TOTAL NHL

CONTENTS

1. SEASON-BY-SEASON REVIEW

2. FRANCHISE HISTORIES

CONTENTS

2. FRANCHISE HISTORIES

continued

3. THE ENTRY DRAFT AND THE BUSINESS OF HOCKEY

4. PLAYER/GOALTENDER/COACH REGISTERS

Year-by-year NHL statistics for more than 5,610 players from 1917–18 to 2002–03

THE ULTIMATE SOURCE ON
THE NATIONAL HOCKEY LEAGUE®

TOTAL NHL®

DAN DIAMOND
EDITOR

PAUL BONTJE RALPH DINGER ERIC ZWEIG
MANAGING EDITORS

JAMES DUPLACEY
ASSISTANT EDITOR

JOHN PASTERNAK
DATA MANAGEMENT

In Memory of
Leslie Duplacey
and Roger Neilson

Published in Canada by:
Dan Diamond and Associates, Inc, 194 Dovercourt Road, Toronto, Ontario M6J 3C8 Canada
ISBN in Canada 0-920445-86-1

Published in the United States by:
Triumph Books, 601 South LaSalle, Suite 500, Chicago, Illinois 60605
ISBN in USA 1-57243-604-2

A conscientious attempt has been made to contact proprietors of the rights in every image used in the book. If through inadvertence the publisher has failed to identify any holder of rights, forgiveness is requested and corrected information will be entered in future printings.

Distribution

Trade sales and distribution in Canada by:
North 49 Books, 35 Prince Andrew Drive, Toronto, Ontario M3C 2H2
416/449-4000; FAX 416/449-9924

Dan Diamond and Associates, Inc., 194 Dovercourt Road, Toronto, Ontario M6J 3C8
416/531-6535; FAX 416/531-3939 e-mail: dda.nhl@sympatico.ca

Trade sales and distribution in the United States by:
Triumph Books, 601 South LaSalle, Suite 500, Chicago, Illinois 60605
312/939-3330; FAX 312/663-3557

Licensed by the National Hockey League®

Data Management and Typesetting: Caledon Data Management, Hillsburgh, Ontario
Film Output and Scanning: Stafford Graphics, Toronto, Ontario
Cover Design: Dan Diamond and Associates
Cover Photos: Hockey Hall of Fame
Printing: Fidelity National Information Solutions Canada, Scarborough, Ontario
Production Management: Dan Diamond and Associates, Inc., Toronto Ontario

Introducing *Total NHL*

Dan Diamond

WELCOME TO THE ULTIMATE SOURCE on the National Hockey League. This ambitious subtitle sets the bar high for *Total NHL*. To this end we set out to create a reading and reference work that covers 86 years of National Hockey League play in a format that's as concise, informative and comprehensive about events from earlier eras as it is about today.

Things that are new often are said to have "started with a clean sheet of paper." Proudly, *Total NHL* can't make that claim as this books reaps the benefit of almost 20 years of study, research and refinement. It's deeply rooted in the passion for hockey and scholarship that created the best-selling *Total Hockey* Encyclopedia that was published in 1998 and 2000, and the *NHL Official Guide & Record*, published annually since 1932 and by the current editorial team since 1984. One covers every corner of the hockey world from the game's origins to its distant future; the other is the book issued by the NHL to reporters, broadcasters, scouts and general managers before the start of each hockey season. Both are acknowledged as being among the best guide and reference books in sports.

Total NHL, then, grows from fertile ground. It has been crafted to mesh with how those of us who care for the game shape our thoughts about the National Hockey League: by season, by franchise, by player, by draft choice and by the business forces that determine much of what occurs in hockey today.

A Season–By–Season Review *(page 13)* describes each campaign from 1917–18 to 2002–03, accompanied by photos and detailed statistics that include top scorers and goaltenders in the regular season and playoffs, leaders in numerous categories such as assists, powerplay goals and shutouts. Each season's trophy winners, all-stars and all-rookie team are listed as are significant trades and records set. The score of every playoff game is listed along with the roster of the Stanley Cup winner.

Extensive Franchise Histories *(page 223)* profile every NHL club, including those no longer in operation, and are supplemented by photos and statistical panels that list season-by-season standings and playoff results.

The Player Register *(page 447)* and the Goaltender Register *(page 864)* provide complete NHL playing statistics for all 5,610 forwards, defensemen and goaltenders to see action in one or more regular-season or playoff games. Player and goaltender panels include birthplace and birthdate, height and weight, shooting or catching side and applicable draft information. Awards, All-Star Team selections, Stanley Cup wins and league leadership in various categories are provided as are extensive notes concerning trades, extraordinary injuries and father/son/brother relationships to other NHLers.

Trades and free agent signing that occur in the few days after *Total NHL* went to press are found on page 446.

A Coach Register *(page 909)* provides similar information for coaches. Coaching statistics consist of wins, losses and ties. Total NHL adds an additional statistic—team points (TP)—for each season coached. You will note that a team's overtime losses—part of the NHL's standings since 1999–2000—are included in their coach's loss column in the coaching register, but the points earned by the club for these losses in overtime are reflected in the team points column for its coach.

The annual NHL Entry Draft *(page 368)* continues to grow in stature, having become the fulcrum upon which one hockey season swings into the next. Since the earliest Amateur Draft in 1963, 8,092 players have been selected. All are presented here accompanied by the career NHL totals, making apparent the link between good drafting and eventual on-ice success.

"Inside the National Hockey League" *(page 425)* is written by NHL vice president of public relations and media services Gary Meagher. It describes how the NHL operates at the nuts-and-bolts level of trades, free agency and standard player contracts. Every aspect of the modern NHL from draft eligibility to marketing to collective bargaining is described in this invaluable guide to understanding the business of hockey.

Other features in Total NHL worth noting include Founding a New League *(page 7)* by Brian McFarlane and Joseph Nieforth. A great deal of boardroom maneuvering took place leading up to the genesis of the National Hockey League in November of 1917. The authors paint a picture of the personalities involved and the conflicts that resulted in the folding of one league (the National Hockey Association) and the creation of the NHL.

A Series of Crossroads *(page 10)* by assistant editor James Duplacey surveys the NHL from its inception to today, zeroing in on those times when tough decisions were required for the league to go forward. Challenges presented by the Depression, wartime, rival leagues, expansion and labor negotiations all have contributed greatly to the league as we know it today.

The Changing Stanley Cup *(page 6)* depicts the evolution of what every NHL player will assure you is the trophy that matters most of all. A complete list of Cup winners and finalists since the NHL was formed in 1917–18 is found on page 12. The NHL's All-Time Playoff Formats *(page 440)* describes the various methods of determining a champion that have been used as the league has grown from three to 30 teams. Hall of Famers are listed by year of induction on page 443 and an All-Time NHL Franchises list is found on page 222.

Contributors are profiled or acknowledged on page 927 where contact information also can be found.

Your comments and suggestions are welcome.

They—and you—make *Total NHL* better.

Dan Diamond

Dan Diamond
July, 2003

The Changing Stanley Cup

THERE ARE MANY WAYS to judge a career in the National Hockey League, but none is as clear-cut as the answer to the question, "Did he win the Stanley Cup?" The act of hoisting the big silver trophy, engraved with the names of hundreds of winning players and of winning teams since 1893, has been the centerpiece of countless hockey dreams, and every year a small number of players experience the joy of having this dream come true.

The changing trophy is depicted here. Clockwise from top left: Lord Stanley, Canada's Governor-General, donated the squat English silver bowl that soon bore his name. The custom of engraving the winners' names on the trophy forced it to grow with the addition of silver bands. By 1932, the trophy had become an ungainly cylinder that grew taller by the time Toronto goaltender Turk Broda posed with the Cup in 1947. The silver bands from this cigar-shaped trophy were remounted in 1948, forming a two-piece trophy that split at the top of the wide barrel. The top part would be presented to each year's winning captain; the barrel remained on the presentation table. A new five-band barrel was added in 1958, forming the one-piece Stanley Cup in use today. The inscribed names of each year's winner filled the five bands in 1991. The top band was removed and a new one added at the base. It, too, will be filled after the names of the 2004 Cup winner have been added.

See NHL Stanley Cup Champions and Finalists, page 12

CHAPTER 1

Founding a New League

Brian McFarlane and Joseph Nieforth

THERE MIGHT NEVER HAVE BEEN A NATIONAL HOCKEY LEAGUE had it not been for a number of quarrels and disputes between owners of teams in the National Hockey Association, the circuit that came just before the NHL. Such disagreements were particularly vitriolic during the 1916–17 season due to unique circumstances dictated by wartime.

In 1916, the NHA comprised six teams: Montreal Canadiens, Montreal Wanderers, Ottawa Senators, Quebec Bulldogs, the Torontos (commonly called the Blueshirts) and an army team made up of enlisted sportsmen stationed in Toronto who represented the 228th Battalion.

Because so many men had joined the armed services as part of the war effort, there was a shortage of skilled players throughout the league. Ottawa sought to withdraw for this reason but was persuaded to stay on operated by a new managing committee. Sam Lichtenhein, owner of the Wanderers, came up with the patriotic idea that the Montreal club would sign only married men and munitions workers. With able-bodied men in short supply because of military commitments throughout the league, it was natural that a khaki-clad army team would be resented by the other owners.

In Toronto, the 228th Battalion team shared the hockey market with Edward J. Livingstone's Blueshirts. "Livvy" had entered the NHA two years before by purchasing a floundering franchise called the Ontarios. By 1916 he was barely tolerated by his fellow owners. He had bucked the professional hockey establishment at almost every opportunity and had recruited the best young talent he could find. He had good contacts from his days as a manager and referee in the amateur Ontario Hockey Association and he made use of them, signing players from eastern and northern Ontario.

Toronto's Eddie Livingstone had a knack for recruiting good players and for exploiting loopholes in league regulations, leaving him unpopular with his fellow owners.

In Livingstone's first season of 1914–15, the bespectacled Toronto owner raised the hackles of Sam Lichtenhein by accusing him of poor sportsmanship for not postponing a game. The passing of George, Harold and Howard McNamara's father left the Ontarios without a full compliment of players in an era where few spares were employed. Lichtenhein, despite pleas on compassionate grounds, demanded the game be forfeited.

The next season, 1915–16, Livingstone made another hockey purchase when he bought the Torontos (Blueshirts) franchise a day after the rival Pacific Coast Hockey Association had raided the team of its players. Livingstone simply folded his first club – the Ontarios – and transferred its players to his newest acquisition. This move did not go over well with his NHA colleagues.

Sam Lichtenhein found another reason, if he needed any more, to be angry with Livingstone after Ken Randall of the Torontos took out Wanderers star Sprague Cleghorn. The two players became entangled in a chase for the puck and slammed into the end boards. Cleghorn was left with a fractured ankle and torn ligaments; the Wanderers went from leading the NHA to recording a 3–13 mark in the remaining games of the season.

The other NHA owners were also miffed when Livingstone played Frank Foyston and Harry Holmes late in the schedule. The two players had jumped from the Torontos to the PCHA at the begining of the season but the NHA had not suspended these players when they left. Livingstone was taking full advantage of this oversight to add firepower to his roster.

In the 1916 offseason, Livingstone was finally able to convince his fellow owners on a radical new split schedule. No longer would the regular-season leader be proclaimed the best team; instead the winner of the first and second half would meet in a playoff to determine the NHA championship. Thus a rudimentary postseason system was created.

Despite his being able to sell them on the split season, Livingston was soon at odds with his fellow owners once again. Prior to the start of the 1916–17 season, the 228th Battalion traded Gordon "Duke" Keats to the Torontos for the rights to goaltender Percy LeSueur. LeSueur had enlisted in a different army group and refused to transfer to the 228th Battalion. The army club declared the trade void but Livingstone protested so vehemently to Major Frank Robinson, the new NHA president, that it was ruled that Keats would play for Livingstone's team when his military duties permitted. (The fact that the Battalion later threw Keats in jail prior to a game was claimed to be entirely co-incidental!)

Livingstone faced further trouble when Ottawa native Cy Denneny demanded a trade to his hometown. Denneny, spurred on by Tommy Gorman, a new member of the Senators managing committee, insisted he had a job in Ottawa that would not permit him to play in Toronto. Livingstone was prepared to release Denneny to Ottawa in exchange for Frank Nighbor or $1,800. The Senators refused, and Denneny sat. His hockey hiatus finally ended in late January of 1917 when Livingstone accepted $750 and goaltender Sammy Hebert in exchange. Still, things would continue to get worse: over the next few years Livingstone was involved in bitter battles with his fellow owners, threatening to start a new league with teams in the United States, initiating lawsuits and injunctions and even offering contracts to players to not play hockey.

Meanwhile, the boys of the 228th were a major attraction around the NHA in 1916–17. Today, their khaki uniforms would be perceived as some sort of fashion statement, but there was more to them than patriotic sentiment on ice. In their opening game, they scored no less than 10 goals to beat Ottawa. George and Howard McNamara, the "Dynamite Twins" from Sault Ste. Marie, had been instrumental in forming the team in the summer of 1916. They were famous for sandwiching opponents who tried to get between them. Howard McNamara (arguably the Battalion's most temperamental player) took two major penalties — including one for rushing the referee — in the return game against Ottawa. He may have been somewhat surprised that the no-nonsense official Cooper Smeaton came out swinging at his aggression.

The 228th Battalion's eventful stay in pro hockey proved brief. Knowing that their future in hockey was unpredictable, the NHA had the team take out a $3,000 bond with Ocean Accident and Guarantee Corporation against the possibility of being called overseas prior to the end of the schedule. By January 27, 1917, the 228th had completed the first half of the NHA split season with a 6–4 record (the Canadiens won the first half with a 7–3 mark), but the rumors of the Battalion being shipped overseas were already swirling. An overhaul in military leadership meant that sporting teams were not being held back from European duty. On February 10 the club withdrew from the NHA when their orders to ship out arrived.

The following day, the league owners met in Montreal to determine what to do with the rest of the season. Eddie Livingstone was unable to attend due to illness yet sent instructions to NHA president Frank Robinson on dealing with his interests. President Robinson could only look on in shock as the other teams chose to erase Toronto from the National Hockey Association. After three years of bucking hockey's traditional Montreal-Ottawa power axis, Livingstone was dumped without compensation and his players redistributed among the remaining clubs. The NHA also chose to go after the $3,000 bond that the 228th Battalion posted. The association took Ocean Accident and Guarantee Corporation to court but lost when the judge ruled the 228th Battalion had a higher calling than playing hockey, and that the war superseded the terms of the policy. An appeal judge confirmed the ruling.

Livingstone, meanwhile, launched his first legal action against his former association partners. This lawsuit, and the ones that followed, would keep the association, and the successor National Hockey League, busy until the early 1930s.

On the ice, the second half of the NHA's 1916–17 split season saw Ottawa emerge victorious and meet Montreal in a two-game, total-goals playoff. After the Canadiens won the first game 5–2, huge crowds waited outside the arena in Ottawa, hoping for a chance to buy tickets for the second. Mounted policemen were required to maintain order. Local recruiting officers worked up and down the line, trying to persuade able-bodied youth to sign up for military service. Not a single one chose to forgo watching hockey for a more serious life in the army. Over 7000 people filed into Dey's Arena in Ottawa to see the Senators win, but by only 4–2. The series went to the Canadiens by seven goals to six.

On the strength of its one-goal advantage, Montreal qualified to go west to play for the Stanley Cup against Seattle, current champions of the Pacific Coast Hockey Association. On the coast, Seattle's Bernie Morris was sensational, scoring 14 goals against the Canadiens in the four-game series, which was won by Seattle three games to one. Game two was especially intense. A Seattle sportswriter wrote: "Harry Mummery threw himself into Jack Walker with such force that the frail forward of the Seattle team had to be stretched out and carried off the ice. Mummery and Rickey swung their sticks on one another's heads so hard that the raps could be heard up in the gods. Then Rickey and Couture staged a bout that would have furnished a lively reel for the movies." And to cap the most exciting scenes ever enacted in the Seattle Arena, Newsy Lalonde swatted referee George Irvine across the face, whereupon judge of play Mickey Ion pitched into Lalonde and chased him off the ice, adding a fine of $25.

Thus ended the last season of play in the NHA. But if the eastern league owners thought they were in for a peaceful offseason, they were badly mistaken. Eddie Livingstone was still fuming, and he certainly wasn't going away.

Even before the Stanley Cup was decided in 1917, Livingstone was demanding the expulsion of the Wanderers from the NHA, charging the team with attempting to lure two of his Toronto players (Alf Skinner and Ken Randall) to Montreal. The incident blew over when the NHA promised to return Livingstone's players to him for the 1917–18 season.

The summer of 1917 saw further tightening of the labor market as the military began drawing more people into the war effort. Unmarried hockey players were forced to scramble for exempt positions in munitions plants and other vital industries. The trouble for the hockey owners was that those same players were barred from playing the professional game by the exemption regulations. Odie Cleghorn was one such player that gave up his playing privilege in return for safe employment.

Most NHA teams had a further manpower problem in that they had not renewed their talent base over the years — the exception being the Torontos as Livingstone continually uncovered new players. (The Toronto owner had introduced fans to a variety of future stars, including Duke Keats, Reg Noble, Alf Skinner and the Denneny brothers.) The Quebec Bulldogs tried to overcome their talent shortage by merging with the Sons of Ireland, the top amateur outfit in that city, but were rejected due to the new military regulations. Meanwhile, Wanderers owner Sam Lichtenhein was hoping to keep the Toronto players who had been sent his way.

At an NHA meeting on September 29, 1917, Major Frank Robinson resigned as president after just one season at the helm. With Robinson's resignation Livingstone lost a potential ally in his battle against his NHA partners. At this point his relationship with the rest of the NHA had deteriorated to the point that he no longer attended association meetings, sending a legal representative in his place. The other owners responded by ordering him to sell his franchise within five days.

Clearly, the NHA owners were now maneuvering to rid themselves of Livingstone. To achieve that end, the Senators, Canadiens, Wanderers and Bulldogs planned to suspend the operations of the NHA and start a new league. A key piece of that business was getting an agreement with the PCHA that the eastern teams would not be raided of players if they reorganized their operations. Frank Patrick, PCHA president, sent a telegram giving his word that all existing agreements would stand; there would be no scooping of players by the PCHA.

Sensing that the 1917–18 season might be lost entirely, the Arena Company, which owned the rinks in Montreal and Toronto, began putting pressure on the parties to find a solution to their woes, threatening to lock out the pro teams if a deal could not be reached. (Senior amateur hockey was still very popular in this era.) To compound the urgency, the Quebec Bulldogs, having failed to merge with the Sons of Ireland, were on the verge of disbanding due to a lack of players.

Livingstone, meanwhile, was actively trying to move himself to the sidelines by negotiating to have the Toronto Arena Gardens take over the management of his team. The deal would leave the Arena Gardens with day-to-day control, but Livingstone would receive a share of profits at the end of the season and retain the rights to all players under contract. If the NHA continued to operate, all control eventually would revert back to Livingstone.

Frank Calder served as NHL president from 1917, the time of the league's formation, until his passing in 1943, the dawn of hockey's modern era.

Regardless of Livingstone's dealings, Toronto may well have been dropped from the new league that was formed at meetings that began November 22, 1917, but the scenario changed when Quebec officially suspended operations (under a guarantee of payment for their remaining players) on November 26. Without Quebec and Toronto, the new league would be reduced to clubs in only Montreal and Ottawa and would not be seen to represent top-level hockey in all of Eastern Canada. Given these circumstances and with Livingstone on the sidelines, the readmittance of a Toronto team became a top priority.

Later on November 26 in Montreal's Windsor Hotel, it was formally announced that a new National Hockey League had been formed. As expected, Frank Calder, the NHA secretary-treasurer, was named president. The loop consisted of four teams: Ottawa, the two Montreal clubs and the "new" Toronto franchise. "A syndicate of Toronto sportsmen purchased the team," Calder stated. "The new owners were thoroughly acceptable" to the other clubs of the league, he added.

Other team owners weren't as polite about the change as their league's new president. "He was always arguing about everything," Ottawa's Tommy Gorman said of Livingstone, remarking that with him gone, the new NHL could get down to business.

Sam Lichtenhein, who had been the first to feud with Livingstone, had seen his Wanderers fade to a shadow of their former NHA glory. The situation was so dire that Lichtenhein threatened to pull out of the new league unless the other teams sent him players. None were forthcoming. Lichtenhein's involvement with the NHL, and all of professional hockey, ended on January 2, 1918, when the Montreal Arena burned to the ground. Unlike the Canadiens, the Wanderers decided not to make the move to the Jubilee rink and soon faded into hockey history.

On the other hand, Livingstone's old team thrived under its new management. The hockey club, which would officially be renamed the Arenas the following season, won the first NHL championship and hosted the Vancouver Millionaires in the 1918 Stanley Cup playoffs, a best-of-five affair. In the final game, a goal by Corbett Denneny proved to be the winner in a 2–1 Toronto victory.

When Livingstone called to collect his profits, Arena Gardens executives balked at paying him, which resulted in more legal action over monies owed and control of player contracts. The dispute lasted almost a decade before Livingstone received compensation. The team, however, fell out of his control.

Following the stormy first season of the NHL and just prior to the second, the league owners entered into two agreements on November 9, 1918, to further protect themselves from Livingstone. The first agreement was a contract that bound the clubs together for the next five years, and the second was a declaration that the National Hockey League was the governing body for professional hockey. George Kennedy, owner of the Montreal Canadiens, declared, "Livingstone has made us a real league. We were more or less disjointed but now we are solid."

Today, the names of Frank Calder and Tommy Gorman are honored in the Hockey Hall of Fame as builders of the game, but their accomplishments would be pale indeed if they did not have an adversary like Edward J. Livingstone to contend with. While Livingstone may have been a stubborn, ambitious and confrontational character, there is little doubt that he played a major role in the new league's formation. If he had not been present in the NHL's early days there would not have been the pressure to unite in the first place or later to expand to the United States of America. (It was Livingstone's American connections that had threatened the NHL with competition from south of the border.) Every move the NHL took in its early days to counter the combative Torontonian aided in the league's development. Livingstone, the man, may be forgotten but the league that developed because of him survived and thrives to this day.

As for his team, Livingstone's Torontos would thrive without him after two further name and ownership changes. In 1919–20, the Arenas became the St. Patricks. Then, in 1926–27 after Conn Smythe and a group of investors bought the club, the St. Pats became the Toronto Maple Leafs. In total, these Toronto NHL teams would win 13 Stanley Cup titles.

CHAPTER 2

A Series of Crossroads

James Duplacey

SINCE ITS INCEPTION IN 1917, the NHL has regularly updated and modified the game in response to new advances in equipment, improved ice and arena technology and the physical conditioning of the athletes who play the sport. This has involved changing existing rules, writing new ones and reconfiguring the playing surface by adding or shifting the on-ice markings that indicate the face-off circles, goal crease, offensive and defensive zones and goal lines.

Even the experience of watching hockey has changed dramatically as arenas have grown from dark chilly barns to bright air-conditioned palaces with seats that have gone from plank to plush. Fans who once watched the action through randomly placed wire mesh and dodged pucks, skates and sticks in unprotected seats now enjoy the game protected by shatterproof glass and netting while watching replays on giant video screens mounted throughout the arena.

Yet, as dramatically as the game has changed on the ice, some of the NHL's most significant victories have occurred on dry land, in boardrooms and meeting halls where tough business decisions were taken in times of crisis.

Here's a round-up of instances when the NHL found itself at a crossroads. The decisions taken at these times contributed greatly to the league as we know it today.

1917 – ADDITION BY SUBTRACTION

A combination of lawsuits and boardroom intrigue resulted in the formation of the National Hockey League. Eastern Canada's elite professional league, the National Hockey Association, was teetering on the brink of extinction in the fall of 1917. The November 6, 1917, edition of the *Toronto Globe* ran a headline that read, "Pro Hockey on Last Legs."

In addition to suffering from dwindling attendance, a talent shortage and the complications of World War I, the organization faced a lengthy legal battle with Eddie Livingstone, the owner of the NHA's Toronto franchise. (See "Founding a New League" page 7.)

The owners of the other NHA clubs chose to switch rather than fight. They disbanded the NHA and formed a "Livingstone-less" National Hockey League and in so doing ceded considerable authority to the new entity. For the first time, club owners recognized that though they were on-ice competitors, they had common interests best served by working as one.

1926 – HOW THE WEST WAS ONE

After struggling to stay in business for a decade, hockey's longest surviving professional league, winner of the Stanley Cup in 1915, 1917 and 1925, folded following the 1925-26 season. The PCHA/WCHL/WHL, which was operated and owned by brothers Lester and Frank Patrick, closed its doors, no longer capable of matching the salaries being offered by the NHL, which was adding new teams in the United States. To maintain this vigorous expansion, the NHL needed fresh talent so the Patricks sold their assets —players and, in some cases, entire teams—to the NHL. It was a good deal for everyone involved. The players got a pay raise, the NHL received an infusion of fresh talent and the Patricks, who sold the Portland franchise to Chicago and the Victoria club to Detroit for $100,000 each, covering their recent losses.

The other players all became free agents, although the Patricks received a fee for each player signed by an NHL club. The result was that the NHL had the talent to add the New York Rangers, Detroit Cougars and Chicago Black Hawks, combining with Boston, Pittsburgh and the New York Americans to make big-league hockey a sports fixture in the United States by the late 1920s.

1930s – ECONOMIC EROSION

The Great Depression took its toll on the National Hockey League during the 1930s, with franchises folding, moving, suspending operations and disappearing. Financial problems and a major decline in the coal industry prompted Pittsburgh to move to Philadelphia and become the Quakers for 1930–31. They lasted only one season.

Despite on-ice success, Ottawa began selling off its high priced talent and fell into the NHL basement. The club did not play in 1931–32 and later relocated to St. Louis in 1934. They lasted only one season as well. Even the Montreal Maroons, Stanley Cup winners in 1935, couldn't keep the customers satisfied and were forced to close their doors in 1938.

Despite these financial woes, the NHL continued to produce high quality entertainment and grow as a league and a sport. The hockey held fans' interest because it was competitive. From 1931 to 1940, seven different franchises—Toronto, the Montreal Canadiens and Maroons, Chicago, Detroit, Boston and New York —won at least one Stanley Cup title as some of the finest athletes to ever play the game displayed their talent. But as tough as the 1930s were, the 1940s posed their own set of challenges.

1940s – HARD TIMES DURING WAR TIME

Over the years, epidemics, World Wars, depressions and recessions have stood in the NHL's path, but the league has always persevered and continued to operate despite the conflicts. However, this resolve was severely tested during World War II. More than 80 players joined the armed services, depleting rosters and diminishing the quality of the on-ice product.

The league responded by altering its rules to keep the game fresh. Overtime was cancelled, the center red line was introduced, creating three zones, and forward passing from zone to zone was permitted for the first time. This had a profound effect on the game, which became quicker and slicker while continuing to reward finesse, speed and inventive play.

The war years also gave many players their chance to play in the

NHL. When the war ended, those players helped rejuvenate the minor leagues and deliver an unprecedented hockey revival. The minor-pro American and the Western leagues became so powerful, many experts argued that the champions of those leagues could have challenged for the Stanley Cup without embarrassment.

Surviving the war and improving the game at the same time prepared the NHL for its golden era, a 25-year "Original Six" voyage that produced many of the game's greatest stars and brought stability and success to the league.

1967 – ICE DREAMS

It was a minor league's quest to become a major league force that prompted the NHL to finally venture into another era of expansion.

The Western Hockey League, which rose from the ashes of the Pacific Coast Hockey League, was formed in 1952 and enjoyed a prosperous boom period for the first four years of its existence. By the end of the decade, however, the loop was on the brink of extinction, forced to the edge of the cliff by fading attendance, folding franchises and constant team relocations.

In a last-ditch effort to regroup, the WHL upped the ante, expanding to San Diego, Los Angeles and San Francisco while announcing a plan to establish itself as a major league and compete for the Stanley Cup. With four teams playing in arenas that held more than 10,000 fans and promises of bigger and better sports palaces on the way, the WHL's aspirations had to be taken seriously. They certainly could ice good teams; with only six clubs in the NHL, the elite minor-pro leagues had no shortage of excellent players.

The NHL kept a close watch on the WHL's California experiment, and when it became clear that the seats were full and the franchises were flourishing, the league decided that it was time to move west as well. In 1965, the NHL announced that it would be adding six new teams in 1967–68, including franchises in Los Angeles and Oakland.

That news stymied the WHL's plans for major league status, although the league did continue exploring new hockey territories in Denver and Phoenix. However, the arrival of the World Hockey Association in 1972 and the continued growth of the NHL eventually forced the league to fold in 1974.

1970s – RIVALS AND SURVIVAL

The 1970s were the most tumultuous decade in hockey history, not just for the NHL, but for every team and league that played the game. Numerous leagues folded, others started and were driven out business but when the dust cleared, the NHL stood resolute. The league withstood the rise and eventual demise of the WHA, even though the rival league created labor woes, turned the salary structure upside down, diluted the talent pool and diminished the quality of the on-ice product.

Yet the NHL soldiered on and, despite the relocation of Oakland, Kansas City and Cleveland during the 1970s, iced 17 franchises in 1978–79, the last season of the WHA.

For much of the decade, NHL hockey was increasingly stagnant, and fight-filled. The Soviet national team shocked NHL fans by their otherworldly display in 1972's eight-game "Summit Series" against an NHL all-star Team Canada. The Canadians would rally to win narrowly, but it was obvious that in almost every technical aspect of hockey, the Russians were dominant.

The NHL and its team general managers responded by adapting. The demise of the WHA brought talented players back to NHL rosters. European players and training drills became an important part of the NHL mix as new teams, fresh faces and fresh legs pumped offensive production, paving the way for the entertaining 1980s.

1992 and 1994 – LABOR AND MANAGEMENT

The NHL's first two league-wide labor disruptions occurred in the 1990s: a players' strike at the end of 1991–92 and an owner's lockout at the beginning of 1994–95. (See Labor Disruptions in "Inside the NHL," page 433.) In both instances, fans of the game returned when games resumed.

Salaries have grown more than 250 percent since the end of the lockout in 1995, making business difficult. (The Buffalo Sabres and Ottawa Senators both filed for bankruptcy protection in 2002–03 and have subsequently found new owners.)

The current collective bargaining agreement between the NHL and its players expires September 15, 2004. The negotiation of a new agreement presents the NHL with one of the greatest challenges it has faced since its formation in 1917.

2003 – THE GRETZKY EFFECT

Is it possible for one player to determine the fate of not only his team, but also, arguably, his entire sport? If you examine the impact that Wayne Gretzky had on the sport of hockey, it would be hard to disagree that he has been the most influential player in the history of professional sports.

By the end of the 1978–79 season—the year before Gretzky made his NHL debut—there were only four professional hockey leagues and 41 teams operating in North America. In the 1970s, seven pro loops closed their doors as the WHA as well as the Eastern, North American, Pacific, Southern, Western and Northeastern leagues all ceased operations.

When Gretzky and his Edmonton teammates were rewriting the NHL record book in the 1980s, Canada enjoyed a hockey renaissance. There were eight Canadian NHL franchises, the Oilers, Canadiens and Flames won six Stanley Cup titles between them and Canada defeated the USSR in a thrilling 1987 Canada Cup. Yet, by the end of the 1987–88 season—Gretzky's last in Edmonton—the American, International and All-American leagues were the only minor-pro circuits left in North America.

However, when Gretzky was dealt to the Los Angeles Kings in the summer of 1988, he almost single-handedly opened America's eyes to the sport. He was hockey's pioneer, superstar, ambassador, entrepreneur and spokesman. The numbers don't lie. In 1998–99, Gretzky's last season in the league, there were eight professional leagues and over 140 teams operating everywhere from Idaho to Alaska to Nevada to New Mexico. There were more pro hockey clubs in Texas than in all of Canada!

Post-Gretzky, the NHL has to deal with the absence of a single mega-superstar and the wide recognition he brought to the league.

The NHL has dealt with these and other challenges since it began play in 1917. It is unlikely that the years ahead will prove any different, so when the tough times occur, the league will find a way to move forward. It always has.

NHL Stanley Cup Champions and Finalists

1918 – 2003

YEAR	WINNER	FINALIST
2003	New Jersey Devils	Mighty Ducks of Anaheim
2002	Detroit Red Wings	Carolina Hurricanes
2001	Colorado Avalanche	New Jersey Devils
2000	New Jersey Devils	Dallas Stars
1999	Dallas Stars	Buffalo Sabres
1998	Detroit Red Wings	Washington Capitals
1997	Detroit Red Wings	Philadelphia Flyers
1996	Colorado Avalanche	Florida Panthers
1995	New Jersey Devils	Detroit Red Wings
1994	New York Rangers	Vancouver Canucks
1993	Montreal Canadiens	Los Angeles Kings
1992	Pittsburgh Penguins	Chicago Blackhawks
1991	Pittsburgh Penguins	Minnesota North Stars
1990	Edmonton Oilers	Boston Bruins
1989	Calgary Flames	Montreal Canadiens
1988	Edmonton Oilers	Boston Bruins
1987	Edmonton Oilers	Philadelphia Flyers
1986	Montreal Canadiens	Calgary Flames
1985	Edmonton Oilers	Philadelphia Flyers
1984	Edmonton Oilers	New York Islanders
1983	New York Islanders	Edmonton Oilers
1982	New York Islanders	Vancouver Canucks
1981	New York Islanders	Minnesota North Stars
1980	New York Islanders	Philadelphia Flyers
1979	Montreal Canadiens	New York Rangers
1978	Montreal Canadiens	Boston Bruins
1977	Montreal Canadiens	Boston Bruins
1976	Montreal Canadiens	Philadelphia Flyers
1975	Philadelphia Flyers	Buffalo Sabres
1974	Philadelphia Flyers	Boston Bruins
1973	Montreal Canadiens	Chicago Black Hawks
1972	Boston Bruins	New York Rangers
1971	Montreal Canadiens	Chicago Black Hawks
1970	Boston Bruins	St. Louis Blues
1969	Montreal Canadiens	St. Louis Blues
1968	Montreal Canadiens	St. Louis Blues
1967	Toronto Maple Leafs	Montreal Canadiens
1966	Montreal Canadiens	Detroit Red Wings
1965	Montreal Canadiens	Chicago Black Hawks
1964	Toronto Maple Leafs	Detroit Red Wings
1963	Toronto Maple Leafs	Detroit Red Wings
1962	Toronto Maple Leafs	Chicago Black Hawks
1961	Chicago Black Hawks	Detroit Red Wings
1960	Montreal Canadiens	Toronto Maple Leafs
1959	Montreal Canadiens	Toronto Maple Leafs

YEAR	WINNER	FINALIST
1958	Montreal Canadiens	Boston Bruins
1957	Montreal Canadiens	Boston Bruins
1956	Montreal Canadiens	Detroit Red Wings
1955	Detroit Red Wings	Montreal Canadiens
1954	Detroit Red Wings	Montreal Canadiens
1953	Montreal Canadiens	Boston Bruins
1952	Detroit Red Wings	Montreal Canadiens
1951	Toronto Maple Leafs	Montreal Canadiens
1950	Detroit Red Wings	New York Rangers
1949	Toronto Maple Leafs	Detroit Red Wings
1948	Toronto Maple Leafs	Detroit Red Wings
1947	Toronto Maple Leafs	Montreal Canadiens
1946	Montreal Canadiens	Boston Bruins
1945	Toronto Maple Leafs	Detroit Red Wings
1944	Montreal Canadiens	Chicago Black Hawks
1943	Detroit Red Wings	Boston Bruins
1942	Toronto Maple Leafs	Detroit Red Wings
1941	Boston Bruins	Detroit Red Wings
1940	New York Rangers	Toronto Maple Leafs
1939	Boston Bruins	Toronto Maple Leafs
1938	Chicago Black Hawks	Toronto Maple Leafs
1937	Detroit Red Wings	New York Rangers
1936	Detroit Red Wings	Toronto Maple Leafs
1935	Montreal Maroons	Toronto Maple Leafs
1934	Chicago Black Hawks	Detroit Red Wings
1933	New York Rangers	Toronto Maple Leafs
1932	Toronto Maple Leafs	New York Rangers
1931	Montreal Canadiens	Chicago Black Hawks
1930	Montreal Canadiens	Boston Bruins
1929	Boston Bruins	New York Rangers
1928	New York Rangers	Montreal Maroons
1927	Ottawa Senators	Boston Bruins

The National Hockey League assumed control of Stanley Cup competition after 1926

YEAR	WINNER	FINALIST
1926	Montreal Maroons	Victoria Cougars
1925	Victoria Cougars (WHL)	Montreal Canadiens
1924	Montreal Canadiens	Calgary Tigers Vancouver Maroons
1923	Ottawa Senators	Edmonton Eskimos Vancouver Maroons
1922	Toronto St. Pats	Vancouver Millionaires
1921	Ottawa Senators	Vancouver Millionaires
1920	Ottawa Senators	Seattle Metropolitans
1919	No decision	
1918	Toronto Arenas	Vancouver Millionaires

Section 1:
Season-By-Season Review
1917-18 to 2002-03

CLASS OF SERVICE | SYMBOL
Day Message |
Day Letter | Blue
Night Message | Nite
Night Letter | N L
If none of these three symbols appears after the check (number of words) this is a day message. Otherwise its character is indicated by the symbol appearing after the check.

GREAT NORTH WESTERN TELEGRAPH AND CABLE

FORM 1 T.W.

TELEGRAM

Z.A.LASH, PRESIDENT — HEAD OFFICE, TORONTO, ONT. — GEO.D.PERRY, GENERAL MANAGER

111 N KB 68 COLL NL NL

SEATTLE WASH APR 3

FRANK CALDER

2053 RES NATL HOCKEY LEAGUE MONTREAL QUE 1919 APR 5 AM 10 47

ALL BOYS EXCEPT HALL ARE DOING NICELY LALONDE BERLANQUETTE COUTURE HAVE BEEN NORMAL FOR TWO DAYS THEY WILL GET OUT SATURDAY KENNEDY HAS SLIGHT TEMPERATURE YET BUT CONSIDER HIM DOING WELL AND NO DANGER HALL DEVELOPED PNEUMONIA TODAY HE IS EASILY WORST CASE BUT WE ARE HOPING FOR THE BEST HAVE BEEN HERE MYSELF FOR THREE DAYS AND EVERYTHING POSSIBLE BEING DONE AM LEAVING FOR VANCOUVER TONIGHT

FRANK A PATRICK.

Telegram from Frank Patrick to NHL president Frank Calder, April 3, 1919, commenting on the health of Montreal Canadiens players stricken with Spansih influenza while in Seattle to play for the Stanley Cup. Despite Patrick's hopes, Joe Hall – mentioned here as having pneumonia – would die in hospital. The Stanley Cup series was abandoned incomplete, marking the only year since the NHL was established that a Cup winner was not declared.

1917-18

Stanley Cup • Toronto Arenas

FINAL STANDINGS

FIRST HALF

Team	GP	W	L	T	GF	GA	PTS
Montreal	14	10	4	0	81	47	20
Toronto	14	8	6	0	71	75	16
Ottawa	14	5	9	0	67	79	10
Mt. Wanderers*	6	1	5	0	17	35	2

* Montreal Arena burned down and Wanderers forced to withdraw. Canadiens and Toronto both awarded a win for defaulted games.

SECOND HALF

Team	GP	W	L	T	GF	GA	PTS
Toronto	8	5	3	0	37	34	10
Ottawa	8	4	4	0	35	35	8
Montreal	8	3	5	0	34	37	6

LEADING SCORERS

Player	Club	GP	G	A	PTS	PIM
Joe Malone	Montreal	20	44	4	48	30
Cy Denneny	Ottawa	20	36	10	46	80
Reg Noble	Toronto	20	30	10	40	35
Newsy Lalonde	Montreal	14	23	7	30	51
Corb Denneny	Toronto	21	20	9	29	14
Harry Cameron	Toronto	21	17	10	27	28
Didier Pitre	Montreal	20	17	6	23	29
Eddie Gerard	Ottawa	20	13	7	20	26
Jack Darragh	Ottawa	18	14	5	19	26
Frank Nighbor	Ottawa	10	11	8	19	6
Harry Meeking	Toronto	21	10	9	19	28
Alf Skinner	Toronto	20	13	5	18	28
Georges Boucher	Ottawa	21	9	8	17	46
Harry Hyland	Mtl.W./Ott.	17	14	2	16	65
Bert Corbeau	Montreal	21	8	8	16	41
Joe Hall	Montreal	21	8	7	15	100

LEADING GOALTENDERS

Goaltender	Club	GPI	MINS	GA	SO	AVG
Georges Vezina	Montreal	21	1282	84	1	3.93
Hap Holmes	Toronto	16	965	76	0	4.73
Clint Benedict	Ottawa	22	1337	114	1	5.12

LEADING NHL PLAYOFF SCORERS

Player	Club	GP	G	A	PTS	PIM
Newsy Lalonde	Montreal	2	4	2	6	17
Harry Meeking	Toronto	2	3	0	3	6
Rusty Crawford	Toronto	2	2	1	3	9
Harry Cameron	Toronto	2	1	2	3	0
Harry Mummery	Toronto	2	1	1	2	17
Reg Noble	Toronto	2	1	1	2	9
Bert Corbeau	Montreal	2	1	1	2	11
Ken Randall	Toronto	2	1	1	2	12

LEADING NHL PLAYOFF GOALTENDERS

Goaltender	Club	GPI	MINS	GA	SO	AVG
Hap Holmes	Toronto	2	120	7	0	3.50
Georges Vezina	Montreal	2	120	10	0	5.00

LEADING STANLEY CUP SCORERS

Player	Club	GP	G	A	PTS	PIM
Alf Skinner	Toronto	5	8	2	10	0
Mickey MacKay	Vancouver	5	5	5	10	12
Cyclone Taylor	Vancouver	5	9	0	9	15
Harry Mummery	Toronto	5	0	6	6	0
Harry Cameron	Toronto	5	3	1	4	0
Corb Denneny	Toronto	5	3	1	4	0

LEADING STANLEY CUP GOALTENDERS

Goaltender	Club	GPI	MINS	GA	SO	AVG
Hugh Lehman	Vancouver	5	300	18	0	3.60
Hap Holmes	Toronto	5	300	21	0	4.20

The Montreal Canadiens' Joe Malone was already an established goal-scoring star by the time the NHL was formed. As a member of the Quebec Bulldogs, he had led the National Hockey Association with 43 goals in 20 games in 1912–13 and with 41 goals in 19 games in 1916–17.

The NHL is born – Joe Malone flies high with 44 goals, the Wanderers lose their rink and the NHL's first Stanley Cup was won by a group of veteran players from Toronto.

In a meeting on November 26, 1917, team owners from the National Hockey Association met to form a new league, the National Hockey League. Former NHA secretary Frank Calder was chosen as the new circuit's first president. Notably absent from the meetings was Toronto owner Eddie Livingstone, who was not popular among his fellow owners; instead, the NHL's Toronto franchise was given to the directors of the Arena Gardens.

In addition to Toronto, the NHL's charter members were two Montreal clubs, the Canadiens and Wanderers, the Ottawa Senators and the Quebec Bulldogs. The Bulldogs, however, elected not to operate their team until the 1919–20 season and the Wanderers withdrew from the league after just six games when their home arena burned down.

The star of the NHL's first season was Joe Malone of the Canadiens, who had 44 goals in just 20 games.

Clubs played a split schedule. The Canadiens won the first half, but were defeated in a playoff for the NHL championship by the leaders of the second half, the Torontos—or the Arenas as they are more commonly known.

In the rival Pacific Coast Hockey Association, Gordie Roberts and Bernie Morris led the Seattle Metropolitans to a first–place finish, but league scoring champion Cyclone Taylor and the Vancouver Millionaires knocked them out in the playoffs, earning the right to travel east to play Toronto for the Stanley Cup.

The Stanley Cup series went the full five-game limit, with Toronto emerging victorious. Incidentally, the PCHA still played seven-man hockey (using a rover) and also allowed limited forward passing, which was not added in the NHL until the following season. To accommodate for the differences, the teams alternated between eastern and western rules during the series. Each team won the games played under its rules.

Leaders, 1917-18

GOALS

Name, Team	G
Joe Malone, Mtl.	44
Cy Denneny, Ott.	36
Reg Noble, Tor.	30
Newsy Lalonde, Mtl.	23
Corb Denneny, Tor.	20
Didier Pitre, Mtl.	17
Harry Cameron, Tor.	17
Harry Hyland, Mtl.W./Ott.	14
Jack Darragh, Ott.	14
Eddie Gerard, Ott.	13
Alf Skinner, Tor.	13

ASSISTS

Name, Team	A
Cy Denneny, Ott.	10
Reg Noble, Tor.	10
Harry Cameron, Tor.	10
Corb Denneny, Tor.	9
Harry Meeking, Tor.	9
Frank Nighbor, Ott.	8
Hamby Shore, Ott.	8
Georges Boucher, Ott.	8
Bert Corbeau, Mtl.	8
Newsy Lalonde, Mtl.	7
Eddie Gerard, Ott.	7
Joe Hall, Mtl.	7

GOALIE WINS

Name, Team	W
Georges Vezina, Mtl.	12
Hap Holmes, Tor.	9
Clint Benedict, Ott.	9
Art Brooks, Tor.	2
Sammy Hebert, Tor.	1
Bert Lindsay, Mtl.W.	1

SHUTOUTS

Name, Team	SO
Georges Vezina, Mtl.	1
Clint Benedict, Ott.	1

PLAYOFF GOALS

Name, Team	G
Newsy Lalonde, Mtl.	4
Harry Meeking, Tor.	3
Rusty Crawford, Tor.	2
Harry Cameron, Tor.	1
Harry Mummery, Tor.	1
Reg Noble, Tor.	1
Bert Corbeau, Mtl.	1
Ken Randall, Tor.	1
Jack McDonald, Mtl.	1
Joe Malone, Mtl.	1

PLAYOFF ASSISTS

Name, Team	A
Newsy Lalonde, Mtl.	2
Harry Cameron, Tor.	2
Rusty Crawford, Tor.	1
Harry Mummery, Tor.	1
Reg Noble, Tor.	1
Bert Corbeau, Mtl.	1
Ken Randall, Tor.	1
Didier Pitre, Mtl.	1
Alf Skinner, Tor.	1
Joe Hall, Mtl.	1

PLAYOFF GOALIE WINS

Name, Team	W
Hap Holmes, Tor.	1
Georges Vezina, Mtl.	1

PLAYOFF SHUTOUTS

Name, Team	SO
none	

STANLEY CUP GOALS

Name, Team	G
Cyclone Taylor, Van.	9
Alf Skinner, Tor.	8
Mickey MacKay, Van.	5
Harry Cameron, Tor.	3
Corb Denneny, Tor.	3

STANLEY CUP ASSISTS

Name, Team	A
Harry Mummery, Tor.	6
Mickey MacKay, Van.	5
Alf Skinner, Tor.	2
Harry Meeking, Tor.	2
Three tied with	1

STANLEY CUP GOALIE WINS

Name, Team	W
Hap Holmes, Tor.	3
Hugh Lehman, Van.	2

STANLEY CUP SHUTOUTS

Name, Team	SO
none	

1918 Playoffs

NHL FINALS

Mar.	11	Montreal	3	at	Toronto	7
Mar.	13	Toronto	3	at	Montreal	4

Montreal won total-goals series 10–7

STANLEY CUP FINALS

Mar.	20	Vancouver	3	at	Toronto	5
Mar.	23	Vancouver	6	at	Toronto	4
Mar.	26	Vancouver	3	at	Toronto	6
Mar.	28	Vancouver	8	at	Toronto	1
Mar.	30	Vancouver	1	at	Toronto	2

Toronto won best-of-five series 3-2

1917-18 – Toronto Arenas – Rusty Crawford, Harry Meeking, Ken Randall (Captain), Corb Denneny, Harry Cameron, Jack Adams, Alf Skinner, Harry Mummery, Hap Holmes, Reg Noble, Sammy Hebert, Jack Marks, Jack Coughlin, Charlie Querrie (Manager), Dick Carroll (Coach), Frank Carroll (Trainer).

Reg Noble's professional career began with the Toronto Blueshirts in 1916–17. The team did not officially become known as the Arenas until 1918–19, then became the St. Pats in 1919–20.

NHL NOTEBOOK

TRANSACTIONS

- Nov. 26, 1917 – Montreal Canadiens retained rights to Newsy Lalonde, Joe Malone, Didier Pitre, and Georges Vezina after NHA folded.
- Nov. 26, 1917 – Ottawa retained rights to Eddie Gerard, Cy Denneny, Jack Darragh, George Boucher, and Clint Benedict after NHA folded.
- Dec. 5, 1917 – Toronto Arenas signed Harry Cameron.
- Dec. 22, 1917 – Ottawa signed Frank Nighbor.

RECORDS

- Jan. 12, 1918 – Ottawa's Dave Ritchie became the first NHL player to score a goal with two teams in one season, in a 9-4 loss to the Canadiens, in Montreal. Ritchie began the season with the Montreal Wanderers, but went to Ottawa when the Wanderers folded.
- Jan. 12, 1918 – Montreal's Joe Malone scored five times to become the first 20 goal scorer in NHL history as the Canadiens won 9-4 over Ottawa.
- Feb. 6, 1918 – Montreal's Joe Malone extended his goal scoring streak to 14 straight games (which began at the start of the NHL's first season two months earlier) with his 35th goal of the season in a 6-3 Canadiens loss at Ottawa.

MILESTONES

- Dec. 19, 1917 – The first two games in NHL history were played. Montreal Canadiens beat Ottawa 7-4 and Montreal Wanderers beat Toronto 10-9.
- Feb. 18, 1918 – Montreal Canadiens goalie Georges Vezina recorded the NHL's first shutout 9-0 over Toronto.
- Mar. 20, 1918 – Toronto became the first NHL team to compete in the Stanley Cup finals, when they beat Vancouver of the PCHA 5-3 in Toronto.
- Mar. 23, 1918 – Alf Skinner of the Toronto Arenas scored the first hat trick by an NHL player in the Stanley Cup finals as the Vancouver Millionaires beat Toronto 6-4 in game two of the 1918 finals, the first Stanley Cup involving an NHL franchise.

1918-19

Stanley Cup • no champion

FINAL STANDINGS

FIRST HALF

Team	GP	W	L	T	GF	GA	PTS
Montreal	10	7	3	0	57	50	14
Ottawa	10	5	5	0	39	39	10
Toronto	10	3	7	0	42	49	6

SECOND HALF

Team	GP	W	L	T	GF	GA	PTS
Ottawa	8	7	1	0	32	14	14
Montreal	8	3	5	0	31	28	6
Toronto	8	2	6	0	22	43	4

LEADING SCORERS

Player	Club	GP	G	A	PTS	PIM
Newsy Lalonde	Montreal	17	22	10	32	40
Odie Cleghorn	Montreal	17	22	6	28	22
Frank Nighbor	Ottawa	18	19	9	28	27
Cy Denneny	Ottawa	18	18	4	22	58
Didier Pitre	Montreal	17	14	5	19	12
Alf Skinner	Toronto	17	12	4	16	26
Reg Noble	Toronto	17	10	5	15	35
Harry Cameron	Tor./Ott.	14	11	3	14	35
Jack Darragh	Ottawa	14	11	3	14	33
Ken Randall	Toronto	14	8	6	14	27
Sprague Cleghorn	Ottawa	18	7	6	13	27
Jack McDonald	Montreal	18	8	4	12	9
Corb Denneny	Toronto	16	8	3	11	15
Rusty Crawford	Toronto	18	7	4	11	51
Harry Meeking	Toronto	14	7	3	10	32
Eddie Gerard	Ottawa	18	4	6	10	17

LEADING GOALTENDERS

Goaltender	Club	GPI	MINS	GA	SO	AVG
Clint Benedict	Ottawa	18	1152	53	2	2.76
Georges Vezina	Montreal	18	1117	78	1	4.19
Bert Lindsay	Toronto	16	998	83	0	4.99

LEADING NHL PLAYOFF SCORERS

Player	Club	GP	G	A	PTS	PIM
Newsy Lalonde	Montreal	5	11	2	13	6
Odie Cleghorn	Montreal	5	7	0	7	0
Joe Malone	Montreal	5	5	0	5	0
Cy Denneny	Ottawa	5	3	2	5	0
Didier Pitre	Montreal	5	2	3	5	3
Harry Cameron	Ottawa	5	4	0	4	6
Eddie Gerard	Ottawa	5	3	0	3	3
Punch Broadbent	Ottawa	5	2	1	3	18

LEADING NHL PLAYOFF GOALTENDERS

Goaltender	Club	GPI	MINS	GA	SO	AVG
Georges Vezina	Montreal	5	300	18	0	3.60
Clint Benedict	Ottawa	5	300	26	0	5.20

LEADING STANLEY CUP SCORERS

Player	Club	GP	G	A	PTS	PIM
Frank Foyston	Seattle	5	9	1	10	0
Newsy Lalonde	Montreal	5	6	0	6	3
Cully Wilson	Seattle	5	1	3	4	6
Jack Walker	Seattle	5	3	0	3	9
Muzz Murray	Seattle	5	3	0	3	3
Didier Pitre	Montreal	5	0	3	3	0
Roy Rickey	Seattle	5	1	2	3	0

LEADING STANLEY CUP GOALTENDERS

Goaltender	Club	GPI	MINS	GA	SO	AVG
Hap Holmes	Seattle	5	336	10	2	1.79
Georges Vezina	Montreal	5	356	19	1	2.74

In addition to his two NHL scoring titles, Newsy Lalonde also won scoring championships in three different major professional leagues that predate the NHL. He later led the Western Canada Hockey League with 30 goals in 1922–23. All tolled, Lalonde scored 453 goals in a major pro career that dated from 1906–07 to 1926–27 — by far the most of this era.

THE NHL FIELDED ONLY THREE TEAMS in the 1918–19 season and a 20-game split schedule was drawn up, with the winners of the two halves to meet for the league title. The Montreal Canadiens, led by Newsy Lalonde (who would claim the league scoring title with 22 goals and 10 assists), were the class of the NHL's first half, posting a 7–3 record. In the second half, the Ottawa Senators had won seven of eight games when the season was cut short because the Toronto Arenas ran into financial difficulties and had to withdraw from the league.

Epidemic Proportions – Newsy made headlines, Montreal sang an Odie to Cleghorn, the Arenas shut their doors and a world-wide epidemic resulted in an abandoned Stanley Cup final.

Left with only two teams, the NHL decided to stage a best-of-seven series between Ottawa and Montreal to determine a league champion. The Canadiens proved to be surprisingly easy winners of this showdown, taking the first three games and winning the series in five.

The NHL championship entitled Montreal to play the Seattle Metropolitans of the Pacific Coast Hockey Association for the Stanley Cup. Reversing the results of the previous season, Seattle had finished second in the PCHA before knocking off the first-place Vancouver Millionaires in the playoffs. The Victoria Aristocrats once again missed the playoffs.

The Stanley Cup finals were played in Seattle, with the Mets taking the opener 7–0 under western rules that included the use of the rover. As was the custom, alternate games were played under eastern and western rules. The series proved hard-fought and evenly matched, as each team had recorded two wins and a tie through five games. The deciding game was scheduled for April 1, but the worldwide epidemic of Spanish influenza intervened. Several Canadiens players were too sick to continue and the series was abandoned. Canadiens star "Bad Joe" Hall lost his life to the illness four days later. It was the only year that no Stanley Cup champion would be declared.

Leaders, 1918-19

GOALS

Name, Team	G
Newsy Lalonde, Mtl.	22
Odie Cleghorn, Mtl.	22
Frank Nighbor, Ott.	19
Cy Denneny, Ott.	18
Didier Pitre, Mtl.	14
Alf Skinner, Tor.	12
Harry Cameron, Tor./Ott.	11
Jack Darragh, Ott.	11
Reg Noble, Tor.	10
Ken Randall, Tor.	8
Corb Denneny, Tor.	8
Jack McDonald, Mtl.	8

ASSISTS

Name, Team	A
Newsy Lalonde, Mtl.	10
Frank Nighbor, Ott.	9
Ken Randall, Tor.	6
Odie Cleghorn, Mtl.	6
Sprague Cleghorn, Ott.	6
Eddie Gerard, Ott.	6
Didier Pitre, Mtl.	5
Reg Noble, Tor.	5
Alf Skinner, Tor.	4
Cy Denneny, Ott.	4
Jack McDonald, Mtl.	4
Rusty Crawford, Tor.	4

GOALIE WINS

Name, Team	W
Clint Benedict, Ott.	12
Georges Vezina, Mtl.	10
Bert Lindsay, Tor.	5

SHUTOUTS

Name, Team	SO
Clint Benedict, Ott.	2
Georges Vezina, Mtl.	1

PLAYOFF GOALS

Name, Team	G
Newsy Lalonde, Mtl.	11
Odie Cleghorn, Mtl.	7
Joe Malone, Mtl.	5
Harry Cameron, Ott.	4
Cy Denneny, Ott.	3
Eddie Gerard, Ott.	3
Didier Pitre, Mtl.	2
Punch Broadbent, Ott.	2
Jack Darragh, Ott.	2
Georges Boucher, Ott.	2
Sprague Cleghorn, Ott.	2

PLAYOFF ASSISTS

Name, Team	A
Didier Pitre, Mtl.	3
Frank Nighbor, Ott.	2
Newsy Lalonde, Mtl.	2
Cy Denneny, Ott.	2
Louis Berlinquette, Mtl.	2
Punch Broadbent, Ott.	1
Bert Corbeau, Mtl.	1
Billy Coutu, Mtl.	1
Jack McDonald, Mtl.	1

PLAYOFF GOALIE WINS

Name, Team	W
Georges Vezina, Mtl.	4
Clint Benedict, Ott.	1

PLAYOFF SHUTOUTS

Name, Team	SO
none	

STANLEY CUP GOALS

Name, Team	G
Frank Foyston, Sea.	9
Newsy Lalonde, Mtl.	6
Muzz Murray, Sea.	3
Jack Walker, Sea.	3
Odie Cleghorn, Mtl.	2

STANLEY CUP ASSISTS

Name, Team	A
Cully Wilson, Sea.	3
Didier Pitre, Mtl.	3
Roy Rickey, Sea.	2
Six tied with	1

STANLEY CUP GOALIE WINS

Name, Team	W
Hap Holmes, Sea.	2
Georges Vezina, Mtl.	2

STANLEY CUP SHUTOUTS

Name, Team	SO
Hap Holmes, Sea.	2
Georges Vezina, Mtl.	1

1919 Playoffs

NHL FINALS

Date	Visitor			Home	
Feb. 22	Ottawa	4	at	Montreal	8
Feb. 27	Montreal	5	at	Ottawa	3
Mar. 1	Ottawa	3	at	Montreal	6
Mar. 3	Montreal	3	at	Ottawa	6
Mar. 6	Ottawa	2	at	Montreal	4

Montreal won best-of-seven series 4–1

STANLEY CUP FINALS

Date	Visitor			Home	
Mar. 19	Montreal	0	at	Seattle	7
Mar. 22	Montreal	4	at	Seattle	2
Mar. 24	Montreal	2	at	Seattle	7
Mar. 26	Montreal	0	at	Seattle	0 OT
Mar. 30	Montreal	4	at	Seattle	3 OT

SERIES CANCELLED DUE TO INFLUENZA EPIDEMIC

Noted as one of the toughest players of his day, Joe Hall was also one of hockey's top defensemen. Sadly, he is best remembered as a victim of the Spanish Influenza epidemic that cancelled the 1919 Stanley Cup finals.

NHL NOTEBOOK

TRANSACTIONS

- Dec. 9, 1918 – Toronto signed Ken Randall.
- Dec. 9, 1918 – Montreal Canadiens signed Odie Cleghorn.
- Jan. 21, 1919 – Ottawa signed Punch Broadbent.
- Jan. 23, 1919 – Montreal Canadiens signed Amos Arbour.

RECORDS

- Dec. 28, 1918 – Montreal Canadiens' Georges Vezina became the first NHL goalie to earn an assist in a 6-3 win over Toronto.
- Feb. 18, 1919 – Ottawa's Cy Denneny scored his 52nd career goal (in a 4-3 win over the Toronto Arenas) to become the NHL's all-time leading goal scorer.
- Feb. 12, 1919 – Ottawa's Clint Benedict became the first goalie in NHL history to record two shutouts in one season, when the Senators won 7-0 over the visiting Montreal Canadiens.
- Mar. 1, 1919 – Montreal's Newsy Lalonde set an NHL playoff record with five goals in a 6-3 win over Ottawa.

MILESTONES

- Nov. 30, 1918 – The NHL modified its penalty rules: From this time forward, teams would play shorthanded for only the first three minutes of a five minute major, and for only the first five minutes of a 20 minute match penalty.
- Mar. 22, 1919 – Montreal center Newsy Lalonde became the first NHL player to score four goals in a Stanley Cup finals game, leading the Canadiens to a 4-2 win against the PCHA's Seattle Metropolitans.
- Mar. 30, 1919 – Montreal Canadiens' Odie Cleghorn scored the first overtime goal by an NHL player, snapping a 3-3 tie with the Seattle Metropolitans at 15:57 of OT for a 4-3 Montreal win.
- Apr. 1, 1919 – The final game for the 1919 Stanley Cup championship was cancelled because of an epidemic of influenza sweeping North America. It remains the only time in its history that the Stanley Cup was not awarded to a team.

1919-20

Stanley Cup • Ottawa Senators

FINAL STANDINGS

FIRST HALF

Team	GP	W	L	T	GF	GA	PTS
Ottawa	12	9	3	0	59	23	18
Montreal	12	8	4	0	62	51	16
Toronto	12	5	7	0	52	62	10
Quebec	12	2	10	0	44	81	4

SECOND HALF

Team	GP	W	L	T	GF	GA	PTS
Ottawa	12	10	2	0	62	41	20
Toronto	12	7	5	0	67	44	14
Montreal	12	5	7	0	67	62	10
Quebec	12	2	10	0	47	96	4

LEADING SCORERS

Player	Club	GP	G	A	PTS	PIM
Joe Malone	Quebec	24	39	10	49	12
Newsy Lalonde	Montreal	23	37	9	46	34
Frank Nighbor	Ottawa	23	26	15	41	18
Corb Denneny	Toronto	24	24	12	36	20
Jack Darragh	Ottawa	23	22	14	36	22
Reg Noble	Toronto	24	24	9	33	52
Amos Arbour	Montreal	22	21	5	26	13
Cully Wilson	Toronto	23	20	6	26	86
Didier Pitre	Montreal	22	14	12	26	6
Punch Broadbent	Ottawa	21	19	6	25	40
Odie Cleghorn	Montreal	21	20	4	24	30
Cy Denneny	Ottawa	24	16	6	22	31
Sprague Cleghorn	Ottawa	21	16	5	21	85
Harry Cameron	Tor./Mtl.	23	15	5	20	42
George Carey	Quebec	20	11	9	20	6
Thomas McCarthy	Quebec	12	12	6	18	0
Ken Randall	Toronto	22	10	8	18	42
Harry Mummery	Quebec	24	9	9	18	42
Bert Corbeau	Montreal	23	11	6	17	65
Georges Boucher	Ottawa	22	9	8	17	55
Louis Berlinquette	Montreal	24	8	9	17	36
Eddie Gerard	Ottawa	22	9	7	16	19

LEADING GOALTENDERS

Goaltender	Club	GPI	MINS	GA	SO	AVG
Clint Benedict	Ottawa	24	1443	64	5	2.66
Ivan Mitchell	Toronto	16	830	60	0	4.34
Georges Vezina	Montreal	24	1456	113	0	4.66
Frank Brophy	Quebec	21	1249	148	0	7.11

LEADING NHL PLAYOFF SCORERS

No NHL Playoffs

LEADING NHL PLAYOFF GOALTENDERS

No NHL Playoffs

LEADING STANLEY CUP SCORERS

Player	Club	GP	G	A	PTS	PIM
Frank Nighbor	Ottawa	5	6	1	7	2
Frank Foyston	Seattle	5	6	1	7	7
Jack Darragh	Ottawa	5	5	2	7	3
Jack Walker	Seattle	5	1	3	4	0
Eddie Gerard	Ottawa	5	2	1	3	3
Roy Rickey	Seattle	5	2	1	3	0
Georges Boucher	Ottawa	5	2	0	2	2
Bobby Rowe	Seattle	5	2	0	2	13
Cy Denneny	Ottawa	5	0	2	2	3
Bernie Morris	Seattle	5	0	2	2	0

LEADING STANLEY CUP GOALTENDERS

Goaltender	Club	GPI	MINS	GA	SO	AVG
Clint Benedict	Ottawa	5	300	11	1	2.20
Hap Holmes	Seattle	5	300	15	0	3.00

Ottawa's Clint Benedict is considered one of the greatest goaltenders of all-time, ranking ahead of even Georges Vezina in most estimates of the players of his era. Benedict's habit of "accidentally" falling to the ice to stop shots and cover loose pucks forced a change to the NHL rule that stated goaltenders must remain standing at all times.

THE 1919–20 SEASON saw the NHL regrouping after a rocky 1918–19 campaign. On the eve of the regular season, the Toronto club found new owners, was renamed the St. Patricks and rejoined the NHL. Meanwhile the Quebec Bulldogs, one of the NHL's founding members, finally exercised its franchise and iced a team. A number of players who'd taken jobs elsewhere returned to Quebec City, most notably forward Joe Malone. Though Quebec would post a dismal record of four wins and 20 losses, Malone was the league's top scorer with 39 goals and 10 assists for 49 points. On January 31, 1920, Malone also set an NHL record that still stands when he scored seven goals in a single game in the Bulldogs' 10–6 victory over Toronto.

Malone Alone – The NHL returned to Quebec, Malone returned to the top of the scoring column, Lalonde remained a laudable leader but the Senators were Lord Stanley's best bet when they sank the Seattle Mets.

The NHL again played a split season, but this year the Ottawa Senators negated the need for a playoff by winning both halves. Led by stars Frank Nighbor, Cy Denneny, Jack Darragh, Punch Broadbent and goalie Clint Benedict, the Senators were 9–3 in the first half and 10–2 in the second.

The competition was much tighter in the Pacific Coast Hockey Association, where just two wins separated the three teams. The Seattle Metropolitans clinched first place on the second-last night of the season and finished 12–10. The Vancouver Millionaires went 11–11, while the Victoria Aristocrats again missed the playoffs with a 10–12 record. Vancouver beat the Mets 3–1 in game one in Seattle, but lost 6–0 at home as the Metropolitans advanced to the Stanley Cup finals with a 7–3 victory in the two-game, total-goals series.

The Stanley Cup finals were slated for Ottawa, but warm weather forced the final two games to be moved to the artificial ice of Toronto's Arena Gardens. Despite the disruption, the Senators prevailed with a 6–1 victory in the fifth and deciding game of the best-of-five affair.

Leaders, 1919-20

GOALS

Name, Team	G
Joe Malone, Que.	39
Newsy Lalonde, Mtl.	37
Frank Nighbor, Ott.	26
Corb Denneny, Tor.	24
Reg Noble, Tor.	24
Jack Darragh, Ott.	22
Amos Arbour, Mtl.	21
Odie Cleghorn, Mtl.	20
Cully Wilson, Tor.	20
Punch Broadbent, Ott.	19

ASSISTS

Name, Team	A
Frank Nighbor, Ott.	15
Jack Darragh, Ott.	14
Didier Pitre, Mtl.	12
Corb Denneny, Tor.	12
Joe Malone, Que.	10
George Carey, Que.	9
Newsy Lalonde, Mtl.	9
Reg Noble, Tor.	9
Harry Mummery, Que.	9
Louis Berlinquette, Mtl.	9

GOALIE WINS

Name, Team	W
Clint Benedict, Ott.	19
Georges Vezina, Mtl.	13
Ivan Mitchell, Tor.	6
Howard Lockhart, Tor./Que.	4
Frank Brophy, Que.	3
Jake Forbes, Tor.	2
Harry Mummery, Que.	1

SHUTOUTS

Name, Team	SO
Clint Benedict, Ott.	5

PLAYOFF GOALS

Name, Team	G
No NHL playoffs	

PLAYOFF ASSISTS

Name, Team	A
No NHL playoffs	

PLAYOFF GOALIE WINS

Name, Team	W
No NHL playoffs	

PLAYOFF SHUTOUTS

Name, Team	SO
No NHL playoffs	

STANLEY CUP GOALS

Name, Team	G
Frank Nighbor, Ott.	6
Frank Foyston, Sea.	6
Jack Darragh, Ott.	5
Four tied with	2

STANLEY CUP ASSISTS

Name, Team	A
Jack Walker, Sea.	3
Jack Darragh, Ott.	2
Cy Denneny, Ott.	2
Bernie Morris, Sea.	2
Five tied with	1

STANLEY CUP GOALIE WINS

Name, Team	W
Clint Benedict, Ott.	3
Hap Holmes, Sea.	2

STANLEY CUP SHUTOUTS

Name, Team	SO
Clint Benedict, Ott.	1

1920 Playoffs

NHL FINALS

No Series played.

Ottawa won both halves of split schedule.

STANLEY CUP FINALS

Mar.	22	Seattle	2	at	Ottawa	3
Mar.	24	Seattle	0	at	Ottawa	3
Mar.	27	Seattle	3	at	Ottawa	1
Mar.	30	Seattle	5	vs	Ottawa	2 *
Apr.	1	Seattle	1	vs	Ottawa	6 *

* played in Toronto

Ottawa won best-of-five series 3-2

1919-20 – Ottawa Senators – Jack MacKell, Jack Darragh, Morley Bruce, Horrace Merrill, Georges Boucher, Eddie Gerard (Captain), Clint Benedict, Sprague Cleghorn, Frank Nighbor, Punch Broadbent, Cy Denneny, Tommy Gorman (Manager), Pete Green (Coach).

Like Newsy Lalonde, Didier Pitre was a member of the original Canadiens back in 1909–10. Except for a season with Vancouver of the PCHA in 1913–14, "Cannonball" Pitre played in Montreal until 1922–23.

NHL NOTEBOOK

TRANSACTIONS

- Nov. 27, 1919 – Toronto signed Cully Wilson.
- Dec. 15, 1919 – Toronto signed Babe Dye.
- Dec. 16, 1919 – Toronto signed Mickey Roach.
- Jan. 14, 1920 – Montreal Canadiens obtained Harry Cameron from Toronto in trade for Goldie Prodgers.

RECORDS

- Jan. 10, 1920 – Montreal's Newsy Lalonde scored six goals as the Canadiens beat Toronto St. Pats 14-7, at the Mount Royal Arena in Montreal. The combined 21 goals by both teams was an NHL record.
- Jan. 28, 1920 – Ottawa's Clint Benedict set an NHL record with his third shutout of the season, in a 7-0 Senators win over Toronto.
- Jan. 31, 1920 – Quebec's Joe Malone set an NHL record with seven goals in a 10-6 win against Toronto.
- Mar. 3, 1920 – Montreal Canadiens set an NHL record with 16 goals in one game, a 16-3 win over the Bulldogs in Quebec City.

MILESTONES

- Dec. 27, 1919 – Ottawa became the first team in NHL history to open a season with two straight shutouts, in a 2-0 win over the Canadiens, in Montreal.
- Feb. 21, 1920 – Ottawa Senators set a new NHL record for most wins by a team in one season, with their 14th of the year, a 5-3 victory at Toronto.
- Mar. 10, 1920 – Quebec Bulldogs' center Joe Malone became the first player in NHL history to score six goals in a game twice during his career. This time he led the Bulldogs to a 10-4 win over Ottawa.
- Mar. 24, 1920 – Ottawa's Clint Benedict recorded the first of his 15 career playoff shutouts, with a 3-0 Senators win over the Seattle Metropolitans, in game two of the Stanley Cup championship, in Ottawa. The record of 15 playoff shutouts wasn't broken until 2001 (Patrick Roy).

1920-21

Stanley Cup • Ottawa Senators

FINAL STANDINGS

FIRST HALF

Team	GP	W	L	T	GF	GA	PTS
Ottawa	10	8	2	0	49	23	16
Toronto	10	5	5	0	39	47	10
Montreal	10	4	6	0	37	51	8
Hamilton	10	3	7	0	34	38	6

SECOND HALF

Team	GP	W	L	T	GF	GA	PTS
Toronto	14	10	4	0	66	53	20
Montreal	14	9	5	0	75	48	18
Ottawa	14	6	8	0	48	52	12
Hamilton	14	3	11	0	58	94	6

LEADING SCORERS

Player	Club	GP	G	A	PTS	PIM
Newsy Lalonde	Montreal	24	33	10	43	36
Babe Dye	Ham./Tor.	24	35	5	40	32
Cy Denneny	Ottawa	24	34	5	39	10
Joe Malone	Hamilton	20	28	9	37	6
Frank Nighbor	Ottawa	24	19	10	29	10
Reg Noble	Toronto	24	19	8	27	54
Harry Cameron	Toronto	24	18	9	27	35
Goldie Prodgers	Hamilton	24	18	9	27	8
Corb Denneny	Toronto	20	19	7	26	29
Jack Darragh	Ottawa	24	11	15	26	20
Leo Reise	Hamilton	24	9	14	23	11
Didier Pitre	Montreal	23	16	5	21	25
Harry Mummery	Montreal	24	15	5	20	69
Louis Berlinquette	Montreal	24	11	9	20	28
Georges Boucher	Ottawa	23	11	8	19	53
Mickey Roach	Tor./Ham.	23	10	9	19	2

LEADING GOALTENDERS

Goaltender	Club	GPI	MINS	GA	SO	AVG
Clint Benedict	Ottawa	24	1462	75	2	3.08
Jake Forbes	Toronto	20	1221	78	0	3.83
Georges Vezina	Montreal	24	1441	99	1	4.12
Howard Lockhart	Hamilton	24	1454	132	1	5.45

LEADING NHL PLAYOFF SCORERS

Player	Club	GP	G	A	PTS	PIM
Frank Nighbor	Ottawa	2	1	3	4	2
Georges Boucher	Ottawa	2	3	0	3	10
Cy Denneny	Ottawa	2	2	0	2	5
Punch Broadbent	Ottawa	2	0	2	2	4
Eddie Gerard	Ottawa	2	1	0	1	50

LEADING NHL PLAYOFF GOALTENDERS

Goaltender	Club	GPI	MINS	GA	SO	AVG
Clint Benedict	Ottawa	2	120	0	2	0.00
Jake Forbes	Toronto	2	120	7	0	3.50

LEADING STANLEY CUP SCORERS

Player	Club	GP	G	A	PTS	PIM
Jack Darragh	Ottawa	5	5	0	5	12
Alf Skinner	Vancouver	3	4	0	4	14
Cy Denneny	Ottawa	5	2	2	4	10
Jack Adams	Vancouver	5	2	1	3	6
Art Duncan	Vancouver	5	2	1	3	3
Smokey Harris	Vancouver	5	2	1	3	6
Sprague Cleghorn	Ottawa	5	1	2	3	44
Punch Broadbent	Ottawa	4	2	0	2	0
Georges Boucher	Ottawa	5	2	0	2	9
Lloyd Cook	Vancouver	5	2	0	2	20

LEADING STANLEY CUP GOALTENDERS

Goaltender	Club	GPI	MINS	GA	SO	AVG
Clint Benedict	Ottawa	5	300	12	0	2.40
Hugh Lehman	Vancouver	5	300	12	0	2.40

Cy Denneny was short, stocky and a slow skater, but he possessed a hard, accurate shot. He scored more goals than any other original Ottawa Senators player, and only Newsy Lalonde and Joe Malone scored more among all players of his era. Denneny was runner-up in the NHL scoring race five times in the league's first nine seasons and led the league in 1923–24.

The first franchise shift in NHL history took place as the Quebec Bulldogs moved to Hamilton and became the Tigers. The change of venue did little to improve the team's fortunes: Though other NHL teams contributed players to bolster Hamilton's roster, the Tigers finished last in both halves of the split season, going 3–7 and 3–11.

Senators Re-Elected – A Babe named Dye scored 35, Lalonde stood atop the scoring ladder, but Ottawa's Jack Darragh was the hero that helped the Cup return to Parliament Hill.

The defending Stanley Cup champions, the Ottawa Senators, were the best team in the NHL's first half, posting an 8–2 record, but they slumped to third place in the second half. Former Senator Sprague Cleghorn helped Toronto post a 10–4 record to win the second half, edging out the 9–5 Canadiens. Toronto's Babe Dye led the league with 35 goals, one better than Ottawa's Cy Denneny. Montreal's Newsy Lalonde had 33 goals, but his 10 assists gave him 43 points to lead the league. Despite poor support, Hamilton's Joe Malone was fourth in both goals and points, with 28 goals and nine assists. It was defense, though, that made the difference in the playoffs, as Ottawa twice blanked Toronto, 5–0 and 2–0, for an easy win in the total-goals series. Clint Benedict was brilliant in net, while Eddie Gerard and George Boucher were solid on defense.

Ottawa traveled west to face the Vancouver Millionaires of the Pacific Coast Hockey Association for the Stanley Cup. For the second straight year, the PCHA had gone down to the wire. The Millionaires were 13–11–0 to Seattle's 12–11–1. The Victoria Aristocrats were in their usual third-place spot at 10–13–1, but the debut this season of Frank Fredrickson offered hope for future improvement. Vancouver crushed the Metropolitans 7–0 and 6–2 in the playoffs.

The first game of the Stanley Cup series drew a record crowd of 11,000 fans, as Vancouver beat Ottawa 3–1. The Senators, though, were able to retain the trophy with a victory in five games that were witnessed by an estimated 51,000 fans.

Leaders, 1920-21

GOALS

Name, Team	G
Babe Dye, Ham./Tor.	35
Cy Denneny, Ott.	34
Newsy Lalonde, Mtl.	33
Joe Malone, Ham.	28
Corb Denneny, Tor.	19
Frank Nighbor, Ott.	19
Reg Noble, Tor.	19
Harry Cameron, Tor.	18
Goldie Prodgers, Ham.	18
Didier Pitre, Mtl.	16

ASSISTS

Name, Team	A
Jack Darragh, Ott.	15
Leo Reise, Ham.	14
Newsy Lalonde, Mtl.	10
Frank Nighbor, Ott.	10
Joe Malone, Ham.	9
Joe Matte, Ham.	9
Mickey Roach, Tor./Ham.	9
Harry Cameron, Tor.	9
Goldie Prodgers, Ham.	9
Louis Berlinquette, Mtl.	9

GOALIE WINS

Name, Team	W
Clint Benedict, Ott.	14
Jake Forbes, Tor.	13
Georges Vezina, Mtl.	13
Howard Lockhart, Ham.	6
Ivan Mitchell, Tor.	2

SHUTOUTS

Name, Team	SO
Clint Benedict, Ott.	2
Georges Vezina, Mtl.	1
Howard Lockhart, Ham.	1

PLAYOFF GOALS

Name, Team	G
Georges Boucher, Ott.	3
Cy Denneny, Ott.	2
Frank Nighbor, Ott.	1
Eddie Gerard, Ott.	1

PLAYOFF ASSISTS

Name, Team	A
Frank Nighbor, Ott.	3
Punch Broadbent, Ott.	2

PLAYOFF GOALIE WINS

Name, Team	W
Clint Benedict, Ott.	2

PLAYOFF SHUTOUTS

Name, Team	SO
Clint Benedict, Ott.	2

STANLEY CUP GOALS

Name, Team	G
Jack Darragh, Ott.	5
Alf Skinner Van	4
Seven tied with	2

STANLEY CUP ASSISTS

Name, Team	A
Cy Denneny, Ott.	2
Sprague Cleghorn, Ott.	2
Five tied with	1

STANLEY CUP GOALIE WINS

Name, Team	W
Clint Benedict, Ott.	3
Hugh Lehman, Van.	2

STANLEY CUP SHUTOUTS

Name, Team	SO
none	

1921 Playoffs

NHL FINALS

Date	Team	Score		Team	Score
Mar. 10	Toronto	0	at	Ottawa	5
Mar. 14	Ottawa	2	at	Toronto	0

Ottawa won total-goals series 7–0

STANLEY CUP FINALS

Date	Team	Score		Team	Score
Mar. 21	Ottawa	1	at	Vancouver	3
Mar. 24	Ottawa	4	at	Vancouver	3
Mar. 28	Ottawa	3	at	Vancouver	2
Mar. 31	Ottawa	2	at	Vancouver	3
Apr. 4	Ottawa	2	at	Vancouver	1

Ottawa won best-of-five series 3-2

1920-21 – Ottawa Senators – Jack MacKell, Jack Darragh, Morley Bruce, Georges Boucher, Eddie Gerard (Captain), Clint Benedict, Sprague Cleghorn, Frank Nighbor, Punch Broadbent, Cy Denneny, Leth Graham, Tommy Gorman (Manager), Pete Green (Coach), F. Dolan (Trainer).

Eddie Gerard was captain of the Ottawa Senators when they won their second straight Stanley Cup title in 1921. He earned a third Stanley Cup championship while on loan to the Toronto St. Pats for the playoffs in 1922, then won yet another Stanley Cup title with Ottawa in 1923.

NHL NOTEBOOK

TRANSACTIONS

- Nov. 27, 1920 – Toronto St. Patricks obtained Harry Cameron from the Montreal Canadiens for Joe Matte and Goldie Prodgers.
- Dec. 16, 1920 – Toronto traded goaltender Howard Lockhart to Hamilton for cash.
- Jan. 21, 1921 – Toronto traded Mickey Roach to Hamilton for cash.
- Feb. 23, 1921 – Hamilton signed Leo Reise.

RECORDS

- Mar. 5, 1921 – Ottawa's Clint Benedict became the first goaltender in NHL history to record 10 career shutouts, in a 1-0 Senators win over the Canadiens, in Montreal.
- Mar. 7, 1921 – Cy Denneny scored six goals when the Senators beat the Hamilton Tigers in Ottawa 12-5 to become part of the first brother combo to each score 6 goals in an NHL game, joining Corbett, who also had 6 goals in a game vs Hamilton six weeks earlier.
- Montreal Canadiens' Bert Corbeau set an NHL record with 86 penalty minutes.

MILESTONES

- Dec. 22, 1920 – Hamilton became the first (and only) NHL team to post a shutout in its debut, when the Tigers (relocated from Quebec City) beat the visiting Canadiens 5-0.
- Mar. 10, 1921 – George Boucher became the first NHL defenseman to score a playoff hat trick, as the Senators beat Toronto 5-0.
- Mar. 21, 1921 – The largest crowd ever to watch a hockey game – more than 11,000 – jammed the Vancouver Arena for the first game of the Stanley Cup series as the Millionaires beat Ottawa Senators 2-1.
- Apr. 4, 1921 – Ottawa Senators became the first NHL team to win consecutive Cup championships when they defeated the Vancouver Millionaires 2-1 in the decisive fifth game of their Stanley Cup series.

1921-22

Stanley Cup • Toronro St. Pats

1921-22

FINAL STANDINGS

Team	GP	W	L	T	GF	GA	PTS
Ottawa	24	14	8	2	106	84	30
Toronto	24	13	10	1	98	97	27
Montreal	24	12	11	1	88	94	25
Hamilton	24	7	17	0	88	105	14

LEADING SCORERS

Player	Club	GP	G	A	PTS	PIM
Punch Broadbent	Ottawa	24	32	14	46	28
Cy Denneny	Ottawa	22	27	12	39	20
Babe Dye	Toronto	24	31	7	38	39
Harry Cameron	Toronto	24	18	17	35	22
Joe Malone	Hamilton	24	24	7	31	4
Corb Denneny	Toronto	24	19	9	28	28
Reg Noble	Toronto	24	17	11	28	19
Sprague Cleghorn	Montreal	24	17	9	26	80
Georges Boucher	Ottawa	23	13	12	25	12
Odie Cleghorn	Montreal	24	21	3	24	26
Leo Reise	Hamilton	24	9	14	23	11
Billy Boucher	Montreal	24	17	5	22	18
Goldie Prodgers	Hamilton	24	15	6	21	4
Mickey Roach	Hamilton	24	14	6	20	7
Louis Berlinquette	Montreal	24	13	5	18	10
Frank Nighbor	Ottawa	20	8	10	18	4
Eddie Gerard	Ottawa	21	7	11	18	16
Ken Randall	Toronto	24	10	6	16	32
Cully Wilson	Hamilton	23	7	9	16	20
Amos Arbour	Hamilton	23	9	6	15	8
Newsy Lalonde	Montreal	20	9	5	14	20

LEADING GOALTENDERS

Goaltender	Club	GPI	MINS	GA	SO	AVG
Clint Benedict	Ottawa	24	1510	84	2	3.34
Georges Vezina	Montreal	24	1469	94	0	3.84
John Ross Roach	Toronto	22	1340	91	0	4.07
Howard Lockhart	Hamilton	24	1409	103	0	4.39

LEADING NHL PLAYOFF SCORERS

Player	Club	GP	G	A	PTS	PIM
Frank Nighbor	Ottawa	2	2	1	3	4
Cy Denneny	Ottawa	2	2	0	2	4
Babe Dye	Toronto	2	2	0	2	2
Billy Stuart	Toronto	2	1	1	2	0
Harry Cameron	Toronto	2	0	2	2	8
Corb Denneny	Toronto	2	1	0	1	0
Ken Randall	Toronto	2	1	0	1	4
Punch Broadbent	Ottawa	2	0	1	1	8

LEADING NHL PLAYOFF GOALTENDERS

Goaltender	Club	GPI	MINS	GA	SO	AVG
John Ross Roach	Toronto	2	120	4	1	2.00
Clint Benedict	Ottawa	2	120	5	1	2.50

LEADING STANLEY CUP SCORERS

Player	Club	GP	G	A	PTS	PIM
Babe Dye	Toronto	5	9	1	10	3
Jack Adams	Vancouver	5	6	1	7	....
Corb Denneny	Toronto	5	3	2	5	2
Rod Smylie	Toronto	5	1	3	4	0
Ernie Parkes	Vancouver	5	0	3	3	....

LEADING STANLEY CUP GOALTENDERS

Goaltender	Club	GPI	MINS	GA	SO	AVG
John Ross Roach	Toronto	5	305	9	1	1.77
Hugh Lehman	Vancouver	5	305	16	1	3.15

A Stanley Cup star in 1922, Babe Dye was a superb stickhandler with a hard, accurate shot. In addition to his immense hockey skills, he played senior football while growing up in Toronto and also played minor league baseball throughout most of his NHL career — hence his nickname. (His real name was Cecil.)

PROFESSIONAL HOCKEY prospered as the 1920s roared. In November 1921 the Montreal Canadiens were sold to Leo Dandurand, Joseph Cattarinich and Louis Letourneau for a reported $11,000. Bigger news came out of the Prairies with the rise of a third professional league to rival the NHL and Pacific Coast Hockey Association. The Western Canada Hockey League boasted teams in Calgary, Edmonton, Regina and Saskatoon.

Luck of the Irish – Punch Broadbent was the NHL's top scorer, but his Senators were unseated by the St. Pats. In the finals, Babe Dye set an NHL record with nine goals in five games as Toronto took the title.

The NHL abandoned the split-season format for 1921–22, adopting the PCHA's playoff scheme that saw the first- and second-place teams meet for the league championship. The defending Stanley Cup champion Ottawa Senators, who added King Clancy and Frank Boucher to a star-studded lineup, were again the NHL's best with a 14–8–2 record. Ottawa's Punch Broadbent led the NHL in scoring with 32 goals and 14 assists and established an NHL record that still stands today, scoring in 16 consecutive games. Still, the second-place Toronto St. Pats pulled off an upset in the two-game, total-goals playoff.

In the west, the PCHA had another tight finish, with Seattle going 12–11–1, Vancouver finishing 12–12–0 and Victoria 11–12–1. The Millionaires then defeated the first-place Metropolitans with a pair of 1–0 shutouts by Hugh Lehman. Edmonton was the first-place club in the WCHL's inaugural season, but the Regina Capitals, having first knocked off the Calgary Tigers in a playoff to determine second place, defeated the Eskimos to claim the first league championship.

Regina and Vancouver met in a two-game, total-goals series to determine the western challenger for the Stanley Cup. After a 2–1 win, Regina was shut out 4–0 and it was the Millionaires who earned the right to go to Toronto to play for the Stanley Cup. The final went a full five games before the St. Patricks emerged victorious. Babe Dye of Toronto was the series star with nine goals.

Leaders, 1921-22

GOALS

Name, Team	G
Punch Broadbent, Ott.	32
Babe Dye, Tor.	31
Cy Denneny, Ott.	27
Joe Malone, Ham.	24
Odie Cleghorn, Mtl.	21
Corb Denneny, Tor.	19
Harry Cameron, Tor.	18
Reg Noble, Tor.	17
Sprague Cleghorn, Mtl.	17
Billy Boucher, Mtl.	17

ASSISTS

Name, Team	A
Harry Cameron, Tor.	17
Punch Broadbent, Ott.	14
Leo Reise, Ham.	14
Cy Denneny, Ott.	12
Georges Boucher, Ott.	12
Eddie Gerard, Ott.	11
Reg Noble, Tor.	11
Frank Nighbor, Ott.	10
Cully Wilson, Ham.	9
Corb Denneny, Tor.	9
Sprague Cleghorn, Mtl.	9

GOALIE WINS

Name, Team	W
Clint Benedict, Ott.	14
Georges Vezina, Mtl.	12
John Ross Roach, Tor.	11
Howard Lockhart, Ham.	6
Ivan Mitchell, Tor.	2
Harry Mummery, Ham.	1

SHUTOUTS

Name, Team	SO
Clint Benedict, Ott.	2

PLAYOFF GOALS

Name, Team	G
Frank Nighbor, Ott.	2
Cy Denneny, Ott.	2
Babe Dye, Tor.	2
Billy Stuart, Tor.	1
Corb Denneny, Tor.	1
Ken Randall, Tor.	1

PLAYOFF ASSISTS

Name, Team	A
Harry Cameron, Tor.	2
Frank Nighbor, Ott.	1
Billy Stuart, Tor.	1
Punch Broadbent, Ott.	1

PLAYOFF GOALIE WINS

Name, Team	W
John Ross Roach, Tor.	1

PLAYOFF SHUTOUTS

Name, Team	SO
John Ross Roach, Tor.	1
Clint Benedict, Ott	1

STANLEY CUP GOALS

Name, Team	G
Babe Dye, Tor.	9
Jack Adams, Van.	6
Corb Denneny, Tor.	3
Lloyd Andrews, Tor.	2
Five tied with	1

STANLEY CUP ASSISTS

Name, Team	A
Rod Smylie, Tor.	3
Ernie Parkes, Van.	3
Harry Cameron, Tor.	2
Corb Denneny, Tor.	2
Red Stuart, Tor.	2

STANLEY CUP GOALIE WINS

Name, Team	W
John Ross Roach, Tor.	3
Hugh Lehman, Van.	2

STANLEY CUP SHUTOUTS

Name, Team	SO
John Ross Roach, Tor.	1
Hugh Lehman, Van.	1

1922 Playoffs

NHL FINALS

Mar.	11	Ottawa	4	at	Toronto	5
Mar.	13	Toronto	0	at	Ottawa	0

Toronto won total-goals series 5–4

PCHA / WCHL PLAYOFF

Mar.	8	Regina	2	at	Vancouver	1
Mar.	11	Vancouver	4	at	Regina	0

Vancouver won total-goals series 5-2

STANLEY CUP FINALS

Mar.	17	Vancouver	4	at	Toronto	3
Mar.	20	Vancouver	1	at	Toronto	2 OT
Mar.	23	Vancouver	3	at	Toronto	0
Mar.	25	Vancouver	0	at	Toronto	6
Mar.	28	Vancouver	1	at	Toronto	5

Toronto won best-of-five series 3-2

1921-22 – Toronto St. Pats – Ted Stackhouse, Corb Denneny, Rod Smylie, Lloyd Andrews, John Ross Roach, Harry Cameron, Billy Stuart, Babe Dye, Ken Randall, Reg Noble (Captain), Eddie Gerard (borrowed for one game from Ottawa), Stan Jackson, Ivan Mitchell, Charlie Querrie (Manager), George O'Donoghue (Coach).

Like Gordie Howe later, Ottawa's Punch Broadbent was a star player who was as talented battling opponents with his elbows as he was scoring goals.

NHL NOTEBOOK

TRANSACTIONS

- Nov. 26, 1921 – Montreal Canadiens traded Amos Arbour and Harry Mummery to Hamilton for Sprague Cleghorn.
- Nov. 26, 1921 – Toronto purchased Harry Cameron from the Montreal Canadiens.
- Dec. 5, 1921 – Toronto signed goal-tender John Ross Roach.
- Dec. 13, 1921 – Montreal Canadiens signed Billy Boucher.
- Dec. 14, 1921 – Ottawa signed King Clancy.

RECORDS

- Feb. 15, 1922 – Ottawa's Harry "Punch" Broadbent extended his NHL-record goal scoring streak to 16 straight games, as the Senators tied the Canadiens 6-6 in Montreal.
- Toronto's Harry Cameron set a new NHL single-season assist record with 17

MILESTONES

- Jan. 14, 1922 – For the first time in NHL history, brothers on the same team scored four goals apiece, as Montreal defenseman Sprague Cleghorn and his brother Odie led the Canadiens to a 10-6 win over the Hamilton Tigers, in Montreal.
- Feb. 11, 1922 – After 20 minutes of overtime Toronto St. Pats and Ottawa Senators settled for a 4-4 tie at Ottawa. It was the first game in NHL history that ended in a tie.
- Mar. 25, 1922 – Toronto St. Pats beat the Vancouver Millionaires 6-0 in the final professional hockey game played with seven men on each side.
- Mar. 25, 1922 – Toronto goaltender John Ross Roach blanked the Vancouver Millionaires 6-0 in the first shutout in Stanley Cup play by an NHL rookie.

1922-23

Stanley Cup • Ottawa Senators

FINAL STANDINGS

Team	GP	W	L	T	GF	GA	PTS
Ottawa	24	14	9	1	77	54	29
Montreal	24	13	9	2	73	61	28
Toronto	24	13	10	1	82	88	27
Hamilton	24	6	18	0	81	110	12

LEADING SCORERS

Player	Club	GP	G	A	PTS	PIM
Babe Dye	Toronto	22	26	11	37	19
Cy Denneny	Ottawa	24	23	11	34	28
Billy Boucher	Montreal	24	24	7	31	55
Jack Adams	Toronto	23	19	9	28	64
Mickey Roach	Hamilton	24	17	10	27	8
Odie Cleghorn	Montreal	24	19	6	25	18
Georges Boucher	Ottawa	24	14	9	23	58
Reg Noble	Toronto	24	12	11	23	47
Cully Wilson	Hamilton	23	16	5	21	46
Aurel Joliat	Montreal	24	12	9	21	37
Eddie Gerard	Ottawa	23	6	13	19	12
Frank Nighbor	Ottawa	22	11	7	18	14
Goldie Prodgers	Hamilton	23	13	4	17	17
Sprague Cleghorn	Montreal	24	9	8	17	34
Edmond Bouchard	Mtl./Ham.	24	5	12	17	44
Harry Cameron	Toronto	22	9	7	16	27
Punch Broadbent	Ottawa	24	14	1	15	34
Jack Darragh	Ottawa	24	6	9	15	10
Bert Corbeau	Hamilton	21	10	4	14	22
Leo Reise	Hamilton	24	6	6	12	35
Billy Stuart	Toronto	23	7	3	10	16

LEADING GOALTENDERS

Goaltender	Club	GPI	MINS	GA	SO	AVG
Clint Benedict	Ottawa	24	1486	54	4	2.18
Georges Vezina	Montreal	24	1488	61	2	2.46
John Ross Roach	Toronto	24	1469	88	1	3.59
Jake Forbes	Hamilton	24	1470	110	0	4.49

LEADING NHL PLAYOFF SCORERS

Player	Club	GP	G	A	PTS	PIM
Cy Denneny	Ottawa	2	2	0	2	2
Louis Berlinquette	Montreal	2	0	2	2	0
Aurel Joliat	Montreal	2	1	0	1	11
Jack Darragh	Ottawa	2	1	0	1	2
Billy Boucher	Montreal	2	1	0	1	2
Frank Nighbor	Ottawa	2	0	1	1	0
Georges Boucher	Ottawa	2	0	1	1	2

LEADING NHL PLAYOFF GOALTENDERS

Goaltender	Club	GPI	MINS	GA	SO	AVG
Clint Benedict	Ottawa	2	120	2	1	1.00
Georges Vezina	Montreal	2	120	3	0	1.50

LEADING STANLEY CUP SCORERS

Player	Club	GP	G	A	PTS	PIM
Punch Broadbent	Ottawa	6	6	1	7	12
Art Duncan	Vancouver	4	2	2	4	0
Georges Boucher	Ottawa	6	2	1	3	6
Frank Boucher	Vancouver	4	2	0	2	0
Alf Skinner	Vancouver	3	1	1	2	4
Cy Denneny	Ottawa	6	1	1	2	8
Frank Nighbor	Ottawa	6	1	1	2	10
Ernie Parkes	Vancouver	4	0	2	2	2

LEADING STANLEY CUP GOALTENDERS

Goaltender	Club	GPI	MINS	GA	SO	AVG
Clint Benedict	Ottawa	6	361	8	1	1.33
Hal Winkler	Edmonton	2	123	3	0	1.46
Hugh Lehman	Vancouver	4	240	10	0	2.50

King Clancy grew up in Ottawa and entered the NHL with the Senators as an 18-year-old in 1921–22. He remained a part of the game until his death on November 8, 1986. His father was also an outstanding athlete, and it was from him that Francis Michael Clancy inherited his regal nickname.

A CONTROVERSIAL DEAL marked the preseason in 1922–23. Veteran star Newsy Lalonde of the Montreal Canadiens was sold to the Western Canada league's Saskatoon Crescents without being offered on waivers to other NHL clubs. The dispute was resolved when NHL president Frank Calder ruled Lalonde would be considered traded for a top Saskatoon prospect named Aurel Joliat. Joliat became an instant star in Montreal and helped the Canadiens edge out the Toronto St. Pats for second place and a playoff spot behind the Ottawa Senators.

What a Babe – A gifted athlete who also played baseball and football, Babe Dye excelled in hockey, where his ripping wrist shot and bulldozer physique helped him lead the league in goals (26) and points (37).

Ottawa won the playoff opener 2–0 despite the dirty play of Montreal defensemen Sprague Cleghorn and Bill Couture. The pair were suspended from game two by Canadiens owner Leo Dandurand. Still, Montreal hung on in the second game, taking a 2–0 lead, but Cy Denneny scored for Ottawa and gave the Senators a 3–2 victory in the total-goals series.

Out west, the Pacific Coast Hockey Association finally made the switch to six-man hockey, abandoning the rover position. The move allowed the PCHA and the WCHL to play an interlocking schedule, though the two leagues would maintain separate standings and playoffs. Vancouver finished first in the PCHA, but the real story was in Victoria where Frank Fredrickson's scoring exploits led the Aristocrats to the playoffs for the first time in 10 years. Still, it was Vancouver, now known as the Maroons, who won the league title in the playoffs. Newsy Lalonde won the WCHL scoring title, though his Saskatoon club finished last. Edmonton's 19–10–1 record had the Eskimos comfortably in first place, though they needed overtime to beat Regina 4–3 in the two-game, total-goals playoff.

The NHL champion Senators first defeated Vancouver three games to one in a best-of-five affair, then swept the WCHL champion Eskimos 2–0 in a best-of-three series to claim their third Stanley Cup title in four years.

Leaders, 1922-23

GOALS

Name, Team	G
Babe Dye, Tor.	26
Billy Boucher, Mtl.	24
Cy Denneny, Ott.	23
Jack Adams, Tor.	19
Odie Cleghorn, Mtl.	19
Mickey Roach, Ham.	17
Cully Wilson, Ham.	16
Georges Boucher, Ott.	14
Punch Broadbent, Ott.	14
Goldie Prodgers, Ham.	13

ASSISTS

Name, Team	A
Eddie Gerard, Ott.	13
Edmond Bouchard, Mtl./Ham.	12
Babe Dye, Tor.	11
Cy Denneny, Ott.	11
Reg Noble, Tor.	11
Mickey Roach, Ham.	10
Jack Adams, Tor.	9
Georges Boucher, Ott.	9
Aurel Joliat, Mtl.	9
Jack Darragh, Ott.	9

GOALIE WINS

Name, Team	W
Clint Benedict, Ott.	14
John Ross Roach, Tor.	13
Georges Vezina, Mtl.	13
Jake Forbes, Ham.	6

SHUTOUTS

Name, Team	SO
Clint Benedict, Ott.	4
Georges Vezina, Mtl.	2
John Ross Roach, Tor.	1

PLAYOFF GOALS

Name, Team	G
Cy Denneny, Ott.	2
Aurel Joliat, Mtl.	1
Jack Darragh, Ott.	1
Billy Boucher, Mtl.	1

PLAYOFF ASSISTS

Name, Team	A
Louis Berlinquette, Mtl.	2
Frank Nighbor, Ott.	1
Georges Boucher, Ott.	1

PLAYOFF GOALIE WINS

Name, Team	W
Clint Benedict, Ott.	1
Georges Vezina, Mtl.	1

PLAYOFF SHUTOUTS

Name, Team	SO
Clint Benedict, Ott.	1

STANLEY CUP GOALS

Name, Team	G
Punch Broadbent, Ott.	6
Art Duncan, Van.	3
Frank Boucher, Van.	2
Georges Boucher, Ott.	2
Nine tied with	1

STANLEY CUP ASSISTS

Name, Team	A
Art Duncan, Van.	2
Ernie Parkes, Van.	2
Seven tied with	1

STANLEY CUP GOALIE WINS

Name, Team	W
Clint Benedict, Ott.	5
Hugh Lehman, Van.	1

STANLEY CUP SHUTOUTS

Name, Team	SO
Clint Benedict, Ott.	1

1923 Playoffs

NHL FINALS

Mar.	7	Ottawa	2	at	Montreal	0
Mar.	9	Montreal	2	at	Ottawa	1

Ottawa won total-goals series 3–2

STANLEY CUP FINALS (TWO SERIES)

Mar.	16	Ottawa	1	at	Vancouver	0
Mar.	19	Ottawa	1	at	Vancouver	4
Mar.	23	Ottawa	3	at	Vancouver	2
Mar.	26	Ottawa	5	at	Vancouver	1

Ottawa won best-of-five series 3-1

Mar.	29	Ottawa	2	vs.	Edmonton	1 OT*
Mar.	31	Ottawa	1	vs.	Edmonton	0 *

* played in Vancouver

Ottawa won best-of-three series 2-0

1922-23 – Ottawa Senators – Georges Boucher, Lionel Hitchman, Frank Nighbor, King Clancy, Harry Helman, Clint Benedict, Jack Darragh, Eddie Gerard (Captain), Cy Denneny, Punch Broadbent, Tommy Gorman (Manager), Pete Green (Coach), F. Dolan (Trainer).

While not quite possessing the fiery temper of his Hall of Fame brother Sprague, Odie Cleghorn was an aggressive player and star scorer. Later, as a coach, he would popularize the changing of lines on the fly.

NHL NOTEBOOK

TRANSACTIONS

- May 27, 1922 – Toronto traded Jake Forbes to Hamilton for cash
- Sept. 18, 1922 – Montreal Canadiens traded veteran Newsy Lalonde to the Saskatoon Sheiks of the WCHL for the rights to amateur Aurel Joliat, and $3,500.
- Jan. 30, 1923 – Hamilton signed Billy Burch.
- Feb. 23, 1923 – Ottawa signed Lionel Hitchman.

RECORDS

- Jan. 6, 1923 – Ottawa's Frank Nighbor played in what was reported to be his sixth complete game (without any time on the bench) in a 2-1 win over the Toronto St. Patricks.
- Jan. 31, 1923 – Canadiens beat Hamilton 5-4 in Montreal in the NHL's first penalty-free game.
- Feb. 17, 1923 – Ottawa's Cy Denneny scored his 144th career goal (in a 2-0 win over Montreal) to pass Joe Malone as the all-time NHL goal scoring leader. Denneny held the record for the next 11 years.

MILESTONES

- Dec. 16, 1922 – Montreal's Aurel Joliat scored two goals in his NHL debut at Toronto, but the Canadiens lost to the St. Pats 7-2.
- Mar. 16, 1923 – Brothers faced each other for the first time in Stanley Cup history as Cy and Corb Denneny, and George and Frank Boucher lined up on opposite sides of the ice with the Senators and the Maroons. None of them scored in the 1-0 Ottawa win.
- Mar. 22, 1923 – Foster Hewitt (hockey's first regular radio announcer) broadcast his first game – an intermediate playoff between Toronto Parkdale and Kitchener at the Mutual Street Arena in Toronto.
- Mar. 31, 1923 – Ottawa's 18-year-old King Clancy played all six positions (including ywo minutes in goal) when the Senators beat Edmonton 1-0 in game two of the finals, to become the 1923 Stanley Cup Champions.

1923-24

Stanley Cup • Montreal Canadiens

FINAL STANDINGS

Team	GP	W	L	T	GF	GA	PTS
Ottawa	24	16	8	0	74	54	32
Montreal	24	13	11	0	59	48	26
Toronto	24	10	14	0	59	85	20
Hamilton	24	9	15	0	63	68	18

LEADING SCORERS

Player	Club	GP	G	A	PTS	PIM
Cy Denneny	Ottawa	22	22	2	24	10
Georges Boucher	Ottawa	21	13	10	23	38
Billy Burch	Hamilton	24	16	6	22	6
Billy Boucher	Montreal	23	16	6	22	48
Aurel Joliat	Montreal	24	15	5	20	27
Babe Dye	Toronto	19	16	3	19	23
Jack Adams	Toronto	22	14	4	18	51
Reg Noble	Toronto	24	12	5	17	79
Frank Nighbor	Ottawa	20	11	6	17	16
Howie Morenz	Montreal	24	13	3	16	20
King Clancy	Ottawa	24	8	8	16	26
Bert Corbeau	Toronto	24	8	6	14	55
Red Green	Hamilton	23	11	2	13	31
Goldie Prodgers	Hamilton	23	9	4	13	6
Punch Broadbent	Ottawa	22	9	4	13	44
Ken Randall	Hamilton	24	7	6	13	58
Shorty Green	Hamilton	22	7	6	13	31
Sprague Cleghorn	Montreal	23	8	4	12	45

LEADING GOALTENDERS

Goaltender	Club	GPI	MINS	GA	SO	AVG
Georges Vezina	Montreal	24	1459	48	3	1.97
Clint Benedict	Ottawa	22	1356	45	3	1.99
Jake Forbes	Hamilton	24	1483	68	1	2.75
John Ross Roach	Toronto	23	1380	80	1	3.48

LEADING NHL PLAYOFF SCORERS

Player	Club	GP	G	A	PTS	PIM
Howie Morenz	Montreal	2	3	1	4	6
Cy Denneny	Ottawa	2	2	0	2	2
Aurel Joliat	Montreal	2	1	1	2	0
Billy Boucher	Montreal	2	1	0	1	9
Frank Nighbor	Ottawa	2	0	1	1	0
Georges Boucher	Ottawa	2	0	1	1	4

LEADING NHL PLAYOFF GOALTENDERS

Goaltender	Club	GPI	MINS	GA	SO	AVG
Georges Vezina	Montreal	2	120	2	1	1.00
Clint Benedict	Ottawa	2	120	5	0	2.50

LEADING STANLEY CUP SCORERS

Player	Club	GP	G	A	PTS	PIM
Billy Boucher	Montreal	4	5	1	6	6
Howie Morenz	Montreal	4	4	2	6	4
Aurel Joliat	Montreal	4	3	1	4	6
Sprague Cleghorn	Montreal	4	2	2	4	2
Frank Boucher	Vancouver	2	1	1	2	2
Helge Bostrum	Vancouver	2	1	0	1	0
Joe Matte	Vancouver	2	1	0	1	2
Herb Gardiner	Calgary	2	1	0	1	0
Bernie Morris	Calgary	2	0	1	1	0
Odie Cleghorn	Montreal	4	0	1	1	0

LEADING STANLEY CUP GOALTENDERS

Goaltender	Club	GPI	MINS	GA	SO	AVG
Georges Vezina	Montreal	4	240	4	1	1.00
Hugh Lehman	Vancouver	2	120	5	0	2.50
Charlie Reid	Calgary	2	120	9	0	4.50

Frank Nighbor was the first recipient the NHL's two oldest individual honors, winning the Hart Trophy in 1923–24 and the Lady Byng Trophy the following year. The stylish center was a great goal scorer and an excellent playmaker, but fans of his day would often debate whether he was more valuable offensively or defensively.

THE DEFENDING STANLEY CUP CHAMPION Ottawa Senators were under new ownership for the 1923–24 season, and moved into the new 11,000-seat Ottawa Auditorium. Longtime star and captain Eddie Gerard was forced to retire because of illness, but the Senators were still the class of the NHL, cruising to a first-place finish with a 16–8–0 record. Ottawa's Frank Nighbor was the first winner of the Hart Trophy—donated by Dr. David Hart, father of Montreal Canadiens coach and manager Cecil Hart, to recognize the league's most valuable player.

The Stratford Streak – Ottawa's Cy Denenny and Georges Boucher were regular-season stars, but the playoff spotlight shone on the Habs' Billy Boucher and a speedy rookie sensation named Howie Morenz.

The Canadiens introduced a talented newcomer named Howie Morenz this season, and finished comfortably ahead of Toronto and Hamilton (who finished last for the fourth straight year) to make the playoffs. Montreal then surprised Ottawa with victories of 1–0 and 4–2 to claim the NHL championship.

On the other side of the continent, the Pacific Coast Hockey Association and Western Canada Hockey League once again played an interlocking schedule, with Seattle proving to be the PCHA's best. As in the NHL, there was a playoff upset as second-place Vancouver eliminated Seattle. In the WCHL, future NHL star Bill Cook led the loop in scoring, but his Saskatoon team finished out of the playoffs behind Calgary and Regina. Calgary was the only first-place team to survive the postseason.

Canadiens owner Leo Dandurand wanted the two western champions to face each other in a playoff to send only one team east, but Frank Patrick of the PCHA insisted the NHL champs play both Vancouver and Calgary. Montreal gave in and swept both teams in two straight games. Howie Morenz scored seven goals in the Canadiens' six playoff games as Montreal won its first Stanley Cup championship since the club was part of the old NHA in 1916.

Leaders, 1923-24

GOALS

Name, Team	G
Cy Denneny, Ott.	22
Babe Dye, Tor.	16
Billy Boucher, Mtl.	16
Billy Burch, Ham.	16
Aurel Joliat, Mtl.	15
Jack Adams, Tor.	14
Georges Boucher, Ott.	13
Howie Morenz, Mtl.	13
Reg Noble, Tor.	12
Frank Nighbor, Ott.	11
Red Green, Ham.	11

ASSISTS

Name, Team	A
Georges Boucher, Ott.	10
King Clancy, Ott.	8
Frank Nighbor, Ott.	6
Shorty Green, Ham.	6
Billy Boucher, Mtl.	6
Billy Burch, Ham.	6
Bert Corbeau, Tor.	6
Ken Randall, Ham.	6
Lionel Hitchman, Ott.	6
Odie Cleghorn, Mtl.	5
Aurel Joliat, Mtl.	5
Reg Noble, Tor.	5

GOALIE WINS

Name, Team	W
Clint Benedict, Ott.	15
Georges Vezina, Mtl.	13
John Ross Roach, Tor.	10
Jake Forbes, Ham.	9
Sammy Hebert, Ott.	1

SHUTOUTS

Name, Team	SO
Clint Benedict, Ott.	3
Georges Vezina, Mtl.	3
John Ross Roach, Tor.	1
Jake Forbes, Ham.	1

PLAYOFF GOALS

Name, Team	G
Howie Morenz, Mtl.	3
Cy Denneny, Ott.	2
Aurel Joliat, Mtl.	1
Billy Boucher, Mtl.	1

PLAYOFF ASSISTS

Name, Team	A
Howie Morenz, Mtl.	1
Aurel Joliat, Mtl.	1
Frank Nighbor, Ott.	1
Georges Boucher, Ott.	1

PLAYOFF GOALIE WINS

Name, Team	W
Georges Vezina, Mtl.	2

PLAYOFF SHUTOUTS

Name, Team	SO
Georges Vezina, Mtl.	1

STANLEY CUP GOALS

Name, Team	G
Billy Boucher, Mtl.	5
Howie Morenz, Mtl.	4
Aurel Joliat, Mtl.	3
Sprague Cleghorn, Mtl.	2
Three tied with	1

STANLEY CUP ASSISTS

Name, Team	A
Howie Morenz, Mtl.	2
Sprague Cleghorn, Mtl.	2
Four tied with	1

STANLEY CUP GOALIE WINS

Name, Team	W
Georges Vezina, Mtl.	4

STANLEY CUP SHUTOUTS

Name, Team	SO
Georges Vezina, Mtl.	1

1924 Playoffs

NHL FINALS

Mar. 8	Ottawa	0	at	Montreal	1
Mar. 11	Montreal	4	at	Ottawa	2

Montreal won total-goals series 5–2

PCHA / WCHL PLAYOFF

Mar. 10	Calgary	1	at	Vancouver	3
Mar. 12	Vancouver	3	at	Calgary	6
Mar. 15	Calgary	3	vs.	Vancouver	1*

* played in Winnipeg

Calgary won best-of-three series 2-1

STANLEY CUP FINALS (TWO SERIES)

Mar. 18	Vancouver	2	at	Montreal	3
Mar. 20	Vancouver	1	at	Montreal	2

Montreal won best-of-three series 2-0

Mar. 22	Calgary	1	at	Montreal	6
Mar. 25	Calgary	0	vs.	Montreal	3 **

** played in Ottawa

Montreal won best-of-three series 2-0

1923-24 – Montreal Canadiens – Georges Vezina, Sprague Cleghorn (Captain), Billy Coutu, Howie Morenz, Aurel Joliat, Billy Boucher, Odie Cleghorn, Sylvio Mantha, Bobby Boucher, Billy Bell, Billy Cameron, Joe Malone, Charles Fortier, Leo Dandurand (Manager/Coach).

TROPHY WINNERS

Trophy	Awarded For	Winner	Team
Hart	MVP	Frank Nighbor	Ott.

NHL NOTEBOOK

TRANSACTIONS

- Sept. 30, 1923 – Montreal Canadiens signed Howie Morenz.
- Dec. 3, 1923 – Montreal Canadiens signed Sylvio Mantha.
- Dec. 14, 1923 – Toronto St. Patricks acquired Amos Arbour, Bert Corbeau and George Carey from Hamilton for Ken Randall and cash.
- Feb. 21, 1924 – Ottawa Senators signed Frank Finnigan.

RECORDS

- Dec. 26, 1923 – A record crowd of 8,300 fans (the most ever to attend a hockey game in Ottawa) turned out to see the Senators beat the Montreal Canadiens 3-2.
- Feb. 9, 1924 – Clint Benedict got his 18th career shutout as Ottawa beat Hamilton 1-0 in just the second penalty free game in NHL history.
- Ottawa's Cy Denneny set a record for scoring leaders with just two assists (to go along with his 22 goals) as he led the NHL with 24 points.

MILESTONES

- Jan. 30, 1924 – Frank Nighbor scored twice, including his 100th career NHL goal when Ottawa won 7-2 over the visiting Toronto Maple Leafs.
- Feb. 20, 1924 – Canadiens fans waited two hours in the Mount Royal Arena for the Senators to arrive for their game. But they never showed! The team was stranded on a snow-bound train 50 miles from Ottawa. The game was played the next night (a 3-0 Habs win).
- Mar. 25, 1924 – Montreal beat Calgary 3-0 in game two of the finals (played in Ottawa), to become the 1924 Stanley Cup Champions. Georges Vezina got the shutout as the Canadiens won their first Cup since the formation of the NHL in 1917-18.
- The NHL awarded its first individual trophy when Ottawa's Frank NIghbor was named the winner of the Hart Trophy (as the NHL MVP) despite finishing ninth in league scoring.

1924-25

Stanley Cup • Victoria Cougars (WCHL)

FINAL STANDINGS

Team	GP	W	L	T	GF	GA	PTS
Hamilton	30	19	10	1	90	60	39
Toronto	30	19	11	0	90	84	38
Montreal	30	17	11	2	93	56	36
Ottawa	30	17	12	1	83	66	35
Mtl. Maroons	30	9	19	2	45	65	20
Boston	30	6	24	0	49	119	12

LEADING SCORERS

Player	Club	GP	G	A	PTS	PIM
Babe Dye	Toronto	29	38	8	46	41
Cy Denneny	Ottawa	29	27	15	42	16
Aurel Joliat	Montreal	25	30	11	41	85
Howie Morenz	Montreal	30	28	11	39	46
Red Green	Hamilton	30	19	15	34	81
Jack Adams	Toronto	27	21	10	31	67
Billy Boucher	Montreal	30	17	13	30	92
Billy Burch	Hamilton	27	20	7	27	10
Shorty Green	Hamilton	28	18	9	27	63
Jimmy Herberts	Boston	30	17	7	24	55
Hooley Smith	Ottawa	30	10	13	23	81
Hap Day	Toronto	26	10	12	22	33
King Clancy	Ottawa	29	14	7	21	61
Georges Boucher	Ottawa	28	15	5	20	95
Punch Broadbent	Mtl. Maroons	30	14	6	20	75
Reg Noble	Tor./Mtl.M	30	9	11	20	64
Ken Randall	Hamilton	30	8	10	18	52
Sprague Cleghorn	Montreal	27	8	10	18	89
Bert McCaffrey	Toronto	30	10	6	16	12
Ed Gorman	Ottawa	28	11	4	15	49
Alex McKinnon	Hamilton	29	8	3	11	47
Mickey Roach	Hamilton	30	6	4	10	8
Frank Nighbor	Ottawa	26	5	5	10	18
Bert Corbeau	Toronto	30	4	6	10	74

LEADING GOALTENDERS

Goaltender	Club	GPI	MINS	GA	SO	AVG
Georges Vezina	Montreal	30	1860	56	5	1.81
Jake Forbes	Hamilton	30	1833	60	6	1.96
Clint Benedict	Mtl. Maroons	30	1843	65	2	2.12
Alex Connell	Ottawa	30	1852	66	7	2.14

LEADING NHL PLAYOFF SCORERS

Player	Club	GP	G	A	PTS	PIM
Howie Morenz	Montreal	2	3	0	3	4
Sprague Cleghorn	Montreal	2	1	2	3	2
Jack Adams	Toronto	2	1	0	1	7
Billy Boucher	Montreal	2	1	0	1	4
Bert McCaffrey	Toronto	2	1	0	1	4
Odie Cleghorn	Montreal	2	0	1	1	0
Sylvio Mantha	Montreal	2	0	1	1	0

LEADING NHL PLAYOFF GOALTENDERS

Goaltender	Club	GPI	MINS	GA	SO	AVG
Georges Vezina	Montreal	2	120	2	1	1.00
John Ross Roach	Toronto	2	120	5	0	2.50

LEADING STANLEY CUP SCORERS

Player	Club	GP	G	A	PTS	PIM
Jack Walker	Victoria	4	4	2	6	0
Frank Fredrickson	Victoria	4	3	3	6	6
Howie Morenz	Montreal	4	4	0	4	4
Gord Fraser	Victoria	4	2	1	3	6
Gizzy Hart	Victoria	4	2	1	3	0
Harold Halderson	Victoria	4	2	1	3	8

LEADING STANLEY CUP GOALTENDERS

Goaltender	Club	GPI	MINS	GA	SO	AVG
Hap Holmes	Victoria	4	240	8	0	2.00
Georges Vezina	Montreal	4	240	16	0	4.00

Pictured in the uniform of the New York Americans, Red Green and his brother Shorty were star players with the Hamilton Tigers. It was considered quite a coup for the league when the brothers were lured to the NHL from the amateur Sudbury Wolves. Red and Shorty helped lead the Tigers to respectability, then helped organize the strike that killed the team.

THERE WERE CHANGES throughout professional hockey in 1924–25. The NHL expanded to six teams, adding its first American club, the Boston Bruins, and a second Montreal team (later known as the Maroons) that would play its home games at the new Montreal Forum. In the west, the Seattle Metropolitans folded, marking the end of the Pacific Coast Hockey Association. Vancouver and Victoria joined Calgary, Edmonton, Regina and Saskatoon in a revamped Western Canada Hockey League.

How the West Won – The duo of Joliat and Morenz hammered home 58 goals, Babe Dye sank 38, but the Victoria Cougars grabbed the headlines when they became the last non-NHL team to win the Cup.

With expansion, the NHL extended its season from 24 to 30 games and changed the playoff structure. The first-place team would now receive a bye into the finals and meet the winner of a series between the second- and third-place teams. The Hamilton Tigers, who'd placed last in each of the previous four seasons, went 19–10–1 this year to finish one point ahead of the Toronto St. Pats for first place. But the Tigers players were upset that the season had been lengthened by 25 percent without a comparable increase in their salaries and they refused to take part in the playoffs unless they received an extra $200 each. President Frank Calder suspended the players and announced that the winner of a playoff between the Canadiens and St. Patricks would receive the new Prince of Wales Trophy as the NHL's regular-season champion. Montreal won and earned the right to play for the Stanley Cup.

In the west, Victoria had added Seattle stars Jack Walker, Frank Foyston and Hap Holmes to a roster that already boasted future Hall of Famer Frank Fredrickson, and though they only finished third, the Cougars (as they were now known) beat Saskatoon and Calgary in the playoffs to earn a chance at hockey's top prize. Victoria then beat Montreal to become the last non-NHL team to win the Stanley Cup.

Leaders, 1924-25

GOALS

Name, Team	G
Babe Dye, Tor.	38
Aurel Joliat, Mtl.	30
Howie Morenz, Mtl.	28
Cy Denneny, Ott.	27
Jack Adams, Tor.	21
Billy Burch, Ham.	20
Red Green, Ham.	19
Shorty Green, Ham.	18
Billy Boucher, Mtl.	17
Jimmy Herberts, Bos.	17

ASSISTS

Name, Team	A
Cy Denneny, Ott.	15
Red Green, Ham.	15
Billy Boucher, Mtl.	13
Hooley Smith, Ott.	13
Hap Day, Tor.	12
Aurel Joliat, Mtl.	11
Howie Morenz, Mtl.	11
Reg Noble, Tor./Mtl.M.	11
Jack Adams, Tor.	10
Sprague Cleghorn, Mtl.	10
Ken Randall, Ham.	10

GOALIE WINS

Name, Team	W
Jake Forbes, Ham.	19
John Ross Roach, Tor.	19
Alex Connell, Ott.	17
Georges Vezina, Mtl.	17
Clint Benedict, Mtl.M.	9
Charles Stewart, Bos.	5
Hec Fowler, Bos.	1

SHUTOUTS

Name, Team	SO
Alex Connell, Ott.	7
Jake Forbes, Ham.	6
Georges Vezina, Mtl.	5
Charles Stewart, Bos.	2
Clint Benedict, Mtl.M.	2
John Ross Roach, Tor.	1

PLAYOFF GOALS

Name, Team	G
Howie Morenz, Mtl.	3
Sprague Cleghorn, Mtl.	1
Jack Adams, Tor.	1
Billy Boucher, Mtl.	1
Bert McCaffrey, Tor.	1

PLAYOFF ASSISTS

Name, Team	A
Sprague Cleghorn, Mtl.	2
Odie Cleghorn, Mtl.	1
Sylvio Mantha, Mtl.	1

PLAYOFF GOALIE WINS

Name, Team	W
Georges Vezina, Mtl.	2

PLAYOFF SHUTOUTS

Name, Team	SO
Georges Vezina, Mtl.	1

STANLEY CUP GOALS

Name, Team	G
Jack Walker, Vic.	4
Howie Morenz, Mtl.	4
Frank Fredrickson, Vic.	3
Four tied with	2

STANLEY CUP ASSISTS

Name, Team	A
Frank Fredrickson, Vic.	3
Jack Walker, Vic.	2
Five tied with	1

STANLEY CUP GOALIE WINS

Name, Team	W
Hap Holmes, Vic.	3
Georges Vezina, Mtl.M.	1

STANLEY CUP SHUTOUTS

Name, Team	SO
none	

1925 Playoffs

NHL SEMI-FINALS

Mar. 11	Toronto	2	at	Montreal	3
Mar. 11	Montreal	2	at	Toronto	0

Montreal won total-goals series 5–2

NHL FINALS

Montreal vs. Hamilton

Montreal declared NHL champion due to Hamilton players' strike.

STANLEY CUP FINALS

Mar. 21	Montreal	2	at	Victoria	5
Mar. 23	Montreal	1	vs.	Victoria	3 *
Mar. 27	Montreal	4	at	Victoria	2
Mar. 30	Montreal	1	at	Victoria	6

* played in Vancouver

Victoria won best-of-five series 3-1

1924-25 – Victoria Cougars – Hap Holmes, Clem Loughlin (Captain), Gord Fraser, Frank Fredrickson, Jack Walker, Gizzy Hart, Harold Halderson, Frank Foyston, Wally Elmer, Harry Meeking, Jocko Anderson, Lester Patrick (Manager-Coach).

TROPHY WINNERS

Trophy	Awarded For	Winner	Team
Hart	MVP	Billy Burch	Ham.
Byng	Gentlemanly Conduct	Frank Nighbor	Ott.

NHL NOTEBOOK

TRANSACTIONS

- Oct. 31, 1924 – Ottawa Sentators signed Hooley Smith.
- Nov. 18, 1924 – Ottawa Senators signed Alex Connell.
- Dec. 9, 1924 – Montreal Maroons purchased Reg Noble from Toronto for $8,000.
- Dec. 9, 1924 – Toronto St. Pats signed Clarence "Hap" Day while the youngster was playing at the University of Toronto.
- Jan. 10, 1925 – Boston Bruins purchased Lionel Hitchman from Ottawa.

RECORDS

- Jan. 20, 1925 – Clint Benedict became the first NHL goaltender to record 20 career shutouts as the Maroons won 2-0 at Boston.
- Feb. 11, 1925 – Georges Vezina became the first goaltender in Montreal history to win 100 career NHL games, as the Canadiens defeated Ottawa 10-3.
- Mar. 7, 1925 – Rookie goalie Alex Connell set an NHL record with his seventh shutout of the season, as the Ottawa Senators won 3-0 over the visiting Toronto St. Pats.

MILESTONES

- Nov. 1, 1924 – Boston Bruins became the first U.S. team to join the NHL when they (and the Montreal Maroons) officially received their NHL franchises.
- Nov. 29, 1924 – The Montreal Forum had its official opening, and the Canadiens beat the Toronto St. Patricks 7-1 before a crowd of 9,000.
- Dec. 17, 1924 – Goalies Jake Forbes of the Hamilton Tigers and Alex Connell of the Ottawa Senators played in the first 0-0 tie in eight seasons of NHL play.
- Mar. 4, 1925 – Ottawa's Cy Denneny scored his 200th career NHL goal and added an assist in a 5-1 victory in Montreal.
- Mar. 30, 1925 – Victoria Cougars of WCHL beat the Canadiens 6-1 to become the last non-NHL team to win the Stanley Cup. Victoria won the best of five series 3-1 over Montreal.

1925-26

Stanley Cup • Montreal Maroons

FINAL STANDINGS

Team	GP	W	L	T	GF	GA	PTS
Ottawa	36	24	8	4	77	42	52
Mtl. Maroons	36	20	11	5	91	73	45
Pittsburgh	36	19	16	1	82	70	39
Boston	36	17	15	4	92	85	38
NY Americans	36	12	20	4	68	89	28
Toronto	36	12	21	3	92	114	27
Montreal	36	11	24	1	79	108	23

LEADING SCORERS

Player	Club	GP	G	A	PTS	PIM
Nels Stewart	Mtl. Maroons	36	34	8	42	119
Cy Denneny	Ottawa	36	24	12	36	18
Carson Cooper	Boston	36	28	3	31	10
Jimmy Herberts	Boston	36	26	5	31	47
Howie Morenz	Montreal	31	23	3	26	39
Jack Adams	Toronto	36	21	5	26	52
Aurel Joliat	Montreal	35	17	9	26	52
Billy Burch	NY Americans	36	22	3	25	33
Hooley Smith	Ottawa	28	16	9	25	53
Frank Nighbor	Ottawa	35	12	13	25	40
Babe Siebert	Mtl. Maroons	35	16	8	24	108
Babe Dye	Toronto	31	18	5	23	26
Bert McCaffrey	Toronto	36	14	7	21	42
Hib Milks	Pittsburgh	36	14	5	19	17
Reg Noble	Mtl. Maroons	33	9	9	18	96
Duke McCurry	Pittsburgh	36	13	4	17	32
Red Green	NY Americans	35	13	4	17	42
Punch Broadbent	Mtl. Maroons	36	12	5	17	112
Harold Darragh	Pittsburgh	35	10	7	17	6

LEADING GOALTENDERS

Goaltender	Club	GPI	MINS	GA	SO	AVG
Alex Connell	Ottawa	36	2251	42	15	1.12
Roy Worters	Pittsburgh	35	2145	68	7	1.90
Clint Benedict	Mtl. Maroons	36	2288	73	6	1.91
Charles Stewart	Boston	35	2173	80	6	2.21
Jake Forbes	NY Americans	36	2240	86	2	2.30
Herb Rheaume	Montreal	31	1889	92	0	2.92
John Ross Roach	Toronto	36	2231	114	2	3.07

LEADING NHL PLAYOFF SCORERS

Player	Club	GP	G	A	PTS	PIM
Merlyn Phillips	Mtl. Maroons	4	3	0	3	4
Punch Broadbent	Mtl. Maroons	4	2	1	3	14
Reg Noble	Mtl. Maroons	4	1	1	2	6
Jesse Spring	Pittsburgh	2	0	2	2	2
Nels Stewart	Mtl. Maroons	4	0	2	2	10
Duke McCurry	Pittsburgh	2	0	2	2	4

LEADING NHL PLAYOFF GOALTENDERS

Goaltender	Club	GPI	MINS	GA	SO	AVG
Alex Connell	Ottawa	2	120	2	0	1.00
Clint Benedict	Mtl. Maroons	4	240	5	1	1.25
Roy Worters	Pittsburgh	2	120	6	0	3.00

LEADING STANLEY CUP SCORERS

Player	Club	GP	G	A	PTS	PIM
Nels Stewart	Mtl. Maroons	4	6	1	7	14
Babe Siebert	Mtl. Maroons	4	1	2	3	4
Frank Fredrickson	Victoria	4	1	1	2	10
Merlyn Phillips	Mtl. Maroons	4	1	1	2	0

LEADING STANLEY CUP GOALTENDERS

Goaltender	Club	GPI	MINS	GA	SO	AVG
Clint Benedict	Mtl. Maroons	4	240	3	3	0.75
Hap Holmes	Victoria	4	240	10	0	2.50

Nels Stewart was the most prolific scorer of his day. His 324 career goals stood as an NHL record from the time of his retirement in 1940 until Maurice Richard scored his 325th in 1952. Stewart was the NHL scoring leader as a rookie in 1925–26 when he and Babe Siebert led the Montreal Maroons to a Stanley Cup championship in just their second season.

On September 22, 1925, the NHL held its first meeting in the United States, when a special session was convened in New York to discuss the admission of a new expansion team for that city. The Hamilton Tigers were being dropped and the New York Americans would take Hamilton's place and employ its players. Another new team, the Pittsburgh Pirates, also joined the league for 1925–26, bringing membership to seven teams. The Pirates were stocked with players from the American amateur champion Pittsburgh Yellow Jackets and included such stars as Lionel Conacher and Roy Worters.

Coached by Odie Cleghorn, the new Pirates finished in third place and made the playoffs in their first season, just ahead of the much-improved Boston Bruins.

But it was the Montreal Maroons who showed even greater improvement. Young stars like Babe Siebert and Nels Stewart (who won the NHL scoring title and the Hart Trophy) helped lift the Maroons into second place, beat Pittsburgh in the playoffs, then knock off the first-place Ottawa Senators for the NHL championship.

In the Western Canada Hockey League, poor fan support in Regina saw the franchise transferred to Portland, Oregon. Consequently, the word "Canada" was dropped from the league's name. The defending Stanley Cup champion Victoria Cougars were hampered by injuries during the first half of the season, but came alive late to finish third. Victoria then knocked off Saskatoon and Edmonton to claim the championship of the Western Hockey League.

Victoria came east to Montreal in what proved to be the last Stanley Cup finals involving a team from a league other than the NHL. The Maroons won the best-of-five series in four games, claiming the first of what would be many Stanley Cup championships won on the ice of the Montreal Forum.

Maroon Magic – The Tigers became Americans, the Pirates invaded the NHL, but Siebert and Stewart were the main men who vanquished Victoria and helped the Maroons win their first Stanley Cup.

Leaders, 1925-26

GOALS

Name, Team	G
Nels Stewart, Mtl.M.	34
Carson Cooper, Bos.	28
Jimmy Herberts, Bos.	26
Cy Denneny, Ott.	24
Howie Morenz, Mtl.	23
Billy Burch, NYA	22
Jack Adams, Tor.	21
Babe Dye, Tor.	18
Aurel Joliat, Mtl.	17
Hooley Smith, Ott.	16
Babe Siebert, Mtl.M.	16

ASSISTS

Name, Team	A
Frank Nighbor, Ott.	13
Cy Denneny, Ott.	12
Hooley Smith, Ott.	9
Reg Noble, Mtl.M.	9
Aurel Joliat, Mtl.	9
Babe Siebert, Mtl.M.	8
Nels Stewart, Mtl.M.	8
Harold Darragh, Pit.	7
Bert McCaffrey, Tor.	7
Dunc Munro, Mtl.M.	6

GOALIE WINS

Name, Team	W
Alex Connell, Ott.	24
Clint Benedict, Mtl.M.	20
Roy Worters, Pit.	18
Charles Stewart, Bos.	16
Jake Forbes, NYA	12
John Ross Roach, Tor.	12
Herb Rheaume, Mtl.	10
Odie Cleghorn, Pit.	1
Moe Roberts, Bos.	1
Frenchy Lacroix, Mtl.	1

SHUTOUTS

Name, Team	SO
Alex Connell, Ott.	15
Roy Worters, Pit.	7
Charles Stewart, Bos.	6
Clint Benedict, Mtl.M.	6
Jake Forbes, NYA	2
John Ross Roach, Tor.	2

PLAYOFF GOALS

Name, Team	G
Merlyn Phillips, Mtl.M.	3
Punch Broadbent, Mtl.M.	2
Herb Drury, Pit.	1
Baldy Cotton, Pit.	1
Harold Darragh, Pit.	1
King Clancy, Ott.	1
Rodger Smith, Pit.	1
Reg Noble, Mtl.M.	1
Chuck Dinsmore, Mtl.M.	1
Babe Siebert, Mtl.M.	1

PLAYOFF ASSISTS

Name, Team	A
Jesse Spring, Pit.	2
Duke McCurry, Pit.	2
Nels Stewart, Mtl.M.	2
Punch Broadbent, Mtl.M.	1
Reg Noble, Mtl.M.	1

PLAYOFF GOALIE WINS

Name, Team	W
Clint Benedict, Mtl.M.	2

PLAYOFF SHUTOUTS

Name, Team	SO
Clint Benedict, Mtl.M.	1

STANLEY CUP GOALS

Name, Team	G
Nels Stewart, Mtl.M.	6
Seven tied with	1

STANLEY CUP ASSISTS

Name, Team	A
Babe Siebert, Mtl.M.	2
Nels Stewart, Mtl.M.	1
Frank Fredrickson, Vic.	1
Merlyn Phillips, Mtl.M.	1

STANLEY CUP GOALIE WINS

Name, Team	W
Clint Benedict, Mtl.M.	3
Hap Holmes, Vic.	1

STANLEY CUP SHUTOUTS

Name, Team	SO
Clint Benedict, Mtl.M.	3

1926 Playoffs

NHL SEMI-FINALS

Mar.	8	Mtl. Maroon	3	at	Pittsburgh	1
Mar.	11	Pittsburgh	3	at	Mtl. Maroons	3

Mtl. Maroons won total-goals series 6–4

NHL FINALS

Mar.	8	Ottawa	1	at	Mtl. Maroons	1
Mar.	11	Mtl. Maroons	1	at	Ottawa	0

Mtl. Maroons won total-goals series 2–1

STANLEY CUP FINALS

Mar.	30	Victoria	0	at	Mtl. Maroons	3
Apr.	1	Victoria	0	at	Mtl. Maroons	3
Apr.	3	Victoria	3	at	Mtl. Maroons	2
Apr.	6	Victoria	0	at	Mtl. Maroons	2

Mtl. Maroons won best-of-five series 3-1

1925-26 – Montreal Maroons – Clint Benedict, Reg Noble, Frank Carson, Dunc Munro (Captain), Nels Stewart, Punch Broadbent, Babe Siebert, Chuck Dinsmore, Merlyn Phillips, Hobie Kitchen, Sam Rothschild, Albert Holway, George Horne, Bernie Brophy, Eddie Gerard (Manager/Coach), Bill O'Brien (Trainer).

TROPHY WINNERS

Trophy	Awarded For	Winner	Team
Hart	MVP	Nels Stewart	Mtl.M.
Byng	Gentlemanly Conduct	Frank Nighbor	Ott

NHL NOTEBOOK

TRANSACTIONS

- June 25, 1925 – Montreal Maroons signed Nels Stewart as a free agent.
- Mar. 26, 1925 – Montreal Maroons signed Albert "Babe" Siebert.
- Nov. 11, 1925 – Pittsburgh Pirates signed Lionel Conacher.
- Nov. 12, 1925 – Ottawa Senators signed Hec Kilrea.

RECORDS

- Dec. 26, 1925 – New York Americans and Pittsburgh Pirates set an NHL record with 141 shots in the Americans 3-1 win. New York held the shot edge, 73-68. Roy Worters made 70 saves for Pittsburgh, and Jake Forbes had 67 for NY.
- Feb. 18, 1926 – Ottawa set a new NHL record for most wins in a season, with their 20th of the year, a 4-2 victory over the Canadiens. The Senators broke the record of 19 wins, set by 3 teams over the NHL's first 8 seasons.
- Mar. 16, 1926 – Ottawa's Alex Connell became the first NHL goalie to record 15 shutouts in one season, as the Senators won 4-0 over the visiting Toronto St. Pats.
- Apr. 1, 1926 – Clint Benedict became the first NHL goalie to record three straight playoff shutouts, when the Montreal Maroons won 3-0 over the visiting Victoria Cougars, in game two of their Stanley Cup championship series.

MILESTONES

- Dec. 15, 1925 – Howie Morenz scored a goal and an assist as the Montreal Canadiens beat the New York Americans 3-1 in the first NHL game played in New York. The contest took place at Madison Square Garden.
- Jan. 5, 1926 – Jimmy Herberts became the first Boston player to score three goals in a game, when he led the Bruins to a 3-0 win over the Pittsburgh Pirates, in Boston.
- Jan. 16, 1926 – Clint Benedict became the first goaltender to record 25 career NHL shutouts, when he led the Montreal Maroons to a 1-0 win over the Montreal Canadiens.
- Nels Stewart leads the NHL in scoring in his first season in the league, finishing with 42 points for the Montreal Maroons.

1926-27

Stanley Cup • Ottawa Senators

FINAL STANDINGS

CANADIAN DIVISION

Team	GP	W	L	T	GF	GA	PTS
Ottawa	44	30	10	4	86	69	64
Montreal	44	28	14	2	99	67	58
Mtl. Maroons	44	20	20	4	71	68	44
NY Americans	44	17	25	2	82	91	36
Toronto	44	15	24	5	79	94	35

AMERICAN DIVISION

Team	GP	W	L	T	GF	GA	PTS
New York	44	25	13	6	95	72	56
Boston	44	21	20	3	97	89	45
Chicago	44	19	22	3	115	116	41
Pittsburgh	44	15	26	3	79	108	33
Detroit	44	12	28	4	76	105	28

LEADING SCORERS

Player	Club	GP	G	A	PTS	PIM
Bill Cook	NY Rangers	44	33	4	37	58
Dick Irvin	Chicago	43	18	18	36	34
Howie Morenz	Montreal	44	25	7	32	49
Frank Fredrickson	Det./Bos.	44	18	13	31	45
Babe Dye	Chicago	41	25	5	30	14
Ace Bailey	Toronto	42	15	13	28	82
Frank Boucher	NY Rangers	44	13	15	28	17
Billy Burch	NY Americans	43	19	8	27	40
Harry Oliver	Boston	42	18	6	24	17
Duke Keats	Bos./Det.	42	16	8	24	52
Cy Denneny	Ottawa	42	17	6	23	16
Bun Cook	NY Rangers	44	14	9	23	42
Hib Milks	Pittsburgh	44	16	6	22	18
Bill Carson	Toronto	40	16	6	22	41
Jimmy Herberts	Boston	34	15	7	22	51
George Hay	Chicago	35	14	8	22	12
Mickey MacKay	Chicago	34	14	8	22	23
Nels Stewart	Mtl. Maroons	43	17	4	21	133
Johnny Sheppard	Detroit	43	13	8	21	60
Gord Fraser	Chicago	44	14	6	20	89
King Clancy	Ottawa	43	9	10	19	78

LEADING GOALTENDERS

Goaltender	Club	GPI	MINS	GA	SO	AVG
Clint Benedict	Mtl. Maroons	43	2748	65	13	1.42
Lorne Chabot	NY Rangers	36	2307	56	10	1.46
George Hainsworth	Montreal	44	2732	67	14	1.47
Alex Connell	Ottawa	44	2782	69	13	1.49
Hal Winkler	NYR/Bos.	31	1959	56	6	1.72
Jake Forbes	NY Americans	44	2715	91	8	2.01
John Ross Roach	Toronto	44	2764	94	4	2.04
Hap Holmes	Detroit	41	2685	100	6	2.23
Roy Worters	Pittsburgh	44	2711	108	4	2.39
Hugh Lehman	Chicago	44	2797	116	5	2.49

LEADING PLAYOFF SCORERS

Player	Club	GP	G	A	PTS	PIM
Harry Oliver	Boston	8	4	2	6	4
Percy Galbraith	Boston	8	3	3	6	2
Cy Denneny	Ottawa	6	5	0	5	0
Frank Fredrickson	Boston	8	2	2	4	20
Jimmy Herberts	Boston	8	3	0	3	8
Frank Finnigan	Ottawa	6	3	0	3	0
George Hay	Chicago	2	1	2	3	2

LEADING PLAYOFF GOALTENDERS

Goaltender	Club	GPI	MINS	GA	SO	AVG
Alex Connell	Ottawa	6	400	4	2	0.60
George Hainsworth	Montreal	4	252	6	1	1.43
Hal Winkler	Boston	8	520	13	2	1.50

Already a longtime star when he entered the NHL with Chicago in 1926–27, Dick Irvin (right) would later hook up with Hap Day (left) in Toronto when he became coach of the Maple Leafs in 1931–32. Irvin was the first captain of the Black Hawks and began his coaching career with the club as a player-coach late in the 1928–29 season.

Building Blocks – After pro hockey died on the Coast, the NHL claimed the Cup, welcomed dozens of superstars into the fold, added three more U.S.-based teams and set its sights on the future.

With American expansion proving successful, the NHL prepared to add three more U.S. teams for the 1926–27 season. Much of that growth was at the expense of the Western Hockey League which, lacking the larger, richer markets of the east, closed its doors. The NHL's new Chicago franchise, the Black Hawks, bought the entire roster of the WHL's Portland Rosebuds. Similarly, the Victoria Cougars were sold to eastern interests and joined the NHL in Michigan as the Detroit Cougars.

The Boston Bruins acquired defenseman Eddie Shore from the Edmonton Eskimos, while the newly formed New York Rangers used such WHL stars as Frank Boucher and brothers Bill and Bun Cook to hit the ground running in the NHL. Conn Smythe was originally hired to build, coach and manage the Rangers, but a clash with management saw him ousted in favor of WHL impresario Lester Patrick. Smythe bought the Toronto St. Patricks later in the 1926–27 season and renamed them the Maple Leafs.

With league membership now at 10 teams, the NHL was split into Canadian and American Divisions. Boston, Pittsburgh, Chicago, Detroit and the Rangers comprised the American Division, while Ottawa, Toronto, the Montreal Maroons and Canadiens and, oddly enough, the New York Americans made up the Canadian Division. The top three teams from each division would make the playoffs, with the first-place teams earning a bye into their division finals.

The Rangers were first in the American Division, but Boston beat Chicago before upsetting New York to become the first U.S.-based NHL team to reach the Stanley Cup finals. Ottawa won the Canadian Division, then beat the Bruins to claim their fourth Cup title of the decade.

Leaders, 1926-27

GOALS

Name, Team	G
Bill Cook, NYR	33
Babe Dye, Chi.	25
Howie Morenz, Mtl.	25
Billy Burch, NYA	19
Harry Oliver, Bos.	18
Dick Irvin, Chi.	18
Frank Fredrickson, Det./Bos.	18
Cy Denneny, Ott.	17
Nels Stewart, Mtl.M.	17
Four tied with	16

ASSISTS

Name, Team	A
Dick Irvin, Chi.	18
Frank Boucher, NYR	15
Ace Bailey, Tor.	13
Frank Fredrickson, Det./Bos.	13
King Clancy, Ott.	10
Lionel Conacher, Pit./NYA	9
Bun Cook, NYR	9
Seven tied with	

GOALIE WINS

Name, Team	W
Alex Connell, Ott.	30
George Hainsworth, Mtl.	28
Lorne Chabot, NYR	22
Clint Benedict, Mtl.M.	20
Hugh Lehman, Chi.	19
Jake Forbes, NYA	17
Hal Winkler, NYR/Bos.	15
John Ross Roach, Tor.	15
Roy Worters, Pit.	15
Hap Holmes, Det.	11

SHUTOUTS

Name, Team	SO
George Hainsworth, Mtl.	14
Clint Benedict, Mtl.M.	13
Alex Connell, Ott.	13
Lorne Chabot, NYR	10
Jake Forbes, NYA	8
Hal Winkler, NYR/Bos.	6
Hap Holmes, Det.	6
Hugh Lehman, Chi.	5
John Ross Roach, Tor.	4
Roy Worters, Pit.	4

PLAYOFF GOALS

Name, Team	G
Cy Denneny, Ott.	5
Harry Oliver, Bos.	4
Frank Finnigan, Ott.	3
Percy Galbraith, Bos.	3
Jimmy Herberts, Bos.	3
Dick Irvin, Chi.	2
Frank Fredrickson, Bos.	2
16 tied with	1

PLAYOFF ASSISTS

Name, Team	A
Percy Galbraith, Bos.	3
George Hay, Chi.	2
Harry Oliver, Bos.	2
Frank Fredrickson, Bos.	2
Eddie Rodden, Chi.	1
Clarence Abel, NYR	1
Frank Nighbor, Ott.	1
Hec Kilrea, Ott.	1
King Clancy, Ott.	1
Eddie Shore, Bos.	1

PLAYOFF GOALIE WINS

Name, Team	W
Alex Connell, Ott.	3
Hal Winkler, Bos.	2
George Hainsworth, Mtl.	1

PLAYOFF SHUTOUTS

Name, Team	SO
Alex Connell, Ott.	2
Hal Winkler, Bos.	2
Lorne Chabot, NYR	1
George Hainsworth, Mtl.	1

1927 Playoffs

QUARTER-FINALS

Mar.	29	Montreal	1	at	Mtl. Maroons	1
Mar.	31	Mtl. Maroons	0	at	Montreal	1 OT

Montreal won total-goals series 2–1

Mar.	29	Boston	6	vs	Chicago	1 *
Mar.	31	Chicago	4	at	Boston	4

* played in New York

Boston won total-goals series 10–5

SEMI-FINALS

Apr.	2	Ottawa	4	at	Montreal	0
Apr.	4	Montreal	1	at	Ottawa	1

Ottawa won total-goals series 5–1

Apr.	2	NY Rangers	0	at	Boston	0
Apr.	4	Boston	3	at	NY Rangers	1

Boston won total-goals series 3–1

FINALS

Apr.	7	Ottawa	0	at	Boston	0 OT
Apr.	9	Ottawa	3	at	Boston	1
Apr.	11	Boston	1	at	Ottawa	1 OT
Apr.	13	Boston	1	at	Ottawa	3

Ottawa won best-of-five series 2-0-2

1926-27 – Ottawa Senators – Alex Connell, King Clancy, Georges Boucher (Captain), Ed Gorman, Frank Finnigan, Alex Smith, Hec Kilrea, Hooley Smith, Cy Denneny, Frank Nighbor, Jack Adams, Milt Halliday, Dave Gill (Manager/Coach).

TROPHY WINNERS

Trophy	Awarded For	Winner	Team
Hart	MVP	Herb Gardiner	Mtl.
Vezina	Fewest Goals Against	George Hainsworth	Mtl.
Byng	Gentlemanly Conduct	Billy Burch	NYA

NHL NOTEBOOK

TRANSACTIONS

- May 4, 1926 – NHL Board of Governors purchased the contracts of all players in the Western Hockey League for $258,000. Most of the former Portland players were sold to the expansion Chicago Black Hawks, and the Victoria players were sold to expansion Detroit.
- Aug. 20, 1926 – Boston Bruins purchased Eddie Shore from the Edmonton Eskimos of the WHL.
- Aug. 23, 1926 – Montreal Canadiens purchased goaltender George Hainsworth from the Saskatoon Crescents of the WHL.
- Oct. 18, 1926 – New York Rangers purchased brothers Bill and Bun Cook from the Saskatoon Crescents of the WHL.

RECORDS

- Dec. 14, 1926 – Ottawa's David Gill extended his NHL record for best start by a rookie coach to 9-0-1 when the Senators beat the Americans 2-0 in New York.
- Mar. 3, 1927 – Ottawa set a new NHL record for most wins in a season, with their 25th of the year, a 2-1 victory at Pittsburgh. The Senators broke the record of 24 wins, set by Ottawa in 1925-26, and finished the season with 30 wins.
- Mar. 19, 1927 – Montreal Canadiens became the first team in NHL history to shut out the same opponent four straight times, with a 5-0 win over the visiting Montreal Maroons.
- Chicago's Dick Irvin set an NHL record with 18 assists during the season.

MILESTONES

- Mar. 19, 1927 – Chicago's Cecil "Babe" Dye became just the second player in NHL history to score 200 career goals in a 3-2 win at Pittsburgh.
- Mar. 26, 1927 – Ottawa's Alex Connell became the first goaltender in NHL history to win 30 games in a season, when the Senators beat the Canadiens 3-2 in Montreal, in their final game of the 1926-27 season.
- Mar. 31, 1927 – Montreal's Howie Morenz scored at 12:05 of overtime as the Canadiens beat the Montreal Maroons 1-0 in the first all NHL Stanley Cup playoff overtime game ever played.
- Apr. 2, 1927 – New York Rangers' Lorne Chabot became the first rookie NHL goalie to record a shutout in his first playoff game, when he and Bruins' Hal Winkler traded shutouts in a scoreless tie, in game one of the Stanley Cup semi-finals.

1927-28

Stanley Cup • New York Rangers

FINAL STANDINGS

CANADIAN DIVISION							
Team	GP	W	L	T	GF	GA	PTS
Montreal	44	26	11	7	116	48	59
Mtl. Maroons	44	24	14	6	96	77	54
Ottawa	44	20	14	10	78	57	50
Toronto	44	18	18	8	89	88	44
NY Americans	44	11	27	6	63	128	28
AMERICAN DIVISION							
Team	GP	W	L	T	GF	GA	PTS
Boston	44	20	13	11	77	70	51
New York	44	19	16	9	94	79	47
Pittsburgh	44	19	17	8	67	76	46
Detroit	44	19	19	6	88	79	44
Chicago	44	7	34	3	68	134	17

LEADING SCORERS

Player	Club	GP	G	A	PTS	PIM
Howie Morenz	Montreal	43	33	18	51	66
Aurel Joliat	Montreal	44	28	11	39	105
Frank Boucher	NY Rangers	44	23	12	35	15
George Hay	Detroit	42	22	13	35	20
Nels Stewart	Mtl. Maroons	41	27	7	34	104
Art Gagne	Montreal	44	20	10	30	75
Bun Cook	NY Rangers	44	14	14	28	45
Bill Carson	Toronto	32	20	6	26	36
Frank Finnigan	Ottawa	38	20	5	25	34
Bill Cook	NY Rangers	43	18	6	24	42
Duke Keats	Det./Chi.	37	14	10	24	61
Hec Kilrea	Ottawa	43	19	4	23	66
Hib Milks	Pittsburgh	44	18	3	21	32
Mickey MacKay	Chicago	36	17	4	21	23
Johnny Sheppard	Detroit	44	10	10	20	40
Jimmy Herberts	Bos./Tor.	43	15	4	19	62
Normie Himes	NY Americans	44	14	5	19	22
Hooley Smith	Mtl. Maroons	34	14	5	19	72
Harry Oliver	Boston	43	13	5	18	20

LEADING GOALTENDERS

Goaltender	Club	GPI	MINS	GA	SO	AVG
George Hainsworth	Montreal	44	2730	48	13	1.05
Alex Connell	Ottawa	44	2760	57	15	1.24
Hal Winkler	Boston	44	2780	70	15	1.51
Roy Worters	Pittsburgh	44	2740	76	11	1.66
Clint Benedict	Mtl. Maroons	44	2690	76	7	1.70
Hap Holmes	Detroit	44	2740	79	11	1.73
Lorne Chabot	NY Rangers	44	2730	79	11	1.74
John Ross Roach	Toronto	43	2690	88	4	1.96
Joe Miller	NYA/NYR	28	1721	77	5	2.68
Charlie Gardiner	Chicago	40	2420	114	3	2.83

LEADING PLAYOFF SCORERS

Player	Club	GP	G	A	PTS	PIM
Frank Boucher	NY Rangers	9	7	3	10	2
Bill Cook	NY Rangers	9	2	3	5	26
Nels Stewart	Mtl. Maroons	9	2	2	4	13
Hooley Smith	Mtl. Maroons	9	2	1	3	23
Merlyn Phillips	Mtl. Maroons	9	2	1	3	9
Bun Cook	NY Rangers	9	2	1	3	10
Murray Murdoch	NY Rangers	9	2	1	3	12
Eight players tied with						2

LEADING PLAYOFF GOALTENDERS

Goaltender	Club	GPI	MINS	GA	SO	AVG
Clint Benedict	Mtl. Maroons	9	555	8	4	0.86
Joe Miller	NY Rangers	3	180	3	1	1.00
Lorne Chabot	NY Rangers	6	321	8	1	1.50

The combination of Bun Cook (left), Frank Boucher (center) and Bill Cook (right) gave the New York Rangers the NHL's first great forward line. The Cook brothers were skilled in the art of scoring by Newsy Lalonde when they played together with Saskatoon of the Western Canada Hockey League. Boucher became the NHL's premier passer.

THE NHL WAS NOW HOCKEY'S undisputed major professional league and business was booming. As a sign of the league's growing confidence, it did away with salary cap restrictions and increased the transfer fee for players on waivers from $2,500 to $5,000. There was, however, one cause for concern. The powerhouse Ottawa Senators, playing in what was now the league's smallest market, were losing money despite their Stanley Cup success, and were forced to sell Hooley Smith to the Montreal Maroons.

Broadway Banquet – Morenz feasted on NHL opponents by leading the league in goals, assists and points, but only the New York Rangers had a pair of Cooks with the recipe for Stanley Cup success.

Stars from the NHL's early days were now retired or reaching the ends of their careers and a new generation of superstars was taking their place. The New York Rangers had Frank Boucher and Bill and Bun Cook. Boston boasted Eddie Shore, Dit Clapper and Cooney Weiland. The Maroons would soon team Hooley Smith with Nels Stewart and Babe Siebert to form the powerful S Line, but the Montreal Canadiens had the greatest star of all in Howie Morenz.

Morenz led the NHL in scoring in 1927–28 with 33 goals and 18 assists in the 44-game regular season and won the Hart Trophy as the Canadiens finished first in the Canadian Division. The Habs were upset, however, by the rival Maroons in the playoffs.

In the American Division, Boston finished first, but the second-place Rangers beat the Pittsburgh Pirates and eliminated the Bruins to advance to the Stanley Cup finals. Because a circus was booked into Madison Square Garden, all five games of the series were played at the Montreal Forum. The second game provided a legendary moment when 44-year-old Ranger coach Lester Patrick took over in goal after an injury to Lorne Chabot. Patrick's Rangers won the game 2–1 in overtime and went on to become only the second American team (after the 1917 Seattle Metropolitans) to win the Stanley Cup with a victory in the full five games.

Leaders, 1927-28

GOALS

Name, Team	G
Howie Morenz, Mtl.	33
Aurel Joliat, Mtl.	28
Nels Stewart, Mtl.M.	27
Frank Boucher, NYR	23
George Hay, Det.	22
Bill Carson, Tor.	20
Frank Finnigan, Ott.	20
Art Gagne, Mtl.	20
Hec Kilrea, Ott.	19
Bill Cook, NYR	18
Hib Milks, Pit.	18

ASSISTS

Name, Team	A
Howie Morenz, Mtl.	18
Bun Cook, NYR	14
George Hay, Det.	13
Frank Boucher, NYR	12
Sylvio Mantha, Mtl.	11
Aurel Joliat, Mtl.	11
Duke Keats, Det./Chi.	10
Art Gagne, Mtl.	10
Johnny Sheppard, Det.	10
Babe Siebert, Mtl.M.	9
Frank Fredrickson, Bos./Pit.	8
Nels Stewart, Mtl.M.	8

GOALIE WINS

Name, Team	W
George Hainsworth, Mtl.	26
Clint Benedict, Mtl.M.	24
Alex Connell, Ott.	20
Hal Winkler, Bos.	20
Lorne Chabot, NYR	19
Hap Holmes, Det.	19
Roy Worters, Pit.	19
John Ross Roach, Tor.	18
Joe Miller, NYA/NYR	8
Charlie Gardiner, Chi.	6

SHUTOUTS

Name, Team	SO
Alex Connell, Ott.	15
Hal Winkler, Bos.	15
George Hainsworth, Mtl.	13
Lorne Chabot, NYR	11
Hap Holmes, Det.	11
Roy Worters, Pit.	11
Clint Benedict, Mtl.M.	7
Joe Miller, NYA/NYR	5
John Ross Roach, Tor.	4
Charlie Gardiner, Chi.	3

PLAYOFF GOALS

Name, Team	G
Frank Boucher, NYR	7
Harry Oliver, Bos.	2
Rodger Smith, Pit.	2
Bill Cook, NYR	2
Nels Stewart, Mtl.M.	2
Hooley Smith, Mtl.M.	2
Merlyn Phillips, Mtl.M.	2
Bun Cook, NYR	2
Murray Murdoch, NYR	2
Babe Siebert, Mtl.M.	2

PLAYOFF ASSISTS

Name, Team	A
Frank Boucher, NYR	3
Bill Cook, NYR	3
Nels Stewart, Mtl.M.	2
Dunc Munro, Mtl.M.	2
14 tied with	1

PLAYOFF GOALIE WINS

Name, Team	W
Clint Benedict, Mtl.M.	5
Joe Miller, NYR	2
Lorne Chabot, NYR	2
Lester Patrick, NYR	1
Roy Worters, Pit.	1

PLAYOFF SHUTOUTS

Name, Team	SO
Clint Benedict, Mtl.M.	4
Joe Miller, NYR	1
Lorne Chabot, NYR	1

1928 Playoffs

QUARTER-FINALS

Date		Team	Score		Team	Score	
Mar.	27	Mtl. Maroons	1	at	Ottawa	0	
Mar.	29	Ottawa	1	at	Mtl. Maroons	2	

Mtl. Maroons won total-goals series 3–1

Date		Team	Score		Team	Score	
Mar.	27	Pittsburgh	0	at	NY Rangers	4	
Mar.	29	Pittsburgh	4	at	NY Rangers	2	

NY Rangers won total-goals series 6–4

SEMI-FINALS

Date		Team	Score		Team	Score	
Mar.	31	Montreal	2	at	Mtl. Maroons	2	
Apr.	3	Mtl. Maroons	1	at	Montreal	0	OT

Mtl. Maroons won total-goals series 3–2

Date		Team	Score		Team	Score	
Mar.	31	Boston	1	at	NY Rangers	1	
Apr.	3	NY Rangers	4	at	Boston	1	

NY Rangers won total-goals series 5–2

FINALS

Date		Team	Score		Team	Score	
Apr.	5	NY Rangers	0	at	Mtl. Maroons	2	
Apr.	7	NY Rangers	2	at	Mtl. Maroons	1	OT
Apr.	10	NY Rangers	0	at	Mtl. Maroons	2	
Apr.	12	NY Rangers	1	at	Mtl. Maroons	0	
Apr.	14	NY Rangers	2	at	Mtl. Maroons	1	

NY Rangers won best-of-five series 3–2

1927-28 – New York Rangers – Lorne Chabot, Clarence Abel, Leo Bourgeault, Ching Johnson, Bill Cook (Captain), Bun Cook, Frank Boucher, Bill Boyd, Murray Murdoch, Paul Thompson, Alex Gray, Joe Miller, Patsy Callighen, Lester Patrick (Manager/Coach), Harry Westerby (Trainer).

TROPHY WINNERS

Trophy	Awarded For	Winner	Team
Hart	MVP	Howie Morenz	Mtl.
Vezina	Fewest Goals Against	George Hainsworth	Mtl.
Byng	Gentlemanly Conduct	Frank Boucher	NYR

NHL NOTEBOOK

TRANSACTIONS

- Sept. 26, 1927 – Detroit claimed Larry Aurie from London (of the Canadian Pro League) in the inter-league draft.
- Oct. 4, 1927 – Detroit purchased Reg Noble from the Montreal Maroons for $7,500.
- Oct 7, 1927 – Montreal Maroons obtained Reg "Hooley" Smith from Ottawa in exchange for Punch Broadbent and $22,000.
- Dec. 23, 1927 – Boston purchased Ralph "Cooney" Weiland from the Minneapolis Millers of the AHA.

RECORDS

- Feb. 18, 1928 – Alex Connell recorded his sixth consecutive shutout, an NHL record, in a 1-0 win over the Montreal Canadiens, in Ottawa.
- Howie Morenz became the first player in NHL history to score 50 points in a season, and finishes with 51, to lead the league in scoring.
- Apr. 10, 1928 – Montreal Maroons' goalie Clint Benedict recorded his 15th (and final) career playoff shutout, with a 2-0 win over the visiting Rangers, in game three of their Stanley Cup championship series. His playoff shutout record stood until Patrick Roy broke it in 2001.
- Apr. 14, 1928 – NY Rangers beat the Montreal Maroons 2-1 in game five of the finals, to become the 1928 Stanley Cup Champions. It was the Rangers' first Stanley Cup, after only two seasons in the NHL.

MILESTONES

- May 17, 1927 – Jack Adams was named the general manager/coach of the Detroit Cougars, replacing Duke Keats.
- Sept. 24, 1927 – NHL passed new rules to allow forward passing in the defensive and neutral zones.
- Mar. 15, 1928 – Hal Winkler became the first goaltender in Boston Bruins history to win 20 games in one season with a 3-1 win against the Black Hawks at Chicago.
- Mar. 22, 1928 – Ottawa's Alex Connell became the first goaltender in NHL history to record 50 career shutouts, when his 15th of the season gave the Senators a 5-0 victory over the visiting New York Americans.

1928-29

Stanley Cup • Boston Bruins

FINAL STANDINGS

Team	GP	W	L	T	GF	GA	PTS
CANADIAN DIVISION							
Montreal	44	22	7	15	71	43	59
NY Americans	44	19	13	12	53	53	50
Toronto	44	21	18	5	85	69	47
Ottawa	44	14	17	13	54	67	41
Mtl. Maroons	44	15	20	9	67	65	39
AMERICAN DIVISION							
Boston	44	26	13	5	89	52	57
New York	44	21	13	10	72	65	52
Detroit	44	19	16	9	72	63	47
Pittsburgh	44	9	27	8	46	80	26
Chicago	44	7	29	8	33	85	22

LEADING SCORERS

Player	Club	GP	G	A	PTS	PIM
Ace Bailey	Toronto	44	22	10	32	78
Nels Stewart	Mtl. Maroons	44	21	8	29	74
Carson Cooper	Detroit	43	18	9	27	14
Howie Morenz	Montreal	42	17	10	27	47
Andy Blair	Toronto	44	12	15	27	41
Frank Boucher	NY Rangers	44	10	16	26	8
Harry Oliver	Boston	43	17	6	23	24
Bill Cook	NY Rangers	43	15	8	23	41
Jimmy Ward	Mtl. Maroons	43	14	8	22	46
Frank Finnigan	Ottawa	44	15	4	19	71
Dutch Gainor	Boston	44	14	5	19	30
Danny Cox	Toronto	42	12	7	19	14
Eddie Shore	Boston	39	12	7	19	96
Bill Carson	Tor./Bos.	43	11	8	19	55
George Hay	Detroit	39	11	8	19	14
Hooley Smith	Mtl. Maroons	41	10	9	19	120
Bun Cook	NY Rangers	43	13	5	18	70
Cooney Weiland	Boston	42	11	7	18	16
Aurel Joliat	Montreal	44	12	5	17	59
Paul Thompson	NY Rangers	44	10	7	17	38
Gerry Lowrey	Tor./Pit.	44	5	12	17	30

LEADING GOALTENDERS

Goaltender	Club	GPI	MINS	GA	SO	AVG
George Hainsworth	Montreal	44	2800	43	22	0.92
Tiny Thompson	Boston	44	2710	52	12	1.15
Roy Worters	NY Americans	38	2390	46	13	1.15
Dolly Dolson	Detroit	44	2750	63	10	1.37
John Ross Roach	NY Rangers	44	2760	65	13	1.41
Alex Connell	Ottawa	44	2820	67	7	1.43
Clint Benedict	Mtl. Maroons	37	2300	57	11	1.49

LEADING PLAYOFF SCORERS

Player	Club	GP	G	A	PTS	PIM
Butch Keeling	NY Rangers	6	3	0	3	2
Andy Blair	Toronto	4	3	0	3	2
Ace Bailey	Toronto	4	1	2	3	4
Cooney Weiland	Boston	5	2	0	2	2
Bill Carson	Boston	5	2	0	2	8
Dutch Gainor	Boston	5	2	0	2	4
Eddie Shore	Boston	5	1	1	2	28
Harry Oliver	Boston	5	1	1	2	8
Art Smith	Toronto	4	1	1	2	8
Aurel Joliat	Montreal	3	1	1	2	10
Paul Thompson	NY Rangers	6	0	2	2	6

LEADING PLAYOFF GOALTENDERS

Goaltender	Club	GPI	MINS	GA	SO	AVG
Tiny Thompson	Boston	5	300	3	3	0.60
John Ross Roach	NY Rangers	6	392	5	3	0.77
Lorne Chabot	Toronto	4	242	5	0	1.24
George Hainsworth	Montreal	3	180	5	0	1.67

Roy Worters joined the New York Americans in 1928–29 and posted a 1.15 goals-against average and 13 shutouts to lead the team into the playoffs after a last-place finish the year before. As a result, Worters became the first goaltender to win the Hart Trophy as the NHL's most valuable player. He won the Vezina Trophy in 1930–31.

IN 1919–20, THE LEAGUE'S FOUR CLUBS had averaged nearly five goals each per game, but during the ensuing decade an emphasis on defense meant only the top-scoring teams approached three per game. But 1928–29 was the year the NHL reached its offensive low point—the 10 teams scored fewer than 1.5 goals per game, with last-place Chicago netting just 33 in 44 games. Ace Bailey of the Toronto Maple Leafs led the league with just 22 goals and 10 assists, and Nels Stewart of the Maroons, with 21, was the only other player in the league to score more than 20.

The Bears' Den – Toronto had an Ace in Bailey and the Habs had a zero-hero in Hainsworth, but the Bruins had a giant netminder in Tiny Thompson, who back-stopped them to the Cup.

Meanwhile, all but two of the league's first-string goalies recorded at least 10 shutouts. The Montreal Canadiens' George Hainsworth led the way, setting a record that still stands with 22 shutouts, and posting a remarkable 0.92 goals-against average on his way to his third consecutive Vezina Trophy win.

The playoff format was altered this year. The top three teams from both the Canadian and American divisions still made the playoffs, but each second- and third-place finisher would meet its counterpart from the other division in a two-game, total-goals series. The winners would compete in a best-of three-series for a berth in the Stanley Cup finals. Meanwhile, the two first-place teams played a best-of-five series for the other spot in the finals.

The Canadiens and Bruins finished atop their respective divisions and engaged in a close-checking semi-final. Boston recorded 1–0 victories in each of the first two games, as Tiny Thompson turned away every shot he faced and Cooney Weiland scored both Bruin goals. They completed the sweep with a 3–2 victory in game three. The Rangers knocked off the Americans and then the Toronto Maple Leafs to provide Boston's opposition in the first all-American Stanley Cup finals. The best-of-three set went to the Bruins in two straight as Boston celebrated its first Stanley Cup victory.

Leaders, 1928-29

GOALS

Name, Team	G
Ace Bailey, Tor.	22
Nels Stewart, Mtl.M.	21
Carson Cooper, Det.	18
Howie Morenz, Mtl.	17
Harry Oliver, Bos.	17
Bill Cook, NYR	15
Frank Finnigan, Ott.	15
Jimmy Ward, Mtl.M.	14
Dutch Gainor, Bos.	14
Bob Connors, Det.	13
Bun Cook, NYR	13
King Clancy, Ott.	13

ASSISTS

Name, Team	A
Frank Boucher, NYR	16
Andy Blair, Tor.	15
Gerry Lowrey, Tor./Pit.	12
Howie Morenz, Mtl.	10
Ace Bailey, Tor.	10
Hooley Smith, Mtl.M.	9
Carson Cooper, Det.	9
George Hay, Det.	8
Bill Cook, NYR	8
Jimmy Ward, Mtl.M.	8
Bill Carson, Tor./Bos.	8

GOALIE WINS

Name, Team	W
Tiny Thompson, Bos.	26
George Hainsworth, Mtl.	22
John Ross Roach, NYR	21
Lorne Chabot, Tor.	20
Dolly Dolson, Det.	19
Roy Worters, NYA	16
Clint Benedict, Mtl.M.	14
Alex Connell, Ott.	14
Joe Miller, Pit.	9
Charlie Gardiner, Chi.	7

SHUTOUTS

Name, Team	SO
George Hainsworth, Mtl.	22
Roy Worters, NYA	13
John Ross Roach, NYR	13
Lorne Chabot, Tor.	12
Tiny Thompson, Bos.	12
Clint Benedict, Mtl.M.	11
Joe Miller, Pit.	11
Dolly Dolson, Det.	10
Alex Connell, Ott.	7
Charlie Gardiner, Chi.	5

PLAYOFF GOALS

Name, Team	G
Andy Blair, Tor.	3
Butch Keeling, NYR	3
Cooney Weiland, Bos.	2
Bill Carson, Bos.	2
Dutch Gainor, Bos.	2
14 tied with	1

PLAYOFF ASSISTS

Name, Team	A
Ace Bailey, Tor.	2
Paul Thompson, NYR	2
Aurel Joliat, Mtl.	1
Art Smith, Tor.	1
Danny Cox, Tor.	1
Eddie Shore, Bos.	1
Harry Oliver, Bos.	1
Lionel Hitchman, Bos.	1

PLAYOFF GOALIE WINS

Name, Team	W
Tiny Thompson, Bos.	5
John Ross Roach, NYR	3
Lorne Chabot, Tor.	2

PLAYOFF SHUTOUTS

Name, Team	SO
Tiny Thompson, Bos.	3
John Ross Roach, NYR	3
Roy Worters, NYA	1

1929 Playoffs

SERIES A - SEMI-FINALS

Mar.	19	Montreal	0	at	Boston	1
Mar.	21	Montreal	0	at	Boston	1
Mar.	23	Boston	3	at	Montreal	2

Boston won best-of-five series 3–0

SERIES B AND C - QUARTER-FINALS

Mar.	19	NY Rangers	0	at	NY Americans	0
Mar.	21	NY Americans	0	at	NY Rangers	1 2OT

NY Rangers won total-goals series 1–0

Mar.	19	Toronto	3	at	Detroit	1
Mar.	21	Detroit	1	at	Toronto	4

Toronto won total-goals series 7–2

SERIES D - SEMI-FINALS

Mar.	24	Toronto	0	at	NY Rangers	1
Mar.	26	NY Rangers	2	at	Toronto	1 OT

NY Rangers won best-of-three series 2–0

SERIES E - FINALS

Mar.	28	NY Rangers	0	at	Boston	2
Mar.	29	Boston	2	at	NY Rangers	1

Boston won best-of-three series 2–0

1928-29 – Boston Bruins – Tiny Thompson, Eddie Shore, Lionel Hitchman (Captain), Percy Galbraith, Frank Fredrickson, Mickey Mackay, Red Green, Dutch Gainor, Harry Oliver, Eddie Rodden, Dit Clapper, Cooney Weiland, Lloyd Klein, Cy Denneny, Bill Carson, George Owen, Myles Lane, Art Ross (Manager/Coach), Win Green (Trainer).

TROPHY WINNERS

Trophy	Awarded For	Winner	Team
Hart	MVP	Roy Worters	NYA
Vezina	Fewest Goals Against	George Hainsworth	Mtl.
Byng	Gentlemanly Conduct	Frank Boucher	NYR

NHL NOTEBOOK

TRANSACTIONS

- May 14, 1928 – Detroit claimed Herbie Lewis from Duluth (AHA) in the inter-league draft.
- July 17, 1928 – Toronto signed Joe Primeau.
- Oct. 17, 1928 – Toronto acquired goaltender Lorne Chabot and Alex Gray from the New York Rangers in exchange for Butch Keeling and John Ross Roach.
- Jan. 20, 1929 – Toronto signed Red Horner.

RECORDS

- Dec.18, 1928 – Goaltender George Hainsworth set an NHL record with his fifth straight road shutout in the Canadiens' 5-0 win at Chicago.
- Jan. 8, 1929 – Boston's Harry Oliver set an NHL record for fastest goal from the start of a game, when he scored ten seconds into a 5-2 win over Toronto.
- Jan. 29, 1929 – Montreal's George Hainsworth set an NHL record with his 6th shutout of the month, a 1-0 win over the New York Americans.
- Feb. 28, 1929 – Chicago Black Hawks were shutout for the 8th straight game, an NHL record, when Rangers' goalie John Ross Roach and Black Hawks' Chuck Gardiner dueled to a 0-0 tie in Chicago.

MILESTONES

- Sept. 22, 1928 – NHL passed new rules changing overtime from 10 minutes of sudden-death, to a full 10 minute extra period (without sudden-death) if games were tied at the end of regulation.
- Feb. 9, 1929 – Maroons' Clint Benedict became the NHL's all-time leader in shutouts, when the 55th of his career moved him one ahead of Alex Connell.
- Mar. 2, 1929 – George Hainsworth became the first NHL goaltender to record 20 shutouts in one season, when the Montreal Canadiens beat the visiting Boston Bruins 3-0.

1929-30

Stanley Cup • Montreal Canadiens

FINAL STANDINGS

Team	GP	W	L	T	GF	GA	PTS
CANADIAN DIVISION							
Mtl. Maroons	44	23	16	5	141	114	51
Montreal	44	21	14	9	142	114	51
Ottawa	44	21	15	8	138	118	50
Toronto	44	17	21	6	116	124	40
NY Americans	44	14	25	5	113	161	33
AMERICAN DIVISION							
Boston	44	38	5	1	179	98	77
Chicago	44	21	18	5	117	111	47
New York	44	17	17	10	136	143	44
Detroit	44	14	24	6	117	133	34
Pittsburgh	44	5	36	3	102	185	13

LEADING SCORERS

Player	Club	GP	G	A	PTS	PIM
Cooney Weiland	Boston	44	43	30	73	27
Frank Boucher	NY Rangers	42	26	36	62	16
Dit Clapper	Boston	44	41	20	61	48
Bill Cook	NY Rangers	44	29	30	59	56
Hec Kilrea	Ottawa	44	36	22	58	72
Nels Stewart	Mtl. Maroons	44	39	16	55	81
Howie Morenz	Montreal	44	40	10	50	72
Normie Himes	NY Americans	44	28	22	50	15
Joe Lamb	Ottawa	44	29	20	49	119
Dutch Gainor	Boston	42	18	31	49	39
Ace Bailey	Toronto	43	22	21	43	69
Bun Cook	NY Rangers	43	24	18	42	55
King Clancy	Ottawa	44	17	23	40	83
Baldy Cotton	Toronto	41	21	17	38	47
Frank Finnigan	Ottawa	43	21	15	36	46
Carson Cooper	Detroit	44	18	18	36	14
Ebbie Goodfellow	Detroit	44	17	17	34	54
Pit Lepine	Montreal	44	24	9	33	47
Marty Barry	Boston	44	18	15	33	34
George Hay	Detroit	44	18	15	33	8
Babe Siebert	Mtl. Maroons	39	14	19	33	94

LEADING GOALTENDERS

Goaltender	Club	GPI	MINS	GA	SO	AVG
Tiny Thompson	Boston	44	2680	98	3	2.19
Flat Walsh	Mtl. Maroons	30	1897	74	2	2.34
George Hainsworth	Montreal	42	2680	108	4	2.42
Charlie Gardiner	Chicago	44	2750	111	3	2.42
Alex Connell	Ottawa	44	2780	118	3	2.55
Lorne Chabot	Toronto	42	2620	113	6	2.59

LEADING PLAYOFF SCORERS

Player	Club	GP	G	A	PTS	PIM
Marty Barry	Boston	6	3	3	6	14
Cooney Weiland	Boston	6	1	5	6	2
Dit Clapper	Boston	6	4	0	4	4
Nick Wasnie	Montreal	6	2	2	4	12
Pit Lepine	Montreal	6	2	2	4	6
Percy Galbraith	Boston	6	1	3	4	8
Albert Leduc	Montreal	6	1	3	4	8
Murray Murdoch	NY Rangers	4	3	0	3	6
Howie Morenz	Montreal	6	3	0	3	10
Harry Oliver	Boston	6	2	1	3	6
Sylvio Mantha	Montreal	6	2	1	3	18
Butch Keeling	NY Rangers	4	0	3	3	8

LEADING PLAYOFF GOALTENDERS

Goaltender	Club	GPI	MINS	GA	SO	AVG
George Hainsworth	Montreal	6	481	6	3	0.75
John Ross Roach	NY Rangers	4	309	7	0	1.36
Tiny Thompson	Boston	6	432	12	0	1.67
Flat Walsh	Mtl. Maroons	4	312	11	1	2.12

Bruins great Eddie Shore is rivaled only by Doug Harvey and Bobby Orr as the greatest defenseman in hockey history. Shore came to personify the rough and tumble NHL game of the late 1920s and 1930s. A supremely talented player with a temper to match, he outscored all fellow defensemen during his era and trailed only Red Horner in terms of penalties.

After the previous season's offensive drought, the NHL made significant rule changes to increase scoring in 1929–30. The most important new rule allowed forward passing in the offensive zone—previously it had only been allowed in a team's neutral and defensive zones. But the changes quickly proved too effective, as forwards began to station themselves in front of the opposition goal and wait for passes. So, on December 21, 1929, the NHL legislated that no attacking player would be allowed to precede the puck across the blue line. The modern off-side rule was born.

Les Glorieux – Boston had an .875 winning percentage and a dominating Dynamite Line but losing back-to-back games for the first time all year in the finals handed the title to the Canadiens.

Bruins coach Art Ross had schooled his players well in the new rules and Boston was by far the best team in the NHL, posting a 38–5–1 record for an .875 winning percentage that still remains a league record. Cooney Weiland's league-leading 43 goals nearly doubled Ace Bailey's high of 22 the year before, and his 73 points were by far a new league record. Linemate Dit Clapper had 41 goals, while Dutch Gainor, the third member of the Dynamite Line, recorded 31 assists, second-best in the league. Boston's Tiny Thompson won the Vezina Trophy, though his 2.19 goals-against average was nearly double what it had been the year before. Veteran goaltender Clint Benedict chose to retire from the NHL late in the season after a crude leather facemask failed to adequately protect his broken nose.

The Bruins cruised into the Stanley Cup finals after sweeping the Montreal Maroons to open the playoffs. The Canadiens provided the opposition after beating the Black Hawks and Rangers. Boston was heavily favored, but Montreal swept the best-of-three series, handing the Bruins consecutive losses for the first time all season. Partly as a result of the surprising sweep, the Stanley Cup finals would be increased to a best-of-five affair in the future.

Leaders, 1929-30

GOALS

Name, Team	G
Cooney Weiland, Bos.	43
Dit Clapper, Bos.	41
Howie Morenz, Mtl.	40
Nels Stewart, Mtl.M.	39
Hec Kilrea, Ott.	36
Bill Cook, NYR	29
Joe Lamb, Ott.	29
Normie Himes, NYA	28
Frank Boucher, NYR	26
Bun Cook, NYR	24
Pit Lepine, Mtl.	24

ASSISTS

Name, Team	A
Frank Boucher, NYR	36
Dutch Gainor, Bos.	31
Cooney Weiland, Bos.	30
Bill Cook, NYR	30
King Clancy, Ott.	23
Hec Kilrea, Ott.	22
Normie Himes, NYA	22
Ace Bailey, Tor.	21
Joe Primeau, Tor.	21
Dit Clapper, Bos.	20
Joe Lamb, Ott.	20

GOALIE WINS

Name, Team	W
Tiny Thompson, Bos.	38
Alex Connell, Ott.	21
Charlie Gardiner, Chi.	21
George Hainsworth, Mtl.	20
John Ross Roach, NYR	17
Flat Walsh, Mtl.M.	16
Lorne Chabot, Tor.	16
Bill Beveridge, Det.	14
Roy Worters, NYA/Mon	12
Clint Benedict, Mtl.M.	6

SHUTOUTS

Name, Team	SO
Lorne Chabot, Tor.	6
George Hainsworth, Mtl.	4
Tiny Thompson, Bos.	3
Alex Connell, Ott.	3
Charlie Gardiner, Chi.	3
Flat Walsh, Mtl.M.	2
Roy Worters, NYR/Mtl.	2
Bill Beveridge, Det.	2
John Ross Roach, NYR	1

PLAYOFF GOALS

Name, Team	G
Dit Clapper, Bos.	4
Murray Murdoch, NYR	3
Marty Barry, Bos.	3
Howie Morenz, Mtl.	3
Dunc Munro, Mtl.M.	2
Bun Cook, NYR	2
Nick Wasnie, Mtl.	2
Pit Lepine, Mtl.	2
Harry Oliver, Bos.	2
Sylvio Mantha, Mtl.	2

PLAYOFF ASSISTS

Name, Team	A
Cooney Weiland, Bos.	5
Butch Keeling, NYR	3
Marty Barry, Bos.	3
Percy Galbraith, Bos.	3
Albert Leduc, Mtl.	3
Dave Trottier, Mtl.M.	2
Nick Wasnie, Mtl.	2
Pit Lepine, Mtl.	2
Aurel Joliat, Mtl.	2
George Owen, Bos.	2

PLAYOFF GOALIE WINS

Name, Team	W
George Hainsworth, Mtl.	5
Tiny Thompson, Bos.	3
John Ross Roach, NYR	1
Flat Walsh, Mtl.M.	1

PLAYOFF SHUTOUTS

Name, Team	SO
George Hainsworth, Mtl.	3
Flat Walsh, Mtl.M.	1

1930 Playoffs

SERIES A - SEMI-FINALS

Date	Visitor			Home		
Mar. 20	Boston	2	at	Mtl. Maroons	1	3OT
Mar. 22	Boston	4	at	Mtl. Maroons	2	
Mar. 25	Mtl. Maroons	1	at	Boston	0	2OT
Mar. 27	Mtl. Maroons	1	at	Boston	5	

Boston won best-of-five series 3–1

SERIES B AND C - QUARTER-FINALS

Date	Visitor			Home		
Mar. 23	Montreal	1	at	Chicago	0	
Mar. 26	Chicago	2	at	Montreal	2	3OT

Montreal won total-goals series 3–2

Date	Visitor			Home	
Mar. 20	NY Rangers	1	at	Ottawa	1
Mar. 23	Ottawa	2	at	NY Rangers	5

NY Rangers won total-goals series 6–3

SERIES D - SEMI-FINALS

Date	Visitor			Home		
Mar. 28	NY Rangers	1	at	Montreal	2	4OT
Mar. 30	Montreal	2	at	NY Rangers	0	

Montreal won best-of-three series 2–0

SERIES E - FINALS

Date	Visitor			Home	
Apr. 1	Montreal	3	at	Boston	0
Apr. 3	Boston	3	at	Montreal	4

Montreal won best-of-three series 2–0

1929-30 – Montreal Canadiens – George Hainsworth, Marty Burke, Sylvio Mantha (Captain), Howie Morenz, Bert McCaffrey, Aurel Joliat, Albert Leduc, Pit Lepine, Wildor Larochelle, Nick Wasnie, Gerry Carson, Armand Mondou, Georges Mantha, Gus Rivers, Léo Dandurand (Manager), Cecil Hart (Coach), Ed Dufour (Trainer).

TROPHY WINNERS

Trophy	Awarded For	Winner	Team
Hart	MVP	Nels Stewart	Mtl.M.
Vezina	Fewest Goals Against	Tiny Thompson	Bos.
Byng	Gentlemanly Conduct	Frank Boucher	NYR

NHL NOTEBOOK

TRANSACTIONS

- Apr. 15, 1929 – New York Rangers traded Clarence "Taffy" Abel to Chicago for $15,000.
- May 13, 1929 – Boston claimed Art Chapman from Providence (CAHL) in the inter-league draft.
- Aug. 23, 1929 – Montreal Maroons purchased Archie Wilcox from Detroit.
- Oct. 7, 1929 – Toronto signed Charlie Conacher, who had been playing for the Toronto Marlboros.
- Dec. 6, 1929 – Toronto Maple Leafs signed Harvey "Busher" Jackson.

RECORDS

- Nov. 19, 1929 – Pittsburgh's Johnny McKinnon and Toronto's Hap Day set a new NHL record for most goals in a game by a defenseman. They had four each as Pittsburgh beat Toronto 10-5.
- Dec. 3, 1929 – Boston Bruins began an NHL-record 14-game winning streak (and an NHL-record 22-game home winning streak) with a 3-1 win over the visiting Montreal Canadiens.
- Feb. 18, 1930 – Boston's Tiny Thompson set an NHL record for most wins in a season, when he picked up his 31st victory of the year, in a 3-2 win over the visiting Montreal Canadiens.
- Ralph "Cooney" Wieland set an NHL scoring record with 73 points; Frank Boucher set a new assist mark with 36.

MILESTONES

- Dec. 16, 1929 – The "off-side" rule had its origin at a Board of Governors meeting in Chicago. The new rule stated: "No attacking player shall be allowed to precede the play when entering the opposing defensive zone."
- Jan. 21, 1930 – Boston became the first team in NHL history to score 100 goals in a season, in a 5-1 win over Chicago, at Boston Garden. Cooney Weiland scored the Bruins' 100th goal of the season in their 26th game of the year.
- Feb. 20, 1930 – Montreal Maroons' goalie Clint Benedict became the first goalie to wear a mask in an NHL game, in a 3-3 tie against the New York Americans. Benedict wore the mask temporarily, during an injury.
- Mar. 25, 1930 – Archie Wilcox became the first rookie defenseman in NHL history to score a playoff overtime goal, when he connected at 6:27 of the second overtime as the Maroons took a 1-0 win at Boston, in game three of the Stanley Cup semi-finals.

1930-31

Stanley Cup • Montreal Canadiens

FINAL STANDINGS

Team	GP	W	L	T	GF	GA	PTS
CANADIAN DIVISION							
Montreal	44	26	10	8	129	89	60
Toronto	44	22	13	9	118	99	53
Mtl. Maroons	44	20	18	6	105	106	46
NY Americans	44	18	16	10	76	74	46
Ottawa	44	10	30	4	91	142	24
AMERICAN DIVISION							
Boston	44	28	10	6	143	90	62
Chicago	44	24	17	3	108	78	51
New York	44	19	16	9	106	87	47
Detroit	44	16	21	7	102	105	39
Philadelphia	44	4	36	4	76	184	12

LEADING SCORERS

Player	Club	GP	G	A	PTS	PIM
Howie Morenz	Montreal	39	28	23	51	49
Ebbie Goodfellow	Detroit	44	25	23	48	32
Charlie Conacher	Toronto	37	31	12	43	78
Bill Cook	NY Rangers	43	30	12	42	39
Ace Bailey	Toronto	40	23	19	42	46
Joe Primeau	Toronto	38	9	32	41	18
Nels Stewart	Mtl. Maroons	42	25	14	39	75
Frank Boucher	NY Rangers	44	12	27	39	20
Cooney Weiland	Boston	44	25	13	38	14
Bun Cook	NY Rangers	44	18	17	35	72
Aurel Joliat	Montreal	43	13	22	35	73
Johnny Gottselig	Chicago	42	20	12	32	14
Marty Barry	Boston	44	20	11	31	26
Busher Jackson	Toronto	43	18	13	31	81
Eddie Shore	Boston	44	15	16	31	105
Dit Clapper	Boston	43	22	8	30	50
Art Gagne	Ottawa	44	19	11	30	50
Harry Oliver	Boston	44	16	14	30	18
Bill Touhey	Ottawa	44	15	15	30	8

LEADING GOALTENDERS

Goaltender	Club	GPI	MINS	GA	SO	AVG
Roy Worters	NY Americans	44	2760	74	8	1.61
Charlie Gardiner	Chicago	44	2710	78	12	1.73
John Ross Roach	NY Rangers	44	2760	87	7	1.89
George Hainsworth	Montreal	44	2740	89	8	1.95
Tiny Thompson	Boston	44	2730	90	3	1.98
Lorne Chabot	Toronto	37	2300	80	6	2.09
Dolly Dolson	Detroit	44	2750	105	6	2.29
Dave Kerr	Mtl. Maroons	29	1769	70	1	2.37
Alex Connell	Ottawa	36	2190	110	3	3.01

LEADING PLAYOFF SCORERS

Player	Club	GP	G	A	PTS	PIM
Cooney Weiland	Boston	5	6	3	9	2
Johnny Gagnon	Montreal	10	6	2	8	8
Georges Mantha	Montreal	10	5	1	6	4
Pit Lepine	Montreal	10	4	2	6	6
Stew Adams	Chicago	9	3	3	6	8
Johnny Gottselig	Chicago	9	3	3	6	2
Dit Clapper	Boston	5	2	4	6	4
Nick Wasnie	Montreal	10	4	1	5	8
George Owen	Boston	5	2	3	5	13
Howie Morenz	Montreal	10	1	4	5	10

LEADING PLAYOFF GOALTENDERS

Goaltender	Club	GPI	MINS	GA	SO	AVG
John Ross Roach	NY Rangers	4	240	4	1	1.00
Charlie Gardiner	Chicago	9	638	14	2	1.32
George Hainsworth	Montreal	10	722	21	2	1.75
Tiny Thompson	Boston	5	343	13	0	2.27

Ebbie Goodfellow began his NHL career as a center, but earned greater fame after being converted to defense in his seventh season. A top scorer with Detroit in the early 1930s, he moved to defense in 1935–36 and helped the Red Wings win back-to-back Stanley Cup titles while earning a pair of All-Star selections for himself. He won the Hart Trophy in 1939–40.

The Great Depression began to take its toll on the NHL by the 1930–31 season. Even in the best of times, the Ottawa Senators had been finding the economic going rough. Now, the situation was even worse. Several Senators were sold off prior to the start of the season, most notably the popular King Clancy, who was purchased by the Toronto Maple Leafs for $35,000 and two players. Toronto immediately improved, finishing in second place in the NHL's Canadian Division, while in Ottawa, the Senators slumped to last place.

Mighty Morenz – The NHL's most inventive, influential, creative and charismatic player, Howie Morenz's talents earned him the distinction of being known as "The Babe Ruth of Hockey."

The Pittsburgh Pirates had also been been in trouble for several years, and, after a 5–36–3 season in 1929–30, the franchise was moved to Philadelphia. Renamed the Quakers, the relocated team proved even worse that year as they limped through a 4–36–4 campaign.

At the other end of the spectrum, the Boston Bruins were the NHL's best for the second year in a row, finishing atop the American Division with a 28–10–6 record. League-leading scorer Howie Morenz powered the Montreal Canadiens to top spot in the Canadian Division and earned the Hart Trophy as MVP for the second time.

In a rematch of the previous season's Stanley Cup finals, the Canadiens beat Boston in five games to open the playoffs. The Chicago Black Hawks made their first appearance in the finals after knocking off the Toronto Maple Leafs and the New York Rangers.

The series opened before huge crowds at the Chicago Stadium, where the teams split two games before concluding the series at the Montreal Forum. The Black Hawks won game three before the Canadiens rallied to defend their Cup title by winning the fourth and fifth games.

Leaders, 1930-31

GOALS

Name, Team	G
Charlie Conacher, Tor.	31
Bill Cook, NYR	30
Howie Morenz, Mtl.	28
Nels Stewart, Mtl.M.	25
Ebbie Goodfellow, Det.	25
Cooney Weiland, Bos.	25
Ace Bailey, Tor.	23
Dit Clapper, Bos.	22
Johnny Gottselig, Chi.	20
Marty Barry, Bos.	20

ASSISTS

Name, Team	A
Joe Primeau, Tor.	32
Frank Boucher, NYR	27
Howie Morenz, Mtl.	23
Ebbie Goodfellow, Det.	23
Aurel Joliat, Mtl.	22
Ace Bailey, Tor.	19
Baldy Cotton, Tor.	17
Bun Cook, NYR	17
Eddie Shore, Bos.	16
Bill Touhey, Ott.	15

GOALIE WINS

Name, Team	W
Tiny Thompson, Bos.	28
George Hainsworth, Mtl.	26
Charlie Gardiner, Chi.	24
Lorne Chabot, Tor.	21
John Ross Roach, NYR	19
Roy Worters, NYA	18
Dolly Dolson, Det.	16
Dave Kerr, Mtl.M.	13
Alex Connell, Ott.	10
Flat Walsh, Mtl.M.	7

SHUTOUTS

Name, Team	SO
Charlie Gardiner, Chi.	12
George Hainsworth, Mtl.	8
Roy Worters, NYA	8
John Ross Roach, NYR	7
Lorne Chabot, Tor.	6
Dolly Dolson, Det.	6
Alex Connell, Ott.	3
Tiny Thompson, Bos.	3
Benny Grant, Tor.	2
Flat Walsh, Mtl.M.	2

PLAYOFF GOALS

Name, Team	G
Cooney Weiland, Bos.	6
Johnny Gagnon, Mtl.	6
Georges Mantha, Mtl.	5
Pit Lepine, Mtl.	4
Nick Wasnie, Mtl.	4
Bill Cook, NYR	3
Paul Thompson, NYR	3
Stew Adams, Chi.	3
Johnny Gottselig, Chi.	3
Mush March, Chi.	3

PLAYOFF ASSISTS

Name, Team	A
Dit Clapper, Bos.	4
Howie Morenz, Mtl.	4
Aurel Joliat, Mtl.	4
Hap Day, Tor.	3
Cooney Weiland, Bos.	3
George Owen, Bos.	3
Stew Adams, Chi.	3
Johnny Gottselig, Chi.	3
Tom Cook, Chi.	3
Rosie Couture, Chi.	3

PLAYOFF GOALIE WINS

Name, Team	W
George Hainsworth, Mtl.	6
Charlie Gardiner, Chi.	5
John Ross Roach, NYR	2
Tiny Thompson, Bos.	2

PLAYOFF SHUTOUTS

Name, Team	SO
Charlie Gardiner, Chi.	2
George Hainsworth, Mtl.	2
John Ross Roach, NYR	1

FIRST TEAM ALL-STARS

Name, Team	Position
Howie Morenz, Mtl.	C
Bill Cook, NYR	RW
Aurel Joliat, Mtl.	LW
Eddie Shore, Bos.	D
King Clancy, Tor.	D
Chuck Gardiner, Chi.	G
Lester Patrick, NYR	Coach

SECOND TEAM ALL-STARS

Name, Team	Position
Frank Boucher, NYR	C
Dit Clapper, Bos.	RW
Bun Cook, NYR	LW
Sylvio Mantha, Mtl.	D
Ching Johnson, NYR	D
Tiny Thompson, Bos.	G
Dick Irvin, Tor	Coach

1931 Playoffs

SERIES A - SEMI-FINALS

Mar. 24	Montreal	4	at	Boston	5	OT
Mar. 26	Montreal	1	at	Boston	0	
Mar. 28	Boston	3	at	Montreal	4	OT
Mar. 30	Boston	3	at	Montreal	1	
Apr. 1	Boston	2	at	Montreal	3	OT

Montreal won best-of-five series 3–2

SERIES B AND C - QUARTER-FINALS

Mar. 24	Chicago	2	at	Toronto	2	
Mar. 26	Toronto	1	at	Chicago	2	OT

Chicago won total-goals series 4–3

Mar. 24	Mtl. Maroons	1	at	NY Rangers	5	
Mar. 26	NY Rangers	3	at	Mtl. Maroons	0	

NY Rangers won total-goals series 8–1

SERIES D - SEMI-FINALS

Mar. 29	NY Rangers	0	at	Chicago	2	
Mar. 31	Chicago	1	at	NY Rangers	0	

Chicago won total-goals series 3–0

SERIES E - FINALS

Apr. 3	Montreal	2	at	Chicago	1	
Apr. 5	Montreal	1	at	Chicago	2	2OT
Apr. 9	Chicago	3	at	Montreal	2	3OT
Apr. 11	Chicago	2	at	Montreal	4	
Apr. 14	Chicago	0	at	Montreal	2	

Montreal won best-of-five series 3–2

1930-31 – Montreal Canadiens – George Hainsworth, Wildor Larochelle, Marty Burke, Sylvio Mantha (Captain), Howie Morenz, Johnny Gagnon, Aurel Joliat, Armand Mondou, Pit Lepine, Albert Leduc, Georges Mantha, Art Lesieur, Nick Wasnie, Bert McCaffrey, Gus Rivers, Jean Pusie, Léo Dandurand (Manager), Cecil Hart (Coach), Ed Dufour (Trainer).

TROPHY WINNERS

Trophy	Awarded For	Winner	Team
Hart	MVP	Howie Morenz	Mtl.
Vezina	Fewest Goals Against	Roy Worters	NYA
Byng	Gentlemanly Conduct	Frank Boucher	NYR

NHL NOTEBOOK

TRANSACTIONS

- Oct. 11, 1930 – Ottawa traded King Clancy to Toronto for Eric Pettinger, Art Smith and $35,000. The cash involved was a record price paid for any hockey player.
- Oct. 21, 1930 – Montreal Canadiens obtained Johnny Gagnon from Providence (Can-Am) in trade for Gerry Carson, Jean Pusie and cash.
- Nov. 6, 1930 – Ottawa traded Al Shields, Wally Kilrea and Syd Howe to Philadelphia for $35,000.
- Nov. 10, 1930 – Detroit obtained John Sorrell from London (IAHL) in exchange for Herb Stuart.
- Jan. 1, 1931 – New York Rangers purchased Cecil Dillon from Springfield (CAHL).

RECORDS

- Nov. 22, 1930 – Toronto became the first team in NHL history to open a season with five straight shutouts, when Lorne Chabot led the Maple Leafs to a 2-0 win over the visiting Ottawa Senators.
- Jan. 3, 1931 – Montreal Maroons' forward Nels Stewart scored two goals four seconds apart in the third period (8:24 and 8:28), to set an NHL record for fastest two goals by one player. Stewart led his team to a 5-3 victory over the Bruins.
- Feb. 14, 1931 – In an historic first, three assists were awarded on one NHL goal! Toronto's Charlie Conacher scored, with assists given to King Clancy, Joe Primeau and Busher Jackson, in a 1-1 tie against Detroit.

MILESTONES

- Nov. 11, 1930 – The city of Philadelphia played host to its first NHL game as the Quakers were shut out 3-0 by the New York Rangers. The Quakers dropped out of the league after posting a 4-36-4 record in their only season.
- Dec. 13, 1930 – Toronto's Rolly Huard scored the opening goal in his first NHL game when the Maple Leafs lost 7-3 to the visiting Boston Bruins. Huard never played another NHL game - the first player in history to play just one NHL game and score a goal in that game.
- Mar. 3, 1931 – Toronto's Lorne Chabot became the first goaltender in franchise history to record 100 victories as a member of the Maple Leafs. The milestone came in a 5-1 win, at Philadelphia.
- Mar. 26, 1931 – Art Ross became the first NHL coach to pull his goalie for an extra attacker, as the Bruins lost 1-0 to the Canadiens, in game two of the Stanley Cup semi-finals.

1931-32

Stanley Cup • Toronto Maple Leafs

FINAL STANDINGS

Team	GP	W	L	T	GF	GA	PTS
CANADIAN DIVISION							
Montreal	48	25	16	7	128	111	57
Toronto	48	23	18	7	155	127	53
Mtl. Maroons	48	19	22	7	142	139	45
NY Americans	48	16	24	8	95	142	40
AMERICAN DIVISION							
New York	48	23	17	8	134	112	54
Chicago	48	18	19	11	86	101	47
Detroit	48	18	20	10	95	108	46
Boston	48	15	21	12	122	117	42

LEADING SCORERS

Player	Club	GP	G	A	PTS	PIM
Busher Jackson	Toronto	48	28	25	53	63
Joe Primeau	Toronto	46	13	37	50	25
Howie Morenz	Montreal	48	24	25	49	46
Bill Cook	NY Rangers	48	34	14	48	33
Charlie Conacher	Toronto	44	34	14	48	66
Dave Trottier	Mtl. Maroons	48	26	18	44	94
Hooley Smith	Mtl. Maroons	43	11	33	44	49
Babe Siebert	Mtl. Maroons	48	21	18	39	64
Dit Clapper	Boston	48	17	22	39	21
Aurel Joliat	Montreal	48	15	24	39	46
Cecil Dillon	NY Rangers	48	23	15	38	22
Marty Barry	Boston	48	21	17	38	22
Jimmy Ward	Mtl. Maroons	48	19	19	38	39
Johnny Gagnon	Montreal	48	19	18	37	40
Frank Boucher	NY Rangers	48	12	23	35	18
Bun Cook	NY Rangers	45	14	20	34	43
Nels Stewart	Mtl. Maroons	38	22	11	33	61
Pit Lepine	Montreal	48	19	11	30	42
Ebbie Goodfellow	Detroit	48	14	16	30	56

LEADING GOALTENDERS

Goaltender	Club	GPI	MINS	GA	SO	AVG
Charlie Gardiner	Chicago	48	2989	92	4	1.85
Alex Connell	Detroit	48	3050	108	6	2.12
George Hainsworth	Montreal	48	2998	110	6	2.20
John Ross Roach	NY Rangers	48	3020	112	9	2.23
Tiny Thompson	Boston	43	2698	103	9	2.29
Lorne Chabot	Toronto	44	2698	106	4	2.36
Roy Worters	NY Americans	40	2459	110	5	2.68
Flat Walsh	Mtl. Maroons	27	1670	77	2	2.77
Normie Smith	Mtl. Maroons	21	1267	62	0	2.94

LEADING PLAYOFF SCORERS

Player	Club	GP	G	A	PTS	PIM
Frank Boucher	NY Rangers	7	3	6	9	0
Charlie Conacher	Toronto	7	6	2	8	6
Bun Cook	NY Rangers	7	6	2	8	12
Busher Jackson	Toronto	7	5	2	7	13
Hap Day	Toronto	7	3	3	6	6
Bill Cook	NY Rangers	7	3	3	6	2
Joe Primeau	Toronto	7	0	6	6	2
Frank Finnigan	Toronto	7	2	3	5	8

LEADING PLAYOFF GOALTENDERS

Goaltender	Club	GPI	MINS	GA	SO	AVG
Flat Walsh	Mtl. Maroons	4	258	5	1	1.16
Lorne Chabot	Toronto	7	438	15	0	2.05
George Hainsworth	Montreal	4	300	13	0	2.60
John Ross Roach	NY Rangers	7	480	27	1	3.38

The Kid Line of Charlie Conacher (left), Joe Primeau (center) and Busher Jackson (right) lifted the Maple Leafs to great heights in the 1930s. All three were products of the Toronto farm system, with Primeau reaching the NHL in 1927–28 while Jackson and Conacher graduated from the Toronto Marlboros after a Memorial Cup win in 1929.

THE NHL'S FORTUNES between the two world wars matched those of the countries it played in. The league had grown from four to 10 teams in the space of just four seasons in the Roaring Twenties, but this season would see it suffering from the impact of the Great Depression. One of the casualties was the Philadelphia Quakers, who closed shop after only one year following five seasons in Pittsburgh as the Pirates. More shocking was the decision of the Ottawa Senators to withdraw from play. Ottawa was a founding member of the NHL, had won its first Stanley Cup in 1903 (long before the NHL even existed) and had won the Cup four times in the 1920s.

Carlton Street Cathedral – Inspired by their new palatial home, Toronto topped the scoring charts with the Kid Line, dominated the defense with Day and Clancy and aced the Rangers in the "tennis" Cup finals.

Meanwhile, Conn Smythe's Toronto Maple Leafs seemed to be the picture of optimism. Against long odds, Conn Smythe had built his hockey palace, Maple Leaf Gardens, which opened on November 12, 1931, with a disappointing 2–1 loss to Chicago. The Leafs rebounded to win a club-record 23 games (23–18–7) in the newly expanded 48-game season and their Kid Line of Joe Primeau, Busher Jackson and Charlie Conacher emerged as full-fledged superstars. Jackson led the league with 53 points on 28 goals and 25 assists and Primeau's 37 assists topped the loop, while Conacher's 34 goals tied him with Bill Cook for top spot in the NHL.

Toronto finished second behind the Montreal Canadiens in the Canadian Division, but advanced to the Stanley Cup finals with playoff victories over the Chicago Black Hawks and Montreal Maroons. Meanwhile, the Canadiens were eliminated by the American Division-winning New York Rangers. The Rangers had a week off before meeting Toronto in the Stanley Cup finals, but the rest was of no benefit. Toronto took the opener 6–4 in New York, won game two 6–2 in Boston after the circus forced the series out of Madison Square Garden, then completed the sweep with a 6–4 victory at home. It was Toronto's first Stanley Cup victory since the St. Patricks won it 10 years before.

Leaders, 1931-32

GOALS

Name, Team	G
Charlie Conacher, Tor.	34
Bill Cook, NYR	34
Busher Jackson, Tor.	28
Dave Trottier, Mtl.M.	26
Howie Morenz, Mtl.	24
Cecil Dillon, NYR	23
Nels Stewart, Mtl.M.	22
Babe Siebert, Mtl.M.	21
Marty Barry, Bos.	21
Four tied with	19

ASSISTS

Name, Team	A
Joe Primeau, Tor.	37
Hooley Smith, Mtl.M.	33
Busher Jackson, Tor.	25
Howie Morenz, Mtl.	25
Aurel Joliat, Mtl.	24
Frank Boucher, NYR	23
Dit Clapper, Bos.	22
Normie Himes, NYA	21
Bun Cook, NYR	20
Jimmy Ward, Mtl.M.	19

GOALIE WINS

Name, Team	W
George Hainsworth, Mtl.	25
John Ross Roach, NYR	23
Lorne Chabot, Tor.	22
Alex Connell, Det.	18
Charlie Gardiner, Chi.	18
Flat Walsh, Mtl.M.	14
Tiny Thompson, Bos.	13
Roy Worters, NYA	12
Normie Smith, Mtl.M.	5
Jake Forbes, NYA	3

SHUTOUTS

Name, Team	SO
Tiny Thompson, Bos.	9
John Ross Roach, NYR	9
George Hainsworth, Mtl.	6
Alex Connell, Det.	6
Roy Worters, NYA	5
Lorne Chabot, Tor.	4
Charlie Gardiner, Chi.	4
Flat Walsh, Mtl.M.	2
Wilf Cude, Bos/Chi.	1
Benny Grant, Tor.	1

PLAYOFF GOALS

Name, Team	G
Charlie Conacher, Tor.	6
Bun Cook, NYR	6
Busher Jackson, Tor.	5
Frank Boucher, NYR	3
Hap Day, Tor.	3
Bill Cook, NYR	3
Ott Heller, NYR	3
Bob Gracie, Tor.	3
12 tied with	2

PLAYOFF ASSISTS

Name, Team	A
Frank Boucher, NYR	6
Joe Primeau, Tor.	6
Hap Day, Tor.	3
Bill Cook, NYR	3
Frank Finnigan, Tor.	3
10 tied with	2

PLAYOFF GOALIE WINS

Name, Team	W
Lorne Chabot, Tor.	5
John Ross Roach, NYR	3
Charlie Gardiner, Chi.	1
Flat Walsh, Mtl.M.	1
George Hainsworth, Mtl.	1

PLAYOFF SHUTOUTS

Name, Team	SO
Charlie Gardiner, Chi.	1
Flat Walsh, Mtl.M.	1
John Ross Roach, NYR	1

FIRST TEAM ALL-STARS

Name, Team	Position
Howie Morenz, Mtl.	C
Bill Cook, NYR	RW
Busher Jackson, Tor.	LW
Eddie Shore, Bos.	D
Ching Johnson, NYR	D
Chuck Gardiner, Chi.	G
Lester Patrick, NYR	Coach

SECOND TEAM ALL-STARS

Name, Team	Position
Hooley Smith, Mtl M	C
Charlie Conacher, Tor.	RW
Aurel Joliat, Mtl.	LW
Sylvio Mantha, Mtl.	D
King Clancy, Tor.	D
Roy Worters, NYA	G
Dick Irvin, Tor.	Coach

1932 Playoffs

SERIES A - SEMI-FINALS

Mar. 24	NY Rangers	3	at	Montreal	4
Mar. 26	NY Rangers	4	at	Montreal	3 3OT
Mar. 27	Montreal	0	at	NY Rangers	1
Mar. 29	Montreal	2	at	NY Rangers	5

NY Rangers won best-of-five series 3–1

SERIES B AND C - QUARTER-FINALS

Mar. 27	Toronto	0	at	Chicago	1
Mar. 29	Chicago	1	at	Toronto	6

Toronto won total-goals series 6–2

Mar. 27	Mtl. Maroons	1	at	Detroit	1
Mar. 29	Detroit	0	at	Mtl. Maroons	2

Mtl. Maroons won total-goals series 3–1

SERIES D - SEMI-FINALS

Mar. 31	Toronto	1	at	Mtl. Maroons	1
Apr. 2	Mtl. Maroons	2	at	Toronto	3 OT

Toronto won total-goals series 4–3

SERIES E - FINALS

Apr. 5	Toronto	6	at	NY Rangers	4
Apr. 7	Toronto	6	vs	NY Rangers	2 *
Apr. 9	NY Rangers	4	at	Toronto	6

* played in Boston

Toronto won best-of-five series 3–0

1931-32 – Toronto Maple Leafs – Charlie Conacher, Busher Jackson, King Clancy, Andy Blair, Red Horner, Lorne Chabot, Alex Levinsky, Joe Primeau, Harold Darragh, Baldy Cotton, Frank Finnigan, Hap Day (Captain), Ace Bailey, Bob Gracie, Fred Robertson, Earl Miller, Conn Smythe (Manager), Dick Irvin (Coach), Tim Daly (Trainer).

TROPHY WINNERS

Trophy	Awarded For	Winner	Team
Hart	MVP	Howie Morenz	Mtl.
Vezina	Fewest Goals Against	Charlie Gardiner	Chi
Byng	Gentlemanly Conduct	Joe Primeau	Tor.

NHL NOTEBOOK

TRANSACTIONS

- May 9, 1931 – New York Rangers purchased Earl Seibert from the Springfield Indians of the CAHL.
- Sept. 26, 1931 – New York Americans obtained Joe Lamb, Len Grovesner, Wally Kilrea and Al Shields in the NHL Dispersal Draft, following the league's suspension of Ottawa and Philadelphia.
- Sept. 26, 1931 – Detroit Falcons obtained Alex Connell, Hec Kilrea, Danny Cox, Art Gagne and Alex Smith in the NHL Dispersal Draft, following the league's suspension of Ottawa and Philadelphia.
- Sept. 26, 1931 – Toronto obtained Frank Finnigan and Syd Howe in the NHL Dispersal Draft, following the league's suspension of Ottawa and Philadelphia.

RECORDS

- Nov. 12, 1931 – A new league penalty record was established in the season opener, a 4-1 Canadiens win over the Rangers at the Forum. 35 minor penalties were handed out, including 22 against New York.
- Jan. 23, 1932 – Detroit's Alex Connell took over the NHL's all-time lead in shutouts, when his 67th career shutout moved him one ahead of George Hainsworth. The milestone came in a 2-0 Detroit victory in Boston Garden.
- Feb. 6, 1932 – Maple Leafs' Charlie Conacher set an NHL record for fastest goal from the start of a game, when he scored just seven seconds into a 6-0 win against Boston.
- Apr. 5, 1932 – Toronto's Busher Jackson became the first player to record a playoff hat trick in one period, with three in the second period of a 6-4 Maple Leafs win over the Rangers, in game one of the Stanley Cup finals at New York.

MILESTONES

- Feb. 11, 1932 – George Owen of the Boston Bruins became the first U.S. born player to score a hat trick in the NHL, when the Bruins lost 7-4 to the Montreal Maroons in Boston.
- Nov. 12, 1931 – The first NHL game at Maple Leaf Gardens in Toronto. saw the Black Hawks defeat the Leafs 2-1. Chicago's Mush March got the first goal in the new rink.
- Feb. 11, 1932 – Boston's George Owen became the first U.S.-born player to record a hat trick in the NHL when the Bruins lost 7-4 at home to the Montreal Maroons.
- Mar. 22, 1932 – With both teams out of playoff contention, experimental rules were tried for the final game of the season between the Bruins and Americans. The blue lines were eliminated with just a center line used to determine off-sides. The Americans won 8-6.

1932-33

Stanley Cup • New York Rangers

FINAL STANDINGS

Team	GP	W	L	T	GF	GA	PTS
CANADIAN DIVISION							
Toronto	48	24	18	6	119	111	54
Mtl. Maroons	48	22	20	6	135	119	50
Montreal	48	18	25	5	92	115	41
NY Americans	48	15	22	11	91	118	41
Ottawa	48	11	27	10	88	131	32
AMERICAN DIVISION							
Boston	48	25	15	8	124	88	58
Detroit	48	25	15	8	111	93	58
New York	48	23	17	8	135	107	54
Chicago	48	16	20	12	88	101	44

LEADING SCORERS

Player	Club	GP	G	A	PTS	PIM
Bill Cook	NY Rangers	48	28	22	50	51
Busher Jackson	Toronto	48	27	17	44	43
Baldy Northcott	Mtl. Maroons	48	22	21	43	30
Hooley Smith	Mtl. Maroons	48	20	21	41	66
Paul Haynes	Mtl. Maroons	48	16	25	41	18
Aurel Joliat	Montreal	48	18	21	39	53
Marty Barry	Boston	47	24	13	37	40
Bun Cook	NY Rangers	48	22	15	37	35
Nels Stewart	Boston	47	18	18	36	62
Howie Morenz	Montreal	46	14	21	35	32
Johnny Gagnon	Montreal	48	12	23	35	64
Eddie Shore	Boston	48	8	27	35	102
Frank Boucher	NY Rangers	46	7	28	35	4
Herbie Lewis	Detroit	48	20	14	34	20
Normie Himes	NY Americans	48	9	25	34	12
Jimmy Ward	Mtl. Maroons	48	16	17	33	52
Charlie Conacher	Toronto	40	14	19	33	64
Paul Thompson	Chicago	48	13	20	33	27
Joe Primeau	Toronto	48	11	21	32	4
Cecil Dillon	NY Rangers	48	21	10	31	12
Dave Trottier	Mtl. Maroons	48	16	15	31	38

LEADING GOALTENDERS

Goaltender	Club	GPI	MINS	GA	SO	AVG
Tiny Thompson	Boston	48	3000	88	11	1.76
John Ross Roach	Detroit	48	2970	93	10	1.88
Charlie Gardiner	Chicago	48	3010	101	5	2.01
Andy Aitkenhead	NY Rangers	48	2970	107	3	2.16
Lorne Chabot	Toronto	48	2946	111	5	2.26
Dave Kerr	Mtl. Maroons	25	1520	58	4	2.29
George Hainsworth	Montreal	48	2980	115	8	2.32
Roy Worters	NY Americans	47	2970	116	5	2.34
Bill Beveridge	Ottawa	35	2195	95	5	2.60

LEADING PLAYOFF SCORERS

Player	Club	GP	G	A	PTS	PIM
Cecil Dillon	NY Rangers	8	8	2	10	6
Murray Murdoch	NY Rangers	8	3	4	7	2
Ken Doraty	Toronto	9	5	0	5	2
Bill Cook	NY Rangers	8	3	2	5	4
Art Somers	NY Rangers	8	1	4	5	8
Busher Jackson	Toronto	9	3	1	4	2
Charlie Sands	Toronto	9	2	2	4	2
Frank Boucher	NY Rangers	8	2	2	4	6
Marty Barry	Boston	5	2	2	4	6
John Sorrell	Detroit	4	2	2	4	4

LEADING PLAYOFF GOALTENDERS

Goaltender	Club	GPI	MINS	GA	SO	AVG
Tiny Thompson	Boston	5	438	9	0	1.23
Lorne Chabot	Toronto	9	686	18	2	1.57
Andy Aitkenhead	NY Rangers	8	488	13	2	1.60
John Ross Roach	Detroit	4	240	8	1	2.00

Bill Cook was one of the top scorers in hockey during a 15-year professional career in Saskatoon and New York. He twice led his league in goals and points during his four seasons out west, then led the NHL in goals three times while winning two scoring titles with the Rangers. He was the captain in New York from 1926–27 to 1936–37.

After a one-year absence, the Ottawa Senators returned to the NHL for the 1932–33 season, but finished last in the league with an 11–27–10 mark. In Toronto, the defending Stanley Cup champions climbed to top spot in the Canadian Division, and starting this year, Foster Hewitt's broadcasts from Maple Leaf Gardens could be heard nationally over a network of 20 radio stations. The Montreal Maroons placed second to Toronto, while their rinkmates, the Canadiens, edged the New York Americans for the final playoff spot.

In the American Division, the Rangers, Boston and Detroit (now under new ownership and renamed the Red Wings) battled for top spot, with only Chicago out of the running. The Black Hawks fired two coaches before settling on Tommy Gorman. A dispute over rent at the Chicago Stadium saw the team spend the first month of the season at the old Chicago Coliseum. Eddie Shore won the Hart Trophy for the first of four times in his career as the Bruins finished on top of the division. Detroit finished second despite an identical 25–15–8 record. The Rangers finished third but came on strong in the postseason, knocking off the Canadiens and Red Wings to advance to the Stanley Cup finals.

Rangers' Revenge – The Bread Line of Cook, Cook and Boucher rose to new heights, feasted on the league, fed their Cup hungry fans and kept alive the drive to the Rangers' second Stanley Cup title.

In the battle of first-place finishers, Toronto beat Boston in five games. The series finale on April 3 was the longest game to date in NHL history, as Ken Doraty scored at 4:46 of the sixth overtime period to give the Maple Leafs a 1–0 victory. The game ended at 1:50 a.m. on the 4th, but the Leafs were in New York later that night to open the Stanley Cup finals. The Rangers breezed to a 5–1 victory and won the series in four games, avenging their sweep at the hands of the Leafs in the previous spring's playoffs.

Leaders, 1932-33

GOALS

Name, Team	G
Bill Cook, NYR	28
Busher Jackson, Tor.	27
Marty Barry, Bos.	24
Baldy Northcott, Mtl.M.	22
Bun Cook, NYR	22
Cecil Dillon, NYR	21
Hooley Smith, Mtl.M.	20
Herbie Lewis, Det.	20
Nels Stewart, Bos.	18
Aurel Joliat, Mtl.	18

ASSISTS

Name, Team	A
Frank Boucher, NYR	28
Eddie Shore, Bos.	27
Paul Haynes, Mtl.M.	25
Normie Himes, NYA	25
Johnny Gagnon, Mtl.	23
Bill Cook, NYR	22
Howie Morenz, Mtl.	21
Lionel Conacher, Mtl.M.	21
Baldy Northcott, Mtl.M.	21
Hooley Smith, Mtl.M.	21
Aurel Joliat, Mtl.	21
Joe Primeau, Tor.	21

GOALIE WINS

Name, Team	W
John Ross Roach, Det.	25
Tiny Thompson, Bos.	25
Lorne Chabot, Tor.	24
Andy Aitkenhead, NYR	23
George Hainsworth, Mtl.	18
Charlie Gardiner, Chi.	16
Roy Worters, NYA	15
Dave Kerr, Mtl.M.	14
Flat Walsh, Mtl.M.	8
Bill Beveridge, Ott.	7

SHUTOUTS

Name, Team	SO
Tiny Thompson, Bos.	11
John Ross Roach, Det.	10
George Hainsworth, Mtl.	8
Bill Beveridge, Ott.	5
Roy Worters, NYA	5
Lorne Chabot, Tor.	5
Charlie Gardiner, Chi.	5
Dave Kerr, Mtl.M.	4
Andy Aitkenhead, NYR	3
Flat Walsh, Mtl.M.	2

PLAYOFF GOALS

Name, Team	G
Cecil Dillon, NYR	8
Ken Doraty, Tor.	5
Murray Murdoch, NYR	3
Bill Cook, NYR	3
Ott Heller, NYR	3
Busher Jackson, Tor.	3
Eight tied with	2

PLAYOFF ASSISTS

Name, Team	A
Murray Murdoch, NYR	4
Art Somers, NYR	4
Howie Morenz, Mtl.	3
King Clancy, Tor.	3
Baldy Cotton, Tor.	3
11 tied with	2

PLAYOFF GOALIE WINS

Name, Team	W
Andy Aitkenhead, NYR	6
Lorne Chabot, Tor.	4
John Ross Roach, Det.	2
Tiny Thompson, Bos.	2

PLAYOFF SHUTOUTS

Name, Team	SO
Andy Aitkenhead, NYR	2
Lorne Chabot, Tor.	2
John Ross Roach, Det.	1

FIRST TEAM ALL-STARS

Name, Team	Position
Frank Boucher, NYR	C
Bill Cook, NYR	RW
Baldy Northcott, Mtl M	LW
Eddie Shore, Bos.	D
Ching Johnson, NYR	D
John Ross Roach, Det.	G
Lester Patrick, NYR	Coach

SECOND TEAM ALL-STARS

Name, Team	Position
Howie Morenz, Mtl.	C
Charlie Conacher, Tor.	RW
Busher Jackson, Tor.	LW
King Clancy, Tor.	D
Lionel Conacher, Chi.	D
Chuck Gardiner, Chi.	G
Dick Irvin, Tor.	Coach

1933 Playoffs

SERIES A - SEMI-FINALS

Date	Visitor	Score		Home	Score
Mar. 25	Toronto	1	at	Boston	2 OT
Mar. 28	Toronto	1	at	Boston	0 OT
Mar. 30	Boston	2	at	Toronto	1 OT
Apr. 1	Boston	3	at	Toronto	5
Apr. 3	Boston	0	at	Toronto	1 6OT

Toronto won best-of-five series 3–2

SERIES B AND C - QUARTER-FINALS

Date	Visitor	Score		Home	Score
Mar. 25	Detroit	2	at	Mtl. Maroons	0
Mar. 28	Mtl. Maroons	2	at	Detroit	3

Detroit won total-goals series 5–2

Date	Visitor	Score		Home	Score
Mar. 26	Montreal	2	at	NY Rangers	5
Mar. 28	NY Rangers	3	at	Montreal	3

NY Rangers won total-goals series 8–5

SERIES D - SEMI-FINALS

Date	Visitor	Score		Home	Score
Mar. 30	Detroit	0	at	NY Rangers	2
Apr. 2	NY Rangers	4	at	Detroit	3

NY Rangers won total-goals series 6–3

SERIES E - FINALS

Date	Visitor	Score		Home	Score
Apr. 4	Toronto	1	at	NY Rangers	5
Apr. 8	NY Rangers	3	at	Toronto	1
Apr. 11	NY Rangers	2	at	Toronto	3
Apr. 13	NY Rangers	1	at	Toronto	0 OT

NY Rangers won best-of-five series 3–1

1932-33 – New York Rangers – Ching Johnson, Butch Keeling, Frank Boucher, Art Somers, Babe Siebert, Bun Cook, Andy Aitkenhead, Ott Heller, Oscar Asmundson, Gord Pettinger, Doug Brennan, Cecil Dillon, Bill Cook (Captain), Murray Murdoch, Earl Seibert, Lester Patrick (Manager/Coach), Harry Westerby (Trainer).

TROPHY WINNERS

Trophy	Awarded For	Winner	Team
Hart	MVP	Eddie Shore	Bos.
Calder	Top Rookie	Carl Voss	Det.
Vezina	Fewest Goals Against	Tiny Thompson	Bos.
Byng	Gentlemanly Conduct	Frank Boucher	NYR

NHL NOTEBOOK

TRANSACTIONS

- May 9, 1932 – New York Rangers purchased Ott Heller from the Springfield Indians (CAHL).
- July 25, 1932 – Boston traded Cooney Weiland to Ottawa for Joe Lamb and $7,000
- Oct. 5, 1932 – Detroit purchased goaltender John Ross Roach from the New York Rangers for $11,000.
- Oct. 24, 1932 – Chicago traded Cy Wentworth to Montreal Maroons for $10,000
- Dec. 11, 1932 – Detroit purchased Carl Voss from the New York Rangers.

RECORDS

- Jan. 31, 1933 – Dit Clapper became the first player in Boston history to score 100 goals as a member of the Bruins, when they lost 5-1 to the visiting Chicago Black Hawks.
- Mar. 12, 1933 – John Ross Roach became the first goaltender in NHL history to record 200 career victories when the Red Wings won 3-1 over the visiting Montreal Canadiens.
- Mar. 18, 1933 – Montreal's George Hainsworth became the first goalie in NHL history to record 75 career shutouts, as the Canadiens tied 0-0 against the visiting Bruins.
- Apr. 3, 1933 – Ken Doraty scored after 104:46 of overtime, and Lorne Chabot recorded his 4th career playoff shutout as Toronto defeated Boston 1-0 in game five of the Stanley Cup semi-finals. It was (at the time) the longest game in playoff history (2nd longest now).

MILESTONES

- May 10, 1932 – NHL Board of Governors decided that no team's payroll would exceed $70,000.
- Oct. 5, 1932 – The new name Red Wings (along with red uniforms with a winged wheel crest) was introduced to Detroit hockey fans. The franchise previously had been known as the Cougars and Falcons.
- Feb. 23, 1933 – John Ross Roach became the first goaltender in Detroit Red Wings history to win 20 games in one season. The milestone 20th victory of the year was a 3-0 win against the visiting New York Rangers.
- Reg Noble (who began his career with Toronto in 1917-18) becomes the last of the original NHL players to retire from the league, after appearing in 25 games with Detroit and the Montreal Maroons.

1933-34

Stanley Cup • Chicago Black Hawks

FINAL STANDINGS

Team	GP	W	L	T	GF	GA	PTS
CANADIAN DIVISION							
Toronto	48	26	13	9	174	119	61
Montreal	48	22	20	6	99	101	50
Mtl. Maroons	48	19	18	11	117	122	49
NY Americans	48	15	23	10	104	132	40
Ottawa	48	13	29	6	115	143	32
AMERICAN DIVISION							
Detroit	48	24	14	10	113	98	58
Chicago	48	20	17	11	88	83	51
New York	48	21	19	8	120	113	50
Boston	48	18	25	5	111	130	41

LEADING SCORERS

Player	Club	GP	G	A	PTS	PIM
Charlie Conacher	Toronto	42	32	20	52	38
Joe Primeau	Toronto	45	14	32	46	8
Frank Boucher	NY Rangers	48	14	30	44	4
Marty Barry	Boston	48	27	12	39	12
Nels Stewart	Boston	48	22	17	39	68
Cecil Dillon	NY Rangers	48	13	26	39	10
Busher Jackson	Toronto	38	20	18	38	38
Aurel Joliat	Montreal	48	22	15	37	27
Hooley Smith	Mtl. Maroons	47	18	19	37	58
Paul Thompson	Chicago	48	20	16	36	17
Larry Aurie	Detroit	48	16	19	35	36
Baldy Northcott	Mtl. Maroons	47	20	13	33	27
Bun Cook	NY Rangers	48	18	15	33	36
Cooney Weiland	Ott./Det.	48	13	19	32	10
John Sorrell	Detroit	47	21	10	31	8
Herbie Lewis	Detroit	43	16	15	31	15
Eddie Burke	NY Americans	46	20	10	30	24
Johnny Gottselig	Chicago	48	16	14	30	4
Earl Roche	Ottawa	45	13	16	29	22
Doc Romnes	Chicago	47	8	21	29	6
Earl Robinson	Mtl. Maroons	47	12	16	28	14
King Clancy	Toronto	46	11	17	28	62
Murray Murdoch	NY Rangers	48	17	10	27	29
Wildor Larochelle	Montreal	48	16	11	27	27
Charley McVeigh	NY Americans	48	15	12	27	4

LEADING GOALTENDERS

Goaltender	Club	GPI	MINS	GA	SO	AVG
Wilf Cude	Mtl./Det.	30	1920	47	5	1.47
Charlie Gardiner	Chicago	48	3050	83	10	1.63
Roy Worters	NY Americans	36	2240	75	4	2.01
Lorne Chabot	Montreal	47	2928	101	8	2.07
Andy Aitkenhead	NY Rangers	48	2990	113	7	2.27
George Hainsworth	Toronto	48	3010	119	3	2.37
Dave Kerr	Mtl. Maroons	48	3060	122	6	2.39

LEADING PLAYOFF SCORERS

Player	Club	GP	G	A	PTS	PIM
Larry Aurie	Detroit	9	3	7	10	2
Doc Romnes	Chicago	8	2	7	9	0
Herbie Lewis	Detroit	9	5	2	7	2
Paul Thompson	Chicago	8	4	3	7	6
Johnny Gottselig	Chicago	8	4	3	7	4
Ebbie Goodfellow	Detroit	9	4	3	7	12
Joe Primeau	Toronto	5	2	4	6	6
Charlie Conacher	Toronto	5	3	2	5	0

LEADING PLAYOFF GOALTENDERS

Goaltender	Club	GPI	MINS	GA	SO	AVG
Charlie Gardiner	Chicago	8	542	12	2	1.33
Dave Kerr	Mtl. Maroons	4	240	7	1	1.75
Wilf Cude	Detroit	9	593	21	1	2.12

Pictured in his All-Star sweater for the Ace Bailey benefit game, Chicago's Charlie Gardiner often played for poor teams but is rated by most as the greatest goaltender of his day, and by many as the greatest of all time. Born in Scotland but raised in Winnipeg, Gardiner was at the height of his career when tragedy cut his life short at the age of 29.

As the Great Depression worsened, so did its effect on the NHL. Although the Detroit Red Wings were now safely under the ownership of multimillionaire James Norris and his son James D. Norris of Olympia Incorporated, the Ottawa Senators were on shaky financial ground after 1932–33, and so were the New York Americans. NHL president Frank Calder quickly put down rumors that the teams might merge. Meanwhile in Montreal, it was beginning to look as if there was room for only one team, as the Montreal Maroons were having trouble drawing fans to the Forum, the rink they shared with the Canadiens.

Gardiner's Goodbye – The Kid Line made headlines, an All-Star Game was played for Ace Bailey but most compelling was Charlie Gardiner's Cup-winning courage for Chicago in his NHL swan song.

Despite league-wide economic hardship, Boston's Eddie Shore refused to accept a pay cut after winning the Hart Trophy and sat out the first three games of the season before agreeing to a $7,500 contract. Shore would be in the hockey headlines again a month later after one of the darkest incidents in NHL history.

On December 12, 1933, the Toronto Maple Leafs were in Boston to play the Bruins. The game got chippy and Shore was tripped by King Clancy after a rink-long rush. Shore retaliated angrily by checking the first Leaf he could see, Ace Bailey, from behind. Bailey's skull was fractured as he fell over backward and his head hit the ice. It was 10 days before doctors were even sure the wounded Maple Leaf would live. As it was, Bailey's hockey career was over. Shore was suspended for 16 games—one-third of the 48-game schedule. On February 14, 1934, an NHL All-Star Game was played to benefit Bailey and his family.

The Chicago Black Hawks, led by the exploits of goaltender Charlie Gardiner, won their first Stanley Cup championship. Gardiner played in the Bailey benefit game and also earned the Vezina Trophy that year for the second time. Shortly after Chicago's Stanley Cup victory, Gardiner died of a brain tumor. He was 29 years old.

Leaders, 1933-34

GOALS

Name, Team	G
Charlie Conacher, Tor.	32
Marty Barry, Bos.	27
Nels Stewart, Bos.	22
Aurel Joliat, Mtl.	22
John Sorrell, Det.	21
Busher Jackson, Tor.	20
Eddie Burke, NYA	20
Baldy Northcott, Mtl.M.	20
Paul Thompson, Chi.	20
Hooley Smith, Mtl.M.	18
Bun Cook, NYR	18

ASSISTS

Name, Team	A
Joe Primeau, Tor.	32
Frank Boucher, NYR	30
Cecil Dillon, NYR	26
Doc Romnes, Chi.	21
Charlie Conacher, Tor.	20
Hooley Smith, Mtl.M.	19
Larry Aurie, Det.	19
Cooney Weiland, Ott./Det.	19
Busher Jackson, Tor.	18
Bill Thoms, Tor.	18
Carl Voss, Det/Ott	18

GOALIE WINS

Name, Team	W
George Hainsworth, Tor.	26
Lorne Chabot, Mtl.	21
Andy Aitkenhead, NYR	21
Charlie Gardiner, Chi.	20
Dave Kerr, Mtl.M.	19
Tiny Thompson, Bos.	18
Wilf Cude, Mtl./Det.	16
Bill Beveridge, Ott.	13
Roy Worters, NYA	12
John Ross Roach, Det.	9

SHUTOUTS

Name, Team	SO
Charlie Gardiner, Chi.	10
Lorne Chabot, Mtl.	8
Andy Aitkenhead, NYR	7
Dave Kerr, Mtl.M.	6
Wilf Cude, Mtl/Det.	5
Tiny Thompson, Bos.	5
Roy Worters, NYA	4
George Hainsworth, Tor.	3
Bill Beveridge, Ott.	3
Benny Grant, NYA	1
John Ross Roach, Det.	1

PLAYOFF GOALS

Name, Team	G
Herbie Lewis, Det.	5
Paul Thompson, Chi.	4
Johnny Gottselig, Chi.	4
Ebbie Goodfellow, Det.	4
Charlie Conacher, Tor.	3
Larry Aurie, Det.	3
Ted Graham, Det.	3
10 tied with	2

PLAYOFF ASSISTS

Name, Team	A
Doc Romnes, Chi.	7
Larry Aurie, Det.	7
Joe Primeau, Tor.	4
Paul Thompson, Chi.	3
Johnny Gottselig, Chi.	3
Ebbie Goodfellow, Det.	3
13 tied with	2

PLAYOFF GOALIE WINS

Name, Team	W
Charlie Gardiner, Chi.	6
Wilf Cude, Det.	4
George Hainsworth, Tor.	2
Dave Kerr, Mtl.M.	1

PLAYOFF SHUTOUTS

Name, Team	SO
Charlie Gardiner, Chi	2
Andy Aitkenhead, NYR	1
Dave Kerr, Mtl.M.	1
Wilf Cude, Det.	1

FIRST TEAM ALL-STARS

Name, Team	Position
Frank Boucher, NYR	C
Charlie Conacher, Tor.	RW
Busher Jackson, Tor.	LW
King Clancy, Tor.	D
Lionel Conacher, Chi.	D
Chuck Gardiner, Chi.	G
Lester Patrick, NYR	Coach

SECOND TEAM ALL-STARS

Name, Team	Position
Joe Primeau, Tor.	C
Bill Cook, NYR	RW
Aurel Joliat, Mtl.	LW
Eddie Shore, Bos.	D
Ching Johnson, NYR	D
Roy Worters, NYA	G
Dick Irvin, Tor.	Coach

1934 Playoffs

SERIES A - SEMI-FINALS

Date	Team	Score		Team	Score
Mar. 22	Detroit	2	at	Toronto	1 OT
Mar. 24	Detroit	6	at	Toronto	3
Mar. 26	Toronto	3	at	Detroit	1
Mar. 28	Toronto	5	at	Detroit	1
Mar. 30	Toronto	0	at	Detroit	1

Detroit won best-of-five series 3–2

SERIES B AND C - QUARTER-FINALS

Date	Team	Score		Team	Score
Mar. 22	Chicago	3	at	Montreal	2
Mar. 25	Montreal	1	at	Chicago	1 OT

Chicago won total-goals series 4–3

Date	Team	Score		Team	Score
Mar. 20	NY Rangers	0	at	Mtl. Maroons	0
Mar. 25	Mtl. Maroons	2	at	NY Rangers	1

Mtl. Maroons won total-goals series 2–1

SERIES D - SEMI-FINALS

Date	Team	Score		Team	Score
Mar. 28	Chicago	3	at	Mtl. Maroons	0
Apr. 1	Mtl. Maroons	2	at	Chicago	3

Chicago won total-goals series 6–2

SERIES E - FINALS

Date	Team	Score		Team	Score
Apr. 3	Chicago	2	at	Detroit	1 2OT
Apr. 5	Chicago	4	at	Detroit	1
Apr. 8	Detroit	5	at	Chicago	2
Apr. 10	Detroit	0	at	Chicago	1 2OT

Chicago won best-of-five series 3–1

1933-34 – Chicago Black Hawks – Clarence Abel, Rosie Couture, Lou Trudel, Lionel Conacher, Paul Thompson, Leroy Goldsworthy, Art Coulter, Roger Jenkins, Don McFadyen, Tom Cook, Doc Romnes, Johnny Gottselig, Mush March, Johnny Sheppard, Charlie Gardiner (Captain), Bill Kendall, Jack Leswick, Tommy Gorman (Manager/Coach), Eddie Froelich (Trainer).

TROPHY WINNERS

Trophy	Awarded For	Winner	Team
Hart	MVP	Aurel Joliat	Mtl.
Calder	Top Rookie	Russ Blinko	Mtl.M.
Vezina	Fewest Goals Against	Charlie Gardiner	Chi
Byng	Gentlemanly Conduct	Frank Boucher	NYR

NHL NOTEBOOK

TRANSACTIONS

- Oct. 1, 1933 – Montreal Canadiens obtained Lorne Chabot from the Toronto Maple Leafs, for George Hainsworth, in a trade of the two goaltenders.
- Oct. 19, 1933 – Montreal Canadiens purchased goaltender Wilf Cude from Philadelphia (CAHL).
- Nov. 26, 1933 – Detroit acquired Cooney Weiland from Ottawa for Carl Voss.
- Dec. 18, 1933 – Boston Bruins acquired Babe Siebert from the NY Rangers for Ray Burmeister and Vic Ripley.

RECORDS

- Jan. 16, 1934 – Ken Doraty scored the only hat trick in NHL overtime history as Toronto defeated the Senators 7-4 at Ottawa. Overtime was a 10 minute mandatory period those days, not sudden death.
- Mar. 11, 1934 – NHL records were set when the Montreal Maroons scored four goals in a 10-minute overtime period, to break a 3-3 tie and beat the Rangers 7-3 in New York.
- Mar. 22, 1934 – Herbie Lewis scored the first powerplay overtime goal in NHL history, at 1:33 of OT to give the Red Wings a 2-1 win in Toronto, in game one of their Stanley Cup semi-final series. It was the first OT goal in Detroit playoff history.

MILESTONES

- Sept. 30, 1933 – At the NHL Board of Governors meeting it was decided that two referees would henceforth be used for each game, instead of one referee and one linesman. This system lasted five years, before it went back to one ref and one linesman.
- Nov. 9, 1933 – Toronto's Charlie Conacher became the first player in franchise history to score 100 goals. The milestone came in a 6-1 win over the visiting Boston Bruins.
- Feb. 14, 1934 – The NHL had its first All-Star game, as a benefit to injured player Ace Bailey. Toronto defeated a team of All Stars from the league's other seven teams 7-3 at Maple Leaf Gardens. Bailey's #6 uniform was the first in NHL history to be retired.
- Mar. 15, 1934 – New York Americans beat the Senators 3-2 in the final NHL game played in Ottawa until the league returned to Canada's capital in 1992-93.

1934-35

Stanley Cup • Montreal Maroons

FINAL STANDINGS

Team	GP	W	L	T	GF	GA	PTS
CANADIAN DIVISION							
Toronto	48	30	14	4	157	111	64
Mtl. Maroons	48	24	19	5	123	92	53
Montreal	48	19	23	6	110	145	44
NY Americans	48	12	27	9	100	142	33
St. Louis	48	11	31	6	86	144	28
AMERICAN DIVISION							
Boston	48	26	16	6	129	112	58
Chicago	48	26	17	5	118	88	57
New York	48	22	20	6	137	139	50
Detroit	48	19	22	7	127	114	45

LEADING SCORERS

Player	Club	GP	G	A	PTS	PIM
Charlie Conacher	Toronto	47	36	21	57	24
Syd Howe	St.L./Det.	50	22	25	47	34
Larry Aurie	Detroit	48	17	29	46	24
Frank Boucher	NY Rangers	48	13	32	45	2
Busher Jackson	Toronto	42	22	22	44	27
Herbie Lewis	Detroit	47	16	27	43	26
Art Chapman	NY Americans	47	9	34	43	4
Marty Barry	Boston	48	20	20	40	33
Sweeney Schriner	NY Americans	48	18	22	40	6
Nels Stewart	Boston	47	21	18	39	45
Paul Thompson	Chicago	48	16	23	39	20
Cooney Weiland	Detroit	48	13	25	38	10
Dit Clapper	Boston	48	21	16	37	21
Johnny Gottselig	Chicago	48	19	18	37	16
Bill Cook	NY Rangers	48	21	15	36	23
John Sorrell	Detroit	47	20	16	36	12
Ebbie Goodfellow	Detroit	48	12	24	36	44
Earl Robinson	Mtl. Maroons	48	17	18	35	23
Cecil Dillon	NY Rangers	48	25	9	34	4
Bun Cook	NY Rangers	48	13	21	34	26
Howie Morenz	Chicago	48	8	26	34	21
Eddie Shore	Boston	48	7	26	33	32
Lorne Carr	NY Americans	48	17	14	31	14
Tom Cook	Chicago	48	13	18	31	33
Carl Voss	St. Louis	48	13	18	31	14
Pit Lepine	Montreal	48	12	19	31	16

LEADING GOALTENDERS

Goaltender	Club	GPI	MINS	GA	SO	AVG
Lorne Chabot	Chicago	48	2940	88	8	1.80
Alex Connell	Mtl. Maroons	48	2970	92	9	1.86
Normie Smith	Detroit	25	1550	52	2	2.01
George Hainsworth	Toronto	48	2957	111	8	2.25
Tiny Thompson	Boston	48	2970	112	8	2.26
Dave Kerr	NY Rangers	37	2290	94	4	2.46
Roy Worters	NY Americans	48	3000	142	3	2.84

LEADING PLAYOFF SCORERS

Player	Club	GP	G	A	PTS	PIM
Baldy Northcott	Mtl. Maroons	7	4	1	5	0
Busher Jackson	Toronto	7	3	2	5	2
Cy Wentworth	Mtl. Maroons	7	3	2	5	0
Charlie Conacher	Toronto	7	1	4	5	6
Earl Robinson	Mtl. Maroons	7	2	2	4	0
Russ Blinco	Mtl. Maroons	7	2	2	4	2
Lynn Patrick	NY Rangers	4	2	2	4	0

LEADING PLAYOFF GOALTENDERS

Goaltender	Club	GPI	MINS	GA	SO	AVG
Alex Connell	Mtl. Maroons	7	429	8	2	1.12
Tiny Thompson	Boston	4	275	7	1	1.53
George Hainsworth	Toronto	7	460	12	2	1.57
Dave Kerr	NY Rangers	4	240	10	0	2.50

Though he was a three-time All-Star and a two-time Stanley Cup champion, hockey was far from Lionel Conacher's best game. Named Canada's athlete of the half-century in 1950, "The Big Train" is a charter member of the Canadian Sports Hall of Fame (elected in 1955), the Canadian Football Hall of Fame (1963) and the Canadian Lacrosse Hall of Fame (1966). He was elected to the Hockey Hall of Fame in 1994.

The Ottawa Senators finally succumbed to financial woes prior to the 1934–35 season, as the once proud franchise abandoned the Canadian capital to become the St. Louis Eagles. The change of venue did not improve the club's fortunes, however, and, after finishing last with an 11–31–6 record, the club folded for good. Meanwhile, driven by hard economic times, the NHL lowered its salary cap to $62,500 per team and a maximum of $7,000 per player. The move didn't help the New York Americans players, who complained that they weren't being paid.

Gorman's Gambit – Senators became Eagles, Morenz became a Hawk and Tommy Gorman became the first coach to win the Cup with two different teams when the Maroons marched past the Leafs.

Because of the salary cap, the Montreal Canadiens were forced to trade aging superstar Howie Morenz to the Chicago Black Hawks. Goalie Lorne Chabot was included in the deal to replace the late Charlie Gardiner. Chabot would enjoy a career year and win the Vezina Trophy. The Canadiens received Lionel Conacher and two other players, then they dealt Conacher to the Montreal Maroons, where he was reunited with coach Tommy Gorman, who, despite winning the Stanley Cup in 1934, had been fired by the Black Hawks.

On the ice, Charlie Conacher led the league in scoring and his Toronto Maple Leafs easily outdistanced the Maroons for top spot in the Canadian Division. The Boston Bruins, who had fallen to last place the previous year, regained their usual perch atop the American Division standings and Eddie Shore took home the Hart Trophy for a second time. The Lady Byng Trophy, for sportsmanship, was won by Frank Boucher of the New York Rangers. It was the seventh time in eight years Boucher had won the award and, in recognition of that fact, he was given permanent possession of the original trophy.

In the playoffs, Toronto knocked off Boston to advance to the Stanley Cup finals, while the Maroons defeated the Black Hawks and Rangers before upsetting the Leafs for the league championship.

Leaders, 1934-35

GOALS

Name, Team	G
Charlie Conacher, Tor.	36
Cecil Dillon, NYR	25
Busher Jackson, Tor.	22
Syd Howe, St.L./Det.	22
Nels Stewart, Bos.	21
Dit Clapper, Bos.	21
Bill Cook, NYR	21
Leroy Goldsworthy, Chi./Mtl.	20
Herb Cain, Mtl.M.	20
John Sorrell, Det.	20
Marty Barry, Bos.	20

ASSISTS

Name, Team	A
Art Chapman, NYA	34
Frank Boucher, NYR	32
Larry Aurie, Det.	29
Herbie Lewis, Det.	27
Howie Morenz, Chi.	26
Eddie Shore, Bos.	26
Cooney Weiland, Det.	25
Syd Howe, St.L./Det.	25
Ebbie Goodfellow, Det.	24
Paul Thompson, Chi.	23

GOALIE WINS

Name, Team	W
George Hainsworth, Tor.	30
Lorne Chabot, Chi.	26
Tiny Thompson, Bos.	26
Alex Connell, Mtl.M.	24
Dave Kerr, NYR	19
Wilf Cude, Mtl.	19
Normie Smith, Det.	12
Roy Worters, NYA	12
Bill Beveridge, St.L.	11
John Ross Roach, Det.	7

SHUTOUTS

Name, Team	SO
Alex Connell, Mtl.M.	9
George Hainsworth, Tor.	8
Lorne Chabot, Chi.	8
Tiny Thompson, Bos.	8
John Ross Roach, Det.	4
Dave Kerr, NYR	4
Roy Worters, NYA	3
Bill Beveridge, St.L.	3
Normie Smith, Det.	2
Andy Aitkenhead, NYR	1
Wilf Cude, Mtl.	1

PLAYOFF GOALS

Name, Team	G
Baldy Northcott, Mtl.M.	4
Busher Jackson, Tor.	3
Cy Wentworth, Mtl.M.	3
Jack McGill, Mtl.	2
Lynn Patrick, NYR	2
Butch Keeling, NYR	2
Cecil Dillon, NYR	2
Bun Cook, NYR	2
Earl Robinson, Mtl.M.	2
Russ Blinco, Mtl.M.	2
Dave Trottier, Mtl.M.	2
Bill Thoms, Tor.	2
Pep Kelly, Tor.	2

PLAYOFF ASSISTS

Name, Team	A
Charlie Conacher, Tor.	4
Frank Boucher, NYR	3
Joe Primeau, Tor.	3
Jack Riley, Mtl.	2
Lynn Patrick, NYR	2
Bill Cook, NYR	2
Murray Murdoch, NYR	2
Busher Jackson, Tor.	2
Cy Wentworth, Mtl.M.	2
Earl Robinson, Mtl.M.	2
Russ Blinco, Mtl.M.	2
Frank Finnigan, Tor.	2
Bob Gracie, Mtl.M.	2

PLAYOFF GOALIE WINS

Name, Team	W
Alex Connell, Mtl.M.	5
George Hainsworth, Tor.	3
Tiny Thompson, Bos.	1
Dave Kerr, NYR	1

PLAYOFF SHUTOUTS

Name, Team	SO
Alex Connell, Mtl.M.	2
George Hainsworth, Tor.	2
Lorne Chabot, Chi.	1
Tiny Thompson, Bos.	1

FIRST TEAM ALL-STARS

Name, Team	Position
Frank Boucher, NYR	C
Charlie Conacher, Tor.	RW
Busher Jackson, Tor	LW
Eddie Shore, Bos.	D
Earl Seibert, NYR	D
Lorne Chabot, Chi.	G
Lester Patrick, NYR	Coach

SECOND TEAM ALL-STARS

Name, Team	Position
Cooney Weiland, Det.	C
Dit Clapper, Bos.	RW
Aurel Joliat, Mtl.	LW
Cy Wentworth, Mtl M	D
Art Coulter, Det.	D
Tiny Thompson, Bos.	G
Dick Irvin, Tor.	Coach

1935 Playoffs

SERIES A - SEMI-FINALS

Mar.	23	Toronto	0	at	Boston	1	2OT
Mar.	26	Toronto	2	at	Boston	0	
Mar.	28	Boston	0	at	Toronto	3	
Mar.	30	Boston	1	at	Toronto	2	OT

Toronto won best-of-five series 3–1

SERIES B AND C - QUARTER-FINALS

Mar.	23	Chicago	0	at	Mtl. Maroons	0	
Mar.	26	Mtl. Maroons	1	at	Chicago	0	OT

Mtl. Maroons won total-goals series 1–0

Mar.	24	Montreal	1	at	NY Rangers	2
Mar.	26	NY Rangers	4	at	Montreal	4

NY Rangers won total-goals series 6–5

SERIES D - SEMI-FINALS

Mar.	28	Mtl. Maroons	2	at	NY Rangers	1
Mar.	30	NY Rangers	3	at	Mtl. Maroons	3

Mtl. Maroons won total-goals series 5–4

SERIES E - FINALS

Apr.	4	Mtl. Maroons	3	at	Toronto	2	OT
Apr.	6	Mtl. Maroons	3	at	Toronto	1	
Apr.	9	Toronto	1	at	Mtl. Maroons	4	

Mtl. Maroons won best-of-five series 3–0

1934-35 – Montreal Maroons – Lionel Conacher, Cy Wentworth, Alex Connell, Toe Blake, Stewart Evans, Earl Robinson, Bill Miller, Dave Trottier, Jimmy Ward, Baldy Northcott, Hooley Smith (Captain), Russ Blinco, Al Shields, Sammy McManus, Gus Marker, Bob Gracie, Herb Cain, Tommy Gorman (Manager/Coach), Bill O'Brien (Trainer).

TROPHY WINNERS

Trophy	Awarded For	Winner	Team
Hart	MVP	Eddie Shore	Bos.
Calder	Top Rookie	Sweeney Schriner	NYA
Vezina	Fewest Goals Against	Lorne Chabot	Chi
Byng	Gentlemanly Conduct	Frank Boucher	NYR

NHL NOTEBOOK

TRANSACTIONS

- Oct. 3, 1934 – Montreal Canadiens traded Howie Morenz, Marty Burke and Lorne Chabot to Chicago in exchange for Lionel Conacher, Roger Jenkins and Leroy Goldsworthy.
- Dec. 14, 1934 – New York Rangers purchased goaltender Dave Kerr from the Montreal Maroons.
- Jan. 16, 1935 – Montreal Canadiens purchased Johnny Gagnon from the Boston Bruins.
- Feb. 21, 1935 – Montreal Maroons signed Toe Blake.

RECORDS

- Dec. 1, 1934 – Toronto beat St. Louis 4-3 at Maple Leaf Gardens, to set an NHL record for most wins (eight) from the start of a season.
- Nov. 18, 1934 – Toronto's George Hainsworth became the first goaltender in NHL history to record 80 career shutouts, as the Maple Leafs won 5-0 at Chicago.
- Nov. 20, 1934 – Toronto's Harvey "Busher" Jackson became the first NHL player to score a hat trick in one period. He finished with four goals in the third period to lead the Leafs to a 5-2 win over the St. Louis Eagles.
- Mar. 19, 1935 – George Hainsworth became the first goaltender in Toronto history to win 30 games in one season. The milestone was a 5-3 win against the visiting St. Louis Eagles.

MILESTONES

- Sept. 22, 1934 – A meeting of the NHL board of governors was held, where it was approved that collective salary limits for all clubs for the 1935 season would not exceed $62,500 with an individual salary limit of $7,000 to any one player.
- Nov. 8, 1934 – NHL hockey made its debut in St. Louis, as 12,600 fans welcomed the Eagles to the Coliseum for the 1934-35 home opener, a 3-1 loss to the Black Hawks.
- Nov. 13, 1934 – St. Louis' Ralph Bowman scored the first penalty shot goal in NHL history. It came during a 2-1 Maroons win over the St. Louis Eagles. It was just the second penalty shot attempt in NHL history.
- Dec. 16, 1934 – For the first time in NHL history, two brothers opposed each other as coaches, when Frank Patrick led the Bruins to a 2-1 win over the Rangers' Lester Patrick.

1935-36

Stanley Cup • Detroit Red Wings

FINAL STANDINGS

Team	GP	W	L	T	GF	GA	PTS
CANADIAN DIVISION							
Mtl. Maroons	48	22	16	10	114	106	54
Toronto	48	23	19	6	126	106	52
NY Americans	48	16	25	7	109	122	39
Montreal	48	11	26	11	82	123	33
AMERICAN DIVISION							
Detroit	48	24	16	8	124	103	56
Boston	48	22	20	6	92	83	50
Chicago	48	21	19	8	93	92	50
New York	48	19	17	12	91	96	50

LEADING SCORERS

Player	Club	GP	G	A	PTS	PIM
Sweeney Schriner	NY Americans	48	19	26	45	8
Marty Barry	Detroit	48	21	19	40	16
Paul Thompson	Chicago	45	17	23	40	19
Bill Thoms	Toronto	48	23	15	38	29
Charlie Conacher	Toronto	44	23	15	38	74
Hooley Smith	Mtl. Maroons	47	19	19	38	75
Doc Romnes	Chicago	48	13	25	38	6
Art Chapman	NY Americans	48	10	28	38	14
Herbie Lewis	Detroit	45	14	23	37	25
Baldy Northcott	Mtl. Maroons	48	15	21	36	41
Mush March	Chicago	48	16	19	35	42
Larry Aurie	Detroit	44	16	18	34	17
Cecil Dillon	NY Rangers	48	18	14	32	12
Red Beattie	Boston	48	14	18	32	27
Jimmy Ward	Mtl. Maroons	48	12	19	31	30
Syd Howe	Detroit	48	16	14	30	26
Nels Stewart	NY Americans	48	14	15	29	16
Johnny Gottselig	Chicago	40	14	15	29	4
Frank Boucher	NY Rangers	48	11	18	29	2
Buzz Boll	Toronto	44	15	13	28	14
John Sorrell	Detroit	48	13	15	28	8
Eddie Wiseman	Det./NYA	45	12	16	28	15
Cooney Weiland	Boston	48	14	13	27	15
Leroy Goldsworthy	Montreal	47	15	11	26	8
Glenn Brydson	NYR/Chi.	52	10	16	26	39

LEADING GOALTENDERS

Goaltender	Club	GPI	MINS	GA	SO	AVG
Tiny Thompson	Boston	48	2930	82	10	1.68
Mike Karakas	Chicago	48	2990	92	9	1.85
Dave Kerr	NY Rangers	47	2980	95	8	1.91
Normie Smith	Detroit	48	3030	103	6	2.04
George Hainsworth	Toronto	48	3000	106	8	2.12
Bill Beveridge	Mtl. Maroons	32	1970	71	1	2.16
Roy Worters	NY Americans	48	3000	122	3	2.44
Wilf Cude	Montreal	47	2940	122	6	2.49

LEADING PLAYOFF SCORERS

Player	Club	GP	G	A	PTS	PIM
Buzz Boll	Toronto	9	7	3	10	2
Bill Thoms	Toronto	9	3	5	8	0
Joe Primeau	Toronto	9	3	4	7	0
John Sorrell	Detroit	7	3	4	7	0
Syd Howe	Detroit	7	3	3	6	2
Marty Barry	Detroit	7	2	4	6	6
Six players tied with					5	

LEADING PLAYOFF GOALTENDERS

Goaltender	Club	GPI	MINS	GA	SO	AVG
Lorne Chabot	Mtl. Maroons	3	297	6	0	1.21
Normie Smith	Detroit	7	538	12	2	1.34
Roy Worters	NY Americans	5	300	11	2	2.20
George Hainsworth	Toronto	9	541	27	0	2.99

Jack Adams acquired Marty Barry for the Detroit Red Wings in 1935 and placed him on a powerhouse offensive line with Larry Aurie and Herbie Lewis. Barry led the Red Wings in scoring thee times and helped Detroit win the Stanley Cup in 1936 and 1937. He also won the Lady Byng Trophy and a First All-Star Team berth for the 1936–37 season.

Despite their Stanley Cup win, the Montreal Maroons continued to struggle at the box office. So did the Canadiens, who were sold by Leo Dandurand and Joseph Cattarinich to the Canadian Arena Company prior to the 1935–36 season.

A dispersal draft was held to distribute the players belonging to the defunct St. Louis Eagles, and the Boston Bruins got a diamond in the rough in Bill Cowley who would blossom into a superstar. Boston also traded Marty Barry to the Detroit Red Wings, where he teamed with Larry Aurie and Herbie Lewis to form one of the league's top lines.

Miracle in Motown – The Eagles folded, Amerk Sweeney Schriner couldn't be finer and Detroit had a top trio in Aurie, Lewis and Barry as the Red Wings won the regular-season and playoff titles.

The Wings emerged as the best in the league this season, winning the American Division with a 24–16–8 record. The Maroons won the Canadian Division with the nearly identical mark of 22–16–10. The teams were so evenly matched in the first game of their playoff series that it took until 16:30 of the sixth overtime period for Mud Bruneteau to beat Lorne Chabot for the game's only goal.

Not only had Detroit's Normie Smith recorded a shutout in the longest game in NHL history, he went on to blank the Maroons for 60 minutes more in game two—another 1–0 victory—then allowed only one goal in a 2–1 win that swept the series. Smith's goals-against average for the series was a minuscule 0.20 – the equivalent of one goal allowed for every five games played.

In New York City, the Americans made the playoffs for the first time since 1929 and beat the Chicago Black Hawks in their first series before falling to the Toronto Maple Leafs. It was the Leafs' fourth trip to the finals in five years, but they would come away empty-handed for the third year in a row as the Red Wings earned their first NHL championship.

Leaders, 1935-36

GOALS

Name, Team	G
Charlie Conacher, Tor.	23
Bill Thoms, Tor.	23
Marty Barry, Det.	21
Hooley Smith, Mtl.M.	19
Sweeney Schriner, NYA	19
Cecil Dillon, NYR	18
Paul Thompson, Chi.	17
Larry Aurie, Det.	16
Mush March, Chi.	16
Syd Howe, Det.	16

ASSISTS

Name, Team	A
Art Chapman, NYA	28
Sweeney Schriner, NYA	26
Doc Romnes, Chi.	25
Paul Thompson, Chi.	23
Herbie Lewis, Det.	23
Baldy Northcott, Mtl.M.	21
Hooley Smith, Mtl.M.	19
Marty Barry, Det.	19
Mush March, Chi.	19
Jimmy Ward, Mtl.M.	19
Paul Haynes, Mtl.	19

GOALIE WINS

Name, Team	W
Normie Smith, Det.	24
George Hainsworth, Tor.	23
Tiny Thompson, Bos.	22
Mike Karakas, Chi.	21
Dave Kerr, NYR	18
Roy Worters, NYA	16
Bill Beveridge, Mtl.M.	14
Wilf Cude, Mtl.	11
Lorne Chabot, Mtl.M.	8
Bert Gardiner, NYR	1

SHUTOUTS

Name, Team	SO
Tiny Thompson, Bos.	10
Mike Karakas, Chi.	9
Dave Kerr, NYR	8
George Hainsworth, Tor.	8
Wilf Cude, Mtl.	6
Normie Smith, Det.	6
Roy Worters, NYA	3
Lorne Chabot, Mtl.M.	2
Bill Beveridge, Mtl.M.	1

PLAYOFF GOALS

Name, Team	G
Buzz Boll, Tor.	7
Sweeney Schriner, NYA	3
John Sorrell, Det.	3
Syd Howe, Det.	3
Bucko McDonald, Det.	3
Bill Thoms, Tor.	3
Joe Primeau, Tor.	3
Charlie Conacher, Tor.	3
Busher Jackson, Tor.	3
13 tied with	2

PLAYOFF ASSISTS

Name, Team	A
Bill Thoms, Tor.	5
John Sorrell, Det.	4
Marty Barry, Det.	4
Joe Primeau, Tor.	4
13 tied with	3

PLAYOFF GOALIE WINS

Name, Team	W
Normie Smith, Det.	6
George Hainsworth, Tor.	4
Roy Worters, NYA	2
Mike Karakas, Chi.	1
Tiny Thompson, Bos.	1

PLAYOFF SHUTOUTS

Name, Team	SO
Roy Worters, NYA	2
Normie Smith, Det.	2
Tiny Thompson, Bos.	1

FIRST TEAM ALL-STARS

Name, Team	Position
Hooley Smith, Mtl M	C
Charlie Conacher, Tor.	RW
Sweeney Schriner, NYA	LW
Eddie Shore, Bos.	D
Babe Siebert, Bos.	D
Tiny Thompson, Bos.	G
Lester Patrick, NYR	Coach

SECOND TEAM ALL-STARS

Name, Team	Position
Bill Thoms, Tor.	C
Cecil Dillon, NYR	RW
Paul Thompson, Chi.	LW
Earl Seibert, Chi.	D
Ebbie Goodfellow, Det.	D
Wilf Cude, Mtl.	G
Tommy Gorman, Mtl M	Coach

1936 Playoffs

SERIES A - SEMI-FINALS

Mar.	24	Detroit	1	at	Mtl. Maroons	0 6OT
Mar.	26	Detroit	3	at	Mtl. Maroons	0
Mar.	28	Mtl. Maroons	1	at	Detroit	2

Detroit won best-of-five series 3–0

SERIES B AND C - QUARTER-FINALS

Mar.	24	Toronto	0	at	Boston	3
Mar.	26	Boston	3	at	Toronto	8

Toronto won total-goals series 8–6

Mar.	24	Chicago	0	at	NY Americans	3
Mar.	26	NY Americans	4	at	Chicago	5

NY Americans won total-goals series 7–5

SERIES D - SEMI-FINALS

Mar.	28	NY Americans	1	at	Toronto	3
Mar.	31	Toronto	0	at	NY Americans	1
Apr.	2	NY Americans	1	at	Toronto	3

Toronto won best-of-three series 2-1

SERIES E - FINALS

Apr.	5	Toronto	1	at	Detroit	3
Apr.	7	Toronto	4	at	Detroit	9
Apr.	9	Detroit	3	at	Toronto	4 OT
Apr.	11	Detroit	3	at	Toronto	2

Detroit won best-of-five series 3–1

1935-36 – Detroit Red Wings – John Sorrell, Syd Howe, Marty Barry, Herbie Lewis, Larry Aurie, Mud Bruneteau, Wally Kilrea, Hec Kilrea, Gord Pettinger, Bucko McDonald, Ralph Bowman, Pete Kelly, Doug Young (Captain), Ebbie Goodfellow, Normie Smith, Jack Adams (Manager/Coach), Honey Walker (Trainer).

TROPHY WINNERS

Trophy	Awarded For	Winner	Team
Hart	MVP	Eddie Shore	Bos.
Calder	Top Rookie	Mike Karakas	Chi.
Vezina	Fewest Goals Against	Tiny Thompson	Bos.
Byng	Gentlemanly Conduct	Doc Romnes	Chi

NHL NOTEBOOK

TRANSACTIONS

- Sept. 24, 1935 – Detroit signed Carl Liscombe.
- Oct. 9, 1935 – Boston signed Woody Dumart and Milt Schmidt.
- Oct. 18, 1935 – New York Rangers signed Babe Pratt, Mac Colville, and Neil Colville.
- Oct. 15, 1935 – Boston purchased Bill Cowley and Teddy Graham from the NHL, which had taken over the defunct St. Louis Eagles franchise.
- Feb. 13, 1936 – Montreal Canadiens obtained Hector "Toe" Blake, Bill Miller and Ken Gravel from the Montreal Maroons for Lorne Chabot.

RECORDS

- Mar. 24, 1936 – Mud Bruneteau scored as Detroit beat the Montreal Maroons 1-0 after 116:30 of overtime – 5 hours and 51 minutes after the opening faceoff, in the longest game in NHL history. Goalie Norm Smith made 92 saves for the Red Wings.
- Mar. 26, 1936 – Toronto set a playoff record for most powerplay goals in one period, with four in the second against Boston. Maple Leafs won 8-3 in game two of the Stanley Cup quarter-finals.
- Apr. 7, 1936 – Johnny Sorrell scored twice and added two assists to lead the Red Wings to a 9-4 win against the Maple Leafs in game two of the Stanley Cup finals in Detroit. Nine goals marked a new record for most goals by one team in a playoff game.
- Toronto's Red Horner set an NHL record with 167 penalty minutes. The record would stand for 20 years.

MILESTONES

- Oct. 15, 1935 – NHL Board of Governors purchased the St. Louis Eagles franchise, players, and rights for $35,000. The league then sold off the players to the remaining NHL clubs.
- Mar. 22, 1936 – NY Rangers won 3-1 at Boston on the final night of the season, to finish with a record of 19-17-12, the first time in NHL history that every team in a division finished with records above .500. The Rangers were in the American Division.
- Apr. 11, 1936 – Detroit coach Jack Adams led the Red Wings to their first Stanley Cup championship with a 3-2 win over Toronto in game four of their best-of-five series. The Red Wings became the last of the NHL's "Original Six" teams to win the Stanley Cup.

1936-37

Stanley Cup • Detroit Red Wings

FINAL STANDINGS

Team	GP	W	L	T	GF	GA	PTS
CANADIAN DIVISION							
Montreal	48	24	18	6	115	111	54
Mtl. Maroons	48	22	17	9	126	110	53
Toronto	48	22	21	5	119	115	49
NY Americans	48	15	29	4	122	161	34
AMERICAN DIVISION							
Detroit	48	25	14	9	128	102	59
Boston	48	23	18	7	120	110	53
New York	48	19	20	9	117	106	47
Chicago	48	14	27	7	99	131	35

LEADING SCORERS

Player	Club	GP	G	A	PTS	PIM
Sweeney Schriner	NY Americans	48	21	25	46	17
Syl Apps	Toronto	48	16	29	45	10
Marty Barry	Detroit	47	17	27	44	6
Larry Aurie	Detroit	45	23	20	43	20
Busher Jackson	Toronto	46	21	19	40	12
Johnny Gagnon	Montreal	48	20	16	36	38
Bob Gracie	Mtl. Maroons	47	11	25	36	18
Nels Stewart	Bos./NYA	43	23	12	35	37
Paul Thompson	Chicago	47	17	18	35	28
Bill Cowley	Boston	46	13	22	35	4
Lorne Carr	NY Americans	48	18	16	34	22
Earl Robinson	Mtl. Maroons	47	16	18	34	19
Gordie Drillon	Toronto	41	16	17	33	2
Eddie Wiseman	NY Americans	44	14	19	33	12
Aurel Joliat	Montreal	47	17	15	32	30
Herbie Lewis	Detroit	45	14	18	32	14
Cecil Dillon	NY Rangers	48	20	11	31	13
Ray Getliffe	Boston	48	16	15	31	28
Art Chapman	NY Americans	43	8	23	31	36
Herb Cain	Mtl. Maroons	42	13	17	30	18
Johnny Gottselig	Chicago	47	9	21	30	10
Baldy Northcott	Mtl. Maroons	46	15	14	29	18

LEADING GOALTENDERS

Goaltender	Club	GPI	MINS	GA	SO	AVG
Normie Smith	Detroit	48	2980	102	6	2.05
Dave Kerr	NY Rangers	48	3020	106	4	2.11
Wilf Cude	Montreal	44	2730	99	5	2.18
Alex Connell	Mtl. Maroons	27	1710	63	2	2.21
Tiny Thompson	Boston	48	2970	110	6	2.22
Turk Broda	Toronto	45	2770	106	3	2.30

LEADING PLAYOFF SCORERS

Player	Club	GP	G	A	PTS	PIM
Marty Barry	Detroit	10	4	7	11	2
Herbie Lewis	Detroit	10	4	3	7	4
Syd Howe	Detroit	10	2	5	7	0
Neil Colville	NY Rangers	9	3	3	6	0
John Sorrell	Detroit	10	2	4	6	2
Butch Keeling	NY Rangers	9	3	2	5	2
Frank Boucher	NY Rangers	9	2	3	5	0
Paul Haynes	Montreal	5	2	3	5	0
Alex Shibicky	NY Rangers	9	1	4	5	0

LEADING PLAYOFF GOALTENDERS

Goaltender	Club	GPI	MINS	GA	SO	AVG
Dave Kerr	NY Rangers	9	553	10	4	1.08
Normie Smith	Detroit	5	282	6	1	1.28
Earl Robertson	Detroit	6	340	8	2	1.41
Bill Beveridge	Mtl. Maroons	5	300	11	0	2.20
Wilf Cude	Montreal	5	352	13	0	2.22

Sweeney Schriner was born in Saratov, Russia, but grew up in Calgary, Alberta. He was an instant success in the NHL with the New York Americans, being named the league's rookie of the year in 1934–35 and leading the league in scoring each of the next two seasons. Traded to Toronto in 1939, he helped the Maple Leafs win the Stanley Cup in 1942 and 1945.

The Toronto Maple Leafs unveiled several new players for the 1936–37 season. Center Syl Apps would earn honors as rookie of the year, as his playmaking skills blended perfectly with first-year sniper Gordie Drillon. Goalie Turk Broda also made his debut this season. In Montreal, it was an old name that made headlines, as Howie Morenz returned to the Canadiens after stints with the Black Hawks and Rangers. Morenz took his place at center between his old linemates Aurel Joliat and Johnny Gagnon. The three were now past their prime, but the Canadiens were showing much improvement over the previous year's last-place finish, thanks largely to youngster Toe Blake, who shouldered most of the offensive load.

Sweet Repeat – Apps, Broda and Drillon debuted for the Leafs, Montreal mourned Morenz and the Wings kept their eyes focused on the prize from opening day to the last whistle to take their second consecutive Stanley Cup title.

Meanwhile, reaching the playoffs the previous season had done little to help the New York Americans' bottom line; the NHL was forced to take over operation of the club before the start of the season.

On January 28, 1937, Morenz caught the tip of his skate in the boards at the Montreal Forum, badly breaking his leg above the ankle. On March 8, the hockey world was stunned to learn that Morenz had died in hospital. A pulmonary embolism was given as the cause of death. Thousands of fans filed past Morenz's body, which lay in state at the Forum, and thousands more lined the route of the funeral procession that took him to the cemetery.

Despite the loss of their great superstar, the Canadiens won the Canadian Division, but were knocked out of the playoffs by the Red Wings. Detroit then became the first American franchise to win consecutive Stanley Cup titles when they defeated the New York Rangers.

Leaders, 1936-37

GOALS

Name, Team	G
Nels Stewart, Bos./NYA	23
Larry Aurie, Det.	23
Butch Keeling, NYR	22
Busher Jackson, Tor.	21
Sweeney Schriner, NYA	21
Johnny Gagnon, Mtl.	20
Cecil Dillon, NYR	20
Charlie Sands, Bos.	18
Lorne Carr, NYA	18
Five tied with	17

ASSISTS

Name, Team	A
Syl Apps, Tor.	29
Marty Barry, Det.	27
Bob Gracie, Mtl.M.	25
Sweeney Schriner, NYA	25
Art Chapman, NYA	23
Bill Cowley, Bos.	22
Johnny Gottselig, Chi.	21
Babe Siebert, Mtl.	20
Larry Aurie, Det.	20
Eddie Wiseman, NYA	19
Busher Jackson, Tor.	19
Lionel Conacher, Mtl.M.	19

GOALIE WINS

Name, Team	W
Normie Smith, Det.	25
Tiny Thompson, Bos.	23
Wilf Cude, Mtl.	22
Turk Broda, Tor.	22
Dave Kerr, NYR	19
Mike Karakas, Chi.	14
Bill Beveridge, Mtl.M.	12
Alex Connell, Mtl.M.	10
Alfie Moore, NYA	7
Roy Worters, NYA	6

SHUTOUTS

Name, Team	SO
Normie Smith, Det.	6
Tiny Thompson, Bos.	6
Wilf Cude, Mtl.	5
Mike Karakas, Chi.	5
Dave Kerr, NYR	4
Turk Broda, Tor.	3
Roy Worters, NYA	2
Alex Connell, Mtl.M.	2
Lorne Chabot, NYA	1
Alfie Moore, NYA	1
Bill Beveridge, Mtl.M.	1

PLAYOFF GOALS

Name, Team	G
Marty Barry, Det.	4
Herbie Lewis, Det.	4
Neil Colville, NYR	3
Butch Keeling, NYR	3
Babe Pratt, NYR	3
Lynn Patrick, NYR	3
Hec Kilrea, Det.	3
10 tied with	2

PLAYOFF ASSISTS

Name, Team	A
Marty Barry, Det.	7
Syd Howe, Det.	5
Alex Shibicky, NYR	4
John Sorrell, Det.	4
Bill Cowley, Bos.	3
Paul Haynes, Mtl.	3
Aurel Joliat, Mtl.	3
Neil Colville, NYR	3
Frank Boucher, NYR	3
Art Coulter, NYR	3
Cecil Dillon, NYR	3
Herbie Lewis, Det.	3

PLAYOFF GOALIE WINS

Name, Team	W
Dave Kerr, NYR	6
Normie Smith, Det.	3
Earl Robertson, Det.	3
Bill Beveridge, Mtl.M.	2
Wilf Cude, Mtl.	2

PLAYOFF SHUTOUTS

Name, Team	SO
Dave Kerr, NYR	4
Earl Robertson, Det.	2
Tiny Thompson, Bos.	1
Normie Smith, Det.	1

FIRST TEAM ALL-STARS

Name, Team	Position
Marty Barry, Det.	C
Larry Aurie, Det.	RW
Busher Jackson, Tor.	LW
Babe Siebert, Mtl.	D
Ebbie Goodfellow, Det.	D
Normie Smith, Det.	G
Jack Adams, Det.	Coach

SECOND TEAM ALL-STARS

Name, Team	Position
Art Chapman, NYA	C
Cecil Dillon, NYR	RW
Sweeney Schriner, NYA	LW
Earl Seibert, Chi.	D
Lionel Conacher, Mtl M	D
Wilf Cude, Mtl.	G
Cecil Hart, Mtl.	Coach

1937 Playoffs

SERIES A - SEMI-FINALS

Mar. 23	Montreal	0	at	Detroit	4	
Mar. 25	Montreal	1	at	Detroit	5	
Mar. 27	Detroit	1	at	Montreal	3	
Mar. 30	Detroit	1	at	Montreal	3	
Apr. 1	Detroit	2	at	Montreal	1	3OT

Detroit won best-of-five series 3–2

SERIES B AND C - QUARTER-FINALS

Mar. 23	Boston	1	at	Mtl. Maroons	4	
Mar. 25	Mtl. Maroons	0	at	Boston	4	
Mar. 28	Mtl. Maroons	4	at	Boston	1	

Mtl. Maroons won best-of-three series 2–1

Mar. 23	NY Rangers	3	at	Toronto	0	
Mar. 25	Toronto	1	at	NY Rangers	2	OT

NY Rangers won best-of-three series 2–0

SERIES D - SEMI-FINALS

Apr. 1	Mtl. Maroons	0	at	NY Rangers	1
Apr. 3	NY Rangers	4	at	Mtl. Maroons	0

NY Rangers won best-of-three series 2–0

SERIES E - FINALS

Apr. 6	Detroit	1	at	NY Rangers	5
Apr. 8	NY Rangers	2	at	Detroit	4
Apr. 11	NY Rangers	1	at	Detroit	0
Apr. 13	NY Rangers	0	at	Detroit	1
Apr. 15	NY Rangers	0	at	Detroit	3

Detroit won best-of-five series 3–2

1936-37 – Detroit Red Wings – Normie Smith, Pete Kelly, Larry Aurie, Herbie Lewis, Hec Kilrea, Mud Bruneteau, Syd Howe, Wally Kilrea, Jimmy Franks, Bucko McDonald, Gord Pettinger, Ebbie Goodfellow, John Gallagher, Ralph Bowman, John Sorrell, Marty Barry, Earl Robertson, John Sherf, Howie Mackie, Rolly Roulston, Doug Young (Captain), Jack Adams (Manager/Coach), Honey Walker (Trainer).

TROPHY WINNERS

Trophy	Awarded For	Winner	Team
Hart	MVP	Babe Siebert	Mtl.
Calder	Top Rookie	Syl Apps	Tor.
Vezina	Fewest Goals Against	Normie Smith	Det
Byng	Gentlemanly Conduct	Marty Barry	Det.

NHL NOTEBOOK

TRANSACTIONS

- May 6, 1936 – Toronto purchased goaltender Walter "Turk" Broda from the Detroit Red Wings for $7,500.
- May 7, 1936 – Toronto claimed Murray Armstrong from Philadelphia (CAHL) in the inter-league draft
- Sept. 10, 1936 – Montreal Canadiens obtained Babe Siebert and Roger Jenkins from Boston for LeRoy Goldsworthy, Sammy McManus and $10,000.
- Dec. 4, 1936 – Boston Bruins obtained Hooley Smith from the Montreal Maroons for Gerry Shannon.
- Dec. 20, 1936 – New York Americans purchased Nels Stewart from the Boston Bruins.

RECORDS

- Jan. 30, 1937 – New York Americans' Nels Stewart became the NHL's All-Time goal scoring leader, when he picked up his 270th career goal to surpass Howie Morenz, as the Americans beat the Montreal Canadiens 4-0.
- Mar. 9, 1937 – NY Rangers center Frank Boucher became the first player in NHL history to amass 250 career assists. #250 came on an Alex Shibicky goal in a 7-5 win against the NY Americans.

MILESTONES

- May 7, 1936 – At the NHL meetings in Detroit it was announced that the Montreal Canadiens had been granted first claim on all French-Canadian amateur hockey players in all of Canada, for a period of three years.
- Nov. 14, 1936 – Toronto's King Clancy scored on a penalty shot as the Maple Leafs beat Chicago 6-2. It was the final goal of his NHL playing career. The future Hall of Famer retired one week later.
- Nov. 19, 1936 – Alex Connell became the second goaltender in NHL history to record 80 career shutouts, as the Montreal Maroons beat the Black Hawks 4-0 at Chicago.
- Nov. 26, 1936 – Boston's Tiny Thompson became the first goaltender in franchise history (and the 4th in NHL history) to record 200 victories as the Bruins won 3-2 over the visiting Montreal Maroons.
- Dec. 5, 1936 – Montreal's Aurel Joliat became the third player in NHL history to score 250 career goals, in the Canadiens' 4-3 win over the visiting Boston Bruins.

1937-38

Stanley Cup • Chicago Black Hawks

Alfie Moore was a long-time minor-leaguer who spent a portion of the 1936–37 season with the New York Americans. He gained fame as an emergency fill-in for the Black Hawks during the 1938 Stanley Cup finals but never played for Chicago again after the Stanley Cup victory. He saw action in only three more NHL games over the final four years of his pro career.

FINAL STANDINGS

Team	GP	W	L	T	GF	GA	PTS
CANADIAN DIVISION							
Toronto	48	24	15	9	151	127	57
NY Americans	48	19	18	11	110	111	49
Montreal	48	18	17	13	123	128	49
Mtl. Maroons	48	12	30	6	101	149	30
AMERICAN DIVISION							
Boston	48	30	11	7	142	89	67
New York	48	27	15	6	149	96	60
Chicago	48	14	25	9	97	139	37
Detroit	48	12	25	11	99	133	35

LEADING SCORERS

Player	Club	GP	G	A	PTS	PIM
Gordie Drillon	Toronto	48	26	26	52	4
Syl Apps	Toronto	47	21	29	50	9
Paul Thompson	Chicago	48	22	22	44	14
Georges Mantha	Montreal	47	23	19	42	12
Cecil Dillon	NY Rangers	48	21	18	39	6
Bill Cowley	Boston	48	17	22	39	8
Sweeney Schriner	NY Americans	48	21	17	38	22
Bill Thoms	Toronto	48	14	24	38	14
Clint Smith	NY Rangers	48	14	23	37	0
Nels Stewart	NY Americans	48	19	17	36	29
Neil Colville	NY Rangers	45	17	19	36	11
Alex Shibicky	NY Rangers	48	17	18	35	26
Paul Haynes	Montreal	48	13	22	35	25
Bobby Bauer	Boston	48	20	14	34	9
Busher Jackson	Toronto	48	17	17	34	18
Lynn Patrick	NY Rangers	48	15	19	34	24
Toe Blake	Montreal	43	17	16	33	33
Eddie Wiseman	NY Americans	48	18	14	32	32
Johnny Gottselig	Chicago	48	13	19	32	22
Rod Lorrain	Montreal	48	13	19	32	14
Doc Romnes	Chicago	44	10	22	32	4
Phil Watson	NY Rangers	48	7	25	32	52

LEADING GOALTENDERS

Goaltender	Club	GPI	MINS	GA	SO	AVG
Tiny Thompson	Boston	48	2970	89	7	1.80
Dave Kerr	NY Rangers	48	2960	96	8	1.95
Earl Robertson	NY Americans	48	3000	111	6	2.22
Wilf Cude	Montreal	47	2990	126	3	2.53
Turk Broda	Toronto	48	2980	127	6	2.56
Normie Smith	Detroit	47	2930	130	3	2.66

LEADING PLAYOFF SCORERS

Player	Club	GP	G	A	PTS	PIM
Gordie Drillon	Toronto	7	7	1	8	2
Johnny Gottselig	Chicago	10	5	3	8	4
Earl Seibert	Chicago	10	5	2	7	12
Paul Thompson	Chicago	10	4	3	7	6
Mush March	Chicago	9	2	4	6	12
Doc Romnes	Chicago	12	2	4	6	2
Roger Jenkins	Chicago	10	0	6	6	8
George Parsons	Toronto	7	3	2	5	11
Carl Voss	Chicago	10	3	2	5	0
Nels Stewart	NY Americans	6	2	3	5	2
Tom Anderson	NY Americans	6	1	4	5	2
Syl Apps	Toronto	7	1	4	5	0

LEADING PLAYOFF GOALTENDERS

Goaltender	Club	GPI	MINS	GA	SO	AVG
Earl Robertson	NY Americans	6	475	12	0	1.52
Tiny Thompson	Boston	3	212	6	0	1.70
Mike Karakas	Chicago	8	525	15	2	1.71
Turk Broda	Toronto	7	452	13	1	1.73
Wilf Cude	Montreal	3	192	11	0	3.44

THE NHL HAD LOST ITS first great superstar the year before and so the 1937–38 season began with a memorial All-Star Game in honor of Howie Morenz. A team made up of Montreal Canadiens and Maroons took on the best from the NHL's other six teams. The event raised over $11,000 for the Morenz family.

Nels Stewart, who'd overtaken Morenz as the NHL's all-time career goal-scoring leader the year before, notched his 300th goal in 1937–38, while Boston's Eddie Shore returned from a serious back injury the previous year to win the Hart Trophy for the fourth and final time.

Shore's Bruins were the best in the NHL in the regular season, winning the American Division over a strong New York Ranger squad. The Chicago Black Hawks snuck into the playoffs with a weak 14–25–9 third-place finish. The Toronto Maple Leafs won the Canadian Division behind the stellar play of scoring leader Gordie Drillon and runner-up Syl Apps. Boston's stronger defense had them favored to beat Toronto in the playoffs, but Turk Broda's stellar goaltending sparked an upset as the Leafs advanced to the Stanley Cup finals for the fifth time in seven years.

Miracle on Madison – Could a team that finished 11 games under .500, scored the fewest goals and allowed the second most not only make the playoffs but also win the Stanley Cup? Hey, you can look it up!

Despite a poor regular season (and spared a last-place finish only by Detroit's shocking collapse from first to worst), the Black Hawks came alive in the playoffs. Chicago upset the Canadiens and Americans, though their win over New York cost them the services of netminder Mike Karakas, who suffered a broken toe. Ex-NHLer Alfie Moore took over in goal and stunned the Leafs with a 3–1 victory in game one. Moore was then declared ineligible and Chicago lost game two 5–1 with farmhand Paul Goodman between the pipes. Karakas subsequently returned, wearing a specially fitted skate, and the Black Hawks won the next two games to take the Stanley Cup. Two facts distinguished the Chicago win: they were the first club with a losing record to win the Cup, and they did it with a roster made up of an equal number of Canadian and American players.

Leaders, 1937-38

GOALS

Name, Team	G
Gordie Drillon, Tor.	26
Georges Mantha, Mtl.	23
Paul Thompson, Chi.	22
Syl Apps, Tor.	21
Cecil Dillon, NYR	21
Sweeney Schriner, NYA	21
Bobby Bauer, Bos.	20
Nels Stewart, NYA	19
Eddie Wiseman, NYA	18
Seven tied with	17

ASSISTS

Name, Team	A
Syl Apps, Tor.	29
Art Chapman, NYA	27
Gordie Drillon, Tor.	26
Phil Watson, NYR	25
Bill Thoms, Tor.	24
Clint Smith, NYR	23
Doc Romnes, Chi.	22
Paul Thompson, Chi.	22
Bill Cowley, Bos.	22
Paul Haynes, Mtl.	22

GOALIE WINS

Name, Team	W
Tiny Thompson, Bos.	30
Dave Kerr, NYR	27
Turk Broda, Tor.	24
Earl Robertson, NYA	19
Wilf Cude, Mtl.	18
Mike Karakas, Chi.	14
Bill Beveridge, Mtl.M.	12
Normie Smith, Det.	11
Jimmy Franks, Det.	1

SHUTOUTS

Name, Team	SO
Dave Kerr, NYR	8
Tiny Thompson, Bos.	7
Turk Broda, Tor.	6
Earl Robertson, NYA	6
Wilf Cude, Mtl.	3
Normie Smith, Det.	3
Bill Beveridge, Mtl.M.	2
Mike Karakas, Chi.	1

PLAYOFF GOALS

Name, Team	G
Gordie Drillon, Tor.	7
Johnny Gottselig, Chi.	5
Earl Seibert, Chi.	5
John Sorrell, NYA	4
Paul Thompson, Chi.	4
Toe Blake, Mtl.	3
Lorne Carr, NYA	3
George Parsons, Tor.	3
Carl Voss, Chi.	3
Cully Dahlstrom, Chi.	3

PLAYOFF ASSISTS

Name, Team	A
Roger Jenkins, Chi.	6
Paul Haynes, Mtl.	4
Tom Anderson, NYA	4
Eddie Wiseman, NYA	4
Syl Apps, Tor.	4
Mush March, Chi.	4
Doc Romnes, Chi.	4
Seven tied with	3

PLAYOFF GOALIE WINS

Name, Team	W
Mike Karakas, Chi.	6
Turk Broda, Tor.	4
Earl Robertson, NYA	3
Alfie Moore, Chi.	1
Dave Kerr, NYR	1
Wilf Cude, Mtl.	1

PLAYOFF SHUTOUTS

Name, Team	SO
Mike Karakas, Chi.	2
Turk Broda, Tor.	1

FIRST TEAM ALL-STARS

Name, Team	Position
Bill Cowley, Bos.	C
Cecil Dillon, NYR - tied	RW
Gordie Drillon, Tor - tied	RW
Paul Thompson, Chi.	LW
Eddie Shore, Bos.	D
Babe Siebert, Chi.	D
Tiny Thompson, Bos.	G
Lester Patrick, NYR	Coach

SECOND TEAM ALL-STARS

Name, Team	Position
Syl Apps Sr., Tor.	C
Cecil Dillon, NYR - tied	RW
Gordie Drillon, Tor - tied	RW
Toe Blake, Mtl.	LW
Art Coulter, NYR	D
Earl Seibert, Chi.	D
Dave Kerr, NYR	G
Art Ross, Bos.	Coach

1938 Playoffs

SERIES A - SEMI-FINALS

Mar.	24	Boston	0	at	Toronto	1 2OT
Mar.	26	Boston	1	at	Toronto	2
Mar.	29	Toronto	3	at	Boston	2 OT

Toronto won best-of-five series 3–0

SERIES B AND C - QUARTER-FINALS

Mar.	22	NY Americans	2	at	NY Rangers	1 2OT
Mar.	24	NY Rangers	4	at	NY Americans	3
Mar.	27	NY Americans	3	at	NY Rangers	2 4OT

NY Americans won best-of-three series 2–1

Mar.	22	Chicago	4	at	Montreal	6
Mar.	24	Montreal	0	at	Chicago	4
Mar.	26	Chicago	3	at	Montreal	2 OT

Chicago won best-of-three series 2–1

SERIES D - SEMI-FINALS

Mar.	29	Chicago	1	at	NY Americans	3
Mar.	31	NY Americans	0	at	Chicago	1 2OT
Apr.	3	Chicago	3	at	NY Americans	2

Chicago won best-of-three series 2–1

SERIES E - FINALS

Apr.	5	Chicago	3	at	Toronto	1
Apr.	7	Chicago	1	at	Toronto	5
Apr.	10	Toronto	1	at	Chicago	2
Apr.	12	Toronto	1	at	Chicago	4

Chicago won best-of-five series 3–1

1937-38 – Chicago Black Hawks – Art Wiebe, Carl Voss, Harold Jackson, Mike Karakas, Mush March, Jack Shill, Earl Seibert, Cully Dahlstrom, Alex Levinsky, Johnny Gottselig (Captain), Lou Trudel, Pete Palangio, Bill MacKenzie, Doc Romnes, Paul Thompson, Roger Jenkins, Alfie Moore, Bert Connelly, Virgil Johnson, Paul Goodman, Bill Stewart (Manager/Coach), Eddie Froelich (Trainer).

TROPHY WINNERS

Trophy	Awarded For	Winner	Team
Hart	MVP	Eddie Shore	Bos.
Calder	Top Rookie	Cully Dahlstrom	Chi.
Vezina	Fewest Goals Against	Tiny Thompson	Bos.
Byng	Gentlemanly Conduct	Gordie Drillon	Tor.

NHL NOTEBOOK

TRANSACTIONS

- May 9, 1937 – Chicago Black Hawks claimed Carl Dahlstrom from St. Paul of the AHA in the inter-league draft.
- Oct. 7, 1937 – Montreal Maroons signed Des Smith.
- Oct. 7, 1937 – Toronto obtained Wally Stanowski from the New York Americans for Jack Shill.
- Oct 26, 1937 – Boston signed Jack Crawford, Red Hamill, Jack Shewchuk and Mel Hill.
- Oct. 27, 1937 – Detroit signed Jack Stewart.

RECORDS

- Mar. 13, 1938 – Detroit rookie Carl Liscombe scored the fastest three goals in NHL history in a 5-1 win over Chicago at the Olympia. His record time was 1:52. The record was broken by Chicago's Bill Mosienko (:21) in 1952.

MILESTONES

- Sept. 24, 1937 – NHL adopted a new "icing rule" whereby a team which deliberately shot the puck out of its defensive zone (when not shorthanded) would have the ensuing face-off brought back to the defensive zone point from where the puck was shot.
- Dec. 21, 1937 – Chicago's Paul Thompson became the first player in NHL history to score a goal against his brother, when he scored on Bruins' goalie Cecil "Tiny" Thompson, at 19:51 of the third period, in a 2-1 loss at Boston Garden.
- Mar. 17, 1938 – New York Americans veteran Nels Stewart became the first player in NHL history to score 300 goals, in a 5-3 loss to the Rangers.
- Mar. 17, 1938 – Montreal Canadiens defeated the Montreal Maroons 6-3 in a penalty free game that was also the final game between the two teams. The Maroons dropped out of the NHL after the 1937-38 season. It was the final game between two Quebec teams until the Nordiques joined the NHL in 1979-80.
- Detroit Red Wings become first NHL team to miss the playoffs the year after winning consecutive Stanley Cup championships.

1938-39

Stanley Cup • Boston Bruins

FINAL STANDINGS

Team	GP	W	L	T	GF	GA	PTS
Boston	48	36	10	2	156	76	74
New York	48	26	16	6	149	105	58
Toronto	48	19	20	9	114	107	47
NY Americans	48	17	21	10	119	157	44
Detroit	48	18	24	6	107	128	42
Montreal	48	15	24	9	115	146	39
Chicago	48	12	28	8	91	132	32

LEADING SCORERS

Player	Club	GP	G	A	PTS	PIM
Toe Blake	Montreal	48	24	23	47	10
Sweeney Schriner	NY Americans	48	13	31	44	20
Bill Cowley	Boston	34	8	34	42	2
Clint Smith	NY Rangers	48	21	20	41	2
Marty Barry	Detroit	48	13	28	41	4
Syl Apps	Toronto	44	15	25	40	4
Tom Anderson	NY Americans	47	13	27	40	14
Johnny Gottselig	Chicago	48	16	23	39	15
Paul Haynes	Montreal	47	5	33	38	27
Roy Conacher	Boston	47	26	11	37	12
Lorne Carr	NY Americans	46	19	18	37	16
Neil Colville	NY Rangers	47	18	19	37	12
Phil Watson	NY Rangers	48	15	22	37	42
Syd Howe	Detroit	48	16	20	36	11
Bryan Hextall	NY Rangers	48	20	15	35	18
Nels Stewart	NY Americans	46	16	19	35	43
Gordie Drillon	Toronto	40	18	16	34	15
Johnny Gagnon	Montreal	45	12	22	34	23
Alex Shibicky	NY Rangers	48	24	9	33	24
Eddie Wiseman	NY Americans	47	12	21	33	8
Milt Schmidt	Boston	41	15	17	32	13
Bobby Bauer	Boston	48	13	18	31	4
Woody Dumart	Boston	46	14	15	29	2
Dutch Hiller	NY Rangers	48	10	19	29	22
Lynn Patrick	NY Rangers	35	8	21	29	25

LEADING GOALTENDERS

Goaltender	Club	GPI	MINS	GA	SO	AVG
Frank Brimsek	Boston	43	2610	68	10	1.56
Dave Kerr	NY Rangers	48	2970	105	6	2.12
Turk Broda	Toronto	48	2990	107	8	2.15
Tiny Thompson	Bos./Det.	44	2707	109	4	2.42
Mike Karakas	Chicago	48	2988	132	5	2.65
Claude Bourque	Montreal	25	1560	69	2	2.65

LEADING PLAYOFF SCORERS

Player	Club	GP	G	A	PTS	PIM
Bill Cowley	Boston	12	3	11	14	2
Gordie Drillon	Toronto	10	7	6	13	4
Roy Conacher	Boston	12	6	4	10	12
Mel Hill	Boston	12	6	3	9	12
Syl Apps	Toronto	10	2	6	8	2
Charlie Conacher	Detroit	5	2	5	7	2
Murph Chamberlain	Toronto	10	2	5	7	4
Milt Schmidt	Boston	12	3	3	6	2
Nick Metz	Toronto	10	3	3	6	6
Bobby Bauer	Boston	12	3	2	5	0
Doc Romnes	Toronto	10	1	4	5	0

LEADING PLAYOFF GOALTENDERS

Goaltender	Club	GPI	MINS	GA	SO	AVG
Frank Brimsek	Boston	12	863	18	1	1.25
Bert Gardiner	NY Rangers	6	433	12	0	1.66
Turk Broda	Toronto	10	617	20	2	1.94
Tiny Thompson	Detroit	6	374	15	1	2.41
Claude Bourque	Montreal	3	188	8	1	2.55

Frank Brimsek was a rookie sensation with the Bruins in 1938–39, earning the nickname "Mr. Zero" after twice recording streaks of three straight shutouts during his first month in Boston. Brimsek was a product of Eveleth High School in Minnesota. He joined the U.S. Coast Guard in 1943 but returned to the NHL after World War II and played until 1950.

THE MONTREAL MAROONS' last-place finish in 1937–38 proved the final nail in their coffin. They suspended operations prior to the 1938–39 season, leaving the NHL with just seven teams. As a result, the league reverted to a single division format for the first time since 1925–26. Six of the seven teams would qualify for the postseason: the first- and second-place clubs would play a seven-game semi-final, while the third- and fourth-place teams would meet in a best-of-three quarter-final, as did the fifth- and sixth-place finishers. The quarter-final winners would then compete in a three-game semi-final series. The Stanley Cup finals would be a best-of-seven series.

Hill's Heroics – Boston boasted overwhelming offense, stingy defense and skilled scorers, but it was the heroics of Mel "Sudden Death" Hill that put Boston on top of Lord Stanley's mountain.

The Detroit Red Wings replaced goaltender Normie Smith at the start of the season. Manager Jack Adams purchased Tiny Thompson from the Boston Bruins. Thompson had won the Vezina Trophy for the fourth time the year before—then a league record—but Bruins manager Art Ross knew he had a worthy replacement in Frank Brimsek. "Mr. Zero," as he became known, led the league with 10 shutouts, won the Vezina Trophy with a 1.56 goals-against average, and was named to the First All-Star Team as the Bruins cruised to a first-place finish.

Though the 36–10–2 Bruins had 10 more victories and 16 more points than the second-place Rangers, it took Boston the full seven games to eliminate New York in the semi-finals. Mel Hill earned the nickname "Sudden Death" by scoring three overtime goals in the series. The third-place Leafs beat the Americans and Red Wings to reach the finals, then lost to the Bruins in five games as the Stanley Cup returned to Boston for the first time in 10 years.

Leaders, 1938-39

GOALS

Name, Team	G
Roy Conacher, Bos.	26
Toe Blake, Mtl.	24
Alex Shibicky, NYR	24
Clint Smith, NYR	21
Bryan Hextall, NYR	20
Lorne Carr, NYA	19
Gordie Drillon, Tor.	18
Neil Colville, NYR	18
Nels Stewart, NYA	16
Johnny Gottselig, Chi.	16
Syd Howe, Det.	16

ASSISTS

Name, Team	A
Bill Cowley, Bos.	34
Paul Haynes, Mtl.	33
Sweeney Schriner, NYA	31
Marty Barry, Det.	28
Tom Anderson, NYA	27
Syl Apps, Tor.	25
Toe Blake, Mtl.	23
Johnny Gottselig, Chi.	23
Ott Heller, NYR	23
Johnny Gagnon, Mtl.	22
Phil Watson, NYR	22

GOALIE WINS

Name, Team	W
Frank Brimsek, Bos.	33
Dave Kerr, NYR	26
Tiny Thompson, Bos./Det.	19
Turk Broda, Tor.	19
Earl Robertson, NYA	17
Mike Karakas, Chi.	12
Wilf Cude, Mtl.	8
Claude Bourque, Mtl.	7
Harvey Teno, Det.	2

SHUTOUTS

Name, Team	SO
Frank Brimsek, Bos.	10
Turk Broda, Tor.	8
Dave Kerr, NYR	6
Mike Karakas, Chi.	5
Tiny Thompson, Bos./Det.	4
Earl Robertson, NYA	3
Wilf Cude, Mtl.	2
Claude Bourque, Mtl.	2

PLAYOFF GOALS

Name, Team	G
Gordie Drillon, Tor.	7
Roy Conacher, Bos.	6
Mel Hill, Bos.	6
Marty Barry, Det.	3
Syd Howe, Det.	3
Alex Shibicky, NYR	3
Nick Metz, Tor.	3
Bill Cowley, Bos.	3
Milt Schmidt, Bos.	3
Bobby Bauer, Bos.	3

PLAYOFF ASSISTS

Name, Team	A
Bill Cowley, Bos.	11
Gordie Drillon, Tor.	6
Syl Apps, Tor.	6
Charlie Conacher, Det.	5
Murph Chamberlain, Tor.	5
Doc Romnes, Tor.	4
Roy Conacher, Bos.	4
Eddie Shore, Bos.	4
Six tied with	3

PLAYOFF GOALIE WINS

Name, Team	W
Frank Brimsek, Bos.	8
Turk Broda, Tor.	5
Bert Gardiner, NYR	3
Tiny Thompson, Det.	3
Claude Bourque, Mtl.	1

PLAYOFF SHUTOUTS

Name, Team	SO
Turk Broda, Tor.	2
Claude Bourque, Mtl.	1
Tiny Thompson, Det.	1
Frank Brimsek, Bos.	1

FIRST TEAM ALL-STARS

Name, Team	Position
Syl Apps Sr., Tor.	C
Gordie Drillon, Tor.	RW
Toe Blake, Mtl.	LW
Eddie Shore, Bos.	D
Dit Clapper, Bos.	D
Frank Brimsek, Bos.	G
Art Ross, Bos.	Coach

SECOND TEAM ALL-STARS

Name, Team	Position
Neil Colville, NYR	C
Bobby Bauer, Bos.	RW
Johnny Gottselig, Chi.	LW
Earl Seibert, Chi.	D
Art Coulter, NYR	D
Earl Robertson, NYA	G
Red Dutton, NYA	Coach

1939 Playoffs

SERIES A - SEMI-FINALS

Mar.	21	Boston	2	at	NY Rangers	1	3OT
Mar.	23	NY Rangers	2	at	Boston	3	OT
Mar.	26	NY Rangers	1	at	Boston	4	
Mar.	28	Boston	1	at	NY Rangers	2	
Mar.	30	NY Rangers	2	at	Boston	1	OT
Apr.	1	Boston	1	at	NY Rangers	3	
Apr.	2	NY Rangers	1	at	Boston	2	3OT

Boston won best-of-seven series 4–3

SERIES B AND C - QUARTER-FINALS

Mar.	21	NY Americans	0	at	Toronto	4
Mar.	23	Toronto	2	at	NY Americans	0

Toronto won best-of-three series 2–0

Mar.	21	Detroit	0	at	Montreal	2	
Mar.	23	Montreal	3	at	Detroit	7	
Mar.	26	Montreal	0	at	Detroit	1	OT

Detroit won best-of-three series 2–1

SERIES D - SEMI-FINALS

Mar.	28	Detroit	1	at	Toronto	4	
Mar.	30	Toronto	1	at	Detroit	3	
Apr.	1	Detroit	4	at	Toronto	5	OT

Toronto won best-of-three series 2–1

SERIES E - FINALS

Apr.	6	Toronto	1	at	Boston	2	
Apr.	9	Toronto	3	at	Boston	2	OT
Apr.	11	Boston	3	at	Toronto	1	
Apr.	13	Boston	2	at	Toronto	0	
Apr.	16	Toronto	1	at	Boston	3	

Boston won best-of-seven series 4–1

1938-39 – Boston Bruins – Bobby Bauer, Mel Hill, Flash Hollett, Roy Conacher, Gord Pettinger, Milt Schmidt, Woody Dumart, Jack Crawford, Ray Getliffe, Frank Brimsek, Eddie Shore, Dit Clapper, Bill Cowley, Jack Portland, Red Hamill, Cooney Weiland (Captain), Charlie Sands, Art Ross (Manager/Coach), Win Green (Trainer).

TROPHY WINNERS

Trophy	Awarded For	Winner	Team
Hart	MVP	Toe Blake	Mtl.
Calder	Top Rookie	Frank Brimsek	Bos.
Vezina	Fewest Goals Against	Frank Brimsek	Bos.
Byng	Gentlemanly Conduct	Clint Smith	NYR

NHL NOTEBOOK

TRANSACTIONS

- Sept. 24, 1938 – Montreal Canadiens purchased Herb Cain and Buddy O'Connor from the Montreal Maroons.
- Sept. 28, 1938 – Chicago signed Ab Demarco.
- Oct. 27, 1938 – Boston Bruins signed goaltender Frank Brimsek.
- Nov. 26, 1938 – Detroit purchased veteran goaltender Cecil "Tiny" Thompson from the Boston Bruins for Norm Smith and $15,000.
- Dec 8, 1938 – Chicago traded Doc Romnes to Toronto for Bill Thoms.
- Dec. 19, 1938 – Toronto purchased Bucko McDonald from Detroit in exhchange for Bill Thomson and $10,000.

RECORDS

- Nov. 15, 1938 – Boston extended their overtime undefeated streak to 37 straight games (10-0-27) with a 1-1 tie against Toronto. The 37 game streak, which began in December 1934, is the longest in NHL history.
- Dec. 18, 1938 – Boston's Frank Brimsek recorded his fourth straight road shutout (an NHL record) in a 2-0 road win over the Red Wings. It was also the fifth shutout in six games for the rookie goalie.
- Mar. 23, 1939 – Detroit's Syd Howe set a playoff record with three powerplay goals as the Red Wings beat the Canadiens 7-3 in game two of the Stanley Cup quarter-finals at the Olympia in Detroit.
- Apr. 2, 1939 – Boston rookie Mel Hill scored after 48 minutes of overtime to lead the Bruins to a 2-1 playoff win over the Rangers in game seven of the Stanley Cup semi-finals. It was Hill's third overtime goal in the semi-final series against New York, an NHL record.

MILESTONES

- June 22, 1938 – Montreal Maroons withdrew from the National Hockey League. The team folded two months later, leaving the NHL with seven remaining clubs - all in one division.
- Nov. 20, 1938 – Boston's Tiny Thompson became the first goaltender in NHL history to record 250 victories, in a 4-1 win over the visiting Detroit Red Wings.
- Apr. 16, 1939 – Boston Bruins defeated the Toronto Maple Leafs 3-1 to win the 1939 Stanley Cup championship in five games, in the first best-of-seven Stanley Cup playoff finals. Previously, the championship series had been best of five.

1939-40

Stanley Cup • New York Rangers

FINAL STANDINGS

Team	GP	W	L	T	GF	GA	PTS
Boston	48	31	12	5	170	98	67
New York	48	27	11	10	136	77	64
Toronto	48	25	17	6	134	110	56
Chicago	48	23	19	6	112	120	52
Detroit	48	16	26	6	91	126	38
NY Americans	48	15	29	4	106	140	34
Montreal	48	10	33	5	90	168	25

LEADING SCORERS

Player	Club	GP	G	A	PTS	PIM
Milt Schmidt	Boston	48	22	30	52	37
Woody Dumart	Boston	48	22	21	43	16
Bobby Bauer	Boston	48	17	26	43	2
Gordie Drillon	Toronto	43	21	19	40	13
Bill Cowley	Boston	48	13	27	40	24
Bryan Hextall	NY Rangers	48	24	15	39	52
Neil Colville	NY Rangers	48	19	19	38	22
Syd Howe	Detroit	46	14	23	37	17
Toe Blake	Montreal	48	17	19	36	48
Murray Armstrong	NY Americans	47	16	20	36	12
Phil Watson	NY Rangers	48	7	28	35	42
Alex Shibicky	NY Rangers	44	11	21	32	33
Herb Cain	Boston	48	21	10	31	30
Dutch Hiller	NY Rangers	48	13	18	31	57
Tom Anderson	NY Americans	48	12	19	31	22
Roy Conacher	Boston	31	18	12	30	9
Syl Apps	Toronto	27	13	17	30	5
Cully Dahlstrom	Chicago	45	11	19	30	15
Charlie Sands	Montreal	47	9	20	29	10
Kilby MacDonald	NY Rangers	44	15	13	28	19
Lynn Patrick	NY Rangers	48	12	16	28	34
Ebbie Goodfellow	Detroit	43	11	17	28	31
Charlie Conacher	NY Americans	47	10	18	28	41
Dit Clapper	Boston	44	10	18	28	25
Flash Hollett	Boston	44	10	18	28	18

LEADING GOALTENDERS

Goaltender	Club	GPI	MINS	GA	SO	AVG
Dave Kerr	NY Rangers	48	3000	77	8	1.54
Paul Goodman	Chicago	31	1920	62	4	1.94
Frank Brimsek	Boston	48	2950	98	6	1.99
Turk Broda	Toronto	47	2900	108	4	2.23
Tiny Thompson	Detroit	46	2830	120	3	2.54
Earl Robertson	NY Americans	48	2960	140	6	2.84
Claude Bourque	Mtl./Det.	37	2270	124	2	3.28

LEADING PLAYOFF SCORERS

Player	Club	GP	G	A	PTS	PIM
Phil Watson	NY Rangers	12	3	6	9	16
Neil Colville	NY Rangers	12	2	7	9	18
Syl Apps	Toronto	10	5	2	7	2
Bryan Hextall	NY Rangers	12	4	3	7	11
Alex Shibicky	NY Rangers	11	2	5	7	4
Hank Goldup	Toronto	10	5	1	6	4
Dutch Hiller	NY Rangers	12	2	4	6	2
Mac Colville	NY Rangers	12	3	2	5	6
Mud Bruneteau	Detroit	5	3	2	5	0
12 players tied with					4	

LEADING PLAYOFF GOALTENDERS

Goaltender	Club	GPI	MINS	GA	SO	AVG
Dave Kerr	NY Rangers	12	770	20	3	1.56
Turk Broda	Toronto	10	657	19	1	1.74
Tiny Thompson	Detroit	5	300	12	0	2.40
Frank Brimsek	Boston	6	360	15	0	2.50
Earl Robertson	NY Americans	3	180	9	0	3.00

Dave Kerr of the New York Rangers was featured on the cover of Time *magazine on March 14, 1938. He enjoyed his best season in 1939–40 when he won the Vezina Trophy and led the Rangers to the Stanley Cup. No one since has posted a goals-against average lower than the mark of 1.54 Kerr recorded that season.*

War broke out in Europe before the NHL started the 1939–40 season, but the league was determined to continue operations with as little disruption as possible. Economic conditions were beginning to improve with the end of the Great Depression, but the New York Americans were still strapped for cash. As a result, they peddled their best player, Sweeney Schriner, to the Toronto Maple Leafs for cash and four players, including the aging Busher Jackson. Jackson would team with ex-Kid Line mate Charlie Conacher on an Americans roster that had become something of a haven for fading stars. Former Bruin great Eddie Shore would play out his career alongside the two ex-Leafs, but the Americans would tumble to sixth place, ahead of only the Montreal Canadiens, who were in the cellar for the first time since 1925–26.

Terrific Trio – Boston's Kraut Line of Schmidt, Bauer and Dumart dominated the scoring parade, but it was the Rangers' knack for magic in overtime and a pair of Patricks that brought the Cup back to Broadway.

The loss of Shore did not hinder the Bruins in 1939–40, as Kraut Line stars Milt Schmidt, Woody Dumart and Bobby Bauer finished 1–2–3 in the league scoring race. Teammate Bill Cowley came in fifth. The defending Stanley Cup champions posted the best record in the NHL for the third consecutive season, but were upset by the second-place New York Rangers in six games in their semi-final. New York's opposition in the finals was third-place Toronto, who had advanced with wins over the Chicago Black Hawks and Detroit Red Wings.

The Stanley Cup series opened in New York, with the Rangers winning the first two games. As happened so many times to the Rangers over the years, the circus at Madison Square Garden forced the rest of the series to be played in Toronto. The Leafs won games three and four, but a pair of overtime victories gave the Rangers their third Stanley Cup title in 13 seasons. It would be 54 years before the Rangers won the Stanley Cup again.

Leaders, 1939-40

GOALS

Name, Team	G
Bryan Hextall, NYR	24
Milt Schmidt, Bos.	22
Woody Dumart, Bos.	22
Gordie Drillon, Tor.	21
Herb Cain, Bos.	21
Neil Colville, NYR	19
Roy Conacher, Bos.	18
Bobby Bauer, Bos.	17
Toe Blake, Mtl.	17
Murray Armstrong, NYA	16

ASSISTS

Name, Team	A
Milt Schmidt, Bos.	30
Phil Watson, NYR	28
Bill Cowley, Bos.	27
Bobby Bauer, Bos.	26
Syd Howe, Det.	23
Alex Shibicky, NYR	21
Woody Dumart, Bos.	21
Murray Armstrong, NYA	20
Charlie Sands, Mtl.	20
Six tied with	19

GOALIE WINS

Name, Team	W
Frank Brimsek, Bos.	31
Dave Kerr, NYR	27
Turk Broda, Tor.	25
Paul Goodman, Chi.	16
Tiny Thompson, Det.	16
Earl Robertson, NYA	15
Claude Bourque, Mtl/Det.	9
Mike Karakas, Chi/Mtl.	7
Wilf Cude, Mtl.	1

SHUTOUTS

Name, Team	SO
Dave Kerr, NYR	8
Frank Brimsek, Bos.	6
Earl Robertson, NYA	6
Paul Goodman, Chi.	4
Turk Broda, Tor.	4
Tiny Thompson, Det.	3
Claude Bourque, Mtl/Det.	2

PLAYOFF GOALS

Name, Team	G
Syl Apps, Tor.	5
Hank Goldup, Tor.	5
Bryan Hextall, NYR	4
Hooley Smith, NYA	3
Mud Bruneteau, Det.	3
Gordie Drillon, Tor.	3
Phil Watson, NYR	3
Mac Colville, NYR	3
Alf Pike, NYR	3
Babe Pratt, NYR	3
Muzz Patrick, NYR	3

PLAYOFF ASSISTS

Name, Team	A
Neil Colville, NYR	7
Phil Watson, NYR	6
Alex Shibicky, NYR	5
Dutch Hiller, NYR	4
12 tied with	3

PLAYOFF GOALIE WINS

Name, Team	W
Dave Kerr, NYR	8
Turk Broda, Tor.	6
Tiny Thompson, Det.	2
Frank Brimsek, Bos.	2
Earl Robertson, NYA	1

PLAYOFF SHUTOUTS

Name, Team	SO
Dave Kerr, NYR	3
Turk Broda, Tor.	1

FIRST TEAM ALL-STARS

Name, Team	Position
Milt Schmidt, Bos.	C
Bryan Hextall Sr., NYR	RW
Toe Blake, Mtl.	LW
Eddie Shore, Bos.	D
Dit Clapper, Bos.	D
Dave Kerr, NYR	G
Paul Thompson, Chi.	Coach

SECOND TEAM ALL-STARS

Name, Team	Position
Neil Colville, NYR	C
Bobby Bauer, Bos.	RW
Woody Dumart, Bos.	LW
Earl Seibert, Chi.	D
Art Coulter, NYR	D
Frank Brimsek, Bos.	G
Frank Boucher, NYR	Coach

1940 Playoffs

SERIES A - SEMI-FINALS

Date	Visitor			Home		
Mar. 19	Boston	0	at	NY Rangers	4	
Mar. 21	NY Rangers	2	at	Boston	4	
Mar. 24	NY Rangers	3	at	Boston	4	
Mar. 26	Boston	0	at	NY Rangers	1	
Mar. 28	NY Rangers	1	at	Boston	0	
Mar. 30	Boston	1	at	NY Rangers	4	

NY Rangers won best-of-seven series 4–2

SERIES B AND C - QUARTER-FINALS

Date	Visitor			Home		
Mar. 19	Chicago	2	at	Toronto	3	OT
Mar. 21	Toronto	2	at	Chicago	1	

Toronto won best-of-three series 2–0

Date	Visitor			Home		
Mar. 19	NY Americans	1	at	Detroit	2	OT
Mar. 22	Detroit	4	at	NY Americans	5	
Mar. 24	NY Americans	1	at	Detroit	3	

Detroit won best-of-three series 2–1

SERIES D - SEMI-FINALS

Date	Visitor			Home		
Mar. 26	Detroit	1	at	Toronto	2	
Mar. 28	Toronto	3	at	Detroit	1	

Toronto won best-of-three series 2–0

SERIES E - FINALS

Date	Visitor			Home		
Apr. 2	Toronto	1	at	NY Rangers	2	OT
Apr. 3	Toronto	2	at	NY Rangers	6	
Apr. 6	NY Rangers	1	at	Toronto	2	
Apr. 9	NY Rangers	0	at	Toronto	3	
Apr. 11	NY Rangers	2	at	Toronto	1	2OT
Apr. 13	NY Rangers	3	at	Toronto	2	OT

NY Rangers won best-of-seven series 4–2

1939-40 – New York Rangers – Dave Kerr, Art Coulter (Captain), Ott Heller, Alex Shibicky, Mac Colville, Neil Colville, Phil Watson, Lynn Patrick, Clint Smith, Muzz Patrick, Babe Pratt, Bryan Hextall, Kilby MacDonald, Dutch Hiller, Alf Pike, Stan Smith, Lester Patrick (Manager), Frank Boucher (Coach), Harry Westerby (Trainer).

TROPHY WINNERS

Trophy	Awarded For	Winner	Team
Hart	MVP	Ebbie Goodfellow	Det.
Calder	Top Rookie	Kilby MacDonald	NYR
Vezina	Fewest Goals Against	Dave Kerr	NYR
Byng	Gentlemanly Conduct	Bobby Bauer	Bos

NHL NOTEBOOK

TRANSACTIONS

- Oct. 2, 1939 – Detroit Red Wings signed Billy Reay.
- Oct. 5, 1939 – Detroit Red Wings signed Joe Carveth.
- Oct. 10, 1939 – Boston Bruins obtained Herb Cain from the Montreal Canadiens for Charlie Sands and Ray Getliffe.
- Jan. 25, 1940 – Eddie Shore was traded from the Boston Bruins to the New York Americans for Eddie Wiseman and $5,000.

RECORDS

- Dec. 16, 1939 – Montreal lost 4-2 to the visiting New York Rangers to begin a 15-game winless streak at home (0-12-3) which tied an NHL record.
- Jan. 28, 1940 – Chicago's Les Cunningham scored five points in one period to set an NHL record. Cunningham had two goals and three assists in a span of 10:04 during the third period of an 8-1 win over Montreal.
- Feb. 29, 1940 – Detroit's Cecil "Tiny" Thompson became the first goaltender in NHL history to play 40 (or more) games for 12 straight seasons. The milestone came in a 3-1 Red Wings loss at Toronto.
- Mar. 19, 1940 – Syd Howe scored 25 seconds into overtime to give the Red Wings a 1-0 win over the New York Americans, in game one of the Stanley Cup quarter-finals. At the time it was the fastest overtime goal in NHL playoff history.

MILESTONES

- May 13, 1939 – At the annual NHL Board of Governors meeting, Boston's Art Ross submitted for consideration a new type of hockey stick with a metal handle and replaceable wooden blade.
- Feb. 25, 1940 – NY Rangers faced the Montreal Canadiens in the first hockey game televised in the U.S. The game aired on station W2XBS in NY, with one camera in a fixed position to 300 TV receivers in New York. Rangers won 6-2 for their 14th straight home win.
- Mar. 17, 1940 – For the first time in history, one line (Milt Schmidt, Woody Dumart and Bobby Bauer) finished 1-2-3 in NHL scoring, when Boston scored five goals in the third period to beat Montreal 7-2. The win gave the Bruins the NHL regular season championship.

1940-41

Stanley Cup • Boston Bruins

FINAL STANDINGS

Team	GP	W	L	T	GF	GA	PTS
Boston	48	27	8	13	168	102	67
Toronto	48	28	14	6	145	99	62
Detroit	48	21	16	11	112	102	53
New York	48	21	19	8	143	125	50
Chicago	48	16	25	7	112	139	39
Montreal	48	16	26	6	121	147	38
NY Americans	48	8	29	11	99	186	27

LEADING SCORERS

Player	Club	GP	G	A	PTS	PIM
Bill Cowley	Boston	46	17	45	62	16
Bryan Hextall	NY Rangers	48	26	18	44	16
Gordie Drillon	Toronto	42	23	21	44	2
Syd Howe	Detroit	48	20	24	44	8
Lynn Patrick	NY Rangers	48	20	24	44	12
Syl Apps	Toronto	41	20	24	44	6
Neil Colville	NY Rangers	48	14	28	42	28
Eddie Wiseman	Boston	48	16	24	40	10
Bobby Bauer	Boston	48	17	22	39	2
Sweeney Schriner	Toronto	48	24	14	38	6
Roy Conacher	Boston	41	24	14	38	7
Milt Schmidt	Boston	45	13	25	38	23
Phil Watson	NY Rangers	40	11	25	36	49
Nick Metz	Toronto	47	14	21	35	10
Billy Taylor	Toronto	47	9	26	35	15
John Quilty	Montreal	48	18	16	34	31
Woody Dumart	Boston	40	18	15	33	2
Sid Abel	Detroit	47	11	22	33	29
Art Jackson	Boston	48	17	15	32	10
Joe Benoit	Montreal	45	16	16	32	32
Lorne Carr	NY Americans	48	13	19	32	10
Bill Thoms	Chicago	47	13	19	32	4
Toe Blake	Montreal	48	12	20	32	49
Mac Colville	NY Rangers	47	14	17	31	18
George Allen	Chicago	44	14	17	31	22

LEADING GOALTENDERS

Goaltender	Club	GPI	MINS	GA	SO	AVG
Turk Broda	Toronto	48	2970	99	5	2.00
Frank Brimsek	Boston	48	3040	102	6	2.01
Johnny Mowers	Detroit	48	3040	102	4	2.01
Dave Kerr	NY Rangers	48	3010	125	2	2.49
Bert Gardiner	Montreal	42	2600	119	2	2.75
Sam LoPresti	Chicago	27	1670	84	1	3.02
Earl Robertson	NY Americans	36	2260	142	1	3.77

LEADING PLAYOFF SCORERS

Player	Club	GP	G	A	PTS	PIM
Milt Schmidt	Boston	11	5	6	11	9
Eddie Wiseman	Boston	11	6	2	8	0
Syd Howe	Detroit	9	1	7	8	0
Carl Liscombe	Detroit	8	4	3	7	12
Flash Hollett	Boston	11	3	4	7	8
Nick Metz	Toronto	7	3	4	7	0
Cully Dahlstrom	Chicago	5	3	3	6	2
Terry Reardon	Boston	11	2	4	6	6
Roy Conacher	Boston	11	1	5	6	0
Six players tied with					5	

LEADING PLAYOFF GOALTENDERS

Goaltender	Club	GPI	MINS	GA	SO	AVG
Frank Brimsek	Boston	11	678	23	1	2.04
Turk Broda	Toronto	7	438	15	0	2.05
Sam LoPresti	Chicago	5	343	12	0	2.10
Johnny Mowers	Detroit	9	561	20	0	2.14

Milt Schmidt was a top scorer playing between Bobby Bauer and Woody Dumart on the Boston Bruins' famed Kraut Line. Tough as well as talented, Schmidt was a strong skater and clever stickhandler. Except for three years lost to military service in World War II, Schmidt was a Bruin as a player, coach, general manager and executive from 1936–37 to 1972–73.

DETERMINED TO REBUILD after their last-place finish in 1939–40, the Canadiens hired a new coach—Dick Irvin, who had enjoyed great success with the Toronto Maple Leafs in the 1930s. Though he would help the Canadiens qualify for the playoffs this season, the return to glory in Montreal was still several seasons in the offing.

At the other end of the spectrum, the Boston Bruins—despite failing to repeat as Stanley Cup champions in 1940—kept their team intact for 1940–41. The patience of Boston general manager Art Ross was rewarded with a fourth consecutive first-place finish and the team's second Stanley Cup title in three years. Bill Cowley led the NHL in scoring with 62 points, 18 more than the five players who finished tied for second. Bruins teammates Eddie Wiseman, Bobby Bauer, Roy Conacher and Milt Schmidt all joined Cowley in the top 10, while Frank Brimsek led the league with six shutouts. The Bruins set an NHL record with a 23-game undefeated streak, and they set another record on March 4, 1941, when they fired 83 shots against the Black Hawks. Chicago goalie Sam LoPresti made 80 saves in a 3–2 loss.

Boston Tops – The Bruins had five of the NHL's top marksmen, superior goaltending by Frank Brimsek and the strength and stamina to outlast the Leafs in seven games and sweep the Wings in the finals.

Several games were marred by bench-clearing brawls this season, resulting in a new rule that called for an automatic $25 fine for any player leaving the bench to join in a fight.

In the playoffs, Boston defeated the second-place Maple Leafs in a thrilling seven-game semi-final that saw teams alternate wins until Boston won its second consecutive game with a 2-1 win in game seven. the winning goal was supplied by Mel "Sudden Death" Hill, albeit in regulation time.

Third-place Detroit supplied the opposition for the Stanley Cup after the Red Wings eliminated the New York Rangers and Chicago. Boston then beat Detroit in the first four-game sweep in Stanley Cup history. The victory would prove to be Boston's last until the Orr-and Esposito-led team of 1970.

Leaders, 1940-41

GOALS

Name, Team	G
Bryan Hextall, NYR	26
Roy Conacher, Bos.	24
Sweeney Schriner, Tor.	24
Gordie Drillon, Tor.	23
Syl Apps, Tor.	20
Syd Howe, Det.	20
Lynn Patrick, NYR	20
Woody Dumart, Bos.	18
John Quilty, Mtl.	18
Bill Cowley, Bos.	17
Bobby Bauer, Bos.	17
Art Jackson, Bos.	17

ASSISTS

Name, Team	A
Bill Cowley, Bos.	45
Neil Colville, NYR	28
Billy Taylor, Tor.	26
Phil Watson, NYR	25
Milt Schmidt, Bos.	25
Syl Apps, Tor.	24
Syd Howe, Det.	24
Lynn Patrick, NYR	24
Eddie Wiseman, Bos.	24
Sid Abel, Det.	22
Bobby Bauer, Bos.	22

GOALIE WINS

Name, Team	W
Turk Broda, Tor.	28
Frank Brimsek, Bos.	27
Dave Kerr, NYR	21
Johnny Mowers, Det.	21
Bert Gardiner, Mtl.	13
Sam LoPresti, Chi.	9
Paul Goodman, Chi.	7
Earl Robertson, NYA	6
Wilf Cude, Mtl.	2
Chuck Rayner, NYA	2

SHUTOUTS

Name, Team	SO
Frank Brimsek, Bos.	6
Turk Broda, Tor.	5
Johnny Mowers, Det.	4
Paul Goodman, Chi.	2
Bert Gardiner, Mtl.	2
Dave Kerr, NYR	2
Sam LoPresti, Chi.	1
Earl Robertson, NYA	1

PLAYOFF GOALS

Name, Team	G
Eddie Wiseman, Bos.	6
Milt Schmidt, Bos.	5
Joe Benoit, Mtl.	4
Carl Liscombe, Det.	4
Cully Dahlstrom, Chi.	3
Nick Metz, Tor.	3
Syl Apps, Tor.	3
Gordie Drillon, Tor.	3
Flash Hollett, Bos.	3
Herb Cain, Bos.	3

PLAYOFF ASSISTS

Name, Team	A
Syd Howe, Det.	7
Milt Schmidt, Bos.	6
Roy Conacher, Bos.	5
Dit Clapper, Bos.	5
Nick Metz, Tor.	4
Don Grosso, Det.	4
Flash Hollett, Bos.	4
Terry Reardon, Bos.	4
10 tied with	3

PLAYOFF GOALIE WINS

Name, Team	W
Frank Brimsek, Bos.	8
Johnny Mowers, Det.	4
Turk Broda, Tor.	3
Sam LoPresti, Chi.	2
Dave Kerr, NYR	1
Bert Gardiner, Mtl.	1

PLAYOFF SHUTOUTS

Name, Team	SO
Frank Brimsek, Bos.	1

FIRST TEAM ALL-STARS

Name, Team	Position
Bill Cowley, Bos.	C
Bryan Hextall, NYR	RW
Sweeny Schriner, Tor.	LW
Dit Clapper, Bos.	D
Wally Stanowski, Tor.	D
Turk Broda, Tor.	G
Cooney Weiland, Bos.	Coach

SECOND TEAM ALL-STARS

Name, Team	Position
Syl Apps Sr., Tor.	C
Bobby Bauer, Bos.	RW
Woody Dumart, Bos.	LW
Earl Seibert, Chi.	D
Ott Heller, NYR	D
Frank Brimsek, Bos.	G
Dick Irvin, Mtl.	Coach

1941 Playoffs

SERIES A - SEMI-FINALS

Mar.	20	Toronto	0	at	Boston	3
Mar.	22	Toronto	5	at	Boston	3
Mar.	25	Boston	2	at	Toronto	7
Mar.	27	Boston	2	at	Toronto	1
Mar.	29	Toronto	2	at	Boston	1 OT
Apr.	1	Boston	2	at	Toronto	1
Apr.	3	Toronto	1	at	Boston	2

Boston won best-of-seven series 4–3

SERIES B AND C - QUARTER-FINALS

Mar.	20	NY Rangers	1	at	Detroit	2 OT
Mar.	23	Detroit	1	at	NY Rangers	3
Mar.	25	NY Rangers	2	at	Detroit	3

Detroit won best-of-three series 2–1

Mar.	20	Montreal	1	at	Chicago	2
Mar.	22	Chicago	3	at	Montreal	4 2OT
Mar.	25	Montreal	2	at	Chicago	3

Chicago won best-of-three series 2–1

SERIES D - SEMI-FINALS

Mar.	27	Chicago	1	at	Detroit	3
Mar.	30	Detroit	2	at	Chicago	1 OT

Detroit won best-of-three series 2–0

SERIES E - FINALS

Apr.	6	Detroit	2	at	Boston	3
Apr.	8	Detroit	1	at	Boston	2
Apr.	10	Boston	4	at	Detroit	2
Apr.	12	Boston	3	at	Detroit	1

Boston won best-of-seven series 4–0

1940-41 – Boston Bruins – Bill Cowley, Des Smith, Dit Clapper (Captain), Frank Brimsek, Flash Hollett, Jack Crawford, Bobby Bauer, Pat McReavy, Herb Cain, Mel Hill, Milt Schmidt, Woody Dumart, Roy Conacher, Terry Reardon, Art Jackson, Eddie Wiseman, Jack Shewchuck, Art Ross (Manager), Cooney Weiland (Coach), Win Green (Trainer).

TROPHY WINNERS

Trophy	Awarded For	Winner	Team
Hart	MVP	Bill Cowley	Bos.
Calder	Top Rookie	Johnny Quilty	Mtl.
Vezina	Fewest Goals Against	Turk Broda	Tor.
Byng	Gentlemanly Conduct	Bobby Bauer	Bos.

NHL NOTEBOOK

TRANSACTIONS

- June 7, 1940 – Montreal Canadiens obtained the rights to Joe Benoit from Toronto in exchange for Frank Eddolls.
- Oct 3, 1940 – Detroit signed Adam Brown.
- Oct 26, 1940 – Montreal Canadiens signed Ken Reardon and John Quilty.
- Nov. 19, 1940 – Montreal Canadiens purchased Jack Portland from the Chicago Black Hawks for $12,500.

RECORDS

- Nov. 2, 1940 – Bryan Hextall had a goal and two assists in the final period, to lead the Rangers to a 4-1 win in Toronto. The win started the Rangers on a record-117 game non-shutout streak.
- Feb. 23, 1941 – Boston set an NHL record by extending their unbeaten streak to 23 games (15-0-8) with a 3-1 win over the NY Americans at Boston Garden.
- Mar. 4, 1941 – Boston set an NHL record with 83 shots on goal against Chicago goalie Sam LoPresti, in a 3-2 win over the visiting Black Hawks. Bruins also set a record with 37 shots in the first period.
- Boston's Bill Cowley becomes the first NHL player to lead the league in scoring despite scoring less than 20 goals; he finished with 17 goals and an NHL-record 45 assists for 62 points.

MILESTONES

- Dec. 15, 1940 – Toronto Maple Leafs became the first team in NHL history to win each of their first seven road games of the season, with a 4-1 victory over the Black Hawks at Chicago.
- Feb. 18, 1941 – Dave Kerr became the first goaltender to record 150 wins as a member of the NY Rangers, in a 5-2 victory over the New York Americans.
- Mar. 16, 1941 – Turk Broda had his 26th career shutout in a 3-0 Toronto win over Chicago. Hawks' Paul Thompson became the first NHL coach to pull the goalie for an extra skater in regulation time but nothing came of the strategy, even though Toronto had a man in the penalty box.
- Apr. 12, 1941 – For the first time since the NHL adopted the best of seven finals format in 1939, a team won the Stanley Cup in four straight games. Boston topped Detroit 3-1 to complete their four game sweep of the 1941 series.

1941-42

Stanley Cup • Toronto Maple Leafs

FINAL STANDINGS

Team	GP	W	L	T	GF	GA	PTS
New York	48	29	17	2	177	143	60
Toronto	48	27	18	3	158	136	57
Boston	48	25	17	6	160	118	56
Chicago	48	22	23	3	145	155	47
Detroit	48	19	25	4	140	147	42
Montreal	48	18	27	3	134	173	39
Brooklyn	48	16	29	3	133	175	35

LEADING SCORERS

Player	Club	GP	G	A	PTS	PIM
Bryan Hextall	NY Rangers	48	24	32	56	30
Lynn Patrick	NY Rangers	47	32	22	54	18
Don Grosso	Detroit	48	23	30	53	13
Phil Watson	NY Rangers	48	15	37	52	58
Sid Abel	Detroit	48	18	31	49	45
Toe Blake	Montreal	48	17	28	45	19
Bill Thoms	Chicago	47	15	30	45	4
Gordie Drillon	Toronto	48	23	18	41	6
Syl Apps	Toronto	38	18	23	41	0
Tom Anderson	Brooklyn	48	12	29	41	54
Billy Taylor	Toronto	48	12	26	38	20
Eddie Wares	Detroit	43	9	29	38	31
Roy Conacher	Boston	43	24	13	37	12
Mel Hill	Brooklyn	47	14	23	37	10
Red Hamill	Bos./Chi.	43	24	12	36	23
Sweeney Schriner	Toronto	47	20	16	36	21
Joe Benoit	Montreal	46	20	16	36	27
Syd Howe	Detroit	48	16	19	35	6
Milt Schmidt	Boston	36	14	21	35	34
Bobby Bauer	Boston	36	13	22	35	11
Alex Shibicky	NY Rangers	45	20	14	34	16
Terry Reardon	Montreal	33	17	17	34	14
Eddie Wiseman	Boston	45	12	22	34	8
Clint Smith	NY Rangers	47	10	24	34	4
Five players tied with					33	

LEADING GOALTENDERS

Goaltender	Club	GPI	MINS	GA	SO	AVG
Frank Brimsek	Boston	47	2930	115	3	2.35
Turk Broda	Toronto	48	2960	136	6	2.76
Jim Henry	NY Rangers	48	2960	143	1	2.90
Johnny Mowers	Detroit	47	2880	144	5	3.00
Sam LoPresti	Chicago	47	2860	152	3	3.19
Paul Bibeault	Montreal	38	2380	131	1	3.30
Chuck Rayner	Brooklyn	36	2230	129	1	3.47

LEADING PLAYOFF SCORERS

Player	Club	GP	G	A	PTS	PIM
Don Grosso	Detroit	12	8	6	14	29
Syl Apps	Toronto	13	5	9	14	2
Carl Liscombe	Detroit	12	6	6	12	2
Wally Stanowski	Toronto	13	2	8	10	2
Billy Taylor	Toronto	13	2	8	10	4
Sweeney Schriner	Toronto	13	6	3	9	10
Nick Metz	Toronto	13	4	4	8	12
Syd Howe	Detroit	12	3	5	8	0
Don Metz	Toronto	4	4	3	7	0
John McCreedy	Toronto	13	4	3	7	6
Eddie Bush	Detroit	11	1	6	7	23

LEADING PLAYOFF GOALTENDERS

Goaltender	Club	GPI	MINS	GA	SO	AVG
Jim Henry	NY Rangers	6	360	13	1	2.17
Turk Broda	Toronto	13	780	31	1	2.38
Frank Brimsek	Boston	5	307	16	0	3.13
Johnny Mowers	Detroit	12	720	38	0	3.17

Syl Apps was captain of the Maple Leafs from 1940–41 to 1942–43, and again from 1945–46 through 1947–48. In addition to his great hockey talent, Apps was an excellent football player at McMaster University in Hamilton. He also won the Canadian and British Empire championship in the pole vault in 1934 and finished sixth at the 1936 Berlin Olympics.

After the 1940–41 season, the NHL turned over ownership of the New York Americans to club manager Red Dutton. He tried to spark local interest by changing the team's name to the Brooklyn Americans, evoking the baseball rivalry between the Giants and Dodgers. Dutton even moved to the borough, and encouraged his players to do the same. Although the club held its practices in Brooklyn, games would continue to be played at Madison Square Garden. Still, the cash-strapped team was forced to sell off its few remaining stars, and the 1941–42 season would prove to be the Amerks' swan song.

Maple Leaf Miracle – The Rangers' firepower led the league and dominated the scoring chart, but it was the Leafs' playoff will and some effective substitutions that enabled them to rebound from a 3-0 Detroit deficit and win the Stanley Cup.

The rival New York Rangers enjoyed much more success than their crosstown cousins. The team had slumped after their 1940 Stanley Cup victory, but rebounded to first place in 1941–42. Bryan Hextall led the way, winning the NHL scoring title. His 54 points were two more than runner-up and linemate Lynn Patrick, and four more than his other linemate, Phil Watson, who finished fourth in the scoring race. The Rangers held off the Toronto Maple Leafs in a tight race for top spot. The Boston Bruins finished a close third despite losing their entire Kraut Line to military service midway through the season.

World War II was having an increasing impact on NHL rosters as more and more players traded in their hockey sweaters for more serious sorts of uniforms.

In the playoffs, the Maple Leafs upset the Rangers in the semifinals, but dropped the first three games of the finals to the Detroit Red Wings. Then coach Hap Day shook up his roster, benching Gordie Drillon and Bucko McDonald in favor of Don Metz and Hank Goldup, and the team roared back to win the next four games and the Stanley Cup. Though this was their seventh trip to the finals since 1932, it was the Maple Leafs' first Stanley Cup title since then.

Leaders, 1941-42

GOALS

Name, Team	G
Lynn Patrick, NYR	32
Roy Conacher, Bos.	24
Red Hamill, Bos./Chi.	24
Bryan Hextall, NYR	24
Don Grosso, Det.	23
Gordie Drillon, Tor.	23
Alex Shibicky, NYR	20
Joe Benoit, Mtl.	20
Sweeney Schriner, Tor.	20
Flash Hollett, Bos.	19

ASSISTS

Name, Team	A
Phil Watson, NYR	37
Bryan Hextall, NYR	32
Sid Abel, Det.	31
Bill Thoms, Chi.	30
Don Grosso, Det.	30
Eddie Wares, Det.	29
Tom Anderson, Bro.	29
Toe Blake, Mtl.	28
Billy Taylor, Tor.	26
Mush March, Chi.	26

GOALIE WINS

Name, Team	W
Jim Henry, NYR	29
Turk Broda, Tor.	27
Frank Brimsek, Bos.	24
Sam LoPresti, Chi.	21
Johnny Mowers, Det.	19
Paul Bibeault, Mtl.	17
Chuck Rayner, Bro.	13
Earl Robertson, Bro.	3
Nick Damore, Bos.	1
Bill Dickie, Chi.	1
Bert Gardiner, Mtl.	1

SHUTOUTS

Name, Team	SO
Turk Broda, Tor.	6
Johnny Mowers, Det.	5
Frank Brimsek, Bos.	3
Sam LoPresti, Chi.	3
Chuck Rayner, Bro.	1
Paul Bibeault, Mtl.	1
Jim Henry, NYR	1

PLAYOFF GOALS

Name, Team	G
Don Grosso, Det.	8
Carl Liscombe, Det.	6
Sweeney Schriner, Tor.	6
Mud Bruneteau, Det.	5
Syl Apps, Tor.	5
Don Metz, Tor.	4
Jack McGill, Bos.	4
Joe Carveth, Det.	4
Sid Abel, Det.	4
Nick Metz, Tor.	4
John McCreedy, Tor.	4

PLAYOFF ASSISTS

Name, Team	A
Syl Apps, Tor.	9
Wally Stanowski, Tor.	8
Billy Taylor, Tor.	8
Eddie Bush, Det.	6
Don Grosso, Det.	6
Carl Liscombe, Det.	6
Neil Colville, NYR	5
Syd Howe, Det.	5
Phil Watson, NYR	4
Jimmy Orlando, Det.	4
Nick Metz, Tor.	4

PLAYOFF GOALIE WINS

Name, Team	W
Turk Broda, Tor.	8
Johnny Mowers, Det.	7
Frank Brimsek, Bos.	2
Jim Henry, NYR	2
Sam LoPresti, Chi.	1
Paul Bibeault, Mtl.	1

PLAYOFF SHUTOUTS

Name, Team	SO
Sam LoPresti, Chi.	1
Paul Bibeault, Mtl.	1
Jim Henry, NYR	1
Turk Broda, Tor.	1

FIRST TEAM ALL-STARS

Name, Team	Position
Syl Apps, Tor.	C
Bryan Hextall, NYR	RW
Lynn Patrick, NYR	LW
Earl Seibert, Chi.	D
Tom Anderson, Bro	D
Frank Brimsek, Bos.	G
Frank Boucher, NYR	Coach

SECOND TEAM ALL-STARS

Name, Team	Position
Phil Watson, NYR	C
Gordie Drillon, Tor.	RW
Sid Abel, Det.	LW
Pat Egan, Bro	D
Bucko McDonald, Tor.	D
Turk Broda, Tor.	G
Paul Thompson, Chi.	Coach

1942 Playoffs

SERIES A - SEMI-FINALS

Mar. 21	NY Rangers	1	at	Toronto	3
Mar. 22	Toronto	4	at	NY Rangers	2
Mar. 24	Toronto	0	at	NY Rangers	3
Mar. 28	NY Rangers	1	at	Toronto	2
Mar. 29	Toronto	1	at	NY Rangers	3
Mar. 31	NY Rangers	2	at	Toronto	3

Toronto won best-of-seven series 4–2

SERIES B AND C - QUARTER-FINALS

Mar. 22	Boston	2	at	Chicago	1 OT
Mar. 24	Chicago	4	at	Boston	0
Mar. 26	Chicago	2	at	Boston	3

Boston won best-of-three series 2–1

Mar. 22	Montreal	1	at	Detroit	2
Mar. 24	Detroit	0	at	Montreal	5
Mar. 26	Montreal	2	at	Detroit	6

Detroit won best-of-three series 2–1

SERIES D - SEMI-FINALS

Mar. 29	Detroit	6	at	Boston	4
Mar. 31	Boston	1	at	Detroit	3

Detroit won best-of-three series 2–0

SERIES E - FINALS

Apr. 4	Detroit	3	at	Toronto	2
Apr. 7	Detroit	4	at	Toronto	2
Apr. 9	Toronto	2	at	Detroit	5
Apr. 12	Toronto	4	at	Detroit	3
Apr. 14	Detroit	3	at	Toronto	9
Apr. 16	Toronto	3	at	Detroit	0
Apr. 18	Detroit	1	at	Toronto	3

Toronto won best-of-seven series 4–3

1941-42 – Toronto Maple Leafs – Wally Stanowski, Syl Apps (Captain), Bob Goldham, Gordie Drillon, Hank Goldup, Ernie Dickens, Sweeney Schriner, Bucko McDonald, Bob Davidson, Nick Metz, Bingo Kampman, Don Metz, Gaye Stewart, Turk Broda, John McCreedy, Lorne Carr, Pete Langelle, Billy Taylor, Reg Hamilton, Conn Smythe (Manager), Hap Day (Coach), Frank Selke (Business Manager), Tim Daly (Trainer).

TROPHY WINNERS

Trophy	Awarded For	Winner	Team
Hart	MVP	Tom Anderson	Bro.
Calder	Top Rookie	Grant Warwick	NYR
Vezina	Fewest Goals Against	Frank Brimsek	Bos.
Byng	Gentlemanly Conduct	Syl Apps	Tor.

NHL NOTEBOOK

TRANSACTIONS

- May 5, 1941 – Chicago Black Hawks obtained Cliff "Fido" Purpur from the St. Louis Flyers (AHA) in exchange for Sammy McManus.
- Oct. 10, 1941 – New York Americans signed Harry Watson.
- Oct. 28, 1941 – Brooklyn signed Jimmy Peters and Ken Mosdell.
- Nov. 24, 1941 – Boston Bruins acquired Dutch Hiller and $5,000 from Detroit for Pat McReavy.
- Jan. 4, 1942 – Boston Bruins purchased Harvey "Busher" Jackson from the New York Americans for $7,500.

RECORDS

- Nov. 27, 1941 – Boston Bruins tied an NHL record by scoring four goals in the 10-minute overtime period, to beat the New York Americans 6-2.
- Apr. 9, 1942 – Eddie Bush set a new NHL record for points by a defenseman in a Stanley Cup finals game with 5 (a goal and 4 assists). Bush, who never scored another point in his career, led Detroit to a 5-2 win over Toronto in game three of the Stanley Cup finals.
- Apr. 14, 1942 – Toronto tied a Stanley Cup finals record for most goals by one in a game, with a 9-3 win Detroit in game five of the Stanley Cup finals.

MILESTONES

- Sept. 12, 1941 – The NHL altered rules to establish "minor" and "major" penalty shots. Under the new rules, a minor shot would be taken from a line 28 feet from the goal.
- Feb. 8, 1942 – Playing in his first NHL game, Chicago rookie Bill Mosienko scored two goals in :21 but the Black Hawks lost to the visiting NY Rangers 4-3. Ten years and one month later, Mosienko set an NHL record with three goals in a span of 21 seconds.
- Feb. 8, 1942 – Frank Brimsek became the first goaltender to record 25 shutouts as a member of the Bruins in a 3-0 win against Detroit, at Boston Garden.
- Apr. 18, 1942 – Toronto completed the greatest comeback in playoff history with their 4th straight win, a 3-1 victory over Detroit, in game seven of the Stanley Cup finals. Leafs goalie Turk Broda allowed the Red Wings just seven goals in the final four games.

1942-43

Stanley Cup • Detroit Red Wings

FINAL STANDINGS

Team	GP	W	L	T	GF	GA	PTS
Detroit	50	25	14	11	169	124	61
Boston	50	24	17	9	195	176	57
Toronto	50	22	19	9	198	159	53
Montreal	50	19	19	12	181	191	50
Chicago	50	17	18	15	179	180	49
New York	50	11	31	8	161	253	30

LEADING SCORERS

Player	Club	GP	G	A	PTS	PIM
Doug Bentley	Chicago	50	33	40	73	18
Bill Cowley	Boston	48	27	45	72	10
Max Bentley	Chicago	47	26	44	70	2
Lynn Patrick	NY Rangers	50	22	39	61	28
Lorne Carr	Toronto	50	27	33	60	15
Billy Taylor	Toronto	50	18	42	60	2
Bryan Hextall	NY Rangers	50	27	32	59	28
Toe Blake	Montreal	48	23	36	59	26
Elmer Lach	Montreal	45	18	40	58	14
Buddy O'Connor	Montreal	50	15	43	58	2
Joe Benoit	Montreal	49	30	27	57	23
Syd Howe	Detroit	50	20	35	55	10
Art Jackson	Boston	50	22	31	53	20
Buzz Boll	Boston	43	25	27	52	20
Gordie Drillon	Montreal	49	28	22	50	14
Gaye Stewart	Toronto	48	24	23	47	20
Ray Getliffe	Montreal	50	18	28	46	26
Mud Bruneteau	Detroit	50	23	22	45	2
Red Hamill	Chicago	50	28	16	44	44
Flash Hollett	Boston	50	19	25	44	19
Mel Hill	Toronto	49	17	27	44	47
Bill Thoms	Chicago	47	15	28	43	3
Carl Liscombe	Detroit	50	19	23	42	19
Sid Abel	Detroit	49	18	24	42	33
Phil Watson	NY Rangers	46	14	28	42	44

LEADING GOALTENDERS

Goaltender	Club	GPI	MINS	GA	SO	AVG
Johnny Mowers	Detroit	50	3010	124	6	2.47
Turk Broda	Toronto	50	3000	159	1	3.18
Frank Brimsek	Boston	50	3000	176	1	3.52
Bert Gardiner	Chicago	50	3020	180	1	3.58
Paul Bibeault	Montreal	50	3010	191	1	3.81

LEADING PLAYOFF SCORERS

Player	Club	GP	G	A	PTS	PIM
Carl Liscombe	Detroit	10	6	8	14	2
Sid Abel	Detroit	10	5	8	13	4
Art Jackson	Boston	9	6	3	9	7
Mud Bruneteau	Detroit	9	5	4	9	0
Buddy O'Connor	Montreal	5	4	5	9	0
Flash Hollett	Boston	9	0	9	9	4
Joe Carveth	Detroit	10	6	2	8	4
Bill Cowley	Boston	9	1	7	8	4
Toe Blake	Montreal	5	4	3	7	0
Six players tied with					6	

LEADING PLAYOFF GOALTENDERS

Goaltender	Club	GPI	MINS	GA	SO	AVG
Johnny Mowers	Detroit	10	679	22	2	1.94
Turk Broda	Toronto	6	439	20	0	2.73
Paul Bibeault	Montreal	5	320	18	1	3.38
Frank Brimsek	Boston	9	560	33	0	3.54

Red Wings boss Jack Adams poses with goaltender Johnny Mowers. Mowers spent four seasons with the Red Wings, interrupted by a hitch in the Air Force during World War II. The 1942–43 season was by far his best, leading the league in several categories and recording shutouts in the final two games to deliver the Stanley Cup to Detroit.

WITH THE DEPARTURE of the Brooklyn Americans, the National Hockey League, after growing to as many as 10 teams, was reduced in 1942–43 to what would become known as the Original Six. There were concerns that even the six surviving teams would be sidelined if the increased Canadian and American participation in World War II forced the cancelation of hockey, but such fears were put to rest by NHL President Frank Calder. On September 28, 1942, he announced that government officials in both the United States and Canada had decided the game should continue "in the interest of public morale."

Original Six Shooters – Chicago's Bentley brothers led the scoring parade, but it was the Wings who were redeemed by a balanced offense and the brilliant performance of goaltender Johnny Mowers.

Still, with at least 80 players serving in the armed forces, the NHL's clubs faced severe manpower shortages. The Boston Bruins had lost their entire Kraut Line of Milt Schmidt, Woody Dumart and Bobby Bauer, while seven Toronto Maple Leaf players were in the army. The New York Rangers were hit particularly hard, losing brothers Neil and Mac Colville, Alex Shibicky, Jim Henry and Art Coulter to wartime service.

On November 21, three weeks after the start of the 1942–43 season, the league announced regular-season overtime was being discontinued because of restrictions on travel imposed by the war effort. It would prove to be the last major decision president Frank Calder would ever make, as he died of heart failure on February 4, 1943. Former New York Americans player and manager Mervyn "Red" Dutton succeeded him as the NHL's second president.

Offense increased during the 1942–43 season, and the Chicago Black Hawks' Doug Bentley led the NHL with 73 points (tying Cooney Weiland's single-season record set back in 1929–30). Though the Detroit Red Wings failed to produce a top-10 scorer, they finished first in the regular-season standings and captured the Stanley Cup, avenging the previous year's defeat when they had lost to Toronto after leading the series three games to none.

Leaders, 1942-43

GOALS

Name, Team	G
Doug Bentley, Chi.	33
Joe Benoit, Mtl.	30
Gordie Drillon, Mtl.	28
Red Hamill, Chi.	28
Bill Cowley, Bos.	27
Lorne Carr, Tor.	27
Bryan Hextall, NYR	27
Max Bentley, Chi.	26
Buzz Boll, Bos.	25
Gaye Stewart, Tor.	24

ASSISTS

Name, Team	A
Bill Cowley, Bos.	45
Max Bentley, Chi.	44
Buddy O'Connor, Mtl.	43
Billy Taylor, Tor.	42
Elmer Lach, Mtl.	40
Doug Bentley, Chi.	40
Lynn Patrick, NYR	39
Toe Blake, Mtl.	36
Syd Howe, Det.	35
Lorne Carr, Tor.	33

GOALIE WINS

Name, Team	W
Johnny Mowers, Det.	25
Frank Brimsek, Bos.	24
Turk Broda, Tor.	22
Paul Bibeault, Mtl.	19
Bert Gardiner, Chi.	17
Jimmy Franks, NYR	5
Bill Beveridge, NYR	4
Steve Buzinski, NYR	2

SHUTOUTS

Name, Team	SO
Johnny Mowers, Det.	6
Bill Beveridge, NYR	1
Frank Brimsek, Bos.	1
Turk Broda, Tor.	1
Paul Bibeault, Mtl.	1
Bert Gardiner, Chi.	1

PLAYOFF GOALS

Name, Team	G
Art Jackson, Bos.	6
Carl Liscombe, Det.	6
Joe Carveth, Det.	6
Mud Bruneteau, Det.	5
Sid Abel, Det.	5
Buddy O'Connor, Mtl.	4
Toe Blake, Mtl.	4
Gordie Drillon, Mtl.	4
Herb Cain, Bos.	4
Don Grosso, Det.	4

PLAYOFF ASSISTS

Name, Team	A
Flash Hollett, Bos.	9
Carl Liscombe, Det.	8
Sid Abel, Det.	8
Bill Cowley, Bos.	7
Buddy O'Connor, Mtl.	5
Elmer Lach, Mtl.	4
Bud Poile, Tor.	4
Mud Bruneteau, Det.	4
Bep Guidolin, Bos.	4
Six tied with	3

PLAYOFF GOALIE WINS

Name, Team	W
Johnny Mowers, Det.	8
Frank Brimsek, Bos.	4
Turk Broda, Tor.	2
Paul Bibeault, Mtl.	1

PLAYOFF SHUTOUTS

Name, Team	SO
Johnny Mowers, Det.	2
Paul Bibeault, Mtl.	1

FIRST TEAM ALL-STARS

Name, Team	Position
Bill Cowley, Bos.	C
Lorne Carr, Tor.	RW
Doug Bentley, Chi.	LW
Earl Seibert, Chi.	D
Jack Stewart, Det.	D
Johnny Mowers, Det.	G
Jack Adams, Det.	Coach

SECOND TEAM ALL-STARS

Name, Team	Position
Syl Apps, Tor.	C
Bryan Hextall, NYR	RW
Lynn Patrick, NYR	LW
Jack Crawford, Bos.	D
Flash Hollett, Bos.	D
Frank Brimsek, Bos.	G
Art Ross, Bos.	Coach

1943 Playoffs

SEMI-FINALS

Mar. 21	Toronto	2	at	Detroit	4
Mar. 23	Toronto	3	at	Detroit	2 4OT
Mar. 25	Detroit	4	at	Toronto	2
Mar. 27	Detroit	3	at	Toronto	6
Mar. 28	Toronto	2	at	Detroit	4
Mar. 30	Detroit	3	at	Toronto	2 OT

Detroit won best-of-seven series 4–2

Mar. 21	Montreal	4	at	Boston	5 OT
Mar. 23	Montreal	3	at	Boston	5
Mar. 25	Boston	3	at	Montreal	2 OT
Mar. 27	Boston	0	at	Montreal	4
Mar. 30	Montreal	4	at	Boston	5 OT

Boston won best-of-seven series 4–1

FINALS

Apr. 1	Boston	2	at	Detroit	6
Apr. 4	Boston	3	at	Detroit	4
Apr. 7	Detroit	4	at	Boston	0
Apr. 8	Detroit	2	at	Boston	0

Detroit won best-of-seven series 4–0

1942-43 – Detroit Red Wings – Jack Stewart, Jimmy Orlando, Sid Abel, Alex Motter, Harry Watson, Joe Carveth, Mud Bruneteau, Eddie Wares, Johnny Mowers, Cully Simon, Don Grosso, Carl Liscombe, Adam Brown, Syd Howe, Les Douglas, Harold Jackson, Joe Fisher, Connie Brown, Jack Adams (Manager), Ebbie Goodfellow (Playing Coach), Honey Walker (Trainer).

TROPHY WINNERS

Trophy	Awarded For	Winner	Team
Hart	MVP	Bill Cowley	Bos.
Calder	Top Rookie	Gaye Stewart	Tor.
Vezina	Fewest Goals Against	Johnny Mowers	Det
Byng	Gentlemanly Conduct	Max Bentley	Chi.

NHL NOTEBOOK

TRANSACTIONS

- Oct. 19, 1942 – Detroit signed Bill Quackenbush.
- Oct. 29, 1942 – Montreal Canadiens signed Maurice Richard.
- Nov. 27, 1942 – Toronto Maple Leafs acquired Babe Pratt from the New York Rangers in exchange for Hank Goldup and Dudley "Red" Garrett.
- Mar. 9, 1943 – Boston Bruins purchased Ab DeMarco from Providence (AHL).

RECORDS

- Nov. 5, 1942 – Carl Liscombe set an NHL record with seven points (three goals and four assists) in one game, a 12-5 Red Wings win against the Rangers at the Olympia in Detroit.
- Nov. 12, 1942 – 16-year-old Armand "Bep" Guidolin became the youngest player in NHL history, when he played his first game for the Boston Bruins, a 3-1 loss at Toronto.
- Nov. 8, 1942 – Montreal's Buddy O'Connor had a goal and five assists (including an NHL-record four assists in the third period) in a 10-4 win over the NY Rangers.
- Jan. 14, 1943 – Montreal's Alex Smart became the first NHL rookie to score a hat trick in his first NHL game. His three goals (and an assist) led the Canadiens to a 5-1 win over Chicago. Smart went on to play just eight games in his NHL career.

MILESTONES

- Nov. 10, 1942 – The Rangers scored twice in overtime to beat the Black Hawks 5-3 at MSG, in the final regular-season overtime game in 41 years.
- Nov. 21, 1942 – The NHL Board of Governors announced that overtime would be discontinued in regular season games because of conflicts with train schedules. Overtime was finally reinstated in the 1983-84 season after a 41-year absence.
- Jan. 3, 1943 – Chicago's Reg Bentley scored a goal, with assists from brothers Max and Doug, in a 3-3 Black Hawks tie at New York. It was the first goal in NHL history with three points from the same family!
- Mar. 25, 1943 – Boston's Harvey "Busher" Jackson scored the first overtime shorthanded goal in playoff history as the Bruins beat Montreal 3-2 in game three of the Stanley Cup semi-finals.

1943-44

Stanley Cup • Montreal Canadiens

FINAL STANDINGS

Team	GP	W	L	T	GF	GA	PTS
Montreal	50	38	5	7	234	109	83
Detroit	50	26	18	6	214	177	58
Toronto	50	23	23	4	214	174	50
Chicago	50	22	23	5	178	187	49
Boston	50	19	26	5	223	268	43
New York	50	6	39	5	162	310	17

LEADING SCORERS

Player	Club	GP	G	A	PTS	PIM
Herb Cain	Boston	48	36	46	82	4
Doug Bentley	Chicago	50	38	39	77	22
Lorne Carr	Toronto	50	36	38	74	9
Carl Liscombe	Detroit	50	36	37	73	17
Elmer Lach	Montreal	48	24	48	72	23
Clint Smith	Chicago	50	23	49	72	4
Bill Cowley	Boston	36	30	41	71	12
Bill Mosienko	Chicago	50	32	38	70	10
Art Jackson	Boston	49	28	41	69	8
Gus Bodnar	Toronto	50	22	40	62	18
Syd Howe	Detroit	46	32	28	60	6
Toe Blake	Montreal	41	26	33	59	10
Babe Pratt	Toronto	50	17	40	57	30
Joe Carveth	Detroit	46	21	35	56	6
Maurice Richard	Montreal	46	32	22	54	45
Bryan Hextall	NY Rangers	50	21	33	54	41
Buddy O'Connor	Montreal	44	12	42	54	6
Mud Bruneteau	Detroit	39	35	18	53	4
Ray Getliffe	Montreal	44	28	25	53	44
Ted Kennedy	Toronto	49	26	23	49	2
Phil Watson	Montreal	44	17	32	49	61
Gerry Heffernan	Montreal	43	28	20	48	12
Bob Davidson	Toronto	47	19	28	47	21
Don Grosso	Detroit	42	16	31	47	13
Murph Chamberlain	Montreal	47	15	32	47	85

LEADING GOALTENDERS

Goaltender	Club	GPI	MINS	GA	SO	AVG
Bill Durnan	Montreal	50	3000	109	2	2.18
Paul Bibeault	Toronto	29	1740	87	5	3.00
Mike Karakas	Chicago	26	1560	79	3	3.04
Connie Dion	Detroit	26	1560	80	1	3.08
Bert Gardiner	Boston	41	2460	212	1	5.17
Ken McAuley	NY Rangers	50	2980	310	0	6.24

LEADING PLAYOFF SCORERS

Player	Club	GP	G	A	PTS	PIM
Toe Blake	Montreal	9	7	11	18	2
Maurice Richard	Montreal	9	12	5	17	10
Elmer Lach	Montreal	9	2	11	13	4
Doug Bentley	Chicago	9	8	4	12	4
Clint Smith	Chicago	9	4	8	12	0
Ray Getliffe	Montreal	9	5	4	9	16
George Allen	Chicago	9	5	4	9	8
Murph Chamberlain	Montreal	9	5	3	8	12
Phil Watson	Montreal	9	3	5	8	16
Four players tied with						4

LEADING PLAYOFF GOALTENDERS

Goaltender	Club	GPI	MINS	GA	SO	AVG
Bill Durnan	Montreal	9	549	14	1	1.53
Mike Karakas	Chicago	9	549	24	1	2.62
Connie Dion	Detroit	5	300	17	0	3.40
Paul Bibeault	Toronto	5	300	23	0	4.60

With goalie Frank Brimsek and the entire Kraut Line absent due to military service, the Boston Bruins missed the playoffs for the first time in 10 years in 1943–44 despite Herb Cain's record-breaking offensive performance. Cain is the only retired NHL scoring champion who has not been inducted into the Hockey Hall of Fame.

THE NATIONAL HOCKEY LEAGUE Board of Governors made a decision at the league meetings in September 1943 that has since been interpreted as the beginning of hockey's modern era: they voted to add a red line at center ice. Players could now pass the puck from their own zone into the neutral zone, as far as the red line. The idea was to reduce the number of off-side calls, thus opening up the defensively oriented style of play that dominated. It was hoped that a game that offered an increase in offense would keep customers clicking through the turnstiles while NHL owners suffered through both player and cash shortages during World War II.

Canadiens Crush – After the Habs – who had six 20-goal scorers and only five losses during the season – lost their playoff opener, they exploded for 38 goals and won their next eight games.

Military obligations continued to take talent from NHL rosters during the 1943–44 campaign. The Stanley Cup champion Detroit Red Wings lost nine starters to military service, while the New York Rangers, already badly depleted, lost five more players, including top scorer Lynn Patrick. The Rangers suffered through a horrendous 6–39–5 season in 1943–44, allowing a then-record 310 goals in just 50 games. Goaltender Ken "Tubby" McAuley's 6.20 goals-against average is still the highest single-season mark in league history among goalies appearing in at least 30 games.

The Rangers' woefully inept defense played a part in a league-wide offensive explosion. Four teams scored 200 or more goals, and three players, led by Herb Cain's 82 points for the Boston Bruins, eclipsed the old single-season scoring record of 73 points. On February 3, 1944, Detroit's Syd Howe scored six goals in a single game. The Montreal Canadiens led the league with a record 234 goals and also posted the NHL's best defensive record as they cruised home as regular-season champions, 25 points ahead of their closest competitor, the Detroit Red Wings.

The Habs' Rocket Richard scored 12 goals in nine postseason games—including five in one game against the Toronto Maple Leafs—to lead the Canadiens to their first Stanley Cup title in 13 years.

Leaders, 1943-44

GOALS

Name, Team	G
Doug Bentley, Chi.	38
Herb Cain, Bos.	36
Lorne Carr, Tor.	36
Carl Liscombe, Det.	36
Mud Bruneteau, Det.	35
Syd Howe, Det.	32
Maurice Richard, Mtl.	32
Bill Mosienko, Chi.	32
Bill Cowley, Bos.	30
Gerry Heffernan, Mtl.	28
Ray Getliffe, Mtl.	28
Art Jackson, Bos.	28

ASSISTS

Name, Team	A
Clint Smith, Chi.	49
Elmer Lach, Mtl.	48
Herb Cain, Bos.	46
Buddy O'Connor, Mtl.	42
Bill Cowley, Bos.	41
Art Jackson, Bos.	41
Gus Bodnar, Tor.	40
Babe Pratt, Tor.	40
Doug Bentley, Chi.	39
Lorne Carr, Tor.	38
Bill Mosienko, Chi.	38

GOALIE WINS

Name, Team	W
Bill Durnan, Mtl.	38
Connie Dion, Det.	17
Bert Gardiner, Bos.	17
Paul Bibeault, Tor.	13
Mike Karakas, Chi.	12
Hec Highton, Chi.	10
Benny Grant, Tor./Bos.	9
Jimmy Franks, Det./Bos.	6
Ken McAuley, NYR	6
Normie Smith, Det.	3

SHUTOUTS

Name, Team	SO
Paul Bibeault, Tor.	5
Mike Karakas, Chi.	3
Bill Durnan, Mtl.	2
Jimmy Franks, Det./Bos.	1
Connie Dion, Det.	1
Bert Gardiner, Bos.	1

PLAYOFF GOALS

Name, Team	G
Maurice Richard, Mtl.	12
Doug Bentley, Chi.	8
Toe Blake, Mtl.	7
Ray Getliffe, Mtl.	5
George Allen, Chi.	5
Murph Chamberlain, Mtl.	5
Clint Smith, Chi.	4
John Harms, Chi.	3
Phil Watson, Mtl.	3
Five tied with	2

PLAYOFF ASSISTS

Name, Team	A
Toe Blake, Mtl.	11
Elmer Lach, Mtl.	11
Clint Smith, Chi.	8
Maurice Richard, Mtl.	5
Phil Watson, Mtl.	5
Doug Bentley, Chi.	4
Ray Getliffe, Mtl.	4
George Allen, Chi.	4
Cully Dahlstrom, Chi.	4
Five tied with	3

PLAYOFF GOALIE WINS

Name, Team	W
Bill Durnan, Mtl.	8
Mike Karakas, Chi.	4
Connie Dion, Det.	1
Paul Bibeault, Tor.	1

PLAYOFF SHUTOUTS

Name, Team	SO
Bill Durnan, Mtl.	1
Mike Karakas, Chi.	1

FIRST TEAM ALL-STARS

Name, Team	Position
Bill Cowley, Bos.	C
Lorne Carr, Tor.	RW
Doug Bentley, Chi.	LW
Earl Seibert, Chi.	D
Babe Pratt, Tor.	D
Bill Durnan, Mtl.	G
Dick Irvin, Mtl.	Coach

SECOND TEAM ALL-STARS

Name, Team	Position
Elmer Lach, Mtl.	C
Maurice Richard, Mtl.	RW
Herb Cain, Bos.	LW
Butch Bouchard, Mtl.	D
Dit Clapper, Bos.	D
Paul Bibeault, Tor.	G
Hap Day, Tor.	Coach

1944 Playoffs

SEMI-FINALS

Date	Team	Score		Team	Score
Mar. 21	Toronto	3	at	Montreal	1
Mar. 23	Toronto	1	at	Montreal	5
Mar. 25	Montreal	2	at	Toronto	1
Mar. 28	Montreal	4	at	Toronto	1
Mar. 30	Toronto	0	at	Montreal	11

Montreal won best-of-seven series 4–1

Date	Team	Score		Team	Score
Mar. 21	Chicago	2	at	Detroit	1
Mar. 23	Chicago	1	at	Detroit	4
Mar. 26	Detroit	0	at	Chicago	2
Mar. 28	Detroit	1	at	Chicago	7
Mar. 30	Chicago	5	at	Detroit	2

Chicago won best-of-seven series 4–1

FINALS

Date	Team	Score		Team	Score
Apr. 4	Chicago	1	at	Montreal	5
Apr. 6	Montreal	3	at	Chicago	1
Apr. 9	Montreal	3	at	Chicago	2
Apr. 13	Chicago	4	at	Montreal	5 OT

Montreal won best-of-seven series 4–0

1943-44 – Montreal Canadiens – Toe Blake (Captain), Maurice Richard, Elmer Lach, Ray Getliffe, Murph Chamberlain, Phil Watson, Butch Bouchard, Glen Harmon, Buddy O'Connor, Gerry Heffernan, Mike McMahon, Leo Lamoureux, Fern Majeau, Bob Fillion, Bill Durnan, Tommy Gorman (Manager), Dick Irvin (Coach), Ernie Cook (Trainer).

TROPHY WINNERS

Trophy	Awarded For	Winner	Team
Hart	MVP	Babe Pratt	Tor.
Calder	Top Rookie	Gus Bodnar	Tor.
Vezina	Fewest Goals Against	Bill Durnan	Mtl.
Byng	Gentlemanly Conduct	Clint Smith	Chi

NHL NOTEBOOK

TRANSACTIONS

- Sept. 10, 1943 – Toronto obtained the rights to Ted Kennedy from Montreal for the rights to Frank Eddolls.
- Oct. 30, 1943 – Montreal Canadiens signed Bill Durnan.
- Jan. 5, 1944 – Detroit Red Wings obtained Bill "Flash" Hollett from the Boston Bruins for Pat Egan.
- Jan. 7, 1944 – Chicago Black Hawks obtained goalie Mike Karakas from Providence (AHL) in a trade for Heck Highton, Gord Buttrey and $10,000.

RECORDS

- Oct. 30, 1943 – Toronto Maple Leafs' Gus Bodnar set an NHL record for fastest goal by a rookie in his first game, by scoring just 15 seconds into his NHL debut, as the Leafs beat the Rangers 5-2 at Maple Leaf Gardens.
- Dec. 4, 1943 – Bill Durnan extended his NHL record for the longest unbeaten streak by a rookie goalie to 14 straight games (12-0-2) with an 8-2 Canadiens win against the Red Wings in Montreal. Durnan's record stood until Patrick Lalime broke it in 1996-97.
- Jan. 23, 1944 – Detroit scored 15 straight goals (an NHL record) to beat the visiting Rangers 15-0.

MILESTONES

- Dec. 19, 1943 – Harry Lumley became the youngest goaltender in NHL history, when he made his first appearance with the Red Wings, a 6-2 loss to the Rangers in New York. Lumley made his NHL debut at the age of 17 years and 38 days.
- Jan. 8, 1944 – Toronto's Babe Pratt became the first defenseman in NHL history to get six assists in a game. They came as the Leafs beat Boston 12-3 at Maple Leaf Garden.
- Feb. 20, 1944 – Black Hawks' Mike Karakas and Maple Leafs' Paul Bibeault dueled to the only scoreless, penalty-free game in NHL history. The 0-0 tie, officiated by referee Bill Chadwick, took only 1:55 to play.
- Mar. 18, 1944 – Montreal Canadiens became the first NHL team to go undefeated for an entire season at home, when they finished their season with an 11-2 win over the NY Rangers. The victory gave the Habs a record of 22-0-3 at the Forum.

1944-45

Stanley Cup • Toronto Maple Leafs

FINAL STANDINGS

Team	GP	W	L	T	GF	GA	PTS
Montreal	50	38	8	4	228	121	80
Detroit	50	31	14	5	218	161	67
Toronto	50	24	22	4	183	161	52
Boston	50	16	30	4	179	219	36
Chicago	50	13	30	7	141	194	33
New York	50	11	29	10	154	247	32

LEADING SCORERS

Player	Club	GP	G	A	PTS	PIM
Elmer Lach	Montreal	50	26	54	80	37
Maurice Richard	Montreal	50	50	23	73	46
Toe Blake	Montreal	49	29	38	67	25
Bill Cowley	Boston	49	25	40	65	12
Ted Kennedy	Toronto	49	29	25	54	14
Bill Mosienko	Chicago	50	28	26	54	0
Joe Carveth	Detroit	50	26	28	54	6
Ab DeMarco	NY Rangers	50	24	30	54	10
Clint Smith	Chicago	50	23	31	54	0
Syd Howe	Detroit	46	17	36	53	6
Mud Bruneteau	Detroit	43	23	24	47	6
Lorne Carr	Toronto	47	21	25	46	7
Herb Cain	Boston	50	32	13	45	16
Buddy O'Connor	Montreal	50	21	23	44	2
Gus Bodnar	Toronto	49	8	36	44	18
Grant Warwick	NY Rangers	42	20	22	42	25
Hank Goldup	NY Rangers	48	17	25	42	25
Flash Hollett	Detroit	50	20	21	41	39
Babe Pratt	Toronto	50	18	23	41	39
Steve Wojciechowski	Detroit	49	19	20	39	17
Murray Armstrong	Detroit	50	15	24	39	31
Sweeney Schriner	Toronto	26	22	15	37	10
Pete Horeck	Chicago	50	20	16	36	44
Dutch Hiller	Montreal	48	20	16	36	20
Five players tied with					35	

LEADING GOALTENDERS

Goaltender	Club	GPI	MINS	GA	SO	AVG
Bill Durnan	Montreal	50	3000	121	1	2.42
Harry Lumley	Detroit	37	2220	119	1	3.22
Frank McCool	Toronto	50	3000	161	4	3.22
Mike Karakas	Chicago	48	2880	187	4	3.90
Harvey Bennett	Boston	25	1470	103	0	4.20
Paul Bibeault	Boston	26	1530	116	0	4.55
Ken McAuley	NY Rangers	46	2760	227	1	4.93

LEADING PLAYOFF SCORERS

Player	Club	GP	G	A	PTS	PIM
Joe Carveth	Detroit	14	5	6	11	2
Ted Kennedy	Toronto	13	7	2	9	2
Maurice Richard	Montreal	6	6	2	8	10
Elmer Lach	Montreal	6	4	4	8	2
Eddie Bruneteau	Detroit	14	5	2	7	0
Herb Cain	Boston	7	5	2	7	0
Ken Smith	Boston	7	3	4	7	0
Butch Bouchard	Montreal	6	3	4	7	4
Flash Hollett	Detroit	14	3	4	7	6
Five players tied with					6	

LEADING PLAYOFF GOALTENDERS

Goaltender	Club	GPI	MINS	GA	SO	AVG
Harry Lumley	Detroit	14	871	31	2	2.14
Frank McCool	Toronto	13	807	30	4	2.23
Bill Durnan	Montreal	6	373	15	0	2.41
Paul Bibeault	Boston	7	437	22	0	3.02

Maurice Richard (left), Elmer Lach (center) and Toe Blake (right) were put together by Canadiens coach Dick Irvin in 1943–44. Dubbed the Punch Line, the trio led Montreal back into the Stanley Cup winner's circle that year, then finished 1–2–3 in scoring in 1944–45. All three players were named First Team All-Stars that season.

With the war in Europe winding down, players who had performed military service slowly began trickling back to NHL rosters in 1944–45, though most teams were still thinly stocked. Picking up the slack were several talented newcomers who made their NHL debuts this season, including Ted Lindsay and Harry Lumley with the Detroit Red Wings, Toronto's Frank McCool, and Bill Moe with the New York Rangers. The undisputed star of the 1944–45 season, though, was Rocket Richard.

Hot Rocket, Calm McCool – The Punch Line finished 1-2-3 in points, Rocket went 50 for 50, Elmer Lach-ed up the scoring title, but Frank McCool blanked the Wings in three straight games as Toronto took the title.

Scoring at a season-long pace of a goal per game, the Canadiens right wing enjoyed a record-setting night on December 28, 1944, scoring five goals and adding three assists in a 9–1 Montreal victory over the Detroit Red Wings. Later in the season, Richard surpassed Joe Malone's single-season scoring record of 44 goals (set during the NHL's 22-game inaugural season of 1917–18) when he scored his 45th on February 25, 1945. By season's end, Richard had scored 50 goals in 50 games.

The Rocket was not the only record-setting player during the 1944–45 campaign. His linemate Elmer Lach set a new standard with 54 assists en route to winning the league scoring title with 80 points. Syd Howe's 516th career point during that season put him ahead of Nels Stewart as the NHL's all-time leader, while his Detroit Red Wings teammate Flash Hollett became the first defenseman to score 20 goals in a season.

Montreal's Bill Durnan won the Vezina Trophy for the second consecutive time, as the Canadiens once again finished first. In the playoffs, however, the Canadiens were the targets of a semi-final upset by the Toronto Maple Leafs. Leaf goalie Frank McCool, 1945's rookie of the year, became the only goaltender to open the finals with three consecutive shutouts. The Red Wings rallied to tie the series, but the Leafs held on to beat Detroit in seven games and win the Stanley Cup.

Leaders, 1944-45

GOALS

Name, Team	G
Maurice Richard, Mtl.	50
Herb Cain, Bos.	32
Toe Blake, Mtl.	29
Ted Kennedy, Tor.	29
Bill Mosienko, Chi.	28
Elmer Lach, Mtl.	26
Joe Carveth, Det.	26
Bill Cowley, Bos.	25
Ab DeMarco, NYR	24
Carl Liscombe, Det.	23
Mud Bruneteau, Det.	23
Clint Smith, Chi.	23

ASSISTS

Name, Team	A
Elmer Lach, Mtl.	54
Bill Cowley, Bos.	40
Toe Blake, Mtl.	38
Syd Howe, Det.	36
Gus Bodnar, Tor.	36
Clint Smith, Chi.	31
Ab DeMarco, NYR	30
Joe Carveth, Det.	28
Bill Mosienko, Chi.	26
Lorne Carr, Tor.	25
Hank Goldup, NYR	25
Ted Kennedy, Tor.	25

GOALIE WINS

Name, Team	W
Bill Durnan, Mtl.	38
Harry Lumley, Det.	24
Frank McCool, Tor.	24
Mike Karakas, Chi.	12
Ken McAuley, NYR	11
Harvey Bennett, Bos.	10
Connie Dion, Det.	6
Paul Bibeault, Bos.	6
Normie Smith, Det.	1
Doug Stevenson, NYR/Chi.	1

SHUTOUTS

Name, Team	SO
Mike Karakas, Chi.	4
Frank McCool, Tor.	4
Harry Lumley, Det.	1
Ken McAuley, NYR	1
Bill Durnan, Mtl.	1

PLAYOFF GOALS

Name, Team	G
Ted Kennedy, Tor.	7
Maurice Richard, Mtl.	6
Herb Cain, Bos.	5
Joe Carveth, Det.	5
Eddie Bruneteau, Det.	5
Elmer Lach, Mtl.	4
Carl Liscombe, Det.	4
Murray Armstrong, Det.	4
10 tied with	3

PLAYOFF ASSISTS

Name, Team	A
Joe Carveth, Det.	6
Jack Crawford, Bos.	5
Elmer Lach, Mtl.	4
Butch Bouchard, Mtl.	4
Ken Smith, Bos.	4
Babe Pratt, Tor.	4
Flash Hollett, Det.	4
Jack McGill, Bos.	3
Bill Cowley, Bos.	3
Mel Hill, Tor.	3

PLAYOFF GOALIE WINS

Name, Team	W
Frank McCool, Tor.	8
Harry Lumley, Det.	7
Paul Bibeault, Bos.	3
Bill Durnan, Mtl.	2

PLAYOFF SHUTOUTS

Name, Team	SO
Frank McCool, Tor.	4
Harry Lumley, Det.	2

FIRST TEAM ALL-STARS

Name, Team	Position
Elmer Lach, Mtl.	C
Maurice Richard, Mtl.	RW
Toe Blake, Mtl.	LW
Butch Bouchard, Mtl.	D
Flash Hollett, Det.	D
Bill Durnan, Mtl.	G
Dick Irvin, Mtl.	Coach

SECOND TEAM ALL-STARS

Name, Team	Position
Bill Cowley, Bos.	C
Bill Mosienko, Chi.	RW
Syd Howe, Det.	LW
Glen Harmon, Mtl.	D
Babe Pratt, Tor.	D
Mike Karakas, Chi.	G
Jack Adams, Det.	Coach

1945 Playoffs

SEMI-FINALS

Date	Visitor	Score		Home	Score	
Mar. 20	Toronto	1	at	Montreal	0	
Mar. 22	Toronto	3	at	Montreal	2	
Mar. 24	Montreal	4	at	Toronto	1	
Mar. 27	Montreal	3	at	Toronto	4	OT
Mar. 29	Toronto	3	at	Montreal	10	
Mar. 31	Montreal	2	at	Toronto	3	

Toronto won best-of-seven series 4–2

Date	Visitor	Score		Home	Score	
Mar. 20	Boston	4	at	Detroit	3	
Mar. 22	Boston	4	at	Detroit	2	
Mar. 25	Detroit	3	at	Boston	2	
Mar. 27	Detroit	3	at	Boston	2	
Mar. 29	Boston	2	at	Detroit	3	OT
Apr. 1	Detroit	3	at	Boston	5	
Apr. 3	Boston	3	at	Detroit	5	

Detroit won best-of-seven series 4–3

FINALS

Date	Visitor	Score		Home	Score	
Apr. 6	Toronto	1	at	Detroit	0	
Apr. 8	Toronto	2	at	Detroit	0	
Apr. 12	Detroit	0	at	Toronto	1	
Apr. 14	Detroit	5	at	Toronto	3	
Apr. 19	Toronto	0	at	Detroit	2	
Apr. 21	Detroit	1	at	Toronto	0	OT
Apr. 22	Toronto	2	at	Detroit	1	

Toronto won best-of-seven series 4–3

1944-45 – Toronto Maple Leafs – Don Metz, Frank McCool, Wally Stanowski, Reg Hamilton, Moe Morris, John McCreedy, Tom O'Neill, Ted Kennedy, Babe Pratt, Gus Bodnar, Art Jackson, Jack McLean, Mel Hill, Nick Metz, Bob Davidson (Captain), Sweeney Schriner, Lorne Carr, Pete Backor, Ross Johnstone, Conn Smythe (Manager), Frank Selke (Business Manager), Hap Day (Coach), Tim Daly (Trainer).

TROPHY WINNERS

Trophy	Awarded For	Winner	Team
Hart	MVP	Elmer Lach	Mtl.
Calder	Top Rookie	Frank McCool	Tor.
Vezina	Fewest Goals Against	Bill Durnan	Mtl.
Byng	Gentlemanly Conduct	Bill Mosienko	Chi.

NHL NOTEBOOK

TRANSACTIONS

- Oct. 18, 1944 – Detroit signed Ted Lindsay.
- Oct. 25, 1944 – Toronto signed Frank McCool.
- Oct. 30, 1944 – Boston traded Pete Leswick to Detroit for Bill Jennings.
- Nov. 16, 1944 – Detroit obtained Eddie Bruneteau from Quebec (QSHL) in exchange for Bob Thorpe.

RECORDS

- Jan. 21, 1945 – Boston set an NHL record for fastest four goals by one team, scoring them in a 1:20 span during the second period of a 14-3 win over the Rangers.
- Feb. 25, 1945 – Maurice Richard set an NHL record with his 45th goal of the year, in a 5-2 Canadiens win over the Maple Leafs. Richard's 45th goal broke the NHL single season mark of 44, set by Joe Malone in 1917-18.
- Mar. 11, 1945 – Montreal's Elmer Lach had a goal and three assists in an 11-5 win over the Rangers at New York. Lach's three assists gave him an NHL record 51 for the season.
- Apr. 12, 1945 – Toronto Maple Leafs rookie goalie Frank McCool set a new Stanley Cup record with his third consecutive playoff shutout, 1-0 over Detroit.

MILESTONES

- Mar. 8, 1945 – Detroit's Syd Howe became the NHL's all time leading scorer, with 516 career points (passing Nels Stewart). He set the record with an assist in a 7-3 win against New York.
- Mar. 17, 1945 – Detroit's Bill "Flash" Hollett became the first NHL defenseman to score 20 goals in a season. His 20th goal came in a 4-3 Red Wings win over Toronto.
- Mar. 18, 1945 – In the final game of the 1944-45 season at Boston, Maurice Richard became the first player in NHL history to score 50 goals in one season. Montreal beat the Bruins 4-2. Richard scored his 50 goals in just 50 games.
- Apr. 6, 1945 – Toronto's Frank McCool and Detroit's Harry Lumley became the first rookie goalies to meet in the Stanley Cup finals. Leafs beat the Wings 1-0 to open the best of seven series. It was the first of three straight shutouts for McCool.

1945-46

Stanley Cup • Montreal Canadiens

FINAL STANDINGS

Team	GP	W	L	T	GF	GA	PTS
Montreal	50	28	17	5	172	134	61
Boston	50	24	18	8	167	156	56
Chicago	50	23	20	7	200	178	53
Detroit	50	20	20	10	146	159	50
Toronto	50	19	24	7	174	185	45
New York	50	13	28	9	144	191	35

LEADING SCORERS

Player	Club	GP	G	A	PTS	PIM
Max Bentley	Chicago	47	31	30	61	6
Gaye Stewart	Toronto	50	37	15	52	8
Toe Blake	Montreal	50	29	21	50	2
Clint Smith	Chicago	50	26	24	50	2
Maurice Richard	Montreal	50	27	21	48	50
Bill Mosienko	Chicago	40	18	30	48	12
Ab DeMarco	NY Rangers	50	20	27	47	20
Elmer Lach	Montreal	50	13	34	47	34
Alex Kaleta	Chicago	49	19	27	46	17
Billy Taylor	Toronto	48	23	18	41	14
Pete Horeck	Chicago	50	20	21	41	34
Syl Apps	Toronto	40	24	16	40	2
Doug Bentley	Chicago	36	19	21	40	16
Don Gallinger	Boston	50	17	23	40	18
Red Hamill	Chicago	38	20	17	37	23
Grant Warwick	NY Rangers	45	19	18	37	19
Gus Bodnar	Toronto	49	14	23	37	14
Joe Carveth	Detroit	48	17	18	35	10
Woody Dumart	Boston	50	22	12	34	2
Edgar Laprade	NY Rangers	49	15	19	34	0
Bep Guidolin	Boston	50	15	17	32	62
Adam Brown	Detroit	48	20	11	31	27
Milt Schmidt	Boston	48	13	18	31	21
Jimmy Peters	Montreal	47	11	19	30	10
Four players tied with					29	

LEADING GOALTENDERS

Goaltender	Club	GPI	MINS	GA	SO	AVG
Bill Durnan	Montreal	40	2400	104	4	2.60
Paul Bibeault	Bos./Mtl.	26	1560	75	2	2.88
Harry Lumley	Detroit	50	3000	159	2	3.18
Frank Brimsek	Boston	34	2040	111	2	3.26
Mike Karakas	Chicago	48	2880	166	1	3.46
Chuck Rayner	NY Rangers	40	2377	149	1	3.76

LEADING PLAYOFF SCORERS

Player	Club	GP	G	A	PTS	PIM
Elmer Lach	Montreal	9	5	12	17	4
Toe Blake	Montreal	9	7	6	13	5
Maurice Richard	Montreal	9	7	4	11	15
Milt Schmidt	Boston	10	3	5	8	2
Bep Guidolin	Boston	10	5	2	7	13
Bobby Bauer	Boston	10	4	3	7	2
Woody Dumart	Boston	10	4	3	7	0
Bob Fillion	Montreal	9	4	3	7	6
Murph Chamberlain	Montreal	9	4	2	6	18
Dutch Hiller	Montreal	9	4	2	6	2
Don Gallinger	Boston	10	2	4	6	2

LEADING PLAYOFF GOALTENDERS

Goaltender	Club	GPI	MINS	GA	SO	AVG
Bill Durnan	Montreal	9	581	20	0	2.07
Frank Brimsek	Boston	10	651	29	0	2.67
Harry Lumley	Detroit	5	310	16	1	3.10
Mike Karakas	Chicago	4	240	26	0	6.50

Edgar Laprade was a long-time amateur star in Port Arthur, Ontario. He helped the Bearcats win the Allan Cup in 1939, and was named the most valuable player in the Thunder Bay Senior Hockey League in both 1938–39 and 1940–41. He did not turn pro until after World War II, signing with the New York Rangers in 1945–46 and winning the Calder Trophy.

With World War II over, more than 40 players returned from military service to their respective NHL rosters in time for the start of training camp in 1945.

The league's governors decided against reinstituting regular-season overtime despite having suspended it "temporarily" in 1942 due to wartime travel restrictions. Regular-season overtime would not return to the NHL until 1983–84. The Boston Bruins welcomed back Milt Schmidt, Woody Dumart, Bobby Bauer and goaltender Frank Brimsek. Art Ross, deciding to concentrate on his role as general manager, turned over the coaching honors to Dit Clapper, who would also continue to play for Boston. The revitalized Bruins battled the Canadiens for much of the 1945–46 season before settling for second place.

The New York Rangers welcomed back stars Lynn and Muzz Patrick, Neil Colville and goalie Chuck Rayner. Their lineup also boasted rookie of the year Edgar Laprade, but hard times continued as the club finished last in every major statistical category for the third year in a row and wound up in last place again. The going was also tough in Toronto, where the Maple Leafs opened the season without goaltender Frank McCool. Even Turk Broda's return from the military in January 1946 could not salvage a season that saw Toronto become just the second NHL team to miss the playoffs the year after winning the Stanley Cup.

Punched Up – Despite not having a top-ten scorer, Boston advanced to the finals only to meet Montreal's point-producing Punch Line, who turned out the Bruins' lights in five games, three of which were decided in overtime.

In Montreal, the Canadiens endured a scoring slump by the Punch Line of Rocket Richard, Elmer Lach and Toe Blake, as well as an injury to goalie Bill Durnan, yet they once again finished first in the regular season. Their top trio regained its scoring touch in the playoffs, finishing 1–2–3 in postseason scoring as the Canadiens won the Stanley Cup for the second time in three seasons, beating Boston in the final.

Leaders, 1945-46

GOALS

Name, Team	G
Gaye Stewart, Tor.	37
Max Bentley, Chi.	31
Toe Blake, Mtl.	29
Maurice Richard, Mtl.	27
Clint Smith, Chi.	26
Syl Apps, Tor.	24
Billy Taylor, Tor.	23
Woody Dumart, Bos.	22
Red Hamill, Chi.	20
Adam Brown, Det.	20
Ab DeMarco, NYR	20
Pete Horeck, Chi.	20

ASSISTS

Name, Team	A
Elmer Lach, Mtl.	34
Bill Mosienko, Chi.	30
Max Bentley, Chi.	30
Alex Kaleta, Chi.	27
Ab DeMarco, NYR	27
Clint Smith, Chi.	24
Gus Bodnar, Tor.	23
Don Gallinger, Bos.	23
Doug Bentley, Chi.	21
Toe Blake, Mtl.	21
Maurice Richard, Mtl.	21
Pete Horeck, Chi.	21

GOALIE WINS

Name, Team	W
Bill Durnan, Mtl.	24
Mike Karakas, Chi.	22
Harry Lumley, Det.	20
Frank Brimsek, Bos.	16
Paul Bibeault, Bos/Mtl.	12
Chuck Rayner, NYR	12
Frank McCool, Tor.	10
Turk Broda, Tor.	6
Gordie Bell, Tor.	3
Doug Stevenson, Chi.	1
Jim Henry, NYR	1

SHUTOUTS

Name, Team	SO
Bill Durnan, Mtl.	4
Paul Bibeault, Bos/Mtl.	2
Frank Brimsek, Bos.	2
Harry Lumley, Det.	2
Jim Henry, NYR	1
Chuck Rayner, NYR	1
Mike Karakas, Chi.	1

PLAYOFF GOALS

Name, Team	G
Toe Blake, Mtl.	7
Maurice Richard, Mtl.	7
Elmer Lach, Mtl.	5
Bep Guidolin, Bos.	5
Bob Fillion, Mtl.	4
Murph Chamberlain, Mtl.	4
Dutch Hiller, Mtl.	4
Ken Mosdell, Mtl.	4
Bobby Bauer, Bos.	4
Woody Dumart, Bos.	4
Terry Reardon, Bos.	4

PLAYOFF ASSISTS

Name, Team	A
Elmer Lach, Mtl.	12
Toe Blake, Mtl.	6
Milt Schmidt, Bos.	5
Ken Smith, Bos.	4
Maurice Richard, Mtl.	4
Glen Harmon, Mtl.	4
Don Gallinger, Bos.	4
Bob Fillion, Mtl.	3
Buddy O'Connor, Mtl.	3
Bobby Bauer, Bos.	3
Woody Dumart, Bos.	3
Bill Cowley, Bos.	3

PLAYOFF GOALIE WINS

Name, Team	W
Bill Durnan, Mtl.	8
Frank Brimsek, Bos.	5
Harry Lumley, Det.	1

PLAYOFF SHUTOUTS

Name, Team	SO
Harry Lumley, Det.	1

FIRST TEAM ALL-STARS

Name, Team	Position
Max Bentley, Chi.	C
Maurice Richard, Mtl.	RW
Gaye Stewart, Tor.	LW
Jack Crawford, Bos.	D
Butch Bouchard, Mtl.	D
Bill Durnan, Mtl.	G
Dick Irvin, Mtl.	Coach

SECOND TEAM ALL-STARS

Name, Team	Position
Elmer Lach, Mtl.	C
Bill Mosienko, Chi.	RW
Toe Blake, Mtl.	LW
Ken Reardon, Mtl.	D
Jack Stewart, Det.	D
Frank Brimsek, Bos.	G
Johnny Gottselig, Chi.	Coach

1946 Playoffs

SEMI-FINALS

Date		Team	Score		Team	Score
Mar.	19	Chicago	2	at	Montreal	6
Mar.	21	Chicago	1	at	Montreal	5
Mar.	24	Montreal	8	at	Chicago	2
Mar.	26	Montreal	7	at	Chicago	2

Montreal won best-of-seven series 4–0

Date		Team	Score		Team	Score
Mar.	19	Detroit	1	at	Boston	3
Mar.	21	Detroit	3	at	Boston	0
Mar.	24	Boston	5	at	Detroit	2
Mar.	26	Boston	4	at	Detroit	1
Mar.	28	Detroit	3	at	Boston	4 OT

Boston won best-of-seven series 4–1

FINALS

Date		Team	Score		Team	Score
Mar.	30	Boston	3	at	Montreal	4 OT
Apr.	2	Boston	2	at	Montreal	3 OT
Apr.	4	Montreal	4	at	Boston	2
Apr.	7	Montreal	2	at	Boston	3 OT
Apr.	9	Boston	3	at	Montreal	6

Montreal won best-of-seven series 4–1

1945-46 – Montreal Canadiens – Elmer Lach, Toe Blake (Captain), Maurice Richard, Bob Fillion, Dutch Hiller, Murph Chamberlain, Ken Mosdell, Buddy O'Connor, Glen Harmon, Jimmy Peters, Butch Bouchard, Billy Reay, Ken Reardon, Leo Lamoureux, Frank Eddolls, Gerry Plamondon, Bill Durnan, Tommy Gorman (Manager), Dick Irvin (Coach), Frnie Cook (Trainer).

TROPHY WINNERS

Trophy	Awarded For	Winner	Team
Hart	MVP	Max Bentley	Chi.
Calder	Top Rookie	Edgar Laprade	NYR
Vezina	Fewest Goals Against	Bill Durnan	Mtl.
Byng	Gentlemanly Conduct	Toe Blake	Mtl.

NHL NOTEBOOK

TRANSACTIONS

- June 14, 1945 – Montreal Canadiens claimed Jimmy Peters from Buffalo (AHL) in the inter-league draft.
- Oct. 14, 1945 – Detroit traded Vic Lynn to Montreal for cash.
- Oct. 15, 1945 – New York Rangers signed Edgar Laprade.
- Oct. 16, 1945 – Toronto Maple Leafs signed Jim Thomson.

RECORDS

- Oct. 24, 1945 – The NHL made the earliest season schedule start in league history, and Chicago's Red Hamill scored two unassisted goals in the final seven minutes to give the Black Hawks a 5-4 win at Boston Garden.
- Dec. 13, 1945 – Chicago's Mike Karakas became the second goal-tender in franchise history to record 100 wins as a member of the Black Hawks. The milestone came in a 7-4 road win against the Rangers.
- Dec. 29, 1945 – Maurice Richard scored twice to give him 100 goals in just 145 NHL games, when the Canadiens lost 5-4 to the visiting Black Hawks. It was the fastest 100 goals in NHL history, a record bettered only by Mike Bossy (129 games) and Teemu Selanne (130 games).
- Jan. 20, 1946 – Max Bentley scored his 4th career hat trick as the Black Hawks beat the Rangers 9-1 before a crowd of 19,749 in Chicago, the largest crowd in NHL history.

MILESTONES

- Sept. 7, 1945 – President Red Dutton announced that, for the first time in the history of hockey, the rules as adopted by the NHL would now be standard in all orgainzed hockey, both professional and amateur.
- Mar. 6, 1946 – Maurice Richard scored the 2,000th goal in Montreal Canadiens history, in a 7-3 win over the Rangers at the Forum.
- Mar. 16, 1946 – Bill Durnan became just the third goaltender in Montreal history to win 100 games, when the Canadiens won 6-3 over the visiting Chicago Black Hawks.
- Mar. 30, 1946 – Maurice Richard scored at 9:08 of OT, the first of his NHL-record three career overtime goals in the finals, to give Montreal a 4-3 win over Boston in game one of the Stanley Cup finals. It was also Richard's 8th straight playoff game with a goal, an NHL record.

1946-47

Stanley Cup • Toronto Maple Leafs

FINAL STANDINGS

Team	GP	W	L	T	GF	GA	PTS
Montreal	60	34	16	10	189	138	78
Toronto	60	31	19	10	209	172	72
Boston	60	26	23	11	190	175	63
Detroit	60	22	27	11	190	193	55
New York	60	22	32	6	167	186	50
Chicago	60	19	37	4	193	274	42

LEADING SCORERS

Player	Club	GP	G	A	PTS	PIM
Max Bentley	Chicago	60	29	43	72	12
Maurice Richard	Montreal	60	45	26	71	69
Billy Taylor	Detroit	60	17	46	63	35
Milt Schmidt	Boston	59	27	35	62	40
Ted Kennedy	Toronto	60	28	32	60	27
Doug Bentley	Chicago	52	21	34	55	18
Roy Conacher	Detroit	60	30	24	54	6
Bobby Bauer	Boston	58	30	24	54	4
Bill Mosienko	Chicago	59	25	27	52	2
Woody Dumart	Boston	60	24	28	52	12
Toe Blake	Montreal	60	21	29	50	6
Syl Apps	Toronto	54	25	24	49	6
Adam Brown	Det./Chi.	64	19	30	49	87
Sid Abel	Detroit	60	19	29	48	29
Howie Meeker	Toronto	55	27	18	45	76
Alex Kaleta	Chicago	57	24	20	44	37
Ted Lindsay	Detroit	59	27	15	42	57
Billy Reay	Montreal	59	22	20	42	17
Tony Leswick	NY Rangers	59	27	14	41	51
Red Hamill	Chicago	60	21	19	40	12
George Gee	Chicago	60	20	20	40	26
Grant Warwick	NY Rangers	54	20	20	40	24
Edgar Laprade	NY Rangers	58	15	25	40	9
Bill Cowley	Boston	51	13	25	38	16
Bill Ezinicki	Toronto	60	17	20	37	93

LEADING GOALTENDERS

Goaltender	Club	GPI	MINS	GA	SO	AVG
Bill Durnan	Montreal	60	3600	138	4	2.30
Turk Broda	Toronto	60	3600	172	4	2.87
Frank Brimsek	Boston	60	3600	175	3	2.92
Chuck Rayner	NY Rangers	58	3480	177	5	3.05
Harry Lumley	Detroit	52	3120	159	3	3.06
Paul Bibeault	Chicago	41	2460	170	1	4.15

LEADING PLAYOFF SCORERS

Player	Club	GP	G	A	PTS	PIM
Maurice Richard	Montreal	10	6	5	11	44
Ted Kennedy	Toronto	11	4	5	9	4
Toe Blake	Montreal	11	2	7	9	0
Roy Conacher	Detroit	5	4	4	8	2
Billy Reay	Montreal	11	6	1	7	14
Buddy O'Connor	Montreal	8	3	4	7	0
Gaye Stewart	Toronto	11	2	5	7	8
Syl Apps	Toronto	11	5	1	6	0
Nick Metz	Toronto	6	4	2	6	0
Howie Meeker	Toronto	11	3	3	6	6
Billy Taylor	Detroit	5	1	5	6	4
Roger Leger	Montreal	11	0	6	6	10

LEADING PLAYOFF GOALTENDERS

Goaltender	Club	GPI	MINS	GA	SO	AVG
Bill Durnan	Montreal	11	720	23	1	1.92
Turk Broda	Toronto	11	680	27	1	2.38
Frank Brimsek	Boston	5	343	16	0	2.80
Red Almas	Detroit	5	263	13	0	2.97

Bruins defenseman Fern Flaman clears the puck away from Montreal's Elmer Lach in front of Frank Brimsek in the Boston net. Defense partner Murray Henderson (#8) and forward Woody Dumart (#14) keep an eye out for trouble. Still, with playoff victories in 1946 and 1947, Montreal launched a lengthy run of postseason success against Boston.

POSTWAR RECONSTRUCTION of the NHL began in earnest prior to the 1946–47 season. Clarence Campbell was named the NHL's third president, succeeding Red Dutton, rosters were replenished with returning veterans, and the regular season was extended from 50 to 60 games.

Boston's gifted and durable rearguard Dit Clapper began his 20th season in the NHL, a record that would not be matched until Gordie Howe would join the 20-year-club in 1965. Clapper's achievement was celebrated in several NHL cities throughout the season

Come on, Teeder! – Max Bentley grounded the Rocket to win the scoring title by a single point, the Kraut Line was realigned and Teeder Kennedy's grit and guts helped the NHL's youngest team grab Lord Stanley's silverware.

In Toronto, Frank Selke, who had guided the Maple Leafs during Conn Smythe's military service, lost a power struggle with the team's board of directors and left to run the Montreal Canadiens where he would go on to enjoy considerable success.

Fully in charge of the Maple Leafs again, Smythe cleared out a number of aging stars to make room for youngsters like Bill Barilko, Sid Smith, Calder Trophy-winner Howie Meeker and Garth Boesch, and hockey's newest dynasty was formed.

Max Bentley, playing on the Chicago Black Hawks' Pony Line with brother Doug and Bill Mosienko, led the NHL with 72 points, and Punch Line star Rocket Richard regained his scoring touch to pot 45 goals. Milt Schmidt and Woody Dumart of Boston's Kraut Line also returned to the NHL's top 10 scorers in 1946–47. On March 16, 1947, Billy Taylor of the Detroit Red Wings collected a record seven assists in a single game, while the Leafs' Howie Meeker set a rookie record on January 8 with five goals in one contest.

The Leafs finished the regular season in second place behind Montreal and knocked off the Red Wings in five games in the semifinals. Toronto dropped the opening game of the finals 6–0 to the Canadiens before winning the Stanley Cup in six games.

Leaders, 1946-47

GOALS

Name, Team	G
Maurice Richard, Mtl.	45
Bobby Bauer, Bos.	30
Roy Conacher, Det.	30
Max Bentley, Chi.	29
Ted Kennedy, Tor.	28
Howie Meeker, Tor.	27
Milt Schmidt, Bos.	27
Ted Lindsay, Det.	27
Tony Leswick, NYR	27
Syl Apps, Tor.	25
Bill Mosienko, Chi.	25

ASSISTS

Name, Team	A
Billy Taylor, Det.	46
Max Bentley, Chi.	43
Milt Schmidt, Bos.	35
Doug Bentley, Chi.	34
Ted Kennedy, Tor.	32
Adam Brown, Det./Chi.	30
Toe Blake, Mtl.	29
Sid Abel, Det.	29
Woody Dumart, Bos.	28
Bill Mosienko, Chi.	27

GOALIE WINS

Name, Team	W
Bill Durnan, Mtl.	34
Turk Broda, Tor.	31
Frank Brimsek, Bos.	26
Harry Lumley, Det.	22
Chuck Rayner, NYR	22
Paul Bibeault, Chi.	13
Emile Francis, Chi.	6

SHUTOUTS

Name, Team	SO
Chuck Rayner, NYR	5
Bill Durnan, Mtl.	4
Turk Broda, Tor.	4
Harry Lumley, Det.	3
Frank Brimsek, Bos.	3
Paul Bibeault, Chi.	1

PLAYOFF GOALS

Name, Team	G
Maurice Richard, Mtl.	6
Billy Reay, Mtl.	6
Syl Apps, Tor.	5
Roy Conacher, Det.	4
Nick Metz, Tor.	4
Ted Kennedy, Tor.	4
Vic Lynn, Tor.	4
Milt Schmidt, Bos.	3
Ken Smith, Bos.	3
John Quilty, Mtl.	3
Buddy O'Connor, Mtl.	3
Howie Meeker, Tor.	3
Harry Watson, Tor.	3

PLAYOFF ASSISTS

Name, Team	A
Toe Blake, Mtl.	7
Roger Leger, Mtl.	6
Billy Taylor, Det.	5
Maurice Richard, Mtl.	5
Ted Kennedy, Tor.	5
Gaye Stewart, Tor.	5
Eddie Bruneteau, Det.	4
Roy Conacher, Det.	4
Buddy O'Connor, Mtl.	4
Eight tied with	3

PLAYOFF GOALIE WINS

Name, Team	W
Turk Broda, Tor.	8
Bill Durnan, Mtl.	6
Frank Brimsek, Bos.	1
Red Almas, Det.	1

PLAYOFF SHUTOUTS

Name, Team	SO
Turk Broda, Tor.	1
Bill Durnan, Mtl.	1

FIRST TEAM ALL-STARS

Name, Team	Position
Milt Schmidt, Bos.	C
Maurice Richard, Mtl.	RW
Doug Bentley, Chi.	LW
Ken Reardon, Mtl.	D
Butch Bouchard, Mtl.	D
Bill Durnan, Mtl.	G

SECOND TEAM ALL-STARS

Name, Team	Position
Max Bentley, Chi.	C
Bobby Bauer, Bos.	RW
Woody Dumart, Bos.	LW
Jack Stewart, Det.	D
Bill Quackenbush, Det.	D
Frank Brimsek, Bos.	G

1947 Playoffs

SEMI-FINALS

Date		Team	Score		Team	Score	
Mar.	25	Boston	1	at	Montreal	3	
Mar.	27	Boston	1	at	Montreal	2	OT
Mar.	29	Montreal	2	at	Boston	4	
Apr.	1	Montreal	5	at	Boston	1	
Apr.	3	Boston	3	at	Montreal	4	2OT

Montreal won best-of-seven series 4–1

Date		Team	Score		Team	Score	
Mar.	26	Detroit	2	at	Toronto	3	OT
Mar.	29	Detroit	9	at	Toronto	1	
Apr.	1	Toronto	4	at	Detroit	1	
Apr.	3	Toronto	4	at	Detroit	1	
Apr.	5	Detroit	1	at	Toronto	6	

Toronto won best-of-seven series 4–1

FINALS

Date		Team	Score		Team	Score	
Apr.	8	Toronto	0	at	Montreal	6	
Apr.	10	Toronto	4	at	Montreal	0	
Apr.	12	Montreal	2	at	Toronto	4	
Apr.	15	Montreal	1	at	Toronto	2	OT
Apr.	17	Toronto	1	at	Montreal	3	
Apr.	19	Montreal	1	at	Toronto	2	

Toronto won best-of-seven series 4–2

1946-47 – Toronto Maple Leafs – Turk Broda, Garth Boesch, Gus Mortson, Jimmy Thomson, Wally Stanowski, Bill Barilko, Harry Watson, Bud Poile, Ted Kennedy, Syl Apps (Captain), Don Metz, Nick Metz, Bill Ezinicki, Vic Lynn, Howie Meeker, Gaye Stewart, Joe Klukay, Gus Bodnar, Bob Goldham, Conn Smythe (Manager), Hap Day (Coach), Tim Daly (Trainer).

TROPHY WINNERS

Trophy	Awarded For	Winner	Team
Hart	MVP	Maurice Richard	Mtl.
Calder	Top Rookie	Howie Meeker	Tor.
Vezina	Fewest Goals Against	Bill Durnan	Mtl.
Byng	Gentlemanly Conduct	Bobby Bauer	Bos.

NHL NOTEBOOK

TRANSACTIONS

- Apr. 30, 1946 – Toronto Maple Leafs signed forward Tod Sloan.
- May 30, 1946 – Toronto Maple Leafs signed amateur Howie Meeker from the Stratford Seniors.
- Sept. 21, 1946 Toronto traded Billy Taylor to Detroit for Harry Watson.
- Oct. 8, 1946 – 18-year-old Gordie Howe signed his first contract with the Detroit Red Wings.

RECORDS

- Jan. 8, 1947 – Toronto forward Howie Meeker scored five times to set an NHL record for most goals in a game by a rookie, as the Maple Leafs beat Chicago 10-4.
- Feb. 12, 1947 – Boston's Bill Cowley picked up a goal and an assist for his 529th point to become the NHL's All-Time point scoring leader. He passed Syd Howe, who had retired one year earlier with 528 points. Bruins beat the Rangers 10-1 at Boston Garden.
- Mar. 16, 1947 – Detroit's Billy Taylor set an NHL record with seven assists in a 10-6 win over the Black Hawks.

MILESTONES

- Oct. 16, 1946 – Gordie Howe scored his first NHL goal in his first career game, as Detroit tied Toronto 3-3. Howe wore uniform #17 and also had two fights.
- Feb. 9, 1947 – 20-year-old goaltender Emile Francis made his NHL debut for Chicago (before a crowd of 20,004), and the Black Hawks won 6-4 over Boston.
- Feb. 12, 1947 – Boston's Dit Clapper officially retired after a 20-year NHL career, in a ceremony at Boston Garden. Clapper was granted immediate induction into the Hall of Fame,and his uniform #5 was retired by the Bruins.
- Mar. 8, 1947 – Turk Broda became the first goaltender in franchise history to record 200 career victories as a member of the Maple Leafs. The milestone came in a 12-4 win against the visiting Chicago Black Hawks.

1947-48

Stanley Cup • Toronto Maple Leafs

FINAL STANDINGS

Team	GP	W	L	T	GF	GA	PTS
Toronto	60	32	15	13	182	143	77
Detroit	60	30	18	12	187	148	72
Boston	60	23	24	13	167	168	59
New York	60	21	26	13	176	201	55
Montreal	60	20	29	11	147	169	51
Chicago	60	20	34	6	195	225	46

LEADING SCORERS

Player	Club	GP	G	A	PTS	PIM
Elmer Lach	Montreal	60	30	31	61	72
Buddy O'Connor	NY Rangers	60	24	36	60	8
Doug Bentley	Chicago	60	20	37	57	16
Gaye Stewart	Tor./Chi.	61	27	29	56	83
Max Bentley	Chi./Tor.	59	26	28	54	14
Bud Poile	Tor./Chi.	58	25	29	54	17
Maurice Richard	Montreal	53	28	25	53	89
Syl Apps	Toronto	55	26	27	53	12
Ted Lindsay	Detroit	60	33	19	52	95
Roy Conacher	Chicago	52	22	27	49	4
Jim McFadden	Detroit	60	24	24	48	12
Edgar Laprade	NY Rangers	59	13	34	47	7
Ted Kennedy	Toronto	60	25	21	46	32
Gordie Howe	Detroit	60	16	28	44	63
Sid Abel	Detroit	60	14	30	44	69
Harry Watson	Toronto	57	21	20	41	16
Tony Leswick	NY Rangers	60	24	16	40	76
Grant Warwick	NYR/Bos.	58	23	17	40	38
Jim Conacher	Detroit	60	17	23	40	2
George Gee	Chicago	60	14	25	39	18
Woody Dumart	Boston	59	21	16	37	14
Gus Bodnar	Chicago	46	13	22	35	23
Pete Babando	Boston	60	23	11	34	52
Howie Meeker	Toronto	58	14	20	34	62
Vic Lynn	Toronto	60	12	22	34	53

LEADING GOALTENDERS

Goaltender	Club	GPI	MINS	GA	SO	AVG
Turk Broda	Toronto	60	3600	143	5	2.38
Harry Lumley	Detroit	60	3592	147	7	2.46
Bill Durnan	Montreal	59	3505	162	5	2.77
Frank Brimsek	Boston	60	3600	168	3	2.80
Jim Henry	NY Rangers	48	2880	153	2	3.19
Emile Francis	Chicago	54	3240	183	1	3.39

LEADING PLAYOFF SCORERS

Player	Club	GP	G	A	PTS	PIM
Ted Kennedy	Toronto	9	8	6	14	0
Max Bentley	Toronto	9	4	7	11	0
Pete Horeck	Detroit	10	3	7	10	12
Jim McFadden	Detroit	10	5	3	8	10
Syl Apps	Toronto	9	4	4	8	0
Harry Watson	Toronto	9	5	2	7	9
Milt Schmidt	Boston	5	2	5	7	2
Vic Lynn	Toronto	9	2	5	7	20
Howie Meeker	Toronto	9	2	4	6	15
Seven players tied with					5	

LEADING PLAYOFF GOALTENDERS

Goaltender	Club	GPI	MINS	GA	SO	AVG
Turk Broda	Toronto	9	557	20	1	2.15
Chuck Rayner	NY Rangers	6	360	17	0	2.83
Harry Lumley	Detroit	10	600	30	0	3.00
Frank Brimsek	Boston	5	317	20	0	3.79

Maple Leafs legends Teeder Kennedy (left), Turk Broda (center) and Syl Apps (right). Kennedy succeeded Apps as captain when the classy veteran retired after the 1947–48 season. He played on Toronto teams that won the Stanley Cup five times in seven years between 1945 and 1951. Broda was also a five-time champion and a great clutch performer.

The 1947–48 NHL season began with the All-Star Game, an idea which had been proposed the previous season. A collection of NHL greats defeated the defending Stanley Cup champion Toronto Maple Leafs 4–3. Unfortunately, this spirited game was marred by an injury to Chicago Black Hawks star Bill Mosienko, who suffered a fractured ankle. A similar injury later in the season ended the career of Toe Blake, thus breaking up the Canadiens' much-feared Punch Line. It was also the end of an era in Boston, where Bobby Bauer's retirement broke up the Kraut Line. Meanwhile Detroit saw the rise of a new offensive force when Red Wings coach Tommy Ivan teamed second-year forward Gordie Howe on a line with Ted Lindsay and Sid Abel, creating the Production Line.

Taps for Apps – Toronto sent the Boxcar Line to Chicago for a Bentley, Lach led the league, Apps scored his 200th goal, guided the Leafs to a second straight championship then hung up the blades for good.

In Toronto, Conn Smythe was not satisfied with the defending Stanley Cup champions' depth. He wanted a third center to complement Syl Apps and Teeder Kennedy, a need made all the more pressing by Apps's talk of retirement. The Leafs opened the season undefeated in six games, but after a loss to the Rangers on November 2, Smythe orchestrated the biggest trade in NHL history, sending Bud Poile, Bob Goldham, Ernie Dickens, Gaye Stewart and Gus Bodnar to the Chicago Black Hawks for perennial All-Star and slick stickhandler Max Bentley along with rookie Cy Thomas.

With Bentley bolstering their attack, the Leafs soared to a 32–15–13 record and a first-place finish. In the playoffs, Toronto eliminated the Bruins in five games before sweeping the Detroit Red Wings for their second consecutive Stanley Cup championship. The Red Wings had qualified for the final by downing the New York Rangers in six games.

On a dark note, two of the league's finest playmakers, Billy Taylor of the Rangers and Boston's Don Gallinger, were handed lifetime suspensions for gambling.

Leaders, 1947-48

GOALS

Name, Team	G
Ted Lindsay, Det.	33
Elmer Lach, Mtl.	30
Maurice Richard, Mtl.	28
Gaye Stewart, Tor./Chi.	27
Syl Apps, Tor.	26
Max Bentley, Chi./Tor.	26
Bud Poile, Tor./Chi.	25
Ted Kennedy, Tor.	25
Buddy O'Connor, NYR	24
Jim McFadden, Det.	24
Tony Leswick, NYR	24

ASSISTS

Name, Team	A
Doug Bentley, Chi.	37
Buddy O'Connor, NYR	36
Edgar Laprade, NYR	34
Elmer Lach, Mtl.	31
Sid Abel, Det.	30
Bud Poile, Tor./Chi.	29
Jimmy Thomson, Tor.	29
Gaye Stewart, Tor./Chi.	29
Max Bentley, Chi./Tor.	28
Gordie Howe, Det.	28
Roy Conacher, Chi.	27
Syl Apps, Tor.	27

GOALIE WINS

Name, Team	W
Turk Broda, Tor.	32
Harry Lumley, Det.	30
Frank Brimsek, Bos.	23
Bill Durnan, Mtl.	20
Emile Francis, Chi.	18
Jim Henry, NYR	17
Chuck Rayner, NYR	4
Doug Jackson, Chi.	2

SHUTOUTS

Name, Team	SO
Harry Lumley, Det.	7
Bill Durnan, Mtl.	5
Turk Broda, Tor.	5
Frank Brimsek, Bos.	3
Jim Henry, NYR	2
Emile Francis, Chi.	1

PLAYOFF GOALS

Name, Team	G
Ted Kennedy, Tor.	8
Harry Watson, Tor.	5
Jim McFadden, Det.	5
Max Bentley, Tor.	4
Syl Apps, Tor.	4
Johnny Peirson, Bos.	3
Tony Leswick, NYR	3
Bill Ezinicki, Tor.	3
Pete Horeck, Det.	3
Red Kelly, Det.	3
Ted Lindsay, Det.	3

PLAYOFF ASSISTS

Name, Team	A
Max Bentley, Tor.	7
Pete Horeck, Det.	7
Ted Kennedy, Tor.	6
Milt Schmidt, Bos.	5
Vic Lynn, Tor.	5
Paul Ronty, Bos.	4
Edgar Laprade, NYR	4
Buddy O'Connor, NYR	4
Syl Apps, Tor.	4
Howie Meeker, Tor.	4

PLAYOFF GOALIE WINS

Name, Team	W
Turk Broda, Tor.	8
Harry Lumley, Det.	4
Chuck Rayner, NYR	2
Frank Brimsek, Bos.	1

PLAYOFF SHUTOUTS

Name, Team	SO
Turk Broda, Tor.	1

FIRST TEAM ALL-STARS

Name, Team	Position
Elmer Lach, Mtl.	C
Maurice Richard, Mtl.	RW
Ted Lindsay, Det.	LW
Bill Quackenbush, Det.	D
Jack Stewart, Det.	D
Turk Broda, Tor.	G

SECOND TEAM ALL-STARS

Name, Team	Position
Buddy O'Connor, NYR	C
Bud Poile, Chi.	RW
Gaye Stewart, Chi.	LW
Ken Reardon, Mtl.	D
Neil Colville, NYR	D
Frank Brimsek, Bos.	G

1948 Playoffs

SEMI-FINALS

Date		Visitor	Score		Home	Score
Mar.	24	Boston	4	at	Toronto	5 OT
Mar.	27	Boston	3	at	Toronto	5
Mar.	30	Toronto	5	at	Boston	1
Apr.	1	Toronto	2	at	Boston	3
Apr.	3	Boston	2	at	Toronto	3

Toronto won best-of-seven series 4–1

Date		Visitor	Score		Home	Score
Mar.	24	NY Rangers	1	at	Detroit	2
Mar.	26	NY Rangers	2	at	Detroit	5
Mar.	28	Detroit	2	at	NY Rangers	3
Mar.	30	Detroit	1	at	NY Rangers	3
Apr.	1	NY Rangers	1	at	Detroit	3
Apr.	4	Detroit	4	at	NY Rangers	2

Detroit won best-of-seven series 4–2

FINALS

Date		Visitor	Score		Home	Score
Apr.	7	Detroit	3	at	Toronto	5
Apr.	10	Detroit	2	at	Toronto	4
Apr.	11	Toronto	2	at	Detroit	0
Apr.	14	Toronto	7	at	Detroit	2

Toronto won best-of-seven series 4–0

1947-48 – Toronto Maple Leafs – Turk Broda, Jimmy Thomson, Wally Stanowski, Garth Boesch, Bill Barilko, Gus Mortson, Phil Samis, Syl Apps (Captain), Bill Ezinicki, Harry Watson, Ted Kennedy, Howie Meeker, Vic Lynn, Nick Metz, Max Bentley, Joe Klukay, Les Costello, Don Metz, Sid Smith, Conn Smythe (Manager), Hap Day (Coach), Tim Daly (Trainer).

TROPHY WINNERS

Trophy	Awarded For	Winner	Team
Hart	MVP	Buddy O'Connor	NYR
Art Ross	Top Scorer	Elmer Lach	Mtl.
Calder	Top Rookie	Jim McFadden	Det.
Vezina	Fewest Goals Against	Turk Broda	Tor.
Byng	Gentlemanly Conduct	Buddy O'Connor	NYR

NHL NOTEBOOK

TRANSACTIONS

- June 1947 – Buffalo (AHL) traded Jim McFadden to Detroit for Harold Jackson and Les Douglas.
- Aug. 19, 1947 – Montreal Canadiens traded Buddy O'Connor and Frank Eddolls to the New York Rangers for Joe Bell, Hal Laycoe and George Robertson.
- Nov. 3, 1947 – Chicago traded Max Bentley (the NHL's leading scorer the previous two seasons) along with Cy Thomas to Toronto in exchange for Gus Bodnar, Bud Poile, Gaye Stewart, Bob Goldham and Ernie Dickens.
- Dec. 17, 1947 – Boston traded Joe Carveth to Montreal Canadiens for John Quilty and Jimmy Peters

RECORDS

- Nov. 16, 1947 – Don Raleigh set an NHL record with three assists in a span of 1:21 during a 4-2 Rangers win over Montreal in New York.
- Mar. 10, 1948 – Harry Lumley became the first goaltender in Detroit history to win 30 games in one season, backstopping the Red Wings to a 7-2 win against the visiting Chicago Black Hawks.

MILESTONES

- Oct. 13, 1947 – Toronto Maple Leafs faced a group of NHL All-Stars in the first All-Star game featuring the Stanley Cup champions against a group of stars from the rest of the league. The All Stars won 4-3 in a benefit for the players' pension fund.
- Nov. 13, 1947 – For the first time in NHL history, the league initiated the policy of having players raise their sticks to signify the scoring of a goal. Montreal's Billy Reay became the first to do so as the Canadiens beat Chicago 5-2 at the Forum.
- Jan. 21, 1948 – Don Gallinger scored twice to lead the Bruins to a 2-1 win against Toronto in Boston. The Bruins used two photographers to film their game, for coaching purposes.
- Mar. 21, 1948 – Montreal's Elmer Lach scored twice in the final game of the season to win the Art Ross Trophy by one point over the Rangers' Buddy O'Connor. But the 4-3 loss at Boston kept the Canadiens out of the playoffs for the first time since 1940.

1948-49

Stanley Cup • Toronto Maple Leafs

FINAL STANDINGS

Team	GP	W	L	T	GF	GA	PTS
Detroit	60	34	19	7	195	145	75
Boston	60	29	23	8	178	163	66
Montreal	60	28	23	9	152	126	65
Toronto	60	22	25	13	147	161	57
Chicago	60	21	31	8	173	211	50
New York	60	18	31	11	133	172	47

LEADING SCORERS

Player	Club	GP	G	A	PTS	PIM
Roy Conacher	Chicago	60	26	42	68	8
Doug Bentley	Chicago	58	23	43	66	38
Sid Abel	Detroit	60	28	26	54	49
Ted Lindsay	Detroit	50	26	28	54	97
Jim Conacher	Det./Chi.	59	26	23	49	43
Paul Ronty	Boston	60	20	29	49	11
Harry Watson	Toronto	60	26	19	45	0
Billy Reay	Montreal	60	22	23	45	33
Gus Bodnar	Chicago	59	19	26	45	14
Johnny Peirson	Boston	59	22	21	43	45
Bud Poile	Chi./Det.	60	21	21	42	8
Bill Mosienko	Chicago	60	17	25	42	6
Max Bentley	Toronto	60	19	22	41	18
Ken Smith	Boston	59	20	20	40	6
Ted Kennedy	Toronto	59	18	21	39	25
Maurice Richard	Montreal	59	20	18	38	110
Gaye Stewart	Chicago	54	20	18	38	57
Grant Warwick	Boston	58	22	15	37	14
Joe Carveth	Montreal	60	15	22	37	8
Gordie Howe	Detroit	40	12	25	37	57
Ed Sandford	Boston	56	16	20	36	57
Cal Gardner	Toronto	53	13	22	35	35
Buddy O'Connor	NY Rangers	46	11	24	35	0
Pete Babando	Boston	58	19	14	33	34
Jim McFadden	Detroit	55	12	20	32	10
Milt Schmidt	Boston	44	10	22	32	25

LEADING GOALTENDERS

Goaltender	Club	GPI	MINS	GA	SO	AVG
Bill Durnan	Montreal	60	3600	126	10	2.10
Harry Lumley	Detroit	60	3600	145	6	2.42
Turk Broda	Toronto	60	3600	161	5	2.68
Frank Brimsek	Boston	54	3240	147	1	2.72
Chuck Rayner	NY Rangers	58	3480	168	7	2.90
Jim Henry	Chicago	60	3600	211	0	3.52

LEADING PLAYOFF SCORERS

Player	Club	GP	G	A	PTS	PIM
Gordie Howe	Detroit	11	8	3	11	19
Ted Lindsay	Detroit	11	2	6	8	31
Ted Kennedy	Toronto	9	2	6	8	2
Sid Smith	Toronto	6	5	2	7	0
Max Bentley	Toronto	9	4	3	7	2
Cal Gardner	Toronto	9	2	5	7	0
Gerry Plamondon	Montreal	7	5	1	6	0
Harry Watson	Toronto	9	4	2	6	2
Ray Timgren	Toronto	9	3	3	6	2
Sid Abel	Detroit	11	3	3	6	6
Fleming MacKell	Toronto	9	2	4	6	4
Billy Reay	Montreal	7	1	5	6	4
Jimmy Thomson	Toronto	9	1	5	6	10

LEADING PLAYOFF GOALTENDERS

Goaltender	Club	GPI	MINS	GA	SO	AVG
Turk Broda	Toronto	9	574	15	1	1.57
Harry Lumley	Detroit	11	726	26	0	2.15
Bill Durnan	Montreal	7	468	17	0	2.18
Frank Brimsek	Boston	5	316	16	0	3.04

Montreal's Bill Durnan played only seven years in the NHL, but won the Vezina Trophy and was selected as the goaltender on the First All-Star Team six times. Durnan was ambidextrous, able to use his stick or catch the puck equally well with either hand, but the pressure of the game's most difficult position forced his retirement in 1950.

THE 1948–49 SEASON OPENED on a sour note for the New York Rangers. The team was enjoying a productive training camp when Bill Moe, Edgar Laprade, Buddy O'Connor, Frank Eddolls and Tony Leswick were all injured in a car accident. Three of the five sustained only minor injuries, but O'Connor and Eddolls would be lost for at least two months. The Rangers opened the season 6–11–6, costing Frank Boucher his coaching job. Lynn Patrick took over behind the bench, but the Rangers still wound up missing the playoffs by 10 points.

Triple Play – Four Black Hawks made the top ten but their club missed the playoffs. Abel, Lindsay and Howe produced in Motown and despite limping into the playoffs, the Leafs romped past their rivals for their third straight title.

Joining New York on the sidelines come postseason were the Chicago Black Hawks, who finished fifth in the six-team league despite the fact that teammates Roy Conacher and Doug Bentley were a comfortable 1–2 atop the NHL scoring leaders.

For much of the season, it appeared the two-time Cup-champion Maple Leafs would miss postseason play. Hurt by the retirements of Nick Metz and Syl Apps, and besieged by injuries all season, only a late-season collapse by the Rangers and Hawks got the Leafs into the playoffs.

The brilliant goaltending of Bill Durnan, who had recorded 10 shutouts during the regular season—including a modern-day record four in a row at one stretch—carried the Montreal Canadiens to a third-place finish.

The Maple Leafs and Canadiens shared a dubious NHL record in November as 10 major penalties were called in a fight-filled tgame.

The Detroit Red Wings easily topped the Boston Bruins to wind up first in the regular-season standings.

In the playoffs, the Leafs came to life. Healthy for the first time all season, Toronto downed Boston in five games, then swept Detroit for the second straight year to win their third consecutive Stanley Cup title. They were the first fourth-place regular-season finisher to win the trophy and the only team to do so in the six-team era.

Leaders, 1948-49

GOALS

Name, Team	G
Sid Abel, Det.	28
Ted Lindsay, Det.	26
Jim Conacher, Det./Chi.	26
Roy Conacher, Chi.	26
Harry Watson, Tor.	26
Doug Bentley, Chi.	23
Grant Warwick, Bos.	22
Johnny Peirson, Bos.	22
Billy Reay, Mtl.	22
Bud Poile, Chi./Det.	21

ASSISTS

Name, Team	A
Bentley, Chi.	43
Roy Conacher, Chi.	42
Paul Ronty, Bos.	29
Ted Lindsay, Det.	28
Gus Bodnar, Chi.	26
Sid Abel, Det.	26
Gordie Howe, Det.	25
Bill Mosienko, Chi.	25
Buddy O'Connor, NYR	24
Jim Conacher, Det./Chi.	23
Billy Reay, Mtl.	23

GOALIE WINS

Name, Team	W
Harry Lumley, Det.	34
Bill Durnan, Mtl.	28
Frank Brimsek, Bos.	26
Turk Broda, Tor.	22
Jim Henry, Chi.	21
Chuck Rayner, NYR	16
Emile Francis, NYR	2
Jack Gelineau, Bos.	2
Gord Henry, Bos.	1

SHUTOUTS

Name, Team	SO
Bill Durnan, Mtl.	10
Chuck Rayner, NYR	7
Harry Lumley, Det.	6
Turk Broda, Tor.	5
Gord Henry, Bos.	1
Frank Brimsek, Bos.	1

PLAYOFF GOALS

Name, Team	G
Gordie Howe, Det.	8
Sid Smith, Tor.	5
Gerry Plamondon, Mtl.	5
Max Bentley, Tor.	4
Harry Watson, Tor.	4
Johnny Peirson, Bos.	3
Woody Dumart, Bos.	3
Ray Timgren, Tor.	3
Sid Abel, Det.	3
10 tied with	2

PLAYOFF ASSISTS

Name, Team	A
Ted Kennedy, Tor.	6
Ted Lindsay, Det.	6
Billy Reay, Mtl.	5
Cal Gardner, Tor.	5
Jimmy Thomson, Tor.	5
Fleming MacKell, Tor.	4
Bill Ezinicki, Tor.	4
Seven tied with	3

PLAYOFF GOALIE WINS

Name, Team	W
Turk Broda, Tor.	8
Harry Lumley, Det.	4
Bill Durnan, Mtl.	3
Frank Brimsek, Bos.	1

PLAYOFF SHUTOUTS

Name, Team	SO
Turk Broda, Tor.	1

FIRST TEAM ALL-STARS

Name, Team	Position
Sid Abel, Det.	C
Maurice Richard, Mtl.	RW
Roy Conacher, Chi.	LW
Bill Quackenbush, Det.	D
Jack Stewart, Det.	D
Bill Durnan, Mtl.	G

SECOND TEAM ALL-STARS

Name, Team	Position
Doug Bentley, Chi.	C
Gordie Howe, Det.	RW
Ted Lindsay, Det.	LW
Glen Harmon, Mtl.	D
Ken Reardon, Mtl.	D
Chuck Rayner, NYR	G

1949 Playoffs

SEMI-FINALS

Date	Team	Score		Team	Score
Mar. 22	Montreal	1	at	Detroit	2 3OT
Mar. 24	Montreal	4	at	Detroit	3 OT
Mar. 26	Detroit	2	at	Montreal	3
Mar. 29	Detroit	3	at	Montreal	1
Mar. 31	Montreal	1	at	Detroit	3
Apr. 2	Detroit	1	at	Montreal	3
Apr. 5	Montreal	1	at	Detroit	3

Detroit won best-of-seven series 4–3

Date	Team	Score		Team	Score
Mar. 22	Toronto	3	at	Boston	0
Mar. 24	Toronto	3	at	Boston	2
Mar. 26	Boston	5	at	Toronto	4 OT
Mar. 29	Boston	1	at	Toronto	3
Mar. 30	Toronto	3	at	Boston	2

Toronto won best-of-seven series 4–1

FINALS

Date	Team	Score		Team	Score
Apr. 8	Toronto	3	at	Detroit	2 OT
Apr. 10	Toronto	3	at	Detroit	1
Apr. 13	Detroit	1	at	Toronto	3
Apr. 16	Detroit	1	at	Toronto	3

Toronto won best-of-seven series 4–0

1948-49 – Toronto Maple Leafs – Turk Broda, Jimmy Thomson, Gus Mortson, Bill Barilko, Garth Boesch, Bill Juzda, Ted Kennedy (Captain), Howie Meeker, Vic Lynn, Harry Watson, Bill Ezinicki, Cal Gardner, Max Bentley, Joe Klukay, Sid Smith, Don Metz, Ray Timgren, Fleming MacKell, Harry Taylor, Bob Dawes, Tod Sloan, Conn Smythe (Manager), Hap Day (Coach), Tim Daly (Trainer).

TROPHY WINNERS

Trophy	Awarded For	Winner	Team
Hart	MVP	Sid Abel	Det.
Art Ross	Top Scorer	Roy Conacher	Chi.
Calder	Top Rookie	Pentti Lund	NYR
Vezina	Fewest Goals Against	Bill Durnan	Mtl.
Byng	Gentlemanly Conduct	Bill Quackenbush	Det.

NHL NOTEBOOK

TRANSACTIONS

- Apr. 26, 1948 – Toronto Maple Leafs obtained Cal Gardner, Bill Juzda, Rene Trudell and Frank Mathers from the New York Rangers for Wally Stanowski and Elwyn "Moe" Morris.
- Oct. 7, 1948 – Chicago traded Jim Henry to New York Rangers for Emile Francis and Alex Kaleta.
- Oct. 25 1948 – Detroit traded Bep Guidolin, Jim Conacher and Doug McCaig to Chicago for Bud Poile and George Gee.
- Dec. 9, 1948 – New York Rangers obtained defenseman Allan Stanley from Providence of the AHL for Ed Kullman, Elwyn Morris, cash and future considerations.

RECORDS

- Nov. 25, 1948 – Goaltender Turk Broda recorded his 43rd career shutout, and Bill Ezinicki scored a goal and added an assist as the Toronto Maple Leafs won 2-0 at Montreal. 10 major penalties were assessed in the game, a new NHL record.
- Apr. 10, 1949 – Toronto's Sid Smith tied a playoff record with three powerplay goals in a 3-1 win over Detroit in game two of the Stanley Cup finals.

MILESTONES

- Oct. 27, 1948 – Detroit's Harry Lumley became the first goaltender in franchise history to record 100 victories as a member of the Red Wings. The milestone came in a 3-2 win over the Rangers at New York.
- Feb. 3, 1949 – Toronto's Turk Broda became the first goaltender in Maple Leafs history to record 250 career victories. The milestone came in a 4-1 win over the Canadiens at Montreal.
- Apr. 16, 1949 – Toronto Maple Leafs became the first NHL team to win three straight Stanley Cups, with a 5-1 win over Detroit in game four of the Stanley Cup finals. The win was also the Leafs' ninth straight in the finals.

1949-50

Stanley Cup • Detroit Red Wings

FINAL STANDINGS

Team	GP	W	L	T	GF	GA	PTS
Detroit	70	37	19	14	229	164	88
Montreal	70	29	22	19	172	150	77
Toronto	70	31	27	12	176	173	74
New York	70	28	31	11	170	189	67
Boston	70	22	32	16	198	228	60
Chicago	70	22	38	10	203	244	54

LEADING SCORERS

Player	Club	GP	G	A	PTS	PIM
Ted Lindsay	Detroit	69	23	55	78	141
Sid Abel	Detroit	69	34	35	69	46
Gordie Howe	Detroit	70	35	33	68	69
Maurice Richard	Montreal	70	43	22	65	114
Paul Ronty	Boston	70	23	36	59	8
Roy Conacher	Chicago	70	25	31	56	16
Doug Bentley	Chicago	64	20	33	53	28
Johnny Peirson	Boston	57	27	25	52	49
Metro Prystai	Chicago	65	29	22	51	31
Bep Guidolin	Chicago	70	17	34	51	42
Bert Olmstead	Chicago	70	20	29	49	40
Elmer Lach	Montreal	64	15	33	48	33
Bill Mosienko	Chicago	69	18	28	46	10
Phil Maloney	Boston	70	15	31	46	6
Sid Smith	Toronto	68	22	23	45	6
Billy Reay	Montreal	68	19	26	45	48
Edgar Laprade	NY Rangers	60	22	22	44	2
Ted Kennedy	Toronto	53	20	24	44	34
Tony Leswick	NY Rangers	69	19	25	44	85
Gaye Stewart	Chicago	70	24	19	43	43
Max Bentley	Toronto	69	23	18	41	14
Milt Schmidt	Boston	68	19	22	41	41
Ken Smith	Boston	66	10	31	41	12
Howie Meeker	Toronto	70	18	22	40	35
Red Kelly	Detroit	70	15	25	40	9

LEADING GOALTENDERS

Goaltender	Club	GPI	MINS	GA	SO	AVG
Bill Durnan	Montreal	64	3840	141	8	2.20
Harry Lumley	Detroit	63	3780	148	7	2.35
Turk Broda	Toronto	68	4040	167	9	2.48
Chuck Rayner	NY Rangers	69	4140	181	6	2.62
Jack Gelineau	Boston	67	4020	220	3	3.28
Frank Brimsek	Chicago	70	4200	244	5	3.49

LEADING PLAYOFF SCORERS

Player	Club	GP	G	A	PTS	PIM
Pentti Lund	NY Rangers	12	6	5	11	0
Gerry Couture	Detroit	14	5	4	9	2
Don Raleigh	NY Rangers	12	4	5	9	4
George Gee	Detroit	14	3	6	9	0
Sid Abel	Detroit	14	6	2	8	6
Ted Lindsay	Detroit	13	4	4	8	16
Edgar Laprade	NY Rangers	12	3	5	8	4
Ed Slowinski	NY Rangers	12	2	6	8	6
Allan Stanley	NY Rangers	12	2	5	7	10
Seven players tied with					6	

LEADING PLAYOFF GOALTENDERS

Goaltender	Club	GPI	MINS	GA	SO	AVG
Turk Broda	Toronto	7	450	10	3	1.33
Harry Lumley	Detroit	14	910	28	3	1.85
Chuck Rayner	NY Rangers	12	775	29	1	2.25

Chuck Rayner was a goalie ahead of his time. He enjoyed leaving his crease to handle the puck and twice during the 1946–47 NHL season he fired shots at the opposing goal. In a game against the Maple Leafs on February 19, 1950, Rayner rushed from his net after Toronto had pulled Turk Broda and fired a shot that just missed the empty cage.

THE EXPANDED SCHEDULE (now 70 games) brought out the best in the first-place Red Wings, who finished with the top three scorers in the league. Remarkably, it seemed to inspire the best and the worst in Chicago, who finished last despite having more top-10 scorers (four) than anyone else. The Rangers had hardly any scoring, but their goalie Chuck Rayner had a big Hart by the end of the season, as his play carried the team to the playoffs and beyond.

Rayner's Rangers – Detroit's Production Line dominated the point-parade, Chicago again had four top-10 scorers but missed the dance and Chuck Rayner was prince of the playoffs, though it was the Wings who soared.

Along with these great accomplishments came some strange events. Three Canadiens were charged with assault and then cleared after fighting with Hawks fans. Chicago coach Charlie Conacher even hit a reporter (perhaps he should have been more forceful with his team's woeful defense). In Toronto, the weighty matter on the sports pages was the expanding physiques of four players, including goalie Turk Broda. Conn Smythe told them all to get thinner, and he sat out Broda for a few games. The Turk lost ten pounds and gained his job back from Al Rollins, who, of course, had never really won it to begin with.

The unluckiest player of the year was Bill Quackenbush, who was hardly rewarded for a penalty-free and Lady Byng Trophy-winning season in 1948–49. Despite his all-star form, he may have been too mild for Jack Adams who sent him to Boston, where he missed the playoffs.

In the playoffs, the Red Wings almost lost their Cup dreams when Gordie Howe was seriously injured. He collided with Toronto's Ted Kennedy, breaking his nose and cheekbone and receiving a severe concussion. Doctors stabilized him and the team regained its balance too, beating Toronto in a low-scoring semi-final series. The Rangers upset Montreal but were forced to play the entire championship round on the road because the circus was firmly planted in Madison Square Garden.

Despite the matchup of the best and the worst offenses in the league, Detroit had trouble with New York. The Rangers kept the games close, stealing the fourth and fifth on overtime goals by Don Raleigh. Rayner was on the verge of achieving a nearly perfect season when the teams went to overtime in game seven. However, Pete Babando, traded for Bill Quackenbush the previous off-season, scored the Cup-winning goal for the Red Wings in double overtime.

Leaders, 1949-50

GOALS

Name, Team	G
Maurice Richard, Mtl.	43
Gordie Howe, Det.	35
Sid Abel, Det.	34
Metro Prystai, Chi.	29
Johnny Peirson, Bos.	27
Roy Conacher, Chi.	25
Gerry Couture, Det.	24
Gaye Stewart, Chi.	24
Ted Lindsay, Det.	23
Max Bentley, Tor.	23
Paul Ronty, Bos.	23

ASSISTS

Name, Team	A
Ted Lindsay, Det.	55
Paul Ronty, Bos.	36
Sid Abel, Det.	35
Bep Guidolin, Chi.	34
Doug Bentley, Chi.	33
Elmer Lach, Mtl.	33
Gordie Howe, Det.	33
Ken Smith, Bos.	31
Roy Conacher, Chi.	31
Phil Maloney, Bos.	31

GOALIE WINS

Name, Team	W
Harry Lumley, Det.	33
Turk Broda, Tor.	30
Chuck Rayner, NYR	28
Bill Durnan, Mtl.	26
Jack Gelineau, Bos.	22
Frank Brimsek, Chi.	22
Terry Sawchuk, Det.	4
Gerry McNeil, Mtl.	3
Al Rollins, Tor.	1

SHUTOUTS

Name, Team	SO
Turk Broda, Tor.	9
Bill Durnan, Mtl.	8
Harry Lumley, Det.	7
Chuck Rayner, NYR	6
Frank Brimsek, Chi.	5
Jack Gelineau, Bos.	3
Al Rollins, Tor.	1
Gerry McNeil, Mtl.	1
Terry Sawchuk, Det.	1

PLAYOFF GOALS

Name, Team	G
Pentti Lund, NYR	6
Sid Abel, Det.	6
Gerry Couture, Det.	5
Don Raleigh, NYR	4
Buddy O'Connor, NYR	4
Ted Lindsay, Det.	4
Marty Pavelich, Det.	4
Seven tied with	3

PLAYOFF ASSISTS

Name, Team	A
Ed Slowinski, NYR	6
George Gee, Det.	6
Pentti Lund, NYR	5
Don Raleigh, NYR	5
Edgar Laprade, NYR	5
Allan Stanley, NYR	5
Nick Mickoski, NYR	5
Ray Timgren, Tor.	4
Tony Leswick, NYR	4
Ted Lindsay, Det.	4
Gerry Couture, Det.	4
Joe Carveth, Det.	4
Jack Stewart, Det.	4

PLAYOFF GOALIE WINS

Name, Team	W
Harry Lumley, Det.	8
Chuck Rayner, NYR	7
Turk Broda, Tor.	3
Gerry McNeil, Mtl.	1

PLAYOFF SHUTOUTS

Name, Team	SO
Turk Broda, Tor.	3
Harry Lumley, Det.	3
Chuck Rayner, NYR	1

FIRST TEAM ALL-STARS

Name, Team	Position
Sid Abel, Det.	C
Maurice Richard, Mtl.	RW
Ted Lindsay, Det.	LW
Gus Mortson, Tor.	D
Ken Reardon, Mtl.	D
Bill Durnan, Mtl.	G

SECOND TEAM ALL-STARS

Name, Team	Position
Ted Kennedy, Tor.	C
Gordie Howe, Det.	RW
Tony Leswick, NYR	LW
Leo Reise, Det.	D
Red Kelly, Det.	D
Chuck Rayner, NYR	G

1950 Playoffs

SEMI-FINALS

Date	Team	Score		Team	Score
Mar. 28	Toronto	5	at	Detroit	0
Mar. 30	Toronto	1	at	Detroit	3
Apr. 1	Detroit	0	at	Toronto	2
Apr. 4	Detroit	2	at	Toronto	1 2OT
Apr. 6	Toronto	2	at	Detroit	0
Apr. 8	Detroit	4	at	Toronto	0
Apr. 9	Toronto	0	at	Detroit	1 OT

Detroit won best-of-seven series 4–3

Date	Team	Score		Team	Score
Mar. 29	Montreal	1	at	NY Rangers	3
Apr. 1	NY Rangers	3	at	Montreal	2
Apr. 2	Montreal	1	at	NY Rangers	4
Apr. 4	NY Rangers	2	at	Montreal	3 OT
Apr. 6	NY Rangers	3	at	Montreal	0

NY Rangers won best-of-seven series 4–1

FINALS

Date	Team	Score		Team	Score
Apr. 11	NY Rangers	1	at	Detroit	4
Apr. 13	Detroit	1	vs.	NY Rangers	3 *
Apr. 15	Detroit	4	vs.	NY Rangers	0 *
Apr. 18	NY Rangers	4	at	Detroit	3 OT
Apr. 20	NY Rangers	2	at	Detroit	1 OT
Apr. 22	NY Rangers	4	at	Detroit	5
Apr. 23	NY Rangers	3	at	Detroit	4 2OT

* played in Toronto

Detroit won best-of-seven series 4–3

1949-50 – Detroit Red Wings – Harry Lumley, Jack Stewart, Leo Reise, Jr., Clare Martin, Al Dewsbury, Lee Fogolin, Marcel Pronovost, Red Kelly, Ted Lindsay, Sid Abel (Captain), Gordie Howe, George Gee, Jimmy Peters, Marty Pavelich, Jim McFadden, Pete Babando, Max McNab, Gerry Couture, Joe Carveth, Steve Black, Johnny Wilson, Larry Wilson, Doug McKay, Jack Adams (Manager), Tommy Ivan (Coach), Carl Mattson (Trainer).

TROPHY WINNERS

Trophy	Awarded For	Winner	Team
Hart	MVP	Chuck Rayner	NYR
Art Ross	Top Scorer	Ted Lindsay	Det.
Calder	Top Rookie	Jack Gelineau	Bos.
Vezina	Fewest Goals Against	Bill Durnan	Mtl.
Byng	Gentlemanly Conduct	Edgar Laprade	NYR

NHL NOTEBOOK

TRANSACTIONS

- Aug. 16, 1949 – Boston traded Pete Babando along with Clare Martin, Lloyd Durham and Jim Peters to Detroit for Bill Quackenbush and Pete Horeck.
- Oct. 7, 1949 – New York Rangers traded Billy Moe and the rights to Lorne Ferguson to Boston for Pat Egan.
- Nov. 29, 1949 – Toronto purchased Al Rollins from Cleveland (AHL) in exchange for Bob Dawes, future considerations and $40,000.

RECORDS

- Jan. 21, 1950 – Bill Durnan became the first goaltender in Montreal Canadiens franchise history to record 200 victories. The milestone came in a 3-1 win at Boston.
- Feb. 5, 1950 – Dick Irvin became the first coach in NHL history to win 500 games, when the Canadiens beat the Bruins 5-3 at the Forum in Montreal.
- Mar. 26, 1950 – Detroit's Ted Lindsay set an NHL record for most assists in a season, when he picked up his 55th of the year in a 5-4 loss to the visiting Chicago Black Hawks. Lindsay broke the record of Elmer Lach, who had 54 assists in 1944-45.
- Mar. 26, 1950 – Maurice Richard scored his 250th career NHL goal as the Canadiens tied 3-3 at Boston. It was the Montreal's 19th tie of the season, a new NHL record.

MILESTONES

- Jan. 8, 1950 – Terry Sawchuk made his NHL debut (replacing an injured Harry Lumley) in a 4-3 Red Wings loss to Boston at the Olympia in Detroit.
- Feb. 23, 1950 – Doug Bentley became the first player to score 200 goals as a member of the Black Hawks. The milestone came in a 7-3 loss to the visiting New York Rangers.
- Apr. 20, 1950 – New York's Don Raleigh became the first player in NHL history to score two straight OT goals in the finals, when he connected at 1:38 of overtime as the Rangers beat Detroit 2-1 in game five.
- Apr. 23, 1950 – In the first game seven overtime of the Stanley Cup finals, Pete Babando scored at 28:31 of OT to give Detroit a 4-3 win over the Rangers – and the 1950 Stanley Cup championship.

1950-51

Stanley Cup • Toronto Maple Leafs

FINAL STANDINGS

Team	GP	W	L	T	GF	GA	PTS
Detroit	70	44	13	13	236	139	101
Toronto	70	41	16	13	212	138	95
Montreal	70	25	30	15	173	184	65
Boston	70	22	30	18	178	197	62
New York	70	20	29	21	169	201	61
Chicago	70	13	47	10	171	280	36

LEADING SCORERS

Player	Club	GP	G	A	PTS	PIM
Gordie Howe	Detroit	70	43	43	86	74
Maurice Richard	Montreal	65	42	24	66	97
Max Bentley	Toronto	67	21	41	62	34
Sid Abel	Detroit	69	23	38	61	30
Milt Schmidt	Boston	62	22	39	61	33
Ted Kennedy	Toronto	63	18	43	61	32
Ted Lindsay	Detroit	67	24	35	59	110
Tod Sloan	Toronto	70	31	25	56	105
Red Kelly	Detroit	70	17	37	54	24
Sid Smith	Toronto	70	30	21	51	10
Cal Gardner	Toronto	66	23	28	51	42
Roy Conacher	Chicago	70	26	24	50	16
Elmer Lach	Montreal	65	21	24	45	48
Woody Dumart	Boston	70	20	21	41	7
Bert Olmstead	Chi./Mtl.	54	18	23	41	50
Reg Sinclair	NY Rangers	70	18	21	39	70
Don Raleigh	NY Rangers	64	15	24	39	18
Johnny Peirson	Boston	70	19	19	38	43
Jimmy Peters	Detroit	68	17	21	38	14
Metro Prystai	Detroit	62	20	17	37	27
Pete Babando	Chicago	70	18	19	37	36
Harry Watson	Toronto	68	18	19	37	18
George Gee	Detroit	70	17	20	37	19
Jim Conacher	Chicago	52	10	27	37	16
Bill Mosienko	Chicago	65	21	15	36	18
Buddy O'Connor	NY Rangers	66	16	20	36	0
Jimmy Thomson	Toronto	69	3	33	36	76

LEADING GOALTENDERS

Goaltender	Club	GPI	MINS	GA	SO	AVG
Al Rollins	Toronto	40	2373	70	5	1.77
Terry Sawchuk	Detroit	70	4200	139	11	1.99
Turk Broda	Toronto	31	1827	68	6	2.23
Gerry McNeil	Montreal	70	4200	184	6	2.63
Jack Gelineau	Boston	70	4200	197	4	2.81
Chuck Rayner	NY Rangers	66	3940	187	2	2.85
Harry Lumley	Chicago	64	3785	246	3	3.90

LEADING PLAYOFF SCORERS

Player	Club	GP	G	A	PTS	PIM
Maurice Richard	Montreal	11	9	4	13	13
Max Bentley	Toronto	11	2	11	13	4
Sid Smith	Toronto	11	7	3	10	0
Ted Kennedy	Toronto	11	4	5	9	6
Tod Sloan	Toronto	11	4	5	9	18
Sid Abel	Detroit	6	4	3	7	0
Gordie Howe	Detroit	6	4	3	7	4
Joe Klukay	Toronto	11	4	3	7	0
Billy Reay	Montreal	11	3	3	6	10
Bert Olmstead	Montreal	11	2	4	6	9

LEADING PLAYOFF GOALTENDERS

Goaltender	Club	GPI	MINS	GA	SO	AVG
Turk Broda	Toronto	8	492	9	2	1.10
Jack Gelineau	Boston	4	260	7	1	1.62
Terry Sawchuk	Detroit	6	463	13	1	1.68
Al Rollins	Toronto	4	210	6	0	1.71
Gerry McNeil	Montreal	11	785	25	1	1.91

Carried away on the shoulders of teammates, Bill Barilko was thought to be on the verge of stardom at the time of his death in a plane crash following Toronto's 1951 victory. A sturdy defenseman and solid checker, Barilko had joined the Maple Leafs late in the 1946–47 season and helped the team win the Stanley Cup four times in five years.

ONCE AGAIN, the Red Wings were the story of the regular season. Gordie Howe rebounded from his head injuries to dominate the scoring race, while the team leaped past the 100-point barrier, setting a new NHL standard. The Wings did this after a huge trade that sent overtime hero Pete Babando, goalie Harry Lumley and three others to Chicago for four players. Detroit's Jack Adams felt that despite his youth, Terry Sawchuk was ready to be a starting goalie. Adams proved to be correct.

Bashin' Billy – Detroit topped the 100-point plateau, Howe won the scoring crown, but the Leafs and Habs made the finals. Each game went into overtime before Bill Barilko's final NHL goal won laurels for the Leafs.

Sawchuk played in all of Detroit's 70 games and recorded each of their 44 victories. He took the Calder Trophy easily. Al Rollins edged him for the Vezina, even though he split time with Turk Broda in Toronto. Sawchuk was so good that his team still gave him the $1000 bonus he would have received for winning the Vezina. Broda's consolation prize was the biggest milestone of the season, his 300th win in December.

The Rangers could not sustain their play of the previous year, forcing coach Neil Colville to try hypnotism on his unfocused players. It didn't help, and neither did Charlie Conacher's resignation from a very poor flock of Hawks. The only challenge to Detroit came from a deep Toronto team led by clever Max Bentley. Montreal was mediocre, yet Maurice Richard made them dangerous. The Wings found out the hard way when they lost to the Canadiens in the semi-finals. Richard scored in quadruple overtime in game one and triple overtime in game two, and the Wings never recovered.

The Leafs easily beat Boston to make the finals, where the closest five-game series in history was fought. Sid Smith won the first game for the Leafs in the sixth minute of overtime, and then Richard notched another overtime winner to even the series. Toronto won the next two in overtime, but the Canadiens refused to give up. In the final game, Tod Sloan tied it in the waning seconds as the Leafs pulled their goalie. The unlikely hero was Bill Barilko, a defenseman who won the Cup with his goal 2:53 into extra time. He never played again: he was lost in a plane crash in the wilderness of Ontario that summer.

Leaders, 1950-51

GOALS

Name, Team	G
Gordie Howe, Det.	43
Maurice Richard, Mtl.	42
Tod Sloan, Tor.	31
Sid Smith, Tor.	30
Roy Conacher, Chi.	26
Ted Lindsay, Det.	24
Cal Gardner, Tor.	23
Sid Abel, Det.	23
Milt Schmidt, Bos.	22
Elmer Lach, Mtl.	21
Bill Mosienko, Chi.	21
Max Bentley, Tor.	21

ASSISTS

Name, Team	A
Ted Kennedy, Tor.	43
Gordie Howe, Det.	43
Max Bentley, Tor.	41
Milt Schmidt, Bos.	39
Sid Abel, Det.	38
Red Kelly, Det.	37
Ted Lindsay, Det.	35
Jimmy Thomson, Tor.	33
Cal Gardner, Tor.	28
Jim Conacher, Chi.	27

GOALIE WINS

Name, Team	W
Terry Sawchuk, Det.	44
Al Rollins, Tor.	27
Gerry McNeil, Mtl.	25
Jack Gelineau, Bos.	22
Chuck Rayner, NYR	19
Turk Broda, Tor.	14
Harry Lumley, Chi.	12
Emile Francis, NYR	1
Marcel Pelletier, Chi.	1

SHUTOUTS

Name, Team	SO
Terry Sawchuk, Det.	11
Turk Broda, Tor.	6
Gerry McNeil, Mtl.	6
Al Rollins, Tor.	5
Jack Gelineau, Bos.	4
Harry Lumley, Chi.	3
Chuck Rayner, NYR	2

PLAYOFF GOALS

Name, Team	G
Maurice Richard, Mtl.	9
Sid Smith, Tor.	7
Sid Abel, Det.	4
Gordie Howe, Det.	4
Ted Kennedy, Tor.	4
Tod Sloan, Tor.	4
Joe Klukay, Tor.	4
Billy Reay, Mtl.	3
Bill Barilko, Tor.	3
Six tied with	2

PLAYOFF ASSISTS

Name, Team	A
Max Bentley, Tor.	11
Ted Kennedy, Tor.	5
Tod Sloan, Tor.	5
Doug Harvey, Mtl.	5
Maurice Richard, Mtl.	4
Bert Olmstead, Mtl.	4
Eight tied with	3

PLAYOFF GOALIE WINS

Name, Team	W
Turk Broda, Tor.	5
Gerry McNeil, Mtl.	5
Al Rollins, Tor.	3
Terry Sawchuk, Det.	2
Jack Gelineau, Bos.	1

PLAYOFF SHUTOUTS

Name, Team	SO
Turk Broda, Tor.	2
Jack Gelineau, Bos.	1
Terry Sawchuk, Det.	1
Gerry McNeil, Mtl.	1

FIRST TEAM ALL-STARS

Name, Team	Position
Milt Schmidt, Bos.	C
Gordie Howe, Det.	RW
Ted Lindsay, Det.	LW
Red Kelly, Det.	D
Bill Quackenbush, Bos.	D
Terry Sawchuk, Det.	G

SECOND TEAM ALL-STARS

Name, Team	Position
Ted Kennedy, Tor (tie)	C
Sid Abel, Det (tie)	C
Maurice Richard, Mtl.	RW
Sid Smith, Tor.	LW
Jim Thomson, Tor.	D
Leo Reise, Det.	D
Chuck Rayner, NYR	G

1951 Playoffs

SEMI-FINALS

Mar.	27	Montreal	3	at	Detroit	2 4OT
Mar.	29	Montreal	1	at	Detroit	0 3OT
Mar.	31	Detroit	2	at	Montreal	0
Apr.	3	Detroit	4	at	Montreal	1
Apr.	5	Montreal	5	at	Detroit	2
Apr.	7	Detroit	2	at	Montreal	3

Montreal won best-of-seven series 4–2

Mar.	28	Boston	2	at	Toronto	0
Mar.	31	Boston	1	at	Toronto	1 OT*
Apr.	1	Toronto	3	at	Boston	0
Apr.	3	Toronto	3	at	Boston	1
Apr.	7	Boston	1	at	Toronto	4
Apr.	8	Toronto	6	at	Boston	0

* game called after one overtime period due to curfew.

Toronto won best-of-seven series 4–1

FINALS

Apr.	11	Montreal	2	at	Toronto	3 OT
Apr.	14	Montreal	3	at	Toronto	2 OT
Apr.	17	Toronto	2	at	Montreal	1 OT
Apr.	19	Toronto	3	at	Montreal	2 OT
Apr.	21	Montreal	2	at	Toronto	3 OT

Toronto won best-of-seven series 4–1

1950-51 – Toronto Maple Leafs – Turk Broda, Al Rollins, Jimmy Thomson, Gus Mortson, Bill Barilko, Bill Juzda, Fern Flaman, Hugh Bolton, Ted Kennedy (Captain), Sid Smith, Tod Sloan, Cal Gardner, Howie Meeker, Harry Watson, Max Bentley, Joe Klukay, Danny Lewicki, Ray Timgren, Fleming MacKell, John McCormack, Bob Hassard, Conn Smythe (Manager), Joe Primeau (Coach), Tim Daly (Trainer).

TROPHY WINNERS

Trophy	Awarded For	Winner	Team
Hart	MVP	Milt Schmidt	Bos.
Art Ross	Top Scorer	Gordie Howe	Det.
Calder	Top Rookie	Terry Sawchuk	Det.
Vezina	Fewest Goals Against	Al Rollins	Tor.
Byng	Gentlemanly Conduct	Red Kelly	Det.

NHL NOTEBOOK

TRANSACTIONS

- July 13, 1950 – Detroit traded Pete Babando, Harry Lumley, Jack Stewart, Al Dewsbury and Don Morrison to Chicago for Jim Henry, Bob Goldham, Gaye Stewart, and Metro Prystai.
- Nov. 16, 1950 – Boston traded Leo Boivin along with Fern Flaman, Ken Smith and Phil Maloney to Toronto for Bill Ezinicki and Vic Lynn.
- Dec. 19, 1950 – Detroit traded Bert Olmstead to Montreal Canadiens for Leo Gravelle.
- Feb. 14, 1951 – Montreal Canadiens traded Hal Laycoe to Boston for Ross Lowe.

RECORDS

- Mar. 7, 1951 – Gordie Howe scored twice during the Red Wings' 3-0 win at Toronto, to give him 75 points for the season - breaking the NHL record for points by a right winger, set by Toronto's Lorne Carr in 1943-44.
- Mar. 11, 1951 – Rookie Terry Sawchuk set an NHL record for most goalie wins in a season with his 39th of the year in a 7-0 Red Wings victory at Chicago. Sawchuk finished the season with 44 victories.
- Mar. 15, 1951 – Detroit Red Wings became the first NHL team to win 40 games in a season with a 4-0 victory over the visiting Boston Bruins.
- Mar. 17, 1951 – Gordie Howe had three goals and an assist in an 8-2 win over Chicago at the Olympia, breaking Herbie Cain's record of 82 points in a season set in 1943-44.

MILESTONES

- Dec. 20, 1950 – Toronto's Turk Broda became the first NHL goaltender to win 300 games with a 6-1 victory over the Canadiens.
- Mar. 31, 1951 – Boston and Toronto played a semi-final game that ended in a tie. The teams were deadlocked 1-1 through one overtime but Toronto's Sunday curfew laws made it illegal to begin another period after midnight.
- Apr. 21, 1951 – Toronto's Bill Barilko scored the Stanley Cup-winning goal at 2:53 of overtime to defeat Montreal 3-2 in game five of the finals. It was the only Stanley Cup series in NHL history in which every game ended in overtime.

1951-52

Stanley Cup • Detroit Red Wings

FINAL STANDINGS

Team	GP	W	L	T	GF	GA	PTS
Detroit	70	44	14	12	215	133	100
Montreal	70	34	26	10	195	164	78
Toronto	70	29	25	16	168	157	74
Boston	70	25	29	16	162	176	66
New York	70	23	34	13	192	219	59
Chicago	70	17	44	9	158	241	43

LEADING SCORERS

Player	Club	GP	G	A	PTS	PIM
Gordie Howe	Detroit	70	47	39	86	78
Ted Lindsay	Detroit	70	30	39	69	123
Elmer Lach	Montreal	70	15	50	65	36
Don Raleigh	NY Rangers	70	19	42	61	14
Sid Smith	Toronto	70	27	30	57	6
Bernie Geoffrion	Montreal	67	30	24	54	66
Bill Mosienko	Chicago	70	31	22	53	10
Sid Abel	Detroit	62	17	36	53	32
Ted Kennedy	Toronto	70	19	33	52	33
Milt Schmidt	Boston	69	21	29	50	57
Johnny Peirson	Boston	68	20	30	50	30
George Gee	Chicago	70	18	31	49	39
Tod Sloan	Toronto	68	25	23	48	89
Red Kelly	Detroit	67	16	31	47	16
Maurice Richard	Montreal	48	27	17	44	44
Metro Prystai	Detroit	69	21	22	43	16
Ed Slowinski	NY Rangers	64	21	22	43	18
Paul Ronty	NY Rangers	65	12	31	43	16
Paul Meger	Montreal	69	24	18	42	44
Max Bentley	Toronto	69	24	17	41	40
Cal Gardner	Toronto	70	15	26	41	40
Billy Reay	Montreal	68	7	34	41	20
Dick Gamble	Montreal	64	23	17	40	8
Gaye Stewart	NY Rangers	69	15	25	40	22
Gus Bodnar	Chicago	69	14	26	40	26

LEADING GOALTENDERS

Goaltender	Club	GPI	MINS	GA	SO	AVG
Terry Sawchuk	Detroit	70	4200	133	12	1.90
Al Rollins	Toronto	70	4170	154	5	2.22
Gerry McNeil	Montreal	70	4200	164	5	2.34
Jim Henry	Boston	70	4200	176	7	2.51
Chuck Rayner	NY Rangers	53	3180	159	2	3.00
Harry Lumley	Chicago	70	4180	241	2	3.46

LEADING PLAYOFF SCORERS

Player	Club	GP	G	A	PTS	PIM
Ted Lindsay	Detroit	8	5	2	7	8
Floyd Curry	Montreal	11	4	3	7	6
Metro Prystai	Detroit	8	2	5	7	0
Gordie Howe	Detroit	8	2	5	7	2
Maurice Richard	Montreal	11	4	2	6	6
Johnny Wilson	Detroit	8	4	1	5	5
Glen Skov	Detroit	8	1	4	5	16
Bernie Geoffrion	Montreal	11	3	1	4	6
Tony Leswick	Detroit	8	3	1	4	22
Sid Abel	Detroit	7	2	2	4	12
Ed Sandford	Boston	7	2	2	4	0
Billy Reay	Montreal	10	2	2	4	7
Marty Pavelich	Detroit	8	2	2	4	2

LEADING PLAYOFF GOALTENDERS

Goaltender	Club	GPI	MINS	GA	SO	AVG
Terry Sawchuk	Detroit	8	480	5	4	0.63
Gerry McNeil	Montreal	11	688	23	1	2.01
Jim Henry	Boston	7	448	18	1	2.41

Terry Sawchuk (left) and Sid Abel kiss the Stanley Cup after Detroit's eight-game romp to the championship in 1952. Abel was sold to Chicago during the offseason and became a playing coach with the Black Hawks. Sawchuk would help the Red Wings win again in 1954 and 1955 before being dealt to Boston.

It was a sign of the difference between the top and bottom teams: Detroit traded six players to Chicago for only one, but the Hawks finished last (again) while the Wings claimed first (of course). Yet another great player debuted for Detroit: Alex Delvecchio. With Terry Sawchuk and Gordie Howe reaching peaks of unparalleled dominance, the men in red seemed to have winged feet as well as jerseys. With an offense that was 20 goals better than any other team and a defense that allowed 24 less than the Leafs, the Wings were, in effect, 44 goals better than the league.

Torment and Talent – Solemn, silent, moody and muted, Terry Sawchuk was also the greatest goalie to put on the pads. He didn't allow a single playoff goal on home ice as the Wings swept their way to the Cup.

Chicago barely managed two goals per game, but Bill Mosienko's three in 21 seconds put a memorable finish on their forgettable season. Even with two members of the famous Conacher family appearing on the roster (plus a third, unrelated Conacher), the Black Hawks only gained four wins over the previous year. Elmer Lach also made headlines this year by becoming top scorer in league history, passing Bill Cowley.

The most exciting part of the year came when Boston faced Montreal in the semi-finals. Maurice Richard was back from injuries, and the Canadiens easily captured the first two matches only to see the Bruins bounce back with three wins in a row. In double overtime of game six, Paul Masnick wrote a place for himself in history by winning the game for the Habs. Not to be outdone, Richard was the story in game seven, as he usually was in the tense moments. After getting checked hard and kneed in the head, he had missed most of the game. He didn't even know what the score was when coach Dick Irvin, needing a goal to win, put "the Rocket" back on the ice. He skated through the Bruins team and scored on an end-to-end rush, then later collapsed in tears in the dressing room.

The Wings, meanwhile, swept Toronto and were too good for the tired Canadiens as well. Sawchuk shut them out in games three and four to finish the series and put his personal stamp on the playoffs. With an average of 0.63, he had played the two best consecutive series of any goalie in modern history.

Leaders, 1951-52

GOALS

Name, Team	G
Gordie Howe, Det.	47
Bill Mosienko, Chi.	31
Bernie Geoffrion, Mtl.	30
Ted Lindsay, Det.	30
Maurice Richard, Mtl.	27
Sid Smith, Tor.	27
Wally Hergesheimer, NYR	26
Tod Sloan, Tor.	25
Paul Meger, Mtl.	24
Max Bentley, Tor.	24

ASSISTS

Name, Team	A
Elmer Lach, Mtl.	50
Don Raleigh, NYR	42
Gordie Howe, Det.	39
Ted Lindsay, Det.	39
Sid Abel, Det.	36
Billy Reay, Mtl.	34
Ted Kennedy, Tor.	33
Paul Ronty, NYR	31
Red Kelly, Det.	31
George Gee, Chi.	31

GOALIE WINS

Name, Team	W
Terry Sawchuk, Det.	44
Gerry McNeil, Mtl.	34
Al Rollins, Tor.	29
Jim Henry, Bos.	25
Chuck Rayner, NYR	18
Harry Lumley, Chi.	17
Emile Francis, NYR	4
Lorne Anderson, NYR	1

SHUTOUTS

Name, Team	SO
Terry Sawchuk, Det.	12
Jim Henry, Bos.	7
Gerry McNeil, Mtl.	5
Al Rollins, Tor.	5
Chuck Rayner, NYR	2
Harry Lumley, Chi.	2

PLAYOFF GOALS

Name, Team	G
Ted Lindsay, Det.	5
Johnny Wilson, Det.	4
Floyd Curry, Mtl.	4
Maurice Richard, Mtl.	4
Tony Leswick, Det.	3
Bernie Geoffrion, Mtl.	3
10 tied with	2

PLAYOFF ASSISTS

Name, Team	A
Metro Prystai, Det.	5
Gordie Howe, Det.	5
Glen Skov, Det.	4
Bill Quackenbush, Bos.	3
Alex Delvecchio, Det.	3
Dollard St. Laurent, Mtl.	3
Floyd Curry, Mtl.	3
Doug Harvey, Mtl.	3
Paul Meger, Mtl.	3
13 tied with	2

PLAYOFF GOALIE WINS

Name, Team	W
Terry Sawchuk, Det.	8
Gerry McNeil, Mtl.	4
Jim Henry, Bos.	3

PLAYOFF SHUTOUTS

Name, Team	SO
Terry Sawchuk, Det.	4
Jim Henry, Bos.	1
Gerry McNeil, Mtl.	1

FIRST TEAM ALL-STARS

Name, Team	Position
Elmer Lach, Mtl.	C
Gordie Howe, Det.	RW
Ted Lindsay, Det.	LW
Red Kelly, Det.	D
Doug Harvey, Mtl.	D
Terry Sawchuk, Det.	G

SECOND TEAM ALL-STARS

Name, Team	Position
Milt Schmidt, Bos.	C
Maurice Richard, Mtl.	RW
Sid Smith, Tor.	LW
Hy Buller, NYR	D
Jim Thomson, Tor.	D
Jim Henry, Bos.	G

1952 Playoffs

SEMI-FINALS

Mar.	25	Toronto	0	at	Detroit	3
Mar.	27	Toronto	0	at	Detroit	1
Mar.	29	Detroit	6	at	Toronto	2
Apr.	1	Detroit	3	at	Toronto	1

Detroit won best-of-seven series 4–0

Mar.	25	Boston	1	at	Montreal	5
Mar.	27	Boston	0	at	Montreal	4
Mar.	30	Montreal	1	at	Boston	4
Apr.	1	Montreal	2	at	Boston	3
Apr.	3	Boston	1	at	Montreal	0
Apr.	6	Montreal	3	at	Boston	2 2OT
Apr.	8	Boston	1	at	Montreal	3

Montreal won best-of-seven series 4–3

FINALS

Apr.	10	Detroit	3	at	Montreal	1
Apr.	12	Detroit	2	at	Montreal	1
Apr.	13	Montreal	0	at	Detroit	3
Apr.	15	Montreal	0	at	Detroit	3

Detroit won best-of-seven series 4–0

1951-52 – Detroit Red Wings – Terry Sawchuk, Bob Goldham, Benny Woit, Red Kelly, Leo Reise, Jr., Marcel Pronovost, Ted Lindsay, Tony Leswick, Gordie Howe, Metro Prystai, Marty Pavelich, Sid Abel (Captain), Glen Skov, Alex Delvecchio, Johnny Wilson, Vic Stasiuk, Larry Zeidel, Glenn Hall, Jack Adams (Manager), Tommy Ivan (Coach), Carl Mattson (Trainer).

TROPHY WINNERS

Trophy	Awarded For	Winner	Team
Hart	MVP	Gordie Howe	Det.
Art Ross	Top Scorer	Gordie Howe	Det.
Calder	Top Rookie	Bernie Geoffrion	Mtl.
Vezina	Fewest Goals Against	Terry Sawchuk	Det
Byng	Gentlemanly Conduct	Sid Smith	Tor.

NHL NOTEBOOK

TRANSACTIONS

- June 8, 1951 – NY Rangers traded Tony Leswick to Detroit for Gaye Stewart.
- Aug. 20, 1951 – Chicago traded Hugh Coflin and $75,000 to Detroit for Jim McFadden, Max McNabb, George Gee, Clare Martin, Jimmy Peters and Rags Raglan.
- Sept. 28, 1951 – Boston Bruins acquired goaltender "Sugar" Jim Henry from the Detroit Red Wings.
- Jan. 9, 1952 – Toronto traded Fleming Mackell to Boston for Jim Morrison

RECORDS

- Feb. 10, 1952 – Detroit Red Wings rookie Johnny Wilson began a streak of 580 straight games played – an NHL record at the time. Red Wings won 2-0 over the Bruins at Boston.
- Feb. 23, 1952 – Montreal's Elmer Lach became the NHL's all time scoring leader, when he got a goal and three assists in a 7-0 win over Chicago. The four points gave Lach 550 career NHL points, two more than Bill Cowley, who had held the record since 1946.
- Mar. 23, 1952 – Chicago's Bill Mosienko set an NHL record for fastest three goals by one player (:21). Black Hawks won 7-6 against the Rangers at New York, before a crowd of just 3,254.
- Mar. 30, 1952 – Boston Bruins scored three goals in a span of 1:02 during the second period (a new playoff record) for a 4-1 playoff win over the Canadiens, in game three of the Stanley Cup semi-finals in Boston.

MILESTONES

- Nov. 24, 1951 – Chicago's 46-year-old trainer Moe Roberts made his first NHL appearance in 18 years (after an injury to goaltender Harry Lumley) and helped the Hawks to a 6-2 win over Detroit.
- Feb. 17, 1952 – Montreal's Elmer Lach picked up his 354th career assist to become the NHL's all-time leader in assists. He broke the mark held by Bill Cowley. Lach's historic assist came in a 3-2 loss to the Rangers.
- Mar. 27, 1952 – Toronto's Turk Broda became the first goaltender in NHL history to appear in 100 career playoff games, when he faced the Red Wings in a 1-0 loss, in game two of the Stanley Cup semi-finals in Detroit.

1952-53

Stanley Cup • Montreal Canadiens

FINAL STANDINGS

Team	GP	W	L	T	GF	GA	PTS
Detroit	70	36	16	18	222	133	90
Montreal	70	28	23	19	155	148	75
Boston	70	28	29	13	152	172	69
Chicago	70	27	28	15	169	175	69
Toronto	70	27	30	13	156	167	67
New York	70	17	37	16	152	211	50

LEADING SCORERS

Player	Club	GP	G	A	PTS	PIM
Gordie Howe	Detroit	70	49	46	95	57
Ted Lindsay	Detroit	70	32	39	71	111
Maurice Richard	Montreal	70	28	33	61	112
Wally Hergesheimer	NY Rangers	70	30	29	59	10
Alex Delvecchio	Detroit	70	16	43	59	28
Paul Ronty	NY Rangers	70	16	38	54	20
Metro Prystai	Detroit	70	16	34	50	12
Red Kelly	Detroit	70	19	27	46	8
Bert Olmstead	Montreal	69	17	28	45	83
Fleming MacKell	Boston	65	27	17	44	63
Jim McFadden	Chicago	70	23	21	44	29
Johnny Wilson	Detroit	70	23	19	42	22
Jimmy Peters	Chicago	69	22	19	41	16
Elmer Lach	Montreal	53	16	25	41	56
Bernie Geoffrion	Montreal	65	22	17	39	37
Sid Smith	Toronto	70	20	19	39	6
George Gee	Chicago	67	18	21	39	99
Gerry Couture	Chicago	70	19	18	37	22
Bill Mosienko	Chicago	65	17	20	37	8
Ted Kennedy	Toronto	43	14	23	37	42
Nick Mickoski	NY Rangers	70	19	16	35	39
Gord Hannigan	Toronto	65	17	18	35	51
Ed Sandford	Boston	61	14	21	35	44
Ron Stewart	Toronto	70	13	22	35	29
Cal Gardner	Chicago	70	11	24	35	60

LEADING GOALTENDERS

Goaltender	Club	GPI	MINS	GA	SO	AVG
Terry Sawchuk	Detroit	63	3780	120	9	1.90
Gerry McNeil	Montreal	66	3960	140	10	2.12
Harry Lumley	Toronto	70	4200	167	10	2.39
Jim Henry	Boston	70	4200	172	7	2.46
Al Rollins	Chicago	70	4200	175	6	2.50
Gump Worsley	NY Rangers	50	3000	153	2	3.06

LEADING PLAYOFF SCORERS

Player	Club	GP	G	A	PTS	PIM
Ed Sandford	Boston	11	8	3	11	11
Bernie Geoffrion	Montreal	12	6	4	10	12
Dave Creighton	Boston	11	4	5	9	10
Johnny Peirson	Boston	11	3	6	9	2
Fleming MacKell	Boston	11	2	7	9	7
Maurice Richard	Montreal	12	7	1	8	2
Ted Lindsay	Detroit	6	4	4	8	6
Metro Prystai	Detroit	6	4	4	8	2
Gordie Howe	Detroit	6	2	5	7	2
Johnny Wilson	Detroit	6	2	5	7	0
Elmer Lach	Montreal	12	1	6	7	6

LEADING PLAYOFF GOALTENDERS

Goaltender	Club	GPI	MINS	GA	SO	AVG
Jacques Plante	Montreal	4	240	7	1	1.75
Gerry McNeil	Montreal	8	486	16	2	1.98
Al Rollins	Chicago	7	425	18	0	2.54
Jim Henry	Boston	9	510	26	0	3.06
Terry Sawchuk	Detroit	6	372	21	1	3.39

Gordie Howe attended his first NHL training camp with the New York Rangers as a 15-year-old in 1943, but left the workouts in Winnipeg because he was homesick. Three years later, he broke into the NHL with the Detroit Red Wings and went on to star for 25 years, setting records that, at the time, seemed unbreakable.

PARITY WAS THE HALLMARK of this season, allowing Chicago to edge into the playoffs at Toronto's expense. With Al Rollins as their new goalie and Sid Abel as their new playing coach, the Black Hawks became competitive for the first time in seven years. The Rangers took the Hawks' usual place at the bottom of the standings despite two top-10 scorers. The Leafs had none, which probably cost them a playoff berth.

Here's Howe – Ambidextrous, athletic, sneaky and shy, Gordie Howe finished one shot away from tying the Rocket's record, but set a new points record with 95 as the Red Wings won again.

Goaltending, always crucial in this era, shone brightly as Harry Lumley and Gerry McNeil both reached 10 shutouts, while Jacques Plante, Glenn Hall and Gump Worsley each began their magnificent careers. McNeil's accomplishment was hardly simple, considering how offensive-minded Montreal was. In November, Maurice Richard passed Nels Stewart on the all-time goal list with number 325. It had taken the Rocket only 10 years to break a record Stewart had needed 15 to compile.

When the playoffs began, the Red Wing showed why they had been first in the regular season with a 7–0 rout of Boston. The Beantowners responded with five goals of their own to win game two and took the next contest in overtime. Boston and Detroit then exchanged high-scoring wins. Finally, this wild series ended with a Bruins upset. Chicago versus Montreal was another exciting matchup. The Hawks lost the first two but rebounded with three straight triumphs. McNeil had been performing well, but he asked to be replaced. Plante showed up and showed off by allowing one goal in two wins.

In the finals, "Jake the Snake" slowed down a little, and coach Dick Irvin threw McNeil back in after game two. Once again, the goaltending change paid off. McNeil was fine and the Habs won three in a row, including the clincher in overtime, courtesy of Elmer Lach. The story might have been different if Boston hadn't been forced to play two goalies as well. Regular "Sugar" Jim Henry was hurt for the first four games, and backup Gordon "Red" Henry (no relation) couldn't repel Richard and company. The Rocket had one hat trick in the finals.

Leaders, 1952-53

GOALS

Name, Team	G
Gordie Howe, Det.	49
Ted Lindsay, Det.	32
Wally Hergesheimer, NYR	30
Maurice Richard, Mtl.	28
Fleming MacKell, Bos.	27
Jim McFadden, Chi.	23
Johnny Wilson, Det.	23
Bernie Geoffrion, Mtl.	22
Jimmy Peters, Chi.	22
Sid Smith, Tor.	20

ASSISTS

Name, Team	A
Gordie Howe, Det.	46
Alex Delvecchio, Det.	43
Ted Lindsay, Det.	39
Paul Ronty, NYR	38
Metro Prystai, Det.	34
Maurice Richard, Mtl.	33
Doug Harvey, Mtl.	30
Wally Hergesheimer, NYR	29
Bert Olmstead, Mtl.	28
Red Kelly, Det.	27

GOALIE WINS

Name, Team	W
Terry Sawchuk, Det.	32
Jim Henry, Bos.	28
Harry Lumley, Tor.	27
Al Rollins, Chi.	27
Gerry McNeil, Mtl.	25
Gump Worsley, NYR	13
Glenn Hall, Det.	4
Chuck Rayner, NYR	4
Jacques Plante, Mtl.	2
Hal Murphy, Mtl.	1

SHUTOUTS

Name, Team	SO
Gerry McNeil, Mtl.	10
Harry Lumley, Tor.	10
Terry Sawchuk, Det.	9
Jim Henry, Bos.	7
Al Rollins, Chi.	6
Gump Worsley, NYR	2
Glenn Hall, Det.	1
Chuck Rayner, NYR	1

PLAYOFF GOALS

Name, Team	G
Ed Sandford, Bos.	8
Maurice Richard, Mtl.	7
Bernie Geoffrion, Mtl.	6
Milt Schmidt, Bos.	5
Ted Lindsay, Det.	4
Metro Prystai, Det.	4
Bill Mosienko, Chi.	4
Jack McIntyre, Bos.	4
Dave Creighton, Bos.	4
Four tied with	3

PLAYOFF ASSISTS

Name, Team	A
Fleming MacKell, Bos.	7
Johnny Peirson, Bos.	6
Elmer Lach, Mtl.	6
Gordie Howe, Det.	5
Johnny Wilson, Det.	5
Dave Creighton, Bos.	5
Doug Harvey, Mtl.	5
Ted Lindsay, Det.	4
Metro Prystai, Det.	4
Alex Delvecchio, Det.	4
Red Kelly, Det.	4
Bill Quackenbush, Bos.	4
Bernie Geoffrion, Mtl.	4

PLAYOFF GOALIE WINS

Name, Team	W
Gerry McNeil, Mtl.	5
Jim Henry, Bos.	5
Jacques Plante, Mtl.	3
Al Rollins, Chi.	3
Terry Sawchuk, Det.	2

PLAYOFF SHUTOUTS

Name, Team	SO
Gerry McNeil, Mtl.	2
Jacques Plante, Mtl.	1
Terry Sawchuk, Det.	1

FIRST TEAM ALL-STARS

Name, Team	Position
Fleming Mackell, Bos.	C
Gordie Howe, Det.	RW
Ted Lindsay, Det.	LW
Red Kelly, Det.	D
Doug Harvey, Mtl.	D
Terry Sawchuk, Det.	G

SECOND TEAM ALL-STARS

Name, Team	Position
Alex Delvecchio, Det.	C
Maurice Richard, Mtl.	RW
Bert Olmstead, Mtl.	LW
Bill Quackenbush, Bos.	D
Bill Gadsby, Chi.	D
Gerry McNeil, Mtl.	G

1953 Playoffs

SEMI-FINALS

Date	Visitor	Score		Home	Score	
Mar. 24	Boston	0	at	Detroit	7	
Mar. 26	Boston	5	at	Detroit	3	
Mar. 29	Detroit	1	at	Boston	2	OT
Mar. 31	Detroit	2	at	Boston	6	
Apr. 2	Boston	4	at	Detroit	6	
Apr. 5	Detroit	2	at	Boston	4	

Boston won best-of-seven series 4–2

Date	Visitor	Score		Home	Score	
Mar. 24	Chicago	1	at	Montreal	3	
Mar. 26	Chicago	3	at	Montreal	4	
Mar. 29	Montreal	1	at	Chicago	2	OT
Mar. 31	Montreal	1	at	Chicago	3	
Apr. 2	Chicago	4	at	Montreal	2	
Apr. 4	Montreal	3	at	Chicago	0	
Apr. 7	Chicago	1	at	Montreal	4	

Montreal won best-of-seven series 4–3

FINALS

Date	Visitor	Score		Home	Score	
Apr. 9	Boston	2	at	Montreal	4	
Apr. 11	Boston	4	at	Montreal	1	
Apr. 12	Montreal	3	at	Boston	0	
Apr. 14	Montreal	7	at	Boston	3	
Apr. 16	Boston	0	at	Montreal	1	OT

Montreal won best-of-seven series 4–1

1952-53 – Montreal Canadiens – Gerry McNeil, Jacques Plante, Doug Harvey, Butch Bouchard (Captain), Tom Johnson, Dollard St. Laurent, Bud MacPherson, Maurice Richard, Elmer Lach, Bert Olmstead, Bernie Geoffrion, Floyd Curry, Paul Masnick, Billy Reay, Dickie Moore, Ken Mosdell, Dick Gamble, John McCormack, Lorne Davis, Calum MacKay, Eddie Mazur, Paul Meger, Frank Selke (Manager), Dick Irvin (Coach), Hector Dubois (Trainer).

TROPHY WINNERS

Trophy	Awarded For	Winner	Team
Hart	MVP	Gordie Howe	Det.
Art Ross	Top Scorer	Gordie Howe	Det.
Calder	Top Rookie	Gump Worsley	NYR
Vezina	Fewest Goals Against	Terry Sawchuk	Det
Byng	Gentlemanly Conduct	Red Kelly	Det.

NHL NOTEBOOK

TRANSACTIONS

- Sept. 11, 1952 Chicago obtained Cal Gardner along with Al Rollins, Ray Hannigan and Gus Mortson from Toronto for Harry Lumley.
- Sept. 16, 1952 – Boston Bruins purchased Joe Klukay from Toronto.
- Sept. 22, 1952 – Montreal Canadiens traded Gerry Couture to Chicago for cash.
- Sept. 24, 1952 – Montreal Canadiens signed Dick Gamble as a free agent.

RECORDS

- Nov. 8, 1952 – Maurice Richard scored his 325th career goal to break the all-time record for NHL goals held by Nels Stewart. It came in a 6-4 win over the Black Hawks in Montreal, exactly 10 years after Richard's first NHL goal.
- Mar. 5, 1953 – Gordie Howe scored twice and added three assists to lead the Red Wings to a 7-1 win against the Rangers at the Olympia. With the five points Howe broke his own NHL record for most points for a single season (86).
- Mar. 24, 1953 – Detroit's Terry Sawchuk tied an NHL record with his third straight playoff shutout, a 7-0 Red Wings win over Boston, in game one of the Stanley Cup semi-finals at the Olympia.

MILESTONES

- Nov. 1, 1952 – Hockey was televised nationally in Canada from Maple Leaf Gardens for the first time on the CBC, as the Leafs beat the Bruins 3-2.
- Dec. 6, 1952 – Detroit's Terry Sawchuk shut out Chicago 2-0 in Indianapolis, the first time since 1928 that a regular-season game was played outside an NHL city. Both teams' arenas were unavailable that night.
- Dec. 21, 1952 – Ted Lindsay became the first player to score 200 goals with the Red Wings in a 5-2 win over the Rangers at New York.
- Jan. 29, 1953 – Maurice Richard became the first NHL player to score 20 (or more) goals in each of his first 10 full seasons, when he picked up his 20th of the year in a 5-2 Canadiens win over the Rangers.
- Mar. 22, 1953 – Gordie Howe finished his season with 49 goals, 46 assists for a record 95 points in a 1-1 tie vs. the Canadiens in Detroit. Howe was first to win the Ross Trophy three times (and in three straight years).

1953-54

Stanley Cup • Detroit Red Wings

FINAL STANDINGS

Team	GP	W	L	T	GF	GA	PTS
Detroit	70	37	19	14	191	132	88
Montreal	70	35	24	11	195	141	81
Toronto	70	32	24	14	152	131	78
Boston	70	32	28	10	177	181	74
New York	70	29	31	10	161	182	68
Chicago	70	12	51	7	133	242	31

LEADING SCORERS

Player	Club	GP	G	A	PTS	PIM
Gordie Howe	Detroit	70	33	48	81	57
Maurice Richard	Montreal	70	37	30	67	125
Ted Lindsay	Detroit	70	26	36	62	58
Bernie Geoffrion	Montreal	54	29	25	54	15
Bert Olmstead	Montreal	70	15	37	52	68
Red Kelly	Detroit	62	16	33	49	51
Dutch Reibel	Detroit	69	15	33	48	103
Ed Sandford	Boston	70	16	31	47	14
Fleming MacKell	Boston	67	15	32	47	82
Ken Mosdell	Montreal	67	22	24	46	8
Paul Ronty	NY Rangers	70	13	33	46	74
Don Raleigh	NY Rangers	70	15	30	45	40
Wally Hergesheimer	NY Rangers	66	27	16	43	58
Tod Sloan	Toronto	67	11	32	43	37
Larry Wilson	Chicago	66	9	33	42	28
Bill Gadsby	Chicago	70	12	29	41	48
Johnny Peirson	Boston	68	21	19	40	75
Dave Creighton	Boston	69	20	20	40	34
Camille Henry	NY Rangers	66	24	15	39	37
Sid Smith	Toronto	70	22	16	38	30
Ted Kennedy	Toronto	67	15	23	38	19
Joe Klukay	Boston	70	20	17	37	85
Doug Harvey	Montreal	68	8	29	37	40
Nick Mickoski	NY Rangers	68	19	16	35	53
Leo Labine	Boston	68	16	19	35	32

LEADING GOALTENDERS

Goaltender	Club	GPI	MINS	GA	SO	AVG
Harry Lumley	Toronto	69	4140	128	13	1.86
Terry Sawchuk	Detroit	67	4004	129	12	1.93
Gerry McNeil	Montreal	53	3180	114	6	2.15
Jim Henry	Boston	70	4200	181	8	2.59
Johnny Bower	NY Rangers	70	4200	182	5	2.60
Al Rollins	Chicago	66	3960	213	5	3.23

LEADING PLAYOFF SCORERS

Player	Club	GP	G	A	PTS	PIM
Dickie Moore	Montreal	11	5	8	13	8
Bernie Geoffrion	Montreal	11	6	5	11	18
Jean Beliveau	Montreal	10	2	8	10	4
Gordie Howe	Detroit	12	4	5	9	31
Alex Delvecchio	Detroit	12	2	7	9	7
Ted Lindsay	Detroit	12	4	4	8	14
Red Kelly	Detroit	12	5	1	6	0
Marcel Pronovost	Detroit	12	2	3	5	12
Metro Prystai	Detroit	12	2	3	5	0
Five players tied with				4		

LEADING PLAYOFF GOALTENDERS

Goaltender	Club	GPI	MINS	GA	SO	AVG
Terry Sawchuk	Detroit	12	751	20	2	1.60
Jacques Plante	Montreal	8	480	15	2	1.88
Harry Lumley	Toronto	5	321	15	0	2.80
Jim Henry	Boston	4	240	16	0	4.00

Maple Leafs scouts thought little of Red Kelly when he was playing junior hockey at St. Michael's College in Toronto. He entered the NHL with the Red Wings in 1947–48 and helped Detroit finish first in the standings for seven straight seasons from 1949 to 1955. Kelly was the first winner of the Norris Trophy as the league's best defenseman in 1953–54.

IT WAS THE ERA OF THE SHUTOUT, and with Terry Sawchuk and Harry Lumley boasting 25 clean slates between them, there wasn't much scoring around the league this year. Not one team broke the 200-goal mark. This made Chicago's record even more incredible, as it allowed 3.46 goals per game. With so little support in front of him, Al Rollins was rewarded with a surprise selection as the Hart Trophy winner for his heroic efforts behind a weak Black Hawks lineup. The team had been suffering poor attendance for years, and had been sold to James D. Norris and Arthur Wirtz before the season.

It was a special year for the Canadiens, as Dick Irvin earned his 600th victory as a coach and Maurice Richard passed linemate Elmer Lach to become the league's all-time leading scorer. Jean Beliveau joined the regular squad after a prolonged flirtation, made complicated by the reluctance of his Quebec City team to release him. As for Boston and New York, it was something of a family affair when Muzz Patrick became the Rangers coach during the campaign, joining his brother Lynn, who ran the Bruins. Muzz reunited Max and Doug Bentley in New York to complete the brotherly theme on the ice. Still, the Rangers didn't win.

Seeing Red – Howe was four-for-four in scoring titles, Lindsay was six-for-six in top 10 finishes, Rocket was a four-time bridesmaid and a resourceful rearguard named Red Kelly was the top blue-liner in the league.

Despite Rocket Richard's on-ice accomplishments, he suffered embarrassment off the ice. In a column he "wrote" for a Quebec newspaper, Richard called league president Campbell a dictator for banning Bernie Geoffrion from any further games against New York that season. Geoffrion's crime had been to break Ron Murphy's jaw, so Richard's judgment was condemned by everyone. He had to forsake the newspaper business, pay $1000 as a bond and apologize.

The playoffs proceeded normally until game five of the finals. After the Wings and Canadiens won routine semi-finals, Detroit had coasted to a 3–1 series lead over Montreal. Since Sawchuk was outplaying Jacques Plante, Dick Irvin decided to go with Gerry McNeil in game five. Montreal won the crucial game 1–0 in overtime and went on to force a game seven. This also went to sudden death. Tony Leswick flipped a harmless clearing shot into Montreal's end. Canadiens defenseman Doug Harvey reached up to glove the puck, but it ticked off him and into the net for a most unlikely Cup winner.

Leaders, 1953-54

GOALS

Name, Team	G
Maurice Richard, Mtl.	37
Gordie Howe, Det.	33
Bernie Geoffrion, Mtl.	29
Wally Hergesheimer, NYR	27
Ted Lindsay, Det.	26
Camille Henry, NYR	24
Ken Mosdell, Mtl.	22
Sid Smith, Tor.	22
Johnny Peirson, Bos.	21
Harry Watson, Tor.	21

ASSISTS

Name, Team	A
Gordie Howe, Det.	48
Bert Olmstead, Mtl.	37
Ted Lindsay, Det.	36
Red Kelly, Det.	33
Larry Wilson, Chi.	33
Dutch Reibel, Det.	33
Paul Ronty, NYR	33
Fleming MacKell, Bos.	32
Tod Sloan, Tor.	32
Ed Sandford, Bos.	31

GOALIE WINS

Name, Team	W
Terry Sawchuk, Det.	35
Harry Lumley, Tor.	32
Jim Henry, Bos.	32
Johnny Bower, NYR	29
Gerry McNeil, Mtl.	28
Al Rollins, Chi.	12
Jacques Plante, Mtl.	7
Dave Gatherum, Det.	2

SHUTOUTS

Name, Team	SO
Harry Lumley, Tor.	13
Terry Sawchuk, Det.	12
Jim Henry, Bos.	8
Gerry McNeil, Mtl.	6
Jacques Plante, Mtl.	5
Al Rollins, Chi.	5
Johnny Bower, NYR	5
Dave Gatherum, Det.	1

PLAYOFF GOALS

Name, Team	G
Bernie Geoffrion, Mtl.	6
Dickie Moore, Mtl.	5
Red Kelly, Det.	5
Floyd Curry, Mtl.	4
Gordie Howe, Det.	4
Ted Lindsay, Det.	4
Maurice Richard, Mtl.	3
Tony Leswick, Det.	3
Johnny Wilson, Det.	3
Eight tied with	2

PLAYOFF ASSISTS

Name, Team	A
Jean Beliveau, Mtl.	8
Dickie Moore, Mtl.	8
Alex Delvecchio, Det.	7
Bernie Geoffrion, Mtl.	5
Gordie Howe, Det.	5
Paul Masnick, Mtl.	4
Ted Lindsay, Det.	4
Dutch Reibel, Det.	3
Eddie Mazur, Mtl.	3
Marcel Pronovost, Det.	3
Metro Prystai, Det.	3

PLAYOFF GOALIE WINS

Name, Team	W
Terry Sawchuk, Det.	8
Jacques Plante, Mtl.	5
Gerry McNeil, Mtl.	2
Harry Lumley, Tor.	1

PLAYOFF SHUTOUTS

Name, Team	SO
Jacques Plante, Mtl.	2
Terry Sawchuk, Det.	2
Gerry McNeil, Mtl.	1

FIRST TEAM ALL-STARS

Name, Team	Position
Ken Mosdell, Mtl.	C
Gordie Howe, Det.	RW
Ted Lindsay, Det.	LW
Red Kelly, Det.	D
Doug Harvey, Mtl.	D
Harry Lumley, Tor.	G

SECOND TEAM ALL-STARS

Name, Team	Position
Ted Kennedy, Tor.	C
Maurice Richard, Mtl.	RW
Ed Sandford, Bos.	LW
Bill Gadsby, Chi.	D
Tim Horton, Tor.	D
Terry Sawchuk, Det.	G

1954 Playoffs

SEMI-FINALS

Mar. 23	Toronto	0	at	Detroit	5	
Mar. 25	Toronto	3	at	Detroit	1	
Mar. 27	Detroit	3	at	Toronto	1	
Mar. 30	Detroit	2	at	Toronto	1	
Apr. 1	Toronto	3	at	Detroit	4	2OT

Detroit won best-of-seven series 4–1

Mar. 23	Boston	0	at	Montreal	2
Mar. 25	Boston	1	at	Montreal	8
Mar. 28	Montreal	4	at	Boston	3
Mar. 30	Montreal	2	at	Boston	0

Montreal won best-of-seven series 4–0

FINALS

Apr. 4	Montreal	1	at	Detroit	3	
Apr. 6	Montreal	3	at	Detroit	1	
Apr. 8	Detroit	5	at	Montreal	2	
Apr. 10	Detroit	2	at	Montreal	0	
Apr. 11	Montreal	1	at	Detroit	0	OT
Apr. 13	Detroit	1	at	Montreal	4	
Apr. 16	Montreal	1	at	Detroit	2	OT

Detroit won best-of-seven series 4–3

1953-54 – Detroit Red Wings – Terry Sawchuk, Red Kelly, Bob Goldham, Benny Woit, Marcel Pronovost, Al Arbour, Keith Allen, Ted Lindsay (Captain), Tony Leswick, Gordie Howe, Marty Pavelich, Alex Delvecchio, Metro Prystai, Glen Skov, Johnny Wilson, Bill Dineen, Jimmy Peters, Dutch Reibel, Gilles Dube, Dave Gatherum, Jack Adams (Manager), Tommy Ivan (Coach), Carl Mattson (Trainer).

TROPHY WINNERS

Trophy	Awarded For	Winner	Team
Hart	MVP	Al Rollins	Chi.
Art Ross	Top Scorer	Gordie Howe	Det.
Norris	Top Defenseman	Red Kelly	Det
Calder	Top Rookie	Camille Henry	NYR
Vezina	Fewest Goals Against	Harry Lumley	Tor.
Byng	Gentlemanly Conduct	Red Kelly	Det

NHL NOTEBOOK

TRANSACTIONS

- June 20, 1953 – New York Rangers acquired goaltender Johnny Bower from Cleveland (AHL) in exchange for Emile Francis and cash.
- Oct. 3, 1953 – Jean Beliveau signed his first contract with the Montreal Canadiens, and was assigned uniform #4 for the first time in his NHL career (after wearing number's 17, 20 and 12 during previous brief stays with the Canadiens).
- Jan. 21, 1954 – Chicago Black Hawks purchased Jack McIntyre from Boston.

RECORDS

- Oct. 8, 1953 – Detroit's Earl Reibel set up four goals to set an NHL record for most assists by a player in his first NHL game, in a 4-1 win over the Rangers in Detroit.
- Mar. 13, 1954 – Rookie Camille Henry set a record with four power-play goals to lead the Rangers to a 5-2 win at Detroit.
- Mar. 25, 1954 – Montreal's Dickie Moore scored two goals and added four assists for an NHL record six points in an 8-1 playoff win over Boston, in game two of the Stanley Cup semi-finals.
- Apr. 1, 1954 – Gordie Howe scored two goals and an assist, and set a Stanley Cup playoff record for fastest goal from the start of a game (:09) in a 4-3 win over Toronto, in game five of the semi-finals.

MILESTONES

- Oct. 10, 1953 – Maurice Richard became the first player in NHL history to score 350 goals as the Canadiens won 4-1 over Detroit, at the Forum.
- Oct. 22, 1953 – Dick Irvin became the first coach in NHL history to win 600 career games, when the Canadiens beat the Black Hawks 3-2.
- Dec. 12, 1953 – Maurice Richard became the NHL's all-time scoring leader, when his goal and two assists in a 7-2 win over the Rangers gave him 611 career NHL points, one more than injured teammate Elmer Lach, who had held the record since February 1952.
- Jan. 30, 1954 – For the first time in 20 years, two brothers opposed each other as coaches – Muzz Patrick's Rangers beat brother Lynn Patrick's Bruins 8-3 in New York.
- Mar. 21, 1954 – Gordie Howe became the first player in NHL history to lead the league in scoring four straight years, winning the scoring title with a goal and two assists in the final game of season, a 6-1 Red Wings win over Toronto.

1954-55

Stanley Cup • Detroit Red Wings

Team	GP	W	L	T	GF	GA	PTS
Detroit	70	42	17	11	204	134	95
Montreal	70	41	18	11	228	157	93
Toronto	70	24	24	22	147	135	70
Boston	70	23	26	21	169	188	67
New York	70	17	35	18	150	210	52
Chicago	70	13	40	17	161	235	43

LEADING SCORERS

Player	Club	GP	G	A	PTS	PIM
Bernie Geoffrion	Montreal	70	38	37	75	57
Maurice Richard	Montreal	67	38	36	74	125
Jean Beliveau	Montreal	70	37	36	73	58
Dutch Reibel	Detroit	70	25	41	66	15
Gordie Howe	Detroit	64	29	33	62	68
Red Sullivan	Chicago	70	19	42	61	51
Bert Olmstead	Montreal	70	10	48	58	103
Sid Smith	Toronto	70	33	21	54	14
Ken Mosdell	Montreal	70	22	32	54	82
Danny Lewicki	NY Rangers	70	29	24	53	8
Ted Kennedy	Toronto	70	10	42	52	74
Ed Litzenberger	Mtl./Chi.	73	23	28	51	40
Doug Harvey	Montreal	70	6	43	49	58
Alex Delvecchio	Detroit	69	17	31	48	37
Red Kelly	Detroit	70	15	30	45	28
Nick Mickoski	NYR/Chi.	70	10	33	43	48
Leo Labine	Boston	67	24	18	42	75
Don McKenney	Boston	69	22	20	42	34
Andy Bathgate	NY Rangers	70	20	20	40	37
Real Chevrefils	Boston	64	18	22	40	30
Don Raleigh	NY Rangers	69	8	32	40	19
Ted Lindsay	Detroit	49	19	19	38	85
Cal Gardner	Boston	70	16	22	38	40
Marcel Bonin	Detroit	69	16	20	36	53
Dickie Moore	Montreal	67	16	20	36	32

LEADING GOALTENDERS

Goaltender	Club	GPI	MINS	GA	SO	AVG
Harry Lumley	Toronto	69	4140	134	8	1.94
Terry Sawchuk	Detroit	68	4040	132	12	1.96
Jacques Plante	Montreal	52	3080	110	5	2.14
John Henderson	Boston	45	2628	109	5	2.49
Jim Henry	Boston	27	1572	79	1	3.02
Gump Worsley	NY Rangers	65	3900	197	4	3.03
Al Rollins	Chicago	44	2640	150	0	3.41

LEADING PLAYOFF SCORERS

Player	Club	GP	G	A	PTS	PIM
Gordie Howe	Detroit	11	9	11	20	24
Ted Lindsay	Detroit	11	7	12	19	12
Alex Delvecchio	Detroit	11	7	8	15	2
Bernie Geoffrion	Montreal	12	8	5	13	8
Jean Beliveau	Montreal	12	6	7	13	18
Floyd Curry	Montreal	12	8	4	12	4
Dutch Reibel	Detroit	11	5	7	12	2
Calum MacKay	Montreal	12	3	8	11	8
Ken Mosdell	Montreal	12	2	7	9	8
Vic Stasiuk	Detroit	11	5	3	8	6
Doug Harvey	Montreal	12	0	8	8	6

LEADING PLAYOFF GOALTENDERS

Goaltender	Club	GPI	MINS	GA	SO	AVG
Terry Sawchuk	Detroit	11	660	26	1	2.36
Jacques Plante	Montreal	12	639	30	0	2.82
Harry Lumley	Toronto	4	240	14	0	3.50
Charlie Hodge	Montreal	4	84	6	0	4.29

Harry Lumley recorded 71 shutouts in 16 NHL seasons between 1943–44 and 1959–60, trailing only Terry Sawchuk's total of 100 during the "Original Six" era. His 13 shutouts for Toronto in 1953–54 were the highest single-season total of the era. Lumley's 331 career victories were an NHL record until surpassed by Sawchuk in 1961–62.

A MERE HOCKEY PLAYER became the focus of social and political upheaval this year. Naturally, the player was Maurice Richard, the most tempestuous star of his time. Turned into a symbol of cultural pride by French Canada, still unsure of itself in an English-dominated land, Richard's every triumph was seen as a victory for his people—even though he never asked for, or wanted, it to be so. Simply by refusing to back down from Anglophone players or league officials, while maintaining his status as the NHL's most dangerous scorer, he became a model for what his people longed to be.

Meltdown in Montreal – The Rocket's fire smoked his best chance of winning a scoring title, fueled riots in the streets of Montreal and burned the Habs hopes of downing Detroit.

The trouble started near the end of the season in a game against the Bruins. Richard was being provoked by very rough Boston tactics, and he finally snapped when Hal Laycoe clipped him near the eye. A huge brawl started, and when Richard went to grab his stick and assault Laycoe, linesman Cliff Thompson restrained him. So the Rocket hit him. President Campbell suspended Richard for the rest of the season (three games) and all of the playoffs, angering all of Quebec. At the next home game, the infamous "Richard Riot" broke out. Tear gas, violence and broken glass filled the arena and the streets. The game had to be forfeited. Richard lost the scoring title by one point and the Canadiens lost the Cup in seven games to Detroit.

Despite the loss, it was clear that Montreal was on the rise and the Wings were levelling out. The two were side by side in the league standings, but Montreal's offense had passed that of the Red Wings. They were both far ahead of everyone else, especially the Black Hawks, who had to be put on life support via player transfers from other clubs.

Gordie Howe was the best player in the postseason, setting a record for points that overshadowed his middling campaign. As for Richard, he did have one happy moment this year thanks to his 400th career goal. He gave the $2000 bonus he received to charity. Other notable developments this year included the preseason decision of Conn Smythe to step down as Maple Leafs general manager and the retirement of longtime Bruins boss Art Ross. Both were legends who virtually defined their organizations.

Leaders, 1954-55

GOALS

Name, Team	G
Maurice Richard, Mtl.	38
Bernie Geoffrion, Mtl.	38
Jean Beliveau, Mtl.	37
Sid Smith, Tor.	33
Gordie Howe, Det.	29
Danny Lewicki, NYR	29
Dutch Reibel, Det.	25
Leo Labine, Bos.	24
Ed Litzenberger, Mtl./Chi.	23
Don McKenney, Bos.	22
Ken Mosdell, Mtl.	22

ASSISTS

Name, Team	A
Bert Olmstead, Mtl.	48
Doug Harvey, Mtl.	43
Red Sullivan, Chi.	42
Ted Kennedy, Tor.	42
Dutch Reibel, Det.	41
Bernie Geoffrion, Mtl.	37
Maurice Richard, Mtl.	36
Jean Beliveau, Mtl.	36
Gordie Howe, Det.	33
Nick Mickoski, NYR/Chi.	33

GOALIE WINS

Name, Team	W
Terry Sawchuk, Det.	40
Jacques Plante, Mtl.	33
Harry Lumley, Tor.	23
John Henderson, Bos.	15
Gump Worsley, NYR	15
Al Rollins, Chi.	9
Jim Henry, Bos.	8
Charlie Hodge, Mtl.	6
Hank Bassen, Chi.	4
Glenn Hall, Det.	2
Johnny Bower, NYR	2

SHUTOUTS

Name, Team	SO
Terry Sawchuk, Det.	12
Harry Lumley, Tor.	8
John Henderson, Bos.	5
Jacques Plante, Mtl.	5
Gump Worsley, NYR	4
Charlie Hodge, Mtl.	1
Jim Henry, Bos.	1

PLAYOFF GOALS

Name, Team	G
Gordie Howe, Det.	9
Bernie Geoffrion, Mtl.	8
Floyd Curry, Mtl.	8
Ted Lindsay, Det.	7
Alex Delvecchio, Det.	7
Jean Beliveau, Mtl.	6
Dutch Reibel, Det.	5
Vic Stasiuk, Det.	5
Jack Leclair, Mtl.	5
Sid Smith, Tor.	3
Calum MacKay, Mtl.	3

PLAYOFF ASSISTS

Name, Team	A
Ted Lindsay, Det.	12
Gordie Howe, Det.	11
Alex Delvecchio, Det.	8
Calum MacKay, Mtl.	8
Doug Harvey, Mtl.	8
Dutch Reibel, Det.	7
Jean Beliveau, Mtl.	7
Ken Mosdell, Mtl.	7
Bill Quackenbush, Bos.	5
Bernie Geoffrion, Mtl.	5
Dickie Moore, Mtl.	5
Dollard St. Laurent, Mtl.	5

PLAYOFF GOALIE WINS

Name, Team	W
Terry Sawchuk, Det.	8
Jacques Plante, Mtl.	6
Jim Henry, Bos.	1
Charlie Hodge, Mtl.	1

PLAYOFF SHUTOUTS

Name, Team	SO
Terry Sawchuk, Det.	1

FIRST TEAM ALL-STARS

Name, Team	Position
Jean Beliveau, Mtl.	C
Maurice Richard, Mtl.	RW
Sid Smith, Tor.	LW
Doug Harvey, Mtl.	D
Red Kelly, Det.	D
Harry Lumley, Tor.	G

SECOND TEAM ALL-STARS

Name, Team	Position
Ken Mosdell, Mtl.	C
Bernie Geoffrion, Mtl.	RW
Danny Lewicki, NYR	LW
Bob Goldham, Det.	D
Fern Flaman, Bos.	D
Terry Sawchuk, Det.	G

1955 Playoffs

SEMI-FINALS

Mar.	22	Toronto	4	at	Detroit	7
Mar.	24	Toronto	1	at	Detroit	2
Mar.	26	Detroit	2	at	Toronto	1
Mar.	29	Detroit	3	at	Toronto	0

Detroit won best-of-seven series 4–0

Mar.	22	Boston	0	at	Montreal	2
Mar.	24	Boston	1	at	Montreal	3
Mar.	27	Montreal	2	at	Boston	4
Mar.	29	Montreal	4	at	Boston	3 OT
Mar.	31	Boston	1	at	Montreal	5

Montreal won best-of-seven series 4–1

FINALS

Apr.	3	Montreal	2	at	Detroit	4
Apr.	5	Montreal	1	at	Detroit	7
Apr.	7	Detroit	2	at	Montreal	4
Apr.	9	Detroit	3	at	Montreal	5
Apr.	10	Montreal	1	at	Detroit	5
Apr.	12	Detroit	3	at	Montreal	6
Apr.	14	Montreal	1	at	Detroit	3

Detroit won best-of-seven series 4–3

1954-55 – Detroit Red Wings – Terry Sawchuk, Red Kelly, Bob Goldham, Marcel Pronovost, Benny Woit, Jim Hay, Larry Hillman, Ted Lindsay (Captain), Tony Leswick, Gordie Howe, Alex Delvecchio, Marty Pavelich, Glen Skov, Dutch Reibel, Johnny Wilson, Bill Dineen, Vic Stasiuk, Marcel Bonin, Jack Adams (Manager), Jimmy Skinner (Coach), Carl Mattson (Trainer).

TROPHY WINNERS

Trophy	Awarded For	Winner	Team
Hart	MVP	Ted Kennedy	Tor.
Art Ross	Top Scorer	Bernie Geoffrion	Mtl.
Norris	Top Defenseman	Doug Harvey	Mtl.
Calder	Top Rookie	Ed Litzenberger	Chi.
Vezina	Fewest Goals Against	Terry Sawchuk	Det
Byng	Gentlemanly Conduct	Sid Smith	Tor.

NHL NOTEBOOK

TRANSACTIONS

- Nov. 9, 1954 – Boston traded Joe Klukay to Toronto in exchange for Leo Boivin.
- Nov. 15, 1954 – New York Rangers obtained Andy Bathgate and Vic Howe from Cleveland (AHL) in trade for Glen Sonmor and Eric Pogue.
- Nov. 23, 1954 – Chicago traded Pete Conacher and Bill Gadsby to NY Rangers in exchange for Allan Stanley, Nick Mickoski and Rich Lamoureux.
- Dec. 10, 1954 – Chicago Black Hawks purchased Ed Litzenberger from the Montreal Canadiens. He went on to win the Calder Trophy in 1954-55.

RECORDS

- Oct. 7, 1954 – Detroit beat the visiting Maple Leafs 2-1 and set an NHL record by extending their Opening Night undefeated streak to 15 games (14-0-1). The streak began in 1940.
- Dec. 9, 1954 – Toronto Maple Leafs and Montreal had a bench-clearing brawl that resulted in 15 misconducts and 36 penalties in all. The 36 penalties set a new NHL record, breaking the old mark of 35 set in 1931.
- Feb. 26, 1955 – Doug Harvey picked up his 41st assist of the season, to set a new NHL record for assists by a defenseman, as the Canadiens won 4-1 over the Bruins at the Forum. Harvey surpassed the old mark of 40 set by Toronto's Babe Pratt in 1943-44.
- Mar. 24, 1955 – Montreal captain Emile Bouchard established a new record by playing in his 102nd career Stanley Cup game, breaking the mark of 101 set by former Toronto goalie Turk Broda. Montreal won 3-1 over Boston, in game two of the semi-finals at the Forum.

MILESTONES

- Nov. 25, 1954 – Bill Mosienko became the first player in Chicago Black Hawks history to get career 250 goals when he scored in a 3-2 loss to the visiting Canadiens.
- Dec. 18, 1954 – Montreal's Maurice Richard became the first player in NHL history to score 400 career goals when the Canadiens defeated the Black Hawks 4-2 at Chicago.
- Mar. 20, 1955 – Detroit's Terry Sawchuk became the first goaltender in NHL history to get 40 (or more) wins three times in his career, when he picked up his 40th victory of the season in a 6-0 shutout over the visiting Montreal Canadiens.
- Apr. 12, 1955 – Dick Irvin became the first coach in NHL history to win 100 career playoff games when the Montreal Canadiens beat Detroit 6-3 in game six of the Stanley Cup finals.

1955-56

Stanley Cup • Montreal Canadiens

FINAL STANDINGS

Team	GP	W	L	T	GF	GA	PTS
Montreal	70	45	15	10	222	131	100
Detroit	70	30	24	16	183	148	76
New York	70	32	28	10	204	203	74
Toronto	70	24	33	13	153	181	61
Boston	70	23	34	13	147	185	59
Chicago	70	19	39	12	155	216	50

LEADING SCORERS

Player	Club	GP	G	A	PTS	PIM
Jean Beliveau	Montreal	70	47	41	88	143
Gordie Howe	Detroit	70	38	41	79	100
Maurice Richard	Montreal	70	38	33	71	89
Bert Olmstead	Montreal	70	14	56	70	94
Tod Sloan	Toronto	70	37	29	66	100
Andy Bathgate	NY Rangers	70	19	47	66	59
Bernie Geoffrion	Montreal	59	29	33	62	66
Dutch Reibel	Detroit	68	17	39	56	10
Alex Delvecchio	Detroit	70	25	26	51	24
Dave Creighton	NY Rangers	70	20	31	51	43
Bill Gadsby	NY Rangers	70	9	42	51	84
Ted Lindsay	Detroit	67	27	23	50	161
Red Kelly	Detroit	70	16	34	50	39
Dickie Moore	Montreal	70	11	39	50	55
George Armstrong	Toronto	67	16	32	48	97
Danny Lewicki	NY Rangers	70	18	27	45	26
Ron Murphy	NY Rangers	66	16	28	44	71
Doug Harvey	Montreal	62	5	39	44	60
Dean Prentice	NY Rangers	70	24	18	42	44
Wally Hergesheimer	NY Rangers	70	22	18	40	26
Henri Richard	Montreal	64	19	21	40	46
Red Sullivan	Chicago	63	14	26	40	58
Nick Mickoski	Chicago	70	19	20	39	52
Larry Popein	NY Rangers	64	14	25	39	37
Ed Litzenberger	Chicago	70	10	29	39	36

LEADING GOALTENDERS

Goaltender	Club	GPI	MINS	GA	SO	AVG
Jacques Plante	Montreal	64	3840	119	7	1.86
Glenn Hall	Detroit	70	4200	147	12	2.10
Terry Sawchuk	Boston	68	4080	177	9	2.60
Harry Lumley	Toronto	59	3527	157	3	2.67
Gump Worsley	NY Rangers	70	4200	198	4	2.83
Al Rollins	Chicago	58	3480	171	3	2.95

LEADING PLAYOFF SCORERS

Player	Club	GP	G	A	PTS	PIM
Jean Beliveau	Montreal	10	12	7	19	22
Bernie Geoffrion	Montreal	10	5	9	14	6
Maurice Richard	Montreal	10	5	9	14	24
Bert Olmstead	Montreal	10	4	10	14	8
Gordie Howe	Detroit	10	3	9	12	8
Alex Delvecchio	Detroit	10	7	3	10	2
Ted Lindsay	Detroit	10	6	3	9	22
Dickie Moore	Montreal	10	3	6	9	12
Henri Richard	Montreal	10	4	4	8	21
Doug Harvey	Montreal	10	2	5	7	10

LEADING PLAYOFF GOALTENDERS

Goaltender	Club	GPI	MINS	GA	SO	AVG
Jacques Plante	Montreal	10	600	18	2	1.80
Harry Lumley	Toronto	5	304	13	1	2.57
Glenn Hall	Detroit	10	604	28	0	2.78

Jean Beliveau (left) led the NHL in both goals and points in 1955–56, while linemate Bert Olmstead (right) led the loop in assists. For Beliveau, this season marked the first of ten Stanley Cup titles. Olmstead had already won one in 1953. He would be dealt to Toronto in 1958 and later helped launch the Leafs dynasty of the early 1960s.

THE SHIFT IN POWER was completed this season, as the Canadiens dominated from start to finish. Probably sensing the change, Detroit's Jack Adams stunned Terry Sawchuk by trading him to Boston, where he did not prosper. Seven other Wings left, but the players who came in return did not inspire the club.

Montreal perfected its awesome lineup with Bob Turner, Henri Richard and Claude Provost, not to mention new coach Toe Blake, who was exactly the right man for the job. As an ex-Canadien and former linemate of the Rocket, he commanded everyone's respect. The offense became so creatively unstoppable that Jean Beliveau scored a hat trick during one powerplay. Fearing that games would get out of hand, the league changed the penalty rule the following year so that minor penalties would end after one goal against the offending team. Defense was perhaps the key to Montreal's rise, though, as Jacques Plante and his blueliners built a wall around their net. The result was a season that arguably eclipsed any of Detroit's feats earlier in the decade.

Le Gros Bill – Since arriving in the NHL, Jean Beliveau faced immense pressure and media scrutiny. He silenced critics by tussling with on-ice tormentors, snagging the scoring title and grabbing the MVP award.

Another team that improved, but far more modestly, was the Rangers. Rookie coach Phil Watson pulled the right strings with fine players such as Andy Bathgate, Dave Creighton and Dean Prentice, while defenseman Bill Gadsby finished in a tie for tenth on the scoring list. The declining Leafs only made the playoffs because Boston and Chicago were weak. The team that never scores a goal—the referees and linesmen—also changed its game. Bill Chadwick devised a series of hand signals to indicate infractions and calls, and the modern craft of refereeing took shape.

In the postseason, the Rangers lost four games to one to Montreal, twice allowing seven goals in a game. Detroit, boosted by rookie netminder Glenn Hall, edged Toronto in five games. The Leafs could hardly score against Hall but Montreal had the talent to do so, netting 11 in the first two games of the finals. The rest of the series featured more defensive hockey, but the damage had been done and Montreal took Lord Stanley's trophy with ease and grace. Beliveau confirmed his scoring title by dominating the playoffs, notching seven goals in the last round, a modern record.

Leaders, 1955-56

GOALS

Name, Team	G
Jean Beliveau, Mtl.	47
Gordie Howe, Det.	38
Maurice Richard, Mtl.	38
Tod Sloan, Tor.	37
Bernie Geoffrion, Mtl.	29
Ted Lindsay, Det.	27
Alex Delvecchio, Det.	25
Dean Prentice, NYR	24
Andy Hebenton, NYR	24
Johnny Wilson, Chi.	24

ASSISTS

Name, Team	A
Bert Olmstead, Mtl.	56
Andy Bathgate, NYR	47
Bill Gadsby, NYR	42
Jean Beliveau, Mtl.	41
Gordie Howe, Det.	41
Doug Harvey, Mtl.	39
Dutch Reibel, Det.	39
Dickie Moore, Mtl.	39
Red Kelly, Det.	34
Bernie Geoffrion, Mtl.	33
Maurice Richard, Mtl.	33

GOALIE WINS

Name, Team	W
Jacques Plante, Mtl.	42
Gump Worsley, NYR	32
Glenn Hall, Det.	30
Terry Sawchuk, Bos.	22
Harry Lumley, Tor.	21
Al Rollins, Chi.	17
Bob Perreault, Mtl.	3
Ed Chadwick, Tor.	2
Hank Bassen, Chi.	2
Claude Pronovost, Bos.	1
Gilles Mayer, Tor.	1

SHUTOUTS

Name, Team	SO
Glenn Hall, Det.	12
Terry Sawchuk, Bos.	9
Jacques Plante, Mtl.	7
Gump Worsley, NYR	4
Al Rollins, Chi.	3
Harry Lumley, Tor.	3
Ed Chadwick, Tor.	2
Claude Pronovost, Bos.	1
Bob Perreault, Mtl.	1
Hank Bassen, Chi.	1

PLAYOFF GOALS

Name, Team	G
Jean Beliveau, Mtl.	12
Alex Delvecchio, Det.	7
Ted Lindsay, Det.	6
Bernie Geoffrion, Mtl.	5
Maurice Richard, Mtl.	5
George Armstrong, Tor.	4
Bert Olmstead, Mtl.	4
Henri Richard, Mtl.	4
Gordie Howe, Det.	3
Dickie Moore, Mtl.	3
Claude Provost, Mtl.	3

PLAYOFF ASSISTS

Name, Team	A
Bert Olmstead, Mtl.	10
Bernie Geoffrion, Mtl.	9
Maurice Richard, Mtl.	9
Gordie Howe, Det.	9
Jean Beliveau, Mtl.	7
Dickie Moore, Mtl.	6
Doug Harvey, Mtl.	5
Floyd Curry, Mtl.	5
Dick Duff, Tor.	4
Henri Richard, Mtl.	4
Red Kelly, Det.	4

PLAYOFF GOALIE WINS

Name, Team	W
Jacques Plante, Mtl.	8
Glenn Hall, Det.	5
Gordie Bell, NYR	1
Harry Lumley, Tor.	1

PLAYOFF SHUTOUTS

Name, Team	SO
Jacques Plante, Mtl.	2
Harry Lumley, Tor.	1

FIRST TEAM ALL-STARS

Name, Team	Position
Jean Beliveau, Mtl.	C
Maurice Richard, Mtl.	RW
Ted Lindsay, Det.	LW
Doug Harvey, Mtl.	D
Bill Gadsby, NYR	D
Jacques Plante, Mtl.	G

SECOND TEAM ALL-STARS

Name, Team	Position
Tod Sloan, Tor.	C
Gordie Howe, Det.	RW
Bert Olmstead, Mtl.	LW
Red Kelly, Det.	D
Tom Johnson, Mtl.	D
Glenn Hall, Det.	G

1956 Playoffs

SEMI-FINALS

Date	Visitor	Score		Home	Score	
Mar. 20	NY Rangers	1	at	Montreal	7	
Mar. 22	NY Rangers	4	at	Montreal	2	
Mar. 24	Montreal	3	at	NY Rangers	1	
Mar. 25	Montreal	5	at	NY Rangers	3	
Mar. 27	NY Rangers	0	at	Montreal	7	

Montreal won best-of-seven series 4–1

Date	Visitor	Score		Home	Score	
Mar. 20	Toronto	2	at	Detroit	3	
Mar. 22	Toronto	1	at	Detroit	3	
Mar. 24	Detroit	5	at	Toronto	4	OT
Mar. 27	Detroit	0	at	Toronto	2	
Mar. 29	Toronto	1	at	Detroit	3	

Detroit won best-of-seven series 4–1

FINALS

Date	Visitor	Score		Home	Score
Mar. 31	Detroit	4	at	Montreal	6
Apr. 3	Detroit	1	at	Montreal	5
Apr. 5	Montreal	1	at	Detroit	3
Apr. 8	Montreal	3	at	Detroit	0
Apr. 10	Detroit	1	at	Montreal	3

Montreal won best-of-seven series 4–1

1955-56 – Montreal Canadiens – Jacques Plante, Doug Harvey, Butch Bouchard (Captain), Bob Turner, Tom Johnson, Jean-Guy Talbot, Dollard St. Laurent, Jean Béliveau, Bernie Geoffrion, Bert Olmstead, Floyd Curry, Jack Leclair, Maurice Richard, Dickie Moore, Henri Richard, Ken Mosdell, Don Marshall, Claude Provost, Charlie Hodge, Frank Selke (Manager), Toe Blake (Coach), Hector Dubois (Trainer).

TROPHY WINNERS

Trophy	Awarded For	Winner	Team
Hart	MVP	Jean Beliveau	Mtl.
Art Ross	Top Scorer	Jean Beliveau	Mtl.
Norris	Top Defenseman	Doug Harvey	Mtl.
Calder	Top Rookie	Glenn Hall	Det.
Vezina	Fewest Goals Against	Jacques Plante	Mtl.
Byng	Gentlemanly Conduct	Earl Reibel	Det

NHL NOTEBOOK

TRANSACTIONS

- Apr. 28, 1955 – New York Rangers purchased Andy Hebenton from the Victoria Cougars (WHL).
- June 3 1955 – Boston obtained Terry Sawchuk, Vic Stasiuk, Marcel Bonin and Lorne Davis from Detroit for Real Chevrefils, Ed Sandford, Norm Corcoran, Gilles Boisvert and Warren Godfrey.
- Oct. 13, 1955 – Montreal signed Henri Richard.

RECORDS

- Oct. 6, 1955 – Detroit goaltender Glenn Hall began an NHL-record 502 complete game streak, when he was in the nets in a 3-2 Red Wings loss to Chicago. The streak ended seven years later.
- Oct. 29, 1955 – Detroit's Ted Lindsay scored his 271st career goal to set a new NHL career scoring record for left wingers. The goal came in a 2-1 loss to the Canadiens in Montreal. Lindsay broke the record of 270 set by Aurel Joliat.
- Feb. 22, 1956 – Toronto Maple Leafs beat the Rangers 4-2 as Lou Fontinato set a new NHL penalty minute record; his 169 PIM for the season broke the old record of 167 set by Red Horner in 1935-36.
- Mar. 4, 1956 – Jean Beliveau scored twice (in a 6-4 Montreal win at Detroit) to give him 45 for the year, a new record for centers. Joe Malone set the original mark in 1917-18, the first NHL season.
- Mar. 18, 1956 – Montreal's Bert Olmstead set an NHL single-season record with his 56th assist as the Canadiens won 3-1 over the Rangers in New York. Olmstead broke the record of 55 set by Ted Lindsay in 1949-50.

MILESTONES

- Nov. 5, 1955 – Jean Beliveau scored four goals, including three during one powerplay in a span of :44 in the second period. Canadiens won the game 4-2 over Boston. After the season, the NHL changed the rules to end a minor powerplay after a goal was scored.
- Dec. 29, 1955 – In a game between Montreal and Toronto, NHL officials wore new vertically striped black and white sweaters for the first time. Canadiens won the game 5-2.
- Mar. 18, 1956 – Dick Irvin won his 692nd (and final) career game as an coach, when the Black Hawks won 3-2 in Boston, on the final night of the season.

1956-57

Stanley Cup • Montreal Canadiens

FINAL STANDINGS

Team	GP	W	L	T	GF	GA	PTS
Detroit	70	38	20	12	198	157	88
Montreal	70	35	23	12	210	155	82
Boston	70	34	24	12	195	174	80
New York	70	26	30	14	184	227	66
Toronto	70	21	34	15	174	192	57
Chicago	70	16	39	15	169	225	47

LEADING SCORERS

Player	Club	GP	G	A	PTS	PIM
Gordie Howe	Detroit	70	44	45	89	72
Ted Lindsay	Detroit	70	30	55	85	103
Jean Beliveau	Montreal	69	33	51	84	105
Andy Bathgate	NY Rangers	70	27	50	77	60
Ed Litzenberger	Chicago	70	32	32	64	48
Maurice Richard	Montreal	63	33	29	62	74
Don McKenney	Boston	69	21	39	60	31
Dickie Moore	Montreal	70	29	29	58	56
Henri Richard	Montreal	63	18	36	54	71
Norm Ullman	Detroit	64	16	36	52	47
Doug Harvey	Montreal	70	6	44	50	92
Real Chevrefils	Boston	70	31	17	48	38
Johnny Wilson	Chicago	70	18	30	48	24
Bert Olmstead	Montreal	64	15	33	48	74
Leo Labine	Boston	67	18	29	47	128
Andy Hebenton	NY Rangers	70	21	23	44	10
George Armstrong	Toronto	54	18	26	44	37
Dean Prentice	NY Rangers	68	19	23	42	38
Glen Skov	Chicago	67	14	28	42	69
Sid Smith	Toronto	70	17	24	41	4
Alex Delvecchio	Detroit	48	16	25	41	8
Bill Gadsby	NY Rangers	70	4	37	41	72
Dick Duff	Toronto	70	26	14	40	50
Vic Stasiuk	Boston	64	24	16	40	69
Bernie Geoffrion	Montreal	41	19	21	40	18
Doug Mohns	Boston	68	6	34	40	89

LEADING GOALTENDERS

Goaltender	Club	GPI	MINS	GA	SO	AVG
Jacques Plante	Montreal	61	3660	122	9	2.00
Glenn Hall	Detroit	70	4200	155	4	2.21
Terry Sawchuk	Boston	34	2040	81	2	2.38
Don Simmons	Boston	26	1560	63	4	2.42
Ed Chadwick	Toronto	70	4200	186	5	2.66
Gump Worsley	NY Rangers	68	4080	216	3	3.18
Al Rollins	Chicago	70	4200	224	3	3.20

LEADING PLAYOFF SCORERS

Player	Club	GP	G	A	PTS	PIM
Bernie Geoffrion	Montreal	10	11	7	18	2
Jean Beliveau	Montreal	10	6	6	12	15
Maurice Richard	Montreal	10	8	3	11	8
Dickie Moore	Montreal	10	3	7	10	4
Bert Olmstead	Montreal	10	0	9	9	13
Fleming MacKell	Boston	10	5	3	8	4
Henri Richard	Montreal	10	2	6	8	10
Gordie Howe	Detroit	5	2	5	7	6
Doug Harvey	Montreal	10	0	7	7	10
Ted Lindsay	Detroit	5	2	4	6	8
Don McKenney	Boston	10	1	5	6	4

LEADING PLAYOFF GOALTENDERS

Goaltender	Club	GPI	MINS	GA	SO	AVG
Jacques Plante	Montreal	10	616	17	1	1.66
Don Simmons	Boston	10	600	29	2	2.90
Glenn Hall	Detroit	5	300	15	0	3.00
Gump Worsley	NY Rangers	5	316	21	0	3.99

Ted Lindsay looks ready to attack Toronto's Rudy Migay in front of the Red Wings net. With 30 goals and a league-leading 55 assists in 1956–57, Lindsay enjoyed the most productive season of his career yet he was dealt to Chicago at year's end because of his role in organizing a players' association.

BOSTON AND NEW YORK provided surprises by both making the playoffs this season. The Bruins did it largely without Terry Sawchuk—Don Simmons was a fine replacement for the ill and temporarily-retired star—while the Rangers succeeded in spite of a shaky defense. Toronto was rebuilding with kids like Bob Baun and Bob Pulford and was not yet ready to win. Coach Howie Meeker asked his friend Ted Kennedy to come out of retirement, and he managed to play 30 games. The Canadiens, slowed by injuries, had only a respectable year, allowing Detroit to take first place.

The Habs Have It – The Rocket, the Pocket, Le Gros Bill and Digger finished in the top ten, Plante won the Vezina again as Montreal vanquished the Rangers and Bruins to win their second straight Cup.

Television coverage of the league extended south of the Canadian border this year when CBS showed a game between New York and Chicago from Madison Square Garden. It was an experiment, not a regular feature. Still the network would have been better served if it had picked a Christmas Day contest in Detroit for the show. In his 26 years on NHL ice, Gordie Howe never had another game like it, piling up three goals and three assists against the Rangers. Ten days earlier, he had passed Nels Stewart for second place on the all-time goal list. Although "Mr. Hockey" was the MVP this year, linemate Ted Lindsay had a superb season and was arguably just as valuable even though his days with the Red Wings were numbered.

When he spearheaded the formation of the players' association in February, Lindsay set the stage for his own exit. The angry owners would not tolerate any threat to their power, so after the season Ted was traded to Chicago along with Glenn Hall. Lindsay would prove to be an immense help to his new teammates on and off the ice. Hall later stated that "Terrible Ted" taught the Hawks how to win.

The semi-finals saw an underdog Boston club triumph over Detroit, while the Canadiens handled New York with little trouble. Maurice Richard scored four against the Bruins in the opener of the finals, tying a playoff record held by none other than Lindsay. Jacques Plante recorded one shutout as the Bruins fell in five matches. Montreal was just beginning its Cup streak.

Leaders, 1956-57

GOALS

Name, Team	G
Gordie Howe, Det.	44
Maurice Richard, Mtl.	33
Jean Beliveau, Mtl.	33
Ed Litzenberger, Chi.	32
Real Chevrefils, Bos.	31
Ted Lindsay, Det.	30
Dickie Moore, Mtl.	29
Andy Bathgate, NYR	27
Dick Duff, Tor.	26
Vic Stasiuk, Bos.	24

ASSISTS

Name, Team	A
Ted Lindsay, Det.	55
Jean Beliveau, Mtl.	51
Andy Bathgate, NYR	50
Gordie Howe, Det.	45
Doug Harvey, Mtl.	44
Don McKenney, Bos.	39
Bill Gadsby, NYR	37
Henri Richard, Mtl.	36
Norm Ullman, Det.	36
Doug Mohns, Bos.	34
Bert Olmstead, Mtl.	33

GOALIE WINS

Name, Team	W
Glenn Hall, Det.	38
Jacques Plante, Mtl.	31
Gump Worsley, NYR	26
Ed Chadwick, Tor.	21
Terry Sawchuk, Bos.	18
Al Rollins, Chi.	16
Don Simmons, Bos.	13
Gerry McNeil, Mtl.	4
Norm Defelice, Bos.	3

SHUTOUTS

Name, Team	SO
Jacques Plante, Mtl.	9
Ed Chadwick, Tor.	5
Don Simmons, Bos.	4
Glenn Hall, Det.	4
Gump Worsley, NYR	3
Al Rollins, Chi.	3
Terry Sawchuk, Bos.	2

PLAYOFF GOALS

Name, Team	G
Bernie Geoffrion, Mtl.	11
Maurice Richard, Mtl.	8
Jean Beliveau, Mtl.	6
Fleming MacKell, Bos.	5
Alex Delvecchio, Det.	3
Dickie Moore, Mtl.	3
Leo Labine, Bos.	3
Floyd Curry, Mtl.	3
15 tied with	2

PLAYOFF ASSISTS

Name, Team	A
Bert Olmstead, Mtl.	9
Bernie Geoffrion, Mtl.	7
Dickie Moore, Mtl.	7
Doug Harvey, Mtl.	7
Jean Beliveau, Mtl.	6
Henri Richard, Mtl.	6
Gordie Howe, Det.	5
Don McKenney, Bos.	5
Ted Lindsay, Det.	4
10 tied with	3

PLAYOFF GOALIE WINS

Name, Team	W
Jacques Plante, Mtl.	8
Don Simmons, Bos.	5
Glenn Hall, Det.	1
Gump Worsley, NYR	1

PLAYOFF SHUTOUTS

Name, Team	SO
Don Simmons, Bos.	2
Jacques Plante, Mtl.	1

FIRST TEAM ALL-STARS

Name, Team	Position
Jean Beliveau, Mtl.	C
Gordie Howe, Det.	RW
Ted Lindsay, Det.	LW
Doug Harvey, Mtl.	D
Red Kelly, Det.	D
Glenn Hall, Det.	G

SECOND TEAM ALL-STARS

Name, Team	Position
Eddie Litzenberger, Chi.	C
Maurice Richard, Mtl.	RW
Real Chevrefils, Bos.	LW
Fern Flaman, Bos.	D
Bill Gadsby, NYR	D
Jacques Plante, Mtl.	G

1957 Playoffs

SEMI-FINALS

Date	Team	Score		Team	Score
Mar. 26	Boston	3	at	Detroit	1
Mar. 28	Boston	2	at	Detroit	7
Mar. 31	Detroit	3	at	Boston	4
Apr. 2	Detroit	0	at	Boston	2
Apr. 4	Boston	4	at	Detroit	3

Boston won best-of-seven series 4–1

Date	Team	Score		Team	Score
Mar. 26	Montreal	4	at	NY Rangers	1
Mar. 28	Montreal	3	at	NY Rangers	4 OT
Mar. 30	NY Rangers	3	at	Montreal	8
Apr. 2	NY Rangers	1	at	Montreal	3
Apr. 4	NY Rangers	3	at	Montreal	4 OT

Montreal won best-of-seven series 4–1

FINALS

Date	Team	Score		Team	Score
Apr. 6	Boston	1	at	Montreal	5
Apr. 9	Boston	0	at	Montreal	1
Apr. 11	Montreal	4	at	Boston	2
Apr. 14	Montreal	0	at	Boston	2
Apr. 16	Boston	1	at	Montreal	5

Montreal won best-of-seven series 4–1

1956-57 – Montreal Canadiens – Jacques Plante, Gerry McNeil, Doug Harvey, Tom Johnson, Bob Turner, Dollard St. Laurent, Jean-Guy Talbot, Jean Béliveau, Bernie Geoffrion, Floyd Curry, Dickie Moore, Maurice Richard (Captain), Claude Provost, Bert Olmstead, Henri Richard, Phil Goyette, Don Marshall, André Pronovost, Connie Broden, Frank Selke (Manager), Toe Blake (Coach), Hector Dubois, Larry Aubut (Trainers).

TROPHY WINNERS

Trophy	Awarded For	Winner	Team
Hart	MVP	Gordie Howe	Det.
Art Ross	Top Scorer	Gordie Howe	Det.
Norris	Top Defenseman	Doug Harvey	Mtl.
Calder	Top Rookie	Larry Regan	Bos.
Vezina	Fewest Goals Against	Jacques Plante	Mtl.
Byng	Gentlemanly Conduct	Andy Hebenton	NYR

NHL NOTEBOOK

TRANSACTIONS

- May 21, 1956 – Chicago Black Hawks purchased Eric Nesterenko and veteran goaltender Harry Lumley from Toronto for $40,000.
- May 24, 1956 – Chicago Black Hawks purchased Ken Mosdell, along with Eddie Mazur and Bud MacPherson from Montreal.
- Sept. 19, 1956 – Chicago obtained Wally Hergesheimer from NY Rangers for Red Sullivan.
- Oct. 8, 1956 – Boston purchased Allan Stanley from Chicago.
- Jan. 22, 1957 – Boston Bruins obtained goaltender Don Simmons from Springfield for Norm Defelice, Jack Bionda and cash.

RECORDS

- Dec. 25, 1956 – Gordie Howe scored his 12th career hat trick and added three assists, as the Red Wings beat the Rangers 8-1 at the Olympia in Detroit. It was the biggest scoring night of Howe's 26-year NHL career.
- Apr. 6, 1957 – Maurice Richard tied Newsy Lalonde and Ted Lindsay for the NHL record with four goals in one Stanley Cup finals game, leading Montreal to 5-1 playoff win over Bruins in game one.

MILESTONES

- Dec. 15, 1956 – When Detroit beat Chicago 5-1 Gordie Howe scored twice to bring his career total to 326 goals, topping the record of Nels Stewart. He was now second to Maurice Richard who had 469 career goals at this date.
- Jan. 5, 1957 – CBS television became the first U.S. network to televise an NHL game as the host New York Rangers beat Chicago 4-1 in an afternoon game, at Madison Square Garden.
- Jan. 6, 1957 – Toronto's Ted Kennedy came out of retirement (after a year and a half) to help the Leafs for the remainder of the 1956-57 season. Kennedy went on to score six goals and 16 assists, for 22 points in 30 games.
- Feb. 11, 1957 – The NHL Players Association was formed, with Detroit's Ted Lindsay elected as the first president.

1957-58

Stanley Cup • Montreal Canadiens

Team	GP	W	L	T	GF	GA	PTS
Montreal	70	43	17	10	250	158	96
New York	70	32	25	13	195	188	77
Detroit	70	29	29	12	176	207	70
Boston	70	27	28	15	199	194	69
Chicago	70	24	39	7	163	202	55
Toronto	70	21	38	11	192	226	53

LEADING SCORERS

Player	Club	GP	G	A	PTS	PIM
Dickie Moore	Montreal	70	36	48	84	65
Henri Richard	Montreal	67	28	52	80	56
Andy Bathgate	NY Rangers	65	30	48	78	42
Gordie Howe	Detroit	64	33	44	77	40
Bronco Horvath	Boston	67	30	36	66	71
Ed Litzenberger	Chicago	70	32	30	62	63
Fleming MacKell	Boston	70	20	40	60	72
Jean Beliveau	Montreal	55	27	32	59	93
Alex Delvecchio	Detroit	70	21	38	59	22
Don McKenney	Boston	70	28	30	58	22
Camille Henry	NY Rangers	70	32	24	56	2
Vic Stasiuk	Boston	70	21	35	56	55
John Bucyk	Boston	68	21	31	52	57
Dave Creighton	NY Rangers	70	17	35	52	40
Norm Ullman	Detroit	69	23	28	51	38
Claude Provost	Montreal	70	19	32	51	71
Bernie Geoffrion	Montreal	42	27	23	50	51
Dick Duff	Toronto	65	26	23	49	79
Jerry Toppazzini	Boston	64	25	24	49	51
Bobby Hull	Chicago	70	13	34	47	62
Bill Gadsby	NY Rangers	65	14	32	46	48
Red Sullivan	NY Rangers	70	11	35	46	61
Phil Goyette	Montreal	70	9	37	46	8
Andy Hebenton	NY Rangers	70	21	24	45	17
Billy Harris	Toronto	68	16	28	44	32

LEADING GOALTENDERS

Goaltender	Club	GPI	MINS	GA	SO	AVG
Jacques Plante	Montreal	57	3386	119	9	2.11
Gump Worsley	NY Rangers	37	2220	86	4	2.32
Don Simmons	Boston	39	2288	92	5	2.41
Glenn Hall	Chicago	70	4200	200	7	2.86
Terry Sawchuk	Detroit	70	4200	206	3	2.94
Marcel Paille	NY Rangers	33	1980	102	1	3.09
Ed Chadwick	Toronto	70	4200	223	4	3.19

1957-58

LEADING PLAYOFF SCORERS

Player	Club	GP	G	A	PTS	PIM
Fleming MacKell	Boston	12	5	14	19	12
Don McKenney	Boston	12	9	8	17	0
Maurice Richard	Montreal	10	11	4	15	10
Doug Mohns	Boston	12	3	10	13	18
Jerry Toppazzini	Boston	12	9	3	12	2
Jean Beliveau	Montreal	10	4	8	12	10
Bernie Geoffrion	Montreal	10	6	5	11	2
Dickie Moore	Montreal	10	4	7	11	4
Larry Regan	Boston	12	3	8	11	6
Doug Harvey	Montreal	10	2	9	11	16

LEADING PLAYOFF GOALTENDERS

Goaltender	Club	GPI	MINS	GA	SO	AVG
Jacques Plante	Montreal	10	618	20	1	1.94
Don Simmons	Boston	11	671	25	1	2.24
Terry Sawchuk	Detroit	4	252	19	0	4.52
Gump Worsley	NY Rangers	6	365	28	0	4.60

Montreal's Doug Harvey was the best defenseman in hockey during his heyday. He could check, block shots, rush the puck, stickhandle and pass, but what made him unique was the way he could combine his skills to control the pace of the game. Here, Harvey corrals a young Frank Mahovlich (who wore #26 early in his career) in front of Jacques Plante.

LABOR ISSUES ROSE TO THE FRONT, taking the focus off the ice at times. The fledgling players' association sued the league, claiming it ran a monopoly, and asking for more rights such as free agency (after five years of service). The owners would not recognize the union, which effectively stopped its development, but they did agree to a $7000 base salary and a few other proposals. One of the most important allowed a player, not his team, to determine when he was healthy enough to skate. It was a step forward for the players, and another breakthrough happened when Willie O'Ree arrived in January, becoming the first black man to play in the NHL. His feat did not receive widespread recognition at the time.

Dickie Gives Moore – A Pocket Rocket exploded, the Habs dominated, but a fiery winger known as "Digging Dicker" won hearts and the scoring crown despite playing three months with a broken wrist.

After missing much of the 1956–57 season, Jack Adams persuaded Terry Sawchuk to play again, thus replacing Glenn Hall with the very player he'd previously traded to clear a spot for. Detroit still couldn't post a winning mark, having lost too many key personnel. The Hawks improved a lot, yet weren't quite good enough, while the Leafs finished sixth and last. Apart from the superb Canadiens squad, the Rangers stood out by jumping to second. With two fine lines and a pair of excellent defensemen, they looked confident and dangerous.

Maurice Richard reached a great milestone in October when he scored goal number 500, making him the first player to do so. He wouldn't add much more to his total this year after a severed tendon caused him to miss over half the season. With the Rocket's career winding down, two players arrived who would challenge his scoring exploits, Frank Mahovlich and Bobby Hull. Mahovlich was the top rookie, although Hull looked just as good or better.

In the playoffs, Montreal exploded for 13 goals in its first two games against Detroit, then coasted to a sweep, while Boston took out New York in a highly offensive semifinal series. The Bruins battled hard in the final series against Montreal, but the Canadiens were simply superior in every department. The turning point was overtime of game five, as Richard's winning goal seemed to mark the end of Boston's bid for an upset. To their credit, the Bruins allowed only 16 goals in six games against the highest-scoring team the league had yet seen. It was now three Cup wins in a row and counting for the bleu, blanc et rouge. Still, Boston made a mark by becoming the first team to travel regularly by air. The era of long train rides was coming to an end.

Leaders, 1957-58

GOALS

Name, Team	G
Dickie Moore, Mtl.	36
Gordie Howe, Det.	33
Ed Litzenberger, Chi.	32
Camille Henry, NYR	32
Andy Bathgate, NYR	30
Bronco Horvath, Bos.	30
Henri Richard, Mtl.	28
Don McKenney, Bos.	28
Bernie Geoffrion, Mtl.	27
Jean Beliveau, Mtl.	27

ASSISTS

Name, Team	A
Henri Richard, Mtl.	52
Andy Bathgate, NYR	48
Dickie Moore, Mtl.	48
Gordie Howe, Det.	44
Fleming MacKell, Bos.	40
Alex Delvecchio, Det.	38
Phil Goyette, Mtl.	37
Bronco Horvath, Bos.	36
Vic Stasiuk, Bos.	35
Dave Creighton, NYR	35
Red Sullivan, NYR	35

GOALIE WINS

Name, Team	W
Jacques Plante, Mtl.	34
Terry Sawchuk, Det.	29
Glenn Hall, Chi.	24
Gump Worsley, NYR	21
Ed Chadwick, Tor.	21
Don Simmons, Bos.	15
Harry Lumley, Bos.	11
Marcel Paille, NYR	11
Charlie Hodge, Mtl.	8
Len Broderick, Mtl.	1
Al Millar, Bos.	1

SHUTOUTS

Name, Team	SO
Jacques Plante, Mtl.	9
Glenn Hall, Chi.	7
Don Simmons, Bos.	5
Gump Worsley, NYR	4
Ed Chadwick, Tor.	4
Harry Lumley, Bos.	3
Terry Sawchuk, Det.	3
Charlie Hodge, Mtl.	1
Marcel Paille, NYR	1

PLAYOFF GOALS

Name, Team	G
Maurice Richard, Mtl.	11
Don McKenney, Bos.	9
Jerry Toppazzini, Bos.	9
Bernie Geoffrion, Mtl.	6
Andy Bathgate, NYR	5
Fleming MacKell, Bos.	5
Bronco Horvath, Bos.	5
Jean Beliveau, Mtl.	4
Dickie Moore, Mtl.	4
Phil Goyette, Mtl.	4
Norm Johnson, Bos.	4

PLAYOFF ASSISTS

Name, Team	A
Fleming MacKell, Bos.	14
Doug Mohns, Bos.	10
Doug Harvey, Mtl.	9
Jean Beliveau, Mtl.	8
Don McKenney, Bos.	8
Larry Regan, Bos.	8
Dickie Moore, Mtl.	7
Henri Richard, Mtl.	7
Bernie Geoffrion, Mtl.	5
Vic Stasiuk, Bos.	5

PLAYOFF GOALIE WINS

Name, Team	W
Jacques Plante, Mtl.	8
Don Simmons, Bos.	6
Gump Worsley, NYR	2

PLAYOFF SHUTOUTS

Name, Team	SO
Jacques Plante, Mtl.	1
Don Simmons, Bos.	1

FIRST TEAM ALL-STARS

Name, Team	Position
Henri Richard, Mtl.	C
Gordie Howe, Det.	RW
Dickie Moore, Mtl.	LW
Doug Harvey, Mtl.	D
Bill Gadsby, NYR	D
Glenn Hall, Chi.	G

SECOND TEAM ALL-STARS

Name, Team	Position
Jean Beliveau, Mtl.	C
Andy Bathgate, NYR	RW
Camille Henry, NYR	LW
Fern Flaman, Bos.	D
Marcel Pronovost, Det.	D
Jacques Plante, Mtl.	G

1958 Playoffs

SEMI-FINALS

Mar. 25	Detroit	1	at	Montreal	8	
Mar. 27	Detroit	1	at	Montreal	5	
Mar. 30	Montreal	2	at	Detroit	1	OT
Apr. 1	Montreal	4	at	Detroit	3	

Montreal won best-of-seven series 4–0

Mar. 25	Boston	3	at	NY Rangers	5	
Mar. 27	Boston	4	at	NY Rangers	3	OT
Mar. 29	NY Rangers	0	at	Boston	5	
Apr. 1	NY Rangers	5	at	Boston	2	
Apr. 3	NY Rangers	1	at	Boston	6	
Apr. 5	NY Rangers	2	at	Boston	8	

Boston won best-of-seven series 4–2

FINALS

Apr. 8	Boston	1	at	Montreal	2	
Apr. 10	Boston	5	at	Montreal	2	
Apr. 13	Montreal	3	at	Boston	0	
Apr. 15	Montreal	1	at	Boston	3	
Apr. 17	Boston	2	at	Montreal	3	OT
Apr. 20	Montreal	5	at	Boston	3	

Montreal won best-of-seven series 4–2

1957-58 – Montreal Canadiens – Jacques Plante, Gerry McNeil, Doug Harvey, Tom Johnson, Bob Turner, Dollard St. Laurent, Jean-Guy Talbot, Albert Langlois, Jean Béliveau, Bernie Geoffrion, Maurice Richard (Captain), Dickie Moore, Claude Provost, Floyd Curry, Bert Olmstead, Henri Richard, Marcel Bonin, Phil Goyette, Don Marshall, André Pronovost, Connie Broden, Ab McDonald, Frank Selke (Manager), Toe Blake (Coach), Hector Dubois, Larry Aubut (Trainers).

TROPHY WINNERS

Trophy	Awarded For	Winner	Team
Hart	MVP	Gordie Howe	Det.
Art Ross	Top Scorer	Dickie Moore	Mtl.
Norris	Top Defenseman	Doug Harvey	Mtl.
Calder	Top Rookie	Frank Mahovlich	Tor.
Vezina	Fewest Goals Against	Jacques Plante	Mtl.
Byng	Gentlemanly Conduct	Camille Henry	NYR

NHL NOTEBOOK

TRANSACTIONS

- June 4, 1957 – Boston Bruins acquired Bronco Horvath from the Montreal Canadiens during the NHL's annual Intra-League Draft.
- July 10, 1957 Detroit Red Wings obtained goalie Terry Sawchuk from Boston for Johnny Bucyk.
- July 23, 1957 Detroit traded Ted Lindsay and Glenn Hall to Chicago in exchange for Johnny Wilson, Hank Bassen, Forbes Kennedy and Bob Preston.
- Dec. 17, 1957 – Chicago traded Nick Mickoski, Jack McIntyre, Bob Bailey and Hec Lalonde to Detroit for Earl Reibel, Billy Dea, Bill Dineen and Lorne Ferguson. At the time it was the largest trade in NHL history.

RECORDS

- Nov. 9, 1957 – Montreal's Claude Provost scored just four seconds into the second period to set an NHL record for fastest goal from start of a period. Canadiens beat Boston 4-2.
- Nov. 28, 1957 – Gordie Howe picked up an assist during Detroit's 3-3 tie against Toronto to become the NHL's all time assist leader, with 409. He broke the record set by Montreal's Elmer Lach.
- Jan. 18, 1958 – Boston's Harry Lumley set an NHL record when his first shutout of the season (a 3-0 win over Montreal) gave him one (or more) shutouts in 14 straight seasons. He broke the record of 13 straight seasons set by John Ross Roach (1922-23 thru 1934-35).

MILESTONES

- Oct. 19, 1957 – Montreal's Maurice Richard became the first player in NHL history to score 500 career goals. It came in his 863rd career game as the Canadiens beat Chicago 3-1.
- Oct. 22, 1957 – Chicago rookie Bobby Hull scored his first career NHL goal in a 2-1 win over the visiting Boston Bruins.
- Jan. 18, 1958 – New Brunswick native Willie O'Ree skated onto the ice at Montreal and became the first player of African descent to appear in an NHL game. He went scoreless as the Bruins beat the Canadiens 3-0.
- Apr. 1, 1958 – Montreal's Maurice Richard scored his seventh (and final) career playoff hat trick as the Canadiens won 4-3 at Detroit, in the 4th and deciding game of their Stanley Cup semi-final series.

1958-59

Stanley Cup • Montreal Canadiens

FINAL STANDINGS

Team	GP	W	L	T	GF	GA	PTS
Montreal	70	39	18	13	258	158	91
Boston	70	32	29	9	205	215	73
Chicago	70	28	29	13	197	208	69
Toronto	70	27	32	11	189	201	65
New York	70	26	32	12	201	217	64
Detroit	70	25	37	8	167	218	58

LEADING SCORERS

Player	Club	GP	G	A	PTS	PIM
Dickie Moore	Montreal	70	41	55	96	61
Jean Beliveau	Montreal	64	45	46	91	67
Andy Bathgate	NY Rangers	70	40	48	88	48
Gordie Howe	Detroit	70	32	46	78	57
Ed Litzenberger	Chicago	70	33	44	77	37
Bernie Geoffrion	Montreal	59	22	44	66	30
Red Sullivan	NY Rangers	70	21	42	63	56
Andy Hebenton	NY Rangers	70	33	29	62	8
Don McKenney	Boston	70	32	30	62	20
Tod Sloan	Chicago	59	27	35	62	79
Vic Stasiuk	Boston	70	27	33	60	63
John Bucyk	Boston	69	24	36	60	36
Camille Henry	NY Rangers	70	23	35	58	2
Ted Lindsay	Chicago	70	22	36	58	184
Norm Ullman	Detroit	69	22	36	58	42
Alex Delvecchio	Detroit	70	19	35	54	6
Dick Duff	Toronto	69	29	24	53	73
Billy Harris	Toronto	70	22	30	52	29
Henri Richard	Montreal	63	21	30	51	33
Bill Gadsby	NY Rangers	70	5	46	51	56
Bobby Hull	Chicago	70	18	32	50	50
Dean Prentice	NY Rangers	70	17	33	50	11
Frank Mahovlich	Toronto	63	22	27	49	94
Ron Murphy	Chicago	59	17	30	47	52
Jerry Toppazzini	Boston	70	21	23	44	61

LEADING GOALTENDERS

Goaltender	Club	GPI	MINS	GA	SO	AVG
Jacques Plante	Montreal	67	4000	144	9	2.16
Johnny Bower	Toronto	39	2340	106	3	2.72
Ed Chadwick	Toronto	31	1860	92	3	2.97
Gump Worsley	NY Rangers	67	4001	198	2	2.97
Glenn Hall	Chicago	70	4200	208	1	2.97
Terry Sawchuk	Detroit	67	4020	207	5	3.09
Don Simmons	Boston	58	3480	183	3	3.16

LEADING PLAYOFF SCORERS

Player	Club	GP	G	A	PTS	PIM
Dickie Moore	Montreal	11	5	12	17	8
Marcel Bonin	Montreal	11	10	5	15	4
Gerry Ehman	Toronto	12	6	7	13	8
Bernie Geoffrion	Montreal	11	5	8	13	10
Doug Harvey	Montreal	11	1	11	12	22
Frank Mahovlich	Toronto	12	6	5	11	18
Henri Richard	Montreal	11	3	8	11	13
Claude Provost	Montreal	11	6	2	8	2
Bob Pulford	Toronto	12	4	4	8	8
Tod Sloan	Chicago	6	3	5	8	0
Ralph Backstrom	Montreal	11	3	5	8	12
Ed Litzenberger	Chicago	6	3	5	8	8
Fleming MacKell	Boston	7	2	6	8	8

LEADING PLAYOFF GOALTENDERS

Goaltender	Club	GPI	MINS	GA	SO	AVG
Jacques Plante	Montreal	11	670	26	0	2.33
Harry Lumley	Boston	7	436	20	0	2.75
Johnny Bower	Toronto	12	746	38	0	3.06
Glenn Hall	Chicago	6	360	21	0	3.50

John Bucyk (right, with Jean-Guy Gendron) stood six feet tall and weighed 190 pounds, which made him the biggest left winger in hockey during his career. Bucyk and the Bruins enjoyed good times in the late 1950s, but missed the playoffs eight years in a row beginning in 1959–60. Bucyk would still be around for Boston's heady days of the early 1970s.

IT WAS A STATISTICAL QUIRK: the Canadiens were far ahead of second-place Boston in goals scored and goals allowed, yet they only had seven more wins. Dickie Moore scored at a record rate for the Habs, but the Hart Trophy went to Andy Bathgate, whose Rangers collapsed in the home stretch and missed the playoffs on the final day of the season. It was almost the only honor Montreal didn't capture.

Aside from the Canadiens, momentum shifted towards Chicago this year. Armed with Glenn Hall, Bobby Hull and an improved defense, the Hawks were respectable. In Toronto, Punch Imlach began his career as general manager of the Maple Leafs. He eventually fired coach Billy Reay and took over that job too. It was his squad that sneaked past New York into the playoffs. This was just the first success in his long but stormy tenure.

The Best of the Best – Dickie Moore set a new points record, Punch Imlach connected in Toronto and the Maple Leafs finally made it back to the Stanley Cup finals only to be humbled by the Habs.

The strange fall of the Rangers, who won three of their last 20 games, happened after Gordie Howe battered Lou Fontinato in a legendary fight. The embarrassment of their tough guy seemed to douse a spark within the club. They still held a seven-point lead over Toronto with five games left, but it wasn't enough. Boston had no such problem, bolstered as it was by the Uke Line of Vic Stasiuk, Bronco Horvath and John Bucyk (so named for their Ukrainian heritage). The team was deep in forwards; top-10 scorer Don McKenney was evidence of that. However, the Bruins eventually ran out of gas in the playoffs.

Ahead by two games, Boston looked stronger than Toronto, but the Leafs somehow won two straight in sudden death. They then won a thriller in game seven. The Black Hawks showed the champs just how good they might become, staying close in every game but one in an intriguing six-match loss. President Campbell was not pleased with referee Red Storey, stating that he should have called a penalty shot against Montreal in the last game. Storey left his job in dismay and never came back.

Montreal had an easier job in the finals thanks to Boston's dismissal, since the Leafs did not have enough depth or scoring prowess. Toronto was fortunate to take one win on Dick Duff's overtime marker, but Montreal set a modern record by racing to its fourth straight Stanley Cup title.

Leaders, 1958-59

GOALS

Name, Team	G
Jean Beliveau, Mtl.	45
Dickie Moore, Mtl.	41
Andy Bathgate, NYR	40
Ed Litzenberger, Chi.	33
Andy Hebenton, NYR	33
Gordie Howe, Det.	32
Don McKenney, Bos.	32
Dick Duff, Tor.	29
Tod Sloan, Chi.	27
Vic Stasiuk, Bos.	27

ASSISTS

Name, Team	A
Dickie Moore, Mtl.	55
Andy Bathgate, NYR	48
Jean Beliveau, Mtl.	46
Gordie Howe, Det.	46
Bill Gadsby, NYR	46
Bernie Geoffrion, Mtl.	44
Ed Litzenberger, Chi.	44
Red Sullivan, NYR	42
John Bucyk, Bos.	36
Norm Ullman, Det.	36
Ted Lindsay, Chi.	36

GOALIE WINS

Name, Team	W
Jacques Plante, Mtl.	38
Glenn Hall, Chi.	28
Gump Worsley, NYR	26
Don Simmons, Bos.	24
Terry Sawchuk, Det.	23
Johnny Bower, Tor.	15
Ed Chadwick, Tor.	12
Harry Lumley, Bos.	8
Bob Perreault, Det.	2
Charlie Hodge, Mtl.	1

SHUTOUTS

Name, Team	SO
Jacques Plante, Mtl.	9
Terry Sawchuk, Det.	5
Ed Chadwick, Tor.	3
Johnny Bower, Tor.	3
Don Simmons, Bos.	3
Gump Worsley, NYR	2
Bob Perreault, Det.	1
Harry Lumley, Bos.	1
Glenn Hall, Chi.	1

PLAYOFF GOALS

Name, Team	G
Marcel Bonin, Mtl.	10
Claude Provost, Mtl.	6
Gerry Ehman, Tor.	6
Frank Mahovlich, Tor.	6
Dickie Moore, Mtl.	5
Bernie Geoffrion, Mtl.	5
Vic Stasiuk, Bos.	4
Jerry Toppazzini, Bos.	4
Bob Pulford, Tor.	4
Dick Duff, Tor.	4
Bert Olmstead, Tor.	4

PLAYOFF ASSISTS

Name, Team	A
Dickie Moore, Mtl.	12
Doug Harvey, Mtl.	11
Bernie Geoffrion, Mtl.	8
Henri Richard, Mtl.	8
Gerry Ehman, Tor.	7
Jim Morrison, Bos.	6
Fleming MacKell, Bos.	6
Carl Brewer, Tor.	6
Six tied with	5

PLAYOFF GOALIE WINS

Name, Team	W
Jacques Plante, Mtl.	8
Johnny Bower, Tor.	5
Harry Lumley, Bos.	3
Glenn Hall, Chi.	2

PLAYOFF SHUTOUTS

Name, Team	SO
none	

FIRST TEAM ALL-STARS

Name, Team	Position
Jean Beliveau, Mtl.	C
Andy Bathgate, NYR	RW
Dickie Moore, Mtl.	LW
Tom Johnson, Mtl.	D
Bill Gadsby, NYR	D
Jacques Plante, Mtl.	G

SECOND TEAM ALL-STARS

Name, Team	Position
Henri Richard, Mtl.	C
Gordie Howe, Det.	RW
Alex Delvecchio, Det.	LW
Marcel Pronovost, Det.	D
Doug Harvey, Mtl.	D
Terry Sawchuk, Det.	G

1959 Playoffs

SEMI-FINALS

Date	Visitor	Score		Home	Score
Mar. 24	Chicago	2	at	Montreal	4
Mar. 26	Chicago	1	at	Montreal	5
Mar. 28	Montreal	2	at	Chicago	4
Mar. 31	Montreal	1	at	Chicago	3
Apr. 2	Chicago	2	at	Montreal	4
Apr. 4	Montreal	5	at	Chicago	4

Montreal won best-of-seven series 4–2

Date	Visitor	Score		Home	Score
Mar. 24	Toronto	1	at	Boston	5
Mar. 26	Toronto	2	at	Boston	4
Mar. 28	Boston	2	at	Toronto	3 OT
Mar. 31	Boston	2	at	Toronto	3 OT
Apr. 2	Toronto	4	at	Boston	1
Apr. 4	Boston	5	at	Toronto	4
Apr. 7	Toronto	3	at	Boston	2

Toronto won best-of-seven series 4–3

FINALS

Date	Visitor	Score		Home	Score
Apr. 9	Toronto	3	at	Montreal	5
Apr. 11	Toronto	1	at	Montreal	3
Apr. 14	Montreal	2	at	Toronto	3 OT
Apr. 16	Montreal	3	at	Toronto	2
Apr. 18	Toronto	3	at	Montreal	5

Montreal won best-of-seven series 4–1

1958-59 – Montreal Canadiens – Jacques Plante, Charlie Hodge, Doug Harvey, Tom Johnson, Bob Turner, Jean-Guy Talbot, Albert Langlois, Bernie Geoffrion, Ralph Backstrom, Bill Hicke, Maurice Richard (Captain), Dickie Moore, Claude Provost, Ab McDonald, Henri Richard, Marcel Bonin, Phil Goyette, Don Marshall, André Pronovost, Jean Béliveau, Ken Mosdell, Frank Selke (Manager), Toe Blake (Coach), Hector Dubois, Larry Aubut (Trainers)

TROPHY WINNERS

Trophy	Awarded For	Winner	Team
Hart	MVP	Andy Bathgate	NYR
Art Ross	Top Scorer	Dickie Moore	Mtl.
Norris	Top Defenseman	Tom Johnson	Mtl.
Calder	Top Rookie	Ralph Backstrom	Mtl.
Vezina	Fewest Goals Against	Jacques Plante	Mtl.
Byng	Gentlemanly Conduct	Alex Delvecchio	Det.

NHL NOTEBOOK

TRANSACTIONS

- June 3, 1958 – Toronto Maple Leafs drafted goalie Johnny Bower from the NY Rangers' farm team in Cleveland (of the AHL).
- June 3, 1958 – Chicago purchased Dollard St. Laurent from the Montreal Canadiens for cash and future considerations.
- June 4, 1958 – Chicago Black Hawks purchased Tod Sloan from Toronto.
- Oct. 8, 1958 – Toronto Maple Leafs acquired Allan Stanley from Boston for Jim Morrison.

RECORDS

- Mar. 15, 1959 – Chicago veteran Ted Lindsay became the NHL's all-time leader in career games played, in a 4-1 loss to the visiting Detroit Red Wings. Linday's 928th career NHL game moved him one ahead of Montreal's Maurice Richard.
- Mar. 17, 1959 – John Wilson played in his 509th consecutive game to break the NHL record set by Murray Murdoch, when the Red Wings beat Chicago 2-0. Terry Sawchuk got the shutout.
- Mar. 22, 1959 – Jean Beliveau scored two goals and had an assist during a Canadiens 4-2 win at New York. This gave Beliveau a league-leading 45 goals for the season and 91 points, breaking his record for most points in a season by a center.
- Mar. 22, 1959 – Montreal's Dickie Moore set an NHL record for most points in a season when he scored a goal and an assist for his 96th point of the year, in a 4-2 win at New York. Moore broke Gordie Howe's record of 95 points, set in 1952-53.

MILESTONES

- Dec. 13, 1958 – Gordie Howe became the the second player in NHL history to score 400 goals; the milestone came in a 2-2 Red Wings tie in Montreal.
- Mar. 15, 1959 – Terry Sawchuk became the first goaltender in history to win 250 games with the Detroit Red Wings. The milestone came in a 4-1 win at Chicago.
- Apr. 18, 1959 – Montreal Canadiens became the first team to win four consecutive Stanley Cup championships, with a 5-3 win over Toronto in game five of the finals.

1959-60

Stanley Cup • Montreal Canadiens

1959-60

FINAL STANDINGS

Team	GP	W	L	T	GF	GA	PTS
Montreal	70	40	18	12	255	178	92
Toronto	70	35	26	9	199	195	79
Chicago	70	28	29	13	191	180	69
Detroit	70	26	29	15	186	197	67
Boston	70	28	34	8	220	241	64
New York	70	17	38	15	187	247	49

LEADING SCORERS

Player	Club	GP	G	A	PTS	PIM
Bobby Hull	Chicago	70	39	42	81	68
Bronco Horvath	Boston	68	39	41	80	60
Jean Beliveau	Montreal	60	34	40	74	57
Andy Bathgate	NY Rangers	70	26	48	74	28
Henri Richard	Montreal	70	30	43	73	66
Gordie Howe	Detroit	70	28	45	73	46
Bernie Geoffrion	Montreal	59	30	41	71	36
Don McKenney	Boston	70	20	49	69	28
Vic Stasiuk	Boston	69	29	39	68	121
Dean Prentice	NY Rangers	70	32	34	66	43
Dickie Moore	Montreal	62	22	42	64	54
Norm Ullman	Detroit	70	24	34	58	46
Bill Hay	Chicago	70	18	37	55	31
Bob Pulford	Toronto	70	24	28	52	81
John Bucyk	Boston	56	16	36	52	26
George Armstrong	Toronto	70	23	28	51	60
Gary Aldcorn	Detroit	70	22	29	51	32
Marcel Bonin	Montreal	59	17	34	51	59
Alex Delvecchio	Detroit	70	19	28	47	8
Andy Hebenton	NY Rangers	70	19	27	46	4
Claude Provost	Montreal	70	17	29	46	42
Doug Mohns	Boston	65	20	25	45	62
Jerry Toppazzini	Boston	69	12	33	45	26
Pierre Pilote	Chicago	70	7	38	45	100
Leo Labine	Boston	63	16	28	44	58

LEADING GOALTENDERS

Goaltender	Club	GPI	MINS	GA	SO	AVG
Jacques Plante	Montreal	69	4140	175	3	2.54
Glenn Hall	Chicago	70	4200	179	6	2.56
Terry Sawchuk	Detroit	58	3480	155	5	2.67
Johnny Bower	Toronto	66	3960	177	5	2.68
Don Simmons	Boston	28	1680	91	2	3.25
Harry Lumley	Boston	42	2520	146	2	3.48
Gump Worsley	NY Rangers	39	2301	135	0	3.52

LEADING PLAYOFF SCORERS

Player	Club	GP	G	A	PTS	PIM
Henri Richard	Montreal	8	3	9	12	9
Bernie Geoffrion	Montreal	8	2	10	12	4
Red Kelly	Toronto	10	3	8	11	2
Dickie Moore	Montreal	8	6	4	10	4
Alex Delvecchio	Detroit	6	2	6	8	0
Jean Beliveau	Montreal	8	5	2	7	6
Bert Olmstead	Toronto	10	3	4	7	0
Larry Regan	Toronto	10	3	3	6	0
Dick Duff	Toronto	10	2	4	6	6
Gordie Howe	Detroit	6	1	5	6	4

LEADING PLAYOFF GOALTENDERS

Goaltender	Club	GPI	MINS	GA	SO	AVG
Jacques Plante	Montreal	8	489	11	3	1.35
Johnny Bower	Toronto	10	645	31	0	2.88
Terry Sawchuk	Detroit	6	405	20	0	2.96
Glenn Hall	Chicago	4	249	14	0	3.37

Jacques Plante, wearing the mask he pioneered during the 1959–60 season. A product of the Montreal farm system, Plante made brief but spectacular appearances with the Canadiens in 1952–53 and 1953–54 before becoming the club's regular goaltender in 1954–55. The 1959–60 campaign capped five straight Stanley Cup and Vezina Trophy-winning seasons.

In a year of important changes, perhaps the most significant was the one that didn't happen: Red Kelly becoming a Ranger. New York had continued its collapse of the previous spring, and when Detroit tried to trade Kelly and Billy McNeil for Bill Gadsby and Eddie Shack, the two Wings refused to join the sinking ship. Punch Imlach stepped in, got Kelly without losing any stars, and the Leafs would be smiling about it for the rest of the 1960s.

Helped by injuries to Jean Beliveau and Bernie Geoffrion, young Bobby Hull and surprising Bronco Horvath fought an absorbing duel for the scoring title. The Bruins just missed the playoffs and Horvath did the same with the Art Ross Trophy. A future scoring champion, rookie winger Stan Mikita watched teammate Hull take the prize.

The Rocket's Last Glare – A Golden Jet landed atop the scoring runway, the Uke Line was untouchable in Boston, Montreal completed a five-year Cup run and the Rocket scored his final NHL goal.

Jacques Plante, one of the most influential goalies of all time, changed the face of hockey history this season. Plante was plagued with asthma throughout his career and missed 13 games during the 1957–58 season because of a sinus operation. He then began using a mask in practice. He first wore it in a game against the Rangers on November 1, 1959 after being cut on the face by a shot from Andy Bathgate. Montreal management did not approve—tradition and machismo were at work—but after the Canadiens went undefeated for 10 games, Plante was permitted to retain his new piece of equipment. New York's Muzz Patrick, whose family had seemingly come up with every innovation in the first half-century, instructed his minor league netminders to wear masks. Don Simmons soon followed suit in Boston.

Five years into their dynasty, the Canadiens showed no signs of weakness. Younger players like Ralph Backstrom and Phil Goyette were added to the mix of star veterans and rarely faltered. Chicago could not overcome Montreal's great defensive skill in the semi-finals. Hull only scored once as the Canadiens won two close matches, then two with shutouts, on their way to a sweep. The budding Leafs took out fading Detroit, thanks partly to a triple overtime win. Montreal showed who was boss with three goals in the first 12 minutes of the finals and two more early in game two. The club rode to another championship in style, winning eight straight playoff games. It was Montreal's tenth straight appearance in the Stanley Cup final, and ten players had been part of the entire five Cup winning streak. However, this year marked the final chapter in Maurice Richard's brilliant career.

Leaders, 1959-60

GOALS

Name, Team	G
Bronco Horvath, Bos.	39
Bobby Hull, Chi.	39
Jean Beliveau, Mtl.	34
Dean Prentice, NYR	32
Bernie Geoffrion, Mtl.	30
Henri Richard, Mtl.	30
Vic Stasiuk, Bos.	29
Gordie Howe, Det.	28
Andy Bathgate, NYR	26
Jean-Guy Gendron, Bos.	24
Norm Ullman, Det.	24
Bob Pulford, Tor.	24

ASSISTS

Name, Team	A
Don McKenney, Bos.	49
Andy Bathgate, NYR	48
Gordie Howe, Det.	45
Henri Richard, Mtl.	43
Dickie Moore, Mtl.	42
Bobby Hull, Chi.	42
Bernie Geoffrion, Mtl.	41
Bronco Horvath, Bos.	41
Jean Beliveau, Mtl.	40
Vic Stasiuk, Bos.	39

GOALIE WINS

Name, Team	W
Jacques Plante, Mtl.	40
Johnny Bower, Tor.	34
Glenn Hall, Chi.	28
Terry Sawchuk, Det.	24
Harry Lumley, Bos.	16
Don Simmons, Bos.	12
Gump Worsley, NYR	7
Marcel Paille, NYR	6
Al Rollins, NYR	3
Dennis Riggin, Det.	2

SHUTOUTS

Name, Team	SO
Glenn Hall, Chi.	6
Terry Sawchuk, Det.	5
Johnny Bower, Tor.	5
Jacques Plante, Mtl.	3
Don Simmons, Bos.	2
Harry Lumley, Bos.	2
Dennis Riggin, Det.	1
Marcel Paille, NYR	1

PLAYOFF GOALS

Name, Team	G
Dickie Moore, Mtl.	6
Jean Beliveau, Mtl.	5
Bob Pulford, Tor.	4
Gerry Melnyk, Det.	3
Henri Richard, Mtl.	3
Doug Harvey, Mtl.	3
Red Kelly, Tor.	3
Bert Olmstead, Tor.	3
Larry Regan, Tor.	3
Frank Mahovlich, Tor.	3

PLAYOFF ASSISTS

Name, Team	A
Bernie Geoffrion, Mtl.	10
Henri Richard, Mtl.	9
Red Kelly, Tor.	8
Alex Delvecchio, Det.	6
Gordie Howe, Det.	5
Val Fonteyne, Det.	4
Dickie Moore, Mtl.	4
Marcel Bonin, Mtl.	4
Bert Olmstead, Tor.	4
Dick Duff, Tor.	4
George Armstrong, Tor.	4

PLAYOFF GOALIE WINS

Name, Team	W
Jacques Plante, Mtl.	8
Johnny Bower, Tor.	4
Terry Sawchuk, Det.	2

PLAYOFF SHUTOUTS

Name, Team	SO
Jacques Plante, Mtl.	3

FIRST TEAM ALL-STARS

Name, Team	Position
Jean Beliveau, Mtl.	C
Gordie Howe, Det.	RW
Bobby Hull, Chi.	LW
Doug Harvey, Mtl.	D
Marcel Pronovost, Det.	D
Glenn Hall, Chi.	G

SECOND TEAM ALL-STARS

Name, Team	Position
Bronco Horvath, Bos.	C
Bernie Geoffrion, Mtl.	RW
Dean Prentice, NYR	LW
Allan Stanley, Tor.	D
Pierre Pilote, Chi.	D
Jacques Plante, Mtl.	G

1960 Playoffs

SEMI-FINALS

Date	Team	Score		Team	Score
Mar. 24	Chicago	3	at	Montreal	4
Mar. 26	Chicago	3	at	Montreal	4 OT
Mar. 29	Montreal	4	at	Chicago	0
Mar. 31	Montreal	2	at	Chicago	0

Montreal won best-of-seven series 4–0

Date	Team	Score		Team	Score
Mar. 23	Detroit	2	at	Toronto	1
Mar. 26	Detroit	2	at	Toronto	4
Mar. 27	Toronto	5	at	Detroit	4 3OT
Mar. 29	Toronto	1	at	Detroit	2 OT
Apr. 2	Detroit	4	at	Toronto	5
Apr. 3	Toronto	4	at	Detroit	2

Toronto won best-of-seven series 4–2

FINALS

Date	Team	Score		Team	Score
Apr. 7	Toronto	2	at	Montreal	4
Apr. 9	Toronto	1	at	Montreal	2
Apr. 12	Montreal	5	at	Toronto	2
Apr. 14	Montreal	4	at	Toronto	0

Montreal won best-of-seven series 4–0

1959-60 – Montreal Canadiens – Jacques Plante, Charlie Hodge, Doug Harvey, Tom Johnson, Bob Turner, Jean-Guy Talbot, Albert Langlois, Ralph Backstrom, Jean Béliveau, Marcel Bonin, Bernie Geoffrion, Phil Goyette, Bill Hicke, Don Marshall, Ab McDonald, Dickie Moore, André Pronovost, Claude Provost, Henri Richard, Maurice Richard (Captain), Frank Selke (Manager), Toe Blake (Coach), Hector Dubois, Larry Aubut (Trainers).

TROPHY WINNERS

Trophy	Awarded For	Winner	Team
Hart	MVP	Gordie Howe	Det.
Art Ross	Top Scorer	Bobby Hull	Chi.
Norris	Top Defenseman	Doug Harvey	Mtl.
Calder	Top Rookie	Bill Hay	Chi.
Vezina	Fewest Goals Against	Jacques Plante	Mtl.
Byng	Gentlemanly Conduct	Don McKenney	Bos

NHL NOTEBOOK

TRANSACTIONS

- June 9, 1959 – Chicago purchased veteran Murray Balfour from Montreal.
- June 9, 1959 – Toronto traded Barry Cullen to Detroit in exchange for Johnny Wilson.
- June 10, 1959 – Boston Bruins selected Detroit's Charlie Burns and NY Rangers' goalie Bruce Gamble at the inter-league draft held during the annual NHL meetings, in Montreal.
- Feb. 10, 1960 – Detroit Red Wings traded Red Kelly to the Toronto Maple Leafs in exchange for Marc Reaume.

RECORDS

- Dec. 27, 1959 – Boston's Bronco Horvath began an NHL-record 22-game point-scoring streak in a 6-1 loss at Chicago.
- Jan. 27, 1960 – Chicago's Glenn Hall set a new NHL record for consecutive games played by a goaltender, when he appeared in his 329th straight game, a 2-1 loss to the Maple Leafs. Hall broke the mark set by Montreal's Georges Vezina.
- Jan. 28, 1960 – Montreal's Jacques Plante became the first goaltender in NHL history to record six consecutive 30-win seasons, when his 30th victory of the year gave the Canadiens a 4-2 win at Detroit.
- Mar. 20, 1960 – New York Rangers' Johnny Wilson extended his NHL record for consecutive games to 580 in a 3-1 win over the Canadiens, in New York.

MILESTONES

- Nov. 1, 1959 – Montreal goalie Jacques Plante returned to the ice wearing a mask after being hit in the face with a shot by Andy Bathgate in New York. It marked the beginning of a new era in hockey. Plante led the Canadiens to a 3-1 win over the Rangers.
- Jan. 16, 1960 – Gordie Howe scored a goal and an assist in his 888th career game to become the NHL's all time leading scorer, with 947 points. He broke the record held by Maurice Richard as the Red Wings beat Chicago 3-1 in Detroit.
- Apr. 12, 1960 – Maurice Richard scored his 82nd (and final) NHL playoff goal when Montreal beat Toronto 5-2 in game three of the finals.
- Apr. 14, 1960 – Jean Beliveau scored twice as the Montreal Canadiens became the first team to win five consecutive Stanley Cup championships with a 4-0 win over Toronto.

1960-61

Stanley Cup • Chicago Black Hawks

FINAL STANDINGS

Team	GP	W	L	T	GF	GA	PTS
Montreal	70	41	19	10	254	188	92
Toronto	70	39	19	12	234	176	90
Chicago	70	29	24	17	198	180	75
Detroit	70	25	29	16	195	215	66
New York	70	22	38	10	204	248	54
Boston	70	15	42	13	176	254	43

LEADING SCORERS

Player	Club	GP	G	A	PTS	PIM
Bernie Geoffrion	Montreal	64	50	45	95	29
Jean Beliveau	Montreal	69	32	58	90	57
Frank Mahovlich	Toronto	70	48	36	84	131
Andy Bathgate	NY Rangers	70	29	48	77	22
Gordie Howe	Detroit	64	23	49	72	30
Norm Ullman	Detroit	70	28	42	70	34
Red Kelly	Toronto	64	20	50	70	12
Dickie Moore	Montreal	57	35	34	69	62
Henri Richard	Montreal	70	24	44	68	91
Alex Delvecchio	Detroit	70	27	35	62	26
Bill Hay	Chicago	69	11	48	59	45
Bob Nevin	Toronto	68	21	37	58	13
Bobby Hull	Chicago	67	31	25	56	43
Andy Hebenton	NY Rangers	70	26	28	54	10
Camille Henry	NY Rangers	53	28	25	53	8
Stan Mikita	Chicago	66	19	34	53	100
Vic Stasiuk	Bos./Det.	69	15	38	53	51
Bert Olmstead	Toronto	67	18	34	52	84
Marcel Bonin	Montreal	65	16	35	51	45
Jerry Toppazzini	Boston	67	15	35	50	35
Don McKenney	Boston	68	26	23	49	22
Murray Balfour	Chicago	70	21	27	48	123
Dave Keon	Toronto	70	20	25	45	6
Dean Prentice	NY Rangers	56	20	25	45	17
Bill Hicke	Montreal	70	18	27	45	31
Kenny Wharram	Chicago	64	16	29	45	12

LEADING GOALTENDERS

Goaltender	Club	GPI	MINS	GA	SO	AVG
Charlie Hodge	Montreal	30	1800	74	4	2.47
Johnny Bower	Toronto	58	3480	145	2	2.50
Glenn Hall	Chicago	70	4200	176	6	2.51
Jacques Plante	Montreal	40	2400	112	2	2.80
Hank Bassen	Detroit	35	2050	100	0	2.93
Terry Sawchuk	Detroit	37	2150	112	2	3.13
Gump Worsley	NY Rangers	59	3473	190	1	3.28
Bruce Gamble	Boston	52	3120	193	0	3.71

LEADING PLAYOFF SCORERS

Player	Club	GP	G	A	PTS	PIM
Gordie Howe	Detroit	11	4	11	15	10
Pierre Pilote	Chicago	12	3	12	15	8
Bobby Hull	Chicago	12	4	10	14	4
Stan Mikita	Chicago	12	6	5	11	21
Murray Balfour	Chicago	11	5	5	10	14
Alex Delvecchio	Detroit	11	4	5	9	0
Kenny Wharram	Chicago	12	3	5	8	12
Bill Hay	Chicago	12	2	5	7	20
Vic Stasiuk	Detroit	11	2	5	7	4
Phil Goyette	Montreal	6	3	3	6	0
Henri Richard	Montreal	6	2	4	6	22

LEADING PLAYOFF GOALTENDERS

Goaltender	Club	GPI	MINS	GA	SO	AVG
Glenn Hall	Chicago	12	772	26	2	2.02
Terry Sawchuk	Detroit	8	465	18	1	2.32
Jacques Plante	Montreal	6	412	16	0	2.33
Hank Bassen	Detroit	4	220	9	0	2.45

Glenn Hall was known as "Mr. Goalie" and was one of the greatest netminders in NHL history, though the stress of puckstopping often made him ill before games. With 84 career shutouts, he is third on the NHL's all-time list, trailing only Terry Sawchuk and George Hainsworth. He led the NHL in shutouts six times in his career.

One of the NHL's most exciting and unpredictable seasons ended with a new champion and the resurrection of an old one. Along the way, Bernie Geoffrion had the best offensive display yet seen, tying the retired Rocket Richard's 50-goal mark and landing one short of Dickie Moore's record of 96 points despite missing six games during the season.

The rebirth happened in Toronto, where English Canada's team became a power again. Punch Imlach had shown his innovative genius by moving Red Kelly from defense to center. Teamed with left winger Frank Mahovlich, the two instantly began to score. Goaltender Johnny Bower became a force in net, and Dave Keon turned out to be the league's best rookie. The Leafs looked and played better than Chicago, but it was the third-place Blackhawks who wound up winning the laurels. The Scooter Line was fast and shifty, while the defense solidified very nicely in front of the ultra-consistent Glenn Hall. Boston took Chicago's place as the cellar dwellers, much to the dismay of true-hearted Bruin Milt Schmidt, the coach.

Poetic Justice – The Hawks soared and Boom-Boom scored, but Montreal hit a wall and couldn't go past Chicago as the Hawks go on to win the Cup.

Offensive hockey evolved through the introduction of curved sticks, born in the minds of Andy Bathgate and Stan Mikita, who discovered independently that a bent blade made life uncomfortable for goalies. It gave the forehand more speed and accuracy and caused the puck to dip at times. Bobby Hull was the first to follow them. Eventually, almost no one in hockey would use a straight blade anymore.

The Black Hawks began the playoffs against the perennial champions, and when they lost the first semi-final game 6–2, it seemed Montreal was going to do it again. Chicago bounced back with tight checking and only had one more lapse, in game four. Hall led the way with two shutouts to end the series and the great upset. Detroit demonstrated that the Leafs weren't ready to win quite yet by upending them in five matches. Although the two teams split the first four games of the finals, Chicago wasn't about to lose to Detroit, and its offense fired on all cylinders in the last two games, ending the series and the Cup drought (23 years) in impressive style.

In the offseason, the original Hockey Hall of Fame building opened in Toronto. Richard and Schmidt were among the new members elected.

Leaders, 1960-61

GOALS

Name, Team	G
Bernie Geoffrion, Mtl.	50
Frank Mahovlich, Tor.	48
Dickie Moore, Mtl.	35
Jean Beliveau, Mtl.	32
Bobby Hull, Chi.	31
Andy Bathgate, NYR	29
Camille Henry, NYR	28
Norm Ullman, Det.	28
Alex Delvecchio, Det.	27
Don McKenney, Bos.	26
Andy Hebenton, NYR	26

ASSISTS

Name, Team	A
Jean Beliveau, Mtl.	58
Red Kelly, Tor.	50
Gordie Howe, Det.	49
Bill Hay, Chi.	48
Andy Bathgate, NYR	48
Bernie Geoffrion, Mtl.	45
Henri Richard, Mtl.	44
Norm Ullman, Det.	42
Vic Stasiuk, Bos./Det.	38
Bob Nevin, Tor.	37

GOALIE WINS

Name, Team	W
Johnny Bower, Tor.	33
Glenn Hall, Chi.	29
Jacques Plante, Mtl.	23
Gump Worsley, NYR	20
Charlie Hodge, Mtl.	18
Hank Bassen, Det.	13
Terry Sawchuk, Det.	12
Bruce Gamble, Bos.	12
Cesare Maniago, Tor.	4
Don Simmons, Bos.	3

SHUTOUTS

Name, Team	SO
Glenn Hall, Chi.	6
Charlie Hodge, Mtl.	4
Terry Sawchuk, Det.	2
Jacques Plante, Mtl.	2
Johnny Bower, Tor.	2
Jack McCartan, NYR	1
Don Simmons, Bos.	1
Gump Worsley, NYR	1

PLAYOFF GOALS

Name, Team	G
Stan Mikita, Chi.	6
Murray Balfour, Chi.	5
Gordie Howe, Det.	4
Alex Delvecchio, Det.	4
Bobby Hull, Chi.	4
Phil Goyette, Mtl.	3
Dickie Moore, Mtl.	3
Leo Labine, Det.	3
Pierre Pilote, Chi.	3
Kenny Wharram, Chi.	3

PLAYOFF ASSISTS

Name, Team	A
Pierre Pilote, Chi.	12
Gordie Howe, Det.	11
Bobby Hull, Chi.	10
Jean Beliveau, Mtl.	5
Murray Balfour, Chi.	5
Alex Delvecchio, Det.	5
Vic Stasiuk, Det.	5
Stan Mikita, Chi.	5
Kenny Wharram, Chi.	5
Bill Hay, Chi.	5

PLAYOFF GOALIE WINS

Name, Team	W
Glenn Hall, Chi.	8
Terry Sawchuk, Det.	5
Jacques Plante, Mtl.	2
Cesare Maniago, Tor.	1
Hank Bassen, Det.	1

PLAYOFF SHUTOUTS

Name, Team	SO
Glenn Hall, Chi.	2
Terry Sawchuk, Det.	1

FIRST TEAM ALL-STARS

Name, Team	Position
Jean Beliveau, Mtl.	C
Frank Mahovlich, Tor.	RW
Bernie Geoffrion, Mtl.	LW
Doug Harvey, Mtl.	D
Marcel Pronovost, Det.	D
Johnny Bower, Tor.	G

SECOND TEAM ALL-STARS

Name, Team	Position
Henri Richard, Mtl.	C
Gordie Howe, Det.	RW
Dickie Moore, Mtl.	LW
Allan Stanley, Tor.	D
Pierre Pilote, Chi.	D
Glenn Hall, Chi.	G

1961 Playoffs

SEMI-FINALS

Date		Team	Score		Team	Score	
Mar.	21	Chicago	2	at	Montreal	6	
Mar.	23	Chicago	4	at	Montreal	3	
Mar.	26	Montreal	1	at	Chicago	2	2OT
Mar.	28	Montreal	5	at	Chicago	2	
Apr.	1	Chicago	3	at	Montreal	0	
Apr.	4	Montreal	0	at	Chicago	3	

Chicago won best-of-seven series 4–2

Date		Team	Score		Team	Score	
Mar.	22	Detroit	2	at	Toronto	3	2OT
Mar.	25	Detroit	4	at	Toronto	2	
Mar.	26	Toronto	0	at	Detroit	2	
Mar.	28	Toronto	1	at	Detroit	4	
Apr.	1	Detroit	3	at	Toronto	2	

Detroit won best-of-seven series 4–1

FINALS

Date		Team	Score		Team	Score
Apr.	6	Detroit	2	at	Chicago	3
Apr.	8	Chicago	1	at	Detroit	3
Apr.	10	Detroit	1	at	Chicago	3
Apr.	12	Chicago	1	at	Detroit	2
Apr.	14	Detroit	3	at	Chicago	6
Apr.	16	Chicago	5	at	Detroit	1

Chicago won best-of-seven series 4–2

1960-61 – Chicago Black Hawks – Glenn Hall, Al Arbour, Pierre Pilote (Captain), Moose Vasko, Jack Evans, Dollard St. Laurent, Reggie Fleming, Tod Sloan, Ron Murphy, Ed Litzenberger, Bill Hay, Bobby Hull, Ab McDonald, Eric Nesterenko, Kenny Wharram, Earl Balfour, Stan Mikita, Murray Balfour, Chico Maki, Wayne Hicks, Wayne Hillman, Denis DeJordy, Tommy Ivan (Manager), Rudy Pilous (Coach), Nick Garen (Trainer).

TROPHY WINNERS

Trophy	Awarded For	Winner	Team
Hart	MVP	Bernie Geoffrion	Mtl.
Art Ross	Top Scorer	Bernie Geoffrion	Mtl.
Norris	Top Defenseman	Doug Harvey	Mtl.
Calder	Top Rookie	Dave Keon	Tor.
Vezina	Fewest Goals Against	Johnny Bower	Tor.
Byng	Gentlemanly Conduct	Red Kelly	Tor.

NHL NOTEBOOK

TRANSACTIONS

- June 7, 1960 – Boston obtained Ted Green from Montreal in the inter-league draft.
- Nov. 7, 1960 – Toronto obtained Eddie Shack from the New York Rangers for Pat Hannigan and John Wilson.
- Jan. 23, 1961 – Detroit traded Murray Oliver, Gary Aldcorn and Tom McCarthy to Boston in exchange for Leo Labine and Vic Stasiuk.

RECORDS

- Oct. 19, 1960 – Chicago rookie Reggie Fleming set an NHL record with 37 penalty minutes in a 2-0 loss against the Rangers at NY. Fleming picked up a minor, three majors, a misconduct, and a game misconduct.
- Nov. 24, 1960 – Montreal's Dickie Moore scored his 20th goal of the season in his 21st game (a 3-1 loss at Detroit) to equal an NHL record for fastest 20 goals in a season (set by Maurice Richard in 1944-45).
- Mar. 16, 1961 – Montreal's Jean Beliveau set an NHL record for most assists in one season, when he picked up his 57th and 58th of the year, as the Canadiens won 5-2 over the visiting Maple Leafs. Beliveau broke the mark of 56 set by Bert Olmstead in 1955-56.
- Apr. 8, 1961 – Gordie Howe set a playoff record for most career assists during a 3-1 Red Wings win over Chicago, in game two of the Stanley Cup finals. Howe's two assists in the game gave him 61 in his career career, two more than Doug Harvey.

MILESTONES

- Sept. 15, 1960 – Maurice Richard announced his NHL retirement at the Queen Elizabeth Hotel in Montreal, after a career that saw him score a team-record 544 regular-season goals along with 82 playoff goals.
- Nov. 27, 1960 – Gordie Howe became the first player in NHL history to score 1,000 career points as the Red Wings won 2-0 over Toronto. Howe's 1,000th point came in his 938th NHL game.
- Mar. 16, 1961 – Montreal's Bernie Geoffrion became the second player in NHL history to score 50 goals in a season, in a 5-2 win over Toronto. His 50 goals tied a mark set in 1945 by Maurice Richard.
- Aug. 26, 1961 – The Hockey Hall of Fame had its official opening in Toronto, and its first annual induction dinner. New members included Syl Apps, Charlie Conacher, Hap Day, George Hainsworth, Joe Hall, Percy LeSueur, Maurice Richard, Milt Schmidt and Oliver Seibert.

1961-62

Stanley Cup • Toronto Maple Leafs

FINAL STANDINGS

Team	GP	W	L	T	GF	GA	PTS
Montreal	70	42	14	14	259	166	98
Toronto	70	37	22	11	232	180	85
Chicago	70	31	26	13	217	186	75
New York	70	26	32	12	195	207	64
Detroit	70	23	33	14	184	219	60
Boston	70	15	47	8	177	306	38

LEADING SCORERS

Player	Club	GP	G	A	PTS	PIM
Bobby Hull	Chicago	70	50	34	84	35
Andy Bathgate	NY Rangers	70	28	56	84	44
Gordie Howe	Detroit	70	33	44	77	54
Stan Mikita	Chicago	70	25	52	77	97
Frank Mahovlich	Toronto	70	33	38	71	87
Alex Delvecchio	Detroit	70	26	43	69	18
Ralph Backstrom	Montreal	66	27	38	65	29
Norm Ullman	Detroit	70	26	38	64	54
Bill Hay	Chicago	60	11	52	63	34
Claude Provost	Montreal	70	33	29	62	22
Dave Keon	Toronto	64	26	35	61	2
Dean Prentice	NY Rangers	68	22	38	60	20
John Bucyk	Boston	67	20	40	60	32
Bernie Geoffrion	Montreal	62	23	36	59	36
Earl Ingarfield	NY Rangers	70	26	31	57	18
Don McKenney	Boston	70	22	33	55	10
Gilles Tremblay	Montreal	70	32	22	54	28
George Armstrong	Toronto	70	21	32	53	27
Bill Hicke	Montreal	70	20	31	51	42
Henri Richard	Montreal	54	21	29	50	48
Jerry Toppazzini	Boston	70	19	31	50	26
Red Kelly	Toronto	58	22	27	49	6
Jean-Guy Talbot	Montreal	70	5	42	47	90
Don Marshall	Montreal	66	18	28	46	12
Murray Oliver	Boston	70	17	29	46	21
Bronco Horvath	Chicago	68	17	29	46	21

LEADING GOALTENDERS

Goaltender	Club	GPI	MINS	GA	SO	AVG
Jacques Plante	Montreal	70	4200	166	4	2.37
Johnny Bower	Toronto	59	3540	151	2	2.56
Glenn Hall	Chicago	70	4200	184	9	2.63
Hank Bassen	Detroit	27	1620	75	3	2.78
Gump Worsley	NY Rangers	60	3531	172	2	2.92
Terry Sawchuk	Detroit	43	2580	141	5	3.28
Don Head	Boston	38	2280	158	2	4.16
Bruce Gamble	Boston	28	1680	121	1	4.32

LEADING PLAYOFF SCORERS

Player	Club	GP	G	A	PTS	PIM
Stan Mikita	Chicago	12	6	15	21	19
Tim Horton	Toronto	12	3	13	16	16
Bobby Hull	Chicago	12	8	6	14	12
Dick Duff	Toronto	12	3	10	13	20
George Armstrong	Toronto	12	7	5	12	2
Ab McDonald	Chicago	12	6	6	12	0
Frank Mahovlich	Toronto	12	6	6	12	29
Red Kelly	Toronto	12	4	6	10	0
Bill Hay	Chicago	12	3	7	10	18
Bob Pulford	Toronto	12	7	1	8	24
Dave Keon	Toronto	12	5	3	8	0

LEADING PLAYOFF GOALTENDERS

Goaltender	Club	GPI	MINS	GA	SO	AVG
Johnny Bower	Toronto	10	579	20	0	2.07
Glenn Hall	Chicago	12	720	31	2	2.58
Jacques Plante	Montreal	6	360	19	0	3.17
Gump Worsley	NY Rangers	6	384	21	0	3.28

Dave Keon, buzzing around Terry Sawchuk, joined the Maple Leafs in 1960–61 and won the Calder Trophy. He went on to help the Leafs win the Stanley Cup in 1962, 1963 and 1964, and won the Conn Smythe Trophy when Toronto won the Cup again in 1967.

CHICAGO LOOKED READY to be a contender, but it was the beginning of Toronto's era instead. With a huge, tough defense, smart checking, one great star (Frank Mahovlich) and Johnny Bower in goal, the Maple Leafs were a complete team. Punch Imlach was always ready to push them harder if he saw any complacency, which often bothered Mahovlich, a sensitive man. But the team usually won.

The season standings were deceptive, as Montreal appeared to be the best by a clear margin. However, the core players were slightly past their prime and the overall balance had been subtly lost. Jacques Plante concealed some of the problems by winning the Hart and Vezina trophies in his finest hour. Doug Harvey was no longer in Montreal, having moved to New York to become a playing coach with the Rangers. Jean Ratelle and Vic Hadfield impressed him as rookies. Andy Bathgate did well as usual, and the Rangers finished fourth. Boston fell almost as far as it could go, especially defensively and in goal. Detroit also had a tough campaign.

Leafs in Spring – The Jet matched the Rocket and Boom-Boom, Harvey was a hero in the Big Apple, the Big M was the big man in Toronto and a gritty group of Leafs clipped Chicago to take the trophy.

Bobby Hull found himself in another wild scoring race, this time with Bathgate. In the final 31 games, Hull seemed to score every night (35 goals), and in the very last game he hit the prized 50-goal mark. Though he finished with the same amount of points as Bathgate, Hull won the Art Ross Trophy because he had scored more goals. He had now won two scoring titles by just a single point altogether. Career-wise, Gordie Howe was still many goals ahead of him, having reached his 500th. Hull would hit the milestone eventually.

The Canadiens captured the first two games of their semi-final series against Chicago before the Hawks scored nine times at home to level the set. They slowly pulled past Montreal and shut them out to win in six. Toronto also needed six games to down New York, then showed Chicago just how good its checking could be, allowing only one goal in game one. George Armstrong stunned the Hawks with a late winner in game two. Chicago responded by holding the Leafs to just one goal in the next two games and the series was tied. Bower was injured for the next match, but his teammates scored eight to ensure victory. Two late goals in game six brought the more consistent Leafs their first Cup victory since Bill Barilko's game five overtime winner against the Canadiens in 1951.

Leaders, 1961-62

GOALS

Name, Team	G
Bobby Hull, Chi.	50
Gordie Howe, Det.	33
Frank Mahovlich, Tor.	33
Claude Provost, Mtl.	33
Gilles Tremblay, Mtl.	32
Andy Bathgate, NYR	28
Ralph Backstrom, Mtl.	27
Dave Keon, Tor.	26
Alex Delvecchio, Det.	26
Norm Ullman, Det.	26
Earl Ingarfield, NYR	26

ASSISTS

Name, Team	A
Andy Bathgate, NYR	56
Bill Hay, Chi.	52
Stan Mikita, Chi.	52
Gordie Howe, Det.	44
Alex Delvecchio, Det.	43
Jean-Guy Talbot, Mtl.	42
John Bucyk, Bos.	40
Ralph Backstrom, Mtl.	38
Dean Prentice, NYR	38
Frank Mahovlich, Tor.	38
Norm Ullman, Det.	38

GOALIE WINS

Name, Team	W
Jacques Plante, Mtl.	42
Johnny Bower, Tor.	31
Glenn Hall, Chi.	31
Gump Worsley, NYR	22
Terry Sawchuk, Det.	14
Hank Bassen, Det.	9
Don Head, Bos.	9
Bruce Gamble, Bos.	6
Don Simmons, Tor.	5
Marcel Paille, NYR	4

SHUTOUTS

Name, Team	SO
Glenn Hall, Chi.	9
Terry Sawchuk, Det.	5
Jacques Plante, Mtl.	4
Hank Bassen, Det.	3
Don Head, Bos.	2
Johnny Bower, Tor.	2
Gump Worsley, NYR	2
Don Simmons, Tor.	1
Bruce Gamble, Bos.	1

PLAYOFF GOALS

Name, Team	G
Bobby Hull, Chi.	8
George Armstrong, Tor.	7
Bob Pulford, Tor.	7
Stan Mikita, Chi.	6
Ab McDonald, Chi.	6
Frank Mahovlich, Tor.	6
Dave Keon, Tor.	5
Dickie Moore, Mtl.	4
Red Kelly, Tor.	4
Bronco Horvath, Chi.	4

PLAYOFF ASSISTS

Name, Team	A
Stan Mikita, Chi.	15
Tim Horton, Tor.	13
Dick Duff, Tor.	10
Bill Hay, Chi.	7
Pierre Pilote, Chi.	7
Ron Stewart, Tor.	6
Bobby Hull, Chi.	6
Ab McDonald, Chi.	6
Frank Mahovlich, Tor.	6
Red Kelly, Tor.	6

PLAYOFF GOALIE WINS

Name, Team	W
Johnny Bower, Tor.	6
Glenn Hall, Chi.	6
Don Simmons, Tor.	2
Jacques Plante, Mtl.	2
Gump Worsley, NYR	2

PLAYOFF SHUTOUTS

Name, Team	SO
Glenn Hall, Chi.	2

FIRST TEAM ALL-STARS

Name, Team	Position
Stan Mikita, Chi.	C
Andy Bathgate, NYR	RW
Bobby Hull, Chi.	LW
Doug Harvey, NYR	D
Jean-Guy Talbot, Mtl.	D
Jacques Plante, Mtl.	G

SECOND TEAM ALL-STARS

Name, Team	Position
Dave Keon, Tor.	C
Gordie Howe, Det.	RW
Frank Mahovlich, Tor.	LW
Carl Brewer, Tor.	D
Pierre Pilote, Chi.	D
Glenn Hall, Chi.	G

1962 Playoffs

SEMI-FINALS

Date	Visitor	Score		Home	Score
Mar. 27	Chicago	1	at	Montreal	2
Mar. 29	Chicago	3	at	Montreal	4
Apr. 1	Montreal	1	at	Chicago	4
Apr. 3	Montreal	3	at	Chicago	5
Apr. 5	Chicago	4	at	Montreal	3
Apr. 8	Montreal	0	at	Chicago	2

Chicago won best-of-seven series 4–2

Date	Visitor	Score		Home	Score
Mar. 27	NY Rangers	2	at	Toronto	4
Mar. 29	NY Rangers	1	at	Toronto	2
Apr. 1	Toronto	4	at	NY Rangers	5
Apr. 3	Toronto	2	at	NY Rangers	4
Apr. 5	NY Rangers	2	at	Toronto	3 2OT
Apr. 7	NY Rangers	1	at	Toronto	7

Toronto won best-of-seven series 4–2

FINALS

Date	Visitor	Score		Home	Score
Apr. 10	Chicago	1	at	Toronto	4
Apr. 12	Chicago	2	at	Toronto	3
Apr. 15	Toronto	0	at	Chicago	3
Apr. 17	Toronto	1	at	Chicago	4
Apr. 19	Chicago	4	at	Toronto	8
Apr. 22	Toronto	2	at	Chicago	1

Toronto won best-of-seven series 4–2

1961-62 – Toronto Maple Leafs – Johnny Bower, Don Simmons, Carl Brewer, Tim Horton, Bob Baun, Allan Stanley, Al Arbour, Larry Hillman, Red Kelly, Dick Duff, George Armstrong (Captain), Frank Mahovlich, Bob Nevin, Ron Stewart, Billy Harris, Bert Olmstead, Bob Pulford, Eddie Shack, Dave Keon, Ed Litzenberger, John MacMillan, Punch Imlach (General Manager/Coach), Bob Haggert (Trainer).

TROPHY WINNERS

Trophy	Awarded For	Winner	Team
Hart	MVP	Jacques Plante	Mtl.
Art Ross	Top Scorer	Bobby Hull	Chi.
Norris	Top Defenseman	Doug Harvey	NYR
Calder	Top Rookie	Bobby Rousseau	Mtl.
Vezina	Fewest Goals Against	Jacques Plante	Mtl.
Byng	Gentlemanly Conduct	Dave Keon	Tor.

NHL NOTEBOOK

TRANSACTIONS

- June 13, 1961 – Detroit Red Wings acquired defenseman Bill Gadsby from the New York Rangers for Les Hunt and cash.
- June 13, 1961 – Montreal Canadiens traded Doug Harvey to New York Rangers for Lou Fontinato.
- June 13, 1961 – NY Rangers acquired Vic Hadfield from Chicago during the NHL's Intra-League Draft.
- June 13, 1961 – Toronto Maple Leafs acquired defenseman Al Arbour from the Chicago Black Hawks, during the NHL's annual Intra-League Draft.
- June 13, 1961 – Boston acquired Orland Kurtenbach from the New York Rangers, during the NHL's Intra-League Draft.

RECORDS

- Oct. 14, 1961 – Montreal Canadiens had their 9th straight opening game victory, an NHL record, with a 3-1 win over the Rangers at the Forum.
- Feb. 10, 1962 – Montreal's Jacques Plante became the first goaltender in history to record seven 30-win seasons in the NHL. The milestone (his 30th victory of 1961-62) came in a 4-2 win at Toronto.
- Mar. 25, 1962 – Bobby Hull scored his 50th goal of the season to tie the NHL record held by Maurice Richard and Bernie Geoffrion. Chicago lost 4-1 to the Rangers at New York.
- Apr. 19, 1962 – Chicago's Stan Mikita picked up two assists to set two new playoff records: his 21 points broke Gordie Howe's record of 20 set in 1955, and his 15 assists set a new record. Chicago lost 8-4 at Toronto, in game five of the Stanley Cup finals.

MILESTONES

- Nov. 26, 1961 – Gordie Howe became the first player in NHL history to play in 1,000 career regular season games, when the Red Wings lost 4-1 at Chicago.
- Jan. 17, 1962 – Chicago goaltender Glenn Hall played in his 500th consecutive game (including the playoffs), and received a station wagon and other gifts from team management. But the Black Hawks lost the game 7-3 to Montreal.
- Mar. 17, 1962 – Glenn Hall became the first goaltender in Chicago Black Hawks history to win 30 games in one season. The milestone victory was a 3-1 win against the Maple Leafs at Toronto.

1962-63

Stanley Cup • Toronto Maple Leafs

FINAL STANDINGS

Team	GP	W	L	T	GF	GA	PTS
Toronto	70	35	23	12	221	180	82
Chicago	70	32	21	17	194	178	81
Montreal	70	28	19	23	225	183	79
Detroit	70	32	25	13	200	194	77
New York	70	22	36	12	211	233	56
Boston	70	14	39	17	198	281	45

LEADING SCORERS

Player	Club	GP	G	A	PTS	PIM
Gordie Howe	Detroit	70	38	48	86	100
Andy Bathgate	NY Rangers	70	35	46	81	54
Stan Mikita	Chicago	65	31	45	76	69
Frank Mahovlich	Toronto	67	36	37	73	56
Henri Richard	Montreal	67	23	50	73	57
Jean Beliveau	Montreal	69	18	49	67	68
John Bucyk	Boston	69	27	39	66	36
Alex Delvecchio	Detroit	70	20	44	64	8
Bobby Hull	Chicago	65	31	31	62	27
Murray Oliver	Boston	65	22	40	62	38
Parker MacDonald	Detroit	69	33	28	61	32
Ab McDonald	Chicago	69	20	41	61	12
Camille Henry	NY Rangers	60	37	23	60	8
Red Kelly	Toronto	66	20	40	60	8
Don McKenney	Bos./NYR	62	22	35	57	6
Dave Keon	Toronto	68	28	28	56	2
Norm Ullman	Detroit	70	26	30	56	53
Dean Prentice	NYR/Bos.	68	19	34	53	22
Dickie Moore	Montreal	67	24	26	50	61
Claude Provost	Montreal	67	20	30	50	26
Gilles Tremblay	Montreal	60	25	24	49	42
Bill Hay	Chicago	64	12	33	45	36
Bob Pulford	Toronto	70	19	25	44	49
Tommy Williams	Boston	69	23	20	43	11
Jean-Guy Gendron	Boston	66	21	22	43	42
George Armstrong	Toronto	70	19	24	43	27
Earl Ingarfield	NY Rangers	69	19	24	43	40

LEADING GOALTENDERS

Goaltender	Club	GPI	MINS	GA	SO	AVG
Don Simmons	Toronto	28	1680	69	1	2.46
Glenn Hall	Chicago	66	3910	161	5	2.47
Jacques Plante	Montreal	56	3320	138	5	2.49
Terry Sawchuk	Detroit	48	2781	118	3	2.55
Johnny Bower	Toronto	42	2520	109	1	2.60
Gump Worsley	NY Rangers	67	3980	217	2	3.27
Eddie Johnston	Boston	50	2913	193	1	3.98

LEADING PLAYOFF SCORERS

Player	Club	GP	G	A	PTS	PIM
Gordie Howe	Detroit	11	7	9	16	22
Norm Ullman	Detroit	11	4	12	16	14
Dave Keon	Toronto	10	7	5	12	0
Bobby Hull	Chicago	5	8	2	10	4
Alex Delvecchio	Detroit	11	3	6	9	2
George Armstrong	Toronto	10	3	6	9	4
Red Kelly	Toronto	10	2	6	8	6
Pierre Pilote	Chicago	6	0	8	8	8
Bob Pulford	Toronto	10	2	5	7	14
Allan Stanley	Toronto	10	1	6	7	8

LEADING PLAYOFF GOALTENDERS

Goaltender	Club	GPI	MINS	GA	SO	AVG
Johnny Bower	Toronto	10	600	16	2	1.60
Jacques Plante	Montreal	5	300	14	0	2.80
Terry Sawchuk	Detroit	11	660	35	0	3.18
Glenn Hall	Chicago	6	360	25	0	4.17

Gordie Howe, accepting the silverware from NHL president Clarence Campbell, won both the Hart and Art Ross trophies for the sixth time in 1962–63. While those totals have been surpassed, his record total of 21 selections to the NHL All-Star Team (12 to the First Team, nine to the Second) has not been beaten.

IN AN EFFORT TO BETTER DISTRIBUTE young prospects, the NHL created the Amateur Draft at the end of this season. At this point, the system was still far from perfect as players on NHL-sponsored junior teams were exempt and Montreal was allowed to claim the top two French Canadian prospects before anyone else made a pick. Still, June 5, 1963 was the day of the first NHL draft. The last-place teams in 1962–63, Boston and New York, were indeed far behind the pack, but the top four finished in a log-jam atop the standings. The statistical similarities were uncanny, although the Canadiens and Leafs had a lead over Chicago and Detroit in goals scored.

And Howe – Gordie Howe collected his final NHL scoring title but the Leafs topped the standings for the first time in 15 years then methodically wore down their playoff foes to capture a second consecutive Cup.

An epic performance came to a sudden end on November 7, 1962, when Glenn Hall missed a game. He had played 502 in a row before that, an unthinkable number in today's game. How he had done it was a mystery, given his nervous temperament. Hall said that if he knew another way to support his family, he would have taken it. The Hawks were glad he didn't. Gordie Howe showed he was still the NHL's most complete and useful player by capturing the scoring title and the Hart Trophy, both for the sixth time. Only Wayne Gretzky would top those achievements. It was the last time Howe was quite this dominant, but he remained great into the early 1970s. Still, it was Frank Mahovlich who discovered he was worth $1 million. That was the figure Chicago's James D. Norris offered Stafford Smythe for the Leafs top sniper. However, once Smythe realized that the deal would never be approved by the committee that ran the Toronto team, nothing came of the trade talk.

In the postseason, Chicago looked ready to do special things in its first two games against Detroit, then lost four straight, culminating with a 7–4 loss to the Red Wings. It was these strange lapses that prevented this talented team from winning the Cup again after 1961. Toronto was able to shut down Montreal's forwards in their semi-final set. Johnny Bower, who was approximately 38 (no one really knew for sure), was at his peak. In the Stanley Cup final, the Leafs' diverse scoring and harmonious teamwork took care of the Wings in five games.

Leaders, 1962-63

GOALS

Name, Team	G
Gordie Howe, Det.	38
Camille Henry, NYR	37
Frank Mahovlich, Tor.	36
Andy Bathgate, NYR	35
Parker MacDonald, Det.	33
Stan Mikita, Chi.	31
Bobby Hull, Chi.	31
Dave Keon, Tor.	28
John Bucyk, Bos.	27
Norm Ullman, Det.	26

ASSISTS

Name, Team	A
Henri Richard, Mtl.	50
Jean Beliveau, Mtl.	49
Gordie Howe, Det.	48
Andy Bathgate, NYR	46
Stan Mikita, Chi.	45
Alex Delvecchio, Det.	44
Ab McDonald, Chi.	41
Murray Oliver, Bos.	40
Red Kelly, Tor.	40
John Bucyk, Bos.	39

GOALIE WINS

Name, Team	W
Glenn Hall, Chi.	30
Terry Sawchuk, Det.	22
Jacques Plante, Mtl.	22
Gump Worsley, NYR	22
Johnny Bower, Tor.	20
Don Simmons, Tor.	15
Eddie Johnston, Bos.	11
Hank Bassen, Det.	6
Cesare Maniago, Mtl.	5
Dennis Riggin, Det.	4

SHUTOUTS

Name, Team	SO
Jacques Plante, Mtl.	5
Glenn Hall, Chi.	5
Terry Sawchuk, Det.	3
Gump Worsley, NYR	2
Bob Perreault, Bos.	1
Don Simmons, Tor.	1
Johnny Bower, Tor.	1
Eddie Johnston, Bos.	1

PLAYOFF GOALS

Name, Team	G
Bobby Hull, Chi.	8
Dave Keon, Tor.	7
Gordie Howe, Det.	7
Alex Faulkner, Det.	5
Dick Duff, Tor.	4
Ron Stewart, Tor.	4
Norm Ullman, Det.	4
Eight tied with	3

PLAYOFF ASSISTS

Name, Team	A
Norm Ullman, Det.	12
Gordie Howe, Det.	9
Pierre Pilote, Chi.	8
George Armstrong, Tor.	6
Red Kelly, Tor.	6
Allan Stanley, Tor.	6
Alex Delvecchio, Det.	6
Kenny Wharram, Chi.	5
Dave Keon, Tor.	5
Bob Pulford, Tor.	5

PLAYOFF GOALIE WINS

Name, Team	W
Johnny Bower, Tor.	8
Terry Sawchuk, Det.	5
Glenn Hall, Chi.	2
Jacques Plante, Mtl.	1

PLAYOFF SHUTOUTS

Name, Team	SO
Johnny Bower, Tor.	2

FIRST TEAM ALL-STARS

Name, Team	Position
Stan Mikita, Chi.	C
Gordie Howe, Det.	RW
Frank Mahovlich, Tor.	LW
Pierre Pilote, Chi.	D
Carl Brewer, Tor.	D
Glenn Hall, Chi.	G

SECOND TEAM ALL-STARS

Name, Team	Position
Henri Richard, Mtl.	C
Andy Bathgate, NYR	RW
Bobby Hull, Chi.	LW
Tim Horton, Tor.	D
Elmer Vasko, Chi.	D
Terry Sawchuk, Det.	G

1963 Playoffs

SEMI-FINALS

Date		Team	Score		Team	Score
Mar.	26	Montreal	1	at	Toronto	3
Mar.	28	Montreal	2	at	Toronto	3
Mar.	30	Toronto	2	at	Montreal	0
Apr.	2	Toronto	1	at	Montreal	3
Apr.	4	Montreal	0	at	Toronto	5

Toronto won best-of-seven series 4–1

Date		Team	Score		Team	Score
Mar.	26	Detroit	4	at	Chicago	5
Mar.	28	Detroit	2	at	Chicago	5
Mar.	31	Chicago	2	at	Detroit	4
Apr.	2	Chicago	1	at	Detroit	4
Apr.	4	Detroit	4	at	Chicago	2
Apr.	7	Chicago	4	at	Detroit	7

Detroit won best-of-seven series 4–2

FINALS

Date		Team	Score		Team	Score
Apr.	9	Detroit	2	at	Toronto	4
Apr.	11	Detroit	2	at	Toronto	4
Apr.	14	Toronto	2	at	Detroit	3
Apr.	16	Toronto	4	at	Detroit	2
Apr.	18	Detroit	1	at	Toronto	3

Toronto won best-of-seven series 4–1

1962-63 – Toronto Maple Leafs – Johnny Bower, Don Simmons, Carl Brewer, Tim Horton, Kent Douglas, Allan Stanley, Bob Baun, Larry Hillman, Red Kelly, Dick Duff, George Armstrong (Captain), Bob Nevin, Ron Stewart, Dave Keon, Billy Harris, Bob Pulford, Eddie Shack, Ed Litzenberger, Frank Mahovlich, John MacMillan, Punch Imlach (General Manager/Coach), Bob Haggert (Trainer).

TROPHY WINNERS

Trophy	Awarded For	Winner	Team
Hart	MVP	Gordie Howe	Det.
Art Ross	Top Scorer	Gordie Howe	Det.
Norris	Top Defenseman	Pierre Pilote	Chi
Calder	Top Rookie	Kent Douglas	Tor.
Vezina	Fewest Goals Against	Glenn Hall	Chi
Byng	Gentlemanly Conduct	Dave Keon	Tor.
Amateur Draft	First Overall Selection	Garry Monahan	Mtl.

NHL NOTEBOOK

TRANSACTIONS

- June 6, 1962 – Chicago obtained John McKenzie and Len Lunde from Detroit for Doug Barkley.
- June 6, 1962 – Boston Bruins drafted goaltender Eddie Johnston from the Montreal Canadiens' minor league system, during the NHL meetings in Montreal.
- Dec. 3, 1962 – Boston Bruins obtained Forbes Kennedy from the Detroit Red Wings in exchange for Andre Pronovost.
- Feb. 4, 1963 – New York Rangers traded Dean Prentice to Boston for Don McKenney and Dick Meissner.

RECORDS

- Feb. 17, 1963 – Detroit's Howie Young picked up 27 penalty minutes, giving him a season total of 208 – a new NHL record, in a 6-1 loss to Montreal; he finished the season with 273 PIM.
- Apr. 9, 1963 – Toronto's Dick Duff set a Stanley Cup playoff record for fastest two goals from the start of a game. He scored twice in the first 1:08 of the game against Terry Sawchuk as Toronto beat Detroit 4-2 in game one of the finals.
- Apr. 18, 1963 – Toronto's Dave Keon set a playoff record for most short handed goals in one game – he scored twice during a 3-1 win over Detroit in game five of the finals. The victory gave the Maple Leafs the 1963 Stanley Cup championship.

MILESTONES

- Nov. 4, 1962 – Detroit's Bill Gadsby became the first defenseman in NHL history to score 500 career NHL points. He reached the milestone in a 3-1 win over Chicago, in his 17th NHL season.
- Nov. 7, 1962 – Chicago goalie Glenn Hall was removed from a game against Boston due to a back injury in the first period. It came after he had played in 502 consecutive regular season games for Chicago. Black Hawks tied 3-3 with the Bruins.
- Nov. 22, 1962 – Toronto's Red Kelly became just the third player in NHL history to appear in 1,000 NHL games. The milestone came in a 1-0 loss at Chicago. (Bill Gadsby would play his 1,000th game later this same season.)
- June 5, 1963 – The NHL held its first Amateur Draft at the Queen Elizabeth Hotel in Montreal. 21 players were selected. Montreal chose first and selected Garry Monahan.

1963-64

Stanley Cup • Toronto Maple Leafs

1963-64

FINAL STANDINGS

Team	GP	W	L	T	GF	GA	PTS
Montreal	70	36	21	13	209	167	85
Chicago	70	36	22	12	218	169	84
Toronto	70	33	25	12	192	172	78
Detroit	70	30	29	11	191	204	71
New York	70	22	38	10	186	242	54
Boston	70	18	40	12	170	212	48

LEADING SCORERS

Player	Club	GP	G	A	PTS	PIM
Stan Mikita	Chicago	70	39	50	89	146
Bobby Hull	Chicago	70	43	44	87	50
Jean Beliveau	Montreal	68	28	50	78	42
Andy Bathgate	NYR/Tor.	71	19	58	77	34
Gordie Howe	Detroit	69	26	47	73	70
Kenny Wharram	Chicago	70	39	32	71	18
Murray Oliver	Boston	70	24	44	68	41
Phil Goyette	NY Rangers	67	24	41	65	15
Rod Gilbert	NY Rangers	70	24	40	64	62
Dave Keon	Toronto	70	23	37	60	6
Bobby Rousseau	Montreal	70	25	31	56	32
Bill Hay	Chicago	70	23	33	56	30
Camille Henry	NY Rangers	68	29	26	55	8
Frank Mahovlich	Toronto	70	26	29	55	66
John Bucyk	Boston	62	18	36	54	36
Alex Delvecchio	Detroit	70	23	30	53	11
Henri Richard	Montreal	66	14	39	53	73
Pierre Pilote	Chicago	70	7	46	53	84
Norm Ullman	Detroit	61	21	30	51	55
Bob Pulford	Toronto	70	18	30	48	73
Parker MacDonald	Detroit	68	21	25	46	25
Ab McDonald	Chicago	70	14	32	46	19
John Ferguson	Montreal	59	18	27	45	125
Red Kelly	Toronto	70	11	34	45	16
Dave Balon	Montreal	70	24	18	42	80

LEADING GOALTENDERS

Goaltender	Club	GPI	MINS	GA	SO	AVG
Johnny Bower	Toronto	51	3009	106	5	2.11
Charlie Hodge	Montreal	62	3720	140	8	2.26
Glenn Hall	Chicago	65	3860	148	7	2.30
Terry Sawchuk	Detroit	53	3140	138	5	2.64
Eddie Johnston	Boston	70	4200	211	6	3.01
Jacques Plante	NY Rangers	65	3900	220	3	3.38

LEADING PLAYOFF SCORERS

Player	Club	GP	G	A	PTS	PIM
Gordie Howe	Detroit	14	9	10	19	16
Norm Ullman	Detroit	14	7	10	17	6
Frank Mahovlich	Toronto	14	4	11	15	20
George Armstrong	Toronto	14	5	8	13	10
Red Kelly	Toronto	14	4	9	13	4
Don McKenney	Toronto	12	4	8	12	0
Alex Delvecchio	Detroit	14	3	8	11	0
Dave Keon	Toronto	14	7	2	9	2
Andy Bathgate	Toronto	14	5	4	9	25
Stan Mikita	Chicago	7	3	6	9	8

LEADING PLAYOFF GOALTENDERS

Goaltender	Club	GPI	MINS	GA	SO	AVG
Johnny Bower	Toronto	14	850	30	2	2.12
Charlie Hodge	Montreal	7	420	16	1	2.29
Terry Sawchuk	Detroit	13	677	31	1	2.75
Glenn Hall	Chicago	7	408	22	0	3.24

Johnny Bower spent eight seasons with the Cleveland Barons of the AHL before he got his first opportunity to play in the NHL in 1953–54. Finally, in 1958, Bower made the NHL to stay after Punch Imlach drafted him for the Maple Leafs. Bower backstopped Toronto to four Stanley Cup titles in the 1960s.

TORONTO, BOSTON, MONTREAL and New York all decided to make significant changes, the most unexpected being the goalie exchange between the latter two. Sensing that their core players were no longer strong enough, the Canadiens sent Jacques Plante, Phil Goyette and Don Marshall to New York for Gump Worsley and three others. They also sold Tom Johnson to Boston. Another loss came when Dickie Moore retired. Montreal did manage to hang on to first place, but could not find postseason success. Worsley never made a difference, as his serious injuries turned Charlie Hodge into the starter and a surprise Vezina winner as well.

Lucky Break – Stan Mikita Czeched-out his first scoring title, Ullman and Howe helped the Wings fly but Bob Baun's broken bone and bouncing shot in overtime deflated Detroit as the Leafs turned a Stanley Cup hat-trick.

The key trade of the year, though, sent Andy Bathgate and Don McKenney to Toronto for five Leafs, including Dick Duff. Punch Imlach knew that injuries to Frank Mahovlich, Bob Baun and Johnny Bower, plus a lack of creativity, could hurt him in the playoffs, and he was smart enough to pluck two of the best forwards from Ranger soil. With little separating the top three teams, this was the move that put Toronto ahead.

Terry Sawchuk and Gordie Howe reminded everyone they were the best in history by reaching the top of more lists. Howe passed Maurice Richard for first on the goal chart, while Sawchuk claimed number-one status in shutouts and games played.

This playoff year would be remembered as the most intense and well-fought in a long time. Chicago and Detroit battled for seven games. When the Hawks defense fell in during game six, Detroit took charge and won the series. Toronto also came back from the edge of elimination, winning games six and seven against Montreal. Bob Pulford won the opener in the finals with two seconds left, stealing a Detroit pass. Larry Jeffrey tied the series with an overtime winner and Detroit moved ahead with another last-minute winner in game three. Facing elimination in game six, Toronto's Bob Baun scored the sudden-death winner, even though it was later revealed that he'd broken his ankle earlier. The Leafs recorded a shutout in game seven to finish their three-peat.

Leaders, 1963-64

GOALS

Name, Team	G
Bobby Hull, Chi.	43
Stan Mikita, Chi.	39
Kenny Wharram, Chi.	39
Camille Henry, NYR	29
Jean Beliveau, Mtl.	28
Gordie Howe, Det.	26
Frank Mahovlich, Tor.	26
Bobby Rousseau, Mtl.	25
Phil Goyette, NYR	24
Murray Oliver, Bos.	24
Rod Gilbert, NYR	24
Dave Balon, Mtl.	24

ASSISTS

Name, Team	A
Andy Bathgate, NYR/Tor.	58
Jean Beliveau, Mtl.	50
Stan Mikita, Chi.	50
Gordie Howe, Det.	47
Pierre Pilote, Chi.	46
Bobby Hull, Chi.	44
Murray Oliver, Bos.	44
Phil Goyette, NYR	41
Rod Gilbert, NYR	40
Henri Richard, Mtl.	39

GOALIE WINS

Name, Team	W
Glenn Hall, Chi.	34
Charlie Hodge, Mtl.	33
Terry Sawchuk, Det.	25
Johnny Bower, Tor.	24
Jacques Plante, NYR	22
Eddie Johnston, Bos.	18
Don Simmons, Tor.	9
Roger Crozier, Det.	5
Gump Worsley, Mtl.	3
Denis DeJordy, Chi.	2

SHUTOUTS

Name, Team	SO
Charlie Hodge, Mtl.	8
Glenn Hall, Chi.	7
Eddie Johnston, Bos.	6
Johnny Bower, Tor.	5
Terry Sawchuk, Det.	5
Don Simmons, Tor.	3
Jacques Plante, NYR	3
Roger Crozier, Det.	2
Gump Worsley, Mtl.	1

PLAYOFF GOALS

Name, Team	G
Gordie Howe, Det.	9
Norm Ullman, Det.	7
Dave Keon, Tor.	7
George Armstrong, Tor.	5
Andy Bathgate, Tor.	5
Bob Pulford, Tor.	5
Bruce MacGregor, Det.	5
Don McKenney, Tor.	4
Frank Mahovlich, Tor.	4
Red Kelly, Tor.	4
Floyd Smith, Det.	4
Andre Pronovost, Det.	4

PLAYOFF ASSISTS

Name, Team	A
Frank Mahovlich, Tor.	11
Gordie Howe, Det.	10
Norm Ullman, Det.	10
Red Kelly, Tor.	9
Don McKenney, Tor.	8
George Armstrong, Tor.	8
Alex Delvecchio, Det.	8
Stan Mikita, Chi.	6
Pierre Pilote, Chi.	6
Larry Jeffrey, Det.	6
Allan Stanley, Tor.	6

PLAYOFF GOALIE WINS

Name, Team	W
Johnny Bower, Tor.	0
Terry Sawchuk, Det.	6
Charlie Hodge, Mtl.	3
Glenn Hall, Chi.	3
Bob Champoux, Det.	1

PLAYOFF SHUTOUTS

Name, Team	SO
Johnny Bower, Tor.	2
Charlie Hodge, Mtl.	1
Terry Sawchuk, Det.	1

FIRST TEAM ALL-STARS

Name, Team	Position
Stan Mikita, Chi.	C
Ken Wharram, Chi.	RW
Bobby Hull, Chi.	LW
Pierre Pilote, Chi.	D
Tim Horton, Tor.	D
Glenn Hall, Chi.	G

SECOND TEAM ALL-STARS

Name, Team	Position
Jean Beliveau, Mtl.	C
Gordie Howe, Det.	RW
Frank Mahovlich, Tor.	LW
Elmer Vasko, Chi.	D
Jacques Laperriere, Mtl.	D
Charlie Hodge, Mtl.	G

1964 Playoffs

SEMI-FINALS

Mar.	26	Toronto	0	at	Montreal	2
Mar.	28	Toronto	2	at	Montreal	1
Mar.	31	Montreal	3	at	Toronto	2
Apr.	2	Montreal	3	at	Toronto	5
Apr.	4	Toronto	2	at	Montreal	4
Apr.	7	Montreal	0	at	Toronto	3
Apr.	9	Toronto	3	at	Montreal	1

Toronto won best-of-seven series 4–3

Mar.	26	Detroit	1	at	Chicago	4
Mar.	29	Detroit	5	at	Chicago	4
Mar.	31	Chicago	0	at	Detroit	3
Apr.	2	Chicago	3	at	Detroit	2 OT
Apr.	5	Detroit	2	at	Chicago	3
Apr.	7	Chicago	2	at	Detroit	7
Apr.	9	Detroit	4	at	Chicago	2

Detroit won best-of-seven series 4–3

FINALS

Apr.	11	Detroit	2	at	Toronto	3
Apr.	14	Detroit	4	at	Toronto	3 OT
Apr.	16	Toronto	3	at	Detroit	4
Apr.	18	Toronto	4	at	Detroit	2
Apr.	21	Detroit	2	at	Toronto	1
Apr.	23	Toronto	4	at	Detroit	3 OT
Apr.	25	Detroit	0	at	Toronto	4

Toronto won best-of-seven series 4–3

1963-64 – Toronto Maple Leafs – Johnny Bower, Don Simmons, Carl Brewer, Tim Horton, Bob Baun, Allan Stanley, Larry Hillman, Al Arbour, Red Kelly, Gerry Ehman, Andy Bathgate, George Armstrong (Captain), Ron Stewart, Dave Keon, Billy Harris, Don McKenney, Jim Pappin, Bob Pulford, Eddie Shack, Frank Mahovlich, Ed Litzenberger, Punch Imlach (General Manager/Coach), Bob Haggert (Trainer).

TROPHY WINNERS

Trophy	Awarded For	Winner	Team
Hart	MVP	Jean Beliveau	Mtl.
Art Ross	Top Scorer	Stan Mikita	Chi.
Norris	Top Defenseman	Pierre Pilote	Chi
Calder	Top Rookie	Jacques Laperriere	Mtl.
Vezina	Fewest Goals Against	Charlie Hodge	Mtl.
Byng	Gentlemanly Conduct	Ken Wharram	Chi
Amateur Draft	First Overall Selection	Claude Gauthier	Det.

NHL NOTEBOOK

TRANSACTIONS

- June 4, 1963 – New York traded Dave Balon, Leon Rochefort, Len Ronson and Gump Worsley to Montreal in exchange for Phil Goyette, Don Marshall and Jacques Plante.
- June 4, 1963 – Boston Bruins claimed Tom Johnson from the Montreal Canadiens for the waiver price of $20,000.
- June 4, 1963 – Detroit obtained Roger Crozier and Ron Ingram from Chicago for Howie Young.
- Feb. 22, 1964 – Toronto sent Arnie Brown, Bill Collins, Dick Duff, Bob Nevin, and Rod Seiling to the New York Rangers for Andy Bathgate and Don McKenny.

RECORDS

- Nov. 10, 1963 – Gordie Howe became the NHL's all time leading goal scorer when he scored #545 to move past Maurice "Rocket" Richard as the Red Wings beat Montreal 3-0.
- Jan. 18, 1964 – Terry Sawchuk led the Red Wings to a 2-0 win against Montreal, to become the NHL's all time shutout leader with 95.
- Feb. 8, 1964 – Detroit's Terry Sawchuk set an NHL record for most career games by a goaltender, when he appeared in the 804th of his career, a 3-2 victory at Boston.
- Mar. 22, 1964 – Rangers' Andy Hebenton played in his final NHL game – the 630th consecutive of his career, a league record that stood until Garry Unger broke it in the 1970s. Hebenton played all 70 games each season during his nine years in the NHL.

MILESTONES

- Nov. 8, 1963 – Maple Leafs Gardens became the first NHL arena to install separate penalty-box doors for each team. The move came a week after Leafs' Bob Pulford the Canadiens' Terry Harper had a fight in their shared penalty box after an earlier fight on the ice.
- Dec. 22, 1963 – Jean Beliveau scored his 325th career goal to become the highest goal scoring center in NHL history (passing Nels Stewart) when Montreal beat Detroit 6-1.
- Mar. 22, 1964 – Chicago won 4-3 at Boston, as Bruins goalie Ed Johnston became the final goalie in NHL history to play every minute of every game for an entire 70-game NHL season.
- Apr. 5, 1964 – Gordie Howe became the highest career point scorer in Stanley Cup playoff history when his goal (in a 3-2 loss at Chicago) gave him 127 career playoff points (in 122 games). Howe broke the mark set by Maurice Richard.

1964-65

Stanley Cup • Montreal Canadiens

FINAL STANDINGS

Team	GP	W	L	T	GF	GA	PTS
Detroit	70	40	23	7	224	175	87
Montreal	70	36	23	11	211	185	83
Chicago	70	34	28	8	224	176	76
Toronto	70	30	26	14	204	173	74
New York	70	20	38	12	179	246	52
Boston	70	21	43	6	166	253	48

LEADING SCORERS

Player	Club	GP	G	A	PTS	PIM
Stan Mikita	Chicago	70	28	59	87	154
Norm Ullman	Detroit	70	42	41	83	70
Gordie Howe	Detroit	70	29	47	76	104
Bobby Hull	Chicago	61	39	32	71	32
Alex Delvecchio	Detroit	68	25	42	67	16
Claude Provost	Montreal	70	27	37	64	28
Rod Gilbert	NY Rangers	70	25	36	61	52
Pierre Pilote	Chicago	68	14	45	59	162
John Bucyk	Boston	68	26	29	55	24
Ralph Backstrom	Montreal	70	25	30	55	41
Phil Esposito	Chicago	70	23	32	55	44
Henri Richard	Montreal	53	23	29	52	43
Frank Mahovlich	Toronto	59	23	28	51	76
Dave Keon	Toronto	65	21	29	50	10
Bobby Rousseau	Montreal	66	12	35	47	26
Red Kelly	Toronto	70	18	28	46	8
Parker MacDonald	Detroit	69	13	33	46	38
Phil Goyette	NY Rangers	52	12	34	46	6
Floyd Smith	Detroit	67	16	29	45	44
Andy Bathgate	Toronto	55	16	29	45	34
Camille Henry	NYR/Chi.	70	26	18	44	22
Kenny Wharram	Chicago	68	24	20	44	27
John Ferguson	Montreal	69	17	27	44	156
Murray Oliver	Boston	65	20	23	43	30
Jean Beliveau	Montreal	58	20	23	43	76

LEADING GOALTENDERS

Goaltender	Club	GPI	MINS	GA	SO	AVG
Johnny Bower	Toronto	34	2040	81	3	2.38
Roger Crozier	Detroit	70	4168	168	6	2.42
Glenn Hall	Chicago	41	2440	99	4	2.43
Denis DeJordy	Chicago	30	1760	74	3	2.52
Charlie Hodge	Montreal	53	3180	135	3	2.55
Terry Sawchuk	Toronto	36	2160	92	1	2.56
Jacques Plante	NY Rangers	33	1938	109	2	3.37
Eddie Johnston	Boston	47	2820	163	3	3.47
Marcel Paille	NY Rangers	39	2262	135	0	3.58

LEADING PLAYOFF SCORERS

Player	Club	GP	G	A	PTS	PIM
Bobby Hull	Chicago	14	10	7	17	27
Jean Beliveau	Montreal	13	8	8	16	34
Bobby Rousseau	Montreal	13	5	8	13	24
Chico Maki	Chicago	14	3	9	12	8
Henri Richard	Montreal	13	7	4	11	24
Norm Ullman	Detroit	7	6	4	10	2
Stan Mikita	Chicago	14	3	7	10	53
J.C. Tremblay	Montreal	13	1	9	10	18
Dick Duff	Montreal	13	3	6	9	17
Claude Provost	Montreal	13	2	6	8	12

LEADING PLAYOFF GOALTENDERS

Goaltender	Club	GPI	MINS	GA	SO	AVG
Gump Worsley	Montreal	8	501	14	2	1.68
Charlie Hodge	Montreal	5	300	10	1	2.00
Glenn Hall	Chicago	13	760	28	1	2.21
Johnny Bower	Toronto	5	321	13	0	2.43
Roger Crozier	Detroit	7	420	23	0	3.29

Roger Crozier enjoyed great success early in his NHL career and might have become one of the game's great goalies if not for injuries and a serious illness (pancreatitis). Crozier replaced Terry Sawchuk in the Red Wings goal in 1964–65, playing all 70 games for Detroit which makes him the last NHL netminder to play in every one of his team's games in a season.

THE THEME THIS SEASON was the return of old warriors. Ted Lindsay skated for Detroit after four years of retirement. Dickie Moore disappointed Montreal fans by making a comeback with Toronto. Terry Sawchuk moved to the Leafs too; Detroit thought Roger Crozier was ready to take his place. One veteran did leave. It was Doug Harvey, who left the Rangers but continued to play in the American Hockey League. Off the ice, Frank Selke, the mastermind behind Montreal's success, decided to retire. Sam Pollock took over the general manager's job and began to set the stage for Montreal's dynasty of the 1970s while ensuring the club stayed on top for the rest of this decade as well.

Conn Smythe Delight – Ullman, Howe and Delvecchio produced in the Motor City, Mikita repeated and Claude Provost surprised but Jean Beliveau's crafty captaincy earned him the NHL's newest trophy.

Detroit prospered with its additions, and its threesome of Gordie Howe, Alex Delvecchio and Norman Ullman all reached the top five in scoring. Montreal was strong yet again, thanks to Jean Beliveau and Henri Richard. Toronto did not look as good. Statistically sound, with two excellent goalies, the Leafs just couldn't win as much, prompting Punch Imlach to play defenseman Tim Horton as a winger. He even sent Don McKenney to the minors for a spell. Frank Mahovlich's unhappiness under Imlach reached a peak when he went to the hospital for stress problems. His great potential was not being realized. Boston and the Rangers seemed to be mired in the basement, though John Bucyk and Rod Gilbert were stalwarts for the two teams.

Chicago upset the Red Wings in the semifinals, paced by Bobby Hull's eight goals. The Black Hawks opponent in the finals was Montreal, who knocked out Toronto 4–2. As was often the case, the home team, Montreal, won the first two matches in the final, then went on the road and lost two in a row. Beliveau dominated game five with four points and Chicago lost its momentum. The Hawks managed one more forward push in a 2–1 win in game six, but Beliveau scored 14 seconds into game seven and that was that. Gump Worsley and Charlie Hodge, who shared netminding duties, had their first championship. Beliveau was named the first winner of the Conn Smythe Trophy as playoff MVP.

Leaders, 1964-65

GOALS

Name, Team	G
Norm Ullman, Det.	42
Bobby Hull, Chi.	39
Gordie Howe, Det.	29
Stan Mikita, Chi.	28
Claude Provost, Mtl.	27
John Bucyk, Bos.	26
Camille Henry, NYR/Chi.	26
Alex Delvecchio, Det.	25
Rod Gilbert, NYR	25
Ralph Backstrom, Mtl.	25

ASSISTS

Name, Team	A
Stan Mikita, Chi.	59
Gordie Howe, Det.	47
Pierre Pilote, Chi.	45
Alex Delvecchio, Det.	42
Norm Ullman, Det.	41
Claude Provost, Mtl.	37
Rod Gilbert, NYR	36
Bobby Rousseau, Mtl.	35
Phil Goyette, NYR	34
Parker MacDonald, Det.	33

POWERPLAY GOALS

Name, Team	PPG
Camille Henry, NYR/Chi.	13
Gordie Howe, Det.	12
Claude Provost, Mtl.	11
Ron Murphy, Det.	10
Bobby Hull, Chi.	10
Rod Gilbert, NYR	10
Norm Ullman, Det.	9
Stan Mikita, Chi.	8
Five tied with	7

SHORTHAND GOALS

Name, Team	SHG
Eric Nesterenko, Chi.	6
Forbes Kennedy, Bos.	4
Bob Pulford, Tor.	4
Gordie Howe, Det.	4
Bobby Hull, Chi.	2
Bob Nevin, NYR	2
Reg Fleming, Bos.	2
Ed Westfall, Bos.	2
Don Marshall, NYR	2
Bill Hay, Chi.	2

GAME-WINNING GOALS

Name, Team	GWG
Norm Ullman, Det.	10
Phil Esposito, Chi.	9
Alex Delvecchio, Det.	7
Stan Mikita, Chi.	6
Henri Richard, Mtl.	5
Bobby Hull, Chi.	5
Dave Balon, Mtl.	5
Ron Stewart, Tor.	5
Floyd Smith, Det.	5
Claude Provost, Mtl.	5
Camille Henry, NYR/Chi.	5

GOALIE WINS

Name, Team	W
Roger Crozier, Det.	40
Charlie Hodge, Mtl.	26
Glenn Hall, Chi.	18
Terry Sawchuk, Tor.	17
Denis DeJordy, Chi.	16

SHUTOUTS

Name, Team	SO
Roger Crozier, Det.	6
Glenn Hall, Chi.	4
Denis DeJordy, Chi.	3
Johnny Bower, Tor.	3
Eddie Johnston, Bos.	3
Charlie Hodge, Mtl.	3

PLAYOFF GOALS

Name, Team	G
Bobby Hull, Chi.	10
Jean Beliveau, Mtl.	8
Henri Richard, Mtl.	7
Norm Ullman, Det.	6
Bobby Rousseau, Mtl.	5
Gordie Howe, Det.	4
11 tied with	3

PLAYOFF ASSISTS

Name, Team	A
J.C. Tremblay, Mtl.	9
Chico Maki, Chi.	9
Jean Beliveau, Mtl.	8
Bobby Rousseau, Mtl.	8
Pierre Pilote, Chi.	7
Bobby Hull, Chi.	7
Stan Mikita, Chi.	7

PLAYOFF GOALIE WINS

Name, Team	W
Glenn Hall, Chi.	7
Gump Worsley, Mtl.	5
Charlie Hodge, Mtl.	3
Roger Crozier, Det.	3
Johnny Bower, Tor.	2

PLAYOFF SHUTOUTS

Team	SO
Gump Worsley, Mtl.	2
Charlie Hodge, Mtl.	1
Glenn Hall, Chi.	1

FIRST TEAM ALL-STARS

Name, Team	Position
Norm Ullman, Det.	C
Claude Provost, Mtl.	RW
Bobby Hull, Chi.	LW
Pierre Pilote, Chi.	D
Jacques Laperriere, Mtl.	D
Roger Crozier, Det.	G

SECOND TEAM ALL-STARS

Name, Team	Position
Stan Mikita, Chi.	C
Gordie Howe, Det.	RW
Frank Mahovlich, Tor.	LW
Bill Gadsby, Det.	D
Carl Brewer, Tor.	D
Charlie Hodge, Mtl.	G

1965 Playoffs

SEMI-FINALS

Apr.	1	Chicago	3	at	Detroit	4
Apr.	4	Chicago	3	at	Detroit	6
Apr.	6	Detroit	2	at	Chicago	5
Apr.	8	Detroit	1	at	Chicago	2
Apr.	11	Chicago	2	at	Detroit	4
Apr.	13	Detroit	0	at	Chicago	4
Apr.	15	Chicago	4	at	Detroit	2

Chicago won best-of-seven series 4–3

Apr.	1	Toronto	2	at	Montreal	3
Apr.	3	Toronto	1	at	Montreal	3
Apr.	6	Montreal	2	at	Toronto	3 OT
Apr.	8	Montreal	2	at	Toronto	4
Apr.	10	Toronto	1	at	Montreal	3
Apr.	13	Montreal	4	at	Toronto	3 OT

Montreal won best-of-seven series 4–2

FINALS

Apr.	17	Chicago	2	at	Montreal	3
Apr.	20	Chicago	0	at	Montreal	2
Apr.	22	Montreal	1	at	Chicago	3
Apr.	25	Montreal	1	at	Chicago	5
Apr.	27	Chicago	0	at	Montreal	6
Apr.	29	Montreal	1	at	Chicago	2
May	1	Chicago	0	at	Montreal	4

Montreal won best-of-seven series 4–3

1964-65 – Montreal Canadiens – Gump Worsley, Charlie Hodge, J.C. Tremblay, Ted Harris, Jean-Guy Talbot, Terry Harper, Jacques Laperrière, Jean Gauthier, Noel Picard, Jean Béliveau (Captain), Ralph Backstrom, Dick Duff, Claude Larose, Yvan Cournoyer, Claude Provost, Bobby Rousseau, Henri Richard, Dave Balon, John Ferguson, Red Berenson, Jimmy Roberts, Toe Blake (Coach), Sam Pollock (General Manager), Larry Aubut, Andy Galley (Trainers).

TROPHY WINNERS

Trophy	Awarded For	Winner	Team
Hart	MVP	Bobby Hull	Chi.
Art Ross	Top Scorer	Stan Mikita	Chi.
Norris	Top Defenseman	Pierre Pilote	Chi
Calder	Top Rookie	Roger Crozier	Det.
Vezina	Fewest Goals Against	Terry Sawchuk	Tor.
		Johnny Bower	Tor.
Byng	Gentlemanly Conduct	Bobby Hull	Chi.
Conn Smythe	Playoff MVP	Jean Beliveau	Mtl.
Amateur Draft	First Overall Selection	Andre Veilleux	NYR

NHL NOTEBOOK

TRANSACTIONS

- June 10, 1964 – Toronto Maple Leafs selected Terry Sawchuk from Detroit and Dickie Moore from Montreal in the annual NHL Intra-League Draft.
- June 10, 1964 – Detroit selected Gary Bergman from Montreal and Murray Hall from Chicago in the annual NHL Intra-League Draft.
- June 28, 1964 – Montreal Canadiens made a trade with the Boston Bruins to obtain the rights to 16-year-old amateur goaltender Ken Dryden.
- Dec. 22, 1964 – NY Rangers traded Dick Duff to Montreal in exchange for Bill Hicke.

RECORDS

- Nov. 21, 1964 – Terry Sawchuk became the first goaltender in NHL history to get record a shutout in 16 straight seasons, with a 1-0 Toronto win over the visiting Black Hawks.
- Mar. 20, 1965 – Chicago's Pierre Pilote picked up two assists to give him 58 points for the year, a new record for points by a defenseman.
- Mar. 23, 1965 – Chicago's Stan Mikita set an NHL record with his 59th assist of the season, in a 3-2 loss to the visiting New York Rangers.
- Apr. 6, 1965 – Gordie Howe had three minors in the third game of the Stanley Cup semi-finals against Chicago, to boost his playoff penalty minute total to a record 194, breaking Maurice Richard's mark of 188.
- Apr. 11, 1965 – Detroit's Norm Ullman set a Stanley Cup playoff record for fastest two goals – five seconds. Ullman scored at 17:35 and 17:40 of second period as Red Wings beat Chicago 4-2 in game five of the semi-finals.

MILESTONES

- Jan. 27, 1965 – Ulf Sterner became the first Swedish-born player to make the NHL. He played his first game as the Rangers beat Boston 5-2. Sterner's NHL career lasted only four games – all with the Rangers.
- Feb. 4, 1965 – Toronto's Terry Sawchuk became the first goaltender in NHL history to record 400 career victories as the Maple Leafs won 5-2 at Montreal.
- Mar. 11, 1965 – NHL Board of Governors announced (at a special meeting in New York) that the league would be expanding with the formation of a second six-team division.
- May 1, 1965 – Jean Beliveau became the first winner of the Conn Smythe Trophy (awarded to the playoff MVP) when the Canadiens beat Chicago 4-0 in game seven of the finals in Montreal to win the Stanley Cup for 1965.

1965-66

Stanley Cup • Montreal Canadiens

FINAL STANDINGS

Team	GP	W	L	T	GF	GA	PTS
Montreal	70	41	21	8	239	173	90
Chicago	70	37	25	8	240	187	82
Toronto	70	34	25	11	208	187	79
Detroit	70	31	27	12	221	194	74
Boston	70	21	43	6	174	275	48
New York	70	18	41	11	195	261	47

LEADING SCORERS

Player	Club	GP	G	A	PTS	PIM
Bobby Hull	Chicago	65	54	43	97	70
Bobby Rousseau	Montreal	70	30	48	78	20
Stan Mikita	Chicago	68	30	48	78	58
Jean Beliveau	Montreal	67	29	48	77	50
Gordie Howe	Detroit	70	29	46	75	83
Norm Ullman	Detroit	70	31	41	72	35
Alex Delvecchio	Detroit	70	31	38	69	16
Bob Nevin	NY Rangers	69	29	33	62	10
Henri Richard	Montreal	62	22	39	61	47
Murray Oliver	Boston	70	18	42	60	30
John Bucyk	Boston	63	27	30	57	12
Frank Mahovlich	Toronto	68	32	24	56	68
Bob Pulford	Toronto	70	28	28	56	51
Claude Provost	Montreal	70	19	36	55	38
Don Marshall	NY Rangers	69	26	28	54	6
Dave Keon	Toronto	69	24	30	54	4
Phil Esposito	Chicago	69	27	26	53	49
Jean Ratelle	NY Rangers	67	21	30	51	10
Bill Hay	Chicago	68	20	31	51	20
George Armstrong	Toronto	70	16	35	51	12
Doug Mohns	Chicago	70	22	27	49	63
Floyd Smith	Detroit	66	21	28	49	20
Gilles Tremblay	Montreal	70	27	21	48	24
Chico Maki	Chicago	68	17	31	48	41

LEADING GOALTENDERS

Goaltender	Club	GPI	MINS	GA	SO	AVG
Johnny Bower	Toronto	35	1998	75	3	2.25
Gump Worsley	Montreal	51	2899	114	2	2.36
Charlie Hodge	Montreal	26	1301	56	1	2.58
Glenn Hall	Chicago	64	3747	164	4	2.63
Roger Crozier	Detroit	64	3734	173	7	2.78
Terry Sawchuk	Toronto	27	1521	80	1	3.16
Cesare Maniago	NY Rangers	28	1613	94	2	3.50
Ed Giacomin	NY Rangers	35	2036	125	0	3.68
Bernie Parent	Boston	39	2083	128	1	3.69
Eddie Johnston	Boston	33	1744	108	1	3.72

LEADING PLAYOFF SCORERS

Player	Club	GP	G	A	PTS	PIM
Norm Ullman	Detroit	12	6	9	15	12
J.C. Tremblay	Montreal	10	2	9	11	2
Alex Delvecchio	Detroit	12	0	11	11	4
Jean Beliveau	Montreal	10	5	5	10	6
Dean Prentice	Detroit	12	5	5	10	4
Gordie Howe	Detroit	12	4	6	10	12
Andy Bathgate	Detroit	12	6	3	9	6
Gilles Tremblay	Montreal	10	4	5	9	0
Bobby Rousseau	Montreal	10	4	4	8	6
Three players tied with					7	

LEADING PLAYOFF GOALTENDERS

Goaltender	Club	GPI	MINS	GA	SO	AVG
Gump Worsley	Montreal	10	602	20	1	1.99
Roger Crozier	Detroit	12	668	26	1	2.34
Glenn Hall	Chicago	6	347	22	0	3.80

Henri Richard battles Pierre Pilote in front of goalie Glenn Hall and Moose Vasko. Henri did not possess the fiery temper of his famous older brother Maurice, but he proved to be an aggressive player who could not be intimidated despite his small size. He lasted 20 years in the NHL and played for a record 11 Stanley Cup champions.

Bobby Hull re-wrote the NHL record book this year. Not only did he become the first player to score more than 50 goals in a season when he reached 54, his 97 points broke the scoring record held by Dickie Moore—and he did it all while playing in only 65 games. With Stan Mikita backing him up, the Black Hawks were very impressive, but not quite balanced enough.

The big trade of the year sent Andy Bathgate and two others players from Toronto to Detroit for defender Marcel Pronovost and four other skaters. The Red Wings, as always, were happy to shake up their roster, especially when they didn't win the Cup. Sadly, they lost Doug Barkley to an eye injury that ended his playing days.

The standings were no different than usual, but Boston finally looked to have some hope with youngsters like Bernie Parent, Gerry Cheevers, Gilles Marotte and a few more showing up. On the horizon, a shooting star named Bobby Orr could be glimpsed, but he wasn't there yet. New York found their goalie of the future in Ed Giacomin.

Since the advent of air travel to games, it was realistic to think about a league that stretched beyond the northeast United States and southern Canada. February of 1966 brought confirmation of the first expansion, with six new teams scheduled to start in 1967–68. The old and the new teams would each have their own divisions, with a playoff format that ensured one expansion team of a place in the Stanley Cup final. Some wondered where the talent for six new teams would come from, but there had always been excellent players in the minors who were either out of favor in the NHL or denied a place by deep major-league rosters.

This year's Stanley Cup final featured Detroit and Montreal. Roger Crozier had been a revelation in the Red Wings' net. He continued to amaze as he captured the opening games, 3–2 and 5–2. Montreal bounced back to take the next match and then receiving a big stroke of luck when Crozier was hurt in game four. Hank Bassen allowed the game-winning goal and the series was even. Crozier returned, only to allow five goals in a game five loss. Game six was very tight. The Red Wings pushed it to overtime at home, but Henri Richard notched the Cup winner. Despite Detroit's loss, Crozier won the Conn Smythe Trophy as playoff MVP, the first of several outstanding netminders to capture it.

> **Rocket Leaped – 54 goals rewrite the record book in Chicago, but it was the reliable Pocket Rocket who delivered the goods as the Canadiens won their second straight Stanley Cup title.**

Leaders, 1965-66

GOALS

Name, Team	G
Bobby Hull, Chi.	54
Frank Mahovlich, Tor.	32
Norm Ullman, Det.	31
Alex Delvecchio, Det.	31
Stan Mikita, Chi.	30
Bobby Rousseau, Mtl.	30
Jean Beliveau, Mtl.	29
Bob Nevin, NYR	29
Gordie Howe, Det.	29
Bob Pulford, Tor.	28

ASSISTS

Name, Team	A
Jean Beliveau, Mtl.	48
Stan Mikita, Chi.	48
Bobby Rousseau, Mtl.	48
Gordie Howe, Det.	46
Bobby Hull, Chi.	43
Murray Oliver, Bos.	42
Norm Ullman, Det.	41
Henri Richard, Mtl.	39
Alex Delvecchio, Det.	38
Claude Provost, Mtl.	36

POWERPLAY GOALS

Name, Team	PPG
Bobby Hull, Chi.	22
Jean Beliveau, Mtl.	13
Stan Mikita, Chi.	11
Bob Pulford, Tor.	11
Frank Mahovlich, Tor.	10
Don Marshall, NYR	10
Doug Mohns, Chi.	10
Bobby Rousseau, Mtl.	10
Ken Wharram, Chi.	9
Alex Delvecchio, Det.	9

SHORTHAND GOALS

Name, Team	SHG
Alex Delvecchio, Det.	4
Bill Hay, Chi.	2
Chico Maki, Chi.	2
Bob Pulford, Tor.	2
George Armstrong, Tor.	2
16 tied with	1

GAME-WINNING GOALS

Name, Team	GWG
Paul Henderson, Det.	9
Henri Richard, Mtl.	7
Bobby Hull, Chi.	7
Jean Beliveau, Mtl.	7
Ken Wharram, Chi.	7
Ed Shack, Tor.	6
Frank Mahovlich, Tor.	6
Phil Esposito, Chi.	6
Dave Keon, Tor.	6
Alex Delvecchio, Det.	6
John Bucyk, Bos.	5
Claude Provost, Mtl.	5

GOALIE WINS

Name, Team	W
Glenn Hall, Chi.	34
Gump Worsley, Mtl.	29
Roger Crozier, Det.	27
Johnny Bower, Tor.	18
Charlie Hodge, Mtl.	12
Bernie Parent, Bos.	11

SHUTOUTS

Name, Team	SO
Roger Crozier, Det.	7
Bruce Gamble, Tor.	4
Glenn Hall, Chi.	4
Johnny Bower, Tor.	3
Three tied with	2

PLAYOFF GOALS

Name, Team	G
Norm Ullman, Det.	6
Andy Bathgate, Det.	6
Jean Beliveau, Mtl.	5
Dean Prentice, Det.	5
Floyd Smith, Det.	5

PLAYOFF ASSISTS

Name, Team	A
Alex Delvecchio, Det.	11
J.C. Tremblay, Mtl.	9
Norm Ullman, Det.	9
Gordie Howe, Det.	6
Jean Beliveau, Mtl.	5
Gilles Tremblay, Mtl.	5
Dick Duff, Mtl.	5
Dean Prentice, Det.	5

PLAYOFF GOALIE WINS

Name, Team	W
Gump Worsley, Mtl.	8
Roger Crozier, Det.	6
Glenn Hall, Chi.	2

PLAYOFF SHUTOUTS

Team	SO
Gump Worsley, Mtl.	1
Roger Crozier, Det.	1

FIRST TEAM ALL-STARS

Name, Team	Position
Stan Mikita, Chi.	C
Gordie Howe, Det.	RW
Bobby Hull, Chi.	LW
Jacques Laperriere, Mtl.	D
Pierre Pilote, Chi.	D
Glenn Hall, Chi.	G

SECOND TEAM ALL-STARS

Name, Team	Position
Jean Beliveau, Mtl.	C
Bobby Rousseau, Mtl.	RW
Frank Mahovlich, Tor.	LW
Allan Stanley, Tor.	D
Pat Stapleton, Chi.	D
Lorne Worsley, Mtl.	G

1966 Playoffs

SEMI-FINALS

Apr.	7	Toronto	3	at	Montreal	4
Apr.	9	Toronto	0	at	Montreal	2
Apr.	12	Montreal	5	at	Toronto	2
Apr.	14	Montreal	4	at	Toronto	1

Montreal won best-of-seven series 4–0

Apr.	7	Detroit	1	at	Chicago	2
Apr.	10	Detroit	7	at	Chicago	0
Apr.	12	Chicago	2	at	Detroit	1
Apr.	14	Chicago	1	at	Detroit	5
Apr.	17	Detroit	5	at	Chicago	3
Apr.	19	Chicago	2	at	Detroit	3

Detroit won best-of-seven series 4–2

FINALS

Apr.	24	Detroit	3	at	Montreal	2
Apr.	26	Detroit	5	at	Montreal	2
Apr.	28	Montreal	4	at	Detroit	2
May	1	Montreal	2	at	Detroit	1
May	3	Detroit	1	at	Montreal	5
May	5	Montreal	3	at	Detroit	2 OT

Montreal won best-of-seven series 4–2

1965-66 – Montreal Canadiens – Gump Worsley, Charlie Hodge, J.C. Tremblay, Ted Harris, Jean-Guy Talbot, Terry Harper, Jacques Laperrière, Noel Price, Jean Béliveau (Captain), Ralph Backstrom, Dick Duff, Gilles Tremblay, Claude Larose, Yvan Cournoyer, Claude Provost, Bobby Rousseau, Henri Richard, Dave Balon, John Ferguson, Leon Rochefort, Jimmy Roberts, Toe Blake (Coach), Sam Pollock (General Manager), Larry Aubut, Andy Galley (Trainers).

TROPHY WINNERS

Trophy	Awarded For	Winner	Team
Hart	MVP	Bobby Hull	Chi.
Art Ross	Top Scorer	Bobby Hull	Chi.
Norris	Top Defenseman	Jacques Laperriere	Mtl.
Calder	Top Rookie	Brit Selby	Tor.
Vezina	Fewest Goals Against	Gump Worsley	Mtl.
		Charlie Hodge	Mtl.
Byng	Gentlemanly Conduct	Alex Delvecchio	Det
Conn Smythe	Playoff MVP	Roger Crozier	Det.
Patrick	Service to Hockey in U.S.	J.J. "Jack" Adams	
Amateur Draft	First Overall Selection	Barry Gibbs	Bos.

NHL NOTEBOOK

TRANSACTIONS

- May 17, 1965 – New York Rangers obtained minor league goaltender Eddie Giacomin in trade from Providence of the AHL for Marcel Paille, Aldo Guidolin, Don McGregor and Jim Mikol.
- May 20, 1965 – Detroit Red Wings acquired Andy Bathgate, Billy Harris and Gary Jarrett from the Toronto Maple Leafs for Marcel Pronovost, Aut Erickson, Larry Jeffrey, Ed Joyal, and Lowell MacDonald.
- Jan. 10, 1966 – Boston obtained John McKenzie from the Rangers in exchange for Reggie Fleming.

RECORDS

- Mar. 16, 1966 – Montreal and the Maple Leafs combined to set an NHL record by scoring four goals in a span of 1:05 during a 7-2 Canadiens win at Toronto.
- Apr. 3, 1966 – In the final game of the 1965-66 season, Chicago's Bobby Hull picked up an assist (during a 4-2 loss at Boston) to give him 97 points, the most ever by a player in one season. Hull broke Dickie Moore's NHL record of 96 points set in 1958-59.

MILESTONES

- Oct. 30, 1965 – Chicago's Bobby Hull scored twice and added two assists as the Black Hawks became the first team in NHL history to open a season with four straight games on the road and four straight road victories, with a 6-4 win at Montreal.
- Feb. 5, 1966 – Detroit's Bill Gadsby became the first NHL player to appear in 300 or more games with three different teams, when he picked up an assist in a 2-2 tie against in Montreal. Gadsby had previously played for Chicago and the New York Rangers.
- Feb. 9, 1966 – Hockey's expansion era began as the governors of the NHL announced that six conditional franchises had been granted to Los Angeles, San Francisco, St. Louis, Philadelphia, Pittsburgh, and Minneapolis for the 1967-68 season.
- Feb. 26, 1966 – Toronto's Frank Mahovlich became the first player in franchise history to score 250 goals as a member of the Maple Leafs. The milestone came in a 3-2 win over the visiting Bruins.
- Mar. 12, 1966 – Bobby Hull became the first player in NHL history to score more than 50 goals in a season when he picked up #51 in a 4-2 win over the Rangers. Hull broke the record shared by Maurice Richard and Bernie Geoffrion in front of 22,000 fans in Chicago.

1966-67

Stanley Cup • Toronto Maple Leafs

FINAL STANDINGS

Team	GP	W	L	T	GF	GA	PTS
Chicago	70	41	17	12	264	170	94
Montreal	70	32	25	13	202	188	77
Toronto	70	32	27	11	204	211	75
New York	70	30	28	12	188	189	72
Detroit	70	27	39	4	212	241	58
Boston	70	17	43	10	182	253	44

LEADING SCORERS

Player	Club	GP	G	A	PTS	PIM
Stan Mikita	Chicago	70	35	62	97	12
Bobby Hull	Chicago	66	52	28	80	52
Norm Ullman	Detroit	68	26	44	70	26
Kenny Wharram	Chicago	70	31	34	65	21
Gordie Howe	Detroit	69	25	40	65	53
Bobby Rousseau	Montreal	68	19	44	63	58
Phil Esposito	Chicago	69	21	40	61	40
Phil Goyette	NY Rangers	70	12	49	61	6
Doug Mohns	Chicago	61	25	35	60	58
Henri Richard	Montreal	65	21	34	55	28
Alex Delvecchio	Detroit	70	17	38	55	10
Dave Keon	Toronto	66	19	33	52	2
Pierre Pilote	Chicago	70	6	46	52	90
John Bucyk	Boston	59	18	30	48	12
Ted Hampson	Detroit	65	13	35	48	4
Bruce MacGregor	Detroit	70	28	19	47	14
Rod Gilbert	NY Rangers	64	28	18	46	12
Don Marshall	NY Rangers	70	24	22	46	4
Frank Mahovlich	Toronto	63	18	28	46	44
Dean Prentice	Detroit	68	23	22	45	18
Ron Ellis	Toronto	67	22	23	45	14
Bob Pulford	Toronto	67	17	28	45	28
Bob Nevin	NY Rangers	67	20	24	44	6
Dennis Hull	Chicago	70	25	17	42	33
Pit Martin	Boston	70	20	22	42	40
John Ferguson	Montreal	67	20	22	42	177
Bernie Geoffrion	NY Rangers	58	17	25	42	42

LEADING GOALTENDERS

Goaltender	Club	GPI	MINS	GA	SO	AVG
Glenn Hall	Chicago	32	1664	66	2	2.38
Denis DeJordy	Chicago	44	2536	104	4	2.46
Charlie Hodge	Montreal	37	2055	88	3	2.57
Ed Giacomin	NY Rangers	68	3981	173	9	2.61
Johnny Bower	Toronto	27	1431	63	2	2.64
Terry Sawchuk	Toronto	28	1409	66	2	2.81
Roger Crozier	Detroit	58	3256	182	4	3.35
Eddie Johnston	Boston	34	1880	116	0	3.70

LEADING PLAYOFF SCORERS

Player	Club	GP	G	A	PTS	PIM
Jim Pappin	Toronto	12	7	8	15	12
Pete Stemkowski	Toronto	12	5	7	12	20
Jean Beliveau	Montreal	10	6	5	11	26
Bob Pulford	Toronto	12	1	10	11	12
Henri Richard	Montreal	10	4	6	10	2
Frank Mahovlich	Toronto	12	3	7	10	8
Dave Keon	Toronto	12	3	5	8	0
Tim Horton	Toronto	12	3	5	8	25
Bobby Rousseau	Montreal	10	1	7	8	4
Ralph Backstrom	Montreal	10	5	2	7	6
Mike Walton	Toronto	12	4	3	7	2

LEADING PLAYOFF GOALTENDERS

Goaltender	Club	GPI	MINS	GA	SO	AVG
Rogie Vachon	Montreal	9	555	22	0	2.38
Terry Sawchuk	Toronto	10	565	25	0	2.65
Ed Giacomin	NY Rangers	4	246	14	0	3.41

Frank Mahovlich (left) was the main offensive weapon on Toronto teams that won the Stanley Cup in 1962, 1963, 1964 and 1967. Red Kelly (right) had already won the Stanley Cup four times in Detroit before winning four more in Toronto. His eight Cup victories are the most by any player who never skated for the Montreal Canadiens.

THIS WAS CHICAGO'S TIME TO SHINE. Stan Mikita was the best player in the league and Bobby Hull scoring prodigiously. With youngsters like Phil Esposito and a fabulous defense led by Pierre Pilote, the Hawks were the best from wire to wire—until the playoffs began. Mikita had even sacrificed his chippy play for the good of the team. The son of Czech parents who sent him to Canada, he had been an outsider as a boy, and he needed a mean streak to survive. Now he was old enough to change his ways, and he went from an explosion waiting to happen to the Lady Byng Trophy winner.

Another welcome change was the play of the Rangers. Ed Giacomin was a force in goal and Harry Howell won the Norris Trophy as the league's top defenseman. Rod Gilbert inspired his teammates with a difficult return from back surgery, while Bernie Geoffrion amazingly decided to make a comeback and put on the Broadway colors.

Maple Leaf Magic – Mikita grabbed the hardware as the Black Hawks ruled the roost but Punch Imlach's proud "Old Pappies" won the Silverware in Canada's Centennial Year showdown with Montreal.

The Canadian teams were more troubled than usual. Montreal's offense dipped, and Toe Blake blamed it on excessive experimentation with curved sticks. At this point, there was still no law regulating their curve. However, the Habs reached into their well of endless great goalies and came out with Rogie Vachon. The Leafs were so poor at one stage that Punch Imlach left the team and went into hospital, afflicted by stress and exhaustion. King Clancy took over, and the happy-go-lucky replacement brought out the best in his players.

Boston didn't appear much better than usual, though Bobby Orr had arrived and the league would never be the same. His points were relatively few this year when compared to his prime, but Orr skated like the wind and did things with the puck no one had even dreamed of.

The Leafs came to life in the semi-finals. Their tight-checking style was more suited to the playoffs than Chicago's offensive approach and won the day. The Black Hawks only had one high-scoring game, falling in six. Terry Sawchuk and Johnny Bower had a combined age that gave them a grandfatherly air, but they were still a fine tandem in the Leaf net. Montreal swept the young Rangers to make it to the finals. Canada celebrated its 100th birthday by watching the series, which featured two blowout wins by Montreal over Sawchuk. He rebounded to win games five and six, taking the series. It had been a memorable show by the oldest team ever to win the Cup.

Leaders, 1966-67

GOALS

Name, Team	G
Bobby Hull, Chi.	52
Stan Mikita, Chi.	35
Kenny Wharram, Chi.	31
Rod Gilbert, NYR	28
Bruce MacGregor, Det.	28
Norm Ullman, Det.	26
Doug Mohns, Chi.	25
Gordie Howe, Det.	25
Yvan Cournoyer, Mtl.	25
Dennis Hull, Chi.	25

ASSISTS

Name, Team	A
Stan Mikita, Chi.	62
Phil Goyette, NYR	49
Pierre Pilote, Chi.	46
Norm Ullman, Det.	44
Bobby Rousseau, Mtl.	44
Gordie Howe, Det.	40
Phil Esposito, Chi.	40
Alex Delvecchio, Det.	38
Doug Mohns, Chi.	35
Ted Hampson, Det.	35

POWERPLAY GOALS

Name, Team	PPG
Yvan Cournoyer, Mtl.	20
Bobby Hull, Chi.	18
Stan Mikita, Chi.	8
Ken Wharram, Chi.	8
Don Marshall, NYR	8
Jim Pappin, Tor.	6
Seven tied with	5

SHORTHAND GOALS

Name, Team	SHG
Eric Nesterenko, Chi.	3
Bobby Hull, Chi.	2
Doug Mohns, Chi.	2
Jean-Guy Talbot, Mtl.	2
Ken Schinkel, NYR	2
Ron Ellis, Tor.	2
19 tied with	1

GAME-WINNING GOALS

Name, Team	GWG
Yvan Cournoyer, Mtl.	7
Ron Ellis, Tor.	7
Jim Pappin, Tor.	7
John McKenzie, Bos.	5
Bobby Hull, Chi.	5
Doug Mohns, Chi.	5
Stan Mikita, Chi.	5
Chico Maki, Chi.	5
Paul Henderson, Det.	5
Dave Balon, Mtl.	5
Rod Gilbert, NYR	5

GOALIE WINS

Name, Team	W
Ed Giacomin, NYR	30
Denis DeJordy, Chi.	22
Roger Crozier, Det.	22
Glenn Hall, Chi.	19
Terry Sawchuk, Tor.	15

SHUTOUTS

Name, Team	SO
Ed Giacomin, NYR	9
Denis DeJordy, Chi.	4
Roger Crozier, Det.	4
Charlie Hodge, Mtl.	3
Three tied with	2

PLAYOFF GOALS

Name, Team	G
Jim Pappin, Tor.	7
Jean Beliveau, Mtl.	6
Ralph Backstrom, Mtl.	5
Pete Stemkowski, Tor.	5
Four tied with	4

PLAYOFF ASSISTS

Name, Team	A
Bob Pulford, Tor.	10
Jim Pappin, Tor.	8
Bobby Rousseau, Mtl.	7
Pete Stemkowski, Tor.	7
Frank Mahovlich, Tor.	7

PLAYOFF GOALIE WINS

Name, Team	W
Rogie Vachon, Mtl.	6
Terry Sawchuk, Tor.	6
Johnny Bower, Tor.	2
Glenn Hall, Chi.	1
Denis DeJordy, Chi.	1

PLAYOFF SHUTOUTS

Team	SO
Johnny Bower, Tor.	1

FIRST TEAM ALL-STARS

Name, Team	Position
Stan Mikita, Chi.	C
Ken Wharram, Chi.	RW
Bobby Hull, Chi.	LW
Pierre Pilote, Chi.	D
Harry Howell, NYR	D
Ed Giacomin, NYR	G

SECOND TEAM ALL-STARS

Name, Team	Position
Norm Ulman, Det.	C
Gordie Howe, Det.	RW
Don Marshall, NYR	LW
Tim Horton, Tor.	D
Bobby Orr, Bos.	D
Glenn Hall, Chi.	G

1967 Playoffs

SEMI-FINALS

Apr. 6	Toronto	2	at	Chicago	5	
Apr. 9	Toronto	3	at	Chicago	1	
Apr. 11	Chicago	1	at	Toronto	3	
Apr. 13	Chicago	4	at	Toronto	3	
Apr. 15	Toronto	4	at	Chicago	2	
Apr. 18	Chicago	1	at	Toronto	3	

Toronto won best-of-seven series 4–2

Apr. 6	NY Rangers	4	at	Montreal	6	
Apr. 8	NY Rangers	1	at	Montreal	3	
Apr. 11	Montreal	3	at	NY Rangers	2	
Apr. 13	Montreal	2	at	NY Rangers	1	OT

Montreal won best-of-seven series 4–0

FINALS

Apr. 20	Toronto	2	at	Montreal	6	
Apr. 22	Toronto	3	at	Montreal	0	
Apr. 25	Montreal	2	at	Toronto	3	2OT
Apr. 27	Montreal	6	at	Toronto	2	
Apr. 29	Toronto	4	at	Montreal	1	
May 2	Montreal	1	at	Toronto	3	

Toronto won best-of-seven series 4–2

1966-67 – Toronto Maple Leafs – Johnny Bower, Terry Sawchuk, Larry Hillman, Marcel Pronovost, Tim Horton, Bob Baun, Aut Erickson, Allan Stanley, Red Kelly, Ron Ellis, George Armstrong (Captain), Pete Stemkowski, Dave Keon, Mike Walton, Jim Pappin, Bob Pulford, Brian Conacher, Eddie Shack, Frank Mahovlich, Milan Marcetta, Larry Jeffrey, Bruce Gamble, Punch Imlach (General Manager/Coach), Bob Haggart (Trainer).

TROPHY WINNERS

Trophy	Awarded For	Winner	Team
Hart	MVP	Stan Mikita	Chi.
Art Ross	Top Scorer	Stan Mikita	Chi.
Norris	Top Defenseman	Harry Howell	NYR
Calder	Top Rookie	Bobby Orr	Bos.
Vezina	Fewest Goals Against	Glenn Hall	Chi
		Denis Dejordy	Chi
Byng	Gentlemanly Conduct	Stan Mikita	Chi.
Conn Smythe	Playoff MVP	Dave Keon	Tor.
Patrick	Service to Hockey in U.S.	Gordie Howe	
		Charles F. Adams	
		James Norris, Sr.	
Amateur Draft	First Overall Selection	Rick Pagnutti	L.A.

NHL NOTEBOOK

TRANSACTIONS

- June 9, 1966 – Bernie Geoffrion was claimed on waivers by the NY Rangers from the Montreal Canadiens.
- June 15, 1966 – New York Rangers claimed Orland Kurtenbach from Toronto at the Intra-League draft.
- June 15, 1966 – New York Rangers received Al MacNeil from the Montreal Canadiens in the NHL's Intra-League draft.
- Sept. 3, 1966 – Bobby Orr signed his first NHL contract with the Boston Bruins, a two-year deal paying $70,000 plus a signing bonus – the top salary in the game.

RECORDS

- Oct. 19, 1966 – Detroit's Gordie Howe played in the first game of his 21st consecutive season in the NHL, breaking the old league record of 20 years held by Dit Clapper and Bill Gadsby. He picked up an assist in a 6-2 loss at Boston.
- Mar. 4, 1967 – Terry Sawchuk became the first NHL goaltender to record 100 career shutouts, when Toronto beat Chicago 3-0 at Maple Leaf Gardens.
- Mar. 18, 1967 – Chicago's Bobby Hull became the first NHL player to record back-to-back 50-goal seasons, when he scored his 50th in a 9-5 loss at Toronto.
- Mar. 28, 1967 – Chicago's Stan Mikita set an NHL record for most assists in a season, when he picked up #60 in a 7-2 win over the visiting Detroit Red Wings. Mikita broke his own record of 59 set in 1964-65.

MILESTONES

- Dec. 7, 1966 – Montreal's Henri Richard joined Maurice as the first set of brothers to score 250 career NHL goals when he scored in a 6-3 win over the visiting Maple Leafs.
- Jan. 18, 1967 – The All-Star game was held mid-season for the first time. The Cup-champion Canadiens beat the All Stars 3-0 at the Forum.
- Jan. 21, 1967 – Defenseman Harry Howell became the first player to appear in 1,000 games in a New York Rangers uniform. The milestone came in a 6-2 loss at Boston.
- May 2, 1967 – Toronto beat Montreal 3-1 in game six of the finals to become the 1967 Stanley Cup champions – in the last Stanley Cup series among the "Original Six" NHL teams.

1967-68

Stanley Cup • Montreal Canadiens

FINAL STANDINGS

EAST DIVISION

Team	GP	W	L	T	GF	GA	PTS
Montreal	74	42	22	10	236	167	94
New York	74	39	23	12	226	183	90
Boston	74	37	27	10	259	216	84
Chicago	74	32	26	16	212	222	80
Toronto	74	33	31	10	209	176	76
Detroit	74	27	35	12	245	257	66

WEST DIVISION

Team	GP	W	L	T	GF	GA	PTS
Philadelphia	74	31	32	11	173	179	73
Los Angeles	74	31	33	10	200	224	72
St. Louis	74	27	31	16	177	191	70
Minnesota	74	27	32	15	191	226	69
Pittsburgh	74	27	34	13	195	216	67
Oakland	74	15	42	17	153	219	47

LEADING SCORERS

Player	Club	GP	G	A	PTS	PIM
Stan Mikita	Chicago	72	40	47	87	14
Phil Esposito	Boston	74	35	49	84	21
Gordie Howe	Detroit	74	39	43	82	53
Jean Ratelle	NY Rangers	74	32	46	78	18
Rod Gilbert	NY Rangers	73	29	48	77	12
Bobby Hull	Chicago	71	44	31	75	39
Norm Ullman	Det./Tor.	71	35	37	72	28
Alex Delvecchio	Detroit	74	22	48	70	14
John Bucyk	Boston	72	30	39	69	8
Kenny Wharram	Chicago	74	27	42	69	18
Jean Beliveau	Montreal	59	31	37	68	28
John McKenzie	Boston	74	28	38	66	107
Phil Goyette	NY Rangers	73	25	40	65	10
Bobby Rousseau	Montreal	74	19	46	65	47
Fred Stanfield	Boston	73	20	44	64	10
Yvan Cournoyer	Montreal	64	28	32	60	23
Mike Walton	Toronto	73	30	29	59	48
Andy Bathgate	Pittsburgh	74	20	39	59	55
Bob Nevin	NY Rangers	74	28	30	58	20
Eddie Joyal	Los Angeles	74	23	34	57	20
Wayne Connelly	Minnesota	74	35	21	56	40
Ken Hodge	Boston	74	25	31	56	31
Dean Prentice	Detroit	69	17	38	55	42
Red Berenson	NYR/St.L.	74	24	30	54	24
Ted Hampson	Det./Oak.	71	17	37	54	14

LEADING GOALTENDERS

Goaltender	Club	GPI	MINS	GA	SO	AVG
Gump Worsley	Montreal	40	2213	73	6	1.98
Johnny Bower	Toronto	43	2239	84	4	2.25
Doug Favell	Philadelphia	37	2192	83	4	2.27
Bruce Gamble	Toronto	41	2201	85	5	2.32
Ed Giacomin	NY Rangers	66	3940	160	8	2.44
Glenn Hall	St. Louis	49	2858	118	5	2.48
Rogie Vachon	Montreal	39	2227	92	4	2.48
Bernie Parent	Philadelphia	38	2248	93	4	2.48
Seth Martin	St. Louis	30	1552	67	1	2.59
Denis DeJordy	Chicago	50	2838	128	4	2.71

Minnesota's Bill Masterton had played junior hockey in the Canadiens system in the 1950s before making the then unusual decision to attend an American college (the University of Denver). Acquired by the North Stars in June of 1967, Masterton played just 38 games in the NHL before hitting his head on the ice on January 13, 1968. He died two days later.

IT WAS NOT ONLY THE AGE OF EXPANSION but the era of inflating salaries. Bobby Orr had started the money flowing by negotiating a $75,000 deal for his first two years through new agent Alan Eagleson. He had been offered $13,000. The NHLPA hired Eagleson, and he gained a new minimum salary of $10,000, higher playoff cuts for players and more opportunities to make endorsement money.

The expansion draft meant many players changed teams, but Chicago and Boston made a trade that trumped all. Phil Esposito, Ken Hodge and Fred Stanfield went to Boston for Gilles Marotte, Pit Martin and Jack Norris. The deal—plus the presence of Orr—provided the foundation for Boston's dominance a few years later. The Bruins improved instantly, becoming the NHL's highest-scoring team. In another big deal involving seven players, Frank Mahovlich went from Toronto to Detroit.

Doubling Up – There was something new – six new clubs in the NHL – something borrowed – the Bruins "stole" Phil Esposito from Chicago – and something blue as St. Louis lost four one-goal games in the finals.

Expect for Oakland, the new teams all enjoyed moderate success. In St. Louis, the Blues had an intriguing lineup: Glenn Hall, Red Berenson and Dickie Moore all skated for them. Doug Harvey returned to the league in April and signed with St. Louis. One tragic note was the accidental death of Bill Masterton, a Minnesota North Stars player who hit his head on the ice and never recovered. This caused quite a few players, including Stan Mikita, to begin wearing helmets. A new trophy was instituted in Masterton's honor.

After solid seasons, Boston and the Rangers did not win a playoff round, while Chicago was a disappointment against Montreal in the semi-finals. Toronto and Detroit hadn't managed to qualify for the postseason. In the newly created West Division, St. Louis squeezed through two long series to make it to the finals. The Blues' semi-final win had been truly epic, with four overtimes, including double overtime in game seven. Montreal looked strong with Serge Savard and a young defense that had improved considerably since midseason, when it was last in the East.

Hall was spectacular against the superior Canadiens, but Scotty Bowman's Blues did not have enough scoring power to get and hold a lead. Montreal's Jacques Lemaire took game one on an overtime goal. Savard won the next match in the third period. Bobby Rousseau broke the Blues in the second minute of sudden death to give Montreal a 3–0 series lead. The Canadiens eked out another third-period win to regain the Cup, though Hall was named playoff MVP.

Paul Henderson battles Flyers goalie Doug Favell for the puck following the blockbuster trade that sent him from Detroit to Toronto on March 3, 1968. Henderson enjoyed four solid seasons with the Maple Leafs, but seemed unable to live up to the high expectations created by his three consecutive winning goals to end the 1972 Canada/Russia series.

Leaders, 1967-68

GOALS

Name, Team	G
Bobby Hull, Chi.	44
Stan Mikita, Chi.	40
Gordie Howe, Det.	39
Norm Ullman, Det./Tor.	35
Phil Esposito, Bos.	35
Wayne Connelly, Min.	35
Jean Ratelle, NYR	32
Jean Beliveau, Mtl.	31
John Bucyk, Bos.	30
Mike Walton, Tor.	30

ASSISTS

Name, Team	A
Phil Esposito, Bos.	49
Rod Gilbert, NYR	48
Alex Delvecchio, Det.	48
Stan Mikita, Chi.	47
Jean Ratelle, NYR	46
Bobby Rousseau, Mtl.	46
Fred Stanfield, Bos.	44
Gordie Howe, Det.	43
Kenny Wharram, Chi.	42
Phil Goyette, NYR	40

POWERPLAY GOALS

Name, Team	PPG
Wayne Connelly, Min.	14
Stan Mikita, Chi.	13
Bill Hicke, Oak.	12
Ray Cullen, Min.	11
Mike Walton, Tor.	11
Jean Ratelle, NYR	10
Gordie Howe, Det.	10
Jean Beliveau, Mtl.	9
Parker MacDonald, Min.	9
Phil Esposito, Bos.	9
Kenny Wharram, Chi.	9

SHORTHAND GOALS

Name, Team	SHG
Bill McCreary, St.L.	4
Skip Krake, Bos.	3
Claude Provost, Mtl.	3
Bob Pulford, Tor.	3
11 tied with	2

GAME-WINNING GOALS

Name, Team	GWG
Dick Duff, Mtl.	8
Stan Mikita, Chi.	8
Wayne Connelly, Min.	8
Vic Hadfield, NYR	7
Phil Goyette, NYR	7
Red Berenson, NYR/St.L.	7
Ray Cullen, Min.	6
Eddie Shack, Bos.	6
Bobby Hull, Chi.	6
Derek Sanderson, Bos.	6
Rod Gilbert, NYR	6
Bill Flett, L.A.	6

GOALIE WINS

Name, Team	W
Ed Giacomin, NYR	36
Rogie Vachon, Mtl.	23
Gerry Cheevers, Bos.	23
Denis DeJordy, Chi.	23
Cesare Maniago, Min.	21
Wayne Rutledge, L.A.	20
Les Binkley, Pit.	20
Gump Worsley, Mtl.	19
Bruce Gamble, Tor.	19
Glenn Hall, St.L.	19

SHUTOUTS

Name, Team	SO
Ed Giacomin, NYR	8
Gump Worsley, Mtl.	6
Cesare Maniago, Min.	6
Les Binkley, Pit.	6
Bruce Gamble, Tor.	5
Glenn Hall, St.L.	5

FIRST TEAM ALL-STARS

Name, Team	Position
Stan Mikita, Chi.	C
Gordie Howe, Det.	RW
Bobby Hull, Chi.	LW
Bobby Orr, Bos.	D
Tim Horton, Tor.	D
Lorne Worsley, Mtl.	G

SECOND TEAM ALL-STARS

Name, Team	Position
Phil Esposito, Bos.	C
Rod Gilbert, NYR	RW
Johnny Bucyk, Bos.	LW
J.C. Tremblay, Mtl.	D
Jim Neilson, NYR	D
Ed Giacomin, NYR	G

TROPHY WINNERS

Trophy	Awarded For	Winner	Team
Hart	MVP	Stan Mikita	Chi.
Art Ross	Top Scorer	Stan Mikita	Chi.
Norris	Top Defenseman	Bobby Orr	Bos.
Calder	Top Rookie	Derek Sanderson	Bos.
Vezina	Fewest Goals Against	Gump Worsley	Mtl.
		Rogie Vachon	Mtl.
Byng	Gentlemanly Conduct	Stan Mikita	Chi
Masterton	Perseverance, Sportmanship	Claude Provost	Mtl.
Conn Smythe	Playoff MVP	Glenn Hall	St.L.
Patrick	Service to Hockey in U.S.	Thomas F. Lockhart	
		Walter A. Brown	
		Gen. John R. Kilpatrick	
Amateur Draft	First Overall Selection	Michel Plasse	Mtl.

NHL NOTEBOOK

TRANSACTIONS

- May 15, 1967 – Toronto Maple Leafs traded Eddie Shack to the Boston Bruins for Murray Oliver.
- May 15, 1967 – Phil Esposito, Ken Hodge and Fred Stanfield were traded from Chicago to Boston for Gilles Marotte, Pit Martin and Jack Norris.
- Nov. 29, 1967 – St. Louis traded Ron Stewart and Ron Atwell to the NY Rangers for Barclay Plager and Red Berenson, both of whom went on to star with the Blues.
- Mar. 3, 1968 – Detroit Red Wings traded Paul Henderson, Norm Ullman and Floyd Smith to Toronto for Frank Mahovlich, Pete Stemkowski, Garry Unger and the rights to Carl Brewer.

RECORDS

- Jan. 28, 1968 – Terry Sawchuk got his 101st career shutout as the Kings beat the Flyers 2-0 at Philadelphia. Sawchuk also extended his NHL record when his first shutout of the season gave him one (or more) shutouts in 19 straight years.
- Feb. 24, 1968 – Garry Unger began a 914 consecutive-game playing streak when Toronto beat Boston 1-0. It would stand as an NHL record until broken by Doug Jarvis in 1986-87.
- Feb. 24, 1968 – Rod Gilbert set an NHL record with 16 shots – and scored four goals to lead the Rangers to a 6-1 win at Montreal.
- Apr. 6, 1968 – Los Angeles became the first club in NHL history to win its first two playoff games, beating the Minnesota North Stars 2-0 in game two of the Stanley Cup quarter-finals.

MILESTONES

- Nov. 22, 1967 – 34-year-old Scotty Bowman was named the new coach of the St. Louis Blues, replacing Lynn Patrick, who resigned. It was Bowman's first head coaching job in the NHL. He lost in his debut behind the bench that same night 3-1 to Montreal.
- Dec. 7, 1967 – Montreal's John Ferguson became the first player in NHL history to be assessed a triple minor penalty, in a 2-2 tie against Detroit in Montreal.
- Apr. 9, 1968 – Minnesota's Wayne Connelly became the first player in NHL history to score a penalty shot goal in the playoffs (after two others missed) when he beat Terry Sawchuk during a 7-5 North Stars win over Los Angeles.
- May 10, 1968 – Bobby Orr was named winner of the Norris Memorial Trophy (as the NHL's outstanding defenseman) for the first of what would prove to be an NHL record eight consecutive seasons.

1968 Playoffs

QUARTER-FINALS

Apr.	4	Boston	1	at	Montreal	2
Apr.	6	Boston	3	at	Montreal	5
Apr.	9	Montreal	5	at	Boston	2
Apr.	11	Montreal	3	at	Boston	2

Montreal won best-of-seven series 4–0

Apr.	4	Chicago	1	at	NY Rangers	3
Apr.	9	Chicago	1	at	NY Rangers	2
Apr.	11	NY Rangers	4	at	Chicago	7
Apr.	13	NY Rangers	1	at	Chicago	3
Apr.	14	Chicago	2	at	NY Rangers	1
Apr.	16	NY Rangers	1	at	Chicago	4

Chicago won best-of-seven series 4–2

Apr.	4	St. Louis	1	at	Philadelphia	0
Apr.	6	St. Louis	3	at	Philadelphia	4
Apr.	10	Philadelphia	2	at	St. Louis	3 2OT
Apr.	11	Philadelphia	2	at	St. Louis	5
Apr.	13	St. Louis	1	at	Philadelphia	6
Apr.	16	Philadephia	2	at	St. Louis	1 2OT
Apr.	18	St. Louis	3	at	Philadelphia	1

St. Louis won best-of-seven series 4–3

Apr.	4	Minnesota	1	at	Los Angeles	2
Apr.	6	Minnesota	0	at	Los Angeles	2
Apr.	9	Los Angeles	5	at	Minnesota	7
Apr.	11	Los Angeles	2	at	Minnesota	3
Apr.	13	Minnesota	2	at	Los Angeles	3
Apr.	16	Los Angeles	3	at	Minnesota	4 OT
Apr.	18	Minnesota	9	at	Los Angeles	4

Minnesota won best-of-seven series 4–3

SEMI-FINALS

Apr.	18	Chicago	2	at	Montreal	9
Apr.	20	Chicago	1	at	Montreal	4
Apr.	23	Montreal	4	at	Chicago	2
Apr.	25	Montreal	1	at	Chicago	2
Apr.	28	Chicago	3	at	Montreal	4 OT

Montreal won best-of-seven series 4–1

Apr.	21	Minnesota	3	at	St. Louis	5
Apr.	22	St. Louis	2	at	Minnesota	3 OT
Apr.	25	Minnesota	5	at	St. Louis	1
Apr.	27	Minnesota	3	at	St. Louis	4 OT
Apr.	29	Minnesota	2	at	St. Louis	3 OT
May	1	St. Louis	1	at	Minnesota	5
May	3	Minnesota	1	at	St. Louis	2 2OT

St. Louis won best-of-seven series 4–3

FINALS

May	5	Montreal	3	at	St. Louis	2 OT
May	7	Montreal	1	at	St. Louis	0
May	9	St. Louis	3	at	Montreal	4 OT
May	11	St. Louis	2	at	Montreal	3

Montreal won best-of-seven series 4–0

1967-68 – Montreal Canadiens – Gump Worsley, Rogie Vachon, Jacques Laperrière, J.C. Tremblay, Ted Harris, Serge Savard, Terry Harper, Carol Vadnais, Jean Béliveau (Captain), Gilles Tremblay, Ralph Backstrom, Dick Duff, Claude Larose, Yvan Cournoyer, Claude Provost, Bobby Rousseau, Henri Richard, John Ferguson, Danny Grant, Jacques Lemaire, Mickey Redmond, Toe Blake (Coach), Sam Pollock (General Manager), Larry Aubut, Eddy Palchak (Trainers).

Montreal's Gump Worsley and Serge Savard defend against the St. Louis Blues. Rogie Vachon saw the bulk of action in goal for the Canadiens during the 1967–68 season, but it was Worsley who sparkled in the playoffs.

LEADING PLAYOFF SCORERS

Player	Club	GP	G	A	PTS	PIM
Bill Goldsworthy	Minnesota	14	8	7	15	12
Dickie Moore	St. Louis	18	7	7	14	15
Milan Marcetta	Minnesota	14	7	7	14	4
Yvan Cournoyer	Montreal	13	6	8	14	4
Jacques Lemaire	Montreal	13	7	6	13	6
Frank St. Marseille	St. Louis	18	5	8	13	0
Dave Balon	Minnesota	14	4	9	13	14
Stan Mikita	Chicago	11	5	7	12	6
Wayne Connelly	Minnesota	14	8	3	11	2
Jean Beliveau	Montreal	10	7	4	11	6

LEADING PLAYOFF GOALTENDERS

Goaltender	Club	GPI	Mins	GA	SO	Avg.
Bernie Parent	Philadelphia	5	355	8	0	1.35
Gump Worsley	Montreal	12	672	21	1	1.88
Glenn Hall	St. Louis	18	1111	45	1	2.43
Cesare Maniago	Minnesota	14	893	39	0	2.62
Ed Giacomin	NY Rangers	6	360	18	0	3.00

PLAYOFF GOALS

Name, Team	G
Bill Goldsworthy, Min.	8
Wayne Connelly, Min.	8
Jean Beliveau, Mtl.	7
Jacques Lemaire, Mtl.	7
Milan Marcetta, Min.	7
Dickie Moore, St.L.	7

PLAYOFF ASSISTS

Name, Team	A
Dave Balon, Min.	9
Yvan Cournoyer, Mtl.	8
Claude Provost, Mtl.	8
Frank St. Marseille, St.L.	8
Five tied with	7

PLAYOFF POWERPLAY GOALS

Name, Team	PPG
Frank St. Marseille, St.L.	4
Eddie Joyal, L.A.	3
Jean Beliveau, Mtl.	3
Yvan Cournoyer, Mtl.	3
Wayne Connelly, Min.	3

PLAYOFF SHORTHAND GOALS

Name, Team	SHG
Serge Savard, Mtl.	2
Mike McMahon, Min.	2
Bill McCreary, St.L.	2
Eight tied with	1

PLAYOFF GAME-WINNING GOALS

Name, Team	GWG
Jacques Lemaire, Mtl.	2
Ralph Backstrom, Mtl.	2
Parker MacDonald, Min.	2
Bill McCreary, St.L.	2
Larry Keenan, St.L.	2

PLAYOFF GOALIE WINS

Name, Team	W
Gump Worsley, Mtl.	11
Glenn Hall, St.L.	8
Cesare Maniago, Min.	7
Denis DeJordy, Chi.	5
Three tied with	2

PLAYOFF SHUTOUTS

Name, Team	SO
Terry Sawchuk, L.A.	1
Gump Worsley, Mtl.	1
Glenn Hall, St.L.	1

1968-69

Stanley Cup • Montreal Canadiens

FINAL STANDINGS

EAST DIVISION

Team	GP	W	L	T	GF	GA	PTS
Montreal	76	46	19	11	271	202	103
Boston	76	42	18	16	303	221	100
New York	76	41	26	9	231	196	91
Toronto	76	35	26	15	234	217	85
Detroit	76	33	31	12	239	221	78
Chicago	76	34	33	9	280	246	77

WEST DIVISION

Team	GP	W	L	T	GF	GA	PTS
St. Louis	76	37	25	14	204	157	88
Oakland	76	29	36	11	219	251	69
Philadelphia	76	20	35	21	174	225	61
Los Angeles	76	24	42	10	185	260	58
Pittsburgh	76	20	45	11	189	252	51
Minnesota	76	18	43	15	189	270	51

LEADING SCORERS

Player	Club	GP	G	A	PTS	PIM
Phil Esposito	Boston	74	49	77	126	79
Bobby Hull	Chicago	74	58	49	107	48
Gordie Howe	Detroit	76	44	59	103	58
Stan Mikita	Chicago	74	30	67	97	52
Ken Hodge	Boston	75	45	45	90	75
Yvan Cournoyer	Montreal	76	43	44	87	31
Alex Delvecchio	Detroit	72	25	58	83	8
Red Berenson	St. Louis	76	35	47	82	43
Jean Beliveau	Montreal	69	33	49	82	55
Frank Mahovlich	Detroit	76	49	29	78	38
Jean Ratelle	NY Rangers	75	32	46	78	26
Norm Ullman	Toronto	75	35	42	77	41
Rod Gilbert	NY Rangers	66	28	49	77	22
Ted Hampson	Oakland	76	26	49	75	6
Bobby Rousseau	Montreal	76	30	40	70	59
Jim Pappin	Chicago	75	30	40	70	49
Kenny Wharram	Chicago	76	30	39	69	19
Vic Hadfield	NY Rangers	73	26	40	66	108
John Bucyk	Boston	70	24	42	66	18
Danny Grant	Minnesota	75	34	31	65	46
Dennis Hull	Chicago	72	30	34	64	25
Ray Cullen	Minnesota	67	26	38	64	44
Bobby Orr	Boston	67	21	43	64	133
Jacques Lemaire	Montreal	75	29	34	63	29
Claude Larose	Minnesota	67	25	37	62	106

LEADING GOALTENDERS

Goaltender	Club	GPI	MINS	GA	SO	AVG
Jacques Plante	St. Louis	37	2139	70	5	1.96
Glenn Hall	St. Louis	41	2354	85	8	2.17
Gump Worsley	Montreal	30	1703	64	5	2.25
Roy Edwards	Detroit	40	2099	89	4	2.54
Ed Giacomin	NY Rangers	70	4114	175	7	2.55
Bernie Parent	Philadelphia	58	3365	151	1	2.69
Gerry Cheevers	Boston	52	3112	145	3	2.80
Bruce Gamble	Toronto	61	3446	161	3	2.80
Rogie Vachon	Montreal	36	2051	98	2	2.87
Gary Smith	Oakland	54	2993	148	4	2.97

Red Berenson was the first Canadian hockey player to go directly from an American college (the University of Michigan) to the NHL, joining the Montreal Canadiens late in the 1961–62 season. He later became a star with the St. Louis Blues and was the first player from an expansion team to crack the top-10 in scoring in 1968–69.

OFFENSE PROSPERED and defense suffered. Expansion meant there were fewer experienced blueliners, goalies and players who understood the art of checking. Also, Bobby Orr was leading a revolution in team play. Clubs saw that it was possible to have an all-out attack featuring a defenseman. Brad Park and others came along to emulate number four's style.

Although Phil Esposito and Boston both set scoring records, Montreal was first in the East Division. Yvan Cournoyer, Jean Beliveau and a superb defense made the defending champs the team to beat. Toe Blake had finally retired, ending the most successful coaching career to date. Claude Ruel took his seat. New York flexed its muscles with Park on defense plus Jean Ratelle, Rod Gilbert and Vic Hadfield, the so-called "Goal-A-Game Line," up front. None of them were paid as well as Bobby Hull who received $100,000 and set a new scoring mark with 58 goals. Another old-timer, Gordie Howe, had a remarkable season, joining Esposito and Hull as the league's first 100-point players. Howe was now up to 700 goals for his career. Still, Detroit and Chicago finished the season out of playoff contention.

 # 4 – Defeseman Bobby Orr redefined the role of the rearguard, the Holy Trinity of Hull, Esposito and Howe broke the century mark in points but the Stanley Cup remained in Montreal.

St. Louis was the only dominant team out west. With the most talented goaltending duo in history, Glenn Hall and the unretired Jacques Plante, the Blues easily led the league in fewest goals allowed. The western and eastern teams were now playing each other six times a year, so this feat was accomplished against all the league's best scorers. The highlight of the Blues season was Red Berenson's six-goal game, which gained him a cover shot on Sports Illustrated.

The playoffs went according to form, even if Montreal needed three overtime wins to edge Boston in the semi-finals. The Bruins had outscored Toronto 17–0 in their first two quarter-final games, which led to Punch Imlach being fired. St. Louis allowed just eight goals in two playoff sweeps on its way to a rematch with the Habs. Montreal took the opening two games fairly easily before Vachon shut out the Blues in game three. John Ferguson's goal in the final frame was the Cup winner as Montreal swept St. Louis again. Serge Savard won the Conn Smythe Trophy, setting the precedent for future winners from the blueline.

Leaders, 1968-69

Ken Hodge, bearing down on Leafs goalie Bruce Gamble, blossomed quickly after the big trade that sent Phil Esposito, Fred Stanfield and him from Chicago to Boston in 1967. His 45 goals in 1968–69 were four more than his entire career total from the previous three seasons.

GOALS

Name, Team	G
Bobby Hull, Chi.	58
Phil Esposito, Bos.	49
Frank Mahovlich, Det.	49
Ken Hodge, Bos.	45
Gordie Howe, Det.	44
Yvan Cournoyer, Mtl.	43
Norm Ullman, Tor.	35
Red Berenson, St.L.	35
Danny Grant, Min.	34
Norm Ferguson, Oak.	34

ASSISTS

Name, Team	A
Phil Esposito, Bos.	77
Stan Mikita, Chi.	67
Gordie Howe, Det.	59
Alex Delvecchio, Det.	58
Pat Stapleton, Chi.	50
Rod Gilbert, NYR	49
Jean Beliveau, Mtl.	49
Bobby Hull, Chi.	49
Ted Hampson, Oak.	49
Red Berenson, St.L.	47

POWERPLAY GOALS

Name, Team	PPG
Bobby Hull, Chi.	20
Yvan Cournoyer, Mtl.	14
Norm Ullman, Tor.	13
Andre Lacroix, Phi.	13
John Bucyk, Bos.	11
Bob Nevin, NYR	11
Danny Grant, Min.	11
Vic Hadfield, NYR	10
Phil Esposito, Bos.	10
Four tied with	9

SHORTHAND GOALS

Name, Team	SHG
Dave Keon, Tor.	6
Ed Westfall, Bos.	4
Derek Sanderson, Bos.	3
Bruce MacGregor, Det.	3
Eric Nesterenko, Chi.	3
Stan Mikita, Chi.	3
Gerry Odrowski, Oak.	3
Eight tied with	2

GAME-WINNING GOALS

Name, Team	GWG
Bobby Hull, Chi.	11
Phil Esposito, Bos.	9
Yvan Cournoyer, Mtl.	8
Bobby Rousseau, Mtl.	8
John McKenzie, Bos.	7
John Ferguson, Mtl.	7
Ken Hodge, Bos.	7
Bob Nevin, NYR	6
Bill Flett, L.A.	6
Dave Keon, Tor.	6
Red Berenson, St.L.	6
Gordie Howe, Det.	6

GOALIE WINS

Name, Team	W
Ed Giacomin, NYR	37
Gerry Cheevers, Bos.	28
Bruce Gamble, Tor.	28
Rogie Vachon, Mtl.	22
Denis DeJordy, Chi.	22
Gary Smith, Oak.	21
Gump Worsley, Mtl.	19
Glenn Hall, St.L.	19
Jacques Plante, St.L.	18
Roy Edwards, Det.	18
Gerry Desjardins, L.A.	18
Cesare Maniago, Min.	18

TROPHY WINNERS

Trophy	Awarded For	Winner	Team
Hart	MVP	Phil Esposito	Bos.
Art Ross	Top Scorer	Phil Esposito	Bos.
Norris	Top Defenseman	Bobby Orr	Bos.
Calder	Top Rookie	Danny Grant	Min.
Vezina	Fewest Goals Against	Jacques Plante	St.L.
		Glenn Hall	St.L.
Byng	Gentlemanly Conduct	Alex Delvecchio	Det.
Masterton	Perseverance, Sportsmanship	Ted Hampson	Oak.
Conn Smythe	Playoff MVP	Serge Savard	Mtl.
Patrick	Service to Hockey in U.S.	Bobby Hull	
		Edward J. Jeremiah	
Amateur Draft	First Overall Selection	Rejean Houle	Mtl.

SHUTOUTS

Name, Team	SO
Glenn Hall, St.L.	8
Ed Giacomin, NYR	7
Gump Worsley, Mtl.	5
Jacques Plante, St.L.	5
Roy Edwards, Det.	4
Gary Smith, Oak.	4
Gerry Desjardins, L.A.	4
Dave Dryden, Chi.	3
Gerry Cheevers, Bos.	3
Bruce Gamble, Tor.	3

FIRST TEAM ALL-STARS

Name, Team	Position
Phil Esposito, Bos.	C
Gordie Howe, Det.	RW
Bobby Hull, Chi.	LW
Bobby Orr, Bos.	D
Tim Horton, Tor.	D
Glenn Hall, St.L.	G

SECOND TEAM ALL-STARS

Name, Team	Position
Jean Beliveau, Mtl.	C
Yvan Cournoyer, Mtl.	RW
Frank Mahovlich, Det.	LW
Ted Green, Bos.	D
Ted Harris, Mtl.	D
Ed Giacomin, NYR	G

NHL NOTEBOOK

TRANSACTIONS

- May 21, 1968 – Pittsburgh Penguins purchased Jean Pronovost from Boston.
- May 23, 1968 – Toronto Maple Leafs acquired defenseman Pierre Pilote from Chicago in exchange for forward Jim Pappin.
- June 11, 1968 – Minnesota North Stars obtained Danny Grant and Claude Larose from Montreal in exchange for a 1st choice in the 1972 Entry Draft.
- June 12, 1968 – St. Louis Blues obtained veteran goaltender Jacques Plante from the NY Rangers in the NHL Intra-League Draft.

RECORDS

- Oct. 16, 1968 – Toronto rookie defenseman Jim Dorey picked up 48 penalty minutes in his first NHL game – four minors, two majors, two misconducts and a game misconduct. Maple Leafs tied 2-2 with the Penguins in Toronto.
- Mar. 1, 1969 – Phil Esposito had a goal and an assist to give him 99 points for the season – breaking the old NHL record for most points in a season (97) held by Stan Mikita. His two points helped Bruins to an 8-5 win over the Rangers in Boston.
- Mar. 30, 1969 – Boston won 6-3 over the Canadiens in Boston as Bobby Orr finished the regular season with 21 goals and 64 points, both NHL records for defensemen.
- Apr. 2, 1969 – Bruins set a playoff record with six powerplay goals in a 10-0 win against Toronto in Boston.

MILESTONES

- Oct. 27, 1968 – Gordie Howe became the first NHL player with 900 career assists and 600 career goals when he picked up three assists in the Red Wings 7-5 win over the visiting Boston Bruins.
- Nov. 7, 1968 – St. Louis Blues' Red Berenson scored six goals and an assist in an 8-0 win over the visiting Flyers. It was the NHL's first six-goal game since Detroit's Syd Howe did it in 1944.
- Mar. 2, 1969 – Boston's Phil Esposito scored twice to become the first player in NHL history to score 100 points in a season. His two goals came in a 4-0 shutout win over Pittsburgh in Boston.
- Apr. 17, 1969 – Gerry Cheevers became the first goaltender in playoff history to get three straight shutouts at home, in a 5-0 win against the visiting Montreal Canadiens in game three of the Stanley Cup semi-finals.

1969 Playoffs

QUARTER-FINALS

Apr.	2	NY Rangers	1	at	Montreal	3
Apr.	3	NY Rangers	2	at	Montreal	5
Apr.	5	Montreal	4	at	NY Rangers	1
Apr.	6	Montreal	4	at	NY Rangers	3

Montreal won best-of-seven series 4–0

Apr.	2	Toronto	0	at	Boston	10
Apr.	3	Toronto	0	at	Boston	7
Apr.	5	Boston	4	at	Toronto	3
Apr.	6	Boston	3	at	Toronto	2

Boston won best-of-seven series 4–0

Apr.	2	Philadelphia	2	at	St. Louis	5
Apr.	3	Philadelphia	0	at	St. Louis	5
Apr.	5	St. Louis	3	at	Philadelphia	0
Apr.	6	St. Louis	4	at	Philadelphia	1

St. Louis won best-of-seven series 4–0

Apr.	2	Los Angeles	5	at	Oakland	4 OT
Apr.	3	Los Angeles	2	at	Oakland	4
Apr.	5	Oakland	5	at	Los Angeles	2
Apr.	6	Oakland	2	at	Los Angeles	4
Apr.	9	Los Angeles	1	at	Oakland	4
Apr.	10	Oakland	3	at	Los Angeles	4
Apr.	13	Los Angeles	5	at	Oakland	3

Los Angeles won best-of-seven series 4–3

SEMI-FINALS

Apr.	10	Boston	2	at	Montreal	3 OT
Apr.	13	Boston	3	at	Montreal	4 OT
Apr.	17	Montreal	0	at	Boston	5
Apr.	20	Montreal	2	at	Boston	3
Apr.	22	Boston	2	at	Montreal	4
Apr.	24	Montreal	2	at	Boston	1 2OT

Montreal won best-of-seven series 4–2

Apr.	15	Los Angeles	0	at	St. Louis	4
Apr.	17	Los Angeles	2	at	St. Louis	3
Apr.	19	St. Louis	5	at	Los Angeles	2
Apr.	20	St. Louis	4	at	Los Angeles	1

St. Louis won best-of-seven series 4–0

FINALS

Apr.	27	St. Louis	1	at	Montreal	3
Apr.	29	St. Louis	1	at	Montreal	3
May	1	Montreal	4	at	St. Louis	0
May	4	Montreal	2	at	St. Louis	1

Montreal won best-of-seven series 4–0

1968-69 – Montreal Canadiens – Gump Worsley, Rogie Vachon, Jacques Laperrière, J.C. Tremblay, Ted Harris, Serge Savard, Terry Harper, Larry Hillman, Jean Béliveau (Captain), Ralph Backstrom, Dick Duff, Yvan Cournoyer, Claude Provost, Bobby Rousseau, Henri Richard, John Ferguson, Christian Bordeleau, Mickey Redmond, Jacques Lemaire, Lucien Grenier, Tony Esposito, Claude Ruel (Coach), Sam Pollock (General Manager), Larry Aubut, Eddy Palchak (Trainers).

Yvan Cournoyer stood just 5'7" and weighed 178 pounds. He was considered too small to play regularly in the NHL until his blazing speed and puck-handling skill convinced people otherwise. Used mainly on the powerplay in his early years in the NHL, Cournoyer reached the 40-goal plateau for the first of four times in 1968–69.

LEADING PLAYOFF SCORERS

Player	Club	GP	G	A	PTS	PIM
Phil Esposito	Boston	10	8	10	18	8
Jean Beliveau	Montreal	14	5	10	15	8
Dick Duff	Montreal	14	6	8	14	11
Ken Hodge	Boston	10	5	7	12	4
Gary Sabourin	St. Louis	12	6	5	11	12
John Bucyk	Boston	10	5	6	11	0
Yvan Cournoyer	Montreal	14	4	7	11	5
Derek Sanderson	Boston	9	8	2	10	36
Red Berenson	St. Louis	12	7	3	10	20
Serge Savard	Montreal	14	4	6	10	24
Earl Ingarfield	Oakland	7	4	6	10	2
Ed Westfall	Boston	10	3	7	10	11

LEADING PLAYOFF GOALTENDERS

Goaltender	Club	GPI	Mins	GA	SO	Avg.
Rogie Vachon	Montreal	8	507	12	1	1.42
Jacques Plante	St. Louis	10	589	14	3	1.43
Gerry Cheevers	Boston	9	572	16	3	1.68
Gump Worsley	Montreal	7	370	14	0	2.27
Glenn Hall	St. Louis	3	131	5	0	2.29

PLAYOFF GOALS

Name, Team	G
Derek Sanderson, Bos.	8
Phil Esposito, Bos.	8
Red Berenson, St.L.	7
Gary Sabourin, St.L.	6
Dick Duff, Mtl.	6
Four tied with	5

PLAYOFF ASSISTS

Name, Team	A
Phil Esposito, Bos.	10
Jean Beliveau, Mtl.	10
Dick Duff, Mtl.	8
Six tied with	7

PLAYOFF POWERPLAY GOALS

Name, Team	PPG
Phil Esposito, Bos.	5
Dick Duff, Mtl.	3
Ted Hampson, Oak.	2
Ken Hodge, Bos.	2
John Bucyk, Bos.	2
Red Berenson, St.L.	2
John Ferguson, Mtl.	2

PLAYOFF SHORTHAND GOALS

Name, Team	SHG
Derek Sanderson, Bos.	3
Ed Westfall, Bos.	2
Six tied with	1

PLAYOFF GAME-WINNING GOALS

Name, Team	GWG
Derek Sanderson, Bos.	2
Phil Esposito, Bos.	2
Gary Sabourin, St.L.	2
Larry Keenan, St.L.	2
Terry Crisp, St.L.	2
John Ferguson, Mtl.	2
Yvan Cournoyer, Mtl.	2
Bobby Rousseau, Mtl.	2

PLAYOFF GOALIE WINS

Name, Team	G
Jacques Plante, St.L.	8
Rogie Vachon, Mtl.	7
Gerry Cheevers, Bos.	6
Gump Worsley, Mtl.	5
Gary Smith, Oak.	3
Gerry Desjardins, L.A.	3

PLAYOFF SHUTOUTS

Name, Team	G
Gerry Cheevers, Bos.	3
Jacques Plante, St.L.	3
Rogie Vachon, Mtl.	1

1969-70

Stanley Cup • Boston Bruins

Tony Esposito was often referred to as Phil's kid brother when he broke into the NHL with the Stanley Cup champion Montreal Canadiens in 1968–69. His skill as a goaltender very quickly earned him recognition in his own right when he set a modern NHL record with 15 shutouts for the Chicago Black Hawks in 1969–70

FINAL STANDINGS

EAST DIVISION

Team	GP	W	L	T	GF	GA	PTS
Chicago	76	45	22	9	250	170	99
Boston	76	40	17	19	277	216	99
Detroit	76	40	21	15	246	199	95
New York	76	38	22	16	246	189	92
Montreal	76	38	22	16	244	201	92
Toronto	76	29	34	13	222	242	71

WEST DIVISION

Team	GP	W	L	T	GF	GA	PTS
St. Louis	76	37	27	12	224	179	86
Pittsburgh	76	26	38	12	182	238	64
Minnesota	76	19	35	22	224	257	60
Oakland	76	22	40	14	169	243	58
Philadelphia	76	17	35	24	197	225	58
Los Angeles	76	14	52	10	168	290	38

LEADING SCORERS

Player	Club	GP	G	A	PTS	PIM
Bobby Orr	Boston	76	33	87	120	125
Phil Esposito	Boston	76	43	56	99	50
Stan Mikita	Chicago	76	39	47	86	50
Phil Goyette	St. Louis	72	29	49	78	16
Walt Tkaczuk	NY Rangers	76	27	50	77	38
Jean Ratelle	NY Rangers	75	32	42	74	28
Red Berenson	St. Louis	67	33	39	72	38
J.P. Parise	Minnesota	74	24	48	72	72
Gordie Howe	Detroit	76	31	40	71	58
Frank Mahovlich	Detroit	74	38	32	70	59
Dave Balon	NY Rangers	76	33	37	70	100
John McKenzie	Boston	72	29	41	70	114
John Bucyk	Boston	76	31	38	69	13
Alex Delvecchio	Detroit	73	21	47	68	24
Bobby Hull	Chicago	61	38	29	67	8
Tommy Williams	Minnesota	75	15	52	67	18
Garry Unger	Detroit	76	42	24	66	67
Bill Goldsworthy	Minnesota	75	36	29	65	89
Pit Martin	Chicago	73	30	33	63	61
Yvan Cournoyer	Montreal	72	27	36	63	23
Dave Keon	Toronto	72	32	30	62	6
Jacques Lemaire	Montreal	69	32	28	60	16
Norm Ullman	Toronto	74	18	42	60	37
Wayne Connelly	Detroit	76	23	36	59	10
Frank St. Marseille	St. Louis	74	16	43	59	18

LEADING GOALTENDERS

Goaltender	Club	GPI	MINS	GA	SO	AVG
Ernie Wakely	St. Louis	30	1651	58	4	2.11
Tony Esposito	Chicago	63	3763	136	15	2.17
Jacques Plante	St. Louis	32	1839	67	5	2.19
Ed Giacomin	NY Rangers	70	4148	163	6	2.36
Roy Edwards	Detroit	47	2683	116	2	2.59
Rogie Vachon	Montreal	64	3697	162	4	2.63
Roger Crozier	Detroit	34	1877	83	0	2.65
Gerry Cheevers	Boston	41	2384	108	4	2.72
Bernie Parent	Philadelphia	62	3680	171	3	2.79
Eddie Johnston	Boston	37	2176	108	3	2.98

AMERICAN TEAMS WERE THE STORY, capturing all the playoff berths this year and leaving Montreal and Toronto with unexpectedly long holidays. Chicago relaunched itself with three ex-college players, Tony Esposito, Cliff Koroll and Keith Magnuson. Esposito recorded 15 shutouts, becoming the newest star and giving brother Phil something to think about. As a team, Boston scored fewer goals than the previous year, but Bobby Orr didn't. His dream-like numbers and Art Ross Trophy win (something no other defender has done) took Boston to a virtual tie for first place.

Brewin' in Boston – Esposito scored and Bobby Orr soared as the Big, Bad Bruins crashed their way to the top of the standings, carrying the Cup back to the Hub.

Montreal suffered at the hands of fate when it lost a playoff berth on goal difference to New York. Just three more goals would have been enough to change the verdict. The East was very strong, featuring only one team below 90 points, while the West had only one above 70. That club, St. Louis, would not have made the playoffs in the East. This imbalance was creating lopsided Cup finals, but the format would change in 1971.

The first universal Amateur Draft was held at the end of the 1968-69 season. With the NHL's old sponsorship system now phased out, the draft was open to all prospects aged 20 and older. However, Montreal still had the right to select the top French-Canadian prospects for one last year in 1969. Sam Pollock had selected Rejean Houle and Marc Tardif. In 1970, he had to watch as Gilbert Perreault and others went to competing cities—though his shrewd trading would land Guy Lafleur for Montreal in 1971. Since 1969, the draft has become one of the most successful features of the modern NHL.

This year's first playoff round had an odd result, as Chicago won four straight games 4–2 over Detroit. Boston's stiffest opponent on rout to the finals was New York, who won the middle games of their opening set before getting knocked out in six. Tony and Phil Esposito faced off in the semi-finals, bringing a lot of fanfare, but Tony couldn't do much with the Beantown army. St. Louis won the West with more difficulty than usual. The Blues problems increased exponentially with three straight one-sided losses to Boston. Glenn Hall was benched for one game, but Jacques Plante left with a concussion after taking a shot off the top of his mask. Boston overwhelmed the net with shots in a game three win, but St. Louis fought well in the deciding match. The Bruins were forced into overtime before Orr scored a dramatic series winner. He also added to the Conn Smythe Trophy to a yearly haul that included the Art Ross, the Hart and the Norris and made him the NHL's first four-trophy winner.

Canadiens captain Jean Beliveau battles Blues defenseman Noel Picard in front of Jacques Plante in the St. Louis goal. Picard is the player who would send Bobby Orr flying after his Stanley Cup-winning goal in the 1970 finals.

Leaders, 1969-70

GOALS

Name, Team	G
Phil Esposito, Bos.	43
Garry Unger, Det.	42
Stan Mikita, Chi.	39
Bobby Hull, Chi.	38
Frank Mahovlich, Det.	38
Bill Goldsworthy, Min.	36
Ron Ellis, Tor.	35
Red Berenson, St.L.	33
Bobby Orr, Bos.	33
Dave Balon, NYR	33

ASSISTS

Name, Team	A
Bobby Orr, Bos.	87
Phil Esposito, Bos.	56
Tommy Williams, Min.	52
Walt Tkaczuk, NYR	50
Phil Goyette, St.L.	49
J.P. Parise, Min.	48
Alex Delvecchio, Det.	47
Stan Mikita, Chi.	47
Frank St. Marseille, St.L.	43
Norm Ullman, Tor.	42
Jean Ratelle, NYR	42

POWERPLAY GOALS

Name, Team	PPG
Phil Esposito, Bos.	18
Red Berenson, St.L.	16
Frank Mahovlich, Det.	15
John Bucyk, Bos.	14
Danny Grant, Min.	14
Jacques Lemaire, Mtl.	13
Phil Goyette, St.L.	13
Fred Stanfield, Bos.	13
Dean Prentice, Pit.	12
Garry Unger, Det.	12

SHORTHAND GOALS

Name, Team	SHG
Bill Collins, Min.	6
Derek Sanderson, Bos.	5
Bobby Orr, Bos.	4
Gordie Howe, Det.	4
Ron Stewart, NYR	4
Serge Savard, Mtl.	3
Jimmy Jr. Peters, L.A.	3
Seven tied with	2

GAME-WINNING GOALS

Name, Team	GWG
Bobby Hull, Chi.	8
Red Berenson, St.L.	8
Stan Mikita, Chi.	8
John Ferguson, Mtl.	7
Jim Pappin, Chi.	7
Mike Walton, Tor.	6
John McKenzie, Bos.	6
Jean Pronovost, Pit.	6
Jean Ratelle, NYR	6
John Bucyk, Bos.	6
Pete Stemkowski, Det.	6

GOALIE WINS

Name, Team	W
Tony Esposito, Chi.	38
Ed Giacomin, NYR	35
Rogie Vachon, Mtl.	31
Gerry Cheevers, Bos.	24
Roy Edwards, Det.	24
Bruce Gamble, Tor.	19
Gary Smith, Oak.	19
Jacques Plante, St.L.	18
Roger Crozier, Det.	16
Eddie Johnston, Bos.	16

TROPHY WINNERS

Trophy	Awarded For	Winner	Team
Hart	MVP	Bobby Orr	Bos.
Art Ross	Top Scorer	Bobby Orr	Bos.
Norris	Top Defenseman	Bobby Orr	Bos.
Calder	Top Rookie	Tony Esposito	Chi.
Vezina	Fewest Goals Against	Tony Esposito	Chi
Byng	Gentlemanly Conduct	Phil Goyette	St L.
Masterton	Perseverance, Sportmanship	Pit Martin	Chi.
Conn Smythe	Playoff MVP	Bobby Orr	Bos.
Patrick	Service to Hockey in U.S.	Eddie Shore	
		Jim Hendy	
Amateur Draft	First Overall Selection	Gilbert Perreault	Buf.

SHUTOUTS

Name, Team	SO
Tony Esposito, Chi.	15
Ed Giacomin, NYR	6
Jacques Plante, St.L.	5
Bruce Gamble, Tor.	5
Ernie Wakely, St.L.	4
Gerry Cheevers, Bos.	4
Rogie Vachon, Mtl.	4
Les Binkley, Pit.	3
Eddie Johnston, Bos.	3
Gerry Desjardins, LA/Chi.	3
Bernie Parent, Phi.	3

FIRST TEAM ALL-STARS

Name, Team	Position
Phil Esposito, Bos.	C
Gordie Howe, Det.	RW
Bobby Hull, Chi.	LW
Bobby Orr, Bos.	D
Brad Park, NYR	D
Tony Esposito, Chi.	G

SECOND TEAM ALL-STARS

Name, Team	Position
Stan Mikita, Chi.	C
John McKenzie, Bos.	RW
Frank Mahovlich, Det	LW
Carl Brewer, Det.	D
Jacques Laperriere, Mtl.	D
Ed Giacomin, NYR	G

NHL NOTEBOOK

TRANSACTIONS

- June 6, 1969 – Montreal Canadiens acquired Peter Mahovlich from Detroit in exchange for Garry Monahan.
- June 11, 1969 – In the annual NHL Interleague Draft, the Chicago Black Hawks claimed rookie goalie Tony Esposito from the Montreal Canadiens.
- Feb. 20, 1970 – Los Angeles Kings traded Bryan Campbell, Bill White and Gerry Desjardins to Chicago in exchange for Dennis DeJordy, Gilles Marotte and Jim Stanfield.
- Feb. 27, 1970 – Minnesota North Stars purchased 41-year-old goal-tender Gump Worsley from the Montreal Canadiens.

RECORDS

- Nov. 8, 1969 – Detroit's Billy Dea scored in a 3-2 win over Boston to set an NHL record for longest gap between goals with one team. His previous goal for the Wings was on Nov. 28, 1957 (11 years, 11 months, and 11 days). Randy Cunneyworth would break the mark in 1998-99.
- Jan. 15, 1970 – Boston's Bobby Orr recorded two assists to set a new NHL single-season assist record (51) for defensemen. It came in a 6-3 win over the Kings and broke the mark of 50 set by Chicago's Pat Stapleton in 1968-69.
- Mar. 29, 1970 – Rookie goalie Tony Esposito recorded his 15th shutout of the season, an NHL record for rookie goaltenders, when the Black Hawks beat Toronto 4-0 at Chicago Stadium.
- May 5, 1970 – Bobby Orr had two assists to raise his playoff total to 18 points, a new record for defensemen in one year (breaking Tim Horton's mark of 16). Boston won the game 6-2 in game two of the Stanley Cup finals at St. Louis.

MILESTONES

- Jan. 3, 1970 – Detroit's Gordie Howe and Toronto's George Armstrong became the first two players to appear in the NHL in four different decades.
- Mar. 1, 1970 – Minnesota coach Charlie Burns became the final player/coach in NHL history, when he dressed and played in an 8-0 North Stars win over the Maple Leafs.
- Apr. 5, 1970 – Boston's Bobby Orr had an assist in the final game of the season (a 3-1 win over Toronto) and became the first defenseman in NHL history to lead the league in scoring. Orr finished the season with 33 goals, 87 assists and 120 points in 76 games.
- Apr. 12, 1970 – Pittsburgh Penguins became the first team in NHL history to win its first four playoff games when Michel Briere scored at 8:28 of overtime for a 3-2 win over the Seals in game four of the quarter-finals at Oakland.

1970 Playoffs

QUARTER-FINALS

Apr.	8	Detroit	2	at	Chicago	4
Apr.	9	Detroit	2	at	Chicago	4
Apr.	11	Chicago	4	at	Detroit	2
Apr.	12	Chicago	4	at	Detroit	2

Chicago won best-of-seven series 4–0

Apr.	8	NY Rangers	2	at	Boston	8
Apr.	9	NY Rangers	3	at	Boston	5
Apr.	11	Boston	3	at	NY Rangers	4
Apr.	12	Boston	2	at	NY Rangers	4
Apr.	14	NY Rangers	2	at	Boston	3
Apr.	16	Boston	4	at	NY Rangers	1

Boston won best-of-seven series 4–2

Apr.	8	Minnesota	2	at	St. Louis	6
Apr.	9	Minnesota	1	at	St. Louis	2
Apr.	11	St. Louis	2	at	Minnesota	4
Apr.	12	St. Louis	0	at	Minnesota	4
Apr.	14	Minnesota	3	at	St. Louis	6
Apr.	16	St. Louis	4	at	Minnesota	2

St. Louis won best-of-seven series 4–2

Apr.	8	Oakland	1	at	Pittsburgh	2
Apr.	9	Oakland	1	at	Pittsburgh	3
Apr.	11	Pittsburgh	5	at	Oakland	2
Apr.	12	Pittsburgh	3	at	Oakland	2 OT

Pittsburgh won best-of-seven series 4–0

SEMI-FINALS

Apr.	19	Boston	6	at	Chicago	3
Apr.	21	Boston	4	at	Chicago	1
Apr.	23	Chicago	2	at	Boston	5
Apr.	26	Chicago	4	at	Boston	5

Boston won best-of-seven series 4–0

Apr.	19	Pittsburgh	1	at	St. Louis	3
Apr.	21	Pittsburgh	1	at	St. Louis	4
Apr.	23	St. Louis	2	at	Pittsburgh	3
Apr.	26	St. Louis	1	at	Pittsburgh	2
Apr.	28	Pittsburgh	0	at	St. Louis	5
Apr.	30	St. Louis	4	at	Pittsburgh	3

St. Louis won best-of-seven series 4–2

FINALS

May	3	Boston	6	at	St. Louis	1
May	5	Boston	6	at	St. Louis	2
May	7	St. Louis	1	at	Boston	4
May	10	St. Louis	3	at	Boston	4 OT

Boston won best-of-seven series 4–0

1969-70 – Boston Bruins – Gerry Cheevers, Eddie Johnston, Bobby Orr, Rick Smith, Dallas Smith, Bill Speer, Gary Doak, Don Awrey, Phil Esposito, Ken Hodge, John Bucyk, Wayne Carleton, Wayne Cashman, Derek Sanderson, Fred Stanfield, Ed Westfall, John McKenzie, Jim Lorentz, Don Marcotte, Bill Lesuk, Danny Schock, Harry Sinden (Coach), Milt Schmidt (General Manager), Dan Canney, John Forristall (Trainers).

Bobby Orr began to rewrite the record book during the 1969–70 season when he became the first defenseman to win the NHL scoring title. He scored eight goals in ten games through the first two rounds of the playoffs, but was held scoreless in the finals until his overtime series winner in game four.

LEADING PLAYOFF SCORERS

Player	Club	GP	G	A	PTS	PIM
Phil Esposito	Boston	14	13	14	27	16
Bobby Orr	Boston	14	9	11	20	14
John Bucyk	Boston	14	11	8	19	2
John McKenzie	Boston	14	5	12	17	35
Fred Stanfield	Boston	14	4	12	16	6
Ab McDonald	St. Louis	16	5	10	15	13
Phil Goyette	St. Louis	16	3	11	14	6
Larry Keenan	St. Louis	16	7	6	13	0
Frank St. Marseille	St. Louis	15	6	7	13	4
Ken Hodge	Boston	14	3	10	13	7

LEADING PLAYOFF GOALTENDERS

Goaltender	Club	GPI	Mins	GA	SO	Avg.
Jacques Plante	St. Louis	6	324	8	1	1.48
Les Binkley	Pittsburgh	7	428	15	0	2.10
Gerry Cheevers	Boston	13	781	29	0	2.23
Glenn Hall	St. Louis	7	421	21	0	2.99
Gary Smith	Oakland	4	248	13	0	3.15

PLAYOFF GOALS

Name, Team	G
Phil Esposito, Bos.	13
John Bucyk, Bos.	11
Bobby Orr, Bos.	9
Larry Keenan, St.L.	7
Red Berenson, St.L.	7
Frank St. Marseille, St.L.	6

PLAYOFF ASSISTS

Name, Team	A
Phil Esposito, Bos.	14
John McKenzie, Bos.	12
Fred Stanfield, Bos.	12
Bobby Orr, Bos.	11
Phil Goyette, St.L.	11
Two tied with	10

PLAYOFF POWERPLAY GOALS

Name, Team	PPG
Phil Esposito, Bos.	4
John Bucyk, Bos.	4
Larry Keenan, St.L.	4
Seven tied with	3

PLAYOFF SHORTHAND GOALS

Name, Team	SHG
Derek Sanderson, Bos.	2
Pete Stemkowski, Det.	1
Earl Ingarfield, Oak	1
Bobby Orr, Bos.	1
Ed Westfall, Bos.	1
Don Marcotte, Bos.	1
Red Berenson, St.L.	1
Tim Ecclestone, St.L.	1

PLAYOFF GAME-WINNING GOALS

Name, Team	GWG
Michel Briere, Pit.	3
John McKenzie, Bos.	3
Bill Goldsworthy, Min.	2
Phil Esposito, Bos.	2
Bobby Orr, Bos.	2
Wayne Cashman, Bos.	2
Larry Keenan, St.L.	2
Phil Goyette, St.L.	2

PLAYOFF GOALIE WINS

Name, Team	W
Gerry Cheevers, Bos.	12
Les Binkley, Pit.	5
Jacques Plante, St.L.	4
Glenn Hall, St.L.	4
Tony Esposito, Chi.	4

PLAYOFF SHUTOUTS

Name, Team	SO
Cesare Maniago, Min.	1
Jacques Plante, St.L.	1

1970-71

Stanley Cup • Montreal Canadiens

Phil Esposito's size and strength made it difficult for defensemen to clear him out of the slot in front of the net. The stocky center had established himself as an effective scorer and playmaker over four seasons with the Chicago Black Hawks and became the NHL's dominant offensive force with the Big, Bad Bruins.

FINAL STANDINGS

EAST DIVISION

Team	GP	W	L	T	GF	GA	PTS
Boston	78	57	14	7	399	207	121
New York	78	49	18	11	259	177	109
Montreal	78	42	23	13	291	216	97
Toronto	78	37	33	8	248	211	82
Buffalo	78	24	39	15	217	291	63
Vancouver	78	24	46	8	229	296	56
Detroit	78	22	45	11	209	308	55

WEST DIVISION

Team	GP	W	L	T	GF	GA	PTS
Chicago	78	49	20	9	277	184	107
St. Louis	78	34	25	19	223	208	87
Philadelphia	78	28	33	17	207	225	73
Minnesota	78	28	34	16	191	223	72
Los Angeles	78	25	40	13	239	303	63
Pittsburgh	78	21	37	20	221	240	62
California	78	20	53	5	199	320	45

LEADING SCORERS

Player	Club	GP	G	A	PTS	PIM
Phil Esposito	Boston	78	76	76	152	71
Bobby Orr	Boston	78	37	102	139	91
John Bucyk	Boston	78	51	65	116	8
Ken Hodge	Boston	78	43	62	105	113
Bobby Hull	Chicago	78	44	52	96	32
Norm Ullman	Toronto	73	34	51	85	24
Wayne Cashman	Boston	77	21	58	79	100
John McKenzie	Boston	65	31	46	77	120
Dave Keon	Toronto	76	38	38	76	4
Jean Beliveau	Montreal	70	25	51	76	40
Fred Stanfield	Boston	75	24	52	76	12
Walt Tkaczuk	NY Rangers	77	26	49	75	48
Yvan Cournoyer	Montreal	65	37	36	73	21
Frank Mahovlich	Det./Mtl.	73	31	42	73	41
Gilbert Perreault	Buffalo	78	38	34	72	19
Jean Ratelle	NY Rangers	78	26	46	72	14
Stan Mikita	Chicago	74	24	48	72	85
Jude Drouin	Minnesota	75	16	52	68	49
Tom Webster	Detroit	78	30	37	67	40
Dennis Hull	Chicago	78	40	26	66	16
Andre Boudrias	Vancouver	77	25	41	66	16
Bill Goldsworthy	Minnesota	77	34	31	65	85
Juha Widing	Los Angeles	78	25	40	65	24
Derek Sanderson	Boston	71	29	34	63	130
Bobby Clarke	Philadelphia	77	27	36	63	78
Wayne Maki	Vancouver	78	25	38	63	99
Bob Berry	Los Angeles	77	25	38	63	52
J.C. Tremblay	Montreal	76	11	52	63	23

LEADING GOALTENDERS

Goaltender	Club	GPI	MINS	GA	SO	AVG
Jacques Plante	Toronto	40	2329	73	4	1.88
Ed Giacomin	NY Rangers	45	2641	95	8	2.16
Tony Esposito	Chicago	57	3325	126	6	2.27
Gilles Villemure	NY Rangers	34	2039	78	4	2.3
Glenn Hall	St. Louis	32	1761	71	2	2.42
Eddie Johnston	Boston	38	2280	96	4	2.53
Rogie Vachon	Montreal	47	2676	118	2	2.65
Doug Favell	Philadelphia	44	2434	108	2	2.66
Cesare Maniago	Minnesota	40	2380	107	5	2.70
Bernie Parent	Phi./Tor.	48	2626	119	2	2.72

TWO CITIES THAT NARROWLY MISSED joining the NHL in 1967 were added to the league in 1970–71. Despite the geographic contradiction, the Buffalo Sabres and Vancouver Canucks were both placed in the East Division. To improve the competitive balance between the two divisions, the Chicago Black Hawks moved into the West, and the season, extended to 78 games, featured a balanced schedule. The playoff format was also altered so that teams would cross divisional lines after the opening round.

A Tale of Two Seasons – Phil Esposito and the Bruins rewrote the regular-season record book but in the playoffs a rookie goalie named Ken Dryden authored one of the most amazing stories in NHL history.

The Boston Bruins, as their Stanley Cup predecessors had done in 1929, followed up their championship with a record-breaking season. The 1970–71 edition of the Bruins set NHL all-time single-season records with 57 victories, 121 points and 399 goals. Phil Esposito set new records with 76 goals and 152 points, while Bobby Orr established a new mark with 102 assists. Esposito, Orr, John Bucyk and Ken Hodge finished 1–2–3–4 in the NHL scoring race as all four topped 100 points, while Espo and Bucyk became the first teammates to top 50 goals in a single season. Unfortunately, these Bruins were also like that 1929–30 team in that they couldn't get past the Montreal Canadiens.

Though he had played just six games late in the regular season, Montreal made Ken Dryden their number-one goalie for their quarter-final series against Boston. Dryden completely stymied the powerful Bruins as Montreal pulled off a stunning seven-game upset. The Canadiens then defeated the Minnesota North Stars to advance to the finals. Chicago provided the opposition, but the Stanley Cup returned to Montreal in a tight seven-game series. Henri Richard scored the Cup-winning goal after feuding with coach Al MacNeil earlier in the series. Dryden earned the Conn Smythe Trophy as playoff MVP.

The NHL lost two of its greats when Jean Beliveau and Gordie Howe announced their retirements—although Howe, it would turn out, was not done just yet.

Dave Dryden spent four seasons with the Buffalo Sabres from 1970–71 to 1973–74. His NHL career began back in 1961–62 when he was summoned to serve as an injury replacement for Gump Worsley during a game between the New York Rangers and Toronto Maple Leafs on February 3, 1962.

Leaders, 1970-71

GOALS

Name, Team	G
Phil Esposito, Bos.	76
John Bucyk, Bos.	51
Bobby Hull, Chi.	44
Ken Hodge, Bos.	43
Dennis Hull, Chi.	40
Dave Keon, Tor.	38
Gilbert Perreault, Buf.	38
Yvan Cournoyer, Mtl.	37
Bobby Orr, Bos.	37
Dave Balon, NYR	36

ASSISTS

Name, Team	A
Bobby Orr, Bos.	102
Phil Esposito, Bos.	76
John Bucyk, Bos.	65
Ken Hodge, Bos.	62
Wayne Cashman, Bos.	58
Fred Stanfield, Bos.	52
Jude Drouin, Min.	52
J.C. Tremblay, Mtl.	52
Bobby Hull, Chi.	52
Jean Beliveau, Mtl.	51
Norm Ullman, Tor.	51

POWERPLAY GOALS

Name, Team	PPG
Phil Esposito, Bos.	25
John Bucyk, Bos.	22
Yvan Cournoyer, Mtl.	18
Gilbert Perreault, Buf.	14
Pete Mahovlich, Mtl.	12
Danny Grant, Min.	12
John McKenzie, Bos.	11
Bill Sutherland, Phi./St.L.	11
Norm Ullman, Tor.	11
Bobby Hull, Chi.	11

SHORTHAND GOALS

Name, Team	SHG
Dave Keon, Tor.	8
Ed Westfall, Bos.	7
Derek Sanderson, Bos.	6
Don Marcotte, Bos.	6
Ted Hampson, Cal./Min.	4
Leon Rochefort, Mtl.	3
Bill McCreary, St.L.	3
Pete Mahovlich, Mtl.	3
Bobby Orr, Bos.	3
Nine tied with	2

GAME-WINNING GOALS

Name, Team	GWG
Phil Esposito, Bos.	16
Bobby Hull, Chi.	11
Dave Keon, Tor.	9
Bill Goldsworthy, Min.	7
Dennis Hull, Chi.	7
Ken Hodge, Bos.	7
Dave Balon, NYR	7
Christian Bordeleau, St.L.	7
Ted Irvine, NYR	6
14 tied with	5

GOALIE WINS

Name, Team	W
Tony Esposito, Chi.	35
Eddie Johnston, Bos.	30
Gerry Cheevers, Bos.	27
Ed Giacomin, NYR	27
Jacques Plante, Tor.	24
Rogie Vachon, Mtl.	23
Gilles Villemure, NYR	22
Ernie Wakely, St.L.	20
Cesare Maniago, Min.	19
Gary Smith, Cal.	19

SHUTOUTS

Name, Team	SO
Ed Giacomin, NYR	8
Tony Esposito, Chi.	6
Cesare Maniago, Min.	5
Gilles Villemure, NYR	4
Eddie Johnston, Bos.	4
Jacques Plante, Tor.	4
Gerry Cheevers, Bos.	3
Ernie Wakely, St.L.	3
Eight tied with	2

FIRST TEAM ALL-STARS

Name, Team	Position
Phil Esposito, Bos.	C
Ken Hodge, Bos.	RW
John Bucyk, Bos.	LW
Bobby Orr, Bos.	D
J.C. Tremblay, Mtl.	D
Ed Giacomin, NYR	G

SECOND TEAM ALL-STARS

Name, Team	Position
Dave Keon, Tor.	C
Yvan Cournoyer, Mtl.	RW
Bobby Hull, Chi.	LW
Brad Park, NYR	D
Pat Stapleton, Chi.	D
Jacques Plante, Tor.	G

TROPHY WINNERS

Trophy	Awarded For	Winner	Team
Hart	MVP	Bobby Orr	Bos.
Art Ross	Top Scorer	Phil Esposito	Bos.
Norris	Top Defenseman	Bobby Orr	Bos.
Calder	Top Rookie	Gilbert Perreault	Buf.
Vezina	Fewest Goals Against	Ed Giacomin	NYR
		Gilles Villemure	NYR
Byng	Gentlemanly Conduct	John Bucyk	Bos.
Masterton	Perseverance, Sportmanship	Jean Ratelle	NYR
Conn Smythe	Playoff MVP	Ken Dryden	Mtl.
Patrick	Service to Hockey in U.S.	William M. Jennings	
		John B. Sollenberger	
		Terry Sawchuk	
Amateur Draft	First Overall Selection	Guy Lafleur	Mtl.

NHL NOTEBOOK

TRANSACTIONS

- June 10, 1970 – Oakland Seals traded Francois Lacombe, cash and a first-round draft choice in 1971 to Montreal for Ernie Hicke and Montreal's 1st choice (Chris Oddleifson). One year later, this pick was used to select Guy Lafleur.
- June 10,1970 – Buffalo Sabres traded Tom Webster to Detroit in exchange for Roger Crozier.
- Oct. 31, 1970 – New York Rangers obtained center Pete Stemkowski from the Detroit Red Wings for defenseman Larry Brown.
- Jan. 13, 1971 – Montreal Canadiens obtained Frank Mahovlich from Detroit for Bill Collins, Guy Charron and Mickey Redmond.
- Jan. 26, 1971 – Pittsburgh Penguins acquired center Syl Apps Jr. and Sheldon Kannegiesser from the NY Rangers in exchange for left winger Glen Sather.

RECORDS

- Feb. 25, 1971 – Boston set an NHL record for the fastest three goals by a team. En route to an 8-3 win over the Canucks, John Bucyk, Ed Westfall and Ted Green scored goals in a span of 20 seconds during the third period.
- Mar. 11, 1971 – Boston's Phil Esposito scored twice and had an assist in a 7-2 win in L.A. to set a new NHL record for most goals in a season. His 59th of the year broke the mark of 58 set by Bobby Hull. Esposito finished the year with 76.
- Mar. 18, 1971 – Gil Perreault scored his 35th goal of the season to set a new NHL record for rookies as the Sabres won 5-3 over the Blues. Perreault broke the record of 34 shared by Oakland's Norm Ferguson, Minnesota's Danny Grant and the Montreal Maroons' Nels Stewart.

MILESTONES

- Oct. 29, 1970 – Gordie Howe became the first player in NHL history to record 1,000 career assists when he picked up two (along with a goal) in a 5-3 Red Wings victory over Boston at the Olympia in Detroit.
- Mar. 2, 1971 – Wayne Cashman scored to make the Boston Bruins the first team in NHL history to have nine 20+ goal scorers in one season. The milestone came in a 6-0 win over the North Stars in Minnesota.
- Mar. 20, 1971 – NHL history was made as two brothers faced each other in goal for the first time ever. Ken Dryden's Canadiens beat Dave Dryden's Sabres 5-2 at the Montreal Forum.
- Apr. 4, 1971 – Boston's Bobby Orr had two assists to finish the 1970-71 season with an NHL-record 102 assists along with two records for NHL defensemen: 37 goals and 139 points. Bruins won 7-2 over the visiting Montreal Canadiens.

1971 Playoffs

QUARTER-FINALS

Apr.	7	Montreal	1	at	Boston	3
Apr.	8	Montreal	7	at	Boston	5
Apr.	10	Boston	1	at	Montreal	3
Apr.	11	Boston	5	at	Montreal	2
Apr.	13	Montreal	3	at	Boston	7
Apr.	15	Boston	3	at	Montreal	8
Apr.	18	Montreal	4	at	Boston	2

Montreal won best-of-seven series 4–3

Apr.	7	Toronto	4	at	NY Rangers	5
Apr.	8	Toronto	4	at	NY Rangers	1
Apr.	10	NY Rangers	1	at	Toronto	3
Apr.	11	NY Rangers	4	at	Toronto	2
Apr.	13	Toronto	1	at	NY Rangers	3
Apr.	15	NY Rangers	2	at	Toronto	1 OT

NY Rangers won best-of-seven series 4–2

Apr.	7	Philadelphia	2	at	Chicago	5
Apr.	8	Philadelphia	2	at	Chicago	6
Apr.	10	Chicago	3	at	Philadelphia	2
Apr.	11	Chicago	6	at	Philadelphia	2

Chicago won best-of-seven series 4–0

Apr.	7	Minnesota	3	at	St. Louis	2
Apr.	8	Minnesota	2	at	St. Louis	4
Apr.	10	St. Louis	3	at	Minnesota	0
Apr.	11	St. Louis	1	at	Minnesota	2
Apr.	13	Minnesota	4	at	St. Louis	3
Apr.	15	St. Louis	2	at	Minnesota	5

Minnesota won best-of-seven series 4–2

SEMI-FINALS

Apr.	20	Minnesota	2	at	Montreal	7
Apr.	22	Minnesota	6	at	Montreal	3
Apr.	24	Montreal	6	at	Minnesota	3
Apr.	25	Montreal	2	at	Minnesota	5
Apr.	27	Minnesota	1	at	Montreal	6
Apr.	29	Montreal	3	at	Minnesota	2

Montreal won best-of-seven series 4–2

Apr.	18	NY Rangers	2	at	Chicago	1 OT
Apr.	20	NY Rangers	0	at	Chicago	3
Apr.	22	Chicago	1	at	NY Rangers	4
Apr.	25	Chicago	7	at	NY Rangers	1
Apr.	27	NY Rangers	2	at	Chicago	3 OT
Apr.	29	Chicago	2	at	NY Rangers	3 3OT
May	2	NY Rangers	2	at	Chicago	4

Chicago won best-of-seven series 4–3

FINALS

May	4	Montreal	1	at	Chicago	2 OT
May	6	Montreal	3	at	Chicago	5
May	9	Chicago	2	at	Montreal	4
May	11	Chicago	2	at	Montreal	5
May	13	Montreal	0	at	Chicago	2
May	16	Chicago	3	at	Montreal	4
May	18	Montreal	3	at	Chicago	2

Montreal won best-of-seven series 4–3

1970-71 – Montreal Canadiens – Ken Dryden, Rogie Vachon, Phil Myre, Jacques Laperrière, J.C. Tremblay, Guy Lapointe, Terry Harper, Pierre Bouchard, Jean Beliveau (Captain), Marc Tardif, Yvan Cournoyer, Réjean Houle, Claude Larose, Henri Richard, Phil Roberto, Pete Mahovlich, Leon Rochefort, John Ferguson, Bobby Sheehan, Jacques Lemaire, Frank Mahovlich, Bob Murdoch, Chuck Lefley, Al MacNeil (Coach), Sam Pollock (General Manager), Eddy Palchak, Yvon Belanger (Trainers).

Ken Dryden was selected originally by the Boston Bruins in the 1964 Amateur Draft, but opted to attend Cornell University instead. He also played for the Canadian national team before joining the Montreal Canadiens organization in 1970–71. His playoff run that season is the stuff of hockey legend.

LEADING PLAYOFF SCORERS

Player	Club	GP	G	A	PTS	PIM
Frank Mahovlich	Montreal	20	14	13	27	18
Bobby Hull	Chicago	18	11	14	25	16
Yvan Cournoyer	Montreal	20	10	12	22	6
Jean Beliveau	Montreal	20	6	16	22	28
Jacques Lemaire	Montreal	20	9	10	19	17
Stan Mikita	Chicago	18	5	13	18	16
J.C. Tremblay	Montreal	20	3	14	17	15
Pat Stapleton	Chicago	18	3	14	17	4
Pete Mahovlich	Montreal	20	10	6	16	43
Cliff Koroll	Chicago	18	7	9	16	18

LEADING PLAYOFF GOALTENDERS

Goaltender	Club	GPI	Mins	GA	SO	Avg.
Tony Esposito	Chicago	18	1151	42	2	2.19
Ed Giacomin	NY Rangers	12	759	28	0	2.21
Ken Dryden	Montreal	20	1221	61	0	3.00
Gump Worsley	Minnesota	4	240	13	0	3.25
Cesare Maniago	Minnesota	8	480	28	0	3.50

PLAYOFF GOALS

Name, Team	G
Frank Mahovlich, Mtl.	14
Bobby Hull, Chi.	11
Jim Pappin, Chi.	10
Yvan Cournoyer, Mtl.	10
Pete Mahovlich, Mtl.	10
Jacques Lemaire, Mtl.	9

PLAYOFF ASSISTS

Name, Team	A
Jean Beliveau, Mtl.	16
Bobby Hull, Chi.	14
Pat Stapleton, Chi.	14
J.C. Tremblay, Mtl.	14
Stan Mikita, Chi.	13
Frank Mahovlich, Mtl.	13

PLAYOFF POWERPLAY GOALS

Name, Team	PPG
Bobby Hull, Chi.	6
Jacques Lemaire, Mtl.	4
Danny Grant, Min.	3
Cliff Koroll, Chi.	3
Nine tied with	2

PLAYOFF SHORTHAND GOALS

Name, Team	SHG
Garry Unger, St.L.	1
Bobby Orr, Bos.	1
Ed Westfall, Bos.	1
Ron Stewart, NYR	1
Pat Stapleton, Chi.	1
Pete Mahovlich, Mtl.	1

PLAYOFF GAME-WINNING GOALS

Name, Team	GWG
Bobby Hull, Chi.	4
J.C. Tremblay, Mtl.	3
Paul Henderson, Tor.	2
Lou Nanne, Min.	2
Pete Stemkowski, NYR	2
Guy Lapointe, Mtl.	2

PLAYOFF GOALIE WINS

Name, Team	W
Ken Dryden, Mtl.	12
Tony Esposito, Chi.	11
Ed Giacomin, NYR	7
Gump Worsley, Min.	3
Gerry Cheevers, Bos.	3
Cesare Maniago, Min.	3

PLAYOFF SHUTOUTS

Name, Team	SO
Tony Esposito, Chi.	2
Ernie Wakely, St.L.	1

1971-72

Stanley Cup • Boston Bruins

With 139 goals between them, the GAG Line of Jean Ratelle (left, 46 goals), Vic Hadfield (center, 50 goals) and Rod Gilbert (right, 43 goals) averaged far more than a goal a game during the 1971–72 season. Here they celebrate one of many in front of Keith Magnuson of the Chicago Black Hawks.

FINAL STANDINGS

EAST DIVISION

Team	GP	W	L	T	GF	GA	PTS
Boston	78	54	13	11	330	204	119
New York	78	48	17	13	317	192	109
Montreal	78	46	16	16	307	205	108
Toronto	78	33	31	14	209	208	80
Detroit	78	33	35	10	261	262	76
Buffalo	78	16	43	19	203	289	51
Vancouver	78	20	50	8	203	297	48

WEST DIVISION

Team	GP	W	L	T	GF	GA	PTS
Chicago	78	46	17	15	256	166	107
Minnesota	78	37	29	12	212	191	86
St. Louis	78	28	39	11	208	247	67
Pittsburgh	78	26	38	14	220	258	66
Philadelphia	78	26	38	14	200	236	66
California	78	21	39	18	216	288	60
Los Angeles	78	20	49	9	206	305	49

LEADING SCORERS

Player	Club	GP	G	A	PTS	PIM
Phil Esposito	Boston	76	66	67	133	76
Bobby Orr	Boston	76	37	80	117	106
Jean Ratelle	NY Rangers	63	46	63	109	4
Vic Hadfield	NY Rangers	78	50	56	106	142
Rod Gilbert	NY Rangers	73	43	54	97	64
Frank Mahovlich	Montreal	76	43	53	96	36
Bobby Hull	Chicago	78	50	43	93	24
Yvan Cournoyer	Montreal	73	47	36	83	15
John Bucyk	Boston	78	32	51	83	4
Bobby Clarke	Philadelphia	78	35	46	81	87
Jacques Lemaire	Montreal	77	32	49	81	26
Fred Stanfield	Boston	78	23	56	79	12
Marcel Dionne	Detroit	78	28	49	77	14
Pit Martin	Chicago	78	24	51	75	56
Rick Martin	Buffalo	73	44	30	74	36
Gilbert Perreault	Buffalo	76	26	48	74	24
Brad Park	NY Rangers	75	24	49	73	130
Norm Ullman	Toronto	77	23	50	73	26
Mickey Redmond	Detroit	78	42	29	71	34
Garry Unger	St. Louis	78	36	34	70	104
Dennis Hull	Chicago	78	30	39	69	10
Red Berenson	Detroit	78	28	41	69	16
John McKenzie	Boston	77	22	47	69	126
Pete Mahovlich	Montreal	75	35	32	67	103
Walt Tkaczuk	NY Rangers	76	24	42	66	65

LEADING GOALTENDERS

Goaltender	Club	GPI	MINS	GA	SO	AVG
Tony Esposito	Chicago	48	2780	82	9	1.77
Gilles Villemure	NY Rangers	37	2129	74	3	2.09
Gump Worsley	Minnesota	34	1923	68	2	2.12
Ken Dryden	Montreal	64	3800	142	8	2.24
Gary Smith	Chicago	28	1540	62	5	2.42
Gerry Cheevers	Boston	41	2420	101	2	2.50
Jacques Caron	St. Louis	28	1619	68	1	2.52
Bernie Parent	Toronto	47	2715	116	3	2.56
Jacques Plante	Toronto	34	1965	86	2	2.63
Cesare Maniago	Minnesota	43	2539	112	3	2.65

The Montreal Canadiens made two moves before the 1971–72 season that ensured the success of the franchise for years to come. Scotty Bowman was hired as coach and, after a series of trades to ensure they landed the number-one pick, Guy Lafleur was selected in the draft.

"The Flower" would slowly blossom into the league's top star, but Rick Martin, selected fifth overall by Buffalo, provided the Sabres with more immediate benefits. Martin set a rookie record with 44 goals, but didn't win the Calder Trophy awarded to the NHL's top freshman. The award instead went to Montreal netminder Ken Dryden who, despie his playoff exploits and Conn Smythe Trophy win in the spring of 1971, had not played enough regular-season games in 1970–71 to lose his rookie status.

'da Bruins – Jean Ratelle and Vic Hadfield of the NY Rangers were the darlings of Broadway, Ken Dryden was the champion of the crease but the Boston Bruins were crowned Kings of the Hill.

For the second straight year, the Boston Bruins and New York Rangers proved to be the top teams in the regular season.

Boston's Phil Esposito and Bobby Orr finished 1–2 in the NHL scoring race, while New York's Goal-A-Game Line of Jean Ratelle, Vic Hadfield and Rod Gilbert finished 3–4–5. Bobby Clarke of the Philadelphia Flyers was establishing himself as a star and was the only player from an expansion team to crack the top 10 in scoring.

For the first time in the history of the NHL, nine players finished with 40-or-more goals in regular-season play. The 40-goal scorers represented six different clubs, though Rick Martin of the Sabres was the only one who didn't wear an "Original Six" jersey.

With the previous year's playoff upset still in mind, the Bruins downed the Toronto Maple Leafs in five games, then swept the St. Louis Blues in four to advance to the Stanley Cup finals. The Rangers, who had edged Montreal by just one point in the regular-season standings, knocked off the Canadiens in six games, then swept the West Division-leading Chicago Black Hawks to reach the Stanley Cup finals for the first time since 1950.

The Boston–New York Stanley Cup matchup was the first since 1960 to feature the NHL's top two finishers in the regular-season, and the first-place Bruins emerged victorious in six games. Bobby Orr became the first two-time winner of the Conn Smythe Trophy, earning playoff MVP honors as he had in 1970.

Vancouver's Bobby Schmautz eyes a loose puck bouncing off the blocker of Canadiens goalie Ken Dryden. A junior scoring star with some minor league success, Schmautz would finally establish himself at the NHL level with 38 goals for the Canucks in 1972–73.

Leaders, 1971-72

GOALS

Name, Team	G
Phil Esposito, Bos.	66
Vic Hadfield, NYR	50
Bobby Hull, Chi.	50
Yvan Cournoyer, Mtl.	47
Jean Ratelle, NYR	46
Rick Martin, Buf.	44
Rod Gilbert, NYR	43
Frank Mahovlich, Mtl.	43
Mickey Redmond, Det.	42
Paul Henderson, Tor.	38

ASSISTS

Name, Team	A
Bobby Orr, Bos.	80
Phil Esposito, Bos.	67
Jean Ratelle, NYR	63
Vic Hadfield, NYR	56
Fred Stanfield, Bos.	56
Rod Gilbert, NYR	54
Frank Mahovlich, Mtl.	53
J.C. Tremblay, Mtl.	51
John Bucyk, Bos.	51
Pit Martin, Chi.	51

POWERPLAY GOALS

Name, Team	PPG
Phil Esposito, Bos.	28
Vic Hadfield, NYR	23
Rick Martin, Buf.	19
Yvan Cournoyer, Mtl.	18
Frank Mahovlich, Mtl.	14
Garry Unger, St.L.	14
John Bucyk, Bos.	13
Paul Henderson, Tor.	12
Dale Tallon, Van.	11
Bobby Orr, Bos.	11
Gilbert Perreault, Buf.	11
Bobby Clarke, Phi.	11

SHORTHAND GOALS

Name, Team	SHG
Derek Sanderson, Bos.	7
Terry Crisp, St.L.	6
Jimmy Roberts, St.L./Mtl.	5
Jim Johnson, Phi./L.A.	4
Pete Mahovlich, Mtl.	4
Frank Mahovlich, Mtl.	4
Bobby Orr, Bos.	4
Bill Fairbairn, NYR	4
Six tied with	3

GAME-WINNING GOALS

Name, Team	GWG
Phil Esposito, Bos.	16
Bobby Hull, Chi.	9
Bill Goldsworthy, Min.	8
Gary Sabourin, St.L.	7
Jacques Lemaire, Mtl.	7
John Bucyk, Bos.	7
Vic Hadfield, NYR	7
Pit Martin, Chi.	7
Ron Ellis, Tor.	7
Seven tied with	6

GOALIE WINS

Name, Team	W
Ken Dryden, Mtl.	39
Tony Esposito, Chi.	31
Eddie Johnston, Bos.	27
Gerry Cheevers, Bos.	27
Gilles Villemure, NYR	24
Ed Giacomin, NYR	24
Cesare Maniago, Min.	20
Al Smith, Det.	18
Doug Favell, Phi.	18
Jim Rutherford, Pit.	17
Bernie Parent, Tor.	17

SHUTOUTS

Name, Team	SO
Tony Esposito, Chi.	9
Ken Dryden, Mtl.	8
Gary Smith, Chi.	5
Doug Favell, Phi.	5
Al Smith, Det.	4
Gilles Meloche, Cal.	4
Gilles Villemure, NYR	3
Cesare Maniago, Min.	3
Bernie Parent, Tor.	3
Seven tied with	2

FIRST TEAM ALL-STARS

Name, Team	Position
Phil Esposito, Bos.	C
Rod Gilbert, NYR	RW
Bobby Hull, Chi.	LW
Bobby Orr, Bos.	D
Brad Park, NYR	D
Tony Esposito, Chi.	G

SECOND TEAM ALL-STARS

Name, Team	Position
Jean Ratelle, NYR	C
Yvan Cournoyer, Mtl.	RW
Vic Hadfield, NYR	LW
Bill White, Chi.	D
Pat Stapleton, Chi.	D
Ken Dryden, Mtl.	G

TROPHY WINNERS

Trophy	Awarded For	Winner	Team
Hart	MVP	Bobby Orr	Bos.
Art Ross	Top Scorer	Phil Esposito	Bos.
Norris	Top Defenseman	Bobby Orr	Bos.
Calder	Top Rookie	Ken Dryden	Mtl.
Vezina	Fewest Goals Against	Tony Esposito	Chi
		Gary Smith	Chi
Byng	Gentlemanly Conduct	Jean Ratelle	NYR
Masterton	Perseverance, Sportsmanship	Bobby Clarke	Phi.
Pearson	NHLPA MVP	Jean Ratelle	NYR
Conn Smythe	Playoff MVP	Bobby Orr	Bos.
Patrick	Service to Hockey in U.S.	Clarence S. Campbell	
		John A. "Snooks" Kelly	
		Cooney Weiland	
		James D. Norris	
Amateur Draft	First Overall Selection	Bill Harris	NYI

NHL NOTEBOOK

TRANSACTIONS

- Nov. 4, 1971 – L.A. Kings traded Dale Hoganson, Dennis DeJordy, Noel Price and Doug Robinson to Montreal for goalie Rogie Vachon.
- Jan. 14, 1972 – Buffalo Sabres obtained Jim Lorentz from the Rangers, for Buffalo's second-round choice in the 1972 draft.
- Feb. 23, 1972 – Boston Bruins obtained defenseman Carol Vadnais (along with Don O'Donoghue) from the Oakland Seals for Reggie Leach, Rick Smith and Bob Stewart.
- Mar. 4, 1972 – Buffalo Sabres traded Eddie Shack to Pittsburgh for rookie Rene Robert.

RECORDS

- Mar. 8, 1972 – Derek Sanderson picked up three assists as the Bruins set an NHL record with their eighth straight road victory, a 5-4 win over the North Stars at Minnesota.
- Mar. 22, 1972 – Detroit's Marcel Dionne scored two goals and two assists to reach 75 points, a new NHL record for rookies, as the Red Wings won 6-3 at Los Angeles. Dionne broke the old mark of 72 points, set by Buffalo's Gil Perreault the previous season.
- Mar. 25, 1972 – Goalie Gerry Cheevers extended his NHL-record unbeaten streak to 32 straight games (24-0-8) when the Bruins tied the Black Hawks 5-5 at Boston Garden.
- May 4, 1972 – Bobby Orr scored a goal to break the career record for playoff goals by a defenseman. Goal #17 came in only his 47th playoff game and broke the mark held by Red Kelly (16) in 94 playoff games.

MILESTONES

- Oct. 31, 1971 – Fred Glover became the first in NHL history to coach two NHL teams in one season, when he was named coach of the Los Angeles Kings just 12 days after being fired by the Oakland Seals. He lost in his Kings debut 5-1 to the visiting Chicago Black Hawks.
- Feb. 10, 1972 – Montreal's Guy Lafleur had three goals to become the first rookie in the modern NHL era to score three hat tricks in a season, as the Canadiens won 7-1 over the Black Hawks at the Forum. Lafleur also had an assist in the game.
- Feb. 19, 1972 – Boston's Phil Esposito became the first player in NHL history to score 100 points in a season three times in his career, when he picked up an assist in a 6-4 win over the North Stars at Minnesota.
- May 5, 1972 – Boston's Bobby Orr became the first player in NHL history to win the Hart Trophy (as the NHL's MVP) three straight seasons. He also became the first NHL player to win the Norris Trophy five straight years.

1972 Playoffs

QUARTER-FINALS

Apr.	5	Toronto	0	at	Boston	5
Apr.	6	Toronto	4	at	Boston	3 OT
Apr.	8	Boston	2	at	Toronto	0
Apr.	9	Boston	5	at	Toronto	4
Apr.	11	Toronto	2	at	Boston	3

Boston won best-of-seven series 4–1

Apr.	5	Montreal	2	at	NY Rangers	3
Apr.	6	Montreal	2	at	NY Rangers	5
Apr.	8	NY Rangers	1	at	Montreal	2
Apr.	9	NY Rangers	6	at	Montreal	4
Apr.	11	Montreal	2	at	NY Rangers	1
Apr.	13	NY Rangers	3	at	Montreal	2

NY Rangers won best-of-seven series 4–2

Apr.	5	Pittsburgh	1	at	Chicago	3
Apr.	6	Pittsburgh	2	at	Chicago	3
Apr.	8	Chicago	2	at	Pittsburgh	0
Apr.	9	Chicago	6	at	Pittsburgh	5 OT

Chicago won best-of-seven series 4–0

Apr.	5	St. Louis	0	at	Minnesota	3
Apr.	6	St. Louis	5	at	Minnesota	6 OT
Apr.	8	Minnesota	1	at	St. Louis	2
Apr.	9	Minnesota	2	at	St. Louis	3
Apr.	11	St. Louis	3	at	Minnesota	4
Apr.	13	Minnesota	2	at	St. Louis	4
Apr.	16	St. Louis	2	at	Minnesota	1 OT

St. Louis won best-of-seven series 4–3

SEMI-FINALS

Apr.	18	St. Louis	1	at	Boston	6
Apr.	20	St. Louis	2	at	Boston	10
Apr.	23	Boston	7	at	St. Louis	2
Apr.	25	Boston	5	at	St. Louis	3

Boston won best-of-seven series 4–0

Apr.	16	NY Rangers	3	at	Chicago	2
Apr.	18	NY Rangers	5	at	Chicago	3
Apr.	20	Chicago	2	at	NY Rangers	3
Apr.	23	Chicago	2	at	NY Rangers	6

NY Rangers won best-of-seven series 4–0

FINALS

Apr.	30	NY Rangers	5	at	Boston	6
May	2	NY Rangers	1	at	Boston	2
May	4	Boston	2	at	NY Rangers	5
May	7	Boston	3	at	NY Rangers	2
May	9	NY Rangers	3	at	Boston	2
May	11	Boston	3	at	NY Rangers	0

Boston won best-of-seven series 4–2

1971-72 – Boston Bruins – Gerry Cheevers, Eddie Johnston, Bobby Orr, Ted Green, Carol Vadnais, Dallas Smith, Don Awrey, Phil Esposito, Ken Hodge, John Bucyk, Mike Walton, Wayne Cashman, Garnet Bailey, Derek Sanderson, Fred Stanfield, Ed Westfall, John McKenzie, Don Marcotte, Garry Peters, Chris Hayes, Tom Johnson (Coach), Milt Schmidt (General Manager), Dan Canney, John Forristall (Trainers).

Gerry Cheevers was at his best in big games. Sharing netminding duties with Ed Johnston, Cheevers helped the Bruins emerge from a terrible decade in the 1960s to become an NHL powerhouse during the 1970s. He was perhaps the greatest clutch goaltender in the NHL during that time, helping Boston win the Stanley Cup in 1970 and 1972.

LEADING PLAYOFF SCORERS

Player	Club	GP	G	A	PTS	PIM
Phil Esposito	Boston	15	9	15	24	24
Bobby Orr	Boston	15	5	19	24	19
John Bucyk	Boston	15	9	11	20	6
Ken Hodge	Boston	15	9	8	17	62
Bobby Rousseau	NY Rangers	16	6	11	17	7
John McKenzie	Boston	15	5	12	17	37
Vic Hadfield	NY Rangers	16	7	9	16	22
Fred Stanfield	Boston	15	7	9	16	0
Rod Gilbert	NY Rangers	16	7	8	15	11
Phil Roberto	St. Louis	11	7	6	13	29

LEADING PLAYOFF GOALTENDERS

Goaltender	Club	GPI	Mins	GA	SO	Avg.
Eddie Johnston	Boston	7	420	13	1	1.86
Gilles Villemure	NY Rangers	6	360	14	0	2.33
Gerry Cheevers	Boston	8	483	21	2	2.61
Ed Giacomin	NY Rangers	10	600	27	0	2.70
Ken Dryden	Montreal	6	360	17	0	2.83

PLAYOFF GOALS

Name, Team	G
Phil Esposito, Bos.	9
John Bucyk, Bos.	9
Ken Hodge, Bos.	9
Phil Roberto, St.L.	7
Fred Stanfield, Bos.	7
Vic Hadfield, NYR	7
Rod Gilbert, NYR	7

PLAYOFF ASSISTS

Name, Team	A
Bobby Orr, Bos.	19
Phil Esposito, Bos.	15
John McKenzie, Bos.	12
John Bucyk, Bos.	11
Bobby Rousseau, NYR	11
Fred Stanfield, Bos.	9
Vic Hadfield, NYR	9

PLAYOFF POWERPLAY GOALS

Name, Team	PPG
Bobby Orr, Bos.	4
Rod Gilbert, NYR	4
Phil Roberto, St.L.	3
John McKenzie, Bos.	3
Nine tied with	2

PLAYOFF SHORTHAND GOALS

Name, Team	SHG
Ed Westfall, Bos.	2
Eight tied with	1

PLAYOFF GAME-WINNING GOALS

Name, Team	GWG
Ken Hodge, Bos.	3
Phil Esposito, Bos.	3
Mike Walton, Bos.	2
Rod Gilbert, NYR	2
Walt Tkaczuk, NYR	2

PLAYOFF GOALIE WINS

Name, Team	W
Eddie Johnston, Bos.	6
Gerry Cheevers, Bos.	6
Ed Giacomin, NYR	6
Gilles Villemure, NYR	4
Jacques Caron, St.L.	4

PLAYOFF SHUTOUTS

Name, Team	SO
Gerry Cheevers, Bos.	2
Gary Smith, Chi.	1
Gump Worsley, Min.	1
Eddie Johnston, Bos.	1

1972-73

Stanley Cup • Montreal Canadiens

FINAL STANDINGS

Team	GP	W	L	T	GF	GA	PTS
EAST DIVISION							
Montreal	78	52	10	16	329	184	120
Boston	78	51	22	5	330	235	107
NY Rangers	78	47	23	8	297	208	102
Buffalo	78	37	27	14	257	219	88
Detroit	78	37	29	12	265	243	86
Toronto	78	27	41	10	247	279	64
Vancouver	78	22	47	9	233	339	53
NY Islanders	78	12	60	6	170	347	30
WEST DIVISION							
Team	**GP**	**W**	**L**	**T**	**GF**	**GA**	**PTS**
Chicago	78	42	27	9	284	225	93
Philadelphia	78	37	30	11	296	256	85
Minnesota	78	37	30	11	254	230	85
St. Louis	78	32	34	12	233	251	76
Pittsburgh	78	32	37	9	257	265	73
Los Angeles	78	31	36	11	232	245	73
Atlanta	78	25	38	15	191	239	65
California	78	16	46	16	213	323	48

LEADING SCORERS

Player	Club	GP	G	A	PTS	PIM
Phil Esposito	Boston	78	55	75	130	87
Bobby Clarke	Philadelphia	78	37	67	104	80
Bobby Orr	Boston	63	29	72	101	99
Rick MacLeish	Philadelphia	78	50	50	100	69
Jacques Lemaire	Montreal	77	44	51	95	16
Jean Ratelle	NY Rangers	78	41	53	94	12
Mickey Redmond	Detroit	76	52	41	93	24
John Bucyk	Boston	78	40	53	93	12
Frank Mahovlich	Montreal	78	38	55	93	51
Jim Pappin	Chicago	76	41	51	92	82
Marcel Dionne	Detroit	77	40	50	90	21
Dennis Hull	Chicago	78	39	51	90	27
Pit Martin	Chicago	78	29	61	90	30
Gilbert Perreault	Buffalo	78	28	60	88	10
Syl Apps Jr.	Pittsburgh	77	29	56	85	18
Rod Gilbert	NY Rangers	76	25	59	84	25
Rene Robert	Buffalo	75	40	43	83	83
Stan Mikita	Chicago	57	27	56	83	32
Dennis Hextall	Minnesota	78	30	52	82	140
Ken Hodge	Boston	73	37	44	81	58
Garry Unger	St. Louis	78	41	39	80	119
Yvan Cournoyer	Montreal	67	40	39	79	18
Gary Dornhoefer	Philadelphia	77	30	49	79	168
Fred Stanfield	Boston	78	20	58	78	10
Darryl Sittler	Toronto	78	29	48	77	69

LEADING GOALTENDERS

Goaltender	Club	GPI	MINS	GA	SO	AVG
Ken Dryden	Montreal	54	3165	119	6	2.26
Gilles Villemure	NY Rangers	34	2040	78	3	2.29
Tony Esposito	Chicago	56	3340	140	4	2.51
Roy Edwards	Detroit	52	3012	132	6	2.63
Dave Dryden	Buffalo	37	2018	89	3	2.65
Roger Crozier	Buffalo	49	2633	121	3	2.76
Jacques Plante	Tor./Bos.	40	2197	103	3	2.81
Doug Favell	Philadelphia	44	2419	114	3	2.83
Rogie Vachon	Los Angeles	53	3120	148	4	2.85
Cesare Maniago	Minnesota	47	2736	132	5	2.89

Shaking off the coverage of Jacques Laperriere, Mickey Redmond broke the Red Wings team record of 49 goal shared by Gordie Howe and Frank Mahovlich when he scored 52 in 1972–73. At the time, only six other players in hockey history had reached the 50-goal plateau. Redmond scored 51 goals the following season.

THE HOCKEY UNIVERSE CHANGED forever in 1972. The NHL had a major professional rival for the first time since the 1926 demise of the old Western Hockey League with the establishment of the World Hockey Association. The new 12-team league featured the Alberta Oilers, Winnipeg Jets, Chicago Cougars, Houston Aeros, Los Angeles Sharks and Minnesota Fighting Saints in the Western Division, while the Eastern Division was comprised of the Cleveland Crusaders, New England Whalers, Quebec Nordiques, Ottawa Nationals, Philadelphia Blazers and New York Raiders.

Summit and Plummet – Canada downed Russia in a preseason Series of the Century, the Canadiens regained their glory and the championship but the rival WHA began to sign the NHL's stars.

The WHA raided NHL rosters of talent, securing such players as Bernie Parent, Gerry Cheevers and J.C. Tremblay, though the real coup was Winnipeg's signing of Bobby Hull to a 10-year deal worth $2.75 million. The league was also a place for NHL journeymen such as Andre Lacroix and Danny Lawson to shine. Lawson scored a league-leading 61 goals, while Lacroix topped the loop with 124 points. The Whalers beat Hull's Jets in the Avco Cup finals to claim the first WHA championship.

Before either league opened its 1972–73 schedule, hockey fans around the world focused their attention on an eight-game series pitting an all-NHL Team Canada against the Soviet Union's national team. The Soviets were perennial amateur champions, but Canadian fans were confident their top professionals would put the Russians in their place. The Canadians quickly found that the Soviets were a superb team and struggled valiantly to raise their play to meet the challenge. Only Paul Henderson's goal with 34 seconds to play in game eight secured a narrow victory for Team Canada. The Soviets' superior training techniques and strong skating and passing skills would influence the NHL game for years to come.

The NHL responded to the WHA's challenge by adding the New York Islanders and Atlanta Flames this year, but the season's best performances came from traditional favorites. The Boston Bruins' Phil Esposito won his third consecutive scoring title, while the Montreal Canadiens finished first overall in the regular season and later beat the Chicago Black Hawks in six games in the finals to win the Stanley Cup. A one-game challenge issued by the WHA champion Whalers went unheeded by the NHL.

Jacques Lemaire never achieved all-star status because of the tough competition at his position of center, but he was a key contributor to eight Stanley Cup champions during a 12-year career with the Montreal Canadiens. He scored a career-high 44 goals in 1972–73.

Leaders, 1972-73

GOALS

Name, Team	G
Phil Esposito, Bos.	55
Mickey Redmond, Det.	52
Rick MacLeish, Phi.	50
Jacques Lemaire, Mtl.	44
Bill Flett, Phi.	43
Jim Pappin, Chi.	41
Jean Ratelle, NYR	41
Garry Unger, St.L.	41
Yvan Cournoyer, Mtl.	40
Rene Robert, Buf.	40
Marcel Dionne, Det.	40
John Bucyk, Bos.	40

ASSISTS

Name, Team	A
Phil Esposito, Bos.	75
Bobby Orr, Bos.	72
Bobby Clarke, Phi.	67
Pit Martin, Chi.	61
Gilbert Perreault, Buf.	60
Rod Gilbert, NYR	59
Fred Stanfield, Bos.	58
Stan Mikita, Chi.	56
Syl Apps Jr., Pit.	56
Frank Mahovlich, Mtl.	55

POWERPLAY GOALS

Name, Team	PPG
Rick MacLeish, Phi.	21
Phil Esposito, Bos.	19
Ken Hodge, Bos.	16
Mickey Redmond, Det.	15
Mike Corrigan, L.A.	14
Bob Berry, L.A.	14
Garry Unger, St.L.	13
Bill Flett, Phi.	11
Rick Martin, Buf.	11
Jean Ratelle, NYR	11
Jim Lorentz, Buf.	11

SHORTHAND GOALS

Name, Team	SHG
Phil Esposito, Bos.	5
Pete Mahovlich, Mtl.	4
Bill Flett, Phi.	3
Garnet Bailey, Bos./Det.	3
Ron Schock, Pit.	3
Don Luce, Buf.	3
15 tied with	2

GAME-WINNING GOALS

Name, Team	GWG
Phil Esposito, Bos.	11
John Bucyk, Bos.	10
Chuck Lefley, Mtl.	7
Guy Lafleur, Mtl.	7
Walt Tkaczuk, NYR	7
Mickey Redmond, Det.	7
Dennis Hull, Chi.	7
Gilbert Perreault, Buf.	7
12 tied with	6

GOALIE WINS

Name, Team	W
Ken Dryden, Mtl.	33
Tony Esposito, Chi.	32
Roy Edwards, Det.	27
Ed Giacomin, NYR	26
Eddie Johnston, Bos.	24
Roger Crozier, Buf.	23
Rogie Vachon, L.A.	22
Cesare Maniago, Min.	21
Gilles Villemure, NYR	20
Doug Favell, Phi.	20
Jim Rutherford, Pit.	20

SHUTOUTS

Name, Team	SO
Roy Edwards, Det.	6
Ken Dryden, Mtl.	6
Eddie Johnston, Bos.	5
Cesare Maniago, Min.	5
Ed Giacomin, NYR	4
Rogie Vachon, L.A.	4
Tony Esposito, Chi.	4
Gilles Villemure, NYR	3
Dave Dryden, Buf.	3
Jacques Plante, Tor./Bos.	3
Doug Favell, Phi.	3
Roger Crozier, Buf.	3
Jim Rutherford, Pit.	3

FIRST TEAM ALL-STARS

Name, Team	Position
Phil Esposito, Bos.	C
Mickey Redmond, Det.	RW
Frank Mahovlich, Mtl.	LW
Bobby Orr, Bos.	D
Guy Lapointe, Mtl.	D
Ken Dryden, Mtl.	G

SECOND TEAM ALL-STARS

Name, Team	Position
Bobby Clarke, Phi.	C
Yvan Cournoyer, Mtl.	RW
Dennis Hull, Chi.	LW
Brad Park, NYR	D
Bill White, Chi.	D
Tony Esposito, Chi.	G

TROPHY WINNERS

Trophy	Awarded For	Winner	Team
Hart	MVP	Bobby Clarke	Phi.
Art Ross	Top Scorer	Phil Esposito	Bos.
Norris	Top Defenseman	Bobby Orr	Bos.
Calder	Top Rookie	Steve Vickers	NYR
Vezina	Fewest Goals Against	Ken Dryden	Mtl.
Byng	Gentlemanly Conduct	Gilbert Perreault	Buf.
Masterton	Perseverance, Sportmanship	Lowell MacDonald	Pit.
Pearson	NHLPA MVP	Bobby Clarke	Phi.
Conn Smythe	Playoff MVP	Yvan Cournoyer	Mtl.
Patrick	Service to Hockey in U.S.	Walter L. Bush Jr.	
Amateur Draft	First Overall Selection	Denis Potvin	NYI

NHL NOTEBOOK

TRANSACTIONS

- June 26, 1972 – New York Islanders purchased goaltender Glenn "Chico" Resch from the Montreal Canadiens.
- Aug. 22, 1972 – Los Angeles Kings obtained Terry Harper from Montreal in exchange for future draft picks.
- Dec. 5, 1972 – Chicago obtained Dick Redmond and Bobby Sheehan from the Oakland Seals in trade for Darryl Maggs.
- Feb. 26, 1973 – Los Angeles Kings traded veteran Ralph Backstrom to Chicago in exchange for left wing Dan Maloney.

RECORDS

- Nov. 22, 1972 – Penguins set an NHL record with five goals in 2:07 during a 10-4 win over the Blues.
- Jan. 28, 1973 – Detroit's Henry Boucha set an NHL record for the fastest goal scored from the start of a game when he scored at the six-second mark against Montreal in a 4-2 Red Wings win over the Canadiens.
- May 3, 1973 – Henri Richard set an NHL Stanley Cup record for most career playoff games as the Canadiens lost 7-4 to Chicago in game three of the Stanley Cup finals. Richard broke the record of 164 held by Red Kelly.
- May 8, 1973 – Chicago and Montreal combined to set an NHL record with 15 goals in one Stanley Cup finals game. Black Hawks won 8-7 in game five, at Montreal.

MILESTONES

- Feb. 6, 1973 – Playing his first NHL game at the age of 38, Connie Madigan became the oldest rookie in NHL history when he suited up for the St. Louis Blues in a 5-1 win over the visiting Vancouver Canucks.
- Mar. 1, 1973 – Philadelphia Flyers set a single-season penalty minute record when Bob Kelly's hooking minor during a game against L.A. broke the old NHL mark of 1,371 set by Vancouver in 1970-71.
- Mar. 29, 1973 – Flyers' Bobby Clarke became the first player from a post-67 team to score 100 points in a season. His 100th point was a goal that led the Flyers over the Atlanta Flames 4-2 at the Spectrum.
- May 18, 1973 – Boston's Bobby Orr was named winner of the Norris Trophy. It was the first time in NHL history that a player had won an individual award six consecutive seasons.

1973 Playoffs

QUARTER-FINALS

Apr.	4	Buffalo	1	at	Montreal	2
Apr.	5	Buffalo	3	at	Montreal	7
Apr.	7	Montreal	5	at	Buffalo	2
Apr.	8	Montreal	1	at	Buffalo	5
Apr.	10	Buffalo	3	at	Montreal	2 OT
Apr.	12	Montreal	4	at	Buffalo	2

Montreal won best-of-seven series 4–2

Apr.	4	NY Rangers	6	at	Boston	2
Apr.	5	NY Rangers	4	at	Boston	2
Apr.	7	Boston	4	at	NY Rangers	2
Apr.	8	Boston	0	at	NY Rangers	4
Apr.	10	NY Rangers	6	at	Boston	3

NY Rangers won best-of-seven series 4–1

Apr.	4	St. Louis	1	at	Chicago	7
Apr.	5	St. Louis	0	at	Chicago	1
Apr.	7	Chicago	5	at	St. Louis	2
Apr.	8	Chicago	3	at	St. Louis	5
Apr.	10	St. Louis	1	at	Chicago	6

Chicago won best-of-seven series 4–1

Apr.	4	Minnesota	3	at	Philadelphia	0
Apr.	5	Minnesota	1	at	Philadelphia	4
Apr.	7	Philadelphia	0	at	Minnesota	5
Apr.	8	Philadelphia	3	at	Minnesota	0
Apr.	10	Minnesota	2	at	Philadelphia	3 OT
Apr.	12	Philadelphia	4	at	Minnesota	1

Philadelphia won best-of-seven series 4–2

SEMI-FINALS

Apr.	14	Philadelphia	5	at	Montreal	4 OT
Apr.	17	Philadelphia	3	at	Montreal	4 OT
Apr.	19	Montreal	2	at	Philadelphia	1
Apr.	22	Montreal	4	at	Philadelphia	1
Apr.	24	Philadelphia	3	at	Montreal	5

Montreal won best-of-seven series 4–1

Apr.	12	NY Rangers	4	at	Chicago	1
Apr.	15	NY Rangers	4	at	Chicago	5
Apr.	17	Chicago	2	at	NY Rangers	1
Apr.	19	Chicago	3	at	NY Rangers	1
Apr.	24	NY Rangers	1	at	Chicago	4

Chicago won best-of-seven series 4–1

FINALS

Apr.	29	Chicago	3	at	Montreal	8
May	1	Chicago	1	at	Montreal	4
May	3	Montreal	4	at	Chicago	7
May	6	Montreal	4	at	Chicago	0
May	8	Chicago	8	at	Montreal	7
May	10	Montreal	6	at	Chicago	4

Montreal won best-of-seven series 4–2

1972-73 – Montreal Canadiens – Ken Dryden, Guy Lapointe, Serge Savard, Larry Robinson, Jacques Laperrière, Bob Murdoch, Pierre Bouchard, Jimmy Roberts, Yvan Cournoyer, Frank Mahovlich, Jacques Lemaire, Pete Mahovlich, Marc Tardif, Henri Richard (Captain), Réjean Houle, Guy Lafleur, Chuck Lefley, Claude Larose, Murray Wilson, Steve Shutt, Michel Plasse, Scotty Bowman (Coach), Sam Pollock (General Manager), Eddy Palchak, Bob Williams (Trainers).

Guy Lapointe established himself as one of the NHL's best defensemen over a 16-year career, playing on six Stanley Cup winners with the Montreal Canadiens during the 1970s. Lapointe was a member of "The Big Three" on the Canadiens defense with Serge Savard and Larry Robinson. He was a punishing checker who could join in the offensive rush.

LEADING PLAYOFF SCORERS

Player	Club	GP	G	A	PTS	PIM
Yvan Cournoyer	Montreal	17	15	10	25	2
Dennis Hull	Chicago	16	9	15	24	4
Frank Mahovlich	Montreal	17	9	14	23	6
Stan Mikita	Chicago	15	7	13	20	8
Jacques Lemaire	Montreal	17	7	13	20	2
Pat Stapleton	Chicago	16	2	15	17	10
Pit Martin	Chicago	15	10	6	16	6
Jim Pappin	Chicago	16	8	7	15	24
Guy Lapointe	Montreal	17	6	7	13	20
Pete Mahovlich	Montreal	17	4	9	13	22
Marc Tardif	Montreal	14	6	6	12	6

LEADING PLAYOFF GOALTENDERS

Goaltender	Club	GPI	Mins	GA	SO	Avg.
Cesare Maniago	Minnesota	5	309	9	2	1.75
Ed Giacomin	NY Rangers	10	539	23	1	2.56
Doug Favell	Philadelphia	11	669	29	1	2.60
Roger Crozier	Buffalo	4	249	11	0	2.65
Ken Dryden	Montreal	17	1039	50	1	2.89

PLAYOFF GOALS

Name, Team	G
Yvan Cournoyer, Mtl.	15
Pit Martin, Chi.	10
Dennis Hull, Chi.	9
Frank Mahovlich, Mtl.	9
Jim Pappin, Chi.	8
Three tied with	7

PLAYOFF ASSISTS

Name, Team	A
Dennis Hull, Chi.	15
Pat Stapleton, Chi.	15
Frank Mahovlich, Mtl.	14
Stan Mikita, Chi.	13
Jacques Lemaire, Mtl.	13
Yvan Cournoyer, Mtl.	10

PLAYOFF POWERPLAY GOALS

Name, Team	PPG
Pit Martin, Chi.	4
Dennis Hull, Chi.	4
Jacques Lemaire, Mtl.	3
Yvan Cournoyer, Mtl.	3
Seven tied with	2

PLAYOFF SHORTHAND GOALS

Name, Team	SHG
Gregg Sheppard, Bos.	1
Bill Flett, Phi.	1
Ralph Backstrom, Chi.	1
Bill White, Chi.	1
Pete Mahovlich, Mtl.	1

PLAYOFF GAME-WINNING GOALS

Name, Team	GWG
Yvan Cournoyer, Mtl.	3
Dennis Hextall, Min.	2
Dick Redmond, Chi.	2
Marc Tardif, Mtl.	2
Stan Mikita, Chi.	2
Lou Angotti, Chi.	2
Henri Richard, Mtl.	2

PLAYOFF GOALIE WINS

Name, Team	W
Ken Dryden, Mtl.	12
Tony Esposito, Chi.	10
Ed Giacomin, NYR	5
Doug Favell, Phi.	5
Roger Crozier, Buf.	2
Cesare Maniago, Min.	2

PLAYOFF SHUTOUTS

Name, Team	SO
Cesare Maniago, Min.	2
Ed Giacomin, NYR	1
Doug Favell, Phi.	1
Tony Esposito, Chi.	1
Ken Dryden, Mtl.	1

1973-74

Stanley Cup • Philadelphia Flyers

Defenseman Brad Park and goalie Ed Giacomin were two key reasons why the New York Rangers rose to respectability in the 1970s after decades of despair. Though Park never won the Norris Trophy, he was the runner-up six times in his career. Giacomin shared the Vezina Trophy with Gilles Villemure in 1970–71.

FINAL STANDINGS

EAST DIVISION

Team	GP	W	L	T	GF	GA	PTS
Boston	78	52	17	9	349	221	113
Montreal	78	45	24	9	293	240	99
NY Rangers	78	40	24	14	300	251	94
Toronto	78	35	27	16	274	230	86
Buffalo	78	32	34	12	242	250	76
Detroit	78	29	39	10	255	319	68
Vancouver	78	24	43	11	224	296	59
NY Islanders	78	19	41	18	182	247	56

WEST DIVISION

Team	GP	W	L	T	GF	GA	PTS
Philadelphia	78	50	16	12	273	164	112
Chicago	78	41	14	23	272	164	105
Los Angeles	78	33	33	12	233	231	78
Atlanta	78	30	34	14	214	238	74
Pittsburgh	78	28	41	9	242	273	65
St. Louis	78	26	40	12	206	248	64
Minnesota	78	23	38	17	235	275	63
California	78	13	55	10	195	342	36

LEADING SCORERS

Player	Club	GP	G	A	PTS	PIM
Phil Esposito	Boston	78	68	77	145	58
Bobby Orr	Boston	74	32	90	122	82
Ken Hodge	Boston	76	50	55	105	43
Wayne Cashman	Boston	78	30	59	89	111
Bobby Clarke	Philadelphia	77	35	52	87	113
Rick Martin	Buffalo	78	52	34	86	38
Syl Apps Jr.	Pittsburgh	75	24	61	85	37
Darryl Sittler	Toronto	78	38	46	84	55
Lowell MacDonald	Pittsburgh	78	43	39	82	14
Brad Park	NY Rangers	78	25	57	82	148
Dennis Hextall	Minnesota	78	20	62	82	138
Frank Mahovlich	Montreal	71	31	49	80	47
Stan Mikita	Chicago	76	30	50	80	46
Marcel Dionne	Detroit	74	24	54	78	10
Mickey Redmond	Detroit	76	51	26	77	14
Rod Gilbert	NY Rangers	75	36	41	77	20
Rick MacLeish	Philadelphia	78	32	45	77	42
Pit Martin	Chicago	78	30	47	77	43
John Bucyk	Boston	76	31	44	75	8
Andre Boudrias	Vancouver	78	16	59	75	18
Bill Goldsworthy	Minnesota	74	48	26	74	73
Yvan Cournoyer	Montreal	67	40	33	73	18
Pete Mahovlich	Montreal	78	36	37	73	122
Jim Pappin	Chicago	78	32	41	73	76
Jean Pronovost	Pittsburgh	77	40	32	72	22

LEADING GOALTENDERS

Goaltender	Club	GPI	MINS	GA	SO	AVG
Bernie Parent	Philadelphia	73	4314	136	12	1.89
Tony Esposito	Chicago	70	4143	141	10	2.04
Doug Favell	Toronto	32	1752	79	0	2.71
Wayne Thomas	Montreal	42	2410	111	1	2.76
Dan Bouchard	Atlanta	46	2660	123	5	2.77
Rogie Vachon	Los Angeles	65	3751	175	5	2.80
Michel Larocque	Montreal	27	1431	69	0	2.89
Gilles Gilbert	Boston	54	3210	158	6	2.95
Dave Dryden	Buffalo	53	2987	148	1	2.97
Ed Giacomin	NY Rangers	56	3286	168	5	3.07

During the 1972–73 season, Bobby Clarke had finished second to Phil Esposito in NHL scoring with 104 points, making him the first player from an expansion team to top the 100-point plateau. His Philadelphia Flyers had finished 37–30–11 for their first winning season, and the Flyers' captain was the first member of a non-Original Six team to win the Hart Trophy as most valuable player. During the 1973–74 campaign, the Flyers would emerge as the new NHL powerhouse.

Known as "The Broad Street Bullies" for their intimidating play, the Flyers featured offensive talent in Clarke, Bill Barber and Rick MacLeish, a strong defense boasting Tom Bladon and Andre "Moose" Dupont, and prototypical tough guys like Dave Schultz and Don Saleski, all extremely well coached by Fred Shero. Bernie Parent, back with the Flyers after a season in the with the Philadelphia Blazers of the WHA, provided excellent goaltending, sharing the Vezina Trophy with Tony Esposito of the Chicago Black Hawks. The Flyers recorded a 50–16–12 mark to lead the West Division with 112 points, just one point behind the Boston Bruins for top spot overall. Boston's Phil Esposito, Bobby Orr, Ken Hodge and Wayne Cashman finished 1–2–3–4 on the NHL scoring list.

> **The Broad Street Bullies – The Philadelphia Flyers built a championship squad around a charismatic captain, tough defense, opportunistic scoring and a hardworking bunch who came to play every shift.**

Meanwhile, the World Hockey Association was back with a 12-team lineup for the 1973–74 season, although franchise shifts had landed teams in Toronto (the Toros, formerly the Ottawa Nationals) and Vancouver (the former Philadelphia Blazers). The rival league dropped another bombshell when Gordie Howe ended a two-year retirement to join sons Mark and Marty with the Houston Aeros. The 45-year-old wonder scored 31 goals and added 69 assists and helped Houston win the Avco Cup. Former NHLer Mike Walton led WHA scorers with 57 goals and 117 points.

The NHL postseason was similar to the regular season in that the Bruins and Philadelphia continued to be the league's best teams, marching through the playoffs toward a showdown for the Stanley Cup. Boston won game one of the final 3–2 on a late goal by Bobby Orr, but the Flyers became the first expansion team to win a Stanley Cup final-series game with a 3–2 victory of their own in game two. By game six, with Kate Smith belting out *God Bless America*, Philadelphia was the NHL's first expansion champion after a 1–0 triumph. Rick MacLeish had the game's only goal, while Bernie Parent's shutout sealed his selection as Conn Smythe Trophy winner.

Like father, like sons. At the age of 45, Gordie Howe ended his two-year retirement in order to join Mark and Marty with the Houston Aeros of the World Hockey Association..

Leaders, 1973-74

GOALS

Name, Team	G
Phil Esposito, Bos.	68
Rick Martin, Buf.	52
Mickey Redmond, Det.	51
Ken Hodge, Bos.	50
Bill Goldsworthy, Min.	48
Lowell MacDonald, Pit.	43
Yvan Cournoyer, Mtl.	40
Jean Pronovost, Pit.	40
Darryl Sittler, Tor.	38
Rod Gilbert, NYR	36
Pete Mahovlich, Mtl.	36

ASSISTS

Name, Team	A
Bobby Orr, Bos.	90
Phil Esposito, Bos.	77
Dennis Hextall, Min.	62
Syl Apps Jr., Pit.	61
Wayne Cashman, Bos.	59
Andre Boudrias, Van.	59
Brad Park, NYR	57
Ken Hodge, Bos.	55
Marcel Dionne, Det.	54
Bobby Clarke, Phi.	52

POWERPLAY GOALS

Name, Team	PPG
Mickey Redmond, Det.	21
Rod Gilbert, NYR	16
Ken Hodge, Bos.	15
Phil Esposito, Bos.	14
Rick MacLeish, Phi.	13
Bill Goldsworthy, Min.	12
John Bucyk, Bos.	12
Vic Hadfield, NYR	12
Jim Lorentz, Buf.	12
Bobby Orr, Bos.	11
Darryl Sittler, Tor.	11

SHORTHAND GOALS

Name, Team	SHG
Ralph Stewart, NYI	5
Bobby Clarke, Phi.	5
Syl Apps Jr., Pit.	4
Jean Pronovost, Pit.	4
Phil Esposito, Bos.	4
Rick MacLeish, Phi.	4
Pete Mahovlich, Mtl.	4
Eight tied with	3

GAME-WINNING GOALS

Name, Team	GWG
Ken Hodge, Bos.	11
Yvan Cournoyer, Mtl.	9
John Bucyk, Bos.	9
Mickey Redmond, Det.	9
Phil Esposito, Bos.	9
Rod Gilbert, NYR	8
Jim Pappin, Chi.	8
Gilbert Perreault, Buf.	7
Jacques Lemaire, Mtl.	7
Pete Mahovlich, Mtl.	7

GOALIE WINS

Name, Team	W
Bernie Parent, Phi.	47
Gilles Gilbert, Bos.	34
Tony Esposito, Chi.	34
Ed Giacomin, NYR	30
Rogie Vachon, L.A.	28
Wayne Thomas, Mtl.	23
Dave Dryden, Buf.	23
Gary Smith, Van.	20
Dan Bouchard, Atl.	19
Ross Brooks, Bos.	16
Jim Rutherford, Pit/Det.	16

SHUTOUTS

Name, Team	SO
Bernie Parent, Phi.	12
Tony Esposito, Chi.	10
Gilles Gilbert, Bos.	6
Dan Bouchard, Atl.	5
Ed Giacomin, NYR	5
Rogie Vachon, L.A.	5
Ross Brooks, Bos.	3
Gary Smith, Van.	3
Wayne Stephenson, St.L.	2
12 tied with	1

FIRST TEAM ALL-STARS

Name, Team	Position
Phil Esposito, Bos.	C
Ken Hodge, Bos.	RW
Rick Martin, Buf.	LW
Bobby Orr, Bos.	D
Brad Park, NYR	D
Bernie Parent, Phi.	G

SECOND TEAM ALL-STARS

Name, Team	Position
Bobby Clarke, Phi.	C
Mickey Redmond, Det.	RW
Wayne Cashman, Bos.	LW
Bill White, Chi.	D
Barry Ashbee, Phi.	D
Tony Esposito, Chi.	G

TROPHY WINNERS

Trophy	Awarded For	Winner	Team
Hart	MVP	Phil Esposito	Bos.
Art Ross	Top Scorer	Phil Esposito	Bos.
Norris	Top Defenseman	Bobby Orr	Bos.
Calder	Top Rookie	Denis Potvin	NYI
Vezina	Fewest Goals Against	Bernie Parent (tie)	Phi.
		Tony Esposito (tie)	Chi.
Adams	Top Coach	Fred Shero	Phi.
Byng	Gentlemanly Conduct	John Bucyk	Bos.
Masterton	Perseverance, Sportmanship	Henri Richard	Mtl.
Pearson	NHLPA MVP	Phil Esposito	Bos.
Conn Smythe	Playoff MVP	Bernie Parent	Phi.
Patrick	Service to Hockey in U.S.	Alex Delvecchio	
		Murray Murdoch	
		Weston W. Adams, Sr.	
		Charles L. Crovat	
Amateur Draft	First Overall Selection	Greg Joly	Wsh.

NHL NOTEBOOK

TRANSACTIONS

- May 12, 1973 – Toronto Maple Leafs signed Swedish defenseman Borje Salming and forward Inge Hammarstrom as free agents.
- May 15, 1973 – Philadelphia Flyers obtained Bernie Parent from Toronto for a draft pick and future considerations.
- May 22, 1973 – Boston traded Fred Stanfield to the Minnesota North Stars for goaltender Gilles Gilbert.
- Nov. 30, 1973 – Los Angeles Kings traded Gilles Marotte and Real Lemieux to the NY Rangers in exchange for Sheldon Kannegiesser, Tommy Williams, and Mike Murphy.

RECORDS

- Mar. 30, 1974 – Philadelphia's Bernie Parent set an NHL record for most wins in a season, when he picked up his 45th victory of the year, 5-3 over the visiting Boston Bruins. Parent broke the mark of 44 held by Terry Sawchuk, and finished the season with 47 wins.
- Apr. 6, 1974 – Rookie Denis Potvin scored a goal and three assists in the final game of the season, to give him NHL records for most goals (17), assists (54), and points (71) by a rookie defenseman. Islanders won 4-2 over the Minnesota North Stars in New York.
- Apr. 13, 1974 – Chicago Black Hawks set an NHL playoff record for fewest shots in a playoff game, with just 10 in a 1-0 win at Los Angeles, in game three of the quarter-finals.

MILESTONES

- Dec. 9, 1973 – Rick Martin became the first player in Buffalo Sabres history to score 100 goals. The milestone came in Martin's 174th career game, a 5-2 win over Toronto.
- Feb. 20, 1974 – Phil Esposito became the first player to record four straight 50 goal seasons, and had his 22nd career hat trick in a 5-5 Bruins tie in Minnesota.
- Mar. 12, 1974 – Boston's Bobby Orr became the first player to score 100 points for five straight seasons, when he picked up an assist in a 4-0 win over the Sabres.
- Mar. 27, 1974 – Boston Bruins became the first team in NHL history to win 50 (or more) games four straight seasons, when they got their 50th victory of the 1973-74 season 3-2 over the Rangers, in New York.
- Apr. 7, 1974 – Pittsburgh's Andy Brown became the final NHL goaltender to play without a mask, when he played his final league game for the Penguins, a 6-3 loss to the Flames at Atlanta.

1974 Playoffs

QUARTER-FINALS

Apr. 10	Toronto	0	at	Boston	1
Apr. 11	Toronto	3	at	Boston	6
Apr. 13	Boston	6	at	Toronto	3
Apr. 14	Boston	4	at	Toronto	3 OT

Boston won best-of-seven series 4–0

Apr. 10	NY Rangers	4	at	Montreal	1
Apr. 11	NY Rangers	1	at	Montreal	4
Apr. 13	Montreal	4	at	NY Rangers	2
Apr. 14	Montreal	4	at	NY Rangers	6
Apr. 16	NY Rangers	3	at	Montreal	2 OT
Apr. 18	Montreal	2	at	NY Rangers	5

NY Rangers won best-of-seven series 4–2

Apr. 9	Atlanta	1	at	Philadelphia	4
Apr. 11	Atlanta	1	at	Philadelphia	5
Apr. 12	Philadelphia	4	at	Atlanta	1
Apr. 14	Philadelphia	4	at	Atlanta	3 OT

Philadelphia won best-of-seven series 4–0

Apr. 10	Los Angeles	1	at	Chicago	3
Apr. 11	Los Angeles	1	at	Chicago	4
Apr. 13	Chicago	1	at	Los Angeles	0
Apr. 14	Chicago	1	at	Los Angeles	5
Apr. 16	Los Angeles	0	at	Chicago	1

Chicago won best-of-seven series 4–1

SEMI-FINALS

Apr. 18	Chicago	4	at	Boston	2
Apr. 21	Chicago	6	at	Boston	8
Apr. 23	Boston	3	at	Chicago	4 OT
Apr. 25	Boston	5	at	Chicago	2
Apr. 28	Chicago	2	at	Boston	6
Apr. 30	Boston	4	at	Chicago	2

Boston won best-of-seven series 4–2

Apr. 20	NY Rangers	0	at	Philadelphia	4
Apr. 23	NY Rangers	2	at	Philadelphia	5
Apr. 25	Philadelphia	3	at	NY Rangers	5
Apr. 28	Philadelphia	1	at	NY Rangers	2 OT
Apr. 30	NY Rangers	1	at	Philadelphia	4
May 2	Philadelphia	1	at	NY Rangers	4
May 5	NY Rangers	3	at	Philadelphia	4

Philadelphia won best-of-seven series 4–3

FINALS

May 7	Philadelphia	2	at	Boston	3
May 9	Philadelphia	3	at	Boston	2 OT
May 12	Boston	1	at	Philadelphia	4
May 14	Boston	2	at	Philadelphia	4
May 16	Philadelphia	1	at	Boston	5
May 19	Boston	0	at	Philadelphia	1

Philadelphia won best-of-seven series 4–2

1973-74 – Philadelphia Flyers – Bernie Parent, Ed Van Impe, Tom Bladon, André Dupont, Joe Watson, Jimmy Watson, Barry Ashbee, Bill Barber, Dave Schultz, Don Saleski, Gary Dornhoefer, Terry Crisp, Bobby Clarke (Captain), Simon Nolet, Ross Lonsberry, Rick MacLeish, Bill Flett, Orest Kindrachuk, Bill Clement, Bob Kelly, Bruce Cowick, Al MacAdam, Bobby Taylor, Fred Shero (Coach), Keith Allen (General Manager), Frank Lewis, Jim McKenzie (Trainers).

Bernie Parent was a native of Montreal who grew up watching Jacques Plante play goal for the Canadiens on television. He would later play with Plante on the Toronto Maple Leafs, and their time together would help Parent develop into one of the great goaltenders in the NHL. He led the Flyers to the first to two straight Stanley Cup titles in 1974.

LEADING PLAYOFF SCORERS

Player	Club	GP	G	A	PTS	PIM
Rick MacLeish	Philadelphia	17	13	9	22	20
Gregg Sheppard	Boston	16	11	8	19	4
John Bucyk	Boston	16	8	10	18	4
Bobby Orr	Boston	16	4	14	18	28
Ken Hodge	Boston	16	6	10	16	16
Bobby Clarke	Philadelphia	17	5	11	16	42
Phil Esposito	Boston	16	9	5	14	25
Wayne Cashman	Boston	16	5	9	14	46
Ross Lonsberry	Philadelphia	17	4	9	13	18
Carol Vadnais	Boston	16	1	12	13	42

LEADING PLAYOFF GOALTENDERS

Goaltender	Club	GPI	Mins	GA	SO	Avg.
Rogie Vachon	Los Angeles	4	240	7	0	1.75
Bernie Parent	Philadelphia	17	1042	35	2	2.02
Gilles Gilbert	Boston	16	977	43	1	2.64
Ed Giacomin	NY Rangers	13	788	37	0	2.82
Tony Esposito	Chicago	10	584	28	2	2.88

PLAYOFF GOALS

Name, Team	G
Rick MacLeish, Phi.	13
Gregg Sheppard, Bos.	11
Phil Esposito, Bos.	9
John Bucyk, Bos.	8
Dennis Hull, Chi.	6
Pete Stemkowski, NYR	6
Bruce MacGregor, NYR	6
Ken Hodge, Bos.	6

PLAYOFF ASSISTS

Name, Team	A
Bobby Orr, Bos.	14
Carol Vadnais, Bos.	12
Bobby Clarke, Phi.	11
John Bucyk, Bos.	10
Ken Hodge, Bos.	10
Wayne Cashman, Bos.	9
Rick MacLeish, Phi.	9
Ross Lonsberry, Phi.	9

PLAYOFF POWERPLAY GOALS

Name, Team	PPG
Rick MacLeish, Phi.	5
Phil Esposito, Bos.	4
John Bucyk, Bos.	3
Tom Bladon, Phi.	3
Steve Vickers, NYR	2
Gary Dornhoefer, Phi.	2

PLAYOFF SHORTHAND GOALS

Name, Team	SHG
Gregg Sheppard, Bos.	2
Gary Dornhoefer, Phi.	1
Ross Lonsberry, Phi.	1
Terry Crisp, Phi.	1

PLAYOFF GAME-WINNING GOALS

Name, Team	GWG
Rick MacLeish, Phi.	4
Eight tied with	2

PLAYOFF GOALIE WINS

Name, Team	W
Bernie Parent, Phi.	12
Gilles Gilbert, Bos.	10
Ed Giacomin, NYR	7
Tony Esposito, Chi.	6
Michel Larocque, Mtl.	2

PLAYOFF SHUTOUTS

Name, Team	SO
Tony Esposito, Chi.	2
Bernie Parent, Phi.	2
Gilles Gilbert, Bos.	1

1974-75

Stanley Cup • Philadelphia Flyers

FINAL STANDINGS

PRINCE OF WALES CONFERENCE

Team	GP	W	L	T	GF	GA	PTS
Norris Division							
Montreal	80	47	14	19	374	225	113
Los Angeles	80	42	17	21	269	185	105
Pittsburgh	80	37	28	15	326	289	89
Detroit	80	23	45	12	259	335	58
Washington	80	8	67	5	181	446	21
Adams Division							
Buffalo	80	49	16	15	354	240	113
Boston	80	40	26	14	345	245	94
Toronto	80	31	33	16	280	309	78
California	80	19	48	13	212	316	51
CLARENCE CAMPBELL CONFERENCE							
Patrick Division							
Philadelphia	80	51	18	11	293	181	113
NY Rangers	80	37	29	14	319	276	88
NY Islanders	80	33	25	22	264	221	88
Atlanta	80	34	31	15	243	233	83
Smythe Division							
Vancouver	80	38	32	10	271	254	86
St. Louis	80	35	31	14	269	267	84
Chicago	80	37	35	8	268	241	82
Minnesota	80	23	50	7	221	341	53
Kansas City	80	15	54	11	184	328	41

LEADING SCORERS

Player	Club	GP	G	A	PTS	PIM
Bobby Orr	Boston	80	46	89	135	101
Phil Esposito	Boston	79	61	66	127	62
Marcel Dionne	Detroit	80	47	74	121	14
Guy Lafleur	Montreal	70	53	66	119	37
Pete Mahovlich	Montreal	80	35	82	117	64
Bobby Clarke	Philadelphia	80	27	89	116	125
Rene Robert	Buffalo	74	40	60	100	75
Rod Gilbert	NY Rangers	76	36	61	97	22
Gilbert Perreault	Buffalo	68	39	57	96	36
Rick Martin	Buffalo	68	52	43	95	72
Jacques Lemaire	Montreal	80	36	56	92	20
Jean Ratelle	NY Rangers	79	36	55	91	26
Steve Vickers	NY Rangers	80	41	48	89	64
Danny Grant	Detroit	80	50	37	87	28
Stan Mikita	Chicago	79	36	50	86	48
Ron Schock	Pittsburgh	80	23	63	86	36
John Bucyk	Boston	78	29	52	81	10
Garry Unger	St. Louis	80	36	44	80	123
Darryl Sittler	Toronto	72	36	44	80	47
Rick MacLeish	Philadelphia	80	38	41	79	50
Syl Apps Jr.	Pittsburgh	79	24	55	79	43
Reggie Leach	Philadelphia	80	45	33	78	63
Gregg Sheppard	Boston	76	30	48	78	19
Andre Boudrias	Vancouver	77	16	62	78	46
Tom Lysiak	Atlanta	77	25	52	77	73

LEADING GOALTENDERS

Goaltender	Club	GPI	MINS	GA	SO	AVG
Bernie Parent	Philadelphia	68	4041	137	12	2.03
Rogie Vachon	Los Angeles	54	3239	121	6	2.24
Gary Edwards	Los Angeles	27	1561	61	3	2.34
Glenn Resch	NY Islanders	25	1432	59	3	2.47
Ken Dryden	Montreal	56	3320	149	4	2.69
Tony Esposito	Chicago	71	4219	193	6	2.74
Dan Bouchard	Atlanta	40	2400	111	3	2.78
Billy Smith	NY Islanders	58	3368	156	3	2.78
Phil Myre	Atlanta	40	2400	114	5	2.85
Michel Larocque	Montreal	25	1480	74	3	3.00

Bobby Clarke was diagnosed with diabetes at age 15, but still became a junior hockey star in his hometown of Flin Flon, Manitoba. He went on to a 15-year NHL playing career as the heart and soul of the Philadelphia Flyers. Clarke's 89 assists in both 1974–75 and 1975–76 were a single-season record for centers until being broken by Wayne Gretzky in the 1980s.

It was another expansion year for the NHL, which added the Kansas City Scouts and Washington Capitals and the 18-team league was reorganized into four divisions named after some of the game's builders. The Norris and Adams divisions made up the Prince of Wales Conference, while the Clarence Campbell Conference housed the Patrick and Smythe divisions. The Philadelphia Flyers, Buffalo Sabres and Montreal Canadiens led the Patrick, Adams and Norris divisions respectively, each finishing with 113 points, while the Vancouver Canucks were the surprise winners of the Smythe Division with 86 points in the newly expanded 80-game season. Under a new playoff format, the top three teams in each division qualified, with the four first-place teams receiving a bye into the quarter-finals. The eight other playoff teams played a preliminary round.

Captain Courageous – Orr and Esposito continued to dominate but Bobby Clarke's leadership and MVP credentials led the Philadelphia Flyers into the Stanley Cup winner's circle again.

The WHA also expanded this year, adding Phoenix and Indianapolis, although several of the 12 "established" franchises moved before (and even during) the season. The innovative league created a Canadian Division of Vancouver, Edmonton, Winnipeg, Toronto and Quebec. Bobby Hull set a pro hockey record with 77 goals for Winnipeg, while Andre Lacroix of San Diego had a record 106 assists. Still, it was Gordie Howe's Houston Aeros who emerged on top, winning their second Avco Cup title.

In the NHL postseason, the 1975 Stanley Cup finals marked the first battle between two expansion teams. The Flyers, buoyed by Bobby Clarke's second Hart Trophy performance in as many years, as well as Bernie Parent's Vezina Trophy title, led the league with 51 wins and eliminated the Toronto Maple Leafs and New York Islanders to reach the finals for the second year in a row. The Islanders had battled back from a 3–0 deficit to beat Pittsburgh in the quarter-finals, and nearly duplicated the feat against the Flyers. Meanwhile, the Sabres knocked off the Black Hawks and the Canadiens to play for the Stanley Cup in only their fifth season. The Flyers successfully defended their Cup title in a six-game final series remembered for the fog that rose from the ice at Buffalo's Memorial Auditorium, requiring frequent interruptions to allow the mist to disperse.

The regular season also saw the emergence of new individual talents. Veterans Bobby Orr and Phil Esposito finished 1–2 atop the NHL scoring list, but right behind them were Marcel Dionne and Guy Lafleur, who were finally showing the promise that had made them the top two selections in the 1971 Amateur Draft.

Pat Quinn of the Atlanta Flames and Ed Westfall of the New York Islanders. Both players brought on-ice leadership to their young franchises.

Leaders, 1974-75

GOALS

Name, Team	G
Phil Esposito, Bos.	61
Guy Lafleur, Mtl.	53
Rick Martin, Buf.	52
Danny Grant, Det.	50
Marcel Dionne, Det.	47
Bobby Orr, Bos.	46
Reggie Leach, Phi.	45
Jean Pronovost, Pit.	43
Steve Vickers, NYR	41
Rene Robert, Buf.	40

ASSISTS

Name, Team	A
Bobby Orr, Bos.	89
Bobby Clarke, Phi.	89
Pete Mahovlich, Mtl.	82
Marcel Dionne, Det.	74
Guy Lafleur, Mtl.	66
Phil Esposito, Bos.	66
Ron Schock, Pit.	63
Andre Boudrias, Van.	62
Rod Gilbert, NYR	61
Rene Robert, Buf.	60

POWERPLAY GOALS

Name, Team	PPG
Phil Esposito, Bos.	27
Rick Martin, Buf.	21
Danny Grant, Det.	19
Ken Hodge, Bos.	16
Bobby Orr, Bos.	16
Steve Vickers, NYR	16
Guy Lafleur, Mtl.	15
Jean Ratelle, NYR	15
Marcel Dionne, Det.	15
Rene Robert, Buf.	14

SHORTHAND GOALS

Name, Team	SHG
Marcel Dionne, Det.	10
Don Luce, Buf.	8
Gregg Sheppard, Bos.	7
Craig Ramsay, Buf.	7
Bill Barber, Phi.	5
Lorne Henning, NYI	4
Vic Hadfield, Pit.	4
Phil Esposito, Bos.	4
Five tied with	3

GAME-WINNING GOALS

Name, Team	GWG
Guy Lafleur, Mtl.	11
Reggie Leach, Phi.	10
Jean Pronovost, Pit.	9
Cliff Koroll, Chi.	9
Gilbert Perreault, Buf.	8
Phil Esposito, Bos.	8
Rick MacLeish, Phi.	8
Jacques Lemaire, Mtl.	8
Garry Unger, St.L.	8
Butch Goring, L.A.	7
Craig Ramsay, Buf.	7
Bob Berry, L.A.	7

GOALIE WINS

Name, Team	W
Bernie Parent, Phi.	44
Tony Esposito, Chi.	34
Gary Smith, Van.	32
Ken Dryden, Mtl.	30
Rogie Vachon, L.A.	27
Gary Bromley, Buf.	26
Gary Inness, Pit.	24
Gilles Gilbert, Bos.	23
Gilles Villemure, NYR	22
Billy Smith, NYI	21

SHUTOUTS

Name, Team	SO
Bernie Parent, Phi.	12
Rogie Vachon, L.A.	6
Tony Esposito, Chi.	6
Gary Smith, Van.	6
Phil Myre, Atl.	5
Gary Bromley, Buf.	4
Ken Dryden, Mtl.	4
Seven tied with	3

FIRST TEAM ALL-STARS

Name, Team	Position
Bobby Clarke, Phi.	C
Guy Lafleur, Mtl.	RW
Rick Martin, Buf.	LW
Bobby Orr, Bos.	D
Denis Potvin, NYI	D
Bernie Parent, Phi.	G

SECOND TEAM ALL-STARS

Name, Team	Position
Phil Esposito, Bos.	C
Rene Robert, Buf.	RW
Steve Vickers, NYR	LW
Guy Lapointe, Mtl.	D
Borje Salming, Tor.	D
Rogie Vachon, L.A.	G

TROPHY WINNERS

Trophy	Awarded For	Winner	Team
Hart	MVP	Bobby Clarke	Phi.
Art Ross	Top Scorer	Bobby Orr	Bos.
Norris	Top Defenseman	Bobby Orr	Bos.
Calder	Top Rookie	Eric Vail	Atl.
Vezina	Fewest Goals Against	Bernie Parent	Phi.
Adams	Top Coach	Bob Pulford	L.A.
Byng	Gentlemanly Conduct	Marcel Dionne	Det.
Masterton	Perseverance, Sportsmanship	Don Luce	Buf.
Pearson	NHLPA MVP	Bobby Orr	Bos.
Conn Smythe	Playoff MVP	Bernie Parent	Phi.
Patrick	Service to Hockey in U.S.	Donald M. Clark	
		Bill Chadwick	
		Tommy Ivan	
Amateur Draft	First Overall Selection	Mel Bridgman	Phi.

NHL NOTEBOOK

TRANSACTIONS

- May 24, 1974 – Philadelphia Flyers acquired Reggie Leach from the Oakland Seals for Larry Wright, Al MacAdam and a first-round draft pick in 1974.
- May 27, 1974 – NY Rangers traded Vic Hadfield to Pittsburgh in exchange for defenseman Nick Beverley.
- Sept. 13, 1974 – Pittsburgh Penguins acquired right wing Rick Kehoe from Toronto in exchange for left winger Blaine Stoughton and future considerations.
- Nov. 5, 1974 – Boston Bruins signed free agent Mike Milbury, out of Colgate University.

RECORDS

- Mar. 9, 1975 – Montreal Canadiens broke the NHL record for most powerplay goals in one year with their 82nd of the season in a 5-3 win over the Rangers at New York.
- Mar. 12, 1975 – Montreal Canadiens extended their NHL-record road undefeated streak to 23 straight games (14-0-9) with a 3-3 tie against the Maple Leafs at Toronto. The streak ended with a loss in the next road game.
- Mar. 26, 1975 – The first-year Washington Capitals extended their NHL-record losing streak to 17 straight games with a 5-1 loss to the Los Angeles Kings.
- Mar. 28, 1975 – Washington Capitals recorded the only road victory in their first season, a 5-3 win at Oakland. The win ended their record 37-game road losing streak. They finished the year 1-39-0 on the road.

MILESTONES

- Oct. 9, 1974 – Toronto's Dave Keon became the first player in franchise history to score 350 goals as a member of the Maple Leafs. The milestone goal came in a 6-2 win over the visiting Kansas City Scouts.
- Oct. 19, 1974 – Chicago's Grant Mulvey became the youngest player since World War II to score an NHL goal when the Black Hawks beat the Blues 3-1. Mulvey was 18 years, one month and two days old.
- Apr. 6, 1975 – Chicago's Billy Reay became just the third NHL coach to reach the 500-win milestone, when the Black Hawks won their 1,200th NHL game 3-0 over the visiting Minnesota North Stars.
- Apr. 26, 1975 – New York Islanders beat Pittsburgh 1-0 in game seven of the Stanley Cup quarter-finals to become the second team in NHL history to win a best-of-7 series after losing the first three games.

1975 Playoffs

PRELIMINARY ROUND

Apr.	8	Toronto	2	at	Los Angeles	3 OT
Apr.	10	Los Angeles	2	at	Toronto	3 OT
Apr.	11	Toronto	2	at	Los Angeles	1

Toronto won best-of-three series 2–1

Apr.	8	Chicago	2	at	Boston	8
Apr.	10	Boston	3	at	Chicago	4 OT
Apr.	11	Chicago	6	at	Boston	4

Chicago won best-of-three series 2–1

Apr.	8	St. Louis	3	at	Pittsburgh	4
Apr.	10	Pittsburgh	5	at	St. Louis	3

Pittsburgh won best-of-three series 2–0

Apr.	8	NY Islanders	3	at	NY Rangers	2
Apr.	10	NY Rangers	8	at	NY Islanders	3
Apr.	11	NY Islanders	4	at	NY Rangers	3 OT

NY Islanders won best-of-three series 2–1

QUARTER-FINALS

Apr.	13	Toronto	3	at	Philadelphia	6
Apr.	15	Toronto	0	at	Philadelphia	3
Apr.	17	Philadelphia	2	at	Toronto	0
Apr.	19	Philadelphia	4	at	Toronto	3 OT

Philadelphia won best-of-seven series 4–0

Apr.	13	Chicago	1	at	Buffalo	4
Apr.	15	Chicago	1	at	Buffalo	3
Apr.	17	Buffalo	4	at	Chicago	5 OT
Apr.	20	Buffalo	6	at	Chicago	2
Apr.	22	Chicago	1	at	Buffalo	3

Buffalo won best-of-seven series 4–1

Apr.	13	Vancouver	2	at	Montreal	6
Apr.	15	Vancouver	2	at	Montreal	1
Apr.	17	Montreal	4	at	Vancouver	1
Apr.	19	Montreal	4	at	Vancouver	0
Apr.	22	Vancouver	4	at	Montreal	5 OT

Montreal won best-of-seven series 4–1

Apr.	13	NY Islanders	4	at	Pittsburgh	5
Apr.	15	NY Islanders	1	at	Pittsburgh	3
Apr.	17	Pittsburgh	6	at	NY Islanders	4
Apr.	20	Pittsburgh	1	at	NY Islanders	3
Apr.	22	NY Islanders	4	at	Pittsburgh	2
Apr.	24	Pittsburgh	1	at	NY Islanders	4
Apr.	26	NY Islanders	1	at	Pittsburgh	0

NY Islanders won best-of-seven series 4–3

SEMI-FINALS

Apr.	29	NY Islanders	0	at	Philadelphia	4
May	1	NY Islanders	4	at	Philadelphia	5 OT
May	4	Philadelphia	1	at	NY Islanders	0
May	7	Philadelphia	3	at	NY Islanders	4 OT
May	8	NY Islanders	5	at	Philadelphia	1
May	11	Philadelphia	1	at	NY Islanders	2
May	13	NY Islanders	1	at	Philadelphia	4

Philadelphia won best-of-seven series 4–3

Apr.	27	Montreal	5	at	Buffalo	6 OT
Apr.	29	Montreal	2	at	Buffalo	4
May	1	Buffalo	0	at	Montreal	7
May	3	Buffalo	2	at	Montreal	8
May	6	Montreal	4	at	Buffalo	5 OT
May	8	Buffalo	4	at	Montreal	3

Buffalo won best-of-seven series 4–2

FINALS

May	15	Buffalo	1	at	Philadelphia	4
May	18	Buffalo	1	at	Philadelphia	2
May	20	Philadelphia	4	at	Buffalo	5 OT
May	22	Philadelphia	2	at	Buffalo	4
May	25	Buffalo	1	at	Philadelphia	5
May	27	Philadelphia	2	at	Buffalo	0

Philadelphia won best-of-seven series 4–2

1974-75 – Philadelphia Flyers – Bernie Parent, Wayne Stephenson, Ed Van Impe, Tom Bladon, André Dupont, Joe Watson, Jimmy Watson, Ted Harris, Larry Goodenough, Rick MacLeish, Bobby Clarke (Captain), Bill Barber, Reggie Leach, Gary Dornhoefer, Ross Lonsberry, Bob Kelly, Terry Crisp, Don Saleski, Dave Schultz, Orest Kindrachuk, Bill Clement, Fred Shero (Coach), Keith Allen (General Manager), Frank Lewis, Jim McKenzie (Trainers).

Rick MacLeish became the first player from an NHL expansion team to score 50 goals in 1972–73. His goal in game six of the 1974 finals gave the Flyers a 1–0 win over Boston, enabling Philadelphia to become the first club from the NHL's 1967 expansion to win the Stanley Cup.

LEADING PLAYOFF SCORERS

Player	Club	GP	G	A	PTS	PIM
Rick MacLeish	Philadelphia	17	11	9	20	8
Guy Lafleur	Montreal	11	12	7	19	15
Jude Drouin	NY Islanders	17	6	12	18	6
J.P. Parise	NY Islanders	17	8	8	16	22
Pete Mahovlich	Montreal	11	6	10	16	10
Bobby Clarke	Philadelphia	17	4	12	16	16
Rick Martin	Buffalo	17	7	8	15	20
Gilbert Perreault	Buffalo	17	6	9	15	10
Bill Barber	Philadelphia	17	6	9	15	8
Ed Westfall	NY Islanders	17	5	10	15	12

LEADING PLAYOFF GOALTENDERS

Goaltender	Club	GPI	Mins	GA	SO	Avg.
Bernie Parent	Philadelphia	15	922	29	4	1.89
Glenn Resch	NY Islanders	12	692	25	1	2.17
Ken Dryden	Montreal	11	688	29	2	2.53
Gary Inness	Pittsburgh	9	540	24	0	2.67
Gord McRae	Toronto	7	441	21	0	2.86

PLAYOFF GOALS

Name, Team	G
Guy Lafleur, Mtl.	12
Rick MacLeish, Phi.	11
J.P. Parise, NYI	8
Reggie Leach, Phi.	8
Rick Martin, Buf.	7
Danny Gare, Buf.	7

PLAYOFF ASSISTS

Name, Team	A
Jude Drouin, NYI	12
Bobby Clarke, Phi.	12
Pete Mahovlich, Mtl.	10
Ed Westfall, NYI	10
Rick MacLeish, Phi.	9
Gilbert Perreault, Buf.	9
Bill Barber, Phi.	9
Denis Potvin, NYI	9

PLAYOFF POWERPLAY GOALS

Name, Team	PPG
Rick Martin, Buf.	5
Guy Lafleur, Mtl.	4
Rick MacLeish, Phi.	4
Gilbert Perreault, Buf.	4
J.P. Parise, NYI	4

PLAYOFF SHORTHAND GOALS

Name, Team	SHG
Ten tied with	1

Bill Fairbairn, NYR; Bobby Orr, Bos.; Colin Campbell, Pit.; Vic Hadfield, Pit.; Guy Lapointe, Mtl.; Don Luce, Buf.; Denis Potvin, NYI; Bobby Clarke, Phi.; Ed Westfall, NYI; Craig Ramsay, Buf.

PLAYOFF GAME-WINNING GOALS

Name, Team	GWG
Guy Lafleur, Mtl.	4
Rene Robert, Buf.	3
Jim Lorentz, Buf.	2
Bobby Clarke, Phi.	2
Ed Westfall, NYI	2
Reggie Leach, Phi.	2
Andre Dupont, Phi.	2
Gary Dornhoefer, Phi.	2
Clark Gillies, NYI	2

PLAYOFF GOALIE WINS

Name, Team	W
Bernie Parent, Phi.	10
Glenn Resch, NYI	8
Gerry Desjardins, Buf.	7
Ken Dryden, Mtl.	6
Gary Inness, Pit.	5

PLAYOFF SHUTOUTS

Name, Team	SO
Bernie Parent, Phi.	4
Ken Dryden, Mtl.	2
Wayne Stephenson, Phi.	1
Glenn Resch, NYI	1

1975-76

Stanley Cup • Montreal Canadiens

Gilbert Perreault was the first draft pick in the history of the Buffalo Sabres, chosen first overall in the 1970 Amateur Draft. He went on to become the Sabres career leader in virtually every major category. Perreault established career highs with 44 goals, 69 assists and 113 points in 1975–76.

FINAL STANDINGS

PRINCE OF WALES CONFERENCE

Team	GP	W	L	T	GF	GA	PTS
Norris Division							
Montreal	80	58	11	11	337	174	127
Los Angeles	80	38	33	9	263	265	85
Pittsburgh	80	35	33	12	339	303	82
Detroit	80	26	44	10	226	300	62
Washington	80	11	59	10	224	394	32
Adams Division							
Boston	80	48	15	17	313	237	113
Buffalo	80	46	21	13	339	240	105
Toronto	80	34	31	15	294	276	83
California	80	27	42	11	250	278	65
CLARENCE CAMPBELL CONFERENCE							
Patrick Division							
Philadelphia	80	51	13	16	348	209	118
NY Islanders	80	42	21	17	297	190	101
Atlanta	80	35	33	12	262	237	82
NY Rangers	80	29	42	9	262	333	67
Smythe Division							
Chicago	80	32	30	18	254	261	82
Vancouver	80	33	32	15	271	272	81
St. Louis	80	29	37	14	249	290	72
Minnesota	80	20	53	7	195	303	47
Kansas City	80	12	56	12	190	351	36

LEADING SCORERS

Player	Club	GP	G	A	PTS	PIM
Guy Lafleur	Montreal	80	56	69	125	36
Bobby Clarke	Philadelphia	76	30	89	119	136
Gilbert Perreault	Buffalo	80	44	69	113	36
Bill Barber	Philadelphia	80	50	62	112	104
Pierre Larouche	Pittsburgh	76	53	58	111	33
Jean Ratelle	NYR/Bos.	80	36	69	105	18
Pete Mahovlich	Montreal	80	34	71	105	76
Jean Pronovost	Pittsburgh	80	52	52	104	24
Darryl Sittler	Toronto	79	41	59	100	90
Syl Apps Jr.	Pittsburgh	80	32	67	99	24
Denis Potvin	NY Islanders	78	31	67	98	100
Bryan Trottier	NY Islanders	80	32	63	95	21
Marcel Dionne	Los Angeles	80	40	54	94	38
Lanny McDonald	Toronto	75	37	56	93	70
Reggie Leach	Philadelphia	80	61	30	91	41
Rene Robert	Buffalo	72	35	52	87	53
Rick Martin	Buffalo	80	49	37	86	67
Rod Gilbert	NY Rangers	70	36	50	86	32
Chuck Lefley	St. Louis	75	43	42	85	41
Garry Unger	St. Louis	80	39	44	83	95
John Bucyk	Boston	77	36	47	83	20
Phil Esposito	Bos./NYR	74	35	48	83	36
Steve Vickers	NY Rangers	80	30	53	83	40
Tom Lysiak	Atlanta	80	31	51	82	60
Walt McKechnie	Detroit	80	26	56	82	85

LEADING GOALTENDERS

Goaltender	Club	GPI	MINS	GA	SO	AVG
Ken Dryden	Montreal	62	3580	121	8	2.03
Glenn Resch	NY Islanders	44	2546	88	7	2.07
Dan Bouchard	Atlanta	47	2671	113	2	2.54
Wayne Stephenson	Philadelphia	66	3819	164	1	2.58
Billy Smith	NY Islanders	39	2254	98	3	2.61
Gilles Gilbert	Boston	55	3123	151	3	2.90
Gerry Desjardins	Buffalo	55	3280	161	2	2.95
Tony Esposito	Chicago	68	4003	198	4	2.97
Rogie Vachon	Los Angeles	51	3060	160	5	3.14
Wayne Thomas	Toronto	64	3684	196	2	3.19

THE MONTREAL CANADIENS returned to the NHL's summit in 1975–76, collecting a league-record 58 wins and 127 points. Guy Lafleur won the first of three consecutive scoring titles, leading the league with 56 goals and 125 points, while Ken Dryden earned the Vezina Trophy with a 2.03 goals-against average. The Norris Trophy this year went to Denis Potvin of the New York Islanders, ending Bobby Orr's streak of eight straight years as the league's best defenseman. Orr was forced to undergo two knee operations and played just 10 games during the 1975–76 season.

Orr's was not the only significant absence from the Boston Bruins' lineup. In November, Harry Sinden stunned the hockey world by dealing stars Phil Esposito and Carol Vadnais to the New York Rangers for Jean Ratelle, Brad Park and Joe Zanussi. The blockbuster helped revitalize an aging roster, allowing Boston to claim top spot in the Adams Division and to remain one of the NHL's top clubs for years to come. In another surprising move, Marcel Dionne left the Detroit Red Wings as a free agent. He was signed by the Los Angeles Kings, who sent Dan Maloney, Terry Harper and a draft choice to Detroit as compensation.

Tenacious "D" – With the Big Three (Robinson, Lapointe and Savard) on the blueline, Dryden in the crease and a wish list full of whiz kids on the roster, the Habs reigned over Philly's parade.

The two-time defending Stanley Cup champion Philadelphia Flyers enjoyed another outstanding season, leading the Patrick Division with 118 points. Philadelphia beat the Toronto Maple Leafs in a quarter-final series that saw Toronto's Darryl Sittler tie the playoff record of five goals in a game. Philadelphia's Reggie Leach also enjoyed a five-goal game when the Flyers defeated Boston in the semi-finals. Montreal advanced with wins over the Chicago Black Hawks and the Islanders, then capped their season with a Stanley Cup sweep of Philadelphia.

The WHA had once again opened the season with 14 teams playing in the Canadian, Eastern and Western divisions, though the Cincinnati Stingers and Denver Spurs replaced teams in Chicago and Baltimore, and the Vancouver Blazers became the Calgary Cowboys. The season ended with only 12 teams as both the Spurs and the Minnesota Fighting Saints folded during the year. Quebec enjoyed the season's best individual performances, as Marc Tardif led the league with 71 goals and 148 points and tied teammate J.C. Tremblay with 77 assists. Nordiques goaltender Richard Brodeur had 44 wins. Still, the Winnipeg Jets, led by Bobby Hull, Ulf Nilsson and Anders Hedberg, won the Avco Cup, denying Houston a third straight title with a four-game sweep in the finals.

At just 20 years and five months old, Pierre Larouche was the NHL's youngest 50-goal scorer when he notched 53 goals for the Penguins in 1975–76. His 50-goal season with Montreal in 1979–80 made him the first to reach the milestone for two different teams.

TROPHY WINNERS

Trophy	Awarded For	Winner	Team
Hart	MVP	Bobby Clarke	Phi.
Art Ross	Top Scorer	Guy Lafleur	Mtl.
Norris	Top Defenseman	Denis Potvin	NYI
Calder	Top Rookie	Bryan Trottier	NYI
Vezina	Fewest Goals Against	Ken Dryden	Mtl.
Adams	Top Coach	Don Cherry	Bos.
Byng	Gentlemanly Conduct	Jean Ratelle	NYR/Bos.
Masterton	Perseverance, Sportsmanship	Rod Gilbert	NYR
Pearson	NHLPA MVP	Guy Lafleur	Mtl.
Conn Smythe	Playoff MVP	Reggie Leach	Phi.
Patrick	Service to Hockey in U.S.	Stan Mikita	
		George Leader	
		Bruce A. Norris	
Amateur Draft	First Overall Selection	Rick Green	Wsh.

Leaders, 1975-76

GOALS

Name, Team	G
Reggie Leach, Phi.	61
Guy Lafleur, Mtl.	56
Pierre Larouche, Pit.	53
Jean Pronovost, Pit.	52
Danny Gare, Buf.	50
Bill Barber, Phi.	50
Rick Martin, Buf.	49
Steve Shutt, Mtl.	45
Gilbert Perreault, Buf.	44
Chuck Lefley, St.L.	43
Errol Thompson, Tor.	43

ASSISTS

Name, Team	A
Bobby Clarke, Phi.	89
Pete Mahovlich, Mtl.	71
Guy Lafleur, Mtl.	69
Gilbert Perreault, Buf.	69
Jean Ratelle, NYR/Bos.	69
Denis Potvin, NYI	67
Syl Apps Jr., Pit.	67
Bryan Trottier, NYI	63
Bill Barber, Phi.	62

POWERPLAY GOALS

Name, Team	PPG
Phil Esposito, Bos./NYR	19
Pierre Larouche, Pit.	18
Denis Potvin, NYI	18
Guy Lafleur, Mtl.	18
Rick Martin, Buf.	18
Jean Ratelle, NYR/Bos.	17
Billy Harris, NYI	16
Bill Barber, Phi.	15
Clark Gillies, NYI	15
Gilbert Perreault, Buf.	14

SHORTHAND GOALS

Name, Team	SHG
Chuck Lefley, St.L.	8
Derek Sanderson, NYR/St.L.	6
Lanny McDonald, Tor.	5
Dennis Maruk, Cal.	5
Butch Goring, L.A.	5
Bobby Clarke, Phi.	4
Dave Forbes, Bos.	4
Bill Barber, Phi.	4
Al MacAdam, Cal.	4
Dennis Hull, Chi.	4
Lorne Henning, NYI	4

GAME-WINNING GOALS

Name, Team	GWG
Yvan Cournoyer, Mtl.	12
Guy Lafleur, Mtl.	12
Reggie Leach, Phi.	11
Bill Barber, Phi.	10
Chuck Lefley, St.L.	9
John Bucyk, Bos.	9
Danny Gare, Buf.	9
Curt Bennett, Atl.	8
Six tied with	7

GOALIE WINS

Name, Team	W
Ken Dryden, Mtl.	42
Wayne Stephenson, Phi.	40
Gilles Gilbert, Bos.	33
Tony Esposito, Chi.	30
Gerry Desjardins, Buf.	29
Wayne Thomas, Tor.	28
Rogie Vachon, L.A.	26
Michel Plasse, Pit.	24
Glenn Resch, NYI	23
John Davidson, NYR	22

SHUTOUTS

Name, Team	SO
Ken Dryden, Mtl.	8
Glenn Resch, NYI	7
Rogie Vachon, L.A	5
Jim Rutherford, Det.	4
Tony Esposito, Chi.	4
Billy Smith, NYI	3
Gilles Gilbert, Bos.	3
John Davidson, NYR	3
10 tied with	2

FIRST TEAM ALL-STARS

Name, Team	Position
Bobby Clarke, Phi.	C
Guy Lafleur, Mtl.	RW
Bill Barber, Phi.	LW
Denis Potvin, NYI	D
Brad Park, Bos.	D
Ken Dryden, Mtl.	G

SECOND TEAM ALL-STARS

Name, Team	Position
Gilbert Perreault, Buf.	C
Reggie Leach, Phi.	RW
Rick Martin, Buf.	LW
Guy Lapointe, Mtl.	D
Borje Salming, Tor.	D
Glenn Resch, NYI	G

NHL NOTEBOOK

TRANSACTIONS

- June 23, 1975 – Los Angeles Kings signed free agent Marcel Dionne from Detroit. The Red Wings obtained Dan Maloney and veteran defenseman Terry Harper as compensation from the Kings.
- June 26, 1975 – Montreal Canadiens obtained Doug Jarvis from Toronto for Greg Hubick.
- Nov. 7, 1975 – Phil Esposito and Carol Vadnais were traded from Boston to the Rangers in exchange for Brad Park, Jean Ratelle and Joe Zanussi.

RECORDS

- Oct. 8, 1975 – Doug Jarvis of the Canadiens played the first of his NHL record 964 consecutive games (with three teams over a span of 12 years).
- Oct. 26, 1975 – Buffalo Sabres beat the Oakland Seals 3-2 in Buffalo to tie an NHL record for consecutive wins at the start of a season with their eighth in a row. The record was broken by the 1993-94 Maple Leafs, winners of 10 straight.
- Nov. 13, 1975 – Chicago's John Marks set an NHL record for fastest two goals from the start of a game when he scored twice in the first 33 seconds of a 5-5 tie at Philadelphia. Marks broke the old NHL record of :37 set in 1943 by Boston.
- Feb. 7, 1976 – Darryl Sittler set an NHL record with 10 points in one game – he scored six goals and added four assists in an 11-4 Toronto win over Boston at Maple Leaf Garden. It was the 5th game with three-or-more goals for Sittler.
- May 9, 1976 – Philadelphia's Reggie Leach extended his Stanley Cup playoff-record consecutive goal scoring streak to 10 straight games, when the Flyers lost 4-3 in Montreal in game one of the Stanley Cup finals.

MILESTONES

- Oct. 15, 1975 – Minnesota's Bill Goldsworthy became the first player from a 1967 expansion team to score 250 career goals as the North Stars won 4-1 over the visiting Oakland Seals.
- Dec. 28, 1975 – New York Rangers became first team in NHL history to face a touring Soviet hockey squad. The Soviet Army beat the Rangers 7-3 at Madison Square Garden.
- Mar. 13, 1976 – Chicago's Billy Reay became the winningest coach with one team in NHL history, when he registered his 501st coaching victory as the Black Hawks beat the North Stars 4-1 at Minnesota. Toe Blake had previously collected 500 wins with Montreal.
- Apr. 4, 1976 – Chicago's Tony Esposito became the first goaltender in NHL history to record 30 (or more) wins for seven straight seasons when the Blackhawks won 7-2 over the visiting St. Louis Blues.

1976 Playoffs

PRELIMINARY ROUND

Apr.	6	Buffalo	2	at	St. Louis	5
Apr.	8	St. Louis	2	at	Buffalo	3 OT
Apr.	9	St. Louis	1	at	Buffalo	2 OT

Buffalo won best-of-three series 2–1

Apr.	6	Vancouver	3	at	NY Islanders	5
Apr.	8	NY Islanders	3	at	Vancouver	1

NY Islanders won best-of-three series 2–0

Apr.	6	Atlanta	1	at	Los Angeles	2
Apr.	8	Los Angeles	1	at	Atlanta	0

Los Angeles won best-of-three series 2–0

Apr.	6	Pittsburgh	1	at	Toronto	4
Apr.	8	Toronto	0	at	Pittsburgh	2
Apr.	9	Pittsburgh	0	at	Toronto	4

Toronto won best-of-three series 2–1

QUARTER-FINALS

Apr.	11	Chicago	0	at	Montreal	4
Apr.	13	Chicago	1	at	Montreal	3
Apr.	15	Montreal	2	at	Chicago	1
Apr.	18	Montreal	4	at	Chicago	1

Montreal won best-of-seven series 4–0

Apr.	12	Toronto	1	at	Philadelphia	4
Apr.	13	Toronto	1	at	Philadelphia	3
Apr.	15	Philadelphia	4	at	Toronto	5
Apr.	17	Philadelphia	3	at	Toronto	4
Apr.	20	Toronto	1	at	Philadelphia	7
Apr.	22	Philadelphia	5	at	Toronto	8
Apr.	25	Toronto	3	at	Philadelphia	7

Philadelphia won best-of-seven series 4–3

Apr.	11	Los Angeles	0	at	Boston	4
Apr.	13	Los Angeles	3	at	Boston	2 OT
Apr.	15	Boston	4	at	Los Angeles	6
Apr.	17	Boston	3	at	Los Angeles	0
Apr.	20	Los Angeles	1	at	Boston	7
Apr.	22	Boston	3	at	Los Angeles	4 OT
Apr.	25	Los Angeles	0	at	Boston	3

Boston won best-of-seven series 4–3

Apr.	11	NY Islanders	3	at	Buffalo	5
Apr.	13	NY Islanders	2	at	Buffalo	3 OT
Apr.	15	Buffalo	3	at	NY Islanders	5
Apr.	17	Buffalo	2	at	NY Islanders	4
Apr.	20	NY Islanders	4	at	Buffalo	3
Apr.	22	Buffalo	2	at	NY Islanders	3

NY Islanders won best-of-seven series 4–2

SEMI-FINALS

Apr.	27	NY Islanders	2	at	Montreal	3
Apr.	29	NY Islanders	3	at	Montreal	4
May	1	Montreal	3	at	NY Islanders	2
May	4	Montreal	2	at	NY Islanders	5
May	6	NY Islanders	2	at	Montreal	5

Montreal won best-of-seven series 4–1

Apr.	27	Boston	4	at	Philadelphia	2
Apr.	29	Boston	1	at	Philadelphia	2 OT
May	2	Philadelphia	5	at	Boston	2
May	4	Philadelphia	4	at	Boston	2
May	6	Boston	3	at	Philadelphia	6

Philadelphia won best-of-seven series 4–1

FINALS

May	9	Philadelphia	3	at	Montreal	4
May	11	Philadelphia	1	at	Montreal	2
May	13	Montreal	3	at	Philadelphia	2
May	16	Montreal	5	at	Philadelphia	3

Montreal won best-of-seven series 4–0

1975-76 – Montreal Canadiens – Ken Dryden, Serge Savard, Guy Lapointe, Larry Robinson, Bill Nyrop, Pierre Bouchard, Jimmy Roberts, Guy Lafleur, Steve Shutt, Pete Mahovlich, Yvan Cournoyer (Captain), Jacques Lemaire, Yvon Lambert, Bob Gainey, Doug Jarvis, Doug Risebrough, Murray Wilson, Mario Tremblay, Rick Chartraw, Michel Larocque, Scotty Bowman (Coach), Sam Pollock (General Manager), Eddy Palchak, Pierre Meilleur (Trainers).

LEADING PLAYOFF SCORERS

Player	Club	GP	G	A	PTS	PIM
Reggie Leach	Philadelphia	16	19	5	24	8
Denis Potvin	NY Islanders	13	5	14	19	32
Guy Lafleur	Montreal	13	7	10	17	2
Jean Ratelle	Boston	12	8	8	16	4
Bobby Clarke	Philadelphia	16	2	14	16	28
Steve Shutt	Montreal	13	7	8	15	2
Jude Drouin	NY Islanders	13	6	9	15	0
Mel Bridgman	Philadelphia	16	6	8	14	31
Larry Goodenough	Philadelphia	16	3	11	14	6
Bill Barber	Philadelphia	16	6	7	13	18

LEADING PLAYOFF GOALTENDERS

Goaltender	Club	GPI	Mins	GA	SO	Avg.
Ken Dryden	Montreal	13	780	25	1	1.92
Gerry Cheevers	Boston	6	392	14	1	2.14
Rogie Vachon	Los Angeles	7	438	17	1	2.33
Wayne Stephenson	Philadelphia	8	494	22	0	2.67
Billy Smith	NY Islanders	8	437	21	0	2.88

PLAYOFF GOALS

Name, Team	G
Reggie Leach, Phi.	19
Jean Ratelle, Bos.	8
Guy Lafleur, Mtl.	7
Steve Shutt, Mtl.	7
Five tied with	6

PLAYOFF ASSISTS

Name, Team	A
Denis Potvin, NYI	14
Bobby Clarke, Phi.	14
Larry Goodenough, Phi.	11
Guy Lafleur, Mtl.	10
Ian Turnbull, Tor.	9
Jude Drouin, NYI	9

PLAYOFF POWERPLAY GOALS

Name, Team	PPG
Jean Ratelle, Bos.	5
Ken Hodge, Bos.	4
Marcel Dionne, L.A.	3
Steve Shutt, Mtl.	3
Bill Barber, Phi.	3

PLAYOFF SHORTHAND GOALS

Name, Team	SHG
11 tied with	1

Chuck Lefley, St.L.; John Gould, Van.; Craig Ramsay, Buf.; Errol Thompson, Tor.; Brad Park, Bos.; Dave Forbes, Bos.; Serge Savard, Mtl.; Jacques Lemaire; Mtl.; Lorne Henning, NYI; Jimmy Roberts, St.L.; Don Saleski, Phi.

PLAYOFF GAME-WINNING GOALS

Name, Team	GWG
Guy Lafleur, Mtl.	3
Butch Goring, L.A.	2
Danny Gare, Buf.	2
Serge Savard, Mtl.	2
Billy MacMillan, NYI	2
Reggie Leach, Phi.	2
Orest Kindrachuk, Phi.	2
Mel Bridgman, Phi.	2

PLAYOFF GOALIE WINS

Name, Team	W
Ken Dryden, Mtl.	12
Wayne Thomas, Tor.	5
Rogie Vachon, L.A.	4
Wayne Stephenson, Phi.	4
Billy Smith, NYI	4
Bernie Parent, Phi.	4
Gerry Desjardins, Buf.	4

PLAYOFF SHUTOUTS

Name, Team	SO
Gilles Gilbert, Bos.	2
Michel Plasse, Pit.	1
Gerry Cheevers, Bos.	1
Rogie Vachon, L.A.	1
Wayne Thomas, Tor.	1
Ken Dryden, Mtl.	1

The calender year of 1976 was certainly a special one for Darryl Sittler. He collected an NHL-record 10 points (six goals, four assists) in a game against Boston on February 7, tied a playoff record with five goals in a game against Philadelphia on April 22 and scored the winner for Team Canada against Czechoslovakia at the first Canada Cup tournament in September.

1976-77

Stanley Cup • Montreal Canadiens

FINAL STANDINGS

PRINCE OF WALES CONFERENCE

Norris Division

Team	GP	W	L	T	GF	GA	PTS
Montreal	80	60	8	12	387	171	132
Los Angeles	80	34	31	15	271	241	83
Pittsburgh	80	34	33	13	240	252	81
Washington	80	24	42	14	221	307	62
Detroit	80	16	55	9	183	309	41
Adams Division							
Boston	80	49	23	8	312	240	106
Buffalo	80	48	24	8	301	220	104
Toronto	80	33	32	15	301	285	81
Cleveland	80	25	42	13	240	292	63
CLARENCE CAMPBELL CONFERENCE							
Patrick Division							
Philadelphia	80	48	16	16	323	213	112
NY Islanders	80	47	21	12	288	193	106
Atlanta	80	34	34	12	264	265	80
NY Rangers	80	29	37	14	272	310	72
Smythe Division							
St. Louis	80	32	39	9	239	276	73
Minnesota	80	23	39	18	240	310	64
Chicago	80	26	43	11	240	298	63
Vancouver	80	25	42	13	235	294	63
Colorado	80	20	46	14	226	307	54

LEADING SCORERS

Player	Club	GP	G	A	PTS	PIM
Guy Lafleur	Montreal	80	56	80	136	20
Marcel Dionne	Los Angeles	80	53	69	122	12
Steve Shutt	Montreal	80	60	45	105	28
Rick MacLeish	Philadelphia	79	49	48	97	42
Gilbert Perreault	Buffalo	80	39	56	95	30
Tim Young	Minnesota	80	29	66	95	58
Jean Ratelle	Boston	78	33	61	94	22
Lanny McDonald	Toronto	80	46	44	90	77
Darryl Sittler	Toronto	73	38	52	90	89
Bobby Clarke	Philadelphia	80	27	63	90	71
Peter McNab	Boston	80	38	48	86	11
Butch Goring	Los Angeles	78	30	55	85	6
Larry Robinson	Montreal	77	19	66	85	45
Guy Charron	Washington	80	36	46	82	10
Wilf Paiement	Colorado	78	41	40	81	101
Tom Lysiak	Atlanta	79	30	51	81	52
Phil Esposito	NY Rangers	80	34	46	80	52
Denis Potvin	NY Islanders	80	25	55	80	103
Ian Turnbull	Toronto	80	22	57	79	84
Dennis Maruk	Cleveland	80	28	50	78	68
Borje Salming	Toronto	76	12	66	78	46
Guy Lapointe	Montreal	77	25	51	76	53
Jacques Lemaire	Montreal	75	34	41	75	22
Rod Gilbert	NY Rangers	77	27	48	75	50
Tom Williams	Los Angeles	80	35	39	74	14

LEADING GOALTENDERS

Goaltender	Club	GPI	MINS	GA	SO	AVG
Michel Larocque	Montreal	26	1525	53	4	2.09
Ken Dryden	Montreal	56	3275	117	10	2.14
Glenn Resch	NY Islanders	46	2711	103	4	2.28
Billy Smith	NY Islanders	36	2089	87	2	2.50
Don Edwards	Buffalo	25	1480	62	2	2.51
Gerry Desjardins	Buffalo	49	2871	126	3	2.63
Bernie Parent	Philadelphia	61	3525	159	5	2.71
Rogie Vachon	Los Angeles	68	4059	184	8	2.72
Gilles Gilbert	Boston	34	2040	97	1	2.85
Denis Herron	Pittsburgh	34	1920	94	1	2.94

Known as "Big Bird," the 6'4", 225-pound Larry Robinson was a forward in junior hockey, but was converted to defense in the minors. He played on his first of six Stanley Cup-winning teams as a rookie in 1973, and went on to win the Norris Trophy twice. He was also an NHL all-star five years in a row between 1976–77 and 1980–81.

Two of the NHL's weakest clubs found new homes for the 1976–77 season—the league's first franchise shifts since the Ottawa Senators moved to St. Louis in 1934–35. The Kansas City Scouts headed for Denver, where they would now be known as the Colorado Rockies, while the California Golden Seals left Oakland for the Rust Belt, setting up shop as the Cleveland Barons. Wilf Paiement scored 41 goals for the Rockies, who improved by 18 points over their last year in Kansas City, but both Colorado and Cleveland finished last in their respective divisions. Only the woeful 41-point effort by the Detroit Red Wings kept the two transplanted clubs out of the NHL cellar.

Flower Power – Guy Lafleur blossomed and provided Les Canadiens with the ingredient that every team coveted: an emotional leader who was swift, shifty and "glorieux" gifted.

Franchise shifts and failures would reduce the WHA to 11 clubs by the end of the season. The Quebec Nordiques – eventual playoff champions – and the Winnipeg Jets were the league's top franchises. Anders Hedberg of the Jets led the WHA with 70 goals, while teammate Ulf Nilsson was tops with 85 assists. The scoring title went to Quebec's Real Cloutier, who had 141 points (66 goals and 75 assists).

In the NHL, the Montreal Canadiens were at the top of their game. The Canadiens surpassed their brilliant record of the previous season by setting NHL marks with 60 wins (60–8–12) and 132 points. The Canadiens lost just once on home ice, going 33–1–6 at the Forum. Guy Lafleur won his second straight scoring title with 136 points and also won the Hart Trophy as MVP. Steve Shutt led the NHL with 60 goals, Larry Robinson won the Norris Trophy as best defenseman, and Ken Dryden and Michel "Bunny" Larocque shared the Vezina Trophy. The Philadelphia Flyers also had another great year, leading the Patrick Division with 112 points. The New York Islanders were second with 106, a point total that was good enough for Boston to win the Adams Division title. The Bruins and New York Rangers made another trade—though not as sensational as the previous year's Esposito deal—as Rick Middleton wen to to Boston for Ken Hodge. Still, the deal would pay dividends for the Bruins.

St. Louis, with just 73 points in 80 games, finished first in the Smythe Division but was swept out of the playoffs by the Canadiens, who then beat the Islanders to return to the Stanley Cup finals. Boston provided the opposition after eliminating the Los Angeles Kings and Philadelphia Flyers. The Canadiens won the first three games, with Boston then playing its best hockey of the series in game four before Jacques Lemaire scored in overtime to complete the series sweep.

Marcel Dionne was the NHL's first free agent, signing with Los Angeles in 1975–76. He went on to star with the Kings for 12 seasons, ranking among the NHL's top-10 scorers seven times.

Leaders, 1976-77

GOALS

Name, Team	G
Steve Shutt, Mtl.	60
Guy Lafleur, Mtl.	56
Marcel Dionne, L.A.	53
Rick MacLeish, Phi.	49
Lanny McDonald, Tor.	46
Wilf Paiement, Col.	41
Gilbert Perreault, Buf.	39
Darryl Sittler, Tor.	38
Peter McNab, Bos.	38
Rick Martin, Buf.	36
Guy Charron, Wsh.	36

ASSISTS

Name, Team	A
Guy Lafleur, Mtl.	80
Marcel Dionne, L.A.	69
Borje Salming, Tor.	66
Larry Robinson, Mtl.	66
Tim Young, Min.	66
Bobby Clarke, Phi.	63
Jean Ratelle, Bos.	61
Ian Turnbull, Tor.	57
Gilbert Perreault, Buf.	56
Four tied with	55

POWERPLAY GOALS

Name, Team	PPG
Lanny McDonald, Tor.	16
Phil Esposito, NYR	15
Tom Williams, L.A.	15
Guy Lafleur, Mtl.	14
Marcel Dionne, L.A.	14
Butch Goring, L.A.	13
Rick Martin, Buf.	12
Clark Gillies, NYI	12
Darryl Sittler, Tor.	12
Eric Vail, Atl.	12

SHORTHAND GOALS

Name, Team	SHG
Bobby Clarke, Phi.	6
Lorne Henning, NYI	6
Bill Clement, Atl.	5
Wilf Paiement, Col.	5
Lanny McDonald, Tor.	4
Buster Harvey, Det.	3
Denis Dupere, Col.	3
Jack Valiquette, Tor.	3
Mike Murphy, L.A.	3
Tom Younghans, Min.	3
Ed Westfall, NYI	3
Walt McKechnie, Det.	3
Craig Ramsay, Buf.	3

GAME-WINNING GOALS

Name, Team	GWG
Steve Shutt, Mtl.	9
Gilbert Perreault, Buf.	9
Rick MacLeish, Phi.	8
Guy Lafleur, Mtl.	8
Peter McNab, Bos.	8
J.P. Parise, NYI	7
13 tied with	6

GOALIE WINS

Name, Team	W
Ken Dryden, Mtl.	41
Bernie Parent, Phi.	35
Rogie Vachon, L.A.	33
Gerry Desjardins, Buf.	31
Gerry Cheevers, Bos.	30
Glenn Resch, NYI	26
Tony Esposito, Chi.	25
Mike Palmateer, Tor.	23
Billy Smith, NYI	21
Michel Larocque, Mtl.	19
Gilles Meloche, Cle.	19

SHUTOUTS

Name, Team	SO
Ken Dryden, Mtl.	10
Rogie Vachon, L.A.	8
Dunc Wilson, Pit.	5
Bernie Parent, Phi.	5
Michel Larocque, Mtl.	4
Glenn Resch, NYI	4
Mike Palmateer, Tor.	4
Wayne Stephenson, Phi.	3
Ed Giacomin, Det.	3
Phil Myre, Atl.	3
Gerry Cheevers, Bos.	3
Gerry Desjardins, Buf.	3

FIRST TEAM ALL-STARS

Name, Team	Position
Marcel Dionne, L.A.	C
Guy Lafleur, Mtl.	RW
Steve Shutt, Mtl.	LW
Larry Robinson, Mtl.	D
Borje Salming, Tor.	D
Ken Dryden, Mtl.	G

SECOND TEAM ALL-STARS

Name, Team	Position
Gilbert Perreault, Buf.	C
Lanny McDonald, Tor.	RW
Rick Martin, Buf.	LW
Denis Potvin, NYI	D
Guy Lapointe, Mtl.	D
Rogie Vachon, L.A.	G

TROPHY WINNERS

Trophy	Awarded For	Winner	Team
Hart	MVP	Guy Lafleur	Mtl.
Art Ross	Top Scorer	Guy Lafleur	Mtl.
Norris	Top Defenseman	Larry Robinson	Mtl.
Calder	Top Rookie	Willi Plett	Atl.
Vezina	Fewest Goals Against	Ken Dryden	Mtl.
		Michel Larocque	Mtl.
Adams	Top Coach	Scotty Bowman	Mtl.
Byng	Gentlemanly Conduct	Marcel Dionne	L.A.
Masterton	Perseverance, Sportmanship	Ed Westfall	NYI
Pearson	NHLPA MVP	Guy Lafleur	Mtl.
Conn Smythe	Playoff MVP	Guy Lafleur	Mtl.
Patrick	Service to Hockey in U.S.	John Bucyk	
		Murray Armstrong	
		John Mariucci	
Amateur Draft	First Overall Selection	Dale McCourt	Det.

NHL NOTEBOOK

TRANSACTIONS

- May 26, 1976 – New York Rangers traded center Rick Middleton to the Boston Bruins for Ken Hodge.
- June 24, 1976 – Defenseman Bobby Orr signed with the Chicago Black Hawks as a free agent after 11 seasons with Boston.
- July 23, 1976 – NY Rangers signed native New Yorker Nick Fotiu as a free agent.
- Oct. 12, 1976 – Boston signed John Wensink as free agent.

RECORDS

- Feb. 14, 1977 – Philadelphia's Al Hill scored on his first two shots and added three assists to tie the NHL record for most points in a player's first career game as the Flyers beat St. Louis 6-4.
- Mar. 10, 1977 – Guy Lafleur had four assists as the Canadiens set an NHL-record for longest home unbeaten streak – 28 games (23-0-5) with a 7-1 win against the Colorado Rockies.
- Apr. 3, 1977 – Guy Lafleur extended his NHL-record point-scoring streak to 28 straight games as Montreal won 2-1 at Washington. (Wayne Gretzky would later break the record with a 51-game streak.
- Apr. 17, 1977 – L.A. Kings' right wing Don Kozak set an NHL record for fastest goal from the start of a playoff game, scoring at the :06 mark of a 7-4 win over Boston in game four of the Stanley Cup quarter-finals.

MILESTONES

- Oct. 7, 1976 – Chicago's Stan Mikita became just the third player in NHL history to score 1,300 career points; the milestone came with a goal in a 6-5 win over the Blues in St. Louis.
- Jan. 20, 1977 – For just the third time in NHL history (and the first time in 23 years), two brothers opposed each other as coaches when Johnny Wilson's Colorado Rockies beat brother Larry Wilson's Red Wings 3-1 at Detroit.
- Mar. 9, 1977 – New York Rangers retired Rod Gilbert's uniform #7 before a 6-4 win over the Minnesota North Stars. Gilbert became the first player in Rangers history to have his uniform number retired.
- Apr. 3, 1977 – The Montreal Canadiens beat the Capitals 2-1 at Washington to finish the season with a record of 60-8-12 and 132 points, an NHL record. The Canadiens became the first NHL team to win 60 games in a season.

1977 Playoffs

PRELIMINARY ROUND

Apr.	5	Chicago	2	at	NY Islanders	5	
Apr.	7	Chicago	1	at	NY Islanders	2	

NY Islanders won best-of-three series 2–0

Apr.	5	Minnesota	2	at	Buffalo	4	
Apr.	7	Buffalo	7	at	Minnesota	1	

Buffalo won best-of-three series 2–0

Apr.	5	Atlanta	2	at	Los Angeles	5	
Apr.	7	Los Angeles	2	at	Atlanta	3	
Apr.	9	Atlanta	2	at	Los Angeles	4	

Los Angeles won best-of-three series 2–1

Apr.	5	Toronto	4	at	Pittsburgh	2	
Apr.	7	Pittsburgh	6	at	Toronto	4	
Apr.	9	Toronto	5	at	Pittsburgh	2	

Toronto won best-of-three series 2–1

QUARTER-FINALS

Apr.	11	St. Louis	2	at	Montreal	7	
Apr.	13	St. Louis	0	at	Montreal	3	
Apr.	16	Montreal	5	at	St. Louis	1	
Apr.	17	Montreal	4	at	St. Louis	1	

Montreal won best-of-seven series 4–0

Apr.	11	Toronto	3	at	Philadelphia	2	
Apr.	13	Toronto	4	at	Philadelphia	1	
Apr.	15	Philadelphia	4	at	Toronto	3	OT
Apr.	17	Philadelphia	6	at	Toronto	5	OT
Apr.	19	Toronto	0	at	Philadelphia	2	
Apr.	21	Philadelphia	4	at	Toronto	3	

Philadelphia won best-of-seven series 4–2

Apr.	11	Los Angeles	3	at	Boston	8	
Apr.	13	Los Angeles	2	at	Boston	6	
Apr.	15	Boston	7	at	Los Angeles	6	
Apr.	17	Boston	4	at	Los Angeles	7	
Apr.	19	Los Angeles	3	at	Boston	1	
Apr.	21	Boston	4	at	Los Angeles	3	

Boston won best-of-seven series 4–2

Apr.	11	Buffalo	2	at	NY Islanders	4	
Apr.	13	Buffalo	2	at	NY Islanders	4	
Apr.	15	NY Islanders	4	at	Buffalo	3	
Apr.	17	NY Islanders	4	at	Buffalo	3	

NY Islanders won best-of-seven series 4–0

SEMI-FINALS

Apr.	23	NY Islanders	3	at	Montreal	4	
Apr.	26	NY Islanders	0	at	Montreal	3	
Apr.	28	Montreal	3	at	NY Islanders	5	
Apr.	30	Montreal	4	at	NY Islanders	0	
May	3	NY Islanders	4	at	Montreal	3	OT
May	5	Montreal	2	at	NY Islanders	1	

Montreal won best-of-seven series 4–2

Apr.	24	Boston	4	at	Philadelphia	3	OT
Apr.	26	Boston	5	at	Philadelphia	4	2OT
Apr.	28	Philadelphia	1	at	Boston	2	
May	1	Philadelphia	0	at	Boston	3	

Boston won best-of-seven series 4–0

FINALS

May	7	Boston	3	at	Montreal	7	
May	10	Boston	0	at	Montreal	3	
May	12	Montreal	4	at	Boston	2	
May	14	Montreal	2	at	Boston	1	OT

Montreal won best-of-seven series 4–0

1976-77 – Montreal Canadiens – Ken Dryden, Guy Lapointe, Larry Robinson, Serge Savard, Jimmy Roberts, Rick Chartraw, Bill Nyrop, Pierre Bouchard, Brian Engblom, Yvan Cournoyer (Captain), Guy Lafleur, Jacques Lemaire, Steve Shutt, Pete Mahovlich, Murray Wilson, Doug Jarvis, Yvon Lambert, Bob Gainey, Doug Risebrough, Mario Tremblay, Rejean Houle, Pierre Mondou, Mike Polich, Michel Larocque, Scotty Bowman (Coach), Sam Pollock (General Manager), Eddy Palchak, Pierre Meilleur (Trainers).

Steve Shutt was a minor contributor to Montreal's Stanley Cup victory in his rookie season of 1972–73, but he was one of the team's top offensive threats when the Canadiens won the Stanley Cup four years in a row from 1976 to 1979. His 60 goals in 1976–77 were a record for left wingers until Luc Robitaille scored 63 in 1992–93.

LEADING PLAYOFF SCORERS

Player	Club	GP	G	A	PTS	PIM
Guy Lafleur	Montreal	14	9	17	26	6
Darryl Sittler	Toronto	9	5	16	21	4
Jacques Lemaire	Montreal	14	7	12	19	6
Steve Shutt	Montreal	14	8	10	18	2
Lanny McDonald	Toronto	9	10	7	17	6
Jean Ratelle	Boston	14	5	12	17	4
Billy Harris	NY Islanders	12	7	7	14	8
Marcel Dionne	Los Angeles	9	5	9	14	2
Rick MacLeish	Philadelphia	10	4	9	13	2
Mike Murphy	Los Angeles	9	4	9	13	4
Bob Dailey	Philadelphia	10	4	9	13	15

LEADING PLAYOFF GOALTENDERS

Goaltender	Club	GPI	Mins	GA	SO	Avg.
Ken Dryden	Montreal	14	849	22	4	1.55
Wayne Stephenson	Philadelphia	9	532	23	1	2.59
Billy Smith	NY Islanders	10	580	27	0	2.79
Gerry Cheevers	Boston	14	858	44	1	3.08
Rogie Vachon	Los Angeles	9	520	36	0	4.15

PLAYOFF GOALS

Name, Team	G
Bobby Schmautz, Bos.	11
Lanny McDonald, Tor.	10
Guy Lafleur, Mtl.	9
Steve Shutt, Mtl.	8
Butch Goring, L.A.	7
Billy Harris, NYI	7
Jacques Lemaire, Mtl.	7

PLAYOFF ASSISTS

Name, Team	A
Guy Lafleur, Mtl.	17
Darryl Sittler, Tor.	16
Jacques Lemaire, Mtl.	12
Jean Ratelle, Bos.	12
Steve Shutt, Mtl.	10
Brad Park, Bos.	10
Larry Robinson, Mtl.	10

PLAYOFF POWERPLAY GOALS

Name, Team	PPG
Ian Turnbull, Tor.	4
Bobby Schmautz, Bos.	4
Darryl Sittler, Tor.	3
Lanny McDonald, Tor.	3
Butch Goring, L.A.	3

PLAYOFF SHORTHAND GOALS

Name, Team	SHG
Bill Clement, Atl.	1
Mel Bridgman, Phi.	1
Ed Westfall, NYI	1
Gregg Sheppard, Bos.	1
Don Marcotte, Bos.	1
Bob Gainey, Mtl.	1
Jimmy Roberts, Mtl.	1

PLAYOFF GAME-WINNING GOALS

Name, Team	GWG
Clark Gillies, NYI	4
Steve Shutt, Mtl.	3
Jacques Lemaire, Mtl.	3
Butch Goring, L.A.	2
Reggie Leach, Phi.	2
Billy MacMillan, NYI	2
Gregg Sheppard, Bos.	2
Guy Lafleur, Mtl.	2

PLAYOFF GOALIE WINS

Name, Team	W
Ken Dryden, Mtl.	12
Gerry Cheevers, Bos.	8
Billy Smith, NYI	7
Wayne Stephenson, Phi.	4
Rogie Vachon, L.A.	4

PLAYOFF SHUTOUTS

Name, Team	SO
Ken Dryden, Mtl.	4
Wayne Stephenson, Phi.	1
Gerry Cheevers, Bos.	1

1977-78

Stanley Cup • Montreal Canadiens

Thought of mainly as a tough guy, Terry O'Reilly had plenty of offensive talent too. He topped 200 penalty minutes five years in a row from 1977–78 to 1981–82, but he also reached the 20-goal plateau four times. The 1977–78 campaign marked his best offensive season as he had 29 goals and 61 assists for 90 points. All three totals were career highs.

FINAL STANDINGS

Team	GP	W	L	T	GF	GA	PTS
PRINCE OF WALES CONFERENCE							
NORRIS DIVISION							
Montreal	80	59	10	11	359	183	129
Detroit	80	32	34	14	252	266	78
Los Angeles	80	31	34	15	243	245	77
Pittsburgh	80	25	37	18	254	321	68
Washington	80	17	49	14	195	321	48
Adams Division							
Boston	80	51	18	11	333	218	113
Buffalo	80	44	19	17	288	215	105
Toronto	80	41	29	10	271	237	92
Cleveland	80	22	45	13	230	325	57
CLARENCE CAMPBELL CONFERENCE							
Patrick Division							
NY Islanders	80	48	17	15	334	210	111
Philadelphia	80	45	20	15	296	200	105
Atlanta	80	34	27	19	274	252	87
NY Rangers	80	30	37	13	279	280	73
Smythe Division							
Chicago	80	32	29	19	230	220	83
Colorado	80	19	40	21	257	305	59
Vancouver	80	20	43	17	239	320	57
St. Louis	80	20	47	13	195	304	53
Minnesota	80	18	53	9	218	325	45

LEADING SCORERS

Player	Club	GP	G	A	PTS	PIM
Guy Lafleur	Montreal	78	60	72	132	26
Bryan Trottier	NY Islanders	77	46	77	123	46
Darryl Sittler	Toronto	80	45	72	117	100
Jacques Lemaire	Montreal	76	36	61	97	14
Denis Potvin	NY Islanders	80	30	64	94	81
Mike Bossy	NY Islanders	73	53	38	91	6
Terry O'Reilly	Boston	77	29	61	90	211
Gilbert Perreault	Buffalo	79	41	48	89	20
Bobby Clarke	Philadelphia	71	21	68	89	83
Lanny McDonald	Toronto	74	47	40	87	54
Wilf Paiement	Colorado	80	31	56	87	114
Steve Shutt	Montreal	80	49	37	86	24
Clark Gillies	NY Islanders	80	35	50	85	76
Jean Ratelle	Boston	80	25	59	84	10
Phil Esposito	NY Rangers	79	38	43	81	53
Peter McNab	Boston	79	41	39	80	4
Ivan Boldirev	Chicago	80	35	45	80	34
Marcel Dionne	Los Angeles	70	36	43	79	37
Brad Park	Boston	80	22	57	79	79
Danny Gare	Buffalo	69	39	38	77	95
Borje Salming	Toronto	80	16	60	76	70
Pat Hickey	NY Rangers	80	40	33	73	47
Guy Charron	Washington	80	38	35	73	12
Butch Goring	Los Angeles	80	37	36	73	2
Rene Robert	Buffalo	67	25	48	73	25

LEADING GOALTENDERS

Goaltender	Club	GPI	MINS	GA	SO	AVG
Ken Dryden	Montreal	52	3071	105	5	2.05
Bernie Parent	Philadelphia	49	2923	108	7	2.22
Gilles Gilbert	Boston	25	1326	56	2	2.53
Glenn Resch	NY Islanders	45	2637	112	3	2.55
Tony Esposito	Chicago	64	3840	168	5	2.63
Don Edwards	Buffalo	72	4209	185	5	2.64
Billy Smith	NY Islanders	38	2154	95	2	2.65
Michel Larocque	Montreal	30	1729	77	1	2.67
Mike Palmateer	Toronto	63	3760	172	5	2.74
Dan Bouchard	Atlanta	58	3340	153	2	2.75

THE OFFSEASON WAS EVENTFUL for the World Hockey Association, as six teams applied for entry into the NHL. The vote among NHL owners was close, but not close enough, and with Phoenix, Calgary and San Diego ceasing operations, the WHA entered its sixth season with just eight teams. The rival league did not have much longer to live. The Houston Aeros, a perennial power, were weakened this year by the departure of Marty, Mark and Gordie Howe to the New England Whalers. They would also fold in the spring of 1978.

In the NHL, the Montreal Canadiens dominated play for the third consecutive season. The Canadiens were 59–10–11 on the year and their 129 points led the Norris Division by 51 points over a much-improved Detroit Red Wings team. Guy Lafleur won the Art Ross Trophy for the third year in succession and won the Hart Trophy for the second straight year. Ken Dryden and Bunny Larocque again shared the Vezina Trophy. Bob Gainey won the newly created Selke Trophy as the NHL's best defensive forward. It was an honor he would win again in each of the next three seasons.

Master Mind – With Scotty Bowman plucking Montreal's emotional strings like a maestro accompanied by an on-ice orchestra with a dozen future Hall of Fame members, what chance did the Bruins have?

The New York Islanders won their first Patrick Division title this year with 111 points. Bryan Trottier's 123 points were second behind Lafleur's 132 in the NHL scoring race, while teammate Mike Bossy set a rookie record with 53 goals. Denis Potvin finished fifth in scoring with 30 goals and 64 assists and earned his second Norris Trophy win as the league's best defenseman. But despite their great regular season, the Islanders' year ended in disappointment when Lanny McDonald's seventh-game overtime goal gave the Toronto Maple Leafs a quarter-final series upset. Toronto had enjoyed a 92-point year under rookie coach Roger Neilson, but couldn't get past Montreal in the semi-finals as the Canadiens swept Toronto en route to the finals.

For the second year in a row, Don Cherry's Bruins faced Montreal in the final. Boston had won the Adams Division with 113 points and had needed just nine games to eliminate the Chicago Black Hawks and Philadelphia Flyers. Boston provided much tougher competition this year, but the Canadiens still made it three straight Stanley Cup titles with a six-game victory. Larry Robinson and Guy Lafleur tied for the postseason scoring lead, with the big defenseman taking home the Conn Smythe Trophy as playoff MVP. For Boston-area hockey fans, it was little consolation that Gordie Howe and sons had led New England to the WHA title over the Winnipeg Jets.

Don Edwards' first full season in the NHL (1977–78) was his best, yet he always remained a favorite among Sabres fans and is a member of the Greater Buffalo Sports Hall of Fame.

Leaders, 1977-78

GOALS

Name, Team	G
Guy Lafleur, Mtl.	60
Mike Bossy, NYI	53
Steve Shutt, Mtl.	49
Lanny McDonald, Tor.	47
Bryan Trottier, NYI	46
Darryl Sittler, Tor.	45
Gilbert Perreault, Buf.	41
Peter McNab, Bos.	41
Bill Barber, Phi.	41
Jean Pronovost, Pit.	40
Pat Hickey, NYR	40

ASSISTS

Name, Team	A
Bryan Trottier, NYI	77
Guy Lafleur, Mtl.	72
Darryl Sittler, Tor.	72
Bobby Clarke, Phi.	68
Denis Potvin, NYI	64
Jacques Lemaire, Mtl.	61
Terry O'Reilly, Bos.	61
Borje Salming, Tor.	60
Jean Ratelle, Bos.	59
Brad Park, Bos.	57

POWERPLAY GOALS

Name, Team	PPG
Mike Bossy, NYI	25
Phil Esposito, NYR	21
Steve Shutt, Mtl.	16
Guy Lafleur, Mtl.	15
Mike Walton, Van.	14
Darryl Sittler, Tor.	14
Paul Gardner, Col.	13
Bryan Trottier, NYI	13
Brad Maxwell, Min.	12
Jean Pronovost, Pit.	12

SHORTHAND GOALS

Name, Team	SHG
Craig Ramsay, Buf.	5
Greg Polis, NYR	4
Don Saleski, Phi.	4
Bill Barber, Phi.	4
Bobby Schmautz, Bos.	3
Bill Clement, Atl.	3
Dale McCourt, Det.	3
Butch Goring, L.A.	3
21 tied with	2

GAME-WINNING GOALS

Name, Team	GWG
Guy Lafleur, Mtl.	12
Bill Barber, Phi.	9
Darryl Sittler, Tor.	8
Bob Bourne, NYI	8
Gregg Sheppard, Bos.	7
Rick MacLeish, Phi.	7
Gilbert Perreault, Buf.	7
Steve Shutt, Mtl.	7
Nine tied with	6

GOALIE WINS

Name, Team	W
Don Edwards, Buf.	38
Ken Dryden, Mtl.	37
Mike Palmateer, Tor.	34
Bernie Parent, Phi.	29
Rogie Vachon, L.A.	29
Glenn Resch, NYI	28
Tony Esposito, Chi.	28
Ron Grahame, Bos.	26
Dan Bouchard, Atl.	25
Michel Larocque, Mtl.	22

SHUTOUTS

Name, Team	SO
Bernie Parent, Phi.	7
Ken Dryden, Mtl.	5
Mike Palmateer, Tor.	5
Tony Esposito, Chi.	5
Don Edwards, Buf.	5
Wayne Thomas, NYR	4
Rogie Vachon, L.A.	4
Wayne Stephenson, Phi.	3
Ron Grahame, Bos.	3
Glenn Resch, NYI	3

FIRST TEAM ALL-STARS

Name, Team	Position
Bryan Trottier, NYI	C
Guy Lafleur, Mtl.	RW
Clark Gillies, NYI	LW
Denis Potvin, NYI	D
Brad Park, Bos.	D
Ken Dryden, Mtl.	G

SECOND TEAM ALL-STARS

Name, Team	Position
Darryl Sittler, Tor.	C
Mike Bossy, NYI	RW
Steve Shutt, Mtl.	LW
Larry Robinson, Mtl.	D
Borje Salming, Tor.	D
Don Edwards, Buf.	G

TROPHY WINNERS

Trophy	Awarded For	Winner	Team
Hart	MVP	Guy Lafleur	Mtl.
Art Ross	Top Scorer	Guy Lafleur	Mtl.
Norris	Top Defenseman	Denis Potvin	NYI
Calder	Top Rookie	Mike Bossy	NYI
Selke	Top Defensive Forward	Bob Gainey	Mtl.
Vezina	Fewest Goals Against	Ken Dryden	Mtl.
		Michel Larocque	Mtl.
Adams	Top Coach	Bobby Kromm	Det.
Byng	Gentlemanly Conduct	Butch Goring	L.A.
Masterton	Perseverance, Sportmanship	Butch Goring	L.A.
Pearson	NHLPA MVP	Guy Lafleur	Mtl.
Conn Smythe	Playoff MVP	Larry Robinson	Mtl.
Patrick	Service to Hockey in U.S.	Phil Esposito	
		Tom Fitzgerald	
		William T. Tutt	
		William W. Wirtz	
Amateur Draft	First Overall Selection	Bobby Smith	Min.

NHL NOTEBOOK

TRANSACTIONS

- Aug. 8, 1977 – Los Angeles Kings signed free agent left wing Charlie Simmer.
- Nov. 2, 1977 – Pittsburgh Penguins acquired Dave Schultz and Gene Carr from the L.A. Kings, in trade for Syl Apps Jr. and Hartland Monahan.
- Nov. 29, 1977 – Pittsburgh Penguins traded Pierre Larouche to Montreal for Pete Mahovlich and Peter Lee.
- Mar. 13, 1978 – Detroit Red Wings traded Dan Maloney and a draft pick to the Toronto Maple Leafs in exchange for Errol Thompson and two draft choices.

RECORDS

- Dec. 11, 1977 – Tom Bladon set an NHL record for most points in a game by a defenseman. His eight points (four goals and four assists) led Philadelphia to an 11-1 win over the Cleveland Barons. Bladon also set an NHL record by going +10.
- Feb. 24, 1978 – Colorado Rockies' Barry Beck scored his 18th goal to set an NHL rookie goal-scoring record for defensemen. Colorado won 3-2 over the visiting Minnesota North Stars.
- Mar. 24, 1978 – Phil Esposito set an NHL record with his 29th career hat trick and added an assist as the Rangers beat Washington 11-4. Espo broke the mark of 28 hat tricks set by Bobby Hull.
- Apr. 8, 1978 – Boston rookie Bob Miller scored his 20th goal of the season to give the Bruins eleven 20-goal scorers on the team, a new NHL record. They broke the old mark of ten 20 goal scorers, held by the 1970-71 Bruins and 1974-75 Canadiens.

MILESTONES

- Oct. 12, 1977 – Johnny Wilson became the first man in history to coach four different NHL teams when he led Pittsburgh to a 4-2 win over the visiting St. Louis Blues.
- Feb. 15, 1978 – Montreal won 6-2 at St. Louis to extend their undefeated streak to 24 games (19-0-5) breaking the NHL record of 23 set by the Bruins in 1940-41 and tied by Philadelphia in 1975-76.
- Apr. 1, 1978 – Mike Bossy became the first NHL rookie to score 50 goals in a season in a 3-2 Islanders win over Washington.
- Apr. 9, 1978 – Bob Bourne and Denis Potvin scored their 30th goals of the season (in a 5-2 win at Boston) as the Islanders tied the NHL record for most 30-goal scorers with six.

1978 Playoffs

PRELIMINARY ROUND

Apr.	11	Colorado	2	at	Philadelphia	3 OT
Apr.	13	Philadelphia	3	at	Colorado	1

Philadelphia won best-of-three series 2–0

Apr.	11	NY Rangers	1	at	Buffalo	4
Apr.	13	Buffalo	3	at	NY Rangers	4 OT
Apr.	15	NY Rangers	1	at	Buffalo	4

Buffalo won best-of-three series 2–1

Apr.	11	Los Angeles	3	at	Toronto	7
Apr.	13	Toronto	4	at	Los Angeles	0

Toronto won best-of-three series 2–0

Apr.	11	Detroit	5	at	Atlanta	3
Apr.	13	Atlanta	2	at	Detroit	3

Detroit won best-of-three series 2–0

QUARTER-FINALS

Apr.	17	Detroit	2	at	Montreal	6
Apr.	19	Detroit	4	at	Montreal	2
Apr.	21	Montreal	4	at	Detroit	2
Apr.	23	Montreal	8	at	Detroit	0
Apr.	25	Detroit	2	at	Montreal	4

Montreal won best-of-seven series 4–1

Apr.	17	Chicago	1	at	Boston	6
Apr.	19	Chicago	3	at	Boston	4 OT
Apr.	21	Boston	4	at	Chicago	3 OT
Apr.	23	Boston	5	at	Chicago	2

Boston won best-of-seven series 4–0

Apr.	17	Toronto	1	at	NY Islanders	4
Apr.	19	Toronto	2	at	NY Islanders	3 OT
Apr.	21	NY Islanders	0	at	Toronto	2
Apr.	23	NY Islanders	1	at	Toronto	3
Apr.	25	Toronto	1	at	NY Islanders	2 OT
Apr.	27	NY Islanders	2	at	Toronto	5
Apr.	29	Toronto	2	at	NY Islanders	1 OT

Toronto won best-of-seven series 4–3

Apr.	17	Buffalo	1	at	Philadelphia	4
Apr.	19	Buffalo	2	at	Philadelphia	3
Apr.	22	Philadelphia	1	at	Buffalo	4
Apr.	23	Philadelphia	4	at	Buffalo	2
Apr.	25	Buffalo	2	at	Philadelphia	4

Philadelphia won best-of-seven series 4–1

SEMI-FINALS

May	2	Toronto	3	at	Montreal	5
May	4	Toronto	2	at	Montreal	3
May	6	Montreal	6	at	Toronto	1
May	9	Montreal	2	at	Toronto	0

Montreal won best-of-seven series 4–0

May	2	Philadelphia	2	at	Boston	3 OT
May	4	Philadelphia	5	at	Boston	7
May	7	Boston	1	at	Philadelphia	3
May	9	Boston	4	at	Philadelphia	2
May	11	Philadelphia	3	at	Boston	6

Boston won best-of-seven series 4–1

FINALS

May	13	Boston	1	at	Montreal	4
May	16	Boston	2	at	Montreal	3 OT
May	18	Montreal	0	at	Boston	4
May	21	Montreal	3	at	Boston	4 OT
May	23	Boston	1	at	Montreal	4
May	25	Montreal	4	at	Boston	1

Montreal won best-of-seven series 4–2

1977-78 – Montreal Canadiens – Ken Dryden, Larry Robinson, Serge Savard, Guy Lapointe, Bill Nyrop, Pierre Bouchard, Brian Engblom, Gilles Lupien, Rick Chartraw, Guy Lafleur, Steve Shutt, Jacques Lemaire, Yvan Cournoyer (Captain), Réjean Houle, Pierre Mondou, Bob Gainey, Doug Jarvis, Yvon Lambert, Doug Risebrough, Pierre Larouche, Mario Tremblay, Michel Larocque, Murray Wilson, Scotty Bowman (Coach), Sam Pollock (General Manager), Eddy Palchak, Pierre Meilleur (Trainers).

Guy Lafleur had a combination of speed, style and scoring skill that made him the most exciting player in the NHL during his prime with the Montreal Canadiens. His six consecutive 50-goal seasons from 1974–75 to 1979–80 were a record at the time, and he played on five Stanley Cup champions in Montreal, including four in a row between 1976 and 1979.

LEADING PLAYOFF SCORERS

Player	Club	GP	G	A	PTS	PIM
Guy Lafleur	Montreal	15	10	11	21	16
Larry Robinson	Montreal	15	4	17	21	6
Brad Park	Boston	15	9	11	20	14
Peter McNab	Boston	15	8	11	19	2
Steve Shutt	Montreal	15	9	8	17	20
Rick MacLeish	Philadelphia	12	7	9	16	4
Ian Turnbull	Toronto	13	6	10	16	10
Bobby Schmautz	Boston	15	7	8	15	11
Terry O'Reilly	Boston	15	5	10	15	40
Jacques Lemaire	Montreal	15	6	8	14	10

LEADING PLAYOFF GOALTENDERS

Goaltender	Club	GPI	Mins	GA	SO	Avg.
Ken Dryden	Montreal	15	919	29	2	1.89
Mike Palmateer	Toronto	13	795	32	2	2.42
Don Edwards	Buffalo	8	482	22	0	2.74
Bernie Parent	Philadelphia	12	722	33	0	2.74
Gerry Cheevers	Boston	12	731	35	1	2.87

PLAYOFF GOALS

Name, Team	G
Guy Lafleur, Mtl.	10
Brad Park, Bos.	9
Steve Shutt, Mtl.	9
Peter McNab, Bos.	8
Rick MacLeish, Phi.	7
Bobby Schmautz, Bos.	7
Yvan Cournoyer, Mtl.	7

PLAYOFF ASSISTS

Name, Team	A
Larry Robinson, Mtl.	17
Guy Lafleur, Mtl.	11
Brad Park, Bos.	11
Peter McNab, Bos.	11
Ian Turnbull, Tor.	10
Terry O'Reilly, Bos.	10
Gregg Sheppard, Bos.	10

PLAYOFF POWERPLAY GOALS

Name, Team	PPG
Brad Park, Bos.	4
Rick MacLeish, Phi.	3
Guy Lafleur, Mtl.	3
Steve Shutt, Mtl.	3
Wayne Cashman, Bos.	3

PLAYOFF SHORTHAND GOALS

Name, Team	SHG
Dennis Hextall, Det.	1
Bob Gainey, Mtl.	1
Doug Risebrough, Mtl.	1

PLAYOFF GAME-WINNING GOALS

Name, Team	GWG
Rick MacLeish, Phi.	3
Bob Nystrom, NYI	2
Lanny McDonald, Tor.	2
Ron Ellis, Tor.	2
Guy Lafleur, Mtl.	2
Wayne Cashman, Bos.	2
Peter McNab, Bos.	2
Yvan Cournoyer, Mtl.	2
Rick Middleton, Bos.	2

PLAYOFF GOALIE WINS

Name, Team	W
Ken Dryden, Mtl.	12
Gerry Cheevers, Bos.	8
Bernie Parent, Phi.	7
Mike Palmateer, Tor.	6
Glenn Resch, NYI	3
Don Edwards, Buf.	3

PLAYOFF SHUTOUTS

Name, Team	SO
Mike Palmateer, Tor.	2
Ken Dryden, Mtl.	2
Gerry Cheevers, Bos.	1

1978-79

Stanley Cup • Montreal Canadiens

Bryan Trottier was selected by the New York Islanders in the second round of the 1974 Amateur Draft and entered the NHL in 1975–76. He promptly set an NHL rookie scoring record with 95 points and won the Calder Trophy. He won both the Art Ross and Hart trophies in 1978–79 as the Islanders were on the verge of a dynasty.

FINAL STANDINGS

PRINCE OF WALES CONFERENCE

Team	GP	W	L	T	GF	GA	PTS
Norris Division							
Montreal	80	52	17	11	337	204	115
Pittsburgh	80	36	31	13	281	279	85
Los Angeles	80	34	34	12	292	286	80
Washington	80	24	41	15	273	338	63
Detroit	80	23	41	16	252	295	62
Adams Division							
Boston	80	43	23	14	316	270	100
Buffalo	80	36	28	16	280	263	88
Toronto	80	34	33	13	267	252	81
Minnesota	80	28	40	12	257	289	68
CLARENCE CAMPBELL CONFERENCE							
Patrick Division							
NY Islanders	80	51	15	14	358	214	116
Philadelphia	80	40	25	15	281	248	95
NY Rangers	80	40	29	11	316	292	91
Atlanta	80	41	31	8	327	280	90
Smythe Division							
Chicago	80	29	36	15	244	277	73
Vancouver	80	25	42	13	217	291	63
St. Louis	80	18	50	12	249	348	48
Colorado	80	15	53	12	210	331	42

LEADING SCORERS

Player	Club	GP	G	A	PTS	PIM
Bryan Trottier	NY Islanders	76	47	87	134	50
Marcel Dionne	Los Angeles	80	59	71	130	30
Guy Lafleur	Montreal	80	52	77	129	28
Mike Bossy	NY Islanders	80	69	57	126	25
Bob MacMillan	Atlanta	79	37	71	108	14
Guy Chouinard	Atlanta	80	50	57	107	14
Denis Potvin	NY Islanders	73	31	70	101	58
Bernie Federko	St. Louis	74	31	64	95	14
Dave Taylor	Los Angeles	78	43	48	91	124
Clark Gillies	NY Islanders	75	35	56	91	68
Dennis Maruk	Min./Wsh.	78	31	59	90	71
Butch Goring	Los Angeles	80	36	51	87	16
Darryl Sittler	Toronto	70	36	51	87	69
Rick Middleton	Boston	71	38	48	86	7
Lanny McDonald	Toronto	79	43	42	85	32
Gilbert Perreault	Buffalo	79	27	58	85	20
Eric Vail	Atlanta	80	35	48	83	53
Brian Sutter	St. Louis	77	41	39	80	165
Peter McNab	Boston	76	35	45	80	10
Bill Barber	Philadelphia	79	34	46	80	22
Phil Esposito	NY Rangers	80	42	36	78	37
Ivan Boldirev	Chi./Atl.	79	35	43	78	31
Anders Hedberg	NY Rangers	80	33	45	78	33
Steve Shutt	Montreal	72	37	40	77	31
Terry O'Reilly	Boston	80	26	51	77	205

LEADING GOALTENDERS

Goaltender	Club	GPI	MINS	GA	SO	AVG
Ken Dryden	Montreal	47	2814	108	5	2.30
Glenn Resch	NY Islanders	43	2539	106	2	2.50
Bernie Parent	Philadelphia	36	1979	89	4	2.70
Michel Larocque	Montreal	34	1986	94	3	2.84
Billy Smith	NY Islanders	40	2261	108	1	2.87
Mike Palmateer	Toronto	58	3396	167	4	2.95
Don Edwards	Buffalo	54	3160	159	2	3.02
Glen Hanlon	Vancouver	31	1821	94	3	3.10
Mario Lessard	Los Angeles	49	2860	148	4	3.10
Gerry Cheevers	Boston	43	2509	132	1	3.16

The instability of the World Hockey Association had many of its top players rushing to sign with NHL clubs prior to the 1978–79 season. Most notably, the New York Rangers doled out big bucks for Swedish stars Ulf Nilsson and Anders Hedberg, who got two-year contracts worth $1 million to leave the Winnipeg Jets for the Big Apple. Another summer of fruitless merger talks with the NHL had left the WHA preparing for its seventh season with just seven teams lumped into a single division.

In addition to their purchase of Hedberg and Nilsson, the Rangers had hired former Philadelphia Flyers coach Fred Shero to fill the dual role of coach and general manager. New York's 91 points this season were 18 better than the previous year, but good for only third place in the Patrick Division. First place in the Patrick belonged to the New York Islanders, whose 116 points edged out the Montreal Canadiens at 115 for top spot in the overall standings. Bryan Trottier earned both the Art Ross and Hart trophies, but once again a great Islanders season would end in playoff disappointment. Center Phil Esposito had led the Rangers to playoff victories over the Los Angeles Kings and Philadelphia, but it was goalie John Davidson who made the difference when the team knocked off the Islanders in a six-game semi-final.

The End of an Era – The tumultuous 70s closed with the NY Islanders on the verge, the NHL about to merge, a Broadway revival by the Blueshirts and a Stanley Cup curtain call by the Canadiens.

The Rangers' opponent for the Stanley Cup was Montreal, who had reached the final for the fourth consecutive year after a thrilling seven-game semi-final series with the Bruins. The deciding game had turned on a late Boston bench minor for having too many men on the ice. On the ensuing powerplay, Montreal tied the score and went on to win in overtime. The Rangers took full advantage of the Canadiens' fatigue for a 4–1 series-opening victory, but Montreal stormed back to take the next four games for their fourth consecutive Stanley Cup championship. Bob Gainey earned the Conn Smythe Trophy as playoff MVP.

On March 29, 1979, two weeks before the start of the playoffs, the NHL had announced that it would take in four WHA teams for the 1979–80 season: Edmonton, Winnipeg, Quebec, and New England. The two remaining clubs, the Cincinnati Stingers and Birmingham Bulls, were paid to go out of business. A seventh WHA club, the Indianapolis Racers, had already gone out of business early in the season. The Racers made one significant contribution to hockey before folding, selling the contract of 17-year-old Wayne Gretzky to the Edmonton Oilers. Gretzky scored 46 goals and added 64 assists as a rookie and led Edmonton to a first-place finish in the regular-season standings. His 110 points had ranked him third in WHA scoring behind Real Cloutier (129) and Robbie Ftorek (116). Gretzky and the Oilers were beaten by the Jets for the last-ever Avco Cup championship, but they would reach much higher heights in the years to come.

His best years were behind him by the time he arrived in New York, but Phil Esposito still led the Rangers in scoring four years in a row and helped them reach the Stanley Cup finals in 1979.

Leaders, 1978-79

GOALS

Name, Team	G
Mike Bossy, NYI	69
Marcel Dionne, L.A.	59
Guy Lafleur, Mtl.	52
Guy Chouinard, Atl.	50
Bryan Trottier, NYI	47
Dave Taylor, L.A.	43
Lanny McDonald, Tor.	43
Phil Esposito, NYR	42
Brian Sutter, St.L.	41
Ron Sedlbauer, Van.	40

ASSISTS

Name, Team	A
Bryan Trottier, NYI	87
Guy Lafleur, Mtl.	77
Bob MacMillan, Atl.	71
Marcel Dionne, L.A.	71
Denis Potvin, NYI	70
Bernie Federko, St.L.	64
Dennis Maruk, Min./Wsh.	59
Gilbert Perreault, Buf.	58
Mike Bossy, NYI	57
Guy Chouinard, Atl.	57
Bobby Clarke, Phi.	57

POWERPLAY GOALS

Name, Team	PPG
Mike Bossy, NYI	27
Marcel Dionne, L.A.	19
Paul Gardner, Col./Tor.	16
Lanny McDonald, Tor.	16
Bryan Trottier, NYI	15
Ron Sedlbauer, Van.	15
Ivan Boldirev, Chi./Atl.	14
Dale McCourt, Det.	14
Phil Esposito, NYR	14
Five tied with	13

SHORTHAND GOALS

Name, Team	SHG
Bill Barber, Phi.	6
Rick MacLeish, Phi.	5
Don Marcotte, Bos.	4
Butch Goring, L.A.	4
Denis Potvin, NYI	3
Craig Ramsay, Buf.	3
Paul Woods, Det.	3
George Ferguson, Pit.	3
22 tied with	2

GAME-WINNING GOALS

Name, Team	GWG
Guy Lafleur, Mtl.	12
Mike Bossy, NYI	9
Jean Pronovost, Atl.	8
Ted Bulley, Chi.	8
Bryan Trottier, NYI	8
Pierre Mondou, Mtl.	7
Yvon Lambert, Mtl.	7
Don Luce, Buf.	7
Phil Esposito, NYR	7
Peter Lee, Pit.	7
Marcel Dionne, L.A.	7

GOALIE WINS

Name, Team	W
Dan Bouchard, Atl.	32
Ken Dryden, Mtl.	30
Glenn Resch, NYI	26
Don Edwards, Buf.	26
Mike Palmateer, Tor.	26
Billy Smith, NYI	25
Tony Esposito, Chi.	24
Gerry Cheevers, Bos.	23
Mario Lessard, L.A.	23
Michel Larocque, Mtl.	22
Denis Herron, Pit.	22

SHUTOUTS

Name, Team	SO
Ken Dryden, Mtl.	5
Bernie Parent, Phi.	4
Mario Lessard, L.A.	4
Mike Palmateer, Tor.	4
Tony Esposito, Chi.	4
Glen Hanlon, Van.	3
Michel Larocque, Mtl.	3
Dan Bouchard, Atl.	3
Seven tied with	2

FIRST TEAM ALL-STARS

Name, Team	Position
Bryan Trottier, NYI	C
Guy Lafleur, Mtl.	RW
Clark Gillies, NYI	LW
Denis Potvin, NYI	D
Larry Robinson, Mtl.	D
Ken Dryden, Mtl.	G

SECOND TEAM ALL-STARS

Name, Team	Position
Marcel Dionne, L.A.	C
Mike Bossy, NYI	LW
Bill Barber, Phi.	RW
Borje Salming, Tor.	D
Serge Savard, Mtl.	D
Glenn Resch, NYI	G

TROPHY WINNERS

Trophy	Awarded For	Winner	Team
Hart	MVP	Bryan Trottier	NYI
Art Ross	Top Scorer	Bryan Trottier	NYI
Norris	Top Defenseman	Denis Potvin	NYI
Calder	Top Rookie	Bobby Smith	Min.
Selke	Top Defensive Forward	Bob Gainey	Mtl.
Vezina	Fewest Goals Against	Ken Dryden	Mtl.
		Michel Larocque	Mtl.
Adams	Top Coach	Al Arbour	NYI
Byng	Gentlemanly Conduct	Bob MacMillan	Atl.
Masterton	Perseverance, Sportmanship	Serge Savard	Mtl.
Pearson	NHLPA MVP	Marcel Dionne	L.A.
Conn Smythe	Playoff MVP	Bob Gainey	Mtl.
Patrick	Service to Hockey in U.S.	Bobby Orr	
Entry Draft	First Overall Selection	Rob Ramage	Col.

NHL NOTEBOOK

TRANSACTIONS

- June 14, 1978 – Toronto traded Randy Carlyle and George Ferguson to Pittsburgh in exchange for Dave Burrows.
- June 15, 1978 – Vancouver obtained the rights to Thomas Gradin from Chicago for a future draft pick.
- July 26, 1978 – New York Islanders signed free agent John Tonelli.
- Oct. 18, 1978 – Washington Capitals obtained Dennis Maruk from Washington for a future draft pick.

RECORDS

- Dec. 23, 1978 – Bryan Trottier set an NHL record with six points in the second period, and finished the night with five goals and three assists in a 9-4 Islanders win over the Rangers.
- Feb. 19, 1979 – Mike Bossy scored his 100th career NHL goal (in an 8-3 Islanders win at Los Angeles) in just his 129th career game, to break Maurice Richard's NHL record (145 games) for fastest 100 goals.
- Mar. 11, 1979 – Los Angeles' Randy Holt picked up an NHL-record nine penalties and 67 penalty minutes in one game. They all came in the first period of a 6-3 loss at Philadelphia.
- Apr. 24, 1979 – Rangers and Flyers set an NHL playoff record for most goals in one period with nine in the third period. New York won the period 6-3 and the game 8-3 in game five of the quarter-finals.

MILESTONES

- Nov. 11, 1978 – Dennis Kearns became first player in Vancouver Canucks history to play in 500 games during a 6-4 win at Detroit.
- Apr. 4, 1979 – Ken Dryden became the first goaltender in history to win 30-or-more games in each of his first seven NHL seasons when he led the Canadiens to a 4-1 victory over the visiting Detroit Red Wings.
- Apr. 8, 1979 – Denis Potvin scored two assists to become the second defenseman in NHL history to score 100 points in a season as the Islanders won 5-2 over the Rangers at Madison Square Garden.
- Apr. 22, 1979 – Montreal goaltender Ken Dryden became the NHL's all-time leader in playoff victories in a 5-4 win at Toronto in game four of the Stanley Cup quarter-finals. Dryden's 72nd career playoff win moved him ahead of Jacques Plante.

1979 Playoffs

PRELIMINARY ROUND

Apr.	10	Vancouver	3	at	Philadelphia	2
Apr.	12	Philadelphia	6	at	Vancouver	4
Apr.	14	Vancouver	2	at	Philadelphia	7

Philadelphia won best-of-three series 2–1

Apr.	10	Los Angeles	1	at	NY Rangers	7
Apr.	12	NY Rangers	2	at	Los Angeles	1 OT

NY Rangers won best-of-three series 2–0

Apr.	10	Toronto	2	at	Atlanta	1
Apr.	12	Atlanta	4	at	Toronto	7

Toronto won best-of-three series 2–0

Apr.	10	Pittsburgh	4	at	Buffalo	3
Apr.	12	Buffalo	3	at	Pittsburgh	1
Apr.	14	Pittsburgh	4	at	Buffalo	3 OT

Pittsburgh won best-of-three series 2–1

QUARTER-FINALS

Apr.	16	Chicago	2	at	NY Islanders	6
Apr.	18	Chicago	0	at	NY Islanders	1 OT
Apr.	20	NY Islanders	4	at	Chicago	0
Apr.	22	NY Islanders	3	at	Chicago	1

NY Islanders won best-of-seven series 4–0

Apr.	16	Toronto	2	at	Montreal	5
Apr.	18	Toronto	1	at	Montreal	5
Apr.	21	Montreal	4	at	Toronto	3 2OT
Apr.	22	Montreal	5	at	Toronto	4 OT

Montreal won best-of-seven series 4–0

Apr.	16	Pittsburgh	2	at	Boston	6
Apr.	18	Pittsburgh	3	at	Boston	4
Apr.	21	Boston	2	at	Pittsburgh	1
Apr.	22	Boston	4	at	Pittsburgh	1

Boston won best-of-seven series 4–0

Apr.	16	NY Rangers	2	at	Philadelphia	3 OT
Apr.	18	NY Rangers	7	at	Philadelphia	1
Apr.	20	Philadelphia	1	at	NY Rangers	5
Apr.	22	Philadelphia	0	at	NY Rangers	6
Apr.	24	NY Rangers	8	at	Philadelphia	3

NY Rangers won best-of-seven series 4–1

SEMI-FINALS

Apr.	26	NY Rangers	4	at	NY Islanders	1
Apr.	28	NY Rangers	3	at	NY Islanders	4 OT
May	1	NY Islanders	1	at	NY Rangers	3
May	3	NY Islanders	3	at	NY Rangers	2 OT
May	5	NY Rangers	4	at	NY Islanders	3
May	8	NY Islanders	1	at	NY Rangers	2

NY Rangers won best-of-seven series 4–2

Apr.	26	Boston	2	at	Montreal	4
Apr.	28	Boston	2	at	Montreal	5
May	1	Montreal	1	at	Boston	2
May	3	Montreal	3	at	Boston	4 OT
May	5	Boston	1	at	Montreal	5
May	8	Montreal	2	at	Boston	5
May	10	Boston	4	at	Montreal	5 OT

Montreal won best-of-seven series 4–3

FINALS

May	13	NY Rangers	4	at	Montreal	1
May	15	NY Rangers	2	at	Montreal	6
May	17	Montreal	4	at	NY Rangers	1
May	19	Montreal	4	at	NY Rangers	3 OT
May	21	NY Rangers	1	at	Montreal	4

Montreal won best-of-seven series 4–1

1978-79 – Montreal Canadiens – Ken Dryden, Larry Robinson, Serge Savard, Guy Lapointe, Brian Engblom, Gilles Lupien, Rick Chartraw, Guy Lafleur, Steve Shutt, Jacques Lemaire, Yvan Cournoyer (Captain), Réjean Houle, Pierre Mondou, Bob Gainey, Doug Jarvis, Yvon Lambert, Doug Risebrough, Pierre Larouche, Mario Tremblay, Cam Connor, Pat Hughes, Rod Langway, Mark Napier, Michel Larocque, Richard Sévigny, Scotty Bowman (Coach), Irving Grundman (Managing Director), Eddy Palchak, Pierre Meilleur (Trainers).

Pictured in his 1979 Challenge Cup uniform (the series between the Soviet national team and top NHL stars replaced the All-Star Game that year), Bob Gainey was described by Soviet coach Viktor Tikhonov as technically the world's best hockey player. Gainey won the Stanley Cup five times in his 16-year career with the Montreal Canadiens.

LEADING PLAYOFF SCORERS

Player	Club	GP	G	A	PTS	PIM
Jacques Lemaire	Montreal	16	11	12	23	6
Guy Lafleur	Montreal	16	10	13	23	0
Phil Esposito	NY Rangers	18	8	12	20	20
Don Maloney	NY Rangers	18	7	13	20	19
Bob Gainey	Montreal	16	6	10	16	10
Larry Robinson	Montreal	16	6	9	15	8
Jean Ratelle	Boston	11	7	6	13	2
Mike McEwen	NY Rangers	18	2	11	13	8
Don Murdoch	NY Rangers	18	7	5	12	12
Ron Greschner	NY Rangers	18	7	5	12	16
Rick Middleton	Boston	11	4	8	12	0

LEADING PLAYOFF GOALTENDERS

Goaltender	Club	GPI	Mins	GA	SO	Avg.
Billy Smith	NY Islanders	5	315	10	1	1.90
Glenn Resch	NY Islanders	5	300	11	1	2.20
John Davidson	NY Rangers	18	1106	42	1	2.28
Ken Dryden	Montreal	16	990	41	0	2.48
Gerry Cheevers	Boston	6	360	15	0	2.50

PLAYOFF GOALS

Name, Team	G
Jacques Lemaire, Mtl.	11
Guy Lafleur, Mtl.	10
Phil Esposito, NYR	8
Jean Ratelle, Bos.	7
Don Maloney, NYR	7
Don Murdoch, NYR	7
Ron Greschner, NYR	7

PLAYOFF ASSISTS

Name, Team	A
Guy Lafleur, Mtl.	13
Don Maloney, NYR	13
Jacques Lemaire, Mtl.	12
Phil Esposito, NYR	12
Mike McEwen, NYR	11
Bob Gainey, Mtl.	10
Larry Robinson, Mtl.	9
Carol Vadnais, NYR	9

PLAYOFF POWERPLAY GOALS

Name, Team	PPG
Jacques Lemaire, Mtl.	6
Ron Greschner, NYR	4
Reggie Leach, Phi.	3
Don Murdoch, NYR	3
Eight tied with	2

PLAYOFF SHORTHAND GOALS

Name, Team	SHG
Walt McKechnie, Tor.	1
Lorne Henning, NYI	1
Dick Redmond, Bos.	1
Dave Maloney, NYR	1
Eddie Johnstone, NYR	1
Ron Greschner, NYR	1
Walt Tkaczuk, NYR	1
Anders Hedberg, NYR	1
Ron Duguay, NYR	1

PLAYOFF GAME-WINNING GOALS

Name, Team	GWG
Ron Greschner, NYR	3
Reggie Leach, Phi.	2
Jean Ratelle, Bos.	2
Jacques Lemaire, Mtl.	2
Guy Lafleur, Mtl.	2
Phil Esposito, NYR	2

PLAYOFF GOALIE WINS

Name, Team	W
Ken Dryden, Mtl.	12
John Davidson, NYR	11
Billy Smith, NYI	4
Gerry Cheevers, Bos.	4
Gilles Gilbert, Bos.	3
Robbie Moore, Phi.	3

PLAYOFF SHUTOUTS

Name, Team	SO
Billy Smith, NYI	1
Glenn Resch, NYI	1
John Davidson, NYR	1

1979-80

Stanley Cup • New York Islanders

FINAL STANDINGS

PRINCE OF WALES CONFERENCE

Team	GP	W	L	T	GF	GA	PTS
Norris Division							
Montreal	80	47	20	13	328	240	107
Los Angeles	80	30	36	14	290	313	74
Pittsburgh	80	30	37	13	251	303	73
Hartford	80	27	34	19	303	312	73
Detroit	80	26	43	11	268	306	63
Adams Division							
Buffalo	80	47	17	16	318	201	110
Boston	80	46	21	13	310	234	105
Minnesota	80	36	28	16	311	253	88
Toronto	80	35	40	5	304	327	75
Quebec	80	25	44	11	248	313	61
CLARENCE CAMPBELL CONFERENCE							
Patrick Division							
Philadelphia	80	48	12	20	327	254	116
NY Islanders	80	39	28	13	281	247	91
NY Rangers	80	38	32	10	308	284	86
Atlanta	80	35	32	13	282	269	83
Washington	80	27	40	13	261	293	67
Smythe Division							
Chicago	80	34	27	19	241	250	87
St. Louis	80	34	34	12	266	278	80
Vancouver	80	27	37	16	256	281	70
Edmonton	80	28	39	13	301	322	69
Winnipeg	80	20	49	11	214	314	51
Colorado	80	19	48	13	234	308	51

LEADING SCORERS

Player	Club	GP	G	A	PTS	PIM
Marcel Dionne	Los Angeles	80	53	84	137	32
Wayne Gretzky	Edmonton	79	51	86	137	21
Guy Lafleur	Montreal	74	50	75	125	12
Gilbert Perreault	Buffalo	80	40	66	106	57
Mike Rogers	Hartford	80	44	61	105	10
Bryan Trottier	NY Islanders	78	42	62	104	68
Charlie Simmer	Los Angeles	64	56	45	101	65
Blaine Stoughton	Hartford	80	56	44	100	16
Darryl Sittler	Toronto	73	40	57	97	62
Blair MacDonald	Edmonton	80	46	48	94	6
Bernie Federko	St. Louis	79	38	56	94	24
Al MacAdam	Minnesota	80	42	51	93	24
Kent Nilsson	Atlanta	80	40	53	93	10
Mike Bossy	NY Islanders	75	51	41	92	12
Rick Middleton	Boston	80	40	52	92	24
Pierre Larouche	Montreal	73	50	41	91	16
Dave Taylor	Los Angeles	61	37	53	90	72
Danny Gare	Buffalo	76	56	33	89	90
Steve Shutt	Montreal	77	47	42	89	34
Real Cloutier	Quebec	67	42	47	89	12
Steve Payne	Minnesota	80	42	43	85	40
Bobby Smith	Minnesota	61	27	56	83	24
Dale McCourt	Detroit	80	30	51	81	12
Mark Howe	Hartford	74	24	56	80	20

LEADING GOALTENDERS

Goaltender	Club	GPI	MINS	GA	SO	AVG
Bob Sauve	Buffalo	32	1880	74	4	2.36
Denis Herron	Montreal	34	1909	80	0	2.51
Don Edwards	Buffalo	49	2920	125	2	2.57
Pete Peeters	Philadelphia	40	2373	108	1	2.73
Gilles Gilbert	Boston	33	1933	88	1	2.73
Gerry Cheevers	Boston	42	2479	116	4	2.81
Billy Smith	NY Islanders	38	2114	104	2	2.95
Tony Esposito	Chicago	69	4140	205	6	2.97
Glenn Resch	NY Islanders	45	2606	132	3	3.04
Gilles Meloche	Minnesota	54	3141	160	1	3.06

Wayne Gretzky was marked for stardom almost from the time he began to play organized hockey, particularly after the 1971–72 season when he collected 378 goals and 139 assists as an 11-year-old. He made his junior hockey debut in 1976–77 at age 15, played pro hockey in the WHA at age 17 and entered the NHL as an 18-year-old in 1979–80.

A YEAR AFTER the struggling Cleveland Barons merged with the Minnesota North Stars, reducing the NHL to 17 teams, the league was growing again as it absorbed the four survivors of the World Hockey Association: the Edmonton Oilers, Winnipeg Jets, Quebec Nordiques and Hartford (formerly New England) Whalers.

The National Hockey League benefited from an influx of talent created by the WHA's demise. Most notable was the return of legends Bobby Hull, Dave Keon and 51-year-old Gordie Howe, who would score 15 goals for Hartford. At the other end of their careers were young players like Mike Gartner, Rick Vaive, Michel Goulet and Mark Messier, who'd played in the WHA as underage pros. But it was the youngest of the WHA's former stars who would prove to be the greatest NHL player of all.

"The Great One" Cometh – Two brilliant stars (Howe and Hull) returned for one final bow, but the spotlight belonged to the dominant (Gretzky), the dynamo (Dionne) and the dynasty (New York Islanders).

Beginning his pro career at the age of 17, Wayne Gretzky had finished third in WHA scoring in 1978–79. He had been a point-scoring machine all his young life, but few expected his WHA performance to translate into NHL success. Getting better as the year progressed, Gretzky proved the doubters wrong, enjoying a late-season surge that saw him tie Marcel Dionne for the league lead with 137 points. The Art Ross Trophy, however, went to the Los Angeles Kings superstar because his 53 goals were two more than Gretzky's 51. "The Great One", as Gretzky would become known, was also denied the Calder Trophy because the season he spent in the WHA meant he wasn't considered an NHL rookie, but his brilliance was recognized with both the Hart and Lady Byng trophies. Gretzky's great play also managed to sneak Edmonton into the 16th and final playoff spot, though the Oilers were knocked off in three straight games by Philadelphia. The Flyers set a professional sports record during the season with a 35-game unbeaten streak en route to a first-place finish in the overall standings.

The four-time defending Stanley Cup champion Montreal Canadiens underwent a major overhaul before the 1979–80 season. Goalie Ken Dryden announced his retirement and Scotty Bowman resigned as coach to run the Buffalo Sabres. Bowman was replaced by Canadiens legend Bernie "Boom-Boom" Geoffrion, who in turn gave way to Claude Ruel during the season. Montreal managed to finish atop the Norris Division with 107 points, but a quarter-final defeat at the hands of the Minnesota North Stars ended the team's quest for a record-tying fifth straight Stanley Cup championship. The Cup wound up instead with the New York Islanders when Bob Nystrom's overtime goal upset favored Philadelphia in a six-game final.

Toronto's Borje Salming was the first European-trained player to become a star in the NHL. Salming excelled at blocking shots and was a strong skater who could rush the puck and set up plays.

Leaders, 1979-80

GOALS

Name, Team	G
Charlie Simmer, L.A.	56
Danny Gare, Buf.	56
Blaine Stoughton, Hfd.	56
Marcel Dionne, L.A.	53
Mike Bossy, NYI	51
Wayne Gretzky, Edm.	51
Pierre Larouche, Mtl.	50
Guy Lafleur, Mtl.	50
Reggie Leach, Phi.	50
Steve Shutt, Mtl.	47

ASSISTS

Name, Team	A
Wayne Gretzky, Edm.	86
Marcel Dionne, L.A.	84
Guy Lafleur, Mtl.	75
Gilbert Perreault, Buf.	66
Bryan Trottier, NYI	62
Larry Robinson, Mtl.	61
Mike Rogers, Hfd.	61
Darryl Sittler, Tor.	57
Bobby Clarke, Phi.	57
Ken Linseman, Phi.	57

POWERPLAY GOALS

Name, Team	PPG
Charlie Simmer, L.A.	21
Darryl Sittler, Tor.	17
Danny Gare, Buf.	17
Steve Shutt, Mtl.	17
Marcel Dionne, L.A.	17
Mike Bossy, NYI	16
Blaine Stoughton, Hfd.	16
Steve Payne, Min.	16
Guy Lafleur, Mtl.	15
Bryan Trottier, NYI	15

SHORTHAND GOALS

Name, Team	SHG
Anders Kallur, NYI	4
Reggie Leach, Phi.	4
Ron Duguay, NYR	3
George Ferguson, Pit.	3
Bob MacMillan, Atl.	3
Rick MacLeish, Phi.	3
Larry Patey, St.L.	3
Mike Murphy, L.A.	3
24 tied with	2

GAME-WINNING GOALS

Name, Team	GWG
Danny Gare, Buf.	11
Peter McNab, Bos.	9
Blaine Stoughton, Hfd.	9
Charlie Simmer, L.A.	8
Mike Bossy, NYI	8
Nine tied with	7

GOALIE WINS

Name, Team	W
Mike Liut, St.L.	32
Tony Esposito, Chi.	31
Pete Peeters, Phi.	29
Don Edwards, Buf.	27
Gilles Meloche, Min.	27
Denis Herron, Mtl.	25
Gerry Cheevers, Bos.	24
Glenn Resch, NYI	23
Dan Bouchard, Atl.	23
Four tied with	20

SHUTOUTS

Name, Team	SO
Tony Esposito, Chi.	6
Bob Sauve, Buf.	4
Gerry Cheevers, Bos.	4
Rogie Vachon, Det.	4
Michel Larocque, Mtl.	3
Glenn Resch, NYI	3
12 tied with	2

FIRST TEAM ALL-STARS

Name, Team	Position
Marcel Dionne, L.A.	C
Guy Lafleur, Mtl.	RW
Charlie Simmer, L.A.	LW
Larry Robinson, Mtl.	D
Raymond Bourque, Bos.	D
Tony Esposito, Chi.	G

SECOND TEAM ALL-STARS

Name, Team	Position
Wayne Gretzky, Edm.	C
Danny Gare, Buf.	RW
Steve Shutt, Mtl.	LW
Borje Salming, Tor.	D
Jim Schoenfeld, Buf.	D
Don Edwards, Buf.	G

TROPHY WINNERS

Trophy	Awarded For	Winner	Team
Hart	MVP	Wayne Gretzky	Edm.
Art Ross	Top Scorer	Marcel Dionne	L.A.
Norris	Top Defenseman	Larry Robinson	Mtl.
Calder	Top Rookie	Ray Bourque	Bos.
Selke	Top Defensive Forward	Bob Gainey	Mtl.
Vezina	Fewest Goals Against	Bob Sauve	Buf
		Don Edwards	Buf
Adams	Top Coach	Pat Quinn	Phi.
Byng	Gentlemanly Conduct	Wayne Gretzky	Edm
Masterton	Perseverance, Sportmanship	Al MacAdam	Min.
Pearson	NHLPA MVP	Marcel Dionne	L.A.
Conn Smythe	Playoff MVP	Bryan Trottier	NYI
Patrick	Service to Hockey in U.S.	Bobby Clarke	
		Ed Snider	
		Fred Shero	
		1980 U.S. Olympic Team	
Entry Draft	First Overall Selection	Doug Wickenheiser	Mtl.

NHL NOTEBOOK

TRANSACTIONS

- Aug. 9, 1979 – Edmonton Oilers obtained Dave Semenko from the Minnesota North Stars for two future draft choices.
- Aug. 16, 1979 – St. Louis Blues signed Joe Mullen as a free agent after his college career at Boston College.
- Sept. 28, 1979 – Minnesota North Stars signed free agent Dino Ciccarelli from the London Knights of the OHA.
- Mar. 10, 1980 – NY Islanders obtained center Butch Goring from the L.A. Kings for defenseman Dave Lewis and forward Billy Harris. The Islanders then went undefeated in their last 12 regular-season games, and went on to win the Stanley Cup.

RECORDS

- Philadelphia set an NHL record with a 35-game (25-0-10) unbeaten streak.
- Chicago set an NHL playoff -record with a 16-game losing streak (which began in 1975).
- Gordie Howe set an NHL record for most years in the playoffs (20).
- Charlie Simmer set a modern NHL record with a 13-game goal scoring streak.

MILESTONES

- Oct. 10, 1979 – Gary Smith became the first goaltender in NHL history to play for seven different NHL teams when he suited up for the Winnipeg Jets in a 4-2 loss at Pittsburgh.
- Nov. 28, 1979 – Billy Smith became the first goalie in NHL history to get credit for a goal when he was the last Islander to touch the puck before Colorado's Rob Ramage shot the puck into his own net. But the Islanders lost 7-4 to the Rockies at Denver.
- Jan. 2, 1980 – Gordie Howe became the first player in league history to appear in an NHL game in five different decades when he played for the Hartford Whalers in a 3-3 tie against the Oilers, in Edmonton.
- Feb. 24, 1980 – Edmonton rookie Wayne Gretzky became the first player in NHL history to score 100 points in a season prior to his 20th birthday. His 100th career point came as an assist in just his 61st career game, a 4-2 Oilers loss to the Bruins.
- Mar. 25, 1980 – Montreal's Pierre Larouche became the first player in NHL history to score 50 goals with two different NHL teams. He notched #50 for the Canadiens in an 8-4 win over Chicago after previously scoring 53 goals for Pittsburgh in 1975-76.

1980 Playoffs

PRELIMINARY ROUND

Apr.	8	Edmonton	3	at	Philadelphia	4 OT
Apr.	9	Edmonton	1	at	Philadelphia	5
Apr.	11	Philadelphia	3	at	Edmonton	2 2OT

Philadelphia won best-of-five series 3–0

Apr.	8	Vancouver	1	at	Buffalo	2
Apr.	9	Vancouver	0	at	Buffalo	6
Apr.	11	Buffalo	4	at	Vancouver	5
Apr.	12	Buffalo	3	at	Vancouver	1

Buffalo won best-of-five series 3–1

Apr.	8	Hartford	1	at	Montreal	6
Apr.	9	Hartford	4	at	Montreal	8
Apr.	11	Montreal	4	at	Hartford	3 OT

Montreal won best-of-five series 3–0

Apr.	8	Pittsburgh	4	at	Boston	2
Apr.	10	Pittsburgh	1	at	Boston	4
Apr.	12	Boston	1	at	Pittsburgh	4
Apr.	13	Boston	8	at	Pittsburgh	3
Apr.	14	Pittsburgh	2	at	Boston	6

Boston won best-of-five series 3–2

Apr.	8	Los Angeles	1	at	NY Islanders	8
Apr.	9	Los Angeles	6	at	NY Islanders	3
Apr.	11	NY Islanders	4	at	Los Angeles	3 OT
Apr.	12	NY Islanders	6	at	Los Angeles	0

NY Islanders won best-of-five series 3–1

Apr.	8	Toronto	3	at	Minnesota	6
Apr.	9	Toronto	2	at	Minnesota	7
Apr.	11	Minnesota	4	at	Toronto	3 OT

Minnesota won best-of-five series 3–0

Apr.	8	St. Louis	2	at	Chicago	3 OT
Apr.	9	St. Louis	1	at	Chicago	5
Apr.	11	Chicago	4	at	St. Louis	1

Chicago won best-of-five series 3–0

Apr.	8	Atlanta	1	at	NY Rangers	2 OT
Apr.	9	Atlanta	1	at	NY Rangers	5
Apr.	11	NY Rangers	2	at	Atlanta	4
Apr.	12	NY Rangers	5	at	Atlanta	2

NY Rangers won best-of-five series 3–1

QUARTER-FINALS

Apr.	16	NY Rangers	1	at	Philadelphia	2
Apr.	17	NY Rangers	1	at	Philadelphia	4
Apr.	19	Philadelphia	3	at	NY Rangers	0
Apr.	20	Philadelphia	3	at	NY Rangers	4
Apr.	22	NY Rangers	1	at	Philadelphia	3

Philadelphia won best-of-seven series 4–1

Apr.	16	Chicago	0	at	Buffalo	5
Apr.	17	Chicago	4	at	Buffalo	6
Apr.	19	Buffalo	2	at	Chicago	1
Apr.	20	Buffalo	3	at	Chicago	2

Buffalo won best-of-seven series 4–0

Apr.	16	Minnesota	3	at	Montreal	0
Apr.	17	Minnesota	4	at	Montreal	1
Apr.	19	Montreal	5	at	Minnesota	0
Apr.	20	Montreal	5	at	Minnesota	1
Apr.	22	Minnesota	2	at	Montreal	6
Apr.	24	Montreal	2	at	Minnesota	5
Apr.	27	Minnesota	3	at	Montreal	2

Minnesota won best-of-seven series 4–3

Apr.	16	NY Islanders	2	at	Boston	1 OT
Apr.	17	NY Islanders	5	at	Boston	4 OT
Apr.	19	Boston	3	at	NY Islanders	5
Apr.	21	Boston	4	at	NY Islanders	3 OT
Apr.	22	NY Islanders	4	at	Boston	2

NY Islanders won best-of-seven series 4–1

SEMI-FINALS

Apr.	29	Minnesota	6	at	Philadelphia	5
May	1	Minnesota	0	at	Philadelphia	7
May	4	Philadelphia	5	at	Minnesota	3
May	6	Philadelphia	3	at	Minnesota	2
May	8	Minnesota	3	at	Philadelphia	7

Philadelphia won best-of-seven series 4–1

Apr.	29	NY Islanders	4	at	Buffalo	1
May	1	NY Islanders	2	at	Buffalo	1 2OT
May	3	Buffalo	4	at	NY Islanders	7
May	6	Buffalo	7	at	NY Islanders	4
May	8	NY Islanders	0	at	Buffalo	2
May	10	Buffalo	2	at	NY Islanders	5

NY Islanders won best-of-seven series 4–2

FINALS

May	13	NY Islanders	4	at	Philadelphia	3 OT
May	15	NY Islanders	3	at	Philadelphia	8
May	17	Philadelphia	2	at	NY Islanders	6
May	19	Philadelphia	2	at	NY Islanders	5
May	22	NY Islanders	3	at	Philadelphia	6
May	24	Philadelphia	4	at	NY Islanders	5 OT

NY Islanders won best-of-seven series 4–2

1979-80 – New York Islanders – Gord Lane, Jean Potvin, Bob Lorimer, Denis Potvin (Captain), Stefan Persson, Ken Morrow, Dave Langevin, Duane Sutter, Garry Howatt, Clark Gillies, Lorne Henning, Wayne Merrick, Bob Bourne, Steve Tambellini, Bryan Trottier, Mike Bossy, Bob Nystrom, John Tonelli, Anders Kallur, Butch Goring, Alex McKendry, Glenn Resch, Billy Smith, Al Arbour (Coach), Bill Torrey (General Manager), Jim Devellano (Chief Scout), Ron Waske, Jim Pickard (Trainers).

LEADING PLAYOFF SCORERS

Player	Club	GP	G	A	PTS	PIM
Bryan Trottier	NY Islanders	21	12	17	29	16
Mike Bossy	NY Islanders	16	10	13	23	8
Ken Linseman	Philadelphia	17	4	18	22	40
Bill Barber	Philadelphia	19	12	9	21	23
Gilbert Perreault	Buffalo	14	10	11	21	8
Paul Holmgren	Philadelphia	18	10	10	20	47
Bob Bourne	NY Islanders	21	10	10	20	10
Bobby Clarke	Philadelphia	19	8	12	20	16
Butch Goring	NY Islanders	21	7	12	19	2
Denis Potvin	NY Islanders	21	6	13	19	24

LEADING PLAYOFF GOALTENDERS

Goaltender	Club	GPI	Mins	GA	SO	Avg.
Bob Sauve	Buffalo	8	501	17	2	2.04
John Davidson	NY Rangers	9	541	21	0	2.33
Pete Peeters	Philadelphia	13	799	37	1	2.78
Billy Smith	NY Islanders	20	1198	56	1	2.80
Don Edwards	Buffalo	6	360	17	1	2.83

PLAYOFF GOALS

Name, Team	G
Bill Barber, Phi.	12
Bryan Trottier, NYI	12
Gilbert Perreault, Buf.	10
Mike Bossy, NYI	10
Paul Holmgren, Phi.	10
Bob Bourne, NYI	10

PLAYOFF ASSISTS

Name, Team	A
Ken Linseman, Phi.	18
Bryan Trottier, NYI	17
Bobby Smith, Min.	13
Mike Bossy, NYI	13
Bob Dailey, Phi.	13
Denis Potvin, NYI	13

PLAYOFF POWERPLAY GOALS

Name, Team	PPG
Mike Bossy, NYI	6
Bob Bourne, NYI	5
Tom Lysiak, Chi.	4
Danny Gare, Buf.	4
Bryan Trottier, NYI	4
Denis Potvin, NYI	4
Stefan Persson, NYI	4

PLAYOFF SHORTHAND GOALS

Name, Team	SHG
Bill Barber, Phi.	3
Lorne Henning, NYI	3
Tom Younghans, Min.	2
Bob Bourne, NYI	2
Bryan Trottier, NYI	2

PLAYOFF GAME-WINNING GOALS

Name, Team	GWG
Bill Barber, Phi.	4
Steve Payne, Min.	3
Bob Nystrom, NYI	3
Nine tied with	2

PLAYOFF GOALIE WINS

Name, Team	W
Billy Smith, NYI	15
Pete Peeters, Phi.	8
Bob Sauve, Buf.	6
Phil Myre, Phi.	5
Gilles Meloche, Min.	5

PLAYOFF SHUTOUTS

Name, Team	SO
Bob Sauve, Buf.	2
Michel Larocque, Mtl.	1
Phil Myre, Phi.	1
Don Edwards, Buf.	1
Gilles Meloche, Min.	1
Pete Peeters, Phi.	1
Billy Smith, NYI	1

1980-81

Stanley Cup • New York Islanders

FINAL STANDINGS

PRINCE OF WALES CONFERENCE

Norris Division

Team	GP	W	L	T	GF	GA	PTS
Montreal	80	45	22	13	332	232	103
Los Angeles	80	43	24	13	337	290	99
Pittsburgh	80	30	37	13	302	345	73
Hartford	80	21	41	18	292	372	60
Detroit	80	19	43	18	252	339	56
Adams Division							
Buffalo	80	39	20	21	327	250	99
Boston	80	37	30	13	316	272	87
Minnesota	80	35	28	17	291	263	87
Quebec	80	30	32	18	314	318	78
Toronto	80	28	37	15	322	367	71
CLARENCE CAMPBELL CONFERENCE							
Patrick Division							
NY Islanders	80	48	18	14	355	260	110
Philadelphia	80	41	24	15	313	249	97
Calgary	80	39	27	14	329	298	92
NY Rangers	80	30	36	14	312	317	74
Washington	80	26	36	18	286	317	70
Smythe Division							
St. Louis	80	45	18	17	352	281	107
Chicago	80	31	33	16	304	315	78
Vancouver	80	28	32	20	289	301	76
Edmonton	80	29	35	16	328	327	74
Colorado	80	22	45	13	258	344	57
Winnipeg	80	9	57	14	246	400	32

LEADING SCORERS

Player	Club	GP	G	A	PTS	PIM
Wayne Gretzky	Edmonton	80	55	109	164	28
Marcel Dionne	Los Angeles	80	58	77	135	70
Kent Nilsson	Calgary	80	49	82	131	26
Mike Bossy	NY Islanders	79	68	51	119	32
Dave Taylor	Los Angeles	72	47	65	112	130
Peter Stastny	Quebec	77	39	70	109	37
Charlie Simmer	Los Angeles	65	56	49	105	62
Mike Rogers	Hartford	80	40	65	105	32
Bernie Federko	St. Louis	78	31	73	104	47
Jacques Richard	Quebec	78	52	51	103	39
Rick Middleton	Boston	80	44	59	103	16
Bryan Trottier	NY Islanders	73	31	72	103	74
Dennis Maruk	Washington	80	50	47	97	87
Wilf Paiement	Toronto	77	40	57	97	145
Wayne Babych	St. Louis	78	54	42	96	93
Darryl Sittler	Toronto	80	43	53	96	77
Mike Gartner	Washington	80	48	46	94	100
Bobby Smith	Minnesota	78	29	64	93	73
Rick Kehoe	Pittsburgh	80	55	33	88	6
Blake Dunlop	St. Louis	80	20	67	87	40
Dale McCourt	Detroit	80	30	56	86	50
Danny Gare	Buffalo	73	46	39	85	109
Bill Barber	Philadelphia	80	43	42	85	69
Anton Stastny	Quebec	80	39	46	85	12

LEADING GOALTENDERS

Goaltender	Club	GPI	MINS	GA	SO	AVG
Richard Sevigny	Montreal	33	1777	71	2	2.40
Rick St. Croix	Philadelphia	27	1567	65	2	2.49
Don Edwards	Buffalo	45	2700	133	3	2.96
Pete Peeters	Philadelphia	40	2333	115	2	2.96
Bob Sauve	Buffalo	35	2100	111	2	3.17
Don Beaupre	Minnesota	44	2585	138	0	3.20
Glenn Resch	NYI/Col.	40	2266	121	3	3.20
Reggie Lemelin	Calgary	29	1629	88	2	3.24
Gilles Meloche	Minnesota	38	2215	120	2	3.25
Mario Lessard	Los Angeles	64	3746	203	2	3.25

Mike Liut was a graduate of Bowling Green University who spent two seasons with the Cincinnati Stingers of the World Hockey Association before joining the St. Louis Blues for the 1979–80 season. The following year, he led the Blues to the second-best record in the NHL with 107 points and was runner-up to Wayne Gretzky in voting for the Hart Trophy.

The defending Stanley Cup champion New York Islanders proved to be the best again during the 1980–81 season. The Islanders' 110 points topped both the Patrick Division and the overall NHL standings, just three points ahead of the Smythe Division's surprising St. Louis Blues. The Canadiens were the NHL's third-best team with 103 points, but Montreal was stunned in the first round of the playoffs when the Edmonton Oilers eliminated them in three straight games. The victory was a clear sign that the balance of power in the NHL had shifted from the older, established teams. Edmonton's playoff success continued as they lasted six games in the second round before bowing out against the Islanders.

The Oilers featured a host of talented young players—Glenn Anderson, Jari Kurri, Paul Coffey, Kevin Lowe and Mark Messier—but the undisputed leader was #99, Wayne Gretzky, who began to rewrite the NHL record book this year. He broke Bobby's Orr's single-season assist record by seven with 109, and his 55 goals gave him 164 points, easily breaking Phil Esposito's record of 152. It was the first of seven consecutive Art Ross Trophy wins for Gretzky, and the second of eight straight Hart Trophy selections. The Oilers had a provincial rival this season, as the Atlanta Flames moved north to Calgary.

Swede Czech – Two Europeans (Kent Nilsson and Peter Stastny) were top-ten hits, Gretzky won his first scoring crown, Winnipeg won only nine games and the Isles soared to a second straight Cup title.

Two of Edmonton's fellow WHA refugees did not fare as well in 1980–81. The Hartford Whalers, now without the retired Gordie Howe, fell out of the playoffs, while the Jets suffered through one of the worst season's in hockey history. Winnipeg's 9–57–14 mark was the worst in the NHL since the Washington Capitals went 8–67–5 in 1974–75. The Jets suffered through 30 games without a victory at one point, establishing a new NHL record for futility.

Meanwhile, the Quebec Nordiques unveiled brothers Anton and Peter Stastny this season, with 25-year-old Peter setting a rookie scoring record with 109 points. A third Stastny brother, Marian, would join Quebec in 1981–82. Another new name appeared among the NHL scoring leaders this season, as Calgary's Kent Nilsson placed third with 131 points. The NHL goal-scoring crown went to Mike Bossy of the Islanders, who netted 68 goals and equaled Rocket Richard's legendary feat of 50 goals in 50 games.

After eliminating the Oilers in the quarter-finals, Bossy and the Islanders swept the Rangers to return to the Stanley Cup finals. Their opponents were the upstart Minnesota North Stars, but the Islanders proved too powerful, needing only five games to win their second consecutive Cup title. Bossy, Bryan Trottier and Denis Potvin were the offensive stars, but the determined hustle of Butch Goring was rewarded with the Conn Smythe Trophy.

Undrafted out of junior hockey because of a serious knee injury, Dino Ciccarelli set a rookie record by scoring 14 goals in the 1981 playoffs as Minnesota reached the Stanley Cup finals.

Leaders, 1980-81

GOALS

Name, Team	G
Mike Bossy, NYI	68
Marcel Dionne, L.A.	58
Charlie Simmer, L.A.	56
Wayne Gretzky, Edm.	55
Rick Kehoe, Pit.	55
Wayne Babych, St.L.	54
Jacques Richard, Que.	52
Dennis Maruk, Wsh.	50
Kent Nilsson, Cgy.	49
Mike Gartner, Wsh.	48

ASSISTS

Name, Team	A
Wayne Gretzky, Edm.	109
Kent Nilsson, Cgy.	82
Marcel Dionne, L.A.	77
Bernie Federko, St.L.	73
Bryan Trottier, NYI	72
Peter Stastny, Que.	70
Randy Carlyle, Pit.	67
Blake Dunlop, St.L.	67
Dave Taylor, L.A.	65
Mike Rogers, Hfd.	65

POWERPLAY GOALS

Name, Team	PPG
Mike Bossy, NYI	28
Charlie Simmer, L.A.	23
Marcel Dionne, L.A.	23
Kent Nilsson, Cgy.	20
Rick Kehoe, Pit.	20
Paul Gardner, Pit.	18
Brian Sutter, St.L.	17
Jacques Richard, Que.	16
Rick Middleton, Bos.	16
Dennis Maruk, Wsh.	16
Peter McNab, Bos.	16
Bill Barber, Phi.	16

SHORTHAND GOALS

Name, Team	SHG
Larry Patey, St.L.	8
Bob Bourne, NYI	7
Gerry Minor, Van.	6
Anders Kallur, NYI	6
Don Maloney, NYR	5
Nine tied with	4

GAME-WINNING GOALS

Name, Team	GWG
Mike Bossy, NYI	10
Don Maloney, NYR	9
Charlie Simmer, L.A.	9
Marcel Dionne, L.A.	9
Kent Nilsson, Cgy.	8
Guy Lafleur, Mtl.	7
Tim Kerr, Phi.	7
Danny Gare, Buf.	7
Bobby Smith, Min.	7
Al MacAdam, Min.	7
Wayne Babych, St.L.	7
Rick Middleton, Bos.	7

GOALIE WINS

Name, Team	W
Mario Lessard, L.A.	35
Mike Liut, St.L.	33
Tony Esposito, Chi.	29
Rogie Vachon, Bos.	25
Greg Millen, Pit.	25
Dan Bouchard, Cgy/Que	23
Don Edwards, Buf.	23
Pete Peeters, Phi.	22
Billy Smith, NYI	22
Pat Riggin, Cgy.	21

SHUTOUTS

Name, Team	SO
Glenn Resch, NYI/Col.	3
Don Edwards, Buf.	3
Steve Baker, NYR	2
Rick St. Croix, Phi.	2
Reggie Lemelin, Cgy.	2
Richard Sevigny, Mtl.	2
Bob Sauve, Buf.	2
Gilles Meloche, Min.	2
Pete Peeters, Phi.	2
Billy Smith, NYI	2
Dan Bouchard, Cgy./Que.	2
Mike Palmateer, Wsh.	2
Mario Lessard, L.A.	2

FIRST TEAM ALL-STARS

Name, Team	Position
Wayne Gretzky, Edm.	C
Mike Bossy, NYI	RW
Charlie Simmer, L.A.	LW
Denis Potvin, NYI	D
Randy Carlyle, Pit.	D
Mike Liut, St.L.	G

SECOND TEAM ALL-STARS

Name, Team	Position
Marcel Dionne, L.A.	C
Dave Taylor, L.A.	RW
Bill Barber, Phi.	LW
Larry Robinson, Mtl.	D
Raymond Bourque, Bos.	D
Mario Lessard, L.A.	G

TROPHY WINNERS

Trophy	Awarded For	Winner	Team
Hart	MVP	Wayne Gretzky	Edm.
Art Ross	Top Scorer	Wayne Gretzky	Edm.
Norris	Top Defenseman	Randy Carlyle	Pit
Calder	Top Rookie	Peter Stastny	Que.
Selke	Top Defensive Forward	Bob Gainey	Mtl.
Vezina	Fewest Goals Against	Richard Sevigny	Mtl.
		Denis Herron	Mtl.
		Michel Larocque	Mtl.
Adams	Top Coach	Red Berenson	St.L.
Byng	Gentlemanly Conduct	Rick Kehoe	Pit.
Masterton	Perseverance, Sportmanship	Blake Dunlop	St.L.
Pearson	NHLPA MVP	Mike Liut	St.L.
Conn Smythe	Playoff MVP	Butch Goring	NYI
Patrick	Service to Hockey in U.S.	Charles M. Schulz	
Entry Draft	First Overall Selection	Dale Hawerchuk	Wpg.

NHL NOTEBOOK

TRANSACTIONS

- Oct. 6, 1980 – Vancouver obtained goaltender Richard Brodeur in trade from the NY Islanders.
- Nov. 18, 1980 – Toronto Maple Leafs traded Dave Burrows and Paul Gardner to Pittsburgh for Kim Davis and Paul Marshall.
- Dec. 18, 1980 – Chicago Black Hawks traded Mike O'Connell to Boston in exchange for Al Secord.
- Mar. 10, 1981 – Pittsburgh Penguins acquired Pat Price from the Edmonton Oilers in exchange for Pat Hughes.

RECORDS

- Feb. 22, 1981 – Rookies Peter and Anton Stastny of the Quebec Nordiques scored eight points apiece to set a new rookie record for points in one game as Quebec beat the Capitals 11-7 at Washington.
- Mar. 11, 1981 – Los Angeles' Larry Murphy set a new NHL record for most points by a rookie defenseman. His 66th point (in a 4-4 tie against the Black Hawks) broke the record of 65 set by Raymond Bourque the previous season. Murphy finished the season with 76 points.
- Apr. 1, 1981 – Wayne Gretzky broke Bobby Orr's single-season record for assists with his 103rd and 104th of the season in a 4-4 Oilers tie against the Colorado Rockies. Gretzky finished the season with a new NHL record of 109 assists.
- May 17, 1981 – Minnesota's Dino Ciccarelli set an NHL playoff scoring record for rookies with his 21st point of the playoffs (a goal) in a 7-5 North Stars loss to the Islanders in game three of the Stanley Cup finals.

MILESTONES

- Nov. 2, 1980 – Philadelphia Flyers recorded the 500th win in team history, a 4-2 victory over the visiting Boston Bruins. The win came at a time when no other expansion team had reached the 400-victory plateau.
- Feb. 18, 1981 – 20-year-old Wayne Gretzky became the first player in NHL history to score five career hat tricks before the age of 21 when he had five goals and two assists in a 9-2 Oilers win against St. Louis.
- Mar. 22, 1981 – Jim Rutherford became the first goalie in NHL history to play for three teams in one season when he led the Kings to a 7-5 win over the Jets at Winnipeg. Rutherford started the season with Detroit before being traded to Toronto, and finally L.A.
- May 17, 1981 – Butch Goring became the first player in NHL history to score a playoff hat trick with two teams when he led the Islanders to a 7-5 win over Minnesota North Stars in game three of the Stanley Cup finals. Goring had a previous playoff hat trick with the Kings.

1981 Playoffs

PRELIMINARY ROUND

Apr.	8	Toronto	2	at	NY Islanders	9	
Apr.	9	Toronto	1	at	NY Islanders	5	
Apr.	11	NY Islanders	6	at	Toronto	1	

NY Islanders won best-of-five series 3–0

Apr.	8	Pittsburgh	2	at	St. Louis	4	
Apr.	9	Pittsburgh	6	at	St. Louis	4	
Apr.	11	St. Louis	5	at	Pittsburgh	4	
Apr.	12	St. Louis	3	at	Pittsburgh	6	
Apr.	14	Pittsburgh	3	at	St. Louis	4	2OT

St. Louis won best-of-five series 3–2

Apr.	8	Edmonton	6	at	Montreal	3	
Apr.	9	Edmonton	3	at	Montreal	1	
Apr.	11	Montreal	2	at	Edmonton	6	

Edmonton won best-of-five series 3–0

Apr.	8	NY Rangers	3	at	Los Angeles	1	
Apr.	9	NY Rangers	4	at	Los Angeles	5	
Apr.	11	Los Angeles	3	at	NY Rangers	10	
Apr.	12	Los Angeles	3	at	NY Rangers	6	

NY Rangers won best-of-five series 3–1

Apr.	8	Vancouver	2	at	Buffalo	3	OT
Apr.	9	Vancouver	2	at	Buffalo	5	
Apr.	11	Buffalo	5	at	Vancouver	3	

Buffalo won best-of-five series 3–0

Apr.	8	Quebec	4	at	Philadelphia	6	
Apr.	9	Quebec	5	at	Philadelphia	8	
Apr.	11	Philadelphia	0	at	Quebec	2	
Apr.	12	Philadelphia	3	at	Quebec	4	OT
Apr.	14	Quebec	2	at	Philadelphia	5	

Philadelphia won best-of-five series 3–2

Apr.	8	Chicago	3	at	Calgary	4	
Apr.	9	Chicago	2	at	Calgary	6	
Apr.	11	Calgary	5	at	Chicago	4	2OT

Calgary won best-of-five series 3–0

Apr.	8	Minnesota	5	at	Boston	4	OT
Apr.	9	Minnesota	9	at	Boston	6	
Apr.	11	Boston	3	at	Minnesota	6	

Minnesota won best-of-five series 3–0

QUARTER-FINALS

Apr.	16	Edmonton	2	at	NY Islanders	8	
Apr.	17	Edmonton	3	at	NY Islanders	6	
Apr.	19	NY Islanders	2	at	Edmonton	5	
Apr.	20	NY Islanders	5	at	Edmonton	4	OT
Apr.	22	Edmonton	4	at	NY Islanders	3	
Apr.	24	NY Islanders	5	at	Edmonton	2	

NY Islanders won best-of-seven series 4–2

Apr.	16	NY Rangers	3	at	St. Louis	6	
Apr.	17	NY Rangers	6	at	St. Louis	4	
Apr.	19	St. Louis	3	at	NY Rangers	6	
Apr.	20	St. Louis	1	at	NY Rangers	4	
Apr.	22	NY Rangers	3	at	St. Louis	4	
Apr.	24	St. Louis	4	at	NY Rangers	7	

NY Rangers won best-of-seven series 4–2

Apr.	16	Minnesota	4	at	Buffalo	3	OT
Apr.	17	Minnesota	5	at	Buffalo	2	
Apr.	19	Buffalo	4	at	Minnesota	6	
Apr.	20	Buffalo	5	at	Minnesota	4	OT
Apr.	22	Minnesota	4	at	Buffalo	3	

Minnesota won best-of-seven series 4–1

Apr.	16	Calgary	0	at	Philadelphia	4	
Apr.	17	Calgary	5	at	Philadelphia	4	
Apr.	19	Philadelphia	1	at	Calgary	2	
Apr.	20	Philadelphia	4	at	Calgary	5	
Apr.	22	Calgary	4	at	Philadelphia	9	
Apr.	24	Philadelphia	3	at	Calgary	2	
Apr.	26	Calgary	4	at	Philadelphia	1	

Calgary won best-of-seven series 4–3

SEMI-FINALS

Apr.	28	NY Rangers	2	at	NY Islanders	5
Apr.	30	NY Rangers	3	at	NY Islanders	7
May	2	NY Islanders	5	at	NY Rangers	1
May	5	NY Islanders	5	at	NY Rangers	2

NY Islanders won best-of-seven series 4–0

Apr.	28	Minnesota	4	at	Calgary	1
Apr.	30	Minnesota	2	at	Calgary	3
May	3	Calgary	4	at	Minnesota	6
May	5	Calgary	4	at	Minnesota	7
May	7	Minnesota	1	at	Calgary	3
May	9	Calgary	3	at	Minnesota	5

Minnesota won best-of-seven series 4–2

FINALS

May	12	Minnesota	3	at	NY Islanders	6
May	14	Minnesota	3	at	NY Islanders	6
May	17	NY Islanders	7	at	Minnesota	5
May	19	NY Islanders	2	at	Minnesota	4
May	21	Minnesota	1	at	NY Islanders	5

NY Islanders won best-of-seven series 4–1

1980-81 – New York Islanders – Denis Potvin (Captain), Mike McEwen, Ken Morrow, Gord Lane, Bob Lorimer, Stefan Persson, Dave Langevin, Mike Bossy, Bryan Trottier, Butch Goring, Wayne Merrick, Clark Gillies, John Tonelli, Bob Nystrom, Billy Carroll, Bob Bourne, Hector Marini, Anders Kallur, Duane Sutter, Garry Howatt, Lorne Henning, Billy Smith, Roland Melanson, Al Arbour (Coach), Bill Torrey (General Manager), Jim Devellano (Chief Scout), Ron Waske, Jim Pickard (Trainers).

LEADING PLAYOFF SCORERS

Player	Club	GP	G	A	PTS	PIM
Mike Bossy	NY Islanders	18	17	18	35	4
Steve Payne	Minnesota	19	17	12	29	6
Bryan Trottier	NY Islanders	18	11	18	29	34
Bobby Smith	Minnesota	19	8	17	25	13
Denis Potvin	NY Islanders	18	8	17	25	16
Dino Ciccarelli	Minnesota	19	14	7	21	25
Wayne Gretzky	Edmonton	9	7	14	21	4
Butch Goring	NY Islanders	18	10	10	20	6
Ken Linseman	Philadelphia	12	4	16	20	67
Al MacAdam	Minnesota	19	9	10	19	4

LEADING PLAYOFF GOALTENDERS

Goaltender	Club	GPI	Mins	GA	SO	Avg.
Billy Smith	NY Islanders	17	994	42	0	2.54
Rick St. Croix	Philadelphia	9	541	27	1	2.99
Don Edwards	Buffalo	8	503	28	0	3.34
Gilles Meloche	Minnesota	13	802	47	0	3.52
Pat Riggin	Calgary	11	629	37	0	3.53

PLAYOFF GOALS

Name, Team	G
Mike Bossy, NYI	17
Steve Payne, Min.	17
Dino Ciccarelli, Min.	14
Bill Barber, Phi.	11
Bryan Trottier, NYI	11
Butch Goring, NYI	10

PLAYOFF ASSISTS

Name, Team	A
Mike Bossy, NYI	18
Bryan Trottier, NYI	18
Denis Potvin, NYI	17
Bobby Smith, Min.	17
Ken Linseman, Phi.	16
Four tied with	14

PLAYOFF POWERPLAY GOALS

Name, Team	PPG
Mike Bossy, NYI	9
Denis Potvin, NYI	6
Steve Payne, Min.	6
Willi Plett, Cgy.	5
Ken Houston, Cgy.	5
Steve Christoff, Min.	5
Dino Ciccarelli, Min.	5

PLAYOFF SHORTHAND GOALS

Name, Team	SHG
Bobby Lalonde, Bos.	2
Anders Kallur, NYI	2
Bryan Trottier, NYI	2
Butch Goring, NYI	2
Brad Palmer, Min.	2

PLAYOFF GAME-WINNING GOALS

Name, Team	GWG
Steve Payne, Min.	4
Ken Linseman, Phi.	3
Willi Plett, Cgy.	3
Mike Bossy, NYI	3
Dino Ciccarelli, Min.	3

PLAYOFF GOALIE WINS

Name, Team	W
Billy Smith, NYI	14
Gilles Meloche, Min.	8
Steve Baker, NYR	7
Pat Riggin, Cgy.	6
Andy Moog, Edm.	5
Mike Liut, St.L.	5

PLAYOFF SHUTOUTS

Name, Team	SO
Dan Bouchard, Que.	1
Rick St. Croix, Phi.	1

1981-82

Stanley Cup • New York Islanders

FINAL STANDINGS

CLARENCE CAMPBELL CONFERENCE

Team	GP	W	L	T	GF	GA	PTS
Norris Division							
Minnesota	80	37	23	20	346	288	94
Winnipeg	80	33	33	14	319	332	80
St. Louis	80	32	40	8	315	349	72
Chicago	80	30	38	12	332	363	72
Toronto	80	20	44	16	298	380	56
Detroit	80	21	47	12	270	351	54
Smythe Division							
Edmonton	80	48	17	15	417	295	111
Vancouver	80	30	33	17	290	286	77
Calgary	80	29	34	17	334	345	75
Los Angeles	80	24	41	15	314	369	63
Colorado	80	18	49	13	241	362	49
PRINCE OF WALES CONFERENCE							
Adams Division							
Montreal	80	46	17	17	360	223	109
Boston	80	43	27	10	323	285	96
Buffalo	80	39	26	15	307	273	93
Quebec	80	33	31	16	356	345	82
Hartford	80	21	41	18	264	351	60
Patrick Division							
NY Islanders	80	54	16	10	385	250	118
NY Rangers	80	39	27	14	316	306	92
Philadelphia	80	38	31	11	325	313	87
Pittsburgh	80	31	36	13	310	337	75
Washington	80	26	41	13	319	338	65

LEADING SCORERS

Player	Club	GP	G	A	PTS	PIM
Wayne Gretzky	Edmonton	80	92	120	212	26
Mike Bossy	NY Islanders	80	64	83	147	22
Peter Stastny	Quebec	80	46	93	139	91
Dennis Maruk	Washington	80	60	76	136	128
Bryan Trottier	NY Islanders	80	50	79	129	88
Denis Savard	Chicago	80	32	87	119	82
Marcel Dionne	Los Angeles	78	50	67	117	50
Bobby Smith	Minnesota	80	43	71	114	82
Dino Ciccarelli	Minnesota	76	55	51	106	138
Dave Taylor	Los Angeles	78	39	67	106	130
Glenn Anderson	Edmonton	80	38	67	105	71
Dale Hawerchuk	Winnipeg	80	45	58	103	47
Mike Rogers	NY Rangers	80	38	65	103	43
Neal Broten	Minnesota	73	38	60	98	42
Real Cloutier	Quebec	67	37	60	97	34
Rick Middleton	Boston	75	51	43	94	12
John Tonelli	NY Islanders	80	35	58	93	57
Barry Pederson	Boston	80	44	48	92	53
Morris Lukowich	Winnipeg	77	43	49	92	102
Bernie Federko	St. Louis	74	30	62	92	70
Ken Linseman	Philadelphia	79	24	68	92	275
Blaine Stoughton	Hartford	80	52	39	91	57
Brian Propp	Philadelphia	80	44	47	91	117
Four players tied with					89	

LEADING GOALTENDERS

Goaltender	Club	GPI	MINS	GA	SO	AVG
Denis Herron	Montreal	27	1547	68	3	2.64
Rick Wamsley	Montreal	38	2206	101	2	2.75
Billy Smith	NY Islanders	46	2685	133	0	2.97
Roland Melanson	NY Islanders	36	2115	114	0	3.23
Grant Fuhr	Edmonton	48	2847	157	0	3.31
Richard Brodeur	Vancouver	52	3010	168	2	3.35
Marco Baron	Boston	44	2515	144	1	3.44
Gilles Meloche	Minnesota	51	3026	175	1	3.47
Don Edwards	Buffalo	62	3500	205	0	3.51
Eddie Mio	NY Rangers	25	1500	89	0	3.56

Peter Stastny accepts congratulations from a young Michel Goulet and Gary Lariviere. Brothers Anton and Marian also made an impact in Quebec as the Nordiques improved steadily in the early 1980s, but it was Peter who emerged as an NHL superstar. Only Wayne Gretzky had more points during the decade.

IN JUST THEIR THIRD SEASON in the NHL, the Edmonton Oilers arrived as a powerhouse in 1981–82, winning the Smythe Division with 111 points and finishing second overall to the two-time defending Stanley Cup champion New York Islanders. Wayne Gretzky was the story of the regular season, collecting goals and assists in bunches from the very beginning of the schedule. A year after Mike Bossy had duplicated Rocket Richard's mark of 50 goals in 50 games, Gretzky obliterated this record. His five-goal performance on December 30, 1981, gave him 50 in just 39 games. On February 24, 1982, Gretzky broke Phil Esposito's single-season record with his 77th goal and pushed his total to 92 by season's end. The Great One also broke his own record with 120 assists, giving him an astounding total of 212 points. The Oilers set a new NHL record with 417 goals this year, though none of their other improving young stars managed to join Gretzky in the league's top 10. Edmonton unveiled goalie Grant Fuhr this season and his netminding would soon prove the perfect complement to the team's high-powered offense.

Ravished Records – Gretzky erased Esposito, humbled Howe and obliterated Orr, but when the Oilers were halted in Hollywood, the Islanders stole the show and made it three in a row.

The NHL realigned geographically this year and changed its playoff format to emphasize divisional play. Teams played for division, then conference titles, to determine the two Stanley Cup finalists. The Oilers finished 48 points ahead of fourth-place Los Angeles, but were eliminated by the Kings in the first round of the Smythe Division playoffs. The third game of the best-of-five series saw the Kings rebound from a 5–0 deficit to win in overtime in a game that became known as "The Miracle on Manchester" after the site of the Los Angeles Forum.

There were plenty of other playoff upsets in the Campbell Conference this year, with the Vancouver Canucks (third in the Smythe) and Chicago Black Hawks (fourth in the Norris) advancing to the conference final. In the Prince of Wales Conference, the fourth-place Nordiques eliminated the first-place Montreal Canadiens in "The Battle of Quebec," then beat the Boston Bruins for the Adams Division title. Only in the Patrick Division did things go according to expectations, as the Islanders emerged victorious. The New York club then swept Quebec to return to the Stanley Cup finals against Vancouver.

Game one found the Canucks leading 5–4 with only seven minutes to play before Mike Bossy tied it up and then won it in overtime. Richard Brodeur provided Vancouver with excellent goaltending, which kept the games close, but the Islanders claimed their third straight Stanley Cup title with a series sweep. The Conn Smythe Trophy for playoff MVP went to Bossy, whose 17 postseason goals led all scorers.

A large part of Wayne Gretzky's success stemmed from the fact that no player outworked him in practice. Though much of what he did on the ice looked improvised, Gretzky left very little to chance.

Leaders, 1981-82

GOALS

Name, Team	G
Wayne Gretzky, Edm.	92
Mike Bossy, NYI	64
Dennis Maruk, Wsh.	60
Dino Ciccarelli, Min.	55
Rick Vaive, Tor.	54
Blaine Stoughton, Hfd.	52
Rick Middleton, Bos.	51
Marcel Dionne, L.A.	50
Mark Messier, Edm.	50
Bryan Trottier, NYI	50

ASSISTS

Name, Team	A
Wayne Gretzky, Edm.	120
Peter Stastny, Que.	93
Denis Savard, Chi.	87
Mike Bossy, NYI	83
Bryan Trottier, NYI	79
Dennis Maruk, Wsh.	76
Bobby Smith, Min.	71
Ken Linseman, Phi.	68
Marcel Dionne, L.A.	67
Dave Taylor, L.A.	67
Glenn Anderson, Edm.	67

POWERPLAY GOALS

Name, Team	PPG
Paul Gardner, Pit.	21
Dino Ciccarelli, Min.	20
Dennis Maruk, Wsh.	20
Bobby Smith, Min.	20
Rick Middleton, Bos.	19
Ryan Walter, Wsh.	19
Chris Valentine, Wsh.	18
Wayne Gretzky, Edm.	18
Bryan Trottier, NYI	18
Rick Kehoe, Pit.	17
Marcel Dionne, L.A.	17
Mike Bossy, NYI	17

SHORTHAND GOALS

Name, Team	SHG
Wayne Gretzky, Edm.	6
Michel Goulet, Que.	6
Butch Goring, NYI	5
Rick Vaive, Tor.	5
Bill Gardner, Chi.	4
Larry Patey, St.L.	4
Anders Hakansson, Min.	4
Barry Pederson, Bos.	4
Bill Barber, Phi.	4
14 tied with	3

GAME-WINNING GOALS

Name, Team	GWG
Wayne Gretzky, Edm.	12
Bryan Trottier, NYI	10
Mike Bossy, NYI	10
Rick Middleton, Bos.	9
Glenn Anderson, Edm.	8
Barry Pederson, Bos.	7
Nine tied with	6

GOALIE WINS

Name, Team	W
Billy Smith, NYI	32
Grant Fuhr, Edm.	28
Mike Liut, St.L.	28
Dan Bouchard, Que.	27
Gilles Meloche, Min.	26
Don Edwards, Buf.	26
Michel Dion, Pit.	25
Rick Wamsley, Mtl.	23
Pete Peeters, Phi.	23
Steve Weeks, NYR	23

SHUTOUTS

Name, Team	SO
Denis Herron, Mtl.	3
Rick Wamsley, Mtl.	2
Doug Soetaert, Wpg.	2
Richard Brodeur, Van.	2
Pat Riggin, Cgy.	2
Mario Lessard, L.A.	2
Mike Liut, St.L.	2
13 tied with	1

FIRST TEAM ALL-STARS

Name, Team	Position
Wayne Gretzky, Edm.	C
Mike Bossy, NYI	RW
Mark Messier, Edm.	LW
Doug Wilson, Chi.	D
Raymond Bourque, Bos.	D
Bill Smith, NYI	G

SECOND TEAM ALL-STARS

Name, Team	Position
Bryan Trottier, NYI	C
Rick Middleton, Bos.	RW
John Tonelli, NYI	LW
Paul Coffey, Edm.	D
Brian Engblom, Mtl.	D
Grant Fuhr, Edm.	G

TROPHY WINNERS

Trophy	Awarded For	Winner	Team
Hart	MVP	Wayne Gretzky	Edm.
Art Ross	Top Scorer	Wayne Gretzky	Edm.
Norris	Top Defenseman	Doug Wilson	Chi.
Calder	Top Rookie	Dale Hawerchuk	Wpg.
Selke	Top Defensive Forward	Steve Kasper	Bos.
Vezina	Top Goaltender	Billy Smith	NYI
Jennings	Fewest Goals Against	Rick Wamsley	Mtl.
		Denis Herron	Mtl.
Adams	Top Coach	Tom Watt	Wpg.
Byng	Gentlemanly Conduct	Rick Middleton	Bos.
Masterton	Perseverance, Sportsmanship	Glenn Resch	Col.
Pearson	NHLPA MVP	Wayne Gretzky	Edm.
Conn Smythe	Playoff MVP	Mike Bossy	NYI
Patrick	Service to Hockey in U.S.	Emile P. Francis	
Entry Draft	First Overall Selection	Gord Kluzak	Bos.

NHL NOTEBOOK

TRANSACTIONS

- Nov. 11, 1981 – Flames acquired Mel Bridgeman from Philadelphia in exchange for Brad Marsh.
- Nov. 25, 1981 – Calgary Flames traded Bob MacMillan and Don Lever to the Colorado Rockies in exchange for Lanny McDonald.
- Dec. 2, 1981 – Buffalo Sabres traded Danny Gare, Jim Schoenfeld and Derek Smith to Detroit in exchange for Mike Foligno, Dale McCourt and Brent Peterson.
- Mar. 8, 1982 – Toronto traded Laurie Boschman to Edmonton in exchange for Walt Poddubny.

RECORDS

- Dec. 27, 1981 – In his 38th game of the season, Wayne Gretzky scored a hat trick to record the fastest 100 points in NHL history. It came in a 10-3 Oilers win over the Kings in Edmonton.
- Mar. 28, 1982 – Wayne Gretzky scored his 92nd goal of the season, an NHL record, as the Oilers won 6-2 at Los Angeles.
- Apr. 7, 1982 – Los Angeles and Edmonton set a Stanley Cup playoff record for most goals in a game, with 18, when the Kings beat the Oilers 10-8 in game one of the Smythe Division semi-finals (at Edmonton).
- Apr. 8, 1982 – New York Rangers' Mikko Leinonen set a Stanley Cup playoff record for most assists in one game, with six during a 7-3 win over Philadelphia in game two of the Patrick Division semi-finals.

MILESTONES

- Oct. 10, 1981 – Toronto's Borje Salming became the first European-trained player to score 500 career points, in a 9-8 win over the visiting Chicago Black Hawks.
- Feb. 11, 1982 – NHL history was made when referee Kerry Fraser awarded penalty shots to two Vancouver players in the same period! Thomas Gradin and Ivan Hlinka both scored on Gilles Gilbert in the third period of a 4-4 Canucks tie at Detroit.
- Feb. 15, 1982 – Chicago's Tony Esposito became the first goaltender in NHL history to play 40 (or more) games in 13 straight seasons. The milestone came in a 5-1 Black Hawks loss to Vancouver. Esposito broke the mark set by Tiny Thompson in 1939-40.
- Mar. 25, 1982 – Wayne Gretzky scored two goals and two assists to become the first player in NHL history to score 200 points in a season. The four points gave Gretzky 203 points for the 1981-82 season, and came in a 7-2 Oilers win at Calgary.

1982 Playoffs

DIVISION SEMI-FINALS

Apr.	7	Quebec	1	at	Montreal	5
Apr.	8	Quebec	3	at	Montreal	2
Apr.	10	Montreal	1	at	Quebec	2
Apr.	11	Montreal	6	at	Quebec	2
Apr.	13	Quebec	3	at	Montreal	2 OT

Quebec won best-of-five series 3–2

Apr.	7	Buffalo	1	at	Boston	3
Apr.	8	Buffalo	3	at	Boston	7
Apr.	10	Boston	2	at	Buffalo	5
Apr.	11	Boston	5	at	Buffalo	2

Boston won best-of-five series 3–1

Apr.	7	Chicago	3	at	Minnesota	2 OT
Apr.	8	Chicago	5	at	Minnesota	3
Apr.	10	Minnesota	7	at	Chicago	1
Apr.	11	Minnesota	2	at	Chicago	5

Chicago won best-of-five series 3–1

Apr.	7	St. Louis	4	at	Winnipeg	3
Apr.	8	St. Louis	2	at	Winnipeg	5
Apr.	10	Winnipeg	3	at	St. Louis	6
Apr.	11	Winnipeg	2	at	St. Louis	8

St. Louis won best-of-five series 3–1

Apr.	7	Pittsburgh	1	at	NY Islanders	8
Apr.	8	Pittsburgh	2	at	NY Islanders	7
Apr.	10	NY Islanders	1	at	Pittsburgh	2 OT
Apr.	11	NY Islanders	2	at	Pittsburgh	5
Apr.	13	Pittsburgh	3	at	NY Islanders	4 OT

NY Islanders won best-of-five series 3–2

Apr.	7	Philadelphia	4	at	NY Rangers	1
Apr.	8	Philadelphia	3	at	NY Rangers	7
Apr.	10	NY Rangers	4	at	Philadelphia	3
Apr.	11	NY Rangers	7	at	Philadelphia	5

NY Rangers won best-of-five series 3–1

Apr.	7	Los Angeles	10	at	Edmonton	8
Apr.	8	Los Angeles	2	at	Edmonton	3 OT
Apr.	10	Edmonton	5	at	Los Angeles	6 OT
Apr.	12	Edmonton	3	at	Los Angeles	2
Apr.	13	Los Angeles	7	at	Edmonton	4

Los Angeles won best-of-five series 3–2

Apr.	7	Calgary	3	at	Vancouver	5
Apr.	8	Calgary	1	at	Vancouver	2 OT
Apr.	10	Vancouver	3	at	Calgary	1

Vancouver won best-of-five series 3–0

DIVISION FINALS

Apr.	15	Quebec	3	at	Boston	4
Apr.	16	Quebec	4	at	Boston	8
Apr.	18	Boston	2	at	Quebec	3 OT
Apr.	19	Boston	2	at	Quebec	7
Apr.	21	Quebec	4	at	Boston	3
Apr.	23	Boston	6	at	Quebec	5 OT
Apr.	25	Quebec	2	at	Boston	1

Quebec won best-of-seven series 4–3

Apr.	15	Chicago	5	at	St. Louis	4
Apr.	16	Chicago	1	at	St. Louis	3
Apr.	18	St. Louis	5	at	Chicago	6
Apr.	19	St. Louis	4	at	Chicago	7
Apr.	21	Chicago	2	at	St. Louis	3 OT
Apr.	23	St. Louis	0	at	Chicago	2

Chicago won best-of-seven series 4–2

Apr.	15	NY Rangers	5	at	NY Islanders	4
Apr.	16	NY Rangers	2	at	NY Islanders	7
Apr.	18	NY Islanders	4	at	NY Rangers	3 OT
Apr.	19	NY Islanders	5	at	NY Rangers	3
Apr.	21	NY Rangers	4	at	NY Islanders	2
Apr.	23	NY Islanders	5	at	NY Rangers	3

NY Islanders won best-of-seven series 4–2

Apr.	15	Los Angeles	2	at	Vancouver	3
Apr.	16	Los Angeles	3	at	Vancouver	2 OT
Apr.	18	Vancouver	4	at	Los Angeles	3 OT
Apr.	19	Vancouver	5	at	Los Angeles	4
Apr.	21	Los Angeles	2	at	Vancouver	5

Vancouver won best-of-seven series 4–1

CONFERENCE FINALS

Apr.	27	Quebec	1	at	NY Islanders	4
Apr.	29	Quebec	2	at	NY Islanders	5
May	1	NY Islanders	5	at	Quebec	4 OT
May	4	NY Islanders	4	at	Quebec	2

NY Islanders won best-of-seven series 4–0

Apr.	27	Vancouver	2	at	Chicago	1 2OT
Apr.	29	Vancouver	1	at	Chicago	4
May	1	Chicago	3	at	Vancouver	4
May	4	Chicago	3	at	Vancouver	5
May	6	Vancouver	6	at	Chicago	2

Vancouver won best-of-seven series 4–1

FINALS

May	8	Vancouver	5	at	NY Islanders	6 OT
May	11	Vancouver	4	at	NY Islanders	6
May	13	NY Islanders	3	at	Vancouver	0
May	16	NY Islanders	3	at	Vancouver	1

NY Islanders won best-of-seven series 4–0

1981-82 – New York Islanders – Mike Bossy, Bob Bourne, Billy Carroll, Butch Goring, Greg Gilbert, Clark Gillies, Tomas Jonsson, Anders Kallur, Gord Lane, Dave Langevin, Hector Marini, Mike McEwen, Roland Melanson, Wayne Merrick, Ken Morrow, Bob Nystrom, Stefan Persson, Denis Potvin (Captain), Billy Smith, Brent Sutter, Duane Sutter, John Tonelli, Bryan Trottier, Al Arbour (Coach), Lorne Henning (Assisant Coach), Bill Torrey (General Manager), Jim Devellano (Assistant General Manager/Director of Scouting), Ron Waske, Jim Pickard (Trainers).

LEADING PLAYOFF SCORERS

Player	Club	GP	G	A	PTS	PIM
Bryan Trottier	NY Islanders	19	6	23	29	40
Mike Bossy	NY Islanders	19	17	10	27	0
Denis Potvin	NY Islanders	19	5	16	21	30
Thomas Gradin	Vancouver	17	9	10	19	10
Denis Savard	Chicago	15	11	7	18	52
Stan Smyl	Vancouver	17	9	9	18	25
Barry Pederson	Boston	11	7	11	18	2
Joe Mullen	St. Louis	10	7	11	18	4
Peter Stastny	Quebec	12	7	11	18	10
Bernie Federko	St. Louis	10	3	15	18	10

LEADING PLAYOFF GOALTENDERS

Goaltender	Club	GPI	Mins	GA	SO	Avg.
Billy Smith	NY Islanders	18	1120	47	1	2.52
Richard Brodeur	Vancouver	17	1089	49	0	2.70
Mike Liut	St. Louis	10	494	27	0	3.28
Dan Bouchard	Quebec	11	677	38	0	3.37
Mike Moffat	Boston	11	663	38	0	3.44

PLAYOFF GOALS

Name, Team	G
Mike Bossy, NYI	17
Denis Savard, Chi.	11
Thomas Gradin, Van.	9
Stan Smyl, Van.	9
Bob Bourne, NYI	9
Brian Sutter, St.L.	8
Michel Goulet, Que.	8
Ivan Boldirev, Van.	8
Clark Gillies, NYI	8

PLAYOFF ASSISTS

Name, Team	A
Bryan Trottier, NYI	23
Denis Potvin, NYI	16
Bernie Federko, St.L.	15
Stefan Persson, NYI	14
Marian Stastny, Que.	14
Joe Mullen, St.L.	11
Barry Pederson, Bos.	11
Peter Stastny, Que.	11
Five tied with	10

PLAYOFF POWERPLAY GOALS

Name, Team	PPG
Mike Bossy, NYI	6
Denis Savard, Chi.	5
Marcel Dionne, L.A.	4
Robbie Ftorek, NYR	4
Peter Stastny, Que.	4
Thomas Gradin, Van.	4
Clark Gillies, NYI	4

PLAYOFF SHORTHAND GOALS

Name, Team	SHG
Michel Goulet, Que.	2
Billy Carroll, NYI	2
12 tied with	1

PLAYOFF GAME-WINNING GOALS

Name, Team	GWG
Mike Bossy, NYI	3
Clark Gillies, NYI	3
Nine tied with	2

PLAYOFF GOALIE WINS

Name, Team	W
Billy Smith, NYI	15
Richard Brodeur, Van.	11
Mike Moffat, Bos.	6
Mike Liut, St.L.	5
Murray Bannerman, Chi.	5

PLAYOFF SHUTOUTS

Name, Team	SO
Tony Esposito, Chi.	1
Billy Smith, NYI	1

1982-83

Stanley Cup • New York Islanders

FINAL STANDINGS

CLARENCE CAMPBELL CONFERENCE

Team	GP	W	L	T	GF	GA	PTS
Norris Division							
Chicago	80	47	23	10	338	268	104
Minnesota	80	40	24	16	321	290	96
Toronto	80	28	40	12	293	330	68
St. Louis	80	25	40	15	285	316	65
Detroit	80	21	44	15	263	344	57
Smythe Division							
Edmonton	80	47	21	12	424	315	106
Calgary	80	32	34	14	321	317	78
Vancouver	80	30	35	15	303	309	75
Winnipeg	80	33	39	8	311	333	74
Los Angeles	80	27	41	12	308	365	66
PRINCE OF WALES CONFERENCE							
Adams Division							
Boston	80	50	20	10	327	228	110
Montreal	80	42	24	14	350	286	98
Buffalo	80	38	29	13	318	285	89
Quebec	80	34	34	12	343	336	80
Hartford	80	19	54	7	261	403	45
Patrick Division							
Philadelphia	80	49	23	8	326	240	106
NY Islanders	80	42	26	12	302	226	96
Washington	80	39	25	16	306	283	94
NY Rangers	80	35	35	10	306	287	80
New Jersey	80	17	49	14	230	338	48
Pittsburgh	80	18	53	9	257	394	45

LEADING SCORERS

Player	Club	GP	G	A	PTS	PIM
Wayne Gretzky	Edmonton	80	71	125	196	59
Peter Stastny	Quebec	75	47	77	124	78
Denis Savard	Chicago	78	35	86	121	99
Mike Bossy	NY Islanders	79	60	58	118	20
Marcel Dionne	Los Angeles	80	56	51	107	22
Barry Pederson	Boston	77	46	61	107	47
Mark Messier	Edmonton	77	48	58	106	72
Michel Goulet	Quebec	80	57	48	105	51
Glenn Anderson	Edmonton	72	48	56	104	70
Kent Nilsson	Calgary	80	46	58	104	10
Jari Kurri	Edmonton	80	45	59	104	22
Lanny McDonald	Calgary	80	66	32	98	90
Rick Middleton	Boston	80	49	47	96	8
Paul Coffey	Edmonton	80	29	67	96	87
Anton Stastny	Quebec	79	32	60	92	25
Dale Hawerchuk	Winnipeg	79	40	51	91	31
Steve Larmer	Chicago	80	43	47	90	28
Ron Francis	Hartford	79	31	59	90	60
Bryan Trottier	NY Islanders	80	34	55	89	68
Stan Smyl	Vancouver	74	38	50	88	114
Al Secord	Chicago	80	54	32	86	180
Thomas Gradin	Vancouver	80	32	54	86	61
John Ogrodnick	Detroit	80	41	44	85	30
Bobby Clarke	Philadelphia	80	23	62	85	115

LEADING GOALTENDERS

Goaltender	Club	GPI	MINS	GA	SO	AVG
Pete Peeters	Boston	62	3611	142	8	2.36
Bob Froese	Philadelphia	25	1407	59	4	2.52
Roland Melanson	NY Islanders	44	2460	109	1	2.66
Billy Smith	NY Islanders	41	2340	112	1	2.87
Pelle Lindbergh	Philadelphia	40	2333	116	3	2.98
Murray Bannerman	Chicago	41	2460	127	4	3.10
Pat Riggin	Washington	38	2161	121	0	3.36
Al Jensen	Washington	40	2358	135	1	3.44
Richard Sevigny	Montreal	38	2130	122	1	3.44
Eddie Mio	NY Rangers	41	2365	136	2	3.45

Denis Savard was a high-scoring junior star in Montreal who was passed over by the Canadiens for Doug Wickenheiser as the top choice in the 1980 Entry Draft. Savard was selected third overall by Chicago, and went on to become one of the top offensive stars in the NHL, finishing among the top 10 in scoring five times.

THE BOSTON BRUINS returned to the top of the NHL standings for the first time since 1973–74 with 110 points. Barry Pederson's 46 goals and 61 assists placed him among the NHL's top 10 in scoring and Rick Middleton's 49 goals led the team, but defense was the key to the Bruins' success. Raymond Bourque was named to the Second All-Star Team—the fourth all-star selection of his four-year career—while Pete Peeters earned the Vezina Trophy with 40 wins and a 2.36 goals-against average. His eight shutouts this season would prove to be the best single-season total of the 1980s. A sad note in Boston this season was the brain hemorrhage suffered by second-year wing Normand Leveille. He survived the illness, but his hockey career was over.

Class Dismissed – The Oilers, led by Gretzky, Messier and Jari Kurri were the NHL's top students but they failed their finals exam because of the class and commitment of the Islanders.

The three-time defending Stanley Cup champions, the New York Islanders, started the season slowly, but came on strong. Still, they wound up in second place in the Patrick Division behind the Philadelphia Flyers. (The Patrick Division included a new team this year, as the Colorado Rockies had become the New Jersey Devils.) In the playoffs, Philadelphia lost to the New York Rangers in the first round, while the Islanders beat the Washington Capitals and then the Rangers to set up a Wales Conference showdown with Boston. The Bruins had defeated the Quebec Nordiques and Buffalo Sabres, but after a six-game conference final, the Islanders were headed back to the Stanley Cup finals for the fourth year in a row.

In the Campbell Conference, the Chicago Black Hawks enjoyed an excellent season. Denis Savard finished third in the league with 121 points, Al Secord scored 54 goals, and rookie of the year Steve Larmer notched 43. Chicago topped the Norris Division with 104 points and beat the St. Louis Blues and Minnesota North Stars in the playoffs before falling to the Edmonton Oilers in the conference final.

After the playoff disappointment of the previous season, the Oilers had rebounded. Although Wayne Gretzky "slumped" to 71 goals, his 125 assists were a new league high and his 196 points were 72 more than runner-up Peter Stastny—the widest gap ever between first and second place in the scoring derby. Gretzky's teammates Mark Messier, Glenn Anderson and Jari Kurri each collected at least 40 goals and 100 points and joined him among the top 10 scorers this season as the Oilers broke their own league record with 424 goals.

The Stanley Cup finals between the Oilers and Islanders was much anticipated, but the high-flying newcomers did not yet have the experience necessary to better the defending champions. The Islanders kept Gretzky off the scoresheet and held the Oilers to just six goals as they won their fourth consecutive

Mike Bossy scored 60 goals or more five times in his career (a mark equaled only by Wayne Gretzky). His career goals-per-game ratio of .762 (573 goals in 752 games) trails only Mario Lemieux's mark of .776 entering the 2003–04 season.

Leaders, 1982-83

GOALS

Name, Team	G
Wayne Gretzky, Edm.	71
Lanny McDonald, Cgy.	66
Mike Bossy, NYI	60
Michel Goulet, Que.	57
Marcel Dionne, L.A.	56
Al Secord, Chi.	54
Rick Vaive, Tor.	51
Rick Middleton, Bos.	49
Glenn Anderson, Edm.	48
Mark Messier, Edm.	48

ASSISTS

Name, Team	A
Wayne Gretzky, Edm.	125
Denis Savard, Chi.	86
Peter Stastny, Que.	77
Paul Coffey, Edm.	67
Bobby Clarke, Phi.	62
Barry Pederson, Bos.	61
Dave Babych, Wpg.	61
Bernie Federko, St.L.	60
Anton Stastny, Que.	60
Ron Francis, Hfd.	59
Jari Kurri, Edm.	59
Guy Chouinard, Cgy.	59

POWERPLAY GOALS

Name, Team	PPG
Paul Gardner, Pit.	20
Al Secord, Chi.	20
Mike Bossy, NYI	19
Rick Vaive, Tor.	18
Wayne Gretzky, Edm.	18
Marcel Dionne, L.A.	17
Lanny McDonald, Cgy.	17
Kent Nilsson, Cgy.	16
Stan Smyl, Van.	15
Rick Kehoe, Pit.	15
Barry Pederson, Bos.	15
Brian Bellows, Min.	15
Paul MacLean, Wpg.	15

SHORTHAND GOALS

Name, Team	SHG
Wayne Gretzky, Edm.	6
Mike Rogers, NYR	5
Mike Murphy, L.A.	5
Butch Goring, NYI	5
Mike Eaves, Min.	5
Mark Howe, Phi.	5
Guy Carbonneau, Mtl.	5
Pat Hughes, Edm.	5
Ken Linseman, Edm.	4
Kent Nilsson, Cgy.	4
Michel Goulet, Que.	4

GAME-WINNING GOALS

Name, Team	GWG
Brian Propp, Phi.	12
Glenn Anderson, Edm.	10
Barry Pederson, Bos.	10
Wayne Gretzky, Edm.	9
Steve Larmer, Chi.	9
Blaine Stoughton, Hfd.	8
Rick Vaive, Tor.	8
Mike Bossy, NYI	8
Lanny McDonald, Cgy.	8
Darryl Sittler, Phi.	8

GOALIE WINS

Name, Team	W
Pete Peeters, Bos.	40
Andy Moog, Edm.	33
Rick Wamsley, Mtl.	27
Bob Sauve, Buf.	25
Murray Bannerman, Chi.	24
Roland Melanson, NYI	24
Tony Esposito, Chi.	23
Pelle Lindbergh, Phi.	23
Al Jensen, Wsh.	22
Mike Palmateer, Tor.	21
Richard Brodeur, Van.	21
Mike Liut, St.L.	21

SHUTOUTS

Name, Team	SO
Pete Peeters, Bos.	8
Bob Froese, Phi.	4
Murray Bannerman, Chi.	4
Pelle Lindbergh, Phi.	3
Three tied with	2

SAVE PERCENTAGE

Name, Team	SV%
Roland Melanson, NYI	.910
Billy Smith, NYI	.906
Pete Peeters, Bos.	.904
Murray Bannerman, Chi.	.901
Bob Froese, Phi.	.896

FIRST TEAM ALL-STARS

Name, Team	Position
Peter Stastny, Que.	C
Marian Stastny, Que.	RW
Ryan Walter, Mtl.	LW
Denis Potvin, NYI	D
Mark Howe, Phi.	D
Pete Peeters, Bos.	G

SECOND TEAM ALL-STARS

Name, Team	Position
Barry Pederson, Bos.	C
Mike Bossy, NYI	RW
Michel Goulet, Que.	LW
Rod Langway, Wsh.	D
Raymond Bourque, Bos.	D
Pelle Lindbergh, Phi.	G

ALL-ROOKIE TEAM

Name, Team	Position
Dan Daoust, Mtl./Tor.	C
Steve Larmer, Chi.	RW
Mats Naslund, Mtl.	LW
Scott Stevens, Wsh.	D
Phil Housley, Buf.	D
Pelle Lindbergh, Phi.	G

TROPHY WINNERS

Trophy	Awarded For	Winner	Team
Hart	MVP	Wayne Gretzky	Edm.
Art Ross	Top Scorer	Wayne Gretzky	Edm.
Norris	Top Defenseman	Rod Langway	Wsh
Calder	Top Rookie	Steve Larmer	Chi.
Selke	Top Defensive Forward	Bobby Clarke	Phi.
Vezina	Top Goaltender	Pete Peeters	Bos.
Jennings	Fewest Goals Against	Rollie Melanson	NYI
		Billy Smith	NYI
Adams	Top Coach	Orval Tessier	Chi.
Byng	Gentlemanly Conduct	Mike Bossy	NYI
Masterton	Perseverance, Sportmanship	Lanny McDonald	Cgy.
Pearson	NHLPA MVP	Wayne Gretzky	Edm.
Conn Smythe	Playoff MVP	Billy Smith	NYI
Patrick	Service to Hockey in U.S.	Bill Torrey	
Entry Draft	First Overall Selection	Brian Lawton	Min.

NHL NOTEBOOK

TRANSACTIONS

- July 30, 1982 – Pittsburgh Penguins signed Marty McSorley as a free agent.
- Sept. 9, 1982 – Montreal traded Rod Langway, Doug Jarvis, Craig Laughlin and Brian Engblom to Washington in exchange for Ryan Walter and Rick Green.
- Jan. 6, 1983 – Chicago traded Curt Fraser to Vancouver for Tony Tanti.
- Mar. 8, 1983 – Philadelphia Flyers signed free agent Dave Poulin after his career at Notre Dame and one season in Sweden.

RECORDS

- Jan. 11, 1983 – Edmonton's Pat Hughes became the first player to break a Gretzky record when he set an NHL record for fastest two short-handed goals (25 seconds) during a 7-5 win at St. Louis.
- Feb. 8, 1983 – Wayne Gretzky set an All-Star Game record with four goals (all in the third period) as the Campbell Conference All-Stars defeated the Wales 9-3 at Nassau Coliseum. Gretzky won the MVP honors.
- Feb. 10, 1983 – Buffalo's Craig Ramsay played in his 776th straight game with the Sabres – an NHL record for most consecutive games with one team. But he broke a bone in his foot that night and missed the next game.
- Apr. 17, 1983 – Wayne Gretzky set a playoff record for most points in a game with seven (on four goals and three assists) in a 10-2 Oilers win at Calgary.

MILESTONES

- Sept. 9, 1982 – Washington coach Bryan Murray named younger brother Terry as his assistant, making it the first time in NHL history that a brother combination coached the same team at the same time.
- Apr. 2, 1983 – New York Islanders' Mike Bossy scored a third-period goal to become the first player in NHL history to get 60 or more goals for three straight seasons. The Islanders beat Pittsburgh 6-1.
- Apr. 14, 1983 – For the first time in NHL playoff history players from both teams scored hat tricks when Mark Messier's four goals led the Oilers to a 6-3 win over Calgary despite three goals from Flames defenseman Paul Reinhart.
- Apr. 22, 1983 – Islanders beat the Rangers 5-2 in game six of the Patrick Division finals in Manhattan to win their 14th consecutive playoff series, an NHL record. (They ran the streak to 19 straight series wins before losing to Edmonton in the 1984 finals).

1983 Playoffs

DIVISION SEMI-FINALS

Apr.	5	Quebec	3	at	Boston	4 OT
Apr.	7	Quebec	2	at	Boston	4
Apr.	9	Boston	1	at	Quebec	2
Apr.	10	Boston	2	at	Quebec	1

Boston won best-of-five series 3–1

Apr.	6	Buffalo	1	at	Montreal	0
Apr.	7	Buffalo	3	at	Montreal	0
Apr.	9	Montreal	2	at	Buffalo	4

Buffalo won best-of-five series 3–0

Apr.	5	NY Rangers	5	at	Philadelphia	3
Apr.	7	NY Rangers	4	at	Philadelphia	3
Apr.	9	Philadelphia	3	at	NY Rangers	9

NY Rangers won best-of-five series 3–0

Apr.	6	Washington	2	at	NY Islanders	5
Apr.	7	Washington	4	at	NY Islanders	2
Apr.	9	NY Islanders	6	at	Washington	2
Apr.	10	NY Islanders	6	at	Washington	3

NY Islanders won best-of-five series 3–1

Apr.	6	St. Louis	4	at	Chicago	2
Apr.	7	St. Louis	2	at	Chicago	7
Apr.	9	Chicago	2	at	St. Louis	1
Apr.	10	Chicago	5	at	St. Louis	3

Chicago won best-of-five series 3–1

Apr.	6	Toronto	4	at	Minnesota	5
Apr.	7	Toronto	4	at	Minnesota	5 OT
Apr.	9	Minnesota	3	at	Toronto	6
Apr.	10	Minnesota	5	at	Toronto	4 OT

Minnesota won best-of-five series 3–1

Apr.	6	Winnipeg	3	at	Edmonton	6
Apr.	7	Winnipeg	3	at	Edmonton	4
Apr.	9	Edmonton	4	at	Winnipeg	3

Edmonton won best-of-five series 3–0

Apr.	6	Vancouver	3	at	Calgary	4 OT
Apr.	7	Vancouver	3	at	Calgary	5
Apr.	9	Calgary	4	at	Vancouver	5
Apr.	10	Calgary	4	at	Vancouver	3 OT

Calgary won best-of-five series 3–1

DIVISION FINALS

Apr.	14	Buffalo	7	at	Boston	4
Apr.	15	Buffalo	3	at	Boston	5
Apr.	17	Boston	3	at	Buffalo	4
Apr.	18	Boston	6	at	Buffalo	2
Apr.	20	Buffalo	0	at	Boston	9
Apr.	22	Boston	3	at	Buffalo	5
Apr.	24	Buffalo	2	at	Boston	3 OT

Boston won best-of-seven series 4–3

Apr.	14	NY Rangers	1	at	NY Islanders	4
Apr.	15	NY Rangers	0	at	NY Islanders	5
Apr.	17	NY Islanders	6	at	NY Rangers	7
Apr.	18	NY Islanders	1	at	NY Rangers	3
Apr.	20	NY Rangers	2	at	NY Islanders	7
Apr.	22	NY Islanders	5	at	NY Rangers	2

NY Islanders won best-of-seven series 4–2

Apr.	14	Minnesota	2	at	Chicago	5
Apr.	15	Minnesota	4	at	Chicago	7
Apr.	17	Chicago	1	at	Minnesota	5
Apr.	18	Chicago	4	at	Minnesota	3 OT
Apr.	20	Minnesota	2	at	Chicago	5

Chicago won best-of-seven series 4–1

Apr.	14	Calgary	3	at	Edmonton	6
Apr.	15	Calgary	1	at	Edmonton	5
Apr.	17	Edmonton	10	at	Calgary	2
Apr.	18	Edmonton	5	at	Calgary	6
Apr.	20	Calgary	1	at	Edmonton	9

Edmonton won best-of-seven series 4–1

CONFERENCE FINALS

Apr.	26	NY Islanders	5	at	Boston	2
Apr.	28	NY Islanders	1	at	Boston	4
Apr.	30	Boston	3	at	NY Islanders	7
May	3	Boston	3	at	NY Islanders	8
May	5	NY Islanders	1	at	Boston	5
May	7	Boston	4	at	NY Islanders	8

NY Islanders won best-of-seven series 4–2

Apr.	24	Chicago	4	at	Edmonton	8
Apr.	26	Chicago	2	at	Edmonton	8
May	1	Edmonton	3	at	Chicago	2
May	3	Edmonton	6	at	Chicago	3

Edmonton won best-of-seven series 4–0

FINALS

May	10	NY Islanders	2	at	Edmonton	0
May	12	NY Islanders	6	at	Edmonton	3
May	14	Edmonton	1	at	NY Islanders	5
May	17	Edmonton	2	at	NY Islanders	4

NY Islanders won best-of-seven series 4–0

1982-83 – New York Islanders – Mike Bossy, Bob Bourne, Paul Boutilier, Billy Carroll, Greg Gilbert, Clark Gillies, Butch Goring, Mats Hallin, Tomas Jonsson, Anders Kallur, Gord Lane, Dave Langevin, Mike McEwen, Roland Melanson, Wayne Merrick, Ken Morrow, Bob Nystrom, Stefan Persson, Denis Potvin (Captain), Billy Smith, Brent Sutter, Duane Sutter, John Tonelli, Bryan Trottier, Al Arbour (Coach), Lorne Henning (Assistant Coach), Bill Torrey (General Manager), Ron Waske, Jim Pickard (Trainers).

LEADING PLAYOFF SCORERS

Player	Club	GP	G	A	PTS	PIM
Wayne Gretzky	Edmonton	16	12	26	38	4
Rick Middleton	Boston	17	11	22	33	6
Barry Pederson	Boston	17	14	18	32	21
Bob Bourne	NY Islanders	20	8	20	28	14
Mike Bossy	NY Islanders	19	17	9	26	10
Raymond Bourque	Boston	17	8	15	23	10
Jari Kurri	Edmonton	16	8	15	23	8
Mark Messier	Edmonton	15	15	6	21	14
Brent Sutter	NY Islanders	20	10	11	21	26
Duane Sutter	NY Islanders	20	9	12	21	43

LEADING PLAYOFF GOALTENDERS

Goaltender	Club	GPI	Mins	GA	SO	Avg.
Roland Melanson	NY Islanders	5	238	10	0	2.52
Billy Smith	NY Islanders	17	962	43	2	2.68
Andy Moog	Edmonton	16	949	48	0	3.03
Bob Sauve	Buffalo	10	545	28	2	3.08
Pete Peeters	Boston	17	1024	61	1	3.57

PLAYOFF GOALS

Name, Team	G
Mike Bossy, NYI	17
Mark Messier, Edm.	15
Barry Pederson, Bos.	14
Wayne Gretzky, Edm.	12
Rick Middleton, Bos.	11
Glenn Anderson, Edm.	10
Brent Sutter, NYI	10

PLAYOFF ASSISTS

Name, Team	A
Wayne Gretzky, Edm.	26
Rick Middleton, Bos.	22
Bob Bourne, NYI	20
Barry Pederson, Bos.	18
Jari Kurri, Edm.	15
Raymond Bourque, Bos.	15
Bryan Trottier, NYI	12
Duane Sutter, NYI	12
Denis Potvin, NYI	12
Anders Kallur, NYI	12

PLAYOFF POWERPLAY GOALS

Name, Team	PPG
Mike Bossy, NYI	6
Paul Reinhart, Cgy.	4
Mark Messier, Edm.	4
Rick Middleton, Bos.	4
Denis Potvin, NYI	4

PLAYOFF SHORTHAND GOALS

Name, Team	SHG
Wayne Gretzky, Edm.	3
Mark Messier, Edm.	2
Jari Kurri, Edm.	2
Paul Coffey, Edm.	2
14 tied with	1

PLAYOFF GAME-WINNING GOALS

Name, Team	GWG
Mike Bossy, NYI	5
Wayne Gretzky, Edm.	3
10 tied with	2

PLAYOFF GOALIE WINS

Name, Team	W
Billy Smith, NYI	13
Andy Moog, Edm.	11
Pete Peeters, Bos.	9
Bob Sauve, Buf.	6
Eddie Mio, NYR	5

PLAYOFF SHUTOUTS

Name, Team	SO
Bob Sauve, Buf.	2
Billy Smith, NYI	2
Pete Peeters, Bos.	1

1983-84

Stanley Cup • Edmonton Oilers

FINAL STANDINGS

CLARENCE CAMPBELL CONFERENCE

Norris Division

Team	GP	W	L	T	GF	GA	PTS
Minnesota	80	39	31	10	345	344	88
St. Louis	80	32	41	7	293	316	71
Detroit	80	31	42	7	298	323	69
Chicago	80	30	42	8	277	311	68
Toronto	80	26	45	9	303	387	61
Smythe Division							
Edmonton	80	57	18	5	446	314	119
Calgary	80	34	32	14	311	314	82
Vancouver	80	32	39	9	306	328	73
Winnipeg	80	31	38	11	340	374	73
Los Angeles	80	23	44	13	309	376	59
PRINCE OF WALES CONFERENCE							
Adams Division							
Boston	80	49	25	6	336	261	104
Buffalo	80	48	25	7	315	257	103
Quebec	80	42	28	10	360	278	94
Montreal	80	35	40	5	286	295	75
Hartford	80	28	42	10	288	320	66
Patrick Division							
NY Islanders	80	50	26	4	357	269	104
Washington	80	48	27	5	308	226	101
Philadelphia	80	44	26	10	350	290	98
NY Rangers	80	42	29	9	314	304	93
New Jersey	80	17	56	7	231	350	41
Pittsburgh	80	16	58	6	254	390	38

LEADING SCORERS

Player	Club	GP	G	A	PTS	PIM
Wayne Gretzky	Edmonton	74	87	118	205	39
Paul Coffey	Edmonton	80	40	86	126	104
Michel Goulet	Quebec	75	56	65	121	76
Peter Stastny	Quebec	80	46	73	119	73
Mike Bossy	NY Islanders	67	51	67	118	8
Barry Pederson	Boston	80	39	77	116	64
Jari Kurri	Edmonton	64	52	61	113	14
Bryan Trottier	NY Islanders	68	40	71	111	59
Bernie Federko	St. Louis	79	41	66	107	43
Rick Middleton	Boston	80	47	58	105	14
Dale Hawerchuk	Winnipeg	80	37	65	102	73
Mark Messier	Edmonton	73	37	64	101	165
Glenn Anderson	Edmonton	80	54	45	99	65
Raymond Bourque	Boston	78	31	65	96	57
Bernie Nicholls	Los Angeles	78	41	54	95	83
Denis Savard	Chicago	75	37	57	94	71
Tim Kerr	Philadelphia	79	54	39	93	29
Rick Vaive	Toronto	76	52	41	93	114
Mike Bullard	Pittsburgh	76	51	41	92	57
Charlie Simmer	Los Angeles	79	44	48	92	78
Brian Propp	Philadelphia	79	39	53	92	37
Marcel Dionne	Los Angeles	66	39	53	92	28
Patrik Sundstrom	Vancouver	78	38	53	91	37
Gilbert Perreault	Buffalo	73	31	59	90	32

LEADING GOALTENDERS

Goaltender	Club	GPI	MINS	GA	SO	AVG
Pat Riggin	Washington	41	2299	102	4	2.66
Tom Barrasso	Buffalo	42	2475	117	2	2.84
Al Jensen	Washington	43	2414	117	4	2.91
Doug Keans	Boston	33	1779	92	2	3.10
Bob Froese	Philadelphia	48	2863	150	2	3.14
Pete Peeters	Boston	50	2868	151	0	3.16
Dan Bouchard	Quebec	57	3373	180	1	3.20
Roland Melanson	NY Islanders	37	2019	110	0	3.27
Richard Sevigny	Montreal	40	2203	124	1	3.38
Murray Bannerman	Chicago	56	3335	188	2	3.38

Rod Langway was born in Formosa (Taiwan) but was raised in Randolph, Massachusetts, and grew up to become the first American to win the Norris Trophy as the NHL's best defenseman. Langway earned the honor in 1982–83 and again in 1983–84.

Overtime returned to the NHL regular season for the first time since 1942, when wartime travel restrictions had curtailed the practice. In the event of a tie after 60 minutes, teams would play a five-minute sudden-death session. If no one scored, the game would remain a tie.

Following their Stanley Cup loss to the New York Islanders the previous year, the Edmonton Oilers posted a 119-point season in 1983–84 and, for the third year in a row, set an all-time record with 446 goals. Not surprisingly, it was Wayne Gretzky who led the way as he tallied 87 goals and 118 assists for 205 points. Paul Coffey emerged as the best offensive defenseman since Bobby Orr, collecting 40 goals and 86 assists to finish second to Gretzky in the league scoring race. Jari Kurri had 52 goals and 61 assists to finish seventh in scoring, while right winger Glenn Anderson had 54 goals as the Oilers become the first team to boast three 50-goal scorers in one season.

Lesson Learned – With a new dedication to defense plus a freewheeling offense, the Oilers proved able to win games 1–0 or 5–4 en route to their first championship.

The New York Islanders showed every indication in the regular season that they were a legitimate threat to equal the Montreal Canadiens' record of five consecutive Stanley Cup championships. The Islanders posted 104 points to lead the Patrick Division after a tight race with the much-improved Washington Capitals, who set a franchise high with 101 points. The Boston Bruins, also with 104 points, won the Adams Division by a single point over the Buffalo Sabres. Buffalo was sparked by 18-year-old goalie Tom Barrasso, who won both the Calder and Vezina trophies. The Montreal Canadiens tumbled to fourth place in the division with their first sub-.500 season since 1948–49.

In a move reminiscent of their 1971 decision to go with Ken Dryden, the Habs elected to open the playoffs with rookie Steve Penney in goal, even though he had played only four games during the season. Penney responded by leading Montreal to upsets of Boston and the Quebec Nordiques. His hot hand even carried the Canadiens to two wins to open the Prince of Wales Conference championship before the Islanders recovered to win four in a row and advance to play for the Stanley Cup once again.

Playoff victories over the Winnipeg Jets, Calgary Flames and Minnesota North Stars meant Edmonton would face the Islanders in the finals for the second year in a row. The teams split the first two games before the Oilers' offense clicked into high gear. Edmonton won three in a row, outscoring the Isles 19–6, to take the series in five and deny the Islanders a fifth straight Stanley Cup title. Wayne Gretzky led all playoff performers with 35 points, but the Conn Smythe Trophy for playoff MVP went to rugged teammate Mark Messier.

Playoff rookie sensation Steve Penney of Montreal receives congratulations from an old pro — Canadiens legend Jacques Plante.

TROPHY WINNERS

Trophy	Awarded For	Winner	Team
Hart	MVP	Wayne Gretzky	Edm.
Art Ross	Top Scorer	Wayne Gretzky	Edm.
Norris	Top Defenseman	Rod Langway	Wsh.
Calder	Top Rookie	Tom Barrasso	Buf.
Selke	Top Defensive Forward	Doug Jarvis	Wsh.
Vezina	Top Goaltender	Tom Barrasso	Buf
Jennings	Fewest Goals Against	Al Jensen	Wsh
Jennings	Fewest Goals Against	Pat Riggin	Wsh.
Adams	Top Coach	Bryan Murray	Wsh.
Byng	Gentlemanly Conduct	Mike Bossy	NYI
Masterton	Perseverance, Sportmanship	Brad Park	Det.
Pearson	NHLPA MVP	Wayne Gretzky	Edm.
Conn Smythe	Playoff MVP	Mark Messier	Edm.
Patrick	Service to Hockey in U.S.	John A. Ziegler, Jr. Art Ross	
Entry Draft	First Overall Selection	Mario Lemieux	Pit.

Leaders, 1983-84

GOALS

Name, Team	G
Wayne Gretzky, Edm.	87
Michel Goulet, Que.	56
Tim Kerr, Phi.	54
Glenn Anderson, Edm.	54
Jari Kurri, Edm.	52
Rick Vaive, Tor.	52
Mike Bossy, NYI	51
Mike Bullard, Pit.	51
Pierre Larouche, NYR	48
Rick Middleton, Bos.	47

ASSISTS

Name, Team	A
Wayne Gretzky, Edm.	118
Paul Coffey, Edm.	86
Barry Pederson, Bos.	77
Peter Stastny, Que.	73
Bryan Trottier, NYI	71
Mike Bossy, NYI	67
Bernie Federko, St.L.	66
Michel Goulet, Que.	65
Raymond Bourque, Bos.	65
Dale Hawerchuk, Wpg.	65

POWERPLAY GOALS

Name, Team	PPG
Wayne Gretzky, Edm.	20
John Ogrodnick, Det.	19
Pierre Larouche, NYR	19
Tony Tanti, Van.	19
Sylvain Turgeon, Hfd.	18
Rick Vaive, Tor.	17
Tom McCarthy, Min.	16
Eddy Beers, Cgy.	16
Dino Ciccarelli, Min.	16
Rick Middleton, Bos.	16

SHORTHAND GOALS

Name, Team	SHG
Wayne Gretzky, Edm.	12
Kent Nilsson, Cgy.	9
Guy Carbonneau, Mtl.	7
Jari Kurri, Edm.	5
Butch Goring, NYI	5
Brian Bellows, Min.	5
Bob Bourne, NYI	5
Eight tied with	4

GAME-WINNING GOALS

Name, Team	GWG
Michel Goulet, Que.	16
Mike Bossy, NYI	11
Wayne Gretzky, Edm.	11
Glenn Anderson, Edm.	11
Tom McCarthy, Min.	7
Mark Messier, Edm.	7
John Tonelli, NYI	7
Gilbert Perreault, Buf.	7
Jorgen Pettersson, St.L.	7
Dave Andreychuk, Buf.	7
Patrik Sundstrom, Van.	7
Mike Gartner, Wsh.	7
Barry Pederson, Bos.	7

GOALIE WINS

Name, Team	W
Grant Fuhr, Edm.	30
Pete Peeters, Bos.	29
Dan Bouchard, Que.	29
Bob Froese, Phi.	28
Glen Hanlon, NYR	28
Andy Moog, Edm.	27
Tom Barrasso, Buf.	26
Al Jensen, Wsh.	25
Mike Liut, St.L.	25
Billy Smith, NYI	23
Murray Bannerman, Chi.	23

SHUTOUTS

Name, Team	SO
Pat Riggin, Wsh.	4
Al Jensen, Wsh.	4
Mike Liut, St.L.	3
Nine tied with	2

SAVE PERCENTAGE

Name, Team	SV%
Roland Melanson, NYI	.903
Billy Smith, NYI	.896
Tom Barrasso, Buf.	.893
Reggie Lemelin, Cgy.	.893
Glen Hanlon, NYR	.890
Pat Riggin, Wsh.	.890

FIRST TEAM ALL-STARS

Name, Team	Position
Wayne Gretzky, Edm.	C
Mike Bossy, NYI	RW
Michel Goulet, Que.	LW
Rod Langway, Wsh.	D
Raymond Bourque, Bos.	D
Tom Barrasso, Buf.	G

SECOND TEAM ALL-STARS

Name, Team	Position
Bryan Trottier, NYI	C
Jari Kurri, Edm.	RW
Mark Messier, Edm.	LW
Paul Coffey, Edm.	D
Denis Potvin, NYI	D
Pat Riggin, Wsh.	G

ALL-ROOKIE TEAM

Name, Team	Position
Steve Yzerman, Det.	C
Hakan Loob, Cgy.	RW
Sylvain Turgeon, Hfd.	LW
Thomas Ericksson, Phi.	D
Jamie Macoun, Cgy.	D
Tom Barrasso, Buf.	G

NHL NOTEBOOK

TRANSACTIONS

- June 20, 1983 – Calgary traded Phil Russell along with Mel Bridgman to New Jersey in exchange for Steve Tambellini and Joel Quenneville.
- July 6, 1983 – Boston Bruins signed free agent Geoff Courtnall after his WHL career with Victoria.
- Aug. 17, 1983 – Minnesota North Stars signed Dirk Graham as a free agent.
- Oct. 18, 1983 – Los Angeles traded defenseman Larry Murphy to the Washington Capitals for defenseman Brian Engblom and right wing Ken Houston.

RECORDS

- Oct 15, 1983 – Chicago and Toronto combined to score five goals in a span of 1:24, an NHL record for fastest five goals by two teams. The Black Hawks won the mini-battle 3-2 but the Leafs won the game 10-8.
- Jan. 4, 1984 – Edmonton Oilers beat the Minnesota North Stars 12-8 to set a modern-day NHL record for most goals by two teams in a game.
- Jan. 27, 1984 – Wayne Gretzky extended his NHL record consecutive point-scoring streak to 51 straight games in a 3-3 Oilers tie with New Jersey. The streak began October 5, 1983. In total, Gretzky scored 61 goals and 92 assists in the 51 games.
- Mar. 6, 1984 – Winnipeg's Dale Hawerchuk set an NHL record with five assists in one period (the second), as the Jets won in Los Angeles 7-3.

MILESTONES

- Oct. 23, 1983 – Philadelphia rookie Rich Sutter scored a goal in his first NHL game, making the Sutters the first family in NHL history with six brothers to all score a goal!
- Nov. 19, 1983 – Bruce Hood became the first referee to officiate 1,000 NHL games when Toronto beat Detroit 5-4 at Maple Leaf Gardens
- Jan. 23, 1984 – Buffalo Sabres became the first team in NHL history to win 10 straight road games with a 5-3 victory at Boston.
- Apr. 8, 1984 – Calgary's Paul Reinhart became the first NHL defenseman to score two career playoff hat tricks as the Flames beat Vancouver 5-1 in game four of the Smythe Division semi-finals.

1984 Playoffs

DIVISION SEMI-FINALS

Apr. 4	Montreal	2	at	Boston	1	
Apr. 5	Montreal	3	at	Boston	1	
Apr. 7	Boston	0	at	Montreal	5	

Montreal won best-of-five series 3–0

Apr. 4	Quebec	3	at	Buffalo	2	
Apr. 5	Quebec	6	at	Buffalo	2	
Apr. 7	Buffalo	1	at	Quebec	4	

Quebec won best-of-five series 3–0

Apr. 4	NY Rangers	1	at	NY Islanders	4	
Apr. 5	NY Rangers	3	at	NY Islanders	0	
Apr. 7	NY Islanders	2	at	NY Rangers	7	
Apr. 8	NY Islanders	4	at	NY Rangers	1	
Apr. 10	NY Rangers	2	at	NY Islanders	3	OT

NY Islanders won best-of-five series 3–2

Apr. 4	Philadelphia	2	at	Washington	4	
Apr. 5	Philadelphia	2	at	Washington	6	
Apr. 7	Washington	5	at	Philadelphia	1	

Washington won best-of-five series 3–0

Apr. 4	Chicago	3	at	Minnesota	1	
Apr. 5	Chicago	5	at	Minnesota	6	
Apr. 7	Minnesota	4	at	Chicago	1	
Apr. 8	Minnesota	3	at	Chicago	4	
Apr. 10	Chicago	1	at	Minnesota	4	

Minnesota won best-of-five series 3–2

Apr. 4	Detroit	2	at	St. Louis	3	
Apr. 5	Detroit	5	at	St. Louis	3	
Apr. 7	St. Louis	4	at	Detroit	3	2OT
Apr. 8	St. Louis	3	at	Detroit	2	OT

St. Louis won best-of-five series 3–1

Apr. 4	Winnipeg	2	at	Edmonton	9	
Apr. 5	Winnipeg	4	at	Edmonton	5	OT
Apr. 7	Edmonton	4	at	Winnipeg	1	

Edmonton won best-of-five series 3–0

Apr. 4	Vancouver	3	at	Calgary	5	
Apr. 5	Vancouver	2	at	Calgary	4	
Apr. 7	Calgary	0	at	Vancouver	7	
Apr. 8	Calgary	5	at	Vancouver	1	

Calgary won best-of-five series 3–1

DIVISION FINALS

Apr. 12	Montreal	2	at	Quebec	4	
Apr. 13	Montreal	4	at	Quebec	1	
Apr. 15	Quebec	1	at	Montreal	2	
Apr. 16	Quebec	4	at	Montreal	3	OT
Apr. 18	Montreal	4	at	Quebec	0	
Apr. 20	Quebec	3	at	Montreal	5	

Montreal won best-of-seven series 4–2

Apr. 12	Washington	3	at	NY Islanders	2	
Apr. 13	Washington	4	at	NY Islanders	5	OT
Apr. 15	NY Islanders	3	at	Washington	1	
Apr. 16	NY Islanders	5	at	Washington	2	
Apr. 18	Washington	3	at	NY Islanders	5	

NY Islanders won best-of-seven series 4–1

Apr. 12	St. Louis	1	at	Minnesota	2	
Apr. 13	St. Louis	4	at	Minnesota	3	OT
Apr. 15	Minnesota	1	at	St. Louis	3	
Apr. 16	Minnesota	3	at	St. Louis	2	
Apr. 18	St. Louis	0	at	Minnesota	6	
Apr. 20	Minnesota	0	at	St. Louis	4	
Apr. 22	St. Louis	3	at	Minnesota	4	OT

Minnesota won best-of-seven series 4–3

Apr. 12	Calgary	2	at	Edmonton	5	
Apr. 13	Calgary	6	at	Edmonton	5	OT
Apr. 15	Edmonton	3	at	Calgary	2	
Apr. 16	Edmonton	5	at	Calgary	3	
Apr. 18	Calgary	5	at	Edmonton	4	
Apr. 20	Edmonton	4	at	Calgary	5	OT
Apr. 22	Calgary	4	at	Edmonton	7	

Edmonton won best-of-seven series 4–3

CONFERENCE FINALS

Apr. 24	NY Islanders	0	at	Montreal	3	
Apr. 26	NY Islanders	2	at	Montreal	4	
Apr. 28	Montreal	2	at	NY Islanders	5	
May 1	Montreal	1	at	NY Islanders	3	
May 3	NY Islanders	3	at	Montreal	1	
May 5	Montreal	1	at	NY Islanders	4	

NY Islanders won best-of-seven series 4–2

Apr. 24	Minnesota	1	at	Edmonton	7	
Apr. 26	Minnesota	3	at	Edmonton	4	
Apr. 28	Edmonton	8	at	Minnesota	5	
May 1	Edmonton	3	at	Minnesota	1	

Edmonton won best-of-seven series 4–0

FINALS

May 10	Edmonton	1	at	NY Islanders	0	
May 12	Edmonton	1	at	NY Islanders	6	
May 15	NY Islanders	2	at	Edmonton	7	
May 17	NY Islanders	2	at	Edmonton	7	
May 19	NY Islanders	2	at	Edmonton	5	

Edmonton won best-of-seven series 4–1

1983-84 – Edmonton Oilers – Glenn Anderson, Paul Coffey, Pat Conacher, Lee Fogolin, Jr., Grant Fuhr, Randy Gregg, Wayne Gretzky (Captain), Charlie Huddy, Pat Hughes, Dave Hunter, Don Jackson, Jari Kurri, Willy Lindstrom, Ken Linseman, Kevin Lowe, Dave Lumley, Kevin McClelland, Mark Messier, Andy Moog, Jaroslav Pouzar, Dave Semenko, Peter Pocklington (Owner), Glen Sather (General Manager/Coach), John Muckler, Ted Green (Assistant Coaches), Bruce MacGregor (Assistant General Manager), Barry Fraser (Director of Player Personnel/Chief Scout), Peter Millar (Athletic Therapist), Barrie Stafford (Trainer).

LEADING PLAYOFF SCORERS

Player	Club	GP	G	A	PTS	PIM
Wayne Gretzky	Edmonton	19	13	22	35	12
Jari Kurri	Edmonton	19	14	14	28	13
Mark Messier	Edmonton	19	8	18	26	19
Paul Coffey	Edmonton	19	8	14	22	21
Clark Gillies	NY Islanders	21	12	7	19	19
Mike Bossy	NY Islanders	21	8	10	18	4
Glenn Anderson	Edmonton	19	6	11	17	33
Paul Reinhart	Calgary	11	6	11	17	2
Pat Flatley	NY Islanders	21	9	6	15	14
Six players tied with					14	

LEADING PLAYOFF GOALTENDERS

Goaltender	Club	GPI	Mins	GA	SO	Avg.
Steve Penney	Montreal	15	871	32	3	2.20
Mike Liut	St. Louis	11	714	29	1	2.44
Billy Smith	NY Islanders	21	1190	54	0	2.72
Dan Bouchard	Quebec	9	543	25	0	2.76
Grant Fuhr	Edmonton	16	883	44	1	2.99

PLAYOFF GOALS

Name, Team	G
Jari Kurri, Edm.	14
Wayne Gretzky, Edm.	13
Clark Gillies, NYI	12
Ken Linseman, Edm.	10
Pat Flatley, NYI	9
Mark Messier, Edm.	8
Paul Coffey, Edm.	8
Mike Bossy, NYI	8
Bryan Trottier, NYI	8
Jorgen Pettersson, St.L.	7
Steve Shutt, Mtl.	7

PLAYOFF ASSISTS

Name, Team	A
Wayne Gretzky, Edm.	22
Mark Messier, Edm.	18
Jari Kurri, Edm.	14
Paul Coffey, Edm.	14
Al MacInnis, Cgy.	12
Brian Bellows, Min.	12
Paul Reinhart, Cgy.	11
Brad Maxwell, Min.	11
Glenn Anderson, Edm.	11
Pat Hughes, Edm.	11

PLAYOFF POWERPLAY GOALS

Name, Team	PPG
Jari Kurri, Edm.	4
Lanny McDonald, Cgy.	3
Mark Napier, Min.	3
Mats Naslund, Mtl.	3
Willy Lindstrom, Edm.	3
Ken Linseman, Edm.	3
Clark Gillies, NYI	3

PLAYOFF SHORTHAND GOALS

Name, Team	SHG
Andre Savard, Que.	2
19 tied with	1

PLAYOFF GAME-WINNING GOALS

Name, Team	GWG
Ken Linseman, Edm.	4
Craig Laughlin, Wsh.	3
Mats Naslund, Mtl.	3
Wayne Gretzky, Edm.	3
Brent Sutter, NYI	3
Mike Bossy, NYI	3

PLAYOFF GOALIE WINS

Name, Team	W
Billy Smith, NYI	12
Grant Fuhr, Edm.	11
Steve Penney, Mtl.	9
Mike Liut, St.L.	6
Don Beaupre, Min.	6

PLAYOFF SHUTOUTS

Name, Team	SO
Steve Penney, Mtl.	3
Richard Brodeur, Van.	1
Glen Hanlon, NYR	1
Mike Liut, St.L.	1
Don Beaupre, Min.	1
Grant Fuhr, Edm.	1

PLAYOFF SAVE PERCENTAGE

Name, Team	SV%
Mike Liut, St.L.	.920
Grant Fuhr, Edm.	.910
Steve Penney, Mtl.	.910
Billy Smith, NYI	.905
Don Beaupre, Min.	.895

1984-85

Stanley Cup • Edmonton Oilers

Paul Coffey helped the Edmonton Oilers become the greatest offensive team in hockey history. He finished second to Wayne Gretzky in scoring in 1983–84 and won the Norris Trophy as the NHL's best defenseman for the first of three times in 1984–85.

FINAL STANDINGS

CLARENCE CAMPBELL CONFERENCE

Team	GP	W	L	T	GF	GA	PTS
Norris Division							
St. Louis	80	37	31	12	299	288	86
Chicago	80	38	35	7	309	299	83
Detroit	80	27	41	12	313	357	66
Minnesota	80	25	43	12	268	321	62
Toronto	80	20	52	8	253	358	48
Smythe Division							
Edmonton	80	49	20	11	401	298	109
Winnipeg	80	43	27	10	358	332	96
Calgary	80	41	27	12	363	302	94
Los Angeles	80	34	32	14	339	326	82
Vancouver	80	25	46	9	284	401	59
PRINCE OF WALES CONFERENCE							
Adams Division							
Montreal	80	41	27	12	309	262	94
Quebec	80	41	30	9	323	275	91
Buffalo	80	38	28	14	290	237	90
Boston	80	36	34	10	303	287	82
Hartford	80	30	41	9	268	318	69
Patrick Division							
Philadelphia	80	53	20	7	348	241	113
Washington	80	46	25	9	322	240	101
NY Islanders	80	40	34	6	345	312	86
NY Rangers	80	26	44	10	295	345	62
New Jersey	80	22	48	10	264	346	54
Pittsburgh	80	24	51	5	276	385	53

LEADING SCORERS

Player	Club	GP	G	A	PTS	PIM
Wayne Gretzky	Edmonton	80	73	135	208	52
Jari Kurri	Edmonton	73	71	64	135	30
Dale Hawerchuk	Winnipeg	80	53	77	130	74
Marcel Dionne	Los Angeles	80	46	80	126	46
Paul Coffey	Edmonton	80	37	84	121	97
Mike Bossy	NY Islanders	76	58	59	117	38
John Ogrodnick	Detroit	79	55	50	105	30
Denis Savard	Chicago	79	38	67	105	56
Bernie Federko	St. Louis	76	30	73	103	27
Mike Gartner	Washington	80	50	52	102	71
Brent Sutter	NY Islanders	72	42	60	102	51
Paul MacLean	Winnipeg	79	41	60	101	119
Bernie Nicholls	Los Angeles	80	46	54	100	76
Mario Lemieux	Pittsburgh	73	43	57	100	54
John Tonelli	NY Islanders	80	42	58	100	95
Peter Stastny	Quebec	75	32	68	100	95
Kent Nilsson	Calgary	77	37	62	99	14
Tim Kerr	Philadelphia	74	54	44	98	57
Brian Propp	Philadelphia	76	43	54	97	43
Michel Goulet	Quebec	69	55	40	95	55
Bob Carpenter	Washington	80	53	42	95	87
Dave Taylor	Los Angeles	79	41	51	92	132
Joe Mullen	St. Louis	79	40	52	92	6

LEADING GOALTENDERS

Goaltender	Club	GPI	MINS	GA	SO	AVG
Tom Barrasso	Buffalo	54	3248	144	5	2.66
Pat Riggin	Washington	57	3388	168	2	2.98
Pelle Lindbergh	Philadelphia	65	3858	194	2	3.02
Steve Penney	Montreal	54	3252	167	1	3.08
Bob Sauve	Buffalo	27	1564	84	0	3.22
Warren Skorodenski	Chicago	27	1396	75	2	3.22
Rick Wamsley	St. Louis	40	2319	126	0	3.26
Doug Keans	Boston	25	1497	82	1	3.29
Andy Moog	Edmonton	39	2019	111	1	3.30
Mario Gosselin	Quebec	35	1960	109	1	3.34

CHOSEN FIRST OVERALL in the 1984 Entry Draft, Pittsburgh center Mario Lemieux recorded 43 goals and 57 assists en route to winning the Calder Trophy as rookie of the year. Within a few seasons, Lemieux would be credited with saving the Penguins franchise and would rival Wayne Gretzky as the greatest player in the game. This year, however, the Penguins recorded just 53 points and finished ahead of only the Toronto Maple Leafs in the NHL's overall standings.

Meanwhile, Gretzky and his Edmonton Oilers continued to dominate the league. Gretzky set yet another single-season record with 135 assists, and he added 73 goals for a total of 208 points. Linemate Jari Kurri's 71 goals and 135 points trailed only Gretzky in the league scoring race. Edmonton's Smythe Division rivals, the Winnipeg Jets and Calgary Flames, were also among the league's best this season and the league's top five scorers were all from the Smythe Division: Gretzky, Kurri, Winnipeg's Dale Hawerchuk, Marcel Dionne of Los Angeles and Oiler defenseman Paul Coffey.

Well-Oiled Machine – Gretzky set a single-season assist record, Mario Lemieux made a magnificent debut, the Flyers soared, but the Cup stayed in Edmonton thanks to Jari Kurri's record-tying 19 goals in the playoffs.

The top team overall, however, was the Philadelphia Flyers. Former captain Bobby Clarke was now the general manager and new coach Mike Keenan got 53 wins and 113 points out of his troops. Tim Kerr led the team with 54 goals, but it was a stingy defense, led by Mark Howe and the Vezina Trophy-winning goaltending of Pelle Lindbergh, that was key to Philadelphia's success. The Flyers outdistanced the Washington Capitals for top spot in the Patrick Division, while the New York Islanders slipped to third place. The Islanders upset Washington in the playoffs, but suffered their earliest postseason ouster since 1979 when they lost to Philadelphia in the second round. The Montreal Canadiens survived the midseason retirement of Guy Lafleur to lead the Adams Division, but lost to Quebec in the playoffs. The Nordiques then fell to the Flyers in the Wales Conference final.

Bernie Federko's 103 points led the St. Louis Blues to first place in the Norris Division, but it was the Chicago Black Hawks who survived the playoffs before falling to Edmonton in a six-game Campbell Conference final that saw the powerful Oilers score a record 44 goals. Philadelphia beat Edmonton 4–1 in game one of the finals, before the Oilers won three tight games to take a commanding lead in the series. The Oilers wrapped it up with an offensive explosion that resulted in an 8–3 victory in game five and their second straight Stanley Cup title. Jari Kurri tied former Flyer Reggie Leach's record with 19 goals in the postseason, while Wayne Gretzky had 17 goals and 30 assists for a playoff-record 47 points, earning him the Conn Smythe Trophy.

Tim Kerr stood 6'3" and weighed 230 pounds but he took a physical pounding from defensemen in front of the net. Three knee injuries and a broken leg limited him to just 54 goals in his first three seasons, but he then topped the 50-goal plateau four years in a row.

Leaders, 1984-85

GOALS

Name, Team	G
Wayne Gretzky, Edm.	73
Jari Kurri, Edm.	71
Mike Bossy, NYI	58
Michel Goulet, Que.	55
John Ogrodnick, Det.	55
Tim Kerr, Phi.	54
Dale Hawerchuk, Wpg.	53
Bob Carpenter, Wsh.	53
Mike Gartner, Wsh.	50
Marcel Dionne, L.A.	46
Bernie Nicholls, L.A.	46
Steve Larmer, Chi.	46

ASSISTS

Name, Team	A
Wayne Gretzky, Edm.	135
Paul Coffey, Edm.	84
Marcel Dionne, L.A.	80
Dale Hawerchuk, Wpg.	77
Bernie Federko, St.L.	73
Peter Stastny, Que.	68
Denis Savard, Chi.	67
Raymond Bourque, Bos.	66
Jari Kurri, Edm.	64
Kent Nilsson, Cgy.	62

POWERPLAY GOALS

Name, Team	PPG
Tim Kerr, Phi.	21
Michel Goulet, Que.	17
Dale Hawerchuk, Wpg.	17
Mike Gartner, Wsh.	17
Marcel Dionne, L.A.	16
Scott Stevens, Wsh.	16
John Ogrodnick, Det.	15
Bernie Nicholls, L.A.	15
12 tied with	14

SHORTHAND GOALS

Name, Team	SHG
Wayne Gretzky, Edm.	11
Brian Propp, Phi.	7
Mark Messier, Edm.	5
Bill Derlago, Tor.	5
Bryan Trottier, NYI	5
Steve Kasper, Bos.	5
Kevin Dineen, Hfd.	4
Greg Terrion, Tor.	4
Dave Poulin, Phi.	4
Mike Bossy, NYI	4
Guy Carbonneau, Mtl.	4
Troy Murray, Chi.	4

GAME-WINNING GOALS

Name, Team	GWG
Jari Kurri, Edm.	13
Mike Gartner, Wsh.	11
Tim Kerr, Phi.	9
Peter Stastny, Que.	9
Ilkka Sinisalo, Phi.	8
Mats Naslund, Mtl.	8
Mike Bossy, NYI	7
Brian Sutter, St.L.	7
Wayne Gretzky, Edm.	7
Bob Carpenter, Wsh.	7

GOALIE WINS

Name, Team	W
Pelle Lindbergh, Phi.	40
Brian Hayward, Wpg.	33
Reggie Lemelin, Cgy.	30
Pat Riggin, Wsh.	28
Murray Bannerman, Chi.	27
Grant Fuhr, Edm.	26
Steve Penney, Mtl.	26
Tom Barrasso, Buf.	25
Rick Wamsley, St.L.	23
Andy Moog, Edm.	22
Bob Janecyk, L.A.	22

SHUTOUTS

Name, Team	SO
Tom Barrasso, Buf.	5
Seven tied with	2

SAVE PERCENTAGE

Name, Team	SV%
Warren Skorodenski, Chi.	.903
Pelle Lindbergh, Phi.	.899
Andy Moog, Edm.	.894
Mike Liut, St.L./Hfd.	.889
Reggie Lemelin, Cgy.	.888
Tom Barrasso, Buf.	.887
Pat Riggin, Wsh.	.886
Kelly Hrudey, NYI	.886

FIRST TEAM ALL-STARS

Name, Team	Position
Wayne Gretzky, Edm.	C
Jari Kurri, Edm.	RW
John Ogrodnick, Det.	LW
Paul Coffey, Edm.	D
Raymond Bourque, Bos.	D
Pelle Lindbergh, Phi.	G

SECOND TEAM ALL-STARS

Name, Team	Position
Dale Hawerchuk, Wpg.	C
Mike Bossy, NYI	RW
John Tonelli, NYI	LW
Rod Langway, Wsh.	D
Doug Wilson, Chi.	D
Tom Barrasso, Buf.	G

ALL-ROOKIE TEAM

Name, Team	Position
Mario Lemieux, Pit.	C
Tomas Sandstrom, NYR	RW
Warren Young, Pit.	LW
Chris Chelios, Mtl.	D
Bruce Bell, Que.	D
Steve Penney, Mtl.	G

TROPHY WINNERS

Trophy	Awarded For	Winner	Team
Hart	MVP	Wayne Gretzky	Edm.
Art Ross	Top Scorer	Wayne Gretzky	Edm.
Norris	Top Defenseman	Paul Coffey	Edm
Calder	Top Rookie	Mario Lemieux	Pit.
Selke	Top Defensive Forward	Craig Ramsay	Buf.
Vezina	Top Goaltender	Pelle Lindbergh	Phi.
Jennings	Fewest Goals Against	Tom Barrasso	Buf
		Bob Sauve	Buf.
Adams	Top Coach	Mike Keenan	Phi.
Byng	Gentlemanly Conduct	Jari Kurri	Edm.
Masterton	Perseverance, Sportmanship	Anders Hedberg	NYR
Pearson	NHLPA MVP	Wayne Gretzky	Edm.
Conn Smythe	Playoff MVP	Wayne Gretzky	Edm.
Patrick	Service to Hockey in U.S.	Jack Butterfield	
		Arthur M. Wirtz	
Entry Draft	First Overall Selection	Wendel Clark, LW/D	Tor.

NHL NOTEBOOK

TRANSACTIONS

- May 12, 1984 – Toronto Maple Leafs signed free agent Steve Thomas.
- Sept. 11, 1984 – Calgary Flames signed Joel Otto as a free agent.
- Oct. 1, 1984 – Los Angeles Kings signed free agent Steve Duchesne.
- Feb. 1, 1985 – Edmonton Oilers signed free agent Craig MacTavish.

RECORDS

- Oct. 11, 1984 – In his first NHL game…in his first shift…on his first shot…rookie Mario Lemieux scored his first NHL goal, and later added an assist, but the Penguins lost 4-3 to the Bruins in their season opener at Boston.
- Nov. 9, 1984 – Edmonton beat the Capitals 8-5 at Washington to set an NHL record for longest undefeated streak from the start of the season (12-0-3). The previous record of 14 games (11-0-3) was set by the 1943-44 Montreal Canadiens.
- Apr. 2, 1985 – Edmonton's Wayne Gretzky set an NHL record with his 34th career hat trick as the Oilers beat the Kings 6-4 at Los Angeles. Gretzky broke the record of 33 career hat tricks, set by Mike Bossy two months earlier.
- Apr. 10, 1985 – Detroit defenseman Brad Park set an NHL record by appearing in the Stanley Cup playoffs for the 17th consecutive year.
- May 16, 1985 – Jari Kurri set a new playoff record with his third hat trick of the 1985 playoffs, then added a fourth goal as the Oilers won 8-2 at Chicago in game six of the Conference championships.

MILESTONES

- Nov. 13, 1984 – L.A.'s Bernie Nicholls became the first player in NHL history to score a goal in all four periods of a game. He scored once in each period, plus the overtime winner when the Kings beat the Nordiques 5-4 in Quebec City.
- Dec. 19, 1984 – While playing in his 424th career game, Edmonton's Wayne Gretzky had two goals and four assists to become the fastest player to reach 1,000 career points (breaking Guy Lafleur's record of 720 games). Oilers won 7-3 against the visiting Kings.
- Apr. 6, 1985 – Pittsburgh Penguins became the first team in NHL history to lose 50 (or more) games for three straight years when they dropped their 50th of the 1984-85 season 7-4 to the visiting Washington Capitals.

1985 Playoffs

DIVISION SEMI-FINALS

Date		Team	Score		Team	Score
Apr.	10	Boston	5	at	Montreal	3
Apr.	11	Boston	3	at	Montreal	5
Apr.	13	Montreal	4	at	Boston	2
Apr.	14	Montreal	6	at	Boston	7
Apr.	16	Boston	0	at	Montreal	1

Montreal won best-of-five series 3–2

Date		Team	Score		Team	Score
Apr.	10	Buffalo	2	at	Quebec	5
Apr.	11	Buffalo	2	at	Quebec	3
Apr.	13	Quebec	4	at	Buffalo	6
Apr.	14	Quebec	4	at	Buffalo	7
Apr.	16	Buffalo	5	at	Quebec	6

Quebec won best-of-five series 3–2

Date		Team	Score		Team	Score
Apr.	10	NY Rangers	4	at	Philadelphia	5 OT
Apr.	11	NY Rangers	1	at	Philadelphia	3
Apr.	13	Philadelphia	6	at	NY Rangers	5

Philadelphia won best-of-five series 3–0

Date		Team	Score		Team	Score
Apr.	10	NY Islanders	3	at	Washington	4 OT
Apr.	11	NY Islanders	1	at	Washington	2 2OT
Apr.	13	Washington	1	at	NY Islanders	2
Apr.	14	Washington	4	at	NY Islanders	6
Apr.	16	NY Islanders	2	at	Washington	1

NY Islanders won best-of-five series 3–2

Date		Team	Score		Team	Score
Apr.	10	Minnesota	3	at	St. Louis	2
Apr.	11	Minnesota	4	at	St. Louis	3
Apr.	13	St. Louis	0	at	Minnesota	2

Minnesota won best-of-five series 3–0

Date		Team	Score		Team	Score
Apr.	10	Detroit	5	at	Chicago	9
Apr.	11	Detroit	1	at	Chicago	8
Apr.	13	Chicago	8	at	Detroit	2

Chicago won best-of-five series 3–0

Date		Team	Score		Team	Score
Apr.	10	Los Angeles	2	at	Edmonton	3 OT
Apr.	11	Los Angeles	2	at	Edmonton	4
Apr.	13	Edmonton	4	at	Los Angeles	3 OT

Edmonton won best-of-five series 3–0

Date		Team	Score		Team	Score
Apr.	10	Calgary	4	at	Winnipeg	5 OT
Apr.	11	Calgary	2	at	Winnipeg	5
Apr.	13	Winnipeg	0	at	Calgary	4
Apr.	14	Winnipeg	5	at	Calgary	3

Winnipeg won best-of-five series 3–1

DIVISION FINALS

Date		Team	Score		Team	Score
Apr.	18	Quebec	2	at	Montreal	1 OT
Apr.	21	Quebec	4	at	Montreal	6
Apr.	23	Montreal	6	at	Quebec	7 OT
Apr.	25	Montreal	3	at	Quebec	1
Apr.	27	Quebec	5	at	Montreal	1
Apr.	30	Montreal	5	at	Quebec	2
May	2	Quebec	3	at	Montreal	2 OT

Quebec won best-of-seven series 4–3

Date		Team	Score		Team	Score
Apr.	18	NY Islanders	0	at	Philadelphia	3
Apr.	21	NY Islanders	2	at	Philadelphia	5
Apr.	23	Philadelphia	5	at	NY Islanders	3
Apr.	25	Philadelphia	2	at	NY Islanders	6
Apr.	28	NY Islanders	0	at	Philadelphia	1

Philadelphia won best-of-seven series 4–1

Date		Team	Score		Team	Score
Apr.	18	Minnesota	8	at	Chicago	5
Apr.	21	Minnesota	2	at	Chicago	6
Apr.	23	Chicago	5	at	Minnesota	3
Apr.	25	Chicago	7	at	Minnesota	6 2OT
Apr.	28	Minnesota	5	at	Chicago	4 OT
Apr.	30	Chicago	6	at	Minnesota	5 OT

Chicago won best-of-seven series 4–2

Date		Team	Score		Team	Score
Apr.	18	Winnipeg	2	at	Edmonton	4
Apr.	20	Winnipeg	2	at	Edmonton	5
Apr.	23	Edmonton	5	at	Winnipeg	4
Apr.	25	Edmonton	8	at	Winnipeg	3

Edmonton won best-of-seven series 4–0

CONFERENCE FINALS

Date		Team	Score		Team	Score
May	5	Philadelphia	1	at	Quebec	2 OT
May	7	Philadelphia	4	at	Quebec	2
May	9	Quebec	2	at	Philadelphia	4
May	12	Quebec	5	at	Philadelphia	3
May	14	Philadelphia	2	at	Quebec	1
May	16	Quebec	0	at	Philadelphia	3

Philadelphia won best-of-seven series 4–2

Date		Team	Score		Team	Score
May	4	Chicago	2	at	Edmonton	11
May	7	Chicago	3	at	Edmonton	7
May	9	Edmonton	2	at	Chicago	5
May	12	Edmonton	6	at	Chicago	8
May	14	Chicago	5	at	Edmonton	10
May	16	Edmonton	8	at	Chicago	2

Edmonton won best-of-seven series 4–2

FINALS

Date		Team	Score		Team	Score
May	21	Edmonton	1	at	Philadelphia	4
May	23	Edmonton	3	at	Philadelphia	1
May	25	Philadelphia	3	at	Edmonton	4
May	28	Philadelphia	3	at	Edmonton	5
May	30	Philadelphia	3	at	Edmonton	8

Edmonton won best-of-seven series 4–1

1984-85 – Edmonton Oilers – Glenn Anderson, Billy Carroll, Paul Coffey, Lee Fogolin, Jr., Grant Fuhr, Randy Gregg, Wayne Gretzky (Captain), Charlie Huddy, Pat Hughes, Dave Hunter, Don Jackson, Mike Krushelnyski, Jari Kurri, Willy Lindstrom, Kevin Lowe, Dave Lumley, Kevin McClelland, Larry Melnyk, Mark Messier, Andy Moog, Mark Napier, Jaroslav Pouzar, Dave Semenko, Esa Tikkanen, Peter Pocklington (Owner), Glen Sather (General Manager/Coach), John Muckler, Ted Green (Assistant Coaches), Bruce MacGregor (Assistant General Manager), Barry Fraser (Director of Player Personnel/Chief Scout), Peter Millar (Athletic Therapist), Barrie Stafford, Lyle Kulchisky (Trainers).

LEADING PLAYOFF SCORERS

Player	Club	GP	G	A	PTS	PIM
Wayne Gretzky	Edmonton	18	17	30	47	4
Paul Coffey	Edmonton	18	12	25	37	44
Jari Kurri	Edmonton	18	19	12	31	6
Denis Savard	Chicago	15	9	20	29	20
Glenn Anderson	Edmonton	18	10	16	26	38
Mark Messier	Edmonton	18	12	13	25	12
Peter Stastny	Quebec	18	4	19	23	24
Steve Larmer	Chicago	15	9	13	22	14
Michel Goulet	Quebec	17	11	10	21	17
Charlie Huddy	Edmonton	18	3	17	20	17

LEADING PLAYOFF GOALTENDERS

Goaltender	Club	GPI	Mins	GA	SO	Avg.
Pelle Lindbergh	Philadelphia	18	1008	42	3	2.50
Mario Gosselin	Quebec	17	1059	54	0	3.06
Grant Fuhr	Edmonton	18	1064	55	0	3.10
Steve Penney	Montreal	12	733	40	1	3.27
Murray Bannerman	Chicago	15	906	72	0	4.77

PLAYOFF GOALS

Name, Team	G
Jari Kurri, Edm.	19
Wayne Gretzky, Edm.	17
Darryl Sutter, Chi.	12
Paul Coffey, Edm.	12
Mark Messier, Edm.	12
Michel Goulet, Que.	11

PLAYOFF ASSISTS

Name, Team	A
Wayne Gretzky, Edm.	30
Paul Coffey, Edm.	25
Denis Savard, Chi.	20
Peter Stastny, Que.	19
Charlie Huddy, Edm.	17
Glenn Anderson, Edm.	16

PLAYOFF POWERPLAY GOALS

Name, Team	PPG
Michel Goulet, Que.	7
Steve Larmer, Chi.	5
Tim Kerr, Phi.	4
Wayne Gretzky, Edm.	4
Brian Propp, Phi.	4

PLAYOFF SHORTHAND GOALS

Name, Team	SHG
Bengt Lundholm, Wpg.	2
Dave Poulin, Phi.	2
Wayne Gretzky, Edm.	2
Jari Kurri, Edm.	2
14 tied with	1

PLAYOFF GAME-WINNING GOALS

Name, Team	GWG
Darryl Sutter, Chi.	4
Paul Coffey, Edm.	4
Wayne Gretzky, Edm.	3
Ilkka Sinisalo, Phi.	3
10 tied with	2

PLAYOFF GOALIE WINS

Name, Team	W
Grant Fuhr, Edm.	15
Pelle Lindbergh, Phi.	12
Murray Bannerman, Chi.	9
Mario Gosselin, Que.	9
Steve Penney, Mtl.	6

PLAYOFF SHUTOUTS

Name, Team	SO
Pelle Lindbergh, Phi.	3
Reggie Lemelin, Cgy.	1
Gilles Meloche, Min.	1
Steve Penney, Mtl.	1

PLAYOFF SAVE PERCENTAGE

Name, Team	SV%
Pelle Lindbergh, Phi.	.914
Grant Fuhr, Edm.	.895
Mario Gosselin, Que.	.886
Murray Bannerman, Chi.	.868
Steve Penney, Mtl.	.867

1985-86

Patrick Roy made his NHL debut with the Montreal Canadiens on February 23, 1985, and became a regular during the 1985–86 season. He earned a spot on the NHL All-Rookie Team that year, but it was during the 1986 playoffs that Roy first displayed how great he would be.

Stanley Cup • Montreal Canadiens

FINAL STANDINGS

CLARENCE CAMPBELL CONFERENCE

Team	GP	W	L	T	GF	GA	PTS
Norris Division							
Chicago	80	39	33	8	351	349	86
Minnesota	80	38	33	9	327	305	85
St. Louis	80	37	34	9	302	291	83
Toronto	80	25	48	7	311	386	57
Detroit	80	17	57	6	266	415	40
Smythe Division							
Edmonton	80	56	17	7	426	310	119
Calgary	80	40	31	9	354	315	89
Winnipeg	80	26	47	7	295	372	59
Vancouver	80	23	44	13	282	333	59
Los Angeles	80	23	49	8	284	389	54
PRINCE OF WALES CONFERENCE							
Adams Division							
Quebec	80	43	31	6	330	289	92
Montreal	80	40	33	7	330	280	87
Boston	80	37	31	12	311	288	86
Hartford	80	40	36	4	332	302	84
Buffalo	80	37	37	6	296	291	80
Patrick Division							
Philadelphia	80	53	23	4	335	241	110
Washington	80	50	23	7	315	272	107
NY Islanders	80	39	29	12	327	284	90
NY Rangers	80	36	38	6	280	276	78
Pittsburgh	80	34	38	8	313	305	76
New Jersey	80	28	49	3	300	374	59

LEADING SCORERS

Player	Club	GP	G	A	PTS	PIM
Wayne Gretzky	Edmonton	80	52	163	215	46
Mario Lemieux	Pittsburgh	79	48	93	141	43
Paul Coffey	Edmonton	79	48	90	138	120
Jari Kurri	Edmonton	78	68	63	131	22
Mike Bossy	NY Islanders	80	61	62	123	14
Peter Stastny	Quebec	76	41	81	122	60
Denis Savard	Chicago	80	47	69	116	111
Mats Naslund	Montreal	80	43	67	110	16
Dale Hawerchuk	Winnipeg	80	46	59	105	44
Neal Broten	Minnesota	80	29	76	105	47
Michel Goulet	Quebec	75	53	51	104	64
Glenn Anderson	Edmonton	72	54	48	102	90
Bernie Federko	St. Louis	80	34	68	102	34
Troy Murray	Chicago	80	45	54	99	94
Brian Propp	Philadelphia	72	40	57	97	47
Bernie Nicholls	Los Angeles	80	36	61	97	78
Bryan Trottier	NY Islanders	78	37	59	96	72
Marcel Dionne	Los Angeles	80	36	58	94	42
Joe Mullen	St.L./Cgy	77	44	46	90	21
Dino Ciccarelli	Minnesota	75	44	45	89	51
Dave Andreychuk	Buffalo	80	36	51	87	61
Bobby Smith	Montreal	79	31	55	86	55
Three tied with				84		

LEADING GOALTENDERS

Goaltender	Club	GPI	MINS	GA	SO	AVG
Bob Froese	Philadelphia	51	2728	116	5	2.55
Al Jensen	Washington	44	2437	129	2	3.18
Clint Malarchuk	Quebec	46	2657	142	4	3.21
Kelly Hrudey	NY Islanders	45	2563	137	1	3.21
John Vanbiesbrouck	NY Rangers	61	3326	184	3	3.32
Patrick Roy	Montreal	47	2651	148	1	3.35
Pat Riggin	Wsh./Bos.	46	2641	150	1	3.41
Rick Wamsley	St. Louis	42	2517	144	1	3.43
Pete Peeters	Bos./Wsh.	42	2506	144	1	3.45
Don Beaupre	Minnesota	52	3073	182	1	3.55

JUST AS THE EXPLOSIVE MONTREAL CANADIENS powerplay of the late 1950s had caused the NHL to change its rules (allowing a penalized player to return to the ice before the two minutes expired if a goal was scored), the Edmonton Oilers' abundance of firepower caused the league to allow player substitutions on coincidental minor penalties, virtually eliminating the four-on-four situations that favored teams with superior skill.

The rule change did little to put the brakes on the Oilers, as the two-time defending Stanley Cup champions wrapped up their fifth consecutive Smythe Division title. The Oilers also returned to the top spot in the overall standings with 119 points and became the inaugural winners of the Presidents' Trophy for finishing in first place. Wayne Gretzky broke his own single-season record with 215 points, mainly by shattering his assist record with an astounding total of 163. Gretzky's assist total alone would have been enough to win the scoring title, as Mario Lemieux of the Pittsburgh Penguins finished second with 141 points. Paul Coffey also enjoyed a record-breaking year, surpassing Bobby Orr's standard of 46 goals by a defenseman with 48. Coffey added 90 assists to finish third in the scoring race. Jari Kurri's tally of 68 goals and 63 assists saw him finish fourth.

As in Wayne Gretzky's 212-point campaign of 1981–82, regular-season records didn't translate into playoff prosperity as the rival Calgary Flames eliminated the Oilers in a seven-game Smythe Division final. The series-winning goal came when Edmonton defenseman Steve Smith bounced a clearing pass off goalie Grant Fuhr into his own net. Calgary then defeated the Norris Division champion St. Louis Blues in seven games to reach the Stanley Cup finals.

Upsets also abounded in the Prince of Wales Conference, where the Montreal Canadiens prevailed, setting up the first all-Canadian final since 1967. Mats Naslund's 110 points made him the first Hab to crack the top 10 in scoring since Guy Lafleur in 1980. Rookie Brian Skrudland scored the fastest overtime goal in history after just nine seconds for a 3–2 win over Calgary in game two of the Stanley Cup finals, and newcomer Claude Lemieux had 10 goals in the playoffs. But the most important rookie of all was Patrick Roy. He posted a 1.92 goals-against average in the playoffs and backstopped Montreal to a five-game Stanley Cup victory. Roy was the first rookie since Harry Lumley in 1945 to register a shutout in the finals when he blanked the Flames for a 1–0 victory in game four and was a deserving recipient of the Conn Smythe Trophy as playoff MVP.

Flukes and the Forum – Steve Smith's "own goal" eliminated the Oilers and fired up the Flames, but a rookie-laden Montreal club harnessed "the ghosts of Cups past" to clip Calgary in five.

With 45 goals and 54 assists, Troy Murray was rewarded with the Selke Trophy as the top defensive forward after the best offensive season of his career.

Leaders, 1985-86

GOALS

Name, Team	G
Jari Kurri, Edm.	68
Mike Bossy, NYI	61
Tim Kerr, Phi.	58
Glenn Anderson, Edm.	54
Michel Goulet, Que.	53
Wayne Gretzky, Edm.	52
Mario Lemieux, Pit.	48
Paul Coffey, Edm.	48
Denis Savard, Chi.	47
Dale Hawerchuk, Wpg.	46

ASSISTS

Name, Team	A
Wayne Gretzky, Edm.	163
Mario Lemieux, Pit.	93
Paul Coffey, Edm.	90
Peter Stastny, Que.	81
Neal Broten, Min.	76
Denis Savard, Chi.	69
Bernie Federko, St.L.	68
Mats Naslund, Mtl.	67
Jari Kurri, Edm.	63
Larry Robinson, Mtl.	63

POWERPLAY GOALS

Name, Team	PPG
Tim Kerr, Phi.	34
Michel Goulet, Que.	28
Doug Shedden, Pit/Det.	21
Mike Bossy, NYI	21
Keith Crowder, Bos.	20
Ilkka Sinisalo, Phi.	19
Dino Ciccarelli, Min.	19
Mats Naslund, Mtl.	19
Glenn Anderson, Edm.	18
Dale Hawerchuk, Wpg.	18
Dave Christian, Wsh.	18

SHORTHAND GOALS

Name, Team	SHG
Paul Coffey, Edm.	9
Mark Howe, Phi.	7
Jari Kurri, Edm.	6
Dave Poulin, Phi.	6
Mark Messier, Edm.	5
Rick Paterson, Chi.	5
Troy Murray, Chi.	5
Steve Bozek, Cgy.	4
Bengt-Ake Gustafsson, Wsh.	4
Stan Smyl, Van.	4
Bernie Nicholls, L.A.	4
Dirk Graham, Min.	4

GAME-WINNING GOALS

Name, Team	GWG
Glenn Anderson, Edm.	9
Jari Kurri, Edm.	9
Mike Bossy, NYI	9
Kevin Dineen, Hfd.	8
Tim Kerr, Phi.	8
Peter Stastny, Que.	8
Joe Mullen, St.L/Cgy	8
Denis Savard, Chi.	8
Seven tied with	7

GOALIE WINS

Name, Team	W
Bob Froese, Phi.	31
John Vanbiesbrouck, NYR	31
Grant Fuhr, Edm.	29
Tom Barrasso, Buf.	29
Reggie Lemelin, Cgy.	29
Al Jensen, Wsh.	28
Andy Moog, Edm.	27
Mike Liut, Hfd.	27
Clint Malarchuk, Que.	26
Don Beaupre, Min.	25

SHUTOUTS

Name, Team	SO
Bob Froese, Phi.	5
Clint Malarchuk, Que.	4
Doug Soetaert, Mtl.	3
John Vanbiesbrouck, NYR	3
Eight tied with	2

SAVE PERCENTAGE

Name, Team	SV%
Bob Froese, Phi.	.909
Kelly Hrudey, NYI	.906
Clint Malarchuk, Que.	.895
Rick Wamsley, St.L.	.894
Don Beaupre, Min.	.892

FIRST TEAM ALL-STARS

Name, Team	Position
Wayne Gretzky, Edm.	C
Mike Bossy, NYI	RW
Michel Goulet, Que.	LW
Paul Coffey, Edm.	D
Mark Howe, Phi.	D
John Vanbiesbrouck, NYR	G

SECOND TEAM ALL-STARS

Name, Team	Position
Mario Lemieux, Pit.	C
Jari Kurri, Edm.	RW
Mats Naslund, Mtl.	LW
Larry Robinson, Mtl.	D
Raymond Bourque, Bos.	D
Bob Froese, Phi.	G

ALL-ROOKIE TEAM

Name, Team	Position
Mike Ridley, NYR	C
Kjell Dahlin, Mtl.	RW
Wendel Clark, Tor.	LW
Gary Suter, Cgy.	D
Dana Murzyn, Hfd.	D
Patrick Roy, Mtl.	G

TROPHY WINNERS

Trophy	Awarded For	Winner	Team
Hart	MVP	Wayne Gretzky	Edm.
Art Ross	Top Scorer	Wayne Gretzky	Edm.
Norris	Top Defenseman	Paul Coffey	Edm
Calder	Top Rookie	Gary Suter	Cgy.
Selke	Top Defensive Forward	Troy Murray	Chi.
Vezina	Top Goaltender	John Vanbiesbrouck	NYR
Jennings	Fewest Goals Against	Bob Froese	Phi.
		Darren Jensen	Phi.
Adams	Top Coach	Glen Sather	Edm.
Byng	Gentlemanly Conduct	Mike Bossy	NYI
Masterton	Perseverance, Sportsmanship	Charlie Simmer	Bos.
Pearson	NHLPA MVP	Mario Lemieux	Pit.
Conn Smythe	Playoff MVP	Patrick Roy	Mtl.
Patrick	Service to Hockey in U.S.	John MacInnes	
		Jack Riley	
Entry Draft	First Overall Selection	Joe Murphy	Det.

NHL NOTEBOOK

TRANSACTIONS

- Oct. 7, 1985 – New York Rangers signed free agent Mike Ridley.
- Nov. 27, 1985 – Winnipeg Jets traded defenseman Robert Picard to the Quebec Nordiques in exchange for Mario Marois.
- Dec. 6, 1985 – Washington traded Doug Jarvis to the Hartford Whalers for Jorgen Pettersson.
- Feb. 1, 1986 – Calgary Flames traded Eddy Beers, Gino Cavallini and Charlie Bourgeois to the St. Louis Blues in exchange for Joey Mullen, Terry Johnson and Rik Wilson.

RECORDS

- Oct. 10, 1985 – New Jersey's Greg Adams set an NHL record for most assists (five) in an opening night game as the Devils won 6-5 at Philadelphia.
- Dec. 11, 1985 – Edmonton Oilers beat the Blackhawks 12-9 in Chicago in the highest scoring game in modern NHL history. The teams set another record with 12 goals scored in the second period.
- Jan. 28, 1986 – Denis Potvin scored his 271st NHL goal to break Bobby Orr's record for most career goals by a defenseman. Goal #271 helped the Islanders to a 9-2 win over Toronto.
- Apr. 12, 1986 – Mike Bossy scored his 83rd career playoff goal to break Maurice Richard's long held NHL record of 82. #83 came in a 3-1 Islanders loss to Washington in game three of the Patrick Division semi-finals.

MILESTONES

- Jan. 11, 1986 – Marcel Dionne became the first player in NHL history to get 20 goals in each of his first 15 seasons when he scored twice (and added an assist) in a 4-4 Kings tie at St. Louis.
- Mar. 26, 1986 – Minnesota center Neal Broten became the first U.S. born player to score 100 points in a season. He reached the century mark with two assists in a 6-1 North Stars victory at Toronto.
- May 18, 1986 – Montreal center Brian Skrudland scored the fastest overtime goal in Stanley Cup playoff history (just :09 into overtime) to give Montreal a 3-2 win over Calgary, in game two of the Stanley Cup finals.
- May 22, 1986 – Montreal Canadiens became the first team to win 100 games in the Stanley Cup finals with a 1-0 win over the Calgary Flames in game four of the Stanley Cup finals. Rookie Patrick Roy recorded his first career playoff shutout.

1986 Playoffs

DIVISION SEMI-FINALS

Apr.	9	Hartford	3	at	Quebec	2 OT
Apr.	10	Hartford	4	at	Quebec	1
Apr.	12	Quebec	4	at	Hartford	9

Hartford won best-of-five series 3–0

Apr.	9	Boston	1	at	Montreal	3
Apr.	10	Boston	2	at	Montreal	3
Apr.	12	Montreal	4	at	Boston	3

Montreal won best-of-five series 3–0

Apr.	9	NY Rangers	6	at	Philadelphia	2
Apr.	10	NY Rangers	1	at	Philadelphia	2
Apr.	12	Philadelphia	2	at	NY Rangers	5
Apr.	13	Philadelphia	7	at	NY Rangers	1
Apr.	15	NY Rangers	5	at	Philadelphia	2

NY Rangers won best-of-five series 3–2

Apr.	9	NY Islanders	1	at	Washington	3
Apr.	10	NY Islanders	2	at	Washington	5
Apr.	12	Washington	3	at	NY Islanders	1

Washington won best-of-five series 3–0

Apr.	9	Toronto	5	at	Chicago	3
Apr.	10	Toronto	6	at	Chicago	4
Apr.	12	Chicago	2	at	Toronto	7

Toronto won best-of-five series 3–0

Apr.	9	St. Louis	2	at	Minnesota	1
Apr.	10	St. Louis	2	at	Minnesota	6
Apr.	12	Minnesota	3	at	St. Louis	4
Apr.	13	Minnesota	7	at	St. Louis	4
Apr.	15	St. Louis	6	at	Minnesota	3

St. Louis won best-of-five series 3–2

Apr.	9	Vancouver	3	at	Edmonton	7
Apr.	10	Vancouver	1	at	Edmonton	5
Apr.	12	Edmonton	5	at	Vancouver	1

Edmonton won best-of-five series 3–0

Apr.	9	Winnipeg	1	at	Calgary	5
Apr.	10	Winnipeg	4	at	Calgary	6
Apr.	12	Calgary	4	at	Winnipeg	3 OT

Calgary won best-of-five series 3–0

DIVISION FINALS

Apr.	17	Hartford	4	at	Montreal	1
Apr.	19	Hartford	1	at	Montreal	3
Apr.	21	Montreal	4	at	Hartford	1
Apr.	23	Montreal	1	at	Hartford	2 OT
Apr.	25	Hartford	3	at	Montreal	5
Apr.	27	Montreal	0	at	Hartford	1
Apr.	29	Hartford	1	at	Montreal	2 OT

Montreal won best-of-seven series 4–3

Apr.	17	NY Rangers	4	at	Washington	3 OT
Apr.	19	NY Rangers	1	at	Washington	8
Apr.	21	Washington	6	at	NY Rangers	3
Apr.	23	Washington	5	at	NY Rangers	6 OT
Apr.	25	NY Rangers	4	at	Washington	2
Apr.	27	Washington	1	at	NY Rangers	2

NY Rangers won best-of-seven series 4–2

Apr.	18	Toronto	1	at	St. Louis	6
Apr.	20	Toronto	3	at	St. Louis	0
Apr.	22	St. Louis	2	at	Toronto	5
Apr.	24	St. Louis	7	at	Toronto	4
Apr.	26	Toronto	3	at	St. Louis	4 OT
Apr.	28	St. Louis	3	at	Toronto	5
Apr.	30	Toronto	1	at	St. Louis	2

St. Louis won best-of-seven series 4–3

Apr.	18	Calgary	4	at	Edmonton	1
Apr.	20	Calgary	5	at	Edmonton	6 OT
Apr.	22	Edmonton	2	at	Calgary	3
Apr.	24	Edmonton	7	at	Calgary	4
Apr.	26	Calgary	4	at	Edmonton	1
Apr.	28	Edmonton	5	at	Calgary	2
Apr.	30	Calgary	3	at	Edmonton	2

Calgary won best-of-seven series 4–3

CONFERENCE FINALS

May	1	NY Rangers	1	at	Montreal	2
May	3	NY Rangers	2	at	Montreal	6
May	5	Montreal	4	at	NY Rangers	3 OT
May	7	Montreal	0	at	NY Rangers	2
May	9	NY Rangers	1	at	Montreal	3

Montreal won best-of-seven series 4–1

May	2	St. Louis	3	at	Calgary	2
May	4	St. Louis	2	at	Calgary	8
May	6	Calgary	5	at	St. Louis	3
May	8	Calgary	2	at	St. Louis	5
May	10	St. Louis	2	at	Calgary	4
May	12	Calgary	5	at	St. Louis	6 OT
May	14	St. Louis	1	at	Calgary	2

Calgary won best-of-seven series 4–3

FINALS

May	16	Montreal	2	at	Calgary	5
May	18	Montreal	3	at	Calgary	2 OT
May	20	Calgary	3	at	Montreal	5
May	22	Calgary	0	at	Montreal	1
May	24	Montreal	4	at	Calgary	3

Montreal won best-of-seven series 4–1

1985-86 – Montreal Canadiens – Bob Gainey (Captain), Doug Soetaert, Patrick Roy, Rick Green, David Maley, Ryan Walter, Serge Boisvert, Mario Tremblay, Bobby Smith, Craig Ludwig, Tom Kurvers, Kjell Dahlin, Larry Robinson, Guy Carbonneau, Chris Chelios, Petr Svoboda, Mats Naslund, Lucien DeBlois, Steve Rooney, Gaston Gingras, Mike Lalor, Chris Nilan, John Kordic, Claude Lemieux, Mike McPhee, Brian Skrudland, Stephane Richer, Ronald Corey (President), Serge Savard (General Manager), Jean Perron (Coach), Jacques Laperrière (Assistant Coach), Jean Béliveau, Francois-Xavier Seigneur, Fred Steer (Vice Presidents), Jacques Lemaire, André Boudrias (Assistant General Managers), Claude Ruel (Scout), Yves Belanger (Athletic Therapist), Gaetan Lefebvre (Assistant Athletic Therapist), Eddy Palchak (Trainer), Sylvain Toupin (Assistant Trainer).

LEADING PLAYOFF SCORERS

Player	Club	GP	G	A	PTS	PIM
Doug Gilmour	St. Louis	19	9	12	21	25
Bernie Federko	St. Louis	19	7	14	21	17
Joe Mullen	Calgary	21	12	7	19	4
Mats Naslund	Montreal	20	8	11	19	4
Wayne Gretzky	Edmonton	10	8	11	19	2
Al MacInnis	Calgary	21	4	15	19	30
Lanny McDonald	Calgary	22	11	7	18	30
Paul Reinhart	Calgary	21	5	13	18	4
Greg Paslawski	St. Louis	17	10	7	17	13
Pierre Larouche	NY Rangers	16	8	9	17	2

LEADING PLAYOFF GOALTENDERS

Goaltender	Club	GPI	Mins	GA	SO	Avg.
Mike Liut	Hartford	8	441	14	1	1.90
Patrick Roy	Montreal	20	1218	39	1	1.92
Pete Peeters	Washington	9	544	24	0	2.65
Mike Vernon	Calgary	21	1229	60	0	2.93
Greg Millen	St. Louis	10	586	29	0	2.97

PLAYOFF GOALS

Name, Team	G
Joe Mullen, Cgy.	12
Lanny McDonald, Cgy.	11
Greg Paslawski, St.L.	10
Claude Lemieux, Mtl.	10
Doug Gilmour, St.L.	9
Five tied with	8

PLAYOFF ASSISTS

Name, Team	A
Al MacInnis, Cgy.	15
Bernie Federko, St.L.	14
Larry Robinson, Mtl.	13
Paul Reinhart, Cgy.	13
Doug Gilmour, St.L.	12
Two tied with	11

PLAYOFF POWERPLAY GOALS

Name, Team	PPG
Dan Quinn, Cgy.	5
Wayne Gretzky, Edm.	4
Pierre Larouche, NYR	4
Wilf Paiement, NYR	4
Mats Naslund, Mtl.	4
Claude Lemieux, Mtl.	4
Paul Reinhart, Cgy.	4
Joe Mullen, Cgy.	4
Lanny McDonald, Cgy.	4

PLAYOFF SHORTHAND GOALS

Name, Team	SHG
Mark Messier, Edm.	2
Bob Brooke, NYR	2
Doug Gilmour, St.L.	2
Guy Carbonneau, Mtl.	2
Hakan Loob, Cgy.	2

PLAYOFF GAME-WINNING GOALS

Name, Team	GWG
Claude Lemieux, Mtl.	4
Walt Poddubny, Tor.	3
Bob Gainey, Mtl.	3
Bobby Smith, Mtl.	3
12 tied with	2

PLAYOFF GOALIE WINS

Name, Team	W
Patrick Roy, Mtl.	15
Mike Vernon, Cgy.	12
John Vanbiesbrouck, NYR	8
Greg Millen, St.L.	6
Ken Wregget, Tor.	6

PLAYOFF SHUTOUTS

Name, Team	SO
Mike Liut, Hfd.	1
Ken Wregget, Tor.	1
John Vanbiesbrouck, NYR	1
Patrick Roy, Mtl.	1

PLAYOFF SAVE PERCENTAGE

Name, Team	SV%
Mike Liut, Hfd.	.938
Patrick Roy, Mtl.	.923
Greg Millen, St.L.	.912
Pete Peeters, Wsh.	.905
Ken Wregget, Tor.	.901

1986-87

Stanley Cup • Edmonton Oilers

FINAL STANDINGS

CLARENCE CAMPBELL CONFERENCE

Team	GP	W	L	T	GF	GA	PTS
Norris Division							
St. Louis	80	32	33	15	281	293	79
Detroit	80	34	36	10	260	274	78
Chicago	80	29	37	14	290	310	72
Toronto	80	32	42	6	286	319	70
Minnesota	80	30	40	10	296	314	70
Smythe Division							
Edmonton	80	50	24	6	372	284	106
Calgary	80	46	31	3	318	289	95
Winnipeg	80	40	32	8	279	271	88
Los Angeles	80	31	41	8	318	341	70
Vancouver	80	29	43	8	282	314	66
PRINCE OF WALES CONFERENCE							
Adams Division							
Hartford	80	43	30	7	287	270	93
Montreal	80	41	29	10	277	241	92
Boston	80	39	34	7	301	276	85
Quebec	80	31	39	10	267	276	72
Buffalo	80	28	44	8	280	308	64
Patrick Division							
Philadelphia	80	46	26	8	310	245	100
Washington	80	38	32	10	285	278	86
NY Islanders	80	35	33	12	279	281	82
NY Rangers	80	34	38	8	307	323	76
Pittsburgh	80	30	38	12	297	290	72
New Jersey	80	29	45	6	293	368	64

LEADING SCORERS

Player	Club	GP	G	A	PTS	PIM
Wayne Gretzky	Edmonton	79	62	121	183	28
Jari Kurri	Edmonton	79	54	54	108	41
Mario Lemieux	Pittsburgh	63	54	53	107	57
Mark Messier	Edmonton	77	37	70	107	73
Doug Gilmour	St. Louis	80	42	63	105	58
Dino Ciccarelli	Minnesota	80	52	51	103	88
Dale Hawerchuk	Winnipeg	80	47	53	100	52
Michel Goulet	Quebec	75	49	47	96	61
Tim Kerr	Philadelphia	75	58	37	95	57
Raymond Bourque	Boston	78	23	72	95	36
Ron Francis	Hartford	75	30	63	93	45
Denis Savard	Chicago	70	40	50	90	108
Steve Yzerman	Detroit	80	31	59	90	43
Joe Mullen	Calgary	79	47	40	87	14
Walt Poddubny	NY Rangers	75	40	47	87	49
Bryan Trottier	NY Islanders	80	23	64	87	50
Luc Robitaille	Los Angeles	79	45	39	84	28
Marcel Dionne	L.A./NYR	81	28	56	84	60
Steve Larmer	Chicago	80	28	56	84	22
Bernie Nicholls	Los Angeles	80	33	48	81	101
Larry Murphy	Washington	80	23	58	81	39
Dan Quinn	Cgy./Pit.	80	31	49	80	54
Mats Naslund	Montreal	79	25	55	80	16
Four players tied with					79	

LEADING GOALTENDERS

Goaltender	Club	GPI	MINS	GA	SO	AVG
Brian Hayward	Montreal	37	2178	102	1	2.81
Patrick Roy	Montreal	46	2686	131	1	2.93
Ron Hextall	Philadelphia	66	3799	190	1	3.00
Daniel Berthiaume	Winnipeg	31	1758	93	1	3.17
Mario Gosselin	Quebec	30	1625	86	0	3.18
Glen Hanlon	Detroit	36	1963	104	1	3.18
Pete Peeters	Washington	37	2002	107	0	3.21
Mike Liut	Hartford	59	3476	187	4	3.23
Pokey Reddick	Winnipeg	48	2762	149	0	3.24
Bob Mason	Washington	45	2536	137	0	3.24

Rookie sensation Ron Hextall handled the puck like no goaltender before him. Perhaps offensive talent was in his genes, being the grandson of Hockey Hall of Famer Bryan Hextall and the son of former NHL player Bryan Hextall Jr.

Numerous coaching changes took place before and during the 1986–87 season. The New York Islanders named Terry Simpson their new head coach and promoted four-time Stanley Cup winner Al Arbour to vice president. The New York Rangers named Phil Esposito their new general manager, and he made 19 trades during the course of the year. He also fired coach Ted Sator after just 19 games and took over the chores himself when an inner-ear infection sidelined Sator's replacement, Tom Webster. Sator was hired by the Buffalo Sabres, replacing Craig Ramsay, who had replaced Scotty Bowman. In Boston, the Bruins fired Butch Goring and hired Terry O'Reilly.

Four of the five Norris Division teams made coaching changes. Jacques Demers left St. Louis for the Detroit. Jacques Martin, a successful junior coach, took the job in St. Louis.

In Minnesota, the North Stars sacked Glen Sonmor in favor of Lorne Henning and the Toronto Maple Leafs turned to John Brophy after firing Dan Maloney. Bob Pulford stayed on as Chicago's coach, but the team did change the spelling of its nickname from Black Hawks to Blackhawks after discovering that the moniker had been spelled as one word in the club's original NHL charter.

In an attempt to limit upsets, the first round of the playoffs was extended to a best-of-seven series. The New York Islanders and Washington Capitals took the new format to its limit—and then some. Pat LaFontaine's goal in the fourth overtime period of game seven provided the Islanders with the victory.

Fueled by their playoff defeat in 1986, the Edmonton Oilers again led the regular season, though their 106 points were the fewest by a first-place team since 1969–70. Wayne Gretzky won the Art Ross Trophy for the seventh consecutive season with 62 goals and 121 assists. He was awarded the Hart Trophy as MVP for an eighth consecutive season as well. After playoff victories over the Los Angeles Kings, Winnipeg Jets and Detroit Red Wings, Edmonton faced Philadelphia, the NHL's only other 100-point team, for the Stanley Cup.

The Oilers jumped out to a three-games-to-one lead in the finals, but the Flyers rallied to tie the series. It was Edmonton's turn to come back in game seven as they turned an early 1–0 deficit into a 3–1 victory and their third Cup championship. Wayne Gretzky hoisted the Stanley Cup and then passed it to Steve Smith, whose errant clearing pass the year before had knocked Edmonton out of the playoffs. Flyers goalie Ron Hextall played well enough in defeat to win the Conn Smythe Trophy as, for the second year in a row, a rookie goalie was named playoff MVP. Hextall also won the Vezina Trophy as the NHL's top goaltender.

Back on Track – Demers brought respect to Detroit, "The Great One" took home his eighth straight Hart Trophy, Ron Hextall was Herculean in goal for Philly, but the Oilers outlasted the Flyers in the finals.

An overtime hero in 1987, Pat LaFontaine had tied Mike Bossy for the Islanders lead with 38 goals during the regular season. He would reach a high of 54 in 1989–90.

Leaders, 1986-87

GOALS

Name, Team	G
Wayne Gretzky, Edm.	62
Tim Kerr, Phi.	58
Mario Lemieux, Pit.	54
Jari Kurri, Edm.	54
Dino Ciccarelli, Min.	52
Michel Goulet, Que.	49
Joe Mullen, Cgy.	47
Dale Hawerchuk, Wpg.	47
Luc Robitaille, L.A.	45
Doug Gilmour, St.L.	42

ASSISTS

Name, Team	A
Wayne Gretzky, Edm.	121
Raymond Bourque, Bos.	72
Mark Messier, Edm.	70
Bryan Trottier, NYI	64
Ron Francis, Hfd.	63
Doug Gilmour, St.L.	63
Steve Yzerman, Det.	59
Larry Murphy, Wsh.	58
Al MacInnis, Cgy.	56
Steve Larmer, Chi.	56
Marcel Dionne, LA/NYR	56

POWERPLAY GOALS

Name, Team	PPG
Tim Kerr, Phi.	26
Dino Ciccarelli, Min.	22
Mario Lemieux, Pit.	19
Pat LaFontaine, NYI	19
Luc Robitaille, L.A.	18
Jimmy Carson, L.A.	18
Pat Verbeek, N.J.	17
Michel Goulet, Que.	17
Doug Gilmour, St.L.	17
Gerard Gallant, Det.	17

SHORTHAND GOALS

Name, Team	SHG
Wayne Gretzky, Edm.	7
Petri Skriko, Van.	6
Mike Gartner, Wsh.	6
Russ Courtnall, Tor.	6
Brian Propp, Phi.	5
Dirk Graham, Min.	5
Mark Howe, Phi.	4
Rick Middleton, Bos.	4
Mark Messier, Edm.	4
Craig MacTavish, Edm.	4

GAME-WINNING GOALS

Name, Team	GWG
Joe Mullen, Cgy.	12
Tim Kerr, Phi.	10
Mike Gartner, Wsh.	10
Brent Sutter, NYI	8
Denis Savard, Chi.	7
Peter Zezel, Phi.	7
Ron Francis, Hfd.	7
Greg Paslawski, St.L.	7
Tony Tanti, Van.	7
Steve Thomas, Tor.	7
Kevin Dineen, Hfd.	7
Bobby Smith, Mtl.	7

GOALIE WINS

Name, Team	W
Ron Hextall, Phi.	37
Mike Liut, Hfd.	31
Mike Vernon, Cgy.	30
Andy Moog, Edm.	28
Alain Chevrier, N.J.	24
Grant Fuhr, Edm.	22
Patrick Roy, Mtl.	22
Ken Wregget, Tor.	22
Kelly Hrudey, NYI	21
Pokey Reddick, Wpg.	21

SHUTOUTS

Name, Team	SO
Mike Liut, Hfd.	4
Bill Ranford, Bos.	3
Reggie Lemelin, Cgy.	2
Allan Bester, Tor.	2
Tom Barrasso, Buf.	2

SAVE PERCENTAGE

Name, Team	SV%
Ron Hextall, Phi.	.902
Bob Sauve, Chi.	.894
Brian Hayward, Mtl.	.894
Glen Hanlon, Det.	.893
Patrick Roy, Mtl.	.892

FIRST TEAM ALL-STARS

Name, Team	Position
Wayne Gretzky, Edm.	C
Jari Kurri, Edm.	RW
Michel Goulet, Que.	LW
Raymond Bourque, Bos.	D
Mark Howe, Phi.	D
Ron Hextall, Phi.	G

SECOND TEAM ALL-STARS

Name, Team	Position
Mario Lemieux, Pit.	C
Tim Kerr, Phi.	RW
Luc Robitaille, L.A.	LW
Larry Murphy, Wsh.	D
Al MacInnis, Cgy.	D
Mike Liut, Hfd.	G

ALL-ROOKIE TEAM

Name, Team	Position
Jimmy Carson, L.A.	C
Jim Sandlak, Van.	RW
Luc Robitaille, L.A.	LW
Steve Duchesne, L.A.	D
Brian Benning, St.L.	D
Ron Hextall, Phi.	G

TROPHY WINNERS

Trophy	Awarded For	Winner	Team
Hart	MVP	Wayne Gretzky	Edm.
Art Ross	Top Scorer	Wayne Gretzky	Edm.
Norris	Top Defenseman	Raymond Bourque	Bos.
Calder	Top Rookie	Luc Robitaille	L.A.
Selke	Top Defensive Forward	Dave Poulin	Phi.
Vezina	Top Goaltender	Ron Hextall	Phi.
Jennings	Fewest Goals Against	Patrick Roy	Mtl.
		Brian Hayward	Mtl.
Adams	Top Coach	Jacques Demers	Det.
Byng	Gentlemanly Conduct	Joe Mullen	Cgy.
Masterton	Perseverance, Sportsmanship	Doug Jarvis	Hfd.
Pearson	NHLPA MVP	Wayne Gretzky	Edm.
Conn Smythe	Playoff MVP	Ron Hextall	Phi.
Patrick	Service to Hockey in U.S.	Hobey Baker	
		Frank Mathers	
Entry Draft	First Overall Selection	Pierre Turgeon	Buf.

NHL NOTEBOOK

TRANSACTIONS

- June 6, 1986 – Boston Bruins obtained Cam Neely and Vancouver's first-round choice in the 1987 Entry Draft from Vancouver in exchange for Barry Pederson.
- July 28, 1986 – Free agent Dave Lewis signed a contract with the Detroit Red Wings after leaving the New Jersey Devils.
- Sept. 24, 1986 – Montreal Canadiens signed Sylvain Lefebvre as a free agent.
- Mar. 10, 1987 – L.A. Kings traded Marcel Dionne to the New York Rangers in exchange for Tom Laidlaw and Bobby Carpenter.

RECORDS

- Apr. 5, 1987 – Hartford Whalers' Doug Jarvis completed his 12th NHL season by playing in his 962nd straight game. Jarvis went on to play the first two games of the 1987-88 season before retiring with an NHL record 964 straight games.
- Apr. 9, 1987 – Edmonton set a Stanley Cup playoff record for most goals in a game when they beat L.A. 13-3 in game two of the Smythe Division semi-finals.
- Apr. 12, 1987 – Montreal completed their sweep of the Bruins in the Adams Division semi-finals with a 4-2 win in game four at Boston. It was the Canadiens' 18th straight playoff series victory over Boston (a playoff record dating back to 1946).
- May 22, 1987 – Edmonton's Mark Messier set a new playoff record with his eighth career shorthanded goal. It came in a 5-3 loss to Philadelphia, in game three of the Stanley Cup finals.

MILESTONES

- Feb. 6, 1987 – Mike Bossy became the first player in NHL history to get 30 goals in each of his first 10 seasons when he scored his 30th of the year for the Islanders in a 3-3 tie at Edmonton.
- Mar. 8, 1987 – Mike Keenan became the first coach in NHL history to win 40 games in each of his first three seasons as the Flyers won 7-3 over the New Jersey Devils in Philadelphia.
- Apr. 4, 1987 – Denis Potvin scored twice to become the first defenseman in NHL history to score 1,000 career points. It came on a goal as the Islanders tied Buffalo 6-6.
- Apr. 9, 1987 – Wayne Gretzky had six assists, including his 177th career playoff point, to pass Jean Beliveau and put him into first place on the all-time playoff scoring list, as the Oilers beat the Kings 13-3 in Edmonton.

1987 Playoffs

DIVISION SEMI-FINALS

Apr.	8	Quebec	2	at	Hartford	3 OT
Apr.	9	Quebec	4	at	Hartford	5
Apr.	11	Hartford	1	at	Quebec	5
Apr.	12	Hartford	1	at	Quebec	4
Apr.	14	Quebec	7	at	Hartford	5
Apr.	16	Hartford	4	at	Quebec	5 OT

Quebec won best-of-seven series 4–2

Apr.	8	Boston	2	at	Montreal	6
Apr.	9	Boston	3	at	Montreal	4 OT
Apr.	11	Montreal	5	at	Boston	4
Apr.	12	Montreal	4	at	Boston	2

Montreal won best-of-seven series 4–0

Apr.	8	NY Rangers	3	at	Philadelphia	0
Apr.	9	NY Rangers	3	at	Philadelphia	8
Apr.	11	Philadelphia	3	at	NY Rangers	0
Apr.	12	Philadelphia	3	at	NY Rangers	6
Apr.	14	NY Rangers	1	at	Philadelphia	3
Apr.	16	Philadelphia	5	at	NY Rangers	0

Philadelphia won best-of-seven series 4–2

Apr.	8	NY Islanders	3	at	Washington	4
Apr.	9	NY Islanders	3	at	Washington	1
Apr.	11	Washington	2	at	NY Islanders	0
Apr.	12	Washington	4	at	NY Islanders	1
Apr.	14	NY Islanders	4	at	Washington	2
Apr.	16	Washington	4	at	NY Islanders	5
Apr.	18	NY Islanders	3	at	Washington	2 4OT

NY Islanders won best-of-seven series 4–3

Apr.	8	Toronto	1	at	St. Louis	3
Apr.	9	Toronto	3	at	St. Louis	2 OT
Apr.	11	St. Louis	5	at	Toronto	3
Apr.	12	St. Louis	1	at	Toronto	2
Apr.	14	Toronto	2	at	St. Louis	1
Apr.	16	St. Louis	0	at	Toronto	4

Toronto won best-of-seven series 4–2

Apr.	8	Chicago	1	at	Detroit	3
Apr.	9	Chicago	1	at	Detroit	5
Apr.	11	Detroit	4	at	Chicago	3 OT
Apr.	12	Detroit	3	at	Chicago	1

Detroit won best-of-seven series 4–0

Apr.	8	Los Angeles	5	at	Edmonton	2
Apr.	9	Los Angeles	3	at	Edmonton	13
Apr.	11	Edmonton	6	at	Los Angeles	5
Apr.	12	Edmonton	6	at	Los Angeles	3
Apr.	14	Los Angeles	4	at	Edmonton	5

Edmonton won best-of-seven series 4–1

Apr.	8	Winnipeg	4	at	Calgary	2
Apr.	9	Winnipeg	3	at	Calgary	2
Apr.	11	Calgary	3	at	Winnipeg	2 OT
Apr.	12	Calgary	3	at	Winnipeg	4
Apr.	14	Winnipeg	3	at	Calgary	4
Apr.	16	Calgary	1	at	Winnipeg	6

Winnipeg won best-of-seven series 4–2

DIVISION FINALS

Apr.	20	Quebec	7	at	Montreal	5
Apr.	22	Quebec	2	at	Montreal	1
Apr.	24	Montreal	7	at	Quebec	2
Apr.	26	Montreal	3	at	Quebec	2 OT
Apr.	28	Quebec	2	at	Montreal	3
Apr.	30	Montreal	2	at	Quebec	3
May	2	Quebec	3	at	Montreal	5

Montreal won best-of-seven series 4–3

Apr.	20	NY Islanders	2	at	Philadelphia	4
Apr.	22	NY Islanders	2	at	Philadelphia	1
Apr.	24	Philadelphia	4	at	NY Islanders	1
Apr.	26	Philadelphia	6	at	NY Islanders	4
Apr.	28	NY Islanders	2	at	Philadelphia	1
Apr.	30	Philadelphia	2	at	NY Islanders	4
May	2	NY Islanders	1	at	Philadelphia	5

Philadelphia won best-of-seven series 4–3

Apr.	21	Toronto	4	at	Detroit	2
Apr.	23	Toronto	7	at	Detroit	2
Apr.	25	Detroit	4	at	Toronto	2
Apr.	27	Detroit	2	at	Toronto	3 OT
Apr.	29	Toronto	0	at	Detroit	3
May	1	Detroit	4	at	Toronto	2
May	3	Toronto	0	at	Detroit	3

Detroit won best-of-seven series 4–3

Apr.	21	Winnipeg	2	at	Edmonton	3 OT
Apr.	23	Winnipeg	3	at	Edmonton	5
Apr.	25	Edmonton	5	at	Winnipeg	2
Apr.	27	Edmonton	4	at	Winnipeg	2

Edmonton won best-of-seven series 4–0

CONFERENCE FINALS

May	4	Montreal	3	at	Philadelphia	4 OT
May	6	Montreal	5	at	Philadelphia	2
May	8	Philadelphia	4	at	Montreal	3
May	10	Philadelphia	6	at	Montreal	3
May	12	Montreal	5	at	Philadelphia	2
May	14	Philadelphia	4	at	Montreal	3

Philadelphia won best-of-seven series 4–2

May	5	Detroit	3	at	Edmonton	1
May	7	Detroit	1	at	Edmonton	4
May	9	Edmonton	2	at	Detroit	1
May	11	Edmonton	3	at	Detroit	2
May	13	Detroit	3	at	Edmonton	6

Edmonton won best-of-seven series 4–1

FINALS

May	17	Philadelphia	2	at	Edmonton	4
May	20	Philadelphia	2	at	Edmonton	3 OT
May	22	Edmonton	3	at	Philadelphia	5
May	24	Edmonton	4	at	Philadelphia	1
May	26	Philadelphia	4	at	Edmonton	3
May	28	Edmonton	2	at	Philadelphia	3
May	31	Philadelphia	1	at	Edmonton	3

Edmonton won best-of-seven series 4–3

1986-87 – Edmonton Oilers – Glenn Anderson, Jeff Beukeboom, Kelly Buchberger, Paul Coffey, Grant Fuhr, Randy Gregg, Wayne Gretzky (Captain), Charlie Huddy, Dave Hunter, Mike Krushelnyski, Jari Kurri, Moe Lemay, Kevin Lowe, Craig MacTavish, Kevin McClelland, Marty McSorley, Mark Messier, Andy Moog, Craig Muni, Kent Nilsson, Jaroslav Pouzar, Reijo Ruotsalainen, Steve Smith, Esa Tikkanen, Peter Pocklington (Owner), Glen Sather (General Manager/Coach), John Muckler (Co-Coach), Ted Green, Ron Low (Assistant Coaches), Bruce MacGregor (Assistant General Manager), Barry Fraser (Director of Player Personnel), Peter Millar (Athletic Therapist), Barrie Stafford (Trainer), Lyle Kulchisky (Assistant Trainer).

LEADING PLAYOFF SCORERS

Player	Club	GP	G	A	PTS	PIM
Wayne Gretzky	Edmonton	21	5	29	34	6
Brian Propp	Philadelphia	26	12	16	28	10
Mark Messier	Edmonton	21	12	16	28	16
Glenn Anderson	Edmonton	21	14	13	27	59
Pelle Eklund	Philadelphia	26	7	20	27	2
Jari Kurri	Edmonton	21	15	10	25	20
Mats Naslund	Montreal	17	7	15	22	11
Rick Tocchet	Philadelphia	26	11	10	21	72
Larry Robinson	Montreal	17	3	17	20	6
Ryan Walter	Montreal	17	7	12	19	10
Kent Nilsson	Edmonton	21	6	13	19	6

LEADING PLAYOFF GOALTENDERS

Goaltender	Club	GPI	Mins	GA	SO	Avg.
Glen Hanlon	Detroit	8	467	13	2	1.67
Ken Wregget	Toronto	13	761	29	1	2.29
Grant Fuhr	Edmonton	19	1148	47	0	2.46
Kelly Hrudey	NY Islanders	14	842	38	0	2.71
Brian Hayward	Montreal	13	708	32	0	2.71

PLAYOFF GOALS

Name, Team	G
Jari Kurri, Edm.	15
Glenn Anderson, Edm.	14
Mark Messier, Edm.	12
Brian Propp, Phi.	12
Rick Tocchet, Phi.	11
Michel Goulet, Que.	9
John Ogrodnick, Que.	9
Bobby Smith, Mtl.	9

PLAYOFF ASSISTS

Name, Team	A
Wayne Gretzky, Edm.	29
Pelle Eklund, Phi.	20
Larry Robinson, Mtl.	17
Mark Messier, Edm.	16
Brian Propp, Phi.	16
Mats Naslund, Mtl.	15
Doug Crossman, Phi.	14
Steve Yzerman, Det.	13
Glenn Anderson, Edm.	13
Kent Nilsson, Edm.	13

PLAYOFF POWERPLAY GOALS

Name, Team	PPG
Tim Kerr, Phi.	5
Brian Propp, Phi.	5
Michel Goulet, Que.	4
Mats Naslund, Mtl.	4
Glenn Anderson, Edm.	4
Jari Kurri, Edm.	4

PLAYOFF SHORTHAND GOALS

Name, Team	SHG
Mark Messier, Edm.	2
Kevin Lowe, Edm.	2
15 tied with	1

PLAYOFF GAME-WINNING GOALS

Name, Team	GWG
Jari Kurri, Edm.	5
Tim Kerr, Phi.	3
Mats Naslund, Mtl.	3
Brian Propp, Phi.	3
12 tied with	2

PLAYOFF GOALIE WINS

Name, Team	W
Ron Hextall, Phi.	15
Grant Fuhr, Edm.	14
Mario Gosselin, Que.	7
Ken Wregget, Tor.	7
Kelly Hrudey, NYI	7

PLAYOFF SHUTOUTS

Name, Team	SO
Glen Hanlon, Det.	2
Ron Hextall, Phi.	2
Bob Mason, Wsh.	1
John Vanbiesbrouck, NYR	1
Ken Wregget, Tor.	1

PLAYOFF SAVE PERCENTAGE

Name, Team	SV%
Glen Hanlon, Det.	.943
Ken Wregget, Tor.	.921
Kelly Hrudey, NYI	.918
Grant Fuhr, Edm.	.908
Ron Hextall, Phi.	.908

1987-88

Stanley Cup • Edmonton Oilers

FINAL STANDINGS

CLARENCE CAMPBELL CONFERENCE

Team	GP	W	L	T	GF	GA	PTS
Norris Division							
Detroit	80	41	28	11	322	269	93
St. Louis	80	34	38	8	278	294	76
Chicago	80	30	41	9	284	328	69
Toronto	80	21	49	10	273	345	52
Minnesota	80	19	48	13	242	349	51
Smythe Division							
Calgary	80	48	23	9	397	305	105
Edmonton	80	44	25	11	363	288	99
Winnipeg	80	33	36	11	292	310	77
Los Angeles	80	30	42	8	318	359	68
Vancouver	80	25	46	9	272	320	59
PRINCE OF WALES CONFERENCE							
Adams Division							
Montreal	80	45	22	13	298	238	103
Boston	80	44	30	6	300	251	94
Buffalo	80	37	32	11	283	305	85
Hartford	80	35	38	7	249	267	77
Quebec	80	32	43	5	271	306	69
Patrick Division							
NY Islanders	80	39	31	10	308	267	88
Washington	80	38	33	9	281	249	85
Philadelphia	80	38	33	9	292	292	85
New Jersey	80	38	36	6	295	296	82
NY Rangers	80	36	34	10	300	283	82
Pittsburgh	80	36	35	9	319	316	81

LEADING SCORERS

Player	Club	GP	G	A	PTS	PIM
Mario Lemieux	Pittsburgh	77	70	98	168	92
Wayne Gretzky	Edmonton	64	40	109	149	24
Denis Savard	Chicago	80	44	87	131	95
Dale Hawerchuk	Winnipeg	80	44	77	121	59
Luc Robitaille	Los Angeles	80	53	58	111	82
Peter Stastny	Quebec	76	46	65	111	69
Mark Messier	Edmonton	77	37	74	111	103
Jimmy Carson	Los Angeles	80	55	52	107	45
Hakan Loob	Calgary	80	50	56	106	47
Michel Goulet	Quebec	80	48	58	106	56
Mike Bullard	Calgary	79	48	55	103	68
Steve Yzerman	Detroit	64	50	52	102	44
Jari Kurri	Edmonton	80	43	53	96	30
Kirk Muller	New Jersey	80	37	57	94	114
Bobby Smith	Montreal	78	27	66	93	78
Joe Nieuwendyk	Calgary	75	51	41	92	23
Pat LaFontaine	NY Islanders	75	47	45	92	52
Gary Suter	Calgary	75	21	70	91	124
Craig Simpson	Pit./Edm	80	56	34	90	77
Steve Larmer	Chicago	80	41	48	89	42
Bernie Federko	St. Louis	79	20	69	89	52
Glenn Anderson	Edmonton	80	38	50	88	58
Walt Poddubny	NY Rangers	77	38	50	88	76
Two players tied with					86	

LEADING GOALTENDERS

Goaltender	Club	GPI	MINS	GA	SO	AVG
Pete Peeters	Washington	35	1896	88	2	2.78
Brian Hayward	Montreal	39	2247	107	2	2.86
Patrick Roy	Montreal	45	2586	125	3	2.90
Reggie Lemelin	Boston	49	2828	138	3	2.93
Greg Stefan	Detroit	33	1854	96	1	3.11
Clint Malarchuk	Washington	54	2926	154	4	3.16
Mike Liut	Hartford	60	3532	187	2	3.18
Billy Smith	NY Islanders	38	2107	113	2	3.22
Glen Hanlon	Detroit	47	2623	141	4	3.23
Doug Keans	Boston	30	1660	90	1	3.25

Dale Hawerchuk was a junior superstar who enjoyed immediate success in the NHL after being selected first overall by the Winnipeg Jets in the 1981 Entry Draft. He went on to collect 518 goals and 891 assists in a 16-year career and was a top-10 scorer four times.

During the late summer of 1987, the fourth Canada Cup tournament took place and it marked the rise of Mario Lemieux as a true superstar. Playing on a line with Wayne Gretzky, Lemieux's work ethic and mental approach finally caught up with his immense physical skills. He was the tournament's top goal scorer and netted the dramatic series-winning goal against the Soviets on a feed from Gretzky late in the final game. By the end of the regular season, Lemieux had unseated Gretzky as NHL scoring champion and ended his eight-year hold on the Hart Trophy.

Lemieux's brilliant play and the acquisition of Paul Coffey from the Edmonton Oilers saw Pittsburgh post its best record in 10 years, but the Penguins' tally of 81 points was still not enough to make the playoffs in the tight Patrick Division where only seven points separated the six teams. The New York Islanders finished first, followed by the Washington Capitals and Philadelphia Flyers. In a game against Boston on December 8, 1987, Flyers goalie Ron Hextall became the first NHL netminder to shoot the puck the length of the ice for a goal into an empty net.

A Cup and a Shock – A perfect season that ended with Edmonton winning its fourth Cup turned from mirth to misery when Gretzky was traded to the Los Angeles Kings.

Fourth place in the Patrick Division went to the New Jersey Devils, who made the playoffs for the first time in 10 years and just the second time in franchise history. Led by the goaltending of Canadian national team star Sean Burke, the surprising Devils reached the Wales Conference final before they fell to the Bruins. Boston had finished second behind the Montreal Canadiens—who boasted the league's best defensive record as well as 50-goal scorer Stephane Richer—in the Adams Division, but the Bruins prevailed in the division final, beating Montreal for the first time in 18 playoff series dating back to 1945.

The Presidents' Trophy for first place overall went to Calgary with 105 points, but their Alberta rivals, the defending Stanley Cup champion Edmonton Oilers, made easy work of the Flames in the Smythe Division final, sweeping the series in four games.

The Oilers went on to beat the Detroit Red Wings, the Norris Division champions, to play Boston for the Stanley Cup. Edmonton swept the Bruins to win their fourth Stanley Cup championship in five years, although the series actually went five games—late in the second period of game four, with the score tied 3–3, a power failure at Boston Garden forced the game's suspension. Wayne Gretzky won the Conn Smythe Trophy after setting a new record with 13 points in the finals. The Oilers celebrated their Stanley Cup triumph with what proved to be an instant NHL tradition – an impromptu and informal group photo at center ice. Little did anyone know that the picture documented the end of an era.

One of the best defensemen of all time, Raymond Bourque switched his uniform to number 77 when the Bruins honored Phil Esposito by retiring number seven on December 3, 1987.

Leaders, 1987-88

GOALS

Name, Team	G
Mario Lemieux, Pit.	70
Craig Simpson, Pit./Edm.	56
Jimmy Carson, L.A.	55
Luc Robitaille, L.A.	53
Joe Nieuwendyk, Cgy.	51
Steve Yzerman, Det.	50
Stephane Richer, Mtl.	50
Hakan Loob, Cgy.	50
Mike Bullard, Cgy.	48
Michel Goulet, Que.	48
Mike Gartner, Wsh.	48

ASSISTS

Name, Team	A
Wayne Gretzky, Edm.	109
Mario Lemieux, Pit.	98
Denis Savard, Chi.	87
Dale Hawerchuk, Wpg.	77
Mark Messier, Edm.	74
Gary Suter, Cgy.	70
Bernie Federko, St.L.	69
Bobby Smith, Mtl.	66
Peter Stastny, Que.	65
Raymond Bourque, Bos.	64

POWERPLAY GOALS

Name, Team	PPG
Joe Nieuwendyk, Cgy.	31
Michel Goulet, Que.	29
Marcel Dionne, NYR	22
Mario Lemieux, Pit.	22
Paul MacLean, Wpg.	22
Jimmy Carson, L.A.	22
Craig Simpson, Pit./Edm.	22
Dan Quinn, Pit.	21
Brian Bellows, Min.	21
Mike Bullard, Cgy.	21
Steve Larmer, Chi.	21

SHORTHAND GOALS

Name, Team	SHG
Mario Lemieux, Pit.	10
Hakan Loob, Cgy.	8
Bernie Nicholls, L.A.	7
Steve Larmer, Chi.	7
Denis Savard, Chi.	7
Steve Yzerman, Det.	6
Wayne Gretzky, Edm.	5
Dave Poulin, Phi.	5
Rick Meagher, St.L.	5
Bengt-Ake Gustafsson, Wsh.	5
Petr Klima, Det.	5

GAME-WINNING GOALS

Name, Team	GWG
Stephane Richer, Mtl.	11
Carey Wilson, Cgy./Hfd.	9
Pat Verbeek, N.J.	8
Joe Nieuwendyk, Cgy.	8
Craig Simpson, Pit./Edm.	8
Mike Foligno, Buf.	7
Pat LaFontaine, NYI	7
Mark Messier, Edm.	7
Mario Lemieux, Pit.	7
Bob Sweeney, Bos.	7
Jimmy Carson, L.A.	7
Mike Gartner, Wsh.	7

GOALIE WINS

Name, Team	W
Grant Fuhr, Edm.	40
Mike Vernon, Cgy.	39
Ron Hextall, Phi.	30
John Vanbiesbrouck, NYR	27
Tom Barrasso, Buf.	25
Mike Liut, Hfd.	25
Reggie Lemelin, Bos.	24
Clint Malarchuk, Wsh.	24
Patrick Roy, Mtl.	23
Four tied with	22

SHUTOUTS

Name, Team	SO
Glen Hanlon, Det.	4
Clint Malarchuk, Wsh.	4
Grant Fuhr, Edm.	4
Patrick Roy, Mtl.	3
Kelly Hrudey, NYI	3
Reggie Lemelin, Bos.	3

SAVE PERCENTAGE

Name, Team	SV%
Patrick Roy, Mtl.	.900
Pete Peeters, Wsh.	.898
Brian Hayward, Mtl.	.896
Greg Stefan, Det.	.896
Kelly Hrudey, NYI	.896
Tom Barrasso, Buf.	.896

FIRST TEAM ALL-STARS

Name, Team	Position
Mario Lemieux, Pit.	C
Hakan Loob, Cgy.	RW
Luc Robitaille, L.A.	LW
Raymond Bourque, Bos.	D
Scott Stevens, Wsh.	D
Grant Fuhr, Edm.	G

SECOND TEAM ALL-STARS

Name, Team	Position
Wayne Gretzky, Edm.	C
Cam Neely, Bos.	RW
Michel Goulet, Que.	LW
Gary Suter, Cgy.	D
Brad McCrimmon, Cgy.	D
Patrick Roy, Mtl.	G

ALL-ROOKIE TEAM

Name, Team	Position
Joe Nieuwendyk, Cgy.	C
Ray Sheppard, Buf.	RW
Iain Duncan, Wpg.	LW
Glen Wesley, Bos.	D
Calle Johansson, Buf.	D
Darren Pang, Chi.	G

TROPHY WINNERS

Trophy	Awarded For	Winner	Team
Hart	MVP	Mario Lemieux	Pit.
Art Ross	Top Scorer	Mario Lemieux	Pit.
Norris	Top Defenseman	Raymond Bourque	Bos.
Calder	Top Rookie	Joe Nieuwendyk	Cgy.
Selke	Top Defensive Forward	Guy Carbonneau	Mtl.
Vezina	Top Goaltender	Grant Fuhr	Edm
Jennings	Fewest Goals Against	Patrick Roy	Mtl.
		Brian Hayward	Mtl.
Adams	Top Coach	Jacques Demers	Det.
Byng	Gentlemanly Conduct	Mats Naslund	Mtl.
Masterton	Perseverance, Sportmanship	Bob Bourne	L.A.
Pearson	NHLPA MVP	Mario Lemieux	Pit.
Conn Smythe	Playoff MVP	Wayne Gretzky	Edm.
Patrick	Service to Hockey in U.S.	Keith Allen	
		Fred Cusick	
		Bob Johnson	
Clancy	Leadership On and Off Ice	Lanny McDonald	Cgy.
Entry Draft	First Overall Selection	Mike Modano	Min.

NHL NOTEBOOK

TRANSACTIONS

- June 18, 1987 – Chicago Blackhawks signed two free agent goalies: Bob Mason (from the Washington Capitals) and 22-year-old Eddie Belfour, from University of North Dakota.
- Nov. 24, 1987 – Pittsburgh Penguins traded Dave Hannan, Chris Joseph, Moe Mantha and Craig Simpson to Edmonton for Paul Coffey, Dave Hunter and Wayne Van Dorp.
- Mar. 7, 1988 – St. Louis Blues obtained right winger Brett Hull and Steve Bozek from Calgary for defenseman Rob Ramage and goaltender Rick Wamsley.
- Mar. 26, 1988 – Boston Bruins obtained goaltender Andy Moog from Edmonton for Bill Ranford and Geoff Courtnall.

RECORDS

- Dec. 19, 1987 – Boston's Ken Linseman and St. Louis' Doug Gilmour scored goals just two seconds apart in the third period to set an NHL record for fastest two goals in the Blues' 7-5 win over the Bruins. Gilmour's came off a center-ice face-off into an empty net.
- Mar. 1, 1988 – Edmonton's Wayne Gretzky picked up a first period assist to move ahead of Gordie Howe as the NHL's all-time leader in career assists. Howe had 1,049 assists in 26 years, Gretzky 1,050 in 9 years. Oilers beat the Kings 5-3.
- Mar. 30, 1988 – Edmonton's Grant Fuhr set an NHL record for games played by a goalie in a season when he appeared in his 74th game of 1987-88, breaking Bernie Parent's mark of 73 set in 1973-74 with the Flyers. Oilers won 6-3 over the Minnesota North Stars.
- Apr. 22, 1988 – New Jersey's Patrick Sundstrom set an NHL playoff record with eight points (three goals and five assists) to give the Devils a 10-4 win over Washington in game three of the Patrick Division finals.

MILESTONES

- Dec. 8, 1987 – Ron Hextall became the second goalie in NHL history to get credit for scoring a goal but the first to actually shoot and score as the Flyers beat the Bruins 5-2 at the Spectrum. His goal went into an empty net at 18:48 of the third period.
- Jan. 4, 1988 – Toronto defenseman Borje Salming became the first European-trained player to appear in 1,000 career NHL games in a 7-7 Maple Leafs tie against Vancouver.
- Jan. 14, 1988 – Denis Potvin became the first defenseman in NHL history to score 300 career goals when he scored in the Islanders' 8-5 win over the visiting Quebec Nordiques.
- Jan. 28, 1988 – New York's Marcel Dionne became the first player in NHL history to get 20 goals in each of his first 17 seasons when he scored for the Rangers in a 5-2 win over the Flyers, in Philadelphia.

1988 Playoffs

DIVISION SEMI-FINALS

Apr.	6	Hartford	3	at	Montreal	4
Apr.	7	Hartford	3	at	Montreal	7
Apr.	9	Montreal	4	at	Hartford	3
Apr.	10	Montreal	5	at	Hartford	7
Apr.	12	Hartford	3	at	Montreal	1
Apr.	14	Montreal	2	at	Hartford	1

Montreal won best-of-seven series 4–2

Apr.	6	Buffalo	3	at	Boston	7
Apr.	7	Buffalo	1	at	Boston	4
Apr.	9	Boston	2	at	Buffalo	6
Apr.	10	Boston	5	at	Buffalo	6 OT
Apr.	12	Buffalo	4	at	Boston	5
Apr.	14	Boston	5	at	Buffalo	2

Boston won best-of-seven series 4–2

Apr.	6	New Jersey	3	at	NY Islanders	4 OT
Apr.	7	New Jersey	3	at	NY Islanders	2
Apr.	9	NY Islanders	0	at	New Jersey	3
Apr.	10	NY Islanders	5	at	New Jersey	4 OT
Apr.	12	New Jersey	4	at	NY Islanders	2
Apr.	14	NY Islanders	5	at	New Jersey	6

New Jersey won best-of-seven series 4–2

Apr.	6	Philadelphia	4	at	Washington	2
Apr.	7	Philadelphia	4	at	Washington	5
Apr.	9	Washington	3	at	Philadelphia	4
Apr.	10	Washington	4	at	Philadelphia	5 OT
Apr.	12	Philadelphia	2	at	Washington	5
Apr.	14	Washington	7	at	Philadelphia	2
Apr.	16	Philadelphia	4	at	Washington	5 OT

Washington won best-of-seven series 4–3

Apr.	6	Toronto	6	at	Detroit	2
Apr.	7	Toronto	2	at	Detroit	6
Apr.	9	Detroit	6	at	Toronto	3
Apr.	10	Detroit	8	at	Toronto	0
Apr.	12	Toronto	6	at	Detroit	5 OT
Apr.	14	Detroit	5	at	Toronto	3

Detroit won best-of-seven series 4–2

Apr.	6	Chicago	1	at	St. Louis	5
Apr.	7	Chicago	2	at	St. Louis	3
Apr.	9	St. Louis	3	at	Chicago	6
Apr.	10	St. Louis	6	at	Chicago	5
Apr.	12	Chicago	3	at	St. Louis	5

St. Louis won best-of-seven series 4–1

Apr.	6	Los Angeles	2	at	Calgary	9
Apr.	7	Los Angeles	4	at	Calgary	6
Apr.	9	Calgary	2	at	Los Angeles	5
Apr.	10	Calgary	7	at	Los Angeles	3
Apr.	12	Los Angeles	4	at	Calgary	6

Calgary won best-of-seven series 4–1

Apr.	6	Winnipeg	4	at	Edmonton	7
Apr.	7	Winnipeg	2	at	Edmonton	3
Apr.	9	Edmonton	4	at	Winnipeg	6
Apr.	10	Edmonton	5	at	Winnipeg	3
Apr.	12	Winnipeg	2	at	Edmonton	6

Edmonton won best-of-seven series 4–1

DIVISION FINALS

Apr.	18	Boston	2	at	Montreal	5
Apr.	20	Boston	4	at	Montreal	3
Apr.	22	Montreal	1	at	Boston	3
Apr.	24	Montreal	0	at	Boston	2
Apr.	26	Boston	4	at	Montreal	1

Boston won best-of-seven series 4–1

Apr.	18	New Jersey	1	at	Washington	3
Apr.	20	New Jersey	5	at	Washington	2
Apr.	22	Washington	4	at	New Jersey	10
Apr.	24	Washington	4	at	New Jersey	1
Apr.	26	New Jersey	3	at	Washington	1
Apr.	28	Washington	7	at	New Jersey	2
Apr.	30	New Jersey	3	at	Washington	2

New Jersey won best-of-seven series 4–3

Apr.	19	St. Louis	4	at	Detroit	5
Apr.	21	St. Louis	0	at	Detroit	6
Apr.	23	Detroit	3	at	St. Louis	6
Apr.	25	Detroit	3	at	St. Louis	1
Apr.	27	St. Louis	3	at	Detroit	4

Detroit won best-of-seven series 4–1

Apr.	19	Edmonton	3	at	Calgary	1
Apr.	21	Edmonton	5	at	Calgary	4 OT
Apr.	23	Calgary	2	at	Edmonton	4
Apr.	25	Calgary	4	at	Edmonton	6

Edmonton won best-of-seven series 4–0

CONFERENCE FINALS

May	2	New Jersey	3	at	Boston	5
May	4	New Jersey	3	at	Boston	2 OT
May	6	Boston	6	at	New Jersey	1
May	8	Boston	1	at	New Jersey	3
May	10	New Jersey	1	at	Boston	7
May	12	Boston	3	at	New Jersey	6
May	14	New Jersey	2	at	Boston	6

Boston won best-of-seven series 4–3

May	3	Detroit	1	at	Edmonton	4
May	5	Detroit	3	at	Edmonton	5
May	7	Edmonton	2	at	Detroit	5
May	9	Edmonton	4	at	Detroit	3 OT
May	11	Detroit	4	at	Edmonton	8

Edmonton won best-of-seven series 4–1

FINALS

May	18	Boston	1	at	Edmonton	2
May	20	Boston	2	at	Edmonton	4
May	22	Edmonton	6	at	Boston	3
May	24	Edmonton	3	at	Boston	3 *
May	26	Boston	3	at	Edmonton	6

** Game suspended at 16:37 of second period due to power failure.*

Edmonton won best-of-seven series 4–0

1987-88 – Edmonton Oilers – Keith Acton, Glenn Anderson, Jeff Beukeboom, Geoff Courtnall, Grant Fuhr, Randy Gregg, Wayne Gretzky (Captain), Dave Hannan, Charlie Huddy, Mike Krushelnyski, Jari Kurri, Normand Lacombe, Kevin Lowe, Craig MacTavish, Kevin McClelland, Marty McSorley, Mark Messier, Craig Muni, Bill Ranford, Craig Simpson, Steve Smith, Esa Tikkanen, Peter Pocklington (Owner), Glen Sather (General Manager/Coach), John Muckler (Co-Coach), Ted Green (Assistant Coach), Bruce MacGregor (Assistant General Manager), Barry Fraser (Director of Player Personnel), Bill Tuele (Director of Public Relations), Dr. Gordon Cameron (Team Physician), Peter Millar (Athletic Therapist), Barrie Stafford (Trainer), Juergen Mers (Massage Therapist), Lyle Kulchisky (Assistant Trainer).

LEADING PLAYOFF SCORERS

Player	Club	GP	G	A	PTS	PIM
Wayne Gretzky	Edmonton	19	12	31	43	16
Mark Messier	Edmonton	19	11	23	34	29
Jari Kurri	Edmonton	19	14	17	31	12
Esa Tikkanen	Edmonton	19	10	17	27	72
Ken Linseman	Boston	23	11	14	25	56
Glenn Anderson	Edmonton	19	9	16	25	49
Bob Probert	Detroit	16	8	13	21	51
Raymond Bourque	Boston	23	3	18	21	26
Adam Oates	Detroit	16	8	12	20	6
Patrik Sundstrom	New Jersey	18	7	13	20	14

LEADING PLAYOFF GOALTENDERS

Goaltender	Club	GPI	Mins	GA	SO	Avg.
Reggie Lemelin	Boston	17	1027	45	1	2.63
Grant Fuhr	Edmonton	19	1136	55	0	2.90
Glen Hanlon	Detroit	8	431	22	1	3.06
Pete Peeters	Washington	12	654	34	0	3.12
Patrick Roy	Montreal	8	430	24	0	3.35

PLAYOFF GOALS

Name, Team	G
Jari Kurri, Edm.	14
Craig Simpson, Edm.	13
Wayne Gretzky, Edm.	12
Mark Messier, Edm.	11
Ken Linseman, Bos.	11
Petr Klima, Det.	10
Mark Johnson, N.J.	10
Esa Tikkanen, Edm.	10

PLAYOFF ASSISTS

Name, Team	A
Wayne Gretzky, Edm.	31
Mark Messier, Edm.	23
Raymond Bourque, Bos.	18
Jari Kurri, Edm.	17
Esa Tikkanen, Edm.	17
Glenn Anderson, Edm.	16
John Chabot, Det.	15
Doug Gilmour, St.L.	14
Ken Linseman, Bos.	14

PLAYOFF POWERPLAY GOALS

Name, Team	PPG
Mark Messier, Edm.	7
Rick Vaive, Chi.	5
Bob Probert, Det.	5
Mark Johnson, N.J.	5
Wayne Gretzky, Edm.	5
Jari Kurri, Edm.	5
Esa Tikkanen, Edm.	5

PLAYOFF SHORTHAND GOALS

Name, Team	SHG
Hakan Loob, Cgy.	2
Bobby Gould, Wsh.	2
Claude Loiselle, N.J.	2
29 tied with	1

PLAYOFF GAME-WINNING GOALS

Name, Team	GWG
Petr Klima, Det.	4
Brett Hull, St.L.	3
Wayne Gretzky, Edm.	3
Rick Middleton, Bos.	3
Jari Kurri, Edm.	3
Craig Simpson, Edm.	3

PLAYOFF GOALIE WINS

Name, Team	W
Grant Fuhr, Edm.	16
Reggie Lemelin, Bos.	11
Sean Burke, N.J.	9
Pete Peeters, Wsh.	7
Greg Stefan, Det.	5
Greg Millen, St.L.	5

PLAYOFF SHUTOUTS

Name, Team	SO
Glen Hanlon, Det.	1
Greg Stefan, Det.	1
Reggie Lemelin, Bos.	1
Sean Burke, N.J.	1

PLAYOFF SAVE PERCENTAGE

Name, Team	SV%
Pete Peeters, Wsh.	.896
Reggie Lemelin, Bos.	.895
Patrick Roy, Mtl.	.890
Sean Burke, N.J.	.889
Grant Fuhr, Edm.	.883

1988-89

Stanley Cup • Calgary Flames

FINAL STANDINGS

CLARENCE CAMPBELL CONFERENCE

Norris Division

Team	GP	W	L	T	GF	GA	PTS
Detroit	80	34	34	12	313	316	80
St. Louis	80	33	35	12	275	285	78
Minnesota	80	27	37	16	258	278	70
Chicago	80	27	41	12	297	335	66
Toronto	80	28	46	6	259	342	62
Smythe Division							
Calgary	80	54	17	9	354	226	117
Los Angeles	80	42	31	7	376	335	91
Edmonton	80	38	34	8	325	306	84
Vancouver	80	33	39	8	251	253	74
Winnipeg	80	26	42	12	300	355	64
PRINCE OF WALES CONFERENCE							
Adams Division							
Montreal	80	53	18	9	315	218	115
Boston	80	37	29	14	289	256	88
Buffalo	80	38	35	7	291	299	83
Hartford	80	37	38	5	299	290	79
Quebec	80	27	46	7	269	342	61
Patrick Division							
Washington	80	41	29	10	305	259	92
Pittsburgh	80	40	33	7	347	349	87
NY Rangers	80	37	35	8	310	307	82
Philadelphia	80	36	36	8	307	285	80
New Jersey	80	27	41	12	281	325	66
NY Islanders	80	28	47	5	265	325	61

LEADING SCORERS

Player	Club	GP	G	A	PTS	PIM
Mario Lemieux	Pittsburgh	76	85	114	199	100
Wayne Gretzky	Los Angeles	78	54	114	168	26
Steve Yzerman	Detroit	80	65	90	155	61
Bernie Nicholls	Los Angeles	79	70	80	150	96
Rob Brown	Pittsburgh	68	49	66	115	118
Paul Coffey	Pittsburgh	75	30	83	113	195
Joe Mullen	Calgary	79	51	59	110	16
Jari Kurri	Edmonton	76	44	58	102	69
Jimmy Carson	Edmonton	80	49	51	100	36
Luc Robitaille	Los Angeles	78	46	52	98	65
Dale Hawerchuk	Winnipeg	75	41	55	96	28
Dan Quinn	Pittsburgh	79	34	60	94	102
Mark Messier	Edmonton	72	33	61	94	130
Gerard Gallant	Detroit	76	39	54	93	230
Ed Olczyk	Toronto	80	38	52	90	75
Kevin Dineen	Hartford	79	45	44	89	167
Mike Ridley	Washington	80	41	48	89	49
Tim Kerr	Philadelphia	69	48	40	88	73
Pat LaFontaine	NY Islanders	79	45	43	88	26
Pierre Turgeon	Buffalo	80	34	54	88	26
Tomas Sandstrom	NY Rangers	79	32	56	88	148
Thomas Steen	Winnipeg	80	27	61	88	80
Steve Larmer	Chicago	80	43	44	87	54
John MacLean	New Jersey	74	42	45	87	122
Three players tied with					85	

LEADING GOALTENDERS

Goaltender	Club	GPI	MINS	GA	SO	AVG
Patrick Roy	Montreal	48	2744	113	4	2.47
Mike Vernon	Calgary	52	2938	130	0	2.65
Pete Peeters	Washington	33	1854	88	4	2.85
Brian Hayward	Montreal	36	2091	101	1	2.90
Rick Wamsley	Calgary	35	1927	95	2	2.96
Steve Weeks	Vancouver	35	2056	102	0	2.98
Reggie Lemelin	Boston	40	2392	120	0	3.01
Peter Sidorkiewicz	Hartford	44	2635	133	4	3.03
Jon Casey	Minnesota	55	2961	151	1	3.06
Kirk McLean	Vancouver	42	2477	127	4	3.08

Wayne Gretzky's arrival in Los Angeles finally made hockey a hit in Southern California and helped to promote the game all across the United States.

THE HOCKEY WORLD WAS SHOCKED on August 9, 1988, when the Edmonton Oilers and Los Angeles Kings announced a trade virtually without parallel in sports history. Wayne Gretzky, Mike Krushelnyski and Marty McSorley were L.A.-bound, while the Oilers would receive Jimmy Carson, Martin Gelinas, the Kings' first-round draft choices in 1989, 1991 and 1993, plus a reported $15 million in cash. Fans in Edmonton, and across Canada, bemoaned the loss of "The Great One," while the citizens of southern California would be turned on to hockey as never before.

Showing a flair for the dramatic worthy of his Hollywood surroundings, Gretzky scored a goal on his very first shot of the 1988–89 season. He led the Kings to a 91-point season, good for second place in the Smythe Division and the team's best showing since 1981. His 114 assists tied Mario Lemieux for top spot in the NHL, and though Lemieux's 85 goals to Gretzky's 54 meant Mario again won the Art Ross Trophy, Gretzky was awarded the Hart Trophy as MVP for the ninth time. Gretzky also brought out the greatest in his Los Angeles teammates—Bernie Nicholls, with 70 goals and 80 assists, and Luc Robitaille, with 46 goals and 52 assists, were also among the top 10 in scoring.

Lanny's Legacy – Calgary's Lanny MacDonald, one of hockey's most colorful, classy and best-loved characters, nailed hockey's triple play – 500 goals, 1000 points and a Stanley Cup championship ring.

Los Angeles faced Edmonton in the first round of the playoffs and defeated Gretzky's former teammates in seven games. The Kings were swept aside in the Smythe Division final, however, by the Calgary Flames, the NHL's best team during the regular season with 117 points. Joe Mullen set career highs with 51 goals and 110 points, while Joe Nieuwendyk followed up his 51-goal rookie performance with another 51 goals this season. In the Norris Division, Flames castoff Brett Hull emerged as a star, scoring 41 goals for the St. Louis Blues, while in Detroit, Steve Yzerman led the Red Wings with 65 goals and 90 assists. Still, it was the Chicago Blackhawks who emerged from the Norris Division before falling to the Flames in five games.

Led by Mario Lemieux, Pittsburgh was back in the playoffs after six years. The Penguins took on the New York Rangers—who boasted rookie stars Brian Leetch and Tony Granato, and who had convinced Guy Lafleur to come out of retirement—and eliminated the Blueshirts in the first round. The Philadelphia Flyers knocked Pittsburgh out, then went on to lose to the Montreal Canadiens—led by rookie coach Pat Burns to the league's second-best record with 115 points—in the Prince of Wales Conference final.

Calgary opened the Cup finals at home with a 3–2 victory and, after splitting the next four games, took a one-game series lead back to Montreal for game six. The Canadiens had never allowed an opponent to beat them for the Stanley Cup on Forum ice, but the Flames defied history, claiming victory by a 4–2 score.

With his booming slapshot, Al MacInnis quickly became one of the top defensemen in the NHL. He helped Calgary reach the Stanley Cup finals in 1986 and win it all in 1989.

Leaders, 1988-89

GOALS

Name, Team	G
Mario Lemieux, Pit.	85
Bernie Nicholls, L.A.	70
Steve Yzerman, Det.	65
Wayne Gretzky, L.A.	54
Joe Nieuwendyk, Cgy.	51
Joe Mullen, Cgy.	51
Rob Brown, Pit.	49
Jimmy Carson, Edm.	49
Tim Kerr, Phi.	48
Luc Robitaille, L.A.	46

ASSISTS

Name, Team	A
Mario Lemieux, Pit.	114
Wayne Gretzky, L.A.	114
Steve Yzerman, Det.	90
Paul Coffey, Pit.	83
Bernie Nicholls, L.A.	80
Rob Brown, Pit.	66
Adam Oates, Det.	62
Mark Messier, Edm.	61
Thomas Steen, Wpg.	61
Scott Stevens, Wsh.	61

POWERPLAY GOALS

Name, Team	PPG
Mario Lemieux, Pit.	31
Tim Kerr, Phi.	25
Rob Brown, Pit.	24
Bernie Nicholls, L.A.	21
Kevin Dineen, Hfd.	20
Andrew McBain, Wpg.	20
Joe Nieuwendyk, Cgy.	19
Pierre Turgeon, Buf.	19
Jimmy Carson, Edm.	19
Steve Larmer, Chi.	19

SHORTHAND GOALS

Name, Team	SHG
Mario Lemieux, Pit.	13
Dirk Graham, Chi.	10
Esa Tikkanen, Edm.	8
Bernie Nicholls, L.A.	8
Mark Messier, Edm.	6
Denis Savard, Chi.	5
Neal Broten, Min.	5
Dave Poulin, Phi.	5
Jari Kurri, Edm.	5
Wayne Gretzky, L.A.	5
Steve Duchesne, L.A.	5

GAME-WINNING GOALS

Name, Team	GWG
Joe Nieuwendyk, Cgy.	11
Guy Carbonneau, Mtl.	10
Mike Ridley, Wsh.	9
Mario Lemieux, Pit.	8
Jari Kurri, Edm.	8
Dino Ciccarelli, Min./Wsh.	8
Mike Krushelnyski, L.A.	8
Gerard Gallant, Det.	7
David Volek, NYI	7
Joe Mullen, Cgy.	7
Steve Yzerman, Det.	7
Ray Ferraro, Hfd.	7

GOALIE WINS

Name, Team	W
Mike Vernon, Cgy.	37
Patrick Roy, Mtl.	33
Ron Hextall, Phi.	30
John Vanbiesbrouck, NYR	28
Kelly Hrudey, NYI/L.A.	28
Glenn Healy, L.A.	25
Grant Fuhr, Edm.	23
Peter Sidorkiewicz, Hfd.	22
Greg Millen, St.L.	22
Sean Burke, N.J.	22

SHUTOUTS

Name, Team	SO
Greg Millen, St.L.	6
Pete Peeters, Wsh.	4
Kirk McLean, Van.	4
Peter Sidorkiewicz, Hfd.	4
Patrick Roy, Mtl.	4
Sean Burke, N.J.	3

SAVE PERCENTAGE

Name, Team	SV%
Patrick Roy, Mtl.	.908
Jon Casey, Min.	.900
Kari Takko, Min.	.899
Mike Vernon, Cgy.	.897
Steve Weeks, Van.	.893

FIRST TEAM ALL-STARS

Name, Team	Position
Mario Lemieux, Pit.	C
Joe Mullen, Cgy.	RW
Luc Robitaille, L.A.	LW
Chris Chelios, Mtl.	D
Paul Coffey, Pit.	D
Patrick Roy, Mtl.	G

SECOND TEAM ALL-STARS

Name, Team	Position
Wayne Gretzky, L.A.	C
Jari Kurri, Edm.	RW
Gerard Gallant, Det.	LW
Al MacInnis, Cgy.	D
Raymond Bourque, Bos.	D
Mike Vernon, Cgy.	G

ALL-ROOKIE TEAM

Name, Team	Position
Trevor Linden, Van.	C
Tony Granato, NYR	RW
David Volek, NYI	LW
Brian Leetch, NYR	D
Zarley Zalapski, Pit.	D
Peter Sidorkiewicz, Hfd.	G

TROPHY WINNERS

Trophy	Awarded For	Winner	Team
Hart	MVP	Wayne Gretzky	L.A.
Art Ross	Top Scorer	Mario Lemieux	Pit.
Norris	Top Defenseman	Chris Chelios	Mtl.
Calder	Top Rookie	Brian Leetch	NYR
Selke	Top Defensive Forward	Guy Carbonneau	Mtl.
Vezina	Top Goaltender	Patrick Roy	Mtl.
Jennings	Fewest Goals Against	Patrick Roy	Mtl.
		Brian Hayward	Mtl.
Adams	Top Coach	Pat Burns	Mtl.
Byng	Gentlemanly Conduct	Joe Mullen	Cgy.
Masterton	Perseverance, Sportmanship	Tim Kerr	Phi.
Pearson	NHLPA MVP	Steve Yzerman	Det.
Conn Smythe	Playoff MVP	Al MacInnis	Cgy.
Patrick	Service to Hockey in U.S.	Dan Kelly	
		Lou Nanne	
		Lynn Patrick	
		Bud Poile	
Clancy	Leadership On and Off Ice	Bryan Trottier	NYI
Entry Draft	First Overall Selection	Mats Sundin, Que.	Que.

NHL NOTEBOOK

TRANSACTIONS

- Aug. 9, 1988 – Wayne Gretzky, Mike Krushelnyski and Marty McSorley were traded to the Kings from Edmonton in exchange for Jimmy Carson, Martin Gelinas, three first-round draft choices (1989, 1991, 1993) and cash.
- Sept. 6, 1988 – Calgary Flames obtained Doug Gilmour, Steve Bozek, and Mark Hunter from St. Louis for Mike Bullard and Craig Coxe.
- Nov. 12, 1988 – Pittsburgh Penguins obtained goalie Tom Barrasso from Buffalo in trade for Doug Bodger and Darrin Shannon.

RECORDS

- Jan. 25, 1989 – Mario Lemieux set an NHL record by picking up a point on the 14th consecutive Penguins goal during a 5-4 win over the Winnipeg Jets in Pittsburgh.
- Mar. 29, 1989 – New York Rangers' Brian Leetch set an NHL record for most goals by a rookie defenseman when he scored his 23rd of the season (breaking the mark of 22 set by Barry Beck in 1977-78) in a 4-3 loss at Detroit.
- Mar. 30, 1989 – Mario Lemieux set a new NHL record with his 13th shorthanded goal of the year (breaking the mark of 12 by Wayne Gretzky) as the Penguins lost 9-5 to the visiting Hartford Whalers.
- Apr. 1, 1989 – Paul Coffey scored a goal to become the first defenseman in NHL history to record 30-goal seasons with two different teams. He also added two assists as the Penguins won 5-2 over the visiting New York Rangers.

MILESTONES

- Dec 31, 1988 – Mario Lemieux scored five goals (one on the powerplay, one shorthanded, one even strength, one on a penalty shot and an empty netter) and added three assists for eight points in an 8-6 Penguins win over New Jersey.
- Apr. 2, 1989 – Kelly Hrudey became the first goaltender in NHL history to win 10+ games with two teams in one season when he got his 10th victory with the Kings, a 5-4 win at Vancouver. Hrudey had won 18 games with the NY Islanders before being traded to L.A.
- May 19, 1989 – Montreal's Larry Robinson became the first player in NHL history to play in 200 Stanley Cup playoff games as the Canadiens beat Calgary 4-3 in overtime in game three of the Stanley Cup finals in Montreal.
- June 6, 1989 – Wayne Gretzky became the first player in NHL history to win the same award nine times when he was named the recipient of the Hart Trophy after his first season with the Los Angeles Kings.

1989 Playoffs

DIVISION SEMI-FINALS

Apr.	5	Hartford	2	at	Montreal	6
Apr.	6	Hartford	2	at	Montreal	3
Apr.	8	Montreal	5	at	Hartford	4 OT
Apr.	9	Montreal	4	at	Hartford	3 OT

Montreal won best-of-seven series 4–0

Apr.	5	Buffalo	6	at	Boston	0
Apr.	6	Buffalo	3	at	Boston	5
Apr.	8	Boston	4	at	Buffalo	2
Apr.	9	Boston	3	at	Buffalo	2
Apr.	11	Buffalo	1	at	Boston	4

Boston won best-of-seven series 4–1

Apr.	5	Philadelphia	2	at	Washington	3
Apr.	6	Philadelphia	3	at	Washington	2
Apr.	8	Washington	4	at	Philadelphia	3 OT
Apr.	9	Washington	2	at	Philadelphia	5
Apr.	11	Philadelphia	8	at	Washington	5
Apr.	13	Washington	3	at	Philadelphia	4

Philadelphia won best-of-seven series 4–2

Apr.	5	NY Rangers	1	at	Pittsburgh	3
Apr.	6	NY Rangers	4	at	Pittsburgh	7
Apr.	8	Pittsburgh	5	at	NY Rangers	3
Apr.	9	Pittsburgh	4	at	NY Rangers	3

Pittsburgh won best-of-seven series 4–0

Apr.	5	Chicago	2	at	Detroit	3
Apr.	6	Chicago	5	at	Detroit	4 OT
Apr.	8	Detroit	2	at	Chicago	4
Apr.	9	Detroit	2	at	Chicago	3
Apr.	11	Chicago	4	at	Detroit	6
Apr.	13	Detroit	1	at	Chicago	7

Chicago won best-of-seven series 4–2

Apr.	5	Minnesota	3	at	St. Louis	4 OT
Apr.	6	Minnesota	3	at	St. Louis	4 OT
Apr.	8	St. Louis	5	at	Minnesota	3
Apr.	9	St. Louis	4	at	Minnesota	5
Apr.	11	Minnesota	1	at	St. Louis	6

St. Louis won best-of-seven series 4–1

Apr.	5	Vancouver	4	at	Calgary	3 OT
Apr.	6	Vancouver	2	at	Calgary	5
Apr.	8	Calgary	4	at	Vancouver	0
Apr.	9	Calgary	3	at	Vancouver	5
Apr.	11	Vancouver	0	at	Calgary	4
Apr.	13	Calgary	3	at	Vancouver	6
Apr.	15	Vancouver	3	at	Calgary	4 OT

Calgary won best-of-seven series 4–3

Apr.	5	Edmonton	4	at	Los Angeles	3
Apr.	6	Edmonton	2	at	Los Angeles	5
Apr.	8	Los Angeles	0	at	Edmonton	4
Apr.	9	Los Angeles	3	at	Edmonton	4
Apr.	11	Edmonton	2	at	Los Angeles	4
Apr.	13	Los Angeles	4	at	Edmonton	1
Apr.	15	Edmonton	3	at	Los Angeles	6

Los Angeles won best-of-seven series 4–3

DIVISION FINALS

Apr.	17	Boston	2	at	Montreal	3
Apr.	19	Boston	2	at	Montreal	3 OT
Apr.	21	Montreal	5	at	Boston	4
Apr.	23	Montreal	2	at	Boston	3
Apr.	25	Boston	2	at	Montreal	3

Montreal won best-of-seven series 4–1

Apr.	17	Philadelphia	3	at	Pittsburgh	4
Apr.	19	Philadelphia	4	at	Pittsburgh	2
Apr.	21	Pittsburgh	4	at	Philadelphia	3 OT
Apr.	23	Pittsburgh	1	at	Philadelphia	4
Apr.	25	Philadelphia	7	at	Pittsburgh	10
Apr.	27	Pittsburgh	2	at	Philadelphia	6
Apr.	29	Philadelphia	4	at	Pittsburgh	1

Philadelphia won best-of-seven series 4–3

Apr.	18	Chicago	3	at	St. Louis	1
Apr.	20	Chicago	4	at	St. Louis	5 2OT
Apr.	22	St. Louis	2	at	Chicago	5
Apr.	24	St. Louis	2	at	Chicago	3
Apr.	26	Chicago	4	at	St. Louis	2

Chicago won best-of-seven series 4–1

Apr.	18	Los Angeles	3	at	Calgary	4 OT
Apr.	20	Los Angeles	3	at	Calgary	8
Apr.	22	Calgary	5	at	Los Angeles	2
Apr.	24	Calgary	5	at	Los Angeles	3

Calgary won best-of-seven series 4–0

CONFERENCE FINALS

May	1	Philadelphia	3	at	Montreal	1
May	3	Philadelphia	0	at	Montreal	3
May	5	Montreal	5	at	Philadelphia	1
May	7	Montreal	3	at	Philadelphia	0
May	9	Philadelphia	2	at	Montreal	1 OT
May	11	Montreal	4	at	Philadelphia	2

Montreal won best-of-seven series 4–2

May	2	Chicago	0	at	Calgary	3
May	4	Chicago	4	at	Calgary	2
May	6	Calgary	5	at	Chicago	2
May	8	Calgary	2	at	Chicago	1 OT
May	10	Chicago	1	at	Calgary	3

Calgary won best-of-seven series 4–1

FINALS

May	14	Montreal	2	at	Calgary	3
May	17	Montreal	4	at	Calgary	2
May	19	Calgary	3	at	Montreal	4 2OT
May	21	Calgary	4	at	Montreal	2
May	23	Montreal	2	at	Calgary	3
May	25	Calgary	4	at	Montreal	2

Calgary won best-of-seven series 4–2

1988-89 – Calgary Flames – Mike Vernon, Rick Wamsley, Al MacInnis, Brad McCrimmon, Dana Murzyn, Ric Nattress, Joe Mullen, Lanny McDonald (Co-Captain), Gary Roberts, Colin Patterson, Hakan Loob, Theoren Fleury, Jiri Hrdina, Tim Hunter (Assistant Captain), Gary Suter, Mark Hunter, Jim Peplinski (Co-Captain), Joe Nieuwendyk, Brian MacLellan, Joel Otto, Jamie Macoun, Doug Gilmour, Rob Ramage, Norman Green, Harley Hotchkiss, Norman Kwong, Sonia Scurfield, B.J. Seaman, D.K. Seaman (Owners), Cliff Fletcher (President/General Manager), Al MacNeil (Assistant General Manager), Al Coates (Assistant to the President), Terry Crisp (Head Coach), Doug Risebrough, Tom Watt (Assistant Coaches), Glenn Hall (Goaltending Consultant), Jim Murray (Trainer), Bob Stewart (Equipment Manager), Al Murray (Assistant Trainer).

LEADING PLAYOFF SCORERS

Player	Club	GP	G	A	PTS	PIM
Al MacInnis	Calgary	22	7	24	31	46
Tim Kerr	Philadelphia	19	14	11	25	27
Joe Mullen	Calgary	21	16	8	24	4
Brian Propp	Philadelphia	18	14	9	23	14
Doug Gilmour	Calgary	22	11	11	22	20
Wayne Gretzky	Los Angeles	11	5	17	22	0
Mario Lemieux	Pittsburgh	11	12	7	19	16
Bobby Smith	Montreal	21	11	8	19	46
Denis Savard	Chicago	16	8	11	19	10
Joel Otto	Calgary	22	6	13	19	46
Chris Chelios	Montreal	21	4	15	19	28

LEADING PLAYOFF GOALTENDERS

Goaltender	Club	GPI	Mins	GA	SO	Avg.
Patrick Roy	Montreal	19	1206	42	2	2.09
Mike Vernon	Calgary	22	1381	52	3	2.26
Alain Chevrier	Chicago	16	1013	44	0	2.61
Greg Millen	St. Louis	10	649	34	0	3.14
Ron Hextall	Philadelphia	15	886	49	0	3.32

PLAYOFF GOALS

Name, Team	G
Joe Mullen, Cgy.	16
Brian Propp, Phi.	14
Tim Kerr, Phi.	14
Mario Lemieux, Pit.	12
Bobby Smith, Mtl.	11
Doug Gilmour, Cgy.	11

PLAYOFF ASSISTS

Name, Team	A
Al MacInnis, Cgy.	24
Wayne Gretzky, L.A.	17
Mark Howe, Phi.	15
Chris Chelios, Mtl.	15
Paul Coffey, Pit.	13
Joel Otto, Cgy.	13

PLAYOFF POWERPLAY GOALS

Name, Team	PPG
Tim Kerr, Phi.	8
Mario Lemieux, Pit.	7
Chris Kontos, L.A.	6
Joe Mullen, Cgy.	6
Joe Nieuwendyk, Cgy.	6

PLAYOFF SHORTHAND GOALS

Name, Team	SHG
Wayne Presley, Chi.	3
Dave Poulin, Phi.	2
Derrick Smith, Phi.	2
Hakan Loob, Cgy.	2
22 tied with	1

PLAYOFF GAME-WINNING GOALS

Name, Team	GWG
Al MacInnis, Cgy.	4
Rob Brown, Pit.	3
Stephane Richer, Mtl.	3
Doug Gilmour, Cgy.	3
Theoren Fleury, Cgy.	3

PLAYOFF GOALIE WINS

Name, Team	W
Mike Vernon, Cgy.	16
Patrick Roy, Mtl.	13
Alain Chevrier, Chi.	9
Ron Hextall, Phi.	8
Tom Barrasso, Pit.	7

PLAYOFF SHUTOUTS

Name, Team	SO
Mike Vernon, Cgy.	3
Patrick Roy, Mtl.	2
Jacques Cloutier, Buf.	1
Grant Fuhr, Edm.	1

PLAYOFF SAVE PERCENTAGE

Name, Team	SV%
Patrick Roy, Mtl.	.920
Alain Chevrier, Chi.	.909
Mike Vernon, Cgy.	.905
Tom Barrasso, Pit.	.897
Ron Hextall, Phi.	.890

1989-90

Stanley Cup • Edmonton Oilers

Mark Messier, Esa Tikkanen and Joe Murphy celebrate a Stanley Cup victory for Edmonton just two years after Wayne Gretzky moved to Los Angeles. Messier also won the Hart Trophy.

FINAL STANDINGS

Team	GP	W	L	T	GF	GA	PTS
CLARENCE CAMPBELL CONFERENCE							
Norris Division							
Chicago	80	41	33	6	316	294	88
St. Louis	80	37	34	9	295	279	83
Toronto	80	38	38	4	337	358	80
Minnesota	80	36	40	4	284	291	76
Detroit	80	28	38	14	288	323	70
Smythe Division							
Calgary	80	42	23	15	348	265	99
Edmonton	80	38	28	14	315	283	90
Winnipeg	80	37	32	11	298	290	85
Los Angeles	80	34	39	7	338	337	75
Vancouver	80	25	41	14	245	306	64
PRINCE OF WALES CONFERENCE							
Adams Division							
Boston	80	46	25	9	289	232	101
Buffalo	80	45	27	8	286	248	98
Montreal	80	41	28	11	288	234	93
Hartford	80	38	33	9	275	268	85
Quebec	80	12	61	7	240	407	31
Patrick Division							
NY Rangers	80	36	31	13	279	267	85
New Jersey	80	37	34	9	295	288	83
Washington	80	36	38	6	284	275	78
NY Islanders	80	31	38	11	281	288	73
Pittsburgh	80	32	40	8	318	359	72
Philadelphia	80	30	39	11	290	297	71

LEADING SCORERS

Player	Club	GP	G	A	PTS	PIM
Wayne Gretzky	Los Angeles	73	40	102	142	42
Mark Messier	Edmonton	79	45	84	129	79
Steve Yzerman	Detroit	79	62	65	127	79
Mario Lemieux	Pittsburgh	59	45	78	123	78
Brett Hull	St. Louis	80	72	41	113	24
Bernie Nicholls	L.A./NYR	79	39	73	112	86
Pierre Turgeon	Buffalo	80	40	66	106	29
Pat LaFontaine	NY Islanders	74	54	51	105	38
Paul Coffey	Pittsburgh	80	29	74	103	95
Joe Sakic	Quebec	80	39	63	102	27
Adam Oates	St. Louis	80	23	79	102	30
Luc Robitaille	Los Angeles	80	52	49	101	38
Ron Francis	Hartford	80	32	69	101	73
Brian Bellows	Minnesota	80	55	44	99	72
Rick Tocchet	Philadelphia	75	37	59	96	196
Gary Leeman	Toronto	80	51	44	95	63
Joe Nieuwendyk	Calgary	79	45	50	95	40
Vincent Damphousse	Toronto	80	33	61	94	56
Jari Kurri	Edmonton	78	33	60	93	48
Cam Neely	Boston	76	55	37	92	117
John Cullen	Pittsburgh	72	32	60	92	138
Stephane Richer	Montreal	75	51	40	91	46
Doug Gilmour	Calgary	78	24	67	91	54
Two players ties with					90	

LEADING GOALTENDERS

Goaltender	Club	GPI	MINS	GA	SO	AVG
Mike Liut	Hfd./Wsh.	37	2161	91	4	2.53
Patrick Roy	Montreal	54	3173	134	3	2.53
Reggie Lemelin	Boston	43	2310	108	2	2.81
Andy Moog	Boston	46	2536	122	3	2.89
Daren Puppa	Buffalo	56	3241	156	1	2.89
Jacques Cloutier	Chicago	43	2178	112	2	3.09
Mike Vernon	Calgary	47	2795	146	0	3.13
Bob Essensa	Winnipeg	36	2035	107	1	3.15
Bill Ranford	Edmonton	56	3107	165	1	3.19
Jon Casey	Minnesota	61	3407	183	3	3.22

The NHL enjoyed unprecedented box-office success in 1989–90, as attendance was up for the 11th year in a row. But the story this season was growing parity and tight divisional races. Under rookie coach Mike Milbury, the Boston Bruins won the Presidents' Trophy with 101 points, marking the first season since 1970–71 that only one team broke the 100-point barrier. Cam Neely led the offense with 55 goals, while Raymond Bourque earned his third Norris Trophy in four years as the NHL's best defenseman. Goalies Reggie Lemelin and Andy Moog allowed the fewest goals in the league and shared the Jennings Trophy. The Bruins survived a seven-game scare from the Hartford Whalers in the first round of playoffs before beating the Montreal Canadiens and Washington Capitals to reach the Stanley Cup finals for the second time in three years. At the other end of the standings, the return of Guy Lafleur to the city where he'd starred in junior hockey couldn't save the Quebec Nordiques, whose 61 losses and 31 points were the worst record the league had seen since 1975.

Youth is Served – Gretzky starred in Hollywood, the youngest Hull became a Golden Brett, Stevie Y was Motown's guy, but the Oilers had Moose, a solid "D", young guns, Bill Ranford and a fifth Cup title.

An injury to Mario Lemieux kept him out of 21 games this season and saw the Pittsburgh Penguins miss the playoffs. His absence made it possible for Wayne Gretzky to reclaim the Art Ross Trophy. Although his 142 points represented his lowest total since his first NHL season, Gretzky continued his assault on the record book. On October 15, 1989, Gretzky became the NHL's all-time scoring leader when he surpassed Gordie Howe's career total of 1,850 points—fittingly enough, in a game at Edmonton's Northlands Coliseum. His former Oilers teammate Mark Messier established a career high with 129 points on 45 goals and 84 assists, earning him the Hart Trophy as most valuable player. Brett Hull of the St. Louis Blues led the NHL, and set a new record for right wingers, with 72 goals.

Fourth-place Los Angeles upset the defending Stanley Cup champion Calgary Flames in the Smythe Division semi-finals before falling to Messier and the Oilers in four straight. Edmonton advanced to play for the Stanley Cup after a six-game Campbell Conference final victory over the Chicago Blackhawks, who had won the Norris Division in their second year under former Philadelphia Flyers coach Mike Keenan.

Game one of the Stanley Cup finals needed 55 minutes of overtime before Petr Klima gave Edmonton a 3–2 victory. A 7–2 win followed in game two, and the Oilers rolled to victory in five games. Messier, Glenn Anderson, Jari Kurri and Kevin Lowe all earned their fifth Stanley Cup rings, and the play of youngsters Adam Graves, Joe Murphy and Martin Gelinas had also figured prominently. The Conn Smythe Trophy for playoff MVP went to goalie Bill Ranford, who was in net for all 16 of Edmonton's postseason victories and was a model of sound positional play.

Pictured in the uniform of Moscow's Central Red Army, the rules governing the Calder Trophy were changed after Soviet national team veteran Sergei Makarov won it in 1990.

Leaders, 1989-90

GOALS

Name, Team	G
Brett Hull, St.L.	72
Steve Yzerman, Det.	62
Cam Neely, Bos.	55
Brian Bellows, Min.	55
Pat LaFontaine, NYI	54
Luc Robitaille, L.A.	52
Stephane Richer, Mtl.	51
Gary Leeman, Tor.	51
Mario Lemieux, Pit.	45
Mark Messier, Edm.	45
Joe Nieuwendyk, Cgy.	45
Mike Gartner, Min./NYR	45

ASSISTS

Name, Team	A
Wayne Gretzky, L.A.	102
Mark Messier, Edm.	84
Adam Oates, St.L.	79
Mario Lemieux, Pit.	78
Paul Coffey, Pit.	74
Bernie Nicholls, L.A./NYR	73
Ron Francis, Hfd.	69
Doug Gilmour, Cgy.	67
Pierre Turgeon, Buf.	66
Raymond Bourque, Bos.	65
Steve Yzerman, Det.	65

POWERPLAY GOALS

Name, Team	PPG
Brett Hull, St.L.	27
Cam Neely, Bos.	25
Mike Gartner, Min./NYR	21
Brian Bellows, Min.	21
Luc Robitaille, L.A.	20
John Ogrodnick, NYR	19
Dave Andreychuk, Buf.	18
Joe Nieuwendyk, Cgy.	18
Brent Sutter, NYI	17
Glenn Anderson, Edm.	17
Pierre Turgeon, Buf.	17

SHORTHAND GOALS

Name, Team	SHG
Steve Yzerman, Det.	7
Dave McLlwain, Wpg.	7
Mark Messier, Edm.	6
Craig MacTavish, Edm.	6
Dan Daoust, Tor.	4
Dave Reid, Tor.	4
Wayne Gretzky, L.A.	4
Mike Gartner, Min./NYR	4
Esa Tikkanen, Edm.	4
20 tied with	3

GAME-WINNING GOALS

Name, Team	GWG
Cam Neely, Bos.	12
Brett Hull, St.L.	12
John MacLean, N.J.	11
Pierre Turgeon, Buf.	10
Brian Bellows, Min.	9
Pat LaFontaine, NYI	8
Stephane Richer, Mtl.	8
Steve Yzerman, Det.	8
John Ogrodnick, NYR	8
Glenn Anderson, Edm.	7
Steve Thomas, Chi.	7
Luc Robitaille, L.A.	7

GOALIE WINS

Name, Team	W
Patrick Roy, Mtl.	31
Daren Puppa, Buf.	31
Jon Casey, Min.	31
Andy Moog, Bos.	24
Bill Ranford, Edm.	24
Mike Vernon, Cgy.	23
Don Beaupre, Wsh.	23
Reggie Lemelin, Bos.	22
Ken Wregget, Phi.	22
Sean Burke, N.J.	22
Kelly Hrudey, L.A.	22

SHUTOUTS

Name, Team	SO
Mike Liut, Hfd./Wsh.	4
Andy Moog, Bos.	3
Mark Fitzpatrick, NYI	3
Patrick Roy, Mtl.	3
Jon Casey, Min.	3

SAVE PERCENTAGE

Name, Team	SV%
Patrick Roy, Mtl.	.912
Mike Liut, Hfd./Wsh.	.905
Daren Puppa, Buf.	.903
Clint Malarchuk, Buf.	.903
Mark Fitzpatrick, NYI	.898

FIRST TEAM ALL-STARS

Name, Team	Position
Mark Messier, Edm.	C
Brett Hull, St.L.	RW
Luc Robitaille, L.A.	LW
Raymond Bourque, Bos.	D
Al MacInnis, Cgy.	D
Patrick Roy, Mtl.	G

SECOND TEAM ALL-STARS

Name, Team	Position
Wayne Gretzky, L.A.	C
Cam Neely, Bos.	RW
Brian Bellows, Min.	LW
Paul Coffey, Pit.	D
Doug Wilson, Chi.	D
Daren Puppa, Buf.	G

ALL-ROOKIE TEAM

Name, Team	Position
Mike Modano, Min.	C
Sergei Makarov, Cgy.	RW
Rod Brind'Amour, St.L.	LW
Brad Shaw, Hfd.	D
Geoff Smith, Edm.	D
Bob Essensa, Wpg.	G

TROPHY WINNERS

Trophy	Awarded For	Winner	Team
Hart	MVP	Mark Messier	Edm.
Art Ross	Top Scorer	Wayne Gretzky	L.A.
Norris	Top Defenseman	Raymond Bourque	Bos.
Calder	Top Rookie	Sergei Makarov	Cgy.
Selke	Top Defensive Forward	Rick Meagher	St.L.
Vezina	Top Goaltender	Patrick Roy	Mtl.
Jennings	Fewest Goals Against	Andy Moog	Bos.
		Reggie Lemelin	Bos.
Adams	Top Coach	Bob Murdoch	Wpg.
Byng	Gentlemanly Conduct	Brett Hull	St L
Masterton	Perseverance, Sportmanship	Gord Kluzak	Bos.
Pearson	NHLPA MVP	Mark Messier	Edm.
Conn Smythe	Playoff MVP	Bill Ranford	Edm.
Patrick	Service to Hockey in U.S.	Len Ceglarski	
Clancy	Leadership On and Off Ice	Kevin Lowe	Edm.
Entry Draft	First Overall Selection	Owen Nolan	Que.

NHL NOTEBOOK

TRANSACTIONS

- June 15, 1989 – Detroit traded Adam Oates and Paul MacLean to St. Louis in exchange for Bernie Federko and Tony McKegney.
- June 16, 1989 – St. Louis Blues signed free agent goaltender Curtis Joseph following one season of collegiate hockey at the University of Wisconsin.
- June 26, 1989 – New Jersey Devils signed veteran Soviet defenseman Viacheslav Fetisov.
- Jan. 20, 1990 – Los Angeles Kings traded Bernie Nicholls to the New York Rangers in exchange for Tomas Sandstrom and Tony Granato.

RECORDS

- Oct. 17, 1989 – Calgary's Doug Gilmour and Paul Ranheim set an NHL record for fastest two short-handed goals, scoring just four seconds apart. They came in an 8-8 tie against the Nordiques at Quebec.
- Jan. 30, 1990 – L.A.'s Wayne Gretzky set an NHL record by scoring his 100th point of the season for the 11th straight season; the milestone came in a 5-2 win over the visiting New Jersey Devils.
- Mar. 31, 1990 – Brett Hull scored twice to set a new NHL record for most goals by a right wing (72) when the Blues lost 6-3 to the Minnesota North Stars. Hull's 72 were one more than Jari Kurri, who scored 71 for the Oilers in 1984-85.
- Apr. 4, 1990 – Edmonton's Mark Messier set a new Stanley Cup record with his 11th career playoff shorthanded goal as the Oilers lost 7-5 to the Winnipeg Jets in game one of the Smythe Division semi-finals. Messier broke the record he shared with Wayne Gretzky.

MILESTONES

- Oct. 15, 1989 – Wayne Gretzky picked up a first-period assist for point #1,850 to tie Gordie Howe, then scored in the final minute to become the NHL's all-time leading point scorer. He scored again in over-time to lead the Kings to a 5-4 win at Edmonton.
- Dec. 6, 1989 – Defenseman Larry Robinson became the first NHL player to score 200 career goals without ever getting as many as 20 in one season when he scored his 200th career goal as the Kings won 5-4 over the Canucks.
- Mar. 31, 1990 – Quebec Nordiques' Joe Sakic became the first player in NHL history to score 100 points in a season while playing on a last-place team when he scored a goal in a 3-2 loss to the visiting Hartford Whalers.
- Mar. 31, 1990 – John Tanner made his NHL debut in goal for the Nordiques (in a 3-2 loss to the Hartford Whalers) to make Quebec the first team in NHL history to use seven goalies in one season. The 1934 Americans and 1980 Oilers had each used six goalies in one season.

1990 Playoffs

DIVISION SEMI-FINALS

Apr.	5	Hartford	4	at	Boston	3
Apr.	7	Hartford	1	at	Boston	3
Apr.	9	Boston	3	at	Hartford	5
Apr.	11	Boston	6	at	Hartford	5
Apr.	13	Hartford	2	at	Boston	3
Apr.	15	Boston	2	at	Hartford	3 OT
Apr.	17	Hartford	1	at	Boston	3

Boston won best-of-seven series 4–3

Apr.	5	Montreal	1	at	Buffalo	4
Apr.	7	Montreal	3	at	Buffalo	0
Apr.	9	Buffalo	1	at	Montreal	2 OT
Apr.	11	Buffalo	4	at	Montreal	2
Apr.	13	Montreal	4	at	Buffalo	2
Apr.	15	Buffalo	2	at	Montreal	5

Montreal won best-of-seven series 4–2

Apr.	5	NY Islanders	1	at	NY Rangers	2
Apr.	7	NY Islanders	2	at	NY Rangers	5
Apr.	9	NY Rangers	3	at	NY Islanders	4 2OT
Apr.	11	NY Rangers	6	at	NY Islanders	1
Apr.	13	NY Islanders	5	at	NY Rangers	6

NY Rangers won best-of-seven series 4–1

Apr.	5	Washington	5	at	New Jersey	4 OT
Apr.	7	Washington	5	at	New Jersey	6
Apr.	9	New Jersey	2	at	Washington	1
Apr.	11	New Jersey	1	at	Washington	3
Apr.	13	Washington	4	at	New Jersey	3
Apr.	15	New Jersey	2	at	Washington	3

Washington won best-of-seven series 4–2

Apr.	4	Minnesota	2	at	Chicago	1
Apr.	6	Minnesota	3	at	Chicago	5
Apr.	8	Chicago	2	at	Minnesota	1
Apr.	10	Chicago	0	at	Minnesota	4
Apr.	12	Minnesota	1	at	Chicago	5
Apr.	14	Chicago	3	at	Minnesota	5
Apr.	16	Minnesota	2	at	Chicago	5

Chicago won best-of-seven series 4–3

Apr.	4	Toronto	2	at	St. Louis	4
Apr.	6	Toronto	2	at	St. Louis	4
Apr.	8	St. Louis	6	at	Toronto	5 OT
Apr.	10	St. Louis	2	at	Toronto	4
Apr.	12	Toronto	3	at	St. Louis	4

St. Louis won best-of-seven series 4–1

Apr.	4	Los Angeles	5	at	Calgary	3
Apr.	6	Los Angeles	5	at	Calgary	8
Apr.	8	Calgary	1	at	Los Angeles	2 OT
Apr.	10	Calgary	4	at	Los Angeles	12
Apr.	12	Los Angeles	1	at	Calgary	5
Apr.	14	Calgary	3	at	Los Angeles	4 2OT

Los Angeles won best-of-seven series 4–2

Apr.	4	Winnipeg	7	at	Edmonton	5
Apr.	6	Winnipeg	2	at	Edmonton	3 OT
Apr.	8	Edmonton	1	at	Winnipeg	2
Apr.	10	Edmonton	3	at	Winnipeg	4 2OT
Apr.	12	Winnipeg	3	at	Edmonton	4
Apr.	14	Edmonton	4	at	Winnipeg	3
Apr.	16	Winnipeg	1	at	Edmonton	4

Edmonton won best-of-seven series 4–3

DIVISION FINALS

Apr.	19	Montreal	0	at	Boston	1
Apr.	21	Montreal	4	at	Boston	5 OT
Apr.	23	Boston	6	at	Montreal	3
Apr.	25	Boston	1	at	Montreal	4
Apr.	27	Montreal	1	at	Boston	3

Boston won best-of-seven series 4–1

Apr.	19	Washington	3	at	NY Rangers	7
Apr.	21	Washington	6	at	NY Rangers	3
Apr.	23	NY Rangers	1	at	Washington	7
Apr.	25	NY Rangers	3	at	Washington	4 OT
Apr.	27	Washington	2	at	NY Rangers	1 OT

Washington won best-of-seven series 4–1

Apr.	18	St. Louis	4	at	Chicago	3
Apr.	20	St. Louis	3	at	Chicago	5
Apr.	22	Chicago	4	at	St. Louis	5
Apr.	24	Chicago	3	at	St. Louis	2
Apr.	26	St. Louis	2	at	Chicago	3
Apr.	28	Chicago	2	at	St. Louis	4
Apr.	30	St. Louis	2	at	Chicago	8

Chicago won best-of-seven series 4–3

Apr.	18	Los Angeles	0	at	Edmonton	7
Apr.	20	Los Angeles	1	at	Edmonton	6
Apr.	22	Edmonton	5	at	Los Angeles	4
Apr.	24	Edmonton	6	at	Los Angeles	5 OT

Edmonton won best-of-seven series 4–0

CONFERENCE FINALS

May	3	Washington	3	at	Boston	5
May	5	Washington	0	at	Boston	3
May	7	Boston	4	at	Washington	1
May	9	Boston	3	at	Washington	2

Boston won best-of-seven series 4–0

May	2	Chicago	2	at	Edmonton	5
May	4	Chicago	4	at	Edmonton	3
May	6	Edmonton	1	at	Chicago	5
May	8	Edmonton	4	at	Chicago	2
May	10	Chicago	3	at	Edmonton	4
May	12	Edmonton	8	at	Chicago	4

Edmonton won best-of-seven series 4–2

FINALS

May	15	Edmonton	3	at	Boston	2 3OT
May	18	Edmonton	7	at	Boston	2
May	20	Boston	2	at	Edmonton	1
May	22	Boston	1	at	Edmonton	5
May	24	Edmonton	4	at	Boston	1

Edmonton won best-of-seven series 4–1

1989-90 – Edmonton Oilers – Kevin Lowe, Steve Smith, Jeff Beukeboom, Mark Lamb, Joe Murphy, Glenn Anderson, Mark Messier (Captain), Adam Graves, Craig MacTavish, Kelly Buchberger, Jari Kurri, Craig Simpson, Martin Gelinas, Randy Gregg, Charlie Huddy, Geoff Smith, Reijo Ruotsalainen, Craig Muni, Bill Ranford, Dave Brown, Pokey Reddick, Petr Klima, Esa Tikkanen, Grant Fuhr, Peter Pocklington (Owner), Glen Sather (President/General Manager), John Muckler (Coach), Ted Green (Co-Coach), Ron Low (Assistant Coach), Bruce MacGregor (Assistant General Manager), Barry Fraser (Director of Player Personnel), John Blackwell (Director of Operations, AHL), Ace Bailey, Ed Chadwick, Lorne Davis, Harry Howell, Matti Vaisanen, Albert Reeves (Scouts), Bill Tuele (Director of Public Relations), Werner Baum (Controller), Dr. Gordon Cameron (Medical Chief of Staff), Dr. David Reid (Team Physician), Barrie Stafford (Athletic Trainer), Ken Lowe (Athletic Therapist), Stuart Poirier (Massage Therapist), Lyle Kulchisky (Assistant Trainer).

LEADING PLAYOFF SCORERS

Player	Club	GP	G	A	PTS	PIM
Craig Simpson	Edmonton	22	16	15	31	8
Mark Messier	Edmonton	22	9	22	31	20
Cam Neely	Boston	21	12	16	28	51
Jari Kurri	Edmonton	22	10	15	25	18
Esa Tikkanen	Edmonton	22	13	11	24	26
Glenn Anderson	Edmonton	22	10	12	22	20
Denis Savard	Chicago	20	7	15	22	41
Steve Larmer	Chicago	20	7	15	22	2
Craig Janney	Boston	18	3	19	22	2
Brett Hull	St. Louis	12	13	8	21	17

LEADING PLAYOFF GOALTENDERS

Goaltender	Club	GPI	Mins	GA	SO	Avg.
Andy Moog	Boston	20	1195	44	2	2.21
Daren Puppa	Buffalo	6	370	15	0	2.43
Patrick Roy	Montreal	11	641	26	1	2.43
Ed Belfour	Chicago	9	409	17	0	2.49
Bill Ranford	Edmonton	22	1401	59	1	2.53

PLAYOFF GOALS

Name, Team	G
Craig Simpson, Edm.	16
John Druce, Wsh.	14
Brett Hull, St.L.	13
Esa Tikkanen, Edm.	13
Cam Neely, Bos.	12
Jeremy Roenick, Chi.	11
Jari Kurri, Edm.	10
Glenn Anderson, Edm.	10

PLAYOFF ASSISTS

Name, Team	A
Mark Messier, Edm.	22
Craig Janney, Bos.	19
Cam Neely, Bos.	16
Denis Savard, Chi.	15
Steve Larmer, Chi.	15
Craig Simpson, Edm.	15
Jari Kurri, Edm.	15
Four tied with	12

PLAYOFF POWERPLAY GOALS

Name, Team	PPG
John Druce, Wsh.	8
Brett Hull, St.L.	7
Craig Simpson, Edm.	6
Jari Kurri, Edm.	6
Five tied with	4

PLAYOFF SHORTHAND GOALS

Name, Team	SHG
Steve Larmer, Chi.	2
Esa Tikkanen, Edm.	2
22 tied with	1

PLAYOFF GAME-WINNING GOALS

Name, Team	GWG
John Druce, Wsh.	4
Brett Hull, St.L.	3
Steve Thomas, Chi.	3
Craig Simpson, Edm.	3
Jari Kurri, Edm.	3

PLAYOFF GOALIE WINS

Name, Team	W
Bill Ranford, Edm.	16
Andy Moog, Bos.	13
Greg Millen, Chi.	6
Patrick Roy, Mtl.	5
Five tied with	4

PLAYOFF SHUTOUTS

Name, Team	SO
Andy Moog, Bos.	2
Jon Casey, Min.	1
Patrick Roy, Mtl.	1
Bill Ranford, Edm.	1

PLAYOFF SAVE PERCENTAGE

Name, Team	SV%
Daren Puppa, Buf.	.922
Ed Belfour, Chi.	.915
Bill Ranford, Edm.	.912
Patrick Roy, Mtl.	.911
Andy Moog, Bos.	.909

1990-91

Stanley Cup • Pittsburgh Penguins

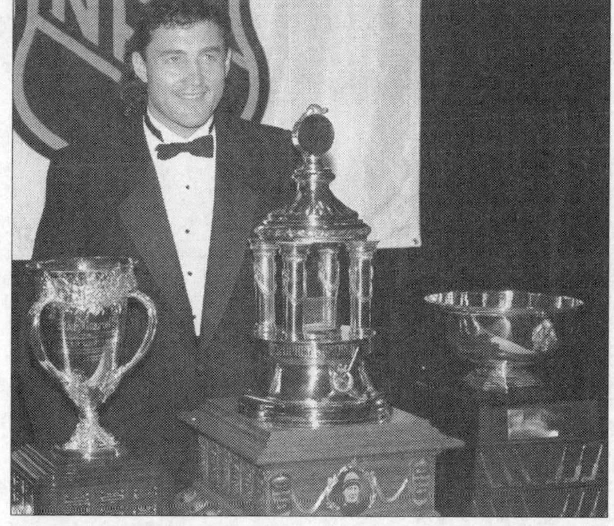

Ed Belfour joined Tony Esposito, Frank Brimsek and Tom Barrasso as the only goaltenders to be awarded the Vezina and Calder trophies in the same season. "The Eagle" also won the Jennings Trophy for the fewest goals allowed by his team.

FINAL STANDINGS

CLARENCE CAMPBELL CONFERENCE

Team	GP	W	L	T	GF	GA	PTS
Norris Division							
Chicago	80	49	23	8	284	211	106
St. Louis	80	47	22	11	310	250	105
Detroit	80	34	38	8	273	298	76
Minnesota	80	27	39	14	256	266	68
Toronto	80	23	46	11	241	318	57
Smythe Division							
Los Angeles	80	46	24	10	340	254	102
Calgary	80	46	26	8	344	263	100
Edmonton	80	37	37	6	272	272	80
Vancouver	80	28	43	9	243	315	65
Winnipeg	80	26	43	11	260	288	63
PRINCE OF WALES CONFERENCE							
Adams Division							
Boston	80	44	24	12	299	264	100
Montreal	80	39	30	11	273	249	89
Buffalo	80	31	30	19	292	278	81
Hartford	80	31	38	11	238	276	73
Quebec	80	16	50	14	236	354	46
Patrick Division							
Pittsburgh	80	41	33	6	342	305	88
NY Rangers	80	36	31	13	297	265	85
Washington	80	37	36	7	258	258	81
New Jersey	80	32	33	15	272	264	79
Philadelphia	80	33	37	10	252	267	76
NY Islanders	80	25	45	10	223	290	60

LEADING SCORERS

Player	Club	GP	G	A	PTS	PIM
Wayne Gretzky	Los Angeles	78	41	122	163	16
Brett Hull	St. Louis	78	86	45	131	22
Adam Oates	St. Louis	61	25	90	115	29
Mark Recchi	Pittsburgh	78	40	73	113	48
John Cullen	Pit./Hfd.	78	39	71	110	101
Joe Sakic	Quebec	80	48	61	109	24
Steve Yzerman	Detroit	80	51	57	108	34
Theoren Fleury	Calgary	79	51	53	104	136
Al MacInnis	Calgary	78	28	75	103	90
Steve Larmer	Chicago	80	44	57	101	79
Jeremy Roenick	Chicago	79	41	53	94	80
Raymond Bourque	Boston	76	21	73	94	75
Paul Coffey	Pittsburgh	76	24	69	93	128
Craig Janney	Boston	77	26	66	92	8
Cam Neely	Boston	69	51	40	91	98
Luc Robitaille	Los Angeles	76	45	46	91	68
Tomas Sandstrom	Los Angeles	68	45	44	89	106
Dale Hawerchuk	Buffalo	80	31	58	89	32
Brian Leetch	NY Rangers	80	16	72	88	42
Ron Francis	Hfd./Pit.	81	23	64	87	72
Kevin Stevens	Pittsburgh	80	40	46	86	133
Joe Nieuwendyk	Calgary	79	45	40	85	36
Pat LaFontaine	NY Islanders	75	41	44	85	42

LEADING GOALTENDERS

Goaltender	Club	GPI	MINS	GA	SO	AVG
Ed Belfour	Chicago	74	4127	170	4	2.47
Don Beaupre	Washington	45	2572	113	5	2.64
Patrick Roy	Montreal	48	2835	128	1	2.71
Andy Moog	Boston	51	2844	136	4	2.87
Pete Peeters	Philadelphia	26	1270	61	1	2.88
Kelly Hrudey	Los Angeles	47	2730	132	3	2.90
Chris Terreri	New Jersey	53	2970	144	1	2.91
Jon Casey	Minnesota	55	3185	158	3	2.98
Vincent Riendeau	St. Louis	44	2671	134	3	3.01
Rick Wamsley	Calgary	29	1670	85	0	3.05

THE 1990–91 SEASON featured a great race for the Presidents' Trophy, with five teams, representing three of the league's four divisions, in the hunt for first place overall. The Boston Bruins again proved the best in the Adams Division with 100 points. Raymond Bourque won the Norris Trophy for the fourth time and Cam Neely scored 51 goals. The Calgary Flames also had 100 points this season, but top spot in the Smythe Division went to the Los Angeles Kings, first-place finishers for the first time in franchise history with 102 points. The Kings were led by Wayne Gretzky, who earned his ninth scoring title with 41 goals and 122 assists. Gretzky also took home the Lady Byng Trophy.

But the battle for first place overall came down to two Norris Division rivals, St. Louis and Chicago. The Blues had Hart Trophy winner Brett Hull's 86 goals on their side, but the Blackhawks edged them out with 106 points to the Blues' 105. Defense was the key in Chicago, where goalie Ed Belfour won the Vezina Trophy as well as the Calder as rookie of the year. In the playoffs, both Norris Division titans were eliminated by the surprising Minnesota North Stars, who racked up a third playoff upset when they knocked off the Edmonton Oilers in the Campbell Conference finals. The defending Stanley Cup champions, who'd slipped to a third-place .500 record, had upset Calgary and Los Angeles before falling to Minnesota.

> **"It's Great Day for Hockey" – Badger Bob Johnson brought a quiet efficiency and calm confidence to the Pittsburgh Penguins and guided them to the Stanley Cup only months before he died.**

In the Patrick Division, the Pittsburgh Penguins opened the season without Mario Lemieux (who missed 54 games because of back surgery), but developed a balanced attack led by Mark Recchi, Kevin Stevens and Paul Coffey. Lemieux's late-season return, and a trade that brought Ron Francis and Ulf Samuelsson from Hartford, propelled the Penguins to their first-ever division title with 88 points. Pittsburgh defeated the New Jersey Devils and Washington Capitals to reach the Wales Conference final for the first time. After dropping the first two games to Boston, the Penguins won four in a row and advanced to play Minnesota for the Stanley Cup.

The matchup of the Penguins and North Stars marked the first time since 1934, when the Detroit Red Wings faced Chicago, that neither finalist had ever won the Stanley Cup. The North Stars won games one and three of the series, but Pittsburgh held a 3–2 lead after five games. The Penguins' offense finally proved to be too much in game six, and Pittsburgh claimed its first Cup title with an 8–0 victory. Mario Lemieux led all postseason performers with 44 points to win the Conn Smythe Trophy as playoff MVP.

Brett Hull's 86 goals in 1990–91 rank as the third-highest single-season total in history behind Wayne Gretzky's 92- and 87-goal seasons.

Leaders, 1990-91

GOALS

Name, Team	G
Brett Hull, St.L.	86
Cam Neely, Bos.	51
Theoren Fleury, Cgy.	51
Steve Yzerman, Det.	51
Mike Gartner, NYR	49
Joe Sakic, Que.	48
Tomas Sandstrom, L.A.	45
Luc Robitaille, L.A.	45
John MacLean, N.J.	45
Joe Nieuwendyk, Cgy.	45

ASSISTS

Name, Team	A
Wayne Gretzky, L.A.	122
Adam Oates, St.L.	90
Al MacInnis, Cgy.	75
Raymond Bourque, Bos.	73
Mark Recchi, Pit.	73
Brian Leetch, NYR	72
John Cullen, Pit./Hfd.	71
Paul Coffey, Pit.	69
Craig Janney, Bos.	66
Ron Francis, Hfd./Pit.	64

POWERPLAY GOALS

Name, Team	PPG
Brett Hull, St.L.	29
Joe Nieuwendyk, Cgy.	22
Mike Gartner, NYR	22
Dave Gagner, Min.	20
John MacLean, N.J.	19
Cam Neely, Bos.	18
Kevin Stevens, Pit.	18
Al MacInnis, Cgy.	17
Steve Larmer, Chi.	17
Brian Bellows, Min.	17

SHORTHAND GOALS

Name, Team	SHG
Dave Reid, Tor.	8
Theoren Fleury, Cgy.	7
Steve Yzerman, Det.	6
Dirk Graham, Chi.	6
Craig MacTavish, Edm.	6
Mike Ridley, Wsh.	5
Marc Habscheid, Det.	4
Phil Bourque, Pit.	4
Joe Nieuwendyk, Cgy.	4
Jeremy Roenick, Chi.	4
Dave Snuggerud, Buf.	4

GAME-WINNING GOALS

Name, Team	GWG
Brett Hull, St.L.	11
Jeremy Roenick, Chi.	10
Mark Recchi, Pit.	9
Theoren Fleury, Cgy.	9
Steve Larmer, Chi.	9
Cam Neely, Bos.	8
Geoff Courtnall, St.L./Van.	8
John MacLean, N.J.	7
Dirk Graham, Chi.	7
Joe Sakic, Que.	7
Ron Francis, Hfd./Pit.	7

GOALIE WINS

Name, Team	W
Ed Belfour, Chi.	43
Mike Vernon, Cgy.	31
Tim Cheveldae, Det.	30
Vincent Riendeau, St.L.	29
Tom Barrasso, Pit.	27
Bill Ranford, Edm.	27
Kelly Hrudey, L.A.	26
Patrick Roy, Mtl.	25
Andy Moog, Bos.	25
Chris Terreri, N.J.	24

SHUTOUTS

Name, Team	SO
Don Beaupre, Wsh.	5
Andy Moog, Bos.	4
Bob Essensa, Wpg.	4
Ed Belfour, Chi.	4
Four tied with	3

SAVE PERCENTAGE

Name, Team	SV%
Ed Belfour, Chi.	.910
Patrick Roy, Mtl.	.906
Mike Richter, NYR	.903
Pete Peeters, Phi.	.902
Kelly Hrudey, L.A.	.900

FIRST TEAM ALL-STARS

Name, Team	Position
Wayne Gretzky, L.A.	C
Brett Hull, St.L.	RW
Luc Robitaille, L.A.	LW
Raymond Bourque, Bos.	D
Al MacInnis, Cgy.	D
Ed Belfour, Chi.	G

SECOND TEAM ALL-STARS

Name, Team	Position
Adam Oates, St.L.	C
Cam Neely, Bos.	RW
Kevin Stevens, Pit.	LW
Chris Chelios, Chi.	D
Brian Leetch, NYR	D
Patrick Roy, Mtl.	G

ALL-ROOKIE TEAM

Name, Team	Position
Sergei Fedorov, Det.	C
Ken Hodge, Bos.	RW
Jaromir Jagr, Pit.	LW
Eric Weinrich, N.J.	D
Rob Blake, L.A.	D
Ed Belfour, Chi.	G

TROPHY WINNERS

Trophy	Awarded For	Winner	Team
Hart	MVP	Brett Hull	St.L.
Art Ross	Top Scorer	Wayne Gretzky	L.A.
Norris	Top Defenseman	Raymond Bourque	Bos.
Calder	Top Rookie	Ed Belfour	Chi.
Selke	Top Defensive Forward	Dirk Graham	Chi.
Vezina	Top Goaltender	Ed Belfour	Chi
Jennings	Fewest Goals Against	Ed Belfour	Chi
Adams	Top Coach	Brian Sutter	St.L.
Byng	Gentlemanly Conduct	Wayne Gretzky	L.A.
Masterton	Perseverance, Sportmanship	Dave Taylor	L.A.
Pearson	NHLPA MVP	Brett Hull	St.L.
Conn Smythe	Playoff MVP	Mario Lemieux	Pit.
Patrick	Service to Hockey in U.S.	Rod Gilbert Mike Ilitch	
Clancy	Leadership On and Off Ice	Dave Taylor	L.A.
Entry Draft	First Overall Selection	Eric Lindros	Que.

NHL NOTEBOOK

TRANSACTIONS

- June 16, 1990 – Calgary traded Joey Mullen to Pittsburgh in exchange for the Penguins' second-round choice in the 1990 Entry Draft.
- Sept. 4, 1990 – Montreal Canadiens traded Claude Lemieux to New Jersey in exchange for Sylvain Turgeon.
- Dec. 11, 1990 – Pittsburgh Penguins obtained defensemen Larry Murphy and Peter Taglianetti from the Minnesota North Stars in exchange for Jim Johnson and Chris Dahlquist.
- Mar. 4, 1991 – Hartford Whalers traded Ron Francis, Grant Jennings and Ulf Samuelsson to the Pittsburgh Penguins in exchange for John Cullen, Jeff Parker and Zarley Zalapski.

RECORDS

- Jan. 17, 1991 – Andy Van Hellemond set an NHL record for most games worked by a referee when he appeared in his 1,173rd regular season game as the St. Louis Blues hosted Montreal. Van Hellemond broke the record set by Dave Newell.
- Mar. 14, 1991 – Los Angeles' Wayne Gretzky set an NHL record with an assist in his 18th consecutive game, breaking the mark of 17 that he shared with Paul Coffey. It came in a 6-3 loss to Chicago.
- Mar. 31, 1991 – Boston's Chris Nilan set an NHL record with 10 penalties in one game (six minors, two majors, a misconduct and a game misconduct) in a 7-3 win over the Hartford Whalers at Boston Garden.
- Apr. 24, 1991 – Minnesota North Stars and the St. Louis Blues scored four powerplay goals each to set an NHL record for most PPG's in a playoff game. North Stars won the game 8-4 to take a 3-1 lead in their Norris Division finals.

MILESTONES

- Oct. 26, 1990 – Wayne Gretzky became the first player in NHL history to hit the 2,000-point milestone with an assist as the Kings lost 6-2 to the Jets at Winnipeg. He upped his career stats to 684 goals, 1,316 assists, for 2,000 points in 857 NHL games.
- Dec. 27, 1990 – Edmonton Oilers recorded their 500th all-time NHL victory 4-1 over the Flames in Edmonton. The win gave the Oilers a lifetime record of 500-295-120, for a winning percentage of .612, the best of any NHL team.
- Apr. 12, 1991 – Wayne Gretzky had four assists to give him 200 in his playoff career. His milestone came as the Kings beat Vancouver 7-4 in game five of the Smythe Division semi-finals.
- June 5, 1991 – Brett Hull became part of the first father-and-son team to win the Hart Trophy when the St. Louis star won the NHL's MVP award in Toronto.

1991 Playoffs

DIVISION SEMI-FINALS

Date	Visitor			Home		
Apr. 3	Hartford	5	at	Boston	2	
Apr. 5	Hartford	3	at	Boston	4	
Apr. 7	Boston	6	at	Hartford	3	
Apr. 9	Boston	3	at	Hartford	4	
Apr. 11	Hartford	1	at	Boston	6	
Apr. 13	Boston	3	at	Hartford	1	

Boston won best-of-seven series 4–2

Date	Visitor			Home		
Apr. 3	Buffalo	5	at	Montreal	7	
Apr. 5	Buffalo	4	at	Montreal	5	
Apr. 7	Montreal	4	at	Buffalo	5	
Apr. 9	Montreal	4	at	Buffalo	6	
Apr. 11	Buffalo	3	at	Montreal	4	OT
Apr. 13	Montreal	5	at	Buffalo	1	

Montreal won best-of-seven series 4–2

Date	Visitor			Home		
Apr. 3	New Jersey	3	at	Pittsburgh	1	
Apr. 5	New Jersey	4	at	Pittsburgh	5	OT
Apr. 7	Pittsburgh	4	at	New Jersey	3	
Apr. 9	Pittsburgh	1	at	New Jersey	4	
Apr. 11	New Jersey	4	at	Pittsburgh	2	
Apr. 13	Pittsburgh	4	at	New Jersey	3	
Apr. 15	New Jersey	0	at	Pittsburgh	4	

Pittsburgh won best-of-seven series 4–3

Date	Visitor			Home		
Apr. 3	Washington	1	at	NY Rangers	2	
Apr. 5	Washington	3	at	NY Rangers	0	
Apr. 7	NY Rangers	6	at	Washington	0	
Apr. 9	NY Rangers	2	at	Washington	3	
Apr. 11	Washington	5	at	NY Rangers	4	OT
Apr. 13	NY Rangers	2	at	Washington	4	

Washington won best-of-seven series 4–2

Date	Visitor			Home		
Apr. 4	Minnesota	4	at	Chicago	3	OT
Apr. 6	Minnesota	2	at	Chicago	5	
Apr. 8	Chicago	6	at	Minnesota	5	
Apr. 10	Chicago	1	at	Minnesota	3	
Apr. 12	Minnesota	6	at	Chicago	0	
Apr. 14	Chicago	1	at	Minnesota	3	

Minnesota won best-of-seven series 4–2

Date	Visitor			Home		
Apr. 4	Detroit	6	at	St. Louis	3	
Apr. 6	Detroit	2	at	St. Louis	4	
Apr. 8	St. Louis	2	at	Detroit	5	
Apr. 10	St. Louis	3	at	Detroit	4	
Apr. 12	Detroit	1	at	St. Louis	6	
Apr. 14	St. Louis	3	at	Detroit	0	
Apr. 16	Detroit	2	at	St. Louis	3	

St. Louis won best-of-seven series 4–3

Date	Visitor			Home		
Apr. 4	Vancouver	6	at	Los Angeles	5	
Apr. 6	Vancouver	2	at	Los Angeles	3	OT
Apr. 8	Los Angeles	1	at	Vancouver	2	OT
Apr. 10	Los Angeles	6	at	Vancouver	1	
Apr. 12	Vancouver	4	at	Los Angeles	7	
Apr. 14	Los Angeles	4	at	Vancouver	1	

Los Angeles won best-of-seven series 4–2

Date	Visitor			Home		
Apr. 4	Edmonton	3	at	Calgary	1	
Apr. 6	Edmonton	1	at	Calgary	3	
Apr. 8	Calgary	3	at	Edmonton	4	
Apr. 10	Calgary	2	at	Edmonton	5	
Apr. 12	Edmonton	3	at	Calgary	5	
Apr. 14	Calgary	2	at	Edmonton	1	OT
Apr. 16	Edmonton	5	at	Calgary	4	OT

Edmonton won best-of-seven series 4–3

DIVISION FINALS

Date	Visitor			Home		
Apr. 17	Montreal	1	at	Boston	2	
Apr. 19	Montreal	4	at	Boston	3	OT
Apr. 21	Boston	3	at	Montreal	2	
Apr 23	Boston	2	at	Montreal	6	
Apr. 25	Montreal	1	at	Boston	4	
Apr. 27	Boston	2	at	Montreal	3	OT
Apr. 29	Montreal	1	at	Boston	2	

Boston won best-of-seven series 4–3

Date	Visitor			Home		
Apr. 17	Washington	4	at	Pittsburgh	2	
Apr. 19	Washington	6	at	Pittsburgh	7	OT
Apr. 21	Pittsburgh	3	at	Washington	1	
Apr. 23	Pittsburgh	3	at	Washington	1	
Apr. 25	Washington	1	at	Pittsburgh	4	

Pittsburgh won best-of-seven series 4–1

Date	Visitor			Home		
Apr. 18	Minnesota	2	at	St. Louis	1	
Apr. 20	Minnesota	2	at	St. Louis	5	
Apr. 22	St. Louis	1	at	Minnesota	5	
Apr. 24	St. Louis	4	at	Minnesota	8	
Apr. 26	Minnesota	2	at	St. Louis	4	
Apr. 28	St. Louis	2	at	Minnesota	3	

Minnesota won best-of-seven series 4–2

Date	Visitor			Home		
Apr. 18	Edmonton	3	at	Los Angeles	4	OT
Apr. 20	Edmonton	4	at	Los Angeles	3	2OT
Apr. 22	Los Angeles	3	at	Edmonton	4	2OT
Apr. 24	Los Angeles	2	at	Edmonton	4	
Apr. 26	Edmonton	2	at	Los Angeles	5	
Apr. 28	Los Angeles	3	at	Edmonton	4	OT

Edmonton won best-of-seven series 4–2

CONFERENCE FINALS

Date	Visitor			Home		
May 1	Pittsburgh	3	at	Boston	6	
May 3	Pittsburgh	4	at	Boston	5	OT
May 5	Boston	1	at	Pittsburgh	4	
May 7	Boston	1	at	Pittsburgh	4	
May 9	Pittsburgh	7	at	Boston	2	
May 11	Boston	3	at	Pittsburgh	5	

Pittsburgh won best-of-seven series 4–2

Date	Visitor			Home		
May 2	Minnesota	3	at	Edmonton	1	
May 4	Minnesota	2	at	Edmonton	7	
May 6	Edmonton	3	at	Minnesota	7	
May 8	Edmonton	1	at	Minnesota	5	
May 10	Minnesota	3	at	Edmonton	2	

Minnesota won best-of-seven series 4–1

FINALS

Date	Visitor			Home		
May 15	Minnesota	5	at	Pittsburgh	4	
May 17	Minnesota	1	at	Pittsburgh	4	
May 19	Pittsburgh	1	at	Minnesota	3	
May 21	Pittsburgh	5	at	Minnesota	3	
May 23	Minnesota	4	at	Pittsburgh	6	
May 25	Pittsburgh	8	at	Minnesota	0	

Pittsburgh won best-of-seven series 4–2

1990-91 – Pittsburgh Penguins – Mario Lemieux (Captain), Paul Coffey, Randy Hillier, Bob Errey, Tom Barrasso, Phil Bourque, Jay Caufield, Ron Francis, Randy Gilhen, Jiri Hrdina, Jaromir Jagr, Grant Jennings, Troy Loney, Joe Mullen, Larry Murphy, Jim Paek, Barry Pederson, Frank Pietrangelo, Mark Recchi, Gordie Roberts, Ulf Samuelsson, Paul Stanton, Kevin Stevens, Peter Taglianetti, Bryan Trottier, Scott Young, Wendell Young, Edward J. DeBartolo, Sr. (Owner), Marie D. DeBartolo York (President), Paul Martha (Vice President/General Counsel), Craig Patrick (General Manager), Scotty Bowman (Director of Player Development & Recruitment), Bob Johnson (Coach), Rick Kehoe (Assistant Coach), Gilles Meloche (Goaltending Coach/Scout), Rick Paterson, Barry Smith (Assistant Coaches), Steve Latin (Equipment Manager), Skip Thayer (Trainer), John Welday (Strength & Conditioning Coach), Greg Malone (Scout).

LEADING PLAYOFF SCORERS

Player	Club	GP	G	A	PTS	PIM
Mario Lemieux	Pittsburgh	23	16	28	44	16
Mark Recchi	Pittsburgh	24	10	24	34	33
Kevin Stevens	Pittsburgh	24	17	16	33	53
Brian Bellows	Minnesota	23	10	19	29	30
Dave Gagner	Minnesota	23	12	15	27	28
Raymond Bourque	Boston	19	7	18	25	12
Brian Propp	Minnesota	23	8	15	23	28
Larry Murphy	Pittsburgh	23	5	18	23	44
Neal Broten	Minnesota	23	9	13	22	6
Craig Janney	Boston	18	4	18	22	11

LEADING PLAYOFF GOALTENDERS

Goaltender	Club	GPI	Mins	GA	SO	Avg.
Tom Barrasso	Pittsburgh	20	1175	51	1	2.60
Kelly Hrudey	Los Angeles	12	798	37	0	2.78
Don Beaupre	Washington	11	624	29	1	2.79
Chris Terreri	New Jersey	7	428	21	0	2.94
Mike Vernon	Calgary	7	427	21	0	2.95

PLAYOFF GOALS

Name, Team	G
Kevin Stevens, Pit.	17
Cam Neely, Bos.	16
Mario Lemieux, Pit.	16
Luc Robitaille, L.A.	12
Esa Tikkanen, Edm.	12
Dave Gagner, Min.	12
Brett Hull, St.L.	11
Brian Bellows, Min.	10
Mark Recchi, Pit.	10

PLAYOFF ASSISTS

Name, Team	A
Mario Lemieux, Pit.	28
Mark Recchi, Pit.	24
Brian Bellows, Min.	19
Craig Janney, Bos.	18
Raymond Bourque, Bos.	18
Larry Murphy, Pit.	18
Kevin Stevens, Pit.	16
Dave Gagner, Min.	15
Brian Propp, Min.	15

PLAYOFF POWERPLAY GOALS

Name, Team	PPG
Cam Neely, Bos.	9
Brian Propp, Min.	8
Kevin Stevens, Pit.	7
Mario Lemieux, Pit.	6
Brian Bellows, Min.	6
Dave Gagner, Min.	6

PLAYOFF SHORTHAND GOALS

Name, Team	SHG
Russ Courtnall, Mtl.	2
Mario Lemieux, Pit.	2
14 tied with	1

PLAYOFF GAME-WINNING GOALS

Name, Team	GWG
Bobby Smith, Min.	5
Cam Neely, Bos.	4
Kevin Stevens, Pit.	4
Ron Francis, Pit.	4
Shayne Corson, Mtl.	3
Esa Tikkanen, Edm.	3
Petr Klima, Edm.	3
Brian Propp, Min.	3

PLAYOFF GOALIE WINS

Name, Team	W
Jon Casey, Min.	14
Tom Barrasso, Pit.	12
Andy Moog, Bos.	10
Grant Fuhr, Edm.	8
Patrick Roy, Mtl.	7

PLAYOFF SHUTOUTS

Name, Team	SO
Frank Pietrangelo, Pit.	1
Mike Richter, NYR	1
Don Beaupre, Wsh.	1
Vincent Riendeau, St.L.	1
Tom Barrasso, Pit.	1

PLAYOFF SAVE PERCENTAGE

Name, Team	SV%
Mike Richter, NYR	.923
Tom Barrasso, Pit.	.919
Kelly Hrudey, L.A.	.903
Chris Terreri, N.J.	.903
Don Beaupre, Wsh.	.901

1991-92

Stanley Cup • Pittsburgh Penguins

FINAL STANDINGS

CLARENCE CAMPBELL CONFERENCE

Team	GP	W	L	T	GF	GA	PTS
Norris Division							
Detroit	80	43	25	12	320	256	98
Chicago	80	36	29	15	257	236	87
St. Louis	80	36	33	11	279	266	83
Minnesota	80	32	42	6	246	278	70
Toronto	80	30	43	7	234	294	67
Smythe Division							
Vancouver	80	42	26	12	285	250	96
Los Angeles	80	35	31	14	287	296	84
Edmonton	80	36	34	10	295	297	82
Winnipeg	80	33	32	15	251	244	81
Calgary	80	31	37	12	296	305	74
San Jose	80	17	58	5	219	359	39
PRINCE OF WALES CONFERENCE							
Adams Division							
Montreal	80	41	28	11	267	207	93
Boston	80	36	32	12	270	275	84
Buffalo	80	31	37	12	289	299	74
Hartford	80	26	41	13	247	283	65
Quebec	80	20	48	12	255	318	52
Patrick Division							
NY Rangers	80	50	25	5	321	246	105
Washington	80	45	27	8	330	275	98
Pittsburgh	80	39	32	9	343	308	87
New Jersey	80	38	31	11	289	259	87
NY Islanders	80	34	35	11	291	299	79
Philadelphia	80	32	37	11	252	273	75

LEADING SCORERS

Player	Club	GP	G	A	PTS	PIM
Mario Lemieux	Pittsburgh	64	44	87	131	94
Kevin Stevens	Pittsburgh	80	54	69	123	254
Wayne Gretzky	Los Angeles	74	31	90	121	34
Brett Hull	St. Louis	73	70	39	109	48
Luc Robitaille	Los Angeles	80	44	63	107	95
Mark Messier	NY Rangers	79	35	72	107	76
Jeremy Roenick	Chicago	80	53	50	103	98
Steve Yzerman	Detroit	79	45	58	103	64
Brian Leetch	NY Rangers	80	22	80	102	26
Adam Oates	St.L./Bos.	80	20	79	99	22
Dale Hawerchuk	Buffalo	77	23	75	98	27
Mark Recchi	Pit./Phi.	80	43	54	97	96
Pierre Turgeon	Buf./NYI	77	40	55	95	20
Joe Sakic	Quebec	69	29	65	94	20
Pat LaFontaine	Buffalo	57	46	47	93	98
Dave Andreychuk	Buffalo	80	41	50	91	71
Gary Roberts	Calgary	76	53	37	90	207
Vincent Damphousse	Edmonton	80	38	51	89	53
Joe Mullen	Pittsburgh	77	42	45	87	30
Doug Gilmour	Calgary	78	26	61	87	78
Craig Janney	Bos./St.L.	78	18	69	87	22
Sergei Fedorov	Detroit	80	32	54	86	72
Phil Housley	Winnipeg	74	23	63	86	92

LEADING GOALTENDERS

Goaltender	Club	GPI	MINS	GA	SO	AVG
Patrick Roy	Montreal	67	3935	155	5	2.36
Ed Belfour	Chicago	52	2928	132	5	2.70
Kirk McLean	Vancouver	65	3852	176	5	2.74
John Vanbiesbrouck	NY Rangers	45	2526	120	2	2.85
Bob Essensa	Winnipeg	47	2627	126	5	2.88
Stephane Beauregard	Winnipeg	26	1267	61	2	2.89
Curtis Joseph	St. Louis	60	3494	175	2	3.01
Craig Billington	New Jersey	26	1363	69	2	3.04
Mike Richter	NY Rangers	41	2298	119	3	3.11
Chris Terreri	New Jersey	54	3186	169	1	3.18

Picked by the Penguins with the first choice in the 1984 NHL Entry Draft, Mario Lemieux would emerge as Pittsburgh's hockey savior. He led the team to back-to-back Stanley Cup championships in 1991 and 1992, winning the Conn Smythe Trophy both years.

The 1991–92 campaign was the league's 75th anniversary season. The Rangers finished with 105 points on a club-record 50 victories, leading the league for the first time since 1941–42. Mark Messier, traded to New York by Edmonton just before the start of the season, won the Hart Trophy, becoming only the second player after former teammate Wayne Gretzky to be named the league's most valuable player with two different teams.

Gretzky and Mario Lemieux both lost time to injuries this season, but Lemieux regained the NHL scoring title with 44 goals and 87 assists. Pittsburgh Penguins teammate Kevin Stevens was second in scoring with 123 points, while #99 was third with 31 goals and 90 assists. For the third season in a row, Brett Hull of the St. Louis Blues led the league in goals, this time with 70.

Mario the Magnificent – A marvelous machine blessed with speed, grace, power and prowess, Lemieux dominated the spotlight with a second scoring title and his second straight playoff MVP award.

A 10-day players' strike late in the year jeopardized the conclusion of the season and pushed back the start of the playoffs to April 18, the latest date in history. The delayed first round proved to be an exciting one as six of the eight series went to seven games. Boston, Detroit, Pittsburgh and Vancouver all rebounded from 3–1 deficits to win their series. For the first time since 1980, all four division leaders (Montreal, the Rangers, Detroit and Vancouver) advanced to the second round, though each team lost its division final. Chicago got past Edmonton to advance to the Stanley Cup finals from the Campbell Conference, while Pittsburgh beat Boston for the Wales Conference championship.

The Penguins' season had been eventful: new owners had taken over and popular coach Bob Johnson had died in November 1991. The team was not to be denied under interim coach Scotty Bowman, even though the Blackhawks had set a playoff record with 11 consecutive postseason wins en route to the finals, and took an early 3–0 lead in game one before Pittsburgh rallied to win 5–4. The Penguins went on to sweep the series, finally matching Chicago's mark of 11 straight playoff wins. The Conn Smythe Trophy for playoff MVP went to Mario Lemieux, who joined Bernie Parent of the Philadelphia Flyers as the only players to win the award two years in a row.

The league awarded its first new franchise since 1979, adding the San Jose Sharks, as NHL hockey returned to the San Francisco Bay area for the first time since 1976. The Sharks' teal and black jersey with its shark-biting-stick logo quickly became a top seller, ushering in a new era of marketing and merchandising consciousness around the NHL.

Brian Leetch established career highs with 80 assists and 102 points in 1991–92 and won the Norris Trophy as best defenseman. He won the award again in 1997.

TROPHY WINNERS

Trophy	Awarded For	Winner	Team
Hart	MVP	Mark Messier	NYR
Art Ross	Top Scorer	Mario Lemieux	Pit.
Norris	Top Defenseman	Brian Leetch	NYR
Calder	Top Rookie	Pavel Bure	Van.
Selke	Top Defensive Forward	Guy Carbonneau	Mtl.
Vezina	Top Goaltender	Patrick Roy	Mtl.
Jennings	Fewest Goals Against	Patrick Roy	Mtl.
Adams	Top Coach	Pat Quinn	Van.
Byng	Gentlemanly Conduct	Wayne Gretzky	L.A.
Masterton	Perseverance, Sportmanship	Mark Fitzpatrick	NYI
Pearson	NHLPA MVP	Mark Messier	NYR
Conn Smythe	Playoff MVP	Mario Lemieux	Pit.
Patrick	Service to Hockey in U.S.	Al Arbour	
		Art Berglund	
		Lou Lamoriello	
Clancy	Leadership On and Off Ice	Ray Bourque	Bos.
Entry Draft	First Overall Selection	Roman Hamrlik	T.B.

Leaders, 1991-92

GOALS

Name, Team	G
Brett Hull, St.L.	70
Kevin Stevens, Pit.	54
Gary Roberts, Cgy.	53
Jeremy Roenick, Chi.	53
Pat LaFontaine, Buf.	46
Steve Yzerman, Det.	45
Mario Lemieux, Pit.	44
Luc Robitaille, L.A.	44
Mark Recchi, Pit./Phi.	43
Owen Nolan, Que.	42
Joe Mullen, Pit.	42

ASSISTS

Name, Team	A
Wayne Gretzky, L.A.	90
Mario Lemieux, Pit.	87
Brian Leetch, NYR	80
Adam Oates, St.L./Bos.	79
Dale Hawerchuk, Buf.	75
Mark Messier, NYR	72
Craig Janney, Bos./St.L.	69
Kevin Stevens, Pit.	69
Joe Sakic, Que.	65
Phil Housley, Wpg.	63
Luc Robitaille, L.A.	63

POWERPLAY GOALS

Name, Team	PPG
Dave Andreychuk, Buf.	28
Luc Robitaille, L.A.	26
Pat LaFontaine, Buf.	23
Jeremy Roenick, Chi.	22
Derek King, NYI	21
Brett Hull, St.L.	20
Mark Recchi, Pit./Phi.	20
Kevin Stevens, Pit.	19
Vladimir Ruzicka, Bos.	18
Owen Nolan, Que.	17
Dave Gagner, Min.	17

SHORTHAND GOALS

Name, Team	SHG
Steve Yzerman, Det.	8
Brett Hull, St.L.	5
Mike Ridley, Wsh.	5
Mario Lemieux, Pit.	4
Ron Sutter, St.L.	4
Murray Craven, Phi./Hfd.	4
Mark Messier, NYR	4
Paul Ysebaert, Det.	4
Kelly Buchberger, Edm.	4
Rod Brind'Amour, Phi.	4
Michal Pivonka, Wsh.	4
Adam Graves, NYR	4

GAME-WINNING GOALS

Name, Team	GWG
Jeremy Roenick, Chi.	13
Brett Hull, St.L.	9
Steve Yzerman, Det.	9
Claude Lemieux, N.J.	8
Mike Modano, Min.	8
Vincent Damphousse, Edm.	8
Tony Granato, L.A.	8
Ed Olczyk, Wpg.	7
Dino Ciccarelli, Wsh.	7
Kirk Muller, Mtl.	7
Dmitri Khristich, Wsh.	7

GOALIE WINS

Name, Team	W
Kirk McLean, Van.	38
Tim Cheveldae, Det.	38
Patrick Roy, Mtl.	36
Don Beaupre, Wsh.	29
Andy Moog, Bos.	28
John Vanbiesbrouck, NYR	27
Curtis Joseph, St.L.	27
Bill Ranford, Edm.	27
Kelly Hrudey, L.A.	26
Tom Barrasso, Pit.	25
Grant Fuhr, Tor.	25

SHUTOUTS

Name, Team	SO
Bob Essensa, Wpg.	5
Ed Belfour, Chi.	5
Kirk McLean, Van.	5
Patrick Roy, Mtl.	5
Three tied with	3

SAVE PERCENTAGE

Name, Team	SV%
Patrick Roy, Mtl.	.914
Bob Essensa, Wpg.	.910
Curtis Joseph, St.L.	.910
John Vanbiesbrouck, NYR	.910
Mark Fitzpatrick, NYI	.902
Two tied with	.901

FIRST TEAM ALL-STARS

Name, Team	Position
Mark Messier, NYR	C
Brett Hull, St.L.	RW
Kevin Stevens, Pit.	LW
Brian Leetch, NYR	D
Raymond Bourque, Bos.	D
Patrick Roy, Mtl.	G

SECOND TEAM ALL-STARS

Name, Team	Position
Mario Lemieux, Pit.	C
Mark Recchi, Pit.-Phi.	RW
Luc Robitaille, L.A.	LW
Phil Housley, Wpg.	D
Scott Stevens, N.J.	D
Kirk McLean, Van.	G

ALL-ROOKIE TEAM

Name, Team	Position
Kevin Todd, N.J.	C
Tony Amonte, NYR	RW
Gilbert Dionne, Mtl.	LW
Nicklas Lidstrom, Det.	D
Vladimir Konstantinov, Det.	D
Dominik Hasek, Chi.	G

NHL NOTEBOOK

TRANSACTIONS

- Sept. 3, 1991 – New Jersey Devils were awarded St. Louis defenseman Scott Stevens as compensation for the Blues signing Brendan Shanahan.
- Oct. 4, 1991 – Edmonton Oilers traded Mark Messier to the New York Rangers for Bernie Nicholls, Steven Rice and Louie DeBrusk.
- Oct. 25, 1991 – Buffalo Sabres obtained Pat LaFontaine, Randy Hillier and Randy Wood from the NY Islanders for Pierre Turgeon, Benoit Hogue, Uwe Krupp and Dave McLlwain.
- Jan. 2, 1992 – In the largest trade in NHL history, Calgary sent Doug Gilmour, Ric Nattress, Jamie Macoun, Rick Wamsley and Kent Manderville to Toronto for Gary Leeman, Michel Petit, Craig Berube, Jeff Reese and Alexander Godynyuk.

RECORDS

- Oct. 17, 1991 – Paul Coffey had two assists to become the highest scoring defenseman in NHL history, with 1,053 career points (passing Denis Potvin), when the Penguins beat the Islanders 8-5 in Pittsburgh.
- Feb. 13, 1992 – Chicago's Steve Larmer set an NHL record for most consecutive games played with one team, when he appeared in his 777th straight game with the Blackhawks.
- May 22, 1992 – Chicago goaltender Ed Belfour set an NHL record with his 11th consecutive playoff victory, a 5-1 win over the Oilers, in game four of the Conference championships.

MILESTONES

- Mar. 7, 1992 – Pittsburgh's Kevin Stevens became the first player with 100 points and 200 penalty minutes in the same season. His 100th point was an assist in a 5-3 loss to the Kings in Los Angeles.
- Apr. 16, 1992 – Mike Gartner picked up his 500th career NHL assist in a 7-1 Rangers win over Pittsburgh to become the first player in NHL history to get his 500th goal, 500th assist, 1,000th point and 1,000th NHL game all in the same season.
- Apr. 27, 1992 – Pittsburgh's Scotty Bowman became the leader in career playoff games coached when he was behind the bench for a 5-2 win over Washington in game five of the Patrick Division semi-finals. It was his 191st career playoff game, one more than Dick Irvin.
- May 1, 1992 – Buffalo's Pat LaFontaine became the first player in NHL history to score a goal in each of his team's first seven playoff games in one year. The milestone came in a 3-2 loss at Boston in game seven of the Adams Division semi-finals.

1992 Playoffs

DIVISION SEMI-FINALS

Date		Team	G		Team	G	
Apr.	19	Hartford	0	at	Montreal	2	
Apr.	21	Hartford	2	at	Montreal	5	
Apr.	23	Montreal	2	at	Hartford	5	
Apr.	25	Montreal	1	at	Hartford	3	
Apr.	27	Hartford	4	at	Montreal	7	
Apr.	29	Montreal	1	at	Hartford	2	OT
May	1	Hartford	2	at	Montreal	3	2OT

Montreal won best-of-seven series 4–3

Date		Team	G		Team	G	
Apr.	19	Buffalo	3	at	Boston	2	
Apr.	21	Buffalo	2	at	Boston	3	OT
Apr.	23	Boston	3	at	Buffalo	2	
Apr.	25	Boston	5	at	Buffalo	4	OT
Apr.	27	Buffalo	2	at	Boston	0	
Apr.	29	Boston	3	at	Buffalo	9	
May	1	Buffalo	2	at	Boston	3	

Boston won best-of-seven series 4–3

Date		Team	G		Team	G	
Apr.	19	New Jersey	1	at	NY Rangers	2	
Apr.	21	New Jersey	7	at	NY Rangers	3	
Apr.	23	NY Rangers	1	at	New Jersey	3	
Apr.	25	NY Rangers	3	at	New Jersey	0	
Apr.	27	New Jersey	5	at	NY Rangers	6	
Apr.	29	NY Rangers	3	at	New Jersey	5	
May	1	New Jersey	4	at	NY Rangers	8	

NY Rangers won best-of-seven series 4–3

Date		Team	G		Team	G	
Apr.	19	Pittsburgh	1	at	Washington	3	
Apr.	21	Pittsburgh	2	at	Washington	6	
Apr.	23	Washington	4	at	Pittsburgh	6	
Apr.	25	Washington	7	at	Pittsburgh	2	
Apr.	27	Pittsburgh	5	at	Washington	2	
Apr.	29	Washington	4	at	Pittsburgh	6	
May	1	Pittsburgh	3	at	Washington	1	

Pittsburgh won best-of-seven series 4–3

Date		Team	G		Team	G	
Apr.	18	Minnesota	4	at	Detroit	3	
Apr.	20	Minnesota	4	at	Detroit	2	
Apr.	22	Detroit	5	at	Minnesota	4	OT
Apr.	24	Detroit	4	at	Minnesota	5	
Apr.	26	Minnesota	0	at	Detroit	3	
Apr.	28	Detroit	1	at	Minnesota	0	OT
Apr.	30	Minnesota	2	at	Detroit	5	

Detroit won best-of-seven series 4–3

Date		Team	G		Team	G	
Apr.	18	St. Louis	1	at	Chicago	3	
Apr.	20	St. Louis	5	at	Chicago	3	
Apr.	22	Chicago	4	at	St. Louis	5	2OT
Apr.	24	Chicago	5	at	St. Louis	3	
Apr.	26	St. Louis	4	at	Chicago	6	
Apr.	28	Chicago	2	at	St. Louis	1	

Chicago won best-of-seven series 4–2

Date		Team	G		Team	G	
Apr.	18	Winnipeg	3	at	Vancouver	2	
Apr.	20	Winnipeg	2	at	Vancouver	3	
Apr.	22	Vancouver	2	at	Winnipeg	4	
Apr.	24	Vancouver	1	at	Winnipeg	3	
Apr.	26	Winnipeg	2	at	Vancouver	8	
Apr.	28	Vancouver	8	at	Winnipeg	3	
Apr.	30	Winnipeg	0	at	Vancouver	5	

Vancouver won best-of-seven series 4–3

Date		Team	G		Team	G	
Apr.	18	Edmonton	3	at	Los Angeles	1	
Apr.	20	Edmonton	5	at	Los Angeles	8	
Apr.	22	Los Angeles	3	at	Edmonton	4	
Apr.	24	Los Angeles	4	at	Edmonton	3	
Apr.	26	Edmonton	5	at	Los Angeles	2	
Apr.	28	Los Angeles	0	at	Edmonton	3	

Edmonton won best-of-seven series 4–2

DIVISION FINALS

Date		Team	G		Team	G	
May	3	Boston	6	at	Montreal	4	
May	5	Boston	3	at	Montreal	2	OT
May	7	Montreal	2	at	Boston	3	
May	9	Montreal	0	at	Boston	2	

Boston won best-of-seven series 4–0

Date		Team	G		Team	G	
May	3	Pittsburgh	4	at	NY Rangers	2	
May	5	Pittsburgh	2	at	NY Rangers	4	
May	7	NY Rangers	6	at	Pittsburgh	5	OT
May	9	NY Rangers	4	at	Pittsburgh	5	OT
May	11	Pittsburgh	3	at	NY Rangers	2	
May	13	NY Rangers	1	at	Pittsburgh	5	

Pittsburgh won best-of-seven series 4–2

Date		Team	G		Team	G	
May	2	Chicago	2	at	Detroit	1	
May	4	Chicago	3	at	Detroit	1	
May	6	Detroit	4	at	Chicago	5	
May	8	Detroit	0	at	Chicago	1	

Chicago won best-of-seven series 4–0

Date		Team	G		Team	G	
May	3	Edmonton	4	at	Vancouver	3	OT
May	4	Edmonton	0	at	Vancouver	4	
May	6	Vancouver	2	at	Edmonton	5	
May	8	Vancouver	2	at	Edmonton	3	
May	10	Edmonton	3	at	Vancouver	4	
May	12	Vancouver	0	at	Edmonton	3	

Edmonton won best-of-seven series 4–2

CONFERENCE FINALS

Date		Team	G		Team	G	
May	17	Boston	3	at	Pittsburgh	4	OT
May	19	Boston	2	at	Pittsburgh	5	
May	21	Pittsburgh	5	at	Boston	1	
May	23	Pittsburgh	5	at	Boston	1	

Pittsburgh won best-of-seven series 4–0

Date		Team	G		Team	G	
May	16	Edmonton	2	at	Chicago	8	
May	18	Edmonton	2	at	Chicago	4	
May	20	Chicago	4	at	Edmonton	3	OT
May	22	Chicago	5	at	Edmonton	1	

Chicago won best-of-seven series 4–0

FINALS

Date		Team	G		Team	G
May	26	Chicago	4	at	Pittsburgh	5
May	28	Chicago	1	at	Pittsburgh	3
May	30	Pittsburgh	1	at	Chicago	0
June	1	Pittsburgh	6	at	Chicago	5

Pittsburgh won best-of-seven series 4–0

1991-92 – Pittsburgh Penguins – Mario Lemieux (Captain), Ron Francis, Bryan Trottier, Kevin Stevens, Bob Errey, Phil Bourque, Troy Loney, Rick Tocchet, Joe Mullen, Jaromir Jagr, Jiri Hrdina, Shawn McEachern, Ulf Samuelsson, Kjell Samuelsson, Larry Murphy, Gordie Roberts, Jim Paek, Paul Stanton, Tom Barrasso, Ken Wregget, Jay Caufield, Jamie Leach, Wendell Young, Grant Jennings, Peter Taglianetti, Jock Callander, Dave Michayluk, Mike Needham, Jeff Chychrun, Ken Priestlay, Jeff Daniels, Howard Baldwin (Owner/President), Morris Belzberg, Thomas Ruta (Owners), Donn Patton (Executive Vice President/Chief Financial Officer), Paul Martha (Executive Vice President/General Counsel), Craig Patrick (Executive Vice President/General Manager), Bob Johnson (Coach), Scotty Bowman (Director of Player Development/Coach), Barry Smith, Rick Kehoe, Pierre McGuire, Gilles Meloche, Rick Paterson (Assistant Coaches), Steve Latin (Equipment Manager), Skip Thayer (Trainer), John Welday (Strength and Conditioning Coach), Greg Malone, Les Binkley, Charlie Hodge, John Gill, Ralph Cox (Scouts).

LEADING PLAYOFF SCORERS

Player	Club	GP	G	A	PTS	PIM
Mario Lemieux	Pittsburgh	15	16	18	34	2
Kevin Stevens	Pittsburgh	21	13	15	28	28
Ron Francis	Pittsburgh	21	8	19	27	6
Jaromir Jagr	Pittsburgh	21	11	13	24	6
Joe Murphy	Edmonton	16	8	16	24	12
Jeremy Roenick	Chicago	18	12	10	22	12
Chris Chelios	Chicago	18	6	15	21	37
Bernie Nicholls	Edmonton	16	8	11	19	25
Rick Tocchet	Pittsburgh	14	6	13	19	24
Adam Oates	Boston	15	5	14	19	4

LEADING PLAYOFF GOALTENDERS

Goaltender	Club	GPI	Mins	GA	SO	Avg.
Ed Belfour	Chicago	18	949	39	1	2.47
Tim Cheveldae	Detroit	11	597	25	2	2.51
Kirk McLean	Vancouver	13	785	33	2	2.52
Patrick Roy	Montreal	11	686	30	1	2.62
Tom Draper	Buffalo	7	433	19	1	2.63

PLAYOFF GOALS

Name, Team	G
Mario Lemieux, Pit.	16
Kevin Stevens, Pit.	13
Jeremy Roenick, Chi.	12
Jaromir Jagr, Pit.	11
Pat LaFontaine, Buf.	8
Mike Gartner, NYR	8
Cliff Ronning, Van.	8
Joe Murphy, Edm.	8
Bernie Nicholls, Edm.	8
Steve Larmer, Chi.	8
Ron Francis, Pit.	8

PLAYOFF ASSISTS

Name, Team	A
Ron Francis, Pit.	19
Mario Lemieux, Pit.	18
Joe Murphy, Edm.	16
Chris Chelios, Chi.	15
Kevin Stevens, Pit.	15
Adam Oates, Bos.	14
Rick Tocchet, Pit.	13
Jaromir Jagr, Pit.	13
Four tied with	11

PLAYOFF POWERPLAY GOALS

Name, Team	PPG
Mario Lemieux, Pit.	8
Pat LaFontaine, Buf.	5
Joe Murphy, Edm.	4
Bernie Nicholls, Edm.	4
Jeremy Roenick, Chi.	4
Kevin Stevens, Pit.	4

PLAYOFF SHORTHAND GOALS

Name, Team	SHG
Mark Messier, NYR	2
Sergei Fedorov, Det.	2
Mario Lemieux, Pit.	2
17 tied with	1

PLAYOFF GAME-WINNING GOALS

Name, Team	GWG
Mario Lemieux, Pit.	5
Jaromir Jagr, Pit.	4
Kris King, NYR	3
Jeremy Roenick, Chi.	3
Kevin Stevens, Pit.	3

PLAYOFF GOALIE WINS

Name, Team	W
Tom Barrasso, Pit.	16
Ed Belfour, Chi.	12
Andy Moog, Bos.	8
Bill Ranford, Edm.	8
Kirk McLean, Van.	6

PLAYOFF SHUTOUTS

Name, Team	SO
Tim Cheveldae, Det.	2
Kirk McLean, Van.	2
Bill Ranford, Edm.	2
Six tied with	1

PLAYOFF SAVE PERCENTAGE

Name, Team	SV%
Tim Cheveldae, Det.	.910
Kirk McLean, Van.	.909
Tom Barrasso, Pit.	.907
Patrick Roy, Mtl.	.904
Ed Belfour, Chi.	.902

1992-93

Stanley Cup • Montreal Canadiens

FINAL STANDINGS

CLARENCE CAMPBELL CONFERENCE

Team	GP	W	L	T	GF	GA	PTS
Norris Division							
Chicago	84	47	25	12	279	230	106
Detroit	84	47	28	9	369	280	103
Toronto	84	44	29	11	288	241	99
St. Louis	84	37	36	11	282	278	85
Minnesota	84	36	38	10	272	293	82
Tampa Bay	84	23	54	7	245	332	53
Smythe Division							
Vancouver	84	46	29	9	346	278	101
Calgary	84	43	30	11	322	282	97
Los Angeles	84	39	35	10	338	340	88
Winnipeg	84	40	37	7	322	320	87
Edmonton	84	26	50	8	242	337	60
San Jose	84	11	71	2	218	414	24

PRINCE OF WALES CONFERENCE

Team	GP	W	L	T	GF	GA	PTS
Adams Division							
Boston	84	51	26	7	332	268	109
Quebec	84	47	27	10	351	300	104
Montreal	84	48	30	6	326	280	102
Buffalo	84	38	36	10	335	297	86
Hartford	84	26	52	6	284	369	58
Ottawa	84	10	70	4	202	395	24
Patrick Division							
Pittsburgh	84	56	21	7	367	268	119
Washington	84	43	34	7	325	286	93
NY Islanders	84	40	37	7	335	297	87
New Jersey	84	40	37	7	308	299	87
Philadelphia	84	36	37	11	319	319	83
NY Rangers	84	34	39	11	304	308	79

LEADING SCORERS

Player	Club	GP	G	A	PTS	PIM
Mario Lemieux	Pittsburgh	60	69	91	160	38
Pat LaFontaine	Buffalo	84	53	95	148	63
Adam Oates	Boston	84	45	97	142	32
Steve Yzerman	Detroit	84	58	79	137	44
Teemu Selanne	Winnipeg	84	76	56	132	45
Pierre Turgeon	NY Islanders	83	58	74	132	26
Alexander Mogilny	Buffalo	77	76	51	127	40
Doug Gilmour	Toronto	83	32	95	127	100
Luc Robitaille	Los Angeles	84	63	62	125	100
Mark Recchi	Philadelphia	84	53	70	123	95
Mats Sundin	Quebec	80	47	67	114	96
Kevin Stevens	Pittsburgh	72	55	56	111	177
Pavel Bure	Vancouver	83	60	50	110	69
Rick Tocchet	Pittsburgh	80	48	61	109	252
Jeremy Roenick	Chicago	84	50	57	107	86
Craig Janney	St. Louis	84	24	82	106	12
Joe Sakic	Quebec	78	48	57	105	40
Joe Juneau	Boston	84	32	70	102	33
Brett Hull	St. Louis	80	54	47	101	41
Theoren Fleury	Calgary	83	34	66	100	88
Ron Francis	Pittsburgh	84	24	76	100	68

LEADING GOALTENDERS

Goaltender	Club	GPI	MINS	GA	SO	AVG
Felix Potvin	Toronto	48	2781	116	2	2.50
Ed Belfour	Chicago	71	4106	177	7	2.59
Tom Barrasso	Pittsburgh	63	3702	186	4	3.01
Curtis Joseph	St. Louis	68	3890	196	1	3.02
Kay Whitmore	Vancouver	31	1817	94	1	3.10
Dominik Hasek	Buffalo	28	1429	75	0	3.15
Andy Moog	Boston	55	3194	168	3	3.16
Jeff Reese	Calgary	26	1311	70	1	3.20
Patrick Roy	Montreal	62	3595	192	2	3.20
Daren Puppa	Buf./Tor.	32	1785	96	2	3.23

Both Teemu Selanne (left) and Alexander Mogilny scored 76 goals in 1992–93. Selanne's 76 obliterated Mike Bossy's rookie record of 53 goals.

MAJOR CHANGES TOOK PLACE during the summer of 1992. League president John Ziegler resigned and was replaced for a short time by Gil Stein. A new position of commissioner was created in December 1992 with the election of Gary Bettman. Meanwhile, NHL membership reached 24 teams with the addition of the Tampa Bay Lightning and Ottawa Senators. The Senators' home opener marked the first NHL game played in the Canadian capital since 1934, but there were even more amazing resurrections during the Stanley Cup's 100th-anniversary season.

The Toronto Maple Leafs repaid their long-suffering fans with a return to the upper echelon under former Montreal Canadiens coach Pat Burns. Longtime Atlanta/Calgary Flames executive Cliff Fletcher had taken over as president and general manager the year before and acquired Doug Gilmour and Grant Fuhr in a pair of blockbuster trades. With Felix Potvin now ready to emerge as the number-one goalie, Fletcher traded Fuhr to the Buffalo Sabres during the 1992–93 season for sniper Dave Andreychuk. With Andreychuk converting his passes, Gilmour enjoyed career highs with 95 assists and 127 points, and with the Leafs adhering to Burns's defensive philosophy, Toronto set club records with 44 wins and 99 points during the expanded 84-game season.

In Awe of Roy – Toronto toasted Gilmour, Gretzky teased Tinsletown but the hockey heavens belonged to St. Patrick of Roy, who won 10 straight overtime games in leading Montreal to the Stanley Cup.

In the playoffs, the Leafs knocked off the Detroit Red Wings in a thrilling seven-game Norris Division semi-final, then beat the St. Louis Blues to win the division final.

Wayne Gretzky also enjoyed a brilliant comeback. He was forced to miss the first 39 games of the season due to a career-threatening back injury, but returned to action on January 6, 1993, and collected 65 points in 45 games. Gretzky was in top form by the playoffs, leading the Los Angeles Kings to victories over the Calgary Flames and Vancouver Canucks before eliminating the Leafs in seven games to reach the Stanley Cup finals for the first time in franchise history.

One day before Gretzky's return to the Kings, the Pittsburgh Penguins announced that Mario Lemieux had Hodgkin's disease, a form of cancer. Lemieux missed 24 games while receiving treatment, then returned to claim the NHL scoring title and spark Pittsburgh to a record 17-game winning streak that led the Penguins to first place overall. Lemieux was bothered by back spasms in the playoffs and the New York Islanders stunned the Penguins in the Patrick Division final before falling to the Montreal Canadiens in the Wales Conference championship.

The 100th anniversary of the Stanley Cup matched the game's greatest franchise against arguably its greatest player and it was the Montreal Canadiens who came out ahead of Wayne Gretzky and the Los Angeles Kings in five games. Montreal won its 24th Stanley Cup title on Patrick Roy's brilliant playoff goaltending and an amazing streak of victories in 10 consecutive overtime games, including three against Los Angeles.

Adam Oates set career highs with 45 goals and a league-leading 97 assists with Boston in 1992–93. He helped Cam Neely score 50 goals in just 44 games the following season.

Leaders, 1992-93

GOALS

Name, Team	G
Alexander Mogilny, Buf.	76
Teemu Selanne, Wpg.	76
Mario Lemieux, Pit.	69
Luc Robitaille, L.A.	63
Pavel Bure, Van.	60
Pierre Turgeon, NYI	58
Steve Yzerman, Det.	58
Kevin Stevens, Pit.	55
Brett Hull, St.L.	54
Dave Andreychuk, Buf./Tor.	54

ASSISTS

Name, Team	A
Adam Oates, Bos.	97
Doug Gilmour, Tor.	95
Pat LaFontaine, Buf.	95
Mario Lemieux, Pit.	91
Craig Janney, St.L.	82
Dale Hawerchuk, Buf.	80
Phil Housley, Wpg.	79
Steve Yzerman, Det.	79
Ron Francis, Pit.	76
Paul Coffey, L.A./Det.	75

POWERPLAY GOALS

Name, Team	PPG
Dave Andreychuk, Buf./Tor.	32
Brett Hull, St.L.	29
Alexander Mogilny, Buf.	27
Kevin Stevens, Pit.	26
Pierre Turgeon, NYI	24
Adam Oates, Bos.	24
Luc Robitaille, L.A.	24
Teemu Selanne, Wpg.	24
Jeremy Roenick, Chi.	22
Derek King, NYI	21
Dino Ciccarelli, Det.	21
Geoff Sanderson, Hfd.	21

SHORTHAND GOALS

Name, Team	SHG
Pavel Bure, Van.	7
Steve Yzerman, Det.	7
Mario Lemieux, Pit.	6
Scott Young, Que.	6
Dave Reid, Bos.	5
Dave Poulin, Bos.	5
Eight tied with	4

GAME-WINNING GOALS

Name, Team	GWG
Alexander Mogilny, Buf.	11
Geoff Courtnall, Van.	11
Adam Oates, Bos.	11
Mario Lemieux, Pit.	10
Mike Ricci, Que.	10
Pierre Turgeon, NYI	10
Mats Sundin, Que.	9
Jaromir Jagr, Pit.	9
Pavel Bure, Van.	9
Five tied with	8

GOALIE WINS

Name, Team	W
Tom Barrasso, Pit.	43
Ed Belfour, Chi.	41
Andy Moog, Bos.	37
Tim Cheveldae, Det.	34
Bob Essensa, Wpg.	33
Patrick Roy, Mtl.	31
Ron Hextall, Que.	29
Mike Vernon, Cgy.	29
Curtis Joseph, St.L.	29
Kirk McLean, Van.	28

SHUTOUTS

Name, Team	SO
Ed Belfour, Chi.	7
Tommy Soderstrom, Phi.	5
John Vanbiesbrouck, NYR	4
Tom Barrasso, Pit.	4
Tim Cheveldae, Det.	4
Three tied with	3

SAVE PERCENTAGE

Name, Team	SV%
Curtis Joseph, St.L.	.911
Felix Potvin, Tor.	.910
Ed Belfour, Chi.	.906
Tom Barrasso, Pit.	.901
John Vanbiesbrouck, NYR	.900

FIRST TEAM ALL-STARS

Name, Team	Position
Mario Lemieux, Pit.	C
Teemu Selanne, Wpg.	RW
Luc Robitaille, L.A.	LW
Chris Chelios, Chi.	D
Raymond Bourque, Bos.	D
Ed Belfour, Chi.	G

SECOND TEAM ALL-STARS

Name, Team	Position
Pat LaFontaine, Buf.	C
Alexander Mogilny, Buf.	RW
Kevin Stevens, Pit.	LW
Larry Murphy, Pit.	D
Al Iafrate, Wsh.	D
Tom Barrasso, Pit.	G

ALL-ROOKIE TEAM

Name, Team	Position
Eric Lindros, Phi.	C
Teemu Selanne, Wpg.	W
Joe Juneau, Bos.	W
Vladimir Malakhov, NYI	D
Scott Niedermayer, N.J.	D
Felix Potvin, Tor.	G

TROPHY WINNERS

Trophy	Awarded For	Winner	Team
Hart	MVP	Mario Lemieux	Pit.
Art Ross	Top Scorer	Mario Lemieux	Pit.
Norris	Top Defenseman	Chris Chelios	Chi
Calder	Top Rookie	Teemu Selanne	Wpg.
Selke	Top Defensive Forward	Doug Gilmour	Tor.
Vezina	Top Goaltender	Ed Belfour	Chi
Jennings	Fewest Goals Against	Ed Belfour	Chi
Adams	Top Coach	Pat Burns	Tor.
Byng	Gentlemanly Conduct	Pierre Turgeon	NYI
Masterton	Perseverance, Sportmanship	Mario Lemieux	Pit.
Pearson	NHLPA MVP	Mario Lemieux	Pit.
Conn Smythe	Playoff MVP	Patrick Roy	Mtl.
Patrick	Service to Hockey in U.S.	Frank Boucher	
		Mervyn Red Dutton	
		Bruce McNall	
		Gil Stein	
Clancy	Leadership On and Off Ice	Dave Poulin	Bos.
Entry Draft	First Overall Selection	Alexandre Daigle	Ott.

NHL NOTEBOOK

TRANSACTIONS

- June 30, 1992 – After an arbritation victory Philadelphia officially acquired Eric Lindros from the Quebec Nordiques for Peter Forsberg, Ron Hextall, Mike Ricci, Steve Duchesne, Kerry Huffman, a 1993 first-round pick and cash.
- Aug. 7, 1992 – Chicago Blackhawks traded goalie Dominik Hasek to Buffalo for goalie Stephane Beauregard and a fourth-round draft choice in 1993.
- Aug. 27, 1992 – Montreal obtained Vince Damphousse from the Edmonton Oilers for Shayne Corson and Brent Gilchrist.
- Aug. 28, 1992 – Hartford Whalers traded Bobby Holik and a future draft pick to New Jersey in exchange for goalie Sean Burke and defenseman Eric Weinrich.

RECORDS

- Winnipeg Jets' Teemu Selanne set NHL rookie records with 76 goals and 132 points.
- Pittsburgh Penguins set an NHL playoff record with 14 straight wins in the postseason over two years.
- Montreal Canadiens set a Stanley Cup record with 10 overtime victories (in 20 games) during the playoffs.
- Wayne Gretzky set a record with his 19th career playoff game-winning-goal during the Smythe Division finals.

MILESTONES

- Oct. 17, 1992 – Jari Kurri became the the first European-trained player to score 500 goals when he picked up an empty netter to clinch an 8-6 home win for the Kings over Boston.
- Dec. 9, 1992 – Boston's Gordie Roberts became the first U.S. born player to play in 1,000 NHL games. The milestone came in a 5-2 Bruins loss at Buffalo.
- Apr. 8, 1993 – Washington Capitals became the first team in NHL history to have three defensemen score 20 goals in one season when Sylvain Cote scored his 20th of the year (joining Kevin Hatcher and Al Iafrate). #20 for Cote came in a 4-3 loss at Philadelphia.
- May 7, 1993 – Wayne Gretzky scored twice to become the first player in NHL history to score 100 playoff goals. Gretzky also added an assist to lead the Kings to a 7-4 win over the Canucks in game three of the Smythe Division finals at the Forum.

1993 Playoffs

DIVISION SEMI-FINALS

Apr.	18	Buffalo	5	at	Boston	4 OT
Apr.	20	Buffalo	4	at	Boston	0
Apr.	22	Boston	3	at	Buffalo	4 OT
Apr.	24	Boston	5	at	Buffalo	6 OT

Buffalo won best-of-seven series 4–0

Apr.	18	Montreal	2	at	Quebec	3 OT
Apr.	20	Montreal	1	at	Quebec	4
Apr.	22	Quebec	1	at	Montreal	2 OT
Apr.	24	Quebec	2	at	Montreal	3
Apr.	26	Montreal	5	at	Quebec	4 OT
Apr.	28	Quebec	2	at	Montreal	6

Montreal won best-of-seven series 4–2

Apr.	18	New Jersey	3	at	Pittsburgh	6
Apr.	20	New Jersey	0	at	Pittsburgh	7
Apr.	22	Pittsburgh	4	at	New Jersey	3
Apr.	25	Pittsburgh	1	at	New Jersey	4
Apr.	26	New Jersey	3	at	Pittsburgh	5

Pittsburgh won best-of-seven series 4–1

Apr.	18	NY Islanders	1	at	Washington	3
Apr.	20	NY Islanders	5	at	Washington	4 2OT
Apr.	22	Washington	3	at	NY Islanders	4 OT
Apr.	24	Washington	3	at	NY Islanders	4 2OT
Apr.	26	NY Islanders	4	at	Washington	6
Apr.	28	Washington	3	at	NY Islanders	5

NY Islanders won best-of-seven series 4–2

Apr.	18	St. Louis	4	at	Chicago	3
Apr.	21	St. Louis	2	at	Chicago	0
Apr.	23	Chicago	0	at	St. Louis	3
Apr.	25	Chicago	3	at	St. Louis	4 OT

St. Louis won best-of-seven series 4–0

Apr.	19	Toronto	3	at	Detroit	6
Apr.	21	Toronto	2	at	Detroit	6
Apr.	23	Detroit	2	at	Toronto	4
Apr.	25	Detroit	2	at	Toronto	3
Apr.	27	Toronto	5	at	Detroit	4 OT
Apr.	29	Detroit	7	at	Toronto	3
May	1	Toronto	4	at	Detroit	3 OT

Toronto won best-of-seven series 4–3

Apr.	19	Winnipeg	2	at	Vancouver	4
Apr.	21	Winnipeg	2	at	Vancouver	3
Apr.	23	Vancouver	4	at	Winnipeg	5
Apr.	25	Vancouver	3	at	Winnipeg	1
Apr.	27	Winnipeg	4	at	Vancouver	3 OT
Apr.	29	Vancouver	4	at	Winnipeg	3 OT

Vancouver won best-of-seven series 4–2

Apr.	18	Los Angeles	6	at	Calgary	3
Apr.	21	Los Angeles	4	at	Calgary	9
Apr.	23	Calgary	5	at	Los Angeles	2
Apr.	25	Calgary	1	at	Los Angeles	3
Apr.	27	Los Angeles	9	at	Calgary	4
Apr.	29	Calgary	6	at	Los Angeles	9

Los Angeles won best-of-seven series 4–2

DIVISION FINALS

May	2	Buffalo	3	at	Montreal	4
May	4	Buffalo	3	at	Montreal	4 OT
May	6	Montreal	4	at	Buffalo	3 OT
May	8	Montreal	4	at	Buffalo	3 OT

Montreal won best-of-seven series 4–0

May	2	NY Islanders	3	at	Pittsburgh	2
May	4	NY Islanders	0	at	Pittsburgh	3
May	6	Pittsburgh	3	at	NY Islanders	1
May	8	Pittsburgh	5	at	NY Islanders	6
May	10	NY Islanders	3	at	Pittsburgh	6
May	12	Pittsburgh	5	at	NY Islanders	7
May	14	NY Islanders	4	at	Pittsburgh	3 OT

NY Islanders won best-of-seven series 4–3

May	3	St. Louis	1	at	Toronto	2 2OT
May	5	St. Louis	2	at	Toronto	1 2OT
May	7	Toronto	3	at	St. Louis	4
May	9	Toronto	4	at	St. Louis	1
May	11	St. Louis	1	at	Toronto	5
May	13	Toronto	1	at	St. Louis	2
May	15	St. Louis	0	at	Toronto	6

Toronto won best-of-seven series 4–3

May	2	Los Angeles	2	at	Vancouver	5
May	5	Los Angeles	6	at	Vancouver	3
May	7	Vancouver	4	at	Los Angeles	7
May	9	Vancouver	7	at	Los Angeles	2
May	11	Los Angeles	4	at	Vancouver	3 2OT
May	13	Vancouver	3	at	Los Angeles	5

Los Angeles won best-of-seven series 4–2

CONFERENCE FINALS

May	16	NY Islanders	1	at	Montreal	4
May	18	NY Islanders	3	at	Montreal	4 2OT
May	20	Montreal	2	at	NY Islanders	1 OT
May	22	Montreal	1	at	NY Islanders	4
May	24	NY Islanders	2	at	Montreal	5

Montreal won best-of-seven series 4–1

May	17	Los Angeles	1	at	Toronto	4
May	19	Los Angeles	3	at	Toronto	2
May	21	Toronto	2	at	Los Angeles	4
May	23	Toronto	4	at	Los Angeles	2
May	25	Los Angeles	2	at	Toronto	3 OT
May	27	Toronto	4	at	Los Angeles	5 OT
May	29	Los Angeles	5	at	Toronto	4

Los Angeles won best-of-seven series 4–3

FINALS

June	1	Los Angeles	4	at	Montreal	1
June	3	Los Angeles	2	at	Montreal	3 OT
June	5	Montreal	4	at	Los Angeles	3 OT
June	7	Montreal	3	at	Los Angeles	2 OT
June	9	Los Angeles	1	at	Montreal	4

Montreal won best-of-seven series 4–1

1992-93 – Montreal Canadiens – Guy Carbonneau (Captain), Patrick Roy, Mike Keane, Eric Desjardins, Stephan Lebeau, Mathieu Schneider, J.J. Daigneault, Denis Savard, Lyle Odelein, Todd Ewen, Kirk Muller, John LeClair, Gilbert Dionne, Benoit Brunet, Patrice Brisebois, Paul Di Pietro, Andre Racicot, Donald Dufresne, Mario Roberge, Sean Hill, Ed Ronan, Kevin Haller, Vincent Damphousse, Brian Bellows, Gary Leeman, Rob Ramage, Ronald Corey (President), Serge Savard (Managing Director/Vice President, Hockey), Jacques Demers (Head Coach), Jacques Laperriere, Charles Thiffault (Assistant Coaches), Francois Allaire (Goaltending Instructor), Jean Béliveau (Senior Vice President, Corporate Affairs), Fred Steer (Vice President, Finance & Adminstration), Aldo Giampaolo (Vice President, Operations), Bernard Brisset (Vice President, Marketing & Communications), André Boudrias (Assistant to the Managing Director/Director of Scouting), Jacques Lemaire (Assistant to the Managing Director), Gaeten Lefebvre (Athletic Trainer), John Shipman (Assistant to the Athletic Trainer), Eddy Palchak (Equipment Manager), Pierre Gervais, Robert Boulanger, Pierre Ouellete (Assistants to the Equipment Manager).

LEADING PLAYOFF SCORERS

Player	Club	GP	G	A	PTS	PIM
Wayne Gretzky	Los Angeles	24	15	25	40	4
Doug Gilmour	Toronto	21	10	25	35	30
Tomas Sandstrom	Los Angeles	24	8	17	25	12
Vincent Damphousse	Montreal	20	11	12	23	16
Luc Robitaille	Los Angeles	24	9	13	22	28
Ray Ferraro	NY Islanders	18	13	7	20	18
Wendel Clark	Toronto	21	10	10	20	51
Dave Andreychuk	Toronto	21	12	7	19	35
Mario Lemieux	Pittsburgh	11	8	10	18	10
Glenn Anderson	Toronto	21	7	11	18	31

LEADING PLAYOFF GOALTENDERS

Goaltender	Club	GPI	Mins	GA	SO	Avg.
Patrick Roy	Montreal	20	1293	46	0	2.13
Curtis Joseph	St. Louis	11	715	27	2	2.27
Felix Potvin	Toronto	21	1308	62	1	2.84
Tom Barrasso	Pittsburgh	12	722	35	2	2.91
Glenn Healy	NY Islanders	18	1109	59	0	3.19

PLAYOFF GOALS

Name, Team	G
Wayne Gretzky, L.A.	15
Ray Ferraro, NYI	13
Dave Andreychuk, Tor.	12
Vincent Damphousse, Mtl.	11
Kirk Muller, Mtl.	10
Doug Gilmour, Tor.	10
Wendel Clark, Tor.	10
Steve Thomas, NYI	9
Luc Robitaille, L.A.	9
Jari Kurri, L.A.	9

PLAYOFF ASSISTS

Name, Team	A
Doug Gilmour, Tor.	25
Wayne Gretzky, L.A.	25
Tomas Sandstrom, L.A.	17
Mike Keane, Mtl.	13
Luc Robitaille, L.A.	13
Vincent Damphousse, Mtl.	12
Six tied with.	11

PLAYOFF POWERPLAY GOALS

Name, Team	PPG
Brett Hull, St.L.	5
Greg Adams, Van.	5
Vincent Damphousse, Mtl.	5
Dale Hunter, Wsh.	4
Kevin Stevens, Pit.	4
Doug Gilmour, Tor.	4
Dave Andreychuk, Tor.	4
Luc Robitaille, L.A.	4

PLAYOFF SHORTHAND GOALS

Name, Team	SHG
Dave Taylor, L.A.	2
Jari Kurri, L.A.	2
18 tied with	1

PLAYOFF GAME-WINNING GOALS

Name, Team	GWG
Vincent Damphousse, Mtl.	3
Kirk Muller, Mtl.	3
John LeClair, Mtl.	3
Dave Andreychuk, Tor.	3
Wayne Gretzky, L.A.	3

PLAYOFF GOALIE WINS

Name, Team	W
Patrick Roy, Mtl.	16
Felix Potvin, Tor.	11
Kelly Hrudey, L.A.	10
Glenn Healy, NYI	9
Curtis Joseph, St.L.	7
Tom Barrasso, Pit.	7

PLAYOFF SHUTOUTS

Name, Team	SO
Curtis Joseph, St.L.	2
Tom Barrasso, Pit.	2
Grant Fuhr, Buf.	1
Felix Potvin, Tor.	1

PLAYOFF SAVE PERCENTAGE

Name, Team	SV%
Curtis Joseph, St.L.	.938
Patrick Roy, Mtl.	.929
Tom Barrasso, Pit.	.905
Felix Potvin, Tor.	.903
Glenn Healy, NYI	.887

1993-94

Pavel Bure became the first Vancouver player to top 50 goals and 100 points in a season when he scored 60 times and added 50 assists in 1992–93. He led the league when he scored 60 goals again in 1993–94.

Stanley Cup • New York Rangers

FINAL STANDINGS

Team	GP	W	L	T	GF	GA	PTS
EASTERN CONFERENCE							
Northeast Division							
Pittsburgh	84	44	27	13	299	285	101
Boston	84	42	29	13	289	252	97
Montreal	84	41	29	14	283	248	96
Buffalo	84	43	32	9	282	218	95
Quebec	84	34	42	8	277	292	76
Hartford	84	27	48	9	227	288	63
Ottawa	84	14	61	9	201	397	37
Atlantic Division							
NY Rangers	84	52	24	8	299	231	112
New Jersey	84	47	25	12	306	220	106
Washington	84	39	35	10	277	263	88
NY Islanders	84	36	36	12	282	264	84
Florida	84	33	34	17	233	233	83
Philadelphia	84	35	39	10	294	314	80
Tampa Bay	84	30	43	11	224	251	71
WESTERN CONFERENCE							
Central Division							
Detroit	84	46	30	8	356	275	100
Toronto	84	43	29	12	280	243	98
Dallas	84	42	29	13	286	265	97
St. Louis	84	40	33	11	270	283	91
Chicago	84	39	36	9	254	240	87
Winnipeg	84	24	51	9	245	344	57
Pacific Division							
Calgary	84	42	29	13	302	256	97
Vancouver	84	41	40	3	279	276	85
San Jose	84	33	35	16	252	265	82
Anaheim	84	33	46	5	229	251	71
Los Angeles	84	27	45	12	294	322	66
Edmonton	84	25	45	14	261	305	64

LEADING SCORERS

Player	Club	GP	G	A	PTS	PIM
Wayne Gretzky	Los Angeles	81	38	92	130	20
Sergei Fedorov	Detroit	82	56	64	120	34
Adam Oates	Boston	77	32	80	112	45
Doug Gilmour	Toronto	83	27	84	111	105
Pavel Bure	Vancouver	76	60	47	107	86
Jeremy Roenick	Chicago	84	46	61	107	125
Mark Recchi	Philadelphia	84	40	67	107	46
Brendan Shanahan	St. Louis	81	52	50	102	211
Dave Andreychuk	Toronto	83	53	46	99	98
Jaromir Jagr	Pittsburgh	80	32	67	99	61
Brett Hull	St. Louis	81	57	40	97	38
Eric Lindros	Philadelphia	65	44	53	97	103
Rod Brind'Amour	Philadelphia	84	35	62	97	85
Pierre Turgeon	NY Islanders	69	38	56	94	18
Ray Sheppard	Detroit	82	52	41	93	26
Mike Modano	Dallas	76	50	43	93	54
Robert Reichel	Calgary	84	40	53	93	58
Ron Francis	Pittsburgh	82	27	66	93	62
Joe Sakic	Quebec	84	28	64	92	18
Vincent Damphousse	Montreal	84	40	51	91	75
Raymond Bourque	Boston	72	20	71	91	58

LEADING GOALTENDERS

Goaltender	Club	GPI	MINS	GA	SO	AVG
Dominik Hasek	Buffalo	58	3358	109	7	1.95
Martin Brodeur	New Jersey	47	2625	105	3	2.40
Patrick Roy	Montreal	68	3867	161	7	2.50
John Vanbiesbrouck	Florida	57	3440	145	1	2.53
Mike Richter	NY Rangers	68	3710	159	5	2.57
Darcy Wakaluk	Dallas	36	2000	88	3	2.64
Ed Belfour	Chicago	70	3998	178	7	2.67
Daren Puppa	Tampa Bay	63	3653	165	4	2.71

THE 1993–94 SEASON was the NHL's third consecutive expansion year as the Miami-based Florida Panthers and the Mighty Ducks of Anaheim joined the fold. The league moved into another southern city as the Minnesota North Stars relocated to Texas, becoming the Dallas Stars. The division and conference names were also changed to geographic designations: the Adams, Patrick, Norris and Smythe divisions became the Northeast, Atlantic, Central and Pacific. The Prince of Wales and Clarence Campbell conferences were now known respectively as the Eastern and Western.

Previous expansions had all produced an explosion of offense, but defense came to the forefront in the new 26-team NHL. In 1992–93 only two goaltenders had posted goals-against averages below 3.00; in 1993–94, 19 goalies broke that barrier, led by Vezina Trophy winner Dominik Hasek of the Buffalo Sabres, whose 1.95 average made him the first netminder below 2.00 since Bernie Parent of the Philadelphia Flyers in 1973–74.

Broadway Revival – The Russian Rocket roared, Brett Hull scored, Eric Lindros became the Next One but Mark Messier's actions spoke louder than his words as the Rangers erased their 54-year curse.

Pittsburgh Penguins superstar Mario Lemieux did not figure in the scoring race this season, as injuries and illness limited him to just 22 games. Pat LaFontaine of the Buffalo Sabres, runner-up to Lemieux in 1992–93, missed 68 games with a knee injury. Teemu Selanne of the Winnipeg Jets, who scored 76 goals as a rookie the year before, played just 51 games, while budding superstar Eric Lindros of the Philadelphia Flyers missed 19 games with injuries.

Despite the drop in offense, Wayne Gretzky still managed to become the greatest goal scorer in NHL history. On March 23, 1994, the Los Angeles Kings superstar was set up by teammates Marty McSorley and Luc Robitaille and beat Kirk McLean of the Vancouver Canucks for his 802nd career goal, breaking Gordie Howe's record of 801. Gretzky finished the year with 38 goals and 92 assists, earning his 10th scoring title. The Hart Trophy went to Sergei Fedorov of the Detroit Red Wings, who was runner-up to Gretzky for the Art Ross and also earned the Selke Trophy as the NHL's best defensive forward.

The New York Rangers proved to be the best in the NHL this year, setting franchise records with 52 wins and 112 points under coach Mike Keenan. They beat the New York Islanders and Washington Capitals before defeating the New Jersey Devils in a thrilling seven-game Eastern Conference final. The Vancouver Canucks provided the opposition for the Stanley Cup. Vancouver won game one, but the Rangers took the next three in a row. The Canucks rallied for two wins to force a seventh game, but the Rangers finally snapped their 54-year Stanley Cup jinx with a 3–2 victory.

Alexei Yashin was a virtual unknown when Ottawa chose him second overall behind Roman Hamrlik in the 1992 Entry Draft. He had 30 goals and 49 assists as a rookie in 1993–94.

Leaders, 1993-94

GOALS

Name, Team	G
Pavel Bure, Van.	60
Brett Hull, St.L.	57
Sergei Fedorov, Det.	56
Dave Andreychuk, Tor.	53
Brendan Shanahan, St.L.	52
Ray Sheppard, Det.	52
Adam Graves, NYR	52
Cam Neely, Bos.	50
Mike Modano, Dal.	50
Wendel Clark, Tor.	46
Jeremy Roenick, Chi.	46

ASSISTS

Name, Team	A
Wayne Gretzky, L.A.	92
Doug Gilmour, Tor.	84
Adam Oates, Bos.	80
Sergei Zubov, NYR	77
Raymond Bourque, Bos.	71
Craig Janney, St.L.	68
Jaromir Jagr, Pit.	67
Mark Recchi, Phi.	67
Joe Juneau, Bos./Wsh.	66
Ron Francis, Pit.	66

POWERPLAY GOALS

Name, Team	PPG
Pavel Bure, Van.	25
Brett Hull, St.L.	25
Luc Robitaille, L.A.	24
Jeremy Roenick, Chi.	24
Keith Tkachuk, Wpg.	22
Wendel Clark, Tor.	21
Kevin Stevens, Pit.	21
Dave Andreychuk, Tor.	21
Cam Neely, Bos.	20
Adam Graves, NYR	20

SHORTHAND GOALS

Name, Team	SHG
Brendan Shanahan, St.L.	7
Wayne Presley, Buf.	5
Shawn McEachern, LA/Pit	5
Mike Gartner, NYR/Tor.	5
Marty McInnis, NYI	5
Dave Andreychuk, Tor.	5
Benoit Hogue, NYI	5
Nelson Emerson, Wpg.	5
Jeremy Roenick, Chi.	5
Nine tied with	4

GAME-WINNING GOALS

Name, Team	GWG
Cam Neely, Bos.	13
Sergei Fedorov, Det.	10
Vincent Damphousse, Mtl.	10
Eric Lindros, Phi.	9
Pavel Bure, Van.	9
Stephane Richer, N.J.	9
Joe Mullen, Pit.	9
Joe Sakic, Que.	9
Wendel Clark, Tor.	8
Brendan Shanahan, St.L.	8
Dave Andreychuk, Tor.	8

GOALIE WINS

Name, Team	W
Mike Richter, NYR	42
Ed Belfour, Chi.	37
Curtis Joseph, St.L.	36
Patrick Roy, Mtl.	35
Felix Potvin, Tor.	34
Jon Casey, Bos.	30
Dominik Hasek, Buf.	30
Arturs Irbe, S.J.	30
Dominic Roussel, Phi.	29
Martin Brodeur, N.J.	27
Ron Hextall, NYI	27

SHUTOUTS

Name, Team	SO
Dominik Hasek, Buf.	7
Patrick Roy, Mtl.	7
Ed Belfour, Chi.	7
Ron Hextall, NYI	5
Mike Richter, NYR	5

SAVE PERCENTAGE

Name, Team	SV%
Dominik Hasek, Buf.	.930
John Vanbiesbrouck, Fla.	.924
Patrick Roy, Mtl.	.918
Martin Brodeur, N.J.	.915
Mark Fitzpatrick, Fla.	.914
Curtis Joseph, St.L.	.911

FIRST TEAM ALL-STARS

Name, Team	Position
Sergei Fedorov, Det.	C
Pavel Bure, Van.	RW
Brendan Shanahan, St.L.	LW
Raymond Bourque, Bos.	D
Scott Stevens, N.J.	D
Dominik Hasek, Buf	G

SECOND TEAM ALL-STARS

Name, Team	Position
Wayne Gretzky, L.A.	C
Cam Neely, Bos.	RW
Adam Graves, NYR	LW
Al MacInnis, Cgy.	D
Brian Leetch, NYR	D
John Vanbiesbrouck, Fla.	G

ALL-ROOKIE TEAM

Name, Team	Position
Jason Arnott, Edm.	C
Mikael Renberg, Phi.	W
Oleg Petrov, Mtl.	W
Chris Pronger, Hfd.	D
Boris Mironov, Wpg./Edm.	D
Martin Brodeur, N.J.	G

TROPHY WINNERS

Trophy	Awarded For	Winner	Team
Hart	MVP	Sergei Fedorov	Det.
Art Ross	Top Scorer	Wayne Gretzky	L.A.
Norris	Top Defenseman	Raymond Bourque	Bos.
Calder	Top Rookie	Martin Brodeur	N.J.
Selke	Top Defensive Forward	Sergei Fedorov	Det.
Vezina	Top Goaltender	Dominik Hasek	Buf
Jennings	Fewest Goals Against	Dominik Hasek	Buf
Jennings	Fewest Goals Against	Grant Fuhr	Buf.
Adams	Top Coach	Jacques Lemaire	N.J.
Byng	Gentlemanly Conduct	Wayne Gretzky	L.A.
Masterton	Perseverance, Sportmanship	Cam Neely	Bos.
Pearson	NHLPA MVP	Sergei Fedorov	Det.
Conn Smythe	Playoff MVP	Brian Leetch	NYR
Patrick	Service to Hockey in U.S.	Wayne Gretzky Robert Ridder	
Clancy	Leadership On and Off Ice	Adam Graves	NYR
Entry Draft	First Overall Selection	Ed Jovanovski	Fla.

NHL NOTEBOOK

TRANSACTIONS

- June 30, 1993 – Detroit Red Wings acquired Kris Draper from the Winnipeg Jets for future considerations.
- Mar. 21, 1994 – New York Rangers traded Tony Amonte and the rights to Matt Oates to the Chicago Blackhawks in exchange for Stephane Matteau and Brian Noonan.
- Mar. 21, 1994 – Edmonton Oilers traded Craig MacTavish to the New York Rangers in exchange for Todd Marchant.
- Jan. 15, 1994 – Vancouver Canucks claimed Martin Gelinas off waivers from the Quebec Nordiques.

RECORDS

- Oct. 28, 1993 – Toronto Maple Leafs extended their NHL record to ten straight wins from the start of the season with a 4-2 win over the Blackhawks at Chicago.
- Feb. 5, 1994 – Peter Bondra scored four goals on four straight shots in a span of 4:12 in the first period to set an NHL record for fastest four goals by one player. Bondra added another goal in the second period as the Capitals won 6-3 over visiting Tampa Bay.
- Mar. 10, 1994 – Doug Gilmour became the first NHL player to get 200 assists with three different teams when he picked up his 71st of the year to give him 200 with Toronto in a 4-2 win at Pittsburgh. He earlier had 200+ assists with St. Louis and Calgary.
- Mar. 23, 1994 – Wayne Gretzky scored career goal #802 to break Gordie Howe's record for all-time NHL goals. The record came in his 15th NHL season as the Kings lost 6-3 to Vancouver at the Forum.

MILESTONES

- Oct. 6, 1993 – Roger Neilson became the first man in history to coach six different NHL teams when he led the Florida Panthers to a 4-4 tie at Chicago in the first game for the new franchise.
- Dec. 8, 1993 – L.A.'s Jari Kurri became the highest-scoring European player in NHL history, when he scored his 1,223rd career point in a 6-5 loss to the Florida Panthers. Kurri replaced Peter Stastny, who had retired with 1,222 points.
- Mar. 26, 1994 – Toronto's Mike Gartner scored twice to become the first player in NHL history to get 30 or more goals in 15 straight seasons. They came in the 6-3 win over the visiting Quebec Nordiques.
- June 16, 1994 – Boston's Raymond Bourque set an NHL record for defensemen when he was named to the First All-Star team for the 11th time in his career.

1994 Playoffs

CONFERENCE QUARTER-FINALS

Apr.	17	NY Islanders	0	at	NY Rangers	6	
Apr.	18	NY Islanders	0	at	NY Rangers	6	
Apr.	21	NY Rangers	5	at	NY Islanders	1	
Apr.	24	NY Rangers	5	at	NY Islanders	2	

NY Rangers won best-of-seven series 4-0

Apr.	17	Washington	5	at	Pittsburgh	3	
Apr.	19	Washington	1	at	Pittsburgh	2	
Apr.	21	Pittsburgh	0	at	Washington	2	
Apr.	23	Pittsburgh	1	at	Washington	4	
Apr.	25	Washington	2	at	Pittsburgh	3	
Apr.	27	Pittsburgh	3	at	Washington	6	

Washington won best-of-seven series 4-2

Apr.	17	Buffalo	2	at	New Jersey	0	
Apr.	19	Buffalo	1	at	New Jersey	2	
Apr.	21	New Jersey	2	at	Buffalo	1	
Apr.	23	New Jersey	3	at	Buffalo	5	
Apr.	25	Buffalo	3	at	New Jersey	5	
Apr.	27	New Jersey	0	at	Buffalo	1	4OT
Apr.	29	Buffalo	1	at	New Jersey	2	

New Jersey won best-of-seven series 4-3

Apr.	16	Montreal	2	at	Boston	3	
Apr.	18	Montreal	3	at	Boston	2	
Apr.	21	Boston	6	at	Montreal	3	
Apr.	23	Boston	2	at	Montreal	5	
Apr.	25	Montreal	2	at	Boston	1	OT
Apr.	27	Boston	3	at	Montreal	2	
Apr.	29	Montreal	3	at	Boston	5	

Boston won best-of-seven series 4-3

Apr.	18	San Jose	5	at	Detroit	4	
Apr.	20	San Jose	0	at	Detroit	4	
Apr.	22	Detroit	3	at	San Jose	2	
Apr.	23	Detroit	3	at	San Jose	4	
Apr.	26	Detroit	4	at	San Jose	6	
Apr.	28	San Jose	1	at	Detroit	7	
Apr.	30	San Jose	3	at	Detroit	2	

San Jose won best-of-seven series 4-3

Apr.	18	Vancouver	5	at	Calgary	0	
Apr.	20	Vancouver	5	at	Calgary	7	
Apr.	22	Calgary	4	at	Vancouver	2	
Apr.	24	Calgary	3	at	Vancouver	2	
Apr.	26	Vancouver	2	at	Calgary	1	OT
Apr.	28	Calgary	2	at	Vancouver	3	OT
Apr.	30	Vancouver	4	at	Calgary	3	2OT

Vancouver won best-of-seven series 4-3

Apr.	18	Chicago	1	at	Toronto	5	
Apr.	20	Chicago	0	at	Toronto	1	OT
Apr.	23	Toronto	4	at	Chicago	5	
Apr.	24	Toronto	3	at	Chicago	4	OT
Apr.	26	Chicago	0	at	Toronto	1	
Apr.	28	Toronto	1	at	Chicago	0	

Toronto won best-of-seven series 4-2

Apr.	17	St. Louis	3	at	Dallas	5	
Apr.	20	St. Louis	2	at	Dallas	4	
Apr.	22	Dallas	5	at	St. Louis	4	OT
Apr.	24	Dallas	2	at	St. Louis	1	

Dallas won best-of-seven series 4-0

CONFERENCE SEMI-FINALS

May	1	Washington	3	at	NY Rangers	6	
May	3	Washington	2	at	NY Rangers	5	
May	5	NY Rangers	3	at	Washington	0	
May	7	NY Rangers	2	at	Washington	4	
May	9	Washington	3	at	NY Rangers	4	

NY Rangers won best-of-seven series 4-1

May	1	Boston	2	at	New Jersey	1	
May	3	Boston	6	at	New Jersey	5	OT
May	5	New Jersey	4	at	Boston	2	
May	7	New Jersey	5	at	Boston	4	OT
May	9	Boston	0	at	New Jersey	2	
May	11	New Jersey	5	at	Boston	3	

New Jersey won best-of-seven series 4-2

May	2	San Jose	3	at	Toronto	2	
May	4	San Jose	1	at	Toronto	5	
May	6	Toronto	2	at	San Jose	5	
May	8	Toronto	8	at	San Jose	3	
May	10	Toronto	2	at	San Jose	5	
May	12	San Jose	2	at	Toronto	3	OT
May	14	San Jose	2	at	Toronto	4	

Toronto won best-of-seven series 4-3

May	2	Vancouver	6	at	Dallas	4	
May	4	Vancouver	3	at	Dallas	0	
May	6	Dallas	4	at	Vancouver	3	
May	8	Dallas	1	at	Vancouver	2	OT
May	10	Dallas	2	at	Vancouver	4	

Vancouver won best-of-seven series 4-1

CONFERENCE FINALS

May	15	New Jersey	4	at	NY Rangers	3	2OT
May	17	New Jersey	0	at	NY Rangers	4	
May	19	NY Rangers	3	at	New Jersey	2	2OT
May	21	NY Rangers	1	at	New Jersey	3	
May	23	New Jersey	4	at	NY Rangers	1	
May	25	NY Rangers	4	at	New Jersey	2	
May	27	New Jersey	1	at	NY Rangers	2	2OT

NY Rangers won best-of-seven series 4-3

May	16	Vancouver	2	at	Toronto	3	OT
May	18	Vancouver	4	at	Toronto	3	
May	20	Toronto	0	at	Vancouver	4	
May	22	Toronto	0	at	Vancouver	2	
May	24	Toronto	3	at	Vancouver	4	2OT

Vancouver won best-of-seven series 4-1

FINALS

May	31	Vancouver	3	at	NY Rangers	2	OT
June	2	Vancouver	1	at	NY Rangers	3	
June	4	NY Rangers	5	at	Vancouver	1	
June	7	NY Rangers	4	at	Vancouver	2	
June	9	Vancouver	6	at	NY Rangers	3	
June	11	NY Rangers	1	at	Vancouver	4	
June	14	Vancouver	2	at	NY Rangers	3	

NY Rangers won best-of-seven series 4-3

1993-94 – New York Rangers – Mark Messier (Captain), Brian Leetch, Kevin Lowe, Adam Graves, Steve Larmer, Glenn Anderson, Jeff Beukeboom, Greg Gilbert, Mike Hartman, Glenn Healy, Mike Hudson, Alexander Karpovtsev, Joe Kocur, Alexei Kovalev, Nick Kypreos, Doug Lidster, Stephane Matteau, Craig MacTavish, Sergei Nemchinov, Brian Noonan, Ed Olczyk, Mike Richter, Esa Tikkanen, Jay Wells, Sergei Zubov, Robert Gutkowski, Stanley Jaffe, Kenneth Munoz (Governors), Neil Smith (President/General Manager/Governor), Larry Pleau (Assistant General Manager), Mike Keenan (Head Coach), Colin Campbell (Associate Coach), Dick Todd (Assistant Coach), Matthew Loughren (Manager, Team Operations), Barry Watkins (Dir., Communications), Christer Rockstrom, Tony Feltrin, Martin Madden, Herb Hammond, Darwin Bennett (Scouts), Dave Smith, Joe Murphy, Mike Folga, Bruce Lifrieri (Trainers).

LEADING PLAYOFF SCORERS

Player	Club	GP	G	A	PTS	PIM
Brian Leetch	NY Rangers	23	11	23	34	6
Pavel Bure	Vancouver	24	16	15	31	40
Mark Messier	NY Rangers	23	12	18	30	33
Doug Gilmour	Toronto	18	6	22	28	42
Trevor Linden	Vancouver	24	12	13	25	18
Alexei Kovalev	NY Rangers	23	9	12	21	18
Geoff Courtnall	Vancouver	24	9	10	19	51
Sergei Zubov	NY Rangers	22	5	14	19	0
Claude Lemieux	New Jersey	20	7	11	18	44
Igor Larionov	San Jose	14	5	13	18	10
Dave Ellett	Toronto	18	3	15	18	31

LEADING PLAYOFF GOALTENDERS

Goaltender	Club	GPI	Mins	GA	SO	Avg.
Dominik Hasek	Buffalo	7	484	13	2	1.61
Martin Brodeur	New Jersey	17	1171	38	1	1.95
Mike Richter	NY Rangers	23	1417	49	4	2.07
Kirk McLean	Vancouver	24	1544	59	4	2.29
Felix Potvin	Toronto	18	1124	46	3	2.46

PLAYOFF GOALS

Name, Team	G
Pavel Bure, Van.	16
Mark Messier, NYR	12
Trevor Linden, Van.	12
Brian Leetch, NYR	11
Adam Graves, NYR	10
Wendel Clark, Tor.	9
Alexei Kovalev, NYR	9
Steve Larmer, NYR	9
Geoff Courtnall, Van.	9

PLAYOFF ASSISTS

Name, Team	A
Brian Leetch, NYR	23
Doug Gilmour, Tor.	22
Mark Messier, NYR	18
Dave Ellett, Tor.	15
Pavel Bure, Van.	15
Sergei Zubov, NYR	14
Igor Larionov, S.J.	13
Trevor Linden, Van.	13
Alexei Kovalev, NYR	12

PLAYOFF POWERPLAY GOALS

Name, Team	PPG
Dmitri Mironov, Tor.	6
Doug Gilmour, Tor.	5
Alexei Kovalev, NYR	5
Trevor Linden, Van.	5
Brian Leetch, NYR	4

PLAYOFF SHORTHAND GOALS

Name, Team	SHG
Mark Osborne, Tor.	2
17 tied with	1

PLAYOFF GAME-WINNING GOALS

Name, Team	GWG
Mark Messier, NYR	4
Brian Leetch, NYR	4
Mike Gartner, Tor.	3
Geoff Courtnall, Van.	3
14 tied with	2

PLAYOFF GOALIE WINS

Name, Team	W
Mike Richter, NYR	16
Kirk McLean, Van.	15
Felix Potvin, Tor.	9
Martin Brodeur, N.J.	8
Arturs Irbe, S.J.	7

PLAYOFF SHUTOUTS

Name, Team	SO
Mike Richter, NYR	4
Kirk McLean, Van.	4
Felix Potvin, Tor.	3
Dominik Hasek, Buf.	2
Three tied with.	1

PLAYOFF SAVE PERCENTAGE

Name, Team	SV%
Dominik Hasek, Buf.	.950
Martin Brodeur, N.J.	.928
Kirk McLean, Van.	.928
Mike Richter, NYR	.921
Felix Potvin, Tor.	.912

1994-95

Stanley Cup • New Jersey Devils

FINAL STANDINGS

Team	GP	W	L	T	GF	GA	PTS
EASTERN CONFERENCE							
Northeast Division							
Quebec	48	30	13	5	185	134	65
Pittsburgh	48	29	16	3	181	158	61
Boston	48	27	18	3	150	127	57
Buffalo	48	22	19	7	130	119	51
Hartford	48	19	24	5	127	141	43
Montreal	48	18	23	7	125	148	43
Ottawa	48	9	34	5	117	174	23
Atlantic Division							
Philadelphia	48	28	16	4	150	132	60
New Jersey	48	22	18	8	136	121	52
Washington	48	22	18	8	136	120	52
NY Rangers	48	22	23	3	139	134	47
Florida	48	20	22	6	115	127	46
Tampa Bay	48	17	28	3	120	144	37
NY Islanders	48	15	28	5	126	158	35
WESTERN CONFERENCE							
Central Division							
Detroit	48	33	11	4	180	117	70
St. Louis	48	28	15	5	178	135	61
Chicago	48	24	19	5	156	115	53
Toronto	48	21	19	8	135	146	50
Dallas	48	17	23	8	136	135	42
Winnipeg	48	16	25	7	157	177	39
Pacific Division							
Calgary	48	24	17	7	163	135	55
Vancouver	48	18	18	12	153	148	48
San Jose	48	19	25	4	129	161	42
Los Angeles	48	16	23	9	142	174	41
Edmonton	48	17	27	4	136	183	38
Anaheim	48	16	27	5	125	164	37

LEADING SCORERS

Player	Club	GP	G	A	PTS	PIM
Jaromir Jagr		48	32	38	70	37
Eric Lindros	Philadelphia	46	29	41	70	60
Alexei Zhamnov	Winnipeg	48	30	35	65	20
Joe Sakic	Quebec	47	19	43	62	30
Ron Francis	Pittsburgh	44	11	48	59	18
Theoren Fleury	Calgary	47	29	29	58	112
Paul Coffey	Detroit	45	14	44	58	72
Mikael Renberg	Philadelphia	47	26	31	57	20
John LeClair	Mtl./Phi.	46	26	28	54	30
Mark Messier	NY Rangers	46	14	39	53	40
Adam Oates	Boston	48	12	41	53	8
Bernie Nicholls	Chicago	48	22	29	51	32
Keith Tkachuk	Winnipeg	48	22	29	51	152
Brett Hull	St. Louis	48	29	21	50	10
Joe Nieuwendyk	Calgary	46	21	29	50	33
Sergei Fedorov	Detroit	42	20	30	50	24
Peter Forsberg	Quebec	47	15	35	50	16
Owen Nolan	Quebec	46	30	19	49	46
Teemu Selanne	Winnipeg	45	22	26	48	2
Mark Recchi	Phi./Mtl.	49	16	32	48	28
Wayne Gretzky	Los Angeles	48	11	37	48	6

LEADING GOALTENDERS

Goaltender	Club	GPI	MINS	GA	SO	AVG
Dominik Hasek	Buffalo	41	2416	85	5	2.11
Rick Tabaracci	Wsh./Cgy	13	596	21	0	2.11
Jim Carey	Washington	28	1604	57	4	2.13
Chris Osgood	Detroit	19	1087	41	1	2.26
Ed Belfour	Chicago	42	2450	93	5	2.28
Jocelyn Thibault	Quebec	18	898	35	1	2.34
Dominic Roussel	Philadelphia	19	1075	42	1	2.34

Martin Brodeur made his NHL debut with the New Jersey Devils as an emergency injury replacement late in the 1991–92 schedule. He won the Calder Trophy as rookie of the year in 1993–94 and led the Devils to the first Stanley Cup title in franchise history in 1995.

A 103-DAY LOCKOUT resulted in the NHL's shortest regular season in 53 years. The 1994–95 season did not begin until January 20, 1995, but the abbreviated 48-game schedule was packed with plenty of excitement.

The Pittsburgh Penguins were without Mario Lemieux for the entire year, as he took the season off to recuperate from the lingering effects of back injuries and his battle with cancer, but the team remained in fine form, opening the season with a 12–0–1 mark. The Quebec Nordiques, not to be outdone, streaked out of the gate at 12–1–0 and the two teams battled for top spot in the Northeast Division until the final night of the season. Quebec, who had swapped Mats Sundin to Toronto in a deal for Wendel Clark and Sylvain Lefebvre, emerged victorious with 65 points to Pittsburgh's 61.

Dark Days, Devilish Nights – Labor woes darkened the rinks but Lindros's MVP year, Jagr's on-ice magic and New Jersey's rise from the swamp to the Stanley Cup gave the season a brighter glow.

The Penguins' Jaromir Jagr broke through as a superstar, leading the NHL with 70 points on 32 goals and 38 assists. Eric Lindros earned the Hart Trophy after leading the Flyers to top spot in the Atlantic Division. Lindros equaled Jagr's 70 points, but missed out on the Art Ross Trophy because he had only scored 29 goals.

The defending Stanley Cup champion New York Rangers battled all season just to earn a berth in the playoffs. They snuck in as the eighth and final qualifier in the Eastern Conference. Montreal wasn't so lucky. Despite acquiring Mark Recchi for John LeClair in a blockbuster deal with Philadelphia, and swapping captain Kirk Muller to the New York Islanders for Pierre Turgeon, the Canadiens missed the playoffs for the first time in 25 years. The Rangers managed to upset the Nordiques in the first round before losing to Philadelphia. Pittsburgh reached the second round before falling to the New Jersey Devils, who then beat the Flyers to advance to the Stanley Cup finals for the first time in franchise history.

In the Western Conference, the Detroit Red Wings cruised to top spot in the Central Division with a record of 33–11–4 and finished first overall in the NHL standings for the first time since 1964–65. The Red Wings then beat the Dallas Stars before avenging the previous year's first-round loss to the San Jose Sharks with a four-game sweep. After a five-game victory over the Chicago Blackhawks for the Western Conference title, Detroit was back in the finals for the first time in 29 years.

Under coach Jacques Lemaire, the Devils had successfully employed a defensive scheme known as the "neutral-zone trap" throughout the Eastern Conference playoffs, but their detractors doubted they could stymie the powerful Red Wings. The Devils proved these critics wrong, completely closing down Detroit's attack in a surprising final series sweep, bringing the Cup to the Meadowlands for the first time.

At 6'4" and 236 pounds, Eric Lindros boasted a combination of strength and skill that had never been seen before. However, his physical style left him very susceptible to injuries.

Leaders, 1994-95

GOALS

Name, Team	G
Peter Bondra, Wsh.	34
Jaromir Jagr, Pit.	32
Ray Sheppard, Det.	30
Owen Nolan, Que.	30
Alexei Zhamnov, Wpg.	30
Eric Lindros, Phi.	29
Theoren Fleury, Cgy.	29
Brett Hull, St.L.	29
Cam Neely, Bos.	27
John LeClair, Mtl./Phi.	26
Mikael Renberg, Phi.	26

ASSISTS

Name, Team	A
Ron Francis, Pit.	48
Paul Coffey, Det.	44
Joe Sakic, Que.	43
Eric Lindros, Phi.	41
Adam Oates, Bos.	41
Mark Messier, NYR	39
Joe Juneau, Wsh.	38
Jaromir Jagr, Pit.	38
Wayne Gretzky, L.A.	37
Phil Housley, Cgy.	35
Peter Forsberg, Que.	35
Alexei Zhamnov, Wpg.	35

POWERPLAY GOALS

Name, Team	PPG
Cam Neely, Bos.	16
Owen Nolan, Que.	13
Donald Audette, Buf.	13
Alexander Mogilny, Buf.	12
Peter Bondra, Wsh.	12
Ray Sheppard, Det.	11
Alexei Yashin, Ott.	11
Bernie Nicholls, Chi.	11
David Oliver, Edm.	10
Nine tied with	9

SHORTHAND GOALS

Name, Team	SHG
Peter Bondra, Wsh.	6
Wayne Presley, Buf.	5
Brent Gilchrist, Dal.	3
Sergei Fedorov, Det.	3
Rob Zamuner, T.B.	3
Mark Messier, NYR	3
Steve Konowalchuk, Wsh.	3
Brett Hull, St.L.	3
Jaromir Jagr, Pit.	3
Scott Young, Que.	3

GAME-WINNING GOALS

Name, Team	GWG
Owen Nolan, Que.	8
John LeClair, Mtl./Phi.	7
Donald Audette, Buf.	7
Jaromir Jagr, Pit.	7
Brendan Shanahan, St.L.	6
Brett Hull, St.L.	6
11 tied with	5

GOALIE WINS

Name, Team	W
Ken Wregget, Pit.	25
Ed Belfour, Chi.	22
Trevor Kidd, Cgy.	22
Curtis Joseph, St.L.	20
Mike Vernon, Det.	19
Blaine Lacher, Bos.	19
Martin Brodeur, N.J.	19
Dominik Hasek, Buf.	19
Jim Carey, Wsh.	18
Kirk McLean, Van.	18

SHUTOUTS

Name, Team	SO
Dominik Hasek, Buf.	5
Ed Belfour, Chi.	5
Jim Carey, Wsh.	4
Blaine Lacher, Bos.	4
John Vanbiesbrouck, Fla.	4
Arturs Irbe, S.J.	4

SAVE PERCENTAGE

Name, Team	SV%
Dominik Hasek, Buf.	.930
Chris Osgood, Det.	.917
Jocelyn Thibault, Que.	.917
Damian Rhodes, Tor.	.916
Andy Moog, Dal.	.915

FIRST TEAM ALL-STARS

Name, Team	Position
Eric Lindros, Phi.	C
Jaromir Jagr, Pit.	RW
John LeClair, Mtl./Phi.	LW
Paul Coffey, Det.	D
Chris Chelios, Chi.	D
Dominik Hasek, Buf.	G

SECOND TEAM ALL-STARS

Name, Team	Position
Alexei Zhamnov, Wpg	C
Theoren Fleury, Cgy.	RW
Keith Tkachuk, Wpg.	LW
Raymond Bourque, Bos.	D
Larry Murphy, Pit.	D
Ed Belfour, Chi.	G

ALL-ROOKIE TEAM

Name, Team	Position
Peter Forsberg, Col.	F
Jeff Friesen, S.J.	F
Paul Karyia, Ana.	F
Chris Therien, Phi.	D
Kenny Jonsson, Tor.	D
Jim Carey, Wsh.	G

TROPHY WINNERS

Trophy	Awarded For	Winner	Team
Hart	MVP	Eric Lindros	Phi.
Art Ross	Top Scorer	Jaromir Jagr	Pit.
Norris	Top Defenseman	Paul Coffey	Det
Calder	Top Rookie	Peter Forsberg	Que.
Selke	Top Defensive Forward	Ron Francis	Pit.
Vezina	Top Goaltender	Dominik Hasek	Buf
Jennings	Fewest Goals Against	Ed Belfour	Chi
Adams	Top Coach	Marc Crawford	Que.
Byng	Gentlemanly Conduct	Ron Francis	Pit.
Masterton	Perseverance, Sportmanship	Pat LaFontaine	Buf.
Pearson	NHLPA MVP	Eric Lindros	Phi.
Conn Smythe	Playoff MVP	Claude Lemieux	N.J.
Patrick	Service to Hockey in U.S.	Joe Mullen Brian Mullen Bob Fleming	
Clancy	Leadership On and Off Ice	Joe Nieuwendyk	Cgy.
Entry Draft	First Overall Selection	Bryan Berard	Ott.

NHL NOTEBOOK

TRANSACTIONS

- June 28, 1994 – Toronto Maple Leafs traded Wendel Clark, Sylvain Lefebvre, Landon Wilson and a 1994 first-round draft pick to Quebec for Mats Sundin, Garth Butcher, Todd Warriner, and the Nordiques' first-round draft in 1994.
- June 28, 1994 – Mighty Ducks of Anaheim selected Steve Rucchin with the second overall pick in the 1994 NHL Supplemental Draft.
- July 4, 1994 – Calgary Flames traded Al MacInnis to St. Louis for Phil Housley.
- Feb. 9, 1995 – Philadelphia obtained John LeClair, Eric Desjardins and Gilbert Dionne from Montreal for Mark Recchi and Philadelphia's third-round pick in the 1995 Entry Draft.

RECORDS

- Mar. 25, 1995 – Detroit's Scotty Bowman became the first coach in NHL history to record 900 career victories when the Red Wings beat the Canucks 2-1 in Vancouver.
- May 15, 1995 – Vancouver set an NHL playoff record for fastest two shorthanded goals by one team when Christian Ruutu and Geoff Courtnall scored in a span 0:17 during a 6-5 win over the Blues.
- May 27, 1995 – Detroit's Scotty Bowman set a coaching record by gaining his 46th career playoff series win when the Red Wings beat the Sharks 6-2 in San Jose to sweep their Western Conference semi-final. Bowman broke Toe Blake's record.
- June 17, 1995 – The Devils set an NHL record with their ninth road playoff win of the year a 2-1 win at Detroit in game one of the finals.

MILESTONES

- Mar. 8, 1995 – Montreal's Mark Recchi became the first player in history to take penalty shots for two different NHL teams in one season when he missed against Dominik Hasek in a 2-2 tie against the Sabres. One month earlier, Recchi had missed with the Flyers against Ottawa.
- Apr. 28, 1995 – San Jose's Arturs Irbe played in his 158th career NHL game, the most by a European born goaltender, as the Sharks shut out the visiting Los Angeles Kings 4-0.
- May 3, 1995 – Jaromir Jagr became the first European player to lead the NHL in scoring as the Penguins lost 4-3 to the visiting Panthers. Jagr and Flyers' Lindros tied with 70 points apiece in the shortened 48-game season but Jagr led, 32-29, in goals to win the Art Ross Trophy.
- June 17, 1995 – Scotty Bowman became the first coach in NHL history to appear in the Stanley Cup finals with four teams when the Red Wings lost to New Jersey in game one of the finals. Bowman had previously appeared with St. Louis, Montreal and Pittsburgh.

1995 Playoffs

CONFERENCE QUARTER-FINALS

May	6	NY Rangers	4	at	Quebec	5	
May	8	NY Rangers	8	at	Quebec	3	
May	10	Quebec	3	at	NY Rangers	4	
May	12	Quebec	2	at	NY Rangers	3	OT
May	14	NY Rangers	2	at	Quebec	4	
May	16	Quebec	2	at	NY Rangers	4	

NY Rangers won best-of-seven series 4-2

May	7	Buffalo	3	at	Philadelphia	4	OT
May	8	Buffalo	1	at	Philadelphia	3	
May	10	Philadelphia	1	at	Buffalo	3	
May	12	Philadelphia	4	at	Buffalo	2	
May	14	Buffalo	4	at	Philadelphia	6	

Philadelphia won best-of-seven series 4-1

May	6	Washington	5	at	Pittsburgh	4	
May	8	Washington	3	at	Pittsburgh	5	
May	10	Pittsburgh	2	at	Washington	6	
May	12	Pittsburgh	2	at	Washington	6	
May	14	Washington	5	at	Pittsburgh	6	OT
May	16	Pittsburgh	7	at	Washington	1	
May	18	Washington	0	at	Pittsburgh	3	

Pittsburgh won best-of-seven series 4-3

May	7	New Jersey	5	at	Boston	0	
May	8	New Jersey	3	at	Boston	0	
May	10	Boston	3	at	New Jersey	2	
May	12	Boston	0	at	New Jersey	1	OT
May	14	New Jersey	3	at	Boston	2	

New Jersey won best-of-seven series 4-1

May	7	Dallas	3	at	Detroit	4	
May	9	Dallas	1	at	Detroit	4	
May	11	Detroit	5	at	Dallas	1	
May	14	Detroit	1	at	Dallas	4	
May	15	Dallas	1	at	Detroit	3	

Detroit won best-of-seven series 4-1

May	7	San Jose	5	at	Calgary	4	
May	9	San Jose	5	at	Calgary	4	OT
May	11	Calgary	9	at	San Jose	2	
May	13	Calgary	6	at	San Jose	4	
May	15	San Jose	0	at	Calgary	5	
May	17	Calgary	3	at	San Jose	5	
May	19	San Jose	5	at	Calgary	4	2OT

San Jose won best-of-seven series 4-3

May	7	Vancouver	1	at	St. Louis	2	
May	9	Vancouver	5	at	St. Louis	3	
May	11	St. Louis	1	at	Vancouver	6	
May	13	St. Louis	5	at	Vancouver	2	
May	15	Vancouver	6	at	St. Louis	5	OT
May	17	St. Louis	8	at	Vancouver	2	
May	19	Vancouver	5	at	St. Louis	3	

Vancouver won best-of-seven series 4-3

May	7	Toronto	5	at	Chicago	3	
May	9	Toronto	3	at	Chicago	0	
May	11	Chicago	3	at	Toronto	2	
May	13	Chicago	3	at	Toronto	1	
May	15	Toronto	2	at	Chicago	4	
May	17	Chicago	4	at	Toronto	5	OT
May	19	Toronto	2	at	Chicago	5	

Chicago won best-of-seven series 4-3

CONFERENCE SEMI-FINALS

May	21	NY Rangers	4	at	Philadelphia	5	OT
May	22	NY Rangers	3	at	Philadelphia	4	OT
May	24	Philadelphia	5	at	NY Rangers	2	
May	26	Philadelphia	4	at	NY Rangers	1	

Philadelphia won best-of-seven series 4-0

May	20	New Jersey	2	at	Pittsburgh	3	
May	22	New Jersey	4	at	Pittsburgh	2	
May	24	Pittsburgh	1	at	New Jersey	5	
May	26	Pittsburgh	1	at	New Jersey	2	OT
May	28	New Jersey	4	at	Pittsburgh	1	

New Jersey won best-of-seven series 4-1

May	21	San Jose	0	at	Detroit	6	
May	23	San Jose	2	at	Detroit	6	
May	25	Detroit	6	at	San Jose	2	
May	27	Detroit	6	at	San Jose	2	

Detroit won best-of-seven series 4-0

May	21	Vancouver	1	at	Chicago	2	OT
May	23	Vancouver	0	at	Chicago	2	
May	25	Chicago	3	at	Vancouver	2	OT
May	27	Chicago	4	at	Vancouver	3	OT

Chicago won best-of-seven series 4-0

CONFERENCE FINALS

June	3	New Jersey	4	at	Philadelphia	1	
June	5	New Jersey	5	at	Philadelphia	2	
June	7	Philadelphia	3	at	New Jersey	2	OT
June	10	Philadelphia	4	at	New Jersey	2	
June	11	New Jersey	3	at	Philadelphia	2	
June	13	Philadelphia	2	at	New Jersey	4	

New Jersey won best-of-seven series 4-2

June	1	Chicago	1	at	Detroit	2	OT
June	4	Chicago	2	at	Detroit	3	
June	6	Detroit	4	at	Chicago	3	2OT
June	8	Detroit	2	at	Chicago	5	
June	11	Chicago	1	at	Detroit	2	2OT

Detroit won best-of-seven series 4-1

FINALS

June	17	New Jersey	2	at	Detroit	1
June	20	New Jersey	4	at	Detroit	2
June	22	Detroit	2	at	New Jersey	5
June	24	Detroit	2	at	New Jersey	5

New Jersey won best-of-seven series 4-0

1994-95 – New Jersey Devils – Scott Stevens (Captain), Tommy Albelin, Martin Brodeur, Neal Broten, Sergei Brylin, Bob Carpenter, Shawn Chambers, Tom Chorske, Danton Cole, Ken Daneyko, Kevin Dean, Jim Dowd, Bruce Driver (Alternate Captain), Bill Guerin, Bobby Holik, Claude Lemieux, John MacLean (Alternate Captain), Chris McAlpine, Randy McKay, Scott Niedermayer, Mike Peluso, Stephane Richer, Brian Rolston, Chris Terreri, Valeri Zelepukin, Dr. John J. McMullen (Owner/Chairman), Peter S. McMullen (Owner), Lou Lamoriello (President/General Manager), Jacques Lemaire (Head Coach), Jacques Caron (Goaltender Coach), Dennis Gendron, Larry Robinson (Assistant Coaches), Robbie Ftorek (AHL Coach), Alex Abasto (Assistant Equipment Manager), Bob Huddleston (Massage Therapist), David Nichols (Equipment Manager), Ted Schuch (Medical Trainer), Mike Vasalani (Strength Coach), David Conte (Director of Scouting), Claude Carrier, Milt Fisher, Dan Labraaten, Marcel Pronovost (Scouts).

LEADING PLAYOFF SCORERS

Player	Club	GP	G	A	PTS	PIM
Sergei Fedorov	Detroit	17	7	17	24	6
Stephane Richer	New Jersey	19	6	15	21	2
Neal Broten	New Jersey	20	7	12	19	6
Ron Francis	Pittsburgh	12	6	13	19	4
Denis Savard	Chicago	16	7	11	18	10
Paul Coffey	Detroit	18	6	12	18	10
John MacLean	New Jersey	20	5	13	18	14
Claude Lemieux	New Jersey	20	13	3	16	20
Vyacheslav Kozlov	Detroit	18	9	7	16	10
Nicklas Lidstrom	Detroit	18	4	12	16	8

LEADING PLAYOFF GOALTENDERS

Goaltender	Club	GPI	Mins	GA	SO	Avg.
Martin Brodeur	New Jersey	20	1222	34	3	1.67
Ed Belfour	Chicago	16	1014	37	1	2.19
Mike Vernon	Detroit	18	1063	41	1	2.31
Ron Hextall	Philadelphia	15	897	42	0	2.81
Felix Potvin	Toronto	7	424	20	1	2.83

PLAYOFF GOALS

Name, Team	G
Claude Lemieux, N.J.	13
Jaromir Jagr, Pit.	10
Joe Murphy, Chi.	9
Dino Ciccarelli, Det.	9
Vyacheslav Kozlov, Det.	9
Randy McKay, N.J.	8
Theoren Fleury, Cgy.	7
Pavel Bure, Van.	7
Luc Robitaille, Pit.	7
Denis Savard, Chi.	7
Sergei Fedorov, Det.	7
Neal Broten, N.J.	7

PLAYOFF ASSISTS

Name, Team	A
Sergei Fedorov, Det.	17
Stephane Richer, N.J.	15
Ron Francis, Pit.	13
Larry Murphy, Pit.	13
John MacLean, N.J.	13
Paul Coffey, Det.	12
Nicklas Lidstrom, Det.	12
Neal Broten, N.J.	12
Eric Lindros, Phi.	11
Denis Savard, Chi.	11
Bernie Nicholls, Chi.	11

PLAYOFF POWERPLAY GOALS

Name, Team	PPG
Dino Ciccarelli, Det.	6
Mike Rathje, S.J.	5
10 tied with	3

PLAYOFF SHORTHAND GOALS

Name, Team	SHG
Pavel Bure, Van.	2
Russ Courtnall, Van.	2
25 tied with	1

PLAYOFF GAME-WINNING GOALS

Name, Team	GWG
Vyacheslav Kozlov, Det.	4
Neal Broten, N.J.	4
Chris Chelios, Chi.	3
Joe Murphy, Chi.	3
Claude Lemieux, N.J.	3

PLAYOFF GOALIE WINS

Name, Team	W
Martin Brodeur, N.J.	16
Mike Vernon, Det.	12
Ron Hextall, Phi.	10
Ed Belfour, Chi.	9
Ken Wregget, Pit.	5

PLAYOFF SHUTOUTS

Name, Team	SO
Martin Brodeur, N.J.	3
Felix Potvin, Tor.	1
Trevor Kidd, Cgy.	1
Ken Wregget, Pit.	1
Ed Belfour, Chi.	1
Mike Vernon, Det.	1

PLAYOFF SAVE PERCENTAGE

Name, Team	SV%
Martin Brodeur, N.J.	.927
Ed Belfour, Chi.	.923
Felix Potvin, Tor.	.921
Ken Wregget, Pit.	.905
Ron Hextall, Phi.	.904

1995-96

Stanley Cup • Colorado Avalanche

FINAL STANDINGS

EASTERN CONFERENCE

Northeast Division

Team	GP	W	L	T	GF	GA	PTS
Pittsburgh	82	49	29	4	362	284	102
Boston	82	40	31	11	282	269	91
Montreal	82	40	32	10	265	248	90
Hartford	82	34	39	9	237	259	77
Buffalo	82	33	42	7	247	262	73
Ottawa	82	18	59	5	191	291	41
Atlantic Division							
Philadelphia	82	45	24	13	282	208	103
NY Rangers	82	41	27	14	272	237	96
Florida	82	41	31	10	254	234	92
Washington	82	39	32	11	234	204	89
Tampa Bay	82	38	32	12	238	248	88
New Jersey	82	37	33	12	215	202	86
NY Islanders	82	22	50	10	229	315	54
WESTERN CONFERENCE							
Central Division							
Detroit	82	62	13	7	325	181	131
Chicago	82	40	28	14	273	220	94
Toronto	82	34	36	12	247	252	80
St. Louis	82	32	34	16	219	248	80
Winnipeg	82	36	40	6	275	291	78
Dallas	82	26	42	14	227	280	66
Pacific Division							
Colorado	82	47	25	10	326	240	104
Calgary	82	34	37	11	241	240	79
Vancouver	82	32	35	15	278	278	79
Anaheim	82	35	39	8	234	247	78
Edmonton	82	30	44	8	240	304	68
Los Angeles	82	24	40	18	256	302	66
San Jose	82	20	55	7	252	357	47

LEADING SCORERS

Player	Club	GP	G	A	PTS	PIM
Mario Lemieux	Pittsburgh	70	69	92	161	54
Jaromir Jagr	Pittsburgh	82	62	87	149	96
Joe Sakic	Colorado	82	51	69	120	44
Ron Francis	Pittsburgh	77	27	92	119	56
Peter Forsberg	Colorado	82	30	86	116	47
Eric Lindros	Philadelphia	73	47	68	115	163
Paul Kariya	Anaheim	82	50	58	108	20
Teemu Selanne	Wpg./Ana.	79	40	68	108	22
Alexander Mogilny	Vancouver	79	55	52	107	16
Sergei Fedorov	Detroit	78	39	68	107	48
Doug Weight	Edmonton	82	25	79	104	95
Wayne Gretzky	L.A./St.L.	80	23	79	102	34
Mark Messier	NY Rangers	74	47	52	99	122
Petr Nedved	Pittsburgh	80	45	54	99	68
Keith Tkachuk	Winnipeg	76	50	48	98	156
John LeClair	Philadelphia	82	51	46	97	64
Theoren Fleury	Calgary	80	46	50	96	112
Pierre Turgeon	Montreal	80	38	58	96	44
Steve Yzerman	Detroit	80	36	59	95	64
Vincent Damphousse	Montreal	80	38	56	94	158
Adam Oates	Boston	70	25	67	92	18
Pat LaFontaine	Buffalo	76	40	51	91	36

LEADING GOALTENDERS

Goaltender	Club	GPI	MINS	GA	SO	AVG
Ron Hextall	Philadelphia	53	3102	112	4	2.17
Chris Osgood	Detroit	50	2933	106	5	2.17
Jim Carey	Washington	71	4069	153	9	2.26
Mike Vernon	Detroit	32	1855	70	3	2.26
Martin Brodeur	New Jersey	77	4433	173	6	2.34
Jeff Hackett	Chicago	35	2000	80	4	2.40
Daren Puppa	Tampa Bay	57	3189	131	5	2.46

Chris Chelios won the Norris Trophy for the third time in 1995–96. With 14 goals and 58 assists, the Chicago native became the first defenseman in Blackhawks history to lead the team in scoring. He was also named team captain that season.

After their first-place finish the year before, most expected the Detroit Red Wings to come out flying in 1995–96 and they didn't disappoint. Coach Scotty Bowman's squad exceeded even his great Montreal Canadiens teams of the late 1970s with an NHL-record 62 victories, though Detroit's 62–13–7 mark produced one fewer point than the record 132 collected by Bowman's 60–8–12 Canadiens of 1976–77. Meanwhile, 1994–95's top Eastern Conference team, the Quebec Nordiques, moved to Denver, becoming the Colorado Avalanche and playing in the Pacific Division. The Avalanche would beat the Wings in a six-game Western Conference final.

An Amazing Avalanche – Exiled from Quebec, adopted by Denver, the Nordiques became the Avalanche, acquired Patrick Roy and snowed under their competition to become Stanley Cup champions.

After sitting out the 1994–95 season, Mario Lemieux came back to score 69 goals in 70 games and win his fifth scoring title with 161 points. Lemieux won the Hart Trophy as most valuable player for the third time. Things did not go as well for Wayne Gretzky this season. The Great One and his Los Angeles Kings were both slumping when he was dealt to the St. Louis Blues in February. Another significant trade this season saw Patrick Roy swapped to Colorado after a dispute with Canadiens coach Mario Tremblay.

Several young players took their place among the NHL's elite. Jaromir Jagr followed up his Art Ross performance of the previous season with 149 points, while Joe Sakic of the Avalanche finished third in league scoring with 120 points. Teammate Peter Forsberg (rookie of the year in 1994–95) collected 116 points, while Eric Lindros of the Philadelphia Flyers had 115. Paul Kariya fulfilled the promise expected of him with 50 goals and 58 assists for the Mighty Ducks of Anaheim and was teamed with a linemate who complemented his talents when Teemu Selanne was acquired from the Winnipeg Jets.

In the Eastern Conference, the Florida Panthers made the playoffs in just their third season and rode the hot goaltending of John Vanbiesbrouck past the Boston Bruins, Philadelphia Flyers and Pittsburgh Penguins to the Stanley Cup finals, which opened in Denver with the Avalanche scoring 3–1 and 8–1 victories. The Panthers played better when the series moved to Miami, but Colorado completed the sweep with 3–2 and 1–0 wins. Uwe Krupp scored the Stanley Cup-winning goal at 4:31 of the third overtime period. Joe Sakic won the Conn Smythe Trophy, while Claude Lemieux (previously a winner in Montreal and New Jersey) became only the fourth player in history to celebrate Stanley Cup titles with three different teams.

The Red Wings set an NHL record with 62 wins in 1995–96, enabling goalies Chris Osgood and Mike Vernon, coach Scotty Bowman and center Sergei Fedorov to take home plenty of silverware.

Leaders, 1995-96

GOALS

Name, Team	G
Mario Lemieux, Pit.	69
Jaromir Jagr, Pit.	62
Alexander Mogilny, Van.	55
Peter Bondra, Wsh.	52
Joe Sakic, Col.	51
John LeClair, Phi.	51
Keith Tkachuk, Wpg.	50
Paul Kariya, Ana.	50
Eric Lindros, Phi.	47
Mark Messier, NYR	47

ASSISTS

Name, Team	A
Mario Lemieux, Pit.	92
Ron Francis, Pit.	92
Jaromir Jagr, Pit.	87
Peter Forsberg, Col.	86
Wayne Gretzky, L.A./St.L.	79
Doug Weight, Edm.	79
Brian Leetch, NYR	70
Joe Sakic, Col.	69
Eric Lindros, Phi.	68
Sergei Fedorov, Det.	68
Teemu Selanne, Wpg./Ana.	68

POWERPLAY GOALS

Name, Team	PPG
Mario Lemieux, Pit.	31
Keith Tkachuk, Wpg.	20
Jaromir Jagr, Pit.	20
Paul Kariya, Ana.	20
Scott Mellanby, Fla.	19
John LeClair, Phi.	19
Valeri Kamensky, Col.	18
Seven tied with	17

SHORTHAND GOALS

Name, Team	SHG
Mario Lemieux, Pit.	8
Dave Reid, Bos.	6
Mats Sundin, Tor.	6
Jamie Baker, S.J.	6
Joe Sakic, Col.	6
Tom Fitzgerald, Fla.	6
Brett Hull, St.L.	5
Alexander Mogilny, Van.	5
Theoren Fleury, Cgy.	5
11 tied with	4

GAME-WINNING GOALS

Name, Team	GWG
Jaromir Jagr, Pit.	12
Sergei Fedorov, Det.	11
Claude Lemieux, Col.	10
John LeClair, Phi.	10
Paul Kariya, Ana.	9
Mario Lemieux, Pit.	8
Steve Yzerman, Det.	8
12 tied with	7

GOALIE WINS

Name, Team	W
Chris Osgood, Det.	39
Jim Carey, Wsh.	35
Patrick Roy, Mtl./Col.	34
Martin Brodeur, N.J.	34
Bill Ranford, Edm./Bos.	34
Ron Hextall, Phi.	31
Felix Potvin, Tor.	30
Grant Fuhr, St.L.	30
Tom Barrasso, Pit.	29
Daren Puppa, T.B.	29

SHUTOUTS

Name, Team	SO
Jim Carey, Wsh.	9
Martin Brodeur, N.J.	6
Chris Osgood, Det.	5
Daren Puppa, T.B.	5
Four tied with	4

SAVE PERCENTAGE

Name, Team	SV%
Dominik Hasek, Buf.	.920
Daren Puppa, T.B.	.918
Jeff Hackett, Chi.	.916
Guy Hebert, Ana.	.914
Ron Hextall, Phi.	.913
Mike Richter, NYR	.912

FIRST TEAM ALL-STARS

Name, Team	Position
Mario Lemieux, Pit.	C
Jaromir Jagr, Pit.	RW
Paul Kariya, Ana.	LW
Chris Chelios, Chi.	D
Raymond Bourque, Bos.	D
Jim Carey, Wsh.	G

SECOND TEAM ALL-STARS

Name, Team	Position
Eric Lindros, Phi.	C
Alexander Mogilny, Van.	RW
John LeClair, Phi.	LW
Brian Leetch, NYR	D
Vladimir Konstantinov, Det.	D
Chris Osgood, Det.	G

ALL-ROOKIE TEAM

Name, Team	Position
Daniel Alfredsson, Ott.	F
Eric Daze, Chi.	F
Petr Sykora, N.J.	F
Ed Jovanovski, Fla.	D
Kyle McLaren, Bos.	D
Corey Hirsch, Van.	G

TROPHY WINNERS

Trophy	Awarded For	Winner	Team
Hart	MVP	Mario Lemieux	Pit.
Art Ross	Top Scorer	Mario Lemieux	Pit.
Norris	Top Defenseman	Chris Chelios	Chi
Calder	Top Rookie	Daniel Alfredsson	Ott.
Selke	Top Defensive Forward	Sergei Fedorov	Det.
Vezina	Top Goaltender	Jim Carey	Wsh
Jennings	Fewest Goals Against	Chris Osgood	Det
Adams	Top Coach	Scotty Bowman	Det.
Byng	Gentlemanly Conduct	Paul Kariya	Ana
Masterton	Perseverance, Sportmanship	Gary Roberts	Cgy.
Pearson	NHLPA MVP	Mario Lemieux	Pit.
Conn Smythe	Playoff MVP	Joe Sakic	Col.
Patrick	Service to Hockey in U.S.	George Gund Ken Morrow Milt Schmidt	
Clancy	Leadership On and Off Ice	Kris King	Wpg.
Entry Draft	First Overall Selection	Chris Phillips	Ott.

NHL NOTEBOOK

TRANSACTIONS

- July 27, 1995 – St. Louis Blues traded Brendan Shanahan to the Hartford Whalers for Chris Pronger.
- Aug. 31, 1995 – Pittsburgh Penguins traded Luc Robitaille and Ulf Samuelsson to the New York Rangers for Sergei Zubov and Petr Nedved.
- Dec. 19, 1995 – Calgary Flames traded Joe Nieuwendyk to the Dallas Stars in exchange for Corey Millen and Jarome Iginla.
- Mar. 20, 1996 – Vancouver Canucks obtained Markus Naslund from the Pittsburgh Penguins for Alek Stojanov.

RECORDS

- Jan. 29, 1996 – Senators beat the Blues 4-2 at the Palladium in Ottawa to end their NHL record for consecutive winless games at home – 17 (0-15-2). It was also Jacques Martin's first victory with Ottawa.
- Mar. 31, 1996 – St. Louis Blues' Grant Fuhr extended his NHL record for consecutive starts in goal and set an NHL record with his 76th appearance of the season, but then left the game with a third-period injury in an 8-1 loss at Detroit.
- Apr. 12, 1996 – Detroit set an NHL record with its 61st win of the year, a 5-3 win over the visiting Blackhawks. The Wings broke the record of 60 set by Montreal in 1976-77. Detroit's 36th home win also tied an NHL record set by Philadelphia in 1975-76.
- June 8, 1996 – Colorado's Joe Sakic set a record with his sixth game-winning goal of the 1996 playoffs as the Avalanche won 3-2 at Florida in game three of the Stanley Cup finals.

MILESTONES

- Dec. 13, 1995 – Detroit's Paul Coffey became the first NHL defenseman to get 1,000 career assists as the Red Wings won 3-1 over the visiting Chicago Blackhawks. Coffey joined Wayne Gretzky, Gordie Howe and Marcel Dionne as the only NHL players with 1,000 assists.
- Mar. 5, 1996 – Tampa Bay's Terry Crisp became the first coach in NHL history to win 100 games with an expansion team when the Lightning won 2-0 on the road in Chicago.
- Apr. 21, 1996 – Tampa Bay became the first NHL team to win its first two playoff games in overtime when Alexander Selivanov scored at 2:13 of OT for a 5-4 win over the Flyers before a record crowd of 25,945 in Tampa Bay in game three of the Eastern Conf. quarter-finals.
- June 4, 1996 – Patrick Roy became NHL's all-time leader in playoff games by a goalie when he appeared in his 133rd game, a 3-1 Avalanche win over the visiting Panthers, in game one of the Stanley Cup finals.

1996 Playoffs

CONFERENCE QUARTER-FINALS

Apr.	16	Tampa Bay	3	at	Philadelphia	7	
Apr.	18	Tampa Bay	2	at	Philadelphia	1	OT
Apr.	21	Philadelphia	4	at	Tampa Bay	5	OT
Apr.	23	Philadelphia	4	at	Tampa Bay	1	
Apr.	25	Tampa Bay	1	at	Philadelphia	4	
Apr.	27	Philadelphia	6	at	Tampa Bay	1	

Philadelphia won best-of-seven series 4-2

Apr.	17	Washington	6	at	Pittsburgh	4	
Apr.	19	Washington	5	at	Pittsburgh	3	
Apr.	22	Pittsburgh	4	at	Washington	1	
Apr.	24	Pittsburgh	3	at	Washington	2	4OT
Apr.	26	Washington	1	at	Pittsburgh	4	
Apr.	28	Pittsburgh	3	at	Washington	2	

Pittsburgh won best-of-seven series 4-2

Apr.	16	Montreal	3	at	NY Rangers	2	OT
Apr.	18	Montreal	5	at	NY Rangers	3	
Apr.	21	NY Rangers	2	at	Montreal	1	
Apr.	23	NY Rangers	4	at	Montreal	3	
Apr.	26	Montreal	2	at	NY Rangers	3	
Apr.	28	NY Rangers	5	at	Montreal	3	

NY Rangers won best-of-seven series 4-2

Apr.	17	Boston	3	at	Florida	6
Apr.	22	Boston	2	at	Florida	6
Apr.	24	Florida	4	at	Boston	2
Apr.	25	Florida	2	at	Boston	6
Apr.	27	Boston	3	at	Florida	4

Florida won best-of-seven series 4-1

Apr.	17	Winnipeg	1	at	Detroit	4
Apr.	19	Winnipeg	0	at	Detroit	4
Apr.	21	Detroit	1	at	Winnipeg	4
Apr.	23	Detroit	6	at	Winnipeg	1
Apr.	26	Winnipeg	3	at	Detroit	1
Apr.	28	Detroit	4	at	Winnipeg	1

Detroit won best-of-seven series 4-2

Apr.	16	Vancouver	2	at	Colorado	5	
Apr.	18	Vancouver	5	at	Colorado	4	
Apr.	20	Colorado	4	at	Vancouver	0	
Apr.	22	Colorado	3	at	Vancouver	4	
Apr.	25	Vancouver	4	at	Colorado	5	OT
Apr.	27	Colorado	3	at	Vancouver	2	

Colorado won best-of-seven series 4-2

Apr.	17	Calgary	1	at	Chicago	4	
Apr.	19	Calgary	0	at	Chicago	3	
Apr.	21	Chicago	7	at	Calgary	5	
Apr.	23	Chicago	2	at	Calgary	1	3OT

Chicago won best-of-seven series 4-0

Apr.	16	St. Louis	3	at	Toronto	1	
Apr.	18	St. Louis	4	at	Toronto	5	OT
Apr.	21	Toronto	2	at	St. Louis	3	OT
Apr.	23	Toronto	1	at	St. Louis	5	
Apr.	25	St. Louis	4	at	Toronto	5	OT
Apr.	27	Toronto	1	at	St. Louis	2	

St. Louis won best-of-seven series 4-2

CONFERENCE SEMI-FINALS

May	2	Florida	2	at	Philadelphia	0	
May	4	Florida	2	at	Philadelphia	3	
May	7	Philadelphia	3	at	Florida	1	
May	9	Philadelphia	3	at	Florida	4	OT
May	12	Florida	2	at	Philadelphia	1	2OT
May	14	Philadelphia	1	at	Florida	4	

Florida won best-of-seven series 4-2

May	3	NY Rangers	3	at	Pittsburgh	4
May	5	NY Rangers	6	at	Pittsburgh	3
May	7	Pittsburgh	3	at	NY Rangers	2
May	9	Pittsburgh	4	at	NY Rangers	1
May	11	NY Rangers	3	at	Pittsburgh	7

Pittsburgh won best-of-seven series 4-1

May	3	St. Louis	2	at	Detroit	3	
May	5	St. Louis	3	at	Detroit	8	
May	8	Detroit	4	at	St. Louis	5	OT
May	10	Detroit	0	at	St. Louis	1	
May	12	St. Louis	3	at	Detroit	2	
May	14	Detroit	4	at	St. Louis	2	
May	16	St. Louis	0	at	Detroit	1	2OT

Detroit won best-of-seven series 4-3

May	2	Chicago	3	at	Colorado	2	OT
May	4	Chicago	1	at	Colorado	5	
May	6	Colorado	3	at	Chicago	4	OT
May	8	Colorado	3	at	Chicago	2	3OT
May	11	Chicago	1	at	Colorado	4	
May	13	Colorado	4	at	Chicago	3	2OT

Colorado won best-of-seven series 4-2

CONFERENCE FINALS

May	18	Florida	5	at	Pittsburgh	1
May	20	Florida	2	at	Pittsburgh	3
May	24	Pittsburgh	2	at	Florida	5
May	26	Pittsburgh	2	at	Florida	1
May	28	Florida	0	at	Pittsburgh	3
May	30	Pittsburgh	3	at	Florida	4
June	1	Florida	3	at	Pittsburgh	1

Florida won best-of-seven series 4-3

May	19	Colorado	3	at	Detroit	2	OT
May	21	Colorado	3	at	Detroit	0	
May	23	Detroit	6	at	Colorado	4	
May	25	Detroit	2	at	Colorado	4	
May	27	Colorado	2	at	Detroit	5	
May	29	Detroit	1	at	Colorado	4	

Colorado won best-of-seven series 4-2

FINALS

June	4	Florida	1	at	Colorado	3	
June	6	Florida	1	at	Colorado	8	
June	8	Colorado	3	at	Florida	2	
June	10	Colorado	1	at	Florida	0	3OT

Colorado won best-of-seven series 4-0

1995-96 – Colorado Avalanche – Joe Sakic (Captain), Rene Corbet, Adam Deadmarsh, Stephane Fiset, Adam Foote, Peter Forsberg, Alexei Gusarov, Dave Hannan, Valeri Kamensky, Mike Keane, Jon Klemm, Uwe Krupp, Sylvain Lefebvre, Claude Lemieux, Curtis Leschyshyn, Troy Murray, Sandis Ozolinsh, Mike Ricci, Patrick Roy, Warren Rychel, Chris Simon, Craig Wolanin, Stephane Yelle, Scott Young, Charlie Lyons (Chairman/CEO), Pierre Lacroix (Executive Vice President/General Manager), Marc Crawford (Head Coach), Joel Quenneville, Jacques Cloutier (Assistant Coaches), Francois Giguere (Assistant General Manager), Michel Goulet (Director of Player Personnel), Dave Draper (Chief Scout), Jean Martineau (Director of Public Relations), Pat Karns (Trainer), Matthew Sokolowski (Assistant Trainer), Rob McLean (Equipment Manager), Mike Kramer, Brock Gibbins (Assistant Equipment Managers), Skip Allen (Strength and Conditioning Coach), Paul Fixter (Video Coordinator), Leo Vyssokov (Massage Therapist).

LEADING PLAYOFF SCORERS

Player	Club	GP	G	A	PTS	PIM
Joe Sakic	Colorado	22	18	16	34	14
Mario Lemieux	Pittsburgh	18	11	16	27	33
Jaromir Jagr	Pittsburgh	18	11	12	23	18
Valeri Kamensky	Colorado	22	10	12	22	28
Peter Forsberg	Colorado	22	10	11	21	18
Petr Nedved	Pittsburgh	18	10	10	20	16
Steve Yzerman	Detroit	18	8	12	20	4
Sergei Fedorov	Detroit	19	2	18	20	10
Sandis Ozolinsh	Colorado	22	5	14	19	16
Dave Lowry	Florida	22	10	7	17	39
Mike Ricci	Colorado	22	6	11	17	18
Adam Deadmarsh	Colorado	22	5	12	17	25

LEADING PLAYOFF GOALTENDERS

Goaltender	Club	GPI	Mins	GA	SO	Avg.
Ed Belfour	Chicago	9	666	23	1	2.07
Patrick Roy	Colorado	22	1454	51	3	2.10
Chris Osgood	Detroit	15	936	33	2	2.12
Ron Hextall	Philadelphia	12	760	27	0	2.13
John Vanbiesbrouck	Florida	22	1332	50	1	2.25

PLAYOFF GOALS

Name, Team	G
Joe Sakic, Col.	18
Mario Lemieux, Pit.	11
Jaromir Jagr, Pit.	11
Petr Nedved, Pit.	10
Valeri Kamensky, Col.	10
Peter Forsberg, Col.	10
Dave Lowry, Fla.	10
Shayne Corson, St.L.	8
Steve Yzerman, Det.	8
Ray Sheppard, Fla.	8

PLAYOFF ASSISTS

Name, Team	A
Sergei Fedorov, Det.	18
Mario Lemieux, Pit.	16
Joe Sakic, Col.	16
Wayne Gretzky, St.L.	14
Sergei Zubov, Pit.	14
Sandis Ozolinsh, Col.	14
Jaromir Jagr, Pit.	12
Steve Yzerman, Det.	12
Valeri Kamensky, Col.	12
Adam Deadmarsh, Col.	12
Uwe Krupp, Col.	12
Scott Young, Col.	12

PLAYOFF POWERPLAY GOALS

Name, Team	PPG
Adam Graves, NYR	6
Shayne Corson, St.L.	6
Dino Ciccarelli, Det.	6
Joe Sakic, Col.	6
Jaromir Jagr, Pit.	5

PLAYOFF SHORTHAND GOALS

Name, Team	SHG
Paul Coffey, Det.	2
19 tied with	1

PLAYOFF GAME-WINNING GOALS

Name, Team	GWG
Joe Sakic, Col.	6
16 tied with	2

PLAYOFF GOALIE WINS

Name, Team	W
Patrick Roy, Col.	16
John Vanbiesbrouck, Fla.	12
Chris Osgood, Det.	8
Ken Wregget, Pit.	7
Three tied with	6

PLAYOFF SHUTOUTS

Name, Team	SO
Patrick Roy, Col.	3
Chris Osgood, Det.	2
Ed Belfour, Chi.	1
Tom Barrasso, Pit.	1
Jon Casey, St.L.	1

PLAYOFF SAVE PERCENTAGE

Name, Team	SV%
John Vanbiesbrouck, Fla.	.932
Ken Wregget, Pit.	.930
Ed Belfour, Chi.	.929
Tom Barrasso, Pit.	.923
Patrick Roy, Col.	.921

1996-97

Stanley Cup • Detroit Red Wings

Keith Tkachuk (left) was the first U.S.-born player to lead the NHL in goals when he scored 52 in 1996–97. He also joined John LeClair, Kevin Stevens and Jeremy Roenick (right) as the only players born in the USA to score 50 goals two years in a row.

FINAL STANDINGS

EASTERN CONFERENCE

Team	GP	W	L	T	GF	GA	PTS
Northeast Division							
Buffalo	82	40	30	12	237	208	92
Pittsburgh	82	38	36	8	285	280	84
Ottawa	82	31	36	15	226	234	77
Montreal	82	31	36	15	249	276	77
Hartford	82	32	39	11	226	256	75
Boston	82	26	47	9	234	300	61
Atlantic Division							
New Jersey	82	45	23	14	231	182	104
Philadelphia	82	45	24	13	274	217	103
Florida	82	35	28	19	221	201	89
NY Rangers	82	38	34	10	258	231	86
Washington	82	33	40	9	214	231	75
Tampa Bay	82	32	40	10	217	247	74
NY Islanders	82	29	41	12	240	250	70

WESTERN CONFERENCE

Team	GP	W	L	T	GF	GA	PTS
Central Division							
Dallas	82	48	26	8	252	198	104
Detroit	82	38	26	18	253	197	94
Phoenix	82	38	37	7	240	243	83
St. Louis	82	36	35	11	236	239	83
Chicago	82	34	35	13	223	210	81
Toronto	82	30	44	8	230	273	68
Pacific Division							
Colorado	82	49	24	9	277	205	107
Anaheim	82	36	33	13	245	233	85
Edmonton	82	36	37	9	252	247	81
Vancouver	82	35	40	7	257	273	77
Calgary	82	32	41	9	214	239	73
Los Angeles	82	28	43	11	214	268	67
San Jose	82	27	47	8	211	278	62

LEADING SCORERS

Player	Club	GP	G	A	PTS	PIM
Mario Lemieux	Pittsburgh	76	50	72	122	65
Teemu Selanne	Anaheim	78	51	58	109	34
Paul Kariya	Anaheim	69	44	55	99	6
John LeClair	Philadelphia	82	50	47	97	58
Wayne Gretzky	NY Rangers	82	25	72	97	28
Jaromir Jagr	Pittsburgh	63	47	48	95	40
Mats Sundin	Toronto	82	41	53	94	59
Ziggy Palffy	NY Islanders	80	48	42	90	43
Ron Francis	Pittsburgh	81	27	63	90	20
Brendan Shanahan	Hfd./Det.	81	47	41	88	131
Keith Tkachuk	Phoenix	81	52	34	86	228
Peter Forsberg	Colorado	65	28	58	86	73
Pierre Turgeon	Mtl./St.L.	78	26	59	85	14
Steve Yzerman	Detroit	81	22	63	85	78
Mark Messier	NY Rangers	71	36	48	84	88
Mike Modano	Dallas	80	35	48	83	42
Brett Hull	St. Louis	77	42	40	82	10
Doug Gilmour	Tor./N.J.	81	22	60	82	68
Adam Oates	Bos./Wsh.	80	22	60	82	14
Doug Weight	Edmonton	80	21	61	82	80
Vincent Damphousse	Montreal	82	27	54	81	82
Mark Recchi	Montreal	82	34	46	80	58

LEADING GOALTENDERS

Goaltender	Club	GPI	MINS	GA	SO	AVG
Martin Brodeur	New Jersey	67	3838	120	10	1.88
Andy Moog	Dallas	48	2738	98	3	2.15
Jeff Hackett	Chicago	41	2473	89	2	2.16
Dominik Hasek	Buffalo	67	4037	153	5	2.27
John Vanbiesbrouck	Florida	57	3347	128	2	2.29
Chris Osgood	Detroit	47	2769	106	6	2.30
Patrick Roy	Colorado	62	3698	143	7	2.32

THERE WERE MANY CHANGES throughout the 1996–97 season, beginning with the United States dethroning Canada as the top hockey nation at the inaugural World Cup of Hockey. Major trades this season involved Jeremy Roenick, Brendan Shanahan, Paul Coffey, Adam Oates, Bill Ranford, Ed Belfour and Doug Gilmour. Wayne Gretzky took his act to Broadway, signing as a free agent with the New York Rangers, and Mario Lemieux staged a farewell tour, retiring at season's end at the age of 31. Lemieux went out in style, winning the Art Ross Trophy for a sixth time with 122 points. Wayne Gretzky tied Lemieux for the league lead with 72 assists and added 25 goals to lead the Rangers in scoring with 97 points. Lemieux and Teemu Selanne were the only players to top 100 points in a season dominated by defense. The southward migration of NHL franchises also continued this year as the Winnipeg Jets moved to Phoenix, setting up shop as the Coyotes.

Goalies Galore – Marty Brodeur excelled with 10 shutouts, Dominik Hasek won the NHL's MVP award and Mike Vernon shone in the playoffs, helping Hockeytown USA erase 42 without a Cup title.

Goaltenders all around the league posted outstanding numbers, but Martin Brodeur of the New Jersey Devils was the most impressive. His 1.88 goals-against average was the lowest in the NHL since Tony Esposito's 1.77 in 1971–72 and his 10 shutouts made him the first to reach double digits since Ken Dryden in 1976–77. Brodeur and backup Mike Dunham shared the Jennings Trophy, but the Vezina Trophy went to Dominik Hasek. The Buffalo star also became the first goaltender since Jacques Plante in 1962 to win the Hart Trophy after leading the Sabres to a surprising first place finish in the Northeast.

The Sabres needed overtime in the seventh game to subdue an improved Ottawa Senators team in the first round of the playoffs. The Philadelphia Flyers—en route to the Stanley Cup finals—then eliminated the Sabres and the Rangers to advance.

In the Western Conference, the defending Stanley Cup champion Colorado Avalanche topped the NHL standings with 107 points. The Detroit Red Wings followed up their record-breaking season with an "ordinary" 94-point campaign and they had trouble getting past the St. Louis Blues to open the playoffs. A four-game sweep of the Mighty Ducks of Anaheim followed before the Red Wings avenged the previous spring's loss to the Avalanche with a six-game victory for the Western Conference championship. The Stanley Cup then returned to Detroit for the first time since 1955 as the Red Wings defeated the Philadelphia Flyers in four consecutive games. Goalie Mike Vernon won the Conn Smythe Trophy as playoff MVP.

Paul Kariya earned both the Lady Byng Trophy and a berth on the First All-Star Team for the second straight season in 1996–97. He also finished as the runner-up to Dominik Hasek for the Hart Trophy after leading Anaheim to the play-offs for the first time.

Leaders, 1996-97

GOALS

Name, Team	G
Keith Tkachuk, Phx.	52
Teemu Selanne, Ana.	51
Mario Lemieux, Pit.	50
John LeClair, Phi.	50
Ziggy Palffy, NYI	48
Jaromir Jagr, Pit.	47
Brendan Shanahan, Hfd./Det.	47
Peter Bondra, Wsh.	46
Paul Kariya, Ana.	44
Brett Hull, St.L.	42

ASSISTS

Name, Team	A
Mario Lemieux, Pit.	72
Wayne Gretzky, NYR	72
Ron Francis, Pit.	63
Steve Yzerman, Det.	63
Doug Weight, Edm.	61
Adam Oates, Bos./Wsh.	60
Doug Gilmour, Tor./N.J.	60
Pierre Turgeon, Mtl./St.L.	59
Peter Forsberg, Col.	58
Teemu Selanne, Ana.	58
Brian Leetch, NYR	58

POWERPLAY GOALS

Name, Team	PPG
Brendan Shanahan, Hfd./Det.	20
Ryan Smyth, Edm.	20
Paul Kariya, Ana.	15
Mario Lemieux, Pit.	15
Andrei Kovalenko, Edm.	14
Keith Jones, Wsh./Col.	14
Ray Sheppard, Fla.	13
Sandis Ozolinsh, Col.	13
Mike Gartner, Phx.	13
Five tied with	12

SHORTHAND GOALS

Name, Team	SHG
Michael Peca, Buf.	6
Mark Messier, NYR	5
Trent Klatt, Phi.	5
Mike Modano, Dal.	5
Sheldon Kennedy, Bos.	4
Peter Forsberg, Col.	4
Peter Bondra, Wsh.	4
Todd Marchant, Edm.	4
Ziggy Palffy, NYI	4
Adam Graves, NYR	4
Mats Sundin, Tor.	4
Rob Zamuner, T.B.	4

GAME-WINNING GOALS

Name, Team	GWG
Paul Kariya, Ana.	10
Mark Messier, NYR	9
Mike Modano, Dal.	9
Bill Guerin, N.J.	9
Teemu Selanne, Ana.	8
Mats Sundin, Tor.	8
Nine tied with	7

GOALIE WINS

Name, Team	W
Patrick Roy, Col.	38
Martin Brodeur, N.J.	37
Dominik Hasek, Buf.	37
Mike Richter, NYR	33
Grant Fuhr, St.L.	33
Curtis Joseph, Edm.	32
Ron Hextall, Phi.	31
Nikolai Khabibulin, Phx.	30
Guy Hebert, Ana.	29
Andy Moog, Dal.	28

SHUTOUTS

Name, Team	SO
Martin Brodeur, N.J.	10
Patrick Roy, Col.	7
Nikolai Khabibulin, Phx.	7
Chris Osgood, Det.	6
Curtis Joseph, Edm.	6

SAVE PERCENTAGE

Name, Team	SV%
Dominik Hasek, Buf.	.930
Jeff Hackett, Chi.	.927
Martin Brodeur, N.J.	.927
Patrick Roy, Col.	.923
Guy Hebert, Ana.	.919
John Vanbiesbrouck, Fla.	.919

FIRST TEAM ALL-STARS

Name, Team	Position
Mario Lemieux, Pit.	C
Teemu Selanne, Ana.	RW
Paul Kariya, Ana.	LW
Brian Leetch, NYR	D
Sandis Ozolinsh, Col.	D
Dominik Hasek, Buf.	G

SECOND TEAM ALL-STARS

Name, Team	Position
Wayne Gretzky, NYR	C
Jaromir Jagr, Pit.	RW
John LeClair, Phi.	LW
Chris Chelios, Chi.	D
Scott Stevens, N.J.	D
Martin Brodeur, N.J.	G

ALL-ROOKIE TEAM

Name, Team	Position
Jarome Iginla, Cgy.	F
Jim Campbell, St.L.	F
Sergei Berezin, Tor.	F
Bryan Berard, NYI	D
Janne Niinimaa, Phi.	D
Patrick Lalime, Pit.	G

TROPHY WINNERS

Trophy	Awarded For	Winner	Team
Hart	MVP	Dominik Hasek	Buf.
Art Ross	Top Scorer	Mario Lemieux	Pit.
Norris	Top Defenseman	Brian Leetch	NYR
Calder	Top Rookie	Bryan Berard	NYI
Selke	Top Defensive Forward	Michael Peca	Buf.
Vezina	Top Goaltender	Dominik Hasek	Buf
Jennings	Fewest Goals Against	Martin Brodeur	N.J.
		Mike Dunham	N.J.
Adams	Top Coach	Ted Nolan	Buf.
Byng	Gentlemanly Conduct	Paul Kariya	Ana.
Masterton	Perseverance, Sportmanship	Tony Granato	S.J.
Pearson	NHLPA MVP	Dominik Hasek	Buf.
Conn Smythe	Playoff MVP	Mike Vernon	Det.
Patrick	Service to Hockey in U.S.	Seymour H. Knox III	
		Bill Cleary	
		Pat LaFontaine	
Clancy	Leadership On and Off Ice	Trevor Linden	Van.
Entry Draft	First Overall Selection	Joe Thornton	Bos.

NHL NOTEBOOK

TRANSACTIONS

- July 21, 1996 – New York Rangers announced the signing of free agent Wayne Gretzky.
- Oct. 9, 1996 – Detroit obtained Brendan Shanahan and Brian Glynn from Whalers for Keith Primeau, Paul Coffey and a 1997 first-round pick.
- Nov. 27, 1996 – Blues obtained Pavol Demitra from the Ottawa Senators in exchange for Christer Olsson.
- Mar. 1, 1997 – Washington obtained Adam Oates, Bill Ranford and Rick Tocchet from Boston for Jim Carey, Anson Carter, Jason Allison and Washington's third-round pick in 1997 Entry Draft.

RECORDS

- Jan. 15, 1997 – Rookie Patrick Lalime improved his career won-loss record to 13-0-2 as Pittsburgh defeated the Whalers 3-0 in Hartford. Lalime broke Bill Durnan's record for best start by a rookie goalie.
- Feb. 8, 1997 – Scotty Bowman became the first coach in history to win 1,000 NHL games as the Red Wings won 6-5 in overtime at Pittsburgh.
- Apr. 5, 1997 – Neal Broten set an all-time record for most career NHL games by a U.S.-born player as Dallas tied 3-3 at Los Angeles. Broten appeared in his 1,098th game, eclipsing Gordie Roberts' mark.
- Apr. 24, 1997 – Patrick Roy set an NHL record with his 89th career playoff win, passing former NY Islander Billy Smith as Colorado won 7-0 over the visiting Blackhawks in game five of the Western Conference quarter-finals.
- May 4, 1997 – Mark Messier broke Larry Robinson's NHL record for most playoff game when he appeared in his 228th career game in the Rangers 2-0 win over the Devils in game two of the Eastern Conference semi-finals in New Jersey.

MILESTONES

- Jan. 21, 1997 – Veteran defenseman Michel Petit set an NHL record by playing for his ninth different team when he suited up for his first game with the Flyers, a 3-3 tie against the Dallas Stars in Philadelphia.
- Oct. 12, 1996 – Washington's Dale Hunter became the first player in NHL history to record 300 goals and 3,000 penalty minutes in his career when he scored in a 4-3 loss to the visiting Los Angeles Kings.
- Dec. 22, 1996 – St. Louis' Brett Hull became part of the first father/son combo to each score 500 career goals when his 26th career hat trick led the Blues to a 7-4 win over the visiting Los Angeles Kings.
- Apr. 18, 1997 – Red Wings' Larry Murphy became the first defenseman to score playoff goals for five different NHL teams as Detroit won 2-1 over the visiting St. Louis Blues in game two of the Western Conference quarter-finals.

1997 Playoffs

CONFERENCE QUARTER-FINALS

Apr.	17	Montreal	2	at	New Jersey	5	
Apr.	19	Montreal	1	at	New Jersey	4	
Apr.	22	New Jersey	6	at	Montreal	4	
Apr.	24	New Jersey	3	at	Montreal	4	3OT
Apr.	26	Montreal	0	at	New Jersey	4	

New Jersey won best-of-seven series 4-1

Apr.	17	Ottawa	1	at	Buffalo	3	
Apr.	19	Ottawa	3	at	Buffalo	1	
Apr.	21	Buffalo	3	at	Ottawa	2	
Apr.	23	Buffalo	0	at	Ottawa	1	OT
Apr.	25	Ottawa	4	at	Buffalo	1	
Apr.	27	Buffalo	3	at	Ottawa	0	
Apr.	29	Ottawa	2	at	Buffalo	3	OT

Buffalo won best-of-seven series 4-3

Apr.	17	Pittsburgh	1	at	Philadelphia	5	
Apr.	19	Pittsburgh	2	at	Philadelphia	3	
Apr.	21	Philadelphia	5	at	Pittsburgh	3	
Apr.	23	Philadelphia	1	at	Pittsburgh	4	
Apr.	26	Pittsburgh	3	at	Philadelphia	6	

Philadelphia won best-of-seven series 4-1

Apr.	17	NY Rangers	0	at	Florida	3	
Apr.	20	NY Rangers	3	at	Florida	0	
Apr.	22	Florida	3	at	NY Rangers	4	OT
Apr.	23	Florida	2	at	NY Rangers	3	
Apr.	25	NY Rangers	3	at	Florida	2	OT

NY Rangers won best-of-seven series 4-1

Apr.	16	Chicago	0	at	Colorado	6	
Apr.	18	Chicago	1	at	Colorado	3	
Apr.	20	Colorado	3	at	Chicago	4	2OT
Apr.	22	Colorado	3	at	Chicago	6	
Apr.	24	Chicago	0	at	Colorado	7	
Apr.	26	Colorado	6	at	Chicago	3	

Colorado won best-of-seven series 4-2

Apr.	16	Edmonton	3	at	Dallas	5	
Apr.	18	Edmonton	4	at	Dallas	0	
Apr.	20	Dallas	3	at	Edmonton	4	OT
Apr.	22	Dallas	4	at	Edmonton	3	
Apr.	25	Edmonton	1	at	Dallas	0	2OT
Apr.	27	Dallas	3	at	Edmonton	2	
Apr.	29	Edmonton	4	at	Dallas	3	OT

Edmonton won best-of-seven series 4-3

Apr.	16	St. Louis	2	at	Detroit	0	
Apr.	18	St. Louis	1	at	Detroit	2	
Apr.	20	Detroit	3	at	St. Louis	2	
Apr.	22	Detroit	0	at	St. Louis	4	
Apr.	25	St. Louis	2	at	Detroit	5	
Apr.	27	Detroit	3	at	St. Louis	1	

Detroit won best-of-seven series 4-2

Apr.	16	Phoenix	2	at	Anaheim	4	
Apr.	18	Phoenix	2	at	Anaheim	4	
Apr.	20	Anaheim	1	at	Phoenix	4	
Apr.	22	Anaheim	0	at	Phoenix	2	
Apr.	24	Phoenix	5	at	Anaheim	2	
Apr.	27	Anaheim	3	at	Phoenix	2	OT
Apr.	29	Phoenix	0	at	Anaheim	3	

Anaheim won best-of-seven series 4-3

CONFERENCE SEMI-FINALS

May	2	NY Rangers	0	at	New Jersey	2	
May	4	NY Rangers	2	at	New Jersey	0	
May	6	New Jersey	2	at	NY Rangers	3	
May	8	New Jersey	0	at	NY Rangers	3	
May	11	NY Rangers	2	at	New Jersey	1	OT

NY Rangers won best-of-seven series 4-1

May	3	Philadelphia	5	at	Buffalo	3	
May	5	Philadelphia	2	at	Buffalo	1	
May	7	Buffalo	1	at	Philadelphia	4	
May	9	Buffalo	5	at	Philadelphia	4	OT
May	11	Philadelphia	6	at	Buffalo	3	

Philadelphia won best-of-seven series 4-1

May	2	Edmonton	1	at	Colorado	5	
May	4	Edmonton	1	at	Colorado	4	
May	7	Colorado	3	at	Edmonton	4	
May	9	Colorado	3	at	Edmonton	2	OT
May	11	Edmonton	3	at	Colorado	4	

Colorado won best-of-seven series 4-1

May	2	Anaheim	1	at	Detroit	2	OT
May	4	Anaheim	2	at	Detroit	3	3OT
May	6	Detroit	5	at	Anaheim	3	
May	8	Detroit	3	at	Anaheim	2	2OT

Detroit won best-of-seven series 4-0

CONFERENCE FINALS

May	16	NY Rangers	1	at	Philadelphia	3	
May	18	NY Rangers	5	at	Philadelphia	4	
May	20	Philadelphia	6	at	NY Rangers	3	
May	23	Philadelphia	3	at	NY Rangers	2	
May	25	NY Rangers	2	at	Philadelphia	4	

Philadelphia won best-of-seven series 4-1

May	15	Detroit	1	at	Colorado	2	
May	17	Detroit	4	at	Colorado	2	
May	19	Colorado	1	at	Detroit	2	
May	22	Colorado	0	at	Detroit	6	
May	24	Detroit	0	at	Colorado	6	
May	26	Colorado	1	at	Detroit	3	

Detroit won best-of-seven series 4-2

FINALS

May	31	Detroit	4	at	Philadelphia	2	
June	3	Detroit	4	at	Philadelphia	2	
June	5	Philadelphia	1	at	Detroit	6	
June	7	Philadelphia	1	at	Detroit	2	

Detroit won best-of-seven series 4-0

1996-97 – Detroit Red Wings – Steve Yzerman (Captain), Doug Brown, Mathieu Dandenault, Kris Draper, Sergei Fedorov, Viacheslav Fetisov, Kevin Hodson, Tomas Holmstrom, Joe Kocur, Vladimir Konstantinov, Vyacheslav Kozlov, Martin Lapointe, Igor Larionov, Nicklas Lidstrom, Kirk Maltby, Darren McCarty, Larry Murphy, Chris Osgood, Jamie Pushor, Bob Rouse, Tomas Sandstrom, Brendan Shanahan, Tim Taylor, Mike Vernon, Aaron Ward, Mike Ilitch (Owner/Chairman), Marian Ilitch (Owner), Atanas Ilitch, Christopher Ilitch (Vice Presidents), Denise Ilitch Lites, Ronald Ilitch, Michael Ilitch, Jr., Lisa Ilitch Murray, Carole Ilitch Trepeck, Jim Devellano (Senior Vice President), Scotty Bowman (Head Coach/Director of Player Personnel), Ken Holland (Assistant General Manager), Barry Smith, Dave Lewis (Associate Coaches), Mike Krushelnyski (Assistant Coach), Jim Nill (Director of Player Development), Dan Belisle, Mark Howe (Pro Scouts), Hakan Andersson (Director of European Scouting), John Wharton (Athletic Trainer), Paul Boyer (Equipment Manager), Tim Abbott (Assistant Equipment Manager), Sergei Mnatsakanov (Masseur).

LEADING PLAYOFF SCORERS

Player	Club	GP	G	A	PTS	PIM
Eric Lindros	Philadelphia	19	12	14	26	40
Joe Sakic	Colorado	17	8	17	25	14
Claude Lemieux	Colorado	17	13	10	23	32
Valeri Kamensky	Colorado	17	8	14	22	16
Rod Brind'Amour	Philadelphia	19	13	8	21	10
John LeClair	Philadelphia	19	9	12	21	10
Wayne Gretzky	NY Rangers	15	10	10	20	2
Sergei Fedorov	Detroit	20	8	12	20	12
Brendan Shanahan	Detroit	20	9	8	17	43
Peter Forsberg	Colorado	14	5	12	17	10
Sandis Ozolinsh	Colorado	17	4	13	17	24

LEADING PLAYOFF GOALTENDERS

Goaltender	Club	GPI	Mins	GA	SO	Avg.
Martin Brodeur	New Jersey	10	659	19	2	1.73
Mike Vernon	Detroit	20	1229	36	1	1.76
Ron Tugnutt	Ottawa	7	425	14	1	1.98
Guy Hebert	Anaheim	9	534	18	1	2.02
Mike Richter	NY Rangers	15	939	33	3	2.11

PLAYOFF GOALS

Name, Team	G
Claude Lemieux, Col.	13
Rod Brind'Amour, Phi.	13
Eric Lindros, Phi.	12
Wayne Gretzky, NYR	10
Esa Tikkanen, NYR	9
John LeClair, Phi.	9
Brendan Shanahan, Det.	9
Four tied with	8

PLAYOFF ASSISTS

Name, Team	A
Joe Sakic, Col.	17
Valeri Kamensky, Col.	14
Eric Lindros, Phi.	14
Sandis Ozolinsh, Col.	13
Peter Forsberg, Col.	12
John LeClair, Phi.	12
Janne Niinimaa, Phi.	12
Sergei Fedorov, Det.	12

PLAYOFF POWERPLAY GOALS

Name, Team	PPG
Valeri Kamensky, Col.	5
Paul Kariya, Ana.	4
Claude Lemieux, Col.	4
Eric Lindros, Phi.	4
John LeClair, Phi.	4
Rod Brind'Amour, Phi.	4
Vyacheslav Kozlov, Det.	4

PLAYOFF SHORTHAND GOALS

Name, Team	SHG
Todd Marchant, Edm.	3
Brian Rolston, N.J.	2
Rod Brind'Amour, Phi.	2
11 tied with	1

PLAYOFF GAME-WINNING GOALS

Name, Team	GWG
Claude Lemieux, Col.	4
Sergei Fedorov, Det.	4
Esa Tikkanen, NYR	3
John LeClair, Phi.	3
13 tied with	2

PLAYOFF GOALIE WINS

Name, Team	W
Mike Vernon, Det.	16
Patrick Roy, Col.	10
Mike Richter, NYR	9
Garth Snow, Phi.	8
Martin Brodeur, N.J.	5
Curtis Joseph, Edm.	5

PLAYOFF SHUTOUTS

Name, Team	SO
Mike Richter, NYR	3
Patrick Roy, Col.	3
Grant Fuhr, St.L.	2
Martin Brodeur, N.J.	2
Curtis Joseph, Edm.	2

PLAYOFF SAVE PERCENTAGE

Name, Team	SV%
Mike Richter, NYR	.932
Patrick Roy, Col.	.932
Guy Hebert, Ana.	.929
Martin Brodeur, N.J.	.929
Mike Vernon, Det.	.927

1997-98

Stanley Cup • Detroit Red Wings

FINAL STANDINGS

Team	GP	W	L	T	GF	GA	PTS
EASTERN CONFERENCE							
Northeast Division							
Pittsburgh	82	40	24	18	228	188	98
Boston	82	39	30	13	221	194	91
Buffalo	82	36	29	17	211	187	89
Montreal	82	37	32	13	235	208	87
Ottawa	82	34	33	15	193	200	83
Carolina	82	33	41	8	200	219	74
Atlantic Division							
New Jersey	82	48	23	11	225	166	107
Philadelphia	82	42	29	11	242	193	95
Washington	82	40	30	12	219	202	92
NY Islanders	82	30	41	11	212	225	71
NY Rangers	82	25	39	18	197	231	68
Florida	82	24	43	15	203	256	63
Tampa Bay	82	17	55	10	151	269	44
WESTERN CONFERENCE							
Central Division							
Dallas	82	49	22	11	242	167	109
Detroit	82	44	23	15	250	196	103
St. Louis	82	45	29	8	256	204	98
Phoenix	82	35	35	12	224	227	82
Chicago	82	30	39	13	192	199	73
Toronto	82	30	43	9	194	237	69
Pacific Division							
Colorado	82	39	26	17	231	205	95
Los Angeles	82	38	33	11	227	225	87
Edmonton	82	35	37	10	215	224	80
San Jose	82	34	38	10	210	216	78
Calgary	82	26	41	15	217	252	67
Anaheim	82	26	43	13	205	261	65
Vancouver	82	25	43	14	224	273	64

LEADING SCORERS

Player	Club	GP	G	A	PTS	PIM
Jaromir Jagr	Pittsburgh	77	35	67	102	64
Peter Forsberg	Colorado	72	25	66	91	94
Pavel Bure	Vancouver	82	51	39	90	48
Wayne Gretzky	NY Rangers	82	23	67	90	28
John LeClair	Philadelphia	82	51	36	87	32
Ziggy Palffy	NY Islanders	82	45	42	87	34
Ron Francis	Pittsburgh	81	25	62	87	20
Teemu Selanne	Anaheim	73	52	34	86	30
Jason Allison	Boston	81	33	50	83	60
Jozef Stumpel	Los Angeles	77	21	58	79	53
Peter Bondra	Washington	76	52	26	78	44
Theoren Fleury	Calgary	82	27	51	78	197
Adam Oates	Washington	82	18	58	76	36
Rod Brind'Amour	Philadelphia	82	36	38	74	54
Mats Sundin	Toronto	82	33	41	74	49
Mark Recchi	Montreal	82	32	42	74	51
Tony Amonte	Chicago	82	31	42	73	66
Alexei Yashin	Ottawa	82	33	39	72	24
Brett Hull	St. Louis	66	27	45	72	26
Eric Lindros	Philadelphia	63	30	41	71	134
Doug Weight	Edmonton	79	26	44	70	69

LEADING GOALTENDERS

Goaltender	Club	GPI	MINS	GA	SO	AVG
Ed Belfour	Dallas	61	3581	112	9	1.88
Martin Brodeur	New Jersey	70	4128	130	10	1.89
Tom Barrasso	Pittsburgh	63	3542	122	7	2.07
Dominik Hasek	Buffalo	72	4220	147	13	2.09
Ron Hextall	Philadelphia	46	2688	97	4	2.17
Trevor Kidd	Carolina	47	2685	97	3	2.17
Jamie McLennan	St. Louis	30	1658	60	2	2.17
Jeff Hackett	Chicago	58	3441	126	8	2.20

Steve Yzerman (left, with Sergei Fedorov) was a prolific scorer early in his career. In 1988–89, he established career highs and Red Wings single-season records with 65 goals, 90 assists and 155 points. The Wings improved as a club as Yzerman upgraded his defensive game.

THE 1997-98 SEASON saw the Red Wings win their second consecutive Stanley Cup title with a four-game sweep of the Washington Capitals. The Red Wings had been the third-best team during the regular season, posting 103 points to trail both the Dallas Stars and New Jersey Devils. Detroit's success had been a true team effort; their team total of 250 goals was the second-highest in the NHL (behind the St. Louis Blues' 256) despite the fact that no Detroit player finished among the NHL's top 20 scorers.

Jaromir Jagr was the league's leading scorer with 102 points. His total was the lowest to top the NHL in a full season since Stan Mikita's 87 points in 1967–68 and marked the first time since Bobby Orr in 1969–70 that only one NHL player had more than 100 points. Jagr's strong play helped the Pitts-burgh Penguins to a surprising first-place finish in the Northeast Division in the first season following the retirement of Mario Lemieux. Jagr also helped the Czech Republic win a gold medal in hockey at the Winter Olympics in Nagano, Japan.

Little Stevie Y – After years of standing in the shadows in Motown, Steve Yzerman's unselfish and determined leadership brought another Cup title to Detroit.

The participation of NHL players at the Winter Olympics resulted in the most evenly matched hockey competition in Winter Games history. North American fans were disappointed by the early elimination of the United States and by Canada's fourth-place finish. The Russians, led by Pavel Bure, appeared headed for the gold until they ran into Dominik Hasek in the championship game. Hasek blanked Russia 1–0 to clinch the Czech Republic's first Olympic gold medal.

Hasek enjoyed another brilliant season in 1997–98. He shook off a slow start to lead the NHL with 13 shutouts, and his 33 wins and 2.09 goals-against average also ranked among the leaders. With his second consecutive Hart Trophy win, he became the first goalie to earn multiple MVP awards. Hasek's play led Buffalo to the Eastern Conference finals, where the Sabres lost to Washington in six games. Upsets had marked the Eastern playoffs, particularly in the first round where the Sabres knocked off the Philadelphia Flyers, the Canadiens surprised Pittsburgh, and the Ottawa Senators stunned the Devils.

The playoffs went more according to form in the west, as Detroit defeated Phoenix and St. Louis to meet a Dallas team that had knocked off the San Jose Sharks and Edmonton Oilers. The Western Conference final matchup of the defending Cup champion (Detroit) against the league's best club in the regular season (Dallas) was compelling, but the Red Wings, led by captain Steve Yzerman, eliminated the Stars in six games.

The Buffalo Sabres saluted Dominik Hasek's gold medal victory with the Czech Republic when NHL action resumed following the Olympic break in late February of 1998.

Leaders, 1997-98

GOALS

Name, Team	G
Teemu Selanne, Ana.	52
Peter Bondra, Wsh.	52
Pavel Bure, Van.	51
John LeClair, Phi.	51
Ziggy Palffy, NYI	45
Keith Tkachuk, Phx.	40
Joe Nieuwendyk, Dal.	39
Rod Brind'Amour, Phi.	36
Jaromir Jagr, Pit.	35
Four tied with	33

ASSISTS

Name, Team	A
Jaromir Jagr, Pit.	67
Wayne Gretzky, NYR	67
Peter Forsberg, Col.	66
Ron Francis, Pit.	62
Jozef Stumpel, L.A.	58
Adam Oates, Wsh.	58
Theoren Fleury, Cgy.	51
Jason Allison, Bos.	50
Sergei Zubov, Dal.	47
Pierre Turgeon, St.L.	46

POWERPLAY GOALS

Name, Team	PPG
Ziggy Palffy, NYI	17
John LeClair, Phi.	16
Brendan Shanahan, Det.	15
Stu Barnes, Pit.	15
Shayne Corson, Mtl.	14
Joe Nieuwendyk, Dal.	14
Kevin Hatcher, Pit.	13
Pavel Bure, Van.	13
Dmitri Khristich, Bos.	13
Joe Sakic, Col.	12
Ray Whitney, Edm./Fla.	12

SHORTHAND GOALS

Name, Team	SHG
Jeff Friesen, S.J.	6
Pavel Bure, Van.	6
Mike Modano, Dal.	5
Michael Peca, Buf.	5
Peter Bondra, Wsh.	5
Bob Corkum, Phx.	5
Seven tied with	4

GAME-WINNING GOALS

Name, Team	GWG
Peter Bondra, Wsh.	13
Joe Nieuwendyk, Dal.	11
Teemu Selanne, Ana.	10
Brendan Shanahan, Det.	9
John LeClair, Phi.	9
Keith Tkachuk, Phx.	8
Jaromir Jagr, Pit.	8
Jason Allison, Bos.	8
Pat Verbeek, Dal.	8
Rod Brind'Amour, Phi.	8
Bobby Holik, N.J.	8

GOALIE WINS

Name, Team	W
Martin Brodeur, N.J.	43
Ed Belfour, Dal.	37
Olaf Kolzig, Wsh.	33
Chris Osgood, Det.	33
Dominik Hasek, Buf.	33
Tom Barrasso, Pit.	31
Patrick Roy, Col.	31
Mike Vernon, S.J.	30
Byron Dafoe, Bos.	30
Nikolai Khabibulin, Phx.	30
John Vanbiesbrouck, Phi.	27
Mike Richter, NYR	27

SHUTOUTS

Name, Team	SO
Dominik Hasek, Buf	13
Martin Brodeur, N.J.	10
Ed Belfour, Dal.	9
Jeff Hackett, Chi.	8
Curtis Joseph, Edm.	8

SAVE PERCENTAGE

Name, Team	SV%
Dominik Hasek, Buf.	.932
Tom Barrasso, Pit.	.922
Trevor Kidd, Car.	.922
Olaf Kolzig, Wsh.	.920
Martin Brodeur, N.J.	.917
Jeff Hackett, Chi.	.917

FIRST TEAM ALL-STARS

Name, Team	Position
Peter Forsberg, Col.	C
Jaromir Jagr, Pit.	RW
John LeClair, Phi.	LW
Nicklas Lidstrom, Det.	D
Rob Blake, L.A.	D
Dominik Hasek, Buf.	G

SECOND TEAM ALL-STARS

Name, Team	Position
Wayne Gretzky, NYR	C
Teemu Selanne, Ana.	RW
Keith Tkachuk, Phx.	LW
Chris Pronger, St.L.	D
Scott Niedermayer, N.J.	D
Martin Brodeur, N.J.	G

ALL-ROOKIE TEAM

Name, Team	Position
Patrik Elias, N.J.	F
Mike Johnson, Tor.	F
Sergei Samsonov, Bos.	F
Derek Morris, Cgy.	D
Mattias Ohlund, Van.	D
Jamie Storr, L.A.	G

TROPHY WINNERS

Trophy	Awarded For	Winner	Team
Hart	MVP	Dominik Hasek	Buf.
Art Ross	Top Scorer	Jaromir Jagr	Pit.
Norris	Top Defenseman	Rob Blake	L.A.
Calder	Top Rookie	Sergei Samsonov	Bos.
Selke	Top Defensive Forward	Jere Lehtinen	Dal.
Vezina	Top Goaltender	Dominik Hasek	Buf
Jennings	Fewest Goals Against	Martin Brodeur	N.J.
Adams	Top Coach	Pat Burns	Bos.
Byng	Gentlemanly Conduct	Ron Francis	Pit
Masterton	Perseverance, Sportmanship	Jamie McLennan	St.L.
Pearson	NHLPA MVP	Dominik Hasek	Buf.
Conn Smythe	Playoff MVP	Steve Yzerman	Det
Patrick	Service to Hockey in U.S.	Peter Karmanos	
		Neal Broten	
		John Mayasich	
		Max McNab	
Clancy	Leadership On and Off Ice	Kelly Chase	St.L.
Bud Light	Best Plus/Minus	Chris Pronger	St.L.
Entry Draft	First Overall Selection	Vincent Lecavalier	T.B.

NHL NOTEBOOK

TRANSACTIONS

- June 26, 1997 – New Jersey Devils signed free agent John Madden.
- July 2, 1997 – Dallas Stars signed free agent Eddie Belfour.
- Aug. 7, 1997 – Pittsburgh Penguins signed Martin Straka as a free agent.
- Feb. 6, 1998 – Vancouver Canucks obtained Todd Bertuzzi, Bryan McCabe and a 1998 third-round draft pick from the Islanders in exchange for Trevor Linden.

RECORDS

- Oct. 19, 1997 – Pittsburgh goalie Tom Barrasso became the first U.S.-born goaltender to record 300 career wins; the milestone came in a 4-1 victory at Florida.
- Oct. 26, 1997 – Steve Yzerman passed Alex Delvecchio as the longest serving captain in NHL history (11 years, 12 games) as the Red Wings recorded a 5-1 win at Vancouver.
- Feb. 5, 1998 – Mike Gartner became the NHL's all-time leader in career games by a player who never won a Stanley Cup when he appeared in his 1,412th NHL game, a 6-2 Phoenix loss to the Flyers. Gartner broke the record set by Harry Howell (1,411 NHL games).
- Feb. 28, 1998 – Vancouver's Pavel Bure set an NHL record by scoring his third penalty shot goal of the season. It came in a 6-4 win over the visiting Ottawa Senators.

MILESTONES

- Oct. 3, 1997 – Vancouver beat Anaheim 3-2 at at Tokyo's Yoyogi Arena,in the first NHL game played outside North America.
- Nov. 27, 1997 – Michel Petit became the first player in NHL history to play for 10 different teams when he made his first appearance with the Phoenix Coyotes in a 4-1 loss to Dallas.
- Dec. 1, 1997 – Montreal Canadiens became the first team in history to play 5,000 NHL games when they took on the Pittsburgh Penguins in a 1-0 loss in Montreal. The loss gave the Canadiens a record of 2,625 wins, 1,603 losses and 772 ties since 1917.
- Dec. 22, 1997 – Detroit's Scotty Bowman became the first coach in NHL history to win 200 games with three different teams when the Red Wings beat the Bruins 4-2 at Boston. Bowman had previously won 200+ games with Montreal and Buffalo.

1998 Playoffs

CONFERENCE QUARTER-FINALS

Date	Visitor			Home	
Apr. 22	Ottawa	2	at	New Jersey	1 OT
Apr. 24	Ottawa	1	at	New Jersey	3
Apr. 26	New Jersey	1	at	Ottawa	2 OT
Apr. 28	New Jersey	3	at	Ottawa	4
Apr. 30	Ottawa	1	at	New Jersey	3
May 2	New Jersey	1	at	Ottawa	4

Ottawa won best-of-seven series 4-2

Date	Visitor			Home	
Apr. 23	Montreal	3	at	Pittsburgh	2 OT
Apr. 25	Montreal	1	at	Pittsburgh	4
Apr. 27	Pittsburgh	1	at	Montreal	3
Apr. 29	Pittsburgh	6	at	Montreal	3
May 1	Montreal	5	at	Pittsburgh	2
May 3	Pittsburgh	0	at	Montreal	3

Montreal won best-of-seven series 4-2

Date	Visitor			Home	
Apr. 22	Buffalo	3	at	Philadelphia	2
Apr. 24	Buffalo	2	at	Philadelphia	3
Apr. 27	Philadelphia	1	at	Buffalo	6
Apr. 29	Philadelphia	1	at	Buffalo	4
May 1	Buffalo	3	at	Philadelphia	2 OT

Buffalo won best-of-seven series 4-1

Date	Visitor			Home	
Apr. 22	Boston	1	at	Washington	3
Apr. 24	Boston	4	at	Washington	3 2OT
Apr. 26	Washington	3	at	Boston	2 2OT
Apr. 28	Washington	3	at	Boston	0
May 1	Boston	4	at	Washington	0
May 3	Washington	3	at	Boston	2 OT

Washington won best-of-seven series 4-2

Date	Visitor			Home	
Apr. 22	San Jose	1	at	Dallas	4
Apr. 24	San Jose	2	at	Dallas	5
Apr. 26	Dallas	1	at	San Jose	4
Apr. 28	Dallas	0	at	San Jose	1 OT
Apr. 30	San Jose	2	at	Dallas	3
May 2	Dallas	3	at	San Jose	2 OT

Dallas won best-of-seven series 4-2

Date	Visitor			Home	
Apr. 22	Edmonton	3	at	Colorado	2
Apr. 24	Edmonton	2	at	Colorado	5
Apr. 26	Colorado	5	at	Edmonton	4 OT
Apr. 28	Colorado	3	at	Edmonton	1
Apr. 30	Edmonton	3	at	Colorado	1
May 2	Colorado	0	at	Edmonton	2
May 4	Edmonton	4	at	Colorado	0

Edmonton won best-of-seven series 4-3

Date	Visitor			Home	
Apr. 22	Phoenix	3	at	Detroit	6
Apr. 24	Phoenix	7	at	Detroit	4
Apr. 26	Detroit	2	at	Phoenix	3
Apr. 28	Detroit	4	at	Phoenix	2
Apr. 30	Phoenix	1	at	Detroit	3
May 3	Detroit	5	at	Phoenix	2

Detroit won best-of-seven series 4-2

Date	Visitor			Home	
Apr. 23	Los Angeles	3	at	St. Louis	8
Apr. 25	Los Angeles	1	at	St. Louis	2
Apr. 27	St. Louis	4	at	Los Angeles	3
Apr. 30	St. Louis	2	at	Los Angeles	1

St. Louis won best-of-seven series 4-0

CONFERENCE SEMI-FINALS

Date	Visitor			Home	
May 7	Ottawa	2	at	Washington	4
May 9	Ottawa	1	at	Washington	6
May 11	Washington	3	at	Ottawa	4
May 13	Washington	2	at	Ottawa	0
May 15	Ottawa	0	at	Washington	3

Washington won best-of-seven series 4-1

Date	Visitor			Home	
May 8	Montreal	2	at	Buffalo	3 OT
May 10	Montreal	3	at	Buffalo	6
May 12	Buffalo	5	at	Montreal	4 2OT
May 14	Buffalo	3	at	Montreal	1

Buffalo won best-of-seven series 4-0

Date	Visitor			Home	
May 7	Edmonton	1	at	Dallas	3
May 9	Edmonton	2	at	Dallas	0
May 11	Dallas	1	at	Edmonton	0 OT
May 13	Dallas	3	at	Edmonton	1 May
16Edmonton		1	at	Dallas	2

Dallas won best-of-seven series 4-1

Date	Visitor			Home	
May 8	St. Louis	4	at	Detroit	2
May 10	St. Louis	1	at	Detroit	6
May 12	Detroit	3	at	St. Louis	2 2OT
May 14	Detroit	5	at	St. Louis	2
May 17	St. Louis	3	at	Detroit	1
May 19	Detroit	6	at	St. Louis	1

Detroit won best-of-seven series 4-2

CONFERENCE FINALS

Date	Visitor			Home	
May 23	Buffalo	2	at	Washington	0
May 25	Buffalo	2	at	Washington	3 OT
May 28	Washington	4	at	Buffalo	3 OT
May 30	Washington	2	at	Buffalo	0
June 2	Buffalo	2	at	Washington	1
June 4	Washington	3	at	Buffalo	2 OT

Washington won best-of-seven series 4-2

Date	Visitor			Home	
May 24	Detroit	2	at	Dallas	0
May 26	Detroit	1	at	Dallas	3
May 29	Dallas	3	at	Detroit	5
May 31	Dallas	2	at	Detroit	3
June 3	Detroit	2	at	Dallas	3 OT
June 5	Dallas	0	at	Detroit	2

Detroit won best-of-seven series 4-2

FINALS

Date	Visitor			Home	
June 9	Washington	1	at	Detroit	2
June 11	Washington	4	at	Detroit	5 OT
June 13	Detroit	2	at	Washington	1
June 16	Detroit	4	at	Washington	1

Detroit won best-of-seven series 4-0

1997-98 – Detroit Red Wings – Steve Yzerman (Captain), Doug Brown, Mathieu Dandenault, Kris Draper, Anders Eriksson, Sergei Fedorov, Viacheslav Fetisov, Brent Gilchrist, Kevin Hodson, Tomas Holmstrom, Mike Knuble, Joe Kocur, Vyacheslav Kozlov, Martin Lapointe, Igor Larionov, Nicklas Lidstrom, Jamie Macoun, Kirk Maltby, Darren McCarty, Dmitri Mironov, Larry Murphy, Chris Osgood, Bob Rouse, Brendan Shanahan, Aaron Ward, Mike Ilitch, (Owner/Chairman), Marian Ilitch (Owner), Atanas Ilitch, Christopher Ilitch (Vice Presidents), Denise Ilitch, Ronald Ilitch, Michael Ilitch, Jr., Lisa Ilitch Murray, Carole Ilitch Trepeck, Jim Devellano (Senior Vice President), Scotty Bowman (Head Coach), Ken Holland (General Manager), Don Waddell (Assistant General Manager), Barry Smith, Dave Lewis (Associate Coaches), Jim Bedard (Goaltending Consultant), Jim Nill (Director of Player Development), Dan Belisle, Mark Howe (Pro Scouts), Hakan Andersson (Director of European Scouting), Mark Leach (USA Scout), Moe McDonnell (Eastern Scout), Bruce Haralson (Western Scout), John Wharton (Athletic Trainer), Paul Boyer (Equipment Manager), Tim Abbott (Assistant Equipment Manager), Bob Huddleston (Masseur), Wally Crossman (Dressing Room Assistant).

LEADING PLAYOFF SCORERS

Player	Club	GP	G	A	PTS	PIM
Steve Yzerman	Detroit	22	6	18	24	22
Sergei Fedorov	Detroit	22	10	10	20	12
Tomas Holmstrom	Detroit	22	7	12	19	16
Nicklas Lidstrom	Detroit	22	6	13	19	8
Joe Juneau	Washington	21	7	10	17	8
Adam Oates	Washington	21	6	11	17	8
Martin Lapointe	Detroit	21	9	6	15	20
Larry Murphy	Detroit	22	3	12	15	2
Vyacheslav Kozlov	Detroit	22	6	8	14	10
Mike Modano	Dallas	17	4	10	14	12
Andrei Nikolishin	Washington	21	1	13	14	12

LEADING PLAYOFF GOALTENDERS

Goaltender	Club	GPI	Mins	GA	SO	Avg.
Ed Belfour	Dallas	17	1039	31	1	1.79
Curtis Joseph	Edmonton	12	716	23	3	1.93
Olaf Kolzig	Washington	21	1351	44	4	1.95
Dominik Hasek	Buffalo	15	948	32	1	2.03
Chris Osgood	Detroit	22	1361	48	2	2.12

PLAYOFF GOALS

Name, Team	G
Sergei Fedorov, Det.	10
Martin Lapointe, Det.	9
Jim Campbell, St.L.	7
Daniel Alfredsson, Ott.	7
Bill Guerin, Edm.	7
Matthew Barnaby, Buf.	7
Peter Bondra, Wsh.	7
Richard Zednik, Wsh.	7
Joe Juneau, Wsh.	7
Sergei Gonchar, Wsh.	7
Tomas Holmstrom, Det.	7

PLAYOFF ASSISTS

Name, Team	A
Steve Yzerman, Det.	18
Andrei Nikolishin, Wsh.	13
Nicklas Lidstrom, Det.	13
Tomas Holmstrom, Det.	12
Larry Murphy, Det.	12
Adam Oates, Wsh.	11
Mike Modano, Dal.	10
Joe Juneau, Wsh.	10
Sergei Fedorov, Det.	10
Igor Larionov, Det.	10

PLAYOFF POWERPLAY GOALS

Name, Team	PPG
Jim Campbell, St.L.	4
Bill Guerin, Edm.	4
Miroslav Satan, Buf.	4
10 tied with	3

PLAYOFF SHORTHAND GOALS

Name, Team	SHG
Jeremy Roenick, Phx.	2
Larry Murphy, Det.	2
18 tied with	1

PLAYOFF GAME-WINNING GOALS

Name, Team	GWG
Joe Juneau, Wsh.	4
Vyacheslav Kozlov, Det.	4
Michal Grosek, Buf.	3
13 tied with	2

PLAYOFF GOALIE WINS

Name, Team	W
Chris Osgood, Det.	16
Olaf Kolzig, Wsh.	12
Dominik Hasek, Buf.	10
Ed Belfour, Dal.	10
Grant Fuhr, St.L.	6

PLAYOFF SHUTOUTS

Name, Team	SO
Olaf Kolzig, Wsh.	4
Curtis Joseph, Edm.	3
Chris Osgood, Det.	2
Five tied with	1

PLAYOFF SAVE PERCENTAGE

Name, Team	SV%
Olaf Kolzig, Wsh.	.941
Dominik Hasek, Buf.	.938
Curtis Joseph, Edm.	.928
Ed Belfour, Dal.	.922
Chris Osgood, Det.	.918

1998-99

Stanley Cup • Dallas Stars

FINAL STANDINGS

Team	GP	W	L	T	GF	GA	PTS
EASTERN CONFERENCE							
Northeast Division							
Ottawa	82	44	23	15	239	179	103
Toronto	82	45	30	7	268	231	97
Boston	82	39	30	13	214	181	91
Buffalo	82	37	28	17	207	175	91
Montreal	82	32	39	11	184	209	75
Atlantic Division							
New Jersey	82	47	24	11	248	196	105
Philadelphia	82	37	26	19	231	196	93
Pittsburgh	82	38	30	14	242	225	90
NY Rangers	82	33	38	11	217	227	77
NY Islanders	82	24	48	10	194	244	58
Southeast Division							
Carolina	82	34	30	18	210	202	86
Florida	82	30	34	18	210	228	78
Washington	82	31	45	6	200	218	68
Tampa Bay	82	19	54	9	179	292	47
WESTERN CONFERENCE							
Central Division							
Detroit	82	43	32	7	245	202	93
St. Louis	82	37	32	13	237	209	87
Chicago	82	29	41	12	202	248	70
Nashville	82	28	47	7	190	261	63
Pacific Division							
Dallas	82	51	19	12	236	168	114
Phoenix	82	39	31	12	205	197	90
Anaheim	82	35	34	13	215	206	83
San Jose	82	31	33	18	196	191	80
Los Angeles	82	32	45	5	189	222	69
Northwest Division							
Colorado	82	44	28	10	239	205	98
Edmonton	82	33	37	12	230	226	78
Calgary	82	30	40	12	211	234	72
Vancouver	82	23	47	12	192	258	58

LEADING SCORERS

Player	Club	GP	G	A	PTS	PIM
Jaromir Jagr	Pittsburgh	81	44	83	127	66
Teemu Selanne	Anaheim	75	47	60	107	30
Paul Kariya	Anaheim	82	39	62	101	40
Peter Forsberg	Colorado	78	30	67	97	108
Joe Sakic	Colorado	73	41	55	96	29
Alexei Yashin	Ottawa	82	44	50	94	54
Theoren Fleury	Cgy./Col.	75	40	53	93	86
Eric Lindros	Philadelphia	71	40	53	93	120
John LeClair	Philadelphia	76	43	47	90	30
Pavol Demitra	St. Louis	82	37	52	89	16
Martin Straka	Pittsburgh	80	35	48	83	26
Mats Sundin	Toronto	82	31	52	83	58
Mike Modano	Dallas	77	34	47	81	44
Jason Allison	Boston	82	23	53	76	68
Tony Amonte	Chicago	82	44	31	75	60
Luc Robitaille	Los Angeles	82	39	35	74	54
Steve Yzerman	Detroit	80	29	45	74	42
Rod Brind'Amour	Philadelphia	82	24	50	74	47
Steve Thomas	Toronto	78	28	45	73	33

LEADING GOALTENDERS

Goaltender	Club	GPI	MINS	GA	SO	AVG
Ron Tugnutt	Ottawa	43	2508	75	3	1.79
Dominik Hasek	Buffalo	64	3817	119	9	1.87
Ed Belfour	Dallas	61	3536	117	5	1.99
Byron Dafoe	Boston	68	4001	133	10	1.99
Roman Turek	Dallas	26	1382	48	1	2.08
Nikolai Khabibulin	Phoenix	63	3657	130	8	2.13
John Vanbiesbrouck	Philadelphia	62	3712	135	6	2.18

Jaromir Jagr had been the first European player to win the Art Ross Trophy in 1994–95. He won it again four years in a row from 1998 through 2001, adding the Hart Trophy in 1999.

There were many compelling plot lines during the 1998-99 regular season: the realignment of the league into six divisions; the rebirth of the Toronto Maple Leafs; the rise to prominence of the Ottawa Senators; and the season-long excellence of the Dallas Stars. But, come the final week of the regular season, one story overshadowed them all.

On April 16, 1999, Wayne Gretzky announced his retirement from the NHL. He played his final game two days later. Gretzky retired with 894 goals and 1,963 assists for a total of 2,857 points. Those totals represent just three of the 61 NHL records that Wayne Gretzky holds or shares. His final goal on March 29, 1999, gave Gretzky 1,072 in his career (NHL and WHA, regular season and playoffs combined)—one more than Gordie Howe scored during his career.

Wayne Gretzky's New York Rangers lost the final game of The Great One's career, dropping 2–1 to the Pittsburgh Penguins. Jaromir Jagr scored the winning goal in overtime, and a gracious Gretzky spoke of the torch being passed. Jagr had a brilliant season, winning the Art Ross Trophy for the second straight season with 127 points (44 goals, 83 assists). He also knocked off Dominik Hasek for the Hart Trophy as MVP. Trailing Jagr in the scoring race were Mighty Ducks teammates Teemu Selanne (107 points) and Paul Kariya (101). Selanne's total included a league-leading 47 goals, which made him the first recipient of the new Maurice "Rocket" Richard Trophy. Kariya's season represented a significant comeback from serious injuries that had kept him out almost all of 1997–98.

> **Great One Gone – Gretzky retired, Jagr was a scoring sensation, Teemu Selanne won the first Maurice Richard Trophy and a determined Dallas team became Stars by bouncing Buffalo in the finals.**

The NHL's realignment for the 1998-99 season brought Toronto back into the Eastern Conference, where the surprising Maple Leafs battled the Ottawa Senators for top spot in the Northeast Division. Ottawa won out, topped only in the Conference by the Atlantic Division-leading New Jersey Devils. The new Southeast Division was won by the Carolina Hurricanes. Out west, the Detroit Red Wings won the Central Division, while the Colorado Avalanche topped the Northwest. The best team in the league was the Dallas Stars, who took the Pacific Division with a team-record 51 wins and 114 points. This marked the second straight year Dallas won the Presidents' Trophy.

It had been five years since the NHL's best regular-season team was also the league's playoff champion, but this year the Stars would not be denied. Dallas swept the Edmonton Oilers to open the playoffs, then defeated the St. Louis Blues before taking on Colorado. The Avalanche had knocked off the two-time defending Stanley Cup champions from Detroit in the second round, but then fell to Dallas in seven games.

The Eastern Conference playoffs saw Buffalo upset Ottawa, then beat Boston before toppling Toronto in five games. Dallas and Buffalo produced a competitive final series with the Stars needing six games to win. Brett Hull scored the Stanley Cup-winning goal with 5:09 left in the third overtime session, ending the second-longest game in the history of the Stanley Cup finals.

Mike Modano helped the Stars win the Stanley Cup in 1999. The next season, he finished among the NHL's top-10 scorers for the first time in his career.

Leaders, 1998-99

GOALS

Name, Team	G
Teemu Selanne, Ana.	47
Jaromir Jagr, Pit.	44
Alexei Yashin, Ott.	44
Tony Amonte, Chi.	44
John LeClair, Phi.	43
Joe Sakic, Col.	41
Eric Lindros, Phi.	40
Theoren Fleury, Cgy./Col.	40
Miroslav Satan, Buf.	40
Paul Kariya, Ana.	39
Luc Robitaille, L.A.	39

ASSISTS

Name, Team	A
Jaromir Jagr, Pit.	83
Peter Forsberg, Col.	67
Paul Kariya, Ana.	62
Teemu Selanne, Ana.	60
Joe Sakic, Col.	55
Wayne Gretzky, NYR	53
Eric Lindros, Phi.	53
Theoren Fleury, Cgy./Col.	53
Jason Allison, Bos.	53
Pavol Demitra, St.L.	52
Mats Sundin, Tor.	52

POWERPLAY GOALS

Name, Team	PPG
Teemu Selanne, Ana.	25
Alexei Yashin, Ott.	19
Adrian Aucoin, Van.	18
John LeClair, Phi.	16
Brett Hull, Dal.	15
Petr Sykora, N.J.	15
Markus Naslund, Van.	15
Pavol Demitra, St.L.	14
Tony Amonte, Chi.	14
Adam Graves, NYR	14

SHORTHAND GOALS

Name, Team	SHG
Joe Sakic, Col.	5
Scott Pellerin, St.L.	5
Brian Rolston, N.J.	5
Mike Modano, Dal.	4
Martin Straka, Pit.	4
Magnus Arvedson, Ott.	4
Radek Dvorak, Fla.	4
Nine tied with	3

GAME-WINNING GOALS

Name, Team	GWG
Brett Hull, Dal.	11
Pavol Demitra, St.L.	10
Joe Nieuwendyk, Dal.	8
Bobby Holik, N.J.	8
Sergei Samsonov, Bos.	8
Claude Lemieux, Col.	8
Michael Peca, Buf.	8
Tony Amonte, Chi.	8
11 tied with	7

GOALIE WINS

Name, Team	W
Martin Brodeur, N.J.	39
Ed Belfour, Dal.	35
Curtis Joseph, Tor.	35
Chris Osgood, Det.	34
Patrick Roy, Col.	32
Nikolai Khabibulin, Phx.	32
Byron Dafoe, Bos.	32
Guy Hebert, Ana.	31
Dominik Hasek, Buf.	30
Arturs Irbe, Car.	27
Tommy Salo, Edm.	27

SHUTOUTS

Name, Team	SO
Byron Dafoe, Bos.	10
Dominik Hasek, Buf.	9
Nikolai Khabibulin, Phx.	8
Arturs Irbe, Car.	6
John Vanbiesbrouck, Phi.	6
Garth Snow, Van.	6
Guy Hebert, Ana.	6

SAVE PERCENTAGE

Name, Team	SV%
Dominik Hasek, Buf.	.937
Byron Dafoe, Bos.	.926
Ron Tugnutt, Ott.	.925
Arturs Irbe, Car.	.923
Nikolai Khabibulin, Phx.	.923

FIRST TEAM ALL-STARS

Name, Team	Position
Peter Forsberg, Col.	C
Jaromir Jagr, Pit.	RW
Paul Kariya, Ana.	LW
Al MacInnis, St.L.	D
Nicklas Lidstrom, Det.	D
Dominik Hasek, Buf.	G

SECOND TEAM ALL-STARS

Name, Team	Position
Alexei Yashin, Ott	C
Teemu Selanne, Ana.	RW
John LeClair, Phi.	LW
Raymond Bourque, Bos.	D
Eric Desjardins, Phi.	D
Byron Dafoe, Bos.	G

ALL-ROOKIE TEAM

Name, Team	Position
Marian Hossa, Ott.	F
Tom Poti, Edm.	F
Sami Salo, Ott.	F
Chris Drury, Col.	D
Milan Hejduk, Col.	D
Jamie Storr, L.A.	G

TROPHY WINNERS

Trophy	Awarded For	Winner	Team
Hart	MVP	Jaromir Jagr	Pit.
Art Ross	Top Scorer	Jaromir Jagr	Pit.
Richard	Top Goal Scorer	Teemu Selanne	Ana.
Norris	Top Defenseman	Al MacInnis	St L
Calder	Top Rookie	Chris Drury	Col.
Selke	Top Defensive Forward	Jere Lehtinen	Dal.
Vezina	Top Goaltender	Dominik Hasek	Buf
Jennings	Fewest Goals Against	Ed Belfour Roman Turek	Dal
Adams	Top Coach	Jacques Martin	Ott.
Byng	Gentlemanly Conduct	Wayne Gretzky	NYR
Masterton	Perseverance, Sportmanship	John Cullen	T.B.
Pearson	NHLPA MVP	Jaromir Jagr	Pit.
Conn Smythe	Playoff MVP	Joe Nieuwendyk	Dal.
Patrick	Service to Hockey in U.S.	Harry Sinden 1998 U.S. Olympic Women's Team	
Clancy	Leadership On and Off Ice	Rob Ray	Buf.
Bud Light	Best Plus/Minus	John LeClair	Phi.
Entry Draft	First Overall Selection	Patrik Stefan	Atl.

NHL NOTEBOOK

TRANSACTIONS

- July 3, 1998 – Dallas Stars signed free agent Brett Hull.
- July 13, 1998 – Carolina Hurricanes signed free agent Ron Francis.
- July 15, 1998 – Toronto Maple Leafs signed free agent Curtis Joseph.
- Jan. 17, 1999 – Florida Panthers acquired Pavel Bure, Bret Hedican, Brad Ference and a conditional third-round draft pick from the Vancouver Canucks for Dave Gagner, Ed Jovanovski, Mike Brown, goaltender Kevin Weekes and a first-round draft pick.

RECORDS

- Oct. 10, 1998 – Detroit's Scotty Bowman matched an NHL record for coaches when he began his 27th year behind the bench (in a 2-1 Red Wings loss at Toronto). Bowman equaled the longevity mark of Dick Irvin.
- Feb. 5, 1999 – Larry Murphy played in his 1,447th game, breaking Tim Horton's NHL record for career games by a defenseman, as the Red Wings lost 3-1 to the visiting Colorado Avalanche.
- Feb. 11, 1999 – Buffalo's Randy Cunneyworth scored in a 5-2 win vs Montreal to set an NHL record for longest gap between goals with one team. His previous goal for the Sabres had been on Nov. 15, 1981 (a span of 17 years, two months, 27 days).
- Apr. 17, 1999 – New Jersey Devils set an NHL record with their 28th road win of the season, a 4-1 victory at Nashville. Devils broke the record of 27 road wins Montreal set in 1976-77 and 1977-78.

MILESTONES

- Feb. 10, 1999 – Los Angeles' Russ Courtnall played in his 1,000th NHL game in a 3-0 Kings loss at Phoenix. The milestone made Russ (along with Geoff) the first set of brothers in history to each play 1,000 career NHL games.
- Feb. 15, 1999 – Wayne Gretzky picked up five assists in the Rangers' 7-4 win against the Predators at Nashville to take a 1,000-point lead over Gordie Howe, the NHL's second all-time leading scorer.
- Feb. 21, 1999 – Ray Sheppard became the first player in NHL history to score 20 or more goals in a season for six different teams when he scored his 20th of the year for the Carolina Hurricanes in a 4-1 win over the visiting New York Islanders.
- Apr. 24, 1999 – Patrick Roy became the first goaltender in NHL history to win 100 playoff games as the Colorado Avalanche beat the Sharks 3-1 at San Jose in game one of the Western Conference quarter-finals.

1999 Playoffs

CONFERENCE QUARTER-FINALS

Apr.	22	Pittsburgh	1	at	New Jersey	3	
Apr.	24	Pittsburgh	4	at	New Jersey	1	
Apr.	25	New Jersey	2	at	Pittsburgh	4	
Apr.	27	New Jersey	4	at	Pittsburgh	2	
Apr.	30	Pittsburgh	3	at	New Jersey	4	
May	2	New Jersey	2	at	Pittsburgh	3	OT
May	4	Pittsburgh	4	at	New Jersey	2	

Pittsburgh won best-of-seven series 4-3

Apr.	21	Buffalo	2	at	Ottawa	1	
Apr.	23	Buffalo	3	at	Ottawa	2	2OT
Apr.	25	Ottawa	0	at	Buffalo	3	
Apr.	27	Ottawa	3	at	Buffalo	4	

Buffalo won best-of-seven series 4-0

Apr.	22	Boston	2	at	Carolina	0	
Apr.	24	Boston	2	at	Carolina	3	OT
Apr.	26	Carolina	3	at	Boston	2	
Apr.	28	Carolina	1	at	Boston	4	
Apr.	30	Boston	4	at	Carolina	3	2OT
May	2	Carolina	0	at	Boston	2	

Boston won best-of-seven series 4-2

Apr.	22	Philadelphia	3	at	Toronto	0	
Apr.	24	Philadelphia	1	at	Toronto	2	
Apr.	26	Toronto	2	at	Philadelphia	1	
Apr.	28	Toronto	2	at	Philadelphia	5	
Apr.	30	Philadelphia	1	at	Toronto	2	OT
May	2	Toronto	1	at	Philadelphia	0	

Toronto won best-of seven series 4-2

Apr.	21	Edmonton	1	at	Dallas	2	
Apr.	23	Edmonton	2	at	Dallas	3	
Apr.	25	Dallas	3	at	Edmonton	2	
Apr.	27	Dallas	3	at	Edmonton	2	3OT

Dallas won best-of-seven series 4-0

Apr.	24	Colorado	3	at	San Jose	1	
Apr.	26	Colorado	2	at	San Jose	1	OT
Apr.	28	San Jose	4	at	Colorado	2	
Apr.	30	San Jose	7	at	Colorado	3	
May	1	San Jose	2	at	Colorado	6	
May	3	Colorado	3	at	San Jose	2	OT

Colorado won best-of-seven series 4-2

Apr.	21	Anaheim	3	at	Detroit	5	
Apr.	23	Anaheim	1	at	Detroit	5	
Apr.	25	Detroit	4	at	Anaheim	2	
Apr.	27	Detroit	3	at	Anaheim	0	

Detroit won best-of-seven series 4-0

Apr.	22	St. Louis	3	at	Phoenix	1	
Apr.	24	St. Louis	3	at	Phoenix	4	OT
Apr.	25	Phoenix	5	at	St. Louis	4	
Apr.	27	Phoenix	2	at	St. Louis	1	
Apr.	30	St. Louis	2	at	Phoenix	1	OT
May	2	Phoenix	3	at	St. Louis	5	
May	4	St. Louis	1	at	Phoenix	0	OT

St. Louis won best-of-seven series 4-3

CONFERENCE SEMI-FINALS

May	7	Pittsburgh	2	at	Toronto	0	
May	9	Pittsburgh	2	at	Toronto	4	
May	11	Toronto	3	at	Pittsburgh	4	
May	13	Toronto	3	at	Pittsburgh	2	OT
May	15	Pittsburgh	1	at	Toronto	4	
May	17	Toronto	4	at	Pittsburgh	3	OT

Toronto won best-of-seven series 4-2

May	6	Buffalo	2	at	Boston	4	
May	9	Buffalo	3	at	Boston	1	
May	12	Boston	2	at	Buffalo	3	
May	14	Boston	0	at	Buffalo	3	
May	16	Buffalo	3	at	Boston	5	
May	18	Boston	2	at	Buffalo	3	

Buffalo won best-of-seven series 4-2

May	6	St. Louis	0	at	Dallas	3	
May	8	St. Louis	4	at	Dallas	5	OT
May	10	Dallas	2	at	St. Louis	3	OT
May	12	Dallas	2	at	St. Louis	3	OT
May	15	St. Louis	1	at	Dallas	3	
May	17	Dallas	2	at	St. Louis	1	OT

Dallas won best-of-seven series 4-2

May	7	Detroit	3	at	Colorado	2	OT
May	9	Detroit	4	at	Colorado	0	
May	11	Colorado	5	at	Detroit	3	
May	13	Colorado	6	at	Detroit	2	
May	16	Detroit	0	at	Colorado	3	
May	18	Colorado	5	at	Detroit	2	

Colorado won best-of-seven series 4-2

CONFERENCE FINALS

May	23	Buffalo	5	at	Toronto	4	
May	25	Buffalo	3	at	Toronto	6	
May	27	Toronto	2	at	Buffalo	4	
May	29	Toronto	2	at	Buffalo	5	
May	31	Buffalo	4	at	Toronto	2	

Buffalo won best-of-seven series 4-1

May	22	Colorado	2	at	Dallas	1	
May	24	Colorado	2	at	Dallas	4	
May	26	Dallas	3	at	Colorado	0	
May	28	Dallas	2	at	Colorado	3	OT
May	30	Colorado	7	at	Dallas	5	
June	1	Dallas	4	at	Colorado	1	
June	4	Colorado	1	at	Dallas	4	

Dallas won best-of-seven series 4-3

FINALS

June	8	Buffalo	3	at	Dallas	2	OT
June	10	Buffalo	2	at	Dallas	4	
June	12	Dallas	2	at	Buffalo	1	
June	15	Dallas	1	at	Buffalo	2	
June	17	Buffalo	0	at	Dallas	2	
June	19	Dallas	2	at	Buffalo	1	3OT

Dallas won best-of-seven series 4-2

1998-99 – Dallas Stars – Derian Hatcher (Captain), Ed Belfour, Guy Carbonneau, Shawn Chambers, Benoit Hogue, Tony Hrkac, Brett Hull, Mike Keane, Jamie Langenbrunner, Jere Lehtinen, Craig Ludwig, Grant Marshall, Richard Matvichuk, Mike Modano, Joe Nieuwendyk, Derek Plante, Dave Reid, Jon Sim, Brian Skrudland, Blake Sloan, Darryl Sydor, Roman Turek, Pat Verbeek, Sergei Zubov, Thomas Hicks (Chairman of the Board/Owner), Jim Lites (Pres.), Bob Gainey (V.P., Hockey Ops/G.M.), Doug Armstrong (Asst. G.M.), Craig Button (Dir. of Player Personnel), Ken Hitchcock (Head Coach), Doug Jarvis, Rick Wilson (Asst. Coaches), Rick McLaughlin (V.P./CFO), Jeff Cogen (V.P., Marketing and Promotion), Bill Strong (V.P., Marketing and Broadcasting), Tim Bernhardt (Dir. of Amateur Scouting), Doug Overton (Dir. of Pro Scouting), Bob Gernander (Chief Scout), Stu MacGregor (Western Scout), Dave Suprenant (Medical Trainer), Dave Smith, Rich Matthews (Equipment Mgrs.), J.J. McQueen (Strength and Conditioning Coach), Rick St. Croix (Goaltending Consultant), Dan Stuchal (Dir. of Team Services), Larry Kelly (Dir. of Public Relations).

LEADING PLAYOFF SCORERS

Player	Club	GP	G	A	PTS	PIM
Peter Forsberg	Colorado	19	8	16	24	31
Mike Modano	Dallas	23	5	18	23	16
Joe Nieuwendyk	Dallas	23	11	10	21	19
Joe Sakic	Colorado	19	6	13	19	8
Jamie Langenbrunner	Dallas	23	10	7	17	16
Theoren Fleury	Colorado	18	5	12	17	20
Mats Sundin	Toronto	17	8	8	16	16
Brett Hull	Dallas	22	8	7	15	4
Martin Straka	Pittsburgh	13	6	9	15	6
Jason Woolley	Buffalo	21	4	11	15	10
Alexei Zhitnik	Buffalo	21	4	11	15	52

LEADING PLAYOFF GOALTENDERS

Goaltender	Club	GPI	Mins	GA	SO	Avg.
Ed Belfour	Dallas	23	1544	43	3	1.67
Dominik Hasek	Buffalo	19	1217	36	2	1.77
Byron Dafoe	Boston	12	768	26	2	2.03
Grant Fuhr	St. Louis	13	790	31	1	2.35
Curtis Joseph	Toronto	17	1011	41	1	2.43

PLAYOFF GOALS

Name, Team	G
Joe Nieuwendyk, Dal.	11
Jamie Langenbrunner, Dal.	10
Jere Lehtinen, Dal.	10
Steve Yzerman, Det.	9
Mats Sundin, Tor.	8
Peter Forsberg, Col.	8
Adam Deadmarsh, Col.	8
Brett Hull, Dal.	8
Curtis Brown, Buf.	7
Dixon Ward, Buf.	7
Stu Barnes, Buf.	7

PLAYOFF ASSISTS

Name, Team	A
Mike Modano, Dal.	18
Peter Forsberg, Col.	16
Joe Sakic, Col.	13
Theoren Fleury, Col.	12
Sergei Zubov, Dal.	12
Claude Lemieux, Col.	11
Jason Woolley, Buf.	11
Alexei Zhitnik, Buf.	11
Joe Nieuwendyk, Dal.	10
Six tied with	9

PLAYOFF POWERPLAY GOALS

Name, Team	PPG
Steve Yzerman, Det.	4
Alexei Zhitnik, Buf.	4
Stu Barnes, Buf.	4
Jamie Langenbrunner, Dal.	4
Nine tied with	3

PLAYOFF SHORTHAND GOALS

Name, Team	SHG
Vincent Damphousse, S.J.	2
Dixon Ward, Buf.	2
Eight tied with	1

PLAYOFF GAME-WINNING GOALS

Name, Team	GWG
Joe Nieuwendyk, Dal.	6
Chris Drury, Col.	4
Milan Hejduk, Col.	3
Dixon Ward, Buf.	3
Curtis Brown, Buf.	3
Jamie Langenbrunner, Dal.	3

PLAYOFF GOALIE WINS

Name, Team	W
Ed Belfour, Dal.	16
Dominik Hasek, Buf.	13
Patrick Roy, Col.	11
Curtis Joseph, Tor.	9
Byron Dafoe, Bos.	6
Grant Fuhr, St.L.	6
Tom Barrasso, Pit.	6

PLAYOFF SHUTOUTS

Name, Team	SO
Ed Belfour, Dal.	3
Byron Dafoe, Bos.	2
Dominik Hasek, Buf.	2
Seven tied with	1

PLAYOFF SAVE PERCENTAGE

Name, Team	SV%
Dominik Hasek, Buf.	.939
Ed Belfour, Dal.	.930
Byron Dafoe, Bos.	.921
Patrick Roy, Col.	.920
Curtis Joseph, Tor.	.907

99-2000

Stanley Cup • New Jersey Devils

FINAL STANDINGS

EASTERN CONFERENCE

Team	GP	W	L	T	OTL	GF	GA	PTS
Northeast Division								
Toronto	82	45	27	7	3	246	222	100
Ottawa	82	41	28	11	2	244	210	95
Buffalo	82	35	32	11	4	213	204	85
Montreal	82	35	34	9	4	196	194	83
Boston	82	24	33	19	6	210	248	73
Atlantic Division								
Philadelphia	82	45	22	12	3	237	179	105
New Jersey	82	45	24	8	5	251	203	103
Pittsburgh	82	37	31	8	6	241	236	88
NY Rangers	82	29	38	12	3	218	246	73
NY Islanders	82	24	48	9	1	194	275	58
Southeast Division								
Washington	82	44	24	12	2	227	194	102
Florida	82	43	27	6	6	244	209	98
Carolina	82	37	35	10	0	217	216	84
Tampa Bay	82	19	47	9	7	204	310	54
Atlanta	82	14	57	7	4	170	313	39

WESTERN CONFERENCE

Team	GP	W	L	T	OTL	GF	GA	PTS
Central Division								
St. Louis	82	51	19	11	1	248	165	114
Detroit	82	48	22	10	2	278	210	108
Chicago	82	33	37	10	2	242	245	78
Nashville	82	28	40	7	7	199	240	70
Pacific Division								
Dallas	82	43	23	10	6	211	184	102
Los Angeles	82	39	27	12	4	245	228	94
Phoenix	82	39	31	8	4	232	228	90
San Jose	82	35	30	10	7	225	214	87
Anaheim	82	34	33	12	3	217	227	83
Northwest Division								
Colorado	82	42	28	11	1	233	201	96
Edmonton	82	32	26	16	8	226	212	88
Vancouver	82	30	29	15	8	227	237	83
Calgary	82	31	36	10	5	211	256	77

LEADING SCORERS

Player	Club	GP	G	A	PTS	PIM
Jaromir Jagr	Pittsburgh	63	42	54	96	50
Pavel Bure	Florida	74	58	36	94	16
Mark Recchi	Philadelphia	82	28	63	91	50
Paul Kariya	Anaheim	74	42	44	86	24
Teemu Selanne	Anaheim	79	33	52	85	12
Owen Nolan	San Jose	78	44	40	84	110
Tony Amonte	Chicago	82	43	41	84	48
Mike Modano	Dallas	77	38	43	81	48
Joe Sakic	Colorado	60	28	53	81	28
Steve Yzerman	Detroit	78	35	44	79	34
Brendan Shanahan	Detroit	78	41	37	78	105
Jeremy Roenick	Phoenix	75	34	44	78	102
John LeClair	Philadelphia	82	40	37	77	36
Valeri Bure	Calgary	82	35	40	75	50
Pavol Demitra	St. Louis	71	28	47	75	8
Luc Robitaille	Los Angeles	71	36	38	74	68
Four players tied with					73	

LEADING GOALTENDERS

Goaltender	Club	GPI	MINS	GA	SO	AVG
Brian Boucher	Philadelphia	35	2038	65	4	1.91
Roman Turek	St. Louis	67	3960	129	7	1.95
Jose Theodore	Montreal	30	1655	58	5	2.10
Ed Belfour	Dallas	62	3620	127	4	2.10
John Vanbiesbrouck	Philadelphia	50	2950	108	3	2.20
Dominik Hasek	Buffalo	35	2066	76	3	2.21
Olaf Kolzig	Washington	73	4371	163	5	2.24
Martin Brodeur	New Jersey	72	4312	161	6	2.24

Scott Stevens was awarded to the New Jersey Devils as compensation when St. Louis signed Devils free agent Brendan Shanahan in 1991. Stevens was named captain of the Devils in 1992–93 and has led the team to three Stanley Cup titles. His hard hitting defensive style earned him the Conn Smythe Trophy in 2000.

In the first NHL season of the post-Gretzky era, Jaromir Jagr became the first player to lead the league in scoring for three consecutive seasons since Wayne won the Art Ross Trophy eight times in a row, starting in 1980–81. Though injuries limited Jagr to just 63 games, his 96 points were still two more than Pavel Bure, who led the league with 58 goals. The Russian Rocket won the Maurice "Rocket" Richard Trophy by a margin of 14 goals over Owen Nolan. Maurice Richard, the NHL's first 50-goal scorer, an icon in the province of Quebec and perhaps the game's most potent finisher, passed away on May 27, 2000 and was accorded a massive and dignified funeral in Montreal.

The Devils You Say – Scott Stevens anchored the blueline for an offensively weak but defensively dominant New Jersey club that overcame adversity and coaching controversy to win the championship.

Among the netminding fraternity, several new names emerged to join more familiar ones atop the 1999–2000 goaltenders statistics. Brian Boucher (1.91), Roman Turek (1.95) and Jose Theodore (2.10) finished 1–2–3 in goals-against average. Turek also topped the league with seven shutouts. Martin Brodeur led the league in wins (43) for the second straight season, while Ed Belfour edged out Theodore for the NHL's best save percentage at .919. Patrick Roy won 32 games to give him 444 victories in his career, three short of Terry Sawchuk's all-time record.

Philadelphia, New Jersey, Toronto and Washington were the top teams in the Eastern Conference. The Flyers edged out the Devils for top spot in the regular season but New Jersey rallied from a three-games-to-one deficit to eliminate Philadelphia in the Conference final. Earlier in the playoffs, the Flyers had defeated Pittsburgh 2–1 in a marathon game that needed 92 minutes of overtime before Keith Primeau potted the winner in a suddenly silent Igloo in Pittsburgh.

Out west, St. Louis won the Presidents' Trophy for the first time, but was eliminated by San Jose in the first round of the playoffs. Dallas won the Pacific Division, while Colorado added Raymond Bourque from Boston at the trade deadline and went on to finish first in the Northwest. The teams met in the Western Conference final with Dallas again winning in seven games. The Stanley Cup finals between the Devils and Stars opened with a 7–3 New Jersey win in game one and ended with New Jersey taking the series in six games. Jason Arnott scored the Cup-winning goal for the Devils in double overtime.

Not only did Chris Pronger win the Norris Trophy for 1999–2000, he became the first defenseman since Bobby Orr in 1972 to win the Hart Trophy as the NHL's MVP.

Leaders, 1999-2000

GOALS

Name, Team	G
Pavel Bure, Fla.	58
Owen Nolan, S.J.	44
Tony Amonte, Chi.	43
Jaromir Jagr, Pit.	42
Paul Kariya, Ana.	42
Brendan Shanahan, Det.	41
John LeClair, Phi.	40
Mike Modano, Dal.	38
Luc Robitaille, L.A.	36
Milan Hejduk, Col.	36

ASSISTS

Name, Team	A
Mark Recchi, Phi.	63
Adam Oates, Wsh.	56
Jaromir Jagr, Pit.	54
Joe Sakic, Col.	53
Viktor Kozlov, Fla.	53
Nicklas Lidstrom, Det.	53
Teemu Selanne, Ana.	52
Doug Weight, Edm.	51
Scott Gomez, N.J.	51
Ron Francis, Car.	50

POWERPLAY GOALS

Name, Team	PPG
Owen Nolan, S.J.	18
Mariusz Czerkawski, NYI	16
Steve Yzerman, Det.	15
Luc Robitaille, L.A.	13
Robert Lang, Pit.	13
Brendan Shanahan, Det.	13
Raymond Bourque, Bos./Col.	13
Valeri Bure, Cgy.	13
John LeClair, Phi.	13
Milan Hejduk, Col.	13

SHORTHAND GOALS

Name, Team	SHG
John Madden, N.J.	6
Tony Amonte, Chi.	5
Sergei Fedorov, Det.	4
Marco Sturm, S.J.	4
Owen Nolan, S.J.	4
Jeff Halpern, Wsh.	4
Nicklas Lidstrom, Det.	4
Michal Handzus, St.L.	4
Mike Keane, Dal.	4
Trevor Letowski, Phx.	4

GAME-WINNING GOALS

Name, Team	GWG
Pavel Bure, Fla.	14
Jeremy Roenick, Phx.	12
Patrik Elias, N.J.	9
Brendan Shanahan, Det.	9
Steve Thomas, Tor.	9
Milan Hejduk, Col.	9
Mike Modano, Dal.	8
12 tied with	7

GOALIE WINS

Name, Team	W
Martin Brodeur, N.J.	43
Roman Turek, St.L.	42
Olaf Kolzig, Wsh.	41
Curtis Joseph, Tor.	36
Arturs Irbe, Car.	34
Ed Belfour, Dal.	32
Patrick Roy, Col.	32
Chris Osgood, Det.	30
Guy Hebert, Ana.	28
Steve Shields, S.J.	27

SHUTOUTS

Name, Team	SO
Roman Turek, St.L.	7
Chris Osgood, Det.	6
Martin Brodeur, N.J.	6
Jose Theodore, Mtl.	5
Martin Biron, Buf.	5
Fred Brathwaite, Cgy.	5
Olaf Kolzig, Wsh.	5
Arturs Irbe, Car.	5

SAVE PERCENTAGE

Name, Team	SV%
Ed Belfour, Dal.	.919
Jose Theodore, Mtl.	.919
Dominik Hasek, Buf.	.919
Brian Boucher, Phi.	.918
Olaf Kolzig, Wsh.	.917
Mike Vernon, S.J./Fla.	.917

FIRST TEAM ALL-STARS

Name, Team	Position
Steve Yzerman, Det.	C
Jaromir Jagr, Pit.	RW
Brendan Shanahan, Det.	LW
Chris Pronger, St.L.	D
Nicklas Lidstrom, Det.	D
Olaf Kolzig, Wsh.	G

SECOND TEAM ALL-STARS

Name, Team	Position
Mike Modano, Dal	C
Pavel Bure, Fla.	RW
Paul Kariya, Ana.	LW
Rob Blake, L.A.	D
Eric Desjardins, Phi.	D
Roman Turek, St.L.	G

ALL-ROOKIE TEAM

Name, Team	Position
Simon Gagne, Phi.	F
Scott Gomez, N.J.	F
Michael York, NYR	F
Brian Rafalski, N.J.	D
Brad Stuart, S.J.	D
Brian Boucher, Phi.	G

TROPHY WINNERS

Trophy	Awarded For	Winner	Team
Hart	MVP	Chris Pronger	St.L.
Art Ross	Top Scorer	Jaromir Jagr	Pit.
Richard	Top Goal Scorer	Pavel Bure	FL.A.
Norris	Top Defenseman	Chris Pronger	St L
Calder	Top Rookie	Scott Gomez	N.J.
Selke	Top Defensive Forward	Steve Yzerman	Det.
Vezina	Top Goaltender	Olaf Kolzig	Wsh
Jennings	Fewest Goals Against	Roman Turek	St L
Crozier	Best Save %	Ed Belfour	Dal.
Adams	Top Coach	Joel Quenneville	St.L.
Byng	Gentlemanly Conduct	Pavol Demitra	St L
Masterton	Perseverance, Sportmanship	Ken Daneyko	N.J.
Pearson	NHLPA MVP	Jaromir Jagr	Pit.
Conn Smythe	Playoff MVP	Scott Stevens	N.J.
Patrick	Service to Hockey in U.S.	Mario Lemieux Craig Patrick Lou Vairo	
Clancy	Leadership On and Off Ice	Curtis Joseph	Tor.
Bud Light	Best Plus/Minus	Chris Pronger	St.L.
Entry Draft	First Overall Selection	Rick DiPietro	NYI

NHL NOTEBOOK

TRANSACTIONS

- June 18, 1999 – New Jersey Devils signed free agent defenseman Brian Rafalski.
- June 20, 1999 – L.A. Kings acquired Zigmund Palffy, Bryan Smolinski, Marcel Cousineau and a 1999 4th Rd Draft Pick from the NY Islanders for Olli Jokinen, Josh Green, Mathieu Biron and the Kings' first-round pick in the 1999 NHL Draft.
- Nov. 19, 1999 – Phoenix Coyotes acquired goaltender Sean Burke from the Florida Panthers in exchange for goaltender Mikhail Shtalenkov.
- Mar. 6, 2000 – Boston traded Raymond Bourque and Dave Andreychuk to Colorado in exchange for Brian Rolston, Martin Grenier, center Sammy Pahlsson and a future first-round draft pick.

RECORDS

- Dec. 6, 1999 – Toronto's Steve Thomas set an NHL record with his 10th career regular-season overtime goal when he scored at 1:05 of OT in a 3-2 win over the Buffalo Sabres. Thomas broke the record of nine OT goals held by Mario Lemieux.
- Feb. 21, 2000 – Buffalo's Dominik Hasek became the first European-trained goaltender to record 200 career NHL victories in a 3-2 win over the visiting New Jersey Devils.
- Apr. 15, 2000 – Red Wings won 8-5 over the visiting Kings in game two of the Western Conference quarter-finals. The teams combined for six goals in the first 6:56 of play, the fastest six goals to start a playoff game since modern record-keeping began in 1943-44.
- May 19, 2000 – Patrick Roy tied an NHL record with his 15th career play-off shutout (set by Clint Benedict in the 1920s) as the Avalanche won 2-0 over the visiting Dallas Stars in game three of the Western Conference finals.

MILESTONES

- June 21, 1999 – The NHL announced new rule changes for regular season overtime games (starting in 1999-2000): from now teams would play OT 4-on-4 (skaters) and each team would get one point for the tie, with an additional point going to the overtime winner.
- Oct. 2, 1999 – Boston's Raymond Bourque became the highest goal-scoring defenseman in NHL history when his 386th career goal moved him one ahead of Paul Coffey. The milestone came in a 3-1 loss to the visiting Carolina Hurricanes.
- Oct. 11, 1999 – Scott Stevens became the first player in NHL history to appear in 600 games with two different teams when he played for the Devils in a 2-2 tie at Ottawa.
- Jan. 2, 2000 – Scotty Bowman became the first coach in NHL history to coach in five different decades when his Detroit Red Wings lost to Pittsburgh 4-3.

2000 Playoffs

CONFERENCE QUARTER-FINALS

Apr. 13	Buffalo	2	at	Philadelphia	3	
Apr. 14	Buffalo	1	at	Philadelphia	2	
Apr. 16	Philadelphia	2	at	Buffalo	0	
Apr. 18	Philadelphia	2	at	Buffalo	3	OT
Apr. 20	Buffalo	2	at	Philadelphia	5	

Philadelphia won best-of-seven series 4-1

Apr. 13	Pittsburgh	7	at	Washington	0	
Apr. 15	Washington	1	at	Pittsburgh	2	OT
Apr. 17	Washington	3	at	Pittsburgh	4	
Apr. 19	Pittsburgh	2	at	Washington	3	
Apr. 21	Pittsburgh	2	at	Washington	1	

Pittsburgh won best-of-seven series 4-1

Apr. 12	Ottawa	0	at	Toronto	2	
Apr. 15	Ottawa	1	at	Toronto	5	
Apr. 17	Toronto	3	at	Ottawa	4	
Apr. 19	Toronto	1	at	Ottawa	2	
Apr. 22	Ottawa	1	at	Toronto	2	OT
Apr. 24	Toronto	4	at	Ottawa	2	

Toronto won best-of-seven series 4-2

Apr. 13	Florida	3	at	New Jersey	4
Apr. 16	Florida	1	at	New Jersey	2
Apr. 18	New Jersey	2	at	Florida	1
Apr. 20	New Jersey	4	at	Florida	1

New Jersey won best-of-seven series 4-0

Apr. 12	San Jose	3	at	St. Louis	5
Apr. 15	San Jose	4	at	St. Louis	2
Apr. 17	St. Louis	1	at	San Jose	2
Apr. 19	St. Louis	2	at	San Jose	3
Apr. 21	San Jose	3	at	St. Louis	5
Apr. 23	St. Louis	6	at	San Jose	2
Apr. 25	San Jose	3	at	St. Louis	1

San Jose won best-of-seven series 4-3

Apr. 12	Edmonton	1	at	Dallas	2
Apr. 13	Edmonton	0	at	Dallas	3
Apr. 16	Dallas	2	at	Edmonton	5
Apr. 18	Dallas	4	at	Edmonton	3
Apr. 21	Edmonton	2	at	Dallas	3

Dallas won best-of-seven series 4-1

Apr. 13	Phoenix	3	at	Colorado	6
Apr. 15	Phoenix	1	at	Colorado	3
Apr. 17	Colorado	4	at	Phoenix	2
Apr. 19	Colorado	2	at	Phoenix	3
Apr. 21	Phoenix	1	at	Colorado	2

Colorado won best-of-seven series 4-1

Apr. 13	Los Angeles	0	at	Detroit	2
Apr. 15	Los Angeles	5	at	Detroit	8
Apr. 17	Detroit	2	at	Los Angeles	1
Apr. 19	Detroit	3	at	Los Angeles	0

Detroit won best-of-seven series 4-0

CONFERENCE SEMI-FINALS

Apr. 27	Pittsburgh	2	at	Philadelphia	0	
Apr. 29	Pittsburgh	4	at	Philadelphia	1	
May 2	Philadelphia	4	at	Pittsburgh	3	OT
May 4	Philadelphia	2	at	Pittsburgh	1	5OT
May 7	Pittsburgh	3	at	Philadelphia	6	
May 9	Philadelphia	2	at	Pittsburgh	1	

Philadelphia won best-of-seven series 4-2

Apr. 27	New Jersey	1	at	Toronto	2
Apr. 29	New Jersey	1	at	Toronto	0
May 1	Toronto	1	at	New Jersey	5
May 3	Toronto	3	at	New Jersey	2
May 6	New Jersey	4	at	Toronto	3
May 8	Toronto	0	at	New Jersey	3

New Jersey won best-of-seven series 4-2

Apr. 28	San Jose	0	at	Dallas	4
Apr. 30	San Jose	0	at	Dallas	1
May 2	Dallas	1	at	San Jose	2
May 5	Dallas	5	at	San Jose	4
May 7	San Jose	1	at	Dallas	4

Dallas won best-of-seven series 4-1

Apr. 27	Detroit	0	at	Colorado	2	
Apr. 29	Detroit	1	at	Colorado	3	
May 1	Colorado	1	at	Detroit	3	
May 3	Colorado	3	at	Detroit	2	OT
May 5	Detroit	2	at	Colorado	4	

Colorado won best-of-seven series 4-1

CONFERENCE FINALS

May 14	New Jersey	4	at	Philadelphia	1
May 16	New Jersey	3	at	Philadelphia	4
May 18	Philadelphia	4	at	New Jersey	2
May 20	Philadelphia	3	at	New Jersey	1
May 22	New Jersey	4	at	Philadelphia	1
May 24	Philadelphia	1	at	New Jersey	2
May 26	New Jersey	2	at	Philadelphia	1

New Jersey won best-of-seven series 4-3

May 13	Colorado	2	at	Dallas	0	
May 15	Colorado	2	at	Dallas	3	
May 19	Dallas	0	at	Colorado	2	
May 21	Dallas	4	at	Colorado	1	
May 23	Colorado	2	at	Dallas	3	OT
May 25	Dallas	1	at	Colorado	2	
May 27	Colorado	2	at	Dallas	3	

Dallas won best-of-seven series 4-3

FINALS

May 30	Dallas	3	at	New Jersey	7	
June 1	Dallas	2	at	New Jersey	1	
June 3	New Jersey	2	at	Dallas	1	
June 5	New Jersey	3	at	Dallas	1	
June 8	Dallas	1	at	New Jersey	0	3OT
June 10	New Jersey	2	at	Dallas	1	2OT

New Jersey won best-of-seven series 4-2

1999-2000 – New Jersey Devils – Scott Stevens (Captain), Jason Arnott, Brad Bombardir, Martin Brodeur, Steve Brule, Sergei Brylin, Ken Daneyko, Patrik Elias, Scott Gomez, Bobby Holik, Steve Kelly, Claude Lemieux, John Madden, Vladimir Malakhov, Randy McKay, Alexander Mogilny, Sergei Nemchinov, Scott Niedermayer, Krzysztof Oliwa, Jay Pandolfo, Brian Rafalski, Ken Sutton, Petr Sykora, Chris Terreri, Colin White, Dr. John J. McMullen (Owner/Chairman), Peter S. McMullen (Owner), Lou Lamoriello (Pres./G.M.), Larry Robinson (Head Coach), Viacheslav Fetisov, Bob Carpenter (Asst. Coaches), Jacques Caron (Goaltending Coach), John Cuniff (AHL Coach), David Conte (Dir. of Scouting), Claude Carrier (Asst. Dir. of Scouting), Milt Fisher, Dan Labraaten, Marcel Pronovost (Scouts), Bob Hoffmeyer (Pro Scout), Dr. Barry Fisher (Orthopedist), Dennis Gendron (AHL Asst. Coach), Robbie Ftorek (Coach), Vladimir Bure (Consultant), Taran Singleton, Marie Carnevale, Callie Smith (Hockey Ops.), Bill Murray (Medical Trainer), Michael Vasalani (Strength/Conditioning Coord.), Dana McGuane (Equipment Mgr.), Juergen Merz (Massage Therapist), Harry Bricker, Lou Centanni (Asst. Equipment Mgrs.).

LEADING PLAYOFF SCORERS

Player	Club	GP	G	A	PTS	PIM
Brett Hull	Dallas	23	11	13	24	4
Mike Modano	Dallas	23	10	13	23	10
Jason Arnott	New Jersey	23	8	12	20	18
Patrik Elias	New Jersey	23	7	13	20	9
Mark Recchi	Philadelphia	18	6	12	18	6
Petr Sykora	New Jersey	23	9	8	17	10
Jaromir Jagr	Pittsburgh	11	8	8	16	6
Peter Forsberg	Colorado	16	7	8	15	12
Adam Deadmarsh	Colorado	17	4	11	15	21
Chris Drury	Colorado	17	4	10	14	4

LEADING PLAYOFF GOALTENDERS

Goaltender	Club	GPI	Mins	GA	SO	Avg.
Martin Brodeur	New Jersey	23	1450	39	2	1.61
Ron Tugnutt	Pittsburgh	11	746	22	2	1.77
Patrick Roy	Colorado	17	1039	31	3	1.79
Ed Belfour	Dallas	23	1443	45	4	1.87
Chris Osgood	Detroit	9	547	18	2	1.97

PLAYOFF GOALS

Name, Team	G
Brett Hull, Dal.	11
Mike Modano, Dal.	10
Petr Sykora, N.J.	9
Owen Nolan, S.J.	8
Jaromir Jagr, Pit.	8
Jason Arnott, N.J.	8
Peter Forsberg, Col.	7
Patrik Elias, N.J.	7
Joe Nieuwendyk, Dal.	7

PLAYOFF ASSISTS

Name, Team	A
Brett Hull, Dal.	13
Mike Modano, Dal.	13
Patrik Elias, N.J.	13
Mark Recchi, Phi.	12
Jason Arnott, N.J.	12
Adam Deadmarsh, Col.	11
Keith Primeau, Phi.	11
Chris Drury, Col.	10
Eric Desjardins, Phi.	10

PLAYOFF POWERPLAY GOALS

Name, Team	PPG
John LeClair, Phi.	4
Mike Modano, Dal.	4
Scott Young, St.L.	3
Mike Ricci, S.J.	3
Sandis Ozolinsh, Col.	3
Milan Hejduk, Col.	3
Brett Hull, Dal.	3
Joe Nieuwendyk, Dal.	3

PLAYOFF SHORTHAND GOALS

Name, Team	SHG
Owen Nolan, S.J.	2
Scott Niedermayer, N.J.	2
10 tied with	1

PLAYOFF GAME-WINNING GOALS

Name, Team	GWG
Jaromir Jagr, Pit.	4
Peter Forsberg, Col.	4
Brett Hull, Dal.	4
Owen Nolan, S.J.	3
Petr Sykora, N.J.	3

PLAYOFF GOALIE WINS

Name, Team	W
Martin Brodeur, N.J.	16
Ed Belfour, Dal.	14
Patrick Roy, Col.	11
Brian Boucher, Phi.	11
Ron Tugnutt, Pit.	6
Curtis Joseph, Tor.	6

PLAYOFF SHUTOUTS

Name, Team	SO
Ed Belfour, Dal.	4
Patrick Roy, Col.	3
Chris Osgood, Det.	2
Ron Tugnutt, Pit.	2
Martin Brodeur, N.J.	2

PLAYOFF SAVE PERCENTAGE

Name, Team	SV%
Ron Tugnutt, Pit.	.945
Curtis Joseph, Tor.	.932
Ed Belfour, Dal.	.931
Patrick Roy, Col.	.928
Martin Brodeur, N.J.	.927

2000-01

Stanley Cup • Colorado Avalanche

FINAL STANDINGS

EASTERN CONFERENCE

Team	GP	W	L	T	OTL	GF	GA	PTS
Northeast Division								
Ottawa	82	48	21	9	4	274	205	109
Buffalo	82	46	30	5	1	218	184	98
Toronto	82	37	29	11	5	232	207	90
Boston	82	36	30	8	8	227	249	88
Montreal	82	28	40	8	6	206	232	70
Atlantic Division								
New Jersey	82	48	19	12	3	295	195	111
Philadelphia	82	43	25	11	3	240	207	100
Pittsburgh	82	42	28	9	3	281	256	96
NY Rangers	82	33	43	5	1	250	290	72
NY Islanders	82	21	51	7	3	185	268	52
Southeast Division								
Washington	82	41	27	10	4	233	211	96
Carolina	82	38	32	9	3	212	225	88
Florida	82	22	38	13	9	200	246	66
Atlanta	82	23	45	12	2	211	289	60
Tampa Bay	82	24	47	6	5	201	280	59
WESTERN CONFERENCE								
Central Division								
Detroit	82	49	20	9	4	253	202	111
St. Louis	82	43	22	12	5	249	195	103
Nashville	82	34	36	9	3	186	200	80
Chicago	82	29	40	8	5	210	246	71
Columbus	82	28	39	9	6	190	233	71
Pacific Division								
Dallas	82	48	24	8	2	241	187	106
San Jose	82	40	27	12	3	217	192	95
Los Angeles	82	38	28	13	3	252	228	92
Phoenix	82	35	27	17	3	214	212	90
Anaheim	82	25	41	11	5	188	245	66
Northwest Division								
Colorado	82	52	16	10	4	270	192	118
Edmonton	82	39	28	12	3	243	222	93
Vancouver	82	36	28	11	7	239	238	90
Calgary	82	27	36	15	4	197	236	73
Minnesota	82	25	39	13	5	168	210	68

LEADING SCORERS

Player	Club	GP	G	A	PTS	PIM
Jaromir Jagr	Pittsburgh	81	52	69	121	42
Joe Sakic	Colorado	82	54	64	118	30
Patrik Elias	New Jersey	82	40	56	96	51
Alexei Kovalev	Pittsburgh	79	44	51	95	96
Jason Allison	Boston	82	36	59	95	85
Martin Straka	Pittsburgh	82	27	68	95	38
Pavel Bure	Florida	82	59	33	92	58
Doug Weight	Edmonton	82	25	65	90	91
Ziggy Palffy	Los Angeles	73	38	51	89	20
Peter Forsberg	Colorado	73	27	62	89	54
Alexei Yashin	Ottawa	82	40	48	88	30
Luc Robitaille	Los Angeles	82	37	51	88	66
Bill Guerin	Edm./Bos.	85	40	45	85	140
Mike Modano	Dallas	81	33	51	84	52
Alexander Mogilny	New Jersey	75	43	40	83	43
Pierre Turgeon	St. Louis	79	30	52	82	37
Adam Oates	Washington	81	13	69	82	28

LEADING GOALTENDERS

Goaltender	Club	GPI	MINS	GA	SO	AVG
Marty Turco	Dallas	26	1266	40	3	1.90
Roman Cechmanek	Philadelphia	59	3431	115	10	2.01
Manny Legace	Detroit	39	2136	73	2	2.05
Dominik Hasek	Buffalo	67	3904	137	11	2.11
Brent Johnson	St. Louis	31	1744	63	4	2.17
Evgeni Nabokov	San Jose	66	3700	135	6	2.19
Patrick Roy	Colorado	62	3585	132	4	2.21

Joe Sakic (seen here with Aaron Miller) has firmly established himself among the game's top players with the Avalanche. He finished third in scoring in 1995–96 when Colorado first won the Stanley Cup and was second in the league when the Avalanche won again in 2000–01.

It was a season of major milestones, achievements and accomplishments for many of the NHL's most respected veterans, capped off by a Stanley Cup victory for Raymond Bourque and the Colorado Avalanche. Bourque's first championship in the final season of his brilliant 22-year career was a fine finish to a campaign which had seen him surpass Paul Coffey as the top scoring defenseman in NHL history and joined Gordie Howe and Larry Murphy to become just the third player to take part in 1,600 regular-season games. Teammate Joe Sakic also enjoyed an excellent year, joining Mark Messier, Wayne Gretzky and Bobby Clarke as only the fourth man to captain his team to a Stanley Cup title and win the Hart Trophy in the same year. Sakic earned MVP honors in his 13th season. No other player in NHL history has captured the award for the first time so late in his career.

With 54 goals and 64 assists, Sakic finished just three points behind Jaromir Jagr (52 goals, 69 assists) in the race for the Art Ross Trophy. However, Jagr's fourth straight scoring title was only the second biggest story in Pittsburgh this year. On December 27, 2000, Mario Lemieux came down from the owner's box and returned to action as an active player. He set up a goal just 33 seconds into his first game and finished with a goal and two assists as the Penguins dumped the Maple Leafs 5–0. Lemieux played in just 43 games, but finished the year with 35 goals and 41 assists.

Goaltenders also made their mark in 2000–01, beginning with Patrick Roy who broke Terry Sawchuk's all-time record with his 448th regular-season victory on October 17. Roy won a career-high 40 games, second in the league behind Martin Brodeur's 42 victories, yet the Vezina Trophy went to Dominik Hasek for the sixth time. Hasek led the NHL with 11 shutouts and ranked high among the leaders in every other category.

Still, it was Roy and the Avalanche who were the NHL's best team with 118 points during the season. Inspired by Bourque's "Mission 16-W" (for the 16 victories needed to win the Cup), Colorado swept the Vancouver Canucks, then outlasted the surprising Los Angeles Kings in a tough seven-game series. A five-game victory over St. Louis in the Western Conference finals set up a Stanley Cup date with the defending champion Devils. New Jersey had finished first in the east with 111 points and had knocked off Carolina, Toronto and Pittsburgh. After absorbing a 5–0 defeat in game one of the finals, the Devils rebounded to take a 3–2 series lead, only to have Colorado storm back to win games six and seven. Raymond Bourque had his Cup, and Patrick Roy earned the Conn Smythe Trophy for a record third time.

Raymond's Reward – The NHL's all-time leading scorer among defensemen, Bourque left his heart in Boston, but experienced a Colorado hockey high by winning a Stanley Cup title with the Avalanche.

Sharks goalie Evgeni Nabokov was a rookie sensation during the 2000–01 season and a big reason why the Sharks won their first Pacific Division title in 2001–02.

Leaders, 2000-01

GOALS

Name, Team	G
Pavel Bure, Fla.	59
Joe Sakic, Col.	54
Jaromir Jagr, Pit.	52
Peter Bondra, Wsh.	45
Alexei Kovalev, Pit.	44
Alexander Mogilny, N.J.	43
Markus Naslund, Van.	41
Milan Hejduk, Col.	41
Jeff O'Neill, Car.	41
Four tied with	40

ASSISTS

Name, Team	A
Jaromir Jagr, Pit.	69
Adam Oates, Wsh.	69
Martin Straka, Pit.	68
Doug Weight, Edm.	65
Joe Sakic, Col.	64
Peter Forsberg, Col.	62
Jason Allison, Bos.	59
Brian Leetch, NYR	58
Patrik Elias, N.J.	56
Nicklas Lidstrom, Det.	56

POWERPLAY GOALS

Name, Team	PPG
Peter Bondra, Wsh.	22
Joe Thornton, Bos.	19
Joe Sakic, Col.	19
Pavel Bure, Fla.	19
Paul Kariya, Ana.	18
Markus Naslund, Van.	18
Keith Tkachuk, Phx./St.L.	17
Jeff O'Neill, Car.	17
Mario Lemieux, Pit.	16
Valeri Bure, Cgy.	16
Luc Robitaille, L.A.	16

SHORTHAND GOALS

Name, Team	SHG
Steve Sullivan, Chi.	8
Theoren Fleury, NYR	7
Wes Walz, Min.	7
Pavel Bure, Fla.	5
Todd Marchant, Edm.	4
Ziggy Palffy, L.A.	4
Peter Bondra, Wsh.	4
Peter Schaefer, Van.	4
Craig Conroy, St.L./Cgy.	4
20 tied with	3

GAME-WINNING GOALS

Name, Team	GWG
Joe Sakic, Col.	12
Jaromir Jagr, Pit.	10
Alexei Yashin, Ott.	10
Alexei Kovalev, Pit.	9
Milan Hejduk, Col.	9
Mark Recchi, Phi.	8
Ziggy Palffy, L.A.	8
Brett Hull, Dal.	8
Eric Daze, Chi.	8
Peter Bondra, Wsh.	8
Martin Lapointe, Det.	8
Pavel Bure, Fla.	8

GOALIE WINS

Name, Team	W
Martin Brodeur, N.J.	42
Patrick Roy, Col.	40
Dominik Hasek, Buf.	37
Olaf Kolzig, Wsh.	37
Arturs Irbe, Car.	37
Patrick Lalime, Ott.	36
Tommy Salo, Edm.	36
Roman Cechmanek, Phi.	35
Ed Belfour, Dal.	35
Curtis Joseph, Tor.	33

SHUTOUTS

Name, Team	SO
Dominik Hasek, Buf.	11
Roman Cechmanek, Phi.	10
Martin Brodeur, N.J.	9
Ed Belfour, Dal.	8
Tommy Salo, Edm.	8

SAVE PERCENTAGE

Name, Team	SV%
Marty Turco, Dal.	.925
Mike Dunham, Nsh.	.923
Sean Burke, Phx.	.922
Roman Cechmanek, Phi.	.921
Dominik Hasek, Buf.	.921

FIRST TEAM ALL-STARS

Name, Team	Position
Joe Sakic, Col.	C
Jaromir Jagr, Pit.	RW
Patrik Elias, N.J.	LW
Raymond Bourque, Col.	D
Nicklas Lidstrom, Det.	D
Dominik Hasek, Buf.	G

SECOND TEAM ALL-STARS

Name, Team	Position
Mario Lemieux, Pit.	C
Pavel Bure, Fla.	RW
Luc Robitaille, L.A.	LW
Rob Blake, L.A./Col.	D
Scott Stevens, N.J.	D
Roman Cechmanek, Phi.	G

ALL-ROOKIE TEAM

Name, Team	Position
Martin Havlat, Ott.	F
Brad Richards, T.B.	F
Shane Willis, Car.	F
Lubomir Visnovsky, L.A.	D
Colin White, N.J.	D
Evgeny Nabokov, S.J.	G

TROPHY WINNERS

Trophy	Awarded For	Winner	Team
Hart	MVP	Joe Sakic	Col.
Art Ross	Top Scorer	Jaromir Jagr	Pit.
Richard	Top Goal Scorer	Pavel Bure	FLA.
Norris	Top Defenseman	Nicklas Lidstrom	Det.
Calder	Top Rookie	Evgeni Nabokov	S.J.
Selke	Top Defensive Forward	John Madden	N.J.
Vezina	Top Goaltender	Dominik Hasek	Buf
Jennings	Fewest Goals Against	Dominik Hasek	Buf
Crozier	Best Save %	Marty Turco	Dal.
Adams	Top Coach	Bill Barber	Phi.
Byng	Gentlemanly Conduct	Joe Sakic	Col.
Masterton	Perseverance, Sportmanship	Adam Graves	NYR
Pearson	NHLPA MVP	Joe Sakic	Col.
Conn Smythe	Playoff MVP	Patrick Roy	Col.
Patrick	Service to Hockey in U.S.	Gary Bettman	
		Scotty Bowman	
		David Poile	
Clancy	Leadership On and Off Ice	Shjon Podein	Col.
Bud Light	Best Plus/Minus	Patrik Elias (tie)	N.J.
		Joe Sakic (tie)	Col.
Entry Draft	First Overall Selection	Ilya Kovalchuk	Atl.

NHL NOTEBOOK

TRANSACTIONS

- June 24, 2000 – New York Islanders traded Olli Jokinen and Roberto Luongo to the Florida Panthers in exchange for Oleg Kvasha and Mark Parrish.
- Feb. 21, 2001 – Colorado Avalanche obtained Rob Blake and Steven Reinprecht from the Los Angeles Kings for Adam Deadmarsh, Aaron Miller, two future draft picks and a player to be named later (Jared Aulin).
- Mar. 5, 2001 – Phoenix Coyotes traded goaltender Nikolai Khabibulin and Stan Neckar to Tampa Bay for Paul Mara, Mike Johnson, Ruslan Zainullin and a second-round draft choice.
- Mar. 13, 2001 – Phoenix Coyotes traded left wing Keith Tkachuk to the St. Louis Blues in exchange for center Michal Handzus, center Ladislav Nagy, the rights to center Jeff Taffe and a first-round pick.

RECORDS

- Oct. 17, 2000 – Patrick Roy set an NHL record for most wins by a goaltender, breaking Terry Sawchuk's record of 447, as Colorado won 4-3 in overtime at Washington.
- Apr. 5, 2001 – Adam Oates set an NHL record for most points (82) by a player age 38 or older in a 3-0 Capitals win over the visiting Florida Panthers. He broke the mark of 81 set by Johnny Bucyk at age 39.
- Apr. 16, 2001 – Colorado's Raymond Bourque set an NHL record by appearing in the playoffs for the 21st year as the Avalanche beat the Canucks 4-3 at Vancouver, in game three of the Western Conference quarter-finals. Bourque broke the mark of 20 years shared by Gordie Howe and Larry Robinson.

MILESTONES

- Oct. 25, 2000 – Raymond Bourque picked up two assists to become the highest scoring defenseman in NHL history. His 1,529th career point (in a 2-1 Colorado win over the visiting Nashville Predators) moved him ahead of Paul Coffey.
- Feb. 25, 2001 – Buffalo's Dominik Hasek became the first European goaltender to play in 500 career NHL games as he led the Sabres to a 5-2 win over the visiting Tampa Bay Lightning.
- May 29, 2001 – Patrick Roy became the first goaltender in NHL history to start in 100 straight playoff games for one team when the Avalanche lost 2-1 against the visiting New Jersey Devils, in game two of the Stanley Cup finals.

2001 Playoffs

CONFERENCE QUARTER-FINALS

Apr. 12 Carolina 1 at New Jersey 5
Apr. 15 Carolina 0 at New Jersey 2
Apr. 17 New Jersey 4 at Carolina 0
Apr. 18 New Jersey 2 at Carolina 3 OT
Apr. 20 Carolina 3 at New Jersey 2
Apr. 22 New Jersey 5 at Carolina 1
New Jersey won best-of-seven series 4-2

Apr. 13 Toronto 1 at Ottawa 0 OT
Apr. 14 Toronto 3 at Ottawa 0
Apr. 16 Ottawa 2 at Toronto 3 OT
Apr. 18 Ottawa 1 at Toronto 3
Toronto won best-of-seven series 4-0

Apr. 12 Pittsburgh 0 at Washington 1
Apr. 14 Pittsburgh 2 at Washington 1
Apr. 16 Washington 0 at Pittsburgh 3
Apr. 18 Washington 4 at Pittsburgh 3 OT
Apr. 21 Pittsburgh 2 at Washington 1
Apr. 23 Washington 3 at Pittsburgh 4 OT
Pittsburgh won best-of-seven series 4-2

Apr. 11 Buffalo 2 at Philadelphia 1
Apr. 14 Buffalo 4 at Philadelphia 3 OT
Apr. 16 Philadelphia 3 at Buffalo 2
Apr. 17 Philadelphia 3 at Buffalo 4 OT
Apr. 19 Buffalo 1 at Philadelphia 3
Apr. 21 Philadelphia 0 at Buffalo 8
Buffalo won best-of-seven series 4-2

Apr. 12 Vancouver 4 at Colorado 5
Apr. 14 Vancouver 1 at Colorado 2
Apr. 16 Colorado 4 at Vancouver 3 OT
Apr. 18 Colorado 5 at Vancouver 1
Colorado won best-of-seven series 4-0

Apr. 11 Los Angeles 3 at Detroit 5
Apr. 14 Los Angeles 0 at Detroit 4
Apr. 15 Detroit 1 at Los Angeles 2
Apr. 18 Detroit 3 at Los Angeles 4 OT
Apr. 21 Los Angeles 3 at Detroit 2
Apr. 23 Detroit 2 at Los Angeles 3 OT
Los Angeles won best-of-seven series 4-2

Apr. 11 Edmonton 1 at Dallas 2 OT
Apr. 14 Edmonton 4 at Dallas 3
Apr. 15 Dallas 3 at Edmonton 2 OT
Apr. 17 Dallas 1 at Edmonton 2
Apr. 19 Edmonton 3 at Dallas 4 OT
Apr. 21 Dallas 3 at Edmonton 1
Dallas won best-of-seven series 4-2

Apr. 12 San Jose 1 at St. Louis 3
Apr. 14 San Jose 1 at St. Louis 0
Apr. 16 St. Louis 6 at San Jose 3
Apr. 17 St. Louis 2 at San Jose 3
Apr. 19 San Jose 2 at St. Louis 3 OT
Apr. 21 St. Louis 2 at San Jose 1
St. Louis won best-of-seven series 4-2

CONFERENCE SEMI-FINALS

Apr. 26 Toronto 2 at New Jersey 0
Apr. 28 Toronto 5 at New Jersey 6 OT
May 1 New Jersey 3 at Toronto 2 OT
May 3 New Jersey 1 at Toronto 3
May 5 Toronto 3 at New Jersey 2
May 7 New Jersey 4 at Toronto 2
May 9 Toronto 1 at New Jersey 5
New Jersey won best-of-seven series 4-3

Apr. 26 Pittsburgh 3 at Buffalo 0
Apr. 28 Pittsburgh 3 at Buffalo 1
Apr. 30 Buffalo 4 at Pittsburgh 1
May 2 Buffalo 5 at Pittsburgh 2
May 5 Pittsburgh 2 at Buffalo 3 OT
May 8 Buffalo 2 at Pittsburgh 3 OT
May 10 Pittsburgh 3 at Buffalo 2 OT
Pittsburgh won best-of-seven series 4-3

Apr. 26 Los Angeles 4 at Colorado 3 OT
Apr. 28 Los Angeles 0 at Colorado 2
Apr. 30 Colorado 4 at Los Angeles 3
May 2 Colorado 3 at Los Angeles 0
May 4 Los Angeles 1 at Colorado 0
May 6 Colorado 0 at Los Angeles 1 2OT
May 9 Los Angeles 1 at Colorado 5
Colorado won best-of-seven series 4-3

Apr. 27 St. Louis 4 at Dallas 2
Apr. 29 St. Louis 2 at Dallas 1
May 1 Dallas 2 at St. Louis 3 2OT
May 3 Dallas 1 at St. Louis 4
St. Louis won best-of-seven series 4-0

May 12 Pittsburgh 1 at New Jersey 3
May 15 Pittsburgh 4 at New Jersey 2
May 17 New Jersey 3 at Pittsburgh 0
May 19 New Jersey 5 at Pittsburgh 0
May 22 Pittsburgh 2 at New Jersey 4
New Jersey won best-of-seven series 4-1

May 12 St. Louis 1 at Colorado 4
May 14 St. Louis 2 at Colorado 4
May 16 Colorado 3 at St. Louis 4 2OT
May 18 Colorado 4 at St. Louis 3 OT
May 21 St. Louis 1 at Colorado 2 OT
Colorado won best-of-seven series 4-1

FINALS

May 26 New Jersey 0 at Colorado 5
May 29 New Jersey 2 at Colorado 1
May 31 Colorado 3 at New Jersey 1
June 2 Colorado 2 at New Jersey 3
June 4 New Jersey 4 at Colorado 1
June 7 Colorado 4 at New Jersey 0
June 9 New Jersey 1 at Colorado 3
Colorado won best-of-seven series 4-3

2000-01 – Colorado Avalanche – Joe Sakic (Captain), David Aebischer, Rob Blake, Raymond Bourque, Greg de Vries, Chris Dingman, Chris Drury, Adam Foote, Peter Forsberg, Milan Hejduk, Dan Hinote, Jon Klemm, Eric Messier, Bryan Muir, Ville Nieminen, Scott Parker, Shjon Podein, Nolan Pratt, Dave Reid, Steve Reinprecht, Patrick Roy, Martin Skoula, Alex Tanguay, Stephane Yelle, E. Stanley Kroenke (Owner/Gov.), Pierre Lacroix (Pres./G.M.), Bob Hartley (Head Coach), Bryan Trottier, Jacques Cloutier (Asst. Coaches), Paul Fixter (Video Coach), Francois Giguere (V.P., Hockey Ops.), Brian McDonald (Asst. G.M.), Michel Goulet (V.P., Player Personnel), Jean Martineau (V.P., Communications/Team Services), Pat Karns (Head Trainer), Matthew Sokolowski (Asst. Trainer), Wayne Flemming, Mark Miller (Equipment Mgrs.), Dave Randolph (Assistant Equipment Mgr.), Paul Goldberg (Strength and Conditioning Coach), Gregorio Pradera (Massage Therapist), Brad Smith (Pro Scout), Jim Hammett (Chief Scout), Garth Joy, Steve Lyons, Joni Lehto, Orval Tessier (Scouts), Charlotte Grahame (Dir. of Hockey Admin.).

LEADING PLAYOFF SCORERS

Player	Club	GP	G	A	PTS	PIM
Joe Sakic	Colorado	21	13	13	26	6
Patrik Elias	New Jersey	25	9	14	23	10
Milan Hejduk	Colorado	23	7	16	23	6
Petr Sykora	New Jersey	25	10	12	22	12
Alex Tanguay	Colorado	23	6	15	21	8
Rob Blake	Colorado	23	6	13	19	16
Brian Rafalski	New Jersey	25	7	11	18	7
Mario Lemieux	Pittsburgh	18	6	11	17	4
Chris Drury	Colorado	23	11	5	16	4
Bobby Holik	New Jersey	25	6	10	16	37
Alexander Mogilny	New Jersey	25	5	11	16	8

LEADING PLAYOFF GOALTENDERS

Goaltender	Club	GPI	Mins	GA	SO	Avg.
Patrick Roy	Colorado	23	1451	41	4	1.70
Roman Turek	St. Louis	14	908	31	0	2.05
Martin Brodeur	New Jersey	25	1505	52	4	2.07
Dominik Hasek	Buffalo	13	833	29	1	2.09
Curtis Joseph	Toronto	11	685	24	3	2.10

PLAYOFF GOALS

Name, Team	G
Joe Sakic, Col.	13
Chris Drury, Col.	11
Petr Sykora, N.J.	10
Patrik Elias, N.J.	9
Jason Arnott, N.J.	8
Milan Hejduk, Col.	7
Brian Rafalski, N.J.	7
Nine tied with	6

PLAYOFF ASSISTS

Name, Team	A
Milan Hejduk, Col.	16
Alex Tanguay, Col.	15
Patrik Elias, N.J.	14
Joe Sakic, Col.	13
Rob Blake, Col.	13
Petr Sykora, N.J.	12
Mario Lemieux, Pit.	11
Brian Rafalski, N.J.	11
Alexander Mogilny, N.J.	11
Five tied with	10

PLAYOFF POWERPLAY GOALS

Name, Team	PPG
Joe Sakic, Col.	5
Jason Arnott, N.J.	5
Steve Thomas, Tor.	4
Milan Hejduk, Col.	4
Six tied with	3

PLAYOFF SHORTHAND GOALS

Name, Team	SHG
Curtis Brown, Buf.	2
Scott Young, St.L.	2
Petr Sykora, N.J.	2
Four tied with	1

PLAYOFF GAME-WINNING GOALS

Name, Team	GWG
Scott Young, St.L.	3
Mario Lemieux, Pit.	3
Joe Sakic, Col.	3
Brian Rafalski, N.J.	3
Bobby Holik, N.J.	3

PLAYOFF GOALIE WINS

Name, Team	W
Patrick Roy, Col.	16
Martin Brodeur, N.J.	15
Roman Turek, St.L.	9
Johan Hedberg, Pit.	9
Curtis Joseph, Tor.	7
Dominik Hasek, Buf.	7
Felix Potvin, L.A.	7

PLAYOFF SHUTOUTS

Name, Team	SO
Patrick Roy, Col.	4
Martin Brodeur, N.J.	4
Curtis Joseph, Tor.	3
Felix Potvin, L.A.	2
Johan Hedberg, Pit.	2

PLAYOFF SAVE PERCENTAGE

Name, Team	SV%
Patrick Roy, Col.	.934
Curtis Joseph, Tor.	.927
Roman Turek, St.L.	.919
Dominik Hasek, Buf.	.916
Johan Hedberg, Pit.	.911

2001-02

Stanley Cup • Detroit Red Wings

FINAL STANDINGS

EASTERN CONFERENCE

Team	GP	W	L	T	OTL	GF	GA	PTS
Northeast Division								
Boston	82	43	24	6	9	236	201	101
Toronto	82	43	25	10	4	249	207	100
Ottawa	82	39	27	9	7	243	208	94
Montreal	82	36	31	12	3	207	209	87
Buffalo	82	35	35	11	1	213	200	82
Atlantic Division								
Philedelphia	82	42	27	10	3	234	192	97
NY Islanders	82	42	28	8	4	239	220	96
New Jersey	82	41	28	9	4	205	187	95
NY Rangers	82	36	38	4	4	227	258	80
Pittsburgh	82	28	41	8	5	198	249	69
Southeast Division								
Carolina	82	35	26	16	5	217	217	91
Washington	82	36	33	11	2	228	240	85
Tampa Bay	82	27	40	11	4	178	219	69
Florida	82	22	44	10	6	180	250	60
Atlanta	82	19	47	11	5	187	288	54

WESTERN CONFERENCE

Team	GP	W	L	T	OTL	GF	GA	PTS
Central Division								
Detroit	82	51	17	10	4	251	187	116
St. Louis	82	43	27	8	4	227	188	98
Chicago	82	41	27	13	1	216	207	96
Nashville	82	28	41	13	0	196	230	69
Columbus	82	22	47	8	5	164	255	57
Pacific Division								
San Jose	82	44	27	8	3	248	199	99
Phoenix	82	40	27	9	6	228	210	95
Los Angeles	82	40	27	11	4	214	190	95
Dallas	82	36	28	13	5	215	213	90
Anaheim	82	29	42	8	3	175	198	69
Northwest Division								
Colorado	82	45	28	8	1	212	169	99
Vancouver	82	42	30	7	3	254	211	94
Edmonton	82	38	28	12	4	205	182	92
Calgary	82	32	35	12	3	201	220	79
Minnesota	82	26	35	12	9	195	238	73

LEADING SCORERS

Player	Club	GP	G	A	PTS	PIM
Jarome Iginla	Calgary	82	52	44	96	77
Markus Naslund	Vancouver	81	40	50	90	50
Todd Bertuzzi	Vancouver	72	36	49	85	110
Mats Sundin	Toronto	82	41	39	80	94
Jaromir Jagr	Washington	69	31	48	79	30
Joe Sakic	Colorado	82	26	53	79	18
Pavol Demitra	St. Louis	82	35	43	78	46
Adam Oates	Wsh./Phi.	80	14	64	78	28
Mike Modano	Dallas	78	34	43	77	38
Ron Francis	Carolina	80	27	50	77	18
Alexei Kovalev	Pittsburgh	67	32	44	76	80
Keith Tkachuk	St. Louis	73	38	37	75	117
Brendan Shanahan	Detroit	80	37	38	75	118
Alexei Yashin	NY Islanders	78	32	43	75	25
Craig Conroy	Calgary	81	27	48	75	32
Jason Allison	Los Angeles	73	19	55	74	68
Miroslav Satan	Buffalo	82	37	36	73	33
Eric Lindros	NY Rangers	72	37	36	73	138

LEADING GOALTENDERS

Goaltender	Club	GPI	MINS	GA	SO	AVG
Patrick Roy	Colorado	63	3773	122	9	1.94
Roman Cechmanek	Philadelphia	46	2603	89	4	2.05
Marty Turco	Dallas	31	1519	53	2	2.09
Jose Theodore	Montreal	67	3864	136	7	2.11
Jean-Sebastien Giguere	Anaheim	53	3127	111	4	2.13
Martin Brodeur	New Jersey	73	4347	156	4	2.15

Calgary's Jarome Iginla became the first player other than Jaromir Jagr, Mario Lemieux or Wayne Gretzky to win the Art Ross Trophy since Marcel Dionne won it in 1979–80. Iginla had 18 goals in his first 20 games in 2001–02, and nine in his last 10 en route to 52 overall.

Several new names emerged as the NHL's top individual stars in 2001–02, but it was a veteran-laden Detroit Red Wings team that took home the ultimate prize.

Following a shocking first-round playoff defeat at the hands of Los Angeles after a 111-point season in 2000–01, the Red Wings chose not to rebuild but to reload. Through trades and free agent signings, Detroit added Dominik Hasek, Brett Hull and Luke Robitaille to a line-up that already included aging stars like Steve Yzerman, Chris Chelios, Igor Larionov plus other veterans like Brendan Shanahan, Sergei Fedorov and Nicklas Lidstrom. Injuries limited Yzerman to just 52 games, but Robitaille, Hull, Fedorov and Shanahan all enjoyed 30-goal seasons. Hasek won a league-leading 41 games as Detroit finished 51–17–10–4 to take the Presidents' Trophy with 116 points. Still, Hasek's play was overshadowed by the performances of Patrick Roy and Jose Theodore. Roy led the league with nine shutouts and a 1.94 goals-against average. Theodore had a .931 save percentage and his brilliant play down the stretch almost single-handedly returned Montreal to the playoffs for the first time since 1998. When it came time to hand out the NHL awards, Theodore edged Roy for the Vezina Trophy and also took home the Hart Trophy as MVP. In both cases, the balloting actually ended in a tie with Theodore being declared the winner due to the fact that he had received more first-place votes.

Full House – Four 500-goal scorers (Hull, Yzerman, Shanahan, Robitaille), a Hall of Fame coach (Bowman) and a two-time MVP goalie (Hasek) helped Detroit demonstrate that best on paper meant best on the ice.

Finishing runner-up to Theodore for the Hart Trophy was Jarome Iginla of the Calgary Flames. After several strong seasons, Iginla rocketed to prominence, winning both the Maurice Richard Trophy with 52 goals and the Art Ross Trophy with 96 points. Still, Calgary missed the playoffs for the sixth straight season. At least Iginla had a chance to celebrate at the Olympics, as Team Canada took home the gold medal in hockey for the first time since 1952. The team Wayne Gretzky had put together started the tournament slowly but came on strong, defeating the Americans 5–2 in the gold medal game. Joe Sakic, Steve Yzerman and Mario Lemieux were the key contributors.

Yzerman saw little action after the Olympic break, but returned to spark the Red Wings in the playoffs. Detroit dropped two games at home to open the post-season, but bounced back to beat Vancouver. After a win over St. Louis, the Red Wings faced Colorado in the Western Conference final. After six tight games, Detroit romped to a 7–0 victory in game seven. In the east, the Carolina Hurricanes emerged as surprise contenders, knocking off New Jersey, Montreal and Toronto in six games apiece. Ron Francis, the heart and soul of the Hurricanes, scored the overtime winner in game one of the finals, but Detroit gained the series lead when Igor Larionov scored in triple overtime in game three. The Red Wings went on to score a five-game victory for their third Stanley Cup title in six years.

Nicklas Lidstrom won the Norris Trophy for the second time after three straight seasons as runner-up. In 2002 he became the first European player to win the Conn Smythe Trophy as playoff MVP.

Leaders, 2001-02

GOALS

Name, Team	G
Jarome Iginla, Cgy.	52
Bill Guerin, Bos.	41
Mats Sundin, Tor.	41
Glen Murray, L.A./Bos.	41
Markus Naslund, Van.	40
Peter Bondra, Wsh.	39
Keith Tkachuk, St.L.	38
Eric Daze, Chi.	38
Eric Lindros, NYR	37
Daniel Alfredsson, Ott.	37
Brendan Shanahan, Det.	37
Miroslav Satan, Buf.	37

ASSISTS

Name, Team	A
Adam Oates, Wsh./Phi.	64
Jason Allison, L.A.	55
Joe Sakic, Col.	53
Nicklas Lidstrom, Det.	50
Ron Francis, Car.	50
Markus Naslund, Van.	50
Jozef Stumpel, L.A./Bos.	50
Todd Bertuzzi, Van.	49
Jaromir Jagr, Wsh.	48
Craig Conroy, Cgy.	48
Andrew Brunette, Min.	48

POWERPLAY GOALS

Name, Team	PPG
Peter Bondra, Wsh.	17
Jarome Iginla, Cgy.	16
Ziggy Palffy, L.A.	15
Alexei Yashin, NYI	15
Miroslav Satan, Buf.	15
Todd Bertuzzi, Van.	14
Ron Francis, Car.	14
Keith Tkachuk, St.L.	13
Luc Robitaille, Det.	13
Seven tied with	12

SHORTHAND GOALS

Name, Team	SHG
Brian Rolston, Bos.	9
Michael Peca, NYI	6
Miroslav Satan, Buf.	5
Stacy Roest, Min.	4
Shawn Bates, NYI	4
10 tied with	3

GAME-WINNING GOALS

Name, Team	GWG
Pavol Demitra, St.L.	10
Mats Sundin, Tor.	9
Glen Murray, L.A./Bos.	9
Patrik Elias, N.J.	8
Peter Bondra, Wsh.	8
Steve Sullivan, Chi.	8
Teemu Selanne, S.J.	8
Paul Kariya, Ana.	8
Seven tied with	7

GOALIE WINS

Name, Team	W
Dominik Hasek, Det.	41
Martin Brodeur, N.J.	38
Evgeni Nabokov, S.J.	37
Byron Dafoe, Bos.	35
Brent Johnson, St.L.	34
Sean Burke, Phx.	33
Jocelyn Thibault, Chi.	33
Patrick Roy, Col.	32
Chris Osgood, NYI	32
Four tied with	31

SHUTOUTS

Name, Team	SO
Patrick Roy, Col.	9
Patrick Lalime, Ott.	7
Dan Cloutier, Van.	7
Evgeni Nabokov, S.J.	7
Jose Theodore, Mtl.	7
Nikolai Khabibulin, T.B.	7

SAVE PERCENTAGE

Name, Team	SV%
Jose Theodore, Mtl.	.931
Patrick Roy, Col.	.925
Roman Cechmanek, Phi.	.921
Marty Turco, Dal.	.921
Three tied with	.920

FIRST TEAM ALL-STARS

Name, Team	Position
Joe Sakic, Col.	C
Jarome Iginla, Cgy.	RW
Markus Naslund, Van.	LW
Nicklas Lidstrom, Det.	D
Chris Chelios, Det.	D
Patrick Roy, Col.	G

SECOND TEAM ALL-STARS

Name, Team	Position
Mats Sundin, Tor.	C
Bill Guerin, Bos.	RW
Brendan Shanahan, Det.	LW
Rob Blake, Col.	D
Sergei Gonchar, Wsh.	D
Jose Theodore, Mtl.	G

ALL-ROOKIE TEAM

Name, Team	Position
Dany Heatley, Atl.	F
Ilya Kovalchuk, Atl.	F
Kristian Huselius, Fla.	F
Nick Boynton, Bos.	D
Rostislav Klesla, CBJ	D
Dan Blackburn, NYR	G

TROPHY WINNERS

Trophy	Awarded For	Winner	Team
Hart	MVP	Jose Theodore	Mtl.
Art Ross	Top Scorer	Jarome Iginla	Cgy.
Richard	Top Goal Scorer	Jarome Iginla	Cgy.
Norris	Top Defenseman	Nicklas Lidstrom	Det.
Calder	Top Rookie	Dany Heatley	Atl.
Selke	Top Defensive Forward	Michael Peca	NYI
Vezina	Top Goaltender	Jose Theodore	Mtl.
Jennings	Fewest Goals Against	Patrick Roy	Col
Crozier	Best Save %	Jose Theodore	Mtl.
Adams	Top Coach	Bob Francis	Phx.
Byng	Gentlemanly Conduct	Ron Francis	Car.
Masterton	Perseverance, Sportmanship	Saku Koivu	Mtl.
Pearson	NHLPA MVP	Jarome Iginla	Cgy.
Conn Smythe	Playoff MVP	Nicklas Lidstrom	Det.
Patrick	Service to Hockey in U.S.	1960 U.S. Olympic Team	
		Herb Brooks	
		Larry Pleau	
Clancy	Leadership On and Off Ice	Ron Francis	Car.
Bud Light	Best Plus/Minus	Chris Chelios	Det.
Entry Draft	First Overall Selection	Rick Nash, LW	CBJ

NHL NOTEBOOK

TRANSACTIONS

- June 23, 2001 – Ottawa Senators traded Alexei Yashin to the New York Islanders for Zdeno Chara, Bill Muckalt and a first-round draft pick.
- June 24, 2001 – Buffalo Sabres traded Michael Peca to the New York Islanders for Tim Connolly and Taylor Pyatt.
- June 30, 2001 – Buffalo Sabres traded goaltender Dominik Hasek to the Detroit Red Wings in exchange for left wing Vyacheslav Kozlov, a 2002 first-round draft pick and future considerations.
- July 11, 2001 – Pittsburgh Penguins traded Jaromir Jagr and Frantisek Kucera to the Washington Capitals for Kris Beech, Michael Sivek, Ross Lupaschuk and future considerations.
- Aug. 22, 2001 – Detroit Red Wings signed unrestricted free agent Brett Hull.
- Aug. 20, 2001 – New York Rangers acquired Eric Lindros from the Philadelphia Flyers for Jan Hlavac, Kim Johnsson, Pavel Brendl a middle-round draft pick and other future considerations.

RECORDS

- Mar. 12, 2002 – Vancouver center Artem Chubarov scored to become the first player in NHL history whose first four career goals were all game winners in a 5-0 win at Nashville.
- Apr. 23, 2002 – Patrick Roy became the first goaltender in NHL history to record 20 career playoff shutouts as the Avalanche beat the Kings 1-0 in Los Angeles in game four of the Western Conference quarter-finals.
- May 25, 2002 – Patrick Roy set a record for most career playoff games (among all players) with his 237th appearance as the Avalanche won 3-2 over the visiting Detroit Red Wings in game four of the Western Conference finals. He broke the mark of 236 set by Mark Messier.

MILESTONES

- Oct. 11, 2001 – Peter Laviolette became the first coach in NHL history to start his career with four straight road victories when the Islanders picked up a 6-4 win over the Devils at New Jersey.
- Dec. 26, 2001 – Colorado's Patrick Roy became the first goaltender in NHL history to record 500 career wins in a 2-0 Avalanche victory at Dallas.
- Apr. 11, 2002 – Roger Neilson became the first man in history to coach eight NHL teams when he went behind the bench for the Ottawa Senators in a 4-0 win over Boston. It was also Neilson's 999th career game as an NHL head coach.
- Apr. 27, 2002 – Brett Hull became the all-time playoff leader in power-play goals, when he scored his 36th career playoff PPG in a 6-4 win at Vancouver in game six of the Western Conference quarter-finals. Hull broke the mark of 35 set by Mike Bossy.

2002 Playoffs

CONFERENCE QUARTER-FINALS

Apr. 18 Montreal 5 at Boston 2
Apr. 21 Montreal 4 at Boston 6
Apr. 23 Boston 3 at Montreal 5
Apr. 25 Boston 5 at Montreal 2
Apr. 27 Montreal 2 at Boston 1
Apr. 29 Boston 1 at Montreal 2

Montreal won best-of-seven series 4-2

Apr. 17 Ottawa 0 at Philadelphia 1 OT
Apr. 20 Ottawa 3 at Philadelphia 0
Apr. 22 Philadelphia 0 at Ottawa 3
Apr. 24 Philadelphia 0 at Ottawa 3
Apr. 26 Ottawa 2 at Philadelphia 1 OT

Ottawa won best-of-seven series 4-1

Apr. 17 New Jersey 1 at Carolina 2
Apr. 19 New Jersey 1 at Carolina 2 OT
Apr. 21 Carolina 0 at New Jersey 4
Apr. 23 Carolina 1 at New Jersey 3
Apr. 24 New Jersey 2 at Carolina 3 OT
Apr. 27 Carolina 1 at New Jersey 0

Carolina won best-of-seven series 4-2

Apr. 18 NY Islanders 1 at Toronto 3
Apr. 20 NY Islanders 0 at Toronto 2
Apr. 23 Toronto 1 at NY Islanders 6
Apr. 24 Toronto 3 at NY Islanders 4
Apr. 26 NY Islanders 3 at Toronto 6
Apr. 28 Toronto 3 at NY Islanders 5
Apr. 30 NY Islanders 2 at Toronto 4

Toronto won best-of-seven series 4-3

Apr. 17 Vancouver 4 at Detroit 3 OT
Apr. 19 Vancouver 5 at Detroit 2
Apr. 21 Detroit 3 at Vancouver 1
Apr. 23 Detroit 4 at Vancouver 2
Apr. 25 Vancouver 0 at Detroit 4
Apr. 27 Detroit 6 at Vancouver 4

Detroit won best-of-seven series 4-2

Apr. 18 Los Angeles 3 at Colorado 4
Apr. 20 Los Angeles 3 at Colorado 5
Apr. 22 Colorado 1 at Los Angeles 3
Apr. 23 Colorado 1 at Los Angeles 0
Apr. 25 Los Angeles 1 at Colorado 0 OT
Apr. 27 Colorado 1 at Los Angeles 3
Apr. 29 Los Angeles 0 at Colorado 4

Colorado won best-of-seven series 4-3

Apr. 17 Phoenix 1 at San Jose 2
Apr. 20 Phoenix 3 at San Jose 1
Apr. 22 San Jose 4 at Phoenix 1
Apr. 24 San Jose 2 at Phoenix 1
Apr. 26 Phoenix 1 at San Jose 4

San Jose won best-of-seven series 4-1

Apr. 18 Chicago 2 at St. Louis 1
Apr. 20 Chicago 0 at St. Louis 2
Apr. 21 St. Louis 4 at Chicago 0
Apr. 23 St. Louis 1 at Chicago 0
Apr. 25 Chicago 3 at St. Louis 5

St. Louis won best-of-seven series 4-1

CONFERENCE SEMI-FINALS

May 3 Montreal 0 at Carolina 2
May 5 Montreal 4 at Carolina 1
May 7 Carolina 1 at Montreal 2 OT
May 9 Carolina 4 at Montreal 3 OT
May 12 Montreal 1 at Carolina 5
May 13 Carolina 8 at Montreal 2

Carolina won best-of-seven series 4-2

May 2 Ottawa 5 at Toronto 0
May 4 Ottawa 2 at Toronto 3 3OT
May 6 Toronto 2 at Ottawa 3
May 8 Toronto 2 at Ottawa 1
May 10 Ottawa 4 at Toronto 2
May 12 Toronto 4 at Ottawa 3
May 14 Ottawa 0 at Toronto 3

Toronto won best-of-seven series 4-3

May 1 San Jose 6 at Colorado 3
May 4 San Jose 2 at Colorado 8
May 6 Colorado 4 at San Jose 6
May 8 Colorado 4 at San Jose 1
May 11 San Jose 5 at Colorado 3
May 13 Colorado 2 at San Jose 1 OT
May 15 San Jose 0 at Colorado 1

Colorado won best-of-seven series 4-3

May 2 St. Louis 0 at Detroit 2
May 4 St. Louis 2 at Detroit 3
May 7 Detroit 1 at St. Louis 6
May 9 Detroit 4 at St. Louis 3
May 11 St. Louis 0 at Detroit 4

Detroit won best-of-seven series 4-1

CONFERENCE FINALS

May 16 Toronto 2 at Carolina 1
May 19 Toronto 1 at Carolina 2 OT
May 21 Carolina 2 at Toronto 1 OT
May 23 Carolina 3 at Toronto 0
May 25 Toronto 1 at Carolina 0
May 28 Carolina 2 at Toronto 1 OT

Carolina won best-of-seven series 4-2

May 18 Colorado 3 at Detroit 5
May 20 Colorado 4 at Detroit 3 OT
May 22 Detroit 2 at Colorado 1 OT
May 25 Detroit 2 at Colorado 3
May 27 Colorado 2 at Detroit 1 OT
May 29 Detroit 2 at Colorado 0
May 31 Colorado 0 at Detroit 7

Detroit won best-of-seven series 4-3

FINALS

June 4 Carolina 3 at Detroit 2 OT
June 6 Carolina 1 at Detroit 3
June 8 Detroit 3 at Carolina 2 3OT
June 10 Detroit 3 at Carolina 0
June 13 Carolina 1 at Detroit 3

Detroit won best-of-seven series 4-1

2001-02 – Detroit Red Wings – Steve Yzerman (Captain), Chris Chelios, Mathieu Dandenault, Pavel Datsyuk, Boyd Devereaux, Kris Draper, Steve Duchesne, Sergei Fedorov, Jiri Fischer, Dominik Hasek, Tomas Holmstrom, Brett Hull, Igor Larionov, Manny Legace, Nicklas Lidstrom, Kirk Maltby, Darren McCarty, Fredrik Olausson, Luc Robitaille, Brendan Shanahan, Jiri Slegr, Jason Williams, Michael Illitch (Owner/Gov.), Marian Illitch (Owner/Sec.-Tres.), Ronald Illitch, Michael Illitch, Jr., Lisa Illitch Murray, Atanas Illitch, Carole Illitch Trepeck, Jim Devellano (Sr. V.P.), Christoper Illitch (V.P.), Denise Illitch (Alt. Governor), Ken Holland (G.M.), Jim Nill (Asst. G.M.), Scotty Bowman (Head Coach), Dave Lewis, Barry Smith (Assoc. Coaches), Jim Berard (Goaltending Consultant), Joe Kocur (Video Coord.), John Wharton (Trainer), Paul Boyer, Mark Miller (Equipment Mgrs.), Piet Van Zant (Asst. Trainer), Tim Abbott (Asst. Equipment Mgr.), Sergei Tchekmarev (Masseur), Dan Belisle, Mark Howe, Bob McCammon (Pro Scouts), Hakan Andersson (Dir. of European Scouting), Mark Leach, Bruce Haralson, Joe McDonnell, Glenn Merkosky (Scouts).

LEADING PLAYOFF SCORERS

Player	Club	GP	G	A	PTS	PIM
Peter Forsberg	Colorado	20	9	18	27	20
Steve Yzerman	Detroit	23	6	17	23	10
Joe Sakic	Colorado	21	9	10	19	4
Brendan Shanahan	Detroit	23	8	11	19	20
Gary Roberts	Toronto	19	7	12	19	56
Sergei Fedorov	Detroit	23	5	14	19	20
Brett Hull	Detroit	23	10	8	18	4
Ron Francis	Carolina	23	6	10	16	6
Nicklas Lidstrom	Detroit	23	5	11	16	2
Alyn McCauley	Toronto	20	5	10	15	4

LEADING PLAYOFF GOALTENDERS

Goaltender	Club	GPI	Mins	GA	SO	Avg.
Patrick Lalime	Ottawa	12	778	18	4	1.39
Kevin Weekes	Carolina	8	408	11	2	1.62
Arturs Irbe	Carolina	18	1078	30	1	1.67
Brent Johnson	St. Louis	10	590	18	3	1.83
Dominik Hasek	Detroit	23	1455	45	6	1.86

PLAYOFF GOALS

Name, Team	G
Brett Hull, Det.	10
Peter Forsberg, Col.	9
Joe Sakic, Col.	9
Alexander Mogilny, Tor.	8
Jeff O'Neill, Car.	8
Brendan Shanahan, Det.	8
Tomas Holmstrom, Det.	8
Scott Mellanby, St.L.	7
Daniel Alfredsson, Ott.	7
Gary Roberts, Tor.	7
Steve Reinprecht, Col.	7

PLAYOFF ASSISTS

Name, Team	A
Peter Forsberg, Col.	18
Steve Yzerman, Det.	17
Sergei Fedorov, Det.	14
Chris Chelios, Det.	13
Gary Roberts, Tor.	12
Brendan Shanahan, Det.	11
Nicklas Lidstrom, Det.	11
Alyn McCauley, Tor.	10
Joe Sakic, Col.	10
Ron Francis, Car.	10

PLAYOFF POWERPLAY GOALS

Name, Team	PPG
Scott Mellanby, St.L.	4
Joe Sakic, Col.	4
Steve Yzerman, Det.	4
Ron Francis, Car.	4
Sean Hill, Car.	4

PLAYOFF SHORTHAND GOALS

Name, Team	SHG
Brett Hull, Det.	2
Kirk Maltby, Det.	2
Nine tied with	1

PLAYOFF GAME-WINNING GOALS

Name, Team	GWG
Peter Forsberg, Col.	4
Daniel Alfredsson, Ott.	3
Patrick Marleau, S.J.	3
Chris Drury, Col.	3
Ron Francis, Car.	3

PLAYOFF GOALIE WINS

Name, Team	W
Dominik Hasek, Det.	16
Patrick Roy, Col.	11
Arturs Irbe, Car.	10
Curtis Joseph, Tor.	10
Patrick Lalime, Ott.	7
Evgeni Nabokov, S.J.	7

PLAYOFF SHUTOUTS

Name, Team	SO
Dominik Hasek, Det.	6
Patrick Lalime, Ott.	4
Brent Johnson, St.L.	3
Curtis Joseph, Tor.	3
Patrick Roy, Col.	3

PLAYOFF SAVE PERCENTAGE

Name, Team	SV%
Patrick Lalime, Ott.	.946
Kevin Weekes, Car.	.939
Arturs Irbe, Car.	.938
Brent Johnson, St.L.	.929
Felix Potvin, L.A.	.925

2002-03

Stanley Cup • New Jersey Devils

A national hero in his homeland, Peter Forsberg was depicted on a Swedish postage stamp after his 1992 Olympic gold medal-winning goal. Already a two-time Stanley Cup champion, Forsberg became the first Swede to win the Hart and Art Ross trophies, edging out Markus Naslund (who hails from the same home town) for both honors in 2002–03.

FINAL STANDINGS

EASTERN CONFERENCE

Team	GP	W	L	T	OTL	GF	GA	PTS
Northeast Division								
Ottawa	82	52	21	8	1	263	182	113
Toronto	82	44	28	7	3	236	208	98
Boston	82	36	31	11	4	245	237	87
Montreal	82	30	35	8	9	206	234	77
Buffalo	82	27	37	10	8	190	219	72
Atlantic Division								
New Jersey	82	46	20	10	6	216	166	108
Philadelphia	82	45	20	13	4	211	166	107
NY Islanders	82	35	34	11	2	224	231	83
NY Rangers	82	32	36	10	4	210	231	78
Pittsburgh	82	27	44	6	5	189	255	65
Southeast Division								
Tampa Bay	82	36	25	16	5	219	210	93
Washington	82	39	29	8	6	224	220	92
Atlanta	82	31	39	7	5	226	284	74
Florida	82	24	36	13	9	176	237	70
Carolina	82	22	43	11	6	171	240	61
WESTERN CONFERENCE								
Central Division								
Detroit	82	48	20	10	4	269	203	110
St. Louis	82	41	24	11	6	253	222	99
Chicago	82	30	33	13	6	207	226	79
Nashville	82	27	35	13	7	183	206	74
Columbus	82	29	42	8	3	213	263	69
Pacific Division								
Dallas	82	46	17	15	4	245	169	111
Anaheim	82	40	27	9	6	203	193	95
Los Angeles	82	33	37	6	6	203	221	78
Phoenix	82	31	35	11	5	204	230	78
San Jose	82	28	37	9	8	214	239	73
Northwest Division								
Colorado	82	42	19	13	8	251	194	105
Vancouver	82	45	23	13	1	264	208	104
Minnesota	82	42	29	10	1	198	178	95
Edmonton	82	36	26	11	9	231	230	92
Calgary	82	29	36	13	4	186	228	75

LEADING SCORERS

Player	Club	GP	G	A	PTS	PIM
Peter Forsberg	Colorado	75	29	77	106	70
Markus Naslund	Vancouver	82	48	56	104	52
Joe Thornton	Boston	77	36	65	101	109
Milan Hejduk	Colorado	82	50	48	98	32
Todd Bertuzzi	Vancouver	82	46	51	97	144
Pavol Demitra	St Louis	78	36	57	93	32
Glen Murray	Boston	82	44	48	92	64
Mario Lemieux	Pittsburgh	67	28	63	91	43
Dany Heatley	Atlanta	77	41	48	89	58
Zigmund Palffy	Los Angeles	76	37	48	85	47
Mike Modano	Dallas	79	28	57	85	30
Sergei Fedorov	Detroit	80	36	47	83	52
Paul Kariya	Anaheim	82	25	56	81	48
Marian Hossa	Ottawa	80	45	35	80	34
Alexander Mogilny	Toronto	73	33	46	79	12
Vaclav Prospal	Tampa Bay	80	22	57	79	53

LEADING GOALTENDERS

Goaltender	Club	GPI	MINS	GA	SO	AVG
Marty Turco	Dallas	55	3203	92	7	1.72
Roman Cechmanek	Philadelphia	58	3350	102	6	1.83
Dwayne Roloson	Minnesota	50	2945	98	4	2.00
Martin Brodeur	New Jersey	73	4374	147	9	2.02
Patrick Lalime	Ottawa	67	3943	142	8	2.16
Manny Legace	Detroit	25	1406	51	0	2.18
Patrick Roy	Colorado	63	3769	137	5	2.18

THE NHL TOOK A HARD LINE on interference and obstructionin the neutral zone for 2002-03 and also adopted a "hurry-up" line change rule. These changes improved the flow while reducing the time required to play a game to two hours, 20 minutes, the lowest it had been in 40 years.

The NHL's top-scoring team was the Detroit Red Wings, who led the league with 269 goals, but had just one player (Sergei Fedorov, who placed 12th with 36 goals and 47 assists) rank among the top 30 individual scorers. Vancouver's Markus Naslund (48 goals, 56 assists, 104 points) was the top scorer for much of the season, but had to settle for second place in the scoring race behind Peter Forsberg (29-77-106). Forsberg passed Naslund to claim the Art Ross Trophy on the last day of the NHL season, just as the Colorado Avalanche passed the Canucks for top spot in the Northwest Division to claim their record ninth straight divisional title.

Colorado's Milan Hejduk scored two goals in the season finale to become the league's only 50-goal shooter.

In Detroit, Steve Yzerman would miss much of the season due to injuries, but the key change was in goal, where Curtis Joseph replaced Dominik Hasek.

With the Dominator in retirement, other goaltenders had a chance to shine. Marty Turco of Dallas posted a 1.72 goals-against average for the lowest mark since 1939–40. New Jersey's Martin Brodeur had his record-setting fourth 40-win season, topping the league for the fifth time with 41. He also led with nine shutouts and won the Vezina Trophy for the first time in his career. However, Jean-Sebastien Giguere stole the goaltending limelight in the playoffs. He was brilliant in leading the Mighty Ducks of Anaheim to upsets of Detroit and Dallas (the top two teams in the Western Conference) during the first two rounds of the playoffs, then posted three straight shutouts to help Anaheim sweep the equally surprising Minnesota Wild. As the Stanley Cup final began, Patrick Roy, perhaps the greatest goaltender of them all, announced his retirement. He left the game with 551 wins in the regular season and 151 more in the playoffs.

> **From Pond to Meadowlands – Upsets ruled the Western Conference as Anaheim and Minnesota defeated the favorites, with the Ducks advancing to a seven-game final where home ice gave the Devils their due.**

Despite the distraction of an ongoing search for new ownership, the Ottawa Senators soared. Led by Marian Hossa (who set a club record with 45 goals), captain Daniel Alfredsson and solid goaltender Patrick Lalime, the Senators set club records for wins (52) and points (113) to capture the Presidents' Trophy. They reached the Eastern Conference final, but fell to the Devils in seven games as New Jersey reached the Stanley Cup final for the third time in four years. The Devils defeated the Ducks in seven more games, with each team winning every game at home for the first time since the 1965 final. For the Devils, it was their third Stanley Cup title in nine seasons.

Wes Walz helped spark the surprising Minnesota Wild to the third round of the playoffs in the team's third year in the NHL.

Leaders, 2002-03

GOALS

Name, Team	G
Milan Hejduk, Col.	50
Markus Naslund, Van.	48
Todd Bertuzzi, Van.	46
Marian Hossa, Ott.	45
Glen Murray, Bos.	44
Dany Heatley, Atl.	41
Ilya Kovalchuk, Atl.	38
Mats Sundin, Tor.	37
Zigmund Palffy, L.A.	37
Alex Kovalev, Pit./NYR	37
Brett Hull, Det.	37

ASSISTS

Name, Team	A
Peter Forsberg, Col.	77
Joe Thornton, Bos.	65
Mario Lemieux, Pit.	63
Pavol Demitra, St.L.	57
Mike Modano, Dal.	57
Vaclav Prospal, T.B.	57
Brad Richards, T.B.	57
Markus Naslund, Van.	56
Paul Kariya, Ana.	56
Doug Weight, St.L.	52
Al Macinnis, St.L.	52
Ray Whitney, CBJ	52

POWERPLAY GOALS

Name, Team	PPG
Todd Bertuzzi, Van.	25
Markus Naslund, Van.	24
Dany Heatley, Atl.	19
Milan Hejduk, Col.	18
Mats Sundin, Tor.	16
Dave Andreychuk, T.B.	15
Vincent Damphousse, S.J.	15
Geoff Sanderson, CBJ	15
Petr Sykora, Ana.	15
Five players tied with	14

SHORTHAND GOALS

Name, Team	SHG
Shawn Bates, NYI	6
Brian Rolston, Bos.	5
Martin Rucinsky, St.L.	4
Curtis Brown, Buf.	4
Kirk Maltby, Det.	4
Matt Cooke, Van.	4
14 tied with	3

GAME-WINNING GOALS

Name, Team	GWG
Markus Naslund, Van.	12
Sergei Fedorov, Det.	11
Marian Hossa, Ott.	10
Alexander Mogilny, Tor.	9
Jaromir Jagr, Wsh.	9
Michal Handzus, Phi.	9
Bryan Smolinski, L.A./Ott.	8
Mats Sundin, Tor.	8
Marian Gaborik, Min.	8
Brendan Morrison, Van.	8

GOALIE WINS

Name, Team	W
Martin Brodeur, N.J.	41
Patrick Lalime, Ott.	39
Ed Belfour, Tor.	37
Patrick Roy, Col.	35
Curtis Joseph, Det.	34
J-S Giguere, Ana.	34
Dan Cloutier, Van.	33
Roman Cechmanek, Phi.	33
Olaf Kolzig, Wsh.	33
Marty Turco, Dal.	31

SHUTOUTS

Name, Team	SO
Martin Brodeur, N.J.	9
Jocelyn Thibault, Chi.	8
J-S Giguere, Ana.	8
Patrick Lalime, Ott.	8
Marty Turco, Dal.	7
Ed Belfour, Tor.	7

SAVE PERCENTAGE

Name, Team	SV%
Marty Turco, Dal.	.932
Dwayne Roloson, Min.	.927
Roman Cechmanek, Phi.	.925
Manny Legace, Det.	.925
Mike Dunham, NYR	.924
Manny Fernandez, Min.	.924

FIRST TEAM ALL-STARS

Name, Team	Position
Peter Forsberg, Col.	C
Todd Bertuzzi, Van.	RW
Markus Naslund, Van.	LW
Nicklas Lidstrom, Det.	D
Al MacInnis, St.L.	D
Martin Brodeur, N.J.	G

SECOND TEAM ALL-STARS

Name, Team	Position
Joe Thornton, Bos.	C
Milan Hejduk, Col.	RW
Paul Kariya, Ana.	LW
Sergei Gonchar, Wsh.	D
Derian Hatcher, Dal.	D
Marty Turco, Dal.	G

ALL-ROOKIE TEAM

Name, Team	Position
Tyler Arnason, Chi.	F
Rick Nash, CBJ	F
Henrik Zetterberg	F
Jay Bouwmeester, Fla.	D
Barret Jackman, St.L.	D
Sebastien Caron, Pit.	G

TROPHY WINNERS

Trophy	Awarded For	Winner	Team
Hart	MVP	Peter Forsberg	Col.
Art Ross	Top Scorer	Peter Forsberg	Col.
Richard	Top Goal Scorer	Milan Hejduk	Col.
Norris	Top Defenseman	Nicklas Lidstrom	Det.
Calder	Top Rookie	Barret Jackman	St.L.
Selke	Top Defensive Forward	Jere Lehtinen	Dal.
Vezina	Top Goaltender	Martin Brodeur	N.J.
Jennings	Fewest Goals Against	Martin Brodeur (tie)	N.J.
		Roman Cechmanek (tie),	Phi.
		Robert Esche	Phi.
Crozier	Best Save %	Marty Turco	Dal.
Adams	Top Coach	Jacques Lemaire	N.J.
Byng	Gentlemanly Conduct	Alexander Mogilny	Tor.
Masterton	Perseverance, Sportmanship	Steve Yzerman	Det.
Pearson	NHLPA MVP	Markus Naslund	Van.
Conn Smythe	Playoff MVP	Jean-Sebastien Giguere	Ana.
Patrick	Service to Hockey in U.S.	Raymond Bourque	
		Ron DeGregorio	
		Willie O'Ree	
Clancy	Leadership On and Off Ice	Brendan Shanahan	Det.
Bud Light	Best Plus/Minus	Peter Forsberg (tie)	Col.
		Milan Hejduk (tie)	Col.
Entry Draft	First Overall Selection	Marc-Andre Fleury	Pit.

NHL NOTEBOOK

TRANSACTIONS

- July 1, 2003 – Mighty Ducks of Anaheim signed free agent Adam Oates.
- July 2, 2003 – Toronto Maple Leafs signed free agent Eddie Belfour.
- July 3, 2003 – Dallas Stars signed free agent Bill Guerin.
- July 6, 2003 – New Jersey Devils traded Petr Sykora, Igor Pohanka, Mike Commodore and Jean-Francois Damphousse to the Mighty Ducks of Anaheim for Jeff Friesen, Oleg Tverdovsky and Maxim Balmochnykh.

RECORDS

- Oct. 24, 2002 – Patrick Roy set an NHL record for goaltenders by playing in his 972nd career game, a 3-2 Colorado win at Phoenix. Roy broke the mark of 971 set by Terry Sawchuk.
- Nov. 15, 2002 – Dave Andreychuk set an NHL record by scoring his 250th career powerplay goal (breaking the record held by Phil Esposito) as the Lightning won 4-2 over the visiting San Jose Sharks.
- Mar. 1, 2003 – Nashville's Barry Trotz set an NHL record for most games coached with an expansion team from its inception when he had his 392nd game with the Predators, a 5-4 OT win over the visiting Chicago Blackhawks. He broke Terry Crisp's record of 391 with Tampa Bay.
- Apr. 4, 2003 – Columbus Blue Jackets goaltender Marc Denis set an NHL record for most minutes played in one season (with 4,451) in a 5-5 tie against the visiting Detroit Red Wings. He broke the mark of 4,443 set by Martin Brodeur in 1995-96 and would finish the season with 4,511 minutes played.

MILESTONES

- Jan. 22, 2003 – Detroit's Brett Hull became just the second player in NHL history to score 20 goals in each of his first 16 NHL seasons, when he connected in the a 4-3 loss in overtime to the Oilers at Edmonton.
- Oct. 12, 2002 – Ron Tugnutt became the first goaltender in NHL history to play for eight different NHL teams, when he led the Dallas Stars to a 5-2 win over the Phoenix Coyotes.
- Feb. 12, 2003 – Anaheim set an NHL record with their 10th consecutive one-goal victory when Mike Leclerc scored 10 seconds into overtime to give the Mighty Ducks a 4-3 win over the visiting Calgary Flames. They broke the record for one-goal wins set by Ottawa in 1926-27.
- Apr. 2, 2003 – Carolina Hurricanes became the first team since the 1925-26 Montreal Canadiens to finish last overall in the NHL one year after making the Stanley Cup finals, when they lost 3-2 to Pittsburgh.

2003 Playoffs

CONFERENCE QUARTER-FINALS

Apr.	9	NY Islanders	3	at	Ottawa	0	
Apr.	12	NY Islanders	0	at	Ottawa	3	
Apr.	14	Ottawa	3	at	NY Islanders	2	2OT
Apr.	16	Ottawa	3	at	NY Islanders	1	
Apr.	17	NY Islanders	1	at	Ottawa	4	

Ottawa won best-of-seven series 4-1

Apr.	9	Boston	1	at	New Jersey	2	
Apr.	11	Boston	2	at	New Jersey	4	
Apr.	13	New Jersey	3	at	Boston	0	
Apr.	15	New Jersey	1	at	Boston	5	
Apr.	17	Boston	0	at	New Jersey	3	

New Jersey won best-of-seven series 4-1

Apr.	10	Washington	3	at	Tampa Bay	0	
Apr.	12	Washington	6	at	Tampa Bay	3	
Apr.	15	Tampa Bay	4	at	Washington	3	OT
Apr.	16	Tampa Bay	3	at	Washington	1	
Apr.	18	Washington	1	at	Tampa Bay	2	
Apr.	20	Tampa Bay	2	at	Washington	1	3OT

Tampa Bay won best-of-seven series 4-2

Apr.	9	Toronto	5	at	Philadelphia	3	
Apr.	11	Toronto	1	at	Philadelphia	4	
Apr.	14	Philadelphia	3	at	Toronto	4	2OT
Apr.	16	Philadelphia	3	at	Toronto	2	3OT
Apr.	19	Toronto	1	at	Philadelphia	4	2OT
Apr.	21	Philadelphia	1	at	Toronto	2	
Apr.	22	Toronto	1	at	Philadelphia	6	

Philadelphia won best-of-seven series 4-3

Apr.	9	Edmonton	2	at	Dallas	1	
Apr.	11	Edmonton	1	at	Dallas	6	
Apr.	13	Dallas	2	at	Edmonton	3	
Apr.	15	Dallas	3	at	Edmonton	1	
Apr.	17	Edmonton	2	at	Dallas	5	
Apr.	19	Dallas	3	at	Edmonton	2	

Dallas won best-of-seven series 4-2

Apr.	10	Anaheim	2	at	Detroit	1	3OT
Apr.	12	Anaheim	3	at	Detroit	2	
Apr.	14	Detroit	1	at	Anaheim	2	
Apr.	16	Detroit	2	at	Anaheim	3	OT

Anaheim won best-of-seven series 4-0

Apr.	10	Minnesota	4	at	Colorado	2	
Apr.	12	Minnesota	2	at	Colorado	3	
Apr.	14	Colorado	3	at	Minnesota	0	
Apr.	16	Colorado	3	at	Minnesota	1	
Apr.	19	Minnesota	3	at	Colorado	2	
Apr.	21	Colorado	2	at	Minnesota	3	OT
Apr.	22	Minnesota	3	at	Colorado	2	OT

Minnesota won best-of-seven series 4-3

Apr.	10	St. Louis	6	at	Vancouver	0	
Apr.	12	St. Louis	1	at	Vancouver	2	
Apr.	14	Vancouver	1	at	St. Louis	3	
Apr.	16	Vancouver	1	at	St. Louis	4	
Apr.	18	St. Louis	3	at	Vancouver	5	
Apr.	20	Vancouver	4	at	St. Louis	3	
Apr.	22	St. Louis	1	at	Vancouver	4	

Vancouver won best-of-seven series 4-3

CONFERENCE SEMI-FINALS

Apr.	25	Philadelphia	2	at	Ottawa	4	
Apr.	27	Philadelphia	2	at	Ottawa	0	
Apr.	29	Ottawa	3	at	Philadelphia	2	OT
May	1	Ottawa	0	at	Philadelphia	1	
May	3	Philadelphia	2	at	Ottawa	5	
May	5	Ottawa	5	at	Philadelphia	1	

Ottawa won best-of-seven series 4-2

Apr.	24	Tampa Bay	0	at	New Jersey	3	
Apr.	26	Tampa Bay	2	at	New Jersey	3	OT
Apr.	28	New Jersey	3	at	Tampa Bay	4	
Apr.	30	New Jersey	3	at	Tampa Bay	1	
May	2	Tampa Bay	1	at	New Jersey	2	3OT

New Jersey won best-of-seven series 4-1

Apr.	24	Anaheim	4	at	Dallas	3	5OT
Apr.	26	Anaheim	3	at	Dallas	2	OT
Apr.	28	Dallas	2	at	Anaheim	1	
Apr.	30	Dallas	0	at	Anaheim	1	
May	3	Anaheim	1	at	Dallas	4	
May	5	Dallas	3	at	Anaheim	4	

Anaheim won best-of-seven series 4-2

Apr.	25	Minnesota	3	at	Vancouver	4	OT
Apr.	27	Minnesota	3	at	Vancouver	2	
Apr.	29	Vancouver	3	at	Minnesota	2	
May	2	Vancouver	3	at	Minnesota	2	OT
May	5	Minnesota	7	at	Vancouver	2	
May	7	Vancouver	1	at	Minnesota	5	
May	8	Minnesota	4	at	Vancouver	2	

Minnesota won best-of-seven series 4-3

CONFERENCE FINALS

May	10	New Jersey	2	at	Ottawa	3	OT
May	13	New Jersey	4	at	Ottawa	1	
May	15	Ottawa	0	at	New Jersey	1	
May	17	Ottawa	2	at	New Jersey	5	
May	19	New Jersey	1	at	Ottawa	3	
May	21	Ottawa	2	at	New Jersey	1	OT
May	23	New Jersey	3	at	Ottawa	2	

New Jersey won best-of-seven series 4-3

May	10	Anaheim	1	at	Minnesota	0	2OT
May	12	Anaheim	2	at	Minnesota	0	
May	14	Minnesota	0	at	Anaheim	4	
May	16	Minnesota	1	at	Anaheim	2	

Anaheim won best-of-seven series 4-0

FINALS

May	27	Anaheim	0	at	New Jersey	3	
May	29	Anaheim	0	at	New Jersey	3	
May	31	New Jersey	2	at	Anaheim	3	OT
June	2	New Jersey	0	at	Anaheim	1	OT
June	5	Anaheim	3	at	New Jersey	6	
June	7	New Jersey	2	at	Anaheim	5	
June	9	Anaheim	0	at	New Jersey	3	

New Jersey won best-of-seven series 4-3

2002-03* – New Jersey Devils – Scott Stevens (Captain), Tommy Albelin, Martin Brodeur, Jiri Bicek, Sergei Brylin, Ken Daneyko, Patrik Elias, Jeff Friesen, Brian Gionta, Scott Gomez, Jamie Langenbrunner, John Madden, Grant Marshall, Jim McKenzie, Scott Niedermayer, Joe Nieuwendyk, Jay Pandolfo, Brian Rafalski, Pascal Rheaume, Michael Rupp, Corey Schwab, Richard Smehlik, Turner Stevenson, Oleg Tverdovsky, Colin White, Raymond G. Chambers (Chairman), Lou Lamoriello (Pres./G.M.), Pat Burns (Head Coach), Bob Carpenter (Asst. Coach), Jacques Caron (Goaltending Coach), Dennis Gendron (AHL Coach), David Conte (Dir. of Scouting), Claude Carrier (Asst. Dir. of Scouting), Milt Fisher, Dan Labraaten, Marcel Pronovost (Scouts), Bob Hoffmeyer (Pro Scout), Dr. Barry Fisher (Orthopedist), Chris Terreri, Geordie Kinnear, Gates Orlando Dennis Gendron (AHL Asst. Coaches), Vladimir Bure (Consultant), Taran Singleton, Marie Carnevale, Callie Smith (Hockey Ops.), Bill Murray (Medical Trainer), Michael Vasalani (Strength/Conditioning Coord.), Rich Matthews (Equipment Mgr.), Juergen Merz (Massage Therapist), Alex Abasto, Joe Murray (Asst. Equipment Mgrs.).

* Final list of names for 2003 not finalized at press time.

LEADING PLAYOFF SCORERS

Player	Club	GP	G	A	PTS	PIM
Jamie Langenbrunner	New Jersey	24	11	7	18	16
Scott Niedermayer	New Jersey	24	2	16	18	16
Marian Gaborik	Minnesota	18	9	8	17	6
John Madden	New Jersey	24	6	10	16	2
Marian Hossa	Ottawa	18	5	11	16	6
Mike Modano	Dallas	12	5	10	15	4
Jeff Friesen	New Jersey	24	10	4	14	6
Markus Naslund	Vancouver	14	5	9	14	18
Sergei Zubov	Dallas	12	4	10	14	4
Nine players tied with					13	

LEADING PLAYOFF GOALTENDERS

Goaltender	Club	GPI	Mins	GA	SO	Avg.
J-S Giguere	Anaheim	21	1407	38	5	1.62
Martin Brodeur	New Jersey	24	1491	41	7	1.65
Patrick Lalime	Ottawa	18	1122	34	1	1.82
Marty Turco	Dallas	12	798	25	0	1.88
Manny Fernandez	Minnesota	9	552	18	0	1.96

PLAYOFF GOALS

Name, Team	G
Jamie Langenbrunner, N.J.	11
Jeff Friesen, N.J.	10
Marian Gaborik, Min.	9
Martin St. Louis, T.B.	7
Mark Recchi, Phi.	7
Ed Jovanovski, Van.	7
Wes Walz, Min.	7
Andrew Brunette, Min.	7
Steve Rucchin, Ana.	7
Six tied with	6

PLAYOFF ASSISTS

Name, Team	A
Scott Niedermayer, N.J.	16
Sergei Zholtok, Min.	11
Marian Hossa, Ott.	11
Mike Modano, Dal.	10
Sergei Zubov, Dal.	10
John Madden, N.J.	10
Markus Naslund, Van.	9
Adam Oates, Ana.	9
Petr Sykora, Ana.	9
Mike Leclerc, Ana.	9
Brian Rafalski, N.J.	9
Scott Gomez, N.J.	9

PLAYOFF POWERPLAY GOALS

Name, Team	PPG
Doug Weight, St.L.	5
Ed Jovanovski, Van.	4
Andrew Brunette, Min.	4
Daniel Alfredsson, Ott.	4
Marian Gaborik, Min.	4

PLAYOFF SHORTHAND GOALS

Name, Team	SHG
Martin St. Louis, T.B.	2
Wes Walz, Min.	2
Rob Niedermayer, Ana.	2
12 tied with	1

PLAYOFF GAME-WINNING GOALS

Name, Team	GWG
Jamie Langenbrunner, N.J.	4
Jeff Friesen, N.J.	4
Martin St. Louis, T.B.	3
Steve Thomas, Ana.	3
10 tied with	2

PLAYOFF GOALIE WINS

Name, Team	W
Martin Brodeur, N.J.	16
J-S Giguere, Ana.	15
Patrick Lalime, Ott.	11
Dan Cloutier, Van.	7
Marty Turco, Dal.	6
Roman Cechmanek, Phi.	6

PLAYOFF SHUTOUTS

Name, Team	SO
Martin Brodeur, N.J.	7
J-S Giguere, Ana.	5
Roman Cechmanek, Phi.	2
Four tied with	1

PLAYOFF SAVE PERCENTAGE

Name, Team	SV%
J-S Giguere, Ana.	.945
Martin Brodeur, N.J.	.934
Manny Fernandez, Min.	.929
Patrick Lalime, Ott.	.924
Marty Turco, Dal.	.919

All-Time NHL Franchises
1917-18 – 2003-04

NHL Franchise	Entered NHL	Last NHL Season	NHL Stanley Cup Wins
Mighty Ducks of Anaheim	1993–94		–
Atlanta Flames (e)	1972–73	1979–80	–
Atlanta Thrashers	1999–2000		–
Boston Bruins	1924–25		5
Brooklyn Americans (c)	1941–42	1941–42	–
Buffalo Sabres	1970–71		–
Calgary Flames (e)	1980–81		1
California Seals (d)	1967–68	1975–76	–
Carolina Hurricanes (j)	1997–98		–
Chicago Blackhawks	1926–27		3
Cleveland Barons (d)	1976–77	1977–78	–
Colorado Avalanche (h)	1995–96		2
Colorado Rockies (f)	1976–77	1981–82	–
Columbus Blue Jackets	2000–01		–
Dallas Stars (g)	1993–94		1
Detroit Cougars (b)	1926–27	1929–30	–
Detroit Falcons (b)	193–310	1931–32	–
Detroit Red Wings	1932–33		10
Edmonton Oilers	1979–80		5
Florida Panthers	1993–94		–
Hamilton Tigers	1920–21	1924–25	–
Hartford Whalers (j)	1979–80	1996–97	–
Kansas City Scouts (f)	1974–75	1975–76	–
Los Angeles Kings	1967–68		–
Minnesota North Stars (g)	1967–68	1992–93	–
Minnesota Wild	2000–01		–
Montreal Canadiens	1917–18		23
Montreal Maroons	1924–25	1937–38	2
Montreal Wanderers	1917–18	1917–18	–
Nashville Predators	1998–99		–
New Jersey Devils (f)	1982–83		3
New York Americans (c)	1925–26	1940–41	–
New York Islanders	1972–73		4
New York Rangers	1926–27		4
Ottawa Senators	1917–18	1930–31	4
Ottawa Senators	1932–33	1933–34	–
Ottawa Senators	1992–93		–
Philadelphia Flyers	1967–68		2
Philadelphia Quakers	1930–31	1930–31	–
Phoenix Coyotes (i)	1996–97		–
Pittsburgh Penguins	1967–68		2
Pittsburgh Pirates	1925–26	1929–30	–
Quebec Bulldogs	1919–20	1919–20	–
Quebec Nordiques (h)	1979–80	1994–95	–
St. Louis Blues	1967–68		–
St. Louis Eagles	1934–35	1934–35	–
San Jose Sharks	1991–92		–
Tampa Bay Lightning	1992–93		–
Toronto Arenas (a)	1917–18	1918–19	1
Toronto Maple Leafs (a)	1926–27		11
Toronto St. Patricks (a)	1919–20	1926–27	1
Vancouver Canucks	1970–71		–
Washington Capitals	1974–75		–
Winnipeg Jets (i)	1979–80	1995–96	–

NOTES:

(a) Toronto Arenas name changed to St. Patricks in 1919–20. St. Patricks changed to Maple Leafs partway through 1926–27.

(b) Detroit Cougars name changed to Falcons in 1930–31. Falcons name changed to Red Wings in 1932–33.

(c) New York Americans name changed to Brooklyn Americans in 1941–42.

(d) Oakland Seals 1967–68 to 1969–70. California Seals 1970–71. California Golden Seals 1971–72 to 1976–76. Cleveland Barons 1976–77 to 1977–78. Cleveland franchise merged with Minnesota before 1978–79 season.

(e) Atlanta franchise transferred to Calgary prior to 1980–81 season.

(f) Kansas City franchise moved to Denver and became the Colorado Rockies in 1976–77. Franchise transferred to East Rutherford, New Jersey and became the New Jersey Devils in 1982–83.

(g) Minnesota franchise transferred to Dallas prior to 1993–94 season.

(h) Quebec franchise transferred to Colorado prior to 1995–96 season.

(i) Winnipeg franchise transferred to Phoenix prior to 1996–97 season.

(j) Hartford franchise transferred to Carolina prior to 1997–98 season.

TOTAL NHL

Section 2: Franchise Histories

1917-18 to 2002-03

NATIONAL HOCKEY LEAGUE

Referee's Report of Match

Chicago vs. Toronto

Played in Arena Rink Toronto City, Date Nov 12/31

No.	Club Chicago	Position	Club Leafs	No.
1	Gardiner	Goal	Chabot	1
2	Abel	Defence	Horner	2
3	Bostrom	"	Levinsky	3
4		"		4
5		Forward	Blair	5
6		"	Bailey	6
7	Couture	"	Clancy	7
8		Spare	Cotton	8
9		"	Conacher	9
10	Wentworth	"	Primeau	10
11	Cook	"	Jackson	11
12	Graham	"	Finnigan	12
14		"		14
16	Adams	"	Horne	15
17				16

Match Started at 8 55 Finished 11 05

Won by Chicago Score 2 to 1

Penalty Recorder

Umpires

Timekeeper

Scorer

REMARKS

Signed Referee

Referees are requested to fill in this report and mail or deliver same immediately after each match to the President of the League, FRANK CALDER, 80 Hospital St. Room 203, MONTREAL.

All matches must start at the advertised time of 8.15 P.M. and if there is more than fifteen minutes, delay, state cause of same and name of club at fault. Undue rough play and name of offending players must be included in this report.

The referee's report of match for the first game played in Maple Leaf Gardens. Chicago defeated Toronto 2–1 on November 12, 1931. Note the start time of 8:55. The pregame ceremonies were lengthy and involved bagpipers and a live orchestra.

Mighty Ducks of Anaheim

THE TRADE THAT SENT WAYNE GRETZKY to the Los Angeles Kings in 1988 did more than anyone could have imagined to spark hockey interest in the United States. Still, the prospect of more than one team at that time in Southern California seemed unimaginable.

But, that was prior to 1992, when a $103-million arena began taking shape in the city of Anaheim. Once a small town better known as the butt of Jack Benny jokes, Anaheim had grown into prominence as the home of Disneyland, as well as one of the major satellite communities of Greater Los Angeles. Anaheim badly wanted to be known as a metropolis in Orange County and the arena would help enhance that image. Once the building was in place, a team would be sought. With that in mind, the city fathers erected a major-league facility that rivaled that of any city on the continent.

For a time, it appeared Anaheim's rink would turn into a white elephant bigger than Dumbo, but Michael Eisner would change all that. Eisner conferred with Bruce McNall, then-owner of the Kings, and learned the NHL might look kindly on a second major-league hockey team in Southern California. Since the building was there and Eisner—whose passion for hockey was deeply rooted—envisioned several positive possibilities for integrating it into his film business, all the pieces began to fall into place.

One of the first pieces was Disney's film The Mighty Ducks, which preceded the arena and became an instant hit. Grossing more than $50 million, the movie whetted Eisner's appetite for an NHL franchise. This coincided with the transfer of NHL power from the conservative regime of president John Ziegler to Gary Bettman, who was named the league's first commissioner late in 1992.

Known as "The Grim Reaper" for his tough style of play, Stu Grimson was an early fan favorite in Anaheim.

Under Bettman, the NHL was encouraging strong ownership and, at the Board of Governors meetings in December, 1992, both Disney (Anaheim) and Wayne Huizenga (South Florida) were awarded expansion franchises. The expansion fee was $50 million. In the case of Anaheim, $25 million went to the NHL and the rest to McNall because of territorial indemnification.

"There's great growth in hockey," Eisner enthused. "In the way hockey is shot (on television), we can be creative in creating stars. We do it in the movie business."

That very "movie business" intruded heavily into hockey thinking from the very beginning in Anaheim, as, to the dismay of traditionalists, Eisner's team became the Mighty Ducks of Anaheim.

Tony Tavares, who had much experience in the arena business and had worked briefly with McNall, became point man for the management team and he, in turn, hired Jack Ferreira as g.m. and Pierre Gauthier as Ferreira's assistant.

A onetime goaltender for Boston University, Ferreira had considerable scouting and front-office experience with the New England Whalers, Calgary Flames and New York Rangers. The Montreal-born Gauthier won his spurs as scouting director for the Quebec Nordiques. Together they attended the NHL Expansion Draft in Quebec City in June, 1993, and picked goaltender Guy Hebert with their first choice after Florida had selected John Vanbiesbrouck. The Ducks' braintrust made an even more important first selection in the Entry Draft that immediately followed when they landed Paul Kariya from the University of Maine. The first freshman to win the Hobey Baker Award as the best collegiate player in the USA, Kariya had played for the NCAA titlists and was projected as a superstar despite his smallish physique, though he would spend a year with the Canadian national team before signing with the Ducks for their second season. For head coach, Anaheim chose Ron Wilson, an assistant with the Vancouver Canucks, who earlier had been an offensive-minded defenseman at Providence College and later in the pros.

The Mighty Ducks played their first exhibition game at Anaheim on September 18, 1993, against the Pittsburgh Penguins. A crowd of 16,673 proved a good barometer of sellouts to come: more than 12,000 season tickets had been sold along with more than 40 luxury boxes. Ducks fans began filling Arrowhead Pond early in the season and remained loyal throughout.

On the ice, the Mighty Ducks were just what had been expected of an expansion team: mediocre but promising. In fact, as the season progressed, it became evident that Wilson had devised a workable system to produce a competitive team. As late as March 6, 1994, the Mighty Ducks still had a shot at a playoff berth. Not surprisingly, they faded in the stretch and officially were eliminated from the race with five games remaining on the slate. But, there was one consolation; they did finish ahead of Los Angeles. "That gave us a great feeling," Wilson admitted.

The Mighty Ducks concluded 1993–94 with 71 points (33–46–5), setting a first-year record with Florida for most wins in a season. They had 19 road wins, most ever by a first-year club in

Franchise Histories prepared with contributions from Mike Board, Tim Campbell, Bob Duff, Stan Fischler, Bruce Garrioch, Jeff Gordon, Chrys Goyens, Jay Greenberg, Brian McFarlane, Ross McKeon and Eric Zweig.

the NHL. Of greater importance, the club captured the attention of Southern California hockey fans, while the rival Kings were in a tailspin.

There was no diminishing of popularity in 1994–95, although the NHL lockout permitted only a 48-game season that didn't begin until January, 1995. In the shortened schedule the Mighty Ducks were a microcosm of the 1993–94 team. They were competitive, staying in the playoff hunt through the homestretch, but were eliminated from contention with only two games remaining, although a strong finish provided optimism for the future. So did Kariya who, as a rookie, led the team in scoring with 39 points (18 goals, 21 assists) in 47 games. Rookie defenseman Oleg Tverdovsky blossomed into an offensive threat, while Guy Hebert's goaltending proved solid. A testimony to fan loyalty was the 24 consecutive home sellouts at Arrowhead Pond.

Disney marketing—not to mention a sequel to the original Mighty Ducks movie—was copied by other teams. Despite the Ducks' low standing, they managed to attract large crowds wherever they played, partly because of the Disney connection and the attraction of the jerseys. But, by far the most significant landmark in the team's evolution was a trade completed on February 7, 1996. Ferreira dealt potential stars Tverdovsky and Chad Kilger to Winnipeg for Finnish whiz Teemu Selanne.

Teamed with Kariya, Selanne averaged more than a point a game in the stretch and was a prime reason why the Ducks nearly qualified for a Western Conference playoff spot. They finished tied for eighth in the conference with Winnipeg, but lost the tie-breaker because the Jets had more wins. Nevertheless, Anaheim's 35 wins and 78 points were club records for one season and the combination of Selanne and Kariya virtually guaranteed that the upswing would continue into 1996–97.

By now Wilson had established himself as a first-rate coach and the playoff berth obtained in the spring of 1997 underlined the point. Judiciously employing Selanne and Kariya—Steve Rucchin usually was third man on the first line—Wilson energized Anaheim to a 7–3–4 record for 18 points in March, 1997, when his team needed it most. They followed that with an undefeated April (3–0–2) before qualifying for the playoffs.

With an overall mark of 36–33–13, the Mighty Ducks celebrated their first winning season. Selanne's 109 points trailed only Mario Lemieux in the NHL scoring race, while Kariya's 99 points in just 69 games ranked him third. Appropriately, the Ducks collided with Phoenix—formerly the Winnipeg Jets—in the opening playoff round, which exceeded dramatic expectations. After taking a two-games-to-none lead, Anaheim lost the next three in a row before rebounding for a 3–2 overtime win in game six. Kariya, on a pass from Selanne, scored at 7:29 of sudden death to send the series to a seventh game. This time Hebert stopped all 31 shots he faced in earning his first playoff shutout.

Advancing to the second round, Anaheim faced the eventual Stanley Cup-winning Detroit Red Wings. Three out of the four games went into overtime but each time the Motor City sextet won and they swept the series. Still it had been a highly successful season in Anaheim—though it would have a bitter aftermath.

A dispute between Wilson and upper management resulted in the hiring of Pierre Page as Wilson's replacement. (The latter moved on to become head coach of the Washington Capitals.) In addition, a contract dispute between Kariya and the high command left the superstar home in Vancouver while Selanne was compelled to carry the scoring load.

The disruptions left the Mighty Ducks in disarray, although Selanne nobly performed extraordinary feats of skill to at least keep his club competitive. Eventually, Kariya returned with a new, enlarged pact but his comeback would be aborted because of a serious concussion following a post-scoring hit delivered by Gary Suter of the Chicago Blackhawks.

Offseason changes prior to the 1998–99 campaign saw Pierre Gauthier succeed Jack Ferreira as general manager after two-plus seasons in Ottawa. Former Blackhawks coach Craig Hartsburg took over behind the bench. Most importantly, Kariya was able to defy doomsayers who thought he might never play again. With 101 points in 1998–99, he again finished third in the league, while Teemu Selanne placed second with 109 points—including a league-leading 47 goals that won him the Maurice Richard Trophy. The Ducks returned to the playoffs, but were ousted in four straight by the Red Wings.

Anaheim had a difficult season in 1999–2000 and failed to make the playoffs. Both Paul Kariya and Teemu Selanne saw their offensive totals decline, though both continued to rank among the league's top scorers. Lack of production from the rest of the lineup, and an uneven season from the usually reliable Guy Hebert in goal, hurt the Mighty Ducks. A powerplay that had ranked first in the NHL the season before tumbled to 27th in the league midway through the 1999–2000 campaign. Traditionally slow starters throughout the brief history of the franchise, Anaheim was not able to make a late run for the playoffs in 1999–2000.

The 2000–01 season was a year of upheaval as Anaheim missed the playoffs for the second season in a row and fell to just 66 points. Coach Craig Hartsburg was fired in December. Assistant coach Guy Charron took over the Ducks on December 14, but could only guide the club to a record of 14–26–7–2 over the final 49 games. With the team out of playoff contention, the decision was made to trade Teemu Selanne. He was dealt to the San Jose Sharks for Jeff Friesen, Steve Shields and future considerations on March 5, 2001. Hampered by injuries once again, Paul Kariya played just 66 games but led the Ducks in goals (33) and points (67) for the fourth time in seven seasons.

Among the club's few bright spots was the play of Jean-Sebastien Giguere, who succeeded Guy Hebert as the club's top goaltender in February. Giguere ranked among the NHL leaders in several categories during the second half of the season and continued to star under new head coach Bryan Murray during the 2001–02 campaign. Giguere set a club record with a 2.13 goals-against average (fifth in the NHL). His save percentage of .920 tied

Mighty Ducks of Anaheim

Year-by-Year Record

Season	GP	W	L	T	OL	GF	GA	Pts.	Finish	Division	Playoff Result\
1993-94	84	33	46	5	...	229	251	71	4th	Pacific Div.	Out of Playoffs
1994-95	48	16	27	5	...	125	164	37	6th	Pacific Div.	Out of Playoffs
1995-96	82	35	39	8	...	234	247	78	4th	Pacific Div.	Out of Playoffs
1996-97	82	36	33	13	...	245	233	85	2nd	Pacific Div.	Lost Conf. Semifinal
1997-98	82	26	43	13	...	205	261	65	6th	Pacific Div.	Out of Playoffs
1998-99	82	35	34	13	...	215	206	83	3rd	Pacific Div.	Lost Conf. Quarterfinal
99-2000	82	34	33	12	3	217	227	83	5th	Pacific Div.	Out of Playoffs
2000-01	82	25	41	11	5	188	245	66	5th	Pacific Div.	Out of Playoffs
2001-02	82	29	42	8	3	175	198	69	5th	Pacific Div.	Out of Playoffs
2002-03	82	40	27	9	6	203	193	95	2nd	Pacific Div.	Lost Final

for fifth in the league. Paul Kariya played the entire 82-game schedule and once again led the Ducks in goals (32) and points (57). Though the team finished 13th in the Western Conference with 69 points, at least Kariya had the satisfaction of contributing to Canada's gold medal victory at the 2002 Olympics.

Anaheim's poor performance in 2001–02 cost club president and general manager Pierre Gauthier his job. Bryan Murray was bumped upstairs and promptly hired Mike Babcock as the Ducks' new coach. Babcock had spent the two previous seasons as coach of the team's American Hockey League affiliate in Cincinnati. Murray also engineered a blockbuster deal that sent Jeff Friesen and Oleg Tverdovsky to New Jersey for four players, including Petr Sykora. During the season, Sandis Ozolinsh was acquired from Florida to add offensive punch to a blueline corps anchored by Keith Carney. Adam Oates had already come on board as a free agent. He missed 15 games due to injuries, but still helped spark an offense that was led by Sykora (34 goals) and Kariya, whose 56 assists and 81 points ranked among the league leaders. Another free agent pickup, Jason Krog, proved to be a valuable addition.

Late in the season, Murray picked up Steve Thomas from Chicago. The former sniper re-discovered his old form and scored 10 goals in 12 games down the stretch. However, it was the goaltending of Giguere (eight shutouts, 2.30 GAA) that may have been most responsible for the Ducks reaching the playoffs for just the third time in their 10-year history. During a five-game span in mid-December, Giguere made 100 consecutive saves while recording three straight shutouts and playing scoreless hockey for 237 minutes and seven seconds. It was the third-longest regular-season streak in modern NHL history, behind only Bill Durnan of the Montreal Canadiens (309:21 in 1949) and Turk Broda of the Toronto Maple Leafs (245:33 in 1950). Durnan is the only goaltender in modern history to have recorded four consecutive shutouts—though Giguere would take another run at his mark during the playoffs.

The Ducks had performed poorly during the first half of the 2002–03 season, but were one of the NHL's best teams over the second half, posting a record of 24–10–2–3 in their final 39 games. They wound up setting team records for wins (40) and points (95) and their 26-point improvement over 2001–02 was the league's best. Still, few people gave them much of a chance against the defending champion Detroit Red Wings in the first round of the playoffs. However, they wound up sweeping the series for a stunning upset behind the brilliant goaltending of Giguere who was making his first playoff appearance. He stopped 165 of 171 shots in the series for a .965 save percentage and a 1.24 goals-against average. Giguere stopped 63 of 64 shots as the Ducks beat the Red Wings 2–1 in triple overtime in the series opener. Steve Thomas capped a late rally in game two as Anaheim shocked Detroit again. Giguere and rookie Stanislav Chistov sparkled in game three as the Ducks scored another 2–1 victory. Steve Rucchin was the overtime hero as the Ducks capped the series with a 3–2 win in game four.

The hot streak continued against top-seeded Dallas in round two, although this time the Ducks needed five overtime periods to pull off their game-one upset. It was the fourth-longest game in NHL history. After surrendering the game-tying goal late in the third period, and having the apparent game-winner called back late in the third overtime session, Petr Sykora gave the plucky Ducks a 4–3 victory 48 seconds into the game's eighth frame. Giguere made 60 saves in yet another stellar performance, making him the first netminder in NHL history to make 60 saves or more in two games in the one playoff year. Game two also required overtime, but this time the Ducks needed just 1:44 before Mike Leclerc gave them a 3–2 win. Rob Niedermayer had tied the game with 1:09 left in the third when his attempted pass deflected off the skate of Stu Barnes and past Marty Turco.

Anaheim suffered its first loss of the playoffs with a 2–1 defeat in game three, but bounced back to take a commanding 3–1 series lead when Giguere recorded his first shutout of the playoffs. Leclerc again scored the game winner, this time with 1:47 left in regulation time, as the Ducks scored a 1–0 victory. Dallas staved off elimination in game five, chasing Giguere after two periods and going on to win 4–1, but the Ducks wrapped up the series with a 4–3 win back at home in game six. Sandis Ozolinsh scored the series winner on a setup from Leclerc with 1:06 remaining in the third period. Steve Thomas had led the way with a goal and two assists. Anaheim had become the first team in the history of the Conference playoff format to knock off the top two seeds in the first two rounds. The Ducks would now play in the Western Conference final for the first time in franchise history . "The plan was to find a way to win and get the job done," said coach Mike

Paul Kariya made his debut with Anaheim in 1994–95 and quickly developed into one of the league's top talents.

Babcock. "It doesn't matter what you do or how you do it, but this is beyond our wildest dreams." They would now be facing the NHL's other Cinderella playoff team—the Minnesota Wild.

Once again in round three, the Ducks were required to go into multiple overtime in the opening game. This time, it 'only' took until 8:06 of the second extra session before Petr Sykora converted a nice feed from Mike Leclerc to give Anaheim a 1–0 victory. Giguere stopped all 39 shots he faced and ran his overtime shutout streak to 160 minutes and 49 seconds, second longest all-time in the NHL and just 1:57 shy of the record set by his boyhood hero Patrick Roy from 1993 through 1997. Giguere recorded another shutout in game two as the Ducks scored a 2–0 win which gave them victories in the first two games on the road for the third consecutive playoff series. Back at home in game three, Giguere notched his third straight shutout in a 4–0 win, making him the first goaltender to open a playoff series with three consecutive scoreless games since Frank McCool of the Maple Leafs in 1945. He stopped 35 shots in the game, including 16 in the first period, as his shutout streak reached 213 minutes and 17 seconds dating back to the third period of game six against Dallas. The Stanley Cup playoff record of 270:08 was set by the Canadiens' George Hainsworth in 1930. Just as importantly for the Ducks, Paul Kariya, who had been playing effective defensive hockey, finally seemed to break out offensively. Kariya had two goals in the second period of game three after having scored just twice since netting the overtime winner in Anaheim's first playoff victory over Detroit.

The chance at a playoff shutout record fell by the wayside when Minnesota scored early in the first period of game four (Giguere's streak reached 217:44, fifth longest in history), but the Ducks bounced back with a pair of powerplay goals from Adam Oates and swept the series with a 2–1 victory. The team's first berth in the Stanley Cup finals was more than enough of a present for Giguere, who was celebrating his 26th birthday. "It's something I've been dreaming of since I was a kid," said the goalie. "Just to be part of this is exceptional, but it's only the beginning. Every game (of the finals) is going to be exciting."

Because they had swept their series, and the Devils needed a full seven gamed to dispose of Ottawa, the Ducks had 10 days off before facing New Jersey in game one of the Stanley Cup finals. They looked rusty in dropping a 3–0 decision to the Devils in the opener, but coach Mike Babcock refused to use the layoff as an excuse. The Devils gave the Ducks more of their same medicine in game two, blanking them again for another 3–0 victory. Giguere challenged his teammates to step up in game three and they did so, outshooting their opponents (33–31) for the first time in the postseason. Still, it took one flukey goal by Sandis Ozolinsh then a goal by Ruslan Salei right from a face-off victory by Adam Oates at 6:59 of overtime to give the Ducks a 3–2 victory. Anaheim improved its overtime record to 6–0 in the playoffs and Giguere ran his scoreless streak to a record 167:48. The Ducks tied the series with another overtime victory in game four. Steve Thomas got the winner after just 39 seconds and Giguere made 24 saves in a 1–0 win.

Game five was back in New Jersey, but the Ducks got on the scoreboard first when Petr Sykora scored after just 42 seconds from a face-off won by Adam Oates. The first goal had been key for Anaheim throughout the playoffs (the Ducks were 10–0 when scoring first), but not this time as the Devils bounced back for a

Though he'd already had a solid season in 2001–02, Jean-Sebastien Giguere skyrocketed into the limelight during a brilliant run in the 2003 playoffs.

6–3 win in by far the highest-scoring game of the series. The goals scoring splurge continued back in Anaheim for game six, as the Ducks stayed alive with an impressive 5–2 victory. Having been silent for much of the series, Paul Kariya set up two goals as the Ducks raced to a 3–0 lead after one period. He had to be helped off the ice after a devastating hit from Scott Stevens midway through the second period, but Kariya returned just a few minutes later and blew a shot past Martin Brodeur to restore the three-goal lead at 4–1. "It was an incredible play," said longtime teammate Steve Rucchin, who scored twice in the first period. "What a sign of leadership. I can't say enough about that play. What a competitor."

Unfortunately for the Ducks, game seven marked midnight on their Cinderella season. The Devils came out strong on home ice once again and scored yet another 3–0 victory. As in the opener, ex-Duck Jeff Friesen scored twice. For Martin Brodeur, it was his third shutout of the series and his record-setting seventh in the playoffs, but it was J.S. Giguere who took home the Conn Smythe Trophy as MVP of the postseason. "I don't think there was any question that he was the single person that did the most for his team," said Ducks general manager Bryan Murray. Still, "This is not the one you want," said Giguere, who was in tears when the game ended. "You want the big silver one; that's the one you're aiming for." He became the fifth player from a losing team to win the Conn Smythe Trophy, joining goaltenders Roger Crozier (Detroit, 1966), Glenn Hall (St. Louis, 1968) and Ron Hextall, (Philadelphia 1987) as well as the Flyers' Reggie Leach (1976). "He was a real rock for us," said Paul Kariya.

Atlanta Thrashers

On June 25, 1997, the National Hockey League awarded expansion teams to Nashville, Columbus, Minnesota and Atlanta. The awarding of the Atlanta franchise saw NHL hockey return to Georgia, which had first entered the league in 1972–73. The lack of a major television contract and a crumbling real estate empire saw the Atlanta Flames sold to Calgary in 1980. Fan support was never seen as an issue in Atlanta, and TV and ownership shouldn't be a problem this time under Ted Turner and Turner Broadcasting System, Inc.

Turner Sports president Dr. Harvey Schiller, former executive director of the United States Olympic Committee, became club president when the franchise was obtained. The nickname Thrashers for the Atlanta hockey club was announced on February16, 1998. It was taken from the state bird of Georgia—the Brown Thrasher. The team logo communicates the characteristics of fierce determination and speed.

Almost a year to the day after the franchise was awarded, Don Waddell was hired as the Thrashers' general manager on June 23, 1998. An assistant g.m. in Detroit during the 1997–98 season, Waddell had previously served as the vice president and general manager of the International Hockey League's Orlando Solar Bears from 1995 to 1997. Prior to the Solar Bears, he held the same role with the IHL's San Diego Gulls from 1990 to 1995. Waddell's playing career included three seasons in the Los Angeles Kings' farm system. He was a member of the United States national team in 1983. An injury kept him from appearing with the 1980 "Miracle on Ice" United States Olympic hockey team.

Selected second overall in the 2000 Entry Draft, Dany Heatley won the Calder Trophy in 2001–02 and was named MVP of the 2003 All-Star Game after a four-goal performance.

For the first head coach in Atlanta, Waddell turned to former NHL player Curt Fraser, who had coached for him previously with Orlando. In fact, the Solar Bears reached the Turner Cup finals under Fraser as a first-year expansion team in 1995–96.

Waddell had begun the process of building his team before hiring Fraser on July 14, 1999. Slightly less than one month earlier (June 18) the club had acquired its first player when goaltender Damian Rhodes was obtained from the Ottawa Senators for future considerations. Andrew Brunette was picked up from Nashville three days later. The bulk of the first-year roster was obtained in the Expansion Draft on June 25. Players picked up that day included Yannick Tremblay from Toronto, Johan Garpenlov from Florida, Kelly Buchberger from Edmonton and David Harlock from the New York Islanders. However, the player on which the Atlanta brass has pinned its hopes for the future was acquired in the Entry Draft on June 26, 1999.

Though the concussion he had suffered while playing for the IHL's Long Beach Ice Dogs scared off some teams, Waddell was determined to land Patrik Stefan for the Thrashers. A series of draft-day deals saw Atlanta move up from the second choice to the first, which they used to obtain the player who was seen as the most physically mature prospect available. The youngest member of the Thrashers would soon be joined by veterans like Nelson Emerson and Ray Ferraro, who were acquired as free agents in July and August respectively.

The NHL was a 28-team league (on its way to 30) when the Thrashers came on board for the 1999–2000 season. Playing out of the Southeast Division of the Eastern Conference with the Carolina Hurricanes, Florida Panthers, Tampa Bay Lightning and Washington Capitals, Atlanta played its first regular-season game on October 2, 1999. A capacity crowd of 18,545 filled the Philips Arena, the new facility the Thrashers share with the NBA's Atlanta Hawks to watch the New Jersey Devils beat the home side 4–1. Captain Kelly Buchberger scored the Thrashers' goal.

After a 7–1 loss to the Detroit Red Wings in their second game, Atlanta picked up its first point in a 5–5 tie with Buffalo on October 9. Stefan starred in that contest, collecting two goals against Sabres goalie—and fellow Czech native—Dominik Hasek. He also picked up an assist. Stefan set up a key goal in a road game five nights later when the Thrashers scored the first win in franchise history. He set up Buchberger for the clinching goal in a 2–0 win over the New York Islanders. The Thrashers picked up their first home-ice victory on October 26 against Atlanta's prior incarnation the Calgary Flames. Nelson Emerson and Andrew Brunette had the goals, but it was Damian Rhodes who was the hero that night in a 2–1 victory. Unfortunately for Atlanta, injuries would keep Rhodes out for much of the season. Norm Maracle assumed the number-one role.

Still, crowds flocked to Philips Arena—the Thrashers became the first NHL expansion team to average better than 17,000 per

Atlanta Thrashers

Year-by-Year Record

Season	GP	W	L	T	OL	GF	GA	Pts.	Finish	Division	Playoff Result
99-2000	82	14	57	7	4	170	313	39	5th	Southeast Div.	Out of Playoffs
2000-01	82	23	45	12	2	211	289	60	4th	Southeast Div.	Out of Playoffs
2001-02	82	19	47	11	5	187	288	54	5th	Southeast Div.	Out of Playoffs
2002-03	82	31	39	7	5	226	284	74	3rd	Southeast Div.	Out of Playoffs

game—but it was a long season for Atlanta hockey fans. Particularly trying was a record-tying 17-game home winless streak (two ties, 15 losses) that lasted until April 2. In all, the team won just 14 games—and six of those were against either the Islanders or the Tampa Bay Lightning. Bright spots for the team included the play of Andrew Brunette, who led the club in goals (23) and assists (27) and Ray Ferraro, who matched his totals of the two previous seasons combined when he scored 19 goals, including a team-leading 10 on the powerplay. Patrik Stefan suffered through a prolonged scoring drought and finished the season with just five goals and 20 assists, but it was young players like him who would offer hope for the future.

Veterans Ray Ferraro and Andrew Brunette were the team leaders once again in 2000–01 as the Thrashers showed great improvement over their inaugural campaign. Ferraro's 29 goals were the most he'd scored since netting 40 in 1991–92, while his 47 assists tied a career high established back in 1985–86. Donald Audette enjoyed a career year, but was traded to Buffalo late in the season. As a team, the Thrashers improved their offense by 41 goals and increased their wins from 14 to 23 and their points from 39 to 60. Still, the greatest moments for the team continued to come at the drafting table. Having claimed Patrik Stefan first overall at the 1999 NHL Entry Draft, the Thrashers grabbed Dany Heatley with the second choice in 2000 and selected Ilya Kovalchuk with the number one pick in 2001.

Though the team seemed to take a step back during the 2001–02 campaign, improvements in the second half augered well for the future. Of course, nothing held out more promise than the play of Heatley and Kovalchuk, who both enjoyed brilliant debuts. Despite missing the last 16 games of the season, Kovalchuk led all rookies with 29 goals, while Heatley topped all freshmen with 41 assists and 67 points and was named rookie of the year. The dynamic duo became the first teammates to finish 1–2 in rookie scoring since Brian Leetch and Tony Granato with the Rangers in 1988–89 and the first to finish 1–2 in Calder Trophy voting since Bryan Trottier and Glenn Resch of the Islanders in 1975–76.

Despite the enthusiasm (and offensive production) generated by Heatley and Kovalchuk, the Thrashers struggled out of the gate in 2002–03. Atlanta had a record of just 8–20–1–4 when coach Curt Fraser was fired in December. Former Colorado Avalanche coach Bob Hartley was hired on January 14 and immediately began to install a winning attitude. (The team had a record of 19–14–5–1 after Hartley took over). Already the team's top scorer, Heatley seemed to elevate his game under Hartley. On February 2, 2003, he tied a record with four goals at the NHL All-Star Game. He finished the year among the NHL leaders with 41 goals and 89 points. Heatley was the hottest player in the league over the last quarter of the season, as his 15 goals and 15 assists in his final 18 games gave him more goals and points than anyone else—including Art Ross Trophy winner Peter Forsberg and Maurice Richard Trophy winner Milan Hejduk. Ilya Kovalchuk scored 38 times on the season for the Thrashers, while Vyacheslav Kozlov had a team-best 49 assists. Pasi Nurminen established himself as the club's top goaltender as the Thrashers set team records with 31 wins and 74 points and climbed to third place in the Southeast Division standings. Heatley's star continued to rise even after the season when he was Team Canada's top scorer (seven goals and three assists in nine games) during a gold medal performance at the 2003 World Championship.

Picked number one overall in 2001, Ilya Kovalchuk led all rookies with 29 goals in 2001–02 and improved his total to 38 in 2002–03.

Boston Bruins

When the NHL was formed in 1917, the Boston Athletic Association was the defending American Amateur Hockey League champion. Boston was already a hockey hub, and it was appropriate that the Bruins would become the first American team in the National Hockey League.

Grocery store magnate Charles Adams had sponsored an amateur club in Boston, but became disenchanted after discovering that several rivals were spreading rather large gratuities among their players. Ripe for a professional franchise, Adams was lobbied by a group that included Tom Duggan, Frank Sullivan and Russ Layton who insisted that a firsthand view of an NHL game would persuade the millionaire to invest his money in professional hockey. Adams agreed to attend the 1924 Stanley Cup finals between the Calgary Tigers and a Montreal Canadiens club loaded with such legends as Georges Vezina, Howie Morenz, Aurel Joliat and Sprague Cleghorn. He was hooked.

Adams wasted little time organizing his new enterprise. During his Canadian excursion he had met early hockey legend Art Ross. Adams liked the man and promptly named him coach, general manager and scout of the new team. However, when the 1924–25 season ended, the Bruins' only claim to fame was that they were America's first NHL team. They barely held up the bottom of the six-team league with a feeble record of six wins and 24 losses.

Despite their misfortune, the Bruins made a singular impact on Bostonians, who began filling Boston Arena. Adams responded after two years by spending $50,000 on a massive infusion of talent. He landed Duke Keats, Perk Galbraith, Harry Oliver and Harry Meeking as well as the inimitable Eddie Shore from the folding Western Hockey League. With Shore as its centerpiece, the Bruins began muscling their way to a more prominent place in the NHL. Within three seasons of the Bruins' birth, Boston had a Stanley Cup contender. Although Art Ross's team lost to Ottawa in the 1927 finals, more than 29,000 applications were received by the Bruins for tickets.

Responding to the hockey mania, and with the backing of Madison Square Garden money, promoters built a new arena for the 1928–29 season. Originally named "Boston Madison Square Garden," the rink opened on November 20, 1928. By season's end, the Bruins had reached the finals again, this time against the Rangers. On March 29, 1929, the visiting Bostonians defeated New York 2–1 to bring the Stanley Cup to the Hub for the first time.

The Dynamite line of Dit Clapper (left), Cooney Weiland (center) and Dutch Gainor (right). The high-scoring trio took full advantage of the NHL's new forward passing rules in 1929–30.

Having acquired Cecil "Tiny" Thompson from the Minneapolis Millers, Ross's Bruins boasted some of the best goaltending the league had ever seen. Thompson twice blanked the Canadiens in a three-game semifinal series, and then held New York to only one goal in two games in the finals. He finished with a 0.60 goals-against average through the five playoff games and would eventually win the Vezina Trophy four times before being dealt to the Detroit Red Wings.

Nevertheless, Shore was the draw at Boston Garden. The defenseman—equally renowned for his end-to-end rushes and bruising physical play—symbolized the macho hockey man of the early NHL days. After an injury left his ear hanging tenuously from the side of his head, Shore insisted on sewing it back on while an incredulous doctor held the mirror for him. Despite his heroics, Shore's career was marred by an ugly episode that nearly resulted in the death of Toronto Maple Leafs stickhandling expert Ace Bailey. The game, played at Boston Garden on the night of December 12, 1933, was a typically robust Toronto/Boston encounter, aggravated by the intense rivalry between Ross and Leafs boss Conn Smythe. The incident, which to this day remains one of the most discussed in league history, began when King Clancy and Red Horner of Toronto simultaneously checked Shore into the boards near the Maple Leafs net.

"I looked back," Clancy recalled, "saw Shore scrambling to his feet and then hit Bailey across the back of the legs. Eddie thought he was retaliating against me. I know he never meant it to be that bad." It was worse. Bailey nearly died in the hospital. After two delicate brain operations, Ace's recuperation was miraculous but he never played hockey again. Shore was suspended for 16 games, which Clancy called "fitting."

Shore's marquee personality tended to overshadow other Bruins who were outstanding in their own right. Aubrey "Dit" Clapper was a star forward who would conclude his 20-year Boston career as a defenseman of equal ability. Lionel Hitchman was every bit as good as Shore on the blue line but less belligerent. Frank Fredrickson, Harry Oliver, Norman "Dutch" Gainor and Ralph "Cooney" Weiland were among the other starry Bruins in their early years. Boston's "Dynamite Line" of Weiland, Clapper and Gainor was one of the better trios ever to don a Bruins uniform. They helped Boston finish first five times in the American Division in the nine seasons between 1929–30 and 1937–38.

Ever the insightful thinker, Art Ross was the first NHL coach to pull his goaltender in a Stanley Cup playoff game. Unheard of at the time, the tactic was employed on March 26, 1931. Ross pulled

Tiny Thompson for a sixth attacker in the last minute but the Montreal Canadiens were able to hold their 1–0 lead. By 1934, Ross had decided he wanted to concentrate on managing and hired Frank Patrick as coach. The salary of $10,500 was considered high for the time. Patrick lasted two seasons behind the bench, doing well in the regular season but losing the first playoff round in successive years. Ross removed Patrick at the start of the 1936–37 season and returned to the bench himself. His sense of timing was excellent. The Bruins had signed a hard-nosed center from Kitchener, Ontario, named Milt Schmidt and soon would add the kid's two pals, Bobby Bauer and Woody Dumart, who would form the outstanding Kraut Line.

When the NHL's two divisions amalgamated in 1938–39, Boston became the scourge of big-league hockey. Frank Brimsek replaced Tiny Thompson in goal and blossomed into one of the best goalies of all time. Another hero of what would prove to be Boston's second Stanley Cup-winning season was "Sudden Death" Mel Hill, who specialized for a brief 12 days in beating the Rangers in overtime. Boston won the best-of-seven semifinal series with New York four games to three; Hill secured three of the wins with overtime goals. He didn't provide any heroics in the Cup finals against Toronto, but none were needed. The Bruins dispatched the Leafs in five games and the team was hailed by many critics as the greatest of all time.

Even after Shore left Boston to play for the New York Americans in 1940, the Bostonians continued to rule. In 1940–41, paced by the Krauts and Brimsek, the Bruins were coached by Cooney Weiland, who had moved behind the bench to replace Ross the year before. Weiland directed his club to a seven-game semifinal playoff win over Toronto and then whipped Detroit four straight. The Krauts were magnificent, but no one was better than a deft center named Bill Cowley, who had won the scoring championship and reached new levels of stickhandling agility.

Cowley would play consecutively through the 1946–47 season, but the club's core soon would be demolished by World War II enlistments. Brimsek enlisted in the U.S. Coast Guard, while Schmidt, Dumart and Bauer signed up as a unit in the Royal Canadian Air Force. The Bruins would never be the same. At war's end, the four veterans returned to Boston, each having lost an edge during their service stint. Brimsek eventually was traded to Chicago and Bauer hung up his skates after the 1946–47 season—he returned for a one-game cameo appearance in 1951–52—leaving Schmidt and Dumart to carry the load. The former was superb for several years while the latter played a workmanlike checking role, which climaxed in the 1953 playoffs when Woody shadowed Gordie Howe efficiently enough to gain Boston an upset of the defending Stanley Cup champion Red Wings.

After retiring, Schmidt became Bruins coach in 1954–55 —with

Boston Bruins

Year-by-Year Record

Season	GP	W	L	T	OL	GF	GA	Pts.	Finish	Division	Playoff Result
1924-25	30	6	24	0	...	49	119	12	6th		Out of Playoffs
1925-26	36	17	15	4	...	92	85	38	4th	...	Out of Playoffs
1926-27	44	21	20	3	...	97	89	45	2nd	Amn. Div.	Lost Final
1927-28	44	20	13	11	...	77	70	51	1st	Amn. Div.	Lost Semifinal
1928-29	44	26	13	5	...	89	52	57	1st	Amn. Div.	Won Stanley Cup
1929-30	44	38	5	1	...	179	98	77	1st	Amn. Div.	Lost Final
1930-31	44	28	10	6	...	143	90	62	1st	Amn. Div.	Lost Semifinal
1931-32	48	15	21	12	...	122	117	42	4th	Amn. Div.	Out of Playoffs
1932-33	48	25	15	8	...	124	88	58	1st	Amn. Div.	Lost Semifinal
1933-34	48	18	25	5	...	111	130	41	4th	Amn. Div.	Out of Playoffs
1934-35	48	26	16	6	...	129	112	58	1st	Amn. Div.	Lost Semifinal
1935-36	48	22	20	6	...	92	83	50	2nd	Amn. Div.	Lost Quarterfinal
1936-37	48	23	18	7	...	120	110	53	2nd	Amn. Div.	Lost Quarterfinal
1937-38	48	30	11	7	...	142	89	67	1st	Amn. Div.	Lost Semifinal
1938-39	48	36	10	2	...	156	76	74	1st	...	Won Stanley Cup
1939-40	48	31	12	5	...	170	98	67	1st	...	Lost Semifinal
1940-41	48	27	8	13	...	168	102	67	1st	...	Won Stanley Cup
1941-42	48	25	17	6	...	160	118	56	3rd	...	Lost Semifinal
1942-43	50	24	17	9	...	195	176	57	2nd	...	Lost Final
1943-44	50	19	26	5	...	223	268	43	5th	...	Out of Playoffs
1944-45	50	16	30	4	...	179	219	36	4th	...	Lost Semifinal
1945-46	50	24	18	8	...	167	156	56	2nd	...	Lost Final
1946-47	60	26	23	11	...	190	175	63	3rd	...	Lost Semifinal
1947-48	60	23	24	13	...	167	168	59	3rd	...	Lost Semifinal
1948-49	60	29	23	8	...	178	163	66	2nd	...	Lost Semifinal
1949-50	70	22	32	16	...	198	228	60	5th	...	Out of Playoffs
1950-51	70	22	30	18	...	178	197	62	4th	...	Lost Semifinal
1951-52	70	25	29	16	...	162	176	66	4th	...	Lost Semifinal
1952-53	70	28	29	13	...	152	172	69	3rd	...	Lost Final
1953-54	70	32	28	10	...	177	181	74	4th	...	Lost Semifinal
1954-55	70	23	26	21	...	169	188	67	4th	...	Lost Semifinal
1955-56	70	23	34	13	...	147	185	59	5th	...	Out of Playoffs
1956-57	70	34	24	12	...	195	174	80	3rd	...	Lost Final
1957-58	70	27	28	15	...	199	194	69	4th	...	Lost Final
1958-59	70	32	29	9	...	205	215	73	2nd	...	Lost Semifinal
1959-60	70	28	34	8	...	220	241	64	5th	...	Out of Playoffs
1960-61	70	15	42	13	...	176	254	43	6th	...	Out of Playoffs
1961-62	70	15	47	8	...	177	306	38	6th	...	Out of Playoffs
1962-63	70	14	39	17	...	198	281	45	6th	...	Out of Playoffs
1963-64	70	18	40	12	...	170	212	48	6th	...	Out of Playoffs
1964-65	70	21	43	6	...	166	253	48	6th	...	Out of Playoffs
1965-66	70	21	43	6	...	174	275	48	5th	...	Out of Playoffs
1966-67	70	17	43	10	...	182	253	44	6th	...	Out of Playoffs
1967-68	74	37	27	10	...	259	216	84	3rd	East Div.	Lost Quarterfinal
1968-69	76	42	18	16	...	303	221	100	2nd	East Div.	Lost Semifinal
1969-70	76	40	17	19	...	277	216	99	2nd	East Div.	Won Stanley Cup
1970-71	78	57	14	7	...	399	207	121	1st	East Div.	Lost Quarterfinal
1971-72	78	54	13	11	...	330	204	119	1st	East Div.	Won Stanley Cup
1972-73	78	51	22	5	...	330	235	107	2nd	East Div.	Lost Quarterfinal
1973-74	78	52	17	9	...	349	221	113	1st	East Div.	Lost Final
1974-75	80	40	26	14	...	345	245	94	2nd	Adams Div.	Lost Prelim. Round
1975-76	80	48	15	17	...	313	237	113	1st	Adams Div.	Lost Semifinal
1976-77	80	49	23	8	...	312	240	106	1st	Adams Div.	Lost Final
1977-78	80	51	18	11	...	333	218	113	1st	Adams Div.	Lost Final
1978-79	80	43	23	14	...	316	270	100	1st	Adams Div.	Lost Semifinal
1979-80	80	46	21	13	...	310	234	105	2nd	Adams Div.	Lost Quarterfinal
1980-81	80	37	30	13	...	316	272	87	2nd	Adams Div.	Lost Prelim. Round
1981-82	80	43	27	10	...	323	285	96	2nd	Adams Div.	Lost Div. Final
1982-83	80	50	20	10	...	327	228	110	1st	Adams Div.	Lost Conf. Finals
1983-84	80	49	25	6	...	336	261	104	1st	Adams Div.	Lost Div. Semifinal
1984-85	80	36	34	10	...	303	287	82	4th	Adams Div.	Lost Div. Semifinal
1985-86	80	37	31	12	...	311	288	86	3rd	Adams Div.	Lost Div. Semifinal
1986-87	80	39	34	7	...	301	276	85	3rd	Adams Div.	Lost Div. Semifinal
1987-88	80	44	30	6	...	300	251	94	2nd	Adams Div.	Lost Final
1988-89	80	37	29	14	...	289	256	88	2nd	Adams Div.	Lost Div. Final
1989-90	80	46	25	9	...	289	232	101	1st	Adams Div.	Lost Final
1990-91	80	44	24	12	...	299	264	100	1st	Adams Div.	Lost Conf. Finals
1991-92	80	36	32	12	...	270	275	84	2nd	Adams Div.	Lost Conf. Finals
1992-93	84	51	26	7	...	332	268	109	1st	Adams Div.	Lost Div. Semifinal
1993-94	84	42	29	13	...	289	252	97	2nd	Northeast Div.	Lost Conf. Semifinal
1994-95	48	27	18	3	...	150	127	57	3rd	Northeast Div.	Lost Conf. Quarterfinal
1995-96	82	40	31	11	...	282	269	91	2nd	Northeast Div.	Lost Conf. Quarterfinal
1996-97	82	26	47	9	...	234	300	61	6th	Northeast Div.	Out of Playoffs
1997-98	82	39	30	13	...	221	194	91	2nd	Northeast Div.	Lost Conf. Quarterfinal
1998-99	82	39	30	13	...	214	181	91	3rd	Northeast Div.	Lost Conf. Semifinal
99-2000	82	24	33	19	6	210	248	73	5th	Northeast Div.	Out of Playoffs
2000-01	82	36	30	8	8	227	249	88	4th	Northeast Div.	Out of Playoffs
2001-02	82	43	24	6	9	236	201	101	1st	Northeast Div.	Lost Conf. Quarterfinal
2002-03	82	36	31	11	4	245	237	87	3rd	Northeast Div.	Lost Conf. Quarterfinal

modest success. By the early 1960s, Uke Line stars Bronco Horvath, Vic Stasiuk and Johnny Bucyk ranked among the league's best, but the Bruins missed the playoffs eight years in a row through 1966–67. That season, Harry Sinden, an intense 34-year-old coach who never played a game in the NHL, was given control of the club. When Schmidt became general manager in 1967–68, he produced one of the most one-sided trades ever. From the Chicago Black Hawks, the Bruins obtained Phil Esposito, Fred Stanfield and Ken Hodge for Jack Norris, Pit Martin and Gilles Marotte. That year, the Bruins began their ascent, abetted by the maturing wunderkind Bobby Orr, who was in the process of revolutionizing the game.

A Boston farmhand since the age of 14, Orr had joined the Bruins as an 18-year-old in 1966–67. Listed as a defenseman, Orr employed extraordinary speed, puck control and shooting ability. Rather than stick to defensive play, he would lead attack after attack, combining like perfectly meshed gears with the finishing genius, Esposito. Together, Orr and Espo helped end the Bruins' Stanley Cup drought with a four-straight sweep of St. Louis in the 1970 finals. The feat was minimized by some because Boston's opponent, the Blues, was an expansion team loaded with retreads and assorted castaways. Yet the image that remains firmly set in the minds of Bostonians is that of an exuberant Orr flying through the air past St. Louis defenseman Noel Picard after the Beantown hero had fired the Cup-winning sudden-death goal past goalie Glenn Hall.

The triumph was partially marred by Sinden's unexpected resignation over a salary dispute. He was replaced by Tom Johnson, the Hall of Fame defenseman who had been Boston's assistant general manager. Although Johnson coached the Bruins to a first-place finish in the East Division, there were concerns about the team's country-club attitude. Favored to repeat as Cup champs, Esposito, Orr & Co. encountered a Montreal team that started an inexperienced rookie goalie named Ken Dryden. As expected, Boston won the opener, but Dryden grew progressively stronger as the series unfolded, while the Bruins became more and more frustrated by the tall Cornell grad. The series ran a full seven games, ending with a remarkable Montreal victory.

Few teams ever have been more determined to atone for a humiliation than the 1971–72 Bruins, one of the most powerful teams ever assembled. They finished the season with the best record—Esposito was leading scorer and Orr the most valuable player—and then marched all the way to the finals where they collided with a mighty Rangers team thirsting for New York's first Cup in 32 years. At times the Rangers appeared on the verge of a breakthrough but, with the series three games to two in Boston's favor, the Bruins came to Madison Square Garden and let Orr do the skating and shooting. He ended a scoreless tie with a dazzling pirouette and then fired what would be the winning goal in what ultimately was a 3–0 decision for the Bruins.

The Bruins had the makings of a dynasty. Eddie Johnston and Gerry Cheevers provided splendid goaltending, while the Orr-centered defense was balanced and robust. Esposito, Ken Hodge, Derek Sanderson and Ed Westfall each provided diverse ingredients necessary to win a Stanley Cup championship.

But, few could have forecast the upheaval that was ahead. The simultaneous arrival of the World Hockey Association and NHL expansion would rob the Bruins of pivotal players. Cheevers, Sanderson and Ted Green immigrated to the new WHA, while Westfall was claimed by the expansion New York Islanders in 1972. The results were devastating for Boston. Johnson was fired in midseason and replaced by former Bruin Armand "Bep" Guidolin. The Canadiens swept past them in the regular-season race, although Esposito won the scoring championship and Orr won the Norris Trophy as the best defenseman. But, the playoffs were a disaster. Esposito was crippled by a knee injury, leaving the Bruins without a top sniper, and the Rangers knocked Boston out of the first round in five games.

The shock was almost as bad as it had been two years earlier and once again the Bruins vowed to regroup. True to their word, they finished an impressive first (52–17–9) in 1973–74 with the usual prizes. Esposito took both the Hart and Art Ross trophies, while Orr again earned the Norris Trophy and Johnny Bucyk won the Lady Byng Trophy. Most of the hockey world expected the Bruins to annex the Stanley Cup when they took on the expansion Philadelphia Flyers in the finals. But, once again a hot goaltender—this time Bernie Parent—did them in and Boston exited in six games. Despite Orr's heroics, the would-be dynasty was no more. Orr won the Norris Trophy yet again in 1975, but when the finals arrived it was Philadelphia versus Buffalo with Boston long gone.

Slowly yet relentlessly the Bruins lost their luster, and eventually lost Phil Esposito and Bobby Orr as well. Esposito was traded to the Rangers with Carol Vadnais for Brad Park, Jean Ratelle and Joe Zanussi on November 7, 1975. On June 24, 1976, Orr, the defenseman who symbolized Bruins hockey as much as Eddie Shore had in an earlier era, signed as a free agent with the Chicago Black Hawks.

Devastating as the losses may have been, the Bruins were revitalized in a curious way. New owners—Sports Systems Corp., led by brothers Jeremy, Max and Lawrence Jacobs of Eggerts, New York—assumed control of the club on August 28, 1975. A career minor-leaguer, Don Cherry, was hired as coach and infused an already rugged Boston squad with

A young Bobby Orr (wearing #27) talks things over with Bruins coach Harry Sinden.

even more fire. They finished first in the Adams Division in 1976–77 and went all the way to the Stanley Cup finals before being dispatched by the Canadiens in four straight. Cherry again brought them to the last round of the playoffs against Montreal the following spring and even managed to win the first two games played at Boston Garden—tying the series at two apiece—before losing in six games.

By now Cherry's exuberance had made him the coaching toast of the league. Everyone seemed to love him except g.m. Harry Sinden. A simmering feud was kept from exploding because Cherry delivered another first-place finish in 1978–79 and a four-game playoff sweep of Pittsburgh in the quarterfinals. He peaked in the semifinals, bringing Boston back from a three-games-to-two deficit against Montreal. Game seven was a classic, with the Bruins leading until late in the third period when a too-many-men-on-the-ice penalty was called against them. Guy Lafleur scored for the Habs to tie it up, and Montreal won the game and the series in overtime.

Cherry was fired. A year later, the Bruins were eliminated from playoff contention by the Islanders, in 1981 by Minnesota and in 1982 by Quebec. They did have the 1982 Lady Byng Trophy winner in Rick Middleton, a top scorer in Barry Pederson and solid goaltending from Pete Peeters, but the Islanders proved too formidable in the playoffs. Over the years, Sinden's adroit managing kept the Bruins in contention and they gained a playoff berth every season for 29 years until 1996–97, when their record streak was ended. They were able to remain a top club because of Orr's successor as defense hero, Raymond Bourque.

Less flamboyant than Orr or Shore, Bourque nevertheless was exceptionally skilled as a skater, shooter and stickhandler and, unlike Orr, was miraculously durable. He helped Boston to the Stanley Cup finals in 1988—a four-games-to-none loss to Edmonton—and again in 1990 when they took one game from a strong Oilers squad. Even though Bourque was a perpetual Norris Trophy candidate, his supporting cast was never sufficient to win the silver mug.

The deteriorating state of Boston Garden was never more apparent then on the night of May 24, 1988, when an electrical failure plunged the building into darkness and forced postponement of the fourth game of the Stanley Cup finals. Construction would begin less than five years later on a modern replacement, FleetCenter. The new facility opened prior to the 1995-96 season and played host to the NHL All-Star Game in January, 1996.

Following a non-playoff year in 1996–97, Sinden fired coach Steve Kasper and replaced him with the veteran Pat Burns. The new coach was presented with two first-round draft picks Joe Thornton and Sergei Samsonov—as well as good goaltending from former second-stringer Byron Dafoe.

While most critics believed that the Bostonians were too shallow to even reach a playoff berth in 1997–98, they surprised almost everyone by quickly moving over the .500 mark and remaining there throughout the season. Thornton initially was a disappointment, but Samsonov—the Calder Trophy winner—led all rookies in scoring with 22 goals and 47 points while Jason Allison emerged as top-10 talent with 83 points. Mostly, though, it was the improved defense credited to Pat Burns's coaching system that saw the Bruins climb to fifth in the Eastern Conference. A succession of bad breaks, as much as anything, saw Boston fall to the Washington Capitals in six games in the opening round of the 1998 playoffs.

The Bruins posted a 39–30–13 record in 1998–99 in their second season under Burns, with Allison, Samsonov and Dmitri Khristich enjoying strong seasons and Joe Thornton beginning to deliver on his promise as a first-overall draft choice. However, it was a defense led by Bourque and Dafoe that remained the team's strength. Dafoe led the league with 10 shutouts, and his 1.99 goals-against average made him just the fourth netminder in Bruins history to post an average below 2.00 and the first since Frank Brimsek 60 years before. In the playoffs, Boston eliminated the Carolina Hurricanes before being knocked out by the Buffalo Sabres. It was the second year in a row that the Bruins had been defeated by the team that would go on to represent the Eastern Conference in the Stanley Cup finals.

Despite his having led the Bruins with 29 goals in each of the previous two seasons, Harry Sinden refused to meet Dmitri Khristich's multi-million dollar arbitration award prior to the 1999–2000 season. Byron Dafoe also presented problems, holding out for a better contract. Khristich was eventually dealt to Toronto, while Dafoe was re-signed after the team's slow start. Unfortunately, the team never seemed to recover. A wrist injury to Jason Allison eventually sidelined him for much of the season, which only added to the Bruins' woes. Among the bright spots of a disappointing season was the play of Joe Thornton. The first-overall draft choice in 1997 wound up leading the team in scoring.

The 1999–2000 season marked the end of an era in Boston. Hoping to finally add a Stanley Cup victory to his Hall of Fame resumé, Raymond Bourque asked for a trade to a contending team. Harry Sinden granted his star defenseman's request and dealt him to the Colorado Avalanche. After 20-plus seasons, Bourque left Boston as the Bruins' all-time leader in games played, assists and points. He would, of course, get his Stanley Cup ring in Colorado, but not until the next season.

There was another change in Boston early in the 2000–01 campaign. This one came in the front office as long-time general manager Harry Sinden relinquished the job to Mike O'Connell, who had served as his assistant since 1994. O'Connell became just the sixth g.m. in Bruins history on November 1, 2000, a short time after head coach Pat Burns was fired just eight games (3–4–1) into the season. Mike Keenan took over behind the bench, but was let go after the season when the team's drive for the playoffs came up just short. (Both the Bruins and Hurricanes had 88 points, but Carolina had 38 victories to Boston's 36).

In something of a surprise move, the Bruins turned to Massachusetts native Robbie Ftorek as coach for the 2001–02 campaign. The team responded with a 101-point season and the top spot in the Eastern Conference. After scoring 37 goals the season before, Joe Thornton continued to develop into a top star. He managed to collected 68 points (22 goals, 46 assists) despite being limited to 66 games due to injuries. Sergei Samsonov delivered another fine offensive performance (29 goals, 41 assists), and Bill Guerin notched 41 goals in his first (and what would prove to be only) full season in a Boston uniform. Glen Murray also scored 41 goals (35 as a Bruin) after being acquired from Los Angeles in a deal for Jason Allison.

Despite their solid regular season, the Bruins ran into an old playoff nemesis when they hooked up with the Montreal

The Bruins selected Joe Thornton first overall at the 1997 Entry Draft and though they put him in the NHL immediately as an 18-year-old, he was allowed to develop slowly. He has become one of the NHL's best players.

Canadiens in the opening round. Byron Dafoe took much of the heat following Boston's six-game defeat and was not re-signed as a free agent. (He eventually caught on with the Atlanta Thrashers). Steve Shields and John Grahame shared netminding duties during the first half of 2002–03, but the team was inconsistent despite the continued brilliance of Thornton and Murray. Thornton had the best season of his career, finishing third in the NHL with 101 points (36 goals, 65 assists). Murray's 44 goals ranked him fifth in the league. Hampering the Bruins was the fact that Sergei Samsonov played only eight games. After missing a huge portion of the schedule, he did return to action for the last game of the season.

It was hoped that the Bruins' goaltending position had been solidified in late January when holdout defenseman Kyle McLaren was dealt to San Jose for Jeff Hackett after the Sharks had acquired him from Montreal. Still, the Bruins continued to struggle and with just nine games to go in the season, general manager Mike O'Connell fired Ftorek and took over behind the bench himself. (Mike Sullivan, coach of the team's Providence farm club was summoned to serve as an assistant, and would be hired as the new head coach during the offseason.) The Bruins had never really been in danger of missing the playoffs, but could finish no better than seventh in the Eastern Conference. That forced a first-round matchup with the New Jersey Devils, whose smothering defense proved too much for Boston. After scoring just three goals in the first three games of the series, the Bruins drove Martin Brodeur from the nets in a 5–1 victory that kept them alive in game four. Two nights later, Brodeur bounced back for his second shutout of the series and the Bruins were bounced from the playoffs. The Devils were able to completely shut down the Bruins big guns, holding Thornton and Murray to just one goal apiece. Four of the eight goals Boston managed in the series came from defensemen, with Dan McGillis netting three of them and Bryan Berard the other.

Buffalo Sabres

THE STORY OF THE BUFFALO SABRES begins in the mid-1960s. Seymour Knox III and Northrup Knox spearheaded a drive for a Buffalo franchise when the NHL announced a doubling of the number of teams for the 1967–68 season. Despite a splendid written and oral presentation to the NHL Board of Governors at that time, the city was not included in the list of six new franchises.

Discouraged but unwilling to give up, the Knoxes joined the fraternity of NHL owners by buying shares in the Oakland Seals. When the NHL decided to add two clubs for the 1970–71 season—at triple the 1967 cost—the Knoxes were still interested on behalf of Buffalo. On December 2, 1969, for a fee of $6 million apiece, Buffalo and Vancouver were named the newest members of the NHL. On January 16, 1970, the yet-to-be-named Buffalo club announced the signing of George "Punch" Imlach as general manager and coach of the new franchise. Imlach had been fired by the Toronto Maple Leafs in 1969 after guiding the club to four Stanley Cup titles. "Running the Buffalo club will be the toughest job in pro hockey," Imlach said. "But, the tougher it is, the better I like it."

Imlach could not resist a dig at his former employers in Toronto. He chose uniforms similar to those worn by his old Cup-winning Maple Leaf teams, but instead of blue and white he wanted blue and gold because, "We're classier than the Leafs."

A "Name the Team" contest in the spring of 1970 brought forth 13,000 suggestions. The club rejected candidates like Mugwumps and Flying Zeppelins before settling on Sabres, because the name reflected the steely determination to succeed at a lightning quick pace. Next came the annual June draft in Montreal and the dispersal of the best amateur talent. The two most coveted players were Gilbert Perreault from the Montreal Junior Canadiens and Dale Tallon of the Toronto Marlboros. A "spin of the wheel" gave Buffalo first choice, and Imlach selected Perreault. (Perreault's number 11 commemorated the result of that fateful spin of the wheel. Vancouver would get first pick if an even number came up; but when the pointer clicked to a stop on 11, Perreault was headed for Buffalo.)

During the Sabres' first season of 1970–71, the Boston Bruins set 37 team records and topped the NHL standings with 57 wins and 121 points. The Sabres turned in a respectable 24 wins and 63 points and finished ahead of Vancouver (56 points) and Detroit (55) for fifth place in the East Division. Perreault proved he needed no further seasoning in the minors, as he set a goal-scoring record for rookies with 38 and earned the Calder Trophy.

Left wing Rick Martin was the Sabres' top pick in the 1971 draft. In a normal year, Martin's 44 goals and 74 points would have made him a shoo-in as rookie of the year. But, Ken Dryden's great goaltending for Montreal, in the eyes of the voters, was even more impressive. The 1971 Amateur Draft also produced Craig Ramsay and Bill Hajt. That year, general manager and coach Punch Imlach suffered heart problems and was persuaded to hand over the coaching duties to his longtime friend, Joe Crozier.

Martin and Perreault played brilliantly together while a search went on to find a right wing to fit their style. It ended in 1972, when the Sabres sent Eddie Shack to Pittsburgh for unheralded Rene Robert and the French Connection Line was born. Defenseman Jim Schoenfeld was the team's number-one draft choice in 1972, and the 1972–73 season saw the Sabres reach the playoffs in just their third year. They qualified by defeating the St. Louis Blues

Rick Martin was runner-up to Ken Dryden for the Calder Trophy despite setting a rookie record with 44 goals in 1971–72. The trigger man on the Sabres' famed French Connection line with Gilbert Perreault and Rene Robert, Martin had 52 goals in 1973–74 and 1974–75.

3–1 in the final game of the regular season, then went on to give Montreal a fright in the first round before bowing out in six games.

Floyd Smith replaced Joe Crozier as the Sabres' coach for the 1974–75 season and guided the club to 49 wins and 113 points, still the best numbers in the history of the franchise. Danny Gare joined the club that season and scored 31 goals. His first came 18 seconds after the opening whistle in his first NHL game, three seconds shy of the fastest goal by a rookie (Gus Bodnar in 1943). The following year, Gare would jump to 50 goals.

The Sabres remained hot in the 1975 playoffs, ousting the Chicago Black Hawks in five games, then eliminating a powerful Montreal club to earn a ticket to the Stanley Cup finals against the Philadelphia Flyers, the defending champions.

The final series matched the French Connection against the Flyers' potent combination of Bobby Clarke, Bill Barber and Reggie Leach. The Flyers captured the first two games, but the Sabres rebounded for a pair of wins on home ice. The Sabres, who had never won at the Philadelphia Spectrum, lost game five by a 5–1 score. Back in Buffalo for game six, Roger Crozier replaced Gerry Desjardins in the Sabres goal, but was outdueled by Bernie Parent in a 2–0 Flyers victory. "We were a good young team then," forward Craig Ramsay would say later. "We thought we'd be back every year, taking a run at the Stanley Cup."

But, it was not to be. A team that boasted five 30-plus goal scorers and a powerful defense remained one of the NHL's elite, but this group would never again generate enough playoff wins to reach the Stanley Cup finals. Despite its string of playoff disappointments, Buffalo remained near the top of the NHL regular-season standings from the mid 1970s onward. From 1974–75 through 1977–78 the team never failed to top the 100-point plateau. One of the highlights of the Sabres' first decade would come from the All-Star Game, held in Buffalo in 1978. Rick Martin and Gilbert Perreault led the Wales Conference to an exciting 3–2 victory. Martin scored the tying goal with 1:39 left in the third period, and Perreault scored the winner after 3:55 of overtime.

Punch Imlach was fired after the 1978 playoffs, and coach Marcel Pronovost also lost his job when the Sabres got off to a slow start in 1978–79. John Anderson was named interim manager until the Sabres were able to land renowned hockey man Scotty Bowman in 1979. Bowman just had coached the Montreal Canadiens to four consecutive Stanley Cup titles and wanted to add general manager's duties to his portfolio.

Bowman spent the next few seasons making widespread changes. He added players Mike Ramsey, Lindy Ruff, Hannu Virta, Phil Housley, Mike Foligno, Dave Andreychuk and goalies Tom Barrasso and Daren Puppa. Bowman's maneuvers and coaching acumen bore results. In 1979–80 the Sabres had 110 points, and from 1980–81 through 1984–85 they never had fewer than 89 points. The club missed the playoffs with 80 points in 1985–86 and sputtered in 1986–87, resulting in Bowman's dismissal. He was replaced as g.m. by Gerry Meehan. Ted Sator took over as coach.

In 1987, after 17 years, 512 goals and 1,326 points, Gilbert Perreault announced his retirement. Despite an offer from the club, he passed up a front office job, returned home to Quebec and would become a successful junior team owner and coach. At the NHL Entry Draft in 1987, Gerry Meehan snared Pierre Turgeon with the number-one pick, hoping that he'd landed a player of Perreault's stature. Turgeon rewarded Meehan with 88 and 106 points in his second and third seasons, but never quite replaced Perreault in the hearts of Sabres fans. In October, 1991, he would be traded to the Islanders, the key player in a deal that would bring Pat LaFontaine to Buffalo.

Meanwhile, with Ted Sator at the helm for the 1987–88 season, the team improved by 21 points. Sator would guide the team to two third-place finishes in the Adams Division and two first-round playoff eliminations. Former Sabre Rick Dudley became the club's coach in 1989, and Buffalo made another impressive leap forward, finishing third overall with 45 wins and 98 points in 1989–90. During the season, the club sought the help of a psychologist for talented Soviet defector Alexander Mogilny, who revealed he had a fear of flying. There was more playoff disappointment in Buffalo this year when the Sabres, who'd finished with more wins, more points and more goals than Montreal, fell to the Canadiens in six games in the first round.

Prior to the 1991–92 season, former Edmonton Oilers coach John Muckler was hired as director of hockey operations. Islanders star Pat LaFontaine, involved in a contract dispute with his team, was acquired by Buffalo in a multiplayer deal, yet the Sabres were ousted in the first round of the playoffs for the fifth year in a row. Muckler took over as coach of the Sabres for 1992–93. Mogilny set a club record with 76 goals, while LaFontaine had 95 assists and 148 points. In the playoffs, the Sabres surprised the Boston

Buffalo Sabres

Year-by-Year Record

Season	GP	W	L	T	OL	GF	GA	Pts.	Finish	Division	Playoff Result
1970-71	78	24	39	15	...	217	291	63	5th	East Div.	Out of Playoffs
1971-72	78	16	43	19	...	203	289	51	6th	East Div.	Out of Playoffs
1972-73	78	37	27	14	...	257	219	88	4th	East Div.	Lost Quarterfinal
1973-74	78	32	34	12	...	242	250	76	5th	East Div.	Out of Playoffs
1974-75	80	49	16	15	...	354	240	113	1st	Adams Div.	Lost Final
1975-76	80	46	21	13	...	339	240	105	2nd	Adams Div.	Lost Quarterfinal
1976-77	80	48	24	8	...	301	220	104	2nd	Adams Div.	Lost Quarterfinal
1977-78	80	44	19	17	...	288	215	105	2nd	Adams Div.	Lost Quarterfinal
1978-79	80	36	28	16	...	280	263	88	2nd	Adams Div.	Lost Prelim. Round
1979-80	80	47	17	16	...	318	201	110	1st	Adams Div.	Lost Semifinal
1980-81	80	39	20	21	...	327	250	99	1st	Adams Div.	Lost Quarterfinal
1981-82	80	39	26	15	...	307	273	93	3rd	Adams Div.	Lost Div. Semifinal
1982-83	80	38	29	13	...	318	285	89	3rd	Adams Div.	Lost Div. Final
1983-84	80	48	25	7	...	315	257	103	2nd	Adams Div.	Lost Div. Semifinal
1984-85	80	38	28	14	...	290	237	90	3rd	Adams Div.	Lost Div. Semifinal
1985-86	80	37	37	6	...	296	291	80	5th	Adams Div.	Out of Playoffs
1986-87	80	28	44	8	...	280	308	64	5th	Adams Div.	Out of Playoffs
1987-88	80	37	32	11	...	283	305	85	3rd	Adams Div.	Lost Div. Semifinal
1988-89	80	38	35	7	...	291	299	83	3rd	Adams Div.	Lost Div. Semifinal
1989-90	80	45	27	8	...	286	248	98	2nd	Adams Div.	Lost Div. Semifinal
1990-91	80	31	30	19	...	292	278	81	3rd	Adams Div.	Lost Div. Semifinal
1991-92	80	31	37	12	...	289	299	74	3rd	Adams Div.	Lost Div. Semifinal
1992-93	84	38	36	10	...	335	297	86	4th	Adams Div.	Lost Div. Final
1993-94	84	43	32	9	...	282	218	95	4th	Northeast Div.	Lost Conf. Quarterfinal
1994-95	48	22	19	7	...	130	119	51	4th	Northeast Div.	Lost Conf. Quarterfinal
1995-96	82	33	42	7	...	247	262	73	5th	Northeast Div.	Out of Playoffs
1996-97	82	40	30	12	...	237	208	92	1st	Northeast Div.	Lost Conf. Semifinal
1997-98	82	36	29	17	...	211	187	89	3rd	Northeast Div.	Lost Conf. Final
1998-99	82	37	28	17	...	207	175	91	4th	Northeast Div.	Lost Final
99-2000	82	35	32	11	4	213	204	85	3rd	Northeast Div.	Lost Conf. Quarterfinal
2000-01	82	46	30	5	1	218	184	98	2nd	Northeast Div.	Lost Conf. Semifinal
2001-02	82	35	35	11	1	213	200	82	5th	Northeast Div.	Out of Playoffs
2002-03	82	27	37	10	8	190	219	72	5th	Northeast Div.	Out of Playoffs

Bruins with a four-game sweep and advanced past the first round for the first time since 1983. In round two, Mogilny suffered a broken leg and the Canadiens swept the series, then defeated the Islanders and the Los Angeles Kings to capture the Stanley Cup.

Dominik Hasek, who had been named the top player in Czechoslovakia in 1987, 1989 and 1990, had joined the Sabres prior to the 1992–93 season. After playing 28 games in that first campaign, he became Buffalo's number-one goaltender in 1993–94. "The Dominator" responded by recording a 1.95 goal-against average, the lowest mark seen in the NHL since Bernie Parent's 1.89 in 1973–74. Hasek's .930 save percentage was the highest recorded since the NHL began to keep this statistic in the early 1980s. He was rewarded with the Vezina Trophy and a First All-Star Team selection.

Hasek's unorthodox and acrobatic goaltending made him a sensation in Buffalo and throughout the NHL. In the 1994 playoffs, he made 70 saves in game six of a first-round playoff matchup against New Jersey. The game was decided in the fourth overtime period, with Buffalo winning on Dave Hannan's goal. It was the longest game in Sabres' history and ranked as the sixth-longest ever played in the NHL to that time. However, the Devils went on to win the series in the seventh game by a 2–1 score.

Pat LaFontaine had ranked second in the NHL behind Mario Lemieux with his 148 points in 1992–93, but missed most of the next two seasons with a serious knee injury. He returned in time to help Buffalo reach the playoffs in 1994–95, but the Sabres suffered yet another first-round defeat—this time to Philadelphia. Hasek continued to frustrate the NHL's best scorers, winning the Vezina Trophy for the second straight year, while Pat LaFontaine was awarded the Bill Masterton Trophy for sportsmanship and dedication to hockey.

Tony McKegney topped the 30-goal plateau twice in his four full seasons in Buffalo. He later had a career-high 40 goals with the St. Louis Blues

On July 8, 1995, the Sabres traded Alexander Mogilny to Vancouver in a deal that brought Michael Peca to Buffalo. Ted Nolan left the St. Louis Blues to join the Sabres in 1995–96, but the team missed the playoffs that year.

On May 22, 1996, Seymour Knox III passed away at age 70. Among his many legacies to the city of Buffalo was the new Marine Midland Arena, which would open that fall. The opening of the new facility (later to become the HSBC Center), plus new team colors, logo and uniforms, coincided with on-ice improvement in 1996–97. With Ted Nolan in his second season as coach, the Sabres leaped to the top of the Northeast Division standings and finished with 92 points. For spearheading the turnaround, Dominik Hasek would become the first goalie since Jacques Plante in 1962 to be awarded the Hart Trophy as the NHL's most valuable player. In the playoffs, however, Hasek sustained a knee injury in the opening round against Ottawa. The Sabres called on backup goalie Steve Shields and survived the Senators in seven games before Philadelphia eliminated them in the second round.

Despite a measure of on-ice success, antagonism had developed between Hasek and coach Nolan and between Nolan and g.m. John Muckler. Both Nolan and Muckler were replaced before the 1997–98 campaign. With Darcy Regier in the front office and ex-Sabre Lindy Ruff behind the bench, Buffalo started the new season poorly but when Hasek moved his game into high gear in December, the Sabres became one of the league's best teams in the second half of the schedule. Hasek also starred for his native Czech Republic in a gold medal performance at the Nagano Olympics.

Though only eight teams would score fewer goals than Buffalo in 1997–98, Hasek's brilliance was enough to get the Sabres into the playoffs with plenty of room to spare. His 13 shutouts were the most since Tony Esposito posted 15 in 1969–70, and he again earned both the Hart and Vezina trophies. In the postseason, Hasek's fine play, and the Sabres overall team speed, saw Buffalo upset the Philadelphia Flyers in the first round. The Sabres then swept the Montreal Canadiens before bowing out against the Washington Capitals in a six-game Eastern Conference final. A groin injury cut into Hasek's playing time in 1998–99, and he relinquished his hold on the Hart, though he again won the Vezina Trophy. He also helped the Sabres reach the Stanley Cup finals for just the second time in team history. Buffalo pushed the Dallas Stars to six games before losing the series in triple overtime.

During the offseason, Dominik Hasek announced that the 1999–2000 campaign would be his last in the NHL. Still bothered by his tender groin, both Hasek and the Sabres got off to a slow start. The Dominator was forced out of the lineup on October 29 and did not return until February 1. On February 14, he announced he would return to Buffalo for one more year.

Though Martin Biron had posted five shutouts in Hasek's absence, the Sabres struggled. Michael Peca was playing below the form of recent years and Miroslav Satan was below the pace that had seen him score 40 goals the year before. He would eventually net 33, and Peca did pick up the pace; however, it was the acquisition of Doug Gilmour at the trade deadline that seemed to breathe new life into the Sabres. Chris Gratton was also a late addition as the defending Stanley Cup finalists came on strong and nailed down the final Eastern Conference playoff berth on the last day of the season. Buffalo carried a full head of steam into the postseason and many felt they were poised to do some damage, but there would be no return to the finals this year. Philadelphia ended the Sabres' season early with a five-game victory in the first round of the playoffs.

The Sabres played the entire 2000–01 season without captain Michael Peca, who sat out in a contract dispute. Still, the team showed an 11-win improvement over the previous season, posting a record of 46–30–5–1 and 98 points. The Sabres came within moments of reaching the Eastern Conference final for the third time in four years, losing game seven of their second-round series with Pittsburgh 3–2 in overtime. Once again, the team was led by Dominik Hasek, who won the Vezina Trophy for the sixth time in eight years during what would turn out to be his final season in a Sabres uniform. Hasek led the NHL with 11 shutouts and also ranked among the league leaders in wins (37), goals-against average (2.11) and save percentage (.921).

The rights to Peca were traded to the Islanders for Tim Connolly and Taylor Pyatt after the 2000–01 season, and Hasek was dealt to Detroit for Slava Kozlov. Martin Biron did well as the new number-one netminder, but the team struggled during the first half and ultimately missed the playoffs despite strong performances from Miroslav Satan, J.P. Dumont and Maxim Afinogenov.

Sadly, all problems of the previous two seasons paled in comparison to what faced the Sabres in 2002–03. The NHL took over ownership of the club from the Rigas family after owner John Rigas and his sons, Michael and Timothy, were charged with fraud.

The club reorganized financially under the protection of federal bankruptcy law, then was acquired by Rochester billionaire B. Thomas Golisano on March 14, 2003. The spirits of the Sabres, who had been struggling on the ice, clearly were buoyed by the purchase. The team played better late in the season, but Buffalo's 72 points represented the lowest total in a full season since they had 64 in 1986–87. As usual, Miroslav Satan was the club's top performer, leading the team in goals (26), assists (49) and points (75).

Martin Biron was selected 16th overall in the 1995 NHL Entry Draft after being selected the Canadian major junior goaltender of the year. After a stellar season in the American Hockey League in 1998–99, Biron saw his first extended action in Buffalo when Dominik Hasek was injured for much of the 1999–2000 season.

Calgary/Atlanta Flames

When the Atlanta Flames became the Calgary Flames in 1980, hockey immediately became the main sport and the hottest ticket in town. The flaming "A" was replaced by a flaming "C" and there was hardly a heartbeat missed. The NHL officially arrived on October 9, 1980, when the newborn Calgary Flames tied the Quebec Nordiques, 5–5.

Playing to raucous crowds in the 6,500-seat Stampede Corral rink that first year, it looked as though the city had inherited a pretty good team to cheer for. "Nobody could beat us in the Corral," recalls then-general manager Cliff Fletcher, the silver-haired wheeler-dealer who was with the organization for 20 years. "It was a very successful first season." With a 25–5–10 record in the Corral and a 39–27–14 record overall, the Flames finished third in the Patrick Division and seventh overall in the league. They then defeated Chicago and Philadelphia before losing to Minnesota in the Stanley Cup semifinals.

With a new 20,000-seat rink being built across the street from the Corral, the future looked bright. Kent Nilsson, the supremely talented Swede, had a franchise-record 82 assists and 131 points that first season in Calgary and just missed the 50-goal plateau, scoring 49. Pat Riggin had 21 wins in net. Jim Peplinski was a rookie, just beginning his famous glove-in-the-face rubs en route to becoming one of the captains on Calgary's championship team of the future. Willi Plett hacked his way to 239 penalty minutes, but also scored 38 goals. Guy Chouinard had 83 points.

The Flames franchise had begun playing in the league in Atlanta in 1972–73. It appeared that Omni Sports group, a consortium of businessmen from the area headed by Tom Cousins, was on solid ground, but that same year the wildcat World Hockey Association began operation and players were jumping from the NHL to the WHA for the big money being offered by the new league. That, in turn, threw a big wrench into the financing of the Atlanta franchise. Still, the team persevered for eight seasons, missing the playoffs only during its first and third years of operation. These early Flames were competitive, too. Teams that probably should have done better in the postseason instead lost every first-round playoff matchup they entered.

As time went on, the businessmen that Cousins had recruited faded from the picture, unwilling to put more money into the operation of a hockey franchise. When he sold the team to Nelson Skalbania, a Vancouver-based businessman, Cousins' stake in the team had increased from 20 percent to 89 percent. But, Cousins sold the team for $16 million U.S., a record amount for an NHL team at the time. "It turned his whole experience into a profitable one," says Fletcher.

Skalbania had, in fact, jumped into the bidding late, had gone high on his bid, and basically had undermined what three Calgary businessmen had been negotiating. Doc and B.J. Seaman were the two instigators in placing an NHL team in Calgary. Harley Hotchkiss, another local businessman with ties to the oil patch that makes Calgary go around, was brought into the picture very early.

Behind the scenes, the Calgary group headed by the Seamans was well along in brokering the deal to purchase the Atlanta franchise, when Canadian financier Skalbania entered the fray. In the end, Skalbania would play a major bartering role in the Calgary franchise, but one that drove the cost of the team much higher than what it probably was worth. Using a $6-million deal with Molson that gave them television rights for 10 years, Skalbania was able to make his deal. However, being based in Vancouver, he immediately found it difficult to negotiate with the parties that the Seamans had been dealing with and called upon Norm Green, a Calgary businessman with whom he had previously dealt. In May, 1980, Green brought the two parties together and a deal was struck: Calgary interests would own 50 percent of the team and Skalbania the other 50 percent.

After a stellar season in the American Hockey League, the Atlanta Flames claimed Daniel Bouchard from Boston in the 1972 Expansion Draft. He played with the team through to the move to Calgary in 1980–81.

The Calgary owners were the Seamans, Hotchkiss, Green, Ralph Scurfield, then owner of the Banff ski area called Sunshine Village, and Norm Kwong, a former running back with the Edmonton Eskimos who had a one-percent share. By August, 1981, the local ownership had bought out Skalbania in two separate transactions. When all was settled, the two Seamans, Hotchkiss, Scurfield and Green equally shared 90 percent of the team while Kwong increased his share to 10 percent. Skalbania had paid $16 million U.S., but by the time the dust had settled, the Calgary owners had spent between $20 and $30 million to complete the deal. With the raging success of the first season, however, there were few complaints.

The Flames moved from the Patrick Division to the Smythe Division for their second season in Calgary, one that began with much optimism but ended in disappointment. It was the year the man with hockey's best-known moustache, Lanny McDonald, joined the team in a trade with the Colorado Rockies. McDonald would finish his playing career in Calgary, scoring a club record 66 goals in 1982–83 and serving as co-captain of the Stanley Cup champion team in 1989.

McDonald retired that summer and has since had his jersey raised to the roof of the current rink, the Saddledome, the only Flames jersey to be retired. McDonald would continue to work in the Flames front office for years, but not even his presence could help the team in its second Alberta season as they finished the 1981–82 season with a 29–34–17 record and then bowed out in the first round of the playoffs to Vancouver, who went on to the Stanley Cup finals.

That would be a trend for Calgary, losing to teams that reached the Stanley Cup finals after beating the Flames in the first round of the playoffs. Usually it was Edmonton. But, Vancouver in 1994 and Los Angeles in 1993 also handed Calgary first-round playoff defeats and proceeded all the way to the Stanley Cup finals.

After that second-year disappointment, the Flames changed direction on the ice. "That's when we realized we really did have a long way to go to build a winner," says Fletcher. "We only had to look 180 miles north to Edmonton to see an emerging dynasty." The 1982–83 season became a rebuilding year. The ultra-positive "Badger Bob" Johnson replaced Al MacNeil as coach. With Johnson's college background, the Flames began recruiting college free agents such as Neil Sheehy, Joel Otto and Colin Patterson, later drafting future captain and 50-goal scorer Joe Nieuwendyk out of Cornell.

Riding Nilsson's 104-point season and McDonald's 66 goals, the Flames reached the playoffs in 1982–83, defeated Vancouver in the first round and then lost to nemesis Edmonton in the division final. The Oilers would win the Stanley Cup the next two seasons, while Fletcher and his staff hustled, traded and pieced together a team that could score, skate and hit with the Oilers. For toughness and grit he added Doug Risebrough. In the skill department he added a young Dan Quinn, Al MacInnis and Hakan Loob. Calgary-born Mike Vernon was added to the goaltending mix and the beginnings of the championship team were born.

In the fall of 1983, the Flames moved into what was then called the Olympic Saddledome, a unique-looking building that fit into the western flavor of the city, as the roof is shaped like the saddle of a horse. In the 1984 playoffs, the Flames extended Edmonton to seven games in the Smythe Division finals. This was the closest

Calgary Flames

Year-by-Year Record

Season	GP	W	L	T	OL	GF	GA	Pts.	Finish	Division	Playoff Result
1972-73*	78	25	38	15	...	191	239	65	7th	West Div.	Out of Playoffs
1973-74*	78	30	34	14	...	214	238	74	4th	West Div.	Lost Quarterfinal
1974-75*	80	34	31	15	...	243	233	83	4th	Patrick Div.	Out of Playoffs
1975-76*	80	35	33	12	...	262	237	82	3rd	Patrick Div.	Lost Prelim. Round
1976-77*	80	34	34	12	...	264	265	80	3rd	Patrick Div.	Lost Prelim. Round
1977-78*	80	34	27	19	...	274	252	87	3rd	Patrick Div.	Lost Prelim. Round
1978-79*	80	41	31	8	...	327	280	90	4th	Patrick Div.	Lost Prelim. Round
1979-80*	80	35	32	13	...	282	269	83	4th	Patrick Div.	Lost Prelim. Round
1980-81	80	39	27	14	...	329	298	92	3rd	Patrick Div.	Lost Semifinal
1981-82	80	29	34	17	...	334	345	75	3rd	Smythe Div.	Lost Div. Semifinal
1982-83	80	32	34	14	...	321	317	78	2nd	Smythe Div.	Lost Div. Final
1983-84	80	34	32	14	...	311	314	82	2nd	Smythe Div.	Lost Div. Final
1984-85	80	41	27	12	...	363	302	94	3rd	Smythe Div.	Lost Div. Semifinal
1985-86	80	40	31	9	...	354	315	89	2nd	Smythe Div.	Lost Final
1986-87	80	46	31	3	...	318	289	95	2nd	Smythe Div.	Lost Div. Semifinal
1987-88	80	48	23	9	...	397	305	105	1st	Smythe Div.	Lost Div. Final
1988-89	80	54	17	9	...	354	226	117	1st	Smythe Div.	Won Stanley Cup
1989-90	80	42	23	15	...	348	265	99	1st	Smythe Div.	Lost Div. Semifinal
1990-91	80	46	26	8	...	344	263	100	2nd	Smythe Div.	Lost Div. Semifinal
1991-92	80	31	37	12	...	296	305	74	5th	Smythe Div.	Out of Playoffs
1992-93	84	43	30	11	...	322	282	97	2nd	Smythe Div.	Lost Div. Semifinal
1993-94	84	42	29	13	...	302	256	97	1st	Pacific Div.	Lost Conf. Quarterfinal
1994-95	48	24	17	7	...	163	135	55	1st	Pacific Div.	Lost Conf. Quarterfinal
1995-96	82	34	37	11	...	241	240	79	2nd	Pacific Div.	Lost Conf. Quarterfinal
1996-97	82	32	41	9	...	214	239	73	5th	Pacific Div.	Out of Playoffs
1997-98	82	26	41	15	...	217	252	67	5th	Pacific Div.	Out of Playoffs
1998-99	82	30	40	12	...	211	234	72	3rd	Northwest Div.	Out of Playoffs
99-2000	82	31	36	10	5	211	256	77	4th	Northwest Div.	Out of Playoffs
2000-01	82	27	36	15	4	197	236	73	4th	Northwest Div.	Out of Playoffs
2001-02	82	32	35	12	3	201	220	79	4th	Northwest Div.	Out of Playoffs
2002-03	82	29	36	13	4	186	228	75	5th	Northwest Div.	Out of Playoffs

* Atlanta Flames

Calgary had come to beating the Oilers, who would go on to win the Stanley Cup for the first time that season.

It was then, perhaps, that one of the greatest hockey rivalries of the modern era developed. Those games were wars. As Wayne Gretzky and Paul Coffey and Hakan Loob, Kent Nilsson and Lanny McDonald battled on the skill side of the game, the likes of Doug Risebrough, Neil Sheehy, Tim Hunter and Jim Peplinski fought against Ken Linesman, Dave Semenko and Don Jackson in the trenches. They were games that meant everything to both teams. "It was tremendous. Anytime you played the Oilers you could feel the electricity in the building, playoffs or regular season," says Fletcher.

In 1984–85, the team achieved a high in points with 94, but bowed out disappointingly in the first round to Winnipeg. The next season was the turning point. "That's when we caught the Oilers and went to the finals," says Fletcher, who dealt for scorer Joe Mullen, the first American-born player to score 500 goals. Gary Suter, a late-round draft pick, won the Calder Trophy, scoring 68 points from the blue line. Late in the season, Fletcher acquired the gritty John Tonelli. Mike Vernon won 12 playoff games.

The key for the organization was that they had found a way to beat the Oilers, winning game seven in Edmonton on a goal that rookie Oiler defenseman Steve Smith put in his own net. Coincidentally, Smith would return to Calgary as a coach in 1997 before making a comeback as a player with the Flames in 1998–99.

"It was the most exhilarating experience in my hockey career," says Fletcher of that win in Edmonton and the short, 30-minute fight home. "We got to the airport and there were 25,000 people there. It was quite a scene. We felt a sense of accomplishment. In the minds of the southern Albertans, it was probably better than winning the Stanley Cup."

Which Calgary didn't do in 1986 as Montreal, led by Larry Robinson and a young Chris Chelios and Patrick Roy, eliminated the Flames in a five-game final.

In 1986, one of the team's original owners, Ralph Scurfield, died in an avalanche. His wife, Sonia took over his share of the Flames. Since that time, a number have ownership changes have occurred.

In 1991, Green bought the Minnesota North Stars and the remaining Calgary owners bought up his shares. In 1994, the ownership again underwent a restructuring. By 1995, the owners, the city and the federal government had combined to spend $40 million in renovations to the Saddledome as a way of increasing revenue for the team. As well, the owners took control of the building on a long-term lease, no longer having to deal with the intermediary Calgary Stampede, which had operated the building since its inception in 1983. By 1998, there were nine owners in the Flames operation. Hotchkiss, the Seamans, local private merchant banker Murray Edwards and Tim Horton Donuts owner Ronald Joyce each own about 23 percent. The remainder is divided evenly among businessmen from Calgary: Allan Markin, Alvin Libin, Grant Bartlett and J.R. McCaig.

On the ice, the Edmonton Oilers would win the Stanley Cup in 1987 and 1988, although the Flames won the Presidents' Trophy in 1987–88 with a 48–23–9 regular season record, the same year Joe Nieuwendyk won the Calder Trophy. Edmonton, however, disposed of Calgary in four games in the Smythe Division finals. From 1986 to 1991, the Flames had one of the best records in the NHL, and twice captured the Presidents' Trophy. Their playoff puzzle came together with a Stanley Cup win in 1989.

Coach Bob Johnson had left Calgary in 1987 to join the Amateur Hockey Association of the United States in Colorado Springs. ("Badger Bob" would later return to the NHL and coach Pittsburgh to a Stanley Cup title before passing away after a battle with cancer.) Terry Crisp took over as coach while Fletcher continued to assemble a winning roster.

Doug Gilmour was brought on in a trade with St. Louis in 1988–89. Theo Fleury, who would become the team's franchise player, was a rookie fourth-liner.

Gilmour, Mullen, Loob, Nieuwendyk, Suter and MacInnis formed perhaps the best power play the Flames have ever assembled. It had all the ingredients, including the rocket from the blue line that was MacInnis's shot. Oddly, the year they won the Cup they did not have to go through Edmonton, instead squeaking by Vancouver, thumping Los Angeles, grinding it out against Chicago and, finally, defeating Montreal at the Forum in game six to claim the Cup. It was the first time the Canadiens had lost a Stanley Cup final series on home ice.

Lanny McDonald scored the final goal of his Hall of Fame career in game six at 4:24 of the second period, giving Calgary a 2–1 lead. Doug Gilmour scored the game winner at 11:02 on the powerplay before adding an empty-netter for the 4–2 Calgary win. They had reached the pinnacle. And since then they have not come close. Crisp, the coach who took them to the Holy Grail of hockey, was fired a year later.

Crisp was replaced on the bench by Doug Risebrough in 1990–91, a season that would be the last for Fletcher in the Flames organization. Fittingly, the team lost to Edmonton in the first round of the playoffs. The team Fletcher had chased all those years had chased him, too.

Fletcher's leaving caused quite the stir in Calgary. After all, he was the only architect the team had known. "It had been 19 years. I just thought it was time for a change to get the juices going to 100 percent again," says Fletcher, who moved to Toronto as president and general manager. Risebrough, who had been under Fletcher's wing in the front office, took on the dual role of g.m. and coach. Fletcher then picked the pocket of his pupil in January, 1992, acquiring Doug Gilmour, who had walked out on the Flames in a contract dispute, Jamie Macoun, Ric Nattress, Kent Manderville and Rick Wamsley for Gary Leeman, Alexander Godynyuk, Jeff Reese, Michel Petit and Craig Berube. It was the largest trade in NHL history at the time and one that turned out to highly favor Toronto. Two seasons later, not one of the players Calgary had acquired was with the team and only Craig Berube, who by then was playing with Washington, was taking a regular shift in the league. The Flames missed the playoffs that season, although Gary Roberts scored 53 goals and vowed to name his next child after setup man Sergei Makarov.

The Flames had broken new ground in bringing Russian players to the NHL when they signed Sergei Priakin to a contract in 1988–89. "What we were trying to do was set up things for down the road but eventually they eased the restrictions," recalls Fletcher. Makarov, a veteran Soviet star, won the Calder Trophy as NHL rookie of the year in 1989–90.

Having missed the playoffs for the first time since moving to Calgary, the Flames gave Dave

The Flames called their three veteran leaders "tri-captains." Tim Hunter (left), Lanny McDonald (center) and Jim Peplinski (right) hoist the Stanley Cup after Calgary's victory over Montreal in 1989.

King, the former Canadian national team coach, his first NHL coaching job in 1992–93. In his three seasons behind the bench, he directed the Flames to very credible regular-season records—all in the top 10 overall. But, the team failed miserably in the playoffs, losing in the first round three consecutive seasons. It was also during these seasons that salaries began to rise, the league went through the lockout and running a small-market team became a very different proposition.

One by one the Flames watched superstars depart: Mike Vernon to Detroit, Al MacInnis to St. Louis, Joe Nieuwendyk to Dallas, Gary Suter to Chicago, Gary Roberts, after two neck surgeries, to Carolina. Pierre Page replaced King behind the bench in 1995–96. After a terrible start to the season, Risebrough was fired as general manager and replaced by Al Coates. The Flames scraped into the playoffs but were swept by Chicago. Rebuilding was the order of the day.

The Flames missed the playoffs in Page's second year, finishing 21st overall in the league. Albertan and taskmaster Brian Sutter was named coach for 1997–98 as the rebuilding and the on-ice struggles continued. Calgary actually finished six points worse (with 67) under Sutter than they had under Page, and though they remained within hailing distance of eighth place in the Western Conference for much of the season, the Flames were never really playoff contenders.

The Flames would show only modest improvement under Sutter in his second season of 1998–99, though they surprised many by remaining in playoff contention after dealing Fleury to the Colorado Avalanche late in the season. Injuries forced the Flames to use six goaltenders during the year. Former nemesis Grant Fuhr was signed for the 1999–2000 season to shore up the goaltending, and to lend experience to promising youngsters like Fred Brathwaite and Jean-Sebastien Giguere (both of whom would later be traded). Unfortunately, injuries limited Fuhr to just 23 games. Once again in 1999–2000, the Flames remained on the edge of playoff contention but ultimately came up short. On the ice Phil Housley provided a veteran example for defensemen like Derek Morris and Cale Hulse, while offensive leadership came from Valeri Bure, who enjoyed a breakthrough season, and Jarome Iginla. (All but Iginla would be traded over waived over the next few seasons.)

Having missed the playoffs for four straight years, the Flames front office went in a new direction for the 2000–01 campaign, hiring Craig Button as general manager. Though only 37 years old, Button came from a hockey family and had already spent 12 seasons in the Dallas Stars organization. He hired former Phoenix coach Don Hay as his man behind the bench, but fired him late in the season and turned the job over to assistant Greg Gilbert. On the ice, the team was led by Jarome Iginla who topped the Flames in both goals (31) and points (71). Still, Calgary missed the playoffs for the fifth straight year.

Iginla made the leap from up-and-comer to true superstar in 2001–02, leading the NHL with 52 goals and 96 points. He also won an Olympic gold medal with Team Canada. Iginla earned the Lester Pearson Award as the players' choice for MVP but was runner-up to Jose Theodore for the Hart Trophy. He scored 18 goals in Calgary's first 20 games, and combined with newly acquired goaltender Roman Turek to lead the team to a 13–2–3–2 start. Craig Conroy (27 goals, 48 assists) also had a solid season, but the Flames went just 19–33–9–1 over the final 62 games and missed the playoffs once again.

With Iginla struggling at the start of the 2002–03 season, Calgary got off to just a 6–13–3–3 start. The poor performance cost Greg Gilbert his job. He was replaced in the interim by veteran Flames front office man Al MacNeil. A few weeks later, the Flames named Darryl Sutter (recently fired by San Jose) as their new head man. The team showed improvement under their new coach (19–18–8–1 in 46 games) but still failed to make the playoffs for the seventh year in a row. Iginla shook off the slow start to finish the year with 35 goals, while newcomers Chris Drury (23), Martin Gelinas (21) and captain Craig Conroy (22) all topped the 20-goal plateau. Within a week of the season's end, the Flames announced they would not offer a contract extension to general manager Craig Button. Darryl Sutter added the g.m. position to his coaching responsibilities.

With 52 goals and 96 points, Jarome Iginla won the Maurice Richard and Art Ross trophies in 2001–02 and also received the Lester B. Pearson Award after being voted the NHL's outstanding player by the members of the NHL Players' Association.

California/Oakland Seals and Cleveland Barons

WITH ITS LONG TRADITION OF MINOR LEAGUE HOCKEY, the state of California was a natural target of growth for NHL expansion in 1967. The Los Angeles entry went to Jack Kent Cooke, while the leader in Northern California was a 28-year-old friend of New York Rangers president William Jennings. Barend (Barry) Van Gerbig was a jet-setting beachboy who owned pieces of Standard Oil and Union Carbide.

On 1966-67, the seemingly well-heeled Van Gerbig and his partners purchased the San Francisco Seals of the Western Hockey League and moved their home games across the Bay to the brand-new Oakland-Alameda County Coliseum. The decision to leave San Francisco would prove a mistake.

Gary Smith set a single-season record for losses when he went 19–48–4 with the Seals in 1970–71.

Bert Olmstead was hired as general manager and coach of the new Oakland team, and he selected what looked like a winning lineup in the 1967 Expansion Draft. Goalie Charlie Hodge had considerable NHL experience with the Canadiens, while Bob Baun and Kent Douglas had skated for Stanley Cup winners in Toronto. Gerry Ehman had been a proven goal scorer, and Bill Hicke once had been touted as the natural heir to Maurice Richard in Montreal. The Seals also drafted the young sons of former stars King Clancy, Babe Pratt and Bryan Hextall. However, Olmstead's crew was a dismal 11–37–16 when he was fired late in the 1967–68 season.

The Seals were the only club in the newly created West Division that was never in playoff contention. Even worse, attendance was terrible. Early in the season Van Gerbig had threatened to move the team if more fans didn't show up. By the time the NHL Board of Governors convened for its March meeting, there were changes afoot. Labatt Breweries of Canada offered a loan of $680,000 (the amount that the league specified the Seals had to come up with by May 15) in order to move the franchise to Vancouver. Other interested parties included Ralph Wilson, owner of the Buffalo Bills football team. A move to Vancouver was vetoed by an 8–4 vote, as the league was in no mood to depart from a large population area so vital to any television plans. (The CBS TV contract specifically stipulated the inclusion of the Bay Area.)

Aided by the loan from Labatt, the Seals were purchased in August by the owners of the Harlem Globetrotters—Potter Palmer and George Gillett of Chicago, and John O'Neil Jr. of Miami. The three also had financial interests in the Atlanta Braves, the Miami Dolphins and the Atlanta Chiefs soccer team. Palmer and O'Neil had been partners of Van Gerbig, who would now serve the team in an advisory capacity only. President Frank Selke Jr. became the general manager. Fred Glover was the new coach.

Glover was not the only new face in the Seals dressing room for the 1968–69 season. Only seven of the 20 players originally drafted by the club remained. It was hoped that newcomers like Bryan Watson, Carol Vadnais, Gary Jarrett and Doug Roberts would help Glover move the Seals upward. In goal, the new coach inherited Charlie Hodge and Gary Smith who, while promising, had shown an alarming tendency to stickhandle the puck across the blue line in his first season. Few NHL goalies have been bombarded the way Smith would be during the 1969–70 and 1970–71 seasons.

Prior to the 1970–71 campaign, flamboyant Oakland A's baseball owner Charles Finley bought the hockey club and changed its name to the California Golden Seals. Finley added colored skates, new jerseys and several other gimmicks, but the Seals finished with the worst record in the league. One disaster led to another until February 1974, when the team was purchased by the NHL. League president Clarence Campbell named Munson Campbell as club president. Campbell was a man with over 30 years experience in the inner workings of professional hockey. He had been named vice president of the California Seals under Finley in 1971, but left a year later to return to private business.

As president, Campbell attempted to find new ownership for the foundering Seals. He eventually came up with hotelier Mel Swig, a former owner of the San Francisco Seals and another suitor who had been interested in purchasing the club during its original troubles in 1968. The hope now was that a proposed new arena would be built in San Francisco for the Seals, but when it became apparent that the plans never would become reality, the club moved to Cleveland in 1976. Swig's ownership gave way to the Gund family in June, 1977, but the Gunds could not solve the arena problem that had bedeviled the Seals in San Francisco.

The new Cleveland Barons played their home games at the Coliseum in Richfield, Ohio. While it listed the largest seating capacity in the NHL at the time (18,544), the Coliseum was located in farm country far from downtown Cleveland and suffered sparse crowds. Of course, the Barons' record hardly encouraged sellouts. Under coach Jack Evans, Cleveland finished the 1977–78 season with a 22–45–13 record and last place in the Adams Division. So poor was the club's financial condition that prior to the 1978–79 season the Gunds merged with the Minnesota North Stars. In 1990, the Gunds would agree to sell the North Stars in exchange for the rights to an expansion team that would return hockey to Northern California—the San Jose Sharks.

California/Oakland/Cleveland

Year-by-Year Record

Season	GP	W	L	T	GF	GA	Pts	Finish	Division	Playoff Results
1967–68	74	15	42	17	153	219	47	6th	West	Out of Playoffs
1968–69	76	29	36	11	219	251	69	2nd	West	Lost Quarterfinal
1969–70	76	22	40	14	169	243	58	4th	West	Lost Quarterfinal
1970–71	78	20	53	5	199	320	45	7th	West	Out of Playoffs
1971–72	78	21	39	18	216	288	60	6th	West	Out of Playoffs
1972–73	78	16	46	16	213	323	48	8th	West	Out of Playoffs
1973–74	78	13	55	10	195	342	36	8th	West	Out of Playoffs
1974–75	80	19	48	13	212	316	51	4th	Adams	Out of Playoffs
1975–76	80	27	42	11	250	278	65	4th	Adams	Out of Playoffs
1976–77	80	25	42	13	240	292	63	4th	Adams	Out of Playoffs
1977–78	80	22	45	13	230	325	57	4th	Adams	Out of Playoffs

Carolina Hurricanes and Hartford Whalers

THE CAROLINA HURRICANES started their existence as the New England Whalers and are the culmination of a saga that has moved from Boston to Springfield to Hartford to Greensboro and, finally, to Raleigh. The seeds of the franchise were planted in October, 1971, by a pair of young sportsmen, Howard Baldwin and John Coburn Jr., who originally had planned to build a small hockey arena near Cape Cod. Out of this blueprint emerged one of the most powerful teams in the World Hockey Association. Baldwin, a former business manager of the Jersey Devils of the old Eastern Hockey League, hired Jack Kelley, the Boston University coach, to manage and coach the Whalers.

Former Montreal Canadiens center Larry Pleau of Lynn, Massachusetts, was the first Whaler signed by Kelley, followed by NHL regulars Brad Selwood, Rick Ley and Jim Dorey, all former Toronto Maple Leafs. On July 27, 1972, the Whalers signed former Boston Bruins defenseman Ted Green as captain, and then signed other NHL aces such as Tom Webster, Al Smith and Tom Williams. On October 12, 1972, the Whalers played their first home game at Boston Garden before a crowd of 14,442, defeating the Philadelphia Blazers, 4–3. The Whalers went on to finish first and win the Avco World Cup.

Kelley gave assistant coach Ron Ryan the head coaching position in 1973–74, and once again the Whalers moved to the top of the East Division. However, the team was encountering financial problems because of competition from the NHL's Boston Bruins.

The Whalers selected Sylvain Turgeon second overall in the 1983 Entry Draft. Though he scored 40 goals as a rookie that season, and 45 two years later, he never really enjoyed the same success as brother Pierre, selected first overall by the Sabres in 1987.

Attendance was less than satisfactory at Boston Garden in the second season, so Baldwin began entertaining offers from other cities that coveted the franchise. He finally selected Hartford, which was building a new arena in the Connecticut city's civic center.

Instead of waiting until the end of the 1973–74 season, the Whalers moved their home games to the Eastern States Coliseum in Springfield, Massachusetts, because their new home in Hartford had yet to be completed. Playing their final games in Springfield late in the 1973–74 season had a negative effect on the Whalers, who were eliminated from the playoffs in a first-round upset by the Chicago Cougars.

The Whalers continued to excel during the 1974–75 campaign, which was launched in Springfield and continued in Hartford late in the season upon completion of the 10,400-seat Civic Center arena. Once again they finished first in their division, but not without problems. En route to a match in Toronto on March 30, coach Ryan collapsed and was rushed to a hospital. He was replaced behind the bench by Kelley. On the plus side, the Whalers became an instant hit in Hartford, frequently selling out the new building.

During their WHA existence, the Whalers boasted several luminaries, not the least of whom were Gordie Howe and Dave Keon. Baldwin would become president of the league and was the prime architect in hammering out the deal that saw the Whalers, Edmonton Oilers, Winnipeg Jets and Quebec Nordiques become NHL members. The venerable Gordie Howe returned to the NHL at the age of 51 in 1979–80 as a member of Hartford. He finished his 32nd and final NHL season with 15 goals, including his 800th career regular-season tally. That same year, the Whalers traded for another Hall of Famer, Bobby Hull, and the two played on the same line for nine games.

The 1980–81 season saw first-ever Whalers player Larry Pleau take over as coach, replacing the fired Don Blackburn. Also that summer, Pleau drafted an 18-year-old center fourth overall. Less than six months after being selected, Ron Francis was brought up to Hartford. He made an immediate impact, finishing the year third in team scoring with 68 points in 56 games and helping to turn the 21st-ranked power-play into the best in the league for a three-month stretch. Despite missing the playoffs for the second straight year, the Whalers seemed destined for greatness. But, the 1982–83 campaign saw Larry Pleau return as bench boss, replacing another fired coach, Larry Kish, and the Whalers did not qualify for postseason play, finishing with only 19 wins.

The 1983 offseason saw a total overhaul to the Hartford front office. Now coaching was Jack Evans, and hired as general manager was Emile "the Cat" Francis. In two years, this tandem would eventually lead the hapless Whalers to unseen heights in the NHL. After missing the playoffs yet again in the 1984–85 season, the Whalers traded for goalie (and Ron Francis's first cousin) Mike Liut. Liut helped the Whale to their first winning finish in seven years and put them in the playoffs for the first time since their initial NHL season. Hartford then upset the Quebec Nordiques before pushing the Montreal Canadiens to seven games in a thrilling Adams Division final. Emile Francis was named NHL executive of the year by both The Hockey News and The Sporting News.

The next season, 1986–87, saw the Whalers capture their first and only regular-season Adams Division championship. The celebration, however, was short-lived as the Nordiques upset the Whalers in the first playoff round. Hartford returned to the postseason the following year, but was again ousted in the first round, this time by rival Montreal. Following 1988–89, and another first-round loss to the Canadiens, Emile Francis was made team president and former goaltender Ed Johnston was named g.m. Pleau, who had returned to the bench for a third time the previous season, was fired and replaced by former Whaler Rick Ley. But, the next two seasons saw little excitement as the Whalers still could not win a playoff round.

En route to their worst finish in seven seasons, in March, 1991, Ron Francis, owner of most Hartford Whalers offensive records, was traded to Pittsburgh in a multiplayer deal. Francis would go on to win the Stanley Cup that year and the next, and the Whalers never seemed to recover. The next three years saw three separate coaches: Jimmy Roberts, Paul Holmgren and Pierre Maguire. Emile Francis retired after a 47-year hockey career. Brian Burke replaced Johnston as g.m., but soon resigned to become senior vice president and director of hockey operations for the NHL. He was replaced by Holmgren. On the day the 1994 NHL Entry Draft was held in Hartford, the team was sold to Compuware owner Peter Karmanos, Thomas Thewes and former NHL goaltender Jim Rutherford for $47.5 million. Rutherford became g.m. and president, and Holmgren was named head coach.

Two more non-playoff seasons followed, and the end was near for the Hartford Whalers. On March 26, 1997, near the end of yet another lackluster season, Peter Karmanos confirmed suspicions as he announced that the franchise would be playing elsewhere come the 1997–98 season. While some die-hard fans did their best to prevent the move, launching a "Save the Whale" campaign in an effort to sell more tickets, it was announced that the Whalers would relocate to Raleigh, North Carolina. A new arena would be built there for the Hurricanes, but meanwhile the team would be playing at Greensboro Coliseum, which overnight became one of the NHL's largest arenas. Kevin Dineen scored the last Whaler goal in history as Hartford defeated the Tampa Bay Lightning, 2–1, in an emotional game on April 13, 1997. The Whalers finished out of the playoffs, but Karmanos predicted that the move to Carolina would be good for another 10 to 15 points.

Carolina Hurricanes

Year-by-Year Record

Season	GP	W	L	T	OL	GF	GA	Pts.	Finish	Division	Playoff Result
1979-80*	80	27	34	19	...	303	312	73	4th	Norris Div.	Lost Prelim. Round
1980-81*	80	21	41	18	...	292	372	60	4th	Norris Div.	Out of Playoffs
1981-82*	80	21	41	18	...	264	351	60	5th	Adams Div.	Out of Playoffs
1982-83*	80	19	54	7	...	261	403	45	5th	Adams Div.	Out of Playoffs
1983-84*	80	28	42	10	...	288	320	66	5th	Adams Div.	Out of Playoffs
1984-85*	80	30	41	9	...	268	318	69	5th	Adams Div.	Out of Playoffs
1985-86*	80	40	36	4	...	332	302	84	4th	Adams Div.	Lost Div. Final
1986-87*	80	43	30	7	...	287	270	93	1st	Adams Div.	Lost Div. Semifinal
1987-88*	80	35	38	7		249	267	77	4th	Adams Div.	Lost Div. Semifinal
1988-89*	80	37	38	5	...	299	290	79	4th	Adams Div.	Lost Div. Semifinal
1989-90*	80	38	33	9	...	275	268	85	4th	Adams Div.	Lost Div. Semifinal
1990-91*	80	31	38	11	...	238	276	73	4th	Adams Div.	Lost Div. Semifinal
1991-92*	80	26	41	13	...	247	283	65	4th	Adams Div.	Lost Div. Semifinal
1992-93*	84	26	52	6	...	284	369	58	5th	Adams Div.	Out of Playoffs
1993-94*	84	27	48	9	...	227	288	63	6th	Northeast Div.	Out of Playoffs
1994-95*	48	19	24	5	...	127	141	43	5th	Northeast Div.	Out of Playoffs
1995-96*	82	34	39	9	...	237	259	77	4th	Northeast Div.	Out of Playoffs
1996-97*	82	32	39	11	...	226	256	75	5th	Northeast Div.	Out of Playoffs
1997-98	82	33	41	8	...	200	219	74	6th	Northeast Div.	Out of Playoffs
1998-99	82	34	30	18	...	210	202	86	1st	Southeast Div.	Lost Conf. Quarterfinal
99-2000	82	37	35	10	0	217	216	84	3rd	Southeast Div.	Out of Playoffs
2000-01	82	38	32	9	3	212	225	88	2nd	Southeast Div.	Lost Conf. Quarterfinal
2001-02	82	35	26	16	5	217	217	91	1st	Southeast Div.	Lost Final
2002-03	82	22	43	11	6	171	240	61	5th	Southeast Div.	Out of Playoffs

* Hartford Whalers

It wasn't to be. The Carolina Hurricanes' first season was, to put it mildly, a stormy one. Deep in the heart of college basketball and NASCAR country in Greensboro, the Hurricanes did not attract as much attention as they had wished. There were problems with the personnel as well. Geoff Sanderson, the leading scorer of the 1996–97 team, was unhappy. He was traded away. Goalie Sean Burke, who had won four consecutive awards as the team MVP, did not play up to his usual standards. Plagued by this, as well as some off-ice problems, the successful goaltender also was traded. And finally, the team owners tried to lure all-star Sergei Fedorov away from the Detroit Red Wings with a $38 million offer sheet designed to sink the Wings' chances of matching. But, match they did, leaving Carolina without the superstar center.

But, there were some silver linings among the gray storm clouds that hung over the transferred franchise. Captain and team leader Keith Primeau was an important part of Canada's entry at the 1998 Nagano Olympics and led the Hurricanes in scoring. Power forward Gary Roberts, who had played only 43 games since the end of the 1993–94 season because of injuries, joined the team after one year of retirement and went on to be the third-leading scorer with 20 goals and 29 assists in only 61 games. And forward Sami Kapanen had a breakthrough year, amassing 63 points for a share of first place in team scoring, and turning a few heads in the league in the process.

Still commuting to Greensboro for games, Primeau and Kapanen led the Hurricanes again in 1998–99. With the addition of goaltender Arturs Irbe and the free-agent acquisition of former Whalers great Ron Francis, Carolina won the newly created Southeast Division and made the playoffs for the first time in six years. In 1999–2000, the Hurricanes began the season with nine straight road games before finally opening their brand-new arena in Raleigh on October 29, 1999. A sellout crowd of 18,730 saw the party spoiled by the New Jersey Devils, who scored a 4–2 victory. The Hurricanes averaged 12,400 fans per game at the Raleigh Entertainment and Sports Arena for an increase of over 4,000 per game from the season before in Greensboro. Despite the move to their new home, the dominant story for the first half of the Hurricanes' season was the holdout of Keith Primeau, who was eventually traded to the Philadelphia Flyers for Rod Brind'amour.

With a final record of 37–35–10–0, Carolina posted back-to-back .500-plus seasons for the first time since 1985–86 and 1986–87. Unfortunately, the Hurricanes were eliminated from playoff contention on the final day of the regular season as they finished one point behind the eighth-place Buffalo Sabres. Highlights of the season included Arturs Irbe setting franchise records for games (75) and wins (34) by a goaltender and Paul Maurice becoming the franchise's winningest coach. Ron Francis and Paul Coffey became the first teammates to top the 1,500-point plateau in the same season. They were just the sixth and eighth players, respectively, in NHL history to score 1,500 points. Francis led the team in scoring with 73 points, with Gary Roberts, Jeff O'Neill and Sami Kapanen each also scoring at least 23 goals.

After being eliminated from playoff contention on the final night of the 1999–2000 season, the Carolina Hurricanes edged out the Boston Bruins for the eighth and final spot in the Eastern Conference playoffs in 2000–01. Both teams had 88 points, but Carolina had 38 wins to Boston's 36. However—as had been the case throughout most of their postseason history—the Hurricanes were knocked out in the first round, eliminated by New Jersey in six games.

Carolina came back with another solid season in 2001–02, winning the Southeast Division with 91 points, the second-best regular-season total in franchise history. The Hurricanes also reached the Stanley Cup final for the first time.

Carolina got a team-leading 31 goals from Jeff O'Neill, who had scored 41 the year before, as well as 20-goal performances from Sami Kapanen, Rod Brind'Amour and Bates Battaglia. Still, the offensive star was the ageless Ron Francis. His 27 goals equalled his best output since scoring 32 back in 1989–90, while his 50 assists tied him for fourth in the NHL. His 77 points tied him for ninth. Francis reached the 500-goal plateau for his career on January 2, 2002, surpassed Raymond Bourque for second place all-time in NHL assists and became just the fifth player in history to reach 1,700 points. With just 18 penalty minutes, Francis earned his third Lady Byng Trophy. He also received the King Clancy Trophy for his many charitable contributions off the ice.

Ron Francis has quietly become one of the NHL's all-time leaders in assists and points. One of the league's top young stars in his days with Hartford, he has provided veteran leadership since rejoining the franchise in Carolina in 1998.

In goal, Arturs Irbe surpassed Mike Liut as the winningest netminder in franchise history yet he saw much less action than he'd been accustomed to. Irbe shared the nets with Tom Barrasso for much of the season. Kevin Weekes was acquired from Tampa Bay late in the year and would play a key role in the playoffs. Trades also brought in Bret Hedican and Sean Hill, who helped to solidify the defense during the Hurricanes' surprising playoff run.

Though they had earned the third seed in the playoffs thanks to their Southeast Division title, Carolina actually had four points less than the sixth-seeded Devils. New Jersey had come on strong late in the season, and most experts favored them to dispose of the Hurricanes for the second year in a row. The Hurricanes won the first two games at home, but let the Devils back into the series with wins in games three and four in New Jersey. It was then that the Hurricanes turned to Weekes, who backstopped the team to a 3–2 overtime victory in game five and a 1–0 victory in game six. Weekes earned his second straight shutout with a 2–0 win over Montreal to open the second round, but the Canadiens came back with two straight wins. Irbe returned to the nets after the first period of game four, but the Canadiens threatened to take a stranglehold on the series with a 3–0 lead through two frames. However, third period goals by Hill, Battaglia and rookie Erik Cole, plus an overtime winner by Niclas Wallin, turned the series around. The Hurricanes wrapped it up with a pair of one-sided victories (5–1 and 8–2) and advanced to face the Toronto Maple Leafs in the Eastern Conference final.

The Leafs opened the series with a 2–1 victory. Carolina evened matters with a 2–1 win of its own thanks to another Wallin overtime goal. Jeff O'Neill's winner in extra time put the Hurricanes on top with another 2–1 victory in game three. They went on to win the series in six games, scoring yet another 2–1 overtime win in the final contest. Carolina's luck in extra time continued when Ron Francis scored after just 58 seconds to give the Hurricanes a 3–2 win over Detroit in game one of the Stanley Cup final. However, the Red Wings gained control of the series when Igor Larionov scored in triple overtime to give Detroit a 3–2 win in game three. The Wings went on to take the series in five games.

Much was expected of the Hurricanes in 2002–03, but instead they became the first team in the NHL's modern era to go from the Stanley Cup final in one year to last place overall the next. Injuries played a big part in Carolina's demise, though both Jeff O'Neill (30 goals, 31 assists) and Ron Francis (22, 35) played in all 82 games.

Goaltender Arturs Irbe, so important to the club's success in the previous season, had a record of 7–24–2 and was sent to the minors for a stretch in March. Kevin Weekes put up better numbers than his record of 14–24–9 indicated, but he was one of several Hurricanes whose year ended early because of injury. The Hurricanes' bad luck continued even after the season ended, as Florida beat them out in the lottery for the first choice at the 2003 Entry Draft. Carolina had to settle for the second pick. However, after Florida swapped first round picks with the Penguins, Carolina was able to land top-rated prospect Eric Staal of the Peterborough Petes after Pittsburgh decided to make goaltender Marc-Andre Fleury the first player selected in the 2003 Entry Draft.

Jeff O'Neill, seen here fighting off the coverage of Boston's P.J. Axelsson, scored a key overtime goal in game three of Carolina's 2002 Eastern Conference final with Toronto. O'Neill's eight playoff goals led the Hurricanes during their surprising postseason run.

Chicago Blackhawks

THE SAGA OF THE CHICAGO BLACKHAWKS began during the mid-1920s with a telephone call to Major Frederic McLaughlin, a millionaire coffee baron and prominent American polo player. The Patrick brothers, Frank and Lester, who were disbanding the Western Hockey League, were on the other end of the wire. The WHL no longer could compete with the higher-salaried NHL and the Patricks were holding a fire sale. They convinced McLaughlin that there was money to be made out of hockey and that Chicago could have a ready-made team by purchasing the Portland (Oregon) Rosebuds for $200,000. Fortified with about one hundred of his aristocratic Windy City friends, including H.R. Hardwick, the Major formed a consortium, bought the franchise, moved the Rosebuds to Illinois and changed their name.

As a commander of the 333rd Machine Gun Battalion of the U.S. Army's World War I Expeditionary Force, the Major belonged to the 85th Blackhawk Division and felt a many-faceted affection for the name. He also was aware that a Chief Blackhawk headed an Indian tribe that roamed the plains of the Midwest. After McLaughlin named the team, his wife Irene Castle—a world-renowned ballroom dancer who had teamed with her former husband Vernon before he had died—designed the unique black-and-white striped uniforms with the head of Chief Blackhawk on the logo.

McLaughlin and friends found a home for their hockey team at the 6,000-seat Chicago Coliseum. More often than not the arena was home to cattle shows, but with the aid of an ice plant, the Black Hawks were ready for play in the 1926–27 season. (Until 1985–86, the name "Black Hawks" usually was written as two words.)

Paul Thompson was the brother of Hockey Hall of Fame goaltender Tiny Thompson, and a top left winger during the 1920s and 1930s. He helped the Black Hawks win the Stanley Cup in 1934 and 1938 and coached the club to the Stanley Cup finals in 1944.

Thanks to the Patricks, McLaughlin not only acquired a coach in Pete Muldoon but a package of players that included coach-in-waiting Dick Irvin, Rabbit McVeigh, Mickey MacKay, George Hay, Percy Traub and Bob Trapp. For added scoring power, Babe Dye was obtained from the Toronto St. Pats. Dye was a poor skater, but was reputed to have the hardest shot in hockey and had been a top goal scorer throughout the 1920s. With 25 goals in 1926–27, Dye tied for second in the NHL and helped the Black Hawks finish third in the new American Division, whereupon McLaughlin—displaying an impatience that would be his hallmark—promptly fired coach Muldoon.

Whether the story is apocryphal remains debatable to this day, but legend has it that when Muldoon was fired he warned the Major that he would be sorry. "The Hawks will never finish first!" Muldoon hollered. "I'll put a curse on this team that will hoodoo it."

True hoodoo or not, the Chicagoans did seem cursed. During the 1927–28 training camp, Dye broke his leg in a scrimmage prank and the injury virtually ended his playing career. Without Dye to bolster their attack, the Hawks finished fifth in the American Division and wound up out of the playoffs. If they had anything worth cheering about, it was a young goaltender imported from the Winnipeg Maroons. His name was Charlie Gardiner, and he was slowly developing into one of the finds of the decade.

The 1928–29 season was another poor one for the Black Hawks, who scored just 33 goals in 44 games and were shut out in eight straight late in the season. With the Chicago Stadium slated to open the following season, Major McLaughlin managed to let his lease with the Coliseum lapse, and the Black Hawks were forced to close out the year by playing home games on the road in Buffalo, Fort Erie, Detroit and Windsor. Things finally began to look up in 1929–30 when the Black Hawks moved their home base to the mammoth new structure on West Madison Street. The Chicago Stadium would hold more than 18,000 people, making it the largest rink in the NHL. By that season, Gardiner had improved so much that he finished second to Tiny Thompson of the Boston Bruins in the race for the Vezina Trophy. In 1932, he finally would win the coveted prize. The 1929–30 season saw the Black Hawks finish second to Boston, albeit a distant second, but they were eliminated by the Canadiens in the Stanley Cup semifinals. A year later they were runners-up to the Bruins again. However, this time they eliminated Toronto in the first round, New York in the second round, and advanced to the Cup finals before losing to the Canadiens. After coaching the team in 1930–31, Dick Irvin was released and later accepted a similar job with the Maple Leafs. It was too much to expect Major McLaughlin to follow Irvin with an equally competent coach. Instead, the Major chose a chap named Godfrey Matheson, who had absolutely no big-league hockey coaching experience.

Despite the Major's machinations, the Black Hawks had sold Chicagoans on big-league hockey and the NHL was so popular that grain millionaire James Norris, a Canadian with ties to the Montreal Athletic Association, applied for a second Windy City franchise to share Chicago with the Black Hawks. The Major wanted no part of that and stopped the Norris bid. But, Norris went to war and organized a competitive team, the Chicago Shamrocks, and entered them in the American Hockey Association in 1930–31. Norris further embarrassed McLaughlin by hiring Tom Shaughnessy—recently fired by the Major—as Shamrocks coach.

Playing at the Chicago Stadium (which was owned by Norris), the Shamrocks drew healthy crowds and won the AHA title in 1931–32. At season's end, Norris even issued a challenge for the Stanley Cup but was rejected by the NHL. Prior to the 1932–33 season, Norris bought into the Detroit Red Wings and folded the Shamrocks. McLaughlin and his Black Hawks now had the run of the Stadium, and they continued their futile pursuit of the Stanley Cup.

Charlie Gardiner's superlative goaltending kept the Hawks competitive. In 1933–34, Chicago finished second to Detroit in the American Division while Gardiner allowed only 83 goals in 48 games and posted 10 shutouts. In 14 other games, he permitted just one goal. But, astute Gardiner-watchers perceived that there was something unusual about the goalie's deportment. The goaltender had lost his jovial manner and appeared melancholy. There were many explanations, but it soon became apparent that Gardiner had been gravely ill all season. Two months after his heroic goaltending had led Chicago to its first Stanley Cup title, Gardiner collapsed and died of a brain hemorrhage in his hometown of Winnipeg. He was 29 years old.

Without Gardiner, the Black Hawks were no longer a Stanley Cup contender. But, McLaughlin had an arresting idea for bringing glory back to his hockey club. An ardent nationalist, he resented Canada's grip on hockey and believed that a team of all American-born players could well represent Chicago in the NHL.

He started with Mike Karakas (Aurora, Minnesota), Alex Levinsky (Syracuse, New York), Doc Romnes (White Bear, Minnesota) and Lou Trudel (Salem, Massachusetts). Although Canadian-born managers throughout the league mocked him, the Major urged his high command to add Americans whenever possible. By the 1937–38 season even the coach, Bill Stewart, was American.

The Americanized Black Hawks managed to plod along through the schedule at a slightly quicker pace than the Red Wings. The result was that Chicago finished third in the American Division, just two points ahead of its Detroit pursuers, but a good 30 points behind division-leading Boston. Their chances for winning the Stanley Cup were considered no better than 100–1. To begin with, the Hawks were the only one of the six qualifying teams to have less than a .500 record (14–25–9), and their first-round opponents were the Montreal Canadiens. Further complicating matters for Chicago was the fact that two of the three games would be played in the Montreal Forum.

Predictably, the Canadiens won the first match, 6–4. But, when the series shifted to Chicago, goalie Karakas shut out the Montrealers, 4–0. Suddenly the Black Hawks were coming on strong. The final game was tied 2–2 after regulation time. It was decided in Chicago's favor when Lou Trudel's shot bounced off Paul Thompson and into Montreal's cage, although some observers insist that the puck was shot home by Mush March.

Now the Black Hawks were to face an equally aroused New York American sextet that had just routed the arch-rival Rangers in three games. Once again, the Hawks would have the benefit of only one home game in the best-of-three series, but once again the Chicago team prevailed and advanced into the Stanley Cup finals against the Toronto Maple Leafs.

By now the betting odds had dropped considerably in Chicago's favor. But, they soared again when it was learned that Karakas had suffered a broken big toe in the final game with the Americans. Karakas didn't realize the extent of the damage until he attempted to lace on his skates for the game with Toronto. He just couldn't make it, and the Hawks suddenly became desperate for a goaltender. With the Leafs blocking Chicago's efforts to borrow Rangers goalie Dave Kerr, the Black Hawks turned to Alfie Moore, a minor-league goalie who purportedly was quaffing liquid refreshment in a Toronto pub when he was drafted to climb into the barrel for the Chicagoans. Moore answered the call and went into the Chicago nets on April 5, 1938, defeating Toronto 4–1 in the opening game of the series at Maple Leaf Gardens. Moore was deemed ineligible for game two, but with Karakas back by the third game, Chicago went on to defeat Toronto in what was one of the singular upsets in Cup history.

Stewart was the coaching hero of Chicago until the following season when McLaughlin fired him after 21 games. From that point on, for more than two decades, the Windy City's hockey fortunes dipped. There would not be another championship at Chicago Stadium for almost a quarter of a century. There were, however, some fun years, particularly at the outset of World War II, when a pair of fleet youngsters named Max and Doug Bentley teamed with Bill Mosienko to form the Pony Line, one of the best offensive trios the league has known.

In both 1945–46 and 1946–47, Max Bentley led the league in scoring, but Chicago was going nowhere and, early in the 1947–48 season, the Black Hawks sent Bentley to the Toronto Maple Leafs. The Leafs dispatched Gaye Stewart, Gus Bodnar, and Bud Poile—an entire forward line—as well as defensemen Bob Goldham and Ernie Dickens, to Chicago in return for Bentley and an unobtrusive forward named Cy Thomas. The deal correctly was called one of the most extraordinary ever made. Conn Smythe, the Toronto boss, immediately claimed the trade would become the basis for a hockey dynasty—and he was right. With centers such as Syl Apps, Ted Kennedy and Bentley, he had the best offense in the league. The Leafs finished first that season and romped to the Cup.

In contrast, the Hawks, even augmented with the ex-Leafs, continued to struggle. They always seemed to come up with adequate scorers, but defense never seemed to be part of their vocabulary. The team acquired new ownership on September 11, 1952, when James Norris Sr., James D. Norris Jr. and Arthur Wirtz obtained control of the team. The Norrises already owned the Detroit Red Wings and had an interest in Madison Square Garden. By 1954, brothers Arthur and Michael Wirtz held controlling interest. Bill Wirtz also joined his father and uncle in reinvigorating the Black Hawks organization.

The Red Wings and Black Hawks became frequent trading partners, and in 1952–53 a collection of ex-Detroiters including Jim McFadden, Jimmy Peters, George Gee, Gerry Couture and Lidio

"Lee" Fogolin lifted Chicago to a fourth-place finish. With ex-Red Wing Sid Abel coaching while also doing considerable work at center, the Black Hawks marched into the Stanley Cup playoffs for the first time since the Bentley trade. The Black Hawks' most important asset was the goaltending of angular Al Rollins, perhaps the most underrated goalie the NHL has known. A former Maple Leaf, Rollins would win the Hart Trophy in 1953–54 despite Chicago's last-place finish that season. That season marked the first of five consecutive non-playoff years.

The decline of the Hawks nearly caused owner Jim Norris to forsake the game for more lucrative ventures. But, Norris finally was persuaded to invest a few million dollars in the rejuvenation of the franchise. He imported Tommy Ivan from the Detroit system and ordered him to develop a farm system from which Chicago could obtain a constant flow of young players. In the meantime, a few members of the league sympathized enough with the Chicago plight to promise help in some form or other. The talent-rich Canadiens finally cooperated by dealing the Hawks Ed Litzenberger, a muscular young forward of great promise.

By the 1955–56 season, the first trickles of new talent began flowing into Chicago Stadium. Such youngsters as Ken Wharram and Pierre Pilote pulled on Black Hawk jerseys and hardly seemed out of place against their more accomplished opponents. Soon the St. Catharines farm club began funneling such young talents as Bobby Hull and Hank Ciesla, and veterans were traded for hopefully better prospects. Chicago finished fifth in 1957–58, but the signs were clear that better days were ahead. The next season, they leaped into third place and gave Montreal a six-game run in the playoffs.

With Rudy Pilous at the helm, guiding the likes of Litzenberger, Hull, Pilote and Stan Mikita, Chicago remained a solid third-place team without making any playoff progress until 1961, when they again ran head-long into the Canadiens. Led by Glenn Hall's exceptional goaltending, Chicago captured the series, 4–2, and then defeated Detroit in six games. It had taken 23 long and often miserable years for the Hawks to win the Stanley Cup.

With the Stanley Cup finally returned to Chicago, the Hawks appeared ready for an assault on "The Muldoon Jinx." Certainly, with such stars as Hull, Hall, Mikita, and Pilote, they were the equal of any club in the league. But, when the chips were down, they didn't produce. They looked like sure champs in 1962–63, but they bowed out in the stretch, and as a result coach Pilous was fired. His successor, Billy Reay, who had once been fired by the Leafs, was imported from Buffalo in the American Hockey League. But, the next season the Black Hawks missed again and landed in second place, just a solitary point behind the champion Canadiens. In fact, the Black Hawks would not finish first in the NHL standings until the 1966–67 season. But, there were some

Chicago Blackhawks

Year-by-Year Record

Season	GP	W	L	T	OL	GF	GA	Pts.	Finish	Division	Playoff Result
1926-27	44	19	22	3	...	115	116	41	3rd	Amn. Div.	Lost Quarterfinal
1927-28	44	7	34	3	...	68	134	17	5th	Amn. Div.	Out of Playoffs
1928-29	44	7	29	8	...	33	85	22	5th	Amn. Div.	Out of Playoffs
1929-30	44	21	18	5	...	117	111	47	2nd	Amn. Div.	Lost Quarterfinal
1930-31	44	24	17	3	...	108	78	51	2nd	Amn. Div.	Lost Final
1931-32	48	18	19	11	...	86	101	47	2nd	Amn. Div.	Lost Quarterfinal
1932-33	48	16	20	12	...	88	101	44	4th	Amn. Div.	Out of Playoffs
1933-34	48	20	17	11	...	88	83	51	2nd	Amn. Div.	Won Stanley Cup
1934-35	48	26	17	5	...	118	88	57	2nd	Amn. Div.	Lost Quarterfinal
1935-36	48	21	19	8	...	93	92	50	3rd	Amn. Div.	Lost Quarterfinal
1936-37	48	14	27	7	...	99	131	35	4th	Amn. Div.	Out of Playoffs
1937-38	48	14	25	9	...	97	139	37	3rd	Amn. Div.	Won Stanley Cup
1938-39	48	12	28	8	...	91	132	32	7th	...	Out of Playoffs
1939-40	48	23	19	6	...	112	120	52	4th	...	Lost Quarterfinal
1940-41	48	16	25	7	...	112	139	39	5th	...	Lost Semifinal
1941-42	48	22	23	3	...	145	155	47	4th	...	Lost Quarterfinal
1942-43	50	17	18	15	...	179	180	49	5th	...	Out of Playoffs
1943-44	50	22	23	5	...	178	187	49	4th	...	Lost Final
1944-45	50	13	30	7	...	141	194	33	5th	...	Out of Playoffs
1945-46	50	23	20	7	...	200	178	53	3rd	...	Lost Semifinal
1946-47	60	19	37	4	...	193	274	42	6th	...	Out of Playoffs
1947-48	60	20	34	6	...	195	225	46	6th	...	Out of Playoffs
1948-49	60	21	31	8	...	173	211	50	5th	...	Out of Playoffs
1949-50	70	22	38	10	...	203	244	54	6th	...	Out of Playoffs
1950-51	70	13	47	10	...	171	280	36	6th	...	Out of Playoffs
1951-52	70	17	44	9	...	158	241	43	6th	...	Out of Playoffs
1952-53	70	27	28	15	...	169	175	69	4th	...	Lost Semifinal
1953-54	70	12	51	7	...	133	242	31	6th	...	Out of Playoffs
1954-55	70	13	40	17	...	161	235	43	6th	...	Out of Playoffs
1955-56	70	19	39	12	...	155	216	50	6th	...	Out of Playoffs
1956-57	70	16	39	15	...	169	225	47	6th	...	Out of Playoffs
1957-58	70	24	39	7	...	163	202	55	5th	...	Out of Playoffs
1958-59	70	28	29	13	...	197	208	69	3rd	...	Lost Semifinal
1959-60	70	28	29	13	...	191	180	69	3rd	...	Lost Semifinal
1960-61	70	29	24	17	...	198	180	75	3rd	...	Won Stanley Cup
1961-62	70	31	26	13	...	217	186	75	3rd	...	Lost Final
1962-63	70	32	21	17	...	194	178	81	2nd	...	Lost Semifinal
1963-64	70	36	22	12	...	218	169	84	2nd	...	Lost Semifinal
1964-65	70	34	28	8	...	224	176	76	3rd	...	Lost Final
1965-66	70	37	25	8	...	240	187	82	2nd	...	Lost Semifinal
1966-67	70	41	17	12	...	264	170	94	1st	...	Lost Semifinal
1967-68	74	32	26	16	...	212	222	80	4th	East Div.	Lost Semifinal
1968-69	76	34	33	9	...	280	246	77	6th	East Div.	Out of Playoffs
1969-70	76	45	22	9	...	250	170	99	1st	East Div.	Lost Semifinal
1970-71	78	49	20	9	...	277	184	107	1st	West Div.	Lost Final
1971-72	78	46	17	15	...	256	166	107	1st	West Div.	Lost Semifinal
1972-73	78	42	27	9	...	284	225	93	1st	West Div.	Lost Final
1973-74	78	41	14	23	...	272	164	105	2nd	West Div.	Lost Semifinal
1974-75	80	37	35	8	...	268	241	82	3rd	Smythe Div.	Lost Quarterfinal
1975-76	80	32	30	18	...	254	261	82	1st	Smythe Div.	Lost Quarterfinal
1976-77	80	26	43	11	...	240	298	63	3rd	Smythe Div.	Lost Prelim. Round
1977-78	80	32	29	19	...	230	220	83	1st	Smythe Div.	Lost Quarterfinal
1978-79	80	29	36	15	...	244	277	73	1st	Smythe Div.	Lost Quarterfinal
1979-80	80	34	27	19	...	241	250	87	1st	Smythe Div.	Lost Quarterfinal
1980-81	80	31	33	16	...	304	315	78	2nd	Smythe Div.	Lost Prelim. Round
1981-82	80	30	38	12	...	332	363	72	4th	Norris Div.	Lost Conf. Finals
1982-83	80	47	23	10	...	338	268	104	1st	Norris Div.	Lost Conf. Finals
1983-84	80	30	42	8	...	277	311	68	4th	Norris Div.	Lost Div. Semifinal
1984-85	80	38	35	7	...	309	299	83	2nd	Norris Div.	Lost Conf. Finals
1985-86	80	39	33	8	...	351	349	86	1st	Norris Div.	Lost Div. Semifinal
1986-87	80	29	37	14	...	290	310	72	3rd	Norris Div.	Lost Div. Semifinal
1987-88	80	30	41	9	...	284	328	69	3rd	Norris Div.	Lost Div. Semifinal
1988-89	80	27	41	12	...	297	335	66	4th	Norris Div.	Lost Conf. Finals
1989-90	80	41	33	6	...	316	294	88	1st	Norris Div.	Lost Conf. Finals
1990-91	80	49	23	8	...	284	211	106	1st	Norris Div.	Lost Div. Semifinal
1991-92	80	36	29	15	...	257	236	87	2nd	Norris Div.	Lost Final
1992-93	84	47	25	12	...	279	230	106	1st	Norris Div.	Lost Div. Semifinal
1993-94	84	39	36	9	...	254	240	87	5th	Central Div.	Lost Conf. Quarterfinal
1994-95	48	24	19	5	...	156	115	53	3rd	Central Div.	Lost Conf. Finals
1995-96	82	40	28	14	...	273	220	94	2nd	Central Div.	Lost Conf. Semifinal
1996-97	82	34	35	13	...	223	210	81	5th	Central Div.	Lost Conf. Quarterfinal
1997-98	82	30	39	13	...	192	199	73	5th	Central Div.	Out of Playoffs
1998-99	82	29	41	12	...	202	248	70	3rd	Central Div.	Out of Playoffs
99-2000	82	33	37	10	2	242	245	78	3rd	Central Div.	Out of Playoffs
2000-01	82	29	40	8	5	210	246	71	4th	Central Div.	Out of Playoffs
2001-02	82	41	27	13	1	216	207	96	3rd	Central Div.	Lost Conf. Quarterfinal
2002-03	82	30	33	13	6	207	226	79	3rd	Central Div.	Out of Playoffs

highlights along the way, most notably in the 1965–66 season when Bobby Hull became the first player to break the 50-goal barrier when he collected his 51st against Cesare Maniago on March 12, 1966. He finished with 54 goals and broke the league points record with 97.

Following the NHL's expansion from six to 12 teams in 1967, one of the most damaging events in franchise history occurred when Black Hawks general manager Tommy Ivan dealt Phil Esposito, Ken Hodge and Fred Stanfield to Boston for Gilles Marotte, Pit Martin and a minor-league goalie named Jack Norris. The three ex-Hawks, all young forwards, were responsible for a Boston surge. The rangy Esposito set an NHL record for points in a single season with 126 for the Bruins in 1968–69, while the Black Hawks fell into last place in the East Division. But, the Black Hawks weren't dead for long. With Phil's brother Tony Esposito starring in goal, Chicago finished first in the East in 1969–70, and then were transferred to the West Division after further expansion in 1970–71 and finished on top once more. In the playoffs, they went all the way to the seventh game of the Stanley Cup finals before being defeated by the Montreal Canadiens.

With players like Bobby Hull (left) and Stan Mikita, the Black Hawks became an offensive force in the 1960s. Between them, Hull and Mikita won the Art Ross Trophy seven times in nine seasons from 1959–60 to 1967–68.

Another telling blow occurred in 1972 when a contract dispute with the Wirtz family resulted in Windy City hero Bobby Hull bolting to the newly organized World Hockey Association. Despite NHL assertions that the WHA would quickly fold—causing Hull to return to the Black Hawks—it remained in business through the 1970s and Chicago lost its most colorful drawing card. But, once again the Black Hawks survived and, in some cases, thrived. Thanks to productive performers such as Stan Mikita, Jim Pappin and Ivan Boldirev, the Black Hawks remained competitive throughout the WHA years.

Stars like Denis Savard and Doug Wilson kept the club strong throughout the 1980s, but it wasn't until the 1991–92 season under coach Mike Keenan that the Blackhawks reached the Stanley Cup finals again. Despite the heroics of Ed Belfour, Jeremy Roenick, Steve Larmer and Chicago native Chris Chelios, they were eliminated by Pittsburgh in four straight games and have yet to reach similar heights again.

After 65 years in the historic Chicago Stadium, the Hawks moved across Madison Street for the 1994–95 season and into their new home, the United Center. However, by 1997–98, only Chelios remained of the Blackhawks' all-star nucleus from the early 1990s. Bob Pulford had departed as general manager after 20 years at the helm, turning over the position to Bob Murray. After a disastrous start to the season, the Blackhawks appeared to have their new house in order, but a weak finish saw the club miss postseason play for the first time since 1968–69. Third-year coach Craig Hartsburg lost his job, and the rebuilding process began anew with the hiring of former Blackhawk captain Dirk Graham to coach the team. However, Graham did not even last the entire 1998–99 season. The Blackhawks improved under new coach Lorne Molleken, who led them to a 13–6–4 record, but the team was never really in playoff contention. Tony Amonte had a fine season, leading the club in scoring for the third straight year, but expensive free-agent acquisition Doug Gilmour was less effective than hoped in a season cut short by injuries. Late in the year, Chelios was sent to the Detroit Red Wings for a package of prospects.

Eric Daze had 30 goals as a rookie in 1995–96 and a career-high 38 goals in 2001–02.

The club's hot finish under Molleken in 1998–99 did not carry over to the start of the 1999–2000 season. In December, Bob Pulford was brought out of semi-retirement in the upper levels of the front office to replace both Murray and Molleken, though Molleken stayed on as an associate coach. Mike Smith was added to the management team following a power struggle that had seen him lose his job in Toronto after the 1998–99 season. The changes led to only minimal improvements on the ice and the Blackhawks were never in playoff contention. Hampered by goaltending problems early in the season and the holdout of defenseman Boris Mironov, Chicago had slumped to last in the Western Conference at the midway point in the season, though once again they finished the year strongly. Amonte enjoyed another excellent year, ranking third in the NHL with 43 goals and seventh in scoring with 84 points.

Having missed the playoffs three seasons in a row, Mike Smith got an early start on the rebuilding process when he dealt Gilmour to the Buffalo Sabres at the 2000 trade deadline. Shortly after the season ended, he fired Lorne Molleken and made Alpo Suhonen, who had worked under him in both Winnipeg and Toronto, the first man born and raised in Europe to become a head coach in the NHL. Smith was formally given the title of general manager in Chicago on September 22, 2000, but the turnaround he hoped to achieve would have to wait one more year as the Blackhawks failed to reach the playoffs for the fourth straight season in 2000–01. Tony Amonte scored 35 goals to top the team in that department for the fifth year in a row, but Steve Sullivan ended Amonte's four-year reign as the team's top point-getter. Sullivan collected 34 goals and 41 assists.

The decision to make Alpo Suhonen the head coach had not worked out well, and Suhonen left the Blackhawks after the season due to health reasons. On May 3, 2001, Smith turned to Brian Sutter, making him the second of the six Sutter brothers to go behind the bench in Chicago. Sutter engineered a 25-point turnaround as the Hawks produced 41 wins and 96 points for their best performance since Darryl Sutter's first year as coach in 1992–93. The Blackhawks were back in the playoffs for the first time since 1996–97, but bowed out to St. Louis in five games.

Though both Amonte and Sullivan had seen their offensive output decline in 2001–02, both Alexei Zhamnov (22 goals, 45 assists) and Eric Daze (38 goals, 32 assists) helped pick up the slack. Phil Housley was acquired from Calgary in the Waiver Draft and rediscovered his scoring touch with 15 goals. (He was traded to Toronto late the next year). Better team defense, though, was the key to success in Chicago in 2001–02. In recent years, Chicago had allowed more than 240 goals per season. The Hawks surrendered just 207 in 2001–02. Jocelyn Thibault established himself among the game's top goaltenders, a position he solidified in 2002–03. His eight shutouts tied him for second in the NHL that year, while his save percentage (.915) and goals-against average (2.37) were also impressive. However, the Blackhawks slipped back to just 30 wins and 79 points and missed the playoffs for the fifth time in six years. The Hawks were led offensively by Steve Sullivan (26 goals, 35 assists), Eric Daze (22 goals), and Alexei Zhamnov (43 assists). Tyler Arnason ranked third among NHL rookies with 19 goals and was second in points with 39. He finished fourth in voting for the Calder Trophy and was named to the NHL All-Rookie team.

Colorado Avalanche and Quebec Nordiques

THE QUEBEC NORDIQUES strived for equal billing with the Montreal Canadiens in the province of Quebec for 23 years, seven of them spent in the World Hockey Association and 16 in the NHL. No matter how arduous the task, the Nordiques would enjoy their share of success in "The Battle of Quebec." Ironically, when the franchise relocated to Colorado, the influence of the Montreal Canadiens would be felt in a much more positive way.

In 1971, Guy Lafleur was the latest in a long line of homegrown superstars who had excelled in junior hockey in Quebec City and then graduated to the Canadiens. This grated on the provincial capital. Lafleur was in the second month of his rookie season with Montreal when news came on November 1, 1971, of a new professional league. The World Hockey Association would begin play the following October with 12 franchises. In February, a group of six Quebec businessmen purchased the rights of the San Francisco franchise and moved it to Quebec, where they would play as the Nordiques, a term that roughly translates to "North-men."

The Montreal influence was all pervasive, even as the infant franchise took its first steps. Veteran Montreal defenseman Jean-Claude Tremblay was the first player signed by the new team, on July 20, 1972, and Maurice Richard joined him as the team's first coach. The new team even managed a $1 million offer for Jean Beliveau to come out of retirement, but the former Quebec City star and Canadiens legend opted to remain in the Montreal head office. The Nordiques played their first WHA game on October 11, 1972, a 3–0 loss to Gerry Cheevers and the Cleveland Crusaders. Three days later, Richard admitted that he wasn't suited to coaching and resigned. Shortly thereafter, Hall of Fame netminder Jacques Plante joined the team as general manager.

Other former Canadiens, including the young duo of Marc Tardif and Rejean Houle (the team's top two draft picks in 1969), joined a mix of veteran NHL and minor pro stars that made Quebec a competitive team in its first seasons. Le Colisee was one of the best-attended WHA arenas. While other franchises in Canada and the United States foundered, the Nordiques built a loyal following in the province. Young stars in the Quebec Junior League now had an alternative to the Canadiens and the NHL when draft time came. The Nordiques scored a coup in 1974 when they signed 18-year-old Quebec Remparts star Real Cloutier.

The Nordiques challenged for the Avco Cup in their third season of 1974–75, but were swept in the finals by the Houston Aeros, who boasted the unique trio of Gordie Howe and his two sons, Mark and Marty. Two years later a local brewery invested $2 million in the team, and rookie coach Marc Boileau led the Nordiques to their first championship when the team edged out the Winnipeg Jets and Bobby Hull in seven games. That victory was savored in Quebec City, but paled against the exploits of the Canadiens. With Guy Lafleur in a six-year run of 50-goal seasons, the Canadiens captured the second of four straight Stanley Cup titles and were recognized as the power in hockey.

Although some fans cried out for a championship series between the Stanley Cup and Avco Cup winners, few executives in pro hockey paid much mind. Though they didn't know it, the fans were a lot closer to a reunification championship than they dared hope, as talks of a merger between the leagues, which had begun in 1974, were now being taken seriously. With the WHA providing a windfall in players' salaries, and the new league siphoning off junior-aged talents such as Wayne Gretzky, Mark Messier and Rod Langway, as well as opening the doors wide to such skilled Europeans as Ulf and Kent Nilsson and Anders Hedberg of Sweden, the NHL sought to institute damage control. During the 1978–79 season it was announced that four WHA teams would enter the NHL the following September. Although six WHA teams remained, only Quebec, Winnipeg, New England and Edmonton would join the league. The Cincinnati Stingers and the Birmingham Bulls would be dissolved. Significant talent was involved, and dispersed throughout the newly expanded NHL via the Entry Draft.

Coach Jacques Demers had several veterans available to him in Quebec's first NHL season, among them Marc Tardif, Real Cloutier, Robbie Ftorek, Dale Hoganson, Gerry Hart and Serge Bernier, and the team was astute in its inaugural pass at the drafting table, picking up Michel Goulet as well as junior stalwarts Dale Hunter and Lee Norwood. A more significant draft was that of

Michel Goulet established a career high with 57 goals in 1982–83 and topped 50 again in each of the next three seasons. He had over 100 points four times and finished among the top 10 in scoring on three occasions.

Czech star Anton Stastny, although it seemed the big wing might never make it across the Atlantic because the powerhouses of Eastern Europe jealously protected their talent. Still, at season's end, none of the former WHA teams had a winning record. Only Edmonton and Hartford made the playoffs, but both were swept in their best-of-five division semifinals, although the Whalers may have cost the Canadiens a second shot at five straight championships when wing Pat Boutette downed Lafleur with a season-ending knee injury.

The Nordiques showed great improvement during the 1980–81 season and gave indications of future greatness. Quebec's success was the result of several factors: the hiring of a feisty coach from Quebec's junior league, Michel Bergeron; some judicious draft choices; and a special scouting expedition to Europe by team president Marcel Aubut and chief scout Gilles Leger. With the suspense and secrecy of a spy thriller, the Nordiques braintrust spirited away 1979 draft choice Anton Stastny—and netted a bigger prize, older brother Peter—from Czechoslovakia in the summer of 1980.

With the emergence of Jacques Richard (52 goals) and Goulet (32 goals), the arrival of Hunter (19 goals), young defensemen Mario Marois and Normand Rochefort and newly acquired goalie Daniel Bouchard, the Nordiques surged immediately. But the biggest influence by far was the Stastny brothers. Both scored 39 goals, and Peter added 70 assists to finish his Calder Trophy-winning season with 109 points. The Nordiques were now seen as a rising force, while Montreal apparently was floundering, both on the ice and in the front office.

"The Battle of Quebec" emerged as a premier NHL matchup in 1981–82 for several reasons. First and foremost, the Canadiens and Nordiques found themselves in the same division, the Adams, which meant a full slate of games at the Forum and Le Colisee each winter. Each game was no-holds-barred, and the same could be said for their first postseason meeting in April, 1982. The Canadiens had rebounded to claim first in the Adams with 118 points, 43 better than the fourth-place Nordiques, but all observers agreed that regular-season statistics would have little bearing on the playoffs.

The Canadiens handily defeated Quebec, 5–1, in the series opener, but the Nords rebounded 3–2 in the second game at the Forum and returned to Quebec with home-ice advantage to bounce the Canadiens, 2–1. With Montreal on the ropes, it was Quebec's turn to falter and Montreal silenced a boisterous Colisee crowd with a 6–2 walkover. Game five was the stuff of legend, with the Nordiques taking a 2–0 lead into the third period, even though they had been outplayed significantly by the home team. Mario Tremblay, a fiery wing who became famous for his confrontations with Nordiques coach Bergeron, pulled the Habs within one at 10:49, and then Robert Picard drew Montreal even 80 seconds later.

The teams were tied 2–2 after regulation play, although the Canadiens had swarmed the Quebec net. Early in overtime, Montreal attacked the Quebec zone but it was the Nordiques who would emerge victorious on a goal by Dale Hunter. From that point on, the two teams would meet as equals.

The Canadiens and Nordiques would face off in 113 regular-season games between 1979 and 1995. The Canadiens won 62, lost 39 and played 12 ties. The teams would meet five times in the playoffs. The Canadiens eliminated Quebec on three occasions (twice going on to win the Stanley Cup), while the Nordiques got the best of the Canadiens on the two other occasions but never went on to win the NHL's top prize. Nords–Habs playoffs were fraught with drama, including Peter Stastny's overtime goal in game seven of the 1985 division finals and Montreal's seven-game victory in 1987. The series that may have hurt the Quebec franchise the most came in 1993, the year Montreal would go on to win its 24th Stanley Cup title.

After missing the playoffs for five straight seasons, which enabled the Nordiques to stockpile an impressive inventory of draft choices, Quebec fought the Bruins and Canadiens tooth-and-nail in the Adams Division, finishing second with 104 points—five behind Boston and two ahead of Montreal. Those five years had been torture for the Nordiques' faithful, and they sought vindication when the Adams Division semifinals began. The only relief of sorts during the five-year power outage had been the return of Guy Lafleur to Quebec. "The Flower" had retired from Montreal during the 1984–85 season, despondent over his apparently waning talent. After sitting out three seasons, during which he was inducted into the Hockey Hall of Fame, Lafleur came back for a single season with the Rangers and coach Michel Bergeron, and then the two were reunited in Quebec the following season. Lafleur would play two seasons for Quebec before putting a proper close to his playing career.

Lining up for the Nordiques against Montreal in 1993 were the harvests of so many rich draft years: Joe Sakic (1987, #15), Valeri Kamensky (1987, #129), Mats Sundin (1989, #1), Adam Foote (1989, #22) and Owen Nolan (1990, #1). Not in the lineup, however, was the biggest draft prize, Eric Lindros. Lindros had told the hockey world that he would not play in Quebec, but the Nordiques made him the top choice in 1991, anyway. Both sides became involved in a year-long soap opera that finally came to a head at the 1992 Entry Draft when Aubut entertained offers from all comers. He eventually decided on a five-player package plus cash,

Colorado Avalanche

Year-by-Year Record

Season	GP	W	L	T	OL	GF	GA	Pts.	Finish	Division	Playoff Result
1979-80*	80	25	44	11	...	248	313	61	5th	Adams Div.	Out of Playoffs
1980-81*	80	30	32	18	...	314	318	78	4th	Adams Div.	Lost Prelim. Round
1981-82*	80	33	31	16	...	356	345	82	4th	Adams Div.	Lost Conf. Finals
1982-83*	80	34	34	12	...	343	336	80	4th	Adams Div.	Lost Div. Semifinal
1983-84*	80	42	28	10	...	360	278	94	3th	Adams Div.	Lost Div. Final
1984-85*	80	41	30	9	...	323	275	91	2nd	Adams Div.	Lost Conf. Finals
1985-86*	80	43	31	6	...	330	289	92	1st	Adams Div.	Lost Div. Semifinal
1986-87*	80	31	39	10	...	267	276	72	4th	Adams Div.	Lost Div. Final
1987-88*	80	32	43	5	...	271	306	69	5th	Adams Div.	Out of Playoffs
1988-89*	80	27	46	7	...	269	342	61	5th	Adams Div.	Out of Playoffs
1989-90*	80	12	61	7	...	240	407	31	5th	Adams Div.	Out of Playoffs
1990-91*	80	16	50	14	...	236	354	46	5th	Adams Div.	Out of Playoffs
1991-92*	80	20	48	12	...	255	318	52	5th	Adams Div.	Out of Playoffs
1992-93*	84	47	27	10	...	351	300	104	2nd	Adams Div.	Lost Div. Semifinal
1993-94*	84	34	42	8	...	277	292	76	5th	Northeast Div.	Out of Playoffs
1994-95*	48	30	13	5	...	185	134	65	1st	Northeast Div.	Lost Conf. Quarterfinal
1995-96	82	47	25	10	...	326	240	104	1st	Pacific Div.	Won Stanley Cup
1996-97	82	49	24	9	...	277	205	107	1st	Pacific Div.	Lost Conf. Finals
1997-98	82	39	26	17	...	231	205	95	1st	Pacific Div.	Lost Conf. Quarterfinal
1998-99	82	44	28	10	...	239	205	98	1st	Northwest Div.	Lost Conf. Finals
99-2000	82	42	28	11	1	233	201	96	1st	Northwest Div.	Lost Conf. Finals
2000-01	82	52	16	10	4	270	192	118	1st	Northwest Div.	Won Stanley Cup
2001-02	82	45	28	8	1	212	169	99	1st	Northwest Div.	Lost Conf. Finals
2002-03	82	42	19	13	8	251	194	105	1st	Northwest Div.	Lost Conf. Quarterfinal

* Quebec Nordiques

offered by the New York Rangers.

At this point, Philadelphia vice president Jay Snider complained his team's offer had been verbally accepted by the Nordiques, and he took his contention to the league. Independent arbitrator Larry Bertuzzi, a Toronto-based lawyer, was appointed and he eventually ruled in favor of Philadelphia. While that decision may have been embarrassing to the Nordiques president, the decision definitely would help the team. Coming to Quebec were forwards Peter Forsberg, Chris Simon and Mike Ricci, defensemen Kerry Huffman and Steve Duchesne, goalie Ron Hextall, draft choices in 1993 (Jocelyn Thibault) and 1994 (traded) and $15 million cash.

The franchise leader in most significant categories, Joe Sakic was already a top scorer before the club relocated to Colorado. Though the Nordiques only made the playoffs twice in Sakic's seven seasons in Quebec, he was able to establish himself as a star.

All but Huffman and Thibault were in the Quebec lineup against Montreal in 1993, as were other solid players such as Czech Martin Rucinsky and Russian Andrei Kovalenko. The Nordiques immediately jumped to a 2–0 series lead, but Montreal got back into the series with a 2–1 overtime win, then evened things with a 3–2 victory at the Forum. The game that took Quebec out of the series was played at Le Colisee, a 5–4 win by Montreal on Kirk Muller's overtime goal through Ron Hextall's legs. Two nights later, the aroused Habs thumped the dispirited Nords, 6–2, at the Forum and their season was over. It was the last playoff meeting between the teams.

While the Nordiques players were struggling on the ice in the 1993–94 season, dropping to fifth place in the Adams and out of the playoffs, a similar uphill battle was being waged off the ice by their president. Marcel Aubut, who represented a consortium of owners of the team, had taken his case to his community as well as the city and provincial governments.

The Nordiques were victims of the 1990s disease in sports, an outdated facility and too few revenue streams, and the only cure would be a state-of-the-art new building, with control of concessions and parking, and tax breaks. The war of words was waged for two years, and the spirits and hopes of Quebec fans were raised in 1994–95 when the team, under new coach Marc Crawford, soared to the top of the Adams Division in a lockout-shortened season. Mats Sundin had been moved to Toronto for veteran wing Wendel Clark and defenseman Sylvain Lefebvre, and the young goaltending tandem of Jocelyn Thibault and Stephane Fiset showed poise beyond its years.

And then the bad news came all at once. The Nordiques were swept aside in six games by the Rangers, and three levels of government said no. Quebec's last game was a 4–2 loss at Madison Square Garden on May 16.

Nine days later, the Nordiques ownership group signed an agreement in principle with COMSAT Entertainment Group to sell the team. Ironically, it was on Canada Day, July 1, 1995, that the Nordiques announced that they were moving to Colorado. The Battle of Quebec was stilled forever. Despite the move, the long-reaching shadow of the Forum and the Montreal Canadiens would touch the hockey team once again, albeit in a positive manner.

The team's new home, Denver, had a tenuous connection with professional hockey, playing host to a succession of minor league teams and a WHA franchise called the Spurs over the years before the Kansas City Scouts moved to the Mile High City in 1976 and became the Colorado Rockies. A succession of coaches, including the colorful Don Cherry, led the team, and talented young stars like Rob Ramage, Barry Beck, Wilf Paiement and Lanny McDonald plied their trade with the Rockies until the franchise was moved to New Jersey after the 1981–82 season. Denver attempted half-hearted efforts at pro hockey after that until the Grizzlies entered the International Hockey League in 1993. A strong entry in the "I," the Grizzlies captured the Calder Cup championship in their inaugural season and averaged 12,000 fans per game at McNichols Arena. When the Avalanche came to town two years later, the Grizzlies moved to Salt Lake City.

It is rare that a team in a new city is competitive, and unlike the case of the Scouts/Rockies, this time Denver was getting a serious Stanley Cup contender. The team became a threat during the season, thanks to the influence of the Montreal Canadiens. The first move was made October 3, 1995, when former Montreal winger Claude Lemieux was acquired from New Jersey in a three-way deal. Lemieux had debuted with the Canadiens late in the 1985–86 season and scored 10 goals during the playoffs. Four months before joining Colorado, he had led New Jersey to its first Stanley Cup title and won the Conn Smythe Trophy as playoff MVP. Three weeks later, the Avalanche traded power forward Owen Nolan to San Jose to acquire the defensive quarterback they needed in Sandis Ozolinsh, but the team's biggest move still was two months away and came in the form of an early Christmas present from Montreal. On December 6, 1995, four days after a feud with coach Mario Tremblay became public knowledge, Patrick Roy was dealt to the Avalanche along with Canadiens captain Mike Keane in a blockbuster deal engineered by g.m. Pierre Lacroix. Goalie Jocelyn Thibault and forwards Andrei Kovalenko and Martin Rucinsky were sent to Montreal. Avalanche defenseman Uwe Krupp was driving around Denver when he heard the news and said to himself, "We've got a great chance to win the whole thing now."

On June 10, 1996, less than a year after acquiring an NHL franchise, Colorado won the Stanley Cup on a goal by Krupp in the third overtime period after a masterful postseason by Roy. While the Colorado sweep over the Florida Panthers in the finals was the stuff of champions, the real victory came in the conference finals when the Avalanche bested favored Detroit, a team that had won an NHL-record 62 games during the regular season, in a masterful six-game set.

The Avalanche have remained at the top of their conference with Detroit and the Dallas Stars since 1996. Led by the likes of Sakic, Forsberg, Roy, Ozolinsh, Kamensky, Lemieux and Adam Deadmarsh, Colorado followed up its Stanley Cup championship with a Presidents' Trophy win in 1996–97, but dropped the Western Conference championship to the rival Red Wings, who finally went on to win the Stanley Cup. A year later, the Avalanche suffered a shocking first-round playoff loss to Edmonton.

NHL realignment saw Colorado shifted into the newly created Northwest Division in 1998–99, and the club won its fifth straight division title. The emergence of rookies Milan Hejduk and Chris Drury (the Calder Trophy winner) as stars, and the late-season acquisition of Theo Fleury in a deal with Calgary made the Avalanche a Stanley Cup favorite heading into the playoffs. The Avalanche downed San Jose in six games before dropping the first two games of their second-round series with Detroit. The Avalanche rallied for four straight victories to eliminate the Red Wings, then took a three-games-to-two lead over Dallas in the Western Conference final before falling to the eventual Stanley Cup winners in seven games.

The offseason prior to the 1999–2000 season was an eventful one, as the Avalanche lost Fleury and Kamensky to the New York Rangers via free agency, but gained a new owner in Donald L. Strum of Liberty Media, who purchased the Avalanche, the Denver Nuggets basketball team and the Pepsi Center. (The entire package would later be sold again to Wal-Mart heir Stanley Kroenke) The Avalanche made their debut in the new 18,129-seat Pepsi Center on October 15, 1999, but with Peter Forsberg out because of off-season shoulder surgery and Joe Sakic also sidelined by injuries, Colorado started the new season slowly. Hedjuk and Drury continued to shine, as did rookie Alex Tanguay, but by early March, the Avalanche trailed Edmonton in the Northwest Division standings.

On March 6, 2000, Colorado acquired Ray Bourque from the Bruins. After 20-plus seasons in Boston, Bourque had asked for a trade to a contender—though Colorado hardly looked like potential Stanley Cup champions when he arrived. However, the future Hockey Hall of Famer collected eight goals and six assists in his first 13 games with the Avalanche, sparking the team to a 10–2–1 record and its sixth straight division crown. Colorado carried an eight-game winning streak into the playoffs and wiped out the Phoenix Coyotes in five games. Facing Detroit in the second round for the second straight year, the Avalanche disposed of their rivals with relative ease in another five-game series. Bourque was hurt during the fourth game, and did not return until game three of the Conference final against Dallas. Bourque was key in a game-six victory that kept Colorado alive, but for the second year in a row the Avalanche fell to the Stars in seven games. Shortly after their season ended, Bourque, who could have become a free agent, signed a one-year deal to stay in Colorado.

On July 6, 2000, two weeks after the purchase was completed, E. Stanley Kroenke was officially introduced as the new owner of the Avalanche, the Denver Nuggets and the Pepsi Center. Already a co-owner of the 2000 Super Bowl champion St. Louis Rams of the National Football League, Kroenke added the Stanley Cup to his list of accomplishments in 2000–01. Colorado's Stanley Cup title was a fitting send-off for Raymond Bourque, who announced his retirement shortly after the victory. "Mission 16-W" (for the 16 wins it would take to make the 22-year veteran a champion for the first time) had been the team's rallying cry throughout the playoffs.

The Avalanche had been the NHL's best team throughout the 2000–01 season, posting a record of 52–16–10–4 for 118 points and the Presidents' Trophy. Significant offensive contributions came from Peter Forsberg (89 points), Milan Hejduk (41 goals), Alex Tanguay and Chris Drury. Defensively, the team was led by Bourque, Jon Klemm and Adam Foote. Late in the season, Rob Blake was added in a deal that sent Adam Deadmarsh to Los Angeles. Still, the undisputed leader of the Avalanche was captain Joe Sakic.

Sakic's 54 goals established a new career high and ranked him second in the NHL behind Pavel Bure (59). His 118 points represented the second-best total of his career and left him just three points behind Jaromir Jagr for the league lead. The 13-year NHL veteran was rewarded with both the Lady Byng Trophy for sportsmanship and the Hart Trophy as MVP. It was the first time he had won either award. No other player in the 78-year history of the Hart Trophy had ever played as many seasons before winning the award for the first time. Sakic also joined Bobby Clarke, Wayne Gretzky and Mark Messier in an elite group as he became only the fourth player in history to win the Hart Trophy and captain his team to a Stanley Cup championship in the same year.

Despite their strong regular season, Colorado's route through the Stanley Cup playoffs was not always smooth. After a four-game sweep of Vancouver in the opening round, the Avalanche jumped out to a 3–1 lead in games over Los Angeles but were forced to go to a seventh game before eliminating the Kings. Peter Forsberg suffered an injury in this series that resulted in the loss of his spleen and knocked him out of the rest of the playoffs. (This injury, plus problems with his ankle, would also keep Forsberg out of the 2001–02 regular season.) After a five-game victory over St. Louis in the Western Conference final, Colorado needed another seven games to defeat New Jersey for the Stanley Cup.

Patrick Roy won the Conn Smythe Trophy as playoff MVP for a record third time in the spring of 2001. He went on to enjoy the best season of his stellar career in 2001–02. Not only did he surpass Terry Sawchuk as the NHL's all-time winningest goaltender, he also posted a career-best 1.94 goals-against average and a career-high nine shutouts. Roy led the Avalanche to the franchise's eighth straight division title, tying a record set by the Montreal Canadiens between 1975 and 1982. He earned the Jennings Trophy for the fifth time as Colorado allowed the fewest goals in the league, but he lost out to Montreal's Jose Theodore in voting for both the Hart and Vezina trophies. Joe Sakic was not nearly as dominant as he had been the year before, but he did lead Team Canada in scoring during their gold medal performance at the Olympics.

Peter Forsberg returned to the team for the playoffs and was nothing short of spectacular. He led all playoff performers with 27 points (nine goals, 18 assists) in 20 games. However, Colorado's hopes of a Stanley Cup repeat ended when the Red Wings beat the Avalanche in a seven-game Western Conference final.

After the season, assistant coach Bryan Trottier left Colorado to take over as the head man with the New York Rangers. (He would later be fired). Tony Granato was brought in to replace Trottier. On December 18, 2002, Granato was elevated to head coach after the decision to fire Bob Hartley, who had guided the team since the 1998–99 season. Among the few highlights for the club in the first half of the 2002–03 season was Patrick Roy becoming the first goaltender in NHL history to reach the 1,000-games plateau. At the time, the Avalanche were struggling just to hold down a playoff spot, and their hopes of a record-setting ninth straight divisional title seemed lost. However, with Roy returning to his usual form (he ended the year with 35 wins, a 2.18 goals-against average and a .920 save percentage), the team posted a record of 32–11–4–4 in 51 games under Granato. Joe Sakic was limited to just 58 games due to injuries, but Forsberg and Milan Hejduk picked up the offensive slack. On the last day of the regular season, Forsberg pulled ahead of Vancouver's Markus Naslund to win the scoring title (106 points to 104), while Colorado passed the Canucks to win the Northwest Division (105 points to 104). Forsberg would also beat out Naslund for the Hart Trophy. Hedjuk scored twice to become the league's only 50-goal scorer and the winner of the Maurice Richard Trophy. Both Forsberg and Hedjuk were responsible in their own ends as well, tying for the NHL lead in plus-minus at +52. On defense, Adam Foote had a plus-minus rating of +30, while Rob Blake scored 17 goals and was a +20. Derek Morris (acquired from Calgary for Chris Drury) topped the team's blueliners with 48 points (11 goals, 37 assists).

Colorado opened the playoffs against the surprising Minnesota Wild, and even though they dropped the opening game of the series to the third year team most people still saw the Avalanche as a legitimate threat to go all the way. That feeling was reinforced when the team rattled off three wins in a row while their rivals in Detroit were being swept out of the playoffs by the Mighty Ducks of Anaheim. However, the Avalanche failed to wrap up the series on home ice in game five, then were beaten again in Minnesota and were forced to head to a seventh game for the fifth straight series dating back to their Stanley Cup victory in 2001. Against the Wild, the team that scored first had won each of the first six games, but despite holding leads of 1–0 and 2–1, the Avalanche lost game seven 3–2 in overtime.

"We played with fire and burned ourselves," said Patrick Roy. "We've done that a couple of years in a row and this year, we paid for it."

Shortly after the Avalanche were eliminated, rumors began to circulate that Roy was ready to announce his retirement. He confirmed the story on May 28, 2003, leaving the game but beginning the debate as to whether he was the greatest goaltender of all time. Roy retired with many records to his credit, including most games played by a goaltender (1,029) and most wins (551). Avalanche g.m. Pierre Lacroix stunned the hockey world in early July announcing that the talented duo of Paul Kariya and Teemu Selanne, former teammates in Anaheim, would play in Colorado in 2003–04.

Though his fierce playing style has made him somewhat injury prone, a healthy Peter Forsberg is one of the most dangerous players in the NHL.

Columbus Blue Jackets

THE ADDITION OF TEAMS in Columbus and Minnesota to the National Hockey League for the 2000–2001 season saw the league become a 30-club circuit and completed a wave of expansion that began on June 25, 1997, when those two cities were formally admitted into the NHL along with Nashville and Atlanta. Columbus was placed in the Central Division of the Western Conference with the Chicago Blackhawks, Detroit Red Wings, Nashville Predators and St. Louis Blues.

Principal owner of the NHL's Columbus franchise is John H. McConnell, who announced the selection of the team name Blue Jackets on November 11, 1997. "We wanted a name that reflected the spirit and pride that exists in Columbus," McConnell said. "The Blue Jacket [an insect] is aggressive, industrious, multi-tasked, resourceful and fast—many of the qualities exemplified by our community." The name was selected after a name-the-team contest which drew over 14,000 entries and thousands of different suggestions.

The Blue Jackets were quick to start the process of putting some sting in their on-ice activities, hiring former Florida Panthers head coach Doug MacLean in February, 1998 as the franchise's first general manager. MacLean assembled a staff of scouts and consultants that includes former Los Angeles Kings general manager Sam McMaster and former NHL goaltender Rick Wamsley. Guiding the team on the ice will be Dave King, former coach of the Canadian national team whose previous NHL experience includes a head coaching job with the Calgary Flames and an assistant's role with the Montreal Canadiens.

The Blue Jackets play out of Nationwide Arena, a $150-million facility privately financed by Nationwide Insurance Enterprises and the Dispatch Printing Company. Excavation for the arena began in June, 1998, with a formal groundbreaking ceremony on July 23. The mixed-use glass, brick and steel structure seats 18,500 for hockey and also houses an adjoining practice rink, an office building, retail space and restaurants.

The Blue Jackets enjoyed one of the NHL's most successful inaugural seasons when they took to the ice at the Nationwide Arena in 2000–01, becoming just the third expansion team (excluding the 1967–68 season) to top the 70-point plateau. The Blue Jackets posted a record of 28–39–9–6 for 71 points. Only the Mighty Ducks (33 wins, 71 points) and the Florida Panthers (33 wins, 83 points) have enjoyed better debut seasons. Ron Tugnutt tied a career high with 22 wins, a total which set a new record for expansion team goalies. He recorded the club's first win (in its third game) with a 3–2 victory over Calgary on October 12, 2000. Offensively, Columbus was led by Geoff Sanderson in their inaugural season. He collected 30 goals in just 68 games, leaving him 12 goals behind Brian Bradley's expansion team record of 42 set with Tampa Bay in 1992–93. The Blue Jackets had an average attendance of 17,452 in 2000–01, including 26 sellouts (18,136). Columbus ended the season with 15 straight sellouts.

Despite a drop-off in performance in 2001–02 (22–47–8–5, 57 points), Columbus sold out all 41 home games at Nationwide Arena. Injuries limited Geoff Sanderson to just 11 goals, but Ray Whitney bounced back from a back injury to lead the team in goals (20), assists (41) and points (61) in his first full season with the Blue Jackets. Sanderson returned to form in 2002–03, while Whitney continued to shine, earning a selection to the Western Conference All-Star Team. Sanderson led the Blue Jackets with 34 goals. Whitney was tops with 52 assists and 76 points. Andrew Cassels and David Vyborny both scored 20 times. Goaltender Marc Denis started all but five of Columbus's games during the season. His 77 games played tied him for the second most by a goaltender in one year, while his total of more than 4,510 minutes played set a new record. Denis faced a league-high 2,404 shots and made a league-leading 2,172 saves for a percentage of .903

Geoff Sanderson (left) has been the Blue Jackets best scorer, but it is players like Rick Nash (right) who offer the most hope for the future.

Though coach Dave King was fired midway through the 2002–03 season (president and general manager Doug MacLean took over behind the bench), players like Rostislav Klesla and Rick Nash give the Blue Jackets considerable upside. Klesla was the club's first draft choice in 2000. He was named to the NHL All-Rookie team in 2001–02. Columbus traded up in the draft in order to claim Nash with the top pick in 2002. He was the youngest player in the NHL during the 2002–03 season and ranked among the rookie leaders in goals (17), assists (22) and points (39). He finished third in voting for the Calder Trophy behind winner Barret Jackman of St. Louis and Henrik Zetterberg of Detroit and, like Klesla before him, was named to the All-Rookie team.

Columbus Blue Jackets

Year-by-Year Record

Season	GP	W	L	T	OL	GF	GA	Pts.	Finish	Division	Playoff Result
2000-01	82	28	39	9	6	190	233	71	5th	Central Div.	Out of Playoffs
2001-02	82	22	47	8	5	164	255	57	5th	Central Div.	Out of Playoffs
2002-03	82	29	42	8	3	213	263	69	5th	Central Div.	Out of Playoffs

Dallas Stars and Minnesota North Stars

WITH THE EXCEPTION of the Canadian provinces, no similar region produces as many hockey players, nor is the game played as much per square mile, as in Minnesota. So when the NHL decided to expand to 12 teams in 1967, it was not surprising that the state was included.

In order to enter the NHL, Minnesota had to produce a suitable arena. This requirement was fulfilled when the splendid Metropolitan Sports Center was completed in Bloomington just prior to the start of the 1967–68 season. And with such eminent sportsmen as Gordon Ritz, Walter Bush, W. John Driscoll, Robert McNulty, Robert Ridder and Harry McNeely, Jr. on the North Stars' board, success was virtually guaranteed. Wren Blair, a veteran hockey organizer, was named coach and general manager and the building of the North Stars was under way. The first game of the season was held at Bloomington on October 21, 1967. The North Stars beat the Oakland Seals 3–1.

The young franchise was was dealt a stunning blow early in its existence with the death of 29-year-old Bill Masterton on January 15, 1968, two days after he sustained a brain injury in a game against Oakland. "Because he had the habit of giving everything he had for every second he was on the ice, Bill was the type of player who didn't have to score a lot of goals to help a club," said Wren Blair. Soon after the 1967–68 season, the NHL inaugurated a memorial award, the Bill Masterton Trophy, for perseverance, sportsmanship and dedication to hockey.

The North Stars finished fourth in the West Division and reached the NHL playoffs in their rookie season. They eliminated the Los Angeles Kings in a rugged seven-game first-round series, fighting back from 2–0 and 3–2 deficits. In the semifinals, Minnesota went up against the St. Louis Blues and carried the foe to seven games before losing 2–1 in double overtime.

The North Stars fell to the worst record in the NHL in their second season, but a complete house-cleaning by Blair turned things around in 1969–70. In 1970–71, he turned over coaching duties to Jack Gordon, and also infused the playing roster with significant names: defenseman Ted Harris, a hardrock ex-Canadien who became the team captain, veterans Doug Mohns and Lorne "Gump" Worsley, plus youngsters Jude Drouin and Barry Gibbs. Despite a fourth-place finish, the North Stars played mightily in the Stanley Cup competition, defeating the heavily favored St. Louis Blues in the first round.

Every young franchise requires a significant series to make it respectable. For the North Stars, it came in April, 1971 in a series with the fabled Montreal Canadiens. Conspicuous underdogs, the North Stars lost the series in six games, but not before giving the Montrealers considerable consternation. "None of us realized that the North Stars were that good," said Peter Mahovlich of the Canadiens. The Minnesotans obtained another measure of glory in the 1971–72 season, challenging Chicago for first place in the West before settling for a strong second-place position. Their eventual defeat by the Blues in the seventh game of the opening Cup round has gone down as a Stanley Cup classic.

Computations revealed that the North Stars' average attendance was 11,800 fans

Bill Goldsworthy was Minnesota's first star player. His 48 goals in 1973–74 were a club record for eight years and he was the first player to score 200 goals for a 1967 expansion team. Goldsworthy celebrated his goals with a move known as the "Goldy Shuffle."

in their first NHL season, in a rink with a seating capacity of 15,095. By the third season the average had jumped to 14,351, and in the 1971–72 season it was next to impossible to find an empty seat in the building at any time. One reason for the club's popularity was its cast of characters.

It is doubtful that any NHL team ever boasted two such competent yet contrasting goaltenders as the Mutt and Jeff combination of Gump Worsley and Cesare Maniago. Worsley was short and round and tended his goal without the benefit of a protective face mask; tall and lean, Maniago wore a white mask with huge openings around the eyes that was suggestive of a World War I gas mask. Another marquee player was big, blond right wing Bill Goldsworthy, who played with flair and a shuffle that endeared him to rooters at the Met Center.

Led by Dennis Hextall, who tallied 30 goals and 52 assists, and all-stars Barry Gibbs and J.P. Parise, the North Stars enjoyed another solid season in 1972–73, but were defeated in the opening round of the playoffs by Philadelphia. The next five seasons were disappointing, as the North Stars were transformed into also-rans. The 1976–77 season did offer some hope, as Tim Young led the team in scoring with 95 points and Roland Eriksson (Minnesota's first Swedish import) added some scoring punch. Minnesota managed to finish second in the Smythe despite a mediocre 23–39–18 record, but whatever high hopes fans could have for a gallant playoff run reminiscent of the early 1970s was extinguished in the first round when the Buffalo Sabres swept a best-of-three series. The Stars' fell back to the bottom of the NHL pack in 1977–78. They managed just 18 wins and nine ties—and a whopping 53 losses.

Popular player Lou Nanne took over as coach and general manager late in the 1977–78 season. As g.m., he would soon help turn the franchise around, but things looked bleak for the financially struggling North Stars until an unprecedented merger with another cash-strapped franchise breathed some life into their roster.

The Minnesota franchise had been owned by a group of investors led by team president Gordon Ritz since the club's inception. With the team fighting for its fiscal life, Ritz and company looked to cut their losses and sell to new investors, who, it so happened, were already owners of another struggling NHL franchise. Brothers George and Gordon Gund had also been suffering heavy monetary losses since they purchased the former Oakland Seals and moved them to Cleveland in 1976.

The Gunds knew it would be economic suicide to manage two losing hockey clubs at once. The solution? The two franchises merged and the Gunds assumed ownership of the Minnesota club while Cleveland folded. More significantly, all the players who had a contract with Cleveland were transferred to Minnesota, and the 1978–79 North Stars hit the ice with eight former Cleveland Barons. Right wing Al MacAdam and goaltender Gilles Meloche proved to be the best of a bunch.

But the most promising newcomer of 1978-79 was first-round draft choice Bobby Smith, a talented young center who burst on the scene in Minnesota with 30 goals and 44 assists that season. Smith's production earned him the team lead in scoring and the Calder Trophy as the NHL's rookie of the year.

These new players left the North Stars much improved. In 1980, they ended Montreal's bid for a fifth straight Stanley Cup title with a thrilling four-games-to-three victory in the quarterfinals. In 1981, they were demonstrating their proficiency by advancing to the Stanley Cup finals against the defending champion New York Islanders. Badly outgunned, the Minnesotans played gamely and averted a sweep with a 4–2 win in game four at home. The Islanders would clinch their second consecutive Cup title in with a 5–1 win in game five. The North Stars followed up their Stanley Cup appearance with a 94-point season to lead the Norris Division in 1981–82, but dropped an opening-round playoff series to Chicago. The Black Hawks would eliminate Minnesota again one year later, this time in the second round.

Bobby Smith was traded to Montreal 10 games into the 1983–84 season, but still the Stars regained the Norris Division title. Helping to fill the void created by Smith's absence was Brian Bellows, who contributed 44 goals. In the first round of the playoffs, the Stars faced and defeated their nemesis from Chicago in a tough five-game series. The second-round series against the St. Louis Blues also went the distance, with Minnesota prevailing at 6:00 of overtime in game seven on a goal by Steve Payne. But the powerhouse Edmonton Oilers steamrollered the Stars with a fast four-game sweep in the Campbell Conference finals.

The North Stars' loss seemed to affect them the following sea-

Dallas Stars

Year-by-Year Record

Season	GP	W	L	T	OL	GF	GA	Pts.	Finish	Division	Playoff Result
1967-68*	**74**	**27**	**32**	**15**	**...**	**191**	**226**	**69**	**4th**	**West Div.**	**Lost Semifinal**
1968-69*	76	18	43	15	...	189	270	51	6th	West Div.	Out of Playoffs
1969-70*	76	19	35	22	...	224	257	60	3rd	West Div.	Lost Quarterfinal
1970-71*	78	28	34	16	...	191	223	72	4th	West Div.	Lost Semifinal
1971-72*	78	37	29	12	...	212	191	86	2nd	West Div.	Lost Quarterfinal
1972-73*	78	37	30	11	...	254	230	85	3rd	West Div.	Lost Quarterfinal
1973-74*	78	23	38	17	...	235	275	63	7th	West Div.	Out of Playoffs
1974-75*	80	23	50	7	...	221	341	53	4th	Smythe Div.	Out of Playoffs
1975-76*	80	20	53	7	...	195	303	47	4th	Smythe Div.	Out of Playoffs
1976-77*	80	23	39	18	...	240	310	64	2nd	Smythe Div.	Lost Prelim. Round
1977-78*	80	18	53	9	...	218	325	45	5th	Smythe Div.	Out of Playoffs
1978-79*	80	28	40	12	...	257	289	68	4th	Adams Div.	Out Of Playoffs
1979-80*	80	36	28	16	...	311	253	88	3rd	Adams Div.	Lost Semifinal
1980-81*	80	35	28	17	...	291	263	87	3rd	Adams Div.	Lost Final
1981-82*	80	37	23	20	...	346	288	94	1st	Norris Div.	Lost Div. Semifinal
1982-83*	80	40	24	16	...	321	290	96	2nd	Norris Div.	Lost Div. Final
1983-84*	80	39	31	10	...	345	344	88	1st	Norris Div.	Lost Conf. Finals
1984-85*	80	25	43	12	...	268	321	62	4th	Norris Div.	Lost Div. Final
1985-86*	80	38	33	9	...	327	305	85	2nd	Norris Div.	Lost Div. Semifinal
1986-87*	80	30	40	10	...	296	314	70	5th	Norris Div.	Out of Playoffs
1987-88*	80	19	48	13	...	242	349	51	5th	Norris Div.	Out of Playoffs
1988-89*	80	27	37	16	...	258	278	70	3rd	Norris Div.	Lost Div. Semifinal
1989-90*	80	36	40	4	...	284	291	76	4th	Norris Div.	Lost Div. Semifinal
1990-91*	80	27	39	14	...	256	266	68	4th	Norris Div.	Lost Final
1991-92*	80	32	42	6	...	246	278	70	4th	Norris Div.	Lost Div. Semifinal
1992-93*	84	36	38	10	...	272	293	82	5th	Norris Div.	Out of Playoffs
1993-94	84	42	29	13	...	286	265	97	3rd	Central Div.	Lost Conf. Semifinal
1994-95	48	17	23	8	...	136	135	42	5th	Central Div.	Lost Conf. Quarterfinal
1995-96	82	26	42	14	...	227	280	66	6th	Central Div.	Out of Playoffs
1996-97	82	48	26	8	...	252	198	104	1st	Central Div.	Lost Conf. Quarterfinal
1997-98	82	49	22	11	...	242	167	109	1st	Central Div.	Lost Conf. Final
1998-99	82	51	19	12	...	236	168	114	1st	Pacific Div.	Won Stanley Cup
99-2000	82	43	23	10	6	211	184	102	1st	Pacific Div.	Lost Final
2000-01	82	48	24	8	2	241	187	106	1st	Pacific Div.	Lost Conf. Semifinal
2001-02	82	36	28	13	5	215	213	90	4th	Pacific Div.	Out of Playoffs
2002-03	82	46	17	15	4	245	169	111	1st	Pacific Div.	Lost Conf. Semifinal

* Minnesota North Stars

son. They finished 18 games under .500, but did earn a playoff berth, albeit against first-place St. Louis. Most were anticipating a quick series. And indeed it was—but it was Minnesota that blindsided the Blues with a sweep in the best-of-five first round. Keith Acton, who had been acquired from Montreal in the Bobby Smith trade, scored two game-winners in the series. The Stars were brought back down to earth in round two by—who else?—the Chicago Black Hawks.

The 1985–86 season was something of a bounce-back year. Broten bumped his numbers over 100 points for the first time in his career, Dino Ciccarelli, who had scored 55 goals in 1981–82 but just 15 in 51 games in 1984–85, was back with 44 goals. Bellows popped in 31 more. The Stars finished in second in their division, but this year St. Louis would turn the tables and eliminate them in the opening round of the playoffs. It would be the last postseason action the Stars would see for some time.

Thanks to a pair of key trades, the North Stars found themselves back in the pack for the playoffs of 1989. Dave Gagner, who had been acquired from the New York Rangers in 1987, came out of nowhere to lead the Stars in scoring in 1988–89 with 78 points. Mike Gartner, on the other hand, was already an established star in Washington when Minnesota traded fan-favorite Dino Ciccarelli for him in March, 1989. Also coming into prominence with the North Stars that year was goaltender Jon Casey. Led by this new corps—and, of course, Broten and Bellows—the Stars locked up third place in the Norris Division. Once again, however, they were knocked out of the playoffs by St. Louis. Making matters worse, the Gartner gamble didn't pay off; he went scoreless in the series and the Stars traded him to the Rangers for Ulf Dahlen next season.

In 1989–90, Minnesota fans got their first true glimpse of the man who would ultimately become their team's biggest star. Speedy center Mike Modano had 29 goals and 46 assists in his rookie campaign, earning him kudos as the rookie of the year as chosen by The Hockey News.

Meanwhile, Bellows banged home an impressive 55 goals that season and Broten's playmaking was as good as ever. But once again an old nemesis was there to ground the Stars: Chicago ousted them in the first round of a hard-fought seven-game series.

But the 1989–90 season was tumultuous in other ways for the Stars. Owners George and Gordon Gund threatened to move the team elsewhere (San Jose) if they didn't find a buyer who would pay $50 million. At the 11th hour Howard Baldwin and Norm Green pulled together the resources and purchased the team. The Gunds were granted an NHL expansion franchise for San Jose and reached an agreement that would see them retain a portion of the players on the Minnesota reserve list. The new San Jose team—later called the Sharks—would select players from the Minnesota system at a dispersal draft after the 1990-91 season.

The old regime, headed by general manager Jack Ferreira and coach Pierre Page, was replaced by a new one featuring former Flyers captain Bob Clarke as g.m. and ex-Montreal hero Bob Gainey as coach, but the 1990–91 season began ominously for the North Stars. They managed only one win in their first nine contests and continued to play poorly until January. A late-season slump nearly cost them a playoff spot, but the North Stars managed to hold on. What followed can only be described as a miracle run.

A native of Roseau, Minnesota, and a product of the University of Minnesota, Neal Broten was a member of the "Miracle on Ice" U.S. Olympic team that won the gold medal in Lake Placid in 1980. He was a high-scoring star in both Minnesota and Dallas.

The North Stars—a fourth-place team that had finished 12 games under .500—defeated their traditional playoff foes in the next three rounds. First it was a 4–2 series win over Norris Division champs Chicago, then a 4–2 win over St. Louis in round two. Goalie Jon Casey outplayed rookie of the year counterpart Ed Belfour in round one, and shut down the deadly duo of 86-goal scorer Brett Hull and super-playmaker Adam Oates in round two. Minnesota hadn't won in Edmonton in more than 11 years, but needed only five games to defeat the Oilers for the Campbell Conference championship.

The Stanley Cup finals pitted two surprise American teams: Minnesota, who had finished 16th overall in the 21-team NHL, and Mario Lemieux's Pittsburgh Penguins, playoff participants only once in the previous eight years. The teams split the first two games before Minnesota took the third 3–1. Lemieux had sat out the match with recurring back spasms, but when he returned to the lineup in time for game four the Penguins' offense kicked into high gear. Behind Super Mario, the Pens took control of the series with a pair of victories before Lemieux's four-point outburst triggered an 8–0 victory over the shell-shocked Stars in game six. The 1991 trip to the finals would prove to be the North Stars' final flirtation with a Stanley Cup title.

The dispersal draft to stock the new San Jose franchise was held on May 30, 1991. As per prior agreement the Sharks claimed four players from the Stars' NHL roster and 10 from their farm system.

As compensation, the North Stars were allowed to select players from other NHL clubs in the 1991 Expansion Draft.

By this time, owner Norman Green's stewardship of the club had become ensnared with financial and legal problems, and the North Stars followed up their gallant playoff run by finishing in fourth place in the Norris Division in 1991–92 and losing to Detroit in seven games in the first playoff round. As if to add to the troubles, the Met Center itself, once a jewel among ice rinks, suddenly became an also-ran among arenas when the Target Center opened in downtown Minneapolis. Arrangements to move the North Stars from Bloomington's suburbs to the inner city failed.

After 1991–92, Bob Clarke returned to Philadelphia (before moving on to run the expansion Florida Panthers), leaving Bob Gainey to add general manager's duties to his coaching role. Despite Gainey's competence and Hall of Fame status, the Stars finished out of the playoffs in 1992–93.

Minnesota lost its NHL franchise in 1993. The North Stars were transferred to Dallas and became the first Texas-based team in the league. The word "North" was erased from the name. Thus truncated, the Dallas Stars' home games would be played at the 16,924-seat Reunion Arena, home of the NBA Mavericks. Before the season began the Stars made one more drastic change, sending goalie Jon Casey to Boston for Andy Moog to complete an earlier deal.

The Stars enjoyed a stellar first season in Texas, but showed signs of weakness one season later during the lockout-shortened 1994–95 campaign. Norman Green sold the club to media mogul Tom Hicks in December, 1995, but despite the infusion of cash and new blood, the Stars gave a harsh welcome to their new bosses when they finished with a 26–42–14 mark and didn't qualify for the 1995–96 postseason. On January 8, 1996, Gainey formally stepped down as coach to concentrate on his g.m. duties and brought Ken Hitchcock in to replace him. A highly successful junior coach, Hitchcock was guiding the Stars' International Hockey League affiliate in Kalamazoo when he got the call.

The addition of Hitchcock and dependable veterans like Guy Carbonneau and Joe Nieuwendyk couldn't help the Stars in what was ultimately a lost season—but they did lay the groundwork for a dramatic franchise turnaround. Dallas won the Central Division crown with a 38-point jump in 1996–97, but the Stars were upset in the first round of the playoffs by a red-hot Curtis Joseph in net for the Edmonton Oilers.

Taking much of the blame for the crushing upset was Moog, who was not re-signed by the Stars. For a new goaltender, Gainey looked to Ed Belfour, who had been traded by Chicago to San Jose and had no intentions of re-signing with the struggling Sharks. Gainey also signed free-agent defenseman Shawn Chambers, late of the 1995 New Jersey Cup-winning team. Later in the season, Dallas obtained forwards Mike Keane and Brian Skrudland from the Rangers. Both had prior experience as team captains, and both had played on Stanley Cup champions.

In a neck-and-neck race with the Devils and Red Wings for the best overall points record in 1997-98, the Stars won the Presidents' Trophy with 109 points (49–22–11) before taking a more determined run at the Stanley Cup. The road to the top wasn't easy, though. The Stars battled injuries during the entire season and at one time or another were missing such potent offensive forces as Nieuwendyk, Selke Trophy winner Jere Lehtinen and superstar Mike Modano. Leading the way in spite of those potentially disastrous absences were defensemen Sergei Zubov and Derian Hatcher.

With Belfour playing some of the best hockey of his life, Dallas eliminated San Jose in six games in the first round before exacting revenge on the Oilers in a five-game second-round test. But more injuries, particularly to Nieuwendyk (who was hurt in the first game against San Jose) caught up with the Stars in the Western Conference final. The Red Wings defeated Dallas in six games and went on to capture their second straight Stanley Cup championship. However the Stars would not be denied in 1998–99.

With Modano's 34 goals and 81 points leading the way, Dallas established club records with 51 wins and 114 points and captured the Presidents' Trophy for the second straight year. A four-game sweep of the Oilers was followed up with a tough six-game victory over the St. Louis Blues that featured four overtime games, including Dallas's 2–1 win in the clincher. Belfour, who had combined with Roman Turek to win the Jennings Trophy, then outdueled Patrick Roy as the Stars defeated Colorado in seven games to win the Western Conference championship. Belfour got the better of Dominik Hasek in the Stanley Cup finals, as Dallas captured the franchise's first NHL title in six games. Free-agent acquisition Brett Hull scored the Cup-winning goal for Dallas in triple overtime. Nieuwendyk led all playoff performers with 11 goals and won the Conn Smythe Trophy.

A rush of injuries led to a slow start to the 1999–2000 season and saw both Brett Hull and Mike Modano question Ken Hitchcock's defensive system. Though Modano ended the year with 38 goals (his most since scoring 50 in 1993–94) and Hull matched his father with 610 career scores, it was defense that continued to win in Dallas as the Stars soon got back on the winning track and topped 100 points for the fifth straight year in cruising to their fifth consecutive division title. Remarkably, Ed Belfour's 2.10 goals-against average was the highest of this three seasons with the Stars, but his .919 save percentage was the NHL's best by a thread over Jose Theodore of Montreal.

In the playoffs, the defending Stanley Cup champions once again knocked off the Edmonton Oilers in the first round (this time in five games), then beat the San Jose Sharks in five to set up a Western Conference final rematch with Colorado. Once again the series went seven tough games before Dallas emerged victorious. The Stars then dropped three of the first four games of the Stanley Cup final to New Jersey. For game five, Belfour dug out the skates he had not worn since game six against Buffalo the year before and, in a contest that was remarkably similar, he blanked the Devils through more than 100 minutes of playing time before Mike Modano scored at 6:21 of triple overtime to give the Stars a 1–0 victory. But the Stars run as Stanley Cup champions ended at home two nights later when Jason Arnott scored for the Devils in double overtime.

The loss to New Jersey proved just how difficult it is to stay on top in the modern NHL—a point that was proven again with a second-round playoff loss to the St. Louis Blues in the spring of 2001. Though it marked the first time in three years that they had failed to reach at least the Western Conference final, the Stars had enjoyed another solid season in 2000–01. They won their fifth straight division title with a record of 48–24–8–2 and 106 points. They also topped both the 40-win and 100-point plateaus for the fifth year in a row, a feat equaled only by the New Jersey Devils over the same time span. Offensively, the Stars were led by Mike Modano, Brett Hull and Joe Nieuwendyk. Hull topped the team with 39 goals, while Modano was best with 51 assists and 84 points. Both Modano and Nieuwendyk reached the 900-point plateau during the season.

Defensively, the group of Derian Hatcher, Sergei Zubov, Darryl Sydor, Richard Matvichuk and Brad Lukowich helped goaltenders Ed Belfour and Marty Turco allow the league's second fewest goals against. During one stretch in March, the Stars allowed one goal or less in eight straight games, the best defensive run in the NHL since 1932–33. Belfour recorded three straight shutouts during November and became just the fifth goalie in NHL history to post at least seven 30-win seasons. Marty Turco played in 26 games and led the NHL with a 1.90 goals-against average. His average was the second-best to be turned in by a rookie netminder in the "modern" era (since 1943–44), topped only by Al Rollins' mark of 1.77 back in 1950–51.

The season of 2001–02 saw several changes in Dallas, including the opening of the new American Airlines Center. Brett Hull left the team as a free agent in the offseason, and Joe Nieuwendyk was dealt to the Devils for Jason Arnott late in the year. In between, coach Ken Hitchcock and general manager Bob Gainey were let go. Mike Modano enjoyed a top-10 scoring season (34 goals, 43 assists), and Jere Lehtinen had a career-high 25 goals, but Ed Belfour slumped badly. Though the Stars finished the season with a winning record and a respectable 90 points, they were tenth in the Western Conference and failed to qualify for the playoffs.

Mike Modano scored 50 goals during the Stars first season in Dallas in 1993–94. Since then, he has continued to rank as the Stars' top scorer, but has also developed into a solid defensive player.

Several moves were made to change the team's fortunes for 2002–03. Among the first was new general manager Doug Armstrong's decision to hire Los Angeles Kings assistant Dave Tippett as the Stars' head coach. The former NHL player had enjoyed success as a head coach in the minors and had helped turn the Kings into perennial playoff contenders. Dallas also decided to make Marty Turco its number-one goaltender, allowing Ed Belfour to leave as a free agent. Though he missed a stretch due to injuries late in the season, Turco responded with a record of 35–10–10 and a 1.72 goals-against average that was the lowest in the NHL since the 1939–40 season. He earned his seventh shutout with a 2–0 victory over Nashville on the last day of the season. The win enabled Dallas to climb ahead of Detroit for top spot in the Western Conference (111 points to 110).

Offensively, the Stars were led once again by Mike Modano who topped the team with 57 assists and 85 points while posting a plus-minus rating of +34. Jere Lehtinen led the team with a new career-high of 31 goals and was a +39. (He would win the Selke Trophy as best defensive forward for the third time.) Free agent Bill Guerin had 25 goals in just 64 games. Sergei Zubov led the club's blueliners with 11 goals and 44 assists, while Derian Hatcher bounced back from a poor season with eight goals, 22 assists and a plus-minus rating of +37.

The Stars opened the playoffs against Edmonton for the fifth time in seven years (they had also played them in the second round in 1998), and when the Oilers won the first game it rekindled memories of their 1997 upset. However, the Stars bounced back with a 6–1 rout in game two and took the series in six.

Next up for Dallas was the Mighty Ducks of Anaheim, who had shocked the Red Wings in a four-game sweep of their opening-round series. The Ducks stayed hot in game one when Peter Sykora's goal 48 seconds into the fifth overtime period gave them a 4–3 win over the Stars in the fourth-longest game in NHL history. Game two required just 1:44 of extra time, but Dallas again came out on the wrong end as Mike Leclerc gave the Ducks a 3–2 victory. After a 2–1 Stars victory in game three, Leclerc scored the winner again, this time with 1:47 left in regulation time as the Ducks scored a 1–0 victory to take a 3–1 series lead.

Dallas staved off elimination with a 4–1 win in game five, but the Ducks wrapped up the series with a 4–3 win back at home in game six. Sandis Ozolinsh scored the series winner with 1:06 remaining in the third period. Anaheim had led 3–2 midway through the third when an apparent tying goal by Stu Barnes was disallowed. Dallas did tie the game less than three minutes later when Brenden Morrow redirected defenseman Sergei Zubov's pass into the net with his right skate at 14:49, but the Ducks would not be denied. "There's certainly a lot of ways you can look at the series," said Marty Turco, "but the bottom line is we lost. We had our chances, but we didn't get it done."

Detroit Red Wings
(includes Cougars and Falcons)

The Motor City's passion for the game is etched at center ice of Joe Louis Arena. Detroit is Hockeytown. Has been for more than three-quarters of a century.

As the most successful American-based franchise in National Hockey League history, only the Montreal Canadiens and Toronto Maple Leafs have won more Stanley Cup titles in NHL competition than the nine captured by the Red Wings. The Detroit franchise has been part of the NHL since 1926. American expansion by the NHL brought the Boston Bruins into the fold in 1924, with the Pittsburgh Pirates and the New York Americans joining the following year.

The success of these moves led to more U.S. cities clamoring for NHL hockey, and the league had no fewer than 11 bids for NHL franchises from American-based groups at its 1926 spring meetings, including five from Detroit. As early as March, 1926, one of the groups made a bold attempt to acquire the rights to Edmonton's franchise in the Western Hockey League and move it to Detroit. "Detroit will have professional hockey, of that there is no doubt," said James Connors, a representative of the Detroit Hockey Club.

On May 15, a group that included former pro netminder Percy LeSueur was awarded the franchise. Charles King was named club president. Players were secured when the roster of the WHL's Victoria Cougars was purchased for $100,000. Art Duncan, who led the Pacific Coast Hockey Association in scoring with Vancouver in 1923–24, was signed and named player-manager.

On paper, it appeared Detroit had bought itself instant status as a contender. Victoria had won the Stanley Cup in 1925 and was the losing finalist in 1926. Among the players acquired were goaltender Harry "Hap" Holmes, who had backstopped four teams to Stanley Cup victories, and Frank Fredrickson, Jack Walker and Frank Foyston, superstars of the western circuits.

But, the Stanley Cup is won on the ice and the Detroit club, which kept the Cougars nickname, soon found the nucleus of its roster was past its prime and no longer had what it took to contend. Detroit played its home games in Windsor, Ontario, making it the first professional franchise to have a foreign country as home base. A disappointing first campaign concluded with a 12–28–4 record and a last-place finish in the NHL's five-team American Division. Financially, the team was more than $80,000 in the hole after just one season.

There would be plenty of changes before the puck would drop again. The most significant came May 16, 1927, when the Cougars announced that Jack Adams had been signed as manager. A star player who had just helped Ottawa win the Stanley Cup, Adams was chosen after the owners failed to lure Lester Patrick, who had coached the Cougars in the WHL, away from the New York Rangers. The Olympia, Detroit's new rink, finally debuted on November 22, 1927. Johnny Sheppard scored for the Cougars, who lost, 2–1, to the Stanley Cup champion Senators.

Like Gordie Howe (to whom he is not related), Syd Howe had a long NHL career starring with the Detroit Red Wings before retiring as the NHL's all-time scoring leader. Howe is also one of only seven players in history to score six goals in one NHL game.

Tight-fisted, indecisive ownership would be the trademark of Detroit's early years. Detroit made the playoffs just twice in its first seven seasons, losing in the first round on both occasions. The club tried changing players, changing sweaters and changing names, going from the Cougars to the Falcons in 1930, but where the Cougars hadn't roared, the Falcons couldn't soar.

Distraught during one of his team's many slumps, Adams concluded that it was because the Cougars had loaned backup goalie Porky Levine to Seattle of the Pacific Coast League, thus leaving his club with only one goalie to shoot at during practice. Team officials would not allow him to sign another netminder, so Adams had a wooden effigy of Porky constructed and outfitted in goalie equipment, including skates. The Detroit players pushed their pine Porky into place in front of the net during practice and sometimes took it out for pregame warmups.

Carving goaltenders out of plywood was a fact of life for Adams until the summer of 1932, when grain millionaire James Norris purchased the Detroit franchise. Norris had been a member of the Montreal Amateur Athletic Association, a sporting club with cycling roots. The MAAA's teams were known by their club emblem and these Winged Wheelers were the first winners of the Stanley Cup in 1893. Norris decided a version of their logo was perfect for a team playing in the Motor City and on October 5, 1932, the club was renamed the Red Wings.

The winged wheel also was suitable, because this was a franchise that was about to turn things around and take off. Adams had used his eye for talent to methodically assemble the basis of a decent club. He added defenseman Doug Young and forwards Herbie Lewis, John Sorrell and Larry Aurie from the minor leagues, and acquired the rights to amateur Ebbie Goodfellow from the New York Americans.

Detroit reached the Stanley Cup semifinals the first season with Norris as owner and in 1933–34, bolstered by the midseason acquisition of goalie Wilf Cude on loan from the Montreal Canadiens, Detroit reached the Stanley Cup finals for the first time. Although the Red Wings lost the final to the Chicago Black Hawks, excitement finally was gripping the hockey fans of Detroit. But, just when everything seemed rosy, a large hole was cut in the lineup when Cude was recalled by the Habs.

Minus its goalie, Detroit fell out of the playoff picture again in 1934–35, but Adams still was looking ahead. He dispatched $50,000 and defenseman Teddy Graham to the St. Louis Eagles for forward Syd Howe and defenseman Ralph (Scotty) Bowman. Adams also acquired Normie Smith from the Eagles to fill the void in net. He converted Goodfellow, who had been the club's scoring leader, from forward to defense.

The final piece of the puzzle fell into place when Adams met with Boston coach Frank Patrick during the 1935 Cup finals in Montreal. "If I had Cooney Weiland, my club would be here," Patrick said of the Detroit wing. "If I had Marty Barry," responded Adams, referring to Boston's number-one center, "we'd win the Cup." On June 30, 1935, the deal was consummated—Barry and Art Giroux to Detroit for Weiland and Walt Buswell.

Adams proved a prophet. With Barry playing between Lewis and Aurie on the club's top forward unit, the Wings soared to the top of the NHL standings in 1935–36. Under the playoff format of the day, the first-place finishers from the league's two divisions would meet in the first round of the playoffs, with the winner advancing to the final. That meant Detroit would open at Montreal against the defending champion Maroons on March 24.

The game was scoreless after 60 minutes and through five overtime periods neither goaltender—Smith or Montreal's Lorne Chabot—had faltered. At 4:47 of the sixth overtime period, the game became the longest in NHL history, surpassing the 164:46 mark set by Boston and Toronto in 1933.

Late in the sixth overtime, winger Mud Bruneteau, recalled from the minors just two weeks earlier, came over the boards with Howe and Hec Kilrea. After Smith thwarted a Montreal rush, Kilrea

Detroit Red Wings

Year-by-Year Record

Season	GP	W	L	T	OL	GF	GA	Pts.	Finish	Division	Playoff Result
1926-27*	44	12	28	4	...	76	105	28	5th	Amn. Div.	Out of Playoffs
1927-28	44	19	19	6	...	88	79	44	4th	Amn. Div.	Out of Playoffs
1928-29	44	19	16	9	...	72	63	47	3rd	Amn. Div.	Lost Quarterfinal
1929-30	44	14	24	6	...	117	133	34	4th	Amn. Div.	Out of Playoffs
1930-31§	44	16	21	7	...	102	105	39	4th	Amn. Div.	Out of Playoffs
1931-32	48	18	20	10	...	95	108	46	3rd	Amn. Div.	Lost Quarterfinal
1932-33•	48	25	15	8	...	111	93	58	2nd	Amn. Div.	Lost Semifinal
1933-34	48	24	14	10	...	113	98	58	1st	Amn. Div.	Lost Final
1934-35	48	19	22	7	...	127	114	45	4th	Amn. Div.	Out of Playoffs
1935-36	48	24	16	8	...	124	103	56	1st	Amn. Div.	Won Stanley Cup
1936-37	48	25	14	9	...	128	102	59	1st	Amn. Div.	Won Stanley Cup
1937-38	48	12	25	11	...	99	133	35	4th	Amn. Div.	Out of Playoffs
1938-39	48	18	24	6	...	107	128	42	5th	...	Lost Semifinal
1939-40	48	16	26	6	...	91	126	38	5th	...	Lost Semifinal
1940-41	48	21	16	11	...	112	102	53	3rd	...	Lost Final
1941-42	48	19	25	4	...	140	147	42	5th	...	Lost Final
1942-43	50	25	14	11	...	169	124	61	1st	...	Won Stanley Cup
1943-44	50	26	18	6	...	214	177	58	2nd	...	Lost Semifinal
1944-45	50	31	14	5	...	218	161	67	2nd	...	Lost Final
1945-46	50	20	20	10	...	146	159	50	4th	...	Lost Semifinal
1946-47	60	22	27	11	...	190	193	55	4th	...	Lost Semifinal
1947-48	60	30	18	12	...	187	148	72	2nd	...	Lost Final
1948-49	60	34	19	7	...	195	145	75	1st	...	Lost Final
1949-50	70	37	19	14	...	229	164	88	1st	...	Won Stanley Cup
1950-51	70	44	13	13	...	236	139	101	1st	...	Lost Semifinal
1951-52	70	44	14	12	...	215	133	100	1st	...	Won Stanley Cup
1952-53	70	36	16	18	...	222	133	90	1st	...	Lost Semifinal
1953-54	70	37	19	14	...	191	132	88	1st	...	Won Stanley Cup
1954-55	70	42	17	11	...	204	134	95	1st	...	Won Stanley Cup
1955-56	70	30	24	16	...	183	148	76	2nd	...	Lost Final
1956-57	70	38	20	12	...	198	157	88	1st	...	Lost Semifinal
1957-58	70	29	29	12	...	176	207	70	3rd	...	Lost Semifinal
1958-59	70	25	37	8	...	167	218	58	6th	...	Out of Playoffs
1959-60	70	26	29	15	...	186	197	67	4th	...	Lost Semifinal
1960-61	70	25	29	16	...	195	215	66	4th	...	Lost Final
1961-62	70	23	33	14	...	184	219	60	5th	...	Out of Playoffs
1962-63	70	32	25	13	...	200	194	77	4th	...	Lost Final
1963-64	70	30	29	11	...	191	204	71	4th	...	Lost Final
1964-65	70	40	23	7	...	224	175	87	1st	...	Lost Semifinal
1965-66	70	31	27	12	...	221	194	74	4th	...	Lost Final
1966-67	70	27	39	4	...	212	241	58	5th	...	Out of Playoffs
1967-68	74	27	35	12	...	245	257	66	6th	East Div.	Out of Playoffs
1968-69	76	33	31	12	...	239	221	78	5th	East Div.	Out of Playoffs
1969-70	76	40	21	15	...	246	199	95	3rd	East Div.	Lost Quarterfinal
1970-71	78	22	45	11	...	209	308	55	7th	East Div.	Out of Playoffs
1971-72	78	33	35	10	...	261	262	76	5th	East Div.	Out of Playoffs
1972-73	78	37	29	12	...	265	243	86	5th	East Div.	Out of Playoffs
1973-74	78	29	39	10	...	255	319	68	6th	East Div.	Out of Playoffs
1974-75	80	23	45	12	...	259	335	58	4th	Norris Div.	Out of Playoffs
1975-76	80	26	44	10	...	226	300	62	4th	Norris Div.	Out of Playoffs
1976-77	80	16	55	9	...	183	309	41	5th	Norris Div.	Out of Playoffs
1977-78	80	32	34	14	...	252	266	78	2nd	Norris Div.	Lost Quarterfinal
1978-79	80	23	41	16	...	252	295	62	5th	Norris Div.	Out of Playoffs
1979-80	80	26	43	11	...	268	306	63	5th	Norris Div.	Out of Playoffs
1980-81	80	19	43	18	...	252	339	56	5th	Norris Div.	Out of Playoffs
1981-82	80	21	47	12	...	270	351	54	6th	Norris Div.	Out of Playoffs
1982-83	80	21	44	15	...	263	344	57	5th	Norris Div.	Out of Playoffs
1983-84	80	31	42	7	...	298	323	69	3rd	Norris Div.	Lost Div. Semifinal
1984-85	80	27	41	12	...	313	357	66	3rd	Norris Div.	Lost Div. Semifinal
1985-86	80	17	57	6	...	266	415	40	5th	Norris Div.	Out of Playoffs
1986-87	80	34	36	10	...	260	274	78	2nd	Norris Div.	Lost Conf. Finals
1987-88	80	41	28	11	...	322	269	93	1st	Norris Div.	Lost Conf. Finals
1988-89	80	34	34	12	...	313	316	80	1st	Norris Div.	Lost Div. Semifinal
1989-90	80	28	38	14	...	288	323	70	5th	Norris Div.	Out of Playoffs
1990-91	80	34	38	8	...	273	298	76	3rd	Norris Div.	Lost Div. Semifinal
1991-92	80	43	25	12	...	320	256	98	1st	Norris Div.	Lost Div. Final
1992-93	84	47	28	9	...	369	280	103	2nd	Norris Div.	Lost Div. Semifinal
1993-94	84	46	30	8	...	356	275	100	1st	Central Div.	Lost Conf. Quarterfinal
1994-95	48	33	11	4	...	180	117	70	1st	Central Div.	Lost Final
1995-96	82	62	13	7	...	325	181	131	1st	Central Div.	Lost Conf. Finals
1996-97	82	38	26	18	...	253	197	94	2nd	Central Div.	Won Stanley Cup
1997-98	82	44	23	15	...	250	196	103	2nd	Central Div.	Won Stanley Cup
1998-99	82	43	32	7	...	245	202	93	1st	Central Div.	Lost Conf. Semifinal
99-2000	82	48	22	10	2	278	210	108	2nd	Central Div.	Lost Conf. Semifinal
2000-01	82	49	20	9	4	253	202	111	1st	Central Div.	Lost Conf. Quarterfinal
2001-02	82	51	17	10	4	251	187	116	1st	Central Div.	Won Stanley Cup
2002-03	82	48	20	10	4	269	203	110	1st	Central Div.	Lost Conf. Quarterfinal

* Team named Cougars.
§ Team name changed to Falcons.
• Team name changed to Red Wings.

broke down ice, Bruneteau at his side. He fed Bruneteau, who deked the sliding Chabot and ended hockey's longest game after 176 minutes and 30 seconds.

Smith stopped 89 shots in the game, which ended at 2:25 a.m. on March 25. He also shut out the Maroons in game two and his shutout sequence of 248:32 remains a playoff record. After sweeping the Maroons, the Red Wings bounced the Toronto Maple Leafs in the finals to win their first Stanley Cup title.

Detroit became the first American-based franchise to win consecutive Stanley Cup championships when the Wings downed the New York Rangers in 1937, even though minor-league goalie Earl Robertson, filling in for an injured Smith, played the final series. Buoyed by Robertson's performance, Adams sold minor-league goalie Turk Broda to Toronto shortly after the playoffs. It was a move he would live to regret.

The 1937–38 season would play a large role in mapping out Adams's future plans. Sticking with the same nucleus, he watched as his two-time Cup champs slipped out of the playoffs. Afterwards, Adams developed a theory that championship-caliber squads had a shelf life of approximately five years—a theory he would continue to put into practice.

The war years saw Detroit play in three straight finals. The Wings lost in 1941, won in 1943 and gained infamy in 1942. Taking a 3–0 lead in the best-of-seven series, Detroit lost game four and its coach when Adams was suspended by the NHL after assaulting referee Mel Harwood. Amazingly, Toronto—behind the goaltending of Broda—won four straight, the only time a team has rallied from a 3–0 deficit to win a best-of-seven Stanley Cup final.

Goaltender John Mowers, defenseman Black Jack Stewart and center Syd Howe were Detroit stars of this era. In a club-record 15–0 win over the Rangers on January 23, 1944, Howe posted a hat trick to surpass Lewis (148) as Detroit's career goal-scoring leader. Eleven days later, also against the Rangers, Howe set another club mark, scoring six times in a 12–2 win. "I wonder what the boys in the shop will say now," pondered the soft-spoken Howe, who, like many U.S.-based NHLers during World War II, worked a day job at a war plant.

By now, the face of the NHL had changed—shrinking from 10 teams to six. Sponsorship of amateur teams by NHL clubs was now being employed to develop future talent. The league allotted each club the rights to all players playing within a 50-mile radius of that NHL city. That was good news for Toronto and Montreal and even Detroit, which could grab players from Southwestern Ontario. It didn't do much good at all for Boston, New York or Chicago, which might explain why the Maple Leafs, Canadiens and Red Wings were the only teams to win the Stanley Cup from 1942 to 1960.

Detroit reached the finals in 1945 and nearly turned the tables on Toronto. The Leafs won the first three games, Detroit the next three, but Toronto rallied to take the deciding contest. Even though his club had played in four Stanley Cup finals in five seasons, Adams stuck to his five-year plan. Harry Lumley replaced Mowers in goal. A rugged winger named Ted Lindsay and a slick center named Sid Abel also moved into the lineup.

If the NHL's modern era is designated by the advent of the red line in 1943, the golden era of the Detroit franchise is earmarked by the arrival of Gordie Howe in 1946. Labeled "the best prospect I've seen in 20 years" by Adams, Howe had a goal in his first NHL game against Toronto and two games later displayed his legendary mean streak for the first time, running Chicago goalie Paul Bibeault when he wandered from his net to play the puck.

Detroit finished first in 1948–49, starting a streak of seven first-place finishes—an NHL record. The Wings reached the finals in both 1948 and 1949, but both times were vanquished by their nemesis Broda and the Maple Leafs.

By this time, Howe was considered the NHL's most complete player and Detroit's Production Line of Lindsay, Abel and Howe finished 1–2–3 in NHL scoring in 1949–50. This time, Detroit got the better of Broda and the Leafs in the playoffs, even though they had to do so without Howe. Howe suffered a severe head injury—but not a fractured skull, as is often reported—in Detroit's first playoff game in Toronto when he tried to hit Toronto's Teeder Kennedy, but miscalculated and put himself head-first into the boards.

"I enjoyed my last three Stanley Cups," reflected Howe, a six-time Hart Trophy winner, who captured the first of four consecutive NHL scoring crowns in 1950–51. "I don't remember much about the first one." Terry Sawchuk replaced Lumley in goal after the 1950 victory, and Red Kelly, veteran Bob Goldham and Marcel Pronovost, pilfered out of Quebec from right under the Canadiens' noses, anchored the defense. Classy forward Alex Delvecchio, who would play 24 seasons in Detroit, was added to the mix.

Detroit beat the New York Rangers in the 1950 final, and had Stanley Cup wins over Montreal in 1952, 1954 and 1955. In 1952, the Red Wings became the first team to sweep through the playoffs, going 8–0. Sawchuk, considered by many to be the greatest goaltender in the game, posted four shutouts.

Wins in 1950 and 1954 had come in more dramatic fashion—game-seven overtime goals. Pete Babando (1950) and Tony Leswick (1954) were the scorers. Detroit also vanquished the Canadiens in a seven-game final in 1955, prompting The Hockey News to predict that Detroit was plotting "to imprison the Stanley Cup for all time." Ever the wheeler-dealer, Adams went to work on another rebuilding project shortly after the 1955 Cup win. He made a nine-player deal with Chicago and an eight-player trade with Boston, which sent Sawchuk to the Bruins.

This time, the moves backfired. "He definitely took the heart and character out of that team with those trades and he didn't get much in return," said Hall of Fame defenseman Pronovost. Adams took issue with Lindsay's attempts to organize a player's union in 1957 and shipped him and goalie Glenn Hall to Chicago. He dealt talented young forward John Bucyk to Boston to get Sawchuk back. By 1958–59, the once-mighty Wings were a last-place club. Adams was gone in 1962, retiring to take over as president of the Central Hockey League.

The Red Wings reached the finals again in 1961, 1963, 1964 and 1966, but each time came out a loser, blowing the 1966 series after winning the first two games in Montreal. From 1967 to 1986, Detroit would reach the playoffs just four times. "They just got rid of so much great talent," said Howe, who retired in 1971 as the NHL's all-time scoring leader, having worn the winged wheel for a quarter-century. "They made bad trades, the people didn't come up through the system and they made more bad trades trying to fill the holes."

Another Detroit revival was launched in 1982, when Mike and Marian Ilitch purchased the club from the Norris family, installing Jim Devellano as general manager. Devellano picked center Steve Yzerman in the first round of the 1983 NHL draft. Yzerman remains the pillar of the franchise to this day.

Under coach Jacques Demers, workmanlike Detroit clubs reached the Stanley Cup semifinals in 1987 and 1988, reviving fan interest. But, the best was yet to come. In the 1989 draft, the Wings raided Europe for defensemen Nicklas Lidstrom and Vladimir Konstantinov and forward Sergei Fedorov. All were playing key roles in Detroit by the early 1990s.

Scotty Bowman, the NHL's winningest coach, was hired in 1993. A year later, the club acquired veteran goalie Mike Vernon from Calgary and reached the Stanley Cup finals for the first time since the 1966 fiasco. Although swept by New Jersey, the Wings rebounded to set an NHL record with 62 wins (62–13–7) in 1995–96. Bowman picked up legends Igor Larionov and Slava Fetisov to play with Fedorov, Konstantinov and Slava Kozlov as part of an all-Russian unit. Rugged wing Brendan Shanahan and skilled defender Larry Murphy came aboard in 1997, and in a

Veteran Sid Abel (center) was first teamed with right winger Gordie Howe (left) and left winger Ted Lindsay (right) during the 1946–47 season, but it was not until 1948–49 that the threesome was dubbed the Production Line. Lindsay, Abel and Howe finished 1–2–3 in the NHL in scoring in 1949–50.

sweep of Philadelphia, returned the Stanley Cup to the Motor City for the first time in 42 years.

The euphoria was short-lived. Konstantinov and team masseur Sergei Mnatsakanov suffered life-threatening head injuries in an automobile accident just a week after the final game. Vernon, who won the Conn Smythe Trophy as the most valuable player in the playoffs, was dealt to San Jose, following in the tradition of Jack Adams who had dealt away Harry Lumley (1950) and Sawchuk (1955) shortly after they'd won Cup titles.

In 1997–98, the Red Wings finished behind the Dallas Stars and the New Jersey Devils with the third-best record overall. In the playoffs, Chris Osgood provided steady goaltending and rebounded heroically from the occasional weak goal. The Red Wings won 16 games to match Konstantinov's jersey number 16, concluding the postseason on June 16 with a sweep of the Washington Capitals for their second straight Stanley Cup title. After he accepted the NHL's top prize (and his first major individual honor, the Conn Smythe Trophy as playoff MVP), captain Steve Yzerman placed the Stanley Cup in the lap of Konstantinov, who had been brought onto the ice in his wheelchair.

The Red Wings entered the 1998–99 season as favorites to win the Stanley Cup once again. Detroit got off to a quick start under the guidance of associate coaches Dave Lewis and Barry Smith while Scotty Bowman recovered from offseason surgery, but the Red Wings were a very ordinary team for most of the season. Not until deals at the trade deadline added Wendel Clark and Bill Ranford from Tampa Bay, Chris Chelios from Chicago and Ulf Samuelsson from the Rangers did Detroit finally look capable of winning a third straight Stanley Cup title. The Red Wings ended the regular season with 93 points and the top spot in the Central Division. They opened the playoffs with a convincing four-game sweep of Anaheim, and though Chris Osgood hurt his knee in the clinching victory over the Mighty Ducks, Ranford stepped in to score two straight victories over the Avalanche in Colorado. Heading back to Detroit, the Red Wings seemed poised for a sweep of their fierce Western Conference rivals. Suddenly Ranford seemed to lose the magic and the Avalanche evened the series. Even the return of Osgood for game five couldn't stop the sudden and surprising slide, and Colorado wrapped up the series in six.

Anxious to atone in 1999–2000, the Red Wings came out strongly and had the NHL's best record through the first half of the season. Year's end would find them with 48 wins for their best total since their record-breaking 62-win campaign, though their 108 points were only good for second overall, and second place in the Central Division, behind the St. Louis Blues. Detroit did lead the NHL with 279 goals—the league's highest total in four years. The Red Wings were led by captain Steve Yzerman, who topped the team with 79 points and cracked the top 10 in the NHL for the first time since 1992–93. (Yzerman would also be named a First Team All-Star, the first all-star honor of his career.) Brendan Shanahan led Detroit with 41 goals. Pat Verbeek, picked up after he was released by the Dallas Stars, added 22 tallies to the Red Wings total, including the 500th of his career. Chris Chelios proved a good fit among a veteran defense corp led by Nicklas Lidstrom. The former Blackhawk recorded a +48 to trail only Chris Pronger of St. Louis among the league leaders. But, the true measure of success in Detroit these days comes in the playoffs, and after sweeping the Los Angeles Kings in the opening round, the Red Wings were ousted by the Avalanche in the second round for the second straight year—this time in only five games.

After his brilliant season in 1999–2000, Steve Yzerman suffered yet another knee injury in 2000–01. Though they had their captain for just 54 games, the Red Wings had yet another banner year. With a record of 49–20–9–4 and 111 points, Detroit won the Central Division for the fifth time in eight years. Only the Colorado Avalanche (118 points) finished ahead of the Red Wings in the overall standings. Brendan Shanahan was the team's top scorer with 76 points (31 goals, 45 assists) and Sergei Fedorov collected 32 goals, but the team's top performer was Nicklas Lidstrom. Lidstrom was second on the team, and second among NHL defensemen, in scoring with 15 goals and a career-high 56 assists. He was finally rewarded with the Norris Trophy as the league's best defenseman after finishing as the runner-up for three straight seasons.

Despite their solid season, Detroit was knocked out of the playoffs by Los Angeles in the first round. Some critics believed it was finally time for the most successful team of the 1990s to launch a youth movement. Instead, the team got even older with the free-agent acquisitions of Dominik Hasek, Brett Hull and Luc Robitaille. The moves paid off brilliantly, as Hasek led the NHL with 41 victories and Hull and Robitaille both scored 30 goals. More importantly, Detroit raced from the gate in 2001–02, winning eight of their first ten games and posting a record of 22–3–1–1 after 27. Critics warned that the veteran squad might burn out, especially when 10 Red Wings were named to various Olympic teams (Yzerman and Shanahan, Canada; Hull and Chris Chelios, USA; Fedorov, Igor Larionov and Pavel Datsyuk, Russia; Lidstrom and Tomas Holmstrom, Sweden; and Hasek, Czech Republic). After helping Canada win gold, Steve Yzerman was sidelined for much of the stretch drive, but Detroit finished up the season as both the league's best home team (28–7–5–1) and the best road team (23–10–5–3) and won the Presidents' Trophy with 116 points, the second-highest total in team history.

Still, there were those who doubted that the Red Wings would have the staying power needed to survive the marathon that is the playoffs. Things looked bad when the Vancouver Canucks came into Detroit and won the first two games of the playoffs, but the Red Wings rallied to take the series in six games. They needed only five to dispose of the St. Louis Blues and advanced to the Western Conference final where they would face the Colorado Avalanche.

Colorado and Detroit had been fierce rivals since the Avalanche upset the Red Wings in the 1996 Conference final. Their 2002 meeting was a classic—through six games. Detroit won the opener 5–3 on the strength of Darren McCarty's hat trick. Colorado drew even on Chris Drury's overtime winner in game two, but an overtime goal by Fredrik Olausson put Detroit back on top in game three. Colorado won the next two games. The Avalanche had a chance to wrap up the series at home in game six, but Detroit stayed alive with a 2–0 victory. The seventh game was highly anticipated, but it turned out to be a laugher. The Red Wings scored two goals in the first three minutes and went on to a 7–0 victory. It was the largest margin of victory in a game seven in NHL history.

The surprising Carolina Hurricanes faced Detroit in the Stanley Cup final and opened the series with a 3–2 victory when Ron Francis scored just 58 seconds into overtime. The Red Wings evened matters with a 3–1 win in game two and took command of the series when Igor Larionov scored at 14:47 of triple overtime to give Detroit a 3–2 victory in game three. They wrapped up the series in five. Dominik Hasek had set a new playoff record with six shutouts, but the Conn Smythe Trophy went to Nicklas Lidstrom. He was the first European player to be named playoff MVP.

Scotty Bowman chose the on-ice celebrations after his NHL-record ninth Stanley Cup coaching victory to announce his retirement. Associate coach Dave Lewis was moved up to head man. Dominik Hasek also retired. Curtis Joseph was brought in as a free agent to replace him. Offensively, Brett Hull led the Wings with 37 goals in 2002–03. Sergei Fedorov scored 36 times and topped the team with 47 assists and 83 points. Brendan Shanahan also reached the 30-goal plateau. Henrik Zetterberg led all NHL rookies with 22 goals and 44 points and was second in voting for the Calder Trophy behind Barret Jackman of St. Louis. Nicklas Lidstrom tied for first among defensemen with 18 goal (his 62 points ranked third) and led all blueliners with a plus-minus rating of +40. He won the Norris Trophy for the third year in a row, giving him the most consecutive selections as the top defenseman since Bobby Orr won the award eight years in a row.

The longest-serving captain in NHL history, Steve Yzerman finally lifted the Stanley Cup for the first time in 1997. Yzerman won the Conn Smythe Trophy when the Red Wings repeated as champions in 1998.

Joseph seemed to struggle for a while in his new environment, and the Wings were without Steve Yzerman for much of the 2002–03 season, but a second-half surge saw them rank among the league's best teams once again—though they fell a point behind Dallas (111–110) for top spot in the Western Conference on the last day of the season. Still their first-round playoff matchup with the Mighty Ducks of Anaheim was seen as little more than a tune-up for the defending Stanley Cup champions.

Detroit had swept the Ducks out of the postseason in both 1997 and 1999, but this year Anaheim turned the tables in a stunning upset, getting superior goaltending from Jean-Sebastien Giguere. Giguere set the tone for the series early, stopping 63 of 64 shots for a 2–1 triple overtime victory in game one. Over the course of four games he stopped 165 of 171 shots for a .965 save percentage and a 1.24 goals-against average.

Detroit was held to six goals as regular-season scoring stars like Fedorov, Shanahan and Zetterberg scored just once each during the series, while players like Hull, Yzerman, Datsyuk, Lidstrom and Larionov were never able to get untracked. With the loss, the Red Wings became the first defending champs to be swept out of the first round of the playoffs since the Toronto Maple Leafs in 1952.

For 2003–04, the Red Wings will again have Dominik Hasek in net as the six-time Vezina winner pronounced his batteries recharged after a year away from hockey.

Edmonton Oilers

The history of the Oilers franchise dates back to 1972 and the inaugural season of the World Hockey Association. Despite predictions by NHL moguls that "a rival league will never get off the ground or on the ice," the WHA opened for business as a 12-team circuit with Eastern and Western divisions. The Alberta Oilers, with Bill Hunter as spokesman, Ray Kinasewich as coach and Jim Harrison as the new league's early scoring leader, were named for the province because initially the franchise was to split its games between Calgary and Edmonton. This idea was abandoned before the WHA opened for business. In 1973–74, the team name was changed to Edmonton Oilers. Later, Edmonton and Calgary would become fierce rivals in the NHL.

Prior to the 1977–78 season, six WHA cities—Edmonton, Quebec, Hartford, Winnipeg, Houston and Cincinnati—were told they would be welcomed into the NHL fold—for $2.9 million apiece. But, at a subsequent meeting, Toronto Maple Leafs owner Harold Ballard persuaded some of the NHL governors to kill any merger plans. The war between the two leagues continued. The Oilers could not decide whether to continue operating or to fold. Two weeks before the season opener, two schedules were in place: one including the Oilers and one without. New owner Peter

Kevin Lowe was the first player ever selected by the Edmonton Oilers in the NHL Entry Draft when he was chosen 21st overall in 1979. He went on to play more games for the Oilers than any player in franchise history. Lowe became coach of the Oilers in 1999–2000, then took over as general manager after the season.

Pocklington was said to be trying to buy the NHL's Colorado Rockies. Meanwhile, the Oilers decided to continue playing and finished in fifth place in the revamped eight-team league. The Oilers were eliminated in the playoffs by New England, whose most famous player, Gordie Howe, became a grandfather during the series.

Early in the 1978–79 season, the Edmonton Oilers announced the acquisition of teenage sensation Wayne Gretzky from the Indianapolis Racers. The announced price for Gretzky, Eddie Mio and Peter Driscoll was $850,000. In Edmonton, Gretzky signed a 21-year personal services contract with Peter Pocklington, the longest player agreement in hockey history, and one said to be worth between $4 and $5 million. The pact was signed at center ice before 12,000 fans on January 26, 1979—Gretzky's 18th birthday.

The NHL, by a vote of 14–3, agreed to accept four WHA clubs for the 1979–80 season. Edmonton was one of them. Cost of entry was $6 million. During the final WHA season of 1978–79, the Oilers led all clubs with 48 wins and 98 points. Gretzky was third in league scoring with 46 goals and 110 points. Edmonton was upset by the Winnipeg Jets in the final series for the Avco Cup, and fans wondered if Wayne Gretzky would find life more difficult in the NHL.

Upon entry into the NHL, the Oilers used one of their two Expansion Draft priority selections to retain Gretzky. In the annual NHL Entry Draft, the Oilers selected teenager Mark Messier who had jumped from Tier II junior hockey to the Cincinnati Stingers of the WHA the previous season. Edmonton was placed in the Smythe Division of the NHL in 1979–80, along with its fellow WHA refugees from Winnipeg. Gretzky set a scoring record for first-year players with 137 points, but was declared ineligible for the Calder Trophy because of his WHA service. Gretzky's 137 points tied the Kings' Marcel Dionne atop the NHL scoring list, but Dionne won the Art Ross Trophy by virtue of having scored 53 goals to Gretzky's 51. The Oilers finished the season in fourth place in their division, but were swept aside by Philadelphia in the first round of the playoffs.

Bryan Watson was behind the Oilers bench for the 1980–81 season, but was fired after just 18 games and replaced by team president and general manager Glen Sather, who had coached the club in its first year. Gretzky finished the 1980–81 season with a league-record 164 points, then led the Oilers to a major playoff upset as the 14th-place club stunned the third-place Montreal Canadiens in three straight games. "I guess we've come of age," chuckled rookie defenseman Paul Coffey. The Oilers then carried the New York Islanders to six games before bowing out in the quarterfinals. Gretzky won both the Art Ross and Hart trophies.

Edmonton Oilers

Year-by-Year Record

Season	GP	W	L	T	OL	GF	GA	Pts.	Finish	Division	Playoff Result
1979-80	80	28	39	13	...	301	322	69	4th	Smythe Div.	Lost Prelim. Round
1980-81	80	29	35	16	...	328	327	74	4th	Smythe Div.	Lost Quarterfinal
1981-82	80	48	17	15	...	417	295	111	1st	Smythe Div.	Lost Div. Semifinal
1982-83	80	47	21	12	...	424	315	106	1st	Smythe Div.	Lost Final
1983-84	80	57	18	5	...	446	314	119	1st	Smythe Div.	Won Stanley Cup
1984-85	80	49	20	11	...	401	298	109	1st	Smythe Div.	Won Stanley Cup
1985-86	80	56	17	7	...	426	310	119	1st	Smythe Div.	Lost Div. Final
1086 87	00	50	24	0	...	372	284	106	1st	Smythe Div.	Won Stanley Cup
1987-88	80	44	25	11	...	363	288	99	2nd	Smythe Div.	Won Stanley Cup
1988-89	80	38	34	8	...	325	306	84	3rd	Smythe Div.	Lost Div. Semifinal
1989-90	80	38	28	14	...	315	283	90	2nd	Smythe Div.	Won Stanley Cup
1990-91	80	37	37	6	...	272	272	80	3rd	Smythe Div.	Lost Conf. Finals
1991-92	80	36	34	10	...	295	297	82	3rd	Smythe Div.	Lost Conf. Finals
1992 93	04	26	50	8	...	242	337	60	5th	Smythe Div.	Out of Playoffs
1993-94	84	25	45	14	...	261	305	64	6th	Pacific Div.	Out of Playoffs
1994-95	48	17	27	4	...	136	183	38	5th	Pacific Div.	Out of Playoffs
1995-96	82	30	44	8	...	240	304	68	5th	Pacific Div.	Out of Playoffs
1996-97	82	36	37	9	...	252	247	81	3rd	Pacific Div.	Lost Conf. Semifinal
1997-98	82	35	37	10	...	215	224	80	3rd	Pacific Div.	Lost Conf. Semifinal
1998-99	82	33	37	12	...	230	226	78	2nd	Northwest Div.	Lost Conf. Quarterfinal
99-2000	82	32	26	16	8	226	212	88	2nd	Northwest Div.	Lost Conf. Quarterfinal
2000-01	82	39	28	12	3	243	222	93	2nd	Northwest Div.	Lost Conf. Quarterfinal
2001-02	82	38	28	12	4	205	182	92	3rd	Northwest Div.	Out of Playoffs
2002-03	82	36	26	11	9	231	230	92	4th	Northwest Div.	Lost Conf. Quarterfinal

During the 1981–82 season, Wayne Gretzky signed a new contract calling for $20 million over the next 15 years and making him the NHL's highest-paid player. Gretzky scored 50 goals through the first 39 games of the season and broke Phil Esposito's record of 76 goals in his 64th game. His year-end accomplishments included a record 92 goals, 120 assists and 212 points. The Oilers cruised to top spot in the Smythe Division but were then shocked when the lowly Los Angeles Kings eliminated them in the first round of the playoffs.

Gretzky captured most of the headlines again in 1982–83, winning the scoring crown for the third straight season. The Oilers finished third overall with 106 points, but they amassed a record number of goals—424—and Gretzky, Messier and Glenn Anderson all topped 100 points. The Oilers reached the Stanley Cup finals, only to be ousted in four games by the Islanders.

They would not be denied in 1983–84.

Gretzky had yet another remarkable season with 87 goals, 118 assists and 205 points as the Oilers smashed their own record for goals in a season with 446. In the spring of 1984, the Oilers overpowered the Islanders to win the Stanley Cup in five games. Peter Pocklington said: "No question. I can see we're going to keep the Cup in Edmonton." On May 30, 1985, at Northlands Coliseum, the Oilers bounced the Philadelphia Flyers, 8–3, in game five of the final series and captured their second Stanley Cup title. Gretzky compiled a record 30 assists and 47 playoff points in just 18 games.

The 1985–86 season saw Gretzky collect an amazing 215 points, breaking his own record. His 163 assists represented more points than any other player had ever scored in a season. Paul Coffey, with 48 goals, broke Bobby Orr's record for most goals by a defenseman. Jari Kurri became the first European player to win the goal-scoring title with 68. The Oilers finished on top of the standings with 119 points, but lost to Calgary in the playoffs when rookie defenseman Steve Smith's clearing attempt resulted in an accidental goal against the Oilers in game seven. Intent on redeeming themselves, the Oilers finished on top of the overall standings with 106 points in 1986–87, and advanced to the Stanley Cup finals against the Philadelphia Flyers. The Oilers won the series in seven games and celebrated their third Stanley Cup victory.

Prior to the 1987–88 season, Paul Coffey announced: "It will be impossible for me to wear the Oiler jersey ever again." He was irate over remarks made by Peter Pocklington that allegedly questioned the two-time Norris Trophy winner's courage. Coffey was traded to Pittsburgh in return for Craig Simpson and defenseman Chris Joseph.

That season, Gretzky scored a goal to tie Mike Bossy for fifth place in career goals (573) but on the play he injured a knee and missed 13 games. Later, Gretzky passed Gordie Howe to become the National Hockey League's all-time assists leader. The Oilers slipped to second place behind Calgary in the Smythe Division, but managed to eliminate the Flames in four games in the division final. The Oilers moved on to oust the Detroit Red Wings in the conference final. In the Cup finals, they easily defeated Boston in four games to win their fourth Cup title in five years. Gretzky won the Conn Smythe Trophy after compiling 43 playoff points, but Mario Lemieux captured the Hart Trophy, ending Gretzky's eight-year reign as hockey's top player.

Hockey's most publicized wedding took place in Edmonton on July 16, 1988, when Gretzky married Hollywood actress Janet Jones. On August 9, 1988, news of the greatest trade in history rocked the hockey world as Gretzky was dealt to the Los Angeles Kings. The Oilers received $15 million as part of the multiplayer deal. Without Gretzky, Edmonton slid to third place in the Smythe Division behind Los Angeles and first-place Calgary. In the first round of the playoffs, the Oilers blew a 3–1 lead in games and lost to Gretzky and the Kings.

The 1989–90 season got under way with John Muckler behind the Oilers bench. On October 15, 1989, Gretzky returned to Edmonton as a visiting player with the Kings and scored the tying goal against Bill Ranford late in the game. The goal marked his 1,851st regular-season point and broke Gordie Howe's record of 1,850. He then scored the game-winning goal in overtime. That same week, Jimmy Carson (a 100-point scorer for the Oilers in 1988–89 after coming over in the Gretzky trade) announced his retirement from hockey because he "can't get mentally up for the games." Glen Sather suspended him, then traded him to Detroit in a deal that brought Joe Murphy, Adam Graves and Petr Klima to Edmonton. All three would be key contributors when the Oilers beat Boston to win the Stanley Cup in 1990. Goalie Bill Ranford captured the Conn Smythe Trophy. At the victory celebration, Mark Messier said: "This one's for you, Gretz." Messier was named winner of the Hart Trophy for 1989–90.

Prior to the 1990–91 season, Jari Kurri returned to Europe to play hockey. Goalie Grant Fuhr received a one-year suspension after admitting to past substance abuse. Later, Fuhr's suspension was reduced to 60 games. The Oilers won just two of their first 15 games and almost slid into the basement. Come the playoffs, the Oilers, with Fuhr back in goal, ousted Calgary in seven games and the Kings in six. Mark Messier was severely hobbled by injuries in the Conference finals and the Oilers lost to the Minnesota North Stars in six games.

In 1991–92, Ted Green replaced John Muckler as coach, but after Fuhr and Anderson were traded to Toronto, the Oilers were only a pale imitation of their former selves. In 1992–93, they missed the playoffs for the first time. Owner Peter Pocklington announced he'd move the Oilers to Hamilton if he didn't get a better lease arrangement. He later filed a letter with the league requesting permission to move the Oilers.

In 1993–94, the Oilers slipped to the bottom of the renamed Pacific Division with a 25–45–14 record. Rookie coach George Burnett took over in 1994–95, but was fired after 35 games and replaced by Ron Low. Still, the Oilers finished just one point ahead of the expansion Mighty Ducks of Anaheim during the lockout-shortened 48-game season. In 1995–96, the Oilers missed the playoffs for the fourth year in a row.

In September, 1996, NHL commissioner Gary Bettman announced that Oilers season ticket sales must rise from 6,800 to 13,000 for the team to qualify for the NHL's Canadian Assistance Plan. Oiler fans bought the tickets. They were rewarded when the

Mike Vernon stopped Wayne Gretzky on this play, but "The Great One" scored a memorable overtime goal against the Calgary netminder in game two of the 1988 Smythe Division final.

Oilers crept close to .500 hockey with a 36–37–9 record and a third-place finish in the Pacific Division. In the playoffs, Curtis Joseph starred as the Oilers ousted the Dallas Stars (second overall) in seven games. But, the Oilers couldn't match the speed and scoring of the Colorado Avalanche in round two and fell in five games. Coach Low was rewarded with a contract extension.

The Oilers were again facing an uncertain future by the spring of 1998. The team was up for sale. Local sportsmen were scrambling around, talking to bank managers, financial wizards and potential investors, attempting to raise millions of dollars in time to meet a Friday, March 13 deadline. Their goal was to save the team and keep it in Edmonton. On deadline day, a local ownership group of 17 investors did rescue the franchise by announcing its decision to purchase. The sale was approved by the NHL on April 27. By the 1999–2000 season, the team was headed up by a 37-person ownership group.

Meanwhile, led by Doug Weight, the Oilers qualified for the 1998 playoffs and proceeded to engineer another upset, defeating the Colorado Avalanche in seven games after trailing three games to one. Goaltending by Joseph and strong team defense held the Avalanche to just one goal over the final three games of the series. Facing the Stars in the second round, Edmonton could not continue the Cinderella story and was dropped by Dallas in five games.

Ryan Smyth's 20 powerplay goals in 1996–97 tied Wayne Gretzky's club record.

Curtis Joseph had been the star of two great Oilers playoff runs, but after the 1997–98 season, he signed with the Toronto Maple Leafs as a free agent. Mikhail Shtalenkov and Bob Essensa shared goaltending duties, but it was not until Tommy Salo was acquired from the Islanders on March 20, 1999, that Edmonton was able to outdistance Calgary for the final playoff spot in the West. There would be no playoff miracles, as the Stars swept the Oilers in the opening round.

Under new coach (and former Oilers star) Kevin Lowe, Edmonton opened the 1999–2000 season without sniper Bill Guerin, who was holding out for a new contract. Guerin slumped after returning to the lineup, but the scoring slack was picked up by Alexander Selivanov, who emerged as one of the NHL's most productive goal-getters in the early going. Selivanov's production would decline, be he would still wind up with 27 goals, second on the club behind Ryan Smyth's 28. Guerin rebounded to net 24, but the top offensive player in Edmonton was Doug Weight. He recovered from an injury-plagued 1998–99 campaign to lead the club in scoring for the sixth time in seven years with 72 points. Jason Smith anchored the Oilers blueline, but the club's key performer was netminder Tommy Salo. His solid play was the main reason Edmonton battled Colorado for top spot in the Northeast Division for much of the season. A strong finish by the Avalanche relegated the Oilers to a battle with the Phoenix Coyotes and San Jose Sharks for the sixth, seventh and eighth seeds in the Western Conference playoffs. Edmonton wound up seventh and had to face Dallas once again in the first round of the playoffs. Though they battled hard, the Oilers were defeated in five games.

Shortly after the Oilers were eliminated from the playoffs, stories began to spread that Wayne Gretzky was going to become a minority owner of the Phoenix Coyotes (which he did) and that Glen Sather might join him in the desert (which he did not). There were also reports that Sather might wind up in Calgary, though the most persistent talk was that Sather would wind up in New York with the Rangers. He made the move on June 1, 2000. Though there were also reports that Kevin Lowe would follow Sather to New York, he remained in Edmonton where he was named the club's new general manager on June 9. Assistant coach Craig MacTavish was bumped up to head man behind the bench.

In his first year as general manager, Lowe engineered trades that brought Anson Carter and Eric Brewer to Edmonton. He also signed Ryan Smyth and goaltender Tommy Salo to long-term contracts. With 39 wins and 93 points in 2000–01, the Oilers enjoyed their best season since the glory days of the 1980s. Still, they were beaten out in the first round of the playoffs by the Dallas Stars for the third year in a row. Doug Weight led the team in scoring (25 goals, 65 assists) for the seventh time in eight years, but Lowe dealt him to St. Louis after the season because he knew he would not be able to meet his contract demands. Defensive defenseman Jason Smith took over as team captain in 2001–02.

Ryan Smyth had been the team's top goal scorer (31) in 2000–01 and was among the league's best players early in 2001–02 until an ankle injury sidelined him for 21 games. He returned in time to play at the Olympics (along with teammate Brewer) and helped Team Canada win a gold medal (Smyth, Brewer and Anson Carter—by then a member of the New York Rangers—would help Canada win gold again at the 2003 World Championship). Edmonton native Mike Comrie supplanted Smyth as the team's top goal-getter during the 2001–02 campaign. The former Hobey Baker Award finalist notched 33 goals in his first full NHL season. Tommy Salo anchored the NHL's second-stingiest defense. Still Edmonton missed the playoffs for the first time since 1996 despite posting 92 points.

The Oilers had 92 points again in 2002–03, but this time the total was good enough for a return to the playoffs. A slump in February, combined with a hot streak by Nashville, seemed to threaten Edmonton's hold on eighth place in the Western Conference. Deadline deals saw Anson Carter depart for the Rangers and Janne Niinimaa go to the Islanders, but still the Oilers wound up with a 13-point bulge over ninth-place Chicago. Ryan Smyth led the team with 27 goals and 61 points, while Todd Marchant had 20 goals and 40 assists. Mike York and Mike Comrie also reached the 20-goal plateau.

Edmonton opened the playoffs against Dallas for the fifth time in seven years (they had also played them in the second round in 1998), and when the Oilers won the first game 2–1 it rekindled memories of their 1997 upset. However, the Stars bounced back with a 6–1 rout in game two. Edmonton won game three 3–2 on home ice, but Dallas took the next three in a row to wrap up the series in six games.

Florida Panthers

IN 1972, THE WORLD HOCKEY ASSOCIATION granted a franchise to Miami for its inaugural season. But, the Screaming Eagles never got off the ground. Twenty years later, in November, 1992, H. Wayne Huizenga launched his NHL project.

Huizenga, who spent his early years in Chicago, was part-owner of the National Football League Miami Dolphins and also had purchased the expansion Florida Marlins baseball team. As chairman of Blockbuster Entertainment, he already had established himself as a major player in merchandising, but he had no interest in hockey until a chance meeting with then-NHL board chairman and Los Angeles Kings head Bruce McNall. McNall and interim NHL president Gil Stein informed Huizenga that Disney soon would be admitted to the league as owners of an Anaheim franchise and another nationally known company like Blockbuster would be welcome at the same time. Although Huizenga may have had doubts about including a major-league hockey team in his portfolio, he took the gamble and on December 10, 1992, NHL owners approved both the Miami and Anaheim applications. The new franchises would begin operations for the 1993–94 season, which meant there was precious little time to organize an office staff and no time to build a new rink for the team-to-be. The club would play out of the Miami Arena, home to the NBA Heat, until a state-of-the-art facility could be constructed.

As for the club's high command, the key selection would be the team's general manager and the race narrowed to Washington Capitals g.m. David Poile and Philadelphia Flyers senior vice president Bob Clarke, whose position was largely ceremonial. Clarke was hired on March 1, 1993. Needing a president to oversee the operation, Huizenga opted for Bill Torrey, architect of the New York Islanders Stanley Cup dynasty of the early 1980s. As a nickname, Huizenga settled on "Panthers," in part because the Florida panther had been designated the official state animal—even though there were fewer than 100 left in the wild.

For the team's first coach, Clarke selected Roger Neilson, who had directed the New York Rangers to their most productive record in a half-century in 1991–92. When it came to stocking the team, the Panthers were fortunate. The NHL created more favorable rules—better than those accorded Ottawa and Tampa Bay—for Miami and Anaheim, and the Panthers hit the ground running. With Torrey and Clarke masterminding the selections, Neilson got the tough defensive team he wanted. Brian Skrudland, who would become team captain, was renowned for his work ethic, as were players such as Bill Lindsay, Tom Fitzgerald, Mike Hough and Dave Lowry. Others such as Gord Murphy and Scott Mellanby also were proven big leaguers.

A Stanley Cup hero with the Canadiens as a rookie in 1986, Brian Skrudland became the first captain of the Panthers and led Florida to the finals in 1996 after just three seasons.

Goaltending can make or break a club, and in that department Neilson got a big break. Onetime Rangers hero John Vanbiesbrouck was made available and was promptly snapped up by the Panthers. To serve as backup, the Panthers picked former Islander Mark Fitzpatrick. Torrey made further use of his Long Island past when he landed Billy Smith as a goaltending coach.

Surrounding the veterans with first-rate young players was the next objective, which meant adroit scouting among the Canadian junior ranks. Clarke's prize selection was Rob Niedermayer, a big, highly touted forward (and kid brother of New Jersey Devils ace defenseman Scott Niedermayer) who was believed to be ready to make the difficult jump to the NHL directly from amateur hockey.

The brand-new Panthers opened training camp on September 10, 1993, and kicked off their first season on October 6 against the Blackhawks at Chicago Stadium. Despite suggestions that the new club could not help but be overwhelmed by one of the Original Six, the final score was 4–4. A loss to St. Louis in game two was followed by a match at Tampa Bay's ThunderDome, viewed by an NHL record 27,227. Vanbiesbrouck registered a 2–0 shutout and Florida had posted its first NHL victory. More important than wins and losses, South Florida sports fans had instantly taken to the team. They jammed Miami Arena all season long.

Past the halfway mark and into the home stretch, the Panthers continued to be competitive. At one point they were five games over .500, but then the dreaded slump occurred and the Panthers plummeted. They were knocked out of playoff contention during the final week of the season. Still, the first-year results were impressive. The Panthers won 33 games and finished with 83 points. Their .494 won-lost percentage was the best for a first-year team in modern pro sports history. However, the front office suffered a blow when Clarke returned to Philadelphia once again to run the Flyers organization. His replacement would be Bryan Murray, who had established a good reputation in both coaching (for Washington) and managing (for Detroit).

With first pick in the 1994 Entry Draft, the Panthers selected Ed Jovanovski, a rugged defenseman from the Windsor Spitfires. Murray also obtained productive veterans such as Ray Sheppard, but in a lockout-shortened 1994–95 season, the Panthers didn't begin play until January 21, 1995, when they opened against the Islanders at Nassau Coliseum. The 2–1 loss would set a tone for the rest of the season. Neilson brought his club to the brink in the final days of the schedule but had to settle for another non-playoff year. Granted, the Panthers missed by only one point, but that fact rankled management and the scapegoat was Neilson. Doug MacLean was appointed coach on July 24, 1995. Management claimed Neilson's defense-first orientation had slowed the club's progress.

Under Neilson, the Panthers were lacking something to set them apart from the NHL's other new franchises. This would change in the second game of the 1995–96 season at Miami Arena. A few minutes before game time, a rat darted into the Panthers locker room, heading straight for Scott Mellanby. The Florida forward grabbed his stick and used the rat as a puck, slapping it so hard it catapulted across the room and off the wall—dead. An hour later, he starred in the Panthers' 4–3 win over Calgary, scoring two goals. Following the victory, several reporters approached Mellanby, who was being kidded by Vanbiesbrouck. The three-goal hat trick was replaced at Miami Arena by the two-goal "rat trick."

Newspapers reported the rodent assault a day later, and a number of fans picked up on it. When Mellanby registered another hot night, his goals were greeted with a shower of plastic and rubber rats. "Pretty soon they were throwing rats no matter who scored," Mellanby recalled, "and all of a sudden, we had an identity." And because the club was enjoying its best season yet, the population of ersatz rats increased as the wins multiplied and enthusiasm grew

Under MacLean's direction, the Panthers had become a better team than they had been in their previous two seasons. After 50 games, the club boasted a 31–14–5 mark and ranked among the NHL elite. Although a slump followed, the Panthers managed to stumble to the finish line with enough points to earn a playoff berth.

They were not expected to advance beyond the opening playoff round, since their first-round foe was the Boston Bruins, then the league's hottest team. But, a three-goal outburst in the first period of the Panthers' initial playoff game set a tone for the series. They stunned Boston with a four-games-to-one upset and next faced a daunting challenge in the Philadelphia Flyers. The series would not prove as easy as the opener with Boston, but Florida prevailed again, this time in six games. Among the highlights was the neutralizing of Philadelphia behemoth Eric Lindros by rookie sensation Ed Jovanovski.

Having disposed of the Broad Street Bullies, the Panthers then

The term "rat trick" was coined for Scott Mellanby when he scored two goals for the Panthers after killing a rat in the dressing room before a game early in the 1995–96 season.

stunned Mario Lemieux and the Pittsburgh Penguins in seven games.The main man for the Panthers, as he had been throughout the playoffs, was Vanbiesbrouck. He thwarted the best Lemieux had to offer in a throbbing seventh match that was tied 1–1 early in the third period. Instead of faltering, the Panthers went on to score an improbable 3–1 victory. In only its third year, the expansion club was headed for the Stanley Cup finals.

Facing the Panthers for the Cup were the transplanted Quebec Nordiques, now playing out of Denver as the Colorado Avalanche. The series lasted only four games, but the fact that Florida went down in a sweep was deceptive. In game four, which went into three sudden-death overtime periods, the Panthers hurled 63 shots at Avalanche goalie Patrick Roy. Deadlocked at 0–0, the game lasted beyond 1 a.m. on a damp Miami morning before Uwe Krupp, the hulking Colorado defenseman, blasted a slapshot past Vanbiesbrouck at 4:31 of the sixth period of play.

Disheartened though they were, South Floridians had become dedicated to their club. Approval had been given for construction of a new arena in the city of Sunrise, which would be home to the Panthers by the start of the 1998–99 season. In the meantime, the team continued filling Miami Arena through 1996–97 with a zestful brand of hockey that was good enough for a second straight playoff berth. Optimism prevailed as the Panthers entered the playoffs against Wayne Gretzky, Mark Messier and the rest of the New York Rangers. For a brief moment, it appeared that the 1996 playoff success would be repeated. Vanbiesbrouck thwarted New York 3–0 in the opener at Miami Arena, but the Rangers rebounded for four wins in a row.

Overall, two playoffs in two years was a major positive for the young franchise, which appeared on the rise—until its high command changed in the offseason. When Lindy Ruff resigned as assistant coach to become head coach of the Buffalo Sabres in

Florida Panthers

Year-by-Year Record

Season	GP	W	L	T	OL	GF	GA	Pts.	Finish	Division	Playoff Result
1993-94	84	33	34	17	...	233	233	83	5th	Atlantic Div.	Out of Playoffs
1994-95	48	20	22	6	...	115	127	46	5th	Atlantic Div.	Out of Playoffs
1995-96	82	41	31	10	...	254	234	92	3rd	Atlantic Div.	Lost Final
1996-97	82	35	28	19	...	221	201	89	3rd	Atlantic Div.	Lost Conf. Quarterfinal
1997-98	82	24	43	15	...	203	256	63	6th	Atlantic Div.	Out of Playoffs
1998-99	82	30	34	18	...	210	228	78	2nd	Southeast Div.	Out of Playoffs
99-2000	82	43	27	6	6	244	209	98	2nd	Southeast Div.	Lost Conf. Quarterfinal
2000-01	82	22	38	13	9	200	246	66	3rd	Southeast Div.	Out of Playoffs
2001-02	82	22	44	10	6	180	250	60	4th	Southeast Div.	Out of Playoffs
2002-03	82	24	36	13	9	176	237	70	4th	Southeast Div.	Out of Playoff

1997–98, the Panthers lost a valuable resource behind the bench. Once the season began, the evidence suggested problems. Jovanovski's declining play continued to be a problem, Vanbiesbrouck could not hold the club together on his own, and a perilous slump produced a major shakeup in the front office. Murray fired MacLean and assumed the coach's role while remaining the manager. (After the season he would hire his brother, Terry, who had previously been an NHL head coach in Washington and Philadelphia.) By late March, 1998, the Panthers had lost 13 consecutive games. "The underdog team that charmed South Florida and reached the Stanley Cup Finals only two years ago is no more," commented Miami Herald columnist Greg Cote.

Olli Jokinen scored 36 goals for the Panthers in 2002–03.

Florida was eliminated from playoff contention long before the season's end, leaving a bitter taste with fans. But, if there was a sweet use of the adversity, it was the prospect that starting in October, 1998, the still-young franchise would play its home games at a spanking new rink in suburban Sunrise—the National Car Rental Center (later to be known as the Office Depot Center). The Panthers did lose John Vanbiesbrouck to free agency, but the 1998–99 season saw the team pick up its first offensive superstar. On January 17, 1999, Florida sent a package of players including Ed Jovanovski to Vancouver in a deal that brought them Pavel Bure. "The Russian Rocket" scored 13 goals in just 11 games for Florida before a knee injury cut short his season. The loss of Bure effectively ended any chances of catching the Carolina Hurricanes in the newly created Southeast Division, and once again the Panthers missed the playoffs.

Though Bure battled injuries early in the 1999–2000 campaign, he certainly delivered everything the Panthers could have hoped for. His 58 goals were 14 more than anyone else in the NHL and represented the league's best total since Mario Lemieux scored 69 in 1995–96. Bure won the Maurice Richard Trophy as the league's top goal scorer and his 94 points saw him finish just two behind Jaromir Jagr in the battle for the Art Ross Trophy. Goaltender Trevor Kidd was another reason why the Panthers got off to a fast start. His shoulder injury in December could have been a severe blow, but the acquisition of Mike Vernon from the San Jose Sharks kept the Panthers in contention not only for the Southeast Division title but also for the best-overall record in the Eastern Conference. The Panthers eventually recorded the fifth-best record with a franchise high 43 wins and 98 points. There would be no miracle run to the Stanley Cup finals this time, though. Scott Stevens did an effective job of shutting down Bure, and the New Jersey Devils scored three straight one-goal victories en route to a series sweep in the first round of the playoffs that sent them on their way to an eventual Stanley Cup championship.

On June 24, 2000, the Florida Panthers dealt Mark Parrish and Oleg Kvasha to the New York Islanders. In return, they received Roberto Luongo and Olli Jokinen. Luongo went on to set a club record with five shutouts during the 2000–01 season. He also set a rookie record with a save percentage of .920. Unfortunately, the play of Luongo was one of very few high points for the Panthers. Another was the performance of Pavel Bure. His 59 goals broke the club record of 58 he had set the year before and made him just the 12th player in NHL history to capture goal-scoring titles in back-to-back years. Bure accounted for 29.5 percent of Florida's 200 goals, easily the highest percentage of the NHL's modern era. No other Panthers player scored more than 14.

Valeri Bure was acquired from Calgary before the 2001–02 season, but both he and Pavel were slowed by injuries and the Panthers played even more poorly than the year before. Duane Sutter, who had taken over as head coach when Terry Murray was fired early in the 2000–01 season, was himself replaced by Mike Keenan early in 2001–02. Keenan could do little to improve the club's fortunes. With the Panthers out of contention by the trade deadline, general manager Chuck Fletcher dealt Pavel Bure to the Rangers for a package of prospects and draft choices. (Valeri Bure was traded to St. Louis in 2002–03). Rick Dudley joined the team as their new g.m. shortly after the end of the 2001–02 season.

After scoring just 15 goals in his first two seasons with the Panthers, Olli Jokinen established himself among the league's top snipers when the club celebrated its tenth season in 2002–03. Unfortunately, Jokinen's 36 goals were one of few bright spots as the Panthers failed to reach the playoffs for the third year in a row and the seventh time in team history. Despite his poor win/loss record, Roberto Luongo continued to prove he was one of the top netminders in the game. He faced 2,011 shots in 2002–03 (second only to the 2,404 against Columbus's Marc Denis) and made 1,847 stops for a save percentage of .918. Kristian Huselius followed his fine rookie season with another 20-goal campaign, while Viktor Kozlov led the team with 34 assists.

The Panthers luck improved after the season when they won the top selection in the lottery for the 2003 Entry Draft. Florida had also won the top choice in 2002, but then swapped picks with Columbus and selected Jay Bouwmeester third overall. Bouwmeester played in all 82 games as a rookie in 2002–03 and averaged over 20 minutes of ice time per game. After the season, he starred for Team Canada at the World Championship, earning a selection as the tournament's best defenseman and helping Canada win a gold medal. He was also named to the NHL All-Rookie team. Luongo also played a key role, stopping 37 of 39 shots in a 3–2 overtime victory against Sweden in the gold medal game.

Once again at the 2003 Draft, Florida swapped the first pick (this time to Pittsburgh), but the Panthers were still able to get the player they wanted at number three, selecting Nathan Horton of the Oshawa Generals.

Hamilton Tigers

HAMILTON'S FIRST ATTEMPT to attract an NHL franchise came during the league's inaugural season of 1917–18. Arena owners in the city offered to take in the Montreal Wanderers after fire destroyed the Montreal Arena on January 2, 1918, but Wanderers' owner Sam Lichtenhein chose to withdraw his franchise instead. Hamilton would have to wait three more years before attracting another unwanted franchise. Amid rumors that a rival league with teams in Toronto, Hamilton and Cleveland was being organized by E.J. Livingstone (the former Toronto owner who had been frozen out when the NHL was created), the owners of the Abso-Pure Ice Company paid $5,000 for the NHL franchise in Quebec City. Abso-Pure recently had built a 3,800-seat artificial ice rink in Hamilton, and was looking for a hockey team to fill it.

The Quebec club that became the Hamilton Tigers had recorded just four wins against 20 losses during the 1919–20 season. Former Quebec players Eddie Carpenter, George Carey, Tom McCarthy and goalie Howie Lockhart were retained, but the NHL recognized that more than a new name was needed to attract fans in the new city. The Montreal Canadiens provided Billy Coutu, while the Toronto St. Pats supplied Joe Matte, Goldie Prodgers and Babe Dye (though they quickly recalled Dye and sent Mickey Roach to Hamilton instead). Four games into the 1920–21 season, Quebec star Joe Malone signed with the Tigers. He went on to rank among the league leaders with 28 goals, but Hamilton finished last in both halves of the NHL season, going 3–7–0 and 3–11–0. The Tigers showed little improvement with a record of 7–17–0 when the split schedule was abandoned in 1921–22.

After being gassed at Passchendaele in the First World War, Wilfred "Shorty" Green was able to resume his Hall of Fame hockey career.

Percy Thompson originally had been hired by the Abso-Pure Ice Company to coach and manage its hockey team, but he gave up his coaching duties after the 1921–22 season. Concentrating on building the Hamilton team, Thompson made several astute moves heading into the 1922–23 season—although improvement would still take time. Thompson signed former Toronto St. Pats goalie Jake Forbes to replace "Holes" Lockhart, and inked amateur star Billy Burch to his first pro contract. His most controversial move was trading Joe Malone to the Montreal Canadiens for Bert Corbeau and Edmond Bouchard. This deal worked out to the Tigers' advantage, as Malone scored just one goal in 20 games in Montreal while Bouchard led the NHL with 12 assists. Unfortunately, Hamilton posted a 6–18–0 record under coach Art Ross for yet another last-place finish. In 1923–24, the Tigers finished last again under Percy LeSueur. However, two newcomers to the Hamilton lineup that year would help make the difference in 1924–25.

Brothers Red and Shorty Green had been amateur stars in their hometown of Sudbury, Ontario. Thompson convinced them to turn pro with two-year deals reportedly worth $6,000—about twice the going rate—and placed them on a line with Billy Burch. The NHL had been courting Shorty Green since 1920, and Hamilton's acquisition of the brothers was seen as a major coup. When Thompson signed ex-Sudbury stars Alex McKinnon and Charlie Langlois for the Tigers' defense in 1924–25, Hamilton was poised for a breakthrough.

In an era when a team's starting players still played almost the entire game, having the four long-time Sudbury teammates in Hamilton made all the difference to the Tigers' teamwork. Under new coach Jimmy Gardiner, the Tigers raced out to a 10–4–1 record by the season's midpoint, then held off the hard-charging Toronto St. Pats to finish in first place by one point with a record of 19–10–1. Billy Burch earned the Hart Trophy as the most valuable player as Hamilton went from worst to first. But, on March 9, 1925, the 10 Tigers players promptly informed Percy Thompson that they would not take part in the upcoming playoffs unless each man received an additional $200. The dispute became public two days later when the St. Pats and the Montreal Canadiens began the semifinal series that was supposed to determine the Tigers' playoff opponent.

The Hamilton players had legitimate reasons to feel they were entitled to additional money. The NHL had undergone significant changes prior to the 1924–25 campaign. Expanding for the first time, the league had added a second franchise in Montreal and made its first foray into the United States with the admission of the Boston Bruins. With six teams instead of four, NHL owners had decided to increase the length of the season from 24 to 30 games and to increase the playoffs from one round to two. All the profits from the expanded playoffs would be divided evenly among the six NHL owners, with no money guaranteed to go to the players. The Hamilton owners had already turned a record profit due to the Tigers' first winning season, while the players had worked harder than ever under contracts originally signed for a 24-game schedule. Other teams had given raises to their players, or had provided generous Christmas bonuses. Hamilton had not. And now the Tigers would have to play at least two unpaid playoff games.

NHL president Frank Calder was not sympathetic. He stated that

Hamilton Tigers

Year-by-Year Record

Season	GP	W	L	T	GF	GA	Pts	Finish	Division	Playoff Results
1920–21	24	6	18	0	92	132	12	4th	...	Out of Playoffs
1921–22	24	7	17	0	88	105	14	4th	...	Out of Playoffs
1922–23	24	6	18	0	81	110	12	4th	...	Out of Playoffs
1923–24	24	9	15	0	63	68	18	4th	...	Out of Playoffs
1924–25	30	19	10	1	90	60	39	1st	...	Suspended

their contracts required players to make their services available from December 1 to March 31, regardless of the length of the season. (It is interesting to note, however, that the 1924–25 NHL season had actually begun on November 29.) Calder announced that the players would be fined or suspended if they refused to play, but the players stated they would quit the sport rather than be taken advantage of. Shorty Green met with Calder on March 13, 1925, during the final game of the Toronto–Montreal playoff series, but no compromise could be reached. The players were suspended and fined $200, and Hamilton was disqualified from the NHL finals. A plan to have the fourth-place Ottawa Senators meet the victorious Canadiens proved unpopular, so Montreal was simply declared league champions and sent to meet the winners of the Western Canada Hockey League. The Canadiens proved no match for the Victoria Cougars, who became the last non-NHL team to win the Stanley Cup.

On April 17, 1925, the NHL announced it would place a team in New York for the 1925–26 season. "Big Bill" Dwyer, New York's most-celebrated Prohibition bootlegger, would own the team. Tommy Gorman would operate it out of the newly completed 18,000-seat Madison Square Garden. In order to assure a solid showing in the most important American market, Dwyer bought the Hamilton franchise from Percy Thompson and Abso-Pure for $75,000. The Hamilton owners were only too happy to sell, having become convinced the league had outgrown their 3,800-seat arena and knowing that their players had stated publicly that they would never play for them again.

Now known as the New York Americans, the former Hamilton players all received raises, with Shorty Green's salary reportedly bumped from $3,000 to $5,000. Billy Burch signed a three-year deal said to be worth between $18,000 and $25,000. Born in Yonkers, New York, and being the league's reigning MVP, Burch was promoted as "The Babe Ruth of Hockey." However, before the former Hamilton players could suit up in New York there was the matter of their fines and suspensions. Frank Calder required every player to offer an apology, and to request readmission to the league in writing. After a series of letters in which most players began by maintaining that they had been right to strike, Calder finally received the apologies he wanted. As for the fines, it remains unclear whether they were paid by the players, by Tommy Gorman, or at all.

The NHL has yet to return to Canada's Steel City, but Hamilton's loss ultimately proved to be hockey's gain. Though the New York Americans would prove unsuccessful, they did help to sell the sport in the United States at a time when the NHL was struggling to establish itself south of the border.

The 1924–25 Hamilton Tigers. After four straight seasons of last-place finishes, the Tigers topped the NHL standings this year but refused to take part in the playoffs.

Los Angeles Kings

AT ONE TIME, the thriving Pacific Coast Hockey League (later the Western Hockey League) embraced teams in Los Angeles. During the immediate postwar years, the PCHL's Hollywood Wolves were linked with the NHL's Toronto Maple Leafs. The Wolves' most significant contribution as a farm team was defenseman Bill Barilko, who would in time score the 1951 Stanley Cup-winning goal for Toronto against the Montreal Canadiens. Despite the rapid growth of Southern California in the 1940s and 1950s, the NHL ignored the area for several reasons, not the least of which was the absence of a major-league arena in which to hold games.

By the early 1960s, Canadian-born entrepreneur Jack Kent Cooke recognized the potential for major-league hockey in the Los Angeles area. He paid $2 million for an expansion franchise for the 1967–68 season when the NHL doubled in size from six to 12 teams. Asked where he proposed to play home games, Cooke replied, "I'm going to build the most beautiful arena in the world, and it will be ready sometime in the opening season." True to his word, Cooke supervised construction of his "Fabulous Forum" in suburban Inglewood, and the $20 million project opened to rave reviews.

After enjoying success in Montreal, Rogie Vachon was traded to Los Angeles on November 4, 1971. He remained with the Kings through 1977–78, and emerged as one of the league's top goalies while leading Los Angeles to respectability.

For his first coach, Cooke hired Leonard "Red" Kelly, the former Detroit Red Wings and Toronto Maple Leafs star. He also purchased the Springfield Indians of the American Hockey League in order to develop minor-leaguers for his organization. In addition to Kelly, Cooke surrounded himself with top personnel, including Larry Regan, a former Leafs center, as general manager. Los Angeles finished its first season in the expansion West Division only one point out of first place, and Cooke was voted executive of the year by The Hockey News.

The Kings were fourth in the West during their sophomore year, but managed to make it to the semifinals. By this time the best-laid plans of Cooke had become damaged by fate and mismanagement. The Kings then missed the playoffs for four years straight, as Cooke proved more a problem than a blessing. Because of his brash style, he angered key members of the NHL Board of Governors, none of whom would do him any favors in the draft or anywhere else. In 1969, Kelly quit the club to coach in Pittsburgh, and in 1971–72 Regan was replaced by Fred Glover, who had been fired recently by the California Seals.

The result was a last-place finish in the seven-team West Division, with their 49 points ranking 11 back of even the sixth-place Seals. There were major changes the next year. Veteran center Bob Pulford retired to go behind the bench, while the defense was boosted by ex-Canadien Terry Harper and former Black Hawk Gilles Marotte. Los Angeles returned to playoff competition in 1973–74, but lacked a marquee superstar to tantalize the demanding California fans. A dispute a couple of thousand miles away turned out to be the solution to the Kings' quest for a big-name player.

Marcel Dionne had been the captain and foremost scorer on the Detroit Red Wings. In 1974–75 he had his finest season as a Red Wing, amassing 47 goals and 74 assists. His 121 points placed him behind only Phil Esposito and Bobby Orr in the NHL scoring race.

Despite his productive campaign, Dionne still felt under-appreciated in Detroit; so, once the season ended, Marcel's agent Alan Eagleson informed the Red Wings that Dionne would be taking his services elsewhere. Six teams were in the early running—the Kings, the Canadiens, the Blues, the Sabres, the Maple Leafs and the Edmonton Oilers (of the World Hockey Association). Dionne's demands were high, as were those of the Red Wings, who were entitled to compensation from the team that signed him. Ultimately, the Kings, whose owner Jack Kent Cooke had just acquired Kareem Abdul-Jabbar for his basketball Lakers, offered the most money.

The Kings won the bidding war, and surrendered veteran

defenseman Terry Harper and rugged forward Dan Maloney to Detroit. Cooke signed Marcel to a five-year, $1.5 million pact. Although Dionne and Cooke were pleased, Kings coach Bob Pulford wondered how well the newcomer would fit in with the team's disciplined defensive style. The Kings previously had enjoyed an extremely successful season. Los Angeles had the fourth-best won-lost record in the league, and only the Stanley Cup champion Philadelphia Flyers allowed fewer goals.

Pulford explained the situation: "I told Marcel that he couldn't float around center ice here the way he had in Detroit. He should retreat into the defensive end and work with the defensemen to get the puck out. That type of discipline was new to him, and I knew it would take time for him to learn our system."

"The Little Beaver" was up to the new challenge. After a brief period of adjustment with his new team, Dionne scored 40 goals and 54 assists for 94 points. However, the Kings no longer were the stingy defensive team they had been the year before. They gave up more goals, and instead of battling Montreal for first place in the NHL's Norris Division, the club found itself far back of the leader.

Marcel Dionne never played on a Stanley Cup winner in 18 seasons, but with 1,771 career points he ranks as one of the top players in NHL history. At the time of his retirement in 1989, Dionne's 731 goals trailed only Gordie Howe.

It was a tough adjustment for Dionne to adapt to the Kings' style, but he made the necessary changes and was ready for the 1976–77 season, playing both at center and right wing. Dionne became a new man, scoring goals and setting up teammates unselfishly, while diligently attending to the less-glamorous job on defense. He was the only player to stay close to the Canadiens' Guy Lafleur in the scoring race. Marcel finished the 1976–77 season with 53 goals and 69 assists, and, for a pleasant change, earned rave reviews for his positive attitude.

"He was the complete opposite of everything the Detroit people said he was," said former Kings general manager Jake Milford. "In our games in Los Angeles he never wanted to be picked a star of the game and I don't even think he ever worried about the scoring race. He had become that much of a team player."

Unfortunately, Dionne's improvement failed to help the Kings cope with the powerful Canadiens in the 1976–77 Norris Division race. In the playoffs, the Kings again failed to get past the quarter-final round, although they hung tough against the feisty Boston Bruins after losing the first three games, finally bowing out in six.

Dionne won the Lady Byng Trophy and was named to the First All-Star Team in 1976–77. He was a Second Team All-Star in 1978–79 and went on to his best season in 1979–80, leading the NHL in scoring with 53 goals and 84 assists for a career-high 137 points. He also was named a First Team All-Star and won the Lester Pearson Award as the NHL player of the year as selected by his fellow players.

A prime reason for Dionne's point surplus was the quality of his linemates. Until the 1979–80 season, left wing Charlie Simmer bounced between the minors and the NHL, making no significant impact. But in 1979–80, Simmer became Dionne's regular linemate and tallied a league-leading 56 goals in only 64 games. Filling out the Triple Crown Line was big right wing Dave Taylor who had been drafted by the Kings in June, 1975. Taylor was chosen in the 15th round, 210th overall. Taylor's grit and artistry produced 37 goals and 53 assists over 61 games in 1979–80 and set the stage for his great leap forward. In 72 games a season later, he produced 47 goals and 65 assists for 112 points.

Taylor, who would become general manager of the Kings after the 1996–97 season, emerged as one of the NHL's most appealing athletes. When he was in his early years in California, Dave battled and eventually licked a stuttering problem. Beloved by his teammates, he was recognized by the NHL in 1991, when he became the only player to win the King Clancy Trophy for outstanding community service and the Masterton Trophy for dedication to hockey in the same season. He also reached the 1,000-point milestone in 1990-91.

In addition to the members of the Triple Crown Line, another King with extraordinary appeal was goalie Rogatien Vachon. Vachon came to Los Angeles in 1971–72 after winning Stanley Cup championships with Montreal in 1968, 1969 and 1971. Almost minuscule between the pipes, Vachon emerged as a heroic figure to the audience at Inglewood and would become one of California's most popular athletes. "When you're my size," said Vachon, "you've got to be a stand-up kind of person. I take my bruises but I won't back down. Never."

Unquestionably, Vachon ranks as the most competent goaltender in Kings history. He was especially effective in the 1976 playoffs. The Kings eliminated Atlanta two games to none and then faced a powerful Boston Bruins team. Despite a 4–0 drubbing in the opening match at Boston Garden, Los Angeles rebounded with a 3–2 overtime win on the road and extended the favorites to a seventh game before succumbing.

Vachon remained with Los Angeles through the 1977–78 season, during which time the Kings earned regular berths in the playoffs but never developed significant headway. He was traded to Detroit for the 1978–79 campaign without ever being adequately replaced.

Dionne notwithstanding, the Kings remained a club mired in mediocrity during the early 1980s. They missed the playoffs in 1982–83 and 1983–84 as well as 1985–86. But, better days and nights were on the horizon when Bruce McNall became co-owner of the Kings during the 1986–87 season and was named club president in September, 1987. With gifted youngsters such as Luc Robitaille and Steve Duchesne, the Kings were positioned for a leap forward if they could obtain a major scorer and leader. That would happen on August 9, 1988, when Wayne Gretzky was acquired by Los Angeles along with Marty McSorley and Mike Krushelnyski for Jimmy Carson, Martin Gelinas, three first-round draft picks over the next five years and $15 million.

The Gretzky era in Los Angeles produced unprecedented attention for the NHL, as well as a few successful years for the Kings. "The Great One" still possessed enormous scoring skills, as demonstrated by his Art Ross Trophy wins in 1989–90 and 1990–91. In the spring of 1993, Gretzky actually orchestrated a march to the Stanley Cup finals, a first in Los Angeles hockey history. After defeating Montreal in game one, the Kings led the Canadiens late in game two when McSorley was penalized for carrying an illegal stick. The Habs capitalized on the powerplay, sending the game into overtime. Montreal scored the winner and went on to capture the Cup. That launched the downfall of Gretzky in California and the Kings as a contender. They missed the playoffs in the next four seasons, during which time Gretzky moved on to St. Louis and, eventually, New York. It was during this same time that charges of fraud against Bruce McNall were made public. He would eventually do jail time.

Although it wasn't readily apparent at the time, another turning point in the Kings history took place on July 25, 1989. On that date, the team signed Hall of Fame defenseman Larry Robinson as a free agent. He anchored the Kings defense in 1989–90 and spent three seasons on the blue line for Los Angeles. He was the second-highest scoring defenseman on the Kings in 1989–90 with 39 points (seven goals and 32 assists) and helped the team to a first-place finish in the Smythe Division in 1990–91. During his three years with the Kings, Robinson made an indelible imprint not only because of his playing ability but also because of his character. After his retirement, he was named assistant coach of the New Jersey Devils beginning in 1993–94. Working with coach Jacques Lemaire, Robinson helped turn the Devils into a contender and, in 1995, into a Stanley Cup champion. It was evident that he was head coaching material and on July 26, 1995, the Kings gave him the opportunity to prove himself.

Another epoch of redevelopment began in October, 1995, when Philip Anschutz and Edward Roski Jr. assumed ownership of the team. Apart from putting a winning product on the ice, the new ownership began thinking long-range—well into the 21st century. The cornerstone of their planning would be a new, state-of-the-art arena, located not in the suburbs but rather in downtown Los Angeles. Plans for the new arena were unveiled late in the 1997–98 season, thus ushering in a truly new era of major-league hockey.

Meanwhile, Robinson had patiently put a foundering ship on an even keel and by 1997–98 had turned the Kings into a playoff contender once more. Under his guidance, Los Angeles finished with a plus-.500 record for the first time since 1992–93 and earned a playoff berth. Nothing underlined the value of Robinson's coaching ability more than the improvement he brought about in defenseman Rob Blake, who had been named team captain prior to the 1996–97 campaign.

If Robinson was symbolic of one aspect of the franchise's rebound, Blake was part of another. A fourth-round pick in the 1988 Entry Draft, Blake joined the Kings at the end of the 1989–90 season and had one goal and three assists for four points in eight

Los Angeles Kings

Year-by-Year Record

Season	GP	W	L	T	OL	GF	GA	Pts.	Finish	Division	Playoff Result
1967-68	74	31	33	10	...	200	224	72	2nd	West Div.	Lost Quarterfinal
1968-69	76	24	42	10	...	185	260	58	4th	West Div.	Lost Semifinal
1969-70	76	14	52	10	...	168	290	38	6th	West Div.	Out of Playoffs
1970-71	78	25	40	13	...	239	303	63	5th	West Div.	Out of Playoffs
1971-72	78	20	49	9	...	206	305	49	7th	West Div.	Out of Playoffs
1972-73	78	31	36	11	...	232	245	73	6th	West Div.	Out of Playoffs
1973-74	78	33	33	12	...	233	231	78	3rd	West Div.	Lost Quarterfinal
1974-75	80	42	17	21	...	269	185	105	2nd	Norris Div.	Lost Prelim. Round
1975-76	80	38	33	9	...	263	265	85	2nd	Norris Div.	Lost Quarterfinal
1976-77	80	34	31	15	...	271	241	83	2nd	Norris Div.	Lost Quarterfinal
1977-78	80	31	34	15	...	243	245	77	3rd	Norris Div.	Lost Prelim. Round
1978-79	80	34	34	12	...	292	286	80	3rd	Norris Div.	Lost Prelim. Round
1979-80	80	30	36	14	...	290	313	74	2nd	Norris Div.	Lost Prelim. Round
1980-81	80	43	24	13	...	337	290	99	2nd	Norris Div.	Lost Prelim. Round
1981-82	80	24	41	15	...	314	369	63	4th	Smythe Div.	Lost Div. Final
1982-83	80	27	41	12	...	308	365	66	5th	Smythe Div.	Out of Playoffs
1983-84	80	23	44	13	...	309	376	59	5th	Smythe Div.	Out of Playoffs
1984-85	80	34	32	14	...	339	326	82	4th	Smythe Div.	Lost Div. Semifinal
1985-86	80	23	49	8	...	284	389	54	5th	Smythe Div.	Out of Playoffs
1986-87	80	31	41	8	...	318	341	70	4th	Smythe Div.	Lost Div. Semifinal
1987-88	80	30	42	8	...	318	359	68	4th	Smythe Div.	Lost Div. Semifinal
1988-89	80	42	31	7	...	376	335	91	2nd	Smythe Div.	Lost Div. Final
1989-90	80	34	39	7	...	338	337	75	4th	Smythe Div.	Lost Div. Final
1990-91	80	46	24	10	...	340	254	102	1st	Smythe Div	Lost Div. Final
1991-92	80	35	31	14	...	287	296	84	2nd	Smythe Div.	Lost Div. Semifinal
1992-93	84	39	35	10	...	338	340	88	3rd	Smythe Div.	Lost Final
1993-94	84	27	45	12	...	294	322	66	5th	Pacific Div.	Out of Playoffs
1994-95	48	16	23	9	...	142	174	41	4th	Pacific Div.	Out of Playoffs
1995-96	82	24	40	18	...	256	302	66	6th	Pacific Div.	Out of Playoffs
1996-97	82	28	43	11	...	214	268	67	6th	Pacific Div.	Out of Playoffs
1997-98	82	38	33	11	...	227	225	87	2nd	Pacific Div.	Lost Conf. Quaterfinal
1998-99	82	32	45	5	...	189	222	69	5th	Pacific Div.	Out of Playoffs
99-2000	82	39	27	12	4	245	228	94	2nd	Pacific Div.	Lost Conf. Quaterfinal
2000-01	82	38	28	13	3	252	228	92	3rd	Pacific Div.	Lost Conf. Semifinal
2001-02	82	40	27	11	4	214	190	95	3rd	Pacific Div.	Lost Conf. Quarterfinal
2002-03	82	33	37	6	6	203	221	78	3rd	Pacific Div.	Out of Playoffs

playoff games. In his first full season as a King, Blake was named to the NHL's All-Rookie Team, as he led all rookie defensemen in scoring with 12 goals and 34 assists for 46 points. He has paced Kings defensemen in scoring in every season in which he has been healthy enough to play most of the year. Blake would play only 30 games over the 1994–95 and 1995–96 seasons due to a host of injuries, from a nagging groin to a torn ligament in his left knee. His spirited comeback was slow but in the end it was well worth the wait.

The addition of Robinson, Blake's childhood idol, as head coach pushed him to the next level, as he was named winner of the Norris Trophy after the 1997–98 season. Rob Blake had finally arrived. Blake and Robinson were not the only elements of the Kings renaissance that season. New g.m. Dave Taylor worked closely with Robinson, bringing in younger talent. Three 1997 deals had a major impact on the franchise, starting with a March 18, 1997, trade that brought Glen Murray to Los Angeles for Ed Olczyk. Subsequent trades were made for Jozef Stumpel, Sandy Moger and Luc Robitaille (on his second tour of duty with the Kings). Each played a role in the Kings' resurgence in 1997–98. An even earlier trade paid benefits as Mattias Norstrom became a dependable everyday defenseman.

Slovakian sniper Ziggy Palffy topped the 30-goal plateau three times in his first four seasons with Los Angeles. Back in 1994, Palffy was the top scorer (three goals, seven assists) at the Lillehammer Olympics.

Robitaille returned to the upper echelons of NHL scorers in 1998–99, collecting 39 goals, but Rob Blake was again bothered by injuries and the Kings slumped to 69 points. Robinson was fired the day after the season ended and the team turned to Andy Murray, a former Canadian national team coach who had spent seven seasons as an NHL assistant. Murray had coached Shattuck-St. Mary's prep school to the Midget Triple A USA Hockey national championship in 1998–99, and he brought a high school-like enthusiasm to the Kings in 1999–2000. The team was further aided by the addition of Ziggy Palffy in an offseason deal and the opening of the brand new Staples Center. Year's end found the Kings with 39 wins and 94 points—the most since they topped 100 back in 1990–91. Robitaille led the club with 36 goals and combined with Palffy and Jozef Stumpel to give the Kings a potent first line that helped the team rank fifth in the league with 245 goals. Meanwhile, a healthy Rob Blake once again proved to be among the NHL's best defensemen. However, having reached the playoffs for just the second time in seven seasons, the Kings were swept aside in the first round by Detroit, just as they had been in 1998.

The 2000–01 season was a watershed year. Knowing that the team's longtime captain was going to explore free agency after the season, general manager Dave Taylor decided to deal Rob Blake nearly a month before the trade deadline. Blake had been the subject of trade rumors all year, but it came as a bit of a surprise that he was dealt to Colorado. The Avalanche gave up Adam Deadmarsh, Aaron Miller, Jared Aulin and a pair of first-round draft choices. That same week, the Kings acquired struggling goaltender Felix Potvin from Vancouver. Potvin recaptured his lost form in Los Angeles, posting a record of 13–5–5 with a 1.96 goals-against average and five shutouts in just 23 games. Ziggy Palffy (38 goals, 51 assists) and Luc Robitaille (37 and 51) led the offense. The Kings finished the season with 92 points, recording back-to-back 90-point seasons for the first time in club history.

Los Angeles faced Detroit in the opening round of the playoffs. Down two games to one and trailing 3–0 with eight minutes to go in game four, the Kings rallied to win 4–3 in overtime. They went on to win the next two games as well, wrapping up the series when Adam Deadmarsh scored in overtime in game six. The Kings then pushed Colorado to seven games in the second round before succumbing to the eventual Stanley Cup champions.

Having lost Luc Robitaille to free agency, Dave Taylor upgraded the Kings offense when he swung another blockbuster trade early in the 2001–02 season. This deal brought in Jason Allison from Boston. Allison centered a powerful line with Palffy (32 goals) and Deadmarsh (29 goals), and he went on to lead the Kings with 74 points (19 goals, 55 assists) in 73 games. Los Angeles finished the year with 95 points, but was eliminated in the first round of the playoffs after another tough seven-game series with Colorado. Working under Andy Murray for three years, assistant coach Dave Tippett had built the Kings powerplay into the best in the NHL in 2001–02. After the season, Tippett was hired by Dallas to be the Stars' new head coach.

Jason Allison was limited to just 26 games and Adam Deadmarsh to only 20 as a rash of injuries hit the Kings in 2002–03. The team tumbled out of the playoff picture and dealt Bryan Smolinski and Mathieu Schneider at the trade deadline. Still, Ziggy Palffy enjoyed another fine season, leading the team in goals (37), assists (48) and points (85). With goaltender Felix Potvin eligible for free agency over the summer, addressing the club's goaltending situation was one of general manager Dave Taylor's top priorities for 2003–04. "After looking at all the options we had available, we felt that making a trade and acquiring Roman Cechmanek in particular was our best course of action. Roman will help stabilize this position for the Kings as he has proven to be one of the NHL's top goaltenders for the past three seasons." Despite his success in the regular season, Cechmanek had fallen out of favor in Philadelphia and took the brunt of the criticism for the Flyers playoff failures. The Kings were able to acquire him up for a second-round pick in the 2004 Entry Draft.

Minnesota Wild

The National Hockey League announced its return to the Minneapolis–St. Paul area on June 25, 1997, when the league also welcomed Nashville, Atlanta and Columbus as new expansion cities. The hotbed of American high school and college hockey once again became part of the NHL scene, beginning with the 2000–01 season. Minnesota joined the Calgary Flames, Colorado Avalanche, Edmonton Oilers and Vancouver Canucks in the Northwest Division of the Western Conference in the 30-team NHL.

The team name Wild for the Minnesota franchise was announced on January 22, 1998, following a name-the-team contest that ran for six months. The Minnesota Wild word logo was introduced in January, 1997, and adorns the shoulders of the club's jersey. The home sweater, which was unveiled on November 18, 1999, quickly became a bestseller. The crest incorporates a wild animal, the North Star, evergreen trees, a red sky, the sun and/or moon and a stream. "The Wild home sweater reflects the power, energy and speed prevalent in both the Minnesota wilderness and the sport of hockey," stated club CEO Jac K. Sperling.

A native of Minnesota, the Wild selected Darby Hendrickson from the Vancouver Canucks in the 2000 Expansion Draft.

The home of the Minnesota Wild is the Xcel Energy Center. Plans for the 18,600-seat arena were unveiled on June 17, 1998, with the groundbreaking ceremony held six days later. Overseeing construction of the on-ice product is Doug Risebrough. The former Montreal Canadiens star and front office employee in Calgary and Edmonton was hired as the club's executive vice president and general manager on September 2, 1999. Risebrough was made responsible for the entire Minnesota Wild hockey operation, overseeing a scouting department headed up by Tom Thompson and his former Montreal teammate, Guy Lapointe. Another former Canadiens teammate, Jacques Lemaire, was hired as the club's first head coach on June 19, 2000. Lemaire's past successes behind the bench in Montreal and, particularly, New Jersey, ensured that the Wild were well-schooled in the fundamentals when they took to the ice for their inaugural season.

The NHL made a highly successful return to Minnesota in 2000–01. The team was respectable on the ice with 68 points and drew crowds in record numbers for an expansion team. Every game was sold out at the Xcel Energy Center, with the average attendance of 18,329 actually exceeding the rink's official capacity of 18,064. Wild jerseys were the league's number-one seller and sales of overall merchandise ranked second behind the Detroit Red Wings.

Though they were the NHL's lowest-scoring team, the Wild posted a winning record (14–13–10–4) at home in 2000–01 and went unbeaten in nine games at one stretch (five wins, four ties) for the league's fourth-longest home unbeaten streak. The team's success on the ice was attributed to coach Jacques Lemaire's defensive strategy. The Wild surrendered just 210 goals (12th best in the NHL) and goaltender Manny Fernandez set an expansion team record with a 2.24 goals-against average. The previous mark of 2.27 had been established by Doug Favell in 1967–68. Offensively, the club was led by Wes Walz, Darby Hendrickson and Marian Gaborik, each of whom scored 18 goals. Gaborik also had 18 assists to lead the team with 36 points.

Marian Gaborik had been the team's first ever draft choice (third overall) at the 2000 Entry Draft. After his impressive rookie season, he improved to 30 goals and 37 assists in 2001–02. Andrew Brunette was the team's leading scorer in year number two (21 goals, 48 assists) and rookie defenseman Nick Schultz showed great promise for the future. The Wild again sold out every home game, but showed only modest improvement (73 points) in the standings. Still, Minnesota's two-year total of 141 points put them well ahead of the two-year totals of the other recent expansion teams in Columbus, Nashville and Atlanta. The news was even better in 2002–03 when the Wild reached the playoffs with 95 points in just their third season.

The sellout streak continued in a 2002–03 season that saw Marian Gaborik become firmly established among the game's top young stars. The Wild opened the season with a mark of 8–1–2–0 in October and were never out of postseason contention after that. Though Gaborik slumped in the second half, he still led Minnesota with 30 goals, 35 assists and 65 points. However, it was the commitment to Jacques Lemaire's defensive system that allowed the Wild to shine – and would see Lemaire win the Jack Adams Award as coach of the year. The defense was led by players like Filip Kuba, Brad Bombardir, Willie Mitchell and Nick Schultz, but it was a total team effort that resulted in the league's fourth-best defensive record of just 178 goals against. Dwayne Roloson had a record of 23–16–8 with a goals-against average of 2.00 in 50 games. His save percentage of .927 trailed only Marty Turco of Dallas (.932). Manny Fernandez was 19–13–2 with an average of 2.24 and a save percentage of .924 in 35 games as the Wild relied on a 1970s-style two-man system in goal.

The Wild opened their first playoff series in Colorado, where they were winless in eight previous visits. However, Marian Gaborik and Wes Walz scored 25 seconds apart in the second period and Dwayne Roloson made 39 saves to lead Minnesota to a 4–2 victory over the Avalanche in game one. Colorado bounced back for a 3–2 victory. Game three marked the first playoff game in

Minnesota Wild

Year-by-Year Record

Season	GP	W	L	T	OL	GF	GA	Pts.	Finish	Division	Playoff Result
2000-01	82	25	39	13	5	168	210	68	5th	Northwest Div.	Out of Playoffs
2001-02	82	26	35	12	9	195	238	73	5th	Northwest Div.	Out of Playoffs
2002-03	82	42	29	10	1	198	178	95	3rd	Northwest Div.	Lost Conf. Finals

Minnesota in 11 years. The crowd of 19,354 at the Xcel Energy Center was the largest to see a game in what the Wild have dubbed the "State of Hockey." What they saw was Patrick Roy record his 23rd career playoff shutout as the Avalanche scored a 3–0 victory. Manny Fernandez took over in goal from Roloson (who had been battling a groin injury) after Colorado took an early 2–0 lead in game four, but the Avalanche took a 3–1 series lead with a 3–1 victory. However, the Wild bounced back with a pair of 3–2 victories to force a seventh game.

Like game six, game seven was 2–2 after regulation time before the Wild completed their remarkable comeback with an overtime winner. Gaborik, who had a goal and two assists in game six, had scored the tying goal in game seven with just 4:28 remaining, but it was Andrew Brunette who netted the series winner at 3:25 of OT. Manny Fernandez was the real hero, outdueling his illustrious Colorado counterpart by making 43 saves to Roy's 27. Minnesota became just the 17th team to bounce back from down 3–1 in a series, but of the 193 teams that had faced the deficit before them only seven had managed to win both games five and seven while on the road.

Next up for Minnesota was the Vancouver Canucks, who had also bounced back from a 3–1 deficit to win their opening-round series against St. Louis. The Wild took a 1–0 lead in the first period of game one (they were 21–0–1 during the regular season when leading after one) and were ahead 3–1 late in the third only to see the Canucks storm back for two late goals and a 4–3 win in overtime. With Roloson back in goal for game two, the Wild again led 3–1 in the third period. This time they held on for a 3–2 victory, but they dropped the next two games by identical 3–2 scores and once again found themselves on the road facing a three-games-to-one deficit.

"We're a better team when we're desperate," said Andrew Brunette, and Minnesota proved it with a 7–2 victory in game five. Cliff Ronning's first two goals of the playoffs and Marian Gaborik's ninth sparked a five-goal third period as the Wild enjoyed their biggest offensive performance in franchise history. Brunette scored two goals in game six as the Wild continued their offensive onslaught with a 5–1 victory. As in the Colorado series, the Wild would have only 24 hours to prepare for game seven the following evening. They entered the game in Vancouver seeking to become the first team in history to bounce back from a pair of 3–1 deficits.

Much like game six, Vancouver took control of game seven in the first period but could not score. The Canucks did get two quick goals midway through the second period, but a flukey goal by Pascal Dupuis cut the score to 2–1 before the end of the frame. Using their team speed to counter the Vancouver attack, the Wild fired only six shots at Daniel Cloutier in the third period (they had just 16 in the game) but scored on three of them. Dwayne Roloson stopped 24 of 26 Canucks shots on the night as the Wild rallied for a 4–2 victory that capped yet another amazing upset. Minnesota's best players had simply outperformed the Canucks' best during the series. Though he was held off the scoresheet in game seven, Marian Gaborik had 11 points (five goals, six assists) in seven games. Wes Walz's fifth goal of the series had tied the game at 8:05 of the third. He also had five assists during the series.

After scoring 18 goals as an 18-year-old rookie in 2000–01, Marian Gaborik scored 30 in each of the next two seasons. He has led (or shared the team lead) in goal scoring in each of the Wild's first three seasons.

In just their third season, the Minnesota Wild had advanced to the Western Conference final, where they would face the year's other Cinderella playoff team—the Mighty Ducks of Anaheim. Once again there wasn't much time to rest, as game one faced off less than 48 hours after the victory over Vancouver. Still, the Wild seemed to have more life in their legs then the Ducks ... until the game stretched into double overtime. Manny Fernandez (starting once again in place of the ailing Roloson) went save for save with Anaheim playoff hero Jean-Sebastien Giguere until 8:06 of the second extra session when he was beaten on a nifty move by Petr Sykora. Roloson was back in game two, but he too was outperformed by Giguere who posted his second consecutive shutout for a 2–0 victory. The Wild were pushed to the brink in game three when Giguere joined Frank McCool of the 1945 Toronto Maple Leafs as the only goaltenders to open a playoff series with three straight shutouts. The Ducks won the game 3–0.

During their amazing playoff run, the Wild had posted a record of 6–0 when facing elimination. However, only twice before in playoff history had teams come back to win from down three games to nothing. Minnesota was not about to make it three. Though they finally ended Giguere's shutout streak on a Minnesota goal by Andrew Burnette at 4:37 of the first period, the Wild went down to a 2–1 defeat in game four.

"We went in the playoffs and we were not supposed to win one game," said coach Jacques Lemaire. "I look at this team as a group of guys that didn't have a lot of experience, but they lived through a lot in these playoffs and learned a lot. We had a great season, and these guys battled."

Montreal Canadiens

The Montreal Canadiens Hockey Club was born on December 4, 1909—designed to add a French face to hockey in Montreal, until then predominantly the preserve of the mercantile English with clubs like the Shamrocks, Wanderers and Victorias. Ironically, the first owner, J. Ambrose O'Brien, was neither a Montrealer nor a French Canadian. The scion of a wealthy mine-owning family, he sought to establish a French-Canadian club in the National Hockey Association, where he already had an interest in a team in his hometown of Renfrew, Ontario. It was agreed that when French-speaking owners from Montreal could be found, ownership would be transferred as soon as possible. Jack Laviolette was hired to form and manage the team, and the first lineup included stars such as Newsy Lalonde, Didier Pitre, Art Bernier and Skinner Poulin.

Early in its history, the club acquired the nickname "les Habitants" or "the Habs," a French term first used to describe rugged farmer-settlers in New France, the 17th-century predecessor of what is now Quebec. The French usage of the word "Canadien" at the time the team was formed had a similar meaning, and referred to the hard-working local people of Montreal.

The Canadiens played their first National Hockey Association game on natural ice at the Jubilee Arena on January 5, 1910, defeating the Cobalt Silver Kings 7–6. They were the real bleu-blanc-rouge (blue, white and red, the colors of the French flag). They wore blue sweaters featuring a simple "C" of white; short, white pants, and long, red wool socks. O'Brien's right to call his team les Canadiens was challenged by George Kennedy, owner of a sporting association known as le Club Athlétique Canadien. The resulting out-of-court settlement saw ownership of the hockey team transferred to Kennedy's athletic club. (Kennedy's real name was George Kendall, and it is occasionally listed as such—most notably in the 1915–16 Canadiens team photo. He took the name Kennedy during a wrestling career as a young man because his family disapproved of the sport) Within three years, the team petitioned the league and was given the right to hire English-speaking players—homegrown French players being in short supply.

The Canadiens, now sporting the red, white and blue uniforms they wear to this day, but with a "CA" crest (Club Athlétique), won the franchise's first Stanley Cup title on March 30, 1916, defeating the Portland Rosebuds of the Pacific Coast Hockey Association in a five-game series. Upon joining the fledgling National Hockey League as a founding member in November, 1917, the team officially changed its name to le club de hockey Canadien and added the now-famous letters "CH" to its familiar uniform.

Two years later, the Canadiens were poised for a second Stanley Cup victory when tragedy struck. After winning the National Hockey League title in a five-game series with Ottawa, Montreal journeyed west to challenge the Seattle Metropolitans of the PCHA. After five games, the spirited series was deadlocked at two wins and a tie for each team, when fate intervened in the form of the Spanish Influenza pandemic that would kill an estimated 25 million between 1918 and 1920. The final game of the 1919 series was scheduled for April 1, but with Newsy Lalonde, Billy Coutu, Louis Berlinquette, Jack McDonald, Joe Hall and manager Kennedy all down with the flu, the Canadiens were unable to ice a team. The game was canceled and, for the only time in Stanley Cup history, no champion was declared. Four days later, "Bad" Joe Hall died in a Seattle hospital. Within a year, Kennedy was dead of complications related to influenza.

While O'Brien put the first team on the ice, and Kennedy nursed it through its first decade, the Canadiens did not acquire much of their mythic aura until a Franco-American from Bourbonnais, Illinois, came along to take control of the franchise. He was Leo Dandurand, a dandy who made and lost several fortunes in the sports world, especially in horse racing, where he was an owner of famous thoroughbreds, as well as head of the Montreal Jockey Club for years.

Best known as "The Stratford Streak," Howie Morenz was also called "The Babe Ruth of Hockey" for his box office appeal as the NHL expanded into the United States.

Dandurand plus partners Joseph Cattarinich and Louis Letourneau purchased the Canadiens from the widow of Kennedy in 1921. Cecil Hart, who would serve as a club director and later the coach, represented Dandurand *et al.* at the sale. Tommy Duggan, who ran the Mount Royal Arena, where the Canadiens were now playing, also wanted the team, as did a group based in Ottawa. According to stories, Duggan arrived at the negotiating session with ten $1,000 bills. Hart made a phone call to Dandurand and convinced him to go to $11,000. When the Ottawa group could not go above $8,500, the team was sold to the trio that would become known as the Three Musketeers of Sport. (When Dandurand and Cattarinich sold the club in 1935—they had previously bought out Letourneau—the price was $165,000.)

With the fledgling NHL attempting to break out of its eastern Canadian niche and into the northeastern United States, Dandurand was the right man in the right spot. He was a promoter extraordinaire who traveled in the same circles as New York's legendary Tex Rickard and Chicago's Major Frederic McLaughlin. If hockey was to make a go in markets such as New York, Boston and Chicago, the visiting teams would have to capture the imagination of the American fans who were new to the game. Dandurand's Flying Frenchmen—a term first used to describe some of the earliest Canadiens teams—were up to the task.

The Montreal Canadiens of this era boasted Aurel Joliat and Johnny "Black Cat" Gagnon, as well as Georges Vezina, Billy Boucher, the Mantha brothers Sylvio and Georges, and the hardrock Cleghorn brothers, Odie and Sprague, but the man who would become professional hockey's superstar in the Roaring Twenties was Howie Morenz.

William Howard Morenz, a German-Canadian born in Mitchell, Ontario, was spirited away by Cecil Hart and Leo Dandurand from under the noses of the Toronto St. Pats after representing a team from Stratford, Ontario, in a railway league final in Montreal. Morenz was signed for the 1923–24 season for $850, but as training camp approached, he tried to get out of the deal. Morenz was afraid that he wasn't good enough for the NHL and that he would lose his amateur standing because there was no minor professional league at the time. Dandurand stuck to his guns and a tearful Morenz was forced to join the Canadiens. The following March, he led all playoff scorers as the Canadiens won the Stanley Cup.

Montreal Canadiens

Year-by-Year Record

Season GP W L T OL GF GA Pts. Finish Division Playoff Result

Season	GP	W	L	T	OL	GF	GA	Pts.	Finish	Division	Playoff Result
1917-18	22	13	9	0	...	115	84	26	1st and 3rd*		Lost NHL Final
1918-19	18	10	8	0	...	88	78	20	1st and 2nd*		Cup Final/No Decision
1919-20	24	13	11	0	...	129	113	26	2nd and 3rd*		Out of Playoffs
1920-21	24	13	11	0	...	112	99	26	3rd and 2nd*		Out of Playoffs
1921-22	24	12	11	1	...	88	94	25	3rd	...	Out of Playoffs
1922-23	24	13	9	2	...	73	61	28	2nd	...	Lost NHL Final
1923-24	24	13	11	0	...	59	48	26	2nd	...	Won Stanley Cup
1924-25	30	17	11	2	...	93	56	36	3rd	...	Lost Final
1925-26	36	11	24	1	...	79	108	23	7th	...	Out of Playoffs
1926-27	44	28	14	2	...	99	67	58	2nd	Cdn. Div.	Lost Semifinal
1927-28	44	26	11	7	...	116	48	59	1st	Cdn. Div.	Lost Semifinal
1928-29	44	22	7	15	...	71	43	59	1st	Cdn. Div.	Lost Semifinal
1929-30	44	21	14	9	...	142	114	51	2nd	Cdn. Div.	Won Stanley Cup
1930-31	44	26	10	8	...	129	89	60	1st	Cdn. Div.	Won Stanley Cup
1931-32	48	25	16	7	...	128	111	57	1st	Cdn. Div.	Lost Semifinal
1932-33	48	18	25	5	...	92	115	41	3rd	Cdn. Div.	Lost Quarterfinal
1933-34	48	22	20	6	...	99	101	50	2nd	Cdn. Div.	Lost Quarterfinal
1934-35	48	19	23	6	...	110	145	44	3rd	Cdn. Div.	Lost Quarterfinal
1935-36	48	11	26	11	...	82	123	33	4th	Cdn. Div.	Out of Playoffs
1936-37	48	24	18	6	...	115	111	54	1st	Cdn. Div.	Lost Semifinal
1937-38	48	18	17	13	...	123	128	49	3rd	Cdn. Div.	Lost Quarterfinal
1938-39	48	15	24	9	...	115	146	39	6th	...	Lost Quarterfinal
1939-40	48	10	33	5	...	90	167	25	7th	...	Out of Playoffs
1940-41	48	16	26	6	...	121	147	38	6th	...	Lost Quarterfinal
1941-42	48	18	27	3	...	134	173	39	6th	...	Lost Quarterfinal
1942-43	50	19	19	12	...	181	191	50	4th	...	Lost Semifinal
1943-44	50	38	5	7	...	234	109	83	1st	...	Won Stanley Cup
1944-45	50	38	8	4	...	228	121	80	1st	...	Lost Semifinal
1945-46	50	28	17	5	...	172	134	61	1st	...	Won Stanley Cup
1946-47	60	34	16	10	...	189	138	78	1st	...	Lost Final
1947-48	60	20	29	11	...	147	169	51	5th	...	Out of Playoffs
1948-49	60	28	23	9	...	152	126	65	3rd	...	Lost Semifinal
1949-50	70	29	22	19	...	172	150	77	2nd	...	Lost Semifinal
1950-51	70	25	30	15	...	173	184	65	3rd	...	Lost Final
1951-52	70	34	26	10	...	195	164	78	2nd	...	Lost Final
1952-53	70	28	23	19	...	155	148	75	2nd	...	Won Stanley Cup
1953-54	70	35	24	11	...	195	141	81	2nd	...	Lost Final
1954-55	70	41	18	11	...	228	157	93	2nd	...	Lost Final
1955-56	70	45	15	10	...	222	131	100	1st	...	Won Stanley Cup
1956-57	70	35	23	12	...	210	155	82	2nd	...	Won Stanley Cup
1957-58	70	43	17	10	...	250	158	96	1st	...	Won Stanley Cup
1958-59	70	39	18	13	...	258	158	91	1st	...	Won Stanley Cup
1959-60	70	40	18	12	...	255	178	92	1st	...	Won Stanley Cup
1960-61	70	41	19	10	...	254	188	92	1st	...	Lost Semifinal
1961-62	70	42	14	14	...	259	166	98	1st	...	Lost Semifinal
1962-63	70	28	19	23	...	225	183	79	3rd	...	Lost Semifinal
1963-64	70	36	21	13	...	209	167	85	1st	...	Lost Semifinal
1964-65	70	36	23	11	...	211	185	83	2nd	...	Won Stanley Cup
1965-66	70	41	21	8	...	239	173	90	1st	...	Won Stanley Cup
1966-67	70	32	25	13	...	202	188	77	2nd	...	Lost Final
1967-68	74	42	22	10	...	236	167	94	1st	East Div.	Won Stanley Cup
1968-69	76	46	19	11	...	271	202	103	1st	East Div.	Won Stanley Cup
1969-70	76	38	22	16	...	244	201	92	5th	East Div.	Out of Playoffs
1970-71	78	42	23	13	...	291	216	97	3rd	East Div.	Won Stanley Cup
1971-72	78	46	16	16	...	307	205	108	3rd	East Div.	Lost Quarterfinal
1972-73	78	52	10	16	...	329	184	120	1st	East Div.	Won Stanley Cup
1973-74	78	45	24	9	...	293	240	99	2nd	East Div.	Lost Quarter-inal
1974-75	80	47	14	19	...	374	225	113	1st	Norris Div.	Lost Semifinal
1975-76	80	58	11	11	...	337	174	127	1st	Norris Div.	Won Stanley Cup
1976-77	80	60	8	12	...	387	171	132	1st	Norris Div.	Won Stanley Cup
1977-78	80	59	10	11	...	359	183	129	1st	Norris Div.	Won Stanley Cup
1978-79	80	52	17	11	...	337	204	115	1st	Norris Div.	Won Stanley Cup
1979-80	80	47	20	13	...	328	240	107	1st	Norris Div.	Lost Quarterfinal
1980-81	80	45	22	13	...	332	232	103	1st	Norris Div.	Lost Prelim. Round
1981-82	80	46	17	17	...	360	223	109	1st	Adams Div.	Lost Div. Semifinal
1982-83	80	42	24	14	...	350	286	98	2nd	Adams Div.	Lost Div. Semifinal
1983-84	80	35	40	5	...	286	295	75	4th	Adams Div.	Lost Conf. Finals
1984-85	80	41	27	12	...	309	262	94	1st	Adams Div.	Lost Div. Final
1985-86	80	40	33	7	...	330	280	87	2nd	Adams Div.	Won Stanley Cup
1986-87	80	41	29	10	...	277	241	92	2nd	Adams Div.	Lost Conf. Finals
1987-88	80	45	22	13	...	298	238	103	1st	Adams Div.	Lost Div. Final
1988-89	80	53	18	9	...	315	218	115	1st	Adams Div.	Lost Final
1989-90	80	41	28	11	...	288	234	93	3rd	Adams Div.	Lost Div. Final
1990-91	80	39	30	11	...	273	249	89	2nd	Adams Div.	Lost Div. Final
1991-92	80	41	28	11	...	267	207	93	1st	Adams Div.	Lost Div. Final
1992-93	84	48	30	6	...	326	280	102	3rd	Adams Div.	Won Stanley Cup
1993-94	84	41	29	14	...	283	248	96	3rd	Northeast Div.	Lost Conf. Quarterfinal
1994-95	48	18	23	7	...	125	148	43	6th	Northeast Div.	Out of Playoffs
1995-96	82	40	32	10	...	265	248	90	3rd	Northeast Div.	Lost Conf. Quarterfinal
1996-97	82	31	36	15	...	249	276	77	4th	Northeast Div.	Lost Conf. Quarterfinal
1997-98	82	37	32	13	...	235	208	87	4th	Northeast Div.	Lost Conf. Semifinal
1998-99	82	32	39	11	...	184	209	75	5th	Northeast Div.	Out of Playoffs
99-2000	82	35	34	9	4	196	194	83	4th	Northeast Div.	Out of Playoffs
2000-01	82	28	40	8	6	206	232	70	5th	Northeast Div.	Out of Playoffs
2001-02	82	36	31	12	3	207	209	87	4th	Northeast Div.	Lost Conf. Semifinal
2002-03	82	30	35	8	9	206	234	77	4th	Northeast Div.	Out of Playoffs

* Season played in two halves with no combined standing at end. From 1917-18 through 1925-26, NHL champions played against PCHA/WCHL champions for Stanley Cup.

Morenz, Joliat, Gagnon and the rest sold hockey on both sides of the border in the 1920s, helping new franchises take root in Boston, New York, Detroit and Chicago. As well, Dandurand's skill as a promoter and Morenz's on-ice heroics helped in the creation of another franchise in Montreal, the Maroons, who would represent English Montreal against the darlings of French Montreal, les Canadiens.

A modern ice palace with the latest in artificial-ice technology would accompany the Maroons' arrival in the NHL. Called the Forum, it was constructed in 159 days in 1924 and was ready for action in late November when the new National Hockey League season got under way. Ironically, it would be inaugurated by the Canadiens, whose own Mount Royal Arena and its newly installed artificial-ice plant was plagued by electrical problems. On November 29, 1924, the Canadiens took part in the first game ever played at the Forum, thumping the Toronto St. Pats, 7–1. It took Billy Boucher only 56 seconds to score the first goal at what would become hockey's most venerated shrine.

For its first two seasons, the Forum was home to the Maroons exclusively. The Canadiens joined them starting with the 1926–27 season and would play there for another 70 years. The Maroons-Canadiens rivalry would galvanize Montreal hockey fans for more than a decade. The Maroons would win the Stanley Cup in 1926 and 1935, but by the late 1930s, Montreal no longer could support two teams during The Great Depression and the Maroons were sold.

In the meantime, the Maroons era made Montreal the hockey hotbed of the league. Morenz and the Flying Frenchmen returned to prominence when they won consecutive Stanley Cup championships in 1930 and 1931. With the win in 1924, and the two titles by the Maroons, Montreal was the summer home to the Cup for five of 11 seasons. That kind of success could not prepare Montreal fans for what would become known as the grand noirceur or "great darkness" of the period between the Maroons' Cup in 1935 and the next success by a Montreal team in 1944. And nothing could prepare the hockey world for the unspeakable tragedy that would befall Howie Morenz in 1937.

As age gained on "The Stratford Streak," the rocketing speed and rink-long dashes that had thrilled fans in all NHL cities was being displayed less and less often. In 1934, he was traded to Chicago. After a year-and-a-half with the Black Hawks and half a season with the Rangers, Morenz rejoined the Canadiens late in the summer of 1936.

On January 28, 1937, in a rush that evoked Morenz at the peak of his powers, he burst into the Chicago zone at full speed. Chicago defenseman Earl Seibert caught the Canadiens center with a hip check and Morenz lost his balance. He fell toward the boards and, somehow, his skate jammed in a crack in the boards. When Seibert collided with him again, the sound of the leg breaking could be heard throughout the Forum.

Hospitalized, Howie Morenz kept up a brave appearance, but told teammate Aurel Joliat he never would skate again. Still in hospital nearly two months later, weak and depressed, Morenz died suddenly on March 8, 1937, of a coronary embolism. Three days later, more than 10,000 people sat in silence in a jam-packed Forum during Morenz's funeral service. The city of Montreal was in mourning for Morenz for months. On the ice, the mourning period was extended some seven more years, until the arrival of the next Montreal superhero.

Montreal's previous superstar had come out of the machine shops of the Grand Trunk Railway. The next one was the son of a machinist in the Montreal shops of the Canadian Pacific Railway. Born Joseph Henri Maurice Richard, he would come to be known as "The Rocket" and would carry professional hockey and the NHL through the World War II era and into the modern age. After suffering a season-ending ankle injury in his first campaign, Richard settled into the NHL during the 1943–44 season. Significantly, that ankle injury would keep him out of military service.

A bone of contention in English Canada during the 1940s was French Quebec's reluctance to embrace the war, which involved the entire British Commonwealth. Anti-conscription riots broke out in Montreal and other Quebec centers, and local draft boards were seen from outside the province as notoriously lax. And although the Canadiens had their share of players in the country's uniform, the team was to all intents and purposes left intact. Veterans Hector "Toe" Blake and Elmer Lach teamed up with a "Rocket" right wing in 1943–44, and the Canadiens took off, posting an astonishing 38–5–7 record in a 50-game schedule. In nine playoff games, Richard scored 12 goals and the Canadiens had their first Stanley Cup victory since 1931.

A year later, with the war winding down in Europe, Richard's scoring exploits began taking over the front pages, as the fiery competitor maintained a goal-a-game clip into January and then February. War-depleted lineups or not, opposing teams tried everything to stop Montreal's scoring machine, and the superstar spent a significant amount of playing time in the penalty box for defending himself against all comers. Late in February, his two goals against Detroit gave Montreal a 5–2 win and Richard 43 in 38 games, tying Cooney Weiland for the second highest season total in league history. A week later, a score against Toronto tied the legendary Joe Malone at 44, and he passed Malone in a Forum encounter against the Leafs several days later. With eight games remaining in the season, could Richard possibly tally five more for a magical 50?

By game 49, Richard had 49 goals and an emotional crowd was crammed into every nook and cranny of the Forum on the last Saturday of the season. Late in the game, a Chicago defenseman tripped Richard and the Rocket was awarded a penalty shot... and missed. It was not to be—at home, anyway. The following night, Richard scored his 50th goal of the season in Boston.

The arrival of Richard heralded a new era for the Canadiens, and though the team would win another Stanley Cup in 1946, Montreal's leap into the upper echelons of the league was the result of another new recruit. On August 1, 1946, the victim of a Toronto purge by Conn Smythe began work at the Forum as the Canadiens' manager. The diminutive new leader was Frank Selke, and he would build the farm system that would allow the team to rival the Leafs and Red Wings during the late 1940s and then surpass all comers in the golden 1950s. Not only did Selke's wide-reaching farm system ensure the Canadiens a rich bounty each season, it soon began to pay for itself with the sales of prospects to other NHL teams.

Richard had joined a team that included veterans Blake and Lach, as well as Ken Reardon and Butch Bouchard. It soon added goalie Bill Durnan and defenseman Doug Harvey, arguably the greatest rearguard of his era. However, the Montreal team that would emerge in the mid-1950s was based on Selke's star harvests, and future Hall of Famers, Bernard "Boom Boom" Geoffrion, Jean Beliveau, Richard's younger brother Henri, Dickie Moore, Bert Olmstead, Jean-Guy Talbot, Phil Goyette, Don Marshall, Ralph Backstrom and the greatest character of them all, goaltender Jacques Plante.

Elements of the old and the new came together to win the Stanley Cup in 1953, but it would not be until the spring of 1956 that the team would take off in postseason play, setting a raft of records in the process. Local fans argue that the Canadiens might have won eight Cup titles in a row if not for a bit of bad luck and a decision by NHL president Clarence Campbell that ignited Montreal in 1955. In 1954, the Canadiens and Red Wings played to overtime in the seventh game of the finals, with Detroit's Tony Leswick sealing the issue. In 1955, although the team would go down in a seventh game at Detroit, the Cup actually had been lost weeks before, in Boston and Montreal. Late that season, with the Canadiens and Wings battling neck-and-neck for first place, Rocket Richard attacked Hal Laycoe after the Bruins defenseman cut him with a swinging stick. During the ensuing brawl, Richard twice punched linesman Cliff Thompson. He was ejected immediately with a match penalty and was ordered to a meeting at league headquarters in Montreal two days later.

Maurice Richard (left), Toe Blake (center) and Jean Beliveau (right). Blake was a former linemate of Richard who coached the Canadiens to eight Stanley Cup titles in 13 years.

A year earlier, Richard had emerged unscathed from a similar incident with an official in Toronto, and Conn Smythe of the Leafs and Detroit's Jack Adams took great pains to remind Campbell of the results of his previous clemency. This time, the president suspended Richard for the rest of the regular season (three games) and all of the playoffs. Montreal went into shock, and then, rage, with the French media and French-speaking mayor Jean Drapeau accusing Campbell of anti-French bias. The English media adopted a law-and-order stance.

A restive crowd thronged the Forum on March 17 for a first-place showdown with the visiting Wings, with another 10,000 or so fans milling about outside the building. Late in the first period, with Detroit leading the dispirited Canadiens 4–1, Campbell sat down at his seat and was attacked in short order by a fan. Then a tear-gas canister was set off, driving fans out of the building as the first period came to an end. Inside the Forum, a fire marshal declared that the game was over. (It would be forfeited to the Red Wings.) Outside the Forum, Montreal erupted into a riot that trashed the downtown core and had the city seething for more than 24 hours. It took a special radio appeal by the Rocket to call an end to what would become known as "The Richard Riot." Detroit went on to capture first place and home-ice advantage in the playoffs, and Boom Boom Geoffrion won the scoring title, only to be vilified by his own fans for surpassing their beloved Rocket.

Montreal would not win the Cup that year, but it would be the last loss during Maurice Richard's career. On April 12, 1960, Richard scored on a backhand against Toronto's Johnny Bower as Montreal went on to a fifth straight Stanley Cup title. It was his 82nd playoff goal, 34th in the finals and the last of his career. Eventually all of his scoring records, 544 regular-season goals, 988 points, would be surpassed. But, no player would match the Rocket's impact during his era.

It was a testament to Frank Selke's skill as a hockey manager and administrator that his team took the powerful Red Wings to seven games in 1954 and 1955 minus several important players. Selke had built a juggernaut by then, and team leadership was moving from Maurice Richard and Butch Bouchard to Doug Harvey, Jean Beliveau, Henri Richard and Dickie Moore. The most distinctive of all was the 6'3" Beliveau, an elegant center with soft hands who had the strength to fight off opposing defensemen while scoring spectacular goals. The Canadiens had the luxury of two all-star lines. The Richard brothers and Moore terrorized opposition defenses, only to be replaced by the trio of Beliveau, Geoffrion and Olmstead. With Hall of Famers like Harvey and Tom Johnson plus Jean-Guy Talbot on the blue line and five-time Vezina Trophy winner Plante in nets, the Canadiens were challenged rarely as they won the Stanley Cup five times in a row. These championships were won under Toe Blake, who replaced Dick Irvin as coach after the 1954–55 season because it was believed that Blake would have a calming influence on his former linemate, the Rocket.

With Geoffrion winning the scoring title in 1954–55 and Beliveau winning it the following year, the Montreal offense proved so powerful during the team's Stanley Cup run that the league was forced to change the rule governing minor penalties. Previous to the change, minors were served in their entirety even if a goal was scored on the shorthanded team. The Canadiens offense was so potent that the team sometimes scored two or three goals per opposition minor, putting games out of reach in the first period. The amended rule allowed the penalized player to return to the ice if a goal was scored against his team. Rule change notwithstanding, Dickie Moore managed to win the scoring title in 1957–58 and 1958–59. At the other end of the ice, the Canadiens allowed the fewest goals for five years running.

The Canadiens finally relinquished the Stanley Cup to Chicago in 1961, but after Punch Imlach's Leafs captured three straight championships, the Habs were back in contention in 1965. Although many veterans of the five-straight team remained, direction of the team had moved from Frank Selke to Sam Pollock, and the astute managing director would guide the team into the modern era.

Montreal won the Cup in 1965 and 1966 with a team built primarily through its farm system, and then came back with victories in 1968, 1969, 1971 and 1973 with teams built by trades and draft choices acquired by Pollock. By the time the league had welcomed six new teams with the Expansion Draft in 1967, Pollock had dismantled Selke's vast farm system and shipped more that 70 players throughout the league, stockpiling draft selections as he went. Teams like St. Louis, Minnesota and Oakland immediately were competitive thanks to former Canadiens farmhands, but Montreal's future throughout the coming decade was assured. Stars like Guy Lafleur, Larry Robinson and Steve Shutt were all accumulated in this fashion. Occasionally, "Trader Sam" got lucky as well, such as when he acquired goalie Ken Dryden from the Boston farm system.

The acquisition of Guy Lafleur provides a classic example of Pollock's foresight. The Canadiens owned Oakland's first pick for the 1971 draft, and with the Seals in last place in the Western Division, it appeared that the selection would be first overall. Late in the season, however, the Los Angeles Kings began to falter and threatened to sink below the Seals in the standings. Pollock immediately dispatched veteran center Ralph Backstrom to Los Angeles and his leadership got the Kings over the hump. On June 9, 1971, Jean Beliveau announced his retirement, but a day later, the Canadiens obtained his replacement in Lafleur by using the Oakland draft choice. For good measure, the team also picked up future Hall of Fame defenseman Larry Robinson in the same draft.

In the mid-1960s, the Canadiens had been a veteran team that included Beliveau, Henri Richard, Talbot, Ralph Backstrom and Claude Provost, bolstered by a large and strong defense corps that included newcomers Jacques Laperriere, Terry Harper and Ted Harris. They were strengthened up front by the addition of tough wings Claude Larose and John Ferguson and the sheer explosiveness of Yvan Cournoyer.

Pollock tinkered with his team yearly. The club that won in 1965 and 1966 saw players like Jean-Guy Talbot, Leon Rochefort, Charlie Hodge and Dave Balon moved to make room for newcomers Rogatien Vachon, Serge Savard, Guy Lapointe, Jacques Lemaire, Pete Mahovlich and Mickey Redmond. The reconstructed Canadiens then turned around and burned the rising Bruins and Black Hawks in the 1968 and 1969 playoffs. By 1971, Gump Worsley had departed from the goal, as had scorers Redmond and Danny Grant. These moves made room for Ken Dryden and Frank Mahovlich, who would both star in the team's 1971 Stanley Cup triumph. Dryden, who had played just six games late in the regular season, almost singlehandedly eliminated the first-place Bruins to open the playoffs and went on to win the Conn Smythe Trophy before he had even qualified as an NHL rookie.

In the period between the 1964–65 and 1972–73 seasons, Pollock managed to remake his entire team and still win the Stanley Cup six times. Only five players, Henri Richard, Yvan Cournoyer, Jacques Laperriere, Jim Roberts and Claude Larose, played for both the 1965 and 1973 Cup winners, and the latter two had been traded away and reacquired in the interim. Yet some Canadiens players accumulated individual postseason statistics that are staggering in today's context: Henri Richard won 11 championships, while Beliveau and Cournoyer each won 10. Provost was a part of nine Cup teams; Lemaire, eight; Talbot, seven, and a raft of others won six or five championships.

Ice generalship was not a factor. When the popular and demanding Toe Blake asked to be replaced behind the Canadiens bench in 1968 after eight titles in 13 years, Pollock's team was strong enough to win the 1969 championship with rookie coach Claude Ruel calling the shots. Two years later, another rookie coach, Al MacNeil, replaced Ruel midway through the season and led the team to a championship, only to be replaced by Scotty Bowman the following September. Bowman would win five titles with Montreal in the 1970s before shuffling off to Buffalo.

The onset of the World Hockey Association in 1972 saw the Canadiens lose some players (Rejean Houle, Marc Tardif, J.C. Tremblay and Frank Mahovlich) to the new league, but the team was in better shape than most NHL entries. Lafleur struggled in his first three seasons, alternating between right wing and center on different lines, but finally emerged a top-rank superstar in 1974–75. A cross between the elegance of Beliveau and the fire of the Rocket, he electrified NHL audiences with his rink-long dashes, blond hair streaming behind him. Pollock put together a stellar supporting cast that included Cournoyer, Shutt, Lemaire, Peter Mahovlich, Doug Risebrough, Yvon Lambert, Mario Tremblay and the incomparable Bob Gainey on the forward lines, and "The Big Three" of Larry Robinson, Guy Lapointe and Serge Savard anchoring an airtight defense backstopped by Dryden.

That Montreal team ended the "three-peat" aspirations of the Philadelphia Flyers in May, 1976, outdueling the Broad Street Bullies in the corners, with bangers like Pierre Bouchard, Lambert and Rick Chartraw, and outfinessing them with the likes of Lafleur, Shutt and Mahovlich. Four straight championships resulted, as the Habs fended off strong teams in Boston, Buffalo and New York (Islanders) until injury and age caught up with them in 1980. The last Canadiens dynasty came to an end on April 27, 1980, in a 3–2 Forum loss to the youthful Minnesota North Stars. Gone a year earlier to retirement were young Jacques Lemaire, 33, and Ken Dryden, 31. Gone also was Scotty Bowman, miffed because Sam Pollock would not name him as his own replacement. Pollock selected Irving Grundman, his assistant in the previous decade, who was not a hockey man. Although Grundman managed a Cup winner in his "rookie" season of 1978–79, his leadership was under perpetual challenge by the strident Montreal media.

Grundman made a major mistake when he attempted to replace

Captain Serge Savard has a chat with Guy Lapointe. Savard was an eight-time Stanley Cup champion as a player in Montreal and won twice more as the Canadiens general manager.

Bowman with the colorful Bernie Geoffrion, who had coached the Rangers and later the expansion Atlanta Flames, stepping down both times for health reasons. Boomer lasted just 30 games in Montreal and was replaced, as Toe Blake had been, by Claude Ruel. The team still was competitive, but the early 1980s belonged to the Islanders and the Edmonton Oilers. A nucleus of talent that included Robinson, Savard and Gainey, and quality additions like Ryan Walter, Bobby Smith, Rick Green, Chris Chelios and Mats Naslund kept the team near the top of the league standings. Montreal could not afford to dwell on the successes of the Oilers and Islanders, however, because the challenge to their hegemony came from their own backyard. In 1979, the NHL expanded to include four teams from the WHA, and suddenly the province of Quebec was no longer the exclusive preserve of the Canadiens, with the Nordiques challenging them from the provincial capital.

When Quebec managed to eliminate Montreal in their first playoff confrontation, a best-of-five series in 1982, the second floor at the Forum went into shock. With Quebec now claiming to be the province's "French" team, the Canadiens responded with the hiring of Ronald Corey as team president, and his decision was to replace Grundman with former star Serge Savard.

In the spring of 1984, the Canadiens gained a measure of revenge by ousting the Nordiques in the bitterly fought six-game Adams Division finals, which included a huge Good Friday brawl in the final contest. Montreal went on to lose to the Islanders in six games in the conference finals, but the Canadiens had given notice that they were back in the chase. In June, 1984, Savard and the Canadiens had a dream draft, selecting Czech defector Petr Svoboda and Shayne Corson in the first round, adding Stephane Richer in the second and goaltender Patrick Roy in the third. They once again lost to the Nordiques in the playoffs, but were poised to challenge the league in 1985–86, when Svoboda, Richer and Roy, joined the team as regulars.

When Montreal had fallen to Quebec in 1985, the scapegoat was goaltender Steve Penney, a journeyman who had enjoyed two decent seasons in Montreal but was unable to provide the championship backstopping the team needed. That changed in 1986 with Patrick Roy.

Roy was a cross between Jacques Plante and Ken Dryden, impressive credentials indeed in Montreal. And like Plante and Dryden before him, he took the team to a Stanley Cup triumph in his rookie season. Roy was unbeatable in the playoffs, helping the Canadiens to sweep the Bruins 3–0 in their best-of-five division semifinals, and then out-battling Hartford's Mike Liut in a division final that went to overtime in game seven before rookie Claude Lemieux ended it. The Canadiens disposed of the Rangers in five games, including a spectacular overtime win in game three (again on a goal by Lemieux) that saw Roy hold off the aroused Rangers single-handedly, including 13 stops (44 overall) in extra time. The final was a formality. Montreal defeated Calgary in five close games, and Roy posed happily in the team's dressing room at the Saddledome with his arms around the Conn Smythe Trophy and the Stanley Cup.

Roy remained one of the league's best goaltenders over the years, but was truly at his best seven years later when he led a much-changed team—only he and Guy Carbonneau remained from the 1986 champions—to the franchise's 24th Stanley Cup and 23rd in the team's NHL history. The 1986 and 1993 victories gave Montreal a unique and enviable record in professional sports in North America at the time as it made them the only long-established team to win a league championship in each decade in which it has played. However, just two seasons later, Montreal would miss the playoffs for the first time since 1970 and just the second time since 1948.

In March, 1996, the fabulous Forum closed its doors with a touching ceremony after a 4–1 win over the Dallas Stars. The team moved across town to the spanking-new Molson Centre (later the Bell Centre), but the team that made the move had few connections with the Stanley Cup, including the championship won less than three years before. In the fashion of professional sport in the 1990s and the new world of free agency and liberal player movement, only four Canadiens remained from the team that had won Cup #24.

Gone to Philadelphia were John LeClair and the memories of his two overtime goals in "The Fabulous Forum" in Inglewood that eviscerated Wayne Gretzky and the Kings. Joining "Marmaduke" in the Philly shuffle was Eric Desjardins, whose three goals, including one in overtime, in the pivotal second game of the Kings series, set Montreal on the road to the championship.

Gone were longtime NHL stars Kirk Muller, Brian Bellows, Denis Savard, Guy Carbonneau and Mathieu Schneider. Gone, too, were players who had huge roles in the 1993 conquest: Lyle Odelein, Jean-Jacques Daigneault, Gilbert Dionne, Paul DiPietro, Mike Keane, Andre Racicot and Kevin Haller. Farthest gone was King Patrick, in a spectacular and very public tantrum against rookie coach Mario Tremblay seen nationwide on Hockey Night in Canada during an 11–1 Forum shellacking at the hands of Detroit. Roy's snubbing of his coach and embarrassing of team president Ronald Corey forced the reluctant Canadiens to trade him to Colorado, where he won the Stanley Cup six months later.

Montreal's 1993 champions were an all-North American aggregation, not a whiff of Europe to them. That would change quickly. Not only would Andrei Kovalenko, Martin Rucinsky and Vladimir Malakhov arrive by trades, the Canadiens would find European-trained talent on both sides of the Atlantic, adding Valeri Bure, brother of Vancouver's Pavel, who played his junior hockey in Spokane, and a feisty Finnish centre, Saku Koivu, from Turku's TPS team. All but Koivu would later be traded as the late 1990s proved to be turbulent times in Montreal. Such popular players as Pierre Turgeon, Vincent Damphousse and Mike Recchi were all shipped out as the team's fortunes took a turn for the worse. The club fell out of the playoff picture in 1998–99. Ronald Corey resigned. He was replaced as president by Pierre Boivin, who joined the team from the sporting goods industry.

With top players like Shayne Corson, Brian Savage, Saku Koivu and Trevor Linden all missing significant time due to injuries, the Canadiens appeared to tumble hopelessly out of contention in the first half of the 1999–2000 season. Among the most serious of Montreal's many injuries was that of Trent McCleary, who was struck in the throat by a puck, damaging his windpipe. Though the injuries continued to pile up, the Canadiens were able to turn around their season in the second half. Led by the spectacular goaltending of Jose Theodore and Jeff Hackett, Montreal climbed to as high as seventh overall in the Eastern Conference standings. However, when returning players such as Koivu and Linden were again knocked out of the lineup, the rally lost steam and the Canadiens were eliminated from playoff contention on the final

Saturday night of the regular season. It marked the first time that Montreal had failed to reach the playoffs in consecutive years since the early 1920s. With eight seasons between Stanley Cup victories, Montreal was also in the midst of its longest championship drought since before World War II. When the club missed the playoffs again in 2000–01, it marked the third year in a row in which the Canadiens had failed to qualify for the postseason, the longest such streak since 1922.

Named captain of the Canadiens prior to the 1999–2000 season, Saku Koivu missed most of the 2001–02 season battling cancer. He returned late in the year to help lift the Canadiens into the playoffs.

Not surprisingly, changes were made. Both coach Alain Vigneault and general manager Réjean Houle were let go, replaced by Michel Therrien and Andre Savard on November 20, 2000. Bigger changes came two months later. On January 31, 2001, Molson Inc. announced that it had sold 80.1 percent of the team to George Gillett, Jr. The Molson family had owned the Canadiens since 1957, and the sale of Canada's most storied sports franchise to someone from outside Montreal was viewed as a significant event. Gillett also purchased 100 percent of the Molson Centre (soon renamed the Bell Centre) and maintained that he was committed to making the Canadiens a success in Montreal once again. The team did manage to end its playoff drought in 2001–02.

On the ice, the 2001–02 Canadiens were led offensively by Savard acquisitions Yanic Perreault and Richard Zednik. Newly acquired Doug Gilmour was no longer the playmaker he had once been, but added much-needed leadership—especially with the loss of captain Saku Koivu. Diagnosed with non-Hodgkin's lymphoma cancer in early September, Koivu missed all but the last three games of the regular season. His battle with the life-threatening disease was truly inspirational. Koivu maintained a strong leadership role in the Montreal dressing room and participated in numerous club activities while undergoing treatment and rehabilitation. Once he did return, Koivu performed brilliantly in the playoffs, as the Canadiens upset Boston in the first round before falling to the surprising Carolina Hurricanes. Still, the Canadiens would not even have qualified for the playoffs if it had not been for netminder Jose Theodore.

Theodore, who had first risen to prominence in 1999–2000, was brilliant throughout the 2001–02 season. His save percentage of .931 was tops in the NHL and his seven shutouts and 2.11 goals-against average also ranked him among the leaders. He was at his very best late in the season when a seven-game winning streak finally allowed the Canadiens to nail down the final playoff berth in the Eastern Conference. After the season, Theodore was rewarded with both the Vezina Trophy as the league's top goaltender and the Hart Trophy as NHL MVP. In both cases, the voting had actually ended in a tie but Theodore received the trophies because he had more first-place votes than Patrick Roy and Jarome Iginla.

Playing behind Theodore, Jeff Hackett had been the subject of trade rumors for several seasons. However, with Theodore playing below form for the first half of 2002–03, Hackett saw more action then he had seen for several years. Still, facing the prospect of losing him for nothing as a free agent, Savard finally dealt Hackett in January. A few weeks earlier, the struggling Canadiens had fired Michel Therrien and replaced him with successful minor league coach Claude Julien. Still, the Canadiens never really posed a serious playoff threat in 2002–03, though there were some good performances. Saku Koivu played in all 82 games and led the team with 50 assists and 71 points. Richard Zdenik had 31 goals. Yanic Perreault had 24 goals, but had a plus-minus rating of -11. Typical of the trying times in Montreal was the fact that the Canadiens were 0–28–0–0 in games they were trailing after two periods. They were the only team in the NHL without a single come-from-behind victory during the season.

Though there had been little word of such a move being in the works, on June 2, 2003, the Canadiens announced that former captain (and former Dallas Stars g.m.) Bob Gainey was returning to Montreal in the position of general manager and executive vice president. (Andre Savard would stay on as his assistant.) "My presence is not about the past," said Gainey. "It's about the present, which is today, and about the future, which is tomorrow. This is a new challenge for me—one that I welcome. It will be tough but it will also be fun and exciting and this is where it's going to happen."

Montreal Maroons

During 14 seasons in the NHL, the Montreal Maroons boasted some of the top stars of the era, including Nels Stewart, the NHL's first 300-goal scorer. They won the Stanley Cup twice. But, the Maroons' greatest legacy to their city and the NHL was the Montreal Forum.

Montreal had been left without a top-rate hockey facility, and without a team to represent its anglophone population, when fire destroyed the Montreal Arena on January 2, 1918. The Mount Royal Arena was built to house the Montreal Canadiens in 1920, but its natural ice surface was unreliable in mild weather. By March, 1922, English Montreal was mobilizing to build a new hockey showcase and to return to the NHL. Ironically, French Canadian Donat Raymond would make it happen. He and William Northey appealed to Canadian Pacific Railway Chairman Edward W. Beatty, whose influence and financial support led to the creation of the Canadian Arena Company in January, 1924. Construction began in late spring, and by fall the Montreal Forum stood at the corner of St. Catherine and Atwater.

To provide a team for the new arena, Raymond and Northey turned to James Strachan who had created the Montreal Wanderers in 1903. On October 12, 1924, it was reported that Strachan and Raymond would be granted an NHL franchise for $15,000. The NHL formally admitted the new Montreal team, along with its first American entry, the Boston Bruins, on November 1, 1924. Yet another French Canadian had been instrumental behind the scenes. Leo Dandurand facilitated the admittance of the English Montreal team as part of a gentlemen's agreement that would allow him to move his Canadiens into the Forum when the lease expired at the Mount Royal Arena in 1926. In fact, the Canadiens played the first game at the Forum on November 29, 1924, because the natural ice surface at the Arena was not ready for the 1924–25 season opener.

The new Montreal team was formally known as the Montreal Professional Hockey Club during its first season. The owners had

Five of the 11 players on the 1925–26 Montreal Maroons (Reg Noble, Clint Benedict, Punch Broadbent, Nels Stewart and Babe Siebert) were later inducted into the Hockey Hall of Fame. Coach Eddie Gerard was also inducted, as was club director Donat Raymond.

hoped to use the Wanderers name, but the rights apparently belonged to former Wanderers player and manager Dickie Boon. The Montreal roster comprised mostly veteran castoffs, though Clint Benedict, Punch Broadbent and Reg Noble would prove they had some life left. Rookies included Dunc Munro, a prized acquisition from the Toronto Granites, who had won an Olympic gold medal in February 1924. Still, the team was only spared from last place by the woeful record of its expansion cousins in Boston. However, with sellout crowds flocking to the Forum, success would come as quickly.

By January of the club's first season, newspapers had taken to calling Montreal's new hockey team the Maroons. In 1925–26, the team officially became known by the color of its uniforms. Two players acquired to wear those uniforms—Nels Stewart and Babe Siebert—led the Montreal Maroons from second last to second place in the club's second season. Stewart was a slow, plodding skater, but he had size and strength and would become known as "Old Poison" for the deadly accuracy of his shot. It found the net a league-leading 34 times in 1925–26, not only earning Stewart a scoring title but also the Hart Trophy as the NHL's most valuable player.

The Maroons defeated the Pittsburgh Pirates in their playoff debut, but the first-place Ottawa Senators were favored to defeat them in the NHL championship series. However ex-Senator Punch Broadbent scored for Montreal in a 1–1 tie in the first game, while former Ottawa star Clint Benedict recorded a shutout in game two. Babe Siebert's goal gave the Maroons a 2–1 total-goals series victory that entitled them to play the Western Hockey League's Victoria Cougars for the Stanley Cup. Nels Stewart fired six goals in four games against Victoria, including both goals in the 2–0 victory that gave the Maroons the series three games to one.

Montreal Maroons

Year-by-Year Record

Season	GP	W	L	T	GF	GA	Pts	Finish	Division	Playoff Results
1924–25	30	9	19	2	45	65	20	5th	...	Out of Playoffs
1925–26	36	20	11	5	91	73	45	2nd	...	Won Stanley Cup
1926–27	44	20	20	4	71	68	44	3rd	Canadian	Lost Quarterfinal
1927–28	44	24	14	6	96	77	54	2nd	Canadian	Lost Final
1928–29	44	15	20	9	67	65	30	5th	Canadian	Out of Playoffs
1929–30	44	23	16	5	141	114	51	1st	Canadian	Lost Semifinal
1930–31	44	20	18	6	105	106	46	3rd	Canadian	Lost Quarterfinal
1931–32	48	19	22	7	142	139	45	3rd	Canadian	Lost Semifinal
1932–33	48	22	20	6	135	119	50	2nd	Canadian	Lost Quarterfinal
1933–34	48	19	18	11	117	122	49	3rd	Canadian	Lost Semifinal
1934–35	48	24	19	5	123	92	53	2nd	Canadian	Won Stanley Cup
1935–36	48	22	16	10	114	106	54	1st	Canadian	Lost Semifinal
1936–37	48	22	17	9	126	110	53	2nd	Canadian	Lost Semifinal
1937–38	48	12	30	6	101	149	30	4th	Canadian	Out of Playoffs

The NHL expanded to 10 teams in 1926–27, and split into Canadian and American divisions. The defending Stanley Cup champion Maroons slumped to third place in the Canadian Division and were knocked out of the playoffs by their fellow Forum tenants. Crowds of more than 11,000 fans jammed the arena—whose capacity was said to be only 10,000—for each of the two-game quarterfinal series. Howie Morenz won it for the Canadiens with an overtime goal in game two. The Maroons got their revenge the following year with a semifinal victory over the Canadiens that put them into the Stanley Cup finals against the New York Rangers. Though every game of the 1928 final was played at the Forum because the circus was performing at Madison Square Garden, the Rangers beat the Maroons three games to two. This was the series in which Rangers coach Lester Patrick made an emergency appearance in goal.

The Maroons fell to last place in the Canadian Division in 1928–29, but rebounded to remain a power in the league well into the 1930s. Nels Stewart again was the most valuable player in 1929–30, and the S-Line of Stewart, Babe Siebert and Hooley Smith remained among the league's most dangerous units until Stewart and Siebert were traded in 1932. By then, Baldy Northcott, Dave Trottier and Jimmy Ward had emerged as new stars, and with Russ Blinco named rookie of the year in 1933–34, the Maroons were able to compensate for the loss of the two future Hall of Famers.

Tommy Gorman joined the club in 1934–35 after winning the Stanley Cup in Chicago. The new coach and general manager acquired Alex Connell, who gave the Maroons their first star goaltender since Clint Benedict's departure in 1930. (Ironically, it was Connell's arrival in Ottawa in 1924 that had convinced the Senators to sell Benedict to Montreal.) Connell led the league with nine shutouts, then sparkled in the playoffs as the Maroons won the Stanley Cup again. With the line of Hooley Smith, Baldy Northcott and Jimmy Ward leading the way, the Maroons followed up their Stanley Cup victory with a Canadian Division title in 1935–36. But, attendance had been in decline in Montreal and around the league since the onset of the Depression, and now the Maroons began to feel the economic pinch.

Hooley Smith was an all-star in 1935–36, but salary concerns saw him peddled to the Boston Bruins. Without him, the Maroons opened the 1936–37 season poorly and attendance suffered all the more. The retirement of Lionel Conacher and Alex Connell further weakened the team in 1937–38, but Gorman hoped that hiring King Clancy as coach would fill the Maroons with a fighting spirit. It didn't. Clancy resigned on December 31, 1937, with the team in last place. At the time it was said that Clancy hadn't enforced enough discipline; others put the blame for the team's poor play on the low wages Gorman was paying. The Maroons continued to slump with Gorman behind the bench, and attendance worsened amid talk the city might be better served by just one professional hockey team. A 6–3 loss to the Canadiens on March 17, 1938, saw the Maroons finish the season with the league's worst record and miss the playoffs for the first time in nine years. It was the last game they ever played.

With the threat of war in Europe making the economic future even more uncertain, the team requested permission to suspend operations for one year, which the NHL granted on August 25, 1938. On May 13, 1939, the Montreal Maroons advised the NHL that they would no longer operate a franchise. Within a year, the Canadian Arena Company acquired the complete stock and assets of the Montreal Canadiens. The city's French team was also drawing poorly, but Donat Raymond would assure that at least one Montreal club survived. While the man who had built the Forum and created the Maroons continued to absorb financial losses, Tommy Gorman and coach Dick Irvin rebuilt the Canadiens into the team that would become the most successful franchise in hockey history.

Montreal Wanderers

THOUGH THEY HAVE BEEN GONE FOR MORE THAN 80 YEARS, the Montreal Wanderers remain one of the legendary teams in hockey history. Sixteen future Hockey Hall of Famers played for the Wanderers during the club's 15-year existence. The team won Stanley Cup championships in 1906, 1907, 1908 and 1910. But, even more than success, controversy defined the Montreal Wanderers.

The Wanderers were charter members of the Federal Amateur Hockey League, which was formed on December 5, 1903, to accommodate Wanderers founder James Strachan (a member of a prominent Montreal bakery family who would later help form the Montreal Maroons). Strachan's team was not welcome in the Canadian Amateur Hockey League because he had raided the roster of the Montreal Amateur Athletic Association hockey club. Jack Marshall, Jimmy Gardner, Cecil Blachford, Dickie Boon, Billy Bellingham and Billy Nicholson all had been with the rival Montreal organization the previous season. All except Blachford also had been members of the AAA's Stanley Cup-winning team of 1902. That team had been dubbed "The Little Men of Iron" for the tenacious way they hung on to defeat the Winnipeg Victorias. In later years the nickname was applied frequently to the Wanderers.

The Wanderers' powerful aggregation of former champions had little trouble with the competition in the FAHL, romping to the championship with a perfect 6–0 record. A two-game, total-goals Stanley Cup challenge match then was arranged between the Wanderers and the Ottawa Silver Seven. Ottawa, too, had seen its share of controversy that year, as the club had resigned from the

The Montreal Wanderers were four-time Stanley Cup champions before the NHL was formed. This 1907 team included five Hall of Famers: Moose Johnson (standing, second from left), Hod Stuart (standing, third from left), Riley Hern (seated, third from left), Lester Patrick (seated, third from right) and Ernie Russell (seated, second from right).

CAHL in midseason. The Stanley Cup series between the season's two most troublesome teams provided even more problems after an extremely physical game on March 2, 1904 ended in a 5–5 tie after 60 minutes. Unhappy with the refereeing, the Wanderers refused to play overtime. The Stanley Cup trustees ordered a new two-game set with both games to be played in Ottawa. The Wanderers refused to take part unless the tied game was replayed in Montreal, and the series had to be abandoned.

The Silver Seven joined the Wanderers in the Federal League in 1904–05, although there were rumors that both teams would abandon the FAHL if the CAHL would accept them. The rumors heated up again prior to the 1905–06 season, but the Wanderers would be in on a much more surprising development when a new league was formed on December 11, 1906. The Eastern Canada Amateur Hockey Association consisted of the Wanderers and Ottawa from the FAHL, and the Montreal Victorias, Quebec Bulldogs, Montreal AAA and Montreal Shamrocks of the CAHL.

Bolstered by the addition of future Hall of Famers Lester Patrick, Moose Johnson and Ernie Russell, the Wanderers proved the equal of the defending Stanley Cup champions from Ottawa and the two teams finished the first ECAHA season with identical 9–1 records. To break the tie, a two-game, total-goals playoff was scheduled. The winner would not only claim the league title but also the Stanley Cup. The first game was played in Montreal on March 14, 1906, and resulted in a 9–1 victory for the Wanderers. Game two was played in Ottawa three nights later. Amazingly, Ottawa stormed back to even the series score at 10–10 before Lester Patrick ended the Silver Seven's Stanley Cup reign with a pair of late goals.

Not content to rest on their championship laurels, James Strachan and the Wanderers began to stir up new trouble at the annual meeting of the Eastern Canada Amateur Hockey Association on November 11, 1906. Strachan led the move to allow professional players into the ECAHA along with amateurs, then threatened to withdraw from the league unless the Wanderers were permitted to meet a team from New Glasgow, Nova Scotia, in a preseason Stanley Cup challenge match in December. Permission was granted, and the Wanderers scored easy 10–3 and 7–2 victories. Strachan's team then took time out from the ECAHA season in mid-January to entertain another Stanley Cup challenge. This time, however, the Wanderers were defeated by the Kenora Thistles, 4–2 and 8–6.

Spurred on by the desire to win back the trophy, the Wanderers blazed through the remainder of the regular season. With Ernie Russell scoring 42 goals in nine league games, the Wanderers romped to a 10–0 record and headed west to Winnipeg for a Stanley Cup rematch with Kenora. The Wanderers scored a 7–2 victory in the first game on March 23, 1907, and though the Thistles won the second game, 6–5, the Wanderers took the total-goals series, 12–8, and were Stanley Cup champions once again. Another ECAHA title in 1907–08, and successful defenses against teams from Ottawa, Toronto, Winnipeg and Edmonton kept the Stanley Cup in Montreal through one more year. Lester Patrick had gone west to British Columbia to work in the family lumber business and Hod Stuart had drowned during the summer of 1907, but the addition of Art Ross and Hod's brother, Bruce Stuart, helped the Wanderers offset their losses.

The 1908–09 season saw the Eastern Canada Amateur Hockey Association become the Eastern Canada Hockey Association after the withdrawal of the strictly amateur Montreal Victorias and Montreal AAA. Ottawa (now known as the Senators) beat the Wanderers in the final game of the season to win the ECHA title and the Stanley Cup, but the Wanderers would return to the top in 1910—though not without more controversy.

By this time the Wanderers had been sold to P.J. Doran, who owned the Jubilee Arena in Montreal. Although his arena had about half the capacity of the team's previous home, Doran proposed to move the Wanderers into his rink for the 1909–10 season. Facing a dwindling share of the gate receipts, Doran's fellow owners voted the ECHA out of existence on November 25, 1909, and created the new Canadian Hockey Association. This league would not include the Wanderers, nor the team from Renfrew, Ontario, that the Wanderers supported for inclusion in the ECHA.

Having both been snubbed, the Wanderers and Renfrew joined to form a rival hockey league—the National Hockey Association. Backed by Renfrew millionaire M.J. O'Brien and run by his son Ambrose, the NHA proved more viable than the CHA and by mid-January, 1910, the Montreal Shamrocks and Ottawa Senators abandoned the CHA for the new league. The Wanderers posted an 11–1 record during the 1909–10 season to win both the NHA title and the Stanley Cup.

Ownership of the Wanderers again changed hands for the 1910–11 season, and the team moved back to the larger Montreal Arena. However, the glory days of the franchise were over. The period of Sam Lichtenhein's ownership was marked by financial struggles. The war over players with the rival Pacific Coast Hockey Association drove up salaries, while the war in Europe depleted rosters and lessened hockey's box-office appeal. The Wanderers were included when the teams of the NHA reorganized to form the NHL in November, 1917, but Lichtenhein's team was clearly in trouble. As late as December 12, 1917, it appeared the Wanderers might not be able to produce a team because of injuries and military commitments. However, when the NHL season opened seven days later, the Wanderers' cast of aging veterans and unproven youngsters defeated Toronto 10–9—though only 700 fans saw the game. Two nights later, the rival Canadiens crushed the Wanderers, 11–2, and Lichtenhein threatened to withdraw from the NHL unless he could get more players. Two more lopsided losses followed.

On January 2, 1918, fire destroyed the Montreal Arena. The blaze was attributed to an unknown cause in the Wanderers dressing room. The Montreal Canadiens announced they would play out the season in the Wanderers' old home, the Jubilee Arena. Hamilton, Ontario, offered to provide a home for the Wanderers, but when the other NHL teams refused to provide additional players, Lichtenhein withdrew his club on January 4, 1918. A colorful and controversial era in hockey history was over.

Montreal Wanderers

Year-by-Year Record

Season	GP	W	L	T	GF	GA	Pts	Finish	Division	Playoff Results
1917–18	*6	1	*5	0	17	35	2	Withdrew	...	...

* includes two defaulted games

Nashville Predators

NASHVILLE WAS THE FIRST TEAM TO BEGIN PLAY after being welcomed into the National Hockey League with Atlanta, Minnesota and Columbus as expansion clubs on June 25, 1997. The Predators were placed in the Central Division of the Western Conference along with the Chicago Blackhawks, Detroit Red Wings and St. Louis Blues for the 1997–98 season. (The Columbus Blue Jackets were added to the division for the 2000–2001 campaign.) Their home rink is the Gaylord Entertainment Center, which was known as the Nashville Arena when it opened for the club's inaugural year.

The first major order of business for team president Jack Diller was to hire David Poile as executive vice president of hockey operations and general manager on July 9, 1997. Poile had served as general manager of the Washington Capitals since 1982, and had helped build the team into a perennial contender. He had begun his career in hockey administration with the expansion Atlanta Flames in 1972, and worked himself up to the position of assistant general manager in both Atlanta and Calgary. His father, Bud Poile, had played seven years in the NHL and was the general manager of expansion teams in both Philadelphia and Vancouver. A little less than a month after his own hiring in Nashville, Poile signed Barry Trotz as the team's first head coach. Trotz had spent four seasons as the head coach of the Portland Pirates, Washington's farm club in the American Hockey League.

The Predators braintrust with David Legwand (in team sweater), the club's first choice, second overall, at their first NHL Entry Draft in 1998.

The Predators name was announced for Nashville's first major-league sports franchise on November 13, 1997, by club chairman and majority owner Craig Leipold and Diller. "Given the intense nature of hockey, combined with the game's speed and skill, Predators is a natural fit," said Leipold, "and it is the name Nashville fans chose for their team." Added Diller: "The image of a predator is one who succeeds and wins, something we hope our team will do often when we begin play." For a logo, the team chose a dramatic profile of a saber-toothed cat, which was native in prehistoric times to the region that is now Nashville.

On June 1, 1998, the Predators acquired their first player when they obtained Marian Cisar from the Los Angeles Kings for future considerations. (Cisar was later assigned to Nashville's AHL farm club in Milwaukee.) Free agents Jayson More, Rob Valicevic and Mark Mowers, who were signed later in June, all saw action for Nashville during the inaugural 1998–99 season, but roster-building began in earnest on June 26, 1998, at the Expansion Draft in Buffalo. Greg Johnson and Andrew Brunette, as well as goaltenders Mike Dunham and Tomas Vokoun, were key members of the inaugural club. Such players as Sergei Krivokrasov, Jan Vopat and Sebastien Bordeleau were picked up in trades later in the day.

One day after the Expansion Draft, a trade with the San Jose Sharks landed Nashville the second pick in the NHL Entry Draft. The Predators chose highly regarded junior prospect David Legwand. A rookie in the Ontario Hockey League in 1997–98, Legwand had 54 goals and 51 assists in just 59 games for the Plymouth Whalers and became the first rookie (and second American-born player) to be named the OHL's most valuable player. Tom Fitzgerald, who had been the first forward selected by the Florida Panthers in the 1993 Expansion Draft, joined the Predators as a free agent on July 6, 1998, and became the club's first captain.

The Nashville Predators played their first game on October 10, 1998, entering the arena on a red carpet in front of a sellout crowd of 17,298. Even a 1–0 loss to the Florida Panthers couldn't dampen the enthusiasm generated that evening. Three nights later, the Predators had their first victory when they defeated the Carolina Hurricanes 3–2 on home ice. Andrew Brunette scored the club's first goal, while Mike Dunham earned the first victory. By month's end, the team had a respectable record of 3–5–1, including a 3–2 victory over the Colorado Avalanche on October 31. Even more important than a victory over one of the NHL's top clubs was the trade that day that brought Cliff Ronning to Nashville from the Phoenix Coyotes. Ronning's 35 assists and 53 points in 72 games as a Predator led all Nashville players during the club's first season. Krivokrasov's 25 goals were also tops on the team.

Among the highlights of the Predators' first season was the one and only visit by Wayne Gretzky to Nashville. Gretzky had four assists as the New York Rangers raced out to a 6–0 lead midway through the second period and, despite the lopsided score, the performance of "The Great One" had the crowd buzzing. Live country music being played in the aisles added to the festive atmosphere, which reached frenzied proportions when the Predators scored four straight goals. A fifth assist by Gretzky capped an eventual 7–4 Rangers win.

Though Nashville ended its inaugural season with four straight losses to drop its record to 28–47–7, the club attracted sellout

Nashville Predators

Year-by-Year Record

Season	GP	W	L	T	OL	GF	GA	Pts.	Finish	Division	Playoff Result
1998-99	82	28	47	7	...	190	261	63	4th	Central Div.	Out of Playoffs
99-2000	82	28	40	7	7	199	240	70	4th	Central Div.	Out of Playoffs
2000-01	82	34	36	9	3	186	200	80	3rd	Central Div.	Out of Playoffs
2001-02	82	28	41	13	0	196	230	69	4th	Central Div.	Out of Playoffs
2002-03	82	27	35	13	7	183	206	74	4th	Central Div.	Out of Playoffs

crowds for six straight games to close out the schedule. The Predators drew 664,000 fans during their first season for an average attendance of 16,202 (94% of capacity). The season finale, on April 18, 1999, featured the NHL debut of David Legwand, who had signed with the team two days earlier after playing out the season in Plymouth. Legwand had two shots on goal in a game won 4–1 by the Devils. The success of the Predators' inaugural campaign was reflected in the contract extensions offered to Barry Trotz and his assistant coaches, Paul Gardner and Brent Peterson, a month after the season ended.

Few personnel changes were made prior to the 1999–2000 season, as the Predators kept the core of the first-year team together. David Legwand, still only 19 years old, earned a spot on the Nashville roster to start the 1999–2000 season. He had a landmark game in Toronto on October 11, 1999, when he collected the first goal and the first assist of his NHL career. Legwand's goal against the Maple Leafs goaltender Glenn Healy came with 1:03 remaining in the third period. It broke a 2–2 tie and sparked the Predators to a 4–2 victory. The win was the first of the season for the second-year club. Legwand wound up playing 71 games for the Predators and ranked among the rookie scoring leaders with 28 points. Once again Cliff Ronning was the team's top scorer, but fans new the future of the club lay in players like Legwand and Denis Arkhipov. Among the most pleasant surprises of 1999–2000 was the play of rookie defenseman Karlis Skrastins.

Like their inaugural season, the Predators were able to play consistent hockey through the first half of the schedule—and even dreamed of the postseason—until the club hit a February swoon. They wound up the 1999–2000 campaign with an identical won-loss-tied record of 28–47–7, but did gain seven extra points in the standings due to the new rule providing a point for losses in overtime.

The Predators enjoyed the best season in their brief history in 2000–01, establishing club records with 34 wins and 80 points. Nashville's 10-point improvement over the previous season was the second-biggest in the Western Conference (Colorado improved its performance by 22 points), yet still left the club 10 points out of a playoff spot. More attention to defense was the key to success as the Predators cut their goals against from 240 to 200. Kimmo Timonen was the team's top defenseman, but goaltenders Mike Dunham and Tomas Vokoun deserved most of the credit. Their combined save percentage of .915 was second best in the NHL behind Buffalo's mark of .916. Individually, Dunham's .923 save percentage trailed only Marty Turco of Dallas.

The Predators opened the 2001–02 season in Japan, scoring a 3–1 victory over Pittsburgh on October 7 but dropping a 3–1 decision to the Penguins the following night. Though it was hoped that Nashville might contend for a playoff spot in its fourth season, the young team (17 players on the final roster had less than 200 games experience in the NHL) slipped in the standings. Original Predator Greg Johnson led the team in scoring with 44 points (18 goals, 26 assists) and players like Denis Arkhipov and Scott Hartnell showed promise for the future. Once again there were expectations that the Predators would make the playoffs in 2002–03, but once again the team struggled. A hot streak had Nashville near contention in late February, but an injury to David Legwand seemed to deflate the team's chances and they limped to the finish with a franchise-low 27 wins.

Vokoun was Nashville's biggest star in 2002–03 posting 25 of the Predators' 27 wins while recording a goals-against average of 2.20 and a .918 save percentage. His emergence as a number-one goaltender allowed the Predators to trade Mike Dunham to the Rangers. Legwand was the team's top points producer with 17 goals and 31 assists in 64 games. Andy Delmore scored 18 goals to tie Nicklas Lidstrom and Sergei Gonchar for the league league among defensemen. Andreas Johansson led the team with 20 goals in just 56 games while Kimmo Timonen topped the team with 34 assists in 72 games. Rem Murray, who joined the Predators from the Rangers, wound up playing 85 games on the season.

A veteran of seven seasons in the Finnish Elite League, Kimmo Timonen joined the Predators in their first season and has become the club's best offensive defenseman.

New Jersey Devils, Colorado Rockies and Kansas City Scouts

During the 1990s, the New Jersey Devils were able to erase their image as the league's laughing stock and establish themselves as Stanley Cup champions and a consistent challenger for the Presidents' Trophy as the NHL's regular-season leader.

The Devils began their existence not in New Jersey, but in Missouri as the Kansas City Scouts. They entered the league with the Washington Capitals in 1974–75. Playing out of the brand-new Kemper Arena, the Scouts had little to offer in their rookie season. Facing competition from the two-year-old World Hockey Association, the Scouts scrambled for talent and had little apart from the solid goaltending of Denis Herron, the power shooting of Simon Nolet and the hope that high-priced rookie Wilf Paiement would make his three-year, $500,000 contract pay off.

Former Detroit Red Wings hero Sid Abel was named general manager, and he did the best with what he had but, admittedly, it was not much. "Neither the Capitals nor ourselves were exactly overloaded with stars," said Abel. By comparison with the Capitals, the Scouts did relatively well. Kansas City finished with 41 points, 20 more than Washington, but that was the extent of the jubilation. A year later Kansas City slipped to 36 points while attendance slipped to the point of no return. With the NHL's approval, the franchise was moved to Denver, where it was rechristened the Colorado Rockies and continued to lose hockey games.

Wilf Paiement, in the uniform of the Colorado Rockies. Paiement had entered the NHL as a 19-year-old when the franchise began life as the Kansas City Scouts in 1974–75. He was traded to Toronto in the deal that delivered Lanny McDonald to Denver in 1979.

Under coach Johnny Wilson, the Rockies finished last in the Smythe Division and offered little to attract the Rocky Mountain fans other than Paiement, who began fulfilling his early notices. There was little difference between the franchise in Kansas City and Denver other than the fact that Rockies lasted six years rather than two and for a brief, colorful period had Don Cherry as their coach.

By the 1980–81 season it had become obvious that Denver was not buying into the Rockies. New Jersey trucking executive Arthur Imperatore, who had purchased the team, threatened to move the franchise to a new arena in his home state's Meadowlands within view of the Manhattan skyline. But the Rangers, Islanders and Flyers—each of whom had veto power—nixed the idea, whereupon Imperatore sold the club to Buffalo cable television magnate Peter Gilbert and former Colorado lieutenant governor Mark Hogan.

After another dreadful season in 1981–82, Gilbert wanted out and found a buyer in Dr. John J. McMullen. Renowned in sporting circles, Dr. McMullen first ventured into baseball as a partner in the New York Yankees and later would own the Houston Astros.

A New Jersey native, McMullen became convinced that his native state could support an NHL team at The Meadowlands. On May 27, 1982, it became official. McMullen, along with John C. Whitehead, now the chairman of AEA Investors, Inc., and former New Jersey governor Brendan T. Byrne, purchased the Rockies and received NHL approval to shift the franchise to The Meadowlands. It was not, however, a simple transaction. McMullen had to indemnify the Flyers, Rangers and Islanders handsomely for "invading" their territory. McMullen named longtime hockey executive Max McNab vice president in charge of hockey operations and Billy MacMillan as general manager and coach.

The New Jersey Devils played their first home game on September 21, 1982, in a preseason contest with the New York Rangers. Dr. McMullen accelerated the future rivalry by twitting the denizens of Madison Square Garden in a pregame comment that was well-covered by the media. "I believe we're going to be a lot more aggressive than the Rangers," said McMullen. "They're complacent because they're sold out." Seizing on the observation, the New York Post headlined the story "Rangers Angry Over McMullen Remark."

Perhaps they were, but McMullen couldn't have cared less. He wanted his team to put on a good showing against the 56-year-old franchise from across the Hudson River. The Devils did not win, but the 9,193 fans were well entertained. Billy MacMillan was disappointed with the result. "We still have a long way to go," he opined.

It is doubtful that McMullen realized precisely how long it

would take for his Devils to become a playoff contender. They finished their first season with a record of 17–49–14, placing them fifth in the six-team Patrick Division. "We're making some progress," said Aaron Broten. "Last year we didn't know if the team would be in Denver or wherever. Now we know we're going to be in New Jersey next year."

But 1983–84 was no kinder to New Jersey's franchise. If one episode could encapsulate the club's futility, it would be a game at Northlands Coliseum in Edmonton on November 19, 1983. Ron Low started in goal for New Jersey. He was well-known to Edmonton fans and players, having played for the Oilers over four seasons before being traded to the Devils. Much as they liked Low, the Oilers were merciless in their treatment of him that evening. They pumped eight goals past him through two periods of play and were so overwhelming that MacMillan felt obligated to pull his starter and replace Ron with Glenn "Chico" Resch for the third period. The final tally was 13–4, representing the largest score ever run up against the franchise. And the swarming was not over.

Reporters descended on the Oilers dressing room for comments, especially from Wayne Gretzky who had recorded three goals and five assists. Prodded with leading questions from the newsmen, Gretzky was lured into a denunciation that he might have avoided. But he answered spontaneously when queried about the bombardment of his buddy Low. "It got to a point where it wasn't even funny," said Gretzky. "They're ruining the whole league. They had better stop running a Mickey Mouse operation and put somebody on ice."

The 13–4 game took place on Saturday night in Edmonton, after most of the New Jersey-New York newspapers had their last editions put to bed. Little other than the scoring results appeared in most Sunday papers, but by Monday the headlines were blaring all over the country. "Gretzky Takes a Slap at Devils Organization" barked the headline in USA Today. The New York Post was more direct: "Gretzky: Devils are a Mickey Mouse Team."

To his surprise, Gretzky began feeling the heat. He was surprised by the groundswell of public opinion against his tirade. "You'd have thought I'd criticized Miss Newark or something," said Gretzky. "The fans went crazy against me."

The fallout from the Gretzky fiasco led to MacMillan being dismissed. Max McNab was named general manager and Tom McVie, who had been coaching the Maine Mariners, was promoted to head coach. The results were insignificant. Not only did the Devils finish fifth again, now they had the stigma of Gretzky's insult tarnishing their image. If there was hope, it was provided by draft choices such as Kirk Muller and John MacLean, who infused energy into the machine if not sufficient wins. Soon rugged, young defenseman Ken Daneyko would established himself as a fan favorite.

Management appointed Doug Carpenter as head coach in 1985–86, and while the redhead provided a sense of discipline and purpose in the young club, the coveted playoff berth was still beyond reach. The club's turning point began on April 24, 1987, when president Bob Butera resigned and McMullen named Lou Lamoriello as his successor. For two decades Lamoriello had been the guiding force behind Providence College's hockey success. When Max McNab was moved up to a vice presidency, Lamoriello became general manager as well. On January 26, 1988, he introduced Jim Schoenfeld as the Devils' new bench boss.

Schoenfeld was one of two key additions who would transform the Devils from perennial losers to a playoff team. The other was goaltender Sean Burke, who had been drafted by New Jersey in 1985 and had come to the team following the 1988 Winter Olympic Games at Calgary. In his first game as a Devil at Boston Garden, Burke defeated the Bruins 7–6 in overtime. Although nobody knew it for sure at the time, this was the start of something big. Slowly, relentlessly, the Devils began a long climb toward a playoff berth that culminated with a decisive game at Chicago Stadium on April 3, 1988. Trailing the Rangers throughout the homestretch, the Devils could oust their rivals by defeating the Blackhawks. The game went into overtime before John MacLean beat goalie Darren Pang at 2:21 to give New Jersey its victory and first taste of postseason play.

The Devils then upset the first-place Islanders in the opening round and followed that with a seven-game series win—again MacLean scored the decisive goal—over favored Washington. Facing Boston in the third round, the Devils unexpectedly became involved in a brouhaha at the end of game three at Byrne Arena. Coach Jim Schoenfeld engaged in a verbal bout with referee Don Koharski that continued in a hallway leading from the ice to the dressing rooms. When NHL vice president Brian O'Neill—NHL president John Ziegler was reportedly out-of-town—suspended Schoenfeld, the Devils charged that no hearing had been held and the right of appeal should be honored.

Taking their case to court, the Devils won a temporary restrain-

New Jersey Devils

Year-by-Year Record

Season	GP	W	L	T	OL	GF	GA	Pts.	Finish	Division	Playoff Result
1974-75*	80	15	54	11	...	184	328	41	5th	Smythe Div.	Out of Playoffs
1975-76*	80	12	56	12	...	190	351	36	5th	Smythe Div.	Out of Playoffs
1976-77**	80	20	46	14	...	226	307	54	5th	Smythe Div.	Out of Playoffs
1977 78**	80	19	40	21	...	257	305	59	2nd	Smythe Div.	Lost Prelim. Round
1978-79**	80	15	53	12	...	210	331	42	4th	Smythe Div.	Out of Playoffs
1979-80**	80	19	48	13	...	234	308	51	6th	Smythe Div.	Out of Playoffs
1980-81**	80	22	45	13	...	258	344	57	5th	Smythe Div.	Out of Playoffs
1981-82**	80	18	49	13	...	241	362	49	5th	Smythe Div.	Out of Playoffs
1982-83	80	17	49	14	...	230	338	48	5th	Patrick Div.	Out of Playoffs
1983-84	80	17	56	7	...	231	350	41	5th	Patrick Div.	Out of Playoffs
1984-85	80	22	48	10	...	264	346	54	5th	Patrick Div.	Out of Playoffs
1985-86	80	28	49	3	...	300	374	59	6th	Patrick Div.	Out of Playoffs
1986-87	80	29	45	6	...	293	368	64	6th	Patrick Div.	Out of Playoffs
1987-88	80	38	36	6	...	295	296	82	4th	Patrick Div.	Lost Conf. Finals
1988-89	80	27	41	12	...	281	325	66	5th	Patrick Div.	Out of Playoffs
1989-90	80	37	34	9	...	295	288	83	2nd	Patrick Div.	Lost Div. Semifinal
1990-91	80	32	33	15	...	272	264	79	4th	Patrick Div.	Lost Div. Semifinal
1991-92	80	38	31	11	...	289	259	87	4th	Patrick Div.	Lost Div. Semifinal
1992-93	84	40	37	7	...	308	299	87	4th	Patrick Div.	Lost Div. Semifinal
1993-94	84	47	25	12	...	306	220	106	2nd	Atlantic Div.	Lost Conf. Finals
1994-95	48	22	18	8	...	136	121	52	2nd	Atlantic Div.	Won Stanley Cup
1995-96	82	37	33	12	...	215	202	86	6th	Atlantic Div.	Out of Playoffs
1996-97	82	45	23	14	...	231	182	104	1st	Atlantic Div.	Lost Conf. Semifinal
1997-98	82	48	23	11	...	225	166	107	1st	Atlantic Div.	Lost Conf. Quarterfinal
1998-99	82	47	24	11	...	248	196	105	1st	Atlantic Div.	Lost Conf. Quarterfinal
99-2000	82	45	24	8	5	251	203	103	2nd	Atlantic Div.	Won Stanley Cup
2000-01	82	48	19	12	3	295	195	111	1st	Atlantic Div.	Lost Final
2001-02	82	41	28	9	4	205	187	95	3rd	Atlantic Div.	Lost Conf. Quarterfinal
2002-03	82	46	20	10	6	216	166	108	1st	Atlantic Div.	Won Stanley Cup

* Kansas City Scouts. ** Colorado Rockies.

ing order that lifted Schoenfeld's suspension. The decision was rendered minutes before game time on Mother's Day, May 8, the night on which game four was to be played. Upon hearing of the judge's decision, the referee and linesmen refused to take the ice. The NHL responded by hiring three off-ice officials—Paul McInnis, Vin Godleski and Jim Sullivan—to officiate the game. Skates were found for all three. Only one had a striped shirt. The other two donned yellow practice jerseys and took the ice one hour and six minutes after the scheduled start of the game. (Two more striped shirts were found for the start of period two.) The Devils won 3–1 and the replacement officials won praise for their efforts.

New Jersey took Boston to seven games before succumbing 6–2 in the finale at Boston Garden. "Our club has proven that we no longer will be two easy points for every opponent," said Lamoriello. But instead of providing an impetus for bigger things, the big run to the playoffs proved illusory. In 1988–89, the Devils missed the postseason again, but they rebounded the following season with a second-place finish after John Cunniff had replaced Schoenfeld as coach. A first-round exit dimmed the luster, and Cunniff exited in the middle of the 1990–91 season in favor of Tom McVie. The Devils continued to play competitively, reaching the playoffs but never advancing past the first round, even after Herb Brooks succeeded McVie for the 1992–93 campaign.

A new era dawned on June 28, 1993, when Jacques Lemaire, a member of eight Stanley Cup-winning Montreal Canadiens teams, was named New Jersey's seventh head coach, with former teammate Larry Robinson coming aboard as assistant. Lemaire introduced a defensive system that would become known as the neutral zone trap, and the results were remarkable. The Devils recorded their best-ever record, 47–25–12, good for second place in the division. They then defeated Boston and Buffalo in the first two playoff rounds before extending the Rangers to double-overtime of the seventh game of a thrilling Eastern Conference championship.

John MacLean played in New Jersey from 1983 to 1997, setting franchise records for goals (347), assists (354) and points (701). He topped the 40-goal plateau for three straight seasons beginning in 1988–89.

A year later, in a lockout-shortened season, the Devils finished second again and entered the playoffs as distinct underdogs to the Boston Bruins. Paced by Claude Lemieux and Stephane Richer, New Jersey opened with a 5–0 win on the road and demolished the Bruins in five games. Facing Pittsburgh, the Devils fell behind by a game, then closed out the series with four wins in a row.

Next on the agenda was Philadelphia, with the Devils again opening on the road. It hardly mattered. They beat the Flyers in two straight at the Spectrum and won the series in six. Lemieux, Richer and goalie Martin Brodeur continued to excel as New Jersey reached the finals against the Red Wings at Joe Louis Arena. Employing their trap to perfection, the Devils shut down the high-flying Wings in a surprising four-game sweep, wrapping up the series with consecutive 5–2 victories before capacity crowds of 19,040 at the Meadowlands. NHL commissioner Gary Bettman presented the Cup to captain Scott Stevens and then congratulated John McMullen. The new NHL champs boasted 12 American-born players in their lineup, a record for a Stanley Cup winner.

But the days of celebration were clouded in uncertainty. In a dispute with the New Jersey Sports and Exposition Authority—the landlord of Byrne Arena—McMullen threatened to move his club to Nashville where a brand-new rink was being completed and financial enticements were difficult to refuse. After a summer of intense negotiations with the involvement of Bettman, a compromise was hammered out which included a new lease at what would become known as Continental Airlines Arena.

In their defense of the Stanley Cup, the Devils proved a disappointment. Although their record in 1995–96 was 37–33–12, good for 86 points, New Jersey was eliminated from playoff contention on the final weekend of the season, losing to Ottawa at home and thus enabling the Tampa Bay Lightning to earn their first playoff berth. However, Lemaire was able to galvanize his team the following year, lifting New Jersey to first place both in the division and the conference. Martin Brodeur had established himself as one of the league's foremost goaltenders while Scott Stevens was a rock on the blue line. Lacking a gunner, the Devils nevertheless spread the goals among four well-balanced lines led by the likes of Bobby Holik, Dave Andreychuk and Randy McKay.

The Devils seemed on course for another long playoff run in the spring of 1997 until Andreychuk—the club's best two-way forward—badly broke his ankle in the final game of the season at Philadelphia. Although New Jersey defeated Montreal in a five-game opening playoff round, they went down to the Rangers in round two—losing four in a row after a game-one victory.

Lamoriello made some lineup alterations for 1997–98, dipping into his Albany River Rats farm club for reinforcements. Youngsters such as Brad Bombardier, Patrik Elias and Sheldon Souray were added to the lineup and paid off handsomely. New Jersey finished with a club record 107 points (48–23–11), falling just short of winning the Presidents' Trophy. First in their division and first in their conference, the Devils were rated among the

Stanley Cup favorites. However, New Jersey was stunned by an Ottawa Senators team that eliminated them in six games. Jacques Lemaire stepped down as coach after the season and was replaced by Robbie Ftorek.

Despite the disappointing finish, New Jersey had established itself as a formidable organization. Attendance reached an all-time high during the 1997–98 season with an average of more than 17,000 per game, and the Albany farm club continued to excel in the American Hockey League. Ftorek would relax the Devils' tight defensive system in 1998–99, and for the first time in three years the team did not allow the fewest goals against, although Martin Brodeur did lead the league with 39 victories. The Devils set an NHL road record with 28 wins away from home (28–10–3) and led the Eastern Conference with 105 points. However, the season ended almost identically to the year before, as once again the Devils were eliminated in the first round of the playoffs, this time by Pittsburgh.

Patrick Elias and Hispanic-Alaskan rookie Scott Gomez fueled the Devils offense in 1999–2000, but once again the team's top performer was Martin Brodeur who led the NHL with 43 victories. Scott Stevens continued to lead a defense that was among the league's stingiest. Rookies John Madden and Brian Rafalski proved to be key additions. Rafalski had played four years in Europe after being undrafted out of the University of Wisconsin. Another rookie, Colin White, would prove his value in the playoffs as a blueliner in the Stevens image.

The Devils topped the Eastern Conference standings for much of the year, but a late slump cost Robbie Ftorek his job with just eight games left in the season. The Devils limped to a 4–4 finish under new coach Larry Robinson and allowed Philadelphia to slip past them for first place in both the Atlantic Division and the East. Though New Jersey's 103 points was the second-best total in the conference they were seeded fourth in the playoffs behind the division-winning Capitals and Toronto Maple Leafs.

The Devils seemed to shake off their late-season slide when they swept the Florida Panthers in the opening round of the playoffs. New Jersey's stifling defense shut down Pavel Bure, and was even more effective against Toronto's top line of Mats Sundin, Steve Thomas and Jonas Hogland in round two. That victory required six games, but the Maple Leafs were limited to just six shots in the series finale, an all-time playoff low. New Jersey's hot playoff run seemed about to end when they fell behind the Flyers three games to one in the Eastern Conference final, but the Devils rallied for three straight wins and advanced to meet the defending champion Dallas Stars for the Stanley Cup. After stunning the Stars with a 7–3 victory in game one, it was the Devils who jumped out to a 3–1 series lead this time. With a chance to wrap up the series on home ice in game five, the Devils were instead shut out through more than five periods of hockey before Mike Modano finally gave Dallas a 1–0 victory in triple overtime. Two nights later in Dallas, the two teams battled into double overtime before Jason Arnott beat Ed Belfour to make the Devils Stanley Cup champions for the first time since 1995. Scott Stevens, whose crushing bodychecks had neutralized opposition scorers throughout the playoffs, earned the Conn Smythe Trophy as playoff MVP. The Stanley Cup victory marked a fitting send off for John McMullen, whose effective ownership had allowed Lou Lamoriello to build the Devils.

The Devils followed up their championship of 1999–2000 with another stellar season in 2000–01. In fact, they reached the seventh game of the Stanley Cup final before finally relinquishing their title. Back on opening night, October 6, 2000, the Devils had raised their second Stanley Cup banner and paid tribute to Dr. John McMullen. McMullen had brought NHL hockey to New Jersey in 1982 and had owned the club for 18 years before selling to Puck Holdings, an affiliate of the YankeeNets organization. In their first full year under new ownership, the Devils set a club record with 111 points and won the Atlantic Division for the fourth time in five seasons. Though Scott Stevens and company were still regarded as a defensive team, the Devils led the NHL with 295 goals scored. Alexander Mogilny led the way with 43 goals, and Patrik Elias set a new team record with 96 points (40 goals, 56 assists). Petr Sykora scored 35 times while Jason Arnott, Sergei Brylin, Randy McKay and John Madden each topped 20. In a 9–0 win over Pittsburgh on October 28, Madden and McKay both scored four goals, marking the first time that two teammates had scored four goals in a game since brothers Sprague and Odie Cleghorn accomplished the feat with the Montreal Canadiens on January 14, 1922. Of course, the Devils were still strong in their own end of the rink, with a defensive crew led by Stevens, Brian Rafalski, Scott Niedermayer and Colin White. John Madden won the Selke Trophy as the NHL's best defensive forward. Martin Brodeur was as busy as ever in goal, playing in 72 games and winning 42. He led the league in wins for the fourth year in a row.

In the playoffs, New Jersey downed Carolina to set up a second-round rematch with Toronto. The Maple Leafs pushed the Devils harder this year, but were dispatched in seven games. Mario Lemieux and the Pittsburgh Penguins fell in five games in the Eastern Conference final and the Devils advanced to face the Avalanche for the Stanley Cup. Colorado scored a surprising 5–0 victory in the opener, but New Jersey bounced back for a 3–2 series lead after five games. The Devils had a chance to wrap up the series on home ice in game six, but Colorado scored a 4–0 win and went on to take the series back in Denver two nights later.

The 2001–02 season saw the Devils underperform for much of the year. The team dropped its first four games of the season and struggled to stay around the .500 mark. Still, it came as a surprise when coach Larry Robinson was let go on January 28, 2002. The Devils responded by going 20–8–2–1 under Kevin Constantine. New Jersey seemed to be peaking just in time for the playoffs, but the team was defeated by the Carolina Hurricanes in the opening round. The poor postseason performance likely contributed to the decision not to keep Constantine. Pat Burns was hired to coach the team in 2002–03.

Once again, the Devils started slowly, as new additions Jeff Friesen and Joe Nieuwendyk as well as homegrown talent like Elias and Scott Gomez struggled offensively. Still, Burns' attention to defense had the Devils battling the Ottawa Senators for top spot in the Eastern Conference by the All-Star Game. In the end, the Devils wound up second in the Conference with 108 points but held off the Flyers for first place in the Atlantic Division. The team had continued to struggle offensively all season, and was last in the NHL in powerplay efficiency. They made up for it by ranking first in penalty killing. In the end, Elias, Friesen and Jamie Langenbrunner all topped the 20-goal plateau but it was a defense still anchored by Scott Stevens, Scott Niedermayer and Bryan Rafalski that made the difference. Martin Brodeur won 41 games, setting an NHL record with his fourth career 40-win season, while posting a goals-against average of 2.02 and a save percentage of .914. As a team, the Devils allowed just 166 goals, tying the Flyers for the Jennings Trophy as the NHL's best defensive team. Brodeur would also receive the Vezina Trophy for the first time in his career.

New Jersey was at its defensive best as they opened the playoffs with three straight wins over the Bruins. After a 5–1 defeat in game four at Boston, the Devils bounced back for a 3–0 victory that wrapped up the series at home. It was Brodeur's second shutout of the five-game set. Next up was the surprising Tampa Bay Lightning, who had held off Washington for top spot in the Southeast Division then knocked them out of the postseason with four straight wins after dropping the first two games of the series. The Devils had had a week off between games and though their offense was slow to respond, the defense was at its smothering best in game one. The Lightning managed only 15 shots on goal, and the red hot Jamie Langenbrunner finally broke a scoreless tie with a goal and an assist in the third period to spark the Devils to a 3–0 victory. New Jersey went on to take the series in five hard-fought games, typified by the 2–1 triple overtime victory in the finale. Grant Marshall, who prior to game two had never scored a playoff goal in 65 career postseason games (a record among NHL forwards) netted the game winner at 11:12 of the third extra session.

The Devils were back in the Eastern Conference final for the third time in four years, this time taking on the Ottawa Senators. The two teams had not hooked up in a postseason series since the opening round of 1998 when the Senators stunned New Jersey in the franchise's first playoff appearance. After an eight-day layoff following their victory over Tampa, the Devils came out quickly against Ottawa in game one, but two quick goals gave the Senators a 2–0 lead after 20 minutes. New Jersey scored twice in the second, but after a scoreless third period, Shaun Van Allen gave Ottawa a 3–2 victory on a neat give-and-go with Martin Havlat at 3:08 of overtime.

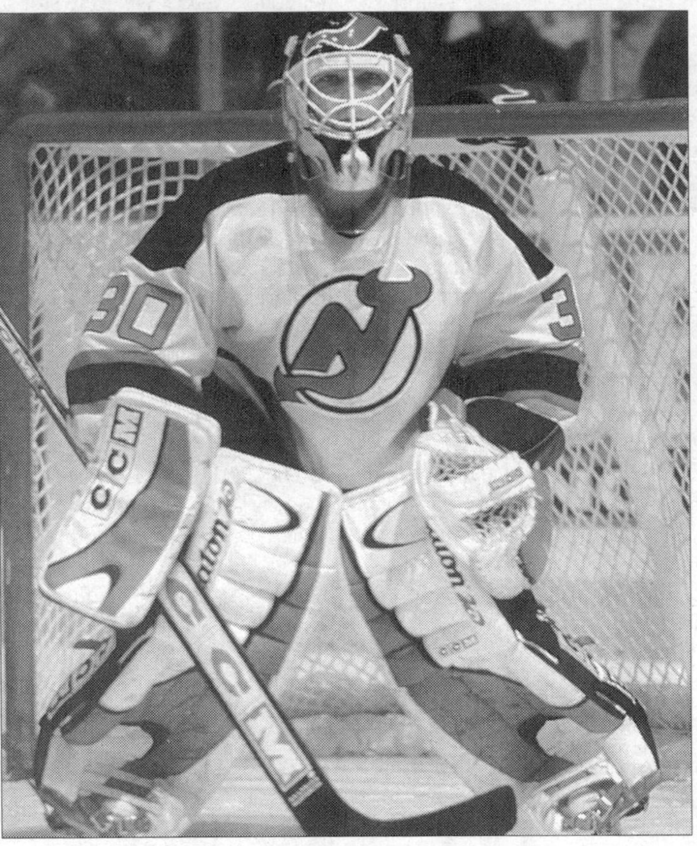

Martin Brodeur set a playoff record with seven shutouts in the 2003 postseason. With 64 regular-season shutouts in his career, Brodeur has a shot at Terry Sawchuk's record of 103.

New Jersey bounced back with a 4–1 win in game two and headed home to the Meadowlands where they were a perfect 6–0 in the playoffs. They kept their streak alive with a 1–0 victory in game three. Sergei Brylin scored the only goal of the game in the first period and Martin Brodeur finished with 24 saves in a game the Devils dominated more than the scoreboard indicates. Coach Pat Burns called it "probably one of the best games we've played defensively in the playoffs." After a 2–2 tie through 40 minutes in game four, the Devils scored three third-period goals for a 5–2 victory and a 3–1 series lead. New Jersey had a chance to wrap up the series in Ottawa in game five, but the Senators stayed a live with a 3–1 win and sent the series back to New Jersey. This time, home ice failed them as the Devils dropped a 2–1 decision in overtime and had to head back to the Corel Centre for a final showdown. Ottawa scored early in game seven, but the Devils scored twice in the second. Jamie Langenbrunner, who'd scored seven times in the playoffs but not once in this series, notched both goals just 1:54 apart early in the frame. Ottawa got the equalizer early in the third period, but Jeff Friesen's goal with 2:14 left in regulation time lifted the Devils to a wild 3-2 win.

New Jersey would be making its third appearance in the Stanley Cup finals in four years, and its fourth in nine. Facing the Devils were the surprising Mighty Ducks of Anaheim, who had romped through the playoffs with upsets of Detroit and Dallas, then swept the Minnesota Wild in the Western Conference final. Anaheim had 10 days off before game one of the Stanley Cup, and were perhaps a bit rusty in the opener. As in game seven against the Senators, Jeff Friesen was the goal-scoring hero. The former Duck broke a scoreless tie early in the second period, then iced a 3–0 win with an open-net goal late in the third. Oleg Tverdovsky, another former Duck who had come to New Jersey in the same trade for Petr Sykora that delivered Friesen, set up two goals in game two as the Devils scored another 3–0 victory. The Ducks, who had opened their Minnesota series with three straight shutouts, had now been blanked twice in a row. The Devils had held them to just 16 shots in each game as Martin Brodeur tied Dominik Hasek's postseason record with six playoff shutouts. The Ducks finally put some pucks past Brodeur in game three, including a fluky goal midway through the second period that bounced in off Brodeur's stick when he dropped it while trying to play a dump-in from Sandis Ozolinsh. Still, it took an overtime goal for Anaheim to emerge with a 3–2 victory. The Ducks then tied the series with another overtime victory. Steve Thomas netted the game winner after just 39 seconds and Ducks playoff hero Jean-Sebastien Giguere made 24 saves in a 1–0 win.

A tight, defensive series broke open in game five when the

Devils scored a 6–3 victory to move within one win of the Stanley Cup. Petr Sykora had put the Ducks on top just 42 seconds into the game, but the Devils responded with two quick goals. The first period ended 2–2, and the Devils scored twice more in the second to take a 4–3 lead. New Jersey had won 27 straight playoff games when leading after two periods. Jamie Langenbrunner made sure the streak reached 28, icing the game with two third-period goals and moving into top spot among playoff point scorers. (Langenbrunner would lead all postseason performers with 11 goals, and tied teammate Scott Niedermayer with 18 points.)

The Devils had a chance to wrap up the series at Anaheim in game six, but home ice continued to rule the series as the Ducks scored an impressive 5–2 victory. Each team had won three games on home ice, with the edge returning to the Devils for game seven. "We had a great opportunity to finish the series," said defenseman Scott Niedermayer, "and we let it slip away. Now, we have to settle down and get it going at home." New Jersey had let a 3–2 series lead slip away in the Stanley Cup final versus Colorado in 2001, but this time the Devils would be in the Meadowlands for game seven, where they were 11–1 during the playoffs. They made it a record 12 wins at home with a 3–0 victory that capped the first final since 1965 to see the home team win every game.

One of the NHL's best defensive forwards, John Madden has helped the Devils win the Stanley Cup twice in his first four full seasons.

Martin Brodeur tied a record with his third shutout of the final, and set a new one with his seventh of the playoffs. Scott Stevens, Scott Niedermayer, Sergei Brylin and Ken Daneyko were also members of all three Devils champions. Daneyko had taken part in every playoff game in Devils history until coach Pat Burns decided to sit him down during the Ottawa series. He finally returned to action in game seven of the finals, and was on the ice in the final minute. Joe Nieuwendyk also became a three-time champion, though he became just the ninth player in NHL history to win the Cup with three different teams (Calgary in 1989 and Dallas in 1999). Nieuwendyk was an emotional catalyst for the Devils, even though he could not play a game in the finals due to a torn oblique muscle in his left side. Nieuwendyk's absence created a spot in the lineup for Mike Rupp, who had suited up in game four against the Ducks and was a hero in game seven. The 6'5", 235-pound forward tipped in a drive from Niedermayer to break a scoreless tie early in the second period, then helped set up Jeff Friesen for the game's other two goals.

"This is so hard to win," said captain Scott Stevens. "I never would have thought this would have happened again, but we started at the beginning of the year and we built and worked hard as a team. We've got a lot of character and guys worked hard together. All year, we found a way to win. It was never easy for us to win all the games we won. We had 108 points, but all of those were close games, hard-fought games. Once again, we found a way to win, we found a way to win this last game of the year."

New York Americans

(includes Brooklyn Americans)

Though they were the first NHL team in Manhattan, the New York Americans played second-fiddle to the New York Rangers during most of their run on Broadway. Yet in their own bizarre way, the star-spangled skaters generated excitement both on the ice and off. They entered the NHL for the 1925–26 season, one year before the Rangers were granted a franchise, and became a barometer for future NHL expansion.

At a time when journalist Damon Runyon was glorifying the guys and dolls of Broadway, the New York Americans boasted a list of characters that could have filled Runyon's columns. By far the best was William V. Dwyer, founder of the Amerks (as the newspapers called them), who also happened to be one of America's most notorious bootleggers during the Prohibition years of the Roaring Twenties.

Not especially versed in hockey, Dwyer happened upon the Americans in a curious way. Having already expanded to Boston, the NHL targeted Manhattan as its next site but lacked a buyer. William MacBeth, a Canadian who wrote for the New York Herald-Tribune, knew about the NHL's interest and believed that hockey would become a cash cow in America's largest city. Friendly with Dwyer, MacBeth persuaded the liquor boss to buy the waiting New York franchise, knowing that George "Tex" Rickard, impresario of the new Madison Square Garden, had been persuaded to include ice-making facilities in his arena. Since Rickard was lukewarm to hockey, Dwyer made his move.

Understanding the importance of a strong Broadway opening, Dwyer purchased the Hamilton Tigers and moved them to New York. The Tigers had finished in first place during the 1924–25 season, but the franchise was ripe for relocation because the Hamilton players had pulled a protest walkout during the playoffs. For $75,000 Dwyer was able to obtain a team that was primed to be instantly competitive, with top talents like Billy Burch and brothers Red and Shorty Green—plus a speedy addition from Western Canada who would immediately catch the fans' fancy, "Bullet" Joe Simpson.

The Americans played their first NHL game at the Garden on December 15, 1925, against the Montreal Canadiens. Although they lost, 3–1, the Amerks impressed everyone, including the legion of New York City bluebloods who graced the arena. With MacBeth handling their publicity and Tommy Gorman managing them, the Americans became an instant hit. Unfortunately, the press agent overplayed his hand in touting Simpson as "The Blue Streak from Saskatoon" and Burch as "The Babe Ruth of Hockey." Unschooled in the fundamentals, New York fans seized upon the nicknames. They immediately made these two players their favorites, and demanded goals from them.

"Every time one of them passed to another player," wrote Frank Graham Sr., who covered sports for the New York Sun, "the spectators howled in rage and disappointment. Seeking to please the customers, Billy and Joe did as little passing as possible. This resulted in spectacular but futile one-man raids on enemy nets and a rapid disintegration of the team play necessary to ensure victories."

Still, the Americans proved so popular that Madison Square Garden ownership decided to obtain a big-league team of its own despite the fact that Dwyer had an unwritten "guarantee" from the Garden that his club would have sole rights to the New York area. Unfortunately, the bootlegger was in no position to take issue with Garden president Colonel John Hammond. Dwyer had been nailed by the feds over an elaborate rum-running scheme. (He would be

The first New York Americans team doesn't quite seem ready to pose for a team picture outside of Madison Square Garden in October of 1925.

dispatched to Atlanta Penitentiary for two years in June, 1927.) Meanwhile, what infuriated Dwyer most about the Garden's New York Rangers was the rent-free status enjoyed by the new franchise compared with his Amerks, whose own rent bill grew steeper by the season. These indignities sparked a rivalry that quickly flamed into one of the best in a city that featured the Brooklyn Dodgers versus the New York Giants and, if a World Series meeting took place, either of these clubs against the New York Yankees.

Despite Roy Worters' peerless goaltending, the Americans rarely were as good as the Rangers. When the Broadway Blueshirts won their first Stanley Cup in their second season (1927–28), they instantly became the darlings of New York hockey while the Amerks took on the image of also-rans. By 1933, the Americans were still Cup-less while the Rangers had won their second championship. Although Dwyer remained a member of the NHL Board of Governors until 1937, his fiscal infusions into his hockey club had ended. Big Bill went broke after the government won a $3.7 million action against him, causing the league to take over the team in 1936–37. That, plus the end of Prohibition, finished Dwyer but not the Amerks.

Mervyn "Red" Dutton, who had become playing coach, was the scion of a wealthy western Canadian contracting family. With the Great Depression playing havoc with finances, Dutton occasionally had shelled out money to Dwyer. Now the team was his to run. Despite the Depression and other hardships, Dutton managed to keep the Americans afloat. Deft trades for veteran castoffs and the addition of unproven rookies enabled him to ice a competitive team that nearly challenged for the Stanley Cup in 1937–38. That year the Americans finished second in the Canadian Division and faced the Rangers in a best-of-three series to open the playoffs. The clubs split the first two games before the largest crowd of the season (16,340) jammed the arena for the deciding contest. The Rangers jumped into a 2–0 lead, but Lorne Carr and Nels Stewart tied the game for the Amerks and sent it into overtime. Neither team could break the tie for three sudden-death periods until Carr finally scored the winner for the Americans 40 seconds into the fourth overtime period.

Playing on the Americans' top forward line with Lorne Carr and Sweeney Schriner, Art Chapman led the NHL in assists in 1934–35 and 1935–36.

"That," Dutton stated, "was the greatest thrill I ever got in hockey. The Rangers had a high-priced team then, and beating them was like winning the Stanley Cup to us."

Unfortunately, the Americans were knocked out of the playoffs by Chicago in the next round and were never to achieve such lofty heights again. They did reach the playoffs in each of the next two seasons, but they finished dead last in 1940–41. By then World War II had broken out, and many Canadian-born players quit hockey to join the armed forces. Dutton lost 14 of 16 players to the Canadian army and other branches of the services.

When the 1941–42 season started, Dutton changed the club's name to the Brooklyn Americans. "We had fans mostly from Brooklyn," he said, "while the Rangers had the hotsy-totsy ones from New York." However, all Americans' home games were still played at the Garden and this token gesture did little to stimulate a Brooklyn–New York rivalry. The Amerks finished last again, but had come up with young players like goalie Chuck Rayner and defenseman Pat Egan, who showed considerable promise. However, the war effort soon took Rayner and several other Americans, and at the start of the 1942–43 season, Dutton was forced to fold the club just when he was starting to pull out from under the debris of the Dwyer days. "It looked as though we were going to come out of it all right. A couple more years and we would have run the Rangers right out of the rink." Instead, the Americans vanished and a glorious hockey era came to a sad close.

New York Americans

Year-by-Year Record

Season	GP	W	L	T	GF	GA	Pts	Finish	Division	Playoff Results
1925–26	36	12	20	4	68	89	28	4th	Canadian	Out of Playoffs
1926–27	44	17	25	2	82	91	36	4th	Canadian	Out of Playoffs
1927–28	44	11	27	6	63	128	28	5th	Canadian	Out of Playoffs
1928–29	44	19	13	12	53	53	50	2nd	Canadian	Lost Quarterfinal
1929–30	44	14	25	5	113	161	33	5th	Canadian	Out of Playoffs
1930–31	44	18	16	10	76	74	46	4th	Canadian	Out of Playoffs
1931–32	48	16	24	8	95	142	40	4th	Canadian	Out of Playoffs
1932–33	48	15	22	11	91	118	41	4th	Canadian	Out of Playoffs
1933–34	48	15	23	10	104	132	40	4th	Canadian	Out of Playoffs
1934–35	48	12	27	9	100	142	33	4th	Canadian	Out of Playoffs
1935–36	48	16	25	7	109	122	39	3rd	Canadian	Lost Semifinal
1936–37	48	15	29	4	122	161	34	4th	Canadian	Out of Playoffs
1937–38	48	19	18	11	110	111	49	2nd	Canadian	Lost Semifinal
1938–39	48	17	21	10	119	157	44	4th	...	Lost Quarterfinal
1939–40	48	15	29	4	106	140	34	6th	...	Lost Quarterfinal
1940–41	48	8	29	11	99	186	27	7th	...	Out of Playoffs
1941–42	48	16	29	3	133	175	35	7th	...	Out of Playoffs

New York Islanders

THE HISTORY OF HOCKEY in Nassau and Suffolk counties, which comprise Long Island, dates back to amateur leagues of the 1930s and various minor pro clubs that emerged in the years after World War II. When Nassau Veterans' Memorial Coliseum was designed in 1970, the NHL decided to place an expansion franchise on Long Island as well as another in Atlanta. Businessman Roy Boe, who already owned the New York Nets of the infant American Basketball Association, badly wanted to add big-league hockey to his portfolio.

The NHL was asking $6 million per franchise, so Boe persuaded 19 other investors besides him to purchase the franchise and pay off a $4 million territorial fee to the Rangers, who were a mere 25 miles away. He also hired William Arthur (Bill) Torrey, who had previously been chief executive of the Oakland Seals, as his general manager. Torrey's task was daunting because the World Hockey Association was also set to debut in October, 1972.

Torrey's opening season nucleus included coach Phil Goyette, a former Montreal Canadiens and Rangers ace; top draft pick Billy Harris, a fleet right wing with a powerful shot; versatile checking forward Ed Westfall, who had played for two Stanley Cup-winning Bruins teams; and rugged defenseman Gerry Hart.

Other members of the first-year club included Gerry Desjardins, the former Chicago goalie who had a permanently bent arm following an injury, and flame-haired Terry Crisp, who had been an effective utility player with the St. Louis Blues. One of Torrey's most colorful additions would be a 24-year-old out of the U.S. hockey system—goaltender Glenn "Chico" Resch, though Resch would not reach the NHL for a few seasons yet.

The Islanders' first season opened on October 7, 1972, when a crowd of 12,221 turned out to see the Islanders lose 3–2 to the Flames. Westfall scored the first goal in Islanders' history and would prove to be a formidable captain during the team's formative years. On October 12, 1972, the Isles won their first NHL game, beating the Kings 3–2 at Inglewood, but after 25 games, the Islanders had only three wins, two ties and 20 losses. Although the club admittedly was weak, it had hoped to be more competitive. After considerable review, Torrey decided in midseason to replace Goyette with Earl Ingarfield.

Ingarfield replaced Goyette as coach on January 29, 1973, but the results were hardly encouraging. No fewer than 32 players would wear the blue and orange that first season, and none of them would collect more than 50 points. As expected, Billy Harris, the Long Island hunk, led the team with 28 goals; no one else had more than 19. At one point, the team lost 12 straight games, never won more than three in a row, and in one particularly futile stretch compiled a 1–20–1 record on the road.

The team's overall won-lost record showed that the Islanders had captured only 12 games, a record low, and lost 60, a record high. They finished 72 points behind the Rangers, who nevertheless had helped the Islanders forge the kind of white-hot rivalry Boe had envisioned—even though the Rangers won all six regular-season meetings by outscoring the upstarts from Long Island, 25–5. Among the rookies, the most encouraging were pugnacious Garry Howatt and hard-working Bob Nystrom, who were elevated to the big club in March, 1973.

The Islanders' last-place finish guaranteed them the first pick in the Amateur Draft, which was one of the best in history. Torrey resisted several offers from Canadiens general manager Sam Pollock, and made Denis Potvin of the Ottawa 67's his top choice. When Ingarfield asked to be relieved of the coaching job, Torrey offered the position to bespectacled Al Arbour.

A junior scoring sensation, Billy Harris was the first player drafted by the Islanders in 1972. He was traded to Los Angeles for Butch Goring late in the 1979–80 campaign.

The addition of Arbour to his general staff was one of Torrey's most meaningful moves. Arbour quickly brought discipline and toughness to the sophomore—and sometimes sophomoric—Islanders. Under Goyette, the team regularly had broken training rules, but Arbour changed all that. An 11 p.m. curfew on the eve of games was instituted and rigorously enforced, and Arbour began fining players who were late, whether it was for the bus, the plane or practice. The strict new regime began on the first day of training camp, when Arbour insisted that each and every player jog from the motel to the practice rink.

Even with Arbour, Potvin and Westfall, the Islanders struggled in 1973–74, finishing last (19–41–18) in the Eastern Division with the second-worst record in the entire league. They did gain respect in goal. Billy Smith had emerged as a combative netminder with a knack of making the hardest saves at the most critical moments. Smith and Resch would become a tandem through the club's first Stanley Cup season.

It wasn't until the autumn of 1974 that the Isles began turning the competitive corner. Torrey had selected Clark Gillies, a big left wing, as his first draft pick and later added Gillies' pal, Bob Bourne, a swift left wing. At midseason, Torrey completed a landmark trade with Minnesota, obtaining left wing J.P. Parise and center Jude Drouin. Working with Westfall, Parise and Drouin provided New York with a dependable scoring and checking line. In a neck-and-neck battle with Atlanta for a final playoff berth, the Islanders prevailed in the homestretch, finishing with 33 wins compared to 19 the previous season.

The 1975 playoff experience figured to be remarkably short. Facing the Islanders in the first round was a powerful Rangers squad sprinkled with future Hall of Famers such as Rod Gilbert, Brad Park and Ed Giacomin. The best-of-three series was expected to be completed with a two-straight Rangers rout because of experience and talent.

Instead, the Islanders won with a stirring sudden-death victory on Parise's goal—on a pass from Drouin—with only 11 seconds elapsed in overtime. They advanced to the second round against a Pittsburgh Penguins franchise that also was rated a prohibitive favorite. For three games, the Isles appeared lost, but, facing elimination, they won three in a row. Not only did they tie the series but a folk hero was born after goalie Chico Resch smothered a shot by Ron Schock that had rebounded to him after it had hit the goal post. Resch pulled himself to his feet and kissed the red piping, an act that forever endeared him to the fans.

In another melodramatic moment, Westfall ended the series by breaking a 0–0 tie late in the third period of the seventh game with a backhand past goalie Gary Inness. Thus the Isles found their place in history alongside the 1942 Toronto Maple Leafs, as the only NHL clubs to have surmounted a three-game deficit in the playoffs to win four straight. Defying all odds, the Islanders next took on the defending champion Philadelphia Flyers, lost three straight and then rebounded for another remarkable comeback. With the series tied at three and the deciding game in Philadelphia, the Flyers took no chances, producing their club's ultimate good luck charm.

Kate Smith had sung "God Bless America" before many Flyers games—either in person or on tape—and Philadelphia had a record of 40–3–1 on those occasions. Islanders captain Ed Westfall attempted to change the luck by presenting Kate with a bouquet of yellow roses. It didn't work; Philadelphia triumphed, 4–1. But, the Isles' miracle run had a long-term benefit for the team. Beating the Rangers gave them bragging rights in the New York Metropolitan area, and the two separate comeback performances captured the imagination of NHL fans, while boosting the young club's confidence. Meanwhile, Torrey continued building the foundation of what eventually would be a dynasty.

To his promising attacking corps Torrey added rugged center Bryan Trottier for the 1975–76 season and a year later Mike Bossy was picked first (15th overall) in the 1977 draft. Gillies, Trottier and Bossy would in time become Trio Grande, the best line ever to skate in Nassau. Gifted though they were, the Islanders were missing a key element in team chemistry and balance. This was evident when underdog Toronto eliminated them in a vicious, seven-game 1978 playoff that was followed a year later by a humiliating six-game series loss to the Rangers after the Isles had become the first expansion team to lead the NHL with a 51–15–14 mark.

Torrey made changes. He added World Hockey Association defenseman Dave Langevin and gold medal Olympian Ken Morrow after the U.S. won at Lake Placid in 1980, but his most important move was obtaining center Butch Goring from Los Angeles.

"With Butchie at center," said Denis Potvin, "there was a sense of hope we didn't have before." Sure enough, the revitalized Islanders reached the Stanley Cup finals against the Flyers. Leading three games to two, the Isles hosted the sixth game on a warm spring afternoon. The game was tied 4–4 when the biggest goal in franchise history was scored. Bob Nystrom took a pass from John Tonelli and beat Pete Peeters at 7:11 of overtime.

Nystrom's goal was the start of something big. The Islanders won additional Stanley Cup titles in 1981, 1982 and 1983. The victims, successively, were Minnesota, Vancouver and Edmonton, the latter two exiting in four straight games while the North Stars lasted five.

To maintain the dynasty, Torrey continually juggled his roster. Additions such as defensemen Gord Lane and Mike McEwen played pivotal roles in the Cup years, as did forwards Wayne Merrick and Anders Kallur. But, the steady work of tempestuous goalie Billy Smith provided the last line of defense so necessary to a champion. For grit there was the Sutter brothers, Duane and Brent, as well as underrated defensemen Stefan Persson and fellow Swede Tomas Jonsson.

In their "Drive for Five," the Islanders came close. They etched their names in the history book by completing a total of 19 consecutive playoff series victories when they won the first three rounds of the 1984 playoffs. But, by the time they reached the finals against a young, healthy Edmonton team, Al Arbour's

New York Islanders

Year-by-Year Record

Season	GP	W	L	T	OL	GF	GA	Pts.	Finish	Division	Playoff Result
1972-73	78	12	60	6	...	170	347	30	8th	East Div.	Out of Playoffs
1973-74	78	19	41	18	...	182	247	56	8th	East Div.	Out of Playoffs
1974-75	80	33	25	22	...	264	221	88	3rd	Patrick Div.	Lost Semifinal
1975-76	80	42	21	17	...	297	190	101	2nd	Patrick Div.	Lost Semifinal
1976-77	80	47	21	12	...	288	193	106	2nd	Patrick Div.	Lost Semifinal
1977-78	80	48	17	15	...	334	210	111	1st	Patrick Div.	Lost Quarterfinal
1978-79	80	51	15	14	...	358	214	116	1st	Patrick Div.	Lost Semifinal
1979-80	80	39	28	13	...	281	247	91	2nd	Patrick Div.	Won Stanley Cup
1980-81	80	48	18	14	...	355	260	110	1st	Patrick Div.	Won Stanley Cup
1981-82	80	54	16	10	...	385	250	118	1st	Patrick Div.	Won Stanley Cup
1982-83	80	42	26	12	...	302	226	96	2nd	Patrick Div.	Won Stanley Cup
1983-84	80	50	26	4	...	357	269	104	1st	Patrick Div.	Lost Final
1984-85	80	40	34	6	...	345	312	86	3rd	Patrick Div.	Lost Div. Final
1985-86	80	39	29	12	...	327	284	90	3rd	Patrick Div.	Lost Div. Semifinal
1986-87	80	35	33	12	...	279	281	82	3rd	Patrick Div.	Lost Div. Final
1987-88	80	39	31	10	...	308	267	88	1st	Patrick Div.	Lost Div. Semifinal
1988-89	80	28	47	5	...	265	325	61	6th	Patrick Div.	Out of Playoffs
1989-90	80	31	38	11	...	281	288	73	4th	Patrick Div.	Lost Div. Semifinal
1990-91	80	25	45	10	...	223	290	60	6th	Patrick Div.	Out of Playoffs
1991-92	80	34	35	11	...	291	299	79	5th	Patrick Div.	Out of Playoffs
1992-93	84	40	37	7	...	335	297	87	3rd	Patrick Div.	Lost Conf. Finals
1993-94	84	36	36	12	...	282	264	84	4th	Atlantic Div.	Lost Conf. Quarterfinal
1994-95	48	15	28	5	...	126	158	35	7th	Atlantic Div.	Out of Playoffs
1995-96	82	22	50	10	...	229	315	54	7th	Atlantic Div.	Out of Playoffs
1996-97	82	29	41	12	...	240	250	70	7th	Atlantic Div.	Out of Playoffs
1997-98	82	30	41	11	...	212	225	71	4th	Atlantic Div.	Out of Playoffs
1998-99	82	24	48	10	...	194	244	58	5th	Atlantic Div.	Out of Playoffs
99-2000	82	24	48	9	1	194	275	58	5th	Atlantic Div.	Out of Playoffs
2000-01	82	21	51	7	3	185	268	52	5th	Atlantic Div.	Out of Playoffs
2001-02	82	42	28	8	4	239	220	96	2nd	Atlantic Div.	Lost Conf. Quarterfinal
2002-03	82	35	34	11	2	224	231	83	3rd	Atlantic Div.	Lost Conf. Quarterfinal

skaters were wounded beyond repair. They split the first two games on Long Island before flying to Edmonton and three straight games at Northlands Coliseum. By the end of the fifth game, the league had a new champion and Torrey returned to the drawing board to reshape his squad.

Two key additions—forwards Pat LaFontaine and Patrick Flatley—fortified the attack, while Kelly Hrudey was designated the number-two goalie behind Bill Smith. But, the shocker was Arbour's decision to retire after 13 seasons behind the Islanders bench. He was replaced by Terry Simpson, who was pacing the matting on April 18–19, 1987, when the Islanders participated in their longest game. Played at Capital Centre in Landover, Maryland, the seventh game of the Washington–Islanders series lasted until 8:47 of the fourth overtime period when LaFontaine beat goalie Bob Mason just seconds before 2 a.m.

The Islanders remained competitive through the late 1980s under the ownership of John Pickett. In 1987–88, they won the Patrick Division title and faced New Jersey in the opening playoff round. The Devils had gained a playoff berth on the final night of the season and seemed to be easy pickings, but New Jersey physically manhandled the Islanders and wiped them out in six games. Not only were the Isles eliminated but they lost their best defenseman, Denis Potvin, to retirement, and a severe depression settled over the club in 1988–89 when they finished with a record of 28–47–5, their worst season since the second year of the franchise. Bill Smith retired, leaving youthful Mark Fitzpatrick and Jeff Hackett to battle for the goaltending job.

Denis Potvin ties up the Flyers' Reggie Leach in front of Billy Smith. Potvin was selected first overall by the Islanders in the 1973 Amateur Draft to become the foundation for their developing team. He later captained the Islanders to four straight Stanley Cup victories.

Torrey persuaded Arbour to come out of retirement, but there was little improvement until late in the 1989–90 season when the Isles were able to clinch a playoff berth on the final night of the season by beating Philadelphia while Buffalo toppled Pittsburgh. It was the next-to-last high point of what would become a terribly disappointing decade. Only in 1992–93 was there a renaissance, as a gutsy team including Ray Ferraro, Steve Thomas, Benoit Hogue and Tom Fitzgerald kept them competitive, while Pierre Turgeon—obtained from Buffalo in a deal for Pat LaFontaine—led the scoring and ebullient Glenn Healy surfaced as the new netminding favorite.

The Islanders beat Washington in six games to open the playoffs, but the bad news was a blindside cheap shot delivered by Dale Hunter of the Capitals against Turgeon that left the star with a shoulder separation and concussion. Undaunted, the Isles next took favored Pittsburgh to a seventh game and won it at the Igloo when Czech-born David Volek steered a Ferraro pass behind Tom Barrasso at 5:16 of overtime to complete the upset. The dream ended in the next round as the eventual Stanley Cup-winning Montreal Canadiens ousted the Islanders in five games.

A number of personnel moves changed the team's chemistry, although it did manage another playoff berth in 1994. With Healy moved to the Rangers, Ron Hextall became the resident goaltender. On some nights he was peerless and others powerless. But, in a tense stretch drive, he enabled his new club to gain a playoff berth with a 2–0 win over the Lightning at Tampa Bay during the last week of the regular season.

Facing the Rangers in the first round, the Islanders—especially Hextall—disintegrated, losing four straight and setting the stage for a dismal playoff drought through the remainder of the 1990s. Adding insult to injury was Pickett's decision to sell the team to so-called tycoon John Spano. Before the sale could be consummated, Spano was indicted on several fraud counts and eventually sentenced to prison.

Pickett regained control of the team and in 1997 sold the Islanders to New York Sports Ventures, a group headed by Steven Gluckstern, Howard Milstein, Edward Milstein and David Seldin. The new owners took command during the 1997–98 season, another disappointing year during which general manager Mike Milbury fired coach Rick Bowness and finished the year behind the bench himself. Trades dominated the Islanders agenda in 1998–99 and 1999–2000, with players such as 1997 Calder Trophy winner Bryan Berard, scoring star Ziggy Palffy and captain Trevor Linden all shipped out. Hope for the future existed in former Stanley Cup star Butch Goring, who was hired to coach the team on April 30, 1999, and in the first-overall 2000 Entry Draft selection of Boston University goaltending Rick DiPietro. Most important of all, the Islanders' ownership was resolved with the $175 million sale of the team to software billionaire Charles Wang of Long Island-based Computer Associates in April 2000. The NHL Board of Governors approved the sale to Wang and Sanjay Kumar on June 20, 2000. Said NHL commissioner Gary Bettman: "We are optimistic we will see some positive steps that will begin to put the franchise back on the firm footing it had for so many years."

Though better times really were on the horizon, the Islanders missed the playoffs for the seventh straight season in 2000–01. In fact, with just 52 points, the Islanders struggled through their worst season since the club's inaugural campaign of 1972–73. The poor performance cost an Islanders legend his coaching job, as Butch Goring was let go after less than two full seasons on the job.

Given the increased resources now at his disposal, general manager Mike Milbury moved quickly to address the team's problems for 2001–02. The result was a 44-point improvement that ranks as the fourth-biggest single-season turnaround in NHL history. Among Milbury's first moves was the hiring of Peter Laviolette as his new man behind the bench. A successful minor league coach, Laviolette had spent one year as an assistant in Boston before joining the Islanders. Like Al Arbour before him, Laviolette instilled a new positive attitude and a fierce work ethic from the first day of training camp. Milbury's most important player acquisitions came in deals made during the 2001 NHL Draft. On June 23, 2001, he sent Zdeno Chara, Bill Muckalt and two draft picks to Ottawa for Alexei Yashin. A day later, Milbury acquired Michael Peca from the Sabres for Tim Connolly and Taylor Pyatt. Just prior to the start of the 2001–02 season, goaltender Chris Osgood was claimed from Detroit in the Waiver Draft.

Peca was named the team captain just days before the season began. He scored 25 goals and established career highs in assists (35) and points (60). Still as good a two-way player as ever, Peca earned the Selke Trophy as the NHL's best defensive forward. Alexei Yashin proved to be the offensive catalyst the Islanders needed, leading the club with 32 goals, 43 assists and 75 points. Mark Parrish, acquired by Milbury the year before, established career highs in goals (30), assists (30) and points (60). Roman Hamrlik, Adrian Aucoin and Kenny Jonsson anchored a much-improved defense. The Islanders finished the year with a record of 42–28–8–4 and 96 points. They returned to the playoffs for the first time since 1993–94, but were eliminated in seven games in a fierce first-round matchup with the Toronto Maple Leafs.

Michael Peca suffered a serious knee injury during the Leafs series. He was still on the sidelines to start the 2002–03 season and the Islanders struggled without their captain. Peca returned to action on November 14, only to hurt his knee again. However, he was back in the lineup two days later and the team began to improve its play. Still, the Islanders went right down to the wire before finally holding off the Rangers for the eighth and final playoff spot in the Eastern Conference. Alexei Yashin slumped for much of the season, but got hot down the stretch and wound up as the team's top scorer with 65 points (26 goals, 39 assists). Dave Scatchard led the team with 27 goals, while Jason Blake and Mark Parrish also topped the 20-goal plateau. Chris Osgood was the only Islanders goaltender to post a winning record, but the emergence of Rick DiPietro allowed the Isles to ship Osgood to St. Louis at the trade deadline. Garth Snow sparkled in the opening game of the playoffs, making 25 saves for his first career postseason shutout as the Islanders shocked the first-overall Ottawa Senators with a 3–0 victory. Ottawa players had seemed to go out of their way to run at former Senator Yashin, who scored the second goal of the opening game and was the best player on the ice.

Michael Peca was a high-scoring center in junior hockey who has become one of the NHL's top defensive forwards. He brought new on-ice leadership to the Islanders in 2001–02.

The Islanders were 22–2 in their playoff history when they won the first game of a series. However, Ottawa played the rest of the series like the team that had finished the season 30 points ahead of the Islanders (113–83) and wrapped it up with four straight wins. "The overtime loss (in game three) in New York kind of gave them control," said Yashin. "I feel we played some good games, but we just couldn't get any goals."

The positive feelings after the team's seven-game loss to Toronto were definitely missing after the five-game loss to Ottawa, and despite the team's success over the past two seasons, Mike Milbury decided to make a coaching change. It would mark the seventh time in his seven-plus seasons as the club's g.m. that Milbury had fired his coach, including himself twice. "Ultimately this decision was made because the line of communication between the players and the coach snapped," Milbury explained. "When that line of communication is snapped, it is impossible to secure it again."

The new man behind the bench for the Islanders in 2003–04 will be Steve Stirling, who had spent the previous two seasons with the club's AHL farm team.

New York Rangers

The Rangers were born out of a New York City hockey boom that was rooted in a popular series of exhibition games played at the old St. Nicholas Arena on Manhattan's Upper West Side shortly after the turn of the century. But, it wasn't until the ice game's popularity was confirmed on a big-league level in 1925–26 by the New York Americans that the Broadway Blueshirts finally were awarded an NHL franchise.

None of this would have been possible had a Kansas City-born, Texas-bred entrepreneur named George Lewis Rickard not made a fortune promoting fights in New York. By 1924, when the New York Life Insurance Company decided to raze old Madison Square Garden and build a 40-story office building, Rickard had become Manhattan's most renowned sportsman. He rounded up a syndicate of businessmen—his self-proclaimed "600 millionaires"—and organized the Madison Square Garden Corporation. By December 15, 1925, the new Garden was up and flourishing, with its lone NHL tenant, the New York Americans, playing the Montreal Canadiens.

Once Rickard realized that hockey was a hit on Broadway, he concluded that the Garden should organize its own team—the Americans were merely renting the arena—and, along with MSG president Colonel John S. Hammond, laid the groundwork for a second New York franchise. Rickard and Hammond designated Conn Smythe, a bright, young Torontonian who already had a reputation for successfully managing hockey teams, to organize the Rangers. Since the strong-willed Hammond paid close attention to the hockey club, the Colonel and Smythe developed a strong but stormy relationship.

Smythe adroitly signed a nucleus of superb players, including the amateur defense pair of Ivan "Ching" Johnson and Clarence "Taffy" Abel, names soon to become bywords among New York sports fans. By far Smythe's best moves were the acquisitions of center Frank Boucher, left wing Fred "Bun" Cook and right wing Bill Cook. The brothers Cook and Boucher—all future Hall of Famers—would comprise one of the finest forward lines ever to grace the NHL.

Smythe also chose wisely in goal with Lorne Chabot and when the Rangers gathered for their first training camp at Toronto's little Ravina rink in the fall of 1926, their roster appeared competitive if not downright formidable. Unfortunately for Smythe, Hammond disagreed. He wanted more recognizable names for the New York club. Hammond wanted Smythe to sign Babe Dye, a leading scorer throughout the 1920s, but Smythe didn't feel Dye would fit in with the team-first approach he wanted his players to take. His refusal to sign Dye led to him being fired before training camp was finished.

The Colonel had been well prepared for this moment, having already summoned former Pacific Coast Hockey Association co-organizer and former player Lester Patrick to Toronto. The moment Smythe departed, Patrick became coach of the Rangers for the then astronomical fee of $18,000 a year. It marked the beginning of a long and lovely relationship.

Patrick not only oozed the kind of class that Rickard revered, he also knew as much about hockey as Smythe and proved it by taking over the Rangers without missing a beat. Beginning with an opening night 1–0 victory over the powerful Montreal Maroons on November 17, 1926, the Rangers obliged Patrick by recording a first-place finish in the newly created American Division. They also proved Smythe had been correct in his assessment of the team.

Stanley Cup hero Bryan Hextall shakes hands with coach Frank Boucher while Dutch Hiller looks on. The Rangers' victory in 1940 marked the third championship in 13 seasons. The fourth one would take a little bit longer!

Paced by the Boucher-Cook line, as well as stout defense and solid goaltending, the Rangers became immediate contenders, while coach Patrick emerged as a major personality in the Big Apple along with Babe Ruth and Lou Gehrig. "Lester didn't adjust to New York," said Americans manager Tommy Gorman, "New York adjusted to him." In only their second NHL season, the Rangers reached the Stanley Cup finals against the Maroons. They had achieved a rare balance from goal through defense to the forward lines but they had one obstacle that was unconquerable: they couldn't defeat Ringling Brothers and Barnum and Bailey.

The appearance of the elephants at playoff time would haunt the Blueshirts for nearly four decades, but playing all games on the Maroons' home ice in 1928 was hardly daunting for the Rangers. More challenging was the search for a goaltender after Chabot was injured during the second game. In an era when NHL clubs carried only one goalie, it was commonplace for teams to "borrow" a neutral netminder. Patrick asked permission to use either Alex Connell of the Ottawa Senators or a minor-leaguer, Hughie McCormick, both of whom were in the stands. When Maroons manager Eddie Gerard refused, Patrick went to his dressing room, huddled with Bun Cook and Boucher, then decided to play goal himself.

Already down one game to none, the Rangers desperately needed this win and Patrick heroically stopped all but one shot as the teams completed regulation time tied 1–1. According to Montreal Star columnist Baz O'Meara, Patrick performed "prodigious feats of netminding." The climax to the remarkable evening came when Boucher scored the game winner in overtime.

For the remainder of the series, Patrick was replaced in goal by an obscure netminder named Joe Miller, on loan from the Americans. Tied at two games apiece, the Rangers and Maroons met in game five to decide the championship. As coach Patrick had earlier, Miller held Montreal to one goal while Boucher managed both scores for New York. The final score was 2–1. In their second NHL season, the Rangers had won their first Stanley Cup. Upon returning to Manhattan, the Blueshirts were suitably hailed as conquering heroes. They were greeted on the steps of City Hall by a beaming Mayor Jimmy Walker, who was a regular at Madison Square Garden games, and a crowd of proud New Yorkers. The Rangers had arrived.

Under Patrick's orchestration, the Rangers' standard of excellence was maintained through the early 1930s, although they didn't win another Stanley Cup title until 1933. The core of the original Cup-winners was intact except for Chabot and Abel, who had been traded, when they faced Toronto in the 1933 finals. Ironically, Smythe, who was running the Maple Leafs, watched in frustration as the very players he had signed for New York dominated his Toronto skaters. Bill Cook led the Rangers to a 1–0 victory in the fourth and final game, although he was now 35 years old and supposedly past his prime.

Two Stanley Cup titles in only seven seasons were a laudable achievement for Patrick and his Rangers, who were feted in a glittering victory party at the Astor Hotel in the center of Times Square. The celebration was significant in another way because it served as an introductory platform for the Rangers' new president, General John Reed Kilpatrick. A World War I hero, Kilpatrick was the ideal boss for Patrick and the two set out to rejuvenate what was an aging hockey team. The feat was accomplished by means of an elaborate farm system that would eventually comprise the Three Rs—New Haven Ramblers, New York Rovers and Lake Placid Roamers.

However, the original revivifying sources came from Patrick's American League farm club in Philadelphia, not to mention Lester's own family. His sons, Lynn—the eldest and most productive as a scorer—and Murray had been outstanding athletes in

New York Rangers

Year-by-Year Record

Season	GP	W	L	T	OL	GF	GA	Pts.	Finish	Division	Playoff Result
1926-27	44	25	13	6	...	95	72	56	1st	Amn. Div.	Lost Quarterfinal
1927-28	44	19	16	9	...	94	79	47	2nd	Amn. Div.	Won Stanley Cup
1928-29	44	21	13	10	...	72	65	52	2nd	Amn. Div	Lost Final
1929-30	44	17	17	10	...	136	143	44	3rd	Amn. Div.	Lost Semifinal
1930-31	44	19	16	9	...	106	87	47	3rd	Amn. Div.	Lost Semifinal
1931-32	48	23	17	8	...	134	112	54	1st	Amn. Div.	Lost Final
1932-33	48	23	17	8	...	135	107	54	3rd	Amn. Div.	Won Stanley Cup
1933-34	48	21	19	8	...	120	113	50	3rd	Amn. Div.	Lost Quarterfinal
1934-35	48	22	20	6	...	137	139	50	3rd	Amn. Div.	Lost Semifinal
1935-36	48	19	17	12	...	91	96	50	4th	Amn. Div.	Out of Playoffs
1936-37	48	19	20	9	...	117	106	47	3rd	Amn. Div.	Lost Final
1937-38	48	27	15	6	...	149	96	60	2nd	Amn. Div.	Lost Quarterfinal
1938-39	48	26	16	6	...	149	105	58	2nd	...	Lost Semifinal
1939-40	48	27	11	10	...	136	77	64	2nd	...	Won Stanley Cup
1940-41	48	21	19	8	...	143	125	50	4th	...	Lost Quarterfinal
1941-42	48	29	17	2	...	177	143	60	1st	...	Lost Semifinal
1942-43	50	11	31	8	...	161	253	30	6th	...	Out of Playoffs
1943-44	50	6	39	5	...	162	310	17	6th	...	Out of Playoffs
1944-45	50	11	29	10	...	154	247	32	6th	...	Out of Playoffs
1945-46	50	13	28	9	...	144	191	35	6th	...	Out of Playoffs
1946-47	60	22	32	6	...	167	186	50	5th	...	Out of Playoffs
1947-48	60	21	26	13	...	176	201	55	4th	...	Lost Semifinal
1948-49	60	18	31	11	...	133	172	47	6th	...	Out of Playoffs
1949-50	70	28	31	11	...	170	189	67	4th	...	Lost Final
1950-51	70	20	29	21	...	169	201	61	5th	...	Out of Playoffs
1951-52	70	23	34	13	...	192	219	59	5th	...	Out of Playoffs
1952-53	70	17	37	16	...	152	211	50	6th	...	Out of Playoffs
1953-54	70	29	31	10	...	161	182	68	5th	...	Out of Playoffs
1954-55	70	17	35	18	...	150	210	52	5th	...	Out of Playoffs
1955-56	70	32	28	10	...	204	203	74	3rd	...	Lost Semifinal
1956-57	70	26	30	14	...	184	227	66	4th	...	Lost Semifinal
1957-58	70	32	25	13	...	195	188	77	2nd	...	Lost Semifinal
1958-59	70	26	32	12	...	201	217	64	5th	...	Out of Playoffs
1959-60	70	17	38	15	...	187	247	49	6th	...	Out of Playoffs
1960-61	70	22	38	10	...	204	248	54	5th	...	Out of Playoffs
1961-62	70	26	32	12	...	195	207	64	4th	...	Lost Semifinal
1962-63	70	22	36	12	...	211	233	56	5th	...	Out of Playoffs
1963-64	70	22	38	10	...	186	242	54	5th	...	Out of Playoffs
1964-65	70	20	38	12	...	179	246	52	5th	...	Out of Playoffs
1965-66	70	18	41	11	...	195	261	47	6th	...	Out of Playoffs
1966-67	70	30	28	12	...	188	189	72	4th	...	Lost Semifinal
1967-68	74	39	23	12	...	226	183	90	2nd	East Div.	Lost Quarterfinal
1968-69	76	41	26	9	...	231	196	91	3rd	East Div.	Lost Quarterfinal
1969-70	76	38	22	16	...	246	189	92	4th	East Div.	Lost Quarterfinal
1970-71	78	49	18	11	...	259	177	109	2nd	East Div.	Lost Semifinal
1971-72	78	48	17	13	...	317	192	109	2nd	East Div.	Lost Final
1972-73	78	47	23	8	...	297	208	102	3rd	East Div.	Lost Semifinal
1973-74	78	40	24	14	...	300	251	94	3rd	East Div.	Lost Semifinal
1974-75	80	37	29	14	...	319	276	88	2nd	Patrick Div.	Lost Prelim. Round
1975-76	80	29	42	9	...	262	333	67	4th	Patrick Div.	Out of Playoffs
1976-77	80	29	37	14	...	272	310	72	4th	Patrick Div.	Out of Playoffs
1977-78	80	30	37	13	...	279	280	73	4th	Patrick Div.	Lost Prelim. Round
1978-79	80	40	29	11	...	316	292	91	3rd	Patrick Div.	Lost Final
1979-80	80	38	32	10	...	308	284	86	3rd	Patrick Div.	Lost Quarterfinal
1980-81	80	30	36	14	...	312	317	74	4th	Patrick Div.	Lost Semifinal
1981-82	80	39	27	14	...	316	306	92	2nd	Patrick Div.	Lost Div. Final
1982-83	80	35	35	10	...	306	287	80	4th	Patrick Div.	Lost Div. Final
1983-84	80	42	29	9	...	314	304	93	4th	Patrick Div.	Lost Div. Semifinal
1984-85	80	26	44	10	...	295	345	62	4th	Patrick Div.	Lost Div. Semifinal
1985-86	80	36	38	6	...	280	276	78	4th	Patick Div.	Lost Conf. Finals
1986-87	80	34	38	8	...	307	323	76	4th	Patrick Div.	Lost Div. Semifinal
1987-88	80	36	34	10	...	300	283	82	5th	Patrick Div.	Out of Playoffs
1988-89	80	37	35	8	...	310	307	82	3rd	Patrick Div.	Lost Div. Semifinal
1989-90	80	36	31	13	...	279	267	85	1st	Patrick Div.	Lost Div. Final
1990-91	80	36	31	13	...	297	265	85	2nd	Patrick Div.	Lost Div. Semifinal
1991-92	80	50	25	5	...	321	246	105	1st	Patrick Div.	Lost Div. Final
1992-93	84	34	39	11	...	304	308	79	6th	Patrick Div.	Out of Playoffs
1993-94	84	52	24	8	...	299	231	112	1st	Atlantic Div.	Won Stanley Cup
1994-95	48	22	23	3	...	139	134	47	4th	Atlantic Div.	Lost Conf. Semifinal
1995-96	82	41	27	14	...	272	237	96	2nd	Atlantic Div.	Lost Conf. Semifinal
1996-97	82	38	34	10	...	258	231	86	4th	Atlantic Div.	Lost Conf. Final
1997-98	82	25	39	18	...	197	231	68	5th	Atlantic Div.	Out of Playoffs
1998-99	82	33	38	11	...	217	227	77	4th	Atlantic Div.	Out of Playoffs
99-2000	82	29	38	12	3	218	246	73	4th	Atlantic Div.	Out of Playoffs
2000-01	82	33	43	5	1	250	290	72	4th	Atlantic Div.	Out of Playoffs
2001-02	82	36	38	4	4	227	258	80	4th	Atlantic Div.	Out of Playoffs
2002-03	82	32	36	10	4	210	231	78	4th	Atlantic Div.	Out of Playoffs

hockey, track, bicycling, baseball, rugby, football and basketball. Murray, better known as Muzz, was so adept in the ring that he became an amateur boxing champion. As the Cooks and Boucher were phased out of the lineup, the likes of Bryan Hextall, Phil Watson, Dutch Hiller, the Colville Brothers (Neil and Mac), Alex Shibicky and goalie Davey Kerr moved in, along with Lynn up front and Muzz on defense. By the time World War II had exploded in the fall of 1939, Patrick's Rangers were as powerful as his club of a dozen years earlier. Only this time, Boucher was behind the bench coaching instead of occupying his familiar spot on the ice at center.

The 1939–40 Rangers were an extraordinary group of players. At one point they had recorded 24 victories or ties in 25 games. They developed the strategy of offensive penalty-killing and popularized pulling the goalie for a sixth attacker in the final minute of play. With exquisite irony, they advanced to the Stanley Cup finals against Smythe's Maple Leafs once more and defeated them in six games. Forced out of their Madison Square Garden home by the circus, the Rangers played the last two games at Maple Leaf Gardens, winning both in overtime. Lester accepted the Stanley Cup from NHL president Frank Calder and then posed for an historic picture: a father and two sons on a Cup-winner at the same time.

Since their inception, the Rangers now had won the Stanley Cup three times and, with a young roster, it appeared that more championships were in the offing. But, World War II would change that. Within months, the Blueshirts roster was decimated by armed forces enlistments and by 1942, both Muzz and Lynn were in uniform. It was the beginning of a long and dismal run for the Rangers, with relief not coming until well after the war's end. By that time Lester had retired and Boucher took over both managing and coaching. New York's only bright season was 1949–50 when some adroit trades elevated the Rangers to playoff contention. They reached the finals—naturally playing all home games on the road—against Detroit and forced the Red Wings to double overtime in the seventh game before losing on a Pete Babando goal.

The Frank Boucher era ended with his dismissal at the end of the 1954–55 season, just after he had successfully reorganized the farm system, centered on the Guelph Biltmore Madhatters of the Ontario Hockey Association. Future Hall of Famers such as Harry Howell and Andy Bathgate graduated to the Blueshirts, along with goalie Lorne "Gump" Worsley, who had been developed on the Rangers' Eastern League farm club, the Rovers.

With Muzz Patrick managing and Phil Watson coaching, the club enjoyed a few bright moments in the late 1950s before fading again under Watson's tyrannical rule. By 1964, Patrick was gone, replaced by onetime—though only briefly—Ranger goalie Emile "the Cat" Francis. A native of North Battleford, Saskatchewan, Francis restored the franchise to a modicum of dignity and championship potential.

Francis's goaltending discovery Ed Giacomin anchored an impressive lineup that included the G-A-G (Goal-A-Game) Line centered by Jean Ratelle and flanked by Rod Gilbert on the right and Vic Hadfield on the left. Although not as popular as Patrick, Francis became a Big Apple favorite who enjoyed innovation as much as his predecessor. "The Cat" even lured onetime NHL scoring champion Bernie "Boom Boom" Geoffrion out of retirement in a move that paid immediate dividends: a second playoff berth in two years in 1967–68. Try as he might, Francis could not craft a Cup-winner, although the 1971–72 team reached the finals before losing to Bobby Orr and the Boston Bruins in six games. Unable to replenish his aging lineup with young stars, Francis lost favor with management and soon was replaced by former Ranger-basher John Ferguson.

This was a trying time for Rangers fans. An expansion franchise in adjoining Nassau County had become a winner faster than anyone had expected. In the 1974–75 season—only the third in franchise history—the New York Islanders not only reached the playoffs but unceremoniously ousted the vaunted Rangers in the opening round. Revenge, of sorts, was obtained four seasons later when the Blueshirts, now guided by former Philadelphia Flyers coach Fred Shero, upset the Islanders in a six-game series and reached the Stanley Cup finals against the defending champion Montreal Canadiens. A New York victory in the opener at the Forum was followed by a two-goal Rangers lead in game two, but the Habs soon counterattacked and won four straight games and another Cup title. Of course, the Islanders followed up this most Rangers success by winning four Stanley Cup titles in a row!

Rod Gilbert overcame a broken back in junior hockey and more back surgery later in his career to become one of the best players in the NHL. He spent 15 full seasons with the Rangers during the 1960s and '70s and set 20 club scoring records.

One by one, New York coaches and managers came and went, but that coveted fourth Stanley Cup appeared more distant than ever. Craig Patrick—Lynn's son and grandson of Lester—provided hope in the early 1980s, along with Lake Placid Olympic hero Herb Brooks. With the latter behind the bench, the Blueshirts introduced a revolutionary game plan that blended European and North American hockey styles. During the 1983–84 playoffs, Brooks's Rangers extended the four-time Cup-champion Islanders to a full five games before losing in sudden-death overtime. Again, the team crested and then plummeted while management desperately searched for a Cup-winning formula. Meanwhile, expansion teams were passing them by. Philadelphia had already won two and the Islanders four before Edmonton crafted a late 1980s Stanley Cup dynasty and Calgary won a title before the decade was over. The likes of Phil Esposito in the front office and Michel Bergeron behind the bench did little to bring the club closer to a championship.

The gloom over Broadway was lifted at the start of the 1990s when Craig Patrick draftee Brian Leetch established himself as a premier defenseman on the Rangers blue line. "He's reminiscent of the great Doug Harvey," said Esposito. Leetch won the Norris Trophy in 1992, not coincidentally in the same season that Mark Messier was lured away from Edmonton in a colossal deal that saw the Rangers' young general manager Neil Smith dispatch minor-league prospects Louie DeBrusk and Steven Rice to the Oilers along with popular center Bernie Nicholls and an unnamed but substantial amount of cash.

For the first time in 50 years, the Rangers had the best NHL record in 1991–92 (50–25–5), thanks in large part to Messier's leadership, his 107 points and an all-round performance that earned him the Hart Trophy. Still, it wasn't enough. Pittsburgh won the Stanley Cup for the second straight year. Messier's presence notwithstanding, the Rangers fell to the bottom of the division in 1992–93 and missed the playoffs as injuries and personnel strife disrupted the organization. Messier was openly critical of coach Roger Neilson, who was fired and replaced by Mike Keenan.

The turnabout was dramatic. Under Keenan's rule, the Rangers rebounded to the top, finishing with the league's best regular-season record (52–24–8) before embarking on a relentless march through the playoffs. They stumbled in a third-round encounter with the New Jersey Devils, falling behind three games to two. But, Messier scored a hat trick in game six and third-liner Stephane Matteau put them in the finals with an overtime goal in the seventh match.

After 54 years of waiting, Ranger fans were finally rewarded in 1994 when captain Mark Messier received the Stanley Cup from commissioner Gary Bettman after a nerve-wracking seven-game series with the Vancouver Canucks.

New York required seven games before disposing of Vancouver in the 1994 finals. Leetch, who tallied 34 points and won the Conn Smythe Trophy, detonated the seventh-game win with a goal in the first period. Goalie Mike Richter withstood a late-game Canucks assault to preserve the victory and give the Big Apple its first Stanley Cup since 1940. A sign carried by one fan in the stands read "Now I can die in peace." There was, however, no peace in the Rangers front office.

Keenan and Smith had been feuding all season and, instead of bringing the high command together, the Cup triumph pulled them farther apart. By mid-summer, 1994, Keenan had left New York to become general manager and coach of the St. Louis Blues. Smith replaced him with assistant coach Colin Campbell.

In a lockout-shortened 1994–95 season, the Rangers betrayed their age by playoff time. Messier proved no match for the younger, stronger Eric Lindros, and his teammates saw their one-year reign collapse. Smith moved quickly, obtaining Wayne Gretzky—"The Great One" had moved from Edmonton, to Los Angeles, to St. Louis—and suddenly Broadway was abuzz with hockey frenzy. The former Oilers cronies, Gretzky and Messier, infused the Rangers with new life. Along with Adam Graves, Alexei Kovalev, Ulf Samuelsson, Richter and Leetch, the Rangers had elite written all over them, although their regular-season record was less than awesome. But, once the playoffs began, the old pros delivered. Gretzky personally took over the opening-round series against Florida and delivered a five-game victory. Second-round opponent New Jersey looked impressive, shutting out the Rangers in game one, but Richter turned impregnable and again the New Yorkers annexed a series in five.

An opening-game win in round three against Philadelphia suggested that the finals—and even the Cup—were reachable. But, injuries and age combined to enervate the Blueshirts. Lindros and company rolled over them in the next four games, ending hopes for a Gretzky-Messier return to the finals. As captain, Messier had been an unqualified leader on Broadway, but the general staff had more and more come to the conclusion that he was overstepping his power base. A dismal performance in the Philadelphia series led general manager Smith to conclude that Messier's value would diminish in the seasons ahead. The Rangers did make the captain an offer to return, but it was not deemed suitable by Messier. Instead, he chose a more lucrative Canucks contract and signed with Vancouver.

The decision caused shockwaves up and down Seventh Avenue. Garden officials were assailed for failing to retain the captain, but Smith and others countered that a reasonable offer was made and rejected by the Messier camp. Instead, the Rangers obtained Pat LaFontaine from Buffalo, sending a second-round draft pick to the Sabres. Smith also obtained free agent veterans Brian Skrudland and Mike Keane. Prior to the opening game, fellow general managers told Smith that he had a potential Stanley Cup-winner if LaFontaine had fully recovered from the concussions that had sidelined him in Buffalo. Unfortunately, another head injury to LaFontaine late in the 1997–98 campaign not only ended his season early, it ended his career. John Muckler replaced Colin Campbell as coach in February, but despite strong play by Wayne Gretzky over the last two months of the season, the Rangers missed the playoffs. Skrudland and Keane were shipped out to Dallas before the year was through.

The 1998–99 season proved to be another disappointing one in New York, with the club missing the playoffs for the second year in a row. As Gretzky struggled through injuries, rumors began to spread that he would retire. "The Great One" confirmed this during the season's final week. He formally announced his retirement on April 16, 1999, and played his final game two days later. The Rangers lost, 2–1, to Pittsburgh in overtime.

Looking to retool for 1999–2000, the Rangers signed free agents Theo Fleury, Valeri Kamensky, Sylvain Lefebvre and Kirk McLean, which bloated the payroll to an NHL-high $61 million. Not one made the contribution that was expected of him. Though injuries to Brian Leetch and Mike Richter also contributed, the Rangers' disappointing play again in 1999–2000 cost John Muckler and g.m. Neil Smith their jobs with four games left in the regular season. On June 1, 2000, the Rangers announced that former Edmonton Oilers president and g.m. Glen Sather had been hired to serve the same dual role in New York. In July, 2000, Ron Low was hired as coach and Mark Messier returned as captain after a three-year absence. Petr Nedved had led the club in points in 1999–2000, but the team's best player was rookie Michael York who led the club with 26 goals.

Despite some impressive individual performances during the 2000–01 season, the New York Rangers disappointed in Glen Sather's first year on Broadway, missing the playoffs for the fourth year in a row. Brian Leetch was the top-scoring defenseman in the NHL, and the Rangers leading points producer with 79 (21 goals, 58 assists). Petr Nedved, Radek Dvorak and Theo Fleury all reached the 30-goal plateau. Fleury had 30 goals and 44 assists in just 62 games, but missed the last quarter of the season after entering a league-sponsored addiction program. Mark Messier played all 82 games during his first year back with the Rangers. He scored 24 goals but had a plus-minus rating of -25. Defense was a problem, as the Rangers allowed a league-high 290 goals. Injuries and inconsistency hobbled Mike Richter. Kirk McLean, Guy Hebert and three rookie netminders all saw some time in the Rangers goal.

During the offseason, Glen Sather sent three players and a draft pick to the Philadelphia Flyers for Eric Lindros. Though there were still some concerns about his health, Lindros managed to play in 72 games in 2001–02 and led the Rangers with 73 points (37 goals, 36 assists). Pavel Bure was brought in from Florida at the trade deadline, and collected 12 goals and eight assists in just 12 games with the Rangers. With 36 wins and 80 points, the Rangers had their best season in five years but still finished 11th in the Eastern Conference. Another year out of the playoffs cost Ron Low his coaching job.

Glen Sather continued to add to the team's growing payroll in the offseason prior to the 2002–03 campaign. Sather made several moves in the offseason in an attempt to improve his club, signing free agents Bobby Holik and Darius Kasparaitis. Former New York Islanders superstar Bryan Trottier was brought in as the club's new head coach. Though he had been highly successful as an assistant coach for four years in Colorado, Trottier had trouble getting through to the veteran Rangers team and was fired with the team just 21–26–6–1 after 54 games. Former headmen Ted Green, Jim Schoenfeld and Terry O'Reilly were all on the coaching staff, but Glen Sather elected to go behind the bench himself in an effort to get the Rangers back into the playoff picture. Within two weeks of becoming coach, Sather the g.m. pulled off an eight-player swap with the Pittsburgh Penguins that brought Alexei Kovalev to New York on February 11, 2003. Earlier in the year he had acquired Mike Dunham from Nashville following an injury to Mike Richter. At the deadline in March, he picked up Anson Carter from Edmonton.

Though the team played better under Sather (11–10–4–3) they lost several key games down the stretch and were eliminated on the final Friday night of the season. Injuries throughout the year to key players such as Brian Leetch and Pavel Bure had not helped the Rangers as they missed the playoffs for the sixth year in a row.

Ottawa Senators

1917–18 to 1933–34

TEAMS FROM CANADA'S CAPITAL have brought honor and distinction to the city almost from the beginning of hockey history. At the second Montreal Winter Carnival in 1884, an Ottawa team competed against four Montreal squads and beat McGill University in the finals. After Lord Stanley arrived in Ottawa in 1888 to begin his term as Canada's Governor-General, the excitement of the hockey scene he found there inspired him to donate the Stanley Cup. Though it would take 10 years for an Ottawa team to win it after the Stanley Cup was first presented in 1893, Ottawa's team enjoyed nine championship seasons through 1927—a mark unprecedented at the time.

The famed Ottawa Silver Seven won the Stanley Cup in 1903, and retained it until being dethroned by the Montreal Wanderers in 1906. The Silver Seven boasted six future members of the Hockey Hall of Fame, including the legendary Frank McGee. The Silver Seven became known as the Ottawa Senators after their Stanley Cup reign ended, and, by 1909, the great Cyclone Taylor had led the team to another championship. Stars like Percy LeSueur, Marty Walsh and Dubbie Kerr brought the Stanley Cup back to Ottawa again in 1911.

The Senators were charter members of the National Hockey League when it was formed in 1917, and Ottawa quickly established itself as the NHL's best team. Boasting such stars as Clint Benedict, Eddie Gerard, Frank Nighbor and Cy Denneny, the Senators won both halves of the 1919–20 season's split schedule to eliminate the need for a playoff to determine the NHL champion.

The Senators won the Stanley Cup four times in eight years from 1920 to 1927. Of the 11 players on the 1920 team, eight would be enshrined in the Hockey Hall of Fame. Only part-time players Horace Merrill, Morley Bruce and Jack MacKell missed out.

The Senators then hosted the Pacific Coast Hockey Association's Seattle Metropolitans for the Stanley Cup, and defeated them in five games—though mild weather in Ottawa saw the final two games moved to the artificial ice surface of Toronto's Mutual Street Arena.

In 1921, Ottawa won the first half of the NHL's split-season schedule, but slumped to third place in the second half before catching fire in the playoffs and winning the right to meet the Vancouver Millionaires in Vancouver for the Stanley Cup. An estimated 51,000 fans saw the five games played in the West Coast city. Thousands had to be turned away from the final game on April 4, which Ottawa won, 2–1, on a pair of goals by Jack Darragh. Cyclone Taylor, the star of Ottawa's 1909 Stanley Cup victory, suited up for the Millionaires that night in one of the final games of his brilliant career.

The 1921–22 season saw the Senators top the standings in the year in which the NHL did away with its split-season format. However, Ottawa was defeated by the second-place Toronto St. Pats under the new NHL playoff format. A year later, the Senators edged out the Montreal Canadiens by a single point to finish first again, then scored a 3–2 victory in a two-game, total-goals playoff. The victory entitled the banged-up Ottawa team to face Vancouver once again in the 1923 Stanley Cup playoffs. The Senators took the series three games to one, and were described by Vancouver's Frank Patrick as "the greatest team I have ever seen." However, there still was the matter of the Western Canada Hockey League's Edmonton Eskimos, whom the Senators beat in two straight games to claim the Stanley Cup championship.

It was in game two of the Edmonton series that Ottawa star Frank "King" Clancy is said to have played every position on the ice, including goal. In that era, goaltenders served their own penalties and when Senator netminder Clint Benedict was banished to the box for two minutes, he casually handed his goal stick to Clancy, who guarded the net until Benedict returned.

Artificial ice finally came to Ottawa on November 30, 1923, when the Auditorium opened for hockey business. Playing at their new arena, the Senators topped the NHL standings again for three of the next four seasons. By 1926–27, the rival professional leagues of the west had collapsed and the Stanley Cup had become exclusively an NHL trophy. The final Stanley Cup championship won by an Ottawa team came from a tight 1927 playoff series that saw the Senators beat the Boston Bruins two games to nothing, although two other games ended in ties. After the fourth and final game, Boston's Billy Coutu assaulted one of the game officials in the corridor and received a lifetime suspension from the NHL.

Ottawa newspaperman Tommy Gorman was heavily involved in Senators management.

Despite the Senators' success on the ice, NHL expansion into the United States had left Ottawa as the smallest market in the NHL by far. Owner Frank Ahearn had been absorbing financial losses for years, but the first official notice of the difficulties the team was facing came at the NHL meetings in September, 1927, when Ottawa management requested that the team receive a larger percentage of the box office receipts from road games. (As perennial champions, the Senators were always a large draw on the road.) Next, the Senators sold Hooley Smith to the Montreal Maroons. Ed Gorman was sold to Toronto, and Jack Adams was permitted to retire. The defending Stanley Cup champions slipped to third in the standings of the NHL's Canadian Division, and were eliminated by the Montreal Maroons in the first round of the playoffs.

The Senators continued to ship out expensive talent in 1928–29 when they sent Cy Denneny to the Bruins and Punch Broadbent to the New York Americans. Ottawa fell to fourth in the standings and missed the playoffs. Prior to the 1929–30 season, the Senators again requested an increased share of the road receipts. In January, they shipped an aging Frank Nighbor to the Toronto Maple Leafs. With King Clancy and Alex Connell as the only stars left in Ottawa, the Senators managed to slip into the playoffs that year, but were handled easily by the New York Rangers in the opening round.

Prior to the 1930–31 season, one of hockey's biggest deals took place when Conn Smythe purchased Clancy from the Senators. The $35,000 Ottawa received wasn't enough to solve the Senators' financial woes, and reports began circulating that the team might be sold. Before the start of the 1931–32 season, the Senators requested a year's leave of absence from the NHL. Ottawa players were distributed around the league. The Senators returned under new management in 1932–33, but finished with the worst record in the league the next two years. Arrangements were made to transfer the once-proud franchise to St. Louis.

The original Ottawa Senators played their final home game on March 15, 1934. The New York Americans defeated the Senators 3–2. When Americans goalie Roy Worters received a deep gash over the eye in this match, Ottawa loaned the visitors Alex Connell, who had been relegated to a backup role earlier in the season. Connell played brilliantly for the visitors and was the number-one star of the contest. Over 6,500 fans applauded Connell, then left the Auditorium with solemn faces, knowing it was the end of a memorable era in Canadian hockey.

Ottawa Senators, 1917–1934

Year-by-Year Record

Season	GP	W	L	T	GF	GA	Pts	Finish	Division	Playoff Results
1917–18	22	9	13	0	102	114	18	3rd	…	Out of Playoffs
1918–19	18	12	6	0	71	53	24	1st	…	Lost NHL Final
1919–20	24	19	5	0	121	64	38	1st	…	Won Stanley Cup
1920–21	24	14	10	0	97	75	28	2nd	…	Won Stanley Cup
1921–22	24	14	8	2	106	84	30	1st	…	Lost NHL Final
1922–23	24	14	9	1	77	54	29	1st	…	Won Stanley Cup
1923–24	24	16	8	0	74	54	32	1st	…	Lost NHL Final
1924–25	30	17	12	1	83	66	35	4th	…	Out of Playoffs
1925–26	36	24	8	4	77	42	52	1st	…	Lost NHL Final
1926–27	44	30	10	4	86	69	64	1st	Canadian	Won Stanley Cup
1927–28	44	20	14	10	78	57	50	3rd	Canadian	Lost Quarterfinal
1928–29	44	14	17	13	54	67	41	4th	Canadian	Out of Playoffs
1929–30	44	21	15	8	138	118	50	3rd	Canadian	Lost Quarterfinal
1930–31	44	10	30	4	91	142	24	5th	Canadian	Out of Playoffs
1931–32	Suspended operations for one season									
1932–33	48	11	27	10	88	131	32	5th	Canadian	Out of Playoffs
1933–34	48	13	29	6	115	143	32	5th	Canadian	Out of Playoffs

Brad Marsh spent his 15th and final NHL season as a member of the expansion Ottawa Senators in their inaugural season of 1992–93. The gritty blueliner was a fan favorite.

Ottawa Senators

THOUGH THE HISTORY OF HOCKEY in Ottawa is long and rich, the original attempt by Terrace Investments to bring the NHL back to Canada's capital city was given little chance of success. "It's not that the area isn't big enough to support a professional hockey team," said former Ottawa mayor Jim Durrell, who later joined the Senators as team president. "It's just that we're not going to get it."

For a year, Bruce Firestone, Randy Sexton and Cyril Leeder lobbied NHL owners, governors and general managers in an attempt to get them to believe in the city as an appropriate home for the NHL. They fought political types constantly, trying to get land re-zoned in order to build the Ottawa Palladium (later the Corel Centre). The battle proved difficult. It was obvious the city wanted hockey, but nobody wanted to say for sure that these were the men who could make it happen. Firestone was ripped in the media. People wondered if he actually had the backing to get the job done.

Armed with an impressive hardcover book outlining their bid, the Senators made their way to the NHL Board of Governors meeting at The Breakers in West Palm Beach, Florida. The Ottawa group received little indication that its bid had been well-received, but on December 6, 1990, with the announcement imminent, Firestone was summoned to a room where the governors were gathered prior to a press conference. He was handed a piece of paper that contained just two words—"Tampa" and "Ottawa." With that simple gesture, Firestone burst into tears. Ottawa had scored.

There was joy at the announcement and season tickets were snapped up by fans immediately after they went on sale. Still, raising the $50 million (U.S.) franchise fee and getting the funding for the $150 million Palladium—which had been downsized from 22,500 to 18,500 seats—would prove difficult. That's when Rod Bryden entered the picture. A local businessman and friend of Firestone's, Bryden was brought on board to find investors in the team.

Once the expansion fee was paid and the franchise's future secured, the team began to build its hockey department. Sexton was the man in charge. Mel Bridgman, a 14-year NHL player with an impressive education from the Wharton School of Business, was assigned the tough job of building the team with the help of former Montreal Canadiens great John Ferguson. Only days before the Expansion Draft, highly touted coach Rick Bowness was fired by the Boston Bruins and immediately hired as the Senators' first coach.

The first mistake by Bridgman, and one of the

most embarrassing for the franchise, came at the Expansion Draft in a downtown hotel in Montreal. The final list was misplaced by Ferguson, and the Senators attempted to draft two players who were ineligible. Twice they were told to make a new selection. It left the organization looking bad from the start. "Ottawa apologizes," said Bridgman.

Only days later, at the Entry Draft in Montreal, fans could have cut the silence with a knife after the club made relative unknown Alexei Yashin from the Moscow Dynamo its number-one pick and the second overall selection. The top-rated player in the draft, Roman Hamrlik, went to Tampa Bay. A trainload of people from Ottawa clapped politely. Ferguson talked about Yashin's star potential. Nobody knew it would become a reality.

The new Ottawa Senators played their first NHL game on October 8, 1992, against the Montreal Canadiens. Fans packed the cozy 10,500-seat Civic Centre—the club's temporary home—and with a national television audience watching on Hockey Night in Canada, the Senators beat the Habs, 5–3. It was a special night, though it would be the last bit of joy for the season. The team finished with a 10–70–4 record for 24 points, which made them one of the worst expansion teams of all time. Yashin had decided to stay in Russia an extra year. Laurie Boschman, the man assigned the captaincy, showed he could not do it anymore. Instead, the player who carried the torch was defenseman Brad Marsh.

Asked to breakfast by Bryden—who had been installed as chief operating officer—the morning after getting a vote of confidence on local television, Bridgman was fired unceremoniously. What was the meeting like? "Well, I didn't eat my breakfast," said Bridgman. Sexton was installed as g.m.—the job he always had coveted—and a new era in Ottawa NHL hockey began.

Ottawa Senators

Year-by-Year Record

Season	GP	W	L	T	OL	GF	GA	Pts.	Finish	Division	Playoff Result
1992-93	84	10	70	4	...	202	395	24	6th	Adams Div.	Out of Playoffs
1993-94	84	14	61	9	...	201	397	37	7th	Northeast Div.	Out of Playoffs
1994-95	48	9	34	5	...	117	174	23	7th	Northeast Div.	Out of Playoffs
1995-96	82	18	59	5	...	191	291	41	6th	Northeast Div.	Out of Playoffs
1996-97	82	31	36	15	...	226	234	77	3rd	Northeast Div.	Lost Conf. Quarterfinal
1997-98	82	34	33	15	...	193	200	83	5th	Northeast Div.	Lost Conf. Semifinal
1998-99	82	44	23	15	...	239	179	103	1st	Northeast Div.	Lost Conf. Quarterfinal
99-2000	82	41	28	11	2	244	210	95	2nd	Northeast Div.	Lost Conf. Quarterfinal
2000-01	82	48	21	9	4	274	205	109	1st	Northeast Div.	Lost Conf. Quarterfinal
2001-02	82	39	27	9	7	243	208	94	3rd	Northeast Div.	Lost Conf. Semifinal
2002-03	82	52	21	8	1	263	182	113	1st	Northeast Div.	Lost Conf. Finals

Ottawa's last-place finish had sealed up the number-one pick at the 1993 NHL Entry Draft, and the Senators made no secret of the fact they would use the selection for highly touted Victoriaville Tigres superstar Alexandre Daigle. Daigle was young, French and had superstar quality. Believing he would be just the tonic the franchise needed, management handed him an unprecedented five-year, $12.5 million contract.

The next season started with promise and hope. Yashin reported to camp and looked brilliant. Daigle had his flashy speed. It couldn't get worse than the season before. The team looked like it was going places. Even financing for the Palladium was falling into place and there was a belief in the region the rink was going to get built. The Senators actually were surrounded by excitement.

Yashin finished with 77 points—including 35 goals—and was voted to play in the NHL All-Star Game, while Daigle had 20 goals and 31 assists. Unfortunately, the record didn't get much better on the ice. The team finished with 37 points. Questions started about Sexton's leadership because Yashin and agent Mark Gandler claimed the organization had made a verbal promise to renegotiate Yashin's contract.

A war of words stretched through the summer. Yashin didn't report to training camp and 1995 number-one selection Bryan Berard walked out because Sexton didn't make him a contract offer. While the NHL lockout stole the headlines, Yashin worked out with the Ottawa 67's junior team. A deal was struck to bring Yashin back into the fold just hours before the team left to play its first game of the shortened 48-game schedule in January when the lockout was settled. Again, all seemed well in the world.

But, another disappointing season passed under Sexton and Bowness. Then, another battle with Yashin broke out and confidence in management reached an all-time low. Ferguson walked out on the team because he didn't agree with the club's position to trade Yashin. "Just get the guy signed and get him into camp," said Ferguson. "You don't trade talent like that."

On opening night of the 1995–96 season, Yashin was on the front page of the local newspaper with his sticks packed up and headed for Russia. He practiced for a week with Moscow Dynamo and suited up for a couple of games before the International Ice Hockey Federation suspended him. An attempt to have his contract declared null and void by an NHL arbitrator was turned down. Twenty games into the year, Bowness was fired and Dave Allison—a career minor-leaguer with no NHL coaching experience—was Sexton's hand-picked successor. The move didn't work. Only weeks later, Sexton was shown the door by Bryden, with Anaheim Mighty Ducks assistant g.m. Pierre Gauthier hired to take over the hockey operation. He moved swiftly by bringing Yashin back into the fold—signing him to a five-year, $13 million U.S. contract. Excitement was building, the team was ready to move into the Palladium in January, 1996, and there was a sense of direction to the franchise. But, Gauthier wasn't finished.

Allison, who had only two victories since taking over from Bowness, was fired on January 24 and replaced by Colorado Avalanche assistant Jacques Martin. The move came only hours after Gauthier pulled off an important three-way trade with the Toronto Maple Leafs and New York Islanders that brought the club young defenseman Wade Redden and goaltender Damian Rhodes. It was a move that signalled there was a new era in Ottawa. The move to get Rhodes injected life into the team. Swede Daniel Alfredsson was selected the NHL's rookie of the year, and by the time the season ended, fans had confidence. Former L.A. Kings president Roy Mlakar, who carried a strong background in marketing, was installed to take over in Ottawa.

The summer of 1996 was a flurry of activity. By the time training camp ended, Gauthier and Martin had made 10 changes to the roster. The only consistency in the lineup was Yashin, Alfredsson, Daigle, Redden and Rhodes, along with 1994 number-one selection Radek Bonk and veteran captain Randy Cunneyworth. Virtually every other part had changed, but the Senators were expected to compete for a playoff spot.

Goaltender Ron Tugnutt, signed in the offseason to back up

Rhodes, emerged as the hero down the stretch when the latter went down with a season-ending ankle injury in late February. The Senators needed help getting into the playoffs, but did themselves a favor by going 9–3–1 down the stretch to seal up seventh place in the Eastern Conference on the final night of the season. Defenseman Steve Duchesne fired the shot heard around Ottawa with a late goal that broke a 0–0 tie with Buffalo and vaulted the Senators into the playoffs.

Backed by Tugnutt, the "Cinderella" Senators faced the Sabres in the first round. With Dominik Hasek injured, it appeared Ottawa was going to knock off Buffalo after taking a 3–2 lead in the series, but a 3–0 loss at home in the sixth game set the stage for a dramatic game seven at the Marine Midland Arena. The Senators lost, 3–2, in overtime. After the initial disappointment passed, the Senators viewed their run to the playoffs as a good sign for the future. Changes were kept to a minimum in the summer. Tugnutt was signed to a new three-year deal. Defenseman Chris Phillips, the club's top draft pick in 1996 from the Western Hockey League's Prince Albert Raiders, was added to the roster at the start of the 1997–98 season. Alfredsson joined the club six games into the season after signing a new five-year, $10 million U.S. deal. The average attendance in the building leaped by more than 2,000 additional tickets sold per game.

Not everything stayed the same. Daigle left. Gauthier shipped him to the Philadelphia Flyers for Pat Falloon and prospect Vaclav Prospal. Carrying the weight of the rookie contract he had signed, Daigle never had success in Ottawa.

Marian Hossa proved he was fully recovered from a serious knee injury in junior hockey when he scored 29 goals in 1999–2000. He set a club record with 45 goals in 2002–03.

After finishing the regular schedule with a franchise-record 83 points, the Senators faced the powerful New Jersey Devils in the opening round of the 1998 playoffs. Although some insiders thought the speedy Senators were capable of beating the older, slower Devils, Ottawa's domination during a six-game playoff victory was considered a major upset. Though a five-game loss to the Washington Capitals followed, 1997–98 had been a very successful season.

Shortly after the 1998 NHL Entry Draft, Pierre Gauthier announced his resignation. Soon he would resurface in Anaheim. Rick Dudley, who previously was g.m. of the successful Detroit Vipers franchise in the International Hockey League, was hired as the Senators' fourth general manager.

Ottawa had come of age when they knocked off the Devils in the playoffs, but their improvement in 1998-99 went beyond most predictions. Alexei Yashin showed that he belonged among the league's elite, collecting 44 goals and 50 assists. With players like Marian Hossa and Magnus Arvedson emerging among the team's corp of young stars, the Senators had excellent team speed and solid defense backed up by the stellar goaltending of Ron Tugnutt (whose league-leading goals-against average of 1.79 was the lowest in the NHL since Tony Esposito's 1.77 in 1971-72). Ottawa was also the least-penalized team in the NHL. The Senators not only led the Northeast Division with 103 points, they topped the entire Eastern Conference for much of the year. Only a late-season slump allowed the New Jersey Devils to claim top spot with 105 points. However, the season ended in disappointment when the Buffalo Sabres swept the Senators to open the playoffs.

Though the 1999–2000 season would be another productive one on the ice, there were plenty of distractions off of it. Dudley bolted the team for a similar job in Tampa Bay, and Marshall Johnston became the club's fifth general manager in its eight-year history. Once again Yashin refused to report unless the club agreed to renegotiate his contract, and this time his holdout/suspension played out as a season-long soap opera. Many expected Ottawa to deal him at the trade deadline, but the Senators held firm to their position that he would not be moved.

Most problematic of all for Ottawa was the possibility that owner Rod Bryden would be forced to sell and/or relocate the franchise unless the Canadian government agreed to provide financial assistance and/or tax concessions. The Canadian government did announce a subsidy plan on January 18, 2000, but revoked the plan after public protest just two days later. A show of support by Ottawa fans when Bryden announced the team needed to sell more tickets convinced him not to put the club on the market.

With the absence of Alexei Yashin, Daniel Alfredsson was named team captain. Radek Bonk and Marian Hossa helped pick up the offensive slack, as Bonk led the team with 60 points and Hossa topped all scorers with 29 goals. Wade Redden continued to develop into one of the NHL's best young defensemen. The decision to deal Damian Rhodes to the expansion Atlanta Thrashers before the season left Tugnutt to assume the role of the number-one goaltender, but he was dealt to the Pittsburgh Penguins for Tom Barrasso at the trade deadline.

While not quite able to live up to the previous year's performance, Ottawa was able to keep the pressure on Toronto in the race for first place in the Northeast Division. Though the Maple Leafs wound up on top, the Senators had their chance for revenge in the first round of the playoffs, as the teams hooked up in "The Battle of Ontario." After losing the first two games in Toronto, Ottawa fought back to make a series of it before eventually surrendering in six. The Senators could only manage 10 goals against Curtis Joseph, with their top line of Bonk, Hossa and Arvedson being held without a point.

After missing the entire 1999–2000 season over a contract dispute, Alexei Yashin returned to Ottawa in 2000–01 and led the team back into first place in the Northeast Division. Yashin topped the team with 40 goals and 48 assists as the Senators set numerous club records, including most wins (48) and most points (109). Marian Hossa and Shawn McEachern both tallied 32 goals, while Daniel Alfredsson and Radek Bonk each topped the 20-goal plateau. Nineteen-year-old rookie Martin Havlat contributed 19 goals. Defensively, Wade Redden continued to improve. Come the playoffs, however, the Senators were knocked out in the first round by the Toronto Maple Leafs for the second year in a row. This time, they were swept aside in four straight.

The Senators dealt Yashin to the New York Islanders in the offseason, then slumped somewhat in 2001–02. Still, they ranked as the league's fifth-best offensive team with Alfredsson leading the way. He had a career-high 37 goals and topped the team with 71 points. Hossa had 31 goals while Bonk, Havlat and Todd White each had at least 20. Zdeno Chara, acquired in the Yashin trade, added size and toughness to the defense. Patrick Lalime sparkled in the playoffs, recording three straight shutouts versus Philadelphia and allowing just two goals in five games as the Senators dumped the Flyers. Once again, though, they could not get past Toronto as the Leafs eliminated the Senators in a hard-fought seven-game, second-round series. John Muckler then replaced Marshall Johnston as the club's general manager during the offseason.

Wade Redden scored his first NHL goal for the Senators on his first shot in his first game on October 5, 1996. Since his rookie season of 1996–97, he has developed into one of the league's top young defensemen.

The 2002–03 season saw Marian Hossa establish himself among the game's top snipers, and with Patrick Lalime supplying top-notch goaltending the Senators soared to the top of the Eastern Conference standings during the first half of the 2002–03 season.

Unfortunately, while the Senators were succeeding on the ice, the team continued to struggle financially and ultimately required protection through a bankruptcy filing before Canadian billionaire Eugene Melnyk purchased the club and made a separate deal to secure the Corel Centre.

Meanwhile, the Senators continued to excel on the ice. They broke the club records set just two years before by recording 52 victories and 113 points and became the first Canadian team to win the Presidents' Trophy since the 1988–89 Calgary Flames. Hossa ranked fourth in the NHL with 45 goals (one more than Alexei Yashin's previous team record). His 80 points ranked 14th in the league. Daniel Alfredsson was 14th in the NHL with 51 assists and 17th in points with 78. Todd White, Martin Havlat, Radek Bonk and Bryan Smolinski (acquired from Los Angeles at the trade deadline) all topped the 20-goal plateau as well. Most importantly, the Senators seemed to play with a passion and toughness not seen before in previous Ottawa teams. Late seasons trades for Vaclav Varada and Rob Ray added further grit.

With their potential sale still playing out, Ottawa began the playoffs against the Islanders, a team they had finished 30 points ahead of in the regular-season standings. When the Senators dropped a 3–0 decision it sparked fears of the disappointments of playoffs past. Ottawa players had seemed to go out of their way to run at former Senator Yashin, who scored the second goal of the opening game and was the best player on the ice. From that point on, however, they returned to the form that had seen them finish first overall. They outscored the Islanders 13–4 in winning the next four in a row, including a key double-overtime victory in game three. The series wrapped up amid reports that Eugene Melnyk had all but wrapped up his negotiations to purchase the club—with a separate deal for the arena still pending. (A court-appointed monitor representing the team's creditors would approve the deal on May 9, but the sale was not finalized until after the playoffs.)

Next up on the ice was Philadelphia, who figured to be much tougher than the team Ottawa had completely shut down the year before. Indeed, the Flyers equaled their two-goal performance of 2002 within 11 minutes of the first period, but the Senators stormed back for a 4–2 victory. Roman Cechmanek stopped 33 shots in game two as Philadelphia bounced back for a 2–0 victory. He looked shaky again in Ottawa's 3–2 overtime win in game three, but rebounded with a 28-save performance for a 1–0 Flyers win in game four. However, the unorthodox netminder appeared off his game again two days later as the Senators took a 3–2 lead in the series with a 5–2 victory.

Cleary, Philadelphia was running out of gas after a tough seven-game series with Toronto in the opening round. The Senators also had the Maple Leafs to thank for their steely resolve not to let game six slip away as they had in the second round one year before. Peter Schaefer scored 2:41 into the contest, and Mike Fisher made it 2–0 at the seven-minute mark. Ottawa went on to a 5–1 victory that moved the Senators into the Eastern Conference final for the first time in franchise history.

Facing the Senators for a berth in the Stanley Cup final were the New Jersey Devils. The two teams had not hooked up in the post-season since 1998, when Ottawa was a surprise winner in its very first playoff appearance. Two quick goals gave Ottawa a 2–0 lead after 20 minutes of game one. New Jersey scored twice in the second, but after a scoreless third period, Shaun Van Allen gave the Senators a 3–2 victory when he scored his first career playoff goal on a neat give-and-go with Martin Havlat at 3:08 of overtime. The Devils scored a 4–1 win in game two, and the series headed to the Meadowlands tied 1–1.

Daniel Alfredsson won the Calder Trophy as rookie of the year in 1995–96 and has been the Senators captain since the 1999–2000 season. He had a career-high 37 goals in 2001–02 and a career-best 51 assists and 78 points in 2002–03.

The Senators had not lost two straight games in the playoffs, but New Jersey had not been defeated at home and they ran their streak to seven straight wins with a 1–0 victory in game three. Sergei Brylin scored the only goal of the game in the first period and Martin Brodeur finished with 24 saves, including 13 in a wild third-period onslaught by the desperate Senators. Until that point, Ottawa had been completely stifled by the Devils defense. The Senators were much more effective through the first 40 minutes of game four, but New Jersey broke a 2–2 tie with three third-period goals and took a 3–1 series lead back to Ottawa for game five.

General manager John Muckler had stated that the Senators needed their stars to step up, but neither Alfredsson, Hossa nor Havlat had scored during the Devils series. Desperate for an offensive spark, coach Jacques Martin inserted Jason Spezza into the lineup in game five. The team's top draft pick (second overall) in 2001, Spezza had spent his first professional season bouncing back and forth between Ottawa and Binghamton of the American Hockey League. He had yet to suit up during the playoffs, but he did add the necessary spark in game five, helping to set up Havlat for the game-winning goal midway through the third period, then icing the game with Ottawa's first powerplay goal after an 0-for-20 stretch. The Senators stayed alive with a 3–1 victory. It was the first time in team history (after six defeats) that Ottawa had won when facing elimination. Then they did it again with a 2–1 victory in game six. Chris Phillips capitalized on a fine play by Hossa to score the winner in overtime and send the series back to the Corel Centre for a final showdown.

Game seven was a thriller, with Ottawa taking an early first-period lead only to see New Jersey wipe it out with two quick goals early in the second. Radek Bonk tied the game on a feed from Hossa at 1:53 of the third period, but Jeff Friesen's goal with just 2:14 left in regulation lifted the Devils to a 3–2 victory.

"I'm proud of our players," said coach Jacques Martin, "but obviously it's a failure because we lost the game. The business that we're in is to win the Stanley Cup." With new ownership in place (ironically, the announcement that Melnyk had finally completed negotiations for the Corel Centre came on the same day the Devils won the Stanley Cup), and a deep core of talented youngsters, the Senators may not have to wait too much longer.

Philadelphia Flyers

Ed Snider was a football executive talking business with team banker Bill Putnam in 1965 when he got the tip that led to the birth of one of the NHL's most enduringly successful franchises. Putnam mentioned he would soon be leaving to prepare Jack Kent Cooke's bid for an NHL franchise for Los Angeles and referred Snider to Bill Jennings, the president of the New York Rangers and chairman of the expansion committee.

Jennings was both intrigued by the nation's fourth-largest market and skeptical of its historically poor support of a variety of minor-league teams. The last, the Ramblers of the Eastern Hockey League, had abandoned the ramshackle Philadelphia Arena in 1964 for another shabby arena in the New Jersey suburbs.

Meanwhile, Snider, who was the Philadelphia Eagles' point man for a proposed baseball/football stadium in South Philadelphia, was asked by Ike Richman, part-owner of the NBA's Philadelphia 76ers, whether Jerry Wolman, the wildly successful developer who owned the Eagles, had any interest in building an arena. Snider went to Wolman, who agreed that a building with twin hockey/basketball tenants could be viable.

When Putnam subsequently decided to leave Cooke, he joined the Snider-Wolman partnership and began the bid for an NHL franchise. It was granted, to the surprise of many who expected a team to go to Baltimore, on February 9, 1966. Ground was broken for the arena (the Spectrum) in May at the corner of Broad Street and Pattison Avenue. Team colors of orange, black and white were selected by Putnam, both because of their boldness and because of his old loyalties to the University of Texas, where he had played football. Snider's sister, Phyllis, came up with the name Flyers, as did enough voters in a name-the-team contest that the franchise could justify its selection over suggestions like Quakers and Liberty Bells.

Before payment of the $2-million franchise fee was due in June, 1967, Snider acquired Wolman's 22 percent stake in the team in exchange for his own 40 percent share in the Spectrum. Snider also bought out Jerry Schiff, giving him 60 percent of the Flyers. Wolman reiterated his pledge to put up half of the $2 million franchise fee, but with less than two weeks to go before the money was due at the expansion draft, he admitted he didn't have it. Snider and Putnam had to scramble. The last $500,000 was not procured until 48 hours before the deadline. A 15 percent share in the team later was sold to Joe Scott, a well-known local beer baron who would work tirelessly to sell tickets and open doors to a business community that was slow to respond to a perceived foreign sport.

Doug Favell was the first goalie to give his mask a custom paint job while playing with the Flyers.

On June 6, 1967, general manager Bud Poile, a longtime minor-league executive in the Detroit organization hired by Putnam on the advice of Jack Adams, and coach Keith Allen supervised the Flyers in a drafting approach that differed from the other five new teams. Starting with their two goaltender selections, Bernie Parent and Doug Favell, the Flyers focused on young players, only four of whom—Joe Watson, Ed Van Impe, Lou Angotti and Brit Selby—had spent more than token time in the NHL.

The Flyers debuted with a 5–1 loss at Oakland on October 11, 1967. The team's first victory was a 2–1 win in St. Louis on October 18. The following night, with signs of unfinished construction all around the Spectrum, they drew 7,812 for their initial home game, a 1–0 victory over Pittsburgh. Winger Bill Sutherland, who had to sneak into the building after an overzealous usher refused to believe he was a player, scored the winning goal in the third period.

With a base of only 2,100 season tickets and no radio contract, the team endured crowds as embarrassingly low as 4,203 in the early weeks. But, momentum began to build. In February, the team had just drawn consecutive sellouts of home games against Toronto and Chicago when high winds tore portions of tarpaper off the Spectrum roof during a performance of the Ice Capades. The building was quickly repaired, but 12 days later more wind did greater damage to a building that, it was learned, had never received a final safety inspection before opening.

The Flyers were orphaned, moving the first two of seven remaining home games to Madison Square Garden and Maple Leaf Gardens before settling in Quebec City, where they owned their farm club. Nevertheless, the team persevered to be crowned champions of the expansion West Division and returned home to the re-opened Spectrum for the playoffs. They lost a tough seven-game series to St. Louis, but left to a standing ovation that was symbolic of how they had captured the city's heart. A year later, after the Flyers were physically abused by the Blues in four straight, the team prioritized size in the draft. But first, they struck gold with the selection of center Bobby Clarke. Though a dominating junior player, Clarke had been passed over by ten teams, including the Flyers, in the 1969 draft because he had been diagnosed as a diabetic.

By this time, Poile was losing favor with Snider, who had become increasingly impressed with Allen. Bumped up to assistant general manager at the end of the second season, Allen was elevated to g.m. when Poile was fired midway through the third. With the departure of the g.m. he had selected, Putnam sold his shares and left.

When a late-season slump cost the Flyers a playoff spot in 1970–71, the decision was made to move one of the team's young goalies for some scoring. Allen traded Parent to Toronto in a three-way deal with the Leafs and Bruins for Rick MacLeish. Philadelphia made the playoffs in their fourth year, but were uncompetitive in a first-round sweep by Chicago. In 1971–72, an eight-player trade with Los Angeles brought a player of lasting impact, left wing Ross Lonsberry, but the team missed the playoffs after losing the last game of the season. The loss seemed a devastating setback to the modest progress the team had made in the second half under first-year coach Fred Shero, but Allen and Snider stayed the course.

The next season, the heretofore disappointing MacLeish blossomed dramatically into a 50-goal scorer while Bill Barber added offensive punch and poise well beyond his years. Also, the organization's bulk-up plan, four years in the works, came to fruition with the promotion of enforcer Dave Schultz. A trade with St. Louis for defenseman Andre Dupont added a bouncer to a defense anchored by Watson and Van Impe and bolstered by the development of Barry Ashbee. Rambunctious wing Bob Kelly now had some muscle on his side, and Shero showed no hesitation to use it. The scrawny little Flyers had become "The Broad Street Bullies" and, with Clarke breaking 100 points and winning the Hart Trophy, they completed their first winning season in 1972–73. Philadelphia had emerged not only as the NHL's most notorious team, but also as one of its best.

Allen reacquired Parent, who had matured under the tutelage of Jacques Plante in Toronto, and with the balance of excellent goaltending, the discipline of Shero's dump-and-chase system, large doses of terror tactics, and a charmed home record whenever Kate Smith sang "God Bless America," the 1973–74 Flyers rolled to a division title and then past the Atlanta Flames into the semifinals.

In seven ferocious games with the New York Rangers, during which Ashbee lost his playing career to a puck in the eye, Philadelphia held off the Rangers 4–3 in a desperate seventh game at the Spectrum and became the first expansion team to beat an old guard club. After losing game one of the finals to the heavily favored Bruins at Boston Garden, the Flyers won game two when Clarke put in his own rebound 12:01 into overtime. Having obtained their first victory in Boston in six-plus seasons, the Flyers then scored a 4–1 victory over the suddenly passive Bruins in game three. The series went to six, but with Kate Smith making her second live appearance at the Spectrum, the Flyers played the game of their lives. They won the Cup in a 1–0 classic on a first-period tip-in by MacLeish, relentless bumping and checking of Orr, and a flawless performance by Parent. The Flyers made it two in a row in 1975, beating the Sabres in six. Once again, Bernie Parent blanked the opposition in the decisive game as Philadelphia scored a 2–0 victory. Parent won the Conn Smythe Trophy for the second time.

Five months later, the best goaltender in the game had to leave training camp for neck disc surgery. Still, the well-oiled Flyers rolled to their best-yet regular-season record (51–13–16, 118 points). They also scored a victory in one of the most storied international sports events in history, beating the Central Red Army, 4–1, after the visiting Soviet League champions had gone undefeated through the first three games of an unprecedented four-game tour of NHL teams.

Parent was back by playoff time, but struggled during the team's unexpectedly difficult seven-game first-round triumph over Toronto. He was benched, and backup Wayne Stephenson led the Flyers past Boston in five games and into one of the most anticipated finals in years against a swift and powerful Montreal team

Philadelphia Flyers

Year-by-Year Record

Season	GP	W	L	T	OL	GF	GA	Pts.	Finish	Division	Playoff Result
1967-68	74	31	32	11	...	173	179	73	1st	West Div.	Lost Quarterfinal
1968-69	76	20	35	21	...	174	225	61	3rd	West Div.	Lost Quarterfinal
1969-70	76	17	35	24	...	197	225	58	5th	West Div.	Out of Playoffs
1970-71	78	28	33	17	...	207	225	73	3rd	West Div.	Lost Quarterfinal
1971-72	78	26	38	14	...	200	236	66	5th	West Div.	Out of Playoffs
1972-73	78	37	30	11	...	296	256	85	2nd	West Div.	Lost Semifinal
1973-74	78	50	16	12	...	273	164	112	1st	West Div.	Won Stanley Cup
1974-75	80	51	18	11	...	293	181	113	1st	Patrick Div.	Won Stanley Cup
1975-76	80	51	13	16	...	348	209	118	1st	Patrick Div.	Lost Final
1976-77	80	48	16	16	...	323	213	112	1st	Patrick Div.	Lost Semifinal
1977-78	80	45	20	15	...	296	200	105	2nd	Patrick Div.	Lost Semifinal
1978-79	80	40	25	15	...	281	248	95	2nd	Patrick Div.	Lost Quarterfinal
1979-80	80	48	12	20	...	327	254	116	1st	Patrick Div.	Lost Final
1980-81	80	41	24	15	...	313	249	97	2nd	Patrick Div.	Lost Quarterfinal
1981-82	80	38	31	11	...	325	313	87	3rd.	Patrick Div.	Lost Div. Semifinal
1982-83	80	49	23	8	...	326	240	106	1st	Patrick Div.	Lost Div. Semifinal
1983-84	80	44	26	10	...	350	290	98	3rd	Patrick Div.	Lost Div. Semifinal
1984-85	80	53	20	7	...	348	241	113	1st	Patrick Div.	Lost Final
1985-86	80	53	23	4	...	335	241	110	1st	Patrick Div.	Lost Div. Semifinal
1986-87	80	46	26	8	...	310	245	100	1st	Patrick Div.	Lost Final
1987-88	80	38	33	9	...	292	292	85	3rd	Patrick Div.	Lost Div. Semifinal
1988-89	80	36	36	8	...	307	285	80	4th	Patrick Div.	Lost Conf. Finals
1989-90	80	30	39	11	...	290	297	71	6th	Patrick Div.	Out of Playoffs
1990-91	80	33	37	10	...	252	267	76	5th	Patrick Div.	Out of Playoffs
1991-92	80	32	37	11	...	252	273	75	6th	Patrick Div.	Out of Playoffs
1992-93	84	36	37	11	...	319	319	83	5th	Patrick Div.	Out of Playoffs
1993-94	84	35	39	10	...	294	314	80	6th	Atlantic Div.	Out of Playoffs
1994-95	48	28	16	4	...	150	132	60	1st	Atlantic Div.	Lost Conf. Finals
1995-96	82	45	24	13	...	282	208	103	1st	Atlantic Div.	Lost Conf. Semifinal
1996-97	82	45	24	13	...	274	217	103	2nd	Atlantic Div.	Lost Final
1997-98	82	42	29	11	...	242	193	95	2nd	Atlantic Div.	Lost Conf. Quarterfinal
1998-99	82	37	26	19	...	231	196	93	2nd	Atlantic Div.	Lost Conf. Quarterfinal
99-2000	82	45	22	12	3	237	179	105	1st	Atlantic Div.	Lost Conf. Finals
2000-01	82	43	25	11	3	240	207	100	2nd	Atlantic Div.	Lost Conf. Quarterfinal
2001-02	82	42	27	10	3	234	192	97	1st	Atlantic Div.	Lost Conf. Quarterfinal
2002-03	82	45	20	13	4	211	166	107	2nd	Atlantic Div.	Lost Conf. Semifinal

that had outlasted Philadelphia for the league's best record. Without Parent or MacLeish, who had suffered a season-ending knee injury in February, and with Clarke hobbled by a bad knee, Montreal won four straight games by a total margin of five goals to end the Flyers' reign, despite a record 19-goal playoff by Reggie Leach.

Another Patrick Division title followed in 1976–77, but the Flyers were emotionally worn by the death of Barry Ashbee (now an assistant coach) from leukemia in the spring of 1977, and were swept by the Bruins in the semifinals. When Boston eliminated Philadelphia one step short of the finals again in 1978, Allen made the decision to rebuild.

Shero, who wanted more control over personnel decisions, left to become the coach and general manager of the Rangers, who routed the rebuilding Flyers and rookie head coach Pat Quinn in the 1979 quarterfinals. But, two high draft picks, center Ken Linseman and defenseman Behn Wilson, plus the emergence of bedrock right wing Paul Holmgren as a scorer and leader, brought the Flyers back strong the following season.

After dropping the second contest of the year, the Flyers did not lose again for 84 days, running their mind-boggling streak to 35 games (25–0–10). During a tough playoff run, the battered Flyers ultimately proved deeper in enthusiasm than they were on defense, and the Islanders defeated them for the Stanley Cup on Bob Nystrom's overtime goal in game six.

More major changes followed a 1981 upset by Calgary in the quarterfinals, and a 1982 first-round loss to the Rangers. The acquisition of defenseman Mark Howe from Hartford in a trade for Linseman stabilized a defense that was hanging in tatters. Under coach Bob McCammon, who had succeeded the fired Quinn late in the 1981–82 season, the Flyers bounced back strongly with a 106-point season and a Patrick Division championship. After the speedier Rangers took them apart in three straight first-round games, Allen was pushed upstairs and McCammon was given the dual role of coach and general manager. He then was let go by new team president Jay Snider, the owner's son, after a third consecutive first-round loss in 1984.

Bobby Clarke retired to become general manager, and Bill Barber's career ended with a knee injury. Nevertheless, in what was expected to be a rebuilding season, the youngest team in the NHL was directed by rookie coach Mike Keenan to the NHL's best record (53–20–7, 113 points). Keyed by the emergence of a new 50-goal scorer, Tim Kerr, anchored by the flawless defense of Howe and brilliant goaltending by Swedish import Pelle Lindbergh, plus injected with three energetic rookies—Rick Tocchet, Peter Zezel and Derrick Smith—the Flyers ended their playoff misery by advancing all the way to the Stanley Cup finals. Their loss there to the defending champion Oilers became inconsequential five months later when Lindbergh, the Vezina Trophy winner, was killed in an automobile accident.

Despite the loss of Lindbergh, the Flyers came within three points of the previous season's total before a first-round playoff loss to the Rangers brought the season to a crashing halt. The following year, Keenan turned over the goaltending duties from Bob

Flyers Hall of Famers: Bill Barber (right) holds the Flyers career record with 420 goals. He scored 30 playing alongside Bobby Clarke (left) as a rookie in 1972–73. Clarke was named captain of the Flyers that season and became the first player from an NHL expansion team to top 100 points, finishing second in the league to Phil Esposito with 104.

Froese to rookie Ron Hextall, whose unprecedented puck-handling skills and fiery demeanor carried an injury-racked team to another 100-point season. A brilliant playoff performance by Hextall saw the Flyers return to the finals for a second crack at Edmonton and the Cup in three years. This time Philadelphia rallied from a three-games-to-one deficit before falling to the Oilers in seven.

The Flyers began the 1987–88 season looking burned out from their record 26-game playoff ordeal, and struggled in the continuing absence of Kerr, who needed multiple operations on a shoulder that had forced him out of the final two series. They started to come on in late November and made history on December 8 against Boston when Hextall became the first NHL goalie to shoot and score a goal. But, they struggled down the stretch and blew a 3–1 series lead in the first round to Washington, failing to hold a 3–0 edge in a 5–4 overtime loss in game seven at the Capital Centre.

Clarke perceived mental fatigue from four years under the hard-driving Keenan and fired the coach, promoting assistant Holmgren. The Flyers suffered through their first losing season in 17 years, but got hot in the playoffs and advanced to the semifinals. However, this turned out to be the last hurrah for the era. In 1989–90, the team missed the playoffs for the first time in 18 seasons. Clarke, who had lost the confidence of Jay Snider over a perceived reluctance to rebuild, was fired and new g.m. Russ Farwell struggled to right the team's direction after years of poor drafting. After two more years of missing the playoffs, the Sniders and Farwell decided it was time to do something bold. They pursued a trade with the Quebec Nordiques for Eric Lindros, heralded as the prospect of the decade.

The Flyers agreed to give up six players—including the injury-racked Hextall and their last two number-one draft picks, center Mike Ricci and Peter Forsberg. They spiced the package with two future first-round picks, plus $15 million. When Nordiques president Marcel Aubut claimed he had never finalized the deal and announced he had reached an agreement for Lindros with the New York Rangers, Jay Snider protested to the league and arbitrator Larry Bertuzzi decided in favor of the Flyers, consummating one of the biggest deals in sports.

Despite missing 40 games with various injuries in his first two seasons, Lindros performed well. Still, the lineup gaps left by the massive trade doomed the Flyers to fourth and fifth consecutive seasons without a playoff spot. Jay Snider resigned to go into private business, and Ed Snider, returned to an active role in running the team as he negotiated to build a new arena, brought back Clarke as general manager. His trade of Mark Recchi to Montreal late in the lockout-shortened 1994–95 season brought defenseman Eric Desjardins and left wing John LeClair and reestablished the Flyers as an elite team.

With a reacquired Hextall, the Flyers, under coach Terry Murray, reached the conference finals before losing to the eventual champion New Jersey Devils in six games, but Lindros joined Clarke to become just the second Flyer to win the Hart Trophy. Two years later, in 1996–97, the Flyers returned to the Stanley Cup finals, but were overwhelmed in four straight by Detroit, leading to the firing of Murray. That same season saw the opening of the new 19,519-seat CoreStates Center (later renamed the First Union Center). The next year, Lindros missed 18 games just before the 1998 playoffs due to a concussion. He returned but was ineffective as the Flyers, under veteran coach Roger Neilson, lost in the first round to Buffalo. In 1998–99, Lindros was having his most complete season when he suffered a collapsed lung that left the Flyers without him for the playoffs, where they lost in six games to Toronto.

After backing up John Vanbiesbrouck for a year, Ron Hextall retired prior to the 1999–2000 campaign, but the Flyers entered the new season with few changes to the lineup. The club started poorly, but was in top form by December when it was learned coach Roger Neilson had bone-marrow cancer. Though he continued to coach while undergoing treatment, he was forced to step aside on February 20, 2000, and was replaced by assistant coach Craig Ramsay. (Ramsay would be formally named the club's new head coach after the playoffs.) On the ice, meanwhile, Mark Recchi (who had been reacquired late in the 1998–99 season) reestablished himself as a top-notch NHL star, leading the league with 63 assists and finishing third in scoring behind Jaromir Jagr and Pavel Bure. John LeClair scored 40 goals. Simon Gagne, the club's first draft choice in 1998, proved to have a scoring touch with 20 goals, while fellow rookie Brian Boucher, the club's top pick in 1997, emerged as the number-one goaltender. In 35 games played, Boucher posted a 1.91 goals-against average to lead the league and become the first rookie netminder with an average below 2.00 since 1950–51.

All was not well with Eric Lindros, however. Having already missed some time due to back spasms, Lindros was sidelined by a concussion late in the season. (He would suffer yet another head injury when he returned to action against New Jersey in the playoffs.) While he was out, Eric Desjardins replaced Lindros as captain. The club played well down the stretch, riding a hot finish to overhaul the Devils for first place overall in the Eastern Conference. Though some thought the eighth-seeded Buffalo Sabres had a chance to do some damage in the playoffs, the Flyers handled them easily for an opening-round victory in five games. Roger Neilson received medical clearance to rejoin the team for the conference semifinals and returned to assist Craig Ramsay and the coaching staff for the series with Pittsburgh. The Flyers dropped the first two games of the second-round set on home ice and the Penguins seemed poised for an upset before the Flyers won two in a row on the road, including a 2–1 victory in game four that required five overtime periods. After winning the third-longest game in NHL history, Philadelphia posted two more wins to take the series in six and advance to play New Jersey in the Conference final. Though the Flyers raced to a 3–1 series lead, the Devils got their revenge for the regular season when they stormed back to take the series in seven games.

Bill Barber, a member of the Flyers organization since he was selected in the first round of the 1972 Amateur Draft, took over as the club's head coach 28 games into the 2000–01 season. Barber had spent four seasons as the head coach with the team's AHL affiliate before being named an assistant coach with the Flyers at the start of the season. With the team floundering at the .500 mark, Barber took over the top job from Craig Ramsay on December 10, 2000. The team responded with an eight-game unbeaten streak (five wins, three ties) and went on to post a mark of 31–13–7–3 in 54 games and finish the year with 100 points. In the playoffs, however, the Flyers were knocked out by Buffalo in the first round, losing the sixth and final game of the series 8–0. Still, Barber became the eighth man to win the Jack Adams Award as coach of the year

John LeClair (left) is a three-time 50-goal scorer. Simon Gagne (center) gives the Flyers speed and skill, while Keith Primeau (right) adds size and strength.

in his first year as a head coach. He was the first to win the honor after taking over behind the bench in midseason.

On the ice, the team was led by the play of another first-year performer, goaltender Roman Cechmanek. A veteran of the Elite League in the Czech Republic, Cechmanek was too old to qualify as an NHL rookie, but his 10 shutouts were the most by a first-year netminder since Tony Esposito had 15 in 1969–70. Cechmanek ranked second in the NHL in both shutouts and goals-against average (2.01) and finished second to Dominik Hasek in voting for the Vezina Trophy. Offensively, Mark Recchi reached the 1,000-point plateau during the season and led the club with 77 points (27 goals, 50 assists). Keith Primeau (34 goals) and Simon Gagne (27 goals) also had good years. John LeClair was limited to just 16 games because of a back injury. Eric Lindros missed the entire season while recovering from injuries and because of a contract dispute.

During the offseason, the Flyers traded Lindros to the Rangers for three players and a draft pick. They also signed Jeremy Roenick as a free agent and inked LeClair to a new long-term contract. LeClair returned to play all 82 games and was second on the club with 25 goals. Gagne was tops with 33, while Roenick led the team with 67 points (21 goals, 47 assists). Kim Johnsson, who was acquired in the Lindros trade, topped Philly blueliners with 11 goals and 30 assists. Once again, Cechmanek ranked second in the NHL in goals-against average (2.05). Seven Flyers (Gagne, Roenick, LeClair, Johnsson, Cechmanek, Jiri Dopita and Ruslan Fedotenko) took part in the Winter Olympics at Salt Lake City, with Simon Gagne helping Team Canada win gold.

The Flyers won the Atlantic Division with 97 points in 2001–02. They added Adam Oates in a deal with Washington late in the season, but once again they were beaten in the first round of the playoffs. Philadelphia was shutout in three straight games and scored only two goals overall in their five-game loss to the Ottawa Senators. The poor postseason performance cost Barber his job, as the Flyers turned to former Dallas coach Ken Hitchcock for the 2002–03 season.

The team struggled for goals under their new defensive-minded bench boss, but were very difficult to score against. Philadelphia surrendered just 166 goals, tying New Jersey for the Jennings Trophy. The Flyers also battled the Devils for top spot in the Atlantic Division, but fell short by a single point (108–107). Roman Cechmanek posted a record of 35–15–10 while ranking second behind the Stars' Marty Turco with a 1.83 goals-against average and third behind Turco and Minnesota's Dwayne Roloson with a .925 save percentage. Offensively, the Flyers were hurt by injuries that sidelined John LeClair and Simon Gagne for much of the season. The club was led by Jeremy Roenick (27 goals, 32 assists), Mark Recchi (20 goals, 32 assists) and Michal Handzus (23 goals). Tony Amonte was acquired from Phoenix at the trade deadline and had seven goals in just 13 games with the Flyers after scoring only 13 times in 59 games with Phoenix. However, he would score just once in 13 playoff games.

Philadelphia opened the playoffs against Toronto, and though they were the dominant team for much of the series (they outshot the Leafs 282–189) they needed the full seven games to win it. They also had to survive the loss of Eric Desjardins, who broke his foot late in game five. The series was just the second in NHL history (Rangers vs. Devils, 1994) to feature as many as three multiple-overtime games. The total playing time of 532 minutes and five seconds was nearly the equivalent of nine full games and ranked second all time to the clocking of 553:08 in a matchup between the Bruins and Rangers way back in 1939.

The Flyers' victory marked the first time in three years they had gotten out of the first round, but Philadelphia could not survive the second. Cechmanek was sharp in shutting out the Senators for victories in games two and four, but the unorthodox netminder looked vulnerable in the next two games as Ottawa scored 5–2 and 5–1 victories to wrap up the series in six. It was obvious that the long Leafs series had taken its toll on the Flyers. Jeremy Roenick had been banged up and Keith Primeau was paying the price for playing with a physical presence.

"Anybody that understands the game of hockey knew we were running out of gas in game five," Ken Hitchcock said. "When they got the lead, our lack of energy started to show. People that had quickness and puck strength earlier in the playoffs had nothing left."

Still, much of the blame for the Flyers' lack of postseason success went to Cechmanek, who was booed by the notoriously tough Philadelphia fans. Despite his stellar numbers during the past three regular seasons, Bobby Clarke indicated that the netminder would not be back. Indeed, he was traded to the Los Angeles Kings for a second-round draft choice in the 2004 draft before the playoffs were even complete.

Philadelphia Quakers

IT WAS 1930 when the NHL first arrived in the City of Brotherly Love. The Pittsburgh Pirates moved across state to become the Philadelphia Quakers, taking their name from the religious community of the Pennsylvania countryside.

Pittsburgh had become the third American city in the NHL (after Boston and New York) when the Pirates were granted a franchise in 1925. Though the city had a long hockey tradition, the Pirates were not a financial success. One year after the stock market crash of October, 1929 weakened the city's steel industry, Benny Leonard, the ex-boxer and fight promoter who had joined the hockey club's ownership group in 1928, decided to relocate. The transfer of Pittsburgh's home games to Philadelphia was accepted by the NHL's Board of Governors on October 18, 1930.

Twelve players who had worn the yellow and black of the Pittsburgh Pirates in 1929–30 suited up in the orange and black of the Philadelphia Quakers in 1930–31. Harry Darragh, Hib Milks, Tex White and Herb Drury had been with the franchise since its NHL debut in 1925–26, though only Milks would suffer through the entire season in Philadelphia. Future Hockey Hall of Fame referee Cooper Smeaton had resigned as the NHL's referee-in-chief to coach the Quakers. The roster was bolstered by future star Syd Howe and new goalie Wilf Cude, but Smeaton would be refereeing again by 1931–32.

The first NHL game in Philadelphia took place on November 11, 1930, with the New York Rangers defeating the Quakers, 3–0. It would take until their third game before the Quakers scored their first goal. Their first victory came in game six against the Toronto Maple Leafs on November 25, but the Quakers' next win would not come until January 10, 1931, when they beat the Montreal Maroons to "improve" to 2–19–1. The Quakers finished the season with a record of 4–36–4. Philadelphia's 76 goals in 1930–31 tied the New York Americans for fewest in the league, while the Quakers' 184 goals against was 42 more than the next worst team (the Ottawa Senators) and almost double the average of 97 goals allowed by the NHL's other nine clubs. Philadelphia's winning percentage of .136 would remain the worst in NHL history until the Washington Capitals went 8–67–5 for a .131 mark in 1974–75.

At the NHL Board of Governors meeting on September 26, 1931, it was announced that both the Ottawa Senators and the Pittsburgh-Philadelphia franchise would suspend operations for 1931–32. The Pennsylvania club continued to receive permission to suspend operations until May 7, 1936, when the franchise was formally canceled. The NHL did not return to Pittsburgh or Philadelphia until 1967.

Herb Drury played 24 games for the dreadful Philadelphia Quakers of 1930–31. Previously, Drury had played hockey in Pittsburgh since the 1916–17 season, including five years with the NHL's Pittsburgh Pirates.

Philadelphia Quakers

Year-by-Year Record

Season	GP	W	L	T	GF	GA	Pts	Finish	Division	Playoff Results
1930–31	44	4	36	4	76	184	12	5th	American	Out of Playoffs

Phoenix Coyotes and Winnipeg Jets

THREE-TIME CHAMPIONS in the seven-year history of the World Hockey Association, the Winnipeg Jets enjoyed good times and bad in the NHL. At their best during the heyday of the Edmonton Oilers, Winnipeg iced strong teams that never could get out of their division in the playoffs. Left in a competitive desert as the smallest of small-market teams, the Jets left Winnipeg for Phoenix in 1996 and rose from the ashes as the Coyotes.

The original Winnipeg Jets franchise began in the Western Canada Junior Hockey League in 1967. Spearheaded by entrepreneur Ben Hatskin, the team was named simply because Hatskin was a friend and admirer of Sonny Werblin, owner of the National Football League's New York Jets. The new hockey team met with only limited success, but Hatskin was hooked on both the game and ownership. When Gary Davidson and Dennis Murphy created a pro league to rival the NHL, Hatskin joined the 12-team World Hockey Association in 1971. The WHA's first games were played in 1972-73.

The rival league wasn't regarded with much interest or credibility by hockey's establishment, until a couple of high-profile signings changed everything. Talented goalie Bernie Parent led the defections to the WHA, and Hatskin was not far behind with his coup de grace. His target was Bobby Hull.

"The Golden Jet" found most of Hatskin's early overtures merely a nuisance, and jokingly told the Winnipeg organization that he needed a million dollars to jump leagues. Hull soon found out that Hatskin and his new partners weren't kidding around.

Some intense negotiations and deal-brokering with other WHA franchises to contribute half of a $2.75 million contract led to Hull's decision to switch leagues. He inked the deal on June 27, 1972, and jetted off to Winnipeg for a symbolic signing at the city's epicenter, the corner of Portage Avenue and Main Street. Hull's signing touched off a flurry of NHL defections that numbered 60 by the time the first WHA schedule had begun.

The defections were followed as quickly by lawsuits from NHL clubs, who held that the reserve clause bound players to teams, even if their contracts had expired. Legal actions continued into August 1972 (costing Hull a spot on Team Canada's 1972 roster), but the Jets did not sit still. Not only did they name Hull as the team's first coach, but they hired Nick Mickoski as his assistant and named Ab McDonald their first captain. Hull did not suit up for the franchise's first pro game, a 6–4 win over the New York Raiders at Madison Square Garden on October 12, 1972. In fact, he missed 15 games before an American judge tossed out the NHL suits as "harassment."

Despite the forced hiatus, "The Golden Jet" fired 51 goals and 103 points that inaugural season. Playing on the Luxury Line with Christian Bordeleau and Normie Beaudin, Hull and the Jets went all the way to the Avco Cup finals before losing to New England. After a mediocre second year, Hatskin dispatched confidant and scout Billy Robinson to Sweden to bolster the club's lineup—a philosophy much ahead of its time. The mission brought Ulf Nilsson, Anders Hedberg, defenseman Lars-Erik Sjoberg and others to Winnipeg, and became the catalyst for a new and high-tempo brand of offensive hockey that made the Jets immensely successful in the remaining WHA years. Playing with Nilsson and Hedberg, Hull scored a pro hockey record 77 goals in 1974–75.

While the Jets were dominating the WHA in the late 1970s, the league eventually ran up against some insurmountable problems, most of them financial. However, as one of the league's strongest entities, the Jets eventually became one of four clubs that were accepted into the NHL's expansion of 1979. About a year earlier, a local lawyer named Barry Shenkarow and Winnipeg businessman Michael Gobuty had become part of the ownership team. The deal cut to admit the Jets, Edmonton, Hartford and Quebec into the NHL came with some harsh conditions attached. Jets general manager John Ferguson was allowed to retain only two skaters and two goaltenders before the Expansion Draft, and the successful hockey team Winnipeggers had come to love was more or less disbanded.

The chance to play with Gordie Howe and sons lured Morris Lukowich to Houston after a stellar junior career in Medicine Hat. Sold to Winnipeg in 1978, he entered the NHL with the Jets in 1979–80 and was one of the the club's top point producers in its early years in the NHL.

Under coach Tom McVie and his assistant Billy Sutherland, the Jets opened their first NHL season in Pittsburgh, October 10, 1979, with a 4–2 loss. Their first NHL goal came from Morris Lukowich, who went on to lead the club in scoring that first rag-tag season. It produced 20 wins, as the Jets managed to tie Colorado for last place with 51 points. The team found the going even rougher in year two. The Jets went 30 games without a victory in one stretch, went through three coaches (McVie, Sutherland and future g.m. Mike Smith) and ended up a distant last in the NHL with only nine wins (9–57–14) and 32 points. The Jets' rebound in the 1981–82 season was one of the most dramatic on record. The club posted a .500 mark that year, 33–33–14, finishing second in the Norris Division to Minnesota.

There were reasons for this turnaround. Having the worst record the year before had allowed the Jets to select Dale Hawerchuk first overall in the 1981 Entry Draft. Hawerchuk's scoring exploits from junior translated instantly into the pro game, amounting to 45 goals and 103 points. Thomas Steen also made his debut in Winnipeg. The Jets had hired career college coach Tom Watt from the University of Toronto, and the additions were enough to bring them immediate respectability. Hawerchuk won the Calder Trophy, and Watt was rewarded with the Jack Adams Award as NHL coach of the year.

An ominous tendency for early playoff exits began in that spring of 1982, when the Jets lost four straight to St. Louis in the first round. In the following two years, it happened against the powerful Oilers. A minor breakthrough occurred in the spring of 1985, when a very balanced Jets team dropped the Calgary Flames in the first round, but lost Hawerchuk to a broken rib. An Edmonton sweep in the second round took away from many of the positives in a season where six different Jets had at least 30 goals. An experienced defense led by Randy Carlyle and Dave Ellett also had been promising. Under coach Barry Long, the Jets had hit a high-water mark of 43 wins and 96 points.

Dale Hawerchuk won back-to-back Memorial Cup championships with the Cornwall Royals before winning the Calder Trophy in 1981–82. He established career highs with 53 goals and 130 points in 1984–85 when he placed third in scoring behind Wayne Gretzky and Jari Kurri.

The Jets fell back to 59 points the very next season, and the yo-yo trend of good season followed by bad was well under way. Long was replaced by Dan Maloney who, as per the script, brought the team back up to 88 points in 1986–87.

That was another exciting spring in Winnipeg. The Jets won a stirring first-round playoff matchup against the Calgary Flames in six games—the last time the team made it past the first round—but it was the same old story against the Oilers. The second-round series lasted the minimum four games, taking the Jets' postseason record against Edmonton to 0–14. From 88 points, the Jets slipped back again the following season to 77 and the 1988 playoffs brought a familiar opponent, the Oilers. A five-game triumph for Edmonton left the overall tally at 1–18. That, as much as anything, cost the always-boisterous Ferguson his job in October, 1988.

Longtime scout and assistant g.m. Mike Smith was brought in as general manager, first on an interim basis and then as a permanent appointment. But, by the time he started rearranging the team's role players and depth, the season was lost. Maloney was a casualty, and the Jets finished under Rick Bowness. Bob Murdoch took over as the new coach in 1989–90, and the team perked up once again. It rebounded to 85 points with a very workmanlike approach. In the playoffs, Winnipeg jumped out to a 3–1 series lead over Edmonton, including Dave Ellett's double-overtime marker that for many Jets fans remains one of the club's greatest NHL moments. But, Jari Kurri, Mark Messier and company still proved too much for Winnipeg in seven games and the Oilers marched on to the Stanley Cup.

Over the years, Smith's management style became the subject of much scrutiny. The introspective and highly educated g.m. made frequent trades (71 during his five-year tenure) and stocked the

Phoenix Coyotes

Year-by-Year Record

Season	GP	W	L	T	OL	GF	GA	Pts.	Finish	Division	Playoff Result
1979-80*	80	20	49	11	...	214	314	51	5th	Smythe Div.	Out of Playoffs
1980-81*	80	9	57	14	...	246	400	32	6th	Smythe Div.	Out of Playoffs
1981-82*	80	33	33	14	...	319	332	80	2nd	Norris Div.	Lost Div. Semifinal
1982-83*	80	33	39	8	...	311	333	74	4th	Smythe Div.	Lost Div. Semifinal
1983-84*	80	31	38	11	...	340	374	73	4th	Smythe Div.	Lost Div. Semifinal
1984-85*	80	43	27	10	...	358	332	96	2nd	Smythe Div.	Lost Div. Final
1985-86*	80	26	47	7	...	295	372	59	3rd	Smythe Div.	Lost Div. Semifinal
1986-87*	80	40	32	8	...	279	271	88	3rd	Smythe Div.	Lost Div. Final
1987-88*	80	33	36	11	...	292	310	77	3rd	Smythe Div.	Lost Div. Semifinal
1988-89*	80	26	42	12	...	300	355	64	5th	Smythe Div.	Out of Playoffs
1989-90*	80	37	32	11	...	298	290	85	3rd	Smythe Div.	Lost Div. Semifinal
1990-91*	80	26	43	11	...	260	288	63	5th	Smythe Div.	Out of Playoffs
1991-92*	80	33	32	15	...	251	244	81	4th	Smythe Div.	Lost Div. Semifinal
1992-93*	84	40	37	7	...	322	320	87	4th	Smythe Div.	Lost Div. Semifinal
1993-94*	84	24	51	9	...	245	344	57	6th	Central Div.	Out of Playoffs
1994-95*	48	16	25	7	...	157	177	39	6th	Central Div.	Out of Playoffs
1995-96*	82	36	40	6	...	275	291	78	5th	Central Div.	Lost Conf. Quarterfinal
1996-97	82	38	37	7	...	240	243	83	3rd	Central Div.	Lost Conf. Quarterfinal
1997-98	82	35	35	12	...	224	227	82	4th	Central Div.	Lost Conf. Quarterfinal
1998-99	82	39	31	12	...	205	197	90	2nd	Pacific Div.	Lost Conf. Quarterfinal
99-2000	82	39	31	8	4	232	228	90	3rd	Pacific Div.	Lost Conf. Quarterfinal
2000-01	82	35	27	17	3	214	212	90	4th	Pacific Div.	Out of Playoffs
2001-02	82	40	27	9	6	228	210	95	2nd	Pacific Div.	Lost Conf. Quarterfinal
2002-03	82	31	35	11	5	204	230	78	4th	Pacific Div.	Out of Playoffs

* Winnipeg Jets

Winnipeg reserve list with European players, mainly Russians. Smith also became known as a frugal manager and formidable negotiator, a trait that may have been good for the team's bottom line but alienated several important players.

Hawerchuk eventually became disgruntled and his trade request was granted by Smith after the seven-game loss to the Oilers in 1990. The haul was Buffalo's highly talented defenseman Phil Housley, who himself became a contractual headache and was traded to St. Louis in September, 1993. The same fate befell goalie Bob Essensa, who was a Vezina Trophy finalist in 1991–92, and later won the first $1 million arbitration award in NHL history. Essensa, however, was traded in March, 1994.

After the Hawerchuk trade, the Jets had sagged to 63 points under Murdoch in 1990-91 and the coach was replaced by Oak River, Manitoba, native John Paddock. Paddock had spent most of his playing time in the minors and had assembled an impressive resume behind the bench of several successful American Hockey League clubs. He took over in the fall of 1991 and moved the team to two straight playoff berths, with improved point totals each year—a first for the franchise. But, the Vancouver Canucks defeated the Jets in the playoffs in both 1992 and 1993.

Paddock had benefited from the introduction of Teemu Selanne to the NHL in the fall of 1992. With speed, skill and charisma, "The Finnish Flash" vaulted to instant stardom in Winnipeg and around the NHL. Selanne smashed records for goals by freshmen with 76 (tying Alexander Mogilny for the overall league lead) and points with 132. He was the unanimous selection (all 50 first-place votes) as the Calder Trophy winner over the likes of Eric Lindros and Felix Potvin.

Mike Smith was responsible for drafting or bringing much of the new wave of talent to the franchise—including Selanne, Teppo Numminen, Alexei Zhamnov, Keith Tkachuk and goalie Nikolai Khabibulin. But Shenkarow, the team's president, could go no further with Smith and dismissed him in January, 1994. Paddock the coach became Paddock the coach/general manager.

The lockout-shortened season of 1994–95 proved to be the beginning of the end for the franchise in Winnipeg. Burdened with the city's decaying arena (built in the 1950s and renovated several times) and escalating NHL salaries, Shenkarow and his private ownership group (holding 64 percent) were caught in a financial squeeze. Provincial and city governments held a 36 percent stake and had a grip on the team's purse strings after agreeing to fund any operating losses in 1991.

The covering of losses was the panacea to Shenkarow to be patient. It also turned out to be a short-sighted guarantee in the wake of rising salaries, and eventually became a political lightning rod that damaged whatever hope there might have been to save the franchise in Winnipeg.

Two distinct groups emerged to try to rescue the situation in 1994 and 1995. Manitoba Entertainment Complex (MEC) was the first group to try to arrange the purchase of the team and construction of a new, revenue-enhancing arena. Shenkarow, in his 1991 agreement with governments, had agreed to sell the franchise to approved buyers for $32 million Canadian by 1996. MEC, however, after first blaming NHL commissioner Gary Bettman, couldn't finalize an agreement with Shenkarow on the sale of the team or with different government bodies on the arena financing, and flew the white flag in early May.

After missing the playoffs, an emotional in-arena funeral to retire the team logo and Thomas Steen's number 25 was held only days before a second group called Spirit of Manitoba surfaced. However, Shenkarow's August deadline to consummate a deal with the group could not be met.

Mostly, the deal was just too complicated, but Bettman's summation of the mess was painfully accurate—that it was a simple case that nobody in the Manitoba capital wanted to step up and own the team. Winnipeg fans and taxpayers had run the emotional gamut from death to life, back to the inevitable and impending departure. Winnipeg was left with a lame-duck team for the 1995–96 season because all the political and financial wrangling went past the league deadline for transferring locations.

Right winger Mike Johnson led the Coyotes in scoring in 2002-03.

And so they played their final season, to poor crowds that eventually averaged 11,316 (74 percent of capacity). The club's 36–40–6 record was overshadowed by Tkachuk's huge new five-year contract, the terms of which were dictated by an offer sheet tendered by the Chicago Blackhawks, and by the unpopular trade of Teemu Selanne to Anaheim.

On the ice, the club struggled to the bitter end to squeeze into the playoffs. Tkachuk's 50th goal in the second-to-last game of the season sparked a final burst of enthusiasm for the team, though the

Jets had drawn the powerful, first-seeded Detroit Red Wings in the first round of the Western Conference playoffs. Winnipeg, with its white-clad, frenzied fans, got in its licks to take the Wings to six games, but Norm Maciver's goal in the 3–1, game six loss on April 28, 1996, closed the book on Winnipeg in the NHL.

Exactly 1,400 regular and postseason NHL games had been played by the Jets, who were turned into the Phoenix Coyotes after a $68-million (U.S.) purchase by Richard Burke and Steven Gluckstern. Coach Terry Simpson lost his job in the transition as ties to Winnipeg were cut by the new owners. Paddock, who had stepped aside as coach in the spring of 1995, also was a casualty just two months into the team's new season in Phoenix. Vice president Bobby Smith, hired by Burke, took over the job of running the team.

With rookie Don Hay running the show, the Coyotes played inconsistently again, but eventually finished at 38–37–7, in spite of a losing record in their new home rink, America West Arena. Tkachuk scored 52 goals to become the first American-born player to lead the league. The team survived a lengthy holdout by Jeremy Roenick, who was acquired for Zhamnov during the offseason, and matched up against the Mighty Ducks of Anaheim in the first playoff round.

From Winnipeg, Phoenix imported the "white-out" tradition of fans all wearing white to home games in the postseason, but all it brought them was the same old grief. The Coyotes were knocked out by the Ducks in a seventh game. The defeat surprisingly prompted Smith to dismiss Hay, and Jim Schoenfeld was brought in to coach year number two in Phoenix. Rick Tocchet was signed as a free agent to add on-ice leadership. Again the club qualified for the playoffs, only to be knocked out in the first round, this time by the eventual Stanley Cup champions from Detroit.

The Coyotes kept pace with the eventual Stanley Cup champions in Dallas in the very early going in 1998–99, but a midseason slump knocked them far out of contention for top spot. Still, the Coyotes enjoyed a 90-point campaign and the club's best season since its move to Phoenix. In the playoffs, the Coyotes jumped out to a 3–1 series lead—only to fall to the St. Louis Blues in seven games. The unsettling playoff departure cost Jim Schoenfeld his job, as the Coyotes turned to Bob Francis, a successful minor-league coach and son of Emile Francis, for the 1999–2000 season.

Since the move to Phoenix, Nikolai Khabibulin had established himself as a front line goaltender in the NHL, yet the Coyotes refused to meet his contract demands and the netminder held out before eventually playing out the season with the Long Beach Ice Dogs of the International Hockey League. Still, with former Jet Bob Essensa and Sean Burke providing solid goaltending, and Jeremy Roenick rediscovering the form from his Chicago days, the Coyotes raced out of the starting blocks. Despite a seven-game losing streak in March that represented the club's worst slide since leaving Winnipeg, Phoenix still was able to match the 39 wins and 90 points of the previous season. Injuries limited Keith Tkachuk to just 22 goals in 50 games.

Though Phoenix had pulled out of its late-season funk by playoff time, the Colorado Avalanche handed the team its ninth consecutive first-round defeat. During the series it was announced that an agreement of terms had been reached in the sale of the club by Richard Burke to The Ellman Companies, a real estate development group that was planning a new arena for the hockey team in neighboring Scottsdale. Construction was due to be completed by the 2002–03 season. Buying in as a minority owner in Steve Ellman's investment was Wayne Gretzky. However, even with Gretzky's presence, the sale was slow to go through and arena plans were delayed. Questions of budgets and ownership continued to surround the team for much of the 2000–01 season, yet the Coyotes enjoyed their third-straight 90-point season—but fell one win short of making the playoffs.

Wayne Gretzky had been introduced as the Coyotes' managing partner in charge of hockey operations back on June 2, 2000. However, the ownership group of Steve Ellman, Gretzky, Jerry Moyes and Shawn Hunter did not complete their purchase of the team from Richard Burke until February 15, 2001. Two days later, Gretzky installed Cliff Fletcher as the team's new general manager, replacing Bobby Smith. Within three weeks, Nikolai Khabibulin (who had refused to sign with the team for nearly two full years) was traded to Tampa Bay and Keith Tkachuk, who was soon to be a free agent, was swapped to St. Louis. Jeremy Roenick, who led the team with 30 goals and 46 assists, signed with the Flyers as a free agent after the season. The star on the ice for Phoenix in 2000–01 was Sean Burke. Touted as a possible Hart Trophy candidate throughout the first half of the season, Burke wound up with the NHL's third-highest save percentage (.922) and tenth-lowest goals-against average (2.27). Both marks represented career bests.

Mike Barnett, Gretzky's former agent, became general manager just before training camp opened in 2001. Little was expected of the club in what was regarded as a rebuilding year, yet the Coyotes won 40 games in 2001–02, and their 95 points represented the second-best total in franchise history. Once again, Sean Burke starred. He was a finalist for both the Vezina Trophy as best goaltender and for the Lester Pearson Award for the NHL MVP as voted on by the players. He also finished fourth in voting for the Hart Trophy. Bob Francis was rewarded for the team's fine season with the Jack Adams Award as coach of the year. Newly acquired Daymond Langkow led the team with 67 points, while former junior scoring sensation Daniel Briere played his first full NHL season and led the club with 32 goals. His shooting percentage of 21.5 was tops in the league. Teppo Numminen broke Thomas Steen's franchise record of 950 games played early in the season (October 16, 2001) and went on to reach the 1,000-game plateau on March 3.

Though the Coyotes were eliminated in the first round of the playoffs, there was still good news in April of 2002 as construction got under way for the team's new arena, now located in suburban Glendale. The building will open during the 2003–04 season. The team will be hoping to rebound from a disappointing 2002–03 campaign, when, despite the addition of free agent Tony Amonte (who was later dealt to Philadelphia at the trade deadline), the team fell out of playoff contention. Much of the team's problems in 2002–03 could be blamed on the fact that Sean Burke was limited to just 22 games due to injuries. Offensively, the club was led by Mike Johnson, Shane Doan, Ladislav Nagy and Daymond Langkow, each of whom reached the 20-goal plateau. Daniel Briere scored 17 goals in 68 games before being traded to Buffalo. Teppo Numminen played in his franchise-record 15th season and was the club's top-scoring defenseman with 30 points on six goals and 24 assists. His tenure with the franchise ended in the offseason when a three-way deal saw him join the Dallas Stars for 2003–04.

Pittsburgh Penguins

PITTSBURGH ENTERED THE NHL during the great expansion of 1967–68. The winning name in the contest to give the team an identifying symbol was Penguins. However, the team symbol, a penguin skating along, stick in hand, flowing scarf from neck, was nowhere to be seen on the uniform. Only the word "Pittsburgh" adorned the front of each jersey. (In 1969, the Penguins symbol, sans scarf, was added in a new uniform design.) One particularly plausible answer as to why "Penguins" was chosen is that the Civic Arena, completed in 1961 at the cost of $22 million, is called "The Igloo" because of its domed roof.

The NHL's first franchise in Pittsburgh had joined the league back in 1925. The Pirates, who took their name from the National League baseball team, moved to Philadelphia after the 1929–30 season, when The Great Depression damaged the city's steel industry. From the mid-1930s, when John H. Harris bought a franchise in the AHL, the Hornets had been symbolic of Pittsburgh hockey and a training ground, first for Detroit but later, and more famously, for Toronto Maple Leafs farmhands. When the old Duquesne Gardens on Craig Street was torn down in the 1950s, there was an absence of hockey in Pittsburgh for five years until the Civic Arena opened and the Hornets returned for the 1961–62 season. The year before the NHL came to town, Pittsburgh won both the AHL title and the Calder Cup. Although they would now see Howe, Hull and Beliveau, the ice fans in the Steel City no longer had a team they identified with and they had to be won over.

Rick Kehoe is still a member of the Penguins organization he joined as a player back in 1974. He had a career-high 55 goals and 88 points in 1980-81, then collected a career-best 52 assists the following season.

In the Expansion Draft of 1967, general manager Jack Riley and coach Red Sullivan sought players with experience and wound up with the oldest club—average age 32. Explained Riley, a popular hockey man who had run the Rochester team of the AHL, and then became president of that league before joining the Penguins: "[Pittsburgh] won the Calder Cup last year. Our fans don't want a building program, they're used to winners. We felt we had to put quality on the ice immediately.... The older players have been winning in hockey in recent years, so that's the way we went."

Three of the important draftees were Earl Ingarfield, Ken Schinkel and Andy Bathgate. All were over 30 and each had something else in common. They had played for the New York Rangers, where the Penguins' coach, Sullivan, had played and coached. In fact, the Pittsburgh roster began to resemble an old Rangers list with defenseman Al MacNeil and forwards Val Fonteyne and Mel Pearson.

Before the 1966–67 season, Pittsburgh had purchased three defensemen—Ted Lanyon, Dick Mattiussi and Bill Speer—and goaltender Les Binkley from the Cleveland Barons. At the time, the Pens had no farm team of their own, so the four were spread around the minors and convened with the rest of the squad at Brantford, Ontario, for the first training camp. A hot battle for the two goaltending jobs developed among Binkley, rookie Joe Daley, veteran Hank Bassen and amateur Marv Edwards. Bassen, who as a Hornet had led his team to the Calder Cup the previous year, was garnered in a trade with Detroit just before the season opened. He figured to do a job and be colorfully popular at the same time. What he hadn't anticipated was just how good Binkley was.

Binkley posted six shutouts in 1967–68, tying him for second place in that department with Lorne Worsley and Cesare Maniago behind Ed Giacomin's eight. In 54 games he compiled a solid 2.87 goals-against average. However, in the futile pursuit of a playoff berth, Binkley broke his finger in a 6–6 tie in Oakland. The Penguins blew a big lead and lost a vital point along with their ace goalie. To their credit, they kept battling to the end of the campaign. Binkley, having recovered, returned in time to lead them to victory in three of their last four winning games. When it was all over, they had as many wins as the North Stars but two fewer points.

Despite missing the playoffs, there were signs of encouragement in the Penguin nest. Pittsburgh fandom, resentful and skeptical at first, had been won over, and late in the season the club's majority interest was sold to a group of Michigan investors, headed by Donald H. Parsons, board chairman of the Bank of the Commonwealth of Detroit, who announced that the Penguins would remain in Pittsburgh. Early in the 1967–68 season, a bid to purchase the team by owners of the baseball Braves had led to rumors that the Penguins might move to Atlanta.

The Pens kept plugging away and gained their first playoff berth in April, 1970, under the coaching of Red Kelly (who would add general managers duties the following year). Pittsburgh moved into the semifinals before being eliminated by St. Louis. Delighted with the play of rookie forward Michel Briere, the Penguins looked forward to next year, but tragedy struck shortly after the 1969–70 season. Briere was seriously injured in an automobile accident in Northern Quebec and never recovered. After a long convalescence, the young player died during the 1971 playoffs. Without Briere, the Penguins had been unable to gain a postseason berth in 1971.

That year did see the team sold again, this time to a Pittsburgh-based group led by Thayer R. "Tad" Potter, who installed himself as general partner and CEO. Other changes included Kelly stepping down as general manager and Jack Riley replacing him, and the acquisition of the flamboyant Eddie Shack in exchange for future Buffalo Sabres star Rene Robert. All these moves didn't help the on-ice product, though, as Pittsburgh was swept in the first round of the playoffs by Chicago. The Penguins continued their hot and cold ways for the next three seasons. Despite setting a still-enduring NHL record for the fastest five goals scored by one team (two minutes, seven seconds) and Greg Polis winning the 1972–73 All-Star Game MVP award, they missed the playoffs that season and the next.

But, there was a turnaround in the 1974–75 campaign. Behind Jean Pronovost, Syl Apps Jr. (that year's All-Star MVP) and rookie Pierre Larouche, Pittsburgh climbed to a 37–28–15 record, third-best in the new Norris Division. After sweeping the Blues in the preliminary round, the Penguins went into the quarterfinals against the New York Islanders and quickly established a three-games-to-none lead going into game four.

It was then that Pittsburgh suffered one of the most ignominious setbacks in playoff history. They lost four games in a row, including a 1–0 defeat in game seven that left Penguins fans in a state of shock. The following seasons didn't help ease the pain, as the Penguins suffered consecutive preliminary-round losses to Toronto in the 1976 and 1977 playoffs and were a no-show in 1978. Although the 1978–79 Penguins finished second in their division, they too didn't fare well, surrendering to the Boston Bruins in straight games in the quarterfinals.

The Penguins unveiled a new uniform in 1979, doffing the old blue-and-white and adopting the black-and-gold color scheme of the baseball Pirates and football Steelers. This didn't sit well with Boston, which had been wearing almost identical hues. The Bruins protested, but to no avail as the Penguins cited a precedent set by the Pittsburgh Hockey Club of the 1920s, similar wearers of black and gold uniforms. First-round playoff losses in 1980, 1981 and 1982 followed in what would prove to be the franchise's only playoff appearances until 1989.

Because of a last-place finish in 1983–84, the Penguins were able to select Mario Lemieux first in the 1984 Entry draft. Considered the finest young player to arrive in the NHL since Wayne Gretzky, Lemieux arrived at training camp in 1984 and immediately dazzled onlookers with his comprehensive talent. Lemieux won the Calder Trophy as rookie of the year in 1984–85, and followed that with nomination to the Second All-Star Team in 1986 and 1987. A season later, he won the Hart Trophy as most valuable player as well as the Art Ross Trophy as leading scorer. Despite these accomplishments, the Penguins missed the playoffs every season through 1987–88. During this time, former goaltenders Ed Johnston and Tony Esposito called the shots as g.m. Bob Berry and Pierre Creamer worked behind the bench. Finally, in 1988–89, Gene Ubriaco coached Pittsburgh to second in the Patrick Division and a berth in the playoffs. Despite this measure of success. Ubriaco and Lemieux never saw eye-to-eye.

When Craig Patrick was named general manager on December 5, 1989, a new era in Pittsburgh hockey leadership was launched. One of Patrick's most crucial moves was made at the 1990 Entry Draft, where Pittsburgh held the fifth selection overall. After Owen Nolan, Petr Nedved, Keith Primeau and Mike Ricci were picked in that order, the Penguins g.m. opted for a tall, gangly Czech named Jaromir Jagr, who would emerge as the second coming of Lemieux.

On June 12, 1990, Patrick hired collegiate legend "Badger" Bob Johnson as head coach. With Johnson at the helm, the Penguins would win their first division title in 1990–91. Patrick's most significant move was a multiplayer trade he completed on March 4, 1991. To the Hartford Whalers went John Cullen, Zarley Zalapski and Jeff Parker; coming to the Igloo were Ulf Samuelsson, Grant Jennings and the symbol of Hartford hockey, Ron Francis. All three players became key components as the Penguins proceeded

Pittsburgh Penguins

Year-by-Year Record

Season	GP	W	L	T	OL	GF	GA	Pts.	Finish	Division	Playoff Result
1967-68	74	27	34	13	...	195	216	67	5th	West Div.	Out of Playoffs
1968-69	76	20	45	11	...	189	252	51	5th	West Div.	Out of Playoffs
1969-70	76	26	38	12	...	182	238	64	2nd	West Div.	Lost Semifinal
1970-71	78	21	37	20	...	221	240	62	6th	West Div.	Out of Playoffs
1971-72	78	26	38	14	...	220	258	66	4th	West Div.	Lost Quarterfinal
1972-73	78	32	37	9	...	257	265	73	5th	West Div.	Out of Playoffs
1973-74	78	28	41	9	...	242	273	65	5th	West Div.	Out of Playoffs
1974-75	80	37	28	15	...	326	289	89	3rd	Norris Div.	Lost Quarterfinal
1975-76	80	35	33	12	...	339	303	82	3rd	Norris Div.	Lost Prelim. Round
1976-77	80	34	33	13	...	240	252	81	3rd	Norris Div.	Lost Prelim. Round
1977-78	80	25	37	18	...	254	321	68	4th	Norris Div.	Out of Playoffs
1978-79	80	36	31	13	...	281	279	85	2nd	Norris Div.	Lost Quarterfinal
1979-80	80	30	37	13	...	251	303	73	3rd	Norris Div.	Lost Prelim. Round
1980-81	80	30	37	13	...	302	345	73	3rd	Norris Div.	Lost Prelim. Round
1981-82	80	31	36	13	...	310	337	75	4th	Patrick Div.	Lost Div. Semifinal
1982-83	80	18	53	9	...	257	394	45	6th	Patrick Div.	Out of Playoffs
1983-84	80	16	58	6	...	254	390	38	6th	Patrick Div.	Out of Playoffs
1984-85	80	24	51	5	...	276	385	53	6th	Patrick Div.	Out of Playoffs
1985-86	80	34	38	8	...	313	305	76	5th	Patrick Div.	Out of Playoffs
1986-87	80	30	38	12	...	297	290	72	5th	Patrick Div.	Out of Playoffs
1987-88	80	36	35	9	...	319	316	81	6th	Patrick Div.	Out of Playoffs
1988-89	80	40	33	7	...	347	349	87	2nd	Patrick Div.	Lost Div. Final
1989-90	80	32	40	8	...	318	359	72	5th	Patrick Div.	Out of Playoffs
1990-91	80	41	33	6	...	342	305	88	1st	Patrick Div.	Won Stanley Cup
1991-92	80	39	32	9	...	343	308	87	3rd	Patrick Div.	Won Stanley Cup
1992-93	84	56	21	7	...	367	268	119	1st	Patrick Div.	Lost Div. Final
1993-94	84	44	27	13	...	299	285	101	1st	Northeast Div.	Lost Conf. Quarterfinal
1994-95	48	29	16	3	...	181	158	61	2nd	Northeast Div.	Lost Conf. Semifinal
1995-96	82	49	29	4	...	362	284	102	1st	Northeast Div.	Lost Conf. Finals
1996-97	82	38	36	8	...	285	280	84	2nd	Northeast Div.	Lost Conf. Quarterfinal
1997-98	82	40	24	18	...	228	188	98	1st	Northeast Div.	Lost Conf. Quarterfinal
1998-99	82	38	30	14	...	242	225	90	3rd	Atlantic Div.	Lost Conf. Semifinal
99-2000	82	37	31	8	6	241	236	88	3rd	Atlantic Div.	Lost Conf. Semifinal
2000-01	82	42	28	9	3	281	256	96	3rd	Atlantic Div.	Lost Conf. Finals
2001-02	82	28	41	8	5	198	249	69	5th	Atlantic Div.	Out of Playoffs
2002-03	82	27	44	6	5	189	255	65	5th	Atlantic Div.	Out of Playoffs

to defeat Minnesota in six games to win the Stanley Cup. Lemieux won the Conn Smythe Trophy as the playoffs' most valuable player and had surpassed Gretzky as the NHL's dominant performer.

A significant ownership change took place in 1991 when the DeBartolo family sold the franchise to a partnership that included Howard Baldwin, Morris Belzberg and Thomas Ruta. Baldwin, who had been president of the World Hockey Association and head of the Hartford Whalers, became the hands-on leader of the hockey club as it was entering its golden era. However, tragedy marred the 1991–92 season for the Penguins. On August 29, 1991, Bob Johnson was diagnosed with brain tumors and was replaced behind the bench on October 1 by Scott Bowman, who had been the club's director of player development and Johnson's consigliere during the first Cup triumph. Johnson died at the age of 60 on November 26, 1991 in Colorado Springs.

Mario Lemieux was a star from childhood who attracted great attention during the 1983–84 season when he set Quebec Major Junior Hockey League records with 133 goals and 282 points in 70 games. Lemieux scored his first NHL goal on his first shift in a game against the Boston Bruins on October 11, 1984.

Despite the loss, Lemieux's dominance continued through 1991–92. He swept the Hart and Art Ross trophies with a combination of stickhandling and shooting artistry. He also was the NHL's plus-minus leader. Not surprisingly, Pittsburgh gained its second consecutive Stanley Cup championship with a four-game sweep of Chicago. The Penguins closed the playoffs with 11 straight victories, tying an NHL record set by the Blackhawks earlier in the postseason.

With Bowman retained to guide the team once again, Pittsburgh expected a third straight Stanley Cup title in 1993. The Penguins underlined the point by finishing first in the Patrick Division and winning the Presidents' Trophy for most points in the league. But, tragedy struck again. Mario Lemieux, who had previously battled debilitating back injuries, was diagnosed with Hodgkin's disease, a form of cancer. Radiation treatments lasted from February 1 to March 2. Amazingly, Lemieux returned to the lineup immediately and won another scoring title.

The Penguins began the playoffs with a five-game opening-round victory over the New Jersey Devils. However, the dynasty was derailed when the New York Islanders scored one of the league's most extraordinary upsets. Game seven proved to be a classic on every level. Rallying to tie the game 3–3 in the final minutes of the third period, the Penguins appeared ready to win the game in overtime until David Volek stunned the capacity crowd by beating Tom Barrasso after 5:16 of extra time.

Although the Penguins finished first again in 1993–94, they were without Lemieux for all but 22 games because of illness. They were eliminated by Washington in the first round and began retooling for the future. This was made even more imperative after Lemieux announced in August, 1994, that he would take a one-year leave of absence from the game. Jagr inherited the leadership role and won the Art Ross Trophy in the lockout-shortened 1994–95 season.

Though Jaromir Jagr has won five scoring titles, his best offensive season was 1995–96 when he established career highs with 62 goals, 87 assists and 149 points but finished second to Mario Lemieux.

Lemieux startled the hockey world with his return from medical leave in October, 1995. He scored his 500th career goal on October 28, 1995, and finished the season with an Art Ross Trophy-winning 69 goals and 92 assists for 161 points in just 70 games. Jagr was runner-up with 149 points.

Uncertainty characterized the Penguins' play during 1996–97, culminating with the firing of coach Ed Johnston on March 3, 1997. He was replaced on an interim basis by g.m. Patrick. Lemieux retired at the conclusion of the 1996–97 season after Pittsburgh was eliminated in a five-game opening-round series with Philadelphia—but Penguins fans had not seen the last of him.

In May, 1997, Roger Marino joined Howard Baldwin as co-owner and co-managing director of the franchise. During the off-season, Craig Patrick named the defense-oriented Kevin Constantine as head coach. Although Constantine occasionally clashed with Jagr over his disciplinary tactics and heavy defensive orientation, the Penguins surprised the critics with a strong performance in 1997–98, finishing first in the Northeast Division with 98 points. Jagr won the Art Ross Trophy while Tom Barrasso turned in a strong comeback effort in goal. The year would end in disappointment, however, as the Montreal Canadiens eliminated the Penguins in six games in the opening round of the 1998 playoffs.

On October 13, 1998, Marino and Baldwin declared bankruptcy, claiming $100 million in debt. Facing the loss of millions of dollars in deferred monies owed to him, Lemieux organized a group of investors. In March, 1999, they filed a plan of reorganization that was acknowledged by the U.S. Bankruptcy court on June 24, leading to several more months of negotiations with partners and creditors. Lemieux would finally be confirmed as the club's new owner nearly a year later, and would make a miraculous return to the ice as a player during the 2000–01 season.

Meanwhile, the Penguins played most of the 1998–99 season in uncertainty. In the competitive Eastern Conference, Pittsburgh's 90 points were good only for the eighth and final playoff position, but the fact the Penguins could compete at all was due mainly to Jaromir Jagr. His 44 goals and 83 assists gave him a league-leading 127 points. Not only did Jagr win the Art Ross Trophy for the second straight season, he also was rewarded with the Hart Trophy as MVP. In the playoffs, he returned from a serious groin injury to engineer a seven-game upset of the conference-leading New Jersey Devils. However, when the Penguins lost their second-round series to Toronto on May 17, 1999, there was the chance that they might have played their last game in Pittsburgh.

On September 3, 1999, Judge Bernard Markovitz approved Lemieux's purchase of the Penguins. Two days earlier, the NHL Board of Governors had voted in favor of Lemieux's bid. A month later, the Penguins opened the 1999–2000 season. Despite Jagr's continued brilliance, the team struggled and in December Craig Patrick replaced Kevin Constantine with Herb Brooks. The former coach of the 1980 "Miracle on Ice" U.S. Olympic team had been a Penguins scout since 1995. Ivan Hlinka, former Czechoslovakian national team star and coach of the 1998 Czech Republic Olympic gold medal team, was brought in as an associate coach. (He would be named the club's head coach after the season.) However, injuries to Jagr almost saw the team fall out of playoff contention.

Though he was only able to play 63 games, Jagr still led the NHL in scoring for the third straight season (96 points) and returned to the lineup in time to help Pittsburgh nail down a playoff spot in the Eastern Conference. Once in the playoffs, Jagr turned in a dominating effort as the seventh-seeded Penguins knocked off the Southeast Division champion Washington Capitals in the first round. Ron Tugnutt, acquired in a deal with Ottawa for Tom Barrasso at the trade deadline, also sparkled. Pittsburgh jumped out to a 2–0 lead in games in a second-round matchup with Philadelphia, but with injuries again hampering Jagr, the Flyers rebounded for four straight wins. The back-breaker for the Penguins was a 2–1 loss in game four that required five overtime periods, the third-longest game in NHL history.

Not surprisingly, in a season that would feature the return of Mario Lemieux, offense was the name of the game in Pittsburgh during the 2000–01 campaign. The season began in Japan, where the Penguins split a pair of 3–1 games with the Nashville Predators. The offensive explosion got under way back in Pittsburgh on October 14 when Jaromir Jagr recorded the first four-goal game of his career. A month later, Jagr scored his 400th career goal. In December, he reached the 1,000-point plateau. Jagr went on to record 52 goals and 69 assists for 121 points in 2000–01, winning the Art Ross Trophy for the fourth straight year and fifth time overall. He had plenty of company atop the scoring charts with Alexei Kovalev (44 goals, 51 assists) finishing fourth in the league and Martin Straka (27 goals, 68 assists) finishing sixth. Robert Lang (32 goals, 48 assists) also cracked the top 20. Still, the biggest story in Pittsburgh was the return of Mario.

While it was known that Lemieux had begun working out early in the season with an eye to making a comeback, there was no official word until he held a press conference on December 11. He played his first game on December 27 and set up Jagr for a goal after just 33 seconds. Lemieux finished with night with a goal and two assists as the Penguins crushed the Toronto Maple Leafs 5–0. He went on to record 35 goals and 41 assists for 76 points in just 43 games. Pittsburgh finished the season second in the NHL in scoring behind New Jersey with 281 goals.

Though the offense was lighting up the scoreboard, the Penguins' defense was having trouble keeping the puck out of the net until a late-season trade brought them little-known goaltender Johan Hedberg. Acquired from San Jose, Hedberg was called up from the Manitoba Moose of the International Hockey League and made 41 saves in his NHL debut on March 16, 2001. He posted a record of 7–1–1 down the stretch and was brilliant in the playoffs as the Penguins reached the Eastern Conference final before bowing out to New Jersey in five games.

Continuing to face financial pressures since Lemieux had bought the team out of bankruptcy, the Penguins traded Jaromir Jagr in the offseason, dealing him to the Washington Capitals for a package of prospects. Pittsburgh dropped the first four games of the 2001–02 season, and decided to fire Ivan Hlinka. He was replaced by Rick Kehoe, the former Penguins star who was in his 27th season with the organization. Still, the team struggled to just 28 wins and missed the playoffs for the first time since 1989–90—the year before they won back-to-back Stanley Cup titles. Compounding the team's problems in 2001–02 was a hip injury that sidelined Lemieux for all but 24 games and kept him out of the entire second half of the schedule after he helped lead Team Canada to a gold medal at the Winter Olympics in Salt Lake City.

Healthy again to begin the 2002–03 season, Lemieux leaped to the top of the scoring charts until a groin injury sidelined him near the midway point of the season. In all, he missed 15 games during the year yet he still finished eighth in the NHL with 91 points (28 goals, 63 assists) he finished the season with two assists as the Penguins rallied for a 3–2 win over Carolina in what many thought might be Mario's final NHL game.

Despite the win, the Penguins closed out the season three days later with a record of just 27–44–6–5—their worst performance since Lemieux was a rookie back in 1984–85. A little more than a week after the season, on April 15, the Penguins relieved Kehoe of his head coaching duties and shuffled him into another front office job. "Rick battled through some difficult circumstances the last two seasons and did a very good job," said Craig Patrick. "However, our organization is moving in a new direction and we needed to make a change." Ed Olczyk was hired as the new head coach on June 11, 2003. A longtime NHL player who had been a broadcaster since retiring in 2000, he became the team's fifth coach in five years despite having no coaching experience.

The 2003 Entry Draft a short time later marked the first time since they had selected Lemieux that Pittsburgh would pick number one after trading up with the Florida Panthers. The Penguins elected to take another French Canadian star, making Marc-Andre Fleury just the second goaltender to be selected number one (after Rick DiPietro in 2000) since the draft became universal in 1969.

Pittsburgh Pirates

THE NHL'S THIRD FRANCHISE in the United States was granted on November 7, 1925, when Pittsburgh formally joined the Boston Bruins and New York Americans in the seven-team circuit. Though there were published reports saying Americans owner William Dwyer would have a hand in Pittsburgh ownership, the team belonged to Henry Townsend, who, with an investment from attorney James F. Callahan, had purchased the Pittsburgh Yellow Jackets—United States Amateur Hockey Association champions in 1924 and 1925.

Lionel Conacher, Canada's greatest all-around athlete, had been the leader of the Yellow Jackets since his formal arrival in Pittsburgh in the fall of 1923. (He had actually come to play football, which he did briefly at Duquesne University in 1924.) Conacher helped recruit friends like goalie Roy Worters, Harry Darragh, and Harold "Baldy" Cotton from top amateur clubs in Toronto and Ottawa to join him in Pittsburgh. They all accepted the offer to turn pro when the NHL arrived in town, as did Yellow Jackets teammates Hib Milks, Duke McCurry, Tex White and Herb Drury. As professionals, they would be known as the Pittsburgh Pirates—the same as the city's baseball team.

Odie Cleghorn left Montreal to operate the Pirates (and would occasionally see ice time as well—including a game in goal when Worters had pneumonia). Because his team did not have the star talent others did, Cleghorn employed three set forward lines at a time when most teams simply used their best players for as long as possible. He also became the first NHL coach to change his players on the fly. Little had been expected from Cleghorn's roster of

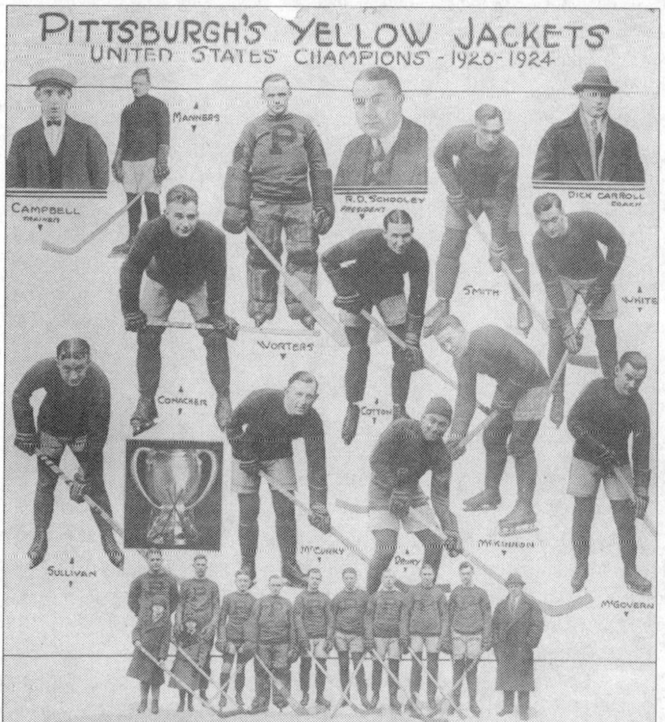

With teams like the Yellow Jackets, Pittsburgh already had a long hockey tradition when the NHL came to town for the first time in 1925.

amateurs, but his innovative coaching tactics—and Worters' great goaltending—saw the Pirates finish in third place with a record of 19–16–1 and beat out the Bruins by one point for the final playoff spot. The Montreal Maroons then defeated the Pirates 6–4 in a two-game, total-goals series, and went on to win the Stanley Cup.

The 1926–27 season saw the NHL add the New York Rangers, Chicago Black Hawks, and Detroit Cougars (later the Falcons, then the Red Wings), who joined Pittsburgh and Boston in the newly created American Division. The league also was bolstered by an influx of talent after the Western Hockey League ceased operations. Most of the western players stocked the rosters of the NHL's newest teams, though future stars like Eddie Shore (Bruins) and George Hainsworth (Montreal Canadiens) found their way onto existing clubs. The Pirates' only acquisition was Ty Arbour from the Vancouver Maroons.

Pittsburgh headed into its second season with virtually the same roster as the year before, but Lionel Conacher was soon traded to the New York Americans. "The Big Train" was sorely missed, as the Pirates' defensive record ballooned to second-worst in the NHL. Pittsburgh finished the year fourth in the American Division and missed the playoffs. A few minor roster adjustments and Roy Worters' return to form saw the Pirates reach the playoffs again in 1927–28. As in 1926, Pittsburgh was beaten in the first round by the team that would go on to win the Stanley Cup—this time the New York Rangers.

Even with their success on the ice, the Pirates were not receiving much fan support in Pittsburgh. Despite new ownership by ex-boxer and fight promoter Benny Leonard (Townsend had died in January, 1927, though the team remained in his family through the 1927–28 season), the Pirates, like the Ottawa Senators, began peddling talent to help their finances—most notably Roy Worters, who joined the New York Americans. The Pirates plummeted to 9–27–8 in 1928–29 and were only spared last place in the NHL by the dreadful Chicago Black Hawks.

Odie Cleghorn resigned after the 1928–29 campaign and became an NHL referee. Frank Fredrickson took over as playing coach in Pittsburgh (though a serious knee injury would limit his playing to just nine games), but he could do nothing to change the team's fortunes. The Pirates suffered through a 5–36–3 season, and the combination of a last-place team plus the stock market crash, which had seriously depressed the steel industry, doomed professional hockey in Pittsburgh. The Pirates were transferred to Philadelphia in 1930, but the results were even worse. After a 4–36–4 season, the Pittsburgh–Philadelphia franchise was given permission to suspend operations at the NHL Board of Governors meeting on September 26, 1931. Not until the NHL meetings on May 7, 1936, was the franchise formally canceled. It would be more than 30 years before the NHL returned to the state of Pennsylvania.

Pittsburgh Pirates

Year-by-Year Record

Season	GP	W	L	T	GF	GA	Pts	Finish	Division	Playoff Results
1925–26	36	19	16	1	82	70	39	3rd	...	Lost NHL Semifinal
1926–27	44	15	26	3	79	108	33	4th	American	Out of Playoffs
1927–28	44	19	17	8	67	76	46	3rd	American	Lost Quarterfinal
1928–29	44	9	27	8	46	80	26	4th	American	Out of Playoffs
1929–30	44	5	36	3	102	185	13	5th	American	Out of Playoffs

Quebec Bulldogs

THE HISTORY OF HOCKEY IN QUEBEC CITY dates back to at least the first Montreal Winter Carnival in 1883. The roots of the Quebec Bulldogs can be traced to 1886 and the formation of the Amateur Hockey Association of Canada (the first national hockey league). Quebec continued to be represented in a variety of top Canadian leagues until 1909–10, when the Bulldogs were left out during the formation of the National Hockey Association. A realignment of the NHA in 1910–11 brought Quebec back into the fold. By 1912, the Bulldogs were Stanley Cup champions. Quebec retained the Stanley Cup in 1913, but the Bulldogs' championship reign came to an end in 1914.

Quebec's roster from the Stanley Cup years boasted future Hall of Famers Joe Malone, Paddy Moran, Joe Hall, Tommy Smith and Russell Crawford. All were of English, Irish, or Scottish descent, as was the entire team. In fact, though it represented the capital city of the province of Quebec, there are no more than a handful of French Canadians who ever played for the team. Even the Bulldogs nickname (which dates to at least 1909) was chosen to evoke the ideals of courage and determination represented by 19th century Britain.

Joe Malone was the greatest star in the history of the Quebec franchise. He joined the club as a 19-year-old in 1908–09, and his goal-scoring feats became legendary during seven seasons in the NHA. His greatest year came in the first season of the NHL, when he scored 44 goals in 20 games for the Montreal Canadiens. The Bulldogs had been charter members when the NHL was formed in November, 1917, but the financially troubled franchise did not operate a team that year and its players were dispersed throughout the NHL. They did reassemble for an exhibition game against the Canadiens in February.

Quebec finally did ice a team during the NHL's third season, 1919–20, and although many of the Bulldogs' star players returned, only Malone proved still capable. He led the NHL with 39 goals (including a record seven in one game on January 31, 1920) and 49 points, but Quebec was a dismal 4–20–0. Prior to the 1920–21 season, the Bulldogs became the Hamilton Tigers. After five seasons in the Ontario city, the team moved again and became the New York Americans. Quebec City did not return to the NHL until 1979 when the Nordiques were absorbed from the World Hockey Association. That team, too, wound up in the United States when it became the Colorado Avalanche in 1995.

Quebec Bulldogs

Year-by-Year Record

Season	GP	W	L	T	GF	GA	Pts	Finish	Division	Playoff Results
1919–20	24	4	20	0	91	177	8	4th	...	Out of Playoffs

The Quebec Bulldogs were Stanley Cup champions in 1912 and 1913. The team's greatest player was future NHL star Joe Malone, seated in the middle of the bottom row between fellow Hall of Famers Paddy Moran (left) and Joe Hall. The mascot is named "Rowdie."

St. Louis Blues

SINCE ENTERING THE NHL, the St. Louis Blues have employed some of the greatest players in history. Such old-time hockey heroes as Dickie Moore, Doug Harvey, Glenn Hall and Jacques Plante helped give the team its start. Later, stars such as Brett Hull, Wayne Gretzky, Dale Hawerchuk and Peter Stastny also would spend time in St. Louis. Legendary architects Lynn Patrick and Emile Francis once ran the Blues, and championship team builders Cliff Fletcher and Jimmy Devellano had stints on the St. Louis hockey staff. Coaches include Stanley Cup champions Scotty Bowman, Al Arbour and Jacques Demers.

The Blues enjoyed some team success, too, reaching the Cup finals in the first three seasons out of the expansion bracket. From 1979–80 through 2002–03, the club has reached the playoffs 24 times in a row…yet the team still seeks its first Stanley Cup title after 36 seasons. The franchise has also been scarred by tragedies. Young defenseman Bobby Gassoff was killed in a motorcycle crash after attending a team function. Broadcaster Dan Kelly lost his battle with cancer while still in his prime. Barclay Plager succumbed to brain tumors while serving as an assistant coach.

Hockey began auspiciously in St. Louis in 1967–68. The Blues were the best of the NHL's six expansion teams, playing a disciplined defensive game that allowed them to outperform the other fledgling franchises. Midway through their inaugural campaign, Scotty Bowman convinced future Hall of Fame forward Dickie Moore to make a comeback. Moore, who hadn't laced up the blades since retiring at the end of the 1964–65 season, quickly established himself as the team leader.

With Moore and, later, Doug Harvey providing the emotional lift, the Blues survived two gruelling seven-game marathons against Los Angeles and Minnesota before reaching the Stanley Cup finals. Waiting there to welcome them were the well-rested Montreal Canadiens, still steaming from their loss to the underdog Toronto Maple Leafs 12 months earlier. The Blues fought hard, losing in four one-goal games, but it was clear the gap in talent was too wide for the Blues to overcome.

Still, the franchise flourished for the game's ultimate players' owner, Sidney J. Salomon Jr. His family had bought the team for $2 million and the St. Louis Arena from Chicago Black Hawks owners Arthur and Bill Wirtz for $4 million. The Original Six teams were run by strict and penurious men, but Salomon provided cars for his players and treated them to Florida vacations. The Blues acquired a bunch of all-stars in the twilight of their careers and they loved St. Louis. "It was unique compared to what was going on in the league," Glenn Hall said. "You were just like cattle, bought and sold and auctioned off. The only way we could return the favor to the Salomons was to go out and give a good effort every night."

Hall and Jacques Plante were stellar in goal and the Plager brothers, Barclay and Bob, led a gritty defense that also featured Al Arbour and Doug Harvey. Red Berenson, Ab McDonald and Gary Sabourin led the offense. Berenson's six-goal game in Philadelphia during the 1968–69 season remains one of the great milestones for the franchise.

Bowman added the general manager's portfolio to his resume in 1968 and he continued to mold his oldtimers into a lovable team that filled the old St. Louis Arena. Alas, the good times would not last. The Blues continued to be the best of the bunch in the West Division, reaching the Stanley Cup finals again in both 1969 and 1970. Once there, however, they were unable to win a game against their Original Six opponents, dropping four-game decisions to Montreal and Boston. Then, in 1971, Sidney Salomon III took a larger role in running his father's franchise and the result was constant upheaval from 1971, when Bowman left, until 1977.

The coaches came and went, with Arbour, Sid Abel, Bill McCreary, Jean-Guy Talbot, Lou Angotti, Garry Young, Leo Boivin and Emile Francis spending time behind the bench. General managers also came and went, with Abel, Charles Catto, Gerry Ehman and Dennis Ball holding the job from 1972 to 1976. Only Garry Unger's flashy scoring kept fans interested until the Salomons' final day. The challenge of the World Hockey Association, escalating costs and declining revenues pushed the franchise to the brink of financial ruin. Out of the gloom came Emile "The Cat" Francis, who took over as general manager, caretaker, security guard and saviour. If "The Cat" was going to save the Blues, he would need all of his nine lives to do it.

Early Blues heroes Barclay Plager (left) and Garry Unger surround Bobby Orr.

After a financially devastating 1976–77 season that saw the Blues pare down their staff to three employees, Francis was able to convince Ralston Purina chairman R. Hal Dean to invest in the team. On July 27, 1977, Francis announced the St. Louis Blues had been reborn. On paper, at least. In 1978–79, the Blues slipped off the bottom rung of the NHL ladder, winning just 18 games under coach Barclay Plager. Yet, once again, Francis was able to rebuild the crumbling foundation. Ralston Purina repainted the old bandbox known as the Arena and rechristened it the Checkerdome. In the 1976 Amateur Draft, Francis had selected Bernie Federko, Brian Sutter and Mike Liut, who would go on to become the cornerstones of the team in the 1980s. Such runners-and-gunners as Wayne Babych (picked third overall in 1978) and Perry Turnbull (taken second in 1979) were added to the nucleus and by 1980–81, the Blues had a 107-point juggernaut for Red Berenson, who had taken over as coach during the previous season.

"It was a very exciting time for me," Francis says. "There we were, on the brink of extinction, then to come all the way back the way we did and get the support we needed ... that was like a dream come true." Almost as quickly, it all came tumbling down. The Blues finished eight games under .500 in 1981–82 and slid to 65 points the following season, the fourth-lowest total in club history. Berenson got canned, Dean retired and Ralston Purina soon lost interest in hockey. Citing losses of $1.8 million per year, the company put the team up for sale. When the league blocked the sale of the Blues to Saskatoon interests in 1983, the company padlocked the Checkerdome and left the franchise on the NHL's doorstep. The Blues, with their ownership unresolved, did not participate in the 1983 NHL Entry Draft.

Enter entrepreneur Harry Ornest, who bought the franchise off the scrap heap. He, new general manager Ron Caron and coach Jacques Demers quickly made the Blues profitable and competitive. Federko, Sutter and Doug Gilmour, a gritty two-way center whose desire and determination more than made up for his lack of size, led the charge back up the NHL ladder. Caron traded furiously, shuffling stars (like Liut and Joe Mullen) and draft picks for lots of affordable, competent veterans whose work ethic helped transform the team into the type of blue-collar hockey club that the city had rallied behind so vigorously in the early years.

This regime peaked in the 1986 playoffs with the "Monday Night Miracle" game. After being stretched to the limit to eliminate Minnesota and Toronto, the Blues had their backs against the wall once again in their semifinal series against the Calgary Flames. Needing a home-ice victory to force a seventh game, the Blues trailed 5–2 with less than 12 minutes remaining in the game and their season. The unlikely hero on this madcap Monday night was Greg Paslawski, a hard-plugging foot soldier. "Paws" notched a pair of late third-period goals to even the affair after Brian Sutter had lit the comeback torch at 8:08.

Twenty minutes later, Doug Wickenheiser—who had received his fair share of hard knocks when the Montreal Canadiens selected him ahead of hometown hero Denis Savard in the 1980 Entry Draft—slipped a rebound past Mike Vernon to give the Blues a comeback win for the ages. Paslawski notched 10 playoff goals in the greatest spring of his career, more than he would score in the rest of his postseason career combined. The 6–5 victory forced a decisive seventh game of the Western Conference finals, but the Flames extinguished the Blues' Stanley Cup aspirations with a 2–1 win back in the Saddledome. Doug Gilmour and Bernie Federko tied for the playoff lead in points, becoming the first players to lead the postseason scoring parade without making it to the finals.

Demers left for Detroit after that season and Ornest, like the other owners before him, also decided to move on. He sold the team to a local ownership group led by Michael Shanahan during the 1986–87 season. However, with Ron Caron still aboard, the club remained in capable hands. Within two years, Caron had landed Brett Hull, Adam Oates and Curtis Joseph. Later, through astute trades and eye-opening free agent acquisitions, Caron brought such high-profile names as Scott Stevens, Brendan Shanahan, Phil Housley and Al MacInnis into the St. Louis fold. Still, the manager's coup remained the steal of Brett Hull from the Calgary Flames.

Deemed uncoachable, lazy and uninterested in improving his game, Hull was an enigma to many of the scouts and coaches who took him under their wing. In St. Louis, however, the offensive system was molded around Hull, his deadly accurate shot and his uncanny ability to find open ice, and once there, deliver the goods. With Adam Oates supplying picture-perfect passes, Hull became the NHL's top sniper. Hull reached the 70-goal plateau in three

St. Louis Blues

Year-by-Year Record

Season	GP	W	L	T	OL	GF	GA	Pts.	Finish	Division	Playoff Result
1967-68	74	27	31	16	...	177	191	70	3rd	West Div.	Lost Final
1968-69	76	37	25	14	...	204	157	88	1st	West Div.	Lost Final
1969-70	76	37	27	12	...	224	179	86	1st	West Div.	Lost Final
1970-71	78	34	25	19	...	223	208	87	2nd	West Div.	Lost Quarterfinal
1971-72	78	28	39	11	...	208	247	67	3rd	West Div.	Lost Semifinal
1972-73	78	32	34	12	...	233	251	76	4th	West Div.	Lost Quarterfinal
1973-74	78	26	40	12	...	206	248	64	6th	West Div.	Out of Playoffs
1974-75	80	35	31	14	...	269	267	84	2nd	Smythe Div.	Lost Prelim. Round
1975-76	80	29	37	14	...	249	290	72	3rd	Smythe Div.	Lost Prelim. Round
1976-77	80	32	39	9	...	239	276	73	1st	Smythe Div.	Lost Quarterfinal
1977-78	80	20	47	13	...	195	304	53	4th	Smythe Div.	Out of Playoffs
1978-79	80	18	50	12	...	249	348	48	3rd	Smythe Div.	Out of Playoffs
1979-80	80	34	34	12	...	266	278	80	2nd	Smythe Div.	Lost Prelim. Round
1980-81	80	45	18	17	...	352	281	107	1st	Smythe Div.	Lost Quarterfinal
1981-82	80	32	40	8	...	315	349	72	3rd	Norris Div.	Lost Div. Final
1982-83	80	25	40	15	...	285	316	65	4th	Norris Div.	Lost Div. Semifinal
1983-84	80	32	41	7	...	293	316	71	2nd	Norris Div.	Lost Div. Final
1984-85	80	37	31	12	...	299	288	86	1st	Norris Div.	Lost Div. Semifinal
1985-86	80	37	34	9	...	302	291	83	3rd	Norris Div.	Lost Conf. Finals
1986-87	80	32	33	15	...	281	293	79	1st	Norris Div.	Lost Div. Semifinal
1987-88	80	34	38	8	...	278	294	76	2nd	Norris Div.	Lost Div. Final
1988-89	80	33	35	12	...	275	285	78	2nd	Norris Div.	Lost Div. Final
1989-90	80	37	34	9	...	295	279	83	2nd	Norris Div.	Lost Div. Final
1990-91	80	47	22	11	...	310	250	105	2nd	Norris Div.	Lost Div. Final
1991-92	80	36	33	11	...	279	266	83	3rd	Norris Div.	Lost Div. Semifinal
1992-93	84	37	36	11	...	282	278	85	4th	Norris Div.	Lost Div. Final
1993-94	84	40	33	11	...	270	283	91	4th	Central Div.	Lost Conf. Quarterfinal
1994-95	48	28	15	5	...	178	135	61	2nd	Central Div.	Lost Conf. Quarterfinal
1995-96	82	32	34	16	...	219	248	80	4th	Central Div.	Lost Conf. Semifinal
1996-97	82	36	35	11	...	236	239	83	4th	Central Div.	Lost Conf. Quarterfinal
1997-98	82	45	29	8	...	256	204	98	3rd	Central Div.	Lost Conf. Semifinal
1998-99	82	37	32	13	...	237	209	87	2nd	Central Div.	Lost Conf. Semifinal
99-2000	82	51	19	11	1	248	165	114	1st	Central Div.	Lost Conf. Quarterfinal
2000-01	82	43	22	12	5	249	195	103	2nd	Central Div.	Lost Conf. Finals
2001-02	82	43	27	8	4	227	188	98	2nd	Central Div.	Lost Conf. Semifinal
2002-03	82	41	24	11	6	253	222	99	2nd	Central Div.	Lost Conf. Quarterfinal

consecutive seasons, including his Hart Trophy-winning campaign of 1990–91, when he slipped 86 pucks past enemy goaltenders—the most by any player in NHL history not named Gretzky. Hull's exploits helped to broaden local interest in the team. The Blues filled the arena, made the playoffs every year and began multiplying both their revenue and payroll in a giddy bid for greatness.

In 1990–91, the Blues had a breakout 105-point season behind Hull but the club couldn't get past the second round of the playoffs. Though this front office never got to the final four with coaches Jacques Martin, Brian Sutter, Bob Plager and Bob Berry, it did turn the Blues into a mainstream sports success. The team's success inspired the top St. Louis corporations to come together, buy the team from Shanahan and build the new Kiel Center (now the Savvis Center), which opened in downtown St. Louis in 1994.

Shanahan's last stab at glory was to hire Mike Keenan as general manager and coach. Keenan brought a lot of baggage with him, but he also carried a reputation as a winner. He tested the patience of the Blues fans early, unloading Petr Nedved, Craig Janney and Brendan Shanahan within a year of stepping into the front office. Dedicated St. Louis fans were slow to forgive Keenan for casting off Shanahan, as the player he was traded for (Chris Pronger) was slow to develop. The quick-witted power forward had been a local favorite and one of the most outgoing of all the pro athletes in the city, who generously gave his time and effort to charities and special events. There was another tempest brewing, as well.

Relations between Keenan and Brett Hull were acrimonious at best, and when Iron Mike stripped Hull of his captaincy, the battle of wills was on. In an effort to stem the tide of unrest, Keenan made a bold move, acquiring potential free agent Wayne Gretzky for the final playoff push in the 1995–96 season. Any hopes for a lengthy playoff run were dashed early when Grant Fuhr suffered a season-ending knee injury in the first game of the postseason against the Toronto Maple Leafs. Although backup Jon Casey performed admirably, the Blues lacked the consistent offensive attack

Bernie Federko was the Blues' first choice (seventh overall) in the 1976 Amateur Draft and established himself as the franchise's best player during his time in St. Louis. His 13 seasons, 927 games, 721 assists and 1,073 points are all still Blues career records.

required to reach the highest level. Gretzky came close to resurrecting the club's Stanley Cup hopes with 16 points in 13 games, but in the end, the Blues' lack of firepower caught up to them. The Blues did manage to stretch Detroit to double overtime in the seventh game in the Western Conference semifinal, but a Steve Yzerman goal gave the Wings a 1–0 victory and ended Keenan's quest for the Cup.

After the season, Gretzky joined the New York Rangers via free agency. The war of words between Keenan and Hull escalated and the product on the ice suffered. Finally, on December 19, 1996, the Keenan era ended, with both him and Jack Quinn being ushered out of town. Ron Caron came out of quasi-retirement to serve as interim general manager, helping new team president Mark Sauer hire coach Joel Quenneville and general manager Larry Pleau. Together, they tried to get the franchise back to the basics of drafting talent, grooming players and building up for another run at the Stanley Cup.

The Blues made another remarkable recovery in 1997–98. Even Brett Hull bought into Quenneville's defense-first philosophy, proving himself a better-than-adequate penalty killer and checker. Still, the Blues had enough all-around firepower to lead the NHL with 256 goals and finished with 98 points for the league's fourth-best record. The Blues overwhelmed the Los Angeles Kings with a four-game sweep to open the playoffs and were given an excellent chance of knocking off defending champion Detroit in round two. It was not to be, however, as the Red Wings eliminated St. Louis for the third year in a row en route to their second straight Stanley Cup title.

Acquired in a trade for Brendan Shanahan in 1995–96, Chris Pronger led the Blues in plus-minus in 1996–97, was named captain in 1997–98 and, at 6'6" and 220 pounds, has been a tower of strength on the St. Louis blue line.

The Brett Hull era came to a close in St. Louis, after a decade of highlight reel goals and mile-wide smiles, when Hull signed as a free agent with Dallas. The Blues did re-sign veteran rearguard Al MacInnis, ensuring that the league's most powerful shooter would have a chance to finish his career in St. Louis. MacInnis won the Norris Trophy as the NHL's best defenseman for the first time in his career in 1998–99. The emergence of Chris Pronger as a potential superstar continued that year. Pavol Demitra developed into a top-flight scorer with 37 goals and helped St. Louis overcome the loss of Hull. In the playoffs, the Blues rebounded from a 3–1 deficit in games to eliminate Phoenix, then engaged in a thrilling six-game series with Dallas that featured four overtime matches before the Blues were beaten by the eventual Stanley Cup champions for the third straight season.

In September, 1999, the consortium of 19 St. Louis companies which owned the Blues and the Kiel Center announced that the team and the rink had been sold to Bill and Nancy Laurie. (Nancy is the daughter of Wal-Mart co-founder James "Bud" Walton.) New on the ice that season was Roman Turek, who had been acquired from Dallas within days of the Stars' 1999 Stanley Cup title. He proved to be a dominant netminder in 1999–2000. Turek led the league with seven shutouts, while his 1.95 goals-against average was just edged out by Brian Boucher of the Philadelphia Flyers. He also posted a club-record 42 victories in leading St. Louis to a franchise high 51 wins and 114 points and the first Presidents' Trophy title in club history. With a defense led by Pronger and MacInnis, the Blues also won the Jennings Trophy by allowing the fewest goals in the NHL. In fact, with just 165 goals against, the Blues allowed the fewest goals in any full season since 1973–74 when both Philadelphia and Chicago surrendered 164 goals in 78 games. Offensively, the club was once again led by Pavol Demitra, who collected 28 goals and 75 points (though an injury late in the season would keep him out of the playoffs). Pierre Turgeon had 26 goals and 40 assists in just 52 games. Even with the club's defensive brilliance, only the Red Wings and the New Jersey Devils scored more goals than St. Louis, which netted 248.

Hopes were high for the club's first Stanley Cup championship entering the playoffs. But after taking game one from the San Jose Sharks, St. Louis suddenly lost three in a row and was down three games to one. Things looked good for yet another comeback, especially after the Blues trounced the Sharks 6–2 in San Jose in game six, but a 3–1 loss in game seven made St. Louis the first first-place club to be bounced in the opening round of the playoffs since the 1991 Chicago Blackhawks. At least there was some consolation at the 2000 NHL Awards, where Chris Pronger won the Hart Trophy as the league's most valuable player, Pavol Demitra earned the Lady Byng Trophy for gentlemanly play and Joel Quenneville won the Jack Adams Award as coach of the year.

Though not quite up to their Presidents' Trophy performance of 1999–2000, the Blues bounced back from their surprising playoff defeat with another solid season in 2000–01. With a record of 43–22–12–5, the Blues had 103 points—their second straight 100-point season and just the fourth in team history. In the playoffs, St. Louis advanced to the Western Conference final for the first time since 1986. Offensively, the club was led by Pierre Turgeon, whose 82 points (30 goals, 52 assists) were his best total since 1995–96 and ranked him 16th in the league. Scott Young's 40 goals topped the team and were 10 more than he had ever scored in one season. Keith Tkachuk was added to the team in a late-season trade with Phoenix. Defensively, of course, the Blues were led by MacInnis and Pronger. Rookie Brent Johnson played 31 games in goal as the backup to Roman Turek and ranked fifth in the league with a 2.17 goals-against average.

The Blues finished eight points behind Detroit in the Central Division and earned the fourth seed in the playoffs. Their first-round matchup offered a chance at revenge against San Jose and St. Louis took the series in six games. A sweep of the Stars followed before Colorado eliminated the Blues in five games.

St. Louis lost Turgeon to Dallas as a free agent in the offseason, but acquired Doug Weight from Edmonton. Brent Johnson was installed as the number-one goaltender and Roman Turek was traded to Calgary in a deal that brought in Fred Brathwaite to serve as a backup. The best news, though, was that Pavol Demitra was fully recovered from the eye and leg injuries that had limited him to just 44 games in 2000–01. His 78 points in 2001–02 (35 goals 43 assists) led the Blues and tied him for seventh in the NHL. Demitra's 10 game-winning goals led the league. Keith Tkachuk led the team with 38 goals in his first full season in St. Louis. As always, Pronger and MacInnis anchored the defense. They also helped Team Canada win an Olympic gold medal. As in 2000–01, the Blues finished second to Detroit in the Central Division. This year, the Red Wings also eliminated St. Louis in the second-round of the playoffs.

Despite the absence of Chris Pronger, who missed all but five games of the 2002–03 season with a wrist injury, and a series of other setbacks that forced St. Louis to use six goalies in the first half of the season (and eight in all), the Blues continued to rank among the NHL's best teams. Once again, however, they had to settle for second place behind Detroit in the Central Division, this time with 99 points. Al MacInnis wore the captain's C in Pronger's absence and enjoyed another fine season, scoring 16 goals and leading all NHL defensemen with 52 assists and 68 points. He would finish second to Detroit's Nicklas Lidstrom in voting for the Norris Trophy and was a key reason why Blues rookie defenseman Barret Jackman won the Calder Trophy. Pavol Demitra led the Blues in goals (36), assists (57) and points (93) to rank sixth in the NHL in scoring. Keith Tkachuk had 31 goals, while Scott Mellanby, Cory Stillman, Eric Boguniecki and Dallas Drake all topped the 20-goal plateau. Despite injuries, Brent Johnson and Fred Brathwaite handled most of the goaltending duties in St. Louis until the Blues acquired Chris Osgood from the Islanders at the trade deadline.

Yet again though, another promising season ended with an early playoff defeat. This time the loss came in the first round against the Vancouver Canucks. The Blues opened the series with a 6–0 victory and raced out to a 3–1 lead in games, only to see the Canucks storm back to win it in seven. St. Louis played most of the final six games without MacInnis, who injured his right shoulder early in game two. He returned for the finale but played just under 15 minutes. Game seven started much like the series opener, with St. Louis grabbing a quick lead when Doug Weight set up Martin Rucinsky just a minute into the opening period. Weight was the leading scorer in the opening round of the playoffs with five goals and eight assists. Still, it did no good.

"We had the start we hoped for," said coach Joel Quenneville. But once again the Blues didn't get the end result.

St. Louis Eagles

Despite four Stanley Cup titles during the 1920s, the Ottawa Senators fell victim to the Great Depression. Senators owner Tommy Ahearne absorbed losses for years, but at the NHL Board of Governors meeting on September 22, 1934, the directors of the Ottawa club sought permission to move their team to St. Louis. Permission was granted, even though a franchise application from the city had been rejected at an NHL meeting two years earlier because of excessive travel expenses. Redmond Quinn would continue to guide operations from Ottawa, while Clare Brunton ran the team in Missouri. The Ottawa Senators were now the St. Louis Eagles, but the city was already home to an American Hockey Association team called the Flyers. Owners of this club contended that there was an agreement between the AHA and the NHL that prevented the latter from placing a team west of the Mississippi. However, a threatened $200,000 damage suit was never filed.

The Eagles began the 1934–35 season with much the same roster the Senators had employed in 1933–34, but an NHL team that had gone 13–29–6 the previous season did not excite fans in St. Louis any more than it had in Ottawa. Attendance began at 12,600 on opening night (November 8, 1934) but crowds quickly decreased. By early December, financial concerns saw the Eagles begin to trade away players, and when the team tumbled to 2–11–0 on December 9, coach Eddie Gerard was fired in favor of George Boucher. By February, Brunton and Quinn were denying rumors that home games would be switched back to Ottawa. However, star player Syd Howe was promptly sold to the Detroit Red Wings. Frank Finnigan was bought by the Toronto Maple Leafs. Season's end found the Eagles last overall in the NHL.

The annual NHL meeting on May 11, 1935, left the status of the Ottawa-St. Louis franchise unsettled, but at a league meeting on September 28, Redmond Quinn asked if the team could suspend operations for a year as it had done in Ottawa in 1931–32. On October 15 the NHL governors decided to terminate the team instead, buying out the franchise and distributing the players through the league via draft. The prize pick wound up going to the Boston Bruins, who selected sixth. Bill Cowley had attracted little attention as a rookie in St. Louis, but would go on to become one of the league's top stars. The NHL finally returned to St. Louis in 1967. It was not back in Ottawa until 1992.

St. Louis Eagles

Year-by-Year Record

Season	GP	W	L	T	GF	GA	Pts	Finish	Division	Playoff Results
1934–35	48	11	31	6	86	144	28	5th	Canadian	Out of Playoffs

Fans in the city had already suffered through growing pains with the St. Louis Flyers of the American Hockey Association. They were not about to support another losing team — especially with the Eagles in last place while the Flyers were first in the AHA in 1934–35.

San Jose Sharks

PRO HOCKEY WAS NO STRANGER to the San Francisco Bay Area, but success and longevity never had gone hand-in-hand. A series of minor-league teams had called the area home over a period from 1928 to 1967, when the Oakland Seals entered the NHL, one of six new franchises as the NHL doubled from its Original Six to 12 teams. Struggling at the gate and in the standings, the Seals went through numerous owners before ending a nine-year run in the Bay Area by moving to Cleveland in 1976, where they would be owned by George and Gordon Gund. The franchise merged with the Minnesota North Stars after two more unsuccessful seasons.

On May 9, 1990, the National Hockey League granted approval for the Gund brothers to sell the North Stars in return for the rights to an expansion franchise in the San Francisco Bay Area. The new club would begin to play in the 1991–92 season. Despite past failures, the league was attracted to the region because it had grown to boast eight million residents and represented the fourth-largest media market in the United States.

On September 6, 1990, it was announced that the newest Bay Area franchise would be known as the Sharks. A week later, the team's majority owner George Gund and San Jose mayor Tom McEnery announced that the South Bay city would be the permanent home for the NHL franchise. The Sharks would play two years at the Cow Palace in Daly City, located just outside the San Francisco city limits, before moving to a new arena in downtown San Jose for the 1993–94 campaign. The team colors of Pacific teal, gray, black and white were unveiled on February 12, 1991. Two months later, the Sharks chose George Kingston to be the team's initial head coach. The 52-year-old had little previous NHL experience among his 30 years in hockey.

Nine days after paying the league the balance of a $50-million entrance fee, the Sharks obtained their first 34 players in dispersal and expansion drafts held on May 30, 1991. San Jose inherited 24 players from Minnesota's reserve list, mostly young players from the North Stars affiliate, Kalamazoo of the International Hockey League, or those playing in the college or junior ranks. Among those players were Arturs Irbe, Brian Hayward, Neil Wilkinson, Rob Zettler and Link Gaetz. The Sharks also selected 10 players from other NHL teams' unprotected lists in the Expansion Draft. Goalie Jeff Hackett was among those chosen.

On June 22, 1991, the Sharks participated in their first NHL Entry Draft and selected right wing Pat Falloon from the Western Hockey League's Spokane Chiefs with the second-overall pick. The Sharks also picked Ray Whitney and Sandis Ozolinsh. Just as the team was preparing to begin its first training camp, general manager Jack Ferreira engineered a trade with Chicago to bring popular defenseman Doug Wilson to the Sharks. The 14-year Blackhawk became San Jose's first captain. (He would later go on to a career in Sharks management.)

The Sharks first game, on October 4, 1991, ended in a 4–3 loss at Vancouver. The visitors rallied for three goals in the final period to tie the score before Trevor Linden provided the game winner with just 19 seconds remaining in regulation. Journeyman forward Craig Coxe scored the first goal in club history. In the second game at the Cow Palace on October 8, the Sharks posted their first win against the Calgary Flames.

San Jose faced a lot of adversity in its first season. The Sharks experienced an early-season 13-game losing streak, three four-game skids and two stretches of seven consecutive losses—including one to close out the year. In addition, they surrendered a league-high 359 goals. They led the league with 17 one-goal losses and dropped 13 of 14 two-goal decisions. San Jose finished last in the six-team Smythe Division with a 17–58–5 record in a season that included a 10-day work stoppage.

It didn't take long once the season ended for changes to occur. Jack Ferreira, a highly respected manager around the league, was fired on June 26, 1992. Chuck Grillo, director of player personnel, convinced initial team president Art Savage a change was needed. Besides remaining in his capacity, Grillo was elevated to vice president and given one-third of the general manager's responsibilities to share with Kingston and former assistant g.m. Dean Lombardi.

The Sharks' second season would be their last one in the intimate and sometimes odorous confines of the Cow Palace. An opening-night 4–3 win against visiting Winnipeg in overtime provided a false illusion of how 1992–93 would unfold. The Sharks proceeded to lose their next nine games and were mired in last place, hopelessly out of playoff contention, at 6–31–2 by January 3. The next

Doug Wilson was noted for his booming slapshot, and is the greatest offensive defenseman in the history of the Chicago Blackhawks. On September 6, 1991, Wilson was traded to the expansion San Jose Sharks and was named the team's first captain.

night they would embark on an NHL record-tying 17-game losing streak. Along the way, the Sharks suffered a franchise-worst loss with a 13–1 shellacking in Calgary. The ineptitude finally ended with a 3–2 victory over Winnipeg on February 14, 1993. However, the Sharks would win just four more times in their last 26 outings. Losing 16 of its final 17 games, San Jose ended a miserable second season with an 11–71–2 record to set a league record for most losses in a single campaign. Four days into the offseason, Kingston was fired.

Latvian goaltender Arturs Irbe, who would develop into a fan favorite, won only seven of 33 decisions in his first full season in the NHL. He did provide one of the season's few highlights by stopping 39 Los Angeles shots during a 6–0 victory on November 17, 1992, the first Sharks shutout. Rookie right wing Rob Gaudreau made a splash by recording the team's first hat trick in just his second NHL game. It came during a 7–5 loss to visiting Hartford on December 3, 1992.

The Sharks opened their third season in the San Jose Arena, a state-of-the-art building that featured 64 luxury boxes and seating for 17,190 at a cost of $162.5 million. (The rink was later named the Compaq Center, then the HP Pavilion following the merger of Compaq and Hewlett-Packard.) Replacing Kingston behind the bench in 1993–94 was Kevin Constantine. The 35-year-old entered the season as the league's youngest coach. One year removed from winning the Turner Cup with San Jose's minor-league affiliate, Kansas City of the International Hockey League, Constantine was familiar with San Jose's personnel and direction since he'd been part of the franchise from its inception.

Owen Nolan rebounded from two off-years to establish himself among the NHL's top scorers in 1999–2000. The former first-overall draft choice (1990) ranked second in the league behind Pavel Bure with 44 goals. He had been named captain of the Sharks in 1998-99.

The Sharks would make their initial season in San Jose a memorable one. Despite getting off to an 0–8–1 start, the players rallied behind Constantine's defense-first approach to make the playoffs for the first time, as they established an NHL record for the greatest single-season turnaround—finishing 58 points better than 1992–93's total of 24. The reunion of Russian hockey greats Sergei Makarov and Igor Larionov to form two-thirds of a potent first line, the maturation of young defenseman Sandis Ozolinsh and the workmanlike goaltending of Arturs Irbe sparked the team to a 33–35–16 record and an eighth-place finish in the Western Conference standings. But, the Sharks were not finished there. In the first round of the playoffs they drew top-seed Detroit, a team they had beaten only once in 11 previous meetings. Amazingly, the Sharks took the series in seven games. Against Toronto in the second round, San Jose jumped out to a 3–2 lead in the series before the Cinderella season ended with a seventh-game defeat.

The lovefest in the Bay Area that was now Sharks hockey had to wait until late January, 1995, to resume because of a labor lockout. San Jose picked up where it left off, shooting 5–1–1 out of the gate to raise already high expectations. Qualifying for a second straight postseason would become a challenge, however, as the team slumped by losing 10 of its next 16 before having a home game on March 10 against Detroit postponed because of heavy rain and flooding around San Jose Arena. Knowing a loss in the season finale would preclude an invitation to the playoffs, the Sharks tied Vancouver, 3–3, to sneak into seventh place with an otherwise disappointing 19–25–4 record.

Like its first-round opponent a season ago, the Sharks drew a foe that was ripe for an upset. Calgary had lost six straight first-round matchups since its Stanley Cup triumph in 1989, and the streak reached seven when San Jose scored a seven-game victory. Revenge-seeking Detroit was waiting in round two and they

San Jose Sharks

Year-by-Year Record

Season	GP	W	L	T	OL	GF	GA	Pts.	Finish	Division	Playoff Result
1991-92	80	17	58	5	...	219	359	39	6th	Smythe Div.	Out of Playoffs
1992-93	84	11	71	2	...	218	414	24	6th	Smythe Div.	Out of Playoffs
1993-94	84	33	35	16	...	252	265	82	3rd	Pacific Div.	Lost Conf. Semifinal
1994-95	48	19	25	4	...	129	161	42	3rd	Pacific Div.	Lost Conf. Semifinal
1995-96	82	20	55	7	...	252	357	47	7th	Pacific Div.	Out of Playoffs
1996-97	82	27	47	8	...	211	278	62	7th	Pacific Div.	Out of Playoffs
1997-98	82	34	38	10	...	210	216	78	4th	Pacific Div.	Lost Conf. Quarterfinal
1998-99	82	31	33	18	...	196	191	80	4th	Pacific Div.	Lost Conf. Quarterfinal
99-2000	82	35	30	10	7	225	214	87	4th	Pacific Div.	Lost Conf. Semifinal
2000-01	82	40	27	12	3	217	192	95	2nd	Pacific Div.	Lost Conf. Quarterfinal
2001-02	82	44	27	8	3	248	199	99	1st	Pacific Div.	Lost Conf. Semifinal
2002-03	82	28	37	9	8	214	239	73	5th	Pacific Div.	Out of Playoffs

destroyed the Sharks in four straight games, outscoring them, 24–6. The postseason disappointment was softened by the outstanding showing of rookie Jeff Friesen, who stepped right into the lineup after being selected 11th overall the previous June. He was the first Shark to be named to an NHL All-Rookie Team.

All the success and giddiness that surrounded the seemingly up-and-coming franchise would come crashing down, however. One by one, the heroes fell. His confidence already shaken by the loss of his status as the team's number-one goalie, Irbe experienced an offseason mishap when he was attacked by his dog. He required delicate surgery to repair injuries to his hands and left wrist. He and Wade Flaherty would get off to awful starts in 1995–96. An out-of-shape Makarov never made it out of training camp. A frustrated Larionov had a run-in with Constantine and was traded on October 24. Ozolinsh was dealt two days later to Colorado in return for a much-needed scorer, Owen Nolan. Constantine didn't last much longer. Despite having signed a new three-year deal the first week of the season, he was fired on December 2 after the team managed to win only three of its first 25 games (3–18–4). Interim coach Jim Wiley could do little with a group that quit and malingered throughout the sorry campaign. The team's first draft choice, Pat Falloon, was traded. San Jose gave up on Irbe when it acquired Chris Terreri. Grillo was fired and Dean Lombardi was named general manager. The Sharks finished ahead of only Ottawa in the overall standings at 20–55–7. Surprisingly, they sold out all 41 home games.

Rebuilding would prove tedious, as Lombardi started over from scratch. He had to weed the organization of veterans who had gotten used to losing, evaluate youth to determine who had viable NHL potential, and acquire players who would compete on a nightly basis. Lombardi turned the roster over before the 1996–97 season, securing no fewer than eight seasoned veterans with a winning track record, including Todd Gill, Al Iafrate, Kelly Hrudey, Marty McSorley, Tony Granato and Bernie Nicholls. Once the new campaign began, Lombardi continued adding players. In his boldest move, he gambled on acquiring veteran goalie Ed Belfour from Chicago. Belfour would be an unrestricted free agent at season's end.

The one move by Lombardi that did not pan out was the hiring of ex-Anaheim assistant Al Sims as the team's fourth head coach. Sims's Sharks finished 25th overall again, posting a 27–47–8 record. They produced a league-low 211 goals and fell 19 points short of a playoff spot.

Sims was fired on May 9. Exactly one month later, former Blackhawks coach Darryl Sutter was lured out of retirement and hired to lead San Jose into the 1997–98 season. Though Belfour bolted for Dallas, Lombardi acquired 1997 Conn Smythe Trophy winner Mike Vernon from Detroit. The two-time champion would handle the job of number-one goaltender as the Sharks also welcomed newcomers Murray Craven, Stephane Matteau, Shawn Burr, Bill Houlder and rookies Patrick Marleau and Marco Sturm.

Vincent Damphousse was traded to the San Jose Sharks on March 23, 1999, and regained his scoring touch on a rapidly improving team. He reached the 1,000-point plateau on October 14, 2000.

The 1997–98 season proved to be a success. The Sharks won a franchise-high 34 games and returned to the playoffs after a two-year absence. Unfortunately, San Jose hooked up with the regular season's strongest team when they faced the Dallas Stars to open the postseason. Although they won twice on home ice, the Sharks were eliminated in six games. A six-game loss to the Colorado Avalanche knocked San Jose out of the playoffs in 1998–99.

The Sharks picked up Vincent Damphousse from the Montreal Canadiens late in the 1998–99 season, and the 31-year-old veteran helped bring big changes to a team that never had finished above .500. Damphousse, Nolan, Granato and Mike Ricci gave the Sharks a solid veteran presence, while Friesen and emerging stars like Marleau, Sturm, Alex Korolyuk and Niklas Sundstrom provided a youthful talent core. The need for a greater physical presence was addressed during the 1999–2000 campaign when Mike Vernon was dealt to the Florida Panthers in a three-way deal that brought in Todd Harvey from the New York Rangers. The trade installed Steve Shields as the number-one goaltender in San Jose.

The Sharks started the 1999–2000 season strongly and were battling for top spot in the tough Pacific Division through the first two months until the club began to slide in December. Though Owen Nolan continued to score (his 44 goals were topped only by Pavel Bure's 58), San Jose did not nail down the final playoff berth in the Western Conference until the final week of the season. Finishing eighth meant a playoff matchup with the NHL's best team—the St. Louis Blues—but after dropping the first game, the Sharks won the next three and suddenly seemed to have the series well in hand.

Game five saw St. Louis storm out to an early 3–0 lead, but the Sharks rallied to tie the game before suffering a 5–3 defeat. Heading back home with another chance to wrap up the series, the Sharks were blown out 6–2 and suddenly St. Louis seemed to be in command. But, just like against Detroit back in 1994, San Jose shook off a game-six shellacking and wrapped up the series in seven. The return to form of Steve Shields and an Owen Nolan goal from near center ice with 10 seconds left in the first period were the keys to a 3–1 victory. The Sharks battled hard in round two against the defending Stanley Cup champions from Dallas, but went down to defeat in five games.

Rookie goaltender Evgeni Nabokov was the big story in San Jose during the 2000–01 season. Originally selected 219th overall in the 1994 NHL Entry Draft, Nabokov had been playing with the Sharks' minor league affiliate since 1997. He made a brief NHL appearance during the 1999–2000 season but was still a virtual unknown before posting brilliant numbers during the first half of 2000–01. He finished the year among the NHL leaders with 32 wins, seven shutouts, a 2.17 goals-against average and a .915 save percentage. Just one year after Sharks defenseman Brad Stuart was the runner-up for the Calder Trophy, Nabokov was named rookie of the year and finished fourth in voting for the Vezina Trophy as the league's top goaltender.

Evgeni Nabokov made 39 saves in a 0-0 tie with Colorado in his first NHL start on January 19, 2000. He won the Calder Trophy as rookie of the year in 2000–01 and was fourth in voting for the Vezina Trophy.

Offensively, the Sharks were led by Patrick Marleau, who had 25 goals and 27 assists. Owen Nolan was limited to just 57 games due to an abdominal injury and an 11-game suspension. His production dropped from 44 goals to 24. Mike Ricci scored 22 goals. Vincent Damphousse missed 37 games with a shoulder injury. He had just nine goals, but was second on the team with 37 assists and topped the 1,000-point plateau for his career. Late in the season, the Sharks dealt Steve Shields and Jeff Friesen to Anaheim for Teemu Selanne. He had seven goals and six assists in just 12 games for San Jose, but was held to no goals in six playoff games as the Sharks were beaten by St. Louis in the first round.

The Sharks remarkable resurgence under coach Darryl Sutter reached new heights in 2001–02 as the team set several club records, including most wins (44) and most points (99), and finished first in the Pacific Division. Selanne led the Sharks with 29 goals, while Nolan had a team-best 66 points (23 goals, 43 assists). Both Selanne and Nolan represented their home countries at the Olympics, with Nolan helping Team Canada win the gold medal. Other Sharks who topped 20 goals in 2001–02 were Scott Thornton (26), Patrick Marleau (21), Marco Sturm (21) and Vincent Damphousse (20). Nabokov enjoyed another fine season in goal. In the playoffs, San Jose downed Phoenix in five games before surrendering a seven-game series to the Colorado Avalanche.

Though some experts saw the Sharks as Stanley Cup contenders in 2002–03, it was not to be the case. With both Brad Stuart and Evgeni Nabokov refusing to sign contracts early in the season, the Sharks struggled out of the gate. The team had a record of just 8–12–2–2 through 24 games when Darryl Sutter was fired on December 1. (He would resurface in Calgary a few weeks later.) Former Anaheim and Washington coach Ron Wilson was brought in as the new head man, but he could not turn the team around. After six straight seasons of improved performances, the Sharks slipped back to just 28 wins and 73 points. They finished last in the Pacific Division and 14th overall in the Western Conference. Still, the team received decent offensive performances from Teemu Selanne, Marco Sturm and Patrick Marleau, each of whom scored 28 goals. Vincent Damphousse had 23 and led the team with 38 assists. However, with the team out of contention by the trade deadline, captain Owen Nolan was dealt to Toronto for Alyn McCauley, prospect Brad Boyes and a first round draft pick. A few days later, longtime g.m. Dean Lombardi was fired. He would be replaced by Doug Wilson, who had spent four seasons as the club's director of pro development. Two weeks after the season was over Teemu Selanne announced he would not exercise the option in his contract, leaving him free to explore free agency. He would sign with Colorado.

Tampa Bay Lightning

PRIOR TO THE LATE 1980S, there had been considerable skepticism about the possibility of major-league hockey in steamy Florida. An attempt by the World Hockey Association to establish a foothold in Miami during the early 1970s ended in failure before a game was ever played. But, in December, 1989, the NHL announced a grand plan to expand, and in March of the next year, Hall of Famer Phil Esposito came to the conclusion that the Tampa-St. Petersburg area was prime for NHL expansion.

Teaming with Florida attorney Henry Lee Paul, son of longtime baseball executive Gabe Paul, and Mel Lowell, a former Madison Square Garden official, Esposito laid the groundwork for acceptance. His first move was to promote an exhibition game at the massive Florida Suncoast Dome between the Los Angeles Kings and Pittsburgh Penguins on September 19, 1990. The game drew a crowd of 25,581—the largest in NHL history—and Tampa Coliseum, Inc. agreed to finance construction of a multi-purpose arena next to Tampa Stadium.

Brian Bradley had never had more than 19 goals and 48 points in his seven-year career until he was claimed from Toronto in the 1992 Expansion Draft. His 42 goals and 86 points for Tampa Bay in 1992–93 set scoring records for a first-year team.

Still cautious, the NHL dispatched an expeditionary force to Tampa on November 1, 1990, to gauge interest. Less than five weeks later, Tampa Bay and Ottawa were awarded conditional franchises to play in 1992–93.

It had been expected that the Pritzger family, owner of the Hyatt Corporation among other holdings, would put up the $50 million expansion fee. Pritzger decided to stay out of the hockey business. Esposito then jetted to the Orient in search of funding.

He started with a $2 million infusion and eventually boosted it with support from such Japanese firms as Kokusai Green, Nippon Green and Tokyo Tower. Esposito liked to humorously recall that some of the negotiations took place between drinks. "The more we drank," said Esposito, "the more [the deal] made sense."

Fiscal clouds appeared in June, 1991, when the team missed a $22.5-million franchise installment payment. That moved Kokusai Green into action, and it felt obliged to take a majority stake in the franchise.

In September, 1991, the Lightning received league approval for a restructured partnership with Lightning

Partners—owned by Kokusai Green—assuming the role of general partner. Esposito's group now had been formally replaced by the Japanese majority owners.

In December, 1991, the NHL granted permanent membership status to both the Lightning and Ottawa Senators. On the operating front, Phil Esposito emerged as the general manager, with brother Tony heading the scouting division. Terry Crisp would be the team's first coach. As for a playing venue, the club opted for the Florida State Fairgrounds Expo Hall as a temporary home until a permanent arena was built in Tampa.

During the club's first training camp, Esposito stunned the hockey world by signing female goaltender Manon Rheaume to a tryout form. The attractive French Canadian made history on September 23, 1992, by becoming the first woman to play one of the four major professional sports when she started against St. Louis in a preseason game. Rheaume made seven saves during 20 minutes of action and later was awarded a contract with Atlanta, Tampa Bay's International Hockey League affiliate.

On opening night, a sellout crowd of 10,425 jammed Expo Hall cheering the Lightning to a 7–3 victory over Chicago. Chris Kontos, a reject of several NHL teams, scored four goals for Tampa Bay. As expected, the Lightning played like an expansion team, although there were conspicuous highlights. One of the earliest took place on November 7, 1992, when defenseman Doug Crossman collected six points in a 6–5 win over the New York Islanders. Of all the discards picked up by Esposito, the most impressive was Brian Bradley, who finished the season with a team-leading 42 goals and 44 assists. In the end, Tampa Bay finished sixth in the Norris Division (23–54–7) and missed the playoffs.

For their second season, the Lightning moved out of the drafty, barn-like Expo Hall to St. Petersburg's Florida Suncoast Dome, which was designed as a baseball stadium but was reconfigured to handle hockey. It would have 28,000 seats for NHL games and would later be renamed the Thunderdome.

Underlying all the excitement were negative fiscal currents. Starting in 1992, the club was so cash-strapped that Lightning officials were constantly concerned about failure to make payroll and the potential collapse of the team. Nevertheless, Phil Esposito continued to fortify his lineup. With his first selection (third overall) in the 1993 Entry Draft, Esposito selected Chris Gratton, a big forward. He also acquired five-time 30-goal scorer Petr Klima from Edmonton for future considerations.

Klima led the Lightning in scoring with 28 goals in 1993–94, while Daren Puppa, who was obtained from the Florida Panthers in phase two of the 1993 Expansion Draft, proved to be the formidable goaltender the club required to remain competitive.

Any doubts that the Tampa Bay area was hockey country were dispelled on October 9, 1993, when the club set an NHL single-game attendance mark with 27,227 fans witnessing the Lightning home-opener against Florida. The team's record of 30–43–11 was a further boost, despite a second straight year without making the playoffs. The team drew 805,901 over 41 games, for an average of 19,656, but many of the seats were low-priced or giveaways and the financial woes continued.

During the autumn of 1994, the Internal Revenue Service and the State of Florida were prepared to file liens on the Lightning for $750,000 in past-due taxes. Other debts also were piling up, and to handle them, Kokusai Green borrowed against many of the team's revenue streams. Further financial troubles in 1995 saw Mel Lowell leave his job as executive vice president when his contract was not renewed.

These events coincided with yet another non-playoff season during the lockout-shortened 1994–95 campaign. The turnabout for the Lightning's fortunes took place in October, 1995 when Paul Ysebaert was named the first captain in team history and young defenseman Roman Hamrlik surfaced as one of the best offensive point men in the NHL. Between Puppa's goaltending, Hamrlik's versatility on defense and attack and Terry Crisp's spirited coaching, the Lightning earned their first playoff berth when they edged out the defending champion New Jersey Devils for the final postseason spot.

A powerful Philadelphia club faced the Lightning and won 7–3 at the Spectrum in the opener, but an overtime goal by Brian Bellows provided the underdogs with a 2–1 win in game two. Then came the stunner: returning to the confines of their home rink, the Lightning defeated Philadelphia, 5–4, on Alexander Selivanov's goal in overtime.

It proved to be the Lightning's last gasp, as the Flyers next ran off three straight victories to capture the series. However, fan support was stronger than ever and on April 23, 1996, the Lightning set an all-time NHL attendance record of 28,183 for game four of the playoff series. Even more encouraging was news that the club's new home, the Tampa-based Ice Palace, was ready for occupancy at the start of the 1996–97 season.

Opening night at the new building was October 20, 1996, when the home team defeated the New York Rangers 5–3 in front of 20,543 fans. It was an auspicious debut for a season of disappointment. A troublesome back kayoed Puppa, causing coach Crisp to alternate Corey Schwab and Rick Tabaracci in goal. Strong offensive efforts by Dino Ciccarelli and John Cullen enabled the Lightning to stay in the playoff hunt, but it was not to be.

By this time the Japanese-based ownership had begun a determined effort to sell the team. The organization's debt had passed $50 million and would reach $100 million by 1998. The Las Vegas-based Maloof family spent eight months trying to hammer out a deal but never was able to personally contact the mysterious Japanese owner Takashi Okubo. Instead of buying the Lightning, the Maloofs purchased the NBA Sacramento Kings.

Okubo, who had poured $90 million into the team but had never attended a game, became more and more the subject of scrutiny as the 1997–98 season unfolded. It would be a traumatic year for the Lightning. Among the many misfortunes to face the team was the fact that John Cullen, who had been diagnosed with cancer, learned

Tampa Bay Lightning

Year-by-Year Record

Season	GP	W	L	T	OL	GF	GA	Pts.	Finish	Division	Playoff Result
1992-93	84	23	54	7	...	245	332	53	6th	Norris Div.	Out of Playoffs
1993-94	84	30	43	11	...	224	251	71	7th	Atlantic Div.	Out of Playoffs
1994-95	48	17	28	3	...	120	144	37	6th	Atlantic Div.	Out of Playoffs
1995-96	82	38	32	12	...	238	248	88	5th	Atlantic Div.	Lost Conf. Quarterfinal
1996-97	82	32	40	10	...	217	247	74	6th	Atlantic Div.	Out of Playoffs
1997-98	82	17	55	10	...	151	269	44	7th	Atlantic Div.	Out of Playoffs
1998-99	82	19	54	9	...	179	292	47	4th	Southeast Div.	Out of Playoffs
99-2000	82	19	47	9	7	204	310	54	4th	Southeast Div.	Out of Playoffs
2000-01	82	24	47	6	5	201	280	59	5th	Southeast Div.	Out of Playoffs
2001-02	82	27	40	11	4	178	219	69	3rd	Southeast Div.	Out of Playoffs
2002-03	82	36	25	16	5	219	210	93	1st	Southeast Div.	Lost Conf. Semifinal

in September, 1997 that radiation and chemotherapy treatments had not been successful. He would have to undergo a bone-marrow transplant, and doctors now reported that his chances of recovery—once reported to be better than 90 percent—were no better than 75 percent.

On a purely hockey front, the most egregious loss for Tampa was that of Chris Gratton, the 6'4", 218-pound center who received a five-year, $16.5-million, free-agent offer sheet from the Philadelphia Flyers in the summer of 1997.

Unable to match the bid, Phil Esposito later explained to an arbitrator that he couldn't decipher Philadelphia's proposal because some of the numbers on the fax were smudged. The Lightning escaped a total disaster when Philadelphia agreed to trade Mikael Renberg and Karl Dykhuis to Tampa Bay for the four first-round draft picks that the Flyers would have lost to the Lightning in the original offer sheet plan. But, by December, 1997, Renberg had broken his wrist and was lost for a month. (Gratton would prove to be a bust in Philly, and was traded back to Tampa for Renberg during the 1998–99 season. He was later dealt to the Buffalo Sabres in 1999–2000.)

Meanwhile, Phil Esposito had fired Terry Crisp, placed Rick Paterson in the head coaching slot, and then replaced him with Jacques Demers. No matter who was behind the bench, the Lightning required Puppa's top goaltending to survive, but in a game against Boston in December, 1997, the goalie left complaining of back spasms. He was unable to play for the rest of the season. The club concluded the 1997–98 season with the worst record of its six-year existence. With only 17 wins in 82 games, the Lightning lost 55 matches, one more than in their maiden season.

Nikolai Khabibulin was inspired to become a goaltender at the age of 14 when he read a book about Soviet legend Vladislav Tretiak. By the age of 18 he was playing for the Moscow 's Central Red Army. Khabibulin entered the NHL with Winnipeg in 1995 and joined Tampa Bay in 2001.

At season's end, NHL commissioner Gary Bettman revealed that the league was diligently working to consummate a sale of the team that would eliminate "99.9 percent" of the team's problems. "There are difficulties in having distant ownership," said Bettman, "particularly if that ownership is not familiar with the sports business. At this point I'll define 'local interest' as North America. I'll take somebody within a six-hour flight!"

Insurance magnate Art Williams purchased the club on June 25, 1998, just a few weeks after John Cullen learned that his cancer was in remission. He returned to play briefly in 1998–99 before retiring to become an assistant coach.

The club's on-ice future received a considerable boost in 1998–99, with first overall 1998 draft choice Vincent Lecavalier. Still, the team posted the NHL's worst record amid a season of upheaval. Just two games in, Art Williams fired Phil Esposito and gave his general manager's job to coach Jacques Demers. Later in the year, Williams sold the team to Bill Davidson, owner of the Detroit Pistons of the NBA and the Detroit Vipers of the International Hockey League. After the season, Davidson hired former Vipers coach and g.m. Rick Dudley away from the Ottawa Senators to head up hockey operations in Tampa. (The move cost the

Lightning Rob Zamuner as compensation.) Dudley hired Steve Ludzik, who had coached for him in Detroit, as the Lightning's bench boss

Despite the changes, the Lightning fell below 20 wins (19–47–9–7) for the third year in a row in 1999–2000. Still there was reason for optimism in Tampa. Lecavalier became the youngest captain in NHL history during the season (he would have the C removed after 2000–01 to lessen the pressure on him) and he improved in every facet of his game. Acquisitions like former Toronto Maple Leafs Mike Johnson (later traded to Phoenix in the deal for Nikolai Khabibulin) and Fredrik Modin helped bolster the offense, while youngsters like Ben Clymer and defenseman Pavel Kubina offered more hope for the future. Unfortunately, plans to ease Dan Cloutier into the number-one goaltending job had to be accelerated when Daren Puppa was injured for the fourth straight season. In fact, injuries forced Tampa Bay to use six different goalies in 1999–2000 and the club struggled to the NHL's second-worst defensive record, behind only the expansion Atlanta Thrashers.

Brad Richards, the club's second selection behind Vincent Lecavalier at the 1998 NHL Entry Draft, joined Tampa Bay as a 20-year-old rookie in 2000–01 and made an immediate impact. He was the only Lightning player to take part in all 82 games and led all NHL rookies in goals (21), assists (41) and points (62). Richards finished second to San Jose goaltender Evgeni Nabokov in voting for the Calder Trophy as rookie of the year. Tampa Bay also got impressive performances from Fredrik Modin (32 goals) and Lecavalier (23 goals) but the Lightning suffered through another dismal season, finishing behind even the second-year Thrashers in the Southeast Division. The poor performance cost coach Steve Ludzik his job. He was replaced by John Tortorella midway through the season. Jay Feaster would replace Rick Dudley as the club's general manager during the 2001–02 campaign.

Having dealt Dan Cloutier to Vancouver for defenseman Adrian Aucoin in February of 2001, Tampa Bay acquired Nikolai Khabibulin from Phoenix a month later. He solidified the Lightning's goaltending in 2001–02. After missing almost two full seasons, Khabibulin was once again one of the NHL's busiest netminders, playing in 70 games. He ranked fifth in the NHL with a .920 save percentage. Brad Richards had another solid season (20 goals, 42 assists) and free agent acquisition Dave Andreychuk led the team with 21 goals, but improvement was modest until 2002–03.

With the surprising rise of Martin St. Louis as one of the league's most dangerous scorers, the Lightning ranked among the top teams in the Eastern Conference early in the 2002–03 season. They remained in competition for a playoff spot all season long, holding off the Washington Capitals to win the Southeast Division by a single point (93–92). It was the first divisional title, and just the second playoff berth, in the franchise's 11-year history. Though St. Louis' production had declined in the second half, he still finished tied with Vincent Lecavalier for the team lead with 33 goals. Vaclav Prospal led the team with 79 points (one more than Lecavalier), while tying Brad Richards for top spot with 57 assists. Dan Boyle ranked among the league's top-scoring defensemen with 13 goals and 40 assists. Dave Andreychuk enjoyed another 20-goal season as he continued to climb the all-time scoring charts.

Vincent Lecavalier was just the fifth player from the Quebec Major Junior Hockey League to be selected first overall in the NHL Entry Draft. The other four were Guy Lafleur, Mario Lemieux, Pierre Turgeon and Alexander Daigle.

Surprisingly, Khabibulin was not at his best during much of the 2002–03 season and was occasionally benched in favor of John Grahame. He eventually found his form and rode a career-high 16-game unbeaten streak (12–0–4) from February 11 to April 2 and went on to set a club record with 30 wins. The Lightning as a team enjoyed a franchise-best 13-game unbeaten streak (7–0–6) from March 7 to April 2.

The Lightning opened the playoffs at home against Washington and the Capitals seemed poised to exact their revenge for losing the division title when they won the first two games of the series. However, Tampa took game three 4–3 on Lecavalier's overtime goal with a two-man advantage. A 3–1 win in game four marked the franchise's first postseason victory in regulation time. Tampa then became the first team to win at home in the series with a 2–1 victory in game five. They wrapped up the series with another 2–1 win in game six, this time in triple overtime. Dave Andreychuk had tied the game late in the third period before Martin St. Louis won it with his fifth goal of the series early in the third extra session. St. Louis became just the fourth player in NHL history to score three straight game-winning goals in a series, joining Roy Conacher (1939), Clark Gillies (1977) and Kevin Stevens (1991) in that select group.

Tampa Bay faced New Jersey in the second round, and though they would bow out in five games, the Lightning gave the Devils all they could handle. After four tough games, and with Tampa facing elimination in the series, John Tortorella decided to bench Khabibulin and go with John Grahame. He made 46 saves in his first start since the regular-season finale, but Tampa Bay came out on the wrong end of a triple overtime decision this time, losing the game 2–1 and the series four games to one.

The longest game in Lightning history had capped their most successful season, one which offered plenty of hope for the future. "We've made tremendous steps," said Tortorella. "These are the steps you need to go through to become a model organization."

Toronto Maple Leafs

(includes St. Patricks and Arenas)

TORONTO WAS A CHARTER MEMBER OF THE NHL, joining the league for its inaugural 1917-18 season. An ownership dispute was ongoing when Toronto's first NHL entry, operated by the city's Mutual Street Arena, began play. (See page 7.) This club has come to be known as the Toronto Arenas, though it appears that the Arenas name was not actually formally adopted until the following season.

The club played its first NHL game on December 19, 1917, and lost, 10–9, to the Montreal Wanderers. Despite the fact those original Toronto players quarreled with management and were hit by fines for breaking training, the team won the second half of the NHL's split schedule, defeated the Montreal Canadiens in a playoff series and captured the Stanley Cup by winning a best-of-five series with the Vancouver Millionaires of the Pacific Coast Hockey Association. And they did it on a surface of artificial ice—the only such surface in the NHL.

While the victory in 1918 was Toronto's first Cup win under the NHL banner, a 1914 team playing in the National Hockey Association is credited with first bringing Lord Stanley's basin to the city. The 1914 Toronto Blueshirts featured goaltender Harry Holmes and defenseman Harry Cameron, who also played on the 1918 championship team. Why not? They were well paid for their efforts. By 1918, Holmes was earning $700 per season, Cameron $900. The total payroll for the 10 players on the Toronto roster was $6,150.

Irvine "Ace" Bailey was one of two players with the Toronto St. Pats who would become cornerstones of the Toronto Maple Leafs. The other was Hap Day.

Despite winning the Stanley Cup in the NHL's first season, the Toronto Arenas struggled in 1918–19 and, in fact, withdrew from the league on February 20, 1919. The team was back for the 1919–20 season after having been reorganized as the Toronto St. Patricks. In 1922, the St. Pats squad surprised the hockey world by defeating the Ottawa Senators in the NHL playoffs and then toppling Vancouver in five games in the finals for the Stanley Cup. Toronto's Babe Dye led all playoff scorers with 11 goals in seven games. Dye had been the NHL's top goal scorer in 1920–21 (35 goals) and would top the league again with 26 in 1922–23. His 38 goals in 1924–25 were a career high and his 44 points that season also led the NHL.

By 1926–27 the NHL had expanded to 10 teams. Young Conn Smythe was hired to assemble the original New York Rangers, but was fired before the first game was played. Lester Patrick, older and more experienced, was signed to replace him. New York's loss soon became Toronto's gain.

Following his dismissal in New York, Smythe managed to raise $160,000 and purchased the last-place St. Pats in February, 1927. He promptly renamed the team the Toronto Maple Leafs, and switched the uniform colors from green and white to blue and white.

Meanwhile, in March, 1923, a 20-year old newspaper reporter named Foster Hewitt had begun broadcasting hockey games from Mutual Street Arena on the Toronto Star's new radio station, CFCA. Soon, Hewitt's broadcasts of Maple Leaf games were attracting more and more fans to the Arena and Smythe began formulating plans for a new ice palace—Maple Leaf Gardens.

When financing the project became a major undertaking, Smythe and his energetic assistant Frank Selke turned to the trade unions and bartered Gardens stock in return for labor. In what has been called "a miracle of engineering," the new ice palace was erected in six months and at a bargain price of $1.5 million. It opened for business on November 12, 1931. With Hap Day and King Clancy on defense and the Kid Line of Charlie Conacher, Joe Primeau and Busher Jackson up front, the Leafs became a powerful force in the NHL. Through the decades that followed, the Gardens was always full to overflowing.

In 1931–32, their first year on Gardens ice, the Leafs swept to the Stanley Cup, ousting the Rangers in the finals in three straight games. Early in the season, Smythe had replaced coach Art Duncan with Dick Irvin, who had been fired by Chicago the previous season. Irvin brought the Leafs from last place to first place within a month and would guide the team to the Stanley Cup finals six times in eight years following their victory in 1932.

In 1940, Dick Irvin resigned as Leafs coach and accepted a similar position with the Montreal Canadiens. Hap Day was Irvin's successor and figured prominently in one of hockey's most dramatic comebacks. In 1942, after Detroit took a 3–0 lead in games over Toronto in the Stanley Cup finals, Day made some player changes and the Leafs roared back with three straight wins to tie the series. They won the Cup with a 3–1 victory in a thrilling seventh game. It's the only time a club has come back from such a deficit in the Stanley Cup finals.

Goaltender Frank McCool was a Toronto hero in the Stanley Cup finals of 1945 when he set a record with three shutouts. The Leafs won the series in seven games. One of the stars of that team was defenseman Babe Pratt, who had won the Hart Trophy in 1944. Pratt would be expelled from hockey in 1945–46 for wagering on games and, although he was reinstated on February 14, 1946, his days in Toronto were numbered. Pratt was traded to the Boston Bruins after the season and finished his playing days in the minors.

The Leafs regained the Stanley Cup in the spring of 1947, with Ted Kennedy scoring the winning goal in a 2–1 victory over Montreal in game six of the finals. Early the following season, Conn Smythe traded several players to Chicago in order to land Max Bentley, who helped the Leafs retain the Cup in 1948 and 1949. The 1950–51 season is remembered for Bill Barilko's Stanley Cup-winning goal, capping a series in which all five games required overtime. Barilko perished in a plane crash a few weeks later.

On February 1, 1955, Conn Smythe stepped down as general manager of the Leafs and handed the position to Hap Day. Leaf fans, however, had little to cheer about during this era. The club finished in last place for the first time in history in 1956–57, but things were about to get better.

In August, 1958, Toronto signed 33-year-old minor-league goaltender Johnny Bower and rookie defenseman Carl Brewer. Defenseman Allan Stanley was acquired from Boston and assistant general manager Punch Imlach took over as general manager in November. One of his first moves was to fire Billy Reay and add the coaching job to his own portfolio. Imlach's "Cinderella Leafs" climbed from last place into the playoffs that season but lost in the finals to a powerful Montreal club. In February, 1960, Imlach snared Red Kelly from Detroit and switched him from defense to center. Once again the Leafs reached the finals and once again they lost to Montreal, who captured their fifth straight Stanley Cup championship. Imlach installed rookie Dave Keon at center in 1960–61 (he won the Calder Trophy as rookie of the year) and grabbed roustabout wing Eddie Shack from the Rangers in a deal.

Toronto Maple Leafs

Year-by-Year Record

Season	GP	W	L	T	OL	GF	GA	Pts.	Finish	Division	Playoff Result
1917-18	22	13	9	0	...	108	109	26	2nd and 1st*		Won Stanley Cup
1918-19	18	5	13	0	...	64	92	10	3rd and 3rd*		Out of Playoffs
1919-20§	24	12	12	0	...	119	106	24	3rd and 2nd*		Out of Playoffs
1920-21	24	15	9	0	...	105	100	30	2nd and 1st*		Lost NHL Final
1921-22	24	13	10	1	...	98	97	27	2nd	...	Won Stanley Cup
1922-23	24	13	10	1	...	82	88	27	3rd	...	Out of Playoffs
1923-24	24	10	14	0	...	59	85	20	3rd	...	Out of Playoffs
1924-25	30	19	11	0	...	90	84	38	2nd	...	Lost NHL Sfinal
1925-26	36	12	21	3	...	92	114	27	6th	...	Out of Playoffs
1926-27•	44	15	24	5	...	79	94	35	5th	Cdn. Div.	Out of Playoffs
1927-28	44	18	18	8	...	89	88	44	4th	Cdn. Div.	Out of Playoffs
1928-29	44	21	18	5	...	85	69	47	3rd	Cdn. Div.	Lost Semifinal
1929-30	44	17	21	6	...	116	124	40	4th	Cdn. Div.	Out of Playoffs
1930-31	44	22	13	9	...	118	99	53	2nd	Cdn. Div.	Lost Quarterfinal
1931-32	48	23	18	7	...	155	127	53	2nd	Cdn. Div.	Won Stanley Cup
1932-33	48	24	18	6	...	119	111	54	1st	Cdn. Div.	Lost Final
1933-34	48	26	13	9	...	174	119	61	1st	Cdn. Div.	Lost Semifinal
1934-35	48	30	14	4	...	157	111	64	1st	Cdn. Div.	Lost Final
1935-36	48	23	19	6	...	126	106	52	2nd	Cdn. Div.	Lost Final
1936-37	48	22	21	5	...	119	115	49	3rd	Cdn. Div.	Lost Quarterfinal
1937-38	48	24	15	9	...	151	127	57	1st	Cdn. Div.	Lost Final
1938-39	48	19	20	9	...	114	107	47	3rd	...	Lost Final
1939-40	48	25	17	6	...	134	110	56	3rd	...	Lost Final
1940-41	48	28	14	6	...	145	99	62	2nd	...	Lost Semifinal
1941-42	48	27	18	3	...	158	136	57	2nd	...	Won Stanley Cup
1942-43	50	22	19	9	...	198	159	53	3rd	...	Lost Semifinal
1943-44	50	23	23	4	...	214	174	50	3rd	...	Lost Semifinal
1944-45	50	24	22	4	...	183	161	52	3rd	...	Won Stanley Cup
1945-46	50	19	24	7	...	174	185	45	5th	...	Out of Playoffs
1946-47	60	31	19	10	...	209	172	72	2nd	...	Won Stanley Cup
1947-48	60	32	15	13	...	182	143	77	1st	...	Won Stanley Cup
1948-49	60	22	25	13	...	147	161	57	4th	...	Won Stanley Cup
1949-50	70	31	27	12	...	176	173	74	3rd	...	Lost Semifinal
1950-51	70	41	16	13	...	212	138	95	2nd	...	Won Stanley Cup
1951-52	70	29	25	16	...	168	157	74	3rd	...	Lost Semifinal
1952-53	70	27	30	13	...	156	167	67	5th	...	Out of Playoffs
1953-54	70	32	24	14	...	152	131	78	3rd	...	Lost Semifinal
1954-55	70	24	24	22	...	147	135	70	3rd	...	Lost Semifinal
1955-56	70	24	33	13	...	153	181	61	4th	...	Lost Semifinal
1956-57	70	21	34	15	...	174	192	57	5th	...	Out of Playoffs
1957-58	70	21	38	11	...	192	226	53	6th	...	Out of Playoffs
1958-59	70	27	32	11	...	189	201	65	4th	...	Lost Final
1959-60	70	35	26	9	...	199	195	79	2nd	...	Lost Final
1960-61	70	39	19	12	...	234	176	90	2nd	...	Lost Semifinal
1961-62	70	37	22	11	...	232	180	85	2nd	...	Won Stanley Cup
1962-63	70	35	23	12	...	221	180	82	1st	...	Won Stanley Cup
1963-64	70	33	25	12	...	192	172	78	3rd	...	Won Stanley Cup
1964-65	70	30	26	14	...	204	173	74	4th	...	Lost Semifinal
1965-66	70	34	25	11	...	208	187	79	3rd	...	Lost Semifinal
1966-67	70	32	27	11	...	204	211	75	3rd	...	Won Stanley Cup
1967-68	74	33	31	10	...	209	176	76	5th	East Div.	Out of Playoffs
1968-69	76	35	26	15	...	234	217	85	4th	East Div.	Lost Quarterfinal
1969-70	76	29	34	13	...	222	242	71	6th	East Div.	Out of Playoffs
1970-71	78	37	33	8	...	248	211	82	4th	East Div.	Lost Quarterfinal
1971-72	78	33	31	14	...	209	208	80	4th	East Div.	Lost Quarterfinal
1972-73	78	27	41	10	...	247	279	64	6th	East Div.	Out of Playoffs
1973-74	78	35	27	16	...	274	230	86	4th	East Div.	Lost Quarterfinal
1974-75	80	31	33	16	...	280	309	78	3rd	Adams Div.	Lost Quarterfinal
1975-76	80	34	31	15	...	294	276	83	3rd	Adams Div.	Lost Quarterfinal
1976-77	80	33	32	15	...	301	285	81	3rd	Adams Div.	Lost Quarterfinal
1977-78	80	41	29	10	...	271	237	92	3rd	Adams Div.	Lost Semifinal
1978-79	80	34	33	13	...	267	252	81	3rd	Adams Div.	Lost Quarterfinal
1979-80	80	35	40	5	...	304	327	75	4th	Adams Div.	Lost Prelim. Round
1980-81	80	28	37	15	...	322	367	71	5th	Adams Div.	Lost Prelim. Round
1981-82	80	20	44	16	...	298	380	56	5th	Norris Div.	Out of Playoffs
1982-83	80	28	40	12	...	293	330	68	3rd	Norris Div.	Lost Div. Semifinal
1983-84	80	26	45	9	...	303	387	61	5th	Norris Div.	Out of Playoffs
1984-85	80	20	52	8	...	253	358	48	5th	Norris Div.	Out of Playoffs
1985-86	80	25	48	7	...	311	386	57	4th	Norris Div.	Lost Div. Final
1986-87	80	32	42	6	...	286	319	70	4th	Norris Div.	Lost Div. Final
1987-88	80	21	49	10	...	273	345	52	4th	Norris Div.	Lost Div. Semifinal
1988-89	80	28	46	6	...	259	342	62	5th	Norris Div.	Out of Playoffs
1989-90	80	38	38	4	...	337	358	80	3rd	Norris Div.	Lost Div. Semifinal
1990-91	80	23	46	11	...	241	318	57	5th	Norris Div.	Out of Playoffs
1991-92	80	30	43	7	...	234	294	67	5th	Norris Div.	Out of Playoffs
1992-93	84	44	29	11	...	288	241	99	3rd	Norris Div.	Lost Conf. Finals
1993-94	84	43	29	12	...	280	243	98	2nd	Central Div.	Lost Conf. Finals
1994-95	48	21	19	8	...	135	146	50	4th	Central Div.	Lost Conf. Quarterfinal
1995-96	82	34	36	12	...	247	252	80	3rd	Central Div.	Lost Conf. Quarterfinal
1996-97	82	30	44	8	...	230	273	68	6th	Central Div.	Out of Playoffs
1997-98	82	30	43	9	...	194	237	69	6th	Central Div.	Out of Playoffs
1998-99	82	45	30	7	...	268	231	97	2nd	Northeast Div.	Lost Conf. Finals
99-2000	82	45	27	7	3	246	222	100	1st	Northeast Div.	Lost Conf. Semifinal
2000-01	82	37	29	11	5	232	207	90	3rd	Northeast Div.	Lost Conf. Semifinal
2001-02	82	43	25	10	4	249	207	100	2nd	Northeast Div.	Lost Conf. Finals
2002-03	82	44	28	7	3	236	208	98	2nd	Northeast Div.	Lost Conf. Quarterfinal

* Season played in two halves with no combined standing at end.

§ Name changed from Arenas to St. Patricks.

• Name changed from St. Patricks to Maple Leafs.

* Season played in two halves with no combined standing at end. From 1917-18 through 1925-26, NHL champions played against PCHA/WCHL champions for Stanley Cup.

In November, 1961, Conn Smythe officially stepped aside and sold his 50,000 shares in the Maple Leafs franchise (60 percent of the voting rights) to his son Stafford, Harold Ballard and Toronto Telegram owner John Bassett for $2 million dollars. Under this new ownership group, the Leafs won the Stanley Cup in 1962 and 1963. The following season, Punch Imlach dealt forwards Dick Duff, Bob Nevin and Bill Collins, plus defensemen Arnie Brown and Rod Seiling, to the Rangers in return for Andy Bathgate and Don McKenney. Bathgate and McKenney proved a big help as the Leafs won their third consecutive Cup title in 1964. In the final series against Detroit, hardrock defenseman Bobby Baun scored the winning goal in game six in overtime while playing on a cracked bone in his ankle. Toronto captured the Cup once more in the 1960s. With NHL expansion looming, Imlach's veterans—the oldest club ever to reach the finals—ousted Montreal in six games in 1967 behind the superb goaltending of Terry Sawchuk and Johnny Bower.

When his team slumped in 1967–68, Imlach sent Frank Mahovlich (a player he couldn't get along with), Pete Stemkowski and Garry Unger, along with the rights to retired Carl Brewer (another Leaf who drove Imlach to distraction), to Detroit for Norm Ullman, Paul Henderson and Floyd Smith. But the Leafs were no longer championship material. After they were eliminated by Boston in the 1969 playoffs, Imlach was fired by Stafford Smythe. Jim Gregory took over as general manager and John McLellan was assigned the coaching job.

Relations between Turk Broda and Conn Smythe were not always this good. With the Leafs slumping early in the 1949–50 season, Smythe demanded Broda lose 10 pounds. The move generated plenty of publicity for the team.

In the summer of 1969, Harold Ballard and Stafford Smythe faced charges of tax evasion. John Bassett, unwilling to be associated with partners who faced jail terms, sold his shares to Ballard and Smythe for close to $6 million. Smythe died before he could be sentenced. Ballard then bought Smythe's shares, with help from his friend Don Giffin, who arranged for a loan of $7.4 million. Ballard, now in full control of the franchise and the Gardens, had his jail sentenced postponed until after the Canada–Soviet series of 1972. Then he was whisked off to jail to serve three concurrent three-year terms. He served only a year, and returned to put his personal ruinous stamp on hockey at Maple Leaf Gardens for most of the next two decades.

Upon his return to Toronto, Ballard scoffed at reports the newly formed World Hockey Association would give him any trouble. As a result, his organization lost no fewer than 14 players to the rival loop, including such young stars as Brad Selwood, Rick Ley, Jim Harrison and the brilliant young goaltender Bernie Parent.

Though they were no longer the powerhouse club of the 1960s, Ballard's Leafs played decent hockey throughout most of the 1970s. One of the game's great moments took place on February 7, 1976, when Leaf captain Darryl Sittler scored a record 10 points (six goals and four assists) in a game against Boston. Sittler capped an outstanding year by scoring five goals in a playoff game against Philadelphia, and later scored in overtime for Team Canada against Czechoslovakia in the final of the inaugural Canada Cup tournament in September, 1976. In 1977–78, the Leafs, with new coach Roger Neilson replacing Red Kelly behind the bench, stunned the New York Islanders in the playoff quarterfinals, winning in overtime in game seven on a Lanny McDonald goal.

Late in the 1978–79 season, Ballard fired Neilson after a March 1 loss to Montreal, then found he had nobody to replace him. He rehired Neilson prior to the next game, then fired him a second time a few weeks later. He also fired Jim Gregory and dumped chief scout Bob Davidson. The Leafs were about to head into a steep decline. Ballard talked of hiring Scotty Bowman to run his team. Then it was Don Cherry. Instead, he wound up bringing back Punch Imlach and promising him full control. It proved a huge mistake.

Imlach's dictatorial ways had paid big dividends for the Maple Leafs of the 1960s, but his tactics didn't work with the Leafs of the 1980s. When players raised his ire he got rid of them. He feuded with Darryl Sittler and fumed because Sittler had a no-trade clause in his contract. Maliciously, he traded Sittler's best friend Lanny McDonald to Colorado. He sent Pat Boutette to Hartford, Dave Hutchison to Chicago and Tiger Williams to Vancouver. Imlach brought back retired players in Larry Carriere and Carl Brewer, and installed old pals as coaches, first Floyd Smith and then Joe Crozier. When Imlach suffered two heart attacks and required bypass surgery during the 1980–81 season, Ballard didn't fire him. He simply said his manager wouldn't be back because of ill health. When Imlach did return, his parking spot was gone. That same season, on November 18, 1980, team founder Conn Smythe passed away at the age of 85.

When Imlach was pushed aside, Ballard took over. He appointed Gerry McNamara as general manager. It was another unpopular move, but McNamara remained on the job through the 1987–88 season. Thirty-year-old Gord Stellick (who had begun working for the Leafs while still in high school) and loyal Floyd Smith followed McNamara in the general manager's chair, while Leaf coaches in the 1980s included Joe Crozier, Mike Nykoluk, Dan Maloney, John Brophy, Doug Carpenter and George Armstrong.

Darryl Sittler had resigned as Leaf captain under Imlach, but later was persuaded by Ballard to resume that role. Sittler was grossly underpaid compared to other stars in the league, and when he requested a raise, Ballard told him to think about joining another team. During the 1981–82 season, Sittler agreed to join the Philadelphia Flyers. He had set club records for goals (389), assists (527) and points (916) during his career in Toronto.

Though the club missed the playoffs four times in eight years during the mid-1980s, Leaf fans at least could witness some

Red Kelly (left) with George Armstrong (center) and Tim Horton. Armstrong spent his entire NHL career with the Maple Leafs, playing a club record 1,187 games between 1949–50 and 1970–71. Horton spent 18 years in Toronto and was one of the NHL's best defensemen.

impressive individual efforts. Rick Vaive became the first Leaf player to reach the 50-goal plateau with 54 in 1981–82, and topped 50 again each of the next two years. Later in the decade, Gary Leeman totaled 51 goals.

In November, 1986, King Clancy died after a gall bladder operation. The death of his great friend left Harold Ballard devastated despite the consoling words of Yolanda, the lady in his life. In the later years of his own life, the saga of Harold and Yolanda would play out like a soap opera in the Toronto media. In April, 1990, Ballard passed away at age 86, leaving a once-great hockey franchise in tatters. Donald Giffin, Steve Stavro and Donald Crump stepped in as executors of the Ballard estate to sort out the mess both on and off the ice, which included a debt of $60 million.

On June 4, 1991, Giffin hired Cliff Fletcher as president, chief operating officer and general manager of the Leafs. Fletcher was signed to a five-year, $4 million contract. He immediately reshaped the front office, named popular Wendel Clark as captain, and masterminded a number of shrewd deals to improve the questionable product on the ice. On January 2, 1992, he hit the jackpot by sweet-talking his Calgary counterpart, Doug Risebrough, into giving up Doug Gilmour, Jamie Macoun, Ric Nattress, Kent Manderville and Rick Wamsley in return for Gary Leeman, Michel Petit, Alexander Godynyuk, Craig Berube and Jeff Reese. Gilmour, always a prolific scorer, was the plum in the pudding. He swiftly became a superstar in Toronto.

Fletcher's next major move was to sign Pat Burns as coach, replacing Tom Watt. Burns had resigned from the Montreal Canadiens in May, 1992. Within hours, he was a Maple Leaf. Together, Fletcher and Burns resurrected the franchise. The Leafs recorded a club-record 99 points in 1992–93. Thrilling seven-game playoff victories over Detroit and St. Louis saw Toronto reach the Campbell Conference final, where the most exciting hockey season in Toronto in years ended with a seventh-game loss to Wayne Gretzky and the Los Angeles Kings.

In the playoffs of 1994, the Leafs eliminated Chicago in six and San Jose in seven. But, a five-game playoff loss to Vancouver ended their season. Undaunted, Fletcher kept making moves. At the annual draft sessions in Hartford, Fletcher traded Wendel Clark, Sylvain Lefebvre and Landon Wilson to Quebec for Mats Sundin, Garth Butcher and Todd Warriner. This time, the dealing took its toll and the team began to tumble. Burns was fired late in 1995–96 after a devastating midseason slump.

Ordered by owner Steve Stavro to trim the payroll, on June 22, 1996, Fletcher traded Mike Gartner to Phoenix (Gartner claimed he had a verbal no-trade agreement with the g.m.) and Dave Gagner to Calgary. During the 1996–97 season, Doug Gilmour was traded to New Jersey, along with Dave Ellett, for Steve Sullivan, Jason Smith and junior star Alyn McCauley. At the trade deadline, Fletcher sent Larry Murphy to Detroit and Kirk Muller to the Panthers. Despite the many moves in an attempt to salvage the season, Toronto finished in last place in the Central Division and missed the playoffs. The next move would involve Fletcher himself. He was dismissed on May 24, 1997.

In a surprise move six days after Fletcher's departure, Hall of Fame goaltender Ken Dryden accepted the job as president of the Toronto Maple Leafs. Though he had no managerial experience, Dryden promised everything from a better team on the ice to better hot dogs at the concession stands. "I'm here because it feels right to be here," Dryden said.

On August 20, 1997, Dryden named himself to the position of general manager and named Anders Hedberg, Mike Smith and Bill Watters to his management team. Mike Murphy was retained as coach, but was presented with perhaps an even less-talented roster than the team that had missed the playoffs in Fletcher's final season. With only Mats Sundin proving capable offensively, the Leafs struggled to score goals throughout the 1997–98 season and missed the playoffs for the second year in a row. Dryden fired Murphy on June 23, 1998, and replaced him with Pat Quinn three days later.

An era in NHL history ended during the 1998–99 season when the Toronto Maple Leafs bid farewell to their home of 68 years and moved into the Air Canada Centre (which would also house the NBA's Toronto Raptors, who had been purchased by Maple Leaf Sports and Entertainment). The last remaining Original Six arena played host to its final game on February 13, 1999. Unfortunately for Toronto fans, Maple Leaf Gardens closed much as it opened, with the Chicago Blackhawks scoring a 6–2 victory (Chicago had beaten the Maple Leafs, 2–1, back in 1931).

The loss to the Blackhawks was one of very few disappointments in Toronto during the 1998–99 season, as the Maple Leafs made a surprising return to the upper echelon of the NHL. The good things began in the offseason, when Dryden negotiated Toronto back into the Eastern Conference and into the Northeast Division with Ottawa, Buffalo, Boston and Montreal.

Most important to the Leafs' on-ice success in 1998–99 was the decision to sign Curtis Joseph who would provide clutch goaltending that allowed Quinn to employ an offensive approach and saw the Leafs lead the league with 268 goals while winning a team-record 45 games. Joseph himself established a franchise high with 35 victories. The acquisition of Joseph made Felix Potvin expendable, though associate general manager Mike Smith held on to him until he could get the deal he wanted. Smith was finally able to land talented young defenseman Bryan Berard when he shipped Potvin to the New York Islanders in January. (Berard would find his career in jeopardy when he suffered a serious eye injury against the Ottawa Senators on March 11, 2000. After missing the entire 2000–01 season, he returned to the NHL with the New York Rangers in 2001–02, then joined the Boston Bruins the following year.)

The Maple Leafs finished the 1998–99 season with 97 points, good for second in their division behind the surprising Senators. They then defeated Philadelphia and Pittsburgh in the playoffs before bowing out to the Buffalo Sabres in the Eastern Conference final.

During the offseason, Smith left the team. He would resurface in Chicago. Anders Hedberg also departed, and would work in Edmonton before returning to Europe to manage Sweden's national team program. Pat Quinn was promoted to general manager, making him the first man since Punch Imlach to hold the dual role of coach and g.m. in Toronto.

The club's failure to make significant additions to the on-ice talent worried fans heading into the 1999–2000 season, but newcomer Jonas Hoglund proved a key addition to the club's top line alongside Mats Sundin and Steve Thomas. Nik Antropov, drafted 10th overall out of Kazakhstan in 1997, showed promise as a rookie after being called up early in the season. Deals for Darcy Tucker and Gerald Diduck added to the team's toughness, but the biggest key to Toronto's success continued to be Curtis Joseph. He broke his own team record with 36 victories as Toronto posted the first 100-point season in franchise history. By coming in first in the Northeast Division, Toronto finished atop the standings for the first time since finishing first overall in the six-team NHL back in 1962–63. However, hopes for the franchise's first Stanley Cup title since 1967 were dashed in the second round of the playoffs. After beating the Senators in six games in the opening round, the Leafs were defeated in six games by the New Jersey Devils. They fired an all-time playoff low six shots on goal in the final game.

Following the loss to New Jersey, Maple Leafs coach and general manager Pat Quinn decided his team had to get tougher. Towards that end, Toronto signed free agents Gary Roberts and Shayne Corson in the offseason and later dealt for Bryan McCabe. Corson added grit and McCabe definitely improved the team's blueline corps, but Roberts was the key acquisition. His 29 goals in 2000–01 led the team and were the most he had scored since notching 41 back in 1993–94. Once again though, it was Mats Sundin who was the team's top offensive performer, collecting 28 goals and 46 assists. Yanic Perreault, Sergei Berezin and Jonas Hoglund also topped the 20-goal plateau (though neither Perreault nor Berezin would be back with the team in 2001–02). Still, Toronto fell to 90 points and seventh place overall in the Eastern Conference. All year long, Maple Leafs fans had been told that there team was built for success in the playoffs and the Toronto faithful were rewarded with a stunning first-round sweep of the Ottawa Senators. However, New Jersey proved too tough in the second round once again, though it took the Devils seven games to eliminate the Leafs this year.

Alexander Mogilny, Robert Reichel, Mikael Renberg and Travis Green were newcomers to Toronto for the 2001–02 season. Both Mogilny and Reichel reached the 20-goal plateau, as did Gary Roberts and Darcy Tucker. Mats Sundin demonstrated that he belonged among the league's top stars, tying for second in the NHL with 41 goals and ranking fourth in points with 80. Bryan McCabe and Tomas Kaberle were strong on defense and, despite injuries, Curtis Joseph's 2.23 goals-against average was the lowest of his four-year stay in Toronto. With 100 points on the season, the Maple Leafs had the NHL's third-best record, but finished second behind Boston in the Northeast Division and were thus ranked fourth in the Eastern Conference. Despite a rash of injuries in the playoffs, the Leafs eliminated the New York Islanders in a tough seven-game series, then disposed of the Senators again in seven more. With Sundin among the many casualties, Gary Roberts had emerged as the team leader, while Alyn McCauley became an offensive force. Sundin was finally back for the second game of the Eastern Conference final, but the Leafs fell to the surprising

Wendel Clark fights for position in front of former teammate Felix Potvin in the Vancouver net. Wendel remains a huge fan favorite in Toronto.

Carolina Hurricanes in six games.

During the offseason, it was learned that Roberts required surgery in both shoulders and would be sidelined until February. Curtis Joseph signed with the Red Wings and Toronto was unable to attract any big-name free agents. Ed Belfour was brought in to replace Joseph. He struggled in the early going, but was soon displaying the form that had made him one of the NHL's best netminders. He wound up winning 37 games—a new Leafs record—and topped the 400-win plateau for his career. Robert Svehla was acquired from Florida for Dmitry Yushkevich and was rock-solid on defense. As usual, the offense revolved around Mats Sundin. He led the team with 37 goals, but failed to top the team in scoring for the first time since he arrived in Toronto. That honor went to Alexander Mogilny, who had 33 goals and 46 assists for 79 points—seven more than Sundin. Sundin did reach the 1,000-point plateau for his career and also played in his 1,000th game. Mogilny would be rewarded for his fine season with the Lady Byng Trophy, making him the first Leafs player to win a major award since Doug Gilmour won the Selke Trophy in 1993.

The Leafs were playing their best hockey of the 2002–03 season by the time of the All-Star Game when club chairman Steve Stavro confirmed that he was selling his stake in Maple Leafs Sports and Entertainment (the group that owned the hockey team, the Air Canada Centre and the NBA's Toronto Raptors).

Meanwhile, the team continued to perform well on the ice after the All-Star break and Toronto fans were enthused when the Maple Leafs acquired Owen Nolan, Doug Gilmour, Glen Wesley and Phil Housley in deals at the trade deadline. Production declined somewhat when Gilmour, Wesley, Gary Roberts, Mats Sundin and others were affected by a rash of injuries that hit the team late in the year, but Toronto still managed to finish the season with 98 points. They were seeded fifth overall in the Eastern Conference and would have to start the playoffs on the road in Philadelphia.

Mats Sundin was the first European player ever selected number one in the NHL Entry Draft when the Quebec Nordiques chose him in 1989. He was traded to Toronto in 1994 and has led the Maple Leafs in either goals, assists or points (sometimes all three) in every year since.

After enjoying a breakout season, Nik Antropov was added to the wounded list during the playoffs, and though all of the ailing players (except Gilmour) eventually returned to the lineup, the Leafs were outplayed through much of their series with the Flyers. Still they managed to push Philadelphia to seven games with a gutsy 2–1 overtime victory in game six. However, the tank was empty for game seven the following night and the Leafs suffered a 6–1 defeat. The two teams had played a total of 532 minutes and five seconds during the series, nearly the equivalent of nine full games. The Leafs-Flyers series ranked second all time to the clocking of 553:08 in a matchup between the Bruins and Rangers way back in 1939.

Immediately following the earliest playoff ouster of the Quinn era, speculation over the future of the front office began anew. With new ownership in place headed by chairman Larry Tanenbaum, several changes were made. A three-man committee was formed to search for a new general manager with Quinn to retain the coaching job when the new g.m. was hired. Ken Dryden became vice-chairman and a director of the company that owns the Leafs and their basketball counterparts, the Toronto Raptors.

Vancouver Canucks

WHEN THE VANCOUVER CANUCKS played their first NHL game, a 3–1 loss to the Los Angeles Kings, on October 9, 1970, it marked the first major professional hockey game in the British Columbia city since the 1920s.

The Vancouver Millionaires had played some glorious hockey in the old Pacific Coast Hockey Association, a creation of brothers Frank and Lester Patrick. Featuring future Hockey Hall of Famers Cyclone Taylor, Frank Nighbor and Hugh Lehman, the Millionaires had won Vancouver's one and only Stanley Cup in 1915. The team was known as the Vancouver Maroons by the time pro hockey collapsed in the west in 1926. In the years that followed, Vancouver would be home to several minor pro teams and leagues.

In 1965, when the NHL was getting ready to announce plans to expand into six additional hockey markets, Vancouver representatives were front-and-center seeking a franchise to represent western Canada. Fred Hume, former mayor of the city and owner of the minor-league Vancouver Canucks, announced that he would apply for a franchise.

Initially, Cyrus McLean, chairman of the board of B.C. Telephone, and the legendary broadcaster Foster Hewitt were named as the prospective owners of the Vancouver entry in the NHL. McLean had purchased the minor-league Canucks from Fred Hume, who was then in failing health. But, the McLean/Hewitt presentation to the league governors at a 1966 meeting in New York was sloppily prepared. Another reason the bid for a team failed may have stemmed from Toronto Maple Leafs owner Stafford Smythe's distaste for Vancouver after the city failed to approve a Smythe plan to build an arena on city-owned land a few months earlier. Yet another reason for denial may be attributed to Chicago Black Hawks' influential owner James D. Norris. It was said Norris would have preferred to see some of his personal friends involved in the Vancouver bid—men like Frank McMahon, Max Bell and Red Dutton, all powerful figures in sports and business in western Canada.

Meanwhile, Captain Harry Terry, president of the Pacific National Exhibition, had decided that a new rink should adorn the Vancouver Exhibition grounds. Terry knew that the federal government would come through with low-interest loans and grants for such an edifice because of new legislation promising funding of winter and summer fairs, etc. It was agreed that the federal and provincial governments would put up $2 million each; the city would be liable for another $1 million. Through private funding, the city would also commit another $1 million to the arena project.

The Pacific Coliseum was dedicated on January 8, 1968. A month later, the first hockey game was played between the Montreal Oldtimers and the Western All-Stars. It attracted 16,511 fans—the largest crowd to see a game in Canada at that time. Obviously, Vancouver had a thirst for hockey. Now it hungered for an NHL team.

By the time of the follow-up NHL expansion in 1970–71, the Vancouver ownership picture had changed. Foster Hewitt was no longer involved and Cyrus McLean was thrust into a secondary role among the new majority owners, the Medicor Group of Minneapolis. The new ownership group had bought the minor league Western Hockey League Vancouver Canucks and successfully negotiated with the NHL for an expansion franchise. At a cost of $6 million apiece, both the new Vancouver Canucks and the Buffalo Sabres were admitted into the league. In an effort to maintain the NHL's competitive balance, both Buffalo and Vancouver were placed in the East Division, despite the odd geography.

Orland Kurtenbach began his pro hockey career with the old Vancouver Canucks of the Western Hockey League in 1957–58. After 10 NHL seasons, he was claimed by the new Canucks in the 1970 Expansion Draft and became the team's first captain.

The first general manager of the Canucks was Norman "Bud" Poile, former g.m. of the Philadelphia Flyers, who had entered the league in 1967. There was grumbling in some quarters when Poile was selected over Joe Crozier, who had run the minor-league Canucks with much success. Poile in turn selected Hal Laycoe, formerly of the Los Angeles Kings, to coach the Canucks in their inaugural season.

Despite a restrictive Expansion Draft procedure, the Canucks were relatively pleased with their new talent. Their first choice was Gary Doak, a former Boston Bruin who was thought of as a young defenseman with promise. Also chosen was Orland Kurtenbach, a tough forward and future team leader. Wayne Maki, who scored only seven goals in 66 games with Chicago and St. Louis, contributed a career-high 25 goals (and 63 points) in that first season—a pleasant surprise.

After the June, 1970, Expansion Draft, the

immediate future of the Canucks—and the Sabres—depended largely on the Amateur Draft of junior players. A "spin of the wheel" at the June 9 draft meetings in Montreal determined that the Canucks would pick second. After Buffalo grabbed Gilbert Perreault, Poile selected defenseman Dale Tallon as the Canucks' first choice.

The Canucks finished their first season out of the playoffs, but achieved 56 points in a 78-game schedule. They finished seven points below their expansion cousins in Buffalo, but did manage to finish one point ahead of Detroit, an Original Six team, in the East Division standings.

The Canucks struggled through the next three seasons, finishing with 48, 53 and 59 points. Then, with a happy-go-lucky goaltender named Gary Smith in the net, obtained from Chicago with Jerry Korab in return for Tallon, they soared to first place in the Smythe Division with 86 points in their fifth season of 1974–75. In the playoffs, the Canucks lost in overtime to a powerful Montreal club in the fifth game of the quarterfinals.

Along with Stan Smyl and Richard Brodeur, Thomas Gradin led the Canucks to their first appearance in the Stanley Cup finals in 1982.

Meanwhile, when the Medicor people stepped away from hockey and the club was put up for sale, the Griffiths family moved forward to rescue the organization. Frank Griffiths' wife Emily is often credited with making the final decision to purchase the club in 1974. Griffiths had been highly successful in the broadcast business and he genuinely wanted to put something back into the community.

The new ownership provided a degree of stability and things began to look up on the ice. By 1982 the Canucks found themselves sailing into the Stanley Cup finals. Coach Harry Neale, suspended for 10 games after challenging some fans in Quebec, wasn't around for the fun. His assistant, Roger Neilson, took the spotlight behind the bench, and captured headlines after he waved a white towel at referee Bob Myers in mock surrender during a playoff game in Chicago. Tiger Williams and the other Canucks followed suit, hoisting towels on their hockey sticks. The club was fined $10,000 for ridiculing the game officials. When the team returned home for the next game, almost every Vancouver fan waved a white towel enthusiastically.

The Canucks disposed of the Black Hawks and advanced to the finals against the Islanders, only to lose in four straight games. One day after their defeat, 100,000 Vancouverites honored their underdog heroes with a civic parade. Thomas Gradin, Stan Smyl and Ivan Boldirev were the team's top scorers, but the star of the surprising playoff run had been goaltender Richard Brodeur. Unfortunately, the success of 1982 did not carry over into subsequent seasons, as the team struggled annually to reach the playoffs and failed to advance beyond the first round when it did.

A turning point in team history occurred on January 9, 1987, when the Canucks announced that Pat Quinn had accepted the position of general manager and president in Vancouver. Quinn was under contract as coach of the Los Angeles Kings at the time, and league president John Ziegler issued a fine of $310,000 (later reduced to $10,000 by the B.C. Supreme Court) for tampering. Quinn was not permitted to assume his dual roles until May 1, and soon after, hired Bob McCammon as his coach and Brian Burke as director of hockey operations. After collecting just 59 points during the 80-game 1987–88 season, the Canucks used the second selection overall in the 1988 Entry Draft to obtain Trevor Linden.

Linden entered the NHL as the league's youngest player in 1988–89 after having helped the Medicine Hat Tigers win consecutive Memorial Cup championships. He set a Canucks rookie record with 30 goals and was

Vancouver Canucks

Year-by-Year Record

Season	GP	W	L	T	OL	GF	GA	Pts.	Finish	Division	Playoff Result
1970-71	78	24	46	8	...	229	296	56	6th	East Div.	Out of Playoffs
1971-72	78	20	50	8	...	203	297	48	7th	East Div.	Out of Playoffs
1972-73	78	22	47	9	...	233	339	53	7th	East Div.	Out of Playoffs
1973-74	78	24	43	11	...	224	296	59	7th	East Div.	Out of Playoffs
1974-75	80	38	32	10	...	271	254	86	1st	Smythe Div.	Lost Quarterfinal
1975-76	80	33	32	15	...	271	272	81	2nd	Smythe Div.	Lost Prelim. Round
1976-77	80	25	42	13	...	235	294	63	4th	Smythe Div.	Out of Playoffs
1977-78	80	20	43	17	...	239	320	57	3rd	Smythe Div.	Out of Playoffs
1978-79	80	25	42	13	...	217	291	63	2nd	Smythe Div.	Lost Prelim. Round
1979-80	80	27	37	16	...	256	281	70	3rd	Smythe Div.	Lost Prelim. Round
1980-81	80	28	32	20	...	289	301	76	3rd	Smythe Div.	Lost Prelim. Round
1981-82	80	30	33	17	...	290	286	77	2nd	Smythe Div.	Lost Final
1982-83	80	30	35	15	...	303	309	75	3rd	Smythe Div.	Lost Div. Semifinal
1983-84	80	32	39	9	...	306	328	73	3rd	Smythe Div.	Lost Div. Semifinal
1984-85	80	25	46	9	...	284	401	59	5th	Smythe Div.	Out of Playoffs
1985-86	80	23	44	13	...	282	333	59	4th	Smythe Div.	Lost Div. Semifinal
1986-87	80	29	43	8	...	282	314	66	5th	Smythe Div.	Out of Playoffs
1987-88	80	25	46	9	...	272	320	59	5th	Smythe Div.	Out of Playoffs
1988-89	80	33	39	8	...	251	253	74	4th	Smythe Div.	Lost Div. Semifinal
1989-90	80	25	41	14	...	245	306	64	5th	Smythe Div.	Out of Playoffs
1990-91	80	28	43	9	...	243	315	65	4th	Smythe Div.	Lost Div. Semifinal
1991-92	80	42	26	12	...	285	250	96	1st	Smythe Div.	Lost Div. Final
1992-93	84	46	29	9	...	346	278	101	1st	Smythe Div.	Lost Div. Final
1993-94	84	41	40	3	...	279	276	85	2nd	Pacific Div.	Lost Final
1994-95	48	18	18	12	...	153	148	48	2nd	Pacific Div.	Lost Conf. Semifinal
1995-96	82	32	35	15	...	278	278	79	3rd	Pacific Div.	Lost Conf. Quarterfinal
1996-97	82	35	40	7	...	257	273	77	4th	Pacific Div.	Out of Playoffs
1997-98	82	25	43	14	...	224	273	64	7th	Pacific Div.	Out of Playoffs
1998-99	82	23	47	12	...	192	258	58	4th	Northwest Div.	Out of Playoffs
99-2000	82	30	29	15	8	227	237	83	3rd	Northwest Div.	Out of Playoffs
2000-01	82	36	28	11	7	239	238	90	3rd	Northwest Div.	Lost Conf. Quarterfinal
2001-02	82	42	30	7	3	254	211	94	2nd	Northwest Div.	Lost Conf. Quarterfinal
2002-03	82	45	23	13	1	264	208	104	2nd	Northwest Div.	Lost Conf. Semifinal

named Vancouver's most valuable player while finishing as the runner-up to New York Rangers defenseman Brian Leetch in voting for the Calder Trophy as rookie of the year. In the playoffs, Vancouver was beaten in the first round, but they were the only team to take the eventual Stanley Cup champion Calgary Flames to the seven-game limit, losing 4–3 in overtime in the final game.

On July 1, 1989, the Canucks signed former Soviet star Igor Larionov. The move came just a few days after Vancouver had selected Pavel Bure in the fourth round of the 1989 Entry Draft. Bure's draft eligibility was questioned, but was resolved in the Canucks' favor several months later. He joined the Canucks for the 1991–92 season, scoring 34 goals to break Linden's club rookie record. "The Russian Rocket" also became the first Canucks player to win a major postseason award when he was named the winner of the Calder Trophy. Pat Quinn, who had added coaching duties to his portfolio in January, 1991, joined Bure on the winners' podium as he captured the Jack Adams Award as coach of the year. With a record of 42–26–12, Quinn had guided the Canucks to first place in the Smythe Division for the first time since 1974–75.

It was another first-place finish in 1992–93, as two club records set the preceding season were shattered when the Canucks registered 46 wins and 101 points. Bure became the first Canuck to top 50 goals and 100 points, finishing the season with 60 and 110. On April 2, 1993, team owner Frank Griffiths was inducted into the Hockey Hall of Fame. A year later he passed away after a lengthy illness.

On April 13, 1994, Bure reached 60 goals for the second straight season. Later in the month, Bure scored at 2:20 of the second overtime to give Vancouver a 4–3 win over Calgary. It was the club's third straight overtime win in a come-from-behind, seven-game playoff victory. After eliminating the Dallas Stars, goalie Kirk McLean blanked the Leafs in consecutive playoff games en route to a five-game victory in the Campbell Conference finals. The Canucks advanced to the Stanley Cup finals for the second time in their history.

Greg Adams's goal at 19:26 of overtime gave the Canucks a 3–2 win over the Rangers in game one of the finals before New York reeled off three straight wins. Heading back to Madison Square Garden for game five, the Canucks stayed alive with a 6–3 victory, then forced a seventh game with a 4–1 win at home. Back in New York, the Rangers sweated out a 3–2 victory for their first Cup triumph in 54 years. Bure's 16 goals led all playoff performers.

In March, 1995, Seattle businessman John E. McCaw purchased a majority interest in the Canucks and also gained control of the new $163-million General Motors Place arena and the NBA's Vancouver Grizzlies. The Canucks reunited former junior hockey teammates Alexander Mogilny and Pavel Bure when they acquired Mogilny from Buffalo for the 1995–96 season. He would go on to collect 55 goals and 107 points. On October 9, 1995, the Canucks played their first regular-season game at General Motors Place and lost 5–3 to Detroit. Mike Ridley scored the first regular-season goal in the new ice palace.

After the season, Quinn hired former Canadian national team coach Tom Renney to coach the Canucks. The team had difficulty adjusting to Renney's checking system, and the Canucks finished out of the playoffs. In June, 1997, the club introduced new team colors and a logo of a killer whale breaking through ice shaped in the letter C. Mark Messier was signed as an expensive free agent (three years at more than $20 million) and Linden chose to relinquish the captaincy to the newly acquired team leader. The 1997–98 season, however, proved to be a disaster. Quinn was fired after a poor start and Renney was released a short time later. Mike Keenan was brought in to coach and, by the end of January, was given the authority to make personnel changes. Keenan had feuded with Linden since his arrival and traded the popular player to the New York Islanders in February. Though Keenan's shakeups improved the team marginally, Vancouver still missed the playoffs for the second year in a row. In June, 1998, Brian Burke returned to the Canucks as the club's general manager.

Though Burke and Keenan stated for the record that they would have no problem working together, the club's poor record during the 1998–99 season saw former Colorado Avalanche boss Marc Crawford brought in to coach the Canucks in January. Just a few weeks earlier, Burke had dealt Pavel Bure to the Florida Panthers in a package deal that brought Ed Jovanovski to Vancouver. Bure had refused to suit up for the Canucks after demanding a trade in the offseason. The emergence of Adrian Aucoin was one bright spot during the season, as he led all NHL defensemen with 23 goals. Injuries would limit his effectiveness in 1999–2000.

After a decent start to the new season, the Canucks endured a dismal December that saw them win just twice in 11 games. Though the slump continued through January, the Canucks began to pick up the pace after the All-Star break. Newly acquired Felix Potvin started to flash the form he had displayed earlier in his career. Mark Messier returned from injuries and though there were rumors that he would be dealt at the trade deadline, the team was suddenly in playoff contention and Messier's leadership was key. Alexander Mogilny, however, was dealt to the New Jersey Devils for Brendan Morrison and Denis Pederson. Ultimately, the Canucks came up short of a playoff spot.

Despite the poor results of recent years, Canucks fans were encouraged by the 1999 Entry Draft. It cost him Bryan McCabe and the club's first-round choice in the 2000 draft, but Burke was able to gain the second overall draft position in addition to Vancouver's third choice, which allowed him to select talented Swedish twins Daniel and Henrik Sedin, both of whom began their NHL careers in 2000–2001. However, it was another Swede who would spark the club's resurgence.

Though he had reached a new career high with 36 goals in 1998–99 and established another career best with 38 assists the following season, Markus Naslund was hardly thought of as one of the game's top performers until the 2000–01 season. Naslund was named captain of the Canucks that year (after Mark Messier resigned with the New York Rangers) and led the team back into the playoffs for the first time since 1996. However, the Canucks' return to the postseason lasted just four games, as the eventual Stanley Cup champion Colorado Avalanche swept them out of the first round.

Naslund led the team in scoring with 75 points in 2000–01 and his 41 goals were the most ever scored by a Canucks captain. His numbers would have been even more impressive had he not suffered a broken leg after 72 games. Naslund did get some help from the Sedin twins, both of whom ranked among the game's top-scoring rookies. Ed Jovanovski also had a solid season on the Canucks defense, but goaltending was a problem as veterans Bob Essensa and Felix Potvin both proved ineffective. Dan Cloutier was acquired from Tampa Bay in a deal for Adrian Aucoin. He would take over as the Canucks' number-one netminder in 2001–02. In his first full season in Vancouver, Cloutier shattered all previous career bests with 62 games played, 31 wins and a 2.43 goals-against average. His seven shutouts tied him for second in the NHL behind Patrick Roy's nine. But the biggest story in Vancouver in 2001–02 was the play of Markus Naslund and his linemate, Todd Bertuzzi.

Centered by Brendan Morrison (who reached career highs with 23 goals and 44 assists), Naslund and Bertuzzi shot to second and third respectively in the NHL scoring race. Naslund had 40 goals and 50 assists, while Bertuzzi had 36 and 49. Ed Jovanovski established personal bests in goals (17) and points (48) for the second straight season, ranking among the NHL's top-scoring defensemen. Mattias Ohlund had 10 goals and 28 assists, while Brent Sopel was the team's best defensive defenseman with a plus-minus rating of +21. Meanwhile, former Canucks star Trevor Linden returned to the team early in the season after a trade with Washington.

Markus Naslund (right) finished second in the NHL in scoring in both 2001–02 and 2002–03. Todd Bertuzzi (above) finished third in 2001–02 and fifth in 2002–03. Naslund won the Lester B. Pearson Award as NHLPA's outstanding player for 2002–03.

Though the Canucks' 94 points were their most in a season since 1992–93 they held down just the eighth seed in the Western Conference and were forced to face the Detroit Red Wings in the first round of the playoffs. The Canucks stunned the first-place Red Wings by taking the first two games of the series in Detroit. However, a bad goal against Cloutier scored from center ice by Nicklas Lidstrom in game three seemed to turn the series around. The Canucks were beaten in six games.

With Naslund (48 goals, 56 assists), Bertuzzi (46 and 51) and Morrison (25 and 46) again leading the way in 2002–03, the Canucks took an early lead in the Northwest Division and ranked among the top teams in the NHL all season long. Cloutier bounced back from the playoff disappointment to post 33 wins, though he was sidelined by knee injuries a few times during the season. The Canucks set a new club record with 104 points, but the regular season ended on something of a down note. A win by Colorado combined with a Canucks loss on the final afternoon of the schedule saw the Avalanche edge out Vancouver by a single point for top spot in the Northwest Division. Not only that, but Peter Forsberg passed Naslund to win the scoring title with 106 points to Naslund's 104. (Forsberg would also beat out Naslund for the Hart Trophy, though the Canucks captain was rewarded with the Pearson Award as the players' choice for MVP). Milan Hejduk scored two goals to beat out Naslund for the Maurice Richard Trophy as he became the season's only 50-goal scorer.

The disappointing end to the season seemed to carry over into the playoffs as the Canucks dropped a 6–0 decision to St. Louis in the opener of their first-round matchup, then fell behind three games to one. Vancouver's best players seemed to be slumping, but suddenly Naslund, Bertuzzi, and Morrison started finding the net again and the Canucks stormed back to take the series in seven. Trent Klatt and the Sedin twins were solid in the finale, but the hero was Trevor Linden who had a goal and an assist in the 4–1 victory. Among active players, only Mark Messier and Doug Gilmour had scored more game-seven points in their playoff careers.

Next up for Vancouver was the surprising Minnesota Wild, who, like the Canucks, had stormed back from a three-games-to-one deficit to shock Colorado in the opening round. Vancouver's roll continued in game one, as the Canucks rallied for two goals late in the third period (Matt Cooke tied the game with under two seconds remaining) and pulled out a 4–3 win on Klatt's goal early in overtime. Another late comeback in game four led to a 3–2 overtime victory and a 3–1 Vancouver lead in the series. The Canucks had a chance to wrap things up on home ice in game five, but the Wild stormed back for 7–2 victory, then went home and forced a seventh game with a 5–1 win.

As in game six, Vancouver took control of game seven in the first period but could not score against Dwayne Roloson. The Canucks did get two quick goals midway through the second period, but a flukey goal by Pascal Dupuis cut the score to 2–1 before the end of the frame. Using their team speed to counter the Vancouver attack, the Wild fired only six shots at Daniel Cloutier in the third period (they had just 16 in the game) but scored on three as they rallied for a 4–2 victory that capped yet another amazing upset. The loss marked the first time all season that Vancouver had been beaten three times in a row.

Though the Canucks had gone deeper into the playoffs then they had since 1996, the loss to the Wild was a shocking conclusion to the season. "It's a very empty feeling," said Naslund. "We worked hard all year and it ends up in a finish like this."

"It's very disappointing for us," added coach Marc Crawford, "but sometimes it doesn't work out. You just have to look at the series and learn from it."

Washington Capitals

When Abe Pollin announced in 1972 that he planned to bring an NHL team to America's national capital, the Washington sportsman—who had headed his own construction firm—was advised by a Las Vegas bookmaker that the odds were 600–1 against him. Undaunted, Pollin personally delivered his application to the NHL office in Montreal on the day of the deadline to submit it. He made his presentation at the Board of Governors meetings in May, 1972. Aware that he was an underdog among 10 competitors for two expansion franchise openings, Pollin spent five days in a Montreal hotel, lobbying hockey's power brokers on Washington's behalf. His presentation was impressive enough to get him the franchise, on the condition that a suitable arena would be available by 1974–75.

Pollin, who already owned the NBA Baltimore Bullets, envisioned a new arena that would house both his major-league teams somewhere in the Capital District. But bickering and bureaucratic delays over who—or which city—would build the arena frustrated his plans. Finally he decided to construct the rink with his own funds, on a site he personally would choose. Pollin bypassed both Washington and Baltimore for a tract of former farmland in Landover, Maryland, where he planned to build an $18-million arena to be known as the Capital Centre.

The minimum target date for completion was thought to be two years. Instead, the arena was completed in 15 months. It seated 17,962 for hockey and boasted that every spectator was guaranteed a seat no further than 200 feet from center ice. Furthermore, at a time when other NHL arenas were not even considering premium seating, Pollin arranged for 40 luxury sky suites to be clustered along the upper levels.

For their first season, the Washington Capitals had former American Hockey League star Jimmy Anderson behind the bench and Hall of Famer Milt Schmidt as general manager. However, the Capitals were competing against the three-year-old World Hockey Association and the NHL expansion Kansas City Scouts for players. The result was a patchwork conspicuously lacking in talent on both the attack and defense. Washington's leading scorer, Tommy Williams (22 goals, 36 assists), was a Boston Bruins discard, and the supporting cast, with the notable exception of heroic goalie Ron Low, had even fewer credentials. The team's major hope was an African-Canadian named Mike Marson who had been the top scorer with the Sudbury Wolves in the Ontario Hockey Association. Marson was only the second black to reach the NHL, the first having been Willie O'Ree, who had played briefly for the Boston Bruins beginning in 1957–58. Marson finished as the Caps' third-leading scorer with 16 goals and 28 points.

Mike Marson had 16 goals as a rookie with the Washington Capitals in 1974–75. He was the first black player in the NHL since Willie O'Ree in 1960–61.

Precisely how Washingtonians would respond to hockey was underscored on opening night, October 9, 1974, when a crowd of 17,500 turned out to see the New York Rangers defeat the Caps 6–3. Sellouts were not the norm, but there were enough substantial gates to persuade Pollin he had made a good move despite the fact that the team went just 8–67–5 and set records for fewest wins (minimum 70 games), most losses (since broken), most consecutive losses (17—later tied by San Jose) and most goals-against (446).

It would have been difficult for Pollin's puckchasers to do worse in their second season, but the improvement proved to be minuscule. The Capitals launched the season with Schmidt managing and coaching. After 36 games, his record was three wins, five ties and 28 losses, and Pollin made a wholesale change. Central Hockey League president Max McNab was imported as general manager, and McNab in turn hired Tom McVie to handle the team. The Caps finished the year 11–59–10. McVie, who won eight, tied five and lost 31, was retained to coach the following year.

McNab's regime was marked by a significant improvement. In 1976–77, the team's record leaped to a more reasonable 24–42–14 thanks to key acquisitions such as Guy Charron, Bryan Watson and Gerry Meehan. Unfortunately for McVie, the upward trend didn't continue. In 1977–78, the Caps' record dropped to 17–49–14.

"It was the low point in my career," McVie allowed. "It was my first NHL job and I gave my soul. I put the team ahead of my family and health. I took a day off once with my wife, and when I came back, Danny Belisle was in my coach's chair. They said, 'You're gone!' That taught me a lesson. Ever since then, I take my chair with me and never go on vacations."

With Belisle coaching in their fifth year of existence (1978–79), the Capitals registered their best record yet with 63 points (24–41–15)—but still missed the playoffs. Fleet little Dennis Maruk became an overnight sensation as he led the team in scoring with 90 points.

Belisle's tenure was short-lived. The victim of a poor start (4–10–2) in 1979–80, he was yanked after 16 games in favor of a youthful Gary Green. The 26-year-old Green was the youngest coach in NHL history.

Green produced the best-yet Capitals coaching record (23–30–11), but it was a case of too little, too late and a playoff berth eluded the franchise for the sixth consecutive year in spite of starry efforts by Maruk, Mike Gartner and Ryan Walter that offered hope for the future.

Green could not shake the Capitals' playoffs jinx in 1980–81, either. The club finished with a 26–36–18 record, but Green simply couldn't find the necessary mix. He lasted 13 games into the 1981–82 season, winning but a single game and losing a dozen before he got the hook. Assistant g.m. Roger Crozier handled one game (a tie) until Bryan Murray could be named the head coach.

Still, the ongoing playoff drought finally compelled Pollin to make another change in his general staff. On August 30, 1982, McNab was dropped as general manager in favor of 33-year-old David Poile, who became the youngest g.m. in NHL history. David's father, Norman "Bud" Poile, had been an NHL star and later a top hockey executive, and David had done his front office basic training with Atlanta and Calgary before moving to Landover.

On September 10, 1982, shortly after training camp started, Poile sent defenseman Rick Green and forward Ryan Walter to Montreal for defensemen Rod Langway and Brian Engblom as well as forwards Doug Jarvis and Craig Laughlin. Few deals for any team at any time have ever produced a more dramatic impact. The former Canadiens infused the Capitals with a winning spirit that was translated into the club's first season above .500. Washington finished third in the Patrick Division with a record of 39–25–16 before losing their first playoff series to the Stanley Cup champion New York Islanders. Langway won the Norris Trophy as the NHL's best defenseman and Scott Stevens made an instant impact as a rookie defenseman.

With Langway leading the way on the ice and in the dressing room, Washington improved to second place (48–27–5) in 1983–84. The captain again won the Norris Trophy, Doug Jarvis the Selke Trophy as the NHL's best defensive forward, the goaltending tandem of Al Jensen and Pat Riggin the Jennings Trophy for having the fewest goals against, and to top off Washington's biggest year yet for awards, Murray took the Jack Adams Award as coach of the year. Still, the defending champion Islanders once more eliminated them from the Stanley Cup run, four games to one.

Murray's effervescent coaching continued to keep the Capitals near the top of the Patrick Division. In 1984–85, they finished third overall with 101 points and featured two 50-goal scorers in Bobby Carpenter (53) and Mike Gartner (50). "It was a positive development," says Poile. "But, the problem was that too much of our scoring was concentrated in those two people."

After winning 50 regular-season games for the first time in franchise history in 1985–86, Murray appeared to have a Cup-worthy team. Carpenter, Gartner, Dave Christian and Bengt Gustafsson paced the attack while Al Jensen provided grade-A goaltending. Heavy favorites to defeat the Rangers in the playoffs, the Capitals were upset four games to two and by now had taken on the distinct image of playoff chokers, a state of affairs that moved Poile to action.

Once again he executed an arresting deal. On New Year's Day, 1987, he delivered Carpenter and a second-round draft choice to the Rangers for Kelly Miller, Mike Ridley and Bob Crawford. Carpenter was a bust on Broadway, while Ridley and Miller excelled in a dual capacity as scoring threats and penalty killers. Remarkably, defenseman Larry Murphy led Washington in points (81); Gartner's 41 goals were tops in that department.

Still nothing changed with regard to the playoffs. After a 38–32–10 season, the Caps encountered their traditional nemesis, the Islanders, in the divisional semifinals. The series wound down to an excruciatingly close seventh game at Capital Centre. When the fans finally departed, it was six hours after the opening face-off and they had witnessed the most memorable game of the 1980s—a quadruple-overtime thriller in which the Isles ultimately prevailed, 3–2. It was at 1:56 a.m. on Easter Sunday when Pat LaFontaine launched a turnaround slapshot that put the Caps out of their misery. Washington had suffered another premature season's end.

The pattern of playoff futility continued through the Bryan Murray regime in spite of heartening regular-season efforts. Finally, the 1989–90 campaign brought a breakthrough. After going 18–24–4 in the first half of the season, Poile replaced head coach Bryan Murray with his brother, Terry. This time there was an improvement: Washington reached the third round of the playoffs before losing to Boston in four straight games.

Meanwhile, the face of the Capitals was changing. In 1990–91, rookie Peter Bondra showed flashes of brilliance behind usual point producers Mike Ridley and Michal Pivonka. The blue line was solidified with Kevin Hatcher and smooth-skating Calle Johansson. In 1994, the Caps acquired playmaker Joe Juneau from Boston for defenseman Al Iafrate. Rounding out the new look was goalie Jim Carey, who posted a stunning 18–6–3 record in his rookie year, then went 35–24–9 with nine shutouts the year after and captured the 1996 Vezina Trophy. The final step in the process of change saw the Capital Centre renamed the U.S. Air Arena.

Washington Capitals

Year-by-Year Record

Season	GP	W	L	T	OL	GF	GA	Pts.	Finish	Division	Playoff Result
1974-75	80	8	67	5	...	181	446	21	5th	Norris Div.	Out of Playoffs
1975-76	80	11	59	10	...	224	394	32	5th	Norris Div.	Out of Playoffs
1976-77	80	24	42	14	...	221	307	62	4th	Norris Div.	Out of Playoffs
1977-78	80	17	49	14	...	195	321	48	5th	Norris Div.	Out of Playoffs
1978-79	80	24	41	15	...	273	338	63	4th	Norris Div.	Out of Playoffs
1979-80	80	27	40	13	...	261	293	67	5th	Patrick Div.	Out of Playoffs
1980-81	80	26	36	18	...	286	317	70	5th	Patrick Div.	Out of Playoffs
1981-82	80	26	41	13	...	319	338	65	5th	Patrick Div.	Out of Playoffs
1982-83	80	39	25	16	...	306	283	94	3rd	Patrick Div.	Lost Div. Semifinal
1983-84	80	48	27	5	...	308	226	101	2nd	Patrick Div.	Lost Div. Final
1984-85	80	46	25	9	...	322	240	101	2nd	Patrick Div.	Lost Div. Semifinal
1985-86	80	50	23	7	...	315	272	107	2nd	Patrick Div.	Lost Div. Final
1986-87	80	38	32	10	...	285	278	86	2nd	Patrick Div.	Lost Div. Semifinal
1987-88	80	38	33	9	...	281	249	85	2nd	Patrick Div.	Lost Div. Final
1988-89	80	41	29	10	...	305	259	92	1st	Patrick Div.	Lost Div. Semifinal
1989-90	80	36	38	6	...	284	275	78	3rd	Patrick Div.	Lost Conf. Finals
1990-91	80	37	36	7	...	258	258	81	3rd	Patrick Div.	Lost Div. Final
1991-92	80	45	27	8	...	330	275	98	2nd	Patrick Div.	Lost Div. Semifinal
1992-93	84	43	34	7	...	325	286	93	2nd	Patrick Div.	Lost Div. Semifinal
1993-94	84	39	35	10	...	277	263	88	3rd	Atlantic Div.	Lost Conf. Semifinal
1994-95	48	22	18	8	...	136	120	52	3rd	Atlantic Div.	Lost Conf. Quarterfinal
1995-96	82	39	32	11	...	234	204	89	4th	Atlantic Div.	Lost Conf. Quarterfinal
1996-97	82	33	40	9	...	214	231	75	5th	Atlantic Div.	Out of Playoffs
1997-98	82	40	30	12	...	219	202	92	3rd	Atlantic Div.	Lost Final
1998-99	82	31	45	6	...	200	218	68	3rd	Southeast Div.	Out of Playoffs
99-2000	82	44	24	12	2	227	194	102	1st	Southeast Div.	Lost Conf. Quarterfinal
2000-01	82	41	27	10	4	233	211	96	1st	Southeast Div.	Lost Conf. Quarterfinal
2001-02	82	36	33	11	2	228	240	85	2nd	Southeast Div.	Out of Playoffs
2002-03	82	39	29	8	6	224	220	92	2nd	Southeast Div.	Lost Conf. Quarterfinal

Despite the many alterations, the Caps' legendary lack of luck in the playoffs continued. Every year that Washington failed to reach the Stanley Cup finals brought Poile under more fire from the hometown media. Still, he retained Pollin's confidence until the end of the 1996–97 season. This time, for the first time in 15 years, the Caps didn't even get to the playoffs.

Poile executed a late-season deal that at first seemed to save his job when he sent the suddenly struggling Carey and young forwards Anson Carter and Jason Allison to Boston for top playmaker Adam Oates, former Philadelphia captain Rick Tocchet and one-time Conn Smythe Trophy-winning goalie Bill Ranford. But, it wasn't enough. Pollin replaced Poile with former left wing George McPhee on June 9, 1997. (As many suspected, Poile wasn't out of work long. By the end of the summer, he had been hired as g.m. of the expansion Nashville Predators.) Also released was head coach Jim Schoenfeld, who had replaced Terry Murray in 1993–94.

The first major coup of the McPhee era was hiring Ron Wilson as head coach. Wilson had coached the Mighty Ducks of Anaheim to their first playoff berth in 1996, then guided Team USA to a victory at the World Cup of Hockey. A dispute with Anaheim high command paved the way for Wilson's arrival on Capital Hill, where he discovered a major change in the Capitals' ambience. After playing in Landover for 24 years, the team moved into a spanking-new arena in downtown Washington. Commercially named MCI Center, the rink signaled a gamble that Pollin could lure the suburban fans from Maryland and Virginia into the inner city that had been off-limits to many of them in the past, but the change of venue was temporarily disappointing in terms of attendance. Crowds were smaller than anticipated until the Capitals turned on the heat in the homestretch of 1997–98 and reached the playoffs.

Under Wilson, the Caps suffered through a season pockmarked by injuries but still finished third in the Atlantic Division with a 40–30–12 record and eliminated Boston in the first round of the playoffs. At least part of the success came from Wilson's unorthodox coaching: using popsicle sticks to illustrate plays and having water pistol fights to stimulate his skaters in practice.

Wilson guided Washington into the second playoff round against Ottawa and the battle between the two national capitals went to the American city in five games. Goaltender Olaf Kolzig had enjoyed an excellent season in 1997–98. His 33 wins, five shutouts and 2.20 goals-against average had all ranked among the best in the game, but in the postseason, "Olie the Goalie" truly came into his own. He outplayed Dominik Hasek as Washington beat Buffalo to win the Eastern Conference championship and advance to the Stanley Cup finals for the first time. But, the ultimate mission would not be accomplished. Though Wilson scoffed at speculation that the Detroit Red Wings would complete the Stanley Cup's fourth consecutive sweep, the defending champions did just that and retained their title with four straight wins.

The 1998–99 season proved to be a tremendous disappointment as the Capitals tumbled out of the playoffs with just 68 points, finishing ahead of only the Tampa Bay Lightning in the newly created Southeast Division. Injuries limited the effectiveness of Peter Bondra and Adam Oates, though defenseman Sergei Gonchar helped pick up the slack with 21 goals in just 53 games. Longtime fan favorite Dale Hunter was traded late in the season, but returned to Washington in a front-office capacity for 1999–2000.

Though he had been the guiding force behind the Capitals since the beginning, the Capitals changed hands on May 12, 1999, when Pollin sold the franchise to a small investment group headed by America Online president Ted Leonsis. However, despite the new big-bucks ownership, the struggle continued on the ice through the first half of the 1999–2000 season. At the Christmas break, Washington stood 11th in the Eastern Conference. And then the team started to win. Though Peter Bondra struggled for goals (he would only score 21), Chris Simon picked up much of the slack by almost doubling his previous best with 29. Sergei Gonchar scored 18 times. Adam Oates led the club with 71 points and reached milestones with his 300th career goal and 900th assist. Sparking the turnaround that would see Washington win the Southeast Division with 102 points was the play of Olaf Kolzig. "Olie the Goalie" recaptured his form of 1997–98 and then some. He won the Vezina Trophy after setting club records for games (73), minutes

Mike Gartner topped 30 goals for 15 consecutive years between 1979–80 and 1993–94. He spent his first 10 seasons with the Capitals, leading the team in goals on five occasions and in points four times.

(4,371) and, of greatest importance, wins (41). His 2.24 goals-against average and .917 save percentage also ranked high among the league leaders. However, the Capitals ran into Pittsburgh and a red-hot Jaromir Jagr in the first round of the playoffs. Apparently fully recovered from injuries that had sidelined him for much of the last half of the regular season, Jagr recorded four assists to lead the Pittsburgh Penguins to a 7–0 victory in the playoff opener. The Capitals never seemed to recover. Pittsburgh raced out to a 3–0 series lead and eliminated Washington in five games.

The Capitals won their second straight division title, and just the third in franchise history, in 2000–01, topping the Southeast Division with a record of 41–27–10–4 and 96 points. Again Washington was one of the NHL's top teams in the second half of the season, recording 34 victories after December 1. Offensively, the club was led by Adam Oates and Peter Bondra. Oates had 82 points, including 69 assists to tie Pittsburgh's Jaromir Jagr for the NHL lead in helpers. Bondra had 81 points. His 45 goals ranked him fourth in the NHL, while his 22 powerplay goals led the league. In all, Washington had 11 players who reached double digits in goals, including D.C.-area native Jeff Halpern (21) and Steve Konowalchuk (24). The Capitals had not had three 20-goal scorers since 1993–94. Sergei Gonchar ranked among the league's top-scoring defensemen with 19 goals while setting a new career high with 38 assists. Calle Johansson became Washington's career leader in assists and points by a defenseman and reached the 1,000-games plateau. Olaf Kolzig was not quite up to his Vezina Trophy performance of the year before, yet still tied for third among NHL netminders in both games (72) and wins (37). Despite their solid season, the Capitals were beaten by Jagr and the Penguins in the first round of the playoffs for the second year in a row.

After spending most of his first six seasons in the minors, Olaf Kolzig emerged as a star in 1997–98 and led the Capitals to the Stanley Cup finals for the first time. "Ollie the Goalie" won the Vezina Trophy in 1999–2000.

Having been unable to beat him, the Capitals invited Jaromir Jagr to join them, sending three prospects to Pittsburgh to acquire the five-time NHL scoring champ in the summer of 2001. Jagr was signed to a new contract, paying him $11 million per season for seven years plus an option for an eighth. Expectations were high for 2001–02, but another slow start saw the Capitals miss the playoffs despite the most wins in the Eastern Conference after the All-Star break. Jagr was limited to just 69 games due to injuries, and struggled at times in his new surroundings, but still finished fifth in the NHL in scoring with 79 points (31 goals, 48 assists). Bondra's 39 goals ranked him sixth in the league, while his 17 powerplay tallies were tops once again. He also surpassed the 400-goal plateau for his career and broke Mike Gartner's Capitals record of 397 goals. Sergei Gonchar also had another stellar season, leading all NHL defenseman with a career-best 26 goals and 59 points.

Missing the playoffs cost Ron Wilson his job after five years in Washington, as the Capitals turned to 37-year-old rookie head coach Bruce Cassidy for 2002–03. There were high expectations for the new season, but again the Capitals started slowly. They had finally moved into first place in the Southeast Division by the All-Star break and battled Tampa Bay for the division lead throughout the second half before finally setting for second place and sixth seed in the Eastern Conference. Once again Jaromir Jagr led the team in scoring. He had 36 goals and 41 assists for 77 points. Another former Penguin, Robert Lang, chipped in 22 goals and 47 assists. Sergei Gonchar tied for the NHL lead among defenseman with 18 goals, while his 67 points trailed only Al MacInnis. Peter Bondra scored two goals in the final game of the season to reach 30 goals for the year and 790 points in his career—one more than Mike Gartner's previous franchise record.

After finishing just one point behind Tampa in the regular-season standings (93–92), Washington had a chance for revenge when they were paired up with the Lightning to open the playoffs. The Capitals took the first two games of the series on Tampa ice, only to drop the next four in a row as the Lightning won in the postseason for the first time in franchise history. The final game was a 2–1 Tampa Bay victory in triple overtime. The winning goal was scored with Washington a man short after being penalized for too many men on the ice. For the Capitals, it was the third straight playoff appearance in which they had been eliminated in the first round. It was also the third time they'd blown a two-games-to-none lead in the first round (Pittsburgh in 1992 and 1996; New York Islanders in 1985.)

Section 3: The Entry Draft

1963 to 2003

LEMIEUX, Mario

5 October 1965

6.4 200

C Right

FINAL RANKING **1**

YEAR	CLUB	GP	G	A	PTS	PIM
83/84	Laval	70	133	149	282	92
82/83	Laval	66	84	100	184	76

RATING RANGE 0 – 10 RANKING RANGE 1 – 2

Good speed and quickness...good stride and balance, — tremendous change of pace...good crossovers...quick stops...moves to left or right with ease... good acceleration — very deceptive skater...excellent goal-scorer — very smart around net...excellent wrist and slapshot — hard and accurate; gets it off quickly...good backhand shot — excellent concentration and timing ...excellent passer...soft hands...handles the puck extremely well — holds on to it...rushes the puck well...excellent stickhandler...plays the power play and kills penalties...good forechecker — knows where to go...great anticipation...good face-off man...fair checker — angles the man well; completes his check...at times will check with intensity — occasionally will not work at his checking game...takes out man well in corners and along boards...ties up man...hides puck well well on offence...excellent strength...can play it tough and aggressive in his own way — will not back away in the tough going...great desire and attitude... excellent natural ability and skills...good mobility... great hockey sense...exceptional all around qualities -- is inclined to pace himself at times but this negative factor is minor in comparison to his overall skills.

Game Reports Filed - 85 Plus.

Glowing scouting report filed on Mario Lemieux after a 282-point season with Laval of the Quebec Major Junior Hockey League. Lemieux was selected first overall by the Pittsburgh Penguins at the 1984 Entry Draft.

CHAPTER 5

The NHL Entry Draft

8,092 Dreams of Hockey Glory

THE NHL'S ENTRY DRAFT and its predecessor, the Amateur Draft, have been the gateway to the National Hockey League for players from all over the world. There have been 8,092 valid selections made since the first NHL draft in 1963 including a total of 292 picks at the 2003 Entry Draft.

The Amateur Draft was created by the NHL in 1963 as a means of phasing out the sponsorship of amateur teams by the league's member clubs. However, since most of hockey's top junior players had already been assigned to NHL clubs through sponsored junior teams, few top prospects were eligible in the early years. As a result, even though each of the NHL's "Original Six" clubs was allowed to select four players, not all of the choices would be exercised every year. In 1965, for example, only 11 players where drafted—even though teams from the American Hockey League, the Western Hockey League and the Central Pro league were allowed to select junior prospects as part of the draft. Even after the NHL added six new teams in 1967, no more than 24 players were selected in one season through 1968. The draft in 1968 marked the first time that teams selected in the reverse order of the final standings. Previously, the draft order had rotated on an annual basis.

On June 12, 1969, the National Hockey League staged its first universal Amateur Draft. All junior prospects were eligible to be drafted because the old sponsorship system had been phased out. Every team had an equal opportunity to acquire the best junior talent—with one exception: Since the first draft in 1963, the Montreal Canadiens had held the option of selecting two French-Canadian players before any other NHL team made its first choice. Using this rule, and some clever trading, the Canadiens had acquired the first three picks in the 1968 draft. In 1969, they used the first two picks to land Rejean Houle and Marc Tardif. This territorial exemption was discontinued beginning in 1970.

Eighty-four players were selected in the 1969 Amateur Draft—almost four times more than had ever been picked before. The number of selections reached 115 the following year and, as the NHL continued to expand through the 1970s, topped 200 for the first time in 1978. When, in 1979, the NHL expanded to include four teams that had previously played in the World Hockey Association, the Amateur Draft was renamed the Entry Draft to reflect the fact that young players who previously had played professionally in the WHA now were eligible to be drafted by NHL clubs.

Though Garry Monahan was just 16 years and seven months old when he became the first player drafted in 1963, the eligibility age had risen to 20 by 1967. Competiton from WHA teams in the mid-1970s resulted in the age limit dropping to 18 in certain cases. Between 1980 and 1995, all 18-, 19- and 20-year-old North American players were eligible for the Entry Draft. From 1987 to 1991, the selection of 18- and 19-year-old players was generally restricted to the first three rounds. Since the 1995 Entry Draft, all 18-year-old players are required to declare themselves eligible by signing what is called an "opt-in" form.

Players from outside North America are also draft eligible from the age of 18. Non-North American players over the age of 20 must be drafted as well.

In order to be eligible for the draft, a player must be 18 years old by September 15 of his draft year.

Players have been eligible to re-enter the draft since 1978. League rules state that any North American player age 20 or under who does not receive a bona fide offer from his NHL club within one year, or, has not signed a contract within two years of being selected is eligible to re-enter the draft. If a player is drafted twice, he is not eligible for further re-entry.

Since 1995, the NHL has awarded compensatory picks to clubs in two circumstances: i) if a club is unable to sign a first-round draft choice and ii) if a club loses a player to Group III (unrestricted) free agency. (See Inside the NHL, page 425, for more on compensatory draft selections.)

Though Canadian major junior hockey always has supplied the largest number of players selected, the international flavor of the Entry Draft dates back to its Amateur days. The first player to be selected from an American university was Al Karlander (17th overall in 1967), a Canadian who attended Michigan Tech. The first American-born player drafted into the NHL was another Michigan Tech player, Herb Boxer (17th overall in 1968). Brian Lawton became the first American to be chosen number-one in the draft when the Minnesota North Stars selected him in 1983.

In 1969, the St. Louis Blues made Finnish-born Tommi Salmelainen (66th overall) the first European player to be selected in the draft. By the late 1970s, and throughout the 1980s, many NHL teams used late-round selections to take a chance on Russians and Czechs who would have had to defect in order to enter the NHL. Sergei Priakin, the first Russian to play with permission in the NHL, was the last player drafted in 1988 when the Calgary Flames claimed him with the 252nd choice. One year later, Sweden's Mats Sundin became the first European player selected atop the draft when the Quebec Nordiques chose him first overall.

NOTE: Complete NHL Amateur and Entry Drafts 1963 to 2003 follow. If a player or goaltender has appeared in one or more regular-season NHL games, his lifetime career scoring or goaltending totals are found beside his draft details.

Complete NHL Amateur and Entry Drafts 1963 to 2003

1963

PICK	TEAM	NAME	DRAFTED FROM	NHL PLAYERS: POS / NHL GOALTENDERS: POS	GP / GP	G / W	A / GA	PTS / SO	PIM / AVG
1	Mtl.	Garry Monahan	St. Michael's Juveniles	LW	748	116	169	285	484
2	Det.	Pete Mahovlich	St. Michael's Juveniles	C	884	288	485	773	916
3	Bos.	Orest Romashyma	New Hamburg Jr. C						
4	NYR	Al Osborne	Weston Jr. B	RW					
5	Chi.	Art Hampson	Trenton Midgets						
6	Tor.	Walt McKechnie	London Jr. B	C	955	214	392	606	469
7	Mtl.	Rodney Presswood	Georgetown Midgets						
8	Det.	Bill Cosburn	Bick's Pickles						
9	Bos.	Terrance Lane	Georgetown Midgets						
10	NYR	Terry Jones	Weston Midgets						
11	Chi.	Wayne Davidson	Georgetown Midgets						
12	Tor.	Neil Clairmont	Parry Sound Midgets	LW					
13	Mtl.	Roy Pugh	Aurora Jr. C	C					
14	Bos.	Roger Bamburak	Isaac Brock	RW					
15	NYR	Mike Cummings	Georgetown Midgets						
16	Chi.	Bill Carson	Brampton Midgets	D					
17	Tor.	Jim McKenny	Neil McNeil Jr. A	D	604	82	247	329	294
18	Mtl.	Glen Shirton	Port Colborne Midgets	D					
19	Bos.	Jim Blair	Georgetown Midgets						
20	NYR	Campbell Alleson	Portage la Prairie Jr.						
21	Tor.	Gerry Meehan	Neil McNeil Jr. A	C	670	180	243	423	111

1964

PICK	TEAM	NAME	DRAFTED FROM	POS	GP	G / W	A / GA	PTS / SO	PIM / AVG
1	Det.	Claude Gauthier	Rosemount Midgets						
2	Bos.	Alec Campbell	Strathroy Midgets	RW					
3	NYR	Robert Graham	Toronto Marlboro Midgets	D					
4	Chi.	Richard Bayes	Dixie Midgets	C					
5	Tor.	Tom Martin	Toronto Marlboro Midgets	RW	3	1	0	1	0
6	Mtl.	Claude Chagnon	Rosemount Midgets						
7	Det.	Brian Watts	Toronto Marlboro Midgets	LW	4	0	0	0	0
8	Bos.	Jim Booth	Sault Ste. Marie	LW					
9	NYR	Tim Ecclestone	Etobicoke Jr. B	LW	692	126	233	359	344
10	Chi.	Jan Popiel	Georgetown Midgets	LW					
11	Tor.	Dave Cotey	Aurora Jr. C						
12	Mtl.	Guy Allen	Stamford Jr. B	D					
13	Det.	Ralph Buchanan	Montreal East Intermediates	D					
14	Bos.	Ken Dryden	Etobicoke Jr. B	G	397	23352	870	46	2.24
15	NYR	Gordon Lowe	Toronto Marlboro Midgets	D					
16	Chi.	Carl Hadfield	Dixie Jr. B	RW					
17	Tor.	Mike Pelyk	Toronto Marlboro Midgets	D	441	26	88	114	566
18	Mtl.	Paul Reid	Kingston Midgets						
19	Det.	Rene Leclerc	Hamilton Jr. B	RW	87	10	11	21	105
20	Bos.	Blair Allister	Ingersoll Jr. B						
21	NYR	Syl Apps Jr.	Kingston Midgets	C	727	183	423	606	311
22	Chi.	Moe L'Abbe	Rosemount Midgets	RW	5	0	1	1	0
23	Tor.	Jim Dorey	Stamford Jr. B	D	232	25	74	99	553
24	Mtl.	Michel Jacques	Megantic Jr. B	LW					

1965

PICK	TEAM	NAME	DRAFTED FROM	POS	GP	G / W	A / GA	PTS / SO	PIM / AVG
1	NYR	Andre Veilleux	Montreal Jr. B	RW					
2	Chi.	Andrew Culligan	St. Michael's Jr. B						
3	Det.	George Forgie	Flin Flon	D					
4	Bos.	Joe Bailey	St. Thomas Jr. B						
5	Mtl.	Pierre Bouchard	St. Vincent de Paul Jr. B	D	595	24	82	106	433
6	NYR	George Surmay	Kelvin Juveniles	G					
7	Chi.	Brian McKenney	Smiths Falls Jr.						
8	Det.	Bob Birdsell	Settler	RW					
9	Bos.	Bill Ramsay	Winnipeg						
10	NYR	Michel Parizeau	Montreal Jr. B	C	58	3	14	17	18
11	Pit.(AHL)	Gary Beattie	Gananoque Jr. C						

1966

PICK	TEAM	NAME	DRAFTED FROM	POS	GP	G / W	A / GA	PTS / SO	PIM / AVG
1	Bos.	Barry Gibbs	Estevan	D	797	58	224	282	945
2	NYR	Brad Park	Toronto	D	1113	213	683	896	1429
3	Chi.	Terry Caffery	Toronto	C	14	0	0	0	0
4	Tor.	John Wright	West Clair Jr. B	C	127	16	36	52	67
5	Mtl.	Phil Myre	Shawinigan	G	439	25220	1482	14	3.53
6	Det.	Steve Atkinson	Niagara Falls	RW	302	60	51	111	104
7	Bos.	Rick Smith	Hamilton	D	687	52	167	219	560
8	NYR	Joey Johnston	Peterborough	LW	331	85	106	191	320
9	Chi.	Ron Dussiaume	Oshawa	LW					
10	Tor.	Cam Crosby	Toronto						
11	Mtl.	Maurice St. Jacques	London	C					
12	Det.	Jim Whittaker	Oshawa	D					
13	Bos.	Garnet Bailey	Edmonton	LW	568	107	171	278	633
14	NYR	Don Luce	Kitchener	C	894	225	329	554	364
15	Chi.	Larry Gibbons	Markham Jr. B	D					
16	Tor.	Rick Ley	Niagara Falls	D	310	12	72	84	528
17	Mtl.	Jude Drouin	Verdun	C	666	151	305	456	346
18	Det.	Lee Carpenter	Hamilton Jr. B	D					
19	Bos.	Tom Webster	Niagara Falls	RW	102	33	42	75	61
20	NYR	Jack Egers	Kitchener Jr. B	RW	284	64	69	133	154
21	Chi.	Brian Morenz	Oshawa	LW					
22	Tor.	Dale MacLeish	Peterborough	C					
23	Mtl.	Bob Pate	Montreal	D					
24	Det.	Grant Cole	St. Michael's Jr. B	G					

1967

PICK	TEAM	NAME	DRAFTED FROM	POS	GP	G / W	A / GA	PTS / SO	PIM / AVG
1	L.A.	Rick Pagnutti	Garson	D					
2	Pit.	Steve Rexe	Belleville Sr.	G					
3	Oak.	Ken Hicks	Brandon						
4	Min.	Wayne Cheesman	Whitby Jr. B	D					
5	Phi.	Serge Bernier	Sorel	RW	302	78	119	197	234
6	NYR	Robert Dickson	Chatham Jr. B	LW					
7	Chi.	Bob Tombari	Sault Ste. Marie	LW					
8	Mtl.	Elgin McCann	Weyburn Jr. A	RW					
9	Det.	Ron Barkwell	Flin Flon						
10	Bos.	Meehan Bonnar	St. Thomas Jr. B	RW					
11	Pit.	Bob Smith	Sault Ste. Marie	C					
12	Oak.	Garry Wood	Fort Frances	D					
13	Min.	Larry Mick	Pembroke Jr. A						
14	Phi.	Al Sarault	Pembroke Jr. A	D					
15	NYR	Brian Tosh	Smiths Falls Jr.	D					
16	Tor.	Bob Kelly	Port Arthur Jr.	LW	425	87	109	196	687
17	Det.	Al Karlander	Michigan Tech	C	212	36	56	92	70
18	Oak.	Kevin Smith	Halifax Jr.	D					

1968

PICK	TEAM	NAME	DRAFTED FROM	POS	GP	G / W	A / GA	PTS / SO	PIM / AVG
1	Mtl.	Michel Plasse	Drummondville	G	299	16760	1058	2	3.79
2	Mtl.	Roger Belisle	Montreal North Beavers						
3	Mtl.	Jim Pritchard	Winnipeg	D					
4	Pit.	Garry Swain	Niagara Falls	C	9	1	1	2	0
5	Min.	Jim Benzelock	Winnipeg	RW					
6	St.L.	Gary Edwards	Toronto	G	286	16002	973	10	3.65
7	L.A.	Jim McInally	Hamilton	D					
8	Phi.	Lew Morrison	Flin Flon	RW	564	39	52	91	107
9	Chi.	John Marks	North Dakota	LW	657	112	163	275	330
10	Tor.	Brad Selwood	Niagara Falls	D	163	7	40	47	153
11	Det.	Steve Andrascik	Flin Flon	RW					
12	Bos.	Danny Schock	Estevan	LW	20	1	2	3	0
13	Oak.	Doug Smith	Winnipeg	C					
14	Pit.	Ron Snell	Regina	RW	7	3	2	5	6
15	Min.	Marc Rioux	Verdun	C					
16	St.L.	Curt Bennett	Brown	LW	580	152	182	334	347
17	Det.	Herb Boxer	Michigan Tech	RW					
18	Bos.	Fraser Rice	Halifax Jr.	C					

PICK	TEAM	NAME	DRAFTED FROM	NHL PLAYERS: POS / NHL GOALTENDERS: POS	GP / GP	G / W	A / GA	PTS / SO	PIM / AVG
19	NYR	Bruce Buchanan	Weyburn Jr. A	D					
20	Oak.	Jim Trewin	Flin Flon	D					
21	Pit.	Dave Simpson	Port Arthur Jr.	D					
22	Min.	Glen Lindsay	Saskatoon	G					
23	Mtl.	Don Grierson	North Bay Jr. A	RW					
24	Bos.	Brian St. John	U. of Toronto	C					

1969

FIRST ROUND

PICK	TEAM	NAME	DRAFTED FROM	POS	GP	G / W	A / GA	PTS / SO	PIM / AVG
1	Mtl.	Rejean Houle	Montreal	W	635	161	247	408	395
2	Mtl.	Marc Tardif	Montreal	LW	517	194	207	401	443
3	Bos.	Don Tannahill	Niagara Falls	LW	111	30	33	63	25
4	Bos.	Frank Spring	Edmonton	RW	61	14	20	34	12
5	Min.	Dick Redmond	St. Catharines	D	771	133	312	445	504
6	Phi.	Bob Currier	Cornwall	C					
7	Oak.	Tony Featherstone	Peterborough	RW	130	17	21	38	65
8	NYR	Andre Dupont	Montreal	D	800	59	185	244	1986
9	Tor.	Ernie Moser	Estevan	RW					
10	Det.	Jim Rutherford	Hamilton	G	457	25895	1576	14	3.65
11	Bos.	Ivan Boldirev	Oshawa	C	1052	361	505	866	507
12	NYR	Pierre Jarry	Ottawa	LW	344	88	117	205	142
13	Chi.	J.P. Bordeleau	Montreal	RW	519	97	126	223	143

SECOND ROUND

PICK	TEAM	NAME	DRAFTED FROM	POS	GP	G / W	A / GA	PTS / SO	PIM / AVG
14	Min.	Dennis O'Brien	St. Catharines	D	592	31	91	122	1017
15	Pit.	Rick Kessell	Oshawa	C	135	4	24	28	6
16	L.A.	Dale Hoganson	Estevan	D	343	13	77	90	186
17	Phi.	Bobby Clarke	Flin Flon	C	1144	358	852	1210	1453
18	Oak.	Ron Stackhouse	Peterborough	D	889	87	372	459	824
19	St.L.	Mike Lowe	Loyola College	C					
20	Tor.	Doug Brindley	Niagara Falls	LW/C	3	0	0	0	0
21	Det.	Ron Garwasiuk	Regina	LW					
22	Bos.	Art Quoquochi	Montreal	RW					
23	NYR	Bert Wilson	London	LW	478	37	44	81	646
24	Chi.	Larry Romanchych	Flin Flon	RW	298	68	97	165	102

OTHER ROUNDS

PICK	TEAM	NAME	DRAFTED FROM	POS	GP	G / W	A / GA	PTS / SO	PIM / AVG
25	Min.	Gilles Gilbert	London	G	416	23677	1290	18	3.27
26	Pit.	Michel Briere	Shawinigan	C	76	12	32	44	20
27	L.A.	Gregg Boddy	Edmonton	D	273	23	44	67	263
28	Phi.	Willie Brossart	Estevan	D	129	1	14	15	88
29	Oak.	Don O'Donoghue	St. Catharines	RW	125	18	17	35	35
30	St.L.	Bernard Gagnon	Michigan	C					
31	Tor.	Larry McIntyre	Moose Jaw	D	41	0	3	3	26
32	Mtl.	Bobby Sheehan	St. Catharines	C	310	48	63	111	40
33	Det.	Wayne Hawrysh	Flin Flon	RW					
34	Bos.	Nels Jacobson	Winnipeg	LW					
35	NYR	Kevin Morrison	St-Jerome	D	41	4	11	15	23
36	Chi.	Milt Black	Winnipeg	RW					
37	Min.	Fred O'Donnell	Oshawa	RW	115	15	11	26	98
38	Pit.	Yvon Labre	Toronto	D	371	14	87	101	788
39	L.A.	Bruce Landon	Peterborough	G					
40	Phi.	Michel Belhumeur	Drummondville	G	65	3306	254	0	4.61
41	Oak.	Pierre Farmer	Shawinigan	D					
42	St.L.	Vic Teal	St. Catharines	RW	1	0	0	0	0
43	Tor.	Frank Hughes	Edmonton	LW	5	0	0	0	0
44	Mtl.	Murray Anderson	Flin Flon	D	40	0	1	1	68
45	Det.	Wayne Chernecki	Winnipeg	C					
46	Bos.	Ron Fairbrother	Saskatoon	LW					
47	NYR	Bruce Hellemond	Moose Jaw	LW					
48	Chi.	Daryl Maggs	Calgary	D	135	14	19	33	54
49	Min.	Pierre Jutras	Shawinigan	LW					
50	Pit.	Ed Patenaude	Calgary	RW					
51	L.A.	Butch Goring	Dauphin Jr. A	C	1107	375	513	888	102
52	Phi.	Dave Schultz	Sorel	LW	535	79	121	200	2294
53	Oak.	Warren Harrison	Sorel	C					
54	St.L.	Brian Glenwright	Kitchener	LW					
55	Tor.	Brian Spencer	Swift Current	LW	553	80	143	223	634
56	Mtl.	Garry Doyle	Ottawa	G					
57	Det.	Wally Olds	Minnesota-Duluth	D					
58	Bos.	Jeremy Wright	Calgary	C					
59	NYR	Gordon Smith	Cornwall	D					
60	Chi.	Mike Baumgartner	North Dakota	D	17	0	0	0	0
61	Min.	Bob Walton	Niagara Falls	C					
62	Pit.	Paul Hoganson	Toronto	G	2	57	7	0	7.37
63	Mtl.	Guy Delparte	London	LW	48	1	8	9	18
64	Phi.	Don Saleski	Regina	RW	543	128	125	253	629
65	Oak.	Neil Nicholson	London	D	39	3	1	4	23
66	St.L.	Tommi Salmelainen	HIFK Helsinki	LW					
67	Tor.	Bob Neufeld	Dauphin Jr. A	LW					
68	Mtl.	Lynn Powis	U. of Denver	C	130	19	33	52	25
69	Bos.	Jim Jones	Peterborough	D	2	0	0	0	0
70	St.L.	Dale Yutsyk	Colorado College	LW					
71	Chi.	Dave Hudson	North Dakota	C	409	59	124	183	89
72	Min.	Rick Thompson	Niagara Falls	D					
73	St.L.	Bob Collyard	Colorado College	C	10	1	3	4	4
74	Mtl.	Ian Wilkie	Edmonton	G					
75	Mtl.	Dale Power	Peterborough	C					
76	Oak.	Pete Vipond	Oshawa	LW	3	0	0	0	0
77	St.L.	Dave Pulkkinen	Oshawa	LW/D	2	0	0	0	0
78	Min.	Cal Russell	Hamilton	RW					
79	Mtl.	Frank Hamill	Toronto	RW					
80	St.L.	Pat Lange	Sudbury						
81	Phi.	Claude Chartre	Drummondville	C					
82	St.L.	John Converse	Estevan						
83	Mtl.	Gilles Drolet	Quebec						
84	Mtl.	Darrel Knibbs	Lethbridge	C					

1970

FIRST ROUND

PICK	TEAM	NAME	DRAFTED FROM	POS	GP	G / W	A / GA	PTS / SO	PIM / AVG
1	Buf.	Gilbert Perreault	Montreal	C	1191	512	814	1326	500
2	Van.	Dale Tallon	Toronto	D	642	98	238	336	568
3	Bos.	Reggie Leach	Flin Flon	RW	934	381	285	666	387
4	Bos.	Rick MacLeish	Peterborough	C	846	349	410	759	434
5	Mtl.	Ray Martyniuk	Flin Flon	G					
6	Mtl.	Chuck Lefley	Canadian National	LW	407	128	164	292	137
7	Pit.	Greg Polis	Estevan	LW	615	174	169	343	391
8	Tor.	Darryl Sittler	London	C	1096	484	637	1121	948
9	Bos.	Ron Plumb	Peterborough	D	26	3	4	7	14
10	Cal.	Chris Oddleifson	Winnipeg	C	524	95	191	286	464
11	NYR	Norm Gratton	Montreal	LW	201	39	44	83	64
12	Det.	Serge Lajeunesse	Montreal	D/RW	103	1	4	5	103
13	Bos.	Bob Stewart	Oshawa	D	575	27	101	128	809
14	Chi.	Dan Maloney	London	LW	737	192	259	451	1489

SECOND ROUND

PICK	TEAM	NAME	DRAFTED FROM	POS	GP	G / W	A / GA	PTS / SO	PIM / AVG
15	Buf.	Butch Deadmarsh	Brandon	LW	137	12	5	17	155
16	Van.	Jim Hargreaves	Winnipeg	D	66	1	7	8	105
17	Min.	Buster Harvey	Hamilton	RW	407	90	118	208	131
18	Phi.	Bill Clement	Ottawa	C	719	148	208	356	383
19	Cal.	Pete Laframboise	Ottawa	LW/C	227	33	55	88	70
20	Min.	Fred Barrett	Toronto	D	745	25	123	148	671
21	Pit.	John Stewart	Flin Flon	LW	258	58	60	118	158
22	Tor.	Errol Thompson	Charlottetown Sr.	LW	599	208	185	393	184
23	St.L.	Murray Keogan	Minnesota-Duluth	C					
24	L.A.	Al McDonough	St. Catharines	RW	237	73	88	161	73
25	NYR	Mike Murphy	Toronto	RW	831	238	318	556	514
26	Det.	Bobby Guindon	Montreal	LW	6	0	1	1	0
27	Bos.	Dan Bouchard	London	G	655	37919	2061	27	3.26
28	Chi.	Michel Archambault	Drummondville	LW	3	0	0	0	0

OTHER ROUNDS

PICK	TEAM	NAME	DRAFTED FROM	POS	GP	G / W	A / GA	PTS / SO	PIM / AVG
29	Buf.	Steve Cuddie	Toronto	D					
30	Van.	Ed Dyck	Calgary	G	49	2453	178	1	4.35
31	Mtl.	Steve Carlyle	Red Deer Jr. A	D					
32	Phi.	Bob Kelly	Oshawa	LW	837	154	208	362	1454
33	Cal.	Randy Rota	Calgary	C/LW	212	38	39	77	60
34	Min.	Dennis Patterson	Peterborough	D	138	6	22	28	67
35	Pit.	Larry Bignell	Edmonton	D	20	0	3	3	2
36	Tor.	Gerry O'Flaherty	Kitchener	LW	438	99	95	194	168
37	St.L.	Ron Climie	Hamilton	LW					
38	L.A.	Terry Holbrook	London	RW	43	3	6	9	4
39	NYR	Wendell Bennett	Weyburn Jr. A	D					
40	Det.	Yvon Lambert	Drummondville	LW	683	206	273	479	340
41	Bos.	Ray Brownlee	U. of Brandon	C					
42	Chi.	Len Frig	Calgary	D	311	13	51	64	479
43	Buf.	Randy Wyrozub	Edmonton	C	100	8	10	18	10
44	Van.	Brent Taylor	Estevan	RW					
45	Mtl.	Cal Hammond	Flin Flon	G					
46	Phi.	Jacques Lapierre	Shawinigan	D					
47	Cal.	Ted McAneeley	Edmonton	D	158	8	35	43	141

PICK	TEAM	NAME	DRAFTED FROM	NHL PLAYERS: POS / NHL GOALTENDERS: POS	GP / GP	G / W	A / GA	PTS / SO	PIM / AVG
48	Min.	Dave Cressman	Kitchener	LW	85	6	8	14	37
49	Pit.	Connie Forey	Ottawa	LW	4	0	0	0	2
50	Tor.	Bob Gryp	Boston U.	LW	74	11	13	24	33
51	St.L.	Gord Brooks	London	RW	70	7	18	25	37
52	Mtl.	John French	Toronto	LW					
53	NYR	Andre St. Pierre	Drummondville	D					
54	Det.	Tom Johnston	Toronto	RW					
55	Bos.	Gordon Davies	Toronto	LW					
56	Chi.	Walt Ledingham	Minnesota-Duluth	LW	15	0	2	2	4
57	Buf.	Mike Morton	Shawinigan	RW					
58	Van.	Bill McFadden	Swift Current	F					
59	L.A.	Billy Smith	Cornwall	G	680	38431	2031	22	3.17
60	Phi.	Doug Kerslake	Edmonton	RW					
61	Oak.	Ray Gibbs	Charlottetown Sr.	G					
62	Min.	Henri Lehvonen	Kitchener	D					
63	Pit.	Steve Cardwell	Oshawa	LW	53	9	11	20	35
64	Tor.	Luc Simard	Trois-Rivieres	RW					
65	St.L.	Mike Stevens	Minnesota-Duluth	D					
66	Mtl.	Rick Wilson	North Dakota	D	239	6	26	32	165
67	NYR	Gary Coalter	Hamilton	RW	34	2	4	6	2
68	Det.	Tom Mellor	Boston College	D	26	2	4	6	25
69	Bos.	Robert Roselle	Sorel	LW					
70	Chi.	Gilles Meloche	Verdun	G	788	45401	2756	20	3.64
71	Buf.	Mike Keeler	Niagara Falls	D					
72	Van.	Dave Gilmour	London	LW					
73	L.A.	Gerry Bradbury	London	C					
74	Phi.	Dennis Giannini	London	LW					
75	Oak.	Doug Moyes	Sorel	RW					
76	Min.	Murray McNeill	Calgary	LW					
77	Pit.	Bob Fitchner	Brandon	C	78	12	20	32	59
78	Tor.	Calvin Booth	Weyburn Jr. A	LW					
79	St.L.	Claude Moreau	Montreal	D					
80	Mtl.	Robert Brown	Boston U.	D					
81	NYR	Duane Wylie	St. Catharines	C	14	3	3	6	2
82	Det.	Bernie MacNeil	Espanola Jr.	LW	4	0	0	0	0
83	Bos.	Murray Wing	North Dakota	D	1	0	1	1	0
84	Buf.	Tim Regan	Boston U.	G					
85	St.L.	Jack Taggart	U. of Denver	D					
86	L.A.	Brian Carlin	Calgary	LW	5	1	0	1	0
87	Phi.	Hank Nowak	Oshawa	LW	180	26	29	55	161
88	Oak.	Terry Murray	Ottawa	D	302	4	76	80	199
89	Min.	Gary Geldart	London	D	4	0	0	0	5
90	Pit.	Jim Pearson	St. Catharines	RW					
91	Tor.	Paul Larose	Quebec	RW					
92	St.L.	Terry Marshall	Brandon	D					
93	Mtl.	Bob Fowler	Estevan	RW					
94	NYR	Wayne Bell	Estevan	G					
95	Det.	Ed Hays	U. of Denver	C					
96	Bos.	Glen Siddall	Kitchener	LW					
97	Buf.	Doug Rombough	St. Catharines	C	150	24	27	51	80
98	L.A.	Brian Chinnick	Peterborough	C					
99	Phi.	Garry Cunningham	St. Catharines	D					
100	Oak.	Al Henry	North Dakota	D					
101	Min.	Mickey Donaldson	Peterborough	LW					
102	Pit.	Cam Newton	Kitchener	G	16	814	51	0	3.76
103	Tor.	Ron Low	Dauphin Jr. A	G	382	20502	1463	4	4.28
104	St.L.	Dave Tataryn	Niagara Falls	G	2	80	10	0	7.50
105	Mtl.	Rick Jordan	Boston U.	D					
106	NYR	Pierre Brind'Amour	Montreal	LW					
107	Buf.	Luc Nadeau	Drummondville	C					
108	St.L.	Bob Winograd	Colorado College	D					
109	Phi.	Jean Daigle	Sorel	LW					
110	Pit.	Ron Lemieux	Dauphin Jr. A	RW					
111	St.L.	Mike Lampman	U. of Denver	LW	96	17	20	37	34
112	St.L.	Jeff Rotsch	Wisconsin	D					
113	St.L.	Al Calver	Kitchener	D					
114	St.L.	Gerry MacDonald	St. Francis Xavier	D					
115	St.L.	Gerald Haines	Kenora						

1971

FIRST ROUND

PICK	TEAM	NAME	DRAFTED FROM	NHL PLAYERS: POS / NHL GOALTENDERS: POS	GP / GP	G / W	A / GA	PTS / SO	PIM / AVG
1	Mtl.	Guy Lafleur	Quebec	RW	1126	560	793	1353	399
2	Det.	Marcel Dionne	St. Catharines	C	1348	731	1040	1771	600
3	Van.	Jocelyn Guevremont	Montreal	D	571	84	223	307	319
4	St.L.	Gene Carr	Flin Flon	C	465	79	136	215	365
5	Buf.	Rick Martin	Montreal	LW	685	384	317	701	477
6	Bos.	Ron Jones	Edmonton	D	54	1	4	5	31
7	Mtl.	Chuck Arnason	Flin Flon	RW	401	109	90	199	122
8	Phi.	Larry Wright	Regina	C	106	4	8	12	19
9	Phi.	Pierre Plante	Drummondville	RW	599	125	172	297	599
10	NYR	Steve Vickers	Toronto	LW	698	246	340	586	330
11	Mtl.	Murray Wilson	Ottawa	LW	386	94	95	189	162
12	Chi.	Dan Spring	Edmonton	C					
13	NYR	Steve Durbano	Toronto	D	220	13	60	73	1127
14	Bos.	Terry O'Reilly	Oshawa	RW	891	204	402	606	2095

SECOND ROUND

PICK	TEAM	NAME	DRAFTED FROM	NHL PLAYERS: POS / NHL GOALTENDERS: POS	GP / GP	G / W	A / GA	PTS / SO	PIM / AVG
15	Cal.	Ken Baird	Flin Flon	D	10	0	2	2	15
16	Det.	Henry Boucha	U.S. Nationals	C	247	53	49	102	157
17	Van.	Bobby Lalonde	Montreal	C	641	124	210	334	298
18	Pit.	Brian McKenzie	St. Catharines	LW	6	1	1	2	4
19	Buf.	Craig Ramsay	Peterborough	LW	1070	252	420	672	201
20	Mtl.	Larry Robinson	Kitchener	D	1384	208	750	958	793
21	Min.	Rod Norrish	Regina	LW	21	3	3	6	2
22	Tor.	Rick Kehoe	Hamilton	RW	906	371	396	767	120
23	Tor.	Dave Fortier	St. Catharines	D	205	8	21	29	335
24	Mtl.	Michel Deguise	Sorel	G					
25	Mtl.	Terry French	Ottawa	C					
26	Chi.	Dave Kryskow	Edmonton	LW	231	33	56	89	174
27	NYR	Tom Williams	Hamilton	LW	397	115	138	253	73
28	Bos.	Curt Ridley	Portage la Prairie Jr.	G	104	5498	355	1	3.87

OTHER ROUNDS

PICK	TEAM	NAME	DRAFTED FROM	NHL PLAYERS: POS / NHL GOALTENDERS: POS	GP / GP	G / W	A / GA	PTS / SO	PIM / AVG
29	Cal.	Rich LeDuc	Trois-Rivieres	C	130	28	38	66	69
30	Det.	Ralph Hopiavuouri	Toronto	D					
31	Mtl.	Jim Cahoon	North Dakota	C					
32	Pit.	Joe Noris	Toronto	C/D	55	2	5	7	22
33	Buf.	Bill Hajt	Saskatoon	D	854	42	202	244	433
34	L.A.	Vic Venasky	U. of Denver	C	430	61	101	162	66
35	Min.	Ron Wilson	Flin Flon	D					
36	Phi.	Glen Irwin	Estevan	D					
37	Tor.	Gavin Kirk	Toronto	C					
38	St.L.	John Garrett	Peterborough	G	207	11763	837	1	4.27
39	Van.	Rich Lemieux	Montreal	C	274	39	82	121	132
40	Chi.	Bob Peppler	St. Catharines	LW					
41	NYR	Terry West	London	C					
42	Bos.	Dave Bonter	Estevan	C					
43	Cal.	Hartland Monahan	Montreal	RW	334	61	80	141	163
44	Det.	George Hulme	St. Catharines	G					
45	Mtl.	Ed Sidebottom	Estevan	D					
46	Pit.	Gerald Methe	Oshawa	D					
47	Buf.	Bob Richer	Trois-Rivieres	C	3	0	0	0	0
48	L.A.	Neil Komadoski	Winnipeg	D	502	16	76	92	632
49	Min.	Mike Legge	Winnipeg	LW					
50	Phi.	Ted Scharf	Kitchener	RW					
51	Tor.	Rick Cunningham	Peterborough	D					
52	St.L.	Derek Harker	Edmonton	D					
53	Mtl.	Greg Hubick	Minnesota-Duluth	D	77	6	9	15	10
54	Chi.	Clyde Simon	St. Catharines	RW					
55	NYR	Jerry Butler	Hamilton	RW	641	99	120	219	515
56	Bos.	Dave Hynes	Harvard	LW	22	4	0	4	2
57	Cal.	Ray Belanger	Shawinigan	G					
58	Det.	Earl Anderson	North Dakota	RW	109	19	19	38	22
59	Van.	Mike McNiven	Halifax Jr.	D					
60	Pit.	Dave Murphy	North Dakota	G					
61	Buf.	Steve Warr	Clarkson	D					
62	L.A.	Gary Crosby	Michigan Tech	C					
63	Min.	Brian McBratney	St. Catharines	D					
64	Phi.	Don McCulloch	Niagara Falls	D					
65	Tor.	Bob Sykes	Sudbury	LW	2	0	0	0	0
66	St.L.	Wayne Gibbs	Calgary	D					
67	Mtl.	Mike Busniuk	U. of Denver	D	143	3	23	26	297
68	Chi.	Dean Blais	U. of Minnesota	LW					
69	NYR	Fraser Robertson	Lethbridge	D					
70	Bos.	Bert Scott	Edmonton	C					
71	Cal.	Gerry Egers	Sudbury	D					
72	Det.	Charlie Shaw	Toronto	D					
73	Van.	Tim Steeves	Prince Edward Islanders Jr.	D					
74	Pit.	Ian Williams	U. of Notre Dame	RW					
75	Buf.	Pierre Duguay	Quebec	C					
76	L.A.	Camille Lapierre	Montreal	C					

PICK	TEAM	NAME	DRAFTED FROM	NHL PLAYERS: POS / NHL GOALTENDERS: POS	GP / GP	G / W	A / GA	PTS / SO	PIM / AVG
77	Min.	Al Globensky	Montreal	D					
78	Phi.	Yvon Bilodeau	Estevan	D					
79	Tor.	Mike Ruest	Cornwall	D					
80	St.L.	Bernie Doan	Calgary	D					
81	Mtl.	Ross Butler	Winnipeg	LW					
82	Chi.	Jim Johnston	Wisconsin	C					
83	NYR	Wayne Wood	Montreal	G					
84	Bos.	Bob McMahon	St. Catharines	D					
85	Cal.	Al Simmons	Winnipeg	D	11	0	1	1	21
86	Det.	Jim Nahrgang	Michigan Tech	D	57	5	12	17	34
87	Van.	Bill Green	U. of Notre Dame	D					
88	Pit.	Doug Elliott	Harvard	D					
89	L.A.	Peter Harasym	Clarkson	LW					
90	L.A.	Norm Dube	Sherbrooke	LW	57	8	10	18	54
91	Min.	Bruce Abbey	Peterborough	D					
92	Phi.	Bob Gerrard	Regina	RW					
93	Tor.	Dale Smedsmo	Bemidji State College	LW	4	0	0	0	0
94	St.L.	Dave Smith	Regina	D					
95	Mtl.	Peter Sullivan	Oshawa	C	126	28	54	82	40
96	NYR	Douglas Keeler	Ottawa	C					
97	NYR	Jean Denis Royal	St-Jerome	D					
98	Tor.	Steve Johnson	Verdun	D					
99	Cal.	Angus Beck	Charlottetown Jr.	C					
100	Det.	Bob Boyd	Michigan State	D					
101	Van.	Norm Cherry	Wisconsin	RW					
102	Van.	Bob Murphy	Cornwall	LW					
103	L.A.	Lorne Stamler	Michigan Tech	LW	116	14	11	25	16
104	Cal.	Red Lyons	Halifax Jr.	LW					
105	Min.	Russ Frieson	Hamilton	C					
106	Phi.	Jerome Mrazek	Minnesota-Duluth	G	1	6	1	0	10.00
107	Tor.	Bob Burns	Cdn. Armed Forces	D					
108	St.L.	Jim Collins	Flin Flon	LW					
109	NYR	Gene Sobchuk	Regina	LW/C	1	0	0	0	0
110	NYR	Jim Ivison	Brandon	D					
111	NYR	Andre Peloffy	Rosemount Jr. A	C	9	0	0	0	0
112	NYR	Elston Evoy	Sault Ste. Marie	C					
113	Min.	Mike Antonovich	Minnesota-Duluth	C	87	10	15	25	37
114	NYR	Gerald Lecompte	Sherbrooke	D					
115	NYR	Wayne Forsey	Swift Current	LW					
116	NYR	Bill Forrest	Hamilton	D					
117	Min.	Richard Coutu	Rosemount Jr. A	G					

1972

FIRST ROUND

PICK	TEAM	NAME	DRAFTED FROM	POS	GP	G / W	A / GA	PTS / SO	PIM / AVG
1	NYI	Billy Harris	Toronto	RW	897	231	327	558	394
2	Atl.	Jacques Richard	Quebec	LW	556	160	187	347	307
3	Van.	Don Lever	Niagara Falls	LW	1020	313	367	680	593
4	Mtl.	Steve Shutt	Toronto	LW	930	424	393	817	410
5	Buf.	Jim Schoenfeld	Niagara Falls	D	719	51	204	255	1132
6	Mtl.	Michel Larocque	Ottawa	G	312	17615	978	17	3.33
7	Phi.	Bill Barber	Kitchener	LW	903	420	463	883	623
8	Mtl.	Dave Gardner	Toronto	C	350	75	115	190	41
9	St.L.	Wayne Merrick	Ottawa	C	774	191	265	456	303
10	NYR	Al Blanchard	Kitchener	LW					
11	Tor.	George Ferguson	Toronto	C	797	160	238	398	431
12	Min.	Jerry Byers	Kitchener	LW	43	3	4	7	15
13	Chi.	Phil Russell	Edmonton	D	1016	99	325	424	2038
14	Mtl.	John Van Boxmeer	Guelph	D	588	84	274	358	465
15	NYR	Bob MacMillan	St. Catharines	RW	753	228	349	577	260
16	Bos.	Mike Bloom	St. Catharines	LW	201	30	47	77	215

SECOND ROUND

PICK	TEAM	NAME	DRAFTED FROM	POS	GP	G / W	A / GA	PTS / SO	PIM / AVG
17	NYI	Lorne Henning	New Westminster	C	544	73	111	184	102
18	Atl.	Dwight Bialowas	Regina	D	164	11	46	57	46
19	Van.	Bryan McSheffrey	Ottawa	RW	90	13	7	20	44
20	L.A.	Don Kozak	Edmonton	RW	437	96	86	182	480
21	NYR	Larry Sacharuk	Saskatoon	D	151	29	33	62	42
22	Cal.	Tom Cassidy	Kitchener	C	26	3	4	7	15
23	Phi.	Tom Bladon	Edmonton	D	610	73	197	270	392
24	Pit.	Jack Lynch	Oshawa	D	382	24	106	130	336
25	Buf.	Larry Carriere	Loyola College	D	367	16	74	90	462
26	Det.	Pierre Guite	St. Catharines	LW					
27	Tor.	Randy Osburn	London	LW	27	0	2	2	0
28	Cal.	Stan Weir	Medicine Hat	C	642	139	207	346	183
29	Chi.	Brian Ogilvie	Edmonton	C	90	15	21	36	29
30	Pit.	Bernie Lukowich	New Westminster	RW	79	13	15	28	34
31	NYR	Rene Villemure	Shawinigan	LW					
32	Bos.	Wayne Elder	London	D					

OTHER ROUNDS

PICK	TEAM	NAME	DRAFTED FROM	POS	GP	G / W	A / GA	PTS / SO	PIM / AVG
33	NYI	Bob Nystrom	Calgary	RW	900	235	278	513	1248
34	Atl.	Jean Lemieux	Sherbrooke	D	204	23	63	86	39
35	Van.	Paul Raymer	Peterborough	LW					
36	L.A.	Dave Hutchison	London	D	584	19	97	116	1550
37	Buf.	Jim McMasters	Calgary	D					
38	Cal.	Paul Shakes	St. Catharines	D	21	0	4	4	12
39	Phi.	Jimmy Watson	Calgary	D	613	38	148	186	492
40	Pit.	Denis Herron	Trois-Rivieres	G	462	25608	1579	10	3.70
41	St.L.	Jean Hamel	Drummondville	D	699	26	95	121	766
42	Det.	Bob Krieger	U. of Denver	C					
43	Tor.	Denis Deslauriers	Shawinigan	D					
44	Min.	Terry Ryan	Hamilton	C					
45	Chi.	Mike Veisor	Peterborough	G	139	7806	532	5	4.09
46	Mtl.	Ed Gilbert	Hamilton	C	166	21	31	52	22
47	NYR	Gerry Teeple	Cornwall	C					
48	Bos.	Michel Boudreau	Laval	C					
49	NYI	Ron Smith	Cornwall	D	11	1	1	2	14
50	Atl.	Don Martineau	New Westminster	RW	90	6	10	16	63
51	Van.	Ron Homenuke	Calgary	RW	1	0	0	0	0
52	L.A.	John Dobie	Regina	D					
53	Buf.	Richard Campeau	Sorel	D					
54	Cal.	Claude St. Sauveur	Sherbrooke	C	79	24	24	48	23
55	Phi.	Al MacAdam	University of PEI	RW	864	240	351	591	509
56	Pit.	Ron Lalonde	Peterborough	C	397	45	78	123	106
57	St.L.	Murray Myers	Saskatoon	D					
58	Det.	Danny Gruen	Thunder Bay Jr. A	LW	49	9	13	22	19
59	Tor.	Brian Bowles	Cornwall	D					
60	Min.	Tom Thomson	Toronto	D					
61	Chi.	Tom Peluso	U. of Denver	LW					
62	Mtl.	Dave Ellenbaas	Cornell	G					
63	NYR	Doug Horbul	Calgary	LW	4	1	0	1	2
64	Bos.	Les Jackson	New Westminster	LW					
65	NYI	Richard Grenier	Verdun	C	10	1	1	2	2
66	Mtl.	Bill Nyrop	U. of Notre Dame	D	207	12	51	63	101
67	Van.	Larry Bolonchuk	Winnipeg	D	74	3	9	12	97
68	L.A.	Bernie Germaine	Regina	G					
69	Buf.	Gilles Gratton	Oshawa	G	47	2299	154	0	4.02
70	Cal.	Tim Jacobs	St. Catharines	D	46	0	10	10	35
71	Phi.	Daryl Fedorak	Victoria	G					
72	Pit.	Brian Walker	Calgary	C					
73	St.L.	Dave Johnson	Cornwall	LW					
74	Det.	Dennis Johnson	North Dakota	LW					
75	Tor.	Michel Plante	Drummondville	LW					
76	Min.	Chris Ahrens	Kitchener	D	52	0	3	3	84
77	Chi.	Rejean Giroux	Quebec	RW					
78	Atl.	Jean-Paul Martin	Shawinigan	C					
79	NYR	Martin Gateman	Hamilton	D					
80	Bos.	Brian Coates	Brandon	LW					
81	NYI	Derek Black	Calgary	LW					
82	Atl.	Frank Blum	Sarnia Jr. B	G					
83	Van.	Dave McLelland	Brandon	G	2	120	10	0	5.00
84	L.A.	Mike Usitalo	Michigan Tech	LW					
85	Buf.	Peter McNab	U. of Denver	C	954	363	450	813	179
86	Cal.	Jacques Lefebvre	Shawinigan	G					
87	Phi.	Dave Hastings	Charlottetown Jr.	G					
88	Pit.	Jeff Ablett	Medicine Hat	LW					
89	St.L.	Tom Simpson	Oshawa	RW					
90	Det.	Bill Miller	Medicine Hat	D					
91	Tor.	Dave Shardlow	Flin Flon	LW					
92	Min.	Steve West	Oshawa	C					
93	Chi.	Rob Palmer	U. of Denver	C	16	0	3	3	2
94	Mtl.	D'Arcy Ryan	Yale	LW					
95	NYR	Ken Ireland	New Westminster	C					
96	Bos.	Peter Gaw	Ottawa	RW					
97	NYI	Richard Brodeur	Cornwall	G	385	21968	1410	6	3.85
98	Atl.	Scott Smith	Regina	LW					
99	Van.	Dan Gloor	Peterborough	C	2	0	0	0	0
100	L.A.	Glen Toner	Regina	LW					
101	NYI	Don McLaughlin	Brandon	LW					
102	Cal.	Mike Amodeo	Oshawa	D	19	0	0	0	2
103	Phi.	Serge Beaudoin	Trois-Rivieres	D	3	0	0	0	0

PICK	TEAM	NAME	DRAFTED FROM	NHL PLAYERS: POS	GP	G	A	PTS	PIM
				NHL GOALTENDERS: POS	GP	W	GA	SO	AVG
104	Pit.	D'Arcy Keating	U. of Notre Dame	RW					
105	St.L.	Brian Coughlin	Verdun	D					
106	Det.	Glenn Seperich	Kitchener	G					
107	Tor.	Monte Miron	Clarkson	D					
108	Min.	Chris Meloff	Kitchener	D					
109	Chi.	Terry Smith	Edmonton	C					
110	Mtl.	Yves Archambault	Sorel	G					
111	NYR	Jeff Hunt	Winnipeg	LW					
112	Bos.	Gordie Clark	New Hampshire	RW	8	0	1	1	0
113	NYI	Derek Kuntz	Medicine Hat	LW					
114	Atl.	Dave Murphy	Hamilton	C					
115	Van.	Dennis McCord	London	D	3	0	0	0	6
116	Min.	Scott MacPhail	Montreal	RW					
117	NYI	Rene Lavasseur	Shawinigan	D					
118	Cal.	Brent Meeke	Niagara Falls	D	75	9	22	31	8
119	Phi.	Pat Russell	Vancouver	RW					
120	Pit.	Yves Bergeron	Shawinigan	RW	3	0	0	0	0
121	St.L.	Gary Winchester	Wisconsin	C					
122	Det.	Mike Ford	Brandon	D					
123	Tor.	Peter Williams	University of PEI	D					
124	Min.	Bob Lundeen	Wisconsin	D					
125	Chi.	Billy Reay Jr.	Wisconsin	RW					
126	Mtl.	Graham Parsons	Red Deer Jr. A	G					
127	NYR	Yvon Blais	Cornwall	LW					
128	Bos.	Roy Carmichael	New Westminster	D					
129	NYI	Yvan Rolando	Drummondville	RW					
130	Atl.	Pierre Roy	Quebec	D					
131	Van.	Steve Stone	Niagara Falls	RW	2	0	0	0	0
132	Atl.	Jean Lamarre	Quebec	RW					
133	NYI	Bill Ennos	Vancouver	RW					
134	Cal.	Denis Meloche	Drummondville	C					
135	Phi.	Ray Boutin	Sorel	G					
136	Pit.	Jay Babcock	London	D					
137	NYR	Pierre Archambault	St-Jerome	D					
138	Det.	George Kuzmicz	Cornell	D					
139	Tor.	Pat Boutette	Minnesota Duluth	C/RW	756	171	282	453	1354
140	Min.	Glen Mikkelson	Brandon	RW					
141	Chi.	Gary Donaldson	Victoria	RW	1	0	0	0	0
142	Mtl.	Edward Bumbacco	U. of Notre Dame	LW					
143	Tor.	Gary Schofield	Clarkson	D					
144	NYI	Garry Howatt	Flin Flon	LW	720	112	156	268	1836
145	Min.	Steve Lyon	Peterborough	D/RW	3	0	0	0	2
146	NYI	Rene Lambert	St-Jerome	RW					
147	Min.	Juri Kudrosov	Kitchener	C					
148	Min.	Marcel Comeau	Edmonton	C					
149	Pit.	Don Atchison	Saskatoon	G					
150	Det.	Dave Arundel	Wisconsin	D					
151	Mtl.	Fred Riggall	Dartmouth	RW					
152	Mtl.	Ron Leblanc	U. of Moncton	RW					

1973

FIRST ROUND

PICK	TEAM	NAME	DRAFTED FROM	POS	GP	G/W	A/GA	PTS/SO	PIM/AVG
1	NYI	Denis Potvin	Ottawa	D	1060	310	742	1052	1356
2	Atl.	Tom Lysiak	Medicine Hat	C	919	292	551	843	567
3	Van.	Dennis Ververgaert	London	RW	583	176	216	392	247
4	Tor.	Lanny McDonald	Medicine Hat	RW	1111	500	506	1006	899
5	St.L.	John Davidson	Calgary	G	301	17109	1004	7	3.52
6	Bos.	Andre Savard	Quebec	C	790	211	271	482	411
7	Pit.	Blaine Stoughton	Flin Flon	RW	526	258	191	449	204
8	Mtl.	Bob Gainey	Peterborough	LW	1160	239	262	501	585
9	Van.	Bob Dailey	Toronto	D	561	94	231	325	814
10	Tor.	Bob Neely	Peterborough	LW	283	39	59	98	266
11	Det.	Terry Richardson	New Westminster	G	20	906	85	0	5.63
12	Buf.	Morris Titanic	Sudbury	LW	19	0	0	0	0
13	Chi.	Darcy Rota	Edmonton	LW	794	256	239	495	973
14	NYR	Rick Middleton	Oshawa	RW	1005	448	540	988	157
15	Tor.	Ian Turnbull	Ottawa	D	628	123	317	440	736
16	Atl.	Vic Mercredi	New Westminster	C	2	0	0	0	0

SECOND ROUND

PICK	TEAM	NAME	DRAFTED FROM	POS	GP	G/W	A/GA	PTS/SO	PIM/AVG
17	Mtl.	Glenn Goldup	Toronto	RW	291	52	67	119	303
18	Min.	Blake Dunlop	Ottawa	C	550	130	274	404	172
19	Van.	Paulin Bordeleau	Toronto	RW	183	33	56	89	47
20	Phi.	Larry Goodenough	London	D	242	22	77	99	179
21	Atl.	Eric Vail	Sudbury	LW	591	216	260	476	281
22	Mtl.	Peter Marrin	Toronto	C					
23	Pit.	Wayne Bianchin	Flin Flon	LW	276	68	41	109	137
24	St.L.	George Pesut	Saskatoon	D	92	3	22	25	130
25	Min.	John Rogers	Edmonton	RW	14	2	4	6	0
26	Phi.	Brent Leavins	Swift Current	LW					
27	Pit.	Colin Campbell	Peterborough	D	636	25	103	128	1292
28	Buf.	Jean Landry	Quebec	D					
29	Chi.	Reg Thomas	London	LW	39	9	7	16	6
30	NYR	Pat Hickey	Hamilton	LW	646	192	212	404	351
31	Bos.	Jimmy Jones	Peterborough	RW	148	13	18	31	68
32	Mtl.	Ron Andruff	Flin Flon	C	153	19	36	55	54

OTHER ROUNDS

PICK	TEAM	NAME	DRAFTED FROM	POS	GP	G/W	A/GA	PTS/SO	PIM/AVG
33	NYI	Dave Lewis	Saskatoon	D	1008	36	187	223	953
34	Cal.	Jeff Jacques	St. Catharines	RW					
35	Van.	Paul Sheard	Ottawa	RW					
36	Bos.	Doug Gibson	Peterborough	C	63	9	19	28	0
37	Mtl.	Ed Humphreys	Saskatoon	G					
38	L.A.	Russ Walker	Saskatoon	RW	17	1	0	1	41
39	Det.	Nelson Pyatt	Oshawa	C	296	71	63	134	69
40	Phi.	Bob Stumpf	New Westminster	RW/D	10	1	1	2	20
41	Min.	Rick Chinnick	Peterborough	RW	4	0	2	2	0
42	Phi.	Mike Clarke	Calgary	C					
43	Det.	Robbie Neale	Brandon	LW					
44	Buf.	Andre Deschamps	Quebec	LW					
45	Chi.	Randy Holt	Sudbury	D	395	4	37	41	1438
46	NYR	John Campbell	Sault Ste. Marie	C					
47	Bos.	Al Sims	Cornwall	D	475	49	116	165	286
48	St.L.	Bob Gassoff	Medicine Hat	D	245	11	47	58	866
49	NYI	Andre St. Laurent	Montreal	C	644	129	187	316	749
50	Cal.	Ron Serafini	St. Catharines	D	2	0	0	0	2
51	Van.	Keith Mackie	Edmonton	D					
52	Tor.	Francois Rochon	Sherbrooke	LW					
53	Atl.	Dean Talafous	Wisconsin	RW	497	104	154	258	163
54	L.A.	Jim McCrimmon	Medicine Hat	D	2	0	0	0	0
55	Pit.	Dennis Owchar	Toronto	D	288	30	85	115	200
56	Mtl.	Al Hangsleben	North Dakota	D	185	21	48	69	396
57	Min.	Tom Colley	Sudbury	C	1	0	0	0	2
58	Phi.	Dale Cook	Victoria	LW					
59	Det.	Mike Korney	Winnipeg	RW	77	9	10	19	59
60	Buf.	Yvon Dupuis	Quebec	RW					
61	Chi.	Dave Elliott	Winnipeg	LW					
62	NYR	Brian Molvik	Calgary	D					
63	Bos.	Steve Langdon	London	LW	7	0	1	1	2
64	Mtl.	Richard Latulippe	Quebec	C					
65	NYI	Ron Kennedy	New Westminster	RW					
66	Cal.	Jim Moxey	Hamilton	RW	127	22	27	49	59
67	Van.	Paul O'Neil	Boston U.	C/RW	6	0	0	0	0
68	Tor.	Gord Titcomb	St. Catharines	LW					
69	Atl.	John Flesch	Lake Superior State	LW	124	18	23	41	117
70	L.A.	Dennis Abgrall	Saskatoon	RW	13	0	2	2	4
71	Pit.	Guido Tenesi	Oshawa	D					
72	St.L.	Bill Laing	Saskatoon	LW					
73	Min.	Lowell Ostlund	Saskatoon	D					
74	Phi.	Michel Latreille	Montreal	D					
75	Det.	Blair Stewart	Winnipeg	C	229	34	44	78	326
76	Buf.	Bob Smulders	Peterborough	RW					
77	Chi.	Dan Hinton	Sault Ste. Marie	LW	14	0	0	0	16
78	NYR	Pierre Laganiere	Sherbrooke	RW					
79	Bos.	Peter Crosbie	London	G					
80	Mtl.	Gerry Gibbons	St. Mary's U.	D					
81	NYI	Keith Smith	Brown	D					
82	Cal.	William Trognitz	Thunder Bay Jr. A	LW					
83	Van.	Jim Cowell	Ottawa	C					
84	Tor.	Doug Marit	Regina	D					
85	Atl.	Ken Houston	Chatham Jr. B	RW	570	161	167	328	624
86	L.A.	Blair MacDonald	Cornwall	RW	219	91	100	191	65
87	Pit.	Don Seiling	Oshawa	LW					
88	St.L.	Randy Smith	Edmonton	C	3	0	0	0	0
89	Min.	David Lee	Ottawa	LW					
90	Phi.	Doug Ferguson	Hamilton	D					
91	Det.	Glenn Cickello	Hamilton	D					
92	Buf.	Neil Korzack	Peterborough	LW					
93	Chi.	Gary Doerksen	Winnipeg	C					
94	NYR	Dwayne Pentland	Brandon	D					
95	Bos.	Jean-Pierre Bourgouyne	Shawinigan	D					

PICK	TEAM	NAME	DRAFTED FROM	NHL PLAYERS: POS	GP	G	A	PTS	PIM
				NHL GOALTENDERS: POS	GP	W	GA	SO	AVG
96	Mtl.	Dennis Patry	Drummondville	RW					
97	NYI	Don Cutts	RPI	G	6	269	16	0	3.57
98	Cal.	Paul Tantardini	Downsview Jr.	LW					
99	Van.	Clay Hebenton	Portland	G					
100	Tor.	Dan Follett	Downsview Jr.	G					
101	Atl.	Tom Machowski	Wisconsin	D					
102	L.A.	Roly Kimble	Hamilton	G					
103	Pit.	Terry Ewasiuk	Victoria	LW					
104	St.L.	John Wensink	Cornwall	LW	403	70	68	138	840
105	Min.	Lou Nistico	London	C	3	0	0	0	0
106	Phi.	Tom Young	Sudbury	D					
107	Det.	Brian Middleton	U. of Alberta	D					
108	Buf.	Bob Young	U. of Denver	D					
109	Chi.	Wayne Dye	New Westminster	LW					
110	NYI	Dennis Anderson	New Westminster	D					
111	Bos.	Walter Johnson	Oshawa	RW					
112	Mtl.	Michel Belisle	Montreal	C					
113	NYI	Mike Kennedy	Kitchener	RW					
114	Cal.	Bruce Greig	Vancouver	LW	9	0	1	1	46
115	Van.	John Senkpiel	Vancouver	LW					
116	Tor.	Les Burgess	Kitchener	LW					
117	Atl.	Bob Law	North Dakota	RW					
118	Det.	Dennis Polonich	Flin Flon	C/RW	390	59	82	141	1242
119	Pit.	Fred Comrie	Edmonton	C					
120	St.L.	John Tetreault	Drummondville	LW					
121	Min.	George Beveridge	Kitchener	D					
122	Phi.	Norm Barnes	Michigan State	D	156	6	38	44	178
123	Det.	George Lyle	Michigan Tech	LW	99	24	38	62	51
124	Buf.	Tim O'Connell	Vermont	RW					
125	Chi.	Jim Koleff	Hamilton	C					
126	NYI	Denis Desgagnes	Sorel	C					
127	Bos.	Virgil Gates	Swift Current	D					
128	Mtl.	Mario Desjardins	Sherbrooke	LW					
129	NYI	Bob Lorimer	Michigan Tech	D	529	22	90	112	431
130	Cal.	Larry Patey	Braintree H.S.	C	717	153	163	316	631
131	Van.	Peter Folco	Quebec	D	2	0	0	0	0
132	Tor.	Dave Pay	Wisconsin	LW					
133	Atl.	Bob Bilodeau	New Westminster	D					
134	Pit.	Gord Lane	New Westminster	D	539	19	94	113	1228
135	Det.	Dennis O'Brien	Laurentian	D					
136	Min.	Jim Johnston	Peterborough	C					
137	Phi.	Dan O'Donohue	Sault Ste. Marie	D					
138	Det.	Tom Newman	Kitchener	D					
139	Det.	Ray Bibeau	Montreal	D					
140	Chi.	Jack Johnson	Wisconsin	LW					
141	Chi.	Steve Alley	Wisconsin	LW	15	3	3	6	11
142	Bos.	Jim Pettie	St. Catharines	G	21	1157	71	1	3.68
143	Mtl.	Bob Wright	Pembroke Jr. A						
144	Tor.	Lee Palmer	Clarkson	D					
145	Cal.	Doug Mahood	Sault Ste. Marie	RW					
146	Van.	Terry McDougall	Swift Current	C					
147	Tor.	Bob Peace	Cornell	F					
148	Atl.	Glen Surbey	Loyola College	D					
149	Atl.	Guy Ross	Sherbrooke	D					
150	Pit.	Randy Aimoe	Medicine Hat	D					
151	Det.	Kevin Neville	Toronto	G					
152	Min.	Sam Clegg	Medicine Hat	G					
153	Phi.	Brian Dick	Winnipeg	RW					
154	Det.	Ken Gibb	North Dakota	D					
155	Det.	Mitch Brandt	U. of Denver						
156	Chi.	Rick Clubbe	North Dakota	RW					
157	Bos.	Yvan Bouillon	Cornwall	C					
158	Mtl.	Alain Labrecque	Trois-Rivieres	C					
159	Tor.	Norm McLeod	Ottawa M&W Rangers	LW					
160	Cal.	Angelo Moretto	Michigan	C	5	1	2	3	2
161	Min.	Russ Wiechnik	Calgary	C					
162	Atl.	Greg Fox	Michigan	D	494	14	92	106	637
163	Min.	Max Hansen	Sudbury	LW					
164	Pit.	Don McLeod	Saskatoon	G	18	879	74	0	5.05
165	Chi.	Gene Strate	Edmonton	D					
166	Mtl.	Gord Halliday	U. of Pennsylvania						
167	Mtl.	Cap Raeder	New Hampshire	G					
168	Mtl.	Louis Chiasson	Trois-Rivieres	C					

1974

FIRST ROUND

PICK	TEAM	NAME	DRAFTED FROM	NHL PLAYERS: POS	GP	G	A	PTS	PIM
				NHL GOALTENDERS: POS	GP	W	GA	SO	AVG
1	Wsh.	Greg Joly	Regina	D	365	21	76	97	250
2	K.C.	Wilf Paiement	St. Catharines	RW	946	356	458	814	1757
3	Cal.	Rick Hampton	St. Catharines	LW/D	337	59	113	172	147
4	NYI	Clark Gillies	Regina	LW	958	319	378	697	1023
5	Mtl.	Cam Connor	Flin Flon	RW	89	9	22	31	256
6	Min.	Doug Hicks	Flin Flon	D	561	37	131	168	442
7	Mtl.	Doug Risebrough	Kitchener	C	740	185	286	471	1542
8	Pit.	Pierre Larouche	Sorel	C	812	395	427	822	237
9	Det.	Bill Lochead	Oshawa	LW	330	69	62	131	180
10	Mtl.	Rick Chartraw	Kitchener	D/RW	420	28	64	92	399
11	Buf.	Lee Fogolin Jr.	Oshawa	D	924	44	195	239	1318
12	Mtl.	Mario Tremblay	Montreal	RW	852	258	326	584	1043
13	Tor.	Jack Valiquette	Sault Ste. Marie	C	350	84	134	218	79
14	NYR	Dave Maloney	Kitchener	D	657	71	246	317	1154
15	Mtl.	Gord McTavish	Sudbury	C	11	1	3	4	2
16	Chi.	Grant Mulvey	Calgary	RW	586	149	135	284	816
17	Cal.	Ron Chipperfield	Brandon	C	83	22	24	46	34
18	Bos.	Don Larway	Swift Current	RW					

SECOND ROUND

PICK	TEAM	NAME	DRAFTED FROM	POS	GP	G/W	A/GA	PTS/SO	PIM/AVG
19	Wsh.	Mike Marson	Sudbury	LW	196	24	24	48	233
20	K.C.	Glen Burdon	Regina	C	11	0	2	2	0
21	Cal.	Bruce Affleck	U. of Denver	D	280	14	66	80	86
22	NYI	Bryan Trottier	Swift Current	C	1279	524	901	1425	912
23	Van.	Ron Sedlbauer	Kitchener	LW	430	143	86	229	210
24	Min.	Rich Nantais	Quebec	LW	63	5	4	9	79
25	Bos.	Mark Howe	Toronto	D	929	197	545	742	455
26	St.L.	Bob Hess	New Westminster	D	329	27	95	122	178
27	Pit.	Jacques Cossette	Sorel	RW	64	8	6	14	29
28	Atl.	Guy Chouinard	Quebec	C	578	205	370	575	120
29	Buf.	Danny Gare	Calgary	RW	827	354	331	685	1285
30	Mtl.	Gary MacGregor	Cornwall	C					
31	Tor.	Tiger Williams	Swift Current	LW	962	241	272	513	3966
32	NYR	Ron Greschner	New Westminster	D	982	179	431	610	1226
33	Mtl.	Gilles Lupien	Montreal	D	226	5	25	30	416
34	Chi.	Alain Daigle	Trois-Rivieres	RW	389	56	50	106	122
35	Phi.	Don McLean	Sudbury	D	9	0	0	0	6
36	Bos.	Peter Sturgeon	Kitchener	LW	6	0	1	1	2

OTHER ROUNDS

PICK	TEAM	NAME	DRAFTED FROM	POS	GP	G/W	A/GA	PTS/SO	PIM/AVG
37	Wsh.	John Paddock	Brandon	RW	87	8	14	22	86
38	K.C.	Bob Bourne	Saskatoon	C	964	258	324	582	605
39	Cal.	Charlie Simmer	Sault Ste. Marie	LW	712	342	369	711	544
40	NYI	Brad Anderson	Victoria	C					
41	Van.	John Hughes	Toronto	D	70	2	14	16	211
42	Min.	Pete LoPresti	U. of Denver	G	175	9858	668	5	4.07
43	St.L.	Gord Buynak	Kingston	D	4	0	0	0	2
44	Det.	Dan Mandryk	Calgary	C					
45	Det.	Bill Evo	Peterborough	RW					
46	Atl.	Dick Spannbauer	Minnesota-Duluth	D					
47	Buf.	Michel Deziel	Sorel	LW					
48	L.A.	Gary Sargent	Fargo-Moorhead	D	402	61	161	222	273
49	Tor.	Per Arne Alexandersson	Leksand	C					
50	NYR	Jerry Holland	Calgary	LW	37	8	4	12	6
51	Mtl.	Marty Howe	Toronto	D	197	2	29	31	99
52	Chi.	Bob Murray	Cornwall	D	1008	132	382	514	873
53	Phi.	Bob Sirois	Montreal	RW	286	92	120	212	42
54	Bos.	Tom Edur	Toronto	D	158	17	70	87	67
55	Wsh.	Paul Nicholson	London	LW	62	4	8	12	18
56	K.C.	Roger Lemelin	London	D	36	1	2	3	27
57	Cal.	Tom Price	Ottawa	D	29	0	2	2	12
58	Atl.	Pat Ribble	Oshawa	D	349	19	60	79	365
59	Van.	Harold Snepsts	Edmonton	D	1033	38	195	233	2009
60	Min.	Kim MacDougall	Regina	D	1	0	0	0	0
61	Mtl.	Barry Legge	Winnipeg	D	107	1	11	12	144
62	Pit.	Mario Faubert	St. Louis U.	D	231	21	90	111	292
63	Det.	Michel Bergeron	Sorel	RW	229	80	58	138	165
64	Atl.	Cam Botting	Niagara Falls	RW	2	0	1	1	0
65	Buf.	Paul McIntosh	Peterborough	D	48	0	2	2	66
66	L.A.	Brad Winton	Toronto	C					
67	Tor.	Peter Driscoll	Kingston	LW	60	3	8	11	97
68	NYR	Boyd Anderson	Medicine Hat	LW					
69	Mtl.	Mike McKegney	Kitchener	RW					

PICK	TEAM	NAME	DRAFTED FROM	NHL PLAYERS: POS	GP	G	A	PTS	PIM
				NHL GOALTENDERS: POS	GP	W	GA	SO	AVG
70	Chi.	Terry Ruskowski	Swift Current	C	630	113	313	426	1354
71	Phi.	Randy Andreachuk	Kamloops	C					
72	Bos.	Bill Reed	Sault Ste. Marie	D					
73	Wsh.	Jack Patterson	Kamloops	C					
74	K.C.	Mark Lomenda	Victoria	RW					
75	Cal.	Jim Warden	Michigan Tech	G					
76	NYI	Carlo Torresan	Sorel	D					
77	Van.	Mike Rogers	Calgary	C	484	202	317	519	184
78	Min.	Ron Ashton	Saskatoon	D					
79	St.L.	Mike Zuke	Michigan Tech	C	455	86	196	282	220
80	Pit.	Bruce Aberhart	London	G					
81	Det.	John Taft	Wisconsin	D	15	0	2	2	4
82	Atl.	Jerry Badiuk	Kitchener	D					
83	Buf.	Garry Lariviere	St. Catharines	D	219	6	57	63	167
84	L.A.	John Paul Evans	Kitchener	C	103	14	25	39	34
85	Tor.	Mike Palmateer	Toronto	G	356	20131	1183	17	3.53
86	NYR	Dennis Olmstead	Wisconsin	C					
87	St.L.	Don Wheldon	London	D	2	0	0	0	0
88	Chi.	Dave Logan	Laval	D	218	5	29	34	470
89	Phi.	Dennis Sobchuk	Regina	C	35	5	6	11	2
90	Bos.	Jim Bateman	Quebec	LW					
91	Wsh.	Brian Kinsella	Oshawa	C	10	0	1	1	0
92	K.C.	John Shewchuk	St. Paul Jr. A	C					
93	Cal.	Tom Sundberg	St. Paul Jr. A	C/LW					
94	NYI	Sid Prysunka	New Westminster	W					
95	Van.	Andy Spruce	London	LW	172	31	42	73	111
96	Min.	John Sheridan	Minnesota-Duluth	C					
97	St.L.	Mike Thompson	Victoria	D					
98	Pit.	William Schneider	Minnesota-Duluth	LW					
99	Det.	Don Dufek	Michigan	LW					
100	Atl.	Bill Moen	U. of Minnesota	G					
101	Buf.	Dave Given	Brown	D					
102	L.A.	Marty Mathews	Flin Flon	LW					
103	Tor.	Bill Hassard	Wexford Jr.	C					
104	NYR	Eddie Johnstone	Medicine Hat	RW	426	122	136	258	375
105	Mtl.	John Stewart	Bowling Green	C	2	0	0	0	0
106	Chi.	Bob Volpe	Sudbury	G					
107	Phi.	Willie Friesen	Swift Current	LW					
108	Bos.	Bill Best	Sudbury	LW					
109	Wsh.	Garth Malarchuk	Calgary	G					
110	K.C.	Mike Boland	Sault Ste. Marie	D	23	1	2	3	29
111	Cal.	Tom Anderson	St. Paul Jr. A	D					
112	NYI	Dave Langevin	Minnesota-Duluth	D	513	12	107	119	530
113	Van.	Jim Clarke	Toronto	D					
114	Min.	Dave Heitz	Fargo-Moorhead	G					
115	St.L.	Terry Casey	St. Catharines	RW					
116	Pit.	Robbie Laird	Regina	LW	1	0	0	0	0
117	Det.	Jack Carlson	Marquette Sr.	LW	236	30	15	45	417
118	Atl.	Peter Brown	Boston U.	D					
119	Buf.	Bernard Noreau	Laval	RW					
120	L.A.	Harvey Stewart	Flin Flon	G					
121	Tor.	Kevin Devine	Toronto	LW	2	0	1	1	8
122	NYR	John Memryk	Winnipeg	G					
123	Mtl.	Joe Micheletti	Minnesota-Duluth	D	158	11	60	71	114
124	Chi.	Eddie Mio	Colorado College	G	192	10428	705	4	4.06
125	Phi.	Reggie Lemelin	Sherbrooke	G	507	28006	1613	12	3.46
126	Bos.	Ray Maluta	Flin Flon	D	25	2	3	5	6
127	Wsh.	John Nazar	Cornwall	LW					
128	Cal.	Jim McCabe	Welland Jr. B	C					
129	NYI	David Inkpen	Edmonton	D					
130	Van.	Robbie Watt	Flin Flon	LW					
131	Min.	Roland Eriksson	Tunabro	C	193	48	95	143	26
132	St.L.	Rod Tordoff	Swift Current	D					
133	Pit.	Larry Finck	St. Catharines	D					
134	Det.	Greg Steele	Calgary	D					
135	Atl.	Tom Lindskog	Michigan	D					
136	Buf.	Charles Constantin	Quebec	C					
137	L.A.	John Held	London	D					
138	Tor.	Kevin Kemp	Ottawa	D	3	0	0	0	4
139	NYR	Greg Holst	Kingston	C	11	0	0	0	0
140	Mtl.	Jamie Hislop	New Hampshire	RW	345	75	103	178	86
141	Chi.	Mike St. Cyr	Kitchener	D					
142	Phi.	Steve Short	Minnesota Jr. Stars	LW	6	0	0	0	2
143	Bos.	Darryl Drader	North Dakota	D					
144	Wsh.	Kelvin Erickson	Calgary	G					
145	K.C.	Brian Kurliak	North Bay	LW					
146	NYI	Jim Foubister	Victoria	G					
147	Van.	Marc Gaudreault	Lake Superior State	D					
148	Min.	Dave Staffen	Ottawa	C					
149	St.L.	Paul-Andre Touzin	Shawinigan	G					
150	Pit.	James Chicoyne	Brandon	D					
151	Det.	Glenn McLeod	Sudbury	D					
152	Atl.	Larry Hopkins	Oshawa	LW	60	13	16	29	26
153	Buf.	Rick Jodzio	Hamilton	LW	70	2	8	10	71
154	L.A.	Mario Lessard	Sherbrooke	G	240	13529	843	9	3.74
155	Tor.	Dave Syvret	St. Catharines	D					
156	NYR	Claude Arvisais	Shawinigan	C					
157	Mtl.	Gord Stewart	Kamloops	C					
158	Chi.	Stephen Colp	Michigan State	C					
159	Phi.	Peter McKenzie	St. Francis Xavier	D					
160	Bos.	Peter Roberts	St. Cloud Jr.	C					
161	Wsh.	Tony White	Kitchener	LW	164	37	28	65	104
162	K.C.	Denis Carufel	Sorel	D					
163	NYI	Bob Ferguson	Cornwall	C					
164	Min.	Brian Anderson	New Westminster	D					
165	St.L.	Jack Ahern	Brown	D					
166	Pit.	Rick Uhrich	Regina	RW					
167	Atl.	Louis Loranger	Shawinigan	C					
168	Buf.	Derek Smith	Ottawa	C/LW	335	78	116	194	60
169	L.A.	Derrick Emerson	Montreal	RW					
170	Tor.	Andy Stoesz	Selkirk Jr.	G					
171	NYR	Ken Dodd	New Westminster	LW					
172	Mtl.	Charlie Luksa	Kitchener	D	8	0	1	1	4
173	Chi.	Rick Fraser	Oshawa	D					
174	Phi.	Marcel Labrosse	Shawinigan	C					
175	Bos.	Peter Waselovich	North Dakota	G					
176	Wsh.	Ron Pronchuk	Brandon	D					
177	K.C.	Soren Johansson	Djurgarden	C					
178	NYI	Murray Fleck	Estevan	D					
179	Min.	Duane Bray	Flin Flon	D					
180	St.L.	Mitch Babin	North Bay	C	8	0	0	0	0
181	Pit.	Serge Gamelin	Sorel	RW					
182	Atl.	Randy Montgomery	Welland Jr. B	LW					
184	L.A.	Jacques Locas	Quebec Remparts	C					
185	Tor.	Martin Feschuk	Saskatoon	D					
186	NYR	Ralph Krentz	Brandon	LW					
187	Mtl.	Cliff Cox	New Hampshire	C					
188	Chi.	Jean Bernier	Shawinigan	D					
189	Phi.	Scott Jessee	Michigan Tech	RW					
190	Wsh.	Dave McKee	Oshawa	RW					
191	K.C.	Mats Ulander	Boden	D					
192	NYI	David Rooke	Cornwall	D					
193	Min.	Don Hay	New Westminster	RW					
194	St.L.	Doug Allan	New Westminster	G					
195	Pit.	Richard Perron	Quebec	D					
196	Buf.	Bob Geoffrion	Cornwall	LW					
197	L.A.	Lindsay Thomson	U. of Denver	C					
198	NYR	Larry Jacques	Ottawa	RW					
199	Mtl.	Dave Lumley	New Hampshire	RW	437	98	160	258	680
200	Chi.	Dwane Byers	Sherbrooke	RW					
201	Phi.	Richard Guay	Chicoutimi	G					
202	Wsh.	Scott Mabley	Sault Ste. Marie	D					
203	K.C.	Edward Pizunski	Peterborough	D					
204	NYI	Neil Smith	Brockville Jr. A	D					
205	Min.	Brian Holderness	Saskatoon	G					
206	Pit.	Richard Hindmarch	U. of Calgary	RW					
207	L.A.	Craig Brickley	U. of Pennsylvania	C					
208	NYR	Tom Gastle	Peterborough	LW					
209	Mtl.	Mike Hobin	Hamilton	C					
210	Chi.	Glen Ing	Victoria	RW					
211	Phi.	Brad Morrow	Minnesota-Duluth	D					
212	Wsh.	Bernard Plante	Trois-Rivieres	LW					
213	K.C.	Willie Wing	Hamilton	RW					
214	NYI	Stefan Persson	Brynas Gavle	D	622	52	317	369	574
215	Min.	Frank Taylor	Brandon	D					
216	Pit.	Bill Davis	Colgate	D					
217	L.A.	Brad Kuglin	U. of Pennsylvania	LW					
218	NYR	Eric Brubacher	Kingston	C					
219	Phi.	Craig Arvidson	Minnesota-Duluth	LW					
220	Wsh.	Jacques Chiasson	Drummondville	RW					
221	NYI	Dave Otness	Wisconsin	C					
222	Min.	Jeff Hymanson	St. Cloud Jr.	D					

PICK	TEAM	NAME	DRAFTED FROM	POS	GP	G / W	A / GA	PTS / SO	PIM / AVG
223	Pit.	James Mathers	Northeastern	D					
224	NYR	Russell Hall	Winnipeg	RW					
225	Wsh.	Bill Bell	Regina	LW					
226	NYI	Jim Murray	Michigan State	D					
227	NYR	Bill Kriski	Winnipeg	G					
228	Wsh.	Robert Blanchet	Kitchener	G					
229	NYI	Mike Dibble	Wisconsin	G					
230	NYR	Kevin Treacy	Cornwall	RW					
231	Wsh.	Johnny Bower	Downsview Jr.	G					
232	NYI	Brian Bye	Kitchener	LW					
233	NYR	Ken Gassoff	Medicine Hat	C					
234	Wsh.	Yves Plouffe	Sorel	D					
235	NYI	Martti Jarkko	Tappara Tampere	D					
236	NYR	Cliff Bast	Medicine Hat	D					
237	Wsh.	Terry Bozack	Pembroke Jr. A	D					
238	NYI	Ron Phillips	St. Catharines	D					
239	NYR	Jim Mayer	Michigan Tech	RW	4	0	0	0	0
240	Wsh.	Gord Cole	Brandon	LW					
241	NYR	Warren Miller	Minnesota-Duluth	RW	262	40	50	90	137
242	Wsh.	Mike Cosentino	Hamilton	C					
243	NYR	Kevin Walker	Cornell	D					
244	Wsh.	John Duncan	Cornwall	D					
245	NYR	Jim Warner	Minnesota Jr.	RW	32	0	3	3	10
246	Wsh.	Barry Kerfoot	Smiths Falls Jr.	RW					
247	Wsh.	Ron Poole	Kamloops	C					

1975

FIRST ROUND

PICK	TEAM	NAME	DRAFTED FROM	POS	GP	G / W	A / GA	PTS / SO	PIM / AVG
1	Phi.	Mel Bridgman	Victoria	C	977	252	449	701	1625
2	K.C.	Barry Dean	Medicine Hat	LW	165	25	56	81	146
3	Cal.	Ralph Klassen	Saskatoon	C	497	52	93	145	120
4	Min.	Bryan Maxwell	Medicine Hat	D	331	18	77	95	745
5	Det.	Rick Lapointe	Victoria	D	664	44	176	220	831
6	Tor.	Don Ashby	Calgary	C	188	40	56	96	40
7	Chi.	Greg Vaydik	Medicine Hat	C	5	0	0	0	0
8	Atl.	Richard Mulhern	Sherbrooke	D	303	27	93	120	217
9	Mtl.	Robin Sadler	Edmonton	D					
10	Van.	Rick Blight	Brandon	RW	326	96	125	221	170
11	NYI	Pat Price	Saskatoon (WHL)	D	726	43	218	261	1456
12	NYR	Wayne Dillon	Toronto	C	229	43	66	109	60
13	Pit.	Gord Laxton	New Westminster	G	17	800	74	0	5.55
14	Bos.	Doug Halward	Peterborough	D	653	69	224	293	774
15	Mtl.	Pierre Mondou	Montreal	C	548	194	262	456	179
16	L.A.	Tim Young	Ottawa	C	628	195	341	536	438
17	Buf.	Bob Sauve	Laval	G	420	23711	1377	8	3.48
18	Wsh.	Alex Forsyth	Kingston	C	1	0	0	0	0

SECOND ROUND

PICK	TEAM	NAME	DRAFTED FROM	POS	GP	G / W	A / GA	PTS / SO	PIM / AVG
19	Wsh.	Peter Scamurra	Peterborough	D	132	8	25	33	59
20	K.C.	Don Cairns	Victoria	LW	9	0	1	1	2
21	Cal.	Dennis Maruk	London	C	888	356	522	878	761
22	Mtl.	Brian Engblom	Wisconsin	D	659	29	177	206	599
23	Det.	Jerry Rollins	Winnipeg	D					
24	Tor.	Doug Jarvis	Peterborough	C	964	139	264	403	263
25	Chi.	Daniel Arndt	Saskatoon	LW					
26	Atl.	Rick Bowness	Montreal	RW	173	18	37	55	191
27	St.L.	Ed Staniowski	Regina	G	219	12075	818	2	4.06
28	Van.	Brad Gassoff	Kamloops	LW	122	19	17	36	163
29	NYI	Dave Salvian	St. Catharines	RW					
30	NYR	Doug Soetaert	Edmonton	G	284	15583	1030	6	3.97
31	Pit.	Russ Anderson	Minnesota-Duluth	D	519	22	99	121	1086
32	Bos.	Barry Smith	New Westminster	C	114	7	7	14	10
33	L.A.	Terry Bucyk	Lethbridge	RW					
34	Mtl.	Kelly Greenbank	Winnipeg	RW					
35	Buf.	Ken Breitenbach	St. Catharines	D	68	1	13	14	49
36	St.L.	Jamie Masters	Ottawa	D	33	1	13	14	2

OTHER ROUNDS

PICK	TEAM	NAME	DRAFTED FROM	POS	GP	G / W	A / GA	PTS / SO	PIM / AVG
37	Det.	Al Cameron	New Westminster	D	282	11	44	55	356
38	K.C.	Neil Lyseng	Kamloops	RW					
39	Cal.	John Tweedle	Lake Superior State	RW					
40	Min.	Paul Harrison	Oshawa	G	109	5806	408	2	4.22
41	Min.	Alex Pirus	U. of Notre Dame	RW	159	30	28	58	94
42	Tor.	Bruce Boudreau	Toronto	C	141	28	42	70	46
43	Chi.	Mike O'Connell	Kingston	D	860	105	334	439	605
44	Buf.	Terry Martin	London	LW	479	104	101	205	202
45	Det.	Blair Davidson	Flin Flon	D					
46	Van.	Normand Lapointe	Trois-Rivieres	G					
47	NYI	Joe Fortunato	Kitchener	LW					
48	NYR	Greg Hickey	Hamilton	LW	1	0	0	0	0
49	Pit.	Paul Baxter	Winnipeg	D	472	48	121	169	1564
50	Det.	Clarke Hamilton	U. of Notre Dame	LW					
51	Mtl.	Paul Woods	Sault Ste. Marie	LW	501	72	124	196	276
52	Mtl.	Pat Hughes	Michigan	RW	573	130	128	258	646
53	Buf.	Gary McAdam	St. Catharines	LW	534	96	132	228	243
54	Phi.	Bob Ritchie	Sorel	LW	29	8	4	12	10
55	Wsh.	Blair MacKasey	Montreal	D	1	0	0	0	2
56	K.C.	Ron Delorme	Lethbridge	C	524	83	83	166	667
57	Cal.	Greg Smith	Colorado College	D	829	56	232	288	1110
58	Min.	Steve Jensen	Michigan Tech	LW	438	113	107	220	318
59	Det.	Mike Wirachowsky	Regina	D					
60	Bos.	Rick Adduono	St. Catharines	C	4	0	0	0	2
61	Chi.	Pierre Giroux	Hull	C	6	1	0	1	17
62	Atl.	Dale Ross	Ottawa	LW					
63	St.L.	Rick Bourbonnais	Ottawa	RW	71	9	15	24	29
64	Van.	Glen Richardson	Hamilton	LW	24	3	6	9	19
65	NYI	Andre Lepage	Montreal	G					
66	NYR	Bill Cheropita	St. Catharines	G					
67	Pit.	Stuart Younger	Michigan State	LW					
68	Bos.	Denis Daigle	Montreal	LW					
69	L.A.	Andre Leduc	Sherbrooke	D					
70	Mtl.	Dave Gorman	St. Catharines	RW	3	0	0	0	0
71	Buf.	Greg Neeld	Calgary	D					
72	Phi.	Rick St. Croix	Oshawa	G	130	7295	451	2	3.71
73	Wsh.	Craig Crawford	Toronto	LW					
74	K.C.	Terry McDonald	Kamloops	D	8	0	1	1	6
75	Cal.	Doug Young	Michigan Tech	D					
76	Min.	David Norris	Hamilton	LW					
77	Det.	Mike Wong	Montreal	C	22	1	1	2	12
78	Tor.	Ted Long	Hamilton	D					
79	Chi.	Bob Hoffmeyer	Saskatoon	D	198	14	52	66	325
80	Atl.	Willi Plett	St. Catharines	RW	834	222	215	437	2572
81	St.L.	Jim Gustafson	Victoria	C					
82	Van.	Doug Murray	Brandon	LW					
83	NYI	Denis McLean	Calgary	LW					
84	NYR	Larry Huras	Kitchener	D	2	0	0	0	0
85	Pit.	Kim Clackson	Victoria	D	106	0	8	8	370
86	Bos.	Stan Jonathan	Peterborough	LW	411	91	110	201	751
87	L.A.	Dave Miglia	Trois-Rivieres	D					
88	Mtl.	Jim Turkiewicz	Peterborough	D					
89	Buf.	Don Edwards	Kitchener	G	459	26181	1449	16	3.32
90	Phi.	Gary Morrison	Michigan	RW	43	1	15	16	70
91	Wsh.	Roger Swanson	Flin Flon	G					
92	K.C.	Eric Sanderson	Victoria	LW					
93	Cal.	Larry Hendrick	Calgary	G					
94	Min.	Greg Clause	Hamilton	RW					
95	Det.	Mike Harazny	Regina	D					
96	Tor.	Kevin Campbell	St. Lawrence U.	D					
97	Chi.	Tom Ulseth	Wisconsin	RW					
98	Atl.	Paul Heaver	Oshawa	D					
99	St.L.	Jack Brownschidle	U. of Notre Dame	D	494	39	162	201	151
100	Van.	Bob Watson	Flin Flon	RW					
101	NYI	Mike Sleep	New Westminster	RW					
102	NYR	Randy Koch	Vermont	LW					
103	Pit.	Peter Morris	Victoria	LW					
104	Bos.	Matti Hagman	HIFK Helsinki	C	237	56	89	145	36
105	L.A.	Bob Russell	Sudbury	C					
106	Mtl.	Michel Lachance	Montreal	D	21	0	4	4	22
107	Buf.	Jim Minor	Regina	LW					
108	Phi.	Paul Holmgren	U. of Minnesota	RW	527	144	179	323	1684
109	Wsh.	Clark Jantzie	U. of Alberta	LW					
110	K.C.	Bill Oleschuk	Saskatoon	G	55	2835	188	1	3.98
111	Cal.	Rick Shinske	New Westminster	C	63	5	16	21	10
112	Min.	Francois Robert	Sherbrooke	D					
113	Det.	Jean-Luc Phaneuf	Montreal	C					
114	Tor.	Mario Rouillard	Trois-Rivieres	RW					
115	Chi.	Ted Bulley	Hull	LW	414	101	113	214	704
116	Atl.	Dale McMullin	Brandon	LW					
117	St.L.	Doug Lindskog	Michigan	LW					
118	Van.	Brian Shmyr	New Westminster	C					
119	NYI	Richie Hansen	Sudbury	C	20	2	8	10	4

Column headings as printed: for NHL players, POS, GP, G, A, PTS, PIM; for NHL goaltenders, POS, GP, W, GA, SO, AVG.

PICK	TEAM	NAME	DRAFTED FROM	NHL PLAYERS: POS	GP	G	A	PTS	PIM
				NHL GOALTENDERS: POS	GP	W	GA	SO	AVG
120	NYR	Claude Larose	Sherbrooke	LW	25	4	7	11	2
121	Pit.	Mike Will	Edmonton	C					
122	Bos.	Gary Carr	Toronto	G					
123	L.A.	Dave Faulkner	Regina	C					
124	Mtl.	Tim Burke	New Hampshire	D					
125	Buf.	Grant Rowe	Ottawa	D					
126	Phi.	Dana Decker	Michigan Tech	LW					
127	Wsh.	Mike Fryia	Peterborough	LW					
128	K.C.	Joe Baker	Minnesota-Duluth	D					
129	Cal.	Doug Schoenfeld	Cambridge Sr.	D					
130	Min.	Dean Magee	Colorado College	LW	7	0	0	0	4
131	Det.	Steve Carlson	Johnstown NAHL	C	52	9	12	21	23
132	Tor.	Ron Wilson	Providence	D	177	26	67	93	68
133	Chi.	Paul Jensen	Michigan Tech	D					
134	Atl.	Rick Piche	Brandon	D					
135	St.L.	Dick Lamby	Salem State	D	22	0	5	5	22
136	Van.	Allan Fleck	New Westminster	LW					
137	NYI	Bob Sunderland	Boston U.	D					
138	NYR	Bill Hamilton	St. Catharines	RW					
139	Pit.	Tapio Levo	Assat Pori	D	107	16	53	69	36
140	Bos.	Bo Berglund	Djurgarden	LW					
141	L.A.	Bill Reber	Vermont	RW					
142	Mtl.	Craig Norwich	Wisconsin	D	104	17	58	75	60
143	Buf.	Alex Tidey	Lethbridge	RW	9	0	0	0	8
144	Wsh.	Jim Ofrim	U. of Alberta	C					
145	K.C.	Scott Williams	Flin Flon	LW					
146	Cal.	Jim Weaver	Kingston	G					
147	Min.	Terry Angel	Oshawa	RW					
148	Det.	Gary Vaughn	Medicine Hat	RW					
149	Tor.	Paul Evans	Peterborough	C/LW	11	1	1	2	21
150	Atl.	Nick Sanza	Sherbrooke	G					
151	St.L.	Dave McNab	Wisconsin	G					
152	Van.	Bob McNeice	New Westminster	D					
153	NYI	Don Blair	Ottawa	RW					
154	NYR	Bud Stefanski	Oshawa	C	1	0	0	0	0
155	Pit	Bryan Shutt	Bowling Green	LW					
156	Bos.	Joe Rando	New Hampshire	D					
157	L.A.	Sean Sullivan	Hamilton	D					
158	Mtl.	Paul Clarke	U. of Notre Dame	D					
159	Buf.	Andy Whitby	Oshawa	RW					
160	Phi.	Viktor Khatulev	Dynamo Riga	C					
161	Wsh	Malcolm Zinger	Kamloops	RW					
162	St.L.	Greg Agar	Merritt Jr. A	RW					
163	Min.	Michel Blais	Kingston	D					
164	Det.	Jean Thibodeau	Shawinigan	C					
165	Tor.	Jean Latendresse	Shawinigan	D					
166	Tor.	Paul Crowley	Sudbury	RW					
167	Atl.	Brian O'Connell	St. Louis U.	G					
168	NYI	Joey Girardin	Winnipeg	D					
169	NYR	Daniel Beaulieu	Quebec	LW					
170	Pit.	Frank Salive	Peterborough	G					
171	Bos.	Kevin Nugent	U. of Notre Dame	G					
172	L.A.	Brian Petrovek	Harvard	G					
173	Mtl.	Bob Ferriter	Boston College	C					
174	Buf.	Len Moher	U. of Notre Dame	G					
175	Phi.	Duffy Smith	Bowling Green	D					
176	Det.	David Hanson	Colorado College	D					
177	Min.	Earl Sargent	Fargo-Moorhead	RW					
178	Det.	Robin Larson	Minnesota-Duluth	D					
179	Tor.	Dan D'Alvise	Royal York Jr.	C					
180	Tor.	Jack Laine	Bowling Green	RW					
181	Atl.	Joe Augustine	Austin Prep	D					
182	Van.	Sid Veysey	Sherbrooke	C	1	0	0	0	0
183	NYI	Geoff Green	Sudbury	RW					
184	NYR	John McMorrow	Providence	C					
185	Pit.	John Glynne	Vermont	D					
186	L.A.	Tom Goddard	North Dakota	RW					
187	Mtl.	David Bell	Harvard	C					
188	Tor.	Ken Holland	Medicine Hat	G	4	206	17	0	4.95
189	Tor.	Bob Barnes	Hamilton	D					
190	Min.	Gilles Cloutier	Shawinigan	G					
191	Tor.	Gary Burns	New Hampshire	LW/C	11	2	2	4	18
192	Atl.	Torbjorn Nilsson	Skelleftea	RW					
193	Tor.	Jim Montgomery	Hull	C	1	0	0	0	0
194	NYI	Kari Makkonen	Assat Pori	RW	9	2	2	4	0
195	NYR	Tom McNamara	Vermont	G					
196	Pit.	Lex Hudson	U. of Denver	D	2	0	0	0	0
197	L.A.	Mario Viens	Cornwall	G					
198	Mtl.	Carl Jackson	U. of Pennsylvania	C					
199	Tor.	Rick Martin	London	RW					
200	NYR	Steve Roberts	Providence	D					
201	NYR	Paul Dionne	Princeton	D					
202	Pit.	Dan Tsubouchi	St. Louis U.	RW					
203	L.A.	Chuck Carpenter	Yale	C					
204	Mtl.	Michel Brisebois	Sherbrooke	C					
205	NYR	Cecil Luckern	New Hampshire	LW					
206	Pit.	Bronislav Stankovsky	Fargo-Moorhead	LW					
207	L.A.	Bob Fish	Fargo-Moorhead	LW					
208	Mtl.	Roger Bourque	U. of Notre Dame	D					
209	NYR	John Corriveau	New Hampshire	RW					
210	L.A.	Dave Taylor	Clarkson	RW	1111	431	638	1069	1589
211	Mtl.	Jim Lundquist	Brown	D					
212	NYR	Tom Funke	Fargo-Moorhead	LW					
213	L.A.	Robert Shaw	Clarkson	D					
214	Mtl.	Don Madson	Fargo-Moorhead	C					
215	Mtl.	Bob Bain	New Hampshire	D					
216	Atl.	Gary Gill	Sault Ste. Marie	LW					
217	Pit.	Kelly Secord	New Westminster	RW					

1976

FIRST ROUND

PICK	TEAM	NAME	DRAFTED FROM	POS	GP	G	A	PTS	PIM
1	Wsh.	Rick Green	London	D	845	43	220	263	588
2	Pit.	Blair Chapman	Saskatoon	RW	402	106	125	231	158
3	Min.	Glen Sharpley	Hull	C	389	117	161	278	199
4	Det.	Fred Williams	Saskatoon	C	44	2	5	7	10
5	Cal.	Bjorn Johansson	Orebro	D	15	1	1	2	10
6	NYR	Don Murdoch	Medicine Hat	RW	320	121	117	238	155
7	St.L.	Bernie Federko	Saskatoon	C	1000	369	761	1130	487
8	Atl.	Dave Shand	Peterborough	D	421	19	84	103	544
9	Chi.	Real Cloutier	Quebec	RW	317	146	198	344	119
10	Atl.	Harold Phillipoff	New Westminster	LW	141	26	57	83	267
11	K.C.	Paul Gardner	Oshawa	C	447	201	201	402	207
12	Mtl.	Peter Lee	Ottawa	RW	431	114	131	245	257
13	Mtl.	Rod Schutt	Sudbury	LW	286	77	92	169	177
14	NYI	Alex McKendry	Sudbury	W	46	3	6	9	21
15	Wsh.	Greg Carroll	Medicine Hat	C	131	20	34	54	44
16	Bos.	Clayton Pachal	New Westminster	C/LW	35	2	3	5	95
17	Phi.	Mark Suzor	Kingston	D	64	4	16	20	60
18	Mtl.	Bruce Baker	Ottawa	RW					

SECOND ROUND

PICK	TEAM	NAME	DRAFTED FROM	POS	GP	G	A	PTS	PIM
19	Pit.	Greg Malone	Oshawa	C	704	191	310	501	661
20	St.L.	Brian Sutter	Lethbridge	LW	779	303	333	636	1786
21	L.A.	Steve Clippingdale	New Westminster	LW	19	1	2	3	9
22	Det.	Reed Larson	Minnesota-Duluth	D	904	222	463	685	1391
23	Cal.	Vern Stenlund	London	C	4	0	0	0	0
24	NYR	Dave Farrish	Sudbury	D	430	17	110	127	440
25	St.L.	John Smrke	Toronto	LW	103	11	17	28	33
26	Van.	Bob Manno	St. Catharines	D	371	41	131	172	274
27	Chi.	Jeff McDill	Victoria	RW	1	0	0	0	0
28	Atl.	Bobby Simpson	Sherbrooke	LW	175	35	29	64	98
29	Pit.	Peter Marsh	Sherbrooke	RW	278	48	71	119	224
30	Tor.	Randy Carlyle	Sudbury	D	1055	148	499	647	1400
31	Min.	Jim Roberts	Ottawa	LW	106	17	23	40	33
32	NYI	Mike Kaszycki	Sault Ste. Marie	C	226	42	80	122	108
33	Buf.	Joe Kowal	Hamilton	LW	22	0	5	5	13
34	Bos.	Lorry Gloeckner	Victoria	D	13	0	2	2	6
35	Phi.	Drew Callander	Regina	C/RW	39	6	2	8	7
36	Mtl.	Barry Melrose	Kamloops	D	300	10	23	33	728
37	Ws								

OTHER ROUNDS

PICK	TEAM	NAME	DRAFTED FROM	POS	GP	G	A	PTS	PIM
h.Tom Rowe		London	RW	357	85	100	185	615	
38	K.C.	Mike Kitchen	Toronto	D	474	12	62	74	370
39	Min.	Don Jackson	U. of Notre Dame	D	311	16	52	68	640
40	Det.	Fred Berry	New Westminster	C	3	0	0	0	0
41	Cal.	Mike Fidler	Boston U.	LW	271	84	97	181	124
42	NYR	Mike McEwen	Toronto	D	716	108	296	404	460
43	St.L.	Jim Kirkpatrick	Toronto	D					
44	Van.	Rob Flockhart	Kamloops	LW	55	2	5	7	14
45	Chi.	Thomas Gradin	MoDo Ornskoldsvik	C	677	209	384	593	298
46	Atl.	Rick Hodgson	Calgary	D	6	0	0	0	6

PICK	TEAM	NAME	DRAFTED FROM	NHL PLAYERS: POS / NHL GOALTENDERS: POS	GP / GP	G / W	A / GA	PTS / SO	PIM / AVG
47	Pit.	Morris Lukowich	Medicine Hat	LW	582	199	219	418	584
48	Tor.	Alain Belanger	Sherbrooke	RW	9	0	1	1	6
49	L.A.	Don Moores	Kamloops	C					
50	NYI	Garth MacGuigan	Montreal	C	5	0	1	1	2
51	Min.	Ron Zanussi	London	RW	299	52	83	135	373
52	Tor.	Gary McFayden	Hull	RW					
53	Phi.	Craig Hamner	St. Paul Jr. A	D					
54	Mtl.	Bill Baker	Minnesota-Duluth	D	143	7	25	32	175
55	Wsh.	Al Glendinning	Calgary	D					
56	St.L.	Mike Liut	Bowling Green	G	664	38215	2221	25	3.49
57	Min.	Mike Fedorko	Hamilton	D					
58	Det.	Kevin Schamehorn	New Westminster	RW	10	0	0	0	17
59	Cal.	Warren Young	Michigan Tech	C	236	72	77	149	472
60	NYR	Claude Periard	Trois-Rivieres	LW					
61	St.L.	Paul Skidmore	Boston College	G	2	120	6	0	3.00
62	Van.	Elmer Ray	Calgary	LW					
63	Chi.	Dave Debol	Michigan	C	92	26	26	52	4
64	Atl.	Kent Nilsson	Djurgarden	C	553	264	422	686	116
65	Pit.	Greg Redquest	Oshawa	G	1	13	3	0	13.85
66	Tor.	Tim Williams	Victoria	D					
67	L.A.	Bob Mears	Kingston	G					
68	NYI	Ken Morrow	Bowling Green	D	550	17	88	105	309
69	Buf.	Henry Maze	Edmonton	LW					
70	Bos.	Bob Miller	Ottawa	C	404	75	119	194	220
71	Phi.	Dave Hynek	Kingston	LW					
72	Mtl.	Ed Clarey	Cornwall	RW					
73	Wsh.	Doug Patey	Sault Ste. Marie	RW	45	4	2	6	8
74	K.C.	Rick McIntyre	Oshawa	LW					
75	Min.	Phil Verchota	Minnesota-Duluth	C					
76	Det.	Dwight Schofield	London	D	211	8	22	30	631
77	Cal.	Darcy Regier	Lethbridge	D	26	0	2	2	35
78	NYR	Doug Gaines	St. Catharines	C					
79	Cal.	Cal Sandbeck	U. of Denver	D					
80	Van.	Rick Durston	Victoria	LW					
81	Chi.	Terry McDonald	Edmonton	C					
82	Atl.	Mark Earp	Kamloops	G					
83	Pit.	Brendan Lowe	Sherbrooke	D					
84	Tor.	Greg Hotham	Kingston	D	230	15	74	89	139
85	L.A.	Robert Palmer	Michigan	D	320	9	101	110	115
86	NYI	Mike Hordy	Sault Ste. Marie	D	11	0	0	0	7
87	Buf.	Ron Roscoe	Hamilton	D					
88	Bos.	Peter Vandemark	Oshawa	LW					
89	Phi.	Robin Lang	Cornell	D					
90	Mtl.	Maurice Barrette	Quebec	G					
91	Wsh.	Jim Bedard	Sudbury	G	73	4232	278	1	3.94
92	K.C.	Larry Skinner	Ottawa	C	47	10	12	22	8
93	Min.	Dave Delich	Colorado College	C					
94	Det.	Tony Horvath	Sault Ste. Marie	D					
95	Cal.	Jouni Rinne	Lukko Rauma	RW					
96	NYR	Barry Scully	Kingston	RW					
97	St.L.	Nels Goddard	Michigan Tech	D					
98	Van.	Rob Tudor	Regina	RW/C	28	4	4	8	19
99	Chi.	John Peterson	U. of Notre Dame	G					
100	Wsh.	Don Wilson	St. Catharines	D					
101	Pit.	Vic Sirko	Oshawa	D					
102	Tor.	Dan Djakalovic	Kitchener	C					
103	L.A.	Larry McRae	Windsor	G					
104	NYI	Yvon Vautour	Laval	RW	204	26	33	59	401
105	Buf.	Don Lemieux	Trois-Rivieres	D					
106	Bos.	Ted Olson	Calgary	LW					
107	Phi.	Paul Klasinski	St. Paul Jr. A	LW					
108	Mtl.	Pierre Brassard	Cornwall	LW					
109	Wsh.	Dale Rideout	Flin Flon	G					
110	Min.	Jeff Barr	Michigan State	D					
111	Det.	Fern LeBlanc	Sherbrooke	C	34	5	6	11	0
112	NYR	Remi Levesque	Quebec	C					
113	St.L.	Mike Eaves	Wisconsin	C	324	83	143	226	80
114	Van.	Brad Rhiness	Kingston	C					
115	Chi.	John Rothstein	Minnesota-Duluth	RW					
116	Tor.	Chuck Skjodt	Windsor	C					
117	Phi.	Ray Kurpis	Austin Prep	RW					
118	Mtl.	Rick Gosselin	Flin Flon	C					
119	Wsh.	Allan Dumba	Regina	RW					
120	Det.	Claude Legris	Sorel	G	4	91	4	0	2.64
121	St.L.	Jacques Soguel	Davos, SUI.	C					
122	Van.	Stu Ostlund	Michigan Tech	C					
123	Mtl.	John Gregory	Wisconsin	D					
124	St.L.	David Dornself	Providence	D					
125	Mtl.	Bruce Horsch	Michigan Tech	G					
126	St.L.	Brad Wilson	Providence	C					
127	Mtl.	John Tavella	Sault Ste. Marie	LW					
128	St.L.	Don Hoene	Michigan	RW					
129	Mtl.	Mark Davidson	Flin Flon	RW					
130	St.L.	Goran Lindblom	Skelleftea	D					
131	Mtl.	Bill Wells	Cornwall	LW					
132	St.L.	Jim Bales	U. of Denver	G					
133	Mtl.	Ron Wilson	St. Catharines	C	832	110	216	326	415
134	St.L.	Anders Hakansson	AIK Solna	LW	330	52	46	98	141
135	St.L.	Juhani Wallenius	Lukko Rauma	C					

1977

FIRST ROUND

PICK	TEAM	NAME	DRAFTED FROM	POS	GP	G / W	A / GA	PTS / SO	PIM / AVG
1	Det.	Dale McCourt	St. Catharines	C	532	194	284	478	124
2	Col.	Barry Beck	New Westminster	D	615	104	251	355	1016
3	Wsh.	Robert Picard	Montreal	D	899	104	319	423	1025
4	Van.	Jere Gillis	Sherbrooke	LW	386	78	95	173	230
5	Cle.	Mike Crombeen	Kingston	RW	475	55	68	123	218
6	Chi.	Doug Wilson	Ottawa	D	1024	237	590	827	830
7	Min.	Brad Maxwell	New Westminster	D	612	98	270	368	1292
8	NYR	Lucien DeBlois	Sorel	C	993	249	276	525	814
9	St.L.	Scott Campbell	London	D	80	4	21	25	243
10	Mtl.	Mark Napier	Toronto	RW	767	235	306	541	157
11	Tor.	John Anderson	Toronto	RW	814	282	349	631	263
12	Tor.	Trevor Johansen	Toronto	D	286	11	46	57	282
13	NYR	Ron Duguay	Sudbury	C/RW	864	274	346	620	582
14	Buf.	Ric Seiling	St. Catharines	RW/C	738	179	208	387	573
15	NYI	Mike Bossy	Laval	RW	752	573	553	1126	210
16	Bos.	Dwight Foster	Kitchener	RW	541	111	163	274	420
17	Phi.	Kevin McCarthy	Winnipeg	D	537	67	191	258	527
18	Mtl.	Norm Dupont	Montreal	LW	256	55	85	140	52

SECOND ROUND

PICK	TEAM	NAME	DRAFTED FROM	POS	GP	G / W	A / GA	PTS / SO	PIM / AVG
19	Chi.	Jean Savard	Quebec	C	43	7	12	19	29
20	Atl.	Miles Zaharko	New Westminster	D	129	5	32	37	84
21	Wsh.	Mark Lofthouse	New Westminster	RW/C	181	42	38	80	73
22	Van.	Jeff Bandura	Portland	D	2	0	1	1	0
23	Cle.	Dan Chicoine	Sherbrooke	RW	31	1	2	3	12
24	Tor.	Bob Gladney	Oshawa	D	14	1	5	6	4
25	Min.	Dave Semenko	Brandon	LW	575	65	88	153	1175
26	NYR	Mike Keating	St. Catharines	LW	1	0	0	0	0
27	St.L.	Neil Labatte	Toronto	C/D	26	0	2	2	19
28	Atl.	Don Laurence	Kitchener	C	79	15	22	37	14
29	Tor.	Rocky Saganiuk	Lethbridge	RW/C	259	57	65	122	201
30	Pit.	Jim Hamilton	London	RW	95	14	18	32	28
31	Atl.	Brian Hill	Medicine Hat	RW	19	1	1	2	4
32	Buf.	Ron Areshenkoff	Medicine Hat	C	4	0	0	0	0
33	NYI	John Tonelli	Toronto	LW	1028	325	511	836	911
34	Bos.	Dave Parro	Saskatoon	G	77	4015	274	2	4.09
35	Phi.	Tom Gorence	U. of Minnesota	RW	303	58	53	111	89
36	Mtl.	Rod Langway	New Hampshire	D	994	51	278	329	849

OTHER ROUNDS

PICK	TEAM	NAME	DRAFTED FROM	POS	GP	G / W	A / GA	PTS / SO	PIM / AVG
37	Det.	Rick Vasko	Peterborough	D	31	3	7	10	29
38	Col.	Doug Berry	U. of Denver	C	121	10	33	43	25
39	Wsh.	Eddy Godin	Quebec	RW	27	3	6	9	12
40	Van.	Glen Hanlon	Brandon	G	477	26037	1561	13	3.60
41	Cle.	Reg Kerr	Kamloops	LW	263	66	94	160	169
42	Cle.	Guy Lash	Winnipeg	RW					
43	Mtl.	Alain Cote	Chicoutimi	LW	696	103	190	293	383
44	NYR	Steve Baker	Union College	G	57	3081	190	3	3.70
45	St.L.	Tom Roulston	Winnipeg	C/RW	195	47	49	96	74
46	Mtl.	Pierre Lagace	Quebec	LW					
47	Col.	Randy Pierce	Sudbury	RW	277	62	76	138	223
48	Pit.	Kim Davis	Flin Flon	C	36	5	7	12	51
49	Mtl.	Moe Robinson	Kingston	D	1	0	0	0	0
50	NYI	Hector Marini	Sudbury	RW	154	27	46	73	246
51	NYI	Bruce Andres	New Westminster	LW					
52	Bos.	Mike Forbes	St. Catharines	D	50	1	11	12	41
53	Phi.	Dave Hoyda	Portland	LW	132	6	17	23	299
54	Mtl.	Gordie Roberts	Victoria	D	1097	61	359	420	1582
55	Det.	John Hilworth	Medicine Hat	D	57	1	1	2	89

PICK	TEAM	NAME	DRAFTED FROM	NHL PLAYERS: POS / NHL GOALTENDERS: POS	GP / GP	G / W	A / GA	PTS / SO	PIM / AVG
56	Van.	Dave Morrow	Calgary	C/D					
57	Wsh.	Nelson Burton	Quebec	LW	8	1	0	1	21
58	Van.	Murray Bannerman	Victoria	G	289	16470	1051	8	3.83
59	Cle.	John Baby	Sudbury	D	26	2	8	10	26
60	Chi.	Randy Ireland	Portland	G	Re-entered Draft in 1978				
61	Min.	Kevin McCloskey	Calgary	D					
62	NYR	Mario Marois	Quebec	D	955	76	357	433	1746
63	St.L.	Tony Currie	Portland	RW	290	92	119	211	83
64	Mtl.	Robbie Holland	Montreal	G	44	2513	171	1	4.08
65	Tor.	Dan Eastman	London	C	Re-entered Draft in 1978				
66	Pit.	Mark Johnson	Wisconsin	C	669	203	305	508	260
67	Phi.	Yves Guillemette	Shawinigan	G					
68	Buf.	Bill Stewart	Niagara Falls	D	261	7	64	71	424
69	NYI	Steve Stoyanovich	RPI	C	23	3	5	8	11
70	Bos.	Brian McGregor	Saskatoon	RW					
71	Phi.	Rene Hamelin	Shawinigan	LW					
72	Atl.	Jim Craig	Boston U.	G	30	1588	100	0	3.78
73	Det.	Jim Korn	Providence	D/LW	597	66	122	188	1801
74	Col.	Mike Dwyer	Niagara Falls	LW	31	2	6	8	25
75	Wsh.	Denis Turcotte	Quebec	C					
76	Van.	Steve Hazlett	St. Catharines	LW	1	0	0	0	0
77	Cle.	Owen Lloyd	Medicine Hat	D					
78	Chi.	Gary Platt	Sorel	D					
79	Min.	Robert Parent	Kingston	D					
80	NYR	Benoit Gosselin	Trois-Rivieres	LW	7	0	0	0	33
81	St.L.	Bruce Hamilton	Saskatoon	LW					
82	Atl.	Kurt Christofferson	Colorado College	D					
83	Tor.	John Wilson	Windsor	LW					
84	L.A.	Julian Baretta	Wisconsin	G					
85	L.A.	Warren Holmes	Ottawa	C	45	8	18	26	7
86	Buf.	Richard Sirois	Laval	G	Re-entered Draft in 1978				
87	NYI	Markus Mattsson	Ilves Tampere	G	92	5007	343	6	4.11
88	Bos.	Douglas Butler	St. Louis U.	D					
89	Phi.	Dan Clark	Kamloops	D	Re-entered Draft in 1978				
90	Mtl.	Gaetan Rochette	Shawinigan	LW					
91	Det.	Jim Baxter	Union College	G					
92	Col.	Dan Lempe	Minnesota-Duluth	C					
93	Wsh.	Perry Schnarr	U. of Denver	RW					
94	Van.	Brian Drumm	Peterborough	LW					
95	Cle.	Jeff Allan	Hull	D	4	0	0	0	2
96	Chi.	Jack O'Callahan	Boston U.	D	389	27	104	131	541
97	Min.	Jamie Gallimore	Kamloops	RW	2	0	0	0	0
98	NYR	John Bethel	Boston U.	LW	17	0	2	2	4
99	St.L.	Gary McMonagle	Peterborough	C					
100	Atl.	Bernard Harbec	Laval	C					
101	Tor.	Roy Sommer	Calgary	LW/C	3	1	0	1	7
102	Pit.	Greg Millen	Peterborough	G	604	35377	2281	17	3.87
103	L.A.	Randy Rudnyk	New Westminster	RW					
104	Buf.	Wayne Ramsey	Brandon	D	2	0	0	0	0
105	NYI	Steve Letzgus	Michigan Tech	D					
106	Bos.	Keith Johnson	Saskatoon	D					
107	Phi.	Alain Chaput	Sorel	C					
108	Mtl.	Bill Himmelright	North Dakota	D					
109	Det.	Randy Wilson	Providence	LW					
110	Col.	Rick Doyle	London	LW					
111	Wsh.	Rollie Boutin	Lethbridge	G	22	1137	75	0	3.96
112	Van.	Ray Creasey	New Westminster	C					
113	Cle.	Mark Toffolo	Chicoutimi	D	Re-entered Draft in 1978				
114	Chi.	Floyd Lahache	Sherbrooke	RW					
115	Min.	Jean-Pierre Sanvido	Trois-Rivieres	G					
116	NYR	Bob Sullivan	Chicoutimi	LW	62	18	19	37	18
117	St.L.	Matti Forss	Lukko Rauma	C					
118	Atl.	Bobby Gould	New Hampshire	RW	697	145	159	304	572
119	Tor.	Lynn Jorgensen	Toronto	LW					
120	L.A.	Robert Suter	Wisconsin	D					
121	NYI	Harald Luckner	Farjestad Karlstad	C	Re-entered Draft in 1978				
122	Bos.	Ralph Cox	New Hampshire	RW					
123	Phi.	Richard Dalpe	Trois-Rivieres	C					
124	Mtl.	Richard Sevigny	Sherbrooke	G	176	9485	507	5	3.21
125	Det.	Raymond Roy	Sherbrooke	C					
126	Col.	Joe Contini	St. Catharines	C	68	17	21	38	34
127	Wsh.	Brent Tremblay	Trois-Rivieres	D	10	1	0	1	6
128	Cle.	Grant Eakin	Lethbridge	LW					
129	Chi.	Jeff Geiger	Ottawa	D					
130	Min.	Greg Tebbutt	Victoria	D	26	0	3	3	35
131	NYR	Lance Nethery	Cornell	C	41	11	14	25	14

PICK	TEAM	NAME	DRAFTED FROM	NHL PLAYERS: POS / NHL GOALTENDERS: POS	GP / GP	G / W	A / GA	PTS / SO	PIM / AVG
132	St.L.	Raimo Hirvonen	HIFK Helsinki	C					
133	Atl.	Jim Bennett	Brown	LW					
134	Tor.	Kevin Howe	Sault Ste. Marie	C/D					
135	Phi.	Pete Peeters	Medicine Hat	G	489	27699	1424	21	3.08
136	Phi.	Clint Eccles	Kamloops	LW					
137	Mtl.	Keith Hendrickson	U. of Minnesota	D					
138	Bos.	Mario Claude	Sherbrooke	D					
139	Phi.	Mike Greeder	St. Paul Jr. A	D					
140	Mtl.	Mike Reilly	Colorado College	RW					
141	Det.	Kip Churchill	Union College	C					
142	Col.	Jack Hughes	Harvard	D	46	2	5	7	104
143	Wsh.	Don Michiletti	U. of Minnesota	LW					
144	Chi.	Stephen Ough	Laval	D					
145	Min.	Keith Hanson	Austin Prep (H.S.)	D	25	0	2	2	77
146	NYR	Alex Jeans	U. of Toronto	RW					
147	St.L.	Bjorn Olsson	Farjestad Karlstad	D					
148	Atl.	Tim Harrer	U. of Minnesota	RW	3	0	0	0	2
149	Tor.	Ray Robertson	St. Lawrence U.	D					
150	Phi.	Tom Bauer	Providence	LW					
151	Phi.	Mike Bauman	Hull	LW					
152	Mtl.	Barry Borrett	Cornwall	G					
153	Phi.	Bruce Crowder	New Hampshire	RW	243	47	51	98	156
154	Mtl.	Sid Tanchak	Clarkson	C					
155	Det.	Lance Gatoni	U. of Toronto	D					
156	Wsh.	Archie Henderson	Victoria	RW	23	3	1	4	92
157	NYR	Peter Raps	Western Michigan	LW					
158	Phi.	Rob Nicholson	St. Paul Jr. A	D					
159	Phi.	Dave Isherwood	Winnipeg	C					
160	Mtl.	Mark Holden	Brown	G	8	372	25	0	4.03
161	Phi.	Steve Jones	Ohio State	G					
162	Mtl.	Craig Laughlin	Clarkson	RW	549	136	205	341	364
163	Det.	Rob Plumb	Kingston	LW	14	3	2	5	2
164	NYR	Mike Brown	Western Michigan	RW					
165	Phi.	Jim Trainor	Harvard	D					
166	Phi.	Daniel Duench	Kitchener	D					
167	Mtl.	Daniel Poulin	Chicoutimi	D	3	1	1	2	2
168	Phi.	Rod McNair	Ohio State	D					
169	Mtl.	Tom McDonnell	Ottawa	C					
170	Det.	Alain Belanger	Trois-Rivieres	RW					
171	NYR	Mark Miller	Michigan	LW					
172	Phi.	Mike Laycock	Brown	G					
173	Mtl.	Gary Farelli	Toronto	C/RW					
174	Mtl.	Carey Walker	New Westminster	G					
175	Det.	Dean Willers	Union College	C					
176	Mtl.	Mark Wells	Bowling Green	C					
177	Mtl.	Stan Palmer	U. of Minnesota	D					
178	Det.	Roland Cloutier	Trois-Rivieres	C	34	8	9	17	2
179	Mtl.	Jean Belisle	Chicoutimi	G					
180	Mtl.	Bob Daly	Ottawa	G					
181	Det.	Edward Hill	Vermont	RW					
182	Mtl.	Bob Boileau	Boston U.	RW					
183	Mtl.	John Costello	Lowell Tech College	C					
184	Det.	Val James	Quebec	LW	11	0	0	0	30
185	Det.	Grant Morin	Calgary	RW					

1978

FIRST ROUND

PICK	TEAM	NAME	DRAFTED FROM	POS	GP	G	A	PTS	PIM
1	Min.	Bobby Smith	Ottawa	C	1077	357	679	1036	917
2	Wsh.	Ryan Walter	Seattle	C/LW	1003	264	382	646	946
3	St.L.	Wayne Babych	Portland	RW	519	192	246	438	498
4	Van.	Bill Derlago	Brandon	C	555	189	227	416	247
5	Col.	Mike Gillis	Kingston	LW	246	33	43	76	186
6	Phi.	Behn Wilson	Kingston	D	601	98	260	358	1480
7	Phi.	Ken Linseman	Kingston	C	860	256	551	807	1727
8	Mtl.	Danny Geoffrion	Cornwall	RW	111	20	32	52	99
9	Det.	Willie Huber	Hamilton	D	655	104	217	321	950
10	Chi.	Tim Higgins	Ottawa	RW	706	154	198	352	719
11	Atl.	Brad Marsh	London	D	1086	23	175	198	1241
12	Det.	Brent Peterson	Portland	C	620	72	141	213	484
13	Buf.	Larry Playfair	Portland	D	688	26	94	120	1812
14	Phi.	Danny Lucas	Sault Ste. Marie	RW	6	1	0	1	0
15	NYI	Steve Tambellini	Lethbridge	C	553	160	150	310	105
16	Bos.	Al Secord	Hamilton	LW	766	273	222	495	2093
17	Mtl.	Dave Hunter	Sudbury	LW	746	133	190	323	918
18	Wsh.	Tim Coulis	Hamilton	LW	47	4	5	9	138

PICK	TEAM	NAME	DRAFTED FROM	NHL PLAYERS: POS	GP	G	A	PTS	PIM
				NHL GOALTENDERS: POS	GP	W	GA	SO	AVG

SECOND ROUND

PICK	TEAM	NAME	DRAFTED FROM	POS	GP	G/W	A/GA	PTS/SO	PIM/AVG
19	Min.	Steve Payne	Ottawa	LW	613	228	238	466	435
20	Wsh.	Paul Mulvey	Portland	LW	225	30	51	81	613
21	Tor.	Joel Quenneville	Windsor	D	803	54	136	190	705
22	Van.	Curt Fraser	Victoria	LW	704	193	240	433	1306
23	Wsh.	Paul MacKinnon	Peterborough	D	147	5	23	28	91
24	Min.	Steve Christoff	Minnesota-Duluth	C	248	77	64	141	108
25	Pit.	Mike Meeker	Peterborough	RW	4	0	0	0	5
26	NYR	Don Maloney	Kitchener	LW	765	214	350	564	815
27	Col.	Merlin Malinowski	Medicine Hat	C	282	54	111	165	121
28	Det.	Glenn Hicks	Flin Flon	LW	108	6	12	18	127
29	Chi.	Doug Lecuyer	Portland	LW	126	11	31	42	178
30	Mtl.	Dale Yakiwchuk	Portland	C					
31	Det.	Al Jensen	Hamilton	G	179	9974	557	8	3.35
32	Buf.	Tony McKegney	Kingston	LW	912	320	319	639	517
33	Phi.	Mike Simurda	Kingston	RW					
34	NYI	Randy Johnston	Peterborough	D	4	0	0	0	4
35	Bos.	Graeme Nicolson	Cornwall	D	52	2	7	9	60
36	Mtl.	Ron Carter	Sherbrooke	RW	2	0	0	0	0

OTHER ROUNDS

PICK	TEAM	NAME	DRAFTED FROM	POS	GP	G/W	A/GA	PTS/SO	PIM/AVG
37	Phi.	Gord Salt	Michigan Tech	RW					
38	Wsh.	Glen Currie	Laval	C	326	39	79	118	100
39	St.L.	Steve Harrison	Toronto	D					
40	Van.	Stan Smyl	New Westminster	RW	896	262	411	673	1556
41	Col.	Paul Messier	U. of Denver	C	9	0	0	0	4
42	Mtl.	Richard David	Trois-Rivieres	LW	31	4	4	8	10
43	NYR	Ray Markham	Flin Flon	C	14	1	1	2	21
44	NYR	Dean Turner	Michigan	D	35	1	0	1	59
45	Wsh.	Jay Johnston	Hamilton	D	8	0	0	0	13
46	Chi.	Rick Paterson	Cornwall	C	430	50	43	93	136
47	Atl.	Tim Bernhardt	Cornwall	G	67	3748	267	0	4.27
48	Tor.	Mark Kirton	Peterborough	C	266	57	56	113	121
49	Buf.	Rob McClanahan	Minnesota-Duluth	C	224	38	63	101	126
50	Phi.	Glen Cochrane	Victoria	D	411	17	72	89	1556
51	NYI	Dwayne Lowdermilk	Seattle	D	2	0	1	1	2
52	Bos.	Brad Knelson	Lethbridge	D					
53	Det.	Doug Derkson	New Westminster	C					
54	Min.	Curt Giles	Minnesota-Duluth	D	895	43	199	242	733
55	Wsh.	Bengt-Ake Gustafsson	Farjestad Karlstad	RW	629	196	359	555	196
56	Van.	Harald Luckner	Farjestad Karlstad	C					
57	Van.	Brad Smith	Sudbury	RW	222	28	34	62	591
58	Col.	Dave Watson	Sault Ste. Marie	LW	18	0	1	1	10
59	NYR	Dave Silk	Boston U.	RW	249	54	59	113	271
60	NYR	Andre Dore	Quebec	D	257	14	81	95	261
61	Pit.	Shane Pearsall	Ottawa	LW					
62	Det.	Bjorn Skaare	Ottawa	C	1	0	0	0	0
63	Chi.	Brian Young	New Westminster	D	8	0	2	2	6
64	Atl.	Jim MacRae	London	LW					
65	Tor.	Bob Parent	Kitchener	G	3	160	15	0	5.63
66	Buf.	Mike Gazdic	Sudbury	D					
67	Phi.	Russ Wilderman	Seattle	C					
68	Bos.	George Buat	Seattle	RW					
69	Mtl.	Kevin Reeves	Montreal	C					
70	Min.	Roy Kerling	Cornell	LW					
71	Wsh.	Lou Franceschetti	Niagara Falls	RW	459	59	81	140	747
72	St.L.	Kevin Willison	Billings	D					
73	Col.	Tim Thomlison	Billings	G					
74	Col.	Rod Guimont	Lethbridge	RW					
75	Pit.	Rob Garner	Toronto	C	1	0	0	0	0
76	NYR	Mike McDougal	Port Huron IHL	RW	61	8	10	18	43
77	L.A.	Paul Mancini	Sault Ste. Marie	LW					
78	Det.	Ted Nolan	Sault Ste. Marie	C	78	6	16	22	105
79	Chi.	Mark Murphy	Toronto	LW					
80	Atl.	Gord Wappel	Regina	D	20	1	1	2	10
81	Tor.	Jordy Douglas	Flin Flon	LW	268	76	62	138	160
82	Buf.	Randy Ireland	Portland	G	2	30	3	0	6.00
83	Phi.	Brad Tamblyn	U. of Toronto	D					
84	NYI	Greg Hay	Michigan Tech	LW					
85	Bos.	Darryl MacLeod	Boston U.	LW					
86	Mtl.	Mike Boyd	Sault Ste. Marie	D					
87	Min.	Bob Bergloff	Minnesota-Duluth	D	2	0	0	0	5
88	Wsh.	Vince Magnan	U. of Denver	LW					
89	St.L.	Jim Nill	Medicine Hat	RW	524	58	87	145	854
90	Van.	Gerry Minor	Regina	C	140	11	21	32	173
91	Col.	John Hynes	Harvard	G					
92	Tor.	Mel Hewitt	Calgary	D/LW					
93	NYR	Tom Laidlaw	Northern Michigan	D	705	25	139	164	717
94	L.A.	Doug Keans	Ottawa	G	210	11388	666	4	3.51
95	Det.	Sylvain Locas	Sherbrooke	C					
96	Chi.	Dave Feamster	Colorado College	D	169	13	24	37	154
97	Atl.	Greg Meredith	U. of Notre Dame	RW	38	6	4	10	8
98	Tor.	Normand Lefebvre	Trois-Rivieres	RW					
99	Buf.	Cam MacGregor	Cornwall	LW					
100	Phi.	Mark Taylor	North Dakota	C	209	42	68	110	73
101	NYI	Kelly Davis	Flin Flon	LW/D					
102	Bos.	Jeff Brubaker	Peterborough	LW	178	16	9	25	512
103	Mtl.	Keith Acton	Peterborough	C	1023	226	358	584	1172
104	Min.	Kim Spencer	Victoria	D					
105	Wsh.	Mats Hallin	Sodertalje	LW	152	17	14	31	193
106	St.L.	Steve Stockman	Cornwall	C					
107	Van.	Dave Ross	Portland	W					
108	Col.	Andy Clark	Lake Superior State	D					
109	St.L.	Paul MacLean	Hull	RW	719	324	349	673	968
110	NYR	Dan Clark	Milwaukee (IHL)	D	4	0	1	1	6
111	L.A.	Don Waddell	Northern Michigan	D	1	0	0	0	0
112	Det.	Wes George	Saskatoon	LW					
113	Chi.	Dave Mancuso	Windsor	D					
114	Atl.	Dave Hindmarch	U. of Alberta	RW	99	21	17	38	25
115	Tor.	John Scammel	Lethbridge	D					
116	Buf.	Dan Eastman	Saginaw (IHL)	C					
117	Phi.	Mike Ewanouski	Boston College	RW					
118	NYI	Richard Pepin	Laval	RW					
119	Bos.	Murray Skinner	Lake Superior State	G					
120	Mtl.	Jim Lawson	Brown	RW					
121	Min.	Mike Cotter	Bowling Green	D					
122	Wsh.	Richard Sirois	Milwaukee (IHL)	G					
123	St.L.	Denis Houle	Hamilton	RW					
124	Van.	Steve O'Neill	Providence	LW					
125	Col.	John Olver	Michigan	RW/C					
126	Phi.	Jerry Price	Portland	G					
127	NYR	Greg Kostenko	Ohio State	D					
128	L.A.	Rob Mierkalns	Hamilton	C					
129	Det.	John Barrett	Windsor	D	488	20	77	97	604
130	Chi.	Sandy Ross	Colgate	D					
131	Atl.	Dave Morrison	Calgary	RW					
132	Tor.	Kevin Reinhart	Kitchener	D					
133	Buf.	Eric Strobel	Minnesota-Duluth	C					
134	Phi.	Darre Switzer	Medicine Hat	D					
135	NYI	Dave Cameron	University of PEI	C	168	25	28	53	238
136	Bos.	Richard Hehir	Boston College	C					
137	Mtl.	Larry Landon	RPI	RW	9	0	0	0	2
138	Min.	Brent Gogol	Billings	D					
139	Wsh.	Denis Pomerleau	Trois-Rivieres	RW					
140	St.L.	Tony Meagher	Boston U.	RW					
141	Van.	Charlie Antetomaso	Boston College	D					
142	Col.	Kevin Krook	Regina	D	3	0	0	0	2
143	St.L.	Rick Simpson	Medicine Hat	C/RW					
144	NYR	Brian McDavid	Kitchener	D					
145	L.A.	Ric Scully	Brown	LW					
146	Det.	Jim Malazdrewicz	St. Boniface Jr. A	LW					
147	Chi.	Mark Locken	Niagara Falls	G					
148	Atl.	Doug Todd	Michigan	RW					
149	Tor.	Mike Waghorne	New Hampshire	D					
150	Buf.	Eugene O'Sullivan	Calgary	C					
151	Phi.	Greg Francis	St. Lawrence U.	D					
152	NYI	Paul Joswiak	Minnesota-Duluth	G					
153	Bos.	Craig MacTavish	University of Lowell	C	1093	213	267	480	891
154	Mtl.	Kevin Constantine	RPI	G					
155	Min.	Mark Seide	Bloomington Jr.	LW/D					
156	Wsh.	Barry Heard	London	G					
157	St.L.	Jim Lockhurst	Kingston	G					
158	Van.	Richard Martens	New Westminster	G					
159	Col.	Jeff Jensen	Lake Superior State	LW					
160	St.L.	Bob Froese	Niagara Falls	G	242	13451	694	13	3.10
161	NYR	Mark Rodrigues	Yale	G					
162	L.A.	Brad Thiessen	Toronto	C					
163	Det.	Geoff Shaw	Hamilton	RW					
164	Chi.	Glenn Van	Colorado College	D					
165	Atl.	Mark Green	Sherbrooke	C					
166	Tor.	Laurie Cuvelier	St. Francis Xavier	D					

PICK	TEAM	NAME	DRAFTED FROM	NHL PLAYERS: POS / NHL GOALTENDERS: POS	GP / GP	G / W	A / GA	PTS / SO	PIM / AVG
167	Phi.	Rick Berard	St. Mary's U.	LW/Defens					
168	Phi.	Don Lucia	U. of Notre Dame	D					
169	NYI	Scott Cameron	U. of Notre Dame	D					
170	St.L.	Dan Lerg	Michigan	C					
171	Mtl.	John Swan	McGill University	C					
172	Wsh.	Mark Toffolo	Port Huron (IHL)	D					
173	St.L.	Risto Siltanen	Ilves Tampere	D	562	90	265	355	266
174	Col.	Bo Ericson	AIK Solna	D					
175	St.L.	Dan Hermansson	Karlskoga	LW					
176	NYR	Steve Weeks	Northern Michigan	G	290	15879	989	5	3.74
177	L.A.	Jim Armstrong	Clarkson	LW/C					
178	Det.	Carl Van Harrewyn	New Westminster	D/RW					
179	Chi.	Darryl Sutter	Lethbridge	LW	406	161	118	279	288
180	Atl.	Robert Sullivan	New Haven/Toledo (IHL)	C/LW					
181	St.L.	Jean-Francois Boutin	Verdun	LW					
182	Phi.	Mark Berge	North Dakota	D					
183	Phi.	Ken Moore	Clarkson	G					
184	NYI	Christer Lowdahl	Oreboro	C/LW					
185	St.L.	John Sullivan	Providence	RW					
186	Mtl.	Daniel Metivier	Hull	RW					
187	Wsh.	Paul Hogan	Regina	LW					
188	St.L.	Serge Menard	Montreal	RW					
189	Wsh.	Steve Barger	Boston College	RW					
190	Col.	Jari Viitala	Ilves Tampere	C/LW					
191	St.L.	Don Boyd	RPI	D/C					
192	NYR	Pierre Daigneault	St. Laurent College	LW					
193	L.A.	Claude Larochelle	Hull	C					
194	Det.	Ladislav Svozil	TJ Vitkovice	LW					
195	Phi.	Jim Olson	St. Paul Jr. A	C					
196	Atl.	Bernhard Englbrecht	Landshut, FRG	G					
197	St.L.	Paul Stasiuk	Providence	LW					
198	Phi.	Anton Stastny	Slovan Bratislava	LW	Re-entered Draft in 1979				
199	NYI	Gunnar Persson	Brynas Gavle	D					
200	St.L.	Gerd Truntschka	Landshut, FRG	C/LW					
201	Mtl.	Viacheslav Fetisov	CSKA	D	Re-entered Draft in 1983				
202	Wsh.	Rod Pacholzuk	Michigan	D					
203	St.L.	Viktor Shkurdyuk	SKA Leningrad	RW					
204	Col.	Ulf Zetterstrom	Kiruna	LW					
205	St.L.	Carl Bloomberg	St. Louis U.	G					
206	NYR	Chris McLaughlin	Dartmouth	D					
207	St.L.	Terry Kitching	St. Louis U.	LW					
208	Det.	Tom Bailey	Kingston	RW					
209	St.L.	Brian O'Connor	Boston U.	D					
210	St.L.	Brian Crombeen	Kingston	D					
211	St.L.	Mike Pidgeon	Oshawa	C					
212	Mtl.	Jeff Mars	Michigan	RW					
213	Wsh.	Wes Jarvis	Windsor	C	237	31	55	86	98
214	St.L.	John Cochrane	Harvard	RW					
215	Wsh.	Ray Irwin	Oshawa	D					
216	St.L.	Joe Casey	Boston College	D					
217	NYR	Todd Johnson	Boston U.	C					
218	St.L.	Jim Farrell	Princeton	C					
219	Det.	Larry Lozinski	Flin Flon	G	30	1459	105	0	4.32
220	St.L.	Frank Johnson	Providence	D					
221	St.L.	Blair Wheeler	Yale	D					
222	Mtl.	Greg Tiganelli	Northern Michigan	LW					
223	NYR	Dan McCarthy	Sudbury	C	5	4	0	4	4
224	Det.	Randy Betty	New Westminster	LW					
225	Mtl.	George Goulakos	St. Lawrence U.	LW					
226	Det.	Brian Crawley	St. Lawrence U.	D					
227	Mtl.	Ken Moodie	Colgate	RW					
228	Det.	Doug Feasby	Toronto	C					
229	Mtl.	Serge Leblanc	Vermont	D					
230	Mtl.	Bob Magnuson	Merrimack	C					
231	Mtl.	Chris Nilan	Northeastern	RW	688	110	115	225	3043
232	Mtl.	Rick Wilson	St. Lawrence U.	G					
233	Mtl.	Louis Sleigher	Chicoutimi	RW	194	46	53	99	146
234	Mtl.	Doug Robb	Billings	RW					

1979

FIRST ROUND

PICK	TEAM	NAME	DRAFTED FROM	POS	GP	G / W	A / GA	PTS / SO	PIM / AVG
1	Col.	Rob Ramage	London	D	1044	139	425	564	2226
2	St.L.	Perry Turnbull	Portland	C	608	188	163	351	1245
3	Det.	Mike Foligno	Sudbury	RW	1018	355	372	727	2049
4	Wsh.	Mike Gartner	Niagara Falls	RW	1432	708	627	1335	1159
5	Van.	Rick Vaive	Sherbrooke	RW	876	441	347	788	1445
6	Min.	Craig Hartsburg	Sault Ste. Marie	D	570	98	315	413	818
7	Chi.	Keith Brown	Portland	D	876	68	274	342	916
8	Bos.	Raymond Bourque	Verdun	D	1612	410	1169	1579	1141
9	Tor.	Laurie Boschman	Brandon	C	1009	229	348	577	2265
10	Min.	Tom McCarthy	Oshawa	LW	460	178	221	399	330
11	Buf.	Mike Ramsey	Minnesota-Duluth	D	1070	79	266	345	1012
12	Atl.	Paul Reinhart	Kitchener	D	648	133	426	559	277
13	NYR	Doug Sulliman	Kitchener	RW	631	160	168	328	175
14	Phi.	Brian Propp	Brandon	LW	1016	425	579	1004	830
15	Bos.	Brad McCrimmon	Brandon	D	1222	81	322	403	1416
16	L.A.	Jay Wells	Kingston	D	1098	47	216	263	2359
17	NYI	Duane Sutter	Lethbridge	RW	731	139	203	342	1333
18	Hfd.	Ray Allison	Brandon	RW	238	64	93	157	223
19	Wpg.	Jimmy Mann	Sherbrooke	RW	293	10	20	30	895
20	Que.	Michel Goulet	Quebec	LW	1089	548	604	1152	825
21	Edm.	Kevin Lowe	Quebec	D	1254	84	347	431	1498

SECOND ROUND

PICK	TEAM	NAME	DRAFTED FROM	POS	GP	G / W	A / GA	PTS / SO	PIM / AVG
22	Phi.	Blake Wesley	Portland	D	298	18	46	64	486
23	Atl.	Mike Perovich	Brandon	D					
24	Wsh.	Errol Rausse	Seattle	LW	31	7	3	10	0
25	NYI	Tomas Jonsson	MoDo Ornskoldsvik	D	552	85	259	344	482
26	Van.	Brent Ashton	Saskatoon	LW	998	284	345	629	635
27	Mtl.	Gaston Gingras	Hamilton	D	476	61	174	235	161
28	Chi.	Tim Trimper	Peterborough	LW	190	30	36	66	153
29	L.A.	Dean Hopkins	London	RW	223	23	51	74	306
30	L.A.	Mark Hardy	Montreal	D	915	62	306	368	1293
31	Pit.	Paul Marshall	Brantford	LW	95	15	18	33	17
32	Buf.	Lindy Ruff	Lethbridge	D/LW	691	105	195	300	1264
33	Atl.	Pat Riggin	London	G	350	19872	1135	11	3.43
34	NYR	Ed Hospodar	Ottawa	D	450	17	51	68	1314
35	Phi.	Pelle Lindbergh	AIK Solna	G	157	9150	503	7	3.30
36	Bos.	Doug Morrison	Lethbridge	RW	23	7	3	10	15
37	Mtl.	Mats Naslund	Brynas Gavle	LW	651	251	383	634	111
38	NYI	Billy Carroll	London	C	322	30	54	84	113
39	Hfd.	Stu Smith	Peterborough	D	77	2	10	12	95
40	Wpg.	Dave Christian	North Dakota	RW	1009	340	433	773	284
41	Que.	Dale Hunter	Sudbury	C	1407	323	697	1020	3565
42	Min.	Neal Broten	Minnesota-Duluth	C	1099	289	634	923	569

OTHER ROUNDS

PICK	TEAM	NAME	DRAFTED FROM	POS	GP	G / W	A / GA	PTS / SO	PIM / AVG
43	Mtl.	Craig Levie	Edmonton	D	183	22	53	75	177
44	Mtl.	Guy Carbonneau	Chicoutimi	C	1318	260	403	663	820
45	Det.	Jody Gage	Kitchener	RW	68	14	15	29	26
46	Det.	Boris Fistric	New Westminster	D					
47	Van.	Ken Ellacott	Peterborough	G	12	555	41	0	4.43
48	Edm.	Mark Messier	St. Albert Jr. A	C	1680	676	1168	1844	1868
49	Chi.	Bill Gardner	Peterborough	C	380	73	115	188	68
50	L.A.	John Paul Kelly	New Westminster	LW	400	54	70	124	366
51	Tor.	Norm Aubin	Verdun	C	69	18	13	31	30
52	Pit.	Bennett Wolf	Kitchener	D	30	0	1	1	133
53	Buf.	Mark Robinson	Victoria	D					
54	Atl.	Tim Hunter	Seattle	RW	815	62	76	138	3146
55	Buf.	Jacques Cloutier	Trois-Rivieres	G	255	12826	778	3	3.64
56	Phi.	Lindsay Carson	Billings	C	373	66	80	146	524
57	Bos.	Keith Crowder	Peterborough	RW	662	223	271	494	1354
58	Mtl.	Rick Wamsley	Brantford	G	407	23123	1287	12	3.34
59	NYI	Roland Melanson	Windsor	G	291	16452	995	6	3.63
60	Hfd.	Don Nachbaur	Billings	C	223	23	46	69	465
61	Wpg.	Bill Whelton	North Dakota	D	2	0	0	0	0
62	Que.	Lee Norwood	Oshawa	D	503	58	153	211	1099
63	Min.	Kevin Maxwell	North Dakota	C	66	6	15	21	61
64	Col.	Steve Peters	Oshawa	C	2	0	1	1	0
65	St.L.	Bob Crawford	Cornwall	RW	246	71	71	142	72
66	Det.	John Ogrodnick	New Westminster	LW	928	402	425	827	260
67	Wsh.	Harvie Pocza	Billings	LW	3	0	0	0	2
68	Van.	Art Rutland	Sault Ste. Marie	C					
69	Edm.	Glenn Anderson	U. of Denver	RW	1129	498	601	1099	1120
70	Chi.	Lou Begin	Sherbrooke	LW					
71	L.A.	John Gibson	Niagara Falls	D	48	0	2	2	120
72	Tor.	Vincent Tremblay	Quebec	G	58	2785	223	1	4.80
73	Pit.	Brian Cross	Brantford	D					
74	Buf.	Gilles Hamel	Laval	LW	519	127	147	274	276
75	Atl.	Jim Peplinski	Toronto	RW	711	161	263	424	1467
76	NYR	Pat Conacher	Saskatoon	LW	521	63	76	139	235

PICK	TEAM	NAME	DRAFTED FROM	NHL PLAYERS: POS / NHL GOALTENDERS: POS	GP / GP	G / W	A / GA	PTS / SO	PIM / AVG
77	Phi.	Don Gillen	Brandon	RW	35	2	4	6	22
78	Bos.	Larry Melnyk	New Westminster	D	432	11	63	74	686
79	Mtl.	Dave Orleski	New Westminster	LW	2	0	0	0	0
80	NYI	Tim Lockridge	Brandon	D					
81	Hfd.	Ray Neufeld	Edmonton	RW	595	157	200	357	816
82	Wpg.	Pat Daley	Montreal	LW	12	1	0	1	13
83	Que.	Anton Stastny	Slovan Bratislava	LW	650	252	384	636	150
84	Edm.	Maxwell Kostovich	Portland	LW					
85	Col.	Gary Dillon	Toronto	C	13	1	1	2	29
86	St.L.	Mark Reeds	Peterborough	RW	365	45	114	159	135
87	Det.	Joe Paterson	London	LW	291	19	37	56	829
88	Wsh.	Tim Tookey	Portland	C	106	22	36	58	71
89	Van.	Dirk Graham	Regina	Right/LW	772	219	270	489	917
90	Min.	Jim Dobson	Portland	RW	12	0	0	0	6
91	Chi.	Lowell Loveday	Kingston	D					
92	L.A.	Jim Brown	U. of Notre Dame	D	3	0	1	1	5
93	Tor.	Frank Nigro	London	C	68	8	18	26	39
94	Pit.	Nick Ricci	Niagara Falls	G	19	1087	79	0	4.36
95	Buf.	Alan Haworth	Sherbrooke	C	524	189	211	400	425
96	Atl.	Brad Kempthorne	Brandon	C/RW					
97	NYR	Dan Makuch	Clarkson	RW					
98	Phi.	Thomas Eriksson	Djurgarden	D	208	22	76	98	107
99	Bos.	Marco Baron	Montreal	G	86	4822	292	1	3.63
100	Mtl.	Yvan Joly	Ottawa	RW	2	0	0	0	0
101	NYI	Glenn Duncan	Toronto	LW					
102	Hfd.	Mark Renaud	Niagara Falls	D	152	6	50	56	86
103	Wpg.	Thomas Steen	Leksand	C	950	264	553	817	753
104	Que.	Pierre Lacroix	Trois-Rivieres	D	274	24	108	132	197
105	Edm.	Mike Toal	Portland	C	3	0	0	0	0
106	Col.	Bob Attwell	Peterborough	RW	22	1	5	6	0
107	St.L.	Gilles Leduc	Verdun	LW					
108	Det.	Carmine Cirella	Peterborough	LW					
109	Wsh.	Greg Theberge	Peterborough	D	153	15	63	78	73
110	Van.	Shane Swan	Sudbury	D					
111	Min.	Brian Gualazzi	Sault Ste. Marie	D					
112	Chi.	Doug Crossman	Ottawa	D	914	105	359	464	534
113	L.A.	Jay MacFarlane	Wisconsin	D					
114	Tor.	Bill McCreary Jr.	Colgate	RW	12	1	0	1	4
115	Pit.	Marc Chorney	North Dakota	D	210	8	27	35	209
116	Buf.	Rick Knickle	Brandon	G	14	706	44	0	3.74
117	Atl.	Glenn Johnson	U. of Denver	C					
118	NYR	Stan Adams	Niagara Falls	C					
119	Phi.	Gord Williams	Lethbridge	RW	2	0	0	0	2
120	Bos.	Mike Krushelnyski	Montreal	LW/C	897	241	328	569	699
121	Mtl.	Greg Moffett	New Hampshire	LW					
122	NYI	John Gibb	Bowling Green	D					
123	Hfd.	Dave McDonald	Brandon	LW					
124	Wpg.	Tim Watters	Michigan Tech	D	741	26	151	177	1289
125	Que.	Scott McGeown	Toronto	D					
126	Edm.	Blair Barnes	Windsor	RW	1	0	0	0	0

1980

FIRST ROUND

PICK	TEAM	NAME	DRAFTED FROM	POS	GP	G / W	A / GA	PTS / SO	PIM / AVG
1	Mtl.	Doug Wickenheiser	Regina	C	556	111	165	276	286
2	Wpg.	Dave Babych	Portland	D	1195	142	581	723	970
3	Chi.	Denis Savard	Montreal	C	1196	473	865	1338	1336
4	L.A.	Larry Murphy	Peterborough	D	1615	287	929	1216	1084
5	Wsh.	Darren Veitch	Regina	D	511	48	209	257	296
6	Edm.	Paul Coffey	Kitchener	D	1409	396	1135	1531	1802
7	Van.	Rick Lanz	Oshawa	D	569	65	221	286	448
8	Hfd.	Fred Arthur	Cornwall	D	80	1	8	9	49
9	Pit.	Mike Bullard	Brantford	C	727	329	345	674	703
10	L.A.	Jim Fox	Ottawa	RW	578	186	293	479	143
11	Det.	Mike Blaisdell	Regina	RW	343	70	84	154	166
12	St.L.	Rik Wilson	Kingston	D	251	25	65	90	220
13	Cgy.	Denis Cyr	Montreal	RW	193	41	43	84	36
14	NYR	Jim Malone	Toronto	C					
15	Chi.	Jerome Dupont	Toronto	D	214	7	29	36	468
16	Min.	Brad Palmer	Victoria	LW	168	32	38	70	58
17	NYI	Brent Sutter	Red Deer Jr. A	C	1111	363	466	829	1054
18	Bos.	Barry Pederson	Victoria	C	701	238	416	654	472
19	Col.	Paul Gagne	Windsor	LW	390	110	101	211	127
20	Buf.	Steve Patrick	Brandon	RW	250	40	68	108	242
21	Phi.	Mike Stothers	Kingston	D	30	0	2	2	65

SECOND ROUND

PICK	TEAM	NAME	DRAFTED FROM	POS	GP	G / W	A / GA	PTS / SO	PIM / AVG
22	Col.	Joe Ward	Seattle	C	4	0	0	0	2
23	Wpg.	Moe Mantha	Toronto	D	656	81	289	370	501
24	Que.	Normand Rochefort	Quebec (QMJHL)	D	598	39	119	158	570
25	Tor.	Craig Muni	Kingston	D	819	28	119	147	775
26	Tor.	Bob McGill	Victoria	D	705	17	55	72	1766
27	Mtl.	Ric Nattress	Brantford	D	536	29	135	164	377
28	Chi.	Steve Ludzik	Niagara Falls	C	424	46	93	139	333
29	Hfd.	Michel Galarneau	Hull	C	78	7	10	17	34
30	Chi.	Ken Solheim	Medicine Hat	LW	135	19	20	39	34
31	Cgy.	Tony Curtale	Brantford	D	2	0	0	0	0
32	Cgy.	Kevin LaVallee	Brantford	LW	366	110	125	235	85
33	L.A.	Greg Terrion	Brantford	LW	561	93	150	243	339
34	L.A.	Dave Morrison	Peterborough	RW	39	3	3	6	4
35	NYR	Mike Allison	Sudbury	LW	499	102	166	268	630
36	Chi.	Len Dawes	Victoria	D					
37	Min.	Don Beaupre	Sudbury	G	667	37396	2151	17	3.45
38	NYI	Kelly Hrudey	Medicine Hat	G	677	38084	2174	17	3.43
39	Cgy.	Steve Konroyd	Oshawa	D	895	41	195	236	863
40	Mtl.	John Chabot	Hull	C	508	84	228	312	85
41	Buf.	Mike Moller	Lethbridge	RW	134	15	28	43	41
42	Phi.	Jay Fraser	Ottawa	LW					

OTHER ROUNDS

PICK	TEAM	NAME	DRAFTED FROM	POS	GP	G / W	A / GA	PTS / SO	PIM / AVG
43	Tor.	Fred Boimistruck	Cornwall	D	83	4	14	18	45
44	Wpg.	Murray Eaves	Michigan	C	57	4	13	17	9
45	Mtl.	John Newberry	Nanaimo (BCJHL)	C	22	0	4	4	6
46	Det.	Mark Osborne	Niagara Falls	LW	919	212	319	531	1152
47	Wsh.	Don Miele	Providence	RW					
48	Edm.	Shawn Babcock	Windsor	RW					
49	Van.	Andy Schliebener	Peterborough	D	84	2	11	13	74
50	Hfd.	Mickey Volcan	North Dakota	D	162	8	33	41	146
51	Pit.	Randy Boyd	Ottawa	D	257	20	67	87	328
52	L.A.	Steve Bozek	Northern Michigan	LW	641	164	167	331	309
53	Min.	Randy Velischek	Providence	D	509	21	76	97	401
54	St.L.	Jim Pavese	Kitchener	D	328	13	44	57	689
55	Wsh.	Torrie Robertson	Victoria	LW	442	49	99	148	1751
56	Buf.	Sean McKenna	Sherbrooke	RW	414	82	80	162	181
57	Chi.	Troy Murray	St. Albert Jr. A	C	915	230	354	584	875
58	Chi.	Marcel Frere	Billings	LW					
59	NYI	Dave Simpson	London	C					
60	Bos.	Tom Fergus	Peterborough	C	726	235	346	581	499
61	Mtl.	Craig Ludwig	U. of North dakota (WCHA)	D	1256	38	184	222	1437
62	Buf.	Jay North	Bloomington-Jefferson H.S.	C					
63	Phi.	Paul Mercier	Sudbury	D					
64	Col.	Rick LaFerriere	Peterborough	G	1	20	1	0	3.00
65	Wpg.	Guy Fournier	Shawinigan	C					
66	Que.	Jay Miller	New Hampshire	LW	446	40	44	84	1723
67	Chi.	Carey Wilson	Dartmouth	C	552	169	258	427	314
68	NYI	Monty Trottier	Billings	C					
69	Edm.	Jari Kurri	Jokerit Helsinki	RW	1251	601	797	1398	545
70	Van.	Marc Crawford	Cornwall	LW	176	19	31	50	229
71	Hfd.	Kevin McClelland	Niagara Falls	RW	588	68	112	180	1672
72	Pit.	Tony Feltrin	Victoria	D	48	3	3	6	65
73	L.A.	Bernie Nicholls	Kingston	C	1127	475	734	1209	1292
74	Tor.	Stew Gavin	Toronto	LW	768	130	155	285	584
75	St.L.	Bob Brooke	Yale	C	447	69	97	166	520
76	Cgy.	Marc Roy	Trois-Rivieres	RW					
77	NYR	Kurt Kleinendorst	Providence	C					
78	Chi.	Brian Shaw	Portland	RW					
79	Min.	Mark Huglen	Roseau H.S.	D					
80	NYI	Greg Gilbert	Toronto	LW	837	150	228	378	576
81	Bos.	Steve Kasper	Verdun	C	821	177	291	468	554
82	Mtl.	Jeff Teal	U. of Minnesota	RW	6	0	1	1	0
83	Buf.	Jim Wiemer	Peterborough	D	325	29	72	101	378
84	Phi.	Taras Zytynsky	Montreal	D					
85	Col.	Ed Cooper	Portland	LW	49	8	7	15	46
86	Wpg.	Glen Ostir	Portland	D					
87	Que.	Basil McRae	London	LW	576	53	83	136	2457
88	Det.	Mike Corrigan	Cornwall	RW					
89	Wsh.	Timo Blomqvist	Jokerit Helsinki	D	243	4	53	57	293
90	Edm.	Walt Poddubny	Kingston	LW	468	184	238	422	454
91	Van.	Darrell May	Portland	G	6	364	31	0	5.11
92	Hfd.	Darren Jensen	North Dakota	G	30	1496	95	2	3.81
93	Pit.	Doug Shedden	Sault Ste. Marie	C	416	139	186	325	176
94	L.A.	Alan Graves	Seattle	LW					

PICK	TEAM	NAME	DRAFTED FROM	NHL PLAYERS: POS / NHL GOALTENDERS: POS	GP / GP	G / W	A / GA	PTS / SO	PIM / AVG
95	Tor.	Hugh Larkin	Sault Ste. Marie	RW					
96	St.L.	Alain Lemieux	Chicoutimi	C	119	28	44	72	38
97	Cgy.	Randy Turnbull	Portland	D	1	0	0	0	2
98	NYR	Scot Kleinendorst	Providence	D	281	12	46	58	452
99	Chi.	Kevin Ginnell	Medicine Hat	C					
100	Min.	David Jensen	Minnesota-Duluth	D	18	0	2	2	11
101	NYI	Ken Leiter	Michigan State	D	143	14	36	50	62
102	Bos.	Randy Hillier	Sudbury	D	543	16	110	126	906
103	Mtl.	Remi Gagne	Chicoutimi	RW					
104	Buf.	Dirk Rueter	Sault Ste. Marie	D					
105	Phi.	Dan Held	Seattle	C					
106	Col.	Aaron Broten	Minnesota-Duluth	LW/C	748	186	329	515	441
107	Wpg.	Ron Loustel	Saskatoon	G	1	60	10	0	10.00
108	Que.	Mark Kumpel	University of Lowell	RW	288	38	46	84	113
109	Det.	Wayne Crawford	Toronto	C					
110	Wsh.	Todd Bidner	Toronto	LW	12	2	1	3	7
111	Edm.	Mike Winther	Brandon	C					
112	Van.	Ken Berry	Canadian Olympic	LW	55	8	10	18	30
113	Hfd.	Mario Cerri	Ottawa	C					
114	Pit.	Pat Graham	Niagara Falls	LW	103	11	17	28	136
115	L.A.	Darren Eliot	Cornell	G	89	4931	377	1	4.59
116	Tor.	Ron Dennis	Princeton	G					
117	St.L.	Perry Anderson	Brantford	LW	400	50	59	109	1051
118	Cgy.	John Multan	Portland	RW					
119	NYR	Reijo Ruotsalainen	Karpat Oulu	D	446	107	237	344	180
120	Chi.	Steve Larmer	Niagara Falls	RW	1006	441	571	1012	532
121	Min.	Dan Zavarise	Cornwall	D					
122	NYI	Dan Revell	Oshawa	RW					
123	Bos.	Steve Lyons	Matignon H.S.	LW					
124	Mtl.	Mike McPhee	RPI	LW	744	200	199	399	661
125	Buf.	Daniel Naud	Verdun	D					
126	Phi.	Brian Tutt	Calgary	D	7	1	0	1	2
127	Col.	Dan Fascinato	Ottawa	D					
128	Wpg.	Brian Mullen	U.S. Jr. National Team	RW	832	260	362	622	414
129	Que.	Gaston Therrien	Quebec	D	22	0	8	8	12
130	Det.	Mike Braun	Niagara Falls	D					
131	Wsh.	Frank Perkins	Sudbury	RW					
132	Edm.	Andy Moog	Billings	G	713	40151	2097	28	3.13
133	Van.	Doug Lidster	Colorado College	D	897	75	268	343	679
134	Hfd.	Mike Martin	Sudbury	D					
135	Wpg.	Mike Lauen	Michigan Tech	RW	4	0	1	1	0
136	L.A.	Mike O'Connor	Michigan Tech	D					
137	Tor.	Russ Adam	Kitchener	C	8	1	2	3	11
138	St.L.	Roger Hagglund	Bjorkloven Umea	D	3	0	0	0	0
139	Cgy.	Dave Newsom	Brantford	LW					
140	NYR	Bob Scurfield	Western Michigan	C					
141	Chi.	Sean Simpson	Ottawa	C					
142	Min.	Bill Stewart	U. of Denver	RW					
143	NYI	Mark Hamway	Michigan State	RW	53	5	13	18	9
144	Bos.	Tony McMurchy	New Westminster	C					
145	Mtl.	Bill Norton	Clarkson	LW					
146	Buf.	Jari Paavola	TPS Turku	G					
147	Phi.	Ross Fitzpatrick	Western Michigan	C	20	5	2	7	0
148	Col.	Andre Hidi	Peterborough	LW	7	2	1	3	9
149	Wpg.	Sandy Beadle	Northeastern	LW	6	1	0	1	2
150	Que.	Michel Bolduc	Chicoutimi	D	10	0	0	0	6
151	Det.	John Beukeboom	Peterborough	D					
152	Wsh.	Bruce Raboin	Providence	D					
153	Edm.	Rob Polman Tuin	Michigan Tech	G					
154	Van.	John O'Connor	Vermont	D					
155	Hfd.	Brent Denat	Michigan Tech	LW					
156	Pit.	Bob Geale	Portland	C	1	0	0	0	2
157	L.A.	Bill O'Dwyer	Boston College	C	120	9	13	22	108
158	Tor.	Fred Perlini	Toronto	C	8	2	3	5	0
159	St.L.	Pat Rabbit	Billings	LW					
160	Cgy.	Claude Drouin	Quebec	C					
161	NYR	Bart Wilson	Toronto	D					
162	Chi.	Jim Ralph	Ottawa	G					
163	Min.	Jeff Walters	Peterborough	RW					
164	NYI	Morrison Gare	Penticton Jr. A	RW					
165	Bos.	Mike Moffat	Kingston	G	19	979	70	0	4.29
166	Mtl.	Steve Penney	Shawinigan	G	91	5194	313	1	3.62
167	Buf.	Randy Cunneyworth	Ottawa	LW	866	189	225	414	1280
168	Phi.	Mark Botell	Brantford	D	32	4	10	14	31
169	Col.	Shawn MacKenzie	Windsor	G	4	130	15	0	6.92
170	Wpg.	Edward Christian	Warroad H.S.	LW					
171	Que.	Christian Tanguay	Trois-Rivieres	RW	2	0	0	0	0
172	Det.	Dave Miles	Brantford	RW					
173	Wsh.	Peter Andersson	Timra	D	172	10	41	51	81
174	Edm.	Lars-Gunnar Petterson	Lulea	D					
175	Van.	Patrik Sundstrom	Bjorkloven Umea	C	679	219	369	588	349
176	Hfd.	Paul Fricker	Michigan	G					
177	Pit.	Brian Lundberg	Michigan	D	1	0	0	0	2
178	L.A.	Daryl Evans	Niagara Falls	LW	113	22	30	52	25
179	Tor.	Darwin McCutcheon	Toronto	D	1	0	0	0	2
180	St.L.	Peter Lindgren	Hammarby	D					
181	Cgy.	Hakan Loob	Farjestad Karlstad	RW	450	193	236	429	189
182	NYR	Chris Wray	Boston College	RW					
183	Chi.	Don Dietrich	Brandon	D	28	0	7	7	10
184	Min.	Bob Lakso	Aurora H.S.	LW					
185	NYI	Peter Steblyk	Medicine Hat	D					
186	Bos.	Michael Thelven	Djurgarden	D	207	20	80	100	217
187	Mtl.	John Schmidt	U. of Notre Dame	D					
188	Buf.	Dave Beckon	Peterborough	C					
189	Phi.	Peter Dineen	Kingston	D	13	0	2	2	13
190	Col.	Bob Jansch	Victoria	RW					
191	Wpg.	Dave Chartier	Brandon	C	1	0	0	0	0
192	Que.	William Robinson	Acton-Boxboro H.S.	D					
193	Det.	Brian Rorabeck	Niagara Falls	D					
194	Wsh.	Tony Camazzola	Brandon	D	3	0	0	0	4
195	Phi.	Bob O'Brien	Dixie Jr. B.	RW					
196	Van.	Grant Martin	Kitchener	LW	44	0	4	4	55
197	Hfd.	Lorne Bokshowan	Saskatoon	C					
198	Pit.	Steve McKenzie	St. Albert Jr. A	D					
199	L.A.	Kim Collins	Bowling Green	LW					
200	Tor.	Paul Higgins	Henry Carr H.S.	RW	25	0	0	0	152
201	St.L.	John Smyth	Calgary	D					
202	Cgy.	Steven Fletcher	Hull	LW/D	3	0	0	0	5
203	NYR	Anders Backstrom	Brynas Gavle	D					
204	Chi.	Dan Frawley	Sudbury	RW	273	37	40	77	674
205	Min.	Dave Richter	Michigan	D	365	9	40	49	1030
206	NYI	Glenn Johannesen	Red Deer Jr. A.	LW	2	0	0	0	0
207	Bos.	Jens Ohling	Djurgarden	LW					
208	Mtl.	Scott Robinson	Denver University	G					
209	Buf.	John Bader	Irondale H.S.	LW					
210	Phi.	Andy Brickley	Bowling Green	LW/C	385	82	140	222	81

1981

FIRST ROUND

PICK	TEAM	NAME	DRAFTED FROM	POS	GP	G / W	A / GA	PTS / SO	PIM / AVG
1	Wpg.	Dale Hawerchuk	Cornwall	C	1188	518	891	1409	730
2	L.A.	Doug Smith	Ottawa	C	535	115	138	253	624
3	Wsh.	Bob Carpenter	St. John's Prep.	C	1178	320	408	728	919
4	Hfd.	Ron Francis	Sault Ste. Marie	C	1651	536	1222	1758	965
5	Col.	Joe Cirella	Oshawa	D	828	64	211	275	1446
6	Tor.	Jim Benning	Portland	D	605	52	191	243	461
7	Mtl.	Mark Hunter	Brantford	RW	628	213	171	384	1426
8	Edm.	Grant Fuhr	Victoria	G	868	48945	2756	25	3.38
9	NYR	James Patrick	Prince Albert	D	1225	145	483	628	747
10	Van.	Garth Butcher	Regina	D	897	48	158	206	2302
11	Que.	Randy Moller	Lethbridge	D	815	45	180	225	1692
12	Chi.	Tony Tanti	Oshawa	RW	697	287	273	560	661
13	Min.	Ron Meighan	Niagara Falls	D	48	3	7	10	18
14	Bos.	Normand Leveille	Chicoutimi	LW	75	17	25	42	49
15	Cgy.	Al MacInnis	Kitchener	D	1413	340	932	1272	1495
16	Phi.	Steve Smith	Sault Ste. Marie	D	18	0	1	1	15
17	Buf.	Jiri Dudacek	Poldi SNOP Kladno	RW					
18	Mtl.	Gilbert Delorme	Chicoutimi	D	541	31	92	123	520
19	Mtl.	Jan Ingman	Farjestad Karlstad	LW					
20	St.L.	Marty Ruff	Lethbridge	D					
21	NYI	Paul Boutilier	Sherbrooke	D	288	27	83	110	358

SECOND ROUND

PICK	TEAM	NAME	DRAFTED FROM	POS	GP	G / W	A / GA	PTS / SO	PIM / AVG
22	Wpg.	Scott Arniel	Cornwall	LW	730	149	189	338	599
23	Det.	Claude Loiselle	Windsor	C	616	92	117	209	1149
24	Tor.	Gary Yaremchuk	Portland	C	34	1	4	5	28
25	Chi.	Kevin Griffin	Portland	LW					
26	Col.	Rich Chernomaz	Victoria	RW	51	9	7	16	18
27	Min.	Dave Donnelly	St. Albert Jr. A	C	137	15	24	39	150
28	Pit.	Steve Gatzos	Sault Ste. Marie	RW	89	15	20	35	83
29	Edm.	Todd Strueby	Regina	LW	5	0	1	1	2
30	NYR	Jan Erixon	Skelleftea (Sweden)	LW	556	57	159	216	167

PICK	TEAM	NAME	DRAFTED FROM	NHL PLAYERS: POS / NHL GOALTENDERS: POS	GP / GP	G / W	A / GA	PTS / SO	PIM / AVG
31	Min.	Mike Sands	Sudbury	G	6	302	26	0	5.17
32	Mtl.	Lars Eriksson	Brynas Gavle	G					
33	Min.	Tom Hirsch	Patrick Henry High	D	31	1	7	8	30
34	Min.	Dave Preuss	St. Thomas Academy	RW					
35	Bos.	Luc Dufour	Chicoutimi	LW	167	23	21	44	199
36	St.L.	Hakan Nordin	Farjestad Karlstad	D					
37	Phi.	Rich Costello	Pickering	C	12	2	2	4	2
38	Buf.	Hannu Virta	TPS Turku	D	245	25	101	126	66
39	L.A.	Dean Kennedy	Brandon	D	717	26	108	134	1118
40	Mtl.	Chris Chelios	Moose Jaw	D	1326	176	717	893	2634
41	Min.	Jali Wahlsten	TPS Turku	C					
42	NYI	Gord Dineen	Sault Ste. Marie	D	528	16	90	106	695

OTHER ROUNDS

PICK	TEAM	NAME	DRAFTED FROM	NHL PLAYERS: POS / NHL GOALTENDERS: POS	GP / GP	G / W	A / GA	PTS / SO	PIM / AVG
43	Wpg.	Jyrki Seppa	Ilves Tampere	D	13	0	2	2	6
44	Det.	Corrado Micalef	Sherbrooke	G	113	5794	409	2	4.24
45	Wsh.	Eric Calder	Cornwall	D	2	0	0	0	0
46	Mtl.	Dieter Hegen	ESV Kaufbeuern, FRG	LW					
47	Phi.	Barry Tabobondung	Oshawa	LW					
48	Col.	Uli Hiemer	Fussen, FRG	D	143	19	54	73	176
49	Pit.	Tom Thornbury	Niagara Falls	D	14	1	8	9	16
50	NYR	Peter Sundstrom	Bjorkloven Umea	LW	338	61	83	144	120
51	NYR	Mark Morrison	Victoria	C	10	1	1	2	0
52	Van.	Jean-Marc Lanthier	Sorel	RW	105	16	16	32	29
53	Que.	Jean-Marc Gaulin	Sorel	RW	26	4	3	7	8
54	Chi.	Darrel Anholt	Calgary	D	1	0	0	0	0
55	Tor.	Ernie Godden	Windsor	C	5	1	1	2	6
56	Cgy.	Mike Vernon	Calgary	G	781	44449	2206	27	2.98
57	NYI	Ron Handy	Sault Ste. Marie	LW	14	0	3	3	0
58	Phi.	Ken Strong	Peterborough	LW	15	2	2	4	6
59	Buf.	Jim Aldred	Kingston	LW					
60	Buf.	Colin Chisholm	Calgary	D	1	0	0	0	0
61	Hfd.	Paul MacDermid	Windsor	RW	690	116	142	258	1303
62	St.L.	Gord Donnelly	Sherbrooke	D	554	28	41	69	2069
63	NYI	Neal Coulter	Toronto	RW	26	5	5	10	11
64	Wpg.	Kirk McCaskill	Vermont	C					
65	Phi.	Dave Michayluk	Regina	LW	14	2	6	8	8
66	Col.	Gus Greco	Windsor	C					
67	Hfd.	Mike Hoffman	Brantford	LW	9	1	3	4	2
68	Wsh.	Tony Kellin	Grand Rapids H.S.	D					
69	Min.	Terry Tait	Sault Ste. Marie	C					
70	Pit.	Norm Schmidt	Oshawa	D	125	23	33	56	73
71	Edm.	Paul Houck	Kelowna	RW	16	1	2	3	2
72	NYR	John Vanbiesbrouck	Sault Ste. Marie	G	882	50475	2503	40	2.98
73	Van.	Wendell Young	Kitchener	G	187	9410	618	2	3.94
74	Que.	Clint Malarchuk	Portland	G	338	19030	1100	12	3.47
75	Chi.	Perry Pelensky	Portland	RW	4	0	0	0	5
76	Min.	Jim Malwitz	Grand Rapids H.S.	C					
77	Bos.	Scott McLellan	Niagara Falls	RW	2	0	0	0	0
78	Cgy.	Peter Madach	HV 71 Jonkoping	C					
79	Phi.	Ken Latta	Sault Ste. Marie	RW					
80	Buf.	Jeff Eatough	Cornwall	RW	1	0	0	0	0
81	L.A.	Marty Dallman	RPI	C	6	0	1	1	0
82	Mtl.	Kjell Dahlin	Timra	RW	166	57	59	116	10
83	Buf.	Anders Wikberg	Timra	LW					
84	NYI	Todd Lumbard	Brandon	G					
85	Wpg.	Marc Behrend	Wisconsin	G	39	1991	160	1	4.82
86	Det.	Larry Trader	London	D	91	5	13	18	74
87	Col.	Doug Speck	Peterborough	D					
88	Mtl.	Steve Rooney	Canton H.S.	LW	154	15	13	28	496
89	Wsh.	Mike Siltala	Kingston	RW	7	1	0	1	2
90	Tor.	Normand Lefrancois	Trois-Rivieres	LW					
91	Wsh.	Peter Sidorkiewicz	Oshawa	G	246	13884	832	8	3.60
92	Edm.	Phil Drouillard	Niagara Falls	LW					
93	Hfd.	Bill Maguire	Niagara Falls	D					
94	NYI	Jacques Sylvestre	Sorel	C					
95	Que.	Edward Lee	Princeton	RW	2	0	0	0	5
96	Chi.	Doug Chessell	London	G					
97	Min.	Kelly Hubbard	Portland	D					
98	Bos.	Joe Mantione	Cornwall	G					
99	Cgy.	Mario Simioni	Toronto	RW					
100	Phi.	Justin Hanley	Kingston	C					
101	Buf.	Mauri Eivola	TPS Turku	C					
102	Tor.	Barry Bringley	Calgary	C					
103	Hfd.	Dan Bourbonnais	Calgary	LW	59	3	25	28	11
104	St.L.	Mike Hickey	Sudbury	C					
105	Van.	Moe Lemay	Ottawa	LW	317	72	94	166	442
106	Wpg.	Bob O'Connor	Boston College	G					
107	Det.	Gerard Gallant	Sherbrooke	LW	615	211	269	480	1674
108	Col.	Bruce Driver	Wisconsin	D	922	96	390	486	670
109	Pit.	Paul Edwards	Oshawa	D					
110	Wsh.	Jim McGeough	Billings	C	57	7	10	17	32
111	Edm.	Steve Smith	London	D	804	72	303	375	2139
112	Pit.	Rod Buskas	Medicine Hat	D	556	19	63	82	1294
113	Edm.	Marc Habscheid	Saskatoon	RW/C	345	72	91	163	171
114	NYR	Eric Magnuson	RPI	C					
115	Van.	Stu Kulak	Victoria	RW	90	8	4	12	130
116	Que.	Mike Eagles	Kitchener	C/LW	853	74	122	196	928
117	Chi.	Bill Schafhauser	Northern Michigan	D					
118	Min.	Paul Guay	Mount St. Charles H.S.	RW	117	11	23	34	92
119	Bos.	Bruce Milton	Boston U.	D					
120	Cgy.	Todd Hooey	Windsor	RW					
121	Phi.	Andre Villeneuve	Chicoutimi	D					
122	Buf.	Ali Butorac	Ottawa	D/LW					
123	L.A.	Brad Thompson	London	D					
124	Mtl.	Tom Anastos	Paddock Pool H.S.	RW					
125	St.L.	Peter Aslin	AIK Solna	G					
126	NYI	Chuck Brimmer	Kingston	C					
127	Wpg.	Peter Nilsson	Hammarby	C					
128	Det.	Greg Stefan	Oshawa	G	299	16333	1068	5	3.92
129	Col.	Jeff Larmer	Kitchener	LW	158	37	51	88	57
130	Hfd.	John Mokosak	Victoria	D	41	0	2	2	96
131	Wsh.	Risto Jalo	Ilves Tampere	C	3	0	3	3	0
132	Tor.	Andrew Wright	Peterborough	D					
133	Pit.	Geoff Wilson	Winnipeg	RW					
134	L.A.	Craig Hurley	Saskatoon	D					
135	NYR	Mike Guentzel	Greenway/Coleraine H.S.	D					
136	Van.	Bruce Holloway	Regina	D	2	0	0	0	0
137	Phi.	Vladimir Svitek	VSZ Kosice	RW					
138	Chi.	Marc Centrone	Lethbridge	C/RW					
139	Min.	Jim Archibald	Moose Jaw	RW	16	1	2	3	45
140	Bos.	Mats Thelin	AIK Solna	D	163	8	19	27	107
141	Cgy.	Rick Heppner	Mount View H.S.	D					
142	Phi.	Gil Hudon	Prince Albert	G					
143	Buf.	Heikki Leime	TPS Turku	D					
144	L.A.	Peter Sawkins	St. Paul Academy	D					
145	Mtl.	Tom Kurvers	Minnesota-Duluth	D	659	93	328	421	350
146	St.L.	Erik Holmberg	Sodertalje	C					
147	NYI	Teppo Virta	TPS Turku	RW					
148	Wpg.	Dan McFall	Buffalo Jr. Sabres	D	9	0	1	1	0
149	Det.	Rick Zombo	Austin Prep	D	652	24	130	154	728
150	Col.	Tony Arima	Jokerit Helsinki	LW					
151	Hfd.	Denis Dore	Chicoutimi	RW					
152	Wsh.	Gaetan Duchesne	Quebec	LW	1028	179	254	433	617
153	Tor.	Richard Turmel	Shawinigan	D					
154	Pit.	Mitch Lamoureux	Oshawa	C	73	11	9	20	59
155	Edm.	Mike Sturgeon	Kelowna	D					
156	NYR	Ari Lahtenmaki	HIFK Helsinki	RW					
157	Van.	Petri Skriko	SaiPa Lappeenranta	LW	541	183	222	405	246
158	Que.	Andre Cote	Quebec	RW					
159	Chi.	Johan Mellstrom	Falun	LW					
160	Min.	Kari Kanervo	TPS Turku	C					
161	Bos.	Armel Parisee	Chicoutimi	D					
162	Cgy.	Dale DeGray	Oshawa	D	153	18	47	65	195
163	Phi.	Steve Taylor	Providence	LW					
164	Buf.	Gates Orlando	Providence	C	98	18	26	44	51
165	L.A.	Dan Brennan	North Dakota	LW	8	0	1	1	9
166	Mtl.	Paul Gess	Jefferson H.S.	RW					
167	St.L.	Alain Vigneault	Trois-Rivieres	D	42	2	5	7	82
168	NYI	Bill Dowd	Ottawa	D					
169	Wpg.	Greg Dick	St. Mary's H.S.	G					
170	Det.	Don Leblanc	Moncton Jr.	LW					
171	Col.	Tim Army	Providence	C					
172	Hfd.	Jeff Poeschl	Northern Michigan	G					
173	Wsh.	George White	New Hampshire	LW					
174	Tor.	Greg Barber	Victoria	D					
175	Pit.	Dean Defazio	Brantford	LW	22	0	2	2	28
176	Edm.	Miloslav Horava	Poldi SNOP Kladno	D	80	5	17	22	38
177	NYR	Paul Reifenberger	Anoka H.S.	C					
178	Van.	Frank Caprice	London	G	102	5589	391	1	4.20
179	Que.	Marc Brisebois	Sorel	RW					
180	Chi.	John Benns	Billings	LW					

PICK	TEAM	NAME	DRAFTED FROM	NHL PLAYERS: POS	GP	G	A	PTS	PIM
				NHL GOALTENDERS: POS	GP	W	GA	SO	AVG
181	Min.	Scott Bjugstad	Minnesota-Duluth	RW	317	76	68	144	144
182	Bos.	Don Sylvestri	Clarkson	G	3	102	6	0	3.53
183	Cgy.	George Boudreau	Matignon H.S.	D					
184	Phi.	Len Hachborn	Brantford	C	102	20	39	59	29
185	Buf.	Venci Sebek	Niagara Falls	D					
186	L.A.	Allan Tuer	Regina	D	57	1	1	2	208
187	Mtl.	Scott Ferguson	Edina West H.S.	D	78	3	5	8	120
188	St.L.	Dan Wood	Kingston	RW					
189	NYI	Scott MacLellan	Burlington Jr. B.	RW					
190	Wpg.	Vladimir Kadlec	TJ Vitkovice	D					
191	Det.	Robert Nordmark	Lulea	D					
192	Col.	John Johannson	Wisconsin	C	5	0	0	0	0
193	Hfd.	Larry Power	Kitchener	C					
194	Wsh.	Chris Valentine	Sorel	C	105	43	52	95	127
195	Tor.	Marc Magnan	Lethbridge	LW	4	0	1	1	5
196	Pit.	Dave Hannan	Brantford	C	841	114	191	305	942
197	Edm.	Gord Sherven	Weyburn Jr. A	C	97	13	22	35	33
198	NYR	Mario Proulx	Providence	G					
199	Van.	Rejean Vignola	Shawinigan	C					
200	Que.	Kari Takko	Assat Pori	G	Re-entered Draft in 1984				
201	Chi.	Sylvain Roy	Hull	D					
202	Min.	Steve Kudebeh	Breck H.S.	G					
203	Bos.	Richard Bourque	Sherbrooke	LW					
204	Cgy.	Bruce Eakin	Saskatoon	C	13	2	2	4	4
205	Phi.	Steve Tsujiura	Medicine Hat	C					
206	Buf.	Warren Harper	Prince Albert	RW					
207	L.A.	Jeff Baikie	Cornell	LW					
208	Mtl.	Danny Burrows	Belleville	G					
209	St.L.	Richard Zemlak	Spokane	RW	132	2	12	14	587
210	NYI	Dave Randerson	Stratford Jr. B	RW					
211	Wpg.	Dave Kirwin	Irondale H.S.	D					

1982

FIRST ROUND

PICK	TEAM	NAME	DRAFTED FROM	POS	GP	G	A	PTS	PIM
1	Bos.	Gord Kluzak	Billings	D	299	25	98	123	543
2	Min.	Brian Bellows	Kitchener	LW	1188	485	537	1022	718
3	Tor.	Gary Nylund	Portland	D	608	32	139	171	1235
4	Phi.	Ron Sutter	Lethbridge	C	1093	205	329	534	1352
5	Wsh.	Scott Stevens	Kitchener	D	1597	193	703	896	2763
6	Buf.	Phil Housley	South St. Paul High	D	1495	338	894	1232	822
7	Chi.	Ken Yaremchuk	Portland	C	235	36	56	92	106
8	N.J.	Rocky Trottier	Billings	RW	38	6	4	10	2
9	Buf.	Paul Cyr	Victoria	LW	470	101	140	241	623
10	Pit.	Rich Sutter	Lethbridge	RW	874	149	166	315	1411
11	Van.	Michel Petit	Sherbrooke	D	827	90	238	328	1839
12	Wpg.	Jim Kyte	Cornwall	D	598	17	49	66	1342
13	Que.	David Shaw	Kitchener	D	769	41	153	194	906
14	Hfd.	Paul Lawless	Windsor	LW	239	49	77	126	54
15	NYR	Chris Kontos	Toronto	LW/C	230	54	69	123	103
16	Buf.	Dave Andreychuk	Oshawa	LW	1515	613	668	1281	1067
17	Det.	Murray Craven	Medicine Hat	LW	1071	266	493	759	524
18	N.J.	Ken Daneyko	Seattle	D	1283	36	142	178	2519
19	Mtl.	Alain Heroux	Chicoutimi	LW					
20	Edm.	Jim Playfair	Portland	D	21	2	4	6	51
21	NYI	Pat Flatley	Wisconsin	RW	780	170	340	510	686

SECOND ROUND

PICK	TEAM	NAME	DRAFTED FROM	POS	GP	G	A	PTS	PIM
22	Bos.	Brian Curran	Portland	D	381	7	33	40	1461
23	Det.	Yves Courteau	Laval	RW	22	2	5	7	4
24	Tor.	Gary Leeman	Regina	RW	667	199	267	466	531
25	Tor.	Peter Ihnacak	Sparta Praha	C	417	102	165	267	175
26	Buf.	Mike Anderson	North St. Paul H.S.	C					
27	L.A.	Mike Heidt	Calgary	D	6	0	1	1	7
28	Chi.	Rene Badeau	Quebec	D					
29	Cgy.	Dave Reierson	Prince Albert	D	2	0	0	0	2
30	Buf.	Jens Johansson	Pitea	D					
31	Mtl.	Jocelyn Gauvreau	Granby	D	2	0	0	0	0
32	Mtl.	Kent Carlson	St. Lawrence U.	D	113	7	11	18	148
33	Mtl.	David Maley	Edina High	LW	466	43	81	124	1043
34	Que.	Paul Gillis	Niagara Falls	C	624	88	154	242	1498
35	Hfd.	Mark Paterson	Ottawa	D	29	3	3	6	33
36	NYR	Tomas Sandstrom	Farjestad Karlstad	RW	983	394	462	856	1193
37	Cgy.	Richard Kromm	Portland	LW	372	70	103	173	138
38	Pit.	Tim Hrynewich	Sudbury	LW	55	6	8	14	82
39	Bos.	Lyndon Byers	Regina	RW	279	28	43	71	1081
40	Mtl.	Scott Sandelin	Hibbing High	D	25	0	4	4	2
41	Edm.	Steve Graves	Sault Ste. Marie	LW	35	5	4	9	10
42	NYI	Vern Smith	Lethbridge	D	1	0	0	0	0

OTHER ROUNDS

PICK	TEAM	NAME	DRAFTED FROM	POS	GP	G/W	A/GA	PTS/SO	PIM/AVG
43	N.J.	Pat Verbeek	Sudbury	RW	1424	522	541	1063	2905
44	Det.	Carmine Vani	Kingston	LW					
45	Tor.	Ken Wregget	Lethbridge	G	575	31663	1917	9	3.63
46	Phi.	Miroslav Dvorak	Motor Ceske (Czech.)	D	193	11	74	85	51
47	Phi.	Bill Campbell	Montreal	D					
48	L.A.	Steve Seguin	Kingston	W	5	0	0	0	9
49	Chi.	Tom McMurchy	Brandon	RW	55	8	4	12	65
50	St.L.	Mike Posavad	Peterborough	D	8	0	0	0	0
51	Cgy.	Jim Laing	Clarkson	D					
52	Pit.	Troy Loney	Lethbridge	LW	624	87	110	197	1091
53	Van.	Yves Lapointe	Shawinigan	LW					
54	N.J.	Dave Kasper	Sherbrooke	C					
55	Que.	Mario Gosselin	Shawinigan	G	241	12857	801	6	3.74
56	Hfd.	Kevin Dineen	U. of Denver	RW	1188	355	405	760	2229
57	NYR	Corey Millen	Cloquet H.S.	C	335	90	119	209	236
58	Wsh.	Milan Novy	Poldi SNOP Kladno	C	73	18	30	48	16
59	Min.	Wally Chapman	Edina H.S.	C					
60	Bos.	Dave Reid	Peterborough	LW	961	165	204	369	253
61	Mtl.	Scott Harlow	S.S. Braves H.S.	LW	1	0	1	1	0
62	Edm.	Brent Loney	Cornwall	LW					
63	NYI	Garry Lacey	Toronto	LW					
64	L.A.	Dave Gans	Oshawa	C	6	0	0	0	2
65	Cgy.	Dave Meszaros	Toronto	G					
66	Det.	Craig Coxe	St. Albert Jr. A	LW	235	14	31	45	713
67	Hfd.	Ulf Samuelsson	Leksand	D	1080	57	275	332	2453
68	Buf.	Timo Jutila	Tappara Tampere	D	10	1	5	6	13
69	Mtl.	John Devoe	Edina H.S.	RW					
70	Chi.	Bill Watson	Prince Albert	RW	115	23	36	59	12
71	Van.	Shawn Kilroy	Peterborough	G					
72	Cgy.	Mark Lamb	Billings	C	403	46	100	146	291
73	Tor.	Vladimir Ruzicka	CHZ Litvinov	C	233	82	85	167	129
74	Wpg.	Tom Martin	Kelowna Jr.	LW	92	12	11	23	249
75	Wpg.	Dave Ellett	Ottawa Jr. A	D	1129	153	415	568	985
76	Que.	Jiri Lala	Dukla Jihlava	RW					
77	Phi.	Mikael Hjalm	MoDo Ornskoldsvik	W					
78	NYR	Chris Jensen	Kelowna Packers (BCJHL)	RW	74	9	12	21	27
79	Buf.	Jeff Hamilton	Providence	W					
80	Min.	Bob Rouse	Billings	D	1061	37	181	218	1559
81	Min.	Dusan Pasek	Slovan Bratislava	C	48	4	10	14	30
82	L.A.	Dave Ross	Seattle	G					
83	Edm.	Jaroslav Pouzar	Motor Ceske Budejovice	LW	186	34	48	82	135
84	NYI	Alan Kerr	Seattle	RW	391	72	94	166	826
85	N.J.	Scott Brydges	Mariner H.S.	D					
86	Det.	Brad Shaw	Ottawa	D	377	22	137	159	208
87	Tor.	Eduard Uvira	CHZ Litvinov	D					
88	Hfd.	Ray Ferraro	Penticton Jr. A	C	1258	408	490	898	1288
89	Wsh.	Dean Evason	Kamloops	C	803	139	233	372	1002
90	L.A.	Darcy Roy	Ottawa	LW					
91	Chi.	Brad Beck	Penticton Jr. A	D					
92	St.L.	Scott Machej	Calgary	C/LW					
93	Cgy.	Lou Kiriakou	Toronto	D					
94	Pit.	Grant Sasser	Portland	C	3	0	0	0	0
95	L.A.	Ulf Isaksson	AIK Solna	LW	50	7	15	22	10
96	Wpg.	Tim Mishler	East Grand Forks H.S.	C					
97	Que.	Phil Stanger	Seattle	LW					
98	Phi.	Todd Bergen	Prince Albert	C	14	11	5	16	4
99	Tor.	Sylvain Charland	Shawinigan	LW					
100	Buf.	Robert Logan	West Island Jr.	RW	42	10	5	15	0
101	Min.	Marty Wiitala	Superior H.S.	C					
102	Bos.	Bob Nicholson	London	D					
103	Mtl.	Kevin Houle	Acton-Boxboro H.S.	LW					
104	Edm.	Dwayne Boettger	Toronto	D					
105	NYI	Rene Breton	Granby	C					
106	N.J.	Mike Moher	Kitchener	RW	9	0	1	1	28
107	Det.	Claude Vilgrain	Laval	RW	89	21	32	53	78
108	Tor.	Ron Dreger	Saskatoon	LW					
109	Hfd.	Randy Gilhen	Winnipeg	C	457	55	60	115	314
110	Wsh.	Ed Kastelic	London	W	220	11	10	21	719
111	Buf.	Jeff Parker	Mariner H.S.	RW	141	16	19	35	163
112	Chi.	Mark Hatcher	Niagara Falls	D					
113	St.L.	Perry Ganchar	Saskatoon	RW	42	3	7	10	36

PICK	TEAM	NAME	DRAFTED FROM	NHL PLAYERS: POS / NHL GOALTENDERS: POS	GP / GP	G / W	A / GA	PTS / SO	PIM / AVG
114	Cgy.	Jeff Vaive	Ottawa	C					
115	Tor.	Craig Kales	Niagara Falls	RW					
116	Van.	Taylor Hall	Regina	LW	41	7	9	16	29
117	Mtl.	Ernie Vargas	Coon Rapids H.S.	C					
118	Cgy.	Mats Kihlstrom	Sodertalje	D					
119	Phi.	Ron Hextall	Brandon	G	608	34750	1723	23	2.97
120	NYR	Tony Granato	Northwood Prep.	RW	773	248	244	492	1425
121	Buf.	Jacob Gustavsson	Almtuna	G					
122	Min.	Todd Carlile	North St. Paul H.S.	D					
123	Bos.	Bob Sweeney	Acton-Boxboro H.S.	C/RW	639	125	163	288	799
124	Mtl.	Michael Dark	Sarnia Jr. B	D	43	5	6	11	14
125	Edm.	Raimo Summanen	Reipas Lahti	LW	151	36	40	76	35
126	NYI	Roger Kortko	Saskatoon	C	79	7	17	24	28
127	N.J.	Paul Fulcher	London	LW					
128	Det.	Greg Hudas	Redford Jr.	D					
129	Tor.	Dom Campedelli	Cohasset H.S.	D	2	0	0	0	0
130	Hfd.	Jim Johannson	Rochestor Mayo H.S.	C					
131	Que.	Daniel Poudrier	Shawinigan	D	25	1	5	6	10
132	L.A.	Viktor Nechayev	SKA Leningrad	C	3	1	0	1	0
133	Chi.	Jay Ness	Roseau H.S.	C					
134	St.L.	Doug Gilmour	Cornwall	C	1474	450	964	1414	1301
135	Cgy.	Brad Ramsden	Peterborough	RW					
136	Pit.	Brent Couture	Lethbridge	D					
137	Van.	Parie Proft	Calgary	D					
138	Wpg.	Derek Ray	Seattle Jr. B	LW					
139	Tor.	Jeff Triano	Toronto	D					
140	Phi.	Dave Brown	Saskatoon	RW	729	45	52	97	1789
141	NYR	Sergei Kapustin	Spartak	LW					
142	Buf.	Allen Bishop	Niagara Falls	D					
143	Min.	Viktor Zhluktov	CSKA	LW					
144	Bos.	John Meulenbroeks	Brantford	D					
145	Mtl.	Hannu Jarvenpaa	Karpat Oulu	RW	Re-entered Draft in 1986				
146	Edm.	Brian Small	Ottawa	RW					
147	NYI	John Tiano	Winthrop H.S.	C					
148	N.J.	John Hutchings	Oshawa	D					
149	Det.	Pat Lahey	Windsor	C					
150	Mtl.	Steve Smith	St. Lawrence U.	D					
151	Hfd.	Mickey Kramptoich	Hibbing H.S.	C					
152	Wsh.	Wally Schreiber	Regina	RW	41	8	10	18	12
153	L.A.	Peter Helander	Skelleftea	D	7	0	1	1	0
154	Chi.	Jeff Smith	London	LW					
155	St.L.	Chris Delaney	Boston College	LW					
156	Cgy.	Roy Myllari	Cornwall	D					
157	Pit.	Peter Derksen	Portland	LW					
158	Van.	Newell Brown	Michigan State	C					
159	Wpg.	Guy Gosselin	John Marshall H.S.	D	5	0	0	0	6
160	NYR	Brian Glynn	Buffalo Jr.	C					
161	Phi.	Alain Lavigne	Shawinigan	RW					
162	NYR	Jan Karlsson	Kiruna	D					
163	Buf.	Claude Verret	Trois-Rivieres	C	14	2	5	7	2
164	Min.	Paul Miller	Crookston H.S.	D					
165	Bos.	Tony Fiore	Montreal	C					
166	Mtl.	Tom Koliouspoulos	Fraser H.S.	RW					
167	Edm.	Dean Clark	St. Albert Jr. A	D	1	0	0	0	0
168	NYI	Todd Okerlund	Burnsville H.S.	RW	4	0	0	0	2
169	N.J.	Alan Hepple	Ottawa	D	3	0	0	0	7
170	Det.	Gary Cullen	Cornell	C					
171	Tor.	Miroslav Ihnacak	VSZ Kosice	LW	56	8	9	17	39
172	Hfd.	Kevin Skilliter	Cornwall	D					
173	Wsh.	Jamie Reeve	Saskatoon Jr. A	G					
175	Chi.	Phil Patterson	Ottawa	RW					
176	St.L.	Matt Christensen	Aurora H.S.	C					
177	Cgy.	Ted Pearson	Wisconsin	LW					
178	Pit.	Greg Gravel	Windsor	C					
179	Van.	Don McLaren	Ottawa	RW					
180	Wpg.	Tom Ward	Richfield H.S.	D					
181	Que.	Mike Hough	Kitchener	LW	707	100	156	256	675
182	Phi.	Magnus Roupe	Farjestad Karlstad	LW	40	3	5	8	42
183	NYR	Kelly Miller	Michigan State	LW	1057	181	282	463	512
184	Buf.	Rob Norman	Cornwall	RW					
185	Min.	Pat Micheletti	Hibbing H.S.	C	12	2	0	2	8
186	Bos.	Doug Kostynski	Kamloops	C	15	3	1	4	4
187	Mtl.	Brian Williams	Sioux City Jr. A.	C					
188	Edm.	Ian Wood	Penticton Jr. A	G					
189	NYI	Gord Paddock	Saskatoon Jr. A	D					
190	N.J.	Brent Shaw	Seattle	RW					
191	Det.	Brent Meckling	Calgary Jr. A	D					
192	Tor.	Leigh Verstraete	Calgary	RW	8	0	1	1	14
193	NYR	Simo Saarinen	HIFK Helsinki	D	8	0	0	0	0
194	Wsh.	Juha Nurmi	Tappara Tampere	C					
195	L.A.	John Franzosa	Brown	G					
196	Chi.	James Camazzola	Penticton Jr. A.	LW	3	0	0	0	0
197	St.L.	John Shumski	RPI	C/RW					
198	Cgy.	Jim Uens	Oshawa	C/RW					
199	Pit.	Stu Wenaas	Winnipeg	D					
200	Van.	Alain Raymond	Niagara Falls	LW					
201	Wpg.	Mike Savage	Sudbury	LW					
202	Que.	Vincent Lukac	Dukla Jihlava	RW					
203	Phi.	Tom Allen	Michigan Tech	G					
204	NYR	Bob Lowes	Prince Albert	C					
205	Buf.	Mike Craig	Billings	G					
206	Min.	Arnold Kadlec	CHZ Litvinov	D					
207	Bos.	Tony Gilliard	Niagara Falls	LW					
208	Mtl.	Bob Emery	Matignon H.S.	D					
209	Edm.	Grant Dion	Cowichan Valley Jr.	D					
210	NYI	Eric Faust	Henry Carr Jr. B	D					
211	N.J.	Scott Fusco	Harvard	LW					
212	Det.	Mike Stern	Oshawa	LW					
213	Tor.	Tim Loven	Red River H.S.	D					
214	Hfd.	Martin Linse	Djurgarden	C					
215	Wsh.	Wayne Prestage	Seattle	C					
216	L.A.	Ray Shero	St. Lawrence U.	LW					
217	Chi.	Mike James	Ottawa	D					
218	St.L.	Brian Ahern	West St. Paul H.S.	LW					
219	Cgy.	Rick Erdall	Minnesota-Duluth	C					
220	Pit.	Chris McCauley	London	RW					
221	Van.	Steve Driscoll	Cornwall	LW					
222	Wpg.	Bob Shaw	Penticton Jr. A	RW					
223	Que.	Andre Martin	Montreal	D					
224	Phi.	Rick Gal	Lethbridge	LW					
225	NYR	Andy Otto	Northwood Prep	D					
226	Buf.	Jim Plankers	Cloquet H.S.	D					
227	Min.	Scott Knutson	Warroad H.S.	C					
228	Bos.	Tommy Lehman	Stocksund	C	36	5	5	10	16
229	Mtl.	Darren Acheson	Fort Saskatchewan	C					
230	Edm.	Chris Smith	Regina	G					
231	NYI	Pat Goff	Alexander Ramsey H.S.	D					
232	N.J.	Dan Dorion	Austin Prep	C	4	1	1	2	2
233	Det.	Shaun Reagan	Brantford	RW					
234	Tor.	Jim Appleby	Winnipeg	G					
235	Hfd.	Randy Cameron	Winnipeg	D					
236	Wsh.	Jim Holden	Peterborough	G					
237	L.A.	Mats Ulander	AIK Solna	RW					
238	Chi.	Bob Andrea	Dartmouth Jr.	D					
239	St.L.	Peter Smith	U. of Maine	G					
240	Cgy.	Dale Thompson	Calgary Jr. A.	RW					
241	Pit.	Stan Bautch	Hibbing H.S.	G					
242	Van.	Shawn Green	Victoria	RW					
243	Wpg.	Jan Urban Ericson	AIK Solna	LW					
244	Que.	Jozef Lukac	VSZ Kosice	C					
245	Phi.	Mark Vichorek	Sioux City Jr. A.	D					
246	NYR	Dwayne Robinson	New Hampshire	D					
247	Wsh.	Marco Kallas	St. Louis Jr. B	C					
248	Que.	Jan Jasko	Slovan Bratislava	LW					
249	Bos.	Bruno Campese	Northern Michigan	G					
250	Mtl.	Bill Brauer	Edina H.S.	D					
251	Edm.	Jeff Crawford	Regina	LW					
252	NYI	Jim Koudys	Sudbury	D					

1983

FIRST ROUND

PICK	TEAM	NAME	DRAFTED FROM	POS	GP	G / W	A / GA	PTS / SO	PIM / AVG
1	Min.	Brian Lawton	Mount St. Charles H.S.	LW	483	112	154	266	401
2	Hfd.	Sylvain Turgeon	Hull	LW	669	269	226	495	691
3	NYI	Pat LaFontaine	Verdun	C	865	468	545	1013	552
4	Det.	Steve Yzerman	Peterborough	C	1378	660	1010	1670	860
5	Buf.	Tom Barrasso	Acton-Boxborough	G	777	44180	2385	38	3.24
6	N.J.	John MacLean	Oshawa	RW	1194	413	429	842	1328
7	Tor.	Russ Courtnall	Victoria	RW	1029	297	447	744	557
8	Wpg.	Andrew McBain	North Bay	RW	608	129	172	301	633
9	Van.	Cam Neely	Portland	RW	726	395	299	694	1241
10	Buf.	Normand Lacombe	New Hampshire	RW	319	53	62	115	196

PICK	TEAM	NAME	DRAFTED FROM	NHL PLAYERS: POS	GP	G	A	PTS	PIM
				NHL GOALTENDERS: POS	GP	W	GA	SO	AVG
11	Buf.	Adam Creighton	Ottawa	C	708	187	216	403	1077
12	NYR	Dave Gagner	Brantford	C	946	318	401	719	1018
13	Cgy.	Dan Quinn	Belleville	C	805	266	419	685	533
14	Wpg.	Bobby Dollas	Laval	D	646	42	96	138	467
15	Pit.	Bob Errey	Peterborough	LW	895	170	212	382	1005
16	NYI	Gerald Diduck	Lethbridge	D	932	56	156	212	1612
17	Mtl.	Alfie Turcotte	Portland	C	112	17	29	46	49
18	Chi.	Bruce Cassidy	Ottawa	D	36	4	13	17	10
19	Edm.	Jeff Beukeboom	Sault Ste. Marie	D	804	30	129	159	1890
20	Hfd.	David Jensen	Lawrence Academy	C	69	9	13	22	22
21	Bos.	Nevin Markwart	Regina	LW	309	41	68	109	794

SECOND ROUND

PICK	TEAM	NAME	DRAFTED FROM	POS	GP	G	A	PTS	PIM
22	Pit.	Todd Charlesworth	Oshawa	D	93	3	9	12	47
23	Hfd.	Ville Siren	Ilves Tampere	D	290	14	68	82	276
24	N.J.	Shawn Evans	Peterborough	D	9	1	0	1	2
25	Det.	Lane Lambert	Saskatoon	RW	283	58	66	124	521
26	Mtl.	Claude Lemieux	Trois-Rivieres	RW	1197	379	406	785	1756
27	Mtl.	Sergio Momesso	Shawinigan	LW	710	152	193	345	1557
28	Tor.	Jeff Jackson	Brantford	LW	263	38	48	86	313
29	Wpg.	Brad Berry	St. Albert Jr. A	D	241	4	28	32	323
30	Van.	David Bruce	Kitchener	LW	234	48	39	87	338
31	Buf.	John Tucker	Kitchener	C	656	177	259	436	285
32	Que.	Yves Heroux	Chicoutimi	RW	1	0	0	0	0
33	NYR	Randy Heath	Portland	LW	13	2	4	6	15
34	Buf.	Richard Hajdu	Kamloops	LW	5	0	0	0	4
35	Mtl.	Todd Francis	Brantford	RW					
36	Min.	Malcolm Parks	St. Albert Jr. A	C					
37	NYI	Garnet McKechney	Kitchener	RW					
38	Min.	Frantisek Musil	Tesla Pardubice	D	797	34	106	140	1241
39	Chi.	Wayne Presley	Kitchener	RW	684	155	147	302	953
40	Edm.	Mike Golden	Reading High	C					
41	Phi.	Peter Zezel	Toronto	C	873	219	389	608	435
42	Bos.	Greg Johnston	Toronto	RW	187	26	29	55	124

OTHER ROUNDS

PICK	TEAM	NAME	DRAFTED FROM	POS	GP	G	A	PTS	PIM
43	Wpg.	Peter Taglianetti	Providence	D	451	18	74	92	1106
44	Phi.	Derrick Smith	Peterborough	LW	537	82	92	174	373
45	Mtl.	Daniel Letendre	Quebec	RW					
46	Det.	Bob Probert	Brantford	LW	935	163	221	384	3300
47	L.A.	Bruce Shoebottom	Peterborough	D	35	1	4	5	53
48	St.L.				no selection				
49	Tor.	Allan Bester	Brantford	G	219	11773	786	7	4.01
50	NYR	Vesa Salo	Lukko Rauma	D					
51	Van.	Scott Tottle	Peterborough	RW					
52	Cgy.	Brian Bradley	London	C	651	182	321	503	528
53	Que.	Bruce Bell	Windsor	D	209	12	64	76	113
54	NYR	Gord Walker	Portland	RW	31	3	4	7	23
55	Que.	Iiro Jarvi	HIFK Helsinki	RW	116	18	43	61	58
56	Cgy.	Perry Berezan	St. Albert Jr. A	C	378	61	75	136	279
57	Min.	Mitch Messier	Notre Dame Sask. Juvenile	C	20	0	2	2	11
58	NYI	Mike Neill	Sault Ste. Marie	D					
59	Pit.	Mike Rowe	Toronto	D	11	0	0	0	11
60	Chi.	Marc Bergevin	Chicoutimi	D	1130	35	135	170	1061
61	Edm.	Mike Flanagan	Acton-Boxboro H.S.	D					
62	Hfd.	Leif Karlsson	Mora	D					
63	Bos.	Greg Puhalski	Kitchener	LW					
64	Pit.	Frank Pietrangelo	Minnesota-Duluth	G	141	7141	490	1	4.12
65	Hfd.	Dave MacLean	Belleville	RW					
66	NYI	Mikko Makela	Ilves Tampere	LW	423	118	147	265	139
67	Cgy.	John Bekkers	Regina	C					
68	L.A.	Guy Benoit	Shawinigan	C					
69	St.L.				no selection				
70	Det.	David Korol	Winnipeg	D					
71	Wpg.	Bob Essensa	Henry Carr Jr. B	G	446	24215	1270	18	3.15
72	Van.	Tim Lorentz	Portland	LW					
73	Cgy.	Kevan Guy	Medicine Hat	D	156	5	20	25	138
74	Hfd.	Ron Chyzowski	St. Albert Jr. A	C					
75	NYR	Peter Andersson	Orebro	D	47	6	13	19	20
76	Buf.	Daren Puppa	Kirkland Lake	G	429	23819	1204	19	3.03
77	Wsh.	Tim Bergland	Lincoln H.S.	RW	182	17	26	43	75
78	Min.	Brian Durand	Cloquet H.S.	C					
79	Cgy.	Bill Claviter	Virginia H.S.	LW					
80	Mtl.	John Kordic	Portland	RW	244	17	18	35	997
81	Chi.	Tarek Howard	Olds Jr. A.	D					
82	Edm.	Esa Tikkanen	HIFK Helsinki	LW	877	244	386	630	1077

PICK	TEAM	NAME	DRAFTED FROM	NHL PLAYERS: POS	GP	G	A	PTS	PIM
				NHL GOALTENDERS: POS	GP	W	GA	SO	AVG
83	Phi.	Alan Bourbeau	Acton-Boxboro H.S.	C					
84	Bos.	Alain Larochelle	Saskatoon	G					
85	Tor.	Dan Hodgson	Prince Albert	C	114	29	45	74	64
86	NYI	Bob Caulfield	Detroit Lakes H.S.	RW					
87	N.J.	Chris Terreri	Providence	G	406	22369	1143	9	3.07
88	Det.	Petr Klima	Dukla Jihlava	W	786	313	260	573	671
89	L.A.	Bob LaForest	North Bay	RW	5	1	0	1	2
90	St.L.				no selection				
91	Det.	Joe Kocur	Saskatoon	RW	820	80	82	162	2519
92	Wpg.	Harry Armstrong	Dubuque Jr. A	D					
93	Van.	Doug Quinn	Nanaimo	D					
94	Cgy.	Igor Liba	Dukla Jihlava	LW	37	7	18	25	36
95	Que.	Luc Guenette	Quebec	G					
96	NYR	Jim Andonoff	Belleville	RW					
97	Buf.	Jayson Meyer	Regina	D					
98	Wsh.	Martin Bouliane	Granby	C					
99	Min.	Rich Geist	St. Paul Academy	C					
100	NYI	Ron Viglasi	Victoria	D					
101	Mtl.	Dan Wurst	Edina H.S.	D					
102	Chi.	Kevin Robinson	Toronto	D					
103	L.A.	Garry Galley	Bowling Green	D	1149	125	475	600	1218
104	Phi.	Jerome Carrier	Verdun	D					
105	Bos.	Allen Pedersen	Medicine Hat	D	428	5	36	41	487
106	Pit.	Patrick Emond	Hull	C					
107	Hfd.	Brian Johnson	Silver Bay H.S.	RW	3	0	0	0	5
108	N.J.	Gordon Mark	Kamloops	D	85	3	10	13	187
109	Det.	Chris Pusey	Abbotsford Jr.	G	1	40	3	0	4.50
110	L.A.	Dave Lundmark	Virginia H.S.	D					
111	St.L.				no selection				
112	L.A.	Kevin Stevens	Silver Lake H.S.	LW	874	329	397	726	1470
113	Wpg.	Joel Baillargeon	Hull	LW	20	0	2	2	31
114	Van.	Dave Lowry	London	LW	1066	163	186	349	1180
115	Cgy.	Grant Blair	Harvard	G					
116	Que.	Brad Walcott	Kingston	D					
117	NYR	Bob Alexander	Rosemount H.S.	D					
118	Buf.	Jim Hofford	Windsor	D	18	0	0	0	47
119	Chi.	Jari Torkki	Lukko Rauma	LW	4	1	0	1	0
120	Min.	Tom McComb	Mount St. Charles H.S.	D					
121	NYI	Darin Illikainen	Hermantown H.S.						
122	Mtl.	Arto Javanainen	Assat Pori	RW	Re-entered Draft In 1984				
123	Chi.	Mark LaVarre	Stratford Jr. B	RW	78	9	16	25	58
124	Edm.	Don Barber	Kelowna	W	115	25	32	57	64
125	Phi.	Rick Tocchet	Sault Ste. Marie	RW	1144	440	512	952	2972
126	Bos.	Terry Taillefer	St. Albert Jr. A	G					
127	Pit.	Paul Ames	Billerica H.S.	D					
128	Hfd.	Joe Reekie	North Bay	D	Re-entered Draft in 1985				
129	N.J.	Greg Evtushevski	Kamloops	RW					
130	Det.	Bob Pierson	London	LW					
131	L.A.	Tim Burgess	Oshawa	D					
132	St.L.				no selection				
133	Tor.	Cam Plante	Brandon	D	2	0	0	0	0
134	Wpg.	Iain Duncan	North York Jr. B.	LW	127	34	55	89	149
135	Van.	Terry Maki	Brantford	LW					
136	Cgy.	Jeff Hogg	Oshawa	G					
137	Que.	Craig Mack	East Grand Forks H.S.	D					
138	NYR	Steve Orth	St. Cloud Tech H.S.	C					
139	Buf.	Christian Ruuttu	Assat Pori	C	621	134	298	432	714
140	Wsh.	Dwaine Hutton	Kelowna	C					
141	Min.	Sean Toomey	Cretin H.S.	LW	1	0	0	0	0
142	NYI	Jim Sprenger	Cloquet H.S.	D					
143	Mtl.	Vladislav Tretiak	CSKA	G					
144	Chi.	Scott Birnie	Cornwall	RW					
145	Edm.	Dale Derkatch	Regina	C					
146	Phi.	Bobby Mormina	Longueuil	D					
147	Bos.	Ian Armstrong	Peterborough	D					
148	Hfd.	Chris Duperron	Chicoutimi	D					
149	Hfd.	James Falle	Clarkson	G					
150	N.J.	Viacheslav Fetisov	CSKA	D	546	36	192	228	656
151	Det.	Craig Butz	Kelowna	D					
152	L.A.	Ken Hammond	RPI	D	193	18	29	47	290
153	St.L.				no selection				
154	Tor.	Paul Bifano	Burnaby Jr.	LW					
155	Wpg.	Ron Pessetti	Western Michigan	D					
156	Van.	John Labatt	Minnetonka H.S.	C					
157	Cgy.	Chris MacDonald	Western Michigan	D					
158	Que.	Tommy Albelin	Djurgarden	D	871	43	202	245	411

PICK	TEAM	NAME	DRAFTED FROM	NHL PLAYERS: POS / NHL GOALTENDERS: POS	GP / GP	G / W	A / GA	PTS / SO	PIM / AVG
159	NYR	Peter Marcov	Welland Jr. B	LW					
160	Buf.	Don McSween	Regina Jr. A	D	47	3	10	13	55
161	Wsh.	Marty Abrams	Pembroke Jr. A.	G					
162	Min.	Don Biggs	Oshawa	C	12	2	0	2	8
163	NYI	Dale Henry	Saskatoon	LW	132	13	26	39	263
164	Mtl.	Rob Bryden	Henry Carr Jr. B	LW					
165	Chi.	Kent Paynter	Kitchener	D	37	1	3	4	69
166	Edm.	Ralph Vos	Abbotsford Jr. A	LW					
167	Phi.	Pelle Eklund	AIK Solna	C	594	120	335	455	109
168	Bos.	Francois Olivier	St-Jean	LW					
169	Pit.	Marty Ketola	St. Cloquet H.S.	RW					
170	Hfd.	Bill Fordy	Guelph	LW					
171	N.J.	Jay Octeau	Mount St. Charles H.S.	D					
172	Det.	Dave Sikorski	Cornwall	D					
173	L.A.	Bruce Fishback	Mariner H.S.	C					
174	St.L.				no selection				
175	Tor.	Cliff Albrecht	Princeton	D					
176	Wpg.	Todd Flichel	Gloucester	D	6	0	1	1	4
177	Van.	Allan Measures	Calgary	D					
178	Cgy.	Rob Kivell	Victoria	D					
179	Que.	Wayne Groulx	Sault Ste. Marie	C	1	0	0	0	0
180	NYR	Paul Jerrard	Notre Dame Jr. A	D	5	0	0	0	4
181	Buf.	Tim Hoover	Sault Ste. Marie	D					
182	Wsh.	David Cowan	Washburn H.S.	LW					
183	Min.	Paul Pulis	Hibbing H.S.	RW					
184	NYI	Kevin Vescio	North Bay	D					
185	Mtl.	Grant MacKay	U. of Calgary	D					
186	Chi.	Brian Noonan	Archbishop Williams H.S.	RW	629	116	159	275	518
187	Edm.	Dave Roach	New Westminster	G					
188	Phi.	Rob Nichols	Kitchener	LW					
189	Bos.	Harri Laurila	Reipas Lahti	D					
190	Pit.	Alec Haidy	Sault Ste. Marie	RW					
191	Tor.	Greg Rolston	Michael Power H.S.	RW					
192	N.J.	Alexander Chernykh	Khimik Voskresensk	C					
193	Det.	Stu Grimson	Regina	LW	Re-entered Draft in 1985				
194	L.A.	Thomas Ahlen	Skelleftea	D					
195	St.L.				no selection				
196	Tor.	Brian Ross	Kitchener	D					
197	Wpg.	Cory Wright	Dubuque Jr. A.	RW					
198	Van.	Roger Grillo	U. of Maine	D					
199	Cgy.	Tom Pratt	Kimball Union Academy	D					
200	Que.	Scott Shaunessy	St. John's Prep	D/LW	7	0	0	0	23
201	Hfd.	Reine Karlsson	Sodertalje	LW					
202	Buf.	Mark Ferner	Kamloops	D	91	3	10	13	51
203	Wsh.	Yves Beaudoin	Shawinigan	D	11	0	0	0	5
204	Min.	Milos Riha	TJ Gottwaldov	LW					
205	NYI	Dave Shellington	Cornwall	LW					
206	Mtl.	Thomas Rundqvist	Farjestad Karlstad	C	2	0	1	1	0
207	Chi.	Dominik Hasek	Tesla Pardubice	G	581	33745	1254	61	2.23
208	Edm.	Warren Yadlowski	Calgary	C					
209	Phi.	William McCormick	Westminster Heights H.S.	C					
210	Bos.	Paul Fitzsimmons	Northeastern	D					
211	Pit.	Garth Hildebrand	Calgary	LW					
212	Hfd.	Allan Acton	Saskatoon	LW					
213	N.J.	Allan Stewart	Prince Albert	LW	64	6	4	10	243
214	Det.	Jeff Frank	Regina	RW					
215	L.A.	Miroslav Blaha	Motor Ceske Budejovice	RW					
216	St.L.				no selection				
217	Tor.	Mike Tomlak	Cornwall	C/LW	141	15	22	37	103
218	Wpg.	Eric Cormier	St. Georges	LW					
219	Van.	Steve Kayser	Vermont	D					
220	Cgy.	Jaroslav Benak	Dukla Jihlava	LW					
221	Min.	Oldrich Valek	Dukla Jihlava	RW					
222	NYR	Bryan Walker	Portland	D					
223	Buf.	Uwe Krupp	Koln, FRG	D	729	69	212	281	660
224	Wsh.	Alain Raymond	Trois-Rivieres	G	1	40	2	0	3.00
225	Wsh.	Anders Huss	Brynas Gavle	C					
226	NYI	John Bjorkman	Warroad H.S.	C					
227	Mtl.	Jeff Perpich	Hibbing H.S.	D					
228	Chi.	Steve Pepin	St-Jean	C					
229	Edm.	John Miner	Regina	D	14	2	3	5	16
230	Phi.	Brian Jopling	Williston Academy	G					
231	Bos.	Norm Foster	Penticton Jr. A	G	13	623	34	0	3.27
232	Pit.	Dave Goertz	Regina	D	2	0	0	0	2
233	Hfd.	Darcy Kaminski	Lethbridge	D					
234	N.J.	Alexei Kasatonov	CSKA	D	383	38	122	160	326
235	Det.	Charles Chiatto	Cranbrook H.S.	C					
236	L.A.	Chad Johnson	Roseau H.S.	C					
237	St.L.				no selection				
238	Tor.	Ron Choules	Trois-Rivieres	LW					
239	Wpg.	Jamie Husgen	Des Moines Jr. A	D					
240	Van.	Jay Mazur	Breck H.S.	C/RW	47	11	7	18	20
241	Cgy.	Sergei Makarov	CSKA	RW	424	134	250	384	317
242	Que.	Bo Berglund	Djurgarden	RW	130	28	39	67	40
243	NYR	Ulf Nilsson	Skelleftea	C	170	57	112	169	85
244	Buf.	Marc Hamelin	Shawinigan	G					
245	Buf.	Kermit Salfi	Northwood Prep	LW					
246	Min.	Paul Roff	Edina H.S.	RW					
247	NYI	Peter McGeough	Henricken H.S.	RW					
248	Mtl.	Jean-Guy Bergeron	Shawinigan	D					
249	Que.	Jindrich Kokrment	CHZ Litvinov	C					
250	Edm.	Steve Woodburn	Verdun	D					
251	Phi.	Harold Duvall	Belmont Hill H.S.	LW					
252	Bos.	Greg Murphy	Trinity-Pawling H.S.	D					

1984

FIRST ROUND

PICK	TEAM	NAME	DRAFTED FROM	POS	GP	G / W	A / GA	PTS / SO	PIM / AVG
1	Pit.	Mario Lemieux	Laval	C	879	682	1010	1692	812
2	N.J.	Kirk Muller	Guelph	LW	1349	357	602	959	1223
3	Chi.	Eddie Olczyk	Team USA	C	1031	342	452	794	874
4	Tor.	Al Iafrate	Belleville	D	799	152	311	463	1301
5	Mtl.	Petr Svoboda	CHZ Litvinov	D	1028	58	341	399	1605
6	L.A.	Craig Redmond	U. of Denver	D	191	16	68	84	134
7	Det.	Shawn Burr	Kitchener	LW/C	878	181	259	440	1069
8	Mtl.	Shayne Corson	Brantford	LW	1139	268	415	683	2328
9	Pit.	Doug Bodger	Kamloops	D	1071	106	422	528	1007
10	Van.	J.J. Daigneault	Longueuil	D	899	53	197	250	687
11	Hfd.	Sylvain Cote	Quebec	D	1171	122	313	435	545
12	Cgy.	Gary Roberts	Ottawa	LW	957	369	389	758	2261
13	Min.	David Quinn	Kent High	D					
14	NYR	Terry Carkner	Peterborough	D	858	42	188	230	1588
15	Que.	Trevor Stienburg	Guelph	RW	71	8	4	12	161
16	Pit.	Roger Belanger	Kingston	C	44	3	5	8	32
17	Wsh.	Kevin Hatcher	North Bay	D	1157	227	450	677	1392
18	Buf.	Mikael Andersson	Vastra Frolunda Goteborg	LW	761	95	169	264	134
19	Bos.	Dave Pasin	Prince Albert	RW	76	18	19	37	50
20	NYI	Duncan MacPherson	Saskatoon	D					
21	Edm.	Selmar Odelein	Regina	D	18	0	2	2	35

SECOND ROUND

PICK	TEAM	NAME	DRAFTED FROM	POS	GP	G / W	A / GA	PTS / SO	PIM / AVG
22	Phi.	Greg Smyth	London	D	229	4	16	20	783
23	N.J.	Craig Billington	Belleville	G	332	17097	1034	9	3.63
24	L.A.	Brian Wilks	Kitchener	C	48	4	8	12	27
25	Tor.	Todd Gill	Windsor	D	1007	82	272	354	1214
26	St.L.	Brian Benning	Portland	D	568	63	233	296	963
27	Phi.	Scott Mellanby	Henry Carr Jr. B	RW	1223	326	413	739	2285
28	Det.	Doug Houda	Calgary	D	561	19	63	82	1104
29	Mtl.	Stephane Richer	Granby	RW	1054	421	398	819	614
30	Wpg.	Peter Douris	New Hampshire	RW	321	54	67	121	80
31	Van.	Jeff Rohlicek	Portland	C	9	0	0	0	8
32	St.L.	Tony Hrkac	Orillia Jr. A.	C	758	132	239	371	173
33	Cgy.	Ken Sabourin	Sault Ste. Marie	D	74	2	8	10	201
34	Wsh.	Stephen Leach	Matignon High	RW	702	130	153	283	978
35	NYR	Raimo Helminen	Ilves Tampere	C	117	13	46	59	16
36	Que.	Jeff Brown	Sudbury	D	747	154	430	584	498
37	Phi.	Jeff Chychrun	Kingston	D	262	3	22	25	744
38	Cgy.	Paul Ranheim	Edina H.S.	LW	1013	161	199	360	288
39	Buf.	Doug Trapp	Regina	LW	2	0	0	0	0
40	Bos.	Ray Podloski	Portland	C	8	0	1	1	17
41	NYI	Bruce Melanson	Oshawa	RW					
42	Edm.	Daryl Reaugh	Kamloops	G	27	1246	72	1	3.47

OTHER ROUNDS

PICK	TEAM	NAME	DRAFTED FROM	POS	GP	G / W	A / GA	PTS / SO	PIM / AVG
43	Phi.	David McLay	Kelowna	LW					
44	N.J.	Neil Davey	Michigan State	D					
45	Chi.	Trent Yawney	Saskatoon	D	593	27	102	129	783
46	Min.	Ken Hodge	St. John's Prep	C/RW	142	39	48	87	32
47	Phi.	John Stevens	Oshawa	D	53	0	10	10	48
48	L.A.	John English	Sault Ste. Marie	D	3	1	3	4	4
49	Det.	Milan Chalupa	Dukla Jihlava	D	14	0	5	5	6
50	St.L.	Toby Ducolon	Bellows Academy	RW					

PICK	TEAM	NAME	DRAFTED FROM	NHL PLAYERS: POS	GP	G	A	PTS	PIM
				NHL GOALTENDERS: POS	GP	W	GA	SO	AVG
51	Mtl.	Patrick Roy	Granby	G	1029	60235	2546	66	2.54
52	Van.	David Saunders	St. Lawrence U.	LW	56	7	13	20	10
53	St.L.	Robert Dirk	Regina	D	402	13	29	42	786
54	Mtl.	Graeme Bonar	Sault Ste. Marie	RW					
55	Van.	Landis Chaulk	Calgary	LW					
56	St.L.	Alan Perry	Mount St. Charles H.S.	G					
57	Que.	Steven Finn	Laval	D	725	34	78	112	1724
58	Van.	Mike Stevens	Kitchener	LW	23	1	4	5	29
59	Wsh.	Michal Pivonka	Poldi SNOP Kladno	C	825	181	418	599	478
60	Buf.	Ray Sheppard	Cornwall	RW	817	357	300	657	212
61	Bos.	Jeff Cornelius	Toronto	D					
62	NYI	Jeff Norton	Cushing Academy	D	799	52	332	384	615
63	Edm.	Todd Norman	Hill-Murray H.S.	C					
64	Pit.	Mark Teevens	Peterborough	RW					
65	Mtl.	Lee Brodeur	Grafton H.S.	RW					
66	Chi.	Tommy Eriksson	MoDo Ornskoldsvik	C					
67	Tor.	Jeff Reese	London	G	174	8667	529	5	3.66
68	Wpg.	Chris Mills	Bramalea Jr. B	D					
69	L.A.	Thomas Glavine	Billerica H.S.	C					
70	NYI	Doug Wieck	Rochester Mayo H.S.	LW					
71	St.L.	Graham Herring	Longueuil	D					
72	Wpg.	Sean Clement	Brockville Jr. A	D					
73	Van.	Brian Bertuzzi	Kamloops	C					
74	N.J.	Paul Ysebaert	Petrolia Jr. B	C	532	149	187	336	217
75	Cgy.	Petr Rosol	Dukla Jihlava	LW					
76	Min.	Miroslav Maly	Bayreuth, FRG	D					
77	NYR	Paul Broten	Roseau H.S.	RW	322	46	55	101	264
78	Que.	Terry Perkins	Portland	RW					
79	Phi.	Dave Hanson	Denver University	C					
80	Wsh.	Kris King	Peterborough	LW	849	66	85	151	2030
81	Buf.	Bob Halkidis	London	D	256	8	32	40	825
82	Bos.	Bob Joyce	Notre Dame Jr. A	LW	158	34	49	83	90
83	NYI	Ari Haanpaa	Ilves Tampere	RW	60	6	11	17	37
84	Edm.	Rich Novak	Richmond Jr.	RW					
85	Pit.	Arto Javanainen	Assat Pori	RW	14	4	1	5	2
86	N.J.	Jon Morris	Chelmsford H.S.	C	103	16	33	49	47
87	L.A.	David Grannis	South St. Paul H.S.	RW					
88	Tor.	Jack Capuano	Kent Prep	D	6	0	0	0	0
89	Min.	Jiri Poner	Landshut, FRG	RW					
90	Chi.	Timo Lehkonen	Jokerit Helsinki	D					
91	Det.	Mats Lundstrom	Skelleftea	LW					
92	St.L.	Scott Paluch	Chicago Jr.	D					
93	Wpg.	Scott Schneider	Colorado College	C					
94	Van.	Brett MacDonald	North Bay	D	1	0	0	0	0
95	Mtl.	Gerald Johannson	Swift Current	D					
96	Cgy.	Joel Paunio	HIFK Helsinki	LW					
97	Min.	Kari Takko	Assat Pori	G	142	7317	475	1	3.90
98	NYR	Clark Donatelli	Stratford Jr. B	LW	35	3	4	7	39
99	Wpg.	Brent Severyn	Seattle	LW	328	10	30	40	825
100	Phi.	Brian Dobbin	London	RW	63	7	8	15	61
101	Chi.	Darin Sceviour	Lethbridge	RW	1	0	0	0	0
102	Buf.	Joel Rampton	Sault Ste. Marie	LW					
103	Bos.	Mike Bishop	London Knights	G					
104	NYI	Mike Murray	London	C	1	0	0	0	0
105	Edm.	Richard Lambert	Henry Carr Jr. B	LW					
106	Edm.	Emanuel Viveiros	Prince Albert	D	29	1	11	12	6
107	N.J.	Kirk McLean	Oshawa	G	612	35090	1904	22	3.26
108	L.A.	Greg Strome	North Dakota	G					
109	Tor.	Fabian Joseph	Victoria	C					
110	Hfd.	Mike Millar	Brantford	RW	78	18	18	36	12
111	Chi.	Chris Clifford	Kingston	G	2	24	0	0	0.00
112	Det.	Randy Hansch	Victoria	G					
113	St.L.	Steve Tuttle	Richmond Jr.	RW	144	28	28	56	12
114	Wpg.	Gary Lorden	Bishop Hendricken H.S.	D					
115	Van.	Jeff Korchinski	Clarkson	D					
116	Mtl.	Jim Nesich	Verdun	RW/C					
117	Cgy.	Brett Hull	Penticton Jr. A	RW	1183	716	606	1322	446
118	Min.	Gary McColgan	Oshawa	LW					
119	NYR	Kjell Samuelsson	Leksand	D	813	48	138	186	1225
120	Que.	Darren Cota	Kelowna	RW					
121	Phi.	John Dzikowski	Brandon	LW					
122	Wsh.	Vito Cramarossa	Toronto	RW					
123	Buf.	James Gasseau	Drummondville	D					
124	Bos.	Randy Oswald	Michigan Tech	D					
125	NYI	Jim Wilharm	Minnetonka H.S.	D					
126	Edm.	Ivan Dornic	Dukla Trencin	LW					
127	Pit.	Tom Ryan	Newton North H.S.	D					
128	N.J.	Ian Ferguson	Oshawa	D					
129	L.A.	Timothy Hanley	Deerfield Academy	C					
130	Tor.	Joseph McInnis	Watertown H.S.	C					
131	Hfd.	Mike Vellucci	Belleville	D	2	0	0	0	11
132	Chi.	Mike Stapleton	Cornwall	C	697	71	111	182	342
133	Det.	Stefan Larsson	Vastra Frolunda Goteborg	D					
134	St.L.	Cliff Ronning	New Westminster	C	1097	297	548	845	451
135	Wpg.	Luciano Borsato	Bramalea Jr. B	C	203	35	55	90	113
136	Van.	Blaine Chrest	Portland	C					
137	Mtl.	Scott MacTavish	Fredericton H.S.	D					
138	Cgy.	Kevan Melrose	Red Deer Jr. A	D					
139	Min.	Vladimir Kyhos	CHZ Litvinov	LW					
140	NYR	Thomas Hussey	St. Andrew's H.S.	LW					
141	Que.	Henrik Cedegren	Brynas Gavle	RW					
142	Phi.	Tom Allen	Kitchener	D					
143	Wsh.	Timo Iljima	Karpat Oulu	C					
144	Buf.	Darcy Wakaluk	Kelowna	G	191	9756	524	9	3.22
145	Bos.	Mark Thietke	Saskatoon	C					
146	NYI	Kelly Murphy	Notre Dame Jr. A	D					
147	Edm.	Heikki Riihijarvi	Kiekko-Espoo	D					
148	St.L.	Don Porter	Michigan Tech	LW					
149	N.J.	Vladimir Kames	Dukla Jihlava	C					
150	L.A.	Shannon Deegan	Vermont	C					
151	Tor.	Derek Laxdal	Brandon	RW	67	12	7	19	88
152	Det.	Lars Karlsson	Farjestad Karlstad	LW					
153	Chi.	Glen Greenough	Sudbury	RW					
154	Det.	Urban Nordin	MoDo Ornskoldsvik	C					
155	St.L.	Jim Vesey	CBJ H.S.	C/RW	15	1	2	3	7
156	Wpg.	Brad Jones	Michigan	LW	148	25	31	56	122
157	Van.	Jim Agnew	Brandon	D	81	0	1	1	257
158	Mtl.	Brad McCaughey	Ann Arbor H.S.	RW					
159	Cgy.	Jiri Hrdina	Sparta Praha	C	250	45	85	130	92
160	Min.	Darin MacInnis	Kent Prep	G					
161	NYR	Brian Nelson	Willmar H.S.	C					
162	Que.	Jyrki Maki	Simley H.S.	D					
163	Phi.	Luke Vitale	Henry Carr Jr. B	C					
164	Wsh.	Frank Joo	Regina	D					
165	Buf.	Orvar Stambert	Djurgarden	D					
166	Bos.	Don Sweeney	St. Paul's H.S.	D	1052	52	210	262	663
167	NYI	Franco Desantis	Verdun	D					
168	Edm.	Todd Ewen	New Westminster	RW	518	36	40	76	1911
169	Pit.	John Del Col	Toronto	LW					
170	N.J.	Mike Roth	Hill-Murray H.S.	D					
171	L.A.	Luc Robitaille	Hull	LW	1286	631	688	1319	1069
172	Tor.	Dan Turner	Medicine Hat	LW					
173	Hfd.	John Devereaux	Scituate H.S.	C					
174	Chi.	Ralph Difiore	Shawinigan	D					
175	Det.	Bill Shibicky	Michigan State	C					
176	St.L.	Daniel Jomphe	Granby	LW					
177	Wpg.	Gord Whitaker	Colorado College	RW					
178	Van.	Rex Grant	Kamloops	G					
179	Mtl.	Eric Demers	Shawinigan	LW					
180	Cgy.	Gary Suter	Wisconsin	D	1145	203	641	844	1349
181	Min.	Duane Wahlin	Johnson H.S.	RW					
182	NYR	Ville Kentala	HIFK Helsinki	LW					
183	Que.	Guy Ouellette	Quebec	C					
184	Phi.	Billy Powers	Matignon H.S.	C					
185	Wsh.	Jim Thomson	Toronto	RW	115	4	3	7	416
186	Bos.	Kevin Heffernan	Weymouth H.S.	C					
187	NYI	Tom Warden	North Bay	D					
188	NYR	Heinz Ehlers	Leksand	C					
189	Pit.	Steve Hurt	Hill-Murray H.S.	RW					
190	N.J.	Mike Peluso	Greenway H.S.	LW	458	38	52	90	1951
191	L.A.	Jeff Crossman	Western Michigan	C					
192	Tor.	David Buckley	Trinity-Pawling H.S.	D					
193	Hfd.	Brent Regan	St. Albert Jr. A	RW					
194	Chi.	Joakim Persson	S/G Hockey 83 Gavle	RW					
195	Det.	Jay Rose	New Prep H.S.	D					
196	St.L.	Tom Tilley	Orillia Jr. A.	D	174	4	38	42	89
197	Wpg.	Rick Forst	Melville Jr. A.	LW					
198	Van.	Ed Lowney	Boston U.	RW					
199	Mtl.	Ron Annear	San Diego U.	D					
200	Cgy.	Petr Rucka	Sparta Praha	C					
201	Min.	Michael Orn	Stillwater H.S.	C					
202	NYR	Kevin Miller	Redford Jr.	C	616	150	183	333	429

PICK	TEAM	NAME	DRAFTED FROM	NHL PLAYERS: POS / NHL GOALTENDERS: POS	GP / GP	G / W	A / GA	PTS / SO	PIM / AVG
203	Que.	Ken Quinney	Calgary	RW	59	7	13	20	23
204	Phi.	Daryn Fersovich	St. Albert Jr. A	C					
205	Wsh.	Paul Cavallini	Henry Carr Jr. B	D	564	56	177	233	750
206	Buf.	Brian McKinnon	Ottawa	C					
207	Bos.	J. D. Urbanic	Windsor	LW					
208	NYI	David Volek	Slavia Praha	W	396	95	154	249	201
209	Edm.	Joel Curtis	Oshawa	LW					
210	Pit.	Jim Steen	Moorehead H.S.	C					
211	N.J.	Jarkko Piiparinen	Kiekkoreipas	C					
212	L.A.	Paul Kenny	Cornwall	G					
213	Tor.	Mikael Wurst	Ohio State	LW					
214	Hfd.	Jim Culhane	Western Michigan	D	6	0	1	1	4
215	Chi.	Bill Brown	Simley H.S.	C					
216	Det.	Tim Kaiser	Guelph	RW/D					
217	St.L.	Mark Cupolo	Guelph	LW					
218	Wpg.	Mike Warus	Lake Superior State	RW					
219	Van.	Doug Clarke	Colorado College	D					
220	Mtl.	Dave Tanner	Notre Dame Jr. A	D					
221	Cgy.	Stefan Jonsson	Sodertalje	D					
222	Min.	Tom Terwilliger	Edina H.S.	D					
223	NYR	Tom Lorentz	Brady H.S.	C					
224	Chi.	David Mackey	Victoria	LW	126	8	12	20	305
225	Wsh.	Mikhail Tatarinov	Sokol Kiev	D	161	21	48	69	184
226	Buf.	Grant Delcourt	Kelowna	RW					
227	Bos.	Bill Kopecky	Austin Prep	C					
228	NYI	Russ Becker	Virginia H.S.	D					
229	Edm.	Simon Wheeldon	Victoria	C	15	0	2	2	10
230	Pit.	Mark Ziliotto	Streetsville Jr. B	LW					
231	N.J.	Chris Kiene	Springfield Jr. B	D					
232	L.A.	Brian Martin	Belleville	C					
233	Tor.	Peter Slanina	VSZ Kosice	D					
234	Hfd.	Peter Abric	North Bay	G					
235	Chi.	Dan Williams	Chicago Jr.	D					
236	Det.	Tom Nickolau	Guelph	C					
237	St.L.	Mark Lanigan	U. of Waterloo	D					
238	Wpg.	Jim Edmonds	Cornell	G					
239	Van.	Ed Kister	London	D					
240	Mtl.	Troy Crosby	Verdun	G					
241	Cgy.	Rudolf Suchanek	Motor Ceske Budejovice	D					
242	Min.	Mike Nightengale	Simley H.S.	D					
243	NYR	Scott Brower	Lloydminster Jr.	G					
244	Que.	Peter Loob	Sodertalje	D	8	1	2	3	0
245	Phi.	Juraj Bakos	VSZ Kosice	D					
246	Wsh.	Per Schedrin	Brynas Gavle	D					
247	Buf.	Sean Baker	Seattle	LW					
248	Bos.	Jim Newhouse	Matignon H.S.	LW					
249	NYI	Allister Brown	New Hampshire	D					
250	Edm.	Darren Gani	Belleville	D					

1985

FIRST ROUND

PICK	TEAM	NAME	DRAFTED FROM	NHL PLAYERS: POS / NHL GOALTENDERS: POS	GP / GP	G / W	A / GA	PTS / SO	PIM / AVG
1	Tor.	Wendel Clark	Saskatoon	LW/D	793	330	234	564	1690
2	Pit.	Craig Simpson	Michigan State	LW	634	247	250	497	659
3	N.J.	Craig Wolanin	Kitchener	D	695	40	133	173	894
4	Van.	Jim Sandlak	London	RW	549	110	119	229	821
5	Hfd.	Dana Murzyn	Calgary	D	838	52	152	204	1571
6	NYI	Brad Dalgarno	Hamilton	RW	321	49	71	120	332
7	NYR	Ulf Dahlen	Ostersund	LW	966	301	354	655	230
8	Det.	Brent Fedyk	Regina	LW	470	97	112	209	308
9	L.A.	Craig Duncanson	Sudbury	LW	38	5	4	9	61
10	L.A.	Dan Gratton	Oshawa	C	7	1	0	1	5
11	Chi.	Dave Manson	Prince Albert	D	1103	102	288	390	2792
12	Mtl.	Jose Charbonneau	Drummondville	RW	71	9	13	22	67
13	NYI	Derek King	Sault Ste. Marie	LW	830	261	351	612	417
14	Buf.	Calle Johansson	Vastra Frolunda	D	1101	119	410	529	519
15	Que.	David Latta	Kitchener	LW	36	4	8	12	4
16	Mtl.	Tom Chorske	Minneapolis SW H.S.	LW	596	115	122	237	225
17	Cgy.	Chris Biotti	Belmont Hill H.S.	D					
18	Wpg.	Ryan Stewart	Kamloops	C	3	1	0	1	0
19	Wsh.	Yvon Corriveau	Toronto	LW	280	48	40	88	310
20	Edm.	Scott Metcalfe	Kingston	LW	19	1	2	3	18
21	Phi.	Glen Seabrooke	Peterborough	C	19	1	6	7	4

SECOND ROUND

PICK	TEAM	NAME	DRAFTED FROM	NHL PLAYERS: POS / NHL GOALTENDERS: POS	GP / GP	G / W	A / GA	PTS / SO	PIM / AVG
22	Tor.	Ken Spangler	Calgary	D					
23	Pit.	Lee Giffin	Oshawa	RW	27	1	3	4	9
24	N.J.	Sean Burke	Toronto	G	715	40799	2023	33	2.98
25	Van.	Troy Gamble	Medicine Hat	G	72	3804	229	1	3.61
26	Hfd.	Kay Whitmore	Peterborough	G	155	8596	508	4	3.55
27	Cgy.	Joe Nieuwendyk	Cornell	C	1113	511	501	1012	601
28	NYR	Mike Richter	Northwood Prep	G	666	38183	1840	24	2.89
29	Det.	Jeff Sharples	Kelowna	D	105	14	35	49	70
30	L.A.	Par Edlund	Bjorkloven Umea	RW					
31	Bos.	Alain Cote	Quebec	D	119	2	18	20	124
32	N.J.	Eric Weinrich	North Yarmouth Academy	D	1002	65	287	352	727
33	Mtl.	Todd Richards	Armstrong H.S.	D	8	0	4	4	4
34	NYI	Brad Lauer	Regina	LW	323	44	67	111	218
35	Buf.	Benoit Hogue	St-Jean	C	863	222	321	543	877
36	Que.	Jason Lafreniere	Hamilton	C	146	34	53	87	22
37	St.L.	Herb Raglan	Kingston	RW	343	33	56	89	775
38	Cgy.	Jeff Wenaas	Medicine Hat	C					
39	Wpg.	Roger Ohman	Leksand	D					
40	Wsh.	John Druce	Peterborough	RW	531	113	126	239	347
41	Edm.	Todd Carnelley	Kamloops	D					
42	Phi.	Bruce Rendall	Chatham Jr. B	LW					

OTHER ROUNDS

PICK	TEAM	NAME	DRAFTED FROM	NHL PLAYERS: POS / NHL GOALTENDERS: POS	GP / GP	G / W	A / GA	PTS / SO	PIM / AVG
43	Tor.	Dave Thomlinson	Brandon	LW	42	1	3	4	50
44	St.L.	Nelson Emerson	Stratford Jr. A	RW	771	195	293	488	575
45	N.J.	Myles O'Connor	Notre Dame Jr. A	D	43	3	4	7	69
46	Van.	Shane Doyle	Belleville	D					
47	Mtl.	Rocky Dundas	Spokane	RW	5	0	0	0	14
48	Phi.	Darryl Gilmour	Moose Jaw	G					
49	NYR	Sam Lindstahl	Sodertalje	G					
50	Det.	Steve Chiasson	Guelph	D	751	93	305	398	1107
51	Min.	Stephane Roy	Granby	C	12	1	0	1	0
52	Bos.	Bill Ranford	New Westminster	G	647	35936	2042	15	3.41
53	Chi.	Andy Helmuth	Ottawa	G					
54	St.L.	Ned Desmond	Hotchkiss H.S.	D					
55	NYI	Jeff Finley	Portland	D	655	13	69	82	423
56	Buf.	Keith Gretzky	Windsor	C					
57	Que.	Max Middendorf	Sudbury	RW	13	2	4	6	6
58	Pit.	Bruce Racine	Northeastern	G	11	230	12	0	3.13
59	Cgy.	Lane Macdonald	Harvard	LW					
60	Wpg.	Daniel Berthiaume	Chicoutimi	G	215	11662	714	5	3.67
61	Wsh.	Rob Murray	Peterborough	C	107	4	15	19	111
62	Edm.	Michael Ware	Hamilton	RW	5	0	1	1	15
63	Phi.	Shane Whelan	Oshawa	C					
64	Tor.	Greg Vey	Peterborough	C					
65	Que.	Peter Massey	New Hampton H.S.	LW					
66	N.J.	Gregg Polak	Lincoln H.S.	LW					
67	Van.	Randy Siska	Medicine Hat	C					
68	Hfd.	Gary Callaghan	Belleville	C					
69	Min.	Mike Berger	Lethbridge	D	30	3	1	4	67
70	NYR	Pat Janostin	Notre Dame Jr. A	D					
71	Det.	Mark Gowans	Windsor	G					
72	L.A.	Perry Florio	Kent Prep	D					
73	Bos.	Jaime Kelly	Scituate H.S.	RW					
74	Chi.	Dan Vincelette	Drummondville	LW	193	20	22	42	351
75	Mtl.	Martin Desjardins	Trois-Rivieres	C	8	0	2	2	2
76	NYI	Kevin Herom	Moose Jaw	LW					
77	Buf.	Dave Moylan	Sudbury	D					
78	Que.	David Espe	White Bear Lake H.S.	D					
79	Mtl.	Brent Gilchrist	Kelowna	LW	792	135	170	305	400
80	Cgy.	Roger Johansson	Troja	D	161	9	34	43	163
81	Wpg.	Fredrik Olausson	Farjestad Karlstad	D	1022	147	434	581	450
82	Wsh.	Bill Houlder	North Bay	D	846	59	191	250	412
83	Wsh.	Larry Shaw	Peterborough	D					
84	Phi.	Paul Marshall	Northwood Prep	D					
85	Tor.	Jeff Serowik	Lawrence Academy	D	28	0	6	6	16
86	Pit.	Steve Gotaas	Prince Albert	C	49	6	9	15	53
87	Chi.	Rick Herbert	Portland	D					
88	Van.	Robert Kron	Zetor Brno	LW	771	144	194	338	119
89	NYI	Tommy Hedlund	AIK Solna	D					
90	Min.	Dwight Mullins	Lethbridge	C					
91	NYR	Brad Stephan	Hastings H.S.	LW					
92	Det.	Chris Luongo	St. Clair Shores H.S.	D	218	8	23	31	176
93	L.A.	Petr Prajsler	Tesla Pardubice	D	46	3	10	13	51
94	Bos.	Steve Moore	London Jr. B	D					

PICK	TEAM	NAME	DRAFTED FROM	NHL PLAYERS: POS / NHL GOALTENDERS: POS	GP / GP	G / W	A / GA	PTS / SO	PIM / AVG
95	Chi.	Brad Belland	Sudbury	C					
96	Mtl.	Tom Sagissor	Hastings H.S.	C					
97	NYI	Jeff Sveen	Boston U.	C					
98	Buf.	Ken Priestlay	Victoria	C	168	27	34	61	63
99	Que.	Bruce Major	Richmond Jr.	C	4	0	0	0	0
100	St.L.	Dan Brooks	St. Thomas Academy	D					
101	Cgy.	Esa Keskinen	TPS Turku	C					
102	Wpg.	John Borrell	Burnsville H.S.	RW					
103	Wsh.	Claude Dumas	Granby	C					
104	Edm.	Tomas Kapusta	TJ Gottwaldov	C					
105	Phi.	Daril Holmes	Kingston	RW					
106	Tor.	Jiri Latal	Sparta Praha	D	92	12	36	48	24
107	Pit.	Kevin Clemens	Regina	LW					
108	N.J.	Bill McMillan	Peterborough	RW					
109	Van.	Martin Hrstka	Ingstav Brno	LW					
110	Hfd.	Shane Churla	Medicine Hat	RW	488	26	45	71	2301
111	Min.	Michael Mullowney	Deerfield Academy	D					
112	NYR	Brian McReynolds	Orillia Jr. A	C	30	1	5	6	8
113	Det.	Randy McKay	Michigan Tech	RW	932	162	201	363	1731
114	Pit.	Stuart Marston	Longueuil	D					
115	Bos.	Gord Hynes	Medicine Hat	D	52	3	9	12	22
116	Chi.	Jonas Heed	Sodertalje	D					
117	Mtl.	Donald Dufresne	Trois-Rivieres	D	268	6	36	42	258
118	NYI	Rod Dallman	Prince Albert	LW	6	1	0	1	26
119	Buf.	Joe Reekie	Cornwall	D	902	25	139	164	1326
120	Que.	Andy Akervik	Claire H.S.	C					
121	St.L.	Rich Burchill	Catholic Memorial H.S.	G					
122	Cgy.	Tim Sweeney	Weymouth North H.S.	LW	291	55	83	138	123
123	Wpg.	Danton Cole	Aurora Jr. A	C/RW	318	58	60	118	125
124	Wsh.	Doug Stromback	Kitchener	RW					
125	Edm.	Brian Tessier	North Bay	G					
126	Phi.	Ken Alexander	Kitchener	D					
127	Tor.	Tim Bean	North Bay	LW					
128	Pit.	Steve Titus	Cornwall	G					
129	N.J.	Kevin Schrader	Burnsville H.S.	D					
130	Van.	Brian McFarlane	Seattle	RW					
131	Hfd.	Chris Brant	Sault Ste. Marie	LW					
132	Min.	Michael Kelfer	St. John's Prep	C					
133	NYR	Neil Pilon	Kamloops	D					
134	Det.	Thomas Bjur	AIK Solna	RW					
135	L.A.	Tim Flannigan	Michigan Tech	RW					
136	Bos.	Per Martinelle	AIK Solna	RW					
137	Chi.	Victor Posa	Wisconsin	LW/D	2	0	0	0	2
138	St.L.	Pat Jablonski	Detroit Compuware Jr. A.	G	128	6634	413	1	3.74
139	NYI	Kurt Lackten	Moose Jaw	RW					
140	Buf.	Petri Matikainen	SaPKo Savolinna	D					
141	Que.	Mike Oliverio	Sault Ste. Marie	C					
142	Mtl.	Ed Cristofoli	Penticton Jr. A	RW	9	0	1	1	4
143	Cgy.	Stu Grimson	Regina	LW	729	17	22	39	2113
144	Wpg.	Brent Mowery	Summerland Jr.	LW					
145	Wsh.	Jamie Nadjiwan	Sudbury	LW					
146	Edm.	Shawn Tyers	Kitchener	RW					
147	Phi.	Tony Horacek	Kelowna	LW	154	10	19	29	316
148	Tor.	Andy Donahue	Belmont Hill H.S.	C					
149	Pit.	Paul Stanton	Catholic Memorial H.S.	D	295	14	49	63	262
150	N.J.	Ed Krayer	St. Paul's H.S.	C					
151	Van.	Hakan Ahlund	Orebro	RW					
152	Hfd.	Brian Puhalsky	Notre Dame Jr. A	LW					
153	Min.	Ross Johnson	Mayo H.S.	C					
154	NYR	Larry Bernard	Seattle	LW					
155	Det.	Mike Luckraft	Burnsville H.S.	D					
156	L.A.	John Hyduke	Hibbing H.S.	D					
157	Bos.	Randy Burridge	Peterborough	LW	706	199	251	450	458
158	Chi.	John Reid	Belleville	G					
159	St.L.	Scott Brickey	Port Huron Jr.	RW					
160	NYI	Hank Lammens	St. Lawrence U.	D	27	1	2	3	22
161	Buf.	Trent Kaese	Lethbridge	RW	1	0	0	0	0
162	Que.	Mario Brunetta	Quebec	G	40	1967	128	0	3.90
163	Mtl.	Mike Claringbull	Medicine Hat	D					
164	Cgy.	Nate Smith	Lawrence Academy	D					
165	Wpg.	Tom Draper	Vermont	G	53	2807	173	1	3.70
166	Wsh.	Mark Haarmann	Oshawa	D					
167	Edm.	Tony Fairfield	St. Albert Jr. A	RW					
168	Phi.	Mike Cusack	Dubuque Jr. A	RW					
169	Tor.	Todd Whittemore	Kent Prep	C					
170	Pit.	Jim Paek	Oshawa	D	217	5	29	34	155
171	N.J.	Jamie Huscroft	Seattle	D	352	5	33	38	1065
172	Van.	Curtis Hunt	Prince Albert	D					
173	Hfd.	Greg Dornbach	Miami of Ohio	C					
174	Min.	Tim Helmer	Ottawa	C					
175	NYR	Stephane Brochu	Quebec	D	1	0	0	0	0
176	Det.	Rob Schenna	St. John's Prep	D					
177	L.A.	Steve Horner	Henry Carr Jr. B	RW					
178	Bos.	Gord Cruickshank	Providence	C					
179	Chi.	Richard Laplante	Vermont	C					
180	St.L.	Jeff Urban	Minnetonka H.S.	LW					
181	NYI	Rich Wiest	Lethbridge	C					
182	Buf.	Jiri Sejba	Dukla Jihlava	LW	11	0	2	2	8
183	Que.	Brit Peer	Sault Ste. Marie	RW					
184	Mtl.	Roger Beedon	Sarnia Jr. B	G					
185	Cgy.	Darryl Olsen	St. Albert Jr. A	D	1	0	0	0	0
186	Wpg.	Nevin Kardum	Henry Carr Jr. B	C					
187	Wsh.	Steve Hollett	Sault Ste. Marie	C					
188	Edm.	Kelly Buchberger	Moose Jaw	RW	1111	104	201	305	2188
189	Phi.	Gord Murphy	Oshawa	D	862	85	238	323	668
190	Tor.	Bobby Reynolds	St. Clair Shores H.S.	LW	7	1	1	2	0
191	Pit.	Steve Shaunessy	Reading H.S.	D					
192	N.J.	Terry Shold	International Falls H.S.	LW					
193	Van.	Carl Valimont	University of Lowell	D					
194	Hfd.	Paul Tory	Illinois-Chicago	C					
195	Min.	Gordon Ernst	Cranston East H.S.	C					
196	NYR	Steve Nemeth	Lethbridge	C	12	2	0	2	2
197	Det.	Erik Hamalainen	Lukko Rauma	D					
198	Mtl.	Maurice Mansi	RPI	C					
199	Bos.	Dave Buda	Streetsville Jr. B	LW					
200	Chi.	Brad Hamilton	Aurora Jr. A	D					
201	St.L.	Vince Guidotti	Noble and Greenough H.S.	D					
202	NYI	Real Arsenault	Prince Andrew H.S.	LW					
203	Buf.	Boyd Sutton	Stratford Jr. B.	C					
204	Que.	Tom Sasso	Babson College	C					
205	Mtl.	Chad Arthur	Stratford Jr. B	LW					
206	Cgy.	Peter Romberg	Iserlohn, FRG	D					
207	Wpg.	Dave Quigley	U. of Moncton	G					
208	Wsh.	Dallas Eakins	Peterborough	D	120	0	9	9	208
209	Edm.	Mario Barbe	Chicoutimi	D					
210	Bos.	Bob Beers	Buffalo Jr.	D	258	28	79	107	225
211	Tor.	Tim Armstrong	Toronto	C	11	1	0	1	6
212	Pit.	Doug Greschuk	St. Albert Jr. A	D					
213	N.J.	Jamie McKinley	Guelph	C					
214	Van.	Igor Larionov	CSKA	C	872	168	465	633	454
215	Hfd.	Jerry Pawlowski	Harvard	D					
216	Min.	Ladislav Lubina	Tesla Pardubice	RW					
217	NYR	Robert Burakovsky	Leksand	RW	23	2	3	5	6
218	Det.	Bo Svanberg	Farjestad Karlstad	C					
219	L.A.	Trent Ciprick	Brandon	RW					
220	Bos.	John Byce	Madison Memorial H.S.	C	21	2	3	5	6
221	Chi.	Ian Pound	Kitchener	D					
222	St.L.	Ron Saatzer	Hopkins H.S.	C					
223	NYI	Mike Volpe	St. Mary's U.	G					
224	Buf.	Guy Larose	Guelph	C	70	10	9	19	63
225	Que.	Gary Murphy	Arlington Catholic H.S.	D					
226	Mtl.	Mike Bishop	Sarnia Jr. B	D					
227	Cgy.	Alexander Kozhevnikov	Spartak	LW					
228	Wpg.	Chris Norton	Cornell	D					
229	Wsh.	Steve Hrynewich	Ottawa	LW					
230	Edm.	Peter Headon	Notre Dame Jr. A	C					
231	Phi.	Rod Williams	Kelowna	RW					
232	Tor.	Mitch Murphy	St. Paul's H.S.	G					
233	Pit.	Gregory Choules	Chicoutimi	LW					
234	N.J.	David Williams	Choate	D	173	11	53	64	157
235	Van.	Darren Taylor	Calgary	LW					
236	Hfd.	Bruce Hill	U. of Denver	LW					
237	Min.	Tommy Sjodin	Timra	D	106	8	40	48	52
238	NYR	Rudy Poeschek	Kamloops	RW/D	364	6	25	31	817
239	Det.	Mikael Lindman	AIK Solna	D					
240	L.A.	Marian Horwath	Slovan Bratislava	LW					
241	Bos.	Marc West	Burlington Jr. B	C					
242	Chi.	Rick Braccia	Avon Old Farms H.S.	LW					
243	St.L.	Dave Jecha	Minnetonka H.S.	D					
244	NYI	Tony Grenier	Prince Albert	C					
245	Buf.	Ken Baumgartner	Prince Albert	LW	696	13	41	54	2244
246	Que.	Jean Bois	Trois-Rivieres	LW					

PICK	TEAM	NAME	DRAFTED FROM	NHL PLAYERS: POS / NHL GOALTENDERS: POS	GP / GP	G / W	A / GA	PTS / SO	PIM / AVG
247	Mtl.	John Ferguson Jr.	Winnipeg South Blues Jr.	LW					
248	Cgy.	Bill Gregoire	Victoria	D					
249	Wpg.	Anssi Melametsa	HIFK Helsinki	LW	27	0	3	3	2
250	Wsh.	Frank Di Muzio	Belleville	C					
251	Edm.	John Haley	Hull H.S.	G					
252	Phi.	Paul Maurice	Windsor	D					

1986

FIRST ROUND

PICK	TEAM	NAME	DRAFTED FROM	POS	GP	G / W	A / GA	PTS / SO	PIM / AVG
1	Det.	Joe Murphy	Michigan State	RW	779	233	295	528	810
2	L.A.	Jimmy Carson	Verdun	C	626	275	286	561	254
3	N.J.	Neil Brady	Medicine Hat	C	89	9	22	31	95
4	Pit.	Zarley Zalapski	Canadian National	D	637	99	285	384	684
5	Buf.	Shawn Anderson	Canadian National	D	255	11	51	62	117
6	Tor.	Vincent Damphousse	Laval	C	1296	420	744	1164	1124
7	Van.	Dan Woodley	Portland	RW	5	2	0	2	17
8	Wpg.	Pat Elynuik	Prince Albert	RW	506	154	188	342	459
9	NYR	Brian Leetch	Avon Old Farms H.S.	D	1072	227	718	945	501
10	St.L.	Jocelyn Lemieux	Laval	RW	598	80	84	164	740
11	Hfd.	Scott Young	Boston U.	RW	1049	316	376	692	382
12	Min.	Warren Babe	Lethbridge	LW	21	2	5	7	23
13	Bos.	Craig Janney	Boston College	C	760	188	563	751	170
14	Chi.	Everett Sanipass	Verdun	LW	164	25	34	59	358
15	Mtl.	Mark Pederson	Medicine Hat	LW	169	35	50	85	77
16	Cgy.	George Pelawa	Bemidji High	RW					
17	NYI	Tom Fitzgerald	Austin Prep	RW	957	128	174	302	684
18	Que.	Ken McRae	Sudbury	C	137	14	21	35	364
19	Wsh.	Jeff Greenlaw	Canadian National	LW	57	3	6	9	108
20	Phi.	Kerry Huffman	Guelph	D	401	37	108	145	361
21	Edm.	Kim Issel	Prince Albert	RW	4	0	0	0	0

SECOND ROUND

PICK	TEAM	NAME	DRAFTED FROM	POS	GP	G / W	A / GA	PTS / SO	PIM / AVG
22	Det.	Adam Graves	Windsor	LW	1152	329	287	616	1224
23	Phi.	Jukka Seppo	Sport Vaasa	LW					
24	N.J.	Todd Copeland	Belmont Hill High	D					
25	Pit.	Dave Capuano	Mount St. Charles High	LW	104	17	38	55	56
26	Buf.	Greg Brown	St. Mark's High	D	94	4	14	18	86
27	Mtl.	Benoit Brunet	Hull	LW	539	101	161	262	229
28	Phi.	Kent Hawley	Ottawa	C					
29	Wpg.	Teppo Numminen	Tappara Tampere	D	1098	108	426	534	405
30	Min.	Neil Wilkinson	Selkirk Jr. A	D	460	16	67	83	813
31	St.L.	Mike Posma	Buffalo Jr. A	D					
32	Hfd.	Marc Laforge	Kingston	LW	14	0	0	0	64
33	Min.	Dean Kolstad	Prince Albert	D	40	1	7	8	69
34	Bos.	Pekka Tirkkonen	SaPKo Savolinna	C					
35	Chi.	Mark Kurzawski	Windsor	D					
36	Tor.	Darryl Shannon	Windsor	D	544	28	111	139	523
37	Cgy.	Brian Glynn	Saskatoon	D	431	25	79	104	410
38	NYI	Dennis Vaske	Armstrong High	D	235	5	41	46	253
39	Que.	Jean-Marc Routhier	Hull	RW	8	0	0	0	9
40	Wsh.	Steve Seftel	Kingston	LW	4	0	0	0	2
41	Que.	Stephane Guerard	Shawinigan	D	34	0	0	0	40
42	Edm.	Jamie Nichols	Portland	LW					

OTHER ROUNDS

PICK	TEAM	NAME	DRAFTED FROM	POS	GP	G / W	A / GA	PTS / SO	PIM / AVG
43	Det.	Derek Mayer	U. of Denver	D	17	2	2	4	8
44	L.A.	Denis Larocque	Guelph	D	8	0	1	1	18
45	N.J.	Janne Ojanen	Tappara Tampere	C	98	21	23	44	28
46	Pit.	Brad Aitken	Sault Ste. Marie	LW	14	1	3	4	25
47	Buf.	Bob Corkum	U. of Maine	C	720	97	103	200	281
48	Tor.	Sean Boland	Toronto	D					
49	Van.	Don Gibson	Winkler Jr. A	D	14	0	3	3	20
50	Wpg.	Esa Palosaari	Karpat Oulu	RW					
51	NYR	Bret Walter	U. of Alberta	C					
52	St.L.	Tony Hejna	Nichols H.S.	LW					
53	NYR	Shawn Clouston	U. of Alberta	RW					
54	Min.	Rick Bennett	Wilbraham Monson H.S.	LW	15	1	1	2	13
55	Min.	Rob Zettler	Sault Ste. Marie	D	569	5	65	70	920
56	Buf.	Kevin Kerr	Windsor	RW					
57	Mtl.	Jyrki Lumme	Ilves Tampere	D	985	114	354	468	620
58	Min.	Brad Turner	Calgary	D	3	0	0	0	0
59	NYI	Bill Berg	Toronto	LW	546	55	67	122	488
60	Wsh.	Shawn Simpson	Sault Ste. Marie	G					
61	Wsh.	Jim Hrivnak	Merrimack	G	85	4217	262	0	3.73
62	N.J.	Marc Laniel	Oshawa	D					
63	Edm.	Ron Shudra	Kamloops	D	10	0	5	5	6
64	Det.	Tim Cheveldae	Saskatoon	G	340	19172	1116	10	3.49
65	L.A.	Sylvain Couturier	Laval	C	33	4	5	9	4
66	N.J.	Anders Carlsson	Sodertalje	C	104	7	26	33	34
67	Pit.	Rob Brown	Kamloops	RW	543	190	248	438	599
68	Buf.	David Baseggio	Yale	D					
69	Tor.	Kent Hulst	Windsor	C					
70	Van.	Ron Stern	Longueuil	RW	638	75	86	161	2077
71	Wpg.	Hannu Jarvenpaa	Karpat Oulu	RW	114	11	26	37	83
72	NYR	Mark Janssens	Regina	C	711	40	73	113	1422
73	St.L.	Glen Featherstone	Windsor	D	384	19	61	80	939
74	Hfd.	Brian Chapman	Belleville	D	3	0	0	0	29
75	Min.	Kirk Tomlinson	Hamilton	C	1	0	0	0	0
76	Bos.	Dean Hall	St. James Jr. A	C					
77	Chi.	Frantisek Kucera	Sparta Praha	D	465	24	95	119	251
78	Mtl.	Brent Bobyck	Notre Dame Midgets	LW					
79	Cgy.	Tom Quinlan	Hill-Murray H.S.	RW					
80	NYI	Shawn Byram	Regina	LW	5	0	0	0	14
81	Que.	Ron Tugnutt	Peterborough	G	526	28938	1475	25	3.06
82	Wsh.	Erin Ginnell	Calgary	C					
83	Phi.	Mark Bar	Peterborough	D					
84	Edm.	Dan Currie	Sault Ste. Marie	LW	22	2	1	3	4
85	Det.	Johan Garpenlov	Nacka	LW	609	114	197	311	276
86	L.A.	Dave Guden	Roxbury Latin	LW					
87	St.L.	Michael Wolak	Kitchener	C					
88	Pit.	Sandy Smith	Brainerd H.S.	C					
89	Buf.	Larry Rooney	Thayer Academy	F					
90	Tor.	Scott Taylor	Kitchener	D					
91	Van.	Eric Murano	Calgary	C					
92	Wpg.	Craig Endean	Seattle	LW	2	0	1	1	0
93	NYR	Jeff Bloemberg	North Bay	D	43	3	6	9	25
94	Mtl.	Eric Aubertin	Granby	LW					
95	Hfd.	Bill Horn	Western Michigan	G					
96	Min.	Jari Gronstrand	Tappara Tampere	D	185	8	26	34	135
97	Bos.	Matt Pesklewis	St. Albert Jr. A	LW					
98	Chi.	Lonnie Loach	Guelph	LW	56	10	13	23	29
99	Mtl.	Mario Milani	Verdun	RW					
100	Cgy.	Scott Bloom	Burnsville H.S.	LW					
101	NYI	Dean Sexsmith	Brandon	C					
102	Que.	Gerald Bzdel	Regina	D					
103	Wsh.	John Purves	Hamilton	RW	7	1	0	1	0
104	NYI	Todd McLellan	Saskatoon	C	5	1	1	2	0
105	Edm.	David Haas	London	LW	7	2	1	3	7
106	Det.	Jay Stark	Portland	D					
107	L.A.	Robb Stauber	Duluth Denfield H.S.	G	62	3295	209	1	3.81
108	N.J.	Troy Crowder	Hamilton	RW	150	9	7	16	433
109	Pit.	Jeff Daniels	Oshawa	LW	425	17	26	43	83
110	Buf.	Miguel Baldris	Shawinigan	D					
111	Tor.	Stephane Giguere	St-Jean	LW					
112	Van.	Steve Herniman	Cornwall	D					
113	Wpg.	Robertson Bateman	St. Laurent College	RW					
114	NYR	Darren Turcotte	North Bay	C	635	195	216	411	301
115	St.L.	Mike O' Toole	Markham Jr. B	W					
116	Hfd.	Joe Quinn	Calgary	RW					
117	Que.	Scott White	Michigan Tech	D					
118	Bos.	Garth Premak	New Westminster	D					
119	Chi.	Mario Doyon	Drummondville	D	28	3	4	7	16
120	Mtl.	Steve Bisson	Sault Ste. Marie	D					
121	Cgy.	John Parker	White Bear Lake H.S.	C					
122	NYI	Tony Schmalzbauer	Hill-Murray H.S.	D					
123	Que.	Morgan Samuelsson	Boden	F					
124	Wsh.	Stefan Nilsson	Lulea IF	C	Re-entered Draft in 1988				
125	Phi.	Steve Scheifele	Stratford Jr. B	RW					
126	Edm.	Jim Ennis	Boston U.	D	5	1	0	1	10
127	Det.	Per Djoos	Mora	D	82	2	31	33	58
128	L.A.	Sean Krakiwsky	Calgary	RW					
129	N.J.	Kevin Todd	Prince Albert	C	383	70	133	203	225
130	Pit.	Doug Hobson	Prince Albert	D					
131	Buf.	Mike Hartman	North Bay	LW	397	43	35	78	1388
132	Tor.	Danny Hie	Ottawa	C					
133	Van.	Jon Helgeson	Roseau H.S.	C					
134	Que.	Mark Vermette	Lake Superior State	RW	67	5	13	18	33
135	NYR	Robb Graham	Guelph	RW					
136	St.L.	Andy May	Bramalea Jr. B.						
137	Hfd.	Steve Torrel	Hibbing H.S.	C					
138	NYI	Will Anderson	Victoria						

PICK	TEAM	NAME	DRAFTED FROM	NHL PLAYERS: POS	GP	G	A	PTS	PIM
				NHL GOALTENDERS: POS	GP	W	GA	SO	AVG
139	Bos.	Paul Beraldo	Sault Ste. Marie	RW	10	0	0	0	4
140	Chi.	Mike Hudson	Sudbury	C/LW	416	49	87	136	414
141	Mtl.	Lyle Odelein	Moose Jaw	D	947	46	189	235	2178
142	Cgy.	Rick Lessard	Ottawa	D	15	0	4	4	18
143	NYI	Rich Pilon	Prince Albert AAA	D	631	8	69	77	1745
144	Que.	Jean F. Nault	Granby	C					
145	Wsh.	Peter Choma	Belleville	RW					
146	Phi.	Sami Wahlsten	TPS Turku	W					
147	Edm.	Ivan Matulik	Slovan Bratislava	LW					
148	Det.	Dean Morton	Oshawa	D	1	1	0	1	2
149	L.A.	Rene Chapdelaine	Lake Superior State	D	32	0	2	2	32
150	N.J.	Ryan Pardoski	Calgary	LW					
151	Pit.	Steve Rohlik	Hill-Murray H.S.						
152	Buf.	Francois Guay	Laval	C	1	0	0	0	0
153	Tor.	Stephen Brennan	New Prep H.S.	W					
154	Van.	Jeff Noble	Kitchener	C					
155	Wpg.	Frank Furlan	Sherwood Park Jr. A	G					
156	NYR	Barry Chyzowski	St. Albert Jr. A	C					
157	St.L.	Randy Skarda	St. Thomas Academy	D	26	0	5	5	11
158	Hfd.	Ron Hoover	Western Michigan	C	18	4	0	4	31
159	Min.	Scott Mathias	U. of Denver	C					
160	Bos.	Brian Ferreira	Falmouth H.S.	RW					
161	Chi.	Marty Nanne	Minnesota-Duluth	RW					
162	Mtl.	Rick Hayward	Hull	D	4	0	0	0	5
163	Cgy.	Mark Olsen	Colorado College	D					
164	NYI	Peter Harris	Haverhill H.S.	G					
165	Que.	Keith Miller	Guelph	LW					
166	Wsh.	Lee Davidson	Penticton Jr. A	C					
167	Phi.	Murray Baron	Vernon Jr. A	D	908	34	89	123	1248
168	Edm.	Nicolas Beaulieu	Drummondville	LW					
169	Det.	Marc Potvin	Stratford Jr. B	RW	121	3	5	8	456
170	L.A.	Trevor Pochipinski	Penticton Jr. A	D					
171	N.J.	Scott McCormack	St. Paul's H.S.						
172	Pit.	Dave McLlwain	North Bay	C/RW	501	100	107	207	292
173	Buf.	Shawn Whitham	Providence	D					
174	Tor.	Brian Bellefeuille	Canterbury H.S.	LW					
175	Van.	Matt Merton	Stratford Jr. B	G					
176	Wpg.	Mark Green	New Hampton H.S.	C					
177	NYR	Pat Scanlon	Cretin H.S.						
178	St.L.	Martyn Ball	St. Michael's Jr. B	LW					
179	Hfd.	Robert Glasgow	Sherwood Park Jr. A	RW					
180	Min.	Lance Pitlick	Cooper H.S.	D	393	16	33	49	298
181	Bos.	Jeff Flaherty	Weymouth H.S.	RW					
182	Chi.	Geoff Benic	Windsor	LW					
183	Mtl.	Antonin Routa	Poldi SNOP Kladno	D					
184	Cgy.	Scott Sharples	Penticton Jr. A	G	1	65	4	0	3.69
185	NYI	Jeff Jablonski	London Jr. B	LW					
186	Que.	Pierre Millier	Chicoutimi	D					
187	Wsh.	Tero Toivola	Tappara Tampere	W					
188	Phi.	Blaine Rude	Fergus Falls	RW					
189	Edm.	Mike Greenlay	Calgary Midget AAA	G	2	20	4	0	12.00
190	Det.	Scott King	Vernon Jr. A	G	2	61	3	0	2.95
191	L.A.	Paul Kelly	Guelph	D					
192	N.J.	Frederic Chabot	St. Foy Midget AAA	G	32	1262	62	0	2.95
193	Pit.	Kelly Cain	London	C					
194	Buf.	Kenton Rein	Prince Albert	G					
195	Tor.	Sean Davidson	Toronto	RW					
196	Van.	Marc Lyons	Kingston	D					
197	Wpg.	John Blue	Minnesota-Duluth	G	46	2521	126	1	3.00
198	NYR	Joe Ranger	London	D					
199	St.L.	Rod Thacker	Hamilton	D					
200	Hfd.	Sean Evoy	Cornwall	G					
201	Min.	Dan Keczmer	Detroit Little Caesar's	D	235	8	38	46	212
202	Bos.	Greg Hawgood	Kamloops	D	474	60	164	224	426
203	Chi.	Glen Lowes	Toronto						
204	Mtl.	Eric Bohemier	Hull	G					
205	Cgy.	Doug Pickell	Kamloops	LW					
206	NYI	Kerry Clark	Saskatoon	RW					
207	Que.	Chris Lappin	Canterbury H.S.	D					
208	Wsh.	Bobby Babcock	Sault Ste. Marie	D	2	0	0	0	2
209	Phi.	Shaun Sabol	St. Paul Jr.	D	2	0	0	0	0
210	Edm.	Matt Lanza	Winthrop H.S.	D					
211	Det.	Tom Bissett	Michigan Tech	C	5	0	0	0	0
212	L.A.	Russ Mann	St. Lawrence U.	D					
213	N.J.	John Andersen	Oshawa	LW					
214	Pit.	Stan Drulia	Belleville	RW	126	15	27	42	52
215	Buf.	Tony Arndt	Portland	D					
216	Tor.	Mark Holick	Saskatoon	RW					
217	Van.	Todd Hawkins	Belleville	W	10	0	0	0	15
218	Wpg.	Matt Cote	Lake Superior State						
219	NYR	Russell Parent	South Winnipeg Jr.	D					
220	St.L.	Terry MacLean	Longueuil	C					
221	Hfd.	Cal Brown	Penticton Jr. A	D					
222	Min.	Garth Joy	Hamilton	D					
223	Bos.	Steffan Malmqvist	Leksand	F					
224	Chi.	Chris Thayer	Kent Prep	C					
225	Mtl.	Charlie Moore	Belleville	LW					
226	Cgy.	Anders Lindstrom	Timra	C					
227	NYI	Dan Beaudette	St. Thomas Academy						
228	Que.	Martin Latreille	Laval	D					
229	Wsh.	John Schratz	Amherst Jr. B	D					
230	Phi.	Brett Lawrence	Rochester Jr. B	RW					
231	Edm.	Mojmir Bozik	VSZ Kosice	D					
232	Det.	Peter Ekroth	Sodertalje	D					
233	L.A.	Brian Hayton	Guelph	LW					
234	St.L.	Bill Butler	Northwood Prep	LW					
235	Pit.	Rob Wilson	Sudbury	D					
236	N.J.	Doug Kirton	Orillia Jr. A	W					
237	Tor.	Brian Hoard	Hamilton	D					
238	Van.	Vladimir Krutov	CSKA	LW	61	11	23	34	20
239	Wpg.	Arto Blomsten	Djurgarden	D	25	0	4	4	8
240	NYR	Soren True	Skovbakken, DEN	W					
241	St.L.	David O'Brien	Northeastern	RW					
242	Hfd.	Brian Verbeek	Kingston	C					
243	Min.	Kurt Stahura	Williston Academy	LW					
244	Bos.	Joel Gardner	Sarnia Jr. B	C					
245	Chi.	Sean Williams	Oshawa	C	2	0	0	0	4
246	Mtl.	Karel Svoboda	Skoda Plzen	W					
247	Cgy.	Antonin Stavjana	TJ Gottwaldov	D					
248	NYI	Paul Thompson	Northern Manitoba AAA	D					
249	Que.	Sean Boudreault	Mount St. Charles H.S.	F					
250	Wsh.	Scott McCrory	Oshawa	C					
251	Phi.	Daniel Stephano	Northwood Prep	G					
252	Edm.	Tony Hand	Murrayfield Racers	C					

1987

FIRST ROUND

PICK	TEAM	NAME	DRAFTED FROM	POS	GP	G/W	A/GA	PTS/SO	PIM/AVG
1	Buf.	Pierre Turgeon	Granby	C	1139	480	754	1234	390
2	N.J.	Brendan Shanahan	London	LW	1186	533	565	1098	2156
3	Bos.	Glen Wesley	Portland	D	1173	124	376	500	859
4	L.A.	Wayne McBean	Medicine Hat	D	211	10	39	49	168
5	Pit.	Chris Joseph	Seattle	D	510	39	112	151	567
6	Min.	Dave Archibald	Portland	C/LW	323	57	67	124	139
7	Tor.	Luke Richardson	Peterborough	D	1183	31	142	173	1877
8	Chi.	Jimmy Waite	Chicoutimi	G	106	5253	293	4	3.35
9	Que.	Bryan Fogarty	Kingston	D	156	22	52	74	119
10	NYR	Jay More	New Westminster	D	406	18	54	72	702
11	Det.	Yves Racine	Longueuil	D	508	37	194	231	439
12	St.L.	Keith Osborne	North Bay	RW	16	1	3	4	16
13	NYI	Dean Chynoweth	Medicine Hat	D	241	4	18	22	667
14	Bos.	Stephane Quintal	Granby	D	964	60	175	235	1238
15	Que.	Joe Sakic	Swift Current	C	1074	509	806	1315	440
16	Wpg.	Bryan Marchment	Belleville	D	814	38	137	175	2126
17	Mtl.	Andrew Cassels	Ottawa	C	926	194	500	694	370
18	Hfd.	Jody Hull	Peterborough	RW	830	124	137	261	156
19	Cgy.	Bryan Deasley	U. of Michigan	LW					
20	Phi.	Darren Rumble	Kitchener	D	188	10	26	36	214
21	Edm.	Peter Soberlak	Swift Current	LW					

SECOND ROUND

PICK	TEAM	NAME	DRAFTED FROM	POS	GP	G/W	A/GA	PTS/SO	PIM/AVG
22	Buf.	Brad Miller	Regina	D	82	1	5	6	321
23	N.J.	Ricard Persson	Ostersund	D	229	10	44	54	262
24	Van.	Rob Murphy	Laval	C	125	9	12	21	152
25	Cgy.	Stephane Matteau	Hull	LW	848	144	172	316	742
26	Pit.	Rick Tabaracci	Cornwall	G	286	15255	760	15	2.99
27	L.A.	Mark Fitzpatrick	Medicine Hat	G	329	18329	953	8	3.12
28	Tor.	Daniel Marois	Chicoutimi	RW	350	117	93	210	419
29	Chi.	Ryan McGill	Swift Current	D	151	4	15	19	391
30	Phi.	Jeff Harding	St. Michael's Jr. B	RW	15	0	0	0	47
31	NYR	Daniel Lacroix	Granby	LW	188	11	7	18	379
32	Det.	Gord Kruppke	Prince Albert	D	23	0	0	0	32

PICK	TEAM	NAME	DRAFTED FROM	NHL PLAYERS: POS / NHL GOALTENDERS: POS	GP / GP	G / W	A / GA	PTS / SO	PIM / AVG
33	Mtl.	John LeClair	Bellows Academy	LW	798	359	347	706	377
34	NYI	Jeff Hackett	Oshawa	G	473	26495	1296	23	2.93
35	Min.	Scott McCrady	Medicine Hat	D					
36	Wsh.	Jeff Ballantyne	Ottawa	D					
37	Wpg.	Patrik Ericksson	Brynas Gavle	C					
38	Mtl.	Eric Desjardins	Granby	D	1050	131	408	539	673
39	Hfd.	Adam Burt	North Bay	D	737	37	115	152	961
40	Cgy.	Kevin Grant	Kitchener	D					
41	Det.	Bob Wilkie	Swift Current	D	18	2	5	7	10
42	Edm.	Brad Werenka	Northern Michigan	D	320	19	61	80	299

OTHER ROUNDS

PICK	TEAM	NAME	DRAFTED FROM	POS	GP	G / W	A / GA	PTS / SO	PIM / AVG
43	L.A.	Ross Wilson	Peterborough	RW					
44	Mtl.	Mathieu Schneider	Cornwall	D	914	154	352	506	907
45	Van.	Steve Veilleux	Trois-Rivieres	D					
46	NYR	Simon Gagne	Laval	RW	46	9	18	27	16
47	Pit.	Jamie Leach	Hamilton	RW	81	11	9	20	12
48	Min.	Kevin Kaminski	Saskatoon	C	139	3	10	13	528
49	Tor.	John McIntyre	Guelph	C	351	24	54	78	516
50	Chi.	Cam Russell	Hull	D	396	9	21	30	872
51	Que.	Jim Sprott	London	D					
52	Det.	Dennis Holland	Portland	C					
53	Buf.	Andrew MacVicar	Peterborough	LW					
54	St.L.	Kevin Miehm	Ottawa	C	22	1	4	5	8
55	NYI	Dean Ewen	Spokane	LW					
56	Bos.	Todd Lalonde	Sudbury	LW					
57	Wsh.	Steve Maltais	Cornwall	LW	120	9	18	27	53
58	Mtl.	Francois Gravel	Shawinigan	G					
59	St.L.	Robert Nordmark	Lulea	D	236	13	70	83	254
60	Chi.	Mike Dagenais	Peterborough	D					
61	Cgy.	Scott Mahoney	Oshawa	LW					
62	Phi.	Martin Hostak	Sparta Praha	C	55	3	11	14	24
63	Edm.	Geoff Smith	St. Albert Jr. A	D	462	18	73	91	282
64	Edm.	Peter Eriksson	HV 71 Jonkoping	LW	20	3	3	6	24
65	N.J.	Brian Sullivan	Springfield Jr. B	RW	2	0	1	1	0
66	Van.	Doug Torrel	Hibbing H.S.	C					
67	Bos.	Darwin McPherson	New Westminster	D					
68	Pit.	Risto Kurkinen	JyP HT Jyvaskyla	LW					
69	NYR	Mike Sullivan	Boston U.	C	709	54	82	136	203
70	Cgy.	Tim Harris	Pickering Jr. B.	RW					
71	Tor.	Joe Sacco	Medford H.S.	RW	738	94	119	213	421
72	Que.	Kip Miller	Michigan State	C	383	65	143	208	97
73	Min.	John Weisbrod	Choate	C					
74	Det.	Mark Reimer	Saskatoon	G					
75	St.L.	Darren Smith	North Bay	LW					
76	NYI	George Maneluk	Brandon	G	4	140	15	0	6.43
77	Bos.	Matt DelGuidice	St. Anselm College	G	11	434	28	0	3.87
78	Wsh.	Tyler Larter	Sault Ste. Marie	C	1	0	0	0	0
79	Wpg.	Don McLennan	U. of Denver	D					
80	Mtl.	Kris Miller	Greenway H.S.	D					
81	Hfd.	Terry Yake	Brandon	C	403	77	120	197	220
82	St.L.	Andy Rymsha	Western Michigan	D	6	0	0	0	23
83	Phi.	Tomaz Eriksson	Djurgarden	LW					
84	Buf.	John Bradley	New Hampton H.S.	G					
85	Buf.	David Pergola	Belmont Hill H.S.	RW					
86	N.J.	Kevin Dean	Culver Military Academy	D	331	7	48	55	138
87	Van.	Sean Fabian	Hill-Murray H.S.	D					
88	Min.	Teppo Kivela	Jokerit Helsinki	C					
89	Pit.	Jeff Waver	Hamilton	D					
90	L.A.	Mike Vukonich	Duluth Denfield H.S.	C					
91	Tor.	Mike Eastwood	Pembroke Jr. A	C	701	83	134	217	314
92	Chi.	Ulf Sandstrom	MoDo Ornskoldsvik	RW					
93	Que.	Rob Mendel	Wisconsin	D					
94	NYR	Eric O'Borsky	Yale	C					
95	Det.	Radomir Brazda	Tesla Pardubice	D					
96	Wpg.	Ken Gernander	Greenway H.S.	RW	10	2	3	5	4
97	NYI	Petr Vlk	Dukla Jihlava	LW					
98	Bos.	Ted Donato	Catholic Memorial H.S.	LW	733	144	192	336	378
99	Wsh.	Pat Beauchesne	Moose Jaw	D					
100	Wpg.	Darrin Amundson	Duluth East H.S.	C					
101	Mtl.	Steve McCool	Hill H.S.	D					
102	Hfd.	Marc Rousseau	U. of Denver	D					
103	Cgy.	Tim Corkery	Ferris State	D					
104	Phi.	Bill Gall	New Hampton H.S.	RW					
105	Edm.	Shaun Van Allen	Saskatoon	C	721	82	175	257	401
106	Buf.	Chris Marshall	Boston College H.S.	LW					
107	N.J.	Ben Hankinson	Edina H.S.	RW	43	3	3	6	45
108	Van.	Garry Valk	Sherwood Park Jr. A	RW	777	100	156	256	747
109	Min.	D'arcy Norton	Kamloops	LW					
110	Pit.	Shawn McEachern	Matignon H.S.	RW	801	237	279	516	408
111	L.A.	Greg Batters	Victoria	RW					
112	Tor.	Damian Rhodes	Richfield H.S.	G	309	17339	820	12	2.84
113	Chi.	Mike McCormick	Richmond Jr.	D					
114	Que.	Garth Snow	Mount St. Charles H.S.	G	309	16726	763	15	2.74
115	NYR	Ludek Cajka	Dukla Jihlava	D					
116	Det.	Sean Clifford	Ohio State	D					
117	St.L.	Rob Robinson	Miami of Ohio	D	22	0	1	1	8
118	NYI	Rob DiMaio	Medicine Hat	RW	764	93	143	236	758
119	Bos.	Matt Glennon	Archbishop Williams H.S.	LW	3	0	0	0	2
120	Wsh.	Rich Defreitas	St. Mark's H.S.	D					
121	Wpg.	Joe Harwell	Hill-Murray H.S.	D					
122	Mtl.	Les Kuntar	Nichols H.S.	G	6	302	16	0	3.18
123	Hfd.	Jeff St. Cyr	Michigan Tech	D					
124	Cgy.	Joe Aloi	Hull	D					
125	Phi.	Tony Link	Dimond H.S.	D					
126	Edm.	Radek Toupal	Motor Ceske Budejovice	RW					
127	Buf.	Paul Flanagan	New Hampton H.S.	D					
128	N.J.	Tom Neziol	Miami of Ohio	LW					
129	Van.	Todd Fanning	Ohio State	G					
130	Min.	Timo Kulonen	KalPa Kuopio	D					
131	Pit.	Jim Bodden	Chatham Jr. B	C					
132	L.A.	Kyosti Karjalainen	Brynas Gavle	RW	28	1	8	9	12
133	Tor.	Trevor Jobe	Moose Jaw	LW					
134	Chi.	Stephen Tepper	Westboro H.S.	RW	1	0	0	0	0
135	Que.	Tim Hanus	Minnetonka H.S.	LW					
136	NYR	Clint Thomas	Bartlet H.S.	D					
137	Det.	Mike Gober	Laval	LW					
138	St.L.	Todd Crabtree	Governor Dummer H.S.	D					
139	NYI	Knut Walbye	Furuset Oslo, NOR	C					
140	Bos.	Rob Cheevers	Boston College	C					
141	Wsh.	Devon Oleniuk	Kamloops	D					
142	Wpg.	Todd Hartje	Harvard	C					
143	Mtl.	Rob Kelley	Matignon H.S.	LW					
144	Hfd.	Greg Wolf	Buffalo Regal Midgets	D					
145	Cgy.	Peter Ciavaglia	Nichols H.S.	C	5	0	0	0	0
146	Phi.	Mark Strapon	Hayward H.S.	D					
147	Edm.	Tomas Srsen	Zetor Brno	RW	2	0	0	0	0
148	Buf.	Sean Dooley	Groton	D					
149	N.J.	Jim Dowd	Brick H.S.	C	442	50	124	174	245
150	Van.	Viktor Tyumenev	Spartak	C					
151	Min.	Don Schmidt	Kamloops	D					
152	Pit.	Jiri Kucera	Dukla Jihlava	C					
153	Buf.	Tim Roberts	Deerfield Academy	C					
154	Tor.	Chris Jensen	Northwood Prep	RW					
155	Chi.	John Reilly	Phillips Andover H.S.	LW					
156	Que.	Jake Enebak	Northfield H.S.	LW					
157	NYR	Charles Wiegand	Essex Junction H.S.	C					
158	Det.	Kevin Scott	Vernon Jr. A	C					
159	St.L.	Guy Hebert	Hamilton College	G	491	27889	1307	28	2.81
160	NYI	Jeff Saterdalen	Jefferson H.S.	RW					
161	Bos.	Chris Winnes	Northwood Prep	RW	33	1	6	7	6
162	Wsh.	Thomas Sjogren	Vastra Frolunda Goteborg	RW					
163	Wpg.	Markku Kyllonen	Karpat Oulu	LW	9	0	2	2	2
164	Mtl.	Will Geist	St. Paul Academy	D					
165	Hfd.	John Moore	Yale	C					
166	Cgy.	Theoren Fleury	Moose Jaw	RW	1084	455	633	1088	1840
167	Phi.	Darryl Ingham	U. of Manitoba	RW					
168	Edm.	Age Ellingsen	Storhamar, NOR	D					
169	Buf.	Grant Tkachuk	Saskatoon	LW					
170	N.J.	John Blessman	Toronto	D					
171	Van.	Greg Daly	New Hampton H.S.	D					
172	Min.	Jarmo Myllys	Lukko Rauma	G	39	1846	161	0	5.23
173	Pit.	Jack MacDougall	New Prep H.S.	RW					
174	L.A.	Jeff Gawlicki	Northern Michigan	LW					
175	Tor.	Brian Blad	Belleville	D					
176	Chi.	Lance Werness	Burnsville H.S.	RW					
177	Que.	Jaroslav Sevcik	Zetor Brno	LW	13	0	2	2	2
178	NYR	Eric Burrill	Tartan H.S.	RW					
179	Det.	Mikko Haapakoski	Karpat Oulu	D					
180	St.L.	Robert Dumas	Seattle	D					
181	NYI	Shawn Howard	Penticton Jr. A	D					
182	Bos.	Paul Ohman	St. John's Prep	D					

PICK	TEAM	NAME	DRAFTED FROM	NHL PLAYERS: POS / NHL GOALTENDERS: POS	GP / GP	G / W	A / GA	PTS / SO	PIM / AVG
183	Que.	Ladislav Tresl	Zetor Brno	C					
184	Wpg.	Jim Fernholz	White Bear Lake H.S.	RW					
185	Mtl.	Eric Tremblay	Drummondville	D					
186	Hfd.	Joe Day	St. Lawrence U.	C	72	1	10	11	87
187	Cgy.	Mark Osiecki	Madison Jr. A.	D	93	3	11	14	43
188	Phi.	Bruce McDonald	Loomis-Chaffee H.S.	RW					
189	Edm.	Gavin Armstrong	RPI	G					
190	Buf.	Ian Herbers	Swift Current	D	65	0	5	5	79
191	N.J.	Peter Fry	Victoria	G					
192	Van.	John Fletcher	Clarkson	G					
193	Min.	Larry Olimb	Warroad H.S.	D					
194	Pit.	Daryn McBride	U. of Denver	C					
195	L.A.	John Preston	Boston U.	C					
196	Tor.	Ron Bernacci	Hamilton College	C					
197	Chi.	Dale Marquette	Brandon	LW					
198	Que.	Darren Nauss	North Battleford Jr.	RW					
199	NYR	David Porter	Northern Michigan	LW					
200	Det.	Darin Bannister	Illinois-Chicago	D					
201	St.L.	David Marvin	Warroad H.S.	D					
202	NYI	John Herlihy	Babson College	RW					
203	Bos.	Casey Jones	Cornell	C					
204	Wsh.	Chris Clarke	Pembroke Jr. A.	D					
205	NYR	Brett Barnett	Wexford Jr. B	RW					
206	Mtl.	Barry McKinlay	Illinois-Chicago	D					
207	St.L.	Andy Cesarski	Culver Military Academy	D					
208	Cgy.	William Sedergren	Springfield Jr. B	D					
209	Phi.	Steve Morrow	Westminster H.S.	D					
210	Edm.	Mike Tinkham	Newburyport H.S.	RW					
211	Buf.	David Littman	Boston College	G	3	141	14	0	5.96
212	N.J.	Alain Charland	Drummondville	C					
213	Van.	Roger Hansson	Rogle Angelholm	LW					
214	Min.	Mark Felicio	Northwood Prep	G					
215	Pit.	Mark Carlson	Philadelphia Jr.	LW					
216	L.A.	Rostislav Vlach	TJ Gottwaldov	RW					
217	Tor.	Ken Alexander	Hamilton	LW					
218	Chi.	Bill Lacouture	Natick H.S.	RW					
219	Que.	Mike Williams	Ferris State	G					
220	NYR	Lance Marciano	Choate	D					
221	Det.	Craig Quinlan	Hill-Murray H.S.	D					
222	St.L.	Dan Rolfe	Brockville Jr. A.	D					
223	NYI	Michael Erickson	St. John's Hill H.S.	D					
224	Bos.	Eric Lemarque	Northern Michigan	RW					
225	Wsh.	Milos Vanik	Freiburg, FRG	C					
226	Wpg.	Roger Rougelot	Madison Jr. A.	G					
227	Mtl.	Ed Ronan	Andover Academy	RW	182	13	23	36	101
228	Hfd.	Kevin Sullivan	Princeton	RW					
229	Cgy.	Peter Hasselblad	Orebro	D					
230	Phi.	Darius Rusnak	Slovan Bratislava	C					
231	Edm.	Jeff Pauletti	Minnesota-Duluth	D					
232	Buf.	Allan MacIsaac	Guelph	LW					
233	Van.	Neil Eisenhut	Langley Eagles (BCJHL)	C	16	1	3	4	21
234	Van.	Matt Evo	Country Day H.S.	LW					
235	Min.	Dave Shields	U. of Denver	C					
236	Pit.	Ake Lilljebjorn	Brynas Gavle	G					
237	L.A.	Mikael Lindholm	Brynas Gavle	C	18	2	2	4	2
238	Tor.	Alex Weinrich	North Yarmouth Academy	C					
239	Chi.	Mike Lappin	Northwood Prep	C					
240	Wsh.	Dan Brettschneider	Burnsville H.S.	RW					
241	Edm.	Jesper Duus	Rodovre, DEN	D					
242	Det.	Tomas Jansson	IK Talje	D					
243	St.L.	Ray Savard	Regina	C					
244	NYI	Will Averill	Belmont Hill H.S.	D					
245	Bos.	Sean Gorman	Matignon H.S.	D					
246	Wsh.	Ryan Kummo	RPI	D					
247	Wpg.	Hans Goran Flo	Djurgarden	G					
248	Mtl.	Bryan Herring	Dubuque Jr. A	C					
249	Hfd.	Steve Laurin	Dartmouth	G					
250	Cgy.	Magnus Svensson	Leksand	D	46	4	14	18	31
251	Phi.	Dale Roehl	Minnetonka H.S.	G					
252	Edm.	Igor Vyazmikin	CSKA	W	4	1	0	1	0

1988

FIRST ROUND

PICK	TEAM	NAME	DRAFTED FROM	NHL PLAYERS: POS / NHL GOALTENDERS: POS	GP / GP	G / W	A / GA	PTS / SO	PIM / AVG
1	Min.	Mike Modano	Prince Albert	C	1025	444	618	1062	668
2	Van.	Trevor Linden	Medicine Hat	RW	1079	335	443	778	805
3	Que.	Curtis Leschyshyn	Saskatoon	D	977	46	161	207	653
4	Pit.	Darrin Shannon	Windsor	LW	506	87	163	250	344
5	Que.	Daniel Dore	Drummondville	RW	17	2	3	5	59
6	Tor.	Scott Pearson	Kingston	LW	292	56	42	98	615
7	L.A.	Martin Gelinas	Hull	LW	976	252	268	520	614
8	Chi.	Jeremy Roenick	Thayer Academy	C	1062	456	617	1073	1283
9	St.L.	Rod Brind'Amour	Notre Dame Jr. A	C	1031	339	534	873	848
10	Wpg.	Teemu Selanne	Jokerit Helsinki	RW	801	436	483	919	303
11	Hfd.	Chris Govedaris	Toronto	LW	45	4	6	10	24
12	N.J.	Corey Foster	Peterborough	D	45	5	6	11	24
13	Buf.	Joel Savage	Victoria	RW	3	0	1	1	0
14	Phi.	Claude Boivin	Drummondville	LW	132	12	19	31	364
15	Wsh.	Reggie Savage	Victoriaville	C	34	5	7	12	28
16	NYI	Kevin Cheveldayoff	Brandon	D					
17	Det.	Kory Kocur	Saskatoon	RW					
18	Bos.	Rob Cimetta	Toronto	W	103	16	16	32	66
19	Edm.	Francois Leroux	St-Jean	D	249	3	20	23	577
20	Mtl.	Eric Charron	Trois-Rivieres	D	130	2	7	9	127
21	Cgy.	Jason Muzzatti	Michigan State	G	62	3014	167	1	3.32
		SECOND ROUND							
22	NYR	Troy Mallette	Sault Ste. Marie	LW	456	51	68	119	1226
23	N.J.	Jeff Christian	London	LW	18	2	2	4	17
24	Que.	Stephane Fiset	Victoriaville	G	390	21785	1114	16	3.07
25	Pit.	Mark Major	North Bay	LW	2	0	0	0	5
26	NYR	Murray Duval	Spokane	RW					
27	Tor.	Tie Domi	Peterborough	RW	863	92	117	209	3198
28	L.A.	Paul Holden	London	D					
29	NYI	Wayne Doucet	Hamilton	LW					
30	St.L.	Adrien Plavsic	New Hampshire	D	214	16	56	72	161
31	Wpg.	Russell Romaniuk	St. Boniface Jr. A.	LW	102	13	14	27	63
32	Hfd.	Barry Richter	Culver Military Academy	D	151	11	34	45	76
33	Van.	Leif Rohlin	Vasteras	D	96	8	24	32	40
34	Mtl.	Martin St. Amour	Verdun	LW	1	0	0	0	2
35	Phi.	Pat Murray	Michigan State	LW	25	3	1	4	15
36	Wsh.	Tim Taylor	London	C	511	58	68	126	370
37	NYI	Sean Lebrun	New Westminster	LW					
38	Det.	Serge Anglehart	Drummondville	D					
39	Edm.	Petro Koivunen	Kiekko-Espoo	C					
40	Min.	Link Gaetz	Spokane	D	65	6	8	14	412
41	Wsh.	Wade Bartley	Dauphin Jr. A.	D					
42	Cgy.	Todd Harkins	Miami of Ohio	C	48	3	3	6	78
		OTHER ROUNDS							
43	Min.	Shaun Kane	Springfield Jr. B	D					
44	Van.	Dane Jackson	Vernon Jr. A	RW	45	12	6	18	58
45	Que.	Petri Aaltonen	HIFK Helsinki	C					
46	Mtl.	Neil Carnes	Verdun	C					
47	Det.	Guy Dupuis	Hull	D					
48	Tor.	Peter Ing	Windsor	G	74	3941	266	1	4.05
49	L.A.	John Van Kessel	North Bay	RW					
50	Chi.	Trevor Dam	London	RW					
51	St.L.	Rob Fournier	North Bay	G					
52	Wpg.	Stephane Beauregard	St-Jean	G	90	4402	268	2	3.65
53	Edm.	Trevor Sim	Seattle	RW	3	0	1	1	2
54	N.J.	Zdeno Ciger	ZTS Martin	LW	352	94	134	228	101
55	Buf.	Darcy Loewen	Spokane	LW	135	4	8	12	211
56	Phi.	Craig Fisher	Oshawa Jr. B	C	12	0	0	0	2
57	Wsh.	Duane Derksen	Winkler Jr. A	G					
58	NYI	Danny Lorenz	Seattle	G	8	357	25	0	4.20
59	Det.	Petr Hrbek	Sparta Praha	RW					
60	Bos.	Steve Heinze	Lawrence Academy	RW	694	178	158	336	379
61	Edm.	Collin Bauer	Saskatoon	D					
62	Pit.	Daniel Gauthier	Victoriaville	LW	5	0	0	0	0
63	Phi.	Dominic Roussel	Trois-Rivieres	G	205	10665	555	7	3.12
64	Min.	Jeffrey Stolp	Greenway H.S.	G					
65	N.J.	Matt Ruchty	Bowling Green	LW					
66	Que.	Darin Kimble	Prince Albert	RW	311	23	20	43	1082
67	Pit.	Mark Recchi	Kamloops	RW	1091	430	696	1126	733
68	NYR	Tony Amonte	Thayer Academy	RW	933	372	403	775	631
69	Tor.	Ted Crowley	Lawrence Academy	D	34	2	4	6	12

PICK	TEAM	NAME	DRAFTED FROM	NHL PLAYERS: POS / NHL GOALTENDERS: POS	GP / GP	G / W	A / GA	PTS / SO	PIM / AVG
70	L.A.	Rob Blake	Bowling Green	D	829	173	367	540	1174
71	Chi.	Stefan Elvenas	Rogle Angelholm	RW					
72	St.L.	Jaan Luik	Miami of Ohio	D					
73	Wpg.	Brian Hunt	Oshawa	C					
74	Hfd.	Dean Dyer	Lake Superior State	C					
75	N.J.	Scott Luik	Miami of Ohio	RW					
76	Buf.	Keith Carney	Mount St. Charles H.S.	D	648	32	119	151	635
77	Phi.	Scott Lagrand	Hotchkiss H.S.	G					
78	Wsh.	Bob Krauss	Lethbridge	D					
79	NYI	Andre Brassard	Trois-Rivieres	D					
80	Det.	Sheldon Kennedy	Swift Current	RW	310	49	58	107	233
81	Bos.	Joe Juneau	RPI	C	758	151	406	557	252
82	Edm.	Cam Brauer	RPI	D					
83	Mtl.	Patric Kjellberg	Falun	RW	394	64	96	160	84
84	Cgy.	Gary Socha	Tabor Academy	C					
85	Cgy.	Tomas Forslund	Leksand	RW	44	5	11	16	12
86	Tor.	Len Esau	Humboldt Jr. A	D	27	0	10	10	24
87	Que.	Stephane Venne	Vermont	D					
88	Pit.	Greg Andrusak	Minnesota-Duluth	D	28	0	6	6	16
89	Buf.	Alexander Mogilny	CSKA	RW	919	453	524	977	414
90	Cgy.	Scott Matusovich	Canterbury H.S.	D					
91	L.A.	Jeff Robison	Mount St. Charles H.S.	D					
92	Chi.	Joe Cleary	Stratford Jr. B	D					
93	Mtl.	Peter Popovic	Vasteras	D	485	10	63	73	291
94	Wpg.	Tony Joseph	Oshawa	RW	2	1	0	1	0
95	Hfd.	Scott Morrow	Northwood Prep	LW	4	0	0	0	0
96	N.J.	Chris Nelson	Rochester Jr. A	D					
97	Buf.	Rob Ray	Cornwall	RW	894	40	50	90	3193
98	Phi.	Edward O'Brien	Cushing Academy	LW					
99	NYR	Martin Bergeron	Drummondville	C					
100	NYI	Paul Rutherford	Ohio State	C					
101	Wpg.	Benoit Lebeau	Merrimack	LW					
102	Bos.	Daniel Murphy	Gunnery H.S.	D					
103	Edm.	Don Martin	London	LW					
104	Mtl.	Jean-Claude Bergeron	Verdun	G	72	3772	232	1	3.69
105	St.L.	Dave Lacouture	Natick H.S.	RW					
106	Buf.	David Di Vita	Lake Superior State	G					
107	Van.	Corrie D'Alessio	Cornell	G	1	11	0	0	0.00
108	Que.	Ed Ward	Michigan	RW	278	23	26	49	354
109	L.A.	Micah Aivazoff	Victoria	C	92	4	6	10	46
110	NYR	Dennis Vial	Hamilton	D/LW	242	4	15	19	794
111	NYI	Pavel Gross	Sparta Praha	RW					
112	L.A.	Robert Larsson	Skelleftea	D					
113	Chi.	Justin Lafayette	Ferris State	LW					
114	St.L.	Dan Fowler	U. of Maine	D					
115	Wpg.	Ronald Jones	Windsor	RW					
116	Hfd.	Corey Beaulieu	Seattle	D					
117	N.J.	Chad Johnson	Rochester Jr. A	C					
118	Buf.	Mike McLaughlin	Choate	LW					
119	Phi.	Gordie Frantti	Calumet H.S.	C					
120	Wsh.	Dmitri Khristich	Sokol Kiev	LW/C	811	259	337	596	422
121	NYI	Jason Rathbone	Brookline H.S.	RW					
122	Van.	Phil Von Stefenelli	Boston U.	D	33	0	5	5	23
123	Bos.	Derek Geary	Gloucester	RW					
124	Edm.	Len Barrie	Victoria	C	184	19	45	64	290
125	Mtl.	Patrik Carnback	Vastra Frolunda Goteborg	C	154	24	38	62	122
126	Cgy.	Jonas Bergqvist	Leksand	RW	22	2	5	7	10
127	Wpg.	Markus Akerblom	Bjorkloven Umea	C					
128	Van.	Dixon Ward	Red Deer Jr. A	RW	537	95	129	224	431
129	Que.	Valeri Kamensky	CSKA	LW	637	200	301	501	383
130	Pit.	Troy Mick	Portland	LW					
131	NYR	Mike Rosati	Hamilton	G	1	28	0	0	0.00
132	Tor.	Matt Mallgrave	St. Paul's H.S.	C					
133	L.A.	Jeff Kruesel	John Marshall H.S.	G					
134	Chi.	Craig Woodcroft	Colgate	LW					
135	St.L.	Matt Hayes	New Hampton H.S.	D					
136	Wpg.	Jukka Marttila	Tappara Tampere	D					
137	Hfd.	Kerry Russell	Michigan State	RW					
138	N.J.	Chad Erickson	Warroad H.S.	G	2	120	9	0	4.50
139	Buf.	Mike Griffith	Ottawa	RW					
140	Phi.	Jamie Cooke	Bramalea Jr. B	RW					
141	Wsh.	Keith Jones	Niagara Falls Jr. B	RW	491	117	141	258	765
142	NYI	Yves Gaucher	Chicoutimi	LW					
143	Det.	Kelly Hurd	Michigan Tech	RW					
144	Wsh.	Brad Schlegel	London	D	48	1	8	9	10
145	Edm.	Mike Glover	Sault Ste. Marie	RW					
146	Mtl.	Tim Chase	Tabor Academy	C					
147	Cgy.'s	Stefan Nilsson	HV 71 Jonkoping	C					
148	Min.	Ken MacArthur	U. of Denver	D					
149	Van.	Greg Geldart	St. Albert Jr. A	C					
150	Que.	Sakari Lindfors	HIFK Helsinki	G					
151	Pit.	Jeff Blaeser	St. John's Prep	LW					
152	NYR	Eric Couvrette	St-Jean	LW					
153	Tor.	Peter Elvenas	Rogle Angelholm	C					
154	L.A.	Timo Peltomaa	Ilves Tampere	RW					
155	Chi.	Jon Pojar	Roseville H.S.	LW					
156	St.L.	John McCoy	Edina H.S.	LW					
157	Wpg.	Mark Smith	Trinity-Pawling H.S.	C					
158	Hfd.	Jim Burke	U. of Maine	D					
159	N.J.	Bryan Lafort	Waltham H.S.	G					
160	Buf.	Daniel Ruoho	Madison Memorial H.S.	D					
161	Phi.	Johan Salle	Malmo	D					
162	Wsh.	Todd Hilditch	Penticton Jr. A	D					
163	NYI	Marty McInnis	Milton Academy	RW	796	170	250	420	330
164	Det.	Brian McCormack	St. Paul's H.S.	D					
165	Bos.	Mark Krys	Boston U.	D					
166	Edm.	Shjon Podein	Minnesota-Duluth	LW	699	100	106	206	439
167	Mtl.	Sean Hill	Duluth East H.S.	D	602	44	161	205	702
168	Cgy.	Troy Kennedy	Brandon	RW					
169	Min.	Travis Richards	Armstrong H.S.	D	3	0	0	0	2
170	Van.	Roger Akerstrom	Lulea	D					
171	Que.	Dan Wiebe	U. of Alberta	LW					
172	Pit.	Rob Gaudreau	Bishop Hendricken H.S.	RW	231	51	54	105	69
173	NYI	Shorty Forrest	St. Cloud State	D					
174	Tor.	Mike Delay	Canterbury H.S.	D					
175	L.A.	Jim Larkin	Mount St. Charles H.S.	LW					
176	Chi.	Mathew Hentges	Edina H.S.	D					
177	St.L.	Tony Twist	Saskatoon	LW	445	10	18	28	1121
178	Wpg.	Mike Helber	Ann Arbor H.S.	C					
179	Hfd.	Mark Hirth	Michigan State	C					
180	N.J.	Sergei Svetlov	Dynamo	RW					
181	Buf.	Wade Flaherty	Victoria	G	120	5941	348	5	3.51
182	Phi.	Brian Arthur	Etobicoke Jr. B	D					
183	Wsh.	Petr Pavlas	Dukla Trencin	D					
184	NYI	Jeff Blumer	U. of St. Thomas	RW					
185	Det.	Jody Praznik	Colorado College	D					
186	Bos.	Jon Rohloff	Grand Rapids H.S.	D	150	7	25	32	129
187	Edm.	Tim Cole	Woburn H.S.	G					
188	Mtl.	Harijs Vitolinsh	Dynamo Riga	C	Re-entered Draft in 1993				
189	Cgy.	Brett Peterson	St. Paul Jr. A	D					
190	Min.	Ari Matilainen	Assat Pori	RW					
191	Van.	Paul Constantin	Burlington Jr. B	C					
192	Wsh.	Mark Sorensen	Michigan	D					
193	Pit.	David Pancoe	Hamilton	LW					
194	NYR	Paul Cain	Cornwall	C					
195	Tor.	David Sacco	Medford H.S.	RW	35	5	13	18	22
196	L.A.	Brad Hyatt	Windsor	D					
197	Chi.	Daniel Maurice	Chicoutimi	C					
198	St.L.	Bret Hedican	North St. Paul H.S.	D	717	40	170	210	629
199	Wpg.	Pavel Kostichkin	CSKA	C					
200	Hfd.	Wayde Bucsis	Prince Albert	RW					
201	N.J.	Bob Woods	Brandon	D					
202	NYR	Eric Fenton	North Yarmouth Academy	C					
203	Phi.	Jeff Dandretta	Cushing Academy	RW					
204	Wsh.	Claudio Scremin	U. of Maine	D	17	0	1	1	29
205	NYI	Jeff Kampersal	St. John's Prep	D					
206	Det.	Glen Goodall	Seattle	C					
207	N.J.	Alexander Semak	Dynamo	C	289	83	91	174	187
208	Edm.	Vladimir Zubkov	CSKA	D					
209	Mtl.	Yuri Krivokhizha	Dynamo Minsk	D					
210	Cgy.	Guy Darveau	Victoriaville	D					
211	Min.	Grant Bischoff	Minnesota-Duluth	LW					
212	Van.	Chris Wolanin	Illinois-Chicago	D					
213	Que.	Alexei Gusarov	CSKA	D	607	39	128	167	313
214	Pit.	Cory Laylin	St. Cloud Appollo H.S.	LW					
215	NYR	Peter Fiorentino	Sault Ste. Marie	D	1	0	0	0	0
216	Tor.	Mike Gregorio	Cushing Academy	G					
217	L.A.	Doug Laprade	Lake Superior State	RW					
218	Chi.	Dirk Tenzer	St. Paul's H.S.	D					
219	St.L.	Heath DeBoer	Spring Lake Park H.S.	D					
220	Wpg.	Kevin Heise	Lethbridge	LW					
221	Hfd.	Rob White	St. Lawrence U.	D					

PICK	TEAM	NAME	DRAFTED FROM	NHL PLAYERS: POS / NHL GOALTENDERS: POS	GP / GP	G / W	A / GA	PTS / SO	PIM / AVG
222	N.J.	Charles Hughes	Catholic Memorial H.S.	G					
223	Buf.	Thomas Nieman	Choate	RW					
224	Phi.	Scott Billey	Madison Jr. A	RW					
225	Wsh.	Chris Venkus	Western Michigan	RW					
226	NYI	Phillip Neururer	Osseo H.S.	D					
227	Det.	Darren Colbourne	Cornwall	RW					
228	Bos.	Eric Reisman	Ohio State	D					
229	Edm.	Darin MacDonald	Boston U.	LW					
230	Mtl.	Kevin Dahl	Bowling Green	D	188	7	22	29	153
231	Cgy.	Dave Tretowicz	Clarkson	D					
232	Min.	Trent Andison	Cornwall	LW					
233	Van.	Steffan Nilsson	Troja	LW					
234	Que.	Claude Lapointe	Laval	LW/C	837	122	175	297	689
235	Pit.	Darren Stolk	Lethbridge	D					
236	NYR	Keith Slifstein	Choate	RW					
237	Tor.	Peter DeBoer	Windsor	RW					
238	L.A.	Joe Flanagan	Canterbury H.S.	C					
239	Chi.	Andreas Lupzig	Landshut, FRG	C					
240	St.L.	Michael Francis	Harvard	G					
241	Wpg.	Kyle Galloway	U. of Manitoba	D					
242	Hfd.	Dan Slatalla	Deerfield Academy	LW					
243	Buf.	Michael Pohl	Rosenheim, FRG	C					
244	N.J.	Robert Wallwork	Miami of Ohio	C					
245	Phi.	Drahomir Kadlec	Dukla Jihlava	D					
246	Wsh.	Ron Pascucci	Belmont Hill H.S.	D					
247	NYI	Joe Caprinni	Babson College	G					
248	Det.	Donald Stone	Michigan	C					
249	Bos.	Doug Jones	Kitchener	D					
250	Edm.	Tim Tisdale	Swift Current	C					
251	Mtl.	Dave Kunda	U. of Guelph	D					
252	Cgy.	Sergei Priakin	Krylja Sovetov	RW	46	3	8	11	2

1989

FIRST ROUND

PICK	TEAM	NAME	DRAFTED FROM	POS	GP	G / W	A / GA	PTS / SO	PIM / AVG
1	Que.	Mats Sundin	Nacka	C	1005	421	590	1011	017
2	NYI	Dave Chyzowski	Kamloops	LW	126	15	16	31	144
3	Tor.	Scott Thornton	Belleville	LW	685	109	107	216	1167
4	Wpg.	Stu Barnes	Tri-City	C	820	210	274	484	310
5	N.J.	Bill Guerin	Springfield Jr. B	RW	797	281	273	554	1149
6	Chi.	Adam Bennett	Sudbury	D	69	3	8	11	69
7	Min.	Doug Zmolek	John Marshall H.S.	D	467	11	53	64	905
8	Van.	Jason Herter	North Dakota	D	1	0	1	1	0
9	St.L.	Jason Marshall	Vernon Jr. A.	D	479	15	41	56	944
10	Hfd.	Bobby Holik	Dukla Jihlava	C	942	256	330	586	1006
11	Det.	Mike Sillinger	Regina	C	753	153	221	374	439
12	Tor.	Rob Pearson	Belleville	RW	269	56	54	110	645
13	Mtl.	Lindsay Vallis	Seattle	D	1	0	0	0	0
14	Buf.	Kevin Haller	Regina	D	642	41	97	138	907
15	Edm.	Jason Soules	Niagara Falls	D					
16	Pit.	Jamie Heward	Regina	D	239	25	45	70	116
17	Bos.	Shayne Stevenson	Kitchener	RW	27	0	2	2	35
18	N.J.	Jason Miller	Medicine Hat	LW	6	0	0	0	0
19	Wsh.	Olaf Kolzig	Tri-City	G	481	27679	1162	31	2.52
20	NYR	Steven Rice	Kitchener	RW	329	64	61	125	275
21	Tor.	Steve Bancroft	Belleville	D	6	0	1	1	2

SECOND ROUND

PICK	TEAM	NAME	DRAFTED FROM	POS	GP	G / W	A / GA	PTS / SO	PIM / AVG
22	Que.	Adam Foote	Sault Ste. Marie	D	726	47	157	204	1053
23	NYI	Travis Green	Spokane	C	793	171	244	415	591
24	Cgy.	Kent Manderville	Notre Dame Jr. A	C	646	37	67	104	348
25	Wpg.	Dan Ratushny	Cornell	D	1	0	1	1	2
26	N.J.	Jarrod Skalde	Oshawa	C	115	13	21	34	62
27	Chi.	Michael Speer	Guelph	D					
28	Min.	Mike Craig	Oshawa	RW	423	71	97	168	550
29	Van.	Robert Woodward	Deerfield Academy	LW					
30	Mtl.	Patrice Brisebois	Laval	D	720	75	236	311	479
31	St.L.	Rick Corriveau	London	D	Re-entered Draft in 1991				
32	Det.	Bob Boughner	Sault Ste. Marie	D	535	14	46	60	1240
33	Phi.	Greg Johnson	Thunder Bay Jr. A	C	635	120	198	318	302
34	Phi.	Patrik Juhlin	Vasteras	LW	56	7	6	13	23
35	Wsh.	Byron Dafoe	Portland	G	397	22505	1000	26	2.67
36	Edm.	Richard Borgo	Kitchener	G					
37	Pit.	Paul Laus	Niagara Falls	D	530	14	58	72	1702
38	Bos.	Mike Parson	Guelph	G					
39	L.A.	Brent Thompson	Medicine Hat	D	121	1	10	11	352
40	NYR	Jason Prosofsky	Medicine Hat	RW					
41	Mtl.	Steve Larouche	Trois-Rivieres	C	26	9	9	18	10
42	Cgy.	Ted Drury	Fairfield Prep	C	414	41	52	93	367

OTHER ROUNDS

PICK	TEAM	NAME	DRAFTED FROM	POS	GP	G / W	A / GA	PTS / SO	PIM / AVG
43	Que.	Stephane Morin	Chicoutimi	C	90	16	39	55	52
44	NYI	Jason Zent	Nichols H.S.	LW	27	3	3	6	13
45	NYR	Rob Zamuner	Guelph	LW	741	135	167	302	451
46	Wpg.	Jason Cirone	Cornwall	C	3	0	0	0	2
47	N.J.	Scott Pellerin	U. of Maine	LW	534	72	126	198	318
48	Chi.	Bob Kellogg	Springfield Jr. B	D					
49	NYR	Louie DeBrusk	London	LW	401	24	17	41	1161
50	Cgy.	Veli-Pekka Kautonen	HIFK Helsinki	D					
51	Mtl.	Pierre Sevigny	Trois-Rivieres	LW	78	4	5	9	64
52	Hfd.	Blair Atcheynum	Moose Jaw	RW	196	27	33	60	36
53	Det.	Nicklas Lidstrom	Vasteras	D	935	163	525	688	258
54	Que.	John Tanner	Peterborough	G	21	1084	65	1	3.60
55	St.L.	Denny Felsner	Michigan	LW	18	1	4	5	6
56	Buf.	Scott Thomas	Nichols H.S.	RW	63	6	4	10	32
57	Bos.	Wes Walz	Lethbridge	C	395	68	102	170	214
58	Pit.	John Brill	Grand Rapids H.S.						
59	Wsh.	Jim Mathieson	Regina	D	2	0	0	0	4
60	Min.	Murray Garbutt	Medicine Hat	C					
61	Wsh.	Jason Woolley	Michigan State	D	610	63	213	276	374
62	Wpg.	Kris Draper	Canadian National	C	657	84	112	196	495
63	Cgy.	Corey Lyons	Lethbridge	RW					
64	Wpg.	Mark Brownschidle	Boston U.	D					
65	NYI	Brent Grieve	Oshawa	LW	97	20	16	36	87
66	Tor.	Matt Martin	Avon Old Farms H.S.	D	76	0	5	5	71
67	NYR	Jim Cummins	Michigan State	RW	456	23	34	57	1391
68	Que.	Niklas Andersson	Vastra Frolunda Goteborg	LW	164	29	53	82	85
69	Wpg.	Allain Roy	Harvard	G					
70	Cgy.	Robert Reichel	CHZ Litvinov	C	761	241	359	600	358
71	Van.	Brett Hauer	Richfield H.S.	D	37	4	4	8	38
72	Phi.	Reid Simpson	Prince Albert	LW	299	18	18	36	821
73	Hfd.	Jim McKenzie	Victoria	LW	819	47	49	96	1651
74	Det.	Sergei Fedorov	CSKA	C	908	400	554	954	587
75	Min.	Jean-Francois Quintin	Shawinigan	LW	22	5	5	10	4
76	Que.	Eric Dubois	Laval	D					
77	Buf.	Doug MacDonald	Wisconsin	LW	11	1	0	1	2
78	Edm.	Josef Beranek	CHZ Litvinov	LW/C	531	118	144	262	398
79	Pit.	Todd Nelson	Prince Albert	D	3	1	0	1	2
80	Bos.	Jackson Penney	Victoria	C					
81	L.A.	Jim Maher	Illinois-Chicago	D					
82	Wsh.	Trent Klatt	Osseo H.S.	RW	700	126	174	300	261
83	Mtl.	Andre Racicot	Granby	G	68	3357	196	2	3.50
84	Cgy.	Ryan O'Leary	Hermantown H.S.	C					
85	Que.	Kevin Kaiser	Minnesota-Duluth	LW					
86	NYI	Jace Reed	Grand Rapids H.S.	D					
87	Min.	Pat MacLeod	Kamloops	D	53	5	13	18	14
88	NYR	Aaron Miller	Niagara Jr. A	D	447	23	68	91	271
89	N.J.	Mike Heinke	Avon Old Farms H.S.	G					
90	NYI	Steve Young	Moose Jaw	RW					
91	Min.	Bryan Schoen	Minnetonka H.S.	G					
92	Edm.	Peter White	Michigan State	C	217	23	37	60	34
93	St.L.	Daniel Laperriere	St. Lawrence U.	D	48	2	5	7	27
94	Hfd.	James Black	Portland	LW	352	58	57	115	84
95	Det.	Shawn McCosh	Niagara Falls	C	9	1	0	1	6
96	Tor.	Keith Carney	Mount St. Charles H.S.	D	81	4	18	22	65
97	Min.	Rhys Hollyman	Miami of Ohio	D					
98	Buf.	Ken Sutton	Saskatoon	D	388	23	80	103	338
99	NYI	Kevin O'Sullivan	Catholic Memorial H.S.	D					
100	Pit.	Tom Nevers	Edina H.S.	C					
101	Bos.	Mark Montanari	Kitchener	C					
102	L.A.	Eric Ricard	Granby	D					
103	L.A.	Thomas Newman	Blaine H.S.	G					
104	Mtl.	Marc Deschamps	Cornell	D					
105	Cgy.	Toby Kearney	Belmont Hill H.S.	LW					
106	Que.	Dan Lambert	Swift Current	D	29	6	9	15	22
107	Buf.	Bill Pye	Northern Michigan	G					
108	Tor.	David Burke	Cornell	D					
109	Wpg.	Dan Bylsma	Bowling Green	RW	418	19	43	62	184
110	N.J.	David Emma	Boston College	C	34	5	6	11	2
111	Chi.	Tommi Pullola	Sport Vaasa	C					
112	Min.	Scott Cashman	Kanata Jr.	G					
113	Van.	Pavel Bure	CSKA	RW	702	437	342	779	484

PICK	TEAM	NAME	DRAFTED FROM	NHL PLAYERS: POS / NHL GOALTENDERS: POS	GP / GP	G / W	A / GA	PTS / SO	PIM / AVG
114	St.L.	David Roberts	Avon Old Farms H.S.	LW	125	20	33	53	85
115	Hfd.	Jerome Bechard	Moose Jaw	LW					
116	Det.	Dallas Drake	Northern Michigan	RW	743	153	245	398	682
117	Phi.	Niklas Eriksson	Leksand	C					
118	NYR	Joby Messier	Michigan State	D	25	0	4	4	24
119	Buf.	Mike Barkley	U. of Maine	RW					
120	Edm.	Anatoli Semenov	Dynamo	C/LW	362	68	126	194	122
121	Pit.	Mike Markovich	U. of Denver	D					
122	Bos.	Stephen Foster	Catholic Memorial H.S.	D					
123	L.A.	Daniel Rydmark	Farjestad Karlstad	C					
124	St.L.	Derek Frenette	Ferris State	LW					
125	Tor.	Michael Doers	Northwood Prep.	RW					
126	Pit.	Mike Needham	Kamloops	RW	86	9	5	14	16
127	Que.	Sergei Mylnikov	Traktor Chelyabinsk	G	10	568	47	0	4.96
128	NYI	Jon Larson	Roseau H.S.	D					
129	Tor.	Keith Merkler	Portledge H.S.	LW					
130	Wpg.	Pekka Peltola	HPK Hameenlinna	RW					
131	Wpg.	Doug Evans	Peterborough	D					
132	Chi.	Tracy Egeland	Prince Albert	LW					
133	NYI	Brett Harkins	Detroit Compuware Jr. A	LW	78	6	30	36	22
134	Van.	James Revenberg	Windsor	RW					
135	St.L.	Jeff Batters	Alaska-Anchorage	D	16	0	0	0	28
136	Hfd.	Scott Daniels	Regina	LW	149	8	12	20	667
137	Det.	Scott Zygulski	Culver Military Academy	D					
138	Phi.	John Callahan Jr.	Belmont Hill H.S.	C					
139	NYR	Greg Leahy	Portland	C					
140	Edm.	Davis Payne	Michigan Tech	LW	22	0	1	1	14
141	Edm.	Sergei Yashin	Dynamo	LW					
142	Pit.	Patrick Schafhauser	Hill-Murray H.S.	D					
143	Bos.	Otto Hascak	Dukla Trencin	RW					
144	L.A.	Ted Kramer	Michigan	RW					
145	Wsh.	Dave Lorentz	Peterborough	LW					
146	Mtl.	Craig Ferguson	Yale	C	27	1	1	2	6
147	Cgy.	Alex Nikolic	Cornell	LW					
148	Que.	Paul Krake	Alaska-Anchorage	G					
149	NYI	Phil Huber	Kamloops	LW					
150	Tor.	Derek Langille	North Bay	D					
151	Wpg.	Jim Solly	Bowling Green	C					
152	N.J.	Sergei Starikov	CSKA	D	16	0	1	1	8
153	Chi.	Milan Tichy	Skoda Plzen	D	23	0	5	5	40
154	Min.	Jonathon Pratt	Pingree Prep	C					
155	Van.	Rob Sangster	Kitchener	LW					
156	St.L.	Kevin Plager	Parkway North H.S.	RW					
157	Hfd.	Raymond Saumier	Trois-Rivieres	RW					
158	Det.	Andy Suhy	Western Michigan	D					
159	Phi.	Sverre Sears	Belmont Hill H.S.	D					
160	NYR	Greg Spenrath	Tri-City	LW					
161	Buf.	Derek Plante	Cloquet H.S.	C	450	96	152	248	138
162	Edm.	Darcy Martini	Michigan Tech	D	2	0	0	0	0
163	Pit.	Dave Shute	Victoria	C					
164	Bos.	Rick Allain	Kitchener	D					
165	L.A.	Sean Whyte	Guelph	RW	21	0	2	2	12
166	Wsh.	Dean Holoien	Saskatoon	D					
167	Mtl.	Patrick Lebeau	St-Jean	LW	15	3	2	5	6
168	Cgy.	Kevin Wortman	American Int'l College	D	5	0	0	0	2
169	Que.	Vyacheslav Bykov	CSKA	C					
170	NYI	Matthew Robbins	New Hampton H.S.	C					
171	Tor.	Jeffrey St. Laurent	Berwick H.S.	RW					
172	Wpg.	Stephane Gauvin	Cornell	LW					
173	N.J.	Andre Faust	Princeton	C	47	10	7	17	14
174	Chi.	Jason Greyerbiehl	Colgate	LW					
175	Min.	Kenneth Blum	St. Joseph H.S.	C					
176	Van.	Sandy Moger	Lake Superior State	C	236	41	38	79	212
177	St.L.	John Roderick	Rindge and Latin Academy	D					
178	Hfd.	Michel Picard	Trois-Rivieres	LW	166	28	42	70	103
179	Det.	Bob Jones	Sault Ste. Marie	LW	2	0	0	0	0
180	Phi.	Glen Wisser	Philadelphia Jr.	RW					
181	NYR	Mark Bavis	Cushing Academy	C					
182	L.A.	Jim Giacin	Culver Military Academy	LW					
183	Buf.	Donald Audette	Laval	RW	684	251	237	488	546
184	Pit.	Andrew Wolf	Victoria	D					
185	Bos.	James Lavish	Deerfield Academy	RW					
186	L.A.	Martin Maskarinec	Sparta Praha	D					
187	Wsh.	Victor Gervais	Seattle	C					
188	Mtl.	Roy Mitchell	Portland	D	3	0	0	0	0
189	Cgy.	Sergei Gomolyako	Traktor Chelyabinsk	C					
190	Que.	Andrei Khomutov	CSKA	RW					
191	NYI	Vladimir Malakhov	CSKA	D	621	79	239	318	616
192	Tor.	Justin Tomberlin	Greenway H.S.	C					
193	Wpg.	Joe Larson	Minnetonka H.S.	C					
194	Buf.	Mark Astley	Lake Superior State	D	75	4	19	23	92
195	Chi.	Matt Saunders	Northeastern	LW					
196	Min.	Arturs Irbe	Dynamo Riga	G	558	31502	1490	33	2.84
197	Van.	Gus Morschauser	Kitchener	G					
198	St.L.	John Valo	Detroit Compuware Jr. A	D					
199	Hfd.	Trevor Buchanan	Kamloops	LW					
200	Det.	Greg Bignell	Belleville	D					
201	Phi.	Al Kummu	Humboldt Jr. A	D					
202	NYR	Roman Oksiuta	Khimik Voskresensk	RW	153	46	41	87	100
203	Buf.	John Nelson	Toronto	C					
204	Det.	Rick Judson	Illinois-Chicago	LW					
205	Pit.	Greg Hagen	Hill-Murray H.S.	RW					
206	Bos.	Geoff Simpson	Estevan Jr. A	D					
207	L.A.	Jim Hiller	Melville Jr. A	RW	63	8	12	20	116
208	Wsh.	Jiri Vykoukal	DS Olomouc	D					
209	Mtl.	Ed Henrich	Nichols H.S.	D					
210	Cgy.	Dan Sawyer	Ramapo Jr.	D					
211	Que.	Byron Witkowski	Nipiwan Jr. A	LW					
212	NYI	Kelly Ens	Lethbridge	C					
213	Tor.	Mike Jackson	Toronto	RW					
214	Wpg.	Bradley Podiak	Wayzata H.S.	LW					
215	N.J.	Jason Simon	Windsor	LW	5	0	0	0	34
216	Chi.	Mike Kozak	Clarkson	RW					
217	Min.	Tom Pederson	Minnesota-Duluth	D	240	20	49	69	142
218	Van.	Hayden O'Rear	Lathrop H.S.	D					
219	St.L.	Brian Lukowski	Niagara Jr. A	G					
220	Hfd.	John Battice	London	D					
221	Det.	Vladimir Konstantinov	CSKA	D	446	47	128	175	838
222	Phi.	Matt Brait	St. Michael's Jr. B	D					
223	NYR	Steve Locke	Niagara Falls	LW					
224	Buf.	Todd Henderson	Thunder Bay Jr. A	G					
225	Edm.	Roman Bozek	Motor Ceske Budejovice	RW					
226	Pit.	Scott Farrell	Spokane	D					
227	Bos.	David Franzosa	Boston College	LW					
228	L.A.	Steve Jaques	Tri-City	D					
229	Wsh.	Sidorov Sidorov	Sokol Kiev						
230	Mtl.	Justin Duberman	North Dakota	RW	4	0	0	0	0
231	Cgy.	Alexander Yudin	Dynamo	D					
232	Que.	Noel Rahn	Edina H.S.	C					
233	NYI	Iain Fraser	Oshawa	C	94	23	23	46	31
234	Tor.	Steve Chartrand	Drummondville	LW					
235	Wpg.	Evgeny Davydov	CSKA	LW	155	40	39	79	120
236	N.J.	Peter Larsson	Sodertalje	C					
237	Chi.	Michael Doneghey	Catholic Memorial H.S.	G					
238	Min.	Helmut Balderis	Dynamo Riga	RW	26	3	6	9	2
239	Van.	Darcy Cahill	Cornwall	C					
240	Wpg.	Sergei Kharin	Krylja Sovetov	RW	7	2	3	5	2
241	Hfd.	Peter Kasowski	Swift Current	C					
242	Det.	Joseph Frederick	Madison Jr. A	RW					
243	Phi.	James Pollio	Vermont Academy	LW					
244	NYR	Ken MacDermid	Hull	LW					
245	Buf.	Michael Bavis	Cushing Academy	RW					
246	Det.	Jason Glickman	Hull	G					
247	Pit.	Jason Smart	Saskatoon	C					
248	Van.	Jan Bergman	Sodertalje	D					
249	L.A.	Kevin Sneddon	Harvard	D					
250	Wsh.	Ken House	Miami of Ohio	C					
251	Mtl.	Steve Cadieux	Shawinigan	C					
252	Cgy.	Kenneth Kennholt	Djurgarden	D					

1990

FIRST ROUND

PICK	TEAM	NAME	DRAFTED FROM	POS	GP	G	A	PTS	PIM
1	Que.	Owen Nolan	Cornwall	RW	850	330	357	687	1490
2	Van.	Petr Nedved	Seattle	C	808	282	352	634	564
3	Det.	Keith Primeau	Niagara Falls	C	846	258	332	590	1455
4	Phi.	Mike Ricci	Peterborough	C	943	226	336	562	861
5	Pit.	Jaromir Jagr	Poldi Kladno	RW	950	506	729	1235	661
6	NYI	Scott Scissons	Saskatoon	C	2	0	0	0	0
7	L.A.	Darryl Sydor	Kamloops	D	863	82	323	405	598
8	Min.	Derian Hatcher	North Bay	D	827	71	223	294	1380
9	Wsh.	John Slaney	Cornwall	D	264	22	67	89	99

PICK	TEAM	NAME	DRAFTED FROM	NHL PLAYERS: POS / NHL GOALTENDERS: POS	GP / GP	G / W	A / GA	PTS / SO	PIM / AVG
10	Tor.	Drake Berehowsky	Kingston	D	493	31	94	125	781
11	Cgy.	Trevor Kidd	Brandon	G	372	20543	966	18	2.82
12	Mtl.	Turner Stevenson	Seattle	RW	552	60	99	159	848
13	NYR	Michael Stewart	Michigan State	D					
14	Buf.	Brad May	Niagara Falls	LW	734	115	140	255	1800
15	Hfd.	Mark Greig	Lethbridge	RW	125	13	27	40	90
16	Chi.	Karl Dykhuis	Hull	D	635	42	91	133	493
17	Edm.	Scott Allison	Prince Albert	C					
18	Van.	Shawn Antoski	North Bay	LW	183	3	5	8	599
19	Wpg.	Keith Tkachuk	Malden Catholic H.S.	LW	781	398	363	761	1778
20	N.J.	Martin Brodeur	St-Hyacinthe	G	665	38956	1419	64	2.19
21	Bos.	Bryan Smolinski	Michigan State	C	749	212	276	488	454

SECOND ROUND

PICK	TEAM	NAME	DRAFTED FROM	POS	GP	G / W	A / GA	PTS / SO	PIM / AVG
22	Que.	Ryan Hughes	Cornell	C	3	0	0	0	0
23	Van.	Jiri Slegr	CHZ Litvinov	D	538	45	162	207	747
24	N.J.	David Harlock	Michigan	D	212	2	14	16	188
25	Phi.	Chris Simon	Ottawa	LW	527	108	117	225	1346
26	Cgy.	Nicolas Perreault	Hawkesbury Jr. A	D					
27	NYI	Chris Taylor	London	C	95	5	15	20	26
28	L.A.	Brandy Semchuk	Canadian Olympic	RW	1	0	0	0	2
29	N.J.	Chris Gotziaman	Roseau High	RW					
30	Wsh.	Rod Pasma	Cornwall	D					
31	Tor.	Felix Potvin	Chicoutimi	G	607	35160	1627	28	2.78
32	Cgy.	Vesa Viitakoski	SaiPa Lappeenranta	LW	23	2	4	6	8
33	St.L.	Craig Johnson	Hill-Murray High	LW	493	73	89	162	232
34	NYR	Doug Weight	Lake Superior State	C	837	210	553	763	697
35	Wpg.	Mike Muller	Wayzata High	D					
36	Hfd.	Geoff Sanderson	Swift Current	LW	848	300	276	576	355
37	Chi.	Ivan Droppa	Kosice Jr.	D	19	0	1	1	14
38	Edm.	Alexandre Legault	Boston U.	RW					
39	Mtl.	Ryan Kuwabara	Ottawa	RW					
40	Phi.	Mikael Renberg	Pitea	RW	602	178	261	439	322
41	Cgy.	Etienne Belzile	Cornell U.	D					
42	Phi.	Terran Sandwith	Tri-City	D	8	0	0	0	6

OTHER ROUNDS

PICK	TEAM	NAME	DRAFTED FROM	POS	GP	G / W	A / GA	PTS / SO	PIM / AVG
43	Que.	Brad Zavisha	Seattle	LW	2	0	0	0	0
44	Phi.	Kimbi Daniels	Swift Current	C	27	1	2	3	4
45	Det.	Vyacheslav Kozlov	Khimik Voskresensk	RW	724	232	275	507	458
46	Phi.	Bill Armstrong	Oshawa	D					
47	Phi	Chris Therien	Northwood Prep	D	650	28	117	145	499
48	NYI	Dan Plante	Edina H.S.	RW	159	9	14	23	135
49	L.A.	Bill Berg	Belleville	LW					
50	Min.	Laurie Billeck	Prince Albert	D					
51	Wsh.	Chris Longo	Peterborough	RW					
52	Phi.	Al Kinisky	Seattle	LW					
53	N.J.	Mike Dunham	Canterbury H.S.	G	301	16747	733	16	2.63
54	St.L.	Patrice Tardif	Lennoxville Jr.	C	65	7	11	18	78
55	NYR	John Vary	North Bay	D					
56	N.J.	Brad Bombardir	Powell River Jr. A	D	287	7	44	51	102
57	Hfd.	Mike Lenarduzzi	Sault Ste. Marie	G	4	189	10	0	3.17
58	Mtl.	Charles Poulin	St-Hyacinthe	C					
59	Edm.	Joe Crowley	Lawrence Academy	LW					
60	Mtl.	Robert Guillet	Longueuil	RW					
61	Pit.	Joe Dziedzic	Edison H.S.	LW	130	14	14	28	131
62	Cgy.	Glen Mears	Rochester Jr. A	D					
63	Bos.	Cam Stewart	Elmira Jr. B	LW	202	16	23	39	120
64	N.J.	Mike Bodnarchuk	Kingston	RW					
65	Van.	Darin Bader	Saskatoon	LW					
66	Det.	Stewart Malgunas	Seattle	D	129	1	5	6	144
67	Edm.	Joel Blain	Hull	LW					
68	Pit.	Chris Tamer	Michigan	D	606	19	59	78	1128
69	NYR	Jeff Nielsen	Grand Rapids H.S.	RW	252	20	27	47	70
70	Min.	Cal McGowan	Kamloops	C					
71	Min.	Frank Kovacs	Regina	LW					
72	Wsh.	Randy Pearce	Kitchener	LW					
73	Tor.	Darby Hendrickson	Richfield H.S.	C	484	63	61	124	358
74	Wpg.	Roman Meluzin	Zetor Brno	RW					
75	Wpg.	Scott Levins	Tri-City	C/RW	124	13	20	33	316
76	NYR	Rick Willis	Pingree Prep	LW					
77	Wpg.	Alexei Zhamnov	Dynamo	C	740	237	436	673	610
78	Hfd.	Chris Bright	Moose Jaw	C					
79	Chi.	Chris Tucker	Jefferson H.S.	C					
80	Tor.	Greg Walters	Ottawa	C					
81	Mtl.	Gilbert Dionne	Kitchener	LW	223	61	79	140	108
82	Buf.	Brian McCarthy	Pingree Prep	C					
83	Cgy.	Paul Kruse	Kamloops	LW	423	38	33	71	1074
84	Bos.	Jerome Buckley	Northwood Prep	RW					
85	NYR	Sergei Zubov	CSKA	D	779	116	449	565	233
86	Van.	Gino Odjick	Laval	RW	605	64	73	137	2567
87	Det.	Tony Burns	Duluth Denfield H.S.	D					
88	Phi.	Dan Kordic	Medicine Hat	LW	197	4	8	12	584
89	Pit.	Brian Farrell	Avon Old Farms H.S.	C					
90	NYI	Chris Marinucci	Grand Rapids H.S.	C	13	1	4	5	2
91	L.A.	David Goverde	Sudbury	G	5	278	29	0	6.26
92	Min.	Enrico Ciccone	Trois-Rivieres	D	374	10	18	28	1469
93	Wsh.	Brian Sakic	Tri-City	C					
94	Wsh.	Mark Ouimet	Michigan	C					
95	N.J.	Dean Malkoc	Kamloops	D	116	1	3	4	299
96	St.L.	Jason Ruff	Lethbridge	LW	14	3	3	6	10
97	Buf.	Richard Smehlik	TJ Vitkovice	D	644	49	146	195	415
98	Wpg.	Craig Martin	Hull	RW	21	0	1	1	24
99	NYR	Lubos Rob	Motor Ceske Budejovice	C					
100	Buf.	Todd Bojcun	Peterborough	G					
101	Edm.	Greg Louder	Cushing Academy	G					
102	Mtl.	Paul Di Pietro	Sudbury	C	192	31	49	80	96
103	Buf.	Brad Pascall	North Dakota	D					
104	N.J.	Petr Kuchyna	Dukla Jihlava	D					
105	Bos.	Mike Bales	Ohio State	G	23	1120	77	0	4.13
106	Que.	Jeff Parrott	Minnesota-Duluth	D					
107	Pit.	Ian Moran	Belmont Hill H.S.	D	441	19	45	64	283
108	Det.	Claude Barthe	Victoriaville	D					
109	Phi.	Viacheslav Butsayev	CSKA	C	132	17	26	43	133
110	Pit.	Denis Casey	Colorado College	G					
111	NYI	Joni Lehto	Ottawa	D					
112	L.A.	Erik Andersson	Danderyd	C	Re-entered Draft in 1997				
113	Min.	Roman Turek	VTJ Pisek	G	310	18064	694	24	2.31
114	Wsh.	Andrei Kovalev	Dynamo	RW					
115	Tor.	Alexander Godynyuk	Sokol Kiev	D	223	10	39	49	224
116	N.J.	Lubomir Kolnik	Dukla Trencin	RW					
117	St.L.	Kurtis Miller	Rochester Jr. A	LW					
118	NYR	Jason Weinrich	Springfield Jr. B	D					
119	Wpg.	Daniel Jardemyr	Uppsala	D					
120	Hfd.	Cory Keenan	Kitchener	D					
121	Chi.	Brett Stickney	St. Paul's H.S.	C					
122	Edm.	Keijo Sailynoja	Jokerit Helsinki	LW					
123	Mtl.	Craig Conroy	Northwood Prep	C	546	110	183	293	293
124	Chi.	Derek Edgerly	Stoneham H.S.	C					
125	Cgy.	Chris Tschupp	Trinity-Pawling H.S.	C					
126	Bos.	Mark Woolf	Spokane	RW					
127	Que.	Dwayne Norris	Michigan State	RW	20	2	4	6	8
128	Van.	Daryl Filipek	Ferris State	D					
129	Det.	Jason York	Kitchener	D	641	39	167	206	525
130	Pit.	Mika Valila	Tappara Tampere	C					
131	Pit.	Ken Plaquin	Michigan Tech	D					
132	NYI	Michael Guilbert	Governor Dummer H.S.	D					
133	L.A.	Robert Lang	CHZ Litvinov	C	577	144	244	388	146
134	Min.	Jeff Levy	Rochester Jr. A	G					
135	Wsh.	Roman Kontsek	Dukla Trencin	RW					
136	Tor.	Eric Lacroix	Governor Dummer H.S.	LW	472	67	70	137	361
137	N.J.	Chris McAlpine	Roseville H.S.	D	289	6	24	30	245
138	St.L.	Wayne Conlan	Trinity-Pawling H.S.	C					
139	NYR	Brian Lonsinger	Choate	D					
140	Wpg.	John Lilley	Cushing Academy	RW	23	3	8	11	13
141	Hfd.	Jergus Baca	VSZ Kosice	D	10	0	2	2	14
142	Buf.	Viktor Gordiouk	Krylja Sovetov	LW	26	3	8	11	0
143	Edm.	Mike Power	Western Michigan	G					
144	Mtl.	Stephen Rohr	Culver Military Academy	RW					
145	Pit.	Pat Neaton	Michigan	D	9	1	1	2	12
146	Cgy.	Dimitri Frolov	Dynamo	D					
147	Bos.	Jim Mackey	Hotchkiss H.S.	D					
148	Que.	Andrei Kovalenko	CSKA	RW	620	173	206	379	389
149	Van.	Paul O'Hagan	Oshawa	D					
150	Det.	Wes McCauley	Michigan State	D					
151	Phi.	Patrik Englund	AIK Solna	LW					
152	Pit.	Petteri Koskimaki	Boston U.	C					
153	NYI	Sylvain Fleury	Longueuil	LW					
154	L.A.	Dean Hulett	Lake Superior State	RW					
155	Min.	Doug Barrault	Lethbridge	RW	4	0	0	0	2
156	Wsh.	Peter Bondra	HC Kosice	RW	907	451	339	790	657
157	Tor.	Dan Stiver	Michigan	RW					

PICK	TEAM	NAME	DRAFTED FROM	NHL PLAYERS: POS / NHL GOALTENDERS: POS	GP / GP	G / W	A / GA	PTS / SO	PIM / AVG
158	Que.	Alexander Karpovtsev	VSZ Dynamo	D	563	34	146	180	408
159	Wsh.	Steve Martell	London	RW					
160	NYR	Todd Hedlund	Roseau H.S.	RW					
161	Wpg.	Henrik Andersson	Vasteras	D					
162	Hfd.	Martin D'Orsonnens	Clarkson	D					
163	Chi.	Hugo Belanger	Clarkson	LW					
164	Edm.	Roman Mejzlik	Dukla Jihlava	LW/C					
165	Mtl.	Brent Fleetwood	Portland	LW					
166	Buf.	Milan Nedoma	Zetor Brno	D					
167	Cgy.	Shawn Murray	Hill-Murray H.S.	G					
168	Bos.	John Gruden	Waterloo Jr. A	D	81	0	8	8	40
169	Que.	Pat Mazzoli	Humboldt Jr. A	G					
170	Van.	Mark Cipriano	Victoria	RW					
171	Det.	Anthony Gruba	Hill-Murray H.S.	RW					
172	Phi.	Toni Porkka	Lukko Rauma	D					
173	Pit.	Ladislav Karabin	Slovan Bratislava	LW	9	0	0	0	2
174	NYI	John Joyce	Avon Old Farms H.S.	C					
175	L.A.	Denis Leblanc	St-Hyacinthe	C					
176	Min.	Joe Biondi	Minnesota-Duluth	C					
177	Wsh.	Ken Klee	Bowling Green	D	570	43	68	111	608
178	Tor.	Robert Horyna	Dukla Jihlava	G					
179	N.J.	Jaroslav Modry	Motor Ceske Budejovice	D	411	35	118	153	286
180	St.L.	Parris Duffus	Melfort Jr. A	G	1	29	1	0	2.07
181	NYR	Andrew Silverman	Beverly H.S.	D					
182	Wpg.	Rauli Raitanen	Assat Pori	C					
183	Hfd.	Corey Osmak	Nipiwan Jr. A	C					
184	Chi.	Owen Lessard	Owen Sound	LW					
185	Edm.	Richard Zemlicka	Sparta Praha	W					
186	Mtl.	Derek Maguire	Delbarton H.S.	D					
187	Buf.	Jason Winch	Niagara Falls	LW					
188	Cgy.	Mike Murray	Cushing Academy	RW					
189	Bos.	Darren Wetherill	Minot Jr. A	D					
190	Que.	Scott Davis	U. of Manitoba	D					
191	Van.	Troy Neumier	Prince Albert	D					
192	Det.	Travis Tucker	Avon Old Farms H.S.	D					
193	Phi.	Greg Hanson	Bloomington-Kennedy H.S.	D					
194	Pit.	Timothy Fingerhut	Canterbury H.S.	LW					
195	NYI	Richard Enga	Culver Military Academy	C					
196	L.A.	Patrik Ross	HV-71 Jonkoping	RW					
197	Min.	Troy Binnie	Ottawa	RW					
198	Wsh.	Michael Boback	Providence	C					
199	Tor.	Rob Chebator	Arlington Catholic H.S.	D					
200	N.J.	Corey Schwab	Seattle	G	144	7289	358	5	2.95
201	St.L.	Steve Widmeyer	U. of Maine	RW					
202	NYR	Jon Hillebrandt	Monona Grove H.S.	G					
203	Wpg.	Mika Alatalo	KooKoo Kouvola	LW	152	17	29	46	58
204	Hfd.	Espen Knutsen	Valerengen, NOR	C	193	30	77	107	103
205	Chi.	Erik Peterson	Brockton H.S.	C					
206	Edm.	Petr Korinek	Skoda Plzen	C					
207	Mtl.	Mark Kettelhut	Duluth East H.S.	D					
208	Buf.	Sylvain Naud	Laval	RW					
209	Cgy.	Rob Sumner	Victoria	D					
210	Bos.	Dean Capuano	Mount St. Charles H.S.	D					
211	Que.	Mika Stromberg	Jokerit Helsinki	D					
212	Van.	Tyler Ertel	North Bay	C					
213	Det.	Brett Larson	Duluth Denfield H.S.	D					
214	Phi.	Tommy Soderstrom	Djurgarden	G	156	8189	496	10	3.63
215	Pit.	Michael Thompson	Michigan State	RW					
216	NYI	Martin Lacroix	St. Lawrence U.	RW					
217	L.A.	K.J.(Kevin) White	Windsor	C					
218	Min.	Ole-Eskild Dahlstrom	Furuset Oslo, NOR	C					
219	Wsh.	Alan Brown	Colgate	D					
220	Tor.	Scott Malone	Northfield H.S.	D					
221	N.J.	Valeri Zelepukin	Khimik Voskresensk	LW	595	117	177	294	527
222	St.L.	Joe Hawley	Peterborough	RW					
223	NYR	Brett Lievers	Wayzata H.S.	C					
224	Wpg.	Sergei Selyanin	Khimik Voskresensk	D					
225	Hfd.	Tommie Eriksen	Prince Albert	D					
226	Chi.	Steve Dubinsky	Clarkson	C	375	25	45	70	164
227	Edm.	invalid pick							
228	Mtl.	John Uniac	Kitchener	D					
229	Buf.	Kenneth Martin	Belmont Hill H.S.	LW					
230	Cgy.	invalid pick							
231	Bos.	Andy Bezeau	Niagara Falls	LW					
232	Que.	Wade Klippenstein	Alaska-Fairbanks	LW					
233	Van.	Karri Kivi	Ilves Tampere	D					
234	Det.	John Hendry	Lake Superior State	LW					
235	Phi.	William Lund	Roseau H.S.	C					
236	Pit.	Brian Bruininks	Colorado College	D					
237	NYI	Andy Shier	Detroit Compuware Jr. A	C					
238	L.A.	Troy Mohns	Colgate	D					
239	Min.	John McKersie	West H.S.	G					
240	Wsh.	Todd Hlushko	London	C	79	8	13	21	84
241	Tor.	Nick Vachon	Governor Dummer H.S.	C	1	0	0	0	0
242	N.J.	Todd Reirden	Tabor Academy	D	176	11	33	44	177
243	St.L.	Joe Fleming	Xaverian H.S.	D					
244	NYR	Sergei Nemchinov	Krylja Sovetov	LW	761	152	193	345	251
245	Wpg.	Keith Morris	Alaska-Anchorage	C					
246	Hfd.	Denis Chalifoux	Laval	C					
247	Chi.	Dino Grossi	Northeastern	RW					
248	Edm.	Sami Nuutinen	Kiekko-Espoo	D					
249	Mtl.	Sergei Martynyuk	Torpedo Yaroslavl	LW					
250	Buf.	Brad Rubachuk	Lethbridge	C					
251	Cgy.	Leo Gudas	Sparta Praha	D					
252	Bos.	Ted Miskolczi	Belleville	D					

1991

FIRST ROUND

PICK	TEAM	NAME	DRAFTED FROM	POS	GP	G	A	PTS	PIM
1	Que.	Eric Lindros	Oshawa	C	639	346	439	785	1225
2	S.J.	Pat Falloon	Spokane	RW	575	143	179	322	141
3	N.J.	Scott Niedermayer	Kamloops	D	811	98	324	422	434
4	NYI	Scott Lachance	Boston U.	D	742	31	108	139	523
5	Wpg.	Aaron Ward	Michigan	D	432	22	44	66	402
6	Phi.	Peter Forsberg	MoDo Ornskoldsvik	C	541	198	488	686	514
7	Van.	Alek Stojanov	Hamilton	RW	107	2	5	7	222
8	Min.	Richard Matvichuk	Saskatoon	D	658	37	109	146	548
9	Hfd.	Patrick Poulin	St-Hyacinthe	C	634	101	134	235	299
10	Det.	Martin Lapointe	Laval	RW	679	133	155	288	1076
11	N.J.	Brian Rolston	Detroit Compuware Jr. A	C/RW	654	171	213	384	183
12	Edm.	Tyler Wright	Swift Current	C	502	68	55	123	740
13	Buf.	Philippe Boucher	Granby	D	457	46	113	159	392
14	Wsh.	Pat Peake	Detroit	C	134	28	41	69	105
15	NYR	Alexei Kovalev	Dynamo	RW	771	278	357	635	836
16	Pit.	Markus Naslund	MoDo Ornskoldsvik	LW	712	255	290	545	455
17	Mtl.	Brent Bilodeau	Seattle	D					
18	Bos.	Glen Murray	Sudbury	RW	742	236	227	463	477
19	Cgy.	Niklas Sundblad	AIK Solna	RW	2	0	0	0	0
20	Edm.	Martin Rucinsky	CHZ Litvinov	LW	735	194	269	463	605
21	Wsh.	Trevor Halverson	North Bay	LW	17	0	4	4	28
22	Chi.	Dean McAmmond	Prince Albert	LW	581	118	179	297	336

SECOND ROUND

PICK	TEAM	NAME	DRAFTED FROM	POS	GP	G	A	PTS	PIM
23	S.J.	Ray Whitney	Spokane	LW	633	191	301	492	197
24	Que.	Rene Corbet	Drummondville	LW	362	58	74	132	420
25	Wsh.	Eric Lavigne	Hull	D	1	0	0	0	0
26	NYI	Ziggy Palffy	AC Nitra	RW	607	302	328	630	298
27	St.L.	Steve Staios	Niagara Falls	D	455	27	62	89	690
28	Mtl.	Jim Campbell	Lawrence Prep	RW	284	61	75	136	266
29	Van.	Jassen Cullimore	Peterborough	D	445	17	42	59	446
30	S.J.	Sandis Ozolinsh	Dynamo Riga	D	743	153	356	509	554
31	Hfd.	Martin Hamrlik	TJ Zlin	D					
32	Det.	Jamie Pushor	Lethbridge	D	503	13	44	57	646
33	N.J.	Donevan Hextall	Prince Albert	LW					
34	Edm.	Andrew Verner	Peterborough	G					
35	Buf.	Jason Dawe	Peterborough	RW	366	86	90	176	162
36	Wsh.	Jeff Nelson	Prince Albert	C	52	3	8	11	20
37	NYR	Darcy Werenka	Lethbridge	D					
38	Pit.	Rusty Fitzgerald	East Duluth High	C	25	2	2	4	12
39	Chi.	Michael Pomichter	Springfield Jr. B	C					
40	Bos.	Jozef Stumpel	AC Nitra	C	694	143	368	511	171
41	Cgy.	Francois Groleau	Shawinigan	D	8	0	1	1	6
42	L.A.	Guy Leveque	Cornwall	C	17	2	2	4	21
43	Mtl.	Craig Darby	Albany Academy	C	194	21	35	56	32
44	Chi.	Jamie Matthews	Sudbury	C	Re-entered Draft in 1993				

OTHER ROUNDS

PICK	TEAM	NAME	DRAFTED FROM	POS	GP	G / W	A / GA	PTS / SO	PIM / AVG
45	S.J.	Dody Wood	Seattle	C	106	8	10	18	471
46	Que.	Rich Brennan	Tabor Academy	D	50	2	6	8	33
47	Tor.	Yanic Perreault	Trois-Rivieres	C	602	179	197	376	274
48	NYI	Jamie McLennan	Lethbridge	G	198	10933	486	9	2.67
49	Wpg.	Dmitri Filimonov	Dynamo	D	30	1	4	5	18

PICK	TEAM	NAME	DRAFTED FROM	NHL PLAYERS: POS / NHL GOALTENDERS: POS	GP / GP	G / W	A / GA	PTS / SO	PIM / AVG
50	Phi.	Yanick Dupre	Drummondville	LW	35	2	0	2	16
51	Van.	Sean Pronger	Bowling Green	C	257	23	35	58	155
52	Cgy.	Sandy McCarthy	Laval	RW	686	68	75	143	1504
53	Hfd.	Todd Hall	Hamden H.S.	LW					
54	Det.	Chris Osgood	Medicine Hat	G	501	28743	1180	38	2.46
55	N.J.	Fredrik Lindquist	Djurgarden	C	8	0	0	0	2
56	Edm.	George Breen	Cushing Academy	RW					
57	Buf.	Jason Young	Sudbury	LW					
58	Wsh.	Steve Konowalchuk	Portland	LW	687	146	195	341	619
59	Hfd.	Michael Nylander	Huddinge	C	630	139	294	433	272
60	Pit.	Shane Peacock	Lethbridge	D					
61	Mtl.	Yves Sarault	St-Jean	LW	106	10	10	20	51
62	Bos.	Marcel Cousineau	Beauport	G	26	1047	51	1	2.92
63	Cgy.	Brian Caruso	Minnesota-Duluth	LW					
64	St.L.	Kyle Reeves	Tri-City	RW					
65	St.L.	Nathan LaFayette	Cornwall	C	187	17	20	37	103
66	Chi.	Bobby House	Brandon	RW					
67	S.J.	Kerry Toporowski	Spokane	D					
68	Que.	Dave Karpa	Ferris State	D	557	18	80	98	1374
69	Tor.	Terry Chitaroni	Sudbury	C					
70	NYI	Milan Hnilicka	Poldi Kladno	G	119	6429	354	5	3.30
71	Chi.	Igor Kravchuk	CSKA	D	699	64	210	274	251
72	Buf.	Peter Ambroziak	Ottawa	LW	12	0	1	1	0
73	Mtl.	Vladimir Vujtek	Tri-City	LW	110	7	30	37	38
74	Min.	Mike Torchia	Kitchener	G	6	327	18	0	3.30
75	Hfd.	Jim Storm	Michigan Tech	LW	84	7	15	22	44
76	Det.	Mike Knuble	Kalamazoo Jr. A	RW	428	80	82	162	192
77	N.J.	Bradley Willner	Richfield H.S.	D					
78	Edm.	Mario Nobili	Longueuil	LW					
79	L.A.	Keith Redmond	Bowling Green	LW	12	1	0	1	20
80	Wsh.	Justin Morrison	Kingston	C					
81	L.A.	Alexei Zhitnik	Sokol Kiev	D	814	77	291	368	928
82	Pit.	Joe Tamminen	Virginia H.S.	C					
83	Mtl.	Sylvain Lapointe	Clarkson	D					
84	Bos.	Brad Tiley	Sault Ste. Marie	D	11	0	0	0	0
85	Cgy.	Steven Magnusson	Anoka H.S.	C					
86	Phi.	Aris Brimanis	Bowling Green	D	100	2	12	14	53
87	St.L.	Grayden Reid	Owen Sound	C					
88	Chi.	Zac Boyer	Kamloops	RW	3	0	0	0	0
89	S.J.	Dan Ryder	Sudbury	G					
90	Que.	Patrick Labrecque	St-Jean	G	2	98	7	0	4.29
91	Wpg.	Juha Ylonen	Kiekko Espoo	C	341	26	76	102	90
92	NYI	Steve Junker	Spokane	LW	5	0	0	0	0
93	Edm.	Ryan Haggerty	Westminster H.S.	C					
94	Phi.	Yanick Degrace	Trois-Rivieres	G					
95	Van.	Dan Kesa	Prince Albert	RW	139	8	22	30	66
96	NYR	Corey Machanic	Vermont	D					
97	Min.	Mike Kennedy	U. of British Columbia	C	145	16	36	52	112
98	Det.	Dimitri Motkov	CSKA	D					
99	Wpg.	Yan Kaminsky	Dynamo	RW	26	3	2	5	4
100	Mtl.	Brad Layzell	RPI	D					
101	Buf.	Steve Shields	Michigan	G	225	12632	545	10	2.59
102	Tor.	Alexei Kudashov	Krylja Sovetov	C	25	1	0	1	4
103	Que.	Bill Lindsay	Tri-City	RW	753	83	141	224	897
104	Pit.	Robert Melanson	Hull	D					
105	Mtl.	Tony Prpic	Culver Military Academy	RW					
106	Bos.	Mariusz Czerkawski	GKS Tychy, POL	RW	629	182	194	376	248
107	Cgy.	Jerome Butler	Roseau H.S.	G					
108	L.A.	Pauli Jaks	Ambri-Piotta, SUI	G	1	40	2	0	3.00
109	St.L.	Jeff Callinan	Minnetonka H.S.	G					
110	Chi.	Maco Balkovec	Merritt Jr. A	D					
111	S.J.	Frank Nilsson	Vasteras	C					
112	Chi.	Kevin St. Jacques	Lethbridge	LW					
113	Tor.	Jeff Perry	Owen Sound	LW					
114	NYI	Rob Valicevic	Detroit Red Wings Jr. A	RW	186	28	20	48	59
115	Wpg.	Jeff Sebastian	Seattle	D					
116	Phi.	Clayton Norris	Medicine Hat	RW					
117	Van.	John Namestnikov	Torpedo Nizhny Novogord	D	43	0	9	9	24
118	Min.	Mark Lawrence	Detroit	RW	142	18	26	44	115
119	Hfd.	Mike Harding	Northern Michigan	RW					
120	Tor.	Alexander Kuzminsky	Sokol Kiev	C					
121	N.J.	Curt Regnier	Prince Albert	RW					
122	Phi.	Dmitry Yushkevich	Torpedo Yaroslavl	D	786	43	182	225	659
123	Buf.	Sean O'Donnell	Sudbury	D	611	20	109	129	1125
124	Buf.	Brian Holzinger	Detroit Jr. A	C	473	86	130	216	299
125	NYR	Fredrik Jax	Leksand	RW					
126	Pit.	Brian Clifford	Nichols H.S.	C					
127	Mtl.	Oleg Petrov	CSKA	RW	382	72	115	187	101
128	NYR	Barry Young	Sudbury	D					
129	Cgy.	Bobby Marshall	Miami of Ohio	D					
130	L.A.	Brett Seguin	Ottawa	C					
131	St.L.	Bruce Gardiner	Colgate	RW	312	34	54	88	263
132	Chi.	Jacques Auger	Wisconsin	D					
133	S.J.	Jaroslav Otevrel	TJ Zlin	LW	16	3	4	7	2
134	Que.	Mikael Johansson	Djurgarden	C					
135	Tor.	Martin Prochazka	Poldi Kladno	RW	32	2	5	7	8
136	NYI	Andreas Johansson	Falun	C	330	69	73	142	164
137	Min.	Geoff Finch	Brown	G					
138	Phi.	Andrei Lomakin	Dynamo	RW	215	42	62	104	92
139	Van.	Brent Thurston	Spokane	LW					
140	Cgy.	Matt Hoffman	Oshawa	LW					
141	Hfd.	Brian Mueller	South Kent H.S.	D					
142	Det.	Igor Malykhin	CSKA	D					
143	N.J.	David Craievich	Oshawa	D					
144	Edm.	David Oliver	Michigan	RW	194	42	44	86	72
145	Buf.	Chris Snell	Ottawa	D	34	2	7	9	24
146	Wsh.	Dave Morissette	Shawinigan	LW	11	0	0	0	57
147	NYR	John Rushin	Kennedy H.S.	C					
148	Pit.	Ed Patterson	Kamloops	RW	68	3	3	6	56
149	Mtl.	Brady Kramer	Haverford H.S.	C					
150	Bos.	Gary Golczewski	Trinity-Pawling H.S.	LW					
151	Cgy.	Kelly Harper	Michigan State	C					
152	L.A.	Kelly Fairchild	Grand Rapids H.S.	C	34	2	3	5	6
153	St.L.	Terry Hollinger	Lethbridge	D	7	0	0	0	2
154	Chi.	Scott Kirton	Powell River Jr. A	RW					
155	S.J.	Dean Grillo	Warroad H.S.	RW					
156	Que.	Janne Laukkanen	Reipas Lahti	D	407	22	99	121	335
157	Que.	Aaron Asp	Ferris State	C					
158	NYI	Todd Sparks	Hull	LW					
159	Wpg.	Jeff Ricciardi	Ottawa	D					
160	Tor.	Dmitri Mironov	Krylia Sovetov	D	556	54	206	260	560
161	Van.	Eric Johnson	Armstrong H.S.	RW					
162	Buf.	Jiri Kuntos	Dukla Jihlava	D					
163	Hfd.	Steve Yule	Kamloops	D					
164	Tor.	Robb McIntyre	Dubuque Jr. A	LW					
165	N.J.	Paul Wolanski	Niagara Falls	D					
166	Edm.	Gary Kitching	Thunder Bay Jr. A	C					
167	Tor.	Tomas Kucharcik	Dukla Jihlava	C					
168	Wsh.	Rick Corriveau	London	D					
169	NYR	Corey Hirsch	Kamloops	G	108	5775	301	4	3.13
170	Pit.	Peter McLaughlin	Belmont Hill H.S.	D					
171	Mtl.	Brian Savage	Miami of Ohio	LW	534	167	146	313	255
172	Bos.	Jay Moser	Park H.S.	D					
173	Cgy.	David St-Pierre	Longueuil	C					
174	Min.	Michael Burkett	Michigan State	LW					
175	St.L.	Chris Kenady	St. Paul Jr. A	RW	7	0	2	2	0
176	Chi.	Roch Belley	Niagara Falls	G					
177	S.J.	Corwin Saurdiff	Waterloo Jr. A	G					
178	Que.	Adam Bartell	Niagara Jr. A	D					
179	Tor.	Guy Lehoux	Drummondville	D					
180	NYI	John Johnson	Niagara Falls	C					
181	Wpg.	Sean Gauthier	Kingston	G	1	3	0	0	0.00
182	Phi.	James Bode	Armstrong H.S.	RW					
183	Van.	David Neilson	Prince Albert	LW					
184	Min.	Derek Herlofsky	St. Paul Jr. A	G					
185	Hfd.	Chris Belanger	Western Michigan	D					
186	Det.	Jim Bermingham	Laval	C					
187	N.J.	Daniel Reimann	Anoka H.S.	D					
188	Que.	Brent Brekke	Western Michigan	D					
189	Buf.	Tony Iob	Sault Ste. Marie	LW					
190	Wsh.	Trevor Duhaime	St-Jean	RW					
191	NYR	Vyachesl Uvayev	Spartak	D					
192	Pit.	Jeff Lembke	Omaha Jr. A	G					
193	Mtl.	Scott Fraser	Dartmouth	C	72	16	15	31	24
194	Bos.	Daniel Hodge	Merrimack	D					
195	Cgy.	David Struch	Saskatoon	C	4	0	0	0	4
196	L.A.	Craig Brown	Western Michigan	G					
197	St.L.	Jed Fiebelkorn	Osseo H.S.	RW					
198	Chi.	Scott MacDonald	Choate	D					
199	S.J.	Dale Craigwell	Oshawa	C	98	11	18	29	28
200	Que.	Paul Koch	Omaha Jr. A	D					
201	Tor.	Gary Miller	North Bay	D					

PICK	TEAM	NAME	DRAFTED FROM	NHL PLAYERS: POS / NHL GOALTENDERS: POS	GP / GP	G / W	A / GA	PTS / SO	PIM / AVG
202	NYI	Robert Canavan	Hingham H.S.	LW					
203	Wpg.	Igor Ulanov	Khimik Voskresensk	D	660	19	116	135	1094
204	Phi.	Josh Bartell	Rome Free Academy	D					
205	Van.	Brad Barton	Kitchener	D					
206	Min.	Tom Nemeth	Cornwall	LW					
207	Hfd.	Jason Currie	Clarkson	G					
208	Det.	Jason Firth	Kitchener	C					
209	Wsh.	Rob Leask	Hamilton	D					
210	Edm.	Vegar Barlie	Valerengen, NOR	RW					
211	Buf.	Spencer Meany	St. Lawrence U.	RW					
212	Wsh.	Carl Leblanc	Granby	D					
213	NYR	Jamie Ram	Michigan Tech	G	1	27	0	0	0.00
214	Pit.	Chris Tok	Greenway H.S.	D					
215	Mtl.	Greg MacEachern	Laval	D					
216	Bos.	Steve Norton	Michigan State	D					
217	Cgy.	Sergei Zolotov	Krylja Sovetov	LW					
218	L.A.	Mattias Olsson	Farjestad Karlstad	D					
219	St.L.	Chris MacKenzie	Colgate	LW					
220	Chi.	Alexander Andrievski	Dynamo	RW	1	0	0	0	0
221	S.J.	Aaron Kriss	Cranbrook H.S.	D					
222	Que.	Doug Friedman	Boston U.	LW	18	0	1	1	34
223	Tor.	Johnathon Kelley	Arlington Catholic H.S.	C					
224	NYI	Marcus Thuresson	Leksand	C					
225	Wpg.	Jason Jennings	Western Michigan	RW					
226	Phi.	Neil Little	RPI	G	1	60	4	0	4.00
227	Van.	Jason Fitzsimmons	Moose Jaw	G					
228	Min.	Shayne Green	Kamloops	RW					
229	Hfd.	Mike Santonelli	Matignon H.S.	C					
230	Det.	Bart Turner	Michigan State	LW					
231	N.J.	Kevin Riehl	Medicine Hat	C					
232	Edm.	Yevgeny Belosheiken	CSKA	G					
233	Buf.	Mikhail Volkov	Krylja Sovetov	RW					
234	Wsh.	Rob Puchniak	Lethbridge	D					
235	NYR	Vitali Chinakhov	Torpedo Yaroslavl	C					
236	Pit.	Paul Dyck	Moose Jaw	D					
237	Mtl.	Paul Lepler	Rochester Jr. A	D					
238	Bos.	Stephen Lombardi	Deerfield Academy	C					
239	Cgy.	Marko Jantunen	Reipas Lahti	C	3	0	0	0	0
240	L.A.	Andre Bouliane	Longueuil	G					
241	St.L.	Kevin Rappana	Duluth East H.S.	D					
242	Chi.	Mike Larkin	Rice Memorial H.S.	D					
243	S.J.	Mikhail Kravets	SKA Leningrad	RW	2	0	0	0	0
244	Que.	Eric Meloche	Drummondville	RW	13	5	1	6	4
245	Tor.	Chris O'Rourke	Alaska-Fairbanks	D					
246	NYI	Marty Schriner	North Dakota	C					
247	Wpg.	Sergei Sorokin	Dynamo	D					
248	Phi.	John Porco	Belleville	C					
249	Van.	Xavier Majic	RPI	C					
250	Min.	Jukka Suomalainen	GrIFK Kauniainen	D					
251	Hfd.	Rob Peters	Ohio State	D					
252	Det.	Andrew Miller	Wexford Jr. B	RW					
253	N.J.	Jason Hehr	Kelowna Jr. A	D					
254	Edm.	Juha Riihijarvi	Karpat Oulu	RW					
255	Buf.	Michael Smith	Lake Superior State	D					
256	Wsh.	Bill Kovacs	Sudbury	LW					
257	NYR	Brian Wiseman	Michigan	C	3	0	0	0	0
258	Pit.	Pasi Huura	Ilves Tampere	D					
259	Mtl.	Dale Hooper	Springfield Jr. B	D					
260	Bos.	Torsten Kienass	Dynamo Berlin, FRG	D					
261	Cgy.	Andrei Trefilov	Dynamo	G	54	2663	153	2	3.45
262	L.A.	Mike Gaul	St. Lawrence U.	D	3	0	0	0	4
263	St.L.	Mike Veisor	Springfield Jr. B	G					
264	Chi.	Scott Dean	Lake Forest H.S.	D					

1992

FIRST ROUND

PICK	TEAM	NAME	DRAFTED FROM	POS	GP	G / W	A / GA	PTS / SO	PIM / AVG
1	T.B.	Roman Hamrlik	ZPS Zlin	D	792	110	302	412	917
2	Ott.	Alexei Yashin	Dynamo	C	663	276	355	631	279
3	S.J.	Mike Rathje	Medicine Hat	D	591	25	111	136	393
4	Que.	Todd Warriner	Windsor	LW	453	65	89	154	249
5	NYI	Darius Kasparaitis	Dynamo	D	728	24	119	143	1204
6	Cgy.	Cory Stillman	Windsor	LW	485	135	152	287	234
7	Phi.	Ryan Sittler	Nichols H.S.	LW					
8	Tor.	Brandon Convery	Sudbury	C	72	9	19	28	36
9	Hfd.	Robert Petrovicky	Dukla Trencin	C	208	27	38	65	118
10	S.J.	Andrei Nazarov	Dynamo	LW	536	52	69	121	1278
11	Buf.	David Cooper	Medicine Hat	D	30	3	7	10	24
12	Chi.	Sergei Krivokrasov	CSKA	RW	450	86	109	195	288
13	Edm.	Joe Hulbig	St. Sebastian's	LW	55	4	4	8	16
14	Wsh.	Sergei Gonchar	Traktor Chelyabinsk	D	598	137	230	367	473
15	Phi.	Jason Bowen	Tri-City	D	77	2	6	8	109
16	Bos.	Dmitri Kvartalnov	San Diego IHL	LW	112	42	49	91	26
17	Wpg.	Sergei Bautin	Dynamo	D	132	5	25	30	176
18	N.J.	Jason Smith	Regina	D	574	22	77	99	617
19	Pit.	Martin Straka	HC Skoda Plzen	C	676	182	322	504	252
20	Mtl.	David Wilkie	Kamloops	D	167	10	26	36	165
21	Van.	Libor Polasek	TJ Vitkovice	C					
22	Det.	Curtis Bowen	Ottawa	LW					
23	Tor.	Grant Marshall	Ottawa	RW	559	76	123	199	656
24	NYR	Peter Ferraro	Waterloo Jr. A	LW	92	9	15	24	58

SECOND ROUND

PICK	TEAM	NAME	DRAFTED FROM	POS	GP	G / W	A / GA	PTS / SO	PIM / AVG
25	Ott.	Chad Penney	North Bay	LW	3	0	0	0	2
26	T.B.	Drew Bannister	Sault Ste. Marie	D	164	5	25	30	161
27	Wpg.	Boris Mironov	CSKA	D	641	73	218	291	805
28	Que.	Paul Brousseau	Hull	RW	26	1	3	4	29
29	Que.	Tuomas Gronman	Tacoma	D	38	1	3	4	38
30	Cgy.	Chris O'Sullivan	Catholic Memorial H.S.	D	62	2	17	19	16
31	Phi.	Denis Metlyuk	Lada Togliatti	C					
32	Wsh.	Jim Carey	Catholic Memorial H.S.	G	172	9668	416	16	2.58
33	Mtl.	Valeri Bure	Spokane	RW	553	152	196	348	195
34	Min.	Jarkko Varvio	HPK Hameenlinna	RW	13	3	4	7	4
35	Buf.	Jozef Cierny	ZTK Zvolen	LW	1	0	0	0	0
36	Chi.	Jeff Shantz	Regina	C	642	72	139	211	341
37	Edm.	Martin Reichel	Freiburg	RW					
38	St.L.	Igor Korolev	Dynamo	C	733	116	217	333	308
39	L.A.	Justin Hocking	Spokane	D	1	0	0	0	0
40	Van.	Michael Peca	Ottawa	C	546	140	191	331	489
41	Chi.	Sergei Klimovich	Dynamo	C	1	0	0	0	2
42	N.J.	Sergei Brylin	CSKA	C	437	78	104	182	152
43	Pit.	Marc Hussey	Moose Jaw	D					
44	Mtl.	Keli Corpse	Kingston	C					
45	Van.	Mike Fountain	Oshawa	G	11	483	28	1	3.48
46	Det.	Darren McCarty	Bellevile	RW	600	113	149	262	1225
47	Hfd.	Andrei Nikolishin	Dynamo	C	579	88	180	268	246
48	NYR	Mattias Norstrom	AIK Solna	D	610	9	91	100	471

OTHER ROUNDS

PICK	TEAM	NAME	DRAFTED FROM	POS	GP	G / W	A / GA	PTS / SO	PIM / AVG
49	T.B.	Brent Gretzky	Belleville	C	13	1	3	4	2
50	Ott.	Patrick Traverse	Shawinigan	D	278	14	51	65	113
51	S.J.	Alexander Cherbayev	Khimik Voskresensk	LW					
52	Que.	Manny Fernandez	Laval	G	154	8693	365	8	2.52
53	Wsh.	Stefan Ustorf	ESV Kaufbeuren	C	54	7	10	17	16
54	Cgy.	Mathias Johansson	Farjestad	C	58	5	10	15	16
55	Bos.	Sergei Zholtok	Rigas Stars	C	518	97	130	227	147
56	NYI	Jarrett Deuling	Kamloops	LW	15	0	1	1	11
57	Hfd.	Jan Vopat	HC Chemopetrol Litvinov	D	126	11	20	31	70
58	Min.	Jeff Bes	Guelph	C					
59	Buf.	Ondrej Steiner	HC Skoda Plzen	C					
60	Wpg.	Jeremy Stevenson	Cornwall	LW	Re-entered Draft in 1994				
61	Edm.	Simon Roy	Shawinigan	D					
62	St.L.	Vitali Karamnov	Dynamo	LW	92	12	20	32	65
63	L.A.	Sandy Allan	North Bay	G					
64	St.L.	Vitali Prokhorov	Spartak	LW	83	19	11	30	35
65	Edm.	Kirk Maltby	Owen Sound	RW	638	88	90	178	565
66	N.J.	Cale Hulse	Portland	D	498	13	58	71	814
67	Pit.	Travis Thiessen	Moose Jaw	D					
68	Mtl.	Craig Rivet	Kingston	D	437	22	67	89	531
69	Van.	Jeff Connolly	St. Sebastian's	C					
70	Det.	Sylvain Cloutier	Guelph	C	7	0	0	0	0
71	Wsh.	Martin Gendron	St-Hyacinthe	RW	30	4	2	6	10
72	NYR	Eric Cairns	Detroit	D	334	7	25	32	864
73	Ott.	Radek Hamr	Sparta Praha	D	11	0	0	0	0
74	T.B.	Aaron Gavey	Sault Ste. Marie	C	355	41	50	91	270
75	S.J.	Jan Caloun	HC Chemopetrol Litvinov	RW	24	8	6	14	2
76	Que.	Ian McIntyre	Beauport	D					
77	Tor.	Nikolai Borschevsky	Spartak	RW	162	49	73	122	44
78	Cgy.	Robert Svehla	Dukla Trencin	D	655	68	267	335	649
79	Hfd.	Kevin Smyth	Moose Jaw	LW	58	6	8	14	31
80	Buf.	Dean Melanson	St-Hyacinthe	D	9	0	0	0	8
81	Hfd.	Jason McBain	Portland	D	9	0	0	0	0

PICK	TEAM	NAME	DRAFTED FROM	NHL PLAYERS: POS / NHL GOALTENDERS: POS	GP / GP	G / W	A / GA	PTS / SO	PIM / AVG
82	Mtl.	Louis Bernard	Drummondville	D					
83	Buf.	Matthew Barnaby	Beauport	RW	631	88	136	224	2100
84	Wpg.	Mark Visheau	London	D	29	1	3	4	107
85	NYR	Chris Ferraro	Waterloo Jr. A	C	74	7	9	16	57
86	St.L.	Lee Leslie	Prince Albert	LW					
87	L.A.	Kevin Brown	Belleville	RW	64	7	9	16	28
88	Min.	Jere Lehtinen	Kiekko-Espoo	RW	510	144	171	315	114
89	Chi.	Andy MacIntyre	Saskatoon	LW					
90	N.J.	Vitali Tomilin	Krylja Sovetov	C					
91	Pit.	Todd Klassen	Tri-City	D					
92	Mtl.	Marc Lamothe	Kingston	G	2	116	10	0	5.17
93	Van.	Brent Tully	Peterborough	D					
94	N.J.	Scott McCabe	GPD Midgets	D					
95	Tor.	Mark Raiter	Saskatoon	D					
96	Edm.	Ralph Intranuovo	Sault Ste. Marie	C	22	2	4	6	4
97	T.B.	Brantt Myhres	Lethbridge	RW	154	6	2	8	687
98	Ott.	Daniel Guerard	Victoriaville	RW	2	0	0	0	0
99	S.J.	Marcus Ragnarsson	Djurgarden	D	562	30	131	161	424
100	Que.	Charlie Wasley	St. Paul Jr. A	D					
101	Tor.	Janne Gronvall	Lukko Rauma	D					
102	Cgy.	Sami Helenius	Jokerit Helsinki	D	155	2	4	6	260
103	Phi.	Vladislav Buljin	Dizelist Penza	D					
104	NYI	Thomas Klimt	HC Skoda Plzen	C					
105	NYI	Ryan Duthie	Spokane	C					
106	Tor.	Chris Deruiter	Kingston Jr. A	RW					
107	Buf.	Markus Ketterer	Jokerit Helsinki	G					
108	Buf.	Yuri Khmylev	Krylja Sovetov	LW	263	64	88	152	133
109	Edm.	Joaquin Gage	Portland	G	23	1076	67	0	3.74
110	Van.	Brian Loney	Ohio State	RW	12	2	3	5	6
111	L.A.	Jeff Shevalier	North Bay	LW	32	5	9	14	8
112	Bos.	Scott Bailey	Spokane	G	19	965	55	0	3.42
113	Chi.	Tim Hogan	Michigan	D					
114	N.J.	Ryan Black	Peterborough	LW					
115	Pit.	Philippe DeRouville	Verdun	G	3	171	9	0	3.16
116	Mtl.	Don Chase	Springfield Jr. B	C					
117	Van.	Adrian Aucoin	Boston U.	D	521	70	131	201	402
118	Det.	Mike Sullivan	Reading H.S.	C					
119	Wsh.	John Varga	Tacoma	LW					
120	NYR	Dmitri Starostenko	CSKA	LW					
121	Ott.	Al Sinclair	Michigan	D					
122	T.B.	Martin Tanguay	Verdun	C					
123	S.J.	Michal Sykora	Tacoma	D	267	15	54	69	185
124	Que.	Paxton Schulte	Spokane	LW	2	0	0	0	4
125	Tor.	Mikael Hakansson	Nacka	C					
126	Cgy.	Ravil Yakubov	Dynamo	C					
127	Phi.	Roman Zolotov	Dynamo	D					
128	NYI	Derek Armstrong	Sudbury	C	152	21	36	57	86
129	Cgy.	Joel Bouchard	Verdun	D	311	20	38	58	231
130	Min.	Michael Johnson	Ottawa	D					
131	Buf.	Paul Rushforth	North Bay	C					
132	Wpg.	Alexander Alexeyev	Sokol Kiev	D					
133	Bos.	Jiri Dopita	DS Olomouc	C	Re-entered Draft in 1998				
134	St.L.	Bob Lachance	Springfield Jr. B	RW					
135	L.A.	Rem Murray	Michigan State	LW	512	85	111	196	147
136	Bos.	Grigori Panteleev	Rigas Stars	LW	54	8	6	14	12
137	Chi.	Gerry Skrypec	Ottawa	D					
138	N.J.	Dan Trebil	Bloomington-Jefferson H.S.	D	85	4	4	8	32
139	Pit.	Artem Kopot	Traktor Chelyabinsk	D					
140	Mtl.	Martin Sychra	Zetor Brno	C					
141	Van.	Jason Clark	St. Thomas Jr. B	C					
142	Det.	Jason MacDonald	Owen Sound	RW					
143	Hfd.	Jarrett Reid	Sault Ste. Marie	C					
144	NYR	David Dal Grande	Ottawa Jr. A	D					
145	T.B.	Derek Wilkinson	Detroit	G	22	933	57	0	3.67
146	Ott.	Jaroslav Miklenda	DS Olomouc	G					
147	S.J.	Eric Bellerose	Trois-Rivieres	LW					
148	Que.	Martin Lepage	Hull	D					
149	Tor.	Patrik Augusta	Dukla Jihlava	RW	4	0	0	0	0
150	Cgy.	Pavel Rajnoha	ZPS Zlin	D					
151	Phi.	Kirk Daubenspeck	Culver Military Academy	G					
152	NYI	Vladimir Grachev	Dynamo-2	LW					
153	Hfd.	Ken Belanger	Ottawa	LW	243	11	12	23	688
154	Min.	Kyle Peterson	Thunder Bay Jr. A	C					
155	Wpg.	Artur Oktyabrev	CSKA	D					
156	Wpg.	Andrei Raisky	Torpedo Ust-Kamenogorsk	C					
157	Edm.	Steve Gibson	Windsor	LW					
158	St.L.	Ian Laperriere	Drummondville	C/RW	632	68	114	182	1184
159	NYI	Steve O'Rourke	Tri-City	RW					
160	St.L.	Lance Burns	Lethbridge	C					
161	Chi.	Mike Prokopec	Cornwall	RW	15	0	0	0	11
162	N.J.	Geordie Kinnear	Peterborough	D	4	0	0	0	13
163	Pit.	Jan Alinc	HC Chemopetrol Litvinov	LW					
164	Mtl.	Christian Proulx	St-Jean	D	7	1	2	3	20
165	Van.	Scott Hollis	Oshawa	RW					
166	Det.	Greg Scott	Niagara Falls	G					
167	Wsh.	Mark Matier	Sault Ste. Marie	D					
168	NYR	Matt Oates	Miami of Ohio	LW					
169	Ott.	Jay Kenney	Canterbury H.S.	D					
170	T.B.	Dennis Maxwell	Niagara Falls	C					
171	S.J.	Ryan Smith	Brandon	D					
172	Que.	Mike Jickling	Spokane	C					
173	Tor.	Ryan Vandenbussche	Cornwall	RW	225	5	9	14	540
174	Cgy.	Ryan Mulhern	Canterbury H.S.	C	3	0	0	0	0
175	Phi.	Claude Jr. Jutras	Hull	RW					
176	NYI	Jason Widmer	Lethbridge	D	7	0	1	1	7
177	Hfd.	Konstantin Korotkov	Spartak	C					
178	Min.	Juha Lind	Jokerit Helsinki	C	133	9	13	22	20
179	Buf.	Dean Tiltgen	Tri-City	C					
180	St.L.	Igor Boldin	Spartak	C					
181	Edm.	Kyuin Shim	Sherwood Park Jr. A	RW					
182	St.L.	Nick Naumenko	Dubuque Jr. A	D					
183	Det.	Justin Krall	Omaha Jr. A	D					
184	Bos.	Kurt Seher	Seattle	D					
185	Chi.	Layne Roland	Portland	RW					
186	N.J.	Stephane Yelle	Oshawa	C	587	64	104	168	302
187	Pit.	Fran Bussey	Duluth East H.S.	C					
188	Mtl.	Michael Burman	North Bay	D					
189	Det.	C. J. Denomme	Kitchener	G					
190	Edm.	Colin Schmidt	Regina Midgets	C					
191	Wsh.	Mike Mathers	Kamloops	LW					
192	NYR	Mickey Elick	Wisconsin	D					
193	T.B.	Andrew Kemper	Seattle	D					
194	Ott.	Claude Savoie	Victoriaville	RW					
195	S.J.	Chris Burns	Thunder Bay Jr. A	G					
196	Que.	Steve Passmore	Victoria	G	84	4567	212	2	2.79
197	Tor.	Wayne Clarke	RPI	RW					
198	Cgy.	Brandon Carper	Bowling Green	D					
199	Phi.	Jonas Hakansson	Malmo	LW					
200	NYI	Daniel Paradis	Chicoutimi	C					
201	Hfd.	Greg Zwakman	Edina H.S.	D					
202	Min.	Lars Edstrom	Lulea	LW					
203	Buf.	Todd Simon	Niagara Falls	C	15	0	1	1	0
204	Wpg.	Nikolai Khabibulin	CSKA	G	421	23833	1050	32	2.64
205	Edm.	Marko Tuomainen	Clarkson	RW	79	9	9	18	84
206	St.L.	Todd Harris	Tri-City	D					
207	L.A.	Magnus Wernblom	MoDo Ornskoldsvik	RW					
208	Bos.	Mattias Timander	MoDo Ornskoldsvik	D	380	11	52	63	144
209	Chi.	David Hymovitz	Thayer Academy	LW					
210	N.J.	Jeff Toms	Sault Ste. Marie	C	236	22	33	55	59
211	Pit.	Brian Bonin	White Bear Lake H.S.	C	12	0	0	0	0
212	Mtl.	Earl Cronan	St. Mark's H.S.	LW					
213	Van.	Sonny Mignacca	Medicine Hat	G					
214	Det.	Jeff Walker	Peterborough	D					
215	Wsh.	Brian Stagg	Kingston	RW					
216	NYR	Daniel Brierley	Choate	D					
217	Ott.	Jake Grimes	Belleville	C					
218	T.B.	Marc Tardif	Shawinigan	LW					
219	S.J.	Alexander Kholomeyev	Izoherts St. Petersburg	LW					
220	Que.	Anson Carter	Wexford Jr. A	RW	452	143	167	310	150
221	Tor.	Sergei Simonov	Kristall Saratov	D					
222	Cgy.	Jonas Hoglund	Farjestad Karlstad	LW	545	117	145	262	112
223	Phi.	Chris Herperger	Swift Current	C	169	18	25	43	75
224	NYI	David Wainwright	Thayer Academy	D					
225	Hfd.	Steven Halko	Thornhill Jr. A.	D	155	0	15	15	71
226	Min.	Jeff Romfo	Blaine H.S.	C					
227	Buf.	Rick Kowalsky	Sault Ste. Marie	RW					
228	Wpg.	Yevgeny Garanin	Khimik Voskresensk	C					
229	Wpg.	Teemu Numminen	Stoneham H.S.	C					
230	St.L.	Yuri Gunko	Sokol Kiev	D					
231	L.A.	Ryan Pisiak	Prince Albert	RW					
232	Bos.	Chris Crombie	London	LW					
233	Chi.	Richard Raymond	Cornwall	D					

PICK	TEAM	NAME	DRAFTED FROM	NHL PLAYERS: POS	GP	G	A	PTS	PIM
				NHL GOALTENDERS: POS	GP	W	GA	SO	AVG
234	N.J.	Heath Weenk	Regina	D					
235	Pit.	Brian Callahan	Belmont Hill H.S.	C					
236	Mtl.	Trent Cavicchi	Dartmouth Midgets	G					
237	Van.	Mark Wotton	Saskatoon	D	43	3	6	9	25
238	Det.	Dan McGillis	Hawkesbury Jr. A	D	527	51	153	204	469
239	Wsh.	Gregory Callahan	Belmont Hill H.S.	D					
240	NYR	Vladimir Vorobiev	Metallurg Cherepovets	LW	33	9	7	16	14
241	T.B.	Tom MacDonald	Sault Ste. Marie	C					
242	Ott.	Tomas Jelinek	HPK Hameenlinna	RW	49	7	6	13	52
243	S.J.	Victor Ignatjev	Rigas Stars	D	11	0	1	1	6
244	Que.	Aaron Ellis	Culver Military Academy	G					
245	Tor.	Nathan Dempsey	Regina	D	115	7	35	42	34
246	Cgy.	Andrei Potaichuk	Krylja Sovetov	RW					
247	Phi.	Patrice Paquin	Beauport	LW					
248	NYI	Andrei Vasilyev	CSKA	LW	16	2	5	7	6
249	Hfd.	Joacim Esbjors	Vastra Frolunda Goteborg	D					
250	Min.	Jeffrey Moen	Roseville H.S.	G					
251	Buf.	Chris Clancy	Cornwall	LW					
252	Wpg.	Andrei Karpovstev	Dynamo	RW					
253	Edm.	Bryan Rasmussen	St. Louis Park H.S.	LW					
254	Wpg.	Ivan Vologzhaninov	Sokol Kiev	RW					
255	L.A.	Jukka Tiilikainen	Kiekko-Espoo	LW					
256	Bos.	Denis Chervyakov	Rigas Stars	D	2	0	0	0	2
257	Bos.	Evgeny Pavlov	SKA Leningrad						
258	N.J.	Vladislav Yakovenko	Argus	LW					
259	St.L.	Wade Salzman	Duluth East H.S.	G					
260	Mtl.	Hiroyuki Miura	Kushiro High School, JPN	D					
261	Van.	Aaron Boh	Spokane	D					
262	Det.	Ryan Bach	Notre Dame Jr. A.	G	3	108	8	0	4.44
263	Wsh.	Billy Jo MacPherson	Oshawa	LW					
264	Ott.	Petter Ronnqvist	Nacka	G					

1993

FIRST ROUND

PICK	TEAM	NAME	DRAFTED FROM	POS	GP	G/W	A/GA	PTS/SO	PIM/AVG
1	Ott.	Alexandre Daigle	Victoriaville	C	492	104	144	248	160
2	Hfd.	Chris Pronger	Peterborough	D	642	80	266	346	1010
3	T.B.	Chris Gratton	Kingston	C	770	161	277	438	1240
4	Ana.	Paul Kariya	U. of Maine	LW	606	300	369	669	213
5	Fla.	Rob Niedermayer	Medicine Hat	C	641	117	191	308	541
5	Det.	Benoit Larose	Laval	D					
6	S.J.	Viktor Kozlov	Dynamo	C	540	119	214	333	152
7	Edm.	Jason Arnott	Oshawa	C	670	223	288	511	831
8	NYR	Niklas Sundstrom	MoDo Ornskoldsvik	RW	629	103	211	314	208
9	Dal.	Todd Harvey	Detroit	RW/C	561	82	125	207	880
10	Que.	Jocelyn Thibault	Sherbrooke	G	522	29656	1329	35	2.69
11	Wsh.	Brendan Witt	Seattle	D	496	17	43	60	771
12	Tor.	Kenny Jonsson	Rogle Angelholm	D	607	58	180	238	276
13	N.J.	Denis Pederson	Prince Albert	C/RW	435	57	71	128	398
14	Que.	Adam Deadmarsh	Portland	RW	567	184	189	373	819
15	Wpg.	Mats Lindgren	Skelleftea	C/LW	387	54	74	128	146
16	Edm.	Nick Stajduhar	London	D	2	0	0	0	4
17	Wsh.	Jason Allison	London	C	486	137	288	425	365
18	Cgy.	Jesper Mattsson	Malmo	C					
19	Tor.	Landon Wilson	Dubuque Jr. A.	RW	294	45	56	101	284
20	Van.	Mike Wilson	Sudbury	D	336	16	41	57	264
21	Mtl.	Saku Koivu	TPS Turku	C	429	106	237	343	290
22	Det.	Anders Eriksson	MoDo Ornskoldsvik	D	346	14	89	103	140
23	NYI	Todd Bertuzzi	Guelph	RW	559	181	217	398	789
24	Chi.	Eric Lecompte	Hull	LW					
25	Bos.	Kevyn Adams	Miami of Ohio	C	290	31	46	77	200
26	Pit.	Stefan Bergkvist	Leksand	D	7	0	0	0	9

SECOND ROUND

PICK	TEAM	NAME	DRAFTED FROM	POS	GP	G/W	A/GA	PTS/SO	PIM/AVG
27	Ott.	Radim Bicanek	Dukla Jihlava	D	122	1	11	12	62
28	S.J.	Shean Donovan	Ottawa	RW	536	67	68	135	348
29	T.B.	Tyler Moss	Kingston	G	30	1496	81	0	3.25
30	Ana.	Nikolai Tsulygin	Salavat Yulayev Ufa	D	22	0	1	1	8
31	Wpg.	Scott Langkow	Portland	G	20	943	68	0	4.33
32	N.J.	Jay Pandolfo	Boston U.	LW	406	42	65	107	78
33	Edm.	David Vyborny	Sparta Praha	RW	233	46	63	109	44
34	NYR	Lee Sorochan	Lethbridge	D	3	0	0	0	0
35	Dal.	Jamie Langenbrunner	Cloquet H.S.	RW	524	115	181	296	449
36	Phi.	Janne Niinimaa	Karpat Oulu	D	555	42	230	272	547
37	St.L.	Maxim Bets	Spokane	LW	3	0	0	0	0
38	Buf.	Denis Tsygurov	Lada Togliatti	D	51	1	5	6	45
39	N.J.	Brendan Morrison	Penticton Jr. A	C	389	89	193	282	140
40	NYI	Bryan McCabe	Spokane	D	633	60	157	217	1176
41	Fla.	Kevin Weekes	Owen Sound	G	211	11323	574	13	3.04
42	L.A.	Shayne Toporowski	Prince Albert	RW	3	0	0	0	7
43	Wpg.	Alexei Budayev	Kristall Elektrostal	C					
44	Cgy.	Jamie Allison	Detroit	D	298	7	19	26	507
45	S.J.	Vlastimil Kroupa	HC Chemopetrol Litvinov	D	105	4	19	23	66
46	Van.	Rick Girard	Swift Current	C					
47	Mtl.	Rory Fitzpatrick	Sudbury	D	94	1	6	7	50
48	Det.	Jon Coleman	Andover Academy	D					
49	Que.	Ashley Buckberger	Swift Current	RW					
50	Chi.	Eric Manlow	Kitchener	C	19	2	2	4	6
51	Bos.	Matt Alvey	Springfield Jr. B	RW					
52	Pit.	Domenic Pittis	Lethbridge	C	82	5	11	16	67

OTHER ROUNDS

PICK	TEAM	NAME	DRAFTED FROM	POS	GP	G/W	A/GA	PTS/SO	PIM/AVG
53	Ott.	Patrick Charbonneau	Victoriaville	G					
54	Chi.	Bogdan Savenko	Niagara Falls	RW					
55	T.B.	Allan Egeland	Tacoma	C	17	0	0	0	16
56	Ana.	Valeri Karpov	Traktor Chelyabinsk	RW	76	14	15	29	32
57	Fla.	Chris Armstrong	Moose Jaw	D	3	0	0	0	0
58	S.J.	Ville Peltonen	HIFK Helsinki	LW	175	18	42	60	40
59	Edm.	Kevin Paden	Detroit	C/LW					
60	Edm.	Alexander Kerch	Pardaugava Riga	LW	5	0	0	0	2
61	NYR	Maxim Galanov	Lada Togliatti	D	122	8	12	20	44
62	Pit.	Dave Roche	Peterborough	LW	171	15	15	30	334
63	St.L.	Jamie Rivers	Sudbury	D	340	13	36	49	270
64	Buf.	Ethan Philpott	Andover Academy	RW					
65	N.J.	Krzysztof Oliwa	Welland Jr. B	LW	342	14	26	40	1200
66	NYI	Vladimir Chebaturkin	Kristall Elektrostal	D	62	2	7	9	52
67	Fla.	Mikael Tjallden	MoDo Ornskoldsvik	D					
68	L.A.	Jeff Mitchell	Detroit	C/RW	7	0	0	0	7
69	Wsh.	Patrick Boileau	Laval	D	32	2	7	9	18
70	Cgy.	Dan Tompkins	Omaha Jr. A	LW					
71	Phi.	Vaclav Prospal	Motor Ceske Budejovice	C	467	88	206	294	236
72	Hfd.	Marek Malik	TJ Vitkovice	D	386	24	71	95	343
73	Mtl.	Sebastien Bordeleau	Hull	C	251	37	61	98	118
74	Det.	Kevin Hilton	Michigan	C					
75	Que.	Bill Pierce	Lawrence Academy	C					
76	Chi.	Ryan Huska	Kamloops	LW	1	0	0	0	0
77	Phi.	Milos Holan	TJ Vitkovice	D	49	5	11	16	42
78	Fla.	Steve Washburn	Ottawa	C	93	14	15	29	42
79	Wpg.	Ruslan Batyrshin	Dynamo	D	2	0	0	0	6
80	S.J.	Alexander Osadchy	CSKA	D					
81	T.B.	Marian Kacir	Owen Sound	RW					
82	Ana.	Joel Gagnon	Oshawa	G					
83	Fla.	Bill McCauley	Detroit	C	Re-entered Draft in 1995				
84	Hfd.	Trevor Roenick	Boston Jr.	RW					
85	Mtl.	Adam Wiesel	Springfield Jr. B	D					
86	NYR	Sergei Olimpiyev	Dynamo Minsk	LW					
87	Dal.	Chad Lang	Peterborough	G					
88	Bos.	Charles Paquette	Sherbrooke	D					
89	St.L.	Jamal Mayers	Western Michigan	RW	288	30	42	72	356
90	Chi.	Eric Daze	Beauport	RW	581	222	165	387	174
91	Ott.	Cosmo Dupaul	Victoriaville	C					
92	NYI	Warren Luhning	Calgary Jr. A.	RW	29	0	1	1	21
93	Wpg.	Ravil Gusmanov	Traktor Chelyabinsk	LW	4	0	0	0	0
94	L.A.	Bob Wren	Detroit	C	5	0	0	0	0
95	Cgy.	Jason Smith	Princeton	D					
96	Cgy.	Marty Murray	Brandon	C	176	26	33	59	29
97	Det.	John Jakopin	St. Michael's Jr. B	D	113	1	6	7	145
98	Van.	Dieter Kochan	Kelowna Jr. A.	G	21	849	56	0	3.96
99	Mtl.	Jean-Francois Houle	Northwood Prep	LW					
101	Que.	Ryan Tocher	Niagara Falls	D					
102	Chi.	Patrik Pysz	Augsburg	C					
103	Bos.	Shawn Bates	Medford H.S.	C	280	44	78	122	126
104	Pit.	Jonas Andersson-Junkka	Kiruna	D					
105	L.A.	Frederick Beaubien	St-Hyacinthe	G					
106	S.J.	Andrei Buschan	Sokol Kiev	D					
107	T.B.	Ryan Brown	Swift Current	D					
108	Ana.	Mikhail Shtalenkov	Milwaukee IHL	G	190	9966	480	8	2.89
109	Fla.	Todd MacDonald	Tacoma	G					
110	N.J.	John Guirestante	London	RW					
111	Edm.	Miroslav Satan	Dukla Trencin	LW	622	230	232	462	247
112	NYR	Gary Roach	Sault Ste. Marie	D					
113	Mtl.	Jeff Lank	Prince Albert	D	Re-entered Draft in 1995				

PICK	TEAM	NAME	DRAFTED FROM	NHL PLAYERS: POS	GP	G	A	PTS	PIM
				NHL GOALTENDERS: POS	GP	W	GA	SO	AVG
114	Phi.	Vladimir Krechin	Traktor Chelyabinsk	LW					
115	Hfd.	Nolan Pratt	Portland	D	316	6	31	37	361
116	Buf.	Richard Safarik	AC Nitra	RW					
117	L.A.	Jason Saal	Detroit	G					
118	NYI	Tommy Salo	Vasteras	G	477	27645	1177	34	2.55
119	Wpg.	Larry Courville	Newmarket	LW	Re-entered Draft in 1995				
120	L.A.	Tomas Vlasak	Slavia Praha	C	10	1	3	4	2
121	Cgy.	Darryl Lafrance	Oshawa	C					
122	Cgy.	John Emmons	Yale	C	85	2	4	6	64
123	Tor.	Zdenek Nedved	Sudbury	RW	31	4	6	10	14
124	Van.	Scott Walker	Owen Sound	RW	499	76	132	208	801
125	Mtl.	Dion Darling	Spokane	D					
126	Det.	Norm Maracle	Saskatoon	G	66	3430	177	1	3.10
127	Que.	Anders Myrvold	Farjestad Karlstad	D	25	0	4	4	10
128	Chi.	Jonni Vauhkonen	Reipas Lahti	RW					
129	Bos.	Andrei Sapozhnikov	Traktor Chelyabinsk	D					
130	Pit.	Chris Kelleher	St. Sebastian's	D	1	0	0	0	0
131	Ott.	Rick Bodkin	Sudbury	C					
132	S.J.	Petri Varis	Assat Pori	LW	1	0	0	0	0
133	T.B.	Kiley Hill	Sault Ste. Marie	LW					
134	Ana.	Antti Aalto	TPS Turku	C	151	11	17	28	52
135	Fla.	Alain Nasreddine	Drummondville	D	18	0	0	0	54
136	Dal.	Rick Mrozik	Cloquet H.S.	C	2	0	0	0	0
137	Que.	Nicholas Checco	Bloomington-Jefferson H.S.	C					
138	NYR	Dave Trofimenkoff	Lethbridge	G					
139	Dal.	Per Svartvadet	MoDo Ornskoldsvik	C	247	17	34	51	58
140	Phi.	Mike Crowley	Bloomington-Jefferson H.S.	D	67	5	15	20	44
141	St.L.	Todd Kelman	Vernon Jr. A.	D					
142	Buf.	Kevin Pozzo	Moose Jaw	D					
143	N.J.	Steve Brule	St-Jean	RW	2	0	0	0	0
144	NYI	Peter LeBoutillier	Red Deer	RW	Re-entered Draft in 1995				
145	Wpg.	Michal Grosek	ZPS Zlin	LW	493	81	135	216	476
146	L.A.	Jere Karalahti	HIFK Helsinki	D	149	8	19	27	97
147	Wsh.	Frank Banham	Saskatoon	RW	32	9	2	11	16
148	Cgy.	Andreas Karlsson	Leksand	C	153	11	27	38	50
149	Tor.	Paul Vincent	Cushing Academy	C					
150	Van.	Troy Creurer	Notre Dame Jr. A	D					
151	Mtl.	Darcy Tucker	Kamloops	RW	545	106	160	266	947
152	Det.	Tim Spitzig	Kitchener	RW					
153	Que.	Christian Matte	Granby	RW	25	2	3	5	12
154	S.J.	Fredrik Oduya	Ottawa	LW					
155	Bos.	Milt Mastad	Seattle	D					
156	Pit.	Patrick Lalime	Shawinigan	G	265	15229	611	28	2.41
157	Ott.	Sergei Poleschuk	Krylja Sovetov	D					
158	S.J.	Anatoli Filatov	Torpedo Ust-Kamenogorsk	RW					
159	T.B.	Matthieu Raby	Victoriaville	D					
160	Ana.	Matt Peterson	Osseo H.S.	D					
161	Fla.	Trevor Doyle	Kingston	D					
162	NYR	Sergei Kondrashkin	Metallurg Cherepovets	RW					
163	Edm.	Alexander Zhurik	Dynamo Minsk	D					
164	NYR	Todd Marchant	Clarkson	C	679	136	207	343	490
165	Dal.	Jeremy Stasiuk	Spokane	RW					
166	Phi.	Aaron Israel	Harvard	G					
167	St.L.	Mike Buzak	Michigan State	G					
168	Buf.	Sergei Petrenko	Dynamo	LW	14	0	4	4	0
169	N.J.	Nikolai Zavarukhin	Salavat Yulayev Ufa	C					
170	NYI	Darren Van Impe	Red Deer	D	411	25	90	115	397
171	Wpg.	Martin Woods	Victoriaville	D					
172	L.A.	Justin Martin	Essex Junction H.S.	RW					
173	Wsh.	Daniel Hendrickson	St. Paul Jr. A.	RW					
174	Wsh.	Andrew Brunette	Owen Sound	LW	460	106	189	295	154
175	Tor.	Jeff Andrews	North Bay	LW					
176	Van.	Yevgeni Babariko	Torpedo Nizhny Novogord	C					
177	Mtl.	David Ruhly	Culver Military Academy	LW					
178	Det.	Yuri Yeresko	CSKA	D					
179	Que.	David Ling	Kingston	RW	43	3	2	5	93
180	Chi.	Tom White	Westminster H.S.	C					
181	Bos.	Ryan Golden	Reading H.S.	C					
182	Pit.	Sean Selmser	Red Deer	LW	1	0	0	0	5
183	Ott.	Jason Disher	Kingston	D					
184	S.J.	Todd Holt	Swift Current	RW					
185	T.B.	Ryan Nauss	Peterborough	LW					
186	Ana.	Tom Askey	Ohio State	G	7	273	12	0	2.64
187	Fla.	Briane Thompson	Sault Ste. Marie	D					
188	Hfd.	Manny Legace	Niagara Falls	G	105	5798	219	3	2.27
189	Edm.	Martin Bakula	Alaska-Anchorage	D					
190	NYR	Eddy Campbell	Omaha Jr. A.	D					
191	Dal.	Rob Lurtsema	Burnsville H.S.	LW					
192	Phi.	Paul Healey	Prince Albert	LW	71	6	14	20	30
193	St.L.	Eric Boguniecki	Westminster H.S.	C	93	22	28	50	44
194	Buf.	Mike Barrie	Victoria	C					
195	N.J.	Thomas Cullen	Wexford Jr. A.	D					
196	NYI	Rod Hinks	Sudbury	C					
197	Wpg.	Adrian Murray	Newmarket	D					
198	L.A.	John-Tra Dillabough	Wexford Jr. A.	C					
199	Wsh.	Joel Poirier	Sudbury	LW					
200	Cgy.	Derek Sylvester	Niagara Falls	RW					
201	Tor.	David Brumby	Tri-City	G					
202	Van.	Sean Tallaire	Lake Superior State	RW					
203	Mtl.	Alan Letang	Newmarket	D	14	0	0	0	2
204	Det.	Vitezslav Skuta	TJ Vitkovice	D					
205	Que.	Petr Franek	HC Chemopetrol Litvinov	G					
206	Chi.	Sergei Petrov	Cloquet H.S.	LW					
207	Bos.	Hal Gill	Nashoba H.S.	D	464	17	61	78	365
208	Pit.	Larry McMorran	Seattle	C					
209	Ott.	Toby Kvalevog	Bemidji State College	G					
210	S.J.	Jonas Forsberg	Djurgarden	G					
211	T.B.	Alexandre Laporte	Victoriaville	D					
212	Ana.	Vitali Kozel	Khimik Novopolotsk	C					
213	Fla.	Chad Cabana	Tri-City	LW					
214	Hfd.	Dmitri Gorenko	CSKA	LW					
215	Edm.	Brad Norton	Cushing Academy	D	75	3	5	8	142
216	NYR	Ken Shepard	Oshawa	G					
217	Wpg.	Vladimir Potapov	Kristall Elektrostal	RW					
218	Phi.	Tripp Tracy	Harvard	G					
219	St.L.	Mike Grier	St. Sebastian's	RW	530	96	119	215	328
220	Buf.	Barrie Moore	Sudbury	LW	39	2	6	8	18
221	N.J.	Judd Lambert	Chilliwack Jr. A	G					
222	NYI	Daniel Johansson	Rogle Angelholm	D					
223	Wpg.	Ilja Stashenkov	Krylja Sovetov	D					
224	L.A.	Martin Strbak	ZPA Presov	D					
225	Wsh.	Jason Gladney	Kitchener	D					
226	Phi.	E.J. Bradley	Tabor Academy	C					
227	Ott.	Pavol Demitra	Dukla Trencin	LW	485	193	268	461	152
228	Wpg.	Harijs Vitolinsh	Chur, SUI.	C	8	0	0	0	4
229	Mtl.	Alexandre Duchesne	Drummondville	LW					
230	Det.	Ryan Shanahan	Sudbury	RW					
231	Que.	Vincent Auger	Hawkesbury Jr. A	C					
232	Chi.	Mike Rusk	Guelph	D					
233	Bos.	Joel Prpic	Waterloo Jr. B	C	18	0	3	3	4
234	Pit.	Timothy Harberts	Wayzata H.S.	C					
235	Ott.	Rick Schuwerk	Canterbury H.S.	D					
236	S.J.	Jeff Salajko	Ottawa	G					
237	T.B.	Brett Duncan	Seattle	D					
238	Ana.	Anatoli Fedotov	Moncton AHL	D	4	0	2	2	0
239	Fla.	John Demarco	Archbishop Williams H.S.	D					
240	Hfd.	Wes Swinson	Kitchener	D					
241	Edm.	Oleg Maltsev	Traktor Chelyabinsk	LW					
242	NYR	Andrei Kudinov	Traktor Chelyabinsk	RW					
243	Dal.	Jordan Willis	London	G	1	19	1	0	3.16
244	Phi.	Jeff Staples	Brandon	D					
245	St.L.	Libor Prochazka	Poldi Kladno	D					
246	Buf.	Chris Davis	Calgary Jr. A	G					
247	N.J.	Jimmy Provencher	St-Jean	RW					
248	NYI	Stephane Larocque	Sherbrooke	RW					
249	Dal.	Bill Lang	North Bay	C					
250	L.A.	Kimmo Timonen	KalPa Kuopio	D	337	43	109	152	180
251	Wsh.	Mark Seliger	Rosenheim, FRG	G					
252	Cgy.	German Titov	TPS Turku	LW	624	157	220	377	311
253	Tor.	Kyle Ferguson	Michigan Tech	RW					
254	Van.	Bert Robertsson	Sodertalje	D	123	4	10	14	75
255	Mtl.	Brian Larochelle	Phillips-Exeter H.S.	G					
256	Det.	James Kosecki	Berkshire H.S.	G					
257	Que.	Mark Pivetz	Saskatoon Jr. A	D					
258	Chi.	Mike McGhan	Prince Albert	LW					
259	Bos.	Joakim Persson	Hammarby	G					
260	Pit.	Leonid Toropchenko	Springfield AHL	C					
261	NYR	Pavel Komarov	Torpedo Nizhny Novogord	D					
262	S.J.	Jamie Matthews	Sudbury	C					
263	T.B.	Mark Szoke	Lethbridge	LW					
264	Ana.	David Penney	Worcester Academy	LW					
265	Fla.	Eric Montreuil	Chicoutimi	C					

PICK	TEAM	NAME	DRAFTED FROM	NHL PLAYERS: POS / NHL GOALTENDERS: POS	GP / GP	G / W	A / GA	PTS / SO	PIM / AVG
266	Hfd.	Igor Chibirev	Fort Wayne IHL	C	45	7	12	19	2
267	Edm.	Ilja Byakin	Landshut	D	57	8	25	33	44
268	NYR	Maxim Smelnitsky	Traktor Chelyabinsk	RW					
269	Dal.	Cory Peterson	Bloomington-Jefferson H.S.	D					
270	Phi.	Ken Hemenway	Alaska All-Stars	D					
271	St.L.	Alexander Vasilevski	Victoria	RW	4	0	0	0	2
272	Buf.	Scott Nichol	Portland	C	133	13	14	27	270
273	N.J.	Mike Legg	London Jr. B	RW					
274	NYI	Carl Charland	Hull	LW					
275	St.L.	Christer Olsson	Brynas Gavle	D	56	4	12	16	24
276	L.A.	Patrick Howald	Lugano, SUI	LW					
277	Wsh.	Dany Bousquet	Penticton Jr. A	C					
278	Cgy.	Burke Murphy	St. Lawrence U.	LW					
279	Tor.	Mikhail Lapin	Western Michigan	D					
280	Van.	Sergei Tkachenko	Hamilton AHL	G					
281	Mtl.	Russell Guzior	Culver Military Academy	C					
282	Det.	Gordon Hunt	Detroit Compuware Jr. A	C					
283	Que.	John Hillman	St. Paul Jr. A	C					
284	Chi.	Tom Noble	Catholic Memorial H.S.	G					
285	Wpg.	Russ Hewson	Swift Current	LW					
286	Pit.	Hans Jonsson	MoDo Ornskoldsvik	D	242	10	38	48	92

1994

FIRST ROUND

PICK	TEAM	NAME	DRAFTED FROM	POS	GP	G / W	A / GA	PTS / SO	PIM / AVG
1	Fla.	Ed Jovanovski	Windsor	D	587	71	190	261	963
2	Ana.	Oleg Tverdovsky	Krylja Sovetov	D	615	74	216	290	244
3	Ott.	Radek Bonk	Las Vegas IHL	C	623	140	215	355	335
4	Edm.	Jason Bonsignore	Niagara Falls	C	79	3	13	16	34
5	Hfd.	Jeff O'Neill	Guelph	RW	606	184	198	382	492
6	Edm.	Ryan Smyth	Moose Jaw	LW	560	175	196	371	441
7	L.A.	Jamie Storr	Owen Sound	G	205	10852	456	16	2.52
8	T.B.	Jason Wiemer	Portland	C	602	80	96	176	1187
9	NYI	Brett Lindros	Kingston	RW	51	2	5	7	147
10	Wsh.	Nolan Baumgartner	Kamloops	D	34	1	4	5	12
11	S.J.	Jeff Friesen	Regina	LW	689	191	265	456	396
12	Que.	Wade Belak	Saskatoon	D/RW	241	6	14	20	702
13	Van.	Mattias Ohlund	Pitea	D	398	40	138	178	327
14	Chi.	Ethan Moreau	Niagara Falls	LW	523	85	79	164	637
15	Wsh.	Alexander Kharlamov	CSKA	C					
16	Tor.	Eric Fichaud	Chictoutimi	G	95	4799	251	2	3.14
17	Buf.	Wayne Primeau	Owen Sound	C	427	33	66	99	456
18	Mtl.	Brad Brown	North Bay	D	287	2	24	26	681
19	Cgy.	Chris Dingman	Brandon	LW	277	14	13	27	607
20	Dal.	Jason Botterill	Michigan	LW	69	3	8	11	75
21	Bos.	Evgeni Ryabchikov	Molot Perm	G					
22	Que.	Jeffrey Kealty	Catholic Memorial H.S.	D					
23	Det.	Yan Golubovsky	Dynamo-2	D	56	1	7	8	32
24	Pit.	Chris Wells	Seattle	C	195	9	20	29	193
25	N.J.	Vadim Sharifijanov	Salavat Yulayev Ufa	LW	92	16	21	37	50
26	NYR	Dan Cloutier	Sault Ste. Marie	G	245	12937	591	10	2.74

SECOND ROUND

PICK	TEAM	NAME	DRAFTED FROM	POS	GP	G / W	A / GA	PTS / SO	PIM / AVG
27	Fla.	Rhett Warrener	Saskatoon	D	483	13	56	69	660
28	Ana.	Johan Davidsson	HV 71 Jonkoping	C	83	6	9	15	16
29	Ott.	Stan Neckar	HC Ceske Budejovice	D	509	12	40	52	316
30	Wpg.	Deron Quint	Seattle	D	407	42	90	132	148
31	Fla.	Jason Podollan	Spokane	RW	41	1	5	6	19
32	Edm.	Mike Watt	Stratford Jr. B	LW	157	15	26	41	41
33	L.A.	Matt Johnson	Peterborough	LW	416	16	19	35	1346
34	T.B.	Colin Cloutier	Brandon	C					
35	Que.	Josef Marha	Dukla Jihlava	C	159	21	32	53	32
36	Fla.	Ryan Johnson	Thunder Bay Jr. A	C	275	15	38	53	108
37	S.J.	Angel Nikolov	HC Chemopetrol Litvinov	D					
38	NYI	Jason Holland	Kamloops	D	29	1	2	3	12
39	Van.	Robb Gordon	Powell River Jr. A	C	4	0	0	0	2
40	Chi.	Jean-Yves Leroux	Beauport	LW	220	16	22	38	146
41	Wsh.	Scott Cherrey	North Bay	LW					
42	Van.	Dave Scatchard	Portland	C	465	98	99	197	755
43	Buf.	Curtis Brown	Moose Jaw	C/LW	474	100	131	231	258
44	Mtl.	Jose Theodore	St-Jean	G	248	13979	604	17	2.59
45	Cgy.	Dmitri Ryabykin	Dynamo-2	D					
46	Dal.	Lee Jinman	North Bay	C					
47	Bos.	Daniel Goneau	Laval	LW	Re-entered Draft in 1996				
48	Tor.	Sean Haggerty	Detroit	LW	14	1	2	3	4
49	Det.	Mathieu Dandenault	Sherbrooke	RW/D	551	45	92	137	302
50	Pit.	Richard Park	Belleville	RW	235	29	35	64	82
51	N.J.	Patrik Elias	HC Kladno	C	476	169	209	378	231
52	NYR	Rudolf Vercik	Slovan Bratislava	LW					

OTHER ROUNDS

PICK	TEAM	NAME	DRAFTED FROM	POS	GP	G / W	A / GA	PTS / SO	PIM / AVG
53	Edm.	Corey Neilson	North Bay	D					
54	Mtl.	Chris Murray	Kamloops	RW	242	16	18	34	550
55	T.B.	Vadim Epanchintsev	Spartak	C					
56	Wpg.	Dorian Anneck	Victoria	C					
57	Pit.	Sven Butenschon	Brandon	D	91	1	6	7	46
58	Wpg.	Tavis Hansen	Tacoma	RW	34	2	1	3	16
59	L.A.	Vitali Yachmenev	North Bay	LW	487	83	133	216	88
60	Edm.	Brad Symes	Portland	D					
61	Que.	Sebastien Bety	Drummondville	D					
62	Phi.	Artem Anisimov	Itil Kazan	D					
63	NYI	Jason Strudwick	Kamloops	D	309	6	19	25	497
64	Tor.	Fredrik Modin	Yepandhin Dev Timra	LW	503	123	128	251	227
65	Van.	Chad Allan	Saskatoon	D					
66	S.J.	Alexei Yegorov	SKA St. Petersburg	RW	11	3	3	6	2
67	Ana.	Craig Reichert	Red Deer	RW	3	0	0	0	0
68	St.L.	Stephane Roy	Val d'Or	C					
69	Buf.	Rumun Ndur	Guelph	D	69	2	3	5	137
70	Mtl.	Marko Kiprusoff	TPS Turku	D	51	0	10	10	12
71	N.J.	Sheldon Souray	Tri-City	D	287	13	35	48	466
72	Que.	Chris Drury	Fairfield Prep	C	394	108	167	275	222
73	Pit.	Greg Crozier	Lawrence Academy	LW	1	0	0	0	0
74	Mtl.	Martin Belanger	Granby	D					
75	Det.	Sean Gillam	Spokane	D					
76	Pit.	Alexei Krivchenkov	CSKA	D					
77	Cgy.	Chris Clark	Springfield Jr. B	RW	196	25	21	46	257
78	NYR	Adam Smith	Tacoma	D					
79	Edm.	Adam Copeland	Burlington Jr. B	RW					
80	Ana.	Byron Briske	Red Deer	D					
81	Ott.	Bryan Masotta	Hotchkiss H.S.	G					
82	Wpg.	Steve Cheredaryk	Medicine Hat	D					
83	Hfd.	Hnat Domenichelli	Kamloops	LW	267	52	61	113	104
84	Fla.	David Nemirovsky	Ottawa	RW	91	16	22	38	42
85	Chi.	Steve McLaren	North Bay	D					
86	T.B.	Dmitri Klevakin	Spartak	RW					
87	Que.	Milan Hejduk	HC Pardubice	RW	388	162	179	341	134
88	Phi.	Adam Magarrell	Brandon	D					
89	S.J.	Vaclav Varada	HC Vitkovice	RW	387	48	104	152	334
90	NYI	Brad Lukowich	Kamloops	D	294	10	34	44	233
91	Cgy.	Ryan Duthie	Spokane	C					
92	Van.	Mike Dubinsky	Brandon	RW					
93	Wsh.	Matt Herr	Hotchkiss H.S.	C	58	4	5	9	25
94	St.L.	Tyler Harlton	Vernon Jr. A	D					
95	Edm.	Jussi Tarvainen	KalPa Kuopio	RW					
96	Mtl.	Arto Kuki	Kiekko-Espoo	C					
97	Cgy.	Johan Finnstrom	Rogle Angelholm	D					
98	Dal.	Jamie Wright	Guelph	LW	124	12	20	32	54
99	Bos.	Eric Nickulas	Cushing Academy	RW	37	5	7	12	22
100	NYR	Alexander Korobolin	Traktor Chelyabinsk	D					
101	Phi.	Sebastien Vallee	Victoriaville	LW					
102	Pit.	Tom O'Connor	Springfield Jr. B	D					
103	N.J.	Zdenek Skorepa	HC Chemopetrol Litvinov	RW					
104	NYR	Sylvain Blouin	Laval	LW	115	3	4	7	336
105	Fla.	Dave Geris	Windsor	D					
106	Ana.	Pavel Trnka	HC Skoda Plzen	D	344	11	50	61	272
107	Cgy.	Nils Ekman	Hammarby	LW	71	11	13	24	76
108	Wpg.	Craig Mills	Belleville	RW	31	0	5	5	36
109	Hfd.	Ryan Risidore	Guelph	D					
110	Edm.	Jon Gaskins	Dubuque Jr. B	D					
111	L.A.	Chris Schmidt	Seattle	C	10	0	2	2	5
112	NYI	Mark McArthur	Guelph	G					
113	Que.	Tony Tuzzolino	Michigan State	RW	9	0	0	0	7
114	Det.	Frederic Deschenes	Granby	G					
115	S.J.	Brian Swanson	Omaha Jr. A.	C	68	4	12	16	16
116	NYI	Albert O'Connell	St. Sebastian's	LW					
117	Van.	Yanick Dube	Laval	C					
118	Chi.	Marc Dupuis	Belleville	D					
119	Wsh.	Yanick Jean	Chicoutimi	D					
120	St.L.	Edvin Frylen	Vasteras	D					
121	Buf.	Sergei Klimentiev	Medicine Hat	D					
122	Mtl.	Jimmy Drolet	St-Hyacinthe	D					
123	Cgy.	Frank Appel	Dusseldorf	D					

PICK	TEAM	NAME	DRAFTED FROM	NHL PLAYERS: POS NHL GOALTENDERS: POS	GP GP	G W	A GA	PTS SO	PIM AVG
124	Dal.	Marty Turco	Cambridge Jr. B	G	112	5988	185	12	1.85
125	Bos.	Darren Wright	Prince Albert	D					
126	Tor.	Mark Deyell	Saskatoon	C					
127	Det.	Doug Battaglia	Brockville Jr. A	LW					
128	Pit.	Clint Johnson	Duluth East H.S.	LW					
129	N.J.	Christian Gosselin	St-Hyacinthe	D					
130	NYR	Martin Ethier	Beauport	D					
131	Ott.	Mike Gaffney	St. John's Prep.	D					
132	Ana.	Bates Battaglia	Caledon Jr. A	LW	415	64	92	156	366
133	Ott.	Daniel Alfredsson	Vastra Frolunda Goteborg	RW	552	187	301	488	235
134	N.J.	Ryan Smart	Meadville H.S.	C					
135	NYR	Yuri Litvinov	Krylja Sovetov	C					
136	Edm.	Terry Marchant	Niagara Jr. A.	LW					
137	T.B.	Daniel Juden	Governor Dummer H.S.	RW					
138	T.B.	Bryce Salvador	Lethbridge	D	212	9	23	32	242
139	Que.	Nicholas Windsor	Cornwall	D					
140	Phi.	Alex Selivanov	Spartak	RW	459	121	114	235	379
141	S.J.	Alexander Korolyuk	Krylja Sovetov	LW	233	43	62	105	122
142	NYI	Jason Stewart	Simley H.S.	RW					
143	Wpg.	Steve Vezina	Beauport	G					
144	Chi.	Jim Enson	North Bay	C					
145	Wsh.	Dmitri Mekeshkin	Avangard Omsk	D					
146	Wpg.	Chris Kibermanis	Red Deer	D					
147	Buf.	Cal Benazic	Medicine Hat	D					
148	Mtl.	Joel Irving	Regina Midgets	C					
149	Cgy.	Patrick Haltia	Grums	G					
150	Dal.	Evgeny Petrochinin	Spartak	D					
151	Bos.	Andre Roy	Chicoutimi	RW	277	24	26	50	656
152	Tor.	Kam White	Newmarket	D					
153	Det.	Pavel Agarkov	Krylja Sovetov	RW					
154	Pit.	Valentin Morozov	CSKA	C					
155	N.J.	Luciano Caravaggio	Michigan Tech	G					
156	NYR	David Brosseau	Shawinigan	C					
157	Fla.	Matt O'Dette	Kitchener	LW					
158	Ana.	Rocky Welsing	Wisconsin Jr. A.	D					
159	Ott.	Doug Sproule	Hotchkiss H.S.	LW					
160	Edm.	Curtis Sheptak	Olds Jr. A	LW					
161	Pit.	Serge Aubin	Granby	LW	234	27	32	59	209
162	Edm.	Dmitri Shulga	Tivali Minsk	RW					
163	L.A.	Luc Gagne	Sudbury	RW					
164	T.B.	Chris Maillet	Red Deer	D					
165	Que.	Calvin Elfring	Powell River Jr. A	D					
166	Phi.	Colin Forbes	Sherwood Park Jr. A	C	300	33	28	61	211
167	S.J.	Sergei Gorbachev	Dynamo	RW					
168	Buf.	Steve Plouffe	Granby	G					
169	Van.	Yuri Kuznetsov	Avangard Omsk	C					
170	Chi.	Tyler Prosofsky	Tacoma	C	Re-entered Draft in 1996				
171	Wsh.	Daniel Reja	London	C					
172	St.L.	Roman Vopat	HC Chemopetrol Litvinov	C	133	6	14	20	253
173	Buf.	Shane Hnidy	Prince Albert	D	152	4	11	15	271
174	Mtl.	Jessie Rezansoff	Regina	RW					
175	Cgy.	Ladislav Kohn	Swift Current	RW	186	14	28	42	125
176	Buf.	Steve Webb	Peterborough	RW	311	5	13	18	528
177	Bos.	Jeremy Schaefer	Medicine Hat	LW					
178	Tor.	Tommi Rajamaki	Assat Pori	D					
179	Edm.	Chris Wickenheiser	Red Deer	G					
180	Pit.	Drew Palmer	Seattle	D					
181	N.J.	Jeff Williams	Guelph	C					
182	NYR	Alexei Lazarenko	CSKA-2	LW					
183	Fla.	Jason Boudrias	Laval	C					
184	Ana.	Brad Englehart	Kimball Union Academy	C					
185	Edm.	Rob Guinn	Newmarket	D					
186	Wpg.	Ramil Saifullin	Avangard Omsk	C					
187	Hfd.	Tom Buckley	St. Joseph H.S.	C					
188	Edm.	Jason Reid	St. Andrew's H.S.	D					
189	L.A.	Andrew Dale	Sudbury	RW					
190	T.B.	Alexei Baranov	Dynamo-2	C					
191	Que.	Jay Bertsch	Spokane	RW	Re-entered Draft in 1996				
192	Phi.	Derek Diener	Lethbridge	D					
193	S.J.	Eric Landry	Guelph	RW					
194	NYI	Mike Loach	Windsor	C					
195	Van.	Rob Trumbley	Moose Jaw	C					
196	Chi.	Mike Josephson	Kamloops	LW					
197	Wsh.	Chris Patrick	Kent Prep.	LW					
198	St.L.	Steve Noble	Stratford Jr. B.	C					
199	Buf.	Bob Westerby	Kamloops	LW					
200	Mtl.	Peter Strom	Vastra Frolunda Goteborg	LW					
201	Cgy.	Keith McCambridge	Swift Current	D					
202	Phi.	Raymond Giroux	Powasson Jr.	D	27	0	10	10	18
203	NYI	Peter Hogardh	Vastra Frolunda Goteborg	C					
204	Tor.	Rob Butler	Niagara Jr. A.	LW					
205	Det.	Jason Elliot	Kimberley Jr. A.	G					
206	Pit.	Boris Zelenko	CSKA	RW					
207	N.J.	Eric Bertrand	Granby	LW	15	0	0	0	4
208	NYR	Craig Anderson	Park Center H.S.	D					
209	NYR	Vitali Yeremeyev	Torpedo Ust-Kamenogorsk	G	4	212	16	0	4.53
210	Ott.	Frederic Cassivi	St-Hyacinthe	G	8	430	28	0	3.91
211	Ott.	Danny Dupont	Laval	D					
212	Wpg.	Henrik Smangs	Leksand	G					
213	Hfd.	Ashlin Halfnight	Harvard	D					
214	Edm.	Jeremy Jablonski	Victoria	G					
215	L.A.	Jan Nemecek	HC Ceske Budejovice	D	7	1	0	1	4
216	T.B.	Yuri Smirnov	Spartak	C					
217	Que.	Tim Thomas	Vermont	G	4	220	11	0	3.00
218	Phi.	Johan Hedberg	Leksand	G	116	6832	328	7	2.88
219	S.J.	Evgeni Nabokov	Torpedo Ust-Kamenogorsk	G	199	11242	445	17	2.38
220	NYI	Gord Walsh	Kingston	LW					
221	Van.	Bill Muckalt	Kelowna Jr. A	RW	256	40	57	97	204
222	Chi.	Lubomir Jandera	HC Chemopetrol Litvinov	D					
223	Wsh.	John Tuohy	Kent Prep	D					
224	St.L.	Marc Stephan	Tri-City	C					
225	Buf.	Craig Millar	Swift Current	D	114	8	14	22	73
226	Mtl.	Tomas Vokoun	HC Kladno	G	206	11386	484	9	2.55
227	Cgy.	Jorgen Jonsson	Rogle Angelholm	LW	81	12	19	31	16
228	Dal.	Marty Flichel	Tacoma	RW					
229	Bos.	John Grahame	Sioux City Jr. A.	G	93	5160	230	6	2.67
230	Hfd.	Matt Ball	Detroit	RW					
231	Det.	Jeff Mikesch	Michigan Tech	C					
232	Pit.	Jason Godbout	Hill-Murray H.S.	D					
233	N.J.	Steve Sullivan	Sault Ste. Marie	RW	517	151	225	376	332
234	NYR	Eric Boulton	Oshawa	LW	128	4	10	14	401
235	Fla.	Tero Lehtera	Kiekko-Espoo	LW					
236	Ana.	Tommi Miettinen	KalPa Kuopio	C					
237	Ott.	Stephen MacKinnon	Cushing Academy	LW					
238	Wpg.	Mike Mader	Loomis-Chaffee H.S.	RW					
239	Hfd.	Brian Regan	Westminster H.S.	G					
240	S.J.	Tomas Pisa	HC Pardubice	RW					
241	L.A.	Sergei Shalomai	Spartak	LW					
242	T.B.	Shawn Gervais	Seattle	C					
243	Que.	Chris Pittman	Kitchener	LW					
244	Phi.	Andre Payette	Sault Ste. Marie	C					
245	S.J.	Aniket Dhadphale	Marquette Elec. AAA	LW					
246	NYI	Kirk Dewaele	Lethbridge	D					
247	Van.	Tyson Nash	Kamloops	LW	255	24	26	50	479
248	Chi.	Lars Weibel	Lugano, SUI	G					
249	Wsh.	Richard Zednik	IS Banska Bystrica	Righ W	431	119	100	219	345
250	St.L.	Kevin Harper	Wexford Jr. A	D					
251	Buf.	Mark Polak	Medicine Hat	C					
252	Mtl.	Chris Aldous	Northwood Prep	D					
253	Cgy.	Mike Peluso	Omaha Jr. A	RW	37	4	2	6	19
254	Dal.	Jimmy Roy	Thunder Bay Jr. A	C					
255	Bos.	Neil Savary	Hull	G					
256	Tor.	Sergei Berezin	Khimik Voskresensk	LW	502	160	126	286	54
257	Det.	Tomas Holmstrom	Boden	LW	474	81	125	206	349
258	Pit.	Mikhail Kazakevich	Torpedo Yaroslavl	LW					
259	N.J.	Scott Swanjord	Waterloo Jr. A	G					
260	NYR	Radoslav Kropac	Slovan Bratislava	RW					
261	Fla.	Per Gustafsson	HV 71 Jonkoping	D	89	8	27	35	38
262	Ana.	Jeremy Stevenson	Sault Ste. Marie	LW	100	9	12	21	251
263	Chi.	Rob Mara	Belmont Hill H.S.	RW					
264	Wpg.	Jason Issel	Prince Albert	LW					
265	Hfd.	Steve Nimigon	Niagara Falls	LW					
266	Edm.	Ladislav Benysek	HC Olomouc Jr.	D	161	3	12	15	74
267	NYR	Jamie Butt	Tacoma	LW					
268	T.B.	Brian White	Arlington Catholic H.S.	D	2	0	0	0	0
269	N.J.	Mike Hanson	Minot H.S.	C					
270	Phi.	Jan Lipiansky	Slovan Bratislava	LW					
271	S.J.	David Beauregard	St-Hyacinthe	LW					
272	NYI	Dick Tarnstrom	AIK Solna	D	123	10	50	60	88
273	Van.	Robert Longpre	Medicine Hat	C					
274	Ott.	Antti Tormanen	Jokerit Helsinki	RW	50	7	8	15	28
275	Wsh.	Sergei Tertyshny	Traktor Chelyabinsk	D					

PICK	TEAM	NAME	DRAFTED FROM	NHL PLAYERS: POS / NHL GOALTENDERS: POS	GP / GP	G / W	A / GA	PTS / SO	PIM / AVG
276	St.L.	Scott Fankhouser	Loomis-Chaffe H.S.	G	23	1180	65	0	3.31
277	Buf.	Shayne Wright	Owen Sound	D					
278	Mtl.	Ross Parsons	Regina	D					
279	Cgy.	Pavel Torgaev	TPS Turku	LW	55	6	14	20	20
280	Dal.	Chris Szysky	Swift Current	RW					
281	Bos.	Andrei Yakhanov	Salavat Yulayev Ufa	D					
282	Tor.	Doug Nolan	Catholic Memorial H.S.	LW					
283	Det.	Toivo Suursoo	Krylja Sovetov	LW					
284	Pit.	Brian Leitza	Sioux City Jr. A	G					
285	Que.	Steven Low	Sherbrooke	D					
286	NYR	Kim Johnsson	Malmo	D	315	32	95	127	166

1995

FIRST ROUND

PICK	TEAM	NAME	DRAFTED FROM	POS	GP	G / W	A / GA	PTS / SO	PIM / AVG
1	Ott.	Bryan Berard	Detroit	D	452	46	173	219	359
2	NYI	Wade Redden	Brandon	D	548	61	182	243	338
3	L.A.	Aki Berg	Kiekko-67 Turku	D	452	13	55	68	278
4	Ana.	Chad Kilger	Kingston	C	459	63	76	139	208
5	T.B.	Daymond Langkow	Tri-City	C	544	115	187	302	334
6	Edm.	Steve Kelly	Prince Albert	C	144	9	12	21	83
7	Wpg.	Shane Doan	Kamloops	RW	569	115	168	283	541
8	Mtl.	Terry Ryan	Tri-City	LW	8	0	0	0	36
9	Bos.	Kyle McLaren	Tacoma	D	450	34	98	132	400
10	Fla.	Radek Dvorak	HC Ceske Budejovice	RW	604	138	196	334	192
11	Dal.	Jarome Iginla	Kamloops	RW	545	209	221	430	338
12	S.J.	Teemu Riihijarvi	Kiekko-Espoo	LW					
13	Hfd.	Jean-Sebastien Giguere	Halifax	G	182	10517	428	16	2.44
14	Buf.	Jay McKee	Niagara Falls	D	464	10	67	77	372
15	Tor.	Jeff Ware	Oshawa	D	21	0	1	1	12
16	Buf.	Martin Biron	Beauport	G	194	10802	435	15	2.42
17	Wsh.	Brad Church	Prince Albert	LW	2	0	0	0	0
18	N.J.	Petr Sykora	Detroit	RW	445	145	205	350	182
19	Chi.	Dmitri Nabokov	Krylja Sovetov	C/LW	55	11	13	24	28
20	Cgy.	Denis Gauthier	Drummondville	D	304	12	30	42	402
21	Bos.	Sean Brown	Belleville	D	350	13	29	42	828
22	Phi.	Brian Boucher	Tri-City	G	148	8347	365	7	2.62
23	Wsh.	Miika Elomo	Kiekko-67 Turku	LW	2	0	1	1	2
24	Pit.	Aleksey Morozov	Krylja Sovetov	RW	376	68	101	169	74
25	Col.	Marc Denis	Chicoutimi	G	179	10156	515	9	3.04
26	Det.	Maxim Kuznetsov	Dynamo	D	120	2	7	9	117

SECOND ROUND

PICK	TEAM	NAME	DRAFTED FROM	POS	GP	G / W	A / GA	PTS / SO	PIM / AVG
27	Ott.	Marc Moro	Kingston	D	30	0	0	0	77
28	NYI	Jan Hlavac	Sparta Praha	LW	284	73	90	163	82
29	Ana.	Brian Wesenberg	Guelph	RW	1	0	0	0	5
30	T.B.	Mike McBain	Red Deer	D	64	0	7	7	22
31	Edm.	Georges Laraque	St-Jean	RW	352	35	47	82	654
32	Wpg.	Marc Chouinard	Beauport	C	159	10	13	23	62
33	L.A.	Don MacLean	Beauport	C	25	5	3	8	6
34	Wpg.	Jason Doig	Laval	D	93	4	9	13	180
35	Hfd.	Sergei Fedotov	Dynamo	D					
36	Fla.	Aaron MacDonald	Swift Current	G					
37	Dal.	Patrick Cote	Beauport	LW	105	1	2	3	377
38	S.J.	Peter Roed	White Bear Lake H.S.	C					
39	NYR	Christian Dube	Sherbrooke	C	33	1	1	2	4
40	Van.	Chris McAllister	Saskatoon	D	255	4	16	20	560
41	NYI	D.J. Smith	Windsor	D	45	1	1	2	67
42	Buf.	Mark Dutiaume	Brandon	LW					
43	Wsh.	Dwayne Hay	Guelph	LW	79	2	4	6	22
44	N.J.	Nathan Perrott	Oshawa	RW	23	1	2	3	79
45	Chi.	Christian Laflamme	Beauport	D	308	2	44	46	262
46	Cgy.	Pavel Smirnov	Molot Perm	C/RW					
47	Bos.	Paxton Schafer	Medicine Hat	G	3	77	6	0	4.68
48	Phi.	Shane Kenny	Owen Sound	D					
49	St.L.	Jochen Hecht	Mannheim	LW	269	58	86	144	166
50	L.A.	Pavel Rosa	HC Chemopetrol Litvinov	RW	34	4	12	16	6
51	Col.	Nic Beaudoin	Detroit	LW					
52	Det.	Philippe Audet	Granby	LW	4	0	0	0	0

OTHER ROUNDS

PICK	TEAM	NAME	DRAFTED FROM	POS	GP	G / W	A / GA	PTS / SO	PIM / AVG
53	Ott.	Brad Larsen	Swift Current	LW	Re-entered Draft in 1997				
54	Tor.	Ryan Pepperall	Kitchener	RW					
55	Ana.	Mike Leclerc	Brandon	LW	281	53	75	128	247
56	T.B.	Shane Willis	Prince Albert	RW	Re-entered Draft in 1997				
57	Edm.	Lukas Zib	HC Ceske Budejovice	D					
58	Det.	Darryl Laplante	Moose Jaw	C	35	0	6	6	10
59	L.A.	Vladimir Tsyplakov	Fort Wayne IHL	LW	331	69	101	170	90
60	Mtl.	Miloslav Guren	ZPS Zlin	D	36	1	3	4	16
61	Van.	Larry Courville	Oshawa	LW	33	1	2	3	16
62	Fla.	Mike O'Grady	Lethbridge	D					
63	Dal.	Petr Buzek	Dukla Jihlava	D	157	9	22	31	94
64	S.J.	Marko Makinen	TPS Turku	RW					
65	NYR	Mike Martin	Windsor	D					
66	Van.	Peter Schaefer	Brandon	LW	253	42	56	98	82
67	Wpg.	Brad Isbister	Portland	LW	358	83	82	165	463
68	Buf.	Mathieu Sunderland	Drummondville	RW					
69	Dal.	Sergey Gusev	CSK VVS Samara	D	89	4	10	14	34
70	N.J.	Sergei Vyshedkevich	Dynamo	D	30	2	5	7	16
71	Chi.	Kevin McKay	Moose Jaw	D					
72	Cgy.	Rocky Thompson	Medicine Hat	RW	25	0	0	0	117
73	Bos.	Bill McCauley	Detroit	C					
74	Mtl.	Martin Hohenberger	Prince George	LW					
75	St.L.	Scott Roche	North Bay	G					
76	Pit.	Jean-Sebastien Aubin	Sherbrooke	G	146	7821	379	5	2.91
77	Col.	John Tripp	Oshawa	RW	Re-entered Draft in 1997				
78	N.J.	David Gosselin	Sherbrooke	RW	13	2	1	3	11
79	N.J.	Alyn McCauley	Ottawa	C	320	36	56	92	56
80	Fla.	Dave Duerden	Peterborough	LW	2	0	0	0	0
81	Col.	Tomi Kallio	Kiekko-67 Turku	RW	140	24	31	55	48
82	Chi.	Chris Van Dyk	Windsor	D					
83	Edm.	Mike Minard	Chilliwack Jr. A	G	1	60	3	0	3.00
84	Wpg.	Justin Kurtz	Brandon	D	27	3	5	8	14
85	Hfd.	Ian MacNeil	Oshawa	C	2	0	0	0	0
86	Mtl.	Jonathan Delisle	Hull	RW	1	0	0	0	0
87	Hfd.	Sami Kapanen	HIFK Helsinki	RW	548	149	212	361	111
88	Fla.	Daniel Tjarnqvist	Rogle Angelholm	D	150	5	28	33	40
89	Ott.	Kevin Bolibruck	Peterborough	D	Re-entered Draft in 1997				
90	S.J.	Vesa Toskala	Ilves Tampere	G	12	547	21	1	2.30
91	NYR	Marc Savard	Oshawa	C	376	86	166	252	277
92	Van.	Lloyd Shaw	Seattle	D					
93	Wsh.	Sebastien Charpentier	Laval	G	19	981	45	0	2.75
94	Buf.	Matt Davidson	Portland	RW	56	5	7	12	28
95	Wsh.	Joel Theriault	Beauport	D					
96	N.J.	Henrik Rehnberg	Farjestad Karlstad	D					
97	Chi.	Pavel Kriz	Tri-City	D					
98	Cgy.	Jan Labraaten	Farjestad Karlstad	LW					
99	Bos.	Cameron Mann	Peterborough	RW	93	14	10	24	40
100	Phi.	Radovan Somik	ZTS Martin	RW	60	8	10	18	10
101	St.L.	Michal Handzus	IS Banska Bystrica	C	354	81	109	190	187
102	Pit.	Oleg Belov	CSKA	C					
103	Ott.	Kevin Boyd	London	LW					
104	Det.	Anatoli Ustyugov	Torpedo Yaroslavl	LW					
105	Wsh.	Benoit Gratton	Laval	C	54	6	9	15	54
106	NYI	Vladimir Orszagh	IS Banska Bystrica	RW	191	34	39	73	106
107	Ana.	Igor Nikulin	Severstal Cherepovets	RW					
108	T.B.	Konstantin Golokhvastov	Dynamo	RW					
109	Edm.	Jan Snopek	Oshawa	D					
110	NYR	Alexei Vasiliev	Torpedo-2 Yaroslavl	D	1	0	0	0	2
111	Buf.	Marian Menhart	HC Chemopetrol Litvinov	D					
112	Mtl.	Niklas Anger	Djurgarden	RW					
113	Hfd.	Hugh Hamilton	Spokane	D					
114	Fla.	Francois Cloutier	Hull	LW					
115	Dal.	Wade Strand	Regina	D					
116	S.J.	Miikka Kiprusoff	TPS Turku	G	47	2390	113	3	2.84
117	NYR	Dale Purinton	Tacoma	D	141	3	15	18	461
118	L.A.	Jason Morgan	Kingston	C	14	1	0	1	4
119	Buf.	Kevin Popp	Seattle	D					
120	Van.	Todd Norman	Guelph	LW					
121	Wpg.	Brian Elder	Brandon	G					
122	N.J.	Chris Mason	Prince George	G	4	128	8	0	3.75
123	Buf.	Daniel Bienvenue	Val d'Or	LW					
124	Wsh.	Joel Cort	Guelph	D					
125	Det.	Chad Wilchynski	Regina	D					
126	Det.	David Arsenault	Drummondville	G					
127	St.L.	Jeff Ambrosio	Belleville	LW					
128	Pit.	Jan Hrdina	Seattle	C	370	79	152	231	223
129	Col.	Brent Johnson	Owen Sound	G	133	7563	284	11	2.25
130	S.J.	Michal Bros	HC Olomouc	C					
131	Ott.	David Hruska	Banik Sokolov	RW					
132	Phi.	Dmitri Tertyshny	Traktor Chelyabinsk	D	62	2	8	10	30
133	Ana.	Peter LeBoutillier	Red Deer	RW	35	2	1	3	176

PICK	TEAM	NAME	DRAFTED FROM	NHL PLAYERS: POS / NHL GOALTENDERS: POS	GP / GP	G / W	A / GA	PTS / SO	PIM / AVG
134	T.B.	Eduard Pershin	Dynamo	RW					
135	Phi.	Jamie Sokolsky	Belleville	D					
136	Wpg.	Sylvain Daigle	Shawinigan	G					
137	L.A.	Igor Melyakov	Torpedo Yaroslavl	LW					
138	Mtl.	Boyd Olson	Tri-City	C					
139	Tor.	Doug Bonner	Seattle	G					
140	S.J.	Timo Hakanen	Assat Pori	C					
141	Dal.	Dominic Marleau	Victoriaville	D					
142	S.J.	Jaroslav Kudrna	Penticton Jr. A.	LW					
143	NYR	Peter Slamiar	ZTK Zvolen	LW					
144	Van.	Brent Sopel	Swift Current	D	222	22	61	83	93
145	Tor.	Yannick Tremblay	Beauport	D	340	35	77	112	153
146	Chi.	Marc Magliarditi	Des Moines Jr. A	G					
147	Wsh.	Frederick Jobin	Laval	D					
148	N.J.	Adam Young	Windsor	D					
149	Chi.	Marty Wilford	Oshawa	D					
150	Cgy.	Clarke Wilm	Saskatoon	C	385	36	53	89	286
151	Bos.	Yevgeny Shaldybin	Torpedo Yaroslavl	D	3	1	0	1	0
152	Phi.	Martin Spanhel	ZPS Zlin	LW	10	2	0	2	4
153	St.L.	Denis Hamel	Chicoutimi	LW	130	13	9	22	67
154	Pit.	Alexei Kolkunov	Krylja Sovetov	C					
155	Col.	John Cirjak	Spokane	RW					
156	Det.	Tyler Perry	Seattle	C					
157	L.A.	Benoit Larose	Sherbrooke	D					
158	NYI	Andrew Taylor	Detroit	LW					
159	Ana.	Mike LaPlante	Calgary	D					
160	T.B.	Cory Murphy	Sault Ste. Marie	D					
161	Edm.	Martin Cerven	Dukla Trencin	C					
162	Wpg.	Paul Traynor	Kitchener	D					
163	L.A.	Juha Vuorivirta	Tappara Tampere	C					
164	Mtl.	Stephane Robidas	Shawinigan	D	198	10	23	33	63
165	Hfd.	Byron Ritchie	Lethbridge	C	94	5	11	16	72
166	Fla.	Peter Worrell	Hull	LW	342	16	26	42	1375
167	S.J.	Brad Mehalko	Lethbridge	RW					
168	S.J.	Robert Jindrich	HC Interconex Plzen	D					
169	NYR	Jeff Heil	Wisconsin-River Falls	G					
170	Van.	Stewart Bodtker	Colorado College	C					
171	Tor.	Marek Melenovsky	Dukla Jihlava	C					
172	Buf.	Brian Scott	Kitchener	LW					
173	Dal.	Jeff Dewar	Moose Jaw	RW					
174	N.J.	Richard Rochefort	Sudbury	C					
175	Chi.	Steve Tardif	Drummondville	C					
176	Cgy.	Ryan Gillis	North Bay	D					
177	Bos.	P.J. Axelsson	Vastra Frolunda Goteborg	LW	465	57	96	153	147
178	Phi.	Martin Streit	HC Olomouc	RW					
179	St.L.	Jean-Luc Grand-Pierre	Val d'Or	D	213	4	11	15	259
180	Pit.	Derrick Pyke	Halifax	RW					
181	Col.	Dan Smith	U. of British Columbia	D	15	0	0	0	9
182	Det.	Per Eklund	Djurgarden	LW					
183	Ott.	Kaj Linna	Boston U.	D					
184	Ott.	Ray Schultz	Tri-City	D	45	0	4	4	155
185	Ana.	Igor Karpenko	Sokol Kiev	G					
186	T.B.	Joe Cardarelli	Spokane	LW					
187	Edm.	Stephen Douglas	Niagara Falls	D					
188	Wpg.	Jaroslav Obsut	North Battleford	D	7	0	0	0	2
189	Wpg.	Fredrik Loven	Djurgarden	C					
190	Mtl.	Greg Hart	Kamloops	RW					
191	Hfd.	Milan Kostolny	Detroit	RW					
192	Fla.	Filip Kuba	HC Vitkovice	D	233	23	67	90	91
193	Dal.	Anatoli Koveshnikov	Sokol Kiev	RW					
194	S.J.	Ryan Kraft	Minnesota-Duluth	C	7	0	1	1	0
195	NYR	Ilja Gorokhov	Torpedo Yaroslavl	D					
196	Van.	Tyler Willis	Swift Current	RW					
197	Tor.	Mark Murphy	Stratford Jr. B	LW					
198	Buf.	Mike Zanutto	Oshawa	C					
199	Wsh.	Vasili Turkovsky	CSKA	D					
200	N.J.	Frederic Henry	Granby	G					
201	Chi.	Casey Hankinson	Minnesota-Duluth	LW	14	0	1	1	9
202	Dal.	Sergei Luchinkin	Dynamo	C					
203	Bos.	Sergei Zhukov	Torpedo Yaroslavl	D					
204	Phi.	Ruslan Shafikov	Salavat Yulayev Ufa	C					
205	St.L.	Derek Bekar	Powell River Jr. A	LW	7	0	0	0	4
206	Pit.	Sergei Voronov	Dynamo	D					
207	Col.	Tomi Hirvonen	Ilves Tampere	C					
208	Det.	Andrei Samokhvalov	Torpedo Ust-Kamenogorsk	RW					
209	St.L.	Libor Zabransky	HC Ceske Budejovice	D	40	1	6	7	50
210	NYI	David MacDonald	Sudbury	G					
211	NYI	Mike Broda	Moose Jaw	LW					
212	T.B.	Zac Bierk	Peterborough	G	43	1945	101	1	3.12
213	Edm.	Jiri Antonin	HC Pardubice	D					
214	Wpg.	Rob Deciantis	Kitchener	C					
215	L.A.	Brian Stewart	Sault Ste. Marie	D					
216	Mtl.	Eric Houde	Halifax	C	30	2	3	5	4
217	Hfd.	Mike Rucinski	Detroit	D	26	0	2	2	10
218	Fla.	David Lemanowicz	Spokane	G					
219	Dal.	Stephen Lowe	Sault Ste. Marie	C					
220	S.J.	Mikko Markkanen	TPS Turku	RW					
221	NYR	Bob Maudie	Kamloops	C					
222	Van.	Jason Cugnet	Kelowna Jr. A.	G					
223	Tor.	Danny Markov	Spartak	D	336	19	82	101	240
224	Buf.	Rob Skrlac	Kamloops	LW					
225	Wsh.	Scott Swanson	Omaha Jr. A.	D					
226	N.J.	Colin O'Hara	Winnipeg Jr. A	D					
227	Chi.	Mike Pittman	Guelph	C					
228	Col.	Chris George	Sarnia	RW					
229	Bos.	Jonathon Murphy	Peterborough	D					
230	Phi.	Jeff Lank	Prince Albert	D	2	0	0	0	2
231	Ott.	Erik Kaminski	Cleveland Jr.	RW					
232	Pit.	Frank Ivankovic	Oshawa	G					
233	Cgy.	Steve Shirreffs	Hotchkiss H.S.	D					
234	Det.	David Engblom	Vallentuna	C					

1996

FIRST ROUND

PICK	TEAM	NAME	DRAFTED FROM	POS	GP	G / W	A / GA	PTS / SO	PIM / AVG
1	Ott.	Chris Phillips	Prince Albert	D	385	24	72	96	240
2	S.J.	Andrei Zyuzin	Salavat Yulayev Ufa	D	293	20	50	70	280
3	NYI	J.P. Dumont	Val d'Or	RW	303	79	84	163	168
4	Wsh.	Alexandre Volchkov	Barrie	C	3	0	0	0	0
5	Dal.	Richard Jackman	Sault Ste. Marie	D	82	1	4	5	67
6	Edm.	Boyd Devereaux	Kitchener	C	370	32	62	94	103
7	Buf.	Erik Rasmussen	Minnesota-Duluth	LW/C	338	37	58	95	207
8	Bos.	Johnathan Aitken	Medicine Hat	D	3	0	0	0	0
9	Ana.	Ruslan Salei	Las Vegas IHL	D	434	21	50	71	511
10	N.J.	Lance Ward	Red Deer	D	Re-entered Draft in 1998				
11	Phx.	Dan Focht	Tri-City	D	30	0	3	3	40
12	Van.	Josh Holden	Regina	C	59	5	9	14	16
13	Cgy.	Derek Morris	Regina	D	418	45	166	211	453
14	St.L.	Marty Reasoner	Boston College	C	217	34	55	89	111
15	Phi.	Dainius Zubrus	Pembroke Jr. A	RW	485	79	137	216	265
16	T.B.	Mario Larocque	Hull	D	5	0	0	0	16
17	Wsh.	Jaroslav Svejkovsky	Tri-City	RW	113	23	19	42	56
18	Mtl.	Matt Higgins	Moose Jaw	C	57	1	2	3	6
19	Edm.	Matthieu Descoteaux	Shawinigan	D	5	1	1	2	4
20	Fla.	Marcus Nilson	Djurgarden	LW	258	42	65	107	167
21	S.J.	Marco Sturm	Landshut	LW	466	101	115	216	190
22	NYR	Jeff Brown	Sarnia	D					
23	Pit.	Craig Hillier	Ottawa	G					
24	Phx.	Daniel Briere	Drummondville	C	272	77	81	158	158
25	Col.	Peter Ratchuk	Shattuck St. Mary's H.S.	D	32	1	1	2	10
26	Det.	Jesse Wallin	Red Deer	D	49	0	2	2	34

SECOND ROUND

PICK	TEAM	NAME	DRAFTED FROM	POS	GP	G / W	A / GA	PTS / SO	PIM / AVG
27	Buf.	Cory Sarich	Saskatoon	D	290	6	34	40	351
28	Pit.	Pavel Skrbek	HC Poldi Kladno	D	12	0	0	0	8
29	NYI	Dan LaCouture	Springfield	LW	206	11	21	32	196
30	L.A.	Josh Green	Medicine Hat	LW	182	24	26	50	122
31	Chi.	Remi Royer	St-Hyacinthe	D	18	0	0	0	67
32	Edm.	Chris Hajt	Guelph	D	1	0	0	0	0
33	Buf.	Darren Van Oene	Brandon	LW					
34	Hfd.	Trevor Wasyluk	Medicine Hat	LW					
35	Ana.	Matt Cullen	St. Cloud State	C	457	71	141	212	190
36	Tor.	Marek Posmyk	Dukla Jihlava	D	19	1	2	3	20
37	L.A.	Marian Cisar	Slovan Bratislava	RW	73	13	17	30	57
38	N.J.	Wes Mason	Sarnia	LW					
39	Cgy.	Travis Brigley	Lethbridge	LW	19	0	2	2	6
40	Cgy.	Steve Begin	Val d'Or	C	123	11	7	18	192
41	N.J.	Josh DeWolf	Twin Cities Jr.	D					
42	Chi.	Jeff Paul	Niagara Falls	D	2	0	0	0	7
43	Wsh.	Jan Bulis	Barrie	C	328	51	101	152	118
44	Mtl.	Mathieu Garon	Victoriaville	G	24	1332	59	4	2.66
45	Bos.	Henry Kuster	Medicine Hat	RW					

PICK	TEAM	NAME	DRAFTED FROM	NHL PLAYERS: POS / NHL GOALTENDERS: POS	GP / GP	G / W	A / GA	PTS / SO	PIM / AVG
46	Chi.	Geoff Peters	Niagara Falls	C					
47	N.J.	Pierre Dagenais	Moncton	RW	Re-entered Draft in 1998				
48	NYR	Daniel Goneau	Granby	LW	53	12	3	15	14
49	N.J.	Colin White	Hull	D	248	10	31	41	426
50	Tor.	Francis Larivee	Laval	G					
51	Col.	Yuri Babenko	Krylja Sovetov	C	3	0	0	0	0
52	Det.	Aren Miller	Spokane	G					

OTHER ROUNDS

PICK	TEAM	NAME	DRAFTED FROM	POS	GP	G / W	A / GA	PTS / SO	PIM / AVG
53	Bos.	Eric Naud	St-Hyacinthe	LW					
54	Buf.	Francois Methot	St-Hyacinthe	C					
55	S.J.	Terry Friesen	Swift Current	G					
56	NYI	Zdeno Chara	Dukla Trencin	D	380	25	66	91	619
57	L.A.	Greg Phillips	Saskatoon	RW					
58	Wsh.	Sergei Zimakov	Krylja Sovetov	D					
59	Edm.	Tom Poti	Cushing Academy	D	376	39	122	161	269
60	Fla.	Chris Allen	Kingston	D	2	0	0	0	2
61	Hfd.	Andrei Petrunin	CSKA	RW					
62	Phx.	Per-Anton Lundstrom	MoDo Ornskoldsvik	D					
63	N.J.	Scott Parker	Kelowna	RW	Re-entered Draft in 1998				
64	Phi.	Chester Gallant	Niagara Falls	RW					
65	Fla.	Oleg Kvasha	CSKA	LW/C	348	53	81	134	249
66	Tor.	Mike Lankshear	Guelph	D					
67	St.L.	Gordie Dwyer	Beauport	LW	Re-entered Draft in 1998				
68	Tor.	Konstantin Kalmikov	Detroit	LW					
69	T.B.	Curtis Tipler	Regina	RW					
70	Dal.	Jon Sim	Sarnia	LW	95	10	8	18	57
71	Mtl.	Arron Asham	Red Deer	RW	199	26	28	54	195
72	Pit.	Boyd Kane	Regina	LW	Re-entered Draft in 1998				
73	Cgy.	Dmitri Vlasenkov	Torpedo Yaroslavl	LW					
74	Wsh.	Dave Weninger	Michigan Tech U.	G					
75	Van.	Zenith Komarniski	Tri-City	D	19	1	1	2	10
76	NYR	Dmitri Subbotin	CSKA	LW					
77	Pit.	Boris Protsenko	Calgary	RW					
78	Wsh.	Shawn McNeil	Kamloops	C					
79	Col.	Mark Parrish	St. Cloud State	RW	383	120	99	219	152
80	Bos.	Jason Doyle	Owen Sound	RW	Re-entered Draft in 1998				
81	Ott.	Antti-Jussi Niemi	Jokerit Helsinki	D	29	1	1	2	22
82	Fla.	Joey Tetarenko	Portland	RW	71	4	1	5	176
83	NYI	Tyrone Garner	Oshawa	G	3	139	12	0	5.18
84	L.A.	Mikael Simons	Mora	C					
85	Wsh.	Justin Davis	Kingston	RW					
86	Tor.	Jason Sessa	Lake Superior State	RW					
87	Buf.	Kurt Walsh	Owen Sound	RW					
88	Hfd.	Craig MacDonald	Harvard	LW	58	2	4	6	20
89	Cgy.	Toni Lydman	Reipas Lahti	D	222	15	58	73	110
90	Dal.	Mike Hurley	Tri-City	RW					
91	N.J.	Josef Boumedienne	Huddinge	D	10	2	0	2	6
92	Mtl.	Kim Staal	Malmo	C					
93	Van.	Jonas Soling	Huddinge	RW					
94	Cgy.	Christian Lefebvre	Granby	D	Re-entered Draft in 1998				
95	St.L.	Jonathan Zukiwsky	Red Deer	C					
96	L.A.	Eric Belanger	Beauport	C	177	33	47	80	63
97	St.L.	Andrei Petrakov	Avtomobilist Yekaterinburg	RW					
98	Col.	Ben Storey	Harvard	D					
99	Mtl.	Etienne Drapeau	Beauport	C					
100	Bos.	Trent Whitfield	Spokane	C	100	3	6	9	69
101	N.J.	Josh MacNevin	Vernon Jr. A.	D					
102	S.J.	Matt Bradley	Kingston	RW	121	12	17	29	99
103	Tor.	Vladimir Antipov	Torpedo Yaroslavl	RW					
104	Hfd.	Steve Wasylko	Detroit	C					
105	Pit.	Michal Rozsival	Dukla Jihlava	D	237	18	47	65	161
106	Buf.	Mike Martone	Peterborough	D					
107	Col.	Randy Petruk	Kamloops	G					
108	Det.	Johan Forsander	HV-71 Jonkoping	LW					
109	NYI	Bubba Berenzweig	Michigan	D	37	3	7	10	14
110	Tor.	Peter Cava	Sault Ste. Marie	C					
111	Tor.	Brandon Sugden	London	D					
112	Dal.	Ryan Christie	Owen Sound	LW	7	0	0	0	0
113	Dal.	Yevgeny Tsybuk	Torpedo Yaroslavl	D					
114	Edm.	Brian Urick	U. of Notre Dame	RW					
115	Buf.	Alexei Tezikov	Lada Togliatti	D	30	1	1	2	2
116	Hfd.	Mark McMahon	Kitchener	D					
117	Ana.	Brendan Buckley	Boston College	D					
118	N.J.	Glenn Crawford	Windsor	C					
119	Phx.	Richard Lintner	Dukla Trencin	D	112	8	12	20	54

PICK	TEAM	NAME	DRAFTED FROM	NHL PLAYERS: POS / NHL GOALTENDERS: POS	GP / GP	G / W	A / GA	PTS / SO	PIM / AVG
120	L.A.	Jesse Black	Niagara Falls	D					
121	Van.	Tyler Prosofsky	Kelowna	C					
122	Cgy.	Josef Straka	HC Chemopetrol Litvinov	C					
123	L.A.	Peter Hogan	Oshawa	D					
124	Phi.	Per-Ragna Bergqvist	Leksand	G					
125	T.B.	Jason Robinson	Niagara Falls	D					
126	Wsh.	Matthew Lahey	Peterborough	LW					
127	Mtl.	Daniel Archambault	Val d'Or	D					
128	NYI	Petr Sachl	HC Ceske Budejovice	LW					
129	Fla.	Andrew Long	Guelph	C					
130	Chi.	Andy Johnson	Peterborough	D					
131	NYR	Colin Pepperall	Niagara Falls	LW					
132	Bos.	Elias Abrahamsson	Halifax	D					
133	Phi.	Jesse Boulerice	Detroit	RW	51	2	1	3	113
134	Col.	Luke Curtin	Kelowna	LW					
135	Det.	Michal Podolka	Sault Ste. Marie	G					
136	Ott.	Andreas Dackell	Brynas Gavle	RW	553	87	151	238	152
137	S.J.	Michel Larocque	Boston University	G	3	152	9	0	3.55
138	NYI	Todd Miller	Sarnia	C					
139	Phx.	Robert Esche	Detroit	G	88	4671	210	5	2.70
140	Tor.	Dmitri Yakushin	Pembroke Jr. A	D	2	0	0	0	2
141	Edm.	Bryan Randall	Medicine Hat	C					
142	Buf.	Ryan Davis	Owen Sound	RW					
143	Hfd.	Aaron Baker	Tri-City	G					
144	Det.	Magnus Nilsson	Vita Hasten	RW					
145	N.J.	Sean Ritchlin	Michigan	RW					
146	Col.	Brian Willsie	Guelph	RW	69	7	8	15	29
147	Van.	Nolan McDonald	Vermont	G					
148	Tor.	Chris Bogas	Michigan State	D					
149	Ana.	Blaine Russell	Prince Albert	G					
150	Pit.	Peter Bergman	Kamloops	C					
151	Tor.	Lucio DeMartinis	Shawinigan	LW					
152	T.B.	Nikolai Ignatov	CSKA	D					
153	Wsh.	Andrew Van Bruggen	Northern Michigan	RW					
154	Mtl.	Brett Clark	U. of Maine	D	146	4	5	9	54
155	Bos.	Chris Lane	Spokane	D					
156	Fla.	Gaetan Poirier	Merrimack	LW					
157	T.B.	Xavier Delisle	Granby	C	16	3	2	5	6
158	NYR	Ola Sandberg	Djurgarden	D					
159	St.L.	Stephen Wagner	Olds Jr. A	G					
160	Col.	Kai Fischer	Dusseldorf	G					
161	Buf.	Darren Mortier	Sarnia	C					
162	Det.	Alexandre Jacques	Shawinigan	C					
163	Ott.	Francois Hardy	Val d'Or	D					
164	S.J.	Jake Deadmarsh	Kamloops	D					
165	NYI	J.R. Prestifilippo	Hotchkiss H.S.	G					
166	Dal.	Eoin McInerney	London	G					
167	Col.	Dan Hinote	Army	RW	221	18	23	41	149
168	Edm.	David Bernier	St-Hyacinthe	C	Re-entered Draft in 1998				
169	St.L.	Daniel Corso	Victoriaville	C	70	14	10	24	20
170	Edm.	Brandon Lafrance	Ohio State	RW					
171	Hfd.	Greg Kuznik	Seattle	D	1	0	0	0	0
172	Ana.	Timo Ahmaoja	JyP HT Jyvaskyla	D					
173	N.J.	Daryl Andrews	Melfort Jr. A.	D					
174	Phx.	Trevor Letowski	Sarnia	RW	326	48	67	115	109
175	Van.	Clint Cabana	Medicine Hat	D					
176	Col.	Sami Pahlsson	MoDo Ornskoldsvik	C	190	14	30	44	64
177	St.L.	Reed Low	Moose Jaw	RW	193	3	14	17	553
178	Tor.	Reggie Berg	Minnesota-Duluth	C					
179	T.B.	Pavel Kubina	HC Vitkovice	D	374	43	93	136	482
180	Wsh.	Michael Anderson	Minnesota-Duluth	RW					
181	Mtl.	Timo Vertala	JyP HT Jyvaskyla	LW					
182	Bos.	Thomas Brown	Sarnia	D					
183	Fla.	Alexandre Couture	Victoriaville	D					
184	Chi.	Mike Vellinga	Guelph	D					
185	NYR	Jeff Dessner	Taft H.S.	D					
186	Pit.	Eric Meloche	Cornwall	RW	23	0	1	1	8
187	Phi.	Roman Malov	Avangard Omsk	LW					
188	Col.	Roman Pylner	HC Chemopetrol Litvinov	C					
189	Det.	Colin Beardsmore	North Bay	C					
190	L.A.	Stephen Valiquette	Sudbury	G	6	193	6	0	1.87
191	S.J.	Cory Cyrenne	Brandon	C					
192	NYI	Evgeny Korolev	Peterborough	D	Re-entered Draft in 1998				
193	L.A.	Kai Nurminen	HV-71 Jonkoping	LW	69	17	11	28	24
194	Dal.	Joel Kwiatkowski	Prince George	D	69	1	5	6	30
195	Edm.	Fernando Pisani	St. Albert Jr. A	RW	35	8	5	13	10

PICK	TEAM	NAME	DRAFTED FROM	NHL PLAYERS: POS / NHL GOALTENDERS: POS	GP / GP	G / W	A / GA	PTS / SO	PIM / AVG
196	St.L.	Andrej Podkonicky	ZTK Zvolen	C	6	1	0	1	2
197	Hfd.	Kevin Marsh	Calgary	LW					
198	Ana.	Kevin Kellett	Prince Albert	D					
199	N.J.	Willie Mitchell	Melfort Jr. A.	D	172	6	31	37	192
200	Phx.	Nicholas Lent	Omaha Jr. A	RW					
201	Van.	Jeff Scissons	Vernon Jr. A.	C					
202	Cgy.	Ryan Wade	Kelowna	RW					
203	St.L.	Tony Hutchins	Lawrence Academy	C					
204	Tor.	Tomas Kaberle	HC Poldi Kladno	D	372	38	155	193	92
205	N.J.	Jay Bertsch	Spokane	RW					
206	Wsh.	Oleg Orekhovsky	Dynamo	D					
207	Mtl.	Mattia Baldi	Ambri-Piotta, SUI	F					
208	Bos.	Bob Prier	St. Lawrence U.	RW					
209	Fla.	Denis Khloptonov	CSKA	G					
210	Chi.	Chris Twerdun	Moose Jaw	D					
211	NYR	Ryan McKie	London	D					
212	Ott.	Erich Goldmann	Mannheim	D	1	0	0	0	0
213	Phi.	Jeff Milleker	Moose Jaw	C					
214	Col.	Matt Scorsune	Hotchkiss H.S.	D					
215	Det.	Craig Stahl	Tri-City	RW					
216	Ott.	Ivan Ciernik	HC Nitra	RW	82	11	13	24	32
217	S.J.	David Thibeault	Drummondville	LW					
218	NYI	Mike Muzechka	Calgary	D					
219	L.A.	Sebastien Simard	Drummondville	LW					
220	Dal.	Nick Bootland	Guelph	LW					
221	Edm.	John Hultberg	Kingston	G					
222	Buf.	Scott Buhler	Medicine Hat	G					
223	Hfd.	Craig Adams	Harvard	RW	158	7	13	20	129
224	Ana.	Tobias Johansson	Malmo	LW					
225	N.J.	Pasi Petrilainen	Tappara Tampere	D					
226	Phx.	Marc-Etienne Hubert	Laval	C					
227	Van.	Lubomir Vaic	HC Kosice	C	9	1	1	2	2
228	Cgy.	Ronald Petrovicky	Prince George	RW	173	14	21	35	216
229	St.L.	Konstantin Shafranov	Fort Wayne IHL	RW	5	2	1	3	0
230	Tor.	Jared Hope	Spokane	C					
231	Hfd.	Ashkat Rakhmatullin	Salavat Yulayev Ufa	LW					
232	Wsh.	Chad Cavanagh	London	C					
233	Mtl.	Michel Tremblay	Shawinigan	LW					
234	Bos.	Anders Soderberg	MoDo Ornskoldsvik	RW					
235	Fla.	Russell Smith	Hull	D					
236	Chi.	Andrei Kozyrev	Severstal Cherepovets	D					
237	NYR	Ronnie Sundin	Vastra Frolunda Goteborg	D	1	0	0	0	0
238	Pit.	Timo Seikkula	Junkkarit Kalajoki	LW					
239	Ott.	Sami Salo	TPS Turku	D	274	28	71	99	60
240	Col.	Justin Clark	Michigan	RW					
241	Det.	Eugeny Afanasiev	Detroit L.C. Midgets	LW					

1997

FIRST ROUND

PICK	TEAM	NAME	DRAFTED FROM	POS	GP	G / W	A / GA	PTS / SO	PIM / AVG
1	Bos.	Joe Thornton	Sault Ste. Marie	C	432	137	211	348	513
2	S.J.	Patrick Marleau	Seattle	C	478	125	145	270	169
3	L.A.	Olli Jokinen	HIFK Helsinki	C	395	71	81	152	413
4	NYI	Roberto Luongo	Val d'Or	G	194	10577	481	16	2.73
5	NYI	Eric Brewer	Prince George	D	327	27	61	88	195
6	Cgy.	Daniel Tkaczuk	Barrie	C	19	4	7	11	14
7	T.B.	Paul Mara	Sudbury	D	265	31	58	89	263
8	Bos.	Sergei Samsonov	Detroit	LW	401	129	170	299	77
9	Wsh.	Nick Boynton	Ottawa	D	Re-entered Draft in 1999				
10	Van.	Brad Ference	Spokane	D	182	4	25	29	460
11	Mtl.	Jason Ward	Erie	RW	52	5	3	8	22
12	Ott.	Marian Hossa	Dukla Trencin	RW	386	152	156	308	197
13	Chi.	Daniel Cleary	Belleville	RW	261	35	60	95	151
14	Edm.	Michel Riesen	Biel-Bienne, SUI	RW	12	0	1	1	4
15	L.A.	Matt Zultek	Ottawa	LW	Re-entered Draft in 1999				
16	Chi.	Ty Jones	Spokane	RW	8	0	0	0	12
17	Pit.	Robert Dome	Las Vegas IHL	RW	53	7	7	14	12
18	Ana.	Mikael Holmqvist	Djurgarden	C					
19	NYR	Stefan Cherneski	Brandon	RW					
20	Fla.	Mike Brown	Red Deer	LW	16	0	0	0	77
21	Buf.	Mika Noronen	Tappara Tampere	G	28	1517	64	1	2.53
22	Car.	Nikos Tselios	Belleville	D	2	0	0	0	6
23	S.J.	Scott Hannan	Kelowna	D	266	9	49	58	185
24	N.J.	J-F Damphousse	Moncton	G	6	294	12	0	2.45
25	Dal.	Brenden Morrow	Portland	LW	289	72	83	155	452
26	Col.	Kevin Grimes	Kingston	D					

SECOND ROUND

PICK	TEAM	NAME	DRAFTED FROM	POS	GP	G / W	A / GA	PTS / SO	PIM / AVG
27	Bos.	Ben Clymer	Minnesota-Duluth	LW	229	27	39	66	201
28	Car.	Brad DeFauw	North Dakota	LW	9	3	0	3	2
29	L.A.	Scott Barney	Peterborough	C	5	0	0	0	0
30	Phi.	Jean-Marc Pelletier	Cornell	G	3	179	11	0	3.69
31	NYI	Jeff Zehr	Windsor	LW	4	0	0	0	2
32	Cgy.	Evan Lindsay	Prince Albert	G					
33	T.B.	Kyle Kos	Red Deer	D					
34	Van.	Ryan Bonni	Saskatoon	D	3	0	0	0	0
35	Wsh.	Jean-Francois Fortin	Sherbrooke	D	69	1	4	5	42
36	Van.	Harold Druken	Detroit	C	137	27	32	59	34
37	Mtl.	Gregor Baumgartner	Laval	LW	Re-entered Draft in 1999				
38	N.J.	Stanislav Gron	Slovan Bratislava	RW	1	0	0	0	0
39	Chi.	Jeremy Reich	Seattle	LW					
40	St.L.	Tyler Rennette	North Bay	C					
41	Edm.	Patrick Dovigi	Erie	G					
42	Cgy.	John Tripp	Oshawa	RW	9	1	2	3	2
43	Phx.	Juha Gustafsson	Kiekko-Espoo	D					
44	Pit.	Brian Gaffaney	North Iowa Jr. A.	D					
45	Ana.	Maxim Balmochnykh	Lada Togliatti	LW	6	0	1	1	2
46	NYR	Wes Jarvis	Kitchener	D					
47	Fla.	Kristian Huselius	Farjestad Karlstad	LW	157	43	45	88	34
48	Buf.	Henrik Tallinder	AIK Solna	D	48	3	10	13	28
49	Det.	Yuri Butsayev	Lada Togliatti	LW	99	10	4	14	28
50	Phi.	Pat Kavanagh	Peterborough	RW	3	1	0	1	2
51	Cgy.	Dimitri Kokorev	Dynamo-2	D					
52	Dal.	Roman Lyashenko	Torpedo Yaroslavl	C	139	14	9	23	55
53	Col.	Graham Belak	Edmonton	D					

OTHER ROUNDS

PICK	TEAM	NAME	DRAFTED FROM	POS	GP	G / W	A / GA	PTS / SO	PIM / AVG
54	Bos.	Mattias Karlin	MoDo Ornskoldsvik	C					
55	Col.	Rick Berry	Seattle	D	132	2	7	9	206
56	Fla.	Vratislav Cech	Kitchener	D					
57	Tor.	Jeff Farkas	Boston College	RW	11	0	2	2	6
58	Ott.	Jani Hurme	TPS Turku	G	76	4041	176	6	2.61
59	NYI	Jarrett Smith	Prince George	C					
60	Cgy.	Derek Schutz	Spokane	C					
61	T.B.	Matt Elich	Windsor	RW	16	1	1	2	0
62	Phi.	Kris Mallette	Kelowna	D					
63	Bos.	Lee Goren	North Dakota	RW	35	4	1	5	14
64	Van.	Kyle Freadrich	Regina	LW	23	0	1	1	75
65	Mtl.	Ilkka Mikkola	Karpat Oulu	D					
66	Ott.	Josh Langfeld	Lincoln Jr.	RW	13	0	1	1	6
67	Chi.	Mike Souza	New Hampshire	LW					
68	Edm.	Sergei Yerkovich	Las Vegas IHL	D					
69	Buf.	Maxim Afinogenov	Dynamo	RW	259	56	65	121	171
70	Cgy.	Erik Andersson	U. of Denver	C	12	2	1	3	8
71	Pit.	Josef Melichar	HC Ceske Budejovice	D	86	0	5	5	91
72	Ana.	Jay Legault	London	LW					
73	NYR	Burke Henry	Brandon	D	16	0	2	2	9
74	Fla.	Nick Smith	Barrie	C	15	0	0	0	0
75	Buf.	Jeff Martin	Windsor	C					
76	Det.	Petr Sykora	HC Pojistovna IB Pardubice	C	84	34	25	59	24
77	Dal.	Steve Gainey	Kamloops	LW	6	0	1	1	7
78	Col.	Ville Nieminen	Tappara Tampere	LW	192	34	36	70	169
79	NYI	Robert Schnabel	Slavia Praha	D	Re-entered Draft in 1998				
80	Car.	Francis Lessard	Val d'Or	D/RW	23	0	2	2	87
81	Bos.	Karol Bartanus	Drummondville	RW					
82	S.J.	Adam Colagiacomo	Oshawa	RW					
83	L.A.	Joe Corvo	Western Michigan	D	50	5	7	12	14
84	Tor.	Adam Mair	Owen Sound	C	131	8	14	22	229
85	NYI	Petr Mika	Slavia Praha	LW	3	0	0	0	0
86	St.L.	Didier Tremblay	Halifax	D					
87	Col.	Brad Larsen	Swift Current	LW	66	2	10	12	49
88	Car.	Shane Willis	Lethbridge	RW	162	31	37	68	75
89	Wsh.	Curtis Cruickshank	Kingston	G					
90	Van.	Chris Stanley	Belleville	C					
91	Mtl.	Daniel Tetrault	Brandon	D					
92	Cgy.	Chris St. Croix	Kamloops	D					
93	NYR	Tomi Kallarsson	HPK Hameenlinna	D					
94	Edm.	Jonas Elofsson	Farjestad Karlstad	D					
95	Fla.	Ivan Novoseltsev	Krylja Sovetov	RW	200	28	40	68	98
96	Phx.	Scott McCallum	Tri-City	D					
97	Pit.	Alexandre Mathieu	Halifax	LW					
98	St.L.	Jan Horacek	Slavia Praha	D					

PICK	TEAM	NAME	DRAFTED FROM	NHL PLAYERS: POS NHL GOALTENDERS: POS	GP GP	G W	A GA	PTS SO	PIM AVG
99	L.A.	Sean Blanchard	Ottawa	D					
100	Cgy.	Ryan Ready	Belleville	LW					
101	Buf.	Luc Theoret	Lethbridge	D					
102	Det.	Quintin Laing	Kelowna	LW					
103	Phi.	Mikhail Chernov	Torpedo-2 Yaroslavl	D					
104	N.J.	Lucas Nehrling	Sarnia	D					
105	Dal.	Marcus Kristoffersson	Mora	LW					
106	St.L.	Jame Pollock	Seattle	RW					
107	S.J.	Adam Nittel	Erie	RW					
108	T.B.	Mark Thompson	Regina	D					
109	T.B.	Jan Sulc	HC Chemopetrol Litvinov	C					
110	Chi.	Ben Simon	U. of Notre Dame	LW	16	0	1	1	15
111	Tor.	Frantisek Mrazek	HC Ceske Budejovice	LW					
112	T.B.	Karel Betik	Kelowna	D	3	0	2	2	2
113	Cgy.	Martin Moise	Beauport	LW					
114	Van.	David Darguzas	Edmonton	C					
115	NYI	Adam Edinger	Bowling Green	C					
116	Wsh.	Kevin Caulfield	Boston College	RW					
117	Van.	Matt Cockell	Saskatoon	G					
118	Mtl.	Konstantin Sidulov	Traktor Chelyabinsk	D					
119	Ott.	Magnus Arvedson	Farjestad Karlstad	LW	393	92	118	210	229
120	Chi.	Peter Gardiner	RPI	RW					
121	Edm.	Jason Chimera	Medicine Hat	LW	70	15	9	24	36
122	Mtl.	Gennady Razin	Kamloops	D					
123	Phx.	Curtis Suter	Spokane	LW					
124	Pit.	Harlan Pratt	Prince Albert	D					
125	Ana.	Luc Vaillancourt	Beauport	G					
126	NYR	Jason McLean	Moose Jaw	G					
127	Fla.	Pat Parthenais	Detroit	D					
128	Buf.	Torrey DiRoberto	Seattle	C					
129	Det.	John Wikstrom	Lulea	D					
130	Chi.	Kyle Calder	Regina	LW	214	38	74	112	103
131	N.J.	Jiri Bicek	HC Kosice	RW	50	6	6	12	29
132	Dal.	Teemu Elomo	TPS Turku	LW					
133	Col.	Aaron Miskovich	Green Bay Jr.	C					
134	NYR	Johan Lindbom	HV-71 Jonkoping	LW	38	1	3	4	28
135	Bos.	Denis Timofeev	CSKA-2	D					
136	NYR	Mike York	Michigan State	LW	313	82	111	193	64
137	L.A.	Richard Seeley	Prince Albert	D					
138	Tor.	Eric Gooldy	Detroit	LW					
139	NYI	Bobby Leavins	Brandon	LW					
140	Cgy.	Ilja Demidov	Dynamo-2	D					
141	Edm.	Peter Sarno	Windsor	C					
142	Car.	Kyle Dafoe	Owen Sound	D					
143	Wsh.	Henrik Petre	Djurgarden	D					
144	Van.	Matt Cooke	Windsor	C	326	47	69	116	353
145	Mtl.	Jonathan Desroches	Granby	D					
146	Ott.	Jeff Sullivan	Halifax	D					
147	Chi.	Heath Gordon	Green Bay Jr.	RW					
148	Van.	Larry Shapley	Welland Jr. B	D					
149	St.L.	Nicholas Bilotto	Beauport	D					
150	L.A.	Jeff Katcher	Brandon	D					
151	Phx.	Robert Francz	Peterborough	LW					
152	Pit.	Petr Havelka	Sparta Praha	LW					
153	T.B.	Andrei Skopintsev	TPS Turku	D	40	2	4	6	32
154	NYR	Shawn Degagne	Kitchener	G					
155	Fla.	Keith Delaney	Barrie	C					
156	Buf.	Brian Campbell	Ottawa	D	114	6	24	30	38
157	Det.	B.J. Young	Red Deer	RW	1	0	0	0	0
158	Phi.	Jordon Flodell	Moose Jaw	D					
159	N.J.	Sascha Goc	Schwenningen	D	22	0	0	0	4
160	Dal.	Alexei Timkin	Torpedo-2 Yaroslavl	RW					
161	Col.	David Aebischer	Fribourg-Gotteron, SUI	G	69	3812	139	6	2.19
162	Bos.	Joel Trottier	Ottawa	RW					
163	S.J.	Joe Dusbabek	U. of Notre Dame	RW					
164	Phi.	Todd Fedoruk	Kelowna	LW	171	9	14	23	355
165	Tor.	Hugo Marchand	Victoriaville	D					
166	NYI	Kris Knoblauch	Edmonton	LW					
167	Cgy.	Jeremy Rondeau	Swift Current	LW					
168	T.B.	Justin Jack	Kelowna	RW					
169	Car.	Andrew Merrick	Michigan	C					
170	T.B.	Eero Somervuori	Jokerit Helsinki	RW					
171	Van.	Rod Leroux	Seattle	D					
172	Mtl.	Ben Guite	U. of Maine	RW					
173	Ott.	Robin Bacul	Slavia Praha Jr.	RW					
174	Chi.	Jerad Smith	Portland	D					
175	NYR	Johan Holmqvist	Brynas Gavle	G	4	167	12	0	4.31
176	Edm.	Kevin Bolibruck	Peterborough	D					
177	St.L.	Ladislav Nagy	Dragon Presov	LW	211	55	67	122	166
178	Ana.	Tony Mohagen	Seattle	LW					
179	Pit.	Mark Moore	Harvard	D					
180	Bos.	Jim Baxter	Oshawa	D	Re-entered Draft in 1999				
181	Ana.	Mat Snesrud	North Iowa Jr. A	D					
182	NYR	Mike Mottau	Boston College	D	23	0	3	3	13
183	Fla.	Tyler Palmer	Lake Superior State	D					
184	Buf.	Jeremy Adduono	Sudbury	RW					
185	T.B.	Samuel St-Pierre	Victoriaville	RW					
186	Det.	Mike Laceby	Kingston	C					
187	Edm.	Chad Hinz	Moose Jaw	C					
188	N.J.	Mathieu Benoit	Chicoutimi	RW					
189	Dal.	Jeff McKercher	Barrie	D					
190	Tor.	Shawn Thornton	Peterborough	RW	13	1	1	2	31
191	Bos.	Antti Laaksonen	U. of Denver	LW	284	50	54	104	76
192	S.J.	Cam Severson	Prince Albert	LW	2	0	0	0	8
193	L.A.	Jay Kopischke	North Iowa Jr. A	LW					
194	Tor.	Russ Bartlett	Phillips-Exeter H.S.	C					
195	Car.	Niklas Nordgren	Modo Ornskoldsvik	LW					
196	NYI	Jeremy Symington	Petrolia Jr. B	G					
197	Mtl.	Petr Kubos	Petra Vsetin	D					
198	T.B.	Shawn Skolney	Seattle	D					
199	Car.	Randy Fitzgerald	Detroit	LW					
200	Wsh.	Pierre-Luc Therrien	Drummondville	G					
201	Van.	Denis Martynyuk	CSKA-2	LW					
202	Mtl.	Andrei Sidyakin	Salavat Yulayev Ufa	RW					
203	Ott.	Nick Gillis	Cushing Academy	RW					
204	Chi.	Sergei Shikhanov	Lada Togliatti	RW					
205	Edm.	Chris Kerr	Sudbury	D					
206	St.L.	Bobby Haglund	Des Moines Jr. A	LW					
207	Phx.	Alexander Andreyev	Weyburn	D					
208	Pit.	Andrew Ference	Portland	D	179	11	29	40	163
209	Ana.	Rene Stussi	Thurgau, SUI	C					
210	NYR	Andrew Proskurnicki	Sarnia	LW					
211	Fla.	Doug Schueller	Twin Cities Jr.	D					
212	Buf.	Kamil Piros	Chemopetrol Litvinov	C	11	3	3	6	6
213	Det.	Steve Willejto	Prince Albert	C					
214	Phi.	Marko Kauppinen	JYP HT Jyvaskyla Jr.	D					
215	N.J.	Scott Clemmensen	Des Moines Jr. A	G	2	20	1	0	3.00
216	Dal.	Alexei Komarov	Dynamo-2	D					
217	Col.	Doug Schmidt	Waterloo Jr. A	D					
218	Bos.	Eric Van Acker	Chicoutimi	D					
219	S.J.	Mark Smith	Lethbridge	C	166	9	16	25	187
220	L.A.	Konrad Brand	Medicine Hat	D					
221	Tor.	Jonathan Hedstrom	Skelleftea	RW	4	0	0	0	0
222	NYI	Ryan Clark	Lincoln Jr.	D					
223	Cgy.	Dustin Paul	Moose Jaw	RW					
224	T.B.	Paul Comrie	U. of Denver	C	15	1	2	3	4
225	Car.	Kent McDonell	Guelph	RW	Re-entered Draft in 1999				
226	Wsh.	Matt Oikawa	St. Lawrence U.	RW					
227	Van.	Peter Brady	Powell River Jr. A	G					
228	Mtl.	Jarl Espen Ygranes	Furuset Oslo	D					
229	Ott.	Karel Rachunek	ZPS Zlin Jr.	D	186	10	70	80	116
230	Chi.	Chris Feil	Ohio State	D					
231	Edm.	Alexander Fomitchev	St. Albert Jr. A	G					
232	St.L.	Dmitri Plekhanov	Neftekhimik Nizhnekamsk	D					
233	Phx.	Wyatt Smith	Minnesota-Duluth	C	65	4	7	11	13
234	Pit.	Eric Lind	Avon Old Farms H.S.	D					
235	Ana.	Tommi Degerman	Boston U.	LW					
236	NYR	Richard Miller	Providence	D					
237	Fla.	Benoit Cote	Shawinigan	C					
238	Buf.	Dylan Kemp	Lethbridge	D					
239	Det.	Greg Willers	Kingston	D					
240	Phi.	Par Styf	Modo Ornskoldsvik	D					
241	N.J.	Jan Srdinko	Petra Vsetin	D					
242	Dal.	Brett McLean	Kelowna	C	2	0	0	0	0
243	Col.	Kyle Kidney	Salisbury H.S.	LW					
244	St.L.	Marek Ivan	Lethbridge	C					
245	Col.	Stephen Lafleur	Belleville	D					
246	Bos.	Jay Henderson	Edmonton	LW	33	1	3	4	37

1998

FIRST ROUND

PICK	TEAM	NAME	DRAFTED FROM	NHL PLAYERS: POS / NHL GOALTENDERS: POS	GP / GP	G / W	A / GA	PTS / SO	PIM / AVG
1	T.B.	Vincent Lecavalier	Rimouski	C	386	114	147	261	232
2	Nsh.	David Legwand	Plymouth	C	280	54	93	147	156
3	S.J.	Brad Stuart	Regina	D	277	25	77	102	173
4	Van.	Bryan Allen	Oshawa	D	65	5	3	8	79
5	Ana.	Vitaly Vishnevski	Torpedo-2 Yaroslavl	D	261	4	20	24	261
6	Cgy.	Rico Fata	London	RW	100	7	13	20	26
7	NYR	Manny Malhotra	Guelph	C	281	23	29	52	137
8	Chi.	Mark Bell	Ottawa	C	175	26	32	58	241
9	NYI	Mike Rupp	Erie	RW	Re-entered Draft in 2000				
10	Tor.	Nik Antropov	Torpedo Ust-Kamenogorsk	C	201	35	59	94	199
11	Car.	Jeff Heerema	Sarnia	RW	10	3	0	3	2
12	Col.	Alex Tanguay	Halifax	LW	310	83	160	243	131
13	Edm.	Michael Henrich	Barrie	RW					
14	Phx.	Patrick DesRochers	Sarnia	G	11	540	33	0	3.67
15	Ott.	Mathieu Chouinard	Shawinigan	G	Re-entered Draft in 2000				
16	Mtl.	Eric Chouinard	Quebec	LW	41	5	7	12	8
17	Col.	Martin Skoula	Barrie	D	325	25	72	97	168
18	Buf.	Dmitri Kalinin	Traktor Chelyabinsk	D	206	14	42	56	125
19	Col.	Robyn Regehr	Kamloops	D	281	8	28	36	296
20	Col.	Scott Parker	Kelowna	RW	202	4	10	14	462
21	L.A.	Mathieu Biron	Shawinigan	D	144	5	13	18	76
22	Phi.	Simon Gagne	Quebec	LW	228	80	93	173	72
23	Pit.	Milan Kraft	Keramika Plzen Jr.	C	141	22	20	42	34
24	St.L.	Christian Backman	Vastra Frolunda Jr.	D	4	0	0	0	0
25	Det.	Jiri Fischer	Hull	D	202	4	29	33	187
26	N.J.	Mike Van Ryn	U. of Michigan	D	69	2	11	13	26
27	N.J.	Scott Gomez	Tri-City	C	314	56	180	236	208

SECOND ROUND

PICK	TEAM	NAME	DRAFTED FROM	NHL PLAYERS: POS / NHL GOALTENDERS: POS	GP / GP	G / W	A / GA	PTS / SO	PIM / AVG
28	Col.	Ramzi Abid	Chicoutimi	LW	Re-entered Draft in 2000				
29	S.J.	Jonathan Cheechoo	Belleville	RW	66	9	7	16	39
30	Fla.	Kyle Rossiter	Spokane	D	5	0	0	0	2
31	Van.	Artem Chubarov	Dynamo	C	163	13	26	39	26
32	Ana.	Stephen Peat	Red Deer	D	65	3	2	5	142
33	Cgy.	Blair Betts	Prince George	C	15	2	3	5	2
34	Buf.	Andrew Peters	Oshawa	LW					
35	Tor.	Petr Svoboda	Havlickuv Brod	D	18	1	2	3	10
36	NYI	Chris Nielsen	Calgary	RW	52	6	8	14	8
37	N.J.	Christian Berglund	Farjestad Karlstad Jr.	LW	53	6	12	18	28
38	Col.	Philippe Sauve	Rimouski	G					
39	Dal.	John Erskine	London	D	49	2	1	3	91
40	NYR	Randy Copley	Cape Breton	RW					
41	St.L.	Maxim Linnik	St. Thomas Jr. B	D					
42	Phi.	Jason Beckett	Seattle	D					
43	Phx.	Ossi Vaananen	Jokerit Helsinki Jr.	D	224	8	31	39	246
44	Ott.	Mike Fisher	Sudbury	C	224	44	46	90	170
45	Mtl.	Mike Ribeiro	Rouyn-Noranda	C	116	14	23	37	22
46	L.A.	Justin Papineau	Belleville	C	Re-entered Draft in 2000				
47	Buf.	Norm Milley	Laval	RW	13	0	3	3	6
48	Bos.	Jonathan Girard	Laval	D	150	10	34	44	46
49	Wsh.	Jomar Cruz	Brandon	G					
50	Buf.	Jaroslav Kristek	ZPS Zlin	RW	6	0	0	0	4
51	Phi.	Ian Forbes	Guelph	D					
52	Bos.	Bobby Allen	Boston College	D	1	0	0	0	0
53	Col.	Steve Moore	Harvard	C	12	0	0	0	4
54	Pit.	Alexander Zevakhin	CSKA	LW					
55	Det.	Ryan Barnes	Sudbury	LW					
56	Det.	Tomek Valtonen	Ilves Tampere Jr.	LW					
57	Dal.	Tyler Bouck	Prince George	C	55	2	5	7	33
58	Ott.	Chris Bala	Harvard	LW	6	0	1	1	0

OTHER ROUNDS

PICK	TEAM	NAME	DRAFTED FROM	NHL PLAYERS: POS / NHL GOALTENDERS: POS	GP / GP	G / W	A / GA	PTS / SO	PIM / AVG
59	Wsh.	Todd Hornung	Portland	C					
60	Nsh.	Denis Arkhipov	Ak Bars Kazan	C	201	37	53	90	52
61	Fla.	Joe DiPenta	Boston U.	D	3	1	1	2	0
62	Cgy.	Paul Manning	Colorado College	D	8	0	0	0	2
63	Fla.	Lance Ward	Red Deer	D	163	4	8	12	297
64	T.B.	Brad Richards	Rimouski	C	244	58	140	198	51
65	S.J.	Eric Laplante	Halifax	LW					
66	NYR	Jason Labarbera	Portland	G	1	10	0	0	0.00
67	Edm.	Alex Henry	London	D	41	0	0	0	80
68	Van.	Jarkko Ruutu	HIFK Helsinki	RW	114	7	13	20	178
69	Tor.	Jamie Hodson	Brandon	G					
70	Car.	Kevin Holdridge	Plymouth	D					
71	Car.	Erik Cole	Clarkson	LW	134	30	37	67	107
72	T.B.	Dmitry Afanasenkov	Torpedo-2 Yaroslavl	LW	14	1	1	2	4
73	Phx.	Pat O'Leary	Robbinsdale-Armstrong H.S.	C					
74	Ott.	Julien Vauclair	Lugano	D					
75	Mtl.	Francois Beauchemin	Laval	D	1	0	0	0	0
76	L.A.	Alexei Volkov	Krylja Sovetov-2	G					
77	Buf.	Mike Pandolfo	St. Sebastian's	LW					
78	Bos.	Peter Nordstrom	Farjestad Karlstad Jr.	C	2	0	0	0	0
79	Col.	Yevgeny Lazarev	Kitchener Jr. B	LW					
80	Pit.	David Cameron	Prince Albert	C					
81	Van.	Justin Morrison	Colorado College	RW					
82	N.J.	Brian Gionta	Boston College	RW	91	16	20	36	31
83	St.L.	Matt Walker	Portland	D	16	0	1	1	38
84	Det.	Jake McCracken	Sault Ste. Marie	G					
85	Nsh.	Geoff Koch	U. of Michigan	LW					
86	Dal.	Gabriel Karlsson	HV 71 Jonkoping Jr.	C					
87	Tor.	Alexei Ponikarovsky	Dynamo-2	LW	43	3	6	9	25
88	Nsh.	Kent Sauer	North Iowa Jr. A.	D					
89	Fla.	Ryan Jardine	Sault Ste. Marie	LW	8	0	2	2	2
90	Van.	Regan Darby	Tri-City	D					
91	Car.	Josef Vasicek	Slavia Praha Jr.	C	211	32	40	72	139
92	T.B.	Eric Beaudoin	Guelph	LW	23	1	4	5	29
93	Car.	Tommy Westlund	Brynas Gavle	RW	203	9	13	22	48
94	Chi.	Matthias Trattnig	U. of Maine	C					
95	NYI	Andy Burnham	Windsor	RW					
96	N.J.	Mikko Jokela	HIFK Helsinki	D	1	0	0	0	0
97	Car.	Chris Madden	Guelph	G					
98	S.J.	Rob Davison	North Bay	D	15	1	2	3	22
99	Edm.	Shawn Horcoff	Michigan State	C	188	29	42	71	83
100	Phx.	Ryan Vanbuskirk	Sarnia	D	Re-entered Draft in 2000				
101	Ott.	Petr Schastlivy	Torpedo Yaroslavl	LW	64	14	18	32	12
102	Cgy.	Shaun Sutter	Lethbridge	RW					
103	L.A.	Kip Brennan	Sudbury	LW	23	0	0	0	79
104	S.J.	Miroslav Zalesak	Plastika Nitra	RW	10	1	2	3	0
105	N.J.	Pierre Dagenais	Rouyn-Noranda	RW	60	13	6	19	18
106	Wsh.	Krys Barch	London	LW					
107	Wsh.	Chris Corrinet	Princeton	RW	8	0	1	1	6
108	Cgy.	Dany Sabourin	Sherbrooke	G					
109	Phi.	Jean-Philippe Morin	Drummondville	D					
110	Pit.	Scott Myers	Prince George	G					
111	Det.	Brent Hobday	Moose Jaw	C					
112	Ana.	Viktor Wallin	HV 71 Jonkoping Jr.	D					
113	Edm.	Kristian Antila	Ilves Tampere	G					
114	NYR	Boyd Kane	Regina	LW					
115	Phx.	Jay Leach	Providence College	D					
116	Phx.	Josh Blackburn	Lincoln Jr. A.	G					
117	Fla.	Jaroslav Spacek	Farjestad Karlstad	D	362	34	106	140	232
118	Wsh.	Mike Siklenka	Lloydminster	RW	1	0	0	0	0
119	N.J.	Anton But	Torpedo Yaroslavl 2	LW					
120	Cgy.	Brent Gauvreau	Oshawa	RW	Re-entered Draft in 2000				
121	T.B.	Curtis Rich	Calgary	D					
122	NYR	Patrick Leahy	Miami of Ohio	RW					
123	NYI	Jiri Dopita	DS Olomouc	C	73	12	21	33	19
124	Phi.	Francis Belanger	Rimouski	LW	10	0	0	0	29
125	Wsh.	Erik Wendell	Maple Grove H.S.	C					
126	Tor.	Morgan Warren	Moncton	RW					
127	S.J.	Brandon Coalter	Oshawa	LW					
128	Edm.	Paul Elliott	Medicine Hat	D					
129	Phx.	Robert Schnabel	Slavia Praha	D	2	0	0	0	0
130	Ott.	Gavin McLeod	Kelowna	D					
131	NYR	Tomas Kloucek	Slavia Praha Jr.	D	98	2	7	9	213
132	Mtl.	Andrei Bashkirov	Fort Wayne/Las Vegas	LW	30	0	3	3	0
133	L.A.	Joe Rullier	Rimouski	D					
134	Pit.	Rob Scuderi	Boston College	D					
135	Bos.	Andrew Raycroft	Sudbury	G	21	1014	47	0	2.78
136	Van.	David Ytfeldt	Leksand	D					
137	Buf.	Aaron Goldade	Brandon	C					
138	Nsh.	Martin Beauchesne	Sherbrooke	D					
139	Phi.	Garrett Prosofsky	Saskatoon	C					
140	Van.	Rick Bertran	Kitchener	D					
141	Col.	K.C. Timmons	Tri-City	LW					
142	Det.	Calle Steen	Hammarby	RW					
143	N.J.	Ryan Flinn	Laval	LW	29	1	0	1	79
144	Edm.	Oleg Smirnov	Kristall Elektrostal	LW					
145	S.J.	Mikael Samuelsson	Sodertalje	RW	151	16	24	40	63

PICK	TEAM	NAME	DRAFTED FROM	NHL PLAYERS: POS / NHL GOALTENDERS: POS	GP / GP	G / W	A / GA	PTS / SO	PIM / AVG
146	T.B.	Sergei Kuznetsov	Torpedo Yaroslavl 2	C					
147	Nsh.	Craig Brunel	Prince Albert	RW	Re-entered Draft in 1999				
148	Fla.	Chris Ovington	Red Deer	D					
149	Van.	Paul Cabana	Fort McMurray	LW					
150	Ana.	Trent Hunter	Prince George	RW	8	0	4	4	4
151	Det.	Adam DeLeeuw	Barrie	LW					
152	Mtl.	Gordie Dwyer	Beauport	LW	106	0	5	5	387
153	Dal.	Pavel Patera	AIK Solna	C	32	2	7	9	8
154	Tor.	Allan Rourke	Kitchener	D					
155	NYI	Kevin Clauson	Western Michigan	D					
156	Chi.	Kent Huskins	Clarkson	D					
157	St.L.	Brad Voth	Medicine Hat	D					
158	Chi.	Jari Viuhkola	Karpat Oulu	C					
159	Edm.	Trevor Ettinger	Cape Breton	D					
160	Phx.	Rickard Wallin	Farjestad Karlstad Jr.	C	4	1	0	1	0
161	Ott.	Chris Neil	North Bay	RW	140	16	11	27	378
162	Mtl.	Andrei Markov	Khimik Voskresensk	D	198	24	60	84	76
163	L.A.	Tomas Zizka	ZPS Zlin	D	10	0	3	3	4
164	Buf.	Ales Kotalik	Ceske Budejovice Jr.	RW	81	22	17	39	32
165	Bos.	Ryan Milanovic	Kitchener	LW					
166	Chi.	Jonathan Pelletier	Drummondville	G					
167	Col.	Alexander Riazantsev	Victoriaville	D					
168	Phi.	Antero Niittymaki	TPS Turku Jr.	G					
169	Pit.	Jan Fadrny	Slavia Praha	C					
170	St.L.	Andrei Troschinsky	Kamenogorsk	C					
171	Det.	Pavel Datsyuk	Dynamo-E. Yeka'burg	C	134	23	63	86	20
172	N.J.	Jacques Lariviere	Moncton	LW					
173	Dal.	Niko Kapanen	HPK Hameenlinna	C	91	5	30	35	46
174	T.B.	Brett Allan	Swift Current	C					
175	Phi.	Cam Ondrik	Medicine Hat	G					
176	Fla.	B.J. Ketcheson	Peterborough	D					
177	Van.	Vincent Malts	Hull	RW					
178	Ana.	Jesse Fibiger	U. Minn-Duluth	D	16	0	0	0	2
179	Wsh.	Nate Forster	Seattle	D					
180	NYR	Stefan Lundqvist	Brynas Gavle	RW					
181	Tor.	Jonathan Gagnon	Cape Breton	C					
182	NYI	Evgeny Korolev	London	D	42	1	4	5	20
183	Chi.	Tyler Arnason	St. Cloud St.	C	103	22	21	43	24
184	Car.	Don Smith	Clarkson	C					
185	S.J.	Robert Mulick	Sault Ste. Marie	D					
186	Edm.	Mike Morrison	U. of Maine	G					
187	Phx.	Erik Westrum	U. of Minnesota	C					
188	Ott.	Michel Periard	Shawinigan	D					
189	Mtl.	Andrei Kruchinin	Lada Togliatti	D					
190	L.A.	Tommi Hannus	TPS Turku Jr.	LW					
191	Buf.	Brad Moran	Calgary	C	3	0	0	0	0
192	Cgy.	Radek Duda	Sparta Praha	RW					
193	Wsh.	Ratislav Stana	HC Kosice	G					
194	T.B.	Oak Hewer	North Bay	C					
195	Phi.	Tomas Divisek	Slavia Praha	C	5	1	0	1	0
196	Pit.	Joel Scherban	London	C					
197	St.L.	Brad Twordik	Brandon	C					
198	Det.	Jeremy Goetzinger	Prince Albert	D					
199	N.J.	Erik Jensen	Des Moines (USHL)	RW					
200	Dal.	Scott Perry	Boston U.	C					
201	Mtl.	Craig Murray	U. of Michigan	C					
202	Nsh.	Martin Bartek	Sherbrooke	C					
203	Fla.	Ian Jacobs	Ottawa	RW					
204	Van.	Greg Mischler	Northeastern	C					
205	Ana.	David Bernier	Quebec	C					
206	Cgy.	Jonas Frogren	Farjestad	D					
207	NYR	Johan Witehall	Leksandden	LW	54	2	5	7	16
208	Car.	Jaroslav Svoboda	HC Olomouc	LW	58	5	13	18	34
209	NYI	Frederik Brindamour	Sherbrooke	G					
210	Chi.	Sean Griffin	Kingston	D					
211	Car.	Mark Kosick	U. of Michigan	C					
212	S.J.	Jim Fahey	Northeastern	D	43	1	19	20	33
213	Edm.	Christian Lefebvre	Granby	D					
214	Phx.	Justin Hansen	Prince George	RW					
215	Tor.	Dwight Wolfe	Halifax	D					
216	Mtl.	Michael Ryder	Hull	RW					
217	L.A.	Jim Henkel	Ottawa	C					
218	Buf.	David Moravec	HC Vitkovice	RW	1	0	0	0	0
219	Van.	Curtis Valentine	Bowling Green	LW					
220	Wsh.	Michael Farrell	Providence	RW	12	0	0	0	2
221	T.B.	Daniel Hulak	Swift Current	D					
222	Phi.	Lubomir Pistek	Kelowna	RW					
223	Ott.	Sergei Verenikin	Yaroslavl	RW					
224	Pit.	Mika Lehto	Assat Pori	G					
225	St.L.	Yevgeny Pastukh	Khimik	LW					
226	Det.	David Petrasek	HV 71	D					
227	N.J.	Marko Ahosilta	KalPa	C					
228	Tor.	Michal Travnicek	Litvinov	RW					
229	T.B.	Chris Lyness	Cape Breton	D					
230	Nsh.	Karlis Skrastins	TPS Turku	D	307	13	41	54	130
231	Fla.	Adrian Wichser	EHC Kloten	C					
232	Van.	Jason Metcalfe	London	D					
233	Ana.	Pelle Prestberg	Farjestad	LW					
234	Cgy.	Kevin Mitchell	Guelph	D					
235	NYR	Jan Mertzig	Lulea	D	23	0	2	2	8
236	Tor.	Sergei Rostov	Dynamo-2	D					
237	NYI	Ben Blais	Walpole H.S.	D					
238	Chi.	Alexandre Couture	Sherbrooke	LW					
239	Car.	Brent McDonald	Prince George	C					
240	Chi.	Andrei Yershov	Khimik	D					
241	Edm.	Maxim Spiridonov	London	LW					
242	NYI	Jason Doyle	Sault Ste. Marie	RW					
243	Phi.	Petr Hubacek	Kometa Brno	C	6	1	0	1	2
244	Pit.	Toby Petersen	Colorado College	C	91	10	16	26	8
245	Ana.	Andreas Andersson	HV 71	G					
246	Ott.	Rastislav Pavlikovsky	Dukla Trencin	LW					
247	Mtl.	Darcy Harris	Kitchener	RW					
248	L.A.	Matthew Yeats	Olds Jr. A	G					
249	Buf.	Edo Terglav	Baie-Comeau	RW					
250	NYI	Radek Matejovsky	Slavia Praha	RW					
251	Wsh.	Blake Evans	Tri-City	C					
252	T.B.	Martin Cibak	Medicine Hat	C	26	1	5	6	8
253	Phi.	Bruno St. Jacques	Baie-Comeau	D	31	2	5	7	16
254	Pit.	Matt Hussey	Avon Old Farms H.S.	C					
255	St.L.	John Pohl	U. of Minnesota	C					
256	Det.	Petja Pietilainen	Saskatoon	LW					
257	N.J.	Ryan Held	Kitchener	C					
258	Phi.	Sergei Skrobot	Dynamo-2	D					

1999

FIRST ROUND

PICK	TEAM	NAME	DRAFTED FROM	POS	GP	G / W	A / GA	PTS / SO	PIM / AVG
1	Atl.	Patrik Stefan	Long Beach	C	268	35	78	113	86
2	Van.	Daniel Sedin	MoDo	LW	233	43	54	97	90
3	Van.	Henrik Sedin	MoDo	C	242	33	71	104	112
4	NYR	Pavel Brendl	Calgary	RW	58	6	8	14	8
5	NYI	Tim Connolly	Erie	C	325	46	99	145	152
6	Nsh.	Brian Finley	Barrie	G	1	47	3	0	3.83
7	Wsh.	Kris Beech	Calgary	C	95	10	16	26	53
8	NYI	Taylor Pyatt	Sudbury	LW	204	28	38	66	112
9	NYR	Jamie Lundmark	Moose Jaw	C	55	8	11	19	16
10	NYI	Branislav Mezei	Belleville	D	77	3	6	9	75
11	Cgy.	Oleg Saprykin	Seattle	LW	118	17	30	47	91
12	Fla.	Denis Shvidki	Barrie	RW	74	11	14	25	30
13	Edm.	Jani Rita	Jokerit	LW	13	3	1	4	0
14	S.J.	Jeff Jillson	U. of Michigan	D	74	5	19	24	38
15	Phx.	Scott Kelman	Seattle	C					
16	Car.	David Tanabe	Wisconsin	D	251	15	47	62	115
17	St.L.	Barret Jackman	Regina	D	83	3	16	19	190
18	Pit.	Konstantin Koltsov	Cherepovets	RW	2	0	0	0	0
19	Phx.	Kirill Safronov	St. Petersburg	D	35	2	2	4	16
20	Buf.	Barrett Heisten	U. of Maine	LW	10	0	0	0	2
21	Bos.	Nick Boynton	Ottawa	D	164	11	31	42	206
22	Phi.	Maxime Ouellet	Quebec	G	2	76	3	0	2.37
23	Chi.	Steve McCarthy	Kootenay	D	109	2	10	12	37
24	Tor.	Luca Cereda	Ambri	C					
25	Col.	Mikhail Kuleshov	Cherepovets	LW					
26	Ott.	Martin Havlat	Trinec	LW	212	65	86	151	116
27	N.J.	Ari Ahonen	JyP HT Jr.	G					
28	NYI	Kristian Kudroc	Michalovce	D	24	2	2	4	36

SECOND ROUND

PICK	TEAM	NAME	DRAFTED FROM	POS	GP	G	A	PTS	PIM
29	Wsh.	Michal Sivek	Kladno	C	38	3	3	6	14
30	Atl.	Luke Sellars	Ottawa	D	1	0	0	0	2
31	Wsh.	Charlie Stephens	Guelph	C/RW	Re-entered Draft in 2001				
32	Dal.	Michael Ryan	Boston College H.S.	C					
33	Nsh.	Jonas Andersson	AIK Solna Jr.	RW	5	0	0	0	2

PICK	TEAM	NAME	DRAFTED FROM	NHL PLAYERS: POS / NHL GOALTENDERS: POS	GP / GP	G / W	A / GA	PTS / SO	PIM / AVG
34	Wsh.	Ross Lupaschuk	Prince Albert	D	3	0	0	0	4
35	Buf.	Milan Bartovic	Dukla Trencin Jr.	RW	3	1	0	1	0
36	Edm.	Alexei Semenov	Sudbury	D	46	1	6	7	58
37	Wsh.	Nolan Yonkman	Kelowna	D	11	1	0	1	4
38	Cgy.	Dan Cavanaugh	Boston University	C					
39	Mtl.	Alexander Buturlin	CSKA	RW					
40	Fla.	Alexander Auld	North Bay	G	8	442	12	1	1.63
41	Edm.	Tony Salmelainen	HIFK	LW					
42	N.J.	Mike Commodore	North Dakota	D	63	1	6	7	63
43	L.A.	Andrei Shefer	Cherepovets	LW					
44	Ana.	Jordan Leopold	U. of Minnesota	D	58	4	10	14	12
45	Col.	Martin Grenier	Quebec	D	8	0	0	0	5
46	Chi.	Dimitri Levinski	Cherepovets	LW					
47	T.B.	Sheldon Keefe	Barrie	RW	125	12	12	24	78
48	Ott.	Simon Lajeunesse	Moncton	G	1	24	0	0	0.00
49	Car.	Brett Lysak	Regina	C					
50	N.J.	Brett Clouthier	Kingston	LW					
51	Pit.	Matt Murley	RPI	LW					
52	Nsh.	Adam Hall	Michigan State	RW	80	16	13	29	31
53	Phx.	Brad Ralph	Oshawa	LW	1	0	0	0	0
54	Nsh.	Andrew Hutchinson	Michigan State	D					
55	Buf.	Doug Janik	U. of Maine	D	6	0	0	0	2
56	Bos.	Matt Zultek	Ottawa	LW					
57	Pit.	Jeremy Van Hoof	Ottawa	D	Re-entered Draft in 2001				
58	Mtl.	Matt Carkner	Peterborough	D					
59	NYR	David Inman	U. of Notre Dame	C					
60	Tor.	Peter Reynolds	London	D	Re-entered Draft in 2001				
61	Nsh.	Ed Hill	Barrie	D					
62	Ott.	Teemu Sainomaa	Jokerit Jr.	LW					
63	Chi.	Stepan Mokhov	Cherepovets	D					
64	Buf.	Mike Zigomanis	Kingston	C	Re-entered Draft in 2001				
65	Nsh.	Jan Lasak	Zvolen	G	6	267	18	0	4.04
66	Dal.	Dan Jancevski	London	D					

SECOND ROUND

PICK	TEAM	NAME	DRAFTED FROM	POS	GP	G / W	A / GA	PTS / SO	PIM / AVG
67	T.B.	Evgeny Konstantinov	Kazan 2	G	2	21	1	0	2.86
68	Atl.	Zdenek Blatny	Seattle	LW	4	0	0	0	0
69	Van.	Rene Vydareny	Bratislava Jr.	D					
70	Fla.	Niklas Hagman	HIFK	LW	158	18	33	51	28
71	Phx.	Jason Jaspers	Sudbury	C	6	0	1	1	4
72	Nsh.	Brett Angel	North Bay	D					
73	Buf.	Tim Preston	Seattle	LW					
74	L.A.	Jason Crain	Ohio State	D					
75	T.B.	Brett Scheffelmaier	Medicine Hat	D	Re-entered Draft in 2001				
76	L.A.	Frantisek Kaberle	MoDo	D	242	17	65	82	84
77	Cgy.	Craig Andersson	Guelph	G	Re-entered Draft in 2001				
78	NYI	Mattias Weinhandl	Troja-Ljungby	RW	47	6	17	23	10
79	NYR	Johan Asplund	Brynas Gavle	G					
80	Fla.	Jean-Francois Laniel	Shawinigan	G					
81	Edm.	Adam Hauser	U. of Minnesota	G					
82	S.J.	Mark Concannon	Winchendon H.S.	LW					
83	Ana.	Niclas Havelid	Malmo	D	231	18	41	59	124
84	Car.	Brad Fast	Prince George - TII	D					
85	St.L.	Peter Smrek	Des Moines	D	28	2	4	6	18
86	Pit.	Sebastian Caron	Rimouski	G	24	1408	62	2	2.64
87	NYI	Brian Collins	St. John's H.S.	C					
88	T.B.	Jimmie Olvestad	Djurgarden	LW	111	3	14	17	40
89	Bos.	Kyle Wanvig	Kootenay	RW	Re-entered Draft in 2001				
90	NYR	Patrick Aufiero	Boston University	D					
91	Edm.	Mike Comrie	Michigan	C	192	61	72	133	149
92	L.A.	Cory Campbell	Belleville	G					
93	Col.	Branko Radivojevic	Belleville	RW	97	16	17	33	67
94	Ott.	Chris Kelly	London	C/LW					
95	N.J.	Andre Lakos	Barrie	D					
96	Dal.	Mathias Tjarnqvist	Rogle	RW					
97	Mtl.	Chris Dyment	Boston University	D					
98	Atl.	David Kaczowka	Seattle	LW					
99	Atl.	Rob Zepp	Plymouth	G	Re-entered Draft in 2001				
100	N.J.	Teemu Kesa	Ilves Jr.	D					
101	NYI	Juraj Kolnik	Rimouski	RW	46	6	4	10	12
102	NYI	Johan Halvardsson	HV 71	D					
103	Fla.	Morgan McCormick	Kingston	RW					
104	L.A.	Brian McGrattan	Sudbury	RW					
105	Ana.	Alexandr Chagodayev	HC CSKA	C					
106	Cgy.	Rail Rozakov	Lada Togliatti 2	D					
107	Mtl.	Evan Lindsay	Prince Albert	G					
108	Tor.	Mirko Murovic	Moncton	LW					
109	Fla.	Rod Sarich	Calgary	D					
110	Tor.	Jon Zion	Ottawa	D					
111	S.J.	Willie Levesque	Northeastern	RW					
112	Col.	Sanny Lindstrom	Huddinge	D					
113	Car.	Ryan Murphy	Bowling Green	LW					
114	St.L.	Chad Starling	Kamloops	D					
115	Pit.	Ryan Malone	Omaha	LW					
116	Phx.	Ryan Lauzon	Hull	C					
117	Buf.	Karel Mosovsky	Regina	LW					
118	Bos.	Jaakko Harikkala	Lukko	D					
119	Phi.	Jeff Feniak	Calgary	D					
120	Det.	Jari Tolsa	Frolunda Jr.	C					
121	Nsh.	Yevgeny Pavlov	Lada Togliatti	RW					
122	Col.	Kristian Kovac	Kosice Jr.	RW					
123	Phx.	Preston Mizzi	Peterborough	C					
124	Nsh.	Alexandre Krevsun	Samara	RW					
125	L.A.	Daniel Johansson	MoDo Jr.	C					
126	Dal.	Jeff Bateman	Brampton	C					
127	T.B.	Kaspars Astashenko	Cincinnati (IHL)	D/W	23	1	2	3	8
128	Atl.	Derek MacKenzie	Sudbury	C	1	0	0	0	2
129	Van.	Ryan Thorpe	Spokane	LW					
130	NYI	Justin Mapletoft	Red Deer	C	11	2	2	4	2
131	Nsh.	Konstantin Panov	Kamloops	LW					
132	Wsh.	Roman Tvrdon	Dukla Trencin Jr.	C					
133	L.A.	Jean-Francois Nogues	Victoriaville	G					
134	Chi.	Michael Jacobsen	Belleville	D					
135	Cgy.	Matt Doman	U. of Wisconsin	RW					
136	Mtl.	Dusty Jamieson	Sarnia	LW					
137	NYR	Garrett Bembridge	Saskatoon	RW	Re-entered Draft in 2001				
138	Buf.	Ryan Miller	Soo Indians	G	15	912	40	1	2.63
139	Edm.	Jonathan Fauteux	Val d'Or	D					
140	NYI	Adam Johnson	Greenway	D					
141	Ana.	Maxim Rybin	Spartak	LW					
142	Col.	Will Magnuson	Lake Superior U.	D					
143	St.L.	Trevor Byrne	Deerfield Academy	D					
144	Pit.	Tomas Skvaridlo	Zvolen Jr.	C					
145	Mtl.	Marc-Andre Thinel	Victoriaville	RW					
146	Buf.	Matt Kinch	Calgary	D					
147	Bos.	Seamus Kotyk	Ottawa	G					
148	T.B.	Michal Lanicek	Slavia Praha Jr.	G					
149	Det.	Andrei Maximenko	Soviet Wings	LW					
150	Mtl.	Matt Shasby	Des Moines	D					
151	Tor.	Vaclav Zavoral	Litvinov Jr.	D					
152	Col.	Jordan Krestanovich	Calgary	LW	8	0	2	2	0
153	Cgy.	Jesse Cook	U. of Denver	D					
154	Ott.	Andrew Ianiero	Kingston	LW					
155	S.J.	Nico Dimitrakos	U. of Maine	RW	21	6	7	13	8
156	Dal.	Gregor Baumgartner	Acadie-Bathurst	LW					
157	Pit.	Vladimir Malenkikh	Lada Togliatti	D					
158	Col.	Anders Lovdahl	HV 71 Jr.	C					
159	Atl.	Yuri Dobryshkin	Soviet Wings	LW					
160	Phi.	Konstantin Rudenko	Cherepovets 2	LW					
161	Tor.	Jan Sochor	Slavia Praha	LW					
162	Nsh.	Timo Helbling	Davos	D					
163	NYI	Bjorn Melin	HV 71 Jr.	RW					
164	Ott.	Martin Prusek	HC Vitkovice	G	19	997	40	0	2.41
165	Chi.	Michael Leighton	Windsor	G	8	447	21	1	2.82
166	Cgy.	Cory Pecker	Sault Ste. Marie	C					
167	Mtl.	Sean Dixon	Erie	D					
168	Phx.	Erik Lewerstrom	Grums	D					
169	Fla.	Brad Woods	Brampton	D					
170	Cgy.	Matt Underhill	Cornell	G					
171	Edm.	Chris Legg	London, Jr. B	C					
172	Van.	Josh Reed	Vernon	D					
173	Ana.	Jan Sandstrom	AIK Solna	D					
174	Car.	Damian Surma	Plymouth	C	1	1	0	1	0
175	Wsh.	Kyle Clark	Harvard U.	RW					
176	Pit.	Doug Meyer	U. of Minnesota	LW					
177	NYR	Jay Dardis	Proctor	C					
178	Buf.	Seneque Hyacinthe	Val d'Or	LW					
179	Bos.	Donald Choukalos	Regina	G					
180	St.L.	Tore Vikingstad	Farjestad	LW					
181	Det.	Kent McDonell	Guelph	RW	3	0	0	0	0
182	T.B.	Fedor Fedorov	Port Huron	C	Re-entered Draft in 2001				
183	Col.	Riku Hahl	HPK	C	64	5	7	12	26

PICK	TEAM	NAME	DRAFTED FROM	NHL PLAYERS: POS	GP	G	A	PTS	PIM
				NHL GOALTENDERS: POS	GP	W	GA	SO	AVG
184	Dal.	Justin Cox	Prince George	RW					
185	N.J.	Scott Cameron	Barrie	C					
186	Dal.	Brett Draney	Kamloops	LW					
187	T.B.	Ivan Rachunek	ZPS Zlin Jr.	LW					
188	Atl.	Stephan Baby	Green Bay	RW					
189	Van.	Kevin Swanson	Kelowna	G					
190	Cgy.	Blair Stayzer	Windsor	LW					
191	Nsh.	Martin Erat	ZPS Zlin Jr.	LW	107	10	31	41	46
192	Wsh.	David Bornhammar	AIK Solna Jr.	D					
193	L.A.	Kevin Baker	Belleville	RW					
194	Chi.	Mattias Wennerberg	MoDo Jr.	C					
195	Chi.	Yorick Treille	U. of Mass.-Lowell	RW					
196	Mtl.	Vadim Tarasov	Novokuznetsk	G					
197	NYR	Arto Laatikainen	Espoo	D					
198	Fla.	Travis Eagles	Prince George	RW					
199	Edm.	Chris Chartier	Saskatoon	D					
200	Phi.	Pavel Kasparik	Pisek	C					
201	Ott.	Mikko Ruutu	HIFK	LW					
202	Car.	Jim Baxter	Oshawa	D					
203	St.L.	Phil Osaer	Ferris State	G					
204	Pit.	Tom Kostopoulos	London	RW	19	1	3	4	9
205	Nsh.	Kyle Kettles	Neepawa	G					
206	Buf.	Bret DeCecco	Seattle	RW					
207	Bos.	Greg Barber	Victoria	RW					
208	Phi.	Vaclav Pletka	Trinec	RW	1	0	0	0	0
209	Ott.	Layne Ulmer	Swift Current	C					
210	Det.	Henrik Zetterberg	Timra	LW	79	22	22	44	8
211	Tor.	Vladimir Kulikov	HC CSKA	G					
212	Col.	Radim Vrbata	Hull	RW	128	34	31	65	32
213	Ott.	Alexandre Giroux	Hull	C/LW					
214	N.J.	Chris Hartsburg	Colorado Coll.	RW					
215	Dal.	Jeff MacMillan	Oshawa	D					
216	T.B.	Erkki Rajamaki	HIFK	LW					
217	Atl.	Garnet Exelby	Saskatoon	D	15	0	2	2	41
218	Van.	Markus Kankaanpera	JyP HT	D					
219	Wsh.	Maxim Orlov	CSKA	C					
220	Nsh.	Miroslav Durak	Bratislava Jr.	D					
221	St.L.	Colin Hemingway	Surrey	RW					
222	L.A.	George Parros	Chicago	RW					
223	Chi.	Andrew Carver	Hull	D					
224	Phi.	David Nystrom	Frolunda Jr.	LW					
225	Mtl.	Mikko Hyytia	JyP HT Jr.	C					
226	NYR	Yevgeny Gusakov	Lada Togliatti 2	RW					
227	Fla.	Jonathon Charron	Val d'Or	G					
228	NYI	Radek Martinek	Budejovice	D	89	3	15	18	42
229	S.J.	Eric Betournay	Acadie-Bathurst	C					
230	Ana.	Petr Tenkrat	Kladno	RW	113	13	25	38	50
231	Car.	David Evans	Clarkson	RW					
232	St.L.	Alexander Khavanov	Dynamo	D	236	18	62	80	155
233	Pit.	Darcy Robinson	Saskatoon	D					
234	Phx.	Goran Bezina	Fribourg	D					
235	Buf.	Brad Self	Peterborough	C					
236	Bos.	John Cronin	Boston U.	D					
237	Car.	Antti Jokela	Lukko Jr.	G					
238	Det.	Anton Borodkin	Kamloops	LW					
239	Tor.	Pierre Hedin	MoDo	D					
240	Col.	Jeff Finger	Green Bay	D					
241	S.J.	Doug Murray	Applecore	D					
242	N.J.	Justin Dziama	Nobles Prep.	RW					
243	Dal.	Brian Sullivan	Thayer Acad.	D					
244	T.B.	Mikko Kuparinen	Grand Rapids	D					
245	Atl.	Tommi Santala	Jokerit	C					
246	Atl.	Raymond DiLauro	St. Lawrence	D					
247	Bos.	Mikko Eloranta	TPS Turku	LW	264	32	44	76	186
248	Nsh.	Darren Haydar	New Hampshire	RW	2	0	0	0	0
249	Wsh.	Igor Schadilov	Dynamo	D					
250	L.A.	Noah Clarke	Des Moines	LW					
251	NYR	Petter Henning	MoDo	RW					
252	Cgy.	Dmitri Kirilenko	CSKA	C					
253	Mtl.	Jerome Marois	Quebec	LW					
254	NYR	Alexei Bulatov	Yekaterinburg	RW					
255	NYI	Brett Henning	U. of Notre Dame	C					
256	Edm.	Tamas Groschl	UTE Budapest	RW					
257	S.J.	Hannes Hyvonen	Espoo	RW	42	4	5	9	22
258	Ana.	Brian Gornick	Air Force	C					
259	Car.	Yevgeny Kurilin	Anchorage	C					
260	St.L.	Brian McMeekin	Cornell	D					
261	Pit.	Andrew McPherson	R.P.I.	LW					
262	Phx.	Alexei Litvinenko	Ust-Kamenogorsk	D					
263	Buf.	Craig Brunel	Prince Albert	RW					
264	Bos.	Georgy Pujacs	Dynamo-81 Riga	D					
265	Dal.	Jamie Chamberlain	Peterborough	RW					
266	Det.	Ken Davis	Portland	RW					
267	Tor.	Peter Metcalf	Maine	D					
268	NYI	Tyler Scott	Upper Canada	D					
269	Ott.	Konstantin Gorovikov	St. Petersburg	LW					
270	St.L.	James Desmarais	Rouyn Noranda	C					
271	Van.	Darrell Hay	Tri-City	D					
272	Dal.	Mikhail Donika	Yaroslavl	D					

2000

FIRST ROUND

PICK	TEAM	NAME	DRAFTED FROM	NHL PLAYERS: POS	GP	G	A	PTS	PIM
				NHL GOALTENDERS: POS	GP	W	GA	SO	AVG
1	NYI	Rick DiPietro	Boston University	G	30	1668	92	0	3.31
2	Atl.	Dany Heatley	U. of Wisconsin	RW	159	67	89	156	114
3	Min.	Marian Gaborik	Dukla Trencin	RW	230	78	90	168	112
4	CBJ	Rostislav Klesla	Brampton	D	155	12	22	34	151
5	NYI	Raffi Torres	Brampton	LW	31	0	6	6	16
6	Nsh.	Scott Hartnell	Prince Albert	LW	232	28	63	91	260
7	Bos.	Lars Jonsson	Leksand	D					
8	T.B.	Nikita Alexeev	Erie	RW	81	8	6	14	16
9	Cgy.	Brent Krahn	Calgary	G					
10	Chi.	Mikhail Yakubov	Lada Togliatti	C					
11	Chi.	Pavel Vorobiev	Yaroslavl	RW					
12	Ana.	Alexei Smirnov	Tver	LW	44	3	2	5	18
13	Mtl.	Ron Hainsey	U. of Mass-Lowell	D	21	0	0	0	2
14	Col.	Vaclav Nedorost	Budejovice	C	67	6	7	13	22
15	Buf.	Artem Kryukov	Yaroslavl	C					
16	Mtl.	Marcel Hossa	Portland	LW	44	9	8	17	16
17	Edm.	Alexei Mikhnov	Yaroslavl	LW					
18	Pit.	Brooks Orpik	Boston College	D	6	0	0	0	2
19	Phx.	Krys Kolanos	Boston College	C	59	11	11	22	48
20	L.A.	Alexander Frolov	Yaroslavl 2	LW	79	14	17	31	34
21	Ott.	Anton Volchenkov	HC	D	57	3	13	16	40
22	N.J.	David Hale	Sioux City	D					
23	Van.	Nathan Smith	Swift Current	C					
24	Tor.	Brad Boyes	Erie	C					
25	Dal.	Steve Ott	Windsor	C	26	3	4	7	31
26	Wsh.	Brian Sutherby	Moose Jaw	C	79	2	9	11	95
27	Bos.	Martin Samuelsson	MoDo	RW	8	0	1	1	2
28	Phi.	Justin Williams	Plymouth	RW	179	37	52	89	76
29	Det.	Niklas Kronwall	Djurgarden	D					
30	St.L.	Jeff Taffe	U. of Minnesota	C	20	3	1	4	4

SECOND ROUND

PICK	TEAM	NAME	DRAFTED FROM	NHL PLAYERS: POS	GP	G	A	PTS	PIM
				NHL GOALTENDERS: POS	GP	W	GA	SO	AVG
31	Atl.	Ilja Nikulin	Tver	D					
32	Car.	Tomas Kurka	Plymouth	LW	14	3	2	5	2
33	Min.	Nick Schultz	Prince Albert	D	127	7	13	20	37
34	T.B.	Ruslan Zainullin	Ak Bars	RW					
35	Edm.	Brad Winchester	U. of Wisconsin	LW					
36	Nsh.	Daniel Widing	Leksand	RW					
37	Bos.	Andy Hilbert	U. of Michigan	C/LW	20	1	3	4	9
38	Det.	Tomas Kopecky	Dukla Trencin	C					
39	N.J.	Teemu Laine	Jokerit	RW					
40	Cgy.	Kurtis Foster	Peterborough	D	2	0	0	0	0
41	S.J.	Tero Maatta	Jokerit	D					
42	Atl.	Libor Ustrnul	Plymouth	D					
43	Wsh.	Matt Pettinger	Calgary	LW	72	7	3	10	46
44	Ana.	Ilja Bryzgalov	Lada	G	1	32	1	0	1.88
45	Ott.	Mathieu Chouinard	Shawinigan	G					
46	Cgy.	Jarret Stoll	Kootenay	C	Re-entered Draft in 2002				
47	Col.	Jared Aulin	Kamloops	C/RW	17	2	2	4	0
48	Buf.	Gerard Dicaire	Seattle	D	Re-entered Draft in 2002				
49	Chi.	Jonas Nordqvist	Leksand	C					
50	Col.	Sergei Soin	Krylja Sovetov	C/LW					
51	Tor.	Kris Vernarsky	Plymouth	C	14	1	0	1	2
52	Pit.	Shane Endicott	Seattle	C	4	0	1	1	4
53	Phx.	Alexander Tatarinov	Yaroslavl	RW					
54	L.A.	Andreas Lilja	Malmo	D	101	5	15	20	96
55	Ott.	Antoine Vermette	Victoriaville	C					
56	N.J.	Alexander Suglobov	Yaroslavl	RW					
57	N.J.	Matt DeMarchi	U. of Minnesota	D					

PICK	TEAM	NAME	DRAFTED FROM	NHL PLAYERS: POS / NHL GOALTENDERS: POS	GP / GP	G / W	A / GA	PTS / SO	PIM / AVG
58	Fla.	Vladimir Sapozhnikov	Novokuznetsk	D					
59	Bos.	Ivan Huml	Langley	LW	42	6	12	18	30
60	Dal.	Dan Ellis	Omaha	G					
61	Wsh.	Jakub Cutta	Swift Current	D	5	0	0	0	0
62	N.J.	Paul Martin	Elk River H.S.	D					
63	Col.	Agris Saviels	Owen Sound	D					
64	NYR	Filip Novak	Regina	D					
65	St.L.	Dave Morisset	Seattle	RW	4	0	0	0	5

OTHER ROUNDS

PICK	TEAM	NAME	DRAFTED FROM	NHL PLAYERS: POS / NHL GOALTENDERS: POS	GP / GP	G / W	A / GA	PTS / SO	PIM / AVG
66	Bos.	Tuukka Makela	HIFK	D					
67	N.J.	Max Birbraer	Newmarket	RW					
68	Dal.	Joel Lundqvist	Frolunda	C					
69	CBJ	Ben Knopp	Moose Jaw	RW					
70	Tor.	Mikael Tellqvist	Djurgarden	G	3	86	4	0	2.79
71	Van.	Thatcher Bell	Rimouski	C					
72	Nsh.	Mattias Nilsson	MoDo	D					
73	Bos.	Sergei Zinovjev	Novokuznetsk	C/LW					
74	Chi.	Igor Radulov	Yaroslavl	LW	7	5	0	5	4
75	St.L.	Justin Papineau	Belleville	C	17	3	3	6	4
76	N.J.	Mike Rupp	Erie	RW	26	5	3	8	21
77	Fla.	Robert Fried	Deerfield	RW					
78	Mtl.	Josef Balej	Portland	RW					
79	Mtl.	Tyler Hanchuck	Brampton	D					
80	Car.	Ryan Bayda	U. of North Dakota	LW	25	4	10	14	16
81	T.B.	Alexander Kharitonov	Dynamo	IW	71	7	15	22	12
82	Fla.	Sean O'Connor	Moose Jaw	RW					
83	Edm.	Alexander Liubimov	Lada	D					
84	Pit.	Peter Hamerlik	Skalica	G	Re-entered Draft in 2002				
85	Phx.	Ramzi Abid	Halifax	LW	33	10	8	18	32
86	L.A.	Yanick Lehoux	Baie-Comeau	C					
87	Ott.	Jan Bohac	Slavia Praha	C					
88	Col.	Kurt Sauer	Spokane	D	80	1	2	3	74
89	Nsh.	Libor Pivko	Havirov	IW					
90	Tor.	Jean-Francois Racine	Drummondville	G					
91	Dal.	Alexei Tereshchenko	Dynamo	C					
92	Col.	Sergei Klyazmin	Dynamo	LW					
93	Van.	Tim Branham	Barrie	D					
94	Phi.	Alexander Drozdetsky	St. Petersburg	RW					
95	NYR	Dominic Moore	Harvard	C					
96	St.L.	Antoine Bergeron	Val D'Or	D					
97	Car.	Niclas Wallin	Brynas	D	166	5	13	18	128
98	Ana.	Jonas Ronnqvist	Lulea	RW	38	0	4	4	14
99	Min.	Marc Cavosie	RPI	C					
100	Tor.	Miguel Delisle	Ottawa 67's	RW					
101	NYI	Arto Tukio	Ilves	D					
102	Bos.	Brett Nowak	Harvard	C					
102	Det.	Stefan Liv	HV 71	G					
104	S.J.	Jon Disalvatore	Providence	RW					
105	NYI	Vladimir Gorbunov	HC	RW					
106	Chi.	Scott Balan	Regina	D					
107	Atl.	Carl Mallette	Victoriaville	C					
108	Atl.	Blake Robson	Portland	C					
109	Mtl.	Johan Enegvist	Leksand	LW					
110	Car.	Jared Newman	Plymouth	D					
111	Buf.	Ghyslain Rousseau	Baie-Comeau	G					
112	NYR	Premysl Duben	Jihlava	D					
113	Edm.	Lou Dickenson	Mississauga	C					
114	Mtl.	Christian Larrivee	Chicoutimi	C					
115	Fla.	Chris Eade	North Bay	D					
116	Cgy.	Levente Szuper	Ottawa	G					
117	Chi.	Olli Malmivaara	Jokerit	D					
118	L.A.	Lubomir Visnovsky	Bratislava	D	210	19	65	84	78
119	Col.	Brian Fahey	U. of Wisconsin	D					
120	Fla.	Davis Parley	Kamloops	G					
121	Wsh.	Ryan Vanbuskirk	Sarnia	D					
122	Ott.	Derrick Byfuglien	Fargo	D					
123	Dal.	Vadim Khomitsky	Moscow	D					
124	Pit.	Michel Ouellet	Rimouski	RW					
125	N.J.	Phil Cole	Lethbridge	D					
126	T.B.	Johan Hagglund	MoDo	C					
127	Det.	Dmitri Semenov	Dynamo	RW					
128	Det.	Alexander Seluyanov	Salavat Yulayev	D					
129	St.L.	Troy Riddle	Des Moines	C					
130	Det.	Aaron Van Leusen	Brampton	C					
131	Nsh.	Matt Hendricks	Blaine	C					
132	Min.	Maxim Sushinsky	Omsk	RW	30	7	4	11	29
133	CBJ	Petteri Nummelin	CBJ	D	61	4	12	16	10
134	Ana.	Peter Podhradsky	Bratislava	D					
135	N.J.	Mike Danton	Barrie	C	19	2	0	2	41
136	NYI	Dmitri Upper	Nizhny Novgorod	C					
137	Nsh.	Mike Stuart	Colorado College	D					
138	CBJ	Scott Heffernan	Sarnia	D					
139	Dal.	Ruslan Bernikov	Khabarovsk	RW					
140	NYR	Nathan Martz	Chilliwack	C					
141	Cgy.	Wade Davis	Calgary	D					
142	S.J.	Michal Pinc	Rouyn-Noranda	LW					
143	NYR	Brandon Snee	Union College	G					
144	Van.	Pavel Duma	Nizhnekamsk	C					
145	Mtl.	Ryan Glenn	Walpole	D					
146	Pit.	David Koci	Sparta	D					
147	Atl.	Matt McRae	Cornell University	C					
148	NYI	Kristofer Ottosson	Djurgarden	RW					
149	Buf.	Denis Denisov	Moscow	LW					
150	CBJ	Tyler Kolarik	Deerfield	C					
151	Chi.	Alexander Barkunov	Yaroslavl	D					
152	Edm.	Paul Flache	Brampton	D	Re-entered Draft in 2002				
153	Ana.	Bill Cass	Boston College	D					
154	Nsh.	Matt Koalska	Twin Cities	C					
155	Cgy.	Travis Moen	Kelowna	LW					
156	Ott.	Greg Zanon	U. Nebraska-Omaha	D					
157	Ott.	Grant Potulny	Lincoln	C					
158	Ott.	Sean Connolly	Northern Michigan	D					
159	Col.	John-Michael Liles	Michigan State	D					
160	Phx.	Nate Kiser	Plymouth	D					
161	T.B.	Pavel Sedov	Khimik	RW					
162	Dal.	Artem Chernov	Novokuznetsk	C					
163	Wsh.	Ivan Nepryayev	Yaroslavl	C					
164	N.J.	Matus Kostur	Zvolen	G					
165	L.A.	Nathan Marsters	Chilliwack	G					
166	S.J.	Nolan Schaefer	Providence	G					
167	St.L.	Craig Weller	Calgary	D					
168	Atl.	Zdenek Smid	Karlovy Vary	G					
169	CBJ	Shane Bendera	Red Deer	G					
170	Min.	Erik Reitz	Barrie	D					
171	Phi.	Roman Cechmanek	Vsetin	G	163	9384	306	20	1.96
172	Mtl.	Scott Selig	Thayer Academy	RW					
173	Nsh.	Tomas Harant	Zilina	D					
174	Bos.	Jarno Kultanen	IFK Helsinki	D	102	2	11	13	59
175	NYR	Sven Helfenstein	Kloten Jr.	LW					
176	Cgy.	Jukka Hentunen	HPK	RW	38	4	5	9	4
177	Chi.	Michael Ayers	Dubuque	G					
178	Atl.	Jeff Dwyer	Choate	D					
179	Tor.	Vadim Sozinov	Novokuznetsk 2	C					
180	Atl.	Darcy Hordichuk	Saskatoon	LW	73	1	1	2	276
181	Car.	J.D. Forrest	US National	D					
182	Mtl.	Petr Chvojka	Pizen	D					
183	S.J.	Michal Macho	Martin	C					
184	Edm.	Shaun Norrie	Calgary	RW					
185	Pit.	Patrick Foley	U.of New Hampshire	LW					
186	Phx.	Brent Gauvreau	Oshawa	RW					
187	Det.	Per Backer	Grums	RW					
188	Ott.	Jason Maleyko	Brampton	D					
189	Col.	Chris Bahen	Clarkson	D					
190	Fla.	Josh Olson	Omaha	LW					
191	T.B.	Aaron Gionet	Kamloops	D					
192	Dal.	Ladislav Vlcek	Kladno	RW					
193	Chi.	Joey Martin	Omaha	D					
194	N.J.	Deryk Engelland	Moose Jaw	D					
195	Phi.	Colin Shields	Cleveland	RW					
196	Det.	Paul Ballantyne	Sault Ste. Marie	D					
197	Nsh.	Zbynek Irgl	Vitkovice	C					
198	N.J.	Ken Magowan	Vernon	LW					
199	Min.	Brian Passmore	Oshawa	C					
200	CBJ	Janne Jokila	TPS	LW					
201	L.A.	Yevgeny Fedorov	Molot-Perm	C					
202	NYI	Ryan Caldwell	Thunder Bay	D					
203	Nsh.	Jure Penko	Green Bay	G					
204	Bos.	Chris Berti	Sarnia	C					
205	NYR	Henrik Lundqvist	V. Frolunda	G					
206	L.A.	Tim Eriksson	V. Frolunda	C					
207	Chi.	Cliff Loya	U. of Maine	D					

PICK	TEAM	NAME	DRAFTED FROM	NHL PLAYERS: POS	GP	G	A	PTS	PIM
				NHL GOALTENDERS: POS	GP	W	GA	SO	AVG
208	Van.	Brandon Reid	Halifax	C	7	2	3	5	0
209	Tor.	Markus Seikola	TPS	D					
210	Phi.	John Eichelberger	Green Bay	C					
211	Edm.	Joe Cullen	Colorado College	C					
212	Car.	Magnus Kahnberg	V. Frolunda	LW					
213	Buf.	Vasili Bizyayev	Moscow	RW					
214	Min.	Peter Bartos	Budejovice	LW	13	4	2	6	6
215	Edm.	Matthew Lombardi	Victoriaville	C	Re-entered Draft in 2002				
216	Pit.	Jim Abbott	U. of New Hampshire	LW					
217	Phx.	Igor Samoilov	Yaroslavl	D					
218	L.A.	Craig Olynick	Seattle	D					
219	Dal.	Marco Tuokko	TPS	C					
220	Buf.	Paul Gaustad	Portland	C	1	0	0	0	0
221	Col.	Aaron Molnar	London	G					
222	T.B.	Marek Priechodsky	Trnava	D					
223	Tor.	Lubos Velebny	Zvolen	D					
224	Dal.	Antti Miettinen	HPK	C					
225	Chi.	Vladislav Luchkin	Cherepovets	C					
226	T.B.	Brian Eklund	Brown University	G					
227	Phi.	Guillaume Lefebvre	Rouyn Noranda	LW	29	2	4	6	4
228	Det.	Jimmie Svensson	Vasteras	C					
229	St.L.	Brett Lutes	Montreal	LW					
230	Atl.	Samu Isosalo	North Bay	RW					
231	CBJ	Peter Zingoni	New England	C					
232	Min.	Lubomir Sekeras	Trinec	D	209	17	52	69	120
233	T.B.	Alexander Polukeyev	St. Petersburg	G					
234	Fla.	Janis Sprukts	Lukko	C					
235	Car.	Craig Kowalski	Compuware	G					
236	Nsh.	Mats Christeen	Sodertalje	D					
237	Bos.	Zdenek Kutlak	Budejovice	D	14	1	2	3	4
238	NYR	Dan Eberly	Rensselaer	D					
239	Cgy.	David Hajek	Chomutov	D					
240	Chi.	Adam Berkhoel	Twin Cities	G					
241	Van.	Nathan Barrett	Lethbridge	C					
242	Atl.	Evan Nielsen	U. of Notre Dame	D					
243	Mtl.	Joni Puurula	Hermes	G					
244	Atl.	Eric Bowen	Portland	RW					
245	L.A.	Dan Welch	U. of Minnesota	RW					
246	S.J.	Chad Wiseman	Mississauga	LW	4	0	0	0	4
247	Edm.	Jason Platt	Omaha	D					
248	Pit.	Steve Crampton	Moose Jaw	RW					
249	Phx.	Sami Venalainen	Tappara	RW					
250	L.A.	Flavien Conne	Fribourg, SUI	C					
251	Det.	Todd Jackson	U.S. National	RW					
252	Col.	Darryl Bootland	St. Michael's	RW					
253	Fla.	Mathew Sommerfeld	Swift Current	LW					
254	Tor.	Alexander Shinkar	Cherepovets	RW					
255	Min.	Eric Johansson	Tri-City	C	Re-entered Draft in 2002				
256	S.J.	Pasi Saarinen	Ilves	D					
257	N.J.	Warren McCutcheon	Lethbridge	C					
258	Buf.	Sean McMorrow	Kitchener	LW	1	0	0	0	0
259	Phi.	Regan Kelly	Nipawin	D					
260	Det.	Yevgeny Bumagin	Togliatti	C					
261	St.L.	Reinhard Divis	Leksand	G	3	108	1	0	0.56
262	Chi.	Peter Flache	Guelph	C					
263	T.B.	Thomas Ziegler	Ambri-Piotta	RW	5	0	0	0	0
264	NYI	Dmitri Altarev	Penza	LW					
265	Tor.	Jean-Philippe Cote	Cape Breton	D					
266	Col.	Sean Kotary	Northwood	C					
267	NYI	Tomi Pettinen	Ilves	D	2	0	0	0	0
268	Bos.	Pavel Kolarik	Slavia Praha	D	23	0	0	0	10
269	NYR	Martin Richter	SaiPa	D					
270	Cgy.	Micki DuPont	Kamloops	D	18	1	2	3	6
271	Chi.	Reto Von Arx	Davos	C	19	3	1	4	4
272	Van.	Tim Smith	Spokane	C					
273	Pit.	Roman Simicek	HPK	C	63	7	10	17	59
274	Edm.	Yevgeny Muratov	Nizhnekamsk	LW					
275	Mtl.	Jonathan Gauthier	Rouyn Noranda	D					
276	Car.	Troy Ferguson	Michigan State	RW					
277	Buf.	Ryan Courtney	Windsor	LW					
278	CBJ	Martin Paroulek	Vsetin	RW					
279	Bos.	Andreas Lindstrom	Lulea	RW					
280	Pit.	Nick Boucher	Dartmouth College	G					
281	Phx.	Peter Fabus	Dukla Trencin	C					
282	L.A.	Carl Grahn	KalPa	G					
283	Ott.	James Demone	Portland	D					
284	Nsh.	Martin Hohener	Kloten	D					
285	Col.	Blake Ward	Tri-City	G					
286	CBJ	Andrej Nedorost	Essen	LW	19	0	3	3	6
287	Phi.	Milan Kopecky	Slavia Praha	LW					
288	Atl.	Mark McRae	Cornell University	D					
289	Wsh.	Bjorn Nord	Djurgarden	D					
290	Atl.	Simon Gamache	Val D'Or	C	2	0	0	0	2
291	Chi.	Arne Ramholt	Kloten	D					
292	CBJ	Louis Mandeville	Rouyn Noranda	D					
293	St.L.	Lauri Kinos	Montreal	D					

2001

FIRST ROUND

PICK	TEAM	NAME	DRAFTED FROM	POS	GP	G/W	A/GA	PTS/SO	PIM/AVG
1	Atl.	Ilya Kovalchuk	Krylja Sovetov	LW	146	67	51	118	85
2	Ott.	Jason Spezza	Windsor	C	33	7	14	21	8
3	T.B.	Alexander Svitov	Avangard Omsk	C	63	4	4	8	58
4	Fla.	Stephen Weiss	Plymouth	C	84	7	16	23	17
5	Ana.	Stanislav Chistov	Avangard Omsk	LW	79	12	18	30	54
6	Min.	Mikko Koivu	TPS Turku	C					
7	Mtl.	Mike Komisarek	Michigan	D	21	0	1	1	28
8	CBJ	Pascal Leclaire	Halifax	G					
9	Chi.	Tuomo Ruutu	Jokerit	C/LW					
10	NYR	Dan Blackburn	Kootenay	G	63	3499	188	1	3.22
11	Phx.	Fredrik Sjostrom	Vastra Frolunda	RW					
12	Nsh.	Dan Hamhuis	Prince George	D					
13	Edm.	Ales Hemsky	Hull	RW	59	6	24	30	14
14	Cgy.	Chuck Kobasew	Boston College	C	23	4	2	6	8
15	Car.	Igor Knyazev	Spartak	D					
16	Van.	R.J. Umberger	Ohio State	C					
17	Tor.	Carlo Colaiacovo	Erie	D	2	0	1	1	0
18	L.A.	Jens Karlsson	Vastra Frolunda	RW					
19	Bos.	Shaone Morrisonn	Kamloops	D	11	0	0	0	8
20	S.J.	Marcel Goc	Schwenningen	C					
21	Pit.	Colby Armstrong	Red Deer	RW					
22	Buf.	Jiri Novotny	Budejovice	C					
23	Ott.	Tim Gleason	Windsor	D					
24	Fla.	Lukas Krajicek	Peterborough	D	5	0	0	0	0
25	Mtl.	Alexander Perezhogin	Avangard Omsk	C					
26	Dal.	Jason Bacashihua	Chicago (NAHL)	G					
27	Phi.	Jeff Woywitka	Red Deer	D					
28	N.J.	Adrian Foster	Saskatoon	C					
29	Chi.	Adam Munro	Erie	G					
30	L.A.	Dave Steckel	Ohio State	C					

SECOND ROUND

PICK	TEAM	NAME	DRAFTED FROM	POS	GP	G/W	A/GA	PTS/SO	PIM/AVG
31	Phx.	Matthew Spiller	Seattle	D					
32	Buf.	Derek Roy	Kitchener	C					
33	Nsh.	Timofei Shishkanov	Spartak	LW					
34	Fla.	Greg Watson	Prince Albert	C					
35	Ana.	Mark Popovic	St. Michael's	D					
36	Min.	Kyle Wanvig	Red Deer	RW	7	1	0	1	13
37	Mtl.	Duncan Milroy	Swift Current	RW					
38	CBJ	Tim Jackman	Minnesota State	RW					
39	Tor.	Karel Pilar	Litvinov	D	40	4	7	11	20
40	NYR	Fedor Tutin	St. Petersburg	D					
41	Cgy.	Andrei Taratukhin	Omsk	C					
42	Nsh.	Tomas Slovak	Kosice	D					
43	Edm.	Doug Lynch	Red Deer	D					
44	N.J.	Igor Pohanka	Prince Albert	C					
45	Phx.	Martin Podlesak	Lethbridge	C					
46	Car.	Mike Zigomanis	Kingston	C	19	2	1	3	0
47	T.B.	Alexander Polushin	Tver	C					
48	N.J.	Thomas Pihlman	JYP Jyvaskyla	LW					
49	L.A.	Michael Cammalleri	Michigan	C	28	5	3	8	22
50	Buf.	Chris Thorburn	North Bay	C					
51	L.A.	Jaroslav Bednar	HIFK Helsinki	RW	89	9	24	33	26
52	Edm.	Ed Caron	Phillips-Exeter	C					
53	CBJ	Kiel McLeod	Kelowna	C					
54	Pit.	Noah Welch	St. Sebastian's	D					
55	Buf.	Jason Pominville	Shawinigan	RW					
56	Cgy.	Andrei Medvedev	Spartak	G					
57	St.L.	Jay McClement	Brampton	C					
58	Wsh.	Nathan Paetsch	Moose Jaw	D	Re-entered Draft in 2003				
59	Chi.	Matt Keith	Spokane	RW					
60	N.J.	Victor Uchevatov	Yaroslavl	D					

PICK	TEAM	NAME	DRAFTED FROM	NHL PLAYERS: POS / NHL GOALTENDERS: POS	GP / GP	G / W	A / GA	PTS / SO	PIM / AVG
61	T.B.	Andreas Holmqvist	Hammarby	D					
62	Det.	Igor Grigorenko	Togliatti	RW					
63	Col.	Peter Budaj	St. Michael's	G					
OTHER ROUNDS									
64	Fla.	Tomas Malec	Rimouski	D	41	0	2	2	43
65	Tor.	Brendan Bell	Ottawa	D					
66	Van.	Fedor Fedorov	Sudbury	C	7	0	1	1	4
67	N.J.	Robin Leblanc	Baie Comeau	RW					
68	Fla.	Grant McNeill	Prince Albert	D					
69	Ana.	Joel Stepp	Red Deer	C					
70	Dal.	Yared Hagos	AIK	C					
71	Mtl.	Tomas Plekanec	Kladno	LW					
72	N.J.	Brandon Nolan	Oshawa	C	Re-entered Draft in 2003				
73	Chi.	Craig Andersson	Guelph	G					
74	Min.	Chris Heid	Spokane	D					
75	Nsh.	Denis Platonov	Saratov	RW					
76	Nsh.	Oliver Setzinger	Ilves	C					
77	Bos.	Darren McLachlan	Seattle	LW					
78	Phx.	Beat Forster	Davos	D					
79	NYR	Garth Murray	Regina	C					
80	Atl.	Michael Garnett	Saskatoon	G					
81	Ott.	Neil Komadoski	U. of Notre Dame	D					
82	Tor.	Jay Harrison	Brampton	D					
83	L.A.	Henrik Juntunen	Karpat	RW					
84	Edm.	Kenny Smith	Harvard	D					
85	CBJ	Aaron Johnson	Rimouski	D					
86	Pit.	Drew Fata	St. Michael's	D					
87	CBJ	Per Mars	Brynas	C					
88	Tor.	Nicolas Corbeil	Sherbrooke	C					
89	St.L.	Tuomas Nissinen	Kalpa Jr.	G					
90	Wsh.	Owen Fussey	Calgary	RW					
91	Car.	Kevin Estrada	Chilliwack	RW					
92	Dal.	Anthony Aquino	Merrimack	RW					
93	Min.	Stephane Veilleux	Val d'Or	LW	38	3	2	5	23
94	T.B.	Evgeni Artukhin	Podolsk	RW					
95	Phi.	Patrick Sharp	Vermont	C	3	0	0	0	2
96	Pit.	Alexandre Rouleau	Val d'Or	D					
97	Col.	Danny Bois	London	RW					
98	Nsh.	Jordin Tootoo	Brandon	RW					
99	Ott.	Ray Emery	Sault Ste. Marie	G	3	85	2	0	1.41
100	Atl.	Brian Sipotz	Miami-Ohio	D					
101	NYI	Cory Stillman	Kingston	C	79	24	43	67	56
102	Ana.	Timo Parssinen	HPK	LW	17	0	3	3	2
103	Min.	Tony Virta	TPS Turku	RW	8	2	3	5	0
104	Chi.	Brent MacLellan	Rimouski	D					
105	Ana.	Vladimir Korsunov	Spartak	D					
106	S.J.	Christian Ehrhoff	Krefeld	D					
107	S.J.	Dimitri Patzold	Erding	G					
108	Cgy.	Tomi Maki	Jokerit Jrs.	RW					
109	Mtl.	Martti Jarventie	TPS Turku	D	1	0	0	0	0
110	Car.	Rob Zepp	Plymouth	G					
111	Bos.	Matti Kaltiainen	Blues Espoo Jr.	G					
112	Atl.	Milan Gajic	Burnaby	C					
113	NYR	Bryce Lampman	Omaha	D					
114	Van.	Evgeny Gladskikh	Magnitogorsk	RW					
115	Chi.	Vladimir Gusev	Khabarovsk	D					
116	L.A.	Richard Petiot	Camrose	D					
117	Fla.	Mike Woodford	Cushing Academy	RW					
118	Ana.	Brandon Rogers	Hotchkiss	D					
119	Chi.	Alexei Zotkin	Magnitogorsk	LW					
120	Pit.	Tomas Surovy	Poprad	C	26	4	7	11	10
121	Det.	Drew MacIntyre	Sherbrooke	G					
122	St.L.	Igor Valeyev	North Bay	RW					
123	T.B.	Aaron Lobb	London	RW					
124	Cgy.	Yegor Shastin	Omsk	LW					
125	Wsh.	Jeff Lucky	Spokane	RW					
126	Dal.	Daniel Volrab	Sparta Praha Jrs.	C					
127	Ott.	Christoph Schubert	Munich	D					
128	N.J.	Andrei Posnov	Kryla Sovetov Jrs.	RW					
129	Det.	Miroslav Blatak	Zlin	D					
130	Col.	Colt King	Guelph	LW					
131	Pit.	Ben Eaves	Boston College	C					
132	NYI	Dusan Salficky	Plzen	G					
133	Edm.	Jussi Markkanen	Tappara	G	36	1964	75	5	2.29
134	Tor.	Kyle Wellwood	Belleville	C					
135	Atl.	Colin Stuart	Colorado College	C					
136	Fla.	Billy Thompson	Prince George	G					
137	Ana.	Joel Perreault	Baie Comeau	RW					
138	T.B.	Paul Lynch	Valley Jrs.	D					
139	NYR	Shawn Collymore	Quebec	RW					
140	S.J.	Tomas Plihal	Liberac Jrs.	C					
141	CBJ	Cole Jarrett	Plymouth	D					
142	Chi.	Tommi Jaminki	Espoo Jrs.	LW					
143	Col.	Frantisek Skladany	Boston U.	LW					
144	Col.	Cody McCormick	Belleville	C/RW					
145	Cgy.	James Hakewill	Westminster	D					
146	Phi.	Jussi Timonen	Kalpa Jrs.	D					
147	Bos.	Jiri Jakes	Brandon	RW					
148	Phx.	David Klema	Des Moines	C					
149	Col.	Mikko Viitanen	Ahmat	D					
150	Phi.	Bernd Bruckler	Tri-City	G					
151	Van.	Kevin Bieksa	Bowling Green	D					
152	L.A.	Terry Denike	Weyburn	G					
153	L.A.	Tuukka Mantyla	Tappara	D					
154	Edm.	Jake Brenk	Breck High	C					
155	Buf.	Michal Vondrka	Budejovice Jrs.	LW					
156	Pit.	Andrew Schneider	Lincoln High	D					
157	Det.	Andreas Jamtin	Farjestad Jrs.	RW					
158	Phi.	Roman Malek	Slavia Praha	G					
159	St.L.	Dmitri Semin	Spartak Jrs.	C					
160	Wsh.	Artem Ternavsky	Sherbrooke	D					
161	Dal.	Mike Smith	Sudbury	G					
162	Ott.	Stefan Schauer	Riebersee	D					
163	N.J.	Andreas Salomonsson	Djurgarden	RW	71	5	9	14	36
164	Cgy.	Yuri Trubachev	St. Peterburg	C					
165	Col.	Pierre-Luc Emond	Drummondville	C					
166	NYI	Andy Chiodo	St. Michael's	G	Re-entered Draft in 2003				
167	Dal.	Michal Blazek	Vsetin Jr.	D					
168	Tor.	Maxim Kondratjev	Togliatti Jr.	D					
169	Fla.	Dustin Johner	Seattle	C					
170	Ana.	Jan Tabacek	Martin	D					
171	Mtl.	Eric Himelfarb	Sarnia	C					
172	Phi.	Dennis Seidenberg	Mannheim	D	58	4	9	13	20
173	CBJ	Justin Aikins	Langley	C					
174	Chi.	Alexander Golovin	Omsk-Jr.	LW					
175	S.J.	Ryan Clowe	Rimouski	RW					
176	NYR	Marek Zidlicky	IFK	D					
177	Phi.	Andrei Razin	Magnitogorsk	C					
178	Nsh.	Anton Lavrentiev	Kazan Jr.	D					
179	Bos.	Andrew Alberts	Waterloo	D					
180	Phx.	Scott Polaski	Sioux City	RW					
181	Car.	Daniel Boisclair	Cape Breton	G					
182	S.J.	Tom Cavanagh	Phillips-Exeter	LW					
183	Tor.	Jaroslav Sklenar	Brno	RW					
184	Col.	Scott Horvath	Mass-Amherst	RW					
185	Edm.	Mikael Svensk	Frolunda Jr.	D					
186	Chi.	Petr Puncochar	Karlovy Vary	D					
187	CBJ	Artem Vostrikov	Togliatti Jr.	C					
188	T.B.	Arthur Femenella	Sioux City	D					
189	Atl.	Pasi Nurminen	Jokerit	G	61	3321	165	2	2.98
190	St.L.	Brett Scheffelmaier	Medicine Hat	D					
191	Wsh.	Zbynek Novak	Slavia Praha Jr.	LW					
192	Dal.	Jussi Jokinen	Karpat Jr.	C					
193	Ott.	Brooks Laich	Moose Jaw	C					
194	N.J.	James Massen	Sioux Falls	RW					
195	Det.	Nick Pannoni	Seattle	G					
196	Col.	Charlie Stephens	Guelph	C/RW	2	0	0	0	0
197	NYI	Jan Holub	Liberec Jr.	D					
198	Tor.	Ivan Kolozvary	Trencin Jr.	C					
199	Atl.	Matt Suderman	Saskatoon	D					
200	Fla.	Toni Koivisto	Lukko	LW					
201	Atl.	Colin FitzRandolph	Phillips-Exeter	C					
202	Min.	Derek Boogaard	Prince George	LW					
203	Mtl.	Andrew Archer	Guelph	D					
204	CBJ	Raffaele Sannitz	Lugano	C					
205	Chi.	Teemu Jaaskelainen	Ilves Jr.	D					
206	NYR	Petr Preucil	Quebec	C					
207	Cgy.	Garrett Bembridge	Saskatoon	RW					
208	Phi.	Thierry Douville	Baie Comeau	D					
209	Bos.	Jordan Sigalet	Victoria	G					
210	Phx.	Steve Belanger	Kamloops	G					

PICK	TEAM	NAME	DRAFTED FROM	NHL PLAYERS: POS / NHL GOALTENDERS: POS	GP / GP	G / W	A / GA	PTS / SO	PIM / AVG
211	Car.	Sean Curry	Tri-City	D					
212	Van.	Jason King	Halifax	C	8	0	2	2	0
213	Tor.	Jan Chovan	Belleville	G					
214	L.A.	Cristobal Huet	Lugano	G	12	541	21	1	2.33
215	Edm.	Dan Baum	Prince George	C					
216	Chi.	Oleg Minakov	Elektrostal	RW					
217	Pit.	Tomas Duba	Sparta Praha Jr.	G					
218	Ott.	Jan Platil	Barrie	D					
219	T.B.	Dennis Packard	Harvard	LW					
220	Cgy.	David Moss	Cedar Rapids	LW					
221	Wsh.	John Oduya	Victoriaville	D					
222	T.B.	Jeremy Van Hoof	Ottawa	D					
223	Ott.	Brandon Bochenski	Lincoln	RW					
224	Ana.	Tony Martensson	Brynas	C					
225	Phi.	David Printz	Great Falls	D					
226	NYR	Pontus Petterstrom	Tingsryd	LW					
227	Col.	Marek Svatos	Kootenay	RW					
228	NYI	Mike Bray	Quebec	RW					
229	N.J.	Aaron Voros	Victoria	C					
230	NYR	Leonid Zhvachkin	Podolsk Jr.	D					
231	Fla.	Kyle Bruce	Prince Albert	RW					
232	Ana.	Martin Gerber	Langnau	G	22	1203	39	1	1.95
233	Cgy.	Joe Campbell	Des Moines	D					
234	Buf.	Calle Aslund	Huddinge Jr.	D					
235	Ott.	Neil Petruic	Kindersley	D					
236	CBJ	Ryan Bowness	Brampton	RW					
237	L.A.	Mike Gabinet	Nebraska-Omaha	D					
238	NYR	Ryan Hollweg	Medicine Hat	C					
239	Min.	Jake Riddle	Seattle	LW					
240	Nsh.	Gustav Grasberg	Mora	C					
241	Bos.	Milan Jurcina	Halifax	D					
242	CBJ	Andrew Murray	Selkirk	C					
243	Phx.	Frantisek Lukes	St. Michael's	LW					
244	Car.	Carter Trevisani	Ottawa	D					
245	Van.	Konstantin Mikhailov	Nizhnekamsk Jrs.	C					
246	Tor.	Tomas Mojzis	Moose Jaw	D					
247	Buf.	Marek Dubec	Vsetin Jr.	LW					
248	Edm.	Kari Haakana	Jokerit	D	13	0	0	0	4
249	Wsh.	Matt Maglione	Princeton	D					
250	Pit.	Brandon Crawford-West	Texas Tornado	G					
251	Cgy.	Ville Hamalainen	SaiPa	LW					
252	T.B.	J.F. Soucy	Montreal	C					
253	St.L.	Petr Cajanek	Zlin	RW	51	9	29	38	20
254	Wsh.	Peter Polcik	Nitra	RW					
255	Dal.	Marco Rosa	Merrimack	C					
256	Ott.	Gregg Johnson	Boston U.	C					
257	N.J.	Yevgeny Gamalei	Dynamo-Moscow	D					
258	Det.	Dmitri Bykov	Kazan	D	71	2	10	12	43
259	T.B.	Dmitri Bezrukov	Neftekhimik	LW					
260	NYI	Bryan Perez	Michigan Tech	C					
261	T.B.	Vitali Smolyaninov	Neftechimik	LW					
262	Atl.	Mario Cartelli	Trinec	D					
263	Fla.	Jan Blanar	Trencin Jr.	D					
264	Ana.	Pierre Parenteau	Chicoutimi	C					
265	Dal.	Dale Sullivan	Hull	RW					
266	Mtl.	Viktor Ujcik	Slavia Praha	RW					
267	Fla.	Ivan Majesky	Ilves	D	82	4	8	12	92
268	Chi.	Jeff Miles	U. of Vermont	C					
269	NYR	Juris Stals	Lukko Jr.	LW					
270	St.L.	Grant Jacobsen	Regina	C					
271	Nsh.	Mikko Lehtonen	Karpat	D					
272	Edm.	Ales Pisa	Pardubice	D	53	1	3	4	26
273	Phx.	Severin Blindenbacher	Kloten	D					
274	Car.	Peter Reynolds	North Bay	D					
275	Wsh.	Robert Muller	Mannheim	G					
276	Tor.	Mike Knoepfli	Georgetown	LW					
277	L.A.	Sebastien Laplante	Rayside-Balfour	G					
278	Edm.	Shay Stephenson	Red Deer	LW	Re-entered Draft in 2003				
279	Buf.	Ryan Jorde	Tri-City	D					
280	NYI	Roman Kukhtinov	Novokuznetsk	D					
281	T.B.	Ilja Solarev	Perm	LW					
282	Bos.	Marcel Rodman	Peterborough	RW					
283	St.L.	Simon Skoog	Morrum	D					
284	Wsh.	Viktor Hubl	Slavia Praha	LW					
285	Dal.	Marek Tomica	Slavia	LW					
286	Ott.	Toni Dahlman	Ilves Tampere	RW	22	1	1	2	0
287	NYI	Juha-Pekka Ketola	Lukko Jr.	C					
288	Det.	Francois Senez	R.P.I.	D					
289	T.B.	Henrik Bergfors	Sodertalje	D					

2002

FIRST ROUND

PICK	TEAM	NAME	DRAFTED FROM	NHL PLAYERS: POS / NHL GOALTENDERS: POS	GP / GP	G / W	A / GA	PTS / SO	PIM / AVG
1	CBJ	Rick Nash	London	LW	74	17	22	39	78
2	Atl.	Kari Lehtonen	Jokerit	G					
3	Fla.	Jay Bouwmeester	Medicine Hat	D	82	4	12	16	14
4	Phi.	Joni Pitkanen	Karpat	D					
5	Pit.	Ryan Whitney	Boston U.	D					
6	Nsh.	Scottie Upshall	Kamloops	RW	8	1	0	1	0
7	Ana.	Joffrey Lupul	Medicine Hat	C					
8	Min.	Pierre-Marc Bouchard	Chicoutimi	C	50	7	13	20	18
9	Fla.	Petr Taticek	Sault Ste. Marie	C					
10	Cgy.	Eric Nystrom	U. of Michigan	LW					
11	Buf.	Keith Ballard	U. of Minnesota	D					
12	Wsh.	Steve Eminger	Kitchener	D	17	0	2	2	24
13	Wsh.	Alexander Semin	Chelyabinsk	LW					
14	Mtl.	Christopher Higgins	Yale	C					
15	Edm.	Jesse Niinimaki	Ilves	C					
16	Ott.	Jakub Klepis	Portland	C					
17	Wsh.	Boyd Gordon	Red Deer	RW					
18	L.A.	Denis Grebeshkov	Yaroslavl	D					
19	Phx.	Jakub Koreis	Plzen	C					
20	Buf.	Dan Paille	Guelph	LW					
21	Chi.	Anton Babchuk	Elektrostal	D					
22	NYI	Sean Bergenheim	Jokerit	C					
23	Phx.	Ben Eager	Oshawa	LW					
24	Tor.	Alexander Steen	Vastra Frolunda	C					
25	Car.	Cam Ward	Red Deer	G					
26	Dal.	Martin Vagner	Hull	D					
27	S.J.	Mike Morris	St. Sebastian's	RW					
28	Col.	Jonas Johansson	HV 71 Jonkoping Jr.	RW					
29	Bos.	Hannu Toivonen	HPK-Jr.	G					
30	Atl.	Jim Slater	Michigan State	C					

SECOND ROUND

PICK	TEAM	NAME	DRAFTED FROM	NHL PLAYERS: POS / NHL GOALTENDERS: POS	GP / GP	G / W	A / GA	PTS / SO	PIM / AVG
31	Edm.	Jeff Deslauriers	Chicoutimi	G					
32	Dal.	Janos Vas	Malmo-Jr.	LW					
33	NYR	Lee Falardeau	Michigan State	C					
34	Dal.	Tobias Stephan	Chur	G					
35	Pit.	Ondrej Nemec	Vsetin	D					
36	Edm.	Jarret Stoll	Kootenay	C	4	0	1	1	0
37	Ana.	Tim Brent	St. Michaell's	C					
38	Min.	Josh Harding	Regina	G					
39	Cgy.	Brian McConnell	Boston U.	C					
40	Fla.	Rob Globke	Notre Dame	C					
41	CBJ	Joakim Lindstrom	MoDo	C					
42	Dal.	Marius Holtet	Farjestad Jr.	C					
43	Dal.	Trevor Daley	Sault Ste. Marie	D					
44	Edm.	Matt Greene	Green Bay	D					
45	Mtl.	Tomas Linhart	Pardubice-Jr.	D					
46	Phx.	David Leneveu	Cornell	G					
47	Ott.	Alexei Kaigorodov	Magnitogorsk	C					
48	St.L.	Alexei Shkotov	Elektrostal-Jr.	RW					
49	Van.	Kirill Koltsov	Omsk	D					
50	L.A.	Sergei Anshakov	CSKA	LW					
51	N.J.	Anton Kadeikin	Elektrostal	D					
52	S.J.	Dan Spang	Winchester High	D					
53	N.J.	Barry Tallackson	U. of Minnesota	RW					
54	Chi.	Duncan Keith	Michigan State	D					
55	Van.	Denis Grot	Elektrostal	D					
56	Bos.	Vladislav Yevseyev	CSKA	LW					
57	Tor.	Matt Stajan	Belleville	C	1	1	0	1	0
58	Det.	Jiri Hudler	Vsetin	C					
59	Wsh.	Maxime Daigneault	Val d'Or	G					
60	T.B.	Adam Henrich	Brampton	LW					
61	Col.	Johnny Boychuk	Calgary	D					
62	St.L.	Andrei Mikhnov	Sudbury	C					
63	Det.	Tomas Fleischmann	Vitkovice-Jr.	LW					

OTHER ROUNDS

PICK	TEAM	NAME	DRAFTED FROM	NHL PLAYERS: POS / NHL GOALTENDERS: POS	GP / GP	G / W	A / GA	PTS / SO	PIM / AVG
64	N.J.	Jason Ryznar	U. of Michigan	LW					
65	CBJ	Ole-Kristian Tollefsen	Lillehammer	D					

PICK	TEAM	NAME	DRAFTED FROM	NHL PLAYERS: POS / NHL GOALTENDERS: POS	GP / GP	G / W	A / GA	PTS / SO	PIM / AVG
66	L.A.	Petr Kanko	Kitchener	RW					
67	Fla.	Gregory Campbell	Plymouth	LW					
68	Van.	Brett Skinner	Des Moines	D					
69	Pit.	Erik Christensen	Kamloops	C					
70	Phx.	Joe Callahan	Yale	D					
71	Ana.	Brian Lee	Erie	D					
72	Min.	Mike Erickson	U. of Minnesota	RW					
73	Min.	Barry Brust	Spokane	G					
74	Tor.	Todd Ford	Swift Current	G					
75	Ott.	Arttu Luttinen	HIFK-Jr.	LW					
76	Buf.	Michael Tessier	Acadie-Bathurst	LW					
77	Wsh.	Patrick Wellar	Portland	D					
78	Dal.	Geoff Waugh	Kindersley (MJHL)	D					
79	Edm.	Brock Radunske	Michigan State	LW					
80	Phx.	Matt Jones	North Dakota	D					
81	NYR	Marcus Jonasen	Vasteras	LW					
82	Buf.	John Adams	Boston College	D					
83	Van.	Lukas Mensator	Karlovy Vary	G					
84	N.J.	Marek Chvatal	Trinec	D					
85	N.J.	Ahren Nittel	Windsor	LW					
86	S.J.	Jonas Fiedler	Plymouth	RW					
87	NYI	Frans Nielsen	Malmo	C					
88	Tor.	Dominic D'Amour	Hull	D					
89	St.L.	Tomas Troliga	Nova Ves.	C					
90	Cgy.	Matthew Lombardi	Victoriaville	C					
91	Car.	Jesse Lane	Hull	D					
92	Wsh.	Derek Krestanovich	Moose Jaw	C					
93	Chi.	Alexander Kozhevnikov	Ktylja Sovetov-Jr.	LW					
94	Col.	Eric Lundberg	Providence College	D					
95	Det.	Valtteri Filppula	Jokerit Jr.	C					
96	CBJ	Jeff Genovy	Des Moines	LW					
97	Phx.	Lance Monych	Brandon	RW					
98	CBJ	Ivan Tkachenko	Yaroslavl	LW					
99	Mtl.	Michael Lambert	Montreal	LW					
100	T.B.	Dmitri Kazionov	CSKA	C					
101	Pit.	Daniel Fernholm	Djurgarden	D					
102	Nsh.	Brandon Segal	Calgary (WHL)	RW					
103	Ana.	Joonas Vihko	HIFK Helsinki	C					
104	L.A.	Aaron Rome	Swift Current	D					
105	Phi.	Rosario Ruggeri	Chicoutimi	D					
106	Edm.	Ivan Koltsov	Cherepovets-2	D					
107	Col.	Mikko Kalteva	Jokerit Jr.	D					
108	Buf.	Jakub Hulva	Vitkovice-Jr.	RW					
109	Wsh.	Jevon Desautels	Spokane	LW					
110	Dal.	Jarkko A. Immonen	Blues Espoo-Jr.	C					
111	Edm.	Jonas Almtorp	MoDo-Jr.	C					
112	Cgy.	Yuri Artemenkov	Krylja Sovetov-Jr.	RW					
113	Ott.	Scott Dobben	Erie	C/LW					
114	Van.	John Laliberte	N.H. Jr. Monarchs	RW					
115	L.A.	Mark Rooneem	Kamloops	LW					
116	Atl.	Patrick Dwyer	Western Michigan	RW					
117	N.J.	Cam Janssen	Windsor	RW					
118	Wsh.	Petr Dvorak	Havirov-Jr.	C					
119	CBJ	Jekabs Redlihs	NY Apple Core	D					
120	St.L.	Robin Jonsson	Bofors	D					
121	Buf.	Marty Magers	Omaha (USHL)	G					
122	Tor.	David Turon	Havirov	D					
123	Edm.	invalid pick							
124	Atl.	Lane Manson	Moose Jaw	D					
125	Ott.	Johan Bjork	Malmo-Jr.	D					
126	Phi.	Konstantin Baranov	Togliatti	RW					
127	NYR	Nate Guenin	Green Bay (USHL)	D					
128	Chi.	Matt Ellison	Cowichan (BCJHL)	RW					
129	Col.	Tom Gilbert	Chicago (USHL)	D					
130	Bos.	Jan Kubista	Pardubice-Jr.	RW					
131	Det.	Johan Berggren	Sunne	D					
132	Phx.	John Zeiler	Sioux City	RW					
133	CBJ	Lasse Pirjeta	Karpat	LW	51	11	10	21	12
134	Fla.	Topi Jaakola	Karpat	D					
135	T.B.	Joseph Pearce	N.H. Jr. Monarchs	G					
136	Pit.	Andrew Sertich	Greenway High	LW					
137	Pit.	Cam Paddock	Kelowna	C					
138	Nsh.	Patrick Jarrett	Owen Sound	C					
139	S.J.	Kris Newbury	Sarnia	C					
140	Ana.	George Davis	Cape Breton	RW					
141	Cgy.	Jiri Cetkovsky	Zlin-Jr.	C					
142	Cgy.	Emanuel Peter	Kloten	C					
143	NYR	Mike Walsh	Compuware	LW					
144	Atl.	Paul Flache	Brampton	D					
145	Wsh.	Rob Gherson	Sarnia	G					
146	Cgy.	Viktor Bobrov	CSKA-2	C					
147	Dal.	David Bararuk	Moose Jaw	C					
148	Edm.	Glenn Fisher	Ft-Saskatchewan	G					
149	NYI	Marcus Paulsson	Morrums IK	C					
150	Ott.	Brock Hooton	Quesnel (BCJHL)	RW					
151	Van.	Rob McVicar	Brandon	G					
152	L.A.	Greg Hogeboom	Miami University	RW					
153	Bos.	Peter Hamerlik	Kingston	G					
154	N.J.	Krisjanis Redlihs	Metalurgs Liepaja	D					
155	Min.	Armands Berzins	Shawinigan	C					
156	Chi.	James Wisniewski	Plymouth	D					
157	L.A.	Joel Andresen	St. Albert (AJHL)	D					
158	Fla.	Vince Bellissimo	Topeka (USHL)	C					
159	Cgy.	Kristofer Persson	MoDo-Jr.	RW					
160	Car.	Daniel Manzato	Victoriaville	G					
161	Phi.	Dov Grumet-Morris	Harvard	G					
162	T.B.	Gerard Dicaire	Kootenay	D					
163	S.J.	Tom Walsh	Deerfield (Hi-School)	D					
164	Col.	Tyler Weiman	Tri-City	G					
165	St.L.	Justin Maiser	Boston U.	C					
166	Det.	Logan Koopmans	Lethbridge	G					
167	Atl.	Brad Schell	Spokane	C					
168	CBJ	Tim Konsorada	Brandon	RW					
169	Fla.	Jeremy Swanson	Barrie	D					
170	T.B.	P.J. Atherton	Cedar Rapids	D					
171	Pit.	Robert Goepfert	Cedar Rapids	G					
172	Nsh.	Mike McKenna	St. Lawrence	G					
173	Ana.	Luke Fritshaw	Prince Albert	D					
174	T.B.	Karri Akkanen	Ilves Jr.	C					
175	Min.	Matt Foy	Merrimack	RW					
176	Cgy.	Curtis McElhinney	Colorado College	G					
177	NYR	Jake Taylor	Green Bay	D					
178	Buf.	Maxim Schevjev	Elektrostal	C					
179	Wsh.	Marian Havel	Vancouver (WHL)	C/LW					
180	Dal.	Kirill Sidorenko	Kurgan	C					
181	Edm.	Mikko Luoma	Tappara	D					
182	Mtl.	Andre Deveaux	Belleville	C					
183	T.B.	Paul Ranger	Oshawa	D					
184	CBJ	Jaroslav Balastik	Zlin	RW					
185	L.A.	Ryan Murphy	Boston College	RW					
186	Phx.	Jeff Pietrasiak	Berkshire	G					
187	N.J.	Eric Johansson	Tri-City	C					
188	Chi.	Kevin Kantee	Jokerit Jr.	D					
189	NYI	Alexei Stonkus	Elektrostal	D					
191	Tor.	Ian White	Swift Current	D					
191	St.L.	D.J. King	Lethbridge	C					
192	Phi.	Nikita Korovkin	Kamloops	D					
193	Phi.	Joey Mormina	Colgate	D					
194	NYR	Kim Hirschovits	HIFK Helsinki	C					
195	Col.	Taylor Christie	Bowling Green	D					
196	Fla.	Mikael Vuorio	Lukko Jr.	G					
197	Det.	James Cuddihy	Shawinigan	C					
198	Atl.	Nathan Oystrick	South Surrey	D					
199	CBJ	Greg Mauldin	Mass-Amherst	C					
200	Fla.	Denis Yachmenev	North Bay	LW					
201	Phi.	Mathieu Brunelle	Victoriaville	LW					
202	Pit.	Patrik Bartschi	Kloten	C/RW					
203	Nsh.	Josh Morrow	Tri City	D					
204	Min.	Niklas Eckerblom	Djurgarden Jr.	C					
205	Edm.	J.F. Dufort	Cape Breton	LW					
206	Cgy.	David Van Der Gulik	Chilliwack	RW					
207	Cgy.	Pierre Johnsson	Farjestad Jr.	D					
208	Buf.	Radoslav Hecl	Bratislava	D	14	0	0	0	2
209	Wsh.	Joni Lindlof	Tappara Jr.	LW					
210	Dal.	Bryan Hamm	Peterborough	D					
211	Edm.	Patrick Murphy	Newmarket	LW					
212	Mtl.	Jonathan Ferland	Acadie Bathurst	RW					
213	T.B.	Fredrik Norrena	TPS Turku	G					
214	Van.	Marc-Andre Roy	Baie Comeau	LW					
215	L.A.	Mikhail Lyubushin	Krylja Sovetov	D					
216	Phx.	Ladislav Kouba	Red Deer	LW					
217	S.J.	Tim Conboy	Topeka	D					

PICK	TEAM	NAME	DRAFTED FROM	NHL PLAYERS: POS / NHL GOALTENDERS: POS	GP / GP	G / W	A / GA	PTS / SO	PIM / AVG
218	N.J.	Ilkka Pikkarainen	HIFK Helsinki	RW					
219	Chi.	Tyson Kellerman	North Bay	G					
220	NYI	Brad Topping	Brampton	G					
221	St.L.	Jonas Johnson	Vastra Frolunda	C					
222	Tor.	Scott May	Ohio State	RW					
223	Van.	Ilja Krikunov	Elektrostal	LW					
224	Car.	Adam Taylor	Kootenay	C					
225	CBJ	Steve Goertzen	Seattle	RW					
226	NYR	Joey Crabb	Green Bay	RW					
227	Col.	Ryan Steeves	Yale	C/LW					
228	Bos.	Dmitri Utkin	Yaroslavl 2	LW					
229	Det.	Derek Meech	Red Deer	D					
230	Atl.	Colton Fretter	Chatham	C					
231	CBJ	Jaroslav Kracik	Plzen Jr.	RW					
232	Fla.	Peter Hafner	Taft High School	D					
233	T.B.	Vasily Koshechkin	Togliatti	G					
234	Pit.	Maxime Talbot	Hull	C					
235	Nsh.	Kaleb Betts	Chilliwack	C					
236	Atl.	Tyler Boldt	Kamloops	D					
237	Min.	Christoph Brandner	Krefeld	LW					
238	Cgy.	Jyri Marttinen	JYP Jyvaskyla	D					
239	Pit.	Ryan Lannon	Harvard	D					
240	NYR	Petr Prucha	Pardubice	RW					
241	Buf.	Dennis Wideman	London	D					
242	Wsh.	Igor Ignatushkin	Elektrostal	C					
243	Dal.	Tuomas Mikkonen	JyP Jyvaskyla	LW					
244	Edm.	Dwight Helminen	U. of Michigan	C					
245	Edm.	Tomas Micka	Slavia Praha Jr.	LW					
246	Ott.	Josef Vavra	Vsetin Jr.	LW					
247	Van.	Matt Violin	Lake Superior	G					
248	L.A.	Tuukka Pulliainen	TuTo	RW					
249	Phx.	Marcus Smith	Kitchener	D					
250	N.J.	Dan Glover	Camrose	D					
251	Chi.	Jason Kostadine	Hull	RW					
252	NYI	Martin Chabada	Sparta Praha	LW					
253	St.L.	Tom Koivisto	Jokerit	D	22	2	4	6	10
254	Tor.	Jarkko Immonen	Assat	C					
255	T.B.	Ryan Craig	Brandon	C					
256	T.B.	Darren Reid	Medicine Hat	RW					
257	Atl.	Pauli Levokari	HIFK Helsinki	D					
258	Col.	Sergei Shemetov	Elektrostal	LW					
259	Bos.	Yan Stastny	U of Notre Dame	C					
260	Det.	Pierre-Olivier Beaulieu	Quebec	D					
261	Ana.	Francois Caron	Moncton	D					
262	Det.	Christian Soderstrom	Timra	LW					
263	CBJ	Sergei Mozyakin	CSKA	LW					
264	Nsh.	Matt Davis	Moncton	G					
265	Pit.	Dwight Labrosse	Guelph	G					
266	Nsh.	Steve Spencer	Swift Current	D					
267	Ana.	Chris Petrow	Oshawa	D					
268	Min.	Mikhail Tyulyapkin	Nizhny Novgorod 2	D					
269	Min.	Mika Hannula	Malmo	RW					
270	NYR	Rob Flynn	Harvard	RW					
271	Buf.	Martin Cizek	Slavia Praha Jr.	D					
272	Wsh.	Patric Blomdahl	AIK Solna Jr.	RW					
273	Dal.	Ned Havern	Boston College	LW					
274	Edm.	Fredrik Johansson	Vastra Frolunda Jr.	C					
275	Mtl.	Konstantin Korneyev	Krylja Sovetov 2	D					
276	Ott.	Vitali Atyushov	Perm	D					
277	Van.	Thomas Nussli	Zug	RW					
278	Van.	Matt Gens	St. Cloud State	D					
279	L.A.	Connor James	U. of Denver	RW					
280	Phx.	Russell Spence	Opaskwayak	C					
281	N.J.	Bill Kinkel	Kitchener	LW					
282	Chi.	Adam Burish	Green Bay	RW					
283	NYI	Per Braxenholm	Morrum	D					
284	St.L.	Ryan MacMurchy	Notre Dame	RW					
285	Tor.	Staffan Kronvall	Huddinge	D					
286	T.B.	Alexei Glukhov	Voskresensk 2	RW					
287	T.B.	John Toffey	Ohio State	C					
288	S.J.	Michael Hutchins	Des Moines	D					
289	Col.	Sean Collins	New Hampshire	LW					
290	Bos.	Pavel Frolov	Nizhny Novgorod 2	C					
291	Det.	Jonathan Ericsson	Hasten Jr.	D					

2003

FIRST ROUND

PICK	TEAM	NAME	DRAFTED FROM	NHL PLAYERS: POS / NHL GOALTENDERS: POS	GP / GP	G / W	A / GA	PTS / SO	PIM / AVG
1	Pit.	Marc-Andre Fleury	Cape Breton	G					
2	Car.	Eric Staal	Peterborough	C					
3	Fla.	Nathan Horton	Oshawa	C					
4	CBJ	Nikolai Zherdev	CSKA Moscow	W					
5	Buf.	Thomas Vanek	U. of Minnesota	LW					
6	S.J.	Milan Michalek	Budejovice	RW					
7	Nsh.	Ryan Suter	U.S. National U-18	D					
8	Atl.	Braydon Coburn	Portland	D					
9	Cgy.	Dion Phaneuf	Red Deer	D					
10	Mtl.	Andrei Kostitsyn	CSKA Moscow 2	RW					
11	Phi.	Jeff Carter	Sault Ste. Marie	C					
12	NYR	Hugh Jessiman	Dartmouth	RW					
13	L.A.	Dustin Brown	Guelph	RW					
14	Chi.	Brent Seabrook	Lethbridge	D					
15	NYI	Robert Nilsson	Leksand	RW					
16	S.J.	Steve Bernier	Moncton	RW					
17	N.J.	Zach Parise	North Dakota	C					
18	Wsh.	Eric Fehr	Brandon	RW					
19	Ana.	Ryan Getzlaf	Calgary	C					
20	Min.	Brent Burns	Brampton	RW					
21	Bos.	Mark Stuart	Colorado College	D					
22	Edm.	Marc-Antoine Pouliot	Rimouski	C					
23	Van.	Ryan Kesler	Ohio State	C					
24	Phi.	Mike Richards	Kitchener	C					
25	Fla.	Anthony Stewart	Kingston	C					
26	L.A.	Brian Boyle	St. Sebastian's	C					
27	L.A.	Jeff Tambellini	U. of Michigan	LW					
28	Ana.	Corey Perry	London	RW					
29	Ott.	Patrick Eaves	Boston College	RW					
30	St.L.	Shawn Belle	Tri City	D					

SECOND ROUND

PICK	TEAM	NAME	DRAFTED FROM	NHL PLAYERS: POS / NHL GOALTENDERS: POS	GP / GP	G / W	A / GA	PTS / SO	PIM / AVG
31	Car.	Danny Richmond	U. of Michigan	D					
32	Pit.	Ryan Stone	Brandon	C					
33	Dal.	Loui Eriksson	Vastra Frolunda Jr.	LW					
34	T.B.	Mike Egener	Calgary	D					
35	Nsh.	Konstantin Glazachev	Yaroslavl	LW					
36	Dal.	Vojtech Polak	Karlovy Vary	LW					
37	Nsh.	Kevin Klein	St. Michael's	D					
38	Fla.	Kamil Kreps	Brampton	C					
39	Cgy.	Tim Ramholt	Zurich	D					
40	Mtl.	Cory Urquhart	Montreal	C					
41	T.B.	Matt Smaby	Shattuck-St. Mary's	D					
42	N.J.	Petr Vrana	Halifax	LW					
43	S.J.	Joshua Hennessy	Quebec	C					
44	L.A.	Konstantin Pushkarev	Ust-Kamenogorsk	RW					
45	Bos.	Patrice Bergeron-Cleary	Acadie-Bathurst	C					
46	CBJ	Dan Fritsche	Sarnia	C					
47	S.J.	Matthew Carle	River City	D					
48	NYI	Dmitri Chernykh	Khimik	RW					
49	Nsh.	Shea Weber	Kelowna	D					
50	NYR	Ivan Baranka	Dubnica Jr.	D					
51	Edm.	Colin McDonald	New England	RW					
52	Chi.	Corey Crawford	Moncton	G					
53	NYI	Yevgeni Tunik	Elektrostal	C					
54	Dal.	Brandon Crombeen	Barrie	RW					
55	Fla.	Stefan Meyer	Medicine Hat	LW					
56	Min.	Patrick O'Sullivan	Mississauga	C					
57	Tor.	John Doherty	Phillips-Andover	D					
58	NYI	Jeremy Colliton	Prince Albert	C					
59	Chi.	Michal Barinka	Budejovice	D					
60	Van.	Marc-Andre Bernier	Halifax	RW					
61	Mtl.	Maxim Lapierre	Montreal	C					
62	St.L.	David Backes	Lincoln	C					
63	Col.	David Liffiton	Plymouth	D					
64	Det.	James Howard	U. of Maine	G					
65	Buf.	Branislav Fabry	Bratislava Jr.	LW					
66	Bos.	Masi Marjamaki	Red Deer	LW					
67	Ott.	Igor Mirnov	Dynamo	LW					
68	Edm.	Jean-Francois Jacques	Baie-Comeau	LW					

OTHER ROUNDS

PICK	TEAM	NAME	DRAFTED FROM	NHL PLAYERS: POS	GP	G	A	PTS	PIM
				NHL GOALTENDERS: POS	GP	W	GA	SO	AVG
69	Phi.	Colin Fraser	Red Deer	C					
70	Pit.	Jonathan Filewich	Prince George	RW					
71	CBJ	Dmitri Kosmachev	CSKA Moscow	D					
72	Edm.	Mishail Joukov	Arboga	LW					
73	Pit.	Daniel Carcillo	Sarnia	LW					
74	Buf.	Clarke MacArthur	Medicine Hat	LW					
75	NYR	Ken Roche	St. Sebastian's	C					
76	Nsh.	Richard Stehlik	Sherbrooke	D					
77	Phx.	Tyler Redenbach	Swift Current	C					
78	Min.	Danny Irmen	Lincoln	C					
79	Mtl.	Ryan O'Byrne	Nanaimo	D					
80	Phx.	Dmitri Pestunov	Magnitogorsk	C					
81	Phi.	Stefan Ruzicka	Nitra	LW					
82	L.A.	Ryan Munce	Sarnia	G					
83	Wsh.	Stephen Werner	Mass-Amherst	RW					
84	St.L.	Konstantin Barulin	Tjumen	G					
85	Phi.	Alexandre Picard	Halifax	D					
86	Ana.	Shane Hynes	Cornell U.	RW					
87	Phi.	Ryan Potulny	Lincoln	C					
88	St.L.	Zach Fitzgerald	Seattle	D					
89	Nsh.	Paul Brown	Kamloops	RW					
90	Ana.	Juha Alen	Northern Michigan]	D					
91	Tor.	Martin Sagat	Trencin	LW					
92	Nsh.	Alexander Sulzer	Hamburg	D					
93	N.J.	Ivan Khomutov	Elektrostal	RW					
94	Edm.	Zachery Stortini	Sudbury	RW					
95	Phi.	Rick Kozak	Brandon	RW					
96	T.B.	Jonathan Boutin	Halifax	G					
97	Cgy.	Ryan Donally	Windsor	LW					
98	Nsh.	Grigory Shafigulin	Yaroslavl	C					
99	Dal.	Matt Nickerson	Texas	D					
100	Ott.	Philippe Seydoux	Kloten	D					
101	St.L.	Konstantin Zakharov	Yunost	LW					
102	Car.	Aaron Dawson	Peterborough	D					
103	CBJ	Kevin Jarman	Stouffville	LW					
104	CBJ	Philippe Dupuis	Hull	C					
105	Fla.	Martin Lojek	Brampton	D					
106	Buf.	Jan Hejda	Slavia	D					
107	Bos.	Byron Bitz	Nanaimo	RW					
108	Phi.	Kevin Romy	Geneve	C					
109	Wsh.	Andreas Valdix	Malmo	LW					
110	Atl.	James Sharrow	Halifax	D					
111	Van.	Brandon Nolan	Oshawa	C					
112	Cgy.	Jamie Tardif	Peterborough	RW					
113	Mtl.	Corey Locke	Ottawa	C					
114	Buf.	Denis Yezhov	Samara	D					
115	Phx.	Liam Lindstrom	Mora	C					
116	Atl.	Guillaume Desbiens	Rouyn Noranda	RW					
117	Nsh.	Teemu Lassila	TPS	G					
118	Bos.	Frank Rediker	Windsor	D					
119	Ana.	Nathan Saunders	Moncton	D					
120	NYI	Stefan Blaho	Trencin Jr.	RW					
121	Pit.	Paul Bissonnette	Saginaw	D					
122	NYR	Corey Potter	Michigan State	D					
123	Mtl.	Danny Stewart	Rimouski	LW					
124	Fla.	James Pemberton	Providence College	D					
125	Tor.	Konstantin Volkov	Dynamo 2	RW					
126	Car.	Kevin Nastiuk	Medicine Hat	G					
127	St.L.	Alexandre Bolduc	Rouyn Noranda	C					
128	Van.	Ty Morris	St. Albert	LW					
129	Bos.	Patrik Valcak	Ostrava Jr.	C					
130	Car.	Matej Trojovsky	Regina	D					
131	Col.	David Svagrovsky	Seattle	RW					
132	Det.	Kyle Quincey	London	D					
133	Nsh.	Rustam Sidikov	CSKA Moscow 2	G					
134	Dal.	Alexander Naurov	Yaroslavl 2	RW					
135	Ott.	Mattias Karlsson	Brynas JR.	D					
136	Atl.	Michael Vannelli	Sioux Falls	D					
137	Car.	Tyson Strachan	Vernon	D					
138	CBJ	Arsi Piispanen	Jokerit Jr.	RW					
139	S.J.	Patrick Ehelechner	Hannover	G					
140	Phi.	David Tremblay	Hull	G					
141	Fla.	Dan Travis	Deerfield Academy	RW					
142	Ott.	Tim Cook	River City	D					
143	Cgy.	Greg Moore	U. Of Maine	RW					
144	Dal.	Eero Kilpelainen	Kalpa Jr.	G					
145	Atl.	Brett Sterling	Colorado College	LW					
146	Col.	Mark McCutcheon	New England	C					
147	Edm.	Kalle Olsson	Frolunda Jr.	RW					
148	St.L.	Lee Stempniak	Dartmouth College	RW					
149	NYR	Nigel Dawes	Kootenay	LW					
150	Buf.	Thomas Morrow	Des Moines	D					
151	Chi.	Lasse Kukkonen	Karpat	D					
152	L.A.	Brady Murray	Salmon Arm	C					
153	Bos.	Mike Brown	Saginaw	G					
154	Edm.	David Rohlfs	Compuware	RW					
155	Wsh.	Josh Robertson	Proctor	C					
156	Chi.	Alexei Ivanov	Yaroslavl 2	C					
157	Min.	Marcin Kolusz	Nowy Targ	RW					
158	Tor.	John Mitchell	Plymouth	C					
159	St.L.	Chris Beckford-Tseu	Oshawa	G					
160	Van.	Nicklas Danielsson	Brynas	RW					
161	Pit.	Yevgeny Isakov	Cherepovets	RW					
162	Fla.	Martin Tuma	Litvinov Jr.	D					
163	Col.	Brad Richardson	Owen Sound	C					
164	Det.	Ryan Oulahen	Brampton	C					
165	Dal.	Gino Guyer	U. of Minnesota	C					
166	Ott.	Sergei Gimayev	Cherepovets	D					
167	N.J.	Zach Tarkir	Chilliwack	D					
168	CBJ	Marc Methot	London	D					
169	Pit.	Lukas Bolf	Sparta Jr.	D					
170	Det.	Andreas Sundin	Linkoping	LW					
171	Fla.	Denis Stasyuk	Novokuznetsk	RW					
172	Buf.	Pavel Voroshnin	Mississauga	D					
173	Cgy.	Tyler Johnson	Moose Jaw	C					
174	L.A.	Esa Pirnes	Tappara	C					
175	Atl.	Mike Hamilton	Merritt	F					
176	NYR	Ivan Dornic	Bratislava Jr.	C					
177	Mtl.	Chris Heino-Lindberg	Hammarby Jr.	G					
178	Phx.	Ryan Gibbons	Seattle	RW					
179	NYR	Philippe Furrer	Bern	D					
180	NYR	Chris Holt	U.S. National U-18	G					
181	Chi.	Johan Andersson	Troja/Ljunby	C					
182	NYI	Bruno Gervais	Acadie-Bathurst	D					
183	Bos.	Nate Thompson	Seattle	C					
184	Edm.	Dragan Umicevic	Sodertalje	LW					
185	Dal.	Francis Wathier	Hull	LW					
186	Ana.	Andrew Miller	River City	LW					
187	Min.	Miroslav Kopriva	Kladno Jr.	G					
188	Mtl.	Mark Flood	Peterborough	D					
189	St.L.	Jonathan Lehun	St. Cloud State	C					
190	Van.	Chad Brownlee	Vernon	D					
191	Phi.	Rejean Beauchemin	Prince Albert	G					
192	T.B.	Doug O'Brien	Hull	D					
193	Phi.	Ville Hostikka	Saipa	G					
194	Det.	Stefan Blom	Hammarby Jr.	D					
195	Dal.	Drew Bagnall	Battlefords	D					
196	Dal.	Elias Granath	Leksand Jr.	D					
197	N.J.	Jason Smith	Lennoxville	G					
198	Car.	Shay Stephenson	Red Deer	LW					
199	Pit.	Andy Chiodo	St. Michael's	G					
200	CBJ	Alexander Gusjkov	Yaroslavl	D					
201	S.J.	Jonathan Tremblay	Acadie-Bathurst	RW					
202	Buf.	Nathan Paetsch	Moose Jaw	D					
203	Atl.	Denis Loginov	Kazan 2	C					
204	Col.	Linus Videll	Sodertalje Jr.	LW					
205	S.J.	Joe Pavelski	Waterloo	C					
206	Cgy.	Thomas Bellemare	Drummondville	D					
207	Min.	Grigory Misharin	Yekaterinburg	D					
208	Phx.	Randall Gelech	Kelowna	C					
209	NYR	Dylan Reese	Pittsburgh	D					
210	Nsh.	Andrei Mukhachev	CSKA Moscow	D					
211	Chi.	Mike Brodeur	Camrose	G					
212	NYI	Denis Rehak	Trencin Jr.	D					
213	Nsh.	Miroslav Hanuljak	Litvinov Jr.	G					
214	Edm.	Kyle Brodziak	Moose Jaw	C					
215	Edm.	Mathieu Roy	Val d'Or	D					
216	S.J.	Kai Hospelt	Koln	C					
217	Mtl.	Oskari Korpikari	Karpat	D					
218	Ana.	Dirk Southern	Northern Michigan	C					
219	Min.	Adam Courchaine	Vancouver	C					

PICK	TEAM	NAME	DRAFTED FROM	NHL PLAYERS: POS / NHL GOALTENDERS: POS	GP / GP	G / W	A / GA	PTS / SO	PIM / AVG
220	Tor.	Jeremy Williams	Swift Current	C					
221	St.L.	Yevgeny Skachkov	Kapitan	LW					
222	Van.	Francois-Pierre Guenette	Halifax	C					
223	Fla.	Dany Roussin	Rimouski	C					
224	T.B.	Gerald Coleman	London	G					
225	Col.	Brett Hemingway	Coquitlam	W					
226	Det.	Tomas Kollar	Hammarby	LW					
227	T.B.	Jay Rosehill	Olds	D					
228	Ott.	William Colbert	Ottawa	D					
229	Pit.	Stephen Dixon	Cape Breton	C					
230	Car.	Jamie Hoffmann	Des Moines	C					
231	L.A.	Matt Zaba	Vernon	G					
232	Pit.	Joe Jensen	St. Cloud State	C					
233	CBJ	Mathieu Gravel	Shawinigan	LW					
234	Fla.	Petr Kadlec	Slavia	D					
235	Buf.	Jeff Weber	Plymouth	G					
236	S.J.	Alexander Hult	HV 71 Jr.	C					
237	Tor.	Shaun Landolt	Calgary	RW					
238	NYI	Cody Blanshan	U. Nebraska-Omaha	D					
239	Atl.	Tobias Enstrom	Modo	D					
240	Cgy.	Cam Cunning	Kamloops	LW					
241	Mtl.	Jimmy Bonneau	Montreal	LW					
242	Phx.	Eduard Lewandowski	Koln	LW					
243	NYR	Jan Marek	Trinec	F					
244	L.A.	Mike Sullivan	Stouffville	C					
245	Chi.	Dustin Byfuglien	Prince George	D					
246	NYI	Igor Volkov	Ufa	LW					
247	Bos.	Benoit Mondou	Shawinigan	C					
248	Edm.	Josef Hrabal	Vsetin Jr.	D					
249	Wsh.	Andrew Joudrey	Notre Dame	C					
250	Ana.	Shane O'Brien	St. Michael's	D					
251	Min.	Mathieu Melanson	Chicoutimi	LW					
252	Van.	Sergei Topol	Omsk 2	RW					
253	St.L.	Andrei Pervyshin	Yaroslavl	D					
254	Van.	Nathan Mciver	St. Michael's	D					
255	T.B.	Raimonds Danilics	Stalkers-Juniors	C					
256	T.B.	Brady Greco	Chicago	D					
257	Col.	Darryl Yacboski	Regina	D					
258	Det.	Vladimir Kutny	Quebec	LW					
259	Dal.	Niko Vainio	Jokerit Jr.	D					
260	Ott.	Ossi Louhivaara	Kookoo	RW					
261	N.J.	Joey Tenute	Sarnia	C					
262	Car.	Ryan Rorabeck	St. Michael's	C					
263	Pit.	Matt Moulson	Cornell	LW					
264	Fla.	John Hecimovic	Sarnia	RW					
265	Fla.	Tanner Glass	Nanaimo	LW					
266	Buf.	Louis Philippe Martin	Baie Comeau	RW					
267	S.J.	Brian O'Hanley	Boston College HS	D					
268	Nsh.	Lauris Darzins	Lukko Jr.	RW					
269	Atl.	Rylan Kaip	Notre Dame	C					
270	Cgy.	Kevin Harvey	Georgetown	LW					
271	Mtl.	Jaroslav Halak	Bratislava Jr.	G					
272	Phx.	Sean Sullivan	St. Sebastian's	D					
273	T.B.	Albert Vishnyakov	Kazan	LW					
274	L.A.	Martin Guerin	Des Moines	RW					
275	Chi.	Michael Grenzy	Chicago	D					
276	S.J.	Carter Lee	Canterbury	F					
277	Bos.	Kevin Regan	St. Sebastian's	G					
278	Edm.	Troy Bodie	Kelowna	RW					
279	Wsh.	Mark Olafson	Kelowna	RW					
280	Ana.	Ville Mantymaa	Tappara	D					
281	Min.	Jean-Michel Bolduc	Quebec	D					
282	Chi.	Chris Porter	Lincoln	C					
283	CBJ	Trevor Hendrikx	Peterborough	D					
284	St.L.	Juhamatti Tapi Aaltonen	Karpat Jr.	RW					
285	Van.	Matthew Hansen	Seattle	D					
286	T.B.	Zbynek Hrdel	Rimouski	C					
287	T.B.	Nick Tarnasky	Lethbridge	C					
288	Col.	David Jones	Coquitlam	RW					
289	Det.	Mikael Johansson	Arvika	C					
290	Phx.	Loic Burkhalter	Ambri	C					
291	Ott.	Brian Elliott	Ajax	G					
292	N.J.	Arseny Bondarev	Yaroslavl 2	LW					

Entry Draft Notes

Dark Horse Entry Draft Selections

PLAYER	PICK	YEAR	DRAFTED BY
Dan McGillis, S.J.	238	1992	Detroit
Pavol Demitra, St. L	227	1993	Ottawa
Vladimir Konstantinov, Det*	221	1989	Detroit
Anson Carter, NYR	220	1992	Quebec
Johan Hedberg, Pit	218	1994	Philadelphia
Dave Taylor, L.A.*	210	1975	Los Angeles
Dominik Hasek, Det*	207	1983	Chicago
Vladimir Malakhov, NYR	191	1989	NY Islanders
Luc Robitaille, Det	171	1984	Los Angeles
Roman Cechmanek, L.A.	171	2000	Philadelphia
Peter Bondra, Wsh	156	1990	Washington
Doug Gilmour, Tor	134	1982	St. Louis
Daniel Alfredsson, Ott	133	1994	Ottawa
Steve Larmer, NYR*	120	1980	Chicago
Brett Hull, Det	117	1984	Calgary
Pavel Bure, NYR	113	1989	Vancouver

* retired

Breaking New Ice – European Firsts

1969 – First European Draft Pick The first European-trained player to be selected in the NHL Entry Draft was Finnish-born left winger Tommi Salmelainen, 66th overall, by the St. Louis Blues.

1974 – First Swedish Selection Swedish-born center Per Alexandersson was selected by the Toronto Maple Leafs, 49th overall, becoming the first Swedish player to be drafted into the NHL. There were five Swedish-born players selected in 1974, including defenseman Stefan Persson (214th overall, NY Islanders). Persson became the first European player to have his name engraved on the Stanley Cup (four times, 1980-83).

1975 – First Russian Draft Pick The Philadelphia Flyers became the first NHL club to select a Russian player, picking center Viktor Khatulev, 160th overall.

1976 – First European Taken in the First Round The 1976 Draft saw the first European selected in the first round when the California Seals made Swedish defenseman Bjorn Johansson their first pick, fifth overall. Although he only played 15 games in the NHL, Johansson remained the highest European draft pick until 1989 (Mats Sundin, first overall).

1976 – First Swiss Player Selected – Although Switzerland is just beginning to have an impact in international hockey, the country made its first inroads to the NHL in 1976 when the St. Louis Blues selected Swiss center Jacques Soguel, 121st overall.

1978 – First Czechoslovak in the Entry Draft The Detroit Red Wings made the first selection from the former Czechoslovakia, drafting left wing Ladislav Svozil, 194th overall.

1978 – First German Pick The first German players were also drafted into the NHL in 1978, with the Atlanta Flames' selection of goal-tender Bernard Englbrecht, 196th overall, and St. Louis' choice of forward Gerd Truntschka, 200th overall.

CHAPTER 6

Inside the National Hockey League

Off-ice Action: Understanding the Business Side of Hockey

Gary Meagher

At a meeting of representatives of hockey clubs held at the Windsor Hotel, Montreal, the following present, G.W. Kendall, S.E. Lichtenhein, T.P. Gorman, M.J. Quinn and Frank Calder, it was explained by the last named that in view of the suspension of operations by the National Hockey Association of Canada Limited, he had called the meeting at the suggestion of the Quebec Hockey Club to ascertain if some steps could not be taken to perpetuate the game of hockey.

Frank Calder was elected to the Chair and a discussion ensued after which it was moved by T.P. Gorman, seconded by G.W. Kendall: "That the Canadiens, Wanderers, Ottawa and Quebec Hockey Clubs unite to comprise the National Hockey League". The motion was carried.

It was then moved by M.J. Quinn seconded by G.W. Kendall that: "This League agrees to operate under the rules and conditions governing the game of hockey prescribed by the National Hockey Association of Canada Limited". The motion was carried.

At this stage Mr W.E. Northey, representing the Toronto Arena Company asked to be admitted to the meeting and was admitted. Mr. Northey explained that he was empowered by the interests he represented to say that in the event of a league being formed to contain four clubs, the Toronto Arenas desired to enter a team in the competition.

Upon this assurance M.J. Quinn on behalf of the Quebec Hockey Club declared the latter willing to withdraw provided a suitable arrangement could be made regarding players then the property of the Quebec Hockey Club.

After discussion it was unanimously agreed that the Quebec players be taken over by the league at a cost of $700 of which amount 50% should be paid to the Quebec Hockey Club by the club winning the championship, 30% by the second club and 20% by the third club in the race.

The meeting then proceeded to the election of officers. The following directors were elected S.E. Lichtenhein (Wanderers), Martin Rosenthal (Ottawa), G.W. Kendall (Canadiens) and a director to be named by the Toronto club.

M.J. Quinn was elected Honorary President with power to vote on matters pertaining to the general welfare of the league.

Frank Calder was elected President and Secretary-Treasurer at a salary of $800 on the understanding that there could be no appeal from his decisions.

After a schedule of Wednesday and Saturday games was adopted the meeting was adjourned.

From the Minutes of the
First NHL Board of Governors Meeting
November, 1917

ON THE ICE, the National Hockey League officially had its beginnings on December 19, 1917, as the Montreal Canadiens defeated Ottawa 7–4 and the Montreal Wanderers downed Toronto 10–9. Those historic games, however, were preceded by more than a month of meetings and backroom dealings by a group of gentlemen that were entrusted with the formation of the National Hockey League (NHL) following the demise of the National Hockey Association (NHA).

These meetings began in early November as the National Hockey Association's directors—S.E. Lichtenhein of the Wanderers, G.W. Kendall of the Canadiens, T.P. Gorman of Ottawa and M.J. Quinn of Quebec along with NHA secretary-treasurer Frank Calder—attempted to keep the league afloat. The numerous franchise problems in the preceding season, however, eventually led the NHA executives to start anew.

At the historic Board of Governors meeting in November 1917 at Montreal's Windsor Hotel, the National Hockey League was formed. The crude 25-page constitution of the National Hockey Association, the predecessor of the NHL, was adopted as the governing document of the new league. As president-elect Calder told a sparse gathering of media, the purpose of the new league was "the fostering and furtherance of the game of hockey to be governed by bylaws and rules."

While there were more than 250 owners meetings over the next half century which dealt with all aspects of developing the game, the second most important piece of off-ice business enacted by the Board of Governors took place on June 7, 1967, when the National Hockey League officially recognized the NHL Players' Association as the exclusive bargaining agent "for all of the present and future hockey players employed by the clubs with respect to certain terms and conditions of employment."

Eight years later, on May 4, 1976, the first Collective Bargaining Agreement was printed and distributed.

More than 80 years after its founding, the National Hockey League is still governed by a Board of Governors comprised of owners and club management personnel who establish the policies of the league and who, along with NHL commissioner Gary Bettman, uphold the *Lex Scripta* containing the league's constitution, bylaws and resolutions. Those documents, along with the Collective Bargaining Agreement between the league and the NHL Players' Association, comprise the basis for managing the game off the ice.

Following is an "A-Z" look at the inner workings of today's National Hockey League along with some historical perspective on numerous aspects of the game and business.

AGE OF PLAYER

Today, a player must turn 18 years of age by September 15 of the year in which he is eligible to be drafted by an NHL club. The requirement that a player be 18 years old prior to competing in the NHL was first introduced in 1950 when then NHL president Clarence Campbell negotiated an agreement with all North American professional leagues that moved the age limit for signing players or placing their names on negotiation lists from 16 to 18.

Armand "Bep" Guidolin was the youngest player ever to play in the NHL. Guidolin was only 16 years old when he made his NHL debut for Boston in November 1942. Guidolin would go on to play nine years for Boston, Detroit and Chicago.

Patrick Marleau of the San Jose Sharks was as young as a player can be when he was drafted second overall in 1997. Marleau was born on September 15, 1979, and was the exact minimum age for 1997 draft eligibility. He made his NHL debut less than three weeks after his 18th birthday on October 1, 1997.

BENCHES

In 1978–79, to remove an unfair advantage that some teams had in their home rinks where their player bench was located on the same side of the ice as the penalty bench (thus allowing for a quick substitution for a player when his penalty expired), the NHL introduced a rule that required that the player benches for both teams be located on the same side of the ice. A waiver was provided to teams whose buildings were built prior to 1978 to maintain their benches in their current position. By 1988–89, however, all teams were required to have both the home and visiting benches on the same side of the ice with the penalty bench located on the opposite side. This meant significant renovations in some NHL buildings.

BOARD OF GOVERNORS

The NHL is governed by a Board of Governors which establishes the policies of the league and upholds the constitution and bylaws. Each NHL club appoints a governor as well as alternate governors who are vested with the full power and authority to represent their club and bind it by their vote. The Board of Governors has two scheduled meetings during the year (June and December) as well as special meetings as necessary.

There is also a Chairman of the Board, a position first created in 1953. Harley Hotchkiss of the Calgary Flames is currently serving in his fifth consecutive two-year term as chairman.

CENTRAL REGISTRY

The NHL's Central Registry department is responsible for maintaining all player information. It maintains the NHL clubs' reserve lists which contain the names and vital status information of all players a club has proprietary rights to, either contractual rights or exclusive negotiation rights. It records the status of each player with regard to contracts, waivers, free agency etc. It tracks a player from the first time he is drafted until the completion of his career as a player.

CENTRAL SCOUTING

NHL Central Scouting (CSS) was established prior to the start of the 1975–76 season as a service for the NHL member clubs. CSS supplies the NHL clubs with personal and hockey information and rankings on draft-eligible players throughout the world; schedules, team rosters and directories for amateur leagues; weekly reports on injuries and roster changes of draft-eligible players; and video on draft-eligible players.

CSS consists of nine full-time and six part-time scouts, a director of scouting, and an administrative staff. The scouts file reports from more than 3,000 games throughout North America and Europe during a hockey season as well as coordinating medical and fitness testing for more than 150 draft-eligible players.

Two player rankings are done each season—one in late January and the final ranking in May.

COMMISSIONER

The NHL commissioner, as selected by the Board of Governors, serves as the chief executive officer of the league and is charged with protecting the integrity of the game and preserving public confidence in the league. The commissioner has the responsibility for the general supervision and direction of all business and affairs of the league and has all such powers as may be necessary or appropriate to fulfill his responsibilities.

The office of commissioner was created in December 1992 with the appointment of Gary B. Bettman. Mr. Bettman assumed office on February 1, 1993. Five others have served as the league's chief executive officer under the title of president. The five men are: Frank Calder (1917 to 1943); Mervyn "Red" Dutton (1943 to 1946); Clarence Campbell (1946 to 1977); John Ziegler (1977 to 1992) and Gil Stein (1992–1993).

CONSTITUTION, NHL

The purposes and objects of the National Hockey League, as stated in its constitution are:

a) To perpetuate hockey as one of the national games of the United States and Canada.

b) The promotion of the common interests of the members of the league, each member being an owner of a professional hockey club located in the USA or Canada.

c) The promulgation of rules governing the conduct of play of hockey games between the member clubs in the league, the relationships between players and member clubs, between member clubs and the league and between the member clubs and other hockey clubs, to the end that the public may be assured of a high standard of skill and fair play, integrity and good sportsmanship.

d) The arbitration and settlement of disputes between the member clubs and between member clubs and players.

e) The education of the public, through advertising, radio and other media, to the end that professional hockey, as played according to the standards of the league, may gain popular support and acceptance as a wholesome entertainment.

f) The development of youth in mind and body and the

teaching of fair play and good sportsmanship through the medium of hockey.

CANADIAN SUPPLEMENTARY CURRENCY ASSISTANCE PLAN

The Canadian Supplementary Currency Assistance Plan was adopted on January 5, 1996. The plan has two key features to assist eligible Canadian clubs in addressing the disparity between the United States and Canadian dollars.

Canadian clubs in the bottom half of NHL revenues are eligible for assistance. Eligible clubs must qualify annually for assistance by either having revenues that are at least 80 percent of the NHL average or by selling defined numbers of season tickets, arena suites and dasherboards. Eligible qualifying clubs may receive up to $5 million in United States funds. The precise amount of assistance that eligible qualifying clubs will receive will depend on the magnitude of the currency differential, club revenues and the available pool for distribution.

Eligible Canadian clubs may also receive a subsidy for Group II players to whom they have tendered a qualifying offer and who receive offer sheets from U.S. teams. By way of example, if a player is presently earning $1 million in Canadian funds and is offered $1.5 million in U.S. funds and the currency differential is 30 percent, the subsidy would be calculated as follows:

1. New contract (CDN$) = $1.95 million
2. Old contract (CDN$) = $1 million
3. Difference (CDN$) = $950,000
4. Currency differential = 30 percent
5. Subsidy (CDN$) = $285,000

COLLECTIVE BARGAINING AGREEMENTS

The current Collective Bargaining Agreement between the NHL and the NHL Players' Association runs through September 15, 2004.

The NHL clubs first recognized the National Hockey League Players' Association as the exclusive representative of all players employed by the clubs in June 1967, prior to the NHL's first expansion from six to 12 teams.

From 1967 until the execution of their first formal Collective Bargaining Agreement on May 4, 1976, the clubs and the NHLPA reached agreements on business matters through collective bargaining, which were reflected in minutes of owner-player meetings, in standard players' contracts and in an arbitration agreement relating to said contracts.

On May 4, 1976, the NHLPA and the clubs published their first comprehensive, printed Collective Bargaining Agreement (CBA).

Although the CBA's stated term would not expire until September 30, 1980, one of the points agreed to was that the clubs and the NHLPA would continue the process of collective bargaining throughout its duration, through an "owner-player" council which would meet twice a year.

Through the establishment of this process of continuing negotiations, the players and owners were able to amend the CBA in May 1977, September 1977, January 1978, February 1979, June 1979, August 1979 and November 1979.

On August 1, 1981, a second comprehensive CBA between the clubs and the NHLPA was printed.

The CBA's stated term would expire September 15, 1984 but an ongoing dialogue continued which resulted in numerous changes to the agreement in the interim.

On November 1, 1984, a third comprehensive CBA between the clubs and the NHLPA was printed, which clarified existing terms that had previously been agreed to and incorporated all amendments to the prior CBA then in effect. The next expiry date for the CBA was September 15, 1986.

On June 1, 1988, a fourth comprehensive CBA was printed with the stated term set to expire on September 15, 1991.

The 1991–92 NHL season began without a CBA in place. Negotiations between the NHL and NHLPA were unsuccessful in averting a strike by the players on April 1, 1992. This spurred negotiations and a retroactive two-year CBA was reached on April 10. It would expire before the start of the 1993–94 season. (See Labor Disruptions, page 433.)

The 1993-94 season was also played without a CBA in place. Negotiations of varying levels of intensity took place through September 1994. The NHL's club owners locked out the players, postponing the start of the 1994-95 season for what would prove to be 103 days. Play resumed on January 20, 1995. Teams played a 48-game schedule. (See Labor Disruptions, page 433.)

The CBA that resulted from the lockout had a clause that would have allowed either side to reopen negotiations, but that reopener was waived by both parties in October 1995. On June 25, in connection with the addition of four new expansion franchises on June 25, 1997, the agreement was extended through September 15, 2004.

CONTRACT, STANDARD PLAYER'S

A standard player's contract is an agreement between the club and player for a specified term for a specified salary. Following is a summary of some of the clauses contained in the Standard Player's Contract.

- A player is paid in consecutive semi-monthly installments from the commencement of the regular season until the conclusion of the regular season.
- A player agrees to give his best services to the club that has signed him and to play hockey only for that club unless his contract is released, assigned, exchanged or loaned by his club.
- A player also agrees to provide his services and to play hockey in all regular-season, All-Star, international, exhibition and Stanley Cup playoff games.
- If a player, in the sole judgment of the club's physician, is disabled and unable to perform his duties as a hockey player by reason of an injury sustained during the course of his employment as a hockey player, including travel with his team or on business requested by the club, he shall be entitled to receive his remaining salary due in accordance with the terms of this contract for the remaining stated term of this contract (excluding option period).
- The player and the club recognize and agree that the player's participation in other sports may impair or destroy his ability and skill as a hockey player. Accordingly, the player

agrees that he will not during the period of his contract engage or participate in football, baseball, softball, hockey, lacrosse, boxing, wrestling or other athletic sport without the written consent of the club.

- The club recognizes that the player owns exclusive rights to his individual personality, including his likeness. The player recognizes that the club owns exclusive rights to his name, emblems and uniform which the player wears as a hockey player for the club.

DEVELOPMENT CLUB

Some NHL clubs maintain a player-development club in one of the professional minor leagues, while others either share minor-league clubs or have working agreements to provide a certain number of players to a specific minor-league club. During the 2003–04 season, each NHL club's primary minor-league affiliate is in the American Hockey League.

ENTRY DRAFT, COMPENSATORY DRAFT SELECTION

Compensatory draft selections were introduced for the first time in the 1995 Entry Draft as a means of compensating clubs that are either unable to sign first-round draft choices or lose a Group III free agent who re-signs with another club and the club that lost the Group III free agent fails to sign another Group III free agent of equal or greater value. The determination of the value of these players is based on salary, honors earned, and certain performance achievements. A club may not receive a Group III compensatory pick until at least the 11th pick in the second round of the next following Entry Draft.

In the event that a club loses its draft rights to an unsigned rookie drafted in the first round of the Entry Draft, who is again eligible for the Entry Draft or becomes an unrestricted free agent, a compensatory draft selection is granted to the club (maximum of two compensatory picks per club per year). The compensatory draft selection is the same numerical choice in the second round in the Entry Draft immediately following the date the club loses the rights to the player. For example, if a club cannot sign the third overall choice in the first round, it will receive the third choice in the second round of the next Entry Draft as compensation.

ENTRY DRAFT, DRAWING

The NHL draft drawing is a weighted lottery system that has been used since 1995 to determine the order of selection in the first round only of the Entry Draft for the non-playoff clubs from the previous season as well as expansion clubs (when applicable).

The draft drawing was adopted by the NHL's Board of Governors on March 24, 1994, in order to protect the integrity of the Entry Draft and the regular season, while continuing to ensure that the teams with the poorest records get the best selections. The club winning the draft drawing may not move up more than four positions in the draft order, while no club can fall back more than one position as a result of the draft drawing.

Under the weighted lottery system, the non-playoff team with the fewest regular-season points has the greatest chance of winning the drawing. Fourteen balls, numbered one to 14, are placed in a lottery machine and four are randomly drawn. There are 1,001 possible combinations and each of the clubs involved is assigned a specified number of those combinations. For example, in the 2003 draft drawing, the club with the fewest regular-season points received 25 percent of the possible combinations. The next club had an 18.8% chance of winning the drawing; while clubs three through 14 followed with a 14.2%, 10.7%, 8.1%, 6.2%, 4.7%, 3.6%, 2.7%, 2.1%, 1.5%, 1.1%, 0.8% and 0.5%, respectively, chance of winning. The combinations are assigned to the clubs by a computer on a random basis. Following is a listing of the results of previous draft drawings:

Year	Winner	Effect on Draft Order	Player Selected
1995	Los Angeles	From 7th to 3rd overall	Aki Berg
1996	Ottawa	Retained 1st overall	Chris Phillips
1997	Boston	Retained 1st overall	Joe Thornton
1998	Tampa Bay	From 3rd to 1st via two trades	Vincent Lecavalier
1999	Chicago	From 8th to 4th overall (Traded 4th pick to NY Rangers)	Pavel Brendl
2000	NY Islanders	From 5th to 1st overall	Rick DiPietro
2001	Atlanta	From 3rd to 1st overall	Ilya Kovalchuk
2002	Florida	From 3rd to 1st overall (Traded 1st pick to Columbus)	Rick Nash
2003	Florida	From 4th to 1st overall (Traded 1st pick to Pittsburgh)	Marc-Andre Fleury

ENTRY DRAFT, LENGTH

The annual Entry Draft consists of nine rounds plus compensatory draft selections.

ENTRY DRAFT, ELIGIBILITY

All players age 19 or older are eligible for claim in the Entry Draft except:

- A player on the reserve list of a club, other than as a tryout;
- A player who has been claimed in two prior entry drafts;
- A player who previously played in the league and became a free agent pursuant to the Collective Bargaining Agreement;
- A player age 21 or older who played hockey for at least one season in North America when he was age 18, 19 or 20.

In addition, any player who will be age 18 on or before September 15 in the year in which such Entry Draft is held, or reaches his 19th birthday between September 16 and December 31 inclusive, next following the Entry Draft, can become eligible by providing written notice to the league on an opt-in form.

ENTRY DRAFT, ORDER OF SELECTION

The draft drawing determines the order of selection for the first 14 non-playoff teams in the first round of the Entry Draft. For the remainder of the first round, and subsequent rounds in their entirety, the order of selection is determined as follows: teams not advancing to the playoffs draft in reverse order based on regular-season points; followed by those teams advancing to the playoffs in reverse order based on regular-season points but that had not either won their division or the Stanley Cup that season; followed by regular-season division winners in reverse order of regular-season points; followed by the Stanley Cup winner. This draft order regulation has been in effect since the 2001 Entry Draft.

ENTRY DRAFT, UNSIGNED DRAFT CHOICES

A player selected in the draft is registered on the club's reserve list as an "unsigned draft choice" and the club maintains exclusive right of negotiation up to and including June 1 of the calendar year next following the date of his selection. If a "bona fide offer" is made, the period of exclusive right of negotiation is extended up to and including the second June 1. The offer may be conditioned upon acceptance by the player within 30 days.

An unsigned draft choice who enters into an agreement with any organization or person other than the NHL club or with a club in a league affiliated with the NHL, may be retained on the reserve list as a "defected player." The NHL club may retain such a player on its reserve list for as long as the agreement is in effect.

A player selected in the draft who is either a college student at the time or becomes a college student by the next June 1 following his draft, may be retained on the reserve list of a club so long as he remains a college student and thereafter for a period of 180 days plus the period between the end of said 180 days and the next June 1. A college player may also elect to be tendered a player contract at any time by filing the proper notice.

ENTRY DRAFT PLAYERS, EUROPEANS

All European-trained players must be drafted by an NHL club prior to competing in the NHL. This, however, was not always the case. Beginning in the early 1980s the league began to phase in the process of drafting European players. By the late 1980s, the present-day rule was in place.

Players under contract to teams in International Ice Hockey Federation member countries may be signed by an NHL club in the year in which they are drafted through and including August 15. Once the signing deadline has passed, players under contract to IIHF teams or having signed a contract during the season with an IIHF team may not be signed by a National Hockey League club until the conclusion of the IIHF team's season.

ENTRY LEVEL SYSTEM, ASSIGNING OF 18- AND 19-YEAR-OLDS

During the first two seasons following the drafting of an 18-year-old player, the club he signs a contract with must first offer him to the club from which he was claimed before it may assign him out of the NHL.

During the first season following the drafting of a 19-year-old player or a player who reaches age 19 between September 16 and December 31, inclusive, of the year of his draft, the club he signs a contract with must first offer him to the club from which he was claimed before it may assign him out of the NHL.

A player aged 18 or 19 who was selected in the first three rounds of the Entry Draft and who has not been signed by his NHL club may not be retained by the club and must be returned to his junior team no later than the day prior to the opening of the NHL regular season.

A player aged 18 or 19 who was selected in the fourth or subsequent rounds who has not been signed by his NHL club may not be retained by the club and must be returned to his junior team no later than the fourth day prior to the opening of the NHL regular season (but, in no event, later than Oct. 3).

An NHL club may not retain the services of a junior player signed after the start of the season, except under emergency conditions or after his junior club is no longer in competition.

With respect to forwards, an 18- or 19-year-old junior player may be recalled when the NHL club is in what is known as a third emergency (fewer than 16 skaters available to play). For defensemen, a junior player may be recalled when the NHL club is in a second emergency (fewer than 17 skaters available to play). With goaltenders, a junior may be recalled at any time when the NHL club is in an emergency.

ENTRY LEVEL SYSTEM, COMPENSATION

The Collective Bargaining Agreement has, since 1995, included a salary cap on entry level players as follows:

Draft Year	Entry Level Cap
1995	$850,000
1996	875,000
1997	925,000
1998	975,000
1999	1,025,000
2000	1,075,000
2001	1,130,000
2002	1,185,000
2003	1,240,000
2004	1,295,000

Other provisions of the entry level compensation system include:

- Maximum annual compensation includes salary and all bonuses other than certain specified legitimate performance bonuses. Bonuses, other than performance bonuses, are limited to 50 percent of player's annual compensation.
- Amounts of permitted bonuses can be individually negotiated by players.
- An entry level player has no rights to salary arbitration.
- Mandatory two-way contracts with the maximum minor-league salary component at no more than 50 percent of the NHL minimum. NHL minimum is at $180,000 for the 2003–04 season.

ENTRY LEVEL SYSTEM, PLAYERS

Players 18 through 21 years of age when signing their first NHL contract must sign a three-year contract. Players age 22 and 23 when signing their first NHL contract must sign a two-year contract, while those age 24 when signing their first NHL contract must sign a one-year contract. Players who are 25 or older when they sign their first contract are not subject to the entry level system.

"Age" means a player's age on September 15 of the calendar year in which he signs a player contract regardless of his actual age on the date he signs the contract.

In the event that a signed 18- or 19-year-old player does not play at least 10 NHL games (regular season and/or playoffs) in his first season under contract, the term of his player contract and his number of years in the entry level system will be extended for a period of one year. The exception to this is a 19-year-old player who turns 20 years of age between September 16 and December 31 in his first contract year.

In the event that a player signs his first contract at age 18 and has had his player contract extended pursuant to the above, and such player does not play at least 10 NHL games (regular season and/or playoffs) in the second season under that player's player contract, then the term of his player contract and his number of years in the entry level system shall be extended for one additional year.

EQUIPMENT/UNIFORMS

HELMETS – In 1979, all players entering the NHL were required to wear a helmet approved by the NHL's Rules Committee. Those in the league prior to 1979 were not. Beginning in 1992–93, all players had the option to play without a helmet, though only a handful did so. Craig MacTavish was the last player to go bare-headed.

Beginning in 1997, regulations were amended to require that certified helmets be worn by all players who either already wear a certified helmet or are 25 or younger.

SKATES – In 1960, the Boston Bruins and Montreal Canadiens began wearing an improved skate that featured an injury-reducing plastic guard fitted to the rear end of the blade. At the NHL's annual meeting in 1961, use of the CCM Pro-Guard Heel was made mandatory for all forwards and defensemen commencing with the 1961–62 season.

SWEATERS – In August 1970, the NHL's Board of Governors passed a resolution allowing the home team to put names on the back of player sweaters. Visiting teams could do the same only with the consent of the home club. Beginning with the 1977–78 season, it became mandatory for all players to have names on the backs of their sweaters.

Beginning in 1930, it became mandatory for each player to wear a number, measuring at least 10 inches in height, on the back of his sweater.

STICKS – The league first placed a limit on the maximum curvature of a stick blade in 1966–67 ($^1/_2$"). The maximum curvature was increased in 1968–69 to $1^1/_2$" and reduced to 1" in 1969–70. The current maximum curvature ($^1/_2$") was adopted in 1970–71.

The approval for the use of an aluminum shaft stick by NHL players was first given in the 1981–82 season.

GOALTENDERS' FACEMASK – Journeyman goaltender Andy Brown (who played for Detroit and Pittsburgh in the early 1970s) played his last NHL game on March 31, 1973, against the St. Louis Blues. Brown's appearance marked the last time an NHL goalie appeared in a game without the protection of a facemask.

GOALTENDERS' PADS – Since the 1989–90 season, the maximum width of a goaltender's pads has been 12 inches (before that it was 10 inches). Beginning with the 2003–04 season, the league established, for the first time, a maximum length of a goaltender's pads of 38 inches.

The league began measuring goaltender pads and blockers on December 15, 1996.

EXPANSION

During the 33-year period between 1967 and the year 2000, the NHL expanded its membership from just six teams (in 1966–67) to 30 teams (in 2000–01). The league's most active periods of expansion occurred in 1967, when its grew from six to 12 teams, and during the 1990s when it moved from a 21-club league to its current total of 30 teams.

FIRST EXPANSION—1967: California (Seals), Los Angeles (Kings), Minnesota (North Stars), Philadelphia (Flyers), Pittsburgh (Penguins) and St. Louis (Blues) were added to the league, each paying a membership cost of $2 million.

The 1967 expansion process formally began on March 11, 1965, when then NHL president Clarence Campbell stated that the league "proposes to expand its operations through the formation of a second six-team division." Just under 12 months later the process was completed, when on February 7 and 8, the Board of Governors considered 14 different expansion applications, including five groups from Los Angeles, two from Pittsburgh and one each from San Francisco, Philadelphia, St. Louis, Minneapolis-St. Paul, Baltimore, Buffalo and Vancouver. St Louis was not represented at the meeting as an ownership group had yet to emerge. Cleveland and Louisville, Kentucky, had also expressed interest, but were not represented.

The procedure for stocking the new teams saw each of the "Original Six" teams protect 11 skaters and one goaltender with the expansion teams each drafting 18 skaters and two goaltenders. A "claim and fill" procedure was used during the draft that allowed a team that had had a player claimed by an expansion club to add one more player to its protected list.

SECOND EXPANSION—1970: Buffalo (Sabres) and Vancouver (Canucks) increased the league's membership from 12 to 14 teams. Each paid a membership cost of $6 million.

The origins of the 1970 expansion can be traced to the financial difficulties of the California Seals. In December 1967, only three months into their inaugural season, the NHL began to lend the California franchise money so that it would be able to complete its first season. The financial difficulties of the California franchise led to a request in February 1969 by a Vancouver group to buy and transfer the team to the Canadian west coast city. At the same meeting, a Buffalo group represented by Seymour and Northrup Knox and Robert Swados offered to purchase the franchise and continue to operate it in the Bay area in the event the Vancouver proposal was rejected. By June 1969 they would own a portion of the California club.

The league formally adopted its plan of second expansion in October 1969 with the objective to add two new teams for the 1970–71 season. The plan included a franchise for Vancouver "if an acceptable applicant applies prior to December 1, 1969." Informal applications had been received from Atlanta, Baltimore, Buffalo, Cleveland, Kansas City and Washington D.C. By December 1969, conditional franchises had been awarded to Buffalo and Vancouver.

To stock the two new teams, each of the 12 existing teams protected 15 skaters and two goaltenders, with Buffalo and Vancouver selecting 18 skaters and two goaltenders. The two clubs also received the first two draft positions in the 1970 Amateur Draft.

THIRD EXPANSION—1972: Atlanta (Flames) and New York (Islanders) increased the league from 14 to 16 teams. Each was added at a membership cost of $6 million. In addition, the Islanders had to make a $4 million indemnity payment to the New York Rangers for moving into their home territory.

The 1972 expansion was actually part of a three-phase plan adopted by the Board of Governors on November 8, 1971, to counteract the plans of the newly formed World Hockey Association. In phase one, the league identified Atlanta and Long Island as desirable locations for franchises.

Phase two of the plan called for the admission of two new members for the 1974–75 season. Cities identified by the league as being potential members included Cleveland, Kansas City, Miami, Seattle, Portland (Oregon) and the Washington/Baltimore area. Phase three called for the NHL to expand to at least 24 teams during the 1970s. The league identified the need for additional teams in the Western part of the U.S. and in Canada.

To stock the Atlanta and New York Islanders franchises, each of the existing 14 teams protected 15 skaters and two goaltenders with the new clubs selecting 19 skaters and two goaltenders. The Islanders and Atlanta selected first and second, respectively, in the 1972 Amateur Draft.

FOURTH EXPANSION—1974: Kansas City (Scouts) and Washington (Capitals) each were added for a franchise fee of $6 million, increasing the league's membership from 16 to 18 teams.

The Board of Governors reviewed 11 applications from eight different groups: Kansas City (four applicant groups) and one each from Cincinnati, Cleveland, Dallas, Indianapolis, Phoenix, San Diego and Washington.

The same draft procedures for both the Expansion and Amateur drafts in 1972 were used, with the exception that the two new teams drafted 22 skaters and two goaltenders each.

Following its fourth expansion, the league went about attempting to realize its stated goal of 24 teams by 1979. Prospective ownership groups from Denver, Seattle and San Diego were interviewed with the former two even being granted conditional franchises in June 1974. Both groups, however, failed to meet the conditions of their membership.

FIFTH EXPANSION—1979: The NHL's fifth expansion saw membership grow to 21 teams with Edmonton (Oilers), Hartford (Whalers), Quebec (Nordiques) and Winnipeg (Jets) paying franchise fees of $6 million each.

The addition of the four clubs from the World Hockey Association came in June 1979, after more than a year of discussions in which other WHA teams (Houston and Cincinnati) also attempted to gain entry into the league.

To stock the four former WHA teams now joining the NHL, each of the existing 17 teams protected 15 skaters and two goaltenders. Each of the four expansion teams drafted 15 skaters and two goaltenders and were also permitted a maximum of four priority selections from their 1978–79 WHA playing rosters. In the Entry Draft (formerly known as the Amateur Draft), the four expansion teams selected in the 18th through 21st positions.

SIXTH EXPANSION—1991, 1992, 1993: San Jose (Sharks) was added for the 1991–92 season, bringing NHL membership to 22 teams. Ottawa (Senators) and Tampa Bay (Lightning) were added for the 1992–93 season, bringing NHL membership to 24 teams. Anaheim (Mighty Ducks) and Florida (Panthers) were added for the 1993–94 season, bringing NHL membership to 26 teams. The membership cost of each of the franchises from the sixth expansion was $50 million. The process by which the above teams were added is described here:

1991: In December 1989, the NHL's Board of Governors agreed in principle to become a league of 28 teams by the end of the century. On May 9, 1990, the Board approved the awarding of a conditional expansion franchise to the then owners of the Minnesota North Stars, George and Gordon Gund. On the same day, the Board also approved the sale of the North Stars to a group consisting of Howard Baldwin and Morris Belzberg.

1992: The 1992 expansion process began in June 1990 when the league sent out expansion application forms to 50 interested parties throughout North America. By August, a total of 11 applications representing 10 cities were received. The cities were: Hamilton, Houston, Miami, Milwaukee, Ottawa, Phoenix, San Diego (two), St. Petersburg, Seattle and Tampa Bay. Houston, San Diego, Milwaukee, Seattle and Phoenix would withdraw from the process prior to formal presentations to the Board on December 5, 1990.

1993: The league had already identified Anaheim and South Florida as attractive expansion locations when the Board formally announced the two newest additions on December 10, 1992.

SEVENTH EXPANSION—1998, 1999, 2000: The league began the process of growing to a 30-team league in 1998 with the addition of Nashville (Predators). Atlanta (Thrashers) became the 28th team in 1999–2000, and Columbus (Blue Jackets) and Minnesota (Wild) made their debut in the 2000–01 season.

The league's seventh expansion process began on June 26, 1996, when it was announced that the NHL would begin accepting applications for expansion teams. By November 1, 1996, the league had received 11 applications—Atlanta, Columbus, Hamilton, Houston (three applications), Minneapolis-St. Paul, Nashville, Norfolk/Virginia Beach/Newport News (Hampton Roads), Oklahoma City and Raleigh-Durham.

On January 13–14, expansion applicants' presentations were made to the league's Expansion Committee and on February 19, the NHL announced that the list of active expansion applicants had been reduced from 11 to six. The applicants that remained under consideration were: Atlanta, Columbus, Houston, Minneapolis-St. Paul, Nashville and Oklahoma City. On June 17, 1997, the Expansion Committee formally recommended the addition of Nashville, Atlanta, Columbus and Minneapolis-St. Paul and on June 25, 1997, the league's Board of Governors approved the four new teams at a membership cost of $80 million per franchise.

FREE AGENCY

If a club makes a qualifying offer of contract to a player who does not have sufficient professional experience to qualify for Group II free agency, it maintains exclusive negotiation rights to him and he is not eligible for free agency.

FREE AGENCY, GROUP II PLAYER

Any player who meets the qualifications set forth in the following chart and is not a Group I player or a Group IV player, and is not an unrestricted free agent, becomes a Group II restricted free agent upon the expiration of his contract.

FIRST CONTRACT ELIGIBLE FOR GROUP II FREE AGENCY

SIGNING AGE	
18-21	plus three years professional experience
22-23	plus two years professional experience
24+	plus one year professional experience

Clubs must make qualifying offers to Group II free agents to maintain its right of first refusal and/or draft choice compensation. A club's qualifying offer must be 110 percent of the prior year's NHL salary to players making the NHL average salary or less. For players earning more than the NHL average salary, the qualifying offer must be 100 percent of the prior year's NHL salary. The player's old club shall have the right to match any offer and retain the services of the player or, if it elects not to match, to receive draft choice compensation. A qualifying offer for players aged 26 or older must be at least $727,502 for the old club to retain the right to match, the amount has been indexed annually beginning with the 1997–98 league year based on increases in the NHL average salary.

FREE AGENCY, GROUP II COMPENSATION

The level of draft-pick compensation that a club receives for losing a Group II free agent is determined by the salary offer the player receives from his new club. The following chart depicts the current compensation that the player's old club is entitled to.

SALARY OFFER	DRAFT CHOICE COMPENSATION
$727,502 or below	None
$727,503 to 1,000,315	One 3rd round choice
$1,000316 to 1,182,191	One 2nd round choice
$1,182192 to 1,455,005	One 1st round choice
$1,455,006 to 1,818,754	One 1st round and one 3rd round choice
$1,818,755 to 2,182,505	One 1st round and one 2nd round choice
$2,182,506 to 2,546,256	Two 1st round choices
$2,546,257 to 3,091,882	Two 1st round and one 2nd round choice
Over $3,091,882	Three 1st round choices
Each additional $1,818,754	Additional 1st round choice to maximum of five

Clubs owing one pick must have it available in the next draft. Clubs owing two picks in the same round must have them available within the next three entry drafts. Clubs owing three draft picks in the same round must have them available in the next four drafts and so forth. Clubs owing two draft picks in different rounds must have them available in the next draft. Also, clubs must use their own picks and not picks acquired from other clubs.

FREE AGENCY, GROUP II OFFER AND FIRST REFUSAL PROCEDURE

Once a Group II player signs an offer sheet from a new club, his old club, if applicable, has seven days to match that offer and retain the services of the player.

FREE AGENCY, GROUP III PLAYER

Any player who is 31 years of age or older as of June 30, 2003 or 2004 and who has four accrued seasons shall, if his contract expires, become an unrestricted free agent. Such player shall be completely free to negotiate and sign a contract with any club without restriction.

FREE AGENCY, GROUP IV PLAYER

A Group IV player is defined as a player who has never signed an NHL contract and who becomes a free agent after having met the conditions for a defected player. The NHL club owning his rights must make him a qualifying offer and receives only the right to match any offer sheet signed by the player with another NHL club.

FREE AGENCY, GROUP V PLAYER

A Group V player is defined as a player who has completed 10 or more professional seasons (minor league or NHL, excluding junior) and who did not earn in the final year of his contract more than that year's average league salary. This player may elect, once in his career, to negotiate and sign a contract with any club without restriction.

FREE AGENCY, GROUP VI PLAYER

A Group VI player is defined as a player age 25 or older who has completed three or more professional seasons, whose contract has expired and, in the case of a skater, has played less than 80 NHL games (regular season and/or playoffs), or in the case of a goaltender, less than 28 NHL games. A Group VI player is an unrestricted free agent at the end of his contract.

FREE AGENT, LIST

On July 1 of each year a free agent list is issued setting forth the names of those players who are free agents as of that date.

INJURED RESERVE LIST

A club may place a player on the injured reserve list if such player is injured or disabled and unable to perform his duties as a hockey player by reason of an injury sustained during the course of his employment as a hockey player after having passed the club's initial physical examination in that season.

A player who has an injury that renders him physically unable to play for a minimum of seven days after the date of the injury can be placed on the club's injured reserve list. Once a player is placed on injured reserve, the club may replace said player on its NHL roster with another player. All determinations that a player has suffered an injury warranting injured reserve list status must be made by the club's medical staff and in accordance with the club's medical standards.

A player placed on injured reserve is ineligible to compete in NHL games for a period of not less than seven days from the date of injury. A player will be eligible for activation beginning the eighth day from the date of injury.

Players on injured reserve may attend club meetings and meals, travel with their club and participate in practice sessions.

LABOR DISRUPTIONS

During its more than 86-year history, there have been only two labor disputes that forced the postponement of regular-season games—a 10-day players' strike in April 1992 and a 103-day owners' lockout during the 1994–95 campaign.

There has also been one strike by on-ice officials. On November 15, 1993, the 58 members of the NHL Officials' Association initiated a strike. The strike lasted 16 days. The league and the NHLOA agreed upon a four-year collective bargaining agreement on November 30, 1993. Referees and linesmen returned to duty on December 2.

Details of the 1992 strike and 1994 lockout follow:

1992 Strike

The process which led to the players' strike in 1992 actually began on May 14, 1991, when the NHL owners announced their intention to extend the Collective Bargaining Agreement by one year. This declaration was pursuant to a clause in the CBA which stated that a notice of termination and proposed revisions be provided "not less than 120 days prior to the 15th day of September, 1991." The league claimed that the NHLPA's notice of termination and proposed revisions on May 14 was defective as it did not provide any proposals for a revised CBA. The league later requested that the matter be heard by an arbitrator, while the NHLPA balked at any negotiations as long as the threat of an arbitration loomed.

On August 20, 1991, the league withdrew its request for arbitration thereby meeting the NHLPA's request and a month-long period of negotiating began in earnest. While the season commenced as scheduled in October, bargaining sessions ground to a halt between September 25, 1991, and March 9, 1992.

Numerous bargaining sessions during the month of March 1992 yielded very little in the way of progress, however, and on March 20, with the playoffs imminent, the NHLPA announced a strike deadline of March 30 if no agreement were concluded by that time. Forty minutes before the players were to strike NHLPA executive director Bob Goodenow announced a postponement of the deadline until April 1. On April 1, 1992, at 3:00 p.m. ET, with no agreement in place, the NHL players announced that, by a vote of 560–4, they would commence the first league-wide players' strike in NHL history.

A few moments later, President Ziegler announced at a news conference in the Sutton Place Hotel in Toronto: "It is with deep regret that I advise that effective 3:01 p.m. (EST) April 1, 1992, I have declared the 1991–92 NHL season suspended on a day-to-day basis until further notice. This action is required by reason of the unprecedented and regretful decision of the National Hockey League Players' Association to go on strike. Our concerns are for and with the great fans of hockey who will suffer the most from the action taken today by the NHLPA."

Despite the doom and gloom, little time was wasted getting back to the bargaining table as several negotiating sessions took place between April 1–7. Ziegler delivered a final offer to the NHLPA on April 7, with the provision that the offer be accepted by noon on Friday, April 10. Failing acceptance, the clubs would be unable to conclude their season and there would be no Stanley Cup playoff games. Later that day (April 7), less than four hours after receiving the offer, the NHLPA rejected the league's offer. Nevertheless, the offer remained open for acceptance until 3:00 p.m. on April 9. A marathon 14-hour bargaining session in New York eventually concluded with a new two-year Agreement (1991–92 and 1992–93) shortly before midnight on April 10.

At a news conference beginning at 12:04 a.m. on April 11 at the Plaza Hotel in New York, President Ziegler stated: "I'm pleased to report that after a very long day, at times a very difficult day, a day that demonstrated the spirit that traditionally has been between owners and players, we came to a meeting of the minds with respect to the essential provisions and have reached an agreement in principle."

Goodenow stated, "I guess to me the turning point was on Wednesday (April 1), I'd say about 6:00 p.m. There were some owners who came to Toronto with John Ziegler, and I had a feeling then that there was an ambition, a dedication to get this thing taken care of."

The season resumed on Sunday, April 12, with 11 of the remaining 30 regular-season games played. A full slate of Stanley Cup playoff games then ensued.

1994 Lockout

On May 10, 1993, the NHL Board of Governors voted not to terminate the CBA which was set to expire on September 15, 1993. Instead they wished to allow the agreement to remain in effect for an additional year in order to afford ample opportunity to reach a new comprehensive agreement. Ten days later, on May 20, Bob Goodenow advised Commissioner Bettman that the NHLPA had decided to end the CBA that September. Bettman said at the time: "The clubs had decided that, notwithstanding their unhappiness with numerous aspects of the agreement, the most prudent course was to opt for a year of stability and careful planning, in the hopes of avoiding the possibility of contentious labor negotiations during the summer and fall. We know that there are a great many issues to be resolved and we look forward to working closely with the players on those matters. We are disappointed that the agreement had to be reopened at this time. We will negotiate diligently and in good faith to reach a new CBA as soon as possible."

The league played under an expired Collective Bargaining Agreement for the entire 1993–94 season.

Over the 18 month-period from June 1993 through January 1995, representatives of the NHL and NHLPA would meet formally and informally more than 40 times, but an agreement would not be reached until the NHL had closed its doors for 103 days from October 11, 1994, until January 20, 1995.

There was a five-month hiatus in the talks from March until August 1994, and when the negotiations did resume on August 19, 1994, it was against the backdrop of a series of takebacks in a 19-point plan (valued at $20 million) which the league intended to implement on September 1 in the absence of a new CBA. The intended purpose of the threat of the takebacks was to get the negotiations back on track. But following a two-hour meeting with the union, Commissioner Bettman stated, "We did not make as much progress as I would have hoped. It was a very small step in terms of the substance."

While the threat of a lockout loomed, training camps did open as scheduled on September 4 because of the fact that negotiations were in full swing in an attempt to reach an agreement. By September 30, however, with no agreement in sight, the league announced a two-week postponement of the opening of the regular season. If an agreement was reached by then, a full regular-season complement of games would begin on October 15. By October 11, the NHL's Board of Governors voted to postpone indefinitely the start of the season and less than two weeks later (October 24), announced the cancelation of four games. Ten more games were lopped off the schedule on November 2. NHL stars such as Toronto's Mats Sundin and Doug Gilmour, Pittsburgh's Jaromir Jagr and Quebec's Peter Forsberg made their way overseas to maintain their conditioning in European leagues.

A month of more talks still produced nothing and on December 12 the Board of Governors authorized Commissioner Bettman to cancel the season if a 50-game schedule could not be played. January 16 was identified as the last possible starting date in order to play 50 games.

Finally, after two days of marathon bargaining (January 9–10) between the two principle negotiators—NHL commissioner Gary Bettman and NHLPA executive director Bob Goodenow—the league's offer was accepted, subject to ratification, by the NHLPA. A new six-year CBA was in place through September 15, 2000. Training camps opened on January 13 and a 48-game 1995 regular season began on January 20.

LINE CHANGES

The rule which provides the home team with the last change of players prior to the resumption of play was introduced for the 1990–91 season.

A "hurry-up" line change was adopted for the 2002–03 season which reduced the average length of a regular season game by 14 minutes to two hours and 20 minutes.

"LAST MINUTE OF PLAY"

The NHL first required that a public address announcement be made of the last minute of a period for the 1946–47 season.

MARKETING THE GAME

Over the past decade, the National Hockey League has taken a new view of the marketing of hockey. The key principle in this new approach is to maximize exposure by working with a key group of business partners who will invest in all aspects of the game. Corporate partnership agreements, licensing programs, grass-roots fan development initiatives, broadcasting, publishing ventures and the use of new technology have all combined to increase exposure for hockey, NHL players and the League.

When the NHL signs an agreement with a new corporate partner or extends an agreement with an existing partner, the goal is to have the partner support the game in a variety of ways. No longer do sponsors buy a place in the game without providing support for programs that will help the sport grow.

Working with business partners such as Nextel, Labatt, Anheuser Busch, MBNA, MasterCard, Coca-Cola and Dodge, the NHL has drawn unprecedented exposure over the past 10 years. In that same time span, investment in hockey by the league's partners has increased from $25 million to almost $400 million.

The overall growth of the NHL's licensing business has been reflected in the growth of sales of NHL licensed merchandise and the addition of new partners. In the 2002–03 business year, sales of NHL licensed products increased by more than 7 percent to $1.3 billion, far outpacing the industry trend. The league also announced landmark partnership agreements with The LEGO Company and The Hockey Company.

The broadcast of NHL games on CBC's "Hockey Night in Canada" is the longest running regularly scheduled television program in North America. On cable in Canada, the all sports station TSN is the NHL's carrier. In the United States, ABC Sports is the network broadcaster of NHL games and ESPN holds the cable rights. The NHL Network, a digital cable channel, offers fans in Canada wall-to-wall hockey coverage. The NHL has more games broadcast in the high-definition format than any other professional sports league.

On the Internet, the NHL.com Network has become one of the most popular sports sites in the world. NHL.com gives hockey fans around the world real-time access to statistics, summaries, news, features and video of NHL games and the sport of hockey. The NHL.com Network, which is based on the TV network model, is a 30-plus site league-wide network, which includes the NHL homepage, all 30 official team sites, as well as NHL minor league affiliates and other hockey sites around the world, including German and Italian language sites and the Canadian Hockey Association.

The NHL has developed a growing and thriving wireless and licensed content business, one that has increased by more than 300 percent through the 2002–03 season. The NHL has wireless deals that provide subscribers with a wireless version of NHL.com, along with alerts and java-based video games. The business has become highly profitable for the NHL due to the league's superior technological capabilities and tech-savvy nature of its fan base. The NHL is the only professional sports league to digitize its highlights in-house, allowing the league to maximize revenues.

The NHL has identified fan development as a key area in trying to increase interest in the game of hockey and has instituted a series of off- and on-ice programs to attract new fans. In 2002, the league introduced the NHL Hockey Rules Ice and Inline Hockey Tour presented by Southwest Airlines, a series of weekend indoor ice and inline tournaments for youth in eight-and-under through 17-and-under age categories. The NHL Street program introduces hockey to hundreds of thousands of youngsters across the United States. The NHL Fan Development department has partnered with the likes of Nickelodeon, Radio Disney and S.I. (Sports Illustrated) for Kids to further promote the game of hockey and increase its cultural relevancy among the youth audience. NHL Diversity offers assistance to hockey programs in non-traditional markets and recently had a graduate of the program drafted by an NHL team.

The NHL has truly become a worldwide league with more than 33 percent of its players hailing from outside North America and the league's marketing efforts reflect that global diversity. The NHL has competed in the past two Olympic Winter Games held in Nagano and Salt Lake City to further showcase its athletes, as well as sent teams to Europe for training camps and preseason games. In 2004, the second World Cup of Hockey will feature the best players in the world from eight nations competing for their countries. The event will be held in seven cities in Europe and North America.

NATIONAL ANTHEMS

Although several teams had played their country's national anthem prior to games several years earlier, the NHL first required that the national anthem of the home club be played prior to a game for the 1946–47 season. For the 1987–88 season, the league expanded the regulation to its present-day form which requires, when a U.S. and Canadian club are competing, both national anthems be played.

OFFICIATING

In 1998–99, the league instituted a two-referee system with each team playing 20 regular season games with two referees and a pair of linesmen. In 1999–2000, each team played 50 games with the two-referee system and, beginning in 2000–01, all games featured the two-referee system.

The NHL's Officiating Department is responsible for the recruiting, assigning, training and evaluating of NHL referees and linesmen for preseason, regular season and Stanley Cup playoff games. In addition, the league assigns referees for all games in the American Hockey League. In 2002–03, NHL-assigned officials worked more than 2,500 games.

The 2002–03 staff consisted of 33 NHL referees, 34 NHL linesmen, 12 minor-league referees and nine supervisors.

The development system for officials mirrors that of a player with many of the NHL officials recruited while working junior and collegiate hockey before working their way up through the minor professional system.

During the NHL's inaugural season of 1917–18, local referees (one per game) were employed in each of the three NHL cities at a fee of $12.50 per game. The policy of using local referees for NHL games was discontinued in 1926 when the league appointed a full-time staff of six referees.

OVERTIME

Beginning in the 1983–84 season, the league instituted a five-minute "sudden death" overtime period for regular-season games.

In 1999-2000, the league altered its overtime format to feature "four on four" with four skaters and a goalkeeper.

PER DIEM

A per diem of $5 for players (players also paid their own hotel room and were allotted $2.50) was first introduced in the league during the 1930–31 season. A uniform per diem was introduced for players for the first time during the 1968–69 season ($15 per day with the proviso that on game days when clubs provided players with a steak dinner, only $7.50 was paid). Previously, clubs could decide what their team's per diem would be.

Today, a player's per diem is $85.

PLAYERS, EUROPEANS

Jaroslav Drobny, a member of the Czechoslovakian national team that won the International Ice Hockey Federation World Championships in 1947, was the first European player to appear on an NHL club's reserve list. Drobny was placed on Boston's negotiating list in 1949 but would never play in the NHL.

In 1957, Sweden's Sven "Tumba" Johansson became the first European-trained player to attend an NHL team's training camp (Boston Bruins). He never played in the NHL.

On January 27, 1965, Swede Ulf Sterner became the first European-trained player to appear in the NHL as his New York Rangers defeated Boston 5-2.

The first formal rules governing the transfer of European players to the NHL were adopted on September 24, 1968.

In 1972, Sweden's Thommie Bergman became the first European to play as a regular in the NHL (Detroit Red Wings).

On March 29, 1989, Sergei Priakin, a right winger with the Soviet national team, became the first Soviet player to be permitted by the USSR Ice Hockey Federation to play in the NHL. Priakin signed a contract with the Calgary Flames.

(Also see "Breaking New Ice—European Firsts" on page 424.)

PLAYOFF ELIGIBILITY

The idea of a playoff eligibility list was first introduced for the 1946 Stanley Cup playoffs when clubs were required to submit a list of 25 players (excluding goaltenders) who would be eligible to play in that year's playoffs to the league office by March 1. The only additions to the list after the deadline would be players returning from active military service oversees.

Today, only players on the reserve list of an NHL club at the trading deadline may participate in the Stanley Cup playoffs.

PROTECTIVE GLASS/NETTING

Protective glass surrounding the boards first appeared in the NHL at Toronto's Maple Leaf Gardens in 1948. The use of protective glass in all NHL buildings became mandatory in the 1950s.

The league mandated that protective netting be installed above the end glass in all rinks beginning with the 2002–03 season.

RESERVE LIST

During World War II, NHL team rosters were severely depleted as players fulfilled their military obligations. For that reason, the league had loose restrictions on roster limitations. Beginning on May 15, 1947, however, the league required that a club's reserve list not exceed 40 players.

Today, a member club may have on its reserve list, at any one time, not more than 90 players, which shall include the following:

- Not more than 50 players signed to standard player's contracts and not less than 24 players and three goalkeepers under contract. Age 18 and age 19 players who were returned to Canadian major junior hockey clubs, and who have not played 11 games in the National Hockey League in one season, are exempt from inclusion in the 50 player limit.
- Unsigned draft selections.

RINK-BOARD ADVERTISING

Clubs were first granted the right to advertise on rink boards beginning with the 1978–79 season. Such advertising first appeared in 1980 and by the 1989–90 season, all NHL clubs were using rink-board advertising.

Advertising on the ice surface first appeared in the early 1990s.

ROSTER, 23-MAN

There may be a maximum of 23 players on each club's playing roster at any one time from the commencement of the NHL regular season through the trade deadline. Prior to the start of the season, each club must submit to the NHL its "opening day playing roster" which shall be comprised of not more than 23 players. Each club must have a roster of at least 20 players, composed of 18 skaters and two goaltenders. Players on injured reserve do not count in the 23-man limit.

ROSTER, PLAYING

The current playing roster of 18 skaters and two goaltenders was established for the 1982–83 season. The size of the playing roster has varied considerably in league history. In 1925–26, the playing roster was set at a 12-man maximum; it was increased to 15 players in 1929–30 and varied from 12 to 16 skaters plus goalies until 1971–72. Between 1971–72 and 1981–82, the playing roster was set at 17 skaters and two goalies.

SALARY, ARBITRATION

Salary arbitration is a process pursuant to which a club and a player may resolve a salary dispute by presenting their respective cases to an independent arbitrator in which they seek to establish the value of the player's contract. After each side has presented its case, the arbitrator makes a determination as to the appropriate salary for the player to be paid.

A player is eligible to elect salary arbitration if the player meets the qualifications set forth in the following chart:

FIRST CONTRACT ELIGIBLE FOR SALARY ARBITRATION

SIGNING AGE	
18-20	Five years professional experience
21	Four years professional experience
22-23	Three years professional experience
24	Two years professional experience
25+	One year professional experience

SALARY, CAP

The only salary cap currently in place is for entry level players (see Entry Level System, Compensation).

In the league's formative years there was a salary cap, beginning in 1925–26 when the salary limit for a 12-player team was set at $35,000. That team cap grew to $70,000 (14-man roster plus goalies) in 1932–33 with the further provision that no player's salary could exceed $7,500. The cap was eliminated by the late 1930s after the Great Depression had ended.

SALARY, MINIMUM

A minimum player's salary of $7,000 was first introduced for the 1958–59 season.

For 2003–04 the minimum NHL salary is $180,000.

SALARY, MINOR LEAGUE

The minimum minor-league salary for a player is $30,000 (American Hockey League) for an entry level player; the maximum compensation is 50 percent of the NHL minimum salary for 2003-04. The maximum compensation payable to a player who is playing major junior hockey is $9,500.

SUPPLEMENTARY DISCIPLINE

In accordance with NHL rules (Rule 33A of the Rule Book), an NHL club general manager has 24 hours following the completion of a game to request a review of an on-ice incident. A review may also be initiated by the NHL based on its own video review, the game reports of the officials or supervisor of officials. A match penalty is automatically reviewed by the NHL.

After an initial screening of the videotape, the incident is either deemed not to warrant further action or to be "under review." Before a player can be disciplined he is entitled to a hearing, which may be conducted either in person or by telephone conference call.

All player suspensions are without pay, meaning that a club must remit the player's salary for the period in which he is suspended to the league. Player fine money goes to the NHL's Emergency Assistance Fund to benefit former players. The NHL calculates the amount of money the player must forfeit due to the suspension. This is calculated on the following basis:

a) For first offenders (first incident requiring supplementary discipline in the form of a game suspension), player to forfeit one day's salary for each regular-season game lost (one divided by the total number of days in the season measured from the date of the NHL's first regular-season game to the last, irrespective of the player's club's schedule.

b) For repeat offenders (second or subsequent incidents requiring game suspension), player to forfeit one game's salary for each regular-season game lost (one divided by the number of regular season games for each regular season game suspended).

A player may also be fined up to $1,000, the maximum permitted under the Collective Bargaining Agreement.

SCOREBOARD

The use of scoreboards in all NHL arenas to show scores from out of town games became mandatory beginning in February 1955.

STANLEY CUP, ENGRAVING OF NAMES

The Stanley Cup is the oldest trophy competed for by professional athletes in North America and is the only trophy that provides for each player from the winning team to have his name engraved on it. Prior to the 1976–77 season, only those players who competed in the Stanley Cup playoffs were eligible to have their names engraved on the Stanley Cup. In January 1977, however, the NHL changed the criteria to allow players competing in 40 regular-season games or one final-series game to have their names on the Cup. Since 1994, the league has allowed exceptions to this rule in the case of players who, by reason of injury, do not appear in the sufficient number of games.

TELEVISION

Prior to 1968, all broadcast revenues were divided according to international borders. With the exception of local market revenues that were reserved for the home team, all U.S. broadcast rights revenue was evenly distributed among the U.S.-based member clubs, while all Canadian broadcast rights revenues were evenly divided among the Canadian-based clubs. In 1968, the first version of the Trans-Border TV Rights Agreement was devised which saw the Canadian broadcast rightsholder (Molson) pay the U.S. broadcaster (CBS) for the right to air playoff games between two U.S.-based clubs within Canada. Molson, who owned the rights to cover games that involved two Canadian-based member clubs, did not have the right to cover any playoff games that involved two US-based clubs. The TBA was formed to allow Molson to cover the playoffs, in the event that no Canadian-based teams advance to the Stanley Cup finals. The sum that would be paid to the U.S. broadcaster was evenly split among all U.S. member clubs.

The TBA was altered a few more times, beginning in the early 1980s when Carling O'Keefe acquired the rights to cover home games between Canadian clubs and U.S. teams in Canada, while Molson continued to broadcast all home games between the Canadian teams. Since all broadcast rights were controlled by the clubs and not the NHL, it was possible to sell non-exclusive rights to a variety of broadcasters. However, this was changed in 1986 when it was announced that the league would sell the exclusive rights to broadcast coverage. The home team would reserve the right to provide its own exclusive coverage of home games within its local market, but the league's rightsholder would provide coverage to the rest of the nation. The division of such revenue would follow the previous guidelines of international boundaries.

The agreement was once again altered in accordance with the rise of U.S. cable. The NHL negotiated agreements with the emerging cable companies in the U.S. and revised the TBA so that all broadcast revenue from the sale of exclusive rights to both Canadian and U.S. networks and cable companies would be pooled and equally divided among all member clubs. This process of pooling and equal distribution of national television revenue remains in effect in today's NHL.

TIE-BREAKING PROCEDURE, REGULAR-SEASON STANDINGS

At the conclusion of the regular season, the standing of the teams in each conference shall be determined in accordance with the following priorities in the order listed:

a) The higher number of points earned by the club.

b) The greater number of games won by the club.

c) The higher number of points earned in games against each other among two or more clubs having equal standing under priorities (a) and (b).

NOTE: For the purpose of determining standings under priority (c) for two teams that have not played an equal number of games with each other, points earned in the first game played in the city that has the extra game shall not be included. However, when more than two teams are tied, the percentage of available points earned in games among each other shall be used to determine the standing.

d) The greater differential between goals scored for and against by clubs having equal standing under priority (c).

A tie-breaking formula was first introduced in 1928–29 (most wins followed by better goal differential). In 1940, the criteria was changed to most wins; followed by fewest losses; most goals for; and fewest goals against. In 1970–71, the NHL adopted head-to-head results as the second criteria ahead of goals for and against. The current criteria were adopted beginning in 1984–85.

In 1969–70, the tie-breaking formula led to a bizarre regular-season finish. The New York Rangers, after leading the NHL standings for much of the 1969–70 season, found themselves in a must-win situation on the last day of the regular season in order to have a chance to qualify for the final postseason position in the East Division. They trailed the Montreal Canadiens by two points heading into the final day and also had to overcome a five-goal Montreal advantage that the Canadiens owned in the goals-for criteria. The Canadiens had scored 242 goals as compared to 237 goals for the Rangers heading into the final day of action, Sunday, April 5.

Playing an afternoon game at Madison Square Garden against Detroit, the Rangers gave themselves a chance, scoring nine goals in a 9–5 win, while outshooting the Red Wings 65–22. They pushed their points total to 92 and number of wins to 38 to tie the Canadiens for the last playoff spot and their goals-for total to 246, four better than Montreal.

Montreal still had one game to play—an evening encounter versus the Black Hawks at Chicago Stadium—where any of the following scenarios would get them into the playoffs ahead of the Rangers: a win, a tie or five goals scored.

A wild evening ensued. The Canadiens, trailing 3–2 entering the third period, fell behind 5–2 with less than 10 minutes to go in the game. Canadiens coach Claude Ruel, sensing his team would not get the tie or win, pulled goaltender Rogatien Vachon for an extra attacker at the 11:40 mark of the third period in the hope of scoring the necessary five goals. Five goals were scored—but all by the Black Hawks into an empty Montreal net.

The Canadiens lost the game 10–2, and by failing to score five goals, were eliminated from participating in the Stanley Cup playoffs for the first time in 22 years. During the off-season, the NHL adopted head-to-head results as the second criteria (after wins) for breaking a tie between two clubs in the standings.

TIE-BREAKING PROCEDURE, ART ROSS TROPHY/INDIVIDUAL AWARDS

In 1979–80, Edmonton's Wayne Gretzky and Marcel Dionne of Los Angeles tied for the league lead in scoring with 137 points. Dionne was awarded the Art Ross Trophy based on his having scored 53 goals to Gretzky's 51 goals. The same situation had presented itself 18 years earlier when Bobby Hull and Andy Bathgate shared the scoring lead with 84 points. Hull was awarded the Art Ross Trophy based on his having scored 50 goals to Bathgate's 28.

Additional tie-break criteria were established for the 1987–88 season in the event that the tied players had scored an equal number of goals. The player who had taken part in the fewest games would then be awarded the trophy, with the next tiebreaker (if necessary) being the earliest date of each player's first goal.

For the remainder of the league's individual awards, the number of first-place votes is the determining factor in breaking a tie followed by most second-place votes and so forth.

In 2002, for the first time in league history, two players tied in voting for the Hart Trophy (league MVP) as Montreal's Jose Theodore and Calgary's Jarome Iginla each collected 434 points. Theodore won the award based on more first place votes (26 to Iginla's 23).

TIMING DEVICES

GAME CLOCKS: Visible time clocks were first required in NHL rinks in 1933–34.

GOAL LIGHTS: In November 1938, the league passed a resolution requiring that all rinks be equipped with a "timing-lighting device" behind the goal, showing a green light at the expiry of each period. The new equipment made it impossible for the red goal light to be illuminated once the green light was on. Toronto was the first NHL club to have such a light installed in its rink—in March 1936.

DRESSING ROOM: The league first required clocks in the dressing rooms to alert players of the amount of time remaining before the start of a game or period for the 1986–87 season.

TRANSFER OF PLAYERS

TRADING DEADLINE: NHL players may be traded at any time up to 3:00 p.m. Eastern Time of the 26th day immediately preceding the final day of the regular season. (The trading deadline in 2003–04 is March 9, 2004.)

LOANING PLAYERS: An NHL club may loan players on its reserve list to clubs of any league affiliated with the NHL at any time up to 3:00 p.m. Eastern Time of the 26th day immediately preceding the final day of the regular season.

During the period following noon of the 26th day immediately preceding the final day of the regular season no player may be recalled from loan to a member club of any league affiliated with the league, except that:

a) An NHL club may exercise four recalls from a member club or clubs of a league affiliated with the NHL.

b) Players may be recalled on an emergency basis.

c) Players may be recalled upon completion of the regular season and playoffs of the club to which they were loaned.

EMERGENCY RECALL: A player on loan to a club of any league affiliated with the NHL may be recalled under emergency conditions at any time. Emergency conditions are established when the playing strength of the NHL club, by reason of injury, illness or by league suspension, is reduced below the level of two goaltenders, six defensemen and 12 forwards.

IIHF/NHL: Any player under contract to an International Ice Hockey Federation team may be signed by an NHL club through July 15 of the year in which he will begin play in the NHL (e.g. July 15, 2003 was the signing deadline for a player for the 2003–04 season). For players drafted in the most recent Entry Draft, however, the deadline is August 15. The cost the NHL club must pay to the IIHF for any player signed between July 15 and August 15 is $100,000.

Any player who is under contract to an IIHF team; signs an NHL contract; has not yet reached his 20th birthday; is unable to earn a roster position on his NHL club by the first day of the NHL season and was not selected in the first round of the NHL Entry Draft may not be assigned by his NHL club to a minor-league affiliate but instead must be returned to his IIHF club for the balance of the IIHF season.

Players not under contract to an IIHF team or who were selected in the first round of the NHL Entry Draft or have reached their 20th birthday may be assigned by an NHL team to a minor-league club without restriction. All other players not signed by their NHL club must be returned to their IIHF club.

TRYOUT

An NHL club may enter into a tryout agreement with any amateur player whose eligibility for junior hockey is exhausted (ie. has attained or will have attained his 20th birthday by December 31 next following). Such a tryout may not last for more than eight regular-season games and cannot take place prior to November 1 or after March 1.

VIDEO REPLAY

Video replay was first instituted in the NHL in the 1991–92 season with the following situations subject to review: puck crossing the goal line; puck in the net prior to the goal frame being dislodged; puck in the net prior to, or after expiration of time at the end of the period; puck directed into the net by a hand or foot; puck deflected into the net off an official; puck struck with a high stick (this criteria was actually added after the start of the 1991–92 season on December 6). Prior to the 1994–95 season, an additional criteria was added to establish the correct time on the game clock, while the man in the crease criteria was added in 1996–97 and then eliminated following the 1998–99 season.

Experimentation into using video replay for NHL games was first done in November 1985 in a U.S. collegiate game at Michigan State. Further experiments were conducted by the NHL on February 13-14, 1986, in the International Hockey League.

WAIVERS

Waivers were first introduced in the league in 1922. The new clause in the bylaws read: "No club in this league shall have the right to sell outright, option or otherwise exchange any of its players to any other league without first offering the services of such player or players to all NHL clubs at a price not to exceed $1,500." Today, waivers operate under that basic principle adopted in the league's early days.

WAIVER DRAFT (INTRA-LEAGUE DRAFT), REGULAR-SEASON WAIVERS

Parity in the six-team NHL had become of great concern to the NHL owners in the 1950–51 season when the last-place Chicago Black Hawks finished 65 points behind the league-leading Montreal Canadiens. A number of discussions ensued as to the feasibility of adopting a draft system to assist the weaker clubs with a player (or players) from the stronger clubs. In June 1952, the Intra-League Draft (the forerunner of the Waiver Draft) was adopted. It provided that each club would have the right to protect 25 professional players on its reserve list. In turn, the three lowest clubs in the league standings from the previous season were entitled to draft from the top three clubs two professional players. The top three clubs were then able to draft one professional player (not included on any protected list) from any other club with the draft price for any player established at $7,500.

Each year the NHL holds a Waiver Draft prior to the start of the regular season. The Waiver Draft is organized to allow each club an equal opportunity to acquire unprotected talent from the league's other member clubs. Prior to the start of each year, NHL clubs must submit a protected list consisting of 18 skaters and two goaltenders. The order of selection is based on the inverse order of standing from the previous regular season, beginning with only non-playoff teams selecting in the first round. Each subsequent round offers each member club an opportunity for selection. The draft is concluded when a round is completed without any clubs making a selection. In the first round, a team is not permitted to claim a player from a club in its own division. When a player is claimed he must immediately be placed on the claiming team's protected list, replacing a previously protected player who is now made available for claim by other clubs. A team losing a player is granted the option of receiving a cash payment from the claiming club or the player who is taken off the claiming team's protected list. No team shall lose more than three players, however, each club reserves the right to offer as many players as it so chooses. In addition, this three-man limit will increase according to the number of additional players the team claims in the draft.

Not every player is eligible for claim in the Waiver Draft. Exemptions are based on the players' age and experience in the league. For example, a player 18 years of age will not be eligible for the Waiver Draft for five years or until he has played in 160 NHL games.

Today, the number of years a player is exempt from the Waiver Draft is outlined in the chart that follows. The exemption ends once the player has played in the number of NHL regular-season and playoff games set forth in the applicable column.

Goaltenders				Skaters			
Age	Years from NHL signing		NHL Games Played	Age	Years from NHL signing		NHL Games Played
18	6	or	80	18	5	or	160
19	5	or	80	19	4	or	160
20	4	or	80	20	3	or	160
21	4	or	60	21	3	or	80
22	4	or	60	22	3	or	70
23	3	or	60	23	3	or	60
24	2	or	60	24	2	or	60
25+	1			25+	1		

The rights granted to assign a player who is otherwise required to clear waivers to a minor-league club expire for any player, who, after clearing the Waiver Draft or regular-season waivers:

- Is not sent to a minor-league club, or is recalled from a minor-league club (except on emergency recall) and;
- Remains on an NHL roster for 30 days (cumulative) or plays 10 NHL games (cumulative).

ZAMBONI

A marked improvement in the playing conditions of the ice surface resulted in the early 1950s with the widespread adoption of the Zamboni ice-finishing machine that replaced the old practice of flooding the rink between periods. Instead of merely coating the ice with water, the Zamboni scraped away a layer of the old surface first, resulting in a quicker and smoother freeze.

With more clubs providing fans with between-periods entertainment on the ice, the league adopted a rule in early 1990s that requires teams to use two Zambonis to resurface the ice.

CHAPTER 7

All-Time NHL Playoff Formats

1917-18 – The regular-season was split into two halves. The winners of both halves faced each other in a two-game, total-goals series for the NHL championship and the right to meet the Pacific Coast Hockey Association champion in the best-of-five Stanley Cup Finals.

1918-19 – Same as 1917-18, except that the NHL Finals was extended to a best-of-seven series.

1919-20 – Same as 1917-1918, except that Ottawa won both halves of the split regular-season schedule to earn an automatic berth into the best-of-five Stanley Cup Finals against the PCHA champions.

1921-22 – The top two teams at the conclusion of the regular-season faced each other in a two-game, total-goals series for the NHL championship. The NHL champion then moved on to play the winner of the PCHA-Western Canada Hockey League playoff series in the best-of-five Stanley Cup Finals.

1922-23 – The top two teams at the conclusion of the regular-season faced each other in a two-game, total-goals series for the NHL championship. The NHL champion then moved on to play the PCHA champion in the best-of-three Stanley Cup Semi-Finals, and the winner of the Semi-Finals played the WCHL champion, which had been given a bye, in the best-of-three Stanley Cup Finals.

1923-24 – The top two teams at the conclusion of the regular-season faced each other in a two-game, total-goals series for the NHL championship. The NHL champion then moved on to play the loser of the PCHA-WCHL playoff (the winner of the PCHA-WCHL playoff earned a bye into the Stanley Cup Finals) in the best-of-three Stanley Cup Semi-Finals. The winner of this series met the PCHA-WCHL playoff winner in the best-of-three Stanley Cup Finals.

1924-25 – The first place team (Hamilton) at the conclusion of the regular-season was scheduled to play the winner of a two-game, total goals series between the second (Toronto) and third (Montreal) place clubs. However, Hamilton refused to abide by this new format, demanding greater compensation than offered by the League. Thus, Toronto and Montreal played their two-game, total-goals series, and the winner (Montreal) earned the NHL title and then played the WCHL champion (Victoria) in the best-of-five Stanley Cup Finals.

1925-26 – The format which was intended for 1924-25 went into effect. The winner of the two-game, total-goals series between the second and third place teams squared off against the first place team in the two-game, total-goals NHL championship series. The NHL champion then moved on to play the Western Hockey League champion in the best-of-five Stanley Cup Finals.

After the 1925-26 season, the NHL was the only major professional hockey league still in existence and consequently took over sole control of the Stanley Cup competition.

1926-27 – The 10-team league was divided into two divisions – Canadian and American – of five teams apiece. In each division, the winner of the two-game, total-goals series between the second and third place teams faced the first place team in a two-game, total-goals series for the division title. The two division title winners then met in the best-of-five Stanley Cup Finals.

1928-29 – Both first place teams in the two divisions played each other in a best-of-five series. Both second place teams in the two divisions played each other in a two-game, total-goals series as did the two third place teams. The winners of these latter two series then played each other in a best-of-three series for the right to meet the winner of the series between the two first place clubs. This Stanley Cup Final was a best-of-three.

Series A: First in Canadian Division versus first in American (best-of-five)
Series B: Second in Canadian Division versus second in American (two-game, total-goals)
Series C: Third in Canadian Division versus third in American (two-game, total-goals)
Series D: Winner of Series B versus winner of Series C (best-of-three)
Series E: Winner of Series A versus winner of Series D (best-of-three) for Stanley Cup

1931-32 – Same as 1928-29, except that Series D was changed to a two-game, total-goals format and Series E was changed to best-of-five.

1936-37 – Same as 1931-32, except that Series B, C, and D were each best-of-three.

1938-39 – With the NHL reduced to seven teams, the two-division system was replaced by one seven-team league. Based on final regular-season standings, the following playoff format was adopted:

Series A: First versus Second (best-of-seven)
Series B: Third versus Fourth (best-of-three)
Series C: Fifth versus Sixth (best-of-three)
Series D: Winner of Series B versus winner of Series C (best-of-three)
Series E: Winner of Series A versus winner of Series D (best-of-seven)

1942-43 – With the NHL reduced to six teams (the "original six"), only the top four finishers qualified for playoff action. The best-of-seven Semi-Finals pitted Team #1 vs Team #3 and Team #2 vs Team #4. The winners of each Semi-Final series met in the best-of-seven Stanley Cup Finals.

1967-68 – When it doubled in size from 6 to 12 teams, the NHL once again was divided into two divisions – East and West – of six teams apiece. The top four clubs in each division qualified for the playoffs (all series were best-of-seven):

Series A: Team #1 (East) vs Team #3 (East)
Series B: Team #2 (East) vs Team #4 (East)
Series C: Team #1 (West) vs Team #3 (West)
Series D: Team #2 (West) vs Team #4 (West)
Series E: Winner of Series A vs winner of Series B
Series F: Winner of Series C vs winner of Series D
Series G: Winner of Series E vs Winner of Series F

1970-71 – Same as 1967-68 except that Series E matched the winners of Series A and D, and Series F matched the winners of Series B and C.

1971-72 – Same as 1970-71, except that Series A and C matched Team #1 vs Team #4, and Series B and D matched Team #2 vs Team #3.

1974-75 – With the League now expanded to 18 teams in four divisions, a completely new playoff format was introduced. First, the #2 and #3 teams in each of the four divisions were pooled together in the Preliminary round. These eight (#2 and #3) clubs were ranked #1 to #8 based on regular-season record:

Series A: Team #1 vs Team #8 (best-of-three)
Series B: Team #2 vs Team #7 (best-of-three)
Series C: Team #3 vs Team #6 (best-of-three)
Series D: Team #4 vs Team #5 (best-of-three)

The winners of this Preliminary round then pooled together with the four division winners, which had received byes into this Quarter-Final round. These eight teams were again ranked #1 to #8 based on regular-season record:

Series E: Team #1 vs Team #8 (best-of-seven)
Series F: Team #2 vs Team #7 (best-of-seven)
Series G: Team #3 vs Team #6 (best-of-seven)
Series H: Team #4 vs Team #5 (best-of-seven)

The four Quarter-Finals winners, which moved on to the Semi-Finals, were then ranked #1 to #4 based on regular season record:

Series I: Team #1 vs Team #4 (best-of-seven)
Series J: Team #2 vs Team #3 (best-of-seven)
Series K: Winner of Series I vs winner of Series J (best-of-seven)

1977-78 – Same as 1974-75, except that the Preliminary round consisted of the #2 teams in the four divisions and the next four teams based on regular-season record (not their standings within their divisions).

1979-80 – With the addition of four WHA franchises, the League expanded its playoff structure to include 16 of its 21 teams. The four first place teams in the four divisions automatically earned playoff berths. Among the 17 other clubs, the top 12, according to regular-season record, also earned berths. All 16 teams were then pooled together and ranked #1 to #16 based on regular-season record:

Series A: Team #1 vs Team #16 (best-of-five)
Series B: Team #2 vs Team #15 (best-of-five)
Series C: Team #3 vs Team #14 (best-of-five)
Series D: Team #4 vs Team #13 (best-of-five)
Series E: Team #5 vs Team #12 (best-of-five)
Series F: Team #6 vs Team #11 (best-of-five)
Series G: Team #7 vs Team #10 (best-of-five)
Series H: Team #8 vs Team #9 (best-of-five)

The eight Preliminary round winners, ranked #1 to #8 based on regular-season record, moved on to the Quarter-Finals:

Series I: Team #1 vs Team #8 (best-of-seven)
Series J: Team #2 vs Team #7 (best-of-seven)
Series K: Team #3 vs Team #6 (best-of-seven)
Series L: Team #4 vs Team #5 (best-of-seven)

The four Quarter-Finals winners, ranked #1 to #4 based on regular-season record, moved on to the Semi-Finals:

Series M: Team #1 vs Team #4 (best-of-seven)
Series N: Team #2 vs Team #3 (best-of-seven)
Series O: Winner of Series M vs winner of Series N (best-of-seven)

1981-82 – The first four teams in each division earned playoff berths. In each division, the first-place team opposed the fourth-place team and the second-place team opposed the third-place team in a best-of-five Division Semi-Final (DSF) series. In each division, the two winners of the DSF met in a best-of-seven Division Final (DF) series. The two DF winners in each conference met in a best-of-seven Conference Final (CF) series. In the Prince of Wales Conference, the Adams Division winner opposed the Patrick Division winner; in the Clarence Campbell Conference, the Smythe Division winner opposed the Norris Division winner. The two CF winners met in a best-of-seven Stanley Cup Final (F) series.

1986-87 – Division Semi-Final series changed from best-of-five to best-of-seven.

1993-94 – The NHL's playoff draw was conference-based rather than division-based. At the conclusion of the regular season, the top eight teams in each of the Eastern and Western Conferences qualified for the playoffs. The teams that finished in first place in each of the League's divisions are seeded first and second in each conference's playoff draw and were assured of home ice advantage in the first two playoff rounds.

The remaining teams were seeded based on their regular-season point totals. In each conference, the team seeded #1 plays #8; #2 vs. #7; #3 vs. #6; and #4 vs. #5. All series were best-of-seven with home ice rotating on a 2-2-1-1-1 basis, with the exception of matchups between Central and Pacific Division teams. These matchups were played on a 2-3-2 basis to reduce travel. In a 2-3-2 series, the team with the most points could choose to start the series at home or on the road. The Eastern Conference champion faced the Western Conference champion in the Stanley Cup Final.

1994-95 – Same as 1993-94, except that in first, second or third-round playoff series involving Central and Pacific Division teams, the team with the better record had the choice of using either a 2-3-2 or a 2-2-1-1-1 format. When a 2-3-2 format was selected, the higher-ranked team also had the choice of playing games 1, 2, 6 and 7 at home or playing games 3, 4 and 5 at home. The format for the Stanley Cup Final remained 2-2-1-1-1.

1998-99 – The NHL's clubs were re-aligned into two conferences each consisting of three divisions. The number of teams qualifying for the Stanley Cup Playoffs remained unchanged at 16.

First-round playoff berths were awarded to the first-place team in each division as well as to the next five best teams based on regular-season point totals in each conference. The three division winners in each conference were seeded first through third, in order of points, for the playoffs and the next five best teams, in order of points, were seeded fourth through eighth. In each conference, the team seeded #1 played #8; #2 vs. #7; #3 vs. #6; and #4 vs. #5 in the quarter-final round. Home-ice in the Conference Quarter-Finals was granted to those teams seeded first through fourth in each conference.

In the Conference Semi-Finals and Conference Finals, teams were re-seeded according to the same criteria as the Conference Quarter-Finals. Higher seeded teams gained home-ice advantage.

Home-ice advantage for the Stanley Cup Finals to be determined by points.

All series remain best-of-seven.

2004 NHL Playoff Format

THE NATIONAL HOCKEY LEAGUE'S 30 CLUBS are aligned into two conferences, each consisting of three divisions (Eastern Conference: Atlantic, Northeast, Southeast; Western Conference: Central, Northwest, Pacific). The number of teams qualifying for the 2004 Stanley Cup playoffs remains at 16.

First-round playoff berths will be awarded to the first-place team in each division, as well as to the next five best teams (based on regular-season point totals in each conference). The three division winners in each conference will be seeded first through third (in order of points) and the next five best teams (in order of points) will be seeded fourth through eighth. In each conference, the team seeded #1 will play the team seeded #8; #2 vs. #7; #3 vs. #6 and #4 vs. #5 in the Conference Quarter-Final round. Home-ice in the Conference Quarter-Finals is granted to those teams seeded first through fourth in each conference.

In the Conference Semi-Finals and Conference Finals, teams will be re-seeded according to the same criteria as the Conference Quarter-Finals (division leaders will be seeded first and granted home-ice advantage while the remaining teams will be seeded in order of regular-season points).

Home-ice advantage in the Stanley Cup series will be determined by points.

All series remain best-of-seven.

In the event two or more clubs are tied in points at the conclusion of the regular season, the standing of the clubs in each conference will be determined by a tie-breaking procedure described on page 437.

Conference Quarter-Finals (Series A – H)

The six regular-season division champions will be ranked in the first three positions in their respective conferences, the clubs with the greatest number of points being ranked first in their respective conferences. The remaining five playoff clubs in each conference will be ranked based on regular-season points. Following are the matchups based on the rankings.

Eastern Conference

Series A #1 (Division winner) vs. #8
Series B #2 (Division winner) vs. #7
Series C #3 (Division winner) vs. #6
Series D #4 vs. #5

Western Conference

Series E #1 (Division winner) vs. #8
Series F #2 (Division winner) vs. #7
Series G #3 (Division winner) vs. #6
Series H #4 vs. #5

Conference Semi-Finals (Series I – L)

If one division winner is eliminated in the Conference Quarter-Finals: The remaining division winners would be seeded first and second, followed by the two remaining clubs in order of regular-season points. The #1 seed would face the club with the fewest regular-season points, while the other two clubs would meet.

If two division winners are eliminated in the Conference Quarter-Finals: The remaining division winner would be seeded first, followed by the three remaining clubs in order of regular-season points. The #1 seed would face the club with the fewest regular-season points, while the other two clubs would meet.

If all three division winners are eliminated in the Conference Quarter-Finals: The remaining clubs would be ranked in order of regular-season points. The remaining team with the most regular-season points would be seeded first, followed by the three remaining teams. The #1 seed would face the #4 seed, while the #2 and #3 seeds would meet.

If a division winner meets a non-division winner that compiled more regular-season points: The division winner would receive home-ice advantage.

Conference Finals (Series M and N)

The same criteria used in the selection of order for the Conference Quarter-Finals (Advancing division winners, followed by remaining clubs based on regular-season points) again will be in effect.

If a division winner meets a non-division winner that compiled more regular-season points: The division winner would receive home-ice advantage.

If Conference Semi-Final series end early: Start dates for the Conference Finals may be moved up depending on a number of factors, including building availability and travel schedules.

Stanley Cup Final (Series O)

The Eastern Conference and Western Conference champion will meet in the Stanley Cup Final series. Home ice will be determined by the greater number of regular-season points, subject to the tie-breaking procedures outlined earlier. Games will be played on a 2-2-1-1-1 basis.

CHAPTER 8

The Hockey Hall of Fame

Honoured Members by Year of Induction

The Hockey Hall of Fame was established in 1943. with members first inducted in 1945. On August 26, 1961, the Hall opened its doors to the public in a building located on the grounds of the Canadian National Exhibition in Toronto.

The Hockey Hall of Fame relocated to its present site in downtown Toronto, welcoming the hockey world on June 18, 1993.

There are 332 "Honoured Members" in the Hockey Hall of Fame. 227 have been inducted as players, 91 as builders and 14 as referees or linesmen. In addition to the names listed here, there are 68 media honourees. (Note that the Hall of Fame always uses the Canadian spelling of the word "honoured.")

The Hockey Hall of Fame's 18-person selection committee is responsible for nominating and electing new members in the player, builder and referee/linesman categories. Nominees must receive three-quarters of the committee's votes to be elected. The members of the selection committee are: Jim Gregory (chairman), Al Arbour, Scotty Bowman, Ed Chynoweth, John Davidson, Mike Emrick, Red Fisher, Emile Francis, Dick Irvin Jr., Stan Mikita, Richard M. Patrick, Marty Pavelich, Pat Quinn, Bertrand Raymond, Serge Savard, Frank Selke Jr., Harry Sinden and Frank Udvari.

The maximum number of player inductees permitted in one year is four; for builders, two and for referees/linesmen, one. Players, referees and linesmen become eligible three years after the end of their on-ice careers. Over the years, 10 players have been inducted without the customary waiting period: Dit Clapper, Maurice Richard, Ted Lindsay, Red Kelly, Terry Sawchuk, Jean Beliveau, Gordie Howe, Bobby Orr, Mario Lemieux and Wayne Gretzky. Gretzky will be the last player to be so honored as the Hall of Fame has amended its rules to make the three-year waiting period an absolute requirement.

The Hockey Hall of Fame celebrated 10 years in its downtown Toronto location in June of 2003. More than 300,000 hockey fans visit each year.

1945
* Sir Montaqu Allan. . . . . . . Builder
* Dan Bain . . . . Player
* Hobey Baker. . . . . Player
* Russell Bowie. . . . . Player
* Charlie Gardiner . . . . Player
* Eddie Gerard . . . . Player
* Frank McGee . . . . Player
* Howie Morenz . . . . Player
* Tommy Phillips . . . . Player
* Harvey Pulford . . . . Player
* Art Ross. . . . . Player
* Lord Stanley of Preston . . . Builder
* Hod Stuart . . . . Player
* Georges Vezina. . . . . Player

1947
* Frank Calder. . . . . Builder
* Aubrey "Dit" Clapper . . . . Player
* W.A. Hewitt . . . . Builder
* Aurel Joliat. . . . . Player
* Francis Nelson . . . . Builder
* Frank Nighbor . . . . Player
* William M. Northey. . . . . . Builder
* Lester Patrick . . . . Player
* John Ross Robertson. . . . . Builder
* Claude C. Robinson. . . . . . Builder
* Eddie Shore . . . . Player
* James T. Sutherland. . . . . . Builder
* Frederick "Cyclone" Taylor. Player

1950
* Allan "Scotty" Davidson . . Player
* Charles Drinkwater . . . . . . Player
* Mike Grant. . . . . Player
* Si Griffis. . . . . Player
* Edouard "Newsy" Lalonde. Player
* Joe Malone . . . . Player
* George Richardson . . . . . . Player
* Harry Trihey . . . . Player

1952
* Dickie Boon . . . . Player
* Bill Cook . . . . Player
* F.X. "Moose" Goheen . . . . Player
* Ernest "Moose" Johnson. . Player
* Duncan "Mickey" MacKay. Player

1958
* Frank Boucher . . . . Player
* Francis "King" Clancy . . . . Player
* Sprague Cleghorn . . . . Player
* Alex Connell. . . . . Player
* George Dudley . . . . Builder
* Mervyn "Red" Dutton . . . . Player
* Frank Foyston . . . . Player
* Frank Fredrickson . . . . Player
* Herb Gardiner. . . . . Player
* George Hay . . . . Player
* Dick Irvin . . . . Player
* Ivan "Ching" Johnson . . . . Player
* Gordon "Duke" Keats . . . . Player
* Hugh Lehman. . . . . Player
* George McNamara . . . . . . Player
* Paddy Moran . . . . Player
* James Norris, Sr. . . . . Builder
* Frank Patrick . . . . Builder
* Al Pickard . . . . Builder
* Donat Raymond . . . . Builder
* Conn Smythe . . . . Builder
* Lloyd Turner . . . . Builder

1959
* Jack Adams . . . . Player
* Cy Denneny . . . . Player
* Cecil "Tiny" Thompson . . . Player

1960
* Charles Adams . . . . Builder
* George "Buck" Boucher . . Player
* John Reed Kilpatrick . . . . . Builder
* Sylvio Mantha . . . . Player
* Frank Selke. . . . . Builder
* Jack Walker . . . . Player

1961
* Syl Apps. . . . . Player
* George Brown . . . . Builder
* Charlie Conacher . . . . Player
* Clarence "Hap" Day . . . . . Player
* Chaucer Elliott . . . . Referee
* George Hainsworth. . . . . . Player
* Joe Hall . . . . Player
* Fred "Mickey" Ion. . . . . . . Referee
* Percy LeSueur. . . . . Player
* Paul Loicq . . . . Builder
* Frank Rankin . . . . Player
* Maurice "Rocket" Richard . Player
Milt Schmidt. . . . . Player
* Oliver Seibert . . . . Player
* Cooper Smeaton. . . . . Referee
* Bruce Stuart. . . . . Player
* Fred Waghorn. . . . . Builder

1962
* Frank Ahearn . . . . Builder
* Harry "Punch" Broadbent . Player
* Walter Brown. . . . . Builder
* Harry Cameron. . . . . Player
* Russell "Rusty" Crawford . Player
* Jack Darragh . . . . Player
* Jimmy Gardner. . . . . Player
* Billy Gilmour. . . . . Player
* Wilfred "Shorty" Green. . . Player
* William "Riley" Hern. . . . . Player
* Tom Hooper. . . . . Player
* Fred Hume . . . . Builder
* J.B. "Bouse" Hutton . . . . . Player
* Harry Hyland . . . . Player
* Jack Laviolette . . . . Player
* Fred "Steamer" Maxwell . . Player
* Billy McGimsie . . . . Player
* Reg Noble . . . . Player
* James Norris, Jr. . . . . Builder
* John Ambrose O'Brien. . . . Builder
* Didier Pitre. . . . . Player
* Mike Rodden . . . . Referee
* Jack Ruttan . . . . Player
* David "Sweeney" Schriner. Player
* "Bullet Joe" Simpson . . . . Player
* Al Smith. . . . . Player
* Frank Smith . . . . Builder
* Russell "Barney" Stanley. . Player
* Nels Stewart. . . . . Player

* Marty Walsh . . . . Player
* Harry E. Watson . . . . Player
* Harry Westwick. . . . . Player
* Fred Whitcroft. . . . . Player
* Gordon "Phat" Wilson . . . Player

1963

* Leo Dandurand. . . . . Builder
* Ebbie Goodfellow . . . . Player
* Tommy Gorman . . . . Builder
* Bobby Hewitson . . . . Referee
* Major Frederic McLaughlin. Builder
* Joe Primeau . . . . Player
* Earl Seibert. . . . . Player

1964

* Doug Bentley . . . . Player
* Angus Campbell . . . . Builder
Billy Chadwick . . . . Referee
* Francis Dilio . . . . Builder
* Billy Durnan . . . . Player
* Albert "Babe" Siebert . . . . Player
* John "Black Jack" Stewart. Player

1965

* Marty Barry . . . . Player
* Clint Benedict. . . . . Player
* Arthur Farrell . . . . Player
* Foster Hewitt . . . . Builder
Reginald "Red" Horner . . . Player
* Syd Howe. . . . . Player
* Thomas Lockhart . . . . Builder
* John "Jack" Marshall . . . . Player
* Billy Mosienko . . . . Player
* Blair Russel . . . . Player
* Ernest Russell. . . . . Player
* Fred Scanlan. . . . . Player

1966

* Max Bentley. . . . . Player
* Hector "Toe" Blake. . . . . . . Player
Emile "Butch" Bouchard . . Player
* Frank Brimsek. . . . . Player
* Clarence Campbell . . . . . . Builder
Ted "Teeder" Kennedy. . . . Player
Elmer Lach. . . . . Player
Ted Lindsay . . . . Player
* Walter "Babe" Pratt . . . . . Player
Ken Reardon . . . . Player

1967

* Walter "Turk" Broda . . . . . Player
* Neil Colville . . . . Player
* Harry Oliver . . . . Player
Roy Alvin "Red" Storey . . . Referee

1968

* Billy Cowley . . . . Player
* Jimmie Dunn . . . . Builder
* Jim Hendy . . . . Builder

1969

* Sid Abel. . . . . Player
* Bryan Hextall . . . . Player
Leonard "Red" Kelly . . . . . Player
* George Leader . . . . Builder
* Bruce Norris . . . . Builder
* Roy Worters . . . . Player

1970

* Cecil "Babe" Dye . . . . Player
Bill Gadsby. . . . . Player
Tom Johnson . . . . Player
* Robert LeBel. . . . . Builder

1971

* Harvey "Busher" Jackson. . Player
* Gordon Roberts . . . . Player
* Terry Sawchuk . . . . Player
* Ralph "Cooney" Weiland. . Player
* Arthur Wirtz . . . . Builder

1972

* Weston Adams . . . . Builder
Jean Béliveau . . . . Player
Bernie Geoffrion . . . . Player
* Harry "Hap" Holmes . . . . . Player
Gordon Howe. . . . . Player
* Reginald "Hooley" Smith. . Player
* Doug Harvey . . . . Player

1973

* Hon. Hartland Molson . . . . Builder
* Chuck Rayner . . . . Player
* Thomas Smith. . . . . Player
Frank Udvari. . . . . Referee

1974

* Billy Burch . . . . Player
* Art Coulter. . . . . Player
* Tommy Dunderdale . . . . . . Player
* Charles Hay . . . . Builder
* Tommy Ivan . . . . Builder
Dickie Moore . . . . Player
* Anatoli Tarasov. . . . . Builder
* Carl Voss . . . . Builder

1975

George Armstrong . . . . . . Player
* Irvine "Ace" Bailey . . . . . . Player
* Frank Buckland. . . . . Builder
* Gordie Drillon. . . . . Player
Glenn Hall . . . . Player
* William M. Jennings . . . . . Builder
Pierre Pilote . . . . Player

1976

Johnny Bower. . . . . Player
* Jack Gibson . . . . Builder
* Bill Quackenbush . . . . Player
* Philip Ross . . . . Builder
Bill Wirtz . . . . Builder

1977

* Francis "Bunny" Ahearne. . Builder
* Harold Ballard . . . . Builder
* Joseph Cattarinich . . . . . . Builder
Alex Delvecchio . . . . Player
* Tim Horton. . . . . Player

1978

Andy Bathgate . . . . Player
* John Paris Bickell . . . . Builder
* Jacques Plante . . . . Player
Sam Pollock . . . . Builder
Marcel Pronovost . . . . Player
* William Thayer Tutt . . . . . . Builder

1979

Harry Howell . . . . Player
* Gordon Juckes . . . . Builder
Bobby Orr . . . . Player
Henri Richard . . . . Player

1980

Jack Butterfield. . . . . Builder
* Harry Lumley . . . . Player
* Lynn Patrick . . . . Player
Lorne "Gump" Worsley . . . Player

1981

John Ashley . . . . Referee
John Bucyk. . . . . Player
Frank Mahovlich . . . . Player
Allan Stanley . . . . Player

1982

Yvan Cournoyer . . . . Player
Emile Francis . . . . Builder
Rod Gilbert . . . . Player
Norm Ullman . . . . Player

1983

Ken Dryden . . . . Player
Bobby Hull . . . . Player
Stan Mikita . . . . Player
Harry Sinden. . . . . Builder

1984

Phil Esposito. . . . . Player
* George "Punch" Imlach . . Builder
Jacques Lemaire . . . . Player
* Jake Milford . . . . Builder
Bernie Parent . . . . Player

1985

Gerry Cheevers . . . . Player
* John Mariucci . . . . Builder
Bert Olmstead . . . . Player
* Rudy Pilous . . . . Builder
Jean Ratelle . . . . Player

1986

Leo Boivin . . . . Player
* William Hanley . . . . Builder
Dave Keon . . . . Player
Serge Savard . . . . Player

1987

Bobby Clarke . . . . Player
Eddie Giacomin . . . . Player
Jacques Laperriere . . . . . . Player
Matt Pavelich . . . . Linesman
John A. Ziegler, Jr. . . . . . . Builder

1988

Tony Esposito . . . . Player
* Bill Hayes. . . . . Linesman
Guy Lafleur . . . . Player
* Herbert "Buddy" O'Connor . Player
Brad Park. . . . . Player
Ed Snider . . . . Builder

1989

* Father David Bauer . . . . . . Builder
* Herbie Lewis. . . . . Player
Darryl Sittler . . . . Player
Vladislav Tretiak . . . . Player

1990

Bill Barber . . . . Player
Fern Flaman . . . . Player
Gil Perreault . . . . Player
Norman "Bud" Poile . . . . . Builder

1991

Neil Armstrong . . . . Referee
Mike Bossy. . . . . Player
Scotty Bowman . . . . Builder
Denis Potvin . . . . Player
Bob Pulford . . . . Player
Clint Smith. . . . . Player

1992

Keith Allen . . . . Builder
Marcel Dionne . . . . Player
* Woody Dumart . . . . Player
Bob Gainey . . . . Player
* Bob Johnson . . . . Builder
Frank Mathers . . . . Builder
Lanny McDonald. . . . . Player

1993

John D'Amico. . . . . Linesman
* Frank A. Griffiths. . . . . Builder
* Seymour H. Knox III. . . . . . Builder
Guy Lapointe . . . . Player
Edgar Laprade . . . . Player
* Fred Page. . . . . Builder
Stephen Shutt. . . . . Player
Billy Smith . . . . Player

1994

* Lionel Conacher . . . . Player
Brian O'Neill. . . . . Builder
Harry Watson . . . . Player
* Fred "Bun" Cook . . . . Player

1995

Larry Robinson . . . . Player
* Gunther Sabetzki . . . . Builder
Bill Torrey. . . . . Builder

1996

Al Arbour . . . . Builder
* Bobby Bauer. . . . . Player
Borje Salming. . . . . Player

1997

Mario Lemieux . . . . Player
Glen Sather . . . . Builder
Bryan Trottier . . . . Player

1998

* Roy Conacher. . . . . Player
Michel Goulet. . . . . Player
* Monsignor Athol Murray . . Builder
Peter Stastny . . . . Player

1999

Wayne Gretzky . . . . Player
Ian "Scotty" Morrison . . . . Builder
Andy Van Hellemond. . . . . Referee

2000

Walter Bush, Sr. . . . . Builder
Joe Mullen . . . . Player
Denis Savard . . . . Player

2001

Viacheslav Fetisov. . . . . . . Player
Mike Gartner . . . . Player
Dale Hawerchuk . . . . Player
Jari Kurri . . . . Player
Craig Patrick. . . . . Builder

2002

Bernie Federko . . . . Player
Clark Gillies . . . . Player
Rod Langway . . . . Player
* Roger Neilson. . . . . Builder

2003

Grant Fuhr . . . . Player
Mike Ilitch . . . . Builder
Brian Kilrea . . . . Builder
Pat LaFontaine . . . . Player

TOTAL NHL

Section 4: Player, Goaltender and Coach Registers

296 Sherbrooke Street West,

Montreal, January 16th, 1924.

Mr Frank Calder,
President National Hockey League,
40 Hospital Street,
Montreal.

Dear Sir:-

I understand that both Mr Leo Dandurand and my son have spoken to you in reference to a proposed Trophy to be donated to your League for its most valuable player.

If acceptable to yourself and associates I have much pleasure indeed in offering a Trophy for this purpose, as no doubt it will create a new line of interest and help your League in many ways.

I understand the American League of Baseball Clubs have a Trophy under similar lines and it has proved a huge success.

If the Trophy is accepted I am only too pleased to leave the rules to govern same to your good-self and your Directors, but if I may be permitted to suggest, I think you should act with one Sporting Writer from each of the four cities your League plays in, the final decision being by points.

I may also add that I think it would be fair if the Trophy must be won three times by the same player before becoming his own property, in the meantime it can be held in the custody of the club the player belongs to, while your League may feel inclined to donate some sort of a token to the successful player each year.

I would be glad to hear from you, and wishing you continued success.

Yours very truly

David A. Hart M.D.

Letter from Dr. David A. Hart, dated January 16, 1924, proposing to donate a trophy to be awarded to the NHL's most valuable player. David Hart was the father of Cecil Hart, later coach and general manager of the Montreal Canadiens. The original Hart Trophy was replaced by today's torch-shaped award in 1960, but remains the NHL's ultimate individual accolade.

Late Trades and Transactions

BUCHBERGER, Kelly
Signed as a free agent by Pittsburgh, July 31, 2003.

EASTWOOD, Mike
Signed as a free agent by Pittsburgh, July 31, 2003.

LEETCH, Brian
Signed as a free agent by NY Rangers, July 30, 2003.

MUIR, Bryan
Signed as a free agent by Los Angeles, July 31, 2003.

OLIWA, Krysztof
Signed as a free agent by Calgary, July 30, 2003.

WALLIN, Jesse
Signed as a free agent by Calgary, July 31, 2003.

Notes

CHAPTER 9

All-Time NHL Player Register

NHL Statistics for Every Forward and Defenseman, 1917–18 to 2002–03

Note: The All-Time NHL Player Register lists forwards and defensemen only. Goaltenders are listed separately. The Player Register lists the NHL statistics of every player who has appeared in an NHL regular-season or playoff game from 1917–18 to 2002–03. Trades current as of July 29, 2003.

Abbreviations: GP - games played, **G** - goals, **A** - assists, **Pts** - points, **PIM** - penalties in minutes, ***** - league leading total, **◆** - member of Stanley Cup winning team, **(Cup)** - Stanley Cup games vs. non-NHL opponents, 1917-18 to 1925-26. These statistics not included in career NHL playoff totals.

All-time NHL Goaltender Register begins on page 864.

All-Time NHL Coach Register begins on page 909.

Late Trades and Transactions are found on the facing page.

AALTO, Antti

Center. Shoots left. 6'2", 210 lbs. Born, Lappeenranta, Finland, March 4, 1975.
(Anaheim's 6th choice, 134th overall, in 1993 Entry Draft).

		REGULAR SEASON					PLAYOFFS				
Season	Club	GP	G	A	Pts	PIM	GP	G	A	Pts	PIM
1997-98	Mighty Ducks of Anaheim	3	0	0	0	0	....	....	....	....	....
1998-99	Mighty Ducks of Anaheim	73	3	5	8	24	4	0	0	0	2
99-2000	Mighty Ducks of Anaheim	63	7	11	18	26	....	....	....	....	....
2000-01	Mighty Ducks of Anaheim	12	1	1	2	2	....	....	....	....	....
	NHL Totals	**151**	**11**	**17**	**28**	**52**	**4**	**0**	**0**	**0**	**2**

ABBOTT, Reg

Center. Shoots left. 5'11", 164 lbs. Born, Winnipeg, Man., February 4, 1930.

Season	Club	GP	G	A	Pts	PIM	GP	G	A	Pts	PIM
1952-53	Montreal Canadiens	3	0	0	0	0	....	....	....	....	....
	NHL Totals	**3**	**0**	**0**	**0**	**0**	....	....	....	....	....

ABEL, Clarence

USHOF

Defense. Shoots left. 6'1", 225 lbs. Born, Sault Ste. Marie, MI, May 28, 1900.

Season	Club	GP	G	A	Pts	PIM	GP	G	A	Pts	PIM
1926-27	New York Rangers	44	8	4	12	78	2	0	1	1	8
1927-28 ◆	New York Rangers	23	0	1	1	28	9	1	0	1	14
1928-29	New York Rangers	44	3	1	4	41	6	0	0	0	8
1929-30	Chicago Black Hawks	38	3	3	6	42	2	0	0	0	10
1930-31	Chicago Black Hawks	43	0	1	1	45	9	0	0	0	8
1931-32	Chicago Black Hawks	48	3	3	6	34	2	0	0	0	2
1932-33	Chicago Black Hawks	47	0	4	4	63	....	....	....	....	....
1933-34 ◆	Chicago Black Hawks	46	2	1	3	28	8	0	0	0	8
	NHL Totals	**333**	**19**	**18**	**37**	**359**	**38**	**1**	**1**	**2**	**58**

Signed as a free agent by **NY Rangers**, August 14, 1926. Traded to **Chicago** by **NY Rangers** for $15,000, April 15, 1929.

ABEL, Gerry

Left wing. Shoots left. 6'2", 168 lbs. Born, Detroit, MI, December 25, 1944.

Season	Club	GP	G	A	Pts	PIM	GP	G	A	Pts	PIM
1966-67	Detroit Red Wings	1	0	0	0	0	....	....	....	....	....
	NHL Totals	**1**	**0**	**0**	**0**	**0**	....	....	....	....	....

• Son of Sid

ABEL, Sid

HHOF

Center/Left wing. Shoots left. 5'11", 170 lbs. Born, Melville, Sask., February 22, 1918.

Season	Club	GP	G	A	Pts	PIM	GP	G	A	Pts	PIM
1938-39	Detroit Red Wings	15	1	1	2	0	6	1	1	2	2
1939-40	Detroit Red Wings	24	1	5	6	4	5	0	3	3	21
1940-41	Detroit Red Wings	47	11	22	33	29	9	2	2	4	2
1941-42	Detroit Red Wings	48	18	31	49	45	12	4	2	6	8
1942-43 ◆	Detroit Red Wings	49	18	24	42	33	10	5	8	13	4
1945-46	Detroit Red Wings	7	0	2	2	0	3	0	0	0	0
1946-47	Detroit Red Wings	60	19	29	48	29	3	1	1	2	2
1947-48	Detroit Red Wings	60	14	30	44	69	10	0	3	3	16
1948-49	Detroit Red Wings	60	*28	26	54	49	11	3	3	6	6
1949-50 ◆	Detroit Red Wings	69	34	35	69	46	14	*6	2	8	6
1950-51	Detroit Red Wings	69	23	38	61	30	6	4	3	7	0
1951-52 ◆	Detroit Red Wings	62	17	36	53	32	7	2	2	4	12
1952-53	Chicago Black Hawks	39	5	4	9	6	1	0	0	0	0
1953-54	Chicago Black Hawks	3	0	0	0	4	....	....	....	....	....
	NHL Totals	**612**	**189**	**283**	**472**	**376**	**97**	**28**	**30**	**58**	**79**

• Father of Gerry • NHL Second All-Star Team (1942, 1951) • NHL First All-Star Team (1949, 1950) • Hart Trophy (1949)

Played in NHL All-Star Game (1949, 1950, 1951)

Traded to **Chicago** by **Detroit** for cash, July 22, 1952.

ABGRALL, Dennis

Right wing. Shoots right. 6'1", 180 lbs. Born, Moosomin, Sask., April 24, 1953.
(Los Angeles' 3rd choice, 70th overall, in 1973 Amateur Draft).

Season	Club	GP	G	A	Pts	PIM	GP	G	A	Pts	PIM
1975-76	Los Angeles Kings	13	0	2	2	4	....	....	....	....	....
	NHL Totals	**13**	**0**	**2**	**2**	**4**	....	....	....	....	....

Claimed by **Winnipeg** from **Los Angeles** in 1979 Expansion Draft, June 13, 1979.

ABID, Ramzi

Left wing. Shoots left. 6'2", 210 lbs. Born, Montreal, Que., March 24, 1980.
(Phoenix's 3rd choice, 85th overall, in 2000 Entry Draft).

Season	Club	GP	G	A	Pts	PIM	GP	G	A	Pts	PIM
2002-03	Phoenix Coyotes	30	10	8	18	30	....	....	....	....	....
	Pittsburgh Penguins	3	0	0	0	2	....	....	....	....	....
	NHL Totals	**33**	**10**	**8**	**18**	**32**	....	....	....	....	....

• Re-entered NHL Entry Draft. Originally Colorado's 5th choice, 28th overall, in 1998 Entry Draft.

Traded to **Pittsburgh** by **Phoenix** with Dan Focht and Guillaume Lefebvre for Jan Hrdina and Francois Leroux, March 11, 2003.

ABRAHAMSSON, Thommy

Defense. Shoots left. 6'2", 185 lbs. Born, Umea, Sweden, April 12, 1947.

Season	Club	GP	G	A	Pts	PIM	GP	G	A	Pts	PIM
1980-81	Hartford Whalers	32	6	11	17	16	....	....	....	....	....
	NHL Totals	**32**	**6**	**11**	**17**	**16**	....	....	....	....	....

Signed as a free agent by **Hartford**, May 23, 1980.

ACHTYMICHUK, Gene

Center. Shoots left. 5'11", 170 lbs. Born, Lamont, Alta., September 7, 1932.

Season	Club	GP	G	A	Pts	PIM	GP	G	A	Pts	PIM
1951-52	Montreal Canadiens	1	0	0	0	0	....	....	....	....	....
1956-57	Montreal Canadiens	3	0	0	0	0	....	....	....	....	....
1957-58	Montreal Canadiens	16	3	5	8	2	....	....	....	....	....
1958-59	Detroit Red Wings	12	0	0	0	0	....	....	....	....	....
	NHL Totals	**32**	**3**	**5**	**8**	**2**	....	....	....	....	....

Traded to **Detroit** by **Montreal** with Claude Laforge and Bud MacPherson for cash, June 3, 1958. Traded to **Boston** by **Detroit** for Gord Haworth, August, 1961. Traded to **Portland** (WHL) by **Boston** with Don Ward as part of transaction that sent Don Head to Boston (May, 1961), August, 1961.

ACOMB, Doug

Center. Shoots left. 5'11", 165 lbs. Born, Toronto, Ont., May 15, 1949.

Season	Club	GP	G	A	Pts	PIM	GP	G	A	Pts	PIM
1969-70	Toronto Maple Leafs	2	0	1	1	0	....	....	....	....	....
	NHL Totals	**2**	**0**	**1**	**1**	**0**	....	....	....	....	....

ACTON, Keith

Center. Shoots left. 5'8", 170 lbs. Born, Stouffville, Ont., April 15, 1958.
(Montreal's 8th choice, 103rd overall, in 1978 Amateur Draft).

Season	Club	GP	G	A	Pts	PIM	GP	G	A	Pts	PIM
1980-81	Montreal Canadiens	61	15	24	39	74	2	0	0	0	6
1981-82	Montreal Canadiens	78	36	52	88	88	5	0	4	4	16
1982-83	Montreal Canadiens	78	24	26	50	63	3	0	0	0	0
1983-84	Montreal Canadiens	9	3	7	10	4	....	....	....	....	....
	Minnesota North Stars	62	17	38	55	60	15	4	7	11	12
1984-85	Minnesota North Stars	78	20	38	58	90	9	4	4	8	6
1985-86	Minnesota North Stars	79	26	32	58	100	5	0	3	3	6
1986-87	Minnesota North Stars	78	16	29	45	56	....	....	....	....	....
1987-88	Minnesota North Stars	46	8	11	19	74	....	....	....	....	....
◆	Edmonton Oilers	26	3	6	9	21	7	2	0	2	16
1988-89	Edmonton Oilers	46	11	15	26	47	....	....	....	....	....
	Philadelphia Flyers	25	3	10	13	64	16	2	3	5	18
1989-90	Philadelphia Flyers	69	13	14	27	80	....	....	....	....	....
1990-91	Philadelphia Flyers	76	14	23	37	131	....	....	....	....	....
1991-92	Philadelphia Flyers	50	7	10	17	98	....	....	....	....	....
1992-93	Philadelphia Flyers	83	8	15	23	51	....	....	....	....	....

		REGULAR SEASON					PLAYOFFS				
Season	Club	GP	G	A	Pts	PIM	GP	G	A	Pts	PIM
1993-94	Washington Capitals	6	0	0	0	21	....	....	....	....	....
	New York Islanders	71	2	7	9	50	4	0	0	0	8
	NHL Totals	**1023**	**226**	**358**	**584**	**1172**	**66**	**12**	**21**	**33**	**88**

Played in NHL All-Star Game (1982)

Traded to **Minnesota** by **Montreal** with Mark Napier and Toronto's 3rd round choice (previously acquired, Minnesota selected Ken Hodge Jr.) in 1984 Entry Draft for Bobby Smith, October 28, 1983. Traded to **Edmonton** by **Minnesota** for Moe Mantha, January 22, 1988. Traded to **Philadelphia** by **Edmonton** with Edmonton's 6th round choice (Dmitry Yushkevich) in 1991 Entry Draft for Dave Brown, February 7, 1989. Traded to **Winnipeg** by **Philadelphia** with Pete Peeters for future considerations, September 28, 1989. Traded to **Philadelphia** by **Winnipeg** with Pete Peeters for Toronto's 5th round choice (previously acquired, Winnipeg selected Juha Ylonen) in 1991 Entry Draft and the cancellation of future considerations owed Philadelphia from the Shawn Cronin trade, October 3, 1989. Signed as a free agent by **Washington**, July 27, 1993. Claimed on waivers by **NY Islanders** from **Washington**, October 22, 1993.

ADAM, Douglas

Left wing. Shoots left. 5'11", 165 lbs. Born, Toronto, Ont., September 7, 1923.

Season	Club	GP	G	A	Pts	PIM	GP	G	A	Pts	PIM
1949-50	New York Rangers	4	0	1	1	0	....	....	....	....	....
	NHL Totals	**4**	**0**	**1**	**1**	**0**	....	....	....	....	....

ADAM, Russ

Center. Shoots left. 5'10", 185 lbs. Born, Windsor, Ont., May 5, 1961.
(Toronto's 7th choice, 137th overall, in 1980 Entry Draft).

Season	Club	GP	G	A	Pts	PIM	GP	G	A	Pts	PIM
1982-83	Toronto Maple Leafs	8	1	2	3	11	....	....	....	....	....
	NHL Totals	**8**	**1**	**2**	**3**	**11**	....	....	....	....	....

ADAMS, Bryan

Center. Shoots left. 6', 185 lbs. Born, Fort St. James, B.C., March 20, 1977.

Season	Club	GP	G	A	Pts	PIM	GP	G	A	Pts	PIM
99-2000	Atlanta Thrashers	2	0	0	0	0	....	....	....	....	....
2000-01	Atlanta Thrashers	9	0	1	1	2	....	....	....	....	....
	NHL Totals	**11**	**0**	**1**	**1**	**2**	....	....	....	....	....

Signed as a free agent by **Atlanta**, July 6, 1999. Signed as a free agent by **Detroit**, August 5, 2002.

ADAMS, Craig

Right wing. Shoots right. 6', 200 lbs. Born, Seria, Brunei, April 26, 1977.
(Hartford's 9th choice, 223rd overall, in 1996 Entry Draft).

Season	Club	GP	G	A	Pts	PIM	GP	G	A	Pts	PIM
2000-01	Carolina Hurricanes	44	1	0	1	20	3	0	0	0	0
2001-02	Carolina Hurricanes	33	0	1	1	38	1	0	0	0	0
2002-03	Carolina Hurricanes	81	6	12	18	71	....	....	....	....	....
	NHL Totals	**158**	**7**	**13**	**20**	**129**	**4**	**0**	**0**	**0**	**0**

Rights transferred to **Carolina** after **Hartford** franchise relocated, June 25, 1997.

ADAMS, Greg

Left wing. Shoots left. 6'1", 190 lbs. Born, Duncan, B.C., May 31, 1960.

Season	Club	GP	G	A	Pts	PIM	GP	G	A	Pts	PIM
1980-81	Philadelphia Flyers	6	3	0	3	8	....	....	....	....	....
1981-82	Philadelphia Flyers	33	4	15	19	105	....	....	....	....	....
1982-83	Hartford Whalers	79	10	13	23	216	....	....	....	....	....
1983-84	Washington Capitals	57	2	6	8	133	1	0	0	0	0
1984-85	Washington Capitals	51	6	12	18	72	5	0	0	0	9
1985-86	Washington Capitals	78	18	38	56	152	9	1	3	4	27
1986-87	Washington Capitals	67	14	30	44	184	7	1	3	4	38
1987-88	Washington Capitals	78	15	12	27	153	14	0	5	5	58
1988-89	Edmonton Oilers	49	4	5	9	82	....	....	....	....	....
	Vancouver Canucks	12	4	2	6	35	7	0	0	0	21
1989-90	Quebec Nordiques	7	1	3	4	17	....	....	....	....	....
	Detroit Red Wings	28	3	7	10	16	....	....	....	....	....
	NHL Totals	**545**	**84**	**143**	**227**	**1173**	**43**	**2**	**11**	**13**	**153**

Signed as a free agent by **Philadelphia**, September 28, 1979. Traded to **Hartford** by **Philadelphia** with Ken Linseman and Philadelphia's 1st (David Jensen) and 3rd (Leif Karlsson) round choices in 1983 Entry Draft for Mark Howe and Hartford's 3rd round choice (Derrick Smith) in 1983 Entry Draft, August 19, 1982. Traded to **Washington** by **Hartford** for Torrie Robertson, October 3, 1983. Traded to **Edmonton** by **Washington** for the rights to Geoff Courtnall, July 22, 1988. Traded to **Vancouver** by **Edmonton** with Doug Smith for John LeBlanc and Vancouver's 5th round choice (Peter White) in 1989 Entry Draft, March 7, 1989. Claimed by **Quebec** from **Vancouver** in Waiver Draft, October 2, 1989. Traded to **Detroit** by **Quebec** with Robert Picard for Tony McKegney, December 4, 1989.

ADAMS, Greg

Left wing. Shoots left. 6'3", 195 lbs. Born, Nelson, B.C., August 15, 1963.

Season	Club	GP	G	A	Pts	PIM	GP	G	A	Pts	PIM
1984-85	New Jersey Devils	36	12	9	21	14	....	....	....	....	....
1985-86	New Jersey Devils	78	35	42	77	30	....	....	....	....	....
1986-87	New Jersey Devils	72	20	27	47	19	....	....	....	....	....
1987-88	Vancouver Canucks	80	36	40	76	30	....	....	....	....	....
1988-89	Vancouver Canucks	61	19	14	33	24	7	2	3	5	2
1989-90	Vancouver Canucks	65	30	20	50	18	....	....	....	....	....
1990-91	Vancouver Canucks	55	21	24	45	10	5	0	0	0	2
1991-92	Vancouver Canucks	76	30	27	57	26	6	0	2	2	4
1992-93	Vancouver Canucks	53	25	31	56	14	12	7	6	13	6
1993-94	Vancouver Canucks	68	13	24	37	20	23	6	8	14	2
1994-95	Vancouver Canucks	31	5	10	15	12	....	....	....	....	....
	Dallas Stars	12	3	3	6	4	5	2	0	2	0
1995-96	Dallas Stars	66	22	21	43	33	....	....	....	....	....
1996-97	Dallas Stars	50	21	15	36	2	3	0	1	1	0
1997-98	Dallas Stars	49	14	18	32	20	12	2	2	4	0
1998-99	Phoenix Coyotes	75	19	24	43	26	3	1	0	1	0
99-2000	Phoenix Coyotes	69	19	27	46	14	5	0	0	0	0

		REGULAR SEASON					PLAYOFFS				
Season	Club	GP	G	A	Pts	PIM	GP	G	A	Pts	PIM
2000-01	Florida Panthers	60	11	12	23	10	....	....	....	....	....
	NHL Totals	**1056**	**355**	**388**	**743**	**326**	**81**	**20**	**22**	**42**	**16**

• Family name originally Adamakos

Played in NHL All-Star Game (1988)

Signed as a free agent by **New Jersey**, June 25, 1984. Traded to **Vancouver** by **New Jersey** with Kirk McLean and New Jersey's 2nd round choice (Leif Rohlin) in 1988 Entry Draft for Patrik Sundstrom and Vancouver's 2nd (Jeff Christian) and 4th (Matt Ruchty) round choices in 1988 Entry Draft, September 15, 1987. Traded to **Dallas** by **Vancouver** with Dan Kesa and Vancouver's 5th round choice (later traded to Los Angeles – Los Angeles selected Jason Morgan) in 1995 Entry Draft for Russ Courtnall, April 7, 1995. Signed as a free agent by **Phoenix**, September 1, 1998. Signed as a free agent by **Florida**, November 6, 2000.

ADAMS, Jack

HHOF

Center. Shoots right. 5'9", 175 lbs. Born, Fort William, Ont., June 14, 1895.

Season	Club	GP	G	A	Pts	PIM	GP	G	A	Pts	PIM
1917-18♦	Toronto Arenas	8	0	0	0	31	2	0	0	0	6
1918-19	Toronto Arenas	17	3	3	6	35	....	....	....	....	....
1922-23	Toronto St. Pats	23	19	9	28	*64	....	....	....	....	....
1923-24	Toronto St. Pats	22	14	4	18	51	....	....	....	....	....
1924-25	Toronto St. Pats	27	21	10	31	67	2	1	0	1	7
1925-26	Toronto St. Pats	36	21	5	26	52	....	....	....	....	....
1926-27♦	Ottawa Senators	40	5	1	6	66	6	0	0	0	0
	NHL Totals	**173**	**83**	**32**	**115**	**366**	**10**	**1**	**0**	**1**	**13**

Lester Patrick Trophy (1966)

Signed as a free agent by **Toronto** , February 9, 1918. Traded to **Vancouver** (PCHA) by **Toronto** for cash, December 7, 1919. Traded to **Toronto** by **Vancouver** (PCHA) for the PCHA rights to Corb Denneny, December 18, 1922. Traded to **Ottawa** by **Toronto** for cash, August, 1926.

ADAMS, John

Left wing. Shoots left. 5'10", 163 lbs. Born, Calgary, Alta., May 5, 1920.

Season	Club	GP	G	A	Pts	PIM	GP	G	A	Pts	PIM
1940-41	Montreal Canadiens	42	6	12	18	11	3	0	0	0	0
	NHL Totals	**42**	**6**	**12**	**18**	**11**	**3**	**0**	**0**	**0**	**0**

Traded to **Montreal** by **Vancouver** (PCHL) for cash, May 13, 1940. Traded to **Buffalo** (AHL) by **Montreal** with Moe White for Murdo MacKay with Montreal holding right of recall, January 14, 1946.

ADAMS, Kevyn

Center. Shoots right. 6'1", 195 lbs. Born, Washington, DC, October 8, 1974.
(Boston's 1st choice, 25th overall, in 1993 Entry Draft).

Season	Club	GP	G	A	Pts	PIM	GP	G	A	Pts	PIM
1997-98	Toronto Maple Leafs	5	0	0	0	7	....	....	....	....	....
1998-99	Toronto Maple Leafs	1	0	0	0	0	7	0	2	2	14
99-2000	Toronto Maple Leafs	52	5	8	13	39	12	1	0	1	7
2000-01	Columbus Blue Jackets	66	8	12	20	52	....	....	....	....	....
	Florida Panthers	12	3	6	9	2	....	....	....	....	....
2001-02	Florida Panthers	44	4	8	12	28	....	....	....	....	....
	Carolina Hurricanes	33	2	3	5	15	23	1	0	1	4
2002-03	Carolina Hurricanes	77	9	9	18	57	....	....	....	....	....
	NHL Totals	**290**	**31**	**46**	**77**	**200**	**42**	**2**	**2**	**4**	**25**

Signed as a free agent by **Toronto**, August 7, 1997. Selected by **Columbus** from **Toronto** in Expansion Draft, June 23, 2000. Traded to **Florida** by **Columbus** with Columbus's 4th round choice (Mike Woodford) in 2001 Entry Draft for Ray Whitney and future considerations, March 13, 2001. Traded to **Carolina** by **Florida** with Bret Hedican, Tomas Malec and future considerations for Sandis Ozolinsh and Byron Ritchie, January 16, 2002.

ADAMS, Stew

Left wing. Shoots left. 5'10", 165 lbs. Born, Calgary, Alta., October 16, 1904.

Season	Club	GP	G	A	Pts	PIM	GP	G	A	Pts	PIM
1929-30	Chicago Black Hawks	24	4	6	10	16	2	0	0	0	6
1930-31	Chicago Black Hawks	37	5	13	18	18	9	3	3	6	8
1931-32	Chicago Black Hawks	26	0	5	5	26	....	....	....	....	....
1932-33	Toronto Maple Leafs	8	0	2	2	0	....	....	....	....	....
	NHL Totals	**95**	**9**	**26**	**35**	**60**	**11**	**3**	**3**	**6**	**14**

Traded to **Chicago** by **Minneapolis** (AHA) for Tom Westwick and $15,000, January 4, 1930. Traded to **Toronto** by **Chicago** for cash, November 3, 1932. Traded to **Mtl. Maroons** (Windsor-IHL) by **Toronto** (Syracuse-IHL) for Al Huggins, November 1, 1933.

ADDUONO, Rick

Center. 5'11", 182 lbs. Born, Fort William, Ont., January 25, 1955.
(Boston's 3rd choice, 60th overall, in 1975 Amateur Draft).

Season	Club	GP	G	A	Pts	PIM	GP	G	A	Pts	PIM
1975-76	Boston Bruins	1	0	0	0	0	....	....	....	....	....
1979-80	Atlanta Flames	3	0	0	0	2	....	....	....	....	....
	NHL Totals	**4**	**0**	**0**	**0**	**2**	....	....	....	....	....

Signed as a free agent by **Atlanta**, October 9, 1979.

AFANASENKOV, Dmitry

Left wing. Shoots right. 6'2", 200 lbs. Born, Arkhangelsk, USSR, May 12, 1980.
(Tampa Bay's 3rd choice, 72nd overall, in 1998 Entry Draft).

Season	Club	GP	G	A	Pts	PIM	GP	G	A	Pts	PIM
2000-01	Tampa Bay Lightning	9	1	1	2	4	....	....	....	....	....
2001-02	Tampa Bay Lightning	5	0	0	0	0	....	....	....	....	....
	NHL Totals	**14**	**1**	**1**	**2**	**4**	....	....	....	....	....

AFFLECK, Bruce

Defense. Shoots left. 6', 205 lbs. Born, Salmon Arm, B.C., May 5, 1954.
(California's 3rd choice, 21st overall, in 1974 Amateur Draft).

Season	Club	GP	G	A	Pts	PIM	GP	G	A	Pts	PIM
1974-75	St. Louis Blues	13	0	2	2	4	1	0	0	0	0
1975-76	St. Louis Blues	80	4	26	30	20	3	0	0	0	0
1976-77	St. Louis Blues	80	5	20	25	24	4	0	0	0	0

		Regular Season					Playoffs				
Season	Club	GP	G	A	Pts	PIM	GP	G	A	Pts	PIM
1977-78	St. Louis Blues	75	4	14	18	26	....	....	....	....	....
1978-79	St. Louis Blues	26	1	3	4	12	....	....	....	....	....
1979-80	Vancouver Canucks	5	0	1	1	0	....	....	....	....	....
1983-84	New York Islanders	1	0	0	0	0	....	....	....	....	....
	NHL Totals	**280**	**14**	**66**	**80**	**86**	**8**	**0**	**0**	**0**	**0**

Traded to **St. Louis** by **California** for Frank Spring, January 9, 1975. Traded to **Vancouver** by **St. Louis** with Gord Buynak for cash, November 6, 1979. Traded to **St. Louis** by **Vancouver** with Gord Buynak for cash, February 28, 1980. Signed as a free agent by **NY Islanders**, September 22, 1980.

AFINOGENOV, Maxim

Right wing. Shoots left. 6', 190 lbs. Born, Moscow, USSR, September 4, 1979.
(Buffalo's 3rd choice, 69th overall, in 1997 Entry Draft).

		Regular Season					Playoffs				
Season	Club	GP	G	A	Pts	PIM	GP	G	A	Pts	PIM
99-2000	Buffalo Sabres	65	16	18	34	41	5	0	1	1	2
2000-01	Buffalo Sabres	78	14	22	36	40	11	2	3	5	4
2001-02	Buffalo Sabres	81	21	19	40	69	....	....	....	....	....
2002-03	Buffalo Sabres	35	5	6	11	21	....	....	....	....	....
	NHL Totals	**259**	**56**	**65**	**121**	**171**	**16**	**2**	**4**	**6**	**6**

• Missed majority of 2002-03 season recovering from head injury suffered in training camp, October 8, 2002.

AGNEW, Jim

Defense. Shoots left. 6'1", 190 lbs. Born, Hartney, Man., March 21, 1966.
(Vancouver's 10th choice, 157th overall, in 1984 Entry Draft).

		Regular Season					Playoffs				
Season	Club	GP	G	A	Pts	PIM	GP	G	A	Pts	PIM
1986-87	Vancouver Canucks	4	0	0	0	0	....	....	....	....	....
1987-88	Vancouver Canucks	10	0	1	1	16	....	....	....	....	....
1989-90	Vancouver Canucks	7	0	0	0	36	....	....	....	....	....
1990-91	Vancouver Canucks	20	0	0	0	81	....	....	....	....	....
1991-92	Vancouver Canucks	24	0	0	0	56	4	0	0	0	6
1992-93	Hartford Whalers	16	0	0	0	68	....	....	....	....	....
	NHL Totals	**81**	**0**	**1**	**1**	**257**	**4**	**0**	**0**	**0**	**6**

Signed as a free agent by **Hartford**, July 8, 1992.

AHERN, Fred

Right wing. Shoots right. 6', 180 lbs. Born, Boston, MA, February 12, 1952.

		Regular Season					Playoffs				
Season	Club	GP	G	A	Pts	PIM	GP	G	A	Pts	PIM
1974-75	California Golden Seals	3	2	1	3	0	....	....	....	....	....
1975-76	California Golden Seals	44	17	8	25	43	....	....	....	....	....
1976-77	Cleveland Barons	25	4	4	8	20	....	....	....	....	....
1977-78	Cleveland Barons	36	3	4	7	48	....	....	....	....	....
	Colorado Rockies	38	5	13	18	19	2	0	1	1	2
	NHL Totals	**146**	**31**	**30**	**61**	**130**	**2**	**0**	**1**	**1**	**2**

Signed as a free agent by **California**, September, 1974. Transferred to **Cleveland** after **California** franchise relocated, August 26, 1976. Traded to **Colorado** by **Cleveland** with Ralph Klassen for Rick Jodzio and Chuck Arnason, January 9, 1978. Traded to **Cleveland** by **Colorado** for cash, May 11, 1978. Placed on **Minnesota** reserve list after **Cleveland-Minnesota** Dispersal Draft, June 15, 1979.

AHLIN, Tony

Left wing. Shoots left. 5'11", 176 lbs. Born, Eveleth, MN, December 12, 1914.

		Regular Season					Playoffs				
Season	Club	GP	G	A	Pts	PIM	GP	G	A	Pts	PIM
1937-38	Chicago Black Hawks	1	0	0	0	0	....	....	....	....	....
	NHL Totals	**1**	**0**	**0**	**0**	**0**	....	....	....	....	....

AHOLA, Peter

Defense. Shoots left. 6'3", 205 lbs. Born, Espoo, Finland, May 14, 1968.

		Regular Season					Playoffs				
Season	Club	GP	G	A	Pts	PIM	GP	G	A	Pts	PIM
1991-92	Los Angeles Kings	71	7	12	19	101	6	0	0	0	2
1992-93	Los Angeles Kings	8	1	1	2	6	....	....	....	....	....
	Pittsburgh Penguins	22	0	1	1	14	....	....	....	....	....
	San Jose Sharks	20	2	3	5	16	....	....	....	....	....
1993-94	Calgary Flames	2	0	0	0	0	....	....	....	....	....
	NHL Totals	**123**	**10**	**17**	**27**	**137**	**6**	**0**	**0**	**0**	**2**

Signed as a free agent by **Los Angeles**, April 5, 1991. Traded to **Pittsburgh** by **Los Angeles** for Jeff Chychrun, November 6, 1992. Traded to **San Jose** by **Pittsburgh** for future considerations, February 26, 1993. Traded to **Tampa Bay** by **San Jose** for Dave Capuano, June 19, 1993. Traded to **Calgary** by **Tampa Bay** for cash, October 5, 1993.

AHRENS, Chris

Defense. Shoots right. 6', 185 lbs. Born, San Bernadino, CA, July 31, 1952.
(Minnesota's 4th choice, 76th overall, in 1972 Amateur Draft).

		Regular Season					Playoffs				
Season	Club	GP	G	A	Pts	PIM	GP	G	A	Pts	PIM
1972-73	Minnesota North Stars	....	....	....	....	....	1	0	0	0	0
1973-74	Minnesota North Stars	3	0	1	1	0	....	....	....	....	....
1974-75	Minnesota North Stars	44	0	2	2	77	....	....	....	....	....
1975-76	Minnesota North Stars	2	0	0	0	2	....	....	....	....	....
1976-77	Minnesota North Stars	2	0	0	0	5	....	....	....	....	....
1977-78	Minnesota North Stars	1	0	0	0	0	....	....	....	....	....
	NHL Totals	**52**	**0**	**3**	**3**	**84**	**1**	**0**	**0**	**0**	**0**

Traded to **Edmonton** (WHA) by **Minnesota** with Pierre Jarry for future considerations, March, 1978.

AILSBY, Lloyd

Defense. Shoots left. 5'11", 194 lbs. Born, Lac Pelletier, Sask., May 11, 1917.

		Regular Season					Playoffs				
Season	Club	GP	G	A	Pts	PIM	GP	G	A	Pts	PIM
1951-52	New York Rangers	3	0	0	0	2	....	....	....	....	....
	NHL Totals	**3**	**0**	**0**	**0**	**2**	....	....	....	....	....

Signed as a free agent by **NY Rangers**, October 21, 1940.

AITKEN, Brad

Left wing. Shoots left. 6'2", 200 lbs. Born, Scarborough, Ont., October 30, 1967.
(Pittsburgh's 3rd choice, 46th overall, in 1986 Entry Draft).

		Regular Season					Playoffs				
Season	Club	GP	G	A	Pts	PIM	GP	G	A	Pts	PIM
1987-88	Pittsburgh Penguins	5	1	1	2	0	....	....	....	....	....
1990-91	Pittsburgh Penguins	6	0	1	1	25	....	....	....	....	....
	Edmonton Oilers	3	0	1	1	0	....	....	....	....	....
	NHL Totals	**14**	**1**	**3**	**4**	**25**	....	....	....	....	....

Traded to **Edmonton** by **Pittsburgh** for Kim Issel, March 5, 1991. Signed as a free agent by **Toronto**, July 30, 1991.

AITKEN, Johnathan

Defense. Shoots left. 6'4", 215 lbs. Born, Edmonton, Alta., May 24, 1978.
(Boston's 1st choice, 8th overall, in 1996 Entry Draft).

		Regular Season					Playoffs				
Season	Club	GP	G	A	Pts	PIM	GP	G	A	Pts	PIM
99-2000	Boston Bruins	3	0	0	0	0	....	....	....	....	....
	NHL Totals	**3**	**0**	**0**	**0**	**0**	....	....	....	....	....

Signed as a free agent by **Chicago**, May 22, 2002.

AIVAZOFF, Micah

Center. Shoots left. 6', 195 lbs. Born, Powell River, B.C., May 4, 1969.
(Los Angeles' 6th choice, 109th overall, in 1988 Entry Draft).

		Regular Season					Playoffs				
Season	Club	GP	G	A	Pts	PIM	GP	G	A	Pts	PIM
1993-94	Detroit Red Wings	59	4	4	8	38	....	....	....	....	....
1994-95	Edmonton Oilers	21	0	1	1	2	....	....	....	....	....
1995-96	New York Islanders	12	0	1	1	6	....	....	....	....	....
	NHL Totals	**92**	**4**	**6**	**10**	**46**	....	....	....	....	....

Signed as a free agent by **Detroit**, March 18, 1993. Claimed by **Pittsburgh** from **Detroit** in Waiver Draft, January 18, 1995. Claimed by **Edmonton** from **Pittsburgh** in Waiver Draft, January 18, 1995. Signed as a free agent by **NY Islanders**, August 23, 1995. Signed as a free agent by **NY Rangers**, August 23, 1996.

ALATALO, Mika

Left wing. Shoots left. 6', 202 lbs. Born, Oulu, Finland, June 11, 1971.
(Winnipeg's 11th choice, 203rd overall, in 1990 Entry Draft).

		Regular Season					Playoffs				
Season	Club	GP	G	A	Pts	PIM	GP	G	A	Pts	PIM
99-2000	Phoenix Coyotes	82	10	17	27	36	5	0	0	0	2
2000-01	Phoenix Coyotes	70	7	12	19	22	....	....	....	....	....
	NHL Totals	**152**	**17**	**29**	**46**	**58**	**5**	**0**	**0**	**0**	**2**

Rights transferred to **Phoenix** after **Winnipeg** franchise relocated, July 1, 1996.

ALBELIN, Tommy

Defense. Shoots left. 6'2", 195 lbs. Born, Stockholm, Sweden, May 21, 1964.
(Quebec's 7th choice, 158th overall, in 1983 Entry Draft).

		Regular Season					Playoffs				
Season	Club	GP	G	A	Pts	PIM	GP	G	A	Pts	PIM
1987-88	Quebec Nordiques	60	3	23	26	47	....	....	....	....	....
1988-89	Quebec Nordiques	14	2	4	6	27	....	....	....	....	....
	New Jersey Devils	46	7	24	31	40	....	....	....	....	....
1989-90	New Jersey Devils	68	6	23	29	63	....	....	....	....	....
1990-91	New Jersey Devils	47	2	12	14	44	3	0	1	1	2
1991-92	New Jersey Devils	19	0	4	4	4	1	1	1	2	0
1992-93	New Jersey Devils	36	1	5	6	14	5	2	0	2	0
1993-94	New Jersey Devils	62	2	17	19	36	20	2	5	7	14
1994-95♦	New Jersey Devils	48	5	10	15	20	20	1	7	8	2
1995-96	New Jersey Devils	53	1	12	13	14	....	....	....	....	....
	Calgary Flames	20	0	1	1	4	4	0	0	0	0
1996-97	Calgary Flames	72	4	11	15	14	....	....	....	....	....
1997-98	Calgary Flames	69	2	17	19	32	....	....	....	....	....
1998-99	Calgary Flames	60	1	5	6	8	....	....	....	....	....
99-2000	Calgary Flames	41	4	6	10	12	....	....	....	....	....
2000-01	Calgary Flames	77	1	19	20	22	....	....	....	....	....
2001-02	New Jersey Devils	42	1	3	4	4	6	0	0	0	0
2002-03♦	New Jersey Devils	37	1	6	7	6	16	1	0	1	2
	NHL Totals	**871**	**43**	**202**	**245**	**411**	**75**	**7**	**14**	**21**	**20**

Traded to **New Jersey** by **Quebec** for New Jersey's 4th round choice (Niklas Andersson) in 1989 Entry Draft, December 12, 1988. Traded to **Calgary** by **New Jersey** with Cale Hulse and Jocelyn Lemieux for Phil Housley and Dan Keczmer, February 26, 1996. Signed as a free agent by **New Jersey**, July 9, 2001.

ALBRIGHT, Clint

Center. Shoots left. 6'2", 180 lbs. Born, Winnipeg, Man., February 28, 1926.

		Regular Season					Playoffs				
Season	Club	GP	G	A	Pts	PIM	GP	G	A	Pts	PIM
1948-49	New York Rangers	59	14	5	19	19	....	....	....	....	....
	NHL Totals	**59**	**14**	**5**	**19**	**19**	....	....	....	....	....

ALDCORN, Gary

Left wing. Shoots left. 5'11", 170 lbs. Born, Shaunavon, Sask., March 7, 1935.

		Regular Season					Playoffs				
Season	Club	GP	G	A	Pts	PIM	GP	G	A	Pts	PIM
1956-57	Toronto Maple Leafs	22	5	1	6	4	....	....	....	....	....
1957-58	Toronto Maple Leafs	59	10	14	24	12	....	....	....	....	....
1958-59	Toronto Maple Leafs	5	0	3	3	2	....	....	....	....	....
1959-60	Detroit Red Wings	70	22	29	51	32	6	1	2	3	4
1960-61	Detroit Red Wings	49	2	6	8	16	....	....	....	....	....
	Boston Bruins	21	2	3	5	12	....	....	....	....	....
	NHL Totals	**226**	**41**	**56**	**97**	**78**	**6**	**1**	**2**	**3**	**4**

Claimed by **Toronto** from **Pittsburgh** (AHL) in Inter-League Draft, June 5, 1956. Claimed by **Detroit** from **Toronto** in Intra-League Draft, June 10, 1959. Traded to **Boston** by **Detroit** with Murray Oliver and Tom McCarthy for Vic Stasiuk and Leo Labine, January 23, 1961.

ALDRIDGE, Keith

Defense. Shoots right. 5'11", 185 lbs. Born, Detroit, MI, July 20, 1973.

Season	Club	GP	G	A	Pts	PIM	GP	G	A	Pts	PIM
		REGULAR SEASON					PLAYOFFS				
99-2000	Dallas Stars	4	0	0	0	0	....	....	....	....	....
	NHL Totals	**4**	**0**	**0**	**0**	**0**	....	....	....	....	....

Signed as a free agent by **Dallas**, September 1, 1999.

ALEXANDER, Claire

Defense. Shoots right. 6'1", 175 lbs. Born, Collingwood, Ont., June 16, 1945.

Season	Club	GP	G	A	Pts	PIM	GP	G	A	Pts	PIM
1974-75	Toronto Maple Leafs	42	7	11	18	12	7	0	0	0	0
1975-76	Toronto Maple Leafs	33	2	6	8	6	9	2	4	6	4
1976-77	Toronto Maple Leafs	48	1	12	13	12	....	....	....	....	....
1977-78	Vancouver Canucks	32	8	18	26	6	....	....	....	....	....
	NHL Totals	**155**	**18**	**47**	**65**	**36**	**16**	**2**	**4**	**6**	**4**

Signed as a free agent by **Toronto**, September, 1974. Traded to **Vancouver** by **Toronto** for cash, January 29, 1978.

ALEXANDRE, Art

Left wing. Shoots right. 5'5", 150 lbs. Born, St-Jean, Que., March 2, 1909.

Season	Club	GP	G	A	Pts	PIM	GP	G	A	Pts	PIM
1931-32	Montreal Canadiens	10	0	2	2	8	4	0	0	0	0
1932-33	Montreal Canadiens	1	0	0	0	0	....	....	....	....	....
	NHL Totals	**11**	**0**	**2**	**2**	**8**	**4**	**0**	**0**	**0**	**0**

Traded to **Providence** (Can-Am) by **Montreal** for cash, May 8, 1932. Traded to **Montreal** by **Providence** (Can-Am) for cash, February 6, 1933.

ALEXEEV, Nikita

Right wing. Shoots left. 6'5", 210 lbs. Born, Murmansk, USSR, December 27, 1981.
(Tampa Bay's 1st choice, 8th overall, in 2000 Entry Draft).

Season	Club	GP	G	A	Pts	PIM	GP	G	A	Pts	PIM
2001-02	Tampa Bay Lightning	44	4	4	8	8	....	....	....	....	....
2002-03	Tampa Bay Lightning	37	4	2	6	8	11	1	0	1	0
	NHL Totals	**81**	**8**	**6**	**14**	**16**	**11**	**1**	**0**	**1**	**0**

ALFREDSSON, Daniel

Right wing. Shoots right. 5'11", 195 lbs. Born, Goteborg, Sweden, December 11, 1972.
(Ottawa's 5th choice, 133rd overall, in 1994 Entry Draft).

Season	Club	GP	G	A	Pts	PIM	GP	G	A	Pts	PIM
1995-96	Ottawa Senators	82	26	35	61	28	....	....	....	....	....
1996-97	Ottawa Senators	76	24	47	71	30	7	5	2	7	6
1997-98	Ottawa Senators	55	17	28	45	18	11	7	2	9	20
1998-99	Ottawa Senators	58	11	22	33	14	4	1	2	3	4
99-2000	Ottawa Senators	57	21	38	59	28	6	1	3	4	2
2000-01	Ottawa Senators	68	24	46	70	30	4	1	0	1	2
2001-02	Ottawa Senators	78	37	34	71	45	12	7	6	13	4
2002-03	Ottawa Senators	78	27	51	78	42	18	4	4	8	12
	NHL Totals	**552**	**187**	**301**	**488**	**235**	**62**	**26**	**19**	**45**	**50**

NHL All-Rookie Team (1996) • Calder Memorial Trophy (1996)
Played in NHL All-Star Game (1996, 1997, 1998)

ALLAN, Jeff

Defense. Shoots left. 6' 1", 194 lbs. Born, Hull, Que., May 17, 1957.
(Cleveland's 7th choice, 95th overall, in 1977 Amateur Draft).

Season	Club	GP	G	A	Pts	PIM	GP	G	A	Pts	PIM
1977-78	Cleveland Barons	4	0	0	0	2	....	....	....	....	....
	NHL Totals	**4**	**0**	**0**	**0**	**2**	....	....	....	....	....

ALLEN, Bobby

Defense. Shoots left. 6'1", 205 lbs. Born, Braintree, MA, November 14, 1978.
(Boston's 2nd choice, 52nd overall, in 1998 Entry Draft).

Season	Club	GP	G	A	Pts	PIM	GP	G	A	Pts	PIM
2002-03	Edmonton Oilers	1	0	0	0	0	....	....	....	....	....
	NHL Totals	**1**	**0**	**0**	**0**	**0**	....	....	....	....	....

Traded to **Edmonton** by **Boston** for Sean Brown, March 19, 2002.

ALLEN, Bryan

Defense. Shoots left. 6'4", 215 lbs. Born, Kingston, Ont., August 21, 1980.
(Vancouver's 1st choice, 4th overall, in 1998 Entry Draft).

Season	Club	GP	G	A	Pts	PIM	GP	G	A	Pts	PIM
2000-01	Vancouver Canucks	6	0	0	0	0	2	0	0	0	2
2001-02	Vancouver Canucks	11	0	0	0	6	....	....	....	....	....
2002-03	Vancouver Canucks	48	5	3	8	73	1	0	0	0	2
	NHL Totals	**65**	**5**	**3**	**8**	**79**	**3**	**0**	**0**	**0**	**4**

ALLEN, Chris

Defense. Shoots right. 6'2", 197 lbs. Born, Chatham, Ont., May 8, 1978.
(Florida's 2nd choice, 60th overall, in 1996 Entry Draft).

Season	Club	GP	G	A	Pts	PIM	GP	G	A	Pts	PIM
1997-98	Florida Panthers	1	0	0	0	2	....	....	....	....	....
1998-99	Florida Panthers	1	0	0	0	0	....	....	....	....	....
	NHL Totals	**2**	**0**	**0**	**0**	**2**	....	....	....	....	....

ALLEN, George

Left wing/Defense. Shoots left. 5'10", 162 lbs. Born, Bayfield, N.B., July 27, 1914.

Season	Club	GP	G	A	Pts	PIM	GP	G	A	Pts	PIM
1938-39	New York Rangers	19	6	6	12	10	7	0	0	0	4
1939-40	Chicago Black Hawks	48	10	12	22	26	2	0	0	0	0
1940-41	Chicago Black Hawks	44	14	17	31	22	5	2	2	4	10
1941-42	Chicago Black Hawks	43	7	13	20	31	3	1	1	2	0
1942-43	Chicago Black Hawks	47	10	14	24	26	....	....	....	....	....
1943-44	Chicago Black Hawks	45	17	24	41	36	9	5	4	9	8
1945-46	Chicago Black Hawks	44	11	15	26	16	4	0	0	0	4
1946-47	Montreal Canadiens	49	7	14	21	12	11	1	3	4	6
	NHL Totals	**339**	**82**	**115**	**197**	**179**	**41**	**9**	**10**	**19**	**32**

• Brother of Vivian

Traded to **Chicago** by **NY Rangers** for cash, May 17, 1939. Traded to **Montreal** by **Chicago** for Paul Bibeault with both teams holding right of recall, September 23, 1946. Players returned to original teams, June 2, 1947.

ALLEN, Keith

HHOF

Defense. Shoots left. 5'10", 190 lbs. Born, Saskatoon, Sask., August 21, 1923.

Season	Club	GP	G	A	Pts	PIM	GP	G	A	Pts	PIM
1953-54 ♦	Detroit Red Wings	10	0	4	4	2	5	0	0	0	0
1954-55	Detroit Red Wings	18	0	0	0	6	....	....	....	....	....
	NHL Totals	**28**	**0**	**4**	**4**	**8**	**5**	**0**	**0**	**0**	**0**

Lester Patrick Trophy (1988)
Played in NHL All-Star Game (1954)

Traded to **Detroit** by **Syracuse** (AHL) for cash, February 26, 1954.

ALLEN, Peter

Defense. Shoots right. 6'2", 200 lbs. Born, Calgary, Alta., March 6, 1970.
(Boston's 1st choice, 24th overall, in 1991 Supplemental Draft).

Season	Club	GP	G	A	Pts	PIM	GP	G	A	Pts	PIM
1995-96	Pittsburgh Penguins	8	0	0	0	8	....	....	....	....	....
	NHL Totals	**8**	**0**	**0**	**0**	**8**	....	....	....	....	....

Signed as a free agent by **Pittsburgh**, August 10, 1995. Signed as a free agent by **San Jose**, August 19, 1997.

ALLEN, Viv

Right wing. Shoots right. 5'6", 140 lbs. Born, Bayfield, N.B., September 9, 1916.

Season	Club	GP	G	A	Pts	PIM	GP	G	A	Pts	PIM
1940-41	New York Americans	6	0	1	1	0	....	....	....	....	....
	NHL Totals	**6**	**0**	**1**	**1**	**0**	....	....	....	....	....

• Brother of George

Signed as a free agent by **NY Americans**, October 15, 1940. • Team name changed to **Brooklyn Americans** prior to 1941-42 season. Traded to **Toronto** (Pittsburgh-AHL) by **Brooklyn** with Glenn Brydson for Phil McAtee and the return of Peanuts O'Flaherty (previously on loan), October 8, 1941.

ALLEY, Steve

Left wing. Shoots left. 6', 185 lbs. Born, Anoka, MN, December 29, 1953.
(Chicago's 10th choice, 141st overall, in 1973 Amateur Draft).

Season	Club	GP	G	A	Pts	PIM	GP	G	A	Pts	PIM
1979-80	Hartford Whalers	7	1	1	2	0	3	0	1	1	0
1980-81	Hartford Whalers	8	2	2	4	11	....	....	....	....	....
	NHL Totals	**15**	**3**	**3**	**6**	**11**	**3**	**0**	**1**	**1**	**0**

Claimed by **Hartford** from **Birmingham** (WHA) in 1979 WHA Dispersal Draft, June 9, 1979.

ALLISON, Dave

Defense. Shoots right. 6'1", 200 lbs. Born, Fort Frances, Ont., April 14, 1959.

Season	Club	GP	G	A	Pts	PIM	GP	G	A	Pts	PIM
1983-84	Montreal Canadiens	3	0	0	0	12	....	....	....	....	....
	NHL Totals	**3**	**0**	**0**	**0**	**12**	....	....	....	....	....

• Brother of Mike

Signed as a free agent by **Montreal**, October 4, 1979.

ALLISON, Jamie

Defense. Shoots left. 6'1", 200 lbs. Born, Lindsay, Ont., May 13, 1975.
(Calgary's 2nd choice, 44th overall, in 1993 Entry Draft).

Season	Club	GP	G	A	Pts	PIM	GP	G	A	Pts	PIM
1994-95	Calgary Flames	1	0	0	0	0	....	....	....	....	....
1996-97	Calgary Flames	20	0	0	0	35	....	....	....	....	....
1997-98	Calgary Flames	43	3	8	11	104	....	....	....	....	....
1998-99	Chicago Blackhawks	39	2	2	4	62	....	....	....	....	....
99-2000	Chicago Blackhawks	59	1	3	4	102	....	....	....	....	....
2000-01	Chicago Blackhawks	44	1	3	4	53	....	....	....	....	....
2001-02	Calgary Flames	37	0	2	2	24	....	....	....	....	....
	Columbus Blue Jackets	7	0	0	0	28	....	....	....	....	....
2002-03	Columbus Blue Jackets	48	0	1	1	99	....	....	....	....	....
	NHL Totals	**298**	**7**	**19**	**26**	**507**	....	....	....	....	....

Traded to **Chicago** by **Calgary** with Marty McInnis and Erik Andersson for Jeff Shantz and Steve Dubinsky, October 27, 1998. Claimed by **Calgary** from **Chicago** in Waiver Draft, September 28, 2001. Traded to **Columbus** by **Calgary** for Blake Sloan, March 19, 2002.

ALLISON, Jason

Center. Shoots right. 6'3", 215 lbs. Born, North York, Ont., May 29, 1975.
(Washington's 2nd choice, 17th overall, in 1993 Entry Draft).

Season	Club	GP	G	A	Pts	PIM	GP	G	A	Pts	PIM
1993-94	Washington Capitals	2	0	1	1	0	....	....	....	....	....
1994-95	Washington Capitals	12	2	1	3	6	....	....	....	....	....
1995-96	Washington Capitals	19	0	3	3	2	....	....	....	....	....
1996-97	Washington Capitals	53	5	17	22	25	....	....	....	....	....
	Boston Bruins	19	3	9	12	9	....	....	....	....	....
1997-98	Boston Bruins	81	33	50	83	60	6	2	6	8	4
1998-99	Boston Bruins	82	23	53	76	68	12	2	9	11	6
99-2000	Boston Bruins	37	10	18	28	20	....	....	....	....	....
2000-01	Boston Bruins	82	36	59	95	85	....	....	....	....	....
2001-02	Los Angeles Kings	73	19	55	74	68	7	3	3	6	4

Season	Club	REGULAR SEASON GP	G	A	Pts	PIM	PLAYOFFS GP	G	A	Pts	PIM
2002-03	Los Angeles Kings	26	6	22	28	22	....	....	....	....	....
	NHL Totals	**486**	**137**	**288**	**425**	**365**	**25**	**7**	**18**	**25**	**14**

Played in NHL All-Star Game (2001)

Traded to **Boston** by **Washington** with Jim Carey, Anson Carter and Washington's 3rd round choice (Lee Goren) in 1997 Entry Draft for Bill Ranford, Adam Oates and Rick Tocchet, March 1, 1997. • Missed majority of 1999-2000 season recovering from thumb injury suffered in game vs. NY Islanders, January 8, 2000. Traded to **Los Angeles** by **Boston** with Mikko Eloranta for Jozef Stumpel and Glen Murray, October 24, 2001. • Missed majority of 2002-03 season recovering from knee (October 27, 2002 vs. Columbus) and hip (January 25, 2003 vs. New Jersey) injuries.

ALLISON, Mike

Left wing. Shoots right. 6', 200 lbs. Born, Fort Frances, Ont., March 28, 1961.
(NY Rangers' 2nd choice, 35th overall, in 1980 Entry Draft).

Season	Club	GP	G	A	Pts	PIM	GP	G	A	Pts	PIM
1980-81	New York Rangers	75	26	38	64	83	14	3	1	4	20
1981-82	New York Rangers	48	7	15	22	74	10	1	3	4	18
1982-83	New York Rangers	39	11	9	20	37	8	0	5	5	10
1983-84	New York Rangers	45	8	12	20	64	5	0	1	1	6
1984-85	New York Rangers	31	9	15	24	17	....	....	....	....	....
1985-86	New York Rangers	28	2	13	15	22	16	0	2	2	38
1986-87	Toronto Maple Leafs	71	7	16	23	66	13	3	5	8	15
1987-88	Toronto Maple Leafs	15	0	3	3	10	....	....	....	....	....
	Los Angeles Kings	37	16	12	28	57	5	0	0	0	16
1988-89	Los Angeles Kings	55	14	22	36	122	7	1	0	1	10
1989-90	Los Angeles Kings	55	2	11	13	78	4	1	0	1	2
	NHL Totals	**499**	**102**	**166**	**268**	**630**	**82**	**9**	**17**	**26**	**135**

• Brother of Dave

Traded to **Toronto** by **NY Rangers** for Walt Poddubny, August 18, 1986. Traded to **Los Angeles** by **Toronto** for Sean McKenna, December 14, 1987.

ALLISON, Ray

Right wing. Shoots right. 5'10", 195 lbs. Born, Cranbrook, B.C., March 4, 1959.
(Hartford's 1st choice, 18th overall, in 1979 Entry Draft).

Season	Club	GP	G	A	Pts	PIM	GP	G	A	Pts	PIM
1979-80	Hartford Whalers	64	16	12	28	13	2	0	1	1	0
1980-81	Hartford Whalers	6	1	0	1	0	....	....	....	....	....
1981-82	Philadelphia Flyers	51	17	37	54	104	3	2	0	2	2
1982-83	Philadelphia Flyers	67	21	30	51	57	3	0	1	1	12
1983-84	Philadelphia Flyers	37	8	13	21	47	3	0	1	1	4
1984-85	Philadelphia Flyers	11	1	1	2	2	1	0	0	0	2
1986-87	Philadelphia Flyers	2	0	0	0	0	....	....	....	....	....
	NHL Totals	**238**	**64**	**93**	**157**	**223**	**12**	**2**	**3**	**5**	**20**

Traded to **Philadelphia** by **Hartford** with Fred Arthur and Hartford's 1st (Ron Sutter) and 3rd (Miroslav Dvorak) round choices in 1982 Entry Draft for Rick MacLeish, Blake Wesley, Don Gillen and Philadelphia's 1st (Paul Lawless), 2nd (Mark Paterson) and 3rd (Kevin Dineen) round choices in 1982 Entry Draft, July 3, 1981.

ALLUM, Bill

Defense. Shoots left. 5'11", 194 lbs. Born, Winnipeg, Man., October 9, 1916.

Season	Club	GP	G	A	Pts	PIM	GP	G	A	Pts	PIM
1940-41	New York Rangers	1	0	1	1	0	....	....	....	....	....
	NHL Totals	**1**	**0**	**1**	**1**	**0**	....	....	....	....	....

Signed as a free agent by **NY Rangers**, October 12, 1937. Traded to **Buffalo** (AHL) by **NY Rangers** for cash, September 11, 1941.

AMADIO, Dave

Defense. Shoots right. 6'1", 207 lbs. Born, Glace Bay, N.S., April 23, 1939.

Season	Club	GP	G	A	Pts	PIM	GP	G	A	Pts	PIM
1957-58	Detroit Red Wings	2	0	0	0	2	....	....	....	....	....
1967-68	Los Angeles Kings	58	4	6	10	101	7	0	2	2	8
1968-69	Los Angeles Kings	65	1	5	6	60	9	1	0	1	10
	NHL Totals	**125**	**5**	**11**	**16**	**163**	**16**	**1**	**2**	**3**	**18**

Traded to **Springfield** (AHL) by **Detroit** for cash, June, 1961. NHL rights transferred to **Los Angeles** after NHL club purchased **Springfield** (AHL) franchise, May, 1967.

AMBROZIAK, Peter

Left wing. Shoots left. 6', 206 lbs. Born, Toronto, Ont., September 15, 1971.
(Buffalo's 4th choice, 72nd overall, in 1991 Entry Draft).

Season	Club	GP	G	A	Pts	PIM	GP	G	A	Pts	PIM
1994-95	Buffalo Sabres	12	0	1	1	0	....	....	....	....	....
	NHL Totals	**12**	**0**	**1**	**1**	**0**	....	....	....	....	....

AMODEO, Mike

Defense. Shoots left. 5'10", 190 lbs. Born, Toronto, Ont., June 22, 1952.
(California's 7th choice, 102nd overall, in 1972 Amateur Draft).

Season	Club	GP	G	A	Pts	PIM	GP	G	A	Pts	PIM
1979-80	Winnipeg Jets	19	0	0	0	2	....	....	....	....	....
	NHL Totals	**19**	**0**	**0**	**0**	**2**	....	....	....	....	....

Rights retained by **Winnipeg** prior to Expansion Draft, June 9, 1979.

AMONTE, Tony

Right wing. Shoots left. 6', 200 lbs. Born, Hingham, MA, August 2, 1970.
(NY Rangers' 3rd choice, 68th overall, in 1988 Entry Draft).

Season	Club	GP	G	A	Pts	PIM	GP	G	A	Pts	PIM
1990-91	New York Rangers	....	....	....	....	....	2	0	2	2	2
1991-92	New York Rangers	79	35	34	69	55	13	3	6	9	2
1992-93	New York Rangers	83	33	43	76	49	....	....	....	....	....
1993-94	New York Rangers	72	16	22	38	31	....	....	....	....	....
	Chicago Blackhawks	7	1	3	4	6	6	4	2	6	4
1994-95	Chicago Blackhawks	48	15	20	35	41	16	3	3	6	10
1995-96	Chicago Blackhawks	81	31	32	63	62	7	2	4	6	6
1996-97	Chicago Blackhawks	81	41	36	77	64	6	4	2	6	8
1997-98	Chicago Blackhawks	82	31	42	73	66	....	....	....	....	....
1998-99	Chicago Blackhawks	82	44	31	75	60	....	....	....	....	....
99-2000	Chicago Blackhawks	82	43	41	84	48	....	....	....	....	....
2000-01	Chicago Blackhawks	82	35	29	64	54	....	....	....	....	....
2001-02	Chicago Blackhawks	82	27	39	66	67	5	0	1	1	4
2002-03	Phoenix Coyotes	59	13	23	36	26	....	....	....	....	....
	Philadelphia Flyers	13	7	8	15	2	13	1	6	7	4
	NHL Totals	**933**	**372**	**403**	**775**	**631**	**68**	**17**	**26**	**43**	**40**

NHL All-Rookie Team (1992)

Played in NHL All-Star Game (1997, 1998, 1999, 2000, 2001)

Traded to **Chicago** by **NY Rangers** with the rights to Matt Oates for Stephane Matteau and Brian Noonan, March 21, 1994. Signed as a free agent by **Phoenix**, July 12, 2002. Traded to **Philadelphia** by **Phoenix** for Guillaume Lefebvre, Atlanta's 3rd round choice (previously acquired, Phoenix selected Tyler Redenbach) in 2003 Entry Draft and Philadelphia's 2nd round choice in 2004 Entry Draft, March 10, 2003.

ANDERSON, Bill

Defense. Shoots right. 6', 190 lbs. Born, Tillsonburg, Ont., December 13, 1912.

Season	Club	GP	G	A	Pts	PIM	GP	G	A	Pts	PIM
1942-43	Boston Bruins	....	....	....	....	....	1	0	0	0	0
	NHL Totals	....	....	....	....	....	**1**	**0**	**0**	**0**	**0**

ANDERSON, Dale

Defense. Shoots left. 6'3", 190 lbs. Born, Regina, Sask., March 5, 1932.

Season	Club	GP	G	A	Pts	PIM	GP	G	A	Pts	PIM
1956-57	Detroit Red Wings	13	0	0	0	6	2	0	0	0	0
	NHL Totals	**13**	**0**	**0**	**0**	**6**	**2**	**0**	**0**	**0**	**0**

ANDERSON, Doug

Center. Shoots left. 5'7", 157 lbs. Born, Edmonton, Alta., October 20, 1927.

Season	Club	GP	G	A	Pts	PIM	GP	G	A	Pts	PIM
1952-53 ◆	Montreal Canadiens	....	....	....	....	....	2	0	0	0	0
	NHL Totals	....	....	....	....	....	**2**	**0**	**0**	**0**	**0**

ANDERSON, Earl

Right wing. Shoots right. 6'1", 185 lbs. Born, Roseau, MN, February 24, 1951.
(Detroit's 5th choice, 58th overall, in 1971 Amateur Draft).

Season	Club	GP	G	A	Pts	PIM	GP	G	A	Pts	PIM
1974-75	Detroit Red Wings	45	7	3	10	12	....	....	....	....	....
	Boston Bruins	19	2	4	6	4	3	0	1	1	0
1975-76	Boston Bruins	5	0	1	1	2	....	....	....	....	....
1976-77	Boston Bruins	40	10	11	21	4	2	0	0	0	0
	NHL Totals	**109**	**19**	**19**	**38**	**22**	**5**	**0**	**1**	**1**	**0**

Traded to **Boston** by **Detroit** with Hank Nowak for Walt McKechnie and Boston's 3rd round choice (Clarke Hamilton) in 1975 Amateur Draft, February 18, 1975

ANDERSON, Glenn

Right wing. Shoots left. 6'1", 190 lbs. Born, Vancouver, B.C., October 2, 1960.
(Edmonton's 3rd choice, 69th overall, in 1979 Entry Draft).

Season	Club	GP	G	A	Pts	PIM	GP	G	A	Pts	PIM
1980-81	Edmonton Oilers	58	30	23	53	24	9	5	7	12	12
1981-82	Edmonton Oilers	80	38	67	105	71	5	2	5	7	8
1982-83	Edmonton Oilers	72	48	56	104	70	16	10	10	20	32
1983-84 ◆	Edmonton Oilers	80	54	45	99	65	19	6	11	17	33
1984-85 ◆	Edmonton Oilers	80	42	39	81	69	18	10	16	26	38
1985-86	Edmonton Oilers	72	54	48	102	90	10	8	3	11	14
1986-87 ◆	Edmonton Oilers	80	35	38	73	65	21	14	13	27	59
1987-88 ◆	Edmonton Oilers	80	38	50	88	58	19	9	16	25	49
1988-89	Edmonton Oilers	79	16	48	64	93	7	1	2	3	8
1989-90 ◆	Edmonton Oilers	73	34	38	72	107	22	10	12	22	20
1990-91	Edmonton Oilers	74	24	31	55	59	18	6	7	13	41
1991-92	Toronto Maple Leafs	72	24	33	57	100	....	....	....	....	....
1992-93	Toronto Maple Leafs	76	22	43	65	117	21	7	11	18	31
1993-94	Toronto Maple Leafs	73	17	18	35	50	....	....	....	....	....
	◆ New York Rangers	12	4	2	6	12	23	3	3	6	42
1994-95	St. Louis Blues	36	12	14	26	37	6	1	1	2	*49
1995-96	Edmonton Oilers	17	4	6	10	27	....	....	....	....	....
	St. Louis Blues	15	2	2	4	6	11	1	4	5	6
	NHL Totals	**1129**	**498**	**601**	**1099**	**1120**	**225**	**93**	**121**	**214**	**442**

Played in NHL All-Star Game (1984, 1985, 1986, 1988)

Traded to **Toronto** by **Edmonton** with Grant Fuhr and Craig Berube for Vincent Damphousse, Peter Ing, Scott Thornton and Luke Richardson, September 19, 1991. Traded to **NY Rangers** by **Toronto** with Toronto's 4th round choice (Alexander Korobolin) in 1994 Entry Draft and the rights to Scott Malone for Mike Gartner, March 21, 1994. Signed as a free agent by **St. Louis**, February 13, 1995. Signed as a free agent by **Vancouver**, January 22, 1996. Claimed on waivers by **Edmonton** from **Vancouver**, January 25, 1996. Claimed on waivers by **St. Louis** from **Edmonton**, March 12, 1996.

ANDERSON, Jim

Left wing. Shoots left. 5'10", 165 lbs. Born, Pembroke, Ont., December 1, 1930.

Season	Club	GP	G	A	Pts	PIM	GP	G	A	Pts	PIM
1967-68	Los Angeles Kings	7	1	2	3	2	....	....	....	....	....
	NHL Totals	**7**	**1**	**2**	**3**	**2**	....	....	....	....	....

NHL rights transferred to **Los Angeles** after NHL club purchased **Springfield** (AHL) franchise, May, 1967.

ANDERSON, John

Right wing. Shoots left. 5'11", 200 lbs. Born, Toronto, Ont., March 28, 1957.
(Toronto's 1st choice, 11th overall, in 1977 Amateur Draft).

		REGULAR SEASON					PLAYOFFS				
Season	Club	GP	G	A	Pts	PIM	GP	G	A	Pts	PIM
1977-78	Toronto Maple Leafs	17	1	2	3	2	2	0	0	0	0
1978-79	Toronto Maple Leafs	71	15	11	26	10	6	0	2	2	0
1979-80	Toronto Maple Leafs	74	25	28	53	22	3	1	1	2	0
1980-81	Toronto Maple Leafs	75	17	26	43	31	2	0	0	0	0
1981-82	Toronto Maple Leafs	69	31	26	57	30	....	....	....	....	....
1982-83	Toronto Maple Leafs	80	31	49	80	24	4	2	4	6	0
1983-84	Toronto Maple Leafs	73	37	31	68	22	....	....	....	....	....
1984-85	Toronto Maple Leafs	75	32	31	63	27	....	....	....	....	....
1985-86	Quebec Nordiques	65	21	28	49	26	....	....	....	....	....
	Hartford Whalers	14	8	17	25	2	10	5	8	13	0
1986-87	Hartford Whalers	76	31	44	75	19	6	1	2	3	0
1987-88	Hartford Whalers	63	17	32	49	20	....	....	....	....	....
1988-89	Hartford Whalers	62	16	24	40	28	4	0	1	1	2
	NHL Totals	**814**	**282**	**349**	**631**	**263**	**37**	**9**	**18**	**27**	**2**

Traded to **Quebec** by **Toronto** for Brad Maxwell, August 21, 1985. Traded to **Hartford** by **Quebec** for Risto Siltanen, March 8, 1986.

ANDERSON, Murray

Defense. Shoots left. 5'10", 175 lbs. Born, The Pas, Man., August 28, 1949.
(Montreal's 4th choice, 44th overall, in 1969 Amateur Draft).

		REGULAR SEASON					PLAYOFFS				
Season	Club	GP	G	A	Pts	PIM	GP	G	A	Pts	PIM
1974-75	Washington Capitals	40	0	1	1	68	....	....	....	....	....
	NHL Totals	**40**	**0**	**1**	**1**	**68**	....	....	....	....	....

Traded to **Minnesota** by **Montreal** with Tony Featherstone for cash, May 29, 1973. Claimed by **Washington** from **Minnesota** in Expansion Draft, June 12, 1974

ANDERSON, Perry

Left wing. Shoots left. 6'1", 225 lbs. Born, Barrie, Ont., October 14, 1961.
(St. Louis' 5th choice, 117th overall, in 1980 Entry Draft).

		REGULAR SEASON					PLAYOFFS				
Season	Club	GP	G	A	Pts	PIM	GP	G	A	Pts	PIM
1981-82	St. Louis Blues	5	1	2	3	0	10	2	0	2	4
1982-83	St. Louis Blues	18	5	2	7	14	....	....	....	....	....
1983-84	St. Louis Blues	50	7	5	12	195	9	0	0	0	27
1984-85	St. Louis Blues	71	9	9	18	146	3	0	0	0	7
1985-86	New Jersey Devils	51	7	12	19	91	....	....	....	....	....
1986-87	New Jersey Devils	57	10	9	19	107	....	....	....	....	....
1987-88	New Jersey Devils	60	4	6	10	222	10	0	0	0	113
1988-89	New Jersey Devils	39	3	6	9	128	....	....	....	....	....
1990-91	New Jersey Devils	1	0	0	0	5	4	0	1	1	10
1991-92	San Jose Sharks	48	4	8	12	143	....	....	....	....	....
	NHL Totals	**400**	**50**	**59**	**109**	**1051**	**36**	**2**	**1**	**3**	**161**

Traded to **New Jersey** by **St. Louis** for Rick Meagher and New Jersey's 12th round choice (Bill Butler) in 1986 Entry Draft, August 29, 1985. Signed as a free agent by **San Jose**, July 8, 1991.

ANDERSON, Ron

Right wing. Shoots right. 6', 170 lbs. Born, Red Deer, Alta., July 29, 1945.

		REGULAR SEASON					PLAYOFFS				
Season	Club	GP	G	A	Pts	PIM	GP	G	A	Pts	PIM
1967-68	Detroit Red Wings	18	2	0	2	13	....	....	....	....	....
1968-69	Detroit Red Wings	7	0	0	0	8	....	....	....	....	....
	Los Angeles Kings	56	3	5	8	26	4	0	0	0	2
1969-70	St. Louis Blues	59	9	9	18	36	1	0	0	0	2
1970-71	Buffalo Sabres	74	14	12	26	44	....	....	....	....	....
1971-72	Buffalo Sabres	37	0	4	4	19	....	....	....	....	....
	NHL Totals	**251**	**28**	**30**	**58**	**146**	**5**	**0**	**0**	**0**	**4**

Traded to **Los Angeles** by **Detroit** for Poul Popiel, November 12, 1968. Claimed by **St. Louis** from **Los Angeles** in Intra-League Draft, June 11, 1969. Traded to **Buffalo** by **St. Louis** for Craig Cameron, October 2, 1970. Claimed by **San Diego** (WHL) from **Buffalo** (Salt Lake-WHL) in Reverse Draft, June, 1972.

ANDERSON, Ron

Right wing. Shoots right. 5'10", 165 lbs. Born, Moncton, N.B., January 21, 1950.

		REGULAR SEASON					PLAYOFFS				
Season	Club	GP	G	A	Pts	PIM	GP	G	A	Pts	PIM
1974-75	Washington Capitals	28	9	7	16	8	....	....	....	....	....
	NHL Totals	**28**	**9**	**7**	**16**	**8**	....	....	....	....	....

Signed as a free agent by **Boston**, June, 1972. Claimed by **Washington** from **Boston** in Expansion Draft, June 12, 1974. • Missed majority of 1975-76 season after suffering a knee injury during training camp, September, 1975. Traded to **New Haven** (AHL) by **Washington** with Bob Gryp for Rich Nantais and Alain Langlais, February 23, 1976

ANDERSON, Russ

Defense. Shoots left. 6'3", 210 lbs. Born, Minneapolis, MN, February 12, 1955.
(Pittsburgh's 2nd choice, 31st overall, in 1975 Amateur Draft).

		REGULAR SEASON					PLAYOFFS				
Season	Club	GP	G	A	Pts	PIM	GP	G	A	Pts	PIM
1976-77	Pittsburgh Penguins	66	2	11	13	81	3	0	1	1	14
1977-78	Pittsburgh Penguins	74	2	16	18	150	....	....	....	....	....
1978-79	Pittsburgh Penguins	72	3	13	16	93	2	0	0	0	0
1979-80	Pittsburgh Penguins	76	5	22	27	150	5	0	2	2	14
1980-81	Pittsburgh Penguins	34	3	14	17	112	....	....	....	....	....
1981-82	Pittsburgh Penguins	31	0	1	1	98	....	....	....	....	....
	Hartford Whalers	25	1	3	4	85	....	....	....	....	....
1982-83	Hartford Whalers	57	0	6	6	171	....	....	....	....	....
1983-84	Los Angeles Kings	70	5	12	17	126	....	....	....	....	....
1984-85	Los Angeles Kings	14	1	1	2	20	....	....	....	....	....
	NHL Totals	**519**	**22**	**99**	**121**	**1086**	**10**	**0**	**3**	**3**	**28**

Traded to **Hartford** by **Pittsburgh** with Pittsburgh 8th round choice (Chris Duperron) in 1983 Entry Draft for Rick MacLeish, December 29, 1981. Signed as a free agent by **Los Angeles**, September 2, 1983.

ANDERSON, Shawn

Defense. Shoots left. 6'1", 200 lbs. Born, Montreal, Que., February 7, 1968.
(Buffalo's 1st choice, 5th overall, in 1986 Entry Draft).

		REGULAR SEASON					PLAYOFFS				
Season	Club	GP	G	A	Pts	PIM	GP	G	A	Pts	PIM
1986-87	Buffalo Sabres	41	2	11	13	23	....	....	....	....	....
1987-88	Buffalo Sabres	23	1	2	3	17	....	....	....	....	....
1988-89	Buffalo Sabres	33	2	10	12	18	5	0	1	1	4
1989-90	Buffalo Sabres	16	1	3	4	8	....	....	....	....	....
1990-91	Quebec Nordiques	31	3	10	13	21	....	....	....	....	....
1992-93	Washington Capitals	60	2	6	8	18	6	0	0	0	0
1993-94	Washington Capitals	50	0	9	9	12	8	1	0	1	12
1994-95	Philadelphia Flyers	1	0	0	0	0	....	....	....	....	....
	NHL Totals	**255**	**11**	**51**	**62**	**117**	**19**	**1**	**1**	**2**	**16**

Traded to **Washington** by **Buffalo** for Bill Houlder, September 30, 1990. Claimed by **Quebec** from **Washington** in Waiver Draft, October 1, 1990. Traded to **Winnipeg** by **Quebec** for Sergei Kharin, October 22, 1991. Traded to **Washington** by **Winnipeg** for future considerations, October 23, 1991. Signed as a free agent by **Philadelphia**, August 16, 1994.

ANDERSON, Tom

Left wing/Defense. Shoots left. 5'10", 180 lbs. Born, Edinburgh, Scotland, July 9, 1910.

		REGULAR SEASON					PLAYOFFS				
Season	Club	GP	G	A	Pts	PIM	GP	G	A	Pts	PIM
1934-35	Detroit Red Wings	27	5	2	7	16	....	....	....	....	....
1935-36	New York Americans	24	3	2	5	20	5	0	0	0	6
1936-37	New York Americans	45	10	15	25	24	....	....	....	....	....
1937-38	New York Americans	45	4	21	25	22	6	1	4	5	2
1938-39	New York Americans	47	13	27	40	14	2	0	0	0	0
1939-40	New York Americans	48	12	19	31	22	3	1	3	4	0
1940-41	New York Americans	35	3	12	15	8	....	....	....	....	....
1941-42	Brooklyn Americans	48	12	29	41	54	....	....	....	....	....
	NHL Totals	**319**	**62**	**127**	**189**	**180**	**16**	**2**	**7**	**9**	**8**

NHL First All-Star Team (1942) • Hart Trophy (1942)

Played in NHL All-Star Game (1939)

Traded to **Detroit** by **Philadelphia** (Can-Am) with Irvin Boyd for cash, May 8, 1934. Traded to **NY Americans** by **Detroit** for cash, October 11, 1935. • Team name changed to **Brooklyn Americans** prior to 1941-42 season. Rights transferred to **Chicago** from **Brooklyn** in Special Dispersal Draw, September 11, 1943.

ANDERSSON, Erik

Center. Shoots left. 6'3", 210 lbs. Born, Stockholm, Sweden, August 19, 1971.
(Calgary's 6th choice, 70th overall, in 1997 Entry Draft).

		REGULAR SEASON					PLAYOFFS				
Season	Club	GP	G	A	Pts	PIM	GP	G	A	Pts	PIM
1997-98	Calgary Flames	12	2	1	3	8	....	....	....	....	....
	NHL Totals	**12**	**2**	**1**	**3**	**8**	....	....	....	....	....

• Re-entered NHL Entry Draft. Originally Los Angeles' 5th choice, 112th overall, in 1990 Entry Draft.

Traded to **Chicago** by **Calgary** with Marty McInnis and Jamie Allison for Jeff Shantz and Steve Dubinsky, October 27, 1998.

ANDERSSON, Jonas

Right wing. Shoots left. 6'3", 202 lbs. Born, Stockholm, Sweden, February 24, 1981.
(Nashville's 2nd choice, 33rd overall, in 1999 Entry Draft).

		REGULAR SEASON					PLAYOFFS				
Season	Club	GP	G	A	Pts	PIM	GP	G	A	Pts	PIM
2001-02	Nashville Predators	5	0	0	0	2	....	....	....	....	....
	NHL Totals	**5**	**0**	**0**	**0**	**2**	....	....	....	....	....

ANDERSSON, Kent-Erik

Right wing. 6'2", 185 lbs. Born, Orebro, Sweden, May 24, 1951.

		REGULAR SEASON					PLAYOFFS				
Season	Club	GP	G	A	Pts	PIM	GP	G	A	Pts	PIM
1977-78	Minnesota North Stars	73	15	18	33	4	....	....	....	....	....
1978-79	Minnesota North Stars	41	9	4	13	4	....	....	....	....	....
1979-80	Minnesota North Stars	61	9	10	19	8	13	2	4	6	2
1980-81	Minnesota North Stars	77	17	24	41	22	19	2	4	6	2
1981-82	Minnesota North Stars	70	9	12	21	18	4	0	2	2	0
1982-83	New York Rangers	71	8	20	28	14	9	0	0	0	0
1983-84	New York Rangers	63	5	15	20	8	5	0	1	1	0
	NHL Totals	**456**	**72**	**103**	**175**	**78**	**50**	**4**	**11**	**15**	**4**

Signed as a free agent by **Minnesota**, June 15, 1977. Traded to **Hartford** by **Minnesota** with Mark Johnson for Jordy Douglas and Hartford's 5th round choice (Jiri Poner) in 1984 Entry Draft, October 1, 1982. Traded to **NY Rangers** by **Hartford** for Ed Hospodar, October 1, 1982.

ANDERSSON, Mikael

Left wing. Shoots left. 5'11", 181 lbs. Born, Malmo, Sweden, May 10, 1966.
(Buffalo's 1st choice, 18th overall, in 1984 Entry Draft).

		REGULAR SEASON					PLAYOFFS				
Season	Club	GP	G	A	Pts	PIM	GP	G	A	Pts	PIM
1985-86	Buffalo Sabres	32	1	9	10	4	....	....	....	....	....
1986-87	Buffalo Sabres	16	0	3	3	0	....	....	....	....	....
1987-88	Buffalo Sabres	37	3	20	23	10	1	1	0	1	0
1988-89	Buffalo Sabres	14	0	1	1	4	....	....	....	....	....
1989-90	Hartford Whalers	50	13	24	37	6	5	0	3	3	2
1990-91	Hartford Whalers	41	4	7	11	8	....	....	....	....	....
1991-92	Hartford Whalers	74	18	29	47	14	7	0	2	2	6
1992-93	Tampa Bay Lightning	77	16	11	27	14	....	....	....	....	....
1993-94	Tampa Bay Lightning	76	13	12	25	23	....	....	....	....	....
1994-95	Tampa Bay Lightning	36	4	7	11	4	....	....	....	....	....
1995-96	Tampa Bay Lightning	64	8	11	19	2	6	1	1	2	0
1996-97	Tampa Bay Lightning	70	5	14	19	8	....	....	....	....	....
1997-98	Tampa Bay Lightning	72	6	11	17	29	....	....	....	....	....
1998-99	Tampa Bay Lightning	40	2	3	5	4	....	....	....	....	....
	Philadelphia Flyers	7	0	1	1	0	6	0	1	1	2

Season	Club	GP	G	A	Pts	PIM	GP	G	A	Pts	PIM
		REGULAR SEASON					PLAYOFFS				
99-2000	Philadelphia Flyers	36	2	3	5	0	....	....	....	....	....
	New York Islanders	19	0	3	3	4	....	....	....	....	....
	NHL Totals	**761**	**95**	**169**	**264**	**134**	**25**	**2**	**7**	**9**	**10**

• Brother of Niklas

Claimed by **Hartford** from **Buffalo** in Waiver Draft, October 2, 1989. Signed as a free agent by **Tampa Bay**, June 29, 1992. Traded to **Philadelphia** by **Tampa Bay** with Sandy McCarthy for Colin Forbes and Philadelphia's 4th round choice (Michal Lanicek) in 1999 Entry Draft, March 20, 1999. Traded to **NY Islanders** by **Philadelphia** with Carolina's 5th round choice (previously acquired, NY Islanders selected Kristofer Ottosson) in 2000 Entry Draft for Gino Odjick, February 15, 2000.

ANDERSSON, Niklas

Left wing. Shoots left. 5'9", 180 lbs. Born, Kungalv, Sweden, May 20, 1971.
(Quebec's 5th choice, 68th overall, in 1989 Entry Draft).

Season	Club	GP	G	A	Pts	PIM	GP	G	A	Pts	PIM
1992-93	Quebec Nordiques	3	0	1	1	2	....	....	....	....	....
1995-96	New York Islanders	47	14	12	26	12	....	....	....	....	....
1996-97	New York Islanders	74	12	31	43	57	....	....	....	....	....
1997-98	San Jose Sharks	5	0	0	0	2	....	....	....	....	....
99-2000	New York Islanders	17	3	7	10	8	....	....	....	....	....
	Nashville Predators	7	0	1	1	0	....	....	....	....	....
2000-01	Calgary Flames	11	0	1	1	4	....	....	....	....	....
	NHL Totals	**164**	**29**	**53**	**82**	**85**	....	....	....	....	....

• Brother of Mikael

Signed as a free agent by **NY Islanders**, July 15, 1994. Signed as a free agent by **San Jose**, September 17, 1997. Signed as a free agent by **Toronto**, September 4, 1998. Traded to **NY Islanders** by **Toronto** for Craig Charron, August 17, 1999. Claimed on waivers by **Nashville** from **NY Islanders**, January 20, 2000. Claimed on waivers by **NY Islanders** from **Nashville**, February 19, 2000. Signed as a free agent by **Calgary**, August 29, 2000.

ANDERSSON, Peter

Defense. Shoots right. 6'2", 200 lbs. Born, Sodertalje, Sweden, March 2, 1962.
(Washington's 8th choice, 173rd overall, in 1980 Entry Draft).

Season	Club	GP	G	A	Pts	PIM	GP	G	A	Pts	PIM
1983-84	Washington Capitals	42	3	7	10	20	3	0	1	1	2
1984-85	Washington Capitals	57	0	10	10	21	2	0	0	0	0
1985-86	Washington Capitals	61	6	16	22	36	....	....	....	....	....
	Quebec Nordiques	12	1	8	9	4	2	0	1	1	0
	NHL Totals	**172**	**10**	**41**	**51**	**81**	**7**	**0**	**2**	**2**	**2**

Traded to **Quebec** by **Washington** for Quebec's 3rd round choice (Shawn Simpson) in 1986 Entry Draft, March 10, 1986.

ANDERSSON, Peter

Defense. Shoots left. 6', 196 lbs. Born, Orebro, Sweden, August 29, 1965.
(NY Rangers' 5th choice, 75th overall, in 1983 Entry Draft).

Season	Club	GP	G	A	Pts	PIM	GP	G	A	Pts	PIM
1992-93	New York Rangers	31	4	11	15	18	....	....	....	....	....
1993-94	New York Rangers	8	1	1	2	2	....	....	....	....	....
	Florida Panthers	8	1	1	2	0	....	....	....	....	....
	NHL Totals	**47**	**6**	**13**	**19**	**20**	....	....	....	....	....

Traded to **Florida** by **NY Rangers** for Florida's 9th round choice (Vitali Yeremeyev) in 1994 Entry Draft, March 21, 1994.

ANDRASCIK, Steve

Right wing. Shoots right. 5'11", 200 lbs. Born, Sherridon, Man., November 6, 1948.
(Detroit's 1st choice, 11th overall, in 1968 Amateur Draft).

Season	Club	GP	G	A	Pts	PIM	GP	G	A	Pts	PIM
1971-72	New York Rangers	....	....	....	....	....	1	0	0	0	0
	NHL Totals	....	....	....	....	....	**1**	**0**	**0**	**0**	**0**

Traded to **NY Rangers** by **Detroit** for Don Luce, November 2, 1970. Traded to **Pittsburgh** by **NY Rangers** to complete transaction that sent Sheldon Kannegiesser to NY Rangers (March 2, 1973), May 16, 1973.

ANDREA, Paul

Right wing. Shoots left. 5'10", 174 lbs. Born, North Sydney, N.S., July 31, 1941.

Season	Club	GP	G	A	Pts	PIM	GP	G	A	Pts	PIM
1965-66	New York Rangers	4	1	1	2	0	....	....	....	....	....
1967-68	Pittsburgh Penguins	65	11	21	32	2	....	....	....	....	....
1968-69	Pittsburgh Penguins	25	7	6	13	2	....	....	....	....	....
1970-71	California Seals	9	1	0	1	2	....	....	....	....	....
	Buffalo Sabres	47	11	21	32	4	....	....	....	....	....
	NHL Totals	**150**	**31**	**49**	**80**	**10**	....	....	....	....	....

Traded to **Pittsburgh** by **NY Rangers** with George Konik, Dunc McCallum and Frank Francis for Larry Jeffrey, June 6, 1967. Traded to **Vancouver** (WHL) by **Pittsburgh** with John Arbour and the loan of Andy Bathgate for the 1969-70 season for Bryan Hextall Jr., May 20, 1969. Claimed by **Oakland** from **Vancouver** (WHL) in Intra-League Draft, June 9, 1970. Claimed on waivers by **Buffalo** from **California**, November 4, 1970.

ANDREWS, Lloyd

Left wing. Shoots left. , Born, Tillsonburg, Ont., 1899.

Season	Club	GP	G	A	Pts	PIM	GP	G	A	Pts	PIM
1921-22 ◆	Toronto St. Pats	11	0	0	0	0	2	0	0	0	0
	Toronto St. Pats (Cup)	....	....	....	....	....	*5*	*2*	*0*	*2*	*3*
1922-23	Toronto St. Pats	23	5	4	9	10	....	....	....	....	....
1923-24	Toronto St. Pats	12	2	1	3	0	....	....	....	....	....
1924-25	Toronto St. Pats	7	1	0	1	0	....	....	....	....	....
	NHL Totals	**53**	**8**	**5**	**13**	**10**	**2**	**0**	**0**	**0**	**0**

Signed as a free agent by **Toronto**, January 23, 1922.

ANDREYCHUK, Dave

Left wing. Shoots right. 6'4", 220 lbs. Born, Hamilton, Ont., September 29, 1963.
(Buffalo's 3rd choice, 16th overall, in 1982 Entry Draft).

Season	Club	GP	G	A	Pts	PIM	GP	G	A	Pts	PIM
1982-83	Buffalo Sabres	43	14	23	37	16	4	1	0	1	4
1983-84	Buffalo Sabres	78	38	42	80	42	2	0	1	1	2
1984-85	Buffalo Sabres	64	31	30	61	54	5	4	2	6	4
1985-86	Buffalo Sabres	80	36	51	87	61	....	....	....	....	....
1986-87	Buffalo Sabres	77	25	48	73	46	....	....	....	....	....
1987-88	Buffalo Sabres	80	30	48	78	112	6	2	4	6	0
1988-89	Buffalo Sabres	56	28	24	52	40	5	0	3	3	0
1989-90	Buffalo Sabres	73	40	42	82	42	6	2	5	7	2
1990-91	Buffalo Sabres	80	36	33	69	32	6	2	2	4	8
1991-92	Buffalo Sabres	80	41	50	91	71	7	1	3	4	12
1992-93	Buffalo Sabres	52	29	32	61	48	....	....	....	....	....
	Toronto Maple Leafs	31	25	13	38	8	21	12	7	19	35
1993-94	Toronto Maple Leafs	83	53	46	99	98	18	5	5	10	16
1994-95	Toronto Maple Leafs	48	22	16	38	34	7	3	2	5	25
1995-96	Toronto Maple Leafs	61	20	24	44	54	....	....	....	....	....
	New Jersey Devils	15	8	5	13	10	....	....	....	....	....
1996-97	New Jersey Devils	82	27	34	61	48	1	0	0	0	0
1997-98	New Jersey Devils	75	14	34	48	26	6	1	0	1	4
1998-99	New Jersey Devils	52	15	13	28	20	4	2	0	2	4
99-2000	Boston Bruins	63	19	14	33	28	....	....	....	....	....
	Colorado Avalanche	14	1	2	3	2	17	3	2	5	18
2000-01	Buffalo Sabres	74	20	13	33	32	13	1	2	3	4
2001-02	Tampa Bay Lightning	82	21	17	38	109	....	....	....	....	....
2002-03	Tampa Bay Lightning	72	20	14	34	34	11	3	3	6	10
	NHL Totals	**1515**	**613**	**668**	**1281**	**1067**	**139**	**42**	**41**	**83**	**148**

Played in NHL All-Star Game (1990, 1994)

Traded to **Toronto** by **Buffalo** with Daren Puppa and Buffalo's 1st round choice (Kenny Jonsson) in 1993 Entry Draft for Grant Fuhr and Toronto's 5th round choice (Kevin Popp) in 1995 Entry Draft, February 2, 1993. Traded to **New Jersey** by **Toronto** for New Jersey's 2nd round choice (Marek Posmyk) in 1996 Entry Draft and New Jersey's 3rd round choice (later traded back to New Jersey – New Jersey selected Andre Lakos) in 1999 Entry Draft, March 13, 1996. Signed as a free agent by Boston, July 29, 1999. Traded to **Colorado** by **Boston** with Raymond Bourque for Brian Rolston, Martin Grenier, Samuel Pahlsson and New Jersey's 1st round choice (previously acquired, Boston selected Martin Samuelsson) in 2000 Entry Draft, March 6, 2000. Signed as a free agent by **Buffalo**, July 13, 2000. Signed as a free agent by **Tampa Bay**, July 13, 2001.

ANDRIEVSKI, Alexander

Right wing. Shoots right. 6'5", 211 lbs. Born, Moscow, USSR, August 10, 1968.
(Chicago's 10th choice, 220th overall, in 1991 Entry Draft).

Season	Club	GP	G	A	Pts	PIM	GP	G	A	Pts	PIM
1992-93	Chicago Blackhawks	1	0	0	0	0	....	....	....	....	....
	NHL Totals	**1**	**0**	**0**	**0**	**0**	....	....	....	....	....

ANDRUFF, Ron

Center. Shoots right. 6', 185 lbs. Born, Port Alberni, B.C., July 10, 1953.
(Montreal's 4th choice, 32nd overall, in 1973 Amateur Draft).

Season	Club	GP	G	A	Pts	PIM	GP	G	A	Pts	PIM
1974-75	Montreal Canadiens	5	0	0	0	2	....	....	....	....	....
1975-76	Montreal Canadiens	1	0	0	0	0	....	....	....	....	....
1976-77	Colorado Rockies	66	4	18	22	21	....	....	....	....	....
1977-78	Colorado Rockies	78	15	18	33	31	2	0	0	0	0
1978-79	Colorado Rockies	3	0	0	0	0	....	....	....	....	....
	NHL Totals	**153**	**19**	**36**	**55**	**54**	**2**	**0**	**0**	**0**	**0**

Traded to **Colorado** by **Montreal** with Sean Shanahan for cash, September 13, 1976.

ANDRUSAK, Greg

Defense. Shoots right. 6'1", 195 lbs. Born, Cranbrook, B.C., November 14, 1969.
(Pittsburgh's 5th choice, 88th overall, in 1988 Entry Draft).

Season	Club	GP	G	A	Pts	PIM	GP	G	A	Pts	PIM
1993-94	Pittsburgh Penguins	3	0	0	0	2	....	....	....	....	....
1994-95	Pittsburgh Penguins	7	0	4	4	6	....	....	....	....	....
1995-96	Pittsburgh Penguins	2	0	0	0	0	....	....	....	....	....
1998-99	Pittsburgh Penguins	7	0	1	1	4	12	1	0	1	6
99-2000	Toronto Maple Leafs	9	0	1	1	4	3	0	0	0	2
	NHL Totals	**28**	**0**	**6**	**6**	**16**	**15**	**1**	**0**	**1**	**8**

Signed as a free agent by **Pittsburgh**, March 19, 1999. Signed as a free agent by **Toronto**, July 19, 1999. Signed as a free agent by **San Jose**, August 14, 2000.

ANGOTTI, Lou

Center/Right wing. Shoots right. 5'9", 170 lbs. Born, Toronto, Ont., January 16, 1938.

Season	Club	GP	G	A	Pts	PIM	GP	G	A	Pts	PIM
1964-65	New York Rangers	70	9	8	17	20	....	....	....	....	....
1965-66	New York Rangers	21	2	2	4	2	....	....	....	....	....
	Chicago Black Hawks	30	4	10	14	12	6	0	0	0	2
1966-67	Chicago Black Hawks	63	6	12	18	21	6	2	1	3	2
1967-68	Philadelphia Flyers	70	12	37	49	35	7	0	0	0	2
1968-69	Pittsburgh Penguins	71	17	20	37	36	....	....	....	....	....
1969-70	Chicago Black Hawks	70	12	26	38	25	8	0	0	0	0
1970-71	Chicago Black Hawks	65	9	16	25	19	16	3	3	6	9
1971-72	Chicago Black Hawks	65	5	10	15	23	6	0	0	0	0
1972-73	Chicago Black Hawks	77	15	22	37	26	16	3	4	7	2

Season	Club	GP	G	A	Pts	PIM	GP	G	A	Pts	PIM
		REGULAR SEASON					PLAYOFFS				
1973-74	St. Louis Blues	51	12	23	35	9	....	....	....	....	....
	NHL Totals	**653**	**103**	**186**	**289**	**228**	**65**	**8**	**8**	**16**	**17**

Traded to **NY Rangers** by **Toronto** (Rochester-AHL) with Ed Lawson for Duane Rupp and Ed Ehrenverth, June 25, 1964. Traded to **Chicago** by **NY Rangers** for cash, January 7, 1966. Claimed by **Philadelphia** from **Chicago** in Expansion Draft, June 6, 1967. Traded to **St. Louis** by **Philadelphia** with Ian Campbell for Darryl Edestrand and Gerry Melynk, June 11, 1968. Traded to **Pittsburgh** by **St. Louis** for Ab McDonald, June 11, 1968. Traded to **St. Louis** by **Pittsburgh** with Pittsburgh's 1st round choice (Gene Carr) in 1971 Amateur Draft for Ron Schock, Craig Cameron and St. Louis' 2nd round choice (Brian McKenzie) in 1971 Amateur Draft, June 6, 1969. Claimed by **Chicago** from **St. Louis** in Intra-League Draft, June 11, 1969. Claimed by **St. Louis** from **Chicago** in Intra-League Draft, June 12, 1973.

ANHOLT, Darrel

Defense. Shoots left. 6'2", 230 lbs. Born, Hardisty, Alta., November 23, 1962.
(Chicago's 3rd choice, 54th overall, in 1981 Entry Draft).

Season	Club	GP	G	A	Pts	PIM	GP	G	A	Pts	PIM
1983-84	Chicago Black Hawks	1	0	0	0	0	....	....	....	....	....
	NHL Totals	**1**	**0**	**0**	**0**	**0**	....	....	....	....	....

ANSLOW, Hub

Center. Shoots left. 6', 173 lbs. Born, Pembroke, Ont., March 23, 1926.

Season	Club	GP	G	A	Pts	PIM	GP	G	A	Pts	PIM
1947-48	New York Rangers	2	0	0	0	0	....	....	....	....	....
	NHL Totals	**2**	**0**	**0**	**0**	**0**	....	....	....	....	....

ANTONOVICH, Mike

Center. Shoots left. 5'8", 165 lbs. Born, Calumet, MN, October 18, 1951.
(Minnesota's 8th choice, 113th overall, in 1971 Amateur Draft).

Season	Club	GP	G	A	Pts	PIM	GP	G	A	Pts	PIM
1975-76	Minnesota North Stars	12	0	2	2	8	....	....	....	....	....
1979-80	Hartford Whalers	5	0	1	1	2	....	....	....	....	....
1981-82	Minnesota North Stars	2	0	0	0	0	....	....	....	....	....
1982-83	New Jersey Devils	30	7	7	14	11	....	....	....	....	....
1983-84	New Jersey Devils	38	3	5	8	16	....	....	....	....	....
	NHL Totals	**87**	**10**	**15**	**25**	**37**	....	....	....	....	....

Signed as a free agent by **Minnesota** (NHL) after **Minnesota** (WHA) franchise folded, March 10, 1976. Signed as a free agent by **Hartford**, October 17, 1979. Signed as a free agent by **Minnesota**, November 25, 1981. Signed as a free agent by **New Jersey**, October 1, 1982.

ANTOSKI, Shawn

Left wing. Shoots left. 6'4", 235 lbs. Born, Brantford, Ont., March 25, 1970.
(Vancouver's 2nd choice, 18th overall, in 1990 Entry Draft).

Season	Club	GP	G	A	Pts	PIM	GP	G	A	Pts	PIM
1990-91	Vancouver Canucks	2	0	0	0	0	....	....	....	....	....
1991-92	Vancouver Canucks	4	0	0	0	29	....	....	....	....	....
1992-93	Vancouver Canucks	2	0	0	0	0	....	....	....	....	....
1993-94	Vancouver Canucks	55	1	2	3	190	16	0	1	1	36
1994-95	Vancouver Canucks	7	0	0	0	46	....	....	....	....	....
	Philadelphia Flyers	25	0	0	0	61	13	0	1	1	10
1995-96	Philadelphia Flyers	64	1	3	4	204	7	1	1	2	28
1996-97	Pittsburgh Penguins	13	0	0	0	49	....	....	....	....	....
	Mighty Ducks of Anaheim	2	0	0	0	2	....	....	....	....	....
1997-98	Mighty Ducks of Anaheim	9	1	0	1	18	....	....	....	....	....
	NHL Totals	**183**	**3**	**5**	**8**	**599**	**36**	**1**	**3**	**4**	**74**

Traded to **Philadelphia** by **Vancouver** for Josef Beranek, February 15, 1995. Signed as a free agent by **Pittsburgh**, July 31, 1996. Traded to **Anaheim** by **Pittsburgh** with Dmitri Mironov for Alex Hicks and Fredrik Olausson, November 19, 1996. • Missed majority of 1996-97 season recovering from hernia surgery, February 4, 1997. • Suffered career-ending injuries in automobile accident, November 24, 1997.

ANTROPOV, Nik

Center. Shoots left. 6'5", 203 lbs. Born, Vost, USSR, February 18, 1980.
(Toronto's 1st choice, 10th overall, in 1998 Entry Draft).

Season	Club	GP	G	A	Pts	PIM	GP	G	A	Pts	PIM
99-2000	Toronto Maple Leafs	66	12	18	30	41	3	0	0	0	4
2000-01	Toronto Maple Leafs	52	6	11	17	30	9	2	1	3	12
2001-02	Toronto Maple Leafs	11	1	1	2	4	....	....	....	....	....
2002-03	Toronto Maple Leafs	72	16	29	45	124	3	0	0	0	0
	NHL Totals	**201**	**35**	**59**	**94**	**199**	**15**	**2**	**1**	**3**	**16**

APPS Jr., Syl

Center. Shoots right. 6', 185 lbs. Born, Toronto, Ont., August 1, 1947.
(NY Rangers' 4th choice, 21st overall, in 1964 Amateur Draft).

Season	Club	GP	G	A	Pts	PIM	GP	G	A	Pts	PIM
1970-71	New York Rangers	31	1	2	3	11	....	....	....	....	....
	Pittsburgh Penguins	31	9	16	25	21	....	....	....	....	....
1971-72	Pittsburgh Penguins	72	15	44	59	78	4	1	0	1	2
1972-73	Pittsburgh Penguins	77	29	56	85	18	....	....	....	....	....
1973-74	Pittsburgh Penguins	75	24	61	85	37	....	....	....	....	....
1974-75	Pittsburgh Penguins	79	24	55	79	43	9	2	3	5	9
1975-76	Pittsburgh Penguins	80	32	67	99	24	3	0	1	1	0
1976-77	Pittsburgh Penguins	72	18	43	61	20	3	1	0	1	12
1977-78	Pittsburgh Penguins	9	0	7	7	0	....	....	....	....	....
	Los Angeles Kings	70	19	26	45	18	2	0	1	1	0
1978-79	Los Angeles Kings	80	7	30	37	29	2	1	0	1	0
1979-80	Los Angeles Kings	51	5	16	21	12	....	....	....	....	....
	NHL Totals	**727**	**183**	**423**	**606**	**311**	**23**	**5**	**5**	**10**	**23**

• Son of Syl

Played in NHL All-Star Game (1975)

Traded to **Pittsburgh** by **NY Rangers** with Sheldon Kannegiesser for Glen Sather, January 26, 1971. Traded to **Los Angeles** by **Pittsburgh** with Hartland Monahan for Dave Schultz, Gene Carr and L.A. Kings' 4th round choice (Shane Pearsall) in 1978 Amateur Draft, November 2, 1977.

APPS, Syl

HHOF

Center. Shoots left. 6', 185 lbs. Born, Paris, Ont., January 18, 1915.

Season	Club	GP	G	A	Pts	PIM	GP	G	A	Pts	PIM
1936-37	Toronto Maple Leafs	48	16	*29	45	10	2	0	1	1	0
1937-38	Toronto Maple Leafs	47	21	*29	50	9	7	1	4	5	0
1938-39	Toronto Maple Leafs	44	15	25	40	4	10	2	6	8	2
1939-40	Toronto Maple Leafs	27	13	17	30	5	10	*5	2	7	2
1940-41	Toronto Maple Leafs	41	20	24	44	6	7	3	2	5	2
1941-42 ♦	Toronto Maple Leafs	38	18	23	41	0	13	5	*9	*14	2
1942-43	Toronto Maple Leafs	29	23	17	40	2	....	....	....	....	....
1945-46	Toronto Maple Leafs	40	24	16	40	2	....	....	....	....	....
1946-47 ♦	Toronto Maple Leafs	54	25	24	49	6	11	5	1	6	0
1947-48 ♦	Toronto Maple Leafs	55	26	27	53	12	9	4	4	8	0
	NHL Totals	**423**	**201**	**231**	**432**	**56**	**69**	**25**	**29**	**54**	**8**

• Father of Syl Jr. • Calder Trophy (1937) • NHL Second All-Star Team (1938, 1941, 1943) • NHL First All-Star Team (1939, 1942) • Lady Byng Trophy (1942)

Played in NHL All-Star Game (1939, 1947)

• Missed remainder of 1942-43 season recovering from leg injury suffered in game vs. Boston, January 30, 1943.

ARBOUR, Al

HHOF

Defense. Shoots left. 6', 180 lbs. Born, Sudbury, Ont., November 1, 1932.

Season	Club	GP	G	A	Pts	PIM	GP	G	A	Pts	PIM
1953-54 ♦	Detroit Red Wings	36	0	1	1	18	....	....	....	....	....
1955-56	Detroit Red Wings	....	....	....	....	....	4	0	1	1	0
1956-57	Detroit Red Wings	44	1	6	7	38	5	0	0	0	6
1957-58	Detroit Red Wings	69	1	6	7	104	4	0	1	1	4
1958-59	Chicago Black Hawks	70	2	10	12	86	6	1	2	3	26
1959-60	Chicago Black Hawks	57	1	5	6	66	4	0	0	0	4
1960-61 ♦	Chicago Black Hawks	53	3	2	5	40	7	0	0	0	2
1961-62 ♦	Toronto Maple Leafs	52	1	5	6	68	8	0	0	0	6
1962-63	Toronto Maple Leafs	4	1	0	1	4	....	....	....	....	....
1963-64 ♦	Toronto Maple Leafs	6	0	1	1	0	1	0	0	0	0
1964-65	Toronto Maple Leafs	....	....	....	....	....	1	0	0	0	2
1965-66	Toronto Maple Leafs	4	0	1	1	2	....	....	....	....	....
1967-68	St. Louis Blues	74	1	10	11	50	14	0	3	3	10
1968-69	St. Louis Blues	67	1	6	7	50	12	0	0	0	10
1969-70	St. Louis Blues	68	0	3	3	85	14	0	1	1	16
1970-71	St. Louis Blues	22	0	2	2	6	6	0	0	0	6
	NHL Totals	**626**	**12**	**58**	**70**	**617**	**86**	**1**	**8**	**9**	**92**

Lester Patrick Trophy (1992)

Played in NHL All-Star Game (1969)

Claimed by **Chicago** from **Detroit** in Intra-League Draft, June 3, 1958. Claimed by **Toronto** from **Chicago** in Intra-League Draft, June 13, 1961. Claimed by **St. Louis** from **Toronto** in Expansion Draft, June 6, 1967.

ARBOUR, Amos

Left wing. Shoots left. 5'8", 160 lbs. Born, Waubaushene, Ont., January 26, 1895.

Season	Club	GP	G	A	Pts	PIM	GP	G	A	Pts	PIM
1918-19	Montreal Canadiens	1	0	0	0	0	....	....	....	....	....
1919-20	Montreal Canadiens	22	21	5	26	13	....	....	....	....	....
1920-21	Montreal Canadiens	23	15	3	18	40	....	....	....	....	....
1921-22	Hamilton Tigers	23	9	6	15	8	....	....	....	....	....
1922-23	Hamilton Tigers	23	6	3	9	12	....	....	....	....	....
1923-24	Toronto St. Pats	21	1	3	4	4	....	....	....	....	....
	NHL Totals	**113**	**52**	**20**	**72**	**77**	....	....	....	....	....

Signed as a free agent by **Montreal**, January 23, 1919. Traded to **Hamilton** by **Montreal** with Harry Mummery for Sprague Cleghorn, November 26, 1921. Traded to **Toronto** by **Hamilton** with Bert Corbeau and George Carey for Ken Randall, the NHL rights to Corb Denneny and cash, December 14, 1923.

ARBOUR, Jack

Defense. Shoots left. 5'8", 172 lbs. Born, Waubaushene, Ont., March 7, 1899.

Season	Club	GP	G	A	Pts	PIM	GP	G	A	Pts	PIM
1926-27	Detroit Cougars	37	4	1	5	46	....	....	....	....	....
1928-29	Toronto Maple Leafs	10	1	0	1	10	....	....	....	....	....
	NHL Totals	**47**	**5**	**1**	**6**	**56**	....	....	....	....	....

• Brother of Ty

Traded to **Detroit** by **Calgary** (WHL) for cash, October 27, 1926. Rights traded to **Toronto** by **Detroit** with $12,500 for Jimmy Herberts, April 8, 1928. Traded to **London** (Can-Pro) by **Toronto** for cash, December 12, 1928.

ARBOUR, John

Defense. Shoots left. 5'11", 195 lbs. Born, Niagara Falls, Ont., September 28, 1945.

Season	Club	GP	G	A	Pts	PIM	GP	G	A	Pts	PIM
1965-66	Boston Bruins	2	0	0	0	0	....	....	....	....	....
1967-68	Boston Bruins	4	0	1	1	11	....	....	....	....	....
1968-69	Pittsburgh Penguins	17	0	2	2	35	....	....	....	....	....
1970-71	Vancouver Canucks	13	0	0	0	12	....	....	....	....	....
	St. Louis Blues	53	1	6	7	81	5	0	0	0	0
1971-72	St. Louis Blues	17	0	0	0	10	....	....	....	....	....
	NHL Totals	**106**	**1**	**9**	**10**	**149**	**5**	**0**	**0**	**0**	**0**

Traded to **Pittsburgh** by **Boston** with Jean Pronovost for cash, May 21, 1968. Traded to **Vancouver** (WHL) by **Pittsburgh** with Paul Andrea and the loan of Andy Bathgate for the 1969-70 season for Bryan Hextall Jr., May 20, 1969. Rights transferred to **Vancouver** after NHL franchise purchased WHL club, December 19, 1969. Traded to **St. Louis** by **Vancouver** for cash, December 3, 1970.

ARBOUR, Ty

Left wing. Shoots left. 5'7", 160 lbs. Born, Waubaushene, Ont., June 29, 1896.

Season	Club	Regular Season GP	G	A	Pts	PIM	Playoffs GP	G	A	Pts	PIM
1926-27	Pittsburgh Pirates	41	7	8	15	10	....	....	....	....	....
1927-28	Pittsburgh Pirates	7	0	0	0	0	....	....	....	....	....
	Chicago Black Hawks	32	5	5	10	32	....	....	....	....	....
1928-29	Chicago Black Hawks	44	3	4	7	32	....	....	....	....	....
1929-30	Chicago Black Hawks	42	10	8	18	26	2	1	0	1	0
1930-31	Chicago Black Hawks	41	3	3	6	12	9	1	0	1	6
	NHL Totals	**207**	**28**	**28**	**56**	**112**	**11**	**2**	**0**	**2**	**6**

• Brother of Jack

Traded to **Pittsburgh** by **Vancouver** (WHL) for cash, October 9, 1926. Traded to **Chicago** by **Pittsburgh** to complete three-team transaction that sent Bert McCaffrey to Pittsburgh and Eddie Rodden to Toronto, December, 1927. Traded to **Pittsburgh** (IAHL) by **Chicago** for cash, October 21, 1931.

ARCHAMBAULT, Michel

Left wing. Shoots left. 5'8", 160 lbs. Born, St-Hyacinthe, Que., September 27, 1950.
(Chicago's 2nd choice, 28th overall, in 1970 Amateur Draft).

Season	Club	Regular Season GP	G	A	Pts	PIM	Playoffs GP	G	A	Pts	PIM
1976-77	Chicago Black Hawks	3	0	0	0	0	....	....	....	....	....
	NHL Totals	**3**	**0**	**0**	**0**	**0**	....	....	....	....	....

ARCHIBALD, Dave

Center/Left wing. Shoots left. 6'1", 210 lbs. Born, Chilliwack, B.C., April 14, 1969.
(Minnesota's 1st choice, 6th overall, in 1987 Entry Draft).

Season	Club	Regular Season GP	G	A	Pts	PIM	Playoffs GP	G	A	Pts	PIM
1987-88	Minnesota North Stars	78	13	20	33	26	....	....	....	....	....
1988-89	Minnesota North Stars	72	14	19	33	14	5	0	1	1	0
1989-90	Minnesota North Stars	12	1	5	6	6	....	....	....	....	....
	New York Rangers	19	2	3	5	6	....	....	....	....	....
1992-93	Ottawa Senators	44	9	6	15	32	....	....	....	....	....
1993-94	Ottawa Senators	33	10	8	18	14	....	....	....	....	....
1994-95	Ottawa Senators	14	2	2	4	19	....	....	....	....	....
1995-96	Ottawa Senators	44	6	4	10	18	....	....	....	....	....
1996-97	New York Islanders	7	0	0	0	4	....	....	....	....	....
	NHL Totals	**323**	**57**	**67**	**124**	**139**	**5**	**0**	**1**	**1**	**0**

Traded to **NY Rangers** by **Minnesota** for Jay More, November 1, 1989. Traded to **Ottawa** by **NY Rangers** for Ottawa's 5th round choice (later traded to Los Angeles – Los Angeles selected Frederick Beaubien) in 1993 Entry Draft, November 6, 1992. Signed as a free agent by **NY Islanders**, October 10, 1996.

ARCHIBALD, Jim

Right wing. Shoots right. 5'11", 175 lbs. Born, Craik, Sask., June 6, 1961.
(Minnesota's 11th choice, 139th overall, in 1981 Entry Draft).

Season	Club	Regular Season GP	G	A	Pts	PIM	Playoffs GP	G	A	Pts	PIM
1984-85	Minnesota North Stars	4	1	2	3	11	....	....	....	....	....
1985-86	Minnesota North Stars	11	0	0	0	32	....	....	....	....	....
1986-87	Minnesota North Stars	1	0	0	0	2	....	....	....	....	....
	NHL Totals	**16**	**1**	**2**	**3**	**45**	....	....	....	....	....

ARESHENKOFF, Ron

Center. Shoots left. 6', 175 lbs. Born, Grand Forks, B.C., June 13, 1957.
(Buffalo's 2nd choice, 32nd overall, in 1977 Amateur Draft).

Season	Club	Regular Season GP	G	A	Pts	PIM	Playoffs GP	G	A	Pts	PIM
1979-80	Edmonton Oilers	4	0	0	0	0	....	....	....	....	....
	NHL Totals	**4**	**0**	**0**	**0**	**0**	....	....	....	....	....

Claimed by **Edmonton** from **Buffalo** in Expansion Draft, June 13, 1979. Traded to **Philadelphia** by **Edmonton** with Edmonton's 10th round choice (Bob O'Brien) in 1980 Entry Draft for Barry Dean, June 11, 1980.

ARKHIPOV, Denis

Center. Shoots left. 6'3", 214 lbs. Born, Kazan, USSR, May 19, 1979.
(Nashville's 2nd choice, 60th overall, in 1998 Entry Draft).

Season	Club	Regular Season GP	G	A	Pts	PIM	Playoffs GP	G	A	Pts	PIM
2000-01	Nashville Predators	40	6	7	13	4	....	....	....	....	....
2001-02	Nashville Predators	82	20	22	42	16	....	....	....	....	....
2002-03	Nashville Predators	79	11	24	35	32	....	....	....	....	....
	NHL Totals	**201**	**37**	**53**	**90**	**52**	....	....	....	....	....

ARMSTRONG, Bill

Center. Shoots left. 6'2", 195 lbs. Born, London, Ont., June 25, 1966.

Season	Club	Regular Season GP	G	A	Pts	PIM	Playoffs GP	G	A	Pts	PIM
1990-91	Philadelphia Flyers	1	0	1	1	0	....	....	....	....	....
	NHL Totals	**1**	**0**	**1**	**1**	**0**	....	....	....	....	....

Signed as a free agent by **Philadelphia**, May 16, 1989. Signed as a free agent by **New Jersey**, March 21, 1993.

ARMSTRONG, Bob

Defense. Shoots right. 6'1", 190 lbs. Born, Toronto, Ont., April 7, 1931.

Season	Club	Regular Season GP	G	A	Pts	PIM	Playoffs GP	G	A	Pts	PIM
1950-51	Boston Bruins	2	0	0	0	2	....	....	....	....	....
1951-52	Boston Bruins	....	....	....	....	....	5	0	0	0	2
1952-53	Boston Bruins	55	0	8	8	45	11	1	1	2	10
1953-54	Boston Bruins	64	2	10	12	81	4	0	1	1	0
1954-55	Boston Bruins	57	1	3	4	38	5	0	0	0	2
1955-56	Boston Bruins	68	0	12	12	122	....	....	....	....	....
1956-57	Boston Bruins	57	1	15	16	79	10	0	3	3	10
1957-58	Boston Bruins	47	1	4	5	66	....	....	....	....	....
1958-59	Boston Bruins	60	1	9	10	50	7	0	2	2	4
1959-60	Boston Bruins	69	5	14	19	96	....	....	....	....	....
1960-61	Boston Bruins	54	0	10	10	72	....	....	....	....	....
1961-62	Boston Bruins	9	2	1	3	20	....	....	....	....	....
	NHL Totals	**542**	**13**	**86**	**99**	**671**	**42**	**1**	**7**	**8**	**28**

Played in NHL All-Star Game (1960)

Loaned to **Montreal** (Hull-Ottawa-EPHL) by **Boston** with the loan of Dallas Smith and cash for Wayne Connelly, October 26, 1961.

ARMSTRONG, Chris

Defense. Shoots left. 6', 205 lbs. Born, Regina, Sask., June 26, 1975.
(Florida's 3rd choice, 57th overall, in 1993 Entry Draft).

Season	Club	Regular Season GP	G	A	Pts	PIM	Playoffs GP	G	A	Pts	PIM
2000-01	Minnesota Wild	3	0	0	0	0	....	....	....	....	....
	NHL Totals	**3**	**0**	**0**	**0**	**0**	....	....	....	....	....

Claimed by **Nashville** from **Florida** in Expansion Draft, June 26, 1998. Signed as a free agent by **San Jose**, September 2, 1999. Selected by **Minnesota** from **San Jose** in Expansion Draft, June 23, 2000. Signed as a free agent by **NY Islanders**, August 8, 2001.

ARMSTRONG, Derek

Center. Shoots right. 5'11", 188 lbs. Born, Ottawa, Ont., April 23, 1973.
(NY Islanders' 5th choice, 128th overall, in 1992 Entry Draft).

Season	Club	Regular Season GP	G	A	Pts	PIM	Playoffs GP	G	A	Pts	PIM
1993-94	New York Islanders	1	0	0	0	0	....	....	....	....	....
1995-96	New York Islanders	19	1	3	4	14	....	....	....	....	....
1996-97	New York Islanders	50	6	7	13	33	....	....	....	....	....
1997-98	Ottawa Senators	9	2	0	2	9	....	....	....	....	....
1998-99	New York Rangers	3	0	0	0	0	....	....	....	....	....
99-2000	New York Rangers	1	0	0	0	0	....	....	....	....	....
2000-01	New York Rangers	3	0	0	0	0	....	....	....	....	....
2002-03	Los Angeles Kings	66	12	26	38	30	....	....	....	....	....
	NHL Totals	**152**	**21**	**36**	**57**	**86**	....	....	....	....	....

Signed as a free agent by **Ottawa**, July 28, 1997. Loaned to **Hartford** (AHL) by **Ottawa**, October 28, 1997. Signed as a free agent by **NY Rangers**, August 10, 1998. Traded to **Los Angeles** by **NY Rangers** for Los Angeles' 6th round choice (Chris Holt) in 2003 Entry Draft, July 16, 2002.

ARMSTRONG, George

HHOF

Right wing. Shoots right. 6'1", 184 lbs. Born, Skead, Ont., July 6, 1930.

Season	Club	Regular Season GP	G	A	Pts	PIM	Playoffs GP	G	A	Pts	PIM
1949-50	Toronto Maple Leafs	2	0	0	0	0	....	....	....	....	....
1951-52	Toronto Maple Leafs	20	3	3	6	30	4	0	0	0	2
1952-53	Toronto Maple Leafs	52	14	11	25	54	....	....	....	....	....
1953-54	Toronto Maple Leafs	63	17	15	32	60	5	1	0	1	2
1954-55	Toronto Maple Leafs	66	10	18	28	80	4	1	0	1	4
1955-56	Toronto Maple Leafs	67	16	32	48	97	5	4	2	6	0
1956-57	Toronto Maple Leafs	51	10	20	44	37	....	....	....	....	....
1957-58	Toronto Maple Leafs	59	17	25	42	93	....	....	....	....	....
1958-59	Toronto Maple Leafs	59	20	16	36	37	12	0	4	4	10
1959-60	Toronto Maple Leafs	70	23	28	51	60	10	1	4	5	4
1960-61	Toronto Maple Leafs	47	14	19	33	21	5	1	1	2	0
1961-62 ♦	Toronto Maple Leafs	70	21	32	53	27	12	7	5	12	2
1962-63 ♦	Toronto Maple Leafs	70	19	24	43	27	10	3	6	9	4
1963-64 ♦	Toronto Maple Leafs	66	20	17	37	14	14	5	8	13	10
1964-65	Toronto Maple Leafs	59	15	22	37	14	6	1	0	1	4
1965-66	Toronto Maple Leafs	70	16	35	51	12	4	0	1	1	4
1966-67 ♦	Toronto Maple Leafs	70	9	24	33	26	9	2	1	3	6
1967-68	Toronto Maple Leafs	62	13	21	34	4	....	....	....	....	....
1968-69	Toronto Maple Leafs	53	11	16	27	10	4	0	0	0	0
1969-70	Toronto Maple Leafs	49	13	15	28	12	....	....	....	....	....
1970-71	Toronto Maple Leafs	59	7	18	25	6	6	0	2	2	0
	NHL Totals	**1187**	**296**	**417**	**713**	**721**	**110**	**26**	**34**	**60**	**52**

Played in NHL All-Star Game (1956, 1957, 1959, 1962, 1963, 1964, 1968)

ARMSTRONG, Murray

Center. Shoots left. 5'10", 170 lbs. Born, Manor, Sask., January 1, 1916.

Season	Club	Regular Season GP	G	A	Pts	PIM	Playoffs GP	G	A	Pts	PIM
1937-38	Toronto Maple Leafs	9	0	0	0	0	3	0	0	0	0
1938-39	Toronto Maple Leafs	3	0	1	1	0	....	....	....	....	....
1939-40	New York Americans	47	16	20	36	12	3	0	0	0	0
1940-41	New York Americans	48	10	14	24	6	....	....	....	....	....
1941-42	Brooklyn Americans	45	6	22	28	15	....	....	....	....	....
1943-44	Detroit Red Wings	28	12	22	34	4	5	0	2	2	0
1944-45	Detroit Red Wings	50	15	24	39	31	14	4	2	6	2
1945-46	Detroit Red Wings	40	8	18	26	4	5	0	2	2	0
	NHL Totals	**270**	**67**	**121**	**188**	**72**	**30**	**4**	**6**	**10**	**2**

Lester Patrick Trophy (1977)

Claimed by **Toronto** from **NY Rangers** (Philadelphia-Can-Am) in Inter-League Draft, May 7, 1936. Traded to **NY Americans** by **Toronto** with Buzz Boll, Busher Jackson, Jimmy Fowler and Doc Romnes for Sweeney Schriner, May 18, 1939. • Team name changed to **Brooklyn Americans** prior to 1941-42 season. Rights transferred to **Detroit** from **Brooklyn** in Special Dispersal Draw, September 11, 1943.

ARMSTRONG, Norm

Right wing/Defense. Shoots left. 5'11", 205 lbs. Born, Owen Sound, Ont., October 17, 1938.

Season	Club	Regular Season GP	G	A	Pts	PIM	Playoffs GP	G	A	Pts	PIM
1962-63	Toronto Maple Leafs	7	1	1	2	2	....	....	....	....	....
	NHL Totals	**7**	**1**	**1**	**2**	**2**	....	....	....	....	....

Traded to **Los Angeles** (Springfield-AHL) by **Toronto** for Don Westbrooke, February, 1971. Claimed by **Baltimore** (AHL) from **Los Angeles** in Reverse Draft, June 8, 1971. • Died of injuries suffered in industrial accident, July 23, 1974.

ARMSTRONG, Tim

Center. Shoots right. 5'11", 170 lbs. Born, Toronto, Ont., May 12, 1967.
(Toronto's 11th choice, 211th overall, in 1985 Entry Draft).

Season	Club	GP	G	A	Pts	PIM	GP	G	A	Pts	PIM
		REGULAR SEASON					PLAYOFFS				
1988-89	Toronto Maple Leafs	11	1	0	1	6	....	....	....	....	....
	NHL Totals	**11**	**1**	**0**	**1**	**6**	....	....	....	....	....

ARNASON, Chuck

Right wing. Shoots right. 5'10", 183 lbs. Born, Ashburn, Man., July 15, 1951.
(Montreal's 2nd choice, 7th overall, in 1971 Amateur Draft).

Season	Club	GP	G	A	Pts	PIM	GP	G	A	Pts	PIM
1971-72	Montreal Canadiens	17	3	0	3	4	....	....	....	....	....
1972-73	Montreal Canadiens	19	1	1	2	2	....	....	....	....	....
1973-74	Atlanta Flames	33	7	6	13	13	....	....	....	....	....
	Pittsburgh Penguins	41	13	5	18	4	....	....	....	....	....
1974-75	Pittsburgh Penguins	78	26	32	58	32	9	2	4	6	4
1975-76	Pittsburgh Penguins	30	7	3	10	14	....	....	....	....	....
	Kansas City Scouts	39	14	10	24	21	....	....	....	....	....
1976-77	Colorado Rockies	61	13	10	23	10	....	....	....	....	....
1977-78	Colorado Rockies	29	4	8	12	10	....	....	....	....	....
	Cleveland Barons	40	21	13	34	8	....	....	....	....	....
1978-79	Minnesota North Stars	1	0	0	0	0	....	....	....	....	....
	Washington Capitals	13	0	2	2	4	....	....	....	....	....
	NHL Totals	**401**	**109**	**90**	**199**	**122**	**9**	**2**	**4**	**6**	**4**

Traded to **Atlanta** by **Montreal** for Atlanta's 1st round choice (Rick Chartraw) in 1974 Amateur Draft, May 29, 1973. Traded to **Pittsburgh** by **Atlanta** with Bob Paradise for Al McDonough, January 4, 1974. Traded to **Kansas City** by **Pittsburgh** with Steve Durbano and Pittsburgh's 1st round choice (Paul Gardner) in 1976 Amateur Draft for Simon Nolet, Ed Gilbert and Kansas City's 1st round choice (Blair Chapman) in 1976 Amateur Draft, January 9, 1976. Transferred to **Colorado** after **Kansas City** franchise relocated, July 15, 1976. Traded to **Cleveland** by **Colorado** with Rick Jodzio for Ralph Klassen and Fred Ahern, January 9, 1978. Placed on **Minnesota** Reserve List after **Minnesota-Cleveland** Dispersal Draft, June 15, 1978. Traded to **Washington** by **Minnesota** for future considerations, March 12, 1979. Traded to **Minnesota** by **Washington** for cash, April 24, 1979. Traded to **Vancouver** by **Minnesota** for cash, July 19, 1979.

ARNASON, Tyler

Center. Shoots left. 5'11", 207 lbs. Born, Oklahoma City, OK, March 16, 1979.
(Chicago's 6th choice, 183rd overall, in 1998 Entry Draft).

Season	Club	GP	G	A	Pts	PIM	GP	G	A	Pts	PIM
2001-02	Chicago Blackhawks	21	3	1	4	4	3	0	0	0	0
2002-03	Chicago Blackhawks	82	19	20	39	20	....	....	....	....	....
	NHL Totals	**103**	**22**	**21**	**43**	**24**	**3**	**0**	**0**	**0**	**0**

NHL All-Rookie Team (2003)

ARNIEL, Scott

Left wing. Shoots left. 6'1", 188 lbs. Born, Kingston, Ont., September 17, 1962.
(Winnipeg's 2nd choice, 22nd overall, in 1981 Entry Draft).

Season	Club	GP	G	A	Pts	PIM	GP	G	A	Pts	PIM
1981-82	Winnipeg Jets	17	1	8	9	14	3	0	0	0	0
1982-83	Winnipeg Jets	75	13	5	18	46	2	0	0	0	0
1983-84	Winnipeg Jets	80	21	35	56	68	2	0	0	0	5
1984-85	Winnipeg Jets	79	22	22	44	81	8	1	2	3	9
1985-86	Winnipeg Jets	80	18	25	43	40	3	0	0	0	12
1986-87	Buffalo Sabres	63	11	14	25	59	....	....	....	....	....
1987-88	Buffalo Sabres	73	17	23	40	61	6	0	1	1	5
1988-89	Buffalo Sabres	80	18	23	41	46	5	1	0	1	4
1989-90	Buffalo Sabres	79	18	14	32	77	5	1	0	1	4
1990-91	Winnipeg Jets	75	5	17	22	87	....	....	....	....	....
1991-92	Boston Bruins	29	5	3	8	20	....	....	....	....	....
	NHL Totals	**730**	**149**	**189**	**338**	**599**	**34**	**3**	**3**	**6**	**39**

Traded to **Buffalo** by **Winnipeg** for Gilles Hamel, June 21, 1986. Traded to **Winnipeg** by **Buffalo** with Phil Housley, Jeff Parker and Buffalo's 1st round choice (Keith Tkachuk) in 1990 Entry Draft for Dale Hawerchuk and Winnipeg's 1st round choice (Brad May) in 1990 Entry Draft, June 16, 1990. Traded to **Boston** by **Winnipeg** for future considerations, November 22, 1991.

ARNOTT, Jason

Center. Shoots right. 6'4", 225 lbs. Born, Collingwood, Ont., October 11, 1974.
(Edmonton's 1st choice, 7th overall, in 1993 Entry Draft).

Season	Club	GP	G	A	Pts	PIM	GP	G	A	Pts	PIM
1993-94	Edmonton Oilers	78	33	35	68	104	....	....	....	....	....
1994-95	Edmonton Oilers	42	15	22	37	128	....	....	....	....	....
1995-96	Edmonton Oilers	64	28	31	59	87	....	....	....	....	....
1996-97	Edmonton Oilers	67	19	38	57	92	12	3	6	9	18
1997-98	Edmonton Oilers	35	5	13	18	78	....	....	....	....	....
	New Jersey Devils	35	5	10	15	21	5	0	2	2	0
1998-99	New Jersey Devils	74	27	27	54	79	7	2	2	4	4
99-2000 ♦	New Jersey Devils	76	22	34	56	51	23	8	12	20	18
2000-01	New Jersey Devils	54	21	34	55	75	23	8	7	15	16
2001-02	New Jersey Devils	63	22	19	41	59	....	....	....	....	....
	Dallas Stars	10	3	1	4	6	....	....	....	....	....
2002-03	Dallas Stars	72	23	24	47	51	11	3	2	5	6
	NHL Totals	**670**	**223**	**288**	**511**	**831**	**81**	**24**	**31**	**55**	**62**

NHL All-Rookie Team (1994)

Played in NHL All-Star Game (1997)

Traded to **New Jersey** by **Edmonton** with Bryan Muir for Valeri Zelepukin and Bill Guerin, January 4, 1998. Traded to **Dallas** by **New Jersey** with Randy McKay and New Jersey's 1st round choice (later traded to Columbus – later traded to Buffalo – Buffalo selected Dan Paille) in 2002 Entry Draft for Joe Nieuwendyk and Jamie Langenbrunner, March 19, 2002.

ARTHUR, Fred

Defense. Shoots left. 6'5", 210 lbs. Born, Toronto, Ont., March 6, 1961.
(Hartford's 1st choice, 8th overall, in 1980 Entry Draft).

Season	Club	GP	G	A	Pts	PIM	GP	G	A	Pts	PIM
1980-81	Hartford Whalers	3	0	0	0	0	....	....	....	....	....
1981-82	Philadelphia Flyers	74	1	7	8	47	4	0	0	0	2
1982-83	Philadelphia Flyers	3	0	1	1	2	....	....	....	....	....
	NHL Totals	**80**	**1**	**8**	**9**	**49**	**4**	**0**	**0**	**0**	**2**

Traded to **Philadelphia** by **Hartford** with Ray Allison and Hartford's 1st (Ron Sutter) and 3rd (Miroslav Dvorak) round choices in 1982 Entry Draft for Rick MacLeish, Blake Wesley, Don Gillen and Philadelphia's 1st (Paul Lawless), 2nd (Mark Patterson) and 3rd (Kevin Dineen) round choices in 1982 Entry Draft, July 3, 1981. • Officially announced retirement to attend medical school, October 20, 1982.

ARUNDEL, John

Defense. Shoots left. 5'11", 181 lbs. Born, Winnipeg, Man., November 4, 1927.

Season	Club	GP	G	A	Pts	PIM	GP	G	A	Pts	PIM
1949-50	Toronto Maple Leafs	3	0	0	0	9	....	....	....	....	....
	NHL Totals	**3**	**0**	**0**	**0**	**9**	....	....	....	....	....

ARVEDSON, Magnus

Left wing. Shoots left. 6'2", 198 lbs. Born, Karlstad, Sweden, November 25, 1971.
(Ottawa's 4th choice, 119th overall, in 1997 Entry Draft).

Season	Club	GP	G	A	Pts	PIM	GP	G	A	Pts	PIM
1997-98	Ottawa Senators	61	11	15	26	36	11	0	1	1	6
1998-99	Ottawa Senators	80	21	26	47	50	3	0	1	1	2
99-2000	Ottawa Senators	47	15	13	28	36	6	0	0	0	6
2000-01	Ottawa Senators	51	17	16	33	24	2	0	0	0	0
2001-02	Ottawa Senators	74	12	27	39	35	12	2	1	3	4
2002-03	Ottawa Senators	80	16	21	37	48	18	1	5	6	16
	NHL Totals	**393**	**92**	**118**	**210**	**229**	**52**	**3**	**8**	**11**	**34**

ASHAM, Arron

Right wing. Shoots right. 5'11", 209 lbs. Born, Portage La Prairie, Man., April 13, 1978.
(Montreal's 3rd choice, 71st overall, in 1996 Entry Draft).

Season	Club	GP	G	A	Pts	PIM	GP	G	A	Pts	PIM
1998-99	Montreal Canadiens	7	0	0	0	0	....	....	....	....	....
99-2000	Montreal Canadiens	33	4	2	6	24	....	....	....	....	....
2000-01	Montreal Canadiens	46	2	3	5	59	....	....	....	....	....
2001-02	Montreal Canadiens	35	5	4	9	55	3	0	1	1	0
2002-03	New York Islanders	78	15	19	34	57	5	0	0	0	16
	NHL Totals	**199**	**26**	**28**	**54**	**195**	**8**	**0**	**1**	**1**	**16**

Traded to **NY Islanders** by **Montreal** with Montreal's 5th round choice (Marcus Paulsson) in 2002 Entry Draft for Mariusz Czerkawski, June 22, 2002.

ASHBEE, Barry

Defense. Shoots right. 5'10", 180 lbs. Born, Weston, Ont., July 28, 1939.

Season	Club	GP	G	A	Pts	PIM	GP	G	A	Pts	PIM
1965-66	Boston Bruins	14	0	3	3	14	....	....	....	....	....
1970-71	Philadelphia Flyers	64	4	23	27	44	....	....	....	....	....
1971-72	Philadelphia Flyers	73	6	14	20	75	....	....	....	....	....
1972-73	Philadelphia Flyers	64	1	17	18	106	11	0	4	4	20
1973-74 ♦	Philadelphia Flyers	69	4	13	17	52	6	0	0	0	2
	NHL Totals	**284**	**15**	**70**	**85**	**291**	**17**	**0**	**4**	**4**	**22**

NHL Second All-Star Team (1974)

Traded to **Detroit** (Hershey-AHL) by **Boston** with Ed Chadwick for Bob Perreault, June, 1962. Traded to **Philadelphia** by **Pittsburgh** (Hershey-AHL) for Darryl Edestrand and Larry McKillop, May 22, 1970. • Suffered career-ending eye injury in playoff game vs. NY Rangers, April 28, 1974.

ASHBY, Don

Center. Shoots left. 6'1", 185 lbs. Born, Kamloops, B.C., March 8, 1955.
(Toronto's 1st choice, 6th overall, in 1975 Amateur Draft).

Season	Club	GP	G	A	Pts	PIM	GP	G	A	Pts	PIM
1975-76	Toronto Maple Leafs	50	6	15	21	10	....	....	....	....	....
1976-77	Toronto Maple Leafs	76	19	23	42	24	9	1	0	1	4
1977-78	Toronto Maple Leafs	12	1	2	3	0	....	....	....	....	....
1978-79	Toronto Maple Leafs	3	0	0	0	0	....	....	....	....	....
	Colorado Rockies	12	2	3	5	0	....	....	....	....	....
1979-80	Colorado Rockies	11	0	1	1	4	....	....	....	....	....
	Edmonton Oilers	18	10	9	19	0	3	0	0	0	0
1980-81	Edmonton Oilers	6	2	3	5	2	....	....	....	....	....
	NHL Totals	**188**	**40**	**56**	**96**	**40**	**12**	**1**	**0**	**1**	**4**

• Missed majority of 1978-79 season in retirement. Traded to **Colorado** by **Toronto** with Trevor Johansen for Paul Gardner, March 13, 1979. Traded to **Edmonton** by **Colorado** for Bobby Schmautz, February 25, 1980. • Died of injuries suffered in automobile accident following CHL finals, May 30, 1981.

ASHTON, Brent

Left wing. Shoots left. 6'1", 210 lbs. Born, Saskatoon, Sask., May 18, 1960.
(Vancouver's 2nd choice, 26th overall, in 1979 Entry Draft).

Season	Club	GP	G	A	Pts	PIM	GP	G	A	Pts	PIM
1979-80	Vancouver Canucks	47	5	14	19	11	4	1	0	1	6
1980-81	Vancouver Canucks	77	18	11	29	57	3	0	0	0	0
1981-82	Colorado Rockies	80	24	36	60	26	....	....	....	....	....
1982-83	New Jersey Devils	76	14	19	33	47	....	....	....	....	....
1983-84	Minnesota North Stars	68	7	10	17	54	12	1	2	3	22
1984-85	Minnesota North Stars	29	4	7	11	15	....	....	....	....	....
	Quebec Nordiques	49	27	24	51	38	18	6	4	10	13
1985-86	Quebec Nordiques	77	26	32	58	64	3	2	1	3	9
1986-87	Quebec Nordiques	46	25	19	44	17	....	....	....	....	....
	Detroit Red Wings	35	15	16	31	22	16	4	9	13	6

Season	Club	REGULAR SEASON					PLAYOFFS				
		GP	G	A	Pts	PIM	GP	G	A	Pts	PIM
1987-88	Detroit Red Wings	73	26	27	53	50	16	7	5	12	10
1988-89	Winnipeg Jets	75	31	37	68	36	....	....	....	....	....
1989-90	Winnipeg Jets	79	22	34	56	37	7	3	1	4	2
1990-91	Winnipeg Jets	61	12	24	36	58	....	....	....	....	....
1991-92	Winnipeg Jets	7	1	0	1	4	....	....	....	....	....
	Boston Bruins	61	17	22	39	47	....	....	....	....	....
1992-93	Boston Bruins	26	2	2	4	11	....	....	....	....	....
	Calgary Flames	32	8	11	19	41	6	0	3	3	2
	NHL Totals	**998**	**284**	**345**	**629**	**635**	**85**	**24**	**25**	**49**	**70**

Rights traded to **Winnipeg** by **Vancouver** with Vancouver's 4th round choice (Tom Martin) in 1982 Entry Draft as compensation for Vancouver's signing of free agent Ivan Hlinka, July 15, 1981. Traded to **Colorado** by **Winnipeg** with Winnipeg's 3rd round choice (Dave Kasper) in 1982 Entry Draft for Lucien DeBlois, July 15, 1981. Transferred to **New Jersey** after **Colorado** franchise relocated, June 30, 1982. Traded to **Minnesota** by **New Jersey** for Dave Lewis, October 3, 1983. Traded to **Quebec** by **Minnesota** with Brad Maxwell for Tony McKegney and Bo Berglund, December 14, 1984. Traded to **Detroit** by **Quebec** with Gilbert Delorme and Mark Kumpel for Basil McRae, John Ogrodnick and Doug Shedden, January 17, 1987. Traded to **Winnipeg** by **Detroit** for Paul MacLean, June 13, 1988. Traded to **Boston** by **Winnipeg** for Petri Skriko, October 29, 1991. Traded to **Calgary** by **Boston** for C.J. Young, February 1, 1993.

ASHWORTH, Frank

Center. Shoots left. 5'8", 155 lbs. Born, Moose Jaw, Sask., October 16, 1927.

Season	Club	GP	G	A	Pts	PIM	GP	G	A	Pts	PIM
1946-47	Chicago Black Hawks	18	5	4	9	2	....	....	....	....	....
	NHL Totals	**18**	**5**	**4**	**9**	**2**	....	....	....	....	....

ASMUNDSON, Oscar

Center. Shoots right. 5'11", 170 lbs. Born, Red Deer, Alta., November 17, 1908.

Season	Club	GP	G	A	Pts	PIM	GP	G	A	Pts	PIM
1932-33 ♦	New York Rangers	48	5	10	15	20	8	0	2	2	4
1933-34	New York Rangers	46	2	6	8	8	1	0	0	0	0
1934-35	Detroit Red Wings	3	0	0	0	0	....	....	....	....	....
	St. Louis Eagles	11	4	7	11	2	....	....	....	....	....
1936-37	New York Americans	1	0	0	0	0	....	....	....	....	....
1937-38	Montreal Canadiens	2	0	0	0	0	....	....	....	....	....
	NHL Totals	**111**	**11**	**23**	**34**	**30**	**9**	**0**	**2**	**2**	**4**

Traded to **NY Rangers** by **Vancouver** (PCHL) for cash, October 25, 1931. Traded to **Detroit** by **NY Rangers** for cash, October 1, 1934. Signed as a free agent by **St. Louis** after securing release from **Detroit**, February 6, 1935. Signed as a free agent by **NY Americans**, February 14, 1937. Traded to **Montreal** by **NY Americans** for cash, October 28, 1937. Traded to **Cleveland** (IAHL) by **Montreal** for cash, November, 1938.

ASTASHENKO, Kaspars

Defense/Wing. Shoots left. 6'2", 183 lbs. Born, Riga, Latvia, February 17, 1975.
(Tampa Bay's 5th choice, 127th overall in 1999 Entry Draft).

Season	Club	GP	G	A	Pts	PIM	GP	G	A	Pts	PIM
99-2000	Tampa Bay Lightning	8	0	1	1	4	....	....	....	....	....
2000-01	Tampa Bay Lightning	15	1	1	2	4	....	....	....	....	....
	NHL Totals	**23**	**1**	**2**	**3**	**8**	....	....	....	....	....

Traded to **Carolina** by **Tampa Bay** for Harlan Pratt, December 28, 2001.

ASTLEY, Mark

Defense. Shoots left. 5'11", 185 lbs. Born, Calgary, Alta., March 30, 1969.
(Buffalo's 9th choice, 194th overall, in 1989 Entry Draft).

Season	Club	GP	G	A	Pts	PIM	GP	G	A	Pts	PIM
1993-94	Buffalo Sabres	1	0	0	0	0	....	....	....	....	....
1994-95	Buffalo Sabres	14	2	1	3	12	2	0	0	0	0
1995-96	Buffalo Sabres	60	2	18	20	80	....	....	....	....	....
	NHL Totals	**75**	**4**	**19**	**23**	**92**	**2**	**0**	**0**	**0**	**0**

Signed as a free agent by **Los Angeles**, September 6, 1996.

ATANAS, Walt

Right wing. Shoots right. 5'8", 174 lbs. Born, Hamilton, Ont., December 22, 1923.

Season	Club	GP	G	A	Pts	PIM	GP	G	A	Pts	PIM
1944-45	New York Rangers	49	13	8	21	40	....	....	....	....	....
	NHL Totals	**49**	**13**	**8**	**21**	**40**	....	....	....	....	....

Claimed by **NY Rangers** from **Buffalo** (AHL) in Inter-League Draft, May 12, 1944.

ATCHEYNUM, Blair

Right wing. Shoots right. 6'2", 198 lbs. Born, Estevan, Sask., April 20, 1969.
(Hartford's 2nd choice, 52nd overall, in 1989 Entry Draft).

Season	Club	GP	G	A	Pts	PIM	GP	G	A	Pts	PIM
1992-93	Ottawa Senators	4	0	1	1	0	....	....	....	....	....
1997-98	St. Louis Blues	61	11	15	26	10	10	0	0	0	2
1998-99	Nashville Predators	53	8	6	14	16	....	....	....	....	....
	St. Louis Blues	12	2	2	4	2	13	1	3	4	6
99-2000	Chicago Blackhawks	47	5	7	12	6	....	....	....	....	....
2000-01	Chicago Blackhawks	19	1	2	3	2	....	....	....	....	....
	NHL Totals	**196**	**27**	**33**	**60**	**36**	**23**	**1**	**3**	**4**	**8**

Claimed by **Ottawa** from **Hartford** in Expansion Draft, June 18, 1992. Signed as a free agent by **St. Louis**, September 15, 1997. Claimed by **Nashville** from **St. Louis** in Expansion Draft, June 26, 1998. Traded to **St. Louis** by **Nashville** for St. Louis' 6th round choice (Zbynek Irgl) in 2000 Entry Draft, March 23, 1999. Signed as a free agent by **Chicago**, September 30, 1999.

ATKINSON, Steve

Right wing. Shoots right. 5'11", 170 lbs. Born, Toronto, Ont., October 16, 1948.
(Detroit's 1st choice, 6th overall, in 1966 Amateur Draft).

Season	Club	GP	G	A	Pts	PIM	GP	G	A	Pts	PIM
1968-69	Boston Bruins	1	0	0	0	0	....	....	....	....	....
1970-71	Buffalo Sabres	57	20	18	38	12	....	....	....	....	....
1971-72	Buffalo Sabres	67	14	10	24	26	....	....	....	....	....
1972-73	Buffalo Sabres	61	9	9	18	36	1	0	0	0	0
1973-74	Buffalo Sabres	70	6	10	16	22	....	....	....	....	....
1974-75	Washington Capitals	46	11	4	15	8	....	....	....	....	....
	NHL Totals	**302**	**60**	**51**	**111**	**104**	**1**	**0**	**0**	**0**	**0**

Traded to **Boston** by **Detroit** to complete transaction that sent Leo Boivin and Dean Prentice to Detroit (February 16, 1966), June 6, 1966. Sold to **Hershey** (AHL) by **Boston** for cash, June, 1970. Claimed by **St. Louis** from **Hershey** (AHL) in Intra-League Draft, June 9, 1970. Claimed on waivers by **Buffalo** from **St. Louis**, November 1, 1970. Claimed by **Washington** from **Buffalo** in Expansion Draft, June 12, 1974.

ATTWELL, Bob

Right wing. Shoots right. 6', 192 lbs. Born, Spokane, WA, December 26, 1959.
(Colorado's 4th choice, 106th overall, in 1979 Entry Draft).

Season	Club	GP	G	A	Pts	PIM	GP	G	A	Pts	PIM
1979-80	Colorado Rockies	7	1	1	2	0	....	....	....	....	....
1980-81	Colorado Rockies	15	0	4	4	0	....	....	....	....	....
	NHL Totals	**22**	**1**	**5**	**6**	**0**	....	....	....	....	....

• Son of Ron

Signed as a free agent by **Edmonton**, October 25, 1982.

ATTWELL, Ron

Right wing. Shoots right. 6', 185 lbs. Born, Humber Summit, Ont., February 9, 1935.

Season	Club	GP	G	A	Pts	PIM	GP	G	A	Pts	PIM
1967-68	St. Louis Blues	18	1	7	8	6	....	....	....	....	....
	New York Rangers	4	0	0	0	2	....	....	....	....	....
	NHL Totals	**22**	**1**	**7**	**8**	**8**	....	....	....	....	....

• Father of Bob

Traded to **Montreal** by **Cleveland** (AHL) for cash, June 14, 1967. Traded to **St. Louis** by **Montreal** with Pat Quinn for cash, June 14, 1967. Traded to **NY Rangers** by **St. Louis** with Ron Stewart for Red Berenson and Barclay Plager, November 29, 1967.

AUBIN, Norm

Center. Shoots left. 6', 185 lbs. Born, St-Leonard, Que., July 26, 1960.
(Toronto's 2nd choice, 51st overall, in 1979 Entry Draft).

Season	Club	GP	G	A	Pts	PIM	GP	G	A	Pts	PIM
1981-82	Toronto Maple Leafs	43	14	12	26	22	....	....	....	....	....
1982-83	Toronto Maple Leafs	26	4	1	5	8	1	0	0	0	0
	NHL Totals	**69**	**18**	**13**	**31**	**30**	**1**	**0**	**0**	**0**	**0**

Signed as a free agent by **Edmonton**, December, 1984.

AUBIN, Serge

Left wing. Shoots left. 6'1", 194 lbs. Born, Val-d'Or, Que., February 15, 1975.
(Pittsburgh's 9th choice, 161st overall, in 1994 Entry Draft).

Season	Club	GP	G	A	Pts	PIM	GP	G	A	Pts	PIM
1998-99	Colorado Avalanche	1	0	0	0	0	....	....	....	....	....
99-2000	Colorado Avalanche	15	2	1	3	6	17	0	1	1	6
2000-01	Columbus Blue Jackets	81	13	17	30	107	....	....	....	....	....
2001-02	Columbus Blue Jackets	71	8	8	16	32	....	....	....	....	....
2002-03	Colorado Avalanche	66	4	6	10	64	5	0	0	0	4
	NHL Totals	**234**	**27**	**32**	**59**	**209**	**22**	**0**	**1**	**1**	**10**

Signed as a free agent by **Colorado**, December 22, 1998. Signed as a free agent by **Columbus**, July 11, 2000.

AUBRY, Pierre

Left wing. Shoots left. 5'10", 170 lbs. Born, Cap-de-la-Madeleine, Que., April 15, 1960.

Season	Club	GP	G	A	Pts	PIM	GP	G	A	Pts	PIM
1980-81	Quebec Nordiques	1	0	0	0	0	....	....	....	....	....
1981-82	Quebec Nordiques	62	10	13	23	27	15	1	1	2	30
1982-83	Quebec Nordiques	77	7	9	16	48	2	0	0	0	0
1983-84	Quebec Nordiques	23	1	1	2	17	....	....	....	....	....
	Detroit Red Wings	14	4	1	5	8	3	0	0	0	2
1984-85	Detroit Red Wings	25	2	2	4	33	....	....	....	....	....
	NHL Totals	**202**	**24**	**26**	**50**	**133**	**20**	**1**	**1**	**2**	**32**

Signed as a free agent by **Quebec**, October 10, 1980. Traded to **Detroit** by **Quebec** for cash, February 29, 1984.

AUBUCHON, Ossie

Left wing. Shoots left. 5'10", 175 lbs. Born, St-Hyacinthe, Que., January 1, 1917.

Season	Club	GP	G	A	Pts	PIM	GP	G	A	Pts	PIM
1942-43	Boston Bruins	3	3	0	3	0	6	1	0	1	0
1943-44	Boston Bruins	9	1	0	1	0	....	....	....	....	....
	New York Rangers	38	16	12	28	4	....	....	....	....	....
	NHL Totals	**50**	**20**	**12**	**32**	**4**	**6**	**1**	**0**	**1**	**0**

Traded to **Boston** by **Providence** (AHL) with Norm Calladine and Ab DeMarco for cash, March 8, 1943. Traded to **NY Rangers** by **Boston** for cash, November, 1943.

AUCOIN, Adrian

Defense. Shoots right. 6'2", 214 lbs. Born, Ottawa, Ont., July 3, 1973.
(Vancouver's 7th choice, 117th overall, in 1992 Entry Draft).

Season	Club	GP	G	A	Pts	PIM	GP	G	A	Pts	PIM
1994-95	Vancouver Canucks	1	1	0	1	0	4	1	0	1	0
1995-96	Vancouver Canucks	49	4	14	18	34	6	0	0	0	2
1996-97	Vancouver Canucks	70	5	16	21	63	....	....	....	....	....
1997-98	Vancouver Canucks	35	3	3	6	21	....	....	....	....	....
1998-99	Vancouver Canucks	82	23	11	34	77	....	....	....	....	....
99-2000	Vancouver Canucks	57	10	14	24	30	....	....	....	....	....
2000-01	Vancouver Canucks	47	3	13	16	20	....	....	....	....	....
	Tampa Bay Lightning	26	1	11	12	25	....	....	....	....	....
2001-02	New York Islanders	81	12	22	34	62	7	2	5	7	4

Season	Club	GP	G	A	Pts	PIM	GP	G	A	Pts	PIM
		REGULAR SEASON					PLAYOFFS				
2002-03	New York Islanders	73	8	27	35	70	5	1	2	3	4
	NHL Totals	**521**	**70**	**131**	**201**	**402**	**22**	**4**	**7**	**11**	**10**

• Missed majority of 1997-98 season recovering from ankle (October 4, 1997 vs. Anaheim) and groin (November 1, 1997 vs. Pittsburgh) injuries. Traded to **Tampa Bay** by **Vancouver** with Vancouver's 2nd round choice (Alexander Polushin) in 2001 Entry Draft for Dan Cloutier, February 7, 2001. Traded to **NY Islanders** by **Tampa Bay** with Alexander Kharitonov for Mathieu Biron and NY Islanders' 2nd round choice (later traded to Washington – later traded to Vancouver – Vancouver selected Denis Grot) in 2002 Entry Draft, June 22, 2001.

AUDET, Philippe

Left wing. Shoots left. 6'2", 202 lbs. Born, Ottawa, Ont., June 4, 1977.
(Detroit's 2nd choice, 52nd overall, in 1995 Entry Draft).

Season	Club	GP	G	A	Pts	PIM	GP	G	A	Pts	PIM
1998-99	Detroit Red Wings	4	0	0	0	0	....	....	....	....	....
	NHL Totals	**4**	**0**	**0**	**0**	**0**	....	....	....	....	....

Traded to **Phoenix** by **Detroit** for Todd Gill, March 13, 2000.

AUDETTE, Donald

Right wing. Shoots right. 5'8", 190 lbs. Born, Laval, Que., September 23, 1969.
(Buffalo's 8th choice, 183rd overall, in 1989 Entry Draft).

Season	Club	GP	G	A	Pts	PIM	GP	G	A	Pts	PIM
1989-90	Buffalo Sabres	....	....	....	....	....	2	0	0	0	0
1990-91	Buffalo Sabres	8	4	3	7	4	....	....	....	....	....
1991-92	Buffalo Sabres	63	31	17	48	75	....	....	....	....	....
1992-93	Buffalo Sabres	44	12	7	19	51	8	2	2	4	6
1993-94	Buffalo Sabres	77	29	30	59	41	7	0	1	1	6
1994-95	Buffalo Sabres	46	24	13	37	27	5	1	1	2	4
1995-96	Buffalo Sabres	23	12	13	25	18	....	....	....	....	....
1996-97	Buffalo Sabres	73	28	22	50	48	11	4	5	9	6
1997-98	Buffalo Sabres	75	24	20	44	59	15	5	8	13	10
1998-99	Los Angeles Kings	49	18	18	36	51	....	....	....	....	....
99-2000	Los Angeles Kings	49	12	20	32	45	....	....	....	....	....
	Atlanta Thrashers	14	7	4	11	12	....	....	....	....	....
2000-01	Atlanta Thrashers	64	32	39	71	64	....	....	....	....	....
	Buffalo Sabres	12	2	6	8	12	13	3	6	9	4
2001-02	Dallas Stars	20	4	8	12	12	....	....	....	....	....
	Montreal Canadiens	13	1	5	6	8	12	6	4	10	10
2002-03	Montreal Canadiens	54	11	12	23	19	....	....	....	....	....
	NHL Totals	**684**	**251**	**237**	**488**	**546**	**73**	**21**	**27**	**48**	**46**

Played in NHL ALL-Star Game (2001)

• Missed majority of 1990-91 season recovering from knee injury suffered in game vs. Edmonton, November 16, 1990. • Missed majority of 1995-96 season recovering from knee injury suffered in training camp, September 23, 1995. Traded to **Los Angeles** by **Buffalo** for Los Angeles' 2nd round choice (Milan Bartovic) in 1999 Entry Draft, December 18, 1998. Traded to **Atlanta** by **Los Angeles** with Frantisek Kaberle for Kelly Buchberger and Nelson Emerson, March 13, 2000. Traded to **Buffalo** by **Atlanta** for the rights to Kamil Piros and Buffalo's 4th round choice (later traded to St. Louis – St. Louis selected Igor Valeyev) in 2001 Entry Draft, March 13, 2001. Signed as a free agent by **Dallas**, July 2, 2001. Traded to **Montreal** by **Dallas** with Shaun Van Allen for Martin Rucinsky and Benoit Brunet, November 21, 2001. • Missed majority of 2001-02 season recovering from wrist injury suffered in game vs. NY Rangers, December 1, 2001.

AUGE, Les

Defense. Shoots left. 6'1", 190 lbs. Born, St. Paul, MN, May 16, 1953.

Season	Club	GP	G	A	Pts	PIM	GP	G	A	Pts	PIM
1980-81	Colorado Rockies	6	0	3	3	4	....	....	....	....	....
	NHL Totals	**6**	**0**	**3**	**3**	**4**	....	....	....	....	....

Signed as a free agent by **Colorado**, July 15, 1979.

AUGUSTA, Patrik

Right wing. Shoots left. 5'10", 170 lbs. Born, Jihlava, Czech., November 13, 1969.
(Toronto's 8th choice, 149th overall, in 1992 Entry Draft).

Season	Club	GP	G	A	Pts	PIM	GP	G	A	Pts	PIM
1993-94	Toronto Maple Leafs	2	0	0	0	0	....	....	....	....	....
1998-99	Washington Capitals	2	0	0	0	0	....	....	....	....	....
	NHL Totals	**4**	**0**	**0**	**0**	**0**	....	....	....	....	....

Signed as a free agent by **Washington**, December 11, 1998.

AULIN, Jared

Center/Right wing. Shoots right. 6', 180 lbs. Born, Calgary, Alta., March 15, 1982.
(Colorado's 2nd choice, 47th overall, in 2000 Entry Draft).

Season	Club	GP	G	A	Pts	PIM	GP	G	A	Pts	PIM
2002-03	Los Angeles Kings	17	2	2	4	0	....	....	....	....	....
	NHL Totals	**17**	**2**	**2**	**4**	**0**	....	....	....	....	....

Traded to **Los Angeles** by **Colorado** to complete transaction that sent Rob Blake and Steve Reinprecht to Colorado (February 21, 2001), March 22, 2001.

AURIE, Larry

Right wing. Shoots right. 5'6", 148 lbs. Born, Sudbury, Ont., February 8, 1905.

Season	Club	GP	G	A	Pts	PIM	GP	G	A	Pts	PIM
1927-28	Detroit Cougars	44	13	3	16	43	....	....	....	....	....
1928-29	Detroit Cougars	35	1	1	2	26	2	1	0	1	2
1929-30	Detroit Cougars	43	14	5	19	28	....	....	....	....	....
1930-31	Detroit Falcons	41	12	6	18	23	....	....	....	....	....
1931-32	Detroit Falcons	48	12	8	20	18	2	0	0	0	0
1932-33	Detroit Red Wings	45	12	11	23	25	4	1	0	1	4
1933-34	Detroit Red Wings	48	16	19	35	36	9	3	*7	*10	2
1934-35	Detroit Red Wings	48	17	29	46	24	....	....	....	....	....
1935-36♦	Detroit Red Wings	44	16	18	34	17	7	1	2	3	2
1936-37♦	Detroit Red Wings	45	*23	20	43	20	....	....	....	....	....
1937-38	Detroit Red Wings	47	10	9	19	19	....	....	....	....	....
1938-39	Detroit Red Wings	1	1	0	1	0	....	....	....	....	....
	NHL Totals	**489**	**147**	**129**	**276**	**279**	**24**	**6**	**9**	**15**	**10**

NHL First All-Star Team (1937)

Played in NHL All-Star Game (1934)

Claimed by **Detroit** from **London** (Can-Pro) in Inter-League Draft, September 26, 1927.

AVERY, Sean

Center. Shoots left. 5'10", 185 lbs. Born, North York, Ont., April 10, 1980.

Season	Club	GP	G	A	Pts	PIM	GP	G	A	Pts	PIM
2001-02	Detroit Red Wings	36	2	2	4	68	....	....	....	....	....
2002-03	Detroit Red Wings	39	5	6	11	120	....	....	....	....	....
	Los Angeles Kings	12	1	3	4	33	....	....	....	....	....
	NHL Totals	**87**	**8**	**11**	**19**	**221**	....	....	....	....	....

Signed as a free agent by **Detroit**, September 21, 1999. Traded to **Los Angeles** by **Detroit** with Maxim Kuznetsov, Detroit's 1st round choice (Jeff Tambellini) in 2003 Entry Draft and Detroit's 2nd round choice in 2004 Entry Draft for Mathieu Schneider, March 11, 2003.

AWREY, Don

Defense. Shoots left. 6', 175 lbs. Born, Kitchener, Ont., July 18, 1943.

Season	Club	GP	G	A	Pts	PIM	GP	G	A	Pts	PIM
1963-64	Boston Bruins	16	1	0	1	4	....	....	....	....	....
1964-65	Boston Bruins	47	2	3	5	41	....	....	....	....	....
1965-66	Boston Bruins	70	4	3	7	74	....	....	....	....	....
1966-67	Boston Bruins	4	1	0	1	6	....	....	....	....	....
1967-68	Boston Bruins	74	3	12	15	150	4	0	1	1	4
1968-69	Boston Bruins	73	0	13	13	149	10	0	1	1	28
1969-70♦	Boston Bruins	73	3	10	13	120	14	0	5	5	32
1970-71	Boston Bruins	74	4	21	25	141	7	0	0	0	17
1971-72♦	Boston Bruins	34	1	8	9	52	15	0	4	4	45
1972-73	Boston Bruins	78	2	17	19	90	4	0	0	0	6
1973-74	St. Louis Blues	75	5	16	21	51	....	....	....	....	....
1974-75	St. Louis Blues	20	0	8	8	4	....	....	....	....	....
	Montreal Canadiens	56	1	11	12	58	11	0	6	6	12
1975-76♦	Montreal Canadiens	72	0	12	12	29	....	....	....	....	....
1976-77	Pittsburgh Penguins	79	1	12	13	40	3	0	1	1	0
1977-78	New York Rangers	78	2	8	10	38	3	0	0	0	6
1978-79	Colorado Rockies	56	1	4	5	18	....	....	....	....	....
	NHL Totals	**979**	**31**	**158**	**189**	**1065**	**71**	**0**	**18**	**18**	**150**

Played in NHL All-Star Game (1974)

Traded to **St. Louis** by **Boston** for Jake Rathwell, St. Louis' 2nd round choice (Mark Howe) in 1974 Amateur Draft and cash, October 5, 1973. Traded to **Montreal** by **St. Louis** for Chuck Lefley, November 28, 1974. Traded to **Pittsburgh** by **Montreal** for Pittsburgh's 3rd round choice (Richard David) in 1978 Amateur Draft, August 11, 1976. Rights traded to **Washington** by **Pittsburgh** for Bob Paradise, October 1, 1977. Signed as a free agent by **NY Rangers**, October 4, 1977. Traded to **Colorado** by **NY Rangers** for cash, November, 1978.

AXELSSON, P.J.

Left wing. Shoots left. 6'1", 175 lbs. Born, Kungalv, Sweden, February 26, 1975.
(Boston's 7th choice, 177th overall, in 1995 Entry Draft).

Season	Club	GP	G	A	Pts	PIM	GP	G	A	Pts	PIM
1997-98	Boston Bruins	82	8	19	27	38	6	1	0	1	0
1998-99	Boston Bruins	77	7	10	17	18	12	1	1	2	4
99-2000	Boston Bruins	81	10	16	26	24	....	....	....	....	....
2000-01	Boston Bruins	81	8	15	23	27	....	....	....	....	....
2001-02	Boston Bruins	78	7	17	24	16	6	2	1	3	6
2002-03	Boston Bruins	66	17	19	36	24	5	0	0	0	6
	NHL Totals	**465**	**57**	**96**	**153**	**147**	**29**	**4**	**2**	**6**	**16**

AYRES, Vern

Defense. Shoots left. 6'2", 220 lbs. Born, Toronto, Ont., April 27, 1909.

Season	Club	GP	G	A	Pts	PIM	GP	G	A	Pts	PIM
1930-31	New York Americans	26	2	1	3	54	....	....	....	....	....
1931-32	New York Americans	45	2	4	6	82	....	....	....	....	....
1932-33	New York Americans	48	0	0	0	97	....	....	....	....	....
1933-34	Montreal Maroons	17	0	0	0	19	....	....	....	....	....
1934-35	St. Louis Eagles	47	2	2	4	60	....	....	....	....	....
1935-36	New York Rangers	28	0	4	4	38	....	....	....	....	....
	NHL Totals	**211**	**6**	**11**	**17**	**350**	....	....	....	....	....

Signed as a free agent by **NY Americans**, October 22, 1930. Traded to **Mtl. Maroons** by **NY Americans** for $6,000, June 1, 1933. Traded to **St. Louis** by **Mtl. Maroons** with Normie Smith to complete transaction that sent Al Shields to Mtl. Maroons (September 20, 1934), October 22, 1934. Claimed by **NY Rangers** from **St. Louis** in Dispersal Draft, October 15, 1935.

BABANDO, Pete

Left wing. Shoots left. 5'9", 187 lbs. Born, Braeburn, PA, May 10, 1925.

Season	Club	GP	G	A	Pts	PIM	GP	G	A	Pts	PIM
1947-48	Boston Bruins	60	23	11	34	52	5	1	1	2	2
1948-49	Boston Bruins	58	19	14	33	34	4	0	0	0	2
1949-50♦	Detroit Red Wings	56	6	6	12	25	8	2	2	4	2
1950-51	Chicago Black Hawks	70	18	19	37	36	....	....	....	....	....
1951-52	Chicago Black Hawks	49	11	14	25	29	....	....	....	....	....
1952-53	Chicago Black Hawks	29	5	5	10	14	....	....	....	....	....
	New York Rangers	29	4	4	8	4	....	....	....	....	....
	NHL Totals	**351**	**86**	**73**	**159**	**194**	**17**	**3**	**3**	**6**	**6**

Traded to **Detroit** by **Boston** with Claire Martin, Lloyd Durham and Jimmy Peters for Bill Quackenbush and Pete Horeck, August 16, 1949. Traded to **Chicago** by **Detroit** with Harry Lumley, Jack Stewart, Al Dewsbury and Don Morrison for Jim Henry, Bob Goldham, Gaye Stewart and Metro Prystai, July 13, 1950. Traded to **NY Rangers** by **Chicago** for cash, January 9, 1953. Traded to **Montreal** by **NY Rangers** with Ed Slowinski for Ivan Irwin, August 8, 1953. Traded to **Buffalo** (AHL) by **Montreal** with Gaye Stewart and Ed Slowinski for Jack Leclair and cash, August 17, 1954.

BABCOCK, Bobby

Defense. Shoots left. 6'1", 222 lbs. Born, Agincourt, Ont., August 3, 1968.
(Washington's 11th choice, 208th overall, in 1986 Entry Draft).

Season	Club	Regular Season GP	G	A	Pts	PIM	Playoffs GP	G	A	Pts	PIM
1990-91	Washington Capitals	1	0	0	0	0	....	....	....	....	....
1992-93	Washington Capitals	1	0	0	0	2	....	....	....	....	....
	NHL Totals	**2**	**0**	**0**	**0**	**2**	....	....	....	....	....

BABE, Warren

Left wing. Shoots left. 6'2", 190 lbs. Born, Medicine Hat, Alta., September 7, 1968.
(Minnesota's 1st choice, 12th overall, in 1986 Entry Draft).

Season	Club	Regular Season GP	G	A	Pts	PIM	Playoffs GP	G	A	Pts	PIM
1987-88	Minnesota North Stars	6	0	1	1	4	....	....	....	....	....
1988-89	Minnesota North Stars	14	2	3	5	19	2	0	0	0	0
1990-91	Minnesota North Stars	1	0	1	1	0	....	....	....	....	....
	NHL Totals	**21**	**2**	**5**	**7**	**23**	**2**	**0**	**0**	**0**	**0**

BABENKO, Yuri

Center. Shoots left. 6'1", 200 lbs. Born, Penza, USSR, January 2, 1978.
(Colorado's 2nd choice, 51st overall, in 1996 Entry Draft).

Season	Club	Regular Season GP	G	A	Pts	PIM	Playoffs GP	G	A	Pts	PIM
2000-01	Colorado Avalanche	3	0	0	0	0	....	....	....	....	....
	NHL Totals	**3**	**0**	**0**	**0**	**0**	....	....	....	....	....

BABIN, Mitch

Center. Shoots left. 6'2", 195 lbs. Born, Kapuskasing, Ont., November 1, 1954.
(St. Louis' 10th choice, 180th overall, in 1974 Amateur Draft).

Season	Club	Regular Season GP	G	A	Pts	PIM	Playoffs GP	G	A	Pts	PIM
1975-76	St. Louis Blues	8	0	0	0	0	....	....	....	....	....
	NHL Totals	**8**	**0**	**0**	**0**	**0**	....	....	....	....	....

BABY, John

Defense. Shoots right. 6', 195 lbs. Born, Sudbury, Ont., May 18, 1957.
(Cleveland's 5th choice, 59th overall, in 1977 Amateur Draft).

Season	Club	Regular Season GP	G	A	Pts	PIM	Playoffs GP	G	A	Pts	PIM
1977-78	Cleveland Barons	24	2	7	9	26	....	....	....	....	....
1978-79	Minnesota North Stars	2	0	1	1	0	....	....	....	....	....
	NHL Totals	**26**	**2**	**8**	**10**	**26**	....	....	....	....	....

Placed on **Minnesota** Reserve List after **Cleveland-Minnesota** Dispersal Draft, June 15, 1978. Claimed by **Quebec** from **Minnesota** in Expansion Draft, June 13, 1980.

BABYCH, Dave

Defense. Shoots left. 6'2", 215 lbs. Born, Edmonton, Alta., May 23, 1961.
(Winnipeg's 1st choice, 2nd overall, in 1980 Entry Draft).

Season	Club	Regular Season GP	G	A	Pts	PIM	Playoffs GP	G	A	Pts	PIM
1980-81	Winnipeg Jets	69	6	38	44	90	....	....	....	....	....
1981-82	Winnipeg Jets	79	19	49	68	92	4	1	2	3	29
1982-83	Winnipeg Jets	79	13	61	74	56	3	0	0	0	0
1983-84	Winnipeg Jets	66	18	39	57	62	3	1	1	2	0
1984-85	Winnipeg Jets	78	13	49	62	78	8	2	7	9	6
1985-86	Winnipeg Jets	19	4	12	16	14	....	....	....	....	....
	Hartford Whalers	62	10	43	53	36	8	1	3	4	14
1986-87	Hartford Whalers	66	8	33	41	44	6	1	1	2	14
1987-88	Hartford Whalers	71	14	36	50	54	6	3	2	5	2
1988-89	Hartford Whalers	70	6	41	47	54	4	1	5	6	2
1989-90	Hartford Whalers	72	6	37	43	62	7	1	2	3	0
1990-91	Hartford Whalers	8	0	6	6	4	....	....	....	....	....
1991-92	Vancouver Canucks	75	5	24	29	63	13	2	6	8	10
1992-93	Vancouver Canucks	43	3	16	19	44	12	2	5	7	6
1993-94	Vancouver Canucks	73	4	28	32	52	24	3	5	8	12
1994-95	Vancouver Canucks	40	3	11	14	18	11	2	2	4	14
1995-96	Vancouver Canucks	53	3	21	24	38	....	....	....	....	....
1996-97	Vancouver Canucks	78	5	22	27	38	....	....	....	....	....
1997-98	Vancouver Canucks	47	0	9	9	37	....	....	....	....	....
	Philadelphia Flyers	6	0	0	0	12	5	1	0	1	4
1998-99	Philadelphia Flyers	33	2	4	6	20	....	....	....	....	....
	Los Angeles Kings	8	0	2	2	2	....	....	....	....	....
	NHL Totals	**1195**	**142**	**581**	**723**	**970**	**114**	**21**	**41**	**62**	**113**

• Brother of Wayne

Played in NHL All-Star Game (1983, 1984)

Traded to **Hartford** by **Winnipeg** for Ray Neufeld, November 21, 1985. • Missed majority of 1990-91 season recovering from wrist surgery, October 29, 1990. Claimed by **Minnesota** from **Hartford** in Expansion Draft, May 30, 1991. Traded to **Vancouver** by **Minnesota** for Tom Kurvers, June 22, 1991. Traded to **Philadelphia** by **Vancouver** with Philadelphia's 5th round choice (previously acquired, Philadelphia selected Garrett Prosofsky) in 1998 Entry Draft for Philadelphia's 3rd round choice (Justin Morrison) in 1998 Entry Draft, March 24, 1998. Traded to **Los Angeles** by **Philadelphia** with Philadelphia's 5th round choice (Nathan Marsters) in 2000 Entry Draft for Steve Duchesne, March 23, 1999.

BABYCH, Wayne

Right wing. Shoots right. 5'11", 191 lbs. Born, Edmonton, Alta., June 6, 1958.
(St. Louis' 1st choice, 3rd overall, in 1978 Amateur Draft).

Season	Club	Regular Season GP	G	A	Pts	PIM	Playoffs GP	G	A	Pts	PIM
1978-79	St. Louis Blues	67	27	36	63	75	....	....	....	....	....
1979-80	St. Louis Blues	59	26	35	61	49	3	1	2	3	2
1980-81	St. Louis Blues	78	54	42	96	93	11	2	0	2	8
1981-82	St. Louis Blues	51	19	25	44	51	7	3	2	5	8
1982-83	St. Louis Blues	71	16	23	39	62	....	....	....	....	....
1983-84	St. Louis Blues	70	13	29	42	52	10	1	4	5	4
1984-85	Pittsburgh Penguins	65	20	34	54	35	....	....	....	....	....
1985-86	Pittsburgh Penguins	2	0	0	0	0	....	....	....	....	....
	Quebec Nordiques	15	6	5	11	18	....	....	....	....	....
	Hartford Whalers	37	11	17	28	59	10	0	1	1	2
1986-87	Hartford Whalers	4	0	0	0	4	....	....	....	....	....
	NHL Totals	**519**	**192**	**246**	**438**	**498**	**41**	**7**	**9**	**16**	**24**

• Brother of Dave

Played in NHL All-Star Game (1981)

Claimed by **Pittsburgh** from **St. Louis** in Waiver Draft, October 9, 1984. Traded to **Quebec** by **Pittsburgh** for future considerations, October 20, 1985. Traded to **Hartford** by **Quebec** for Greg Malone, January 17, 1986.

BACA, Jergus

Defense. Shoots left. 6'2", 211 lbs. Born, Liptovsky Mikulas, Czech., January 4, 1965.
(Hartford's 6th choice, 141st overall, in 1990 Entry Draft).

Season	Club	Regular Season GP	G	A	Pts	PIM	Playoffs GP	G	A	Pts	PIM
1990-91	Hartford Whalers	9	0	2	2	14	....	....	....	....	....
1991-92	Hartford Whalers	1	0	0	0	0	....	....	....	....	....
	NHL Totals	**10**	**0**	**2**	**2**	**14**	....	....	....	....	....

BACKMAN, Christian

Defense. Shoots left. 6'4", 198 lbs. Born, Alingsas, Sweden, April 28, 1980.
(St. Louis' 1st choice, 24th overall, in 1998 Entry Draft).

Season	Club	Regular Season GP	G	A	Pts	PIM	Playoffs GP	G	A	Pts	PIM
2002-03	St. Louis Blues	4	0	0	0	0	....	....	....	....	....
	NHL Totals	**4**	**0**	**0**	**0**	**0**	....	....	....	....	....

BACKMAN, Mike

Right wing. Shoots right. 5'10", 175 lbs. Born, Halifax, N.S., January 2, 1955.

Season	Club	Regular Season GP	G	A	Pts	PIM	Playoffs GP	G	A	Pts	PIM
1981-82	New York Rangers	3	0	2	2	4	1	0	0	0	2
1982-83	New York Rangers	7	1	3	4	6	9	2	2	4	0
1983-84	New York Rangers	8	0	1	1	8	....	....	....	....	....
	NHL Totals	**18**	**1**	**6**	**7**	**18**	**10**	**2**	**2**	**4**	**2**

Signed as a free agent by **NY Rangers**, October 11, 1979.

BACKOR, Pete

Defense. Shoots left. 6', 190 lbs. Born, Fort William, Ont., April 29, 1919.

Season	Club	Regular Season GP	G	A	Pts	PIM	Playoffs GP	G	A	Pts	PIM
1944-45 ◆	Toronto Maple Leafs	36	4	5	9	6	....	....	....	....	....
	NHL Totals	**36**	**4**	**5**	**9**	**6**	....	....	....	....	....

BACKSTROM, Ralph

Center. Shoots left. 5'10", 165 lbs. Born, Kirkland Lake, Ont., September 18, 1937.

Season	Club	Regular Season GP	G	A	Pts	PIM	Playoffs GP	G	A	Pts	PIM
1956-57	Montreal Canadiens	3	0	0	0	0	....	....	....	....	....
1957-58	Montreal Canadiens	2	0	1	1	0	....	....	....	....	....
1958-59 ◆	Montreal Canadiens	64	18	22	40	19	11	3	5	8	12
1959-60 ◆	Montreal Canadiens	64	13	15	28	24	7	0	3	3	2
1960-61	Montreal Canadiens	69	12	20	32	44	5	0	0	0	4
1961-62	Montreal Canadiens	66	27	38	65	29	5	0	1	1	6
1962-63	Montreal Canadiens	70	23	12	35	51	5	0	0	0	2
1963-64	Montreal Canadiens	70	8	21	29	41	7	2	1	3	8
1964-65 ◆	Montreal Canadiens	70	25	30	55	41	13	2	3	5	10
1965-66 ◆	Montreal Canadiens	67	22	20	42	10	10	3	4	7	4
1966-67	Montreal Canadiens	69	14	27	41	39	10	5	2	7	6
1967-68 ◆	Montreal Canadiens	70	20	25	45	14	13	4	3	7	4
1968-69 ◆	Montreal Canadiens	72	13	28	41	16	14	3	4	7	10
1969-70	Montreal Canadiens	72	19	24	43	20	....	....	....	....	....
1970-71	Montreal Canadiens	16	1	4	5	0	....	....	....	....	....
	Los Angeles Kings	33	14	13	27	8	....	....	....	....	....
1971-72	Los Angeles Kings	76	23	29	52	22	....	....	....	....	....
1972-73	Los Angeles Kings	63	20	29	49	6	....	....	....	....	....
	Chicago Black Hawks	16	6	3	9	2	16	5	6	11	0
	NHL Totals	**1032**	**278**	**361**	**639**	**386**	**116**	**27**	**32**	**59**	**68**

Calder Memorial Trophy (1959)

Played in NHL All-Star Game (1958, 1959, 1960, 1962, 1965, 1967)

Traded to **Los Angeles** by **Montreal** for Gord Labossiere and Ray Fortin, January 26, 1971.Traded to **Chicago** by **Los Angeles** for Dan Maloney, February 26, 1973.

BAILEY, Ace

HHOF

Right wing. Shoots right. 5'10", 160 lbs. Born, Bracebridge, Ont., July 3, 1903.

Season	Club	Regular Season GP	G	A	Pts	PIM	Playoffs GP	G	A	Pts	PIM
1926-27	Toronto St. Pats/Maple Leafs	42	15	13	28	82	....	....	....	....	....
1927-28	Toronto Maple Leafs	43	9	3	12	72	....	....	....	....	....
1928-29	Toronto Maple Leafs	44	*22	10	*32	78	4	1	*2	*3	4
1929-30	Toronto Maple Leafs	43	22	21	43	69	....	....	....	....	....
1930-31	Toronto Maple Leafs	40	23	19	42	46	2	1	1	2	0
1931-32 ◆	Toronto Maple Leafs	41	8	5	13	62	7	1	0	1	4
1932-33	Toronto Maple Leafs	47	10	8	18	52	8	0	1	1	4
1933-34	Toronto Maple Leafs	13	2	3	5	11	....	....	....	....	....
	NHL Totals	**313**	**111**	**82**	**193**	**472**	**21**	**3**	**4**	**7**	**12**

Signed as a free agent by **Toronto**, November 3, 1926. • Suffered career-ending head injury in game vs. Boston, December 12, 1933.

BAILEY, Bob

Right wing. Shoots right. 5'11", 180 lbs. Born, Kenora, Ont., May 29, 1931.

Season	Club	Regular Season GP	G	A	Pts	PIM	Playoffs GP	G	A	Pts	PIM
1953-54	Toronto Maple Leafs	48	2	7	9	70	5	0	2	2	4
1954-55	Toronto Maple Leafs	32	4	2	6	52	1	0	0	0	0
1955-56	Toronto Maple Leafs	6	0	0	0	6	....	....	....	....	....

Season	Club	REGULAR SEASON GP	G	A	Pts	PIM	PLAYOFFS GP	G	A	Pts	PIM
1956-57	Detroit Red Wings	....	....	....	....	....	5	0	2	2	2
1957-58	Chicago Black Hawks	28	3	6	9	38	....	....	....	....	....
	Detroit Red Wings	36	6	6	12	41	4	0	0	0	16
	NHL Totals	**150**	**15**	**21**	**36**	**207**	**15**	**0**	**4**	**4**	**22**

Traded to **Cleveland** (AHL) by **Detroit** with John Bailey for the rights to Lou Jankowski and Bill Dineen, June, 1951. Traded to **Toronto** by **Cleveland** (AHL) with Gerry Foley for Chuck Blair and $30,000, May 30, 1953. Traded to **Springfield** (AHL) by **Toronto** (Pittsburgh-AHL) with Bob Sabourin for $11,000, May 28, 1956. Traded to **Detroit** by **Springfield** (AHL) for cash, September 22, 1956. Loaned to **Springfield** (AHL) by **Detroit** for 1956-57 season, September, 1956. Claimed by **Chicago** from **Detroit** in Intra-League Draft, June 5, 1957. Traded to **Detroit** by **Chicago** with Jack McIntyre, Nick Mickoski and Hec Lalonde for Earl Reibel, Billy Dea, Lorne Ferguson and Bill Dineen, December 17, 1957. Traded to **Cleveland** (AHL) by **Detroit** for cash, July 31, 1958. Traded to **Buffalo** (AHL) by **Cleveland** (AHL) for Bill Dineen, October 20, 1959. Traded to **Montreal** by **Chicago** (Buffalo-AHL) with Glen Skov, the rights to Danny Lewicki, Terry Gray and Lorne Ferguson for Cec Hoekstra, Reggie Fleming, Ab McDonald and Bob Courcy, June 7, 1960.

BAILEY, Garnet

Left wing. Shoots left. 5'11", 192 lbs. Born, Lloydminster, Sask., June 13, 1948.
(Boston's 3rd choice, 13th overall, in 1966 Amateur Draft).

Season	Club	GP	G	A	Pts	PIM	GP	G	A	Pts	PIM
1968-69	Boston Bruins	8	3	3	6	10	1	0	0	0	2
1969-70 ◆	Boston Bruins	58	11	11	22	82	....	....	....	....	....
1970-71	Boston Bruins	36	0	6	6	44	1	0	0	0	10
1971-72 ◆	Boston Bruins	73	9	13	22	64	13	2	4	6	16
1972-73	Boston Bruins	57	8	13	21	89	....	....	....	....	....
	Detroit Red Wings	13	2	11	13	16	....	....	....	....	....
1973-74	Detroit Red Wings	45	9	14	23	33	....	....	....	....	....
	St. Louis Blues	22	7	3	10	20	....	....	....	....	....
1974-75	St. Louis Blues	49	15	26	41	113	....	....	....	....	....
	Washington Capitals	22	4	13	17	8	....	....	....	....	....
1975-76	Washington Capitals	67	13	19	32	75	....	....	....	....	....
1976-77	Washington Capitals	78	19	27	46	51	....	....	....	....	....
1977-78	Washington Capitals	40	7	12	19	28	....	....	....	....	....
	NHL Totals	**568**	**107**	**171**	**278**	**633**	**15**	**2**	**4**	**6**	**28**

Traded to **Detroit** by **Boston** with future considerations (Murray Wing, June 4, 1973) for Gary Doak, March 1, 1973. Traded to **St. Louis** by **Detroit** with Ted Harris and Bill Collins for Chris Evans, Bryan Watson and Jean Hamel, February 14, 1974. Traded to **Washington** by **St. Louis** with Stan Gilbertson for Denis Dupere, February 10, 1975.

BAILEY, Reid

Defense. Shoots left. 6'2", 200 lbs. Born, Toronto, Ont., May 28, 1956.

Season	Club	GP	G	A	Pts	PIM	GP	G	A	Pts	PIM
1980-81	Philadelphia Flyers	17	1	3	4	55	12	0	2	2	23
1981-82	Philadelphia Flyers	10	0	0	0	23	2	0	0	0	0
1982-83	Toronto Maple Leafs	1	0	0	0	2	2	0	0	0	2
1983-84	Hartford Whalers	12	0	0	0	25	....	....	....	....	....
	NHL Totals	**40**	**1**	**3**	**4**	**105**	**16**	**0**	**2**	**2**	**25**

Signed as a free agent by **Philadelphia**, November 20, 1978. Signed as free agent by **Edmonton**, October 27, 1982. Traded to **Toronto** by **Edmonton** for Serge Boisvert, January 15, 1983. Signed as a free agent by **Hartford**, December 9, 1983.

BAILLARGEON, Joel

Left wing. Shoots left. 6'1", 205 lbs. Born, Quebec City, Que., October 6, 1964.
(Winnipeg's 7th choice, 113th overall, in 1983 Entry Draft).

Season	Club	GP	G	A	Pts	PIM	GP	G	A	Pts	PIM
1986-87	Winnipeg Jets	11	0	1	1	15	....	....	....	....	....
1987-88	Winnipeg Jets	4	0	1	1	12	....	....	....	....	....
1988-89	Quebec Nordiques	5	0	0	0	4	....	....	....	....	....
	NHL Totals	**20**	**0**	**2**	**2**	**31**	....	....	....	....	....

Traded to **Quebec** by **Winnipeg** for future considerations, July 29, 1988.

BAIRD, Ken

Defense. Shoots left. 6', 190 lbs. Born, Flin Flon, Man., February 1, 1951.
(California's 1st choice, 15th overall, in 1971 Amateur Draft).

Season	Club	GP	G	A	Pts	PIM	GP	G	A	Pts	PIM
1971-72	California Golden Seals	10	0	2	2	15	....	....	....	....	....
	NHL Totals	**10**	**0**	**2**	**2**	**15**	....	....	....	....	....

BAKER, Bill

Defense. Shoots left. 6'1", 195 lbs. Born, Grand Rapids, MN, November 29, 1956.
(Montreal's 5th choice, 54th overall, in 1976 Amateur Draft).

Season	Club	GP	G	A	Pts	PIM	GP	G	A	Pts	PIM
1980-81	Montreal Canadiens	11	0	0	0	32	....	....	....	....	....
	Colorado Rockies	13	0	3	3	12	....	....	....	....	....
1981-82	Colorado Rockies	14	0	3	3	17	....	....	....	....	....
	St. Louis Blues	35	3	5	8	50	4	0	0	0	0
1982-83	New York Rangers	70	4	14	18	64	2	0	0	0	0
	NHL Totals	**143**	**7**	**25**	**32**	**175**	**6**	**0**	**0**	**0**	**0**

Traded to **Colorado** by **Montreal** for Colorado's 3rd round choice (Daniel Letendre) in 1983 Entry Draft, March 10, 1981. Traded to **St. Louis** by **Colorado** for Joe Micheletti and Dick Lamby, December 4, 1981. Claimed by **NY Rangers** from **St. Louis** in Waiver Draft, October 4, 1982.

BAKER, Jamie

Center. Shoots left. 6', 195 lbs. Born, Ottawa, Ont., August 31, 1966.
(Quebec's 2nd choice, 8th overall, in 1988 Supplemental Draft).

Season	Club	GP	G	A	Pts	PIM	GP	G	A	Pts	PIM
1989-90	Quebec Nordiques	1	0	0	0	0	....	....	....	....	....
1990-91	Quebec Nordiques	18	2	0	2	8	....	....	....	....	....
1991-92	Quebec Nordiques	52	7	10	17	32	....	....	....	....	....
1992-93	Ottawa Senators	76	19	29	48	54	....	....	....	....	....
1993-94	San Jose Sharks	65	12	5	17	38	14	3	2	5	30
1994-95	San Jose Sharks	43	7	4	11	22	11	2	2	4	12
1995-96	San Jose Sharks	77	16	17	33	79	....	....	....	....	....
1996-97	Toronto Maple Leafs	58	8	8	16	28	....	....	....	....	....
1997-98	Toronto Maple Leafs	13	0	5	5	10	....	....	....	....	....
1998-99	San Jose Sharks	1	0	1	1	0	....	....	....	....	....
	NHL Totals	**404**	**71**	**79**	**150**	**271**	**25**	**5**	**4**	**9**	**42**

Signed as a free agent by **Ottawa**, September 2, 1992. Signed as a free agent by **San Jose**, September 11, 1993. Traded to **Toronto** by **San Jose** with San Jose's 5th round choice (Peter Cava) in 1996 Entry Draft for Todd Gill, June 14, 1996. Signed as a free agent by **San Jose**, September 29, 1998.

BAKOVIC, Peter

Right wing. Shoots right. 6'2", 200 lbs. Born, Port Arthur, Ont., January 31, 1965.

Season	Club	GP	G	A	Pts	PIM	GP	G	A	Pts	PIM
1987-88	Vancouver Canucks	10	2	0	2	48	....	....	....	....	....
	NHL Totals	**10**	**2**	**0**	**2**	**48**	....	....	....	....	....

Signed as a free agent by **Calgary**, October 10, 1985. Traded to **Vancouver** by **Calgary** with Brian Bradley and Kevan Guy for Craig Coxe, March 6, 1988.

BALA, Chris

Left wing. Shoots left. 6'1", 180 lbs. Born, Alexandria, VA, September 24, 1978.
(Ottawa's 3rd choice, 58th overall, in 1998 Entry Draft).

Season	Club	GP	G	A	Pts	PIM	GP	G	A	Pts	PIM
2001-02	Ottawa Senators	6	0	1	1	0	....	....	....	....	....
	NHL Totals	**6**	**0**	**1**	**1**	**0**	....	....	....	....	....

BALDERIS, Helmut

Right wing. Shoots right. 5'11", 190 lbs. Born, Riga, Latvia, June 30, 1952.
(Minnesota's 13th choice, 238th overall, in 1989 Entry Draft).

Season	Club	GP	G	A	Pts	PIM	GP	G	A	Pts	PIM
1989-90	Minnesota North Stars	26	3	6	9	2	....	....	....	....	....
	NHL Totals	**26**	**3**	**6**	**9**	**2**	....	....	....	....	....

BALDWIN, Doug

Defense. Shoots left. 6', 175 lbs. Born, Winnipeg, Man., November 2, 1922.

Season	Club	GP	G	A	Pts	PIM	GP	G	A	Pts	PIM
1945-46	Toronto Maple Leafs	15	0	1	1	6	....	....	....	....	....
1946-47	Detroit Red Wings	4	0	0	0	0	....	....	....	....	....
1947-48	Chicago Black Hawks	5	0	0	0	2	....	....	....	....	....
	NHL Totals	**24**	**0**	**1**	**1**	**8**	....	....	....	....	....

Traded to **Detroit** by **Toronto** with Ray Powell for Gerry Brown, September 21, 1946. Traded to **Chicago** by **Detroit** for cash, June, 1947. Traded to **Cleveland** (AHL) by **Chicago** (Kansas City-USHL) for Ed Wares, January 28, 1949. Traded to **Chicago** (Kansas City-USHL) by **Cleveland** (AHL) with Ralph Wycherley for Al Rollins, September 13, 1949.

BALFOUR, Earl

Left wing. Shoots left. 6'1", 180 lbs. Born, Toronto, Ont., January 4, 1933.

Season	Club	GP	G	A	Pts	PIM	GP	G	A	Pts	PIM
1951-52	Toronto Maple Leafs	3	0	0	0	2	1	0	0	0	0
1953-54	Toronto Maple Leafs	17	0	1	1	6	....	....	....	....	....
1955-56	Toronto Maple Leafs	59	14	5	19	40	3	0	1	1	2
1957-58	Toronto Maple Leafs	1	0	0	0	0	....	....	....	....	....
1958-59	Chicago Black Hawks	70	10	8	18	10	6	0	2	2	0
1959-60	Chicago Black Hawks	70	3	5	8	16	4	0	0	0	0
1960-61 ◆	Chicago Black Hawks	68	3	3	6	4	12	0	0	0	2
	NHL Totals	**288**	**30**	**22**	**52**	**78**	**26**	**0**	**3**	**3**	**4**

Claimed by **Chicago** from **Toronto** in Intra-League Draft, June 3, 1958. Claimed by **Boston** from **Chicago** in Intra-League Draft, June 13, 1961.

BALFOUR, Murray

Right wing. Shoots right. 5'9", 178 lbs. Born, Regina, Sask., August 24, 1936.

Season	Club	GP	G	A	Pts	PIM	GP	G	A	Pts	PIM
1956-57	Montreal Canadiens	2	0	0	0	2	....	....	....	....	....
1957-58	Montreal Canadiens	3	1	1	2	4	....	....	....	....	....
1959-60	Chicago Black Hawks	61	18	12	30	55	4	1	0	1	0
1960-61 ◆	Chicago Black Hawks	70	21	27	48	123	11	5	5	10	14
1961-62	Chicago Black Hawks	49	15	15	30	72	12	1	1	2	15
1962-63	Chicago Black Hawks	65	10	23	33	75	6	0	2	2	12
1963-64	Chicago Black Hawks	41	2	10	12	36	7	2	2	4	4
1964-65	Boston Bruins	15	0	2	2	26	....	....	....	....	....
	NHL Totals	**306**	**67**	**90**	**157**	**393**	**40**	**9**	**10**	**19**	**45**

Traded to **Chicago** by **Montreal** for cash, June 9, 1959. Traded to **Boston** by **Chicago** with Mike Draper for Matt Ravlich and Jerry Toppazzini, June 9, 1964. • Missed remainder of the 1964-65 season after being diagnosed with lung cancer, February 5, 1965.

BALL, Terry

Defense. Shoots right. 5'9", 160 lbs. Born, Selkirk, Man., November 29, 1944.

Season	Club	GP	G	A	Pts	PIM	GP	G	A	Pts	PIM
1967-68	Philadelphia Flyers	1	0	0	0	0	....	....	....	....	....
1969-70	Philadelphia Flyers	61	7	18	25	20	....	....	....	....	....
1970-71	Buffalo Sabres	2	0	0	0	0	....	....	....	....	....
1971-72	Buffalo Sabres	10	0	1	1	6	....	....	....	....	....
	NHL Totals	**74**	**7**	**19**	**26**	**26**	....	....	....	....	....

Claimed by **Philadelphia** from **NY Rangers** in Expansion Draft, June 6, 1967. Traded to **Pittsburgh** by **Philadelphia** for George Swarbrick, June 11, 1970. Traded to **Buffalo** by **Pittsburgh** for Jean-Guy Legace, January 24, 1971.

BALMOCHNYKH, Maxim

Left wing. Shoots left. 6'1", 180 lbs. Born, Lipetsk, USSR, March 7, 1979.
(Anaheim's 2nd choice, 45th overall, in 1997 Entry Draft).

		REGULAR SEASON					PLAYOFFS				
Season	Club	GP	G	A	Pts	PIM	GP	G	A	Pts	PIM
99-2000	Mighty Ducks of Anaheim	6	0	1	1	2	....	....	....	....	....
	NHL Totals	**6**	**0**	**1**	**1**	**2**	....	....	....	....	....

Traded to **New Jersey** by **Anaheim** with Jeff Friesen and Oleg Tverdovsky for Petr Sykora, Mike Commodore, Jean-Francois Damphousse and Igor Pohanka, July 6, 2002.

BALON, Dave

Left wing. Shoots left. 5'10", 180 lbs. Born, Wakaw, Sask., August 2, 1938.

		REGULAR SEASON					PLAYOFFS				
Season	Club	GP	G	A	Pts	PIM	GP	G	A	Pts	PIM
1959-60	New York Rangers	3	0	0	0	0	....	....	....	....	....
1960-61	New York Rangers	13	1	2	3	8	....	....	....	....	....
1961-62	New York Rangers	30	4	11	15	11	6	2	3	5	2
1962-63	New York Rangers	70	11	13	24	72	....	....	....	....	....
1963-64	Montreal Canadiens	70	24	18	42	80	7	1	1	2	25
1964-65 ♦	Montreal Canadiens	63	18	23	41	61	10	0	0	0	10
1965-66 ♦	Montreal Canadiens	45	3	7	10	24	9	2	3	5	16
1966-67	Montreal Canadiens	48	11	8	19	31	9	0	2	2	6
1967-68	Minnesota North Stars	73	15	32	47	84	14	4	*9	13	14
1968-69	New York Rangers	75	10	21	31	57	4	1	0	1	0
1969-70	New York Rangers	76	33	37	70	100	6	1	1	2	32
1970-71	New York Rangers	78	36	24	60	34	13	3	2	5	4
1971-72	New York Rangers	16	4	5	9	2	....	....	....	....	....
	Vancouver Canucks	59	19	19	38	21	....	....	....	....	....
1972-73	Vancouver Canucks	57	3	2	5	22	....	....	....	....	....
	NHL Totals	**776**	**192**	**222**	**414**	**607**	**78**	**14**	**21**	**35**	**109**

Played in NHL All-Star Game (1965, 1967, 1968, 1971)

Traded to **Montreal** by **NY Rangers** with Gump Worsley, Leon Rochefort and Len Ronson for Phil Goyette, Don Marshall and Jacques Plante, June 4, 1963. Selected by **Minnesota** from **Montreal** in Expansion Draft, June 6, 1967. Traded to **NY Rangers** by **Minnesota** for Wayne Hillman, Dan Seguin and Joey Johnston, June 12, 1968. Traded to **Vancouver** by **NY Rangers** with Wayne Connelly and Ron Stewart for Gary Doak and Jim Wiste, November 16, 1971.

BALTIMORE, Bryon

Defense. Shoots right. 6'2", 190 lbs. Born, Whitehorse, Yukon, August 26, 1952.

		REGULAR SEASON					PLAYOFFS				
Season	Club	GP	G	A	Pts	PIM	GP	G	A	Pts	PIM
1979-80	Edmonton Oilers	2	0	0	0	4	....	....	....	....	....
	NHL Totals	**2**	**0**	**0**	**0**	**4**	....	....	....	....	....

Claimed by **Edmonton** from **Cincinnati** (WHA) in WHA Dispersal Draft, June 9, 1979.

BALUIK, Stan

Center. Shoots left. 5'8", 160 lbs. Born, Port Arthur, Ont., October 5, 1935.

		REGULAR SEASON					PLAYOFFS				
Season	Club	GP	G	A	Pts	PIM	GP	G	A	Pts	PIM
1959-60	Boston Bruins	7	0	0	0	2	....	....	....	....	....
	NHL Totals	**7**	**0**	**0**	**0**	**2**	....	....	....	....	....

Claimed by **Boston** from **Chicoutimi** (QHL) in Inter-League Draft, June 4, 1957.

BANCROFT, Steve

Defense. Shoots left. 6'1", 214 lbs. Born, Toronto, Ont., October 6, 1970.
(Toronto's 3rd choice, 21st overall, in 1989 Entry Draft).

		REGULAR SEASON					PLAYOFFS				
Season	Club	GP	G	A	Pts	PIM	GP	G	A	Pts	PIM
1992-93	Chicago Blackhawks	1	0	0	0	0	....	....	....	....	....
2001-02	San Jose Sharks	5	0	1	1	2	....	....	....	....	....
	NHL Totals	**6**	**0**	**1**	**1**	**2**	....	....	....	....	....

Traded to **Boston** by **Toronto** for Rob Cimetta, November 9, 1990. Traded to **Chicago** by **Boston** with Boston's 11th round choice (later traded to Winnipeg – Winnipeg selected Russ Hewson) in 1993 Entry Draft for Chicago's 11th round choice (Evgeny Pavlov) in 1992 Entry Draft, January 8, 1992. Traded to **Winnipeg** by **Chicago** with future considerations for Troy Murray, February 21, 1993. Claimed by **Florida** from **Winnipeg** in Expansion Draft, June 24, 1993. Signed as a free agent by **Pittsburgh**, August 2, 1993. Signed as a free agent by **Los Angeles** (IHL), August 30, 1995. Signed as a free agent by **Carolina**, August 4, 1999.Signed as a free agent by **San Jose**, August 10, 2000. Signed as a free agent by **St. Louis**, July 16, 2002.

BANDURA, Jeff

Defense. Shoots right. 6'1", 195 lbs. Born, White Rock, B.C., February 4, 1957.
(Vancouver's 2nd choice, 22nd overall, in 1977 Amateur Draft).

		REGULAR SEASON					PLAYOFFS				
Season	Club	GP	G	A	Pts	PIM	GP	G	A	Pts	PIM
1980-81	New York Rangers	2	0	1	1	0	....	....	....	....	....
	NHL Totals	**2**	**0**	**1**	**1**	**0**	....	....	....	....	....

Traded to **NY Rangers** by **Vancouver** with Jere Gillis for Mario Marois and Jim Mayer, November 11, 1980.

BANHAM, Frank

Right wing. Shoots right. 6', 190 lbs. Born, Calahoo, Alta., April 14, 1975.
(Washington's 4th choice, 147th overall, in 1993 Entry Draft).

		REGULAR SEASON					PLAYOFFS				
Season	Club	GP	G	A	Pts	PIM	GP	G	A	Pts	PIM
1996-97	Mighty Ducks of Anaheim	3	0	0	0	0	....	....	....	....	....
1997-98	Mighty Ducks of Anaheim	21	9	2	11	12	....	....	....	....	....
99-2000	Mighty Ducks of Anaheim	3	0	0	0	2	....	....	....	....	....
2002-03	Phoenix Coyotes	5	0	0	0	2	....	....	....	....	....
	NHL Totals	**32**	**9**	**2**	**11**	**16**	....	....	....	....	....

Signed as a free agent by **Anaheim**, January 27, 1996. Signed as a free agent by **Phoenix**, November 7, 2002.

BANKS, Darren

Left wing. Shoots left. 6'2", 215 lbs. Born, Toronto, Ont., March 18, 1966.

		REGULAR SEASON					PLAYOFFS				
Season	Club	GP	G	A	Pts	PIM	GP	G	A	Pts	PIM
1992-93	Boston Bruins	16	2	1	3	64	....	....	....	....	....
1993-94	Boston Bruins	4	0	1	1	9	....	....	....	....	....
	NHL Totals	**20**	**2**	**2**	**4**	**73**	....	....	....	....	....

Signed as a free agent by **Calgary**, December 12, 1990. Signed as a free agent by **Boston**, July 16, 1992.

BANNISTER, Drew

Defense. Shoots right. 6'2", 200 lbs. Born, Belleville, Ont., September 4, 1974.
(Tampa Bay's 2nd choice, 26th overall, in 1992 Entry Draft).

		REGULAR SEASON					PLAYOFFS				
Season	Club	GP	G	A	Pts	PIM	GP	G	A	Pts	PIM
1995-96	Tampa Bay Lightning	13	0	1	1	4	....	....	....	....	....
1996-97	Tampa Bay Lightning	64	4	13	17	44	....	....	....	....	....
	Edmonton Oilers	1	0	1	1	0	12	0	0	0	30
1997-98	Edmonton Oilers	34	0	2	2	42	....	....	....	....	....
	Mighty Ducks of Anaheim	27	0	6	6	47	....	....	....	....	....
1998-99	Tampa Bay Lightning	21	1	2	3	24	....	....	....	....	....
2000-01	New York Rangers	3	0	0	0	0	....	....	....	....	....
2001-02	Mighty Ducks of Anaheim	1	0	0	0	0	....	....	....	....	....
	NHL Totals	**164**	**5**	**25**	**30**	**161**	**12**	**0**	**0**	**0**	**30**

Traded to **Edmonton** by **Tampa Bay** with Tampa Bay's 6th round choice (Peter Sarno) in 1997 Entry Draft for Jeff Norton, March 18, 1997. Traded to **Anaheim** by **Edmonton** for Bobby Dollas, January 9, 1998. Traded to **Tampa Bay** by **Anaheim** for Tampa Bay's 5th round choice (Peter Podhradsky) in 2000 Entry Draft, December 10, 1998. Signed as a free agent by **NY Rangers**, October 3, 1999. Signed as a free agent by **Anaheim**, July 27, 2001.

BARAHONA, Ralph

Center. Shoots left. 5'10", 180 lbs. Born, Long Beach, CA, November 16, 1965.

		REGULAR SEASON					PLAYOFFS				
Season	Club	GP	G	A	Pts	PIM	GP	G	A	Pts	PIM
1990-91	Boston Bruins	3	2	1	3	0	....	....	....	....	....
1991-92	Boston Bruins	3	0	1	1	0	....	....	....	....	....
	NHL Totals	**6**	**2**	**2**	**4**	**0**	....	....	....	....	....

Signed as a free agent by **Boston**, September 26, 1990.

BARBE, Andy

Right wing. Shoots right. 6', 170 lbs. Born, Coniston, Ont., July 27, 1923.

		REGULAR SEASON					PLAYOFFS				
Season	Club	GP	G	A	Pts	PIM	GP	G	A	Pts	PIM
1950-51	Toronto Maple Leafs	1	0	0	0	2	....	....	....	....	....
	NHL Totals	**1**	**0**	**0**	**0**	**2**	....	....	....	....	....

BARBER, Bill

HHOF

Left wing. Shoots left. 6', 195 lbs. Born, Callander, Ont., July 11, 1952.
(Philadelphia's 1st choice, 7th overall, in 1972 Amateur Draft).

		REGULAR SEASON					PLAYOFFS				
Season	Club	GP	G	A	Pts	PIM	GP	G	A	Pts	PIM
1972-73	Philadelphia Flyers	69	30	34	64	46	11	3	2	5	22
1973-74 ♦	Philadelphia Flyers	75	34	35	69	54	17	3	6	9	18
1974-75 ♦	Philadelphia Flyers	79	34	37	71	66	17	6	9	15	8
1975-76	Philadelphia Flyers	80	50	62	112	104	16	6	7	13	18
1976-77	Philadelphia Flyers	73	20	35	55	62	10	1	4	5	2
1977-78	Philadelphia Flyers	80	41	31	72	34	12	6	3	9	2
1978-79	Philadelphia Flyers	79	34	46	80	22	8	3	4	7	10
1979-80	Philadelphia Flyers	79	40	32	72	17	19	12	9	21	23
1980-81	Philadelphia Flyers	80	43	42	85	69	12	11	5	16	0
1981-82	Philadelphia Flyers	80	45	44	89	85	4	1	5	6	4
1982-83	Philadelphia Flyers	66	27	33	60	28	3	1	1	2	2
1983-84	Philadelphia Flyers	63	22	32	54	36	....	....	....	....	....
	NHL Totals	**903**	**420**	**463**	**883**	**623**	**129**	**53**	**55**	**108**	**109**

NHL First All-Star Team (1976) • NHL Second All-Star Team (1979, 1981)
Played in NHL All-Star Game (1975, 1976, 1978, 1980, 1981, 1982)

BARBER, Don

Wing. Shoots left. 6'2", 205 lbs. Born, Victoria, B.C., December 2, 1964.
(Edmonton's 5th choice, 124th overall, in 1983 Entry Draft).

		REGULAR SEASON					PLAYOFFS				
Season	Club	GP	G	A	Pts	PIM	GP	G	A	Pts	PIM
1988-89	Minnesota North Stars	23	8	5	13	8	4	1	1	2	2
1989-90	Minnesota North Stars	44	15	19	34	32	7	3	3	6	8
1990-91	Minnesota North Stars	7	0	0	0	4	....	....	....	....	....
	Winnipeg Jets	16	1	2	3	14	....	....	....	....	....
1991-92	Winnipeg Jets	11	0	3	3	4	....	....	....	....	....
	Quebec Nordiques	2	0	0	0	0	....	....	....	....	....
	San Jose Sharks	12	1	3	4	2	....	....	....	....	....
	NHL Totals	**115**	**25**	**32**	**57**	**64**	**11**	**4**	**4**	**8**	**10**

Traded to **Minnesota** by **Edmonton** with Marc Habscheid and Emanuel Viveiros for Gord Sherven and Don Biggs, December 20, 1985. Traded to **Winnipeg** by **Minnesota** for Doug Smail, November 7, 1990. Claimed on waivers by **Quebec** from **Winnipeg**, November 12, 1991. Traded to **San Jose** by **Quebec** for Murray Garbutt, March 7, 1992.

BARILKO, Bill

Defense. Shoots right. 5'11", 180 lbs. Born, Timmins, Ont., March 25, 1927.

		REGULAR SEASON					PLAYOFFS				
Season	Club	GP	G	A	Pts	PIM	GP	G	A	Pts	PIM
1946-47 ♦	Toronto Maple Leafs	18	3	7	10	33	11	0	3	3	18
1947-48 ♦	Toronto Maple Leafs	57	5	9	14	*147	9	1	0	1	17
1948-49 ♦	Toronto Maple Leafs	60	5	4	9	95	9	0	1	1	20
1949-50	Toronto Maple Leafs	59	7	10	17	85	7	1	1	2	18
1950-51 ♦	Toronto Maple Leafs	58	6	6	12	96	11	3	2	5	31
	NHL Totals	**252**	**26**	**36**	**62**	**456**	**47**	**5**	**7**	**12**	**104**

Played in NHL All-Star Game (1947, 1948, 1949)
• Died of injuries suffered in airplane accident, August 26, 1951.

BARKLEY, Doug

Defense. Shoots right. 6'2", 185 lbs. Born, Lethbridge, Alta., January 6, 1937.

		REGULAR SEASON					PLAYOFFS				
Season	Club	GP	G	A	Pts	PIM	GP	G	A	Pts	PIM
1957-58	Chicago Black Hawks	3	0	0	0	0	....	....	....	....	....

		Regular Season					Playoffs				
Season	Club	GP	G	A	Pts	PIM	GP	G	A	Pts	PIM
1959-60	Chicago Black Hawks	3	0	0	0	2	....	....	....	....	....
1962-63	Detroit Red Wings	70	3	24	27	78	11	0	3	3	16
1963-64	Detroit Red Wings	67	11	21	32	115	14	0	5	5	33
1964-65	Detroit Red Wings	67	5	20	25	122	5	0	1	1	14
1965-66	Detroit Red Wings	43	5	15	20	65	....	....	....	....	....
	NHL Totals	**253**	**24**	**80**	**104**	**382**	**30**	**0**	**9**	**9**	**63**

Traded to **Detroit** by **Chicago** for Len Lunde and John McKenzie, June 5, 1962. • Suffered career-ending eye injury in game vs. Chicago, January 30, 1966.

BARLOW, Bob

Left wing. Shoots left. 5'10", 165 lbs. Born, Hamilton, Ont., June 17, 1935.

		Regular Season					Playoffs				
Season	Club	GP	G	A	Pts	PIM	GP	G	A	Pts	PIM
1969-70	Minnesota North Stars	70	16	17	33	10	6	2	2	4	6
1970-71	Minnesota North Stars	7	0	0	0	0	....	....	....	....	....
	NHL Totals	**77**	**16**	**17**	**33**	**10**	**6**	**2**	**2**	**4**	**6**

Claimed by **Toronto** (Rochester-AHL) from **Montreal** in Reverse Draft, June 9, 1965. Rights transferred to **Vancouver** (WHL) after WHL club purchased **Rochester** (AHL) franchise, August 13, 1968. Claimed by **Philadelphia** from **Vancouver** (WHL) in Inter-League Draft, June 10, 1969. Traded to **Minnesota** by **Philadelphia** for cash, June 10, 1969.

BARNABY, Matthew

Right wing. Shoots left. 6', 189 lbs. Born, Ottawa, Ont., May 4, 1973.
(Buffalo's 5th choice, 83rd overall, in 1992 Entry Draft).

		Regular Season					Playoffs				
Season	Club	GP	G	A	Pts	PIM	GP	G	A	Pts	PIM
1992-93	Buffalo Sabres	2	1	0	1	10	1	0	1	1	4
1993-94	Buffalo Sabres	35	2	4	6	106	3	0	0	0	17
1994-95	Buffalo Sabres	23	1	1	2	116	....	....	....	....	....
1995-96	Buffalo Sabres	73	15	16	31	*335	....	....	....	....	....
1996-97	Buffalo Sabres	68	19	24	43	249	8	0	4	4	36
1997-98	Buffalo Sabres	72	5	20	25	289	15	7	6	13	22
1998-99	Buffalo Sabres	44	4	14	18	143	....	....	....	....	....
	Pittsburgh Penguins	18	2	2	4	34	13	0	0	0	35
99-2000	Pittsburgh Penguins	64	12	12	24	197	11	0	2	2	29
2000-01	Pittsburgh Penguins	47	1	4	5	*168	....	....	....	....	....
	Tampa Bay Lightning	29	4	4	8	*97	....	....	....	....	....
2001-02	Tampa Bay Lightning	29	0	0	0	70	....	....	....	....	....
	New York Rangers	48	8	13	21	144	....	....	....	....	....
2002-03	New York Rangers	79	14	22	36	142	....	....	....	....	....
	NHL Totals	**631**	**88**	**136**	**224**	**2100**	**51**	**7**	**13**	**20**	**143**

Traded to **Pittsburgh** by **Buffalo** for Stu Barnes, March 11, 1999. Traded to **Tampa Bay** by **Pittsburgh** for Wayne Primeau, February 1, 2001. Traded to **NY Rangers** by **Tampa Bay** for Zdeno Ciger, December 12, 2001.

BARNES, Blair

Right wing. Shoots right. 5'11", 190 lbs. Born, Windsor, Ont., September 21, 1960.
(Edmonton's 6th choice, 126th overall, in 1979 Entry Draft).

		Regular Season					Playoffs				
Season	Club	GP	G	A	Pts	PIM	GP	G	A	Pts	PIM
1982-83	Los Angeles Kings	1	0	0	0	0	....	....	....	....	....
	NHL Totals	**1**	**0**	**0**	**0**	**0**	....	....	....	....	....

Traded to **Los Angeles** by **Edmonton** for Paul Mulvey, June 22, 1982.

BARNES, Norm

Defense. Shoots left. 6', 190 lbs. Born, Toronto, Ont., August 24, 1953.
(Philadelphia's 9th choice, 122nd overall, in 1973 Amateur Draft).

		Regular Season					Playoffs				
Season	Club	GP	G	A	Pts	PIM	GP	G	A	Pts	PIM
1976-77	Philadelphia Flyers	1	0	0	0	0	....	....	....	....	....
1978-79	Philadelphia Flyers	....	....	....	....	....	2	0	0	0	0
1979-80	Philadelphia Flyers	59	4	21	25	59	10	0	0	0	8
1980-81	Philadelphia Flyers	22	0	3	3	18	....	....	....	....	....
	Hartford Whalers	54	1	10	11	82	....	....	....	....	....
1981-82	Hartford Whalers	20	1	4	5	19	....	....	....	....	....
	NHL Totals	**156**	**6**	**38**	**44**	**178**	**12**	**0**	**0**	**0**	**8**

Played in NHL All-Star Game (1980)

Traded to **Hartford** by **Philadelphia** with Jack McIlhargey for Hartford's 2nd round choice (later traded to Toronto – Toronto selected Peter Ihnacak) in 1982 Entry Draft, November 21, 1980.

BARNES, Stu

Center. Shoots right. 5'11", 180 lbs. Born, Spruce Grove, Alta., December 25, 1970.
(Winnipeg's 1st choice, 4th overall, in 1989 Entry Draft).

		Regular Season					Playoffs				
Season	Club	GP	G	A	Pts	PIM	GP	G	A	Pts	PIM
1991-92	Winnipeg Jets	46	8	9	17	26	....	....	....	....	....
1992-93	Winnipeg Jets	38	12	10	22	10	6	1	3	4	2
1993-94	Winnipeg Jets	18	5	4	9	8	....	....	....	....	....
	Florida Panthers	59	18	20	38	30	....	....	....	....	....
1994-95	Florida Panthers	41	10	19	29	8	....	....	....	....	....
1995-96	Florida Panthers	72	19	25	44	46	22	6	10	16	4
1996-97	Florida Panthers	19	2	8	10	10	....	....	....	....	....
	Pittsburgh Penguins	62	17	22	39	16	5	0	1	1	0
1997-98	Pittsburgh Penguins	78	30	35	65	30	6	3	3	6	2
1998-99	Pittsburgh Penguins	64	20	12	32	20	....	....	....	....	....
	Buffalo Sabres	17	0	4	4	10	21	7	3	10	6
99-2000	Buffalo Sabres	82	20	25	45	16	5	3	0	3	2
2000-01	Buffalo Sabres	75	19	24	43	26	13	4	4	8	2
2001-02	Buffalo Sabres	68	17	31	48	26	....	....	....	....	....
2002-03	Buffalo Sabres	68	11	21	32	20	....	....	....	....	....
	Dallas Stars	13	2	5	7	8	12	2	3	5	0
	NHL Totals	**820**	**210**	**274**	**484**	**310**	**90**	**26**	**27**	**53**	**18**

Traded to **Florida** by **Winnipeg** with St. Louis' 6th round choice (previously acquired, later traded to Edmonton – later traded back to Winnipeg – Winnipeg selected Chris Kibermanis) in 1994 Entry Draft for Randy Gilhen, November 25, 1993. Traded to **Pittsburgh** by **Florida** with Jason Woolley for Chris Wells, November 19, 1996. Traded to **Buffalo** by **Pittsburgh** for Matthew Barnaby, March 11, 1999. Traded to **Dallas** by **Buffalo** for Michael Ryan and Dallas's 2nd round choice (Branislav Fabry) in 2003 Entry Draft, March 10, 2003.

BARNEY, Scott

Center. Shoots right. 6'4", 198 lbs. Born, Oshawa, Ont., March 27, 1979.
(Los Angeles' 3rd choice, 29th overall, in 1997 Entry Draft).

		Regular Season					Playoffs				
Season	Club	GP	G	A	Pts	PIM	GP	G	A	Pts	PIM
2002-03	Los Angeles Kings	5	0	0	0	0	....	....	....	....	....
	NHL Totals	**5**	**0**	**0**	**0**	**0**	....	....	....	....	....

BARON, Murray

Defense. Shoots left. 6'3", 215 lbs. Born, Prince George, B.C., June 1, 1967.
(Philadelphia's 7th choice, 167th overall, in 1986 Entry Draft).

		Regular Season					Playoffs				
Season	Club	GP	G	A	Pts	PIM	GP	G	A	Pts	PIM
1989-90	Philadelphia Flyers	16	2	2	4	12	....	....	....	....	....
1990-91	Philadelphia Flyers	67	8	8	16	74	....	....	....	....	....
1991-92	St. Louis Blues	67	3	8	11	94	2	0	0	0	2
1992-93	St. Louis Blues	53	2	2	4	59	11	0	0	0	12
1993-94	St. Louis Blues	77	5	9	14	123	4	0	0	0	10
1994-95	St. Louis Blues	39	0	5	5	93	7	1	1	2	2
1995-96	St. Louis Blues	82	2	9	11	190	13	1	0	1	20
1996-97	St. Louis Blues	11	0	2	2	11	....	....	....	....	....
	Montreal Canadiens	60	1	5	6	107	....	....	....	....	....
	Phoenix Coyotes	8	0	0	0	4	1	0	0	0	0
1997-98	Phoenix Coyotes	45	1	5	6	106	6	0	2	2	6
1998-99	Vancouver Canucks	81	2	6	8	115	....	....	....	....	....
99-2000	Vancouver Canucks	81	2	10	12	67	....	....	....	....	....
2000-01	Vancouver Canucks	82	3	8	11	63	4	0	0	0	0
2001-02	Vancouver Canucks	61	1	6	7	68	6	0	1	1	10
2002-03	Vancouver Canucks	78	2	4	6	62	14	0	4	4	10
	NHL Totals	**908**	**34**	**89**	**123**	**1248**	**68**	**2**	**8**	**10**	**72**

Traded to **St. Louis** by **Philadelphia** with Ron Sutter for Dan Quinn and Rod Brind'Amour, September 22, 1991. Traded to **Montreal** by **St. Louis** with Shayne Corson and St. Louis' 5th round choice (Gennady Razin) in 1997 Entry Draft for Pierre Turgeon, Rory Fitzpatrick and Craig Conroy, October 29, 1996. Traded to **Phoenix** by **Montreal** with Chris Murray for Dave Manson, March 18, 1997. Signed as a free agent by **Vancouver**, July 14, 1998.

BARON, Normand

Left wing. Shoots left. 6', 205 lbs. Born, Verdun, Que., December 15, 1957.

		Regular Season					Playoffs				
Season	Club	GP	G	A	Pts	PIM	GP	G	A	Pts	PIM
1983-84	Montreal Canadiens	4	0	0	0	12	3	0	0	0	22
1985-86	St. Louis Blues	23	2	0	2	39	....	....	....	....	....
	NHL Totals	**27**	**2**	**0**	**2**	**51**	**3**	**0**	**0**	**0**	**22**

Signed as a free agent by **Montreal**, March 15, 1984. Traded to **St. Louis** by **Montreal** for cash, September 30, 1985.

BARR, Dave

Right wing. Shoots right. 6'1", 195 lbs. Born, Toronto, Ont., November 30, 1960.

		Regular Season					Playoffs				
Season	Club	GP	G	A	Pts	PIM	GP	G	A	Pts	PIM
1981-82	Boston Bruins	2	0	0	0	0	5	1	0	1	0
1982-83	Boston Bruins	10	1	1	2	7	10	0	0	0	2
1983-84	New York Rangers	6	0	0	0	2	....	....	....	....	....
	St. Louis Blues	1	0	0	0	0	....	....	....	....	....
1984-85	St. Louis Blues	75	16	18	34	32	2	0	0	0	2
1985-86	St. Louis Blues	72	13	38	51	70	11	1	1	2	14
1986-87	St. Louis Blues	2	0	0	0	0	....	....	....	....	....
	Hartford Whalers	30	2	4	6	19	....	....	....	....	....
	Detroit Red Wings	37	13	13	26	49	13	1	0	1	14
1987-88	Detroit Red Wings	51	14	26	40	58	16	5	7	12	22
1988-89	Detroit Red Wings	73	27	32	59	69	6	3	1	4	6
1989-90	Detroit Red Wings	62	10	25	35	45	....	....	....	....	....
1990-91	Detroit Red Wings	70	18	22	40	55	....	....	....	....	....
1991-92	New Jersey Devils	41	6	12	18	32	....	....	....	....	....
1992-93	New Jersey Devils	62	6	8	14	61	5	1	0	1	6
1993-94	Dallas Stars	20	2	5	7	21	3	0	1	1	4
	NHL Totals	**614**	**128**	**204**	**332**	**520**	**71**	**12**	**10**	**22**	**70**

Signed as a free agent by **Boston**, September 28, 1981. Traded to **NY Rangers** by **Boston** for Dave Silk, October 5, 1983. Traded to **St. Louis** by **NY Rangers** with NY Rangers' 3rd round choice (Alan Perry) in 1984 Entry Draft and cash for Larry Patey and the rights to Bob Brooke, March 5, 1984. Traded to **Hartford** by **St. Louis** for Tim Bothwell, October 21, 1986. Traded to **Detroit** by **Hartford** for Randy Ladouceur, January 12, 1987. Transferred to **New Jersey** from **Detroit** with Randy McKay as compensation for Detroit's signing of free agent Troy Crowder, September 9, 1991. Signed as a free agent by **Dallas**, August 28, 1993. • Missed majority of 1993-94 season recovering from arthroscopic elbow surgery, October 13, 1993.

BARRAULT, Doug

Right wing. Shoots right. 6'2", 205 lbs. Born, Golden, B.C., April 21, 1970.
(Minnesota's 8th choice, 155th overall, in 1990 Entry Draft).

		Regular Season					Playoffs				
Season	Club	GP	G	A	Pts	PIM	GP	G	A	Pts	PIM
1992-93	Minnesota North Stars	2	0	0	0	2	....	....	....	....	....
1993-94	Florida Panthers	2	0	0	0	0	....	....	....	....	....
	NHL Totals	**4**	**0**	**0**	**0**	**2**	....	....	....	....	....

Transferred to **Dallas** after **Minnesota** franchise relocated, June 9, 1993. Claimed by **Florida** from **Dallas** in Expansion Draft, June 24, 1993.

BARRETT, Fred

Defense. Shoots left. 5'11", 195 lbs. Born, Ottawa, Ont., January 26, 1950.
(Minnesota's 2nd choice, 20th overall, in 1970 Amateur Draft).

Season	Club	GP	G	A	Pts	PIM	GP	G	A	Pts	PIM
		REGULAR SEASON					PLAYOFFS				
1970-71	Minnesota North Stars	57	0	13	13	75	....	....	....	....	....
1972-73	Minnesota North Stars	46	2	4	6	21	6	0	0	0	4
1973-74	Minnesota North Stars	40	0	7	7	12	....	....	....	....	....
1974-75	Minnesota North Stars	62	3	18	21	82	....	....	....	....	....
1975-76	Minnesota North Stars	79	2	9	11	66	....	....	....	....	....
1976-77	Minnesota North Stars	60	1	8	9	46	2	0	0	0	2
1977-78	Minnesota North Stars	79	0	15	15	59	....	....	....	....	....
1978-79	Minnesota North Stars	45	1	9	10	48	....	....	....	....	....
1979-80	Minnesota North Stars	80	8	14	22	71	14	0	0	0	22
1980-81	Minnesota North Stars	62	4	8	12	72	14	0	1	1	16
1981-82	Minnesota North Stars	69	1	15	16	89	4	0	1	1	16
1982-83	Minnesota North Stars	51	1	3	4	22	4	0	0	0	0
1983-84	Los Angeles Kings	15	2	0	2	8	....	....	....	....	....
	NHL Totals	**745**	**25**	**123**	**148**	**671**	**44**	**0**	**2**	**2**	**60**

• Brother of John

Traded to **Los Angeles** by **Minnesota** with Steve Christoff for Dave Lewis, October 3, 1983.

BARRETT, John

Defense. Shoots left. 6'1", 210 lbs. Born, Ottawa, Ont., July 1, 1958.
(Detroit's 10th choice, 129th overall, in 1978 Amateur Draft).

Season	Club	GP	G	A	Pts	PIM	GP	G	A	Pts	PIM
1980-81	Detroit Red Wings	56	3	10	13	60	....	....	....	....	....
1981-82	Detroit Red Wings	69	1	12	13	93	....	....	....	....	....
1982-83	Detroit Red Wings	79	4	10	14	74	....	....	....	....	....
1983-84	Detroit Red Wings	78	2	8	10	78	4	0	0	0	4
1984-85	Detroit Red Wings	71	6	19	25	117	3	0	1	1	11
1985-86	Detroit Red Wings	65	2	12	14	125	....	....	....	....	....
	Washington Capitals	14	0	3	3	12	9	2	1	3	35
1986-87	Washington Capitals	55	2	2	4	43	....	....	....	....	....
1987-88	Minnesota North Stars	1	0	1	1	2	....	....	....	....	....
	NHL Totals	**488**	**20**	**77**	**97**	**604**	**16**	**2**	**2**	**4**	**50**

• Brother of Fred

Traded to **Washington** by **Detroit** with Greg Smith for Darren Veitch, March 10, 1986.
• Suffered eventual career-ending knee injury in game vs. Vancouver, January 20, 1987. Traded to **Minnesota** by **Washington** for future considerations, February 22, 1988.

BARRIE, Doug

Defense. Shoots right. 5'9", 175 lbs. Born, Edmonton, Alta., October 2, 1946

Season	Club	GP	G	A	Pts	PIM	GP	G	A	Pts	PIM
1968-69	Pittsburgh Penguins	8	1	1	2	8	....	....	....	....	....
1970-71	Buffalo Sabres	75	4	23	27	168	....	....	....	....	....
1971-72	Buffalo Sabres	27	2	5	7	45	....	....	....	....	....
	Los Angeles Kings	48	3	13	16	47	....	....	....	....	....
	NHL Totals	**158**	**10**	**42**	**52**	**268**	....	....	....	....	....

Traded to **Toronto** by **Detroit** with Norm Ullman, Paul Henderson and Floyd Smith for Frank Mahovlich, Pete Stemkowski, Garry Unger and the rights to Carl Brewer, March 3, 1968. Traded to **Detroit** by **Toronto** for cash, June 6, 1968. Traded to **Pittsburgh** by **Detroit** for cash, October, 1968. Claimed by **Buffalo** from **Pittsburgh** in Expansion Draft, June 10, 1970. Traded to **Los Angeles** by **Buffalo** with Mike Keeler for Mike Byers and Larry Hillman, December 16, 1971.

BARRIE, Len

Center. Shoots left. 6', 200 lbs. Born, Kimberley, B.C., June 4, 1969.
(Edmonton's 7th choice, 124th overall, in 1988 Entry Draft).

Season	Club	GP	G	A	Pts	PIM	GP	G	A	Pts	PIM
1989-90	Philadelphia Flyers	1	0	0	0	0	....	....	....	....	....
1992-93	Philadelphia Flyers	8	2	2	4	9	....	....	....	....	....
1993-94	Florida Panthers	2	0	0	0	0	....	....	....	....	....
1994-95	Pittsburgh Penguins	48	3	11	14	66	4	1	0	1	8
1995-96	Pittsburgh Penguins	5	0	0	0	18	....	....	....	....	....
99-2000	Los Angeles Kings	46	5	8	13	56	....	....	....	....	....
	Florida Panthers	14	4	6	10	6	4	0	0	0	0
2000-01	Florida Panthers	60	5	18	23	135	....	....	....	....	....
	NHL Totals	**184**	**19**	**45**	**64**	**290**	**8**	**1**	**0**	**1**	**8**

Signed as a free agent by **Philadelphia**, February 28, 1990. Signed as a free agent by **Florida**, July 20, 1993. Signed as a free agent by **Pittsburgh**, August 15, 1994. Signed as a free agent by **Los Angeles**, July 9, 1999. Claimed on waivers by **Florida** from **Los Angeles**, March 10, 2000.

BARRY, Ed

Left wing. Shoots left. 5'10", 180 lbs. Born, Wellesley, MA, October 12, 1919.

Season	Club	GP	G	A	Pts	PIM	GP	G	A	Pts	PIM
1946-47	Boston Bruins	19	1	3	4	2	....	....	....	....	....
	NHL Totals	**19**	**1**	**3**	**4**	**2**	....	....	....	....	....

Signed as a free agent by **Boston**, January 9, 1947.

BARRY, Marty

HHOF

Center. Shoots left. 5'11", 175 lbs. Born, Quebec City, Que., December 8, 1905.

Season	Club	GP	G	A	Pts	PIM	GP	G	A	Pts	PIM
1927-28	New York Americans	9	1	0	1	2	....	....	....	....	....
1929-30	Boston Bruins	44	18	15	33	34	6	3	3	*6	14
1930-31	Boston Bruins	44	20	11	31	26	5	1	1	2	4
1931-32	Boston Bruins	48	21	17	38	22	....	....	....	....	....
1932-33	Boston Bruins	47	24	13	37	40	5	2	2	4	6
1933-34	Boston Bruins	48	27	12	39	12	....	....	....	....	....
1934-35	Boston Bruins	48	20	20	40	33	4	0	0	0	2
1935-36 ♦	Detroit Red Wings	48	21	19	40	16	7	2	4	6	6
1936-37 ♦	Detroit Red Wings	47	17	27	44	6	10	*4	*7	*11	2
1937-38	Detroit Red Wings	48	9	20	29	34	....	....	....	....	....
1938-39	Detroit Red Wings	48	13	28	41	4	6	3	1	4	0
1939-40	Montreal Canadiens	30	4	10	14	2	....	....	....	....	....
	NHL Totals	**509**	**195**	**192**	**387**	**231**	**43**	**15**	**18**	**33**	**34**

NHL First All-Star Team (1937) • Lady Byng Trophy (1937)

Played in NHL All-Star Game (1937)

Signed as a free agent by **NY Americans**, October 27, 1927. Claimed by **Boston** from **NY Americans** (New Haven-Can-Am) in Inter-League Draft, May 13, 1929. Traded to **Detroit** by **Boston** with Art Giroux for Cooney Weiland and Walt Buswell, July 11, 1935. Signed as a free agent by **Montreal**, October 20, 1939.

BARRY, Ray

Center. Shoots left. 5'11", 170 lbs. Born, Boston, MA, October 4, 1928.

Season	Club	GP	G	A	Pts	PIM	GP	G	A	Pts	PIM
1951-52	Boston Bruins	18	1	2	3	6	....	....	....	....	....
	NHL Totals	**18**	**1**	**2**	**3**	**6**	....	....	....	....	....

Signed as a free agent by **Boston**, October 3, 1950.

BARTECKO, Lubos

Left wing. Shoots left. 5'11", 200 lbs. Born, Kezmarok, Czech., July 14, 1976.

Season	Club	GP	G	A	Pts	PIM	GP	G	A	Pts	PIM
1998-99	St. Louis Blues	32	5	11	16	6	5	0	0	0	2
99-2000	St. Louis Blues	67	16	23	39	51	7	1	1	2	0
2000-01	St. Louis Blues	50	5	8	13	12	....	....	....	....	....
2001-02	Atlanta Thrashers	71	13	14	27	30	....	....	....	....	....
2002-03	Atlanta Thrashers	37	7	9	16	8	....	....	....	....	....
	NHL Totals	**257**	**46**	**65**	**111**	**107**	**12**	**1**	**1**	**2**	**2**

Signed as a free agent by **St. Louis**, October 3, 1997. Traded to **Atlanta** by **St. Louis** for Buffalo's 4th round choice (previously acquired, St. Louis selected Igor Valeyev) in 2001 Entry Draft, June 23, 2001. • Missed majority of 2002-03 season recovering from wrist (November 2, 2002 vs. Florida) and groin (January 13, 2003 vs. Philadelphia) injuries.

BARTEL, Robin

Defense. Shoots left. 6', 200 lbs. Born, Drake, Sask., May 16, 1961.

Season	Club	GP	G	A	Pts	PIM	GP	G	A	Pts	PIM
1985-86	Calgary Flames	1	0	0	0	0	6	0	0	0	16
1986-87	Vancouver Canucks	40	0	1	1	14	....	....	....	....	....
	NHL Totals	**41**	**0**	**1**	**1**	**14**	**6**	**0**	**0**	**0**	**16**

Signed as a free agent by **Calgary**, July 1, 1985. Signed as a free agent by **Vancouver**, June 27, 1986.

BARTLETT, Jim

Left wing. Shoots left. 5'9", 165 lbs. Born, Verdun, Que., May 27, 1932.

Season	Club	GP	G	A	Pts	PIM	GP	G	A	Pts	PIM
1954-55	Montreal Canadiens	2	0	0	0	4	2	0	0	0	0
1955-56	New York Rangers	12	0	1	1	8	....	....	....	....	....
1958-59	New York Rangers	70	11	9	20	118	....	....	....	....	....
1959-60	New York Rangers	44	8	4	12	48	....	....	....	....	....
1960-61	Boston Bruins	63	15	9	24	95	....	....	....	....	....
	NHL Totals	**191**	**34**	**23**	**57**	**273**	**2**	**0**	**0**	**0**	**0**

Claimed by **NY Rangers** from **Montreal** in Intra-League Draft, June, 1955. Claimed by **Boston** from **NY Rangers** in Intra-League Draft, June 8, 1960. Traded to **Providence** (AHL) by **Boston** for cash, August, 1961.

BARTON, Cliff

Right wing. Shoots right. 5'7", 155 lbs. Born, Sault Ste. Marie, MI, September 3, 1907.

Season	Club	GP	G	A	Pts	PIM	GP	G	A	Pts	PIM
1929-30	Pittsburgh Pirates	39	4	2	6	4	....	....	....	....	....
1930-31	Philadelphia Quakers	43	6	7	13	18	....	....	....	....	....
1939-40	New York Rangers	3	0	0	0	0	....	....	....	....	....
	NHL Totals	**85**	**10**	**9**	**19**	**22**	....	....	....	....	....

Transferred to **Philadelphia** after **Pittsburgh** franchise relocated, September 27, 1930. Claimed by **NY Rangers** from **Philadelphia** in Dispersal Draft, September 26, 1931. Traded to **Hershey** (IAHL) by **NY Rangers** for cash, April 4, 1940.

BARTOS, Peter

Left wing. Shoots right. 6', 185 lbs. Born, Martin, Czech., September 5, 1973.
(Minnesota's 7th choice, 214th overall, in 2000 Entry Draft).

Season	Club	GP	G	A	Pts	PIM	GP	G	A	Pts	PIM
2000-01	Minnesota Wild	13	4	2	6	6	....	....	....	....	....
	NHL Totals	**13**	**4**	**2**	**6**	**6**	....	....	....	....	....

BARTOVIC, Milan

Right wing. Shoots left. 5'11", 192 lbs. Born, Trencin, Czech., April 9, 1981.
(Buffalo's 2nd choice, 35th overall, in 1999 Entry Draft).

Season	Club	GP	G	A	Pts	PIM	GP	G	A	Pts	PIM
2002-03	Buffalo Sabres	3	1	0	1	0	....	....	....	....	....
	NHL Totals	**3**	**1**	**0**	**1**	**0**	....	....	....	....	....

BASHKIROV, Andrei

Left wing. Shoots left. 6', 215 lbs. Born, Shelekhov, USSR, June 22, 1970.
(Montreal's 4th choice, 132nd overall, in 1998 Entry Draft).

Season	Club	GP	G	A	Pts	PIM	GP	G	A	Pts	PIM
1998-99	Montreal Canadiens	10	0	0	0	0	....	....	....	....	....
99-2000	Montreal Canadiens	2	0	0	0	0	....	....	....	....	....
2000-01	Montreal Canadiens	18	0	3	3	0	....	....	....	....	....
	NHL Totals	**30**	**0**	**3**	**3**	**0**	....	....	....	....	....

BASSEN, Bob

Center. Shoots left. 5'10", 185 lbs. Born, Calgary, Alta., May 6, 1965.

Season	Club	GP	G	A	Pts	PIM	GP	G	A	Pts	PIM
1985-86	New York Islanders	11	2	1	3	6	3	0	1	1	0

Season	Club	REGULAR SEASON					PLAYOFFS				
		GP	G	A	Pts	PIM	GP	G	A	Pts	PIM
1986-87	New York Islanders	77	7	10	17	89	14	1	2	3	21
1987-88	New York Islanders	77	6	16	22	99	6	0	1	1	23
1988-89	New York Islanders	19	1	4	5	21	....	....	....	....	....
	Chicago Blackhawks	49	4	12	16	62	10	1	1	2	34
1989-90	Chicago Blackhawks	6	1	1	2	8	1	0	0	0	2
1990-91	St. Louis Blues	79	16	18	34	183	13	1	3	4	24
1991-92	St. Louis Blues	79	7	25	32	167	6	0	2	2	4
1992-93	St. Louis Blues	53	9	10	19	63	11	0	0	0	10
1993-94	St. Louis Blues	46	2	7	9	44	....	....	....	....	....
	Quebec Nordiques	37	11	8	19	55	....	....	....	....	....
1994-95	Quebec Nordiques	47	12	15	27	33	5	2	4	6	0
1995-96	Dallas Stars	13	0	1	1	15	....	....	....	....	....
1996-97	Dallas Stars	46	5	7	12	41	7	3	1	4	4
1997-98	Dallas Stars	58	3	4	7	57	17	1	0	1	12
1998-99	Calgary Flames	41	1	2	3	35	....	....	....	....	....
99-2000	St. Louis Blues	27	1	3	4	26	....	....	....	....	....
	NHL Totals	**765**	**88**	**144**	**232**	**1004**	**93**	**9**	**15**	**24**	**134**

• Son of Hank

Signed as a free agent by **NY Islanders**, October 19, 1984. Traded to **Chicago** by **NY Islanders** with Steve Konroyd for Marc Bergevin and Gary Nylund, November 25, 1988. Claimed by **St. Louis** from **Chicago** in Waiver Draft, October 1, 1990. Traded to **Quebec** by **St. Louis** with Garth Butcher and Ron Sutter for Steve Duchesne and Denis Chasse, January 23, 1994. Signed as a free agent by **Dallas**, August 10, 1995. Traded to **Calgary** by **Dallas** for Aaron Gavey, July 14, 1998. Signed as a free agent by **Dallas**, December 9, 1999. Claimed on waivers by **St. Louis** from **Dallas**, December 11, 1999.

BAST, Ryan

Defense. Shoots left. 6'2", 190 lbs. Born, Spruce Grove, Alta., August 27, 1975.

Season	Club	GP	G	A	Pts	PIM	GP	G	A	Pts	PIM
1998-99	Philadelphia Flyers	2	0	1	1	0	....	....	....	....	....
	NHL Totals	**2**	**0**	**1**	**1**	**0**	....	....	....	....	....

Signed as a free agent by **Philadelphia**, May 18, 1998. • Calgary Flames filed official protest contesting Philadelphia's signing of Bast under the contention that he was property of AHL's Saint John Flames, May 20, 1998. • NHL ruled that Bast was not under contract to Calgary since he was never drafted and had no NHL clause in contract, May 22, 1998. NHL also ruled that Bast was not property of Philadelphia because Flyers' contract offer exceeded NHL rookie salary cap, May 22, 1998. A compromise was reached that traded Bast to **Philadelphia** by **Calgary** with Calgary's 8th round choice (David Nystrom) in 1999 Entry Draft for Philadelphia's 3rd round choice (later traded to NY Rangers – NY Rangers selected Patrick Aufiero) in 1999 Entry Draft, October 13, 1998. Signed as a free agent by **Carolina**, July 16, 2002. Traded to **Philadelphia** by **Carolina** with Sami Kapanen for Pavel Brendl and Bruno St. Jacques, February 7, 2003.

BATES, Shawn

Center. Shoots right. 6', 205 lbs. Born, Melrose, MA, April 3, 1975.
(Boston's 4th choice, 103rd overall, in 1993 Entry Draft).

Season	Club	GP	G	A	Pts	PIM	GP	G	A	Pts	PIM
1997-98	Boston Bruins	13	2	0	2	2	....	....	....	....	....
1998-99	Boston Bruins	33	5	4	9	2	12	0	0	0	4
99-2000	Boston Bruins	44	5	7	12	14	....	....	....	....	....
2000-01	Boston Bruins	45	2	3	5	26	....	....	....	....	....
2001-02	New York Islanders	71	17	35	52	30	7	2	4	6	11
2002-03	New York Islanders	74	13	29	42	52	5	1	0	1	0
	NHL Totals	**280**	**44**	**78**	**122**	**126**	**24**	**3**	**4**	**7**	**15**

Signed as a free agent by **NY Islanders**, July 8, 2001.

BATHE, Frank

Defense. Shoots left. 6'1", 185 lbs. Born, Oshawa, Ont., September 27, 1954.

Season	Club	GP	G	A	Pts	PIM	GP	G	A	Pts	PIM
1974-75	Detroit Red Wings	19	0	3	3	31	....	....	....	....	....
1975-76	Detroit Red Wings	7	0	1	1	9	....	....	....	....	....
1977-78	Philadelphia Flyers	1	0	0	0	0	....	....	....	....	....
1978-79	Philadelphia Flyers	21	1	3	4	76	6	1	0	1	12
1979-80	Philadelphia Flyers	47	0	7	7	111	1	0	0	0	0
1980-81	Philadelphia Flyers	44	0	3	3	175	12	0	3	3	16
1981-82	Philadelphia Flyers	28	1	3	4	68	4	0	0	0	2
1982-83	Philadelphia Flyers	57	1	8	9	72	3	0	0	0	12
1983-84	Philadelphia Flyers	....	....	....	....	....	1	0	0	0	0
	NHL Totals	**224**	**3**	**28**	**31**	**542**	**27**	**1**	**3**	**4**	**42**

Signed as a free agent by **Detroit**, October 10, 1974. Traded to **Port Huron** (IHL) by **Detroit** (Kalamazoo-IHL) for Henry Lehvonen, November, 1975. Signed as a free agent by **Philadelphia**, October 7, 1977. • Suffered eventual career-ending back injury in training camp, October 15, 1983.

BATHGATE, Andy

HHOF

Right wing. Shoots right. 6', 180 lbs. Born, Winnipeg, Man., August 28, 1932.

Season	Club	GP	G	A	Pts	PIM	GP	G	A	Pts	PIM
1952-53	New York Rangers	18	0	1	1	6	....	....	....	....	....
1953-54	New York Rangers	20	2	2	4	18	....	....	....	....	....
1954-55	New York Rangers	70	20	20	40	37	....	....	....	....	....
1955-56	New York Rangers	70	19	47	66	59	5	1	2	3	2
1956-57	New York Rangers	70	27	50	77	60	5	2	0	2	27
1957-58	New York Rangers	65	30	48	78	42	6	5	3	8	6
1958-59	New York Rangers	70	40	48	88	48	....	....	....	....	....
1959-60	New York Rangers	70	26	48	74	28	....	....	....	....	....
1960-61	New York Rangers	70	29	48	77	22	....	....	....	....	....
1961-62	New York Rangers	70	28	*56	*84	44	6	1	2	3	4
1962-63	New York Rangers	70	35	46	81	54	....	....	....	....	....
1963-64	New York Rangers	56	16	*43	59	26	....	....	....	....	....
	♦ Toronto Maple Leafs	15	3	*15	18	8	14	5	4	9	25
1964-65	Toronto Maple Leafs	55	16	29	45	34	6	1	0	1	6
1965-66	Detroit Red Wings	70	15	32	47	25	12	*6	3	9	6
1966-67	Detroit Red Wings	60	8	23	31	24	....	....	....	....	....
1967-68	Pittsburgh Penguins	74	20	39	59	55	....	....	....	....	....
1970-71	Pittsburgh Penguins	76	15	29	44	34	....	....	....	....	....
	NHL Totals	**1069**	**349**	**624**	**973**	**624**	**54**	**21**	**14**	**35**	**76**

• Brother of Frank • NHL Second All-Star Team (1958, 1963) • NHL First All-Star Team (1959, 1962) • Hart Trophy (1959)

Played in NHL All-Star Game (1957, 1958, 1959, 1960, 1961, 1962, 1963, 1964)

Traded to **NY Rangers** by **Cleveland** (AHL) with Vic Howe for Glen Sonmor and Eric Pogue, November 15, 1954. Traded to **Toronto** by **NY Rangers** with Don McKenney for Dick Duff, Bob Nevin, Arnie Brown, Bill Collins and Rod Seiling, February 22, 1964. Traded to **Detroit** by **Toronto** with Billy Harris and Gary Jarrett for Marcel Pronovost, Eddie Joyal, Larry Jeffrey, Lowell McDonald and Aut Erickson, May 20, 1965. Claimed by **Pittsburgh** from **Detroit** in Expansion Draft, June 6, 1967. Loaned to **Vancouver** (WHL) by **Pittsburgh** for the 1968-69 season for future considerations, October, 1968. Loaned to **Vancouver** (WHL) by **Pittsburgh** for the 1969-70 season with the trade of Paul Andrea and John Arbour for Bryan Hextall Jr., May 20, 1969.

BATHGATE, Frank

Center. Shoots right. 5'10", 162 lbs. Born, Winnipeg, Man., February 14, 1930.

Season	Club	GP	G	A	Pts	PIM	GP	G	A	Pts	PIM
1952-53	New York Rangers	2	0	0	0	2	....	....	....	....	....
	NHL Totals	**2**	**0**	**0**	**0**	**2**	....	....	....	....	....

• Brother of Andy

BATTAGLIA, Bates

Left wing. Shoots left. 6'2", 205 lbs. Born, Chicago, IL, December 13, 1975.
(Anaheim's 6th choice, 132nd overall, in 1994 Entry Draft).

Season	Club	GP	G	A	Pts	PIM	GP	G	A	Pts	PIM
1997-98	Carolina Hurricanes	33	2	4	6	10	....	....	....	....	....
1998-99	Carolina Hurricanes	60	7	11	18	97	6	0	3	3	8
99-2000	Carolina Hurricanes	77	16	18	34	39	....	....	....	....	....
2000-01	Carolina Hurricanes	80	12	15	27	76	6	0	2	2	2
2001-02	Carolina Hurricanes	82	21	25	46	44	23	5	9	14	14
2002-03	Carolina Hurricanes	70	5	14	19	90	....	....	....	....	....
	Colorado Avalanche	13	1	5	6	10	7	0	2	2	4
	NHL Totals	**415**	**64**	**92**	**156**	**366**	**42**	**5**	**16**	**21**	**28**

Traded to **Hartford** by **Anaheim** with Anaheim's 4th round choice (Josef Vasicek) in 1998 Entry Draft for Mark Janssens, March 18, 1997. Rights transferred to **Carolina** after **Hartford** franchise relocated, June 25, 1997. Traded to **Colorado** by **Carolina** for Radim Vrbata, March 11, 2003.

BATTERS, Jeff

Defense. Shoots right. 6'2", 215 lbs. Born, Victoria, B.C., October 23, 1970.
(St. Louis' 7th choice, 135th overall, in 1989 Entry Draft).

Season	Club	GP	G	A	Pts	PIM	GP	G	A	Pts	PIM
1993-94	St. Louis Blues	6	0	0	0	7	....	....	....	....	....
1994-95	St. Louis Blues	10	0	0	0	21	....	....	....	....	....
	NHL Totals	**16**	**0**	**0**	**0**	**28**	....	....	....	....	....

Signed as a free agent by **San Jose**, September 27, 1995. • Died from injuries suffered in automobile accident, August 23, 1996.

BATYRSHIN, Ruslan

Defense. Shoots left. 6'1", 185 lbs. Born, Moscow, USSR, February 19, 1975.
(Winnipeg's 4th choice, 79th overall, in 1993 Entry Draft).

Season	Club	GP	G	A	Pts	PIM	GP	G	A	Pts	PIM
1995-96	Los Angeles Kings	2	0	0	0	6	....	....	....	....	....
	NHL Totals	**2**	**0**	**0**	**0**	**6**	....	....	....	....	....

Rights traded to **Los Angeles** by **Winnipeg** with Winnipeg's 2nd round choice (Marian Cisar) in 1996 Entry Draft for Brent Thompson and cash, August 8, 1994.

BAUER, Bobby

HHOF

Right wing. Shoots right. 5'6", 150 lbs. Born, Waterloo, Ont., February 16, 1915.

Season	Club	GP	G	A	Pts	PIM	GP	G	A	Pts	PIM
1936-37	Boston Bruins	1	1	0	1	0	1	0	0	0	0
1937-38	Boston Bruins	48	20	14	34	9	3	0	0	0	2
1938-39♦	Boston Bruins	48	13	18	31	4	12	3	2	5	0
1939-40	Boston Bruins	48	17	26	43	2	6	1	0	1	2
1940-41♦	Boston Bruins	48	17	22	39	2	11	2	2	4	0
1941-42	Boston Bruins	36	13	22	35	11	....	....	....	....	....
1945-46	Boston Bruins	39	11	10	21	4	10	4	3	7	2
1946-47	Boston Bruins	58	30	24	54	4	5	1	1	2	0
1951-52	Boston Bruins	1	1	1	2	0	....	....	....	....	....
	NHL Totals	**327**	**123**	**137**	**260**	**36**	**48**	**11**	**8**	**19**	**6**

NHL Second All-Star Team (1939, 1940, 1941, 1947) • Lady Byng Trophy (1940, 1941, 1947)

Played in NHL All-Star Game (1939, 1947)

Claimed by **Boston** from **Syracuse** (IHL) in Inter-League Draft, May 11, 1935. • Played in game that Kraut Line had their jersey numbers retired, Boston vs. Chicago, March 18, 1952.

BAUMGARTNER, Ken

Left wing. Shoots left. 6'1", 205 lbs. Born, Flin Flon, Man., March 11, 1966.
(Buffalo's 12th choice, 245th overall, in 1985 Entry Draft).

Season	Club	GP	G	A	Pts	PIM	GP	G	A	Pts	PIM
1987-88	Los Angeles Kings	30	2	3	5	189	5	0	1	1	28
1988-89	Los Angeles Kings	49	1	3	4	288	5	0	0	0	8
1989-90	Los Angeles Kings	12	1	0	1	28	....	....	....	....	....
	New York Islanders	53	0	5	5	194	4	0	0	0	27
1990-91	New York Islanders	78	1	6	7	282	....	....	....	....	....
1991-92	New York Islanders	44	0	1	1	202	....	....	....	....	....
	Toronto Maple Leafs	11	0	0	0	23	....	....	....	....	....
1992-93	Toronto Maple Leafs	63	1	0	1	155	7	1	0	1	0
1993-94	Toronto Maple Leafs	64	4	4	8	185	10	0	0	0	18
1994-95	Toronto Maple Leafs	2	0	0	0	5	....	....	....	....	....

Season	Club	GP	G	A	Pts	PIM	GP	G	A	Pts	PIM
		REGULAR SEASON					PLAYOFFS				
1995-96	Toronto Maple Leafs	60	2	3	5	152	....	....	....	....	....
	Mighty Ducks of Anaheim	12	0	1	1	41	....	....	....	....	....
1996-97	Mighty Ducks of Anaheim	67	0	11	11	182	11	0	1	1	11
1997-98	Boston Bruins	82	0	1	1	199	6	0	0	0	14
1998-99	Boston Bruins	69	1	3	4	119	3	0	0	0	0
	NHL Totals	**696**	**13**	**41**	**54**	**2244**	**51**	**1**	**2**	**3**	**106**

Traded to **Los Angeles** by **Buffalo** with Sean McKenna and Larry Playfair for Brian Engblom and Doug Smith, January 30, 1986. Traded to **NY Islanders** by **Los Angeles** with Hubie McDonough for Mikko Makela, November 29, 1989. Traded to **Toronto** by **NY Islanders** with Dave McLlwain for Daniel Marois and Claude Loiselle, March 10, 1992. Traded to **Anaheim** by **Toronto** for Winnipeg's 4th round choice (previously acquired, later traded to Montreal – Montreal selected Kim Staal) in 1996 Entry Draft, March 20, 1996. Signed as a free agent by **Boston**, July 14, 1997.

BAUMGARTNER, Mike

Defense. Shoots left. 6'2", 195 lbs. Born, Roseau, MN, January 30, 1949.
(Chicago's 5th choice, 60th overall, in 1969 Amateur Draft).

Season	Club	GP	G	A	Pts	PIM	GP	G	A	Pts	PIM
1974-75	Kansas City Scouts	17	0	0	0	0	....	....	....	....	....
	NHL Totals	**17**	**0**	**0**	**0**	**0**	....	....	....	....	....

Traded to **Atlanta** by **Chicago** for Lynn Powis, August 30, 1973. Traded to **Montreal** by **Atlanta** for cash, May 27, 1974. Traded to **Kansas City** by **Montreal** for cash, August 22, 1974.
• Suffered eventual career-ending eye injury in game vs. Vancouver, December 14, 1974.

BAUMGARTNER, Nolan

Defense. Shoots right. 6'2", 205 lbs. Born, Calgary, Alta., March 23, 1976.
(Washington's 1st choice, 10th overall, in 1994 Entry Draft).

Season	Club	GP	G	A	Pts	PIM	GP	G	A	Pts	PIM
1995-96	Washington Capitals	1	0	0	0	0	1	0	0	0	10
1997-98	Washington Capitals	4	0	1	1	0	....	....	....	....	....
1998-99	Washington Capitals	5	0	0	0	0	....	....	....	....	....
99-2000	Washington Capitals	8	0	1	1	2	....	....	....	....	....
2000-01	Chicago Blackhawks	8	0	0	0	6	....	....	....	....	....
2002-03	Vancouver Canucks	8	1	2	3	4	2	0	0	0	0
	NHL Totals	**34**	**1**	**4**	**5**	**12**	**3**	**0**	**0**	**0**	**10**

Traded to **Chicago** by **Washington** for Remi Royer, July 20, 2000. Signed as a free agent by **Vancouver**, July 11, 2002.

BAUN, Bob

Defense. Shoots right. 5'9", 175 lbs. Born, Lanigan, Sask., September 9, 1936.

Season	Club	GP	G	A	Pts	PIM	GP	G	A	Pts	PIM
1956-57	Toronto Maple Leafs	20	0	5	5	37	....	....	....	....	....
1957-58	Toronto Maple Leafs	67	1	9	10	91	....	....	....	....	....
1958-59	Toronto Maple Leafs	51	1	8	9	87	12	0	0	0	24
1959-60	Toronto Maple Leafs	61	8	9	17	59	10	1	0	1	17
1960-61	Toronto Maple Leafs	70	1	14	15	70	3	0	0	0	8
1961-62 ♦	Toronto Maple Leafs	65	4	11	15	94	12	0	3	3	19
1962-63 ♦	Toronto Maple Leafs	48	4	8	12	65	10	0	3	3	6
1963-64 ♦	Toronto Maple Leafs	52	4	14	18	113	14	2	3	5	*42
1964-65	Toronto Maple Leafs	70	0	18	18	160	6	0	1	1	14
1965-66	Toronto Maple Leafs	44	0	6	6	68	4	0	1	1	8
1966-67 ♦	Toronto Maple Leafs	54	2	8	10	83	10	0	0	0	4
1967-68	Oakland Seals	67	3	10	13	81	....	....	....	....	....
1968-69	Detroit Red Wings	76	4	16	20	121	....	....	....	....	....
1969-70	Detroit Red Wings	71	1	18	19	112	4	0	0	0	6
1970-71	Detroit Red Wings	11	0	3	3	24	....	....	....	....	....
	Toronto Maple Leafs	58	1	17	18	123	6	0	1	1	19
1971-72	Toronto Maple Leafs	74	2	12	14	101	5	0	0	0	4
1972-73	Toronto Maple Leafs	5	1	1	2	4	....	....	....	....	....
	NHL Totals	**964**	**37**	**187**	**224**	**1493**	**96**	**3**	**12**	**15**	**171**

Played in NHL All-Star Game (1962, 1963, 1964, 1965, 1968)

Claimed by **California** (Oakland) from **Toronto** in Expansion Draft, June 6, 1967. Traded to **Detroit** by **Oakland** with Ron Harris for Gary Jarrett, Doug Roberts, Howie Young and Chris Worthy, May 27, 1968. Claimed on waivers by **Buffalo** from **Detroit**, November 3, 1970. Traded to **St. Louis** by **Buffalo** for Larry Keenan and Jean-Guy Talbot, November 4, 1970. Traded to **Toronto** by **St. Louis** for Brit Selby, November 13, 1970. • Suffered career-ending neck injury in game vs. Detroit, October 21, 1972.

BAUTIN, Sergei

Defense. Shoots left. 6'3", 200 lbs. Born, Rogachev, USSR, March 11, 1967.
(Winnipeg's 1st choice, 17th overall, in 1992 Entry Draft).

Season	Club	GP	G	A	Pts	PIM	GP	G	A	Pts	PIM
1992-93	Winnipeg Jets	71	5	18	23	96	6	0	0	0	2
1993-94	Winnipeg Jets	59	0	7	7	78	....	....	....	....	....
	Detroit Red Wings	1	0	0	0	0	....	....	....	....	....
1995-96	San Jose Sharks	1	0	0	0	2	....	....	....	....	....
	NHL Totals	**132**	**5**	**25**	**30**	**176**	**6**	**0**	**0**	**0**	**2**

Traded to **Detroit** by **Winnipeg** with Bob Essensa for Tim Cheveldae and Dallas Drake, March 8, 1994. Signed as a free agent by **San Jose**, October 12, 1995.

BAWA, Robin

Right wing. Shoots right. 6'2", 214 lbs. Born, Chemainus, B.C., March 26, 1966.

Season	Club	GP	G	A	Pts	PIM	GP	G	A	Pts	PIM
1989-90	Washington Capitals	5	1	0	1	6	....	....	....	....	....
1991-92	Vancouver Canucks	2	0	0	0	0	1	0	0	0	0
1992-93	San Jose Sharks	42	5	0	5	47	....	....	....	....	....
1993-94	Mighty Ducks of Anaheim	12	0	1	1	7	....	....	....	....	....
	NHL Totals	**61**	**6**	**1**	**7**	**60**	**1**	**0**	**0**	**0**	**0**

Signed as a free agent by **Washington**, May 22, 1987. Traded to **Vancouver** by **Washington** for cash, July 31, 1991. Traded to **San Jose** by **Vancouver** for Rick Lessard, December 15, 1992. Claimed by **Anaheim** from **San Jose** in Expansion Draft, June 24, 1993. Signed as a free agent by **Dallas**, July 22, 1994.

BAXTER, Paul

Defense. Shoots right. 5'11", 200 lbs. Born, Winnipeg, Man., October 28, 1955.
(Pittsburgh's 3rd choice, 49th overall, in 1975 Amateur Draft).

Season	Club	GP	G	A	Pts	PIM	GP	G	A	Pts	PIM
1979-80	Quebec Nordiques	61	7	13	20	145	....	....	....	....	....
1980-81	Pittsburgh Penguins	51	5	14	19	204	5	0	1	1	28
1981-82	Pittsburgh Penguins	76	9	34	43	*409	5	0	0	0	14
1982-83	Pittsburgh Penguins	75	11	21	32	238	....	....	....	....	....
1983-84	Calgary Flames	74	7	20	27	182	11	0	2	2	37
1984-85	Calgary Flames	70	5	14	19	126	4	0	1	1	18
1985-86	Calgary Flames	47	4	3	7	194	13	0	1	1	55
1986-87	Calgary Flames	18	0	2	2	66	2	0	0	0	10
	NHL Totals	**472**	**48**	**121**	**169**	**1564**	**40**	**0**	**5**	**5**	**162**

Reclaimed by **Pittsburgh** from **Quebec** prior to Expansion Draft, June 9, 1979. Claimed as a priority selection by **Quebec** prior to Expansion Draft, June 9, 1979. Signed as a free agent by **Pittsburgh**, August 7, 1980. Signed as a free agent by **Calgary**, September 29, 1983.

BAYDA, Ryan

Left wing. Shoots left. 5'11", 185 lbs. Born, Saskatoon, Sask., December 9, 1980.
(Carolina's 2nd choice, 80th overall, in 2000 Entry Draft).

Season	Club	GP	G	A	Pts	PIM	GP	G	A	Pts	PIM
2002-03	Carolina Hurricanes	25	4	10	14	16	....	....	....	....	....
	NHL Totals	**25**	**4**	**10**	**14**	**16**	....	....	....	....	....

BEADLE, Sandy

Left wing. Shoots left. 6'2", 185 lbs. Born, Regina, Sask., July 12, 1960.
(Winnipeg's 9th choice, 149th overall, in 1980 Entry Draft).

Season	Club	GP	G	A	Pts	PIM	GP	G	A	Pts	PIM
1980-81	Winnipeg Jets	6	1	0	1	2	....	....	....	....	....
	NHL Totals	**6**	**1**	**0**	**1**	**2**	....	....	....	....	....

BEATON, Frank

Left wing. Shoots left. 5'10", 200 lbs. Born, Antigonish, N.S., April 28, 1953.

Season	Club	GP	G	A	Pts	PIM	GP	G	A	Pts	PIM
1978-79	New York Rangers	2	0	0	0	0	....	....	....	....	....
1979-80	New York Rangers	23	1	1	2	43	....	....	....	....	....
	NHL Totals	**25**	**1**	**1**	**2**	**43**	....	....	....	....	....

Signed as a free agent by **NY Rangers**, July 28, 1978. Traded to **Calgary** by **NY Rangers** for Dale Lewis, November 18, 1980. Signed as a free agent by **NY Islanders**, August 25, 1981. Traded to **Minnesota** by **NY Islanders** for future considerations, September 27, 1982.

BEATTIE, Red

Left wing. Shoots left. 5'9", 170 lbs. Born, Ibstock, England, October 2, 1907.

Season	Club	GP	G	A	Pts	PIM	GP	G	A	Pts	PIM
1930-31	Boston Bruins	32	10	11	21	25	4	0	0	0	0
1931-32	Boston Bruins	1	0	0	0	0	....	....	....	....	....
1932-33	Boston Bruins	48	8	12	20	12	5	0	0	0	2
1933-34	Boston Bruins	48	9	13	22	26	....	....	....	....	....
1934-35	Boston Bruins	48	9	18	27	27	4	1	0	1	2
1935-36	Boston Bruins	48	14	18	32	27	2	0	0	0	2
1936-37	Boston Bruins	48	8	7	15	10	3	1	0	1	0
1937-38	Boston Bruins	14	0	0	0	0	....	....	....	....	....
	Detroit Red Wings	11	1	2	3	0	....	....	....	....	....
	New York Americans	19	3	4	7	5	6	2	2	4	2
1938-39	New York Americans	17	0	0	0	5	....	....	....	....	....
	NHL Totals	**334**	**62**	**85**	**147**	**137**	**24**	**4**	**2**	**6**	**8**

Traded to **NY Rangers** by **Vancouver** (PCHL) with Joe Jerwa for $25,000, May 6, 1930. Rights awarded to **Boston** by NHL to settle contract dispute, December 12, 1930. Traded to **Detroit** by **Boston** for Gord Pettinger, December 19, 1937. Traded to **NY Americans** by **Detroit** for Joe Lamb with NY Americans holding right of recall, January 24, 1938. • Lamb was recalled by NY Americans, October 9, 1938.

BEAUCHEMIN, Francois

Defense. Shoots left. 6', 206 lbs. Born, Sorel, Que., June 4, 1980.
(Montreal's 3rd choice, 75th overall, in 1998 Entry Draft).

Season	Club	GP	G	A	Pts	PIM	GP	G	A	Pts	PIM
2002-03	Montreal Canadiens	1	0	0	0	0	....	....	....	....	....
	NHL Totals	**1**	**0**	**0**	**0**	**0**	....	....	....	....	....

BEAUDIN, Norm

Right wing. Shoots right. 5'8", 165 lbs. Born, Montmartre, Sask., November 28, 1941.

Season	Club	GP	G	A	Pts	PIM	GP	G	A	Pts	PIM
1967-68	St. Louis Blues	13	1	1	2	4	....	....	....	....	....
1970-71	Minnesota North Stars	12	0	1	1	0	....	....	....	....	....
	NHL Totals	**25**	**1**	**2**	**3**	**4**	....	....	....	....	....

Claimed by **Detroit** from **Hull-Ottawa** (EPHL) in Inter-League Draft, June 4, 1963. Claimed by **St. Louis** from **Detroit** in Expansion Draft, June 6, 1967. Loaned to **Buffalo** (AHL) by **St. Louis** for the 1968-69 season for cash, September, 1968. Traded to **Buffalo** (AHL) by **St. Louis** with Norm Dennis for cash, May 13, 1969. Traded to **St. Louis** by **NY Rangers** (Buffalo-AHL) with Camille Henry for cash, June 27, 1969. Traded to **Montreal** by **St. Louis** with Bobby Schmautz for Ernie Wakely, June 27, 1969. Traded to **Minnesota** by **Montreal** for cash, June, 1970.

BEAUDOIN, Eric

Left wing. Shoots left. 6'5", 204 lbs. Born, Ottawa, Ont., May 3, 1980.
(Tampa Bay's 4th choice, 92nd overall, in 1998 Entry Draft).

Season	Club	GP	G	A	Pts	PIM	GP	G	A	Pts	PIM
2001-02	Florida Panthers	8	1	3	4	4	....	....	....	....	....
2002-03	Florida Panthers	15	0	1	1	25	....	....	....	....	....
	NHL Totals	**23**	**1**	**4**	**5**	**29**	....	....	....	....	....

Traded to **Florida** by **Tampa Bay** for Florida's 7th round choice (Marek Priechodsky) in 2000 Entry Draft, June 1, 2000.

BEAUDOIN, Serge

Defense. Shoots left. 6'2", 215 lbs. Born, Montreal, Que., November 30, 1952.
(Philadelphia's 7th choice, 103rd overall, in 1972 Amateur Draft).

Season	Club	GP	G	A	Pts	PIM	GP	G	A	Pts	PIM
		REGULAR SEASON					PLAYOFFS				
1979-80	Atlanta Flames	3	0	0	0	0	....	....	....	....	....
	NHL Totals	**3**	**0**	**0**	**0**	**0**	....	....	....	....	....

Signed as a free agent by **Atlanta**, August 15, 1979.

BEAUDOIN, Yves

Defense. Shoots right. 5'11", 180 lbs. Born, Pointe-aux-Trembles, Que., January 7, 1965.
(Washington's 6th choice, 203rd overall, in 1983 Entry Draft).

Season	Club	GP	G	A	Pts	PIM	GP	G	A	Pts	PIM
1985-86	Washington Capitals	4	0	0	0	0	....	....	....	....	....
1986-87	Washington Capitals	6	0	0	0	5	....	....	....	....	....
1987-88	Washington Capitals	1	0	0	0	0	....	....	....	....	....
	NHL Totals	**11**	**0**	**0**	**0**	**5**	....	....	....	....	....

BEAUFAIT, Mark

Center. Shoots right. 5'9", 170 lbs. Born, Livonia, MI, May 13, 1970.
(San Jose's 2nd choice, 7th overall, in 1991 Supplemental Draft).

Season	Club	GP	G	A	Pts	PIM	GP	G	A	Pts	PIM
1992-93	San Jose Sharks	5	1	0	1	0	....	....	....	....	....
	NHL Totals	**5**	**1**	**0**	**1**	**0**	....	....	....	....	....

Signed as a free agent by **Minnesota**, July 16, 2001.

BECK, Barry

Defense. Shoots left. 6'3", 216 lbs. Born, Vancouver, B.C., June 3, 1957.
(Colorado's 1st choice, 2nd overall, in 1977 Amateur Draft).

Season	Club	GP	G	A	Pts	PIM	GP	G	A	Pts	PIM
1977-78	Colorado Rockies	75	22	38	60	89	2	0	1	1	0
1978-79	Colorado Rockies	63	14	28	42	91	....	....	....	....	....
1979-80	Colorado Rockies	10	1	5	6	8	....	....	....	....	....
	New York Rangers	61	14	45	59	98	9	1	4	5	6
1980-81	New York Rangers	75	11	23	34	231	14	5	8	13	32
1981-82	New York Rangers	60	9	29	38	111	10	1	5	6	14
1982-83	New York Rangers	66	12	22	34	112	9	2	4	6	8
1983-84	New York Rangers	72	9	27	36	134	4	1	0	1	6
1984-85	New York Rangers	56	7	19	26	65	3	0	1	1	11
1985-86	New York Rangers	25	4	8	12	24	....	....	....	....	....
1989-90	Los Angeles Kings	52	1	7	8	53	....	....	....	....	....
	NHL Totals	**615**	**104**	**251**	**355**	**1016**	**51**	**10**	**23**	**33**	**77**

Played in NHL All-Star Game (1978, 1979, 1980, 1981, 1982)

Traded to **NY Rangers** by **Colorado** for Pat Hickey, Lucien Deblois, Mike McEwen, Dean Turner and future considerations (Bobby Crawford, January 15, 1980), November 2, 1979. Traded to **Los Angeles** by **NY Rangers** for cash, September 1, 1989.

BECKETT, Bob

Center. Shoots left. 6', 185 lbs. Born, Unionville, Ont., April 8, 1936.

Season	Club	GP	G	A	Pts	PIM	GP	G	A	Pts	PIM
1956-57	Boston Bruins	18	0	3	3	2	....	....	....	....	....
1957-58	Boston Bruins	9	0	0	0	2	....	....	....	....	....
1961-62	Boston Bruins	34	7	2	9	14	....	....	....	....	....
1963-64	Boston Bruins	7	0	1	1	0	....	....	....	....	....
	NHL Totals	**68**	**7**	**6**	**13**	**18**	....	....	....	....	....

BEDARD, James

Defense. Shoots left. 6', 180 lbs. Born, Admiral, Sask., November 19, 1927.

Season	Club	GP	G	A	Pts	PIM	GP	G	A	Pts	PIM
1949-50	Chicago Black Hawks	5	0	0	0	2	....	....	....	....	....
1950-51	Chicago Black Hawks	17	1	1	2	6	....	....	....	....	....
	NHL Totals	**22**	**1**	**1**	**2**	**8**	....	....	....	....	....

BEDDOES, Clayton

Center. Shoots left. 5'11", 190 lbs. Born, Bentley, Alta., November 10, 1970.

Season	Club	GP	G	A	Pts	PIM	GP	G	A	Pts	PIM
1995-96	Boston Bruins	39	1	6	7	44	....	....	....	....	....
1996-97	Boston Bruins	21	1	2	3	13	....	....	....	....	....
	NHL Totals	**60**	**2**	**8**	**10**	**57**	....	....	....	....	....

Signed as a free agent by **Boston**, June 2, 1994. Signed as a free agent by **Ottawa**, July 28, 1997.

BEDNAR, Jaroslav

Right wing. Shoots right. 5'11", 198 lbs. Born, Prague, Czech., November 8, 1976.
(Los Angeles' 4th choice, 51st overall, in 2001 Entry Draft).

Season	Club	GP	G	A	Pts	PIM	GP	G	A	Pts	PIM
2001-02	Los Angeles Kings	22	4	2	6	8	3	0	0	0	0
2002-03	Los Angeles Kings	15	0	9	9	4	....	....	....	....	....
	Florida Panthers	52	5	13	18	14	....	....	....	....	....
	NHL Totals	**89**	**9**	**24**	**33**	**26**	**3**	**0**	**0**	**0**	**0**

Traded to **Florida** by **Los Angeles** with Andreas Lilja for Dmitry Yushkevich and NY Islanders' 5th round choice (previously acquired, Los Angeles selected Brady Murray) in 2003 Entry Draft, November 26, 2002.

BEDNARSKI, John

Defense. Shoots left. 5'10", 195 lbs. Born, Thunder Bay, Ont., July 4, 1952.

Season	Club	GP	G	A	Pts	PIM	GP	G	A	Pts	PIM
1974-75	New York Rangers	35	1	10	11	37	1	0	0	0	17
1975-76	New York Rangers	59	1	8	9	77	....	....	....	....	....
1976-77	New York Rangers	5	0	0	0	0	....	....	....	....	....
1979-80	Edmonton Oilers	1	0	0	0	0	....	....	....	....	....
	NHL Totals	**100**	**2**	**18**	**20**	**114**	**1**	**0**	**0**	**0**	**17**

Signed as a free agent by **NY Rangers**, September, 1972. Signed as a free agent by **Edmonton**, July 15, 1979. Signed as a free agent by **Buffalo**, June 26, 1980.

BEECH, Kris

Center. Shoots left. 6'3", 199 lbs. Born, Salmon Arm, B.C., February 5, 1981.
(Washington's 1st choice, 7th overall, in 1999 Entry Draft).

Season	Club	GP	G	A	Pts	PIM	GP	G	A	Pts	PIM
2000-01	Washington Capitals	4	0	0	0	2	....	....	....	....	....
2001-02	Pittsburgh Penguins	79	10	15	25	45	....	....	....	....	....
2002-03	Pittsburgh Penguins	12	0	1	1	6	....	....	....	....	....
	NHL Totals	**95**	**10**	**16**	**26**	**53**	....	....	....	....	....

Traded to **Pittsburgh** by **Washington** with Michal Sivek, Ross Lupaschuk and future considerations for Jaromir Jagr and Frantisek Kucera, July 11, 2001.

BEERS, Bob

Defense. Shoots right. 6'2", 200 lbs. Born, Pittsburgh, PA, May 20, 1967.
(Boston's 10th choice, 210th overall, in 1985 Entry Draft).

Season	Club	GP	G	A	Pts	PIM	GP	G	A	Pts	PIM
1989-90	Boston Bruins	3	0	1	1	6	14	1	1	2	18
1990-91	Boston Bruins	16	0	1	1	10	6	0	0	0	4
1991-92	Boston Bruins	31	0	5	5	29	1	0	0	0	0
1992-93	Tampa Bay Lightning	64	12	24	36	70	....	....	....	....	....
1993-94	Tampa Bay Lightning	16	1	5	6	12	....	....	....	....	....
	Edmonton Oilers	66	10	27	37	74	....	....	....	....	....
1994-95	New York Islanders	22	2	7	9	6	....	....	....	....	....
1995-96	New York Islanders	13	0	5	5	10	....	....	....	....	....
1996-97	Boston Bruins	27	3	4	7	8	....	....	....	....	....
	NHL Totals	**258**	**28**	**79**	**107**	**225**	**21**	**1**	**1**	**2**	**22**

Traded to **Tampa Bay** by **Boston** for Stephane Richer, October 28, 1992. Traded to **Edmonton** by **Tampa Bay** for Chris Joseph, November 11, 1993. Signed as a free agent by **NY Islanders**, August 29, 1994. Signed as a free agent by **Boston**, August 5, 1996.

BEERS, Eddy

Left wing. Shoots left. 6'2", 195 lbs. Born, Merritt, B.C., October 12, 1959.

Season	Club	GP	G	A	Pts	PIM	GP	G	A	Pts	PIM
1981-82	Calgary Flames	5	1	1	2	21	....	....	....	....	....
1982-83	Calgary Flames	41	11	15	26	21	8	1	1	2	27
1983-84	Calgary Flames	73	36	39	75	88	11	2	5	7	12
1984-85	Calgary Flames	74	28	40	68	94	3	1	0	1	0
1985-86	Calgary Flames	33	11	10	21	8	....	....	....	....	....
	St. Louis Blues	24	7	11	18	24	19	3	4	7	8
	NHL Totals	**250**	**94**	**116**	**210**	**256**	**41**	**7**	**10**	**17**	**47**

Signed as a free agent by **Calgary**, April 1, 1982. Traded to **St. Louis** by **Calgary** with Charlie Bourgeois and Gino Cavallini for Joe Mullen, Terry Johnson and Rik Wilson, February 1, 1986.
• Suffered eventual career-ending back injury in training camp, September 23, 1986.

BEGIN, Steve

Center. Shoots left. 5'11", 190 lbs. Born, Trois-Rivieres, Que., June 14, 1978.
(Calgary's 3rd choice, 40th overall, in 1996 Entry Draft).

Season	Club	GP	G	A	Pts	PIM	GP	G	A	Pts	PIM
1997-98	Calgary Flames	5	0	0	0	23	....	....	....	....	....
99-2000	Calgary Flames	13	1	1	2	18	....	....	....	....	....
2000-01	Calgary Flames	4	0	0	0	21	....	....	....	....	....
2001-02	Calgary Flames	51	7	5	12	79	....	....	....	....	....
2002-03	Calgary Flames	50	3	1	4	51	....	....	....	....	....
	NHL Totals	**123**	**11**	**7**	**18**	**192**	....	....	....	....	....

Traded to **Buffalo** by **Calgary** with Chris Drury for Steve Reinprecht and Rhett Warrener, July 3, 2003.

BEHLING, Dick

Defense. Shoots right. 6'1", 195 lbs. Born, Berlin, Ont., March 16, 1916.

Season	Club	GP	G	A	Pts	PIM	GP	G	A	Pts	PIM
1940-41	Detroit Red Wings	3	0	0	0	0	....	....	....	....	....
1942-43	Detroit Red Wings	2	1	0	1	2	....	....	....	....	....
	NHL Totals	**5**	**1**	**0**	**1**	**2**	....	....	....	....	....

Signed as a free agent by **Detroit**, October 16, 1940.

BEISLER, Frank

Defense. Shoots left. 6'2", 190 lbs. Born, New Haven, CT, October 18, 1913.

Season	Club	GP	G	A	Pts	PIM	GP	G	A	Pts	PIM
1936-37	New York Americans	1	0	0	0	0	....	....	....	....	....
1939-40	New York Americans	1	0	0	0	0	....	....	....	....	....
	NHL Totals	**2**	**0**	**0**	**0**	**0**	....	....	....	....	....

BEKAR, Derek

Left wing. Shoots left. 6'2", 205 lbs. Born, Burnaby, B.C., September 15, 1975.
(St. Louis' 7th choice, 205th overall, in 1995 Entry Draft).

Season	Club	GP	G	A	Pts	PIM	GP	G	A	Pts	PIM
99-2000	St. Louis Blues	1	0	0	0	0	....	....	....	....	....
2002-03	Los Angeles Kings	6	0	0	0	4	....	....	....	....	....
	NHL Totals	**7**	**0**	**0**	**0**	**4**	....	....	....	....	....

Traded to **Washington** by **St. Louis** for Mike Peluso, November 29, 2000. Signed as a free agent by **Los Angeles**, September 25, 2001.

BELAK, Wade

Defense/Right wing. Shoots right. 6'4", 225 lbs. Born, Saskatoon, Sask., July 3, 1976.
(Quebec's 1st choice, 12th overall, in 1994 Entry Draft).

Season	Club	GP	G	A	Pts	PIM	GP	G	A	Pts	PIM
1996-97	Colorado Avalanche	5	0	0	0	11	....	....	....	....	....
1997-98	Colorado Avalanche	8	1	1	2	27	....	....	....	....	....

Season	Club	GP	G	A	Pts	PIM	GP	G	A	Pts	PIM
		REGULAR SEASON					PLAYOFFS				
1998-99	Colorado Avalanche	22	0	0	0	71	....	....	....	....	....
	Calgary Flames	9	0	1	1	23	....	....	....	....	....
99-2000	Calgary Flames	40	0	2	2	122	....	....	....	....	....
2000-01	Calgary Flames	23	0	0	0	79	....	....	....	....	....
	Toronto Maple Leafs	16	1	1	2	31	....	....	....	....	....
2001-02	Toronto Maple Leafs	63	1	3	4	142	16	1	0	1	18
2002-03	Toronto Maple Leafs	55	3	6	9	196	2	0	0	0	4
	NHL Totals	**241**	**6**	**14**	**20**	**702**	**18**	**1**	**0**	**1**	**22**

Rights transferred to **Colorado** after **Quebec** franchise relocated, June 21, 1995. Traded to **Calgary** by **Colorado** with Rene Corbet, Robyn Regehr and Colorado's 2nd round compensatory choice (Jarret Stoll) in 2000 Entry Draft for Theoren Fleury and Chris Dingman, February 28, 1999. • Missed majority of 1999-2000 and 2000-01 seasons recovering from shoulder injury suffered in game vs. Colorado, February 10, 2000. Claimed on waivers by **Toronto** from **Calgary**, February 16, 2001.

BELANGER, Alain

Right wing. Shoots right. 6'1", 190 lbs. Born, St-Janvier, Que., January 18, 1956.
(Toronto's 2nd choice, 48th overall, in 1976 Amateur Draft).

Season	Club	GP	G	A	Pts	PIM	GP	G	A	Pts	PIM
1977-78	Toronto Maple Leafs	9	0	1	1	6	....	....	....	....	....
	NHL Totals	**9**	**0**	**1**	**1**	**6**	....	....	....	....	....

BELANGER, Eric

Center. Shoots left. 6', 185 lbs. Born, Sherbrooke, Que., December 16, 1977.
(Los Angeles' 5th choice, 96th overall, in 1996 Entry Draft).

Season	Club	GP	G	A	Pts	PIM	GP	G	A	Pts	PIM
2000-01	Los Angeles Kings	62	9	12	21	16	13	1	4	5	2
2001-02	Los Angeles Kings	53	8	16	24	21	7	0	0	0	4
2002-03	Los Angeles Kings	62	16	19	35	26	....	....	....	....	....
	NHL Totals	**177**	**33**	**47**	**80**	**63**	**20**	**1**	**4**	**5**	**6**

BELANGER, Francis

Left wing. Shoots left. 6'3", 228 lbs. Born, Bellefeuille, Que., January 15, 1978.
(Philadelphia's 5th choice, 124th overall, in 1998 Entry Draft).

Season	Club	GP	G	A	Pts	PIM	GP	G	A	Pts	PIM
2000-01	Montreal Canadiens	10	0	0	0	29	....	....	....	....	....
	NHL Totals	**10**	**0**	**0**	**0**	**29**	....	....	....	....	....

Signed as a free agent by **Montreal**, February 15, 2001. Signed as a free agent by **Anaheim**, August 22, 2002.

BELANGER, Jesse

Center. Shoots right. 6'1", 190 lbs. Born, St-Georges de Beauce, Que., June 15, 1969.

Season	Club	GP	G	A	Pts	PIM	GP	G	A	Pts	PIM
1991-92	Montreal Canadiens	4	0	0	0	0	....	....	....	....	....
1992-93 ♦	Montreal Canadiens	19	4	2	6	4	9	0	1	1	0
1993-94	Florida Panthers	70	17	33	50	16	....	....	....	....	....
1994-95	Florida Panthers	47	15	14	29	18	....	....	....	....	....
1995-96	Florida Panthers	63	17	21	38	10	....	....	....	....	....
	Vancouver Canucks	9	3	0	3	4	3	0	2	2	2
1996-97	Edmonton Oilers	6	0	0	0	0	....	....	....	....	....
99-2000	Montreal Canadiens	16	3	6	9	2	....	....	....	....	....
2000-01	New York Islanders	12	0	0	0	2	....	....	....	....	....
	NHL Totals	**246**	**59**	**76**	**135**	**56**	**12**	**0**	**3**	**3**	**2**

Signed as a free agent by **Montreal**, October 3, 1990. Claimed by **Florida** from **Montreal** in Expansion Draft, June 24, 1993. Traded to **Vancouver** by **Florida** for Vancouver's 3rd round choice (Oleg Kvasha) in 1996 Entry Draft, March 20, 1996. Signed as a free agent by **Edmonton**, September 16, 1996. Signed as a free agent by **Tampa Bay**, August 18, 1998. Signed as a free agent by **Montreal**, July 23, 1999. Signed as a free agent by **NY Islanders**, July 27, 2000.

BELANGER, Ken

Left wing. Shoots left. 6'4", 225 lbs. Born, Sault Ste. Marie, Ont., May 14, 1974.
(Hartford's 7th choice, 153rd overall, in 1992 Entry Draft).

Season	Club	GP	G	A	Pts	PIM	GP	G	A	Pts	PIM
1994-95	Toronto Maple Leafs	3	0	0	0	9	....	....	....	....	....
1995-96	New York Islanders	7	0	0	0	27	....	....	....	....	....
1996-97	New York Islanders	18	0	2	2	102	....	....	....	....	....
1997-98	New York Islanders	37	3	1	4	101	....	....	....	....	....
1998-99	New York Islanders	9	1	1	2	30	....	....	....	....	....
	Boston Bruins	45	1	4	5	152	12	1	0	1	16
99-2000	Boston Bruins	37	2	2	4	44	....	....	....	....	....
2000-01	Boston Bruins	40	2	2	4	121	....	....	....	....	....
2001-02	Los Angeles Kings	43	2	0	2	85	....	....	....	....	....
2002-03	Los Angeles Kings	4	0	0	0	17	....	....	....	....	....
	NHL Totals	**243**	**11**	**12**	**23**	**688**	**12**	**1**	**0**	**1**	**16**

Traded to **Toronto** by **Hartford** for Toronto's 9th round choice (Matt Ball) in 1994 Entry Draft, March 18, 1994. Traded to **NY Islanders** by **Toronto** with Damian Rhodes for future considerations (Kirk Muller and Don Beaupre, January 23, 1996), January 23, 1996. Traded to **Boston** by **NY Islanders** for Ted Donato, November 7, 1998. • Missed majority of 1999-2000 season recovering from head injury suffered in game vs. Toronto, November 11, 1999. Signed as a free agent by **Los Angeles**, July 2, 2001. • Missed majority of 2002-03 season recovering from head injury suffered in game vs. San Jose, November 5, 2002.

BELANGER, Roger

Center. Shoots right. 6', 190 lbs. Born, St. Catharines, Ont., December 1, 1965.
(Pittsburgh's 3rd choice, 16th overall, in 1984 Entry Draft).

Season	Club	GP	G	A	Pts	PIM	GP	G	A	Pts	PIM
1984-85	Pittsburgh Penguins	44	3	5	8	32	....	....	....	....	....
	NHL Totals	**44**	**3**	**5**	**8**	**32**	....	....	....	....	....

BELISLE, Danny

Right wing. Shoots right. 5'10", 164 lbs. Born, South Porcupine, Ont., May 9, 1937.

Season	Club	GP	G	A	Pts	PIM	GP	G	A	Pts	PIM
1960-61	New York Rangers	4	2	0	2	0	....	....	....	....	....
	NHL Totals	**4**	**2**	**0**	**2**	**0**	....	....	....	....	....

Traded to **San Francisco** (WHL) by **NY Rangers** (Los Angeles-WHL) for Bob Solinger with NY Rangers holding right of recall, July, 1962. Claimed by **Detroit** (Pittsburgh (AHL) from **NY Rangers** in Reverse Draft, June 9, 1965. Claimed by **Springfield** (AHL) from **Detroit** in Reserve Draft, June 15, 1966.

BELIVEAU, Jean

HHOF

Center. Shoots left. 6'3", 205 lbs. Born, Trois-Rivieres, Que., August 31, 1931.

Season	Club	GP	G	A	Pts	PIM	GP	G	A	Pts	PIM
1950-51	Montreal Canadiens	2	1	1	2	0	....	....	....	....	....
1952-53	Montreal Canadiens	3	5	0	5	0	....	....	....	....	....
1953-54	Montreal Canadiens	44	13	21	34	22	10	2	*8	10	4
1954-55	Montreal Canadiens	70	37	36	73	58	12	6	7	13	18
1955-56 ♦	Montreal Canadiens	70	*47	41	*88	143	10	*12	7	*19	22
1956-57 ♦	Montreal Canadiens	69	33	51	84	105	10	6	6	12	15
1957-58 ♦	Montreal Canadiens	55	27	32	59	93	10	4	8	12	10
1958-59 ♦	Montreal Canadiens	64	*45	46	91	67	3	1	4	5	4
1959-60 ♦	Montreal Canadiens	60	34	40	74	57	8	5	2	7	6
1960-61	Montreal Canadiens	69	32	*58	90	57	6	0	5	5	0
1961-62	Montreal Canadiens	43	18	23	41	36	6	2	1	3	4
1962-63	Montreal Canadiens	69	18	49	67	68	5	2	1	3	2
1963-64	Montreal Canadiens	68	28	50	78	42	5	2	0	2	18
1964-65 ♦	Montreal Canadiens	58	20	23	43	76	13	8	8	16	34
1965-66 ♦	Montreal Canadiens	67	29	*48	77	50	10	5	5	10	6
1966-67	Montreal Canadiens	53	12	26	38	22	10	6	5	11	*26
1967-68 ♦	Montreal Canadiens	59	31	37	68	28	10	7	4	11	6
1968-69 ♦	Montreal Canadiens	69	33	49	82	55	14	5	*10	15	8
1969-70	Montreal Canadiens	63	19	30	49	10	....	....	....	....	....
1970-71 ♦	Montreal Canadiens	70	25	51	76	40	20	6	*16	22	28
	NHL Totals	**1125**	**507**	**712**	**1219**	**1029**	**162**	**79**	**97**	**176**	**211**

NHL First All-Star Team (1955, 1956, 1957, 1959, 1960, 1961) • Art Ross Trophy (1956) • Hart Trophy (1956, 1964) • NHL Second All-Star Team (1958, 1964, 1966, 1969) • Conn Smythe Trophy (1965)

Played in NHL All-Star Game (1953, 1954, 1955, 1956, 1957, 1958, 1959, 1960, 1963, 1964, 1965, 1968, 1969)

Signed as a free agent by **Montreal**, October 3, 1953. • Missed start of 1961-62 season recovering from knee injury suffered in exhibition game vs. Spokane (OSHL), September 30, 1961.

BELL, Billy

Center/Right wing. Shoots right. 5'10", 180 lbs. Born, Lachine, Que., June 10, 1891.

Season	Club	GP	G	A	Pts	PIM	GP	G	A	Pts	PIM
1917-18	Montreal Wanderers	2	1	0	1	0	....	....	....	....	....
	Montreal Canadiens	6	0	0	0	6	....	....	....	....	....
1918-19	Montreal Canadiens	1	0	0	0	0	....	....	....	....	....
1920-21	Montreal Canadiens	4	0	0	0	2	....	....	....	....	....
1921-22	Montreal Canadiens	6	1	0	1	0	....	....	....	....	....
	Ottawa Senators	23	2	2	4	4	1	0	0	0	0
1922-23	Montreal Canadiens	19	0	0	0	2	2	0	0	0	0
1923-24 ♦	Montreal Canadiens	11	0	0	0	0	2	0	0	0	0
	Montreal Canadiens (Cup)	....	....	....	....	....	*3*	*0*	*0*	*0*	*0*
	NHL Totals	**72**	**4**	**2**	**6**	**14**	**5**	**0**	**0**	**0**	**0**

Rights retained by **Mtl. Wanderers** after NHA folded, November 26, 1917. Claimed by **Montreal** from **Mtl. Wanderers** in Dispersal Draft, January 4, 1918. Transferred to **Ottawa** by **Montreal** for the remainder of the 1921-22 season as compensation for Montreal acquiring the rights to Sprague Cleghorn (November 26, 1921), January 6, 1922. • 1923-24 Stanley Cup totals includes series with Calgary (WCHL) and Vancouver (PCHA).

BELL, Bruce

Defense. Shoots left. 6'1", 190 lbs. Born, Toronto, Ont., February 15, 1965.
(Quebec's 2nd choice, 53rd overall, in 1983 Entry Draft).

Season	Club	GP	G	A	Pts	PIM	GP	G	A	Pts	PIM
1984-85	Quebec Nordiques	75	6	31	37	44	16	2	2	4	21
1985-86	St. Louis Blues	75	2	18	20	43	14	0	2	2	13
1986-87	St. Louis Blues	45	3	13	16	18	4	1	1	2	7
1987-88	New York Rangers	13	1	2	3	8	....	....	....	....	....
1989-90	Edmonton Oilers	1	0	0	0	0	....	....	....	....	....
	NHL Totals	**209**	**12**	**64**	**76**	**113**	**34**	**3**	**5**	**8**	**41**

NHL All-Rookie Team (1985)

Traded to **St. Louis** by **Quebec** for Gilbert Delorme, October 2, 1985. Traded to **NY Rangers** by **St. Louis** with future considerations for Tony McKegney and Rob Whistle, May 28, 1987. Traded to **Quebec** by **NY Rangers** with Jari Gronstrand, Walt Poddubny and NY Rangers' 4th round choice (Eric Dubois) in 1989 Entry Draft for Jason Lafreniere and Normand Rochefort, August 1, 1988. Claimed on waivers by **Detroit** from **Quebec**, December 20, 1988. Signed as a free agent by **Edmonton**, February 1, 1990. Traded to **Minnesota** by **Edmonton** for Kari Takko, November, 22, 1990.

BELL, Harry

Right wing/Defense. Shoots right. 5'9", 176 lbs. Born, Regina, Sask., October 31, 1925.

Season	Club	GP	G	A	Pts	PIM	GP	G	A	Pts	PIM
1946-47	New York Rangers	1	0	1	1	0	....	....	....	....	....
	NHL Totals	**1**	**0**	**1**	**1**	**0**	....	....	....	....	....

Signed as a free agent by **NY Rangers**, October 10, 1944.

BELL, Joe

Left wing. Shoots left. 5'9", 165 lbs. Born, Portage la Prairie, Man., November 27, 1923.

Season	Club	GP	G	A	Pts	PIM	GP	G	A	Pts	PIM
1942-43	New York Rangers	15	2	5	7	6	....	....	....	....	....

Season	Club	Regular Season GP	G	A	Pts	PIM	Playoffs GP	G	A	Pts	PIM
1946-47	New York Rangers	47	6	4	10	12	....	....	....	....	....
	NHL Totals	**62**	**8**	**9**	**17**	**18**	....	....	....	....	....

• Brother of Gordie

Signed as a free agent by **NY Rangers**, October 30, 1942. Traded to **Montreal** by **NY Rangers** with Hal Laycoe and George Robertson for Buddy O'Connor and Frank Eddolls, August 19, 1947.

BELL, Mark

Center. Shoots left. 6'3", 198 lbs. Born, St. Paul's, Ont., August 5, 1980.
(Chicago's 1st choice, 8th overall, in 1998 Entry Draft).

Season	Club	GP	G	A	Pts	PIM	GP	G	A	Pts	PIM
2000-01	Chicago Blackhawks	13	0	1	1	4	....	....	....	....	....
2001-02	Chicago Blackhawks	80	12	16	28	124	5	0	0	0	8
2002-03	Chicago Blackhawks	82	14	15	29	113	....	....	....	....	....
	NHL Totals	**175**	**26**	**32**	**58**	**241**	**5**	**0**	**0**	**0**	**8**

BELLAND, Neil

Defense. Shoots left. 5'11", 180 lbs. Born, Parry Sound, Ont., April 3, 1961.

Season	Club	GP	G	A	Pts	PIM	GP	G	A	Pts	PIM
1981-82	Vancouver Canucks	28	3	6	9	16	17	1	7	8	16
1982-83	Vancouver Canucks	14	2	4	6	4	....	....	....	....	....
1983-84	Vancouver Canucks	44	7	13	20	24	4	1	2	3	7
1984-85	Vancouver Canucks	13	0	6	6	6	....	....	....	....	....
1985-86	Vancouver Canucks	7	1	2	3	4	....	....	....	....	....
1986-87	Pittsburgh Penguins	3	0	1	1	0	....	....	....	....	....
	NHL Totals	**109**	**13**	**32**	**45**	**54**	**21**	**2**	**9**	**11**	**23**

Signed as a free agent by **Vancouver**, October 1, 1980. Signed as a free agent by **Pittsburgh**, September 29, 1986.

BELLEFEUILLE, Blake

Center. Shoots right. 5'10", 208 lbs. Born, Framingham, MA, December 27, 1977.

Season	Club	GP	G	A	Pts	PIM	GP	G	A	Pts	PIM
2001-02	Columbus Blue Jackets	2	0	1	1	0	....	....	....	....	....
2002-03	Columbus Blue Jackets	3	0	0	0	0	....	....	....	....	....
	NHL Totals	**5**	**0**	**1**	**1**	**0**	....	....	....	....	....

Signed as a free agent by **Columbus**, May 26, 2000.

BELLEFEUILLE, Pete

Right wing. Shoots right. 5'10", 180 lbs. Born, Trois-Rivieres, Que., October 19, 1901.

Season	Club	GP	G	A	Pts	PIM	GP	G	A	Pts	PIM
1925-26	Toronto St. Pats	36	14	2	16	22	....	....	....	....	....
1926-27	Toronto St. Pats/Maple Leafs	13	0	0	0	12	....	....	....	....	....
	Detroit Cougars	18	6	0	6	14	....	....	....	....	....
1928-29	Detroit Cougars	1	1	0	1	0	....	....	....	....	....
1929-30	Detroit Cougars	24	5	2	7	10	....	....	....	....	....
	NHL Totals	**92**	**26**	**4**	**30**	**58**	....	....	....	....	....

Signed as a free agent by **Toronto**, September 21, 1925. Traded to **Detroit** by **Toronto** for Harold Halderson, January 7, 1927. Traded to **Seattle** (PCHL) by **Detroit** with Bob Connors for cash, September 12, 1930.

BELLEMER, Andy

Defense. Shoots left. 5'11", 185 lbs. Born, Penetanguishene, Ont., July 3, 1903.

Season	Club	GP	G	A	Pts	PIM	GP	G	A	Pts	PIM
1932-33	Montreal Maroons	15	0	0	0	0	....	....	....	....	....
	NHL Totals	**15**	**0**	**0**	**0**	**0**	....	....	....	....	....

Traded to **Mtl. Maroons** by **Windsor** (IHL) for cash, November 28, 1932.

BELLOWS, Brian

Left wing. Shoots right. 5'11", 210 lbs. Born, St. Catharines, Ont., September 1, 1964.
(Minnesota's 1st choice, 2nd overall, in 1982 Entry Draft).

Season	Club	GP	G	A	Pts	PIM	GP	G	A	Pts	PIM
1982-83	Minnesota North Stars	78	35	30	65	27	9	5	4	9	18
1983-84	Minnesota North Stars	78	41	42	83	66	16	2	12	14	6
1984-85	Minnesota North Stars	78	26	36	62	72	9	2	4	6	9
1985-86	Minnesota North Stars	77	31	48	79	46	5	5	0	5	16
1986-87	Minnesota North Stars	65	26	27	53	34	....	....	....	....	....
1987-88	Minnesota North Stars	77	40	41	81	81	....	....	....	....	....
1988-89	Minnesota North Stars	60	23	27	50	55	5	2	3	5	8
1989-90	Minnesota North Stars	80	55	44	99	72	7	4	3	7	10
1990-91	Minnesota North Stars	80	35	40	75	43	23	10	19	29	30
1991-92	Minnesota North Stars	80	30	45	75	41	7	4	4	8	14
1992-93 ♦	Montreal Canadiens	82	40	48	88	44	18	6	9	15	18
1993-94	Montreal Canadiens	77	33	38	71	36	6	1	2	3	2
1994-95	Montreal Canadiens	41	8	8	16	8	....	....	....	....	....
1995-96	Tampa Bay Lightning	79	23	26	49	39	6	2	0	2	4
1996-97	Tampa Bay Lightning	7	1	2	3	0	....	....	....	....	....
	Mighty Ducks of Anaheim	62	15	13	28	22	11	2	4	6	2
1997-98	Washington Capitals	11	6	3	9	6	21	6	7	13	6
1998-99	Washington Capitals	76	17	19	36	26	....	....	....	....	....
	NHL Totals	**1188**	**485**	**537**	**1022**	**718**	**143**	**51**	**71**	**122**	**143**

NHL Second All-Star Team (1990)

Played in NHL All-Star Game (1984, 1988, 1992)

Traded to **Montreal** by **Minnesota** for Russ Courtnall, August 31, 1992. Traded to **Tampa Bay** by **Montreal** for Marc Bureau, June 30, 1995. Traded to **Anaheim** by **Tampa Bay** for Anaheim's 6th round choice (Andrei Skopintsev) in 1997 Entry Draft, November 19, 1996. Signed as a free agent by **Washington**, March 21, 1998.

BEND, Lin

Center. Shoots left. 5'10", 165 lbs. Born, Poplar Point, Man., December 20, 1922.

Season	Club	GP	G	A	Pts	PIM	GP	G	A	Pts	PIM
1942-43	New York Rangers	8	3	1	4	2	....	....	....	....	....
	NHL Totals	**8**	**3**	**1**	**4**	**2**	....	....	....	....	....

Signed as a free agent by **NY Rangers**, October 30, 1942. Traded to **St. Paul** (USHL) by **NY Rangers** for cash, October 7, 1947.

BENDA, Jan

Center. Shoots right. 6'3", 215 lbs. Born, Reef, Belgium, March 28, 1972.

Season	Club	GP	G	A	Pts	PIM	GP	G	A	Pts	PIM
1997-98	Washington Capitals	9	0	3	3	6	....	....	....	....	....
	NHL Totals	**9**	**0**	**3**	**3**	**6**	....	....	....	....	....

Signed as a free agent by **Washington**, October 1, 1997. Signed as a free agent by **Edmonton**, July 17, 2001.

BENNETT, Adam

Defense. Shoots right. 6'4", 206 lbs. Born, Georgetown, Ont., March 30, 1971.
(Chicago's 1st choice, 6th overall, in 1989 Entry Draft).

Season	Club	GP	G	A	Pts	PIM	GP	G	A	Pts	PIM
1991-92	Chicago Blackhawks	5	0	0	0	12	....	....	....	....	....
1992-93	Chicago Blackhawks	16	0	2	2	8	....	....	....	....	....
1993-94	Edmonton Oilers	48	3	6	9	49	....	....	....	....	....
	NHL Totals	**69**	**3**	**8**	**11**	**69**	....	....	....	....	....

Traded to **Edmonton** by **Chicago** for Kevin Todd, October 7, 1993.

BENNETT, Bill

Left wing. Shoots left. 6'5", 235 lbs. Born, Warwick, RI, May 31, 1953.

Season	Club	GP	G	A	Pts	PIM	GP	G	A	Pts	PIM
1978-79	Boston Bruins	7	1	4	5	2	....	....	....	....	....
1979-80	Hartford Whalers	24	3	3	6	63	....	....	....	....	....
	NHL Totals	**31**	**4**	**7**	**11**	**65**	....	....	....	....	....

• Son of Harvey • Brother of Curt and Harvey Jr.

Signed as a free agent by **Boston**, October, 1976. Claimed by **Hartford** from **Boston** in Expansion Draft, June 13, 1979.

BENNETT, Curt

Left wing. Shoots left. 6'3", 195 lbs. Born, Regina, Sask., March 27, 1948.
(St. Louis' 2nd choice, 16th overall, in 1968 Amateur Draft).

Season	Club	GP	G	A	Pts	PIM	GP	G	A	Pts	PIM
1970-71	St. Louis Blues	4	2	0	2	0	2	0	0	0	0
1971-72	St. Louis Blues	31	3	5	8	30	10	0	0	0	12
1972-73	New York Rangers	16	0	1	1	11	....	....	....	....	....
	Atlanta Flames	52	18	17	35	9	....	....	....	....	....
1973-74	Atlanta Flames	71	17	24	41	34	4	0	1	1	34
1974-75	Atlanta Flames	80	31	33	64	40	....	....	....	....	....
1975-76	Atlanta Flames	80	34	31	65	61	2	0	0	0	4
1976-77	Atlanta Flames	76	22	25	47	36	3	1	0	1	7
1977-78	Atlanta Flames	25	3	7	10	10	....	....	....	....	....
	St. Louis Blues	50	7	17	24	54	....	....	....	....	....
1978-79	St. Louis Blues	74	14	19	33	62	....	....	....	....	....
1979-80	Atlanta Flames	21	1	3	4	0	....	....	....	....	....
	NHL Totals	**580**	**152**	**182**	**334**	**347**	**21**	**1**	**1**	**2**	**57**

• Son of Harvey • Brother of Harvey Jr. and Bill

Played in NHL All-Star Game (1975, 1976)

Traded to **NY Rangers** by **St. Louis** with Peter McDuffe to complete transaction that sent Steve Durbano to St. Louis (May 24, 1972), June 7, 1972. Traded to **Atlanta** by **NY Rangers** for Ron Harris, November 28, 1972. Traded to **St. Louis** by **Atlanta** with Phil Myre and Barry Gibbs for Yves Belanger, Dick Redmond, Bob MacMillan and St. Louis' 2nd round choice (Mike Perovich) in 1979 Amateur Draft, December 12, 1977. Traded to **Atlanta** by **St. Louis** for Bobby Simpson, May 24, 1979.

BENNETT, Frank

Left wing/Defense. Shoots right. 5'11", 182 lbs. Born, Toronto, Ont., March 4, 1922.

Season	Club	GP	G	A	Pts	PIM	GP	G	A	Pts	PIM
1943-44	Detroit Red Wings	7	0	1	1	2	....	....	....	....	....
	NHL Totals	**7**	**0**	**1**	**1**	**2**	....	....	....	....	....

BENNETT Jr., Harvey

Center. Shoots left. 6'4", 215 lbs. Born, Cranston, RI, August 9, 1952.

Season	Club	GP	G	A	Pts	PIM	GP	G	A	Pts	PIM
1974-75	Pittsburgh Penguins	7	0	0	0	0	....	....	....	....	....
1975-76	Pittsburgh Penguins	25	3	3	6	53	....	....	....	....	....
	Washington Capitals	49	12	10	22	39	....	....	....	....	....
1976-77	Washington Capitals	18	2	6	8	34	....	....	....	....	....
	Philadelphia Flyers	51	12	8	20	60	4	0	0	0	2
1977-78	Philadelphia Flyers	2	1	0	1	7	....	....	....	....	....
	Minnesota North Stars	64	11	10	21	91	....	....	....	....	....
1978-79	St. Louis Blues	52	3	9	12	63	....	....	....	....	....
	NHL Totals	**268**	**44**	**46**	**90**	**347**	**4**	**0**	**0**	**0**	**2**

• Son of Harvey • Brother of Curt and Bill

Signed as a free agent by **Pittsburgh**, June 25, 1974. Traded to **Washington** by **Pittsburgh** for Stan Gilbertson, December 16, 1975. Traded to **Philadelphia** by **Washington** for cash, November 24, 1976. Traded to **Minnesota** by **Philadelphia** for Blake Dunlop and Minnesota's 3rd round choice (Gord Salt) in 1978 Amateur Draft, October 28, 1977. Traded to **St. Louis** by **Minnesota** for St. Louis' 2nd round choice (Jali Wahlsten) in 1981 Entry Draft, August 28, 1978. Traded to **Atlanta** by **St. Louis** for cash, November 6, 1979.

BENNETT, Max

Right wing. Shoots right. 5'6", 157 lbs. Born, Cobalt, Ont., November 4, 1912.

Season	Club	REGULAR SEASON GP	G	A	Pts	PIM	PLAYOFFS GP	G	A	Pts	PIM
1935-36	Montreal Canadiens	1	0	0	0	0	....	....	....	....	....
	NHL Totals	**1**	**0**	**0**	**0**	**0**	....	....	....	....	....

Signed as a free agent by **Montreal**, May 27, 1935.

BENNETT, Rick

Left wing. Shoots left. 6'4", 215 lbs. Born, Springfield, MA, July 24, 1967.
(Minnesota's 4th choice, 54th overall, in 1986 Entry Draft).

Season	Club	REGULAR SEASON GP	G	A	Pts	PIM	PLAYOFFS GP	G	A	Pts	PIM
1989-90	New York Rangers	6	1	0	1	5	....	....	....	....	....
1990-91	New York Rangers	6	0	0	0	6	....	....	....	....	....
1991-92	New York Rangers	3	0	1	1	2	....	....	....	....	....
	NHL Totals	**15**	**1**	**1**	**2**	**13**	....	....	....	....	....

Rights traded to **NY Rangers** by **Minnesota** with Brian Lawton and Igor Liba for Paul Jerrard, Mark Tinordi, Mike Sullivan, the rights to Bret Barnett and Los Angeles' 3rd round choice (previously acquired, Minnesota selected Murray Garbutt) in 1989 Entry Draft, October 11, 1988.

BENNING, Brian

Defense. Shoots left. 6', 195 lbs. Born, Edmonton, Alta., June 10, 1966.
(St. Louis' 1st choice, 26th overall, in 1984 Entry Draft).

Season	Club	REGULAR SEASON GP	G	A	Pts	PIM	PLAYOFFS GP	G	A	Pts	PIM
1984-85	St. Louis Blues	4	0	2	2	0	....	....	....	....	....
1985-86	St. Louis Blues	....	....	....	....	....	6	1	2	3	13
1986-87	St. Louis Blues	78	13	36	49	110	6	0	4	4	9
1987-88	St. Louis Blues	77	8	29	37	107	10	1	6	7	25
1988-89	St. Louis Blues	66	8	26	34	102	7	1	1	2	11
1989-90	St. Louis Blues	7	1	1	2	2	....	....	....	....	....
	Los Angeles Kings	48	5	18	23	104	7	0	2	2	10
1990-91	Los Angeles Kings	61	7	24	31	127	12	0	5	5	6
1991-92	Los Angeles Kings	53	2	30	32	99	....	....	....	....	....
	Philadelphia Flyers	22	2	12	14	35	....	....	....	....	....
1992-93	Philadelphia Flyers	37	9	17	26	93	....	....	....	....	....
	Edmonton Oilers	18	1	7	8	59	....	....	....	....	....
1993-94	Florida Panthers	73	6	24	30	107	....	....	....	....	....
1994-95	Florida Panthers	24	1	7	8	18	....	....	....	....	....
	NHL Totals	**568**	**63**	**233**	**296**	**963**	**48**	**3**	**20**	**23**	**74**

• Brother of Jim • NHL All-Rookie Team (1987)

Traded to **Los Angeles** by **St. Louis** for Los Angeles' 3rd round choice (Kyle Reeves) in 1991 Entry Draft, November 10, 1989. Traded to **Pittsburgh** by **Los Angeles** with Jeff Chychrun and Los Angeles' 1st round choice (later traded to Philadelphia – Philadelphia selected Jason Bowen) in 1992 Entry Draft for Paul Coffey, February 19, 1992. Traded to **Philadelphia** by **Pittsburgh** with Mark Recchi and Los Angeles' 1st round choice (previously acquired, Philadelphia selected Jason Bowen) in 1992 Entry Draft for Rick Tocchet, Kjell Samuelsson, Ken Wregget and Philadelphia's 3rd round choice (Dave Roche) in 1993 Entry Draft, February 19, 1992. Traded to **Edmonton** by **Philadelphia** for Greg Hawgood and Josef Beranek, January 16, 1993. Signed as a free agent by **Florida**, July 13, 1993.

BENNING, Jim

Defense. Shoots left. 6', 180 lbs. Born, Edmonton, Alta., April 29, 1963.
(Toronto's 1st choice, 6th overall, in 1981 Entry Draft).

Season	Club	REGULAR SEASON GP	G	A	Pts	PIM	PLAYOFFS GP	G	A	Pts	PIM
1981-82	Toronto Maple Leafs	74	7	24	31	46	....	....	....	....	....
1982-83	Toronto Maple Leafs	74	5	17	22	47	4	1	1	2	2
1983-84	Toronto Maple Leafs	79	12	39	51	66	....	....	....	....	....
1984-85	Toronto Maple Leafs	80	9	35	44	55	....	....	....	....	....
1985-86	Toronto Maple Leafs	52	4	21	25	71	....	....	....	....	....
1986-87	Toronto Maple Leafs	5	0	0	0	4	....	....	....	....	....
	Vancouver Canucks	54	2	11	13	40	....	....	....	....	....
1987-88	Vancouver Canucks	77	7	26	33	58	....	....	....	....	....
1988-89	Vancouver Canucks	65	3	9	12	48	3	0	0	0	0
1989-90	Vancouver Canucks	45	3	9	12	26	....	....	....	....	....
	NHL Totals	**605**	**52**	**191**	**243**	**461**	**7**	**1**	**1**	**2**	**2**

• Brother of Brian

Traded to **Vancouver** by **Toronto** with Dan Hodgson for Rick Lanz, December 2, 1986.

BENOIT, Joe

Right wing. Shoots right. 5'10", 160 lbs. Born, St. Albert, Alta., February 27, 1916.

Season	Club	REGULAR SEASON GP	G	A	Pts	PIM	PLAYOFFS GP	G	A	Pts	PIM
1940-41	Montreal Canadiens	45	16	16	32	32	3	4	0	4	2
1941-42	Montreal Canadiens	46	20	16	36	27	3	1	0	1	5
1942-43	Montreal Canadiens	49	30	27	57	23	5	1	3	4	4
1945-46 ♦	Montreal Canadiens	39	9	10	19	8	....	....	....	....	....
1946-47	Montreal Canadiens	6	0	0	0	4	....	....	....	....	....
	NHL Totals	**185**	**75**	**69**	**144**	**94**	**11**	**6**	**3**	**9**	**11**

Rights traded to **Montreal** by **Toronto** for the rights to Frank Eddolls, June 7, 1940.

BENSON, Bill

Center. Shoots left. 5'11", 165 lbs. Born, Winnipeg, Man., July 29, 1920.

Season	Club	REGULAR SEASON GP	G	A	Pts	PIM	PLAYOFFS GP	G	A	Pts	PIM
1940-41	New York Americans	22	3	4	7	4	....	....	....	....	....
1941-42	Brooklyn Americans	45	8	21	29	31	....	....	....	....	....
	NHL Totals	**67**	**11**	**25**	**36**	**35**	....	....	....	....	....

Signed as a free agent by **NY Americans**, October 11, 1940. • Team name changed to **Brooklyn Americans** prior to 1941-42 season.

BENSON, Bobby

Defense. Shoots left. 5'6", 135 lbs. Born, Winnipeg, Man., May 18, 1894.

Season	Club	REGULAR SEASON GP	G	A	Pts	PIM	PLAYOFFS GP	G	A	Pts	PIM
1924-25	Boston Bruins	8	0	1	1	4	....	....	....	....	....
	NHL Totals	**8**	**0**	**1**	**1**	**4**	....	....	....	....	....

Traded to **Mtl. Maroons** by **Calgary** (WCHL) for cash, January 3, 1925. Traded to **Boston** by **Mtl. Maroons** with Bernie Morris for Alf Skinner, January 3, 1925.

BENTLEY, Doug

HHOF

Left wing. Shoots left. 5'8", 145 lbs. Born, Delisle, Sask., September 3, 1916.

Season	Club	REGULAR SEASON GP	G	A	Pts	PIM	PLAYOFFS GP	G	A	Pts	PIM
1939-40	Chicago Black Hawks	39	12	7	19	12	2	0	0	0	0
1940-41	Chicago Black Hawks	47	8	20	28	12	5	1	1	2	4
1941-42	Chicago Black Hawks	38	12	14	26	11	3	0	1	1	4
1942-43	Chicago Black Hawks	50	*33	40	*73	18	....	....	....	....	....
1943-44	Chicago Black Hawks	50	*38	39	77	22	9	8	4	12	4
1945-46	Chicago Black Hawks	36	19	21	40	16	4	0	2	2	0
1946-47	Chicago Black Hawks	52	21	*34	55	18	....	....	....	....	....
1947-48	Chicago Black Hawks	60	20	*37	57	16	....	....	....	....	....
1948-49	Chicago Black Hawks	58	23	*43	66	38	....	....	....	....	....
1949-50	Chicago Black Hawks	64	20	33	53	28	....	....	....	....	....
1950-51	Chicago Black Hawks	44	9	23	32	20	....	....	....	....	....
1951-52	Chicago Black Hawks	8	2	3	5	4	....	....	....	....	....
1953-54	New York Rangers	20	2	10	12	2	....	....	....	....	....
	NHL Totals	**566**	**219**	**324**	**543**	**217**	**23**	**9**	**8**	**17**	**12**

• Brother of Reg and Max • NHL First All-Star Team (1943, 1944, 1947) • NHL Second All-Star Team (1949)

Played in NHL All-Star Game (1947, 1948, 1949, 1950, 1951)

• Missed entire 1944-45 NHL season after being given permission to stay home and tend family farm by Canadian Armed Forces officials, September, 1944. Traded to **NY Rangers** by **Chicago** for cash, June 30, 1953.

BENTLEY, Max

HHOF

Center. Shoots left. 5'10", 155 lbs. Born, Delisle, Sask., March 1, 1920.

Season	Club	REGULAR SEASON GP	G	A	Pts	PIM	PLAYOFFS GP	G	A	Pts	PIM
1940-41	Chicago Black Hawks	36	7	10	17	6	4	1	3	4	2
1941-42	Chicago Black Hawks	39	13	17	30	2	3	2	0	2	0
1942-43	Chicago Black Hawks	47	26	44	70	2	....	....	....	....	....
1945-46	Chicago Black Hawks	47	31	30	*61	6	4	1	0	1	4
1946-47	Chicago Black Hawks	60	29	43	*72	12	....	....	....	....	....
1947-48	Chicago Black Hawks	6	3	3	6	4	....	....	....	....	....
♦	Toronto Maple Leafs	53	23	25	48	10	9	4	7	11	0
1948-49 ♦	Toronto Maple Leafs	60	19	22	41	18	9	4	3	7	2
1949-50	Toronto Maple Leafs	69	23	18	41	14	7	3	3	6	0
1950-51 ♦	Toronto Maple Leafs	67	21	41	62	34	11	2	*11	*13	4
1951-52	Toronto Maple Leafs	69	24	17	41	40	4	1	0	1	2
1952-53	Toronto Maple Leafs	36	12	11	23	16	....	....	....	....	....
1953-54	New York Rangers	57	14	18	32	15	....	....	....	....	....
	NHL Totals	**646**	**245**	**299**	**544**	**179**	**51**	**18**	**27**	**45**	**14**

• Brother of Reg and Doug • Lady Byng Trophy (1943) • NHL First All-Star Team (1946) • Hart Trophy (1946) • NHL Second All-Star Team (1947)

Played in NHL All-Star Game (1947, 1948, 1949, 1951)

Traded to **Toronto** by **Chicago** with Cy Thomas for Gus Bodnar, Bud Poile, Gaye Stewart, Ernie Dickens and Bob Goldham, November 2, 1947. Traded to **NY Rangers** by **Toronto** for cash, August 11, 1953.

BENTLEY, Reg

Left wing. Shoots left. 5'8", 155 lbs. Born, Delisle, Sask., May 3, 1914.

Season	Club	REGULAR SEASON GP	G	A	Pts	PIM	PLAYOFFS GP	G	A	Pts	PIM
1942-43	Chicago Black Hawks	11	1	2	3	2	....	....	....	....	....
	NHL Totals	**11**	**1**	**2**	**3**	**2**	....	....	....	....	....

• Brother of Doug and Max

BENYSEK, Ladislav

Defense. Shoots left. 6'2", 190 lbs. Born, Olomouc, Czech., March 24, 1975.
(Edmonton's 16th choice, 266th overall, in 1994 Entry Draft).

Season	Club	REGULAR SEASON GP	G	A	Pts	PIM	PLAYOFFS GP	G	A	Pts	PIM
1997-98	Edmonton Oilers	2	0	0	0	0	....	....	....	....	....
2000-01	Minnesota Wild	71	2	5	7	38	....	....	....	....	....
2001-02	Minnesota Wild	74	1	7	8	28	....	....	....	....	....
2002-03	Minnesota Wild	14	0	0	0	8	....	....	....	....	....
	NHL Totals	**161**	**3**	**12**	**15**	**74**	....	....	....	....	....

Claimed by **Anaheim** from **Edmonton** in Waiver Draft, September 27, 1999. Selected by **Minnesota** from **Anaheim** in Expansion Draft, June 23, 2000.

BERALDO, Paul

Right wing. Shoots right. 5'11", 175 lbs. Born, Hamilton, Ont., October 5, 1967.
(Boston's 6th choice, 139th overall, in 1986 Entry Draft).

Season	Club	REGULAR SEASON GP	G	A	Pts	PIM	PLAYOFFS GP	G	A	Pts	PIM
1987-88	Boston Bruins	3	0	0	0	0	....	....	....	....	....
1988-89	Boston Bruins	7	0	0	0	4	....	....	....	....	....
	NHL Totals	**10**	**0**	**0**	**0**	**4**	....	....	....	....	....

BERANEK, Josef

Left wing/Center. Shoots left. 6'2", 195 lbs. Born, Litvinov, Czech., October 25, 1969.
(Edmonton's 3rd choice, 78th overall, in 1989 Entry Draft).

Season	Club	REGULAR SEASON GP	G	A	Pts	PIM	PLAYOFFS GP	G	A	Pts	PIM
1991-92	Edmonton Oilers	58	12	16	28	18	12	2	1	3	0
1992-93	Edmonton Oilers	26	2	6	8	28	....	....	....	....	....
	Philadelphia Flyers	40	13	12	25	50	....	....	....	....	....
1993-94	Philadelphia Flyers	80	28	21	49	85	....	....	....	....	....

Season	Club	GP	G	A	Pts	PIM	GP	G	A	Pts	PIM
		REGULAR SEASON					PLAYOFFS				
1994-95	Philadelphia Flyers	14	5	5	10	2	....	....	....	....	....
	Vancouver Canucks	37	8	13	21	28	11	1	1	2	12
1995-96	Vancouver Canucks	61	6	14	20	60	3	2	1	3	0
1996-97	Pittsburgh Penguins	8	3	1	4	4	5	0	0	0	2
1998-99	Edmonton Oilers	66	19	30	49	23	2	0	0	0	4
99-2000	Edmonton Oilers	58	9	8	17	39	....	....	....	....	....
	Pittsburgh Penguins	13	4	4	8	18	11	0	3	3	4
2000-01	Pittsburgh Penguins	70	9	14	23	43	13	0	2	2	2
	NHL Totals	**531**	**118**	**144**	**262**	**398**	**57**	**5**	**8**	**13**	**24**

Traded to **Philadelphia** by **Edmonton** with Greg Hawgood for Brian Benning, January 16, 1993. Traded to **Vancouver** by **Philadelphia** for Shawn Antoski, February 15, 1995. Traded to **Pittsburgh** by **Vancouver** for future considerations, March 18, 1997. Traded to **Edmonton** by **Pittsburgh** for Bobby Dollas and Tony Hrkac, June 16, 1998. Traded to **Pittsburgh** by **Edmonton** for German Titov, March 14, 2000.

BERARD, Bryan

Defense. Shoots left. 6'2", 195 lbs. Born, Woonsocket, RI, March 5, 1977.
(Ottawa's 1st choice, 1st overall, in 1995 Entry Draft).

Season	Club	GP	G	A	Pts	PIM	GP	G	A	Pts	PIM
1996-97	New York Islanders	82	8	40	48	86	....	....	....	....	....
1997-98	New York Islanders	75	14	32	46	59	....	....	....	....	....
1998-99	New York Islanders	31	4	11	15	26	....	....	....	....	....
	Toronto Maple Leafs	38	5	14	19	22	17	1	8	9	8
99-2000	Toronto Maple Leafs	64	3	27	30	42	....	....	....	....	....
2001-02	New York Rangers	82	2	21	23	60	....	....	....	....	....
2002-03	Boston Bruins	80	10	28	38	64	3	1	0	1	2
	NHL Totals	**452**	**46**	**173**	**219**	**359**	**20**	**2**	**8**	**10**	**10**

NHL All-Rookie Team (1997) • Calder Memorial Trophy (1997)

Traded to **NY Islanders** by **Ottawa** with Don Beaupre and Martin Straka for Damian Rhodes and Wade Redden, January 23, 1996. Traded to **Toronto** by **NY Islanders** with NY Islanders' 6th round choice (Jan Sochor) in 1999 Entry Draft for Felix Potvin and Toronto's 6th round choice (later traded to Tampa Bay – Tampa Bay selected Fedor Fedorov) in 1999 Entry Draft, January 9, 1999. • Missed remainder of 1999-2000 season and entire 2000-01 season recovering from eye injury suffered in game vs. Ottawa, March 11, 2000. Signed as a free agent by **NY Rangers**, October 5, 2001. Signed as a free agent by **Boston**, August 13, 2002.

BEREHOWSKY, Drake

Defense. Shoots right. 6'2", 225 lbs. Born, Toronto, Ont., January 3, 1972.
(Toronto's 1st choice, 10th overall, in 1990 Entry Draft).

Season	Club	GP	G	A	Pts	PIM	GP	G	A	Pts	PIM
1990-91	Toronto Maple Leafs	8	0	1	1	25	....	....	....	....	....
1991-92	Toronto Maple Leafs	1	0	0	0	0	....	....	....	....	....
1992-93	Toronto Maple Leafs	41	4	15	19	61	....	....	....	....	....
1993-94	Toronto Maple Leafs	49	2	8	10	63	....	....	....	....	....
1994-95	Toronto Maple Leafs	25	0	2	2	15	....	....	....	....	....
	Pittsburgh Penguins	4	0	0	0	13	1	0	0	0	0
1995-96	Pittsburgh Penguins	1	0	0	0	0	....	....	....	....	....
1997-98	Edmonton Oilers	67	1	6	7	169	12	1	2	3	14
1998-99	Nashville Predators	74	2	15	17	140	....	....	....	....	....
99-2000	Nashville Predators	79	12	20	32	87	....	....	....	....	....
2000-01	Nashville Predators	66	6	18	24	100	....	....	....	....	....
	Vancouver Canucks	14	1	1	2	21	4	0	0	0	12
2001-02	Vancouver Canucks	25	1	2	3	18	....	....	....	....	....
	Phoenix Coyotes	32	1	4	5	42	5	0	1	1	4
2002-03	Phoenix Coyotes	7	1	2	3	27	....	....	....	....	....
	NHL Totals	**493**	**31**	**94**	**125**	**781**	**22**	**1**	**3**	**4**	**30**

Traded to **Pittsburgh** by **Toronto** for Grant Jennings, April 7, 1995. Signed as a free agent by **Edmonton**, September 30, 1997. Traded to **Nashville** by **Edmonton** with Eric Fichaud and Greg de Vries for Mikhail Shtalenkov and Jim Dowd, October 1, 1998. Traded to **Vancouver** by **Nashville** for Atlanta's 2nd round choice (previously acquired, Nashville selected Timofei Shishkanov) in 2001 Entry Draft, March 9, 2001. Traded to **Phoenix** by **Vancouver** with Denis Pederson for Todd Warriner, Trevor Letowski, Tyler Bouck and Phoenix's 3rd round choice (later traded back to Phoenix – Phoenix selected Dimitri Pestunov) in 2003 Entry Draft, December 28, 2001. • Missed majority of 2002-03 season recovering from knee injury suffered in training camp, September 24, 2002.

BERENSON, Red

Center. Shoots left. 6', 185 lbs. Born, Regina, Sask., December 8, 1939.

Season	Club	GP	G	A	Pts	PIM	GP	G	A	Pts	PIM
1961-62	Montreal Canadiens	4	1	2	3	4	5	2	0	2	0
1962-63	Montreal Canadiens	37	2	6	8	15	5	0	0	0	0
1963-64	Montreal Canadiens	69	7	9	16	12	7	0	0	0	4
1964-65◆	Montreal Canadiens	3	1	2	3	0	9	0	1	1	2
1965-66	Montreal Canadiens	23	3	4	7	12	....	....	....	....	....
1966-67	New York Rangers	30	0	5	5	2	4	0	1	1	2
1967-68	New York Rangers	19	2	1	3	2	....	....	....	....	....
	St. Louis Blues	55	22	29	51	22	18	5	2	7	9
1968-69	St. Louis Blues	76	35	47	82	43	12	7	3	10	20
1969-70	St. Louis Blues	67	33	39	72	38	16	7	5	12	8
1970-71	St. Louis Blues	45	16	26	42	12	....	....	....	....	....
	Detroit Red Wings	24	5	12	17	4	....	....	....	....	....
1971-72	Detroit Red Wings	78	28	41	69	16	....	....	....	....	....
1972-73	Detroit Red Wings	78	13	30	43	8	....	....	....	....	....
1973-74	Detroit Red Wings	76	24	42	66	28	....	....	....	....	....
1974-75	Detroit Red Wings	27	3	3	6	8	....	....	....	....	....
	St. Louis Blues	44	12	19	31	12	2	1	0	1	0
1975-76	St. Louis Blues	72	20	27	47	47	3	1	2	3	0
1976-77	St. Louis Blues	80	21	28	49	8	4	0	0	0	4
1977-78	St. Louis Blues	80	13	25	38	12	....	....	....	....	....
	NHL Totals	**987**	**261**	**397**	**658**	**305**	**85**	**23**	**14**	**37**	**49**

Played in NHL All-Star Game (1965, 1969, 1970, 1971, 1972, 1974)

Traded to **NY Rangers** by **Montreal** for Ted Taylor and Garry Peters, June 13, 1966. Traded to **St. Louis** by **NY Rangers** with Barclay Plager for Ron Stewart and Ron Attwell, November 29, 1967. Traded to **Detroit** by **St. Louis** with Tim Ecclestone for Garry Unger and Wayne Connelly, February 6, 1971. Traded to **St. Louis** by **Detroit** for Phil Roberto and St. Louis' 3rd round choice (Blair Davidson) in 1975 Amateur Draft, December 30, 1974.

BERENZWEIG, Bubba

Defense. Shoots left. 6'1", 217 lbs. Born, Arlington Heights, IL, August 8, 1977.
(NY Islanders' 5th choice, 109th overall, in 1996 Entry Draft).

Season	Club	GP	G	A	Pts	PIM	GP	G	A	Pts	PIM
99-2000	Nashville Predators	2	0	0	0	0	....	....	....	....	....
2000-01	Nashville Predators	5	0	0	0	0	....	....	....	....	....
2001-02	Nashville Predators	26	3	7	10	14	....	....	....	....	....
2002-03	Nashville Predators	4	0	0	0	0	....	....	....	....	....
	NHL Totals	**37**	**3**	**7**	**10**	**14**	....	....	....	....	....

Traded to **Nashville** by **NY Islanders** for Nashville's 4th round choice (Johan Halvardsson) in 1999 Entry Draft, April 14, 1999. Traded to **Dallas** by **Nashvlle** with future considerations for Jon Sim, February 17, 2003.

BEREZAN, Perry

Center. Shoots right. 6'2", 190 lbs. Born, Edmonton, Alta., December 5, 1964.
(Calgary's 3rd choice, 56th overall, in 1983 Entry Draft).

Season	Club	GP	G	A	Pts	PIM	GP	G	A	Pts	PIM
1984-85	Calgary Flames	9	3	2	5	4	2	1	0	1	4
1985-86	Calgary Flames	55	12	21	33	39	8	1	1	2	6
1986-87	Calgary Flames	24	5	3	8	24	2	0	2	2	7
1987-88	Calgary Flames	29	7	12	19	66	8	0	2	2	13
1988-89	Calgary Flames	35	4	4	8	23	....	....	....	....	....
	Minnesota North Stars	16	1	4	5	4	5	1	2	3	4
1989-90	Minnesota North Stars	64	3	12	15	31	5	1	0	1	0
1990-91	Minnesota North Stars	52	11	6	17	30	1	0	0	0	0
1991-92	San Jose Sharks	66	12	7	19	30	....	....	....	....	....
1992-93	San Jose Sharks	28	3	4	7	28	....	....	....	....	....
	NHL Totals	**378**	**61**	**75**	**136**	**279**	**31**	**4**	**7**	**11**	**34**

Traded to **Minnesota** by **Calgary** with Shane Churla for Brian MacLellan and Minnesota's 4th round choice (Robert Reichel) in 1989 Entry Draft, March 4, 1989. Signed as a free agent by **San Jose**, October 10, 1991.

BEREZIN, Sergei

Left wing. Shoots right. 5'10", 200 lbs. Born, Voskresensk, USSR, November 5, 1971.
(Toronto's 8th choice, 256th overall, in 1994 Entry Draft).

Season	Club	GP	G	A	Pts	PIM	GP	G	A	Pts	PIM
1996-97	Toronto Maple Leafs	73	25	16	41	2	....	....	....	....	....
1997-98	Toronto Maple Leafs	68	16	15	31	10	....	....	....	....	....
1998-99	Toronto Maple Leafs	76	37	22	59	12	17	6	6	12	4
99-2000	Toronto Maple Leafs	61	26	13	39	2	12	4	4	8	0
2000-01	Toronto Maple Leafs	79	22	28	50	8	11	2	5	7	2
2001-02	Phoenix Coyotes	41	7	9	16	4	....	....	....	....	....
	Montreal Canadiens	29	4	6	10	4	6	1	1	2	0
2002-03	Chicago Blackhawks	66	18	13	31	8	....	....	....	....	....
	Washington Capitals	9	5	4	9	4	6	0	1	1	0
	NHL Totals	**502**	**160**	**126**	**286**	**54**	**52**	**13**	**17**	**30**	**6**

NHL All-Rookie Team (1997)

Traded to **Phoenix** by **Toronto** for Mikael Renberg, June 23, 2001. Traded to **Montreal** by **Phoenix** for Brian Savage, Montreal's 3rd round choice (Matt Jones) in 2002 Entry Draft and future considerations, January 25, 2002. Traded to **Chicago** by **Montreal** for Chicago's 4th round choice in 2004 Entry Draft, June 30, 2002. Traded to **Washington** by **Chicago** for Washington's 4th round choice in 2004 Entry Draft, March 11, 2003.

BERG, Aki

Defense. Shoots left. 6'3", 220 lbs. Born, Turku, Finland, July 28, 1977.
(Los Angeles' 1st choice, 3rd overall, in 1995 Entry Draft).

Season	Club	GP	G	A	Pts	PIM	GP	G	A	Pts	PIM
1995-96	Los Angeles Kings	51	0	7	7	29	....	....	....	....	....
1996-97	Los Angeles Kings	41	2	6	8	24	....	....	....	....	....
1997-98	Los Angeles Kings	72	0	8	8	61	4	0	3	3	0
99-2000	Los Angeles Kings	70	3	13	16	45	2	0	0	0	2
2000-01	Los Angeles Kings	47	0	4	4	43	....	....	....	....	....
	Toronto Maple Leafs	12	3	0	3	2	11	0	2	2	4
2001-02	Toronto Maple Leafs	81	1	10	11	46	20	0	1	1	37
2002-03	Toronto Maple Leafs	78	4	7	11	28	7	1	1	2	2
	NHL Totals	**452**	**13**	**55**	**68**	**278**	**44**	**1**	**7**	**8**	**45**

Traded to **Toronto** by **Los Angeles** for Adam Mair and Toronto's 2nd round choice (Mike Cammalleri) in 2001 Entry Draft, March 13, 2001.

BERG, Bill

Left wing. Shoots left. 6'1", 205 lbs. Born, St. Catharines, Ont., October 21, 1967.
(NY Islanders' 3rd choice, 59th overall, in 1986 Entry Draft).

Season	Club	GP	G	A	Pts	PIM	GP	G	A	Pts	PIM
1988-89	New York Islanders	7	1	2	3	10	....	....	....	....	....
1990-91	New York Islanders	78	9	14	23	67	....	....	....	....	....
1991-92	New York Islanders	47	5	9	14	28	....	....	....	....	....
1992-93	New York Islanders	22	6	3	9	49	....	....	....	....	....
	Toronto Maple Leafs	58	7	8	15	54	21	1	1	2	18
1993-94	Toronto Maple Leafs	83	8	11	19	93	18	1	2	3	10
1994-95	Toronto Maple Leafs	32	5	1	6	26	7	0	1	1	4
1995-96	Toronto Maple Leafs	23	1	1	2	33	....	....	....	....	....
	New York Rangers	18	2	1	3	8	10	1	0	1	0
1996-97	New York Rangers	67	8	6	14	37	3	0	0	0	2

Season	Club	Regular Season GP	G	A	Pts	PIM	Playoffs GP	G	A	Pts	PIM
1997-98	New York Rangers	67	1	9	10	55	....	....	....	....	....
1998-99	Ottawa Senators	44	2	2	4	28	2	0	0	0	0
	NHL Totals	**546**	**55**	**67**	**122**	**488**	**61**	**3**	**4**	**7**	**34**

Claimed on waivers by **Toronto** from **NY Islanders**, December 3, 1992. Traded to **NY Rangers** by **Toronto** for Nick Kypreos, February 29, 1996. Traded to **Ottawa** by **NY Rangers** with NY Rangers' 2nd round choice (later traded to Anaheim – Anaheim selected Jordan Leopold) in 1999 Entry Draft for Stan Neckar, November 27, 1998.

BERGDINON, Fred

Right wing. Shoots right. 6'1", 170 lbs. Born, Parry Sound, Ont., 1906.

Season	Club	GP	G	A	Pts	PIM	GP	G	A	Pts	PIM
1925-26	Boston Bruins	2	0	0	0	0	....	....	....	....	....
	NHL Totals	**2**	**0**	**0**	**0**	**0**	....	....	....	....	....

Signed as a free agent by **Boston**, December 14, 1925.

BERGEN, Todd

Center. Shoots left. 6'3", 185 lbs. Born, Prince Albert, Sask., July 11, 1963.
(Philadelphia's 5th choice, 98th overall, in 1982 Entry Draft).

Season	Club	GP	G	A	Pts	PIM	GP	G	A	Pts	PIM
1984-85	Philadelphia Flyers	14	11	5	16	4	17	4	9	13	8
	NHL Totals	**14**	**11**	**5**	**16**	**4**	**17**	**4**	**9**	**13**	**8**

• Suspended by **Philadelphia** for refusing to report to training camp, September, 1985.
• Announced retirement to pursue career as a professional golfer, September, 1985. Traded to **Minnesota** by **Philadelphia** with Ed Hospodar for Dave Richter and Bo Berglund, November 29, 1985.

BERGER, Mike

Defense. Shoots right. 6', 195 lbs. Born, Edmonton, Alta., June 2, 1967.
(Minnesota's 2nd choice, 69th overall, in 1985 Entry Draft).

Season	Club	GP	G	A	Pts	PIM	GP	G	A	Pts	PIM
1987-88	Minnesota North Stars	29	3	1	4	65	....	....	....	....	....
1988-89	Minnesota North Stars	1	0	0	0	2	....	....	....	....	....
	NHL Totals	**30**	**3**	**1**	**4**	**67**	....	....	....	....	....

Traded to **Hartford** by **Minnesota** for Kevin Sullivan, October 7, 1989.

BERGERON, Marc-Andre

Defense. Shoots left. 5'9", 185 lbs. Born, St-Louis-de-France, Que., October 13, 1980.

Season	Club	GP	G	A	Pts	PIM	GP	G	A	Pts	PIM
2002-03	Edmonton Oilers	5	1	1	2	9	1	0	1	1	0
	NHL Totals	**5**	**1**	**1**	**2**	**9**	**1**	**0**	**1**	**1**	**0**

Signed as a free agent by **Edmonton**, July 20, 2001.

BERGERON, Michel

Right wing. Shoots right. 5'10", 170 lbs. Born, Chicoutimi, Que., November 11, 1954.
(Detroit's 4th choice, 63rd overall, in 1974 Amateur Draft).

Season	Club	GP	G	A	Pts	PIM	GP	G	A	Pts	PIM
1974-75	Detroit Red Wings	25	10	7	17	10	....	....	....	....	....
1975-76	Detroit Red Wings	72	32	27	59	48	....	....	....	....	....
1976-77	Detroit Red Wings	74	21	12	33	98	....	....	....	....	....
1977-78	Detroit Red Wings	3	1	0	1	0	....	....	....	....	....
	New York Islanders	25	9	6	15	2	....	....	....	....	....
1978-79	Washington Capitals	30	7	6	13	7	....	....	....	....	....
	NHL Totals	**229**	**80**	**58**	**138**	**165**	....	....	....	....	....

Traded to **NY Islanders** by **Detroit** for Andre St. Laurent, October 20, 1977. Traded to **Washington** by **NY Islanders** for Washington's 2nd round choice (Tomas Jonsson) in 1979 Entry Draft, October 19, 1978.

BERGERON, Yves

Right wing. Shoots right. 5'9", 165 lbs. Born, Malartic, Que., January 11, 1952.
(Pittsburgh's 8th choice, 120th overall, in 1972 Amateur Draft).

Season	Club	GP	G	A	Pts	PIM	GP	G	A	Pts	PIM
1974-75	Pittsburgh Penguins	2	0	0	0	0	....	....	....	....	....
1976-77	Pittsburgh Penguins	1	0	0	0	0	....	....	....	....	....
	NHL Totals	**3**	**0**	**0**	**0**	**0**	....	....	....	....	....

BERGEVIN, Marc

Defense. Shoots left. 6'1", 214 lbs. Born, Montreal, Que., August 11, 1965.
(Chicago's 3rd choice, 60th overall, in 1983 Entry Draft).

Season	Club	GP	G	A	Pts	PIM	GP	G	A	Pts	PIM
1984-85	Chicago Black Hawks	60	0	6	6	54	6	0	3	3	2
1985-86	Chicago Black Hawks	71	7	7	14	60	3	0	0	0	0
1986-87	Chicago Blackhawks	66	4	10	14	66	3	1	0	1	2
1987-88	Chicago Blackhawks	58	1	6	7	85	....	....	....	....	....
1988-89	Chicago Blackhawks	11	0	0	0	18	....	....	....	....	....
	New York Islanders	58	2	13	15	62	....	....	....	....	....
1989-90	New York Islanders	18	0	4	4	30	....	....	....	....	....
1990-91	Hartford Whalers	4	0	0	0	4	....	....	....	....	....
1991-92	Hartford Whalers	75	7	17	24	64	5	0	0	0	2
1992-93	Tampa Bay Lightning	78	2	12	14	66	....	....	....	....	....
1993-94	Tampa Bay Lightning	83	1	15	16	87	....	....	....	....	....
1994-95	Tampa Bay Lightning	44	2	4	6	51	....	....	....	....	....
1995-96	Detroit Red Wings	70	1	9	10	33	17	1	0	1	14
1996-97	St. Louis Blues	82	0	4	4	53	6	1	0	1	8
1997-98	St. Louis Blues	81	3	7	10	90	10	0	1	1	8
1998-99	St. Louis Blues	52	1	1	2	99	....	....	....	....	....
99-2000	St. Louis Blues	81	1	8	9	75	7	0	1	1	6
2000-01	St. Louis Blues	2	0	0	0	0	....	....	....	....	....
	Pittsburgh Penguins	36	1	4	5	26	12	0	1	1	2
2001-02	St. Louis Blues	30	0	3	3	2	7	0	0	0	4
2002-03	Pittsburgh Penguins	69	2	5	7	36	....	....	....	....	....
	Tampa Bay Lightning	1	0	0	0	0	....	....	....	....	....
	NHL Totals	**1130**	**35**	**135**	**170**	**1061**	**76**	**3**	**6**	**9**	**48**

Traded to **NY Islanders** by **Chicago** with Gary Nylund for Steve Konroyd and Bob Bassen, November 25, 1988. Traded to **Hartford** by **NY Islanders** for Hartford's 5th round choice (Ryan Duthie) in 1992 Entry Draft, October 30, 1990. Signed as a free agent by **Tampa Bay**, July 9, 1992. Traded to **Detroit** by **Tampa Bay** with Ben Hankinson for Shawn Burr and Detroit's 3rd round choice (later traded to Boston – Boston selected Jason Doyle) in 1996 Entry Draft, August 17, 1995. Signed as a free agent by **St. Louis**, July 31, 1996. Traded to **Pittsburgh** by **St. Louis** for Dan Trebil, December 28, 2000. • Missed majority of 2000-01 season recovering from thumb (October 5, 2000 vs. Phoenix) and knee (February 23, 2001 vs. Detroit) injuries. Signed as a free agent by **St. Louis**, November 6, 2001. Signed as a free agent by **Pittsburgh**, July 18, 2002. Traded to **Tampa Bay** by **Pittsburgh** for Brian Holzinger, March 11, 2003. Traded to **Pittsburgh** by **Tampa Bay** for NY Rangers' 9th round choice (previouslly acquired, Tampa Bay selected Albert Vishnyakov) in 2003 Entry Draft, May 12, 2003.

BERGKVIST, Stefan

Defense. Shoots left. 6'2", 224 lbs. Born, Leksand, Sweden, March 10, 1975.
(Pittsburgh's 1st choice, 26th overall, in 1993 Entry Draft).

Season	Club	GP	G	A	Pts	PIM	GP	G	A	Pts	PIM
1995-96	Pittsburgh Penguins	2	0	0	0	2	4	0	0	0	2
1996-97	Pittsburgh Penguins	5	0	0	0	7	....	....	....	....	....
	NHL Totals	**7**	**0**	**0**	**0**	**9**	**4**	**0**	**0**	**0**	**2**

BERGLAND, Tim

Right wing. Shoots right. 6'3", 194 lbs. Born, Crookston, MN, January 11, 1965.
(Washington's 1st choice, 77th overall, in 1983 Entry Draft).

Season	Club	GP	G	A	Pts	PIM	GP	G	A	Pts	PIM
1989-90	Washington Capitals	32	2	5	7	31	15	1	1	2	10
1990-91	Washington Capitals	47	5	9	14	21	11	1	1	2	12
1991-92	Washington Capitals	22	1	4	5	2	....	....	....	....	....
1992-93	Tampa Bay Lightning	27	3	3	6	11	....	....	....	....	....
1993-94	Tampa Bay Lightning	51	6	5	11	6	....	....	....	....	....
	Washington Capitals	3	0	0	0	4	....	....	....	....	....
	NHL Totals	**182**	**17**	**26**	**43**	**75**	**26**	**2**	**2**	**4**	**22**

Claimed by **Tampa Bay** from **Washington** in Expansion Draft, June 18, 1992. Claimed on waivers by **Washington** from **Tampa Bay**, March 19, 1994.

BERGLOFF, Bob

Defense. Shoots right. 6'1", 185 lbs. Born, Dickinson, ND, July 26, 1958.
(Minnesota's 6th choice, 87th overall, in 1978 Amateur Draft).

Season	Club	GP	G	A	Pts	PIM	GP	G	A	Pts	PIM
1982-83	Minnesota North Stars	2	0	0	0	5	....	....	....	....	....
	NHL Totals	**2**	**0**	**0**	**0**	**5**	....	....	....	....	....

BERGLUND, Bo

Right wing. Shoots left. 5'10", 175 lbs. Born, Sjalevad, Sweden, April 6, 1955.
(Quebec's 10th choice, 242nd overall, in 1983 Entry Draft).

Season	Club	GP	G	A	Pts	PIM	GP	G	A	Pts	PIM
1983-84	Quebec Nordiques	75	16	27	43	20	7	2	0	2	4
1984-85	Quebec Nordiques	12	4	1	5	6	....	....	....	....	....
	Minnesota North Stars	33	6	9	15	8	2	0	0	0	2
1985-86	Minnesota North Stars	3	2	0	2	2	....	....	....	....	....
	Philadelphia Flyers	7	0	2	2	4	....	....	....	....	....
	NHL Totals	**130**	**28**	**39**	**67**	**40**	**9**	**2**	**0**	**2**	**6**

Traded to **Minnesota** by **Quebec** with Tony McKegney for Brad Maxwell and Brent Ashton, December 14, 1984. Traded to **Philadelphia** by **Minnesota** with Dave Richter for Todd Bergen and Ed Hospodar, November 29, 1985.

BERGLUND, Christian

Left wing. Shoots left. 5'11", 195 lbs. Born, Orebro, Sweden, March 12, 1980.
(New Jersey's 3rd choice, 37th overall, in 1998 Entry Draft).

Season	Club	GP	G	A	Pts	PIM	GP	G	A	Pts	PIM
2001-02	New Jersey Devils	15	2	7	9	8	3	0	0	0	2
2002-03	New Jersey Devils	38	4	5	9	20	....	....	....	....	....
	NHL Totals	**53**	**6**	**12**	**18**	**28**	**3**	**0**	**0**	**0**	**2**

BERGMAN, Gary

Defense. Shoots left. 5'11", 188 lbs. Born, Kenora, Ont., October 7, 1938.

Season	Club	GP	G	A	Pts	PIM	GP	G	A	Pts	PIM
1964-65	Detroit Red Wings	58	4	7	11	85	5	0	1	1	4
1965-66	Detroit Red Wings	61	3	16	19	96	12	0	3	3	14
1966-67	Detroit Red Wings	70	5	30	35	129	....	....	....	....	....
1967-68	Detroit Red Wings	74	13	28	41	109	....	....	....	....	....
1968-69	Detroit Red Wings	76	7	30	37	80	....	....	....	....	....
1969-70	Detroit Red Wings	69	6	17	23	122	4	0	1	1	2
1970-71	Detroit Red Wings	68	8	25	33	149	....	....	....	....	....
1971-72	Detroit Red Wings	75	6	31	37	138	....	....	....	....	....
1972-73	Detroit Red Wings	68	3	28	31	71	....	....	....	....	....
1973-74	Detroit Red Wings	11	0	6	6	18	....	....	....	....	....
	Minnesota North Stars	57	3	23	26	66	....	....	....	....	....
1974-75	Detroit Red Wings	76	5	25	30	104	....	....	....	....	....

		REGULAR SEASON					PLAYOFFS				
Season	Club	GP	G	A	Pts	PIM	GP	G	A	Pts	PIM
1975-76	Kansas City Scouts	75	5	33	38	82	....	....	....	....	....
	NHL Totals	**838**	**68**	**299**	**367**	**1249**	**21**	**0**	**5**	**5**	**20**

Played in NHL All-Star Game (1973)

Claimed by **Chicago** from **Winnipeg** (WHL) in Inter-League Draft, June 7, 1960. Traded to **Cleveland** (AHL) by **Chicago** (Buffalo-AHL) for cash, October, 1961. Traded to **Quebec** (AHL) by **Montreal** (Cleveland-AHL) for cash, July, 1962. Traded to **Montreal** (Cleveland-AHL) by **Quebec** (AHL) for Terry Gray with Boston retaining Gray's NHL rights, November 1, 1962. Loaned to **Springfield** (AHL) by **Montreal** with the trade of Brian Smith, Wayne Boddy, Fred Hilts, Lorne O'Donnell and John Rodger for Terry Gray, Bruce Cline, Wayne Larkin, John Chasczewski and Ted Harris, June, 1963. Claimed by **Detroit** from **Montreal** in Intra-League Draft, June 10, 1964. Traded to **Minnesota** by **Detroit** for Ted Harris, November 7, 1973. Traded to **Detroit** by **Minnesota** for Detroit's 3rd round choice (Alex Pirus) in 1975 Amateur Draft, October 1, 1974. Traded to **Kansas City** by **Detroit** with Bill McKenzie for Peter McDuffe and Glen Burdon, August 22, 1975.

BERGMAN, Thommie

Defense. Shoots left. 6'2", 200 lbs. Born, Munkfors, Sweden, December 10, 1947.

Season	Club	GP	G	A	Pts	PIM	GP	G	A	Pts	PIM
1972-73	Detroit Red Wings	75	9	12	21	70	....	....	....	....	....
1973-74	Detroit Red Wings	43	0	3	3	21	....	....	....	....	....
1974-75	Detroit Red Wings	18	0	1	1	27	....	....	....	....	....
1977-78	Detroit Red Wings	14	1	6	7	16	7	0	2	2	2
1978-79	Detroit Red Wings	68	10	17	27	64	....	....	....	....	....
1979-80	Detroit Red Wings	28	1	5	6	45	....	....	....	....	....
	NHL Totals	**246**	**21**	**44**	**65**	**243**	**7**	**0**	**2**	**2**	**2**

Signed as a free agent by **Detroit**, August 31, 1972. Traded to **Winnipeg** (WHA) by **Detroit** for cash, December, 1974. Signed as a free agent by **Detroit**, March 16, 1978.

BERGQVIST, Jonas

Right wing. Shoots left. 6', 185 lbs. Born, Hassleholm, Sweden, September 26, 1962.
(Calgary's 6th choice, 126th overall, in 1988 Entry Draft).

Season	Club	GP	G	A	Pts	PIM	GP	G	A	Pts	PIM
1989-90	Calgary Flames	22	2	5	7	10	....	....	....	....	....
	NHL Totals	**22**	**2**	**5**	**7**	**10**	....	....	....	....	....

BERLINQUETTE, Louis

Left wing. Shoots left. 5'11", 175 lbs. Born, Papineau, Que., 1887.

Season	Club	GP	G	A	Pts	PIM	GP	G	A	Pts	PIM
1917-18	Montreal Canadiens	20	2	1	3	12	2	0	0	0	0
1918-19	Montreal Canadiens	18	5	3	8	9	5	0	2	2	9
	Montreal Canadiens (Cup)	....	....	....	....	....	*5*	*1*	*1*	*2*	*0*
1919-20	Montreal Canadiens	24	8	9	17	36	....	....	....	....	....
1920-21	Montreal Canadiens	24	11	9	20	28	....	....	....	....	....
1921-22	Montreal Canadiens	24	13	5	18	10	....	....	....	....	....
1922-23	Montreal Canadiens	24	2	4	6	4	2	0	2	2	0
1924-25	Montreal Maroons	29	4	2	6	22	....	....	....	....	....
1925-26	Pittsburgh Pirates	30	0	0	0	8	2	0	0	0	0
	NHL Totals	**193**	**45**	**33**	**78**	**129**	**11**	**0**	**4**	**4**	**9**

Rights retained by **Montreal** after NHA folded, November 26, 1917. Traded to **Saskatoon** (WCHL) by **Montreal** for cash, November 1, 1923. Traded to **Mtl. Maroons** by **Saskatoon** (WCHL) for cash, November 26, 1924. Signed as a free agent by **Pittsburgh**, November 10, 1925.

BERNIER, Serge

Right wing. Shoots right. 6'1", 190 lbs. Born, Padoue, Que., April 29, 1947.
(Philadelphia's 1st choice, 5th overall, in 1967 Amateur Draft).

Season	Club	GP	G	A	Pts	PIM	GP	G	A	Pts	PIM
1968-69	Philadelphia Flyers	1	0	0	0	2	....	....	....	....	....
1969-70	Philadelphia Flyers	1	0	1	1	0	....	....	....	....	....
1970-71	Philadelphia Flyers	77	23	28	51	77	4	1	1	2	0
1971-72	Philadelphia Flyers	44	12	11	23	51	....	....	....	....	....
	Los Angeles Kings	26	11	11	22	12	....	....	....	....	....
1972-73	Los Angeles Kings	75	22	46	68	43	....	....	....	....	....
1979-80	Quebec Nordiques	32	8	14	22	31	....	....	....	....	....
1980-81	Quebec Nordiques	46	2	8	10	18	1	0	0	0	0
	NHL Totals	**302**	**78**	**119**	**197**	**234**	**5**	**1**	**1**	**2**	**0**

Traded to **Los Angeles** by **Philadelphia** with Bill Lesuk and Jim Johnson for Bill Flett, Eddie Joyal, Jean Potvin and Ross Lonsberry, January 28, 1972. Rights retained by **Quebec** prior to Expansion Draft, June 9, 1979.

BERRY, Bob

Left wing. Shoots left. 6', 185 lbs. Born, Montreal, Que., November 29, 1943.

Season	Club	GP	G	A	Pts	PIM	GP	G	A	Pts	PIM
1968-69	Montreal Canadiens	2	0	0	0	0	....	....	....	....	....
1970-71	Los Angeles Kings	77	25	38	63	52	....	....	....	....	....
1971-72	Los Angeles Kings	78	17	22	39	44	....	....	....	....	....
1972-73	Los Angeles Kings	78	36	28	64	75	....	....	....	....	....
1973-74	Los Angeles Kings	77	23	33	56	56	5	0	0	0	0
1974-75	Los Angeles Kings	80	25	23	48	60	3	1	2	3	2
1975-76	Los Angeles Kings	80	20	22	42	37	9	1	1	2	0
1976-77	Los Angeles Kings	69	13	25	38	20	9	0	3	3	4
	NHL Totals	**541**	**159**	**191**	**350**	**344**	**26**	**2**	**6**	**8**	**6**

Played in NHL All-Star Game (1973, 1974)

Traded to **Los Angeles** by **Montreal** for cash, October 8, 1970.

BERRY, Brad

Defense. Shoots left. 6'2", 190 lbs. Born, Bashaw, Alta., April 1, 1965.
(Winnipeg's 3rd choice, 29th overall, in 1983 Entry Draft).

Season	Club	GP	G	A	Pts	PIM	GP	G	A	Pts	PIM
1985-86	Winnipeg Jets	13	1	0	1	10	3	0	0	0	0
1986-87	Winnipeg Jets	52	2	8	10	60	7	0	1	1	14
1987-88	Winnipeg Jets	48	0	6	6	75	....	....	....	....	....
1988-89	Winnipeg Jets	38	0	9	9	45	....	....	....	....	....
1989-90	Winnipeg Jets	12	1	2	3	6	1	0	0	0	0
1991-92	Minnesota North Stars	7	0	0	0	6	2	0	0	0	2
1992-93	Minnesota North Stars	63	0	3	3	109	....	....	....	....	....
1993-94	Dallas Stars	8	0	0	0	12	....	....	....	....	....
	NHL Totals	**241**	**4**	**28**	**32**	**323**	**13**	**0**	**1**	**1**	**16**

Signed as a free agent by **Minnesota**, October 4, 1991. Transferred to **Dallas** after **Minnesota** franchise relocated, June 9, 1993.

BERRY, Doug

Center. Shoots left. 6'1", 190 lbs. Born, New Westminster, B.C., June 3, 1957.
(Colorado's 2nd choice, 38th overall, in 1977 Amateur Draft).

Season	Club	GP	G	A	Pts	PIM	GP	G	A	Pts	PIM
1979-80	Colorado Rockies	75	7	23	30	16	....	....	....	....	....
1980-81	Colorado Rockies	46	3	10	13	9	....	....	....	....	....
	NHL Totals	**121**	**10**	**33**	**43**	**25**	....	....	....	....	....

• Brother of Ken

Reclaimed by **Colorado** from **Edmonton** (WHA) prior to Expansion Draft, June 9, 1979.

BERRY, Fred

Center. Shoots left. 5'9", 175 lbs. Born, Edmonton, Alta., March 26, 1956.
(Detroit's 3rd choice, 40th overall, in 1976 Amateur Draft).

Season	Club	GP	G	A	Pts	PIM	GP	G	A	Pts	PIM
1976-77	Detroit Red Wings	3	0	0	0	0	....	....	....	....	....
	NHL Totals	**3**	**0**	**0**	**0**	**0**	....	....	....	....	....

Traded to **Toledo** (IHL) by **Detroit** (Kalamazoo (IHL) with Al Stoneman and Dean Willers for Pete Crawford and Randy Mohns, December, 1978.

BERRY, Ken

Left wing. Shoots left. 5'9", 175 lbs. Born, Burnaby, B.C., June 21, 1960.
(Vancouver's 5th choice, 112th overall, in 1980 Entry Draft).

Season	Club	GP	G	A	Pts	PIM	GP	G	A	Pts	PIM
1981-82	Edmonton Oilers	15	2	3	5	9	....	....	....	....	....
1983-84	Edmonton Oilers	13	2	3	5	10	....	....	....	....	....
1987-88	Vancouver Canucks	14	2	3	5	6	....	....	....	....	....
1988-89	Vancouver Canucks	13	2	1	3	5	....	....	....	....	....
	NHL Totals	**55**	**8**	**10**	**18**	**30**	....	....	....	....	....

• Brother of Doug

Traded to **Edmonton** by **Vancouver** with Garry Lariviere for Blair MacDonald and the rights to Lars-Gunnar Petersson, March 10, 1981. Signed as a free agent by **Vancouver**, March 2, 1988.

BERRY, Rick

Defense. Shoots left. 6'2", 210 lbs. Born, Birtle, Man., November 4, 1978.
(Colorado's 3rd choice, 55th overall, in 1997 Entry Draft).

Season	Club	GP	G	A	Pts	PIM	GP	G	A	Pts	PIM
2000-01	Colorado Avalanche	19	0	4	4	38	....	....	....	....	....
2001-02	Colorado Avalanche	57	0	0	0	60	....	....	....	....	....
	Pittsburgh Penguins	13	0	2	2	21	....	....	....	....	....
2002-03	Washington Capitals	43	2	1	3	87	....	....	....	....	....
	NHL Totals	**132**	**2**	**7**	**9**	**206**	....	....	....	....	....

Traded to **Pittsburgh** by **Colorado** with Ville Nieminen for Darius Kasparaitis, March 19, 2002. Claimed by **Washington** from **Pittsburgh** in Waiver Draft, October 4, 2002.

BERTRAND, Eric

Left wing. Shoots left. 6'1", 2 lbs. Born, St-Ephrem, Que., April 16, 1975.
(New Jersey's 9th choice, 207th overall, in 1994 Entry Draft).

Season	Club	GP	G	A	Pts	PIM	GP	G	A	Pts	PIM
99-2000	New Jersey Devils	4	0	0	0	0	....	....	....	....	....
	Atlanta Thrashers	8	0	0	0	4	....	....	....	....	....
2000-01	Montreal Canadiens	3	0	0	0	0	....	....	....	....	....
	NHL Totals	**15**	**0**	**0**	**0**	**4**	....	....	....	....	....

Traded to **Atlanta** by **New Jersey** with Wes Mason for Sylvain Cloutier, Jeff Williams and Atlanta's 7th round choice (Ken Magowan) in 2000 Entry Draft, November 1, 1999. Traded to **Philadelphia** by **Atlanta** for Brian Wesenberg, December 9, 1999. Traded to **Nashville** by **Philadelphia** for future considerations, February 14, 2000. Signed as a free agent by **Montreal**, July 7, 2000.

BERTUZZI, Todd

Right wing. Shoots left. 6'3", 235 lbs. Born, Sudbury, Ont., February 2, 1975.
(NY Islanders' 1st choice, 23rd overall, in 1993 Entry Draft).

Season	Club	GP	G	A	Pts	PIM	GP	G	A	Pts	PIM
1995-96	New York Islanders	76	18	21	39	83	....	....	....	....	....
1996-97	New York Islanders	64	10	13	23	68	....	....	....	....	....
1997-98	New York Islanders	52	7	11	18	58	....	....	....	....	....
	Vancouver Canucks	22	6	9	15	63	....	....	....	....	....
1998-99	Vancouver Canucks	32	8	8	16	44	....	....	....	....	....
99-2000	Vancouver Canucks	80	25	25	50	126	....	....	....	....	....
2000-01	Vancouver Canucks	79	25	30	55	93	4	2	2	4	8
2001-02	Vancouver Canucks	72	36	49	85	110	6	2	2	4	14
2002-03	Vancouver Canucks	82	46	51	97	144	14	2	4	6	*60
	NHL Totals	**559**	**181**	**217**	**398**	**789**	**24**	**6**	**8**	**14**	**82**

NHL First All-Star Team (2003)

Played in NHL All-Star Game (2003)

Traded to **Vancouver** by **NY Islanders** with Bryan McCabe and NY Islanders' 3rd round choice (Jarkko Ruutu) in 1998 Entry Draft for Trevor Linden, February 6, 1998. • Missed majority of 1998-99 season recovering from leg injury suffered in game vs. Washington, November 1, 1998.

BERUBE, Craig

Left wing. Shoots left. 6'1", 210 lbs. Born, Calahoo, Alta., December 17, 1965.

Season	Club	GP	G	A	Pts	PIM	GP	G	A	Pts	PIM
1986-87	Philadelphia Flyers	7	0	0	0	57	5	0	0	0	17

Season	Club	GP	G	A	Pts	PIM	GP	G	A	Pts	PIM
		REGULAR SEASON					PLAYOFFS				
1987-88	Philadelphia Flyers	27	3	2	5	108	....	....	....	....	....
1988-89	Philadelphia Flyers	53	1	1	2	199	16	0	0	0	56
1989-90	Philadelphia Flyers	74	4	14	18	291	....	....	....	....	....
1990-91	Philadelphia Flyers	74	8	9	17	293	....	....	....	....	....
1991-92	Toronto Maple Leafs	40	5	7	12	109	....	....	....	....	....
	Calgary Flames	36	1	4	5	155	....	....	....	....	....
1992-93	Calgary Flames	77	4	8	12	209	6	0	1	1	21
1993-94	Washington Capitals	84	7	7	14	305	8	0	0	0	21
1994-95	Washington Capitals	43	2	4	6	173	7	0	0	0	29
1995-96	Washington Capitals	50	2	10	12	151	2	0	0	0	19
1996-97	Washington Capitals	80	4	3	7	218	....	....	....	....	....
1997-98	Washington Capitals	74	6	9	15	189	21	1	0	1	21
1998-99	Washington Capitals	66	5	4	9	166	....	....	....	....	....
	Philadelphia Flyers	11	0	0	0	28	6	1	0	1	4
99-2000	Philadelphia Flyers	77	4	8	12	162	18	1	0	1	23
2000-01	Washington Capitals	22	0	1	1	18	....	....	....	....	....
	New York Islanders	38	0	2	2	54	....	....	....	....	....
2001-02	Calgary Flames	66	3	1	4	164	....	....	....	....	....
2002-03	Calgary Flames	55	2	4	6	100	....	....	....	....	....
	NHL Totals	**1054**	**61**	**98**	**159**	**3149**	**89**	**3**	**1**	**4**	**211**

Signed as a free agent by **Philadelphia**, March 19, 1986. Traded to **Edmonton** by **Philadelphia** with Craig Fisher and Scott Mellanby for Dave Brown, Corey Foster and Jari Kurri, May 30, 1991. Traded to **Toronto** by **Edmonton** with Grant Fuhr and Glenn Anderson for Vincent Damphousse, Peter Ing, Scott Thornton and Luke Richardson, September 19, 1991. Traded to **Calgary** by **Toronto** with Alexander Godynyuk, Gary Leeman, Michel Petit and Jeff Reese for Doug Gilmour, Jamie Macoun, Ric Nattress, Rick Wamsley and Kent Manderville, January 2, 1992. Traded to **Washington** by **Calgary** for Washington's 5th round choice (Darryl Lafrance) in 1993 Entry Draft, June 26, 1993. Traded to **Philadelphia** by **Washington** for cash, March 23, 1999. Signed as a free agent by **Washington**, July 7, 2000. Traded to **NY Islanders** by **Washington** for Vancouver's 9th round choice (previously acquired, Washington selected Robert Muller) in 2001 Entry Draft, January 11, 2001. Signed as a free agent by **Calgary**, September 18, 2001.

BESLER, Phil

Right wing. Shoots right. 5'11", 180 lbs. Born, Melville, Sask., December 9, 1913.

Season	Club	GP	G	A	Pts	PIM	GP	G	A	Pts	PIM
1935-36	Boston Bruins	8	0	0	0	0	....	....	....	....	....
1938-39	Chicago Black Hawks	17	1	3	4	16	....	....	....	....	....
	Detroit Red Wings	5	0	1	1	2	....	....	....	....	....
	NHL Totals	**30**	**1**	**4**	**5**	**18**	....	....	....	....	....

Signed as a free agent by **Chicago**, September 29, 1938. Traded to **Detroit** by **Chicago** for Charley Mason, January 27, 1939.

BESSONE, Pete

USHOF

Defense. Shoots left. 5'11", 200 lbs. Born, New Bedford, MA, January 13, 1913.

Season	Club	GP	G	A	Pts	PIM	GP	G	A	Pts	PIM
1937-38	Detroit Red Wings	6	0	1	1	6	....	....	....	....	....
	NHL Totals	**6**	**0**	**1**	**1**	**6**	....	....	....	....	....

Signed as a free agent by **Detroit**, January 15, 1938. Traded to **Pittsburgh** (AHL) by **Detroit** for cash, October 5, 1939.

BETHEL, John

Left wing. Shoots left. 5'11", 185 lbs. Born, Montreal, Que., January 15, 1957.
(NY Rangers' 7th choice, 98th overall, in 1977 Amateur Draft).

Season	Club	GP	G	A	Pts	PIM	GP	G	A	Pts	PIM
1979-80	Winnipeg Jets	17	0	2	2	4	....	....	....	....	....
	NHL Totals	**17**	**0**	**2**	**2**	**4**	....	....	....	....	....

Signed as a free agent by **Winnipeg**, September, 1979.

BETIK, Karel

Defense. Shoots left. 6'2", 208 lbs. Born, Karvina, Czech., October 28, 1978.
(Tampa Bay's 6th choice, 112th overall, in 1997 Entry Draft).

Season	Club	GP	G	A	Pts	PIM	GP	G	A	Pts	PIM
1998-99	Tampa Bay Lightning	3	0	2	2	2	....	....	....	....	....
	NHL Totals	**3**	**0**	**2**	**2**	**2**	....	....	....	....	....

BETS, Maxim

Left wing. Shoots left. 6'1", 185 lbs. Born, Chelyabinsk, USSR, January 31, 1974.
(St. Louis' 1st choice, 37th overall, in 1993 Entry Draft).

Season	Club	GP	G	A	Pts	PIM	GP	G	A	Pts	PIM
1993-94	Mighty Ducks of Anaheim	3	0	0	0	0	....	....	....	....	....
	NHL Totals	**3**	**0**	**0**	**0**	**0**	....	....	....	....	....

Rights traded to **Anaheim** by **St. Louis** with St. Louis' 6th round choice (later traded back to St. Louis – St. Louis selected Denis Hamel) in 1995 Entry Draft for Alexei Kasatonov, March 21, 1994.

BETTIO, Sam

Left wing. Shoots left. 5'8", 175 lbs. Born, Copper Cliff, Ont., December 1, 1928.

Season	Club	GP	G	A	Pts	PIM	GP	G	A	Pts	PIM
1949-50	Boston Bruins	44	9	12	21	32	....	....	....	....	....
	NHL Totals	**44**	**9**	**12**	**21**	**32**	....	....	....	....	....

Traded to **Victoria** (WHL) by **Boston** with Pentti Lund for cash, July 1, 1953.

BETTS, Blair

Center. Shoots left. 6'1", 200 lbs. Born, Edmonton, Alta., February 16, 1980.
(Calgary's 2nd choice, 33rd overall, in 1998 Entry Draft).

Season	Club	GP	G	A	Pts	PIM	GP	G	A	Pts	PIM
2001-02	Calgary Flames	6	1	0	1	2	....	....	....	....	....
2002-03	Calgary Flames	9	1	3	4	0	....	....	....	....	....
	NHL Totals	**15**	**2**	**3**	**5**	**2**	....	....	....	....	....

• Missed majority of 2002-03 season recovering from shoulder and knee surgery, October 1, 2002.

BEUKEBOOM, Jeff

Defense. Shoots right. 6'5", 230 lbs. Born, Ajax, Ont., March 28, 1965.
(Edmonton's 1st choice, 19th overall, in 1983 Entry Draft).

Season	Club	GP	G	A	Pts	PIM	GP	G	A	Pts	PIM
1985-86	Edmonton Oilers	....	....	....	....	....	1	0	0	0	4
1986-87 ♦	Edmonton Oilers	44	3	8	11	124	....	....	....	....	....
1987-88 ♦	Edmonton Oilers	73	5	20	25	201	7	0	0	0	16
1988-89	Edmonton Oilers	36	0	5	5	94	1	0	0	0	2
1989-90 ♦	Edmonton Oilers	46	1	12	13	86	2	0	0	0	0
1990-91	Edmonton Oilers	67	3	7	10	150	18	1	3	4	28
1991-92	Edmonton Oilers	18	0	5	5	78	....	....	....	....	....
	New York Rangers	56	1	10	11	122	13	2	3	5	47
1992-93	New York Rangers	82	2	17	19	153	....	....	....	....	....
1993-94 ♦	New York Rangers	68	8	8	16	170	22	0	6	6	50
1994-95	New York Rangers	44	1	3	4	70	9	0	0	0	10
1995-96	New York Rangers	82	3	11	14	220	11	0	3	3	6
1996-97	New York Rangers	80	3	9	12	167	15	0	1	1	34
1997-98	New York Rangers	63	0	5	5	195	....	....	....	....	....
1998-99	New York Rangers	45	0	9	9	60	....	....	....	....	....
	NHL Totals	**804**	**30**	**129**	**159**	**1890**	**99**	**3**	**16**	**19**	**197**

Traded to **NY Rangers** by **Edmonton** for David Shaw to complete transaction that sent Mark Messier to NY Rangers (October 4, 1991), November 12, 1991. • Suffered eventual career-ending head injury in game vs. Los Angeles, November 19, 1998. • Announced retirement July 15, 1999.

BEVERLEY, Nick

Defense. Shoots right. 6'2", 185 lbs. Born, Toronto, Ont., April 21, 1947.

Season	Club	GP	G	A	Pts	PIM	GP	G	A	Pts	PIM
1966-67	Boston Bruins	2	0	0	0	0	....	....	....	....	....
1969-70	Boston Bruins	2	0	0	0	2	....	....	....	....	....
1971-72	Boston Bruins	1	0	0	0	0	....	....	....	....	....
1972-73	Boston Bruins	76	1	10	11	26	4	0	0	0	0
1973-74	Boston Bruins	1	0	0	0	0	....	....	....	....	....
	Pittsburgh Penguins	67	2	14	16	21	....	....	....	....	....
1974-75	New York Rangers	67	3	15	18	19	3	0	1	1	0
1975-76	New York Rangers	63	1	8	9	46	....	....	....	....	....
1976-77	New York Rangers	9	0	0	0	2	....	....	....	....	....
	Minnesota North Stars	52	2	17	19	6	....	....	....	....	....
1977-78	Minnesota North Stars	57	7	14	21	18	....	....	....	....	....
1978-79	Los Angeles Kings	7	0	3	3	0	....	....	....	....	....
	Colorado Rockies	52	2	4	6	6	....	....	....	....	....
1979-80	Colorado Rockies	46	0	9	9	10	....	....	....	....	....
	NHL Totals	**502**	**18**	**94**	**112**	**156**	**7**	**0**	**1**	**1**	**0**

Traded to **Pittsburgh** by **Boston** for Darryl Edestrand, October 25, 1973. Traded to **NY Rangers** by **Pittsburgh** for Vic Hadfield, May 27, 1974. Traded to **Minnesota** by **NY Rangers** with Bill Fairbairn for Bill Goldsworthy, November 11, 1976. Claimed on waivers by **Los Angeles** from **Minnesota**, September 5, 1978. Traded to **Colorado** by **Los Angeles** for Colorado's (New Jersey's) 4th round choice (Dave Gans) in 1982 Entry Draft, November 18, 1978. Claimed by **Hartford** from **Colorado** in Expansion Draft, June 13, 1979. Signed as a free agent by **Colorado**, September 15, 1979.

BIALOWAS, Dwight

Defense. Shoots right. 6', 185 lbs. Born, Regina, Sask., September 8, 1952.
(Atlanta's 2nd choice, 18th overall, in 1972 Amateur Draft).

Season	Club	GP	G	A	Pts	PIM	GP	G	A	Pts	PIM
1973-74	Atlanta Flames	11	0	0	0	2	....	....	....	....	....
1974-75	Atlanta Flames	37	3	9	12	20	....	....	....	....	....
	Minnesota North Stars	40	2	10	12	2	....	....	....	....	....
1975-76	Minnesota North Stars	58	5	18	23	22	....	....	....	....	....
1976-77	Minnesota North Stars	18	1	9	10	0	....	....	....	....	....
	NHL Totals	**164**	**11**	**46**	**57**	**46**	....	....	....	....	....

Traded to **Minnesota** by **Atlanta** with Dean Talafous for Barry Gibbs, January 3, 1975.

BIALOWAS, Frank

Left wing. Shoots left. 5'11", 220 lbs. Born, Winnipeg, Man., September 25, 1969.

Season	Club	GP	G	A	Pts	PIM	GP	G	A	Pts	PIM
1993-94	Toronto Maple Leafs	3	0	0	0	12	....	....	....	....	....
	NHL Totals	**3**	**0**	**0**	**0**	**12**	....	....	....	....	....

Signed as a free agent by **Toronto**, March 20, 1994. Signed as a free agent by **Washington**, September 8, 1995. Traded to **Philadelphia** by **Washington** for future considerations, July 18, 1996. Traded to **Chicago** by **Philadelphia** for Dennis Bonvie, January 8, 1999.

BIANCHIN, Wayne

Left wing. Shoots left. 5'10", 180 lbs. Born, Nanaimo, B.C., September 6, 1953.
(Pittsburgh's 2nd choice, 23rd overall, in 1973 Amateur Draft).

Season	Club	GP	G	A	Pts	PIM	GP	G	A	Pts	PIM
1973-74	Pittsburgh Penguins	69	12	13	25	38	....	....	....	....	....
1974-75	Pittsburgh Penguins	2	0	0	0	0	....	....	....	....	....
1975-76	Pittsburgh Penguins	14	1	5	6	4	....	....	....	....	....
1976-77	Pittsburgh Penguins	79	28	6	34	28	3	0	1	1	6
1977-78	Pittsburgh Penguins	61	20	13	33	40	....	....	....	....	....
1978-79	Pittsburgh Penguins	40	7	4	11	20	....	....	....	....	....
1979-80	Edmonton Oilers	11	0	0	0	7	....	....	....	....	....
	NHL Totals	**276**	**68**	**41**	**109**	**137**	**3**	**0**	**1**	**1**	**6**

• Missed majority of 1974-75 recovering from neck surgery, April, 1974. Claimed by **Edmonton** from **Pittsburgh** in Expansion Draft, June 13, 1979.

BICANEK, Radim

Defense. Shoots left. 6'1", 209 lbs. Born, Uherske Hradiste, Czech., January 18, 1975.
(Ottawa's 2nd choice, 27th overall, in 1993 Entry Draft).

Season	Club	GP	G	A	Pts	PIM	GP	G	A	Pts	PIM
1994-95	Ottawa Senators	6	0	0	0	0					

Season	Club	Regular Season GP	G	A	Pts	PIM	Playoffs GP	G	A	Pts	PIM
1996-97	Ottawa Senators	21	0	1	1	8	7	0	0	0	8
1997-98	Ottawa Senators	1	0	0	0	0	....	....	....	....	....
1998-99	Ottawa Senators	7	0	0	0	4	....	....	....	....	....
	Chicago Blackhawks	7	0	0	0	6	....	....	....	....	....
99-2000	Chicago Blackhawks	11	0	3	3	4	....	....	....	....	....
2000-01	Columbus Blue Jackets	9	0	2	2	6	....	....	....	....	....
2001-02	Columbus Blue Jackets	60	1	5	6	34	....	....	....	....	....
	NHL Totals	**122**	**1**	**11**	**12**	**62**	**7**	**0**	**0**	**0**	**8**

Traded to **Chicago** by **Ottawa** for Los Angeles' 6th round choice (previously acquired, Ottawa selected Martin Prusek) in 1999 Entry Draft, March 12, 1999. Selected by **Columbus** from **Chicago** in Expansion Draft, June 23, 2000.

BICEK, Jiri

Right wing. Shoots left. 5'10", 190 lbs. Born, Kosice, Czech., December 3, 1978.
(New Jersey's 4th choice, 131st overall, in 1997 Entry Draft).

Season	Club	GP	G	A	Pts	PIM	GP	G	A	Pts	PIM
2000-01	New Jersey Devils	5	1	0	1	4	....	....	....	....	....
2001-02	New Jersey Devils	1	0	0	0	0	....	....	....	....	....
2002-03 ♦	New Jersey Devils	44	5	6	11	25	5	0	0	0	0
	NHL Totals	**50**	**6**	**6**	**12**	**29**	**5**	**0**	**0**	**0**	**0**

BIDNER, Todd

Left wing. Shoots left. 6'2", 205 lbs. Born, Petrolia, Ont., July 5, 1961.
(Washington's 5th choice, 110th overall, in 1980 Entry Draft).

Season	Club	GP	G	A	Pts	PIM	GP	G	A	Pts	PIM
1981-82	Washington Capitals	12	2	1	3	7	....	....	....	....	....
	NHL Totals	**12**	**2**	**1**	**3**	**7**	....	....	....	....	....

Traded to **Edmonton** by **Washington** for Doug Hicks, March 9, 1982. Traded to **Detroit** by **Edmonton** for Rejean Cloutier, October 17, 1984.

BIGGS, Don

Center. Shoots right. 5'8", 185 lbs. Born, Mississauga, Ont., April 7, 1965.
(Minnesota's 9th choice, 162nd overall, in 1983 Entry Draft).

Season	Club	GP	G	A	Pts	PIM	GP	G	A	Pts	PIM
1984-85	Minnesota North Stars	1	0	0	0	0	....	....	....	....	....
1989-90	Philadelphia Flyers	11	2	0	2	8	....	....	....	....	....
	NHL Totals	**12**	**2**	**0**	**2**	**8**	....	....	....	....	....

Traded to **Edmonton** by **Minnesota** with Gord Sherven for Marc Habscheid, Don Barber and Emanuel Viveiros, December 20, 1985. Signed as a free agent by **Philadelphia**, July 17, 1987. Traded to **NY Rangers** by **Philadelphia** for future considerations, August 8, 1991.

BIGNELL, Larry

Defense. Shoots left. 6', 175 lbs. Born, Edmonton, Alta., January 7, 1950.
(Pittsburgh's 3rd choice, 35th overall, in 1970 Amateur Draft).

Season	Club	GP	G	A	Pts	PIM	GP	G	A	Pts	PIM
1973-74	Pittsburgh Penguins	20	0	3	3	2	....	....	....	....	....
1974-75	Pittsburgh Penguins	....	....	....	....	....	3	0	0	0	2
	NHL Totals	**20**	**0**	**3**	**3**	**2**	**3**	**0**	**0**	**0**	**2**

BILODEAU, Gilles

Left wing. Shoots left. 6'1", 220 lbs. Born, St-Prime, Que., July 31, 1955.

Season	Club	GP	G	A	Pts	PIM	GP	G	A	Pts	PIM
1979-80	Quebec Nordiques	9	0	1	1	25	....	....	....	....	....
	NHL Totals	**9**	**0**	**1**	**1**	**25**	....	....	....	....	....

Rights retained by **Quebec** prior to Expansion Draft, June 9, 1979.

BIONDA, Jack

Defense. Shoots left. 6', 180 lbs. Born, Hunstville, Ont., September 18, 1933.

Season	Club	GP	G	A	Pts	PIM	GP	G	A	Pts	PIM
1955-56	Toronto Maple Leafs	13	0	1	1	18	....	....	....	....	....
1956-57	Boston Bruins	35	2	3	5	43	10	0	1	1	14
1957-58	Boston Bruins	42	1	4	5	50	....	....	....	....	....
1958-59	Boston Bruins	3	0	1	1	2	1	0	0	0	0
	NHL Totals	**93**	**3**	**9**	**12**	**113**	**11**	**0**	**1**	**1**	**14**

Claimed by **Boston** from **Toronto** in Intra-League Draft, June 6, 1956. Loaned to **Springfield** (AHL) by **Boston** with the trade of Norm Defelice and future considerations (Floyd Smith, June, 1957) for Don Simmons, January 22, 1957. Traded to **Portland** (WHL) by **Boston** with future considerations (Gene Achtymichuk and Don Ward (August, 1961) and the loan of Bruce Gamble (September, 1961) for Don Head, May, 1961.

BIRON, Mathieu

Defense. Shoots right. 6'6", 226 lbs. Born, Lac-St-Charles, Que., April 29, 1980.
(Los Angeles' 1st choice, 21st overall, in 1998 Entry Draft).

Season	Club	GP	G	A	Pts	PIM	GP	G	A	Pts	PIM
99-2000	New York Islanders	60	4	4	8	38	....	....	....	....	....
2000-01	New York Islanders	14	0	1	1	12	....	....	....	....	....
2001-02	Tampa Bay Lightning	36	0	0	0	12	....	....	....	....	....
2002-03	Florida Panthers	34	1	8	9	14	....	....	....	....	....
	NHL Totals	**144**	**5**	**13**	**18**	**76**	....	....	....	....	....

• Brother of Martin

Traded to **NY Islanders** by **Los Angeles** with Olli Jokinen, Josh Green and Los Angeles' 1st round choice (Taylor Pyatt) in 1999 Entry Draft for Ziggy Palffy, Brian Smolinski, Marcel Cousineau and New Jersey's 4th round choice (previously acquired, Los Angeles selected Daniel Johansson) in 1999 Entry Draft, June 20, 1999. Traded to **Tampa Bay** by **NY Islanders** with NY Islanders' 2nd round choice (later traded to Washington – later traded to Vancouver – Vancouver selected Denis Grot) in 2002 Entry Draft for Adrian Aucoin and Alexander Kharitonov, June 22, 2001. Claimed by **Columbus** from **Tampa Bay** in Waiver Draft, October 4, 2002. Traded to **Florida** by **Columbus** for Petr Tenkrat, October 4, 2002.

BISSETT, Tom

Center. Shoots left. 6', 180 lbs. Born, Seattle, WA, March 13, 1966.
(Detroit's 11th choice, 211th overall, in 1986 Entry Draft).

Season	Club	GP	G	A	Pts	PIM	GP	G	A	Pts	PIM
1990-91	Detroit Red Wings	5	0	0	0	0	....	....	....	....	....
	NHL Totals	**5**	**0**	**0**	**0**	**0**	....	....	....	....	....

BJUGSTAD, Scott

Right wing. Shoots left. 6'1", 185 lbs. Born, St. Paul, MN, June 2, 1961.
(Minnesota's 13th choice, 181st overall, in 1981 Entry Draft).

Season	Club	GP	G	A	Pts	PIM	GP	G	A	Pts	PIM
1983-84	Minnesota North Stars	5	0	0	0	2	....	....	....	....	....
1984-85	Minnesota North Stars	72	11	4	15	32	....	....	....	....	....
1985-86	Minnesota North Stars	80	43	33	76	24	5	0	1	1	0
1986-87	Minnesota North Stars	39	4	9	13	43	....	....	....	....	....
1987-88	Minnesota North Stars	33	10	12	22	15	....	....	....	....	....
1988-89	Pittsburgh Penguins	24	3	0	3	4	....	....	....	....	....
1989-90	Los Angeles Kings	11	1	2	3	2	2	0	0	0	2
1990-91	Los Angeles Kings	31	2	4	6	12	2	0	0	0	0
1991-92	Los Angeles Kings	22	2	4	6	10	....	....	....	....	....
	NHL Totals	**317**	**76**	**68**	**144**	**144**	**9**	**0**	**1**	**1**	**2**

Traded to **Pittsburgh** by **Minnesota** with Gord Dineen for Ville Siren and Steve Gotaas, December 17, 1988. Signed as a free agent by **Los Angeles**, August 24, 1989.

BLACK, James

Left wing. Shoots left. 6', 202 lbs. Born, Regina, Sask., August 15, 1969.
(Hartford's 4th choice, 94th overall, in 1989 Entry Draft).

Season	Club	GP	G	A	Pts	PIM	GP	G	A	Pts	PIM
1989-90	Hartford Whalers	1	0	0	0	0	....	....	....	....	....
1990-91	Hartford Whalers	1	0	0	0	0	....	....	....	....	....
1991-92	Hartford Whalers	30	4	6	10	10	....	....	....	....	....
1992-93	Minnesota North Stars	10	2	1	3	4	....	....	....	....	....
1993-94	Dallas Stars	13	2	3	5	2	....	....	....	....	....
	Buffalo Sabres	2	0	0	0	0	....	....	....	....	....
1995-96	Chicago Blackhawks	13	3	3	6	16	8	1	0	1	2
1996-97	Chicago Blackhawks	64	12	11	23	20	5	1	1	2	2
1997-98	Chicago Blackhawks	52	10	5	15	8	....	....	....	....	....
1998-99	Washington Capitals	75	16	14	30	14	....	....	....	....	....
99-2000	Washington Capitals	49	8	9	17	6	....	....	....	....	....
2000-01	Washington Capitals	42	1	5	6	4	....	....	....	....	....
	NHL Totals	**352**	**58**	**57**	**115**	**84**	**13**	**2**	**1**	**3**	**4**

Traded to **Minnesota** by **Hartford** for Mark Janssens, September 3, 1992. Transferred to **Dallas** after **Minnesota** franchise relocated, June 9, 1993. Traded to **Buffalo** by **Dallas** with Dallas' 7th round choice (Steve Webb) in 1994 Entry Draft for Gord Donnelly, December 15, 1993. Signed as a free agent by **Chicago**, September 18, 1995. Traded to **Washington** by **Chicago** for Washington's 9th round choice (later traded back to Washington – Washington selected Igor Schadilov) in 1999 Entry Draft, October 15, 1998.

BLACK, Steve

Left wing. Shoots left. 6', 185 lbs. Born, Fort William, Ont., March 31, 1927.

Season	Club	GP	G	A	Pts	PIM	GP	G	A	Pts	PIM
1949-50 ♦	Detroit Red Wings	69	7	14	21	53	13	0	0	0	13
1950-51	Detroit Red Wings	5	0	0	0	2	....	....	....	....	....
	Chicago Black Hawks	39	4	6	10	22	....	....	....	....	....
	NHL Totals	**113**	**11**	**20**	**31**	**77**	**13**	**0**	**0**	**0**	**13**

Played in NHL All-Star Game (1950)

Traded to **Detroit** by **St. Louis** (AHL) with Bill Brennan for Fern Gauthier, Cliff Simpson, Ed Nicholson and future considerations, August 29, 1949. Traded to **Chicago** by **Detroit** with Lee Fogolin for Bert Olmstead and Vic Stasiuk, December 2, 1950.

BLACKBURN, Bob

Defense. Shoots left. 5'11", 198 lbs. Born, Rouyn, Que., February 1, 1938.

Season	Club	GP	G	A	Pts	PIM	GP	G	A	Pts	PIM
1968-69	New York Rangers	11	0	0	0	0	....	....	....	....	....
1969-70	Pittsburgh Penguins	60	4	7	11	51	6	0	0	0	4
1970-71	Pittsburgh Penguins	64	4	5	9	54	....	....	....	....	....
	NHL Totals	**135**	**8**	**12**	**20**	**105**	**6**	**0**	**0**	**0**	**4**

Claimed by **Buffalo** (AHL) from **NY Rangers** in Reverse Draft, June 6, 1967. Traded to **NY Rangers** by **Buffalo** (AHL) for cash, August, 1968. Claimed by **Pittsburgh** from **NY Rangers** in Intra-League Draft, June 11, 1969. Traded to **Vancouver** by **Pittsburgh** for cash, October 3, 1971.

BLACKBURN, Don

Left wing. Shoots left. 6', 190 lbs. Born, Kirkland Lake, Ont., May 14, 1938.

Season	Club	GP	G	A	Pts	PIM	GP	G	A	Pts	PIM
1962-63	Boston Bruins	6	0	5	5	4	....	....	....	....	....
1967-68	Philadelphia Flyers	67	9	20	29	23	7	3	0	3	8
1968-69	Philadelphia Flyers	48	7	9	16	36	4	0	0	0	2
1969-70	New York Rangers	3	0	0	0	0	1	0	0	0	0
1970-71	New York Rangers	1	0	0	0	0	....	....	....	....	....
1972-73	New York Islanders	56	7	10	17	20	....	....	....	....	....
	Minnesota North Stars	4	0	0	0	4	....	....	....	....	....
	NHL Totals	**185**	**23**	**44**	**67**	**87**	**12**	**3**	**0**	**3**	**10**

Claimed by **Montreal** from **Boston** (Kingston-EPHL) in Inter-League Draft, June 4, 1963. Claimed by **Toronto** from **Montreal** in Intra-League Draft, June 15, 1966. Claimed by **Philadelphia** from **Toronto** in Expansion Draft, June 6, 1967. Traded to **NY Rangers** by **Philadelphia** with Leon Rochefort for Reggie Fleming, June 6, 1969. Claimed by **NY Islanders** from **NY Rangers** in Intra-League Draft, June 6, 1972.

BLADE, Hank

Left wing. Shoots left. 5'11", 190 lbs. Born, Peterborough, Ont., April 28, 1920.

Season	Club	Regular Season GP	G	A	Pts	PIM	Playoffs GP	G	A	Pts	PIM
1946-47	Chicago Black Hawks	18	1	3	4	2	....	....	....	....	....
1947-48	Chicago Black Hawks	6	1	0	1	0	....	....	....	....	....
	NHL Totals	**24**	**2**	**3**	**5**	**2**	....	....	....	....	....

BLADON, Tom

Defense. Shoots right. 6'1", 195 lbs. Born, Edmonton, Alta., December 29, 1952.
(Philadelphia's 2nd choice, 23rd overall, in 1972 Amateur Draft).

Season	Club	Regular Season GP	G	A	Pts	PIM	Playoffs GP	G	A	Pts	PIM
1972-73	Philadelphia Flyers	78	11	31	42	26	11	0	4	4	2
1973-74 ♦	Philadelphia Flyers	70	12	22	34	37	16	4	6	10	25
1974-75 ♦	Philadelphia Flyers	76	9	20	29	54	13	1	3	4	12
1975-76	Philadelphia Flyers	80	14	23	37	68	16	2	6	8	14
1976-77	Philadelphia Flyers	80	10	43	53	39	10	1	3	4	4
1977-78	Philadelphia Flyers	79	11	24	35	57	12	0	2	2	11
1978-79	Pittsburgh Penguins	78	4	23	27	64	7	0	4	4	2
1979-80	Pittsburgh Penguins	57	2	6	8	35	1	0	1	1	0
1980-81	Edmonton Oilers	1	0	0	0	0	....	....	....	....	....
	Winnipeg Jets	9	0	5	5	10	....	....	....	....	....
	Detroit Red Wings	2	0	0	0	2	....	....	....	....	....
	NHL Totals	**610**	**73**	**197**	**270**	**392**	**86**	**8**	**29**	**37**	**70**

Played in NHL All-Star Game (1977, 1978)

Traded to **Pittsburgh** by **Philadelphia** with Ross Lonsberry and Orest Kindrachuk for Pittsburgh's 1st round choice (Behn Wilson) in 1978 Amateur Draft, June 14, 1978. Signed as a free agent by **Edmonton**, July 10, 1980. Signed as a free agent by **Winnipeg**, December 13, 1980. Signed as a free agent by **Detroit**, January 14, 1981.

BLAINE, Garry

Right wing. Shoots right. 5'11", 190 lbs. Born, St. Boniface, Man., April 19, 1933.

Season	Club	Regular Season GP	G	A	Pts	PIM	Playoffs GP	G	A	Pts	PIM
1954-55	Montreal Canadiens	1	0	0	0	0	....	....	....	....	....
	NHL Totals	**1**	**0**	**0**	**0**	**0**	....	....	....	....	....

BLAIR, Andy

Center. Shoots left. 6'1", 180 lbs. Born, Winnipeg, Man., February 27, 1908.

Season	Club	Regular Season GP	G	A	Pts	PIM	Playoffs GP	G	A	Pts	PIM
1928-29	Toronto Maple Leafs	44	12	15	27	41	4	*3	0	*3	2
1929-30	Toronto Maple Leafs	42	11	10	21	27	....	....	....	....	....
1930-31	Toronto Maple Leafs	44	11	8	19	32	2	1	0	1	0
1931-32 ♦	Toronto Maple Leafs	48	9	14	23	35	7	2	2	4	6
1932-33	Toronto Maple Leafs	43	6	9	15	38	9	0	2	2	4
1933-34	Toronto Maple Leafs	47	14	9	23	35	5	0	2	2	16
1934-35	Toronto Maple Leafs	45	6	14	20	22	2	0	0	0	2
1935-36	Toronto Maple Leafs	45	5	4	9	60	9	0	0	0	2
1936-37	Chicago Black Hawks	44	0	3	3	33	....	....	....	....	....
	NHL Totals	**402**	**74**	**86**	**160**	**323**	**38**	**6**	**6**	**12**	**32**

Played in NHL All-Star Game (1934)

Traded to **Chicago** by **Toronto** for cash, May 7, 1936.

BLAIR, Chuck

Right wing. Shoots right. 5'10", 175 lbs. Born, Edinburgh, Scotland, July 23, 1928.

Season	Club	Regular Season GP	G	A	Pts	PIM	Playoffs GP	G	A	Pts	PIM
1948-49	Toronto Maple Leafs	1	0	0	0	0	....	....	....	....	....
	NHL Totals	**1**	**0**	**0**	**0**	**0**	....	....	....	....	....

• Brother of Dusty

Traded to **Cleveland** (AHL) by **Toronto** with $30,000 for Bob Bailey and Gerry Foley, May 30, 1953.

BLAIR, Dusty

Center. Shoots right. 5'8", 160 lbs. Born, South Porcupine, Ont., September 15, 1929.

Season	Club	Regular Season GP	G	A	Pts	PIM	Playoffs GP	G	A	Pts	PIM
1950-51	Toronto Maple Leafs	2	0	0	0	0	....	....	....	....	....
	NHL Totals	**2**	**0**	**0**	**0**	**0**	....	....	....	....	....

• Brother of Chuck

Traded to **Chicago** (Buffalo-AHL) by **Toronto** with Frank Sullivan and Jack Leclair for Brian Cullen, May 4, 1954. Loaned to **NY Rangers** by **Buffalo** (AHL) with $10,000 and the loan of Gord Pennell for Pete Conacher, August 20, 1956.

BLAISDELL, Mike

Right wing. Shoots right. 6'1", 196 lbs. Born, Moose Jaw, Sask., January 18, 1960.
(Detroit's 1st choice, 11th overall, in 1980 Entry Draft).

Season	Club	Regular Season GP	G	A	Pts	PIM	Playoffs GP	G	A	Pts	PIM
1980-81	Detroit Red Wings	32	3	6	9	10	....	....	....	....	....
1981-82	Detroit Red Wings	80	23	32	55	48	....	....	....	....	....
1982-83	Detroit Red Wings	80	18	23	41	22	....	....	....	....	....
1983-84	New York Rangers	36	5	6	11	31	....	....	....	....	....
1984-85	New York Rangers	12	1	0	1	11	....	....	....	....	....
1985-86	Pittsburgh Penguins	66	15	14	29	36	....	....	....	....	....
1986-87	Pittsburgh Penguins	10	1	1	2	2	....	....	....	....	....
1987-88	Toronto Maple Leafs	18	3	2	5	2	6	1	2	3	10
1988-89	Toronto Maple Leafs	9	1	0	1	4	....	....	....	....	....
	NHL Totals	**343**	**70**	**84**	**154**	**166**	**6**	**1**	**2**	**3**	**10**

Traded to **NY Rangers** by **Detroit** with Willie Huber and Mark Osborne for Ron Duguay, Eddie Mio and Eddie Johnstone, June 13, 1983. Claimed by **Pittsburgh** from **NY Rangers** in Waiver Draft, October 7, 1985. Signed as a free agent by **Toronto**, July 10, 1987.

BLAKE, Bob

Left wing. Shoots left. 6', 200 lbs. Born, Ashland, WI, August 16, 1914.

Season	Club	Regular Season GP	G	A	Pts	PIM	Playoffs GP	G	A	Pts	PIM
1935-36	Boston Bruins	12	0	0	0	0	....	....	....	....	....
	NHL Totals	**12**	**0**	**0**	**0**	**0**	....	....	....	....	....

Signed as a free agent by **Boston**, October, 1934. Traded to **Minneapolis** (AHA) (Cleveland-IAHL) by **Boston** for cash, September, 1936.

BLAKE, Jason

Center. Shoots left. 5'10", 180 lbs. Born, Moorhead, MN, September 2, 1973.

Season	Club	Regular Season GP	G	A	Pts	PIM	Playoffs GP	G	A	Pts	PIM
1998-99	Los Angeles Kings	1	1	0	1	0	....	....	....	....	....
99-2000	Los Angeles Kings	64	5	18	23	26	3	0	0	0	0
2000-01	Los Angeles Kings	17	1	3	4	10	....	....	....	....	....
	New York Islanders	30	4	8	12	24	....	....	....	....	....
2001-02	New York Islanders	82	8	10	18	36	7	0	1	1	13
2002-03	New York Islanders	81	25	30	55	58	5	0	1	1	2
	NHL Totals	**275**	**44**	**69**	**113**	**154**	**15**	**0**	**2**	**2**	**15**

Signed as a free agent by **Los Angeles**, April 20, 1999. Traded to **NY Islanders** by **Los Angeles** for NY Islanders' 5th round choice (Joel Andresen) in 2002 Entry Draft, January 3, 2001.

BLAKE, Mickey

Left wing/Defense. Shoots left. 5'10", 186 lbs. Born, Barriefield, Ont., October 31, 1912.

Season	Club	Regular Season GP	G	A	Pts	PIM	Playoffs GP	G	A	Pts	PIM
1932-33	Montreal Maroons	1	0	0	0	0	....	....	....	....	....
1934-35	St. Louis Eagles	8	1	1	2	2	....	....	....	....	....
1935-36	Toronto Maple Leafs	1	0	0	0	2	....	....	....	....	....
	NHL Totals	**10**	**1**	**1**	**2**	**4**	....	....	....	....	....

Traded to **St. Louis** by **Mtl. Maroons** for cash, October 12, 1934. Traded to **Detroit** by **St. Louis** with $3,500 for George Patterson with Detroit holding right of recall, November 28, 1934. • Returned to St. Louis after 1934-35 season. Claimed by **Toronto** from **St. Louis** in Dispersal Draft, October 15, 1935.

BLAKE, Rob

Defense. Shoots right. 6'4", 225 lbs. Born, Simcoe, Ont., December 10, 1969.
(Los Angeles' 4th choice, 70th overall, in 1988 Entry Draft).

Season	Club	Regular Season GP	G	A	Pts	PIM	Playoffs GP	G	A	Pts	PIM
1989-90	Los Angeles Kings	4	0	0	0	4	8	1	3	4	4
1990-91	Los Angeles Kings	75	12	34	46	125	12	1	4	5	26
1991-92	Los Angeles Kings	57	7	13	20	102	6	2	1	3	12
1992-93	Los Angeles Kings	76	16	43	59	152	23	4	6	10	46
1993-94	Los Angeles Kings	84	20	48	68	137	....	....	....	....	....
1994-95	Los Angeles Kings	24	4	7	11	38	....	....	....	....	....
1995-96	Los Angeles Kings	6	1	2	3	8	....	....	....	....	....
1996-97	Los Angeles Kings	62	8	23	31	82	....	....	....	....	....
1997-98	Los Angeles Kings	81	23	27	50	94	4	0	0	0	6
1998-99	Los Angeles Kings	62	12	23	35	128	....	....	....	....	....
99-2000	Los Angeles Kings	77	18	39	57	112	4	0	2	2	4
2000-01	Los Angeles Kings	54	17	32	49	69	....	....	....	....	....
	♦ Colorado Avalanche	13	2	8	10	8	23	6	13	19	16
2001-02	Colorado Avalanche	75	16	40	56	58	20	6	6	12	16
2002-03	Colorado Avalanche	79	17	28	45	57	7	1	2	3	8
	NHL Totals	**829**	**173**	**367**	**540**	**1174**	**107**	**21**	**37**	**58**	**138**

NHL All-Rookie Team (1991) • NHL First All-Star Team (1998) • James Norris Memorial Trophy (1998) • NHL Second All-Star Team (2000, 2001, 2002)

Played in NHL All-Star Game (1994, 1999, 2000, 2001, 2002, 2003)

• Missed majority of 1995-96 season recovering from knee injury suffered in game vs. Washington, October 20, 1995. Traded to **Colorado** by **Los Angeles** with Steve Reinprecht for Adam Deadmarsh, Aaron Miller, a player to be named later (Jared Aulin, March 22, 2001), Colorado's 1st round choice (Dave Steckel) in 2001 Entry Draft and 1st round choice (Brian Boyle) in 2003 Entry Draft, February 21, 2001.

BLAKE, Toe

HHOF

Left wing. Shoots left. 5'10", 165 lbs. Born, Victoria Mines, Ont., August 21, 1912.

Season	Club	Regular Season GP	G	A	Pts	PIM	Playoffs GP	G	A	Pts	PIM
1934-35 ♦	Montreal Maroons	8	0	0	0	0	1	0	0	0	0
1935-36	Montreal Canadiens	11	1	2	3	28	....	....	....	....	....
1936-37	Montreal Canadiens	43	10	12	22	12	5	1	0	1	0
1937-38	Montreal Canadiens	43	17	16	33	33	3	3	1	4	2
1938-39	Montreal Canadiens	48	24	23	*47	10	3	1	1	2	2
1939-40	Montreal Canadiens	48	17	19	36	48	....	....	....	....	....
1940-41	Montreal Canadiens	48	12	20	32	49	3	0	3	3	5
1941-42	Montreal Canadiens	48	17	28	45	19	3	0	3	3	2
1942-43	Montreal Canadiens	48	23	36	59	26	5	4	3	7	0
1943-44 ♦	Montreal Canadiens	41	26	33	59	10	9	7	*11	*18	2
1944-45	Montreal Canadiens	49	29	38	67	25	6	0	2	2	5
1945-46 ♦	Montreal Canadiens	50	29	21	50	2	9	*7	6	13	5
1946-47	Montreal Canadiens	60	21	29	50	6	11	2	*7	9	0
1947-48	Montreal Canadiens	32	9	15	24	4	....	....	....	....	....
	NHL Totals	**577**	**235**	**292**	**527**	**272**	**58**	**25**	**37**	**62**	**23**

NHL Second All-Star Team (1938, 1946) • NHL First All-Star Team (1939, 1940, 1945) • Hart Trophy (1939) • Lady Byng Trophy (1946)

Played in NHL All-Star Game (1937, 1939)

Signed as a free agent by **Mtl. Maroons**, February 21, 1935. Traded to **Montreal** by **Mtl. Maroons** with Bill Miller and the rights to Ken Grivel for Lorne Chabot, February, 1936. • Missed remainder of 1947-48 season recovering from leg injury suffered in game vs. NY Rangers, January 10, 1948.

BLATNY, Zdenek

Left wing. Shoots left. 6'1", 190 lbs. Born, Brno, Czech., January 14, 1981.
(Atlanta's 3rd choice, 68th overall, in 1999 Entry Draft).

Season	Club	GP	G	A	Pts	PIM	GP (Playoffs)	G	A	Pts	PIM
2002-03	Atlanta Thrashers	4	0	0	0	0	....	....	....	....	....
	NHL Totals	**4**	**0**	**0**	**0**	**0**	....	....	....	....	....

BLIGHT, Rick

Right wing. Shoots right. 6'2", 195 lbs. Born, Portage La Prairie, Man., October 17, 1955.
(Vancouver's 1st choice, 10th overall, in 1975 Amateur Draft).

Season	Club	GP	G	A	Pts	PIM	GP (Playoffs)	G	A	Pts	PIM
1975-76	Vancouver Canucks	74	25	31	56	29	2	0	1	1	0
1976-77	Vancouver Canucks	78	28	40	68	32	....	....	....	....	....
1977-78	Vancouver Canucks	80	25	38	63	33	....	....	....	....	....
1978-79	Vancouver Canucks	56	5	10	15	16	3	0	4	4	2
1979-80	Vancouver Canucks	33	12	6	18	54	....	....	....	....	....
1980-81	Vancouver Canucks	3	1	0	1	4	....	....	....	....	....
1982-83	Los Angeles Kings	2	0	0	0	2	....	....	....	....	....
	NHL Totals	**326**	**96**	**125**	**221**	**170**	**5**	**0**	**5**	**5**	**2**

Signed as a free agent by **Toronto**, August 31, 1981. Signed as a free agent by **Edmonton**, October 25, 1982. Traded to **Los Angeles** by **Edmonton** for Alan Hangsleben, December 7, 1982.

BLINCO, Russ

Center. Shoots left. 5'10", 171 lbs. Born, Grand'Mere, Que., March 12, 1908.

Season	Club	GP	G	A	Pts	PIM	GP (Playoffs)	G	A	Pts	PIM
1933-34	Montreal Maroons	31	14	9	23	2	4	0	1	1	0
1934-35 ◆	Montreal Maroons	48	13	14	27	4	7	2	2	4	2
1935-36	Montreal Maroons	46	13	10	23	10	3	0	0	0	0
1936-37	Montreal Maroons	48	6	12	18	2	5	1	0	1	2
1937-38	Montreal Maroons	47	10	9	19	4	....	....	....	....	....
1938-39	Chicago Black Hawks	48	3	12	15	2	....	....	....	....	....
	NHL Totals	**268**	**59**	**66**	**125**	**24**	**19**	**3**	**3**	**6**	**4**

NHL Rookie of the Year (1934)

Played in NHL All-Star Game (1937)

Traded to **Mtl. Maroons** (Windsor-IHL) by **NY Rangers** after Springfield (Can-Am) franchise folded, December 18, 1932. Traded to **Chicago** by **Mtl. Maroons** with Baldy Northcott and Earl Robinson for $30,000, September 15, 1938.

BLOCK, Ken

Defense. Shoots left. 5'10", 191 lbs. Born, Steinbach, Man., March 18, 1944.

Season	Club	GP	G	A	Pts	PIM	GP (Playoffs)	G	A	Pts	PIM
1970-71	Vancouver Canucks	1	0	0	0	0	....	....	....	....	....
	NHL Totals	**1**	**0**	**0**	**0**	**0**	....	....	....	....	....

Claimed by **Los Angeles** from **NY Rangers** in Expansion Draft, June 6, 1967. Traded to **Toronto** by **Los Angeles** for the rights to Red Kelly, June 8, 1967. Rights transferred to **Vancouver** (WHL) after WHL club purchased **Rochester** (AHL) franchise, August 13, 1968. NHL rights transferred to **Vancouver** after NHL club purchased **Vancouver** (WHL) franchise, December 19, 1969.

BLOEMBERG, Jeff

Defense. Shoots right. 6'2", 205 lbs. Born, Listowel, Ont., January 31, 1968.
(NY Rangers' 5th choice, 93rd overall, in 1986 Entry Draft).

Season	Club	GP	G	A	Pts	PIM	GP (Playoffs)	G	A	Pts	PIM
1988-89	New York Rangers	9	0	0	0	0	....	....	....	....	....
1989-90	New York Rangers	28	3	3	6	25	7	0	3	3	5
1990-91	New York Rangers	3	0	2	2	0	....	....	....	....	....
1991-92	New York Rangers	3	0	1	1	0	....	....	....	....	....
	NHL Totals	**43**	**3**	**6**	**9**	**25**	**7**	**0**	**3**	**3**	**5**

Claimed by **Tampa Bay** from **NY Rangers** in Expansion Draft, June 18, 1992. Traded to **Edmonton** by **Tampa Bay** for future considerations, September 25, 1992. Signed as a free agent by **Hartford**, August 9, 1993. Signed as a free agent by **Detroit**, May 9, 1995.

BLOMQVIST, Timo

Defense. Shoots right. 6', 200 lbs. Born, Helsinki, Finland, January 23, 1961.
(Washington's 4th choice, 89th overall, in 1980 Entry Draft).

Season	Club	GP	G	A	Pts	PIM	GP (Playoffs)	G	A	Pts	PIM
1981-82	Washington Capitals	44	1	11	12	62	....	....	....	....	....
1982-83	Washington Capitals	61	1	17	18	67	3	0	0	0	16
1983-84	Washington Capitals	65	1	19	20	84	8	0	0	0	8
1984-85	Washington Capitals	53	1	4	5	51	2	0	0	0	0
1986-87	New Jersey Devils	20	0	2	2	29	....	....	....	....	....
	NHL Totals	**243**	**4**	**53**	**57**	**293**	**13**	**0**	**0**	**0**	**24**

Signed as a free agent by **New Jersey**, July 2, 1986.

BLOMSTEN, Arto

Defense. Shoots left. 6'3", 210 lbs. Born, Vaasa, Finland, March 16, 1965.
(Winnipeg's 11th choice, 239th overall, in 1986 Entry Draft).

Season	Club	GP	G	A	Pts	PIM	GP (Playoffs)	G	A	Pts	PIM
1993-94	Winnipeg Jets	18	0	2	2	6	....	....	....	....	....
1994-95	Winnipeg Jets	1	0	0	0	2	....	....	....	....	....
	Los Angeles Kings	4	0	1	1	0	....	....	....	....	....
1995-96	Los Angeles Kings	2	0	1	1	0	....	....	....	....	....
	NHL Totals	**25**	**0**	**4**	**4**	**8**	....	....	....	....	....

Traded to **Los Angeles** by **Winnipeg** for Los Angeles' 8th round choice (Fredrik Loven) in 1995 Entry Draft, March 27, 1995.

BLOOM, Mike

Left wing. Shoots left. 6'3", 206 lbs. Born, Ottawa, Ont., April 12, 1952.
(Boston's 1st choice, 16th overall, in 1972 Amateur Draft).

Season	Club	GP	G	A	Pts	PIM	GP (Playoffs)	G	A	Pts	PIM
1974-75	Washington Capitals	67	7	19	26	84	....	....	....	....	....
	Detroit Red Wings	13	4	8	12	10	....	....	....	....	....
1975-76	Detroit Red Wings	76	13	17	30	99	....	....	....	....	....
1976-77	Detroit Red Wings	45	6	3	9	22	....	....	....	....	....
	NHL Totals	**201**	**30**	**47**	**77**	**215**	....	....	....	....	....

Claimed by **Washington** from **Boston** in Expansion Draft, June 12, 1974. Traded to **Detroit** by **Washington** for Blair Stewart, March 9, 1975.

BLOUIN, Sylvain

Left wing. Shoots left. 6'2", 207 lbs. Born, Montreal, Que., May 21, 1974.
(NY Rangers' 5th choice, 104th overall, in 1994 Entry Draft).

Season	Club	GP	G	A	Pts	PIM	GP (Playoffs)	G	A	Pts	PIM
1996-97	New York Rangers	6	0	0	0	18	....	....	....	....	....
1997-98	New York Rangers	1	0	0	0	5	....	....	....	....	....
1998-99	Montreal Canadiens	5	0	0	0	19	....	....	....	....	....
2000-01	Minnesota Wild	41	3	2	5	117	....	....	....	....	....
2001-02	Minnesota Wild	43	0	2	2	130	....	....	....	....	....
2002-03	Minnesota Wild	2	0	0	0	4	....	....	....	....	....
	Montreal Canadiens	17	0	0	0	43	....	....	....	....	....
	NHL Totals	**115**	**3**	**4**	**7**	**336**	....	....	....	....	....

Traded to **Montreal** by **NY Rangers** with NY Rangers' 6th round choice (later traded to Phoenix – Phoenix selected Erik Lewerstrom) in 1999 Entry Draft for Peter Popovic, June 30, 1998. Signed as a free agent by **St. Louis**, August 25, 1999. Signed as a free agent by **Montreal**, July 7, 2000. Claimed by **Minnesota** from **Montreal** in Waiver Draft, September 29, 2000. • Missed majority of 2000-01 season recovering from shoulder injury suffered in game vs. Chicago, December 7, 2000. Traded to **Montreal** by **Minnesota** for Montreal's 7th round choice (Grigory Misharin) in 2003 Entry Draft, October 31, 2002.

BLUM, John

Defense. Shoots right. 6'3", 205 lbs. Born, Detroit, MI, October 8, 1959.

Season	Club	GP	G	A	Pts	PIM	GP (Playoffs)	G	A	Pts	PIM
1982-83	Edmonton Oilers	5	0	3	3	24	....	....	....	....	....
1983-84	Edmonton Oilers	4	0	1	1	2	....	....	....	....	....
	Boston Bruins	12	1	1	2	30	3	0	0	0	4
1984-85	Boston Bruins	75	3	13	16	263	5	0	0	0	13
1985-86	Boston Bruins	61	1	7	8	80	3	0	0	0	6
1986-87	Washington Capitals	66	2	8	10	133	6	0	1	1	4
1987-88	Boston Bruins	19	0	1	1	70	3	0	1	1	0
1988-89	Detroit Red Wings	6	0	0	0	8	....	....	....	....	....
1989-90	Boston Bruins	2	0	0	0	0	....	....	....	....	....
	NHL Totals	**250**	**7**	**34**	**41**	**610**	**20**	**0**	**2**	**2**	**27**

Signed as a free agent by **Edmonton**, May 5, 1981. Traded to **Boston** by **Edmonton** for Larry Melnyk, March 6, 1984. Claimed by **Washington** from **Boston** in Waiver Draft, October 6, 1986. Traded to **Boston** by **Washington** for Boston's 7th round choice (Brad Schlegel) in 1988 Entry Draft, June 1, 1987. Signed as a free agent by **Detroit**, August 12, 1988. Signed as a free agent by **Boston**, July 6, 1989.

BODAK, Bob

Left wing. Shoots left. 6'2", 200 lbs. Born, Thunder Bay, Ont., May 28, 1961.

Season	Club	GP	G	A	Pts	PIM	GP (Playoffs)	G	A	Pts	PIM
1987-88	Calgary Flames	3	0	0	0	22	....	....	....	....	....
1989-90	Hartford Whalers	1	0	0	0	7	....	....	....	....	....
	NHL Totals	**4**	**0**	**0**	**0**	**29**	....	....	....	....	....

Signed as a free agent by **Calgary**, January 28, 1986. Signed as a free agent by **Hartford**, May 10, 1989.

BODDY, Gregg

Defense. Shoots left. 6'2", 200 lbs. Born, Ponoka, Alta., March 19, 1949.
(Los Angeles' 2nd choice, 27th overall, in 1969 Amateur Draft).

Season	Club	GP	G	A	Pts	PIM	GP (Playoffs)	G	A	Pts	PIM
1971-72	Vancouver Canucks	40	2	5	7	45	....	....	....	....	....
1972-73	Vancouver Canucks	74	3	11	14	70	....	....	....	....	....
1973-74	Vancouver Canucks	53	2	10	12	59	....	....	....	....	....
1974-75	Vancouver Canucks	72	11	12	23	56	3	0	0	0	0
1975-76	Vancouver Canucks	34	5	6	11	33	....	....	....	....	....
	NHL Totals	**273**	**23**	**44**	**67**	**263**	**3**	**0**	**0**	**0**	**0**

Traded to **Montreal** by **Los Angeles** with Leon Rochefort and Wayne Thomas for Larry Mickey, Lucien Grenier and Jack Norris, May 22, 1970. Traded to **Vancouver** by **Montreal** for cash and Vancouver's 3rd round choice (Jim Cahoon) in 1971 Amateur Draft, May 25, 1971.

BODGER, Doug

Defense. Shoots left. 6'2", 210 lbs. Born, Chemainus, B.C., June 18, 1966.
(Pittsburgh's 2nd choice, 9th overall, in 1984 Entry Draft).

Season	Club	GP	G	A	Pts	PIM	GP (Playoffs)	G	A	Pts	PIM
1984-85	Pittsburgh Penguins	65	5	26	31	67	....	....	....	....	....
1985-86	Pittsburgh Penguins	79	4	33	37	63	....	....	....	....	....
1986-87	Pittsburgh Penguins	76	11	38	49	52	....	....	....	....	....
1987-88	Pittsburgh Penguins	69	14	31	45	103	....	....	....	....	....
1988-89	Pittsburgh Penguins	10	1	4	5	7	....	....	....	....	....
	Buffalo Sabres	61	7	40	47	52	5	1	1	2	11
1989-90	Buffalo Sabres	71	12	36	48	64	6	1	5	6	6
1990-91	Buffalo Sabres	58	5	23	28	54	4	0	1	1	0
1991-92	Buffalo Sabres	73	11	35	46	108	7	2	1	3	2
1992-93	Buffalo Sabres	81	9	45	54	87	8	2	3	5	0
1993-94	Buffalo Sabres	75	7	32	39	76	7	0	3	3	6
1994-95	Buffalo Sabres	44	3	17	20	47	5	0	4	4	0
1995-96	Buffalo Sabres	16	0	5	5	18	....	....	....	....	....
	San Jose Sharks	57	4	19	23	50	....	....	....	....	....
1996-97	San Jose Sharks	81	1	15	16	64	....	....	....	....	....
1997-98	San Jose Sharks	28	4	6	10	32	....	....	....	....	....
	New Jersey Devils	49	5	5	10	25	5	0	0	0	0
1998-99	Los Angeles Kings	65	3	11	14	34	....	....	....	....	....

Season	Club	REGULAR SEASON GP	G	A	Pts	PIM	PLAYOFFS GP	G	A	Pts	PIM
99-2000	Vancouver Canucks	13	0	1	1	4	....	....	....	....	....
	NHL Totals	**1071**	**106**	**422**	**528**	**1007**	**47**	**6**	**18**	**24**	**25**

Traded to **Buffalo** by **Pittsburgh** wih Darrin Shannon for Tom Barrasso and Buffalo's 3rd round choice (Joe Dziedzic) in 1990 Entry Draft, November 12, 1988. Traded to **San Jose** by **Buffalo** for Vaclav Varada, Martin Spanhel and Philadelphia's 1st (previously acquired, later traded to Phoenix – Phoenix selected Daniel Briere) and 4th (previously acquired, Buffalo selected Mike Martone) round choices in 1996 Entry Draft, November 16, 1995. Traded to **New Jersey** by **San Jose** with Dody Wood for John MacLean and Ken Sutton, December 7, 1997. Traded to **Los Angeles** by **New Jersey** for Boston's 4th round choice (previously acquired, New Jersey selected Pierre Dagenais) in 1998 Entry Draft, June 18, 1998. Signed as a free agent by **Vancouver**, August 18, 1999. • Officially announced NHL retirement, December 14, 1999.

BODNAR, Gus

Center. Shoots right. 5'11", 160 lbs. Born, Fort William, Ont., April 24, 1923.

Season	Club	GP	G	A	Pts	PIM	GP	G	A	Pts	PIM
1943-44	Toronto Maple Leafs	50	22	40	62	18	5	0	0	0	0
1944-45 ♦	Toronto Maple Leafs	49	8	36	44	18	13	3	1	4	4
1945-46	Toronto Maple Leafs	49	14	23	37	14	....	....	....	....	....
1946-47 ♦	Toronto Maple Leafs	39	4	6	10	10	1	0	0	0	0
1947-48	Chicago Black Hawks	46	13	22	35	23	....	....	....	....	....
1948-49	Chicago Black Hawks	59	19	26	45	14	....	....	....	....	....
1949-50	Chicago Black Hawks	70	11	28	39	6	....	....	....	....	....
1950-51	Chicago Black Hawks	44	8	12	20	8	....	....	....	....	....
1951-52	Chicago Black Hawks	69	14	26	40	26	....	....	....	....	....
1952-53	Chicago Black Hawks	66	16	13	29	26	7	1	1	2	2
1953-54	Chicago Black Hawks	45	6	15	21	20	....	....	....	....	....
	Boston Bruins	14	3	3	6	10	1	0	0	0	0
1954-55	Boston Bruins	67	4	4	8	14	5	0	1	1	4
	NHL Totals	**667**	**142**	**254**	**396**	**207**	**32**	**4**	**3**	**7**	**10**

Calder Memorial Trophy (1944)

Played in NHL All-Star Game (1951)

Traded to **Chicago** by **Toronto** with Bud Poile, Gaye Stewart, Ernie Dickens and Bob Goldham for Max Bentley and Cy Thomas, November 2, 1947. Traded to **Boston** by **Chicago** for Jerry Toppazzini, February 16, 1954.

BOEHM, Ron

Left wing. Shoots left. 5'8", 160 lbs. Born, Saskatoon, Sask., August 14, 1943.

Season	Club	GP	G	A	Pts	PIM	GP	G	A	Pts	PIM
1967-68	Oakland Seals	16	2	1	3	10	....	....	....	....	....
	NHL Totals	**16**	**2**	**1**	**3**	**10**	....	....	....	....	....

Claimed by **NY Rangers** (Vancouver-WHL) from **Boston** in Inter-League Draft, June 9, 1965. Claimed by **California** (Oakland) from **NY Rangers** in Expansion Draft, June 6, 1967. Traded to **NY Rangers** by **Oakland** for cash, September 13, 1968. Claimed by **Cleveland** (AHL) from **NY Rangers** in Reverse Draft, June, 1971. Traded to **Boston** by **Cleveland** (AHL) for cash, June, 1971.

BOESCH, Garth

Defense. Shoots right. 6', 180 lbs. Born, Milestone, Sask., October 7, 1920.

Season	Club	GP	G	A	Pts	PIM	GP	G	A	Pts	PIM
1946-47 ♦	Toronto Maple Leafs	35	4	5	9	47	11	0	2	2	6
1947-48 ♦	Toronto Maple Leafs	45	2	7	9	52	8	2	1	3	2
1948-49 ♦	Toronto Maple Leafs	59	1	10	11	43	9	0	2	2	6
1949-50	Toronto Maple Leafs	58	2	6	8	63	6	0	0	0	4
	NHL Totals	**197**	**9**	**28**	**37**	**205**	**34**	**2**	**5**	**7**	**18**

Played in NHL All-Star Game (1948, 1949)

Claimed by **NY Americans** from **Seattle** (PCHL) in Inter-League Draft, June 27, 1941. • Refused permission to leave Canada for NY Americans training camp because of war-time travel restrictions, September, 1941. Rights transferred to **Toronto** from **Brooklyn** in Special Dispersal Draw, September 11, 1943.

BOGUNIECKI, Eric

Center. Shoots right. 5'8", 192 lbs. Born, New Haven, CT, May 6, 1975.
(St. Louis' 6th choice, 193rd overall, in 1993 Entry Draft).

Season	Club	GP	G	A	Pts	PIM	GP	G	A	Pts	PIM
99-2000	Florida Panthers	4	0	0	0	2	....	....	....	....	....
2000-01	St. Louis Blues	1	0	0	0	0	....	....	....	....	....
2001-02	St. Louis Blues	8	0	1	1	4	1	0	1	1	0
2002-03	St. Louis Blues	80	22	27	49	38	7	1	2	3	2
	NHL Totals	**93**	**22**	**28**	**50**	**44**	**8**	**1**	**3**	**4**	**2**

Signed as a free agent by **Florida**, July 7, 1999. Traded to **St. Louis** by **Florida** for Andrei Podkonicky, December 17, 2000.

BOH, Rick

Center. Shoots right. 5'10", 185 lbs. Born, Kamloops, B.C., May 18, 1964.
(Minnesota's 2nd choice, 9th overall, in 1987 Supplemental Draft).

Season	Club	GP	G	A	Pts	PIM	GP	G	A	Pts	PIM
1987-88	Minnesota North Stars	8	2	1	3	4	....	....	....	....	....
	NHL Totals	**8**	**2**	**1**	**3**	**4**	....	....	....	....	....

BOHONOS, Lonny

Right wing. Shoots right. 5'11", 190 lbs. Born, Winnipeg, Man., May 20, 1973.

Season	Club	GP	G	A	Pts	PIM	GP	G	A	Pts	PIM
1995-96	Vancouver Canucks	3	0	1	1	0	....	....	....	....	....
1996-97	Vancouver Canucks	36	11	11	22	10	....	....	....	....	....
1997-98	Vancouver Canucks	31	2	1	3	4	....	....	....	....	....
	Toronto Maple Leafs	6	3	3	6	4	....	....	....	....	....
1998-99	Toronto Maple Leafs	7	3	0	3	4	9	3	6	9	2
	NHL Totals	**83**	**19**	**16**	**35**	**22**	**9**	**3**	**6**	**9**	**2**

Signed as a free agent by **Vancouver**, May 31, 1994. Traded to **Toronto** by **Vancouver** for Brandon Convery, March 7, 1998.

BOIKOV, Alexandre

Defense. Shoots left. 6', 200 lbs. Born, Chelyabinsk, USSR, February 7, 1975.

Season	Club	REGULAR SEASON GP	G	A	Pts	PIM	PLAYOFFS GP	G	A	Pts	PIM
99-2000	Nashville Predators	2	0	0	0	2	....	....	....	....	....
2000-01	Nashville Predators	8	0	0	0	13	....	....	....	....	....
	NHL Totals	**10**	**0**	**0**	**0**	**15**	....	....	....	....	....

Signed as a free agent by **San Jose**, April 22, 1996. Signed as a free agent by **Nashville**, July 26, 1999.

BOILEAU, Marc

Center. Shoots left. 5'11", 170 lbs. Born, Pointe Claire, Que., September 3, 1932.

Season	Club	GP	G	A	Pts	PIM	GP	G	A	Pts	PIM
1961-62	Detroit Red Wings	54	5	6	11	8	....	....	....	....	....
	NHL Totals	**54**	**5**	**6**	**11**	**8**	....	....	....	....	....

• Son of Rene

• Suspended by **Montreal** for refusing assignment to **Fort Wayne** (IHL), September, 1954. Traded to **Detroit** (Seattle-WHL) by **Indianapolis** (IHL) for cash, September, 1958. Traded to **Los Angeles** (WHL) by **Seattle** (WHL) with Frank Arnett for Jim Powers, Terry Slater and Jim Hay, July, 1962. Traded to **Seattle** (WHL) by **Chicago** (LA Blades-WHL) with Bobby Schmautz for cash with Chicago retaining NHL rights, August 10, 1967.

BOILEAU, Patrick

Defense. Shoots right. 6', 202 lbs. Born, Montreal, Que., February 22, 1975.
(Washington's 3rd choice, 69th overall, in 1993 Entry Draft).

Season	Club	GP	G	A	Pts	PIM	GP	G	A	Pts	PIM
1996-97	Washington Capitals	1	0	0	0	0	....	....	....	....	....
1998-99	Washington Capitals	4	0	1	1	2	....	....	....	....	....
2001-02	Washington Capitals	2	0	0	0	2	....	....	....	....	....
2002-03	Detroit Red Wings	25	2	6	8	14	....	....	....	....	....
	NHL Totals	**32**	**2**	**7**	**9**	**18**	....	....	....	....	....

Signed as a free agent by **Detroit**, August 5, 2002.

BOILEAU, Rene

Center. Shoots left. 5'10", 160 lbs. Born, Pointe Claire, Que., May 18, 1904.

Season	Club	GP	G	A	Pts	PIM	GP	G	A	Pts	PIM
1925-26	New York Americans	7	0	0	0	0	....	....	....	....	....
	NHL Totals	**7**	**0**	**0**	**0**	**0**	....	....	....	....	....

• Father of Marc

Signed as a free agent by **NY Americans** (Niagara Falls-Can-Pro), January 15, 1926.

BOIMISTRUCK, Fred

Defense. Shoots right. 5'11", 190 lbs. Born, Sudbury, Ont., January 14, 1962.
(Toronto's 3rd choice, 43rd overall, in 1980 Entry Draft).

Season	Club	GP	G	A	Pts	PIM	GP	G	A	Pts	PIM
1981-82	Toronto Maple Leafs	57	2	11	13	32	....	....	....	....	....
1982-83	Toronto Maple Leafs	26	2	3	5	13	....	....	....	....	....
	NHL Totals	**83**	**4**	**14**	**18**	**45**	....	....	....	....	....

BOISVERT, Serge

Right wing. Shoots right. 5'9", 172 lbs. Born, Drummondville, Que., June 1, 1959.

Season	Club	GP	G	A	Pts	PIM	GP	G	A	Pts	PIM
1982-83	Toronto Maple Leafs	17	0	2	2	4	....	....	....	....	....
1984-85	Montreal Canadiens	14	2	2	4	0	12	3	5	8	2
1985-86 ♦	Montreal Canadiens	9	2	2	4	2	8	0	1	1	0
1986-87	Montreal Canadiens	1	0	0	0	0	....	....	....	....	....
1987-88	Montreal Canadiens	5	1	1	2	2	3	0	1	1	2
	NHL Totals	**46**	**5**	**7**	**12**	**8**	**23**	**3**	**7**	**10**	**4**

Signed as a free agent by **Toronto**, October 9, 1980. Traded to **Edmonton** by **Toronto** for Reid Bailey, January 15, 1983. Signed as a free agent by **Montreal**, February 8, 1985.

BOIVIN, Claude

Left wing. Shoots left. 6'2", 200 lbs. Born, Ste-Foy, Que., March 1, 1970.
(Philadelphia's 1st choice, 14th overall, in 1988 Entry Draft).

Season	Club	GP	G	A	Pts	PIM	GP	G	A	Pts	PIM
1991-92	Philadelphia Flyers	58	5	13	18	187	....	....	....	....	....
1992-93	Philadelphia Flyers	30	5	4	9	76	....	....	....	....	....
1993-94	Philadelphia Flyers	26	1	1	2	57	....	....	....	....	....
	Ottawa Senators	15	1	0	1	38	....	....	....	....	....
1994-95	Ottawa Senators	3	0	1	1	6	....	....	....	....	....
	NHL Totals	**132**	**12**	**19**	**31**	**364**	....	....	....	....	....

Traded to **Ottawa** by **Philadelphia** with Kirk Daubenspeck for Mark Lamb, March 5, 1994.

BOIVIN, Leo

HHOF

Defense. Shoots left. 5'8", 183 lbs. Born, Prescott, Ont., August 2, 1932.

Season	Club	GP	G	A	Pts	PIM	GP	G	A	Pts	PIM
1951-52	Toronto Maple Leafs	2	0	1	1	0	....	....	....	....	....
1952-53	Toronto Maple Leafs	70	2	13	15	97	....	....	....	....	....
1953-54	Toronto Maple Leafs	58	1	6	7	81	5	0	0	0	2
1954-55	Toronto Maple Leafs	7	0	0	0	8	....	....	....	....	....
	Boston Bruins	59	6	11	17	105	5	0	1	1	4
1955-56	Boston Bruins	68	4	16	20	80	....	....	....	....	....
1956-57	Boston Bruins	55	2	8	10	55	10	2	3	5	12
1957-58	Boston Bruins	33	0	4	4	54	12	0	3	3	21
1958-59	Boston Bruins	70	5	16	21	94	7	1	2	3	4
1959-60	Boston Bruins	70	4	21	25	66	....	....	....	....	....
1960-61	Boston Bruins	57	6	17	23	50	....	....	....	....	....
1961-62	Boston Bruins	65	5	18	23	70	....	....	....	....	....
1962-63	Boston Bruins	62	2	24	26	48	....	....	....	....	....
1963-64	Boston Bruins	65	10	14	24	42	....	....	....	....	....
1964-65	Boston Bruins	67	3	10	13	68	....	....	....	....	....

Season	Club	REGULAR SEASON GP	G	A	Pts	PIM	PLAYOFFS GP	G	A	Pts	PIM
1965-66	Boston Bruins	46	0	5	5	34	....	....	....	....	....
	Detroit Red Wings	16	0	5	5	16	12	0	1	1	16
1966-67	Detroit Red Wings	69	4	17	21	78	....	....	....	....	....
1967-68	Pittsburgh Penguins	73	9	13	22	74	....	....	....	....	....
1968-69	Pittsburgh Penguins	41	5	13	18	26	....	....	....	....	....
	Minnesota North Stars	28	1	6	7	16	....	....	....	....	....
1969-70	Minnesota North Stars	69	3	12	15	30	3	0	0	0	0
	NHL Totals	**1150**	**72**	**250**	**322**	**1192**	**54**	**3**	**10**	**13**	**59**

Played in NHL All-Star Game (1961, 1962, 1964)

Traded to **Toronto** by **Boston** with Fern Flaman, Ken Smith and Phil Maloney for Bill Ezinicki and Vic Lynn, November 16, 1950. Traded to **Boston** by **Toronto** for Joe Klukay, November 9, 1954. Traded to **Detroit** by **Boston** with Dean Prentice for Gary Doak, Ron Murphy, Bill Lesuk and future considerations (Steve Atkinson, June 6, 1966), February 16, 1966. Claimed by **Pittsburgh** from **Detroit** in Expansion Draft, June 6, 1967. Traded to **Minnesota** by **Pittsburgh** for Duane Rupp, January 24, 1969.

BOLAND, Mike

Right wing. Shoots right. 5'10", 183 lbs. Born, Montreal, Que., December 16, 1949.

Season	Club	GP	G	A	Pts	PIM	GP	G	A	Pts	PIM
1974-75	Philadelphia Flyers	2	0	0	0	0	....	....	....	....	....
	NHL Totals	**2**	**0**	**0**	**0**	**0**	....	....	....	....	....

Signed as a free agent by **Philadelphia**, September, 1973.

BOLAND, Mike

Defense. Shoots right. 6', 190 lbs. Born, London, Ont., October 29, 1954.
(Kansas City's 7th choice, 110th overall, in 1974 Amateur Draft).

Season	Club	GP	G	A	Pts	PIM	GP	G	A	Pts	PIM
1974-75	Kansas City Scouts	1	0	0	0	0	....	....	....	....	....
1978-79	Buffalo Sabres	22	1	2	3	29	3	1	0	1	2
	NHL Totals	**23**	**1**	**2**	**3**	**29**	**3**	**1**	**0**	**1**	**2**

Signed as a free agent by **Buffalo**, January 5, 1979.

BOLDIREV, Ivan

Center. Shoots left. 6', 190 lbs. Born, Zranjanin, Yugoslavia, August 15, 1949.
(Boston's 3rd choice, 11th overall, in 1969 Amateur Draft).

Season	Club	GP	G	A	Pts	PIM	GP	G	A	Pts	PIM
1970-71	Boston Bruins	2	0	0	0	0	....	....	....	....	....
1971-72	Boston Bruins	11	0	2	2	6	....	....	....	....	....
	California Golden Seals	57	16	23	39	54	....	....	....	....	....
1972-73	California Golden Seals	56	11	23	34	58	....	....	....	....	....
1973-74	California Golden Seals	78	25	31	56	22	....	....	....	....	....
1974-75	Chicago Black Hawks	80	24	43	67	54	8	4	2	6	2
1975-76	Chicago Black Hawks	78	28	34	62	33	4	0	1	1	0
1976-77	Chicago Black Hawks	80	24	38	62	40	2	0	1	1	0
1977-78	Chicago Black Hawks	80	35	45	80	34	4	0	2	2	2
1978-79	Chicago Black Hawks	66	29	35	64	25	....	....	....	....	....
	Atlanta Flames	13	6	8	14	6	2	0	2	2	2
1979-80	Atlanta Flames	52	16	24	40	20	....	....	....	....	....
	Vancouver Canucks	27	16	11	27	14	4	0	2	2	0
1980-81	Vancouver Canucks	72	26	33	59	34	1	1	1	2	0
1981-82	Vancouver Canucks	78	33	40	73	45	17	8	3	11	4
1982-83	Vancouver Canucks	39	5	20	25	12	....	....	....	....	....
	Detroit Red Wings	33	13	17	30	14	....	....	....	....	....
1983-84	Detroit Red Wings	75	35	48	83	20	4	0	5	5	4
1984-85	Detroit Red Wings	75	19	30	49	16	2	0	1	1	0
	NHL Totals	**1052**	**361**	**505**	**866**	**507**	**48**	**13**	**20**	**33**	**14**

Played in NHL All-Star Game (1978)

Traded to **California** by **Boston** for Rich Leduc and Chris Oddleifson, November 17, 1971. Traded to **Chicago** by **California** for Len Frig and Mike Christie, May 24, 1974. Traded to **Atlanta** by **Chicago** with Phil Russell and Darcy Rota for Tom Lysiak, Pat Ribble, Greg Fox, Harold Phillipoff and Miles Zaharko, March 13, 1979. Traded to **Vancouver** by **Atlanta** with Darcy Rota for Don Lever and Brad Smith, February 8, 1980. Traded to **Detroit** by **Vancouver** for Mark Kirton, January 17, 1983.

BOLDUC, Danny

Left wing. Shoots left. 5'9", 180 lbs. Born, Waterville, ME, April 6, 1953.

Season	Club	GP	G	A	Pts	PIM	GP	G	A	Pts	PIM
1978-79	Detroit Red Wings	56	16	13	29	14	....	....	....	....	....
1979-80	Detroit Red Wings	44	6	5	11	19	....	....	....	....	....
1983-84	Calgary Flames	2	0	1	1	0	1	0	0	0	0
	NHL Totals	**102**	**22**	**19**	**41**	**33**	**1**	**0**	**0**	**0**	**0**

Signed as a free agent by **Detroit**, August 24, 1978. Signed as a free agent by **Montreal**, March 9, 1982. Signed as a free agent by **Calgary**, September 1, 1982.

BOLDUC, Michel

Defense. Shoots left. 6'2", 190 lbs. Born, Angegardien, Que., March 13, 1961.
(Quebec's 6th choice, 150th overall, in 1980 Entry Draft).

Season	Club	GP	G	A	Pts	PIM	GP	G	A	Pts	PIM
1981-82	Quebec Nordiques	3	0	0	0	0	....	....	....	....	....
1982-83	Quebec Nordiques	7	0	0	0	6	....	....	....	....	....
	NHL Totals	**10**	**0**	**0**	**0**	**6**	....	....	....	....	....

Claimed on waivers by **New Jersey** from **Quebec**, January 25, 1985.

BOLL, Buzz

Left wing. Shoots left. 5'10", 166 lbs. Born, Filmore, Sask., March 6, 1911.

Season	Club	GP	G	A	Pts	PIM	GP	G	A	Pts	PIM
1932-33	Toronto Maple Leafs	....	....	....	....	....	1	0	0	0	0
1933-34	Toronto Maple Leafs	42	12	8	20	21	5	0	0	0	9
1934-35	Toronto Maple Leafs	47	14	4	18	4	6	0	0	0	0
1935-36	Toronto Maple Leafs	44	15	13	28	14	9	*7	3	*10	2
1936-37	Toronto Maple Leafs	25	6	3	9	12	2	0	0	0	0
1937-38	Toronto Maple Leafs	44	14	11	25	18	7	0	0	0	2
1938-39	Toronto Maple Leafs	11	0	0	0	0	....	....	....	....	....
1939-40	New York Americans	47	5	10	15	18	1	0	0	0	0
1940-41	New York Americans	47	12	14	26	16	....	....	....	....	....
1941-42	Brooklyn Americans	48	11	15	26	23	....	....	....	....	....
1942-43	Boston Bruins	43	25	27	52	20	....	....	....	....	....
1943-44	Boston Bruins	39	19	25	44	2	....	....	....	....	....
	NHL Totals	**437**	**133**	**130**	**263**	**148**	**31**	**7**	**3**	**10**	**13**

Played in NHL All-Star Game (1934)

Traded to **NY Americans** by **Toronto** with Busher Jackson, Doc Romnes, Jimmy Fowler and Murray Armstrong for Sweeney Schriner, May 18, 1939. • Team name changed to **Brooklyn Americans** prior to 1941-42 season. Rights transferred to **Boston** from **Brooklyn** in Special Dispersal Draw, October 9, 1942.

BOLONCHUK, Larry

Defense. Shoots left. 5'10", 190 lbs. Born, Winnipeg, Man., February 26, 1952.
(Vancouver's 5th choice, 67th overall, in 1972 Amateur Draft).

Season	Club	GP	G	A	Pts	PIM	GP	G	A	Pts	PIM
1972-73	Vancouver Canucks	15	0	0	0	6	....	....	....	....	....
1975-76	Washington Capitals	1	0	1	1	0	....	....	....	....	....
1976-77	Washington Capitals	9	0	0	0	12	....	....	....	....	....
1977-78	Washington Capitals	49	3	8	11	79	....	....	....	....	....
	NHL Totals	**74**	**3**	**9**	**12**	**97**	....	....	....	....	....

Claimed by **Washington** from **Vancouver** in Expansion Draft, June 12, 1974.

BOLTON, Hugh

Defense. Shoots left. 6'3", 186 lbs. Born, Toronto, Ont., April 15, 1929.

Season	Club	GP	G	A	Pts	PIM	GP	G	A	Pts	PIM
1949-50	Toronto Maple Leafs	2	0	0	0	2	....	....	....	....	....
1950-51 ♦	Toronto Maple Leafs	13	1	3	4	4	....	....	....	....	....
1951-52	Toronto Maple Leafs	60	3	13	16	73	3	0	0	0	4
1952-53	Toronto Maple Leafs	9	0	0	0	10	....	....	....	....	....
1953-54	Toronto Maple Leafs	9	0	0	0	10	5	0	1	1	4
1954-55	Toronto Maple Leafs	69	2	19	21	55	4	0	3	3	6
1955-56	Toronto Maple Leafs	67	4	16	20	65	5	0	1	1	0
1956-57	Toronto Maple Leafs	6	0	0	0	2	....	....	....	....	....
	NHL Totals	**235**	**10**	**51**	**61**	**221**	**17**	**0**	**5**	**5**	**14**

Played in NHL All-Star Game (1956)

Missed majority of 1953-54 season recovering from shoulder injury suffered in game vs. Detroit, December 25, 1953. • Suffered eventual career-ending leg injury in exhibition game vs. Montreal, September 24, 1956.

BOMBARDIR, Brad

Defense. Shoots left. 6'1", 205 lbs. Born, Powell River, B.C., May 5, 1972.
(New Jersey's 5th choice, 56th overall, in 1990 Entry Draft).

Season	Club	GP	G	A	Pts	PIM	GP	G	A	Pts	PIM
1997-98	New Jersey Devils	43	1	5	6	8	....	....	....	....	....
1998-99	New Jersey Devils	56	1	7	8	16	5	0	0	0	0
99-2000 ♦	New Jersey Devils	32	3	1	4	6	1	0	0	0	0
2000-01	Minnesota Wild	70	0	15	15	42	....	....	....	....	....
2001-02	Minnesota Wild	28	1	2	3	14	....	....	....	....	....
2002-03	Minnesota Wild	58	1	14	15	16	4	0	0	0	0
	NHL Totals	**287**	**7**	**44**	**51**	**102**	**10**	**0**	**0**	**0**	**0**

• Missed majority of 1999-2000 season recovering from esophagus injury suffered in game vs. Philadelphia, October 30, 1999. Traded to **Minnesota** by **New Jersey** for Chris Terreri and Minnesota's 9th round choice (later traded to Tampa Bay – Tampa Bay selected Thomas Ziegler) in 2000 Entry Draft, June 23, 2000. • Missed majority of 2001-02 season recovering from ankle injury suffered in game vs. San Jose, October 16, 2001.

BONAR, Dan

Center. Shoots right. 5'9", 175 lbs. Born, Brandon, Man., September 23, 1956.

Season	Club	GP	G	A	Pts	PIM	GP	G	A	Pts	PIM
1980-81	Los Angeles Kings	71	11	15	26	57	4	1	1	2	11
1981-82	Los Angeles Kings	79	13	23	36	111	10	2	3	5	11
1982-83	Los Angeles Kings	20	1	1	2	40	....	....	....	....	....
	NHL Totals	**170**	**25**	**39**	**64**	**208**	**14**	**3**	**4**	**7**	**22**

Signed as a free agent by **Los Angeles**, August 7, 1978. Traded to **Montreal** by **Los Angeles** for cash, December 20, 1983.

BONDRA, Peter

Right wing. Shoots left. 6', 200 lbs. Born, Luck, USSR, February 7, 1968.
(Washington's 9th choice, 156th overall, in 1990 Entry Draft).

Season	Club	GP	G	A	Pts	PIM	GP	G	A	Pts	PIM
1990-91	Washington Capitals	54	12	16	28	47	4	0	1	1	2
1991-92	Washington Capitals	71	28	28	56	42	7	6	2	8	4
1992-93	Washington Capitals	83	37	48	85	70	6	0	6	6	0
1993-94	Washington Capitals	69	24	19	43	40	9	2	4	6	4
1994-95	Washington Capitals	47	*34	9	43	24	7	5	3	8	10
1995-96	Washington Capitals	67	52	28	80	40	6	3	2	5	8
1996-97	Washington Capitals	77	46	31	77	72	....	....	....	....	....
1997-98	Washington Capitals	76	*52	26	78	44	17	7	5	12	12
1998-99	Washington Capitals	66	31	24	55	56	....	....	....	....	....
99-2000	Washington Capitals	62	21	17	38	30	5	1	1	2	4
2000-01	Washington Capitals	82	45	36	81	60	6	2	0	2	2
2001-02	Washington Capitals	77	39	31	70	80	....	....	....	....	....
2002-03	Washington Capitals	76	30	26	56	52	6	4	2	6	8
	NHL Totals	**907**	**451**	**339**	**790**	**657**	**73**	**30**	**26**	**56**	**54**

Played in NHL All-Star Game (1993, 1996, 1997, 1998, 1999)

BONIN, Brian

Center. Shoots left. 5'10", 186 lbs. Born, St. Paul, MN, November 28, 1973.
(Pittsburgh's 9th choice, 211th overall, in 1992 Entry Draft).

Season	Club	Regular Season GP	G	A	Pts	PIM	Playoffs GP	G	A	Pts	PIM
1998-99	Pittsburgh Penguins	5	0	0	0	0	3	0	0	0	0
2000-01	Minnesota Wild	7	0	0	0	0	....	....	....	....	....
	NHL Totals	**12**	**0**	**0**	**0**	**0**	**3**	**0**	**0**	**0**	**0**

Signed as a free agent by **Vancouver**, September 9, 1999. Signed as a free agent by **Minnesota**, July 6, 2000.

BONIN, Marcel

Wing. Shoots left. 5'10", 170 lbs. Born, Montreal, Que., September 12, 1932.

Season	Club	Regular Season GP	G	A	Pts	PIM	Playoffs GP	G	A	Pts	PIM
1952-53	Detroit Red Wings	37	4	9	13	14	5	0	1	1	0
1953-54	Detroit Red Wings	1	0	0	0	0	....	....	....	....	....
1954-55◆	Detroit Red Wings	69	16	20	36	53	11	0	2	2	4
1955-56	Boston Bruins	67	9	9	18	49	....	....	....	....	....
1957-58◆	Montreal Canadiens	66	15	24	39	37	9	0	1	1	2
1958-59◆	Montreal Canadiens	57	13	30	43	38	11	*10	5	15	4
1959-60◆	Montreal Canadiens	59	17	34	51	59	8	1	4	5	12
1960-61	Montreal Canadiens	65	16	35	51	45	6	0	1	1	29
1961-62	Montreal Canadiens	33	7	14	21	41	....	....	....	....	....
	NHL Totals	**454**	**97**	**175**	**272**	**336**	**50**	**11**	**14**	**25**	**51**

Played in NHL All-Star Game (1954, 1957, 1958, 1959, 1960)

Traded to **Detroit** by **Quebec** (QMHL) for cash, October 22, 1952. Traded to **Boston** by **Detroit** with Lorne Davis, Terry Sawchuk and Vic Stasiuk for Gilles Boisvert, Real Chevrefils, Norm Corcoran, Warren Godfrey and Ed Sandford, June 3, 1955. Claimed by **Montreal** from **Boston** (Springfield-AHL) in Inter-League Draft, June 4, 1957. • Suffered eventual career-ending back injury in game vs. Detroit, February 9, 1962.

BONK, Radek

Center. Shoots left. 6'3", 210 lbs. Born, Krnov, Czech., January 9, 1976.
(Ottawa's 1st choice, 3rd overall, in 1994 Entry Draft).

Season	Club	Regular Season GP	G	A	Pts	PIM	Playoffs GP	G	A	Pts	PIM
1994-95	Ottawa Senators	42	3	8	11	28	....	....	....	....	....
1995-96	Ottawa Senators	76	16	19	35	36	....	....	....	....	....
1996-97	Ottawa Senators	53	5	13	18	14	7	0	1	1	4
1997-98	Ottawa Senators	65	7	9	16	16	5	0	0	0	2
1998-99	Ottawa Senators	81	16	16	32	48	4	0	0	0	6
99-2000	Ottawa Senators	80	23	37	60	53	6	0	0	0	8
2000-01	Ottawa Senators	74	23	36	59	52	2	0	0	0	2
2001-02	Ottawa Senators	82	25	45	70	52	12	3	7	10	6
2002-03	Ottawa Senators	70	22	32	54	36	18	6	5	11	10
	NHL Totals	**623**	**140**	**215**	**355**	**335**	**54**	**9**	**13**	**22**	**38**

Played in NHL All-Star Game (2000, 2001)

BONNI, Ryan

Defense. Shoots left. 6'4", 190 lbs. Born, Winnipeg, Man., February 18, 1979.
(Vancouver's 2nd choice, 34th overall, in 1997 Entry Draft).

Season	Club	Regular Season GP	G	A	Pts	PIM	Playoffs GP	G	A	Pts	PIM
99-2000	Vancouver Canucks	3	0	0	0	0	....	....	....	....	....
	NHL Totals	**3**	**0**	**0**	**0**	**0**	....	....	....	....	....

Traded to **Toronto** by **Vancouver** for Toronto's 8th round choice (Sergei Topol) in 2003 Entry Draft, June 25, 2002.

BONSIGNORE, Jason

Center. Shoots right. 6'4", 220 lbs. Born, Rochester, NY, April 15, 1976.
(Edmonton's 1st choice, 4th overall, in 1994 Entry Draft).

Season	Club	Regular Season GP	G	A	Pts	PIM	Playoffs GP	G	A	Pts	PIM
1994-95	Edmonton Oilers	1	1	0	1	0	....	....	....	....	....
1995-96	Edmonton Oilers	20	0	2	2	4	....	....	....	....	....
1997-98	Tampa Bay Lightning	35	2	8	10	22	....	....	....	....	....
1998-99	Tampa Bay Lightning	23	0	3	3	8	....	....	....	....	....
	NHL Totals	**79**	**3**	**13**	**16**	**34**	....	....	....	....	....

Traded to **Tampa Bay** by **Edmonton** with Bryan Marchment and Steve Kelly for Roman Hamrlik and Paul Comrie, December 30, 1997. Signed as a free agent by **Toronto**, July 15, 1999. Signed as a free agent by **Phoenix**, December 13, 2002.

BONVIE, Dennis

Right wing. Shoots right. 5'11", 205 lbs. Born, Antigonish, N.S., July 23, 1973.

Season	Club	Regular Season GP	G	A	Pts	PIM	Playoffs GP	G	A	Pts	PIM
1994-95	Edmonton Oilers	2	0	0	0	0	....	....	....	....	....
1995-96	Edmonton Oilers	8	0	0	0	47	....	....	....	....	....
1997-98	Edmonton Oilers	4	0	0	0	27	....	....	....	....	....
1998-99	Chicago Blackhawks	11	0	0	0	44	....	....	....	....	....
99-2000	Pittsburgh Penguins	28	0	0	0	80	....	....	....	....	....
2000-01	Pittsburgh Penguins	3	0	0	0	0	....	....	....	....	....
2001-02	Boston Bruins	23	1	2	3	84	1	0	0	0	0
2002-03	Ottawa Senators	12	0	0	0	29	....	....	....	....	....
	NHL Totals	**91**	**1**	**2**	**3**	**311**	**1**	**0**	**0**	**0**	**0**

Signed as a free agent by **Edmonton**, August 25, 1994. Claimed by **Chicago** from **Edmonton** in Waiver Draft, October 5, 1998. Traded to **Philadelphia** by **Chicago** for Frank Bialowas, January 8, 1999. Signed as a free agent by **Pittsburgh**, September 20, 1999. Signed as a free agent by **Boston**, October 5, 2001. Signed as a free agent by **Ottawa**, August 26, 2002.

BOO, Jim

Defense. Shoots right. 6'1", 200 lbs. Born, Rolla, MO, November 12, 1954.

Season	Club	Regular Season GP	G	A	Pts	PIM	Playoffs GP	G	A	Pts	PIM
1977-78	Minnesota North Stars	6	0	0	0	22	....	....	....	....	....
	NHL Totals	**6**	**0**	**0**	**0**	**22**	....	....	....	....	....

Signed as a free agent by **Minnesota**, March 1, 1978.

BOONE, Buddy

Right wing. Shoots right. 5'7", 158 lbs. Born, Kirkland Lake, Ont., September 11, 1932.

Season	Club	Regular Season GP	G	A	Pts	PIM	Playoffs GP	G	A	Pts	PIM
1956-57	Boston Bruins	....	....	....	....	....	10	1	0	1	12
1957-58	Boston Bruins	34	5	3	8	28	12	1	1	2	13
	NHL Totals	**34**	**5**	**3**	**8**	**28**	**22**	**2**	**1**	**3**	**25**

Claimed by **NY Rangers** from **Vancouver** (WHL) in Inter-League Draft, June 9, 1965. Traded to **Los Angeles** (WHL) by **NY Rangers** for Gord Vejprava, November, 1965.

BOOTHMAN, George

Center/Defense. Shoots right. 6'2", 175 lbs. Born, Calgary, Alta., September 25, 1916.

Season	Club	Regular Season GP	G	A	Pts	PIM	Playoffs GP	G	A	Pts	PIM
1942-43	Toronto Maple Leafs	9	1	1	2	4	....	....	....	....	....
1943-44	Toronto Maple Leafs	49	16	18	34	14	5	2	1	3	2
	NHL Totals	**58**	**17**	**19**	**36**	**18**	**5**	**2**	**1**	**3**	**2**

Loaned to **Providence** (AHL) by **Toronto** with the loan of Jack Forsey for Buck Jones and the loan of Ab DeMarco, February 3, 1943. Traded to **Buffalo** (AHL) by **Toronto** with Don Webster for the rights to Bill Ezinicki, October 13, 1944. Traded to **NY Rangers** (Providence-AHL) by **New Haven** (AHL) with cash for Guy Labrie, Paul Courteau and Roland Forget, November 19, 1945.

BORDELEAU, Christian

Center. Shoots left. 5'8", 172 lbs. Born, Noranda, Que., September 23, 1947.

Season	Club	Regular Season GP	G	A	Pts	PIM	Playoffs GP	G	A	Pts	PIM
1968-69◆	Montreal Canadiens	13	1	3	4	4	6	1	0	1	0
1969-70	Montreal Canadiens	48	2	13	15	18	....	....	....	....	....
1970-71	St. Louis Blues	78	21	32	53	48	5	0	1	1	17
1971-72	St. Louis Blues	41	8	9	17	6	....	....	....	....	....
	Chicago Black Hawks	25	6	8	14	6	8	3	6	9	0
	NHL Totals	**205**	**38**	**65**	**103**	**82**	**19**	**4**	**7**	**11**	**17**

• Brother of J.P. and Paulin

Traded to **St. Louis** by **Montreal** for cash, May 22, 1970. Traded to **Chicago** by **St. Louis** with future considerations (John Garrett, September 19, 1972) for Danny O'Shea, February 8, 1972. Traded to **St. Louis** by **Chicago** for rights to John Garrett, September 15, 1972. Reclaimed by **St. Louis** from **Quebec** prior to Expansion Draft, June 9, 1979.

BORDELEAU, J.P.

Right wing. Shoots right. 6'1", 175 lbs. Born, Noranda, Que., June 13, 1949.
(Chicago's 1st choice, 13th overall, in 1969 Amateur Draft).

Season	Club	Regular Season GP	G	A	Pts	PIM	Playoffs GP	G	A	Pts	PIM
1969-70	Chicago Black Hawks	....	....	....	....	....	1	0	0	0	0
1971-72	Chicago Black Hawks	3	0	2	2	2	....	....	....	....	....
1972-73	Chicago Black Hawks	73	15	15	30	6	14	1	0	1	4
1973-74	Chicago Black Hawks	64	11	9	20	11	11	0	2	2	2
1974-75	Chicago Black Hawks	59	7	8	15	4	7	2	2	4	2
1975-76	Chicago Black Hawks	76	12	18	30	6	4	0	0	0	0
1976-77	Chicago Black Hawks	60	15	14	29	20	2	0	0	0	2
1977-78	Chicago Black Hawks	76	15	25	40	32	4	0	1	1	0
1978-79	Chicago Black Hawks	63	15	21	36	34	4	0	1	1	2
1979-80	Chicago Black Hawks	45	7	14	21	28	1	0	0	0	0
	NHL Totals	**519**	**97**	**126**	**223**	**143**	**48**	**3**	**6**	**9**	**12**

• Brother of Paulin and Christian

BORDELEAU, Paulin

Right wing. Shoots right. 5'9", 162 lbs. Born, Noranda, Que., January 29, 1953.
(Vancouver's 3rd choice, 19th overall, in 1973 Amateur Draft).

Season	Club	Regular Season GP	G	A	Pts	PIM	Playoffs GP	G	A	Pts	PIM
1973-74	Vancouver Canucks	68	11	13	24	20	....	....	....	....	....
1974-75	Vancouver Canucks	67	17	31	48	21	5	2	1	3	0
1975-76	Vancouver Canucks	48	5	12	17	6	....	....	....	....	....
	NHL Totals	**183**	**33**	**56**	**89**	**47**	**5**	**2**	**1**	**3**	**0**

• Brother of Christian and J.P. • Father of Sebastien

BORDELEAU, Sebastien

Center. Shoots right. 5'11", 185 lbs. Born, Vancouver, B.C., February 15, 1975.
(Montreal's 3rd choice, 73rd overall, in 1993 Entry Draft).

Season	Club	Regular Season GP	G	A	Pts	PIM	Playoffs GP	G	A	Pts	PIM
1995-96	Montreal Canadiens	4	0	0	0	0	....	....	....	....	....
1996-97	Montreal Canadiens	28	2	9	11	2	....	....	....	....	....
1997-98	Montreal Canadiens	53	6	8	14	36	5	0	0	0	2
1998-99	Nashville Predators	72	16	24	40	26	....	....	....	....	....
99-2000	Nashville Predators	60	10	13	23	30	....	....	....	....	....
2000-01	Nashville Predators	14	2	3	5	14	....	....	....	....	....
2001-02	Minnesota Wild	14	1	4	5	8	....	....	....	....	....
	Phoenix Coyotes	6	0	0	0	2	....	....	....	....	....
	NHL Totals	**251**	**37**	**61**	**98**	**118**	**5**	**0**	**0**	**0**	**2**

• Son of Paulin

Traded to **Nashville** by **Montreal** for future considerations, June 26, 1998. • Missed majority of 2000-01 season recovering from abdominal injury suffered in game vs. Detroit, November 18, 2000. Claimed on waivers by **St. Louis** from **Nashville**, March 13, 2001. Claimed by **Minnesota** from **St. Louis** in Waiver Draft, September 28, 2001. Traded to **Phoenix** by **Minnesota** for David Cullen, January 4, 2002.

BOROTSIK, Jack

Center. Shoots left. 5'9", 180 lbs. Born, Brandon, Man., November 26, 1949.

Season	Club	Regular Season GP	G	A	Pts	PIM	Playoffs GP	G	A	Pts	PIM
1974-75	St. Louis Blues	1	0	0	0	0	....	....	....	....	....
	NHL Totals	**1**	**0**	**0**	**0**	**0**	....	....	....	....	....

Signed as a free agent by **St. Louis**, October 12, 1972.

BORSATO, Luciano

Center. Shoots right. 5'11", 190 lbs. Born, Richmond Hill, Ont., January 7, 1966.
(Winnipeg's 7th choice, 135th overall, in 1984 Entry Draft).

Season	Club	Regular Season GP	G	A	Pts	PIM	Playoffs GP	G	A	Pts	PIM
1990-91	Winnipeg Jets	1	0	1	1	2	....	....	....	....	....
1991-92	Winnipeg Jets	56	15	21	36	45	1	0	0	0	0
1992-93	Winnipeg Jets	67	15	20	35	38	6	1	0	1	4
1993-94	Winnipeg Jets	75	5	13	18	28	....	....	....	....	....
1994-95	Winnipeg Jets	4	0	0	0	0	....	....	....	....	....
	NHL Totals	**203**	**35**	**55**	**90**	**113**	**7**	**1**	**0**	**1**	**4**

BORSCHEVSKY, Nikolai

Right wing. Shoots left. 5'9", 180 lbs. Born, Tomsk, USSR, January 12, 1965.
(Toronto's 3rd choice, 77th overall, in 1992 Entry Draft).

Season	Club	Regular Season GP	G	A	Pts	PIM	Playoffs GP	G	A	Pts	PIM
1992-93	Toronto Maple Leafs	78	34	40	74	28	16	2	7	9	0
1993-94	Toronto Maple Leafs	45	14	20	34	10	15	2	2	4	4
1994-95	Toronto Maple Leafs	19	0	5	5	0	....	....	....	....	....
	Calgary Flames	8	0	5	5	0	....	....	....	....	....
1995-96	Dallas Stars	12	1	3	4	6	....	....	....	....	....
	NHL Totals	**162**	**49**	**73**	**122**	**44**	**31**	**4**	**9**	**13**	**4**

Traded to **Calgary** by **Toronto** for Calgary's 6th round choice (Chris Bogas) in 1996 Entry Draft, April 6, 1995. Signed as a free agent by **Dallas**, September 13, 1995.

BOSCHMAN, Laurie

Center. Shoots left. 6', 185 lbs. Born, Major, Sask., June 4, 1960.
(Toronto's 1st choice, 9th overall, in 1979 Entry Draft).

Season	Club	Regular Season GP	G	A	Pts	PIM	Playoffs GP	G	A	Pts	PIM
1979-80	Toronto Maple Leafs	80	16	32	48	78	3	1	1	2	18
1980-81	Toronto Maple Leafs	53	14	19	33	178	3	0	0	0	7
1981-82	Toronto Maple Leafs	54	9	19	28	150	....	....	....	....	....
	Edmonton Oilers	11	2	3	5	37	3	0	1	1	4
1982-83	Edmonton Oilers	62	8	12	20	183	....	....	....	....	....
	Winnipeg Jets	12	3	5	8	36	3	0	1	1	12
1983-84	Winnipeg Jets	61	28	46	74	234	3	0	1	1	5
1984-85	Winnipeg Jets	80	32	44	76	180	8	2	1	3	21
1985-86	Winnipeg Jets	77	27	42	69	241	3	0	1	1	6
1986-87	Winnipeg Jets	80	17	24	41	152	10	2	3	5	32
1987-88	Winnipeg Jets	80	25	23	48	229	5	1	3	4	9
1988-89	Winnipeg Jets	70	10	26	36	163	....	....	....	....	....
1989-90	Winnipeg Jets	66	10	17	27	103	2	0	0	0	2
1990-91	New Jersey Devils	78	11	9	20	79	7	1	1	2	16
1991-92	New Jersey Devils	75	8	20	28	121	7	1	0	1	8
1992-93	Ottawa Senators	70	9	7	16	101	....	....	....	....	....
	NHL Totals	**1009**	**229**	**348**	**577**	**2265**	**57**	**8**	**13**	**21**	**140**

Traded to **Edmonton** by **Toronto** for Walt Poddubny and Phil Drouillard, March 9, 1982. Traded to **Winnipeg** by **Edmonton** for Willy Lindstrom, March 7, 1983. Traded to **New Jersey** by **Winnipeg** for Bob Brooke, September 6, 1990. • Brooke retired and Winnipeg received New Jersey's 5th round choice (Yan Kaminsky) in 1991 Entry Draft as compensation. Claimed by **Ottawa** from **New Jersey** in Expansion Draft, June 18, 1992.

BOSSY, Mike

HHOF

Right wing. Shoots right. 6', 186 lbs. Born, Montreal, Que., January 22, 1957.
(NY Islanders' 1st choice, 15th overall, in 1977 Amateur Draft).

Season	Club	Regular Season GP	G	A	Pts	PIM	Playoffs GP	G	A	Pts	PIM
1977-78	New York Islanders	73	53	38	91	6	7	2	2	4	2
1978-79	New York Islanders	80	*69	57	126	25	10	6	2	8	2
1979-80♦	New York Islanders	75	51	41	92	12	16	10	13	23	8
1980-81♦	New York Islanders	79	*68	51	119	32	18	*17	*18	*35	4
1981-82♦	New York Islanders	80	64	83	147	22	19	*17	10	27	0
1982-83♦	New York Islanders	79	60	58	118	20	19	*17	9	26	10
1983-84	New York Islanders	67	51	67	118	8	21	8	10	18	4
1984-85	New York Islanders	76	58	59	117	38	10	5	6	11	4
1985-86	New York Islanders	80	61	62	123	14	3	1	2	3	4
1986-87	New York Islanders	63	38	37	75	33	6	2	3	5	0
	NHL Totals	**752**	**573**	**553**	**1126**	**210**	**129**	**85**	**75**	**160**	**38**

NHL Second All-Star Team (1978, 1979, 1985) • Calder Memorial Trophy (1978) • NHL First All-Star Team (1981, 1982, 1983, 1984, 1986) • Conn Smythe Trophy (1982) • Lady Byng Trophy (1983, 1984, 1986)

Played in NHL All-Star Game (1978, 1980, 1981, 1982, 1983, 1985, 1986)

BOSTROM, Helge

Defense. Shoots left. 5'8", 185 lbs. Born, Gimli, Man., January 9, 1894.

Season	Club	Regular Season GP	G	A	Pts	PIM	Playoffs GP	G	A	Pts	PIM
1929-30	Chicago Black Hawks	20	0	1	1	8	2	0	0	0	0
1930-31	Chicago Black Hawks	42	2	2	4	32	9	0	0	0	16
1931-32	Chicago Black Hawks	14	0	0	0	4	2	0	0	0	0
1932-33	Chicago Black Hawks	20	1	0	1	14	....	....	....	....	....
	NHL Totals	**96**	**3**	**3**	**6**	**58**	**13**	**0**	**0**	**0**	**16**

Traded to **Chicago** by **Minneapolis** (AHA) for Bobby Burns, January 15, 1930. Traded to **St. Paul** (AHA) by **Chicago** for Art Wiebe, December 29, 1932.

BOTELL, Mark

Defense. Shoots left. 6'4", 220 lbs. Born, Scarborough, Ont., August 27, 1961.
(Philadelphia's 8th choice, 168th overall, in 1980 Entry Draft).

Season	Club	Regular Season GP	G	A	Pts	PIM	Playoffs GP	G	A	Pts	PIM
1981-82	Philadelphia Flyers	32	4	10	14	31	....	....	....	....	....
	NHL Totals	**32**	**4**	**10**	**14**	**31**	....	....	....	....	....

BOTHWELL, Tim

Defense. Shoots left. 6'3", 190 lbs. Born, Vancouver, B.C., May 6, 1955.

Season	Club	Regular Season GP	G	A	Pts	PIM	Playoffs GP	G	A	Pts	PIM
1978-79	New York Rangers	1	0	0	0	2	....	....	....	....	....
1979-80	New York Rangers	45	4	6	10	20	9	0	0	0	8
1980-81	New York Rangers	3	0	1	1	0	....	....	....	....	....
1981-82	New York Rangers	13	0	3	3	10	....	....	....	....	....
1982-83	St. Louis Blues	61	4	11	15	34	....	....	....	....	....
1983-84	St. Louis Blues	62	2	13	15	65	11	0	2	2	14
1984-85	St. Louis Blues	79	4	22	26	62	3	0	0	0	2
1985-86	Hartford Whalers	62	2	8	10	53	10	0	0	0	8
1986-87	Hartford Whalers	4	1	0	1	0	....	....	....	....	....
	St. Louis Blues	72	5	16	21	46	6	0	0	0	6
1987-88	St. Louis Blues	78	6	13	19	76	10	0	1	1	18
1988-89	St. Louis Blues	22	0	0	0	14	....	....	....	....	....
	NHL Totals	**502**	**28**	**93**	**121**	**382**	**49**	**0**	**3**	**3**	**56**

Signed as a free agent by **NY Rangers**, June 8, 1978. Claimed by **St. Louis** from **NY Rangers** in Waiver Draft, October 4, 1982. Rights traded to **Hartford** by **St. Louis** for cash, October 4, 1985. Traded to **St. Louis** by **Hartford** for Dave Barr, October 21, 1986.

BOTTERILL, Jason

Left wing. Shoots left. 6'4", 220 lbs. Born, Edmonton, Alta., May 19, 1976.
(Dallas' 1st choice, 20th overall, in 1994 Entry Draft).

Season	Club	Regular Season GP	G	A	Pts	PIM	Playoffs GP	G	A	Pts	PIM
1997-98	Dallas Stars	4	0	0	0	19	....	....	....	....	....
1998-99	Dallas Stars	17	0	0	0	23	....	....	....	....	....
99-2000	Atlanta Thrashers	25	1	4	5	17	....	....	....	....	....
	Calgary Flames	2	0	0	0	0	....	....	....	....	....
2001-02	Calgary Flames	4	1	0	1	2	....	....	....	....	....
2002-03	Buffalo Sabres	17	1	4	5	14	....	....	....	....	....
	NHL Totals	**69**	**3**	**8**	**11**	**75**	....	....	....	....	....

Traded to **Atlanta** by **Dallas** for Jamie Pushor, July 15, 1999. Traded to **Calgary** by **Atlanta** with Darryl Shannon for Hnat Domenichelli and Dmitri Vlasenkov, February 11, 2000. Signed as a free agent by **Buffalo**, August 12, 2002.

BOTTING, Cam

Right wing. Shoots right. 6'2", 205 lbs. Born, Kingston, Ont., March 10, 1954.
(Atlanta's 4th choice, 64th overall, in 1974 Amateur Draft).

Season	Club	Regular Season GP	G	A	Pts	PIM	Playoffs GP	G	A	Pts	PIM
1975-76	Atlanta Flames	2	0	1	1	0	....	....	....	....	....
	NHL Totals	**2**	**0**	**1**	**1**	**0**	....	....	....	....	....

BOUCHA, Henry

USHOF

Center. Shoots right. 6', 185 lbs. Born, Warroad, MN, June 1, 1951.
(Detroit's 2nd choice, 16th overall, in 1971 Amateur Draft).

Season	Club	Regular Season GP	G	A	Pts	PIM	Playoffs GP	G	A	Pts	PIM
1971-72	Detroit Red Wings	16	1	0	1	2	....	....	....	....	....
1972-73	Detroit Red Wings	73	14	14	28	82	....	....	....	....	....
1973-74	Detroit Red Wings	70	19	12	31	32	....	....	....	....	....
1974-75	Minnesota North Stars	51	15	14	29	23	....	....	....	....	....
1975-76	Kansas City Scouts	28	4	7	11	14	....	....	....	....	....
1976-77	Colorado Rockies	9	0	2	2	4	....	....	....	....	....
	NHL Totals	**247**	**53**	**49**	**102**	**157**	....	....	....	....	....

Traded to **Minnesota** by **Detroit** for Danny Grant, August 27, 1974. • Suffered eventual career-ending eye injury in game vs. Boston, January 4, 1975. Rights traded to **Kansas City** by **Minnesota** for Kansas City's 2nd round choice (Steve Christoff) in 1978 Amateur Draft, December 9, 1975. Transferred to **Colorado** after **Kansas City** franchise relocated, July 15, 1976.

BOUCHARD, Butch

HHOF

Defense. Shoots right. 6'2", 205 lbs. Born, Montreal, Que., September 11, 1920.

Season	Club	Regular Season GP	G	A	Pts	PIM	Playoffs GP	G	A	Pts	PIM
1941-42	Montreal Canadiens	44	0	6	6	38	3	1	1	2	0
1942-43	Montreal Canadiens	45	2	16	18	47	5	0	1	1	4
1943-44♦	Montreal Canadiens	39	5	14	19	52	9	1	3	4	4
1944-45	Montreal Canadiens	50	11	23	34	34	6	3	4	7	4
1945-46♦	Montreal Canadiens	45	7	10	17	52	9	2	1	3	17
1946-47	Montreal Canadiens	60	5	7	12	60	11	0	3	3	21
1947-48	Montreal Canadiens	60	4	6	10	78	....	....	....	....	....
1948-49	Montreal Canadiens	27	3	3	6	42	7	0	0	0	6
1949-50	Montreal Canadiens	69	1	7	8	88	5	0	2	2	2
1950-51	Montreal Canadiens	52	3	10	13	80	11	1	1	2	2
1951-52	Montreal Canadiens	60	3	9	12	45	11	0	2	2	14
1952-53♦	Montreal Canadiens	58	2	8	10	55	12	1	1	2	6
1953-54	Montreal Canadiens	70	1	10	11	89	11	2	1	3	4
1954-55	Montreal Canadiens	70	2	15	17	81	12	0	1	1	37
1955-56♦	Montreal Canadiens	36	0	0	0	22	1	0	0	0	0
	NHL Totals	**785**	**49**	**144**	**193**	**863**	**113**	**11**	**21**	**32**	**121**

• Father of Pierre • NHL Second All-Star Team (1944) • NHL First All-Star Team (1945, 1946, 1947)

Played in NHL All-Star Game (1947, 1948, 1950, 1951, 1952, 1953)

Signed as a free agent by **Montreal**, February 21, 1941.

BOUCHARD, Dick

Right wing. Shoots right. 5'8", 155 lbs. Born, Lettelier, Man., December 2, 1934.

Season	Club	Regular Season GP	G	A	Pts	PIM	Playoffs GP	G	A	Pts	PIM
1954-55	New York Rangers	1	0	0	0	0	....	....	....	....	....
	NHL Totals	**1**	**0**	**0**	**0**	**0**	....	....	....	....	....

BOUCHARD, Edmond

Left wing/Defense. Shoots left. 5'10", 185 lbs.   Born, St-Etienne, Que., May 24, 1892.

		REGULAR SEASON					PLAYOFFS				
Season	Club	GP	G	A	Pts	PIM	GP	G	A	Pts	PIM
1921-22	Montreal Canadiens	18	1	5	6	4	....	....	....	....	....
1922-23	Montreal Canadiens	2	0	0	0	4	....	....	....	....	....
	Hamilton Tigers	22	5	*12	17	40	....	....	....	....	....
1923-24	Hamilton Tigers	20	5	0	5	2	....	....	....	....	....
1924-25	Hamilton Tigers	24	2	2	4	14	....	....	....	....	....
1925-26	New York Americans	30	3	1	4	10	....	....	....	....	....
1926-27	New York Americans	38	2	1	3	12	....	....	....	....	....
1927-28	New York Americans	39	1	0	1	27	....	....	....	....	....
1928-29	New York Americans	6	0	0	0	2	....	....	....	....	....
	Pittsburgh Pirates	12	0	0	0	2	....	....	....	....	....
	NHL Totals	**211**	**19**	**21**	**40**	**117**	....	....	....	....	....

Signed as a free agent by **Montreal**, January 2, 1922. Traded to **Hamilton** by **Montreal** for Joe Malone, December 22, 1922. Transferred to **NY Americans** after NHL club purchased **Hamilton** franchise, September 26, 1925. Loaned to **Pittsburgh** by **NY Americans** for remainder of 1928-29 season with the trade of Jesse Spring for the loan of Tex White for remainder of 1928-29 season, February 15, 1929.

BOUCHARD, Joel

Defense. Shoots left. 6'1", 209 lbs.   Born, Montreal, Que., January 23, 1974.
(Calgary's 7th choice, 129th overall, in 1992 Entry Draft).

Season	Club	GP	G	A	Pts	PIM	GP	G	A	Pts	PIM
1994-95	Calgary Flames	2	0	0	0	0	....	....	....	....	....
1995-96	Calgary Flames	4	0	0	0	4	....	....	....	....	....
1996-97	Calgary Flames	76	4	5	9	49	....	....	....	....	....
1997-98	Calgary Flames	44	5	7	12	57	....	....	....	....	....
1998-99	Nashville Predators	64	4	11	15	60	....	....	....	....	....
99-2000	Nashville Predators	52	1	4	5	23	....	....	....	....	....
	Dallas Stars	2	0	0	0	2	....	....	....	....	....
2000-01	Phoenix Coyotes	32	1	2	3	22	....	....	....	....	....
2001-02	New Jersey Devils	1	0	1	1	0	....	....	....	....	....
2002-03	New York Rangers	27	5	7	12	14	....	....	....	....	....
	Pittsburgh Penguins	7	0	1	1	0	....	....	....	....	....
	NHL Totals	**311**	**20**	**38**	**58**	**231**	....	....	....	....	....

Claimed by **Nashville** from **Calgary** in Expansion Draft, June 26, 1998. Claimed on waivers by **Dallas** from **Nashville**, March 14, 2000. Signed as a free agent by **Phoenix**, August 31, 2000. Signed as a free agent by **New Jersey**, October 25, 2001. Signed as a free agent by **NY Rangers**, August 5, 2002. Traded to **Pittsburgh** by **NY Rangers** with Richard Lintner, Rico Fata , Mikael Samuelsson and future considerations for Mike Wilson, Alexei Kovalev, Janne Laukkanen and Dan LaCouture, February 10, 2003. Signed as a free agent by **Buffalo**, July 12, 2003.

BOUCHARD, Pierre

Defense. Shoots left. 6'2", 205 lbs.   Born, Montreal, Que., February 20, 1948.
(Montreal's 1st choice, 5th overall, in 1965 Amateur Draft).

Season	Club	GP	G	A	Pts	PIM	GP	G	A	Pts	PIM
1970-71 ◆	Montreal Canadiens	51	0	3	3	50	13	0	1	1	10
1971-72	Montreal Canadiens	60	3	5	8	39	1	0	0	0	0
1972-73 ◆	Montreal Canadiens	41	0	7	7	69	17	1	3	4	13
1973-74	Montreal Canadiens	60	1	14	15	25	6	0	2	2	4
1974-75	Montreal Canadiens	79	3	9	12	65	10	0	2	2	10
1975-76 ◆	Montreal Canadiens	66	1	11	12	50	13	2	0	2	8
1976-77 ◆	Montreal Canadiens	73	4	11	15	52	6	0	1	1	6
1977-78 ◆	Montreal Canadiens	59	4	6	10	29	10	0	1	1	5
1978-79	Washington Capitals	1	0	0	0	0	....	....	....	....	....
1979-80	Washington Capitals	54	5	9	14	16	....	....	....	....	....
1980-81	Washington Capitals	50	3	7	10	28	....	....	....	....	....
1981-82	Washington Capitals	1	0	0	0	10	....	....	....	....	....
	NHL Totals	**595**	**24**	**82**	**106**	**433**	**76**	**3**	**10**	**13**	**56**

• Son of Butch

Claimed by **Washington** from **Montreal** in Waiver Draft, October 9, 1978.

BOUCHARD, Pierre-Marc

Center. Shoots left. 5'10", 165 lbs.   Born, Sherbrooke, Que., April 27, 1984.
(Minnesota's 1st choice, 8th overall, in 2002 Entry Draft).

Season	Club	GP	G	A	Pts	PIM	GP	G	A	Pts	PIM
2002-03	Minnesota Wild	50	7	13	20	18	5	0	1	1	2
	NHL Totals	**50**	**7**	**13**	**20**	**18**	**5**	**0**	**1**	**1**	**2**

BOUCHER, Billy

Right wing. Shoots right. 5'7", 155 lbs.   Born, Ottawa, Ont., November 10, 1899.

Season	Club	GP	G	A	Pts	PIM	GP	G	A	Pts	PIM
1921-22	Montreal Canadiens	24	17	5	22	18	....	....	....	....	....
1922-23	Montreal Canadiens	24	24	7	31	55	2	1	0	1	2
1923-24 ◆	Montreal Canadiens	23	16	6	22	48	2	1	0	1	9
	Montreal Canadiens (Cup)	....	....	....	....	....	*4*	*5*	*1*	*6*	*6*
1924-25	Montreal Canadiens	30	17	13	30	92	2	1	0	1	4
	Montreal Canadiens (Cup)	....	....	....	....	....	*4*	*1*	*1*	*2*	*13*
1925-26	Montreal Canadiens	34	8	5	13	112	....	....	....	....	....
1926-27	Montreal Canadiens	21	4	0	4	14	....	....	....	....	....
	Boston Bruins	14	2	0	2	12	8	0	0	0	2
1927-28	New York Americans	43	5	2	7	58	....	....	....	....	....
	NHL Totals	**213**	**93**	**38**	**131**	**409**	**14**	**3**	**0**	**3**	**17**

• Brother of Georges, Frank and Bobby

Signed as a free agent by **Montreal**, December 13, 1921. • 1923-24 Stanley Cup totals includes series with Calgary (WCHL) and Vancouver (PCHA). Traded to **Boston** by **Montreal** for Carson Cooper with both teams holding right of recall, January 17, 1927. • Players returned to original teams, May 22, 1927. Traded to **NY Americans** by **Montreal** for cash, October 17, 1927.

BOUCHER, Bobby

Center. Shoots right. 5'8", 142 lbs.   Born, Ottawa, Ont., February 14, 1904.

Season	Club	GP	G	A	Pts	PIM	GP	G	A	Pts	PIM
1923-24 ◆	Montreal Canadiens	11	1	0	1	0	2	0	0	0	0
	Montreal Canadiens (Cup)	....	....	....	....	....	*3*	*0*	*0*	*0*	*0*
	NHL Totals	**11**	**1**	**0**	**1**	**0**	**2**	**0**	**0**	**0**	**0**

• Brother of Georges, Billy and Frank

Signed as a free agent by **Montreal**, January 25, 1924. • 1923-24 Stanley Cup totals includes series with Calgary (WCHL) and Vancouver (PCHA). Traded to **Vancouver** (PCHA) by **Montreal** for Charlie Cotch, March 26, 1924.

BOUCHER, Clarence

Defense. Shoots left. 6'1", 195 lbs.   Born, North Bay, Ont., November 1, 1896.

Season	Club	GP	G	A	Pts	PIM	GP	G	A	Pts	PIM
1926-27	New York Americans	11	0	1	1	4	....	....	....	....	....
1927-28	New York Americans	36	2	1	3	129	....	....	....	....	....
	NHL Totals	**47**	**2**	**2**	**4**	**133**	....	....	....	....	....

Signed as a free agent by **NY Americans**, July 14, 1926.

BOUCHER, Frank

HHOF

Center. Shoots left. 5'9", 185 lbs.   Born, Ottawa, Ont., October 7, 1901.

Season	Club	GP	G	A	Pts	PIM	GP	G	A	Pts	PIM
1921-22	Ottawa Senators	24	8	2	10	4	1	0	0	0	0
1926-27	New York Rangers	44	13	15	28	17	2	0	0	0	4
1927-28 ◆	New York Rangers	44	23	12	35	15	9	*7	3	*10	2
1928-29	New York Rangers	44	10	*16	26	8	6	1	0	1	0
1929-30	New York Rangers	42	26	*36	62	16	3	1	1	2	0
1930-31	New York Rangers	44	12	27	39	20	4	0	2	2	0
1931-32	New York Rangers	48	12	23	35	18	7	3	*6	*9	0
1932-33 ◆	New York Rangers	46	7	*28	35	4	8	2	2	4	6
1933-34	New York Rangers	48	14	30	44	4	2	0	0	0	0
1934-35	New York Rangers	48	13	32	45	2	4	0	3	3	0
1935-36	New York Rangers	48	11	18	29	2	....	....	....	....	....
1936-37	New York Rangers	44	7	13	20	5	9	2	3	5	0
1937-38	New York Rangers	18	0	1	1	2	....	....	....	....	....
1943-44	New York Rangers	15	4	10	14	2	....	....	....	....	....
	NHL Totals	**557**	**160**	**263**	**423**	**119**	**55**	**16**	**20**	**36**	**12**

• Brother of Georges, Billy and Bobby • Lady Byng Trophy (1928, 1929, 1930, 1931, 1933, 1934, 1935) • NHL Second All-Star Team (1931) • NHL First All-Star Team (1933, 1934, 1935) • Lester Patrick Trophy (1993)

Played in NHL All-Star Game (1937)

Signed as a free agent by **Ottawa**, December 6, 1921. Traded to **Vancouver** (PCHA) by **Ottawa** for cash, September 19, 1922. Traded to **NY Rangers** by **Vancouver** (WHL) for $15,000, September 28, 1926.

BOUCHER, Georges

HHOF

Defense. Shoots left. 5'9", 169 lbs.   Born, Ottawa, Ont., August 19, 1896.

Season	Club	GP	G	A	Pts	PIM	GP	G	A	Pts	PIM
1917-18	Ottawa Senators	21	9	8	17	46		....	....	....	....
1918-19	Ottawa Senators	17	3	2	5	29	5	2	0	2	9
1919-20 ◆	Ottawa Senators	22	9	8	17	55	....	....	....	....	....
	Ottawa Senators (Cup)	....	....	....	....	....	*5*	*2*	*0*	*2*	*2*
1920-21 ◆	Ottawa Senators	23	11	8	19	53	2	3	0	3	10
	Ottawa Senators (Cup)	....	....	....	....	....	*5*	*2*	*0*	*2*	*9*
1921-22	Ottawa Senators	23	13	12	25	12	2	0	0	0	4
1922-23 ◆	Ottawa Senators	24	14	9	23	*58	2	0	1	1	2
	Ottawa Senators (Cup)	....	....	....	....	....	*6*	*2*	*1*	*3*	*6*
1923-24	Ottawa Senators	21	13	*10	23	38	2	0	1	1	4
1924-25	Ottawa Senators	28	15	5	20	*95	....	....	....	....	....
1925-26	Ottawa Senators	36	8	4	12	64	2	0	0	0	10
1926-27 ◆	Ottawa Senators	40	8	3	11	115	6	0	0	0	43
1927-28	Ottawa Senators	43	7	5	12	78	2	0	0	0	4
1928-29	Ottawa Senators	29	3	1	4	60	....	....	....	....	....
	Montreal Maroons	12	1	1	2	10	....	....	....	....	....
1929-30	Montreal Maroons	37	2	6	8	50	3	0	0	0	2
1930-31	Montreal Maroons	30	0	0	0	25	....	....	....	....	....
1931-32	Chicago Black Hawks	43	1	5	6	50	2	0	1	1	0
	NHL Totals	**449**	**117**	**87**	**204**	**838**	**28**	**5**	**3**	**8**	**88**

• Brother of Billy, Frank and Bobby

Rights retained by **Ottawa** after NHA folded, November 26, 1917. • 1922-23 Stanley Cup totals includes series with Regina (WCHL) and Edmonton (PCHA). Traded to **Mtl. Maroons** by **Ottawa** for Joe Lamb, February 14, 1929. Claimed on waivers by **Chicago** from **Mtl. Maroons**, November 27, 1931.

BOUCHER, Philippe

Defense. Shoots right. 6'2", 221 lbs.   Born, Ste-Apollinaire, Que., March 24, 1973.
(Buffalo's 1st choice, 13th overall, in 1991 Entry Draft).

Season	Club	GP	G	A	Pts	PIM	GP	G	A	Pts	PIM
1992-93	Buffalo Sabres	18	0	4	4	14	....	....	....	....	....
1993-94	Buffalo Sabres	38	6	8	14	29	7	1	1	2	2
1994-95	Buffalo Sabres	9	1	4	5	0	....	....	....	....	....
	Los Angeles Kings	6	1	0	1	4	....	....	....	....	....
1995-96	Los Angeles Kings	53	7	16	23	31	....	....	....	....	....
1996-97	Los Angeles Kings	60	7	18	25	25	....	....	....	....	....
1997-98	Los Angeles Kings	45	6	10	16	49	....	....	....	....	....
1998-99	Los Angeles Kings	45	2	6	8	32	....	....	....	....	....
99-2000	Los Angeles Kings	1	0	0	0	0	....	....	....	....	....
2000-01	Los Angeles Kings	22	2	4	6	20	13	0	1	1	2
2001-02	Los Angeles Kings	80	7	23	30	94	5	0	1	1	2

Season	Club	GP	G	A	Pts	PIM	GP	G	A	Pts	PIM
		REGULAR SEASON					PLAYOFFS				
2002-03	Dallas Stars	80	7	20	27	94	11	1	2	3	11
	NHL Totals	**457**	**46**	**113**	**159**	**392**	**36**	**2**	**5**	**7**	**17**

Traded to **Los Angeles** by **Buffalo** with Denis Tsygurov and Grant Fuhr for Alexei Zhitnik, Robb Stauber, Charlie Huddy and Los Angeles' 5th round choice (Marian Menhart) in 1995 Entry Draft, February 14, 1995. • Missed majority of 1999-2000 season recovering from foot injury suffered in training camp, September, 1999. Signed as a free agent by **Dallas**, July 2, 2002.

BOUCK, Tyler

Center. Shoots left. 6', 196 lbs. Born, Camrose, Alta., January 13, 1980.
(Dallas' 2nd choice, 57th overall, in 1998 Entry Draft).

Season	Club	GP	G	A	Pts	PIM	GP	G	A	Pts	PIM
2000-01	Dallas Stars	48	2	5	7	29	1	0	0	0	0
2001-02	Phoenix Coyotes	7	0	0	0	4	....	....	....	....	....
	NHL Totals	**55**	**2**	**5**	**7**	**33**	**1**	**0**	**0**	**0**	**0**

Traded to **Phoenix** by **Dallas** for Jyrki Lumme, June 23, 2001. Traded to **Vancouver** by **Phoenix** with Todd Warriner, Trevor Letowski and Phoenix's 3rd round choice (later traded back to Phoenix – Phoenix selected Dimitri Pestunov) in 2003 Entry Draft for Drake Berehowsky and Denis Pederson, December 28, 2001.

BOUDREAU, Bruce

Center. Shoots left. 5'9", 170 lbs. Born, Toronto, Ont., January 9, 1955.
(Toronto's 3rd choice, 42nd overall, in 1975 Amateur Draft).

Season	Club	GP	G	A	Pts	PIM	GP	G	A	Pts	PIM
1976-77	Toronto Maple Leafs	15	2	5	7	4	3	0	0	0	0
1977-78	Toronto Maple Leafs	40	11	18	29	12	....	....	....	....	....
1978-79	Toronto Maple Leafs	26	4	3	7	2	....	....	....	....	....
1979-80	Toronto Maple Leafs	2	0	0	0	2	....	....	....	....	....
1980-81	Toronto Maple Leafs	39	10	14	24	18	2	1	0	1	0
1981-82	Toronto Maple Leafs	12	0	2	2	6	....	....	....	....	....
1982-83	Toronto Maple Leafs	....	....	....	....	....	4	1	0	1	0
1985-86	Chicago Black Hawks	7	1	0	1	2	....	....	....	....	....
	NHL Totals	**141**	**28**	**42**	**70**	**46**	**9**	**2**	**0**	**2**	**0**

Claimed by **Toronto** as a fill-in during Expansion Draft, June 13, 1979. Signed as a free agent by **Chicago**, October 10, 1985.

BOUDRIAS, Andre

Left wing. Shoots left. 5'8", 165 lbs. Born, Montreal, Que., September 19, 1943.

Season	Club	GP	G	A	Pts	PIM	GP	G	A	Pts	PIM
1963-64	Montreal Canadiens	4	1	4	5	2	....	....	....	....	....
1964-65	Montreal Canadiens	1	0	0	0	2	....	....	....	....	....
1966-67	Montreal Canadiens	2	0	1	1	0	....	....	....	....	....
1967-68	Minnesota North Stars	74	18	35	53	42	14	3	6	9	8
1968-69	Minnesota North Stars	53	4	9	13	6	....	....	....	....	....
	Chicago Black Hawks	20	4	10	14	4	....	....	....	....	....
1969-70	St. Louis Blues	50	3	14	17	20	14	2	4	6	4
1970-71	Vancouver Canucks	77	25	41	66	16	....	....	....	....	....
1971-72	Vancouver Canucks	78	27	34	61	26	....	....	....	....	....
1972-73	Vancouver Canucks	77	30	40	70	24	....	....	....	....	....
1973-74	Vancouver Canucks	78	16	59	75	18	....	....	....	....	....
1974-75	Vancouver Canucks	77	16	62	78	46	5	1	0	1	0
1975-76	Vancouver Canucks	71	7	31	38	10	1	0	0	0	0
	NHL Totals	**662**	**151**	**340**	**491**	**216**	**34**	**6**	**10**	**16**	**12**

Played in NHL All-Star Game (1967)

Traded to **Minnesota** by **Montreal** with Bob Charlebois and Bernard Cote for Minnesota's 1st round choice (Chuck Arnason) in 1971 Amateur Draft, June 6, 1967. Traded to **Chicago** by **Minnesota** with Mike McMahon Jr. for Tom Reid and Bill Orban, February 14, 1969. Claimed by **St. Louis** from **Chicago** in Intra-League Draft, June 11, 1969. Traded to **Vancouver** by **St. Louis** for Vancouver's 7th (Jack Taggart) and 9th (Bob Winogard) round choices in 1970 Amateur Draft and cash, June 10, 1970.

BOUGHNER, Barry

Left wing. Shoots left. 5'10", 180 lbs. Born, Delhi, Ont., January 29, 1948.

Season	Club	GP	G	A	Pts	PIM	GP	G	A	Pts	PIM
1969-70	Oakland Seals	4	0	0	0	2	....	....	....	....	....
1970-71	California Seals	16	0	0	0	9	....	....	....	....	....
	NHL Totals	**20**	**0**	**0**	**0**	**11**	....	....	....	....	....

Signed as a free agent by **Oakland**, October, 1969.

BOUGHNER, Bob

Defense. Shoots right. 6', 203 lbs. Born, Windsor, Ont., March 8, 1971.
(Detroit's 2nd choice, 32nd overall, in 1989 Entry Draft).

Season	Club	GP	G	A	Pts	PIM	GP	G	A	Pts	PIM
1995-96	Buffalo Sabres	31	0	1	1	104	....	....	....	....	....
1996-97	Buffalo Sabres	77	1	7	8	225	11	0	1	1	9
1997-98	Buffalo Sabres	69	1	3	4	165	14	0	4	4	15
1998-99	Nashville Predators	79	3	10	13	137	....	....	....	....	....
99-2000	Nashville Predators	62	2	4	6	97	....	....	....	....	....
	Pittsburgh Penguins	11	1	0	1	69	11	0	2	2	15
2000-01	Pittsburgh Penguins	58	1	3	4	147	18	0	1	1	22
2001-02	Calgary Flames	79	2	4	6	170	....	....	....	....	....
2002-03	Calgary Flames	69	3	14	17	126	....	....	....	....	....
	NHL Totals	**535**	**14**	**46**	**60**	**1240**	**54**	**0**	**8**	**8**	**61**

Signed as a free agent by **Florida**, July 25, 1994. Traded to **Buffalo** by **Florida** for Buffalo's 3rd round choice (Chris Allen) in 1996 Entry Draft, February 1, 1996. Claimed by **Nashville** from **Buffalo** in Expansion Draft, June 26, 1998. Traded to **Pittsburgh** by **Nashville** for Pavel Skrbek, March 13, 2000. Signed as a free agent by **Calgary**, July 2, 2001. Traded to **Carolina** by **Calgary** for Carolina's 4th round choice in 2004 Entry Draft and future considerations, July 16, 2003.

BOUILLON, Francis

Defense. Shoots left. 5'8", 194 lbs. Born, New York, NY, October 17, 1975.

Season	Club	GP	G	A	Pts	PIM	GP	G	A	Pts	PIM
99-2000	Montreal Canadiens	74	3	13	16	38	....	....	....	....	....
2000-01	Montreal Canadiens	29	0	6	6	26	....	....	....	....	....
2001-02	Montreal Canadiens	28	0	5	5	33	....	....	....	....	....
2002-03	Nashville Predators	4	0	0	0	2	....	....	....	....	....
	Montreal Canadiens	20	3	1	4	2	....	....	....	....	....
	NHL Totals	**155**	**6**	**25**	**31**	**101**	....	....	....	....	....

Signed as a free agent by **Montreal**, August 18, 1998 • Missed majority of 2000-01 season recovering from ankle injury suffered in game vs. Calgary, December 31, 2000. Claimed by **Nashville** from **Montreal** in Waiver Draft, October 4, 2002. Claimed on waivers by **Montreal** from **Nashville**, October 25, 2002.

BOULERICE, Jesse

Right wing. Shoots right. 6'1", 215 lbs. Born, Plattsburgh, NY, August 10, 1978.
(Philadelphia's 4th choice, 133rd overall, in 1996 Entry Draft).

Season	Club	GP	G	A	Pts	PIM	GP	G	A	Pts	PIM
2001-02	Philadelphia Flyers	3	0	0	0	5	....	....	....	....	....
2002-03	Carolina Hurricanes	48	2	1	3	108	....	....	....	....	....
	NHL Totals	**51**	**2**	**1**	**3**	**113**	....	....	....	....	....

Traded to **Carolina** by **Philadelphia** for Greg Koehler, February 13, 2002.

BOULTON, Eric

Left wing. Shoots left. 6', 222 lbs. Born, Halifax, N.S., August 17, 1976.
(NY Rangers' 12th choice, 234th overall, in 1994 Entry Draft).

Season	Club	GP	G	A	Pts	PIM	GP	G	A	Pts	PIM
2000-01	Buffalo Sabres	35	1	2	3	94	....	....	....	....	....
2001-02	Buffalo Sabres	35	2	3	5	129	....	....	....	....	....
2002-03	Buffalo Sabres	58	1	5	6	178	....	....	....	....	....
	NHL Totals	**128**	**4**	**10**	**14**	**401**	....	....	....	....	....

Signed as a free agent by **Buffalo**, September 14, 1999.

BOUMEDIENNE, Josef

Defense. Shoots left. 6'1", 200 lbs. Born, Stockholm, Sweden, January 12, 1978.
(New Jersey's 7th choice, 91st overall, in 1996 Entry Draft).

Season	Club	GP	G	A	Pts	PIM	GP	G	A	Pts	PIM
2001-02	New Jersey Devils	1	1	0	1	2	....	....	....	....	....
	Tampa Bay Lightning	3	0	0	0	4	....	....	....	....	....
2002-03	Washington Capitals	6	1	0	1	0	....	....	....	....	....
	NHL Totals	**10**	**2**	**0**	**2**	**6**	....	....	....	....	....

Traded to **Tampa Bay** by **New Jersey** with Sascha Goc and the rights to Anton But for Andrei Zyuzin, November 9, 2001. Traded to **Ottawa** by **Tampa Bay** for Ottawa's 7th round choice (Fredrik Norrena) in 2002 Entry Draft, June 23, 2002. Traded to **Washington** by **Ottawa** for Dean Melanson, December 16, 2002.

BOURBONNAIS, Dan

Left wing. Shoots left. 5'10", 185 lbs. Born, Winnipeg, Man., March 6, 1962.
(Hartford's 5th choice, 103rd overall, in 1981 Entry Draft).

Season	Club	GP	G	A	Pts	PIM	GP	G	A	Pts	PIM
1981-82	Hartford Whalers	24	3	9	12	11	....	....	....	....	....
1983-84	Hartford Whalers	35	0	16	16	0	....	....	....	....	....
	NHL Totals	**59**	**3**	**25**	**28**	**11**	....	....	....	....	....

BOURBONNAIS, Rick

Right wing. Shoots right. 6', 186 lbs. Born, Toronto, Ont., April 20, 1955.
(St. Louis' 3rd choice, 63rd overall, in 1975 Amateur Draft).

Season	Club	GP	G	A	Pts	PIM	GP	G	A	Pts	PIM
1975-76	St. Louis Blues	7	0	0	0	8	....	....	....	....	....
1976-77	St. Louis Blues	33	6	8	14	10	4	0	1	1	0
1977-78	St. Louis Blues	31	3	7	10	11	....	....	....	....	....
	NHL Totals	**71**	**9**	**15**	**24**	**29**	**4**	**0**	**1**	**1**	**0**

BOURCIER, Conrad

Center. Shoots left. 5'6", 155 lbs. Born, Montreal, Que., May 28, 1916.

Season	Club	GP	G	A	Pts	PIM	GP	G	A	Pts	PIM
1935-36	Montreal Canadiens	6	0	0	0	0	....	....	....	....	....
	NHL Totals	**6**	**0**	**0**	**0**	**0**	....	....	....	....	....

• Brother of Jean

Signed as a free agent by **Montreal**, December 18, 1935.

BOURCIER, Jean

Left wing. Shoots left. 5'11", 175 lbs. Born, Montreal, Que., January 3, 1911.

Season	Club	GP	G	A	Pts	PIM	GP	G	A	Pts	PIM
1935-36	Montreal Canadiens	9	0	1	1	0	....	....	....	....	....
	NHL Totals	**9**	**0**	**1**	**1**	**0**	....	....	....	....	....

• Brother of Conrad

Signed as a free agent by **Montreal**, October 11, 1935.

BOURGEAULT, Leo

Defense. Shoots left. 5'6", 165 lbs. Born, Sturgeon Falls, Ont., January 17, 1903.

Season	Club	GP	G	A	Pts	PIM	GP	G	A	Pts	PIM
1926-27	Toronto St. Pats/Maple Leafs	22	0	0	0	44	....	....	....	....	....
	New York Rangers	20	2	1	3	28	2	0	0	0	4
1927-28 ◆	New York Rangers	37	7	0	7	7	9	0	0	0	8
1928-29	New York Rangers	44	2	3	5	59	6	0	0	0	0
1929-30	New York Rangers	44	7	6	13	54	3	1	1	2	6
1930-31	New York Rangers	10	0	1	1	12	....	....	....	....	....
	Ottawa Senators	28	0	4	4	28	....	....	....	....	....
1932-33	Ottawa Senators	35	1	1	2	18	....	....	....	....	....
	Montreal Canadiens	15	1	1	2	9	2	0	0	0	0
1933-34	Montreal Canadiens	48	4	3	7	10	2	0	0	0	0

Season	Club	REGULAR SEASON GP	G	A	Pts	PIM	PLAYOFFS GP	G	A	Pts	PIM
1934-35	Montreal Canadiens	4	0	0	0	0	....	....	....	....	....
	NHL Totals	**307**	**24**	**20**	**44**	**269**	**24**	**1**	**1**	**2**	**18**

Traded to **Toronto** by **Saskatoon** (PrHL) with Corb Denneny and Laurie Scott for cash, September 27, 1926. Traded to **NY Rangers** by **Toronto** for cash, January, 1927. Traded to **Ottawa** by **NY Rangers** for cash, December 7, 1930. Traded to **Montreal** by **Ottawa** with Harold Starr for Marty Burke and future considerations (Nick Wasnie, March 23, 1933), February 14, 1933.

BOURGEOIS, Charlie

Defense. Shoots right. 6'4", 220 lbs. Born, Moncton, N.B., November 19, 1959.

Season	Club	GP	G	A	Pts	PIM	GP	G	A	Pts	PIM
1981-82	Calgary Flames	54	2	13	15	112	3	0	0	0	7
1982-83	Calgary Flames	15	2	3	5	21	....	....	....	....	....
1983-84	Calgary Flames	17	1	3	4	35	8	0	1	1	27
1984-85	Calgary Flames	47	2	10	12	134	4	0	0	0	17
1985-86	Calgary Flames	29	5	5	10	128	....	....	....	....	....
	St. Louis Blues	31	2	7	9	116	19	2	2	4	116
1986-87	St. Louis Blues	66	2	12	14	164	6	0	0	0	27
1987-88	St. Louis Blues	30	0	1	1	78	....	....	....	....	....
	Hartford Whalers	1	0	0	0	0	....	....	....	....	....
	NHL Totals	**290**	**16**	**54**	**70**	**788**	**40**	**2**	**3**	**5**	**194**

Signed as a free agent by **Calgary**, April 19, 1981. Traded to **St. Louis** by **Calgary** with Eddy Beers and Gino Cavallini for Joe Mullen, Terry Johnson and Rik Wilson, February 1, 1986. Traded to **Hartford** by **St. Louis** with Hartford's 3rd round choice (previously acquired, Hartford selected Blair Atcheynum) in 1989 Entry Draft for Hartford's 2nd round choice (Rick Corriveau) in 1989 Entry Draft, March 8, 1988.

BOURNE, Bob

Center. Shoots left. 6'3", 200 lbs. Born, Kindersley, Sask., June 21, 1954.
(Kansas City's 3rd choice, 38th overall, in 1974 Amateur Draft).

Season	Club	GP	G	A	Pts	PIM	GP	G	A	Pts	PIM
1974-75	New York Islanders	77	16	23	39	12	9	1	2	3	4
1975-76	New York Islanders	14	2	3	5	13	....	....	....	....	....
1976-77	New York Islanders	75	16	19	35	30	8	2	0	2	4
1977-78	New York Islanders	80	30	33	63	31	7	2	3	5	2
1978-79	New York Islanders	80	30	31	61	48	10	1	3	4	6
1979-80 ♦	New York Islanders	73	15	25	40	52	21	10	10	20	10
1980-81 ♦	New York Islanders	78	35	41	76	62	14	4	6	10	19
1981-82 ♦	New York Islanders	76	27	26	53	77	19	9	7	16	36
1982-83 ♦	New York Islanders	77	20	42	62	55	20	8	20	28	14
1983-84	New York Islanders	78	22	34	56	75	8	1	1	2	7
1984-85	New York Islanders	44	8	12	20	51	10	0	2	2	6
1985-86	New York Islanders	62	17	15	32	36	3	0	0	0	0
1986-87	Los Angeles Kings	78	13	9	22	35	5	2	1	3	0
1987-88	Los Angeles Kings	72	7	11	18	28	5	0	1	1	0
	NHL Totals	**964**	**258**	**324**	**582**	**605**	**139**	**40**	**56**	**96**	**108**

Bill Masterton Trophy (1988)

Played in NHL All-Star Game (1981)

Traded to **NY Islanders** by **Kansas City** for the rights to Larry Hornung and future considerations (Bart Crashley, September 16, 1974), September 10, 1974. Claimed by **Los Angeles** from **NY Islanders** in Waiver Draft, October 6, 1986.

BOURQUE, Phil

Left wing. Shoots left. 6'1", 196 lbs. Born, Chelmsford, MA, June 8, 1962.

Season	Club	GP	G	A	Pts	PIM	GP	G	A	Pts	PIM
1983-84	Pittsburgh Penguins	5	0	1	1	12	....	....	....	....	....
1985-86	Pittsburgh Penguins	4	0	0	0	2	....	....	....	....	....
1986-87	Pittsburgh Penguins	22	2	3	5	32	....	....	....	....	....
1987-88	Pittsburgh Penguins	21	4	12	16	20	....	....	....	....	....
1988-89	Pittsburgh Penguins	80	17	26	43	97	11	4	1	5	66
1989-90	Pittsburgh Penguins	76	22	17	39	108	....	....	....	....	....
1990-91 ♦	Pittsburgh Penguins	78	20	14	34	106	24	6	7	13	16
1991-92 ♦	Pittsburgh Penguins	58	10	16	26	58	21	3	4	7	25
1992-93	New York Rangers	55	6	14	20	39	....	....	....	....	....
1993-94	New York Rangers	16	0	1	1	8	....	....	....	....	....
	Ottawa Senators	11	2	3	5	0	....	....	....	....	....
1994-95	Ottawa Senators	38	4	3	7	20	....	....	....	....	....
1995-96	Ottawa Senators	13	1	1	2	14	....	....	....	....	....
	NHL Totals	**477**	**88**	**111**	**199**	**516**	**56**	**13**	**12**	**25**	**107**

Signed as a free agent by **Pittsburgh**, October 4, 1982. Signed as a free agent by **NY Rangers**, August 31, 1992. Traded to **Ottawa** by **NY Rangers** for future considerations, March 21, 1994.

BOURQUE, Raymond

Defense. Shoots left. 5'11", 219 lbs. Born, Montreal, Que., December 28, 1960.
(Boston's 1st choice, 8th overall, in 1979 Entry Draft).

Season	Club	GP	G	A	Pts	PIM	GP	G	A	Pts	PIM
1979-80	Boston Bruins	80	17	48	65	73	10	2	9	11	27
1980-81	Boston Bruins	67	27	29	56	96	3	0	1	1	2
1981-82	Boston Bruins	65	17	49	66	51	9	1	5	6	16
1982-83	Boston Bruins	65	22	51	73	20	17	8	15	23	10
1983-84	Boston Bruins	78	31	65	96	57	3	0	2	2	0
1984-85	Boston Bruins	73	20	66	86	53	5	0	3	3	4
1985-86	Boston Bruins	74	19	58	77	68	3	0	0	0	0
1986-87	Boston Bruins	78	23	72	95	36	4	1	2	3	0
1987-88	Boston Bruins	78	17	64	81	72	23	3	18	21	26
1988-89	Boston Bruins	60	18	43	61	52	10	0	4	4	6
1989-90	Boston Bruins	76	19	65	84	50	17	5	12	17	16
1990-91	Boston Bruins	76	21	73	94	75	19	7	18	25	12
1991-92	Boston Bruins	80	21	60	81	56	12	3	6	9	12
1992-93	Boston Bruins	78	19	63	82	40	4	1	0	1	2
1993-94	Boston Bruins	72	20	71	91	58	13	2	8	10	0
1994-95	Boston Bruins	46	12	31	43	20	5	0	3	3	0
1995-96	Boston Bruins	82	20	62	82	58	5	1	6	7	2
1996-97	Boston Bruins	62	19	31	50	18	....	....	....	....	....
1997-98	Boston Bruins	82	13	35	48	80	6	1	4	5	2
1998-99	Boston Bruins	81	10	47	57	34	12	1	9	10	14
99-2000	Boston Bruins	65	10	28	38	20	....	....	....	....	....
	Colorado Avalanche	14	8	6	14	6	13	1	8	9	8
2000-01 ♦	Colorado Avalanche	80	7	52	59	48	21	4	6	10	12
	NHL Totals	**1612**	**410**	**1169**	**1579**	**1141**	**214**	**41**	**139**	**180**	**171**

Calder Memorial Trophy (1980) • NHL First All-Star Team (1980, 1982, 1984, 1985, 1987, 1988, 1990, 1991, 1992, 1993, 1994, 1996, 2001) • NHL Second All-Star Team (1981, 1983, 1986, 1989, 1995, 1999) • James Norris Memorial Trophy (1987, 1988, 1990, 1991, 1994) • King Clancy Memorial Trophy (1992)

Played in NHL All-Star Game (1981, 1982, 1983, 1984, 1985, 1986, 1988, 1989, 1990, 1991, 1992, 1993, 1994, 1996, 1997, 1998, 1999, 2000, 2001)

Traded to **Colorado** by **Boston** with Dave Andreychuk for Brian Rolston, Martin Grenier, Samuel Pahlsson and New Jersey's 1st round choice (previously acquired, Boston selected Martin Samuelsson) in 2000 Entry Draft, March 6, 2000. • Officially announced retirement, June 26, 2001.

BOUTETTE, Pat

Center/Right wing. Shoots left. 5'8", 175 lbs. Born, Windsor, Ont., March 1, 1952.
(Toronto's 9th choice, 139th overall, in 1972 Amateur Draft).

Season	Club	GP	G	A	Pts	PIM	GP	G	A	Pts	PIM
1975-76	Toronto Maple Leafs	77	10	22	32	140	10	1	4	5	16
1976-77	Toronto Maple Leafs	80	18	18	36	107	9	0	4	4	17
1977-78	Toronto Maple Leafs	80	17	19	36	120	13	3	3	6	40
1978-79	Toronto Maple Leafs	80	14	19	33	136	6	2	2	4	22
1979-80	Toronto Maple Leafs	32	0	4	4	17	....	....	....	....	....
	Hartford Whalers	47	13	31	44	75	3	1	0	1	6
1980-81	Hartford Whalers	80	28	52	80	160	....	....	....	....	....
1981-82	Pittsburgh Penguins	80	23	51	74	230	5	3	1	4	8
1982-83	Pittsburgh Penguins	80	27	29	56	152	....	....	....	....	....
1983-84	Pittsburgh Penguins	73	14	26	40	142	....	....	....	....	....
1984-85	Pittsburgh Penguins	14	1	3	4	24	....	....	....	....	....
	Hartford Whalers	33	6	8	14	51	....	....	....	....	....
	NHL Totals	**756**	**171**	**282**	**453**	**1354**	**46**	**10**	**14**	**24**	**109**

Traded to **Hartford** by **Toronto** for Bob Stephenson, December 24, 1979. Transferred to **Pittsburgh** by **Hartford** with Kevin McClelland as compensation for Hartford's signing of free agent Greg Millen, June 29, 1981. Traded to **Hartford** by **Pittsburgh** for the rights to Ville Siren, November 16, 1984.

BOUTILIER, Paul

Defense. Shoots left. 6', 200 lbs. Born, Sydney, N.S., May 3, 1963.
(NY Islanders' 1st choice, 21st overall, in 1981 Entry Draft).

Season	Club	GP	G	A	Pts	PIM	GP	G	A	Pts	PIM
1981-82	New York Islanders	1	0	0	0	0	....	....	....	....	....
1982-83 ♦	New York Islanders	29	4	5	9	24	2	0	0	0	2
1983-84	New York Islanders	28	0	11	11	36	21	1	7	8	10
1984-85	New York Islanders	78	12	23	35	90	10	0	2	2	16
1985-86	New York Islanders	77	4	30	34	100	3	0	0	0	2
1986-87	Boston Bruins	52	5	9	14	84	....	....	....	....	....
	Minnesota North Stars	10	2	4	6	8	....	....	....	....	....
1987-88	New York Rangers	4	0	1	1	6	....	....	....	....	....
	Winnipeg Jets	6	0	0	0	6	5	0	0	0	15
1988-89	Winnipeg Jets	3	0	0	0	4	....	....	....	....	....
	NHL Totals	**288**	**27**	**83**	**110**	**358**	**41**	**1**	**9**	**10**	**45**

Transferred to **Boston** by **NY Islanders** as compensation for the NY Islanders' signing of free agent Brian Curran, August 6, 1986. Traded to **Minnesota** by **Boston** for Minnesota's 4th round choice (Darwin McPherson) in 1987 Entry Draft, March 10, 1987. Traded to **NY Rangers** by **Minnesota** with Jari Gronstrand for Jay Caufield and Dave Gagner, October 8, 1987. Traded to **Winnipeg** by **NY Rangers** for future considerations, December 16, 1987.

BOUWMEESTER, Jay

Defense. Shoots left. 6'4", 210 lbs. Born, Edmonton, Alta., September 27, 1983.
(Florida's 1st choice, 3rd overall, in 2002 Entry Draft).

Season	Club	GP	G	A	Pts	PIM	GP	G	A	Pts	PIM
2002-03	Florida Panthers	82	4	12	16	14	....	....	....	....	....
	NHL Totals	**82**	**4**	**12**	**16**	**14**	....	....	....	....	....

NHL All-Rookie Team (2003)

BOWEN, Jason

Defense. Shoots left. 6'4", 220 lbs. Born, Port Alice, B.C., November 9, 1973.
(Philadelphia's 2nd choice, 15th overall, in 1992 Entry Draft).

Season	Club	GP	G	A	Pts	PIM	GP	G	A	Pts	PIM
1992-93	Philadelphia Flyers	7	1	0	1	2	....	....	....	....	....
1993-94	Philadelphia Flyers	56	1	5	6	87	....	....	....	....	....
1994-95	Philadelphia Flyers	4	0	0	0	0	....	....	....	....	....
1995-96	Philadelphia Flyers	2	0	0	0	2	....	....	....	....	....
1996-97	Philadelphia Flyers	4	0	1	1	8	....	....	....	....	....
1997-98	Edmonton Oilers	4	0	0	0	10	....	....	....	....	....
	NHL Totals	**77**	**2**	**6**	**8**	**109**	....	....	....	....	....

Traded to **Edmonton** by **Philadelphia** for Brantt Myhres, October 15, 1997. Signed as a free agent by **Colorado**, August 26, 1999.

BOWLER, Bill

Center. Shoots left. 5'9", 180 lbs. Born, Toronto, Ont., September 25, 1974.

Season	Club	Regular Season GP	G	A	Pts	PIM	Playoffs GP	G	A	Pts	PIM
2000-01	Columbus Blue Jackets	9	0	2	2	8	....	....	....	....	....
	NHL Totals	**9**	**0**	**2**	**2**	**8**	....	....	....	....	....

Signed as a free agent by **Columbus**, August 3, 2000. Claimed on waivers by **Nashville** from **Columbus**, June 1, 2001. Signed as a free agent by **Boston**, July 18, 2002.

BOWMAN, Kirk

Left wing. Shoots left. 5'9", 178 lbs. Born, Leamington, Ont., September 30, 1952.

Season	Club	Regular Season GP	G	A	Pts	PIM	Playoffs GP	G	A	Pts	PIM
1976-77	Chicago Black Hawks	55	10	13	23	6	2	1	0	1	0
1977-78	Chicago Black Hawks	33	1	4	5	13	3	0	0	0	0
1978-79	Chicago Black Hawks	....	....	....	....	....	2	0	0	0	0
	NHL Totals	**88**	**11**	**17**	**28**	**19**	**7**	**1**	**0**	**1**	**0**

Signed as a free agent by **Chicago**, September, 1974.

BOWMAN, Ralph

Defense. Shoots left. 5'11", 190 lbs. Born, Winnipeg, Man., June 20, 1911.

Season	Club	Regular Season GP	G	A	Pts	PIM	Playoffs GP	G	A	Pts	PIM
1933-34	Ottawa Senators	46	0	2	2	64	....	....	....	....	....
1934-35	St. Louis Eagles	31	2	2	4	51	....	....	....	....	....
	Detroit Red Wings	13	1	3	4	21	....	....	....	....	....
1935-36♦	Detroit Red Wings	48	3	2	5	44	7	2	1	3	2
1936-37♦	Detroit Red Wings	37	0	1	1	24	10	0	1	1	4
1937-38	Detroit Red Wings	45	0	2	2	26	....	....	....	....	....
1938-39	Detroit Red Wings	43	2	3	5	26	5	0	0	0	0
1939-40	Detroit Red Wings	11	0	2	2	4	....	....	....	....	....
	NHL Totals	**274**	**8**	**17**	**25**	**260**	**22**	**2**	**2**	**4**	**6**

Transferred to **St. Louis** after **Ottawa** franchise relocated, September 22, 1934. Traded to **Detroit** by **St. Louis** with Syd Howe for Teddy Graham and $50,000, February 11, 1935.

BOWNASS, Jack

Defense. Shoots left. 6'1", 190 lbs. Born, Winnipeg, Man., July 27, 1930.

Season	Club	Regular Season GP	G	A	Pts	PIM	Playoffs GP	G	A	Pts	PIM
1957-58	Montreal Canadiens	4	0	1	1	0	....	....	....	....	....
1958-59	New York Rangers	35	1	2	3	20	....	....	....	....	....
1959-60	New York Rangers	37	2	5	7	34	....	....	....	....	....
1961-62	New York Rangers	4	0	0	0	4	....	....	....	....	....
	NHL Totals	**80**	**3**	**8**	**11**	**58**	....	....	....	....	....

Signed as a free agent by **Montreal**, October 21, 1954. Loaned to **Seattle** (WHL) by **Montreal** for the 1955-56 season, November, 1955. Claimed by **NY Rangers** (Buffalo-AHL) from **Montreal** (Montreal Royals-QHL) in Inter-League Draft, June 3, 1958. Traded to **LA Blades** (WHL) by **NY Rangers** for cash, September, 1962.

BOWNESS, Rick

Right wing. Shoots right. 6'1", 185 lbs. Born, Moncton, N.B., January 25, 1955.
(Atlanta's 2nd choice, 26th overall, in 1975 Amateur Draft).

Season	Club	Regular Season GP	G	A	Pts	PIM	Playoffs GP	G	A	Pts	PIM
1975-76	Atlanta Flames	5	0	0	0	0	....	....	....	....	....
1976-77	Atlanta Flames	28	0	4	4	29	....	....	....	....	....
1977-78	Detroit Red Wings	61	8	11	19	76	4	0	0	0	2
1978-79	St. Louis Blues	24	1	3	4	30	....	....	....	....	....
1979-80	St. Louis Blues	10	1	2	3	11	....	....	....	....	....
1980-81	Winnipeg Jets	45	8	17	25	45	....	....	....	....	....
1981-82	Winnipeg Jets	....	....	....	....	....	1	0	0	0	0
	NHL Totals	**173**	**18**	**37**	**55**	**191**	**5**	**0**	**0**	**0**	**2**

Traded to **Detroit** by **Atlanta** for cash, August 18, 1977. Traded to **St. Louis** by **Detroit** for cash, October 10, 1978. Traded to **Winnipeg** by **St. Louis** for Craig Norwich, June 19, 1980.

BOYD, Bill

Right wing. Shoots right. 5'10", 185 lbs. Born, Belleville, Ont., May 15, 1898.

Season	Club	Regular Season GP	G	A	Pts	PIM	Playoffs GP	G	A	Pts	PIM
1926-27	New York Rangers	41	4	1	5	40	....	....	....	....	....
1927-28♦	New York Rangers	43	4	0	4	11	9	0	0	0	4
1928-29	New York Rangers	11	0	0	0	5	1	0	0	0	0
1929-30	New York Americans	43	7	6	13	16	....	....	....	....	....
	NHL Totals	**138**	**15**	**7**	**22**	**72**	**10**	**0**	**0**	**0**	**4**

Signed as a free agent by **NY Rangers**, November 9, 1926. Claimed by **NY Americans** from **Springfield** (Can-Am) in Inter-League Draft, May 13, 1929.

BOYD, Irvin

Right wing. Shoots right. 5'10", 152 lbs. Born, Ardmore, PA, November 13, 1908.

Season	Club	Regular Season GP	G	A	Pts	PIM	Playoffs GP	G	A	Pts	PIM
1931-32	Boston Bruins	29	2	1	3	10	....	....	....	....	....
1934-35	Detroit Red Wings	42	2	3	5	14	....	....	....	....	....
1942-43	Boston Bruins	20	6	5	11	6	5	0	1	1	4
1943-44	Boston Bruins	5	0	1	1	0	....	....	....	....	....
	NHL Totals	**96**	**10**	**10**	**20**	**30**	**5**	**0**	**1**	**1**	**4**

Traded to **Philadelphia** (Can-Am) by **Boston** for cash, October, 1932. Traded to **Detroit** by **Philadelphia** (Can-Am) with Tom Anderson for cash, May 8, 1934. Signed as a free agent by **Boston**, December 18, 1942.

BOYD, Randy

Defense. Shoots left. 5'11", 190 lbs. Born, Coniston, Ont., January 23, 1962.
(Pittsburgh's 2nd choice, 51st overall, in 1980 Entry Draft).

Season	Club	Regular Season GP	G	A	Pts	PIM	Playoffs GP	G	A	Pts	PIM
1981-82	Pittsburgh Penguins	23	0	2	2	49	3	0	0	0	11
1982-83	Pittsburgh Penguins	56	4	14	18	71	....	....	....	....	....
1983-84	Pittsburgh Penguins	5	0	1	1	6	....	....	....	....	....
	Chicago Black Hawks	23	0	4	4	16	....	....	....	....	....
1984-85	Chicago Black Hawks	3	0	0	0	6	3	0	1	1	7
1985-86	New York Islanders	55	2	12	14	79	3	0	0	0	2
1986-87	New York Islanders	30	7	17	24	37	4	0	1	1	6
1987-88	Vancouver Canucks	60	7	16	23	64	....	....	....	....	....
1988-89	Vancouver Canucks	2	0	1	1	0	....	....	....	....	....
	NHL Totals	**257**	**20**	**67**	**87**	**328**	**13**	**0**	**2**	**2**	**26**

Traded to **Chicago** by **Pittsburgh** for Greg Fox, December 6, 1983. Claimed by **NY Islanders** from **Chicago** in Waiver Draft, October 7, 1985. Claimed by **Vancouver** from **NY Islanders** in Waiver Draft, October 5, 1987.

BOYER, Wally

Center. Shoots left. 5'8", 165 lbs. Born, Cowan, Man., September 27, 1937.

Season	Club	Regular Season GP	G	A	Pts	PIM	Playoffs GP	G	A	Pts	PIM
1965-66	Toronto Maple Leafs	46	4	17	21	23	4	0	1	1	0
1966-67	Chicago Black Hawks	42	5	6	11	15	1	0	0	0	0
1967-68	Oakland Seals	74	13	20	33	44	....	....	....	....	....
1968-69	Pittsburgh Penguins	62	10	19	29	17	....	....	....	....	....
1969-70	Pittsburgh Penguins	72	11	12	23	34	10	1	2	3	0
1970-71	Pittsburgh Penguins	68	11	30	41	30	....	....	....	....	....
1971-72	Pittsburgh Penguins	1	0	1	1	0	....	....	....	....	....
	NHL Totals	**365**	**54**	**105**	**159**	**163**	**15**	**1**	**3**	**4**	**0**

Loaned to **Hershey** (AHL) by **Toronto** for the 1958-59 and 1959-60 seasons with the trade of Mike Nykolyk and Ron Hurst for Willie Marshall, April 29, 1958. Toronto retains right of recall. Loaned to **Springfield** (AHL) by **Toronto** (Rochester-AHL) with the trade of Jim Wilcox, Roger Cote, Bill White and Dick Mattiussi for Kent Douglas, June 7, 1962. Claimed by **Montreal** from **Toronto** in Intra-League Draft, June 15, 1966. Claimed by **Chicago** from **Montreal** in Intra-League Draft, June 15, 1966. Claimed by **California** (Oakland) from **Chicago** in Expansion Draft, June 6, 1967. Traded to **Montreal** by **Oakland** with Alain Caron, Oakland's 1st round choices in 1968 (Jim Pritchard) and 1970 (Ray Martynuik) Amateur Drafts and future considerations (Lyle Bradley, June, 1968) for Norm Ferguson, Stan Fuller and future considerations (Francois Lacombe and Michel Jacques, June, 1968), May 21, 1968. Traded to **Pittsburgh** by **Montreal** for Al MacNeil, June 12, 1968.

BOYER, Zac

Right wing. Shoots right. 6'1", 199 lbs. Born, Inuvik, N.W.T., October 25, 1971.
(Chicago's 6th choice, 88th overall, in 1991 Entry Draft).

Season	Club	Regular Season GP	G	A	Pts	PIM	Playoffs GP	G	A	Pts	PIM
1994-95	Dallas Stars	1	0	0	0	0	2	0	0	0	0
1995-96	Dallas Stars	2	0	0	0	0	....	....	....	....	....
	NHL Totals	**3**	**0**	**0**	**0**	**0**	**2**	**0**	**0**	**0**	**0**

Signed as a free agent by **Dallas**, July 25, 1994.

BOYKO, Darren

Center. Shoots right. 5'9", 169 lbs. Born, Winnipeg, Man., January 16, 1964.

Season	Club	Regular Season GP	G	A	Pts	PIM	Playoffs GP	G	A	Pts	PIM
1988-89	Winnipeg Jets	1	0	0	0	0	....	....	....	....	....
	NHL Totals	**1**	**0**	**0**	**0**	**0**	....	....	....	....	....

Signed as a free agent by **Winnipeg**, May 16, 1988.

BOYLE, Dan

Defense. Shoots right. 5'11", 190 lbs. Born, Ottawa, Ont., July 12, 1976.

Season	Club	Regular Season GP	G	A	Pts	PIM	Playoffs GP	G	A	Pts	PIM
1998-99	Florida Panthers	22	3	5	8	6	....	....	....	....	....
99-2000	Florida Panthers	13	0	3	3	4	....	....	....	....	....
2000-01	Florida Panthers	69	4	18	22	28	....	....	....	....	....
2001-02	Florida Panthers	25	3	3	6	12	....	....	....	....	....
	Tampa Bay Lightning	41	5	15	20	27	....	....	....	....	....
2002-03	Tampa Bay Lightning	77	13	40	53	44	11	0	7	7	6
	NHL Totals	**247**	**28**	**84**	**112**	**121**	**11**	**0**	**7**	**7**	**6**

Signed as a free agent by **Florida**, March 30, 1998. Traded to **Tampa Bay** by **Florida** for Tampa Bay's 5th round choice (Martin Tuma) in 2003 Entry Draft, January 7, 2002.

BOYNTON, Nick

Defense. Shoots right. 6'2", 210 lbs. Born, Nobleton, Ont., January 14, 1979.
(Boston's 1st choice, 21st overall, in 1999 Entry Draft).

Season	Club	Regular Season GP	G	A	Pts	PIM	Playoffs GP	G	A	Pts	PIM
99-2000	Boston Bruins	5	0	0	0	0	....	....	....	....	....
2000-01	Boston Bruins	1	0	0	0	0	....	....	....	....	....
2001-02	Boston Bruins	80	4	14	18	107	6	1	2	3	8
2002-03	Boston Bruins	78	7	17	24	99	5	0	1	1	4
	NHL Totals	**164**	**11**	**31**	**42**	**206**	**11**	**1**	**3**	**4**	**12**

• Re-entered NHL Entry Draft. Originally Washington's 1st choice, 9th overall, in 1997 Entry Draft.
NHL All-Rookie Team (2002)

BOZEK, Steve

Left wing. Shoots left. 5'11", 180 lbs. Born, Kelowna, B.C., November 26, 1960.
(Los Angeles' 5th choice, 52nd overall, in 1980 Entry Draft).

Season	Club	Regular Season GP	G	A	Pts	PIM	Playoffs GP	G	A	Pts	PIM
1981-82	Los Angeles Kings	71	33	23	56	68	10	4	1	5	6
1982-83	Los Angeles Kings	53	13	13	26	14	....	....	....	....	....
1983-84	Calgary Flames	46	10	10	20	16	10	3	1	4	15
1984-85	Calgary Flames	54	13	22	35	6	3	1	0	1	4
1985-86	Calgary Flames	64	21	22	43	24	14	2	6	8	32
1986-87	Calgary Flames	71	17	18	35	22	4	1	0	1	2
1987-88	Calgary Flames	26	3	7	10	12	....	....	....	....	....
	St. Louis Blues	7	0	0	0	2	7	1	1	2	6
1988-89	Vancouver Canucks	71	17	18	35	64	7	0	2	2	4
1989-90	Vancouver Canucks	58	14	9	23	32	....	....	....	....	....
1990-91	Vancouver Canucks	62	15	17	32	22	3	0	0	0	0

Season	Club	GP	G	A	Pts	PIM	GP	G	A	Pts	PIM
		REGULAR SEASON					PLAYOFFS				
1991-92	San Jose Sharks	58	8	8	16	27	....	....	....	....	....
	NHL Totals	**641**	**164**	**167**	**331**	**309**	**58**	**12**	**11**	**23**	**69**

Traded to **Calgary** by **Los Angeles** for Carl Mokosak and Kevin LaVallee, June 20, 1983. • Missed majority of 1987-88 season due to knee injury, October, 1987. Traded to **St. Louis** by **Calgary** with Brett Hull for Rob Ramage and Rick Wamsley, March 7, 1988. Traded to **Calgary** by **St. Louis** with Mark Hunter, Doug Gilmour and Michael Dark for Craig Coxe, Mike Bullard and Tim Corkery, September 6, 1988. Traded to **Vancouver** by **Calgary** with Paul Reinhart for Vancouver's 3rd round choice (Veli-Pekka Kautonen) in 1989 Entry Draft, September 6, 1988. Signed as a free agent by **San Jose**, August 9, 1991.

BOZON, Philippe

Left wing. Shoots left. 5'10", 185 lbs. Born, Chamonix, France, November 30, 1966.

Season	Club	GP	G	A	Pts	PIM	GP	G	A	Pts	PIM
1991-92	St. Louis Blues	9	1	3	4	4	6	1	0	1	27
1992-93	St. Louis Blues	54	6	6	12	55	9	1	0	1	0
1993-94	St. Louis Blues	80	9	16	25	42	4	0	0	0	4
1994-95	St. Louis Blues	1	0	0	0	0	....	....	....	....	....
	NHL Totals	**144**	**16**	**25**	**41**	**101**	**19**	**2**	**0**	**2**	**31**

Signed as a free agent by **St. Louis**, September 29, 1985.

BRACKENBOROUGH, John

Left wing/Center. Shoots left. 5'11", 170 lbs. Born, Parry Sound, Ont., February 9, 1897.

Season	Club	GP	G	A	Pts	PIM	GP	G	A	Pts	PIM
1925-26	Boston Bruins	7	0	0	0	0	....	....	....	....	....
	NHL Totals	**7**	**0**	**0**	**0**	**0**	....	....	....	....	....

• Lost sight and use of right eye in game vs. University of Toronto, February 28, 1924. Signed as a free agent by **Boston**, November 16, 1925.

BRACKENBURY, Curt

Right wing. Shoots right. 5'10", 200 lbs. Born, Kapuskasing, Ont., January 31, 1952.

Season	Club	GP	G	A	Pts	PIM	GP	G	A	Pts	PIM
1979-80	Quebec Nordiques	63	6	8	14	55	....	....	....	....	....
1980-81	Edmonton Oilers	58	2	7	9	153	2	0	0	0	0
1981-82	Edmonton Oilers	14	0	2	2	12	....	....	....	....	....
1982-83	St. Louis Blues	6	1	0	1	6	....	....	....	....	....
	NHL Totals	**141**	**9**	**17**	**26**	**226**	**2**	**0**	**0**	**0**	**0**

Claimed by **Edmonton** from **Quebec** in Waiver Draft, October 10, 1980. Signed as a free agent by **St. Louis**, October 1, 1982.

BRADLEY, Bart

Center. Shoots left. 5'8", 150 lbs. Born, Fort William, Ont., July 29, 1930.

Season	Club	GP	G	A	Pts	PIM	GP	G	A	Pts	PIM
1949-50	Boston Bruins	1	0	0	0	0	....	....	....	....	....
	NHL Totals	**1**	**0**	**0**	**0**	**0**	....	....	....	....	....

BRADLEY, Brian

Center. Shoots right. 5'10", 180 lbs. Born, Kitchener, Ont., January 21, 1965.
(Calgary's 2nd choice, 52nd overall, in 1983 Entry Draft).

Season	Club	GP	G	A	Pts	PIM	GP	G	A	Pts	PIM
1985-86	Calgary Flames	5	0	1	1	0	1	0	0	0	0
1986-87	Calgary Flames	40	10	18	28	16	....	....	....	....	....
1987-88	Vancouver Canucks	11	3	5	8	6	....	....	....	....	....
1988-89	Vancouver Canucks	71	18	27	45	42	7	3	4	7	10
1989-90	Vancouver Canucks	67	19	29	48	65	....	....	....	....	....
1990-91	Vancouver Canucks	44	11	20	31	42	....	....	....	....	....
	Toronto Maple Leafs	26	0	11	11	20	....	....	....	....	....
1991-92	Toronto Maple Leafs	59	10	21	31	48	....	....	....	....	....
1992-93	Tampa Bay Lightning	80	42	44	86	92	....	....	....	....	....
1993-94	Tampa Bay Lightning	78	24	40	64	56	....	....	....	....	....
1994-95	Tampa Bay Lightning	46	13	27	40	42	....	....	....	....	....
1995-96	Tampa Bay Lightning	75	23	56	79	77	5	0	3	3	6
1996-97	Tampa Bay Lightning	35	7	17	24	16	....	....	....	....	....
1997-98	Tampa Bay Lightning	14	2	5	7	6	....	....	....	....	....
	NHL Totals	**651**	**182**	**321**	**503**	**528**	**13**	**3**	**7**	**10**	**16**

Played in NHL All-Star Game (1993, 1994)

Traded to **Vancouver** by **Calgary** with Peter Bakovic and Kevan Guy for Craig Coxe, March 6, 1988. Traded to **Toronto** by **Vancouver** for Tom Kurvers, January 12, 1991. Claimed by **Tampa Bay** from **Toronto** in Expansion Draft, June 18, 1992. • Missed majority of 1997-98 season and entire 1998-99 season recovering from head injury suffered in game vs. Los Angeles, November 11, 1997. • Officially announced retirement, October 23, 1999.

BRADLEY, Lyle

Center/Right wing. Shoots right. 5'9", 160 lbs. Born, Lloydminster, Sask., July 31, 1943.

Season	Club	GP	G	A	Pts	PIM	GP	G	A	Pts	PIM
1973-74	California Golden Seals	4	1	0	1	2	....	....	....	....	....
1976-77	Cleveland Barons	2	0	0	0	0	....	....	....	....	....
	NHL Totals	**6**	**1**	**0**	**1**	**2**	....	....	....	....	....

Traded to **Montreal** by **Oakland** to complete transaction that sent Norm Ferguson to Oakland (May 21, 1968), June, 1968. Traded to **Portland** (WHL) by **Montreal** for cash, June, 1971. Traded to **California** (Salt Lake-WHL) by **Portland** (WHL) with Fred Hilts for Guyle Fielder and John Rathwell, January, 1972. Transferred to **Cleveland** after **California** franchise relocated, August 26, 1976.

BRADLEY, Matt

Right wing. Shoots right. 6'2", 195 lbs. Born, Stittsville, Ont., June 13, 1978.
(San Jose's 4th choice, 102nd overall, in 1996 Entry Draft).

Season	Club	GP	G	A	Pts	PIM	GP	G	A	Pts	PIM
2000-01	San Jose Sharks	21	1	1	2	19	....	....	....	....	....
2001-02	San Jose Sharks	54	9	13	22	43	10	0	0	0	0
2002-03	San Jose Sharks	46	2	3	5	37	....	....	....	....	....
	NHL Totals	**121**	**12**	**17**	**29**	**99**	**10**	**0**	**0**	**0**	**0**

Traded to **Pittsburgh** by **San Jose** for Wayne Primeau, March 11, 2003.

BRADY, Neil

Center. Shoots left. 6'2", 200 lbs. Born, Montreal, Que., April 12, 1968.
(New Jersey's 1st choice, 3rd overall, in 1986 Entry Draft).

Season	Club	GP	G	A	Pts	PIM	GP	G	A	Pts	PIM
1989-90	New Jersey Devils	19	1	4	5	13	....	....	....	....	....
1990-91	New Jersey Devils	3	0	0	0	0	....	....	....	....	....
1991-92	New Jersey Devils	7	1	0	1	4	....	....	....	....	....
1992-93	Ottawa Senators	55	7	17	24	57	....	....	....	....	....
1993-94	Dallas Stars	5	0	1	1	21	....	....	....	....	....
	NHL Totals	**89**	**9**	**22**	**31**	**95**	....	....	....	....	....

Traded to **Ottawa** by **New Jersey** for future considerations, September 3, 1992. Signed as a free agent by **Dallas**, December 3, 1993. Signed as a free agent by **Utah** (IHL), August 18, 1999.

BRAGNALO, Rick

Center. Shoots left. 5'8", 160 lbs. Born, Fort William, Ont., December 1, 1951.

Season	Club	GP	G	A	Pts	PIM	GP	G	A	Pts	PIM
1975-76	Washington Capitals	19	2	10	12	8	....	....	....	....	....
1976-77	Washington Capitals	80	11	12	23	16	....	....	....	....	....
1977-78	Washington Capitals	44	2	13	15	22	....	....	....	....	....
1978-79	Washington Capitals	2	0	0	0	0	....	....	....	....	....
	NHL Totals	**145**	**15**	**35**	**50**	**46**	....	....	....	....	....

Signed as a free agent by **Washington**, March 1, 1976.

BRANIGAN, Andy

Defense. Shoots left. 5'11", 190 lbs. Born, Winnipeg, Man., April 11, 1922.

Season	Club	GP	G	A	Pts	PIM	GP	G	A	Pts	PIM
1940-41	New York Americans	6	1	0	1	5	....	....	....	....	....
1941-42	Brooklyn Americans	21	0	2	2	26	....	....	....	....	....
	NHL Totals	**27**	**1**	**2**	**3**	**31**	....	....	....	....	....

Signed as a free agent by **NY Americans**, October 15, 1940. • Team name changed to **Brooklyn Americans** prior to 1941-42 season. Rights transferred to **Detroit** from **Brooklyn** in Special Dispersal Draw, September 11, 1943.

BRASAR, Per-Olov

Left wing. Shoots left. 5'8", 172 lbs. Born, Falun, Sweden, September 30, 1950.

Season	Club	GP	G	A	Pts	PIM	GP	G	A	Pts	PIM
1977-78	Minnesota North Stars	77	20	37	57	6	....	....	....	....	....
1978-79	Minnesota North Stars	68	6	28	34	6	....	....	....	....	....
1979-80	Minnesota North Stars	22	1	14	15	0	....	....	....	....	....
	Vancouver Canucks	48	9	10	19	7	4	1	2	3	0
1980-81	Vancouver Canucks	80	22	41	63	8	3	0	0	0	0
1981-82	Vancouver Canucks	53	6	12	18	6	6	0	0	0	0
	NHL Totals	**348**	**64**	**142**	**206**	**33**	**13**	**1**	**2**	**3**	**0**

Signed as a free agent by **Minnesota**, August, 1977. Traded to **Vancouver** by **Minnesota** for Vancouver's 2nd round choice (Mike Sands) in 1981 Entry Draft, December 10, 1979.

BRASHEAR, Donald

Left wing. Shoots left. 6'2", 225 lbs. Born, Bedford, IN, January 7, 1972.

Season	Club	GP	G	A	Pts	PIM	GP	G	A	Pts	PIM
1993-94	Montreal Canadiens	14	2	2	4	34	2	0	0	0	0
1994-95	Montreal Canadiens	20	1	1	2	63	....	....	....	....	....
1995-96	Montreal Canadiens	67	0	4	4	223	6	0	0	0	2
1996-97	Montreal Canadiens	10	0	0	0	38	....	....	....	....	....
	Vancouver Canucks	59	8	5	13	207	....	....	....	....	....
1997-98	Vancouver Canucks	77	9	9	18	*372	....	....	....	....	....
1998-99	Vancouver Canucks	82	8	10	18	209	....	....	....	....	....
99-2000	Vancouver Canucks	60	11	2	13	136	....	....	....	....	....
2000-01	Vancouver Canucks	79	9	19	28	145	4	0	0	0	0
2001-02	Vancouver Canucks	31	5	8	13	90	....	....	....	....	....
	Philadelphia Flyers	50	4	15	19	109	5	0	0	0	19
2002-03	Philadelphia Flyers	80	8	17	25	161	13	1	2	3	21
	NHL Totals	**629**	**65**	**92**	**157**	**1787**	**30**	**1**	**2**	**3**	**42**

Signed as a free agent by **Montreal**, July 28, 1992. Traded to **Vancouver** by **Montreal** for Jassen Cullimore, November 13, 1996. Traded to **Philadelphia** by **Vancouver** with Vancouver's 6th round choice (later traded to Columbus – Columbus selected Jaroslav Balastik) in 2002 Entry Draft for Jan Hlavac and Tampa Bay's 3rd round choice (previously acquired, Vancouver selected Brett Skinner) in 2002 Entry Draft, December 17, 2001.

BRAYSHAW, Russ

Left wing. Shoots left. 5'10", 170 lbs. Born, Saskatoon, Sask., January 17, 1918.

Season	Club	GP	G	A	Pts	PIM	GP	G	A	Pts	PIM
1944-45	Chicago Black Hawks	43	5	9	14	24	....	....	....	....	....
	NHL Totals	**43**	**5**	**9**	**14**	**24**	....	....	....	....	....

BREAULT, Francois

Right wing. Shoots left. 5'11", 185 lbs. Born, Acton Vale, Que., May 11, 1967.

Season	Club	GP	G	A	Pts	PIM	GP	G	A	Pts	PIM
1990-91	Los Angeles Kings	17	1	4	5	6	....	....	....	....	....
1991-92	Los Angeles Kings	6	1	0	1	30	....	....	....	....	....
1992-93	Los Angeles Kings	4	0	0	0	6	....	....	....	....	....
	NHL Totals	**27**	**2**	**4**	**6**	**42**	....	....	....	....	....

Signed as a free agent by **Los Angeles**, July, 1988. • Missed remainder of 1990-91 season recovering from knee injury suffered in game vs. Calgary, December 13, 1990.

BREITENBACH, Ken

Defense. Shoots left. 6'1", 190 lbs. Born, Welland, Ont., January 9, 1955.
(Buffalo's 2nd choice, 35th overall, in 1975 Amateur Draft).

Season	Club	GP	G	A	Pts	PIM	GP	G	A	Pts	PIM
1975-76	Buffalo Sabres	7	0	0	0	6	1	0	0	0	0
1976-77	Buffalo Sabres	31	0	5	5	18	4	0	0	0	0

Season	Club	GP	G	A	Pts	PIM	GP	G	A	Pts	PIM
		REGULAR SEASON					PLAYOFFS				
1978-79	Buffalo Sabres	30	1	8	9	25	3	0	1	1	4
	NHL Totals	**68**	**1**	**13**	**14**	**49**	**8**	**0**	**1**	**1**	**4**

• Missed entire 1977-78 season recovering from broken leg suffered in training camp, September, 1977.

BRENDL, Pavel

Right wing. Shoots right. 6'1", 204 lbs. Born, Opocno, Czech., March 23, 1981.
(NY Rangers' 1st choice, 4th overall, in 1999 Entry Draft).

Season	Club	GP	G	A	Pts	PIM	GP	G	A	Pts	PIM
2001-02	Philadelphia Flyers	8	1	0	1	2	2	0	0	0	0
2002-03	Philadelphia Flyers	42	5	7	12	4	....	....	....	....	....
	Carolina Hurricanes	8	0	1	1	2	....	....	....	....	....
	NHL Totals	**58**	**6**	**8**	**14**	**8**	**2**	**0**	**0**	**0**	**0**

Traded to **Philadelphia** by **NY Rangers** with Jan Hlavac, Kim Johnsson and NY Rangers' 3rd round choice (Stefan Ruzicka) in 2003 Entry Draft for Eric Lindros, August 20, 2001. Traded to **Carolina** by **Philadelphia** with Bruno St. Jacques for Sami Kapanen and Ryan Bast, February 7, 2003.

BRENNAN, Dan

Left wing. Shoots left. 6'3", 210 lbs. Born, Dawson Creek, B.C., October 1, 1962.
(Los Angeles' 7th choice, 165th overall, in 1981 Entry Draft).

Season	Club	GP	G	A	Pts	PIM	GP	G	A	Pts	PIM
1983-84	Los Angeles Kings	2	0	0	0	0	....	....	....	....	....
1985-86	Los Angeles Kings	6	0	1	1	9	....	....	....	....	....
	NHL Totals	**8**	**0**	**1**	**1**	**9**	....	....	....	....	....

BRENNAN, Doug

Defense. Shoots left. 5'11", 180 lbs. Born, Peterborough, Ont., January 10, 1905.

Season	Club	GP	G	A	Pts	PIM	GP	G	A	Pts	PIM
1931-32	New York Rangers	38	4	3	7	40	7	1	0	1	10
1932-33♦	New York Rangers	48	5	4	9	94	8	0	0	0	11
1933-34	New York Rangers	37	0	0	0	18	1	0	0	0	0
	NHL Totals	**123**	**9**	**7**	**16**	**152**	**16**	**1**	**0**	**1**	**21**

Traded to **NY Rangers** by **Vancouver** (PCHL) for cash, October 30, 1931.

BRENNAN, Kip

Left wing. Shoots left. 6'4", 210 lbs. Born, Kingston, Ont., August 27, 1980.
(Los Angeles' 4th choice, 103rd overall, in 1998 Entry Draft).

Season	Club	GP	G	A	Pts	PIM	GP	G	A	Pts	PIM
2001-02	Los Angeles Kings	4	0	0	0	22	....	....	....	....	....
2002-03	Los Angeles Kings	19	0	0	0	57	....	....	....	....	....
	NHL Totals	**23**	**0**	**0**	**0**	**79**	....	....	....	....	....

BRENNAN, Rich

Defense. Shoots right. 6'2", 200 lbs. Born, Schenectady, NY, November 26, 1972.
(Quebec's 3rd choice, 46th overall, in 1991 Entry Draft).

Season	Club	GP	G	A	Pts	PIM	GP	G	A	Pts	PIM
1996-97	Colorado Avalanche	2	0	0	0	0	....	....	....	....	....
1997-98	San Jose Sharks	11	1	2	3	2	....	....	....	....	....
1998-99	New York Rangers	24	1	3	4	23	....	....	....	....	....
2000-01	Los Angeles Kings	2	0	0	0	0	....	....	....	....	....
2001-02	Nashville Predators	4	0	0	0	2	....	....	....	....	....
2002-03	Boston Bruins	7	0	1	1	6	....	....	....	....	....
	NHL Totals	**50**	**2**	**6**	**8**	**33**	....	....	....	....	....

Rights transferred to **Colorado** after **Quebec** franchise relocated, June 21, 1995. Signed as a free agent by **San Jose**, July 9, 1997. Traded to **NY Rangers** by **San Jose** for Jason Muzzatti, March 24, 1998. Signed as a free agent by **Nashville**, September 23, 1999. Claimed by **Los Angeles** from **Nashville** in Waiver Draft, September 27, 1999. Signed as a free agent by **Nashville**, August 8, 2001. Traded to **Los Angeles** by **Nashville** for Brett Hauer, December 19, 2001. Signed as a free agent by **Boston**, July 18, 2002.

BRENNAN, Tom

Right wing. Shoots right. 5'9", 155 lbs. Born, Philadelphia, PA, January 22, 1922.

Season	Club	GP	G	A	Pts	PIM	GP	G	A	Pts	PIM
1943-44	Boston Bruins	11	2	1	3	2	....	....	....	....	....
1944-45	Boston Bruins	1	0	1	1	0	....	....	....	....	....
	NHL Totals	**12**	**2**	**2**	**4**	**2**	....	....	....	....	....

Signed as a free agent by **Boston**, November 27, 1943.

BRENNEMAN, John

Left wing. Shoots left. 5'10", 175 lbs. Born, Fort Erie, Ont., January 5, 1943.

Season	Club	GP	G	A	Pts	PIM	GP	G	A	Pts	PIM
1964-65	Chicago Black Hawks	17	1	0	1	2	....	....	....	....	....
	New York Rangers	22	3	3	6	6	....	....	....	....	....
1965-66	New York Rangers	11	0	0	0	14	....	....	....	....	....
1966-67♦	Toronto Maple Leafs	41	6	4	10	4	....	....	....	....	....
1967-68	Detroit Red Wings	9	0	2	2	0	....	....	....	....	....
	Oakland Seals	31	10	8	18	14	....	....	....	....	....
1968-69	Oakland Seals	21	1	2	3	6	....	....	....	....	....
	NHL Totals	**152**	**21**	**19**	**40**	**46**	....	....	....	....	....

Traded to **NY Rangers** by **Chicago** with Doug Robinson and Wayne Hillman for Camille Henry, Don Johns, Billy Taylor and Wally Chevrier, February 4, 1965. Claimed by **Toronto** from **NY Rangers** in Intra-League Draft, June 15, 1966. Claimed by **St. Louis** from **Toronto** in Expansion Draft, June 6, 1967. Traded to **Detroit** by **St. Louis** for Craig Cameron, Larry Hornung and Don Giesebrecht, October 9, 1967. Traded to **Oakland** by **Detroit** with Ted Hampson and Bert Marshall for Kent Douglas, January 9, 1968.

BRETTO, Joe

Defense. Shoots left. 6'1", 248 lbs. Born, Hibbing, MN, November 28, 1912.

Season	Club	GP	G	A	Pts	PIM	GP	G	A	Pts	PIM
1944-45	Chicago Black Hawks	3	0	0	0	4	....	....	....	....	....
	NHL Totals	**3**	**0**	**0**	**0**	**4**	....	....	....	....	....

Traded to **Chicago** by **St. Paul** (AHA) for cash, October 15, 1944. Traded to **Cleveland** (AHL) by **Chicago** for cash, November 14, 1944.

BREWER, Carl

Defense. Shoots left. 5'9", 180 lbs. Born, Toronto, Ont., October 21, 1938.

Season	Club	GP	G	A	Pts	PIM	GP	G	A	Pts	PIM
1957-58	Toronto Maple Leafs	2	0	0	0	0	....	....	....	....	....
1958-59	Toronto Maple Leafs	69	3	21	24	125	12	0	6	6	*40
1959-60	Toronto Maple Leafs	67	4	19	23	*150	10	2	3	5	16
1960-61	Toronto Maple Leafs	51	1	14	15	92	5	0	0	0	4
1961-62♦	Toronto Maple Leafs	67	1	22	23	89	8	0	2	2	22
1962-63♦	Toronto Maple Leafs	70	2	23	25	168	10	0	1	1	12
1963-64♦	Toronto Maple Leafs	57	4	9	13	114	12	0	1	1	30
1964-65	Toronto Maple Leafs	70	4	23	27	*177	6	1	2	3	12
1969-70	Detroit Red Wings	70	2	37	39	51	4	0	0	0	2
1970-71	St. Louis Blues	19	2	9	11	29	5	0	2	2	8
1971-72	St. Louis Blues	42	2	16	18	40	....	....	....	....	....
1979-80	Toronto Maple Leafs	20	0	5	5	2	....	....	....	....	....
	NHL Totals	**604**	**25**	**198**	**223**	**1037**	**72**	**3**	**17**	**20**	**146**

NHL Second All-Star Team (1962, 1965, 1970) • NHL First All-Star Team (1963)

Played in NHL All-Star Game (1959, 1962, 1964, 1970)

Rights traded to **Detroit** by **Toronto** with Frank Mahovlich, Pete Stemkowski and Garry Unger for Norm Ullman, Floyd Smith, Paul Henderson and Doug Barrie, March 3, 1968. • Left Detroit's training camp on September 4, 1970 to concentrate on job with the KOHO hockey stick company. Traded to **St. Louis** by **Detroit** for future considerations (Mike Lowe, Ab McDonald and Bob Wall), May 12, 1971), February 22, 1971. Signed as a free agent by **Toronto**, January 2, 1980.

BREWER, Eric

Defense. Shoots left. 6'3", 220 lbs. Born, Vernon, B.C., April 17, 1979.
(NY Islanders' 2nd choice, 5th overall, in 1997 Entry Draft).

Season	Club	GP	G	A	Pts	PIM	GP	G	A	Pts	PIM
1998-99	New York Islanders	63	5	6	11	32	....	....	....	....	....
99-2000	New York Islanders	26	0	2	2	20	....	....	....	....	....
2000-01	Edmonton Oilers	77	7	14	21	53	6	1	5	6	2
2001-02	Edmonton Oilers	81	7	18	25	45	....	....	....	....	....
2002-03	Edmonton Oilers	80	8	21	29	45	6	1	3	4	6
	NHL Totals	**327**	**27**	**61**	**88**	**195**	**12**	**2**	**8**	**10**	**8**

Played in NHL All-Star Game (2003)

Traded to **Edmonton** by **NY Islanders** with Josh Green and NY Islanders' 2nd round choice (Brad Winchester) in 2000 Entry Draft for Roman Hamrlik, June 24, 2000.

BRICKLEY, Andy

Left wing/Center. Shoots left. 5'11", 200 lbs. Born, Melrose, MA, August 9, 1961.
(Philadelphia's 11th choice, 210th overall, in 1980 Entry Draft).

Season	Club	GP	G	A	Pts	PIM	GP	G	A	Pts	PIM
1982-83	Philadelphia Flyers	3	1	1	2	0	....	....	....	....	....
1983-84	Pittsburgh Penguins	50	18	20	38	9	....	....	....	....	....
1984-85	Pittsburgh Penguins	45	7	15	22	10	....	....	....	....	....
1986-87	New Jersey Devils	51	11	12	23	8	....	....	....	....	....
1987-88	New Jersey Devils	45	8	14	22	14	4	0	1	1	4
1988-89	Boston Bruins	71	13	22	35	20	10	0	2	2	0
1989-90	Boston Bruins	43	12	28	40	8	2	0	0	0	0
1990-91	Boston Bruins	40	2	9	11	8	....	....	....	....	....
1991-92	Boston Bruins	23	10	17	27	2	....	....	....	....	....
1992-93	Winnipeg Jets	12	0	2	2	2	1	1	1	2	0
1993-94	Winnipeg Jets	2	0	0	0	0	....	....	....	....	....
	NHL Totals	**385**	**82**	**140**	**222**	**81**	**17**	**1**	**4**	**5**	**4**

Traded to **Pittsburgh** by **Philadelphia** with Ron Flockhart, Mark Taylor and Philadelphia's 1st (Roger Belanger) and 3rd (later traded to Vancouver – Vancouver selected Mike Stevens) round choices in 1984 Entry Draft for Rich Sutter and Pittsburgh's 2nd (Greg Smyth) and 3rd (David McLay) round choices in 1984 Entry Draft, October 23, 1983. Signed as a free agent by **New Jersey**, July 8, 1986. Claimed by **Boston** from **New Jersey** in Waiver Draft, October 3, 1988. Signed as a free agent by **Winnipeg**, November 11, 1992. Signed as a free agent by **NY Islanders**, July 27, 1994.

BRIDEN, Archie

Left wing. Shoots left. 5'8", 170 lbs. Born, Renfrew, Ont., July 16, 1898.

Season	Club	GP	G	A	Pts	PIM	GP	G	A	Pts	PIM
1926-27	Boston Bruins	16	2	2	4	8	....	....	....	....	....
	Detroit Cougars	26	3	0	3	28	....	....	....	....	....
1929-30	Pittsburgh Pirates	29	4	3	7	20	....	....	....	....	....
	NHL Totals	**71**	**9**	**5**	**14**	**56**	....	....	....	....	....

Traded to **Boston** by **Calgary** (WHL) for cash, August 30, 1926. Traded to **Detroit** by **Boston** with Duke Keats for Harry Meeking and Frank Fredrickson, January 7, 1927. Traded to **NY Rangers** by **Detroit** with Harry Meeking for Stan Brown, October 10, 1927. Traded to **Pittsburgh** by **NY Rangers** (Philadelphia – Can-Am) for cash, October 8, 1929. Traded to **London** (IHL) by **Pittsburgh** for cash, January 27, 1930.

BRIDGMAN, Mel

Center. Shoots left. 6', 190 lbs. Born, Trenton, Ont., April 28, 1955.
(Philadelphia's 1st choice, 1st overall, in 1975 Amateur Draft).

Season	Club	GP	G	A	Pts	PIM	GP	G	A	Pts	PIM
1975-76	Philadelphia Flyers	80	23	27	50	86	16	6	8	14	31
1976-77	Philadelphia Flyers	70	19	38	57	120	7	1	0	1	8
1977-78	Philadelphia Flyers	76	16	32	48	203	12	1	7	8	36
1978-79	Philadelphia Flyers	76	24	35	59	184	8	1	2	3	17

Season	Club	GP	G	A	Pts	PIM	GP	G	A	Pts	PIM
		REGULAR SEASON					PLAYOFFS				
1979-80	Philadelphia Flyers	74	16	31	47	136	19	2	9	11	70
1980-81	Philadelphia Flyers	77	14	37	51	195	12	2	4	6	39
1981-82	Philadelphia Flyers	9	7	5	12	47	....	....	....	....	....
	Calgary Flames	63	26	49	75	94	3	2	0	2	14
1982-83	Calgary Flames	79	19	31	50	103	9	3	4	7	33
1983-84	New Jersey Devils	79	23	38	61	121	....	....	....	....	....
1984-85	New Jersey Devils	80	22	39	61	105	....	....	....	....	....
1985-86	New Jersey Devils	78	23	40	63	80	....	....	....	....	....
1986-87	New Jersey Devils	51	8	31	39	80	....	....	....	....	....
	Detroit Red Wings	13	2	2	4	19	16	5	2	7	28
1987-88	Detroit Red Wings	57	6	11	17	42	16	4	1	5	12
1988-89	Vancouver Canucks	15	4	3	7	10	7	1	2	3	10
	NHL Totals	**977**	**252**	**449**	**701**	**1625**	**125**	**28**	**39**	**67**	**298**

Traded to **Calgary** by **Philadelphia** for Brad Marsh, November 11, 1981. Traded to **New Jersey** by **Calgary** with Phil Russell for Steve Tambellini and Joel Quenneville, June 20, 1983. Traded to **Detroit** by **New Jersey** for Chris Cichocki and Detroit's 3rd round choice (later traded to Buffalo – Buffalo selected Andrew MacVicar) in 1987 Entry Draft, March 9, 1987. Signed as a free agent by **Vancouver**, October 4, 1988.

BRIERE, Daniel

Center. Shoots right. 5'10", 178 lbs. Born, Gatineau, Que., October 6, 1977.
(Phoenix's 2nd choice, 24th overall, in 1996 Entry Draft).

Season	Club	GP	G	A	Pts	PIM	GP	G	A	Pts	PIM
1997-98	Phoenix Coyotes	5	1	0	1	2	....	....	....	....	....
1998-99	Phoenix Coyotes	64	8	14	22	30	....	....	....	....	....
99-2000	Phoenix Coyotes	13	1	1	2	0	1	0	0	0	0
2000-01	Phoenix Coyotes	30	11	4	15	12	....	....	....	....	....
2001-02	Phoenix Coyotes	78	32	28	60	52	5	2	1	3	2
2002-03	Phoenix Coyotes	68	17	29	46	50	....	....	....	....	....
	Buffalo Sabres	14	7	5	12	12	....	....	....	....	....
	NHL Totals	**272**	**77**	**81**	**158**	**158**	**6**	**2**	**1**	**3**	**2**

Traded to **Buffalo** by **Phoenix** with Phoenix's 3rd round choice in 2004 Entry Draft for Chris Gratton and Buffalo's 4th round choice in 2004 Entry Draft, March 10, 2003.

BRIERE, Michel

Center. Shoots left. 5'10", 165 lbs. Born, Shawinigan Falls, Que., October 21, 1949.
(Pittsburgh's 2nd choice, 26th overall, in 1969 Amateur Draft).

Season	Club	GP	G	A	Pts	PIM	GP	G	A	Pts	PIM
1969-70	Pittsburgh Penguins	76	12	32	44	20	10	5	3	8	17
	NHL Totals	**76**	**12**	**32**	**44**	**20**	**10**	**5**	**3**	**8**	**17**

Died on April 13, 1971 of injuries originally suffered in automobile accident on May 15, 1970 .

BRIGLEY, Travis

Left wing. Shoots left. 6'1", 200 lbs. Born, Coronation, Alta., June 16, 1977.
(Calgary's 2nd choice, 39th overall, in 1996 Entry Draft).

Season	Club	GP	G	A	Pts	PIM	GP	G	A	Pts	PIM
1997-98	Calgary Flames	2	0	0	0	2	....	....	....	....	....
99-2000	Calgary Flames	17	0	2	2	4	....	....	....	....	....
	NHL Totals	**19**	**0**	**2**	**2**	**6**	....	....	....	....	....

Traded to **Philadelphia** by **Calgary** with Calgary's 6th round choice (Andrei Razin) in 2001 Entry Draft for Marc Bureau, March 6, 2000. Signed as a free agent by **Florida**, December 16, 2000. Signed as a free agent by **Anaheim**, January 22, 2002.

BRIMANIS, Aris

Defense. Shoots right. 6'3", 210 lbs. Born, Cleveland, OH, March 14, 1972.
(Philadelphia's 3rd choice, 86th overall, in 1991 Entry Draft).

Season	Club	GP	G	A	Pts	PIM	GP	G	A	Pts	PIM
1993-94	Philadelphia Flyers	1	0	0	0	0	....	....	....	....	....
1995-96	Philadelphia Flyers	17	0	2	2	12	....	....	....	....	....
1996-97	Philadelphia Flyers	3	0	1	1	0	....	....	....	....	....
99-2000	New York Islanders	18	2	1	3	6	....	....	....	....	....
2000-01	New York Islanders	56	0	8	8	26	....	....	....	....	....
2001-02	Mighty Ducks of Anaheim	5	0	0	0	9	....	....	....	....	....
	NHL Totals	**100**	**2**	**12**	**14**	**53**	....	....	....	....	....

Signed as a free agent by **NY Islanders**, August 16, 1999. Signed as a free agent by **Anaheim**, August 1, 2001. Signed as a free agent by **St. Louis**, August 15, 2002.

BRIND'AMOUR, Rod

Center. Shoots left. 6'1", 202 lbs. Born, Ottawa, Ont., August 9, 1970.
(St. Louis' 1st choice, 9th overall, in 1988 Entry Draft).

Season	Club	GP	G	A	Pts	PIM	GP	G	A	Pts	PIM
1988-89	St. Louis Blues	....	....	....	....	....	5	2	0	2	4
1989-90	St. Louis Blues	79	26	35	61	46	12	5	8	13	6
1990-91	St. Louis Blues	78	17	32	49	93	13	2	5	7	10
1991-92	Philadelphia Flyers	80	33	44	77	100	....	....	....	....	....
1992-93	Philadelphia Flyers	81	37	49	86	89	....	....	....	....	....
1993-94	Philadelphia Flyers	84	35	62	97	85	....	....	....	....	....
1994-95	Philadelphia Flyers	48	12	27	39	33	15	6	9	15	8
1995-96	Philadelphia Flyers	82	26	61	87	110	12	2	5	7	6
1996-97	Philadelphia Flyers	82	27	32	59	41	19	*13	8	21	10
1997-98	Philadelphia Flyers	82	36	38	74	54	5	2	2	4	7
1998-99	Philadelphia Flyers	82	24	50	74	47	6	1	3	4	0
99-2000	Philadelphia Flyers	12	5	3	8	4	....	....	....	....	....
	Carolina Hurricanes	33	4	10	14	22	....	....	....	....	....
2000-01	Carolina Hurricanes	79	20	36	56	47	6	1	3	4	6
2001-02	Carolina Hurricanes	81	23	32	55	40	23	4	8	12	16
2002-03	Carolina Hurricanes	48	14	23	37	37	....	....	....	....	....
	NHL Totals	**1031**	**339**	**534**	**873**	**848**	**116**	**38**	**51**	**89**	**73**

NHL All-Rookie Team (1990)
Played in NHL All-Star Game (1992)

Traded to **Philadelphia** by **St. Louis** with Dan Quinn for Ron Sutter and Murray Baron, September 22, 1991. Traded to **Carolina** by **Philadelphia** with Jean-Marc Pelletier and Philadelphia's 2nd round choice (later traded to Colorado – Colorado selected Agris Saviels) in 2000 Entry Draft for Keith Primeau and Carolina's 5th round choice (later traded to NY Islanders – NY Islanders selected Kristofer Ottosson) in 2000 Entry Draft, January 23, 2000.

BRINDLEY, Doug

Left wing/Center. Shoots left. 6'1", 175 lbs. Born, Walkerton, Ont., June 8, 1949.
(Toronto's 2nd choice, 20th overall, in 1969 Amateur Draft).

Season	Club	GP	G	A	Pts	PIM	GP	G	A	Pts	PIM
1970-71	Toronto Maple Leafs	3	0	0	0	0	....	....	....	....	....
	NHL Totals	**3**	**0**	**0**	**0**	**0**	....	....	....	....	....

Traded to **Vancouver** by **Toronto** for Andre Hinse, September 27, 1971.

BRINK, Milt

Center. Shoots right. 5'10", 165 lbs. Born, Hibbing, MN, November 26, 1910.

Season	Club	GP	G	A	Pts	PIM	GP	G	A	Pts	PIM
1936-37	Chicago Black Hawks	5	0	0	0	0	....	....	....	....	....
	NHL Totals	**5**	**0**	**0**	**0**	**0**	....	....	....	....	....

BRISEBOIS, Patrice

Defense. Shoots right. 6'2", 203 lbs. Born, Montreal, Que., January 27, 1971.
(Montreal's 2nd choice, 30th overall, in 1989 Entry Draft).

Season	Club	GP	G	A	Pts	PIM	GP	G	A	Pts	PIM
1990-91	Montreal Canadiens	10	0	2	2	4	....	....	....	....	....
1991-92	Montreal Canadiens	26	2	8	10	20	11	2	4	6	6
1992-93◆	Montreal Canadiens	70	10	21	31	79	20	0	4	4	18
1993-94	Montreal Canadiens	53	2	21	23	63	7	0	4	4	6
1994-95	Montreal Canadiens	35	4	8	12	26	....	....	....	....	....
1995-96	Montreal Canadiens	69	9	27	36	65	6	1	2	3	6
1996-97	Montreal Canadiens	49	2	13	15	24	3	1	1	2	24
1997-98	Montreal Canadiens	79	10	27	37	67	10	1	0	1	0
1998-99	Montreal Canadiens	54	3	9	12	28	....	....	....	....	....
99-2000	Montreal Canadiens	54	10	25	35	18	....	....	....	....	....
2000-01	Montreal Canadiens	77	15	21	36	28	....	....	....	....	....
2001-02	Montreal Canadiens	71	4	29	33	25	10	1	1	2	2
2002-03	Montreal Canadiens	73	4	25	29	32	....	....	....	....	....
	NHL Totals	**720**	**75**	**236**	**311**	**479**	**67**	**6**	**16**	**22**	**62**

BRISSON, Gerry

Right wing. Shoots left. 5'9", 155 lbs. Born, St. Boniface, Man., September 3, 1937.

Season	Club	GP	G	A	Pts	PIM	GP	G	A	Pts	PIM
1962-63	Montreal Canadiens	4	0	2	2	4	....	....	....	....	....
	NHL Totals	**4**	**0**	**2**	**2**	**4**	....	....	....	....	....

Claimed by **Cleveland** (AHL) (Montreal) from **Montreal** in Reverse Draft, June 9, 1965. Traded to **San Francisco** (WHL) by **Montreal** (Seattle-WHL) for Len Haley, October 22, 1965. Traded to **NY Rangers** (Vancouver-WHL) by **California** (WHL) for Bob Kabel with NY Rangers holding right of recall, October, 1966.

BRITZ, Greg

Right wing. Shoots left. 6', 190 lbs. Born, Buffalo, NY, January 3, 1961.

Season	Club	GP	G	A	Pts	PIM	GP	G	A	Pts	PIM
1983-84	Toronto Maple Leafs	6	0	0	0	2	....	....	....	....	....
1984-85	Toronto Maple Leafs	1	0	0	0	2	....	....	....	....	....
1986-87	Hartford Whalers	1	0	0	0	0	....	....	....	....	....
	NHL Totals	**8**	**0**	**0**	**0**	**4**	....	....	....	....	....

Signed as a free agent by **Toronto**, November 2, 1983. Signed as a free agent by **Hartford**, November, 1986.

BROADBENT, Punch

HHOF

Right wing. Shoots right. 5'7", 183 lbs. Born, Ottawa, Ont., July 13, 1892.

Season	Club	GP	G	A	Pts	PIM	GP	G	A	Pts	PIM
1918-19	Ottawa Senators	8	4	3	7	12	5	2	1	3	*18
1919-20◆	Ottawa Senators	21	19	6	25	40	....	....	....	....	....
	Ottawa Senators (Cup)	....	....	....	....	....	*4*	*0*	*0*	*0*	*3*
1920-21◆	Ottawa Senators	9	4	1	5	10	2	0	2	2	4
	Ottawa Senators (Cup)	....	....	....	....	....	*4*	*2*	*0*	*2*	*0*
1921-22	Ottawa Senators	24	*32	14	*46	28	2	0	1	1	8
1922-23◆	Ottawa Senators	24	14	1	15	34	2	0	0	0	2
	Ottawa Senators (Cup)	....	....	....	....	....	*6*	*6*	*1*	*7*	*12*
1923-24	Ottawa Senators	22	9	4	13	44	2	0	0	0	2
1924-25	Montreal Maroons	30	14	6	20	75	....	....	....	....	....
1925-26◆	Montreal Maroons	36	12	5	17	112	4	2	1	3	14
	Montreal Maroons (Cup)	....	....	....	....	....	*4*	*1*	*0*	*1*	*20*
1926-27	Montreal Maroons	42	9	5	14	88	2	0	0	0	0
1927-28	Ottawa Senators	43	3	2	5	62	2	0	0	0	0

Season	Club	REGULAR SEASON GP	G	A	Pts	PIM	PLAYOFFS GP	G	A	Pts	PIM
1928-29	New York Americans	44	1	4	5	59	2	0	0	0	2
	NHL Totals	**303**	**121**	**51**	**172**	**564**	**23**	**4**	**5**	**9**	**50**

Signed as a free agent by **Ottawa**, January 21, 1919. Rights transferred to **Hamilton** by **NHL** with Sprague Cleghorn, December 30, 1920. • Broadbent and Cleghorn refused to report. Rights traded to **Montreal** by **Hamilton** for cash, January 4, 1921. • Broadbent refused to report. Rights returned to **Ottawa** by **NHL**, February 21, 1921. • Scored at least one goal in 16 consecutive games (NHL record) from December 21, 1921 to February 15, 1922. • 1922-23 Stanley Cup totals includes series with Regina (WCHL) and Edmonton (PCHA). Traded to **Mtl. Maroons** by **Ottawa** with Clint Benedict for cash, October 20, 1924. • 1925-26 Mtl. Maroons playoff totals includes series against Ottawa and Pittsburgh. Traded to **Ottawa** by **Mtl. Maroons** with $22,500 for Hooley Smith, October 7, 1927. Traded to **NY Americans** by **Ottawa** for cash, October 15, 1928.

BROCHU, Stephane

Defense. Shoots left. 6', 185 lbs. Born, Sherbrooke, Que., August 15, 1967.
(NY Rangers' 9th choice, 175th overall, in 1985 Entry Draft).

Season	Club	GP	G	A	Pts	PIM	GP	G	A	Pts	PIM
1988-89	New York Rangers	1	0	0	0	0	....	....	....	....	....
	NHL Totals	**1**	**0**	**0**	**0**	**0**	....	....	....	....	....

BRODEN, Connie

Center. Shoots left. 5'8", 160 lbs. Born, Montreal, Que., April 6, 1932.

Season	Club	GP	G	A	Pts	PIM	GP	G	A	Pts	PIM
1955-56	Montreal Canadiens	3	0	0	0	2	....	....	....	....	....
1956-57 ♦	Montreal Canadiens	....	....	....	....	....	6	0	1	1	0
1957-58 ♦	Montreal Canadiens	3	2	1	3	0	1	0	0	0	0
	NHL Totals	**6**	**2**	**1**	**3**	**2**	**7**	**0**	**1**	**1**	**0**

Claimed by **Springfield** (AHL) from **Montreal** (Shawinigan-QHL) in Inter-League Draft, June 4, 1957.

BROOKE, Bob

Center. Shoots right. 5'11", 195 lbs. Born, Melrose, MA, December 18, 1960.
(St. Louis' 3rd choice, 75th overall, in 1980 Entry Draft).

Season	Club	GP	G	A	Pts	PIM	GP	G	A	Pts	PIM
1983-84	New York Rangers	9	1	2	3	4	5	0	0	0	7
1984-85	New York Rangers	72	7	9	16	79	3	0	0	0	8
1985-86	New York Rangers	79	24	20	44	111	16	6	9	15	28
1986-87	New York Rangers	15	3	5	8	20	....	....	....	....	....
	Minnesota North Stars	65	10	18	28	78	....	....	....	....	....
1987-88	Minnesota North Stars	77	5	20	25	108	....	....	....	....	....
1988-89	Minnesota North Stars	57	7	9	16	57	5	3	0	3	2
1989-90	Minnesota North Stars	38	4	4	8	33	....	....	....	....	....
	New Jersey Devils	35	8	10	18	30	5	0	0	0	14
	NHL Totals	**447**	**69**	**97**	**166**	**520**	**34**	**9**	**9**	**18**	**59**

Rights traded to **NY Rangers** by **St. Louis** with Larry Patey for Dave Barr, NY Rangers' 3rd round choice (Alan Perry) in 1984 Entry Draft and cash, March 5, 1984. Traded to **Minnesota** by **NY Rangers** with Minnesota's 4th round choice (previously acquired, Minnesota selected Jeffrey Stolp) in 1988 Entry Draft for Curt Giles, Tony McKegney and Minnesota's 2nd round choice (Troy Mallette) in 1988 Entry Draft, November 13, 1986. Traded to **New Jersey** by **Minnesota** for Aaron Broten, January 5, 1990. Traded to **Winnipeg** by **New Jersey** for Laurie Boschman, September 6, 1990. • Officially announced retirement on September 7, 1990. • Winnipeg received New Jersey's 5th round choice (Yan Kaminsky) in 1991 Entry Draft as compensation.

BROOKS, Gord

Right wing. Shoots right. 5'8", 168 lbs. Born, Cobourg, Ont., September 11, 1950.
(St. Louis' 3rd choice, 51st overall, in 1970 Amateur Draft).

Season	Club	GP	G	A	Pts	PIM	GP	G	A	Pts	PIM
1971-72	St. Louis Blues	2	0	0	0	0	....	....	....	....	....
1973-74	St. Louis Blues	30	6	8	14	12	....	....	....	....	....
1974-75	Washington Capitals	38	1	10	11	25	....	....	....	....	....
	NHL Totals	**70**	**7**	**18**	**25**	**37**	....	....	....	....	....

Claimed by **Washington** from **St. Louis** in Expansion Draft, June 12, 1974.

BROPHY, Bernie

Left wing. Shoots left. 5'8", 165 lbs. Born, Collingwood, Ont., August 9, 1905.

Season	Club	GP	G	A	Pts	PIM	GP	G	A	Pts	PIM
1925-26 ♦	Montreal Maroons	10	0	0	0	0	....	....	....	....	....
1928-29	Detroit Cougars	37	2	4	6	23	2	0	0	0	2
1929-30	Detroit Cougars	15	2	0	2	2	....	....	....	....	....
	NHL Totals	**62**	**4**	**4**	**8**	**25**	**2**	**0**	**0**	**0**	**2**

Signed as a free agent by **Mtl. Maroons**, January 4, 1926. Signed as a free agent by **Montreal** after release by **Mtl. Maroons**, February 10, 1927. Signed as a free agent by **Mtl. Maroons**, September, 1928. Traded to **Detroit** by **Mtl. Maroons** for cash, October 23, 1928. Traded to **Cleveland** (IHL) by **Detroit** for cash, November 3, 1931.

BROSSART, Willie

Defense. Shoots left. 6', 190 lbs. Born, Allan, Sask., May 29, 1949.
(Philadelphia's 3rd choice, 28th overall, in 1969 Amateur Draft).

Season	Club	GP	G	A	Pts	PIM	GP	G	A	Pts	PIM
1970-71	Philadelphia Flyers	1	0	0	0	0	....	....	....	....	....
1971-72	Philadelphia Flyers	42	0	4	4	12	....	....	....	....	....
1972-73	Philadelphia Flyers	4	0	1	1	0	....	....	....	....	....
1973-74	Toronto Maple Leafs	17	0	1	1	20	1	0	0	0	0
1974-75	Toronto Maple Leafs	4	0	0	0	2	....	....	....	....	....
	Washington Capitals	12	1	0	1	14	....	....	....	....	....
1975-76	Washington Capitals	49	0	8	8	40	....	....	....	....	....
	NHL Totals	**129**	**1**	**14**	**15**	**88**	**1**	**0**	**0**	**0**	**0**

Traded to **Toronto** by **Philadelphia** for cash, May 23, 1973. Traded to **Washington** by **Toronto** with Tim Ecclestone for Rod Seiling, November 2, 1974.

BROTEN, Aaron

Left wing/Center. Shoots left. 5'10", 180 lbs. Born, Roseau, MN, November 14, 1960.
(Colorado's 5th choice, 106th overall, in 1980 Entry Draft).

Season	Club	GP	G	A	Pts	PIM	GP	G	A	Pts	PIM
1980-81	Colorado Rockies	2	0	0	0	0	....	....	....	....	....
1981-82	Colorado Rockies	58	15	24	39	6	....	....	....	....	....
1982-83	New Jersey Devils	73	16	39	55	28	....	....	....	....	....
1983-84	New Jersey Devils	80	13	23	36	36	....	....	....	....	....
1984-85	New Jersey Devils	80	22	35	57	38	....	....	....	....	....
1985-86	New Jersey Devils	66	18	25	43	26	....	....	....	....	....
1986-87	New Jersey Devils	80	26	53	79	36	....	....	....	....	....
1987-88	New Jersey Devils	80	26	57	83	80	20	5	11	16	20
1988-89	New Jersey Devils	80	16	43	59	81	....	....	....	....	....
1989-90	New Jersey Devils	42	10	8	18	36	....	....	....	....	....
	Minnesota North Stars	35	9	9	18	22	7	0	5	5	8
1990-91	Quebec Nordiques	20	5	4	9	6	....	....	....	....	....
	Toronto Maple Leafs	27	6	4	10	32	....	....	....	....	....
1991-92	Winnipeg Jets	25	4	5	9	14	7	2	2	4	12
	NHL Totals	**748**	**186**	**329**	**515**	**441**	**34**	**7**	**18**	**25**	**40**

• Brother of Neal and Paul

Transferred to **New Jersey** after **Colorado** franchise relocated, June 30, 1982. Traded to **Minnesota** by **New Jersey** for Bob Brooke, January 5, 1990. Claimed by **Quebec** from **Minnesota** in Waiver Draft, October 1, 1990. Traded to **Toronto** by **Quebec** with Lucien DeBlois and Michel Petit for Scott Pearson and Toronto's 2nd round choices in 1991 (later traded to Washington – Washington selected Eric Lavigne) and 1992 (Tuomas Gronman) Entry Drafts, November 17, 1990. Signed as a free agent by **Winnipeg**, January 21, 1992.

BROTEN, Neal

USHOF

Center. Shoots left. 5'9", 175 lbs. Born, Roseau, MN, November 29, 1959.
(Minnesota's 3rd choice, 42nd overall, in 1979 Entry Draft).

Season	Club	GP	G	A	Pts	PIM	GP	G	A	Pts	PIM
1980-81	Minnesota North Stars	3	2	0	2	12	19	1	7	8	9
1981-82	Minnesota North Stars	73	38	60	98	42	4	0	2	2	0
1982-83	Minnesota North Stars	79	32	45	77	43	9	1	6	7	10
1983-84	Minnesota North Stars	76	28	61	89	43	16	5	5	10	4
1984-85	Minnesota North Stars	80	19	37	56	39	9	2	5	7	10
1985-86	Minnesota North Stars	80	29	76	105	47	5	3	2	5	2
1986-87	Minnesota North Stars	46	18	35	53	33	....	....	....	....	....
1987-88	Minnesota North Stars	54	9	30	39	32	....	....	....	....	....
1988-89	Minnesota North Stars	68	18	38	56	57	5	2	2	4	4
1989-90	Minnesota North Stars	80	23	62	85	45	7	2	2	4	18
1990-91	Minnesota North Stars	79	13	56	69	26	23	9	13	22	6
1991-92	Minnesota North Stars	76	8	26	34	16	7	1	5	6	2
1992-93	Minnesota North Stars	82	12	21	33	22	....	....	....	....	....
1993-94	Dallas Stars	79	17	35	52	62	9	2	1	3	6
1994-95	Dallas Stars	17	0	4	4	4	....	....	....	....	....
♦	New Jersey Devils	30	8	20	28	20	20	7	12	19	6
1995-96	New Jersey Devils	55	7	16	23	14	....	....	....	....	....
1996-97	New Jersey Devils	3	0	1	1	0	....	....	....	....	....
	Los Angeles Kings	19	0	4	4	0	....	....	....	....	....
	Dallas Stars	20	8	7	15	12	2	0	1	1	0
	NHL Totals	**1099**	**289**	**634**	**923**	**569**	**135**	**35**	**63**	**98**	**77**

• Brother of Aaron and Paul • Lester Patrick Trophy (1998)

Played in NHL All-Star Game (1983, 1986)

Transferred to **Dallas** after **Minnesota** franchise relocated, June 9, 1993. Traded to **New Jersey** by **Dallas** for Corey Millen, February 27, 1995. Traded to **Los Angeles** by **New Jersey** for future considerations, November 22, 1996. Claimed on waivers by **Dallas** from **Los Angeles**, January 28, 1997.

BROTEN, Paul

Right wing. Shoots right. 5'11", 188 lbs. Born, Roseau, MN, October 27, 1965.
(NY Rangers' 3rd choice, 77th overall, in 1984 Entry Draft).

Season	Club	GP	G	A	Pts	PIM	GP	G	A	Pts	PIM
1989-90	New York Rangers	32	5	3	8	26	6	1	1	2	2
1990-91	New York Rangers	28	4	6	10	18	5	0	0	0	2
1991-92	New York Rangers	74	13	15	28	102	13	1	2	3	10
1992-93	New York Rangers	60	5	9	14	48	....	....	....	....	....
1993-94	Dallas Stars	64	12	12	24	30	9	1	1	2	2
1994-95	Dallas Stars	47	7	9	16	36	5	1	2	3	2
1995-96	St. Louis Blues	17	0	1	1	4	....	....	....	....	....
	NHL Totals	**322**	**46**	**55**	**101**	**264**	**38**	**4**	**6**	**10**	**18**

• Brother of Neal and Aaron

Claimed by **Dallas** from **NY Rangers** in Waiver Draft, October 3, 1993. Traded to **St. Louis** by **Dallas** for Guy Carbonneau, October 2, 1995.

BROUSSEAU, Paul

Right wing. Shoots right. 6'2", 203 lbs. Born, Pierrefonds, Que., September 18, 1973.
(Quebec's 2nd choice, 28th overall, in 1992 Entry Draft).

Season	Club	GP	G	A	Pts	PIM	GP	G	A	Pts	PIM
1995-96	Colorado Avalanche	8	1	1	2	2	....	....	....	....	....
1996-97	Tampa Bay Lightning	6	0	0	0	0	....	....	....	....	....
1997-98	Tampa Bay Lightning	11	0	2	2	27	....	....	....	....	....
2000-01	Florida Panthers	1	0	0	0	0	....	....	....	....	....
	NHL Totals	**26**	**1**	**3**	**4**	**29**	....	....	....	....	....

Rights transferred to **Colorado** after **Quebec** franchise relocated, June 21, 1995. Signed as a free agent by **Tampa Bay**, September 10, 1996. Claimed by **Nashville** from **Tampa Bay** in Expansion Draft, June 26, 1998. Signed as a free agent by **Florida**, September 20, 1999.

BROWN, Adam

Left wing. Shoots left. 5'9", 175 lbs. Born, Johnstone, Scotland, February 4, 1920.

Season	Club	Regular Season GP	G	A	Pts	PIM	Playoffs GP	G	A	Pts	PIM
1941-42	Detroit Red Wings	28	6	9	15	15	10	0	2	2	4
1942-43 ◆	Detroit Red Wings	....	....	....	....	....	6	1	1	2	2
1943-44	Detroit Red Wings	50	24	18	42	56	5	0	0	0	8
1945-46	Detroit Red Wings	48	20	11	31	27	5	1	1	2	0
1946-47	Detroit Red Wings	22	8	5	13	30	....	....	....	....	....
	Chicago Black Hawks	42	11	25	36	57	....	....	....	....	....
1947-48	Chicago Black Hawks	32	7	10	17	41	....	....	....	....	....
1948-49	Chicago Black Hawks	58	8	12	20	69	....	....	....	....	....
1949-50	Chicago Black Hawks	25	2	2	4	16	....	....	....	....	....
1950-51	Chicago Black Hawks	53	10	12	22	61	....	....	....	....	....
1951-52	Boston Bruins	33	8	9	17	6	....	....	....	....	....
	NHL Totals	**391**	**104**	**113**	**217**	**378**	**26**	**2**	**4**	**6**	**14**

• Father of Andy

Signed as a free agent by **Detroit**, October 3, 1940. Traded to **Chicago** by **Detroit** with Ray Powell for Leo Reise and Pete Horeck, December 9, 1946. Traded to **Boston** by **Chicago** for cash, August 20, 1951.

BROWN, Arnie

Defense. Shoots left. 6'1", 185 lbs. Born, Oshawa, Ont., January 28, 1942.

Season	Club	Regular Season GP	G	A	Pts	PIM	Playoffs GP	G	A	Pts	PIM
1961-62	Toronto Maple Leafs	2	0	0	0	0	....	....	....	....	....
1963-64	Toronto Maple Leafs	4	0	0	0	6	....	....	....	....	....
1964-65	New York Rangers	58	1	11	12	145	....	....	....	....	....
1965-66	New York Rangers	64	1	7	8	106	....	....	....	....	....
1966-67	New York Rangers	69	2	10	12	61	4	0	0	0	6
1967-68	New York Rangers	74	1	25	26	83	6	0	1	1	8
1968-69	New York Rangers	74	10	12	22	48	4	0	1	1	0
1969-70	New York Rangers	73	15	21	36	78	4	0	4	4	9
1970-71	New York Rangers	48	3	12	15	24	....	....	....	....	....
	Detroit Red Wings	27	2	6	8	30	....	....	....	....	....
1971-72	Detroit Red Wings	77	2	23	25	84	....	....	....	....	....
1972-73	New York Islanders	48	4	8	12	27	....	....	....	....	....
	Atlanta Flames	15	1	0	1	17	....	....	....	....	....
1973-74	Atlanta Flames	48	2	6	8	29	4	0	0	0	0
	NHL Totals	**681**	**44**	**141**	**185**	**738**	**22**	**0**	**6**	**6**	**23**

Traded to **NY Rangers** by **Toronto** with Rod Seiling, Dick Duff, Bob Nevin and Bill Collins for Andy Bathgate and Don McKenney, February 22, 1964. Traded to **Detroit** by **NY Rangers** with Mike Robitaille and Tom Miller for Bruce MacGregor and Larry Brown, February 2, 1971. Traded to **NY Islanders** by **Detroit** with Gerry Gray for Denis DeJordy and Don McLaughlin, October 4 1972. Traded to **Atlanta** by **NY Islanders** for Ernie Hicke and future considerations (Billy MacMillan, May 29, 1973), February 13, 1973.

BROWN, Brad

Defense. Shoots right. 6'4", 220 lbs. Born, Baie Verte, Nfld., December 27, 1975.
(Montreal's 1st choice, 18th overall, in 1994 Entry Draft).

Season	Club	Regular Season GP	G	A	Pts	PIM	Playoffs GP	G	A	Pts	PIM
1996-97	Montreal Canadiens	8	0	0	0	22	....	....	....	....	....
1998-99	Montreal Canadiens	5	0	0	0	21	....	....	....	....	....
	Chicago Blackhawks	61	1	7	8	184	....	....	....	....	....
99-2000	Chicago Blackhawks	57	0	9	9	134	....	....	....	....	....
2000-01	New York Rangers	48	1	3	4	107	....	....	....	....	....
2001-02	Minnesota Wild	51	0	4	4	123	....	....	....	....	....
2002-03	Minnesota Wild	57	0	1	1	90	11	0	0	0	16
	NHL Totals	**287**	**2**	**24**	**26**	**681**	**11**	**0**	**0**	**0**	**16**

Traded to **Chicago** by **Montreal** with Jocelyn Thibault and Dave Manson for Jeff Hackett, Eric Weinrich, Alain Nasreddine and Tampa Bay's 4th round choice (previously acquired, Montreal selected Chris Dyment) in 1999 Entry Draft, November 16, 1998. Traded to **NY Rangers** by **Chicago** with Michal Grosek for future considerations, October 5, 2000. Signed as a free agent by **Minnesota**, July 31, 2001.

BROWN, Cam

Left wing. Shoots left. 6'1", 210 lbs. Born, Saskatoon, Sask., May 15, 1969.

Season	Club	Regular Season GP	G	A	Pts	PIM	Playoffs GP	G	A	Pts	PIM
1990-91	Vancouver Canucks	1	0	0	0	7	....	....	....	....	....
	NHL Totals	**1**	**0**	**0**	**0**	**7**	....	....	....	....	....

Signed as a free agent by **Vancouver**, April 6, 1990.

BROWN, Connie

Center. Shoots left. 5'7", 168 lbs. Born, Vankleek Hill, Ont., January 11, 1917.

Season	Club	Regular Season GP	G	A	Pts	PIM	Playoffs GP	G	A	Pts	PIM
1938-39	Detroit Red Wings	2	1	0	1	0	....	....	....	....	....
1939-40	Detroit Red Wings	36	8	3	11	2	5	2	1	3	0
1940-41	Detroit Red Wings	3	1	2	3	0	9	0	2	2	0
1941-42	Detroit Red Wings	9	0	3	3	4	....	....	....	....	....
1942-43 ◆	Detroit Red Wings	23	5	16	21	6	....	....	....	....	....
	NHL Totals	**73**	**15**	**24**	**39**	**12**	**14**	**2**	**3**	**5**	**0**

BROWN, Curtis

Center/Left wing. Shoots left. 6', 197 lbs. Born, Unity, Sask., February 12, 1976.
(Buffalo's 2nd choice, 43rd overall, in 1994 Entry Draft).

Season	Club	Regular Season GP	G	A	Pts	PIM	Playoffs GP	G	A	Pts	PIM
1994-95	Buffalo Sabres	1	1	1	2	2	....	....	....	....	....
1995-96	Buffalo Sabres	4	0	0	0	0	....	....	....	....	....
1996-97	Buffalo Sabres	28	4	3	7	18	....	....	....	....	....
1997-98	Buffalo Sabres	63	12	12	24	34	13	1	2	3	10
1998-99	Buffalo Sabres	78	16	31	47	56	21	7	6	13	10
99-2000	Buffalo Sabres	74	22	29	51	42	5	1	3	4	6
2000-01	Buffalo Sabres	70	10	22	32	34	13	5	0	5	8
2001-02	Buffalo Sabres	82	20	17	37	32	....	....	....	....	....
2002-03	Buffalo Sabres	74	15	16	31	40	....	....	....	....	....
	NHL Totals	**474**	**100**	**131**	**231**	**258**	**52**	**14**	**11**	**25**	**34**

BROWN, Dave

Right wing. Shoots right. 6'5", 222 lbs. Born, Saskatoon, Sask., October 12, 1962.
(Philadelphia's 7th choice, 140th overall, in 1982 Entry Draft).

Season	Club	Regular Season GP	G	A	Pts	PIM	Playoffs GP	G	A	Pts	PIM
1982-83	Philadelphia Flyers	2	0	0	0	5	....	....	....	....	....
1983-84	Philadelphia Flyers	19	1	5	6	98	2	0	0	0	12
1984-85	Philadelphia Flyers	57	3	6	9	165	11	0	0	0	59
1985-86	Philadelphia Flyers	76	10	7	17	277	5	0	0	0	16
1986-87	Philadelphia Flyers	62	7	3	10	274	26	1	2	3	59
1987-88	Philadelphia Flyers	47	12	5	17	114	7	1	0	1	27
1988-89	Philadelphia Flyers	50	0	3	3	100	....	....	....	....	....
	Edmonton Oilers	22	0	2	2	56	7	0	0	0	6
1989-90 ◆	Edmonton Oilers	60	0	6	6	145	3	0	0	0	0
1990-91	Edmonton Oilers	58	3	4	7	160	16	0	1	1	30
1991-92	Philadelphia Flyers	70	4	2	6	81	....	....	....	....	....
1992-93	Philadelphia Flyers	70	0	2	2	78	....	....	....	....	....
1993-94	Philadelphia Flyers	71	1	4	5	137	....	....	....	....	....
1994-95	Philadelphia Flyers	28	1	2	3	53	3	0	0	0	0
1995-96	San Jose Sharks	37	3	1	4	46	....	....	....	....	....
	NHL Totals	**729**	**45**	**52**	**97**	**1789**	**80**	**2**	**3**	**5**	**209**

Traded to **Edmonton** by **Philadelphia** for Keith Acton and Edmonton's 6th round choice (Dmitry Yushkevich) in 1991 Entry Draft, February 7, 1989. Traded to **Philadelphia** by **Edmonton** with Jari Kurri and Corey Foster for Craig Fisher, Scott Mellanby and Craig Berube, May 30, 1991. Signed as a free agent by **San Jose**, August 10, 1995.

BROWN, Doug

Right wing. Shoots right. 5'10", 185 lbs. Born, Southborough, MA, June 12, 1964.

Season	Club	Regular Season GP	G	A	Pts	PIM	Playoffs GP	G	A	Pts	PIM
1986-87	New Jersey Devils	4	0	1	1	0	....	....	....	....	....
1987-88	New Jersey Devils	70	14	11	25	20	19	5	1	6	6
1988-89	New Jersey Devils	63	15	10	25	15	....	....	....	....	....
1989-90	New Jersey Devils	69	14	20	34	16	6	0	1	1	2
1990-91	New Jersey Devils	58	14	16	30	4	7	2	2	4	2
1991-92	New Jersey Devils	71	11	17	28	27	....	....	....	....	....
1992-93	New Jersey Devils	15	0	5	5	2	....	....	....	....	....
1993-94	Pittsburgh Penguins	77	18	37	55	18	6	0	0	0	2
1994-95	Detroit Red Wings	45	9	12	21	16	18	4	8	12	2
1995-96	Detroit Red Wings	62	12	15	27	4	13	3	3	6	4
1996-97 ◆	Detroit Red Wings	49	6	7	13	8	14	3	3	6	2
1997-98 ◆	Detroit Red Wings	80	19	23	42	12	9	4	2	6	0
1998-99	Detroit Red Wings	80	9	19	28	42	10	2	2	4	4
99-2000	Detroit Red Wings	51	10	8	18	12	3	0	1	1	0
2000-01	Detroit Red Wings	60	9	13	22	14	4	0	0	0	2
	NHL Totals	**854**	**160**	**214**	**374**	**210**	**109**	**23**	**23**	**46**	**26**

• Brother of Greg

Signed as a free agent by **New Jersey**, August 6, 1986. Signed as a free agent by **Pittsburgh**, September 28, 1993. Claimed by **Detroit** from **Pittsburgh** in Waiver Draft, January 18, 1995. Claimed by **Nashville** from **Detroit** in Expansion Draft, June 26, 1998. Traded to **Detroit** by **Nashville** for Petr Sykora, Detroit's 3rd round choice (later traded to Edmonton – Edmonton selected Mike Comrie) and 4th round compensatory choice (Alexander Krevsun) in 1999 Entry Draft), July 14, 1998.

BROWN, Fred

Left wing. Shoots left. 5'8", 155 lbs. Born, Kingston, Ont., September 15, 1900.

Season	Club	Regular Season GP	G	A	Pts	PIM	Playoffs GP	G	A	Pts	PIM
1927-28	Montreal Maroons	19	1	0	1	0	9	0	0	0	0
	NHL Totals	**19**	**1**	**0**	**1**	**0**	**9**	**0**	**0**	**0**	**0**

Traded to **Mtl. Maroons** by **Stratford** (Can-Pro) for Bill Touhey with Mtl. Maroons holding right of recall, February 14, 1928. Traded to **Stratford** (Can-Pro) by **Mtl. Maroons** for cash, April 23, 1928.

BROWN, George

Center. Shoots left. 5'11", 185 lbs. Born, Winnipeg, Man., May 17, 1912.

Season	Club	Regular Season GP	G	A	Pts	PIM	Playoffs GP	G	A	Pts	PIM
1936-37	Montreal Canadiens	27	4	6	10	10	4	0	0	0	0
1937-38	Montreal Canadiens	34	1	7	8	14	3	0	0	0	2
1938-39	Montreal Canadiens	18	1	9	10	10	....	....	....	....	....
	NHL Totals	**79**	**6**	**22**	**28**	**34**	**7**	**0**	**0**	**0**	**2**

Rights traded to **Mtl. Maroons** by **NY Rangers** for Eddie Wares, October 30, 1935. Rights traded to **Montreal** by **Mtl. Maroons** for Gerry Carson, October 7, 1936. • Suspended by **Montreal** for refusing assignment to **New Haven** (IAHL), November 26, 1939. Traded to **Boston** by **Montreal** for cash, November 29, 1939.

BROWN, Gerry

Left wing. Shoots left. 5'9", 170 lbs. Born, Edmonton, Alta., July 7, 1917.

Season	Club	Regular Season GP	G	A	Pts	PIM	Playoffs GP	G	A	Pts	PIM
1941-42	Detroit Red Wings	13	4	4	8	0	12	2	1	3	4
1945-46	Detroit Red Wings	10	0	1	1	2	....	....	....	....	....
	NHL Totals	**23**	**4**	**5**	**9**	**2**	**12**	**2**	**1**	**3**	**4**

Signed as a free agent by **Detroit**, October 14, 1941. Traded to **Toronto** by **Detroit** for Doug Baldwin and Ray Powell, September 21, 1946. Traded to **Montreal** (Buffalo-AHL) by **Toronto** (Pittsburgh-AHL) with John Mahaffy for Dutch Hiller and Vic Lynn, September 21, 1946. Traded to **Boston** (Hershey-AHL) by **Montreal** (Buffalo-AHL) with Hal Jackson for Jack McGill, June 30, 1948.

		REGULAR SEASON					PLAYOFFS				
Season	Club	GP	G	A	Pts	PIM	GP	G	A	Pts	PIM

BROWN, Greg

Defense. Shoots right. 6', 185 lbs. Born, Hartford, CT, March 7, 1968.
(Buffalo's 2nd choice, 26th overall, in 1986 Entry Draft).

Season	Club	GP	G	A	Pts	PIM	GP	G	A	Pts	PIM
1990-91	Buffalo Sabres	39	1	2	3	35	....	....	....	....	....
1992-93	Buffalo Sabres	10	0	1	1	6	....	....	....	....	....
1993-94	Pittsburgh Penguins	36	3	8	11	28	6	0	1	1	4
1994-95	Winnipeg Jets	9	0	3	3	17	....	....	....	....	....
	NHL Totals	**94**	**4**	**14**	**18**	**86**	**6**	**0**	**1**	**1**	**4**

• Brother of Doug

Signed as a free agent by **Pittsburgh**, September 29, 1993. Traded to **Winnipeg** by **Pittsburgh** for cash, April 7, 1995.

BROWN, Harold

Right wing. Shoots left. 5'10", 160 lbs. Born, Brandon, Man., September 14, 1920.

Season	Club	GP	G	A	Pts	PIM	GP	G	A	Pts	PIM
1945-46	New York Rangers	13	2	1	3	2	....	....	....	....	....
	NHL Totals	**13**	**2**	**1**	**3**	**2**	....	....	....	....	....

Traded to **St. Paul** (USHL) by **NY Rangers** for cash, October 7, 1947.

BROWN, Jeff

Defense. Shoots right. 6'1", 204 lbs. Born, Ottawa, Ont., April 30, 1966.
(Quebec's 2nd choice, 36th overall, in 1984 Entry Draft).

Season	Club	GP	G	A	Pts	PIM	GP	G	A	Pts	PIM
1985-86	Quebec Nordiques	8	3	2	5	6	1	0	0	0	0
1986-87	Quebec Nordiques	44	7	22	29	16	13	3	3	6	2
1987-88	Quebec Nordiques	78	16	36	52	64	....	....	....	....	....
1988-89	Quebec Nordiques	78	21	47	68	62	....	....	....	....	....
1989-90	Quebec Nordiques	29	6	10	16	18	....	....	....	....	....
	St. Louis Blues	48	10	28	38	37	12	2	10	12	4
1990-91	St. Louis Blues	67	12	47	59	39	13	3	9	12	6
1991-92	St. Louis Blues	80	20	39	59	38	6	2	1	3	2
1992-93	St. Louis Blues	71	25	53	78	58	11	3	8	11	6
1993-94	St. Louis Blues	63	13	47	60	46	....	....	....	....	....
	Vancouver Canucks	11	1	5	6	10	24	6	9	15	37
1994-95	Vancouver Canucks	33	8	23	31	16	5	1	3	4	2
1995-96	Vancouver Canucks	28	1	16	17	18	....	....	....	....	....
	Hartford Whalers	48	7	31	38	38	....	....	....	....	....
1996-97	Hartford Whalers	1	0	0	0	0	....	....	....	....	....
1997-98	Carolina Hurricanes	32	3	10	13	16	....	....	....	....	....
	Toronto Maple Leafs	19	1	8	9	10	....	....	....	....	....
	Washington Capitals	9	0	6	6	6	2	0	2	2	0
	NHL Totals	**747**	**154**	**430**	**584**	**498**	**87**	**20**	**45**	**65**	**59**

Traded to **St. Louis** by **Quebec** for Tony Hrkac and Greg Millen, December 13, 1989. Traded to **Vancouver** by **St. Louis** with Bret Hedican and Nathan LaFayette for Craig Janney, March 21, 1994. Traded to **Hartford** by **Vancouver** with Vancouver's 3rd round choice (later traded to Calgary – Calgary selected Paul Manning) in 1998 Entry Draft for Jim Dowd, Frantisek Kucera and Hartford's 2nd round choice (Ryan Bonni) in 1997 Entry Draft, December 19, 1995. Transferred to **Carolina** after **Hartford** franchise relocated, June 25, 1997. Traded to **Toronto** by **Carolina** for Toronto's 4th round choice (later traded to Nashville – Nashville selected Yevgeny Pavlov) in 1999 Entry Draft, January 2, 1998. Traded to **Washington** by **Toronto** for Sylvain Cote, March 24, 1998.

BROWN, Jim

Defense. Shoots right. 6'4", 210 lbs. Born, Phoenix, AZ, March 1, 1960.
(Los Angeles' 6th choice, 92nd overall, in 1979 Entry Draft).

Season	Club	GP	G	A	Pts	PIM	GP	G	A	Pts	PIM
1982-83	Los Angeles Kings	3	0	1	1	5	....	....	....	....	....
	NHL Totals	**3**	**0**	**1**	**1**	**5**	....	....	....	....	....

BROWN, Keith

Defense. Shoots right. 6'1", 196 lbs. Born, Corner Brook, Nfld., May 6, 1960.
(Chicago's 1st choice, 7th overall, in 1979 Entry Draft).

Season	Club	GP	G	A	Pts	PIM	GP	G	A	Pts	PIM
1979-80	Chicago Black Hawks	76	2	18	20	27	6	0	0	0	4
1980-81	Chicago Black Hawks	80	9	34	43	80	3	0	2	2	2
1981-82	Chicago Black Hawks	33	4	20	24	26	4	0	2	2	5
1982-83	Chicago Black Hawks	50	4	27	31	20	7	0	0	0	11
1983-84	Chicago Black Hawks	74	10	25	35	94	5	0	1	1	10
1984-85	Chicago Black Hawks	56	1	22	23	55	11	2	7	9	31
1985-86	Chicago Black Hawks	70	11	29	40	87	3	0	1	1	9
1986-87	Chicago Blackhawks	73	4	23	27	86	4	0	1	1	6
1987-88	Chicago Blackhawks	24	3	6	9	45	5	0	2	2	10
1988-89	Chicago Blackhawks	74	2	16	18	84	13	1	3	4	25
1989-90	Chicago Blackhawks	67	5	20	25	87	18	0	4	4	43
1990-91	Chicago Blackhawks	45	1	10	11	55	6	1	0	1	8
1991-92	Chicago Blackhawks	57	6	10	16	69	14	0	8	8	18
1992-93	Chicago Blackhawks	33	2	6	8	39	4	0	1	1	2
1993-94	Florida Panthers	51	4	8	12	60	....	....	....	....	....
1994-95	Florida Panthers	13	0	0	0	2	....	....	....	....	....
	NHL Totals	**876**	**68**	**274**	**342**	**916**	**103**	**4**	**32**	**36**	**184**

• Missed majority of 1981-82 season recovering from knee injury suffered in game vs. Philadelphia, December 23, 1981. • Missed majority of 1987-88 season recovering from knee injury suffered in training camp, October, 1987. • Missed majority of 1992-93 season recovering from shoulder surgery, September 27, 1992. Traded to **Florida** by **Chicago** for Darin Kimble, September 30, 1993.

BROWN, Kevin

Right wing. Shoots right. 6'1", 212 lbs. Born, Birmingham, England, May 11, 1974.
(Los Angeles' 3rd choice, 87th overall, in 1992 Entry Draft).

Season	Club	GP	G	A	Pts	PIM	GP	G	A	Pts	PIM
1994-95	Los Angeles Kings	23	2	3	5	18	....	....	....	....	....
1995-96	Los Angeles Kings	7	1	0	1	4	....	....	....	....	....
1996-97	Hartford Whalers	11	0	4	4	6	....	....	....	....	....
1997-98	Carolina Hurricanes	4	0	0	0	0	....	....	....	....	....
1998-99	Edmonton Oilers	12	4	2	6	0	....	....	....	....	....
99-2000	Edmonton Oilers	7	0	0	0	0	1	0	0	0	0
	NHL Totals	**64**	**7**	**9**	**16**	**28**	**1**	**0**	**0**	**0**	**0**

Traded to **Ottawa** by **Los Angeles** for Jaroslav Modry and Ottawa's 8th round choice (Stephen Valiquette) in 1996 Entry Draft, March 20, 1996. Traded to **Anaheim** by **Ottawa** for Mike Maneluk, July 1, 1996. Traded to **Hartford** by **Anaheim** for the rights to Espen Knutsen, October 1, 1996. Transferred to **Carolina** after **Hartford** franchise relocated, June 25, 1997. Signed as a free agent by **Edmonton**, August 14, 1998. Traded to **NY Rangers** by **Edmonton** for Vladimir Vorobiev, March 23, 1999. Signed as a free agent by **Edmonton**, March 7, 2000.

BROWN, Larry

Defense. Shoots left. 6'2", 210 lbs. Born, Brandon, Man., April 14, 1947.

Season	Club	GP	G	A	Pts	PIM	GP	G	A	Pts	PIM
1969-70	New York Rangers	15	0	3	3	8	....	....	....	....	....
1970-71	Detroit Red Wings	33	1	4	5	8	....	....	....	....	....
	New York Rangers	31	1	1	2	10	11	0	1	1	0
1971-72	Philadelphia Flyers	12	0	0	0	2	....	....	....	....	....
1972-73	Los Angeles Kings	55	0	7	7	8	....	....	....	....	....
1973-74	Los Angeles Kings	45	0	4	4	14	2	0	0	0	0
1974-75	Los Angeles Kings	78	1	15	16	50	3	0	2	2	0
1975-76	Los Angeles Kings	74	2	5	7	33	9	0	0	0	2
1976-77	Los Angeles Kings	55	1	6	7	24	9	0	1	1	6
1977-78	Los Angeles Kings	57	1	8	9	23	1	0	0	0	2
	NHL Totals	**455**	**7**	**53**	**60**	**180**	**35**	**0**	**4**	**4**	**10**

Traded to **Detroit** by **NY Rangers** for Pete Stemkowski, October 31, 1970. Traded to **NY Rangers** by **Detroit** with Bruce MacGregor for Arnie Brown, Mike Robitaille and Tom Miller, February 2, 1971. Claimed by **Philadelphia** from **NY Rangers** in Intra-League Draft, June 8, 1971. • Missed majority of 1971-72 season recovering from mononucleosis. Claimed on waivers by **Los Angeles** from **Philadelphia**, January 28, 1972. Claimed by **Edmonton** from **Los Angeles** in Expansion Draft, June 13, 1979.

BROWN, Mike

Left wing. Shoots left. 6'5", 185 lbs. Born, Surrey, B.C., April 27, 1979.
(Florida's 1st choice, 20th overall, in 1997 Entry Draft).

Season	Club	GP	G	A	Pts	PIM	GP	G	A	Pts	PIM
2000-01	Vancouver Canucks	1	0	0	0	5	....	....	....	....	....
2001-02	Vancouver Canucks	15	0	0	0	72	....	....	....	....	....
	NHL Totals	**16**	**0**	**0**	**0**	**77**	....	....	....	....	....

Traded to **Vancouver** by **Florida** with Ed Jovanovski, Dave Gagner, Kevin Weekes and Florida's 1st round choice (Nathan Smith) in 2000 Entry Draft for Pavel Bure, Bret Hedican, Brad Ference and Vancouver's 3rd round choice (Robert Fried) in 2000 Entry Draft, January 17, 1999. Claimed on waivers by **Anaheim** from **Vancouver**, October 11, 2002.

BROWN, Rob

Right wing. Shoots left. 5'10", 177 lbs. Born, Kingston, Ont., April 10, 1968.
(Pittsburgh's 4th choice, 67th overall, in 1986 Entry Draft).

Season	Club	GP	G	A	Pts	PIM	GP	G	A	Pts	PIM
1987-88	Pittsburgh Penguins	51	24	20	44	56	....	....	....	....	....
1988-89	Pittsburgh Penguins	68	49	66	115	118	11	5	3	8	22
1989-90	Pittsburgh Penguins	80	33	47	80	102	....	....	....	....	....
1990-91	Pittsburgh Penguins	25	6	10	16	31	....	....	....	....	....
	Hartford Whalers	44	18	24	42	101	5	1	0	1	7
1991-92	Hartford Whalers	42	16	15	31	39	....	....	....	....	....
	Chicago Blackhawks	25	5	11	16	34	8	2	4	6	4
1992-93	Chicago Blackhawks	15	1	6	7	33	....	....	....	....	....
1993-94	Dallas Stars	1	0	0	0	0	....	....	....	....	....
1994-95	Los Angeles Kings	2	0	0	0	0	....	....	....	....	....
1997-98	Pittsburgh Penguins	82	15	25	40	59	6	1	0	1	4
1998-99	Pittsburgh Penguins	58	13	11	24	16	13	2	5	7	8
99-2000	Pittsburgh Penguins	50	10	13	23	10	11	1	2	3	0
	NHL Totals	**543**	**190**	**248**	**438**	**599**	**54**	**12**	**14**	**26**	**45**

Played in NHL All-Star Game (1989)

Traded to **Hartford** by **Pittsburgh** for Scott Young, December 21, 1990. Traded to **Chicago** by **Hartford** for Steve Konroyd, January 24, 1992. Signed as a free agent by **Dallas**, August 12, 1993. Signed as a free agent by **Los Angeles**, June 14, 1994. Signed as a free agent by **Pittsburgh**, October 1, 1997.

BROWN, Sean

Defense. Shoots left. 6'3", 205 lbs. Born, Oshawa, Ont., November 5, 1976.
(Boston's 2nd choice, 21st overall, in 1995 Entry Draft).

Season	Club	GP	G	A	Pts	PIM	GP	G	A	Pts	PIM
1996-97	Edmonton Oilers	5	0	0	0	4	....	....	....	....	....
1997-98	Edmonton Oilers	18	0	1	1	43	....	....	....	....	....
1998-99	Edmonton Oilers	51	0	7	7	188	1	0	0	0	10
99-2000	Edmonton Oilers	72	4	8	12	192	3	0	0	0	23
2000-01	Edmonton Oilers	62	2	3	5	110	....	....	....	....	....
2001-02	Edmonton Oilers	61	6	4	10	127	....	....	....	....	....
	Boston Bruins	12	0	1	1	47	4	0	0	0	2
2002-03	Boston Bruins	69	1	5	6	117	....	....	....	....	....
	NHL Totals	**350**	**13**	**29**	**42**	**828**	**8**	**0**	**0**	**0**	**35**

Rights traded to **Edmonton** by **Boston** with Mariusz Czerkawski and Boston's 1st round choice (Matthieu Descoteaux) in 1996 Entry Draft for Bill Ranford, January 11, 1996. Traded to **Boston** by **Edmonton** for Bobby Allen, March 19, 2002. Signed as a free agent by **New Jersey**, July 24, 2003.

BROWN, Stan

Defense. Shoots left. 5'10", 150 lbs. Born, North Bay, Ont., May 9, 1898.

Season	Club	GP	G	A	Pts	PIM	GP	G	A	Pts	PIM
1926-27	New York Rangers	24	6	2	8	14	2	0	0	0	0

Season	Club	REGULAR SEASON GP	G	A	Pts	PIM	PLAYOFFS GP	G	A	Pts	PIM
1927-28	Detroit Cougars	24	2	0	2	4	....	....	....	....	....
	NHL Totals	**48**	**8**	**2**	**10**	**18**	**2**	**0**	**0**	**0**	**0**

Signed as a free agent by **NY Rangers** after **Detroit** (AHA) franchise folded, December 23, 1926. Traded to **Detroit** by **NY Rangers** for Harry Meeking and Archie Briden, October 10, 1927. Traded to **Montreal** (Windsor-Can-Pro) by **Detroit** for cash and the loan of Pete Palangio, February 13, 1928.

BROWN, Wayne

Right wing. Shoots left. 5'8", 150 lbs. Born, Deloro, Ont., November 16, 1930.

Season	Club	GP	G	A	Pts	PIM	GP	G	A	Pts	PIM
1953-54	Boston Bruins	....	....	....	....	....	4	0	0	0	2
	NHL Totals	....	....	....	....	....	**4**	**0**	**0**	**0**	**2**

NHL rights traded to **Boston** by **Seattle** (WHL) for cash, October, 1953.

BROWNE, Cecil

Left wing. Shoots left. 6', 165 lbs. Born, St. James, Man., February 13, 1896.

Season	Club	GP	G	A	Pts	PIM	GP	G	A	Pts	PIM
1927-28	Chicago Black Hawks	13	2	0	2	4	....	....	....	....	....
	NHL Totals	**13**	**2**	**0**	**2**	**4**	....	....	....	....	....

Traded to **Chicago** by **Winnipeg** (AHA) with Chuck Gardiner for cash, April 8, 1927.

BROWNSCHIDLE, Jack

Defense. Shoots left. 6'2", 195 lbs. Born, Buffalo, NY, October 2, 1955.
(St. Louis' 5th choice, 99th overall, in 1975 Amateur Draft).

Season	Club	GP	G	A	Pts	PIM	GP	G	A	Pts	PIM
1977-78	St. Louis Blues	40	2	15	17	23	....	....	....	....	....
1978-79	St. Louis Blues	64	10	24	34	14	....	....	....	....	....
1979-80	St. Louis Blues	77	12	32	44	8	3	0	0	0	0
1980-81	St. Louis Blues	71	5	23	28	12	11	0	3	3	2
1981-82	St. Louis Blues	80	5	33	38	26	8	0	2	2	14
1982-83	St. Louis Blues	72	1	22	23	30	4	0	0	0	2
1983-84	St. Louis Blues	51	1	7	8	19	....	....	....	....	....
	Hartford Whalers	13	2	2	4	10	....	....	....	....	....
1984-85	Hartford Whalers	17	1	4	5	5	....	....	....	....	....
1985-86	Hartford Whalers	9	0	0	0	4	....	....	....	....	....
	NHL Totals	**494**	**39**	**162**	**201**	**151**	**26**	**0**	**5**	**5**	**18**

• Brother of Jeff

Claimed on waivers by **Hartford** from **St. Louis**, March 2, 1984.

BROWNSCHIDLE, Jeff

Defense. Shoots right. 6'2", 200 lbs. Born, Buffalo, NY, March 1, 1959.

Season	Club	GP	G	A	Pts	PIM	GP	G	A	Pts	PIM
1981-82	Hartford Whalers	3	0	1	1	2	....	....	....	....	....
1982-83	Hartford Whalers	4	0	0	0	0	....	....	....	....	....
	NHL Totals	**7**	**0**	**1**	**1**	**2**	....	....	....	....	....

• Brother of Jack

Signed as a free agent by **Hartford**, June 9, 1981.

BRUBAKER, Jeff

Left wing. Shoots left. 6'2", 207 lbs. Born, Frederick, MD, February 24, 1958.
(Boston's 6th choice, 102nd overall, in 1978 Amateur Draft).

Season	Club	GP	G	A	Pts	PIM	GP	G	A	Pts	PIM
1979-80	Hartford Whalers	3	0	1	1	2	....	....	....	....	....
1980-81	Hartford Whalers	43	5	3	8	93	....	....	....	....	....
1981-82	Montreal Canadiens	3	0	1	1	32	2	0	0	0	27
1983-84	Calgary Flames	4	0	0	0	19	....	....	....	....	....
1984-85	Toronto Maple Leafs	68	8	4	12	209	....	....	....	....	....
1985-86	Toronto Maple Leafs	21	0	0	0	67	....	....	....	....	....
	Edmonton Oilers	4	1	0	1	12	....	....	....	....	....
1987-88	New York Rangers	31	2	0	2	78	....	....	....	....	....
1988-89	Detroit Red Wings	1	0	0	0	0	....	....	....	....	....
	NHL Totals	**178**	**16**	**9**	**25**	**512**	**2**	**0**	**0**	**0**	**27**

NHL rights retained by **Hartford** prior to Expansion Draft, June 9, 1979. Claimed by **Montreal** from **Hartford** in Waiver Draft, October 5, 1981. Claimed by **Quebec** from **Montreal** in Waiver Draft, October 3, 1983. Claimed by **Calgary** from **Quebec** in Waiver Draft, October 3, 1983. Signed as a free agent by **Edmonton**, June 21, 1984. Claimed by **Toronto** from **Edmonton** in Waiver Draft, October 9, 1984. Claimed on waivers by **Edmonton** from **Toronto**, December 5, 1985. Traded to **Philadelphia** by **Edmonton** for Dom Campedelli, March 9, 1987. Traded to **NY Rangers** by **Philadelphia** for cash, July 21, 1987. Signed as a free agent by **Detroit**, October, 1988.

BRUCE, David

Left wing. Shoots right. 5'11", 190 lbs. Born, Thunder Bay, Ont., October 7, 1964.
(Vancouver's 2nd choice, 30th overall, in 1983 Entry Draft).

Season	Club	GP	G	A	Pts	PIM	GP	G	A	Pts	PIM
1985-86	Vancouver Canucks	12	0	1	1	14	1	0	0	0	0
1986-87	Vancouver Canucks	50	9	7	16	109	....	....	....	....	....
1987-88	Vancouver Canucks	28	7	3	10	57	....	....	....	....	....
1988-89	Vancouver Canucks	53	7	7	14	65	....	....	....	....	....
1990-91	St. Louis Blues	12	1	2	3	14	2	0	0	0	2
1991-92	San Jose Sharks	60	22	16	38	46	....	....	....	....	....
1992-93	San Jose Sharks	17	2	3	5	33	....	....	....	....	....
1993-94	San Jose Sharks	2	0	0	0	0	....	....	....	....	....
	NHL Totals	**234**	**48**	**39**	**87**	**338**	**3**	**0**	**0**	**0**	**2**

Signed as a free agent by **St. Louis**, July 6, 1990. Claimed by **San Jose** from **St. Louis** in Expansion Draft, May 30, 1991.

BRUCE, Gordie

Left wing. Shoots left. 5'11", 190 lbs. Born, Ottawa, Ont., May 9, 1919.

Season	Club	GP	G	A	Pts	PIM	GP	G	A	Pts	PIM
1940-41	Boston Bruins	8	0	1	1	2	2	0	0	0	0
1941-42	Boston Bruins	15	4	8	12	11	5	2	3	5	4
1945-46	Boston Bruins	5	0	0	0	0	....	....	....	....	....
	NHL Totals	**28**	**4**	**9**	**13**	**13**	**7**	**2**	**3**	**5**	**4**

Signed as a free agent by **Boston**, October 24, 1939.

BRUCE, Morley

Defense/Center. Shoots right. 5'9", 170 lbs. Born, North Gower, Ont., March 7, 1894.

Season	Club	GP	G	A	Pts	PIM	GP	G	A	Pts	PIM
1917-18	Ottawa Senators	7	0	0	0	0	....	....	....	....	....
1919-20 ♦	Ottawa Senators	21	1	1	2	2	....	....	....	....	....
	Ottawa Senators (Cup)	....	....	....	....	....	*5*	*0*	*0*	*0*	*0*
1920-21 ♦	Ottawa Senators	21	3	1	4	23	2	0	0	0	2
1921-22	Ottawa Senators	22	4	1	5	2	1	0	0	0	0
	NHL Totals	**71**	**8**	**3**	**11**	**27**	**3**	**0**	**0**	**0**	**2**

Signed as a free agent by **Ottawa**, December 7, 1917.

BRULE, Steve

Right wing. Shoots right. 6', 200 lbs. Born, Montreal, Que., January 15, 1975.
(New Jersey's 6th choice, 143rd overall, in 1993 Entry Draft).

Season	Club	GP	G	A	Pts	PIM	GP	G	A	Pts	PIM
99-2000 ♦	New Jersey Devils	....	....	....	....	....	1	0	0	0	0
2002-03	Colorado Avalanche	2	0	0	0	0	....	....	....	....	....
	NHL Totals	**2**	**0**	**0**	**0**	**0**	**1**	**0**	**0**	**0**	**0**

Signed as a free agent by **Detroit**, July 20, 2000. Signed as a free agent by **Colorado**, July 22, 2002.

BRUMWELL, Murray

Defense. Shoots left. 6'2", 190 lbs. Born, Calgary, Alta., March 31, 1960.

Season	Club	GP	G	A	Pts	PIM	GP	G	A	Pts	PIM
1980-81	Minnesota North Stars	1	0	0	0	0	....	....	....	....	....
1981-82	Minnesota North Stars	21	0	3	3	18	2	0	0	0	2
1982-83	New Jersey Devils	59	5	14	19	34	....	....	....	....	....
1983-84	New Jersey Devils	42	7	13	20	14	....	....	....	....	....
1985-86	New Jersey Devils	1	0	0	0	0	....	....	....	....	....
1986-87	New Jersey Devils	1	0	0	0	2	....	....	....	....	....
1987-88	New Jersey Devils	3	0	1	1	2	....	....	....	....	....
	NHL Totals	**128**	**12**	**31**	**43**	**70**	**2**	**0**	**0**	**0**	**2**

Signed as a free agent by **Minnesota**, August 7, 1980. Claimed by **New Jersey** from **Minnesota** in Waiver Draft, October 4, 1982.

BRUNET, Benoit

Left wing. Shoots left. 6', 203 lbs. Born, Ste-Anne-de-Bellevue, Que., August 24, 1968.
(Montreal's 2nd choice, 27th overall, in 1986 Entry Draft).

Season	Club	GP	G	A	Pts	PIM	GP	G	A	Pts	PIM
1988-89	Montreal Canadiens	2	0	1	1	0	....	....	....	....	....
1990-91	Montreal Canadiens	17	1	3	4	0	....	....	....	....	....
1991-92	Montreal Canadiens	18	4	6	10	14	....	....	....	....	....
1992-93 ♦	Montreal Canadiens	47	10	15	25	19	20	2	8	10	8
1993-94	Montreal Canadiens	71	10	20	30	20	7	1	4	5	16
1994-95	Montreal Canadiens	45	7	18	25	16	....	....	....	....	....
1995-96	Montreal Canadiens	26	7	8	15	17	3	0	2	2	0
1996-97	Montreal Canadiens	39	10	13	23	14	4	1	3	4	4
1997-98	Montreal Canadiens	68	12	20	32	61	8	1	0	1	4
1998-99	Montreal Canadiens	60	14	17	31	31	....	....	....	....	....
99-2000	Montreal Canadiens	50	14	15	29	13	....	....	....	....	....
2000-01	Montreal Canadiens	35	3	11	14	12	....	....	....	....	....
2001-02	Montreal Canadiens	16	0	2	2	4	....	....	....	....	....
	Dallas Stars	32	4	9	13	8	....	....	....	....	....
	Ottawa Senators	13	5	3	8	0	12	0	3	3	0
	NHL Totals	**539**	**101**	**161**	**262**	**229**	**54**	**5**	**20**	**25**	**32**

• Missed majority of 2000-01 season recovering from knee injury suffered in game vs. Pittsburgh, December 16, 2000. Traded to **Dallas** by **Montreal** with Martin Rucinsky for Donald Audette and Shaun Van Allen, November 21, 2001. Traded to **Ottawa** by **Dallas** for Ottawa's 6th round choice (Elias Granath) in 2003 Entry Draft, March 16, 2002.

BRUNETEAU, Eddie

Right wing. Shoots right. 5'9", 172 lbs. Born, St. Boniface, Man., August 1, 1919.

Season	Club	GP	G	A	Pts	PIM	GP	G	A	Pts	PIM
1940-41	Detroit Red Wings	11	1	1	2	2	3	0	0	0	0
1943-44	Detroit Red Wings	2	0	1	1	0	....	....	....	....	....
1944-45	Detroit Red Wings	42	12	13	25	6	14	5	2	7	0
1945-46	Detroit Red Wings	46	17	12	29	11	4	1	0	1	0
1946-47	Detroit Red Wings	60	9	14	23	14	4	1	4	5	0
1947-48	Detroit Red Wings	18	1	1	2	2	6	0	0	0	0
1948-49	Detroit Red Wings	1	0	0	0	0	....	....	....	....	....
	NHL Totals	**180**	**40**	**42**	**82**	**35**	**31**	**7**	**6**	**13**	**0**

• Brother of Mud

Traded to **Detroit** by **Duluth** (USHL) for cash, October 2, 1939. Signed as a free agent by **Quebec** (QSHL), November 13, 1941. Traded to **Detroit** by **Quebec** (QSHL) for Bob Thorpe, November 16, 1944.

BRUNETEAU, Mud

Right wing. Shoots right. 5'11", 185 lbs. Born, St. Boniface, Man., November 28, 1914.

Season	Club	GP	G	A	Pts	PIM	GP	G	A	Pts	PIM
1935-36 ♦	Detroit Red Wings	24	2	0	2	2	7	2	2	4	4
1936-37 ♦	Detroit Red Wings	42	9	7	16	18	10	2	0	2	6
1937-38	Detroit Red Wings	24	3	6	9	16	....	....	....	....	....
1938-39	Detroit Red Wings	20	3	7	10	0	6	0	0	0	0
1939-40	Detroit Red Wings	48	10	14	24	10	5	3	2	5	0
1940-41	Detroit Red Wings	45	11	17	28	12	9	2	1	3	2

Season	Club	GP	G	A	Pts	PIM	GP	G	A	Pts	PIM
		REGULAR SEASON					PLAYOFFS				
1941-42	Detroit Red Wings	48	14	19	33	8	12	5	1	6	6
1942-43 ◆	Detroit Red Wings	50	23	22	45	2	9	5	4	9	0
1943-44	Detroit Red Wings	39	35	18	53	4	5	1	2	3	2
1944-45	Detroit Red Wings	43	23	24	47	6	14	3	2	5	2
1945-46	Detroit Red Wings	28	6	4	10	2	....	....	....	....	....
	NHL Totals	**411**	**139**	**138**	**277**	**80**	**77**	**23**	**14**	**37**	**22**

• Brother of Eddie

BRUNETTE, Andrew

Left wing. Shoots left. 6'1", 210 lbs. Born, Sudbury, Ont., August 24, 1973.
(Washington's 6th choice, 174th overall, in 1993 Entry Draft).

Season	Club	GP	G	A	Pts	PIM	GP	G	A	Pts	PIM
1995-96	Washington Capitals	11	3	3	6	0	6	1	3	4	0
1996-97	Washington Capitals	23	4	7	11	12	....	....	....	....	....
1997-98	Washington Capitals	28	11	12	23	12	....	....	....	....	....
1998-99	Nashville Predators	77	11	20	31	26	....	....	....	....	....
99-2000	Atlanta Thrashers	81	23	27	50	30	....	....	....	....	....
2000-01	Atlanta Thrashers	77	15	44	59	26	....	....	....	....	....
2001-02	Minnesota Wild	81	21	48	69	18	....	....	....	....	....
2002-03	Minnesota Wild	82	18	28	46	30	18	7	6	13	4
	NHL Totals	**460**	**106**	**189**	**295**	**154**	**24**	**8**	**9**	**17**	**4**

Claimed by **Nashville** from **Washington** in Expansion Draft, June 26, 1998. Traded to **Atlanta** by **Nashville** for Atlanta's 5th round choice (Matt Hendricks) in 2000 Entry Draft, June 21, 1999. Signed as a free agent by **Minnesota**, July 17, 2001.

BRYDGE, Bill

Defense. Shoots right. 5'9", 195 lbs. Born, Renfrew, Ont., October 22, 1901.

Season	Club	GP	G	A	Pts	PIM	GP	G	A	Pts	PIM
1926-27	Toronto St. Pats/Maple Leafs	41	6	3	9	76	....	....	....	....	....
1928-29	Detroit Cougars	31	2	2	4	59	2	0	0	0	4
1929-30	New York Americans	41	2	6	8	64	....	....	....	....	....
1930-31	New York Americans	43	2	5	7	70	....	....	....	....	....
1931-32	New York Americans	48	2	8	10	77	....	....	....	....	....
1932-33	New York Americans	48	4	15	19	60	....	....	....	....	....
1933-34	New York Americans	48	6	7	13	44	....	....	....	....	....
1934-35	New York Americans	47	2	6	8	29	....	....	....	....	....
1935-36	New York Americans	21	0	0	0	27	....	....	....	....	....
	NHL Totals	**368**	**26**	**52**	**78**	**506**	**2**	**0**	**0**	**0**	**4**

Signed as a free agent by **Toronto**, October 13, 1926. Traded to **Detroit** by **Toronto** for Art Duncan, May 16, 1927. Traded to **NY Americans** by **Detroit** for $5,000, November 22, 1929.

BRYDGES, Paul

Center. Shoots right. 5'11", 180 lbs. Born, Guelph, Ont., June 21, 1965.

Season	Club	GP	G	A	Pts	PIM	GP	G	A	Pts	PIM
1986-87	Buffalo Sabres	15	2	2	4	6	....	....	....	....	....
	NHL Totals	**15**	**2**	**2**	**4**	**6**	....	....	....	....	....

Signed as a free agent by **Buffalo**, June 11, 1986.

BRYDSON, Glenn

Right wing. Shoots right. 5'10", 170 lbs. Born, Swansea, Ont., November 7, 1910.

Season	Club	GP	G	A	Pts	PIM	GP	G	A	Pts	PIM
1930-31	Montreal Maroons	14	0	0	0	4	2	0	0	0	0
1931-32	Montreal Maroons	47	12	13	25	44	4	0	0	0	4
1932-33	Montreal Maroons	48	11	17	28	26	2	0	0	0	0
1933-34	Montreal Maroons	37	4	5	9	19	1	0	0	0	0
1934-35	St. Louis Eagles	48	11	18	29	45	....	....	....	....	....
1935-36	New York Rangers	30	4	12	16	7	....	....	....	....	....
	Chicago Black Hawks	22	6	4	10	32	2	0	0	0	4
1936-37	Chicago Black Hawks	34	7	7	14	20	....	....	....	....	....
1937-38	Chicago Black Hawks	19	1	3	4	6	....	....	....	....	....
	NHL Totals	**299**	**56**	**79**	**135**	**203**	**11**	**0**	**0**	**0**	**8**

• Brother of Gord

Signed as a free agent by **Mtl. Maroons**, February 4, 1931. Traded to **Ottawa** by **Mtl. Maroons** to complete transaction that sent Alex Connell to Montreal (October 2, 1934), October 22, 1934. Transferred to **St. Louis** after **Ottawa** franchise relocated, September 22, 1934. Claimed by **NY Rangers** from **St. Louis** in Dispersal Draft, October 15, 1935. Traded to **Chicago** by **NY Rangers** for Howie Morenz, January 26, 1936. Traded to **NY Americans** (New Haven-AHL) by **Chicago** for cash, January 9, 1938. • Team name changed to **Brooklyn Americans** prior to 1941-42 season. Traded to **Toronto** (Pittsburgh-AHL) by **Brooklyn** with Viv Allen for Phil McAtee and the return of Peanuts O'Flaherty (previously on loan), October 8, 1941.

BRYDSON, Gord

Center/Right wing. Shoots right. 5'7", 150 lbs. Born, Toronto, Ont., January 3, 1907.

Season	Club	GP	G	A	Pts	PIM	GP	G	A	Pts	PIM
1929-30	Toronto Maple Leafs	8	2	0	2	8	....	....	....	....	....
	NHL Totals	**8**	**2**	**0**	**2**	**8**	....	....	....	....	....

• Brother of Glenn

Traded to **Toronto** by **Buffalo** (IHL) for Carl Voss and Wes King, October 10, 1929. Traded to **London** (IHL) by **Toronto** for cash, December 6, 1929.

BRYLIN, Sergei

Center. Shoots left. 5'10", 190 lbs. Born, Moscow, USSR, January 13, 1974.
(New Jersey's 2nd choice, 42nd overall, in 1992 Entry Draft).

Season	Club	GP	G	A	Pts	PIM	GP	G	A	Pts	PIM
1994-95 ◆	New Jersey Devils	26	6	8	14	8	12	1	2	3	4
1995-96	New Jersey Devils	50	4	5	9	26	....	....	....	....	....
1996-97	New Jersey Devils	29	2	2	4	20	....	....	....	....	....
1997-98	New Jersey Devils	18	2	3	5	0	....	....	....	....	....
1998-99	New Jersey Devils	47	5	10	15	28	5	3	1	4	4
99-2000 ◆	New Jersey Devils	64	9	11	20	20	17	3	5	8	0
2000-01	New Jersey Devils	75	23	29	52	24	20	3	4	7	6
2001-02	New Jersey Devils	76	16	28	44	10	6	0	2	2	2
2002-03 ◆	New Jersey Devils	52	11	8	19	16	19	1	3	4	8
	NHL Totals	**437**	**78**	**104**	**182**	**152**	**79**	**11**	**17**	**28**	**24**

BUBLA, Jiri

Defense. Shoots left. 5'11", 200 lbs. Born, Usti nad Labem, Czech., January 27, 1950.

Season	Club	GP	G	A	Pts	PIM	GP	G	A	Pts	PIM
1981-82	Vancouver Canucks	23	1	1	2	16	....	....	....	....	....
1982-83	Vancouver Canucks	72	2	28	30	59	1	0	0	0	5
1983-84	Vancouver Canucks	62	6	33	39	43	2	0	0	0	0
1984-85	Vancouver Canucks	56	2	15	17	54	....	....	....	....	....
1985-86	Vancouver Canucks	43	6	24	30	30	3	0	0	0	2
	NHL Totals	**256**	**17**	**101**	**118**	**202**	**6**	**0**	**0**	**0**	**7**

• Father of Jiri Slegr

Claimed in Special Czechoslovakian Entry Draft by **Colorado**, May 28, 1981. Signed to a contract by **Vancouver**, June, 1981. • Colorado received Brent Ashton and Vancouver's 4th round choice (Tom Martin) in 1982 Entry Draft as compensation via earlier Vancouver/Winnipeg transaction involving Lucien Deblois, July 15, 1981.

BUCHANAN, Al

Left wing. Shoots left. 5'8", 160 lbs. Born, Winnipeg, Man., May 17, 1927.

Season	Club	GP	G	A	Pts	PIM	GP	G	A	Pts	PIM
1948-49	Toronto Maple Leafs	3	0	1	1	2	....	....	....	....	....
1949-50	Toronto Maple Leafs	1	0	0	0	0	....	....	....	....	....
	NHL Totals	**4**	**0**	**1**	**1**	**2**	....	....	....	....	....

BUCHANAN, Bucky

Center/Right wing. Shoots right. 5'9", 172 lbs. Born, Bout-de-L'Isle, Que., December 28, 1922.

Season	Club	GP	G	A	Pts	PIM	GP	G	A	Pts	PIM
1948-49	New York Rangers	2	0	0	0	0	....	....	....	....	....
	NHL Totals	**2**	**0**	**0**	**0**	**0**	....	....	....	....	....

• Father of Ron

BUCHANAN, Jeff

Defense. Shoots right. 6'2", 200 lbs. Born, Swift Current, Sask., May 23, 1971.

Season	Club	GP	G	A	Pts	PIM	GP	G	A	Pts	PIM
1998-99	Colorado Avalanche	6	0	0	0	6	....	....	....	....	....
	NHL Totals	**6**	**0**	**0**	**0**	**6**	....	....	....	....	....

Signed as a free agent by **Tampa Bay**, July 13, 1992. Traded to **Chicago** by **Tampa Bay** with Jim Cummins and Tom Tilley for Paul Ysebaert and Rich Sutter, February 22, 1995. Signed as a free agent by **Colorado**, August 25, 1998. • Officially announced retirement to accept position as Financial Consultant, August, 1999.

BUCHANAN, Mike

Defense. Shoots left. 6'1", 185 lbs. Born, Sault Ste. Marie, Ont., March 1, 1932.

Season	Club	GP	G	A	Pts	PIM	GP	G	A	Pts	PIM
1951-52	Chicago Black Hawks	1	0	0	0	0	....	....	....	....	....
	NHL Totals	**1**	**0**	**0**	**0**	**0**	....	....	....	....	....

BUCHANAN, Ron

Center. Shoots left. 6'3", 170 lbs. Born, Montreal, Que., November 15, 1944.

Season	Club	GP	G	A	Pts	PIM	GP	G	A	Pts	PIM
1966-67	Boston Bruins	3	0	0	0	0	....	....	....	....	....
1969-70	St. Louis Blues	2	0	0	0	0	....	....	....	....	....
	NHL Totals	**5**	**0**	**0**	**0**	**0**	....	....	....	....	....

• Son of Bucky

Claimed by **Philadelphia** from **Boston** in Intra-League Draft, June 12, 1968. Traded to **St. Louis** by **Philadelphia** for cash, May 14, 1969.

BUCHBERGER, Kelly

Right wing. Shoots left. 6'2", 210 lbs. Born, Langenburg, Sask., December 2, 1966.
(Edmonton's 8th choice, 188th overall, in 1985 Entry Draft).

Season	Club	GP	G	A	Pts	PIM	GP	G	A	Pts	PIM
1986-87 ◆	Edmonton Oilers	....	....	....	....	....	3	0	1	1	5
1987-88	Edmonton Oilers	19	1	0	1	81	....	....	....	....	....
1988-89	Edmonton Oilers	66	5	9	14	234	....	....	....	....	....
1989-90 ◆	Edmonton Oilers	55	2	6	8	168	19	0	5	5	13
1990-91	Edmonton Oilers	64	3	1	4	160	12	2	1	3	25
1991-92	Edmonton Oilers	79	20	24	44	157	16	1	4	5	32
1992-93	Edmonton Oilers	83	12	18	30	133	....	....	....	....	....
1993-94	Edmonton Oilers	84	3	18	21	199	....	....	....	....	....
1994-95	Edmonton Oilers	48	7	17	24	82	....	....	....	....	....
1995-96	Edmonton Oilers	82	11	14	25	184	....	....	....	....	....
1996-97	Edmonton Oilers	81	8	30	38	159	12	5	2	7	16
1997-98	Edmonton Oilers	82	6	17	23	122	12	1	2	3	25
1998-99	Edmonton Oilers	52	4	4	8	68	4	0	0	0	0
99-2000	Atlanta Thrashers	68	5	12	17	139	....	....	....	....	....
	Los Angeles Kings	13	2	1	3	13	4	0	0	0	4
2000-01	Los Angeles Kings	82	6	14	20	75	8	1	0	1	2
2001-02	Los Angeles Kings	74	6	7	13	105	7	0	0	0	7
2002-03	Phoenix Coyotes	79	3	9	12	109	....	....	....	....	....
	NHL Totals	**1111**	**104**	**201**	**305**	**2188**	**97**	**10**	**15**	**25**	**129**

Claimed by **Atlanta** from **Edmonton** in Expansion Draft, June 25, 1999. Traded to **Los Angeles** by **Atlanta** with Nelson Emerson for Donald Audette and Frantisek Kaberle, March 13, 2000. Signed as a free agent by **Phoenix**, July 7, 2002.

BUCYK, John

HHOF

Left wing. Shoots left. 6', 215 lbs. Born, Edmonton, Alta., May 12, 1935.

Season	Club	GP	G	A	Pts	PIM	GP	G	A	Pts	PIM
1955-56	Detroit Red Wings	38	1	8	9	20	10	1	1	2	8

Season	Club	GP	G	A	Pts	PIM	GP	G	A	Pts	PIM
		REGULAR SEASON					PLAYOFFS				
1956-57	Detroit Red Wings	66	10	11	21	41	5	0	1	1	0
1957-58	Boston Bruins	68	21	31	52	57	12	0	4	4	16
1958-59	Boston Bruins	69	24	36	60	36	7	2	4	6	6
1959-60	Boston Bruins	56	16	36	52	26	....	....	....	....	....
1960-61	Boston Bruins	70	19	20	39	48	....	....	....	....	....
1961-62	Boston Bruins	67	20	40	60	32	....	....	....	....	....
1962-63	Boston Bruins	69	27	39	66	36	....	....	....	....	....
1963-64	Boston Bruins	62	18	36	54	36	....	....	....	....	....
1964-65	Boston Bruins	68	26	29	55	24	....	....	....	....	....
1965-66	Boston Bruins	63	27	30	57	12	....	....	....	....	....
1966-67	Boston Bruins	59	18	30	48	12	....	....	....	....	....
1967-68	Boston Bruins	72	30	39	69	8	3	0	2	2	0
1968-69	Boston Bruins	70	24	42	66	18	10	5	6	11	0
1969-70 ♦	Boston Bruins	76	31	38	69	13	14	11	8	19	2
1970-71	Boston Bruins	78	51	65	116	8	7	2	5	7	0
1971-72 ♦	Boston Bruins	78	32	51	83	4	15	9	11	20	6
1972-73	Boston Bruins	78	40	53	93	12	5	0	3	3	0
1973-74	Boston Bruins	76	31	44	75	8	16	8	10	18	4
1974-75	Boston Bruins	78	29	52	81	10	3	1	0	1	0
1975-76	Boston Bruins	77	36	47	83	20	12	2	7	9	0
1976-77	Boston Bruins	49	20	23	43	12	5	0	0	0	0
1977-78	Boston Bruins	53	5	13	18	4	....	....	....	....	....
	NHL Totals	**1540**	**556**	**813**	**1369**	**497**	**124**	**41**	**62**	**103**	**42**

NHL Second All-Star Team (1968) • NHL First All-Star Team (1971) • Lady Byng Trophy (1971, 1974) • Lester Patrick Trophy (1977)

Played in NHL All-Star Game (1955, 1963, 1964, 1965, 1968, 1970, 1971)

Traded to **Boston** by **Detroit** with cash for Terry Sawchuk, June 10, 1957.

BUCYK, Randy

Center. Shoots left. 5'11", 185 lbs. Born, Edmonton, Alta., November 9, 1962.

Season	Club	GP	G	A	Pts	PIM	GP	G	A	Pts	PIM
1985-86	Montreal Canadiens	17	4	2	6	8	2	0	0	0	0
1987-88	Calgary Flames	2	0	0	0	0	....	....	....	....	....
	NHL Totals	**19**	**4**	**2**	**6**	**8**	**2**	**0**	**0**	**0**	**0**

Signed as a free agent by **Montreal**, January 15, 1986. Signed as a free agent by **Calgary**, June 29, 1987.

BUHR, Doug

Left wing. Shoots left. 6'3", 215 lbs. Born, Vancouver, B.C., June 29, 1949.

Season	Club	GP	G	A	Pts	PIM	GP	G	A	Pts	PIM
1974-75	Kansas City Scouts	6	0	2	2	4	....	....	....	....	....
	NHL Totals	**6**	**0**	**2**	**2**	**4**	....	....	....	....	....

Signed as a free agent by **Los Angeles**, October 2, 1972. Traded to **Kansas City** by **Los Angeles** for cash, February, 1975.

BUKOVICH, Tony

Left wing/Center. Shoots left. 5'11", 160 lbs. Born, Painesdale, MI, August 30, 1917.

Season	Club	GP	G	A	Pts	PIM	GP	G	A	Pts	PIM
1943-44	Detroit Red Wings	3	0	1	1	0	....	....	....	....	....
1944-45	Detroit Red Wings	14	7	2	9	6	6	0	1	1	0
	NHL Totals	**17**	**7**	**3**	**10**	**6**	**6**	**0**	**1**	**1**	**0**

BULIS, Jan

Center. Shoots left. 6'2", 201 lbs. Born, Pardubice, Czech., March 18, 1978.
(Washington's 3rd choice, 43rd overall, in 1996 Entry Draft).

Season	Club	GP	G	A	Pts	PIM	GP	G	A	Pts	PIM
1997-98	Washington Capitals	48	5	11	16	18	....	....	....	....	....
1998-99	Washington Capitals	38	7	16	23	6	....	....	....	....	....
99-2000	Washington Capitals	56	9	22	31	30	....	....	....	....	....
2000-01	Washington Capitals	39	5	13	18	26	....	....	....	....	....
	Montreal Canadiens	12	0	5	5	0	....	....	....	....	....
2001-02	Montreal Canadiens	53	9	10	19	8	6	0	0	0	6
2002-03	Montreal Canadiens	82	16	24	40	30	....	....	....	....	....
	NHL Totals	**328**	**51**	**101**	**152**	**118**	**6**	**0**	**0**	**0**	**6**

Traded to **Montreal** by **Washington** with Richard Zednik and Washington's 1st round choice (Alexander Perezhogin) in 2001 Entry Draft for Trevor Linden, Dainius Zubrus and New Jersey's 2nd round choice (previously acquired, later traded to Tampa Bay – Tampa Bay selected Andreas Holmqvist) in 2001 Entry Draft, March 13, 2001.

BULLARD, Mike

Center. Shoots left. 6', 195 lbs. Born, Ottawa, Ont., March 10, 1961.
(Pittsburgh's 1st choice, 9th overall, in 1980 Entry Draft).

Season	Club	GP	G	A	Pts	PIM	GP	G	A	Pts	PIM
1980-81	Pittsburgh Penguins	15	1	2	3	19	4	3	3	6	0
1981-82	Pittsburgh Penguins	75	36	27	63	91	5	1	1	2	4
1982-83	Pittsburgh Penguins	57	22	22	44	60	....	....	....	....	....
1983-84	Pittsburgh Penguins	76	51	41	92	57	....	....	....	....	....
1984-85	Pittsburgh Penguins	68	32	31	63	75	....	....	....	....	....
1985-86	Pittsburgh Penguins	77	41	42	83	69	....	....	....	....	....
1986-87	Pittsburgh Penguins	14	2	10	12	17	....	....	....	....	....
	Calgary Flames	57	28	26	54	34	6	4	3	7	2
1987-88	Calgary Flames	79	48	55	103	68	6	0	2	2	6
1988-89	St. Louis Blues	20	4	12	16	46	....	....	....	....	....
	Philadelphia Flyers	54	23	26	49	60	19	3	9	12	32
1989-90	Philadelphia Flyers	70	27	37	64	67	....	....	....	....	....
1991-92	Toronto Maple Leafs	65	14	14	28	40	....	....	....	....	....
	NHL Totals	**727**	**329**	**345**	**674**	**703**	**40**	**11**	**18**	**29**	**44**

Played in NHL All-Star Game (1984)

Traded to **Calgary** by **Pittsburgh** for Dan Quinn, November 12, 1986. Traded to **St. Louis** by **Calgary** with Craig Coxe and Tim Corkery for Mark Hunter, Doug Gilmour, Steve Bozek and Michael Dark, September 6, 1988. Traded to **Philadelphia** by **St. Louis** for Peter Zezel, November 29, 1988. Rights traded to **Toronto** by **Philadelphia** for Toronto's 3rd round choice (Vaclav Prospal) in 1993 Entry Draft, July 29, 1991.

BULLER, Hy

Defense. Shoots left. 5'11", 183 lbs. Born, Montreal, Que., March 15, 1926.

Season	Club	GP	G	A	Pts	PIM	GP	G	A	Pts	PIM
1943-44	Detroit Red Wings	7	0	3	3	4	....	....	....	....	....
1944-45	Detroit Red Wings	2	0	0	0	2	....	....	....	....	....
1951-52	New York Rangers	68	12	23	35	96	....	....	....	....	....
1952-53	New York Rangers	70	7	18	25	73	....	....	....	....	....
1953-54	New York Rangers	41	3	14	17	40	....	....	....	....	....
	NHL Totals	**188**	**22**	**58**	**80**	**215**	....	....	....	....	....

NHL Second All-Star Team (1952)

Played in NHL All-Star Game (1952)

Claimed on waivers by **Hershey** (AHL) from **Detroit**, October 22, 1944. Traded to **Cleveland** (AHL) by **Hershey** (AHL) for Babe Pratt and Joe Cooper, December 24, 1947. Traded to **NY Rangers** by **Cleveland** (AHL) with Wally Hergesheimer for Ed Reigle, Jackie Gordon, Fred Shero, Fern Perreault and cash, May 14, 1951. Traded to **Montreal** (Victoria-WHL) by **NY Rangers** for Dick Gamble and the rights to Eddie Dorohoy with Montreal holding right of recall if Dorohoy failed to make NY Rangers roster, June 8, 1954. Transaction cancelled after Buller retired, September, 1954.

BULLEY, Ted

Left wing. Shoots left. 6'1", 192 lbs. Born, Windsor, Ont., March 25, 1955.
(Chicago's 7th choice, 115th overall, in 1975 Amateur Draft).

Season	Club	GP	G	A	Pts	PIM	GP	G	A	Pts	PIM
1976-77	Chicago Black Hawks	2	0	0	0	0	....	....	....	....	....
1977-78	Chicago Black Hawks	79	23	28	51	141	4	1	1	2	2
1978-79	Chicago Black Hawks	75	27	23	50	153	2	0	0	0	0
1979-80	Chicago Black Hawks	66	14	17	31	136	7	2	3	5	10
1980-81	Chicago Black Hawks	68	18	16	34	95	....	....	....	....	....
1981-82	Chicago Black Hawks	59	12	18	30	120	15	2	1	3	12
1982-83	Washington Capitals	39	4	9	13	47	1	0	0	0	0
1983-84	Pittsburgh Penguins	26	3	2	5	12	....	....	....	....	....
	NHL Totals	**414**	**101**	**113**	**214**	**704**	**29**	**5**	**5**	**10**	**24**

Traded to **Washington** by **Chicago** with Dave Hutchinson for Washington's 6th round choice (Jari Torkki) in 1983 Entry Draft and Washington's 5th round choice (Darin Sceviour) in 1984 Entry Draft, August 24, 1982. Signed as a free agent by **Pittsburgh**, September 30, 1983.

BURAKOVSKY, Robert

Right wing. Shoots right. 5'10", 185 lbs. Born, Malmo, Sweden, November 24, 1966.
(NY Rangers' 11th choice, 217th overall, in 1985 Entry Draft).

Season	Club	GP	G	A	Pts	PIM	GP	G	A	Pts	PIM
1993-94	Ottawa Senators	23	2	3	5	6	....	....	....	....	....
	NHL Totals	**23**	**2**	**3**	**5**	**6**	....	....	....	....	....

Rights traded to **Ottawa** by **NY Rangers** for future considerations, May 7, 1993

BURCH, Billy

HHOF

Center/Left wing. Shoots left. 6', 200 lbs. Born, Yonkers, NY, November 20, 1900.

Season	Club	GP	G	A	Pts	PIM	GP	G	A	Pts	PIM
1922-23	Hamilton Tigers	10	6	3	9	4	....	....	....	....	....
1923-24	Hamilton Tigers	24	16	6	22	6	....	....	....	....	....
1924-25	Hamilton Tigers	27	20	7	27	10	....	....	....	....	....
1925-26	New York Americans	36	22	3	25	33	....	....	....	....	....
1926-27	New York Americans	43	19	8	27	40	....	....	....	....	....
1927-28	New York Americans	32	10	2	12	34	....	....	....	....	....
1928-29	New York Americans	44	11	5	16	45	2	0	0	0	0
1929-30	New York Americans	35	7	3	10	22	....	....	....	....	....
1930-31	New York Americans	44	14	8	22	35	....	....	....	....	....
1931-32	New York Americans	48	7	15	22	20	....	....	....	....	....
1932-33	Boston Bruins	23	3	1	4	4	....	....	....	....	....
	Chicago Black Hawks	24	2	0	2	2	....	....	....	....	....
	NHL Totals	**390**	**137**	**61**	**198**	**255**	**2**	**0**	**0**	**0**	**0**

Hart Trophy (1925) • Lady Byng Trophy (1927)

Signed as a free agent by **Hamilton**, January 30, 1923. Transferred to **NY Americans** after NHL club purchased **Hamilton** franchise, September 25, 1925. Traded to **Boston** by **NY Americans** for cash, April 13, 1932. Traded to **Chicago** by **Boston** for Vic Ripley, January 17, 1933.

BURCHELL, Fred

Center. Shoots left. 5'6", 143 lbs. Born, Montreal, Que., January 9, 1931.

Season	Club	GP	G	A	Pts	PIM	GP	G	A	Pts	PIM
1950-51	Montreal Canadiens	2	0	0	0	0	....	....	....	....	....
1953-54	Montreal Canadiens	2	0	0	0	2	....	....	....	....	....
	NHL Totals	**4**	**0**	**0**	**0**	**2**	....	....	....	....	....

Traded to **Chicago** by **Montreal** for Max Quackenbush, July 3, 1955. Transaction voided when Quackenbush officially announced retirement, July 15, 1955.

BURDON, Glen

Center. Shoots left. 6'2", 178 lbs. Born, Regina, Sask., August 4, 1954.
(Kansas City's 2nd choice, 20th overall, in 1974 Amateur Draft).

Season	Club	GP	G	A	Pts	PIM	GP	G	A	Pts	PIM
1974-75	Kansas City Scouts	11	0	2	2	0	....	....	....	....	....
	NHL Totals	**11**	**0**	**2**	**2**	**0**	....	....	....	....	....

Traded to **Detroit** by **Kansas City** with Peter McDuffe for Bill McKenzie and Gary Bergman, August 22, 1975.

BURE, Pavel

Right wing. Shoots left. 5'10", 189 lbs. Born, Moscow, USSR, March 31, 1971.
(Vancouver's 4th choice, 113th overall, in 1989 Entry Draft).

Season	Club	Regular Season GP	G	A	Pts	PIM	Playoffs GP	G	A	Pts	PIM
1991-92	Vancouver Canucks	65	34	26	60	30	13	6	4	10	14
1992-93	Vancouver Canucks	83	60	50	110	69	12	5	7	12	8
1993-94	Vancouver Canucks	76	*60	47	107	86	24	*16	15	31	40
1994-95	Vancouver Canucks	44	20	23	43	47	11	7	6	13	10
1995-96	Vancouver Canucks	15	6	7	13	8	....	....	....	....	....
1996-97	Vancouver Canucks	63	23	32	55	40	....	....	....	....	....
1997-98	Vancouver Canucks	82	51	39	90	48	....	....	....	....	....
1998-99	Florida Panthers	11	13	3	16	4	....	....	....	....	....
99-2000	Florida Panthers	74	*58	36	94	16	4	1	3	4	2
2000-01	Florida Panthers	82	*59	33	92	58	....	....	....	....	....
2001-02	Florida Panthers	56	22	27	49	56	....	....	....	....	....
	New York Rangers	12	12	8	20	6	....	....	....	....	....
2002-03	New York Rangers	39	19	11	30	16	....	....	....	....	....
	NHL Totals	**702**	**437**	**342**	**779**	**484**	**64**	**35**	**35**	**70**	**74**

• Brother of Valeri • Calder Memorial Trophy (1992) • NHL First All-Star Team (1994) • NHL Second All-Star Team (2000, 2001) • Maurice "Rocket" Richard Trophy (2000, 2001)

Played in NHL All-Star Game (1993, 1994, 1997, 1998, 2000, 2001)

Traded to **Florida** by **Vancouver** with Bret Hedican, Brad Ference and Vancouver's 3rd round choice (Robert Fried) in 2000 Entry Draft for Ed Jovanovski, Dave Gagner, Mike Brown, Kevin Weekes and Florida's 1st round choice (Nathan Smith) in 2000 Entry Draft, January 17, 1999. • Missed majority of 1998-99 season after demanding trade (August 10, 1998) and recovering from knee injury suffered in game vs. Pittsburgh, February 5, 1999. Traded to **NY Rangers** by **Florida** with Florida's 2nd round choice (Lee Falardeau) in 2002 Entry Draft for Igor Ulanov, Filip Novak, NY Rangers' 1st (later traded to Calgary – Calgary selected Eric Nystrom) and 2nd (Rob Globke) round choices in 2002 Entry Draft and NY Rangers' 4th round choice (later traded to Atlanta- Atlanta selected Guillaume Desbiens) in 2003 Entry Draft, March 18, 2002. • Missed majority of 2002-03 season recovering from knee injury originally suffered in game vs. Buffalo, December 6, 2002.

BURE, Valeri

Right wing. Shoots right. 5'10", 185 lbs. Born, Moscow, USSR, June 13, 1974.
(Montreal's 2nd choice, 33rd overall, in 1992 Entry Draft).

Season	Club	Regular Season GP	G	A	Pts	PIM	Playoffs GP	G	A	Pts	PIM
1994-95	Montreal Canadiens	24	3	1	4	6	....	....	....	....	....
1995-96	Montreal Canadiens	77	22	20	42	28	6	0	1	1	6
1996-97	Montreal Canadiens	64	14	21	35	6	5	0	1	1	2
1997-98	Montreal Canadiens	50	7	22	29	33	....	....	....	....	....
	Calgary Flames	16	5	4	9	2	....	....	....	....	....
1998-99	Calgary Flames	80	26	27	53	22	....	....	....	....	....
99-2000	Calgary Flames	82	35	40	75	50	....	....	....	....	....
2000-01	Calgary Flames	78	27	28	55	26	....	....	....	....	....
2001-02	Florida Panthers	31	8	10	18	12	....	....	....	....	....
2002-03	Florida Panthers	46	5	21	26	10	....	....	....	....	....
	St. Louis Blues	5	0	2	2	0	6	0	2	2	8
	NHL Totals	**553**	**152**	**196**	**348**	**195**	**17**	**0**	**4**	**4**	**16**

• Brother of Pavel

Played in NHL All-Star Game (2000)

Traded to **Calgary** by **Montreal** with Montreal's 4th round choice (Shaun Sutter) in 1998 Entry Draft for Jonas Hoglund and Zarley Zalapski, February 1, 1998. Traded to **Florida** by **Calgary** with Jason Wiemer for Rob Niedermayer and Philadelphia's 2nd round choice (previously acquired, Calgary selected Andrei Medvedev) in 2001 Entry Draft, June 24, 2001. • Missed majority of 2001-02 season recovering from knee injury suffered in game vs. Vancouver, October 16, 2001. Traded to **St. Louis** by **Florida** with future considerations for Mike Van Ryn, March 11, 2003.

BUREAU, Marc

Center. Shoots right. 6'1", 203 lbs. Born, Trois-Rivieres, Que., May 19, 1966.

Season	Club	Regular Season GP	G	A	Pts	PIM	Playoffs GP	G	A	Pts	PIM
1989-90	Calgary Flames	5	0	0	0	4	....	....	....	....	....
1990-91	Calgary Flames	5	0	0	0	2	....	....	....	....	....
	Minnesota North Stars	9	0	6	6	4	23	3	2	5	20
1991-92	Minnesota North Stars	46	6	4	10	50	5	0	0	0	14
1992-93	Tampa Bay Lightning	63	10	21	31	111	....	....	....	....	....
1993-94	Tampa Bay Lightning	75	8	7	15	30	....	....	....	....	....
1994-95	Tampa Bay Lightning	48	2	12	14	30	....	....	....	....	....
1995-96	Montreal Canadiens	65	3	7	10	46	6	1	1	2	4
1996-97	Montreal Canadiens	43	6	9	15	16	....	....	....	....	....
1997-98	Montreal Canadiens	74	13	6	19	12	10	1	2	3	6
1998-99	Philadelphia Flyers	71	4	6	10	10	6	0	2	2	2
99-2000	Philadelphia Flyers	54	2	2	4	10	....	....	....	....	....
	Calgary Flames	9	1	3	4	2	....	....	....	....	....
	NHL Totals	**567**	**55**	**83**	**138**	**327**	**50**	**5**	**7**	**12**	**46**

Signed as a free agent by **Calgary**, May 19, 1987. Traded to **Minnesota** by **Calgary** for Minnesota's 3rd round choice (Sandy McCarthy) in 1991 Entry Draft, March 5, 1991. Claimed on waivers by **Tampa Bay** from **Minnesota**, October 16, 1992. Traded to **Montreal** by **Tampa Bay** for Brian Bellows, June 30, 1995. Signed as a free agent by **Philadelphia**, July 20, 1998. Traded to **Calgary** by **Philadelphia** for Travis Brigley and Calgary's 6th round choice (Andrei Razin) in 2001 Entry Draft, March 6, 2000.

BUREGA, Bill

Defense. Shoots left. 6', 195 lbs. Born, Winnipeg, Man., March 13, 1932.

Season	Club	Regular Season GP	G	A	Pts	PIM	Playoffs GP	G	A	Pts	PIM
1955-56	Toronto Maple Leafs	4	0	1	1	4	....	....	....	....	....
	NHL Totals	**4**	**0**	**1**	**1**	**4**	....	....	....	....	....

Signed as a free agent by **Toronto** (Pittsburgh-AHL), September 28, 1953. Claimed by **Buffalo** (AHL) from **Toronto** (Winnipeg-WHL) in Inter-League Draft, June 4, 1957.

BURKE, Eddie

Right wing/Center. Shoots right. 5'8", 175 lbs. Born, Toronto, Ont., June 3, 1907.

Season	Club	Regular Season GP	G	A	Pts	PIM	Playoffs GP	G	A	Pts	PIM
1931-32	Boston Bruins	16	3	0	3	12	....	....	....	....	....
1932-33	New York Americans	15	2	0	2	4	....	....	....	....	....
1933-34	New York Americans	46	20	10	30	24	....	....	....	....	....
1934-35	New York Americans	29	4	10	14	15	....	....	....	....	....
	NHL Totals	**106**	**29**	**20**	**49**	**55**	....	....	....	....	....

Traded to **Boston** by **Boston** (Can-Am) for cash, November 4, 1931. Traded to **Philadelphia** (Can-Am) by **Boston** for cash, October 25, 1932. Traded to **NY Americans** by **Philadelphia** (Can-Am) for Hub Wilson and Norm Cloolngs, February 11, 1933.

BURKE, Marty

Defense. Shoots left. 5'8", 160 lbs. Born, Toronto, Ont., January 28, 1905.

Season	Club	Regular Season GP	G	A	Pts	PIM	Playoffs GP	G	A	Pts	PIM
1927-28	Montreal Canadiens	11	0	0	0	10	....	....	....	....	....
	Pittsburgh Pirates	35	2	1	3	51	2	1	0	1	2
1928-29	Montreal Canadiens	44	4	2	6	68	3	0	0	0	8
1929-30 ♦	Montreal Canadiens	44	2	11	13	71	6	0	1	1	6
1930-31 ♦	Montreal Canadiens	44	2	5	7	91	10	1	2	3	10
1931-32	Montreal Canadiens	48	3	6	9	50	4	0	0	0	12
1932-33	Montreal Canadiens	29	2	5	7	36	....	....	....	....	....
	Ottawa Senators	16	0	0	0	10	....	....	....	....	....
1933-34	Montreal Canadiens	45	1	4	5	28	2	0	1	1	2
1934-35	Chicago Black Hawks	47	2	2	4	29	2	0	0	0	2
1935-36	Chicago Black Hawks	40	0	3	3	49	2	0	0	0	2
1936-37	Chicago Black Hawks	41	1	3	4	28	....	....	....	....	....
1937-38	Chicago Black Hawks	12	0	0	0	8	....	....	....	....	....
	Montreal Canadiens	38	0	5	5	31	....	....	....	....	....
	NHL Totals	**494**	**19**	**47**	**66**	**560**	**31**	**2**	**4**	**6**	**44**

Loaned to **Pittsburgh** by **Montreal** for remainder of 1927-28 season for the loan of Charlie Langlois, December 16, 1927. Traded to **Ottawa** by **Montreal** with future considerations (Nick Wasnie, March 23, 1933) for Harold Starr and Leo Bourgeault, February 14, 1933. Traded to **Montreal** by **Ottawa** for Nick Wasnie, March 23, 1933. Traded to **Chicago** by **Montreal** with Lorne Chabot and Howie Morenz for Leroy Goldsworthy, Lionel Conacher and Roger Jenkins, October 3, 1934. Traded to **Montreal** by **Chicago** for Bill MacKenzie, December 10, 1937.

BURMEISTER, Roy

Left wing. Shoots left. 5'10", 155 lbs. Born, Collingwood, Ont., August 12, 1906.

Season	Club	Regular Season GP	G	A	Pts	PIM	Playoffs GP	G	A	Pts	PIM
1929-30	New York Americans	40	1	1	2	0	....	....	....	....	....
1930-31	New York Americans	11	0	0	0	0	....	....	....	....	....
1931-32	New York Americans	16	3	2	5	2	....	....	....	....	....
	NHL Totals	**67**	**4**	**3**	**7**	**2**	....	....	....	....	....

Traded to **Boston** (Boston-Can-Am) by **NY Americans** (New Haven-Can-Am) for Connie King, February 12, 1933. Traded to **NY Rangers** by **Boston** with Vic Ripley for Babe Siebert, December 18, 1933.

BURNETT, Kelly

Center. Shoots left. 5'10", 160 lbs. Born, Lachine, Que., June 16, 1926.

Season	Club	Regular Season GP	G	A	Pts	PIM	Playoffs GP	G	A	Pts	PIM
1952-53	New York Rangers	3	1	0	1	0	....	....	....	....	....
	NHL Totals	**3**	**1**	**0**	**1**	**0**	....	....	....	....	....

Loaned to **NY Rangers** by **Syracuse** (AHL) for cash, November 22, 1952. Traded to **Montreal** by **Springfield** (AHL) for Bob McCord, September 12, 1954.

BURNS, Bobby

Left wing. Shoots left. 5'10", 155 lbs. Born, Gore Bay, Ont., April 4, 1905.

Season	Club	Regular Season GP	G	A	Pts	PIM	Playoffs GP	G	A	Pts	PIM
1927-28	Chicago Black Hawks	1	0	0	0	0	....	....	....	....	....
1928-29	Chicago Black Hawks	7	0	0	0	6	....	....	....	....	....
1929-30	Chicago Black Hawks	12	1	0	1	2	....	....	....	....	....
	NHL Totals	**20**	**1**	**0**	**1**	**8**	....	....	....	....	....

Traded to **Minneapolis** (AHA) by **Chicago** for Helge Bostrom, January 15, 1930.

BURNS, Charlie

Center. Shoots left. 5'11", 170 lbs. Born, Detroit, MI, February 14, 1936.

Season	Club	Regular Season GP	G	A	Pts	PIM	Playoffs GP	G	A	Pts	PIM
1958-59	Detroit Red Wings	70	9	11	20	32	....	....	....	....	....
1959-60	Boston Bruins	62	10	17	27	46	....	....	....	....	....
1960-61	Boston Bruins	62	15	26	41	16	....	....	....	....	....
1961-62	Boston Bruins	70	11	17	28	43	....	....	....	....	....
1962-63	Boston Bruins	68	12	10	22	13	....	....	....	....	....
1967-68	Oakland Seals	73	9	26	35	20	....	....	....	....	....
1968-69	Pittsburgh Penguins	76	13	38	51	22	....	....	....	....	....
1969-70	Minnesota North Stars	50	3	13	16	10	6	1	0	1	2
1970-71	Minnesota North Stars	76	9	19	28	13	12	3	3	6	2
1971-72	Minnesota North Stars	77	11	14	25	24	7	1	1	2	2
1972-73	Minnesota North Stars	65	4	7	11	13	6	0	0	0	0
	NHL Totals	**749**	**106**	**198**	**304**	**252**	**31**	**5**	**4**	**9**	**6**

Claimed by **Boston** from **Detroit** in Intra-League Draft, June 10, 1959. NHL rights transferred to **Oakland** after owners of **San Francisco** (WHL) franchise granted NHL expansion team, April 26, 1966. Claimed by **Pittsburgh** from **Oakland** in Intra-League Draft, June 12, 1968. Claimed by **Minnesota** from **Pittsburgh** in Intra-League Draft, June 11, 1969. • Named playing-coach of **Minnesota**, December 28, 1969.

BURNS, Gary

Left wing/Center. Shoots left. 6'1", 190 lbs. Born, Cambridge, MA, January 16, 1955.
(Toronto's 15th choice, 191st overall, in 1975 Amateur Draft).

Season	Club	Regular Season GP	G	A	Pts	PIM	Playoffs GP	G	A	Pts	PIM
1980-81	New York Rangers	11	2	2	4	18	1	0	0	0	2

Season	Club	GP	G	A	Pts	PIM	GP	G	A	Pts	PIM
		REGULAR SEASON					PLAYOFFS				
1981-82	New York Rangers	....	....	....	....	....	4	0	0	0	0
	NHL Totals	**11**	**2**	**2**	**4**	**18**	**5**	**0**	**0**	**0**	**2**

Signed as a free agent by **Boston**, October 10, 1978. Signed as a free agent by **NY Rangers**, September 16, 1980.

BURNS, Norm

Center. Shoots right. 6', 195 lbs. Born, Youngstown, Alta., February 20, 1918.

Season	Club	GP	G	A	Pts	PIM	GP	G	A	Pts	PIM
1941-42	New York Rangers	11	0	4	4	2	....	....	....	....	....
	NHL Totals	**11**	**0**	**4**	**4**	**2**	....	....	....	....	....

Claimed by **NY Rangers** from **Minneapolis** (AHA) in Inter-League Draft, June 27, 1941.

BURNS, Robin

Left wing. Shoots left. 6', 195 lbs. Born, Montreal, Que., August 27, 1946.

Season	Club	GP	G	A	Pts	PIM	GP	G	A	Pts	PIM
1970-71	Pittsburgh Penguins	10	0	3	3	4	....	....	....	....	....
1971-72	Pittsburgh Penguins	5	0	0	0	8	....	....	....	....	....
1972-73	Pittsburgh Penguins	26	0	2	2	20	....	....	....	....	....
1974-75	Kansas City Scouts	71	18	15	33	70	....	....	....	....	....
1975-76	Kansas City Scouts	78	13	18	31	37	....	....	....	....	....
	NHL Totals	**190**	**31**	**38**	**69**	**139**	....	....	....	....	....

Traded to **Pittsburgh** by **Montreal** for cash, October 2, 1970. Claimed by **Kansas City** from **Pittsburgh** in Expansion Draft, June 12, 1974.

BURR, Shawn

Left wing/Center. Shoots left. 6'1", 205 lbs. Born, Sarnia, Ont., July 1, 1966.
(Detroit's 1st choice, 7th overall, in 1984 Entry Draft).

Season	Club	GP	G	A	Pts	PIM	GP	G	A	Pts	PIM
1984-85	Detroit Red Wings	9	0	0	0	2	....	....	....	....	....
1985-86	Detroit Red Wings	5	1	0	1	4	....	....	....	....	....
1986-87	Detroit Red Wings	80	22	25	47	107	16	7	2	9	20
1987-88	Detroit Red Wings	78	17	23	40	97	9	3	1	4	14
1988-89	Detroit Red Wings	79	19	27	46	78	6	1	2	3	6
1989-90	Detroit Red Wings	76	24	32	56	82	....	....	....	....	....
1990-91	Detroit Red Wings	80	20	30	50	112	7	0	4	4	15
1991-92	Detroit Red Wings	79	19	32	51	118	11	1	5	6	10
1992-93	Detroit Red Wings	80	10	25	35	74	7	2	1	3	2
1993-94	Detroit Red Wings	51	10	12	22	31	7	2	0	2	6
1994-95	Detroit Red Wings	42	6	8	14	60	16	0	2	2	6
1995-96	Tampa Bay Lightning	81	13	15	28	119	6	0	2	2	8
1996-97	Tampa Bay Lightning	74	14	21	35	106	....	....	....	....	....
1997-98	San Jose Sharks	42	6	6	12	50	6	0	0	0	8
1998-99	San Jose Sharks	18	0	1	1	29	....	....	....	....	....
99-2000	Tampa Bay Lightning	4	0	2	2	0	....	....	....	....	....
	NHL Totals	**878**	**181**	**259**	**440**	**1069**	**91**	**16**	**19**	**35**	**95**

Traded to **Tampa Bay** by **Detroit** with Detroit's 3rd round choice (later traded to Boston – Boston selected Jason Doyle) in 1996 Entry Draft for Marc Bergevin and Ben Hankinson, August 17, 1995. Traded to **San Jose** by **Tampa Bay** for San Jose's 5th round choice (Mark Thompson) in 1997 Entry Draft, June 21, 1997. Traded to **Tampa Bay** by **San Jose** with Andrei Zyuzin, Bill Houlder and Steve Guolla for Niklas Sundstrom and NY Rangers' 3rd round choice (previously acquired, later traded to Chicago – Chicago selected Igor Radulov) in 2000 Entry Draft, August 4, 1999. • Officially announced retirement, July 26, 2000.

BURRIDGE, Randy

Left wing. Shoots left. 5'9", 188 lbs. Born, Fort Erie, Ont., January 7, 1966.
(Boston's 7th choice, 157th overall, in 1985 Entry Draft).

Season	Club	GP	G	A	Pts	PIM	GP	G	A	Pts	PIM
1985-86	Boston Bruins	52	17	25	42	28	3	0	4	4	12
1986-87	Boston Bruins	23	1	4	5	16	2	1	0	1	2
1987-88	Boston Bruins	79	27	28	55	105	23	2	10	12	16
1988-89	Boston Bruins	80	31	30	61	39	10	5	2	7	6
1989-90	Boston Bruins	63	17	15	32	47	21	4	11	15	14
1990-91	Boston Bruins	62	15	13	28	40	19	0	3	3	39
1991-92	Washington Capitals	66	23	44	67	50	2	0	1	1	0
1992-93	Washington Capitals	4	0	0	0	0	4	1	0	1	0
1993-94	Washington Capitals	78	25	17	42	73	11	0	2	2	12
1994-95	Washington Capitals	2	0	0	0	2	....	....	....	....	....
	Los Angeles Kings	38	4	15	19	8	....	....	....	....	....
1995-96	Buffalo Sabres	74	25	33	58	30	....	....	....	....	....
1996-97	Buffalo Sabres	55	10	21	31	20	12	5	1	6	2
1997-98	Buffalo Sabres	30	4	6	10	0	....	....	....	....	....
	NHL Totals	**706**	**199**	**251**	**450**	**458**	**107**	**18**	**34**	**52**	**103**

Played in NHL All-Star Game (1992)

Traded to **Washington** by **Boston** for Stephen Leach, June 21, 1991. • Missed majority of 1992-93 season recovering from knee injury suffered in training camp, September 5, 1992. Traded to **Los Angeles** by **Washington** for Warren Rychel, February 10, 1995. Signed as a free agent by **Buffalo**, October 5, 1995.

BURROWS, Dave

Defense. Shoots left. 6'1", 190 lbs. Born, Toronto, Ont., January 11, 1949.

Season	Club	GP	G	A	Pts	PIM	GP	G	A	Pts	PIM
1971-72	Pittsburgh Penguins	77	2	10	12	48	4	0	0	0	4
1972-73	Pittsburgh Penguins	78	3	24	27	42	....	....	....	....	....
1973-74	Pittsburgh Penguins	71	3	14	17	30	....	....	....	....	....
1974-75	Pittsburgh Penguins	78	2	15	17	49	9	1	1	2	12
1975-76	Pittsburgh Penguins	80	7	22	29	51	3	0	0	0	0
1976-77	Pittsburgh Penguins	69	3	6	9	29	3	0	2	2	0
1977-78	Pittsburgh Penguins	67	4	15	19	24	....	....	....	....	....
1978-79	Toronto Maple Leafs	65	2	11	13	28	6	0	1	1	7
1979-80	Toronto Maple Leafs	80	3	16	19	42	3	0	1	1	2
1980-81	Toronto Maple Leafs	6	0	0	0	2	....	....	....	....	....
	Pittsburgh Penguins	53	0	2	2	28	1	0	0	0	0
	NHL Totals	**724**	**29**	**135**	**164**	**373**	**29**	**1**	**5**	**6**	**25**

Played in NHL All-Star Game (1974, 1976, 1980)

Claimed by **Pittsburgh** from **Chicago** in Intra-League Draft, June 8, 1971. Traded to **Toronto** by **Pittsburgh** for Randy Carlyle and George Ferguson, June 14, 1978. Traded to **Pittsburgh** by **Toronto** with Paul Gardner for Kim Davis and Paul Marshall, November 18, 1980.

BURRY, Bert

Defense. Shoots left. 5'9", 180 lbs. Born, Toronto, Ont., 1909.

Season	Club	GP	G	A	Pts	PIM	GP	G	A	Pts	PIM
1932-33	Ottawa Senators	4	0	0	0	0	....	....	....	....	....
	NHL Totals	**4**	**0**	**0**	**0**	**0**	....	....	....	....	....

BURT, Adam

Defense. Shoots left. 6'2", 205 lbs. Born, Detroit, MI, January 15, 1969.
(Hartford's 2nd choice, 39th overall, in 1987 Entry Draft).

Season	Club	GP	G	A	Pts	PIM	GP	G	A	Pts	PIM
1988-89	Hartford Whalers	5	0	0	0	6	....	....	....	....	....
1989-90	Hartford Whalers	63	4	8	12	105	2	0	0	0	0
1990-91	Hartford Whalers	42	2	7	9	63	....	....	....	....	....
1991-92	Hartford Whalers	66	9	15	24	93	2	0	0	0	0
1992-93	Hartford Whalers	65	6	14	20	116	....	....	....	....	....
1993-94	Hartford Whalers	63	1	17	18	75	....	....	....	....	....
1994-95	Hartford Whalers	46	7	11	18	65	....	....	....	....	....
1995-96	Hartford Whalers	78	4	9	13	121	....	....	....	....	....
1996-97	Hartford Whalers	71	2	11	13	79	....	....	....	....	....
1997-98	Carolina Hurricanes	76	1	11	12	106	....	....	....	....	....
1998-99	Carolina Hurricanes	51	0	3	3	46	....	....	....	....	....
	Philadelphia Flyers	17	0	1	1	14	6	0	0	0	4
99-2000	Philadelphia Flyers	67	1	6	7	45	11	0	1	1	4
2000-01	Atlanta Thrashers	27	0	2	2	27	....	....	....	....	....
	NHL Totals	**737**	**37**	**115**	**152**	**961**	**21**	**0**	**1**	**1**	**8**

Transferred to **Carolina** after **Hartford** franchise relocated, June 25, 1997. Traded to **Philadelphia** by **Carolina** for Andrei Kovalenko, March 6, 1999. Signed as a free agent by **Atlanta**, July 14, 2000. • Missed majority of 2000-01 season recovering from back injury suffered in game vs. Washington, January 1, 2001.

BURTON, Cummy

Right wing. Shoots right. 5'10", 170 lbs. Born, Sudbury, Ont., May 12, 1936.

Season	Club	GP	G	A	Pts	PIM	GP	G	A	Pts	PIM
1955-56	Detroit Red Wings	3	0	0	0	0	3	0	0	0	0
1957-58	Detroit Red Wings	26	0	1	1	12	....	....	....	....	....
1958-59	Detroit Red Wings	14	0	1	1	9	....	....	....	....	....
	NHL Totals	**43**	**0**	**2**	**2**	**21**	**3**	**0**	**0**	**0**	**0**

BURTON, Nelson

Left wing. Shoots left. 6', 205 lbs. Born, Sydney, N.S., November 6, 1957.
(Washington's 4th choice, 57th overall, in 1977 Amateur Draft).

Season	Club	GP	G	A	Pts	PIM	GP	G	A	Pts	PIM
1977-78	Washington Capitals	5	1	0	1	8	....	....	....	....	....
1978-79	Washington Capitals	3	0	0	0	13	....	....	....	....	....
	NHL Totals	**8**	**1**	**0**	**1**	**21**	....	....	....	....	....

Traded to **Quebec** by **Washington** for Dave Parro, June 15, 1979. Traded to **Minnesota** by **Quebec** for Dan Chicoine, June 9, 1981.

BUSH, Eddie

Defense. Shoots right. 6'1", 195 lbs. Born, Collingwood, Ont., July 11, 1918.

Season	Club	GP	G	A	Pts	PIM	GP	G	A	Pts	PIM
1938-39	Detroit Red Wings	8	0	0	0	0	....	....	....	....	....
1941-42	Detroit Red Wings	18	4	6	10	40	11	1	6	7	23
	NHL Totals	**26**	**4**	**6**	**10**	**40**	**11**	**1**	**6**	**7**	**23**

Traded to **Providence** (AHL) by **Detroit** with Cecil Dillon for Harold Jackson, December 15, 1940. Traded to **Detroit** by **Providence** (AHL) with future considerations for Buck Jones and Bob Whitelaw, February 3, 1942. Traded to **St. Louis** (AHL) by **Detroit** for cash, August 17, 1946.

BUSKAS, Rod

Defense. Shoots right. 6'1", 206 lbs. Born, Wetaskiwin, Alta., January 7, 1961.
(Pittsburgh's 5th choice, 112th overall, in 1981 Entry Draft).

Season	Club	GP	G	A	Pts	PIM	GP	G	A	Pts	PIM
1982-83	Pittsburgh Penguins	41	2	2	4	102	....	....	....	....	....
1983-84	Pittsburgh Penguins	47	2	4	6	60	....	....	....	....	....
1984-85	Pittsburgh Penguins	69	2	7	9	191	....	....	....	....	....
1985-86	Pittsburgh Penguins	72	2	7	9	159	....	....	....	....	....
1986-87	Pittsburgh Penguins	68	3	15	18	123	....	....	....	....	....
1987-88	Pittsburgh Penguins	76	4	8	12	206	....	....	....	....	....
1988-89	Pittsburgh Penguins	52	1	5	6	105	10	0	0	0	23
1989-90	Vancouver Canucks	17	0	3	3	36	....	....	....	....	....
	Pittsburgh Penguins	6	0	0	0	13	....	....	....	....	....
1990-91	Los Angeles Kings	57	3	8	11	182	2	0	2	2	22
1991-92	Los Angeles Kings	5	0	0	0	11	....	....	....	....	....
	Chicago Blackhawks	42	0	4	4	80	6	0	1	1	0
1992-93	Chicago Blackhawks	4	0	0	0	26	....	....	....	....	....
	NHL Totals	**556**	**19**	**63**	**82**	**1294**	**18**	**0**	**3**	**3**	**45**

Traded to **Vancouver** by **Pittsburgh** for Vancouver's 6th round choice (Ian Moran) in 1990 Entry Draft, October 24, 1989. Traded to **Pittsburgh** by **Vancouver** with Barry Pederson and Tony Tanti for Dave Capuano, Andrew McBain and Dan Quinn, January 8, 1990. Claimed by **Los Angeles** from **Pittsburgh** in Waiver Draft, October 1, 1990. Traded to **Chicago** by **Los Angeles** from Chris Norton and future considerations, October 28, 1991.

BUSNIUK, Mike

Defense. Shoots right. 6'3", 200 lbs. Born, Thunder Bay, Ont., December 13, 1951.
(Montreal's 10th choice, 67th overall, in 1971 Amateur Draft).

		REGULAR SEASON					PLAYOFFS				
Season	Club	GP	G	A	Pts	PIM	GP	G	A	Pts	PIM
1979-80	Philadelphia Flyers	71	2	18	20	93	19	2	4	6	23
1980-81	Philadelphia Flyers	72	1	5	6	204	6	0	1	1	11
	NHL Totals	**143**	**3**	**23**	**26**	**297**	**25**	**2**	**5**	**7**	**34**

• Brother of Ron

Signed as a free agent by **Philadelphia**, October 23, 1977.

BUSNIUK, Ron

Right wing. Shoots right. 5'11", 180 lbs. Born, Fort William, Ont., August 13, 1948.

Season	Club	GP	G	A	Pts	PIM	GP	G	A	Pts	PIM
1972-73	Buffalo Sabres	1	0	0	0	9	....	....	....	....	....
1973-74	Buffalo Sabres	5	0	3	3	4	....	....	....	....	....
	NHL Totals	**6**	**0**	**3**	**3**	**13**	....	....	....	....	....

• Brother of Mike

Traded to **Buffalo** by **Montreal** for cash, June 8, 1972. Claimed by **Detroit** from **Buffalo** in Intra-League Draft, June 10, 1974.

BUSWELL, Walt

Defense. Shoots left. 5'11", 170 lbs. Born, Montreal, Que., November 6, 1907.

Season	Club	GP	G	A	Pts	PIM	GP	G	A	Pts	PIM
1932-33	Detroit Red Wings	46	2	4	6	16	4	0	0	0	4
1933-34	Detroit Red Wings	47	1	2	3	8	9	0	1	1	2
1934-35	Detroit Red Wings	47	1	3	4	32	....	....	....	....	....
1935-36	Montreal Canadiens	44	0	2	2	34	....	....	....	....	....
1936-37	Montreal Canadiens	44	0	4	4	30	5	0	0	0	2
1937-38	Montreal Canadiens	48	2	15	17	24	3	0	0	0	0
1938-39	Montreal Canadiens	46	3	7	10	10	3	2	0	2	2
1939-40	Montreal Canadiens	46	1	3	4	10	....	....	....	....	....
	NHL Totals	**368**	**10**	**40**	**50**	**164**	**24**	**2**	**1**	**3**	**10**

Played in NHL All-Star Game (1937, 1939)

NHL rights transferred to **Detroit** from **Chicago** (AHA) after AHA club owners purchased Detroit (NHL and IAHL) franchises, September 2, 1932. Traded to **Boston** by **Detroit** with Cooney Weiland for Marty Barry and Art Giroux, July 11, 1935. Traded to **Montreal** by **Boston** with Jean Pusie and cash for Roger Jenkins, July 13, 1935.

BUTCHER, Garth

Defense. Shoots right. 6', 204 lbs. Born, Regina, Sask., January 8, 1963.
(Vancouver's 1st choice, 10th overall, in 1981 Entry Draft).

Season	Club	GP	G	A	Pts	PIM	GP	G	A	Pts	PIM
1981-82	Vancouver Canucks	5	0	0	0	9	1	0	0	0	0
1982-83	Vancouver Canucks	55	1	13	14	104	3	1	0	1	2
1983-84	Vancouver Canucks	28	2	0	2	34	....	....	....	....	....
1984-85	Vancouver Canucks	75	3	9	12	152	....	....	....	....	....
1985-86	Vancouver Canucks	70	4	7	11	188	3	0	0	0	0
1986-87	Vancouver Canucks	70	5	15	20	207	....	....	....	....	....
1987-88	Vancouver Canucks	80	6	17	23	285	....	....	....	....	....
1988-89	Vancouver Canucks	78	0	20	20	227	7	1	1	2	22
1989-90	Vancouver Canucks	80	6	14	20	205	....	....	....	....	....
1990-91	Vancouver Canucks	69	6	12	18	257	....	....	....	....	....
	St. Louis Blues	13	0	4	4	32	13	2	1	3	54
1991-92	St. Louis Blues	68	5	15	20	189	5	1	2	3	16
1992-93	St. Louis Blues	84	5	10	15	211	11	1	1	2	20
1993-94	St. Louis Blues	43	1	6	7	76	....	....	....	....	....
	Quebec Nordiques	34	3	9	12	67	....	....	....	....	....
1994-95	Toronto Maple Leafs	45	1	7	8	59	7	0	0	0	8
	NHL Totals	**897**	**48**	**158**	**206**	**2302**	**50**	**6**	**5**	**11**	**122**

Played in NHL All-Star Game (1993)

Traded to **St. Louis** by **Vancouver** with Dan Quinn for Geoff Courtnall, Robert Dirk, Sergio Momesso, Cliff Ronning and St. Louis' 5th round choice (Brian Loney) in 1992 Entry Draft, March 5, 1991. Traded to **Quebec** by **St. Louis** with Ron Sutter and Bob Bassen for Steve Duchesne and Denis Chase, January 23, 1994. Traded to **Toronto** by **Quebec** with Mats Sundin, Todd Warriner and Philadelphia's 1st round choice (previously acquired, later traded to Washington – Washington selected Nolan Baumgartner) in 1994 Entry Draft for Wendel Clark, Sylvain Lefebvre, Landon Wilson and Toronto's 1st round choice (Jeffrey Kealty) in 1994 Entry Draft, June 28, 1994.

BUTENSCHON, Sven

Defense. Shoots left. 6'4", 215 lbs. Born, Itzehoe, West Germany, March 22, 1976.
(Pittsburgh's 3rd choice, 57th overall, in 1994 Entry Draft).

Season	Club	GP	G	A	Pts	PIM	GP	G	A	Pts	PIM
1997-98	Pittsburgh Penguins	8	0	0	0	6	....	....	....	....	....
1998-99	Pittsburgh Penguins	17	0	0	0	6	....	....	....	....	....
99-2000	Pittsburgh Penguins	3	0	0	0	0	....	....	....	....	....
2000-01	Pittsburgh Penguins	5	0	1	1	2	....	....	....	....	....
	Edmonton Oilers	7	1	1	2	2	....	....	....	....	....
2001-02	Edmonton Oilers	14	0	0	0	4	....	....	....	....	....
2002-03	New York Islanders	37	0	4	4	26	....	....	....	....	....
	NHL Totals	**91**	**1**	**6**	**7**	**46**	....	....	....	....	....

Traded to **Edmonton** by **Pittsburgh** for Dan LaCouture, March 13, 2001. Signed as a free agent by **Florida**, July 9, 2002. Traded to **NY Islanders** by **Florida** for Juraj Kolnik and NY Islanders' 9th round choice (later traded to San Jose – San Jose selected Carter Lee) in 2003 Entry Draft, October 11, 2003.

BUTLER, Dick

Right wing. Shoots right. 5'7", 175 lbs. Born, Delisle, Sask., June 2, 1926.

Season	Club	GP	G	A	Pts	PIM	GP	G	A	Pts	PIM
1947-48	Chicago Black Hawks	7	2	0	2	0	....	....	....	....	....
	NHL Totals	**7**	**2**	**0**	**2**	**0**	....	....	....	....	....

BUTLER, Jerry

Right wing. Shoots right. 6', 180 lbs. Born, Sarnia, Ont., February 27, 1951.
(NY Rangers' 5th choice, 55th overall, in 1971 Amateur Draft).

Season	Club	GP	G	A	Pts	PIM	GP	G	A	Pts	PIM
1972-73	New York Rangers	8	1	0	1	4	....	....	....	....	....
1973-74	New York Rangers	26	6	10	16	24	12	0	2	2	25
1974-75	New York Rangers	78	17	16	33	102	3	1	0	1	16
1975-76	St. Louis Blues	66	17	24	41	75	3	0	0	0	0
1976-77	St. Louis Blues	80	12	20	32	65	4	0	0	0	14
1977-78	St. Louis Blues	9	0	2	2	5	....	....	....	....	....
	Toronto Maple Leafs	73	9	7	16	49	13	1	1	2	18
1978-79	Toronto Maple Leafs	76	8	7	15	52	6	0	0	0	4
1979-80	Toronto Maple Leafs	55	7	8	15	29	....	....	....	....	....
	Vancouver Canucks	23	4	4	8	21	4	0	0	0	2
1980-81	Vancouver Canucks	80	12	15	27	60	3	1	0	1	0
1981-82	Vancouver Canucks	25	3	1	4	15	....	....	....	....	....
1982-83	Winnipeg Jets	42	3	6	9	14	....	....	....	....	....
	NHL Totals	**641**	**99**	**120**	**219**	**515**	**48**	**3**	**3**	**6**	**79**

Traded to **St. Louis** by **NY Rangers** with Ted Irvine and Bert Wilson for Bill Collins and John Davidson, June 18, 1975. Traded to **Toronto** by **St. Louis** for Inge Hammarstrom, November 1, 1977. Traded to **Vancouver** by **Toronto** with Tiger Williams for Bill Derlago and Rick Vaive, February 18, 1980. Signed as a free agent by **Winnipeg**, October 8, 1982.

BUTSAYEV, Viacheslav

Center. Shoots left. 6'2", 228 lbs. Born, Togliatti, USSR, June 13, 1970.
(Philadelphia's 10th choice, 109th overall, in 1990 Entry Draft).

Season	Club	GP	G	A	Pts	PIM	GP	G	A	Pts	PIM
1992-93	Philadelphia Flyers	52	2	14	16	61	....	....	....	....	....
1993-94	Philadelphia Flyers	47	12	9	21	58	....	....	....	....	....
	San Jose Sharks	12	0	2	2	10	....	....	....	....	....
1994-95	San Jose Sharks	6	2	0	2	0	....	....	....	....	....
1995-96	Mighty Ducks of Anaheim	7	1	0	1	0	....	....	....	....	....
1998-99	Florida Panthers	1	0	0	0	2	....	....	....	....	....
	Ottawa Senators	2	0	1	1	2	....	....	....	....	....
99-2000	Tampa Bay Lightning	2	0	0	0	0	....	....	....	....	....
	Ottawa Senators	3	0	0	0	0	....	....	....	....	....
	NHL Totals	**132**	**17**	**26**	**43**	**133**	....	....	....	....	....

• Brother of Yuri

Traded to **San Jose** by **Philadelphia** for Rob Zettler, February 1, 1994. Signed as a free agent by **Anaheim**, October 19, 1995. Signed as a free agent by **Florida**, August 1, 1998. Traded to **Ottawa** by **Florida** for Ottawa's 6th round choice (later traded to Dallas – Dallas selected Justin Cox) in 1999 Entry Draft, March 8, 1999. Claimed by **Tampa Bay** from **Ottawa** in Waiver Draft, September 27, 1999. Claimed on waivers by **Ottawa** from **Tampa Bay**, October 28, 1999.

BUTSAYEV, Yuri

Left wing. Shoots left. 6', 195 lbs. Born, Togliatti, USSR, October 11, 1978.
(Detroit's 1st choice, 49th overall, in 1997 Entry Draft).

Season	Club	GP	G	A	Pts	PIM	GP	G	A	Pts	PIM
99-2000	Detroit Red Wings	57	5	3	8	12	....	....	....	....	....
2000-01	Detroit Red Wings	15	1	1	2	4	....	....	....	....	....
2001-02	Detroit Red Wings	3	0	0	0	0	....	....	....	....	....
	Atlanta Thrashers	8	2	0	2	4	....	....	....	....	....
2002-03	Atlanta Thrashers	16	2	0	2	8	....	....	....	....	....
	NHL Totals	**99**	**10**	**4**	**14**	**28**	....	....	....	....	....

• Brother of Viacheslav

Traded to **Atlanta** by **Detroit** with Detroit's 3rd round choice (later traded to Columbus – Columbus selected Jeff Genovy) in 2002 Entry Draft for Jiri Slegr, March 19, 2002.

BUTTERS, Bill

Defense. Shoots right. 5'10", 185 lbs. Born, St. Paul, MN, January 10, 1951.

Season	Club	GP	G	A	Pts	PIM	GP	G	A	Pts	PIM
1977-78	Minnesota North Stars	23	1	0	1	30	....	....	....	....	....
1978-79	Minnesota North Stars	49	0	4	4	47	....	....	....	....	....
	NHL Totals	**72**	**1**	**4**	**5**	**77**	....	....	....	....	....

Signed as a free agent by **Toronto**, September 27, 1973. Rights traded to **Minnesota** (WHA) by **Toronto** for cash, February, 1975. Signed as a free agent by **Minnesota** after clearing WHA waivers, February 16, 1978.

BUTTREY, Gord

Wing. Shoots left. 6'1", 180 lbs. Born, Regina, Sask., March 17, 1926.

Season	Club	GP	G	A	Pts	PIM	GP	G	A	Pts	PIM
1943-44	Chicago Black Hawks	10	0	0	0	0	....	....	....	....	....
	NHL Totals	**10**	**0**	**0**	**0**	**0**	....	....	....	....	....

Traded to **Providence** (AHL) by **Chicago** with Hec Highton and $10,000 for Mike Karakas, January 7, 1944.

BUYNAK, Gord

Defense. Shoots left. 6'1", 180 lbs. Born, Detroit, MI, March 19, 1954.
(St. Louis' 2nd choice, 43rd overall, in 1974 Amateur Draft).

Season	Club	GP	G	A	Pts	PIM	GP	G	A	Pts	PIM
1974-75	St. Louis Blues	4	0	0	0	2	....	....	....	....	....
	NHL Totals	**4**	**0**	**0**	**0**	**2**	....	....	....	....	....

Traded to **Vancouver** by **St. Louis** with Bruce Affleck for cash, November 6, 1979. Traded to **St. Louis** by **Vancouver** with Bruce Affleck for cash, February 28, 1980.

BUZEK, Petr

Defense. Shoots left. 6'1", 220 lbs. Born, Jihlava, Czech., April 26, 1977.
(Dallas' 3rd choice, 63rd overall, in 1995 Entry Draft).

Season	Club	GP	G	A	Pts	PIM	GP	G	A	Pts	PIM
1997-98	Dallas Stars	2	0	0	0	2	....	....	....	....	....
1998-99	Dallas Stars	2	0	0	0	2	....	....	....	....	....
99-2000	Atlanta Thrashers	63	5	14	19	41	....	....	....	....	....

Season	Club	Regular Season GP	G	A	Pts	PIM	Playoffs GP	G	A	Pts	PIM
2000-01	Atlanta Thrashers	5	0	0	0	8	....	....	....	....	....
2001-02	Atlanta Thrashers	9	0	0	0	13	....	....	....	....	....
	Calgary Flames	32	1	3	4	14	....	....	....	....	....
2002-03	Calgary Flames	44	3	5	8	14	....	....	....	....	....
	NHL Totals	**157**	**9**	**22**	**31**	**94**	....	....	....	....	....

Played in NHL All-Star Game (2000)

Claimed by **Atlanta** from **Dallas** in Expansion Draft, June 25, 1999. • Missed majority of 2000-01 season recovering from neck injury suffered in game vs. Anaheim, October 17, 2000. Traded to **Calgary** by **Atlanta** for Jeff Cowan and the rights to Kurtis Foster, December 18, 2001.

BYAKIN, Ilja

Defense. Shoots left. 5'9", 185 lbs. Born, Sverdlovsk, USSR, February 2, 1963.
(Edmonton's 11th choice, 267th overall, in 1993 Entry Draft).

Season	Club	GP	G	A	Pts	PIM	GP	G	A	Pts	PIM
1993-94	Edmonton Oilers	44	8	20	28	30	....	....	....	....	....
1994-95	San Jose Sharks	13	0	5	5	14	....	....	....	....	....
	NHL Totals	**57**	**8**	**25**	**33**	**44**	....	....	....	....	....

Signed as a free agent by **San Jose**, September 18, 1994.

BYCE, John

Center. Shoots left. 6'1", 180 lbs. Born, Madison, WI, August 9, 1967.
(Boston's 11th choice, 220th overall, in 1985 Entry Draft).

Season	Club	GP	G	A	Pts	PIM	GP	G	A	Pts	PIM
1989-90	Boston Bruins	....	....	....	....	....	8	2	0	2	2
1990-91	Boston Bruins	18	1	3	4	6	....	....	....	....	....
1991-92	Boston Bruins	3	1	0	1	0	....	....	....	....	....
	NHL Totals	**21**	**2**	**3**	**5**	**6**	**8**	**2**	**0**	**2**	**2**

Traded to **Washington** by **Boston** with Dennis Smith for Brent Hughes and future considerations, February 24, 1992.

BYERS, Gord

Defense. Shoots right. 5'10", 182 lbs. Born, Eganville, Ont., March 11, 1930.

Season	Club	GP	G	A	Pts	PIM	GP	G	A	Pts	PIM
1949-50	Boston Bruins	1	0	1	1	0	....	....	....	....	....
	NHL Totals	**1**	**0**	**1**	**1**	**0**	....	....	....	....	....

Signed as a free agent by **Boston**, October 3, 1950.

BYERS, Jerry

Left wing. Shoots left. 5'11", 170 lbs. Born, Kentville, N.S., March 29, 1952.
(Minnesota's 1st choice, 12th overall, in 1972 Amateur Draft).

Season	Club	GP	G	A	Pts	PIM	GP	G	A	Pts	PIM
1972-73	Minnesota North Stars	14	0	2	2	6	....	....	....	....	....
1973-74	Minnesota North Stars	10	0	0	0	0	....	....	....	....	....
1974-75	Atlanta Flames	12	1	1	2	9	....	....	....	....	....
1977-78	New York Rangers	7	2	1	3	0	....	....	....	....	....
	NHL Totals	**43**	**3**	**4**	**7**	**15**	....	....	....	....	....

Traded to **Atlanta** by **Minnesota** with Buster Harvey for John Flesch and Don Martineau, May 27, 1974. Traded to **NY Rangers** by **Atlanta** for Curt Ridley, September 9, 1975.

BYERS, Lyndon

Right wing. Shoots right. 6'1", 200 lbs. Born, Nipawin, Sask., February 29, 1964.
(Boston's 3rd choice, 39th overall, in 1982 Entry Draft).

Season	Club	GP	G	A	Pts	PIM	GP	G	A	Pts	PIM
1983-84	Boston Bruins	10	2	4	6	32	....	....	....	....	....
1984-85	Boston Bruins	33	3	8	11	41	....	....	....	....	....
1985-86	Boston Bruins	5	0	2	2	9	....	....	....	....	....
1986-87	Boston Bruins	18	2	3	5	53	1	0	0	0	0
1987-88	Boston Bruins	53	10	14	24	236	11	1	2	3	62
1988-89	Boston Bruins	49	0	4	4	218	2	0	0	0	0
1989-90	Boston Bruins	43	4	4	8	159	17	1	0	1	12
1990-91	Boston Bruins	19	2	2	4	82	1	0	0	0	10
1991-92	Boston Bruins	31	1	1	2	129	5	0	0	0	12
1992-93	San Jose Sharks	18	4	1	5	122	....	....	....	....	....
	NHL Totals	**279**	**28**	**43**	**71**	**1081**	**37**	**2**	**2**	**4**	**96**

Signed as a free agent by **San Jose**, November 7, 1992.

BYERS, Mike

Right wing. Shoots right. 5'10", 185 lbs. Born, Toronto, Ont., September 11, 1946.

Season	Club	GP	G	A	Pts	PIM	GP	G	A	Pts	PIM
1967-68	Toronto Maple Leafs	10	2	2	4	0	....	....	....	....	....
1968-69	Toronto Maple Leafs	5	0	0	0	2	....	....	....	....	....
	Philadelphia Flyers	5	0	2	2	0	4	0	1	1	0
1970-71	Los Angeles Kings	72	27	18	45	14	....	....	....	....	....
1971-72	Los Angeles Kings	28	4	5	9	11	....	....	....	....	....
	Buffalo Sabres	46	9	7	16	12	....	....	....	....	....
	NHL Totals	**166**	**42**	**34**	**76**	**39**	**4**	**0**	**1**	**1**	**0**

Traded to **Philadelphia** by **Toronto** with Bill Sutherland and Gerry Meehan for Brit Selby and Forbes Kennedy, March 2, 1969. Traded to **Los Angeles** by **Philadelphia** for Brent Hughes, May 20, 1970. Traded to **Buffalo** by **Los Angeles** with Larry Hillman for Doug Barrie and Mike Keeler, December 16, 1971.

BYKOV, Dmitri

Defense. Shoots left. 5'10", 169 lbs. Born, Izhevsk, USSR, May 5, 1977.
(Detroit's 6th choice, 258th overall, in 2001 Entry Draft).

Season	Club	GP	G	A	Pts	PIM	GP	G	A	Pts	PIM
2002-03	Detroit Red Wings	71	2	10	12	43	4	0	0	0	0
	NHL Totals	**71**	**2**	**10**	**12**	**43**	**4**	**0**	**0**	**0**	**0**

BYLSMA, Dan

Right wing. Shoots left. 6'2", 212 lbs. Born, Grand Haven, MI, September 19, 1970.
(Winnipeg's 7th choice, 109th overall, in 1989 Entry Draft).

Season	Club	GP	G	A	Pts	PIM	GP	G	A	Pts	PIM
1995-96	Los Angeles Kings	4	0	0	0	0	....	....	....	....	....
1996-97	Los Angeles Kings	79	3	6	9	32	....	....	....	....	....
1997-98	Los Angeles Kings	65	3	9	12	33	2	0	0	0	0
1998-99	Los Angeles Kings	8	0	0	0	2	....	....	....	....	....
99-2000	Los Angeles Kings	64	3	6	9	55	3	0	0	0	0
2000-01	Mighty Ducks of Anaheim	82	1	9	10	22	....	....	....	....	....
2001-02	Mighty Ducks of Anaheim	77	8	9	17	28	....	....	....	....	....
2002-03	Mighty Ducks of Anaheim	39	1	4	5	12	11	0	1	1	2
	NHL Totals	**418**	**19**	**43**	**62**	**184**	**16**	**0**	**1**	**1**	**2**

Signed as a free agent by **Los Angeles**, July 7, 1994. Signed as a free agent by **Anaheim**, July 13, 2000. • Missed majority of 2002-03 season recovering from knee (January 28, 2003 vs. San Jose) and head (February 9, 2003 vs. Carolina) injuries.

BYRAM, Shawn

Left wing. Shoots left. 6'2", 204 lbs. Born, Neepawa, Man., September 12, 1968.
(NY Islanders' 4th choice, 80th overall, in 1986 Entry Draft).

Season	Club	GP	G	A	Pts	PIM	GP	G	A	Pts	PIM
1990-91	New York Islanders	4	0	0	0	14	....	....	....	....	....
1991-92	Chicago Blackhawks	1	0	0	0	0	....	....	....	....	....
	NHL Totals	**5**	**0**	**0**	**0**	**14**	....	....	....	....	....

Signed as a free agent by **Chicago**, August 15, 1991.

CAFFERY, Jack

Center. Shoots right. 6', 165 lbs. Born, Kingston, Ont., June 30, 1934.

Season	Club	GP	G	A	Pts	PIM	GP	G	A	Pts	PIM
1954-55	Toronto Maple Leafs	3	0	0	0	0	....	....	....	....	....
1956-57	Boston Bruins	47	2	2	4	20	10	1	0	1	4
1957-58	Boston Bruins	7	1	0	1	2	....	....	....	....	....
	NHL Totals	**57**	**3**	**2**	**5**	**22**	**10**	**1**	**0**	**1**	**4**

• Brother of Terry

Claimed by **Boston** from **Pittsburgh** (AHL) in Inter-League Draft, June 5, 1956.

CAFFERY, Terry

Center. Shoots right. 5'9", 165 lbs. Born, Toronto, Ont., April 1, 1949.
(Chicago's 1st choice, 3rd overall, in 1966 Amateur Draft).

Season	Club	GP	G	A	Pts	PIM	GP	G	A	Pts	PIM
1969-70	Chicago Black Hawks	6	0	0	0	0	....	....	....	....	....
1970-71	Minnesota North Stars	8	0	0	0	0	1	0	0	0	0
	NHL Totals	**14**	**0**	**0**	**0**	**0**	**1**	**0**	**0**	**0**	**0**

• Brother of Jack

Traded to **Minnesota** by **Chicago** with Doug Mohns for Danny O'Shea, February 22, 1971.

CAHAN, Larry

Defense. Shoots right. 6'2", 222 lbs. Born, Fort William, Ont., December 25, 1933.

Season	Club	GP	G	A	Pts	PIM	GP	G	A	Pts	PIM
1954-55	Toronto Maple Leafs	59	0	6	6	64	4	0	0	0	0
1955-56	Toronto Maple Leafs	21	0	2	2	46	....	....	....	....	....
1956-57	New York Rangers	61	5	4	9	65	3	0	0	0	2
1957-58	New York Rangers	34	1	1	2	20	5	0	0	0	4
1958-59	New York Rangers	16	1	0	1	8	....	....	....	....	....
1961-62	New York Rangers	57	2	7	9	85	6	0	0	0	10
1962-63	New York Rangers	56	6	14	20	47	....	....	....	....	....
1963-64	New York Rangers	53	4	8	12	80	....	....	....	....	....
1964-65	New York Rangers	26	0	5	5	32	....	....	....	....	....
1967-68	Oakland Seals	74	9	15	24	80	....	....	....	....	....
1968-69	Los Angeles Kings	72	3	11	14	76	11	1	1	2	22
1969-70	Los Angeles Kings	70	4	8	12	52	....	....	....	....	....
1970-71	Los Angeles Kings	67	3	11	14	45	....	....	....	....	....
	NHL Totals	**666**	**38**	**92**	**130**	**700**	**29**	**1**	**1**	**2**	**38**

Claimed by **NY Rangers** from **Toronto** in Intra-League Draft, September, 1956. Loaned to **Springfield** (AHL) by **NY Rangers** (Vancouver-WHL) for the loan of Milan Marcetta, January 10, 1959. Claimed by **California** (Oakland) from **NY Rangers** in Expansion Draft, June 6, 1967. Claimed by **Montreal** from **Oakland** in Intra-League Draft, June 12, 1968. Traded to **Los Angeles** by **Montreal** for Brian D. Smith and Yves Locas, July 1, 1968.

CAHILL, Charles

Right wing. Shoots right. 5'10", 180 lbs. Born, Summerside, P.E.I., January 4, 1904.

Season	Club	GP	G	A	Pts	PIM	GP	G	A	Pts	PIM
1925-26	Boston Bruins	31	0	1	1	4	....	....	....	....	....
1926-27	Boston Bruins	1	0	0	0	0	....	....	....	....	....
	NHL Totals	**32**	**0**	**1**	**1**	**4**	....	....	....	....	....

Signed as a free agent by **Boston**, December 1, 1925. Traded to **New Haven** (Can-Am) by **Boston** for cash, January 31, 1927.

CAIN, Francis

Defense. Shoots left. 5'8", 175 lbs. Born, Newmarket, Ont., March 22, 1899.

Season	Club	GP	G	A	Pts	PIM	GP	G	A	Pts	PIM
1924-25	Montreal Maroons	28	4	0	4	27	....	....	....	....	....
1925-26	Montreal Maroons	10	0	0	0	0	....	....	....	....	....
	Toronto St. Pats	23	0	0	0	8	....	....	....	....	....
	NHL Totals	**61**	**4**	**0**	**4**	**35**	....	....	....	....	....

Signed as a free agent by **Mtl. Maroons**, October 23, 1924. Claimed on waivers by **Toronto** from **Mtl. Maroons**, January 7, 1926. Claimed on waivers by **Hamilton** (Can-Pro) from **Toronto**, October 18, 1926.

CAIN, Herb

Left wing. Shoots left. 5'11", 180 lbs. Born, Newmarket, Ont., December 24, 1912.

Season	Club	GP	G	A	Pts	PIM	GP	G	A	Pts	PIM
		REGULAR SEASON					PLAYOFFS				
1933-34	Montreal Maroons	30	4	5	9	14	4	0	0	0	0
1934-35 ◆	Montreal Maroons	44	20	7	27	13	7	1	0	1	2
1935-36	Montreal Maroons	48	5	13	18	16	3	0	1	1	0
1936-37	Montreal Maroons	42	13	17	30	18	5	1	1	2	0
1937-38	Montreal Maroons	47	11	19	30	10	....	....	....	....	....
1938-39	Montreal Canadiens	45	13	14	27	26	3	0	0	0	2
1939-40	Boston Bruins	48	21	10	31	30	6	1	3	4	2
1940-41 ◆	Boston Bruins	41	8	10	18	6	11	3	2	5	5
1941-42	Boston Bruins	34	8	10	18	2	5	1	0	1	0
1942-43	Boston Bruins	45	18	18	36	19	7	4	2	6	0
1943-44	Boston Bruins	48	36	46	*82	4	....	....	....	....	....
1944-45	Boston Bruins	50	32	13	45	16	7	5	2	7	0
1945-46	Boston Bruins	48	17	12	29	4	9	0	2	2	2
	NHL Totals	**570**	**206**	**194**	**400**	**178**	**67**	**16**	**13**	**29**	**13**

NHL Second All-Star Team (1944)

• **Montreal** protested Cain's contract with **Mtl. Maroons**, claiming they owned his rights, October 3, 1934. NHL rights transferred to **Montreal** by **NHL** after ruling by NHL President Frank Calder, October 3, 1934. NHL rights traded to **Mtl. Maroons** by **Montreal** with Lionel Conacher for the rights to Nels Crutchfield, October 3, 1934. Traded to **Montreal** by **Mtl. Maroons** for cash, September 24, 1938. Traded to **Boston** by **Montreal** for Charlie Sands and Ray Getliffe, October 10, 1939.

CAIRNS, Don

Left wing. Shoots left. 6'1", 195 lbs. Born, Calgary, Alta., October 8, 1955.
(Kansas City's 2nd choice, 20th overall, in 1975 Amateur Draft).

Season	Club	GP	G	A	Pts	PIM	GP	G	A	Pts	PIM
1975-76	Kansas City Scouts	7	0	0	0	0	....	....	....	....	....
1976-77	Colorado Rockies	2	0	1	1	2	....	....	....	....	....
	NHL Totals	**9**	**0**	**1**	**1**	**2**	....	....	....	....	....

Transferred to **Colorado** after **Kansas City** franchise relocated, July 15, 1976.

CAIRNS, Eric

Defense. Shoots left. 6'6", 230 lbs. Born, Oakville, Ont., June 27, 1974.
(NY Rangers' 3rd choice, 72nd overall, in 1992 Entry Draft).

Season	Club	GP	G	A	Pts	PIM	GP	G	A	Pts	PIM
1996-97	New York Rangers	40	0	1	1	147	3	0	0	0	0
1997-98	New York Rangers	39	0	3	3	92	....	....	....	....	....
1998-99	New York Islanders	9	0	3	3	23	....	....	....	....	....
99-2000	New York Islanders	67	2	7	9	196	....	....	....	....	....
2000-01	New York Islanders	45	2	2	4	106	....	....	....	....	....
2001-02	New York Islanders	74	2	5	7	176	7	0	0	0	15
2002-03	New York Islanders	60	1	4	5	124	5	0	0	0	13
	NHL Totals	**334**	**7**	**25**	**32**	**864**	**15**	**0**	**0**	**0**	**28**

Claimed on waivers by **NY Islanders** from **NY Rangers**, December 22, 1998.

CAJANEK, Petr

Right wing. Shoots left. 5'11", 176 lbs. Born, Gottwaldov, Czech., August 18, 1975.
(St. Louis' 6th choice, 253rd overall, in 2001 Entry Draft).

Season	Club	GP	G	A	Pts	PIM	GP	G	A	Pts	PIM
2002-03	St. Louis Blues	51	9	29	38	20	2	0	0	0	2
	NHL Totals	**51**	**9**	**29**	**38**	**20**	**2**	**0**	**0**	**0**	**2**

CALDER, Eric

Defense. Shoots right. 6'1", 180 lbs. Born, Kitchener, Ont., July 26, 1963.
(Washington's 2nd choice, 45th overall, in 1981 Entry Draft).

Season	Club	GP	G	A	Pts	PIM	GP	G	A	Pts	PIM
1981-82	Washington Capitals	1	0	0	0	0	....	....	....	....	....
1982-83	Washington Capitals	1	0	0	0	0	....	....	....	....	....
	NHL Totals	**2**	**0**	**0**	**0**	**0**	....	....	....	....	....

CALDER, Kyle

Left wing. Shoots left. 5'11", 180 lbs. Born, Mannville, Alta., January 5, 1979.
(Chicago's 7th choice, 130th overall, in 1997 Entry Draft).

Season	Club	GP	G	A	Pts	PIM	GP	G	A	Pts	PIM
99-2000	Chicago Blackhawks	8	1	1	2	2	....	....	....	....	....
2000-01	Chicago Blackhawks	43	5	10	15	14	....	....	....	....	....
2001-02	Chicago Blackhawks	81	17	36	53	47	5	2	0	2	2
2002-03	Chicago Blackhawks	82	15	27	42	40	....	....	....	....	....
	NHL Totals	**214**	**38**	**74**	**112**	**103**	**5**	**2**	**0**	**2**	**2**

CALLADINE, Norm

Center. Shoots right. 5'9", 155 lbs. Born, Peterborough, Ont., July 30, 1916.

Season	Club	GP	G	A	Pts	PIM	GP	G	A	Pts	PIM
1942-43	Boston Bruins	3	0	1	1	0	....	....	....	....	....
1943-44	Boston Bruins	49	16	27	43	8	....	....	....	....	....
1944-45	Boston Bruins	11	3	1	4	0	....	....	....	....	....
	NHL Totals	**63**	**19**	**29**	**48**	**8**	....	....	....	....	....

Traded to **Providence** (AHL) by **NY Rangers** for cash, September 11, 1941. Traded to **Boston** by **Providence** (AHL) with Ossie Aubuchon and Ab DeMarco for cash, March 8, 1943.

CALLANDER, Drew

Center/Right wing. Shoots right. 6'2", 185 lbs. Born, Regina, Sask., August 17, 1956.
(Philadelphia's 2nd choice, 35th overall, in 1976 Amateur Draft).

Season	Club	GP	G	A	Pts	PIM	GP	G	A	Pts	PIM
1976-77	Philadelphia Flyers	2	1	0	1	0	....	....	....	....	....
1977-78	Philadelphia Flyers	1	0	0	0	0	....	....	....	....	....
1978-79	Philadelphia Flyers	15	2	1	3	5	....	....	....	....	....
	Vancouver Canucks	17	2	0	2	2	....	....	....	....	....
1979-80	Vancouver Canucks	4	1	1	2	0	....	....	....	....	....
	NHL Totals	**39**	**6**	**2**	**8**	**7**	....	....	....	....	....

• Brother of Jock

Traded to **Vancouver** by **Philadelphia** with Kevin McCarthy for Dennis Ververgaert, December 29, 1978.

CALLANDER, Jock

Right wing. Shoots right. 6'1", 188 lbs. Born, Regina, Sask., April 23, 1961.

Season	Club	GP	G	A	Pts	PIM	GP	G	A	Pts	PIM
1987-88	Pittsburgh Penguins	41	11	16	27	45	....	....	....	....	....
1988-89	Pittsburgh Penguins	30	6	5	11	20	10	2	5	7	10
1989-90	Pittsburgh Penguins	30	4	7	11	49	....	....	....	....	....
1991-92 ◆	Pittsburgh Penguins	....	....	....	....	....	12	1	3	4	2
1992-93	Tampa Bay Lightning	8	1	1	2	2	....	....	....	....	....
	NHL Totals	**109**	**22**	**29**	**51**	**116**	**22**	**3**	**8**	**11**	**12**

• Brother of Drew

Signed as a free agent by **St. Louis**, September 28, 1981. Signed as a free agent by **Pittsburgh**, July 31, 1987. Signed as a free agent by **Tampa Bay**, July 29, 1992.

CALLIGHEN, Brett

Center. Shoots left. 5'11", 182 lbs. Born, Toronto, Ont., May 15, 1953.

Season	Club	GP	G	A	Pts	PIM	GP	G	A	Pts	PIM
1979-80	Edmonton Oilers	59	23	35	58	72	3	0	2	2	0
1980-81	Edmonton Oilers	55	25	35	60	32	9	4	4	8	6
1981-82	Edmonton Oilers	46	8	19	27	28	2	0	0	0	2
	NHL Totals	**160**	**56**	**89**	**145**	**132**	**14**	**4**	**6**	**10**	**8**

NHL rights retained by **Edmonton** prior to Expansion Draft, June 9, 1979. • Missed remainder of 1979-80 regular season and start of 1980-81 season recovering from an eye injury suffered in game vs. Boston, February 24, 1980.

CALLIGHEN, Patsy

Defense. Shoots left. 5'6", 175 lbs. Born, Toronto, Ont., February 13, 1906.

Season	Club	GP	G	A	Pts	PIM	GP	G	A	Pts	PIM
1927-28 ◆	New York Rangers	36	0	0	0	32	9	0	0	0	0
	NHL Totals	**36**	**0**	**0**	**0**	**32**	**9**	**0**	**0**	**0**	**0**

Signed as a free agent by **NY Rangers**, August 22, 1926.

CALOUN, Jan

Right wing. Shoots right. 5'10", 190 lbs. Born, Usti-Nad-Labem, Czech., December 20, 1972.
(San Jose's 4th choice, 75th overall, in 1992 Entry Draft).

Season	Club	GP	G	A	Pts	PIM	GP	G	A	Pts	PIM
1995-96	San Jose Sharks	11	8	3	11	0	....	....	....	....	....
1996-97	San Jose Sharks	2	0	0	0	0	....	....	....	....	....
2000-01	Columbus Blue Jackets	11	0	3	3	2	....	....	....	....	....
	NHL Totals	**24**	**8**	**6**	**14**	**2**	....	....	....	....	....

Traded to **Columbus** by **San Jose** with San Jose's 9th round choice (Martin Paroulek) in 2000 Entry Draft for future considerations, June 12, 2000.

CAMAZZOLA, James

Left wing. Shoots left. 5'11", 190 lbs. Born, Vancouver, B.C., January 5, 1964.
(Chicago's 10th choice, 196th overall, in 1982 Entry Draft).

Season	Club	GP	G	A	Pts	PIM	GP	G	A	Pts	PIM
1983-84	Chicago Black Hawks	1	0	0	0	0	....	....	....	....	....
1986-87	Chicago Blackhawks	2	0	0	0	0	....	....	....	....	....
	NHL Totals	**3**	**0**	**0**	**0**	**0**	....	....	....	....	....

• Brother of Tony

CAMAZZOLA, Tony

Defense. Shoots left. 6'2", 210 lbs. Born, Vancouver, B.C., September 11, 1962.
(Washington's 9th choice, 194th overall, in 1980 Entry Draft).

Season	Club	GP	G	A	Pts	PIM	GP	G	A	Pts	PIM
1981-82	Washington Capitals	3	0	0	0	4	....	....	....	....	....
	NHL Totals	**3**	**0**	**0**	**0**	**4**	....	....	....	....	....

• Brother of James

CAMERON, Al

Defense. Shoots left. 6'1", 205 lbs. Born, Edmonton, Alta., October 21, 1955.
(Detroit's 3rd choice, 37th overall, in 1975 Amateur Draft).

Season	Club	GP	G	A	Pts	PIM	GP	G	A	Pts	PIM
1975-76	Detroit Red Wings	38	2	8	10	49	....	....	....	....	....
1976-77	Detroit Red Wings	80	3	13	16	112	....	....	....	....	....
1977-78	Detroit Red Wings	63	2	7	9	94	7	0	1	1	2
1978-79	Detroit Red Wings	9	0	3	3	8	....	....	....	....	....
1979-80	Winnipeg Jets	63	3	11	14	72	....	....	....	....	....
1980-81	Winnipeg Jets	29	1	2	3	21	....	....	....	....	....
	NHL Totals	**282**	**11**	**44**	**55**	**356**	**7**	**0**	**1**	**1**	**2**

Claimed by **Winnipeg** from **Detroit** in Expansion Draft, June 13, 1979.

CAMERON, Billy

Right wing. Shoots left. 5'11", 160 lbs. Born, Timmins, Ont., December 5, 1896.

Season	Club	GP	G	A	Pts	PIM	GP	G	A	Pts	PIM
1923-24 ◆	Montreal Canadiens	18	0	0	0	2	2	0	0	0	0
	Montreal Canadiens (Cup)	....	....	....	....	....	*4*	*0*	*0*	*0*	*0*
1925-26	New York Americans	21	0	0	0	0	....	....	....	....	....
	NHL Totals	**39**	**0**	**0**	**0**	**2**	**2**	**0**	**0**	**0**	**0**

Signed as a free agent by **Montreal**, December 21, 1923. • 1923-24 Stanley Cup totals includes series with Calgary (WCHL) and Vancouver (PCHA). Traded to **Vancouver** (WCHL) by **Montreal** for cash, October 10, 1924. • Suspended for entire 1924-25 season by **Montreal** for refusing to report to Vancouver (WCHL), October 30, 1924. Signed as a free agent by **NY Americans**, November 1, 1925.

CAMERON, Craig

Right wing. Shoots right. 6', 200 lbs. Born, Edmonton, Alta., July 19, 1945.

Season	Club	GP	G	A	Pts	PIM	GP	G	A	Pts	PIM
		REGULAR SEASON					PLAYOFFS				
1966-67	Detroit Red Wings	1	0	0	0	0	....	....	....	....	....
1967-68	St. Louis Blues	32	7	2	9	8	14	1	0	1	11
1968-69	St. Louis Blues	72	11	5	16	40	2	0	0	0	0
1970-71	St. Louis Blues	78	14	6	20	32	6	2	0	2	4
1971-72	Minnesota North Stars	64	2	1	3	11	5	0	1	1	2
1972-73	New York Islanders	72	19	14	33	27	....	....	....	....	....
1973-74	New York Islanders	78	15	14	29	28	....	....	....	....	....
1974-75	New York Islanders	37	1	6	7	4	....	....	....	....	....
	Minnesota North Stars	40	10	7	17	12	....	....	....	....	....
1975-76	Minnesota North Stars	78	8	10	18	34	....	....	....	....	....
	NHL Totals	**552**	**87**	**65**	**152**	**196**	**27**	**3**	**1**	**4**	**17**

Traded to **St. Louis** by **Detroit** with Larry Hornung and Don Giesebrecht for John Brenneman, October 9, 1967. Traded to **Pittsburgh** by **St. Louis** with Ron Schock and St. Louis' 2nd round choice (Brian McKenzie) in 1971 Amateur Draft for Lou Angotti and Pittsburgh's 1st round choice (Gene Carr) in 1971 Amateur Draft, June 6, 1969. Claimed by **Los Angeles** from **Pittsburgh** in Intra-League Draft, June 9, 1970. Claimed by **Buffalo** from **Los Angeles** in Expansion Draft, June 10, 1970. Traded to **St. Louis** by **Buffalo** for Ron Anderson, October 2, 1970. Claimed on waivers by **Minnesota** from **St. Louis**, October 1, 1971. Claimed by **NY Islanders** from **Minnesota** in Expansion Draft, June 6, 1972. Traded to **Minnesota** by **NY Islanders** for Jude Drouin, January 7, 1975.

CAMERON, Dave

Center. Shoots left. 6', 185 lbs. Born, Charlottetown, P.E.I., July 29, 1958.
(NY Islanders' 7th choice, 135th overall, in 1978 Amateur Draft).

Season	Club	GP	G	A	Pts	PIM	GP	G	A	Pts	PIM
1981-82	Colorado Rockies	66	11	12	23	103	....	....	....	....	....
1982-83	New Jersey Devils	35	5	4	9	50	....	....	....	....	....
1983-84	New Jersey Devils	67	9	12	21	85	....	....	....	....	....
	NHL Totals	**168**	**25**	**28**	**53**	**238**	....	....	....	....	....

Traded to **Colorado** by **NY Islanders** with Bob Lorimer for Colorado's 1st round choice (Pat LaFontaine) in 1983 Entry Draft, October 1, 1981. Transferred to **New Jersey** after **Colorado** franchise relocated, June 30, 1982.

CAMERON, Harry

HHOF

Defense. Shoots right. 5'10", 155 lbs. Born, Pembroke, Ont., February 6, 1890.

Season	Club	GP	G	A	Pts	PIM	GP	G	A	Pts	PIM
1917-18 ♦	Toronto Arenas	21	17	*10	27	28	2	1	2	3	0
	Toronto Arenas (Cup)	....	....	....	....	....	*5*	*3*	*1*	*4*	*0*
1918-19	Toronto Arenas	7	6	2	8	9	....	....	....	....	....
	Ottawa Senators	7	5	1	6	26	5	4	0	4	6
1919-20	Toronto St. Pats	7	3	0	3	6	....	....	....	....	....
	Montreal Canadiens	16	12	5	17	36	....	....	....	....	....
1920-21	Toronto St. Pats	24	18	9	27	35	2	0	0	0	2
1921-22 ♦	Toronto St. Pats	24	18	*17	35	22	2	0	2	2	8
	Toronto St. Pats (Cup)	....	....	....	....	....	*4*	*0*	*2*	*2*	*11*
1922-23	Toronto St. Pats	22	9	7	16	27	....	....	....	....	....
	NHL Totals	**128**	**88**	**51**	**139**	**189**	**11**	**5**	**4**	**9**	**16**

Signed as a free agent by **Toronto**, December 5, 1917. Loaned to **Ottawa** by **Toronto** to complete transaction that sent Rusty Crawford to Toronto (December 14, 1918), January 19, 1919. Returned to **Toronto** by **Ottawa**, November 25, 1919. Traded to **Montreal** by **Toronto** for Goldie Prodgers, January 14, 1920. Traded to **Toronto** by **Montreal** for Goldie Prodgers and Joe Matte, November 27, 1920.

CAMERON, Scotty

Center. Shoots left. 6'2", 175 lbs. Born, Prince Albert, Sask., November 5, 1921.

Season	Club	GP	G	A	Pts	PIM	GP	G	A	Pts	PIM
1942-43	New York Rangers	35	8	11	19	0	....	....	....	....	....
	NHL Totals	**35**	**8**	**11**	**19**	**0**	....	....	....	....	....

Claimed by **NY Rangers** from **Philadelphia** (AHA) in Inter-League Draft, June 27, 1941.

CAMMALLERI, Michael

Center. Shoots left. 5'9", 180 lbs. Born, Richmond Hill, Ont., June 8, 1982.
(Los Angeles' 3rd choice, 49th overall, in 2001 Entry Draft).

Season	Club	GP	G	A	Pts	PIM	GP	G	A	Pts	PIM
2002-03	Los Angeles Kings	28	5	3	8	22	....	....	....	....	....
	NHL Totals	**28**	**5**	**3**	**8**	**22**	....	....	....	....	....

• Missed majority of 2002-03 season recovering from head injury suffered in game vs. San Jose, January 28, 2003.

CAMPBELL, Brian

Defense. Shoots left. 6', 190 lbs. Born, Strathroy, Ont., May 23, 1979.
(Buffalo's 7th choice, 156th overall, in 1997 Entry Draft).

Season	Club	GP	G	A	Pts	PIM	GP	G	A	Pts	PIM
99-2000	Buffalo Sabres	12	1	4	5	4	....	....	....	....	....
2000-01	Buffalo Sabres	8	0	0	0	2	....	....	....	....	....
2001-02	Buffalo Sabres	29	3	3	6	12	....	....	....	....	....
2002-03	Buffalo Sabres	65	2	17	19	20	....	....	....	....	....
	NHL Totals	**114**	**6**	**24**	**30**	**38**	....	....	....	....	....

CAMPBELL, Bryan

Center. Shoots left. 6', 173 lbs. Born, Sudbury, Ont., March 27, 1944.

Season	Club	GP	G	A	Pts	PIM	GP	G	A	Pts	PIM
1967-68	Los Angeles Kings	44	6	15	21	16	....	....	....	....	....
1968-69	Los Angeles Kings	18	2	1	3	4	6	2	1	3	0
1969-70	Los Angeles Kings	31	4	4	8	4	....	....	....	....	....
	Chicago Black Hawks	14	1	1	2	2	8	1	2	3	0
1970-71	Chicago Black Hawks	78	17	37	54	26	4	0	1	1	0
1971-72	Chicago Black Hawks	75	5	13	18	22	4	0	0	0	2
	NHL Totals	**260**	**35**	**71**	**106**	**74**	**22**	**3**	**4**	**7**	**2**

Claimed by **NY Rangers** from **Detroit** in Intra-League Draft, June 15, 1966. Claimed by **Los Angeles** from **NY Rangers** in Expansion Draft, June 6, 1967. Traded to **Chicago** by **Los Angeles** with Bill White and Gerry Desjardins for Gilles Marotte, Jim Stanfield and Denis DeJordy, February 20, 1970.

CAMPBELL, Colin

Defense. Shoots left. 5'9", 190 lbs. Born, London, Ont., January 28, 1953.
(Pittsburgh's 3rd choice, 27th overall, in 1973 Amateur Draft).

Season	Club	GP	G	A	Pts	PIM	GP	G	A	Pts	PIM
1974-75	Pittsburgh Penguins	59	4	15	19	172	9	1	3	4	21
1975-76	Pittsburgh Penguins	64	7	10	17	105	3	0	0	0	0
1976-77	Colorado Rockies	54	3	8	11	67	....	....	....	....	....
1977-78	Pittsburgh Penguins	55	1	9	10	103	....	....	....	....	....
1978-79	Pittsburgh Penguins	65	2	18	20	137	7	1	4	5	30
1979-80	Edmonton Oilers	72	2	11	13	196	3	0	0	0	11
1980-81	Vancouver Canucks	42	1	8	9	75	3	0	1	1	9
1981-82	Vancouver Canucks	47	0	8	8	131	16	2	2	4	89
1982-83	Detroit Red Wings	53	1	7	8	74	....	....	....	....	....
1983-84	Detroit Red Wings	68	3	4	7	108	4	0	0	0	21
1984-85	Detroit Red Wings	57	1	5	6	124	....	....	....	....	....
	NHL Totals	**636**	**25**	**103**	**128**	**1292**	**45**	**4**	**10**	**14**	**181**

Loaned to **Colorado** by **Pittsburgh** for the 1976-77 season to complete transaction that sent Simon Nolet and Michel Plasse to Colorado as compensation for Pittsburgh's signing of free agent Dennis Herron, September 1, 1976. Claimed by **Edmonton** from **Pittsburgh** in Expansion Draft, June 13, 1979. Claimed by **Vancouver** from **Edmonton** in Waiver Draft, October 10, 1980. Signed as a free agent by **Detroit**, June 26, 1982.

CAMPBELL, Dave

Defense. Shoots left. 6', 200 lbs. Born, Lachute, Que., April 27, 1896.

Season	Club	GP	G	A	Pts	PIM	GP	G	A	Pts	PIM
1920-21	Montreal Canadiens	2	0	0	0	0	....	....	....	....	....
	NHL Totals	**2**	**0**	**0**	**0**	**0**	....	....	....	....	....

Signed as a free agent by **Montreal**, February 26, 1921.

CAMPBELL, Don

Left wing. Shoots left. 5'10", 175 lbs. Born, Drumheller, Alta., July 12, 1925.

Season	Club	GP	G	A	Pts	PIM	GP	G	A	Pts	PIM
1943-44	Chicago Black Hawks	17	1	3	4	8	....	....	....	....	....
	NHL Totals	**17**	**1**	**3**	**4**	**8**	....	....	....	....	....

CAMPBELL, Earl

Defense. Shoots left. 5'11", 166 lbs. Born, Buckingham, Que., July 23, 1900.

Season	Club	GP	G	A	Pts	PIM	GP	G	A	Pts	PIM
1923-24	Ottawa Senators	18	5	3	8	8	1	0	0	0	6
1924-25	Ottawa Senators	29	0	0	0	0	....	....	....	....	....
1925-26	New York Americans	29	1	0	1	6	....	....	....	....	....
	NHL Totals	**76**	**6**	**3**	**9**	**14**	**1**	**0**	**0**	**0**	**6**

Loaned to **Ottawa** by **Edmonton** (WCHL) for 1923-24 season, December 23, 1923. Traded to **Ottawa** by **Edmonton** (WCHL) for cash, November 19, 1924. Signed as a free agent by **NY Americans**, September 18, 1925.

CAMPBELL, Jim

Right wing. Shoots right. 6'2", 205 lbs. Born, Worcester, MA, April 3, 1973.
(Montreal's 2nd choice, 28th overall, in 1991 Entry Draft).

Season	Club	GP	G	A	Pts	PIM	GP	G	A	Pts	PIM
1995-96	Mighty Ducks of Anaheim	16	2	3	5	36	....	....	....	....	....
1996-97	St. Louis Blues	68	23	20	43	68	4	1	0	1	6
1997-98	St. Louis Blues	76	22	19	41	55	10	7	3	10	12
1998-99	St. Louis Blues	55	4	21	25	41	....	....	....	....	....
99-2000	St. Louis Blues	2	0	0	0	9	....	....	....	....	....
2000-01	Montreal Canadiens	57	9	11	20	53	....	....	....	....	....
2001-02	Chicago Blackhawks	9	1	1	2	4	....	....	....	....	....
2002-03	Florida Panthers	1	0	0	0	0	....	....	....	....	....
	NHL Totals	**284**	**61**	**75**	**136**	**266**	**14**	**8**	**3**	**11**	**18**

NHL All-Rookie Team (1997)

Traded to **Anaheim** by **Montreal** for Robert Dirk, January 21, 1996. Signed as a free agent by **St. Louis**, July 11, 1996. Signed as a free agent by **Montreal**, August 21, 2000. Signed as a free agent by **Chicago**, November 19, 2001. Signed as a free agent by **Florida**, July 19, 2002.

CAMPBELL, Scott

Defense. Shoots left. 6'3", 205 lbs. Born, Toronto, Ont., June 22, 1957.
(St. Louis' 1st choice, 9th overall, in 1977 Amateur Draft).

Season	Club	GP	G	A	Pts	PIM	GP	G	A	Pts	PIM
1979-80	Winnipeg Jets	63	3	17	20	136	....	....	....	....	....
1980-81	Winnipeg Jets	14	1	4	5	55	....	....	....	....	....
1981-82	St. Louis Blues	3	0	0	0	52	....	....	....	....	....
	NHL Totals	**80**	**4**	**21**	**25**	**243**	....	....	....	....	....

Reclaimed by **St. Louis** from **Winnipeg** prior to Expansion Draft, June 9, 1979. Claimed as a priority selection by **Winnipeg**, June 9, 1979. • Missed majority of 1980-81 season recovering from shoulder injury suffered in game vs. Philadelphia, November 24, 1980. Traded to **St. Louis** by **Winnipeg** with John Markell for Bryan Maxwell, Ed Staniowski and Paul MacLean, July 3, 1981. • Retired following the 1981-82 season because of recurring headaches and asthma, July, 1982.

CAMPBELL, Wade

Defense. Shoots right. 6'4", 220 lbs. Born, Peace River, Alta., January 2, 1961.

Season	Club	GP	G	A	Pts	PIM	GP	G	A	Pts	PIM
1982-83	Winnipeg Jets	42	1	2	3	50	....	....	....	....	....
1983-84	Winnipeg Jets	79	7	14	21	147	3	0	0	0	7
1984-85	Winnipeg Jets	40	1	6	7	21	3	0	0	0	2

		REGULAR SEASON					PLAYOFFS				
Season	Club	GP	G	A	Pts	PIM	GP	G	A	Pts	PIM
1985-86	Winnipeg Jets	24	0	1	1	27	....	....	....	....	....
	Boston Bruins	8	0	0	0	15	....	....	....	....	....
1986-87	Boston Bruins	14	0	3	3	24	4	0	0	0	11
1987-88	Boston Bruins	6	0	1	1	21	....	....	....	....	....
	NHL Totals	**213**	**9**	**27**	**36**	**305**	**10**	**0**	**0**	**0**	**20**

Signed as a free agent by **Winnipeg**, October 5, 1982. Traded to **Boston** by **Winnipeg** for Bill Derlago, January 31, 1986.

CAMPEAU, Tod

Center. Shoots left. 5'11", 170 lbs. Born, St-Jerome, Que., June 4, 1923.

Season	Club	GP	G	A	Pts	PIM	GP	G	A	Pts	PIM
1943-44	Montreal Canadiens	2	0	0	0	0	....	....	....	....	....
1947-48	Montreal Canadiens	14	2	2	4	4	....	....	....	....	....
1948-49	Montreal Canadiens	26	3	7	10	12	1	0	0	0	0
	NHL Totals	**42**	**5**	**9**	**14**	**16**	**1**	**0**	**0**	**0**	**0**

Traded to **Pittsburgh** (AHL) by **Montreal** for cash, November 24, 1944.

CAMPEDELLI, Dom

Defense. Shoots right. 6'1", 185 lbs. Born, Cohasset, MA, April 3, 1964.
(Toronto's 10th choice, 129th overall, in 1982 Entry Draft).

Season	Club	GP	G	A	Pts	PIM	GP	G	A	Pts	PIM
1985-86	Montreal Canadiens	2	0	0	0	0	....	....	....	....	....
	NHL Totals	**2**	**0**	**0**	**0**	**0**	....	....	....	....	....

Traded to **Montreal** by **Toronto** for Montreal's 2nd round choice (Darryl Shannon) in 1986 Entry Draft and Toronto's 4th round choice (previously acquired, Toronto selected Kent Hulst) in 1986 Entry Draft, September 18, 1985. Traded to **Philadelphia** by **Montreal** for Andre Villeneuve, October 30, 1986. Traded to **Edmonton** by **Philadelphia** for Jeff Brubaker, March 9, 1987.

CAPUANO, Dave

Left wing. Shoots left. 6'2", 190 lbs. Born, Warwick, RI, July 27, 1968.
(Pittsburgh's 2nd choice, 25th overall, in 1986 Entry Draft).

Season	Club	GP	G	A	Pts	PIM	GP	G	A	Pts	PIM
1989-90	Pittsburgh Penguins	6	0	0	0	2	....	....	....	....	....
	Vancouver Canucks	27	3	5	8	10	....	....	....	....	....
1990-91	Vancouver Canucks	61	13	31	44	42	6	1	1	2	5
1992-93	Tampa Bay Lightning	6	1	1	2	2	....	....	....	....	....
1993-94	San Jose Sharks	4	0	1	1	0	....	....	....	....	....
	NHL Totals	**104**	**17**	**38**	**55**	**56**	**6**	**1**	**1**	**2**	**5**

• Brother of Jack

Traded to **Vancouver** by **Pittsburgh** with Andrew McBain and Dan Quinn for Rod Buskas, Barry Pederson and Tony Tanti, January 8, 1990. Traded to **Tampa Bay** by **Vancouver** with Vancouver's 4th round choice (later traded to New Jersey – later traded to Calgary – Calgary selected Ryan Duthie) in 1994 Entry Draft for Anatoli Semenov, November 3, 1992. Traded to **San Jose** by **Tampa Bay** for Peter Ahola, June 19, 1993. Traded to **Boston** by **San Jose** for cash, November 5, 1993.

CAPUANO, Jack

Defense. Shoots left. 6'2", 210 lbs. Born, Cranston, RI, July 7, 1966.
(Toronto's 4th choice, 88th overall, in 1984 Entry Draft).

Season	Club	GP	G	A	Pts	PIM	GP	G	A	Pts	PIM
1989-90	Toronto Maple Leafs	1	0	0	0	0	....	....	....	....	....
1990-91	Vancouver Canucks	3	0	0	0	0	....	....	....	....	....
1991-92	Boston Bruins	2	0	0	0	0	....	....	....	....	....
	NHL Totals	**6**	**0**	**0**	**0**	**0**	....	....	....	....	....

• Brother of Dave

Traded to **NY Islanders** by **Toronto** with Paul Gagne and Derek Laxdal for Mike Stevens and Gilles Thibaudeau, December 20, 1989. Traded to **Vancouver** by **NY Islanders** for Jeff Rohlicek, March 6, 1990. Signed as a free agent by **Boston**, August 1, 1991.

CARBOL, Leo

Defense. Shoots right. 5'11", 170 lbs. Born, Ottawa, Ont., June 5, 1910.

Season	Club	GP	G	A	Pts	PIM	GP	G	A	Pts	PIM
1942-43	Chicago Black Hawks	6	0	1	1	4	....	....	....	....	....
	NHL Totals	**6**	**0**	**1**	**1**	**4**	....	....	....	....	....

NHL rights transferred to **Detroit** from **Chicago** (AHA) after AHA club owners purchased Detroit (IHL and NHL) franchises, September 2, 1932. Traded to **Chicago** by **St. Louis** (AHA) with Alex Wood for cash, October 9, 1942.

CARBONNEAU, Guy

Center. Shoots right. 5'11", 186 lbs. Born, Sept-Iles, Que., March 18, 1960.
(Montreal's 4th choice, 44th overall, in 1979 Entry Draft).

Season	Club	GP	G	A	Pts	PIM	GP	G	A	Pts	PIM
1980-81	Montreal Canadiens	2	0	1	1	0	....	....	....	....	....
1982-83	Montreal Canadiens	77	18	29	47	68	3	0	0	0	2
1983-84	Montreal Canadiens	78	24	30	54	75	15	4	3	7	12
1984-85	Montreal Canadiens	79	23	34	57	43	12	4	3	7	8
1985-86 ♦	Montreal Canadiens	80	20	36	56	57	20	7	5	12	35
1986-87	Montreal Canadiens	79	18	27	45	68	17	3	8	11	20
1987-88	Montreal Canadiens	80	17	21	38	61	11	0	4	4	2
1988-89	Montreal Canadiens	79	26	30	56	44	21	4	5	9	10
1989-90	Montreal Canadiens	68	19	36	55	37	11	2	3	5	6
1990-91	Montreal Canadiens	78	20	24	44	63	13	1	5	6	10
1991-92	Montreal Canadiens	72	18	21	39	39	11	1	1	2	6
1992-93 ♦	Montreal Canadiens	61	4	13	17	20	20	3	3	6	10
1993-94	Montreal Canadiens	79	14	24	38	48	7	1	3	4	4
1994-95	St. Louis Blues	42	5	11	16	16	7	1	2	3	6
1995-96	Dallas Stars	71	8	15	23	38	....	....	....	....	....
1996-97	Dallas Stars	73	5	16	21	36	7	0	1	1	6
1997-98	Dallas Stars	77	7	17	24	40	16	3	1	4	6
1998-99 ♦	Dallas Stars	74	4	12	16	31	17	2	4	6	6
99-2000	Dallas Stars	69	10	6	16	36	23	2	4	6	12
	NHL Totals	**1318**	**260**	**403**	**663**	**820**	**231**	**38**	**55**	**93**	**161**

Frank J. Selke Trophy (1988, 1989, 1992)

Traded to **St. Louis** by **Montreal** for Jim Montgomery, August 19, 1994. Traded to **Dallas** by **St. Louis** for Paul Broten, October 2, 1995. • Officially announced retirement, June 29, 2000.

CARDIN, Claude

Left wing. Shoots left. 5'10", 178 lbs. Born, Sorel, Que., February 17, 1941.

Season	Club	GP	G	A	Pts	PIM	GP	G	A	Pts	PIM
1967-68	St. Louis Blues	1	0	0	0	0	....	....	....	....	....
	NHL Totals	**1**	**0**	**0**	**0**	**0**	....	....	....	....	....

Traded to **St. Louis** by **Montreal** for cash, June 21, 1967.

CARDWELL, Steve

Left wing. Shoots left. 5'11", 190 lbs. Born, Toronto, Ont., August 13, 1950.
(Pittsburgh's 5th choice, 63rd overall, in 1970 Amateur Draft).

Season	Club	GP	G	A	Pts	PIM	GP	G	A	Pts	PIM
1970-71	Pittsburgh Penguins	5	0	1	1	15	....	....	....	....	....
1971-72	Pittsburgh Penguins	28	7	8	15	18	4	0	0	0	2
1972-73	Pittsburgh Penguins	20	2	2	4	2	....	....	....	....	....
	NHL Totals	**53**	**9**	**11**	**20**	**35**	**4**	**0**	**0**	**0**	**2**

CAREY, George

Right wing. Shoots right. 5'6", 140 lbs. Born,

Season	Club	GP	G	A	Pts	PIM	GP	G	A	Pts	PIM
1919-20	Quebec Bulldogs	20	11	9	20	6	....	....	....	....	....
1920-21	Hamilton Tigers	20	6	1	7	8	....	....	....	....	....
1921-22	Hamilton Tigers	23	3	2	5	6	....	....	....	....	....
1922-23	Hamilton Tigers	5	1	0	1	0	....	....	....	....	....
1923-24	Toronto St. Pats	4	0	0	0	0	....	....	....	....	....
	NHL Totals	**72**	**21**	**12**	**33**	**20**	....	....	....	....	....

Transferred to **Mtl. Wanderers** from **Quebec** in Dispersal Draft, November 26, 1917. • Suspended by **Mtl. Wanderers** for refusing to report to NHL club, November 29, 1917. Transferred to **Quebec** by **NHL** after Quebec franchise returned to NHL, November 25, 1919. Transferred to **Hamilton** after **Quebec** franchise relocated, November 2, 1920. Loaned to **Calgary** (WCHL) by **Hamilton**, January 16, 1923. Traded to **Toronto** by **Hamilton** with Amos Arbour and Bert Corbeau for Ken Randall, the NHL rights to Corb Denneny and cash, December 14, 1923.

CARKNER, Terry

Defense. Shoots left. 6'3", 210 lbs. Born, Smiths Falls, Ont., March 7, 1966.
(NY Rangers' 1st choice, 14th overall, in 1984 Entry Draft).

Season	Club	GP	G	A	Pts	PIM	GP	G	A	Pts	PIM
1986-87	New York Rangers	52	2	13	15	118	1	0	0	0	0
1987-88	Quebec Nordiques	63	3	24	27	159	....	....	....	....	....
1988-89	Philadelphia Flyers	78	11	32	43	149	19	1	5	6	28
1989-90	Philadelphia Flyers	63	4	18	22	169	....	....	....	....	....
1990-91	Philadelphia Flyers	79	7	25	32	204	....	....	....	....	....
1991-92	Philadelphia Flyers	73	4	12	16	195	....	....	....	....	....
1992-93	Philadelphia Flyers	83	3	16	19	150	....	....	....	....	....
1993-94	Detroit Red Wings	68	1	6	7	130	7	0	0	0	4
1994-95	Detroit Red Wings	20	1	2	3	21	....	....	....	....	....
1995-96	Florida Panthers	73	3	10	13	80	22	0	4	4	10
1996-97	Florida Panthers	70	0	14	14	96	5	0	0	0	6
1997-98	Florida Panthers	74	1	7	8	63	....	....	....	....	....
1998-99	Florida Panthers	62	2	9	11	54	....	....	....	....	....
	NHL Totals	**858**	**42**	**188**	**230**	**1588**	**54**	**1**	**9**	**10**	**48**

Traded to **Quebec** by **NY Rangers** with Jeff Jackson for John Ogrodnick and David Shaw, September 30, 1987. Traded to **Philadelphia** by **Quebec** for Greg Smyth and Philadelphia's 3rd round choice (John Tanner) in 1989 Entry Draft, July 25, 1988. Traded to **Detroit** by **Philadelphia** for Yves Racine and Detroit's 4th round choice (Sebastien Vallee) in 1994 Entry Draft, October 5, 1993. Signed as a free agent by **Florida**, August 8, 1995.

CARLETON, Wayne

Left wing. Shoots left. 6'3", 212 lbs. Born, Sudbury, Ont., August 4, 1946.

Season	Club	GP	G	A	Pts	PIM	GP	G	A	Pts	PIM
1965-66	Toronto Maple Leafs	2	0	1	1	0	....	....	....	....	....
1966-67	Toronto Maple Leafs	5	1	0	1	14	....	....	....	....	....
1967-68	Toronto Maple Leafs	65	8	11	19	34	....	....	....	....	....
1968-69	Toronto Maple Leafs	12	1	3	4	6	....	....	....	....	....
1969-70	Toronto Maple Leafs	7	0	1	1	6	....	....	....	....	....
♦	Boston Bruins	42	6	19	25	23	14	2	4	6	14
1970-71	Boston Bruins	69	22	24	46	44	4	0	0	0	0
1971-72	California Golden Seals	76	17	14	31	45	....	....	....	....	....
	NHL Totals	**278**	**55**	**73**	**128**	**172**	**18**	**2**	**4**	**6**	**14**

Played in NHL All-Star Game (1968)

Traded to **Boston** by **Toronto** for Jim Harrison, December 10, 1969. Claimed by **California** from **Boston** in Intra-League Draft, June 8, 1971.

CARLIN, Brian

Left wing. Shoots left. 5'10", 175 lbs. Born, Calgary, Alta., June 13, 1950.
(Los Angeles' 5th choice, 86th overall, in 1970 Amateur Draft).

Season	Club	GP	G	A	Pts	PIM	GP	G	A	Pts	PIM
1971-72	Los Angeles Kings	5	1	0	1	0	....	....	....	....	....
	NHL Totals	**5**	**1**	**0**	**1**	**0**	....	....	....	....	....

CARLSON, Jack

Left wing. Shoots left. 6'3", 205 lbs. Born, Virginia, MN, August 23, 1954.
(Detroit's 7th choice, 117th overall, in 1974 Amateur Draft).

Season	Club	GP	G	A	Pts	PIM	GP	G	A	Pts	PIM
1978-79	Minnesota North Stars	16	3	0	3	40	....	....	....	....	....
1980-81	Minnesota North Stars	43	7	2	9	108	15	1	2	3	50

Season	Club	Regular Season GP	G	A	Pts	PIM	Playoffs GP	G	A	Pts	PIM
1981-82	Minnesota North Stars	57	8	4	12	103	1	0	0	0	15
1982-83	St. Louis Blues	54	6	1	7	58	4	0	0	0	5
1983-84	St. Louis Blues	58	6	8	14	95	5	0	0	0	2
1986-87	Minnesota North Stars	8	0	0	0	13	....	....	....	....	....
	NHL Totals	**236**	**30**	**15**	**45**	**417**	**25**	**1**	**2**	**3**	**72**

• Brother of Steve

Rights traded to **Minnesota** by **Detroit** for future considerations, July 27, 1978. Traded to **Minnesota** by **New England** (WHA) for future considerations, February 1, 1979. • Missed entire 1979-80 season recovering from back surgery. Claimed by **St. Louis** from **Minnesota** in Waiver Draft, October 4, 1982. Signed as a free agent by **Minnesota**, November, 1986.

CARLSON, Kent

Defense. Shoots left. 6'3", 200 lbs. Born, Concord, NH, January 11, 1962.
(Montreal's 3rd choice, 32nd overall, in 1982 Entry Draft).

Season	Club	Regular Season GP	G	A	Pts	PIM	Playoffs GP	G	A	Pts	PIM
1983-84	Montreal Canadiens	65	3	7	10	73	....	....	....	....	....
1984-85	Montreal Canadiens	18	1	1	2	33	....	....	....	....	....
1985-86	Montreal Canadiens	2	0	0	0	0	....	....	....	....	....
	St. Louis Blues	26	2	3	5	42	5	0	0	0	11
1987-88	St. Louis Blues	....	....	....	....	....	3	0	0	0	2
1988-89	Washington Capitals	2	1	0	1	0	....	....	....	....	....
	NHL Totals	**113**	**7**	**11**	**18**	**148**	**8**	**0**	**0**	**0**	**13**

• Missed majority of 1984-85 season recovering from hand injury suffered in game vs. NY Islanders, January 8, 1985. Traded to **St. Louis** by **Montreal** for Graham Herring and St. Louis' 5th round choice (Eric Aubertin) in 1986 Entry Draft, January 31, 1986. • Missed entire 1986-87 season recovering from spinal fusion surgery. Traded to **Winnipeg** by **St. Louis** with St. Louis' 12th round choice (Sergei Kharin) in 1989 Entry Draft and 4th round choice (Scott Levins) in 1990 Entry Draft for Peter Douris, September 29, 1988. Traded to **Washington** by **Winnipeg** for future considerations, October 19, 1988.

CARLSON, Steve

Center. Shoots left. 6'3", 180 lbs. Born, Virginia, MN, August 26, 1955.
(Detroit's 10th choice, 131st overall, in 1975 Amateur Draft).

Season	Club	Regular Season GP	G	A	Pts	PIM	Playoffs GP	G	A	Pts	PIM
1979-80	Los Angeles Kings	52	9	12	21	23	4	1	1	2	7
	NHL Totals	**52**	**9**	**12**	**21**	**23**	**4**	**1**	**1**	**2**	**7**

• Brother of Jack

NHL rights traded to **Los Angeles** by **Detroit** for Steve Short, December 6, 1978. Reclaimed by **Los Angeles** from **Edmonton** prior to Expansion Draft, June 9, 1979. Signed as a free agent by **Minnesota**, August 9, 1982. Signed as a free agent by **Pittsburgh**, August 15, 1983.

CARLSSON, Anders

Center. Shoots left. 5'11", 185 lbs. Born, Gavle, Sweden, November 25, 1960.
(New Jersey's 5th choice, 66th overall, in 1986 Entry Draft).

Season	Club	Regular Season GP	G	A	Pts	PIM	Playoffs GP	G	A	Pts	PIM
1986-87	New Jersey Devils	48	2	18	20	14	....	....	....	....	....
1987-88	New Jersey Devils	9	1	0	1	0	3	1	0	1	2
1988-89	New Jersey Devils	47	4	8	12	20	....	....	....	....	....
	NHL Totals	**104**	**7**	**26**	**33**	**34**	**3**	**1**	**0**	**1**	**2**

CARLYLE, Randy

Defense. Shoots left. 5'10", 200 lbs. Born, Sudbury, Ont., April 19, 1956.
(Toronto's 1st choice, 30th overall, in 1976 Amateur Draft).

Season	Club	Regular Season GP	G	A	Pts	PIM	Playoffs GP	G	A	Pts	PIM
1976-77	Toronto Maple Leafs	45	0	5	5	51	9	0	1	1	20
1977-78	Toronto Maple Leafs	49	2	11	13	31	7	0	1	1	8
1978-79	Pittsburgh Penguins	70	13	34	47	78	7	0	0	0	12
1979-80	Pittsburgh Penguins	67	8	28	36	45	5	1	0	1	4
1980-81	Pittsburgh Penguins	76	16	67	83	136	5	4	5	9	9
1981-82	Pittsburgh Penguins	73	11	64	75	131	5	1	3	4	16
1982-83	Pittsburgh Penguins	61	15	41	56	110	....	....	....	....	....
1983-84	Pittsburgh Penguins	50	3	23	26	82	....	....	....	....	....
	Winnipeg Jets	5	0	3	3	2	3	0	2	2	4
1984-85	Winnipeg Jets	71	13	38	51	98	8	1	5	6	13
1985-86	Winnipeg Jets	68	16	33	49	93	....	....	....	....	....
1986-87	Winnipeg Jets	71	16	26	42	93	10	1	5	6	18
1987-88	Winnipeg Jets	78	15	44	59	210	5	0	2	2	10
1988-89	Winnipeg Jets	78	6	38	44	78	....	....	....	....	....
1989-90	Winnipeg Jets	53	3	15	18	50	....	....	....	....	....
1990-91	Winnipeg Jets	52	9	19	28	44	....	....	....	....	....
1991-92	Winnipeg Jets	66	1	9	10	54	5	1	0	1	6
1992-93	Winnipeg Jets	22	1	1	2	14	....	....	....	....	....
	NHL Totals	**1055**	**148**	**499**	**647**	**1400**	**69**	**9**	**24**	**33**	**120**

NHL First All-Star Team (1981) • James Norris Trophy (1981)

Played in NHL All-Star Game (1981, 1982, 1985, 1993)

Traded to **Pittsburgh** by **Toronto** with George Ferguson for Dave Burrows, June 14, 1978. Traded to **Winnipeg** by **Pittsburgh** for Winnipeg's 1st round choice (Doug Bodger) in 1984 Entry Draft and future considerations (Moe Mantha, May 1, 1984), March 5, 1984.

CARNBACK, Patrik

Center. Shoots left. 6', 187 lbs. Born, Goteborg, Sweden, February 1, 1968.
(Montreal's 7th choice, 125th overall, in 1988 Entry Draft).

Season	Club	Regular Season GP	G	A	Pts	PIM	Playoffs GP	G	A	Pts	PIM
1992-93	Montreal Canadiens	6	0	0	0	2	....	....	....	....	....
1993-94	Mighty Ducks of Anaheim	73	12	11	23	54	....	....	....	....	....
1994-95	Mighty Ducks of Anaheim	41	6	15	21	32	....	....	....	....	....
1995-96	Mighty Ducks of Anaheim	34	6	12	18	34	....	....	....	....	....
	NHL Totals	**154**	**24**	**38**	**62**	**122**	....	....	....	....	....

Traded to **Anaheim** by **Montreal** with Todd Ewen for Anaheim's 3rd round choice (Chris Murray) in 1994 Entry Draft, August 10, 1993.

CARNEY, Keith

Defense. Shoots left. 6'2", 211 lbs. Born, Providence, RI, February 3, 1970.
(Buffalo's 3rd choice, 76th overall, in 1988 Entry Draft).

Season	Club	Regular Season GP	G	A	Pts	PIM	Playoffs GP	G	A	Pts	PIM
1991-92	Buffalo Sabres	14	1	2	3	18	7	0	3	3	0
1992-93	Buffalo Sabres	30	2	4	6	55	8	0	3	3	6
1993-94	Buffalo Sabres	7	1	3	4	4	....	....	....	....	....
	Chicago Blackhawks	30	3	5	8	35	6	0	1	1	4
1994-95	Chicago Blackhawks	18	1	0	1	11	4	0	1	1	0
1995-96	Chicago Blackhawks	82	5	14	19	94	10	0	3	3	4
1996-97	Chicago Blackhawks	81	3	15	18	62	6	1	1	2	2
1997-98	Chicago Blackhawks	60	2	13	15	73	....	....	....	....	....
	Phoenix Coyotes	20	1	6	7	18	6	0	0	0	4
1998-99	Phoenix Coyotes	82	2	14	16	62	7	1	2	3	10
99-2000	Phoenix Coyotes	82	4	20	24	87	5	0	0	0	17
2000-01	Phoenix Coyotes	82	2	14	16	86	....	....	....	....	....
2001-02	Mighty Ducks of Anaheim	60	5	9	14	30	....	....	....	....	....
2002-03	Mighty Ducks of Anaheim	81	4	18	22	65	21	0	4	4	16
	NHL Totals	**729**	**36**	**137**	**173**	**700**	**80**	**2**	**18**	**20**	**63**

Traded to **Chicago** by **Buffalo** with Buffalo's 6th round choice (Marc Magliarditi) in 1995 Entry Draft for Craig Muni and Chicago's 5th round choice (Daniel Bienvenue) in 1995 Entry Draft, October 26, 1993. Traded to **Phoenix** by **Chicago** with Jim Cummins for Chad Kilger and Jayson More, March 4, 1998. Traded to **Anaheim** by **Phoenix** for Calgary's 2nd round choice (previously acquired, later traded back to Calgary – Calgary selected Andrei Taratukhin) in 2001 Entry Draft, June 19, 2001.

CARON, Alain

Right wing. Shoots right. 5'9", 182 lbs. Born, Dolbeau, Que., April 27, 1938.

Season	Club	Regular Season GP	G	A	Pts	PIM	Playoffs GP	G	A	Pts	PIM
1967-68	Oakland Seals	58	9	13	22	18	....	....	....	....	....
1968-69	Montreal Canadiens	2	0	0	0	0	....	....	....	....	....
	NHL Totals	**60**	**9**	**13**	**22**	**18**	....	....	....	....	....

Claimed by **California** (Oakland) from **Chicago** in Expansion Draft, June 6, 1967. Traded to **Montreal** by **Oakland** with Wally Boyer, Oakland's 1st round choices in 1968 (Jim Pritchard) and 1970 (Ray Martynuik) Amateur Drafts and future considerations (Lyle Bradley, June, 1968) for Norm Ferguson, Stan Fuller and future considerations (Francois Lacombe and Michel Jacques, June, 1968), May 21, 1968. Claimed by **Philadelphia** (San Diego-WHL) from **Montreal** in Reverse Draft, June 10, 1970.

CARPENTER, Bob

Center. Shoots left. 6', 200 lbs. Born, Beverly, MA, July 13, 1963.
(Washington's 1st choice, 3rd overall, in 1981 Entry Draft).

Season	Club	Regular Season GP	G	A	Pts	PIM	Playoffs GP	G	A	Pts	PIM
1981-82	Washington Capitals	80	32	35	67	69	....	....	....	....	....
1982-83	Washington Capitals	80	32	37	69	64	4	1	0	1	2
1983-84	Washington Capitals	80	28	40	68	51	8	2	1	3	25
1984-85	Washington Capitals	80	53	42	95	87	5	1	4	5	8
1985-86	Washington Capitals	80	27	29	56	105	9	5	4	9	12
1986-87	Washington Capitals	22	5	7	12	21	....	....	....	....	....
	New York Rangers	28	2	8	10	20	....	....	....	....	....
	Los Angeles Kings	10	2	3	5	6	5	1	2	3	2
1987-88	Los Angeles Kings	71	19	33	52	84	5	1	1	2	0
1988-89	Los Angeles Kings	39	11	15	26	16	....	....	....	....	....
	Boston Bruins	18	5	9	14	10	8	1	1	2	4
1989-90	Boston Bruins	80	25	31	56	97	21	4	6	10	39
1990-91	Boston Bruins	29	8	8	16	22	1	0	1	1	2
1991-92	Boston Bruins	60	25	23	48	46	8	0	1	1	6
1992-93	Washington Capitals	68	11	17	28	65	6	1	4	5	6
1993-94	New Jersey Devils	76	10	23	33	51	20	1	7	8	20
1994-95 ♦	New Jersey Devils	41	5	11	16	19	17	1	4	5	6
1995-96	New Jersey Devils	52	5	5	10	14	....	....	....	....	....
1996-97	New Jersey Devils	62	4	15	19	14	10	1	2	3	2
1997-98	New Jersey Devils	66	9	9	18	22	6	1	0	1	0
1998-99	New Jersey Devils	56	2	8	10	36	7	0	0	0	2
	NHL Totals	**1178**	**320**	**408**	**728**	**919**	**140**	**21**	**38**	**59**	**136**

Played in NHL All-Star Game (1985)

Traded to **NY Rangers** by **Washington** with Washington's 2nd round choice (Jason Prosofsky) in 1989 Entry Draft for Bob Crawford, Kelly Miller and Mike Ridley, January 1, 1987. Traded to **Los Angeles** by **NY Rangers** with Tom Laidlaw for Jeff Crossman, Marcel Dionne and Los Angeles' 3rd round choice (later traded to Minnesota – Minnesota selected Murray Garbutt) in 1989 Entry Draft, March 10, 1987. Traded to **Boston** by **Los Angeles** for Steve Kasper to complete transaction that sent Jay Miller to Los Angeles (January 22, 1989), January 23, 1989. • Missed majority of 1990-91 season recovering from kneecap injury suffered in game vs. Montreal, December 8, 1990. Signed as a free agent by **Washington**, June 30, 1992. Signed as a free agent by **New Jersey**, September 30, 1993. • Officially announced retirement, August 16, 1999.

CARPENTER, Ed

Defense. Shoots right. 6', 170 lbs. Born, Hartford, MI, June 15, 1890.

Season	Club	Regular Season GP	G	A	Pts	PIM	Playoffs GP	G	A	Pts	PIM
1919-20	Quebec Bulldogs	24	8	4	12	24	....	....	....	....	....
1920-21	Hamilton Tigers	21	2	1	3	17	....	....	....	....	....
	NHL Totals	**45**	**10**	**5**	**15**	**41**	....	....	....	....	....

Signed as a free agent by **Montreal**, December 15, 1919. Traded to **Quebec** by **Montreal** for Goldie Prodgers, December 21, 1919. Transferred to **Hamilton** after **Quebec** franchise relocated, November 2, 1920. Traded to **Toronto** by **Hamilton** for Cully Wilson, November 9, 1921.

CARR, Gene

Center. Shoots left. 5'11", 185 lbs. Born, Nanaimo, B.C., September 17, 1951.
(St. Louis' 1st choice, 4th overall, in 1971 Amateur Draft).

Season	Club	Regular Season GP	G	A	Pts	PIM	Playoffs GP	G	A	Pts	PIM
1971-72	St. Louis Blues	15	3	2	5	9	....	....	....	....	....
	New York Rangers	59	8	8	16	25	16	1	3	4	21

Season	Club	GP	G	A	Pts	PIM	GP	G	A	Pts	PIM
		REGULAR SEASON					PLAYOFFS				
1972-73	New York Rangers	50	9	10	19	50	1	0	1	1	0
1973-74	New York Rangers	29	1	5	6	15	....	....	....	....	....
	Los Angeles Kings	21	6	11	17	36	5	2	1	3	14
1974-75	Los Angeles Kings	80	7	32	39	103	3	1	2	3	29
1975-76	Los Angeles Kings	38	8	11	19	16	....	....	....	....	....
1976-77	Los Angeles Kings	68	15	12	27	25	9	1	1	2	2
1977-78	Los Angeles Kings	5	2	0	2	4	....	....	....	....	....
	Pittsburgh Penguins	70	17	37	54	76	....	....	....	....	....
1978-79	Atlanta Flames	30	3	8	11	6	1	0	0	0	0
	NHL Totals	**465**	**79**	**136**	**215**	**365**	**35**	**5**	**8**	**13**	**66**

• Son of Red

Traded to **NY Rangers** by **St. Louis** with Jim Lorentz and Wayne Connelly for Jack Egers, Andre Dupont and Mike Murphy, November 15, 1971. Traded to **Los Angeles** by **NY Rangers** for Los Angeles' 1st round choice (Ron Duguay) in 1977 Amateur Draft, February 15, 1974. Traded to **Pittsburgh** by **Los Angeles** with Dave Schultz and Los Angeles' 4th round choice (Shane Pearsall) in 1978 Amateur Draft for Syl Apps Jr. and Hartland Monahan, November 2, 1977. Signed as a free agent by **Atlanta**, June 6, 1978. Claimed by **Winnipeg** from **Atlanta**, June 13, 1979.

CARR, Lorne

Right wing. Shoots right. 5'8", 161 lbs. Born, Stoughton, Sask., July 2, 1910.

Season	Club	GP	G	A	Pts	PIM	GP	G	A	Pts	PIM
1933-34	New York Rangers	14	0	0	0	0	....	....	....	....	....
1934-35	New York Americans	48	17	14	31	14	....	....	....	....	....
1935-36	New York Americans	44	8	10	18	4	5	1	1	2	0
1936-37	New York Americans	48	18	16	34	22	....	....	....	....	....
1937-38	New York Americans	48	16	7	23	12	6	3	1	4	2
1938-39	New York Americans	46	19	18	37	16	2	0	0	0	0
1939-40	New York Americans	48	8	17	25	17	3	0	0	0	0
1940-41	New York Americans	48	13	19	32	10	....	....	....	....	....
1941-42 ♦	Toronto Maple Leafs	47	16	17	33	4	13	3	2	5	6
1942-43	Toronto Maple Leafs	50	27	33	60	15	6	1	2	3	0
1943-44	Toronto Maple Leafs	50	36	38	74	9	5	0	1	1	0
1944-45 ♦	Toronto Maple Leafs	47	21	25	46	7	13	2	2	4	5
1945-46	Toronto Maple Leafs	42	5	8	13	2	....	....	....	....	....
	NHL Totals	**580**	**204**	**222**	**426**	**132**	**53**	**10**	**9**	**19**	**13**

NHL First All-Star Team (1943, 1944)

Traded to **Buffalo** (IHL) by **NY Rangers** with $15,000 for Carl Voss, October 4, 1932. Traded to **NY Rangers** by **Buffalo** (IHL) for cash, April 8, 1933. Traded to **Syracuse** (IHL) by **NY Rangers** for cash, January 30, 1934. Traded to **NY Americans** by **Syracuse** (IHL) for Ron Martin and the loan of Walter Jackson, November 5, 1934. • Team name changed to **Brooklyn Americans** prior to 1941-42 season. Traded to **Toronto** by **Brooklyn** for the loan of Red Heron, Gus Marker, Nick Knott and future considerations (cash, February 2, 1942), October 30, 1941.

CARR, Red

Left wing. Shoots left. 5'8", 178 lbs. Born, Winnipeg, Man., December 29, 1916.

Season	Club	GP	G	A	Pts	PIM	GP	G	A	Pts	PIM
1943-44	Toronto Maple Leafs	5	0	1	1	2	....	....	....	....	....
	NHL Totals	**5**	**0**	**1**	**1**	**2**	....	....	....	....	....

• Father of Gene

CARRIERE, Larry

Defense. Shoots left. 6'1", 190 lbs. Born, Montreal, Que., January 30, 1952.
(Buffalo's 2nd choice, 25th overall, in 1972 Amateur Draft).

Season	Club	GP	G	A	Pts	PIM	GP	G	A	Pts	PIM
1972-73	Buffalo Sabres	40	2	8	10	52	6	0	1	1	8
1973-74	Buffalo Sabres	78	6	24	30	103	....	....	....	....	....
1974-75	Buffalo Sabres	80	1	11	12	111	17	0	2	2	32
1975-76	Atlanta Flames	75	4	15	19	96	2	0	0	0	2
1976-77	Atlanta Flames	25	2	3	5	16	....	....	....	....	....
	Vancouver Canucks	49	1	9	10	55	....	....	....	....	....
1977-78	Vancouver Canucks	7	0	3	3	11	....	....	....	....	....
	Los Angeles Kings	2	0	0	0	0	....	....	....	....	....
	Buffalo Sabres	9	0	0	0	18	....	....	....	....	....
1979-80	Toronto Maple Leafs	2	0	1	1	0	2	0	0	0	0
	NHL Totals	**367**	**16**	**74**	**90**	**462**	**27**	**0**	**3**	**3**	**42**

Traded to **Atlanta** by **Buffalo** with Buffalo's 1st round choice (later traded to Washington – Washington selected Greg Carroll) in 1976 Amateur Draft and cash for Jacques Richard, October 1, 1975. Traded to **Vancouver** by **Atlanta** with Hilliard Graves for John Gould and Los Angeles' 2nd round choice (previously acquired, Atlanta selected Brian Hill) in 1977 Amateur Draft, December 2, 1976. Traded to **Los Angeles** by **Vancouver** for Sheldon Kannegiesser, November 21, 1977. Signed as a free agent by **Buffalo**, March 12, 1978. Signed as a free agent by **Toronto** to five-game tryout contract, April 5, 1980.

CARRIGAN, Gene

Center. Shoots left. 6'1", 200 lbs. Born, Edmonton, Alta., July 5, 1907.

Season	Club	GP	G	A	Pts	PIM	GP	G	A	Pts	PIM
1930-31	New York Rangers	33	2	0	2	13	....	....	....	....	....
1933-34	Detroit Red Wings	....	....	....	....	....	4	0	0	0	0
1934-35	St. Louis Eagles	4	0	1	1	0	....	....	....	....	....
	NHL Totals	**37**	**2**	**1**	**3**	**13**	**4**	**0**	**0**	**0**	**0**

Claimed by **NY Rangers** from **Hollywood** (Cal-Pro) in Inter-League Draft, May 14, 1928. Traded to **Chicago** (London-IHL) by **NY Rangers** for cash, October 27, 1931. Traded to **Detroit** by **Chicago** (London-IHL) for Frank Waite and Leroy Goldsworthy, October 19, 1933. Traded to **Boston** by **Detroit** for George Patterson, May 12, 1934. Loaned to **St. Louis** by **Boston** to replace injured Frank Jerwa, January 18, 1935 and returned January 30, 1935. Traded to **Detroit** by **Boston** for Lorne Duguid, December 29, 1935.

CARROLL, Billy

Center. Shoots left. 5'10", 190 lbs. Born, Toronto, Ont., January 19, 1959.
(NY Islanders' 3rd choice, 38th overall, in 1979 Entry Draft).

Season	Club	GP	G	A	Pts	PIM	GP	G	A	Pts	PIM
		REGULAR SEASON					PLAYOFFS				
1980-81 ♦	New York Islanders	18	4	4	8	6	18	3	9	12	4
1981-82 ♦	New York Islanders	72	9	20	29	32	19	2	2	4	8
1982-83 ♦	New York Islanders	71	1	11	12	24	20	1	1	2	2
1983-84	New York Islanders	39	5	2	7	12	5	0	0	0	0
1984-85 ♦	Edmonton Oilers	65	8	9	17	22	9	0	0	0	4
1985-86	Edmonton Oilers	5	0	2	2	0	....	....	....	....	....
	Detroit Red Wings	21	2	4	6	11	....	....	....	....	....
1986-87	Detroit Red Wings	31	1	2	3	6	....	....	....	....	....
	NHL Totals	**322**	**30**	**54**	**84**	**113**	**71**	**6**	**12**	**18**	**18**

Claimed by **Edmonton** from **NY Islanders** in Waiver Draft, October 9, 1984. Traded to **Detroit** by **Edmonton** for Bruce Eakin, December 28, 1985.

CARROLL, George

Defense. Shoots right. 6'2", 210 lbs. Born, Moncton, N.B., June 3, 1897.

Season	Club	GP	G	A	Pts	PIM	GP	G	A	Pts	PIM
1924-25	Montreal Maroons	5	0	0	0	2	....	....	....	....	....
	Boston Bruins	11	0	0	0	9	....	....	....	....	....
	NHL Totals	**16**	**0**	**0**	**0**	**11**	....	....	....	....	....

Signed as a free agent by **Mtl. Maroons**, November 13, 1924. Traded to **Boston** by **Mtl. Maroons** for the rights to Ernie Parkes, December 19, 1924. Signed as a free agent by **Mtl. Maroons** folowing release by **Boston**, February 22, 1925.

CARROLL, Greg

Center. Shoots left. 6', 185 lbs. Born, Gimli, Man., November 10, 1956.
(Washington's 2nd choice, 15th overall, in 1976 Amateur Draft).

Season	Club	GP	G	A	Pts	PIM	GP	G	A	Pts	PIM
1978-79	Washington Capitals	24	5	6	11	12	....	....	....	....	....
	Detroit Red Wings	36	2	9	11	8	....	....	....	....	....
1979-80	Hartford Whalers	71	13	19	32	24	....	....	....	....	....
	NHL Totals	**131**	**20**	**34**	**54**	**44**	....	....	....	....	....

Signed as a free agent by **Washington** after being released by **Cincinnati** (WHA), September 21, 1978. Claimed on waivers by **Detroit** from **Washington**, January 6, 1979. Signed by **Hartford** as a free agent, October 30, 1979.

CARRUTHERS, Dwight

Defense. Shoots right. 5'10", 186 lbs. Born, Lashburn, Sask., November 7, 1944.

Season	Club	GP	G	A	Pts	PIM	GP	G	A	Pts	PIM
1965-66	Detroit Red Wings	1	0	0	0	0	....	....	....	....	....
1967-68	Philadelphia Flyers	1	0	0	0	0	....	....	....	....	....
	NHL Totals	**2**	**0**	**0**	**0**	**0**	....	....	....	....	....

Claimed by **Philadelphia** from **Detroit** in Expansion Draft, June 6, 1967.

CARSE, Bill

Center. Shoots left. 5'8", 165 lbs. Born, Edmonton, Alta., May 29, 1914.

Season	Club	GP	G	A	Pts	PIM	GP	G	A	Pts	PIM
1938-39	New York Rangers	1	0	1	1	0	6	1	1	2	0
1939-40	Chicago Black Hawks	48	10	13	23	10	2	1	0	1	0
1940-41	Chicago Black Hawks	32	5	15	20	12	2	0	0	0	0
1941-42	Chicago Black Hawks	43	13	14	27	16	3	1	1	2	0
	NHL Totals	**124**	**28**	**43**	**71**	**38**	**13**	**3**	**2**	**5**	**0**

• Brother of Bob

Traded to **NY Rangers** by **Vancouver** (PCHL) for cash, October 12, 1937. Traded to **Chicago** by **NY Rangers** for cash, May 17, 1939.

CARSE, Bob

Left wing. Shoots left. 5'9", 170 lbs. Born, Edmonton, Alta., July 19, 1919.

Season	Club	GP	G	A	Pts	PIM	GP	G	A	Pts	PIM
1939-40	Chicago Black Hawks	22	3	5	8	11	2	0	0	0	0
1940-41	Chicago Black Hawks	43	9	9	18	9	5	0	0	0	2
1941-42	Chicago Black Hawks	33	7	16	23	10	3	0	2	2	0
1942-43	Chicago Black Hawks	47	10	22	32	6	....	....	....	....	....
1947-48	Montreal Canadiens	22	3	3	6	16	....	....	....	....	....
	NHL Totals	**167**	**32**	**55**	**87**	**52**	**10**	**0**	**2**	**2**	**2**

• Brother of Bill

Signed as a free agent by **Montreal**, October 14, 1947. Traded to **Cleveland** (AHL) by **Montreal** for future considerations, December 16, 1947.

CARSON, Bill

Center. Shoots left. 5'8", 158 lbs. Born, Bracebridge, Ont., November 25, 1900.

Season	Club	GP	G	A	Pts	PIM	GP	G	A	Pts	PIM
1926-27	Toronto St. Pats/Maple Leafs	40	16	6	22	41	....	....	....	....	....
1927-28	Toronto Maple Leafs	32	20	6	26	36	....	....	....	....	....
1928-29	Toronto Maple Leafs	24	7	6	13	45	....	....	....	....	....
	♦ Boston Bruins	19	4	2	6	10	5	2	0	2	8
1929-30	Boston Bruins	44	7	4	11	24	6	1	0	1	6
	NHL Totals	**159**	**54**	**24**	**78**	**156**	**11**	**3**	**0**	**3**	**14**

• Brother of Frank and Gerry

Signed as a free agent by **Toronto**, April 16, 1926. Traded to **Boston** by **Toronto** for cash, January 25, 1929. Traded to **London** (IHL) by **Boston** for cash, November 24, 1930.

CARSON, Frank

Right wing. Shoots right. 5'7", 165 lbs. Born, Bracebridge, Ont., January 12, 1902.

Season	Club	GP	G	A	Pts	PIM	GP	G	A	Pts	PIM
1925-26 ♦	Montreal Maroons	16	2	1	3	6	4	0	0	0	0
	Montreal Maroons (Cup)	....	....	....	....	....	*4*	*0*	*0*	*0*	*0*
1926-27	Montreal Maroons	44	2	3	5	12	2	0	0	0	2
1927-28	Montreal Maroons	21	0	1	1	10	9	0	0	0	0
1930-31	New York Americans	44	6	7	13	36	....	....	....	....	....
1931-32	Detroit Falcons	31	10	14	24	31	2	0	0	0	2
1932-33	Detroit Red Wings	45	12	13	25	35	4	0	1	1	0

Season	Club	GP	G	A	Pts	PIM	GP	G	A	Pts	PIM
		REGULAR SEASON					PLAYOFFS				
1933-34	Detroit Red Wings	47	10	9	19	36	6	0	1	1	5
	NHL Totals	**248**	**42**	**48**	**90**	**166**	**27**	**0**	**2**	**2**	**9**

• Brother of Bill and Gerry

Signed as a free agent by **Mtl. Maroons**, January 26, 1926. • 1925-26 Montreal Maroons playoff totals includes series against Ottawa and Pittsburgh. Traded to **NY Americans** by **Montreal Maroons** (Windsor-IHL) with Mike Neville, Hap Emms and Red Dutton for $35,000, May 14, 1930. Traded to **Detroit** by **NY Americans** with Hap Emms for Bert McInenly and Tommy Filmore, December 29, 1931. • Officially announced retirement, October 15, 1934.

CARSON, Gerry

Defense. Shoots left. 5'10", 175 lbs. Born, Parry Sound, Ont., October 10, 1905.

Season	Club	GP	G	A	Pts	PIM	GP	G	A	Pts	PIM
1928-29	Montreal Canadiens	26	0	0	0	4	....	....	....	....	....
	New York Rangers	14	0	0	0	5	5	0	0	0	0
1929-30◆	Montreal Canadiens	35	1	0	1	8	6	0	0	0	0
1932-33	Montreal Canadiens	48	5	2	7	53	2	0	0	0	2
1933-34	Montreal Canadiens	48	5	1	6	51	2	0	0	0	2
1934-35	Montreal Canadiens	48	0	5	5	56	2	0	0	0	4
1936-37	Montreal Maroons	42	1	3	4	28	5	0	0	0	4
	NHL Totals	**261**	**12**	**11**	**23**	**205**	**22**	**0**	**0**	**0**	**12**

• Brother of Bill and Frank

Loaned to **NY Rangers** by **Montreal** for remainder of 1928-29 season, February 15, 1929. Traded to **Providence** (Can-Am) by **Montreal** with cash and the loan of Jean Pusie for Johnny Gagnon, October 21, 1930. • Missed entire 1935-36 season recovering from knee surgery, September, 1935. Traded to **Mtl. Maroons** by **Montreal** for the rights to George Brown, October 7, 1936.

CARSON, Jimmy

Center. Shoots right. 6'1", 200 lbs. Born, Southfield, MI, July 20, 1968.
(Los Angeles' 1st choice, 2nd overall, in 1986 Entry Draft).

Season	Club	GP	G	A	Pts	PIM	GP	G	A	Pts	PIM
1986-87	Los Angeles Kings	80	37	42	79	22	5	1	2	3	6
1987-88	Los Angeles Kings	80	55	52	107	45	5	5	3	8	4
1988-89	Edmonton Oilers	80	49	51	100	36	7	2	1	3	6
1989-90	Edmonton Oilers	4	1	2	3	0	....	....	....	....	....
	Detroit Red Wings	44	20	16	36	8	....	....	....	....	....
1990-91	Detroit Red Wings	64	21	25	46	28	7	2	1	3	4
1991-92	Detroit Red Wings	80	34	35	69	30	11	2	3	5	0
1992-93	Detroit Red Wings	52	25	26	51	18	....	....	....	....	....
	Los Angeles Kings	34	12	10	22	14	18	5	4	9	2
1993-94	Los Angeles Kings	25	4	7	11	2	....	....	....	....	....
	Vancouver Canucks	34	7	10	17	22	2	0	1	1	0
1994-95	Hartford Whalers	38	9	10	19	20	....	....	....	....	....
1995-96	Hartford Whalers	11	1	0	1	0	....	....	....	....	....
	NHL Totals	**626**	**275**	**286**	**561**	**254**	**55**	**17**	**15**	**32**	**22**

Played in NHL All-Star Game (1989)

Traded to **Edmonton** by **Los Angeles** with Martin Gelinas, Los Angeles' 1st round choices in 1989 (later traded to New Jersey – New Jersey selected Jason Miller), 1991 (Martin Rucinsky) and 1993 (Nick Stajduhar) Entry Drafts and cash for Wayne Gretzky, Mike Krushelnyski and Marty McSorley, August 9, 1988. Traded to **Detroit** by **Edmonton** with Kevin McClelland and Edmonton's 5th round choice (later traded to Montreal – Montreal selected Brad Layzell) in 1991 Entry Draft for Petr Klima, Joe Murphy, Adam Graves and Jeff Sharples, November 2, 1989. Traded to **Los Angeles** by **Detroit** with Marc Potvin and Gary Shuchuk for Paul Coffey, Sylvain Couturier and Jim Hiller, January 29, 1993. Traded to **Vancouver** by **Los Angeles** for Dixon Ward, January 8, 1994. Signed as a free agent by **Hartford**, July 15, 1994.

CARSON, Lindsay

Center. Shoots left. 6'2", 195 lbs. Born, Oxbow, Sask., November 21, 1960.
(Philadelphia's 4th choice, 56th overall, in 1979 Entry Draft).

Season	Club	GP	G	A	Pts	PIM	GP	G	A	Pts	PIM
1981-82	Philadelphia Flyers	18	0	1	1	32	....	....	....	....	....
1982-83	Philadelphia Flyers	78	18	19	37	67	1	0	0	0	0
1983-84	Philadelphia Flyers	16	1	3	4	10	1	0	0	0	5
1984-85	Philadelphia Flyers	77	20	19	39	123	17	0	3	3	24
1985-86	Philadelphia Flyers	50	9	12	21	84	1	0	0	0	5
1986-87	Philadelphia Flyers	71	11	15	26	141	24	3	5	8	22
1987-88	Philadelphia Flyers	36	2	7	9	37	....	....	....	....	....
	Hartford Whalers	27	5	4	9	30	5	1	2	3	0
	NHL Totals	**373**	**66**	**80**	**146**	**524**	**49**	**4**	**10**	**14**	**56**

Traded to **Hartford** by **Philadelphia** for Paul Lawless, January 22, 1988.

CARTER, Anson

Right wing. Shoots right. 6'1", 200 lbs. Born, Toronto, Ont., June 6, 1974.
(Quebec's 11th choice, 220th overall, in 1992 Entry Draft).

Season	Club	GP	G	A	Pts	PIM	GP	G	A	Pts	PIM
1996-97	Washington Capitals	19	3	2	5	7	....	....	....	....	....
	Boston Bruins	19	8	5	13	2	....	....	....	....	....
1997-98	Boston Bruins	78	16	27	43	31	6	1	1	2	0
1998-99	Boston Bruins	55	24	16	40	22	12	4	3	7	0
99-2000	Boston Bruins	59	22	25	47	14	....	....	....	....	....
2000-01	Edmonton Oilers	61	16	26	42	23	6	3	1	4	4
2001-02	Edmonton Oilers	82	28	32	60	25	....	....	....	....	....
2002-03	Edmonton Oilers	68	25	30	55	20	....	....	....	....	....
	New York Rangers	11	1	4	5	6	....	....	....	....	....
	NHL Totals	**452**	**143**	**167**	**310**	**150**	**24**	**8**	**5**	**13**	**4**

Rights transferred to **Colorado** after **Quebec** franchise relocated, June 21, 1995. Traded to **Washington** by **Colorado** for Washington's 4th round choice (Ben Storey) in 1996 Entry Draft, April 3, 1996. Traded to **Boston** by **Washington** with Jim Carey, Jason Allison and Washington's 3rd round choice (Lee Goren) in 1997 Entry Draft for Bill Ranford, Adam Oates and Rick Tocchet, March 1, 1997. Signed as a free agent by **Utah** (IHL) with Boston retaining NHL rights, October 20, 1998. Traded to **Edmonton** by **Boston** with Boston's 1st (Ales Hemsky) and 2nd (Doug Lynch) round choices in 2001 Entry Draft for Bill Guerin and future considerations, November 15, 2000. Traded to **NY Rangers** by **Edmonton** with Ales Pisa for Radek Dvorak and Cory Cross, March 11, 2003.

CARTER, Billy

Center. Shoots left. 5'11", 155 lbs. Born, Cornwall, Ont., December 2, 1937.

Season	Club	GP	G	A	Pts	PIM	GP	G	A	Pts	PIM
1957-58	Montreal Canadiens	1	0	0	0	0	....	....	....	....	....
1960-61	Boston Bruins	8	0	0	0	2	....	....	....	....	....
1961-62	Montreal Canadiens	7	0	0	0	4	....	....	....	....	....
	NHL Totals	**16**	**0**	**0**	**0**	**6**	....	....	....	....	....

Traded to **Boston** by **Montreal** for cash, June 6, 1960. Traded to **Montreal** by **Boston** for cash, November, 1961. Traded to **Detroit** (Pittsburgh-AHL) by **Montreal** (Seattle-WHL) for Chuck Holmes with Detroit holding right of recall, December, 1964.

CARTER, John

Left wing. Shoots left. 5'10", 181 lbs. Born, Winchester, MA, May 3, 1963.

Season	Club	GP	G	A	Pts	PIM	GP	G	A	Pts	PIM
1985-86	Boston Bruins	3	0	0	0	0	....	....	....	....	....
1986-87	Boston Bruins	8	0	1	1	0	....	....	....	....	....
1987-88	Boston Bruins	4	0	1	1	2	....	....	....	....	....
1988-89	Boston Bruins	44	12	10	22	24	10	1	2	3	6
1989-90	Boston Bruins	76	17	22	39	26	21	6	3	9	45
1990-91	Boston Bruins	50	4	7	11	68	....	....	....	....	....
1991-92	San Jose Sharks	4	0	0	0	0	....	....	....	....	....
1992-93	San Jose Sharks	55	7	9	16	81	....	....	....	....	....
	NHL Totals	**244**	**40**	**50**	**90**	**201**	**31**	**7**	**5**	**12**	**51**

Signed as a free agent by **Boston**, March 27, 1986. Signed as a free agent by **San Jose**, August 22, 1991.

CARTER, Ron

Right wing. Shoots left. 6'1", 205 lbs. Born, Montreal, Que., March 14, 1958.
(Montreal's 4th choice, 36th overall, in 1978 Amateur Draft).

Season	Club	GP	G	A	Pts	PIM	GP	G	A	Pts	PIM
1979-80	Edmonton Oilers	2	0	0	0	0	....	....	....	....	....
	NHL Totals	**2**	**0**	**0**	**0**	**0**	....	....	....	....	....

NHL rights retained by **Edmonton** prior to Expansion Draft, June 9, 1979. Claimed on waivers by **Buffalo** from **Edmonton**, July, 1980.

CARVETH, Joe

Right wing. Shoots right. 5'10", 180 lbs. Born, Regina, Sask., March 21, 1918.

Season	Club	GP	G	A	Pts	PIM	GP	G	A	Pts	PIM
1940-41	Detroit Red Wings	19	2	1	3	2	....	....	....	....	....
1941-42	Detroit Red Wings	29	6	11	17	2	9	4	0	4	0
1942-43◆	Detroit Red Wings	43	18	18	36	6	10	*6	2	8	4
1943-44	Detroit Red Wings	46	21	35	56	6	5	2	1	3	8
1944-45	Detroit Red Wings	50	26	28	54	6	14	5	*6	*11	2
1945-46	Detroit Red Wings	48	17	18	35	10	5	0	1	1	0
1946-47	Boston Bruins	51	21	15	36	18	5	2	1	3	0
1947-48	Boston Bruins	22	8	9	17	2	....	....	....	....	....
	Montreal Canadiens	35	1	10	11	6	....	....	....	....	....
1948-49	Montreal Canadiens	60	15	22	37	8	7	0	1	1	8
1949-50	Montreal Canadiens	11	1	1	2	2	....	....	....	....	....
◆	Detroit Red Wings	60	13	17	30	13	14	2	4	6	6
1950-51	Detroit Red Wings	30	1	4	5	0	....	....	....	....	....
	NHL Totals	**504**	**150**	**189**	**339**	**81**	**69**	**21**	**16**	**37**	**28**

Played in NHL All-Star Game (1950)

Signed as a free agent by **Detroit**, October 5, 1939. Traded to **Boston** by **Detroit** for Roy Conacher, August, 1946. Traded to **Montreal** by **Boston** for Jimmy Peters and John Quilty, December 16, 1947. Traded to **Detroit** by **Montreal** for Calum MacKay, November 11, 1949. Traded to **Cleveland** (AHL) by **Detroit** for cash, June 6, 1951.

CASHMAN, Wayne

Left wing. Shoots right. 6'1", 208 lbs. Born, Kingston, Ont., June 24, 1945.

Season	Club	GP	G	A	Pts	PIM	GP	G	A	Pts	PIM
1964-65	Boston Bruins	1	0	0	0	0	....	....	....	....	....
1967-68	Boston Bruins	12	0	4	4	2	1	0	0	0	0
1968-69	Boston Bruins	51	8	23	31	49	6	0	1	1	0
1969-70◆	Boston Bruins	70	9	26	35	79	14	5	4	9	50
1970-71	Boston Bruins	77	21	58	79	100	7	3	2	5	15
1971-72◆	Boston Bruins	74	23	29	52	103	15	4	7	11	42
1972-73	Boston Bruins	76	29	39	68	100	5	1	1	2	4
1973-74	Boston Bruins	78	30	59	89	111	16	5	9	14	46
1974-75	Boston Bruins	42	11	22	33	24	1	0	2	2	0
1975-76	Boston Bruins	80	28	43	71	87	11	1	5	6	16
1976-77	Boston Bruins	65	15	37	52	76	14	1	8	9	18
1977-78	Boston Bruins	76	24	38	62	69	15	4	6	10	13
1978-79	Boston Bruins	75	27	40	67	63	10	4	5	9	8
1979-80	Boston Bruins	44	11	21	32	19	10	3	3	6	32
1980-81	Boston Bruins	77	25	35	60	80	3	0	1	1	0
1981-82	Boston Bruins	64	12	31	43	59	9	0	2	2	6

Season	Club	GP	G	A	Pts	PIM	GP	G	A	Pts	PIM
		REGULAR SEASON					PLAYOFFS				
1982-83	Boston Bruins	65	4	11	15	20	8	0	1	1	0
	NHL Totals	**1027**	**277**	**516**	**793**	**1041**	**145**	**31**	**57**	**88**	**250**

NHL Second All-Star Team (1974)
Played in NHL All-Star Game (1974)

CASSELMAN, Mike

Center. Shoots left. 5'11", 190 lbs. Born, Morrisburg, Ont., August 23, 1968.
(Detroit's 1st choice, 3rd overall, in 1990 Supplemental Draft).

Season	Club	GP	G	A	Pts	PIM	GP	G	A	Pts	PIM
1995-96	Florida Panthers	3	0	0	0	0	....	....	....	....	....
	NHL Totals	**3**	**0**	**0**	**0**	**0**	....	....	....	....	....

Signed as a free agent by **Florida**, October 31, 1995. Signed as a free agent by **San Jose**, September 24, 1997.

CASSELS, Andrew

Center. Shoots left. 6'1", 185 lbs. Born, Bramalea, Ont., July 23, 1969.
(Montreal's 1st choice, 17th overall, in 1987 Entry Draft).

Season	Club	GP	G	A	Pts	PIM	GP	G	A	Pts	PIM
1989-90	Montreal Canadiens	6	2	0	2	2	....	....	....	....	....
1990-91	Montreal Canadiens	54	6	19	25	20	8	0	2	2	2
1991-92	Hartford Whalers	67	11	30	41	18	7	2	4	6	6
1992-93	Hartford Whalers	84	21	64	85	62	....	....	....	....	....
1993-94	Hartford Whalers	79	16	42	58	37	....	....	....	....	....
1994-95	Hartford Whalers	46	7	30	37	18	....	....	....	....	....
1995-96	Hartford Whalers	81	20	43	63	39	....	....	....	....	....
1996-97	Hartford Whalers	81	22	44	66	46	....	....	....	....	....
1997-98	Calgary Flames	81	17	27	44	32	....	....	....	....	....
1998-99	Calgary Flames	70	12	25	37	18	....	....	....	....	....
99-2000	Vancouver Canucks	79	17	45	62	16	....	....	....	....	....
2000-01	Vancouver Canucks	66	12	44	56	10	....	....	....	....	....
2001-02	Vancouver Canucks	53	11	39	50	22	6	2	1	3	0
2002-03	Columbus Blue Jackets	79	20	48	68	30	....	....	....	....	....
	NHL Totals	**926**	**194**	**500**	**694**	**370**	**21**	**4**	**7**	**11**	**8**

Traded to **Hartford** by **Montreal** for Hartford's 2nd round choice (Valeri Bure) in 1992 Entry Draft, September 17, 1991. Transferred to **Carolina** after **Hartford** franchise relocated, June 25, 1997. Traded to **Calgary** by **Carolina** with Jean-Sebastien Giguere for Gary Roberts and Trevor Kidd, August 25, 1997. Signed as a free agent by **Vancouver**, August 19, 1999. Signed as a free agent by **Columbus**, August 15, 2002.

CASSIDY, Bruce

Defense. Shoots left. 5'11", 176 lbs. Born, Ottawa, Ont., May 20, 1965.
(Chicago's 1st choice, 18th overall, in 1983 Entry Draft).

Season	Club	GP	G	A	Pts	PIM	GP	G	A	Pts	PIM
1983-84	Chicago Black Hawks	1	0	0	0	0	....	....	....	....	....
1985-86	Chicago Black Hawks	1	0	0	0	0	....	....	....	....	....
1986-87	Chicago Blackhawks	2	0	0	0	0	....	....	....	....	....
1987-88	Chicago Blackhawks	21	3	10	13	6	....	....	....	....	....
1988-89	Chicago Blackhawks	9	0	2	2	4	1	0	0	0	0
1989-90	Chicago Blackhawks	2	1	1	2	0	....	....	....	....	....
	NHL Totals	**36**	**4**	**13**	**17**	**10**	**1**	**0**	**0**	**0**	**0**

• Missed majority of 1984-85 season recovering from knee injury suffered during summer training, June, 1984. Signed as a free agent by **Chicago**, July 28, 1994.

CASSIDY, Tom

Center. Shoots left. 5'11", 180 lbs. Born, Blind River, Ont., March 15, 1952.
(California's 1st choice, 22nd overall, in 1972 Amateur Draft).

Season	Club	GP	G	A	Pts	PIM	GP	G	A	Pts	PIM
1977-78	Pittsburgh Penguins	26	3	4	7	15	....	....	....	....	....
	NHL Totals	**26**	**3**	**4**	**7**	**15**	....	....	....	....	....

Traded to **Los Angeles** by **California** for cash, March 12, 1974. Traded to **Toronto** by **Los Angeles** for cash, September, 1975. Signed as a free agent by **Boston**, October 30, 1976. Signed as a free agent by **Pittsburgh**, October 11, 1977.

CASSOLATO, Tony

Right wing. Shoots right. 5'11", 180 lbs. Born, Guelph, Ont., May 7, 1956.

Season	Club	GP	G	A	Pts	PIM	GP	G	A	Pts	PIM
1979-80	Washington Capitals	9	0	2	2	0	....	....	....	....	....
1980-81	Washington Capitals	2	0	0	0	0	....	....	....	....	....
1981-82	Washington Capitals	12	1	4	5	4	....	....	....	....	....
	NHL Totals	**23**	**1**	**6**	**7**	**4**	....	....	....	....	....

Signed as a free agent by **Washington**, August 12, 1979.

CAUFIELD, Jay

Right wing. Shoots right. 6'4", 237 lbs. Born, Philadelphia, PA, July 17, 1960.

Season	Club	GP	G	A	Pts	PIM	GP	G	A	Pts	PIM
1986-87	New York Rangers	13	2	1	3	45	3	0	0	0	12
1987-88	Minnesota North Stars	1	0	0	0	0	....	....	....	....	....
1988-89	Pittsburgh Penguins	58	1	4	5	285	9	0	0	0	28
1989-90	Pittsburgh Penguins	37	1	2	3	123	....	....	....	....	....
1990-91 ♦	Pittsburgh Penguins	23	1	1	2	71	....	....	....	....	....
1991-92 ♦	Pittsburgh Penguins	50	0	0	0	175	5	0	0	0	2
1992-93	Pittsburgh Penguins	26	0	0	0	60	....	....	....	....	....
	NHL Totals	**208**	**5**	**8**	**13**	**759**	**17**	**0**	**0**	**0**	**42**

Signed as a free agent by **NY Rangers**, October 8, 1985. Traded to **Minnesota** by **NY Rangers** with Dave Gagner for Jari Gronstrand and Paul Boutilier, October 8, 1987. Claimed by **Pittsburgh** from **Minnesota** in Waiver Draft, October 3, 1988.

CAVALLINI, Gino

Left wing. Shoots left. 6'1", 215 lbs. Born, Toronto, Ont., November 24, 1962.

Season	Club	GP	G	A	Pts	PIM	GP	G	A	Pts	PIM
1984-85	Calgary Flames	27	6	10	16	14	3	0	0	0	4
1985-86	Calgary Flames	27	7	7	14	26	....	....	....	....	....
	St. Louis Blues	30	6	5	11	36	17	4	5	9	10
1986-87	St. Louis Blues	80	18	26	44	54	6	3	1	4	2
1987-88	St. Louis Blues	64	15	17	32	62	10	5	5	10	19
1988-89	St. Louis Blues	74	20	23	43	79	9	0	2	2	17
1989-90	St. Louis Blues	80	15	15	30	77	12	1	3	4	12
1990-91	St. Louis Blues	78	8	27	35	81	13	1	3	4	2
1991-92	St. Louis Blues	48	9	7	16	40	....	....	....	....	....
	Quebec Nordiques	18	1	7	8	4	....	....	....	....	....
1992-93	Quebec Nordiques	67	9	15	24	34	4	0	0	0	0
	NHL Totals	**593**	**114**	**159**	**273**	**507**	**74**	**14**	**19**	**33**	**66**

• Brother of Paul

Signed as a free agent by **Calgary**, May 16, 1984. Traded to **St. Louis** by **Calgary** with Eddy Beers and Charlie Bourgeois for Joe Mullen, Terry Johnson and Rik Wilson, February 1, 1986. Claimed on waivers by **Quebec** from **St Louis**, February 27, 1992.

CAVALLINI, Paul

Defense. Shoots left. 6'1", 202 lbs. Born, Toronto, Ont., October 13, 1965.
(Washington's 9th choice, 205th overall, in 1984 Entry Draft).

Season	Club	GP	G	A	Pts	PIM	GP	G	A	Pts	PIM
1986-87	Washington Capitals	6	0	2	2	8	....	....	....	....	....
1987-88	Washington Capitals	24	2	3	5	66	....	....	....	....	....
	St. Louis Blues	48	4	7	11	86	10	1	6	7	26
1988-89	St. Louis Blues	65	4	20	24	128	10	2	2	4	14
1989-90	St. Louis Blues	80	8	39	47	106	12	2	3	5	20
1990-91	St. Louis Blues	67	10	25	35	89	13	2	3	5	20
1991-92	St. Louis Blues	66	10	25	35	95	4	0	1	1	6
1992-93	St. Louis Blues	11	1	4	5	10	....	....	....	....	....
	Washington Capitals	71	5	8	13	46	6	0	2	2	18
1993-94	Dallas Stars	74	11	33	44	82	9	1	8	9	4
1994-95	Dallas Stars	44	1	11	12	28	5	0	2	2	6
1995-96	Dallas Stars	8	0	0	0	6	....	....	....	....	....
	NHL Totals	**564**	**56**	**177**	**233**	**750**	**69**	**8**	**27**	**35**	**114**

• Brother of Gino • Alka-Seltzer Plus Award (1990)
Played in NHL All-Star Game (1990)

Traded to **St. Louis** by **Washington** for Montreal's 2nd round choice (previously acquired, Washington selected Wade Bartley) in 1988 Entry Draft, December 11, 1987. Traded to **Washington** by **St. Louis** for Kevin Miller, November 2, 1992. Traded to **Dallas** by **Washington** for future considerations (Enrico Ciccone, June 25, 1993), June 20, 1993. • Officially announced retirement, November 7, 1995.

CERESINO, Ray

Right wing. Shoots right. 5'9", 160 lbs. Born, Port Arthur, Ont., April 24, 1929.

Season	Club	GP	G	A	Pts	PIM	GP	G	A	Pts	PIM
1948-49	Toronto Maple Leafs	12	1	1	2	2	....	....	....	....	....
	NHL Totals	**12**	**1**	**1**	**2**	**2**	....	....	....	....	....

Traded to **Cleveland** (AHL) by **Toronto** with Harry Taylor and the loan of Tod Sloan for the 1949-50 season for Bob Solinger, September 6, 1949.

CERNIK, Frantisek

Wing. Shoots right. 5'10", 189 lbs. Born, Novy Jicin, Czech., June 3, 1953.

Season	Club	GP	G	A	Pts	PIM	GP	G	A	Pts	PIM
1984-85	Detroit Red Wings	49	5	4	9	13	....	....	....	....	....
	NHL Totals	**49**	**5**	**4**	**9**	**13**	....	....	....	....	....

Signed as a free agent by **Quebec**, September 17, 1979. Signed as a free agent by **Detroit**, July 5, 1983.

CHABOT, John

Center. Shoots left. 6'2", 200 lbs. Born, Summerside, P.E.I., May 18, 1962.
(Montreal's 3rd choice, 40th overall, in 1980 Entry Draft).

Season	Club	GP	G	A	Pts	PIM	GP	G	A	Pts	PIM
1983-84	Montreal Canadiens	56	18	25	43	13	11	1	4	5	0
1984-85	Montreal Canadiens	10	1	6	7	2	....	....	....	....	....
	Pittsburgh Penguins	67	8	45	53	12	....	....	....	....	....
1985-86	Pittsburgh Penguins	77	14	31	45	6	....	....	....	....	....
1986-87	Pittsburgh Penguins	72	14	22	36	8	....	....	....	....	....
1987-88	Detroit Red Wings	78	13	44	57	10	16	4	15	19	2
1988-89	Detroit Red Wings	52	2	10	12	6	6	1	1	2	0
1989-90	Detroit Red Wings	69	9	40	49	24	....	....	....	....	....
1990-91	Detroit Red Wings	27	5	5	10	4	....	....	....	....	....
	NHL Totals	**508**	**84**	**228**	**312**	**85**	**33**	**6**	**20**	**26**	**2**

Traded to **Pittsburgh** by **Montreal** for Ron Flockhart, November 9, 1984. Signed as a free agent by **Detroit**, June 25, 1987.

CHAD, John

Right wing. Shoots right. 5'10", 167 lbs. Born, Provost, Alta., September 16, 1919.

Season	Club	GP	G	A	Pts	PIM	GP	G	A	Pts	PIM
1939-40	Chicago Black Hawks	22	8	3	11	11	2	0	0	0	0
1940-41	Chicago Black Hawks	45	7	18	25	16	5	0	0	0	2
1945-46	Chicago Black Hawks	13	0	1	1	2	3	0	1	1	0
	NHL Totals	**80**	**15**	**22**	**37**	**29**	**10**	**0**	**1**	**1**	**2**

Signed as a free agent by **Chicago**, October 18, 1939.

CHALMERS, Chick

Center. Shoots left. 6', 180 lbs. Born, Stratford, Ont., January 24, 1934.

Season	Club	GP	G	A	Pts	PIM	GP	G	A	Pts	PIM
1953-54	New York Rangers	1	0	0	0	0	....	....	....	....	....
	NHL Totals	**1**	**0**	**0**	**0**	**0**	....	....	....	....	....

CHALUPA, Milan

Defense. Shoots right. 5'10", 183 lbs. Born, Oudolen, Czech., July 4, 1953.
(Detroit's 3rd choice, 49th overall, in 1984 Entry Draft).

Season	Club	Regular Season GP	G	A	Pts	PIM	Playoffs GP	G	A	Pts	PIM
1984-85	Detroit Red Wings	14	0	5	5	6	....	....	....	....	....
	NHL Totals	**14**	**0**	**5**	**5**	**6**	....	....	....	....	....

CHAMBERLAIN, Murph

Left wing. Shoots left. 5'11", 165 lbs. Born, Shawville, Que., February 14, 1915.

Season	Club	Regular Season GP	G	A	Pts	PIM	Playoffs GP	G	A	Pts	PIM
1937-38	Toronto Maple Leafs	43	4	12	16	51	5	0	0	0	2
1938-39	Toronto Maple Leafs	48	10	16	26	32	10	2	5	7	4
1939-40	Toronto Maple Leafs	40	5	17	22	63	3	0	0	0	0
1940-41	Montreal Canadiens	45	10	15	25	75	3	0	2	2	11
1941-42	Montreal Canadiens	26	6	3	9	30	....	....	....	....	....
	Brooklyn Americans	11	6	9	15	16	....	....	....	....	....
1942-43	Boston Bruins	45	9	24	33	67	6	1	1	2	12
1943-44 ♦	Montreal Canadiens	47	15	32	47	85	9	5	3	8	12
1944-45	Montreal Canadiens	32	2	12	14	38	6	1	1	2	10
1945-46 ♦	Montreal Canadiens	40	12	14	26	42	9	4	2	6	18
1946-47	Montreal Canadiens	49	10	10	20	97	11	1	3	4	19
1947-48	Montreal Canadiens	30	6	3	9	62	....	....	....	....	....
1948-49	Montreal Canadiens	54	5	8	13	111	4	0	0	0	8
	NHL Totals	**510**	**100**	**175**	**275**	**769**	**66**	**14**	**17**	**31**	**96**

Traded to **Montreal** by **Toronto** for $7,500, May 10, 1940. Loaned to **Brooklyn** by **Montreal** for the loan of Red Heron, February 13, 1942. Loaned to **Boston** by **Montreal** for 1942-43 season for cash, September, 1942. • Missed majority of 1947-48 season recovering from leg injury suffered in game vs. Detroit, October 25, 1947.

CHAMBERS, Shawn

Defense. Shoots left. 6'2", 210 lbs. Born, Sterling Hts., MI, October 11, 1966.
(Minnesota's 1st choice, 4th overall, in 1987 Supplemental Draft).

Season	Club	Regular Season GP	G	A	Pts	PIM	Playoffs GP	G	A	Pts	PIM
1987-88	Minnesota North Stars	19	1	7	8	21	....	....	....	....	....
1988-89	Minnesota North Stars	72	5	19	24	80	3	0	2	2	0
1989-90	Minnesota North Stars	78	8	18	26	81	7	2	1	3	10
1990-91	Minnesota North Stars	29	1	3	4	24	23	0	7	7	16
1991-92	Washington Capitals	2	0	0	0	2	....	....	....	....	....
1992-93	Tampa Bay Lightning	55	10	29	39	36	....	....	....	....	....
1993-94	Tampa Bay Lightning	66	11	23	34	23	....	....	....	....	....
1994-95	Tampa Bay Lightning	24	2	12	14	6	....	....	....	....	....
♦	New Jersey Devils	21	2	5	7	6	20	4	5	9	2
1995-96	New Jersey Devils	64	2	21	23	18	....	....	....	....	....
1996-97	New Jersey Devils	73	4	17	21	19	10	1	6	7	6
1997-98	Dallas Stars	57	2	22	24	26	14	0	3	3	20
1998-99 ♦	Dallas Stars	61	2	9	11	18	17	0	2	2	18
99-2000	Dallas Stars	4	0	0	0	4	....	....	....	....	....
	NHL Totals	**625**	**50**	**185**	**235**	**364**	**94**	**7**	**26**	**33**	**72**

Traded to **Washington** by **Minnesota** for Steve Maltais and Trent Klatt, June 21, 1991. • Missed majority of 1990-91 and 1991-92 seasons recovering from knee injury originally suffered in game vs. Toronto, December 5, 1990. Claimed by **Tampa Bay** from **Washington** in Expansion Draft, June 18, 1992. Traded to **New Jersey** by **Tampa Bay** with Danton Cole for Alexander Semak and Ben Hankinson, March 14, 1995. Signed as a free agent by **Dallas**, July 17, 1997. • Missed majority of 1999-2000 season recovering from knee injury suffered in game vs. Anaheim, October 8, 1999.

CHAMPAGNE, Andre

Left wing. Shoots left. 6', 190 lbs. Born, Ottawa, Ont., September 19, 1943.

Season	Club	Regular Season GP	G	A	Pts	PIM	Playoffs GP	G	A	Pts	PIM
1962-63	Toronto Maple Leafs	2	0	0	0	0	....	....	....	....	....
	NHL Totals	**2**	**0**	**0**	**0**	**0**	....	....	....	....	....

CHAPDELAINE, Rene

Defense. Shoots right. 6'1", 195 lbs. Born, Weyburn, Sask., September 27, 1966.
(Los Angeles' 7th choice, 149th overall, in 1986 Entry Draft).

Season	Club	Regular Season GP	G	A	Pts	PIM	Playoffs GP	G	A	Pts	PIM
1990-91	Los Angeles Kings	3	0	1	1	10	....	....	....	....	....
1991-92	Los Angeles Kings	16	0	1	1	10	....	....	....	....	....
1992-93	Los Angeles Kings	13	0	0	0	12	....	....	....	....	....
	NHL Totals	**32**	**0**	**2**	**2**	**32**	....	....	....	....	....

CHAPMAN, Art

Center. Shoots left. 5'10", 170 lbs. Born, Winnipeg, Man., May 29, 1906.

Season	Club	Regular Season GP	G	A	Pts	PIM	Playoffs GP	G	A	Pts	PIM
1930-31	Boston Bruins	44	7	7	14	22	5	0	1	1	7
1931-32	Boston Bruins	48	11	14	25	18	....	....	....	....	....
1932-33	Boston Bruins	46	3	6	9	19	5	0	0	0	2
1933-34	Boston Bruins	21	2	5	7	7	....	....	....	....	....
	New York Americans	25	3	7	10	8	....	....	....	....	....
1934-35	New York Americans	47	9	*34	43	4	....	....	....	....	....
1935-36	New York Americans	48	10	*28	38	14	5	0	3	3	0
1936-37	New York Americans	43	8	23	31	36	....	....	....	....	....
1937-38	New York Americans	45	2	27	29	8	6	0	1	1	0
1938-39	New York Americans	45	3	19	22	2	2	0	0	0	0
1939-40	New York Americans	26	4	6	10	2	3	1	0	1	0
	NHL Totals	**438**	**62**	**176**	**238**	**140**	**26**	**1**	**5**	**6**	**9**

NHL Second All-Star Team (1937)

Played in NHL All-Star Game (1937)

Traded to **NY Rangers** by **Windsor** (Can-Pro) for cash, November 1, 1927. Traded to **Providence** (Can-Am) by **NY Rangers** for cash, October 18, 1928. Claimed by **Boston** from **Providence** (Can-Am) in Inter-League Draft, May 13, 1929. Traded to **NY Americans** by **Boston** with Bob Gracie for Lloyd Gross and George Patterson, January 11, 1934.

CHAPMAN, Blair

Right wing. Shoots right. 6'1", 190 lbs. Born, Lloydminster, Sask., June 13, 1956.
(Pittsburgh's 1st choice, 2nd overall, in 1976 Amateur Draft).

Season	Club	Regular Season GP	G	A	Pts	PIM	Playoffs GP	G	A	Pts	PIM
1976-77	Pittsburgh Penguins	80	14	23	37	16	3	1	1	2	7
1977-78	Pittsburgh Penguins	75	24	20	44	37	....	....	....	....	....
1978-79	Pittsburgh Penguins	71	10	8	18	18	7	1	0	1	2
1979-80	Pittsburgh Penguins	1	0	0	0	0	....	....	....	....	....
	St. Louis Blues	63	25	26	51	28	3	0	0	0	0
1980-81	St. Louis Blues	55	20	26	46	41	9	2	5	7	6
1981-82	St. Louis Blues	18	6	11	17	8	3	0	0	0	0
1982-83	St. Louis Blues	39	7	11	18	10	....	....	....	....	....
	NHL Totals	**402**	**106**	**125**	**231**	**158**	**25**	**4**	**6**	**10**	**15**

Traded to **St. Louis** by **Pittsburgh** for Bob Stewart, November 13, 1979. • Missed majority of 1981-82 season recovering from back injury suffered in game vs. Los Angeles, November 12, 1981.

CHAPMAN, Brian

Defense. Shoots left. 6', 195 lbs. Born, Brockville, Ont., February 10, 1968.
(Hartford's 3rd choice, 74th overall, in 1986 Entry Draft).

Season	Club	Regular Season GP	G	A	Pts	PIM	Playoffs GP	G	A	Pts	PIM
1990-91	Hartford Whalers	3	0	0	0	29	....	....	....	....	....
	NHL Totals	**3**	**0**	**0**	**0**	**29**	....	....	....	....	....

Signed as a free agent by **Los Angeles**, July 15, 1993.

CHARA, Zdeno

Defense. Shoots left. 6'9", 255 lbs. Born, Trencin, Czech., March 18, 1977.
(NY Islanders' 3rd choice, 56th overall, in 1996 Entry Draft).

Season	Club	Regular Season GP	G	A	Pts	PIM	Playoffs GP	G	A	Pts	PIM
1997-98	New York Islanders	25	0	1	1	50	....	....	....	....	....
1998-99	New York Islanders	59	2	6	8	83	....	....	....	....	....
99-2000	New York Islanders	65	2	9	11	57	....	....	....	....	....
2000-01	New York Islanders	82	2	7	9	157	....	....	....	....	....
2001-02	Ottawa Senators	75	10	13	23	156	10	0	1	1	12
2002-03	Ottawa Senators	74	9	30	39	116	18	1	6	7	14
	NHL Totals	**380**	**25**	**66**	**91**	**619**	**28**	**1**	**7**	**8**	**26**

Played in NHL All-Star Game (2003)

Traded to **Ottawa** by **NY Islanders** with Bill Muckalt and NY Islanders' 1st round choice (Jason Spezza) in 2001 Entry Draft for Alexei Yashin, June 23, 2001.

CHARBONNEAU, Jose

Right wing. Shoots right. 6', 195 lbs. Born, Ferme-Neuve, Que., November 21, 1966.
(Montreal's 1st choice, 12th overall, in 1985 Entry Draft).

Season	Club	Regular Season GP	G	A	Pts	PIM	Playoffs GP	G	A	Pts	PIM
1987-88	Montreal Canadiens	16	0	2	2	6	8	0	0	0	4
1988-89	Montreal Canadiens	9	1	3	4	6	....	....	....	....	....
	Vancouver Canucks	13	0	1	1	6	....	....	....	....	....
1993-94	Vancouver Canucks	30	7	7	14	49	3	1	0	1	4
1994-95	Vancouver Canucks	3	1	0	1	0	....	....	....	....	....
	NHL Totals	**71**	**9**	**13**	**22**	**67**	**11**	**1**	**0**	**1**	**8**

Traded to **Vancouver** by **Montreal** for Dan Woodley, January 25, 1989. Signed as a free agent by **Vancouver**, October 3, 1993.

CHARBONNEAU, Stephane

Right wing. Shoots right. 6'2", 195 lbs. Born, Ste-Adele, Que., June 27, 1970.

Season	Club	Regular Season GP	G	A	Pts	PIM	Playoffs GP	G	A	Pts	PIM
1991-92	Quebec Nordiques	2	0	0	0	0	....	....	....	....	....
	NHL Totals	**2**	**0**	**0**	**0**	**0**	....	....	....	....	....

Signed as a free agent by **Quebec**, April 25, 1991.

CHARLEBOIS, Bob

Left wing. Shoots left. 6', 175 lbs. Born, Cornwall, Ont., May 27, 1944.

Season	Club	Regular Season GP	G	A	Pts	PIM	Playoffs GP	G	A	Pts	PIM
1967-68	Minnesota North Stars	7	1	0	1	0	....	....	....	....	....
	NHL Totals	**7**	**1**	**0**	**1**	**0**	....	....	....	....	....

Traded to **Minnesota** by **Montreal** with Andre Boudrias and Bernard Cote for Minnesota's 1st round choice (Chuck Arnason) in 1971 Amateur Draft, June 6, 1967. Traded to **Phoenix** (WHL) by **Minnesota** with Leo Thiffault to complete earlier transaction that sent Walt McKechnie to Minnesota (February 17, 1968), June, 1968.

CHARLESWORTH, Todd

Defense. Shoots left. 6'1", 190 lbs. Born, Calgary, Alta., March 22, 1965.
(Pittsburgh's 2nd choice, 22nd overall, in 1983 Entry Draft).

Season	Club	Regular Season GP	G	A	Pts	PIM	Playoffs GP	G	A	Pts	PIM
1983-84	Pittsburgh Penguins	10	0	0	0	8	....	....	....	....	....
1984-85	Pittsburgh Penguins	67	1	8	9	31	....	....	....	....	....
1985-86	Pittsburgh Penguins	2	0	1	1	0	....	....	....	....	....
1986-87	Pittsburgh Penguins	1	0	0	0	0	....	....	....	....	....
1987-88	Pittsburgh Penguins	6	2	0	2	2	....	....	....	....	....

Season	Club	GP	G	A	Pts	PIM	GP	G	A	Pts	PIM
		REGULAR SEASON					PLAYOFFS				
1989-90	New York Rangers	7	0	0	0	6	....	....	....	....	....
	NHL Totals	**93**	**3**	**9**	**12**	**47**	....	....	....	....	....

Signed as a free agent by **Edmonton**, June 21, 1989. Traded to **NY Rangers** by **Edmonton** for future considerations, January 18, 1990.

CHARRON, Eric

Defense. Shoots left. 6'3", 195 lbs. Born, Verdun, Que., January 14, 1970.
(Montreal's 1st choice, 20th overall, in 1988 Entry Draft).

Season	Club	GP	G	A	Pts	PIM	GP	G	A	Pts	PIM
1992-93	Montreal Canadiens	3	0	0	0	2	....	....	....	....	....
1993-94	Tampa Bay Lightning	4	0	0	0	2	....	....	....	....	....
1994-95	Tampa Bay Lightning	45	1	4	5	26	....	....	....	....	....
1995-96	Tampa Bay Lightning	14	0	0	0	18	....	....	....	....	....
	Washington Capitals	4	0	1	1	4	6	0	0	0	8
1996-97	Washington Capitals	25	1	1	2	20	....	....	....	....	....
1997-98	Calgary Flames	2	0	0	0	4	....	....	....	....	....
1998-99	Calgary Flames	12	0	1	1	14	....	....	....	....	....
99-2000	Calgary Flames	21	0	0	0	37	....	....	....	....	....
	NHL Totals	**130**	**2**	**7**	**9**	**127**	**6**	**0**	**0**	**0**	**8**

Traded to **Tampa Bay** by **Montreal** with Alain Cote and future considerations (Donald Dufresne, June 18, 1993) for Rob Ramage, March 20, 1993. Traded to **Washington** by **Tampa Bay** for Washington's 7th round choice (Eero Somervuori) in 1997 Entry Draft, November 16, 1995. Traded to **Calgary** by **Washington** for Calgary's 7th round choice (Nathan Forster) in 1998 Entry Draft, September 4, 1997. Signed as a free agent by **Minnesota**, August 31, 2000.

CHARRON, Guy

Center. Shoots left. 5'10", 170 lbs. Born, Verdun, Que., January 24, 1949.

Season	Club	GP	G	A	Pts	PIM	GP	G	A	Pts	PIM
1969-70	Montreal Canadiens	5	0	0	0	0	....	....	....	....	....
1970-71	Montreal Canadiens	15	2	2	4	2	....	....	....	....	....
	Detroit Red Wings	24	8	4	12	4	....	....	....	....	....
1971-72	Detroit Red Wings	64	9	16	25	14	....	....	....	....	....
1972-73	Detroit Red Wings	75	18	18	36	23	....	....	....	....	....
1973-74	Detroit Red Wings	76	25	30	55	10	....	....	....	....	....
1974-75	Detroit Red Wings	26	1	10	11	6	....	....	....	....	....
	Kansas City Scouts	51	13	29	42	21	....	....	....	....	....
1975-76	Kansas City Scouts	78	27	44	71	12	....	....	....	....	....
1976-77	Washington Capitals	80	36	46	82	10	....	....	....	....	....
1977-78	Washington Capitals	80	38	35	73	12	....	....	....	....	....
1978-79	Washington Capitals	80	28	42	70	24	....	....	....	....	....
1979-80	Washington Capitals	33	11	20	31	6	....	....	....	....	....
1980-81	Washington Capitals	47	5	13	18	2	....	....	....	....	....
	NHL Totals	**734**	**221**	**309**	**530**	**146**	....	....	....	....	....

Played in NHL All-Star Game (1977)

Traded to **Detroit** by **Montreal** with Mickey Redmond and Bill Collins for Frank Mahovlich, January 13, 1971. Traded to **Kansas City** by **Detroit** with Claude Houde for Bart Crashley, Ted Snell and Larry Giroux, December 14, 1974. Signed as a free agent by **Washington**, September 1, 1976.

CHARTIER, Dave

Center. Shoots right. 5'9", 170 lbs. Born, St. Lazare, Man., February 15, 1961.
(Winnipeg's 11th choice, 191st overall, in 1980 Entry Draft).

Season	Club	GP	G	A	Pts	PIM	GP	G	A	Pts	PIM
1980-81	Winnipeg Jets	1	0	0	0	0	....	....	....	....	....
	NHL Totals	**1**	**0**	**0**	**0**	**0**	....	....	....	....	....

CHARTRAND, Brad

Center. Shoots left. 5'11", 191 lbs. Born, Winnipeg, Man., December 14, 1974.

Season	Club	GP	G	A	Pts	PIM	GP	G	A	Pts	PIM
99-2000	Los Angeles Kings	50	6	6	12	17	4	0	0	0	6
2000-01	Los Angeles Kings	4	1	0	1	2	....	....	....	....	....
2001-02	Los Angeles Kings	46	7	9	16	40	7	1	1	2	2
2002-03	Los Angeles Kings	62	8	6	14	33	....	....	....	....	....
	NHL Totals	**162**	**22**	**21**	**43**	**92**	**11**	**1**	**1**	**2**	**8**

Signed as a free agent by **Los Angeles**, July 15, 1999.

CHARTRAW, Rick

Defense/Right wing. Shoots right. 6'2", 210 lbs. Born, Caracas, Venezuela, July 13, 1954.
(Montreal's 3rd choice, 10th overall, in 1974 Amateur Draft).

Season	Club	GP	G	A	Pts	PIM	GP	G	A	Pts	PIM
1974-75	Montreal Canadiens	12	0	0	0	6	....	....	....	....	....
1975-76◆	Montreal Canadiens	16	1	3	4	25	2	0	0	0	0
1976-77◆	Montreal Canadiens	43	3	4	7	59	13	2	1	3	17
1977-78◆	Montreal Canadiens	68	4	12	16	64	10	1	0	1	10
1978-79◆	Montreal Canadiens	62	5	11	16	29	16	2	1	3	24
1979-80	Montreal Canadiens	66	5	7	12	35	10	2	2	4	0
1980-81	Montreal Canadiens	14	0	0	0	4	....	....	....	....	....
	Los Angeles Kings	21	1	6	7	28	4	0	1	1	4
1981-82	Los Angeles Kings	33	2	8	10	56	10	0	2	2	17
1982-83	Los Angeles Kings	31	3	5	8	31	....	....	....	....	....
	New York Rangers	26	2	2	4	37	9	0	2	2	6
1983-84	New York Rangers	4	0	0	0	4	....	....	....	....	....
	Edmonton Oilers	24	2	6	8	21	1	0	0	0	2
	NHL Totals	**420**	**28**	**64**	**92**	**399**	**75**	**7**	**9**	**16**	**80**

Traded to **Los Angeles** by **Montreal** for Los Angeles' 2nd round choice (Claude Lemieux) in 1983 Entry Draft, February 17, 1981. Claimed on waivers by **NY Rangers** from **Los Angeles**, January 13, 1983. Traded to **Edmonton** by **NY Rangers** for Edmonton's 9th round choice (Heinz Ehlers) in 1984 Entry Draft, January 20, 1984.

CHASE, Kelly

Right wing. Shoots right. 5'11", 201 lbs. Born, Porcupine Plain, Sask., October 25, 1967.

Season	Club	GP	G	A	Pts	PIM	GP	G	A	Pts	PIM
1989-90	St. Louis Blues	43	1	3	4	244	9	1	0	1	46
1990-91	St. Louis Blues	2	1	0	1	15	6	0	0	0	18
1991-92	St. Louis Blues	46	1	2	3	264	1	0	0	0	7
1992-93	St. Louis Blues	49	2	5	7	204	....	....	....	....	....
1993-94	St. Louis Blues	68	2	5	7	278	4	0	1	1	6
1994-95	Hartford Whalers	28	0	4	4	141	....	....	....	....	....
1995-96	Hartford Whalers	55	2	4	6	230	....	....	....	....	....
1996-97	Hartford Whalers	28	1	2	3	122	....	....	....	....	....
	Toronto Maple Leafs	2	0	0	0	27	....	....	....	....	....
1997-98	St. Louis Blues	67	4	3	7	231	7	0	0	0	23
1998-99	St. Louis Blues	45	3	7	10	143	....	....	....	....	....
99-2000	St. Louis Blues	25	0	1	1	118	....	....	....	....	....
	NHL Totals	**458**	**17**	**36**	**53**	**2017**	**27**	**1**	**1**	**2**	**100**

King Clancy Memorial Trophy (1998)

Signed as a free agent by **St. Louis**, February 23, 1988. Claimed by **Hartford** from **St. Louis** in Waiver Draft, January 18, 1995. Traded to **Toronto** by **Hartford** for Toronto's 8th round choice (Hartford/Carolina selected Jaroslav Svoboda) in 1998 Entry Draft, March 18, 1997. Traded to **St. Louis** by **Toronto** for future considerations, September 30, 1997. • Missed majority of 1999-2000 season recovering from knee injury suffered in game vs. Dallas, November 8, 1999.

CHASSE, Denis

Right wing. Shoots right. 6'2", 200 lbs. Born, Montreal, Que., February 7, 1970.

Season	Club	GP	G	A	Pts	PIM	GP	G	A	Pts	PIM
1993-94	St. Louis Blues	3	0	1	1	15	....	....	....	....	....
1994-95	St. Louis Blues	47	7	9	16	133	7	1	7	8	23
1995-96	St. Louis Blues	42	3	0	3	108	....	....	....	....	....
	Washington Capitals	3	0	0	0	5	....	....	....	....	....
	Winnipeg Jets	15	0	0	0	12	....	....	....	....	....
1996-97	Ottawa Senators	22	1	4	5	19	....	....	....	....	....
	NHL Totals	**132**	**11**	**14**	**25**	**292**	**7**	**1**	**7**	**8**	**23**

Signed as a free agent by **Quebec**, May 14, 1991. Traded to **St. Louis** by **Quebec** with Steve Duchesne for Garth Butcher, Ron Sutter and Bob Bassen, January 23, 1994. Traded to **Washington** by **St. Louis** for Rob Pearson, January 29, 1996. Traded to **Winnipeg** by **Washington** for Stewart Malgunas, February 15, 1996. Signed as a free agent by **Ottawa**, September 5, 1996. Traded to **Chicago** by **Ottawa** with the rights to Kevin Bolibruck and Ottawa's 6th round choice (later traded back to Ottawa – Ottawa selected Chris Neil) in 1998 Entry Draft for Mike Prokopec, March 18, 1997.

CHEBATURKIN, Vladimir

Defense. Shoots left. 6'2", 226 lbs. Born, Tyumen, USSR, April 23, 1975.
(NY Islanders' 3rd choice, 66th overall, in 1993 Entry Draft).

Season	Club	GP	G	A	Pts	PIM	GP	G	A	Pts	PIM
1997-98	New York Islanders	2	0	2	2	0	....	....	....	....	....
1998-99	New York Islanders	8	0	0	0	12	....	....	....	....	....
99-2000	New York Islanders	17	1	1	2	8	....	....	....	....	....
2000-01	St. Louis Blues	22	1	2	3	26	....	....	....	....	....
2001-02	Chicago Blackhawks	13	0	2	2	6	3	0	0	0	2
	NHL Totals	**62**	**2**	**7**	**9**	**52**	**3**	**0**	**0**	**0**	**2**

Signed as a free agent by **St. Louis**, June 9, 2000. Signed as a free agent by **Chicago**, September 5, 2001. Signed as a free agent by **NY Rangers**, July 18, 2002.

CHECK, Lude

Left wing. Shoots left. 5'10", 165 lbs. Born, Brandon, Man., May 22, 1919.

Season	Club	GP	G	A	Pts	PIM	GP	G	A	Pts	PIM
1943-44	Detroit Red Wings	1	0	0	0	0	....	....	....	....	....
1944-45	Chicago Black Hawks	26	6	2	8	4	....	....	....	....	....
	NHL Totals	**27**	**6**	**2**	**8**	**4**	....	....	....	....	....

Signed as a free agent by **Montreal**, October 24, 1944. Loaned to **Detroit** by **Montreal** (Quebec-QSHL) as an emergency injury replacement, March 11, 1944. Loaned to **Chicago** by **Montreal** for cash, October 25, 1944. Loaned to **Ottawa** (QSHL) by **Montreal** with Jim McFadden as compensation for Montreal's signing of Mike McMahon, October 24, 1945.

CHEECHOO, Jonathan

Right wing. Shoots right. 6', 205 lbs. Born, Moose Factory, Ont., July 15, 1980.
(San Jose's 2nd choice, 29th overall, in 1998 Entry Draft).

Season	Club	GP	G	A	Pts	PIM	GP	G	A	Pts	PIM
2002-03	San Jose Sharks	66	9	7	16	39	....	....	....	....	....
	NHL Totals	**66**	**9**	**7**	**16**	**39**	....	....	....	....	....

CHELIOS, Chris

Defense. Shoots right. 6'1", 190 lbs. Born, Chicago, IL, January 25, 1962.
(Montreal's 5th choice, 40th overall, in 1981 Entry Draft).

Season	Club	GP	G	A	Pts	PIM	GP	G	A	Pts	PIM
1983-84	Montreal Canadiens	12	0	2	2	12	15	1	9	10	17
1984-85	Montreal Canadiens	74	9	55	64	87	9	2	8	10	17
1985-86◆	Montreal Canadiens	41	8	26	34	67	20	2	9	11	49
1986-87	Montreal Canadiens	71	11	33	44	124	17	4	9	13	38
1987-88	Montreal Canadiens	71	20	41	61	172	11	3	1	4	29
1988-89	Montreal Canadiens	80	15	58	73	185	21	4	15	19	28
1989-90	Montreal Canadiens	53	9	22	31	136	5	0	1	1	8
1990-91	Chicago Blackhawks	77	12	52	64	192	6	1	7	8	46
1991-92	Chicago Blackhawks	80	9	47	56	245	18	6	15	21	37
1992-93	Chicago Blackhawks	84	15	58	73	282	4	0	2	2	14
1993-94	Chicago Blackhawks	76	16	44	60	212	6	1	1	2	8
1994-95	Chicago Blackhawks	48	5	33	38	72	16	4	7	11	12
1995-96	Chicago Blackhawks	81	14	58	72	140	9	0	3	3	8
1996-97	Chicago Blackhawks	72	10	38	48	112	6	0	1	1	8
1997-98	Chicago Blackhawks	81	3	39	42	151	....	....	....	....	....

Season	Club	REGULAR SEASON GP	G	A	Pts	PIM	PLAYOFFS GP	G	A	Pts	PIM
1998-99	Chicago Blackhawks	65	8	26	34	89	....	....	....	....	....
	Detroit Red Wings	10	1	1	2	4	10	0	4	4	14
99-2000	Detroit Red Wings	81	3	31	34	103	9	0	1	1	8
2000-01	Detroit Red Wings	24	0	3	3	45	5	1	0	1	2
2001-02 ◆	Detroit Red Wings	79	6	33	39	126	23	1	13	14	44
2002-03	Detroit Red Wings	66	2	17	19	78	4	0	0	0	2
	NHL Totals	**1326**	**176**	**717**	**893**	**2634**	**214**	**30**	**106**	**136**	**389**

NHL All-Rookie Team (1985) • NHL First All-Star Team (1989, 1993, 1995, 1996, 2002) • James Norris Memorial Trophy (1989, 1993, 1996) • NHL Second All-Star Team (1991, 1997)

Played in NHL All-Star Game (1985, 1990, 1991, 1992, 1993, 1994, 1996, 1997, 1998, 2000, 2002)

Traded to **Chicago** by **Montreal** with Montreal's 2nd round choice (Michael Pomichter) in 1991 Entry Draft for Denis Savard, June 29, 1990. Traded to **Detroit** by **Chicago** for Anders Eriksson and Detroit's 1st round choices in 1999 (Steve McCarthy) and 2001 (Adam Munro) Entry Drafts, March 23, 1999. • Missed majority of 2000-01 season recovering from knee injury suffered in game vs. Dallas, November 17, 2000.

CHERNOFF, Mike

Left wing. Shoots left. 5'10", 175 lbs. Born, Yorkton, Sask., May 13, 1946.

Season	Club	GP	G	A	Pts	PIM	GP	G	A	Pts	PIM
1968-69	Minnesota North Stars	1	0	0	0	0	....	....	....	....	....
	NHL Totals	**1**	**0**	**0**	**0**	**0**	....	....	....	....	....

Signed as a free agent by **Minnesota**, October, 1968.

CHERNOMAZ, Rich

Right wing. Shoots right. 5'8", 185 lbs. Born, Selkirk, Man., September 1, 1963.
(Colorado's 2nd choice, 26th overall, in 1981 Entry Draft).

Season	Club	GP	G	A	Pts	PIM	GP	G	A	Pts	PIM
1981-82	Colorado Rockies	2	0	0	0	0	....	....	....	....	....
1983-84	New Jersey Devils	7	2	1	3	2	....	....	....	....	....
1984-85	New Jersey Devils	3	0	2	2	2	....	....	....	....	....
1986-87	New Jersey Devils	25	6	4	10	8	....	....	....	....	....
1987-88	Calgary Flames	2	1	0	1	0	....	....	....	....	....
1988-89	Calgary Flames	1	0	0	0	0	....	....	....	....	....
1991-92	Calgary Flames	11	0	0	0	6	....	....	....	....	....
	NHL Totals	**51**	**9**	**7**	**16**	**18**	....	....	....	....	....

Transferred to **New Jersey** after **Colorado** franchise relocated, June 30, 1982. Signed as a free agent by **Calgary**, August 4, 1987. Signed as a free agent by **Toronto**, August 3, 1993.

CHERRY, Dick

Defense. Shoots left. 6', 195 lbs. Born, Kingston, Ont., March 28, 1937.

Season	Club	GP	G	A	Pts	PIM	GP	G	A	Pts	PIM
1956-57	Boston Bruins	6	0	0	0	4	....	....	....	....	....
1968-69	Philadelphia Flyers	71	9	6	15	18	4	1	0	1	4
1969-70	Philadelphia Flyers	68	3	4	7	23	....	....	....	....	....
	NHL Totals	**145**	**12**	**10**	**22**	**45**	**4**	**1**	**0**	**1**	**4**

• Brother of Don

• Retired to teach high-school in Kingston, 1963-1965. Claimed by **Philadelphia** from **Boston** in Expansion Draft, June 6, 1967. Claimed by **Boston** from **Philadelphia** in Intra-League Draft, June 9, 1970.

CHERRY, Don

Defense. Shoots left. 5'11", 180 lbs. Born, Kingston, Ont., February 5, 1934.

Season	Club	GP	G	A	Pts	PIM	GP	G	A	Pts	PIM
1954-55	Boston Bruins	....	....	....	....	....	1	0	0	0	0
	NHL Totals	....	....	....	....	....	**1**	**0**	**0**	**0**	**0**

• Brother of Dick

Traded to **Springfield** (AHL) by **Boston** for cash, September, 1957. Traded to **Detroit** by **Springfield** (AHL) for cash, November, 1961. Traded to **Montreal** by **Detroit** for cash, September 13, 1962. Rights transferred to **Toronto** after NHL club purchased **Spokane** (WHL) franchise, June 4, 1963.

CHERVYAKOV, Denis

Defense. Shoots left. 6', 185 lbs. Born, Leningrad, USSR, April 20, 1970.
(Boston's 9th choice, 256th overall, in 1992 Entry Draft).

Season	Club	GP	G	A	Pts	PIM	GP	G	A	Pts	PIM
1992-93	Boston Bruins	2	0	0	0	2	....	....	....	....	....
	NHL Totals	**2**	**0**	**0**	**0**	**2**	....	....	....	....	....

Signed as a free agent by **NY Islanders**, September 12, 1996.

CHEVREFILS, Real

Left wing. Shoots left. 5'10", 180 lbs. Born, Timmins, Ont., May 2, 1932.

Season	Club	GP	G	A	Pts	PIM	GP	G	A	Pts	PIM
1951-52	Boston Bruins	33	8	17	25	8	7	1	1	2	6
1952-53	Boston Bruins	69	19	14	33	44	7	0	1	1	6
1953-54	Boston Bruins	14	4	1	5	2	....	....	....	....	....
1954-55	Boston Bruins	64	18	22	40	30	5	2	1	3	4
1955-56	Detroit Red Wings	38	3	4	7	24	....	....	....	....	....
	Boston Bruins	25	11	8	19	10	....	....	....	....	....
1956-57	Boston Bruins	70	31	17	48	38	10	2	1	3	4
1957-58	Boston Bruins	44	9	9	18	21	1	0	0	0	0
1958-59	Boston Bruins	30	1	5	6	8	....	....	....	....	....
	NHL Totals	**387**	**104**	**97**	**201**	**185**	**30**	**5**	**4**	**9**	**20**

NHL Second All-Star Team (1957)

Played in NHL All-Star Game (1955, 1957)

Traded to **Detroit** by **Boston** with Ed Sandford, Norm Corcoran, Gilles Boisvert and Warren Godfrey for Marcel Bonin, Terry Sawchuk, Vic Stasiuk and Lorne Davis, June 3, 1955. Traded to **Boston** by **Detroit** with Jerry Toppazzini for Lorne Ferguson and Murray Costello, January 17, 1956.

CHIASSON, Steve

Defense. Shoots left. 6'1", 205 lbs. Born, Barrie, Ont., April 14, 1967.
(Detroit's 3rd choice, 50th overall, in 1985 Entry Draft).

Season	Club	GP	G	A	Pts	PIM	GP	G	A	Pts	PIM
1986-87	Detroit Red Wings	45	1	4	5	73	2	0	0	0	19
1987-88	Detroit Red Wings	29	2	9	11	57	9	2	2	4	31
1988-89	Detroit Red Wings	65	12	35	47	149	5	2	1	3	6
1989-90	Detroit Red Wings	67	14	28	42	114	....	....	....	....	....
1990-91	Detroit Red Wings	42	3	17	20	80	5	3	1	4	19
1991-92	Detroit Red Wings	62	10	24	34	136	11	1	5	6	12
1992-93	Detroit Red Wings	79	12	50	62	155	7	2	2	4	19
1993-94	Detroit Red Wings	82	13	33	46	122	7	2	3	5	2
1994-95	Calgary Flames	45	2	23	25	39	7	1	2	3	9
1995-96	Calgary Flames	76	8	25	33	62	4	2	1	3	0
1996-97	Calgary Flames	47	5	11	16	32	....	....	....	....	....
	Hartford Whalers	18	3	11	14	7	....	....	....	....	....
1997-98	Carolina Hurricanes	66	7	27	34	65	....	....	....	....	....
1998-99	Carolina Hurricanes	28	1	8	9	16	6	1	2	3	2
	NHL Totals	**751**	**93**	**305**	**398**	**1107**	**63**	**16**	**19**	**35**	**119**

Played in NHL All-Star Game (1993)

Traded to **Calgary** by **Detroit** for Mike Vernon, June 29, 1994. Traded to **Hartford** by **Calgary** with Colorado's 3rd round choice (previously acquired, Hartford/Carolina selected Francis Lessard) in 1997 Entry Draft for Hnat Domenichelli, Glen Featherstone, New Jersey's 2nd round choice (previously acquired, Calgary selected Dimitri Kokorev) in 1997 Entry Draft and Vancouver's 3rd round choice (previously acquired, Calgary selected Paul Manning) in 1998 Entry Draft, March 5, 1997. Transferred to **Carolina** after **Hartford** franchise relocated, June 25, 1997. • Died of injuries suffered in automobile accident, May 3, 1999.

CHIBIREV, Igor

Center. Shoots left. 6', 180 lbs. Born, Kiev, USSR, April 19, 1968.
(Hartford's 8th choice, 266th overall, in 1993 Entry Draft).

Season	Club	GP	G	A	Pts	PIM	GP	G	A	Pts	PIM
1993-94	Hartford Whalers	37	4	11	15	2	....	....	....	....	....
1994-95	Hartford Whalers	8	3	1	4	0	....	....	....	....	....
	NHL Totals	**45**	**7**	**12**	**19**	**2**	....	....	....	....	....

CHICOINE, Dan

Right wing. Shoots right. 5'11", 192 lbs. Born, Sherbrooke, Que., November 30, 1957.
(Cleveland's 2nd choice, 23rd overall, in 1977 Amateur Draft).

Season	Club	GP	G	A	Pts	PIM	GP	G	A	Pts	PIM
1977-78	Cleveland Barons	6	0	0	0	0	....	....	....	....	....
1978-79	Minnesota North Stars	1	0	0	0	0	....	....	....	....	....
1979-80	Minnesota North Stars	24	1	2	3	12	1	0	0	0	0
	NHL Totals	**31**	**1**	**2**	**3**	**12**	**1**	**0**	**0**	**0**	**0**

Placed on **Minnesota** Reserve List after **Cleveland-Minnesota** Dispersal Draft, June 15, 1978. Claimed by **Minnesota** as a fill-in during Expansion Draft, June 13, 1979. Traded to **Quebec** by **Minnesota** for Nelson Burton, June 9, 1981.

CHIMERA, Jason

Left wing. Shoots left. 6', 215 lbs. Born, Edmonton, Alta., May 2, 1979.
(Edmonton's 5th choice, 121st overall, in 1997 Entry Draft).

Season	Club	GP	G	A	Pts	PIM	GP	G	A	Pts	PIM
2000-01	Edmonton Oilers	1	0	0	0	0	....	....	....	....	....
2001-02	Edmonton Oilers	3	1	0	1	0	....	....	....	....	....
2002-03	Edmonton Oilers	66	14	9	23	36	2	0	2	2	0
	NHL Totals	**70**	**15**	**9**	**24**	**36**	**2**	**0**	**2**	**2**	**0**

CHINNICK, Rick

Right wing. Shoots left. 5'11", 180 lbs. Born, Chatham, Ont., August 15, 1953.
(Minnesota's 3rd choice, 41st overall, in 1973 Amateur Draft).

Season	Club	GP	G	A	Pts	PIM	GP	G	A	Pts	PIM
1973-74	Minnesota North Stars	1	0	1	1	0	....	....	....	....	....
1974-75	Minnesota North Stars	3	0	1	1	0	....	....	....	....	....
	NHL Totals	**4**	**0**	**2**	**2**	**0**	....	....	....	....	....

Traded to **Detroit** by **Minnesota** for Bryan Hextall Jr., November 21, 1975.

CHIPPERFIELD, Ron

Center. Shoots right. 5'11", 186 lbs. Born, Brandon, Man., March 28, 1954.
(California's 2nd choice, 17th overall, in 1974 Amateur Draft).

Season	Club	GP	G	A	Pts	PIM	GP	G	A	Pts	PIM
1979-80	Edmonton Oilers	67	18	19	37	24	....	....	....	....	....
	Quebec Nordiques	12	4	4	8	8	....	....	....	....	....
1980-81	Quebec Nordiques	4	0	1	1	2	....	....	....	....	....
	NHL Totals	**83**	**22**	**24**	**46**	**34**	....	....	....	....	....

Rights traded to **Philadelphia** by **California** for George Pesut, December 11, 1974. Rights retained by **Edmonton** prior to Expansion Draft, June 9,1979. Traded to **Quebec** by **Edmonton** for Ron Low, March 11, 1980

CHISHOLM, Art

Center/Defense. Shoots left. 5'9", 160 lbs. Born, Arlington, MA, November 11, 1934.

Season	Club	GP	G	A	Pts	PIM	GP	G	A	Pts	PIM
1960-61	Boston Bruins	3	0	0	0	0	....	....	....	....	....
	NHL Totals	**3**	**0**	**0**	**0**	**0**	....	....	....	....	....

Signed as a free agent by **Boston** to a 3-game amateur tryout contract, March 15, 1961.

CHISHOLM, Colin

Defense. Shoots right. 6'3", 200 lbs. Born, Edmonton, Alta., February 25, 1963.
(Buffalo's 4th choice, 60th overall, in 1981 Entry Draft).

Season	Club	GP	G	A	Pts	PIM	GP	G	A	Pts	PIM
1986-87	Minnesota North Stars	1	0	0	0	0	....	....	....	....	....
	NHL Totals	**1**	**0**	**0**	**0**	**0**	....	....	....	....	....

Signed as a free agent by **Minnesota**, June 11, 1986.

CHISHOLM, Lex

Center/Right wing. Shoots right. 5'11", 175 lbs. Born, Galt, Ont., April 1, 1915.

Season	Club	Regular Season GP	G	A	Pts	PIM	Playoffs GP	G	A	Pts	PIM
1939-40	Toronto Maple Leafs	28	6	8	14	11	....	....	....	....	....
1940-41	Toronto Maple Leafs	26	4	0	4	8	3	1	0	1	0
	NHL Totals	**54**	**10**	**8**	**18**	**19**	**3**	**1**	**0**	**1**	**0**

CHISTOV, Stanislav

Left wing. Shoots right. 5'10", 178 lbs. Born, Chelyabinsk, USSR, April 17, 1983.
(Anaheim's 1st choice, 5th overall, in 2001 Entry Draft).

Season	Club	Regular Season GP	G	A	Pts	PIM	Playoffs GP	G	A	Pts	PIM
2002-03	Mighty Ducks of Anaheim	79	12	18	30	54	21	4	2	6	8
	NHL Totals	**79**	**12**	**18**	**30**	**54**	**21**	**4**	**2**	**6**	**8**

CHORNEY, Marc

Defense. Shoots left. 6', 200 lbs. Born, Sudbury, Ont., November 8, 1959.
(Pittsburgh's 5th choice, 115th overall, in 1979 Entry Draft).

Season	Club	Regular Season GP	G	A	Pts	PIM	Playoffs GP	G	A	Pts	PIM
1980-81	Pittsburgh Penguins	8	1	6	7	14	2	0	1	1	2
1981-82	Pittsburgh Penguins	60	1	6	7	63	5	0	0	0	0
1982-83	Pittsburgh Penguins	67	3	5	8	66	....	....	....	....	....
1983-84	Pittsburgh Penguins	4	0	1	1	8	....	....	....	....	....
	Los Angeles Kings	71	3	9	12	58	....	....	....	....	....
	NHL Totals	**210**	**8**	**27**	**35**	**209**	**7**	**0**	**1**	**1**	**2**

Traded to **Los Angeles** by **Pittsburgh** for Los Angeles' 6th round choice (Stuart Marston) in 1985 Entry Draft, October 15, 1983. Signed as a free agent by **Washington**, July 11, 1984.

CHORSKE, Tom

Left wing. Shoots right. 6'1", 212 lbs. Born, Minneapolis, MN, September 18, 1966.
(Montreal's 2nd choice, 16th overall, in 1985 Entry Draft).

Season	Club	Regular Season GP	G	A	Pts	PIM	Playoffs GP	G	A	Pts	PIM
1989-90	Montreal Canadiens	14	3	1	4	2	....	....	....	....	....
1990-91	Montreal Canadiens	57	9	11	20	32	....	....	....	....	....
1991-92	New Jersey Devils	76	19	17	36	32	7	0	3	3	4
1992-93	New Jersey Devils	50	7	12	19	25	1	0	0	0	0
1993-94	New Jersey Devils	76	21	20	41	32	20	4	3	7	0
1994-95♦	New Jersey Devils	42	10	8	18	16	17	1	5	6	4
1995-96	Ottawa Senators	72	15	14	29	21	....	....	....	....	....
1996-97	Ottawa Senators	68	18	8	26	16	5	0	1	1	2
1997-98	New York Islanders	82	12	23	35	39	....	....	....	....	....
1998-99	New York Islanders	2	0	1	1	2	....	....	....	....	....
	Washington Capitals	17	0	2	2	4	....	....	....	....	....
	Calgary Flames	7	0	0	0	2	....	....	....	....	....
99-2000	Pittsburgh Penguins	33	1	5	6	2	....	....	....	....	....
	NHL Totals	**596**	**115**	**122**	**237**	**225**	**50**	**5**	**12**	**17**	**10**

Traded to **New Jersey** by **Montreal** with Stephane Richer for Kirk Muller and Roland Melanson, September 20, 1991. Claimed on waivers by **Ottawa** from **New Jersey**, October 5, 1995. Claimed by **NY Islanders** from **Ottawa** in Waiver Draft, September 28, 1997. Traded to **Washington** by **NY Islanders** with NY Islanders' 8th round choice (Maxim Orlov) in 1999 Entry Draft for Washington's 6th round choice (Bjorn Melin) in 1999 Entry Draft, October 16, 1998. Traded to **Calgary** by **Washington** for Calgary's 7th round choice (later traded to Los Angeles – Los Angeles selected Tim Eriksson) in 2000 Entry Draft and Washington's 9th round choice (previously acquired, Washington selected Bjorn Nord) in 2000 Entry Draft, March 22, 1999. Signed as a free agent by **Pittsburgh**, September 2, 1999. • Missed majority of 1999-2000 season recovering from thumb injury suffered in game vs. NY Islanders, February 3, 2000.

CHOUINARD, Eric

Left wing. Shoots left. 6'3", 205 lbs. Born, Atlanta, GA, July 8, 1980.
(Montreal's 1st choice, 16th overall, in 1998 Entry Draft).

Season	Club	Regular Season GP	G	A	Pts	PIM	Playoffs GP	G	A	Pts	PIM
2000-01	Montreal Canadiens	13	1	3	4	0	....	....	....	....	....
2002-03	Philadelphia Flyers	28	4	4	8	8	....	....	....	....	....
	NHL Totals	**41**	**5**	**7**	**12**	**8**	....	....	....	....	....

• Son of Guy

Traded to **Philadelphia** by **Montreal** for Philadelphia's 2nd round choice (Maxim Lapierre) in 2003 Entry Draft, January 29, 2003.

CHOUINARD, Gene

Defense. Shoots left. 5'6", 160 lbs. Born, Ottawa, Ont., January 5, 1907.

Season	Club	Regular Season GP	G	A	Pts	PIM	Playoffs GP	G	A	Pts	PIM
1927-28	Ottawa Senators	8	0	0	0	0	....	....	....	....	....
	NHL Totals	**8**	**0**	**0**	**0**	**0**	....	....	....	....	....

Signed as a free agent by **Ottawa**, December 19, 1927.

CHOUINARD, Guy

Center. Shoots right. 5'11", 182 lbs. Born, Quebec City, Que., October 20, 1956.
(Atlanta's 1st choice, 28th overall, in 1974 Amateur Draft).

Season	Club	Regular Season GP	G	A	Pts	PIM	Playoffs GP	G	A	Pts	PIM
1974-75	Atlanta Flames	5	0	0	0	2	....	....	....	....	....
1975-76	Atlanta Flames	4	0	2	2	2	2	0	0	0	0
1976-77	Atlanta Flames	80	17	33	50	8	3	2	0	2	0
1977-78	Atlanta Flames	73	28	30	58	8	2	1	0	1	0
1978-79	Atlanta Flames	80	50	57	107	14	2	1	2	3	0
1979-80	Atlanta Flames	76	31	46	77	22	4	1	3	4	4
1980-81	Calgary Flames	52	31	52	83	24	16	3	14	17	4
1981-82	Calgary Flames	64	23	57	80	12	3	0	1	1	0
1982-83	Calgary Flames	80	13	59	72	18	9	1	6	7	4
1983-84	St. Louis Blues	64	12	34	46	10	5	0	2	2	0
	NHL Totals	**578**	**205**	**370**	**575**	**120**	**46**	**9**	**28**	**37**	**12**

• Father of Eric

Transferred to **Calgary** after **Atlanta** franchise relocated, June 24, 1980. Traded to **St. Louis** by **Calgary** for future considerations, September 6, 1983.

CHOUINARD, Marc

Center. Shoots right. 6'5", 210 lbs. Born, Charlesbourg, Que., May 6, 1977.
(Winnipeg's 2nd choice, 32nd overall, in 1995 Entry Draft).

Season	Club	Regular Season GP	G	A	Pts	PIM	Playoffs GP	G	A	Pts	PIM
2000-01	Mighty Ducks of Anaheim	44	3	4	7	12	....	....	....	....	....
2001-02	Mighty Ducks of Anaheim	45	4	5	9	10	....	....	....	....	....
2002-03	Mighty Ducks of Anaheim	70	3	4	7	40	15	1	0	1	0
	NHL Totals	**159**	**10**	**13**	**23**	**62**	**15**	**1**	**0**	**1**	**0**

Traded to **Anaheim** by **Winnipeg** with Teemu Selanne and Winnipeg's 4th round choice (later traded to Toronto – later traded to Montreal – Montreal selected Kim Staal) in 1996 Entry Draft for Chad Kilger, Oleg Tverdovsky and Anaheim's 3rd round choice (Per-Anton Lundstrom) in 1996 Entry Draft, February 7, 1996. Signed as a free agent by **Minnesota**, July 28, 2003.

CHRISTIAN, Dave

USHOF

Right wing. Shoots right. 5'11", 175 lbs. Born, Warroad, MN, May 12, 1959.
(Winnipeg's 2nd choice, 40th overall, in 1979 Entry Draft).

Season	Club	Regular Season GP	G	A	Pts	PIM	Playoffs GP	G	A	Pts	PIM
1979-80	Winnipeg Jets	15	8	10	18	2	....	....	....	....	....
1980-81	Winnipeg Jets	80	28	43	71	22	....	....	....	....	....
1981-82	Winnipeg Jets	80	25	51	76	28	4	0	1	1	2
1982-83	Winnipeg Jets	55	18	26	44	23	3	0	0	0	0
1983-84	Washington Capitals	80	29	52	81	28	8	5	4	9	5
1984-85	Washington Capitals	80	26	43	69	14	5	1	1	2	0
1985-86	Washington Capitals	80	41	42	83	15	9	4	4	8	0
1986-87	Washington Capitals	76	23	27	50	8	7	1	3	4	6
1987-88	Washington Capitals	80	37	21	58	26	14	5	6	11	6
1988-89	Washington Capitals	80	34	31	65	12	6	1	1	2	0
1989-90	Washington Capitals	28	3	8	11	4	....	....	....	....	....
	Boston Bruins	50	12	17	29	8	21	4	1	5	4
1990-91	Boston Bruins	78	32	21	53	41	19	8	4	12	4
1991-92	St. Louis Blues	78	20	24	44	41	4	3	0	3	0
1992-93	Chicago Blackhawks	60	4	14	18	12	1	0	0	0	0
1993-94	Chicago Blackhawks	9	0	3	3	0	1	0	0	0	0
	NHL Totals	**1009**	**340**	**433**	**773**	**284**	**102**	**32**	**25**	**57**	**27**

Played in NHL All-Star Game (1991)

Traded to **Washington** by **Winnipeg** for Washington's 1st round choice (Bobby Dollas) in 1983 Entry Draft, June 8, 1983. Traded to **Boston** by **Washington** for Bob Joyce, December 13, 1989. Transferred to **St. Louis** by **Boston** with Boston's 3rd round choice (Vitali Prokhorov) and 7th round choice (Lance Burns) in 1992 Entry Draft as compensation for Boston's signing of free agents Glen Featherstone and Dave Thomlinson, July 30, 1991. Claimed by **Chicago** from **St. Louis** in Waiver Draft, October 4, 1992.

CHRISTIAN, Jeff

Left wing. Shoots left. 6'2", 210 lbs. Born, Burlington, Ont., July 30, 1970.
(New Jersey's 2nd choice, 23rd overall, in 1988 Entry Draft).

Season	Club	Regular Season GP	G	A	Pts	PIM	Playoffs GP	G	A	Pts	PIM
1991-92	New Jersey Devils	2	0	0	0	2	....	....	....	....	....
1994-95	Pittsburgh Penguins	1	0	0	0	0	....	....	....	....	....
1995-96	Pittsburgh Penguins	3	0	0	0	2	....	....	....	....	....
1996-97	Pittsburgh Penguins	11	2	2	4	13	....	....	....	....	....
1997-98	Phoenix Coyotes	1	0	0	0	0	....	....	....	....	....
	NHL Totals	**18**	**2**	**2**	**4**	**17**	....	....	....	....	....

Signed as a free agent by **Pittsburgh**, August 2, 1994. Signed as a free agent by **Phoenix**, July 28, 1997. Signed as a free agent by **Chicago**, August 25, 1999.

CHRISTIE, Mike

Defense. Shoots left. 6', 190 lbs. Born, Big Spring, TX, December 20, 1949.

Season	Club	Regular Season GP	G	A	Pts	PIM	Playoffs GP	G	A	Pts	PIM
1974-75	California Golden Seals	34	0	14	14	76	....	....	....	....	....
1975-76	California Golden Seals	78	3	18	21	152	....	....	....	....	....
1976-77	Cleveland Barons	79	6	27	33	79	....	....	....	....	....
1977-78	Cleveland Barons	34	1	6	7	49	....	....	....	....	....
	Colorado Rockies	35	2	8	10	28	2	0	0	0	0
1978-79	Colorado Rockies	68	1	10	11	88	....	....	....	....	....
1979-80	Colorado Rockies	74	1	17	18	78	....	....	....	....	....
1980-81	Colorado Rockies	1	0	0	0	0	....	....	....	....	....
	Vancouver Canucks	9	1	1	2	0	....	....	....	....	....
	NHL Totals	**412**	**15**	**101**	**116**	**550**	**2**	**0**	**0**	**0**	**0**

Signed as a free agent by **Chicago**, September, 1972. Traded to **California** by **Chicago** with Len Frig for Ivan Boldirev, May 24, 1974. Transferred to **Cleveland** after **California** franchise relocated, August 26, 1976. Traded to **Colorado** by **Cleveland** for Dennis O'Brien, January 12, 1978. Traded to **Vancouver** by **Colorado** for cash, December 8, 1980

CHRISTIE, Ryan

Left wing. Shoots left. 6'3", 200 lbs. Born, Beamsville, Ont., July 3, 1978.
(Dallas' 4th choice, 112th overall, in 1996 Entry Draft).

Season	Club	Regular Season GP	G	A	Pts	PIM	Playoffs GP	G	A	Pts	PIM
99-2000	Dallas Stars	5	0	0	0	0	....	....	....	....	....
2001-02	Calgary Flames	2	0	0	0	0	....	....	....	....	....
	NHL Totals	**7**	**0**	**0**	**0**	**0**	....	....	....	....	....

Signed as a free agent by **Calgary**, July 1, 2001.

CHRISTOFF, Steve

Center. Shoots right. 6'1", 180 lbs. Born, Richfield, MN, January 23, 1958.
(Minnesota's 3rd choice, 24th overall, in 1978 Amateur Draft).

Season	Club	Regular Season GP	G	A	Pts	PIM	Playoffs GP	G	A	Pts	PIM
1979-80	Minnesota North Stars	20	8	7	15	19	14	8	4	12	7
1980-81	Minnesota North Stars	56	26	13	39	58	18	8	8	16	16
1981-82	Minnesota North Stars	69	26	29	55	14	2	0	0	0	2
1982-83	Calgary Flames	45	9	8	17	4	1	0	0	0	0

		Regular Season					Playoffs				
Season	Club	GP	G	A	Pts	PIM	GP	G	A	Pts	PIM
1983-84	Los Angeles Kings	58	8	7	15	13	....	....	....	....	....
	NHL Totals	**248**	**77**	**64**	**141**	**108**	**35**	**16**	**12**	**28**	**25**

Traded to **Calgary** by **Minnesota** with Bill Nyrop and St. Louis' 2nd round choice (previously acquired, Calgary selected Dave Reierson) in 1982 Entry Draft for Willi Plett and Calgary's 4th round choice (Dusan Pasek) in 1982 Entry Draft, June 7, 1982. Traded to **Minnesota** by **Calgary** with Calgary's 2nd round choice (Frantisek Musil) in 1983 Entry Draft for Mike Eaves and Keith Hanson, June 8, 1983. Traded to **Los Angeles** by **Minnesota** with Fred Barrett for Dave Lewis, October 3, 1983.

CHRYSTAL, Bob

Defense. Shoots left. 6', 180 lbs. Born, Winnipeg, Man., April 3, 1930.

		Regular Season					Playoffs				
Season	Club	GP	G	A	Pts	PIM	GP	G	A	Pts	PIM
1953-54	New York Rangers	64	5	5	10	44	....	....	....	....	....
1954-55	New York Rangers	68	6	9	15	68	....	....	....	....	....
	NHL Totals	**132**	**11**	**14**	**25**	**112**	....	....	....	....	....

Traded to **NY Rangers** by **Cleveland** (AHL) for Steve Kraftcheck and cash, June, 1953. Claimed by **Chicago** from **NY Rangers** (Brandon-WHL) in Inter-League Draft, June 4, 1957.

CHUBAROV, Artem

Center. Shoots left. 6'1", 189 lbs. Born, Gorky, USSR, December 12, 1979.
(Vancouver's 2nd choice, 31st overall, in 1998 Entry Draft).

		Regular Season					Playoffs				
Season	Club	GP	G	A	Pts	PIM	GP	G	A	Pts	PIM
99-2000	Vancouver Canucks	49	1	8	9	10	....	....	....	....	....
2000-01	Vancouver Canucks	1	0	0	0	0	....	....	....	....	....
2001-02	Vancouver Canucks	51	5	5	10	10	6	0	1	1	0
2002-03	Vancouver Canucks	62	7	13	20	6	14	0	2	2	4
	NHL Totals	**163**	**13**	**26**	**39**	**26**	**20**	**0**	**3**	**3**	**4**

CHURCH, Brad

Left wing. Shoots left. 6'1", 210 lbs. Born, Dauphin, Man., November 14, 1976.
(Washington's 1st choice, 17th overall, in 1995 Entry Draft).

		Regular Season					Playoffs				
Season	Club	GP	G	A	Pts	PIM	GP	G	A	Pts	PIM
1997-98	Washington Capitals	2	0	0	0	0	....	....	....	....	....
	NHL Totals	**2**	**0**	**0**	**0**	**0**	....	....	....	....	....

Traded to **Edmonton** by **Washington** for the rights to Barrie Moore, February 3, 1999.

CHURCH, Jack

Defense. Shoots right. 5'11", 180 lbs. Born, Kamsack, Sask., May 24, 1915.

		Regular Season					Playoffs				
Season	Club	GP	G	A	Pts	PIM	GP	G	A	Pts	PIM
1938-39	Toronto Maple Leafs	3	0	2	2	2	1	0	0	0	0
1939-40	Toronto Maple Leafs	31	1	4	5	62	10	1	1	2	6
1940-41	Toronto Maple Leafs	11	0	1	1	22	5	0	0	0	8
1941-42	Toronto Maple Leafs	27	0	3	3	30	....	....	....	....	....
	Brooklyn Americans	15	1	3	4	10	....	....	....	....	....
1945-46	Boston Bruins	43	2	6	8	28	9	0	0	0	4
	NHL Totals	**130**	**4**	**19**	**23**	**154**	**25**	**1**	**1**	**2**	**18**

Traded to **Brooklyn** by **Toronto** for cash, February 2, 1942. Rights transferred to **Boston** from **Brooklyn** in Special Dispersal Draw, September 11, 1943. Traded to **NY Rangers** by **Boston** for $5,000, September 17, 1946. Traded to **Providence** (AHL) by **NY Rangers** for cash, October 4, 1947.

CHURLA, Shane

Right wing. Shoots right. 6'1", 200 lbs. Born, Fernie, B.C., June 24, 1965.
(Hartford's 4th choice, 110th overall, in 1985 Entry Draft).

		Regular Season					Playoffs				
Season	Club	GP	G	A	Pts	PIM	GP	G	A	Pts	PIM
1986-87	Hartford Whalers	20	0	1	1	78	2	0	0	0	42
1987-88	Hartford Whalers	2	0	0	0	14	....	....	....	....	....
	Calgary Flames	29	1	5	6	132	7	0	1	1	17
1988-89	Calgary Flames	5	0	0	0	25	....	....	....	....	....
	Minnesota North Stars	13	1	0	1	54	....	....	....	....	....
1989-90	Minnesota North Stars	53	2	3	5	292	7	0	0	0	44
1990-91	Minnesota North Stars	40	2	2	4	286	22	2	1	3	90
1991-92	Minnesota North Stars	57	4	1	5	278	....	....	....	....	....
1992-93	Minnesota North Stars	73	5	16	21	286	....	....	....	....	....
1993-94	Dallas Stars	69	6	7	13	333	9	1	3	4	35
1994-95	Dallas Stars	27	1	3	4	186	5	0	0	0	20
1995-96	Dallas Stars	34	3	4	7	168	....	....	....	....	....
	Los Angeles Kings	11	1	2	3	37	....	....	....	....	....
	New York Rangers	10	0	0	0	26	11	2	2	4	14
1996-97	New York Rangers	45	0	1	1	106	15	0	0	0	20
	NHL Totals	**488**	**26**	**45**	**71**	**2301**	**78**	**5**	**7**	**12**	**282**

Traded to **Calgary** by **Hartford** with Dana Murzyn for Neil Sheehy, Carey Wilson, and the rights to Lane MacDonald, January 3, 1988. Traded to **Minnesota** by **Calgary** with Perry Berezan for Brian MacLellan and Minnesota's 4th round choice (Robert Reichel) in 1989 Entry Draft, March 4, 1989. Claimed by **San Jose** from **Minnesota** in Dispersal Draft, May 30, 1991. Traded to **Minnesota** by **San Jose** for Kelly Kisio, June 3, 1991. Transferred to **Dallas** after **Minnesota** franchise relocated, June 9, 1993. Traded to **Los Angeles** by **Dallas** with Doug Zmolek for Darryl Sydor and Los Angeles' 5th round choice (Ryan Christie) in 1996 Entry Draft, February 17, 1996. Traded to **NY Rangers** by **Los Angeles** with Marty McSorley and Jari Kurri for Ray Ferraro, Ian Laperriere, Mattias Norstrom, Nathan LaFayette and NY Rangers' 4th round choice (Sean Blanchard) in 1997 Entry Draft, March 14, 1996.

CHYCHRUN, Jeff

Defense. Shoots right. 6'4", 215 lbs. Born, LaSalle, Que., May 3, 1966.
(Philadelphia's 3rd choice, 37th overall, in 1984 Entry Draft).

		Regular Season					Playoffs				
Season	Club	GP	G	A	Pts	PIM	GP	G	A	Pts	PIM
1986-87	Philadelphia Flyers	1	0	0	0	4	....	....	....	....	....
1987-88	Philadelphia Flyers	3	0	0	0	4	....	....	....	....	....
1988-89	Philadelphia Flyers	80	1	4	5	245	19	0	2	2	65
1989-90	Philadelphia Flyers	79	2	7	9	250	....	....	....	....	....
1990-91	Philadelphia Flyers	36	0	6	6	105	....	....	....	....	....
1991-92	Los Angeles Kings	26	0	3	3	76	....	....	....	....	....
	♦ Pittsburgh Penguins	17	0	1	1	35	....	....	....	....	....
1992-93	Pittsburgh Penguins	1	0	0	0	2	....	....	....	....	....
	Los Angeles Kings	17	0	1	1	23	....	....	....	....	....
1993-94	Edmonton Oilers	2	0	0	0	0	....	....	....	....	....
	NHL Totals	**262**	**3**	**22**	**25**	**744**	**19**	**0**	**2**	**2**	**65**

• Missed majority of 1990-91 season recovering from wrist injury suffered in game vs. Toronto, November 23, 1990. Traded to **Los Angeles** by **Philadelphia** with Jari Kurri for Steve Duchesne, Steve Kasper and Los Angeles' 4th round choice (Aris Brimanis) in 1991 Entry Draft, May 30, 1991. Traded to **Pittsburgh** by **Los Angeles** with Brian Benning and Los Angeles' 1st round choice (later traded to Philadelphia – Philadelphia selected Jason Bowen) in 1992 Entry Draft for Paul Coffey, February 19, 1992. Traded to **Los Angeles** by **Pittsburgh** for Peter Ahola, November 6, 1992. Traded to **Edmonton** by **Los Angeles** for future considerations, November 2, 1993. Signed as a free agent by **Hartford**, May 27, 1994.

CHYNOWETH, Dean

Defense. Shoots right. 6'1", 191 lbs. Born, Calgary, Alta., October 30, 1968.
(NY Islanders' 1st choice, 13th overall, in 1987 Entry Draft).

		Regular Season					Playoffs				
Season	Club	GP	G	A	Pts	PIM	GP	G	A	Pts	PIM
1988-89	New York Islanders	6	0	0	0	48	....	....	....	....	....
1989-90	New York Islanders	20	0	2	2	39	....	....	....	....	....
1990-91	New York Islanders	25	1	1	2	59	....	....	....	....	....
1991-92	New York Islanders	11	1	0	1	23	....	....	....	....	....
1993-94	New York Islanders	39	0	4	4	122	2	0	0	0	2
1994-95	New York Islanders	32	0	2	2	77	....	....	....	....	....
1995-96	New York Islanders	14	0	1	1	40	....	....	....	....	....
	Boston Bruins	35	2	5	7	88	4	0	0	0	24
1996-97	Boston Bruins	57	0	3	3	171	....	....	....	....	....
1997-98	Boston Bruins	2	0	0	0	0	....	....	....	....	....
	NHL Totals	**241**	**4**	**18**	**22**	**667**	**6**	**0**	**0**	**0**	**26**

Traded to **Boston** by **NY Islanders** for Boston's 5th round choice (Petr Sachl) in 1996 Entry Draft, December 9, 1995.

CHYZOWSKI, Dave

Left wing. Shoots left. 6'1", 190 lbs. Born, Edmonton, Alta., July 11, 1971.
(NY Islanders' 1st choice, 2nd overall, in 1989 Entry Draft).

		Regular Season					Playoffs				
Season	Club	GP	G	A	Pts	PIM	GP	G	A	Pts	PIM
1989-90	New York Islanders	34	8	6	14	45	....	....	....	....	....
1990-91	New York Islanders	56	5	9	14	61	....	....	....	....	....
1991-92	New York Islanders	12	1	1	2	17	....	....	....	....	....
1993-94	New York Islanders	3	1	0	1	4	2	0	0	0	0
1994-95	New York Islanders	13	0	0	0	11	....	....	....	....	....
1996-97	Chicago Blackhawks	8	0	0	0	6	....	....	....	....	....
	NHL Totals	**126**	**15**	**16**	**31**	**144**	**2**	**0**	**0**	**0**	**0**

Signed as a free agent by **Detroit**, August 29, 1995. Signed as a free agent by **Chicago**, September 26, 1996.

CIAVAGLIA, Peter

Center. Shoots left. 5'10", 173 lbs. Born, Albany, NY, July 15, 1969.
(Calgary's 8th choice, 145th overall, in 1987 Entry Draft).

		Regular Season					Playoffs				
Season	Club	GP	G	A	Pts	PIM	GP	G	A	Pts	PIM
1991-92	Buffalo Sabres	2	0	0	0	0	....	....	....	....	....
1992-93	Buffalo Sabres	3	0	0	0	0	....	....	....	....	....
	NHL Totals	**5**	**0**	**0**	**0**	**0**	....	....	....	....	....

Signed as a free agent by **Buffalo**, August 30, 1991.

CIBAK, Martin

Center. Shoots left. 6'1", 195 lbs. Born, Liptovsky Mikulas, Czech., May 17, 1980.
(Tampa Bay's 11th choice, 252nd overall, in 1998 Entry Draft).

		Regular Season					Playoffs				
Season	Club	GP	G	A	Pts	PIM	GP	G	A	Pts	PIM
2001-02	Tampa Bay Lightning	26	1	5	6	8	....	....	....	....	....
	NHL Totals	**26**	**1**	**5**	**6**	**8**	....	....	....	....	....

CICCARELLI, Dino

Right wing. Shoots right. 5'10", 185 lbs. Born, Sarnia, Ont., February 8, 1960.

		Regular Season					Playoffs				
Season	Club	GP	G	A	Pts	PIM	GP	G	A	Pts	PIM
1980-81	Minnesota North Stars	32	18	12	30	29	19	14	7	21	25
1981-82	Minnesota North Stars	76	55	51	106	138	4	3	1	4	2
1982-83	Minnesota North Stars	77	37	38	75	94	9	4	6	10	11
1983-84	Minnesota North Stars	79	38	33	71	58	16	4	5	9	27
1984-85	Minnesota North Stars	51	15	17	32	41	9	3	3	6	8
1985-86	Minnesota North Stars	75	44	45	89	51	5	0	1	1	6
1986-87	Minnesota North Stars	80	52	51	103	88	....	....	....	....	....
1987-88	Minnesota North Stars	67	41	45	86	79	....	....	....	....	....
1988-89	Minnesota North Stars	65	32	27	59	64	....	....	....	....	....
	Washington Capitals	11	12	3	15	12	6	3	3	6	12
1989-90	Washington Capitals	80	41	38	79	122	8	8	3	11	6
1990-91	Washington Capitals	54	21	18	39	66	11	5	4	9	22
1991-92	Washington Capitals	78	38	38	76	78	7	5	4	9	14
1992-93	Detroit Red Wings	82	41	56	97	81	7	4	2	6	16
1993-94	Detroit Red Wings	66	28	29	57	73	7	5	2	7	14
1994-95	Detroit Red Wings	42	16	27	43	39	16	9	2	11	22
1995-96	Detroit Red Wings	64	22	21	43	99	17	6	2	8	26
1996-97	Tampa Bay Lightning	77	35	25	60	116	....	....	....	....	....
1997-98	Tampa Bay Lightning	34	11	6	17	42	....	....	....	....	....
	Florida Panthers	28	5	11	16	28	....	....	....	....	....

Season	Club	REGULAR SEASON					PLAYOFFS				
		GP	G	A	Pts	PIM	GP	G	A	Pts	PIM
1998-99	Florida Panthers	14	6	1	7	27	....	....	....	....	....
	NHL Totals	**1232**	**608**	**592**	**1200**	**1425**	**141**	**73**	**45**	**118**	**211**

Played in NHL All-Star Game (1982, 1983, 1989, 1997)

Signed as a free agent by **Minnesota**, September 28, 1979. Traded to **Washington** by **Minnesota** with Bob Rouse for Mike Gartner and Larry Murphy, March 7, 1989. Traded to **Detroit** by **Washington** for Kevin Miller, June 20, 1992. Traded to **Tampa Bay** by **Detroit** for Tampa Bay's 4th round choice (later traded to Toronto – Toronto selected Alexei Ponikarovsky) in 1998 Entry Draft, August 27, 1996. Traded to **Florida** by **Tampa Bay** with Jeff Norton for Mark Fitzpatrick and Jody Hull, January 15, 1998. • Missed majority of 1998-99 season with back injury suffered in game vs. Chicago, November 4, 1998. • Officially announced retirement, August 31, 1999.

CICCONE, Enrico

Defense. Shoots left. 6'5", 220 lbs. Born, Montreal, Que., April 10, 1970.
(Minnesota's 5th choice, 92nd overall, in 1990 Entry Draft).

Season	Club	GP	G	A	Pts	PIM	GP	G	A	Pts	PIM
1991-92	Minnesota North Stars	11	0	0	0	48	....	....	....	....	....
1992-93	Minnesota North Stars	31	0	1	1	115	....	....	....	....	....
1993-94	Washington Capitals	46	1	1	2	174	....	....	....	....	....
	Tampa Bay Lightning	11	0	1	1	52	....	....	....	....	....
1994-95	Tampa Bay Lightning	41	2	4	6	*225	....	....	....	....	....
1995-96	Tampa Bay Lightning	55	2	3	5	258	....	....	....	....	....
	Chicago Blackhawks	11	0	1	1	48	9	1	0	1	30
1996-97	Chicago Blackhawks	67	2	2	4	233	4	0	0	0	18
1997-98	Carolina Hurricanes	14	0	3	3	83	....	....	....	....	....
	Vancouver Canucks	13	0	1	1	47	....	....	....	....	....
	Tampa Bay Lightning	12	0	0	0	45	....	....	....	....	....
1998-99	Tampa Bay Lightning	16	1	1	2	24	....	....	....	....	....
	Washington Capitals	43	2	0	2	103	....	....	....	....	....
2000-01	Montreal Canadiens	3	0	0	0	14	....	....	....	....	....
	NHL Totals	**374**	**10**	**18**	**28**	**1469**	**13**	**1**	**0**	**1**	**48**

Traded to **Washington** by **Dallas** to complete transaction that sent Paul Cavallini to Dallas (June 20, 1993), June 25, 1993. Traded to **Tampa Bay** by **Washington** with Washington's 3rd round choice (later traded to Anaheim – Anaheim selected Craig Reichert) in 1994 Entry Draft and the return of conditional draft choice transferred in the Pat Elynuik trade for Joe Reekie, March 21, 1994. Traded to **Chicago** by **Tampa Bay** with Tampa Bay's 2nd round choice (Jeff Paul) in 1996 Entry Draft for Patrick Poulin, Igor Ulanov and Chicago's 2nd round choice (later traded to New Jersey – New Jersey selected Pierre Dagenais) in 1996 Entry Draft, March 20, 1996. Traded to **Carolina** by **Chicago** for Ryan Risidore and Carolina's 5th round choice (later traded to Toronto – Toronto selected Morgan Warren) in 1998 Entry Draft, July 25, 1997. Traded to **Vancouver** by **Carolina** with Sean Burke and Geoff Sanderson for Kirk McLean and Martin Gelinas, January 3, 1998. Traded to **Tampa Bay** by **Vancouver** for Jamie Huscroft, March 14, 1998. Traded to **Washington** by **Tampa Bay** for cash, December 28, 1998. Signed as a free agent by **Montreal**, July 7, 2000. • Officially announced retirement, December 8, 2000.

CICHOCKI, Chris

Right wing. Shoots right. 5'11", 185 lbs. Born, Detroit, MI, September 17, 1963.

Season	Club	GP	G	A	Pts	PIM	GP	G	A	Pts	PIM
1985-86	Detroit Red Wings	59	10	11	21	21	....	....	....	....	....
1986-87	Detroit Red Wings	2	0	0	0	2	....	....	....	....	....
1987-88	New Jersey Devils	5	1	0	1	2	....	....	....	....	....
1988-89	New Jersey Devils	2	0	1	1	2	....	....	....	....	....
	NHL Totals	**68**	**11**	**12**	**23**	**27**	....	....	....	....	....

Signed as a free agent by **Detroit**, June 28, 1985. Traded to **New Jersey** by **Detroit** with Detroit's 3rd round choice (later traded to Buffalo – Buffalo selected Andrew MacVicar) in 1987 Entry Draft for Mel Bridgman, March 9, 1987. Traded to **Hartford** by **New Jersey** for Jim Thompson, October 31, 1989.

CIERNIK, Ivan

Right wing. Shoots left. 6'1", 234 lbs. Born, Levice, Czech., October 30, 1977.
(Ottawa's 6th choice, 216th overall, in 1996 Entry Draft).

Season	Club	GP	G	A	Pts	PIM	GP	G	A	Pts	PIM
1997-98	Ottawa Senators	2	0	0	0	0	....	....	....	....	....
2000-01	Ottawa Senators	4	2	0	2	2	....	....	....	....	....
2001-02	Ottawa Senators	23	1	2	3	4	....	....	....	....	....
	Washington Capitals	6	0	1	1	2	....	....	....	....	....
2002-03	Washington Capitals	47	8	10	18	24	2	0	1	1	6
	NHL Totals	**82**	**11**	**13**	**24**	**32**	**2**	**0**	**1**	**1**	**6**

Claimed on waivers by **Washington** from **Ottawa**, January 19, 2002.

CIERNY, Jozef

Left wing. Shoots left. 6'2", 185 lbs. Born, Zvolen, Czech., May 13, 1974.
(Buffalo's 2nd choice, 35th overall, in 1992 Entry Draft).

Season	Club	GP	G	A	Pts	PIM	GP	G	A	Pts	PIM
1993-94	Edmonton Oilers	1	0	0	0	0	....	....	....	....	....
	NHL Totals	**1**	**0**	**0**	**0**	**0**	....	....	....	....	....

Traded to **Edmonton** by **Buffalo** with Buffalo's 4th round choice (Jussi Tarvainen) in 1994 Entry Draft for Craig Simpson, September 1, 1993.

CIESLA, Hank

Center. Shoots left. 6'2", 190 lbs. Born, St. Catharines, Ont., October 15, 1934.

Season	Club	GP	G	A	Pts	PIM	GP	G	A	Pts	PIM
1955-56	Chicago Black Hawks	70	8	23	31	22	....	....	....	....	....
1956-57	Chicago Black Hawks	70	10	8	18	28	....	....	....	....	....
1957-58	New York Rangers	60	2	6	8	16	6	0	2	2	0
1958-59	New York Rangers	69	6	14	20	21	....	....	....	....	....
	NHL Totals	**269**	**26**	**51**	**77**	**87**	**6**	**0**	**2**	**2**	**0**

• Rights claimed by both Montreal and Toronto out of junior. Rights traded to **Chicago** by **Buffalo** (AHL) for $15,000 with Montreal receiving Bob Duncan (Toronto/OHA-Jr.) and Toronto receiving Gary Collins (Kitchener/OHA-Jr.), September, 1955. Traded to **NY Rangers** by **Chicago** for Ron Murphy, June, 1957. Traded to **Toronto** by **NY Rangers** with Bill Kennedy and future considerations for Noel Price, October 3, 1959. Traded to **Cleveland** (AHL) by **Toronto** (Rochester-AHL) for Bill Dineen and cash, August, 1961. Claimed by **Detroit** (Pittsburgh-AHL) from **Cleveland** (AHL) in Inter-League Draft, June 4, 1963. Traded to **Chicago** (Buffalo-AHL) by **Detroit** (Pittsburgh-AHL) for Jerry Toppazzini, October 10, 1964.

CIGER, Zdeno

Left wing. Shoots left. 6'1", 190 lbs. Born, Martin, Czech., October 19, 1969.
(New Jersey's 3rd choice, 54th overall, in 1988 Entry Draft).

Season	Club	GP	G	A	Pts	PIM	GP	G	A	Pts	PIM
1990-91	New Jersey Devils	45	8	17	25	8	6	0	2	2	4
1991-92	New Jersey Devils	20	6	5	11	10	7	2	4	6	0
1992-93	New Jersey Devils	27	4	8	12	2	....	....	....	....	....
	Edmonton Oilers	37	9	15	24	6	....	....	....	....	....
1993-94	Edmonton Oilers	84	22	35	57	8	....	....	....	....	....
1994-95	Edmonton Oilers	5	2	2	4	0	....	....	....	....	....
1995-96	Edmonton Oilers	78	31	39	70	41	....	....	....	....	....
2001-02	New York Rangers	29	6	7	13	16	....	....	....	....	....
	Tampa Bay Lightning	27	6	6	12	10	....	....	....	....	....
	NHL Totals	**352**	**94**	**134**	**228**	**101**	**13**	**2**	**6**	**8**	**4**

Traded to **Edmonton** by **New Jersey** with Kevin Todd for Bernie Nicholls, January 13, 1993. Claimed by **Nashville** from **Edmonton** in Waiver Draft, October 5, 1998. Claimed by **Minnesota** from **Nashville** in Waiver Draft, September 29, 2000. Signed as a free agent by **NY Rangers**, July 17, 2001. Traded to **Tampa Bay** by **NY Rangers** for Matthew Barnaby, December 12, 2001.

CIMELLARO, Tony

Center. Shoots left. 5'11", 180 lbs. Born, Kingston, Ont., June 14, 1971.

Season	Club	GP	G	A	Pts	PIM	GP	G	A	Pts	PIM
1992-93	Ottawa Senators	2	0	0	0	0	....	....	....	....	....
	NHL Totals	**2**	**0**	**0**	**0**	**0**	....	....	....	....	....

Signed as a free agent by **Ottawa**, July 30, 1992.

CIMETTA, Rob

Wing. Shoots left. 6', 190 lbs. Born, Toronto, Ont., February 15, 1970.
(Boston's 1st choice, 18th overall, in 1988 Entry Draft).

Season	Club	GP	G	A	Pts	PIM	GP	G	A	Pts	PIM
1988-89	Boston Bruins	7	2	0	2	0	1	0	0	0	15
1989-90	Boston Bruins	47	8	9	17	33	....	....	....	....	....
1990-91	Toronto Maple Leafs	25	2	4	6	21	....	....	....	....	....
1991-92	Toronto Maple Leafs	24	4	3	7	12	....	....	....	....	....
	NHL Totals	**103**	**16**	**16**	**32**	**66**	**1**	**0**	**0**	**0**	**15**

Traded to **Toronto** by **Boston** for Steve Bancroft, November 9, 1990. Signed as a free agent by **Chicago**, September 8, 1993.

CIRELLA, Joe

Defense. Shoots right. 6'3", 210 lbs. Born, Hamilton, Ont., May 9, 1963.
(Colorado's 1st choice, 5th overall, in 1981 Entry Draft).

Season	Club	GP	G	A	Pts	PIM	GP	G	A	Pts	PIM
1981-82	Colorado Rockies	65	7	12	19	52	....	....	....	....	....
1982-83	New Jersey Devils	2	0	1	1	4	....	....	....	....	....
1983-84	New Jersey Devils	79	11	33	44	137	....	....	....	....	....
1984-85	New Jersey Devils	66	6	18	24	141	....	....	....	....	....
1985-86	New Jersey Devils	66	6	23	29	147	....	....	....	....	....
1986-87	New Jersey Devils	65	9	22	31	111	....	....	....	....	....
1987-88	New Jersey Devils	80	8	31	39	191	19	0	7	7	49
1988-89	New Jersey Devils	80	3	19	22	155	....	....	....	....	....
1989-90	Quebec Nordiques	56	4	14	18	67	....	....	....	....	....
1990-91	Quebec Nordiques	39	2	10	12	59	....	....	....	....	....
	New York Rangers	19	1	0	1	52	6	0	2	2	26
1991-92	New York Rangers	67	3	12	15	121	13	0	4	4	23
1992-93	New York Rangers	55	3	6	9	85	....	....	....	....	....
1993-94	Florida Panthers	63	1	9	10	99	....	....	....	....	....
1994-95	Florida Panthers	20	0	1	1	21	....	....	....	....	....
1995-96	Ottawa Senators	6	0	0	0	4	....	....	....	....	....
	NHL Totals	**828**	**64**	**211**	**275**	**1446**	**38**	**0**	**13**	**13**	**98**

Played in NHL All-Star Game (1984)

Transferred to **New Jersey** after **Colorado** franchise relocated, June 30, 1982. Traded to **Quebec** by **New Jersey** with Claude Loiselle and New Jersey's 8th round choice (Alexander Karpovtsev) in 1990 Entry Draft for Walt Poddubny and Quebec's 4th round choice (Mike Bodnarchuk) in 1990 Entry Draft, June 17, 1989. Traded to **NY Rangers** by **Quebec** for Aaron Miller and NY Rangers' 5th round choice (Bill Lindsay) in 1991 Entry Draft, January 17, 1991. Claimed by **Florida** from **NY Rangers** in Expansion Draft, June 24, 1993. Signed as a free agent by **Ottawa**, October 10, 1995.

CIRONE, Jason

Center. Shoots left. 5'9", 185 lbs. Born, Toronto, Ont., February 21, 1971.
(Winnipeg's 3rd choice, 46th overall, in 1989 Entry Draft).

Season	Club	GP	G	A	Pts	PIM	GP	G	A	Pts	PIM
1991-92	Winnipeg Jets	3	0	0	0	2	....	....	....	....	....
	NHL Totals	**3**	**0**	**0**	**0**	**2**	....	....	....	....	....

Traded to **Florida** by **Winnipeg** for Dave Tomlinson, August 3, 1993.

CISAR, Marian

Right wing. Shoots right. 6', 197 lbs. Born, Bratislava, Czech., February 25, 1978.
(Los Angeles' 2nd choice, 37th overall, in 1996 Entry Draft).

Season	Club	GP	G	A	Pts	PIM	GP	G	A	Pts	PIM
99-2000	Nashville Predators	3	0	0	0	4	....	....	....	....	....
2000-01	Nashville Predators	60	12	15	27	45	....	....	....	....	....

Season	Club	GP	G	A	Pts	PIM	GP	G	A	Pts	PIM
		REGULAR SEASON					PLAYOFFS				
2001-02	Nashville Predators	10	1	2	3	8	....	....	....	....	....
	NHL Totals	**73**	**13**	**17**	**30**	**57**	....	....	....	....	....

Traded to **Nashville** by **Los Angeles** for future considerations, June 1, 1998. • Missed majority of 2001-02 season recovering from hip injury suffered in training camp, September 29, 2001.

CLACKSON, Kim

Defense. Shoots right. 5'11", 195 lbs. Born, Saskatoon, Sask., February 13, 1955.
(Pittsburgh's 5th choice, 85th overall, in 1975 Amateur Draft).

Season	Club	GP	G	A	Pts	PIM	GP	G	A	Pts	PIM
1979-80	Pittsburgh Penguins	45	0	3	3	166	3	0	0	0	37
1980-81	Quebec Nordiques	61	0	5	5	204	5	0	0	0	33
	NHL Totals	**106**	**0**	**8**	**8**	**370**	**8**	**0**	**0**	**0**	**70**

Claimed by **Pittsburgh** as a fill-in during Expansion Draft, June 13, 1979. Transferred to **Quebec** by **Pittsburgh** as compensation for Pittsburgh's signing of free agent Paul Baxter, August 7, 1980.

CLANCY, King — HHOF

Defense. Shoots left. 5'7", 155 lbs. Born, Ottawa, Ont., February 25, 1903.

Season	Club	GP	G	A	Pts	PIM	GP	G	A	Pts	PIM
1921-22	Ottawa Senators	24	4	6	10	21	2	0	0	0	2
1922-23♦	Ottawa Senators	24	3	2	5	20	2	0	0	0	0
	Ottawa Senators (Cup)	....	....	....	....	....	*6*	*1*	*0*	*1*	*4*
1923-24	Ottawa Senators	24	8	8	16	26	2	0	0	0	6
1924-25	Ottawa Senators	29	14	7	21	61	....	....	....	....	....
1925-26	Ottawa Senators	35	8	4	12	80	2	1	0	1	8
1926-27♦	Ottawa Senators	43	9	10	19	78	6	1	1	2	14
1927-28	Ottawa Senators	39	8	7	15	73	2	0	0	0	6
1928-29	Ottawa Senators	44	13	2	15	89	....	....	....	....	....
1929-30	Ottawa Senators	44	17	23	40	83	2	0	1	1	2
1930-31	Toronto Maple Leafs	44	7	14	21	63	2	1	0	1	0
1931-32♦	Toronto Maple Leafs	48	10	9	19	61	7	2	1	3	14
1932-33	Toronto Maple Leafs	48	13	12	25	79	9	0	3	3	14
1933-34	Toronto Maple Leafs	46	11	17	28	62	3	0	0	0	8
1934-35	Toronto Maple Leafs	47	5	16	21	53	7	1	0	1	8
1935-36	Toronto Maple Leafs	47	5	10	15	61	9	2	2	4	10
1936-37	Toronto Maple Leafs	6	1	0	1	4	....	....	....	....	....
	NHL Totals	**592**	**136**	**147**	**283**	**914**	**55**	**8**	**8**	**16**	**92**

• Father of Terry • NHL First All-Star Team (1931, 1934) • NHL Second All-Star Team (1932, 1933)

Played in NHL All-Star Game (1934, 1937)

Signed as a free agent by **Ottawa**, December 14, 1921. • 1922-23 Stanley Cup totals includes series with Regina (WCHL) and Edmonton (PCHA). Traded to **Toronto** by **Ottawa** for Art Smith, Eric Pettinger and $35,000, October 11, 1930. • Officially announced retirement, November 24, 1936. • Came out of retirement to play in Howie Morenz Memorial Game, November 2, 1937.

CLANCY, Terry

Right wing. Shoots left. 5'11", 195 lbs. Born, Ottawa, Ont., April 2, 1943.

Season	Club	GP	G	A	Pts	PIM	GP	G	A	Pts	PIM
1967-68	Oakland Seals	7	0	0	0	2	....	....	....	....	....
1968-69	Toronto Maple Leafs	2	0	0	0	0	....	....	....	....	....
1969-70	Toronto Maple Leafs	52	6	5	11	31	....	....	....	....	....
1972-73	Toronto Maple Leafs	32	0	1	1	6	....	....	....	....	....
	NHL Totals	**93**	**6**	**6**	**12**	**39**	....	....	....	....	....

• Son of King

Signed as a free agent by **Toronto**, October, 1964. Claimed by **California** (Oakland) from **Toronto** in Expansion Draft, June 6, 1967. Traded to **Toronto** by **Oakland** for cash, May 14, 1968. Traded to **Montreal** by **Toronto** for cash, December 23, 1970. Traded to **Toronto** by **Montreal** for cash, August 30, 1971. Traded to **Detroit** by **Toronto** for cash, October 17, 1973.

CLAPPER, Dit — HHOF

Right wing/Defense. Shoots right. 6'2", 195 lbs. Born, Newmarket, Ont., February 9, 1907.

Season	Club	GP	G	A	Pts	PIM	GP	G	A	Pts	PIM
1927-28	Boston Bruins	40	4	1	5	20	2	0	0	0	2
1928-29♦	Boston Bruins	40	9	2	11	48	5	1	0	1	0
1929-30	Boston Bruins	44	41	20	61	48	6	4	0	4	4
1930-31	Boston Bruins	43	22	8	30	50	5	2	4	6	4
1931-32	Boston Bruins	48	17	22	39	21	....	....	....	....	....
1932-33	Boston Bruins	48	14	14	28	42	5	1	1	2	2
1933-34	Boston Bruins	48	10	12	22	6	....	....	....	....	....
1934-35	Boston Bruins	48	21	16	37	21	3	1	0	1	0
1935-36	Boston Bruins	44	12	13	25	14	2	0	1	1	0
1936-37	Boston Bruins	48	17	8	25	25	3	2	0	2	5
1937-38	Boston Bruins	46	6	9	15	24	3	0	0	0	12
1938-39♦	Boston Bruins	42	13	13	26	22	12	0	1	1	6
1939-40	Boston Bruins	44	10	18	28	25	5	0	2	2	2
1940-41♦	Boston Bruins	48	8	18	26	24	11	0	5	5	4
1941-42	Boston Bruins	32	3	12	15	31	....	....	....	....	....
1942-43	Boston Bruins	38	5	18	23	12	9	2	3	5	9
1943-44	Boston Bruins	50	6	25	31	13	....	....	....	....	....
1944-45	Boston Bruins	46	8	14	22	16	7	0	0	0	0
1945-46	Boston Bruins	30	2	3	5	0	4	0	0	0	0
1946-47	Boston Bruins	6	0	0	0	0	....	....	....	....	....
	NHL Totals	**833**	**228**	**246**	**474**	**462**	**82**	**13**	**17**	**30**	**50**

NHL Second All-Star Team (1931, 1935, 1944) • NHL First All-Star Team (1939, 1940, 1941)

Played in NHL All-Star Game (1937, 1939)

Traded to **Boston** by **Boston** (Can-Am) for cash, October 25, 1927.

CLARK, Brett

Defense. Shoots left. 6'1", 195 lbs. Born, Wapella, Sask., December 23, 1976.
(Montreal's 7th choice, 154th overall, in 1996 Entry Draft).

Season	Club	GP	G	A	Pts	PIM	GP	G	A	Pts	PIM
1997-98	Montreal Canadiens	41	1	0	1	20	....	....	....	....	....
1998-99	Montreal Canadiens	61	2	2	4	16	....	....	....	....	....
99-2000	Atlanta Thrashers	14	0	1	1	4	....	....	....	....	....
2000-01	Atlanta Thrashers	28	1	2	3	14	....	....	....	....	....
2001-02	Atlanta Thrashers	2	0	0	0	0	....	....	....	....	....
	NHL Totals	**146**	**4**	**5**	**9**	**54**	....	....	....	....	....

Claimed by **Atlanta** from **Montreal** in Expansion Draft, June 25, 1999. Traded to **Colorado** by **Atlanta** for Frederic Cassivi, January 24, 2002.

CLARK, Chris

Right wing. Shoots right. 6', 200 lbs. Born, South Windsor, CT, March 8, 1976.
(Calgary's 3rd choice, 77th overall, in 1994 Entry Draft).

Season	Club	GP	G	A	Pts	PIM	GP	G	A	Pts	PIM
99-2000	Calgary Flames	22	0	1	1	14	....	....	....	....	....
2000-01	Calgary Flames	29	5	1	6	38	....	....	....	....	....
2001-02	Calgary Flames	64	10	7	17	79	....	....	....	....	....
2002-03	Calgary Flames	81	10	12	22	126	....	....	....	....	....
	NHL Totals	**196**	**25**	**21**	**46**	**257**	....	....	....	....	....

CLARK, Dan

Defense. Shoots left. 6'1", 195 lbs. Born, Toronto, Ont., November 3, 1957.
(NY Rangers' 8th choice, 110th overall, in 1978 Amateur Draft).

Season	Club	GP	G	A	Pts	PIM	GP	G	A	Pts	PIM
1978-79	New York Rangers	4	0	1	1	6	....	....	....	....	....
	NHL Totals	**4**	**0**	**1**	**1**	**6**	....	....	....	....	....

• Re-entered NHL Entry Draft. Originally Philadelphia's 6th choice, 89th overall, in 1977 Amateur Draft.

CLARK, Dean

Defense. Shoots left. 6'1", 180 lbs. Born, Edmonton, Alta., January 10, 1964.
(Edmonton's 8th choice, 167th overall, in 1982 Entry Draft).

Season	Club	GP	G	A	Pts	PIM	GP	G	A	Pts	PIM
1983-84	Edmonton Oilers	1	0	0	0	0	....	....	....	....	....
	NHL Totals	**1**	**0**	**0**	**0**	**0**	....	....	....	....	....

CLARK, Gordie

Right wing. Shoots right. 5'10", 180 lbs. Born, Glasgow, Scotland, May 31, 1952.
(Boston's 7th choice, 112th overall, in 1972 Amateur Draft).

Season	Club	GP	G	A	Pts	PIM	GP	G	A	Pts	PIM
1974-75	Boston Bruins	1	0	0	0	0					....
1975-76	Boston Bruins	7	0	1	1	0	1	0	0	0	0
	NHL Totals	**8**	**0**	**1**	**1**	**0**	**1**	**0**	**0**	**0**	**0**

CLARK, Nobby

Defense. Shoots right. 6'1", 190 lbs. Born, Orillia, Ont., June 18, 1897.

Season	Club	GP	G	A	Pts	PIM	GP	G	A	Pts	PIM
1927-28	Boston Bruins	5	0	0	0	0	....	....	....	....	....
	NHL Totals	**5**	**0**	**0**	**0**	**0**	....	....	....	....	....

Traded to **Boston** by **Minneapolis** (AHA) with Norm Gainor for Billy Stuart, cash and future considerations, October 24, 1927. Traded to **New Haven** (Can-Am) by **Boston** with Billy Coutu for cash, January 5, 1928.

CLARK, Wendel

Left wing/Defense. Shoots left. 5'11", 194 lbs. Born, Kelvington, Sask., October 25, 1966.
(Toronto's 1st choice, 1st overall, in 1985 Entry Draft).

Season	Club	GP	G	A	Pts	PIM	GP	G	A	Pts	PIM
1985-86	Toronto Maple Leafs	66	34	11	45	227	10	5	1	6	47
1986-87	Toronto Maple Leafs	80	37	23	60	271	13	6	5	11	38
1987-88	Toronto Maple Leafs	28	12	11	23	80	....	....	....	....	....
1988-89	Toronto Maple Leafs	15	7	4	11	66	....	....	....	....	....
1989-90	Toronto Maple Leafs	38	18	8	26	116	5	1	1	2	19
1990-91	Toronto Maple Leafs	63	18	16	34	152	....	....	....	....	....
1991-92	Toronto Maple Leafs	43	19	21	40	123	....	....	....	....	....
1992-93	Toronto Maple Leafs	66	17	22	39	193	21	10	10	20	51
1993-94	Toronto Maple Leafs	64	46	30	76	115	18	9	7	16	24
1994-95	Quebec Nordiques	37	12	18	30	45	6	1	2	3	6
1995-96	New York Islanders	58	24	19	43	60	....	....	....	....	....
	Toronto Maple Leafs	13	8	7	15	16	6	2	2	4	2
1996-97	Toronto Maple Leafs	65	30	19	49	75	....	....	....	....	....
1997-98	Toronto Maple Leafs	47	12	7	19	80	....	....	....	....	....
1998-99	Tampa Bay Lightning	65	28	14	42	35	....	....	....	....	....
	Detroit Red Wings	12	4	2	6	2	10	2	3	5	10

Season	Club	GP	G	A	Pts	PIM	GP	G	A	Pts	PIM
		REGULAR SEASON					PLAYOFFS				
99-2000	Chicago Blackhawks	13	2	0	2	13					
	Toronto Maple Leafs	20	2	2	4	21	6	1	1	2	4
	NHL Totals	**793**	**330**	**234**	**564**	**1690**	**95**	**37**	**32**	**69**	**201**

NHL All-Rookie Team (1986)

Played in NHL All-Star Game (1986, 1999)

Traded to **Quebec** by **Toronto** with Sylvain Lefebvre, Landon Wilson and Toronto's 1st round choice (Jeffrey Kealty) in 1994 Entry Draft for Mats Sundin, Garth Butcher, Todd Warriner and Philadelphia's 1st round choice (previously acquired, later traded to Washington – Washington selected Nolan Baumgartner) in 1994 Entry Draft, June 28, 1994. Transferred to **Colorado** after **Quebec** franchise relocated, June 21, 1995. Traded to **NY Islanders** by **Colorado** for Claude Lemieux, October 3, 1995. Traded to **Toronto** by **NY Islanders** with Mathieu Schneider and D.J. Smith for Darby Hendrickson, Sean Haggerty, Kenny Jonsson and Toronto's 1st round choice (Roberto Luongo) in 1997 Entry Draft, March 13, 1996. Signed as a free agent by **Tampa Bay**, July 31, 1998. Traded to **Detroit** by **Tampa Bay** with Detroit's 6th round choice (previously acquired, Detroit selected Kent McDonell) in 1999 Entry Draft for Kevin Hodson and San Jose's 2nd round choice (previously acquired, Tampa Bay selected Sheldon Keefe) in 1999 Entry Draft, March 23, 1999. Signed as a free agent by **Chicago**, August 2, 1999. Signed as a free agent by **Toronto** following release by Chicago, January 14, 2000. • Officially announced retirement, June 29, 2000.

CLARKE, Bobby

HHOF

Center. Shoots left. 5'10", 185 lbs. Born, Flin Flon, Man., August 13, 1949.
(Philadelphia's 2nd choice, 17th overall, in 1969 Amateur Draft).

Season	Club	GP	G	A	Pts	PIM	GP	G	A	Pts	PIM
1969-70	Philadelphia Flyers	76	15	31	46	68					
1970-71	Philadelphia Flyers	77	27	36	63	78	4	0	0	0	2
1971-72	Philadelphia Flyers	78	35	46	81	87					
1972-73	Philadelphia Flyers	78	37	67	104	80	11	2	6	8	6
1973-74◆	Philadelphia Flyers	77	35	52	87	113	17	5	11	16	42
1974-75◆	Philadelphia Flyers	80	27	*89	116	125	17	4	*12	16	16
1975-76	Philadelphia Flyers	76	30	*89	119	136	16	2	*14	16	28
1976-77	Philadelphia Flyers	80	27	63	90	71	10	5	5	10	8
1977-78	Philadelphia Flyers	71	21	68	89	83	12	4	7	11	8
1978-79	Philadelphia Flyers	80	16	57	73	68	8	2	4	6	8
1979-80	Philadelphia Flyers	76	12	57	69	65	19	8	12	20	16
1980-81	Philadelphia Flyers	80	19	46	65	140	12	3	3	6	6
1981-82	Philadelphia Flyers	62	17	46	63	154	4	4	2	6	4
1982-83	Philadelphia Flyers	80	23	62	85	115	3	1	0	1	2
1983-84	Philadelphia Flyers	73	17	43	60	70	3	2	1	3	6
	NHL Totals	**1144**	**358**	**852**	**1210**	**1453**	**136**	**42**	**77**	**119**	**152**

Bill Masterton Trophy (1972) • NHL Second All-Star Team (1973, 1974) • Lester B. Pearson Award (1973) • Hart Trophy (1973, 1975, 1976) • NHL First All-Star Team (1975, 1976) • NHL Plus/Minus Leader (1976) • Lester Patrick Trophy (1980) • Frank J. Selke Trophy (1983)

Played in NHL All-Star Game (1970, 1971, 1972, 1973, 1974, 1975, 1977, 1978)

CLARKE, Dale

Defense. Shoots right. 6'2", 193 lbs. Born, Belleville, Ont., March 23, 1978.

Season	Club	GP	G	A	Pts	PIM	GP	G	A	Pts	PIM
2000-01	St. Louis Blues	3	0	0	0	0					
	NHL Totals	**3**	**0**	**0**	**0**	**0**					

Signed as a free agent by **St. Louis**, July 24, 1999. Traded to **Colorado** by **St. Louis** for future considerations, December 5, 2002.

CLASSEN, Greg

Center. Shoots left. 6'1", 200 lbs. Born, Aylsham, Sask., August 24, 1977.

Season	Club	GP	G	A	Pts	PIM	GP	G	A	Pts	PIM
2000-01	Nashville Predators	27	2	4	6	14					
2001-02	Nashville Predators	55	5	6	11	30					
2002-03	Nashville Predators	8	0	0	0	4					
	NHL Totals	**90**	**7**	**10**	**17**	**48**					

Signed as a free agent by **Nashville**, March 27, 2000.

CLEARY, Daniel

Right wing. Shoots left. 6', 203 lbs. Born, Carbonear, Nfld., December 18, 1978.
(Chicago's 1st choice, 13th overall, in 1997 Entry Draft).

Season	Club	GP	G	A	Pts	PIM	GP	G	A	Pts	PIM
1997-98	Chicago Blackhawks	6	0	0	0	0					
1998-99	Chicago Blackhawks	35	4	5	9	24					
99-2000	Edmonton Oilers	17	3	2	5	8	4	0	1	1	2
2000-01	Edmonton Oilers	81	14	21	35	37	6	1	1	2	8
2001-02	Edmonton Oilers	65	10	19	29	51					
2002-03	Edmonton Oilers	57	4	13	17	31					
	NHL Totals	**261**	**35**	**60**	**95**	**151**	**10**	**1**	**2**	**3**	**10**

Traded to **Edmonton** by **Chicago** with Chad Kilger, Ethan Moreau and Christian Laflamme for Boris Mironov, Dean McAmmond and Jonas Elofsson, March 20, 1999. Signed as a free agent by **Phoenix**, July 15, 2003.

CLEGHORN, Odie

Right wing/Center. Shoots right. 5'9", 195 lbs. Born, Montreal, Que., September 19, 1891.

Season	Club	GP	G	A	Pts	PIM	GP	G	A	Pts	PIM
1918-19	Montreal Canadiens	17	22	6	28	22	5	7	0	7	0
	Montreal Canadiens (Cup)						*5*	*2*	*0*	*2*	*9*
1919-20	Montreal Canadiens	21	20	4	24	30					
1920-21	Montreal Canadiens	21	6	6	12	8					
1921-22	Montreal Canadiens	24	21	3	24	26					
1922-23	Montreal Canadiens	24	19	6	25	18	2	0	0	0	2
1923-24◆	Montreal Canadiens	22	2	5	7	16	2	0	0	0	0
	Montreal Canadiens (Cup)						*4*	*0*	*1*	*1*	*0*
1924-25	Montreal Canadiens	30	3	3	6	14	2	0	1	1	0
	Montreal Canadiens (Cup)						*4*	*0*	*0*	*0*	*0*
1925-26	Pittsburgh Pirates	17	2	1	3	4	1	0	0	0	0
1926-27	Pittsburgh Pirates	3	0	0	0	0					
1927-28	Pittsburgh Pirates	2	0	0	0	4					
	NHL Totals	**181**	**95**	**34**	**129**	**142**	**12**	**7**	**1**	**8**	**2**

• Brother of Sprague

Retained by **Mtl. Wanderers** after NHA folded, November 26, 1917. Signed as a free agent by **Montreal**, December 9, 1918. • 1923-24 Stanley Cup totals includes series with Calgary (WCHL) and Vancouver (PCHA). Signed as a free agent by **Pittsburgh** and named player/coach, October 18, 1925.

CLEGHORN, Sprague

HHOF

Defense. Shoots left. 5'10", 190 lbs. Born, Montreal, Que., March 11, 1890.

Season	Club	GP	G	A	Pts	PIM	GP	G	A	Pts	PIM
1918-19	Ottawa Senators	18	7	6	13	27	5	2	0	2	11
1919-20◆	Ottawa Senators	21	16	5	21	85					
	Ottawa Senators (Cup)						*5*	*0*	*1*	*1*	*4*
1920-21	Toronto St. Pats	13	3	5	8	31	1	0	0	0	0
◆	*Ottawa Senators (Cup)*						*5*	*1*	*2*	*3*	*36*
1921-22	Montreal Canadiens	24	17	9	26	*80					
1922-23	Montreal Canadiens	24	9	8	17	34	1	0	0	0	7
1923-24◆	Montreal Canadiens	23	8	4	12	45	2	0	0	0	0
	Montreal Canadiens (Cup)						*4*	*2*	*2*	*4*	*2*
1924-25	Montreal Canadiens	27	8	10	18	89	2	1	2	3	2
	Montreal Canadiens (Cup)						*4*	*0*	*0*	*0*	*2*
1925-26	Boston Bruins	28	6	5	11	49					
1926-27	Boston Bruins	44	7	1	8	84	8	1	0	1	8
1927-28	Boston Bruins	37	2	2	4	14	2	0	0	0	0
	NHL Totals	**259**	**83**	**55**	**138**	**538**	**21**	**4**	**2**	**6**	**28**

• Brother of Odie

Rights retained by **Mtl. Wanderers** after NHA folded, November 26, 1917. Claimed by **Ottawa** from **Mtl. Wanderers** in Dispersal Draft, January 4, 1918. Rights transferred to **Hamilton** by **NHL** with Punch Broadbent, December 30, 1920. • Broadbent and Cleghorn refused to report. Traded to **Toronto** by **Hamilton** for future considerations, January 25, 1921. Signed as a free agent by **Ottawa** after securing his release from **Toronto**, March 15, 1921. Rights transferred to **Hamilton** by **NHL**, April 6, 1921. Traded to **Montreal** by **Hamilton** for Harry Mummery and Amos Arbour, November 26, 1921. • 1923-24 Stanley Cup totals includes series with Calgary (WCHL) and Vancouver (PCHA). Traded to **Boston** by **Montreal** for $5,000, November 8, 1925.

CLEMENT, Bill

Center. Shoots left. 6'1", 194 lbs. Born, Thurso, Que., December 20, 1950.
(Philadelphia's 1st choice, 18th overall, in 1970 Amateur Draft).

Season	Club	GP	G	A	Pts	PIM	GP	G	A	Pts	PIM
1971-72	Philadelphia Flyers	49	9	14	23	39					
1972-73	Philadelphia Flyers	73	14	14	28	51	2	0	0	0	0
1973-74◆	Philadelphia Flyers	39	9	8	17	34	4	1	0	1	4
1974-75◆	Philadelphia Flyers	68	21	16	37	42	12	1	0	1	8
1975-76	Washington Capitals	46	10	17	27	20					
	Atlanta Flames	31	13	14	27	29	2	0	1	1	0
1976-77	Atlanta Flames	67	17	26	43	27	3	1	1	2	0
1977-78	Atlanta Flames	70	20	30	50	34	2	0	0	0	2
1978-79	Atlanta Flames	65	12	23	35	14	2	0	0	0	0
1979-80	Atlanta Flames	64	7	14	21	32	4	0	0	0	4
1980-81	Calgary Flames	78	12	20	32	33	16	2	1	3	6
1981-82	Calgary Flames	69	4	12	16	28	3	0	0	0	2
	NHL Totals	**719**	**148**	**208**	**356**	**383**	**50**	**5**	**3**	**8**	**26**

Played in NHL All-Star Game (1976, 1978)

Traded to **Washington** by **Philadelphia** with Don McLean and Philadelphia's 1st round choice (Alex Forsyth) in 1975 Amateur Draft for Washington's 1st round choice (Mel Bridgman) in 1975 Amateur Draft, June 4, 1975. Traded to **Atlanta** by **Washington** for Gerry Meehan, Jean Lemieux and Buffalo's 1st round choice (previously acquired, Atlanta selected Greg Carroll) in 1976 Amateur Draft, January 22, 1976. Transferred to **Calgary** after **Atlanta** franchise relocated, June 24, 1980.

CLINE, Bruce

Right wing. Shoots right. 5'7", 137 lbs. Born, Massawippi, Que., November 14, 1931.

Season	Club	GP	G	A	Pts	PIM	GP	G	A	Pts	PIM
1956-57	New York Rangers	30	2	3	5	10					
	NHL Totals	**30**	**2**	**3**	**5**	**10**					

Traded to **Montreal** by **Springfield** (AHL) with Ted Harris, Terry Gray, Wayne Larkin and John Chasczewski for Wayne Boddy, Fred Hilts, Brian Smith, John Rodger, Lorne O'Donnell and the loan of Gary Bergman, June, 1963.

CLIPPINGDALE, Steve

Left wing. Shoots left. 6'2", 195 lbs. Born, Vancouver, B.C., April 29, 1956.
(Los Angeles' 1st choice, 21st overall, in 1976 Amateur Draft).

Season	Club	GP	G	A	Pts	PIM	GP	G	A	Pts	PIM
1976-77	Los Angeles Kings	16	1	2	3	9	1	0	0	0	0
1979-80	Washington Capitals	3	0	0	0	0					
	NHL Totals	**19**	**1**	**2**	**3**	**9**	**1**	**0**	**0**	**0**	**0**

Traded to **Washington** by **Los Angeles** for Mike Marson, June 11, 1979.

CLOUTIER, Real

Right wing. Shoots left. 5'10", 185 lbs. Born, Ste-Emile, Que., July 30, 1956.
(Chicago's 1st choice, 9th overall, in 1976 Amateur Draft).

Season	Club	GP	G	A	Pts	PIM	GP	G	A	Pts	PIM
1979-80	Quebec Nordiques	67	42	47	89	12					
1980-81	Quebec Nordiques	34	15	16	31	18	3	0	0	0	10
1981-82	Quebec Nordiques	67	37	60	97	34	16	7	5	12	10
1982-83	Quebec Nordiques	68	28	39	67	30	4	0	0	0	0
1983-84	Buffalo Sabres	77	24	36	60	25	2	0	0	0	0

Season	Club	GP	G	A	Pts	PIM	GP	G	A	Pts	PIM
		REGULAR SEASON					PLAYOFFS				
1984-85	Buffalo Sabres	4	0	0	0	0	....	....	....	....	....
	NHL Totals	**317**	**146**	**198**	**344**	**119**	**25**	**7**	**5**	**12**	**20**

Played in NHL All-Star Game (1980)

Rights retained by **Quebec** prior to Expansion Draft, June 9, 1979. • Quebec did not list Cloutier as a priority selection in the 1979 Expansion Draft as per their agreement with Chicago. **Quebec** traded their 1st round choice (Denis Savard) in 1980 Entry Draft to **Chicago** for Chicago agreeing not to reclaim Cloutier prior to Expansion Draft, June 9, 1979. Traded to **Buffalo** by **Quebec** with Quebec's 1st round choice (Adam Creighton) in 1983 Entry Draft for Tony McKegney, Andre Savard, Jean-Francois Sauve and Buffalo's 3rd round choice (Iiro Jarvi) in 1983 Entry Draft, June 8, 1983.

CLOUTIER, Rejean

Defense. Shoots left. 6', 185 lbs. Born, Windsor, Que., February 15, 1960.

Season	Club	GP	G	A	Pts	PIM	GP	G	A	Pts	PIM
1979-80	Detroit Red Wings	3	0	1	1	0	....	....	....	....	....
1981-82	Detroit Red Wings	2	0	1	1	2	....	....	....	....	....
	NHL Totals	**5**	**0**	**2**	**2**	**2**	....	....	....	....	....

Signed as a free agent by **Detroit**, October 30, 1979. Traded to **Edmonton** by **Detroit** for Todd Bidner, October 17, 1984. Signed as a free agent by **Montreal**, August, 1985.

CLOUTIER, Roland

Center. Shoots left. 5'8", 157 lbs. Born, Rouyn, Que., October 6, 1957.
(Detroit's 13th choice, 178th overall, in 1977 Amateur Draft).

Season	Club	GP	G	A	Pts	PIM	GP	G	A	Pts	PIM
1977-78	Detroit Red Wings	1	0	0	0	0	....	....	....	....	....
1978-79	Detroit Red Wings	19	6	6	12	2	....	....	....	....	....
1979-80	Quebec Nordiques	14	2	3	5	0	....	....	....	....	....
	NHL Totals	**34**	**8**	**9**	**17**	**2**	....	....	....	....	....

Claimed by **Quebec** from **Detroit** in Expansion Draft, June 13, 1979.

CLOUTIER, Sylvain

Center. Shoots left. 6', 200 lbs. Born, Mont-Laurier, Que., February 13, 1974.
(Detroit's 3rd choice, 70th overall, in 1992 Entry Draft).

Season	Club	GP	G	A	Pts	PIM	GP	G	A	Pts	PIM
1998-99	Chicago Blackhawks	7	0	0	0	0	....	....	....	....	....
	NHL Totals	**7**	**0**	**0**	**0**	**0**	....	....	....	....	....

• Brother of Dan

Signed as a free agent by **Chicago**, August 17, 1998. Claimed by **Atlanta** from **Chicago** in Expansion Draft, June 25, 1999. Traded to **New Jersey** by **Atlanta** with Jeff Williams and Atlanta's 7th round choice (Ken Magowan) in 2000 Entry Draft for Wes Mason and Eric Bertrand, November 1, 1999.

CLUNE, Wally

Defense. Shoots right. 5'9", 150 lbs. Born, Toronto, Ont., February 20, 1930.

Season	Club	GP	G	A	Pts	PIM	GP	G	A	Pts	PIM
1955-56	Montreal Canadiens	5	0	0	0	6	....	....	....	....	....
	NHL Totals	**5**	**0**	**0**	**0**	**6**	....	....	....	....	....

Claimed by **Montreal** from **Montreal** (QMHL) in Intra-League Draft, June 10, 1953.

CLYMER, Ben

Left wing. Shoots right. 6'1", 199 lbs. Born, Edina, MN, April 11, 1978.
(Boston's 3rd choice, 27th overall, in 1997 Entry Draft).

Season	Club	GP	G	A	Pts	PIM	GP	G	A	Pts	PIM
99-2000	Tampa Bay Lightning	60	2	6	8	87	....	....	....	....	....
2000-01	Tampa Bay Lightning	23	5	1	6	21	....	....	....	....	....
2001-02	Tampa Bay Lightning	81	14	20	34	36	....	....	....	....	....
2002-03	Tampa Bay Lightning	65	6	12	18	57	11	0	2	2	6
	NHL Totals	**229**	**27**	**39**	**66**	**201**	**11**	**0**	**2**	**2**	**6**

Signed as a free agent by **Tampa Bay**, October 2, 1999.

COALTER, Gary

Right wing. Shoots right. 5'10", 185 lbs. Born, Toronto, Ont., July 8, 1950.
(NY Rangers' 5th choice, 67th overall, in 1970 Amateur Draft).

Season	Club	GP	G	A	Pts	PIM	GP	G	A	Pts	PIM
1973-74	California Golden Seals	4	0	0	0	0	....	....	....	....	....
1974-75	Kansas City Scouts	30	2	4	6	2	....	....	....	....	....
	NHL Totals	**34**	**2**	**4**	**6**	**2**	....	....	....	....	....

Traded to **California** by **NY Rangers** with Dave Hrechkosy to complete transaction that sent Bert Marshall to NY Rangers (March 4, 1973), May 17, 1973. Claimed by **Kansas City** from **California** in Expansion Draft, June 12, 1974.

COATES, Steve

Right wing. Shoots right. 5'9", 172 lbs. Born, Toronto, Ont., July 2, 1950.

Season	Club	GP	G	A	Pts	PIM	GP	G	A	Pts	PIM
1976-77	Detroit Red Wings	5	1	0	1	24	....	....	....	....	....
	NHL Totals	**5**	**1**	**0**	**1**	**24**	....	....	....	....	....

Signed as a free agent by **Philadelphia**, June, 1973. Traded to **Detroit** by **Philadelphia** with Terry Murray, Bob Ritchie and Dave Kelly for Rick Lapointe and Mike Korney, February 17, 1977.

COCHRANE, Glen

Defense. Shoots left. 6'2", 205 lbs. Born, Cranbrook, B.C., January 29, 1958.
(Philadelphia's 6th choice, 50th overall, in 1978 Amateur Draft).

Season	Club	GP	G	A	Pts	PIM	GP	G	A	Pts	PIM
1978-79	Philadelphia Flyers	1	0	0	0	0	....	....	....	....	....
1980-81	Philadelphia Flyers	31	1	8	9	219	6	1	1	2	18
1981-82	Philadelphia Flyers	63	6	12	18	329	2	0	0	0	2
1982-83	Philadelphia Flyers	77	2	22	24	237	3	0	0	0	4
1983-84	Philadelphia Flyers	67	7	16	23	225	....	....	....	....	....
1984-85	Philadelphia Flyers	18	0	3	3	100	....	....	....	....	....
1985-86	Vancouver Canucks	49	0	3	3	125	2	0	0	0	5
1986-87	Vancouver Canucks	14	0	0	0	52	....	....	....	....	....
1987-88	Chicago Blackhawks	73	1	8	9	204	5	0	0	0	2
1988-89	Chicago Blackhawks	6	0	0	0	13	....	....	....	....	....
	Edmonton Oilers	12	0	0	0	52	....	....	....	....	....
	NHL Totals	**411**	**17**	**72**	**89**	**1556**	**18**	**1**	**1**	**2**	**31**

Traded to **Vancouver** by **Philadelphia** for Vancouver's 3rd round choice (later traded back to Vancouver – Vancouver selected Don Gibson) in 1986 Entry Draft, March 12, 1985. Claimed by **Chicago** from **Vancouver** in Waiver Draft, October 5, 1987. Claimed on waivers by **Edmonton** from **Chicago**, November 7, 1988.

COFFEY, Paul

Defense. Shoots left. 6', 205 lbs. Born, Weston, Ont., June 1, 1961.
(Edmonton's 1st choice, 6th overall, in 1980 Entry Draft).

Season	Club	GP	G	A	Pts	PIM	GP	G	A	Pts	PIM
1980-81	Edmonton Oilers	74	9	23	32	130	9	4	3	7	22
1981-82	Edmonton Oilers	80	29	60	89	106	5	1	1	2	6
1982-83	Edmonton Oilers	80	29	67	96	87	16	7	7	14	14
1983-84 ♦	Edmonton Oilers	80	40	86	126	104	19	8	14	22	21
1984-85 ♦	Edmonton Oilers	80	37	84	121	97	18	12	25	37	44
1985-86	Edmonton Oilers	79	48	90	138	120	10	1	9	10	30
1986-87 ♦	Edmonton Oilers	59	17	50	67	49	17	3	8	11	30
1987-88	Pittsburgh Penguins	46	15	52	67	93	....	....	....	....	....
1988-89	Pittsburgh Penguins	75	30	83	113	195	11	2	13	15	31
1989-90	Pittsburgh Penguins	80	29	74	103	95	....	....	....	....	....
1990-91 ♦	Pittsburgh Penguins	76	24	69	93	128	12	2	9	11	6
1991-92	Pittsburgh Penguins	54	10	54	64	62	....	....	....	....	....
	Los Angeles Kings	10	1	4	5	25	6	4	3	7	2
1992-93	Los Angeles Kings	50	8	49	57	50	....	....	....	....	....
	Detroit Red Wings	30	4	26	30	27	7	2	9	11	2
1993-94	Detroit Red Wings	80	14	63	77	106	7	1	6	7	8
1994-95	Detroit Red Wings	45	14	44	58	72	18	6	12	18	10
1995-96	Detroit Red Wings	76	14	60	74	90	17	5	9	14	30
1996-97	Hartford Whalers	20	3	5	8	18	....	....	....	....	....
	Philadelphia Flyers	37	6	20	26	20	17	1	8	9	6
1997-98	Philadelphia Flyers	57	2	27	29	30	....	....	....	....	....
1998-99	Chicago Blackhawks	10	0	4	4	0	....	....	....	....	....
	Carolina Hurricanes	44	2	8	10	28	5	0	1	1	2
99-2000	Carolina Hurricanes	69	11	29	40	40	....	....	....	....	....
2000-01	Boston Bruins	18	0	4	4	30	....	....	....	....	....
	NHL Totals	**1409**	**396**	**1135**	**1531**	**1802**	**194**	**59**	**137**	**196**	**264**

NHL Second All-Star Team (1982, 1983, 1984, 1990) • James Norris Memorial Trophy (1985, 1986, 1995) • NHL First All-Star Team (1985, 1986, 1989, 1995)

Played in NHL All-Star Game (1982, 1983, 1984, 1985, 1986, 1988, 1989, 1990, 1991, 1992, 1993, 1994, 1996, 1997)

Traded to **Pittsburgh** by **Edmonton** with Dave Hunter and Wayne Van Dorp for Craig Simpson, Dave Hannan, Moe Mantha and Chris Joseph, November 24, 1987. Traded to **Los Angeles** by **Pittsburgh** for Brian Benning, Jeff Chychrun and Los Angeles' 1st round choice (later traded to Philadelphia – Philadelphia selected Jason Bowen) in 1992 Entry Draft, February 19, 1992. Traded to **Detroit** by **Los Angeles** with Sylvain Couturier and Jim Hiller for Jimmy Carson, Marc Potvin and Gary Shuchuk, January 29, 1993. Traded to **Hartford** by **Detroit** with Keith Primeau and Detroit's 1st round choice (Nikos Tselios) in 1997 Entry Draft for Brendan Shanahan and Brian Glynn, October 9, 1996. Traded to **Philadelphia** by **Hartford** with Hartford's 3rd round choice (Kris Mallette) in 1997 Entry Draft for Kevin Haller, Philadelphia's 1st round choice (later traded to San Jose – San Jose selected Scott Hannan) in 1997 Entry Draft and Hartford's 7th round choice (previously acquired, Carolina selected Andrew Merrick) in 1997 Entry Draft, December 15, 1996. Traded to **Chicago** by **Philadelphia** for NY Islanders' 5th round choice (previously acquired, Philadelphia selected Francis Belanger) in 1998 Entry Draft, June 27, 1998. Traded to **Carolina** by **Chicago** for Nelson Emerson, December 29, 1998. Signed as a free agent by **Boston**, July 13, 2000. • Released by **Boston**, December 15, 2000.

COFLIN, Hugh

Defense. Shoots left. 6', 190 lbs. Born, Blaine Lake, Sask., December 15, 1928.

Season	Club	GP	G	A	Pts	PIM	GP	G	A	Pts	PIM
1950-51	Chicago Black Hawks	31	0	3	3	33	....	....	....	....	....
	NHL Totals	**31**	**0**	**3**	**3**	**33**	....	....	....	....	....

Traded to **Detroit** by **Chicago** to complete transaction that sent George Gee, Jimmy Peters Sr., Clare Martin, Rags Raglan, Max McNab and Jim McFadden to Chicago (August 20, 1951), October, 1951. Claimed by **Hershey** (AHL) from **Detroit** (Edmonton-WHL) in Inter-League Draft, June 1, 1955. Traded to **Detroit** (Edmonton-WHL) by **Hershey** (AHL) for Jimmy Uniac and Larry Zeidel, August 14, 1955.

COLAIACOVO, Carlo

Defense. Shoots left. 6'1", 184 lbs. Born, Toronto, Ont., January 27, 1983.
(Toronto's 1st choice, 17th overall, in 2001 Entry Draft).

Season	Club	GP	G	A	Pts	PIM	GP	G	A	Pts	PIM
2002-03	Toronto Maple Leafs	2	0	1	1	0	....	....	....	....	....
	NHL Totals	**2**	**0**	**1**	**1**	**0**	....	....	....	....	....

COLE, Danton

Center/Right wing. Shoots right. 5'11", 185 lbs. Born, Pontiac, MI, January 10, 1967.
(Winnipeg's 6th choice, 123rd overall, in 1985 Entry Draft).

Season	Club	GP	G	A	Pts	PIM	GP	G	A	Pts	PIM
1989-90	Winnipeg Jets	2	1	1	2	0	....	....	....	....	....
1990-91	Winnipeg Jets	66	13	11	24	24	....	....	....	....	....
1991-92	Winnipeg Jets	52	7	5	12	32	....	....	....	....	....
1992-93	Tampa Bay Lightning	67	12	15	27	23	....	....	....	....	....
1993-94	Tampa Bay Lightning	81	20	23	43	32	....	....	....	....	....
1994-95	Tampa Bay Lightning	26	3	3	6	6	....	....	....	....	....
	♦ New Jersey Devils	12	1	2	3	8	1	0	0	0	0

Season	Club	GP	G	A	Pts	PIM	GP	G	A	Pts	PIM
		REGULAR SEASON					PLAYOFFS				
1995-96	New York Islanders	10	1	0	1	0	....	....	....	....	....
	Chicago Blackhawks	2	0	0	0	0	....	....	....	....	....
	NHL Totals	**318**	**58**	**60**	**118**	**125**	**1**	**0**	**0**	**0**	**0**

Traded to **Tampa Bay** by **Winnipeg** for future considerations, June 19, 1992. Traded to **New Jersey** by **Tampa Bay** with Shawn Chambers for Alexander Semak and Ben Hankinson, March 14, 1995. Signed as a free agent by **NY Islanders**, August 26, 1995. Traded to **Chicago** by **NY Islanders** for Bob Halkidis, February 2, 1996.

COLE, Erik

Left wing. Shoots left. 6'1", 200 lbs. Born, Oswego, NY, November 6, 1978.
(Carolina's 3rd choice, 71st overall, in 1998 Entry Draft).

Season	Club	GP	G	A	Pts	PIM	GP	G	A	Pts	PIM
2001-02	Carolina Hurricanes	81	16	24	40	35	23	6	3	9	30
2002-03	Carolina Hurricanes	53	14	13	27	72	....	....	....	....	....
	NHL Totals	**134**	**30**	**37**	**67**	**107**	**23**	**6**	**3**	**9**	**30**

COLLEY, Tom

Center. Shoots left. 5'9", 162 lbs. Born, Toronto, Ont., August 21, 1953.
(Minnesota's 4th choice, 57th overall, in 1973 Amateur Draft).

Season	Club	GP	G	A	Pts	PIM	GP	G	A	Pts	PIM
1974-75	Minnesota North Stars	1	0	0	0	2	....	....	....	....	....
	NHL Totals	**1**	**0**	**0**	**0**	**2**	....	....	....	....	....

COLLINGS, Norm

Forward. Shoots left. 6'2", 175 lbs. Born, Bradford, Ont., May 6, 1910.

Season	Club	GP	G	A	Pts	PIM	GP	G	A	Pts	PIM
1934-35	Montreal Canadiens	1	0	1	1	0	....	....	....	....	....
	NHL Totals	**1**	**0**	**1**	**1**	**0**	....	....	....	....	....

COLLINS, Bill

Right wing. Shoots right. 6'1", 178 lbs. Born, Ottawa, Ont., July 13, 1943.

Season	Club	GP	G	A	Pts	PIM	GP	G	A	Pts	PIM
1967-68	Minnesota North Stars	71	9	11	20	41	10	2	4	6	4
1968-69	Minnesota North Stars	75	9	10	19	24	....	....	....	....	....
1969-70	Minnesota North Stars	74	29	9	38	48	6	0	1	1	8
1970-71	Montreal Canadiens	40	6	2	8	39	....	....	....	....	....
	Detroit Red Wings	36	5	16	21	10	....	....	....	....	....
1971-72	Detroit Red Wings	71	15	25	40	38	....	....	....	....	....
1972-73	Detroit Red Wings	78	21	21	42	44	....	....	....	....	....
1973-74	Detroit Red Wings	54	13	15	28	37	....	....	....	....	....
	St. Louis Blues	12	2	2	4	14	....	....	....	....	....
1974-75	St. Louis Blues	70	22	15	37	34	2	1	0	1	0
1975-76	New York Rangers	50	4	4	8	38	....	....	....	....	....
1976-77	Philadelphia Flyers	9	1	1	2	4	....	....	....	....	....
	Washington Capitals	54	11	14	25	26	....	....	....	....	....
1977-78	Washington Capitals	74	10	9	19	18	....	....	....	....	....
	NHL Totals	**768**	**157**	**154**	**311**	**415**	**18**	**3**	**5**	**8**	**12**

Traded to **NY Rangers** by **Toronto** with Dick Duff, Bob Nevin, Arnie Brown and Rod Seiling for Andy Bathgate and Don McKenney, February 22, 1964. Claimed by **Minnesota** from **NY Rangers** in Expansion Draft, June 6, 1967. Traded to **Montreal** by **Minnesota** to complete transaction that sent Jude Drouin to Minnesota (May 22, 1970), June 10, 1970. Traded to **Detroit** by **Montreal** with Mickey Redmond and Guy Charron for Frank Mahovlich, January 13, 1971. Traded to **St. Louis** by **Detroit** with Ted Harris and Garnet Bailey for Chris Evans, Bryan Watson and Jean Hamel, February 14, 1974. Traded to **NY Rangers** by **St. Louis** with John Davidson for Ted Irvine, Bert Wilson and Jerry Butler, June 18, 1975. Signed as a free agent by **Philadelphia**, October 20, 1976. Traded to **Washington** by **Philadelphia** for cash, December 4, 1976.

COLLINS, Gary

Center. Shoots left. 5'11", 185 lbs. Born, Toronto, Ont., September 27, 1935.

Season	Club	GP	G	A	Pts	PIM	GP	G	A	Pts	PIM
1958-59	Toronto Maple Leafs	....	....	....	....	....	2	0	0	0	0
	NHL Totals	....	....	....	....	....	**2**	**0**	**0**	**0**	**0**

Transferred to **Toronto** by **Chicago** as compensation for Chicago's signing of free agent Hank Ciesla, June, 1955. Loaned to **Providence** (AHL) by **Toronto** (Rochester-AHL) for loan of Ray Cyr for remainder of 1957-58 season, January 2, 1958. Traded to **Montreal** (Quebec-AHL) by **Toronto** (Rochester-AHL) for $10,000, November, 1959.

COLLYARD, Bob

Center. Shoots left. 5'9", 170 lbs. Born, Hibbing, MN, October 16, 1949.
(St. Louis' 7th choice, 73rd overall, in 1969 Amateur Draft).

Season	Club	GP	G	A	Pts	PIM	GP	G	A	Pts	PIM
1973-74	St. Louis Blues	10	1	3	4	4	....	....	....	....	....
	NHL Totals	**10**	**1**	**3**	**4**	**4**	....	....	....	....	....

Claimed by **Washington** from **St. Louis** in Expansion Draft, June 12, 1974.

COLMAN, Michael

Defense. Shoots right. 6'3", 225 lbs. Born, Stoneham, MA, August 4, 1968.

Season	Club	GP	G	A	Pts	PIM	GP	G	A	Pts	PIM
1991-92	San Jose Sharks	15	0	1	1	32	....	....	....	....	....
	NHL Totals	**15**	**0**	**1**	**1**	**32**	....	....	....	....	....

Signed as a free agent by **San Jose**, September 3, 1991. • Died of injuries suffered in automobile accident, April 5, 1994.

COLVILLE, Mac

Right wing/Defense. Shoots right. 5'9", 175 lbs. Born, Edmonton, Alta., January 8, 1916.

Season	Club	GP	G	A	Pts	PIM	GP	G	A	Pts	PIM
1935-36	New York Rangers	18	1	4	5	6	....	....	....	....	....
1936-37	New York Rangers	46	7	12	19	10	9	1	2	3	2
1937-38	New York Rangers	48	14	14	28	18	3	0	2	2	0
1938-39	New York Rangers	48	7	21	28	24	7	1	2	3	4
1939-40 ♦	New York Rangers	47	7	14	21	12	12	3	2	5	6
1940-41	New York Rangers	47	14	17	31	18	3	1	1	2	2
1941-42	New York Rangers	46	14	16	30	26	6	3	1	4	0
1945-46	New York Rangers	39	7	6	13	8	....	....	....	....	....
1946-47	New York Rangers	14	0	0	0	8	....	....	....	....	....
	NHL Totals	**353**	**71**	**104**	**175**	**130**	**40**	**9**	**10**	**19**	**14**

• Brother of Neil

Signed as a free agent by **NY Rangers**, October 18, 1935.

COLVILLE, Neil

HHOF

Center/Defense. Shoots right. 5'11", 175 lbs. Born, Edmonton, Alta., August 4, 1914.

Season	Club	GP	G	A	Pts	PIM	GP	G	A	Pts	PIM
1935-36	New York Rangers	1	0	0	0	0	....	....	....	....	....
1936-37	New York Rangers	45	10	18	28	33	9	3	3	6	0
1937-38	New York Rangers	45	17	19	36	11	3	0	1	1	0
1938-39	New York Rangers	47	18	19	37	12	7	0	2	2	2
1939-40 ♦	New York Rangers	48	19	19	38	22	12	2	*7	*9	18
1940-41	New York Rangers	48	14	28	42	28	3	1	1	2	0
1941-42	New York Rangers	48	8	25	33	37	6	0	5	5	6
1944-45	New York Rangers	4	0	1	1	2	....	....	....	....	....
1945-46	New York Rangers	49	5	4	9	25	....	....	....	....	....
1946-47	New York Rangers	60	4	16	20	16	....	....	....	....	....
1947-48	New York Rangers	55	4	12	16	25	6	1	0	1	6
1948-49	New York Rangers	14	0	5	5	2	....	....	....	....	....
	NHL Totals	**464**	**99**	**166**	**265**	**213**	**46**	**7**	**19**	**26**	**32**

• Brother of Mac • • NHL Second All-Star Team (1939, 1940)

Played in NHL All-Star Game (1939, 1948)

Signed as a free agent by **NY Rangers**, October 18, 1935.

COLWILL, Les

Right wing. Shoots right. 5'11", 170 lbs. Born, Diwide, Sask., January 1, 1935.

Season	Club	GP	G	A	Pts	PIM	GP	G	A	Pts	PIM
1958-59	New York Rangers	69	7	6	13	16	....	....	....	....	....
	NHL Totals	**69**	**7**	**6**	**13**	**16**	....	....	....	....	....

COMEAU, Rey

Center. Shoots left. 5'8", 190 lbs. Born, Montreal, Que., October 25, 1948.

Season	Club	GP	G	A	Pts	PIM	GP	G	A	Pts	PIM
1971-72	Montreal Canadiens	4	0	0	0	0	....	....	....	....	....
1972-73	Atlanta Flames	77	21	21	42	19	....	....	....	....	....
1973-74	Atlanta Flames	78	11	23	34	16	4	2	1	3	6
1974-75	Atlanta Flames	75	14	20	34	40	....	....	....	....	....
1975-76	Atlanta Flames	79	17	22	39	42	....	....	....	....	....
1976-77	Atlanta Flames	80	15	18	33	16	3	0	0	0	2
1977-78	Atlanta Flames	79	10	22	32	20	2	0	0	0	0
1978-79	Colorado Rockies	70	8	10	18	16	....	....	....	....	....
1979-80	Colorado Rockies	22	2	5	7	6	....	....	....	....	....
	NHL Totals	**564**	**98**	**141**	**239**	**175**	**9**	**2**	**1**	**3**	**8**

Traded to **Cleveland** (AHL) by **Montreal** for cash, July, 1969. Rights transferred to **Minnesota** when NHL club established working agreement with **Cleveland** (AHL), July, 1970. Traded to **Montreal** by **Minnesota** for Gord Labossiere, January 26, 1971. Claimed by **Vancouver** from **Montreal** in Intra-League Draft, June 8, 1971. Traded to **Montreal** by **Vancouver** for cash, September 14, 1971. Traded to **Atlanta** by **Montreal** for cash, June 16, 1972. Signed as a free agent by **Colorado**, June 23, 1978.

COMMODORE, Mike

Defense. Shoots right. 6'4", 230 lbs. Born, Fort Saskatchewan, Alta., November 7, 1979.
(New Jersey's 2nd choice, 42nd overall, in 1999 Entry Draft).

Season	Club	GP	G	A	Pts	PIM	GP	G	A	Pts	PIM
2000-01	New Jersey Devils	20	1	4	5	14	....	....	....	....	....
2001-02	New Jersey Devils	37	0	1	1	30	....	....	....	....	....
2002-03	Calgary Flames	6	0	1	1	19	....	....	....	....	....
	NHL Totals	**63**	**1**	**6**	**7**	**63**	....	....	....	....	....

Traded to **Anaheim** by **New Jersey** with Petr Sykora, Jean-Francois Damphousse and Igor Pohanka for Jeff Friesen, Oleg Tverdovsky and Maxim Balmochnykh, July 6, 2002. Traded to **Calgary** by **Anaheim** with Jean-Francois Damphousse for Rob Niedermayer, March 11, 2003.

COMRIE, Mike

Center. Shoots left. 5'9", 175 lbs. Born, Edmonton, Alta., September 11, 1980.
(Edmonton's 5th choice, 91st overall, in 1999 Entry Draft).

Season	Club	GP	G	A	Pts	PIM	GP	G	A	Pts	PIM
2000-01	Edmonton Oilers	41	8	14	22	14	6	1	2	3	0
2001-02	Edmonton Oilers	82	33	27	60	45	....	....	....	....	....
2002-03	Edmonton Oilers	69	20	31	51	90	6	1	0	1	10
	NHL Totals	**192**	**61**	**72**	**133**	**149**	**12**	**2**	**2**	**4**	**10**

• Brother of Paul

COMRIE, Paul

Center. Shoots left. 5'11", 192 lbs. Born, Edmonton, Alta., February 7, 1977.
(Tampa Bay's 12th choice, 224th overall, in 1997 Entry Draft).

Season	Club	GP	G	A	Pts	PIM	GP	G	A	Pts	PIM
99-2000	Edmonton Oilers	15	1	2	3	4	....	....	....	....	....
	NHL Totals	**15**	**1**	**2**	**3**	**4**	....	....	....	....	....

• Brother of Mike

Traded to **Edmonton** by **Tampa Bay** with Roman Hamrlik for Bryan Marchment, Steve Kelly and Jason Bonsignore, December 30, 1997. • Missed remainder of 1999-2000 season and entire 2000-01 season recovering from head injury suffered during game vs. Tampa Bay, January 7, 2000. • Officially announced retirement, August 31, 2001.

CONACHER, Brian

Left wing. Shoots left. 6'3", 197 lbs. Born, Toronto, Ont., August 31, 1941.

Season	Club	GP	G	A	Pts	PIM	GP	G	A	Pts	PIM
1961-62	Toronto Maple Leafs	1	0	0	0	0	....	....	....	....	....
1965-66	Toronto Maple Leafs	2	0	0	0	2	....	....	....	....	....

Season	Club	REGULAR SEASON GP	G	A	Pts	PIM	PLAYOFFS GP	G	A	Pts	PIM
1966-67 ♦	Toronto Maple Leafs	66	14	13	27	47	12	3	2	5	21
1967-68	Toronto Maple Leafs	64	11	14	25	31	....	....	....	....	....
1971-72	Detroit Red Wings	22	3	1	4	4	....	....	....	....	....
	NHL Totals	**155**	**28**	**28**	**56**	**84**	**12**	**3**	**2**	**5**	**21**

• Son of Lionel

Played in NHL All-Star Game (1968)

Claimed by **Detroit** from **Toronto** in Intra-League Draft, June 12, 1968. Rights traded to **Minnesota** by **Detroit** with Danny Lawson for Wayne Connelly, February 15, 1969. Rights traded to **Toronto** by **Minnesota** with Terry O'Malley and cash for Murray Oliver, May 22, 1970. Rights traded to **Detroit** by **Toronto** for cash, August 20, 1971.

CONACHER, Charlie — HHOF

Right wing. Shoots right. 6'1", 195 lbs. Born, Toronto, Ont., December 20, 1909.

Season	Club	REGULAR SEASON GP	G	A	Pts	PIM	PLAYOFFS GP	G	A	Pts	PIM
1929-30	Toronto Maple Leafs	38	20	9	29	48	....	....	....	....	....
1930-31	Toronto Maple Leafs	37	*31	12	43	78	2	0	1	1	0
1931-32 ♦	Toronto Maple Leafs	44	*34	14	48	66	7	*6	2	8	6
1932-33	Toronto Maple Leafs	40	14	19	33	64	9	1	1	2	10
1933-34	Toronto Maple Leafs	42	*32	20	*52	38	5	3	2	5	0
1934-35	Toronto Maple Leafs	47	*36	21	*57	24	7	1	*4	*5	6
1935-36	Toronto Maple Leafs	44	*23	15	38	74	9	3	2	5	12
1936-37	Toronto Maple Leafs	15	3	5	8	13	2	0	0	0	5
1937-38	Toronto Maple Leafs	19	7	9	16	6	....	....	....	....	....
1938-39	Detroit Red Wings	40	8	15	23	39	5	2	5	7	2
1939-40	New York Americans	47	10	18	28	41	3	1	1	2	8
1940-41	New York Americans	46	7	16	23	32	....	....	....	....	....
	NHL Totals	**459**	**225**	**173**	**398**	**523**	**49**	**17**	**18**	**35**	**49**

• Brother of Lionel and Roy • Father of Pete • NHL Second All-Star Team (1932, 1933) • NHL First All-Star Team (1934, 1935, 1936) • NHL Scoring Leader (1934, 1935)

Played in NHL All-Star Game (1934, 1937)

Signed as a free agent by **Toronto**, October 7, 1929. • Missed majority of 1936-37 season recovering from wrist injury originally suffered in training camp and re-injured in game vs. NY Americans , December 17, 1936. Traded to **Detroit** by **Toronto** for $16,000 with Detroit holding option of contract renewal, October 12, 1938. • Rights returned to **Toronto** by **Detroit** after Detroit failed to renew contract, July 1, 1939. Traded to **NY Americans** by **Toronto** for future considerations (cash, May 21, 1940), September 22, 1939.

CONACHER, Jim

Center. Shoots left. 5'10", 155 lbs. Born, Motherwell, Scotland, May 5, 1921.

Season	Club	REGULAR SEASON GP	G	A	Pts	PIM	PLAYOFFS GP	G	A	Pts	PIM
1945-46	Detroit Red Wings	20	1	5	6	10	5	1	1	2	0
1946-47	Detroit Red Wings	33	16	13	29	2	5	2	1	3	2
1947-48	Detroit Red Wings	60	17	23	40	2	9	2	0	2	2
1948-49	Detroit Red Wings	4	1	0	1	2	....	....	....	....	....
	Chicago Black Hawks	55	25	23	48	41	....	....	....	....	....
1949-50	Chicago Black Hawks	66	13	20	33	14	....	....	....	....	....
1950-51	Chicago Black Hawks	52	10	27	37	16	....	....	....	....	....
1951-52	Chicago Black Hawks	5	1	1	2	0	....	....	....	....	....
	New York Rangers	16	0	1	1	2	....	....	....	....	....
1952-53	New York Rangers	17	1	4	5	2	....	....	....	....	....
	NHL Totals	**328**	**85**	**117**	**202**	**91**	**19**	**5**	**2**	**7**	**4**

Signed as a free agent by **Detroit**, October 17, 1941. Traded to **Chicago** by **Detroit** with Bep Guidolin and Doug McCaig for George Gee and Bud Poile, October 25, 1948. Claimed on waivers by **NY Rangers** from **Chicago**, October 26, 1951. Traded to **Buffalo** (AHL) by **NY Rangers** for cash, December 31, 1952.

CONACHER, Lionel — HHOF

Defense. Shoots left. 6'2", 195 lbs. Born, Toronto, Ont., May 24, 1901.

Season	Club	REGULAR SEASON GP	G	A	Pts	PIM	PLAYOFFS GP	G	A	Pts	PIM
1925-26	Pittsburgh Pirates	33	9	4	13	64	2	0	0	0	0
1926-27	Pittsburgh Pirates	9	0	0	0	12	....	....	....	....	....
	New York Americans	30	8	9	17	81	....	....	....	....	....
1927-28	New York Americans	35	11	6	17	82	....	....	....	....	....
1928-29	New York Americans	44	5	2	7	132	2	0	0	0	10
1929-30	New York Americans	40	4	6	10	73	....	....	....	....	....
1930-31	Montreal Maroons	36	4	3	7	57	2	0	0	0	2
1931-32	Montreal Maroons	45	7	9	16	60	4	0	0	0	2
1932-33	Montreal Maroons	47	7	21	28	61	2	0	1	1	0
1933-34 ♦	Chicago Black Hawks	48	10	13	23	87	8	2	0	2	4
1934-35 ♦	Montreal Maroons	38	2	6	8	44	7	0	0	0	14
1935-36	Montreal Maroons	46	7	7	14	65	3	0	0	0	0
1936-37	Montreal Maroons	47	6	19	25	64	5	0	1	1	2
	NHL Totals	**498**	**80**	**105**	**185**	**882**	**35**	**2**	**2**	**4**	**34**

• Brother of Charlie and Roy • Father of Brian • NHL Second All-Star Team (1933, 1937) • NHL First All-Star Team (1934)

Played in NHL All-Star Game (1934)

Signed as a free agent by **Pittsburgh**, November 11, 1925. Traded to **NY Americans** by **Pittsburgh** for Charlie Langlois and $2,000, December 16, 1926. Traded to **Mtl. Maroons** by **NY Americans** for cash, November 5, 1930. Traded to **Chicago** by **Mtl. Maroons** for Teddy Graham, October 1, 1933. Traded to **Montreal** by **Chicago** with Leroy Goldsworthy and Roger Jenkins for Lorne Chabot, Marty Burke and Howie Morenz, October 3, 1934. Traded to **Mtl. Maroons** by **Montreal** with the rights to Herb Cain for the rights to Nels Crutchfield, October 3, 1934.

CONACHER, Pat

Left wing. Shoots left. 5'8", 190 lbs. Born, Edmonton, Alta., May 1, 1959.
(NY Rangers' 3rd choice, 76th overall, in 1979 Entry Draft).

Season	Club	REGULAR SEASON GP	G	A	Pts	PIM	PLAYOFFS GP	G	A	Pts	PIM
1979-80	New York Rangers	17	0	5	5	4	3	0	1	1	2
1982-83	New York Rangers	5	0	1	1	4	....	....	....	....	....
1983-84 ♦	Edmonton Oilers	45	2	8	10	31	3	1	0	1	2
1985-86	New Jersey Devils	2	0	2	2	2	....	....	....	....	....
1987-88	New Jersey Devils	24	2	5	7	12	17	2	2	4	14
1988-89	New Jersey Devils	55	7	5	12	14	....	....	....	....	....
1989-90	New Jersey Devils	19	3	3	6	4	5	1	0	1	10
1990-91	New Jersey Devils	49	5	11	16	27	7	0	2	2	2
1991-92	New Jersey Devils	44	7	3	10	16	7	1	1	2	4
1992-93	Los Angeles Kings	81	9	8	17	20	24	6	4	10	6
1993-94	Los Angeles Kings	77	15	13	28	71	....	....	....	....	....
1994-95	Los Angeles Kings	48	7	9	16	12	....	....	....	....	....
1995-96	Los Angeles Kings	35	5	2	7	18	....	....	....	....	....
	Calgary Flames	7	0	0	0	0	....	....	....	....	....
	New York Islanders	13	1	1	2	0	....	....	....	....	....
	NHL Totals	**521**	**63**	**76**	**139**	**235**	**66**	**11**	**10**	**21**	**40**

• Missed entire 1980-81 season recovering from ankle injury suffered in pre-season rookie game, September, 1980. Signed as a free agent by **Edmonton**, October 4, 1983. Signed as a free agent by **New Jersey**, August 14, 1985. Traded to **Los Angeles** by **New Jersey** for future considerations, September 3, 1992. Traded to **Calgary** by **Los Angeles** for Craig Ferguson, February 10, 1996. Traded to **NY Islanders** by **Calgary** with Calgary's 6th round choice (later traded back to Calgary – Calgary selected Ilja Demidov) in 1997 Entry Draft for Bob Sweeney, March 20, 1996.

CONACHER, Pete

Left wing. Shoots left. 5'10", 165 lbs. Born, Toronto, Ont., July 29, 1932.

Season	Club	REGULAR SEASON GP	G	A	Pts	PIM	PLAYOFFS GP	G	A	Pts	PIM
1951-52	Chicago Black Hawks	2	0	1	1	0	....	....	....	....	....
1952-53	Chicago Black Hawks	41	5	6	11	7	2	0	0	0	0
1953-54	Chicago Black Hawks	70	19	9	28	23	....	....	....	....	....
1954-55	Chicago Black Hawks	18	2	4	6	2	....	....	....	....	....
	New York Rangers	52	10	7	17	10	....	....	....	....	....
1955-56	New York Rangers	41	11	11	22	10	5	0	0	0	0
1957-58	Toronto Maple Leafs	5	0	1	1	5	....	....	....	....	....
	NHL Totals	**229**	**47**	**39**	**86**	**57**	**7**	**0**	**0**	**0**	**0**

• Son of Charlie

Traded to **NY Rangers** by **Chicago** with Bill Gadsby for Rich Lamoureux, Allan Stanley and Nick Mickoski, November 23, 1954. Traded to **Buffalo** (AHL) by **NY Rangers** for $10,000 and the loan of Dusty Blair and Gord Pennell, August 20, 1956. Traded to **Toronto** by **NY Rangers** for $15,000, June 4, 1957. Traded to **NY Rangers** by **Toronto** for $15,000, November 18, 1957. Traded to **Detroit** by **NY Rangers** (Buffalo-AHL) for Barry Cullen, August, 1960. Traded to **Hershey** (AHL) by **Detroit** with Marc Reaume and Jack McIntyre for Howie Young, January, 1961.

CONACHER, Roy — HHOF

Left wing. Shoots left. 6'2", 175 lbs. Born, Toronto, Ont., October 5, 1916.

Season	Club	REGULAR SEASON GP	G	A	Pts	PIM	PLAYOFFS GP	G	A	Pts	PIM
1938-39 ♦	Boston Bruins	47	*26	11	37	12	12	6	4	10	12
1939-40	Boston Bruins	31	18	12	30	9	6	2	1	3	0
1940-41 ♦	Boston Bruins	41	24	14	38	7	11	1	5	6	0
1941-42	Boston Bruins	43	24	13	37	12	5	2	1	3	0
1945-46	Boston Bruins	4	2	1	3	0	3	0	0	0	0
1946-47	Detroit Red Wings	60	30	24	54	6	5	4	4	8	2
1947-48	Chicago Black Hawks	52	22	27	49	4	....	....	....	....	....
1948-49	Chicago Black Hawks	60	26	42	*68	8	....	....	....	....	....
1949-50	Chicago Black Hawks	70	25	31	56	16	....	....	....	....	....
1950-51	Chicago Black Hawks	70	26	24	50	16	....	....	....	....	....
1951-52	Chicago Black Hawks	12	3	1	4	0	....	....	....	....	....
	NHL Totals	**490**	**226**	**200**	**426**	**90**	**42**	**15**	**15**	**30**	**14**

• Brother of Lionel and Charlie • NHL First All-Star Team (1949) • Art Ross Trophy (1949)

Played in NHL All-Star Game (1949)

Traded to **Detroit** by **Boston** for Joe Carveth, August, 1946. Traded to **NY Rangers** by **Detroit** for Eddie Slowinski and future considerations, October 22, 1947. Conacher refused to report and transaction was voided. Traded to **Chicago** by **Detroit** for cash, November 1, 1947.

CONN, Red

Left wing. Shoots left. 5'11", 180 lbs. Born, Hartney, Man., October 25, 1904.

Season	Club	REGULAR SEASON GP	G	A	Pts	PIM	PLAYOFFS GP	G	A	Pts	PIM
1933-34	New York Americans	48	4	17	21	12	....	....	....	....	....
1934-35	New York Americans	48	5	11	16	10	....	....	....	....	....
	NHL Totals	**96**	**9**	**28**	**37**	**22**	....	....	....	....	....

Traded to **Montreal** by **Springfield** (AHL) for Sam Godin, September 30, 1937.

CONN, Rob

Wing. Shoots right. 6'2", 200 lbs. Born, Calgary, Alta., September 3, 1968.

Season	Club	REGULAR SEASON GP	G	A	Pts	PIM	PLAYOFFS GP	G	A	Pts	PIM
1991-92	Chicago Blackhawks	2	0	0	0	2	....	....	....	....	....
1995-96	Buffalo Sabres	28	2	5	7	18	....	....	....	....	....
	NHL Totals	**30**	**2**	**5**	**7**	**20**	....	....	....	....	....

Signed as a free agent by **Chicago**, July 31, 1991. Traded to **New Jersey** by **Chicago** for Dean Malkoc, January 30, 1995. Claimed by **Buffalo** from **New Jersey** in Waiver Draft, October 2, 1995. Signed as a free agent by **Chicago**, September 26, 1996.

CONNELLY, Bert

Left wing. Shoots left. 5'11", 174 lbs. Born, Montreal, Que., April 22, 1909.

Season	Club	REGULAR SEASON GP	G	A	Pts	PIM	PLAYOFFS GP	G	A	Pts	PIM
1934-35	New York Rangers	47	10	11	21	23	4	1	0	1	0
1935-36	New York Rangers	25	2	2	4	10	....	....	....	....	....
1937-38 ♦	Chicago Black Hawks	15	1	2	3	4	10	0	0	0	0
	NHL Totals	**87**	**13**	**15**	**28**	**37**	**14**	**1**	**0**	**1**	**0**

Signed as a free agent by **NY Rangers**, October 26, 1934. Signed as a free agent by **Chicago**, February 7, 1938.

CONNELLY, Wayne

Center. Shoots right. 5'10", 170 lbs. Born, Rouyn, Que., December 16, 1939.

Season	Club	Regular Season GP	G	A	Pts	PIM	Playoffs GP	G	A	Pts	PIM
1960-61	Montreal Canadiens	3	0	0	0	0	....	....	....	....	....
1961-62	Boston Bruins	61	8	12	20	34	....	....	....	....	....
1962-63	Boston Bruins	18	2	6	8	2	....	....	....	....	....
1963-64	Boston Bruins	26	2	3	5	12	....	....	....	....	....
1966-67	Boston Bruins	64	13	17	30	12	....	....	....	....	....
1967-68	Minnesota North Stars	74	35	21	56	40	14	*8	3	11	2
1968-69	Minnesota North Stars	55	14	16	30	11	....	....	....	....	....
	Detroit Red Wings	19	4	9	13	0	....	....	....	....	....
1969-70	Detroit Red Wings	76	23	36	59	10	4	1	3	4	2
1970-71	Detroit Red Wings	51	8	13	21	12	....	....	....	....	....
	St. Louis Blues	28	5	16	21	9	6	2	1	3	0
1971-72	St. Louis Blues	15	5	5	10	2	....	....	....	....	....
	Vancouver Canucks	53	14	20	34	12	....	....	....	....	....
	NHL Totals	**543**	**133**	**174**	**307**	**156**	**24**	**11**	**7**	**18**	**4**

Traded to **Boston** by **Montreal** (Hull-Ottawa-EPHL) for the loan of Bob Armstrong and Dallas Smith and cash, October 26, 1961. Traded to **San Francisco** (WHL) by **Boston** for cash, June 6, 1964. Traded to **Boston** by **San Francisco** (WHL) for cash, June 14, 1966. Claimed by **Minnesota** from **Boston** in Expansion Draft, June 6, 1967. Traded to **Detroit** by **Minnesota** for Danny Lawson and the rights to Brian Conacher, February 15, 1969. Traded to **St. Louis** by **Detroit** with Garry Unger for Red Berenson and Tim Ecclestone, February 6, 1971. Traded to **NY Rangers** by **St. Louis** with Gene Carr and Jim Lorentz for Andre Dupont, Jack Egers and Mike Murphy, November 15, 1971. Traded to **Vancouver** by **NY Rangers** with Dave Balon and Ron Stewart for Gary Doak and Jim Wiste, November 16, 1971.

CONNOLLY, Tim

Center. Shoots right. 6'1", 182 lbs. Born, Syracuse, NY, May 7, 1981.
(NY Islanders' 1st choice, 5th overall, in 1999 Entry Draft).

Season	Club	Regular Season GP	G	A	Pts	PIM	Playoffs GP	G	A	Pts	PIM
99-2000	New York Islanders	81	14	20	34	44	....	....	....	....	....
2000-01	New York Islanders	82	10	31	41	42	....	....	....	....	....
2001-02	Buffalo Sabres	82	10	35	45	34	....	....	....	....	....
2002-03	Buffalo Sabres	80	12	13	25	32	....	....	....	....	....
	NHL Totals	**325**	**46**	**99**	**145**	**152**	....	....	....	....	....

Traded to **Buffalo** by **NY Islanders** with Taylor Pyatt for Michael Peca, June 24, 2001.

CONNOR, Cam

Right wing. Shoots left. 6'2", 200 lbs. Born, Winnipeg, Man., August 10, 1954.
(Montreal's 1st choice, 5th overall, in 1974 Amateur Draft).

Season	Club	Regular Season GP	G	A	Pts	PIM	Playoffs GP	G	A	Pts	PIM
1978-79◆	Montreal Canadiens	23	1	3	4	39	8	1	0	1	0
1979-80	Edmonton Oilers	38	7	13	20	136	....	....	....	....	....
	New York Rangers	12	0	3	3	37	2	0	0	0	2
1980-81	New York Rangers	15	1	3	4	44	....	....	....	....	....
1981-82	New York Rangers	....	....	....	....	....	10	4	0	4	4
1982-83	New York Rangers	1	0	0	0	0	....	....	....	....	....
	NHL Totals	**89**	**9**	**22**	**31**	**256**	**20**	**5**	**0**	**5**	**6**

Claimed by **Edmonton** from **Montreal** in Expansion Draft, June 13, 1979. Traded to **NY Rangers** by **Edmonton** with Edmonton's 3rd round choice (Peter Sundstrom) in 1981 Entry Draft for Don Murdoch, March 11, 1980.

CONNOR, Harry

Left wing. Shoots left. 6', 195 lbs. Born, Ottawa, Ont., December 3, 1904.

Season	Club	Regular Season GP	G	A	Pts	PIM	Playoffs GP	G	A	Pts	PIM
1927-28	Boston Bruins	42	9	1	10	36	2	0	0	0	0
1928-29	New York Americans	43	6	2	8	83	2	0	0	0	2
1929-30	Ottawa Senators	25	1	2	3	22	....	....	....	....	....
	Boston Bruins	13	0	0	0	4	6	0	0	0	0
1930-31	Ottawa Senators	11	0	0	0	4	....	....	....	....	....
	NHL Totals	**134**	**16**	**5**	**21**	**149**	**10**	**0**	**0**	**0**	**2**

Traded to **Boston** by **Saskatoon** (PrHL) for cash, October, 1927. Traded to **NY Americans** by **Boston** for Red Green, May 18, 1928. Claimed on waivers by **Ottawa** from **NY Americans** for $5,000, November 18, 1929. Traded to **Boston** by **Ottawa** for Bill Hutton, January 30, 1930. Traded to **Ottawa** by **Boston** for Bill Hutton, October 16, 1930.

CONNORS, Bob

Left wing/Defense. Shoots left. 5'9", 165 lbs. Born, Glasgow, Scotland, October 19, 1904.

Season	Club	Regular Season GP	G	A	Pts	PIM	Playoffs GP	G	A	Pts	PIM
1926-27	New York Americans	6	1	0	1	0	....	....	....	....	....
1928-29	Detroit Cougars	41	13	3	16	68	2	0	0	0	10
1929-30	Detroit Cougars	31	3	7	10	42	....	....	....	....	....
	NHL Totals	**78**	**17**	**10**	**27**	**110**	**2**	**0**	**0**	**0**	**10**

Traded to **NY Americans** by **Niagara Falls** (Can-Pro) for cash, February 1, 1927. Traded to **Detroit** by **NY Americans** for cash, September, 1928. Traded to **Seattle** (PCHL) by **Detroit** with Pete Bellefeuille for cash, September 12, 1930. • Died in a diving accident near Port Arthur, Ontario, July 27,1931.

CONROY, Al

Center. Shoots right. 5'8", 170 lbs. Born, Calgary, Alta., January 17, 1966.

Season	Club	Regular Season GP	G	A	Pts	PIM	Playoffs GP	G	A	Pts	PIM
1991-92	Philadelphia Flyers	31	2	9	11	74	....	....	....	....	....
1992-93	Philadelphia Flyers	21	3	2	5	17	....	....	....	....	....
1993-94	Philadelphia Flyers	62	4	3	7	65	....	....	....	....	....
	NHL Totals	**114**	**9**	**14**	**23**	**156**	....	....	....	....	....

Signed as a free agent by **Detroit**, August 16, 1989. Signed as a free agent by **Philadelphia**, August 21, 1991.

CONROY, Craig

Center. Shoots right. 6'2", 197 lbs. Born, Potsdam, NY, September 4, 1971.
(Montreal's 7th choice, 123rd overall, in 1990 Entry Draft).

Season	Club	Regular Season GP	G	A	Pts	PIM	Playoffs GP	G	A	Pts	PIM
1994-95	Montreal Canadiens	6	1	0	1	0	....	....	....	....	....
1995-96	Montreal Canadiens	7	0	0	0	2	....	....	....	....	....
1996-97	St. Louis Blues	61	6	11	17	43	6	0	0	0	8
1997-98	St. Louis Blues	81	14	29	43	46	10	1	2	3	8
1998-99	St. Louis Blues	69	14	25	39	38	13	2	1	3	6
99-2000	St. Louis Blues	79	12	15	27	36	7	0	2	2	2
2000-01	St. Louis Blues	69	11	14	25	46	....	....	....	....	....
	Calgary Flames	14	3	4	7	14	....	....	....	....	....
2001-02	Calgary Flames	81	27	48	75	32	....	....	....	....	....
2002-03	Calgary Flames	79	22	37	59	36	....	....	....	....	....
	NHL Totals	**546**	**110**	**183**	**293**	**293**	**36**	**3**	**5**	**8**	**24**

Traded to **St. Louis** by **Montreal** with Pierre Turgeon and Rory Fitzpatrick for Murray Baron, Shayne Corson and St. Louis' 5th round choice (Gennady Razin) in 1997 Entry Draft, October 29, 1996. Traded to **Calgary** by **St. Louis** with St. Louis' 7th round choice (David Moss) in 2001 Entry Draft for Cory Stillman, March 13, 2001.

CONTINI, Joe

Center. Shoots left. 5'10", 178 lbs. Born, Galt, Ont., January 29, 1957.
(Colorado's 7th choice, 126th overall, in 1977 Amateur Draft).

Season	Club	Regular Season GP	G	A	Pts	PIM	Playoffs GP	G	A	Pts	PIM
1977-78	Colorado Rockies	37	12	9	21	28	2	0	0	0	0
1978-79	Colorado Rockies	30	5	12	17	6	....	....	....	....	....
1980-81	Minnesota North Stars	1	0	0	0	0	....	....	....	....	....
	NHL Totals	**68**	**17**	**21**	**38**	**34**	**2**	**0**	**0**	**0**	**0**

Claimed by **Colorado** as a fill-in during Expansion Draft, June 13, 1979. Signed as a free agent by **Minnesota**, February 1, 1980.

CONVERY, Brandon

Center. Shoots right. 6'1", 195 lbs. Born, Kingston, Ont., February 4, 1974.
(Toronto's 1st choice, 8th overall, in 1992 Entry Draft).

Season	Club	Regular Season GP	G	A	Pts	PIM	Playoffs GP	G	A	Pts	PIM
1995-96	Toronto Maple Leafs	11	5	2	7	4	5	0	0	0	2
1996-97	Toronto Maple Leafs	39	2	8	10	20	....	....	....	....	....
1997-98	Vancouver Canucks	7	0	2	2	0	....	....	....	....	....
1998-99	Vancouver Canucks	12	2	7	9	8	....	....	....	....	....
	Los Angeles Kings	3	0	0	0	4	....	....	....	....	....
	NHL Totals	**72**	**9**	**19**	**28**	**36**	**5**	**0**	**0**	**0**	**2**

Traded to **Vancouver** by **Toronto** for Lonny Bohonos, March 7, 1998. Claimed on waivers by **Los Angeles** from **Vancouver**, November 21, 1998.

CONVEY, Eddie

Left wing/Center. Shoots left. 5'11", 165 lbs. Born, Toronto, Ont., December 16, 1910.

Season	Club	Regular Season GP	G	A	Pts	PIM	Playoffs GP	G	A	Pts	PIM
1930-31	New York Americans	2	0	0	0	0	....	....	....	....	....
1931-32	New York Americans	21	1	0	1	21	....	....	....	....	....
1932-33	New York Americans	13	0	1	1	12	....	....	....	....	....
	NHL Totals	**36**	**1**	**1**	**2**	**33**	....	....	....	....	....

COOK, Bill

HHOF

Right wing. Shoots right. 5'10", 170 lbs. Born, Brantford, Ont., October 9, 1896.

Season	Club	Regular Season GP	G	A	Pts	PIM	Playoffs GP	G	A	Pts	PIM
1926-27	New York Rangers	44	*33	4	*37	58	2	1	0	1	6
1927-28◆	New York Rangers	43	18	6	24	42	9	2	3	5	26
1928-29	New York Rangers	43	15	8	23	41	6	0	0	0	6
1929-30	New York Rangers	44	29	30	59	56	4	0	1	1	11
1930-31	New York Rangers	43	30	12	42	39	4	3	0	3	4
1931-32	New York Rangers	48	*34	14	48	33	7	3	3	6	2
1932-33◆	New York Rangers	48	*28	22	*50	51	8	3	2	5	4
1933-34	New York Rangers	48	13	13	26	21	2	0	0	0	2
1934-35	New York Rangers	48	21	15	36	23	4	1	2	3	7
1935-36	New York Rangers	44	7	10	17	16	....	....	....	....	....
1936-37	New York Rangers	21	1	4	5	6	....	....	....	....	....
	NHL Totals	**474**	**229**	**138**	**367**	**386**	**46**	**13**	**11**	**24**	**68**

• Brother of Bun and Bud • NHL First All-Star Team (1931, 1932, 1933) • NHL Second All-Star Team (1934)

Played in NHL All-Star Game (1934)

Traded to **NY Rangers** by **Saskatoon** (WHL) for cash, October 18, 1926.

COOK, Bob

Right wing. Shoots right. 6', 190 lbs. Born, Sudbury, Ont., January 6, 1946.

Season	Club	Regular Season GP	G	A	Pts	PIM	Playoffs GP	G	A	Pts	PIM
1970-71	Vancouver Canucks	2	0	0	0	0	....	....	....	....	....
1972-73	Detroit Red Wings	13	3	1	4	4	....	....	....	....	....
	New York Islanders	33	8	6	14	14	....	....	....	....	....
1973-74	New York Islanders	22	2	1	3	4	....	....	....	....	....
1974-75	Minnesota North Stars	2	0	1	1	0	....	....	....	....	....
	NHL Totals	**72**	**13**	**9**	**22**	**22**	....	....	....	....	....

NHL rights transferred to **Vancouver** after NHL club purchased **Vancouver** (WHL) franchise, December 19, 1969. Traded to **Detroit** by **Vancouver** for cash, November 21, 1971. Traded to **NY Islanders** by **Detroit** with Ralph Stewart for Ken Murray and Brian Lavender, January 17, 1973. Traded to **Minnesota** by **NY Islanders** for cash, January 5, 1975.

COOK, Bud

Center. Shoots left. 5'10", 160 lbs. Born, Kingston, Ont., November 20, 1907.

Season	Club	Regular Season GP	G	A	Pts	PIM	Playoffs GP	G	A	Pts	PIM
1931-32	Boston Bruins	28	4	4	8	14	....	....	....	....	....
1933-34	Ottawa Senators	18	1	0	1	8	....	....	....	....	....

Season	Club	GP	G	A	Pts	PIM	GP	G	A	Pts	PIM
		REGULAR SEASON					PLAYOFFS				
1934-35	St. Louis Eagles	4	0	0	0	0	....	....	....	....	....
	NHL Totals	**50**	**5**	**4**	**9**	**22**	....	....	....	....	....

• Brother of Bill and Bun

Traded to **Montreal** by **Oakland** (Cal-Pro) for cash, February 18, 1930. Traded to **Boston** by **Montreal** for cash, May 13, 1931. Traded to **Ottawa** by **Boston** with Percy Galbraith and Ted Saunders for Bob Gracie, October 4, 1933. Transferred to **St. Louis** after **Ottawa** franchise relocated, September 22, 1934. Traded to **Cleveland** (IHL) by **St. Louis** for cash, November 29, 1934.

COOK, Bun

HHOF

Left wing. Shoots left. 5'11", 180 lbs. Born, Kingston, Ont., September 18, 1903.

Season	Club	GP	G	A	Pts	PIM	GP	G	A	Pts	PIM
1926-27	New York Rangers	44	14	9	23	42	2	0	0	0	6
1927-28 ◆	New York Rangers	44	14	14	28	45	9	2	1	3	10
1928-29	New York Rangers	43	13	5	18	70	6	1	0	1	12
1929-30	New York Rangers	43	24	18	42	55	4	2	0	2	2
1930-31	New York Rangers	44	18	17	35	72	4	0	0	0	2
1931-32	New York Rangers	45	14	20	34	43	7	6	2	8	12
1932-33 ◆	New York Rangers	48	22	15	37	35	8	2	0	2	4
1933-34	New York Rangers	48	18	15	33	36	2	0	0	0	2
1934-35	New York Rangers	48	13	21	34	26	4	2	0	2	0
1935-36	New York Rangers	26	4	5	9	12	....	....	....	....	....
1936-37	Boston Bruins	40	4	5	9	8	....	....	....	....	....
	NHL Totals	**473**	**158**	**144**	**302**	**444**	**46**	**15**	**3**	**18**	**50**

• Brother of Bill and Bud • NHL Second All-Star Team (1931)

Traded to **NY Rangers** by **Saskatoon** (WHL) for cash, October 18, 1926. Traded to **Boston** by **NY Rangers** for cash, September 10, 1936.

COOK, Lloyd

Defense. Shoots left. 6', 170 lbs. Born, Lynden, Ont., March 21, 1890.

Season	Club	GP	G	A	Pts	PIM	GP	G	A	Pts	PIM
1924-25	Boston Bruins	4	1	0	1	0	....	....	....	....	....
	NHL Totals	**4**	**1**	**0**	**1**	**0**	....	....	....	....	....

Traded to **Boston** by **Vancouver** (WCHL) for cash, November 18, 1924.

COOK, Tom

Center. Shoots left. 5'7", 140 lbs. Born, Fort William, Ont., May 7, 1907.

Season	Club	GP	G	A	Pts	PIM	GP	G	A	Pts	PIM
1929-30	Chicago Black Hawks	41	14	16	30	16	2	0	1	1	4
1930-31	Chicago Black Hawks	44	15	14	29	34	9	1	3	4	11
1931-32	Chicago Black Hawks	48	12	13	25	36	2	0	0	0	2
1932-33	Chicago Black Hawks	48	12	14	26	30	....	....	....	....	....
1933-34 ◆	Chicago Black Hawks	37	5	9	14	15	8	1	0	1	0
1934-35	Chicago Black Hawks	48	13	18	31	33	2	0	0	0	2
1935-36	Chicago Black Hawks	47	4	8	12	20	1	0	0	0	0
1936-37	Chicago Black Hawks	15	0	2	2	0	....	....	....	....	....
1937-38	Montreal Maroons	21	2	4	6	0	....	....	....	....	....
	NHL Totals	**349**	**77**	**98**	**175**	**184**	**24**	**2**	**4**	**6**	**19**

Claimed by **Chicago** from **Tulsa** (AHA) in Inter League Draft, May 13, 1929. Traded to **Cleveland** (AHL) by **Chicago** for cash, January 15, 1937. Claimed by **Mtl. Maroons** from **Cleveland** (AHL) in Inter-League Draft, May 9, 1937.

COOKE, Matt

Center. Shoots left. 5'11", 205 lbs. Born, Belleville, Ont., September 7, 1978.
(Vancouver's 8th choice, 144th overall, in 1997 Entry Draft).

Season	Club	GP	G	A	Pts	PIM	GP	G	A	Pts	PIM
1998-99	Vancouver Canucks	30	0	2	2	27	....	....	....	....	....
99-2000	Vancouver Canucks	51	5	7	12	39	....	....	....	....	....
2000-01	Vancouver Canucks	81	14	13	27	94	4	0	0	0	4
2001-02	Vancouver Canucks	82	13	20	33	111	6	3	2	5	0
2002-03	Vancouver Canucks	82	15	27	42	82	14	2	1	3	12
	NHL Totals	**326**	**47**	**69**	**116**	**353**	**24**	**5**	**3**	**8**	**16**

COOPER, Carson

Right wing. Shoots right. 5'7", 160 lbs. Born, Cornwall, Ont., July 17, 1899.

Season	Club	GP	G	A	Pts	PIM	GP	G	A	Pts	PIM
1924-25	Boston Bruins	12	5	3	8	4	....	....	....	....	....
1925-26	Boston Bruins	36	28	3	31	10	....	....	....	....	....
1926-27	Boston Bruins	10	0	0	0	0	....	....	....	....	....
	Montreal Canadiens	14	9	3	12	16	3	0	0	0	0
1927-28	Detroit Cougars	43	15	2	17	32	....	....	....	....	....
1928-29	Detroit Cougars	43	18	9	27	14	2	0	0	0	2
1929-30	Detroit Cougars	44	18	18	36	14	....	....	....	....	....
1930-31	Detroit Falcons	44	14	14	28	10	....	....	....	....	....
1931-32	Detroit Falcons	48	3	5	8	11	2	0	0	0	0
	NHL Totals	**294**	**110**	**57**	**167**	**111**	**7**	**0**	**0**	**0**	**2**

Signed as a free agent by **Boston**, November 2, 1924. • Missed majority of 1924-25 season recovering from knee injury suffered in game vs. Hamilton, December 10, 1924. Traded to **Montreal** by **Boston** for Billy Boucher with both teams holding right of recall, January 17, 1927. • Players returned to original teams, May 22, 1927. Traded to **Detroit** by **Boston** for cash, May 22, 1927.

COOPER, David

Defense. Shoots left. 6'2", 204 lbs. Born, Ottawa, Ont., November 2, 1973.
(Buffalo's 1st choice, 11th overall, in 1992 Entry Draft).

Season	Club	GP	G	A	Pts	PIM	GP	G	A	Pts	PIM
1996-97	Toronto Maple Leafs	19	3	3	6	16	....	....	....	....	....
1997-98	Toronto Maple Leafs	9	0	4	4	8	....	....	....	....	....
2000-01	Toronto Maple Leafs	2	0	0	0	0	....	....	....	....	....
	NHL Totals	**30**	**3**	**7**	**10**	**24**	....	....	....	....	....

Signed as a free agent by **Toronto**, September 26, 1996. Traded to **Calgary** by **Toronto** for Ladislav Kohn, July 2, 1998. Signed as a free agent by **Toronto**, October 16, 2000.

COOPER, Ed

Left wing. Shoots left. 5'10", 188 lbs. Born, Loon Lake, Sask., August 28, 1960.
(Colorado's 4th choice, 85th overall, in 1980 Entry Draft).

Season	Club	GP	G	A	Pts	PIM	GP	G	A	Pts	PIM
1980-81	Colorado Rockies	47	7	7	14	46	....	....	....	....	....
1981-82	Colorado Rockies	2	1	0	1	0	....	....	....	....	....
	NHL Totals	**49**	**8**	**7**	**15**	**46**	....	....	....	....	....

Traded to **Edmonton** by **Colorado** for Stan Weir, March 9, 1982. Traded to **Colorado** by **Edmonton** for Stan Weir, July 2, 1982.

COOPER, Hal

Right wing. Shoots right. 5'5", 155 lbs. Born, New Liskeard, Ont., August 29, 1915.

Season	Club	GP	G	A	Pts	PIM	GP	G	A	Pts	PIM
1944-45	New York Rangers	8	0	0	0	2	....	....	....	....	....
	NHL Totals	**8**	**0**	**0**	**0**	**2**	....	....	....	....	....

Claimed by **NY Rangers** from **Providence** (IAHL) in Inter-League Draft, May 12, 1939.

COOPER, Joe

Defense. Shoots right. 6'2", 200 lbs. Born, Winnipeg, Man., December 14, 1914.

Season	Club	GP	G	A	Pts	PIM	GP	G	A	Pts	PIM
1935-36	New York Rangers	1	0	0	0	0	....	....	....	....	....
1936-37	New York Rangers	48	0	3	3	42	9	1	1	2	12
1937-38	New York Rangers	46	3	2	5	56	3	0	0	0	4
1938-39	Chicago Black Hawks	17	3	3	6	10	....	....	....	....	....
1939-40	Chicago Black Hawks	44	4	7	11	59	2	0	0	0	0
1940-41	Chicago Black Hawks	45	5	5	10	66	5	1	0	1	8
1941-42	Chicago Black Hawks	47	6	14	20	58	3	0	2	2	2
1943-44	Chicago Black Hawks	13	1	0	1	17	9	1	1	2	18
1944-45	Chicago Black Hawks	50	4	17	21	50	....	....	....	....	....
1945-46	Chicago Black Hawks	50	2	7	9	46	4	0	1	1	14
1946-47	New York Rangers	59	2	8	10	38	....	....	....	....	....
	NHL Totals	**420**	**30**	**66**	**96**	**442**	**35**	**3**	**5**	**8**	**58**

Signed as a free agent by **NY Rangers**, October 24, 1935. Traded to **Chicago** by **NY Rangers** for Alex Levinsky and $5,000, January 16, 1939. Claimed on waivers by **Boston** from **Chicago**, September 7, 1945. Traded to **Chicago** by **Boston** for cash, October, 1945. Traded to **NY Rangers** by **Chicago** for cash, November 1, 1946. Traded to **Cleveland** (AHL) by **NY Rangers** with Ab DeMarco for cash, May 5, 1947.

COPP, Bob

Defense. Shoots left. 5'11", 180 lbs. Born, Port Elgin, N.B., November 15, 1918.

Season	Club	GP	G	A	Pts	PIM	GP	G	A	Pts	PIM
1942-43	Toronto Maple Leafs	38	3	9	12	24	....	....	....	....	....
1950-51	Toronto Maple Leafs	2	0	0	0	2	....	....	....	....	....
	NHL Totals	**40**	**3**	**9**	**12**	**26**	....	....	....	....	....

CORBEAU, Bert

Defense. Shoots right. 5'11", 200 lbs. Born, Penetanguishene, Ont., February 9, 1894.

Season	Club	GP	G	A	Pts	PIM	GP	G	A	Pts	PIM
1917-18	Montreal Canadiens	21	8	8	16	41	2	1	1	2	11
1918-19	Montreal Canadiens	16	2	3	5	51	5	1	1	2	17
	Montreal Canadiens (Cup)	....	....	....	....	....	*5*	*0*	*1*	*1*	*3*
1919-20	Montreal Canadiens	23	11	6	17	65	....	....	....	....	....
1920-21	Montreal Canadiens	24	11	2	13	*86	....	....	....	....	....
1921-22	Montreal Canadiens	22	3	7	10	26	....	....	....	....	....
1922-23	Hamilton Tigers	21	10	4	14	22	....	....	....	....	....
1923-24	Toronto St. Pats	24	8	6	14	*55	....	....	....	....	....
1924-25	Toronto St. Pats	30	4	6	10	74	2	0	0	0	10
1925-26	Toronto St. Pats	36	5	5	10	*121	....	....	....	....	....
1926-27	Toronto St. Pats/Maple Leafs	41	1	2	3	88	....	....	....	....	....
	NHL Totals	**258**	**63**	**49**	**112**	**629**	**9**	**2**	**2**	**4**	**38**

Rights retained by **Montreal** after NHA folded, November 26, 1917. Traded to **Hamilton** by **Montreal** for cash, October 1, 1922. Traded to **Toronto** by **Hamilton** with Amos Arbour and George Carey for Ken Randall, the NHL rights to Corb Denneny and cash, December 14, 1923.

CORBET, Rene

Left wing. Shoots left. 6', 195 lbs. Born, Victoriaville, Que., June 25, 1973.
(Quebec's 2nd choice, 24th overall, in 1991 Entry Draft).

Season	Club	GP	G	A	Pts	PIM	GP	G	A	Pts	PIM
1993-94	Quebec Nordiques	9	1	1	2	0	....	....	....	....	....
1994-95	Quebec Nordiques	8	0	3	3	2	2	0	1	1	0
1995-96 ◆	Colorado Avalanche	33	3	6	9	33	8	3	2	5	2
1996-97	Colorado Avalanche	76	12	15	27	67	17	2	2	4	27
1997-98	Colorado Avalanche	68	16	12	28	133	2	0	0	0	2
1998-99	Colorado Avalanche	53	8	14	22	58	....	....	....	....	....
	Calgary Flames	20	5	4	9	10	....	....	....	....	....
99-2000	Calgary Flames	48	4	10	14	60	....	....	....	....	....
	Pittsburgh Penguins	4	1	0	1	0	7	1	1	2	9
2000-01	Pittsburgh Penguins	43	8	9	17	57	17	1	0	1	12
	NHL Totals	**362**	**58**	**74**	**132**	**420**	**53**	**7**	**6**	**13**	**52**

Transferred to **Colorado** after **Quebec** franchise relocated, June 21, 1995. Traded to **Calgary** by **Colorado** with Wade Belak, Robyn Regehr and Colorado's 2nd round compensatory choice (Jarret Stoll) in 2000 Entry Draft for Theoren Fleury and Chris Dingman, February 28, 1999. Traded to **Pittsburgh** by **Calgary** with Tyler Moss for Brad Werenka, March 14, 2000.

CORBETT, Mike

Right wing/Defense. Shoots left. 6'2", 195 lbs. Born, Toronto, Ont., October 4, 1942.

Season	Club	GP	G	A	Pts	PIM	GP	G	A	Pts	PIM
		REGULAR SEASON					PLAYOFFS				
1967-68	Los Angeles Kings	....	....	....	....	....	2	0	1	1	2
	NHL Totals	....	....	....	....	....	**2**	**0**	**1**	**1**	**2**

NHL rights transferred to **Los Angeles** after NHL club purchased **Springfield** (AHL) franchise, May, 1967. Loaned to **Vancouver** (WHL) by **Los Angeles** (Springfield-AHL) with the loan of Larry Mavety and the trade of Bill Sweeney for cash, October, 1967.

CORCORAN, Norm

Center/Right wing. Shoots right. 5'10", 160 lbs. Born, Toronto, Ont., August 15, 1931.

Season	Club	GP	G	A	Pts	PIM	GP	G	A	Pts	PIM
1949-50	Boston Bruins	1	0	0	0	0	....	....	....	....	....
1952-53	Boston Bruins	1	0	0	0	0	....	....	....	....	....
1954-55	Boston Bruins	2	0	0	0	2	4	0	0	0	6
1955-56	Detroit Red Wings	2	0	0	0	0	....	....	....	....	....
	Chicago Black Hawks	23	1	3	4	19	....	....	....	....	....
	NHL Totals	**29**	**1**	**3**	**4**	**21**	**4**	**0**	**0**	**0**	**6**

Played in NHL All-Star Game (1955)

Signed as a free agent by **Boston**, March 23, 1950. Traded to **Detroit** by **Boston** with Gilles Boisvert, Real Chevrefils, Warren Godfrey and Ed Sandford for Vic Stasiuk, Marcel Bonin, Lorne Davis and Terry Sawchuk, June 3, 1955. Traded to **Chicago** by **Detroit** for Wally Blaisdell, October 4, 1955. • Deal was voided when Blaisdell was unable to report. Traded to **Chicago** by **Detroit** (Edmonton-WHL) for cash and the loan of Gord Pennell, January 17, 1956. Traded to **Toronto** (Rochester-AHL) by **Montreal** (Quebec-AHL) for Guy Rousseau, June 1, 1961. Traded to **Pittsburgh** (AHL) by **Toronto** for cash, June 2, 1961. Traded to **Providence** (AHL) by **Detroit** (Pittsburgh-AHL) for cash, August 8, 1963.

CORKUM, Bob

Center. Shoots right. 6'2", 225 lbs. Born, Salisbury, MA, December 18, 1967.
(Buffalo's 3rd choice, 47th overall, in 1986 Entry Draft).

Season	Club	GP	G	A	Pts	PIM	GP	G	A	Pts	PIM
1989-90	Buffalo Sabres	8	2	0	2	4	5	1	0	1	4
1991-92	Buffalo Sabres	20	2	4	6	21	4	1	0	1	0
1992-93	Buffalo Sabres	68	6	4	10	38	5	0	0	0	2
1993-94	Mighty Ducks of Anaheim	76	23	28	51	18	....	....	....	....	....
1994-95	Mighty Ducks of Anaheim	44	10	9	19	25	....	....	....	....	....
1995-96	Mighty Ducks of Anaheim	48	5	7	12	26	....	....	....	....	....
	Philadelphia Flyers	28	4	3	7	8	12	1	2	3	6
1996-97	Phoenix Coyotes	80	9	11	20	40	7	2	2	4	4
1997-98	Phoenix Coyotes	76	12	9	21	28	6	1	0	1	4
1998-99	Phoenix Coyotes	77	9	10	19	17	7	0	1	1	4
99-2000	Los Angeles Kings	45	5	6	11	14	4	0	0	0	0
2000-01	Los Angeles Kings	58	4	6	10	18	....	....	....	....	....
	New Jersey Devils	17	3	1	4	4	12	1	2	3	0
2001-02	Atlanta Thrashers	65	3	4	7	16	....	....	....	....	....
	Buffalo Sabres	10	0	1	1	4	....	....	....	....	....
	NHL Totals	**720**	**97**	**103**	**200**	**281**	**62**	**7**	**7**	**14**	**24**

Claimed by **Anaheim** from **Buffalo** in Expansion Draft, June 24, 1993. Traded to **Philadelphia** by **Anaheim** for Chris Herperger and Winnipeg's 7th round choice (previously acquired, Anaheim selected Tony Mohagen) in 1997 Entry Draft, February 6, 1996. Claimed by **Phoenix** from **Philadelphia** in Waiver Draft, September 30, 1996. Signed as a free agent by **Los Angeles**, December 28, 1999. Traded to **New Jersey** by **Los Angeles** for future considerations (Steve Kelly, February 27, 2001), February 23, 2001. Signed as a free agent by **Atlanta**, July 16, 2001. Traded to **Buffalo** by **Atlanta** for Buffalo's 5th round choice (Paul Flache) in 2002 Entry Draft, March 19, 2002.

CORMIER, Roger

Right wing. Shoots right. 5'10", 167 lbs. Born, Montreal, Que., March 23, 1905.

Season	Club	GP	G	A	Pts	PIM	GP	G	A	Pts	PIM
1925-26	Montreal Canadiens	1	0	0	0	0	....	....	....	....	....
	NHL Totals	**1**	**0**	**0**	**0**	**0**	....	....	....	....	....

Signed as a free agent by **Montreal**, January 15, 1926.

CORNFORTH, Mark

Defense. Shoots left. 6'1", 193 lbs. Born, Montreal, Que., November 13, 1972.

Season	Club	GP	G	A	Pts	PIM	GP	G	A	Pts	PIM
1995-96	Boston Bruins	6	0	0	0	4	....	....	....	....	....
	NHL Totals	**6**	**0**	**0**	**0**	**4**	....	....	....	....	....

Signed as a free agent by **Boston**, October 6, 1995.

CORRIGAN, Chuck

Right wing. Shoots right. 6'2", 192 lbs. Born, Moosomin, Sask., May 22, 1916.

Season	Club	GP	G	A	Pts	PIM	GP	G	A	Pts	PIM
1937-38	Toronto Maple Leafs	3	0	0	0	0	....	....	....	....	....
1940-41	New York Americans	16	2	2	4	2	....	....	....	....	....
	NHL Totals	**19**	**2**	**2**	**4**	**2**	....	....	....	....	....

Signed as a free agent by **Toronto**, October 17, 1937. Signed as a free agent by **NY Americans**, January 30, 1941. • Team name changed to **Brooklyn Americans** prior to 1941-42 season.

CORRIGAN, Mike

Left wing. Shoots left. 5'10", 175 lbs. Born, Ottawa, Ont., January 11, 1946.

Season	Club	GP	G	A	Pts	PIM	GP	G	A	Pts	PIM
1967-68	Los Angeles Kings	5	0	0	0	2	....	....	....	....	....
1969-70	Los Angeles Kings	36	6	4	10	30	....	....	....	....	....
1970-71	Vancouver Canucks	76	21	28	49	103	....	....	....	....	....
1971-72	Vancouver Canucks	19	3	4	7	25	....	....	....	....	....
	Los Angeles Kings	56	12	22	34	95	....	....	....	....	....
1972-73	Los Angeles Kings	78	37	30	67	146	....	....	....	....	....
1973-74	Los Angeles Kings	75	16	26	42	119	3	0	1	1	4
1974-75	Los Angeles Kings	80	13	21	34	61	3	0	0	0	4
1975-76	Los Angeles Kings	71	22	21	43	71	9	2	2	4	12
1976-77	Pittsburgh Penguins	73	14	27	41	36	2	0	0	0	0
1977-78	Pittsburgh Penguins	25	8	12	20	10	....	....	....	....	....
	NHL Totals	**594**	**152**	**195**	**347**	**698**	**17**	**2**	**3**	**5**	**20**

Claimed by **Los Angeles** from **Toronto** in Expansion Draft, June 6, 1967. Claimed by **Vancouver** from **Los Angeles** in Expansion Draft, June 10, 1970. Claimed on waivers by **Los Angeles** from **Vancouver**, November 22, 1971. Traded to **Pittsburgh** by **Los Angeles** for Pittsburgh's 5th round choice (Julian Baretta) in 1977 Amateur Draft, October 18, 1976.

CORRINET, Chris

Right wing. Shoots right. 6'3", 220 lbs. Born, Derby, CT, October 29, 1978.
(Washington's 4th choice, 107th overall, in 1998 Entry Draft).

Season	Club	GP	G	A	Pts	PIM	GP	G	A	Pts	PIM
2001-02	Washington Capitals	8	0	1	1	6	....	....	....	....	....
	NHL Totals	**8**	**0**	**1**	**1**	**6**	....	....	....	....	....

CORRIVEAU, Andre

Right wing. Shoots left. 5'8", 135 lbs. Born, Grand'Mere, Que., May 15, 1928.

Season	Club	GP	G	A	Pts	PIM	GP	G	A	Pts	PIM
1953-54	Montreal Canadiens	3	0	1	1	0	....	....	....	....	....
	NHL Totals	**3**	**0**	**1**	**1**	**0**	....	....	....	....	....

CORRIVEAU, Yvon

Left wing. Shoots left. 6'1", 195 lbs. Born, Welland, Ont., February 8, 1967.
(Washington's 1st choice, 19th overall, in 1985 Entry Draft).

Season	Club	GP	G	A	Pts	PIM	GP	G	A	Pts	PIM
1985-86	Washington Capitals	2	0	0	0	0	4	0	3	3	2
1986-87	Washington Capitals	17	1	1	2	24	....	....	....	....	....
1987-88	Washington Capitals	44	10	9	19	84	13	1	2	3	30
1988-89	Washington Capitals	33	3	2	5	62	1	0	0	0	0
1989-90	Washington Capitals	50	9	6	15	50	....	....	....	....	....
	Hartford Whalers	13	4	1	5	22	4	1	0	1	0
1990-91	Hartford Whalers	23	1	1	2	18	....	....	....	....	....
1991-92	Hartford Whalers	38	12	8	20	36	7	3	2	5	18
1992-93	San Jose Sharks	20	3	7	10	0	....	....	....	....	....
	Hartford Whalers	37	5	5	10	14	....	....	....	....	....
1993-94	Hartford Whalers	3	0	0	0	0	....	....	....	....	....
	NHL Totals	**280**	**48**	**40**	**88**	**310**	**29**	**5**	**7**	**12**	**50**

Traded to **Hartford** by **Washington** for Mike Liut, March 6, 1990. Traded to **Washington** by **Hartford** to complete June 15, 1992 deal in which Mark Hunter and future considerations were traded to Washington for Nick Kypreos, August 20, 1992. Claimed by **San Jose** from **Washington** in Waiver Draft, October 4, 1992. Traded to **Hartford** by **San Jose** to complete October 9, 1992 trade in which Michel Picard was traded to San Jose for future considerations, January 21, 1993.

CORSO, Daniel

Center. Shoots left. 5'10", 187 lbs. Born, Montreal, Que., April 3, 1978.
(St. Louis' 6th choice, 169th overall, in 1996 Entry Draft).

Season	Club	GP	G	A	Pts	PIM	GP	G	A	Pts	PIM
2000-01	St. Louis Blues	28	10	3	13	14	12	0	1	1	0
2001-02	St. Louis Blues	41	4	7	11	6	2	0	0	0	0
2002-03	St. Louis Blues	1	0	0	0	0	....	....	....	....	....
	NHL Totals	**70**	**14**	**10**	**24**	**20**	**14**	**0**	**1**	**1**	**0**

• Spent majority of 2001-02 season on practice roster, October 22, 2001.

CORSON, Shayne

Left wing. Shoots left. 6'1", 202 lbs. Born, Barrie, Ont., August 13, 1966.
(Montreal's 2nd choice, 8th overall, in 1984 Entry Draft).

Season	Club	GP	G	A	Pts	PIM	GP	G	A	Pts	PIM
1985-86	Montreal Canadiens	3	0	0	0	2	....	....	....	....	....
1986-87	Montreal Canadiens	55	12	11	23	144	17	6	5	11	30
1987-88	Montreal Canadiens	71	12	27	39	152	3	1	0	1	12
1988-89	Montreal Canadiens	80	26	24	50	193	21	4	5	9	65
1989-90	Montreal Canadiens	76	31	44	75	144	11	2	8	10	20
1990-91	Montreal Canadiens	71	23	24	47	138	13	9	6	15	36
1991-92	Montreal Canadiens	64	17	36	53	118	10	2	5	7	15
1992-93	Edmonton Oilers	80	16	31	47	209	....	....	....	....	....
1993-94	Edmonton Oilers	64	25	29	54	118	....	....	....	....	....
1994-95	Edmonton Oilers	48	12	24	36	86	....	....	....	....	....
1995-96	St. Louis Blues	77	18	28	46	192	13	8	6	14	22
1996-97	St. Louis Blues	11	2	1	3	24	....	....	....	....	....
	Montreal Canadiens	47	6	15	21	80	5	1	0	1	4
1997-98	Montreal Canadiens	62	21	34	55	108	10	3	6	9	26
1998-99	Montreal Canadiens	63	12	20	32	147	....	....	....	....	....
99-2000	Montreal Canadiens	70	8	20	28	115	....	....	....	....	....
2000-01	Toronto Maple Leafs	77	8	18	26	189	11	1	1	2	14
2001-02	Toronto Maple Leafs	74	12	21	33	120	19	1	6	7	33
2002-03	Toronto Maple Leafs	46	7	8	15	49	2	0	0	0	2
	NHL Totals	**1139**	**268**	**415**	**683**	**2328**	**135**	**38**	**48**	**86**	**279**

Played in NHL All-Star Game (1990, 1994, 1998)

Traded to **Edmonton** by **Montreal** with Brent Gilchrist and Vladimir Vujtek for Vincent Damphousse and Edmonton's 4th round choice (Adam Wiesel) in 1993 Entry Draft, August 27, 1992. Signed as a free agent by **St. Louis**, July 28, 1995. Traded to **Montreal** by **St. Louis** with Murray Baron and St. Louis' 5th round choice (Gennady Razin) in 1997 Entry Draft for Pierre Turgeon, Rory Fitzpatrick and Craig Conroy, October 29, 1996. Signed as a free agent by **Toronto**, July 4, 2000.

CORVO, Joe

Defense. Shoots right. 6', 205 lbs. Born, Oak Park, IL, June 20, 1977.
(Los Angeles' 4th choice, 83rd overall, in 1997 Entry Draft).

Season	Club	GP	G	A	Pts	PIM	GP	G	A	Pts	PIM
2002-03	Los Angeles Kings	50	5	7	12	14	....	....	....	....	....
	NHL Totals	**50**	**5**	**7**	**12**	**14**	....	....	....	....	....

CORY, Ross

Defense. Shoots left. 6'2", 195 lbs. Born, Calgary, Alta., February 4, 1957.

Season	Club	Regular Season GP	G	A	Pts	PIM	Playoffs GP	G	A	Pts	PIM
1979-80	Winnipeg Jets	46	2	9	11	32	....	....	....	....	....
1980-81	Winnipeg Jets	5	0	1	1	9	....	....	....	....	....
	NHL Totals	**51**	**2**	**10**	**12**	**41**	....	....	....	....	....

Signed as a free agent by **Winnipeg**, October 1, 1979.

COSSETTE, Jacques

Right wing. Shoots right. 5'9", 185 lbs. Born, Rouyn, Que., June 20, 1954.
(Pittsburgh's 2nd choice, 27th overall, in 1974 Amateur Draft).

Season	Club	Regular Season GP	G	A	Pts	PIM	Playoffs GP	G	A	Pts	PIM
1975-76	Pittsburgh Penguins	7	0	2	2	9	....	....	....	....	....
1977-78	Pittsburgh Penguins	19	1	2	3	4	....	....	....	....	....
1978-79	Pittsburgh Penguins	38	7	2	9	16	3	0	1	1	4
	NHL Totals	**64**	**8**	**6**	**14**	**29**	**3**	**0**	**1**	**1**	**4**

COSTELLO, Les

Left wing. Shoots left. 5'8", 158 lbs. Born, South Porcupine, Ont., February 16, 1928.

Season	Club	Regular Season GP	G	A	Pts	PIM	Playoffs GP	G	A	Pts	PIM
1947-48 ♦	Toronto Maple Leafs	....	....	....	....	....	5	2	2	4	2
1948-49	Toronto Maple Leafs	15	2	3	5	11	....	....	....	....	....
1949-50	Toronto Maple Leafs	....	....	....	....	....	1	0	0	0	0
	NHL Totals	**15**	**2**	**3**	**5**	**11**	**6**	**2**	**2**	**4**	**2**

• Brother of Murray

Played in NHL All-Star Game (1948)

• Retired from NHL to begin Seminary studies, May, 1950.

COSTELLO, Murray

Center. Shoots right. 6'3", 190 lbs. Born, South Porcupine, Ont., February 24, 1934.

Season	Club	Regular Season GP	G	A	Pts	PIM	Playoffs GP	G	A	Pts	PIM
1953-54	Chicago Black Hawks	40	3	2	5	6	....	....	....	....	....
1954-55	Boston Bruins	54	4	11	15	25	1	0	0	0	2
1955-56	Boston Bruins	41	6	6	12	19	....	....	....	....	....
	Detroit Red Wings	24	0	0	0	4	4	0	0	0	0
1956-57	Detroit Red Wings	3	0	0	0	0	....	....	....	....	....
	NHL Totals	**162**	**13**	**19**	**32**	**54**	**5**	**0**	**0**	**0**	**2**

• Brother of Les

Traded to **Boston** by **Chicago** for Frank Martin, October 4, 1954. Traded to **Detroit** by **Boston** with Lorne Ferguson for Real Chevrefils and Jerry Toppazzini, January 17, 1956.

COSTELLO, Rich

Center. Shoots right. 6', 175 lbs. Born, Farmington, MA, June 27, 1963.
(Philadelphia's 2nd choice, 37th overall, in 1981 Entry Draft).

Season	Club	Regular Season GP	G	A	Pts	PIM	Playoffs GP	G	A	Pts	PIM
1983-84	Toronto Maple Leafs	10	2	1	3	2	....	....	....	....	....
1985-86	Toronto Maple Leafs	2	0	1	1	0	....	....	....	....	....
	NHL Totals	**12**	**2**	**2**	**4**	**2**	....	....	....	....	....

Rights traded to **Toronto** by **Philadelphia** with Hartford's 2nd round choice (previously acquired, Toronto selected Peter Ihnacak) in 1982 Entry Draft and future considerations (Ken Strong, May, 1982) for Darryl Sittler, January 20, 1982.

COTCH, Charlie

Left wing. Shoots left. 5'11", 175 lbs. Born, Sarnia, Ont., 1902.

Season	Club	Regular Season GP	G	A	Pts	PIM	Playoffs GP	G	A	Pts	PIM
1924-25	Hamilton Tigers	7	1	0	1	0	....	....	....	....	....
	Toronto St. Pats	5	0	0	0	0	....	....	....	....	....
	NHL Totals	**12**	**1**	**0**	**1**	**0**	....	....	....	....	....

Traded to **Montreal** by **Vancouver** (PCHA) for Bobby Boucher, March 26, 1924. Rights traded to **Hamilton** by **Montreal** for cash, December 24, 1924. Signed as a free agent by **Toronto**, February 9, 1925.

COTE, Alain

Defense. Shoots right. 6', 207 lbs. Born, Montmagny, Que., April 14, 1967.
(Boston's 1st choice, 31st overall, in 1985 Entry Draft).

Season	Club	Regular Season GP	G	A	Pts	PIM	Playoffs GP	G	A	Pts	PIM
1985-86	Boston Bruins	32	0	6	6	14	....	....	....	....	....
1986-87	Boston Bruins	3	0	0	0	0	....	....	....	....	....
1987-88	Boston Bruins	2	0	0	0	0	....	....	....	....	....
1988-89	Boston Bruins	31	2	3	5	51	....	....	....	....	....
1989-90	Washington Capitals	2	0	0	0	7	....	....	....	....	....
1990-91	Montreal Canadiens	28	0	6	6	26	11	0	2	2	26
1991-92	Montreal Canadiens	13	0	3	3	22	....	....	....	....	....
1992-93	Tampa Bay Lightning	2	0	0	0	0	....	....	....	....	....
1993-94	Quebec Nordiques	6	0	0	0	4	....	....	....	....	....
	NHL Totals	**119**	**2**	**18**	**20**	**124**	**11**	**0**	**2**	**2**	**26**

Traded to **Washington** by **Boston** for Bobby Gould, September 28, 1989. Traded to **Montreal** by **Washington** for Marc Deschamps, June 22, 1990. Traded to **Tampa Bay** by **Montreal** with Eric Charron and future considerations (Donald Dufresne, June 18, 1993) for Rob Ramage, March 20, 1993. Signed as a free agent by **Quebec**, July 2, 1993.

COTE, Alain

Left wing. Shoots left. 5'10", 203 lbs. Born, Matau, Que., May 3, 1957.
(Montreal's 4th choice, 43rd overall, in 1977 Amateur Draft).

Season	Club	Regular Season GP	G	A	Pts	PIM	Playoffs GP	G	A	Pts	PIM
1979-80	Quebec Nordiques	41	5	11	16	13	....	....	....	....	....
1980-81	Quebec Nordiques	51	8	18	26	64	4	0	0	0	6
1981-82	Quebec Nordiques	79	15	16	31	82	16	1	2	3	8
1982-83	Quebec Nordiques	79	12	28	40	45	4	0	3	3	0
1983-84	Quebec Nordiques	77	19	24	43	41	9	0	2	2	17
1984-85	Quebec Nordiques	80	13	22	35	31	18	5	5	10	11
1985-86	Quebec Nordiques	78	13	21	34	29	3	1	0	1	0
1986-87	Quebec Nordiques	80	12	24	36	38	13	2	3	5	2
1987-88	Quebec Nordiques	76	4	18	22	26	....	....	....	....	....
1988-89	Quebec Nordiques	55	2	8	10	14	....	....	....	....	....
	NHL Totals	**696**	**103**	**190**	**293**	**383**	**67**	**9**	**15**	**24**	**44**

Reclaimed by **Montreal** from **Quebec** prior to Expansion Draft, June 9, 1979. Claimed by **Quebec** from **Montreal** in Expansion Draft, June 13, 1979.

COTE, Patrick

Left wing. Shoots left. 6'3", 220 lbs. Born, LaSalle, Que., January 24, 1975.
(Dallas' 2nd choice, 37th overall, in 1995 Entry Draft).

Season	Club	Regular Season GP	G	A	Pts	PIM	Playoffs GP	G	A	Pts	PIM
1995-96	Dallas Stars	2	0	0	0	5	....	....	....	....	....
1996-97	Dallas Stars	3	0	0	0	27	....	....	....	....	....
1997-98	Dallas Stars	3	0	0	0	15	....	....	....	....	....
1998-99	Nashville Predators	70	1	2	3	242	....	....	....	....	....
99-2000	Nashville Predators	21	0	0	0	70	....	....	....	....	....
2000-01	Edmonton Oilers	6	0	0	0	18	....	....	....	....	....
	NHL Totals	**105**	**1**	**2**	**3**	**377**	....	....	....	....	....

Claimed by **Nashville** from **Dallas** in Expansion Draft, June 26, 1998. Traded to **Edmonton** by **Nashville** for Phoenix's 5th round choice (previously acquired, Nashville selected Matt Koalska) in 2000 Entry Draft, June 12, 2000.

COTE, Ray

Center. Shoots right. 5'11", 170 lbs. Born, Pincher Creek, Alta., May 31, 1961.

Season	Club	Regular Season GP	G	A	Pts	PIM	Playoffs GP	G	A	Pts	PIM
1982-83	Edmonton Oilers	....	....	....	....	....	14	3	2	5	0
1983-84	Edmonton Oilers	13	0	0	0	2	....	....	....	....	....
1984-85	Edmonton Oilers	2	0	0	0	2	....	....	....	....	....
	NHL Totals	**15**	**0**	**0**	**0**	**4**	**14**	**3**	**2**	**5**	**0**

Signed as a free agent by **Edmonton**, October 6, 1981.

COTE, Sylvain

Defense. Shoots right. 5'11", 201 lbs. Born, Quebec City, Que., January 19, 1966.
(Hartford's 1st choice, 11th overall, in 1984 Entry Draft).

Season	Club	Regular Season GP	G	A	Pts	PIM	Playoffs GP	G	A	Pts	PIM
1984-85	Hartford Whalers	67	3	9	12	17	....	....	....	....	....
1985-86	Hartford Whalers	2	0	0	0	0	....	....	....	....	....
1986-87	Hartford Whalers	67	2	8	10	20	2	0	2	2	2
1987-88	Hartford Whalers	67	7	21	28	30	6	1	1	2	4
1988-89	Hartford Whalers	78	8	9	17	49	3	0	1	1	4
1989-90	Hartford Whalers	28	4	2	6	14	5	0	0	0	2
1990-91	Hartford Whalers	73	7	12	19	17	6	0	2	2	2
1991-92	Washington Capitals	78	11	29	40	31	7	1	2	3	4
1992-93	Washington Capitals	77	21	29	50	34	6	1	1	2	4
1993-94	Washington Capitals	84	16	35	51	66	9	1	8	9	6
1994-95	Washington Capitals	47	5	14	19	53	7	1	3	4	2
1995-96	Washington Capitals	81	5	33	38	40	6	2	0	2	12
1996-97	Washington Capitals	57	6	18	24	28	....	....	....	....	....
1997-98	Washington Capitals	59	1	15	16	36	....	....	....	....	....
	Toronto Maple Leafs	12	3	6	9	6	....	....	....	....	....
1998-99	Toronto Maple Leafs	79	5	24	29	28	17	2	1	3	10
99-2000	Toronto Maple Leafs	3	0	1	1	0	....	....	....	....	....
	Chicago Blackhawks	45	6	18	24	14	....	....	....	....	....
	Dallas Stars	28	2	8	10	14	23	2	1	3	8
2000-01	Washington Capitals	68	7	11	18	18	5	0	0	0	2
2001-02	Washington Capitals	70	3	11	14	26	....	....	....	....	....
2002-03	Washington Capitals	1	0	0	0	4	....	....	....	....	....
	NHL Totals	**1171**	**122**	**313**	**435**	**545**	**102**	**11**	**22**	**33**	**62**

Traded to **Washington** by **Hartford** for Washington's 2nd round choice (Andrei Nikolishin) in 1992 Entry Draft, September 8, 1991. Traded to **Toronto** by **Washington** for Jeff Brown, March 24, 1998. Traded to **Chicago** by **Toronto** for Chicago's 2nd round choice (Karel Pilar) in 2001 Entry Draft, October 8, 1999. Traded to **Dallas** by **Chicago** with Dave Manson for Kevin Dean, Derek Plante and Dallas' 2nd round choice (Matt Keith) in 2001 Entry Draft, February 8, 2000. Signed as a free agent by **Washington**, July 7, 2000.

COTTON, Baldy

Left wing. Shoots left. 5'10", 155 lbs. Born, Nanticoke, Ont., November 5, 1902.

Season	Club	Regular Season GP	G	A	Pts	PIM	Playoffs GP	G	A	Pts	PIM
1925-26	Pittsburgh Pirates	33	7	1	8	22	2	1	0	1	0
1926-27	Pittsburgh Pirates	37	5	0	5	17	....	....	....	....	....
1927-28	Pittsburgh Pirates	42	9	3	12	40	2	1	1	2	2
1928-29	Pittsburgh Pirates	32	3	2	5	38	....	....	....	....	....
	Toronto Maple Leafs	11	1	2	3	8	4	0	0	0	2
1929-30	Toronto Maple Leafs	41	21	17	38	47	....	....	....	....	....
1930-31	Toronto Maple Leafs	43	12	17	29	45	2	0	0	0	2
1931-32 ♦	Toronto Maple Leafs	48	5	13	18	41	7	2	2	4	8
1932-33	Toronto Maple Leafs	48	10	11	21	29	9	0	3	3	6
1933-34	Toronto Maple Leafs	47	8	14	22	46	5	0	2	2	0
1934-35	Toronto Maple Leafs	47	11	14	25	36	7	0	0	0	17
1935-36	New York Americans	45	7	9	16	27	5	0	1	1	9
1936-37	New York Americans	29	2	0	2	23	....	....	....	....	....
	NHL Totals	**503**	**101**	**103**	**204**	**419**	**43**	**4**	**9**	**13**	**46**

Played in NHL All-Star Game (1934)

Signed as a free agent by **Pittsburgh**, September 26, 1925. Traded to **Toronto** by **Pittsburgh** for Gerry Lowrey and $9,500, February 12, 1929. Traded to **NY Americans** by **Toronto** for cash, October 9, 1935.

COUGHLIN, Jack

Right wing. Shoots right. 5'10", 170 lbs. Born, Douro, Ont., June 6, 1892.

Season	Club	GP	G	A	Pts	PIM	GP	G	A	Pts	PIM
		REGULAR SEASON					PLAYOFFS				
1917-18 ♦	Toronto Arenas	5	2	0	2	3	....	....	....	....	....
1919-20	Quebec Bulldogs	9	0	0	0	0	....	....	....	....	....
	Montreal Canadiens	3	0	0	0	0	....	....	....	....	....
1920-21	Hamilton Tigers	2	0	0	0	0	....	....	....	....	....
	NHL Totals	**19**	**2**	**0**	**2**	**3**	....	....	....	....	....

Signed as a free agent by **Toronto**, December 5, 1917. Signed as a free agent by **Quebec**, January 13, 1920. Signed as a free agent by **Montreal**, February 18, 1920. Traded to **Hamilton** by **Montreal** with Goldie Prodgers, Joe Matte and loan of Billy Coutu for 1920-21 season for Harry Mummery, Jack McDonald and Dave Ritchie, November 27, 1920.

COULIS, Tim

Left wing. Shoots left. 6', 200 lbs. Born, Kenora, Ont., February 24, 1958.
(Washington's 2nd choice, 18th overall, in 1978 Amateur Draft).

Season	Club	GP	G	A	Pts	PIM	GP	G	A	Pts	PIM
1979-80	Washington Capitals	19	1	2	3	27	....	....	....	....	....
1983-84	Minnesota North Stars	2	0	0	0	4	....	....	....	....	....
1984-85	Minnesota North Stars	7	1	1	2	34	3	1	0	1	2
1985-86	Minnesota North Stars	19	2	2	4	73	....	....	....	....	....
	NHL Totals	**47**	**4**	**5**	**9**	**138**	**3**	**1**	**0**	**1**	**2**

Traded to **Toronto** by **Washington** with Robert Picard and Washington's 2nd round choice (Bob McGill) in 1980 Entry Draft for Mike Palmateer and Toronto's 3rd round choice (Torrie Robertson) in 1980 Entry Draft, June 11, 1980. Signed as a free agent by **Vancouver**, October 13, 1981. Signed as a free agent by **Minnesota**, July 2, 1983.

COULSON, D'arcy

Defense. Shoots right. 5'11", 175 lbs. Born, Sudbury, Ont., February 17, 1908.

Season	Club	GP	G	A	Pts	PIM	GP	G	A	Pts	PIM
1930-31	Philadelphia Quakers	28	0	0	0	103	....	....	....	....	....
	NHL Totals	**28**	**0**	**0**	**0**	**103**	....	....	....	....	....

Signed as a free agent by **Philadelphia**, December 15, 1930. Loaned to **Mtl. Maroons** after **Philadelphia** franchise folded, September 12, 1931. Claimed by **Montreal** from **Philadelphia** in Dispersal Draft, November 26, 1931.

COULTER, Art

HHOF

Defense. Shoots right. 5'11", 185 lbs. Born, Winnipeg, Man., May 31, 1909.

Season	Club	GP	G	A	Pts	PIM	GP	G	A	Pts	PIM
1931-32	Chicago Black Hawks	13	0	1	1	23	2	1	0	1	0
1932-33	Chicago Black Hawks	46	3	2	5	53	....	....	....	....	....
1933-34 ♦	Chicago Black Hawks	46	5	2	7	39	8	1	0	1	10
1934-35	Chicago Black Hawks	48	4	8	12	68	2	0	0	0	5
1935-36	Chicago Black Hawks	25	0	2	2	18	....	....	....	....	....
	New York Rangers	23	1	5	6	26	....	....	....	....	....
1936-37	New York Rangers	47	1	5	6	27	9	0	3	3	15
1937-38	New York Rangers	43	5	10	15	90	....	....	....	....	....
1938-39	New York Rangers	44	4	8	12	58	7	1	1	2	6
1939-40 ♦	New York Rangers	48	1	9	10	68	12	1	0	1	21
1940-41	New York Rangers	35	5	14	19	42	3	0	0	0	0
1941-42	New York Rangers	47	1	16	17	31	6	0	1	1	4
	NHL Totals	**465**	**30**	**82**	**112**	**543**	**49**	**4**	**5**	**9**	**61**

NHL Second All-Star Team (1935, 1938, 1939, 1940)
Played in NHL All-Star Game (1939)

Traded to **Chicago** by **Philadelphia** (Can-Am) for cash and the loan of Frank Ingram, February, 1932. Traded to **NY Rangers** by **Chicago** for Earl Seibert, January 15, 1936.

COULTER, Neal

Right wing. Shoots right. 6'2", 190 lbs. Born, London, Ont., January 2, 1963.
(NY Islanders' 4th choice, 63rd overall, in 1981 Entry Draft).

Season	Club	GP	G	A	Pts	PIM	GP	G	A	Pts	PIM
1985-86	New York Islanders	16	3	4	7	4	....	....	....	....	....
1986-87	New York Islanders	9	2	1	3	7	....	....	....	....	....
1987-88	New York Islanders	1	0	0	0	0	....	....	....	....	....
	NHL Totals	**26**	**5**	**5**	**10**	**11**	....	....	....	....	....

COURNOYER, Yvan

HHOF

Right wing. Shoots left. 5'7", 178 lbs. Born, Drummondville, Que., November 22, 1943.

Season	Club	GP	G	A	Pts	PIM	GP	G	A	Pts	PIM
1963-64	Montreal Canadiens	5	4	0	4	0	....	....	....	....	....
1964-65 ♦	Montreal Canadiens	55	7	10	17	10	12	3	1	4	0
1965-66 ♦	Montreal Canadiens	65	18	11	29	8	10	2	3	5	2
1966-67	Montreal Canadiens	69	25	15	40	14	10	2	3	5	6
1967-68 ♦	Montreal Canadiens	64	28	32	60	23	13	6	8	14	4
1968-69 ♦	Montreal Canadiens	76	43	44	87	31	14	4	7	11	5
1969-70	Montreal Canadiens	72	27	36	63	23	....	....	....	....	....
1970-71 ♦	Montreal Canadiens	65	37	36	73	21	20	10	12	22	6
1971-72	Montreal Canadiens	73	47	36	83	15	6	2	1	3	2
1972-73 ♦	Montreal Canadiens	67	40	39	79	18	17	*15	10	*25	2
1973-74	Montreal Canadiens	67	40	33	73	18	6	5	2	7	2
1974-75	Montreal Canadiens	76	29	45	74	32	11	5	6	11	4
1975-76 ♦	Montreal Canadiens	71	32	36	68	20	13	3	6	9	4
1976-77 ♦	Montreal Canadiens	60	25	28	53	8	....	....	....	....	....
1977-78 ♦	Montreal Canadiens	68	24	29	53	12	15	7	4	11	10
1978-79 ♦	Montreal Canadiens	15	2	5	7	2	....	....	....	....	....
	NHL Totals	**968**	**428**	**435**	**863**	**255**	**147**	**64**	**63**	**127**	**47**

NHL Second All-Star Team (1969, 1971, 1972, 1973) • Conn Smythe Trophy (1973)
Played in NHL All-Star Game (1967, 1971, 1972, 1973, 1974, 1978)
• Missed remainder of 1978-79 season recovering from eventual career-ending back surgery, December, 1978.

COURTEAU, Yves

Right wing. Shoots left. 6', 195 lbs. Born, Montreal, Que., April 25, 1964.
(Detroit's 2nd choice, 23rd overall, in 1982 Entry Draft).

Season	Club	GP	G	A	Pts	PIM	GP	G	A	Pts	PIM
1984-85	Calgary Flames	14	1	4	5	4	....	....	....	....	....
1985-86	Calgary Flames	4	1	1	2	0	1	0	0	0	0
1986-87	Hartford Whalers	4	0	0	0	0	....	....	....	....	....
	NHL Totals	**22**	**2**	**5**	**7**	**4**	**1**	**0**	**0**	**0**	**0**

Rights traded to **Calgary** by **Detroit** for Bobby Francis, December 2, 1982. Traded to **Hartford** by **Calgary** for Mark Paterson, October 7, 1986. • Suffered eventual career-ending stomach injury in training camp, October, 1987.

COURTENAY, Ed

Right wing. Shoots right. 6'4", 215 lbs. Born, Verdun, Que., February 2, 1968.

Season	Club	GP	G	A	Pts	PIM	GP	G	A	Pts	PIM
1991-92	San Jose Sharks	5	0	0	0	0	....	....	....	....	....
1992-93	San Jose Sharks	39	7	13	20	10	....	....	....	....	....
	NHL Totals	**44**	**7**	**13**	**20**	**10**	....	....	....	....	....

Signed as a free agent by **Minnesota**, October 1, 1989. Claimed by **San Jose** from **Minnesota** in Dispersal Draft, May 30, 1991.

COURTNALL, Geoff

Left wing. Shoots left. 6'1", 204 lbs. Born, Duncan, B.C., August 18, 1962.

Season	Club	GP	G	A	Pts	PIM	GP	G	A	Pts	PIM
1983-84	Boston Bruins	4	0	0	0	0	....	....	....	....	....
1984-85	Boston Bruins	64	12	16	28	82	5	0	2	2	7
1985-86	Boston Bruins	64	21	16	37	61	3	0	0	0	2
1986-87	Boston Bruins	65	13	23	36	117	1	0	0	0	0
1987-88	Boston Bruins	62	32	26	58	108	....	....	....	....	....
	♦ Edmonton Oilers	12	4	4	8	15	19	0	3	3	23
1988-89	Washington Capitals	79	42	38	80	112	6	2	5	7	12
1989-90	Washington Capitals	80	35	39	74	104	15	4	9	13	32
1990-91	St. Louis Blues	66	27	30	57	56	....	....	....	....	....
	Vancouver Canucks	11	6	2	8	8	6	3	5	8	4
1991-92	Vancouver Canucks	70	23	34	57	116	12	6	8	14	20
1992-93	Vancouver Canucks	84	31	46	77	167	12	4	10	14	12
1993-94	Vancouver Canucks	82	26	44	70	123	24	9	10	19	51
1994-95	Vancouver Canucks	45	16	18	34	81	11	4	2	6	34
1995-96	St. Louis Blues	69	24	16	40	101	13	0	3	3	14
1996-97	St. Louis Blues	82	17	40	57	86	6	3	1	4	23
1997-98	St. Louis Blues	79	31	31	62	94	10	2	8	10	18
1998-99	St. Louis Blues	24	5	7	12	28	13	2	4	6	10
99-2000	St. Louis Blues	6	2	2	4	6	....	....	....	....	....
	NHL Totals	**1048**	**367**	**432**	**799**	**1465**	**156**	**39**	**70**	**109**	**262**

• Brother of Russ

Signed as a free agent by **Boston**, July 6, 1983. Traded to **Edmonton** by **Boston** with Bill Ranford and Boston's 2nd round choice (Petro Koivunen) in 1988 Entry Draft for Andy Moog, March 8, 1988. Rights traded to **Washington** by **Edmonton** for Greg C. Adams, July 22, 1988. Traded to **St. Louis** by **Washington** for Peter Zezel and Mike Lalor, July 13, 1990. Traded to **Vancouver** by **St. Louis** with Robert Dirk, Sergio Momesso, Cliff Ronning and St. Louis' 5th round choice (Brian Loney) in 1992 Entry Draft for Dan Quinn and Garth Butcher, March 5, 1991. Signed as a free agent by **St. Louis**, July 14, 1995. • Suffered eventual career-ending head injury in game vs. San Jose, November 27, 1998. • Officially announced retirement, November 18, 1999.

COURTNALL, Russ

Right wing. Shoots right. 5'11", 185 lbs. Born, Duncan, B.C., June 2, 1965.
(Toronto's 1st choice, 7th overall, in 1983 Entry Draft).

Season	Club	GP	G	A	Pts	PIM	GP	G	A	Pts	PIM
1983-84	Toronto Maple Leafs	14	3	9	12	6	....	....	....	....	....
1984-85	Toronto Maple Leafs	69	12	10	22	44	....	....	....	....	....
1985-86	Toronto Maple Leafs	73	22	38	60	52	10	3	6	9	8
1986-87	Toronto Maple Leafs	79	29	44	73	90	13	3	4	7	11
1987-88	Toronto Maple Leafs	65	23	26	49	47	6	2	1	3	0
1988-89	Toronto Maple Leafs	9	1	1	2	4	....	....	....	....	....
	Montreal Canadiens	64	22	17	39	15	21	8	5	13	18
1989-90	Montreal Canadiens	80	27	32	59	27	11	5	1	6	10
1990-91	Montreal Canadiens	79	26	50	76	29	13	8	3	11	7
1991-92	Montreal Canadiens	27	7	14	21	6	10	1	1	2	4
1992-93	Minnesota North Stars	84	36	43	79	49	....	....	....	....	....
1993-94	Dallas Stars	84	23	57	80	59	9	1	8	9	0
1994-95	Dallas Stars	32	7	10	17	13	....	....	....	....	....
	Vancouver Canucks	13	4	14	18	4	11	4	8	12	21
1995-96	Vancouver Canucks	81	26	39	65	40	6	1	3	4	2
1996-97	Vancouver Canucks	47	9	19	28	24	....	....	....	....	....
	New York Rangers	14	2	5	7	2	15	3	4	7	0
1997-98	Los Angeles Kings	58	12	6	18	27	4	0	0	0	2

Season	Club	Regular Season GP	G	A	Pts	PIM	Playoffs GP	G	A	Pts	PIM
1998-99	Los Angeles Kings	57	6	13	19	19	....	....	....	....	....
	NHL Totals	**1029**	**297**	**447**	**744**	**557**	**129**	**39**	**44**	**83**	**83**

• Brother of Geoff

Played in NHL All-Star Game (1994)

Traded to **Montreal** by **Toronto** for John Kordic and Montreal's 6th round choice (Michael Doers) in 1989 Entry Draft, November 7, 1988. Traded to **Minnesota** by **Montreal** for Brian Bellows, August 31, 1992. Transferred to **Dallas** after **Minnesota** franchise relocated, June 9, 1993. Traded to **Vancouver** by **Dallas** for Greg Adams, Dan Kesa and Vancouver's 5th round choice (later traded to Los Angeles – Los Angeles selected Jason Morgan) in 1995 Entry Draft, April 7, 1995. Traded to **NY Rangers** by **Vancouver** with Esa Tikkanen for Sergei Nemchinov and Brian Noonan, March 8, 1997. Signed as a free agent by **Los Angeles**, November 7, 1997.

COURVILLE, Larry

Left wing. Shoots left. 6'1", 180 lbs. Born, Timmins, Ont., April 2, 1975.
(Vancouver's 2nd choice, 61st overall, in 1995 Entry Draft).

Season	Club	Regular Season GP	G	A	Pts	PIM	Playoffs GP	G	A	Pts	PIM
1995-96	Vancouver Canucks	3	1	0	1	0	....	....	....	....	....
1996-97	Vancouver Canucks	19	0	2	2	11	....	....	....	....	....
1997-98	Vancouver Canucks	11	0	0	0	5	....	....	....	....	....
	NHL Totals	**33**	**1**	**2**	**3**	**16**	....	....	....	....	....

• Re-entered NHL Entry Draft. Originally Winnipeg's 6th choice, 119th overall, in 1993 Entry Draft.

Signed as a free agent by **San Jose**, September 1, 2000.

COUTU, Billy

Defense. Shoots left. 5'11", 190 lbs. Born, North Bay, Ont., March 1, 1892.

Season	Club	Regular Season GP	G	A	Pts	PIM	Playoffs GP	G	A	Pts	PIM
1917-18	Montreal Canadiens	20	2	2	4	49	2	0	0	0	3
1918-19	Montreal Canadiens	15	1	2	3	18	5	0	1	1	6
	Montreal Canadiens (Cup)	....	....	....	....	....	*5*	*0*	*1*	*1*	*0*
1919-20	Montreal Canadiens	20	4	0	4	67	....	....	....	....	....
1920-21	Hamilton Tigers	24	8	4	12	*95	....	....	....	....	....
1921-22	Montreal Canadiens	24	4	3	7	8	....	....	....	....	....
1922-23	Montreal Canadiens	24	5	2	7	37	1	0	0	0	*22
1923-24 ♦	Montreal Canadiens	16	3	1	4	18	2	0	0	0	0
	Montreal Canadiens (Cup)	....	....	....	....	....	*4*	*0*	*0*	*0*	*0*
1924-25	Montreal Canadiens	28	3	2	5	56	2	0	0	0	0
	Montreal Canadiens (Cup)	....	....	....	....	....	*4*	*1*	*0*	*1*	*10*
1925-26	Montreal Canadiens	33	2	4	6	95	....	....	....	....	....
1926-27	Boston Bruins	40	1	1	2	35	7	1	0	1	4
	NHL Totals	**244**	**33**	**21**	**54**	**478**	**19**	**1**	**1**	**2**	**35**

Rights retained by **Montreal** after NHA folded, November 26, 1917. Loaned to **Hamilton** by **Montreal** for 1920-21 season with the trade of Goldie Prodgers, Jack Coughlin and Joe Matte for Jack McDonald, Dave Ritchie and Harry Mummery, November 27, 1920. Returned to **Montreal** by **Hamilton**, November 15, 1921. • 1923-24 Stanley Cup totals includes series with Calgary (WCHL) and Vancouver (PCHA). Traded to **Boston** by **Montreal** for Amby Moran, October 22, 1926. • Suspended for life by NHL for assault on referee Jerry LaFlamme, April 13, 1927. Traded to **New Haven** (Can-Am) by **Boston** with Nobby Clark for cash, January 5, 1928.

COUTURE, Gerry

Right wing. Shoots right. 6'2", 185 lbs. Born, Saskatoon, Sask., August 6, 1925.

Season	Club	Regular Season GP	G	A	Pts	PIM	Playoffs GP	G	A	Pts	PIM
1944-45	Detroit Red Wings	....	....	....	....	....	2	0	0	0	0
1945-46	Detroit Red Wings	43	3	7	10	18	5	0	2	2	0
1946-47	Detroit Red Wings	30	5	10	15	0	1	0	0	0	0
1947-48	Detroit Red Wings	19	3	6	9	2	....	....	....	....	....
1948-49	Detroit Red Wings	51	19	10	29	6	10	2	0	2	2
1949-50 ♦	Detroit Red Wings	69	24	7	31	21	14	5	4	9	2
1950-51	Detroit Red Wings	53	7	6	13	2	6	1	1	2	0
1951-52	Montreal Canadiens	10	0	1	1	4	....	....	....	....	....
1952-53	Chicago Black Hawks	70	19	18	37	22	7	1	0	1	0
1953-54	Chicago Black Hawks	40	6	5	11	14	....	....	....	....	....
	NHL Totals	**385**	**86**	**70**	**156**	**89**	**45**	**9**	**7**	**16**	**4**

Played in NHL All-Star Game (1950)

Traded to **Montreal** by **Detroit** for Bert Hirschfeld, June 19, 1951. Traded to **Chicago** by **Montreal** for cash, September 22, 1952.

COUTURE, Rosie

Right wing. Shoots right. 5'11", 164 lbs. Born, St. Boniface, Man., July 24, 1905.

Season	Club	Regular Season GP	G	A	Pts	PIM	Playoffs GP	G	A	Pts	PIM
1928-29	Chicago Black Hawks	43	1	3	4	22	....	....	....	....	....
1929-30	Chicago Black Hawks	43	8	8	16	63	2	0	0	0	2
1930-31	Chicago Black Hawks	44	8	11	19	30	9	0	3	3	2
1931-32	Chicago Black Hawks	48	9	9	18	8	2	0	0	0	2
1932-33	Chicago Black Hawks	46	10	7	17	26	....	....	....	....	....
1933-34 ♦	Chicago Black Hawks	48	5	8	13	21	8	1	2	3	4
1934-35	Chicago Black Hawks	27	7	9	16	14	2	0	0	0	5
1935-36	Montreal Canadiens	10	0	1	1	0	....	....	....	....	....
	NHL Totals	**309**	**48**	**56**	**104**	**184**	**23**	**1**	**5**	**6**	**15**

Traded to **Cleveland** (IHL) by **Chicago** for cash, June, 1935. Traded to **Montreal** by **Cleveland** (IHL) for $2,500, October 21, 1935.

COUTURIER, Sylvain

Center. Shoots left. 6'2", 205 lbs. Born, Greenfield Park, Que., April 23, 1968.
(Los Angeles' 3rd choice, 65th overall, in 1986 Entry Draft).

Season	Club	Regular Season GP	G	A	Pts	PIM	Playoffs GP	G	A	Pts	PIM
1988-89	Los Angeles Kings	16	1	3	4	2	....	....	....	....	....
1990-91	Los Angeles Kings	3	0	1	1	0	....	....	....	....	....
1991-92	Los Angeles Kings	14	3	1	4	2	....	....	....	....	....
	NHL Totals	**33**	**4**	**5**	**9**	**4**	....	....	....	....	....

Traded to **Detroit** by **Los Angeles** with Paul Coffey and Jim Hiller for Jimmy Carson, Marc Potvin and Gary Shuchuk, January 29, 1993.

COWAN, Jeff

Left wing. Shoots left. 6'2", 215 lbs. Born, Scarborough, Ont., September 27, 1976.

Season	Club	Regular Season GP	G	A	Pts	PIM	Playoffs GP	G	A	Pts	PIM
99-2000	Calgary Flames	13	4	1	5	16	....	....	....	....	....
2000-01	Calgary Flames	51	9	4	13	74	....	....	....	....	....
2001-02	Calgary Flames	19	1	0	1	40	....	....	....	....	....
	Atlanta Thrashers	38	4	1	5	50	....	....	....	....	....
2002-03	Atlanta Thrashers	66	3	5	8	115	....	....	....	....	....
	NHL Totals	**187**	**21**	**11**	**32**	**295**	....	....	....	....	....

Signed as a free agent by **Calgary**, October 2, 1995. Traded to **Atlanta** by **Calgary** with the rights to Kurtis Foster for Petr Buzek, December 18, 2001.

COWICK, Bruce

Left wing. Shoots left. 6'1", 200 lbs. Born, Victoria, B.C., August 18, 1951.

Season	Club	Regular Season GP	G	A	Pts	PIM	Playoffs GP	G	A	Pts	PIM
1973-74 ♦	Philadelphia Flyers	....	....	....	....	....	8	0	0	0	9
1974-75	Washington Capitals	65	5	6	11	41	....	....	....	....	....
1975-76	St. Louis Blues	5	0	0	0	2	....	....	....	....	....
	NHL Totals	**70**	**5**	**6**	**11**	**43**	**8**	**0**	**0**	**0**	**9**

Traded to **Philadelphia** by **San Diego** (WHL) for Jim Stanfield, Tom Trevelyan, Bob Currier and Bob Hurlburt, May 25, 1973. Claimed by **Washington** from **Philadelphia** in Expansion Draft, June 12, 1974. Claimed on waivers by **St. Louis** from **Washington**, May 21, 1975.

COWIE, Rob

Defense. Shoots left. 6', 195 lbs. Born, Toronto, Ont., November 3, 1967.

Season	Club	Regular Season GP	G	A	Pts	PIM	Playoffs GP	G	A	Pts	PIM
1994-95	Los Angeles Kings	32	2	7	9	20	....	....	....	....	....
1995-96	Los Angeles Kings	46	5	5	10	32	....	....	....	....	....
	NHL Totals	**78**	**7**	**12**	**19**	**52**	....	....	....	....	....

Signed as a free agent by **Winnipeg**, July 4, 1991. Signed as a free agent by **Hartford**, August 9, 1993. Signed as a free agent by **Los Angeles**, July 8, 1994.

COWLEY, Bill

HHOF

Center. Shoots left. 5'10", 165 lbs. Born, Bristol, Que., June 12, 1912.

Season	Club	Regular Season GP	G	A	Pts	PIM	Playoffs GP	G	A	Pts	PIM
1934-35	St. Louis Eagles	41	5	7	12	10	....	....	....	....	....
1935-36	Boston Bruins	48	11	10	21	17	2	2	1	3	2
1936-37	Boston Bruins	46	13	22	35	4	3	0	3	3	0
1937-38	Boston Bruins	48	17	22	39	8	3	2	0	2	0
1938-39 ♦	Boston Bruins	34	8	*34	42	2	12	3	11	*14	2
1939-40	Boston Bruins	48	13	27	40	24	6	0	1	1	7
1940-41 ♦	Boston Bruins	46	17	*45	*62	16	2	0	0	0	0
1941-42	Boston Bruins	28	4	23	27	6	5	0	3	3	5
1942-43	Boston Bruins	48	27	*45	72	10	9	1	7	8	4
1943-44	Boston Bruins	36	30	41	71	12	....	....	....	....	....
1944-45	Boston Bruins	49	25	40	65	12	7	3	3	6	0
1945-46	Boston Bruins	26	12	12	24	6	10	1	3	4	2
1946-47	Boston Bruins	51	13	25	38	16	5	0	2	2	0
	NHL Totals	**549**	**195**	**353**	**548**	**143**	**64**	**12**	**34**	**46**	**22**

NHL First All-Star Team (1938, 1941, 1943, 1944) • Hart Trophy (1941, 1943) • NHL Second All-Star Team (1945)

Signed as a free agent by **St. Louis**, October 22, 1934. Claimed by **Boston** from **St. Louis** in Dispersal Draft, October 15, 1935.

COX, Danny

Left wing. Shoots left. 5'10", 180 lbs. Born, Little Current, Ont., October 12, 1903.

Season	Club	Regular Season GP	G	A	Pts	PIM	Playoffs GP	G	A	Pts	PIM
1926-27	Toronto St. Pats/Maple Leafs	14	0	1	1	4	....	....	....	....	....
1927-28	Toronto Maple Leafs	41	9	6	15	27	....	....	....	....	....
1928-29	Toronto Maple Leafs	42	12	7	19	14	4	0	1	1	4
1929-30	Toronto Maple Leafs	18	1	4	5	18	....	....	....	....	....
	Ottawa Senators	24	3	2	5	20	2	0	0	0	0
1930-31	Ottawa Senators	44	9	12	21	12	....	....	....	....	....
1931-32	Detroit Falcons	47	4	6	10	23	2	0	0	0	2
1932-33	Ottawa Senators	47	4	7	11	8	....	....	....	....	....
1933-34	Ottawa Senators	29	0	4	4	0	....	....	....	....	....
	New York Rangers	13	5	0	5	2	2	0	0	0	0
	NHL Totals	**319**	**47**	**49**	**96**	**128**	**10**	**0**	**1**	**1**	**6**

Signed as a free agent by **Toronto**, October 13, 1926. Traded to **Ottawa** by **Toronto** with cash for Frank Nighbor, January 31, 1930. Claimed by **Detroit** from **Ottawa** for 1931-32 season in Dispersal Draft, September 26, 1931. Signed as a free agent by **NY Rangers** after securing release from **Ottawa** (January 30, 1934), February 3, 1934.

COXE, Craig

Left wing. Shoots left. 6'4", 210 lbs. Born, Chula Vista, CA, January 21, 1964.
(Detroit's 4th choice, 66th overall, in 1982 Entry Draft).

Season	Club	Regular Season GP	G	A	Pts	PIM	Playoffs GP	G	A	Pts	PIM
1984-85	Vancouver Canucks	9	0	0	0	49	....	....	....	....	....
1985-86	Vancouver Canucks	57	3	5	8	176	3	0	0	0	2
1986-87	Vancouver Canucks	15	1	0	1	31	....	....	....	....	....
1987-88	Vancouver Canucks	64	5	12	17	186	....	....	....	....	....
	Calgary Flames	7	2	3	5	32	2	1	0	1	16
1988-89	St. Louis Blues	41	0	7	7	127	....	....	....	....	....
1989-90	Vancouver Canucks	25	1	4	5	66	....	....	....	....	....
1990-91	Vancouver Canucks	7	0	0	0	27	....	....	....	....	....

Season	Club	GP	G	A	Pts	PIM	GP	G	A	Pts	PIM
		REGULAR SEASON					PLAYOFFS				
1991-92	San Jose Sharks	10	2	0	2	19	....	....	....	....	....
	NHL Totals	**235**	**14**	**31**	**45**	**713**	**5**	**1**	**0**	**1**	**18**

Signed as a free agent by **Vancouver**, June 26, 1984. Traded to **Calgary** by **Vancouver** for Brian Bradley, Kevan Guy and Peter Bakovic, March 6, 1988. Traded to **St. Louis** by **Calgary** with Mike Bullard and Tim Corkery for Mark Hunter, Doug Gilmour, Steve Bozek and Michael Dark, September 6, 1988. Transferred to **Chicago** by **St. Louis** as compensation for St. Louis' signing of free agent Rik Wilson, September 27, 1989. Claimed by **Vancouver** in Waiver Draft, October 2, 1989. Claimed by **San Jose** from **Vancouver** in Expansion Draft, May 30, 1991.

CRAIG, Mike

Right wing. Shoots right. 6'1", 185 lbs. Born, London, Ont., June 6, 1971.
(Minnesota's 2nd choice, 28th overall, in 1989 Entry Draft).

Season	Club	GP	G	A	Pts	PIM	GP	G	A	Pts	PIM
1990-91	Minnesota North Stars	39	8	4	12	32	10	1	1	2	20
1991-92	Minnesota North Stars	67	15	16	31	155	4	1	0	1	7
1992-93	Minnesota North Stars	70	15	23	38	106	....	....	....	....	....
1993-94	Dallas Stars	72	13	24	37	139	4	0	0	0	2
1994-95	Toronto Maple Leafs	37	5	5	10	12	2	0	1	1	2
1995-96	Toronto Maple Leafs	70	8	12	20	42	6	0	0	0	18
1996-97	Toronto Maple Leafs	65	7	13	20	62	....	....	....	....	....
1998-99	San Jose Sharks	1	0	0	0	0	....	....	....	....	....
2001-02	San Jose Sharks	2	0	0	0	2	....	....	....	....	....
	NHL Totals	**423**	**71**	**97**	**168**	**550**	**26**	**2**	**2**	**4**	**49**

Transferred to **Dallas** after **Minnesota** franchise relocated, June 9, 1993. Signed as a free agent by **Toronto**, July 29, 1994. Signed as a free agent by **San Jose**, July 13, 1998. Signed as a free agent by **Colorado**, August 2, 2000. Signed as a free agent by **San Jose**, September 6, 2001.

CRAIGHEAD, John

Right wing. Shoots right. 6', 195 lbs. Born, Vancouver, B.C., November 23, 1971.

Season	Club	GP	G	A	Pts	PIM	GP	G	A	Pts	PIM
1996-97	Toronto Maple Leafs	5	0	0	0	10	....	....	....	....	....
	NHL Totals	**5**	**0**	**0**	**0**	**10**	....	....	....	....	....

Signed as a free agent by **Toronto**, July 22, 1996.

CRAIGWELL, Dale

Center. Shoots left. 5'11", 180 lbs. Born, Toronto, Ont., April 24, 1971.
(San Jose's 11th choice, 199th overall, in 1991 Entry Draft).

Season	Club	GP	G	A	Pts	PIM	GP	G	A	Pts	PIM
1991-92	San Jose Sharks	32	5	11	16	8	....	....	....	....	....
1992-93	San Jose Sharks	8	3	1	4	4	....	....	....	....	....
1993-94	San Jose Sharks	58	3	6	9	16	....	....	....	....	....
	NHL Totals	**98**	**11**	**18**	**29**	**28**	....	....	....	....	....

CRASHLEY, Bart

Defense. Shoots right. 6', 180 lbs. Born, Toronto, Ont., June 15, 1946.

Season	Club	GP	G	A	Pts	PIM	GP	G	A	Pts	PIM
1965-66	Detroit Red Wings	1	0	0	0	0	....	....	....	....	....
1966-67	Detroit Red Wings	2	0	0	0	2	....	....	....	....	....
1967-68	Detroit Red Wings	57	2	14	16	18	....	....	....	....	....
1968-69	Detroit Red Wings	1	0	0	0	0	....	....	....	....	....
1974-75	Kansas City Scouts	27	3	6	9	10	....	....	....	....	....
	Detroit Red Wings	48	2	15	17	14	....	....	....	....	....
1975-76	Los Angeles Kings	4	0	1	1	6	....	....	....	....	....
	NHL Totals	**140**	**7**	**36**	**43**	**50**	....	....	....	....	....

Traded to **Montreal** by **Detroit** with Pete Mahovlich for Garry Monahan and Doug Piper, June 6, 1969. Claimed by **NY Islanders** from **Montreal** in Expansion Draft, June 6, 1972. Traded to **Kansas City** by **NY Islanders** to complete transaction that sent Bob Bourne to NY Islanders (September 10, 1974), September 16, 1974. Traded to **Detroit** by **Kansas City** with Ted Snell and Larry Giroux for Guy Charron and Claude Houde, December 14, 1974. Traded to **Los Angeles** by **Detroit** with the rights to Marcel Dionne for Dan Maloney, Terry Harper and Los Angeles' 2nd round choice (later traded to Minnesota – Minnesota selected Jim Roberts) in 1976 Amateur Draft, June 23, 1975.

CRAVEN, Murray

Left wing. Shoots left. 6'3", 195 lbs. Born, Medicine Hat, Alta., July 20, 1964.
(Detroit's 1st choice, 17th overall, in 1982 Entry Draft).

Season	Club	GP	G	A	Pts	PIM	GP	G	A	Pts	PIM
1982-83	Detroit Red Wings	31	4	7	11	6	....	....	....	....	....
1983-84	Detroit Red Wings	15	0	4	4	6	....	....	....	....	....
1984-85	Philadelphia Flyers	80	26	35	61	30	19	4	6	10	11
1985-86	Philadelphia Flyers	78	21	33	54	34	5	0	3	3	4
1986-87	Philadelphia Flyers	77	19	30	49	38	12	3	1	4	9
1987-88	Philadelphia Flyers	72	30	46	76	58	7	2	5	7	4
1988-89	Philadelphia Flyers	51	9	28	37	52	1	0	0	0	0
1989-90	Philadelphia Flyers	76	25	50	75	42	....	....	....	....	....
1990-91	Philadelphia Flyers	77	19	47	66	53	....	....	....	....	....
1991-92	Philadelphia Flyers	12	3	3	6	8	....	....	....	....	....
	Hartford Whalers	61	24	30	54	38	7	3	3	6	6
1992-93	Hartford Whalers	67	25	42	67	20	....	....	....	....	....
	Vancouver Canucks	10	0	10	10	12	12	4	6	10	4
1993-94	Vancouver Canucks	78	15	40	55	30	22	4	9	13	18
1994-95	Chicago Blackhawks	16	4	3	7	2	16	5	5	10	4
1995-96	Chicago Blackhawks	66	18	29	47	36	9	1	4	5	2
1996-97	Chicago Blackhawks	75	8	27	35	12	2	0	0	0	2
1997-98	San Jose Sharks	67	12	17	29	25	6	1	1	2	0
1998-99	San Jose Sharks	43	4	10	14	18	....	....	....	....	....
99-2000	San Jose Sharks	19	0	2	2	4	....	....	....	....	....
	NHL Totals	**1071**	**266**	**493**	**759**	**524**	**118**	**27**	**43**	**70**	**64**

Traded to **Philadelphia** by **Detroit** with Joe Paterson for Darryl Sittler, October 10, 1984. Traded to **Hartford** by **Philadelphia** with Philadelphia's 4th round choice (Kevin Smyth) in 1992 Entry Draft for Kevin Dineen, November 13, 1991. Traded to **Vancouver** by **Hartford** with Vancouver's 5th round choice (previously acquired, Vancouver selected Scott Walker) in 1993 Entry Draft for Robert Kron, Vancouver's 3rd round choice (Marek Malik) in 1993 Entry Draft and future considerations (Jim Sandlak, May 17, 1993), March 22, 1993. Traded to **Chicago** by **Vancouver** for Christian Ruutu, March 10, 1995. Traded to **San Jose** by **Chicago** for the rights to Petri Varis and San Jose's 6th round choice (Jari Viuhkola) in 1998 Entry Draft, July 25, 1997. • Missed remainder of 1999-2000 season recovering from abdominal injury suffered in game vs. New Jersey, November 18, 1999. • Officially released by **San Jose**, December 26, 1999.

CRAWFORD, Bob

Right wing. Shoots right. 5'11", 180 lbs. Born, Belleville, Ont., April 6, 1959.
(St. Louis' 2nd choice, 65th overall, in 1979 Entry Draft).

Season	Club	GP	G	A	Pts	PIM	GP	G	A	Pts	PIM
1979-80	St. Louis Blues	8	1	0	1	2	....	....	....	....	....
1981-82	St. Louis Blues	3	0	1	1	0	....	....	....	....	....
1982-83	St. Louis Blues	27	5	9	14	2	4	0	0	0	0
1983-84	Hartford Whalers	80	36	25	61	32	....	....	....	....	....
1984-85	Hartford Whalers	45	14	14	28	8	....	....	....	....	....
1985-86	Hartford Whalers	57	14	20	34	16	....	....	....	....	....
	New York Rangers	11	1	2	3	10	7	0	1	1	8
1986-87	New York Rangers	3	0	0	0	2	....	....	....	....	....
	Washington Capitals	12	0	0	0	0	....	....	....	....	....
	NHL Totals	**246**	**71**	**71**	**142**	**72**	**11**	**0**	**1**	**1**	**8**

• Brother of Marc and Lou

Claimed by **Hartford** from **St. Louis** in Waiver Draft, October 3, 1983. Traded to **NY Rangers** by **Hartford** for Mike McEwen, March 11, 1986. Traded to **Washington** by **NY Rangers** with Kelly Miller and Mike Ridley for Bob Carpenter and Washington's 2nd round choice (Jason Prosofsky) in 1989 Entry Draft, January 1, 1987.

CRAWFORD, Bobby

Right wing. Shoots left. 5'8", 180 lbs. Born, Long Island, NY, May 27, 1960.

Season	Club	GP	G	A	Pts	PIM	GP	G	A	Pts	PIM
1980-81	Colorado Rockies	15	1	3	4	6	....	....	....	....	....
1982-83	Detroit Red Wings	1	0	0	0	0	....	....	....	....	....
	NHL Totals	**16**	**1**	**3**	**4**	**6**	....	....	....	....	....

Signed as a free agent by **NY Rangers**, November 16, 1979. Traded to **Colorado** by **NY Rangers** to complete transaction that sent Barry Beck to NY Rangers (November 2, 1979), January 15, 1980. Signed as a free agent by **Detroit**, June, 1982.

CRAWFORD, Jack

Defense. Shoots right. 5'11", 200 lbs. Born, Dublin, Ont., October 26, 1916.

Season	Club	GP	G	A	Pts	PIM	GP	G	A	Pts	PIM
1937-38	Boston Bruins	2	0	0	0	0	....	....	....	....	....
1938-39 ♦	Boston Bruins	48	4	8	12	12	12	1	1	2	9
1939-40	Boston Bruins	35	1	4	5	26	6	0	0	0	0
1940-41 ♦	Boston Bruins	45	2	8	10	27	11	0	2	2	7
1941-42	Boston Bruins	43	2	9	11	37	5	0	1	1	4
1942-43	Boston Bruins	49	5	18	23	24	6	1	1	2	10
1943-44	Boston Bruins	34	4	16	20	8	....	....	....	....	....
1944-45	Boston Bruins	40	5	19	24	10	7	0	5	5	0
1945-46	Boston Bruins	48	7	9	16	10	10	1	2	3	4
1946-47	Boston Bruins	58	1	17	18	16	2	0	0	0	0
1947-48	Boston Bruins	45	3	11	14	10	4	0	1	1	2
1948-49	Boston Bruins	55	2	13	15	14	3	0	0	0	0
1949-50	Boston Bruins	46	2	8	10	8	....	....	....	....	....
	NHL Totals	**548**	**38**	**140**	**178**	**202**	**66**	**3**	**13**	**16**	**36**

NHL Second All-Star Team (1943) • NHL First All-Star Team (1946)

Signed as a free agent by **Boston**, October 26, 1937.

CRAWFORD, Lou

Left wing. Shoots left. 6', 185 lbs. Born, Belleville, Ont., November 5, 1962.

Season	Club	GP	G	A	Pts	PIM	GP	G	A	Pts	PIM
1989-90	Boston Bruins	7	0	0	0	20	1	0	0	0	0
1991-92	Boston Bruins	19	2	1	3	9	....	....	....	....	....
	NHL Totals	**26**	**2**	**1**	**3**	**29**	**1**	**0**	**0**	**0**	**0**

• Brother of Bob and Marc

Signed as a free agent by **Buffalo**, August 23, 1984. Signed as a free agent by **Detroit**, August 11, 1988. Signed as a free agent by **Boston**, July 6, 1989.

CRAWFORD, Marc

Left wing. Shoots left. 5'11", 185 lbs. Born, Belleville, Ont., February 13, 1961.
(Vancouver's 3rd choice, 70th overall, in 1980 Entry Draft).

Season	Club	GP	G	A	Pts	PIM	GP	G	A	Pts	PIM
1981-82	Vancouver Canucks	40	4	8	12	29	14	1	0	1	11
1982-83	Vancouver Canucks	41	4	5	9	28	3	0	1	1	25
1983-84	Vancouver Canucks	19	0	1	1	9	....	....	....	....	....
1984-85	Vancouver Canucks	1	0	0	0	4	....	....	....	....	....
1985-86	Vancouver Canucks	54	11	14	25	92	3	0	1	1	8
1986-87	Vancouver Canucks	21	0	3	3	67	....	....	....	....	....
	NHL Totals	**176**	**19**	**31**	**50**	**229**	**20**	**1**	**2**	**3**	**44**

• Brother of Bob and Lou

CRAWFORD, Rusty

HHOF

Left wing. Shoots left. 5'11", 165 lbs. Born, Cardinal, Ont., November 7, 1885.

Season	Club	GP	G	A	Pts	PIM	GP	G	A	Pts	PIM
1917-18	Ottawa Senators	12	2	2	4	15	....	....	....	....	....
	♦ Toronto Arenas	8	1	2	3	51	2	2	1	3	9

		REGULAR SEASON					PLAYOFFS				
Season	Club	GP	G	A	Pts	PIM	GP	G	A	Pts	PIM
1918-19	Toronto Arenas	18	7	4	11	51	....	....	....	....	....
	NHL Totals	**38**	**10**	**8**	**18**	**117**	**2**	**2**	**1**	**3**	**9**

Claimed by **Ottawa** from **Quebec** in Dispersal Draft, November 28, 1917. Signed as a free agent by **Toronto**, February 9, 1918. Signed as a free agent by **Ottawa**, December 2, 1918. Traded to **Toronto** by **Ottawa** for future considerations (loan of Harry Cameron, January 19, 1919), December 14, 1918. Rights transferred to **Quebec** by **Toronto** when Quebec franchise returned to NHL, November 25, 1919.

CREIGHTON, Adam

Center. Shoots left. 6'5", 220 lbs. Born, Burlington, Ont., June 2, 1965.
(Buffalo's 3rd choice, 11th overall, in 1983 Entry Draft).

Season	Club	GP	G	A	Pts	PIM	GP	G	A	Pts	PIM
1983-84	Buffalo Sabres	7	2	2	4	4	....	....	....	....	....
1984-85	Buffalo Sabres	30	2	8	10	33	....	....	....	....	....
1985-86	Buffalo Sabres	19	1	1	2	2	....	....	....	....	....
1986-87	Buffalo Sabres	56	18	22	40	26	....	....	....	....	....
1987-88	Buffalo Sabres	36	10	17	27	87	....	....	....	....	....
1988-89	Buffalo Sabres	24	7	10	17	44	....	....	....	....	....
	Chicago Blackhawks	43	15	14	29	92	15	5	6	11	44
1989-90	Chicago Blackhawks	80	34	36	70	224	20	3	6	9	59
1990-91	Chicago Blackhawks	72	22	29	51	135	6	0	1	1	10
1991-92	Chicago Blackhawks	11	6	6	12	16	....	....	....	....	....
	New York Islanders	66	15	9	24	102	....	....	....	....	....
1992-93	Tampa Bay Lightning	83	19	20	39	110	....	....	....	....	....
1993-94	Tampa Bay Lightning	53	10	10	20	37	....	....	....	....	....
1994-95	St. Louis Blues	48	14	20	34	74	7	2	0	2	16
1995-96	St. Louis Blues	61	11	10	21	78	13	1	1	2	8
1996-97	Chicago Blackhawks	19	1	2	3	13	....	....	....	....	....
	NHL Totals	**708**	**187**	**216**	**403**	**1077**	**61**	**11**	**14**	**25**	**137**

• Son of Dave

Traded to **Chicago** by **Buffalo** for Rick Vaive, December 26, 1988. Traded to **NY Islanders** by **Chicago** with Steve Thomas for Brent Sutter and Brad Lauer, October 25, 1991. Claimed by **Tampa Bay** from **NY Islanders** in Waiver Draft, October 4, 1992. Traded to **St. Louis** by **Tampa Bay** for Tom Tilley, October 6, 1994. Signed as a free agent by **Chicago**, October 9, 1996.

CREIGHTON, Dave

Center. Shoots left. 6'1", 195 lbs. Born, Port Arthur, Ont., June 24, 1930.

Season	Club	GP	G	A	Pts	PIM	GP	G	A	Pts	PIM
1948-49	Boston Bruins	12	1	3	4	0	3	0	0	0	0
1949-50	Boston Bruins	64	18	13	31	13	....	....	....	....	....
1950-51	Boston Bruins	56	5	4	9	4	5	0	1	1	0
1951-52	Boston Bruins	49	20	17	37	18	7	2	1	3	2
1952-53	Boston Bruins	45	8	8	16	14	11	4	5	9	10
1953-54	Boston Bruins	69	20	20	40	27	4	0	0	0	0
1954-55	Toronto Maple Leafs	14	2	1	3	8	....	....	....	....	....
	Chicago Black Hawks	49	7	7	14	6	....	....	....	....	....
1955-56	New York Rangers	70	20	31	51	43	5	0	0	0	4
1956-57	New York Rangers	70	18	21	39	42	5	2	2	4	2
1957-58	New York Rangers	70	17	35	52	40	6	3	3	6	2
1958-59	Toronto Maple Leafs	34	3	9	12	4	5	0	1	1	0
1959-60	Toronto Maple Leafs	14	1	5	6	4	....	....	....	....	....
	NHL Totals	**616**	**140**	**174**	**314**	**223**	**51**	**11**	**13**	**24**	**20**

• Father of Adam

Played in NHL All-Star Game (1952, 1953, 1954, 1955, 1956)

Signed as a free agent by **Boston**, October 5, 1948. Traded to **Toronto** by **Boston** for Fern Flaman, July 20, 1954. Traded to **Chicago** by **Toronto** for cash, November 16, 1954. Traded to **Detroit** by **Chicago** with Jerry Toppazzini, John McCormack and Gord Hollingworth for Tony Leswick, Johnny Wilson, Glen Skov and Benny Woit, May 27, 1955. Traded to **NY Rangers** by **Detroit** with Bronco Horvath for Billy Dea, Aggie Kukulowicz and cash, August 18, 1955. Claimed by **Montreal** from **NY Rangers** in Intra-League Draft, June 3, 1958. Claimed by **Toronto** from **Montreal** on waivers, September 25, 1958. Traded to **Buffalo** (AHL) by **Toronto** for Dick Gamble, June, 1961.

CREIGHTON, Jimmy

Forward. Shoots left. 5'9", 150 lbs. Born, Brandon, Man., November 18, 1905.

Season	Club	GP	G	A	Pts	PIM	GP	G	A	Pts	PIM
1930-31	Detroit Falcons	11	1	0	1	2	....	....	....	....	....
	NHL Totals	**11**	**1**	**0**	**1**	**2**	....	....	....	....	....

CRESSMAN, Dave

Left wing. Shoots left. 6'1", 180 lbs. Born, Kitchener, Ont., January 2, 1950.
(Minnesota's 4th choice, 48th overall, in 1970 Amateur Draft).

Season	Club	GP	G	A	Pts	PIM	GP	G	A	Pts	PIM
1974-75	Minnesota North Stars	5	2	0	2	4	....	....	....	....	....
1975-76	Minnesota North Stars	80	4	8	12	33	....	....	....	....	....
	NHL Totals	**85**	**6**	**8**	**14**	**37**	....	....	....	....	....

CRESSMAN, Glen

Center. Shoots right. 5'9", 155 lbs. Born, Petersburg, Ont., August 29, 1934.

Season	Club	GP	G	A	Pts	PIM	GP	G	A	Pts	PIM
1956-57	Montreal Canadiens	4	0	0	0	2	....	....	....	....	....
	NHL Totals	**4**	**0**	**0**	**0**	**2**	....	....	....	....	....

CRISP, Terry

Center. Shoots left. 5'10", 180 lbs. Born, Parry Sound, Ont., May 28, 1943.

Season	Club	GP	G	A	Pts	PIM	GP	G	A	Pts	PIM
1965-66	Boston Bruins	3	0	0	0	0	....	....	....	....	....
1967-68	St. Louis Blues	73	9	20	29	10	18	1	5	6	6
1968-69	St. Louis Blues	57	6	9	15	14	12	3	4	7	20
1969-70	St. Louis Blues	26	5	6	11	2	16	2	3	5	2
1970-71	St. Louis Blues	54	5	11	16	13	6	1	0	1	2
1971-72	St. Louis Blues	75	13	18	31	12	11	1	3	4	2
1972-73	New York Islanders	54	4	16	20	6	....	....	....	....	....
	Philadelphia Flyers	12	1	5	6	2	11	3	2	5	2
1973-74♦	Philadelphia Flyers	71	10	21	31	28	17	2	2	4	4
1974-75♦	Philadelphia Flyers	71	8	19	27	20	9	2	4	6	0
1975-76	Philadelphia Flyers	38	6	9	15	28	10	0	5	5	2
1976-77	Philadelphia Flyers	2	0	0	0	0	....	....	....	....	....
	NHL Totals	**536**	**67**	**134**	**201**	**135**	**110**	**15**	**28**	**43**	**40**

Claimed by **St. Louis** from **Boston** in Expansion Draft, June 6, 1967. Claimed by **NY Islanders** from **St. Louis** in Expansion Draft, June 6, 1972. Traded to **Philadelphia** by **NY Islanders** for Jean Potvin and future considerations (Glen Irwin, May 18, 1973), March 5, 1973.

CRISTOFOLI, Ed

Right wing. Shoots left. 6'2", 205 lbs. Born, Trail, B.C., May 14, 1967.
(Montreal's 9th choice, 142nd overall, in 1985 Entry Draft).

Season	Club	GP	G	A	Pts	PIM	GP	G	A	Pts	PIM
1989-90	Montreal Canadiens	9	0	1	1	4	....	....	....	....	....
	NHL Totals	**9**	**0**	**1**	**1**	**4**	....	....	....	....	....

CROGHAN, Maurice

Defense. Shoots left. 5'11", 185 lbs. Born, Montreal, Que., November 19, 1914.

Season	Club	GP	G	A	Pts	PIM	GP	G	A	Pts	PIM
1937-38	Montreal Maroons	16	0	0	0	4	....	....	....	....	....
	NHL Totals	**16**	**0**	**0**	**0**	**4**	....	....	....	....	....

Signed as a free agent by **Mtl. Maroons**, October 27, 1937.

CROMBEEN, Mike

Right wing. Shoots right. 5'11", 190 lbs. Born, Sarnia, Ont., April 16, 1957.
(Cleveland's 1st choice, 5th overall, in 1977 Amateur Draft).

Season	Club	GP	G	A	Pts	PIM	GP	G	A	Pts	PIM
1977-78	Cleveland Barons	48	3	4	7	13	....	....	....	....	....
1978-79	St. Louis Blues	37	3	8	11	34	....	....	....	....	....
1979-80	St. Louis Blues	71	10	12	22	20	2	0	0	0	0
1980-81	St. Louis Blues	66	9	14	23	58	11	3	0	3	8
1981-82	St. Louis Blues	71	19	8	27	32	10	3	1	4	20
1982-83	St. Louis Blues	80	6	11	17	20	4	0	1	1	4
1983-84	Hartford Whalers	56	1	4	5	25	....	....	....	....	....
1984-85	Hartford Whalers	46	4	7	11	16	....	....	....	....	....
	NHL Totals	**475**	**55**	**68**	**123**	**218**	**27**	**6**	**2**	**8**	**32**

Claimed by **St. Louis** in **Cleveland-Minnesota** Dispersal Draft, June 13, 1978. Claimed by **Hartford** from **St. Louis** in Waiver Draft, October 3, 1983.

CRONIN, Shawn

Defense. Shoots left. 6'2", 225 lbs. Born, Joliet, Il, August 20, 1963.

Season	Club	GP	G	A	Pts	PIM	GP	G	A	Pts	PIM
1988-89	Washington Capitals	1	0	0	0	0	....	....	....	....	....
1989-90	Winnipeg Jets	61	0	4	4	243	5	0	0	0	7
1990-91	Winnipeg Jets	67	1	5	6	189	....	....	....	....	....
1991-92	Winnipeg Jets	65	0	4	4	271	4	0	0	0	6
1992-93	Philadelphia Flyers	35	2	1	3	37	....	....	....	....	....
1993-94	San Jose Sharks	34	0	2	2	76	14	1	0	1	20
1994-95	San Jose Sharks	29	0	2	2	61	9	0	0	0	5
	NHL Totals	**292**	**3**	**18**	**21**	**877**	**32**	**1**	**0**	**1**	**38**

Signed as a free agent by **Hartford**, March, 1986. Signed as a free agent by **Washington**, June 6, 1988. Signed as a free agent by **Philadelphia**, June 12, 1989. Traded to **Winnipeg** by **Philadelphia** for future considerations (later cancelled as part of the trade that sent Keith Acton and Pete Peeters to Philadelphia by Winnipeg, October 3, 1989), July 21, 1989. Traded to **Quebec** by **Winnipeg** for Dan Lambert, August 25, 1992. Claimed by **Philadelphia** from **Quebec** in Waiver Draft, October 4, 1992. Traded to **San Jose** by **Philadelphia** for cash, August 5, 1993.

CROSS, Cory

Defense. Shoots left. 6'5", 220 lbs. Born, Lloydminster, Alta., January 3, 1971.
(Tampa Bay's 1st choice, 1st overall, in 1992 Supplemental Draft).

Season	Club	GP	G	A	Pts	PIM	GP	G	A	Pts	PIM
1993-94	Tampa Bay Lightning	5	0	0	0	6	....	....	....	....	....
1994-95	Tampa Bay Lightning	43	1	5	6	41	....	....	....	....	....
1995-96	Tampa Bay Lightning	75	2	14	16	66	6	0	0	0	22
1996-97	Tampa Bay Lightning	72	4	5	9	95	....	....	....	....	....
1997-98	Tampa Bay Lightning	74	3	6	9	77	....	....	....	....	....
1998-99	Tampa Bay Lightning	67	2	16	18	92	....	....	....	....	....
99-2000	Toronto Maple Leafs	71	4	11	15	64	12	0	2	2	2
2000-01	Toronto Maple Leafs	41	3	5	8	50	11	2	1	3	10
2001-02	Toronto Maple Leafs	50	3	9	12	54	12	0	0	0	8
2002-03	New York Rangers	26	0	4	4	16	....	....	....	....	....
	Edmonton Oilers	11	2	3	5	8	6	0	1	1	20
	NHL Totals	**535**	**24**	**78**	**102**	**569**	**47**	**2**	**4**	**6**	**62**

Traded to **Toronto** by **Tampa Bay** with Tampa Bay's 7th round choice (Ivan Kolozvary) in 2001 Entry Draft for Fredrik Modin, October 1, 1999. Signed as a free agent by **NY Rangers**, December 17, 2002. Traded to **Edmonton** by **NY Rangers** with Radek Dvorak for Anson Carter and Ales Pisa, March 11, 2003.

CROSSETT, Stan

Defense. Shoots right. 6', 200 lbs. Born, Tillsonburg, Ont., April 18, 1900.

Season	Club	GP	G	A	Pts	PIM	GP	G	A	Pts	PIM
1930-31	Philadelphia Quakers	21	0	0	0	10	....	....	....	....	....
	NHL Totals	**21**	**0**	**0**	**0**	**10**	....	....	....	....	....

Signed as a free agent by **Philadelphia**, January 9, 1931.

CROSSMAN, Doug

Defense. Shoots left. 6'2", 190 lbs. Born, Peterborough, Ont., June 13, 1960.
(Chicago's 6th choice, 112th overall, in 1979 Entry Draft).

Season	Club	GP	G	A	Pts	PIM	GP	G	A	Pts	PIM
1980-81	Chicago Black Hawks	9	0	2	2	2	....	....	....	....	....

Season	Club	GP	G	A	Pts	PIM	GP	G	A	Pts	PIM
		REGULAR SEASON					PLAYOFFS				
1981-82	Chicago Black Hawks	70	12	28	40	24	11	0	3	3	4
1982-83	Chicago Black Hawks	80	13	40	53	46	13	3	7	10	6
1983-84	Philadelphia Flyers	78	7	28	35	63	3	0	0	0	0
1984-85	Philadelphia Flyers	80	4	33	37	65	19	4	6	10	38
1985-86	Philadelphia Flyers	80	6	37	43	55	5	0	1	1	4
1986-87	Philadelphia Flyers	78	9	31	40	29	26	4	14	18	31
1987-88	Philadelphia Flyers	76	9	29	38	43	7	1	1	2	8
1988-89	Los Angeles Kings	74	10	15	25	53	2	0	1	1	2
1989-90	New York Islanders	80	15	44	59	54	5	0	1	1	6
1990-91	New York Islanders	16	1	6	7	12	....	....	....	....	....
	Hartford Whalers	41	4	19	23	19	....	....	....	....	....
	Detroit Red Wings	17	3	4	7	17	6	0	5	5	6
1991-92	Detroit Red Wings	26	0	8	8	14	....	....	....	....	....
1992-93	Tampa Bay Lightning	40	8	21	29	18	....	....	....	....	....
	St. Louis Blues	19	2	7	9	10	....	....	....	....	....
1993-94	St. Louis Blues	50	2	7	9	10	....	....	....	....	....
	NHL Totals	**914**	**105**	**359**	**464**	**534**	**97**	**12**	**39**	**51**	**105**

Traded to **Philadelphia** by **Chicago** with Chicago's 2nd round choice (Scott Mellanby) in 1984 Entry Draft for Behn Wilson, June 8, 1983. Traded to **Los Angeles** by **Philadelphia** for Jay Wells, September 29, 1988. Traded to **NY Islanders** by **Los Angeles** to complete transaction that sent Mark Fitzpatrick and Wayne McBean to NY Islanders (February 22, 1989), May 23, 1989. Traded to **Hartford** by **NY Islanders** for Ray Ferraro, November 13, 1990. Traded to **Detroit** by **Hartford** for Doug Houda, February 20, 1991. Traded to **Quebec** by **Detroit** with Dennis Vial for cash, June 15, 1992. Claimed by **Tampa Bay** from **Quebec** in Expansion Draft, June 18, 1992. Traded to **St. Louis** by **Tampa Bay** with Basil McRae and Tampa Bay's 4th round choice (Andrei Petrakov) in 1996 Entry Draft for Jason Ruff, January 28, 1993.

CROTEAU, Gary

Left wing. Shoots left. 6', 205 lbs. Born, Sudbury, Ont., June 20, 1946.

Season	Club	GP	G	A	Pts	PIM	GP	G	A	Pts	PIM
1968-69	Los Angeles Kings	11	5	1	6	6	11	3	2	5	8
1969-70	Los Angeles Kings	3	0	0	0	0	....	....	....	....	....
	Detroit Red Wings	10	0	2	2	2	....	....	....	....	....
1970-71	California Seals	74	15	28	43	12	....	....	....	....	....
1971-72	California Golden Seals	73	12	12	24	11	....	....	....	....	....
1972-73	California Golden Seals	47	6	15	21	8	....	....	....	....	....
1973-74	California Golden Seals	76	14	21	35	16	....	....	....	....	....
1974-75	Kansas City Scouts	77	8	11	19	16	....	....	....	....	....
1975-76	Kansas City Scouts	79	19	14	33	12	....	....	....	....	....
1976-77	Colorado Rockies	78	24	27	51	14	....	....	....	....	....
1977-78	Colorado Rockies	62	17	22	39	24	....	....	....	....	....
1978-79	Colorado Rockies	79	23	18	41	18	....	....	....	....	....
1979-80	Colorado Rockies	15	1	4	5	4	....	....	....	....	....
	NHL Totals	**684**	**144**	**175**	**319**	**143**	**11**	**3**	**2**	**5**	**8**

Traded to **Los Angeles** by **Toronto** with Brian Murphy and Wayne Thomas for Grant Moore and Lou Deveault, October 15, 1968. Traded to **Detroit** by **Los Angeles** with Dale Rolfe and Larry Johnston for Garry Monahan, Matt Ravlich and Brian Gibbons, February 20, 1970. Claimed by **California** from **Detroit** in Intra-League Draft, June 9, 1970. Claimed by **Kansas City** from **California** in Expansion Draft, June 12, 1974. Transferred to **Colorado** after **Kansas City** franchise relocated, July 15, 1976.

CROWDER, Bruce

Right wing. Shoots right. 6', 180 lbs. Born, Essex, Ont., March 25, 1957.
(Philadelphia's 14th choice, 153rd overall, in 1977 Amateur Draft).

Season	Club	GP	G	A	Pts	PIM	GP	G	A	Pts	PIM
1981-82	Boston Bruins	63	16	11	27	31	11	5	3	8	9
1982-83	Boston Bruins	80	21	19	40	58	17	3	1	4	32
1983-84	Boston Bruins	74	6	14	20	44	3	0	0	0	0
1984-85	Pittsburgh Penguins	26	4	7	11	23	....	....	....	....	....
	NHL Totals	**243**	**47**	**51**	**98**	**156**	**31**	**8**	**4**	**12**	**41**

• Brother of Keith

Signed as a free agent by **Boston**, September 28, 1981. Claimed by **Pittsburgh** from **Boston** in Waiver Draft, October 9, 1984. • Officially announced retirement, February 1, 1985.

CROWDER, Keith

Right wing. Shoots right. 6', 190 lbs. Born, Windsor, Ont., January 6, 1959.
(Boston's 4th choice, 57th overall, in 1979 Entry Draft).

Season	Club	GP	G	A	Pts	PIM	GP	G	A	Pts	PIM
1980-81	Boston Bruins	47	13	12	25	172	3	2	0	2	9
1981-82	Boston Bruins	71	23	21	44	101	11	2	2	4	14
1982-83	Boston Bruins	74	35	39	74	105	17	1	6	7	54
1983-84	Boston Bruins	63	24	28	52	128	3	0	0	0	7
1984-85	Boston Bruins	79	32	38	70	152	4	3	2	5	19
1985-86	Boston Bruins	78	38	46	84	177	3	2	0	2	21
1986-87	Boston Bruins	58	22	30	52	106	4	0	1	1	4
1987-88	Boston Bruins	68	17	26	43	173	23	3	9	12	44
1988-89	Boston Bruins	69	15	18	33	147	10	0	2	2	37
1989-90	Los Angeles Kings	55	4	13	17	93	7	1	0	1	9
	NHL Totals	**662**	**223**	**271**	**494**	**1354**	**85**	**14**	**22**	**36**	**218**

• Brother of Bruce

Signed as a free agent by **Los Angeles**, June 28, 1989.

CROWDER, Troy

Right wing. Shoots right. 6'4", 220 lbs. Born, Sudbury, Ont., May 3, 1968.
(New Jersey's 6th choice, 108th overall, in 1986 Entry Draft).

Season	Club	GP	G	A	Pts	PIM	GP	G	A	Pts	PIM
1987-88	New Jersey Devils	....	....	....	....	....	1	0	0	0	12
1989-90	New Jersey Devils	10	0	0	0	23	2	0	0	0	10
1990-91	New Jersey Devils	59	6	3	9	182	....	....	....	....	....
1991-92	Detroit Red Wings	7	0	0	0	35	1	0	0	0	0
1994-95	Los Angeles Kings	29	1	2	3	99	....	....	....	....	....
1995-96	Los Angeles Kings	15	1	0	1	42	....	....	....	....	....
1996-97	Vancouver Canucks	30	1	2	3	52	....	....	....	....	....
	NHL Totals	**150**	**9**	**7**	**16**	**433**	**4**	**0**	**0**	**0**	**22**

• Missed majority of 1989-90 season in retirement. Signed as a free agent by **Detroit**, August 27, 1991. • Missed majority of 1991-92 season and all of 1992-93 and 1993-94 seasons recovering from back injury suffered in game vs. Montreal, October 10, 1991. Signed as a free agent by **Los Angeles**, August 31, 1994. Signed as a free agent by **Vancouver**, October 4, 1996.

CROWE, Phil

Left wing. Shoots right. 6'2", 230 lbs. Born, Nanton, Alta., April 4, 1970.

Season	Club	GP	G	A	Pts	PIM	GP	G	A	Pts	PIM
1993-94	Los Angeles Kings	31	0	2	2	77	....	....	....	....	....
1995-96	Philadelphia Flyers	16	1	1	2	28	....	....	....	....	....
1996-97	Ottawa Senators	26	0	1	1	30	3	0	0	0	16
1997-98	Ottawa Senators	9	3	0	3	24	....	....	....	....	....
1998-99	Ottawa Senators	8	0	1	1	4	....	....	....	....	....
99-2000	Nashville Predators	4	0	0	0	10	....	....	....	....	....
	NHL Totals	**94**	**4**	**5**	**9**	**173**	**3**	**0**	**0**	**0**	**16**

Signed as a free agent by **Los Angeles**, November 8, 1993. Signed as a free agent by **Philadelphia**, July 19, 1994. Signed as a free agent by **Ottawa**, July 29, 1996. Claimed by **Atlanta** from **Ottawa** in Expansion Draft, June 25, 1999. Traded to **Nashville** by **Atlanta** for future considerations, June 26, 1999.

CROWLEY, Mike

Defense. Shoots left. 5'11", 190 lbs. Born, Bloomington, MN, July 4, 1975.
(Philadelphia's 5th choice, 140th overall, in 1993 Entry Draft).

Season	Club	GP	G	A	Pts	PIM	GP	G	A	Pts	PIM
1997-98	Mighty Ducks of Anaheim	8	2	2	4	8	....	....	....	....	....
1998-99	Mighty Ducks of Anaheim	20	2	3	5	16	....	....	....	....	....
2000-01	Mighty Ducks of Anaheim	39	1	10	11	20	....	....	....	....	....
	NHL Totals	**67**	**5**	**15**	**20**	**44**	....	....	....	....	....

Traded to **Anaheim** by **Philadelphia** with Anatoli Semenov for Brian Wesenberg, March 19, 1996. Signed as a free agent by **Anaheim**, December 8, 2000. Signed as a free agent by **Minnesota**, July 25, 2001. • Missed majority of 2001-02 season recovering from Achilles tendon injury suffered in training camp, October 2, 2001.

CROWLEY, Ted

Defense. Shoots right. 6'2", 188 lbs. Born, Concord, MA, May 3, 1970.
(Toronto's 4th choice, 69th overall, in 1988 Entry Draft).

Season	Club	GP	G	A	Pts	PIM	GP	G	A	Pts	PIM
1993-94	Hartford Whalers	21	1	2	3	10	....	....	....	....	....
1998-99	Colorado Avalanche	7	0	1	1	2	....	....	....	....	....
	New York Islanders	6	1	1	2	0	....	....	....	....	....
	NHL Totals	**34**	**2**	**4**	**6**	**12**	....	....	....	....	....

Traded to **Hartford** by **Toronto** for Mark Greig and Hartford's 6th round choice (Doug Bonner) in 1995 Entry Draft, January 25, 1994. Signed as a free agent by **Boston**, August 9, 1995. Signed as a free agent by **Phoenix**, June 27, 1997. Signed as a free agent by **Colorado**, August 14, 1998. Traded to **NY Islanders** by **Colorado** for Michael Gaul, December 15, 1998. Signed as a free agent by **Chicago**, July 22, 1999.

CROZIER, Greg

Left wing. Shoots left. 6'3", 200 lbs. Born, Calgary, Alta., July 6, 1976.
(Pittsburgh's 4th choice, 73rd overall, in 1994 Entry Draft).

Season	Club	GP	G	A	Pts	PIM	GP	G	A	Pts	PIM
2000-01	Pittsburgh Penguins	1	0	0	0	0	....	....	....	....	....
	NHL Totals	**1**	**0**	**0**	**0**	**0**	....	....	....	....	....

Signed as a free agent by **Boston**, August 8, 2001. Traded to **Minnesota** by **Boston** for Darryl Laplante, March 19, 2002.

CROZIER, Joe

Defense. Shoots right. 6', 185 lbs. Born, Winnipeg, Man., February 19, 1929.

Season	Club	GP	G	A	Pts	PIM	GP	G	A	Pts	PIM
1959-60	Toronto Maple Leafs	5	0	3	3	2	....	....	....	....	....
	NHL Totals	**5**	**0**	**3**	**3**	**2**	....	....	....	....	....

CRUTCHFIELD, Nels

Center. Shoots left. 6'1", 175 lbs. Born, Knowlton, Que., July 12, 1911.

Season	Club	GP	G	A	Pts	PIM	GP	G	A	Pts	PIM
1934-35	Montreal Canadiens	41	5	5	10	20	2	0	1	1	22
	NHL Totals	**41**	**5**	**5**	**10**	**20**	**2**	**0**	**1**	**1**	**22**

Rights traded to **Montreal** by **Mtl. Maroons** for Lionel Conacher and the rights to Herb Cain, October 3, 1934. • Suffered career-ending injuries in automobile accident, September 28, 1935.

CULHANE, Jim

Defense. Shoots left. 6', 190 lbs. Born, Haileybury, Ont., March 13, 1965.
(Hartford's 6th choice, 214th overall, in 1984 Entry Draft).

Season	Club	GP	G	A	Pts	PIM	GP	G	A	Pts	PIM
1989-90	Hartford Whalers	6	0	1	1	4	....	....	....	....	....
	NHL Totals	**6**	**0**	**1**	**1**	**4**	....	....	....	....	....

Signed as a free agent by **NY Islanders**, October, 1990.

CULLEN, Barry

Right wing. Shoots right. 6', 183 lbs. Born, Ottawa, Ont., June 16, 1935.

Season	Club	GP	G	A	Pts	PIM	GP	G	A	Pts	PIM
1955-56	Toronto Maple Leafs	3	0	0	0	4	....	....	....	....	....
1956-57	Toronto Maple Leafs	51	6	10	16	30	....	....	....	....	....
1957-58	Toronto Maple Leafs	70	16	25	41	37	....	....	....	....	....
1958-59	Toronto Maple Leafs	40	6	8	14	17	2	0	0	0	0

		REGULAR SEASON					PLAYOFFS				
Season	Club	GP	G	A	Pts	PIM	GP	G	A	Pts	PIM
1959-60	Detroit Red Wings	55	4	9	13	23	4	0	0	0	2
	NHL Totals	**219**	**32**	**52**	**84**	**111**	**6**	**0**	**0**	**0**	**2**

• Brother of Brian and Ray • Father of John

Signed as a free agent by **Toronto**, June, 1955. Traded to **Detroit** by **Toronto** for Frank Roggeveen and Johnny Wilson, June 9, 1959. Traded to **NY Rangers** (Buffalo-AHL) by **Detroit** for Pete Conacher, August, 1960.

CULLEN, Brian

Center. Shoots left. 5'10", 160 lbs. Born, Ottawa, Ont., November 11, 1933.

		REGULAR SEASON					PLAYOFFS				
Season	Club	GP	G	A	Pts	PIM	GP	G	A	Pts	PIM
1954-55	Toronto Maple Leafs	27	3	5	8	6	4	1	0	1	0
1955-56	Toronto Maple Leafs	21	2	6	8	8	5	1	0	1	2
1956-57	Toronto Maple Leafs	46	8	12	20	27	....	....	....	....	....
1957-58	Toronto Maple Leafs	67	20	23	43	29	....	....	....	....	....
1958-59	Toronto Maple Leafs	59	4	14	18	10	10	1	0	1	0
1959-60	New York Rangers	64	8	21	29	6	....	....	....	....	....
1960-61	New York Rangers	42	11	19	30	6	....	....	....	....	....
	NHL Totals	**326**	**56**	**100**	**156**	**92**	**19**	**3**	**0**	**3**	**2**

• Brother of Barry and Ray

Traded to **Toronto** by **Chicago** (Buffalo-AHL) for Dusty Blair, Frank Sullivan and Jack Leclair, May 4, 1954. Claimed by **NY Rangers** from **Toronto** in Intra-League Draft, June 10, 1959.

CULLEN, David

Defense. Shoots right. 6'2", 209 lbs. Born, St. Catharines, Ont., December 30, 1976.

		REGULAR SEASON					PLAYOFFS				
Season	Club	GP	G	A	Pts	PIM	GP	G	A	Pts	PIM
2000-01	Phoenix Coyotes	2	0	0	0	0	....	....	....	....	....
2001-02	Phoenix Coyotes	14	0	0	0	6	....	....	....	....	....
	Minnesota Wild	3	0	0	0	0	....	....	....	....	....
	NHL Totals	**19**	**0**	**0**	**0**	**6**	....	....	....	....	....

Signed as a free agent by **Phoenix**, April 16, 1999. Traded to **Minnesota** by **Phoenix** for Sebastien Bordeleau, January 4, 2002.

CULLEN, John

Center. Shoots right. 5'10", 182 lbs. Born, Puslinch, Ont., August 2, 1964.
(Buffalo's 2nd choice, 10th overall, in 1986 Supplemental Draft)

		REGULAR SEASON					PLAYOFFS				
Season	Club	GP	G	A	Pts	PIM	GP	G	A	Pts	PIM
1988-89	Pittsburgh Penguins	79	12	37	49	112	11	3	6	9	28
1989-90	Pittsburgh Penguins	72	32	60	92	138	....	....	....	....	....
1990-91	Pittsburgh Penguins	65	31	63	94	83	....	....	....	....	....
	Hartford Whalers	13	8	8	16	18	6	2	7	9	10
1991-92	Hartford Whalers	77	26	51	77	141	7	2	1	3	12
1992-93	Hartford Whalers	19	5	4	9	58	....	....	....	....	....
	Toronto Maple Leafs	47	13	28	41	33	12	2	3	5	0
1993-94	Toronto Maple Leafs	53	13	17	30	67	3	0	0	0	0
1994-95	Pittsburgh Penguins	46	13	24	37	66	9	0	2	2	8
1995-96	Tampa Bay Lightning	76	16	34	50	65	5	3	3	6	0
1996-97	Tampa Bay Lightning	70	18	37	55	95	....	....	....	....	....
1997-98	Tampa Bay Lightning					DID NOT PLAY					
1998-99	Tampa Bay Lightning	4	0	0	0	2	....	....	....	....	....
	NHL Totals	**621**	**187**	**363**	**550**	**898**	**53**	**12**	**22**	**34**	**58**

• Son of Barry • Bill Masterton Memorial Trophy (1999)

• Played in NHL All-Star Game (1991, 1992)

Signed as a free agent by **Pittsburgh**, June 21, 1988. Traded to **Hartford** by **Pittsburgh** with Jeff Parker and Zarley Zalapski for Ron Francis, Grant Jennings and Ulf Samuelsson, March 4, 1991. Traded to **Toronto** by **Hartford** for Toronto's 2nd round choice (later traded to San Jose – San Jose selected Vlastimil Kroupa) in 1993 Entry Draft, November 24, 1992. Signed as a free agent by **Pittsburgh**, August 3, 1994. Signed as a free agent by **Tampa Bay**, September 11, 1995. • Missed entire 1997-98 season recovering from treatment and surgery for non-Hodgkins Lymphoma. • Officially announced retirement and named Assistant Coach with **Tampa Bay**, November 27, 1998.

CULLEN, Matt

Center. Shoots left. 6', 205 lbs. Born, Virginia, MN, November 2, 1976.
(Anaheim's 2nd choice, 35th overall, in 1996 Entry Draft).

		REGULAR SEASON					PLAYOFFS				
Season	Club	GP	G	A	Pts	PIM	GP	G	A	Pts	PIM
1997-98	Mighty Ducks of Anaheim	61	6	21	27	23	....	....	....	....	....
1998-99	Mighty Ducks of Anaheim	75	11	14	25	47	4	0	0	0	0
99-2000	Mighty Ducks of Anaheim	80	13	26	39	24	....	....	....	....	....
2000-01	Mighty Ducks of Anaheim	82	10	30	40	38	....	....	....	....	....
2001-02	Mighty Ducks of Anaheim	79	18	30	48	24	....	....	....	....	....
2002-03	Mighty Ducks of Anaheim	50	7	14	21	12	....	....	....	....	....
	Florida Panthers	30	6	6	12	22	....	....	....	....	....
	NHL Totals	**457**	**71**	**141**	**212**	**190**	**4**	**0**	**0**	**0**	**0**

Traded to **Florida** by **Anaheim** with Pavel Trnka and Anaheim's 4th round choice (James Pemberton) in 2003 Entry Draft for Sandis Ozolinsh and Lance Ward, January 30, 2003.

CULLEN, Ray

Center. Shoots right. 5'11", 180 lbs. Born, Ottawa, Ont., September 20, 1941.

		REGULAR SEASON					PLAYOFFS				
Season	Club	GP	G	A	Pts	PIM	GP	G	A	Pts	PIM
1965-66	New York Rangers	8	1	3	4	0	....	....	....	....	....
1966-67	Detroit Red Wings	27	8	8	16	8	....	....	....	....	....
1967-68	Minnesota North Stars	67	28	25	53	18	14	2	6	8	2
1968-69	Minnesota North Stars	67	26	38	64	44	....	....	....	....	....
1969-70	Minnesota North Stars	74	17	28	45	8	6	1	4	5	0
1970-71	Vancouver Canucks	70	12	21	33	42	....	....	....	....	....
	NHL Totals	**313**	**92**	**123**	**215**	**120**	**20**	**3**	**10**	**13**	**2**

• Brother of Brian and Barry

Traded to **NY Rangers** by **Chicago** with John McKenzie for Dick Meissner, Dave Richardson, Tracy Pratt and Mel Pearson, June 4, 1965. Claimed by **Detroit** from **NY Rangers** in Intra-League Draft, June 15, 1966. Claimed by **Minnesota** from **Detroit** in Expansion Draft, June 6, 1967. Claimed by **Vancouver** from **Minnesota** in Expansion Draft, June 10, 1970.

CULLIMORE, Jassen

Defense. Shoots left. 6'5", 244 lbs. Born, Simcoe, Ont., December 4, 1972.
(Vancouver's 2nd choice, 29th overall, in 1991 Entry Draft).

		REGULAR SEASON					PLAYOFFS				
Season	Club	GP	G	A	Pts	PIM	GP	G	A	Pts	PIM
1994-95	Vancouver Canucks	34	1	2	3	39	11	0	0	0	12
1995-96	Vancouver Canucks	27	1	1	2	21	....	....	....	....	....
1996-97	Vancouver Canucks	3	0	0	0	2	....	....	....	....	....
	Montreal Canadiens	49	2	6	8	42	2	0	0	0	2
1997-98	Montreal Canadiens	3	0	0	0	4	....	....	....	....	....
	Tampa Bay Lightning	25	1	2	3	22	....	....	....	....	....
1998-99	Tampa Bay Lightning	78	5	12	17	81	....	....	....	....	....
99-2000	Tampa Bay Lightning	46	1	1	2	66	....	....	....	....	....
2000-01	Tampa Bay Lightning	74	1	6	7	80	....	....	....	....	....
2001-02	Tampa Bay Lightning	78	4	9	13	58	....	....	....	....	....
2002-03	Tampa Bay Lightning	28	1	3	4	31	11	1	1	2	4
	NHL Totals	**445**	**17**	**42**	**59**	**446**	**24**	**1**	**1**	**2**	**18**

Traded to **Montreal** by **Vancouver** for Donald Brashear, November 13, 1996. Claimed on waivers by **Tampa Bay** from **Montreal**, January 22, 1998.• Missed majority of 2002-03 season recovering from elbow injury suffered in game vs. Vancouver, November 29, 2002.

CUMMINS, Barry

Defense. Shoots left. 5'9", 175 lbs. Born, Regina, Sask., January 25, 1949.

		REGULAR SEASON					PLAYOFFS				
Season	Club	GP	G	A	Pts	PIM	GP	G	A	Pts	PIM
1973-74	California Golden Seals	36	1	2	3	39	....	....	....	....	....
	NHL Totals	**36**	**1**	**2**	**3**	**39**	....	....	....	....	....

Claimed by **Portland** (WHL) from **Montreal** in Reverse Draft, June, 1970. Traded to **Seattle** (WHL) by **Portland** (WHL) for cash, June 10, 1970. Traded to **California** (Salt Lake-WHL) by **Seattle** (WHL) for $15,000, June, 1972.

CUMMINS, Jim

Right wing. Shoots right. 6'2", 212 lbs. Born, Dearborn, MI, May 17, 1970.
(NY Rangers' 5th choice, 67th overall, in 1989 Entry Draft).

		REGULAR SEASON					PLAYOFFS				
Season	Club	GP	G	A	Pts	PIM	GP	G	A	Pts	PIM
1991-92	Detroit Red Wings	1	0	0	0	7	....	....	....	....	....
1992-93	Detroit Red Wings	7	1	1	2	58	....	....	....	....	....
1993-94	Philadelphia Flyers	22	1	2	3	71	....	....	....	....	....
	Tampa Bay Lightning	4	0	0	0	13	....	....	....	....	....
1994-95	Tampa Bay Lightning	10	1	0	1	41	....	....	....	....	....
	Chicago Blackhawks	27	3	1	4	117	14	1	1	2	4
1995-96	Chicago Blackhawks	52	2	4	6	180	10	0	0	0	2
1996-97	Chicago Blackhawks	65	6	6	12	199	6	0	0	0	24
1997-98	Chicago Blackhawks	55	0	2	2	178	....	....	....	....	....
	Phoenix Coyotes	20	0	0	0	47	3	0	0	0	4
1998-99	Phoenix Coyotes	55	1	7	8	190	3	0	1	1	0
99-2000	Montreal Canadiens	47	3	5	8	92	....	....	....	....	....
2000-01	Mighty Ducks of Anaheim	79	5	6	11	167	....	....	....	....	....
2001-02	Mighty Ducks of Anaheim	2	0	0	0	0	....	....	....	....	....
	New York Islanders	10	0	0	0	31	1	0	0	0	9
	NHL Totals	**456**	**23**	**34**	**57**	**1391**	**37**	**1**	**2**	**3**	**43**

Traded to **Detroit** by **NY Rangers** with Kevin Miller and Dennis Vial for Joe Kocur and Per Djoos, March 5, 1991. Traded to **Philadelphia** by **Detroit** with Philadelphia's 4th round choice (previously acquired, later traded to Boston – Boston selected Charles Paquette) in 1993 Entry Draft for Greg Johnson and Philadelphia's 5th round choice (Frederic Deschenes) in 1994 Entry Draft, June 20, 1993. Traded to **Tampa Bay** by **Philadelphia** with Philadelphia's 4th round choice (later traded back to Philadelphia – Philadelphia selected Radovan Somik) in 1995 Entry Draft for Rob DiMaio, March 18, 1994. Traded to **Chicago** by **Tampa Bay** with Tom Tilley and Jeff Buchanan for Paul Ysebaert and Rich Sutter, February 22, 1995. Traded to **Phoenix** by **Chicago** with Keith Carney for Chad Kilger and Jayson More, March 4, 1998. Traded to **Montreal** by **Phoenix** for NY Rangers' 6th round choice (previously acquired, Phoenix selected Erik Lewerstrom) in 1999 Entry Draft, June 26, 1999. Signed as a free agent by **Anaheim**, July 5, 2000. Traded to **NY Islanders** by **Anaheim** for Dave Roche, January 14, 2002.

CUNNEYWORTH, Randy

Left wing. Shoots left. 6', 198 lbs. Born, Etobicoke, Ont., May 10, 1961.
(Buffalo's 9th choice, 167th overall, in 1980 Entry Draft).

		REGULAR SEASON					PLAYOFFS				
Season	Club	GP	G	A	Pts	PIM	GP	G	A	Pts	PIM
1980-81	Buffalo Sabres	1	0	0	0	2	....	....	....	....	....
1981-82	Buffalo Sabres	20	2	4	6	47	....	....	....	....	....
1985-86	Pittsburgh Penguins	75	15	30	45	74	....	....	....	....	....
1986-87	Pittsburgh Penguins	79	26	27	53	142	....	....	....	....	....
1987-88	Pittsburgh Penguins	71	35	39	74	141	....	....	....	....	....
1988-89	Pittsburgh Penguins	70	25	19	44	156	11	3	5	8	26
1989-90	Winnipeg Jets	28	5	6	11	34	....	....	....	....	....
	Hartford Whalers	43	9	9	18	41	4	0	0	0	2
1990-91	Hartford Whalers	32	9	5	14	49	1	0	0	0	0
1991-92	Hartford Whalers	39	7	10	17	71	7	3	0	3	9
1992-93	Hartford Whalers	39	5	4	9	63	....	....	....	....	....
1993-94	Hartford Whalers	63	9	8	17	87	....	....	....	....	....
	Chicago Blackhawks	16	4	3	7	13	6	0	0	0	8
1994-95	Ottawa Senators	48	5	5	10	68	....	....	....	....	....
1995-96	Ottawa Senators	81	17	19	36	130	....	....	....	....	....
1996-97	Ottawa Senators	76	12	24	36	99	7	1	1	2	10
1997-98	Ottawa Senators	71	2	11	13	63	6	0	1	1	6
1998-99	Buffalo Sabres	14	2	2	4	0	3	0	0	0	0
	NHL Totals	**866**	**189**	**225**	**414**	**1280**	**45**	**7**	**7**	**14**	**61**

Traded to **Pittsburgh** by **Buffalo** with Mike Moller for Pat Hughes, October 4, 1985. Traded to **Winnipeg** by **Pittsburgh** with Rick Tabaracci and Dave McLlwain for Jim Kyte, Andrew McBain and Randy Gilhen, June 17, 1989. Traded to **Hartford** by **Winnipeg** for Paul MacDermid, December 13, 1989. Traded to **Chicago** by **Hartford** with Gary Suter and Hartford's 3rd round choice (later traded to Vancouver – Vancouver selected Larry Courville) in 1995 Entry Draft for Frantisek Kucera and Jocelyn Lemieux, March 11, 1994. Signed as a free agent by **Ottawa**, July 15, 1994. Signed as a free agent by **Buffalo**, August 27, 1998.

		REGULAR SEASON					PLAYOFFS				
Season	Club	GP	G	A	Pts	PIM	GP	G	A	Pts	PIM

CUNNINGHAM, Bob

Center. Shoots left. 5'11", 168 lbs. Born, Welland, Ont., February 26, 1941.

Season	Club	GP	G	A	Pts	PIM	GP	G	A	Pts	PIM
1960-61	New York Rangers	3	0	1	1	0	....	....	....	....	....
1961-62	New York Rangers	1	0	0	0	0	....	....	....	....	....
	NHL Totals	**4**	**0**	**1**	**1**	**0**	....	....	....	....	....

Traded to **Detroit** (Pittsburgh-AHL) by **NY Rangers** for Dunc McCallum, June, 1965. Claimed by **NY Rangers** (Baltimore-AHL) from **Detroit** in Reverse Draft, June 15, 1966.

CUNNINGHAM, Jim

Left wing. Shoots left. 5'11", 185 lbs. Born, St. Paul, MN, August 15, 1956.

Season	Club	GP	G	A	Pts	PIM	GP	G	A	Pts	PIM
1977-78	Philadelphia Flyers	1	0	0	0	4	....	....	....	....	....
	NHL Totals	**1**	**0**	**0**	**0**	**4**	....	....	....	....	....

Signed as a free agent by **Philadelphia**, September, 1977. Claimed by **Winnipeg** from **Philadelphia** in Expansion Draft, June 13, 1979.

CUNNINGHAM, Les

Center. Shoots left. 5'8", 165 lbs. Born, Calgary, Alta., October 4, 1913.

Season	Club	GP	G	A	Pts	PIM	GP	G	A	Pts	PIM
1936-37	New York Americans	23	1	8	9	19	....	....	....	....	....
1939-40	Chicago Black Hawks	37	6	11	17	2	1	0	0	0	0
	NHL Totals	**60**	**7**	**19**	**26**	**21**	**1**	**0**	**0**	**0**	**0**

Traded to **NY Americans** by **Cleveland** (IAHL) for Lloyd Klein, January 14, 1937. Traded to **Cleveland** (IAHL) by **NY Americans** for cash, October, 1937. Claimed by **Chicago** from **Cleveland** (IAHL) in Inter-League Draft, May 14, 1939. Traded to **Cleveland** (AHL) by **Chicago** for cash, May 12, 1940.

CUPOLO, Bill

Right wing. Shoots right. 5'8", 170 lbs. Born, Niagara Falls, Ont., January 8, 1924.

Season	Club	GP	G	A	Pts	PIM	GP	G	A	Pts	PIM
1944-45	Boston Bruins	47	11	13	24	10	7	1	2	3	0
	NHL Totals	**47**	**11**	**13**	**24**	**10**	**7**	**1**	**2**	**3**	**0**

CURRAN, Brian

Defense. Shoots left. 6'5", 220 lbs. Born, Toronto, Ont., November 5, 1963.
(Boston's 2nd choice, 22nd overall, in 1982 Entry Draft).

Season	Club	GP	G	A	Pts	PIM	GP	G	A	Pts	PIM
1983-84	Boston Bruins	16	1	1	2	57	3	0	0	0	7
1984-85	Boston Bruins	56	0	1	1	158	....	....	....	....	....
1985-86	Boston Bruins	43	2	5	7	192	2	0	0	0	4
1986-87	New York Islanders	68	0	10	10	356	8	0	0	0	51
1987-88	New York Islanders	22	0	1	1	68	....	....	....	....	....
	Toronto Maple Leafs	7	0	1	1	19	6	0	0	0	41
1988-89	Toronto Maple Leafs	47	1	4	5	185	....	....	....	....	....
1989-90	Toronto Maple Leafs	72	2	9	11	301	5	0	1	1	19
1990-91	Toronto Maple Leafs	4	0	0	0	7	....	....	....	....	....
	Buffalo Sabres	17	0	1	1	43	....	....	....	....	....
1991-92	Buffalo Sabres	3	0	0	0	14	....	....	....	....	....
1993-94	Washington Capitals	26	1	0	1	61	....	....	....	....	....
	NHL Totals	**381**	**7**	**33**	**40**	**1461**	**24**	**0**	**1**	**1**	**122**

Signed as a free agent by **NY Islanders**, August 29, 1986. Traded to **Toronto** by **NY Islanders** for Toronto's 6th round choice (Pavel Gross) in 1988 Entry Draft, March 8, 1988. Traded to **Buffalo** by **Toronto** with Lou Franceschetti for Mike Foligno and Buffalo's 8th round choice (Tomas Kucharcik) in 1991 Entry Draft, December 17, 1990. Signed as a free agent by **Edmonton**, October 27, 1992. Signed as a free agent by **Washington**, October 21, 1993.

CURRIE, Dan

Left wing. Shoots left. 6'2", 195 lbs. Born, Burlington, Ont., March 15, 1968.
(Edmonton's 4th choice, 84th overall, in 1986 Entry Draft).

Season	Club	GP	G	A	Pts	PIM	GP	G	A	Pts	PIM
1990-91	Edmonton Oilers	5	0	0	0	0	....	....	....	....	....
1991-92	Edmonton Oilers	7	1	0	1	0	....	....	....	....	....
1992-93	Edmonton Oilers	5	0	0	0	4	....	....	....	....	....
1993-94	Los Angeles Kings	5	1	1	2	0	....	....	....	....	....
	NHL Totals	**22**	**2**	**1**	**3**	**4**	....	....	....	....	....

Signed as a free agent by **Los Angeles**, July 16, 1993.

CURRIE, Glen

Center. Shoots left. 6'2", 180 lbs. Born, Montreal, Que., July 18, 1958.
(Washington's 5th choice, 38th overall, in 1978 Amateur Draft).

Season	Club	GP	G	A	Pts	PIM	GP	G	A	Pts	PIM
1979-80	Washington Capitals	32	2	0	2	2	....	....	....	....	....
1980-81	Washington Capitals	40	5	13	18	16	....	....	....	....	....
1981-82	Washington Capitals	43	7	7	14	14	....	....	....	....	....
1982-83	Washington Capitals	68	11	28	39	20	4	0	3	3	4
1983-84	Washington Capitals	80	12	24	36	20	8	1	0	1	0
1984-85	Washington Capitals	44	1	5	6	19	....	....	....	....	....
1985-86	Los Angeles Kings	12	1	2	3	9	....	....	....	....	....
1987-88	Los Angeles Kings	7	0	0	0	0	....	....	....	....	....
	NHL Totals	**326**	**39**	**79**	**118**	**100**	**12**	**1**	**3**	**4**	**4**

Traded to **Los Angeles** by **Washington** for Daryl Evans, September 9, 1985. • Missed majority of 1985-86 season recovering from back injury suffered in training camp, September, 1985.

CURRIE, Hugh

Defense. Shoots right. 6', 190 lbs. Born, Saskatoon, Sask., October 22, 1925.

Season	Club	GP	G	A	Pts	PIM	GP	G	A	Pts	PIM
1950-51	Montreal Canadiens	1	0	0	0	0	....	....	....	....	....
	NHL Totals	**1**	**0**	**0**	**0**	**0**	....	....	....	....	....

CURRIE, Tony

Right wing. Shoots right. 5'11", 166 lbs. Born, Sydney Mines, N.S., November 12, 1957.
(St. Louis' 4th choice, 63rd overall, in 1977 Amateur Draft).

Season	Club	GP	G	A	Pts	PIM	GP	G	A	Pts	PIM
1977-78	St. Louis Blues	22	4	5	9	4	....	....	....	....	....
1978-79	St. Louis Blues	36	4	15	19	0	....	....	....	....	....
1979-80	St. Louis Blues	40	19	14	33	4	2	0	0	0	0
1980-81	St. Louis Blues	61	23	32	55	38	11	4	12	16	4
1981-82	St. Louis Blues	48	18	22	40	17	....	....	....	....	....
	Vancouver Canucks	12	5	3	8	2	3	0	0	0	10
1982-83	Vancouver Canucks	8	1	1	2	0	....	....	....	....	....
1983-84	Vancouver Canucks	18	3	3	6	2	....	....	....	....	....
	Hartford Whalers	32	12	16	28	4	....	....	....	....	....
1984-85	Hartford Whalers	13	3	8	11	12	....	....	....	....	....
	NHL Totals	**290**	**92**	**119**	**211**	**83**	**16**	**4**	**12**	**16**	**14**

Traded to **Vancouver** by **St. Louis** with Jim Nill, Rick Heinz and St. Louis' 4th round choice (Shawn Kilroy) in 1982 Entry Draft for Glen Hanlon, March 9, 1982. Signed as a free agent by **Hartford**, January 21, 1984. Claimed on waivers by **Edmonton** from **Hartford**, December 5, 1984. Signed as a free agent by **Quebec**, August 25, 1985.

CURRY, Floyd

Right wing. Shoots right. 5'11", 174 lbs. Born, Chapleau, Ont., August 11, 1925.

Season	Club	GP	G	A	Pts	PIM	GP	G	A	Pts	PIM
1947-48	Montreal Canadiens	31	1	5	6	0	....	....	....	....	....
1948-49	Montreal Canadiens	....	....	....	....	....	2	0	0	0	2
1949-50	Montreal Canadiens	49	8	8	16	8	5	1	0	1	2
1950-51	Montreal Canadiens	69	13	14	27	23	11	0	2	2	2
1951-52	Montreal Canadiens	64	20	18	38	10	11	4	3	*7	6
1952-53 ♦	Montreal Canadiens	68	16	6	22	10	12	2	1	3	2
1953-54	Montreal Canadiens	70	13	8	21	22	11	4	0	4	4
1954-55	Montreal Canadiens	68	11	10	21	36	12	8	4	12	4
1955-56 ♦	Montreal Canadiens	70	14	18	32	10	10	1	5	6	12
1956-57 ♦	Montreal Canadiens	70	7	9	16	20	10	3	2	5	2
1957-58 ♦	Montreal Canadiens	42	2	3	5	8	7	0	0	0	2
	NHL Totals	**601**	**105**	**99**	**204**	**147**	**91**	**23**	**17**	**40**	**38**

Played in NHL All-Star Game (1951, 1952, 1953, 1956, 1957)

Signed as a free agent by **Montreal**, October 18, 1945.

CURTALE, Tony

Defense. Shoots left. 6', 185 lbs. Born, Detroit, MI, January 29, 1962.
(Calgary's 2nd choice, 31st overall, in 1980 Entry Draft).

Season	Club	GP	G	A	Pts	PIM	GP	G	A	Pts	PIM
1980-81	Calgary Flames	2	0	0	0	0	....	....	....	....	....
	NHL Totals	**2**	**0**	**0**	**0**	**0**	....	....	....	....	....

CURTIS, Paul

Defense. Shoots left. 6', 185 lbs. Born, Peterborough, Ont., September 29, 1947.

Season	Club	GP	G	A	Pts	PIM	GP	G	A	Pts	PIM
1969-70	Montreal Canadiens	1	0	0	0	0	....	....	....	....	....
1970-71	Los Angeles Kings	64	1	13	14	82	....	....	....	....	....
1971-72	Los Angeles Kings	64	1	12	13	57	....	....	....	....	....
1972-73	Los Angeles Kings	27	0	5	5	16	....	....	....	....	....
	St. Louis Blues	29	1	4	5	6	5	0	0	0	2
	NHL Totals	**185**	**3**	**34**	**37**	**161**	**5**	**0**	**0**	**0**	**2**

Claimed by **Los Angeles** from **Montreal** in Intra-League Draft, June 9, 1970. Traded to **St. Louis** by **Los Angeles** for Frank St. Marseille, January 22, 1973. Traded to **Buffalo** by **St. Louis** for Jake Rathwell, June 14, 1973. Traded to **NY Rangers** by **Buffalo** for Real Lemieux, January 21, 1974.

CUSHENAN, Ian

Defense. Shoots left. 6'2", 195 lbs. Born, Hamilton, Ont., November 29, 1933.

Season	Club	GP	G	A	Pts	PIM	GP	G	A	Pts	PIM
1956-57	Chicago Black Hawks	11	0	0	0	13	....	....	....	....	....
1957-58	Chicago Black Hawks	61	2	8	10	67	....	....	....	....	....
1958-59 ♦	Montreal Canadiens	35	1	2	3	28	....	....	....	....	....
1959-60	New York Rangers	17	0	1	1	22	....	....	....	....	....
1963-64	Detroit Red Wings	5	0	0	0	4	....	....	....	....	....
	NHL Totals	**129**	**3**	**11**	**14**	**134**	....	....	....	....	....

Played in NHL All-Star Game (1958)

Traded to **Chicago** by **Cleveland** (AHL) for Ron Ingram, September 4, 1956. Traded to **Montreal** by **Chicago** for cash, September, 1958. Traded to **Chicago** by **Montreal** for cash, June, 1959. Claimed by **NY Rangers** from **Chicago** in Intra-League Draft, June 10, 1959. Claimed by **Detroit** from **Buffalo** (AHL) in Inter-League Draft, June 4, 1963. Traded to **Chicago** by **Detroit** with John Miszuk and Art Stratton for Ron Murphy and Aut Erickson, June 9, 1964.

CUSSON, Jean

Left wing. Shoots left. 5'10", 170 lbs. Born, Verdun, Que., October 5, 1942.

Season	Club	GP	G	A	Pts	PIM	GP	G	A	Pts	PIM
1967-68	Oakland Seals	2	0	0	0	0	....	....	....	....	....
	NHL Totals	**2**	**0**	**0**	**0**	**0**	....	....	....	....	....

Signed as a free agent by **Oakland** to three-game amateur tryout contract, March, 1968.

CUTTA, Jakub

Defense. Shoots left. 6'3", 217 lbs. Born, Jablonec nad Nisou, Czech., December 29, 1981.
(Washington's 3rd choice, 61st overall, in 2000 Entry Draft).

Season	Club	GP	G	A	Pts	PIM	GP	G	A	Pts	PIM
2000-01	Washington Capitals	3	0	0	0	0	....	....	....	....	....
2001-02	Washington Capitals	2	0	0	0	0	....	....	....	....	....
	NHL Totals	**5**	**0**	**0**	**0**	**0**	....	....	....	....	....

CYR, Denis

Right wing. Shoots left. 5'10", 180 lbs. Born, Verdun, Que., February 4, 1961.
(Calgary's 1st choice, 13th overall, in 1980 Entry Draft).

Season	Club	Regular Season GP	G	A	Pts	PIM	Playoffs GP	G	A	Pts	PIM
1980-81	Calgary Flames	10	1	4	5	0	....	....	....	....	....
1981-82	Calgary Flames	45	12	10	22	13	....	....	....	....	....
1982-83	Calgary Flames	11	1	1	2	0	....	....	....	....	....
	Chicago Black Hawks	41	7	8	15	2	1	0	0	0	0
1983-84	Chicago Black Hawks	46	12	13	25	19	....	....	....	....	....
1984-85	St. Louis Blues	9	5	3	8	0	3	0	0	0	0
1985-86	St. Louis Blues	31	3	4	7	2	....	....	....	....	....
	NHL Totals	**193**	**41**	**43**	**84**	**36**	**4**	**0**	**0**	**0**	**0**

Traded to **Chicago** by **Calgary** for the rights to Carey Wilson, November 8, 1982. Signed as a free agent by **St. Louis**, September 14, 1984.

CYR, Paul

Left wing. Shoots left. 5'10", 180 lbs. Born, Port Alberni, B.C., October 31, 1963.
(Buffalo's 2nd choice, 9th overall, in 1982 Entry Draft).

Season	Club	Regular Season GP	G	A	Pts	PIM	Playoffs GP	G	A	Pts	PIM
1982-83	Buffalo Sabres	36	15	12	27	59	10	1	3	4	6
1983-84	Buffalo Sabres	71	16	27	43	52	3	0	1	1	0
1984-85	Buffalo Sabres	71	22	24	46	63	5	2	2	4	15
1985-86	Buffalo Sabres	71	20	31	51	120	....	....	....	....	....
1986-87	Buffalo Sabres	73	11	16	27	122	....	....	....	....	....
1987-88	Buffalo Sabres	20	1	1	2	38	....	....	....	....	....
	New York Rangers	40	4	13	17	41	....	....	....	....	....
1988-89	New York Rangers	1	0	0	0	2	....	....	....	....	....
1990-91	Hartford Whalers	70	12	13	25	107	6	1	0	1	10
1991-92	Hartford Whalers	17	0	3	3	19	....	....	....	....	....
	NHL Totals	**470**	**101**	**140**	**241**	**623**	**24**	**4**	**6**	**10**	**31**

Traded to **NY Rangers** by **Buffalo** with Buffalo's 10th round choice (Eric Fenton) in 1988 Entry Draft for Mike Donnelly and NY Rangers' 5th round choice (Alexander Mogilny) in 1988 Entry Draft, December 31, 1987. • Missed majority of 1988-89 season and entire 1989-90 season recovering from knee surgery. Signed as a free agent by **Hartford**, September 30, 1990.

CZERKAWSKI, Mariusz

Right wing. Shoots left. 6', 200 lbs. Born, Radomsko, Poland, April 13, 1972.
(Boston's 5th choice, 106th overall, in 1991 Entry Draft).

Season	Club	Regular Season GP	G	A	Pts	PIM	Playoffs GP	G	A	Pts	PIM
1993-94	Boston Bruins	4	2	1	3	0	13	3	3	6	4
1994-95	Boston Bruins	47	12	14	26	31	5	1	0	1	0
1995-96	Boston Bruins	33	5	6	11	10	....	....	....	....	....
	Edmonton Oilers	37	12	17	29	8	....	....	....	....	....
1996-97	Edmonton Oilers	76	26	21	47	16	12	2	1	3	10
1997-98	New York Islanders	68	12	13	25	23	....	....	....	....	....
1998-99	New York Islanders	78	21	17	38	14	....	....	....	....	....
99-2000	New York Islanders	79	35	35	70	34	....	....	....	....	....
2000-01	New York Islanders	82	30	32	62	48	....	....	....	....	....
2001-02	New York Islanders	82	22	29	51	48	7	2	2	4	4
2002-03	Montreal Canadiens	43	5	9	14	16	....	....	....	....	....
	NHL Totals	**629**	**182**	**194**	**376**	**248**	**37**	**8**	**6**	**14**	**18**

Played in NHL All-Star Game (2000)

Traded to **Edmonton** by **Boston** with Sean Brown and Boston's 1st round choice (Matthieu Descoteaux) in 1996 Entry Draft for Bill Ranford, January 11, 1996. Traded to **NY Islanders** by **Edmonton** for Dan LaCouture, August 25, 1997. Traded to **Montreal** by **NY Islanders** for Arron Asham and Montreal's 5th round choice (Marcus Paulsson) in 2002 Entry Draft, June 22, 2002. Signed as a free agent by **NY Islanders**, July 17, 2003.

DACKELL, Andreas

Right wing. Shoots right. 5'11", 194 lbs. Born, Gavle, Sweden, December 29, 1972.
(Ottawa's 3rd choice, 136th overall, in 1996 Entry Draft).

Season	Club	Regular Season GP	G	A	Pts	PIM	Playoffs GP	G	A	Pts	PIM
1996-97	Ottawa Senators	79	12	19	31	8	7	1	0	1	0
1997-98	Ottawa Senators	82	15	18	33	24	11	1	1	2	2
1998-99	Ottawa Senators	77	15	35	50	30	4	0	1	1	0
99-2000	Ottawa Senators	82	10	25	35	18	6	2	1	3	2
2000-01	Ottawa Senators	81	13	18	31	24	4	0	0	0	0
2001-02	Montreal Canadiens	79	15	18	33	24	12	1	2	3	6
2002-03	Montreal Canadiens	73	7	18	25	24	....	....	....	....	....
	NHL Totals	**553**	**87**	**151**	**238**	**152**	**44**	**5**	**5**	**10**	**10**

Traded to **Montreal** by **Ottawa** for Montreal's 8th round choice (Neil Petruic) in 2001 Entry Draft, June 24, 2001.

DAGENAIS, Pierre

Right wing. Shoots left. 6'5", 215 lbs. Born, Blainville, Que., March 4, 1978.
(New Jersey's 6th choice, 105th overall, in 1998 Entry Draft).

Season	Club	Regular Season GP	G	A	Pts	PIM	Playoffs GP	G	A	Pts	PIM
2000-01	New Jersey Devils	9	3	2	5	6	....	....	....	....	....
2001-02	New Jersey Devils	16	3	3	6	4	....	....	....	....	....
	Florida Panthers	26	7	1	8	4	....	....	....	....	....
2002-03	Florida Panthers	9	0	0	0	4	....	....	....	....	....
	NHL Totals	**60**	**13**	**6**	**19**	**18**	....	....	....	....	....

• Re-entered NHL Entry Draft. Originally New Jersey's 4th choice, 47th overall, in 1996 Entry Draft.

Claimed on waivers by **Florida** from **New Jersey**, January 12, 2002. Signed as a free agent by **Montreal**, July 4, 2003.

DAHL, Kevin

Defense. Shoots right. 5'11", 190 lbs. Born, Regina, Sask., December 30, 1968.
(Montreal's 12th choice, 230th overall, in 1988 Entry Draft).

Season	Club	Regular Season GP	G	A	Pts	PIM	Playoffs GP	G	A	Pts	PIM
1992-93	Calgary Flames	61	2	9	11	56	6	0	2	2	8
1993-94	Calgary Flames	33	0	3	3	23	6	0	0	0	4
1994-95	Calgary Flames	34	4	8	12	38	3	0	0	0	0
1995-96	Calgary Flames	32	1	1	2	26	1	0	0	0	0
1996-97	Phoenix Coyotes	2	0	0	0	0	....	....	....	....	....
1997-98	Calgary Flames	19	0	1	1	6	....	....	....	....	....
1998-99	Toronto Maple Leafs	3	0	0	0	2	....	....	....	....	....
2000-01	Columbus Blue Jackets	4	0	0	0	2	....	....	....	....	....
	NHL Totals	**188**	**7**	**22**	**29**	**153**	**16**	**0**	**2**	**2**	**12**

Signed as a free agent by **Calgary**, July 27, 1991. Signed as a free agent by **Phoenix**, September 4, 1996. Signed as a free agent by **Calgary**, September 8, 1997. Signed as a free agent by **St. Louis**, September 4, 1998. Claimed by **Toronto** from **St. Louis** in Waiver Draft, October 5, 1998. Signed as a free agent by **NY Islanders**, August 12, 1999. Signed as a free agent by **Columbus**, August 24, 2000.

DAHLEN, Ulf

Left wing. Shoots left. 6'2", 199 lbs. Born, Ostersund, Sweden, January 12, 1967.
(NY Rangers' 1st choice, 7th overall, in 1985 Entry Draft).

Season	Club	Regular Season GP	G	A	Pts	PIM	Playoffs GP	G	A	Pts	PIM
1987-88	New York Rangers	70	29	23	52	26	....	....	....	....	....
1988-89	New York Rangers	56	24	19	43	50	4	0	0	0	0
1989-90	New York Rangers	63	18	18	36	30	....	....	....	....	....
	Minnesota North Stars	13	2	4	6	0	7	1	4	5	2
1990-91	Minnesota North Stars	66	21	18	39	6	15	2	6	8	4
1991-92	Minnesota North Stars	79	36	30	66	10	7	0	3	3	2
1992-93	Minnesota North Stars	83	35	39	74	6	....	....	....	....	....
1993-94	Dallas Stars	65	19	38	57	10	....	....	....	....	....
	San Jose Sharks	13	6	6	12	0	14	6	2	8	0
1994-95	San Jose Sharks	46	11	23	34	11	11	5	4	9	0
1995-96	San Jose Sharks	59	16	12	28	27	....	....	....	....	....
1996-97	San Jose Sharks	43	8	11	19	8	....	....	....	....	....
	Chicago Blackhawks	30	6	8	14	10	5	0	1	1	0
99-2000	Washington Capitals	75	15	23	38	8	5	0	1	1	2
2000-01	Washington Capitals	73	15	33	48	6	6	0	1	1	2
2001-02	Washington Capitals	69	23	29	52	8	....	....	....	....	....
2002-03	Dallas Stars	63	17	20	37	14	11	1	3	4	0
	NHL Totals	**966**	**301**	**354**	**655**	**230**	**85**	**15**	**25**	**40**	**12**

Traded to **Minnesota** by **NY Rangers** with Los Angeles' 4th round choice (previously acquired, Minnesota selected Cal McGowan) in 1990 Entry Draft for Mike Gartner, March 6, 1990. Transferred to **Dallas** after **Minnesota** franchise relocated, June 9, 1993. Traded to **San Jose** by **Dallas** with Dallas' 7th round choice (Brad Mehalko) in 1995 Entry Draft for Doug Zmolek and Mike Lalor, March 19, 1994. Traded to **Chicago** by **San Jose** with Chris Terreri and Michal Sykora for Ed Belfour, January 25, 1997. Signed as a free agent by **Washington**, August 16, 1999. Signed as a free agent by **Dallas**, August 13, 2002.

DAHLIN, Kjell

Right wing. Shoots left. 6', 175 lbs. Born, Timra, Sweden, February 2, 1963.
(Montreal's 7th choice, 82nd overall, in 1981 Entry Draft).

Season	Club	Regular Season GP	G	A	Pts	PIM	Playoffs GP	G	A	Pts	PIM
1985-86 ◆	Montreal Canadiens	77	32	39	71	4	16	2	3	5	4
1986-87	Montreal Canadiens	41	12	8	20	0	8	2	4	6	0
1987-88	Montreal Canadiens	48	13	12	25	6	11	2	4	6	2
	NHL Totals	**166**	**57**	**59**	**116**	**10**	**35**	**6**	**11**	**17**	**6**

NHL All-Rookie Team (1986)

DAHLMAN, Toni

Right wing. Shoots right. 6', 193 lbs. Born, Helsinki, Finland, September 3, 1979.
(Ottawa's 12th choice, 286th overall, in 2001 Entry Draft).

Season	Club	Regular Season GP	G	A	Pts	PIM	Playoffs GP	G	A	Pts	PIM
2001-02	Ottawa Senators	10	0	1	1	0	....	....	....	....	....
2002-03	Ottawa Senators	12	1	0	1	0	....	....	....	....	....
	NHL Totals	**22**	**1**	**1**	**2**	**0**	....	....	....	....	....

DAHLQUIST, Chris

Defense. Shoots left. 6'1", 195 lbs. Born, Fridley, MN, December 14, 1962.

Season	Club	Regular Season GP	G	A	Pts	PIM	Playoffs GP	G	A	Pts	PIM
1985-86	Pittsburgh Penguins	5	1	2	3	2	....	....	....	....	....
1986-87	Pittsburgh Penguins	19	0	1	1	20	....	....	....	....	....
1987-88	Pittsburgh Penguins	44	3	6	9	69	....	....	....	....	....
1988-89	Pittsburgh Penguins	43	1	5	6	42	2	0	0	0	0
1989-90	Pittsburgh Penguins	62	4	10	14	56	....	....	....	....	....
1990-91	Pittsburgh Penguins	22	1	2	3	30	....	....	....	....	....
	Minnesota North Stars	42	2	6	8	33	23	1	6	7	20
1991-92	Minnesota North Stars	74	1	13	14	68	7	0	0	0	6
1992-93	Calgary Flames	74	3	7	10	66	6	3	1	4	4
1993-94	Calgary Flames	77	1	11	12	52	1	0	0	0	0
1994-95	Ottawa Senators	46	1	7	8	36	....	....	....	....	....
1995-96	Ottawa Senators	24	1	1	2	14	....	....	....	....	....
	NHL Totals	**532**	**19**	**71**	**90**	**488**	**39**	**4**	**7**	**11**	**30**

Signed as a free agent by **Pittsburgh**, May 7, 1985. Traded to **Minnesota** by **Pittsburgh** with Jim Johnson for Larry Murphy and Peter Taglianetti, December 11, 1990. Claimed by **Calgary** from **Minnesota** in NHL Waiver Draft, October 4, 1992. Signed as a free agent by **Ottawa**, July 4, 1994.

DAHLSTROM, Cully

USHOF

Center. Shoots left. 5'11", 175 lbs. Born, Minneapolis, MN, July 3, 1912.

Season	Club	Regular Season GP	G	A	Pts	PIM	Playoffs GP	G	A	Pts	PIM
1937-38 ◆	Chicago Black Hawks	48	10	9	19	11	10	3	1	4	2
1938-39	Chicago Black Hawks	48	6	14	20	2	....	....	....	....	....
1939-40	Chicago Black Hawks	45	11	19	30	15	2	0	0	0	0
1940-41	Chicago Black Hawks	40	11	14	25	6	5	3	3	6	2
1941-42	Chicago Black Hawks	33	13	14	27	6	3	0	0	0	0
1942-43	Chicago Black Hawks	38	11	13	24	10	....	....	....	....	....
1943-44	Chicago Black Hawks	50	20	22	42	8	9	0	4	4	0

Season	Club	REGULAR SEASON GP	G	A	Pts	PIM	PLAYOFFS GP	G	A	Pts	PIM
1944-45	Chicago Black Hawks	40	6	13	19	0	....	....	....	....	....
	NHL Totals	**342**	**88**	**118**	**206**	**58**	**29**	**6**	**8**	**14**	**4**

Calder Trophy (1938)

Traded to **Boston** by **Minneapolis** (CHL) for cash with Minneapolis retaining right to repurchase if he did not make the Bruins, June 27, 1932. Traded to **Chicago** by **St. Paul** (CHL) for cash with St. Paul retaining right to repurchase if he did not make the Black Hawks, January 27, 1935. Claimed by **Chicago** from **St. Paul** (AHA) in Inter-League Draft, May 9, 1937. Traded to **Seattle** (PCHL) by **Chicago** for cash, November 26, 1945.

DAIGLE, Alain

Right wing. Shoots right. 5'10", 180 lbs. Born, Trois-Rivieres, Que., August 24, 1954.
(Chicago's 2nd choice, 34th overall, in 1974 Amateur Draft).

Season	Club	GP	G	A	Pts	PIM	GP	G	A	Pts	PIM
1974-75	Chicago Black Hawks	52	5	4	9	6	2	0	0	0	0
1975-76	Chicago Black Hawks	71	15	9	24	15	4	0	0	0	0
1976-77	Chicago Black Hawks	73	12	8	20	11	1	0	0	0	0
1977-78	Chicago Black Hawks	53	6	6	12	13	4	0	1	1	0
1978-79	Chicago Black Hawks	74	11	14	25	55	4	0	0	0	0
1979-80	Chicago Black Hawks	66	7	9	16	22	2	0	0	0	0
	NHL Totals	**389**	**56**	**50**	**106**	**122**	**17**	**0**	**1**	**1**	**0**

DAIGLE, Alexandre

Center. Shoots left. 6', 195 lbs. Born, Montreal, Que., February 7, 1975.
(Ottawa's 1st choice, 1st overall, in 1993 Entry Draft).

Season	Club	GP	G	A	Pts	PIM	GP	G	A	Pts	PIM
1993-94	Ottawa Senators	84	20	31	51	40	....	....	....	....	....
1994-95	Ottawa Senators	47	16	21	37	14	....	....	....	....	....
1995-96	Ottawa Senators	50	5	12	17	24	....	....	....	....	....
1996-97	Ottawa Senators	82	26	25	51	33	7	0	0	0	2
1997-98	Ottawa Senators	38	7	9	16	8	....	....	....	....	....
	Philadelphia Flyers	37	9	17	26	6	5	0	2	2	0
1998-99	Philadelphia Flyers	31	3	2	5	2	....	....	....	....	....
	Tampa Bay Lightning	32	6	6	12	2	....	....	....	....	....
99-2000	New York Rangers	58	8	18	26	23	....	....	....	....	....
2002-03	Pittsburgh Penguins	33	4	3	7	8	....	....	....	....	....
	NHL Totals	**492**	**104**	**144**	**248**	**160**	**12**	**0**	**2**	**2**	**2**

Traded to **Philadelphia** by **Ottawa** for Vaclav Prospal, Pat Falloon and Dallas' 2nd round choice (previously acquired, Ottawa selected Chris Bala) in 1998 Entry Draft, January 17, 1998. Traded to **Edmonton** by **Philadelphia** for Andrei Kovalenko, January 29, 1999. Traded to **Tampa Bay** by **Edmonton** for Alexander Selivanov, January 29, 1999. Traded to **NY Rangers** by **Tampa Bay** for cash, October 3, 1999. Signed to a free agent tryout contract by **Pittsburgh**, August 13, 2002.

DAIGNEAULT, J.J.

Defense. Shoots left. 5'10", 192 lbs. Born, Montreal, Que., October 12, 1965.
(Vancouver's 1st choice, 10th overall, in 1984 Entry Draft).

Season	Club	GP	G	A	Pts	PIM	GP	G	A	Pts	PIM
1984-85	Vancouver Canucks	67	4	23	27	69	....	....	....	....	....
1985-86	Vancouver Canucks	64	5	23	28	45	3	0	2	2	0
1986-87	Philadelphia Flyers	77	6	16	22	56	9	1	0	1	0
1987-88	Philadelphia Flyers	28	2	2	4	12	....	....	....	....	....
1989-90	Montreal Canadiens	36	2	10	12	14	9	0	0	0	2
1990-91	Montreal Canadiens	51	3	16	19	31	5	0	1	1	0
1991-92	Montreal Canadiens	79	4	14	18	36	11	0	3	3	4
1992-93 ◆	Montreal Canadiens	66	8	10	18	57	20	1	3	4	22
1993-94	Montreal Canadiens	68	2	12	14	73	7	0	1	1	12
1994-95	Montreal Canadiens	45	3	5	8	40	....	....	....	....	....
1995-96	Montreal Canadiens	7	0	1	1	6	....	....	....	....	....
	St. Louis Blues	37	1	3	4	24	....	....	....	....	....
	Pittsburgh Penguins	13	3	3	6	23	17	1	9	10	36
1996-97	Pittsburgh Penguins	53	3	14	17	36	....	....	....	....	....
	Mighty Ducks of Anaheim	13	2	9	11	22	11	2	7	9	16
1997-98	Mighty Ducks of Anaheim	53	2	15	17	28	....	....	....	....	....
	New York Islanders	18	0	6	6	21	....	....	....	....	....
1998-99	Nashville Predators	35	2	2	4	38	....	....	....	....	....
	Phoenix Coyotes	35	0	7	7	32	6	0	0	0	8
99-2000	Phoenix Coyotes	53	1	6	7	22	1	0	0	0	0
2000-01	Minnesota Wild	1	0	0	0	2	....	....	....	....	....
	NHL Totals	**899**	**53**	**197**	**250**	**687**	**99**	**5**	**26**	**31**	**100**

Traded to **Philadelphia** by **Vancouver** with Vancouver's 2nd round choice (Kent Hawley) in 1986 Entry Draft and 5th round choice (later traded back to Vancouver – Vancouver selected Sean Fabian) in 1987 Entry Draft for Dave Richter, Rich Sutter and Vancouver's 3rd round choice (previously acquired, Vancouver selected Don Gibson) in 1986 Entry Draft, June 6, 1986. Traded to **Montreal** by **Philadelphia** for Scott Sandelin, November 7, 1988. Traded to **St. Louis** by **Montreal** for Pat Jablonski, November 7, 1995. Traded to **Pittsburgh** by **St. Louis** for Pittsburgh's 6th round choice (Stephen Wagner) in 1996 Entry Draft, March 20, 1996. Traded to **Anaheim** by **Pittsburgh** for Garry Valk, February 21, 1997. Traded to **NY Islanders** by **Anaheim** with Joe Sacco and Mark Janssens for Travis Green, Doug Houda and Tony Tuzzolino, February 6, 1998. Claimed by **Nashville** from **NY Islanders** in Expansion Draft, June 26, 1998. Traded to **Phoenix** by **Nashville** for future considerations, January 13, 1999. Signed as a free agent by **Minnesota**, July 24, 2000.

DAILEY, Bob

Defense. Shoots right. 6'5", 220 lbs. Born, Kingston, Ont., May 3, 1953.
(Vancouver's 2nd choice, 9th overall, in 1973 Amateur Draft).

Season	Club	GP	G	A	Pts	PIM	GP	G	A	Pts	PIM
1973-74	Vancouver Canucks	76	7	17	24	143	....	....	....	....	....
1974-75	Vancouver Canucks	70	12	36	48	103	5	1	3	4	14
1975-76	Vancouver Canucks	67	15	24	39	119	2	1	1	2	0
1976-77	Vancouver Canucks	44	4	16	20	52	....	....	....	....	....
	Philadelphia Flyers	32	5	14	19	38	10	4	9	13	15
1977-78	Philadelphia Flyers	76	21	36	57	62	12	1	5	6	22
1978-79	Philadelphia Flyers	70	9	30	39	63	8	1	2	3	14
1979-80	Philadelphia Flyers	61	13	26	39	71	19	4	13	17	22
1980-81	Philadelphia Flyers	53	7	27	34	141	7	0	1	1	18
1981-82	Philadelphia Flyers	12	1	5	6	22	....	....	....	....	....
	NHL Totals	**561**	**94**	**231**	**325**	**814**	**63**	**12**	**34**	**46**	**105**

Played in NHL All-Star Game (1978, 1981)

Traded to **Philadelphia** by **Vancouver** for Larry Goodenough and Jack McIlhargey, January 20, 1977. • Missed remainder of 1981-82 recovering from ankle injury suffered in game vs. Buffalo, November 1, 1981. • Officially announced retirement, July, 1982.

DALEY, Frank

Left wing/Center. Shoots left. 5'11", 178 lbs. Born, Port Arthur, Ont., August 22, 1909.

Season	Club	GP	G	A	Pts	PIM	GP	G	A	Pts	PIM
1928-29	Detroit Cougars	5	0	0	0	0	2	0	0	0	0
	NHL Totals	**5**	**0**	**0**	**0**	**0**	**2**	**0**	**0**	**0**	**0**

Traded to **Detroit** by **Houghton** (NMHL) for cash, February 23, 1929. Traded to **Cleveland** (IHL) by **Detroit** for cash, October 28, 1931.

DALEY, Pat

Left wing. Shoots left. 6'1", 176 lbs. Born, Maryville, France, March 27, 1959.
(Winnipeg's 4th choice, 82nd overall, in 1979 Entry Draft).

Season	Club	GP	G	A	Pts	PIM	GP	G	A	Pts	PIM
1979-80	Winnipeg Jets	5	1	0	1	4	....	....	....	....	....
1980-81	Winnipeg Jets	7	0	0	0	9	....	....	....	....	....
	NHL Totals	**12**	**1**	**0**	**1**	**13**	....	....	....	....	....

Signed as a free agent by **Quebec**, July, 1981.

DALGARNO, Brad

Right wing. Shoots right. 6'3", 215 lbs. Born, Vancouver, B.C., August 11, 1967.
(NY Islanders' 1st choice, 6th overall, in 1985 Entry Draft).

Season	Club	GP	G	A	Pts	PIM	GP	G	A	Pts	PIM
1985-86	New York Islanders	2	1	0	1	0	....	....	....	....	....
1986-87	New York Islanders	....	....	....	....	....	1	0	1	1	0
1987-88	New York Islanders	38	2	8	10	58	4	0	0	0	19
1988-89	New York Islanders	55	11	10	21	86	....	....	....	....	....
1990-91	New York Islanders	41	3	12	15	24	....	....	....	....	....
1991-92	New York Islanders	15	2	1	3	12	....	....	....	....	....
1992-93	New York Islanders	57	15	17	32	62	18	2	2	4	14
1993-94	New York Islanders	73	11	19	30	62	4	0	1	1	4
1994-95	New York Islanders	22	3	2	5	14	....	....	....	....	....
1995-96	New York Islanders	18	1	2	3	14	....	....	....	....	....
	NHL Totals	**321**	**49**	**71**	**120**	**332**	**27**	**2**	**4**	**6**	**37**

• Missed remainder of 1988-89 season and entire 1989-90 season recovering from eye injury suffered in game vs. Detroit, February 21, 1989.

DALLMAN, Marty

Center. Shoots right. 5'10", 180 lbs. Born, Niagara Falls, Ont., February 15, 1963.
(Los Angeles' 3rd choice, 81st overall, in 1981 Entry Draft).

Season	Club	GP	G	A	Pts	PIM	GP	G	A	Pts	PIM
1987-88	Toronto Maple Leafs	2	0	1	1	0	....	....	....	....	....
1988-89	Toronto Maple Leafs	4	0	0	0	0	....	....	....	....	....
	NHL Totals	**6**	**0**	**1**	**1**	**0**	....	....	....	....	....

Signed as a free agent by **Toronto**, November, 1986.

DALLMAN, Rod

Left wing. Shoots left. 5'11", 185 lbs. Born, Prince Albert, Sask., January 26, 1967.
(NY Islanders' 8th choice, 118th overall, in 1985 Entry Draft).

Season	Club	GP	G	A	Pts	PIM	GP	G	A	Pts	PIM
1987-88	New York Islanders	3	1	0	1	6	....	....	....	....	....
1988-89	New York Islanders	1	0	0	0	15	....	....	....	....	....
1989-90	New York Islanders	....	....	....	....	....	1	0	1	1	0
1991-92	Philadelphia Flyers	2	0	0	0	5	....	....	....	....	....
	NHL Totals	**6**	**1**	**0**	**1**	**26**	**1**	**0**	**1**	**1**	**0**

Signed as a free agent by **Philadelphia**, July 31, 1990.

DAME, Bunny

Left wing. Shoots left. 5'9", 160 lbs. Born, Edmonton, Alta., December 6, 1913.

Season	Club	GP	G	A	Pts	PIM	GP	G	A	Pts	PIM
1941-42	Montreal Canadiens	34	2	5	7	4	....	....	....	....	....
	NHL Totals	**34**	**2**	**5**	**7**	**4**	....	....	....	....	....

Signed as a free agent by **Montreal**, October 16, 1941.

DAMORE, Hank

Center. Shoots left. 5'6", 200 lbs. Born, Niagara Falls, Ont., July 17, 1919.

Season	Club	GP	G	A	Pts	PIM	GP	G	A	Pts	PIM
1943-44	New York Rangers	4	1	0	1	2	....	....	....	....	....
	NHL Totals	**4**	**1**	**0**	**1**	**2**	....	....	....	....	....

• Brother of Nick

DAMPHOUSSE, Vincent

Center. Shoots left. 6'1", 200 lbs. Born, Montreal, Que., December 17, 1967.
(Toronto's 1st choice, 6th overall, in 1986 Entry Draft).

Season	Club	GP	G	A	Pts	PIM	GP	G	A	Pts	PIM
1986-87	Toronto Maple Leafs	80	21	25	46	26	12	1	5	6	8
1987-88	Toronto Maple Leafs	75	12	36	48	40	6	0	1	1	10
1988-89	Toronto Maple Leafs	80	26	42	68	75	....	....	....	....	....
1989-90	Toronto Maple Leafs	80	33	61	94	56	5	0	2	2	2
1990-91	Toronto Maple Leafs	79	26	47	73	65	....	....	....	....	....
1991-92	Edmonton Oilers	80	38	51	89	53	16	6	8	14	8
1992-93 ◆	Montreal Canadiens	84	39	58	97	98	20	11	12	23	16
1993-94	Montreal Canadiens	84	40	51	91	75	7	1	2	3	8
1994-95	Montreal Canadiens	48	10	30	40	42	....	....	....	....	....

Season	Club	REGULAR SEASON GP	G	A	Pts	PIM	PLAYOFFS GP	G	A	Pts	PIM
1995-96	Montreal Canadiens	80	38	56	94	158	6	4	4	8	0
1996-97	Montreal Canadiens	82	27	54	81	82	5	0	0	0	2
1997-98	Montreal Canadiens	76	18	41	59	58	10	3	6	9	22
1998-99	Montreal Canadiens	65	12	24	36	46	....	....	....	....	....
	San Jose Sharks	12	7	6	13	4	6	3	2	5	6
99-2000	San Jose Sharks	82	21	49	70	58	12	1	7	8	16
2000-01	San Jose Sharks	45	9	37	46	62	6	2	1	3	14
2001-02	San Jose Sharks	82	20	38	58	60	12	2	6	8	12
2002-03	San Jose Sharks	82	23	38	61	66	....	....	....	....	....
	NHL Totals	**1296**	**420**	**744**	**1164**	**1124**	**123**	**34**	**56**	**90**	**124**

Played in NHL All-Star Game (1991, 1992, 2002)

Traded to **Edmonton** by **Toronto** with Peter Ing, Scott Thornton and Luke Richardson for Grant Fuhr, Glenn Anderson and Craig Berube, September 19, 1991. Traded to **Montreal** by **Edmonton** with Edmonton's 4th round choice (Adam Wiesel) in 1993 Entry Draft for Shayne Corson, Brent Gilchrist and Vladimir Vujtek, August 27, 1992. Traded to **San Jose** by **Montreal** for Phoenix's 5th round choice (previously acquired, Montreal selected Marc-Andre Thinel) in 1999 Entry Draft, San Jose's 1st round choice (Marcel Hossa) in 2000 Entry Draft and 2nd round choice (later traded to Columbus – Columbus selected Kiel McLeod) in 2001 Entry Draft, March 23, 1999.

DANDENAULT, Mathieu

Right wing/Defense. Shoots right. 6', 200 lbs. Born, Sherbrooke, Que., February 3, 1976.
(Detroit's 2nd choice, 49th overall, in 1994 Entry Draft).

Season	Club	GP	G	A	Pts	PIM	GP	G	A	Pts	PIM
1995-96	Detroit Red Wings	34	5	7	12	6	....	....	....	....	....
1996-97 ◆	Detroit Red Wings	65	3	9	12	28	....	....	....	....	....
1997-98 ◆	Detroit Red Wings	68	5	12	17	43	3	1	0	1	0
1998-99	Detroit Red Wings	75	4	10	14	59	10	0	1	1	0
99-2000	Detroit Red Wings	81	6	12	18	20	6	0	0	0	2
2000-01	Detroit Red Wings	73	10	15	25	38	6	0	1	1	0
2001-02 ◆	Detroit Red Wings	81	8	12	20	44	23	1	2	3	8
2002-03	Detroit Red Wings	74	4	15	19	64	4	0	0	0	2
	NHL Totals	**551**	**45**	**92**	**137**	**302**	**52**	**2**	**4**	**6**	**12**

DANEYKO, Ken

Defense. Shoots left. 6'1", 215 lbs. Born, Windsor, Ont., April 17, 1964.
(New Jersey's 2nd choice, 18th overall, in 1982 Entry Draft).

Season	Club	GP	G	A	Pts	PIM	GP	G	A	Pts	PIM
1983-84	New Jersey Devils	11	1	4	5	17	....	....	....	....	....
1984-85	New Jersey Devils	1	0	0	0	10	....	....	....	....	....
1985-86	New Jersey Devils	44	0	10	10	100	....	....	....	....	....
1986-87	New Jersey Devils	79	2	12	14	183	....	....	....	....	....
1987-88	New Jersey Devils	80	5	7	12	239	20	1	6	7	83
1988-89	New Jersey Devils	80	5	5	10	283	....	....	....	....	....
1989-90	New Jersey Devils	74	6	15	21	219	6	2	0	2	21
1990-91	New Jersey Devils	80	4	16	20	249	7	0	1	1	10
1991-92	New Jersey Devils	80	1	7	8	170	7	0	3	3	16
1992-93	New Jersey Devils	84	2	11	13	236	5	0	0	0	8
1993-94	New Jersey Devils	78	1	9	10	176	20	0	1	1	45
1994-95 ◆	New Jersey Devils	25	1	2	3	54	20	1	0	1	22
1995-96	New Jersey Devils	80	2	4	6	115	....	....	....	....	....
1996-97	New Jersey Devils	77	2	7	9	70	10	0	0	0	28
1997-98	New Jersey Devils	37	0	1	1	57	6	0	1	1	10
1998-99	New Jersey Devils	82	2	9	11	63	7	0	0	0	8
99-2000 ◆	New Jersey Devils	78	0	6	6	98	23	1	2	3	14
2000-01	New Jersey Devils	77	0	4	4	87	25	0	3	3	21
2001-02	New Jersey Devils	67	0	6	6	60	6	0	0	0	8
2002-03 ◆	New Jersey Devils	69	2	7	9	33	13	0	0	0	2
	NHL Totals	**1283**	**36**	**142**	**178**	**2519**	**175**	**5**	**17**	**22**	**296**

Bill Masterton Memorial Trophy (2000)

• Missed majority of 1997-98 season after voluntarily entering NHL/NHLPA substance abuse program, November 6, 1997.

DANIELS, Jeff

Left wing. Shoots left. 6'1", 200 lbs. Born, Oshawa, Ont., June 24, 1968.
(Pittsburgh's 6th choice, 109th overall, in 1986 Entry Draft).

Season	Club	GP	G	A	Pts	PIM	GP	G	A	Pts	PIM
1990-91	Pittsburgh Penguins	11	0	2	2	2	....	....	....	....	....
1991-92 ◆	Pittsburgh Penguins	2	0	0	0	0	....	....	....	....	....
1992-93	Pittsburgh Penguins	58	5	4	9	14	12	3	2	5	0
1993-94	Pittsburgh Penguins	63	3	5	8	20	....	....	....	....	....
	Florida Panthers	7	0	0	0	0	....	....	....	....	....
1994-95	Florida Panthers	3	0	0	0	0	....	....	....	....	....
1996-97	Hartford Whalers	10	0	2	2	0	....	....	....	....	....
1997-98	Carolina Hurricanes	2	0	0	0	0	....	....	....	....	....
1998-99	Nashville Predators	9	1	3	4	2	....	....	....	....	....
99-2000	Carolina Hurricanes	69	3	4	7	10	....	....	....	....	....
2000-01	Carolina Hurricanes	67	1	1	2	15	6	0	2	2	2
2001-02	Carolina Hurricanes	65	4	1	5	12	23	0	1	1	0
2002-03	Carolina Hurricanes	59	0	4	4	8	....	....	....	....	....
	NHL Totals	**425**	**17**	**26**	**43**	**83**	**41**	**3**	**5**	**8**	**2**

Traded to **Florida** by **Pittsburgh** for Greg Hawgood, March 19, 1994. Signed as a free agent by **Hartford**, August 18, 1995. Transferred to **Carolina** after **Hartford** franchise relocated, June 25, 1997. Claimed by **Nashville** from **Carolina** in Expansion Draft, June 26, 1998. Signed as a free agent by **Carolina**, August 31, 1999.

DANIELS, Kimbi

Center. Shoots right. 5'10", 175 lbs. Born, Brandon, Man., January 19, 1972.
(Philadelphia's 5th choice, 44th overall, in 1990 Entry Draft).

Season	Club	GP	G	A	Pts	PIM	GP	G	A	Pts	PIM
1990-91	Philadelphia Flyers	2	0	1	1	0	....	....	....	....	....
1991-92	Philadelphia Flyers	25	1	1	2	4	....	....	....	....	....
	NHL Totals	**27**	**1**	**2**	**3**	**4**	....	....	....	....	....

DANIELS, Scott

Left wing. Shoots left. 6'3", 215 lbs. Born, Prince Albert, Sask., September 19, 1969.
(Hartford's 6th choice, 136th overall, in 1989 Entry Draft).

Season	Club	GP	G	A	Pts	PIM	GP	G	A	Pts	PIM
1992-93	Hartford Whalers	1	0	0	0	19	....	....	....	....	....
1994-95	Hartford Whalers	12	0	2	2	55	....	....	....	....	....
1995-96	Hartford Whalers	53	3	4	7	254	....	....	....	....	....
1996-97	Philadelphia Flyers	56	5	3	8	237	....	....	....	....	....
1997-98	New Jersey Devils	26	0	3	3	102	1	0	0	0	0
1998-99	New Jersey Devils	1	0	0	0	0	....	....	....	....	....
	NHL Totals	**149**	**8**	**12**	**20**	**667**	**1**	**0**	**0**	**0**	**0**

Signed as a free agent by **Philadelphia**, June 27, 1996. Claimed by **New Jersey** from **Philadelphia** in NHL Waiver Draft, September 28, 1997.

DANTON, Mike

Center. Shoots right. 5'9", 190 lbs. Born, Brampton, Ont., October 21, 1980.
(New Jersey's 8th choice, 135th overall, in 2000 Entry Draft).

Season	Club	GP	G	A	Pts	PIM	GP	G	A	Pts	PIM
2000-01	New Jersey Devils	2	0	0	0	6	....	....	....	....	....
2002-03	New Jersey Devils	17	2	0	2	35	....	....	....	....	....
	NHL Totals	**19**	**2**	**0**	**2**	**41**	....	....	....	....	....

• Legally changed last name from **Jefferson** to **Danton**, July 25, 2002.

• Suspended for 2001-02 season by New Jersey for refusing to report to Albany (AHL), October 2, 2001. • Missed majority of 2002-03 season after being suspended by New Jersey for refusing to report to Albany (AHL), December 3, 2002. Traded to **St. Louis** by **New Jersey** with New Jersey's 3rd round choice (Konstantin Zakharov) in 2003 Entry Draft for St. Louis's 3rd round choice (Ivan Khomutov) in 2003 Entry Draft, June 21, 2003.

DAOUST, Dan

Center. Shoots left. 5'10", 160 lbs. Born, Montreal, Que., February 29, 1960.

Season	Club	GP	G	A	Pts	PIM	GP	G	A	Pts	PIM
1982-83	Montreal Canadiens	4	0	1	1	4	....	....	....	....	....
	Toronto Maple Leafs	48	18	33	51	31	....	....	....	....	....
1983-84	Toronto Maple Leafs	78	18	56	74	88	....	....	....	....	....
1984-85	Toronto Maple Leafs	79	17	37	54	98	....	....	....	....	....
1985-86	Toronto Maple Leafs	80	7	13	20	88	10	2	2	4	19
1986-87	Toronto Maple Leafs	33	4	3	7	35	13	5	2	7	42
1987-88	Toronto Maple Leafs	67	9	8	17	57	4	0	0	0	2
1988-89	Toronto Maple Leafs	68	7	5	12	54	....	....	....	....	....
1989-90	Toronto Maple Leafs	65	7	11	18	89	5	0	1	1	20
	NHL Totals	**522**	**87**	**167**	**254**	**544**	**32**	**7**	**5**	**12**	**83**

NHL All-Rookie Team (1983)

Signed as a free agent by **Montreal**, March 9, 1981. Traded to **Toronto** by **Montreal** for Toronto's 3rd round choice (later traded to Minnesota – Minnesota selected Ken Hodge Jr.) in 1984 Entry Draft, December 17, 1982. • Played w/ RHI's Toronto Planets in 1993 (6-9-10-19-20).

DARBY, Craig

Center. Shoots right. 6'3", 200 lbs. Born, Oneida, NY, September 26, 1972.
(Montreal's 3rd choice, 43rd overall, in 1991 Entry Draft).

Season	Club	GP	G	A	Pts	PIM	GP	G	A	Pts	PIM
1994-95	Montreal Canadiens	10	0	2	2	0	....	....	....	....	....
	New York Islanders	3	0	0	0	0	....	....	....	....	....
1995-96	New York Islanders	10	0	2	2	0	....	....	....	....	....
1996-97	Philadelphia Flyers	9	1	4	5	2	....	....	....	....	....
1997-98	Philadelphia Flyers	3	1	0	1	0	....	....	....	....	....
99-2000	Montreal Canadiens	76	7	10	17	14	....	....	....	....	....
2000-01	Montreal Canadiens	78	12	16	28	16	....	....	....	....	....
2001-02	Montreal Canadiens	2	0	0	0	0	....	....	....	....	....
2002-03	New Jersey Devils	3	0	1	1	0	....	....	....	....	....
	NHL Totals	**194**	**21**	**35**	**56**	**32**	....	....	....	....	....

Traded to **NY Islanders** by **Montreal** with Kirk Muller and Mathieu Schneider for Pierre Turgeon and Vladimir Malakhov, April 5, 1995. Claimed on waivers by **Philadelphia** from **NY Islanders**, June 4, 1996. Claimed by **Nashville** from **Philadelphia** in Expansion Draft, June 26, 1998. Signed as a free agent by **Montreal**, August 4, 1999. Signed as a free agent by **New Jersey**, July 12, 2002.

DARCHE, Mathieu

Left wing. Shoots left. 6'1", 210 lbs. Born, St. Laurent, Que., November 26, 1976.

Season	Club	GP	G	A	Pts	PIM	GP	G	A	Pts	PIM
2000-01	Columbus Blue Jackets	9	0	0	0	0	....	....	....	....	....
2001-02	Columbus Blue Jackets	14	1	1	2	6	....	....	....	....	....
2002-03	Columbus Blue Jackets	1	0	0	0	0	....	....	....	....	....
	NHL Totals	**24**	**1**	**1**	**2**	**6**					

Signed as a free agent by **Columbus**, May 16, 2000.

DARK, Michael

Defense. Shoots right. 6'3", 210 lbs. Born, Sarnia, Ont., September 17, 1963.
(Montreal's 10th choice, 124th overall, in 1982 Entry Draft).

Season	Club	GP	G	A	Pts	PIM	GP	G	A	Pts	PIM
1986-87	St. Louis Blues	13	2	0	2	2	....	....	....	....	....
1987-88	St. Louis Blues	30	3	6	9	12	....	....	....	....	....
	NHL Totals	**43**	**5**	**6**	**11**	**14**					

Traded to **St. Louis** by **Montreal** with Mark Hunter and Montreal's 2nd (Herb Raglan), 3rd (Nelson Emerson), 5th (Dan Brooks) and 6th (Rich Burchill) round choices in 1985 Entry Draft for St. Louis' 1st (Jose Charbonneau), 2nd (Todd Richards), 4th (Martin Desjardins), 5th (Tom Sagissor) and 6th (Donald Dufresne) round choices in 1985 Entry Draft, June 15, 1985. Traded to **Calgary** by **St. Louis** with Doug Gilmour, Steve Bozek and Mark Hunter for Mike Bullard, Craig Coxe and Tim Corkery, September 6, 1988.

DARRAGH, Harold

Left wing. Shoots right. 5'10", 145 lbs. Born, Ottawa, Ont., September 13, 1902.

Season	Club	GP	G	A	Pts	PIM	GP	G	A	Pts	PIM
		REGULAR SEASON					PLAYOFFS				
1925-26	Pittsburgh Pirates	35	10	7	17	6	2	1	0	1	0
1926-27	Pittsburgh Pirates	42	12	3	15	4	....	....	....	....	....
1927-28	Pittsburgh Pirates	44	13	2	15	16	2	0	1	1	0
1928-29	Pittsburgh Pirates	43	9	3	12	6	....	....	....	....	....
1929-30	Pittsburgh Pirates	42	15	17	32	6	....	....	....	....	....
1930-31	Philadelphia Quakers	10	1	1	2	2	....	....	....	....	....
	Boston Bruins	25	2	4	6	4	5	0	1	1	2
1931-32 ♦	Toronto Maple Leafs	48	5	10	15	6	7	0	1	1	2
1932-33	Toronto Maple Leafs	19	1	2	3	0	....	....	....	....	....
	NHL Totals	**308**	**68**	**49**	**117**	**50**	**16**	**1**	**3**	**4**	**4**

• Brother of Jack

Signed as a free agent by **Pittsburgh**, September 26, 1925. Transferred to **Philadelphia** after **Pittsburgh** franchise relocated, October 18, 1930. Traded to **Boston** by **Philadelphia** for Ron Lyons and Bill Hutton, December 8, 1930. Claimed on waivers by **Toronto** from **Boston**, June 8, 1931. Traded to **Syracuse** (IHL) by **Toronto** for Bill Thoms, January 3, 1933.

DARRAGH, Jack HHOF

Right wing. Shoots right. 5'10", 168 lbs. Born, Ottawa, Ont., December 4, 1890.

Season	Club	GP	G	A	Pts	PIM	GP	G	A	Pts	PIM
1917-18	Ottawa Senators	18	14	5	19	26	....	....	....	....	....
1918-19	Ottawa Senators	14	11	3	14	33	5	2	0	2	3
1919-20 ♦	Ottawa Senators	23	22	14	36	22	....	....	....	....	....
	Ottawa Senators (Cup)	....	....	....	....	....	*5*	*5*	*2*	*7*	*3*
1920-21 ♦	Ottawa Senators	24	11	*15	26	20	2	0	0	0	2
	Ottawa Senators (Cup)	....	....	....	....	....	*5*	*5*	*0*	*5*	*12*
1922-23 ♦	Ottawa Senators	24	6	9	15	10	2	1	0	1	2
1923-24	Ottawa Senators	18	2	0	2	2	2	0	0	0	2
	NHL Totals	**121**	**66**	**46**	**112**	**113**	**11**	**3**	**0**	**3**	**9**

• Brother of Harold

Rights retained by **Ottawa** after NHA folded, November 26, 1917. Signed as a free agent by **Ottawa**, December 4, 1922. • Died of peritonitis (ruptured appendix), June 25, 1924.

DATSYUK, Pavel

Center. Shoots left. 5'11", 180 lbs. Born, Sverdlovsk, USSR, July 20, 1978.
(Detroit's 8th choice, 171st overall, in 1998 Entry Draft).

Season	Club	GP	G	A	Pts	PIM	GP	G	A	Pts	PIM
2001-02 ♦	Detroit Red Wings	70	11	24	35	4	21	3	3	6	2
2002-03	Detroit Red Wings	64	12	39	51	16	4	0	0	0	0
	NHL Totals	**134**	**23**	**63**	**86**	**20**	**25**	**3**	**3**	**6**	**2**

DAVID, Richard

Left wing. Shoots left. 6', 195 lbs. Born, Notre Dame de-la-Salette, Que., April 8, 1958.
(Montreal's 5th choice, 42nd overall, in 1978 Amateur Draft).

Season	Club	GP	G	A	Pts	PIM	GP	G	A	Pts	PIM
1979-80	Quebec Nordiques	10	0	0	0	2	....	....	....	....	....
1981-82	Quebec Nordiques	5	1	1	2	4	1	0	0	0	0
1982-83	Quebec Nordiques	16	3	3	6	4	....	....	....	....	....
	NHL Totals	**31**	**4**	**4**	**8**	**10**	**1**	**0**	**0**	**0**	**0**

Rights retained by **Quebec** prior to Expansion Draft, June 9, 1979.

DAVIDSON, Bob

Left wing. Shoots left. 5'11", 185 lbs. Born, Toronto, Ont., February 10, 1912.

Season	Club	GP	G	A	Pts	PIM	GP	G	A	Pts	PIM
1934-35	Toronto Maple Leafs	5	0	0	0	6	....	....	....	....	....
1935-36	Toronto Maple Leafs	35	4	4	8	32	9	1	3	4	2
1936-37	Toronto Maple Leafs	46	8	7	15	43	2	0	0	0	5
1937-38	Toronto Maple Leafs	48	3	17	20	52	4	0	2	2	7
1938-39	Toronto Maple Leafs	47	4	10	14	29	10	1	1	2	6
1939-40	Toronto Maple Leafs	48	8	18	26	56	10	0	3	3	16
1940-41	Toronto Maple Leafs	37	3	6	9	39	7	0	2	2	7
1941-42 ♦	Toronto Maple Leafs	37	6	20	26	39	13	1	2	3	20
1942-43	Toronto Maple Leafs	50	13	23	36	20	6	1	2	3	7
1943-44	Toronto Maple Leafs	47	19	28	47	21	5	0	0	0	4
1944-45 ♦	Toronto Maple Leafs	50	17	18	35	49	13	1	2	3	2
1945-46	Toronto Maple Leafs	41	9	9	18	12	....	....	....	....	....
	NHL Totals	**491**	**94**	**160**	**254**	**398**	**79**	**5**	**17**	**22**	**76**

DAVIDSON, Gord

Defense. Shoots left. 5'11", 188 lbs. Born, Stratford, Ont., August 5, 1918.

Season	Club	GP	G	A	Pts	PIM	GP	G	A	Pts	PIM
1942-43	New York Rangers	35	2	3	5	4	....	....	....	....	....
1943-44	New York Rangers	16	1	3	4	4	....	....	....	....	....
	NHL Totals	**51**	**3**	**6**	**9**	**8**	....	....	....	....	....

Loaned to **Montreal** (Buffalo-AHL) by **NY Rangers** with the trade of Roger Leger for Bob Dill, January 4, 1944. Traded to **Cleveland** (AHL) by **NY Rangers** (New Haven-AHL) for Harvey Fraser, November 25, 1945.

DAVIDSON, Matt

Right wing. Shoots right. 6'3", 196 lbs. Born, Flin Flon, Man., August 9, 1977.
(Buffalo's 5th choice, 94th overall, in 1995 Entry Draft).

Season	Club	GP	G	A	Pts	PIM	GP	G	A	Pts	PIM
2000-01	Columbus Blue Jackets	5	0	0	0	0	....	....	....	....	....
2001-02	Columbus Blue Jackets	17	1	2	3	10	....	....	....	....	....
2002-03	Columbus Blue Jackets	34	4	5	9	18	....	....	....	....	....
	NHL Totals	**56**	**5**	**7**	**12**	**28**	....	....	....	....	....

Traded to **Columbus** by **Buffalo** with Jean-Luc Grand-Pierre, San Jose's 5th round choice (previously acquired, Columbus selected Tyler Kolarik) in 2000 Entry Draft and Buffalo's 5th round choice (later traded to Calgary – later traded to Detroit – Detroit selected Andreas Jamtin) in 2001 Entry Draft to complete Expansion Draft agreement which had Columbus select Geoff Sanderson and Dwayne Roloson from Buffalo, June 23, 2000. Signed as a free agent by **Calgary**, July 15, 2003.

DAVIDSSON, Johan

Center. Shoots right. 6'1", 190 lbs. Born, Jonkoping, Sweden, January 6, 1976.
(Anaheim's 2nd choice, 28th overall, in 1994 Entry Draft).

Season	Club	GP	G	A	Pts	PIM	GP	G	A	Pts	PIM
1998-99	Mighty Ducks of Anaheim	64	3	5	8	14	1	0	0	0	0
99-2000	Mighty Ducks of Anaheim	5	1	0	1	2	....	....	....	....	....
	New York Islanders	14	2	4	6	0	....	....	....	....	....
	NHL Totals	**83**	**6**	**9**	**15**	**16**	**1**	**0**	**0**	**0**	**0**

Traded to **NY Islanders** by **Anaheim** with future considerations for Jorgen Jonsson, March 11, 2000. Signed as a free agent by **Vancouver**, September 6, 2000.

DAVIE, Bob

Defense. Shoots right. 6', 170 lbs. Born, Beausejour, Man., September 12, 1912.

Season	Club	GP	G	A	Pts	PIM	GP	G	A	Pts	PIM
1933-34	Boston Bruins	9	0	0	0	6	....	....	....	....	....
1934-35	Boston Bruins	30	0	1	1	17	....	....	....	....	....
1935-36	Boston Bruins	2	0	0	0	2	....	....	....	....	....
	NHL Totals	**41**	**0**	**1**	**1**	**25**	....	....	....	....	....

DAVIES, Buck

Center. Shoots left. 5'6", 162 lbs. Born, Bowmanville, Ont., August 10, 1922.

Season	Club	GP	G	A	Pts	PIM	GP	G	A	Pts	PIM
1947-48	New York Rangers	....	....	....	....	....	1	0	0	0	0
	NHL Totals	....	....	....	....	....	**1**	**0**	**0**	**0**	**0**

Traded to **Providence** (AHL) by **NY Rangers** to complete transaction that sent Allan Stanley to NY Rangers (December 9, 1948), June, 1949. Traded to **Cleveland** (AHL) by **Boston** (Providence-AHL) with Vic Lynn for Joe Lund and Jean-Paul Gladu, December 10, 1951.

DAVIS, Bob

Right wing. Shoots right. 6', 202 lbs. Born, Lachine, Que., February 2, 1899.

Season	Club	GP	G	A	Pts	PIM	GP	G	A	Pts	PIM
1932-33	Detroit Red Wings	3	0	0	0	0	....	....	....	....	....
	NHL Totals	**3**	**0**	**0**	**0**	**0**	....	....	....	....	....

Signed as a free agent by **Detroit**, December 5, 1932. Traded to **Buffalo** (IAHL) by **Detroit** with Tip O'Neill and John Newman for Gamey Lederman, September 24, 1933.

DAVIS, Kim

Center. Shoots left. 5'11", 170 lbs. Born, Flin Flon, Man., October 31, 1957.
(Pittsburgh's 2nd choice, 48th overall, in 1977 Amateur Draft).

Season	Club	GP	G	A	Pts	PIM	GP	G	A	Pts	PIM
1977-78	Pittsburgh Penguins	1	0	0	0	0	....	....	....	....	....
1978-79	Pittsburgh Penguins	1	1	0	1	0	....	....	....	....	....
1979-80	Pittsburgh Penguins	24	3	7	10	43	4	0	0	0	0
1980-81	Pittsburgh Penguins	8	1	0	1	4	....	....	....	....	....
	Toronto Maple Leafs	2	0	0	0	4	....	....	....	....	....
	NHL Totals	**36**	**5**	**7**	**12**	**51**	**4**	**0**	**0**	**0**	**0**

Traded to **Toronto** by **Pittsburgh** with Paul Marshall for Dave Burrows and Paul Gardner, November 18, 1980.

DAVIS, Lorne

Right wing. Shoots right. 5'11", 190 lbs. Born, Regina, Sask., July 20, 1930.

Season	Club	GP	G	A	Pts	PIM	GP	G	A	Pts	PIM
1951-52	Montreal Canadiens	3	1	1	2	2	....	....	....	....	....
1952-53 ♦	Montreal Canadiens	....	....	....	....	....	7	1	1	2	2
1953-54	Montreal Canadiens	37	6	4	10	2	11	2	0	2	8
1954-55	Chicago Black Hawks	8	0	0	0	4	....	....	....	....	....
	Detroit Red Wings	22	0	5	5	2	....	....	....	....	....
1955-56	Boston Bruins	15	0	1	1	0	....	....	....	....	....
1959-60	Boston Bruins	10	1	1	2	10	....	....	....	....	....
	NHL Totals	**95**	**8**	**12**	**20**	**20**	**18**	**3**	**1**	**4**	**10**

Played in NHL All-Star Game (1953)

Traded to **Chicago** by **Montreal** for Ike Hildebrand and future considerations, October 13, 1954. Traded to **Detroit** by **Chicago** for Metro Prystai, November 9, 1954. Traded to **Boston** by **Detroit** with Terry Sawchuk, Vic Stasiuk and Marcel Bonin for Ed Sandford, Real Chevrefils, Norm Corcoran, Gilles Boisvert and Warren Godfrey, June 3, 1955.

DAVIS, Mal

Left wing. Shoots left. 5'11", 180 lbs. Born, Lockport, N.S., October 10, 1956.

Season	Club	GP	G	A	Pts	PIM	GP	G	A	Pts	PIM
1978-79	Detroit Red Wings	6	0	0	0	0	....	....	....	....	....
1980-81	Detroit Red Wings	5	2	0	2	0	....	....	....	....	....
1982-83	Buffalo Sabres	24	8	12	20	0	6	1	0	1	0
1983-84	Buffalo Sabres	11	2	1	3	4	1	0	0	0	0
1984-85	Buffalo Sabres	47	17	9	26	26	....	....	....	....	....
1985-86	Buffalo Sabres	7	2	0	2	4	....	....	....	....	....
	NHL Totals	**100**	**31**	**22**	**53**	**34**	**7**	**1**	**0**	**1**	**0**

Signed as a free agent by **Detroit**, October 12, 1978. Signed as a free agent by **Buffalo**, September 2, 1981. Claimed by **Los Angeles** from **Buffalo** in Waiver Draft, October 6, 1986.

DAVISON, Murray

Defense. Shoots right. 6'2", 190 lbs. Born, Brantford, Ont., June 10, 1938.

Season	Club	Regular Season					Playoffs				
		GP	G	A	Pts	PIM	GP	G	A	Pts	PIM
1965-66	Boston Bruins	1	0	0	0	0	....	....	....	....	....
	NHL Totals	**1**	**0**	**0**	**0**	**0**	....	....	....	....	....

DAVISON, Rob

Defense. Shoots left. 6'2", 225 lbs. Born, St. Catharines, Ont., May 1, 1980.
(San Jose's 4th choice, 98th overall, in 1998 Entry Draft).

Season	Club	GP	G	A	Pts	PIM	GP	G	A	Pts	PIM
2002-03	San Jose Sharks	15	1	2	3	22	....	....	....	....	....
	NHL Totals	**15**	**1**	**2**	**3**	**22**	....	....	....	....	....

DAVYDOV, Evgeny

Left wing. Shoots right. 6', 200 lbs. Born, Chelyabinsk, USSR, May 27, 1967.
(Winnipeg's 14th choice, 235th overall, in 1989 Entry Draft).

Season	Club	GP	G	A	Pts	PIM	GP	G	A	Pts	PIM
1991-92	Winnipeg Jets	12	4	3	7	8	7	2	2	4	2
1992-93	Winnipeg Jets	79	28	21	49	66	4	0	0	0	0
1993-94	Florida Panthers	21	2	6	8	8	....	....	....	....	....
	Ottawa Senators	40	5	7	12	38	....	....	....	....	....
1994-95	Ottawa Senators	3	1	2	3	0	....	....	....	....	....
	NHL Totals	**155**	**40**	**39**	**79**	**120**	**11**	**2**	**2**	**4**	**2**

Traded to **Florida** by **Winnipeg** for Florida's 4th round draft choice (later traded to Edmonton – Edmonton selected Adam Copeland) in 1994 Entry Draft. September 30, 1993. Traded to **Ottawa** by **Florida** with Scott Levins, Florida's 6th round choice (Mike Gaffney) in 1994 Entry Draft and Dallas' 4th round choice (previously acquired, Ottawa selected Kevin Bolibruck) in 1995 Entry Draft for Bob Kudelski, January 6, 1994.

DAW, Jeff

Center. Shoots right. 6'3", 190 lbs. Born, Carlisle, Ont., February 28, 1972.

Season	Club	GP	G	A	Pts	PIM	GP	G	A	Pts	PIM
2001-02	Colorado Avalanche	1	0	1	1	0	....	....	....	....	....
	NHL Totals	**1**	**0**	**1**	**1**	**0**	....	....	....	....	....

Signed as a free agent by **Edmonton**, August 1, 1996. Signed as a free agent by **Chicago**, July 22, 1999. Selected by **Minnesota** from **Chicago** in Expansion Draft, June 23, 2000. Signed as a free agent by **Colorado**, July 23, 2001. Traded to **Toronto** by **Carolina** for future considerations, May 29, 2003.

DAWE, Jason

Right wing. Shoots left. 5'10", 189 lbs. Born, North York, Ont., May 29, 1973.
(Buffalo's 2nd choice, 35th overall, in 1991 Entry Draft).

Season	Club	GP	G	A	Pts	PIM	GP	G	A	Pts	PIM
1993-94	Buffalo Sabres	32	6	7	13	12	6	0	1	1	6
1994-95	Buffalo Sabres	42	7	4	11	19	5	2	1	3	6
1995-96	Buffalo Sabres	67	25	25	50	33	....	....	....	....	....
1996-97	Buffalo Sabres	81	22	26	48	32	11	2	1	3	6
1997-98	Buffalo Sabres	68	19	17	36	36	....	....	....	....	....
	New York Islanders	13	1	2	3	6	....	....	....	....	....
1998-99	New York Islanders	22	2	3	5	8	....	....	....	....	....
	Montreal Canadiens	37	4	5	9	14	....	....	....	....	....
99-2000	New York Rangers	3	0	1	1	2	....	....	....	....	....
2001-02	New York Rangers	1	0	0	0	0	....	....	....	....	....
	NHL Totals	**366**	**86**	**90**	**176**	**162**	**22**	**4**	**3**	**7**	**18**

Traded to **NY Islanders** by **Buffalo** for Jason Holland and Paul Kruse, March 24, 1998. Claimed on waivers by **Montreal** from **NY Islanders**, December 15, 1998. Signed as a free agent by **Nashville**, October 2, 1999. Traded to **NY Rangers** by **Nashville** for John Namestnikov, February 3, 2000. Signed as a free agent by **St. Louis**, July 23, 2002.

DAWES, Bob

Defense/Center. Shoots left. 6'1", 170 lbs. Born, Saskatoon, Sask., November 29, 1924.

Season	Club	GP	G	A	Pts	PIM	GP	G	A	Pts	PIM
1946-47	Toronto Maple Leafs	1	0	0	0	0	....	....	....	....	....
1948-49 ♦	Toronto Maple Leafs	5	1	0	1	0	9	0	0	0	2
1949-50	Toronto Maple Leafs	11	1	2	3	2	....	....	....	....	....
1950-51	Montreal Canadiens	15	0	5	5	4	1	0	0	0	0
	NHL Totals	**32**	**2**	**7**	**9**	**6**	**10**	**0**	**0**	**0**	**2**

Played in NHL All-Star Game (1949)

Traded to **Cleveland** (AHL) by **Toronto** with $40,000 and future considerations (Phil Samis, Eric Pogue and the rights to Bob Shropshire, April 6, 1950) for Al Rollins, November 29, 1949. Traded to **Buffalo** (AHL) by **Cleveland** (AHL) for Joe McArthur, September 6, 1950. Traded to **Cincinnati** (AHL) by **Buffalo** (AHL) for cash, January 12, 1951. Traded to **Montreal** by **Cincinnati** (AHL) for Paul Masnick, February 13, 1951.

DAY, Hap

HHOF

Defense. Shoots left. 5'11", 175 lbs. Born, Owen Sound, Ont., June 14, 1901.

Season	Club	GP	G	A	Pts	PIM	GP	G	A	Pts	PIM
1924-25	Toronto St. Pats	26	10	12	22	33	2	0	0	0	0
1925-26	Toronto St. Pats	36	14	2	16	26	....	....	....	....	....
1926-27	Toronto St. Pats/Maple Leafs	44	11	5	16	50	....	....	....	....	....
1927-28	Toronto Maple Leafs	22	9	8	17	48	....	....	....	....	....
1928-29	Toronto Maple Leafs	44	6	6	12	84	4	1	0	1	4
1929-30	Toronto Maple Leafs	43	7	14	21	77	....	....	....	....	....
1930-31	Toronto Maple Leafs	44	1	13	14	56	2	0	3	3	7
1931-32 ♦	Toronto Maple Leafs	47	7	8	15	33	7	3	3	6	6
1932-33	Toronto Maple Leafs	47	6	14	20	46	9	0	1	1	*21
1933-34	Toronto Maple Leafs	48	9	10	19	35	5	0	0	0	6
1934-35	Toronto Maple Leafs	45	2	4	6	38	7	0	0	0	4
1935-36	Toronto Maple Leafs	44	1	13	14	41	9	0	0	0	8
1936-37	Toronto Maple Leafs	48	3	4	7	20	2	0	0	0	0
1937-38	New York Americans	43	0	3	3	14	6	0	0	0	0
	NHL Totals	**581**	**86**	**116**	**202**	**601**	**53**	**4**	**7**	**11**	**56**

Played in NHL All-Star Game (1934, 1937)

Signed as a free agent by **Toronto**, December 9, 1924. Traded to **NY Americans** by **Toronto** for cash, September 23, 1937.

DAY, Joe

Center. Shoots left. 5'11", 180 lbs. Born, Chicago, IL, May 11, 1968.
(Hartford's 8th choice, 186th overall, in 1987 Entry Draft).

Season	Club	GP	G	A	Pts	PIM	GP	G	A	Pts	PIM
1991-92	Hartford Whalers	24	0	3	3	10	....	....	....	....	....
1992-93	Hartford Whalers	24	1	7	8	47	....	....	....	....	....
1993-94	New York Islanders	24	0	0	0	30	....	....	....	....	....
	NHL Totals	**72**	**1**	**10**	**11**	**87**	....	....	....	....	....

Signed as a free agent by **NY Islanders**, August 24, 1993.

DAZE, Eric

Right wing. Shoots left. 6'6", 234 lbs. Born, Montreal, Que., July 2, 1975.
(Chicago's 5th choice, 90th overall, in 1993 Entry Draft).

Season	Club	GP	G	A	Pts	PIM	GP	G	A	Pts	PIM
1994-95	Chicago Blackhawks	4	1	1	2	2	16	0	1	1	4
1995-96	Chicago Blackhawks	80	30	23	53	18	10	3	5	8	0
1996-97	Chicago Blackhawks	71	22	19	41	16	6	2	1	3	2
1997-98	Chicago Blackhawks	80	31	11	42	22	....	....	....	....	....
1998-99	Chicago Blackhawks	72	22	20	42	22	....	....	....	....	....
99-2000	Chicago Blackhawks	59	23	13	36	28	....	....	....	....	....
2000-01	Chicago Blackhawks	79	33	24	57	16	....	....	....	....	....
2001-02	Chicago Blackhawks	82	38	32	70	36	5	0	0	0	2
2002-03	Chicago Blackhawks	54	22	22	44	14	....	....	....	....	....
	NHL Totals	**581**	**222**	**165**	**387**	**174**	**37**	**5**	**7**	**12**	**8**

NHL All-Rookie Team (1996)
Played in NHL All-Star Game (2002)

DEA, Billy

Left wing. Shoots left. 5'8", 175 lbs. Born, Edmonton, Alta., April 3, 1933.

Season	Club	GP	G	A	Pts	PIM	GP	G	A	Pts	PIM
1953-54	New York Rangers	14	1	1	2	2	....	....	....	....	....
1956-57	Detroit Red Wings	69	15	15	30	14	5	2	0	2	2
1957-58	Detroit Red Wings	29	4	4	8	6	....	....	....	....	....
	Chicago Black Hawks	34	5	8	13	4	....	....	....	....	....
1966-67	Chicago Black Hawks	....	....	....	....	....	2	0	0	0	2
1967-68	Pittsburgh Penguins	73	16	12	28	6	....	....	....	....	....
1968-69	Pittsburgh Penguins	66	10	8	18	4	....	....	....	....	....
1969-70	Detroit Red Wings	70	10	3	13	6	4	0	1	1	2
1970-71	Detroit Red Wings	42	6	3	9	2	....	....	....	....	....
	NHL Totals	**397**	**67**	**54**	**121**	**44**	**11**	**2**	**1**	**3**	**6**

Traded to **Detroit** by **NY Rangers** with Aggie Kukulowicz and cash for Dave Creighton and Bronco Horvath, August 18, 1955. Traded to **Chicago** by **Detroit** with Bill Dineen, Lorne Ferguson and Earl Reibel for Nick Mickoski, Bob Bailey, Hec Lalande and John McIntyre, December 17, 1957. Claimed by **Pittsburgh** from **Chicago** in Expansion Draft, June 6, 1967. Traded to **Detroit** by **Pittsburgh** for Mike McMahon, October 28, 1969.

DEACON, Don

Left wing. Shoots left. 5'9", 190 lbs. Born, Regina, Sask., June 2, 1913.

Season	Club	GP	G	A	Pts	PIM	GP	G	A	Pts	PIM
1936-37	Detroit Red Wings	4	0	0	0	2	....	....	....	....	....
1938-39	Detroit Red Wings	8	1	3	4	2	2	2	1	3	0
1939-40	Detroit Red Wings	18	5	1	6	2	....	....	....	....	....
	NHL Totals	**30**	**6**	**4**	**10**	**6**	**2**	**2**	**1**	**3**	**0**

Signed as a free agent by **Detroit**, October 11, 1934. Traded to **Cleveland** (IAHL) by **Detroit** (Indianapolis-IAHL) for Bob Gracie and $30,000, February 5, 1940.

DEADMARSH, Adam

Right wing. Shoots right. 6', 195 lbs. Born, Trail, B.C., May 10, 1975.
(Quebec's 2nd choice, 14th overall, in 1993 Entry Draft).

Season	Club	GP	G	A	Pts	PIM	GP	G	A	Pts	PIM
1994-95	Quebec Nordiques	48	9	8	17	56	6	0	1	1	0
1995-96 ♦	Colorado Avalanche	78	21	27	48	142	22	5	12	17	25
1996-97	Colorado Avalanche	78	33	27	60	136	17	3	6	9	24
1997-98	Colorado Avalanche	73	22	21	43	125	7	2	0	2	4
1998-99	Colorado Avalanche	66	22	27	49	99	19	8	4	12	20
99-2000	Colorado Avalanche	71	18	27	45	106	17	4	11	15	21
2000-01	Colorado Avalanche	39	13	13	26	59	....	....	....	....	....
	Los Angeles Kings	18	4	2	6	4	13	3	3	6	4
2001-02	Los Angeles Kings	76	29	33	62	71	4	1	3	4	2
2002-03	Los Angeles Kings	20	13	4	17	21	....	....	....	....	....
	NHL Totals	**567**	**184**	**189**	**373**	**819**	**105**	**26**	**40**	**66**	**100**

Transferred to **Colorado** after **Quebec** franchise relocated, June 21, 1995. Traded to **Los Angeles** by **Colorado** with Aaron Miller, a player to be named later (Jared Aulin, March 22, 2001), Colorado's 1st round choice (Dave Steckel) in 2001 Entry Draft and 1st round choice (Brian Boyle) in 2003 Entry Draft for Rob Blake and Steve Reinprecht, February 21, 2001. • Missed majority of 2002-03 season recovering from head injury suffered in game vs. Vancouver, November 14, 2002.

DEADMARSH, Butch

Left wing. Shoots left. 5'11", 186 lbs. Born, Trail, B.C., April 5, 1950.
(Buffalo's 2nd choice, 15th overall, in 1970 Amateur Draft).

Season	Club	GP	G	A	Pts	PIM	GP	G	A	Pts	PIM
1970-71	Buffalo Sabres	10	0	0	0	9	....	....	....	....	....
1971-72	Buffalo Sabres	12	1	1	2	4	....	....	....	....	....

Season	Club	Regular Season GP	G	A	Pts	PIM	Playoffs GP	G	A	Pts	PIM
1972-73	Buffalo Sabres	34	1	1	2	26	....	....	....	....	....
	Atlanta Flames	19	1	0	1	8	....	....	....	....	....
1973-74	Atlanta Flames	42	6	1	7	89	4	0	0	0	17
1974-75	Kansas City Scouts	20	3	2	5	19	....	....	....	....	....
	NHL Totals	**137**	**12**	**5**	**17**	**155**	**4**	**0**	**0**	**0**	**17**

Traded to **Atlanta** by **Buffalo** for Norm Gratton, February 14, 1973. Claimed by **Kansas City** from **Atlanta** in Expansion Draft, June 12, 1974. Traded to **Vancouver** (WHA) by **Kansas City** for cash, December, 1974.

DEAN, Barry

Left wing. Shoots left. 6'1", 195 lbs. Born, Maple Creek, Sask., February 26, 1955.
(Kansas City's 1st choice, 2nd overall, in 1975 Amateur Draft).

Season	Club	GP	G	A	Pts	PIM	GP	G	A	Pts	PIM
1976-77	Colorado Rockies	79	14	25	39	92	....	....	....	....	....
1977-78	Philadelphia Flyers	56	7	18	25	34	....	....	....	....	....
1978-79	Philadelphia Flyers	30	4	13	17	20	....	....	....	....	....
	NHL Totals	**165**	**25**	**56**	**81**	**146**	....	....	....	....	....

Rights transferred to **Colorado** after **Kansas City** franchise relocated, June, 1976. Traded to **Philadelphia** by **Colorado** for Mark Suzor, August 5, 1977. Claimed by **Philadelphia** as a fill-in during Expansion Draft, June 13, 1979. Traded to **Edmonton** by **Philadelphia** for Ron Areshenkoff and Edmonton's 10th round choice (Bob O'Brien) in 1980 Entry Draft, June 11, 1980.

DEAN, Kevin

Defense. Shoots left. 6'3", 210 lbs. Born, Madison, WI, April 1, 1969.
(New Jersey's 4th choice, 86th overall, in 1987 Entry Draft).

Season	Club	GP	G	A	Pts	PIM	GP	G	A	Pts	PIM
1994-95 ♦	New Jersey Devils	17	0	1	1	4	3	0	2	2	0
1995-96	New Jersey Devils	41	0	6	6	28	....	....	....	....	....
1996-97	New Jersey Devils	28	2	4	6	6	1	1	0	1	0
1997-98	New Jersey Devils	50	1	8	9	12	5	1	0	1	2
1998-99	New Jersey Devils	62	1	10	11	22	7	0	0	0	0
99-2000	Atlanta Thrashers	23	1	0	1	14	....	....	....	....	....
	Dallas Stars	14	0	0	0	10	....	....	....	....	....
	Chicago Blackhawks	27	2	8	10	12	....	....	....	....	....
2000-01	Chicago Blackhawks	69	0	11	11	30	....	....	....	....	....
	NHL Totals	**331**	**7**	**48**	**55**	**138**	**16**	**2**	**2**	**4**	**2**

Claimed by **Atlanta** from **New Jersey** in Expansion Draft, June 25, 1999. Traded to **Dallas** by **Atlanta** for Dallas' 9th round choice (Mark McRae) in 2000 Entry Draft, December 15, 1999. Traded to **Chicago** by **Dallas** with Derek Plante and Dallas' 2nd round choice (Matt Keith) in 2001 Entry Draft for Sylvain Cote and Dave Manson, February 8, 2000.

DEBENEDET, Nelson

Left wing. Shoots left. 6'1", 195 lbs. Born, Cordeno, Italy, December 31, 1947.

Season	Club	GP	G	A	Pts	PIM	GP	G	A	Pts	PIM
1973-74	Detroit Red Wings	15	4	1	5	2	....	....	....	....	....
1974-75	Pittsburgh Penguins	31	6	3	9	11	....	....	....	....	....
	NHL Totals	**46**	**10**	**4**	**14**	**13**	....	....	....	....	....

Signed as a free agent by **Detroit**, September, 1971. Traded to **Pittsburgh** by **Detroit** for Hank Nowak and Pittsburgh's 3rd round choice (Dan Mandryk) in 1974 Amateur Draft, May 27, 1974.

DeBLOIS, Lucien

Center. Shoots right. 5'11", 200 lbs. Born, Joliette, Que., June 21, 1957.
(NY Rangers' 1st choice, 8th overall, in 1977 Amateur Draft).

Season	Club	GP	G	A	Pts	PIM	GP	G	A	Pts	PIM
1977-78	New York Rangers	71	22	8	30	27	3	0	0	0	2
1978-79	New York Rangers	62	11	17	28	26	9	2	0	2	4
1979-80	New York Rangers	6	3	1	4	7	....	....	....	....	....
	Colorado Rockies	70	24	19	43	36	....	....	....	....	....
1980-81	Colorado Rockies	74	26	16	42	78	....	....	....	....	....
1981-82	Winnipeg Jets	65	25	27	52	87	4	2	1	3	4
1982-83	Winnipeg Jets	79	27	27	54	69	3	0	0	0	5
1983-84	Winnipeg Jets	80	34	45	79	50	3	0	1	1	4
1984-85	Montreal Canadiens	51	12	11	23	20	8	2	4	6	4
1985-86 ♦	Montreal Canadiens	61	14	17	31	48	11	0	0	0	7
1986-87	New York Rangers	40	3	8	11	27	2	0	0	0	2
1987-88	New York Rangers	74	9	21	30	103	....	....	....	....	....
1988-89	New York Rangers	73	9	24	33	107	4	0	0	0	4
1989-90	Quebec Nordiques	70	9	8	17	45	....	....	....	....	....
1990-91	Quebec Nordiques	14	2	2	4	13	....	....	....	....	....
	Toronto Maple Leafs	38	10	12	22	30	....	....	....	....	....
1991-92	Toronto Maple Leafs	54	8	11	19	39	....	....	....	....	....
	Winnipeg Jets	11	1	2	3	2	5	1	0	1	2
	NHL Totals	**993**	**249**	**276**	**525**	**814**	**52**	**7**	**6**	**13**	**38**

Traded to **Colorado** by **NY Rangers** with Pat Hickey, Mike McEwen, Dean Turner and future considerations (Bobby Crawford, January 15, 1980) for Barry Beck, November 2, 1979. Traded to **Winnipeg** by **Colorado** for Brent Ashton and Winnipeg's 3rd round choice (Dave Kasper) in 1982 Entry Draft, July 15, 1981. Traded to **Montreal** by **Winnipeg** for Perry Turnbull, June 13, 1984. Signed as a free agent by **NY Rangers**, September 8, 1986. Signed as a free agent by **Quebec**, August 2, 1989. Traded to **Toronto** by **Quebec** with Aaron Broten and Michel Petit for Scott Pearson and Toronto's 2nd round choices in 1991 (later traded to Washington – Washington selected Eric Lavigne) and 1992 (Tuomas Gronman) Entry Drafts, November 17, 1990. Traded to **Winnipeg** by **Toronto** for Mark Osborne, March 10, 1992.

DEBOL, Dave

Center. Shoots right. 5'11", 175 lbs. Born, St. Claire Shores, MI, March 27, 1956.
(Chicago's 4th choice, 63rd overall, in 1976 Amateur Draft).

Season	Club	GP	G	A	Pts	PIM	GP	G	A	Pts	PIM
1979-80	Hartford Whalers	48	12	14	26	4	3	0	0	0	0
1980-81	Hartford Whalers	44	14	12	26	0	....	....	....	....	....
	NHL Totals	**92**	**26**	**26**	**52**	**4**	**3**	**0**	**0**	**0**	**0**

Claimed by **Hartford** from **Cincinnati** (WHA) in WHA Dispersal Draft, June, 1979.

DeBRUSK, Louie

Left wing. Shoots left. 6'2", 238 lbs. Born, Cambridge, Ont., March 19, 1971.
(NY Rangers' 4th choice, 49th overall, in 1989 Entry Draft).

Season	Club	GP	G	A	Pts	PIM	GP	G	A	Pts	PIM
1991-92	Edmonton Oilers	25	2	1	3	124	....	....	....	....	....
1992-93	Edmonton Oilers	51	8	2	10	205	....	....	....	....	....
1993-94	Edmonton Oilers	48	4	6	10	185	....	....	....	....	....
1994-95	Edmonton Oilers	34	2	0	2	93	....	....	....	....	....
1995-96	Edmonton Oilers	38	1	3	4	96	....	....	....	....	....
1996-97	Edmonton Oilers	32	2	0	2	94	6	0	0	0	4
1997-98	Tampa Bay Lightning	54	1	2	3	166	....	....	....	....	....
1998-99	Phoenix Coyotes	15	0	0	0	34	6	2	0	2	6
99-2000	Phoenix Coyotes	61	4	3	7	78	3	0	0	0	0
2000-01	Phoenix Coyotes	39	0	0	0	79	....	....	....	....	....
2002-03	Chicago Blackhawks	4	0	0	0	7	....	....	....	....	....
	NHL Totals	**401**	**24**	**17**	**41**	**1161**	**15**	**2**	**0**	**2**	**10**

Traded to **Edmonton** by **NY Rangers** with Bernie Nicholls and Steven Rice for Mark Messier and future considerations (Jeff Beukeboom for David Shaw, November 12, 1991), October 4, 1991. Signed as a free agent by **Tampa Bay**, September 23, 1997. Traded to **Phoenix** by **Tampa Bay** with Tampa Bay's 5th round choice (Jay Leach) in 1998 Entry Draft for Craig Janney, June 11, 1998. Signed as a free agent by **Chicago**, August 30, 2002.

DEFAUW, Brad

Left wing. Shoots left. 6'2", 210 lbs. Born, Edina, MN, November 10, 1977.
(Carolina's 2nd choice, 28th overall, in 1997 Entry Draft).

Season	Club	GP	G	A	Pts	PIM	GP	G	A	Pts	PIM
2002-03	Carolina Hurricanes	9	3	0	3	2	....	....	....	....	....
	NHL Totals	**9**	**3**	**0**	**3**	**2**	....	....	....	....	....

DEFAZIO, Dean

Left wing. Shoots left. 5'11", 185 lbs. Born, Ottawa, Ont., April 16, 1963.
(Pittsburgh's 8th choice, 175th overall, in 1981 Entry Draft).

Season	Club	GP	G	A	Pts	PIM	GP	G	A	Pts	PIM
1983-84	Pittsburgh Penguins	22	0	2	2	28	....	....	....	....	....
	NHL Totals	**22**	**0**	**2**	**2**	**28**	....	....	....	....	....

DEGRAY, Dale

Defense. Shoots right. 6', 200 lbs. Born, Oshawa, Ont., September 1, 1963.
(Calgary's 7th choice, 162nd overall, in 1981 Entry Draft).

Season	Club	GP	G	A	Pts	PIM	GP	G	A	Pts	PIM
1985-86	Calgary Flames	1	0	0	0	0	....	....	....	....	....
1986-87	Calgary Flames	27	6	7	13	29	....	....	....	....	....
1987-88	Toronto Maple Leafs	56	6	18	24	63	5	0	1	1	16
1988-89	Los Angeles Kings	63	6	22	28	97	8	1	2	3	12
1989-90	Buffalo Sabres	6	0	0	0	6	....	....	....	....	....
	NHL Totals	**153**	**18**	**47**	**65**	**195**	**13**	**1**	**3**	**4**	**28**

Traded to **Toronto** by **Calgary** for Toronto's 5th round choice (Scott Matusovich) in 1988 Entry Draft, September 17, 1987. Claimed by **Los Angeles** from **Toronto** in Waiver Draft, October 3, 1988. Traded to **Buffalo** by **Los Angeles** for Bob Halkidis, November 24, 1989.

DELISLE, Jonathan

Right wing. Shoots right. 5'10", 180 lbs. Born, Ste-Anne-des-Plaines, Que., June 30, 1977.
(Montreal's 4th choice, 86th overall, in 1995 Entry Draft).

Season	Club	GP	G	A	Pts	PIM	GP	G	A	Pts	PIM
1998-99	Montreal Canadiens	1	0	0	0	0	....	....	....	....	....
	NHL Totals	**1**	**0**	**0**	**0**	**0**	....	....	....	....	....

DELISLE, Xavier

Center. Shoots right. 5'11", 193 lbs. Born, Quebec City, Que., May 24, 1977.
(Tampa Bay's 5th choice, 157th overall, in 1996 Entry Draft).

Season	Club	GP	G	A	Pts	PIM	GP	G	A	Pts	PIM
1998-99	Tampa Bay Lightning	2	0	0	0	0	....	....	....	....	....
2000-01	Montreal Canadiens	14	3	2	5	6	....	....	....	....	....
	NHL Totals	**16**	**3**	**2**	**5**	**6**	....	....	....	....	....

Signed as a free agent by **Montreal**, August 8, 2000.

DELMONTE, Armand

Right wing. Shoots right. 5'10", 170 lbs. Born, Timmins, Ont., June 3, 1927.

Season	Club	GP	G	A	Pts	PIM	GP	G	A	Pts	PIM
1945-46	Boston Bruins	1	0	0	0	0	....	....	....	....	....
	NHL Totals	**1**	**0**	**0**	**0**	**0**	....	....	....	....	....

DELMORE, Andy

Defense. Shoots right. 6'1", 200 lbs. Born, LaSalle, Ont., December 26, 1976.

Season	Club	GP	G	A	Pts	PIM	GP	G	A	Pts	PIM
1998-99	Philadelphia Flyers	2	0	1	1	0	....	....	....	....	....
99-2000	Philadelphia Flyers	27	2	5	7	8	18	5	2	7	14
2000-01	Philadelphia Flyers	66	5	9	14	16	2	1	0	1	2
2001-02	Nashville Predators	73	16	22	38	22	....	....	....	....	....
2002-03	Nashville Predators	71	18	16	34	28	....	....	....	....	....
	NHL Totals	**239**	**41**	**53**	**94**	**74**	**20**	**6**	**2**	**8**	**16**

Signed as a free agent by **Philadelphia**, June 9, 1997. Traded to **Nashville** by **Philadelphia** for Nashville's 3rd round choice (later traded to Phoenix – Phoenix selected Joe Callahan) in 2002 Entry Draft, July 31, 2001. Traded to **Buffalo** by **Nashville** for Buffalo's 3rd round choice in 2004 Entry Draft, June 27, 2003.

DELORME, Gilbert

Defense. Shoots right. 6'1", 199 lbs. Born, Boucherville, Que., November 25, 1962.
(Montreal's 2nd choice, 18th overall, in 1981 Entry Draft).

Season	Club	GP	G	A	Pts	PIM	GP	G	A	Pts	PIM
1981-82	Montreal Canadiens	60	3	8	11	55	....	....	....	....	....
1982-83	Montreal Canadiens	78	12	21	33	89	3	0	0	0	2

Season	Club	REGULAR SEASON					PLAYOFFS				
		GP	G	A	Pts	PIM	GP	G	A	Pts	PIM
1983-84	Montreal Canadiens	27	2	7	9	8	....	....	....	....	....
	St. Louis Blues	44	0	5	5	41	11	1	3	4	11
1984-85	St. Louis Blues	74	2	12	14	53	3	0	0	0	0
1985-86	Quebec Nordiques	64	2	18	20	51	2	0	0	0	5
1986-87	Quebec Nordiques	19	2	0	2	14	....	....	....	....	....
	Detroit Red Wings	24	2	3	5	33	16	0	2	2	14
1987-88	Detroit Red Wings	55	2	8	10	81	15	0	3	3	22
1988-89	Detroit Red Wings	42	1	3	4	51	6	0	1	1	2
1989-90	Pittsburgh Penguins	54	3	7	10	44	....	....	....	....	....
	NHL Totals	**541**	**31**	**92**	**123**	**520**	**56**	**1**	**9**	**10**	**56**

Traded to **St. Louis** by **Montreal** with Greg Paslawski and Doug Wickenheiser for Perry Turnbull, December 21, 1983. Traded to **Quebec** by **St. Louis** for Bruce Bell, October 2, 1985. Traded to **Detroit** by **Quebec** with Brent Ashton and Mark Kumpel for Basil McRae, John Ogrodnick and Doug Shedden, January 17, 1987. Signed as a free agent by **Pittsburgh**, June 28, 1989.

DELORME, Ron

Center. Shoots right. 6'2", 185 lbs. Born, North Battleford, Sask., September 3, 1955.
(Kansas City's 4th choice, 56th overall, in 1975 Amateur Draft).

Season	Club	GP	G	A	Pts	PIM	GP	G	A	Pts	PIM
1976-77	Colorado Rockies	29	6	4	10	23	....	....	....	....	....
1977-78	Colorado Rockies	68	10	11	21	47	2	0	0	0	10
1978-79	Colorado Rockies	77	20	8	28	68	....	....	....	....	....
1979-80	Colorado Rockies	75	19	24	43	76	....	....	....	....	....
1980-81	Colorado Rockies	65	11	16	27	70	....	....	....	....	....
1981-82	Vancouver Canucks	59	9	8	17	177	15	0	2	2	31
1982-83	Vancouver Canucks	56	5	8	13	87	4	0	0	0	10
1983-84	Vancouver Canucks	64	2	2	4	68	4	1	0	1	8
1984-85	Vancouver Canucks	31	1	2	3	51	....	....	....	....	....
	NHL Totals	**524**	**83**	**83**	**166**	**667**	**25**	**1**	**2**	**3**	**59**

Rights transferred to **Colorado** after **Kansas City** franchise relocated, July 15, 1976. Claimed by **Vancouver** from **Colorado** in Waiver Draft, October 5, 1981.

DELORY, Val

Left wing. Shoots left. 5'10", 160 lbs. Born, Toronto, Ont., February 14, 1927.

Season	Club	GP	G	A	Pts	PIM	GP	G	A	Pts	PIM
1948-49	New York Rangers	1	0	0	0	0	....	....	....	....	....
	NHL Totals	**1**	**0**	**0**	**0**	**0**	....	....	....	....	....

DELPARTE, Guy

Left wing. Shoots left. 5'10", 175 lbs. Born, Sault Ste. Marie, Ont., August 30, 1949.
(Montreal's 6th choice, 63rd overall, in 1969 Amateur Draft).

Season	Club	GP	G	A	Pts	PIM	GP	G	A	Pts	PIM
1976-77	Colorado Rockies	48	1	8	9	18	....	....	....	....	....
	NHL Totals	**48**	**1**	**8**	**9**	**18**	....	....	....	....	....

Signed as a free agent by **Colorado**, October 4, 1976. Signed as a free agent by **Philadelphia**, September, 1977.

DELVECCHIO, Alex

HHOF

Center/Left wing. Shoots left. 6', 195 lbs. Born, Fort William, Ont., December 4, 1932.

Season	Club	GP	G	A	Pts	PIM	GP	G	A	Pts	PIM
1950-51	Detroit Red Wings	1	0	0	0	0	....	....	....	....	....
1951-52 ♦	Detroit Red Wings	65	15	22	37	22	8	0	3	3	4
1952-53	Detroit Red Wings	70	16	43	59	28	6	2	4	6	2
1953-54 ♦	Detroit Red Wings	69	11	18	29	34	12	2	7	9	7
1954-55 ♦	Detroit Red Wings	69	17	31	48	37	11	7	8	15	2
1955-56	Detroit Red Wings	70	25	26	51	24	10	7	3	10	2
1956-57	Detroit Red Wings	48	16	25	41	8	5	3	2	5	2
1957-58	Detroit Red Wings	70	21	38	59	22	4	0	1	1	0
1958-59	Detroit Red Wings	70	19	35	54	6	....	....	....	....	....
1959-60	Detroit Red Wings	70	19	28	47	8	6	2	6	8	0
1960-61	Detroit Red Wings	70	27	35	62	26	11	4	5	9	0
1961-62	Detroit Red Wings	70	26	43	69	18	....	....	....	....	....
1962-63	Detroit Red Wings	70	20	44	64	8	11	3	6	9	2
1963-64	Detroit Red Wings	70	23	30	53	11	14	3	8	11	0
1964-65	Detroit Red Wings	68	25	42	67	16	7	2	3	5	4
1965-66	Detroit Red Wings	70	31	38	69	16	12	0	*11	11	4
1966-67	Detroit Red Wings	70	17	38	55	10	....	....	....	....	....
1967-68	Detroit Red Wings	74	22	48	70	14	....	....	....	....	....
1968-69	Detroit Red Wings	72	25	58	83	8	....	....	....	....	....
1969-70	Detroit Red Wings	73	21	47	68	24	4	0	2	2	0
1970-71	Detroit Red Wings	77	21	34	55	6	....	....	....	....	....
1971-72	Detroit Red Wings	75	20	45	65	22	....	....	....	....	....
1972-73	Detroit Red Wings	77	18	53	71	13	....	....	....	....	....
1973-74	Detroit Red Wings	11	1	4	5	2	....	....	....	....	....
	NHL Totals	**1549**	**456**	**825**	**1281**	**383**	**121**	**35**	**69**	**104**	**29**

NHL Second All-Star Team (1953, 1959) • Lady Byng Trophy (1959, 1966, 1969) • Lester Patrick Trophy (1974)

Played in NHL All-Star Game (1953, 1954, 1955, 1956, 1957, 1958, 1959, 1961, 1962, 1963, 1964, 1965, 1967)

DeMARCO, Ab

Center. Shoots right. 6', 168 lbs. Born, North Bay, Ont., May 10, 1916.

Season	Club	GP	G	A	Pts	PIM	GP	G	A	Pts	PIM
1938-39	Chicago Black Hawks	2	1	0	1	0	....	....	....	....	....
1939-40	Chicago Black Hawks	17	0	5	5	17	2	0	0	0	0
1942-43	Toronto Maple Leafs	4	0	1	1	0	....	....	....	....	....
	Boston Bruins	3	4	1	5	0	9	3	0	3	2
1943-44	Boston Bruins	3	0	0	0	0	....	....	....	....	....
	New York Rangers	36	14	19	33	2	....	....	....	....	....
1944-45	New York Rangers	50	24	30	54	10	....	....	....	....	....
1945-46	New York Rangers	50	20	27	47	20	....	....	....	....	....
1946-47	New York Rangers	44	9	10	19	4	....	....	....	....	....
	NHL Totals	**209**	**72**	**93**	**165**	**53**	**11**	**3**	**0**	**3**	**2**

• Father of Ab Jr.

Signed as a free agent by **Chicago**, September 28, 1938. Traded to **Providence** (AHL) by **Chicago** for cash, May 14, 1940. Loaned to **Toronto** by **Providence** (AHL) with the trade of Buck Jones for the loan of Jack Forsey and George Boothman, February 3, 1943. Traded to **Boston** by **Providence** (AHL) with Ossie Aubuchon and Norm Calladine for cash, March 8, 1943. Traded to **NY Rangers** by **Boston** for cash, November, 1943. Traded to **Detroit** by **NY Rangers** with Hank Goldup for Flash Hollett, June 19, 1946. Transaction voided when Hollett decided to retire, June, 1946. Traded to **Cleveland** (AHL) by **NY Rangers** with Joe Cooper for cash, May 5, 1947. Traded to **Washington** (AHL) by **Cleveland** (AHL) with Bryan Hextall Sr. for Dan Porteous, Frank Porteous and Ken Schultz, January 20, 1949. Traded to **Montreal** (Buffalo-AHL) by **Washington** (AHL) for George Robertson with Montreal retaining right of recall, January 28, 1949.

DeMARCO Jr., Ab

Defense. Shoots right. 6', 170 lbs. Born, Cleveland, OH, February 27, 1949.

Season	Club	GP	G	A	Pts	PIM	GP	G	A	Pts	PIM
1969-70	New York Rangers	3	0	0	0	0	5	0	0	0	2
1970-71	New York Rangers	2	0	1	1	0	....	....	....	....	....
1971-72	New York Rangers	48	4	7	11	4	4	0	1	1	0
1972-73	New York Rangers	51	4	13	17	15	....	....	....	....	....
	St. Louis Blues	14	4	9	13	2	4	1	1	2	2
1973-74	St. Louis Blues	23	3	9	12	11	....	....	....	....	....
	Pittsburgh Penguins	34	7	12	19	4	....	....	....	....	....
1974-75	Pittsburgh Penguins	8	2	1	3	4	....	....	....	....	....
	Vancouver Canucks	61	10	14	24	21	2	0	0	0	0
1975-76	Vancouver Canucks	34	3	8	11	2	....	....	....	....	....
	Los Angeles Kings	30	4	3	7	6	9	0	0	0	11
1976-77	Los Angeles Kings	33	3	3	6	6	1	0	0	0	2
1978-79	Boston Bruins	3	0	0	0	0	....	....	....	....	....
	NHL Totals	**344**	**44**	**80**	**124**	**75**	**25**	**1**	**2**	**3**	**17**

• Son of Ab

Signed as a free agent by **NY Rangers**, June 10, 1969. Traded to **St. Louis** by **NY Rangers** for Mike Murphy, March 2, 1973. Traded to **Pittsburgh** by **St. Louis** with Steve Durbano and Bob Kelly for Bryan Watson, Greg Polis and Pittsburgh's 2nd round choice (Bob Hess) in 1974 Amateur Draft, January 17, 1974. Traded to **Vancouver** by **Pittsburgh** for Barry Wilkins, November 4, 1974. Traded to **Los Angeles** by **Vancouver** for Los Angeles' 2nd choice (later traded to Atlanta – Atlanta selected Brian Hill) in 1977 Amateur Draft, January 14, 1976. Traded to **Atlanta** by **Los Angeles** for Randy Manery, May 23, 1977. Signed as a free agent by **Boston**, October 23, 1978.

DEMERS, Tony

Right wing. Shoots right. 5'9", 180 lbs. Born, Chambly, Que., July 22, 1917.

Season	Club	GP	G	A	Pts	PIM	GP	G	A	Pts	PIM
1937-38	Montreal Canadiens	6	0	0	0	0	....	....	....	....	....
1939-40	Montreal Canadiens	14	2	3	5	2	....	....	....	....	....
1940-41	Montreal Canadiens	46	13	10	23	17	2	0	0	0	0
1941-42	Montreal Canadiens	7	3	4	7	4	....	....	....	....	....
1942-43	Montreal Canadiens	9	2	5	7	0	....	....	....	....	....
1943-44	New York Rangers	1	0	0	0	0	....	....	....	....	....
	NHL Totals	**83**	**20**	**22**	**42**	**23**	**2**	**0**	**0**	**0**	**0**

Signed as a free agent by **Montreal**, October 30, 1937. Loaned to **NY Rangers** by **Montreal** for the remainder of the 1943-44 season to complete transaction that sent Phil Watson to Montreal (October 27, 1943), December, 1943.

DEMITRA, Pavol

Left wing. Shoots left. 5'11", 203 lbs. Born, Dubnica, Czech., November 29, 1974.
(Ottawa's 9th choice, 227th overall, in 1993 Entry Draft).

Season	Club	GP	G	A	Pts	PIM	GP	G	A	Pts	PIM
1993-94	Ottawa Senators	12	1	1	2	4	....	....	....	....	....
1994-95	Ottawa Senators	16	4	3	7	0	....	....	....	....	....
1995-96	Ottawa Senators	31	7	10	17	6	....	....	....	....	....
1996-97	St. Louis Blues	8	3	0	3	2	6	1	3	4	6
1997-98	St. Louis Blues	61	22	30	52	22	10	3	3	6	2
1998-99	St. Louis Blues	82	37	52	89	16	13	5	4	9	4
99-2000	St. Louis Blues	71	28	47	75	8	....	....	....	....	....
2000-01	St. Louis Blues	44	20	25	45	16	15	2	4	6	2
2001-02	St. Louis Blues	82	35	43	78	46	10	4	7	11	6
2002-03	St. Louis Blues	78	36	57	93	32	7	2	4	6	2
	NHL Totals	**485**	**193**	**268**	**461**	**152**	**61**	**17**	**25**	**42**	**22**

Lady Byng Trophy (2000)

Played in NHL All-Star Game (1999, 2000, 2002)

Traded to **St. Louis** by **Ottawa** for Christer Olsson, November 27, 1996.

DEMPSEY, Nathan

Defense. Shoots right. 6', 190 lbs. Born, Spruce Grove, Alta., July 14, 1974.
(Toronto's 12th choice, 245th overall, in 1992 Entry Draft).

Season	Club	GP	G	A	Pts	PIM	GP	G	A	Pts	PIM
1996-97	Toronto Maple Leafs	14	1	1	2	2	....	....	....	....	....
99-2000	Toronto Maple Leafs	6	0	2	2	2	....	....	....	....	....
2000-01	Toronto Maple Leafs	25	1	9	10	4	....	....	....	....	....
2001-02	Toronto Maple Leafs	3	0	0	0	0	6	0	2	2	0
2002-03	Chicago Blackhawks	67	5	23	28	26	....	....	....	....	....
	NHL Totals	**115**	**7**	**35**	**42**	**34**	**6**	**0**	**2**	**2**	**0**

Signed as a free agent by **Chicago**, July 13, 2002.

DENIS, Jean-Paul

Right wing. Shoots right. 5'8", 170 lbs. Born, Montreal, Que., February 28, 1924.

Season	Club	GP	G	A	Pts	PIM	GP	G	A	Pts	PIM
1946-47	New York Rangers	6	0	1	1	0	....	....	....	....	....

Season	Club	GP	G	A	Pts	PIM	GP	G	A	Pts	PIM
		REGULAR SEASON					PLAYOFFS				
1949-50	New York Rangers	4	0	1	1	2	....	....	....	....	....
	NHL Totals	**10**	**0**	**2**	**2**	**2**	....	....	....	....	....

Traded to **Providence** (AHL) by **NY Rangers** with Zellio Toppazzini and Pat Egan for Jack Stoddard, January 1, 1952.

DENIS, Lulu

Right wing. Shoots right. 5'8", 140 lbs. Born, Vonda, Sask., June 7, 1928.

Season	Club	GP	G	A	Pts	PIM	GP	G	A	Pts	PIM
1949-50	Montreal Canadiens	2	0	1	1	0	....	....	....	....	....
1950-51	Montreal Canadiens	1	0	0	0	0	....	....	....	....	....
	NHL Totals	**3**	**0**	**1**	**1**	**0**	....	....	....	....	....

DENNENY, Corb

Center. Shoots right. 5'8", 160 lbs. Born, Cornwall, Ont., January 25, 1894.

Season	Club	GP	G	A	Pts	PIM	GP	G	A	Pts	PIM
1917-18 ♦	Toronto Arenas	21	20	9	29	14	2	0	0	0	0
	Toronto Arenas (Cup)	....	....	....	....	....	*5*	*3*	*1*	*4*	*0*
1918-19	Toronto Arenas	16	8	3	11	15	....	....	....	....	....
1919-20	Toronto St. Pats	24	24	12	36	20	....	....	....	....	....
1920-21	Toronto St. Pats	20	19	7	26	29	2	0	0	0	4
1921-22 ♦	Toronto St. Pats	24	19	9	28	28	2	1	0	1	0
	Toronto St. Pats (Cup)	....	....	....	....	....	*5*	*3*	*2*	*5*	*2*
1922-23	Toronto St. Pats	1	1	0	1	0	....	....	....	....	....
1923-24	Hamilton Tigers	23	0	1	1	6	....	....	....	....	....
1926-27	Toronto St. Pats/Maple Leafs	29	7	1	8	24	....	....	....	....	....
1927-28	Chicago Black Hawks	18	5	0	5	12	....	....	....	....	....
	NHL Totals	**176**	**103**	**42**	**145**	**148**	**6**	**1**	**0**	**1**	**4**

• Brother of Cy

Signed as a free agent by **Toronto**, December 5, 1917. PCHA rights traded to **Vancouver** (PCHA) by **Toronto** for Jack Adams, December 18, 1922. NHL rights traded to **Hamilton** by **Toronto** with Ken Randall and cash for Amos Arbour, Bert Corbeau and George Carey, December 14, 1923. Claimed on waivers by **Saskatoon** (WCHL) from **Hamilton**, November 21, 1924. Traded to **Toronto** by **Saskatoon** (PrHL) with Leo Bourgeault and Laurie Scott for cash, September 27, 1926. Rights returned to **Saskatoon** (PrHL) by **Toronto** when terms of transaction were voided, February, 1927. Traded to **Chicago** by **Saskatoon** (PrHL) for cash, June, 1927. Traded to **Saskatoon** (PrHL) by **Chicago** with Nick Wasnie for Eddie McCalmon and Earl Miller, January 11, 1928.

DENNENY, Cy

HHOF

Left wing. Shoots left. 5'7", 168 lbs. Born, Farrow's Point, Ont., December 23, 1891.

Season	Club	GP	G	A	Pts	PIM	GP	G	A	Pts	PIM
1917-18	Ottawa Senators	20	36	*10	46	80	....	....	....	....	....
1918-19	Ottawa Senators	18	18	4	22	58	5	3	2	5	0
1919-20 ♦	Ottawa Senators	24	16	6	22	31	....	....	....	....	....
	Ottawa Senators (Cup)	....	....	....	....	....	*5*	*0*	*2*	*2*	*3*
1920-21 ♦	Ottawa Senators	24	34	5	39	10	2	2	0	2	5
	Ottawa Senators (Cup)	....	....	....	....	....	*5*	*2*	*2*	*4*	*10*
1921-22	Ottawa Senators	22	27	12	39	20	2	2	0	2	4
1922-23 ♦	Ottawa Senators	24	23	11	34	28	2	2	0	2	2
	Ottawa Senators (Cup)	....	....	....	....	....	*6*	*1*	*1*	*2*	*8*
1923-24	Ottawa Senators	22	*22	2	*24	10	2	2	0	2	2
1924-25	Ottawa Senators	29	27	*15	42	16	....	....	....	....	....
1925-26	Ottawa Senators	36	24	12	36	18	2	0	0	0	4
1926-27 ♦	Ottawa Senators	42	17	6	23	16	6	*5	0	5	0
1927-28	Ottawa Senators	44	3	0	3	12	2	0	0	0	0
1928-29 ♦	Boston Bruins	23	1	2	3	2	2	0	0	0	0
	NHL Totals	**328**	**248**	**85**	**333**	**301**	**25**	**16**	**2**	**18**	**17**

• Brother of Corb

Rights retained by **Ottawa** after NHA folded, November 26, 1917. • 1922-23 Stanley Cup totals includes series with Regina (WCHL) and Edmonton (PCHA). Traded to **Boston** by **Ottawa** for cash, October 25, 1928.

DENNIS, Norm

Center. Shoots left. 5'10", 175 lbs. Born, Aurora, Ont., December 10, 1942.

Season	Club	GP	G	A	Pts	PIM	GP	G	A	Pts	PIM
1968-69	St. Louis Blues	2	0	0	0	2	....	....	....	....	....
1969-70	St. Louis Blues	5	3	0	3	5	2	0	0	0	2
1970-71	St. Louis Blues	4	0	0	0	0	3	0	0	0	0
1971-72	St. Louis Blues	1	0	0	0	4	....	....	....	....	....
	NHL Totals	**12**	**3**	**0**	**3**	**11**	**5**	**0**	**0**	**0**	**2**

Traded to **St. Louis** by **Montreal** for cash, October 28, 1968. Traded to **Buffalo** (AHL) by **St. Louis** with Norm Beaudin for cash, May 13, 1969. Traded to **NY Rangers** by **St. Louis** with Don Borgeson for Bob Kelly, September 8, 1973.

DENOIRD, Gerry

Center. Shoots right. 5'10", 170 lbs. Born, Toronto, Ont., August 4, 1902.

Season	Club	GP	G	A	Pts	PIM	GP	G	A	Pts	PIM
1922-23	Toronto St. Pats	17	0	1	1	0	....	....	....	....	....
	NHL Totals	**17**	**0**	**1**	**1**	**0**	....	....	....	....	....

Signed as a free agent by **Toronto**, October 25, 1922.

DePALMA, Larry

Left wing. Shoots left. 6', 195 lbs. Born, Trenton, MI, October 27, 1965.

Season	Club	GP	G	A	Pts	PIM	GP	G	A	Pts	PIM
1985-86	Minnesota North Stars	1	0	0	0	0	....	....	....	....	....
1986-87	Minnesota North Stars	56	9	6	15	219	....	....	....	....	....
1987-88	Minnesota North Stars	7	1	1	2	15	....	....	....	....	....
1988-89	Minnesota North Stars	43	5	7	12	102	2	0	0	0	6
1990-91	Minnesota North Stars	14	3	0	3	26	....	....	....	....	....
1992-93	San Jose Sharks	20	2	6	8	41	....	....	....	....	....
1993-94	Pittsburgh Penguins	7	1	0	1	5	1	0	0	0	0
	NHL Totals	**148**	**21**	**20**	**41**	**408**	**3**	**0**	**0**	**0**	**6**

Signed to an amateur try-out contract by **Minnesota**, February 17, 1986. Signed as a free agent by **Minnesota**, May 12, 1986. Signed as a free agent by **San Jose**, August 30, 1991. Signed as a free agent by **NY Islanders**, November 29, 1993. Claimed on waivers by **Pittsburgh** from **NY Islanders**, March 9, 1994.

DERLAGO, Bill

Center. Shoots left. 5'10", 194 lbs. Born, Birtle, Man., August 25, 1958.
(Vancouver's 1st choice, 4th overall, in 1978 Amateur Draft).

Season	Club	GP	G	A	Pts	PIM	GP	G	A	Pts	PIM
1978-79	Vancouver Canucks	9	4	4	8	2	....	....	....	....	....
1979-80	Vancouver Canucks	54	11	15	26	27	....	....	....	....	....
	Toronto Maple Leafs	23	5	12	17	13	3	0	0	0	4
1980-81	Toronto Maple Leafs	80	35	39	74	26	3	1	0	1	2
1981-82	Toronto Maple Leafs	75	34	50	84	42	....	....	....	....	....
1982-83	Toronto Maple Leafs	58	13	24	37	27	4	3	0	3	2
1983-84	Toronto Maple Leafs	79	40	20	60	50	....	....	....	....	....
1984-85	Toronto Maple Leafs	62	31	31	62	21	....	....	....	....	....
1985-86	Toronto Maple Leafs	1	0	0	0	0	....	....	....	....	....
	Boston Bruins	39	5	16	21	15	....	....	....	....	....
	Winnipeg Jets	27	5	5	10	6	3	1	0	1	0
1986-87	Winnipeg Jets	30	3	6	9	12	....	....	....	....	....
	Quebec Nordiques	18	3	5	8	6	....	....	....	....	....
	NHL Totals	**555**	**189**	**227**	**416**	**247**	**13**	**5**	**0**	**5**	**8**

• Missed majority of 1978-79 season recovering from knee injury suffered in practice, December, 1978. Traded to **Toronto** by **Vancouver** with Rick Vaive for Tiger Williams and Jerry Butler, February 18, 1980. Traded to **Boston** by **Toronto** for Tom Fergus, October 11, 1985. Traded to **Winnipeg** by **Boston** for Wade Campbell, January 31, 1986. Traded to **Quebec** by **Winnipeg** for Quebec's 4th round choice (Mark Brownschidle) in 1989 Entry Draft, January 5, 1987.

DESAULNIERS, Gerard

Center. Shoots left. 5'11", 152 lbs. Born, Shawinigan Falls, Que., December 31, 1928.

Season	Club	GP	G	A	Pts	PIM	GP	G	A	Pts	PIM
1950-51	Montreal Canadiens	3	0	1	1	2	....	....	....	....	....
1952-53	Montreal Canadiens	2	0	1	1	2	....	....	....	....	....
1953-54	Montreal Canadiens	3	0	0	0	0	....	....	....	....	....
	NHL Totals	**8**	**0**	**2**	**2**	**4**	....	....	....	....	....

DESCOTEAUX, Matthieu

Defense. Shoots left. 6'3", 216 lbs. Born, Pierreville, Que., September 23, 1977.
(Edmonton's 2nd choice, 19th overall, in 1996 Entry Draft).

Season	Club	GP	G	A	Pts	PIM	GP	G	A	Pts	PIM
2000-01	Montreal Canadiens	5	1	1	2	4	....	....	....	....	....
	NHL Totals	**5**	**1**	**1**	**2**	**4**	....	....	....	....	....

Traded to **Montreal** by **Edmonton** with Christian Laflamme for Igor Ulanov and Alain Nasreddine, March 9, 2000.

DESILETS, Joffre

Right wing. Shoots right. 5'10", 170 lbs. Born, Capreol, Ont., April 16, 1915.

Season	Club	GP	G	A	Pts	PIM	GP	G	A	Pts	PIM
1935-36	Montreal Canadiens	38	7	6	13	0	....	....	....	....	....
1936-37	Montreal Canadiens	48	7	12	19	17	5	1	0	1	0
1937-38	Montreal Canadiens	32	6	7	13	6	2	0	0	0	7
1938-39	Chicago Black Hawks	48	11	13	24	28	....	....	....	....	....
1939-40	Chicago Black Hawks	26	6	7	13	6	....	....	....	....	....
	NHL Totals	**192**	**37**	**45**	**82**	**57**	**7**	**1**	**0**	**1**	**7**

Signed as a free agent by **Montreal**, October 22, 1935. Traded to **Chicago** by **Montreal** for Lou Trudel, August 26, 1938. Traded to **Cleveland** (AHL) by **Chicago** for cash, May 12, 1940.

DESJARDINS, Eric

Defense. Shoots right. 6'1", 205 lbs. Born, Rouyn, Que., June 14, 1969.
(Montreal's 3rd choice, 38th overall, in 1987 Entry Draft).

Season	Club	GP	G	A	Pts	PIM	GP	G	A	Pts	PIM
1988-89	Montreal Canadiens	36	2	12	14	26	14	1	1	2	6
1989-90	Montreal Canadiens	55	3	13	16	51	6	0	0	0	10
1990-91	Montreal Canadiens	62	7	18	25	27	13	1	4	5	8
1991-92	Montreal Canadiens	77	6	32	38	50	11	3	3	6	4
1992-93 ♦	Montreal Canadiens	82	13	32	45	98	20	4	10	14	23
1993-94	Montreal Canadiens	84	12	23	35	97	7	0	2	2	4
1994-95	Montreal Canadiens	9	0	6	6	2	....	....	....	....	....
	Philadelphia Flyers	34	5	18	23	12	15	4	4	8	10
1995-96	Philadelphia Flyers	80	7	40	47	45	12	0	6	6	2
1996-97	Philadelphia Flyers	82	12	34	46	50	19	2	8	10	12
1997-98	Philadelphia Flyers	77	6	27	33	36	5	0	1	1	0
1998-99	Philadelphia Flyers	68	15	36	51	38	6	2	2	4	4
99-2000	Philadelphia Flyers	81	14	41	55	32	18	2	10	12	2
2000-01	Philadelphia Flyers	79	15	33	48	50	6	1	1	2	0
2001-02	Philadelphia Flyers	65	6	19	25	24	5	0	1	1	2
2002-03	Philadelphia Flyers	79	8	24	32	35	5	2	1	3	0
	NHL Totals	**1050**	**131**	**408**	**539**	**673**	**162**	**22**	**54**	**76**	**87**

NHL Second All-Star Team (1999, 2000)

Played in NHL All-Star Game (1992, 1996, 2000)

Traded to **Philadelphia** by **Montreal** with Gilbert Dionne and John LeClair for Mark Recchi and Philadelphia's 3rd round choice (Martin Hohenberger) in 1995 Entry Draft, February 9, 1995.

DESJARDINS, Martin

Center. Shoots left. 6', 180 lbs. Born, Ste-Rose, Que., January 28, 1967.
(Montreal's 5th choice, 75th overall, in 1985 Entry Draft).

Season	Club	Regular Season GP	G	A	Pts	PIM	Playoffs GP	G	A	Pts	PIM
1989-90	Montreal Canadiens	8	0	2	2	2	....	....	....	....	....
	NHL Totals	**8**	**0**	**2**	**2**	**2**	....	....	....	....	....

Traded to **Chicago** by **Montreal** for cash, October 10, 1990.

DESJARDINS, Vic

USHOF

Center. Shoots right. 5'9", 160 lbs. Born, Sault Ste. Marie, MI, July 4, 1900.

Season	Club	GP	G	A	Pts	PIM	GP	G	A	Pts	PIM
1930-31	Chicago Black Hawks	39	3	12	15	11	9	0	0	0	0
1931-32	New York Rangers	48	3	3	6	16	7	0	0	0	0
	NHL Totals	**87**	**6**	**15**	**21**	**27**	**16**	**0**	**0**	**0**	**0**

Traded to **Chicago** by **St. Paul** (AHA) for cash, October 28, 1930. Traded to **NY Rangers** by **Chicago** with Art Somers for Paul Thompson, September 27, 1931.

DESLAURIERS, Jacques

Defense. Shoots left. 6', 170 lbs. Born, Montreal, Que., September 3, 1928.

Season	Club	GP	G	A	Pts	PIM	GP	G	A	Pts	PIM
1955-56	Montreal Canadiens	2	0	0	0	0	....	....	....	....	....
	NHL Totals	**2**	**0**	**0**	**0**	**0**	....	....	....	....	....

Traded to **Chicoutimi** (QHL) by **Montreal** with Jack Leclair and Guy Rousseau for Stan Smrke, October 27, 1957.

DEULING, Jarrett

Left wing. Shoots left. 6', 205 lbs. Born, Vernon, B.C., March 4, 1974.
(NY Islanders' 2nd choice, 56th overall, in 1992 Entry Draft).

Season	Club	GP	G	A	Pts	PIM	GP	G	A	Pts	PIM
1995-96	New York Islanders	14	0	1	1	11	....	....	....	....	....
1996-97	New York Islanders	1	0	0	0	0	....	....	....	....	....
	NHL Totals	**15**	**0**	**1**	**1**	**11**	....	....	....	....	....

Signed as a free agent by **San Jose**, August 27, 1998.

DEVEREAUX, Boyd

Center. Shoots left. 6'2", 195 lbs. Born, Seaforth, Ont., April 16, 1978.
(Edmonton's 1st choice, 6th overall, in 1996 Entry Draft).

Season	Club	GP	G	A	Pts	PIM	GP	G	A	Pts	PIM
1997-98	Edmonton Oilers	38	1	4	5	6	....	....	....	....	....
1998-99	Edmonton Oilers	61	6	8	14	23	1	0	0	0	0
99-2000	Edmonton Oilers	76	8	19	27	20	....	....	....	....	....
2000-01	Detroit Red Wings	55	5	6	11	14	2	0	0	0	0
2001-02 ◆	Detroit Red Wings	79	9	16	25	24	21	2	4	6	4
2002-03	Detroit Red Wings	61	3	9	12	16	....	....	....	....	....
	NHL Totals	**370**	**32**	**62**	**94**	**103**	**24**	**2**	**4**	**6**	**4**

Signed as a free agent by **Detroit**, August 23, 2000.

DEVINE, Kevin

Left wing. Shoots left. 5'8", 165 lbs. Born, Toronto, Ont., December 9, 1954.
(Toronto's 7th choice, 121st overall, in 1974 Amateur Draft).

Season	Club	GP	G	A	Pts	PIM	GP	G	A	Pts	PIM
1982-83	New York Islanders	2	0	1	1	8	....	....	....	....	....
	NHL Totals	**2**	**0**	**1**	**1**	**8**	....	....	....	....	....

Signed as a free agent by **NY Islanders**, October 9, 1979.

de VRIES, Greg

Defense. Shoots left. 6'3", 215 lbs. Born, Sundridge, Ont., January 4, 1973.

Season	Club	GP	G	A	Pts	PIM	GP	G	A	Pts	PIM
1995-96	Edmonton Oilers	13	1	1	2	12	....	....	....	....	....
1996-97	Edmonton Oilers	37	0	4	4	52	12	0	1	1	8
1997-98	Edmonton Oilers	65	7	4	11	80	7	0	0	0	21
1998-99	Nashville Predators	6	0	0	0	4	....	....	....	....	....
	Colorado Avalanche	67	1	3	4	60	19	0	2	2	22
99-2000	Colorado Avalanche	69	2	7	9	73	5	0	0	0	4
2000-01 ◆	Colorado Avalanche	79	5	12	17	51	23	0	1	1	20
2001-02	Colorado Avalanche	82	8	12	20	57	21	4	9	13	2
2002-03	Colorado Avalanche	82	6	26	32	70	7	2	0	2	0
	NHL Totals	**500**	**30**	**69**	**99**	**459**	**94**	**6**	**13**	**19**	**77**

Signed as a free agent by **Edmonton**, March 20, 1994. Traded to **Nashville** by **Edmonton** with Eric Fichaud and Drake Berehowsky for Mikhail Shtalenkov and Jim Dowd, October 1, 1998. Traded to **Colorado** by **Nashville** for Colorado's 2nd round choice (Ed Hill) in 1999 Entry Draft, October 24, 1998. Signed as a free agent by **NY Rangers**, July 14, 2003.

DEWAR, Tom

Defense. Shoots left. 5'9", 170 lbs. Born, Frobisher, Sask., June 10, 1913.

Season	Club	GP	G	A	Pts	PIM	GP	G	A	Pts	PIM
1943-44	New York Rangers	9	0	2	2	4	....	....	....	....	....
	NHL Totals	**9**	**0**	**2**	**2**	**4**	....	....	....	....	....

DEWSBURY, Al

Defense. Shoots left. 6'2", 202 lbs. Born, Goderich, Ont., April 12, 1926.

Season	Club	GP	G	A	Pts	PIM	GP	G	A	Pts	PIM
1946-47	Detroit Red Wings	23	2	1	3	12	2	0	0	0	4
1947-48	Detroit Red Wings	....	....	....	....	....	1	0	0	0	0
1949-50 ◆	Detroit Red Wings	11	2	2	4	2	4	0	3	3	8
1950-51	Chicago Black Hawks	67	5	14	19	79	....	....	....	....	....
1951-52	Chicago Black Hawks	69	7	17	24	99	....	....	....	....	....
1952-53	Chicago Black Hawks	69	5	16	21	97	7	1	2	3	4
1953-54	Chicago Black Hawks	69	6	15	21	44	....	....	....	....	....
1954-55	Chicago Black Hawks	2	0	1	1	10	....	....	....	....	....
1955-56	Chicago Black Hawks	37	3	12	15	22	....	....	....	....	....
	NHL Totals	**347**	**30**	**78**	**108**	**365**	**14**	**1**	**5**	**6**	**16**

Played in NHL All-Star Game (1951)

Traded to **Chicago** by **Detroit** with Harry Lumley, Jack Stewart, Don Morrison and Pete Babando for Jim Henry, Bob Goldham, Gaye Stewart and Metro Prystai, July 13, 1950. Loaned to **Montreal** (Montreal-QHL) by **Chicago** for cash and the loan of Paul Masnick, November 9, 1954. Traded to **Hershey** (AHL) by **Chicago** (Buffalo-AHL) for Bob Hassard, February 14, 1957.

DEZIEL, Michel

Left wing. Shoots left. 5'11", 180 lbs. Born, Sorel, Que., January 31, 1954.
(Buffalo's 3rd choice, 47th overall, in 1974 Amateur Draft).

Season	Club	GP	G	A	Pts	PIM	GP	G	A	Pts	PIM
1974-75	Buffalo Sabres	....	....	....	....	....	1	0	0	0	0
	NHL Totals	....	....	....	....	....	**1**	**0**	**0**	**0**	**0**

DHEERE, Marcel

Left wing. Shoots left. 5'7", 175 lbs. Born, St. Boniface, Man., December 19, 1920.

Season	Club	GP	G	A	Pts	PIM	GP	G	A	Pts	PIM
1942-43	Montreal Canadiens	11	1	2	3	2	5	0	0	0	6
	NHL Totals	**11**	**1**	**2**	**3**	**2**	**5**	**0**	**0**	**0**	**6**

Traded to **Montreal** by **Portland** (PCHL) for cash, December 25, 1940.

DIACHUK, Edward

Left wing. Shoots left. 6'1", 185 lbs. Born, Vegreville, Alta., August 16, 1936.

Season	Club	GP	G	A	Pts	PIM	GP	G	A	Pts	PIM
1960-61	Detroit Red Wings	12	0	0	0	19	....	....	....	....	....
	NHL Totals	**12**	**0**	**0**	**0**	**19**	....	....	....	....	....

Traded to **LA Blades** (WHL) by **Detroit** for cash, July, 1962.

DICK, Harry

Defense. Shoots left. 5'11", 210 lbs. Born, Port Colborne, Ont., November 22, 1922.

Season	Club	GP	G	A	Pts	PIM	GP	G	A	Pts	PIM
1946-47	Chicago Black Hawks	12	0	1	1	12	....	....	....	....	....
	NHL Totals	**12**	**0**	**1**	**1**	**12**	....	....	....	....	....

DICKENS, Ernie

Defense. Shoots left. 6', 175 lbs. Born, Winnipeg, Man., June 25, 1921.

Season	Club	GP	G	A	Pts	PIM	GP	G	A	Pts	PIM
1941-42 ◆	Toronto Maple Leafs	10	2	2	4	6	13	0	0	0	4
1945-46	Toronto Maple Leafs	15	1	3	4	6	....	....	....	....	....
1947-48	Chicago Black Hawks	54	5	15	20	30	....	....	....	....	....
1948-49	Chicago Black Hawks	59	2	3	5	14	....	....	....	....	....
1949-50	Chicago Black Hawks	70	0	13	13	22	....	....	....	....	....
1950-51	Chicago Black Hawks	70	2	8	10	20	....	....	....	....	....
	NHL Totals	**278**	**12**	**44**	**56**	**98**	**13**	**0**	**0**	**0**	**4**

Traded to **Chicago** by **Toronto** with Gus Bodnar, Bud Poile, Gaye Stewart and Bob Goldham for Max Bentley and Cy Thomas, November 2, 1947. Traded to **Calgary** (PCHL) by **Chicago** for Sid Finney, October 1, 1951.

DICKENSON, Herb

Wing. Shoots left. 5'11", 175 lbs. Born, Hamilton, Ont., June 11, 1931.

Season	Club	GP	G	A	Pts	PIM	GP	G	A	Pts	PIM
1951-52	New York Rangers	37	14	13	27	8	....	....	....	....	....
1952-53	New York Rangers	11	4	4	8	2	....	....	....	....	....
	NHL Totals	**48**	**18**	**17**	**35**	**10**	....	....	....	....	....

• Suffered career-ending eye injury during warm-up prior to game vs.Toronto, November 5, 1952.

DIDUCK, Gerald

Defense. Shoots right. 6'1", 216 lbs. Born, Edmonton, Alta., April 6, 1965.
(NY Islanders' 2nd choice, 16th overall, in 1983 Entry Draft).

Season	Club	GP	G	A	Pts	PIM	GP	G	A	Pts	PIM
1984-85	New York Islanders	65	2	8	10	80	....	....	....	....	....
1985-86	New York Islanders	10	1	2	3	2	....	....	....	....	....
1986-87	New York Islanders	30	2	3	5	67	14	0	1	1	35
1987-88	New York Islanders	68	7	12	19	113	6	1	0	1	42
1988-89	New York Islanders	65	11	21	32	155	....	....	....	....	....
1989-90	New York Islanders	76	3	17	20	163	5	0	0	0	12
1990-91	Montreal Canadiens	32	1	2	3	39	....	....	....	....	....
	Vancouver Canucks	31	3	7	10	66	6	1	0	1	11
1991-92	Vancouver Canucks	77	6	21	27	229	5	0	0	0	10
1992-93	Vancouver Canucks	80	6	14	20	171	12	4	2	6	12
1993-94	Vancouver Canucks	55	1	10	11	72	24	1	7	8	22
1994-95	Vancouver Canucks	22	1	3	4	15	....	....	....	....	....
	Chicago Blackhawks	13	1	0	1	48	16	1	3	4	22
1995-96	Hartford Whalers	79	1	9	10	88	....	....	....	....	....
1996-97	Hartford Whalers	56	1	10	11	40	....	....	....	....	....
	Phoenix Coyotes	11	1	2	3	23	7	0	0	0	10
1997-98	Phoenix Coyotes	78	8	10	18	118	6	0	2	2	20
1998-99	Phoenix Coyotes	44	0	2	2	72	3	0	0	0	2
99-2000	Toronto Maple Leafs	26	0	3	3	33	10	0	1	1	14
2000-01	Dallas Stars	14	0	0	0	18	....	....	....	....	....
	NHL Totals	**932**	**56**	**156**	**212**	**1612**	**114**	**8**	**16**	**24**	**212**

Traded to **Montreal** by **NY Islanders** for Craig Ludwig, September 4, 1990. Traded to **Vancouver** by **Montreal** for Vancouver's 4th round choice (Vladimir Vujtek) in 1991 Entry Draft, January 12, 1991. Traded to **Chicago** by **Vancouver** for Bogdan Savenko and Hartford's 3rd round choice (previously acquired, Vancouver selected Larry Courville) in 1995 Entry Draft, April 7, 1995. Signed as a free agent by **Hartford**, August 24, 1995. Traded to **Phoenix** by **Hartford** for Chris Murray, March 18, 1997. Signed as a free agent by **Toronto**, February 3, 2000. Traded to **Dallas** by **Toronto** for future considerations, October 29, 2000. • Missed majority of 2000-01 season recovering from ankle injury suffered in game vs. San Jose, December 6, 2000.

DIETRICH, Don

Defense. Shoots left. 6'1", 195 lbs. Born, Deloraine, Man., April 5, 1961.
(Chicago's 14th choice, 183rd overall, in 1980 Entry Draft).

Season	Club	REGULAR SEASON GP	G	A	Pts	PIM	PLAYOFFS GP	G	A	Pts	PIM
1983-84	Chicago Black Hawks	17	0	5	5	0	....	....	....	....	....
1985-86	New Jersey Devils	11	0	2	2	10	....	....	....	....	....
	NHL Totals	**28**	**0**	**7**	**7**	**10**	....	....	....	....	....

Traded to **New Jersey** by **Chicago** with Rich Preston and Chicago's 2nd round choice (Eric Weinrich) in 1985 Entry Draft for Bob MacMillan and New Jersey's 5th round choice (Rick Herbert) in 1985 Entry Draft, June 19, 1984.

DILL, Bob

USHOF

Defense. Shoots left. 5'8", 185 lbs. Born, St. Paul, MN, April 25, 1920.

Season	Club	REGULAR SEASON GP	G	A	Pts	PIM	PLAYOFFS GP	G	A	Pts	PIM
1943-44	New York Rangers	28	6	10	16	66	....	....	....	....	....
1944-45	New York Rangers	48	9	5	14	69	....	....	....	....	....
	NHL Totals	**76**	**15**	**15**	**30**	**135**	....	....	....	....	....

Traded to **NY Rangers** by **Montreal** (Buffalo-AHL) for Roger Leger and the loan of Gord Davidson, January 4, 1944.

DILLABOUGH, Bob

Center. Shoots left. 5'10", 180 lbs. Born, Belleville, Ont., April 27, 1941.

Season	Club	REGULAR SEASON GP	G	A	Pts	PIM	PLAYOFFS GP	G	A	Pts	PIM
1961-62	Detroit Red Wings	5	0	0	0	2	....	....	....	....	....
1962-63	Detroit Red Wings	....	....	....	....	....	1	0	0	0	0
1963-64	Detroit Red Wings	....	....	....	....	....	1	0	0	0	0
1964-65	Detroit Red Wings	4	0	0	0	2	4	0	0	0	0
1965-66	Boston Bruins	53	7	13	20	18	....	....	....	....	....
1966-67	Boston Bruins	60	6	12	18	14	....	....	....	....	....
1967-68	Pittsburgh Penguins	47	7	12	19	18	....	....	....	....	....
1968-69	Pittsburgh Penguins	14	0	0	0	2	....	....	....	....	....
	Oakland Seals	48	7	12	19	4	7	3	0	3	0
1969-70	Oakland Seals	52	5	5	10	16	4	0	0	0	0
	NHL Totals	**283**	**32**	**54**	**86**	**76**	**17**	**3**	**0**	**3**	**0**

Traded to **Boston** by **Detroit** with Albert Langlois, Ron Harris and Parker MacDonald for Ab McDonald, Bob McCord and Ken Stephanson, May 31, 1965. Claimed by **Pittsburgh** from **Boston** in Expansion Draft, June 6, 1967. Traded to **Oakland** by **Pittsburgh** for Billy Harris, November 29, 1968. Claimed by **Vancouver** from **Oakland** in Expansion Draft, June 10, 1970. Loaned to **Phoenix** (WHL) by **Vancouver** (Rochester-AHL) for cash, November 11, 1970. Traded to **Detroit** by **Vancouver** with Irv Spencer for John Cunniff and Gary Bredin, June 8, 1971.

DILLON, Cecil

Right wing. Shoots left. 5'11", 173 lbs. Born, Toledo, OH, April 26, 1908.

Season	Club	REGULAR SEASON GP	G	A	Pts	PIM	PLAYOFFS GP	G	A	Pts	PIM
1930-31	New York Rangers	25	7	3	10	8	4	0	1	1	2
1931-32	New York Rangers	48	23	15	38	22	7	2	1	3	4
1932-33 ♦	New York Rangers	48	21	10	31	12	8	*8	2	*10	6
1933-34	New York Rangers	48	13	26	39	10	2	0	1	1	2
1934-35	New York Rangers	48	25	9	34	4	4	2	1	3	0
1935-36	New York Rangers	48	18	14	32	12	....	....	....	....	....
1936-37	New York Rangers	48	20	11	31	13	9	0	3	3	0
1937-38	New York Rangers	48	21	18	39	6	3	1	0	1	0
1938-39	New York Rangers	48	12	15	27	6	1	0	0	0	0
1939-40	Detroit Red Wings	44	7	10	17	12	5	1	0	1	0
	NHL Totals	**453**	**167**	**131**	**298**	**105**	**43**	**14**	**9**	**23**	**14**

NHL Second All-Star Team (1936, 1937) • NHL First All-Star Team (1938)

Played in NHL All-Star Game (1937)

Traded to **NY Rangers** by **Springfield** (Can-Am) for cash, January 1, 1931. Traded to **Detroit** by **NY Rangers** for cash, May 17, 1939. Traded to **Providence** (AHL) by **Detroit** with Eddie Bush for Harold Jackson, December 15, 1940.

DILLON, Gary

Center. Shoots left. 5'10", 173 lbs. Born, Toronto, Ont., February 28, 1959.
(Colorado's 3rd choice, 85th overall, in 1979 Entry Draft).

Season	Club	REGULAR SEASON GP	G	A	Pts	PIM	PLAYOFFS GP	G	A	Pts	PIM
1980-81	Colorado Rockies	13	1	1	2	29	....	....	....	....	....
	NHL Totals	**13**	**1**	**1**	**2**	**29**	....	....	....	....	....

• Brother of Wayne

Signed as a free agent by **Quebec**, October 7, 1981.

DILLON, Wayne

Center. Shoots left. 6', 185 lbs. Born, Toronto, Ont., May 25, 1955.
(NY Rangers' 1st choice, 12th overall, in 1975 Amateur Draft).

Season	Club	REGULAR SEASON GP	G	A	Pts	PIM	PLAYOFFS GP	G	A	Pts	PIM
1975-76	New York Rangers	79	21	24	45	10	....	....	....	....	....
1976-77	New York Rangers	78	17	29	46	33	....	....	....	....	....
1977-78	New York Rangers	59	5	13	18	15	3	0	1	1	0
1979-80	Winnipeg Jets	13	0	0	0	2	....	....	....	....	....
	NHL Totals	**229**	**43**	**66**	**109**	**60**	**3**	**0**	**1**	**1**	**0**

• Brother of Gary

Traded to **Winnipeg** by **NY Rangers** for future considerations, July, 25, 1979.

DiMAIO, Rob

Right wing. Shoots right. 5'10", 190 lbs. Born, Calgary, Alta., February 19, 1968.
(NY Islanders' 6th choice, 118th overall, in 1987 Entry Draft).

Season	Club	REGULAR SEASON GP	G	A	Pts	PIM	PLAYOFFS GP	G	A	Pts	PIM
1988-89	New York Islanders	16	1	0	1	30	....	....	....	....	....
1989-90	New York Islanders	7	0	0	0	2	1	1	0	1	4
1990-91	New York Islanders	1	0	0	0	0	....	....	....	....	....
1991-92	New York Islanders	50	5	2	7	43	....	....	....	....	....
1992-93	Tampa Bay Lightning	54	9	15	24	62	....	....	....	....	....
1993-94	Tampa Bay Lightning	39	8	7	15	40	....	....	....	....	....
	Philadelphia Flyers	14	3	5	8	6	....	....	....	....	....
1994-95	Philadelphia Flyers	36	3	1	4	53	15	2	4	6	4
1995-96	Philadelphia Flyers	59	6	15	21	58	3	0	0	0	0
1996-97	Boston Bruins	72	13	15	28	82	....	....	....	....	....
1997-98	Boston Bruins	79	10	17	27	82	6	1	0	1	8
1998-99	Boston Bruins	71	7	14	21	95	12	2	0	2	8
99-2000	Boston Bruins	50	5	16	21	42	....	....	....	....	....
	New York Rangers	12	1	3	4	8	....	....	....	....	....
2000-01	Carolina Hurricanes	74	6	18	24	54	6	0	0	0	4
2001-02	Dallas Stars	61	6	6	12	25	....	....	....	....	....
2002-03	Dallas Stars	69	10	9	19	76	12	1	4	5	10
	NHL Totals	**764**	**93**	**143**	**236**	**758**	**55**	**7**	**8**	**15**	**38**

Claimed by **Tampa Bay** from **NY Islanders** in Expansion Draft, June 18, 1992. Traded to **Philadelphia** by **Tampa Bay** for Jim Cummins and Philadelphia's 4th round choice (later traded back to Philadelphia – Philadelphia selected Radovan Somik) in 1995 Entry Draft, March 18, 1994. Claimed by **San Jose** from **Philadelphia** in Waiver Draft, September 30, 1996. Traded to **Boston** by **San Jose** for Boston's 5th round choice (Adam Nittel) in 1997 Entry Draft, September 30, 1996. Traded to **NY Rangers** by **Boston** for Mike Knuble, March 10, 2000. Traded to **Carolina** by **NY Rangers** with Darren Langdon for Sandy McCarthy and Carolina's 4th round choice (Bryce Lampman) in 2001 Entry Draft, August 4, 2000. Signed as a free agent by **Dallas**, July 1, 2001.

DIMITRAKOS, Nico

Right wing. Shoots right. 5'11", 190 lbs. Born, Boston, MA, May 21, 1979.
(San Jose's 4th choice, 155th overall, in 1999 Entry Draft).

Season	Club	REGULAR SEASON GP	G	A	Pts	PIM	PLAYOFFS GP	G	A	Pts	PIM
2002-03	San Jose Sharks	21	6	7	13	8	....	....	....	....	....
	NHL Totals	**21**	**6**	**7**	**13**	**8**	....	....	....	....	....

DINEEN, Bill

Right wing. Shoots right. 5'11", 180 lbs. Born, Arvida, Que., September 18, 1932.

Season	Club	REGULAR SEASON GP	G	A	Pts	PIM	PLAYOFFS GP	G	A	Pts	PIM
1953-54 ♦	Detroit Red Wings	70	17	8	25	34	12	0	0	0	2
1954-55 ♦	Detroit Red Wings	69	10	9	19	36	11	0	1	1	8
1955-56	Detroit Red Wings	70	12	7	19	30	10	1	0	1	8
1956-57	Detroit Red Wings	51	6	7	13	12	4	0	0	0	0
1957-58	Detroit Red Wings	22	2	4	6	2	....	....	....	....	....
	Chicago Black Hawks	41	4	9	13	8	....	....	....	....	....
	NHL Totals	**323**	**51**	**44**	**95**	**122**	**37**	**1**	**1**	**2**	**18**

• Father of Gord, Kevin and Peter

Played in NHL All-Star Game (1954, 1955)

Rights traded to **Detroit** by **Cleveland** (AHL) with the rights to Lou Jankowski for Bob Bailey and John Bailey, June, 1951. Traded to **Chicago** by **Detroit** with Billy Dea, Lorne Ferguson and Earl Reibel for Nick Mickoski, Bob Bailey, Hec Lalande and Jack McIntyre, December 17, 1957. Traded to **Cleveland** (AHL) by **Buffalo** (AHL) for Bob Bailey, October 20, 1959. Traded to **Toronto** (Rochester-AHL) by **Cleveland** (AHL) with cash for Hank Ciesla, August, 1961. Traded to **Quebec** (AHL) by **Toronto** (Rochester-AHL) for cash, July, 1962.

DINEEN, Gary

Center. Shoots left. 5'10", 175 lbs. Born, Montreal, Que., December 24, 1943.

Season	Club	REGULAR SEASON GP	G	A	Pts	PIM	PLAYOFFS GP	G	A	Pts	PIM
1968-69	Minnesota North Stars	4	0	1	1	0	....	....	....	....	....
	NHL Totals	**4**	**0**	**1**	**1**	**0**	....	....	....	....	....

Rights traded to **Minnesota** by **Toronto** for cash, June, 1967. Claimed by **Los Angeles** (Springfield-AHL) by **Minnesota** in Reverse Draft, June 10, 1970.

DINEEN, Gord

Defense. Shoots right. 6', 195 lbs. Born, Quebec City, Que., September 21, 1962.
(NY Islanders' 2nd choice, 42nd overall, in 1981 Entry Draft).

Season	Club	REGULAR SEASON GP	G	A	Pts	PIM	PLAYOFFS GP	G	A	Pts	PIM
1982-83	New York Islanders	2	0	0	0	4	....	....	....	....	....
1983-84	New York Islanders	43	1	11	12	32	9	1	1	2	28
1984-85	New York Islanders	48	1	12	13	89	10	0	0	0	26
1985-86	New York Islanders	57	1	8	9	81	3	0	0	0	2
1986-87	New York Islanders	71	4	10	14	110	7	0	4	4	4
1987-88	New York Islanders	57	4	12	16	62	....	....	....	....	....
	Minnesota North Stars	13	1	1	2	21	....	....	....	....	....
1988-89	Minnesota North Stars	2	0	1	1	2	....	....	....	....	....
	Pittsburgh Penguins	38	1	2	3	42	11	0	2	2	8
1989-90	Pittsburgh Penguins	69	1	8	9	125	....	....	....	....	....
1990-91	Pittsburgh Penguins	9	0	0	0	6	....	....	....	....	....
1991-92	Pittsburgh Penguins	1	0	0	0	0	....	....	....	....	....
1992-93	Ottawa Senators	32	2	4	6	30	....	....	....	....	....
1993-94	Ottawa Senators	77	0	21	21	89	....	....	....	....	....
1994-95	New York Islanders	9	0	0	0	2	....	....	....	....	....
	NHL Totals	**528**	**16**	**90**	**106**	**695**	**40**	**1**	**7**	**8**	**68**

• Son of Bill • Brother of Kevin and Peter

Traded to **Minnesota** by **NY Islanders** for Chris Pryor and Minnesota's 7th round choice (Brett Harkins) in 1989 Entry Draft, March 8, 1988. Traded to **Pittsburgh** by **Minnesota** with Scott Bjugstad for Ville Siren and Steve Gotaas, December 17, 1988. Signed as a free agent by **Ottawa**, August 31, 1992. Signed as a free agent by **NY Islanders**, July 26, 1994.

DINEEN, Kevin

Right wing. Shoots right. 5'11", 198 lbs. Born, Quebec City, Que., October 28, 1963.
(Hartford's 3rd choice, 56th overall, in 1982 Entry Draft).

Season	Club	REGULAR SEASON GP	G	A	Pts	PIM	PLAYOFFS GP	G	A	Pts	PIM
1984-85	Hartford Whalers	57	25	16	41	120	....	....	....	....	....
1985-86	Hartford Whalers	57	33	35	68	124	10	6	7	13	18
1986-87	Hartford Whalers	78	40	39	79	110	6	2	1	3	31
1987-88	Hartford Whalers	74	25	25	50	217	6	4	4	8	8
1988-89	Hartford Whalers	79	45	44	89	167	4	1	0	1	10
1989-90	Hartford Whalers	67	25	41	66	164	6	3	2	5	18

Season	Club	GP	G	A	Pts	PIM	GP	G	A	Pts	PIM
		REGULAR SEASON					PLAYOFFS				
1990-91	Hartford Whalers	61	17	30	47	104	6	1	0	1	16
1991-92	Hartford Whalers	16	4	2	6	23	....	....	....	....	....
	Philadelphia Flyers	64	26	30	56	130	....	....	....	....	....
1992-93	Philadelphia Flyers	83	35	28	63	201	....	....	....	....	....
1993-94	Philadelphia Flyers	71	19	23	42	113	....	....	....	....	....
1994-95	Philadelphia Flyers	40	8	5	13	39	15	6	4	10	18
1995-96	Philadelphia Flyers	26	0	2	2	50	....	....	....	....	....
	Hartford Whalers	20	2	7	9	67	....	....	....	....	....
1996-97	Hartford Whalers	78	19	29	48	141	....	....	....	....	....
1997-98	Carolina Hurricanes	54	7	16	23	105	....	....	....	....	....
1998-99	Carolina Hurricanes	67	8	10	18	97	6	0	0	0	8
99-2000	Ottawa Senators	67	4	8	12	57	....	....	....	....	....
2000-01	Columbus Blue Jackets	66	8	7	15	126	....	....	....	....	....
2001-02	Columbus Blue Jackets	59	5	8	13	62	....	....	....	....	....
2002-03	Columbus Blue Jackets	4	0	0	0	12	....	....	....	....	....
	NHL Totals	**1188**	**355**	**405**	**760**	**2229**	**59**	**23**	**18**	**41**	**127**

• Son of Bill • Brother of Gord and Peter • Bud Light/NHL Man of the Year Award (1991)

Played in NHL All-Star Game (1988, 1989)

Traded to **Philadelphia** by **Hartford** for Murray Craven and Philadelphia's 4th round choice (Kevin Smyth) in 1992 Entry Draft, November 13, 1991. Traded to **Hartford** by **Philadelphia** for Hartford/Carolina's 3rd (Kris Mallette) and 7th (later traded back to Hartford/Carolina – Carolina selected Andrew Merrick) round choices in 1997 Entry Draft, December 28, 1995. Transferred to **Carolina** after **Hartford** franchise relocated, June 25, 1997. Signed as a free agent by **Ottawa**, September 1, 1999. Selected by **Columbus** from **Ottawa** in Expansion Draft, June 23, 2000. • Officially announced retirement, November 5, 2002.

DINEEN, Peter

Defense. Shoots right. 5'11", 181 lbs. Born, Kingston, Ont., November 19, 1960.
(Philadelphia's 9th choice, 189th overall, in 1980 Entry Draft).

Season	Club	GP	G	A	Pts	PIM	GP	G	A	Pts	PIM
1986-87	Los Angeles Kings	11	0	2	2	8	....	....	....	....	....
1989-90	Detroit Red Wings	2	0	0	0	5	....	....	....	....	....
	NHL Totals	**13**	**0**	**2**	**2**	**13**	....	....	....	....	....

• Son of Bill • Brother of Gord and Kevin

Traded to **Edmonton** by **Philadelphia** for Bob Hoffmeyer, October 22, 1982. Signed as a free agent by **Boston**, July 16, 1984. Signed as a free agent by **Los Angeles**, July 30, 1986. Signed as a free agent by **Detroit**, September 16, 1987.

DINGMAN, Chris

Left wing. Shoots left. 6'4", 225 lbs. Born, Edmonton, Alta., July 6, 1976.
(Calgary's 1st choice, 19th overall, in 1994 Entry Draft).

Season	Club	GP	G	A	Pts	PIM	GP	G	A	Pts	PIM
1997-98	Calgary Flames	70	3	3	6	149	....	....	....		
1998-99	Calgary Flames	2	0	0	0	17	....	....	....	....	....
	Colorado Avalanche	1	0	0	0	7	....	....	....	....	....
99-2000	Colorado Avalanche	68	8	3	11	132	....	....	....	....	....
2000-01 ♦	Colorado Avalanche	41	1	1	2	108	16	0	4	4	14
2001-02	Carolina Hurricanes	30	0	1	1	77	....	....	....	....	....
	Tampa Bay Lightning	14	0	4	4	26	....	....	....	....	....
2002-03	Tampa Bay Lightning	51	2	1	3	91	10	1	0	1	4
	NHL Totals	**277**	**14**	**13**	**27**	**607**	**26**	**1**	**4**	**5**	**18**

Traded to **Colorado** by **Calgary** with Theoren Fleury for Rene Corbet, Wade Belak, Robyn Regehr and Colorado's 2nd round compensatory choice (Jarret Stoll) in 2000 Entry Draft, February 28, 1999. • Missed majority of 2000-01 season recovering from knee injury suffered in game vs. Ottawa, November 15, 2000. Traded to **Carolina** by **Colorado** for Carolina's 5th round choice (Mikko Viitanen) in 2001 Entry Draft, June 24, 2001. Traded to **Tampa Bay** by **Carolina** with Shane Willis for Kevin Weekes, March 5, 2002.

DINSMORE, Chuck

Center. Shoots left. 5'6", 155 lbs. Born, Toronto, Ont., July 23, 1903.

Season	Club	GP	G	A	Pts	PIM	GP	G	A	Pts	PIM
1924-25	Montreal Maroons	30	2	1	3	26	....	....	....	....	....
1925-26 ♦	Montreal Maroons	33	3	1	4	18	4	1	0	1	2
	Montreal Maroons (Cup)	....	....	....	....	....	*4*	*0*	*0*	*0*	*2*
1926-27	Montreal Maroons	28	1	0	1	6	....	....	....	....	....
1929-30	Montreal Maroons	9	0	0	0	0	4	0	0	0	0
	NHL Totals	**100**	**6**	**2**	**8**	**50**	**8**	**1**	**0**	**1**	**2**

Signed as a free agent by **Mtl. Maroons**, November 18, 1924.

DIONNE, Gilbert

Left wing. Shoots left. 6', 194 lbs. Born, Drummondville, Que., September 19, 1970.
(Montreal's 5th choice, 81st overall, in 1990 Entry Draft).

Season	Club	GP	G	A	Pts	PIM	GP	G	A	Pts	PIM
1990-91	Montreal Canadiens	2	0	0	0	0	....	....	....	....	....
1991-92	Montreal Canadiens	39	21	13	34	10	11	3	4	7	10
1992-93 ♦	Montreal Canadiens	75	20	28	48	63	20	6	6	12	20
1993-94	Montreal Canadiens	74	19	26	45	31	5	1	2	3	0
1994-95	Montreal Canadiens	6	0	3	3	2	....	....	....	....	....
	Philadelphia Flyers	20	0	6	6	2	3	0	0	0	4
1995-96	Philadelphia Flyers	2	0	1	1	0	....	....	....	....	....
	Florida Panthers	5	1	2	3	0	....	....	....	....	....
	NHL Totals	**223**	**61**	**79**	**140**	**108**	**39**	**10**	**12**	**22**	**34**

• Brother of Marcel • NHL All-Rookie Team (1992)

Traded to **Philadelphia** by **Montreal** with Eric Desjardins and John LeClair for Mark Recchi and Philadelphia's 3rd round choice (Martin Hohenberger) in 1995 Entry Draft, February 9, 1995. Signed as a free agent by **Florida**, January 29, 1996. Signed as a free agent by **Carolina**, August 31, 1999.

DIONNE, Marcel

HHOF

Center. Shoots right. 5'9", 190 lbs. Born, Drummondville, Que., August 3, 1951.
(Detroit's 1st choice, 2nd overall, in 1971 Amateur Draft).

Season	Club	GP	G	A	Pts	PIM	GP	G	A	Pts	PIM
		REGULAR SEASON					PLAYOFFS				
1971-72	Detroit Red Wings	78	28	49	77	14	....	....	....	....	....
1972-73	Detroit Red Wings	77	40	50	90	21	....	....	....	....	....
1973-74	Detroit Red Wings	74	24	54	78	10	....	....	....	....	....
1974-75	Detroit Red Wings	80	47	74	121	14	....	....	....	....	....
1975-76	Los Angeles Kings	80	40	54	94	38	9	6	1	7	0
1976-77	Los Angeles Kings	80	53	69	122	12	9	5	9	14	2
1977-78	Los Angeles Kings	70	36	43	79	37	2	0	0	0	0
1978-79	Los Angeles Kings	80	59	71	130	30	2	0	1	1	0
1979-80	Los Angeles Kings	80	53	84	*137	32	4	0	3	3	4
1980-81	Los Angeles Kings	80	58	77	135	70	4	1	3	4	7
1981-82	Los Angeles Kings	78	50	67	117	50	10	7	4	11	0
1982-83	Los Angeles Kings	80	56	51	107	22	....	....	....	....	....
1983-84	Los Angeles Kings	66	39	53	92	28	....	....	....	....	....
1984-85	Los Angeles Kings	80	46	80	126	46	3	1	2	3	2
1985-86	Los Angeles Kings	80	36	58	94	42	....	....	....	....	....
1986-87	Los Angeles Kings	67	24	50	74	54	....	....	....	....	....
	New York Rangers	14	4	6	10	6	6	1	1	2	2
1987-88	New York Rangers	67	31	34	65	54	....	....	....	....	....
1988-89	New York Rangers	37	7	16	23	20	....	....	....	....	....
	NHL Totals	**1348**	**731**	**1040**	**1771**	**600**	**49**	**21**	**24**	**45**	**17**

• Brother of Gilbert • Lady Byng Trophy (1975, 1977) • NHL First All-Star Team (1977, 1980) • NHL Second All-Star Team (1979, 1981) • Lester B. Pearson Award (1979, 1980) • Art Ross Trophy (1980)

Played in NHL All-Star Game (1975, 1976, 1977, 1978, 1980, 1981, 1983, 1985)

Signed as a free agent by **Los Angeles**, June 17, 1975. • NHL orchestrated trade to **Los Angeles** by **Detroit** with Bart Crashley for Terry Harper, Dan Maloney and Los Angeles' 2nd round choice (later traded to Minnesota – Minnesota selected Jim Roberts) in 1976 Amateur Draft, June 23, 1975. Traded to **NY Rangers** by **Los Angeles** with Jeff Crossman and Los Angeles' 3rd round choice (later traded to Minnesota – Minnesota selected Murray Garbutt) in 1989 Entry Draft for Bob Carpenter and Tom Laidlaw, March 10, 1987.

DiPENTA, Joe

Defense. Shoots left. 6'2", 235 lbs. Born, Barrie, Ont., February 25, 1979.
(Florida's 2nd choice, 61st overall, in 1998 Entry Draft).

Season	Club	GP	G	A	Pts	PIM	GP	G	A	Pts	PIM
2002-03	Atlanta Thrashers	3	1	1	2	0	....	....	....	....	....
	NHL Totals	**3**	**1**	**1**	**2**	**0**	....	....	....	....	....

Signed as a free agent by **Philadelphia**, July 12, 2000. Traded to **Atlanta** by **Philadelphia** for Jarrod Skalde, March 5, 2002.

Di PIETRO, Paul

Center. Shoots right. 5'9", 181 lbs. Born, Sault Ste. Marie, Ont., September 8, 1970.
(Montreal's 6th choice, 102nd overall, in 1990 Entry Draft).

Season	Club	GP	G	A	Pts	PIM	GP	G	A	Pts	PIM
1991-92	Montreal Canadiens	33	4	6	10	25	....	....	....	....	....
1992-93 ♦	Montreal Canadiens	29	4	13	17	14	17	8	5	13	8
1993-94	Montreal Canadiens	70	13	20	33	37	7	2	4	6	2
1994-95	Montreal Canadiens	22	4	5	9	4	....	....	....	....	....
	Toronto Maple Leafs	12	1	1	2	6	7	1	1	2	0
1995-96	Toronto Maple Leafs	20	4	4	8	4	....	....	....	....	....
1996-97	Los Angeles Kings	6	1	0	1	6	....	....	....	....	....
	NHL Totals	**192**	**31**	**49**	**80**	**96**	**31**	**11**	**10**	**21**	**10**

Traded to **Toronto** by **Montreal** for Phoenix's 4th round choice (previously acquired, Montreal selected Kim Staal) in 1996 Entry Draft, April 6, 1995. Signed as a free agent by **Los Angeles**, July 23, 1996.

DIRK, Robert

Defense. Shoots left. 6'4", 210 lbs. Born, Regina, Sask., August 20, 1966.
(St. Louis' 4th choice, 53rd overall, in 1984 Entry Draft).

Season	Club	GP	G	A	Pts	PIM	GP	G	A	Pts	PIM
1987-88	St. Louis Blues	7	0	1	1	16	6	0	1	1	2
1988-89	St. Louis Blues	9	0	1	1	11	....	....	....	....	....
1989-90	St. Louis Blues	37	1	1	2	128	3	0	0	0	0
1990-91	St. Louis Blues	41	1	3	4	100	....	....	....	....	....
	Vancouver Canucks	11	1	0	1	20	6	0	0	0	13
1991-92	Vancouver Canucks	72	2	7	9	126	13	0	0	0	20
1992-93	Vancouver Canucks	69	4	8	12	150	9	0	0	0	6
1993-94	Vancouver Canucks	65	2	3	5	105	....	....	....	....	....
	Chicago Blackhawks	6	0	0	0	26	2	0	0	0	15
1994-95	Mighty Ducks of Anaheim	38	1	3	4	56	....	....	....	....	....
1995-96	Mighty Ducks of Anaheim	44	1	2	3	42	....	....	....	....	....
	Montreal Canadiens	3	0	0	0	6	....	....	....	....	....
	NHL Totals	**402**	**13**	**29**	**42**	**786**	**39**	**0**	**1**	**1**	**56**

Traded to **Vancouver** by **St. Louis** with Geoff Courtnall, Sergio Momesso, Cliff Ronning and St. Louis' 5th round choice (Brian Loney) in 1992 Entry Draft for Dan Quinn and Garth Butcher, March 5, 1991. Traded to **Chicago** by **Vancouver** for Chicago's 4th round choice (Mike Dubinsky) in 1994 Entry Draft, March 21, 1994. Traded to **Anaheim** by **Chicago** for Tampa Bay's 4th round choice (previously acquired, Chicago selected Chris Van Dyk) in 1995 Entry Draft, July 12, 1994. Traded to **Montreal** by **Anaheim** for Jim Campbell, January 21, 1996.

DIVISEK, Tomas

Center. Shoots left. 6'2", 204 lbs. Born, Most, Czech., July 19, 1979.
(Philadelphia's 9th choice, 195th overall, in 1998 Entry Draft).

Season	Club	GP	G	A	Pts	PIM	GP	G	A	Pts	PIM
2000-01	Philadelphia Flyers	2	0	0	0	0	....	....	....	....	....
2001-02	Philadelphia Flyers	3	1	0	1	0	....	....	....	....	....
	NHL Totals	**5**	**1**	**0**	**1**	**0**	....	....	....	....	....

DJOOS, Per

Defense. Shoots right. 5'11", 176 lbs. Born, Mora, Sweden, May 11, 1968.
(Detroit's 7th choice, 127th overall, in 1986 Entry Draft).

Season	Club	Regular Season GP	G	A	Pts	PIM	Playoffs GP	G	A	Pts	PIM
1990-91	Detroit Red Wings	26	0	12	12	16	....	....	....	....	....
1991-92	New York Rangers	50	1	18	19	40	....	....	....	....	....
1992-93	New York Rangers	6	1	1	2	2	....	....	....	....	....
	NHL Totals	**82**	**2**	**31**	**33**	**58**	....	....	....	....	....

Traded to **NY Rangers** by **Detroit** with Joe Kocur for Kevin Miller, Jim Cummins and Dennis Vial, March 5, 1991.

DOAK, Gary

Defense. Shoots right. 5'11", 175 lbs. Born, Goderich, Ont., February 26, 1946.

Season	Club	Regular Season GP	G	A	Pts	PIM	Playoffs GP	G	A	Pts	PIM
1965-66	Detroit Red Wings	4	0	0	0	12	....	....	....	....	....
	Boston Bruins	20	0	8	8	28	....	....	....	....	....
1966-67	Boston Bruins	29	0	1	1	50	....	....	....	....	....
1967-68	Boston Bruins	59	2	10	12	100	4	0	0	0	4
1968-69	Boston Bruins	22	3	3	6	37	....	....	....	....	....
1969-70♦	Boston Bruins	44	1	7	8	63	8	0	0	0	9
1970-71	Vancouver Canucks	77	2	10	12	112	....	....	....	....	....
1971-72	Vancouver Canucks	6	0	1	1	23	....	....	....	....	....
	New York Rangers	49	1	10	11	54	12	0	0	0	46
1972-73	Detroit Red Wings	44	0	5	5	51	....	....	....	....	....
	Boston Bruins	5	0	0	0	2	2	0	0	0	2
1973-74	Boston Bruins	69	0	4	4	44	....	....	....	....	....
1974-75	Boston Bruins	40	0	0	0	30	3	0	0	0	4
1975-76	Boston Bruins	58	1	6	7	60	12	1	0	1	22
1976-77	Boston Bruins	76	3	13	16	107	14	0	2	2	26
1977-78	Boston Bruins	61	4	13	17	50	12	1	0	1	4
1978-79	Boston Bruins	63	6	11	17	28	7	0	2	2	4
1979-80	Boston Bruins	52	0	5	5	45	4	0	0	0	0
1980-81	Boston Bruins	11	0	0	0	12	....	....	....	....	....
	NHL Totals	**789**	**23**	**107**	**130**	**908**	**78**	**2**	**4**	**6**	**121**

Traded to **Boston** by **Detroit** with Bill Lesuk, Ron Murphy and future considerations (Steve Atkinson, June 6, 1966) for Dean Prentice and Leo Boivin, February 16, 1966. • Missed majority of 1968-69 season recovering from mononucleosis. Claimed by **Vancouver** from **Boston** in Expansion Draft, June 10, 1970. Traded to **NY Rangers** by **Vancouver** with Jim Wiste for Dave Balon, Wayne Connelly and Ron Stewart, November 16, 1971. Traded to **Detroit** by **NY Rangers** with Rick Newell for Joe Zanussi and Detroit's 1st round choice (Albert Blanchard) in 1972 Amateur Draft, May 24, 1972. Traded to **Boston** by **Detroit** for Garnet Bailey and future considerations (Murray Wing, June 4, 1973), March 1, 1973.

DOAN, Shane

Right wing. Shoots right. 6'2", 228 lbs. Born, Halkirk, Alta., October 10, 1976.
(Winnipeg's 1st choice, 7th overall, in 1995 Entry Draft).

Season	Club	Regular Season GP	G	A	Pts	PIM	Playoffs GP	G	A	Pts	PIM
1995-96	Winnipeg Jets	74	7	10	17	101	6	0	0	0	6
1996-97	Phoenix Coyotes	63	4	8	12	49	4	0	0	0	2
1997-98	Phoenix Coyotes	33	5	6	11	35	6	1	0	1	6
1998-99	Phoenix Coyotes	79	6	16	22	54	7	2	2	4	6
99-2000	Phoenix Coyotes	81	26	25	51	66	4	1	2	3	8
2000-01	Phoenix Coyotes	76	26	37	63	89	....	....	....	....	....
2001-02	Phoenix Coyotes	81	20	29	49	61	5	2	2	4	6
2002-03	Phoenix Coyotes	82	21	37	58	86	....	....	....	....	....
	NHL Totals	**569**	**115**	**168**	**283**	**541**	**32**	**6**	**6**	**12**	**34**

Transferred to **Phoenix** after **Winnipeg** franchise relocated, July 1, 1996.

DOBBIN, Brian

Right wing. Shoots right. 5'11", 205 lbs. Born, Petrolia, Ont., August 18, 1966.
(Philadelphia's 7th choice, 100th overall, in 1984 Entry Draft).

Season	Club	Regular Season GP	G	A	Pts	PIM	Playoffs GP	G	A	Pts	PIM
1986-87	Philadelphia Flyers	12	2	1	3	14	....	....	....	....	....
1987-88	Philadelphia Flyers	21	3	5	8	6	....	....	....	....	....
1988-89	Philadelphia Flyers	14	0	1	1	8	2	0	0	0	17
1989-90	Philadelphia Flyers	9	1	1	2	11	....	....	....	....	....
1991-92	Boston Bruins	7	1	0	1	22	....	....	....	....	....
	NHL Totals	**63**	**7**	**8**	**15**	**61**	**2**	**0**	**0**	**0**	**17**

Traded to **Boston** by **Philadelphia** with Gord Murphy, Philadelphia's 3rd round choice (Sergei Zholtok) in 1992 Entry Draft and 4th round choice (Charles Paquette) in 1993 Entry Draft for Garry Galley, Wes Walz and Boston's 3rd round choice (Milos Holan) in 1993 Entry Draft, January 2, 1992.

DOBSON, Jim

Right wing. Shoots right. 6'1", 195 lbs. Born, Winnipeg, Man., February 29, 1960.
(Minnesota's 5th choice, 90th overall, in 1979 Entry Draft).

Season	Club	Regular Season GP	G	A	Pts	PIM	Playoffs GP	G	A	Pts	PIM
1979-80	Minnesota North Stars	1	0	0	0	0	....	....	....	....	....
1980-81	Minnesota North Stars	1	0	0	0	0	....	....	....	....	....
1981-82	Minnesota North Stars	6	0	0	0	4	....	....	....	....	....
	Colorado Rockies	3	0	0	0	2	....	....	....	....	....
1983-84	Quebec Nordiques	1	0	0	0	0	....	....	....	....	....
	NHL Totals	**12**	**0**	**0**	**0**	**6**	....	....	....	....	....

Rights traded to **Colorado** by **Minnesota** with Kevin Maxwell for cash, December 31, 1981. Signed as a free agent by **Minnesota**, September 20, 1982. Traded to **Quebec** by **Minnesota** for Jay Miller, June 29, 1983. Signed as a free agent by **NY Rangers**, December 13, 1985.

DOHERTY, Fred

Right wing. Shoots left. 5'8", 160 lbs. Born, Norwood, Ont.,

Season	Club	Regular Season GP	G	A	Pts	PIM	Playoffs GP	G	A	Pts	PIM
1918-19	Montreal Canadiens	1	0	0	0	0	....	....	....	....	....
	NHL Totals	**1**	**0**	**0**	**0**	**0**	....	....	....	....	....

Signed as a free agent by **Montreal**, December 13, 1918.

DOIG, Jason

Defense. Shoots right. 6'3", 228 lbs. Born, Montreal, Que., January 29, 1977.
(Winnipeg's 3rd choice, 34th overall, in 1995 Entry Draft).

Season	Club	Regular Season GP	G	A	Pts	PIM	Playoffs GP	G	A	Pts	PIM
1995-96	Winnipeg Jets	15	1	1	2	28	....	....	....	....	....
1997-98	Phoenix Coyotes	4	0	1	1	12	....	....	....	....	....
1998-99	Phoenix Coyotes	9	0	1	1	10	....	....	....	....	....
99-2000	New York Rangers	7	0	1	1	22	....	....	....	....	....
2000-01	New York Rangers	3	0	0	0	0	....	....	....	....	....
2002-03	Washington Capitals	55	3	5	8	108	6	0	1	1	6
	NHL Totals	**93**	**4**	**9**	**13**	**180**	**6**	**0**	**1**	**1**	**6**

Transferred to **Phoenix** after **Winnipeg** franchise relocated, July 1, 1996. Traded to **NY Rangers** by **Phoenix** with Phoenix's 6th round choice (Jay Dardis) in 1999 Entry Draft for Stan Neckar, March 23, 1999. Traded to **Ottawa** by **NY Rangers** with Jeff Ulmer for Sean Gagnon, June 29, 2001. Signed as free agent by **Washington**, September 12, 2002.

DOLLAS, Bobby

Defense. Shoots left. 6'2", 212 lbs. Born, Montreal, Que., January 31, 1965.
(Winnipeg's 2nd choice, 14th overall, in 1983 Entry Draft).

Season	Club	Regular Season GP	G	A	Pts	PIM	Playoffs GP	G	A	Pts	PIM
1983-84	Winnipeg Jets	1	0	0	0	0	....	....	....	....	....
1984-85	Winnipeg Jets	9	0	0	0	0	....	....	....	....	....
1985-86	Winnipeg Jets	46	0	5	5	66	3	0	0	0	2
1987-88	Quebec Nordiques	9	0	0	0	2	....	....	....	....	....
1988-89	Quebec Nordiques	16	0	3	3	16	....	....	....	....	....
1990-91	Detroit Red Wings	56	3	5	8	20	7	1	0	1	13
1991-92	Detroit Red Wings	27	3	1	4	20	2	0	1	1	0
1992-93	Detroit Red Wings	6	0	0	0	2	....	....	....	....	....
1993-94	Mighty Ducks of Anaheim	77	9	11	20	55	....	....	....	....	....
1994-95	Mighty Ducks of Anaheim	45	7	13	20	12	....	....	....	....	....
1995-96	Mighty Ducks of Anaheim	82	8	22	30	64	....	....	....	....	....
1996-97	Mighty Ducks of Anaheim	79	4	14	18	55	11	0	0	0	4
1997-98	Mighty Ducks of Anaheim	22	0	1	1	27	....	....	....	....	....
	Edmonton Oilers	30	2	5	7	22	11	0	0	0	16
1998-99	Pittsburgh Penguins	70	2	8	10	60	13	1	0	1	6
99-2000	Ottawa Senators	1	0	0	0	0	....	....	....	....	....
	Calgary Flames	49	3	7	10	28	....	....	....	....	....
2000-01	San Jose Sharks	16	1	1	2	14	....	....	....	....	....
	Pittsburgh Penguins	5	0	0	0	4	....	....	....	....	....
	NHL Totals	**646**	**42**	**96**	**138**	**467**	**47**	**2**	**1**	**3**	**41**

Traded to **Quebec** by **Winnipeg** for Stu Kulak, December 17, 1987. Signed as a free agent by **Detroit**, October 18, 1990. Claimed by **Anaheim** from **Detroit** in Expansion Draft, June 24, 1993. Traded to **Edmonton** by **Anaheim** for Drew Bannister, January 9, 1998. Traded to **Pittsburgh** by **Edmonton** with Tony Hrkac for Josef Beranek, June 16, 1998. Signed as a free agent by **Long Beach**, October 12, 1999. Signed as a free agent by **Ottawa**, November 9, 1999. Claimed on waivers by **Calgary** from **Ottawa**, November 11, 1999. Signed as a free agent by **San Jose**, November 4, 2000. Traded to **Pittsburgh** by **San Jose** with Johan Hedberg for Jeff Norton, March 12, 2001.

DOME, Robert

Right wing. Shoots left. 6', 210 lbs. Born, Skalica, Czech., January 29, 1979.
(Pittsburgh's 1st choice, 17th overall, in 1997 Entry Draft).

Season	Club	Regular Season GP	G	A	Pts	PIM	Playoffs GP	G	A	Pts	PIM
1997-98	Pittsburgh Penguins	30	5	2	7	12	....	....	....	....	....
99-2000	Pittsburgh Penguins	22	2	5	7	0	....	....	....	....	....
2002-03	Calgary Flames	1	0	0	0	0	....	....	....	....	....
	NHL Totals	**53**	**7**	**7**	**14**	**12**	....	....	....	....	....

Signed as a free agent by **Calgary**, July 17, 2002.

DOMENICHELLI, Hnat

Left wing. Shoots left. 6', 195 lbs. Born, Edmonton, Alta., February 17, 1976.
(Hartford's 2nd choice, 83rd overall, in 1994 Entry Draft).

Season	Club	Regular Season GP	G	A	Pts	PIM	Playoffs GP	G	A	Pts	PIM
1996-97	Hartford Whalers	13	2	1	3	7	....	....	....	....	....
	Calgary Flames	10	1	2	3	2	....	....	....	....	....
1997-98	Calgary Flames	31	9	7	16	6	....	....	....	....	....
1998-99	Calgary Flames	23	5	5	10	11	....	....	....	....	....
99-2000	Calgary Flames	32	5	9	14	12	....	....	....	....	....
	Atlanta Thrashers	27	6	9	15	4	....	....	....	....	....
2000-01	Atlanta Thrashers	63	15	12	27	18	....	....	....	....	....
2001-02	Atlanta Thrashers	40	8	11	19	34	....	....	....	....	....
	Minnesota Wild	27	1	5	6	10	....	....	....	....	....
2002-03	Minnesota Wild	1	0	0	0	0	....	....	....	....	....
	NHL Totals	**267**	**52**	**61**	**113**	**104**	....	....	....	....	....

Traded to **Calgary** by **Hartford** with Glen Featherstone, New Jersey's 2nd round choice (previously acquired, Calgary selected Dimitri Kokorev) in 1997 Entry Draft and Vancouver's 3rd round choice (previously acquired, Calgary selected Paul Manning) in 1998 Entry Draft for Steve Chiasson and Colorado's 3rd round choice (previously acquired, Carolina selected Francis Lessard) in 1997 Entry Draft, March 5, 1997. Traded to **Atlanta** by **Calgary** with Dmitri Vlasenkov for Darryl Shannon and Jason Botterill, February 11, 2000. Traded to **Minnesota** by **Atlanta** for Andy Sutton, January 22, 2002.

DOMI, Tie

Right wing. Shoots right. 5'10", 200 lbs. Born, Windsor, Ont., November 1, 1969.
(Toronto's 2nd choice, 27th overall, in 1988 Entry Draft).

		REGULAR SEASON					PLAYOFFS				
Season	Club	GP	G	A	Pts	PIM	GP	G	A	Pts	PIM
1989-90	Toronto Maple Leafs	2	0	0	0	42	....	....	....	....	....
1990-91	New York Rangers	28	1	0	1	185	....	....	....	....	....
1991-92	New York Rangers	42	2	4	6	246	6	1	1	2	32
1992-93	New York Rangers	12	2	0	2	95	....	....	....	....	....
	Winnipeg Jets	49	3	10	13	249	6	1	0	1	23
1993-94	Winnipeg Jets	81	8	11	19	*347	....	....	....	....	....
1994-95	Winnipeg Jets	31	4	4	8	128	....	....	....	....	....
	Toronto Maple Leafs	9	0	1	1	31	7	1	0	1	0
1995-96	Toronto Maple Leafs	72	7	6	13	297	6	0	2	2	4
1996-97	Toronto Maple Leafs	80	11	17	28	275	....	....	....	....	....
1997-98	Toronto Maple Leafs	80	4	10	14	365	....	....	....	....	....
1998-99	Toronto Maple Leafs	72	8	14	22	198	14	0	2	2	24
99-2000	Toronto Maple Leafs	70	5	9	14	198	12	0	1	1	20
2000-01	Toronto Maple Leafs	82	13	7	20	214	8	0	1	1	20
2001-02	Toronto Maple Leafs	74	9	10	19	157	19	1	3	4	*61
2002-03	Toronto Maple Leafs	79	15	14	29	171	7	1	0	1	13
	NHL Totals	**863**	**92**	**117**	**209**	**3198**	**85**	**5**	**10**	**15**	**197**

Traded to **NY Rangers** by **Toronto** with Mark LaForest for Greg Johnston, June 28, 1990. Traded to **Winnipeg** by **NY Rangers** with Kris King for Ed Olczyk, December 28, 1992. Traded to **Toronto** by **Winnipeg** for Mike Eastwood and Toronto's 3rd round choice (Brad Isbister) in 1995 Entry Draft, April 7, 1995. Traded to **Nashville** by **Toronto** for Nashville's 8th round choice (Shaun Landolt) in 2003 Entry Draft, June 30, 2002. Signed as a free agent by **Toronto**, July 14, 2002.

DONALDSON, Gary

Right wing. Shoots right. 5'9", 155 lbs. Born, Trail, B.C., July 15, 1952.
(Chicago's 9th choice, 141st overall, in 1972 Amateur Draft).

Season	Club	GP	G	A	Pts	PIM	GP	G	A	Pts	PIM
1973-74	Chicago Black Hawks	1	0	0	0	0	....	....	....	....	....
	NHL Totals	**1**	**0**	**0**	**0**	**0**	....	....	....	....	....

DONATELLI, Clark

Left wing. Shoots left. 5'10", 180 lbs. Born, Providence, RI, November 22, 1965.
(NY Rangers' 4th choice, 98th overall, in 1984 Entry Draft).

Season	Club	GP	G	A	Pts	PIM	GP	G	A	Pts	PIM
1989-90	Minnesota North Stars	25	3	3	6	17	....	....	....	....	....
1991-92	Boston Bruins	10	0	1	1	22	2	0	0	0	0
	NHL Totals	**35**	**3**	**4**	**7**	**39**	**2**	**0**	**0**	**0**	**0**

Traded to **Edmonton** by **NY Rangers** with Ville Kentala, Reijo Ruotsalainen and Jim Wiemer for Mike Golden, Don Jackson, Miroslav Horava and future considerations (Stu Kulak, March 10, 1987), October 23, 1986. Signed as a free agent by **Minnesota**, June 20, 1989. Signed as a free agent by **Boston**, March 10, 1992.

DONATO, Ted

Left wing. Shoots left. 5'10", 178 lbs. Born, Boston, MA, April 28, 1969.
(Boston's 6th choice, 98th overall, in 1987 Entry Draft).

Season	Club	GP	G	A	Pts	PIM	GP	G	A	Pts	PIM
1991-92	Boston Bruins	10	1	2	3	8	15	3	4	7	4
1992-93	Boston Bruins	82	15	20	35	61	4	0	1	1	0
1993-94	Boston Bruins	84	22	32	54	59	13	4	2	6	10
1994-95	Boston Bruins	47	10	10	20	10	5	0	0	0	4
1995-96	Boston Bruins	82	23	26	49	46	5	1	2	3	2
1996-97	Boston Bruins	67	25	26	51	37	....	....	....	....	....
1997-98	Boston Bruins	79	16	23	39	54	5	0	0	0	2
1998-99	Boston Bruins	14	1	3	4	4	....	....	....	....	....
	New York Islanders	55	7	11	18	27	....	....	....	....	....
	Ottawa Senators	13	3	2	5	10	1	0	0	0	0
99-2000	Mighty Ducks of Anaheim	81	11	19	30	26	....	....	....	....	....
2000-01	Dallas Stars	65	8	17	25	26	8	0	1	1	0
2001-02	New York Islanders	1	0	0	0	0	....	....	....	....	....
	St. Louis Blues	2	0	0	0	2	....	....	....	....	....
	Los Angeles Kings	2	0	0	0	2	....	....	....	....	....
2002-03	New York Rangers	49	2	1	3	6	....	....	....	....	....
	NHL Totals	**733**	**144**	**192**	**336**	**378**	**56**	**8**	**10**	**18**	**22**

Traded to **NY Islanders** by **Boston** for Ken Belanger, November 7, 1998. Traded to **Ottawa** by **NY Islanders** for Ottawa's 4th round choice (later traded to Phoenix – Phoenix selected Preston Mizzi) in 1999 Entry Draft, March 20, 1999. Traded to **Anaheim** by **Ottawa** with the rights to Antti-Jussi Niemi for Patrick Lalime, June 18, 1999. Signed as a free agent by **Dallas**, August 17, 2000. Signed as a free agent by **NY Islanders**, January 16, 2002. Claimed on waivers by **Los Angeles** from **NY Islanders**, January 28, 2002. Claimed on waivers by **St. Louis** from **Los Angeles**, March 6, 2002. Claimed on waivers by **Los Angeles** from **St. Louis**, March 19, 2002. Signed as a free agent by **NY Rangers**, July 8, 2002. Signed as a free agent by **Boston**, July 22, 2003.

DONNELLY, Babe

Defense. Shoots left. 5'7", 180 lbs. Born, Sault Ste. Marie, Ont., December 22, 1895.

Season	Club	GP	G	A	Pts	PIM	GP	G	A	Pts	PIM
1926-27	Montreal Maroons	34	0	1	1	14	2	0	0	0	0
	NHL Totals	**34**	**0**	**1**	**1**	**14**	**2**	**0**	**0**	**0**	**0**

Signed as a free agent by **Mtl. Maroons** and loaned to **Detroit** (AHA), September 30, 1926.

DONNELLY, Dave

Center. Shoots left. 5'11", 185 lbs. Born, Edmonton, Alta., February 2, 1962.
(Minnesota's 2nd choice, 27th overall, in 1981 Entry Draft).

Season	Club	GP	G	A	Pts	PIM	GP	G	A	Pts	PIM
1983-84	Boston Bruins	16	3	4	7	2	3	0	0	0	0
1984-85	Boston Bruins	38	6	8	14	46	1	0	0	0	0
1985-86	Boston Bruins	8	0	0	0	17	....	....	....	....	....
1986-87	Chicago Blackhawks	71	6	12	18	81	1	0	0	0	0
1987-88	Edmonton Oilers	4	0	0	0	4	....	....	....	....	....
	NHL Totals	**137**	**15**	**24**	**39**	**150**	**5**	**0**	**0**	**0**	**0**

Rights traded to **Boston** by **Minnesota** with Brad Palmer for Boston agreeing not to select Brian Bellows in 1982 Entry Draft, June 9, 1982. Traded to **Detroit** by **Boston** for Dwight Foster, March 11, 1986. Signed as a free agent by **Chicago**, September, 1986. Traded to **Edmonton** by **Chicago** for cash, October 19, 1987.

DONNELLY, Gord

Defense. Shoots right. 6'1", 202 lbs. Born, Montreal, Que., April 5, 1962.
(St. Louis' 3rd choice, 62nd overall, in 1981 Entry Draft).

Season	Club	GP	G	A	Pts	PIM	GP	G	A	Pts	PIM
1983-84	Quebec Nordiques	38	0	5	5	60	....	....	....	....	....
1984-85	Quebec Nordiques	22	0	0	0	33	....	....	....	....	....
1985-86	Quebec Nordiques	36	2	2	4	85	1	0	0	0	0
1986-87	Quebec Nordiques	38	0	2	2	143	13	0	0	0	53
1987-88	Quebec Nordiques	63	4	3	7	301	....	....	....	....	....
1988-89	Quebec Nordiques	16	4	0	4	46	....	....	....	....	....
	Winnipeg Jets	57	6	10	16	228	....	....	....	....	....
1989-90	Winnipeg Jets	55	3	3	6	222	6	0	1	1	8
1990-91	Winnipeg Jets	57	3	4	7	265	....	....	....	....	....
1991-92	Winnipeg Jets	4	0	0	0	11	....	....	....	....	....
	Buffalo Sabres	67	2	3	5	305	6	0	1	1	0
1992-93	Buffalo Sabres	60	3	8	11	221	....	....	....	....	....
1993-94	Buffalo Sabres	7	0	0	0	31	....	....	....	....	....
	Dallas Stars	18	0	1	1	66	....	....	....	....	....
1994-95	Dallas Stars	16	1	0	1	52	....	....	....	....	....
	NHL Totals	**554**	**28**	**41**	**69**	**2069**	**26**	**0**	**2**	**2**	**61**

Transferred to **Quebec** by **St. Louis** with Claude Julien as compensation for St. Louis' signing of Jacques Demers as coach, August 19, 1983. Traded to **Winnipeg** by **Quebec** for Mario Marois, December 6, 1988. Traded to **Buffalo** by **Winnipeg** with Dave McLlwain, Winnipeg's 5th round choice (Yuri Khmylev) in 1992 Entry Draft and future considerations for Darrin Shannon, Mike Hartman and Dean Kennedy, October 11, 1991. Traded to **Dallas** by **Buffalo** for James Black and Dallas' 7th round choice (Steve Webb) in 1994 Entry Draft, December 15, 1993.

DONNELLY, Mike

Left wing. Shoots left. 5'11", 185 lbs. Born, Detroit, MI, October 10, 1963.

Season	Club	GP	G	A	Pts	PIM	GP	G	A	Pts	PIM
1986-87	New York Rangers	5	1	1	2	0	....	....	....	....	....
1987-88	New York Rangers	17	2	2	4	8	....	....	....	....	....
	Buffalo Sabres	40	6	8	14	44	....	....	....	....	....
1988-89	Buffalo Sabres	22	4	6	10	10	....	....	....	....	....
1989-90	Buffalo Sabres	12	1	2	3	8	....	....	....	....	....
1990-91	Los Angeles Kings	53	7	5	12	41	12	5	4	9	6
1991-92	Los Angeles Kings	80	29	16	45	20	6	1	0	1	4
1992-93	Los Angeles Kings	84	29	40	69	45	24	6	7	13	14
1993-94	Los Angeles Kings	81	21	21	42	34	....	....	....	....	....
1994-95	Los Angeles Kings	9	1	1	2	4	....	....	....	....	....
	Dallas Stars	35	11	14	25	29	5	0	1	1	6
1995-96	Dallas Stars	24	2	5	7	10	....	....	....	....	....
1996-97	New York Islanders	3	0	0	0	2	....	....	....	....	....
	NHL Totals	**465**	**114**	**121**	**235**	**255**	**47**	**12**	**12**	**24**	**30**

Signed as a free agent by **NY Rangers**, August 15, 1986. Traded to **Buffalo** by **NY Rangers** with NY Rangers' 5th round choice (Alexander Mogilny) in 1988 Entry Draft for Paul Cyr and Buffalo's 10th round choice (Eric Fenton) in 1988 Entry Draft, December 31, 1987. Traded to **Los Angeles** by **Buffalo** for Mikko Makela, September 30, 1990. Traded to **Dallas** by **Los Angeles** with Los Angeles' 7th round choice (Eoin McInerney) in 1996 Entry Draft for Dallas' 4th round choice (later traded to Washington – Washington selected Justin Davis) in 1996 Entry Draft, February 17, 1995. Signed as a free agent by **NY Islanders**, August 19, 1996.

DONOVAN, Shean

Right wing. Shoots right. 6'2", 200 lbs. Born, Timmins, Ont., January 22, 1975.
(San Jose's 2nd choice, 28th overall, in 1993 Entry Draft).

Season	Club	GP	G	A	Pts	PIM	GP	G	A	Pts	PIM
1994-95	San Jose Sharks	14	0	0	0	6	7	0	1	1	6
1995-96	San Jose Sharks	74	13	8	21	39	....	....	....	....	....
1996-97	San Jose Sharks	73	9	6	15	42	....	....	....	....	....
1997-98	San Jose Sharks	20	3	3	6	22	....	....	....	....	....
	Colorado Avalanche	47	5	7	12	48	....	....	....	....	....
1998-99	Colorado Avalanche	68	7	12	19	37	5	0	0	0	2
99-2000	Colorado Avalanche	18	1	0	1	8	....	....	....	....	....
	Atlanta Thrashers	33	4	7	11	18	....	....	....	....	....
2000-01	Atlanta Thrashers	63	12	11	23	47	....	....	....	....	....
2001-02	Atlanta Thrashers	48	6	6	12	40	....	....	....	....	....
	Pittsburgh Penguins	13	2	1	3	4	....	....	....	....	....
2002-03	Pittsburgh Penguins	52	4	5	9	30	....	....	....	....	....
	Calgary Flames	13	1	2	3	7	....	....	....	....	....
	NHL Totals	**536**	**67**	**68**	**135**	**348**	**12**	**0**	**1**	**1**	**8**

Traded to **Colorado** by **San Jose** with San Jose's 1st round choice (Alex Tanguay) in 1998 Entry Draft for Mike Ricci and Colorado's 2nd round choice (later traded to Buffalo – Buffalo selected Jaroslav Kristek), in 1998 Entry Draft, November 21, 1997. Traded to **Atlanta** by **Colorado** for Rick Tabaracci, December 8, 1999. Claimed on waivers by **Pittsburgh** from **Atlanta**, March 15, 2002. Traded to **Calgary** by **Pittsburgh** for Micki Dupont and Mathias Johansson, March 11, 2003.

DOPITA, Jiri

Center. Shoots left. 6'4", 210 lbs. Born, Sumperk, Czech., December 2, 1968.
(NY Islanders' 4th choice, 123rd overall, in 1998 Entry Draft).

Season	Club	GP	G	A	Pts	PIM	GP	G	A	Pts	PIM
2001-02	Philadelphia Flyers	52	11	16	27	8	....	....	....	....	....

Season	Club	REGULAR SEASON GP	G	A	Pts	PIM	PLAYOFFS GP	G	A	Pts	PIM
2002-03	Edmonton Oilers	21	1	5	6	11	....	....	....	....	....
	NHL Totals	**73**	**12**	**21**	**33**	**19**	....	....	....	....	....

• Re-entered NHL Entry Draft. Originally Boston's 4th choice, 133rd overall, in 1992 Entry Draft.

Rights traded to **Florida** by **NY Islanders** for San Jose's 5th round choice (previously acquired, NY Islanders selected Adam Johnson) in 1999 Entry Draft, June 26, 1999. Rights traded to **Philadelphia** by **Florida** for Philadelphia's 2nd round choice (later traded to Calgary – Calgary selected Andrei Medvedev) in 2001 Entry Draft, June 23, 2001. Traded to **Edmonton** by **Philadelphia** for Edmonton's 3rd round choice (Ryan Potulny) in 2003 Entry Draft and future considerations, June 19, 2002.

DORAN, John

Defense. Shoots left. 5'11", 195 lbs. Born, Belleville, Ont., May 24, 1911.

Season	Club	GP	G	A	Pts	PIM	GP	G	A	Pts	PIM
1933-34	New York Americans	39	1	4	5	40	....	....	....	....	....
1935-36	New York Americans	25	4	2	6	44	3	0	0	0	0
1936-37	New York Americans	21	0	1	1	10	....	....	....	....	....
1937-38	Detroit Red Wings	7	0	0	0	10	....	....	....	....	....
1939-40	Montreal Canadiens	6	0	3	3	6	....	....	....	....	....
	NHL Totals	**98**	**5**	**10**	**15**	**110**	**3**	**0**	**0**	**0**	**0**

Traded to **Detroit** by **NY Americans** with $7,500 for Earl Robertson, May 9, 1937. Loaned to **Montreal** by **Providence** (IAHL), January 15, 1940.

DORAN, Lloyd

Center. Shoots left. 6', 175 lbs. Born, South Porcupine, Ont., January 10, 1921.

Season	Club	GP	G	A	Pts	PIM	GP	G	A	Pts	PIM
1946-47	Detroit Red Wings	24	3	2	5	10	....	....	....	....	....
	NHL Totals	**24**	**3**	**2**	**5**	**10**	....	....	....	....	....

Signed as a free agent by **Detroit**, October 21, 1941. Traded to **Chicago** (St. Louis-AHL) by **Detroit** with Red Almas, Tony Licari, Barry Sullivan and Thain Simon for Joe Lund and Hec Highton, September 9, 1948. Traded to **Cleveland** (AHL) by **Chicago** (St. Louis-AHL) for Eric Pogue, November 17, 1950.

DORATY, Ken

Forward. Shoots right. 5'7", 133 lbs. Born, Stittsville, Ont., June 23, 1906.

Season	Club	GP	G	A	Pts	PIM	GP	G	A	Pts	PIM
1926-27	Chicago Black Hawks	18	0	0	0	0	....	....	....	....	....
1932-33	Toronto Maple Leafs	38	5	11	16	16	9	5	0	5	2
1933-34	Toronto Maple Leafs	34	9	10	19	6	5	2	2	4	0
1934-35	Toronto Maple Leafs	11	1	4	5	0	1	0	0	0	0
1937-38	Detroit Red Wings	2	0	1	1	2	....	....	....	....	....
	NHL Totals	**103**	**15**	**26**	**41**	**24**	**15**	**7**	**2**	**9**	**2**

Played in NHL All-Star Game (1934)

Rights transferred to **Chicago** after NHL club purchased **Portland** (WHL) franchise, May 15, 1926. Traded to **Toronto** (Syracuse-IHL) by **Cleveland** (IHL) for cash, October 6, 1932. Traded to **Cleveland** (IHL) by **Toronto** for cash, December 2, 1935. Signed as a free agent by **Detroit**, December 3, 1936.

DORE, Andre

Defense. Shoots right. 6'2", 200 lbs. Born, Montreal, Que., February 11, 1958.
(NY Rangers' 5th choice, 60th overall, in 1978 Amateur Draft).

Season	Club	GP	G	A	Pts	PIM	GP	G	A	Pts	PIM
1978-79	New York Rangers	2	0	0	0	0	....	....	....	....	....
1979-80	New York Rangers	2	0	0	0	0	....	....	....	....	....
1980-81	New York Rangers	15	1	3	4	15	....	....	....	....	....
1981-82	New York Rangers	56	4	16	20	64	10	1	1	2	16
1982-83	New York Rangers	39	3	12	15	39	....	....	....	....	....
	St. Louis Blues	38	2	15	17	25	4	0	1	1	8
1983-84	St. Louis Blues	55	3	12	15	58	....	....	....	....	....
	Quebec Nordiques	25	1	16	17	25	9	0	0	0	8
1984-85	New York Rangers	25	0	7	7	35	....	....	....	....	....
	NHL Totals	**257**	**14**	**81**	**95**	**261**	**23**	**1**	**2**	**3**	**32**

Traded to **St. Louis** by **NY Rangers** for Vaclav Nedomansky and Glen Hanlon, January 4, 1983. Traded to **Quebec** by **St. Louis** for Dave Pichette, February 10, 1984. Claimed by **NY Rangers** from **Quebec** in Waiver Draft, October 9, 1984.

DORE, Daniel

Right wing. Shoots right. 6'3", 202 lbs. Born, Ferme-Neuve, Que., April 9, 1970.
(Quebec's 2nd choice, 5th overall, in 1988 Entry Draft).

Season	Club	GP	G	A	Pts	PIM	GP	G	A	Pts	PIM
1989-90	Quebec Nordiques	16	2	3	5	59	....	....	....	....	....
1990-91	Quebec Nordiques	1	0	0	0	0	....	....	....	....	....
	NHL Totals	**17**	**2**	**3**	**5**	**59**	....	....	....	....	....

Signed as a free agent by **Philadelphia**, December 14, 1992.

DOREY, Jim

Defense. Shoots left. 6'1", 190 lbs. Born, Kingston, Ont., August 17, 1947.
(Toronto's 4th choice, 23rd overall, in 1964 Amateur Draft).

Season	Club	GP	G	A	Pts	PIM	GP	G	A	Pts	PIM
1968-69	Toronto Maple Leafs	61	8	22	30	200	4	0	1	1	21
1969-70	Toronto Maple Leafs	46	6	11	17	99	....	....	....	....	....
1970-71	Toronto Maple Leafs	74	7	22	29	198	6	0	1	1	19
1971-72	Toronto Maple Leafs	50	4	19	23	56	....	....	....	....	....
	New York Rangers	1	0	0	0	0	1	0	0	0	0
	NHL Totals	**232**	**25**	**74**	**99**	**553**	**11**	**0**	**2**	**2**	**40**

Traded to **NY Rangers** by **Toronto** for Pierre Jarry, February 20, 1972.

DORION, Dan

Center. Shoots right. 5'9", 180 lbs. Born, Astoria, NY, March 2, 1963.
(New Jersey's 12th choice, 232nd overall, in 1982 Entry Draft).

Season	Club	GP	G	A	Pts	PIM	GP	G	A	Pts	PIM
1985-86	New Jersey Devils	3	1	1	2	0	....	....	....	....	....
1987-88	New Jersey Devils	1	0	0	0	2	....	....	....	....	....
	NHL Totals	**4**	**1**	**1**	**2**	**2**	....	....	....	....	....

Traded to **Boston** by **New Jersey** for Jean-Marc Lanthier, December 9, 1988.

DORNHOEFER, Gary

Right wing. Shoots right. 6'1", 190 lbs. Born, Kitchener, Ont., February 2, 1943.

Season	Club	GP	G	A	Pts	PIM	GP	G	A	Pts	PIM
1963-64	Boston Bruins	32	12	10	22	20	....	....	....	....	....
1964-65	Boston Bruins	20	0	1	1	13	....	....	....	....	....
1965-66	Boston Bruins	10	0	1	1	2	....	....	....	....	....
1967-68	Philadelphia Flyers	65	13	30	43	134	3	0	0	0	15
1968-69	Philadelphia Flyers	60	8	16	24	80	4	0	1	1	20
1969-70	Philadelphia Flyers	65	26	29	55	96	....	....	....	....	....
1970-71	Philadelphia Flyers	57	20	20	40	93	2	0	0	0	4
1971-72	Philadelphia Flyers	75	17	32	49	183	....	....	....	....	....
1972-73	Philadelphia Flyers	77	30	49	79	168	11	3	3	6	16
1973-74♦	Philadelphia Flyers	57	11	39	50	125	14	5	6	11	43
1974-75♦	Philadelphia Flyers	69	17	27	44	102	17	5	5	10	33
1975-76	Philadelphia Flyers	74	28	35	63	128	16	3	4	7	43
1976-77	Philadelphia Flyers	79	25	34	59	85	9	1	0	1	22
1977-78	Philadelphia Flyers	47	7	5	12	62	4	0	0	0	7
	NHL Totals	**787**	**214**	**328**	**542**	**1291**	**80**	**17**	**19**	**36**	**203**

Played in NHL All-Star Game (1973, 1977)

Claimed by **Philadelphia** from **Boston** in Expansion Draft, June 6, 1967.

DOROHOY, Eddie

Center/Left wing. Shoots left. 5'9", 155 lbs. Born, Medicine Hat, Alta., March 13, 1929.

Season	Club	GP	G	A	Pts	PIM	GP	G	A	Pts	PIM
1948-49	Montreal Canadiens	16	0	0	0	6	....	....	....	....	....
	NHL Totals	**16**	**0**	**0**	**0**	**6**	....	....	....	....	....

Rights traded to **NY Rangers** by **Montreal** (Victoria-WHL) with Dick Gamble for Hy Buller with Montreal holding right of recall if Dorohoy failed to make NY Rangers roster, June 8, 1954. Transaction cancelled after Buller retired, September, 1954. Loaned to **Victoria** (WHL) by **Montreal** for cash, August, 1955. Loan transferred to **Seattle** (WHL) by **Montreal** for cash, September 12, 1955. Traded to **Victoria** (WHL) by **Montreal** (Seattle-WHL) for Bill Davidson and Don Chiupka, September, 1957.

DOUGLAS, Jordy

Left wing. Shoots left. 6', 200 lbs. Born, Winnipeg, Man., January 20, 1958.
(Toronto's 4th choice, 81st overall, in 1978 Amateur Draft).

Season	Club	GP	G	A	Pts	PIM	GP	G	A	Pts	PIM
1979-80	Hartford Whalers	77	33	24	57	39	....	....	....	....	....
1980-81	Hartford Whalers	55	13	9	22	29	....	....	....	....	....
1981-82	Hartford Whalers	30	10	7	17	44	....	....	....	....	....
1982-83	Minnesota North Stars	68	13	14	27	30	5	0	0	0	2
1983-84	Minnesota North Stars	14	3	4	7	10	....	....	....	....	....
	Winnipeg Jets	17	4	2	6	8	1	0	0	0	2
1984-85	Winnipeg Jets	7	0	2	2	0	....	....	....	....	....
	NHL Totals	**268**	**76**	**62**	**138**	**160**	**6**	**0**	**0**	**0**	**4**

Reclaimed by **Toronto** from **Hartford** prior to Expansion Draft, June 9, 1979. Claimed as a priority selection by **Hartford**, June 9, 1979. Traded to **Minnesota** by **Hartford** with Hartford's 5th round choice (Jiri Poner) in 1984 Entry Draft for Mark Johnson and Kent-Erik Andersson, October 1, 1982. Traded to **Winnipeg** by **Minnesota** for Tim Trimper, January 12, 1984.

DOUGLAS, Kent

Defense. Shoots left. 5'10", 180 lbs. Born, Cobalt, Ont., February 6, 1936.

Season	Club	GP	G	A	Pts	PIM	GP	G	A	Pts	PIM
1962-63♦	Toronto Maple Leafs	70	7	15	22	105	10	1	1	2	2
1963-64♦	Toronto Maple Leafs	43	0	1	1	29	....	....	....	....	....
1964-65	Toronto Maple Leafs	67	5	23	28	129	5	0	1	1	19
1965-66	Toronto Maple Leafs	64	6	14	20	97	4	0	1	1	12
1966-67♦	Toronto Maple Leafs	39	2	12	14	48	....	....	....	....	....
1967-68	Oakland Seals	40	4	11	15	80	....	....	....	....	....
	Detroit Red Wings	36	7	10	17	46	....	....	....	....	....
1968-69	Detroit Red Wings	69	2	29	31	97	....	....	....	....	....
	NHL Totals	**428**	**33**	**115**	**148**	**631**	**19**	**1**	**3**	**4**	**33**

Played in NHL All-Star Game (1962, 1963, 1964)

Traded to **Toronto** (Rochester-AHL) by **Springfield** (AHL) for Jim Wilcox, Roger Cote, Bill White, Dick Mattiussi and the loan of Wally Boyer, June 7, 1962. Claimed by **California** (Oakland) from **Toronto** in Expansion Draft, June 6, 1967. Traded to **Detroit** by **Oakland** for John Brenneman, Ted Hampson and Bert Marshall, January 9, 1968. Traded to **Vancouver** (WHL) by **Detroit** for cash, June 20, 1969. • NHL rights transferred to **Vancouver** after NHL club purchased **Vancouver** (WHL) franchise, December 13, 1969. Traded to **Baltimore** (AHL) by **Vancouver** for cash, October 25, 1970.

DOUGLAS, Les

Center. Shoots left. 5'9", 165 lbs. Born, Perth, Ont., December 5, 1918.

Season	Club	GP	G	A	Pts	PIM	GP	G	A	Pts	PIM
1940-41	Detroit Red Wings	18	1	2	3	2	....	....	....	....	....
1942-43♦	Detroit Red Wings	21	5	8	13	4	10	3	2	5	2
1945-46	Detroit Red Wings	1	0	0	0	0	....	....	....	....	....
1946-47	Detroit Red Wings	12	0	2	2	2	....	....	....	....	....
	NHL Totals	**52**	**6**	**12**	**18**	**8**	**10**	**3**	**2**	**5**	**2**

Signed as a free agent by **Detroit**, October 9, 1939. Traded to **Buffalo** (AHL) by **Detroit** with Harold Jackson for Jim McFadden, June, 1947.

DOURIS, Peter

Right wing. Shoots right. 6'1", 195 lbs. Born, Toronto, Ont., February 19, 1966.
(Winnipeg's 1st choice, 30th overall, in 1984 Entry Draft).

Season	Club	GP	G	A	Pts	PIM	GP	G	A	Pts	PIM
1985-86	Winnipeg Jets	11	0	0	0	0	....	....	....	....	....

Season	Club	Regular Season GP	G	A	Pts	PIM	Playoffs GP	G	A	Pts	PIM
1986-87	Winnipeg Jets	6	0	0	0	0	....	....	....	....	....
1987-88	Winnipeg Jets	4	0	2	2	0	1	0	0	0	0
1989-90	Boston Bruins	36	5	6	11	15	8	0	1	1	8
1990-91	Boston Bruins	39	5	2	7	9	7	0	1	1	6
1991-92	Boston Bruins	54	10	13	23	10	7	2	3	5	0
1992-93	Boston Bruins	19	4	4	8	4	4	1	0	1	0
1993-94	Mighty Ducks of Anaheim	74	12	22	34	21	....	....	....	....	....
1994-95	Mighty Ducks of Anaheim	46	10	11	21	12	....	....	....	....	....
1995-96	Mighty Ducks of Anaheim	31	8	7	15	9	....	....	....	....	....
1997-98	Dallas Stars	1	0	0	0	0	....	....	....	....	....
	NHL Totals	**321**	**54**	**67**	**121**	**80**	**27**	**3**	**5**	**8**	**14**

Traded to **St. Louis** by **Winnipeg** for Kent Carlson, St. Louis' 12th round choice (Sergei Kharin) in 1989 Entry Draft and 4th round choice (Scott Levins) in 1990 Entry Draft, September 29, 1988. Signed as a free agent by **Boston**, June 27, 1989. Signed as a free agent by **Anaheim**, July 22, 1993. Signed as a free agent by **Dallas**, July 16, 1997.

DOWD, Jim

Center. Shoots right. 6'1", 190 lbs. Born, Brick, NJ, December 25, 1968.
(New Jersey's 7th choice, 149th overall, in 1987 Entry Draft).

Season	Club	Regular Season GP	G	A	Pts	PIM	Playoffs GP	G	A	Pts	PIM
1991-92	New Jersey Devils	1	0	0	0	0	....	....	....	....	....
1992-93	New Jersey Devils	1	0	0	0	0	....	....	....	....	....
1993-94	New Jersey Devils	15	5	10	15	0	19	2	6	8	8
1994-95 ♦	New Jersey Devils	10	1	4	5	0	11	2	1	3	8
1995-96	New Jersey Devils	28	4	9	13	17	....	....	....	....	....
	Vancouver Canucks	38	1	6	7	6	1	0	0	0	0
1996-97	New York Islanders	3	0	0	0	0	....	....	....	....	....
1997-98	Calgary Flames	48	6	8	14	12	....	....	....	....	....
1998-99	Edmonton Oilers	1	0	0	0	0	....	....	....	....	....
99-2000	Edmonton Oilers	69	5	18	23	45	5	2	1	3	4
2000-01	Minnesota Wild	68	7	22	29	80	....	....	....	....	....
2001-02	Minnesota Wild	82	13	30	43	54	....	....	....	....	....
2002-03	Minnesota Wild	78	8	17	25	31	15	0	2	2	0
	NHL Totals	**442**	**50**	**124**	**174**	**245**	**51**	**6**	**10**	**16**	**20**

• Missed majority of 1994-95 season recovering from shoulder injury suffered in game vs. Quebec, February 2, 1995. Traded to **Hartford** by **New Jersey** with New Jersey's 2nd round choice (later traded to Calgary – Calgary selected Dmitri Kokorev) in 1997 Entry Draft for Jocelyn Lemieux and Hartford's 2nd round choice (later traded to Dallas – Dallas selected John Erskine) in 1998 Entry Draft, December 19, 1995. Traded to **Vancouver** by **Hartford** with Frantisek Kucera and Hartford's 2nd round choice (Ryan Bonni) in 1997 Entry Draft for Jeff Brown and Vancouver's 3rd round choice (later traded to Calgary – Calgary selected Paul Manning) in 1998 Entry Draft, December 19, 1995. Claimed by **NY Islanders** from **Vancouver** in Waiver Draft, September 30, 1996. Signed as a free agent by **Calgary**, August, 1997. Traded to **Nashville** by **Calgary** for future considerations, June 26, 1998. Traded to **Edmonton** by **Nashville** with Mikhail Shtalenkov for Eric Fichaud, Drake Berehowsky and Greg de Vries, October 1, 1998. Selected by **Minnesota** from **Edmonton** in Expansion Draft, June 23, 2000.

DOWNEY, Aaron

Right wing. Shoots right. 6'1", 216 lbs. Born, Shelburne, Ont., August 27, 1974.

Season	Club	Regular Season GP	G	A	Pts	PIM	Playoffs GP	G	A	Pts	PIM
99-2000	Boston Bruins	1	0	0	0	0	....	....	....	....	....
2000-01	Chicago Blackhawks	3	0	0	0	6	....	....	....	....	....
2001-02	Chicago Blackhawks	36	1	0	1	76	4	0	0	0	8
2002-03	Dallas Stars	43	1	1	2	69	....	....	....	....	....
	NHL Totals	**83**	**2**	**1**	**3**	**151**	**4**	**0**	**0**	**0**	**8**

Signed as a free agent by **Boston**, January 20, 1998. Signed as a free agent by **Chicago**, August 13, 2000. Signed as a free agent by **Dallas**, July 3, 2002.

DOWNIE, Dave

Center/Right wing. Shoots right. 5'8", 168 lbs. Born, Burke's Falls, Ont., March 11, 1909.

Season	Club	Regular Season GP	G	A	Pts	PIM	Playoffs GP	G	A	Pts	PIM
1932-33	Toronto Maple Leafs	11	0	1	1	2	....	....	....	....	....
	NHL Totals	**11**	**0**	**1**	**1**	**2**	....	....	....	....	....

Signed as a free agent by **Boston**, November 4, 1931. Loaned to **Toronto** by **Syracuse** (IHL), February 12, 1933.

DOYON, Mario

Defense. Shoots right. 6', 174 lbs. Born, Quebec City, Que., August 27, 1968.
(Chicago's 5th choice, 119th overall, in 1986 Entry Draft).

Season	Club	Regular Season GP	G	A	Pts	PIM	Playoffs GP	G	A	Pts	PIM
1988-89	Chicago Blackhawks	7	1	1	2	6	....	....	....	....	....
1989-90	Quebec Nordiques	9	2	3	5	6	....	....	....	....	....
1990-91	Quebec Nordiques	12	0	0	0	4	....	....	....	....	....
	NHL Totals	**28**	**3**	**4**	**7**	**16**	....	....	....	....	....

Traded to **Quebec** by **Chicago** with Everett Sanipass and Dan Vincelette for Greg Millen, Michel Goulet and Quebec's 6th round choice (Kevin St. Jacques) in 1991 Entry Draft, March 5, 1990.

DRAKE, Dallas

Right wing. Shoots left. 6'1", 187 lbs. Born, Trail, B.C., February 4, 1969.
(Detroit's 6th choice, 116th overall, in 1989 Entry Draft).

Season	Club	Regular Season GP	G	A	Pts	PIM	Playoffs GP	G	A	Pts	PIM
1992-93	Detroit Red Wings	72	18	26	44	93	7	3	3	6	6
1993-94	Detroit Red Wings	47	10	22	32	37	....	....	....	....	....
	Winnipeg Jets	15	3	5	8	12	....	....	....	....	....
1994-95	Winnipeg Jets	43	8	18	26	30	....	....	....	....	....
1995-96	Winnipeg Jets	69	19	20	39	36	3	0	0	0	0
1996-97	Phoenix Coyotes	63	17	19	36	52	7	0	1	1	2
1997-98	Phoenix Coyotes	60	11	29	40	71	4	0	1	1	2
1998-99	Phoenix Coyotes	53	9	22	31	65	7	4	3	7	4
99-2000	Phoenix Coyotes	79	15	30	45	62	5	0	1	1	4
2000-01	St. Louis Blues	82	12	29	41	71	15	4	2	6	16
2001-02	St. Louis Blues	80	11	15	26	87	8	0	0	0	8
2002-03	St. Louis Blues	80	20	10	30	66	7	1	4	5	23
	NHL Totals	**743**	**153**	**245**	**398**	**682**	**63**	**12**	**15**	**27**	**65**

Traded to **Winnipeg** by **Detroit** with Tim Cheveldae for Bob Essensa and Sergei Bautin, March 8, 1994. Transferred to **Phoenix** after **Winnipeg** franchise relocated, July 1, 1996. Selected by **Minnesota** from **Phoenix** in Expansion Draft, June 23, 2000. Signed as a free agent by **St. Louis**, July 1, 2000.

DRAPER, Bruce

Center. Shoots left. 5'10", 157 lbs. Born, Toronto, Ont., October 2, 1940.

Season	Club	Regular Season GP	G	A	Pts	PIM	Playoffs GP	G	A	Pts	PIM
1962-63	Toronto Maple Leafs	1	0	0	0	0	....	....	....	....	....
	NHL Totals	**1**	**0**	**0**	**0**	**0**	....	....	....	....	....

Traded to **Hershey** (AHL) by **Toronto** to complete transaction that sent Les Duff to Toronto (September, 1963), September, 1964.

DRAPER, Kris

Center. Shoots left. 5'11", 190 lbs. Born, Toronto, Ont., May 24, 1971.
(Winnipeg's 4th choice, 62nd overall, in 1989 Entry Draft).

Season	Club	Regular Season GP	G	A	Pts	PIM	Playoffs GP	G	A	Pts	PIM
1990-91	Winnipeg Jets	3	1	0	1	5	....	....	....	....	....
1991-92	Winnipeg Jets	10	2	0	2	2	2	0	0	0	0
1992-93	Winnipeg Jets	7	0	0	0	2	....	....	....	....	....
1993-94	Detroit Red Wings	39	5	8	13	31	7	2	2	4	4
1994-95	Detroit Red Wings	36	2	6	8	22	18	4	1	5	12
1995-96	Detroit Red Wings	52	7	9	16	32	18	4	2	6	18
1996-97 ♦	Detroit Red Wings	76	8	5	13	73	20	2	4	6	12
1997-98 ♦	Detroit Red Wings	64	13	10	23	45	19	1	3	4	12
1998-99	Detroit Red Wings	80	4	14	18	79	10	0	1	1	6
99-2000	Detroit Red Wings	51	5	7	12	28	9	2	0	2	6
2000-01	Detroit Red Wings	75	8	17	25	38	6	0	1	1	2
2001-02 ♦	Detroit Red Wings	82	15	15	30	56	23	2	3	5	20
2002-03	Detroit Red Wings	82	14	21	35	82	4	0	0	0	4
	NHL Totals	**657**	**84**	**112**	**196**	**495**	**136**	**17**	**17**	**34**	**96**

Traded to **Detroit** by **Winnipeg** for future considerations, June 30, 1993.

DRILLON, Gordie

HHOF

Right wing. Shoots right. 6'2", 178 lbs. Born, Moncton, N.B., October 23, 1913.

Season	Club	Regular Season GP	G	A	Pts	PIM	Playoffs GP	G	A	Pts	PIM
1936-37	Toronto Maple Leafs	41	16	17	33	2	2	0	0	0	0
1937-38	Toronto Maple Leafs	48	*26	26	*52	4	7	*7	1	8	2
1938-39	Toronto Maple Leafs	40	18	16	34	15	10	*7	6	13	4
1939-40	Toronto Maple Leafs	43	21	19	40	13	10	3	1	4	0
1940-41	Toronto Maple Leafs	42	23	21	44	2	7	3	2	5	2
1941-42 ♦	Toronto Maple Leafs	48	23	18	41	6	9	2	3	5	2
1942-43	Montreal Canadiens	49	28	22	50	14	5	4	2	6	0
	NHL Totals	**311**	**155**	**139**	**294**	**56**	**50**	**26**	**15**	**41**	**10**

NHL First All-Star Team (1938, 1939) • Lady Byng Trophy (1938) • NHL Second All-Star Team (1942)

Played in NHL All-Star Game (1939)

Traded to **Montreal** by **Toronto** for $30,000, October 4, 1942.

DRISCOLL, Peter

Left wing. Shoots left. 6', 190 lbs. Born, Kingston, Ont., October 27, 1954.
(Toronto's 4th choice, 67th overall, in 1974 Amateur Draft).

Season	Club	Regular Season GP	G	A	Pts	PIM	Playoffs GP	G	A	Pts	PIM
1979-80	Edmonton Oilers	39	1	5	6	54	3	0	0	0	0
1980-81	Edmonton Oilers	21	2	3	5	43	....	....	....	....	....
	NHL Totals	**60**	**3**	**8**	**11**	**97**	**3**	**0**	**0**	**0**	**0**

Rights retained by **Edmonton** prior to Expansion Draft, June 9, 1979.

DRIVER, Bruce

Defense. Shoots left. 6', 185 lbs. Born, Toronto, Ont., April 29, 1962.
(Colorado's 6th choice, 108th overall, in 1981 Entry Draft).

Season	Club	Regular Season GP	G	A	Pts	PIM	Playoffs GP	G	A	Pts	PIM
1983-84	New Jersey Devils	4	0	2	2	0	....	....	....	....	....
1984-85	New Jersey Devils	67	9	23	32	36	....	....	....	....	....
1985-86	New Jersey Devils	40	3	15	18	32	....	....	....	....	....
1986-87	New Jersey Devils	74	6	28	34	36	....	....	....	....	....
1987-88	New Jersey Devils	74	15	40	55	68	20	3	7	10	14
1988-89	New Jersey Devils	27	1	15	16	24	....	....	....	....	....
1989-90	New Jersey Devils	75	7	46	53	63	6	1	5	6	6
1990-91	New Jersey Devils	73	9	36	45	62	7	1	2	3	12
1991-92	New Jersey Devils	78	7	35	42	66	7	0	4	4	2
1992-93	New Jersey Devils	83	14	40	54	66	5	1	3	4	4
1993-94	New Jersey Devils	66	8	24	32	63	20	3	5	8	12
1994-95 ♦	New Jersey Devils	41	4	12	16	18	17	1	6	7	8
1995-96	New York Rangers	66	3	34	37	42	11	0	7	7	4
1996-97	New York Rangers	79	5	25	30	48	15	0	1	1	2
1997-98	New York Rangers	75	5	15	20	46	....	....	....	....	....
	NHL Totals	**922**	**96**	**390**	**486**	**670**	**108**	**10**	**40**	**50**	**64**

Rights transferred to **New Jersey** after **Colorado** franchise relocated, June 30, 1982. Signed as a free agent by **NY Rangers**, September 28, 1995.

DROLET, Rene

Right wing. Shoots right. 5'8", 160 lbs. Born, Quebec City, Que., November 13, 1944.

Season	Club	Regular Season GP	G	A	Pts	PIM	Playoffs GP	G	A	Pts	PIM
1971-72	Philadelphia Flyers	1	0	0	0	0	....	....	....	....	....

Season	Club	GP	G	A	Pts	PIM	GP	G	A	Pts	PIM
		REGULAR SEASON					PLAYOFFS				
1974-75	Detroit Red Wings	1	0	0	0	0	....	....	....	....	....
	NHL Totals	**2**	**0**	**0**	**0**	**0**	....	....	....	....	....

NHL rights transferred to **Philadelphia** after NHL club purchased **Quebec** (AHL) franchise, May 8, 1967. Claimed by **Quebec** (AHL) from **Philadelphia** in Reverse Draft, June 12, 1969. • NHL rights retained by Philadelphia. Claimed by **Detroit** (Tidewater-AHL) from **Philadelphia** in Reverse Draft, June 13, 1974.

DROPPA, Ivan

Defense. Shoots left. 6'2", 209 lbs. Born, Liptovsky Mikulas, Czech., February 1, 1972.
(Chicago's 2nd choice, 37th overall, in 1990 Entry Draft).

Season	Club	GP	G	A	Pts	PIM	GP	G	A	Pts	PIM
1993-94	Chicago Blackhawks	12	0	1	1	12	....	....	....	....	....
1995-96	Chicago Blackhawks	7	0	0	0	2	....	....	....	....	....
	NHL Totals	**19**	**0**	**1**	**1**	**14**	....	....	....	....	....

Traded to **Florida** by **Chicago** for Alain Nasreddine , December 18, 1996.

DROUILLARD, Clarence

Center. Shoots left. 5'7", 150 lbs. Born, Windsor, Ont., March 2, 1914.

Season	Club	GP	G	A	Pts	PIM	GP	G	A	Pts	PIM
1937-38	Detroit Red Wings	10	0	1	1	0	....	....	....	....	....
	NHL Totals	**10**	**0**	**1**	**1**	**0**	....	....	....	....	....

Traded to **Detroit** by **Windsor** (IHL) for cash, February 26, 1936. Traded to **Boston** by **Detroit** with cash for Alex Motter, December 22, 1937. Signed as a free agent by **Toronto** (Pittsburgh-IAHL), September, 1939. Traded to **NY Americans** (Springfield-AHL) by **Toronto** (Pittsburgh-AHL) for Jack Howard and the loan of Peanuts O'Flaherty, January 17, 1941.

DROUIN, Jude

Center. Shoots right. 5'10", 160 lbs. Born, Mont Louis, Que., October 28, 1948.
(Montreal's 3rd choice, 17th overall, in 1966 Amateur Draft).

Season	Club	GP	G	A	Pts	PIM	GP	G	A	Pts	PIM
1968-69	Montreal Canadiens	9	0	1	1	0	....	....	....	....	....
1969-70	Montreal Canadiens	3	0	0	0	2	....	....	....	....	....
1970-71	Minnesota North Stars	75	16	52	68	49	12	5	7	12	10
1971-72	Minnesota North Stars	63	13	43	56	31	7	4	4	8	6
1972-73	Minnesota North Stars	78	27	46	73	61	6	1	3	4	0
1973-74	Minnesota North Stars	65	19	24	43	30	....	....	....	....	....
1974-75	Minnesota North Stars	38	4	18	22	16	....	....	....	....	....
	New York Islanders	40	14	18	32	6	17	6	*12	18	6
1975-76	New York Islanders	76	21	41	62	58	13	6	9	15	0
1976-77	New York Islanders	78	24	29	53	27	12	5	6	11	6
1977-78	New York Islanders	56	5	17	22	12	5	0	0	0	5
1979-80	Winnipeg Jets	78	8	16	24	50	....	....	....	....	....
1980-81	Winnipeg Jets	7	0	0	0	4	....	....	....	....	....
	NHL Totals	**666**	**151**	**305**	**456**	**346**	**72**	**27**	**41**	**68**	**33**

Traded to **Minnesota** by **Montreal** for future considerations (Bill Collins, June 10, 1970), May 22, 1970. Traded to **NY Islanders** by **Minnesota** for Craig Cameron, January 7, 1975. • Sat out entire 1978-79 season to become a free agent. Signed as a free agent by **Winnipeg**, October 5, 1979.

DROUIN, P.C.

Left wing. Shoots left. 6'2", 208 lbs. Born, St-Lambert, Que., April 22, 1974.

Season	Club	GP	G	A	Pts	PIM	GP	G	A	Pts	PIM
1996-97	Boston Bruins	3	0	0	0	0	....	....	....	....	....
	NHL Totals	**3**	**0**	**0**	**0**	**0**	....	....	....	....	....

Signed as a free agent by **Boston**, October 14, 1996.

DROUIN, Polly

Left wing. Shoots left. 5'7", 160 lbs. Born, Verdun, Que., January 16, 1916.

Season	Club	GP	G	A	Pts	PIM	GP	G	A	Pts	PIM
1934-35	Montreal Canadiens	4	0	0	0	0	....	....	....	....	....
1935-36	Montreal Canadiens	30	1	8	9	19	....	....	....	....	....
1936-37	Montreal Canadiens	4	0	0	0	0	....	....	....	....	....
1937-38	Montreal Canadiens	31	7	13	20	8	1	0	0	0	0
1938-39	Montreal Canadiens	28	7	11	18	2	3	0	1	1	5
1939-40	Montreal Canadiens	42	4	11	15	51	1	0	0	0	0
1940-41	Montreal Canadiens	21	4	7	11	0	....	....	....	....	....
	NHL Totals	**160**	**23**	**50**	**73**	**80**	**5**	**0**	**1**	**1**	**5**

Played in NHL All-Star Game (1939)

Claimed by **Montreal** from **St. Louis** in Dispersal Draft, October 13, 1935. Traded to **Washington** (AHL) by **Montreal** for cash, October 9, 1941.

DRUCE, John

Right wing. Shoots right. 6'2", 195 lbs. Born, Peterborough, Ont., February 23, 1966.
(Washington's 2nd choice, 40th overall, in 1985 Entry Draft).

Season	Club	GP	G	A	Pts	PIM	GP	G	A	Pts	PIM
1988-89	Washington Capitals	48	8	7	15	62	1	0	0	0	0
1989-90	Washington Capitals	45	8	3	11	52	15	14	3	17	23
1990-91	Washington Capitals	80	22	36	58	46	11	1	1	2	7
1991-92	Washington Capitals	67	19	18	37	39	7	1	0	1	2
1992-93	Winnipeg Jets	50	6	14	20	37	2	0	0	0	0
1993-94	Los Angeles Kings	55	14	17	31	50	....	....	....	....	....
1994-95	Los Angeles Kings	43	15	5	20	20	....	....	....	....	....
1995-96	Los Angeles Kings	64	9	12	21	14	....	....	....	....	....
	Philadelphia Flyers	13	4	4	8	13	2	0	2	2	2
1996-97	Philadelphia Flyers	43	7	8	15	12	13	1	0	1	2
1997-98	Philadelphia Flyers	23	1	2	3	2	2	0	0	0	2
	NHL Totals	**531**	**113**	**126**	**239**	**347**	**53**	**17**	**6**	**23**	**38**

Traded to **Winnipeg** by **Washington** with Toronto's 4th round choice (previously acquired by Washington – later traded to Detroit – Detroit selected John Jakopin) in 1993 Entry Draft for Pat Elynuik, October 1, 1992. Signed as a free agent by **Los Angeles**, August 2, 1993. Traded to **Philadelphia** by **Los Angeles** with Los Angeles' 7th round choice (Todd Fedoruk) in 1997 Entry Draft for Los Angeles' 4th round choice (previously acquired, Los Angeles selected Mikael Simons) in 1996 Entry Draft, March 19, 1996.

DRUKEN, Harold

Center. Shoots left. 6', 205 lbs. Born, St. John's, Nfld., January 26, 1979.
(Vancouver's 3rd choice, 36th overall, in 1997 Entry Draft).

Season	Club	GP	G	A	Pts	PIM	GP	G	A	Pts	PIM
99-2000	Vancouver Canucks	33	7	9	16	10	....	....	....	....	....
2000-01	Vancouver Canucks	55	15	15	30	14	4	0	1	1	0
2001-02	Vancouver Canucks	27	4	4	8	6	....	....	....	....	....
2002-03	Vancouver Canucks	3	1	1	2	0	....	....	....	....	....
	Carolina Hurricanes	10	0	1	1	2	....	....	....	....	....
	Toronto Maple Leafs	5	0	2	2	2	....	....	....	....	....
	Carolina Hurricanes	4	0	0	0	0	....	....	....	....	....
	NHL Totals	**137**	**27**	**32**	**59**	**34**	**4**	**0**	**1**	**1**	**0**

Missed majority of 2001-02 season recovering from ankle injury suffered in game vs. Dallas, December 2, 2001. Traded to **Carolina** by **Vancouver** with Jan Hlavac for Darren Langdon and Marek Malik, November 1, 2002. Claimed on waivers by **Toronto** from **Carolina**, December 11, 2002. Claimed on waivers by **Carolina** from **Toronto**, January 17, 2003. Traded to **Toronto** by **Carolina** for Allan Rourke, May 29, 2003.

DRULIA, Stan

Right wing. Shoots right. 5'11", 190 lbs. Born, Elmira, NY, January 5, 1968.
(Pittsburgh's 11th choice, 214th overall, in 1986 Entry Draft).

Season	Club	GP	G	A	Pts	PIM	GP	G	A	Pts	PIM
1992-93	Tampa Bay Lightning	24	2	1	3	10	....	....	....	....	....
99-2000	Tampa Bay Lightning	68	11	22	33	24	....	....	....	....	....
2000-01	Tampa Bay Lightning	34	2	4	6	18	....	....	....	....	....
	NHL Totals	**126**	**15**	**27**	**42**	**52**	....	....	....	....	....

Signed as a free agent by **Edmonton**, February 24, 1989. Signed as a free agent by **Tampa Bay**, September 1, 1992. Signed as a free agent by **Tampa Bay**, September 29, 1999. • Missed majority of 2000-01 season recovering from back injury originally suffered in game vs. Detroit, December 2, 2000.

DRUMMOND, Jim

Defense. Shoots left. 5'9", 170 lbs. Born, Toronto, Ont., October 20, 1918.

Season	Club	GP	G	A	Pts	PIM	GP	G	A	Pts	PIM
1944-45	New York Rangers	2	0	0	0	0	....	....	....	....	....
	NHL Totals	**2**	**0**	**0**	**0**	**0**	....	....	....	....	....

Signed as a free agent by **NY Rangers**, December 5, 1944. Traded to **Hershey** (AHL) by **NY Rangers** for cash, January, 1945.

DRURY, Chris

Center. Shoots right. 5'10", 180 lbs. Born, Trumbull, CT, August 20, 1976.
(Quebec's 5th choice, 72nd overall, in 1994 Entry Draft).

Season	Club	GP	G	A	Pts	PIM	GP	G	A	Pts	PIM
1998-99	Colorado Avalanche	79	20	24	44	62	19	6	2	8	4
99-2000	Colorado Avalanche	82	20	47	67	42	17	4	10	14	4
2000-01 ◆	Colorado Avalanche	71	24	41	65	47	23	11	5	16	4
2001-02	Colorado Avalanche	82	21	25	46	38	21	5	7	12	10
2002-03	Calgary Flames	80	23	30	53	33	....	....	....	....	....
	NHL Totals	**394**	**108**	**167**	**275**	**222**	**80**	**26**	**24**	**50**	**22**

• Brother of Ted • NHL All-Rookie Team (1999) • Calder Memorial Trophy (1999)

Rights transferred to **Colorado** after **Quebec** franchise relocated, June 21, 1995. Traded to **Calgary** by **Colorado** with Stephane Yelle for Derek Morris, Jeff Shantz and Dean McAmmond, October 1, 2002. Traded to **Buffalo** by **Calgary** with Steve Begin for Steve Reinprecht and Rhett Warrener, July 3, 2003.

DRURY, Herb

Defense/Right wing. Shoots right. 5'7", 165 lbs. Born, Midland, Ont., March 2, 1895.

Season	Club	GP	G	A	Pts	PIM	GP	G	A	Pts	PIM
1925-26	Pittsburgh Pirates	33	6	2	8	40	2	1	0	1	0
1926-27	Pittsburgh Pirates	42	5	1	6	48	....	....	....	....	....
1927-28	Pittsburgh Pirates	44	6	4	10	44	2	0	1	1	0
1928-29	Pittsburgh Pirates	43	5	4	9	49	....	....	....	....	....
1929-30	Pittsburgh Pirates	27	2	0	2	12	....	....	....	....	....
1930-31	Philadelphia Quakers	24	0	2	2	10	....	....	....	....	....
	NHL Totals	**213**	**24**	**13**	**37**	**203**	**4**	**1**	**1**	**2**	**0**

Signed as a free agent by **Pittsburgh**, September 26, 1925. Transferred to **Philadelphia** after **Pittsburgh** franchise relocated, October 18, 1930.

DRURY, Ted

Center. Shoots left. 6'2", 210 lbs. Born, Boston, MA, September 13, 1971.
(Calgary's 2nd choice, 42nd overall, in 1989 Entry Draft).

Season	Club	GP	G	A	Pts	PIM	GP	G	A	Pts	PIM
1993-94	Calgary Flames	34	5	7	12	26	....	....	....	....	....
	Hartford Whalers	16	1	5	6	10	....	....	....	....	....
1994-95	Hartford Whalers	34	3	6	9	21	....	....	....	....	....
1995-96	Ottawa Senators	42	9	7	16	54	....	....	....	....	....
1996-97	Mighty Ducks of Anaheim	73	9	9	18	54	10	1	0	1	4
1997-98	Mighty Ducks of Anaheim	73	6	10	16	82	....	....	....	....	....
1998-99	Mighty Ducks of Anaheim	75	5	6	11	83	4	0	0	0	0
99-2000	Mighty Ducks of Anaheim	11	1	1	2	6	....	....	....	....	....
	New York Islanders	55	2	1	3	31	....	....	....	....	....

Season	Club	Regular Season GP	G	A	Pts	PIM	Playoffs GP	G	A	Pts	PIM
2000-01	Columbus Blue Jackets	1	0	0	0	0	....	....	....	....	....
	NHL Totals	**414**	**41**	**52**	**93**	**367**	**14**	**1**	**0**	**1**	**4**

• Brother of Chris

Traded to **Hartford** by **Calgary** with Gary Suter and Paul Ranheim for James Patrick, Zarley Zalapski and Michael Nylander, March 10, 1994. Claimed by **Ottawa** from **Hartford** in Waiver Draft, October 2, 1995. Traded to **Anaheim** by **Ottawa** with the rights to Marc Moro for Jason York and Shaun Van Allen, October 1, 1996. Traded to **NY Islanders** by **Anaheim** for Tony Hrkac and Dean Malkoc, October 29, 1999. Selected by **Columbus** from **NY Islanders** in Expansion Draft, June 23, 2000. Signed as a free agent by **New Jersey**, August 21, 2001. Traded to **Carolina** by **New Jersey** for Mike Rucinski, March 4, 2002.

DUBE, Christian

Center. Shoots right. 5'11", 170 lbs. Born, Sherbrooke, Que., April 25, 1977.
(NY Rangers' 1st choice, 39th overall, in 1995 Entry Draft).

Season	Club	GP	G	A	Pts	PIM	GP	G	A	Pts	PIM
1996-97	New York Rangers	27	1	1	2	4	3	0	0	0	0
1998-99	New York Rangers	6	0	0	0	0	....	....	....	....	....
	NHL Totals	**33**	**1**	**1**	**2**	**4**	**3**	**0**	**0**	**0**	**0**

• Son of Norm

DUBE, Gilles

Left wing. Shoots left. 5'10", 165 lbs. Born, Sherbrooke, Que., June 2, 1927.

Season	Club	GP	G	A	Pts	PIM	GP	G	A	Pts	PIM
1949-50	Montreal Canadiens	12	1	2	3	2	....	....	....	....	....
1953-54 ♦	Detroit Red Wings	....	....	....	....	....	2	0	0	0	0
	NHL Totals	**12**	**1**	**2**	**3**	**2**	**2**	**0**	**0**	**0**	**0**

Signed as a free agent by **Montreal**, September 27, 1949. Signed as a free agent by **Detroit** to three game try-out contract, April 10, 1954.

DUBE, Norm

Left wing. Shoots left. 5'11", 185 lbs. Born, Sherbrooke, Que., September 12, 1951.
(Los Angeles' 6th choice, 90th overall, in 1971 Amateur Draft).

Season	Club	GP	G	A	Pts	PIM	GP	G	A	Pts	PIM
1974-75	Kansas City Scouts	56	8	10	18	54	....	....	....	....	....
1975-76	Kansas City Scouts	1	0	0	0	0	....	....	....	....	....
	NHL Totals	**57**	**8**	**10**	**18**	**54**	....	....	....	....	....

• Father of Christian

Claimed by **Kansas City** from **Los Angeles** in Expansion Draft, June 12, 1974.

DUBERMAN, Justin

Right wing. Shoots right. 6'1", 185 lbs. Born, New Haven, CT, March 23, 1970.
(Montreal's 11th choice, 230th overall, in 1989 Entry Draft).

Season	Club	GP	G	A	Pts	PIM	GP	G	A	Pts	PIM
1993-94	Pittsburgh Penguins	4	0	0	0	0	....	....	....	....	....
	NHL Totals	**4**	**0**	**0**	**0**	**0**	....	....	....	....	....

Signed as a free agent by **Pittsburgh**, November 2, 1992.

DUBINSKY, Steve

Center. Shoots left. 6', 190 lbs. Born, Montreal, Que., July 9, 1970.
(Chicago's 9th choice, 226th overall, in 1990 Entry Draft).

Season	Club	GP	G	A	Pts	PIM	GP	G	A	Pts	PIM
1993-94	Chicago Blackhawks	27	2	6	8	16	6	0	0	0	10
1994-95	Chicago Blackhawks	16	0	0	0	8	....	....	....	....	....
1995-96	Chicago Blackhawks	43	2	3	5	14	....	....	....	....	....
1996-97	Chicago Blackhawks	5	0	0	0	0	4	1	0	1	4
1997-98	Chicago Blackhawks	82	5	13	18	57	....	....	....	....	....
1998-99	Chicago Blackhawks	1	0	0	0	0	....	....	....	....	....
	Calgary Flames	61	4	10	14	14	....	....	....	....	....
99-2000	Calgary Flames	23	0	1	1	4	....	....	....	....	....
2000-01	Chicago Blackhawks	60	6	4	10	33	....	....	....	....	....
2001-02	Chicago Blackhawks	3	1	0	1	4	....	....	....	....	....
	Nashville Predators	26	5	2	7	10	....	....	....	....	....
2002-03	St. Louis Blues	28	0	6	6	4	....	....	....	....	....
	NHL Totals	**375**	**25**	**45**	**70**	**164**	**10**	**1**	**0**	**1**	**14**

Traded to **Calgary** by **Chicago** with Jeff Shantz for Marty McInnis, Jamie Allison and Eric Andersson, October 27, 1998. • Missed remainder of 1999-2000 season recovering from knee injury suffered in game vs. Chicago, December 12, 1999. Signed as a free agent by **Chicago**, August 25, 2000. Traded to **Nashville** by **Chicago** for future considerations, February 6, 2002. Signed as a free agent by **St. Louis**, July 16, 2002.

DUCHESNE, Gaetan

Left wing. Shoots left. 5'11", 200 lbs. Born, Les Saulles, Que., July 11, 1962.
(Washington's 8th choice, 152nd overall, in 1981 Entry Draft).

Season	Club	GP	G	A	Pts	PIM	GP	G	A	Pts	PIM
1981-82	Washington Capitals	74	9	14	23	46	....	....	....	....	....
1982-83	Washington Capitals	77	18	19	37	52	4	1	1	2	4
1983-84	Washington Capitals	79	17	19	36	29	8	2	1	3	2
1984-85	Washington Capitals	67	15	23	38	32	5	0	1	1	7
1985-86	Washington Capitals	80	11	28	39	39	9	4	3	7	12
1986-87	Washington Capitals	74	17	35	52	53	7	3	0	3	14
1987-88	Quebec Nordiques	80	24	23	47	83	....	....	....	....	....
1988-89	Quebec Nordiques	70	8	21	29	56	....	....	....	....	....
1989-90	Minnesota North Stars	72	12	8	20	33	7	0	0	0	6
1990-91	Minnesota North Stars	68	9	9	18	18	23	2	3	5	34
1991-92	Minnesota North Stars	73	8	15	23	102	7	1	0	1	6
1992-93	Minnesota North Stars	84	16	13	29	30	....	....	....	....	....
1993-94	San Jose Sharks	84	12	18	30	28	14	1	4	5	12
1994-95	San Jose Sharks	33	2	7	9	16	....	....	....	....	....
	Florida Panthers	13	1	2	3	0	....	....	....	....	....
	NHL Totals	**1028**	**179**	**254**	**433**	**617**	**84**	**14**	**13**	**27**	**97**

Traded to **Quebec** by **Washington** with Alan Haworth and Washington's 1st round choice (Joe Sakic) in 1987 Entry Draft for Clint Malarchuk and Dale Hunter, June 13, 1987. Traded to **Minnesota** by **Quebec** for Kevin Kaminski, June 19, 1989. Transferred to **Dallas** after **Minnesota** franchise relocated, June 9, 1993. Traded to **San Jose** by **Dallas** for San Jose's 6th round choice (later traded back to San Jose – San Jose selected Petri Varis) in 1993 Entry Draft, June 20, 1993. Traded to **Florida** by **San Jose** for Florida's 6th round choice (Timo Hakanen) in 1995 Entry Draft, April 7, 1995.

DUCHESNE, Steve

Defense. Shoots left. 5'11", 195 lbs. Born, Sept-Iles, Que., June 30, 1965.

Season	Club	GP	G	A	Pts	PIM	GP	G	A	Pts	PIM
1986-87	Los Angeles Kings	75	13	25	38	74	5	2	2	4	4
1987-88	Los Angeles Kings	71	16	39	55	109	5	1	3	4	14
1988-89	Los Angeles Kings	79	25	50	75	92	11	4	4	8	12
1989-90	Los Angeles Kings	79	20	42	62	36	10	2	9	11	6
1990-91	Los Angeles Kings	78	21	41	62	66	12	4	8	12	8
1991-92	Philadelphia Flyers	78	18	38	56	86	....	....	....	....	....
1992-93	Quebec Nordiques	82	20	62	82	57	6	0	5	5	6
1993-94	St. Louis Blues	36	12	19	31	14	4	0	2	2	2
1994-95	St. Louis Blues	47	12	26	38	36	7	0	4	4	2
1995-96	Ottawa Senators	62	12	24	36	42	....	....	....	....	....
1996-97	Ottawa Senators	78	19	28	47	38	7	1	4	5	0
1997-98	St. Louis Blues	80	14	42	56	32	10	0	4	4	6
1998-99	Los Angeles Kings	60	4	19	23	22	....	....	....	....	....
	Philadelphia Flyers	11	2	5	7	2	6	0	2	2	2
99-2000	Detroit Red Wings	79	10	31	41	42	9	0	4	4	10
2000-01	Detroit Red Wings	54	6	19	25	48	6	2	4	6	0
2001-02 ♦	Detroit Red Wings	64	3	15	18	28	23	0	6	6	24
	NHL Totals	**1113**	**227**	**525**	**752**	**824**	**121**	**16**	**61**	**77**	**96**

NHL All-Rookie Team (1987)

Played in NHL All-Star Game (1989, 1990, 1993)

Signed as a free agent by **Los Angeles,** October 1, 1984. Traded to **Philadelphia** by **Los Angeles** with Steve Kasper and Los Angeles' 4th round choice (Aris Brimanis) in 1991 Entry Draft for Jari Kurri and Jeff Chychrun, May 30, 1991. Traded to **Quebec** by **Philadelphia** with Peter Forsberg, Kerry Huffman, Mike Ricci, Ron Hextall, Philadelphia's 1st round choice (Jocelyn Thibault) in 1993 Entry Draft, $15,000,000 and future considerations (Chris Simon and Philadelphia's 1st round choice (later traded to Toronto – later traded to Washington – Washington selected Nolan Baumgartner) in 1994 Entry Draft, July 21, 1992) for Eric Lindros, June 30, 1992. Traded to **St. Louis** by **Quebec** with Denis Chasse for Garth Butcher, Ron Sutter and Bob Bassen, January 23, 1994. Traded to **Ottawa** by **St. Louis** for Ottawa's 2nd round choice (later traded to Buffalo – Buffalo selected Cory Sarich) in 1996 Entry Draft, August 4, 1995. Traded to **St. Louis** by **Ottawa** for Igor Kravchuk, August 25, 1997. Signed as a free agent by **Los Angeles**, July 2, 1998. Traded to **Philadelphia** by **Los Angeles** for Dave Babych and Philadelphia's 5th round choice (Nathan Marsters) in 2000 Entry Draft, March 23, 1999. Signed as a free agent by **Detroit**, September 3, 1999.

DUDLEY, Rick

Left wing. Shoots left. 6', 190 lbs. Born, Toronto, Ont., January 31, 1949.

Season	Club	GP	G	A	Pts	PIM	GP	G	A	Pts	PIM
1972-73	Buffalo Sabres	6	0	1	1	7	....	....	....	....	....
1973-74	Buffalo Sabres	67	13	13	26	71	....	....	....	....	....
1974-75	Buffalo Sabres	78	31	39	70	116	10	3	1	4	26
1978-79	Buffalo Sabres	24	5	6	11	2	3	1	1	2	2
1979-80	Buffalo Sabres	66	11	22	33	58	12	3	0	3	41
1980-81	Buffalo Sabres	38	10	13	23	10	....	....	....	....	....
	Winnipeg Jets	30	5	5	10	28	....	....	....	....	....
	NHL Totals	**309**	**75**	**99**	**174**	**292**	**25**	**7**	**2**	**9**	**69**

Signed as a free agent by **Buffalo**, September, 1971. Rights transferred to **Buffalo** by **Cincinnati** (WHA) for NHL club agreeing to buy out remainder of contract, February, 1979. Claimed on waivers by **Winnipeg** from **Buffalo**, January 12, 1981.

DUERDEN, Dave

Left wing. Shoots left. 6'2", 200 lbs. Born, Oshawa, Ont., April 11, 1977.
(Florida's 4th choice, 80th overall, in 1995 Entry Draft).

Season	Club	GP	G	A	Pts	PIM	GP	G	A	Pts	PIM
99-2000	Florida Panthers	2	0	0	0	0	....	....	....	....	....
	NHL Totals	**2**	**0**	**0**	**0**	**0**	....	....	....	....	....

Traded to **NY Rangers** by **Florida** for future considerations, June 29, 2001.

DUFF, Dick

Left wing. Shoots left. 5'9", 166 lbs. Born, Kirkland Lake, Ont., February 18, 1936.

Season	Club	GP	G	A	Pts	PIM	GP	G	A	Pts	PIM
1954-55	Toronto Maple Leafs	3	0	0	0	2	....	....	....	....	....
1955-56	Toronto Maple Leafs	69	18	19	37	74	5	1	4	5	2
1956-57	Toronto Maple Leafs	70	26	14	40	50	....	....	....	....	....
1957-58	Toronto Maple Leafs	65	26	23	49	79	....	....	....	....	....
1958-59	Toronto Maple Leafs	69	29	24	53	73	12	4	3	7	8
1959-60	Toronto Maple Leafs	67	19	22	41	51	10	2	4	6	6
1960-61	Toronto Maple Leafs	67	16	17	33	54	5	0	1	1	2
1961-62 ♦	Toronto Maple Leafs	51	17	20	37	37	12	3	10	13	20
1962-63 ♦	Toronto Maple Leafs	69	16	19	35	56	10	4	1	5	2
1963-64	Toronto Maple Leafs	52	7	10	17	59	....	....	....	....	....
	New York Rangers	14	4	4	8	2	....	....	....	....	....
1964-65	New York Rangers	29	3	9	12	20	....	....	....	....	....
	♦ Montreal Canadiens	40	9	7	16	16	13	3	6	9	17
1965-66 ♦	Montreal Canadiens	63	21	24	45	78	10	2	5	7	2
1966-67	Montreal Canadiens	51	12	11	23	23	10	2	3	5	4
1967-68 ♦	Montreal Canadiens	66	25	21	46	21	13	3	4	7	4
1968-69 ♦	Montreal Canadiens	68	19	21	40	24	14	6	8	14	11

Season	Club	GP	G	A	Pts	PIM	GP	G	A	Pts	PIM
		REGULAR SEASON					PLAYOFFS				
1969-70	Montreal Canadiens	17	1	1	2	4	....	....	....	....	....
	Los Angeles Kings	32	5	8	13	8	....	....	....	....	....
1970-71	Los Angeles Kings	7	1	0	1	0	....	....	....	....	....
	Buffalo Sabres	53	7	13	20	12	....	....	....	....	....
1971-72	Buffalo Sabres	8	2	2	4	0	....	....	....	....	....
	NHL Totals	**1030**	**283**	**289**	**572**	**743**	**114**	**30**	**49**	**79**	**78**

Played in NHL All-Star Game (1956, 1957, 1958, 1962, 1963, 1965, 1967)

Traded to **NY Rangers** by **Toronto** with Arnie Brown, Bob Nevin, Bill Collins and Rod Seiling for Andy Bathgate and Don McKenney, February 22, 1964. Traded to **Montreal** by **NY Rangers** with Dave McComb for Bill Hicke and the loan of Jean-Guy Morissette for remainder of 1964-65 season, December 22, 1964. Traded to **Los Angeles** by **Montreal** for Dennis Hextall, January 23, 1970. Traded to **Buffalo** by **Los Angeles** with Eddie Shack for Mike McMahon Jr. and future considerations, November 24, 1970.

DUFOUR, Luc

Left wing. Shoots left. 5'11", 180 lbs. Born, Chicoutimi, Que., February 13, 1963.
(Boston's 2nd choice, 35th overall, in 1981 Entry Draft).

Season	Club	GP	G	A	Pts	PIM	GP	G	A	Pts	PIM
1982-83	Boston Bruins	73	14	11	25	107	17	1	0	1	30
1983-84	Boston Bruins	41	6	4	10	47	....	....	....	....	....
1984-85	Quebec Nordiques	30	2	3	5	27	....	....	....	....	....
	St. Louis Blues	23	1	3	4	18	1	0	0	0	2
	NHL Totals	**167**	**23**	**21**	**44**	**199**	**18**	**1**	**0**	**1**	**32**

Traded to **Quebec** by **Boston** with Boston's 4th round choice (Peter Massey) in 1985 Entry Draft for Louis Sleigher, October 25, 1984. Traded to **St. Louis** by **Quebec** for Alain Lemieux, January 29, 1985.

DUFOUR, Marc

Right wing. Shoots right. 6', 175 lbs. Born, Trois-Rivieres, Que., September 11, 1941.

Season	Club	GP	G	A	Pts	PIM	GP	G	A	Pts	PIM
1963-64	New York Rangers	10	1	0	1	2	....	....	....	....	....
1964-65	New York Rangers	2	0	0	0	0	....	....	....	....	....
1968-69	Los Angeles Kings	2	0	0	0	0	....	....	....	....	....
	NHL Totals	**14**	**1**	**0**	**1**	**2**	....	....	....	....	....

Claimed by **Los Angeles** from **NY Rangers** in Expansion Draft, June 6, 1967. Claimed by **Baltimore** from **Los Angeles** (Springfield-AHL) in Reverse Draft, June 10, 1970.

DUFRESNE, Donald

Defense. Shoots right. 6'1", 206 lbs. Born, Quebec City, Que., April 10, 1967.
(Montreal's 8th choice, 117th overall, in 1985 Entry Draft).

Season	Club	GP	G	A	Pts	PIM	GP	G	A	Pts	PIM
1988-89	Montreal Canadiens	13	0	1	1	43	6	1	1	2	4
1989-90	Montreal Canadiens	18	0	4	4	23	10	0	1	1	18
1990-91	Montreal Canadiens	53	2	13	15	55	10	0	1	1	21
1991-92	Montreal Canadiens	3	0	0	0	2	....	....	....	....	....
1992-93 ♦	Montreal Canadiens	32	1	2	3	32	2	0	0	0	0
1993-94	Tampa Bay Lightning	51	2	6	8	48	....	....	....	....	....
	Los Angeles Kings	9	0	0	0	10	....	....	....	....	....
1994-95	St. Louis Blues	22	0	3	3	10	3	0	0	0	4
1995-96	St. Louis Blues	3	0	0	0	4	....	....	....	....	....
	Edmonton Oilers	42	1	6	7	16	....	....	....	....	....
1996-97	Edmonton Oilers	22	0	1	1	15	3	0	0	0	0
	NHL Totals	**268**	**6**	**36**	**42**	**258**	**34**	**1**	**3**	**4**	**47**

Traded to **Tampa Bay** by **Montreal** to complete transaction that sent Rob Ramage to Montreal (March 20, 1993), June 18, 1993. Traded to **Los Angeles** by **Tampa Bay** for Los Angeles' 6th round choice (Daniel Juden) in 1994 Entry Draft, March 19, 1994. Claimed by **St. Louis** from **Los Angeles** in NHL Waiver Draft, January 18, 1995. Traded to **Edmonton** by **St. Louis** with Jeff Norton for Igor Kravchuk and Ken Sutton, January 4, 1996.

DUGGAN, John

Left wing. Shoots left. 5'8", 185 lbs. Born, Ottawa, Ont., December 17, 1898.

Season	Club	GP	G	A	Pts	PIM	GP	G	A	Pts	PIM
1925-26	Ottawa Senators	27	0	0	0	0	2	0	0	0	0
	NHL Totals	**27**	**0**	**0**	**0**	**0**	**2**	**0**	**0**	**0**	**0**

Signed as a free agent by **Ottawa**, December 14, 1925. Loaned to **London** (Can-Pro) by **Ottawa** for cash, November, 1926 and November 27, 1927. Traded to **Hamilton** (IHL) by **Ottawa** for cash, November 7, 1929.

DUGGAN, Ken

Defense. Shoots left. 6'3", 210 lbs. Born, Toronto, Ont., February 21, 1963.

Season	Club	GP	G	A	Pts	PIM	GP	G	A	Pts	PIM
1987-88	Minnesota North Stars	1	0	0	0	0	....	....	....	....	....
	NHL Totals	**1**	**0**	**0**	**0**	**0**	....	....	....	....	....

Signed as a free agent by **NY Rangers**, May 22, 1986. Signed as a free agent by **Minnesota**, January, 1988.

DUGUAY, Ron

Center/Right wing. Shoots right. 6'2", 200 lbs. Born, Sudbury, Ont., July 6, 1957.
(NY Rangers' 2nd choice, 13th overall, in 1977 Amateur Draft).

Season	Club	GP	G	A	Pts	PIM	GP	G	A	Pts	PIM
1977-78	New York Rangers	71	20	20	40	43	3	1	1	2	2
1978-79	New York Rangers	79	27	36	63	35	18	5	4	9	11
1979-80	New York Rangers	73	28	22	50	37	9	5	2	7	11
1980-81	New York Rangers	50	17	21	38	83	14	8	9	17	16
1981-82	New York Rangers	72	40	36	76	82	10	5	1	6	31
1982-83	New York Rangers	72	19	25	44	58	9	2	2	4	28
1983-84	Detroit Red Wings	80	33	47	80	34	4	2	3	5	2
1984-85	Detroit Red Wings	80	38	51	89	51	3	1	0	1	7
1985-86	Detroit Red Wings	67	19	29	48	26	....	....	....	....	....
	Pittsburgh Penguins	13	6	7	13	6	....	....	....	....	....
1986-87	Pittsburgh Penguins	40	5	13	18	30	....	....	....	....	....
	New York Rangers	34	9	12	21	9	6	2	0	2	4
1987-88	New York Rangers	48	4	4	8	23	....	....	....	....	....
	Los Angeles Kings	15	2	6	8	17	2	0	0	0	0
1988-89	Los Angeles Kings	70	7	17	24	48	11	0	0	0	6
	NHL Totals	**864**	**274**	**346**	**620**	**582**	**89**	**31**	**22**	**53**	**118**

Played in NHL All-Star Game (1982)

Traded to **Detroit** by **NY Rangers** with Eddie Mio and Eddie Johnstone for Willie Huber, Mark Osborne and Mike Blaisdell, June 13, 1983. Traded to **Pittsburgh** by **Detroit** for Doug Shedden, March 11, 1986. Traded to **NY Rangers** by **Pittsburgh** for Chris Kontos, January 21, 1987. Traded to **Los Angeles** by **NY Rangers** for Mark Hardy, February 23, 1988.

DUGUID, Lorne

Left wing. Shoots left. 5'11", 185 lbs. Born, Bolton, Ont., April 4, 1910.

Season	Club	GP	G	A	Pts	PIM	GP	G	A	Pts	PIM
1931-32	Montreal Maroons	13	0	0	0	6	....	....	....	....	....
1932-33	Montreal Maroons	48	4	7	11	38	2	0	0	0	4
1933-34	Montreal Maroons	5	0	1	1	0	....	....	....	....	....
1934-35	Detroit Red Wings	34	3	3	6	9	....	....	....	....	....
1935-36	Detroit Red Wings	5	0	0	0	0	....	....	....	....	....
	Boston Bruins	29	1	4	5	2	2	1	0	1	2
1936-37	Boston Bruins	1	1	0	1	2	....	....	....	....	....
	NHL Totals	**135**	**9**	**15**	**24**	**57**	**4**	**1**	**0**	**1**	**6**

Signed as a free agent by **Mtl. Maroons**, October 19, 1931. Traded to **Detroit** by **Mtl. Maroons** for cash, October 28, 1934. Traded to **Boston** by **Detroit** for Gene Carrigan, December 29, 1935.

DUKOWSKI, Duke

Defense. Shoots left. 5'10", 185 lbs. Born, Regina, Sask., August 30, 1902.

Season	Club	GP	G	A	Pts	PIM	GP	G	A	Pts	PIM
1926-27	Chicago Black Hawks	28	3	2	5	16	2	0	0	0	0
1929-30	Chicago Black Hawks	44	7	10	17	42	2	0	0	0	6
1930-31	Chicago Black Hawks	25	1	3	4	28	....	....	....	....	....
	New York Americans	12	1	1	2	12	....	....	....	....	....
1932-33	New York Americans	48	4	7	11	43	....	....	....	....	....
1933-34	New York Americans	9	0	1	1	11	....	....	....	....	....
	Chicago Black Hawks	5	0	0	0	2	....	....	....	....	....
	New York Rangers	29	0	6	6	18	2	0	0	0	0
	NHL Totals	**200**	**16**	**30**	**46**	**172**	**6**	**0**	**0**	**0**	**6**

• Also known as Dutkowski. Prior to his death, Mr. Dukowski requested the "t" be dropped from his last name.

Rights transferred to **Chicago** after NHL club purchased **Portland** (WHL) franchise, May 15, 1926. Claimed on waivers by **NY Americans** from **Chicago**, February 13, 1931. Loaned to **Chicago** by **NY Americans** for remainder of 1933-34 season, December 15, 1933. Recalled by **NY Americans** and traded to **NY Rangers** for cash, January 3, 1934.

DUMART, Woody

HHOF

Left wing. Shoots left. 6', 190 lbs. Born, Berlin, Ont., December 23, 1916.

Season	Club	GP	G	A	Pts	PIM	GP	G	A	Pts	PIM
1935-36	Boston Bruins	1	0	0	0	0	....	....	....	....	....
1936-37	Boston Bruins	17	4	4	8	2	3	0	0	0	0
1937-38	Boston Bruins	48	13	14	27	6	3	0	0	0	0
1938-39 ♦	Boston Bruins	46	14	15	29	2	12	1	3	4	6
1939-40	Boston Bruins	48	22	21	43	16	6	1	0	1	0
1940-41 ♦	Boston Bruins	40	18	15	33	2	11	1	3	4	9
1941-42	Boston Bruins	35	14	15	29	8	....	....	....	....	....
1945-46	Boston Bruins	50	22	12	34	2	10	4	3	7	0
1946-47	Boston Bruins	60	24	28	52	12	5	1	1	2	8
1947-48	Boston Bruins	59	21	16	37	14	5	0	0	0	0
1948-49	Boston Bruins	59	11	12	23	6	5	3	0	3	0
1949-50	Boston Bruins	69	14	25	39	14	....	....	....	....	....
1950-51	Boston Bruins	70	20	21	41	7	6	1	2	3	0
1951-52	Boston Bruins	39	5	8	13	0	7	0	1	1	0
1952-53	Boston Bruins	62	5	9	14	2	11	0	2	2	0
1953-54	Boston Bruins	69	4	3	7	6	4	0	0	0	0
	NHL Totals	**772**	**211**	**218**	**429**	**99**	**88**	**12**	**15**	**27**	**23**

NHL Second All-Star Team (1940, 1941, 1947)

Played in NHL All-Star Game (1947, 1948)

Signed as a free agent by **Boston**, October 9, 1935.

DUMONT, J.P.

Right wing. Shoots left. 6'1", 205 lbs. Born, Montreal, Que., April 1, 1978.
(NY Islanders' 1st choice, 3rd overall, in 1996 Entry Draft).

Season	Club	GP	G	A	Pts	PIM	GP	G	A	Pts	PIM
1998-99	Chicago Blackhawks	25	9	6	15	10	....	....	....	....	....
99-2000	Chicago Blackhawks	47	10	8	18	18	....	....	....	....	....
2000-01	Buffalo Sabres	79	23	28	51	54	13	4	3	7	8
2001-02	Buffalo Sabres	76	23	21	44	42	....	....	....	....	....
2002-03	Buffalo Sabres	76	14	21	35	44	....	....	....	....	....
	NHL Totals	**303**	**79**	**84**	**163**	**168**	**13**	**4**	**3**	**7**	**8**

Rights traded to **Chicago** by **NY Islanders** with Chicago's 5th round choice (later traded to Philadelphia – Philadelphia selected Francis Belanger) in 1998 Entry Draft for Dmitri Nabokov, May 30, 1998. Traded to **Buffalo** by **Chicago** with Doug Gilmour for Michal Grosek, March 10, 2000.

DUNBAR, Dale

Defense. Shoots left. 6', 200 lbs. Born, Winthrop, MA, October 14, 1961.

Season	Club	GP	G	A	Pts	PIM	GP	G	A	Pts	PIM
1985-86	Vancouver Canucks	1	0	0	0	2	....	....	....	....	....

Season	Club	REGULAR SEASON					PLAYOFFS				
		GP	G	A	Pts	PIM	GP	G	A	Pts	PIM
1988-89	Boston Bruins	1	0	0	0	0	....	....	....	....	....
	NHL Totals	**2**	**0**	**0**	**0**	**2**	....	....	....	....	....

Signed as a free agent by **Vancouver**, May 10, 1985. Signed as a free agent by **Boston**, August 25, 1987.

DUNCAN, Art

Defense. Shoots right. 6'1", 190 lbs. Born, Sault Ste. Marie, Ont., July 4, 1894.

Season	Club	GP	G	A	Pts	PIM	GP	G	A	Pts	PIM
1926-27	Detroit Cougars	34	3	2	5	26	....	....	....	....	....
1927-28	Toronto Maple Leafs	43	7	5	12	97	....	....	....	....	....
1928-29	Toronto Maple Leafs	39	4	4	8	53	4	0	0	0	4
1929-30	Toronto Maple Leafs	38	4	5	9	49	....	....	....	....	....
1930-31	Toronto Maple Leafs	2	0	0	0	0	1	0	0	0	0
	NHL Totals	**156**	**18**	**16**	**34**	**225**	**5**	**0**	**0**	**0**	**4**

Traded to **Chicago** by **Calgary** (WHL) for cash, May 15, 1926. Rights traded to **Detroit** by **Chicago** for Art Gagne and Gord Fraser, October 18, 1926. Traded to **Toronto** by **Detroit** for Bill Brydge, May 16, 1927.

DUNCAN, Iain

Left wing. Shoots left. 6'1", 200 lbs. Born, Weston, Ont., August 4, 1963.
(Winnipeg's 8th choice, 134th overall, in 1983 Entry Draft).

Season	Club	GP	G	A	Pts	PIM	GP	G	A	Pts	PIM
1986-87	Winnipeg Jets	6	1	2	3	0	7	0	2	2	6
1987-88	Winnipeg Jets	62	19	23	42	73	4	0	1	1	0
1988-89	Winnipeg Jets	57	14	30	44	74	....	....	....	....	....
1990-91	Winnipeg Jets	2	0	0	0	2	....	....	....	....	....
	NHL Totals	**127**	**34**	**55**	**89**	**149**	**11**	**0**	**3**	**3**	**6**

NHL All-Rookie Team (1988)

DUNCANSON, Craig

Left wing. Shoots left. 6', 190 lbs. Born, Sudbury, Ont., March 17, 1967.
(Los Angeles' 1st choice, 9th overall, in 1985 Entry Draft).

Season	Club	GP	G	A	Pts	PIM	GP	G	A	Pts	PIM
1985-86	Los Angeles Kings	2	0	1	1	0	....	....	....	....	....
1986-87	Los Angeles Kings	2	0	0	0	24	....	....	....	....	....
1987-88	Los Angeles Kings	9	0	0	0	12	....	....	....	....	....
1988-89	Los Angeles Kings	5	0	0	0	0	....	....	....	....	....
1989-90	Los Angeles Kings	10	3	2	5	9	....	....	....	....	....
1990-91	Winnipeg Jets	7	2	0	2	16	....	....	....	....	....
1992-93	New York Rangers	3	0	1	1	0	....	....	....	....	....
	NHL Totals	**38**	**5**	**4**	**9**	**61**	....	....	....	....	....

Traded to **Minnesota** by **Los Angeles** for Daniel Berthiaume, September 6, 1990. Traded to **Winnipeg** by **Minnesota** for Brian Hunt, September 6, 1990. Traded to **Washington** by **Winnipeg** with Brent Hughes and Simon Wheeldon for Bob Joyce, Tyler Larter and Kent Paynter, May 21, 1991. Signed as a free agent by **NY Rangers**, September 4, 1992.

DUNDAS, Rocky

Right wing. Shoots right. 6', 195 lbs. Born, Regina, Sask., January 30, 1967.
(Montreal's 4th choice, 47th overall, in 1985 Entry Draft).

Season	Club	GP	G	A	Pts	PIM	GP	G	A	Pts	PIM
1989-90	Toronto Maple Leafs	5	0	0	0	14	....	....	....	....	....
	NHL Totals	**5**	**0**	**0**	**0**	**14**	....	....	....	....	....

Signed as a free agent by **Toronto**, October 4, 1989.

DUNLAP, Frank

Wing. Shoots left. 6', 185 lbs. Born, Ottawa, Ont., August 10, 1924.

Season	Club	GP	G	A	Pts	PIM	GP	G	A	Pts	PIM
1943-44	Toronto Maple Leafs	15	0	1	1	2	....	....	....	....	....
	NHL Totals	**15**	**0**	**1**	**1**	**2**	....	....	....	....	....

• Played NHL home games only w/ St. Michael's (OHA-Jr.) and Toronto during 1943-44 season while attending law school

DUNLOP, Blake

Center. Shoots right. 5'10", 170 lbs. Born, Hamilton, Ont., April 4, 1953.
(Minnesota's 1st choice, 18th overall, in 1973 Amateur Draft).

Season	Club	GP	G	A	Pts	PIM	GP	G	A	Pts	PIM
1973-74	Minnesota North Stars	12	0	0	0	2	....	....	....	....	....
1974-75	Minnesota North Stars	52	9	18	27	8	....	....	....	....	....
1975-76	Minnesota North Stars	33	9	11	20	8	....	....	....	....	....
1976-77	Minnesota North Stars	3	0	1	1	0	....	....	....	....	....
1977-78	Philadelphia Flyers	3	0	1	1	0	....	....	....	....	....
1978-79	Philadelphia Flyers	66	20	28	48	16	8	1	1	2	4
1979-80	St. Louis Blues	72	18	27	45	28	3	0	2	2	2
1980-81	St. Louis Blues	80	20	67	87	40	11	0	3	3	4
1981-82	St. Louis Blues	77	25	53	78	32	10	2	2	4	4
1982-83	St. Louis Blues	78	22	44	66	14	4	1	1	2	0
1983-84	St. Louis Blues	17	1	10	11	4	....	....	....	....	....
	Detroit Red Wings	57	6	14	20	20	4	0	1	1	4
	NHL Totals	**550**	**130**	**274**	**404**	**172**	**40**	**4**	**10**	**14**	**18**

Bill Masterton Trophy (1981)

Traded to **Philadelphia** by **Minnesota** with Minnesota's 3rd round choice (Gord Salt) in 1978 Amateur Draft for Harvey Bennett Jr., October 28, 1977. Traded to **St. Louis** by **Philadelphia** with Rick Lapointe for Phil Myre, June 7, 1979. Signed as a free agent by **Detroit**, December 2, 1983.

DUNN, Dave

Defense. Shoots left. 6'2", 200 lbs. Born, Moosomin, Sask., August 19, 1948.

Season	Club	GP	G	A	Pts	PIM	GP	G	A	Pts	PIM
1973-74	Vancouver Canucks	68	11	22	33	76	....	....	....	....	....
1974-75	Vancouver Canucks	1	0	0	0	11	....	....	....	....	....
	Toronto Maple Leafs	72	3	11	14	142	7	1	1	2	24
1975-76	Toronto Maple Leafs	43	0	8	8	84	3	0	0	0	17
	NHL Totals	**184**	**14**	**41**	**55**	**313**	**10**	**1**	**1**	**2**	**41**

Signed as a free agent by **Vancouver** September 20, 1970. Traded to **Toronto** by **Vancouver** for Garry Monahan and John Grisdale, October 16, 1974.

DUNN, Richie

Defense. Shoots left. 6', 200 lbs. Born, Boston, MA, May 12, 1957.

Season	Club	GP	G	A	Pts	PIM	GP	G	A	Pts	PIM
1977-78	Buffalo Sabres	25	0	3	3	16	1	0	0	0	2
1978-79	Buffalo Sabres	24	0	3	3	14	....	....	....	....	....
1979-80	Buffalo Sabres	80	7	31	38	61	14	2	8	10	8
1980-81	Buffalo Sabres	79	7	42	49	34	8	0	5	5	6
1981-82	Buffalo Sabres	72	7	19	26	73	4	0	1	1	0
1982-83	Calgary Flames	80	3	11	14	47	9	1	1	2	8
1983-84	Hartford Whalers	63	5	20	25	30	....	....	....	....	....
1984-85	Hartford Whalers	13	1	4	5	2	....	....	....	....	....
1985-86	Buffalo Sabres	29	4	5	9	25	....	....	....	....	....
1986-87	Buffalo Sabres	2	0	1	1	2	....	....	....	....	....
1987-88	Buffalo Sabres	12	2	0	2	8	....	....	....	....	....
1988-89	Buffalo Sabres	4	0	1	1	2	....	....	....	....	....
	NHL Totals	**483**	**36**	**140**	**176**	**314**	**36**	**3**	**15**	**18**	**24**

Signed as a free agent by **Buffalo**, October 3, 1977. Traded to **Calgary** by **Buffalo** with Don Edwards and Buffalo's 2nd round choice (Richard Kromm) in 1982 Entry Draft and Buffalo's 1st round choice (Dan Quinn) in 1983 Entry Draft for Calgary's 1st (Paul Cyr) and 2nd (Jens Johansson) round choices in 1982 Entry Draft and Calgary's 1st (Normand Lacombe) and 2nd (John Tucker) round choices in 1983 Entry Draft, June 9, 1982. Traded to **Hartford** by **Calgary** with Joel Quenneville for Mickey Volcan, July 5, 1983. Signed as a free agent by **Buffalo**, July 10, 1986.

DUPERE, Denis

Left wing. Shoots left. 6'1", 200 lbs. Born, Jonquiere, Que., June 21, 1948.

Season	Club	GP	G	A	Pts	PIM	GP	G	A	Pts	PIM
1970-71	Toronto Maple Leafs	20	1	2	3	4	6	0	0	0	0
1971-72	Toronto Maple Leafs	77	7	10	17	4	5	0	0	0	0
1972-73	Toronto Maple Leafs	61	13	23	36	10	....	....	....	....	....
1973-74	Toronto Maple Leafs	34	8	9	17	8	3	0	0	0	0
1974-75	Washington Capitals	53	20	15	35	8	....	....	....	....	....
	St. Louis Blues	22	3	6	9	8	....	....	....	....	....
1975-76	Kansas City Scouts	43	6	8	14	16	....	....	....	....	....
1976-77	Colorado Rockies	57	7	11	18	4	....	....	....	....	....
1977-78	Colorado Rockies	54	15	15	30	4	2	1	0	1	0
	NHL Totals	**421**	**80**	**99**	**179**	**66**	**16**	**1**	**0**	**1**	**0**

Played in NHL All-Star Game (1975)

Traded to **Toronto** by **NY Rangers** to complete transaction that sent Tim Horton to NY Rangers, (March 3, 1970), May 14, 1970. Claimed by **Washington** from **Toronto** in Expansion Draft, June 12, 1974. Traded to **St. Louis** by **Washington** for Garnet Bailey and Stan Gilbertson, February 10, 1975. Traded to **Kansas City** by **St. Louis** with Craig Patrick and cash for Lynn Powis and Kansas City's 2nd round choice (Brian Sutter) in 1976 Amateur Draft, June 18, 1975. Transferred to **Colorado** when **Kansas City** franchise relocated, July 15, 1976.

DUPONT, Andre

Defense. Shoots left. 6', 200 lbs. Born, Trois-Rivieres, Que., July 27, 1949.
(NY Rangers' 1st choice, 8th overall, in 1969 Amateur Draft).

Season	Club	GP	G	A	Pts	PIM	GP	G	A	Pts	PIM
1970-71	New York Rangers	7	1	2	3	21	....	....	....	....	....
1971-72	St. Louis Blues	60	3	10	13	147	11	1	0	1	20
1972-73	St. Louis Blues	25	1	6	7	51	....	....	....	....	....
	Philadelphia Flyers	46	3	20	23	164	11	1	2	3	29
1973-74◆	Philadelphia Flyers	75	3	20	23	216	16	4	3	7	67
1974-75◆	Philadelphia Flyers	80	11	21	32	276	17	3	2	5	49
1975-76	Philadelphia Flyers	75	9	27	36	214	15	2	2	4	46
1976-77	Philadelphia Flyers	59	10	19	29	168	10	1	1	2	35
1977-78	Philadelphia Flyers	69	2	12	14	225	12	2	1	3	13
1978-79	Philadelphia Flyers	77	3	9	12	135	8	0	0	0	17
1979-80	Philadelphia Flyers	58	1	7	8	107	19	0	4	4	50
1980-81	Quebec Nordiques	63	5	8	13	93	1	0	0	0	0
1981-82	Quebec Nordiques	60	4	12	16	100	16	0	3	3	18
1982-83	Quebec Nordiques	46	3	12	15	69	4	0	0	0	8
	NHL Totals	**800**	**59**	**185**	**244**	**1986**	**140**	**14**	**18**	**32**	**352**

Played in NHL All-Star Game (1976)

Traded to **St. Louis** by **NY Rangers** with Jack Egers and Mike Murphy for Gene Carr, Jim Lorentz and Wayne Connelly, November 15, 1971. Traded to **Philadelphia** by **St. Louis** with St. Louis' 3rd round choice (Bob Stumpf) in 1973 Amateur Draft for Brent Hughes and Pierre Plante, December 14, 1972. Traded to **Quebec** by **Philadelphia** for cash and Quebec's 7th round choice (Vladimir Svitek) in 1981 Entry Draft, September 15, 1980.

DUPONT, Jerome

Defense. Shoots left. 6'3", 190 lbs. Born, Ottawa, Ont., February 21, 1962.
(Chicago's 2nd choice, 15th overall, in 1980 Entry Draft).

Season	Club	GP	G	A	Pts	PIM	GP	G	A	Pts	PIM
1981-82	Chicago Black Hawks	34	0	4	4	51	....	....	....	....	....
1982-83	Chicago Black Hawks	1	0	0	0	0	....	....	....	....	....
1983-84	Chicago Black Hawks	36	2	2	4	116	4	0	0	0	15
1984-85	Chicago Black Hawks	55	3	10	13	105	15	0	2	2	41
1985-86	Chicago Black Hawks	75	2	13	15	173	1	0	0	0	0
1986-87	Toronto Maple Leafs	13	0	0	0	23	....	....	....	....	....
	NHL Totals	**214**	**7**	**29**	**36**	**468**	**20**	**0**	**2**	**2**	**56**

Transferred to **Toronto** by **Chicago** with Ken Yaremchuk and Chicago's 4th round choice (Joe Sacco) in 1987 Entry Draft as compensation for Chicago's signing of free agent Gary Nylund, September 6, 1986.

DuPONT, Micki

Defense. Shoots right. 5'9", 186 lbs. Born, Calgary, Alta., April 15, 1980.
(Calgary's 9th choice, 270th overall, in 2000 Entry Draft).

Season	Club	GP	G	A	Pts	PIM	GP	G	A	Pts	PIM
		REGULAR SEASON					PLAYOFFS				
2001-02	Calgary Flames	2	0	0	0	2	....	....	....	....	....
2002-03	Calgary Flames	16	1	2	3	4	....	....	....	....	....
	NHL Totals	**18**	**1**	**2**	**3**	**6**	....	....	....	....	....

Traded to **Pittsburgh** by **Calgary** with Mathias Johansson for Shean Donovan, March 11, 2003.

DUPONT, Norm

Left wing. Shoots left. 5'10", 185 lbs. Born, Montreal, Que., February 5, 1957.
(Montreal's 2nd choice, 18th overall, in 1977 Amateur Draft).

Season	Club	GP	G	A	Pts	PIM	GP	G	A	Pts	PIM
1979-80	Montreal Canadiens	35	1	3	4	4	8	1	1	2	0
1980-81	Winnipeg Jets	80	27	26	53	8	....	....	....	....	....
1981-82	Winnipeg Jets	62	13	25	38	22	4	2	0	2	0
1982-83	Winnipeg Jets	39	7	16	23	6	1	1	1	2	0
1983-84	Hartford Whalers	40	7	15	22	12	....	....	....	....	....
	NHL Totals	**256**	**55**	**85**	**140**	**52**	**13**	**4**	**2**	**6**	**0**

Traded to **Winnipeg** by **Montreal** for Winnipeg's 2nd round choice (David Maley) in 1982 Entry Draft, September 26, 1980. Traded to **Hartford** by **Winnipeg** for Hartford's 4th round choice (Chris Mills) in 1984 Entry Draft, July 4, 1983.

DUPRE, Yanick

Left wing. Shoots left. 6', 189 lbs. Born, Montreal, Que., November 20, 1972.
(Philadelphia's 2nd choice, 50th overall, in 1991 Entry Draft).

Season	Club	GP	G	A	Pts	PIM	GP	G	A	Pts	PIM
1991-92	Philadelphia Flyers	1	0	0	0	0	....	....	....	....	....
1994-95	Philadelphia Flyers	22	0	0	0	8	....	....	....	....	....
1995-96	Philadelphia Flyers	12	2	0	2	8	....	....	....	....	....
	NHL Totals	**35**	**2**	**0**	**2**	**16**	....	....	....	....	....

DUPUIS, Pascal

Left wing. Shoots Right. 6', 195 lbs. Born, Laval, Que., April 7, 1979.

Season	Club	GP	G	A	Pts	PIM	GP	G	A	Pts	PIM
2000-01	Minnesota Wild	4	1	0	1	4	....	....	....	....	....
2001-02	Minnesota Wild	76	15	12	27	16	....	....	....	....	....
2002-03	Minnesota Wild	80	20	28	48	44	16	4	4	8	8
	NHL Totals	**160**	**36**	**40**	**76**	**64**	**16**	**4**	**4**	**8**	**8**

Signed as a free agent by **Minnesota**, August 18, 2000.

DURBANO, Steve

Defense. Shoots left. 6'1", 210 lbs. Born, Toronto, Ont., December 12, 1951.
(NY Rangers' 2nd choice, 13th overall, in 1971 Amateur Draft).

Season	Club	GP	G	A	Pts	PIM	GP	G	A	Pts	PIM
1972-73	St. Louis Blues	49	3	18	21	231	5	0	2	2	8
1973-74	St. Louis Blues	36	4	5	9	146	....	....	....	....	....
	Pittsburgh Penguins	33	4	14	18	138	....	....	....	....	....
1974-75	Pittsburgh Penguins	1	0	1	1	10	....	....	....	....	....
1975-76	Pittsburgh Penguins	32	0	8	8	*161	....	....	....	....	....
	Kansas City Scouts	37	1	11	12	*209	....	....	....	....	....
1976-77	Colorado Rockies	19	0	2	2	129	....	....	....	....	....
1978-79	St. Louis Blues	13	1	1	2	103	....	....	....	....	....
	NHL Totals	**220**	**13**	**60**	**73**	**1127**	**5**	**0**	**2**	**2**	**8**

Traded to **St. Louis** by **NY Rangers** for future considerations (Peter McDuffe and Curt Bennett, June 7, 1972), May 24, 1972. • Missed remainder of 1974-75 season recovering from wrist injury suffered in game vs. Philadelphia, October 18, 1974. Traded to **Pittsburgh** by **St. Louis** with Ab DeMarco Jr. and Bob Kelly for Bryan Watson, Greg Polis and Pittsburgh's 2nd round choice (Bob Hess) in 1974 Amateur Draft, January 17, 1974. Traded to **Kansas City** by **Pittsburgh** with Chuck Arnason and Pittsburgh's 1st round choice (Paul Gardner) in 1976 Amateur Draft for Simon Nolet, Ed Gilbert and Kansas City's 1st round choice (Blair Chapman) in 1976 Amateur Draft, January 9, 1976. Transferred to **Colorado** after **Kansas City** franchise relocated, July 15, 1976. Signed as a free agent by **Detroit**, July 14, 1977. Loaned to **Birmingham** (WHA) by **Detroit** with the loan of Dave Hanson and future considerations for Vaclav Nedomansky and Tim Sheehy, November 18, 1977. Signed as a free agent by **St. Louis**, August 11, 1978.

DURIS, Vitezslav

Defense. Shoots left. 6'1", 185 lbs. Born, Plzen, Czech., January 5, 1954.

Season	Club	GP	G	A	Pts	PIM	GP	G	A	Pts	PIM
1980-81	Toronto Maple Leafs	57	1	12	13	50	3	0	1	1	2
1982-83	Toronto Maple Leafs	32	2	8	10	12	....	....	....	....	....
	NHL Totals	**89**	**3**	**20**	**23**	**62**	**3**	**0**	**1**	**1**	**2**

Signed as a free agent by **Toronto**, September 25, 1980.

DUSSAULT, Norm

Center. Shoots left. 5'8", 165 lbs. Born, Springfield, MA, September 26, 1925.

Season	Club	GP	G	A	Pts	PIM	GP	G	A	Pts	PIM
1947-48	Montreal Canadiens	28	5	10	15	4	....	....	....	....	....
1948-49	Montreal Canadiens	47	9	8	17	6	2	0	0	0	0
1949-50	Montreal Canadiens	67	13	24	37	22	5	3	1	4	0
1950-51	Montreal Canadiens	64	4	20	24	15	....	....	....	....	....
	NHL Totals	**206**	**31**	**62**	**93**	**47**	**7**	**3**	**1**	**4**	**0**

Traded to **Chicoutimi** (QMHL) by **Montreal** for cash, November 21, 1951.

DUTTON, Red

HHOF

Defense. Shoots right. 6', 185 lbs. Born, Russell, Man., July 23, 1898.

Season	Club	GP	G	A	Pts	PIM	GP	G	A	Pts	PIM
1926-27	Montreal Maroons	44	4	4	8	108	2	0	0	0	4
1927-28	Montreal Maroons	42	7	6	13	94	9	1	0	1	27
1928-29	Montreal Maroons	44	1	3	4	*139	....	....	....	....	....
1929-30	Montreal Maroons	43	3	13	16	98	4	0	0	0	2
1930-31	New York Americans	44	1	11	12	71	....	....	....	....	....
1931-32	New York Americans	47	3	5	8	*107	....	....	....	....	....
1932-33	New York Americans	43	0	2	2	74	....	....	....	....	....
1933-34	New York Americans	48	2	8	10	65	....	....	....	....	....
1934-35	New York Americans	48	3	7	10	46	....	....	....	....	....
1935-36	New York Americans	46	5	8	13	69	3	0	0	0	0
	NHL Totals	**449**	**29**	**67**	**96**	**871**	**18**	**1**	**0**	**1**	**33**

Lester Patrick Trophy (1993)
Played in NHL All-Star Game (1934)

Traded to **Mtl. Maroons** by **Calgary** (WHL) for cash, September 11, 1926. Traded to **NY Americans** by **Mtl. Maroons** with Mike Neville, Hap Emms and Frank Carson for $35,000, May 14, 1930.

DVORAK, Miroslav

Defense. Shoots right. 5'10", 195 lbs. Born, Hluboka-nad-Vltavou, Czech., October 11, 1951.
(Philadelphia's 2nd choice, 46th overall, in 1982 Entry Draft).

Season	Club	GP	G	A	Pts	PIM	GP	G	A	Pts	PIM
1982-83	Philadelphia Flyers	80	4	33	37	20	3	0	1	1	0
1983-84	Philadelphia Flyers	66	4	27	31	27	2	0	0	0	2
1984-85	Philadelphia Flyers	47	3	14	17	4	13	0	1	1	4
	NHL Totals	**193**	**11**	**74**	**85**	**51**	**18**	**0**	**2**	**2**	**6**

DVORAK, Radek

Right wing. Shoots right. 6'1", 194 lbs. Born, Tabor, Czech., March 9, 1977.
(Florida's 1st choice, 10th overall, in 1995 Entry Draft).

Season	Club	GP	G	A	Pts	PIM	GP	G	A	Pts	PIM
1995-96	Florida Panthers	77	13	14	27	20	16	1	3	4	0
1996-97	Florida Panthers	78	18	21	39	30	3	0	0	0	0
1997-98	Florida Panthers	64	12	24	36	33	....	....	....	....	....
1998-99	Florida Panthers	82	19	24	43	29	....	....	....	....	....
99-2000	Florida Panthers	35	7	10	17	6	....	....	....	....	....
	New York Rangers	46	11	22	33	10	....	....	....	....	....
2000-01	New York Rangers	82	31	36	67	20	....	....	....	....	....
2001-02	New York Rangers	65	17	20	37	14	....	....	....	....	....
2002-03	New York Rangers	63	6	21	27	16	....	....	....	....	....
	Edmonton Oilers	12	4	4	8	14	4	1	0	1	0
	NHL Totals	**604**	**138**	**196**	**334**	**192**	**23**	**2**	**3**	**5**	**0**

Traded to **San Jose** by **Florida** for Mike Vernon and San Jose's 3rd round choice (Sean O'Connor) in 2000 Entry Draft, December 30, 1999. Traded to **NY Rangers** by **San Jose** for Todd Harvey and NY Rangers' 4th round choice (Dimitri Patzold) in 2001 Entry Draft, December 30, 1999. Traded to **Edmonton** by **NY Rangers** with Cory Cross for Anson Carter and Ales Pisa, March 11, 2003.

DWYER, Gordie

Left wing. Shoots left. 6'3", 215 lbs. Born, Dalhousie, N.B., January 25, 1978.
(Montreal's 5th choice, 152nd overall, in 1998 Entry Draft).

Season	Club	GP	G	A	Pts	PIM	GP	G	A	Pts	PIM
99-2000	Tampa Bay Lightning	24	0	1	1	135	....	....	....	....	....
2000-01	Tampa Bay Lightning	28	0	1	1	96	....	....	....	....	....
2001-02	Tampa Bay Lightning	26	0	2	2	60	....	....	....	....	....
2002-03	New York Rangers	17	0	1	1	50	....	....	....	....	....
	Montreal Canadiens	11	0	0	0	46	....	....	....	....	....
	NHL Totals	**106**	**0**	**5**	**5**	**387**	....	....	....	....	....

• Re-entered NHL Entry Draft. Originally St. Louis' 2nd choice, 67th overall, in 1996 Entry Draft.

Traded to **Tampa Bay** by **Montreal** for Mike McBain, November 26, 1999. Traded to **NY Rangers** by **Tampa Bay** for Boyd Kane, October 10, 2002. Claimed on waivers by **Montreal** from **NY Rangers**, February 21, 2003.

DWYER, Mike

Left wing. Shoots left. 5'11", 172 lbs. Born, Brampton, Ont., September 16, 1957.
(Colorado's 4th choice, 74th overall, in 1977 Amateur Draft).

Season	Club	GP	G	A	Pts	PIM	GP	G	A	Pts	PIM
1978-79	Colorado Rockies	12	2	3	5	2	....	....	....	....	....
1979-80	Colorado Rockies	10	0	0	0	19	....	....	....	....	....
1980-81	Calgary Flames	4	0	1	1	4	1	1	0	1	0
1981-82	Calgary Flames	5	0	2	2	0	....	....	....	....	....
	NHL Totals	**31**	**2**	**6**	**8**	**25**	**1**	**1**	**0**	**1**	**0**

Signed as a free agent by **Calgary**, October 17, 1980.

DYCK, Henry

Center/Left wing. Shoots left. 5'8", 155 lbs. Born, Herbert, Sask., September 5, 1912.

Season	Club	GP	G	A	Pts	PIM	GP	G	A	Pts	PIM
1943-44	New York Rangers	1	0	0	0	0	....	....	....	....	....
	NHL Totals	**1**	**0**	**0**	**0**	**0**	....	....	....	....	....

DYE, Babe

HHOF

Right wing. Shoots right. 5'8", 150 lbs. Born, Hamilton, Ont., May 13, 1898.

Season	Club	GP	G	A	Pts	PIM	GP	G	A	Pts	PIM
1919-20	Toronto St. Pats	23	11	3	14	10	....	....	....	....	....
1920-21	Hamilton Tigers	1	*2	0	2	0	....	....	....	....	....
	Toronto St. Pats	23	*33	5	38	32	2	0	0	0	7
1921-22 ◆	Toronto St. Pats	24	31	7	38	39	2	2	0	2	2
	Toronto St. Pats (Cup)	....	....	....	....	....	*5*	*9*	*1*	*10*	*3*
1922-23	Toronto St. Pats	22	*26	11	*37	19	....	....	....	....	....
1923-24	Toronto St. Pats	19	16	3	19	23	....	....	....	....	....
1924-25	Toronto St. Pats	29	*38	8	*46	41	2	0	0	0	0
1925-26	Toronto St. Pats	31	18	5	23	26	....	....	....	....	....
1926-27	Chicago Black Hawks	41	25	5	30	14	2	0	0	0	2
1927-28	Chicago Black Hawks	10	0	0	0	0	....	....	....	....	....
1928-29	New York Americans	42	1	0	1	17	2	0	0	0	0

Season	Club	GP	G	A	Pts	PIM	GP	G	A	Pts	PIM
		REGULAR SEASON					PLAYOFFS				
1930-31	Toronto Maple Leafs	6	0	0	0	0	....	....	....	....	....
	NHL Totals	**271**	**201**	**47**	**248**	**221**	**10**	**2**	**0**	**2**	**11**

Signed as a free agent by **Toronto**, December 15, 1919. Loaned to **Hamilton** by **Toronto**, December 4, 1920. Recalled by **Toronto** from **Hamilton**, December 24, 1920. • Retired from hockey to play professional baseball, September 6, 1923. Signed as a free agent by **Toronto**, January 2, 1924. Traded to **Chicago** by **Toronto** for $15,000, October 18, 1926. • Missed majority of 1927-28 season recovering from broken leg suffered in training camp, October 30, 1927. Traded to **NY Americans** by **Chicago** for $15,000, October 17, 1928. Traded to **New Haven** (Can-Am) by **NY Americans** for George Massecar, November 13, 1929. Signed as a free agent by **Toronto**, February 10, 1930. • Released by Toronto, December 8, 1930.

DYKHUIS, Karl

Defense. Shoots left. 6'3", 214 lbs. Born, Sept-Iles, Que., July 8, 1972.
(Chicago's 1st choice, 16th overall, in 1990 Entry Draft).

Season	Club	GP	G	A	Pts	PIM	GP	G	A	Pts	PIM
1991-92	Chicago Blackhawks	6	1	3	4	4	....	....	....	....	....
1992-93	Chicago Blackhawks	12	0	5	5	0	....	....	....	....	....
1994-95	Philadelphia Flyers	33	2	6	8	37	15	4	4	8	14
1995-96	Philadelphia Flyers	82	5	15	20	101	12	2	2	4	22
1996-97	Philadelphia Flyers	62	4	15	19	35	18	0	3	3	2
1997-98	Tampa Bay Lightning	78	5	9	14	110	....	....	....	....	....
1998-99	Tampa Bay Lightning	33	2	1	3	18	....	....	....	....	....
	Philadelphia Flyers	45	2	4	6	32	5	1	0	1	4
99-2000	Philadelphia Flyers	5	0	1	1	6	....	....	....	....	....
	Montreal Canadiens	67	7	12	19	40	....	....	....	....	....
2000-01	Montreal Canadiens	67	8	9	17	44	....	....	....	....	....
2001-02	Montreal Canadiens	80	5	7	12	32	12	1	1	2	8
2002-03	Montreal Canadiens	65	1	4	5	34	....	....	....	....	....
	NHL Totals	**635**	**42**	**91**	**133**	**493**	**62**	**8**	**10**	**18**	**50**

Traded to **Philadelphia** by **Chicago** for Bob Wilkie and Philadelphia's 5th round choice (Kyle Calder) in 1997 Entry Draft, February 16, 1995. Traded to **Tampa Bay** by **Philadelphia** with Mikael Renberg for Philadelphia's 1st round choices (previously acquired by Tampa Bay) in 1998 (Simon Gagne), 1999 (Maxime Ouellet), 2000 (Justin Williams) and 2001 (later traded to Ottawa – Ottawa selected Tim Gleason) Entry Drafts, August 20, 1997. Traded to **Philadelphia** by **Tampa Bay** for Petr Svoboda, December 28, 1998. Traded to **Montreal** by **Philadelphia** for cash, October 20, 1999.

DYKSTRA, Steve

Defense. Shoots left. 6'2", 190 lbs. Born, Edmonton, Alta., December 1, 1962.

Season	Club	GP	G	A	Pts	PIM	GP	G	A	Pts	PIM
1985-86	Buffalo Sabres	64	4	21	25	108	....	....	....	....	....
1986-87	Buffalo Sabres	37	0	1	1	179	....	....	....	....	....
1987-88	Buffalo Sabres	27	1	1	2	91	....	....	....	....	....
	Edmonton Oilers	15	2	3	5	39	....	....	....	....	....
1988-89	Pittsburgh Penguins	65	1	6	7	126	1	0	0	0	2
1989-90	Hartford Whalers	9	0	0	0	2	....	....	....	....	....
	NHL Totals	**217**	**8**	**32**	**40**	**545**	**1**	**0**	**0**	**0**	**2**

Signed as a free agent by **Buffalo**, December 10, 1982. Traded to **Edmonton** by **Buffalo** with Buffalo's 7th round choice (Davis Payne) in 1989 Entry Draft for Scott Metcalfe and Edmonton's 9th round choice (Donald Audette) in 1989 Entry Draft, February 11, 1988. Claimed by **Pittsburgh** from **Edmonton** in Waiver Draft, October 3, 1988. Signed as a free agent by **Hartford**, October 9, 1989. Traded to **Boston** by **Hartford** for Jeff Sirkka, March 3, 1990.

DYTE, Jack

Defense. Shoots left. 6', 190 lbs. Born, New Liskeard, Ont., October 13, 1918.

Season	Club	GP	G	A	Pts	PIM	GP	G	A	Pts	PIM
1943-44	Chicago Black Hawks	27	1	0	1	31	....	....	....	....	....
	NHL Totals	**27**	**1**	**0**	**1**	**31**					

Signed as a free agent by **Chicago**, October 7, 1943. Traded to **Buffalo** (AHL) by **Chicago** for cash, June, 1944.

DZIEDZIC, Joe

Left wing. Shoots left. 6'3", 227 lbs. Born, Minneapolis, MN, December 18, 1971.
(Pittsburgh's 2nd choice, 61st overall, in 1990 Entry Draft).

Season	Club	GP	G	A	Pts	PIM	GP	G	A	Pts	PIM
1995-96	Pittsburgh Penguins	69	5	5	10	68	16	1	2	3	19
1996-97	Pittsburgh Penguins	59	9	9	18	63	5	0	1	1	4
1998-99	Phoenix Coyotes	2	0	0	0	0	....	....	....	....	....
	NHL Totals	**130**	**14**	**14**	**28**	**131**	**21**	**1**	**3**	**4**	**23**

Signed as a free agent by **Phoenix**, August 27, 1998.

EAGLES, Mike

Center/Left wing. Shoots left. 5'10", 195 lbs. Born, Sussex, N.B., March 7, 1963.
(Quebec's 5th choice, 116th overall, in 1981 Entry Draft).

Season	Club	GP	G	A	Pts	PIM	GP	G	A	Pts	PIM
1982-83	Quebec Nordiques	2	0	0	0	2	....	....	....	....	....
1985-86	Quebec Nordiques	73	11	12	23	49	3	0	0	0	2
1986-87	Quebec Nordiques	73	13	19	32	55	4	1	0	1	10
1987-88	Quebec Nordiques	76	10	10	20	74	....	....	....	....	....
1988-89	Chicago Blackhawks	47	5	11	16	44	....	....	....	....	....
1989-90	Chicago Blackhawks	23	1	2	3	34	....	....	....	....	....
1990-91	Winnipeg Jets	44	0	9	9	79	....	....	....	....	....
1991-92	Winnipeg Jets	65	7	10	17	118	7	0	0	0	8
1992-93	Winnipeg Jets	84	8	18	26	131	5	0	1	1	6
1993-94	Winnipeg Jets	73	4	8	12	96	....	....	....	....	....
1994-95	Winnipeg Jets	27	2	1	3	40	....	....	....	....	....
	Washington Capitals	13	1	3	4	8	7	0	2	2	4
1995-96	Washington Capitals	70	4	7	11	75	6	1	1	2	2
1996-97	Washington Capitals	70	1	7	8	42	....	....	....	....	....
1997-98	Washington Capitals	36	1	3	4	16	12	0	2	2	2
1998-99	Washington Capitals	52	4	2	6	50	....	....	....	....	....
99-2000	Washington Capitals	25	2	0	2	15	....	....	....	....	....
	NHL Totals	**853**	**74**	**122**	**196**	**928**	**44**	**2**	**6**	**8**	**34**

Traded to **Chicago** by **Quebec** for Bob Mason, July 5, 1988. Traded to **Winnipeg** by **Chicago** for Winnipeg's 4th round choice (Igor Kravchuk) in 1991 Entry Draft, December 14, 1990. Traded to **Washington** by **Winnipeg** with Igor Ulanov for Washington's 3rd (later traded to Dallas – Dallas selected Sergey Gusev) and 5th (Brian Elder) round choices in 1995 Entry Draft, April 7, 1995.

EAKIN, Bruce

Center. Shoots left. 5'11", 190 lbs. Born, Winnipeg, Man., September 28, 1962.
(Calgary's 9th choice, 204th overall, in 1981 Entry Draft).

Season	Club	GP	G	A	Pts	PIM	GP	G	A	Pts	PIM
1981-82	Calgary Flames	1	0	0	0	0	....	....	....	....	....
1983-84	Calgary Flames	7	2	1	3	4	....	....	....	....	....
1984-85	Calgary Flames	1	0	0	0	0	....	....	....	....	....
1985-86	Detroit Red Wings	4	0	1	1	0	....	....	....	....	....
	NHL Totals	**13**	**2**	**2**	**4**	**4**	....	....	....	....	....

Signed as a free agent by **Detroit**, July 18, 1985. Traded to **Edmonton** by **Detroit** for Billy Carroll, December 28, 1985.

EAKINS, Dallas

Defense. Shoots left. 6'2", 195 lbs. Born, Dade City, FL, February 27, 1967.
(Washington's 11th choice, 208th overall, in 1985 Entry Draft).

Season	Club	GP	G	A	Pts	PIM	GP	G	A	Pts	PIM
1992-93	Winnipeg Jets	14	0	2	2	38	....	....	....	....	....
1993-94	Florida Panthers	1	0	0	0	0	....	....	....	....	....
1994-95	Florida Panthers	17	0	1	1	35	....	....	....	....	....
1995-96	St. Louis Blues	16	0	1	1	34	....	....	....	....	....
	Winnipeg Jets	2	0	0	0	0	....	....	....	....	....
1996-97	Phoenix Coyotes	4	0	0	0	10	....	....	....	....	....
	New York Rangers	3	0	0	0	6	4	0	0	0	4
1997-98	Florida Panthers	23	0	1	1	44	....	....	....	....	....
1998-99	Toronto Maple Leafs	18	0	2	2	24	1	0	0	0	0
99-2000	New York Islanders	2	0	1	1	2	....	....	....	....	....
2000-01	Calgary Flames	17	0	1	1	11	....	....	....	....	....
2001-02	Calgary Flames	3	0	0	0	4	....	....	....	....	....
	NHL Totals	**120**	**0**	**9**	**9**	**208**	**5**	**0**	**0**	**0**	**4**

Signed as a free agent by **Winnipeg**, October 17, 1989. Signed as a free agent by **Florida**, July 8, 1993. Traded to **St. Louis** by **Florida** for St. Louis' 4th round choice (Ivan Novoseltsev) in 1997 Entry Draft, September 28, 1995. Claimed on waivers by **Winnipeg** from **St. Louis**, March 20, 1996. Transferred to **Phoenix** after **Winnipeg** franchise relocated, July 1, 1996. Traded to **NY Rangers** by **Phoenix** with Mike Eastwood for Jayson More, February 6, 1997. Signed as a free agent by **Florida**, July 30, 1997. Signed as a free agent by **Toronto**, July 28, 1998. Signed as a free agent by **NY Islanders**, August 17, 1999. Traded to **Chicago** by **NY Islanders** for future considerations, March 3, 2000. Signed as a free agent by **Calgary**, July 27, 2000. Signed as a free agent by **Atlanta**, July 23, 2002.

EASTWOOD, Mike

Center. Shoots right. 6'3", 213 lbs. Born, Ottawa, Ont., July 1, 1967.
(Toronto's 5th choice, 91st overall, in 1987 Entry Draft)

Season	Club	GP	G	A	Pts	PIM	GP	G	A	Pts	PIM
1991-92	Toronto Maple Leafs	9	0	2	2	4	....	....	....	....	....
1992-93	Toronto Maple Leafs	12	1	6	7	21	10	1	2	3	8
1993-94	Toronto Maple Leafs	54	8	10	18	28	18	3	2	5	12
1994-95	Toronto Maple Leafs	36	5	5	10	32	....	....	....	....	....
	Winnipeg Jets	13	3	6	9	4	....	....	....	....	....
1995-96	Winnipeg Jets	80	14	14	28	20	6	0	1	1	2
1996-97	Phoenix Coyotes	33	1	3	4	4	....	....	....	....	....
	New York Rangers	27	1	7	8	10	15	1	2	3	22
1997-98	New York Rangers	48	5	5	10	16	....	....	....	....	....
	St. Louis Blues	10	1	0	1	6	3	1	0	1	0
1998-99	St. Louis Blues	82	9	21	30	36	13	1	1	2	6
99-2000	St. Louis Blues	79	19	15	34	32	7	1	1	2	6
2000-01	St. Louis Blues	77	6	17	23	28	15	0	2	2	2
2001-02	St. Louis Blues	71	7	10	17	41	10	0	0	0	6
2002-03	St. Louis Blues	17	1	3	4	8	....	....	....	....	....
	Chicago Blackhawks	53	2	10	12	24	....	....	....	....	....
	NHL Totals	**701**	**83**	**134**	**217**	**314**	**97**	**8**	**11**	**19**	**64**

Traded to **Winnipeg** by **Toronto** with Toronto's 3rd round choice (Brad Isbister) in 1995 Entry Draft for Tie Domi, April 7, 1995. Transferred to **Phoenix** after **Winnipeg** franchise relocated, July 1, 1996. Traded to **NY Rangers** by **Phoenix** with Dallas Eakins for Jayson More, February 6, 1997. Traded to **St. Louis** by **NY Rangers** for Harry York, March 24, 1998. Claimed on waivers by **Chicago** from **St. Louis**, December 11, 2002.

EATON, Mark

Defense. Shoots left. 6'2", 205 lbs. Born, Wilmington, DE, May 6, 1977.

Season	Club	GP	G	A	Pts	PIM	GP	G	A	Pts	PIM
99-2000	Philadelphia Flyers	27	1	1	2	8	7	0	0	0	0
2000-01	Nashville Predators	34	3	8	11	14	....	....	....	....	....
2001-02	Nashville Predators	58	3	5	8	24	....	....	....	....	....
2002-03	Nashville Predators	50	2	7	9	22	....	....	....	....	....
	NHL Totals	**169**	**9**	**21**	**30**	**68**	**7**	**0**	**0**	**0**	**0**

Signed as a free agent by **Philadelphia**, August 4, 1998. Traded to **Nashville** by **Philadelphia** for Detroit's 3rd round choice (previously acquired, Philadelphia selected Patrick Sharp) in 2001 Entry Draft, September 29, 2000.

EATOUGH, Jeff

Right wing. Shoots right. 5'9", 168 lbs. Born, Toronto, Ont., June 2, 1963.
(Buffalo's 5th choice, 80th overall, in 1981 Entry Draft).

Season	Club	GP	G	A	Pts	PIM	GP	G	A	Pts	PIM
1981-82	Buffalo Sabres	1	0	0	0	0	....	....	....	....	....
	NHL Totals	**1**	**0**	**0**	**0**	**0**	....	....	....	....	....

EAVES, Mike

Center. Shoots right. 5'10", 180 lbs. Born, Denver, CO, June 10, 1956.
(St. Louis' 8th choice, 113th overall, in 1976 Amateur Draft).

Season	Club	GP	G	A	Pts	PIM	GP	G	A	Pts	PIM
		REGULAR SEASON					PLAYOFFS				
1978-79	Minnesota North Stars	3	0	0	0	0	....	....	....	....	....
1979-80	Minnesota North Stars	56	18	28	46	11	15	2	5	7	4
1980-81	Minnesota North Stars	48	10	24	34	18	....	....	....	....	....
1981-82	Minnesota North Stars	25	11	10	21	0	....	....	....	....	....
1982-83	Minnesota North Stars	75	16	16	32	21	9	0	0	0	0
1983-84	Calgary Flames	61	14	36	50	20	11	4	4	8	2
1984-85	Calgary Flames	56	14	29	43	10	....	....	....	....	....
1985-86	Calgary Flames	....	....	....	....	....	8	1	1	2	8
	NHL Totals	**324**	**83**	**143**	**226**	**80**	**43**	**7**	**10**	**17**	**14**

• Brother of Murray

Rights traded to **Cleveland** by **St. Louis** for Len Frig, August 17, 1977. Rights transferred to **Minnesota** Reserve List after **Cleveland-Minnesota** Dispersal Draft, June 15, 1978. Traded to **Calgary** by **Minnesota** with Keith Hanson fror Steve Christoff and Calgary's 2nd round choice (Frantisek Musil) in 1983 Entry Draft, June 8, 1983. • Suffered eventual career-ending head injury in exhibition game vs. Quebec, September 21, 1985. • Officially announced retirement and named Assistant Coach of **Calgary**, October 21, 1985. • Came out of retirement as an emergency injury replacement for Carey Wilson, May 4, 1986.

EAVES, Murray

Center. Shoots right. 5'10", 185 lbs. Born, Calgary, Alta., May 10, 1960.
(Winnipeg's 3rd choice, 44th overall, in 1980 Entry Draft).

Season	Club	GP	G	A	Pts	PIM	GP	G	A	Pts	PIM
1980-81	Winnipeg Jets	12	1	2	3	5	....	....	....	....	....
1981-82	Winnipeg Jets	2	0	0	0	0	....	....	....	....	....
1982-83	Winnipeg Jets	26	2	7	9	2	....	....	....	....	....
1983-84	Winnipeg Jets	2	0	0	0	0	2	0	0	0	2
1984-85	Winnipeg Jets	3	0	3	3	0	2	0	1	1	0
1985-86	Winnipeg Jets	4	1	0	1	0	....	....	....	....	....
1987-88	Detroit Red Wings	7	0	1	1	2	....	....	....	....	....
1989-90	Detroit Red Wings	1	0	0	0	0	....	....	....	....	....
	NHL Totals	**57**	**4**	**13**	**17**	**9**	**4**	**0**	**1**	**1**	**2**

• Brother of Mike

Traded to **Edmonton** by **Winnipeg** for future considerations, July 3, 1986. Signed as a free agent by **Detroit**, July 1, 1987.

ECCLESTONE, Tim

Left wing. Shoots right. 5'10", 195 lbs. Born, Toronto, Ont., September 24, 1947.
(NY Rangers' 2nd choice, 9th overall, in 1964 Amateur Draft).

Season	Club	GP	G	A	Pts	PIM	GP	G	A	Pts	PIM
1967-68	St. Louis Blues	50	6	8	14	16	12	1	2	3	2
1968-69	St. Louis Blues	68	11	23	34	31	12	2	2	4	20
1969-70	St. Louis Blues	65	16	21	37	59	16	3	4	7	48
1970-71	St. Louis Blues	47	15	24	39	34	....	....	....	....	....
	Detroit Red Wings	27	4	10	14	13	....	....	....	....	....
1971-72	Detroit Red Wings	72	18	35	53	33	....	....	....	....	....
1972-73	Detroit Red Wings	78	18	30	48	28	....	....	....	....	....
1973-74	Detroit Red Wings	14	0	5	5	6	....	....	....	....	....
	Toronto Maple Leafs	46	9	14	23	32	4	0	1	1	0
1974-75	Toronto Maple Leafs	5	1	1	2	0	....	....	....	....	....
	Atlanta Flames	62	13	21	34	34	....	....	....	....	....
1975-76	Atlanta Flames	69	6	21	27	30	....	....	....	....	....
1976-77	Atlanta Flames	78	9	18	27	26	3	0	2	2	6
1977-78	Atlanta Flames	11	0	2	2	2	1	0	0	0	0
	NHL Totals	**692**	**126**	**233**	**359**	**344**	**48**	**6**	**11**	**17**	**76**

Played in NHL All-Star Game (1971)

Traded to **St. Louis** by **NY Rangers** with Gary Sabourin, Bob Plager and Gord Kannegiesser for Rod Seiling, June 6, 1967. Traded to **Detroit** by **St. Louis** with Red Berenson for Garry Unger and Wayne Connelly, February 6, 1971. Traded to **Toronto** by **Detroit** for Pierre Jarry, November 29, 1973. Traded to **Washington** by **Toronto** with Willie Brossart for Rod Seiling, November 2, 1974. Traded to **Atlanta** by **Washington** for cash, November 2, 1974.

EDBERG, Rolf

Center. Shoots left. 5'10", 174 lbs. Born, Stockholm, Sweden, September 29, 1950.

Season	Club	GP	G	A	Pts	PIM	GP	G	A	Pts	PIM
1978-79	Washington Capitals	76	14	27	41	6	....	....	....	....	....
1979-80	Washington Capitals	63	23	23	46	12	....	....	....	....	....
1980-81	Washington Capitals	45	8	8	16	6	....	....	....	....	....
	NHL Totals	**184**	**45**	**58**	**103**	**24**	....	....	....	....	....

Signed as a free agent by **Washington**, June 10, 1978.

EDDOLLS, Frank

Defense. Shoots left. 5'8", 180 lbs. Born, Lachine, Que., July 5, 1921.

Season	Club	GP	G	A	Pts	PIM	GP	G	A	Pts	PIM
1944-45	Montreal Canadiens	43	5	8	13	20	3	0	0	0	0
1945-46♦	Montreal Canadiens	8	0	1	1	6	8	0	1	1	2
1946-47	Montreal Canadiens	6	0	0	0	0	7	0	0	0	4
1947-48	New York Rangers	58	6	13	19	16	2	0	0	0	0
1948-49	New York Rangers	34	4	2	6	10	....	....	....	....	....
1949-50	New York Rangers	58	2	6	8	20	11	0	1	1	4
1950-51	New York Rangers	68	3	8	11	24	....	....	....	....	....
1951-52	New York Rangers	42	3	5	8	18	....	....	....	....	....
	NHL Totals	**317**	**23**	**43**	**66**	**114**	**31**	**0**	**2**	**2**	**10**

Played in NHL All-Star Game (1951)

Rights traded to **Toronto** by **Montreal** for the rights to Joe Benoit, June 7, 1940. Rights traded to **Montreal** by **Toronto** for the rights to Ted Kennedy, September 10, 1943. Loaned to **Buffalo** (AHL) by **Montreal** with Wilf Field, Kenny Mosdell and cash for the loan of Lorrain Thibeault, October 24, 1945. Traded to **NY Rangers** by **Montreal** with Buddy O'Connor for Hal Laycoe, Joe Bell and George Robertson, August 19, 1947. • Missed majority of 1948-49 season recovering from knee injury suffered in automobile accident, October 8, 1948. Traded to **Montreal** by **NY Rangers** for cash, October 8, 1952.

EDESTRAND, Darryl

Defense. Shoots left. 5'11", 180 lbs. Born, Strathroy, Ont., November 6, 1945.

Season	Club	GP	G	A	Pts	PIM	GP	G	A	Pts	PIM
1967-68	St. Louis Blues	12	0	0	0	2	....	....	....	....	....
1969-70	Philadelphia Flyers	2	0	0	0	6	....	....	....	....	....
1971-72	Pittsburgh Penguins	77	10	23	33	52	4	0	2	2	0
1972-73	Pittsburgh Penguins	78	15	24	39	88	....	....	....	....	....
1973-74	Pittsburgh Penguins	3	0	0	0	0	....	....	....	....	....
	Boston Bruins	52	3	8	11	20	16	1	2	3	15
1974-75	Boston Bruins	68	1	9	10	56	3	0	1	1	7
1975-76	Boston Bruins	77	4	17	21	103	12	1	3	4	23
1976-77	Boston Bruins	17	0	3	3	16	3	0	0	0	2
1977-78	Boston Bruins	1	0	0	0	0	....	....	....	....	....
	Los Angeles Kings	13	0	2	2	15	2	1	1	2	4
1978-79	Los Angeles Kings	55	1	4	5	46	2	0	0	0	6
	NHL Totals	**455**	**34**	**90**	**124**	**404**	**42**	**3**	**9**	**12**	**57**

Claimed by **St. Louis** from **Toronto** in Expansion Draft, June 6, 1967. Traded to **Philadelphia** by **St. Louis** with Gerry Melynk for Lou Angotti and Ian Campbell, June 11, 1968. Traded to **Pittsburgh** (Hershey-AHL) by **Philadelphia** with Larry McKillop for Barry Ashbee, May 22, 1970. Traded to **Boston** by **Pittsburgh** for Nick Beverley, October 25, 1973. Traded to **Los Angeles** by **Boston** for cash, March 13, 1978. Claimed by **Los Angeles** as a fill-in during Expansion Draft, June 13, 1979.

EDMUNDSON, Garry

Left wing. Shoots left. 6', 173 lbs. Born, Sexsmith, Alta., May 6, 1932.

Season	Club	GP	G	A	Pts	PIM	GP	G	A	Pts	PIM
1951-52	Montreal Canadiens	1	0	0	0	2	2	0	0	0	4
1959-60	Toronto Maple Leafs	39	4	6	10	47	9	0	1	1	4
1960-61	Toronto Maple Leafs	3	0	0	0	0	....	....	....	....	....
	NHL Totals	**43**	**4**	**6**	**10**	**49**	**11**	**0**	**1**	**1**	**8**

Traded to **Toronto** by **Springfield** (AHL) for Frank Roggeveen, June 9, 1959.

EDUR, Tom

Defense. Shoots right. 6'1", 185 lbs. Born, Toronto, Ont., November 18, 1954.
(Boston's 4th choice, 54th overall, in 1974 Amateur Draft).

Season	Club	GP	G	A	Pts	PIM	GP	G	A	Pts	PIM
1976-77	Colorado Rockies	80	7	25	32	39	....	....	....	....	....
1977-78	Colorado Rockies	20	5	7	12	10	....	....	....	....	....
	Pittsburgh Penguins	58	5	38	43	18	....	....	....	....	....
	NHL Totals	**158**	**17**	**70**	**87**	**67**	....	....	....	....	....

Rights traded to **Colorado** by **Boston** for cash, September 7, 1977. Traded to **Pittsburgh** by **Colorado** for Dennis Owchar, December 2, 1977. • Retired following 1977-78 season to study Christianity, July, 1978. Selected by **Edmonton** from **Pittsburgh** in 1979 Expansion Draft, June 13, 1979.

EGAN, Pat

Defense. Shoots right. 5'10", 195 lbs. Born, Blackie, Alta., April 25, 1918.

Season	Club	GP	G	A	Pts	PIM	GP	G	A	Pts	PIM
1939-40	New York Americans	10	4	3	7	6	2	0	0	0	4
1940-41	New York Americans	39	4	9	13	51	....	....	....	....	....
1941-42	Brooklyn Americans	48	8	20	28	*124	....	....	....	....	....
1943-44	Detroit Red Wings	23	4	15	19	40	....	....	....	....	....
	Boston Bruins	25	11	13	24	55	....	....	....	....	....
1944-45	Boston Bruins	48	7	15	22	*86	7	2	0	2	6
1945-46	Boston Bruins	41	8	10	18	32	10	3	0	3	8
1946-47	Boston Bruins	60	7	18	25	89	5	0	2	2	6
1947-48	Boston Bruins	60	8	11	19	81	5	1	1	2	2
1948-49	Boston Bruins	60	6	18	24	92	5	0	0	0	16
1949-50	New York Rangers	70	5	11	16	50	12	3	1	4	6
1950-51	New York Rangers	70	5	10	15	70	....	....	....	....	....
	NHL Totals	**554**	**77**	**153**	**230**	**776**	**46**	**9**	**4**	**13**	**48**

NHL Second All-Star Team (1942)

Played in NHL All-Star Game (1949)

Signed as a free agent by **NY Americans**, October 13, 1939. • Team name changed to **Brooklyn Americans** prior to 1941-42 season. Rights transferred to **Detroit** from **Brooklyn** in Special Dispersal Draw, October 9, 1942. Traded to **Boston** by **Detroit** for Flash Hollett, January 5, 1944. Traded to **NY Rangers** by **Boston** for Bill Moe, the rights to Lorne Ferguson and future considerations, October 7, 1949. Traded to **Providence** (AHL) by **NY Rangers** with Zellio Toppazzini and Jean-Paul Denis for Jack Stoddard, January 1, 1952.

EGELAND, Allan

Center. Shoots left. 6', 175 lbs. Born, Lethbridge, Alta., January 31, 1973.
(Tampa Bay's 3rd choice, 55th overall, in 1993 Entry Draft).

Season	Club	GP	G	A	Pts	PIM	GP	G	A	Pts	PIM
1995-96	Tampa Bay Lightning	5	0	0	0	2	....	....	....	....	....
1996-97	Tampa Bay Lightning	4	0	0	0	5	....	....	....	....	....
1997-98	Tampa Bay Lightning	8	0	0	0	9	....	....	....	....	....
	NHL Totals	**17**	**0**	**0**	**0**	**16**	....	....	....	....	....

Signed as a free agent by **Calgary**, July 20, 1999. Traded to **Los Angeles** by **Calgary** for future considerations, February 18, 2000.

EGERS, Jack

Right wing. Shoots left. 6'1", 175 lbs. Born, Sudbury, Ont., January 28, 1949.
(NY Rangers' 4th choice, 20th overall, in 1966 Amateur Draft).

Season	Club	REGULAR SEASON GP	G	A	Pts	PIM	PLAYOFFS GP	G	A	Pts	PIM
1969-70	New York Rangers	6	3	0	3	2	5	3	1	4	10
1970-71	New York Rangers	60	7	10	17	50	3	0	0	0	2
1971-72	New York Rangers	17	2	1	3	14	....	....	....	....	....
	St. Louis Blues	63	21	25	46	34	11	1	4	5	14
1972-73	St. Louis Blues	78	24	24	48	26	5	0	1	1	2
1973-74	St. Louis Blues	6	0	1	1	6	....	....	....	....	....
	New York Rangers	28	1	3	4	6	8	1	0	1	4
1974-75	Washington Capitals	14	3	2	5	8	....	....	....	....	....
1975-76	Washington Capitals	12	3	3	6	8	....	....	....	....	....
	NHL Totals	**284**	**64**	**69**	**133**	**154**	**32**	**5**	**6**	**11**	**32**

Traded to **St. Louis** by **NY Rangers** with Andre Dupont and Mike Murphy for Gene Carr, Jim Lorentz and Wayne Connelly, November 15, 1971. Traded to **NY Rangers** by **St. Louis** for Glen Sather and Rene Villemure, October 28, 1973. Claimed by **Washington** from **NY Rangers** in Expansion Draft, June 12, 1974.

EHMAN, Gerry

Right wing. Shoots right. 6', 190 lbs. Born, Cudworth, Sask., November 3, 1932.

Season	Club	REGULAR SEASON GP	G	A	Pts	PIM	PLAYOFFS GP	G	A	Pts	PIM
1957-58	Boston Bruins	1	1	0	1	0	....	....	....	....	....
1958-59	Detroit Red Wings	6	0	1	1	4	....	....	....	....	....
	Toronto Maple Leafs	38	12	13	25	12	12	6	7	13	8
1959-60	Toronto Maple Leafs	69	12	16	28	26	9	0	0	0	0
1960-61	Toronto Maple Leafs	14	1	1	2	2	....	....	....	....	....
1963-64 ♦	Toronto Maple Leafs	4	1	1	2	0	9	1	0	1	4
1967-68	Oakland Seals	73	19	25	44	20	....	....	....	....	....
1968-69	Oakland Seals	70	21	24	45	12	7	2	2	4	0
1969-70	Oakland Seals	76	11	19	30	8	4	1	1	2	0
1970-71	California Seals	78	18	18	36	16	....	....	....	....	....
	NHL Totals	**429**	**96**	**118**	**214**	**100**	**41**	**10**	**10**	**20**	**12**

Played in NHL All-Star Game (1964)

Claimed by **Boston** (Springfield-AHL) from **Detroit** (Edmonton-WHL) in Inter-League Draft, June 1, 1953. Traded to **Detroit** by **Springfield** (AHL) for Hank Bassen, Dennis Olson and Bill McCreary, May 1, 1958. Traded to **Toronto** by **Detroit** (Hershey-AHL) for cash and the loan of Willie Marshall, December 23, 1958. Traded to **Oakland** by **Toronto** (Rochester-AHL) for Bryan Hextall Jr. and J.P. Parise, October 12, 1967.

EISENHUT, Neil

Center. Shoots left. 6'1", 190 lbs. Born, Osoyoos, B.C., February 9, 1967.
(Vancouver's 11th choice, 233rd overall, in 1987 Entry Draft).

Season	Club	REGULAR SEASON GP	G	A	Pts	PIM	PLAYOFFS GP	G	A	Pts	PIM
1993-94	Vancouver Canucks	13	1	3	4	21	....	....	....	....	....
1994-95	Calgary Flames	3	0	0	0	0	....	....	....	....	....
	NHL Totals	**16**	**1**	**3**	**4**	**21**	....	....	....	....	....

Signed as a free agent by **Calgary**, June 16, 1994.

EKLUND, Pelle

Center. Shoots left. 5'10", 175 lbs. Born, Stockholm, Sweden, March 22, 1963.
(Philadelphia's 7th choice, 167th overall, in 1983 Entry Draft).

Season	Club	REGULAR SEASON GP	G	A	Pts	PIM	PLAYOFFS GP	G	A	Pts	PIM
1985-86	Philadelphia Flyers	70	15	51	66	12	5	0	2	2	0
1986-87	Philadelphia Flyers	72	14	41	55	2	26	7	20	27	2
1987-88	Philadelphia Flyers	71	10	32	42	12	7	0	3	3	0
1988-89	Philadelphia Flyers	79	18	51	69	23	19	3	8	11	2
1989-90	Philadelphia Flyers	70	23	39	62	16	....	....	....	....	....
1990-91	Philadelphia Flyers	73	19	50	69	14	....	....	....	....	....
1991-92	Philadelphia Flyers	51	7	16	23	4	....	....	....	....	....
1992-93	Philadelphia Flyers	55	11	38	49	16	....	....	....	....	....
1993-94	Philadelphia Flyers	48	1	16	17	8	....	....	....	....	....
	Dallas Stars	5	2	1	3	2	9	0	3	3	4
	NHL Totals	**594**	**120**	**335**	**455**	**109**	**66**	**10**	**36**	**46**	**8**

Traded to **Dallas** by **Philadelphia** for Dallas' 8th round choice (Raymond Giroux) in 1994 Entry Draft, March 21, 1994.

EKMAN, Nils

Left wing. Shoots left. 5'11", 185 lbs. Born, Stockholm, Sweden, March 11, 1976.
(Calgary's 6th choice, 107th overall, in 1994 Entry Draft).

Season	Club	REGULAR SEASON GP	G	A	Pts	PIM	PLAYOFFS GP	G	A	Pts	PIM
99-2000	Tampa Bay Lightning	28	2	2	4	36	....	....	....	....	....
2000-01	Tampa Bay Lightning	43	9	11	20	40	....	....	....	....	....
	NHL Totals	**71**	**11**	**13**	**24**	**76**	....	....	....	....	....

Traded to **Tampa Bay** by **Calgary** with Calgary's 4th round choice (later traded to NY Islanders – NY Islanders selected Vladimir Gorbunov) in 2000 Entry Draft for Andreas Johansson, November 20, 1999. Traded to **NY Rangers** by **Tampa Bay** with Kyle Freadrich for Tim Taylor, June 30, 2001.

ELDEBRINK, Anders

Defense. Shoots right. 5'11", 190 lbs. Born, Kalix, Sweden, December 11, 1960.

Season	Club	REGULAR SEASON GP	G	A	Pts	PIM	PLAYOFFS GP	G	A	Pts	PIM
1981-82	Vancouver Canucks	38	1	8	9	21	13	0	0	0	10
1982-83	Vancouver Canucks	5	1	1	2	0	....	....	....	....	....
	Quebec Nordiques	12	1	2	3	8	1	0	0	0	0
	NHL Totals	**55**	**3**	**11**	**14**	**29**	**14**	**0**	**0**	**0**	**10**

Signed as a free agent by **Vancouver**, May 18, 1981. Traded to **Quebec** by **Vancouver** for John Garrett, February 4, 1983.

ELIAS, Patrik

Center. Shoots left. 6'1", 195 lbs. Born, Trebic, Czech., April 13, 1976.
(New Jersey's 2nd choice, 51st overall, in 1994 Entry Draft).

Season	Club	REGULAR SEASON GP	G	A	Pts	PIM	PLAYOFFS GP	G	A	Pts	PIM
1995-96	New Jersey Devils	1	0	0	0	0	....	....	....	....	....
1996-97	New Jersey Devils	17	2	3	5	2	8	2	3	5	4
1997-98	New Jersey Devils	74	18	19	37	28	4	0	1	1	0
1998-99	New Jersey Devils	74	17	33	50	34	7	0	5	5	6
99-2000 ♦	New Jersey Devils	72	35	37	72	58	23	7	*13	20	9
2000-01	New Jersey Devils	82	40	56	96	51	25	9	14	23	10
2001-02	New Jersey Devils	75	29	32	61	36	6	2	4	6	6
2002-03 ♦	New Jersey Devils	81	28	29	57	22	24	5	8	13	26
	NHL Totals	**476**	**169**	**209**	**378**	**231**	**97**	**25**	**48**	**73**	**61**

NHL All-Rookie Team (1998) • NHL First All-Star Team (2001)

Played in NHL All-Star Game (2000, 2002)

ELICH, Matt

Right wing. Shoots right. 6'3", 196 lbs. Born, Detroit, MI, September 22, 1979.
(Tampa Bay's 3rd choice, 61st overall, in 1997 Entry Draft).

Season	Club	REGULAR SEASON GP	G	A	Pts	PIM	PLAYOFFS GP	G	A	Pts	PIM
99-2000	Tampa Bay Lightning	8	1	1	2	0	....	....	....	....	....
2000-01	Tampa Bay Lightning	8	0	0	0	0	....	....	....	....	....
	NHL Totals	**16**	**1**	**1**	**2**	**0**	....	....	....	....	....

ELIK, Bo

Left wing. Shoots left. 5'11", 190 lbs. Born, Geraldton, Ont., October 17, 1929.

Season	Club	REGULAR SEASON GP	G	A	Pts	PIM	PLAYOFFS GP	G	A	Pts	PIM
1962-63	Detroit Red Wings	3	0	0	0	0	....	....	....	....	....
	NHL Totals	**3**	**0**	**0**	**0**	**0**	....	....	....	....	....

Traded to **Boston** (Providence-AHL) by **Toronto** (Rochester-AHL) for Gord Redahl, November 21, 1958.

ELIK, Todd

Center. Shoots left. 6'2", 195 lbs. Born, Brampton, Ont., April 15, 1966.

Season	Club	REGULAR SEASON GP	G	A	Pts	PIM	PLAYOFFS GP	G	A	Pts	PIM
1989-90	Los Angeles Kings	48	10	23	33	41	10	3	9	12	10
1990-91	Los Angeles Kings	74	21	37	58	58	12	2	7	9	6
1991-92	Minnesota North Stars	62	14	32	46	125	5	1	1	2	2
1992-93	Minnesota North Stars	46	13	18	31	48	....	....	....	....	....
	Edmonton Oilers	14	1	9	10	8	....	....	....	....	....
1993-94	Edmonton Oilers	4	0	0	0	6	....	....	....	....	....
	San Jose Sharks	75	25	41	66	89	14	5	5	10	12
1994-95	San Jose Sharks	22	7	10	17	18	....	....	....	....	....
	St. Louis Blues	13	2	4	6	4	7	4	3	7	2
1995-96	Boston Bruins	59	13	33	46	40	4	0	2	2	16
1996-97	Boston Bruins	31	4	12	16	16	....	....	....	....	....
	NHL Totals	**448**	**110**	**219**	**329**	**453**	**52**	**15**	**27**	**42**	**48**

Signed as a free agent by **NY Rangers**, February 26, 1988. Traded to **Los Angeles** by **NY Rangers** with Igor Liba, Michael Boyce and future considerations for Dean Kennedy and Denis Larocque, December 12, 1988. Traded to **Minnesota** by **Los Angeles** for Randy Gilhen, Charlie Huddy, Jim Thomson and NY Rangers' 4th round choice (previously acquired, Los Angeles selected Alexei Zhitnik) in 1991 Entry Draft, June 22, 1991. Traded to **Edmonton** by **Minnesota** for Brent Gilchrist, March 5, 1993. Claimed on waivers by **San Jose** from **Edmonton**, October 26, 1993. Traded to **St. Louis** by **San Jose** for Kevin Miller, March 23, 1995. Signed as a free agent by **Boston**, August 8, 1995.

ELLETT, Dave

Defense. Shoots left. 6'2", 205 lbs. Born, Cleveland, OH, March 30, 1964.
(Winnipeg's 3rd choice, 75th overall, in 1982 Entry Draft).

Season	Club	REGULAR SEASON GP	G	A	Pts	PIM	PLAYOFFS GP	G	A	Pts	PIM
1984-85	Winnipeg Jets	80	11	27	38	85	8	1	5	6	4
1985-86	Winnipeg Jets	80	15	31	46	96	3	0	1	1	0
1986-87	Winnipeg Jets	78	13	31	44	53	10	0	8	8	2
1987-88	Winnipeg Jets	68	13	45	58	106	5	1	2	3	10
1988-89	Winnipeg Jets	75	22	34	56	62	....	....	....	....	....
1989-90	Winnipeg Jets	77	17	29	46	96	7	2	0	2	6
1990-91	Winnipeg Jets	17	4	7	11	6	....	....	....	....	....
	Toronto Maple Leafs	60	8	30	38	69	....	....	....	....	....
1991-92	Toronto Maple Leafs	79	18	33	51	95	....	....	....	....	....
1992-93	Toronto Maple Leafs	70	6	34	40	46	21	4	8	12	8
1993-94	Toronto Maple Leafs	68	7	36	43	42	18	3	15	18	31
1994-95	Toronto Maple Leafs	33	5	10	15	26	7	0	2	2	0
1995-96	Toronto Maple Leafs	80	3	19	22	59	6	0	0	0	4
1996-97	Toronto Maple Leafs	56	4	10	14	34	....	....	....	....	....
	New Jersey Devils	20	2	5	7	6	10	0	3	3	10
1997-98	Boston Bruins	82	3	20	23	67	6	0	1	1	6
1998-99	Boston Bruins	54	0	6	6	25	8	0	0	0	4
99-2000	St. Louis Blues	52	2	8	10	12	7	0	1	1	2
	NHL Totals	**1129**	**153**	**415**	**568**	**985**	**116**	**11**	**46**	**57**	**87**

Played in NHL All-Star Game (1989, 1992)

Traded to **Toronto** by **Winnipeg** with Paul Fenton for Ed Olczyk and Mark Osborne, November 10, 1990. Traded to **New Jersey** by **Toronto** with Doug Gilmour and New Jersey's 3rd round choice (previously acquired, New Jersey selected Andre Lakos) in 1999 Entry Draft for Jason Smith, Steve Sullivan and the rights to Alyn McCauley, February 25, 1997. Signed as a free agent by **Boston**, July 29, 1997. Signed as a free agent by **St. Louis**, October 22, 1999. • Officially announced retirement, September 8, 2000.

ELLIOTT, Fred

Right wing. Shoots right. 5'8", 165 lbs. Born, Clinton, Ont., February 18, 1903.

Season	Club	Regular Season GP	G	A	Pts	PIM	Playoffs GP	G	A	Pts	PIM
1928-29	Ottawa Senators	43	2	0	2	6	....	....	....	....	....
	NHL Totals	**43**	**2**	**0**	**2**	**6**	....	....	....	....	....

Traded to **Mtl. Maroons** by **Toronto** for George Horne, October 1, 1928. Loaned to **Ottawa** by **Mtl. Maroons** for 1928-29 season for cash, November 13, 1928.

ELLIS, Ron

Right wing. Shoots right. 5'9", 195 lbs. Born, Lindsay, Ont., January 8, 1945.

Season	Club	Regular Season GP	G	A	Pts	PIM	Playoffs GP	G	A	Pts	PIM
1963-64	Toronto Maple Leafs	1	0	0	0	0	....	....	....	....	....
1964-65	Toronto Maple Leafs	62	23	16	39	14	6	3	0	3	2
1965-66	Toronto Maple Leafs	70	19	23	42	24	4	0	0	0	2
1966-67 ♦	Toronto Maple Leafs	67	22	23	45	14	12	2	1	3	4
1967-68	Toronto Maple Leafs	74	28	20	48	8	....	....	....	....	....
1968-69	Toronto Maple Leafs	72	25	21	46	12	4	2	1	3	2
1969-70	Toronto Maple Leafs	76	35	19	54	14	....	....	....	....	....
1970-71	Toronto Maple Leafs	78	24	29	53	10	6	1	1	2	2
1971-72	Toronto Maple Leafs	78	23	24	47	17	5	1	1	2	4
1972-73	Toronto Maple Leafs	78	22	29	51	22	....	....	....	....	....
1973-74	Toronto Maple Leafs	70	23	25	48	12	4	2	1	3	0
1974-75	Toronto Maple Leafs	79	32	29	61	25	7	3	0	3	2
1977-78	Toronto Maple Leafs	80	26	24	50	17	13	3	2	5	0
1978-79	Toronto Maple Leafs	63	16	12	28	10	6	1	1	2	2
1979-80	Toronto Maple Leafs	59	12	11	23	6	3	0	0	0	0
1980-81	Toronto Maple Leafs	27	2	3	5	2	....	....	....	....	....
	NHL Totals	**1034**	**332**	**308**	**640**	**207**	**70**	**18**	**8**	**26**	**20**

Played in NHL All-Star Game (1964, 1965, 1968, 1970)

ELOMO, Miika

Left wing. Shoots left. 6', 200 lbs. Born, Turku, Finland, April 21, 1977.
(Washington's 2nd choice, 23rd overall, in 1995 Entry Draft).

Season	Club	Regular Season GP	G	A	Pts	PIM	Playoffs GP	G	A	Pts	PIM
99-2000	Washington Capitals	2	0	1	1	2	....	....	....	....	....
	NHL Totals	**2**	**0**	**1**	**1**	**2**	....	....	....	....	....

Traded to **Calgary** by **Washington** with Buffalo's compensatory 4th round choice (previously acquired, Calgary selected Levente Szuper) in 2000 Entry Draft for Anaheim's 2nd round choice (previously acquired, Washington selected Matt Pettinger) in 2000 Entry Draft, June 24, 2000.

ELORANTA, Kari

Defense. Shoots left. 6'2", 200 lbs. Born, Lahti, Finland, February 29, 1956.

Season	Club	Regular Season GP	G	A	Pts	PIM	Playoffs GP	G	A	Pts	PIM
1981-82	Calgary Flames	19	0	5	5	14	....	....	....	....	....
	St. Louis Blues	12	1	7	8	6	5	0	0	0	0
1982-83	Calgary Flames	80	4	40	44	43	9	1	3	4	17
1983-84	Calgary Flames	78	5	34	39	44	6	0	2	2	2
1984-85	Calgary Flames	65	2	11	13	39	....	....	....	....	....
1986-87	Calgary Flames	13	1	6	7	9	6	0	2	2	0
	NHL Totals	**267**	**13**	**103**	**116**	**155**	**26**	**1**	**7**	**8**	**19**

Signed as a free agent by **Calgary**, September 15, 1981. Traded to **St. Louis** by **Calgary** for future considerations, March 8, 1982. Traded to **Calgary** by **St. Louis** for cash, June 3, 1982.

ELORANTA, Mikko

Left wing. Shoots left. 6', 190 lbs. Born, Turku, Finland, August 24, 1972.
(Boston's 9th choice, 247th overall, in 1999 Entry Draft).

Season	Club	Regular Season GP	G	A	Pts	PIM	Playoffs GP	G	A	Pts	PIM
99-2000	Boston Bruins	50	6	12	18	36	....	....	....	....	....
2000-01	Boston Bruins	62	12	11	23	38	....	....	....	....	....
2001-02	Boston Bruins	6	0	0	0	2	....	....	....	....	....
	Los Angeles Kings	71	9	9	18	54	7	1	1	2	2
2002-03	Los Angeles Kings	75	5	12	17	56	....	....	....	....	....
	NHL Totals	**264**	**32**	**44**	**76**	**186**	**7**	**1**	**1**	**2**	**2**

Traded to **Los Angeles** by **Boston** with Jason Allison for Jozef Stumpel and Glen Murray, October 24, 2001.

ELYNUIK, Pat

Right wing. Shoots right. 6', 185 lbs. Born, Foam Lake, Sask., October 30, 1967.
(Winnipeg's 1st choice, 8th overall, in 1986 Entry Draft).

Season	Club	Regular Season GP	G	A	Pts	PIM	Playoffs GP	G	A	Pts	PIM
1987-88	Winnipeg Jets	13	1	3	4	12	....	....	....	....	....
1988-89	Winnipeg Jets	56	26	25	51	29	....	....	....	....	....
1989-90	Winnipeg Jets	80	32	42	74	83	7	2	4	6	2
1990-91	Winnipeg Jets	80	31	34	65	73	....	....	....	....	....
1991-92	Winnipeg Jets	60	25	25	50	65	7	2	2	4	4
1992-93	Washington Capitals	80	22	35	57	66	6	2	3	5	19
1993-94	Washington Capitals	4	1	1	2	0	....	....	....	....	....
	Tampa Bay Lightning	63	12	14	26	64	....	....	....	....	....
1994-95	Ottawa Senators	41	3	7	10	51	....	....	....	....	....
1995-96	Ottawa Senators	29	1	2	3	16	....	....	....	....	....
	NHL Totals	**506**	**154**	**188**	**342**	**459**	**20**	**6**	**9**	**15**	**25**

Traded to **Washington** by **Winnipeg** for John Druce and Toronto's 4th round choice (previously acquired by Washington – later traded to Detroit – Detroit selected John Jakopin) in 1993 Entry Draft, October 1, 1992. Traded to **Tampa Bay** by **Washington** for a conditional draft choice (later traded back to Tampa Bay in the Joe Reekie trade, March 21, 1994), October 22, 1993. Signed as a free agent by **Ottawa**, June 21, 1994. Signed as a free agent by **Dallas**, September 6, 1996.

EMBERG, Eddie

Center. Shoots left. 5'10", 160 lbs. Born, Montreal, Que., November 18, 1921.

Season	Club	Regular Season GP	G	A	Pts	PIM	Playoffs GP	G	A	Pts	PIM
1944-45	Montreal Canadiens	....	....	....	....	....	2	1	0	1	0
	NHL Totals	....	....	....	....	....	**2**	**1**	**0**	**1**	**0**

EMERSON, Nelson

Right wing. Shoots right. 5'11", 180 lbs. Born, Hamilton, Ont., August 17, 1967.
(St. Louis' 2nd choice, 44th overall, in 1985 Entry Draft).

Season	Club	Regular Season GP	G	A	Pts	PIM	Playoffs GP	G	A	Pts	PIM
1990-91	St. Louis Blues	4	0	3	3	2	....	....	....	....	....
1991-92	St. Louis Blues	79	23	36	59	66	6	3	3	6	21
1992-93	St. Louis Blues	82	22	51	73	62	11	1	6	7	6
1993-94	Winnipeg Jets	83	33	41	74	80	....	....	....	....	....
1994-95	Winnipeg Jets	48	14	23	37	26	....	....	....	....	....
1995-96	Hartford Whalers	81	29	29	58	78	....	....	....	....	....
1996-97	Hartford Whalers	66	9	29	38	34	....	....	....	....	....
1997-98	Carolina Hurricanes	81	21	24	45	50	....	....	....	....	....
1998-99	Carolina Hurricanes	35	8	13	21	36	....	....	....	....	....
	Chicago Blackhawks	27	4	10	14	13	....	....	....	....	....
	Ottawa Senators	3	1	1	2	2	4	1	3	4	0
99-2000	Atlanta Thrashers	58	14	19	33	47	....	....	....	....	....
	Los Angeles Kings	5	1	1	2	0	1	0	0	0	0
2000-01	Los Angeles Kings	78	11	11	22	54	13	2	2	4	4
2001-02	Los Angeles Kings	41	5	2	7	25	5	0	1	1	2
	NHL Totals	**771**	**195**	**293**	**488**	**575**	**40**	**7**	**15**	**22**	**33**

Traded to **Winnipeg** by **St. Louis** with Stephane Quintal for Phil Housley, September 24, 1993. Traded to **Hartford** by **Winnipeg** for Darren Turcotte, October 6, 1995. Transferred to **Carolina** after **Hartford** franchise relocated, June 25, 1997. Traded to **Chicago** by **Carolina** for Paul Coffey, December 29, 1998. Traded to **Ottawa** by **Chicago** for Chris Murray, March 23, 1999. Signed as a free agent by **Atlanta**, August 3, 1999. Traded to **Los Angeles** by **Atlanta** with Kelly Buchberger for Donald Audette and Frantisek Kaberle, March 13, 2000.

EMINGER, Steve

Defense. Shoots right. 6'1", 196 lbs. Born, Woodbridge, Ont., October 31, 1983.
(Washington's 1st choice, 12th overall, in 2002 Entry Draft).

Season	Club	Regular Season GP	G	A	Pts	PIM	Playoffs GP	G	A	Pts	PIM
2002-03	Washington Capitals	17	0	2	2	24	....	....	....	....	....
	NHL Totals	**17**	**0**	**2**	**2**	**24**	....	....	....	....	....

EMMA, David

Center. Shoots left. 5'10", 185 lbs. Born, Cranston, RI, January 14, 1969.
(New Jersey's 6th choice, 110th overall, in 1989 Entry Draft).

Season	Club	Regular Season GP	G	A	Pts	PIM	Playoffs GP	G	A	Pts	PIM
1992-93	New Jersey Devils	2	0	0	0	0	....	....	....	....	....
1993-94	New Jersey Devils	15	5	5	10	2	....	....	....	....	....
1994-95	New Jersey Devils	6	0	1	1	0	....	....	....	....	....
1996-97	Boston Bruins	5	0	0	0	0	....	....	....	....	....
2000-01	Florida Panthers	6	0	0	0	0	....	....	....	....	....
	NHL Totals	**34**	**5**	**6**	**11**	**2**	....	....	....	....	....

Signed as a free agent by **Boston**, August 27, 1996. Signed as a free agent by **Florida**, August 1, 2000. Traded to **Washington** by **Florida** for Remi Royer, March 3, 2001.

EMMONS, Gary

Center. Shoots right. 6', 185 lbs. Born, Winnipeg, Man., December 30, 1963.
(NY Rangers' 1st choice, 14th overall, in 1986 Supplemental Draft).

Season	Club	Regular Season GP	G	A	Pts	PIM	Playoffs GP	G	A	Pts	PIM
1993-94	San Jose Sharks	3	1	0	1	0	....	....	....	....	....
	NHL Totals	**3**	**1**	**0**	**1**	**0**	....	....	....	....	....

Signed as a free agent by **Edmonton**, July 27, 1987. Signed as a free agent by **Minnesota**, July 11, 1989. Signed as a free agent by **San Jose**, October 19, 1993.

EMMONS, John

Center. Shoots left. 6'1", 203 lbs. Born, San Jose, CA, August 17, 1974.
(Calgary's 7th choice, 122nd overall, in 1993 Entry Draft).

Season	Club	Regular Season GP	G	A	Pts	PIM	Playoffs GP	G	A	Pts	PIM
99-2000	Ottawa Senators	10	0	0	0	6	....	....	....	....	....
2000-01	Ottawa Senators	41	1	1	2	20	....	....	....	....	....
	Tampa Bay Lightning	12	1	1	2	22	....	....	....	....	....
2001-02	Boston Bruins	22	0	2	2	16	....	....	....	....	....
	NHL Totals	**85**	**2**	**4**	**6**	**64**	....	....	....	....	....

Signed as a free agent by **Ottawa**, August 7, 1998. Traded to **Tampa Bay** by **Ottawa** for Craig Millar, March 13, 2001. Signed as a free agent by **Boston**, August 8, 2001.

EMMS, Hap

Left wing/Defense. Shoots left. 6', 190 lbs. Born, Barrie, Ont., January 12, 1905.

Season	Club	Regular Season GP	G	A	Pts	PIM	Playoffs GP	G	A	Pts	PIM
1926-27	Montreal Maroons	8	0	0	0	0	....	....	....	....	....
1927-28	Montreal Maroons	10	0	1	1	10	....	....	....	....	....
1930-31	New York Americans	44	5	4	9	56	....	....	....	....	....
1931-32	New York Americans	13	1	0	1	11	....	....	....	....	....
	Detroit Falcons	20	5	9	14	27	2	0	0	0	2
1932-33	Detroit Red Wings	43	9	13	22	63	4	0	0	0	8
1933-34	Detroit Red Wings	45	7	7	14	51	8	0	0	0	2
1934-35	Boston Bruins	11	1	1	2	8	....	....	....	....	....
	New York Americans	28	2	2	4	19	....	....	....	....	....
1935-36	New York Americans	32	1	5	6	12	....	....	....	....	....
1936-37	New York Americans	46	4	8	12	48	....	....	....	....	....

Season	Club	REGULAR SEASON GP	G	A	Pts	PIM	PLAYOFFS GP	G	A	Pts	PIM
1937-38	New York Americans	20	1	3	4	6	....	....	....	....	....
	NHL Totals	**320**	**36**	**53**	**89**	**311**	**14**	**0**	**0**	**0**	**12**

Signed as a free agent by **Mtl. Maroons**, November 10, 1926. Traded to **NY Americans** by **Mtl. Maroons** (Windsor-IHL) with Frank Carson, Red Dutton and Mike Neville for $35,000, May 14, 1930. Traded to **Detroit** by **NY Americans** with Frank Carson for Tommy Filmore and Bert McInenly, December 29, 1931. Signed as a free agent by **Boston** after securing release from **Detroit**, October 28, 1934. Traded to **NY Americans** by **Boston** with Obs Heximer for Walter Jackson, December 14, 1934. Traded to **Detroit** by **NY Americans** for John Sorrell, February 13, 1938.

ENDEAN, Craig

Left wing. Shoots left. 5'11", 170 lbs. Born, Kamloops, B.C., April 13, 1968.
(Winnipeg's 5th choice, 92nd overall, in 1986 Entry Draft).

Season	Club	GP	G	A	Pts	PIM	GP	G	A	Pts	PIM
1986-87	Winnipeg Jets	2	0	1	1	0	....	....	....	....	....
	NHL Totals	**2**	**0**	**1**	**1**	**0**	....	....	....	....	....

ENDICOTT, Shane

Center. Shoots left. 6'4", 200 lbs. Born, Saskatoon, Sask., December 21, 1981.
(Pittsburgh's 2nd choice, 52nd overall, in 2000 Entry Draft).

Season	Club	GP	G	A	Pts	PIM	GP	G	A	Pts	PIM
2001-02	Pittsburgh Penguins	4	0	1	1	4	....	....	....	....	....
	NHL Totals	**4**	**0**	**1**	**1**	**4**	....	....	....	....	....

ENGBLOM, Brian

Defense. Shoots left. 6'2", 200 lbs. Born, Winnipeg, Man., January 27, 1955.
(Montreal's 3rd choice, 22nd overall, in 1975 Amateur Draft).

Season	Club	GP	G	A	Pts	PIM	GP	G	A	Pts	PIM
1976-77 ♦	Montreal Canadiens	....	....	....	....	....	2	0	0	0	2
1977-78 ♦	Montreal Canadiens	28	1	2	3	23	5	0	0	0	2
1978-79 ♦	Montreal Canadiens	62	3	11	14	60	16	0	1	1	11
1979-80	Montreal Canadiens	70	3	20	23	43	10	2	4	6	6
1980-81	Montreal Canadiens	80	3	25	28	96	3	1	0	1	4
1981-82	Montreal Canadiens	76	4	29	33	76	5	0	2	2	14
1982-83	Washington Capitals	73	5	22	27	59	4	0	2	2	2
1983-84	Washington Capitals	6	0	1	1	8	....	....	....	....	....
	Los Angeles Kings	74	2	27	29	59	....	....	....	....	....
1984-85	Los Angeles Kings	79	4	19	23	70	3	0	0	0	2
1985-86	Los Angeles Kings	49	3	13	16	61	....	....	....	....	....
	Buffalo Sabres	30	1	4	5	16	....	....	....	....	....
1986-87	Calgary Flames	32	0	4	4	28	....	....	....	....	....
	NHL Totals	**659**	**29**	**177**	**206**	**599**	**48**	**3**	**9**	**12**	**43**

NHL Plus/Minus Leader (1981) • NHL Second All-Star Team (1982)

Traded to **Washington** by **Montreal** with Rod Langway, Doug Jarvis and Craig Laughlin for Ryan Walter and Rick Green, September 9, 1982. Traded to **Los Angeles** by **Washington** with Ken Houston for Larry Murphy, October 18, 1983. Traded to **Buffalo** by **Los Angeles** with Doug Smith for Larry Playfair, Sean McKenna and Ken Baumgartner, January 30, 1986. Traded to **Calgary** by **Buffalo** for Jim Korn, October 3, 1986. • Suffered eventual career-ending neck injury in game vs. Quebec, December 12, 1986.

ENGELE, Jerry

Defense. Shoots left. 6', 197 lbs. Born, Humboldt, Sask., November 26, 1950.

Season	Club	GP	G	A	Pts	PIM	GP	G	A	Pts	PIM
1975-76	Minnesota North Stars	17	0	1	1	16	....	....	....	....	....
1976-77	Minnesota North Stars	31	1	7	8	41	2	0	1	1	0
1977-78	Minnesota North Stars	52	1	5	6	105	....	....	....	....	....
	NHL Totals	**100**	**2**	**13**	**15**	**162**	**2**	**0**	**1**	**1**	**0**

Signed as a free agent by **Minnesota**, June, 1975. Transferred to **Montreal** by **Minnesota** as compensation for Minnesota's signing of free agent Mike Polich, September 6, 1978.

ENGLISH, John

Defense. Shoots right. 6'2", 190 lbs. Born, Toronto, Ont., May 13, 1966.
(Los Angeles' 3rd choice, 48th overall, in 1984 Entry Draft).

Season	Club	GP	G	A	Pts	PIM	GP	G	A	Pts	PIM
1987-88	Los Angeles Kings	3	1	3	4	4	1	0	0	0	0
	NHL Totals	**3**	**1**	**3**	**4**	**4**	**1**	**0**	**0**	**0**	**0**

Traded to **Edmonton** by **Los Angeles** with Brian Wilks for Jim Wiemer and Alan May, March 7, 1989.

ENNIS, Jim

Defense. Shoots left. 6', 200 lbs. Born, Edmonton, Alta., July 10, 1967.
(Edmonton's 6th choice, 126th overall, in 1986 Entry Draft).

Season	Club	GP	G	A	Pts	PIM	GP	G	A	Pts	PIM
1987-88	Edmonton Oilers	5	1	0	1	10	....	....	....	....	....
	NHL Totals	**5**	**1**	**0**	**1**	**10**	....	....	....	....	....

Traded to **Hartford** by **Edmonton** for Norm MacIver, October 10, 1989.

ERAT, Martin

Left wing. Shoots left. 6', 195 lbs. Born, Trebic, Czech., August 28, 1981.
(Nashville's 12th choice, 191st overall, in 1999 Entry Draft).

Season	Club	GP	G	A	Pts	PIM	GP	G	A	Pts	PIM
2001-02	Nashville Predators	80	9	24	33	32	....	....	....	....	....
2002-03	Nashville Predators	27	1	7	8	14	....	....	....	....	....
	NHL Totals	**107**	**10**	**31**	**41**	**46**	....	....	....	....	....

ERICKSON, Aut

Defense. Shoots left. 6'1", 188 lbs. Born, Lethbridge, Alta., January 25, 1938.

Season	Club	GP	G	A	Pts	PIM	GP	G	A	Pts	PIM
1959-60	Boston Bruins	58	1	6	7	29	....	....	....	....	....
1960-61	Boston Bruins	68	2	6	8	65	....	....	....	....	....
1962-63	Chicago Black Hawks	3	0	0	0	8	....	....	....	....	....
1963-64	Chicago Black Hawks	31	0	1	1	34	6	0	0	0	0
1966-67 ♦	Toronto Maple Leafs	....	....	....	....	....	1	0	0	0	2
1967-68	Oakland Seals	65	4	11	15	46	....	....	....	....	....
1969-70	Oakland Seals	1	0	0	0	0	....	....	....	....	....
	NHL Totals	**226**	**7**	**24**	**31**	**182**	**7**	**0**	**0**	**0**	**2**

Claimed by **Chicago** from **Saskatoon-St. Paul** (WHL) in Inter-League Draft, June 3, 1958. Claimed by **Boston** from **Chicago** in Intra-League Draft, June 10, 1959. Claimed by **Chicago** from **Boston** in Intra-League Draft, June 13, 1961. Traded to **Detroit** by **Chicago** with Ron Murphy for John Miszuk, Art Stratton and Ian Cushenan, June 9, 1964. Traded to **Toronto** by **Detroit** with Marcel Pronovost, Larry Jeffrey, Eddie Joyal and Lowell MacDonald for Billy Harris, Gary Jarrett and Andy Bathgate, May 20, 1965. Claimed by **California** (Oakland) from **Toronto** in Expansion Draft, June 6, 1967. • Underwent career-ending spinal fusion surgery, January, 1970.

ERICKSON, Bryan

Right wing. Shoots right. 5'9", 175 lbs. Born, Roseau, MN, March 7, 1960.

Season	Club	GP	G	A	Pts	PIM	GP	G	A	Pts	PIM
1983-84	Washington Capitals	45	12	17	29	16	8	2	3	5	7
1984-85	Washington Capitals	57	15	13	28	23	....	....	....	....	....
1985-86	Los Angeles Kings	55	20	23	43	36	....	....	....	....	....
1986-87	Los Angeles Kings	68	20	30	50	26	3	1	1	2	0
1987-88	Los Angeles Kings	42	6	15	21	20	....	....	....	....	....
	Pittsburgh Penguins	11	1	4	5	0	....	....	....	....	....
1990-91	Winnipeg Jets	6	0	7	7	0	....	....	....	....	....
1991-92	Winnipeg Jets	10	2	4	6	0	....	....	....	....	....
1992-93	Winnipeg Jets	41	4	12	16	14	3	0	0	0	0
1993-94	Winnipeg Jets	16	0	0	0	6	....	....	....	....	....
	NHL Totals	**351**	**80**	**125**	**205**	**141**	**14**	**3**	**4**	**7**	**7**

Signed as a free agent by **Washington**, April 5, 1983. Traded to **Los Angeles** by **Washington** for Bruce Shoebottom, October 31, 1985. Traded to **Pittsburgh** by **Los Angeles** for Chris Kontos and Pittsburgh's 6th round choice (Micah Aivazoff) in 1988 Entry Draft, February 5, 1988. Signed as a free agent by **Winnipeg**, March 2, 1990. • Missed majority of 1991-92 season recovering from abdominal injury suffered in game vs. Los Angeles, October 12, 1991. • Missed majority of 1993-94 season recovering from groin injury suffered in game vs. Quebec, December 23, 1993.

ERICKSON, Grant

Left wing. 5'9", 165 lbs. Born, Pierceland, Sask., April 28, 1947.

Season	Club	GP	G	A	Pts	PIM	GP	G	A	Pts	PIM
1968-69	Boston Bruins	2	1	0	1	0	....	....	....	....	....
1969-70	Minnesota North Stars	4	0	0	0	0	....	....	....	....	....
	NHL Totals	**6**	**1**	**0**	**1**	**0**	....	....	....	....	....

Claimed by **Minnesota** from **Boston** in Intra-League Draft, June 11, 1969.

ERIKSSON, Anders

Defense. Shoots left. 6'2", 220 lbs. Born, Bollnas, Sweden, January 9, 1975.
(Detroit's 1st choice, 22nd overall, in 1993 Entry Draft).

Season	Club	GP	G	A	Pts	PIM	GP	G	A	Pts	PIM
1995-96	Detroit Red Wings	1	0	0	0	2	3	0	0	0	0
1996-97	Detroit Red Wings	23	0	6	6	10	....	....	....	....	....
1997-98 ♦	Detroit Red Wings	66	7	14	21	32	18	0	5	5	16
1998-99	Detroit Red Wings	61	2	10	12	34	....	....	....	....	....
	Chicago Blackhawks	11	0	8	8	0	....	....	....	....	....
99-2000	Chicago Blackhawks	73	3	25	28	20	....	....	....	....	....
2000-01	Chicago Blackhawks	13	2	3	5	2	....	....	....	....	....
	Florida Panthers	60	0	21	21	28	....	....	....	....	....
2001-02	Toronto Maple Leafs	34	0	2	2	12	10	0	0	0	0
2002-03	Toronto Maple Leafs	4	0	0	0	0	....	....	....	....	....
	NHL Totals	**346**	**14**	**89**	**103**	**140**	**31**	**0**	**5**	**5**	**16**

Traded to **Chicago** by **Detroit** with Detroit's 1st round choices in 1999 (Steve McCarthy) and 2001 (Adam Munro) Entry Drafts for Chris Chelios, March 23, 1999. Traded to **Florida** by **Chicago** for Jaroslav Spacek, November 6, 2000. Signed as a free agent by **Toronto**, July 9, 2001.

ERIKSSON, Peter

Left wing. Shoots right. 6'4", 218 lbs. Born, Kramfors, Sweden, July 12, 1965.
(Edmonton's 4th choice, 64th overall, in 1987 Entry Draft).

Season	Club	GP	G	A	Pts	PIM	GP	G	A	Pts	PIM
1989-90	Edmonton Oilers	20	3	3	6	24	....	....	....	....	....
	NHL Totals	**20**	**3**	**3**	**6**	**24**	....	....	....	....	....

ERIKSSON, Roland

Center. Shoots left. 6'3", 190 lbs. Born, Storatuna, Sweden, March 1, 1954.
(Minnesota's 8th choice, 131st overall, in 1974 Amateur Draft).

Season	Club	GP	G	A	Pts	PIM	GP	G	A	Pts	PIM
1976-77	Minnesota North Stars	80	25	44	69	10	2	1	0	1	0
1977-78	Minnesota North Stars	78	21	39	60	12	....	....	....	....	....
1978-79	Vancouver Canucks	35	2	12	14	4	....	....	....	....	....
	NHL Totals	**193**	**48**	**95**	**143**	**26**	**2**	**1**	**0**	**1**	**0**

Played in NHL All-Star Game (1978)

Signed as a free agent by **Vancouver**, June 7, 1978.

ERIKSSON, Thomas

Defense. Shoots left. 6'2", 182 lbs. Born, Stockholm, Sweden, October 16, 1959.
(Philadelphia's 6th choice, 98th overall, in 1979 Entry Draft).

Season	Club	GP	G	A	Pts	PIM	GP	G	A	Pts	PIM
1980-81	Philadelphia Flyers	24	1	10	11	14	7	0	2	2	6
1981-82	Philadelphia Flyers	1	0	0	0	4	....	....	....	....	....
1983-84	Philadelphia Flyers	68	11	33	44	37	3	0	1	1	0
1984-85	Philadelphia Flyers	72	10	29	39	36	9	0	0	0	6
1985-86	Philadelphia Flyers	43	0	4	4	16	....	....	....	....	....
	NHL Totals	**208**	**22**	**76**	**98**	**107**	**19**	**0**	**3**	**3**	**12**

NHL All-Rookie Team (1984)

ERIXON, Jan

Left wing. Shoots left. 6', 196 lbs. Born, Skelleftea, Sweden, July 8, 1962.
(NY Rangers' 2nd choice, 30th overall, in 1981 Entry Draft).

Season	Club	Regular Season GP	G	A	Pts	PIM	Playoffs GP	G	A	Pts	PIM
1983-84	New York Rangers	75	5	25	30	16	5	2	0	2	4
1984-85	New York Rangers	66	7	22	29	33	2	0	0	0	2
1985-86	New York Rangers	31	2	17	19	4	12	0	1	1	4
1986-87	New York Rangers	68	8	18	26	24	6	1	0	1	0
1987-88	New York Rangers	70	7	19	26	33	....	....	....	....	....
1988-89	New York Rangers	44	4	11	15	27	4	0	1	1	2
1989-90	New York Rangers	58	4	9	13	8	10	1	0	1	2
1990-91	New York Rangers	53	7	18	25	8	6	1	2	3	0
1991-92	New York Rangers	46	8	9	17	4	13	2	3	5	2
1992-93	New York Rangers	45	5	11	16	10	....	....	....	....	....
	NHL Totals	**556**	**57**	**159**	**216**	**167**	**58**	**7**	**7**	**14**	**16**

• Missed majority of 1985-86 season recovering from leg injury suffered in game vs. St. Louis, January 12, 1986.

ERREY, Bob

Left wing. Shoots left. 5'10", 185 lbs. Born, Montreal, Que., September 21, 1964.
(Pittsburgh's 1st choice, 15th overall, in 1983 Entry Draft).

Season	Club	Regular Season GP	G	A	Pts	PIM	Playoffs GP	G	A	Pts	PIM
1983-84	Pittsburgh Penguins	65	9	13	22	29	....	....	....	....	....
1984-85	Pittsburgh Penguins	16	0	2	2	7	....	....	....	....	....
1985-86	Pittsburgh Penguins	37	11	6	17	8	....	....	....	....	....
1986-87	Pittsburgh Penguins	72	16	18	34	46	....	....	....	....	....
1987-88	Pittsburgh Penguins	17	3	6	9	18	....	....	....	....	....
1988-89	Pittsburgh Penguins	76	26	32	58	124	11	1	2	3	12
1989-90	Pittsburgh Penguins	78	20	19	39	109	....	....	....	....	....
1990-91 ◆	Pittsburgh Penguins	79	20	22	42	115	24	5	2	7	29
1991-92 ◆	Pittsburgh Penguins	78	19	16	35	119	14	3	0	3	10
1992-93	Pittsburgh Penguins	54	8	6	14	76	....	....	....	....	....
	Buffalo Sabres	8	1	3	4	4	4	0	1	1	10
1993-94	San Jose Sharks	64	12	18	30	126	14	3	2	5	10
1994-95	San Jose Sharks	13	2	2	4	27	....	....	....	....	....
	Detroit Red Wings	30	6	11	17	31	18	1	5	6	30
1995-96	Detroit Red Wings	71	11	21	32	66	14	0	4	4	8
1996-97	Detroit Red Wings	36	1	2	3	27	....	....	....	....	....
	San Jose Sharks	30	3	6	9	20	....	....	....	....	....
1997-98	Dallas Stars	59	2	9	11	46	....	....	....	....	....
	New York Rangers	12	0	0	0	7	....	....	....	....	....
	NHL Totals	**895**	**170**	**212**	**382**	**1005**	**99**	**13**	**16**	**29**	**109**

Traded to **Buffalo** by **Pittsburgh** for Mike Ramsey, March 22, 1993. Signed as a free agent by **San Jose**, August 17, 1993. Traded to **Detroit** by **San Jose** for Detroit's 5th round choice (Michal Bros) in 1995 Entry Draft, February 27, 1995. Claimed on waivers by **San Jose** from **Detroit**, February 8, 1997. Signed as a free agent by **Dallas**, July 28, 1997. Traded to **NY Rangers** by **Dallas** with Todd Harvey and Dallas' 4th round choice (Boyd Kane) in 1998 Entry Draft for Brian Skrudland, Mike Keane and NY Rangers' 6th round choice (Pavel Patera) in 1998 Entry Draft, March 24, 1998.

ERSKINE, John

Defense. Shoots left. 6'4", 215 lbs. Born, Kingston, Ont., June 26, 1980.
(Dallas' 1st choice, 39th overall, in 1998 Entry Draft).

Season	Club	Regular Season GP	G	A	Pts	PIM	Playoffs GP	G	A	Pts	PIM
2001-02	Dallas Stars	33	0	1	1	62	....	....	....	....	....
2002-03	Dallas Stars	16	2	0	2	29	....	....	....	....	....
	NHL Totals	**49**	**2**	**1**	**3**	**91**	....	....	....	....	....

ESAU, Len

Defense. Shoots right. 6'3", 190 lbs. Born, Meadow Lake, Sask., June 3, 1968.
(Toronto's 5th choice, 86th overall, in 1988 Entry Draft).

Season	Club	Regular Season GP	G	A	Pts	PIM	Playoffs GP	G	A	Pts	PIM
1991-92	Toronto Maple Leafs	2	0	0	0	0	....	....	....	....	....
1992-93	Quebec Nordiques	4	0	1	1	2	....	....	....	....	....
1993-94	Calgary Flames	6	0	3	3	7	....	....	....	....	....
1994-95	Edmonton Oilers	14	0	6	6	15	....	....	....	....	....
	Calgary Flames	1	0	0	0	0	....	....	....	....	....
	NHL Totals	**27**	**0**	**10**	**10**	**24**	....	....	....	....	....

Traded to **Quebec** by **Toronto** for Ken McRae, July 21, 1992. Signed as a free agent by **Calgary**, September 6, 1993. Claimed by **Edmonton** from **Calgary** in NHL Waiver Draft, January 18, 1995. Claimed on waivers by **Calgary** from **Edmonton**, March 7, 1995. Signed as a free agent by **Florida**, August 31, 1995.

ESPOSITO, Phil

HHOF

Center. Shoots left. 6'1", 205 lbs. Born, Sault Ste. Marie, Ont., February 20, 1942.

Season	Club	Regular Season GP	G	A	Pts	PIM	Playoffs GP	G	A	Pts	PIM
1963-64	Chicago Black Hawks	27	3	2	5	2	4	0	0	0	0
1964-65	Chicago Black Hawks	70	23	32	55	44	13	3	3	6	15
1965-66	Chicago Black Hawks	69	27	26	53	49	6	1	1	2	2
1966-67	Chicago Black Hawks	69	21	40	61	40	6	0	0	0	7
1967-68	Boston Bruins	74	35	*49	84	21	4	0	3	3	0
1968-69	Boston Bruins	74	49	*77	*126	79	10	*8	*10	*18	8
1969-70 ◆	Boston Bruins	76	*43	56	99	50	14	*13	*14	*27	16
1970-71	Boston Bruins	78	*76	76	*152	71	7	3	7	10	6
1971-72 ◆	Boston Bruins	76	*66	67	*133	76	15	9	15	*24	24
1972-73	Boston Bruins	78	*55	*75	*130	87	2	0	1	1	2
1973-74	Boston Bruins	78	*68	77	*145	58	16	9	5	14	25
1974-75	Boston Bruins	79	*61	66	127	62	3	4	1	5	0
1975-76	Boston Bruins	12	6	10	16	8	....	....	....	....	....
	New York Rangers	62	29	38	67	28	....	....	....	....	....
1976-77	New York Rangers	80	34	46	80	52	....	....	....	....	....
1977-78	New York Rangers	79	38	43	81	53	3	0	1	1	5
1978-79	New York Rangers	80	42	36	78	37	18	8	12	20	20
1979-80	New York Rangers	80	34	44	78	73	9	3	3	6	8
1980-81	New York Rangers	41	7	13	20	20	....	....	....	....	....
	NHL Totals	**1282**	**717**	**873**	**1590**	**910**	**130**	**61**	**76**	**137**	**138**

• Brother of Tony • NHL Second All-Star Team (1968, 1975) • NHL First All-Star Team (1969, 1970, 1971, 1972, 1973, 1974) • Art Ross Trophy (1969, 1971, 1972, 1973, 1974) • Hart Trophy (1969, 1974) • Lester B. Pearson Award (1971, 1974) • Lester Patrick Trophy (1978)

Played in NHL All-Star Game (1969, 1970, 1971, 1972, 1973, 1974, 1975, 1977, 1978, 1980)

Traded to **Boston** by **Chicago** with Ken Hodge and Fred Stanfield for Pit Martin, Jack Norris, and Gilles Marotte, May 15, 1967. Traded to **NY Rangers** by **Boston** with Carol Vadnais for Brad Park, Jean Ratelle and Joe Zanussi, November 7, 1975.

EVANS, Chris

Defense. Shoots left. 5'9", 180 lbs. Born, Toronto, Ont., September 14, 1946.

Season	Club	Regular Season GP	G	A	Pts	PIM	Playoffs GP	G	A	Pts	PIM
1969-70	Toronto Maple Leafs	2	0	0	0	0	....	....	....	....	....
1971-72	Buffalo Sabres	61	6	18	24	98	....	....	....	....	....
	St. Louis Blues	2	0	0	0	0	7	1	0	1	4
1972-73	St. Louis Blues	77	9	12	21	31	5	0	1	1	4
1973-74	St. Louis Blues	54	4	7	11	8	....	....	....	....	....
	Detroit Red Wings	23	0	2	2	2	....	....	....	....	....
1974-75	Kansas City Scouts	2	0	2	2	2	....	....	....	....	....
	St. Louis Blues	20	0	1	1	2	....	....	....	....	....
	NHL Totals	**241**	**19**	**42**	**61**	**143**	**12**	**1**	**1**	**2**	**8**

Claimed by **St. Louis** from **Phoenix** (WHL) in Intra-League Draft, June 9, 1970. Claimed by **Buffalo** from **St. Louis** in Expansion Draft, June 10, 1970. Traded to **St. Louis** by **Buffalo** for George Morrison and St. Louis' 2nd round choice (Larry Carriere) in 1972 Amateur Draft, March 5, 1972. Traded to **Detroit** by **St. Louis** with Bryan Watson and Jean Hamel for Ted Harris, Bill Collins and Garnet Bailey, February 14, 1974. Claimed by **Kansas City** from **Detroit** in Expansion Draft, June 12, 1974. Traded to **St. Louis** by **Kansas City** with Kansas City's 4th round choice (Mike Liut) in 1976 Amateur Draft for Larry Giroux, October 29, 1974.

EVANS, Daryl

Left wing. Shoots left. 5'9", 185 lbs. Born, Toronto, Ont., January 12, 1961.
(Los Angeles' 11th choice, 178th overall, in 1980 Entry Draft).

Season	Club	Regular Season GP	G	A	Pts	PIM	Playoffs GP	G	A	Pts	PIM
1981-82	Los Angeles Kings	14	2	6	8	2	10	5	8	13	12
1982-83	Los Angeles Kings	80	18	22	40	21	....	....	....	....	....
1983-84	Los Angeles Kings	4	0	1	1	0	....	....	....	....	....
1984-85	Los Angeles Kings	7	1	0	1	2	....	....	....	....	....
1985-86	Washington Capitals	6	0	1	1	0	....	....	....	....	....
1986-87	Toronto Maple Leafs	2	1	0	1	0	1	0	0	0	0
	NHL Totals	**113**	**22**	**30**	**52**	**25**	**11**	**5**	**8**	**13**	**12**

Traded to **Washington** by **Los Angeles** for Glen Currie, September 9, 1985. Signed as a free agent by **Toronto**, August, 1986.

EVANS, Doug

Left wing. Shoots left. 5'9", 185 lbs. Born, Peterborough, Ont., June 2, 1963.

Season	Club	Regular Season GP	G	A	Pts	PIM	Playoffs GP	G	A	Pts	PIM
1985-86	St. Louis Blues	13	1	0	1	2	....	....	....	....	....
1986-87	St. Louis Blues	53	3	13	16	91	5	0	0	0	10
1987-88	St. Louis Blues	41	5	7	12	49	2	0	0	0	0
1988-89	St. Louis Blues	53	7	12	19	81	7	1	2	3	16
1989-90	St. Louis Blues	3	0	0	0	0	....	....	....	....	....
	Winnipeg Jets	27	10	8	18	33	7	2	2	4	10
1990-91	Winnipeg Jets	70	7	27	34	108	....	....	....	....	....
1991-92	Winnipeg Jets	30	7	7	14	68	1	0	0	0	2
1992-93	Philadelphia Flyers	65	8	13	21	70	....	....	....	....	....
	NHL Totals	**355**	**48**	**87**	**135**	**502**	**22**	**3**	**4**	**7**	**38**

• Brother of Paul and Kevin

Signed as a free agent by **St. Louis**, June 10, 1985. Traded to **Winnipeg** by **St. Louis** for Ron Wilson, January 22, 1990. Traded to **Boston** by **Winnipeg** for Daniel Berthiaume, June 10, 1992. Claimed by **Philadelphia** from **Boston** in Waiver Draft, October 4, 1992.

EVANS, Jack

Defense. Shoots left. 6', 185 lbs. Born, Morriston, Wales, April 21, 1928.

Season	Club	Regular Season GP	G	A	Pts	PIM	Playoffs GP	G	A	Pts	PIM
1948-49	New York Rangers	3	0	0	0	4	....	....	....	....	....
1949-50	New York Rangers	2	0	0	0	2	....	....	....	....	....
1950-51	New York Rangers	49	1	0	1	95	....	....	....	....	....
1951-52	New York Rangers	52	1	6	7	83	....	....	....	....	....
1953-54	New York Rangers	44	4	4	8	73	....	....	....	....	....
1954-55	New York Rangers	47	0	5	5	91	....	....	....	....	....
1955-56	New York Rangers	70	2	9	11	104	5	1	0	1	18
1956-57	New York Rangers	70	3	6	9	110	5	0	1	1	4
1957-58	New York Rangers	70	4	8	12	108	6	0	0	0	17
1958-59	Chicago Black Hawks	70	1	8	9	75	6	0	0	0	10
1959-60	Chicago Black Hawks	68	0	4	4	60	4	0	0	0	4
1960-61 ◆	Chicago Black Hawks	69	0	8	8	58	12	1	1	2	14
1961-62	Chicago Black Hawks	70	3	14	17	80	12	0	0	0	26
1962-63	Chicago Black Hawks	68	0	8	8	46	6	0	0	0	4
	NHL Totals	**752**	**19**	**80**	**99**	**989**	**56**	**2**	**2**	**4**	**97**

Played in NHL All-Star Game (1961, 1962)

Claimed by **Chicago** from **NY Rangers** in Intra-League Draft, June 3, 1958. Claimed by **Boston** (Hershey-AHL) from **Chicago** in Reverse Draft, June 15, 1966. Traded to **San Diego** (WHL) by **Boston** for cash, October, 1967.

EVANS, John Paul

Center. Shoots left. 5'9", 185 lbs. Born, Toronto, Ont., May 2, 1954.
(Los Angeles' 3rd choice, 84th overall, in 1974 Amateur Draft).

		REGULAR SEASON					PLAYOFFS				
Season	Club	GP	G	A	Pts	PIM	GP	G	A	Pts	PIM
1978-79	Philadelphia Flyers	44	6	5	11	12	....	....	....	....	....
1980-81	Philadelphia Flyers	1	0	0	0	2	....	....	....	....	....
1982-83	Philadelphia Flyers	58	8	20	28	20	1	0	0	0	0
	NHL Totals	**103**	**14**	**25**	**39**	**34**	**1**	**0**	**0**	**0**	**0**

Traded to **Philadelphia** by **Los Angeles** to complete transaction that sent Steve Short to Los Angeles (June 17, 1977), November 3, 1977.

EVANS, Kevin

Left wing. Shoots left. 5'9", 185 lbs. Born, Peterborough, Ont., July 10, 1965.

Season	Club	GP	G	A	Pts	PIM	GP	G	A	Pts	PIM
1990-91	Minnesota North Stars	4	0	0	0	19	....	....	....	....	....
1991-92	San Jose Sharks	5	0	1	1	25	....	....	....	....	....
	NHL Totals	**9**	**0**	**1**	**1**	**44**	....	....	....	....	....

• Brother of Paul and Doug

Signed as a free agent by **Minnesota**, August 8, 1988. Claimed by **San Jose** from **Minnesota** in Dispersal Draft, May 30, 1991. Signed as a free agent by **Minnesota**, July 20, 1992.

EVANS, Paul

Center/Left wing. Shoots left. 5'11", 175 lbs. Born, Peterborough, Ont., February 24, 1955.
(Toronto's 8th choice, 149th overall, in 1975 Amateur Draft).

Season	Club	GP	G	A	Pts	PIM	GP	G	A	Pts	PIM
1976-77	Toronto Maple Leafs	7	1	1	2	19	2	0	0	0	0
1977-78	Toronto Maple Leafs	4	0	0	0	2	....	....	....	....	....
	NHL Totals	**11**	**1**	**1**	**2**	**21**	**2**	**0**	**0**	**0**	**0**

• Brother of Doug and Kevin

EVANS, Shawn

Defense. Shoots left. 6'3", 195 lbs. Born, Kingston, Ont., September 7, 1965.
(New Jersey's 2nd choice, 24th overall, in 1983 Entry Draft).

Season	Club	GP	G	A	Pts	PIM	GP	G	A	Pts	PIM
1985-86	St. Louis Blues	7	0	0	0	2	....	....	....	....	....
1989-90	New York Islanders	2	1	0	1	0	....	....	....	....	....
	NHL Totals	**9**	**1**	**0**	**1**	**2**	....	....	....	....	....

Traded to **St. Louis** by **New Jersey** with New Jersey's 5th round choice (Michael Wolak) in 1986 Entry Draft for Mark Johnson, September 19, 1985. Traded to **Edmonton** by **St. Louis** for Todd Ewen, October 15, 1986. Signed as a free agent by **NY Islanders**, June 20, 1988. Signed as a free agent by **Boston**, December 17, 1990. Signed as a free agent by **Hartford**, August 15, 1991.

EVANS, Stewart

Defense. Shoots left. 5'10", 170 lbs. Born, Ottawa, Ont., June 19, 1908.

Season	Club	GP	G	A	Pts	PIM	GP	G	A	Pts	PIM
1930-31	Detroit Falcons	43	1	4	5	14	....	....	....	....	....
1932-33	Detroit Red Wings	48	2	6	8	74	4	0	0	0	6
1933-34	Detroit Red Wings	17	0	0	0	20	....	....	....	....	....
	Montreal Maroons	27	4	2	6	35	4	0	0	0	4
1934-35 ♦	Montreal Maroons	46	5	7	12	54	7	0	0	0	8
1935-36	Montreal Maroons	48	3	5	8	57	3	0	0	0	0
1936-37	Montreal Maroons	47	6	7	13	54	5	0	0	0	0
1937-38	Montreal Maroons	48	5	11	16	59	....	....	....	....	....
1938-39	Montreal Canadiens	43	2	7	9	58	3	0	0	0	2
	NHL Totals	**367**	**28**	**49**	**77**	**425**	**26**	**0**	**0**	**0**	**20**

Signed as a free agent by **Detroit**, September 12, 1929. Traded to **Mtl. Maroons** by **Detroit** for Teddy Graham, January 2, 1934. Traded to **Montreal** by **Mtl. Maroons** for cash, September 14, 1938.

EVASON, Dean

Center. Shoots right. 5'10", 180 lbs. Born, Flin Flon, Man., August 22, 1964.
(Washington's 3rd choice, 89th overall, in 1982 Entry Draft).

Season	Club	GP	G	A	Pts	PIM	GP	G	A	Pts	PIM
1983-84	Washington Capitals	2	0	0	0	2	....	....	....	....	....
1984-85	Washington Capitals	15	3	4	7	2	....	....	....	....	....
	Hartford Whalers	2	0	0	0	0	....	....	....	....	....
1985-86	Hartford Whalers	55	20	28	48	65	10	1	4	5	10
1986-87	Hartford Whalers	80	22	37	59	67	5	3	2	5	35
1987-88	Hartford Whalers	77	10	18	28	115	6	1	1	2	2
1988-89	Hartford Whalers	67	11	17	28	60	4	1	2	3	10
1989-90	Hartford Whalers	78	18	25	43	138	7	2	2	4	22
1990-91	Hartford Whalers	75	6	23	29	170	6	0	4	4	29
1991-92	San Jose Sharks	74	11	15	26	99	....	....	....	....	....
1992-93	San Jose Sharks	84	12	19	31	132	....	....	....	....	....
1993-94	Dallas Stars	80	11	33	44	66	9	0	2	2	12
1994-95	Dallas Stars	47	8	7	15	48	5	1	2	3	12
1995-96	Calgary Flames	67	7	7	14	38	3	0	1	1	0
	NHL Totals	**803**	**139**	**233**	**372**	**1002**	**55**	**9**	**20**	**29**	**132**

Traded to **Hartford** by **Washington** with Peter Sidorkiewicz for David Jensen, March 12, 1985. Traded to **San Jose** by **Hartford** for Dan Keczmer, October 2, 1991. Traded to **Dallas** by **San Jose** for San Jose's 6th round choice (previously acquired, San Jose selected Petri Varis) in 1993 Entry Draft, June 26, 1993. Signed as a free agent by **Calgary**, August 1, 1995.

EWEN, Todd

Right wing. Shoots right. 6'2", 230 lbs. Born, Saskatoon, Sask., March 22, 1966.
(Edmonton's 9th choice, 168th overall, in 1984 Entry Draft).

Season	Club	GP	G	A	Pts	PIM	GP	G	A	Pts	PIM
1986-87	St. Louis Blues	23	2	0	2	84	4	0	0	0	23
1987-88	St. Louis Blues	64	4	2	6	227	6	0	0	0	21
1988-89	St. Louis Blues	34	4	5	9	171	2	0	0	0	21
1989-90	St. Louis Blues	3	0	0	0	11	....	....	....	....	....
	Montreal Canadiens	41	4	6	10	158	10	0	0	0	4
1990-91	Montreal Canadiens	28	3	2	5	128	....	....	....	....	....
1991-92	Montreal Canadiens	46	1	2	3	130	3	0	0	0	18
1992-93 ♦	Montreal Canadiens	75	5	9	14	193	1	0	0	0	0
1993-94	Mighty Ducks of Anaheim	76	9	9	18	272	....	....	....	....	....
1994-95	Mighty Ducks of Anaheim	24	0	0	0	90	....	....	....	....	....
1995-96	Mighty Ducks of Anaheim	53	4	3	7	285	....	....	....	....	....
1996-97	San Jose Sharks	51	0	2	2	162	....	....	....	....	....
	NHL Totals	**518**	**36**	**40**	**76**	**1911**	**26**	**0**	**0**	**0**	**87**

Traded to **St. Louis** by **Edmonton** for Shawn Evans, October 15, 1986. Traded to **Montreal** by **St. Louis** for St. Louis' 3rd round choice (previously acquired, St. Louis selected Nathan LaFayette) in 1991 Entry Draft, December 12, 1989. Traded to **Anaheim** by **Montreal** with Patrik Carnback for Anaheim's 3rd round choice (Chris Murray) in 1994 Entry Draft, August 10, 1993. Signed as a free agent by **San Jose**, September 4, 1996.

EXELBY, Garnet

Defense. Shoots left. 6'1", 210 lbs. Born, Craik, Sask., August 16, 1981.
(Atlanta's 9th choice, 217th overall, in 1999 Entry Draft).

Season	Club	GP	G	A	Pts	PIM	GP	G	A	Pts	PIM
2002-03	Atlanta Thrashers	15	0	2	2	41	....	....	....	....	....
	NHL Totals	**15**	**0**	**2**	**2**	**41**	....	....	....	....	....

EZINICKI, Bill

Right wing. Shoots right. 5'10", 170 lbs. Born, Winnipeg, Man., March 11, 1924.

Season	Club	GP	G	A	Pts	PIM	GP	G	A	Pts	PIM
1944-45	Toronto Maple Leafs	8	1	4	5	17	....	....	....	....	....
1945-46	Toronto Maple Leafs	24	4	8	12	29	....	....	....	....	....
1946-47 ♦	Toronto Maple Leafs	60	17	20	37	93	11	0	2	2	30
1947-48 ♦	Toronto Maple Leafs	60	11	20	31	97	9	3	1	4	6
1948-49 ♦	Toronto Maple Leafs	52	13	15	28	*145	9	1	4	5	20
1949-50	Toronto Maple Leafs	67	10	12	22	*144	5	0	0	0	13
1950-51	Boston Bruins	53	16	19	35	119	6	1	1	2	18
1951-52	Boston Bruins	28	5	5	10	47	....	....	....	....	....
1954-55	New York Rangers	16	2	2	4	22	....	....	....	....	....
	NHL Totals	**368**	**79**	**105**	**184**	**713**	**40**	**5**	**8**	**13**	**87**

Played in NHL All-Star Game (1947, 1948)

Rights traded to **Toronto** by **Buffalo** (AHL) for George Boothman and Don Webster, October 13, 1944. Traded to **Boston** by **Toronto** with Vic Lynn for Fern Flaman, Ken Smith, Phil Maloney and Leo Boivin, November 16, 1950. Traded to **Toronto** by **Boston** for cash, January 28, 1952. Traded to **Vancouver** (WHL) by **Toronto** with Phil Maloney and Hugh Barlow for $10,000, December 21, 1954. Traded to **NY Rangers** by **Vancouver** (WHL) for Jackie McLeod and cash, February 12, 1955. Traded to **Providence** (AHL) by **NY Rangers** with cash for Jean-Guy Gendron, May 8, 1955.

FAHEY, Jim

Defense. Shoots right. 6', 215 lbs. Born, Boston, MA, May 11, 1979.
(San Jose's 9th choice, 212th overall, in 1998 Entry Draft).

Season	Club	GP	G	A	Pts	PIM	GP	G	A	Pts	PIM
2002-03	San Jose Sharks	43	1	19	20	33	....	....	....	....	....
	NHL Totals	**43**	**1**	**19**	**20**	**33**	....	....	....	....	....

FAHEY, Trevor

Left wing. Shoots left. 6'1", 175 lbs. Born, New Waterford, N.S., January 4, 1944.

Season	Club	GP	G	A	Pts	PIM	GP	G	A	Pts	PIM
1964-65	New York Rangers	1	0	0	0	0	....	....	....	....	....
	NHL Totals	**1**	**0**	**0**	**0**	**0**	....	....	....	....	....

Traded to **Los Angeles** by **NY Rangers** with Jim Murray and Ken Turlick for Barclay Plager, June 16, 1967.

FAIRBAIRN, Bill

Right wing. Shoots right. 5'10", 170 lbs. Born, Brandon, Man., January 7, 1947.

Season	Club	GP	G	A	Pts	PIM	GP	G	A	Pts	PIM
1968-69	New York Rangers	1	0	0	0	0	....	....	....	....	....
1969-70	New York Rangers	76	23	33	56	23	6	0	1	1	10
1970-71	New York Rangers	56	7	23	30	32	4	0	0	0	0
1971-72	New York Rangers	78	22	37	59	53	16	5	7	12	11
1972-73	New York Rangers	78	30	33	63	23	10	1	8	9	2
1973-74	New York Rangers	78	18	44	62	12	13	3	5	8	6
1974-75	New York Rangers	80	24	37	61	10	3	4	0	4	13
1975-76	New York Rangers	80	13	15	28	8	....	....	....	....	....
1976-77	New York Rangers	9	1	2	3	0	....	....	....	....	....
	Minnesota North Stars	51	9	20	29	2	2	0	1	1	0
1977-78	Minnesota North Stars	6	0	1	1	0	....	....	....	....	....
	St. Louis Blues	60	14	16	30	10	....	....	....	....	....
1978-79	St. Louis Blues	5	1	0	1	0	....	....	....	....	....
	NHL Totals	**658**	**162**	**261**	**423**	**173**	**54**	**13**	**22**	**35**	**42**

Traded to **Minnesota** by **NY Rangers** with Nick Beverley for Bill Goldsworthy, November 11, 1976. Claimed on waivers by **St. Louis** from **Minnesota**, October 24, 1977.

FAIRCHILD, Kelly

Center. Shoots left. 5'11", 180 lbs. Born, Hibbing, MN, April 9, 1973.
(Los Angeles' 6th choice, 152nd overall, in 1991 Entry Draft).

Season	Club	GP	G	A	Pts	PIM	GP	G	A	Pts	PIM
1995-96	Toronto Maple Leafs	1	0	1	1	2	....	....	....	....	....
1996-97	Toronto Maple Leafs	22	0	2	2	2	....	....	....	....	....
1998-99	Dallas Stars	1	0	0	0	0	....	....	....	....	....
2001-02	Colorado Avalanche	10	2	0	2	2	....	....	....	....	....
	NHL Totals	**34**	**2**	**3**	**5**	**6**	....	....	....	....	....

Traded to **Toronto** by **Los Angeles** with Dixon Ward, Guy Leveque and Shayne Toporowski for Eric Lacroix, Chris Snell and Toronto's 4th round choice (Eric Belanger) in 1996 Entry Draft, October 3, 1994. Signed as a free agent by **Dallas**, July 2, 1998. Signed as a free agent by **Colorado**, August 29, 2000.

FALKENBERG, Bob

Defense. Shoots right. 6', 185 lbs. Born, Stettler, Alta., January 1, 1946.

Season	Club	GP	G	A	Pts	PIM	GP	G	A	Pts	PIM
		REGULAR SEASON					PLAYOFFS				
1966-67	Detroit Red Wings	16	1	1	2	10	....	....	....	....	....
1967-68	Detroit Red Wings	20	0	3	3	10	....	....	....	....	....
1968-69	Detroit Red Wings	5	0	0	0	0	....	....	....	....	....
1970-71	Detroit Red Wings	9	0	1	1	6	....	....	....	....	....
1971-72	Detroit Red Wings	4	0	0	0	0	....	....	....	....	....
	NHL Totals	**54**	**1**	**5**	**6**	**26**	....	....	....	....	....

FALLOON, Pat

Right wing. Shoots right. 5'11", 190 lbs. Born, Foxwarren, Man., September 22, 1972.
(San Jose's 1st choice, 2nd overall, in 1991 Entry Draft).

Season	Club	GP	G	A	Pts	PIM	GP	G	A	Pts	PIM
1991-92	San Jose Sharks	79	25	34	59	16	....	....	....	....	....
1992-93	San Jose Sharks	41	14	14	28	12	....	....	....	....	....
1993-94	San Jose Sharks	83	22	31	53	18	14	1	2	3	6
1994-95	San Jose Sharks	46	12	7	19	25	11	3	1	4	0
1995-96	San Jose Sharks	9	3	0	3	4	....	....	....	....	....
	Philadelphia Flyers	62	22	26	48	6	12	3	2	5	2
1996-97	Philadelphia Flyers	52	11	12	23	10	14	3	1	4	2
1997-98	Philadelphia Flyers	30	5	7	12	8	....	....	....	....	....
	Ottawa Senators	28	3	3	6	8	1	0	0	0	0
1998-99	Edmonton Oilers	82	17	23	40	20	4	0	1	1	4
99-2000	Edmonton Oilers	33	5	13	18	4	....	....	....	....	....
	Pittsburgh Penguins	30	4	9	13	10	10	1	0	1	2
	NHL Totals	**575**	**143**	**179**	**322**	**141**	**66**	**11**	**7**	**18**	**16**

Traded to **Philadelphia** by **San Jose** for Martin Spanhel, Philadelphia's 1st round choice (later traded to Buffalo – later traded to Phoenix – Phoenix selected Daniel Briere) in 1996 Entry Draft and Philadelphia's 4th round choice (later traded to Buffalo – Buffalo selected Mike Martone), in 1996 Entry Draft, November 16, 1995. Traded to **Ottawa** by **Philadelphia** with Vaclav Prospal and Dallas' 2nd round choice (previously acquired, Ottawa selected Chris Bala) in 1998 Entry Draft for Alexandre Daigle, January 17, 1998. Signed as a free agent by **Edmonton**, August 21, 1998. Claimed on waivers by **Pittsburgh** from **Edmonton**, February 4, 2000.

FARKAS, Jeff

Right wing. Shoots left. 6', 185 lbs. Born, Amherst, NY, January 24, 1978.
(Toronto's 1st choice, 57th overall, in 1997 Entry Draft).

Season	Club	GP	G	A	Pts	PIM	GP	G	A	Pts	PIM
99-2000	Toronto Maple Leafs	....	....	....	....	....	3	1	0	1	0
2000-01	Toronto Maple Leafs	2	0	0	0	2	....	....	....	....	....
2001-02	Toronto Maple Leafs	6	0	2	2	4	2	0	0	0	0
2002-03	Atlanta Thrashers	3	0	0	0	0	....	....	....	....	....
	NHL Totals	**11**	**0**	**2**	**2**	**6**	**5**	**1**	**0**	**1**	**0**

Traded to **Vancouver** by **Toronto** for Josh Holden, June 23, 2002. Traded to **Atlanta** by **Vancouver** for Chris Herperger and Chris Nielsen, January 20, 2003.

FARRANT, Walt

Right wing. Shoots right. 5'10", 155 lbs. Born, Toronto, Ont., August 12, 1912.

Season	Club	GP	G	A	Pts	PIM	GP	G	A	Pts	PIM
1943-44	Chicago Black Hawks	1	0	0	0	0	....	....	....	....	....
	NHL Totals	**1**	**0**	**0**	**0**	**0**	....	....	....	....	....

Signed as a free agent by **NY Americans**, November, 1936. Loaned to **Chicago** by **Toronto** (TIHL) as an emergency injury replacement, March, 1944.

FARRELL, Mike

Right wing. Shoots right. 6', 222 lbs. Born, Edina, MN, October 20, 1978.
(Washington's 9th choice, 220th overall, in 1998 Entry Draft).

Season	Club	GP	G	A	Pts	PIM	GP	G	A	Pts	PIM
2001-02	Washington Capitals	8	0	0	0	0	....	....	....	....	....
2002-03	Washington Capitals	4	0	0	0	2	....	....	....	....	....
	NHL Totals	**12**	**0**	**0**	**0**	**2**	....	....	....	....	....

Traded to **Nashville** by **Washington** for Alexander Riazantsev, July 14, 2003.

FARRISH, Dave

Defense. Shoots left. 6'1", 195 lbs. Born, Wingham, Ont., August 1, 1956.
(NY Rangers' 2nd choice, 24th overall, in 1976 Amateur Draft).

Season	Club	GP	G	A	Pts	PIM	GP	G	A	Pts	PIM
1976-77	New York Rangers	80	2	17	19	102	....	....	....	....	....
1977-78	New York Rangers	66	3	5	8	62	3	0	0	0	0
1978-79	New York Rangers	71	1	19	20	61	7	0	2	2	14
1979-80	Quebec Nordiques	4	0	0	0	0	....	....	....	....	....
	Toronto Maple Leafs	20	1	8	9	30	3	0	0	0	10
1980-81	Toronto Maple Leafs	74	2	18	20	90	1	0	0	0	0
1982-83	Toronto Maple Leafs	56	4	24	28	38	....	....	....	....	....
1983-84	Toronto Maple Leafs	59	4	19	23	57	....	....	....	....	....
	NHL Totals	**430**	**17**	**110**	**127**	**440**	**14**	**0**	**2**	**2**	**24**

Claimed by **Quebec** from **NY Rangers** in Expansion Draft, June 13, 1979. Traded to **Toronto** by **Quebec** with Terry Martin for Reg Thomas, December 13, 1979. Signed as a free agent by **Philadelphia**, October 7, 1985.

FASHOWAY, Gordie

Left wing. Shoots left. 5'11", 180 lbs. Born, Portage la Prairie, Man., June 16, 1926.

Season	Club	GP	G	A	Pts	PIM	GP	G	A	Pts	PIM
1950-51	Chicago Black Hawks	13	3	2	5	14	....	....	....	....	....
	NHL Totals	**13**	**3**	**2**	**5**	**14**	....	....	....	....	....

FATA, Rico

Right wing. Shoots left. 5'11", 200 lbs. Born, Sault Ste. Marie, Ont., February 12, 1980.
(Calgary's 1st choice, 6th overall, in 1998 Entry Draft).

Season	Club	GP	G	A	Pts	PIM	GP	G	A	Pts	PIM
1998-99	Calgary Flames	20	0	1	1	4	....	....	....	....	....
99-2000	Calgary Flames	2	0	0	0	0	....	....	....	....	....
2000-01	Calgary Flames	5	0	0	0	6	....	....	....	....	....
2001-02	New York Rangers	10	0	0	0	0	....	....	....	....	....
2002-03	New York Rangers	36	2	4	6	6	....	....	....	....	....
	Pittsburgh Penguins	27	5	8	13	10	....	....	....	....	....
	NHL Totals	**100**	**7**	**13**	**20**	**26**	....	....	....	....	....

Claimed on waivers by **NY Rangers** from **Calgary**, October 3, 2001. Traded to **Pittsburgh** by **NY Rangers** with Joel Bouchard, Richard Lintner, Mikael Samuelsson and future considerations for Mike Wilson,, Alexei Kovalev, Janne Laukkanen and Dan LaCouture, February 10, 2003.

FAUBERT, Mario

Defense. Shoots right. 6'1", 175 lbs. Born, Valleyfield, Que., December 2, 1954.
(Pittsburgh's 3rd choice, 62nd overall, in 1974 Amateur Draft).

Season	Club	GP	G	A	Pts	PIM	GP	G	A	Pts	PIM
1974-75	Pittsburgh Penguins	10	1	0	1	6	....	....	....	....	....
1975-76	Pittsburgh Penguins	21	1	8	9	10	....	....	....	....	....
1976-77	Pittsburgh Penguins	47	2	11	13	32	3	1	0	1	2
1977-78	Pittsburgh Penguins	18	0	6	6	11	....	....	....	....	....
1979-80	Pittsburgh Penguins	49	5	13	18	31	2	0	1	1	0
1980-81	Pittsburgh Penguins	72	8	44	52	188	5	1	1	2	4
1981-82	Pittsburgh Penguins	14	4	8	12	14	....	....	....	....	....
	NHL Totals	**231**	**21**	**90**	**111**	**292**	**10**	**2**	**2**	**4**	**6**

• Suffered career-ending leg injury in game vs. St. Louis, November 18, 1981.

FAULKNER, Alex

Center. Shoots left. 5'8", 165 lbs. Born, Bishop Falls, Nfld., May 21, 1936.

Season	Club	GP	G	A	Pts	PIM	GP	G	A	Pts	PIM
1961-62	Toronto Maple Leafs	1	0	0	0	0	....	....	....	....	....
1962-63	Detroit Red Wings	70	10	10	20	6	8	5	0	5	2
1963-64	Detroit Red Wings	30	5	7	12	9	4	0	0	0	0
	NHL Totals	**101**	**15**	**17**	**32**	**15**	**12**	**5**	**0**	**5**	**2**

Signed as a free agent by **Toronto**, December, 1960. Claimed by **Detroit** from **Toronto** in Intra-League Draft, June 4, 1962.

FAUSS, Ted

Defense. Shoots left. 6'2", 205 lbs. Born, Clark Mills, NY, June 30, 1961.

Season	Club	GP	G	A	Pts	PIM	GP	G	A	Pts	PIM
1986-87	Toronto Maple Leafs	15	0	1	1	11	....	....	....	....	....
1987-88	Toronto Maple Leafs	13	0	1	1	4	....	....	....	....	....
	NHL Totals	**28**	**0**	**2**	**2**	**15**	....	....	....	....	....

Signed as a free agent by **Montreal**, March, 1983. Signed as a free agent by **Toronto**, July 21, 1986.

FAUST, Andre

Center. Shoots left. 5'11", 191 lbs. Born, Joliette, Que., October 7, 1969.
(New Jersey's 8th choice, 173rd overall, in 1989 Entry Draft).

Season	Club	GP	G	A	Pts	PIM	GP	G	A	Pts	PIM
1992-93	Philadelphia Flyers	10	2	2	4	4	....	....	....	....	....
1993-94	Philadelphia Flyers	37	8	5	13	10	....	....	....	....	....
	NHL Totals	**47**	**10**	**7**	**17**	**14**	....	....	....	....	....

Signed as a free agent by **Philadelphia**, October 5, 1992. Traded to **Winnipeg** by **Philadelphia** for Winnipeg's 7th round choice (later traded to Carolina – Carolina selected Andrew Merrick) in 1997 Entry Draft, September 20, 1995.

FEAMSTER, Dave

Defense. Shoots left. 5'11", 180 lbs. Born, Detroit, MI, September 10, 1958.
(Chicago's 6th choice, 96th overall, in 1978 Amateur Draft).

Season	Club	GP	G	A	Pts	PIM	GP	G	A	Pts	PIM
1981-82	Chicago Black Hawks	29	0	2	2	29	15	2	4	6	53
1982-83	Chicago Black Hawks	78	6	12	18	69	13	1	0	1	4
1983-84	Chicago Black Hawks	46	6	7	13	42	5	0	1	1	4
1984-85	Chicago Black Hawks	16	1	3	4	14	....	....	....	....	....
	NHL Totals	**169**	**13**	**24**	**37**	**154**	**33**	**3**	**5**	**8**	**61**

FEATHERSTONE, Glen

Defense. Shoots left. 6'4", 209 lbs. Born, Toronto, Ont., July 8, 1968.
(St. Louis' 4th choice, 73rd overall, in 1986 Entry Draft).

Season	Club	GP	G	A	Pts	PIM	GP	G	A	Pts	PIM
1988-89	St. Louis Blues	18	0	2	2	22	6	0	0	0	25
1989-90	St. Louis Blues	58	0	12	12	145	12	0	2	2	47
1990-91	St. Louis Blues	68	5	15	20	204	9	0	0	0	31
1991-92	Boston Bruins	7	1	0	1	20	....	....	....	....	....
1992-93	Boston Bruins	34	5	5	10	102	....	....	....	....	....
1993-94	Boston Bruins	58	1	8	9	152	1	0	0	0	0
1994-95	New York Rangers	6	1	0	1	18	....	....	....	....	....
	Hartford Whalers	13	1	1	2	32	....	....	....	....	....
1995-96	Hartford Whalers	68	2	10	12	138	....	....	....	....	....
1996-97	Hartford Whalers	41	2	5	7	87	....	....	....	....	....
	Calgary Flames	13	1	3	4	19	....	....	....	....	....
	NHL Totals	**384**	**19**	**61**	**80**	**939**	**28**	**0**	**2**	**2**	**103**

Signed as a free agent by **Boston**, July 25, 1991. Traded to **NY Rangers** by **Boston** for Daniel Lacroix, August 19, 1994. Traded to **Hartford** by **NY Rangers** with Michael Stewart, NY Rangers' 1st round choice (Jean-Sebastien Giguere) in 1995 Entry Draft and 4th round choice (Steve Wasylko) in 1996 Entry Draft for Pat Verbeek, March 23, 1995. Traded to **Calgary** by **Hartford** with Hnat Domenichelli, New Jersey's 2nd round choice (previously acquired, Calgary selected Dimitri Kokorev) in 1997 Entry Draft and Vancouver's 3rd round choice (previously acquired, Calgary selected Paul Manning) in 1998 Entry Draft for Steve Chiasson and Colorado's 3rd round choice (previously acquired, Carolina selected Francis Lessard) in 1997 Entry Draft, March 5, 1997.

FEATHERSTONE, Tony

Right wing. Shoots right. 5'11", 187 lbs. Born, Toronto, Ont., July 31, 1949.
(Oakland's 1st choice, 7th overall, in 1969 Amateur Draft).

Season	Club	GP	G	A	Pts	PIM	GP	G	A	Pts	PIM
		REGULAR SEASON					PLAYOFFS				
1969-70	Oakland Seals	9	0	1	1	17	2	0	0	0	0
1970-71	California Seals	67	8	8	16	44	....	....	....	....	....
1973-74	Minnesota North Stars	54	9	12	21	4	....	....	....	....	....
	NHL Totals	**130**	**17**	**21**	**38**	**65**	**2**	**0**	**0**	**0**	**0**

Traded to **Montreal** by **California** for Ray Martyniuk, October 6, 1971. Traded to **Minnesota** by **Montreal** with Murray Anderson for cash, May 29, 1973.

FEDERKO, Bernie

HHOF

Center. Shoots left. 6', 178 lbs. Born, Foam Lake, Sask., May 12, 1956.
(St. Louis' 1st choice, 7th overall, in 1976 Amateur Draft).

Season	Club	GP	G	A	Pts	PIM	GP	G	A	Pts	PIM
		REGULAR SEASON					PLAYOFFS				
1976-77	St. Louis Blues	31	14	9	23	15	4	1	1	2	2
1977-78	St. Louis Blues	72	17	24	41	27	....	....	....	....	....
1978-79	St. Louis Blues	74	31	64	95	14	....	....	....	....	....
1979-80	St. Louis Blues	79	38	56	94	24	3	1	0	1	2
1980-81	St. Louis Blues	78	31	73	104	47	11	8	10	18	2
1981-82	St. Louis Blues	74	30	62	92	70	10	3	15	18	10
1982-83	St. Louis Blues	75	24	60	84	24	4	2	3	5	0
1983-84	St. Louis Blues	79	41	66	107	43	11	4	4	8	10
1984-85	St. Louis Blues	76	30	73	103	27	3	0	2	2	4
1985-86	St. Louis Blues	80	34	68	102	34	19	7	14	*21	17
1986-87	St. Louis Blues	64	20	52	72	32	6	3	3	6	18
1987-88	St. Louis Blues	79	20	69	89	52	10	2	6	8	18
1988-89	St. Louis Blues	66	22	45	67	54	10	4	8	12	0
1989-90	Detroit Red Wings	73	17	40	57	24	....	....	....	....	....
	NHL Totals	**1000**	**369**	**761**	**1130**	**487**	**91**	**35**	**66**	**101**	**83**

Played in NHL All-Star Game (1980, 1981)

Traded to **Detroit** by **St. Louis** with Tony McKegney for Adam Oates and Paul MacLean, June 15, 1989. • First player in NHL history to record at least 50 assists in 10 consecutive seasons (1979 – 1988)

FEDOROV, Fedor

Center. Shoots left. 6'3", 202 lbs. Born, Appatity, USSR, June 11, 1981.
(Vancouver's 2nd choice, 66th overall, in 2001 Entry Draft).

Season	Club	GP	G	A	Pts	PIM	GP	G	A	Pts	PIM
		REGULAR SEASON					PLAYOFFS				
2002-03	Vancouver Canucks	7	0	1	1	4	....	....	....	....	....
	NHL Totals	**7**	**0**	**1**	**1**	**4**	....	....	....	....	....

• Re-entered NHL Entry Draft. Originally Tampa Bay's 7th choice, 182nd overall, in 1999 Entry Draft.

FEDOROV, Sergei

Center. Shoots left. 6'1", 200 lbs. Born, Pskov, USSR, December 13, 1969.
(Detroit's 4th choice, 74th overall, in 1989 Entry Draft).

Season	Club	GP	G	A	Pts	PIM	GP	G	A	Pts	PIM
		REGULAR SEASON					PLAYOFFS				
1990-91	Detroit Red Wings	77	31	48	79	66	7	1	5	6	4
1991-92	Detroit Red Wings	80	32	54	86	72	11	5	5	10	8
1992-93	Detroit Red Wings	73	34	53	87	72	7	3	6	9	23
1993-94	Detroit Red Wings	82	56	64	120	34	7	1	7	8	6
1994-95	Detroit Red Wings	42	20	30	50	24	17	7	*17	*24	6
1995-96	Detroit Red Wings	78	39	68	107	48	19	2	*18	20	10
1996-97♦	Detroit Red Wings	74	30	33	63	30	20	8	12	20	12
1997-98♦	Detroit Red Wings	21	6	11	17	25	22	*10	10	20	12
1998-99	Detroit Red Wings	77	26	37	63	66	10	1	8	9	8
99-2000	Detroit Red Wings	68	27	35	62	22	9	4	4	8	4
2000-01	Detroit Red Wings	75	32	37	69	40	6	2	5	7	0
2001-02♦	Detroit Red Wings	81	31	37	68	36	23	5	14	19	20
2002-03	Detroit Red Wings	80	36	47	83	52	4	1	2	3	0
	NHL Totals	**908**	**400**	**554**	**954**	**587**	**162**	**50**	**113**	**163**	**113**

NHL All-Rookie Team (1991) • NHL First All-Star Team (1994) • Frank J. Selke Trophy (1994, 1996) • Lester B. Pearson Award (1994) • Hart Trophy (1994)

Played in NHL All-Star Game (1992, 1994, 1996, 2001, 2002, 2003)

• Missed majority of 1997-98 season after failing to come to contract terms with **Detroit**. Signed as a free agent by **Anaheim**, July 19, 2003.

FEDORUK, Todd

Left wing. Shoots left. 6'2", 235 lbs. Born, Redwater, Alta., February 13, 1979.
(Philadelphia's 6th choice, 164th overall, in 1997 Entry Draft).

Season	Club	GP	G	A	Pts	PIM	GP	G	A	Pts	PIM
		REGULAR SEASON					PLAYOFFS				
2000-01	Philadelphia Flyers	53	5	5	10	109	2	0	0	0	20
2001-02	Philadelphia Flyers	55	3	4	7	141	3	0	0	0	0
2002-03	Philadelphia Flyers	63	1	5	6	105	1	0	0	0	0
	NHL Totals	**171**	**9**	**14**	**23**	**355**	**6**	**0**	**0**	**0**	**20**

FEDOTENKO, Ruslan

Left wing. Shoots left. 6'2", 195 lbs. Born, Kiev, Ukraine, January 18, 1979.

Season	Club	GP	G	A	Pts	PIM	GP	G	A	Pts	PIM
		REGULAR SEASON					PLAYOFFS				
2000-01	Philadelphia Flyers	74	16	20	36	72	6	0	1	1	4
2001-02	Philadelphia Flyers	78	17	9	26	43	5	1	0	1	2
2002-03	Tampa Bay Lightning	76	19	13	32	44	11	0	1	1	2
	NHL Totals	**228**	**52**	**42**	**94**	**159**	**22**	**1**	**2**	**3**	**8**

Signed as a free agent by **Philadelphia**, August 3, 1999. Traded to **Tampa Bay** by **Philadelphia** with Tampa Bay's 2nd round choice (previously acquired, later traded to Dallas – Dallas selected Tobias Stephan) in 2002 Entry Draft and Phoenix's 2nd round choice (previously acquired, later traded to San Jose – San Jose selected Dan Spang) in 2002 Entry Draft for Tampa Bay's 1st round choice (Joni Pitkanen) in 2002 Entry Draft, June 21, 2002.

FEDOTOV, Anatoli

Defense. Shoots left. 5'11", 178 lbs. Born, Saratov, USSR, May 11, 1966.
(Anaheim's 10th choice, 238th overall, in 1993 Entry Draft).

Season	Club	GP	G	A	Pts	PIM	GP	G	A	Pts	PIM
		REGULAR SEASON					PLAYOFFS				
1992-93	Winnipeg Jets	1	0	2	2	0	....	....	....	....	....
1993-94	Mighty Ducks of Anaheim	3	0	0	0	0	....	....	....	....	....
	NHL Totals	**4**	**0**	**2**	**2**	**0**	....	....	....	....	....

Signed as a free agent by **Winnipeg** to AHL contract, July 4, 1991. • NHL ruled that **Winnipeg** had promoted Fedotov illegally and had no claim to his NHL rights. Fedotov entered NHL Entry Draft and was selected by Anaheim, June 26, 1993.

FEDYK, Brent

Left wing. Shoots right. 6', 194 lbs. Born, Yorkton, Sask., March 8, 1967.
(Detroit's 1st choice, 8th overall, in 1985 Entry Draft).

Season	Club	GP	G	A	Pts	PIM	GP	G	A	Pts	PIM
		REGULAR SEASON					PLAYOFFS				
1987-88	Detroit Red Wings	2	0	1	1	2	....	....	....	....	....
1988-89	Detroit Red Wings	5	2	0	2	0	....	....	....	....	....
1989-90	Detroit Red Wings	27	1	4	5	6	....	....	....	....	....
1990-91	Detroit Red Wings	67	16	19	35	38	6	1	0	1	2
1991-92	Detroit Red Wings	61	5	8	13	42	1	0	0	0	2
1992-93	Philadelphia Flyers	74	21	38	59	48	....	....	....	....	....
1993-94	Philadelphia Flyers	72	20	18	38	74	....	....	....	....	....
1994-95	Philadelphia Flyers	30	8	4	12	14	9	2	2	4	8
1995-96	Philadelphia Flyers	24	10	5	15	24	....	....	....	....	....
	Dallas Stars	41	10	9	19	30	....	....	....	....	....
1998-99	New York Rangers	67	4	6	10	30	....	....	....	....	....
	NHL Totals	**470**	**97**	**112**	**209**	**308**	**16**	**3**	**2**	**5**	**12**

Traded to **Philadelphia** by **Detroit** for Philadelphia's 4th round choice (later traded to Boston – Boston selected Charles Paquette) in 1993 Entry Draft, October 1, 1992. Traded to **Dallas** by **Philadelphia** for Trent Klatt, December 13, 1995. Signed as a free agent by **NY Rangers**, August 13, 1998.

FELIX, Chris

Defense. Shoots right. 5'11", 190 lbs. Born, Bramalea, Ont., May 27, 1964.

Season	Club	GP	G	A	Pts	PIM	GP	G	A	Pts	PIM
		REGULAR SEASON					PLAYOFFS				
1987-88	Washington Capitals	....	....	....	....	....	1	0	0	0	0
1988-89	Washington Capitals	21	0	8	8	8	1	0	1	1	0
1989-90	Washington Capitals	6	1	0	1	2	....	....	....	....	....
1990-91	Washington Capitals	8	0	4	4	0	....	....	....	....	....
	NHL Totals	**35**	**1**	**12**	**13**	**10**	**2**	**0**	**1**	**1**	**0**

Signed as a free agent by **Washington**, March 1, 1988.

FELSNER, Brian

Left wing. Shoots left. 5'11", 189 lbs. Born, Mt. Clemens, MI, November 11, 1972.

Season	Club	GP	G	A	Pts	PIM	GP	G	A	Pts	PIM
		REGULAR SEASON					PLAYOFFS				
1997-98	Chicago Blackhawks	12	1	3	4	12	....	....	....	....	....
	NHL Totals	**12**	**1**	**3**	**4**	**12**	....	....	....	....	....

• Brother of Denny

Signed as a free agent by **Chicago**, September 5, 1997. Traded to **Ottawa** by **Chicago** for Justin Hocking, August 21, 1998. Signed as a free agent by **Carolina**, July 28, 2000.

FELSNER, Denny

Left wing. Shoots left. 6', 195 lbs. Born, Warren, MI, April 29, 1970.
(St. Louis' 3rd choice, 55th overall, in 1989 Entry Draft).

Season	Club	GP	G	A	Pts	PIM	GP	G	A	Pts	PIM
		REGULAR SEASON					PLAYOFFS				
1991-92	St. Louis Blues	3	0	1	1	0	1	0	0	0	0
1992-93	St. Louis Blues	6	0	3	3	2	9	2	3	5	2
1993-94	St. Louis Blues	6	1	0	1	2	....	....	....	....	....
1994-95	St. Louis Blues	3	0	0	0	2	....	....	....	....	....
	NHL Totals	**18**	**1**	**4**	**5**	**6**	**10**	**2**	**3**	**5**	**2**

• Brother of Brian

Signed as a free agent by **Vancouver**, August 31, 1995.

FELTRIN, Tony

Defense. Shoots left. 6'1", 184 lbs. Born, Ladysmith, B.C., December 6, 1961.
(Pittsburgh's 3rd choice, 72nd overall, in 1980 Entry Draft).

Season	Club	GP	G	A	Pts	PIM	GP	G	A	Pts	PIM
		REGULAR SEASON					PLAYOFFS				
1980-81	Pittsburgh Penguins	2	0	0	0	0	....	....	....	....	....
1981-82	Pittsburgh Penguins	4	0	0	0	4	....	....	....	....	....
1982-83	Pittsburgh Penguins	32	3	3	6	40	....	....	....	....	....
1985-86	New York Rangers	10	0	0	0	21	....	....	....	....	....
	NHL Totals	**48**	**3**	**3**	**6**	**65**	....	....	....	....	....

Signed as a free agent by **NY Rangers**, October 8, 1985.

FENTON, Paul

Left wing. Shoots left. 5'11", 180 lbs. Born, Springfield, MA, December 22, 1959.

Season	Club	GP	G	A	Pts	PIM	GP	G	A	Pts	PIM
		REGULAR SEASON					PLAYOFFS				
1984-85	Hartford Whalers	33	7	5	12	10	....	....	....	....	....
1985-86	Hartford Whalers	1	0	0	0	0	....	....	....	....	....
1986-87	New York Rangers	8	0	0	0	2	....	....	....	....	....
1987-88	Los Angeles Kings	71	20	23	43	46	5	2	1	3	2
1988-89	Los Angeles Kings	21	2	3	5	6	....	....	....	....	....
	Winnipeg Jets	59	14	9	23	33	....	....	....	....	....
1989-90	Winnipeg Jets	80	32	18	50	40	7	2	0	2	23
1990-91	Winnipeg Jets	17	4	4	8	18	....	....	....	....	....
	Toronto Maple Leafs	30	5	10	15	0	....	....	....	....	....
	Calgary Flames	31	5	7	12	10	5	0	0	0	2

Season	Club	GP	G	A	Pts	PIM	PO GP	PO G	PO A	PO Pts	PO PIM
		REGULAR SEASON					PLAYOFFS				
1991-92	San Jose Sharks	60	11	4	15	33	....	....	....	....	....
	NHL Totals	**411**	**100**	**83**	**183**	**198**	**17**	**4**	**1**	**5**	**27**

Signed as a free agent by **Hartford**, October 6, 1983. Signed as a free agent by **NY Rangers**, September 11, 1986. Claimed by **Los Angeles** from **NY Rangers** in Waiver Draft, October 5, 1987. Traded to **Winnipeg** by **Los Angeles** for Gilles Hamel, November 25, 1988. Traded to **Toronto** by **Winnipeg** with Dave Ellett for Ed Olczyk and Mark Osborne, November 10, 1989. Traded to **Washington** by **Toronto** with John Kordic for Washington's 5th round choice (Alexei Kudashov) in 1991 Entry Draft, January 24, 1991. Traded to **Calgary** by **Washington** for Ken Sabourin, January 24, 1991. Traded to **Hartford** by **Calgary** for future cash, August 26, 1991. Traded to **San Jose** by **Hartford** for Mike McHugh, October 18, 1991.

FENYVES, David

Defense. Shoots left. 6', 192 lbs. Born, Dunnville, Ont., April 29, 1960.

Season	Club	GP	G	A	Pts	PIM	PO GP	PO G	PO A	PO Pts	PO PIM
1982-83	Buffalo Sabres	24	0	8	8	14	4	0	0	0	0
1983-84	Buffalo Sabres	10	0	4	4	9	2	0	0	0	7
1984-85	Buffalo Sabres	60	1	8	9	27	5	0	0	0	2
1985-86	Buffalo Sabres	47	0	7	7	37	....	....	....	....	....
1986-87	Buffalo Sabres	7	1	0	1	0	....	....	....	....	....
1987-88	Philadelphia Flyers	5	0	0	0	0	....	....	....	....	....
1988-89	Philadelphia Flyers	1	0	1	1	0	....	....	....	....	....
1989-90	Philadelphia Flyers	12	0	0	0	4	....	....	....	....	....
1990-91	Philadelphia Flyers	40	1	4	5	28	....	....	....	....	....
	NHL Totals	**206**	**3**	**32**	**35**	**119**	**11**	**0**	**0**	**0**	**9**

Signed as a free agent by **Buffalo**, October 31, 1979. Claimed by **Philadelphia** from **Buffalo** in Waiver Draft, October 5, 1987.

FERENCE, Andrew

Defense. Shoots left. 5'10", 196 lbs. Born, Edmonton, Alta., March 17, 1979.
(Pittsburgh's 8th choice, 208th overall, in 1997 Entry Draft).

Season	Club	GP	G	A	Pts	PIM	PO GP	PO G	PO A	PO Pts	PO PIM
99-2000	Pittsburgh Penguins	30	2	4	6	20	....	....	....	....	....
2000-01	Pittsburgh Penguins	36	4	11	15	28	18	3	7	10	16
2001-02	Pittsburgh Penguins	75	4	7	11	73	....	....	....	....	....
2002-03	Pittsburgh Penguins	22	1	3	4	36	....	....	....	....	....
	Calgary Flames	16	0	4	4	6	....	....	....	....	....
	NHL Totals	**179**	**11**	**29**	**40**	**163**	**18**	**3**	**7**	**10**	**16**

Traded to **Calgary** by **Pittsburgh** for future considerations, February 10, 2003. • Missed majority of 2002-03 season recovering from groin (November 18, 2002 vs. Montreal) and ankle (March 20, 2003 vs. Los Angeles) injuries.

FERENCE, Brad

Defense. Shoots right. 6'3", 210 lbs. Born, Calgary, Alta., April 2, 1979.
(Vancouver's 1st choice, 10th overall, in 1997 Entry Draft).

Season	Club	GP	G	A	Pts	PIM	PO GP	PO G	PO A	PO Pts	PO PIM
99-2000	Florida Panthers	13	0	2	2	46	....	....	....	....	....
2000-01	Florida Panthers	14	0	1	1	14	....	....	....	....	....
2001-02	Florida Panthers	80	2	15	17	254	....	....	....	....	....
2002-03	Florida Panthers	60	2	6	8	118	....	....	....	....	....
	Phoenix Coyotes	15	0	1	1	28	....	....	....	....	....
	NHL Totals	**182**	**4**	**25**	**29**	**460**	....	....	....	....	....

Traded to **Florida** by **Vancouver** with Pavel Bure, Bret Hedican and Vancouver's 3rd round choice (Robert Fried) in 2000 Entry Draft for Ed Jovanovski, Dave Gagner, Mike Brown, Kevin Weekes and Florida's 1st round choice (Nathan Smith) in 2000 Entry Draft, January 17, 1999. Traded to **Phoenix** by **Florida** for Darcy Hordichuk and Phoenix's 2nd round choice (later traded to Tampa Bay – Tampa Bay selected Matt Smaby) in 2003 Entry Draft, March 8, 2003.

FERGUS, Tom

Center. Shoots left. 6'3", 210 lbs. Born, Chicago, IL, June 16, 1962.
(Boston's 2nd choice, 60th overall, in 1980 Entry Draft).

Season	Club	GP	G	A	Pts	PIM	PO GP	PO G	PO A	PO Pts	PO PIM
1981-82	Boston Bruins	61	15	24	39	12	6	3	0	3	0
1982-83	Boston Bruins	80	28	35	63	39	15	2	2	4	15
1983-84	Boston Bruins	69	25	36	61	12	3	2	0	2	9
1984-85	Boston Bruins	79	30	43	73	75	5	0	0	0	4
1985-86	Toronto Maple Leafs	78	31	42	73	64	10	5	7	12	6
1986-87	Toronto Maple Leafs	57	21	28	49	57	2	0	1	1	2
1987-88	Toronto Maple Leafs	63	19	31	50	81	6	2	3	5	2
1988-89	Toronto Maple Leafs	80	22	45	67	48	....	....	....	....	....
1989-90	Toronto Maple Leafs	54	19	26	45	62	5	2	1	3	4
1990-91	Toronto Maple Leafs	14	5	4	9	8	....	....	....	....	....
1991-92	Toronto Maple Leafs	11	1	3	4	4	....	....	....	....	....
	Vancouver Canucks	44	14	20	34	17	13	5	3	8	6
1992-93	Vancouver Canucks	36	5	9	14	20	....	....	....	....	....
	NHL Totals	**726**	**235**	**346**	**581**	**499**	**65**	**21**	**17**	**38**	**48**

Traded to **Toronto** by **Boston** for Bill Derlago, October 11, 1985. • Missed majority of 1990-91 season recovering from abdominal muscle injury originally suffered in game vs. St. Louis, February 6, 1990. Traded to **Vancouver** by **Toronto** for cash, December 18, 1991.

FERGUSON, Craig

Center. Shoots left. 5'11", 190 lbs. Born, Castro Valley, CA, April 8, 1970.
(Montreal's 6th choice, 146th overall, in 1989 Entry Draft).

Season	Club	GP	G	A	Pts	PIM	PO GP	PO G	PO A	PO Pts	PO PIM
1993-94	Montreal Canadiens	2	0	1	1	0	....	....	....	....	....
1994-95	Montreal Canadiens	1	0	0	0	0	....	....	....	....	....
1995-96	Montreal Canadiens	10	1	0	1	2	....	....	....	....	....
	Calgary Flames	8	0	0	0	4	....	....	....	....	....
1996-97	Florida Panthers	3	0	0	0	0	....	....	....	....	....
99-2000	Florida Panthers	3	0	0	0	0	....	....	....	....	....
	NHL Totals	**27**	**1**	**1**	**2**	**6**	....	....	....	....	....

• Son of Norm

Traded to **Calgary** by **Montreal** with Yves Sarault for Calgary's 8th round choice (Petr Kubos) in 1997 Entry Draft, November 26, 1995. Traded to **Los Angeles** by **Calgary** for Pat Conacher, February 10, 1996. Signed as a free agent by **Florida**, July 24, 1996.

FERGUSON, George

Center. Shoots right. 6', 195 lbs. Born, Trenton, Ont., August 22, 1952.
(Toronto's 1st choice, 11th overall, in 1972 Amateur Draft).

Season	Club	GP	G	A	Pts	PIM	PO GP	PO G	PO A	PO Pts	PO PIM
1972-73	Toronto Maple Leafs	72	10	13	23	34	....	....	....	....	....
1973-74	Toronto Maple Leafs	16	0	4	4	4	3	0	1	1	2
1974-75	Toronto Maple Leafs	69	19	30	49	61	7	1	0	1	7
1975-76	Toronto Maple Leafs	79	12	32	44	76	10	2	4	6	2
1976-77	Toronto Maple Leafs	50	9	15	24	24	9	0	3	3	7
1977-78	Toronto Maple Leafs	73	7	16	23	37	13	5	1	6	7
1978-79	Pittsburgh Penguins	80	21	29	50	37	7	2	1	3	0
1979-80	Pittsburgh Penguins	73	21	28	49	36	5	0	3	3	4
1980-81	Pittsburgh Penguins	79	25	18	43	42	5	2	6	8	9
1981-82	Pittsburgh Penguins	71	22	31	53	45	5	0	1	1	0
1982-83	Pittsburgh Penguins	7	0	0	0	2	....	....	....	....	....
	Minnesota North Stars	65	8	12	20	14	9	0	3	3	4
1983-84	Minnesota North Stars	63	6	10	16	19	13	2	0	2	2
	NHL Totals	**797**	**160**	**238**	**398**	**431**	**86**	**14**	**23**	**37**	**44**

Traded to **Pittsburgh** by **Toronto** with Randy Carlyle for Dave Burrows, June 14, 1978. Traded to **Minnesota** by **Pittsburgh** with Pittsburgh's 1st round choice (Brian Lawton) in 1983 Entry Draft for Ron Meighan, Anders Hakansson and Minnesota's 1st round choice (Bob Errey) in 1983 Entry Draft, October 28, 1982.

FERGUSON, John

Left wing. Shoots left. 5'11", 190 lbs. Born, Vancouver, B.C., September 5, 1938.

Season	Club	GP	G	A	Pts	PIM	PO GP	PO G	PO A	PO Pts	PO PIM
1963-64	Montreal Canadiens	59	18	27	45	125	7	0	1	1	25
1964-65 ◆	Montreal Canadiens	69	17	27	44	156	13	3	1	4	28
1965-66 ◆	Montreal Canadiens	65	11	14	25	153	10	2	0	2	*44
1966-67	Montreal Canadiens	67	20	22	42	*177	10	4	2	6	22
1967-68 ◆	Montreal Canadiens	61	15	18	33	117	13	3	5	8	25
1968-69 ◆	Montreal Canadiens	71	29	23	52	185	14	4	3	7	*80
1969-70	Montreal Canadiens	48	19	13	32	139	....	....	....	....	....
1970-71 ◆	Montreal Canadiens	60	16	14	30	162	18	4	6	10	36
	NHL Totals	**500**	**145**	**158**	**303**	**1214**	**85**	**20**	**18**	**38**	**260**

Played in NHL All-Star Game (1965, 1967)

Traded to **Montreal** by **Cleveland** (AHL) for cash, June, 1963.

FERGUSON, Lorne

Left wing. Shoots left. 6', 175 lbs. Born, Palmerston, Ont., May 26, 1930.

Season	Club	GP	G	A	Pts	PIM	PO GP	PO G	PO A	PO Pts	PO PIM
1949-50	Boston Bruins	3	1	1	2	0	....	....	....	....	....
1950-51	Boston Bruins	70	16	17	33	31	6	1	0	1	2
1951-52	Boston Bruins	27	3	4	7	14	....	....	....	....	....
1954-55	Boston Bruins	69	20	14	34	24	4	1	0	1	2
1955-56	Boston Bruins	32	7	5	12	18	....	....	....	....	....
	Detroit Red Wings	31	8	7	15	12	10	1	2	3	12
1956-57	Detroit Red Wings	70	13	10	23	26	5	1	0	1	6
1957-58	Detroit Red Wings	15	1	3	4	0	....	....	....	....	....
	Chicago Black Hawks	38	6	9	15	24	....	....	....	....	....
1958-59	Chicago Black Hawks	67	7	10	17	44	6	2	1	3	2
	NHL Totals	**422**	**82**	**80**	**162**	**193**	**31**	**6**	**3**	**9**	**24**

Rights traded to **Boston** by **NY Rangers** with Bill Moe and future considerations for Pat Egan, October 7, 1949. Traded to **Detroit** by **Boston** with Murray Costello for Real Chevrefils and Jerry Toppazzini, January 17, 1956. Traded to **Chicago** by **Detroit** with Earl Reibel, Billy Dea and Bill Dineen for Bob Bailey, Nick Mickoski, Jack McIntyre and Hec Lalande, December 17, 1957. Traded to **Montreal** by **Chicago** with Glen Skov, the rights to Danny Lewicki, Terry Gray and Bob Bailey for Cec Hoekstra, Reggie Fleming, Ab McDonald and Bob Courcy, June 7, 1960.

FERGUSON, Norm

Right wing. Shoots right. 5'9", 165 lbs. Born, Sydney, N.S., October 16, 1945.

Season	Club	GP	G	A	Pts	PIM	PO GP	PO G	PO A	PO Pts	PO PIM
1968-69	Oakland Seals	76	34	20	54	31	7	1	4	5	7
1969-70	Oakland Seals	72	11	9	20	19	3	0	0	0	0
1970-71	California Seals	54	14	17	31	9	....	....	....	....	....
1971-72	California Golden Seals	77	14	20	34	13	....	....	....	....	....
	NHL Totals	**279**	**73**	**66**	**139**	**72**	**10**	**1**	**4**	**5**	**7**

• Father of Craig

Traded to **Oakland** by **Montreal** with Stan Fuller and future considerations (Francois Lacombe and Michel Jacques, June, 1968) for Wally Boyer, Alain Caron, Oakland's 1st round choices in 1968 (Jim Pritchard) and 1970 (Ray Martynuik) Amateur Drafts and future considerations (Lyle Bradley, June, 1968), May 21, 1968. Claimed by **NY Islanders** from **California** in Expansion Draft, June 6, 1972.

FERGUSON, Scott

Defense. Shoots left. 6'1", 195 lbs. Born, Camrose, Alta., January 6, 1973.

Season	Club	GP	G	A	Pts	PIM	PO GP	PO G	PO A	PO Pts	PO PIM
1997-98	Edmonton Oilers	1	0	0	0	0	....	....	....	....	....
1998-99	Mighty Ducks of Anaheim	2	0	1	1	0	....	....	....	....	....
2000-01	Edmonton Oilers	20	0	1	1	13	6	0	0	0	0
2001-02	Edmonton Oilers	50	3	2	5	75	....	....	....	....	....

Season	Club	REGULAR SEASON GP	G	A	Pts	PIM	PLAYOFFS GP	G	A	Pts	PIM
2002-03	Edmonton Oilers	78	3	5	8	120	5	0	0	0	8
	NHL Totals	**151**	**6**	**9**	**15**	**208**	**11**	**0**	**0**	**0**	**8**

Signed as a free agent by **Edmonton**, June 2, 1994. Traded to **Ottawa** by **Edmonton** for Frantisek Musil, March 9, 1998. Signed as a free agent by **Anaheim**, July 27, 1998. Signed as a free agent by **Edmonton**, July 5, 2000.

FERNER, Mark

Defense. Shoots left. 6', 193 lbs. Born, Regina, Sask., September 5, 1965.
(Buffalo's 12th choice, 202nd overall, in 1983 Entry Draft).

Season	Club	GP	G	A	Pts	PIM	GP	G	A	Pts	PIM
1986-87	Buffalo Sabres	13	0	3	3	9	....	....	....	....	....
1988-89	Buffalo Sabres	2	0	0	0	2	....	....	....	....	....
1989-90	Washington Capitals	2	0	0	0	0	....	....	....	....	....
1990-91	Washington Capitals	7	0	1	1	4	....	....	....	....	....
1993-94	Mighty Ducks of Anaheim	50	3	5	8	30	....	....	....	....	....
1994-95	Mighty Ducks of Anaheim	14	0	1	1	6	....	....	....	....	....
	Detroit Red Wings	3	0	0	0	0	....	....	....	....	....
	NHL Totals	**91**	**3**	**10**	**13**	**51**	....	....	....	....	....

Traded to **Washington** by **Buffalo** for Scott McCrory, June 1, 1989. Traded to **Toronto** by **Washington** for cash, February 27, 1992. Signed as a free agent by **Ottawa**, August 6, 1992. Claimed by **Anaheim** from **Ottawa** in Expansion Draft, June, 24, 1993. Traded to **Detroit** by **Anaheim** with Stu Grimson and Anaheim's 6th round choice (Magnus Nilsson) in 1996 Entry Draft for Mike Sillinger and Jason York, April 4, 1994.

FERRARO, Chris

Center. Shoots right. 5'9", 175 lbs. Born, Port Jefferson, NY, January 24, 1973.
(NY Rangers' 4th choice, 85th overall, in 1992 Entry Draft).

Season	Club	GP	G	A	Pts	PIM	GP	G	A	Pts	PIM
1995-96	New York Rangers	2	1	0	1	0	....	....	....	....	....
1996-97	New York Rangers	12	1	1	2	6	....	....	....	....	....
1997-98	Pittsburgh Penguins	46	3	4	7	43	....	....	....	....	....
1998-99	Edmonton Oilers	2	1	0	1	0	....	....	....	....	....
99-2000	New York Islanders	11	1	3	4	8	....	....	....	....	....
2001-02	Washington Capitals	1	0	1	1	0	....	....	....	....	....
	NHL Totals	**74**	**7**	**9**	**16**	**57**	....	....	....	....	....

• Brother of Peter

Claimed on waivers by **Pittsburgh** from **NY Rangers**, October 1, 1997. Signed as a free agent by **Edmonton**, August 13, 1998. Signed as a free agent by **NY Islanders**, July 22, 1999. Signed as a free agent by **New Jersey**, July 20, 2000. Traded to **Washington** by **New Jersey** for future considerations, August 22, 2001. Signed as a free agent by **Phoenix**, July 17, 2003.

FERRARO, Peter

Left wing. Shoots right. 5'10", 180 lbs. Born, Port Jefferson, NY, January 24, 1973.
(NY Rangers' 1st choice, 24th overall, in 1992 Entry Draft).

Season	Club	GP	G	A	Pts	PIM	GP	G	A	Pts	PIM
1995-96	New York Rangers	5	0	1	1	0	....	....	....	....	....
1996-97	New York Rangers	2	0	0	0	0	2	0	0	0	0
1997-98	Pittsburgh Penguins	29	3	4	7	12	....	....	....	....	....
	New York Rangers	1	0	0	0	2	....	....	....	....	....
1998-99	Boston Bruins	46	6	8	14	44	....	....	....	....	....
99-2000	Boston Bruins	5	0	1	1	0	....	....	....	....	....
2001-02	Washington Capitals	4	0	1	1	0	....	....	....	....	....
	NHL Totals	**92**	**9**	**15**	**24**	**58**	**2**	**0**	**0**	**0**	**0**

• Brother of Chris

Claimed on waivers by **Pittsburgh** from **NY Rangers**, October 1, 1997. Claimed on waivers by **NY Rangers** from **Pittsburgh**, January 9, 1998. Signed as a free agent by **Boston**, August 5, 1998. Claimed by **Atlanta** from **Boston** in Expansion Draft, June 25, 1999. Traded to **Boston** by **Atlanta** for Randy Robitaille, June 25, 1999. Signed as a free agent by **Washington**, August 1, 2001. Signed as a free agent by **Phoenix**, July 17, 2003.

FERRARO, Ray

Center. Shoots left. 5'9", 200 lbs. Born, Trail, B.C., August 23, 1964.
(Hartford's 5th choice, 88th overall, in 1982 Entry Draft).

Season	Club	GP	G	A	Pts	PIM	GP	G	A	Pts	PIM
1984-85	Hartford Whalers	44	11	17	28	40	....	....	....	....	....
1985-86	Hartford Whalers	76	30	47	77	57	10	3	6	9	4
1986-87	Hartford Whalers	80	27	32	59	42	6	1	1	2	8
1987-88	Hartford Whalers	68	21	29	50	81	6	1	1	2	6
1988-89	Hartford Whalers	80	41	35	76	86	4	2	0	2	4
1989-90	Hartford Whalers	79	25	29	54	109	7	0	3	3	2
1990-91	Hartford Whalers	15	2	5	7	18	....	....	....	....	....
	New York Islanders	61	19	16	35	52	....	....	....	....	....
1991-92	New York Islanders	80	40	40	80	92	....	....	....	....	....
1992-93	New York Islanders	46	14	13	27	40	18	13	7	20	18
1993-94	New York Islanders	82	21	32	53	83	4	1	0	1	6
1994-95	New York Islanders	47	22	21	43	30	....	....	....	....	....
1995-96	New York Rangers	65	25	29	54	82	....	....	....	....	....
	Los Angeles Kings	11	4	2	6	10	....	....	....	....	....
1996-97	Los Angeles Kings	81	25	21	46	112	....	....	....	....	....
1997-98	Los Angeles Kings	40	6	9	15	42	3	0	1	1	2
1998-99	Los Angeles Kings	65	13	18	31	59	....	....	....	....	....
99-2000	Atlanta Thrashers	81	19	25	44	88	....	....	....	....	....
2000-01	Atlanta Thrashers	81	29	47	76	91	....	....	....	....	....
2001-02	Atlanta Thrashers	61	8	19	27	66	....	....	....	....	....
	St. Louis Blues	15	6	4	10	8	10	0	3	3	4
	NHL Totals	**1258**	**408**	**490**	**898**	**1288**	**68**	**21**	**22**	**43**	**54**

Played in NHL All-Star Game (1992)

Traded to **NY Islanders** by **Hartford** for Doug Crossman, November 13, 1990. Signed as a free agent by **NY Rangers**, August 9, 1995. Traded to **Los Angeles** by **NY Rangers** with Ian Laperriere, Mattias Norstrom, Nathan LaFayette and NY Rangers' 4th round choice (Sean Blanchard) in 1997 Entry Draft for Marty McSorley, Jari Kurri and Shane Churla, March 14, 1996. Signed as a free agent by **Atlanta**, August 9, 1999. Traded to **St. Louis** by **Atlanta** for Carolina's 4th round choice (previously acquired, Atlanta selected Lane Manson) in 2002 Entry Draft, March 18, 2002. • Officially announced retirement, August 2, 2002.

FETISOV, Viacheslav HHOF

Defense. Shoots left. 6'1", 220 lbs. Born, Moscow, USSR, April 20, 1958.
(New Jersey's 6th choice, 150th overall, in 1983 Entry Draft).

Season	Club	GP	G	A	Pts	PIM	GP	G	A	Pts	PIM
1989-90	New Jersey Devils	72	8	34	42	52	6	0	2	2	10
1990-91	New Jersey Devils	67	3	16	19	62	7	0	0	0	17
1991-92	New Jersey Devils	70	3	23	26	108	6	0	3	3	8
1992-93	New Jersey Devils	76	4	23	27	158	5	0	2	2	4
1993-94	New Jersey Devils	52	1	14	15	30	14	1	0	1	8
1994-95	New Jersey Devils	4	0	1	1	0	....	....	....	....	....
	Detroit Red Wings	14	3	11	14	2	18	0	8	8	14
1995-96	Detroit Red Wings	69	7	35	42	96	19	1	4	5	34
1996-97 ♦	Detroit Red Wings	64	5	23	28	76	20	0	4	4	42
1997-98 ♦	Detroit Red Wings	58	2	12	14	72	21	0	3	3	10
	NHL Totals	**546**	**36**	**192**	**228**	**656**	**116**	**2**	**26**	**28**	**147**

• Re-entered NHL Entry Draft. Originally Montreal's 15th choice, 201st overall, in 1978 Amateur Draft.

Played in NHL All-Star Game (1997, 1998)

Traded to **Detroit** by **New Jersey** for Detroit's 3rd round choice (David Gosselin) in 1995 Entry Draft, April 3, 1995.

FIBIGER, Jesse

Defense. Shoots left. 6'3", 210 lbs. Born, Victoria, B.C., April 4, 1978.
(Anaheim's 5th choice, 178th overall, in 1998 Entry Draft).

Season	Club	GP	G	A	Pts	PIM	GP	G	A	Pts	PIM
2002-03	San Jose Sharks	16	0	0	0	2	....	....	....	....	....
	NHL Totals	**16**	**0**	**0**	**0**	**2**	....	....	....	....	....

Signed as a free agent by **San Jose**, August 15, 2001.

FIDDLER, Vernon

Center. Shoots left. 5'11", 195 lbs. Born, Edmonton, Alta., May 9, 1980.

Season	Club	GP	G	A	Pts	PIM	GP	G	A	Pts	PIM
2002-03	Nashville Predators	19	4	2	6	14	....	....	....	....	....
	NHL Totals	**19**	**4**	**2**	**6**	**14**	....	....	....	....	....

Signed as a free agent by **Nashville**, May 6, 2002.

FIDLER, Mike

Left wing. Shoots left. 5'11", 195 lbs. Born, Everett, MA, August 19, 1956.
(California's 3rd choice, 41st overall, in 1976 Amateur Draft).

Season	Club	GP	G	A	Pts	PIM	GP	G	A	Pts	PIM
1976-77	Cleveland Barons	46	17	16	33	17	....	....	....	....	....
1977-78	Cleveland Barons	78	23	28	51	38	....	....	....	....	....
1978-79	Minnesota North Stars	59	23	26	49	42	....	....	....	....	....
1979-80	Minnesota North Stars	24	5	4	9	13	....	....	....	....	....
1980-81	Minnesota North Stars	20	5	12	17	6	....	....	....	....	....
	Hartford Whalers	38	9	9	18	4	....	....	....	....	....
1981-82	Hartford Whalers	2	0	1	1	0	....	....	....	....	....
1982-83	Chicago Black Hawks	4	2	1	3	4	....	....	....	....	....
	NHL Totals	**271**	**84**	**97**	**181**	**124**	....	....	....	....	....

Transferred to **Cleveland** after **California** franchise relocated, August 26, 1976. Protected by **Minnesota** prior to **Cleveland-Minnesota** Dispersal Draft, June 15, 1978. • Missed majority of 1979-80 season recovering from shoulder surgery, June, 1979. Traded to **Hartford** by **Minnesota** for Gordie Roberts, December 16, 1980. Signed as a free agent by **Boston**, December 1, 1981. Signed as a free agent by **Chicago**, November 28, 1982.

FIELD, Wilf

Defense. Shoots right. 5'11", 185 lbs. Born, Winnipeg, Man., April 29, 1915.

Season	Club	GP	G	A	Pts	PIM	GP	G	A	Pts	PIM
1936-37	New York Americans	2	0	0	0	0	....	....	....	....	....
1938-39	New York Americans	47	1	3	4	37	2	0	0	0	2
1939-40	New York Americans	45	1	3	4	28	....	....	....	....	....
1940-41	New York Americans	36	5	6	11	31	....	....	....	....	....
1941-42	Brooklyn Americans	41	6	9	15	23	....	....	....	....	....
1944-45	Montreal Canadiens	9	1	0	1	10	....	....	....	....	....
	Chicago Black Hawks	39	3	4	7	22	....	....	....	....	....
	NHL Totals	**219**	**17**	**25**	**42**	**151**	**2**	**0**	**0**	**0**	**2**

Signed as a free agent by **NY Americans**, November, 1936. • Team name changed to **Brooklyn Americans** prior to 1941-42 season. Rights transferred to **Montreal** from **Brooklyn** in Special Dispersal Draw, September 11, 1943. Loaned to **Chicago** by **Montreal** for the remainder of the 1944-45 season, December 7, 1944. Loaned to **Buffalo** (AHL) by **Montreal** with Frank Eddolls, Kenny Mosdell and cash for the loan of Lorrain Thibeault, October 24, 1945.

FIELDER, Guyle

Center. Shoots left. 5'9", 165 lbs. Born, Potlatch, ID, November 21, 1930.

Season	Club	GP	G	A	Pts	PIM	GP	G	A	Pts	PIM
1950-51	Chicago Black Hawks	3	0	0	0	0	....	....	....	....	....
1952-53	Detroit Red Wings	....	....	....	....	....	4	0	0	0	0
1953-54	Boston Bruins	....	....	....	....	....	2	0	0	0	2

Season	Club	Regular Season GP	G	A	Pts	PIM	Playoffs GP	G	A	Pts	PIM
1957-58	Detroit Red Wings	6	0	0	0	2	....	....	....	....	....
	NHL Totals	**9**	**0**	**0**	**0**	**2**	**6**	**0**	**0**	**0**	**2**

Signed as a free agent by **Chicago**, March 9, 1951. Traded to **Detroit** by **Chicago** with Steve Hrymnak and Red Almas for cash, September 23, 1952. Loaned to **Chicago** by **Detroit** (Edmonton-WHL) for 1952-53 season for the loan of Ray Hannigan for 1952-53 season, October 15, 1952. Claimed on waivers by **NY Rangers** from **Detroit**, September 29, 1953. Traded to **Seattle** (WHL) by **NY Rangers** for the rights to Lee Hyssop, October, 1953. NHL rights traded to **Boston** by **Seattle** (WHL) for cash, October, 1953. Claimed by **Boston** from **Seattle** (WHL) in Inter-League Draft, June 5, 1957. Traded to **Detroit** by **Boston** for cash, June 15, 1957. Claimed by **Toronto** from **Seattle** (WHL) in Inter-League Draft, June 3, 1958. • Fielder refused to sign with Toronto and remained the property of Seattle. Traded to **Salt Lake** (WHL) by **Seattle** (WHL) for Bobby Schmautz, November 15, 1969. Traded to **Portland** (WHL) by **California** (Salt Lake-WHL) with the loan of Jake Rathwell for Fred Hilts and Lyle Bradley, January, 1972.

FILIMONOV, Dmitri

Defense. Shoots right. 6'4", 220 lbs. Born, Perm, USSR, October 14, 1971.
(Winnipeg's 2nd choice, 49th overall, in 1991 Entry Draft).

Season	Club	GP	G	A	Pts	PIM	GP	G	A	Pts	PIM
1993-94	Ottawa Senators	30	1	4	5	18	....	....	....	....	....
	NHL Totals	**30**	**1**	**4**	**5**	**18**	....	....	....	....	....

Rights traded to **Ottawa** by **Winnipeg** for Ottawa's 4th round choice (Ruslan Batyrshin) in 1993 Entry Draft, March 4, 1993.

FILLION, Bob

Left wing. Shoots left. 5'10", 170 lbs. Born, Thetford Mines, Que., July 12, 1921.

Season	Club	GP	G	A	Pts	PIM	GP	G	A	Pts	PIM
1943-44 ◆	Montreal Canadiens	41	7	23	30	14	3	0	0	0	0
1944-45	Montreal Canadiens	31	6	8	14	12	1	3	0	3	0
1945-46 ◆	Montreal Canadiens	50	10	6	16	12	9	4	3	7	6
1946-47	Montreal Canadiens	57	6	3	9	16	8	0	0	0	0
1947-48	Montreal Canadiens	32	9	9	18	8	....	....	....	....	....
1948-49	Montreal Canadiens	59	3	9	12	14	7	0	1	1	4
1949-50	Montreal Canadiens	57	1	3	4	8	5	0	0	0	0
	NHL Totals	**327**	**42**	**61**	**103**	**84**	**33**	**7**	**4**	**11**	**10**

• Brother of Marcel

FILLION, Marcel

Left wing. Shoots left. 5'7", 175 lbs. Born, Thetford Mines, Que., May 28, 1923.

Season	Club	GP	G	A	Pts	PIM	GP	G	A	Pts	PIM
1944-45	Boston Bruins	1	0	0	0	0	....	....	....	....	....
	NHL Totals	**1**	**0**	**0**	**0**	**0**	....	....	....	....	....

• Brother of Bob

FILMORE, Tommy

Right wing. Shoots right. 5'11", 189 lbs. Born, Thamesford, Ont.,

Season	Club	GP	G	A	Pts	PIM	GP	G	A	Pts	PIM
1930-31	Detroit Falcons	39	6	2	8	10	....	....	....	....	....
1931-32	Detroit Falcons	9	0	0	0	2	....	....	....	....	....
	New York Americans	31	8	6	14	12	....	....	....	....	....
1932-33	New York Americans	34	1	4	5	9	....	....	....	....	....
	Boston Bruins	1	0	0	0	0	....	....	....	....	....
1933-34	Boston Bruins	3	0	0	0	0	....	....	....	....	....
	NHL Totals	**117**	**15**	**12**	**27**	**33**	....	....	....	....	....

Traded to **NY Americans** by **Detroit** with Bert McInenly for Hap Emms and Frank Carson, December 29, 1931. Traded to **Boston** by **NY Americans** for Lloyd Klein, February 12, 1933. Traded to **Montreal** by **Boston** with cash for Tony Savage, November 5, 1934. Traded to **Springfield** (IAHL) by **Montreal** for cash, April, 1936.

FINKBEINER, Lloyd

Left wing/Defense. Shoots left. 5'10", 175 lbs. Born, Guelph, Ont., April 12, 1920.

Season	Club	GP	G	A	Pts	PIM	GP	G	A	Pts	PIM
1940-41	New York Americans	2	0	0	0	0	....	....	....	....	....
	NHL Totals	**2**	**0**	**0**	**0**	**0**	....	....	....	....	....

Signed as a free agent by **NY Americans**, October 22, 1940.

FINLEY, Jeff

Defense. Shoots left. 6'2", 205 lbs. Born, Edmonton, Alta., April 14, 1967.
(NY Islanders' 4th choice, 55th overall, in 1985 Entry Draft).

Season	Club	GP	G	A	Pts	PIM	GP	G	A	Pts	PIM
1987-88	New York Islanders	10	0	5	5	15	1	0	0	0	2
1988-89	New York Islanders	4	0	0	0	6	....	....	....	....	....
1989-90	New York Islanders	11	0	1	1	0	5	0	2	2	2
1990-91	New York Islanders	11	0	0	0	4	....	....	....	....	....
1991-92	New York Islanders	51	1	10	11	26	....	....	....	....	....
1993-94	Philadelphia Flyers	55	1	8	9	24	....	....	....	....	....
1995-96	Winnipeg Jets	65	1	5	6	81	6	0	0	0	4
1996-97	Phoenix Coyotes	65	3	7	10	40	1	0	0	0	2
1997-98	New York Rangers	63	1	6	7	55	....	....	....	....	....
1998-99	New York Rangers	2	0	0	0	0	....	....	....	....	....
	St. Louis Blues	30	1	2	3	20	13	1	2	3	8
99-2000	St. Louis Blues	74	2	8	10	38	7	0	2	2	4
2000-01	St. Louis Blues	72	2	8	10	38	2	0	0	0	0
2001-02	St. Louis Blues	78	0	6	6	30	10	0	0	0	8
2002-03	St. Louis Blues	64	1	3	4	46	6	0	0	0	6
	NHL Totals	**655**	**13**	**69**	**82**	**423**	**51**	**1**	**6**	**7**	**36**

Rights traded to **Ottawa** by **NY Islanders** for Chris Luongo, June 30, 1993. Signed as a free agent by **Philadelphia**, July 30, 1993. Traded to **Winnipeg** by **Philadelphia** for Russ Romaniuk, June 27, 1995. Transferred to **Phoenix** after **Winnipeg** franchise relocated, July 1, 1996. Signed as a free agent by **NY Rangers**, August 18, 1997. Traded to **St. Louis** by **NY Rangers** with Geoff Smith for future considerations (Chris Kenady, February 22, 1999), February 13, 1999.

FINN, Steven

Defense. Shoots left. 6', 191 lbs. Born, Laval, Que., August 20, 1966.
(Quebec's 3rd choice, 57th overall, in 1984 Entry Draft).

Season	Club	GP	G	A	Pts	PIM	GP	G	A	Pts	PIM
1985-86	Quebec Nordiques	17	0	1	1	28	....	....	....	....	....
1986-87	Quebec Nordiques	36	2	5	7	40	13	0	2	2	29
1987-88	Quebec Nordiques	75	3	7	10	198	....	....	....	....	....
1988-89	Quebec Nordiques	77	2	6	8	235	....	....	....	....	....
1989-90	Quebec Nordiques	64	3	9	12	208	....	....	....	....	....
1990-91	Quebec Nordiques	71	6	13	19	228	....	....	....	....	....
1991-92	Quebec Nordiques	65	4	7	11	194	....	....	....	....	....
1992-93	Quebec Nordiques	80	5	9	14	160	6	0	1	1	8
1993-94	Quebec Nordiques	80	4	13	17	159	....	....	....	....	....
1994-95	Quebec Nordiques	40	0	3	3	64	4	0	1	1	2
1995-96	Tampa Bay Lightning	16	0	0	0	24	....	....	....	....	....
	Los Angeles Kings	50	3	2	5	102	....	....	....	....	....
1996-97	Los Angeles Kings	54	2	3	5	84	....	....	....	....	....
	NHL Totals	**725**	**34**	**78**	**112**	**1724**	**23**	**0**	**4**	**4**	**39**

Transferred to **Colorado** after **Quebec** franchise relocated, June 21, 1995. Traded to **Tampa Bay** by **Colorado** for Tampa Bay's 4th round choice (Brad Larsen) in 1997 Entry Draft, October 5, 1995. Traded to **Los Angeles** by **Tampa Bay** for Michel Petit, November 13, 1995.

FINNEY, Sid

Center. Shoots left. 5'11", 160 lbs. Born, Banbridge, Ireland, May 1, 1929.

Season	Club	GP	G	A	Pts	PIM	GP	G	A	Pts	PIM
1951-52	Chicago Black Hawks	35	6	5	11	0	....	....	....	....	....
1952-53	Chicago Black Hawks	18	4	2	6	4	7	0	2	2	0
1953-54	Chicago Black Hawks	6	0	0	0	0	....	....	....	....	....
	NHL Totals	**59**	**10**	**7**	**17**	**4**	**7**	**0**	**2**	**2**	**0**

Traded to **Chicago** by **Calgary** ((PCHL) for Ernie Dickens, October 1, 1951. Claimed by **Chicago** from **Buffalo** (AHL) in Inter-League Draft, June 4, 1957. Claimed by **Hershey** (AHL) from **Chicago** (Calgary-WHL), June 3, 1958.

FINNIGAN, Ed

Left wing. Shoots left. 5'8", 170 lbs. Born, Shawville, Que., May 23, 1913.

Season	Club	GP	G	A	Pts	PIM	GP	G	A	Pts	PIM
1934-35	St. Louis Eagles	12	1	1	2	2	....	....	....	....	....
1935-36	Boston Bruins	3	0	0	0	0	....	....	....	....	....
	NHL Totals	**15**	**1**	**1**	**2**	**2**	....	....	....	....	....

• Brother of Frank

Claimed by **NY Americans** from **St. Louis** in Dispersal Draft, October 14, 1935. Traded to **Boston** by **NY Americans** for cash, December 19, 1935. Traded to **Providence** (IAHL) by **Boston** for cash, October 7, 1936.

FINNIGAN, Frank

Right wing. Shoots right. 5'9", 165 lbs. Born, Shawville, Que., July 9, 1903.

Season	Club	GP	G	A	Pts	PIM	GP	G	A	Pts	PIM
1923-24	Ottawa Senators	2	0	0	0	0	2	0	0	0	2
1924-25	Ottawa Senators	29	0	0	0	22	....	....	....	....	....
1925-26	Ottawa Senators	36	2	0	2	24	2	0	0	0	0
1926-27 ◆	Ottawa Senators	36	15	1	16	52	6	3	0	3	0
1927-28	Ottawa Senators	38	20	5	25	34	2	0	1	1	6
1928-29	Ottawa Senators	44	15	4	19	71	....	....	....	....	....
1929-30	Ottawa Senators	43	21	15	36	46	1	0	0	0	4
1930-31	Ottawa Senators	44	9	8	17	40	....	....	....	....	....
1931-32 ◆	Toronto Maple Leafs	47	8	13	21	45	7	2	3	5	8
1932-33	Ottawa Senators	45	4	14	18	37	....	....	....	....	....
1933-34	Ottawa Senators	48	10	10	20	10	....	....	....	....	....
1934-35	St. Louis Eagles	34	5	5	10	10	....	....	....	....	....
	Toronto Maple Leafs	11	2	0	2	2	7	1	2	3	2
1935-36	Toronto Maple Leafs	48	2	6	8	10	9	0	3	3	0
1936-37	Toronto Maple Leafs	48	2	7	9	4	2	0	0	0	0
	NHL Totals	**553**	**115**	**88**	**203**	**407**	**38**	**6**	**9**	**15**	**22**

• Brother of Ed

Played in NHL All-Star Game (1934)

Signed as a free agent by **Ottawa**, February 21, 1924. Claimed by **Toronto** from **Ottawa** for 1931-32 season in Dispersal Draft, September 26, 1931. Transferred to **St. Louis** after **Ottawa** franchise relocated, September 30, 1934. Traded to **Toronto** by **St. Louis** for cash, February 13, 1935.

FIORENTINO, Peter

Defense. Shoots right. 6'1", 205 lbs. Born, Niagara Falls, Ont., December 22, 1968.
(NY Rangers' 10th choice, 215th overall, in 1988 Entry Draft).

Season	Club	GP	G	A	Pts	PIM	GP	G	A	Pts	PIM
1991-92	New York Rangers	1	0	0	0	0	....	....	....	....	....
	NHL Totals	**1**	**0**	**0**	**0**	**0**	....	....	....	....	....

FISCHER, Jiri

Defense. Shoots left. 6'5", 225 lbs. Born, Horovice, Czech., July 31, 1980.
(Detroit's 1st choice, 25th overall, in 1998 Entry Draft).

Season	Club	GP	G	A	Pts	PIM	GP	G	A	Pts	PIM
99-2000	Detroit Red Wings	52	0	8	8	45	....	....	....	....	....
2000-01	Detroit Red Wings	55	1	8	9	59	5	0	0	0	9
2001-02 ◆	Detroit Red Wings	80	2	8	10	67	22	3	3	6	30
2002-03	Detroit Red Wings	15	1	5	6	16	....	....	....	....	....
	NHL Totals	**202**	**4**	**29**	**33**	**187**	**27**	**3**	**3**	**6**	**39**

• Missed majority of 2002-03 season recovering from knee injury suffered in game vs. Nashville, November 12, 2002.

FISCHER, Ron

Defense. Shoots right. 6'2", 195 lbs. Born, Merritt, B.C., April 12, 1959.

Season	Club	REGULAR SEASON GP	G	A	Pts	PIM	PLAYOFFS GP	G	A	Pts	PIM
1981-82	Buffalo Sabres	15	0	7	7	6	....	....	....	....	....
1982-83	Buffalo Sabres	3	0	0	0	0	....	....	....	....	....
	NHL Totals	**18**	**0**	**7**	**7**	**6**	....	....	....	....	....

Signed as a free agent by **Buffalo**, March 19, 1981.

FISHER, Alvin

Right wing. Shoots right. 6'1", 175 lbs. Born, Sault Ste. Marie, Ont.,

Season	Club	REGULAR SEASON GP	G	A	Pts	PIM	PLAYOFFS GP	G	A	Pts	PIM
1924-25	Toronto St. Pats	9	1	0	1	4	....	....	....	....	....
	NHL Totals	**9**	**1**	**0**	**1**	**4**	....	....	....	....	....

Signed as a free agent by **Toronto**, November 24, 1925.

FISHER, Craig

Center. Shoots left. 6'3", 180 lbs. Born, Oshawa, Ont., June 30, 1970.
(Philadelphia's 3rd choice, 56th overall, in 1988 Entry Draft).

Season	Club	REGULAR SEASON GP	G	A	Pts	PIM	PLAYOFFS GP	G	A	Pts	PIM
1989-90	Philadelphia Flyers	2	0	0	0	0	....	....	....	....	....
1990-91	Philadelphia Flyers	2	0	0	0	0	....	....	....	....	....
1993-94	Winnipeg Jets	4	0	0	0	2	....	....	....	....	....
1996-97	Florida Panthers	4	0	0	0	0	....	....	....	....	....
	NHL Totals	**12**	**0**	**0**	**0**	**2**	....	....	....	....	....

Traded to **Edmonton** by **Philadelphia** with Scott Mellanby and Craig Berube for Dave Brown, Corey Foster and Jari Kurri, May 30, 1991. Traded to **Winnipeg** by **Edmonton** for cash, December 9, 1993. Signed as a free agent by **Chicago**, June 9, 1994. Signed as a free agent by **NY Islanders**, July 29, 1996. Traded to **Florida** by **NY Islanders** for cash, December 7, 1996. Signed as a free agent by **Buffalo**, August 31, 1998.

FISHER, Dunc

Right wing. Shoots right. 5'7", 170 lbs. Born, Regina, Sask., August 30, 1927.

Season	Club	REGULAR SEASON GP	G	A	Pts	PIM	PLAYOFFS GP	G	A	Pts	PIM
1947-48	New York Rangers	....	....	....	....	....	1	0	1	1	0
1948-49	New York Rangers	60	9	16	25	40	....	....	....	....	....
1949-50	New York Rangers	70	12	21	33	42	12	3	3	6	14
1950-51	New York Rangers	12	0	0	0	0	....	....	....	....	....
	Boston Bruins	53	9	20	29	20	6	1	0	1	0
1951-52	Boston Bruins	65	15	12	27	2	2	0	0	0	0
1952-53	Boston Bruins	7	0	1	1	0	....	....	....	....	....
1958-59	Detroit Red Wings	8	0	0	0	0	....	....	....	....	....
	NHL Totals	**275**	**45**	**70**	**115**	**104**	**21**	**4**	**4**	**8**	**14**

Traded to **Boston** by **NY Rangers** with future considerations (loan of Alan Kaleta to Hershey AHL, November 20, 1950) for Ed Harrison and Zellio Toppazzini, November 16, 1950. Traded to **Hershey** (AHL) by **Boston** with Ellard O'Brien for Ray Gariepy, June, 1953. Traded to **Detroit** by **Hershey** (AHL) for Don Poile, Hec Lalande and cash, April 23, 1958.

FISHER, Joe

Right wing. Shoots right. 6', 175 lbs. Born, Medicine Hat, Alta., July 4, 1916.

Season	Club	REGULAR SEASON GP	G	A	Pts	PIM	PLAYOFFS GP	G	A	Pts	PIM
1939-40	Detroit Red Wings	34	2	4	6	2	5	1	1	2	0
1940-41	Detroit Red Wings	27	5	8	13	11	5	1	0	1	6
1941-42	Detroit Red Wings	3	0	0	0	0	1	0	0	0	0
1942-43◆	Detroit Red Wings	1	1	0	1	0	1	0	0	0	0
	NHL Totals	**65**	**8**	**12**	**20**	**13**	**12**	**2**	**1**	**3**	**6**

FISHER, Mike

Center. Shoots right. 6'1", 193 lbs. Born, Peterborough, Ont., June 5, 1980.
(Ottawa's 2nd choice, 44th overall, in 1998 Entry Draft).

Season	Club	REGULAR SEASON GP	G	A	Pts	PIM	PLAYOFFS GP	G	A	Pts	PIM
99-2000	Ottawa Senators	32	4	5	9	15	....	....	....	....	....
2000-01	Ottawa Senators	60	7	12	19	46	4	0	1	1	4
2001-02	Ottawa Senators	58	15	9	24	55	10	2	1	3	0
2002-03	Ottawa Senators	74	18	20	38	54	18	2	2	4	16
	NHL Totals	**224**	**44**	**46**	**90**	**170**	**32**	**4**	**4**	**8**	**20**

• Missed majority of 1999-2000 season recovering from knee injury suffered in game vs. Boston, December 30, 1999.

FITCHNER, Bob

Center. Shoots left. 6', 190 lbs. Born, Sudbury, Ont., December 22, 1950.
(Pittsburgh's 6th choice, 77th overall, in 1970 Amateur Draft).

Season	Club	REGULAR SEASON GP	G	A	Pts	PIM	PLAYOFFS GP	G	A	Pts	PIM
1979-80	Quebec Nordiques	70	11	20	31	59	....	....	....	....	....
1980-81	Quebec Nordiques	8	1	0	1	0	3	0	0	0	10
	NHL Totals	**78**	**12**	**20**	**32**	**59**	**3**	**0**	**0**	**0**	**10**

Rights retained by **Quebec** prior to Expansion Draft, June 9, 1979.

FITZGERALD, Rusty

Center. Shoots left. 6'1", 210 lbs. Born, Minneapolis, MN, October 4, 1972.
(Pittsburgh's 2nd choice, 38th overall, in 1991 Entry Draft).

Season	Club	REGULAR SEASON GP	G	A	Pts	PIM	PLAYOFFS GP	G	A	Pts	PIM
1994-95	Pittsburgh Penguins	4	1	0	1	0	5	0	0	0	4
1995-96	Pittsburgh Penguins	21	1	2	3	12	....	....	....	....	....
	NHL Totals	**25**	**2**	**2**	**4**	**12**	**5**	**0**	**0**	**0**	**4**

FITZGERALD, Tom

Right wing. Shoots right. 6', 195 lbs. Born, Billerica, MA, August 28, 1968.
(NY Islanders' 1st choice, 17th overall, in 1986 Entry Draft).

Season	Club	REGULAR SEASON GP	G	A	Pts	PIM	PLAYOFFS GP	G	A	Pts	PIM
1988-89	New York Islanders	23	3	5	8	10	....	....	....	....	....
1989-90	New York Islanders	19	2	5	7	4	4	1	0	1	4
1990-91	New York Islanders	41	5	5	10	24	....	....	....	....	....
1991-92	New York Islanders	45	6	11	17	28	....	....	....	....	....
1992-93	New York Islanders	77	9	18	27	34	18	2	5	7	18
1993-94	Florida Panthers	83	18	14	32	54	....	....	....	....	....
1994-95	Florida Panthers	48	3	13	16	31	....	....	....	....	....
1995-96	Florida Panthers	82	13	21	34	75	22	4	4	8	34
1996-97	Florida Panthers	71	10	14	24	64	5	0	1	1	0
1997-98	Florida Panthers	69	10	5	15	57	....	....	....	....	....
	Colorado Avalanche	11	2	1	3	22	7	0	1	1	20
1998-99	Nashville Predators	80	13	19	32	48	....	....	....	....	....
99-2000	Nashville Predators	82	13	9	22	66	....	....	....	....	....
2000-01	Nashville Predators	82	9	9	18	71	....	....	....	....	....
2001-02	Nashville Predators	63	7	9	16	33	....	....	....	....	....
	Chicago Blackhawks	15	1	3	4	6	5	0	0	0	4
2002-03	Toronto Maple Leafs	66	4	13	17	57	7	0	1	1	4
	NHL Totals	**957**	**128**	**174**	**302**	**684**	**68**	**7**	**12**	**19**	**84**

Claimed by **Florida** from **NY Islanders** in Expansion Draft, June 24, 1993. Traded to **Colorado** by **Florida** for the rights to Mark Parrish and Anaheim's 3rd round choice (previously acquired, Florida selected Lance Ward) in 1998 Entry Draft, March 24, 1998. Signed as a free agent by **Nashville**, July 6, 1998. Traded to **Chicago** by **Nashville** for Chicago's 4th round choice (later traded to Anaheim – Anaheim selected Nathan Saunders) in 2003 Entry Draft and future considerations, March 13, 2002. Signed as a free agent by **Toronto**, July 17, 2002.

FITZPATRICK, Rory

Defense. Shoots right. 6'2", 215 lbs. Born, Rochester, NY, January 11, 1975.
(Montreal's 2nd choice, 47th overall, in 1993 Entry Draft).

Season	Club	REGULAR SEASON GP	G	A	Pts	PIM	PLAYOFFS GP	G	A	Pts	PIM
1995-96	Montreal Canadiens	42	0	2	2	18	6	1	1	2	0
1996-97	Montreal Canadiens	6	0	1	1	6	....	....	....	....	....
	St. Louis Blues	2	0	0	0	2	....	....	....	....	....
1998-99	St. Louis Blues	1	0	0	0	2	....	....	....	....	....
2000-01	Nashville Predators	2	0	0	0	2	....	....	....	....	....
2001-02	Buffalo Sabres	5	0	0	0	4	....	....	....	....	....
2002-03	Buffalo Sabres	36	1	3	4	16	....	....	....	....	....
	NHL Totals	**94**	**1**	**6**	**7**	**50**	**6**	**1**	**1**	**2**	**0**

Traded to **St. Louis** by **Montreal** with Pierre Turgeon and Craig Conroy for Murray Baron, Shayne Corson and St. Louis' 5th round choice (Gennady Razin) in 1997 Entry Draft, October 29, 1996. Claimed by **Boston** from **St. Louis** in Waiver Draft, October 5, 1998. Claimed on waivers by **St. Louis** from **Boston**, October 7, 1998. Traded to **Nashville** by **St. Louis** for Dan Keczmer, February 9, 2000. Traded to **Edmonton** by **Nashville** for future considerations, January 12, 2001. Signed as a free agent by **Buffalo**, August 14, 2001.

FITZPATRICK, Ross

Center. Shoots left. 6', 195 lbs. Born, Penticton, B.C., October 7, 1960.
(Philadelphia's 7th choice, 147th overall, in 1980 Entry Draft).

Season	Club	REGULAR SEASON GP	G	A	Pts	PIM	PLAYOFFS GP	G	A	Pts	PIM
1982-83	Philadelphia Flyers	1	0	0	0	0	....	....	....	....	....
1983-84	Philadelphia Flyers	12	4	2	6	0	....	....	....	....	....
1984-85	Philadelphia Flyers	5	1	0	1	0	....	....	....	....	....
1985-86	Philadelphia Flyers	2	0	0	0	0	....	....	....	....	....
	NHL Totals	**20**	**5**	**2**	**7**	**0**	....	....	....	....	....

Signed as a free agent by **NY Rangers**, July 24, 1990.

FITZPATRICK, Sandy

Center. Shoots left. 6'1", 195 lbs. Born, Paisley, Scotland, December 22, 1944.

Season	Club	REGULAR SEASON GP	G	A	Pts	PIM	PLAYOFFS GP	G	A	Pts	PIM
1964-65	New York Rangers	4	0	0	0	2	....	....	....	....	....
1967-68	Minnesota North Stars	18	3	6	9	6	12	0	0	0	0
	NHL Totals	**22**	**3**	**6**	**9**	**8**	**12**	**0**	**0**	**0**	**0**

Claimed by **Minnesota** from **NY Rangers** in Expansion Draft, June 6, 1967. Traded to **San Diego** (WHL) by **Minnesota** for cash, July 15, 1969.

FLAMAN, Fern

HHOF

Defense. Shoots right. 5'10", 190 lbs. Born, Dysart, Sask., January 25, 1927.

Season	Club	REGULAR SEASON GP	G	A	Pts	PIM	PLAYOFFS GP	G	A	Pts	PIM
1944-45	Boston Bruins	1	0	0	0	0	....	....	....	....	....
1945-46	Boston Bruins	1	0	0	0	0	....	....	....	....	....
1946-47	Boston Bruins	23	1	4	5	41	5	0	0	0	8
1947-48	Boston Bruins	56	4	6	10	69	5	0	0	0	12
1948-49	Boston Bruins	60	4	12	16	62	5	0	1	1	8
1949-50	Boston Bruins	69	2	5	7	122	....	....	....	....	....
1950-51	Boston Bruins	14	1	1	2	37	....	....	....	....	....
	◆ Toronto Maple Leafs	39	2	6	8	64	9	1	0	1	8
1951-52	Toronto Maple Leafs	61	0	7	7	110	4	0	2	2	18
1952-53	Toronto Maple Leafs	66	2	6	8	110	....	....	....	....	....
1953-54	Toronto Maple Leafs	62	0	8	8	84	2	0	0	0	0
1954-55	Boston Bruins	70	4	14	18	*150	4	1	0	1	2
1955-56	Boston Bruins	62	4	17	21	70	....	....	....	....	....
1956-57	Boston Bruins	68	6	25	31	108	10	0	3	3	19
1957-58	Boston Bruins	66	0	15	15	71	12	2	2	4	10
1958-59	Boston Bruins	70	0	21	21	101	7	0	0	0	8
1959-60	Boston Bruins	60	2	18	20	112	....	....	....	....	....
1960-61	Boston Bruins	62	2	9	11	59	....	....	....	....	....
	NHL Totals	**910**	**34**	**174**	**208**	**1370**	**63**	**4**	**8**	**12**	**93**

NHL Second All-Star Team (1955, 1957, 1958)

Played in NHL All-Star Game (1952, 1955, 1956, 1957, 1958, 1959)

Traded to **Toronto** by **Boston** with Ken Smith, Phil Maloney and Leo Boivin for Bill Ezinicki and Vic Lynn. November 16, 1950. Traded to **Boston** by **Toronto** for Dave Creighton, July 20, 1954.

FLATLEY, Pat

Right wing. Shoots right. 6'2", 197 lbs. Born, Toronto, Ont., October 3, 1963.
(NY Islanders' 1st choice, 21st overall, in 1982 Entry Draft).

Season	Club	Regular Season GP	G	A	Pts	PIM	Playoffs GP	G	A	Pts	PIM
1983-84	New York Islanders	16	2	7	9	6	21	9	6	15	14
1984-85	New York Islanders	78	20	31	51	106	4	1	0	1	6
1985-86	New York Islanders	73	18	34	52	66	3	0	0	0	21
1986-87	New York Islanders	63	16	35	51	81	11	3	2	5	6
1987-88	New York Islanders	40	9	15	24	28	....	....	....	....	....
1988-89	New York Islanders	41	10	15	25	31	....	....	....	....	....
1989-90	New York Islanders	62	17	32	49	101	5	3	0	3	2
1990-91	New York Islanders	56	20	25	45	74	....	....	....	....	....
1991-92	New York Islanders	38	8	28	36	31	....	....	....	....	....
1992-93	New York Islanders	80	13	47	60	63	15	2	7	9	12
1993-94	New York Islanders	64	12	30	42	40	....	....	....	....	....
1994-95	New York Islanders	45	7	20	27	12	....	....	....	....	....
1995-96	New York Islanders	56	8	9	17	21	....	....	....	....	....
1996-97	New York Rangers	68	10	12	22	26	11	0	0	0	14
	NHL Totals	**780**	**170**	**340**	**510**	**686**	**70**	**18**	**15**	**33**	**75**

Signed as a free agent by **NY Rangers**, September 26, 1996.

FLEMING, Gerry

Left wing. Shoots left. 6'5", 253 lbs. Born, Montreal, Que., October 16, 1967.

Season	Club	Regular Season GP	G	A	Pts	PIM	Playoffs GP	G	A	Pts	PIM
1993-94	Montreal Canadiens	5	0	0	0	25	....	....	....	....	....
1994-95	Montreal Canadiens	6	0	0	0	17	....	....	....	....	....
	NHL Totals	**11**	**0**	**0**	**0**	**42**	....	....	....	....	....

Signed as a free agent by **Montreal**, February 17, 1992.

FLEMING, Reggie

Defense/Left wing. Shoots left. 5'8", 170 lbs. Born, Montreal, Que., April 21, 1936.

Season	Club	Regular Season GP	G	A	Pts	PIM	Playoffs GP	G	A	Pts	PIM
1959-60	Montreal Canadiens	3	0	0	0	2	....	....	....	....	....
1960-61 ♦	Chicago Black Hawks	66	4	4	8	145	12	1	0	1	12
1961-62	Chicago Black Hawks	70	7	9	16	71	12	2	2	4	27
1962-63	Chicago Black Hawks	64	7	7	14	99	6	0	0	0	27
1963-64	Chicago Black Hawks	61	3	6	9	140	7	0	0	0	18
1964-65	Boston Bruins	67	18	23	41	136	....	....	....	....	....
1965-66	Boston Bruins	34	4	6	10	*42	....	....	....	....	....
	New York Rangers	35	10	14	24	*124	....	....	....	....	....
1966-67	New York Rangers	61	15	16	31	146	4	0	2	2	11
1967-68	New York Rangers	73	17	7	24	132	6	0	2	2	4
1968-69	New York Rangers	72	8	12	20	138	3	0	0	0	7
1969-70	Philadelphia Flyers	65	9	18	27	134	....	....	....	....	....
1970-71	Buffalo Sabres	78	6	10	16	159	....	....	....	....	....
	NHL Totals	**749**	**108**	**132**	**240**	**1468**	**50**	**3**	**6**	**9**	**106**

Played in NHL All-Star Game (1961)

Traded to **Chicago** by **Montreal** with Cec Hoekstra, Ab McDonald and Bob Courcy for Terry Gray, Glen Skov and the rights to Danny Lewicki, Lorne Ferguson and Bob Bailey, June 7, 1960. Traded to **Boston** by **Chicago** with Ab McDonald for Doug Mohns, June 8, 1964. Traded to **NY Rangers** by **Boston** for John McKenzie, January 10, 1966. Traded to **Philadelphia** by **NY Rangers** for Leon Rochefort and Don Blackburn, June 6, 1969. Claimed by **Buffalo** from **Philadelphia** in Expansion Draft, June 10, 1970.

FLESCH, John

Left wing. Shoots left. 6'2", 200 lbs. Born, Sudbury, Ont., July 15, 1953.
(Atlanta's 5th choice, 69th overall, in 1973 Amateur Draft).

Season	Club	Regular Season GP	G	A	Pts	PIM	Playoffs GP	G	A	Pts	PIM
1974-75	Minnesota North Stars	57	8	15	23	47	....	....	....	....	....
1975-76	Minnesota North Stars	33	3	2	5	47	....	....	....	....	....
1977-78	Pittsburgh Penguins	29	7	5	12	19	....	....	....	....	....
1979-80	Colorado Rockies	5	0	1	1	4	....	....	....	....	....
	NHL Totals	**124**	**18**	**23**	**41**	**117**	....	....	....	....	....

Traded to **Minnesota** by **Atlanta** with Don Martineau for Buster Harvey and Jerry Byers, May 27, 1974. Signed as a free agent by **Pittsburgh**, February 4, 1978. Signed as a free agent by **Colorado**, January 13, 1980.

FLETCHER, Steven

Left wing/Defense. Shoots left. 6'2", 180 lbs. Born, Montreal, Que., March 31, 1962.
(Calgary's 11th choice, 202nd overall, in 1980 Entry Draft).

Season	Club	Regular Season GP	G	A	Pts	PIM	Playoffs GP	G	A	Pts	PIM
1987-88	Montreal Canadiens	....	....	....	....	....	1	0	0	0	5
1988-89	Winnipeg Jets	3	0	0	0	5	....	....	....	....	....
	NHL Totals	**3**	**0**	**0**	**0**	**5**	**1**	**0**	**0**	**0**	**5**

Signed as a free agent by **Montreal**, August 21, 1984. Signed as a free agent by **Winnipeg**, July 15, 1988. Traded to **Philadelphia** by **Winnipeg** for future considerations, December 12, 1988.

FLETT, Bill

Right wing. Shoots right. 6'1", 205 lbs. Born, Vermillion, Alta., July 21, 1943.

Season	Club	Regular Season GP	G	A	Pts	PIM	Playoffs GP	G	A	Pts	PIM
1967-68	Los Angeles Kings	73	26	20	46	97	7	1	2	3	8
1968-69	Los Angeles Kings	72	24	25	49	53	10	3	4	7	11
1969-70	Los Angeles Kings	69	14	18	32	70	....	....	....	....	....
1970-71	Los Angeles Kings	64	13	24	37	57	....	....	....	....	....
1971-72	Los Angeles Kings	45	7	12	19	18	....	....	....	....	....
	Philadelphia Flyers	31	11	10	21	26	....	....	....	....	....
1972-73	Philadelphia Flyers	69	43	31	74	53	11	3	4	7	0
1973-74 ♦	Philadelphia Flyers	67	17	27	44	51	17	0	6	6	21
1974-75	Toronto Maple Leafs	77	15	25	40	38	5	0	0	0	2
1975-76	Atlanta Flames	78	23	17	40	30	2	0	0	0	0
1976-77	Atlanta Flames	24	4	4	8	6	....	....	....	....	....
1979-80	Edmonton Oilers	20	5	2	7	2	....	....	....	....	....
	NHL Totals	**689**	**202**	**215**	**417**	**501**	**52**	**7**	**16**	**23**	**42**

Played in NHL All-Star Game (1971)

Claimed by **Los Angeles** from **Toronto** in Expansion Draft, June 6, 1967. Traded to **Philadelphia** by **Los Angeles** with Eddie Joyal, Jean Potvin and Ross Lonsberry for Bill Lesuk, Jim Johnson and Serge Bernier, January 28, 1972. Traded to **Toronto** by **Philadelphia** for Dave Fortier and Randy Osburn, May 27, 1974. Claimed on waivers by **Atlanta** from **Toronto**, May 20, 1975. Traded to **Edmonton** (WHA) by **Atlanta** for cash, December, 1976. Rights retained by **Edmonton** prior to Expansion Draft, June 9, 1979.

FLEURY, Theoren

Right wing. Shoots right. 5'6", 180 lbs. Born, Oxbow, Sask., June 29, 1968.
(Calgary's 9th choice, 166th overall, in 1987 Entry Draft).

Season	Club	Regular Season GP	G	A	Pts	PIM	Playoffs GP	G	A	Pts	PIM
1988-89 ♦	Calgary Flames	36	14	20	34	46	22	5	6	11	24
1989-90	Calgary Flames	80	31	35	66	157	6	2	3	5	10
1990-91	Calgary Flames	79	51	53	104	136	7	2	5	7	14
1991-92	Calgary Flames	80	33	40	73	133	....	....	....	....	....
1992-93	Calgary Flames	83	34	66	100	88	6	5	7	12	27
1993-94	Calgary Flames	83	40	45	85	186	7	6	4	10	5
1994-95	Calgary Flames	47	29	29	58	112	7	7	7	14	2
1995-96	Calgary Flames	80	46	50	96	112	4	2	1	3	14
1996-97	Calgary Flames	81	29	38	67	104	....	....	....	....	....
1997-98	Calgary Flames	82	27	51	78	197	....	....	....	....	....
1998-99	Calgary Flames	60	30	39	69	68	....	....	....	....	....
	Colorado Avalanche	15	10	14	24	18	18	5	12	17	20
99-2000	New York Rangers	80	15	49	64	68	....	....	....	....	....
2000-01	New York Rangers	62	30	44	74	122	....	....	....	....	....
2001-02	New York Rangers	82	24	39	63	216	....	....	....	....	....
2002-03	Chicago Blackhawks	54	12	21	33	77	....	....	....	....	....
	NHL Totals	**1084**	**455**	**633**	**1088**	**1840**	**77**	**34**	**45**	**79**	**116**

Shared Alka-Seltzer Plus Award with Marty McSorley (1991) • NHL Second All-Star Team (1995)

Played in NHL All-Star Game (1991, 1992, 1996, 1997, 1998, 1999, 2001)

Traded to **Colorado** by **Calgary** with Chris Dingman for Rene Corbet, Wade Belak, Robyn Regehr and Colorado's 2nd round compensatory choice (Jarret Stoll) in 2000 Entry Draft, February 28, 1999. Signed as a free agent by **NY Rangers**, July 8, 1999. Traded to **San Jose** by **NY Rangers** to complete transaction that sent San Jose's 6th round choice (Kim Hirschovits) in 2002 Entry Draft for NY Rangers' 6th round choice in 2003 Entry Draft (June 23, 2002), June 26, 2002. Signed as a free agent by **Chicago**, August 15, 2002. Suspended indefinitely by NHL for violating terms of his substance abuse aftercare program, October 8, 2002. Reinstated by NHL and cleared to return to active duty, December 5, 2002.

FLICHEL, Todd

Defense. Shoots right. 6'3", 195 lbs. Born, Osgoode, Ont., September 14, 1964.
(Winnipeg's 10th choice, 176th overall, in 1983 Entry Draft).

Season	Club	Regular Season GP	G	A	Pts	PIM	Playoffs GP	G	A	Pts	PIM
1987-88	Winnipeg Jets	2	0	0	0	2	....	....	....	....	....
1988-89	Winnipeg Jets	1	0	0	0	0	....	....	....	....	....
1989-90	Winnipeg Jets	3	0	1	1	2	....	....	....	....	....
	NHL Totals	**6**	**0**	**1**	**1**	**4**	....	....	....	....	....

FLINN, Ryan

Left wing. Shoots left. 6'5", 223 lbs. Born, Halifax, N.S., April 20, 1980.
(New Jersey's 8th choice, 143rd overall, in 1998 Entry Draft).

Season	Club	Regular Season GP	G	A	Pts	PIM	Playoffs GP	G	A	Pts	PIM
2001-02	Los Angeles Kings	10	0	0	0	51	....	....	....	....	....
2002-03	Los Angeles Kings	19	1	0	1	28	....	....	....	....	....
	NHL Totals	**29**	**1**	**0**	**1**	**79**	....	....	....	....	....

Signed as a free agent by **Los Angeles**, January 8, 2002.

FLOCKHART, Rob

Left wing. Shoots left. 6', 185 lbs. Born, Sicamous, B.C., February 6, 1956.
(Vancouver's 2nd choice, 44th overall, in 1976 Amateur Draft).

Season	Club	Regular Season GP	G	A	Pts	PIM	Playoffs GP	G	A	Pts	PIM
1976-77	Vancouver Canucks	5	0	0	0	0	....	....	....	....	....
1977-78	Vancouver Canucks	24	0	1	1	12	....	....	....	....	....
1978-79	Vancouver Canucks	14	1	1	2	0	....	....	....	....	....
1979-80	Minnesota North Stars	10	1	3	4	2	1	1	0	1	2
1980-81	Minnesota North Stars	2	0	0	0	0	....	....	....	....	....
	NHL Totals	**55**	**2**	**5**	**7**	**14**	**1**	**1**	**0**	**1**	**2**

• Brother of Ron

Signed as a free agent by **Minnesota**, October 12, 1979. Signed as a free agent by **Chicago**, December 1, 1982.

FLOCKHART, Ron

Center. Shoots left. 5'11", 190 lbs. Born, Smithers, B.C., October 10, 1960.

Season	Club	Regular Season GP	G	A	Pts	PIM	Playoffs GP	G	A	Pts	PIM
1980-81	Philadelphia Flyers	14	3	7	10	11	3	1	0	1	2
1981-82	Philadelphia Flyers	72	33	39	72	44	4	0	1	1	2
1982-83	Philadelphia Flyers	73	29	31	60	49	2	1	1	2	2
1983-84	Philadelphia Flyers	8	0	3	3	4	....	....	....	....	....
	Pittsburgh Penguins	68	27	18	45	40	....	....	....	....	....
1984-85	Pittsburgh Penguins	12	0	5	5	4	....	....	....	....	....
	Montreal Canadiens	42	10	12	22	14	2	1	1	2	2
1985-86	St. Louis Blues	79	22	45	67	26	8	1	3	4	6
1986-87	St. Louis Blues	60	16	19	35	12	....	....	....	....	....
1987-88	St. Louis Blues	21	5	4	9	4	....	....	....	....	....

Season	Club	Regular Season GP	G	A	Pts	PIM	Playoffs GP	G	A	Pts	PIM
1988-89	Boston Bruins	4	0	0	0	0	....	....	....	....	....
	NHL Totals	**453**	**145**	**183**	**328**	**208**	**19**	**4**	**6**	**10**	**14**

• Brother of Rob

Signed as a free agent by **Philadelphia**, July 2, 1980. Traded to **Pittsburgh** by **Philadelphia** with Andy Brickley, Mark Taylor and Philadelphia's 1st (Roger Belanger) and 3rd (later traded to Vancouver – Vancouver selected Mike Stevens) round choices in 1984 Entry Draft for Rich Sutter and Pittsburgh's 2nd (Greg Smyth) and 3rd (David McLay) round choices in 1984 Entry Draft, October 23, 1983. Traded to **Montreal** by **Pittsburgh** for John Chabot, November 9, 1984. Traded to **St. Louis** by **Montreal** for Perry Ganchar, August 26, 1985. Traded to **Boston** by **St. Louis** for future considerations, February 13, 1989.

FLOYD, Larry

Center. Shoots left. 5'8", 180 lbs. Born, Peterborough, Ont., May 1, 1961.

Season	Club	GP	G	A	Pts	PIM	GP	G	A	Pts	PIM
1982-83	New Jersey Devils	5	1	0	1	2	....	....	....	....	....
1983-84	New Jersey Devils	7	1	3	4	7	....	....	....	....	....
	NHL Totals	**12**	**2**	**3**	**5**	**9**	....	....	....	....	....

Signed as a free agent by **New Jersey**, September 16, 1982.

FOCHT, Dan

Defense. Shoots left. 6'6", 242 lbs. Born, Regina, Sask., December 31, 1977.
(Phoenix's 1st choice, 11th overall, in 1996 Entry Draft).

Season	Club	GP	G	A	Pts	PIM	GP	G	A	Pts	PIM
2001-02	Phoenix Coyotes	8	0	0	0	11	1	0	1	1	0
2002-03	Phoenix Coyotes	10	0	0	0	10	....	....	....	....	....
	Pittsburgh Penguins	12	0	3	3	19	....	....	....	....	....
	NHL Totals	**30**	**0**	**3**	**3**	**40**	**1**	**0**	**1**	**1**	**0**

Traded to **Pittsburgh** by **Phoenix** with Ramzi Abid and Guillaume Lefebvre for Jan Hrdina and Francois Leroux, March 11, 2003.

FOGARTY, Bryan

Defense. Shoots left. 6'2", 206 lbs. Born, Brantford, Ont., June 11, 1969.
(Quebec's 1st choice, 9th overall, in 1987 Entry Draft).

Season	Club	GP	G	A	Pts	PIM	GP	G	A	Pts	PIM
1989-90	Quebec Nordiques	45	4	10	14	31	....	....	....	....	....
1990-91	Quebec Nordiques	45	9	22	31	24	....	....	....	....	....
1991-92	Quebec Nordiques	20	3	12	15	16	....	....	....	....	....
1992-93	Pittsburgh Penguins	12	0	4	4	4	....	....	....	....	....
1993-94	Montreal Canadiens	13	1	2	3	10	....	....	....	....	....
1994-95	Montreal Canadiens	21	5	2	7	34	....	....	....	....	....
	NHL Totals	**156**	**22**	**52**	**74**	**119**	....	....	....	....	....

Traded to **Pittsburgh** by **Quebec** for Scott Young, March 10, 1992. Signed as a free agent by **Tampa Bay**, September 28, 1993. Signed as a free agent by **Montreal**, February 25, 1994. Signed as a free agent by **Buffalo**, September 8, 1995. Signed as a free agent by **Chicago**, September 2, 1998. Signed as a free agent by **Toronto**, September 14, 1999.

FOGOLIN Jr., Lee

Defense. Shoots right. 6', 200 lbs. Born, Chicago, IL, February 7, 1955.
(Buffalo's 1st choice, 11th overall, in 1974 Amateur Draft).

Season	Club	GP	G	A	Pts	PIM	GP	G	A	Pts	PIM
1974-75	Buffalo Sabres	50	2	2	4	59	8	0	0	0	6
1975-76	Buffalo Sabres	58	0	9	9	64	9	0	4	4	23
1976-77	Buffalo Sabres	71	3	15	18	100	4	0	0	0	2
1977-78	Buffalo Sabres	76	0	23	23	98	6	0	2	2	23
1978-79	Buffalo Sabres	74	3	19	22	103	3	0	0	0	4
1979-80	Edmonton Oilers	80	5	10	15	104	3	0	0	0	4
1980-81	Edmonton Oilers	80	13	17	30	139	9	0	0	0	12
1981-82	Edmonton Oilers	80	4	25	29	154	5	1	1	2	14
1982-83	Edmonton Oilers	72	0	18	18	92	16	0	5	5	36
1983-84 ♦	Edmonton Oilers	80	5	16	21	125	19	1	4	5	23
1984-85 ♦	Edmonton Oilers	79	4	14	18	126	18	3	1	4	16
1985-86	Edmonton Oilers	80	4	22	26	129	8	0	2	2	10
1986-87	Edmonton Oilers	35	1	3	4	17	....	....	....	....	....
	Buffalo Sabres	9	0	2	2	8	....	....	....	....	....
	NHL Totals	**924**	**44**	**195**	**239**	**1318**	**108**	**5**	**19**	**24**	**173**

• Son of Lee

Played in NHL All-Star Game (1986)

Claimed by **Edmonton** from **Buffalo** in Expansion Draft, June 13, 1979. Traded to **Buffalo** by **Edmonton** with Mark Napier and Edmonton's 4th round choice (John Bradley) in 1987 Entry Draft for Normand Lacombe, Wayne Van Dorp and Buffalo's 4th round choice (Peter Eriksson) in 1987 Entry Draft, March 6, 1987.

FOGOLIN, Lee

Defense. Shoots left. 5'11", 195 lbs. Born, Fort William, Ont., February 27, 1926.

Season	Club	GP	G	A	Pts	PIM	GP	G	A	Pts	PIM
1947-48	Detroit Red Wings	....	....	....	....	....	2	0	1	1	6
1948-49	Detroit Red Wings	43	1	2	3	59	9	0	0	0	4
1949-50 ♦	Detroit Red Wings	63	4	8	12	63	10	0	0	0	16
1950-51	Detroit Red Wings	19	0	1	1	16	....	....	....	....	....
	Chicago Black Hawks	35	3	10	13	63	....	....	....	....	....
1951-52	Chicago Black Hawks	69	0	9	9	96	....	....	....	....	....
1952-53	Chicago Black Hawks	70	2	8	10	79	7	0	1	1	4
1953-54	Chicago Black Hawks	68	0	1	1	95	....	....	....	....	....
1954-55	Chicago Black Hawks	9	0	1	1	16	....	....	....	....	....
1955-56	Chicago Black Hawks	51	0	8	8	88	....	....	....	....	....
	NHL Totals	**427**	**10**	**48**	**58**	**575**	**28**	**0**	**2**	**2**	**30**

• Father of Lee Jr.

Played in NHL All-Star Game (1950, 1951)

Traded to **Chicago** by **Detroit** with Steve Black for Bert Olmstead and Vic Stasiuk, December 2, 1950. • Missed majority of 1954-55 season recovering from elbow injury originally suffered in training camp, September 30, 1954.

FOLCO, Peter

Defense. Shoots left. 6', 185 lbs. Born, Montreal, Que., August 13, 1953.
(Vancouver's 10th choice, 131st overall, in 1973 Amateur Draft).

Season	Club	GP	G	A	Pts	PIM	GP	G	A	Pts	PIM
1973-74	Vancouver Canucks	2	0	0	0	0	....	....	....	....	....
	NHL Totals	**2**	**0**	**0**	**0**	**0**	....	....	....	....	....

FOLEY, Gerry

Right wing. Shoots right. 5'11", 165 lbs. Born, Ware, MA, September 22, 1932.

Season	Club	GP	G	A	Pts	PIM	GP	G	A	Pts	PIM
1954-55	Toronto Maple Leafs	4	0	0	0	8	....	....	....	....	....
1956-57	New York Rangers	69	7	9	16	48	3	0	0	0	0
1957-58	New York Rangers	68	2	5	7	43	6	0	1	1	2
1968-69	Los Angeles Kings	1	0	0	0	0	....	....	....	....	....
	NHL Totals	**142**	**9**	**14**	**23**	**99**	**9**	**0**	**1**	**1**	**2**

Traded to **Toronto** by **Cleveland** (AHL) with Bob Bailey for Chuck Blair and $30,000, May 30, 1953. Claimed by **NY Rangers** from **Toronto** in Intra-League Draft, June 5, 1956. NHL rights transferred to **Los Angeles** after NHL club purchased **Springfield** (AHL) franchise, May, 1967.

FOLEY, Rick

Defense. Shoots left. 6'4", 223 lbs. Born, Niagara Falls, Ont., September 22, 1945.

Season	Club	GP	G	A	Pts	PIM	GP	G	A	Pts	PIM
1970-71	Chicago Black Hawks	2	0	1	1	8	4	0	1	1	4
1971-72	Philadelphia Flyers	58	11	25	36	168	....	....	....	....	....
1973-74	Detroit Red Wings	7	0	0	0	4	....	....	....	....	....
	NHL Totals	**67**	**11**	**26**	**37**	**180**	**4**	**0**	**1**	**1**	**4**

Claimed by **Portland** (WHL) from **Toronto** in Reverse Draft, June 13, 1968. Traded to **Philadelphia** by **Chicago** for Andre Lacroix, October 15, 1971. Traded to **Detroit** by **Philadelphia** for Serge Lajeunesse, May 15, 1973.

FOLIGNO, Mike

Right wing. Shoots right. 6'2", 195 lbs. Born, Sudbury, Ont., January 29, 1959.
(Detroit's 1st choice, 3rd overall, in 1979 Entry Draft).

Season	Club	GP	G	A	Pts	PIM	GP	G	A	Pts	PIM
1979-80	Detroit Red Wings	80	36	35	71	109	....	....	....	....	....
1980-81	Detroit Red Wings	80	28	35	63	210	....	....	....	....	....
1981-82	Detroit Red Wings	26	13	13	26	28	....	....	....	....	....
	Buffalo Sabres	56	20	31	51	149	4	2	0	2	9
1982-83	Buffalo Sabres	66	22	25	47	135	10	2	3	5	39
1983-84	Buffalo Sabres	70	32	31	63	151	3	2	1	3	19
1984-85	Buffalo Sabres	77	27	29	56	154	5	1	3	4	12
1985-86	Buffalo Sabres	79	41	39	80	168	....	....	....	....	....
1986-87	Buffalo Sabres	75	30	29	59	176	....	....	....	....	....
1987-88	Buffalo Sabres	74	29	28	57	220	6	3	2	5	31
1988-89	Buffalo Sabres	75	27	22	49	156	5	3	1	4	21
1989-90	Buffalo Sabres	61	15	25	40	99	6	0	1	1	12
1990-91	Buffalo Sabres	31	4	5	9	42	....	....	....	....	....
	Toronto Maple Leafs	37	8	7	15	65	....	....	....	....	....
1991-92	Toronto Maple Leafs	33	6	8	14	50	....	....	....	....	....
1992-93	Toronto Maple Leafs	55	13	5	18	84	18	2	6	8	42
1993-94	Toronto Maple Leafs	4	0	0	0	4	....	....	....	....	....
	Florida Panthers	39	4	5	9	49	....	....	....	....	....
	NHL Totals	**1018**	**355**	**372**	**727**	**2049**	**57**	**15**	**17**	**32**	**185**

Traded to **Buffalo** by **Detroit** with Dale McCourt and Brent Peterson for Danny Gare, Jim Schoenfeld and Derek Smith, December 2, 1981. Traded to **Toronto** by **Buffalo** with Buffalo's 8th round choice (Tomas Kucharcik) in 1991 Entry Draft for Brian Curran and Lou Franceschetti, December 17, 1990. • Missed majority of 1991-92 season recovering from broken leg suffered in game vs. Buffalo, December 21, 1991. Traded to **Florida** by **Toronto** for cash, November 5, 1993.

FOLK, Bill

Defense. Shoots left. 5'11", 190 lbs. Born, Regina, Sask., July 11, 1927.

Season	Club	GP	G	A	Pts	PIM	GP	G	A	Pts	PIM
1951-52	Detroit Red Wings	4	0	0	0	2	....	....	....	....	....
1952-53	Detroit Red Wings	8	0	0	0	2	....	....	....	....	....
	NHL Totals	**12**	**0**	**0**	**0**	**4**	....	....	....	....	....

FONTAINE, Len

Right wing. Shoots right. 5'7", 165 lbs. Born, Quebec City, Que., February 25, 1948.

Season	Club	GP	G	A	Pts	PIM	GP	G	A	Pts	PIM
1972-73	Detroit Red Wings	39	8	10	18	6	....	....	....	....	....
1973-74	Detroit Red Wings	7	0	1	1	4	....	....	....	....	....
	NHL Totals	**46**	**8**	**11**	**19**	**10**	....	....	....	....	....

Signed as a free agent by **Detroit**, May 1, 1972.

FONTAS, Jon

Center. Shoots right. 5'10", 185 lbs. Born, Arlington, MA, April 16, 1955.

Season	Club	GP	G	A	Pts	PIM	GP	G	A	Pts	PIM
1979-80	Minnesota North Stars	1	0	0	0	0	....	....	....	....	....
1980-81	Minnesota North Stars	1	0	0	0	0	....	....	....	....	....
	NHL Totals	**2**	**0**	**0**	**0**	**0**	....	....	....	....	....

Signed as a free agent by **Minnesota**, September, 1979.

FONTEYNE, Val

Left wing. Shoots left. 5'10", 160 lbs. Born, Wetaskiwin, Alta., December 2, 1933.

Season	Club	GP	G	A	Pts	PIM	GP	G	A	Pts	PIM
1959-60	Detroit Red Wings	69	4	7	11	2	6	0	4	4	0
1960-61	Detroit Red Wings	66	6	11	17	4	11	2	3	5	0
1961-62	Detroit Red Wings	70	5	5	10	4	....	....	....	....	....
1962-63	Detroit Red Wings	67	6	14	20	2	11	0	0	0	2
1963-64	New York Rangers	69	7	18	25	4	....	....	....	....	....

Season	Club	GP	G	A	Pts	PIM	GP	G	A	Pts	PIM
		REGULAR SEASON					PLAYOFFS				
1964-65	New York Rangers	27	0	1	1	2	....	....	....	....	....
	Detroit Red Wings	16	2	5	7	4	5	0	1	1	0
1965-66	Detroit Red Wings	59	5	10	15	0	12	1	0	1	4
1966-67	Detroit Red Wings	28	1	1	2	0	....	....	....	....	....
1967-68	Pittsburgh Penguins	69	6	28	34	0	....	....	....	....	....
1968-69	Pittsburgh Penguins	74	12	17	29	2	....	....	....	....	....
1969-70	Pittsburgh Penguins	68	11	15	26	2	10	0	2	2	0
1970-71	Pittsburgh Penguins	70	4	9	13	0	....	....	....	....	....
1971-72	Pittsburgh Penguins	68	6	13	19	0	4	0	0	0	2
	NHL Totals	**820**	**75**	**154**	**229**	**26**	**59**	**3**	**10**	**13**	**8**

Claimed by **NY Rangers** from **Detroit** in Intra-League Draft, June 4, 1963. Claimed on waivers by **Detroit** from **NY Rangers**, February 8, 1965. Claimed by **Pittsburgh** from **Detroit** in Expansion Draft, June 6, 1967.

FONTINATO, Lou

Defense. Shoots left. 6'1", 195 lbs. Born, Guelph, Ont., January 20, 1932.

Season	Club	GP	G	A	Pts	PIM	GP	G	A	Pts	PIM
1954-55	New York Rangers	27	2	2	4	60	....	....	....	....	....
1955-56	New York Rangers	70	3	15	18	*202	4	0	0	0	6
1956-57	New York Rangers	70	3	12	15	139	5	0	0	0	7
1957-58	New York Rangers	70	3	8	11	*152	6	0	1	1	6
1958-59	New York Rangers	64	7	6	13	149	....	....	....	....	....
1959-60	New York Rangers	64	2	11	13	137	....	....	....	....	....
1960-61	New York Rangers	53	2	3	5	100	....	....	....	....	....
1961-62	Montreal Canadiens	54	2	13	15	*167	6	0	1	1	23
1962-63	Montreal Canadiens	63	2	8	10	141	....	....	....	....	....
	NHL Totals	**535**	**26**	**78**	**104**	**1247**	**21**	**0**	**2**	**2**	**42**

Traded to **Montreal** by **NY Rangers** for Doug Harvey, June 13, 1961. • Suffered career-ending neck injury in game vs. NY Rangers, March 9, 1963.

FOOTE, Adam

Defense. Shoots right. 6'2", 215 lbs. Born, Toronto, Ont., July 10, 1971.
(Quebec's 2nd choice, 22nd overall, in 1989 Entry Draft).

Season	Club	GP	G	A	Pts	PIM	GP	G	A	Pts	PIM
1991-92	Quebec Nordiques	46	2	5	7	44	....	....	....	....	....
1992-93	Quebec Nordiques	81	4	12	16	168	6	0	1	1	2
1993-94	Quebec Nordiques	45	2	6	8	67	....	....	....	....	....
1994-95	Quebec Nordiques	35	0	7	7	52	6	0	1	1	14
1995-96♦	Colorado Avalanche	73	5	11	16	88	22	1	3	4	36
1996-97	Colorado Avalanche	78	2	19	21	135	17	0	4	4	62
1997-98	Colorado Avalanche	77	3	14	17	124	7	0	0	0	23
1998-99	Colorado Avalanche	64	5	16	21	92	19	2	3	5	24
99-2000	Colorado Avalanche	59	5	13	18	98	16	0	7	7	28
2000-01♦	Colorado Avalanche	35	3	12	15	42	23	3	4	7	*47
2001-02	Colorado Avalanche	55	5	22	27	55	21	1	6	7	28
2002-03	Colorado Avalanche	78	11	20	31	88	6	0	1	1	8
	NHL Totals	**726**	**47**	**157**	**204**	**1053**	**143**	**7**	**30**	**37**	**272**

Transferred to **Colorado** after **Quebec** franchise relocated, June 21, 1995. • Missed majority of 2000-01 season recovering from shoulder injury suffered in game vs. Carolina, January 6, 2001.

FORBES, Colin

Center. Shoots left. 6'3", 205 lbs. Born, New Westminster, B.C., February 16, 1976.
(Philadelphia's 5th choice, 166th overall, in 1994 Entry Draft).

Season	Club	GP	G	A	Pts	PIM	GP	G	A	Pts	PIM
1996-97	Philadelphia Flyers	3	1	0	1	0	3	0	0	0	0
1997-98	Philadelphia Flyers	63	12	7	19	59	5	0	0	0	2
1998-99	Philadelphia Flyers	66	9	7	16	51	....	....	....	....	....
	Tampa Bay Lightning	14	3	1	4	10	....	....	....	....	....
99-2000	Tampa Bay Lightning	8	0	0	0	18	....	....	....	....	....
	Ottawa Senators	45	2	5	7	12	5	1	0	1	14
2000-01	Ottawa Senators	39	0	1	1	31	....	....	....	....	....
	New York Rangers	19	1	4	5	15	....	....	....	....	....
2001-02	Washington Capitals	38	5	3	8	15	....	....	....	....	....
2002-03	Washington Capitals	5	0	0	0	0	....	....	....	....	....
	NHL Totals	**300**	**33**	**28**	**61**	**211**	**13**	**1**	**0**	**1**	**16**

Traded to **Tampa Bay** by **Philadelphia** with Philadelphia's 4th round choice (Michal Lanicek) in 1999 Entry Draft for Mikael Andersson and Sandy McCarthy, March 20, 1999. Traded to **Ottawa** by **Tampa Bay** for Bruce Gardiner, November 11, 1999. Traded to **NY Rangers** by **Ottawa** for Eric Lacroix, March 1, 2001. Signed as a free agent by **Washington**, January 8, 2002.

FORBES, Dave

Left wing. Shoots left. 5'10", 180 lbs. Born, Montreal, Que., November 16, 1948.

Season	Club	GP	G	A	Pts	PIM	GP	G	A	Pts	PIM
1973-74	Boston Bruins	63	10	16	26	41	16	0	2	2	6
1974-75	Boston Bruins	69	18	12	30	80	3	0	0	0	0
1975-76	Boston Bruins	79	16	13	29	52	12	1	1	2	5
1976-77	Boston Bruins	73	9	11	20	47	14	0	1	1	2
1977-78	Washington Capitals	77	11	11	22	119	....	....	....	....	....
1978-79	Washington Capitals	2	0	1	1	2	....	....	....	....	....
	NHL Totals	**363**	**64**	**64**	**128**	**341**	**45**	**1**	**4**	**5**	**13**

Signed as a free agent by **Boston**, September, 1973. Claimed by **Washington** from **Boston** in Waiver Draft, October 10, 1977.

FORBES, Mike

Defense. Shoots right. 6'2", 200 lbs. Born, Brampton, Ont., September 20, 1957.
(Boston's 3rd choice, 52nd overall, in 1977 Amateur Draft).

Season	Club	GP	G	A	Pts	PIM	GP	G	A	Pts	PIM
1977-78	Boston Bruins	32	0	4	4	15	....	....	....	....	....
1979-80	Edmonton Oilers	2	0	0	0	0	....	....	....	....	....
1981-82	Edmonton Oilers	16	1	7	8	26	....	....	....	....	....
	NHL Totals	**50**	**1**	**11**	**12**	**41**	....	....	....	....	....

Claimed by **Edmonton** from **Boston** in Expansion Draft, June 13, 1979.

FOREY, Connie

Left wing. Shoots left. 6'2", 185 lbs. Born, Montreal, Que., October 18, 1950.
(Pittsburgh's 4th choice, 49th overall, in 1970 Amateur Draft).

Season	Club	GP	G	A	Pts	PIM	GP	G	A	Pts	PIM
1973-74	St. Louis Blues	4	0	0	0	2	....	....	....	....	....
	NHL Totals	**4**	**0**	**0**	**0**	**2**	....	....	....	....	....

Claimed by **NY Islanders** from **Hershey** (AHL) in Inter-League Draft, June 6, 1972. Claimed by **St. Louis** (Denver-WHL) from **NY Islanders** in Reverse Draft, June 6, 1973.

FORSBERG, Peter

Center. Shoots left. 6', 205 lbs. Born, Ornskoldsvik, Sweden, July 20, 1973.
(Philadelphia's 1st choice, 6th overall, in 1991 Entry Draft).

Season	Club	GP	G	A	Pts	PIM	GP	G	A	Pts	PIM
1994-95	Quebec Nordiques	47	15	35	50	16	6	2	4	6	4
1995-96♦	Colorado Avalanche	82	30	86	116	47	22	10	11	21	18
1996-97	Colorado Avalanche	65	28	58	86	73	14	5	12	17	10
1997-98	Colorado Avalanche	72	25	66	91	94	7	6	5	11	12
1998-99	Colorado Avalanche	78	30	67	97	108	19	8	16	*24	31
99-2000	Colorado Avalanche	49	14	37	51	52	16	7	8	15	12
2000-01♦	Colorado Avalanche	73	27	62	89	54	11	4	10	14	6
2001-02	Colorado Avalanche	....	....	....	....	....	20	9	*18	*27	20
2002-03	Colorado Avalanche	75	29	*77	*106	70	7	2	6	8	6
	NHL Totals	**541**	**198**	**488**	**686**	**514**	**122**	**53**	**90**	**143**	**119**

NHL All-Rookie Team (1995) • Calder Memorial Trophy (1995) • NHL First All-Star Team (1998, 1999, 2003) • Art Ross Trophy (2003) • Hart Trophy (2003)

Played in NHL All-Star Game (1996, 1998, 1999, 2001, 2003)

Traded to **Quebec** by **Philadelphia** with Steve Duchesne, Kerry Huffman, Mike Ricci, Ron Hextall, Philadelphia's 1st round choice (Jocelyn Thibault) in 1993 Entry Draft, $15,000,000 and future considerations (Chris Simon and Philadelphia's 1st round choice (later traded to Toronto – later traded to Washington – Washington selected Nolan Baumgartner) in 1994 Entry Draft, July 21, 1992) for Eric Lindros, June 30, 1992. Transferred to **Colorado** after **Quebec** franchise relocated, June 21, 1995. • Missed entire 2001-02 regular season recovering from spleen injury suffered in game vs. Los Angeles, May 9, 2001 and ankle injury suffered in practice, January 10, 2002.

FORSEY, Jack

Right wing. Shoots right. 5'11", 170 lbs. Born, Swift Current, Sask., November 7, 1914.

Season	Club	GP	G	A	Pts	PIM	GP	G	A	Pts	PIM
1942-43	Toronto Maple Leafs	19	7	9	16	10	3	0	1	1	0
	NHL Totals	**19**	**7**	**9**	**16**	**10**	**3**	**0**	**1**	**1**	**0**

Loaned to **Providence** (AHL) by **Toronto** with the loan of George Boothman for Buck Jones and the loan of Ab DeMarco, February 3, 1943.

FORSLUND, Gus

Right wing. Shoots right. 5'10", 150 lbs. Born, Umea, Sweden, April 25, 1908.

Season	Club	GP	G	A	Pts	PIM	GP	G	A	Pts	PIM
1932-33	Ottawa Senators	48	4	9	13	2	....	....	....	....	....
	NHL Totals	**48**	**4**	**9**	**13**	**2**	....	....	....	....	....

FORSLUND, Tomas

Right wing. Shoots left. 5'11", 200 lbs. Born, Falun, Sweden, November 24, 1968.
(Calgary's 4th choice, 85th overall, in 1988 Entry Draft).

Season	Club	GP	G	A	Pts	PIM	GP	G	A	Pts	PIM
1991-92	Calgary Flames	38	5	9	14	12	....	....	....	....	....
1992-93	Calgary Flames	6	0	2	2	0	....	....	....	....	....
	NHL Totals	**44**	**5**	**11**	**16**	**12**	....	....	....	....	....

FORSYTH, Alex

Center. Shoots left. 6'2", 195 lbs. Born, Galt, Ont., January 6, 1955.
(Washington's 1st choice, 18th overall, in 1975 Amateur Draft).

Season	Club	GP	G	A	Pts	PIM	GP	G	A	Pts	PIM
1976-77	Washington Capitals	1	0	0	0	0	....	....	....	....	....
	NHL Totals	**1**	**0**	**0**	**0**	**0**	....	....	....	....	....

FORTIER, Dave

Defense. Shoots left. 5'11", 190 lbs. Born, Sudbury, Ont., June 17, 1951.
(Toronto's 2nd choice, 23rd overall, in 1971 Amateur Draft).

Season	Club	GP	G	A	Pts	PIM	GP	G	A	Pts	PIM
1972-73	Toronto Maple Leafs	23	1	4	5	63	....	....	....	....	....
1974-75	New York Islanders	65	6	12	18	79	14	0	2	2	33
1975-76	New York Islanders	59	0	2	2	68	6	0	0	0	0
1976-77	Vancouver Canucks	58	1	3	4	125	....	....	....	....	....
	NHL Totals	**205**	**8**	**21**	**29**	**335**	**20**	**0**	**2**	**2**	**33**

Traded to **Philadelphia** by **Toronto** with Randy Osburn for Bill Flett, May 27, 1974. Claimed by **NY Islanders** from **Philadelphia** in Intra-League Draft, June 10, 1974. Traded to **Vancouver** by **NY Islanders** with Ralph Stewart for cash, October 6, 1976.

FORTIER, Marc

Center. Shoots right. 6', 192 lbs. Born, Windsor, Que., February 26, 1966.

Season	Club	GP	G	A	Pts	PIM	GP	G	A	Pts	PIM
1987-88	Quebec Nordiques	27	4	10	14	12	....	....	....	....	....
1988-89	Quebec Nordiques	57	20	19	39	45	....	....	....	....	....
1989-90	Quebec Nordiques	59	13	17	30	28	....	....	....	....	....
1990-91	Quebec Nordiques	14	0	4	4	6	....	....	....	....	....
1991-92	Quebec Nordiques	39	5	9	14	33	....	....	....	....	....

Season	Club	GP	G	A	Pts	PIM	GP	G	A	Pts	PIM
		REGULAR SEASON					PLAYOFFS				
1992-93	Ottawa Senators	10	0	1	1	6	....	....	....	....	....
	Los Angeles Kings	6	0	0	0	5	....	....	....	....	....
	NHL Totals	**212**	**42**	**60**	**102**	**135**	....	....	....	....	....

Signed as a free agent by **Quebec**, February 3, 1987. Signed as a free agent by **Ottawa**, October 1, 1992. Traded to **Los Angeles** by **Ottawa** with Jim Thomson for Bob Kudelski and Shawn McCosh, December 19, 1992.

FORTIN, Jean-Francois

Defense. Shoots right. 6'2", 205 lbs. Born, Laval, Que., March 15, 1979.
(Washington's 2nd choice, 35th overall, in 1997 Entry Draft).

Season	Club	GP	G	A	Pts	PIM	GP	G	A	Pts	PIM
2001-02	Washington Capitals	36	1	3	4	20	....	....	....	....	....
2002-03	Washington Capitals	33	0	1	1	22	....	....	....	....	....
	NHL Totals	**69**	**1**	**4**	**5**	**42**	....	....	....	....	....

FORTIN, Ray

Defense. Shoots left. 5'8", 180 lbs. Born, Drummondville, Que., March 11, 1941.

Season	Club	GP	G	A	Pts	PIM	GP	G	A	Pts	PIM
1967-68	St. Louis Blues	24	0	2	2	8	3	0	0	0	2
1968-69	St. Louis Blues	11	1	0	1	6	....	....	....	....	....
1969-70	St. Louis Blues	57	1	4	5	19	3	0	0	0	6
	NHL Totals	**92**	**2**	**6**	**8**	**33**	**6**	**0**	**0**	**0**	**8**

Signed as a free agent by **St. Louis**, June, 1967. Traded to **Los Angeles** by **St. Louis** for Bob Wall, May 11, 1970. Traded to **Montreal** by **Los Angeles** with Gord Labossiere for Ralph Backstrom, January 26, 1971. Claimed by **Hershey** (AHL) from **Montreal** in Reverse Draft, June, 1971. Traded to **Boston** by **Hershey** (AHL) for cash, August, 1971.

FOSTER, Corey

Defense. Shoots left. 6'3", 204 lbs. Born, Ottawa, Ont., October 27, 1969.
(New Jersey's 1st choice, 12th overall, in 1988 Entry Draft).

Season	Club	GP	G	A	Pts	PIM	GP	G	A	Pts	PIM
1988-89	New Jersey Devils	2	0	0	0	0	....	....	....	....	....
1991-92	Philadelphia Flyers	25	3	4	7	20	....	....	....	....	....
1995-96	Pittsburgh Penguins	11	2	2	4	2	3	0	0	0	4
1996-97	New York Islanders	7	0	0	0	2	....	....	....	....	....
	NHL Totals	**45**	**5**	**6**	**11**	**24**	**3**	**0**	**0**	**0**	**4**

Traded to **Edmonton** by **New Jersey** for Edmonton's 1st round choice (Jason Miller) in 1989 Entry Draft, June 17, 1989. Traded to **Philadelphia** by **Edmonton** with Dave Brown and Jari Kurri for Craig Fisher, Scott Mellanby and Craig Berube, May 30, 1991. Signed as a free agent by **Ottawa**, June 20, 1994. Signed as a free agent by **Pittsburgh**, August 7, 1995. Claimed by **NY Islanders** from **Pittsburgh** in Waiver Draft, September 30, 1996.

FOSTER, Dwight

Right wing. Shoots right. 5'10", 190 lbs. Born, Toronto, Ont., April 2, 1957.
(Boston's 1st choice, 16th overall, in 1977 Amateur Draft).

Season	Club	GP	G	A	Pts	PIM	GP	G	A	Pts	PIM
1977-78	Boston Bruins	14	2	1	3	6	....	....	....	....	....
1978-79	Boston Bruins	44	11	13	24	14	11	1	3	4	0
1979-80	Boston Bruins	57	10	28	38	42	9	3	5	8	2
1980-81	Boston Bruins	77	24	28	52	62	3	1	1	2	0
1981-82	Colorado Rockies	70	12	19	31	41	....	....	....	....	....
1982-83	New Jersey Devils	4	0	0	0	2	....	....	....	....	....
	Detroit Red Wings	58	17	22	39	58	....	....	....	....	....
1983-84	Detroit Red Wings	52	9	12	21	50	3	0	1	1	0
1984-85	Detroit Red Wings	50	16	16	32	56	3	0	0	0	0
1985-86	Detroit Red Wings	55	6	12	18	48	....	....	....	....	....
	Boston Bruins	13	0	0	0	4	3	0	2	2	2
1986-87	Boston Bruins	47	4	12	16	37	3	0	0	0	0
	NHL Totals	**541**	**111**	**163**	**274**	**420**	**35**	**5**	**12**	**17**	**4**

Signed as a free agent by **Colorado**, July 21, 1981. Transferred to **New Jersey** when **Colorado** franchise relocated, June 30, 1982. Rights traded to **Detroit** by **New Jersey** for cash, October 29, 1982. Traded to **Boston** by **Detroit** for Dave Donnelly, March 11, 1986.

FOSTER, Herb

Left wing. Shoots left. 5'10", 168 lbs. Born, Brockville, Ont., August 9, 1913.

Season	Club	GP	G	A	Pts	PIM	GP	G	A	Pts	PIM
1940-41	New York Rangers	5	1	0	1	5	....	....	....	....	....
1947-48	New York Rangers	1	0	0	0	0	....	....	....	....	....
	NHL Totals	**6**	**1**	**0**	**1**	**5**	....	....	....	....	....

Signed as a free agent by **NY Rangers**, October 21, 1940. Traded to **Cleveland** (AHL) by **NY Rangers** for cash, September 9, 1941.

FOSTER, Kurtis

Defense. Shoots right. 6'5", 230 lbs. Born, Carp, Ont., November 24, 1981.
(Calgary's 2nd choice, 40th overall, in 2000 Entry Draft).

Season	Club	GP	G	A	Pts	PIM	GP	G	A	Pts	PIM
2002-03	Atlanta Thrashers	2	0	0	0	0	....	....	....	....	....
	NHL Totals	**2**	**0**	**0**	**0**	**0**	....	....	....	....	....

Rights traded to **Atlanta** by **Calgary** with Jeff Cowan for Petr Buzek, December 18, 2001.

FOSTER, Yip

Defense. Shoots left. 6'6", 198 lbs. Born, Guelph, Ont., November 25, 1907.

Season	Club	GP	G	A	Pts	PIM	GP	G	A	Pts	PIM
1929-30	New York Rangers	31	0	0	0	10	....	....	....	....	....
1931-32	Boston Bruins	34	1	2	3	12	....	....	....	....	....
1933-34	Detroit Red Wings	6	0	0	0	2	....	....	....	....	....
1934-35	Detroit Red Wings	12	2	0	2	8	....	....	....	....	....
	NHL Totals	**83**	**3**	**2**	**5**	**32**	....	....	....	....	....

Signed as a free agent by **NY Rangers**, September, 1927. • Toronto also claimed to have his rights. NHL arranged for Eric Pettinger to be sent to Toronto as compensation, October, 1927. Traded to **Boston** by **NY Rangers** with $15,000 for Bill Regan, February 17, 1930. Traded to **Tulsa** (AHA) by **Boston** for cash, January 6, 1933. Signed as a free agent by **Detroit**, October 17, 1933. Traded to **Cleveland** (IAHL) by **Detroit** for cash, October 14, 1936.

FOTIU, Nick

Left wing. Shoots left. 6'2", 210 lbs. Born, Staten Island, NY, May 25, 1952.

Season	Club	GP	G	A	Pts	PIM	GP	G	A	Pts	PIM
1976-77	New York Rangers	70	4	8	12	174	....	....	....	....	....
1977-78	New York Rangers	59	2	7	9	105	3	0	0	0	5
1978-79	New York Rangers	71	3	5	8	190	4	0	0	0	6
1979-80	Hartford Whalers	74	10	8	18	107	3	0	0	0	6
1980-81	Hartford Whalers	42	4	3	7	79	....	....	....	....	....
	New York Rangers	27	5	6	11	91	2	0	0	0	4
1981-82	New York Rangers	70	8	10	18	151	10	0	2	2	6
1982-83	New York Rangers	72	8	13	21	90	5	0	1	1	6
1983-84	New York Rangers	40	7	6	13	115	....	....	....	....	....
1984-85	New York Rangers	46	4	7	11	54	....	....	....	....	....
1985-86	Calgary Flames	9	0	1	1	21	11	0	1	1	34
1986-87	Calgary Flames	42	5	3	8	145	....	....	....	....	....
1987-88	Philadelphia Flyers	23	0	0	0	40	....	....	....	....	....
1988-89	Edmonton Oilers	1	0	0	0	0	....	....	....	....	....
	NHL Totals	**646**	**60**	**77**	**137**	**1362**	**38**	**0**	**4**	**4**	**67**

Signed as a free agent by **NY Rangers**, July 23, 1976. Claimed by **Hartford** from **NY Rangers** in Expansion Draft, June 13, 1979. Traded to **NY Rangers** by **Hartford** for NY Rangers' 5th round choice (Bill Maguire) in 1981 Entry Draft, January 15, 1981. Traded to **Calgary** by **NY Rangers** for future considerations, March 11, 1986. Signed as a free agent by **Philadelphia**, October 30, 1987. Signed as a free agent by **Edmonton**, March, 1989.

FOWLER, Jimmy

Defense. Shoots left. 5'11", 168 lbs. Born, Toronto, Ont., April 6, 1915.

Season	Club	GP	G	A	Pts	PIM	GP	G	A	Pts	PIM
1936-37	Toronto Maple Leafs	48	7	11	18	22	2	0	0	0	0
1937-38	Toronto Maple Leafs	48	10	12	22	8	7	0	2	2	0
1938-39	Toronto Maple Leafs	39	1	6	7	9	9	0	1	1	2
	NHL Totals	**135**	**18**	**29**	**47**	**39**	**18**	**0**	**3**	**3**	**2**

Signed as a free agent by **Toronto**, October 22, 1935. Traded to **NY Americans** by **Toronto** with Busher Jackson, Murray Armstrong, Buzz Boll and Doc Romnes for Sweeney Schriner, May 18, 1939.

FOWLER, Tom

Center. Shoots left. 5'11", 165 lbs. Born, Winnipeg, Man., May 18, 1924.

Season	Club	GP	G	A	Pts	PIM	GP	G	A	Pts	PIM
1946-47	Chicago Black Hawks	24	0	1	1	18	....	....	....	....	....
	NHL Totals	**24**	**0**	**1**	**1**	**18**	....	....	....	....	....

FOX, Greg

Defense. Shoots left. 6'2", 190 lbs. Born, Port McNeil, B.C., August 12, 1953.
(Atlanta's 12th choice, 162nd overall, in 1973 Amateur Draft).

Season	Club	GP	G	A	Pts	PIM	GP	G	A	Pts	PIM
1977-78	Atlanta Flames	16	1	2	3	25	2	0	1	1	8
1978-79	Atlanta Flames	64	0	12	12	70	....	....	....	....	....
	Chicago Black Hawks	14	0	5	5	16	4	0	1	1	0
1979-80	Chicago Black Hawks	71	4	11	15	73	7	0	0	0	8
1980-81	Chicago Black Hawks	75	3	16	19	112	3	0	1	1	2
1981-82	Chicago Black Hawks	79	2	19	21	137	15	1	3	4	27
1982-83	Chicago Black Hawks	76	0	12	12	81	13	0	3	3	22
1983-84	Chicago Black Hawks	24	0	5	5	31	....	....	....	....	....
	Pittsburgh Penguins	49	2	5	7	66	....	....	....	....	....
1984-85	Pittsburgh Penguins	26	2	5	7	26	....	....	....	....	....
	NHL Totals	**494**	**14**	**92**	**106**	**637**	**44**	**1**	**9**	**10**	**67**

Traded to **Chicago** by **Atlanta** with Tom Lysiak, Harold Phillipoff, Pat Ribble and Miles Zaharko for Ivan Boldirev, Darcy Rota and Phil Russell, March 13, 1979. Traded to **Pittsburgh** by **Chicago** for Randy Boyd, December 6, 1983.

FOX, Jim

Right wing. Shoots right. 5'8", 185 lbs. Born, Coniston, Ont., May 18, 1960.
(Los Angeles' 2nd choice, 10th overall, in 1980 Entry Draft).

Season	Club	GP	G	A	Pts	PIM	GP	G	A	Pts	PIM
1980-81	Los Angeles Kings	71	18	25	43	8	4	0	1	1	0
1981-82	Los Angeles Kings	77	30	38	68	23	9	1	4	5	0
1982-83	Los Angeles Kings	77	28	40	68	8	....	....	....	....	....
1983-84	Los Angeles Kings	80	30	42	72	26	....	....	....	....	....
1984-85	Los Angeles Kings	79	30	53	83	10	3	0	1	1	0
1985-86	Los Angeles Kings	39	14	17	31	2	....	....	....	....	....
1986-87	Los Angeles Kings	76	19	42	61	48	5	3	2	5	0
1987-88	Los Angeles Kings	68	16	35	51	18	1	0	0	0	0
1989-90	Los Angeles Kings	11	1	1	2	0	....	....	....	....	....
	NHL Totals	**578**	**186**	**293**	**479**	**143**	**22**	**4**	**8**	**12**	**0**

• Missed entire 1988-89 season recovering from knee injury originally suffered in game vs. Boston, March 10, 1988.

FOYSTON, Frank

HHOF

Center/Right wing. Shoots left. 5'9", 158 lbs. Born, Minesing, Ont., February 2, 1891.

Season	Club	GP	G	A	Pts	PIM	GP	G	A	Pts	PIM
1926-27	Detroit Cougars	41	10	5	15	16	....	....	....	....	....

Season	Club	GP	G	A	Pts	PIM	GP	G	A	Pts	PIM
		REGULAR SEASON					PLAYOFFS				
1927-28	Detroit Cougars	23	7	2	9	16	....	....	....	....	....
	NHL Totals	**64**	**17**	**7**	**24**	**32**	....	....	....	....	....

NHL rights transferred to **Detroit** after NHL club purchased **Victoria** (WHL) franchise, May 15, 1926. • Named playing coach of **Detroit Olympics** (Can-Pro), October 11, 1927. Traded to **Detroit** by **Detroit Olympics** (Can-Pro) for cash, January 10, 1928.

FRAMPTON, Bob

Left wing. Shoots left. 5'10", 175 lbs. Born, Toronto, Ont., January 20, 1929.

Season	Club	GP	G	A	Pts	PIM	GP	G	A	Pts	PIM
1949-50	Montreal Canadiens	2	0	0	0	0	3	0	0	0	0
	NHL Totals	**2**	**0**	**0**	**0**	**0**	**3**	**0**	**0**	**0**	**0**

Signed as a free agent by **Montreal**, June 28, 1949. Claimed by **Chicago** from **Mtl. Royals** (QHL) in Reverse Draft, June 10, 1953.

FRANCESCHETTI, Lou

Right wing. Shoots left. 6', 200 lbs. Born, Toronto, Ont., March 28, 1958.
(Washington's 8th choice, 71st overall, in 1978 Amateur Draft).

Season	Club	GP	G	A	Pts	PIM	GP	G	A	Pts	PIM
1981-82	Washington Capitals	30	2	10	12	23	....	....	....	....	....
1983-84	Washington Capitals	2	0	0	0	0	3	0	0	0	8
1984-85	Washington Capitals	22	4	7	11	45	5	1	1	2	15
1985-86	Washington Capitals	76	7	14	21	131	8	0	0	0	15
1986-87	Washington Capitals	75	12	9	21	127	7	0	0	0	23
1987-88	Washington Capitals	59	4	8	12	113	4	0	0	0	14
1988-89	Washington Capitals	63	7	10	17	123	6	1	0	1	8
1989-90	Toronto Maple Leafs	80	21	15	36	127	5	0	1	1	26
1990-91	Toronto Maple Leafs	16	1	1	2	30	....	....	....	....	....
	Buffalo Sabres	35	1	7	8	28	6	1	0	1	2
1991-92	Buffalo Sabres	1	0	0	0	0	....	....	....	....	....
	NHL Totals	**459**	**59**	**81**	**140**	**747**	**44**	**3**	**2**	**5**	**111**

Traded to **Toronto** by **Washington** for Toronto's 5th round choice (Mark Ouimet) in 1990 Entry Draft, June 29, 1989. Traded to **Buffalo** by **Toronto** with Brian Curran for Mike Foligno and Buffalo's 8th round choice (Tomas Kucharcik) in 1991 Entry Draft, December 17, 1990.

FRANCIS, Bobby

Center. Shoots right. 5'9", 175 lbs. Born, North Battleford, Sask., December 5, 1958.

Season	Club	GP	G	A	Pts	PIM	GP	G	A	Pts	PIM
1982-83	Detroit Red Wings	14	2	0	2	0	....	....	....	....	....
	NHL Totals	**14**	**2**	**0**	**2**	**0**	....	....	....	....	....

• Son of Emile

Signed as a free agent by **Calgary**, October 27, 1980. Traded to **Detroit** by **Calgary** for the rights to Yves Courteau, December 2, 1982.

FRANCIS, Ron

Center. Shoots left. 6'3", 200 lbs. Born, Sault Ste. Marie, Ont., March 1, 1963.
(Hartford's 1st choice, 4th overall, in 1981 Entry Draft).

Season	Club	GP	G	A	Pts	PIM	GP	G	A	Pts	PIM
1981-82	Hartford Whalers	59	25	43	68	51	....	....	....	....	....
1982-83	Hartford Whalers	79	31	59	90	60	....	....	....	....	....
1983-84	Hartford Whalers	72	23	60	83	45	....	....	....	....	....
1984-85	Hartford Whalers	80	24	57	81	66	....	....	....	....	....
1985-86	Hartford Whalers	53	24	53	77	24	10	1	2	3	4
1986-87	Hartford Whalers	75	30	63	93	45	6	2	2	4	6
1987-88	Hartford Whalers	80	25	50	75	87	6	2	5	7	2
1988-89	Hartford Whalers	69	29	48	77	36	4	0	2	2	0
1989-90	Hartford Whalers	80	32	69	101	73	7	3	3	6	8
1990-91	Hartford Whalers	67	21	55	76	51	....	....	....	....	....
	◆ Pittsburgh Penguins	14	2	9	11	21	24	7	10	17	24
1991-92	◆ Pittsburgh Penguins	70	21	33	54	30	21	8	*19	27	6
1992-93	Pittsburgh Penguins	84	24	76	100	68	12	6	11	17	19
1993-94	Pittsburgh Penguins	82	27	66	93	62	6	0	2	2	6
1994-95	Pittsburgh Penguins	44	11	*48	59	18	12	6	13	19	4
1995-96	Pittsburgh Penguins	77	27	*92	119	56	11	3	6	9	4
1996-97	Pittsburgh Penguins	81	27	63	90	20	5	1	2	3	2
1997-98	Pittsburgh Penguins	81	25	62	87	20	6	1	5	6	2
1998-99	Carolina Hurricanes	82	21	31	52	34	3	0	1	1	0
99-2000	Carolina Hurricanes	78	23	50	73	18	....	....	....	....	....
2000-01	Carolina Hurricanes	82	15	50	65	32	3	0	0	0	0
2001-02	Carolina Hurricanes	80	27	50	77	18	23	6	10	16	6
2002-03	Carolina Hurricanes	82	22	35	57	30	....	....	....	....	....
	NHL Totals	**1651**	**536**	**1222**	**1758**	**965**	**159**	**46**	**93**	**139**	**93**

Alka-Seltzer Plus Award (1995) • Frank J. Selke Trophy (1995) • Lady Byng Trophy (1995, 1998, 2002) • King Clancy Memorial Trophy (2002)

Played in NHL All-Star Game (1983, 1985, 1990, 1996)

Traded to **Pittsburgh** by **Hartford** with Grant Jennings and Ulf Samuelsson for John Cullen, Jeff Parker and Zarley Zalapski, March 4, 1991. Signed as a free agent by **Carolina**, July 13, 1998.

FRASER, Archie

Center. Shoots left. 5'11", 160 lbs. Born, Souris, Man., February 9, 1914.

Season	Club	GP	G	A	Pts	PIM	GP	G	A	Pts	PIM
1943-44	New York Rangers	3	0	1	1	0	....	....	....	....	....
	NHL Totals	**3**	**0**	**1**	**1**	**0**	....	....	....	....	....

• Brother of Harvey

FRASER, Charles

Defense. Shoots left. , Born, Stellarton, N.S.,

Season	Club	GP	G	A	Pts	PIM	GP	G	A	Pts	PIM
1923-24	Hamilton Tigers	1	0	0	0	0	....	....	....	....	....
	NHL Totals	**1**	**0**	**0**	**0**	**0**	....	....	....	....	....

Signed as a free agent by **Hamilton**, December 14, 1923.

FRASER, Curt

Left wing. Shoots left. 6'1", 200 lbs. Born, Cincinnati, OH, January 12, 1958.
(Vancouver's 2nd choice, 22nd overall, in 1978 Amateur Draft).

Season	Club	GP	G	A	Pts	PIM	GP	G	A	Pts	PIM
1978-79	Vancouver Canucks	78	16	19	35	116	3	0	2	2	6
1979-80	Vancouver Canucks	78	17	25	42	143	4	0	0	0	2
1980-81	Vancouver Canucks	77	25	24	49	118	3	1	0	1	2
1981-82	Vancouver Canucks	79	28	39	67	175	17	3	7	10	98
1982-83	Vancouver Canucks	36	6	7	13	99	....	....	....	....	....
	Chicago Black Hawks	38	6	13	19	77	13	4	4	8	18
1983-84	Chicago Black Hawks	29	5	12	17	28	5	0	0	0	14
1984-85	Chicago Black Hawks	73	25	25	50	109	15	6	3	9	36
1985-86	Chicago Black Hawks	61	29	39	68	84	3	0	1	1	12
1986-87	Chicago Blackhawks	75	25	25	50	182	2	1	1	2	10
1987-88	Chicago Blackhawks	27	4	6	10	57	....	....	....	....	....
	Minnesota North Stars	10	1	1	2	20	....	....	....	....	....
1988-89	Minnesota North Stars	35	5	5	10	76	....	....	....	....	....
1989-90	Minnesota North Stars	8	1	0	1	22	....	....	....	....	....
	NHL Totals	**704**	**193**	**240**	**433**	**1306**	**65**	**15**	**18**	**33**	**198**

Traded to **Chicago** by **Vancouver** for Tony Tanti, January 6, 1983. • Missed majority of 1983-84 season recovering from knee injury suffered in game vs. Minnesota, November 5, 1983. Traded to **Minnesota** by **Chicago** for Dirk Graham, January 4, 1988.

FRASER, Gord

Defense. Shoots left. 6', 180 lbs. Born, Pembroke, Ont., January 3, 1902.

Season	Club	GP	G	A	Pts	PIM	GP	G	A	Pts	PIM
1926-27	Chicago Black Hawks	44	14	6	20	89	2	1	0	1	6
1927-28	Chicago Black Hawks	11	1	1	2	10	....	....	....	....	....
	Detroit Cougars	30	3	1	4	50	....	....	....	....	....
1928-29	Detroit Cougars	14	0	0	0	12	....	....	....	....	....
1929-30	Montreal Canadiens	10	0	0	0	4	....	....	....	....	....
	Pittsburgh Pirates	30	6	4	10	37	....	....	....	....	....
1930-31	Philadelphia Quakers	5	0	0	0	22	....	....	....	....	....
	NHL Totals	**144**	**24**	**12**	**36**	**224**	**2**	**1**	**0**	**1**	**6**

NHL rights transferred to **Detroit** after NHL club purchased **Victoria** (WHL) franchise, May 15, 1926. Traded to **Chicago** by **Detroit** with Art Gagne for the rights to Art Duncan, October 18, 1926. Traded to **Detroit** by **Chicago** with $5,000 for Duke Keats, December 16, 1927. Traded to **Montreal** by **Detroit** for cash, October 10, 1929. Loaned to **Providence** (Can-Am) by **Montreal** for cash, December 12, 1929. Traded to **Pittsburgh** by **Montreal** for Bert McCaffery, December 23, 1929. Transferred to **Philadelphia** after **Pittsburgh** franchise relocated, October 18, 1930. Traded to **Pittsburgh** (IHL) by **Philadelphia** for cash, November 28, 1930.

FRASER, Harvey

Center. Shoots right. 5'10", 168 lbs. Born, Souris, Man., October 14, 1918.

Season	Club	GP	G	A	Pts	PIM	GP	G	A	Pts	PIM
1944-45	Chicago Black Hawks	21	5	4	9	0	....	....	....	....	....
	NHL Totals	**21**	**5**	**4**	**9**	**0**	....	....	....	....	....

• Brother of Archie

Signed as a free agent by **Chicago**, October 14, 1944. Traded to **Cleveland** (AHL) by **Chicago** for cash, February 6, 1945. Traded to **NY Rangers** (New Haven-AHL) by **Cleveland** (AHL) for Gord Davidson, November 25, 1945. Traded to **St. Louis** (AHL) by **NY Rangers** (New Haven-AHL) for cash, February 3, 1946.

FRASER, Iain

Center. Shoots left. 5'10", 175 lbs. Born, Scarborough, Ont., August 10, 1969.
(NY Islanders' 14th choice, 233rd overall, in 1989 Entry Draft).

Season	Club	GP	G	A	Pts	PIM	GP	G	A	Pts	PIM
1992-93	New York Islanders	7	2	2	4	2	....	....	....	....	....
1993-94	Quebec Nordiques	60	17	20	37	23	....	....	....	....	....
1994-95	Dallas Stars	4	0	0	0	0	....	....	....	....	....
	Edmonton Oilers	9	3	0	3	0	....	....	....	....	....
1995-96	Winnipeg Jets	12	1	1	2	4	4	0	0	0	0
1996-97	San Jose Sharks	2	0	0	0	2	....	....	....	....	....
	NHL Totals	**94**	**23**	**23**	**46**	**31**	**4**	**0**	**0**	**0**	**0**

Signed as a free agent by **Quebec**, August 3, 1993. Traded to **Dallas** by **Quebec** for Dallas' 7th round choice (Dan Hinote) in 1996 Entry Draft, January 31, 1995. Claimed on waivers by **Edmonton** from **Dallas**, March 3, 1995. Signed as a free agent by **Winnipeg**, October 11, 1995. Signed as a free agent by **San Jose**, September 1, 1996.

FRASER, Scott

Center. Shoots right. 6'1", 178 lbs. Born, Moncton, N.B., May 3, 1972.
(Montreal's 12th choice, 193rd overall, in 1991 Entry Draft).

Season	Club	GP	G	A	Pts	PIM	GP	G	A	Pts	PIM
1995-96	Montreal Canadiens	15	2	0	2	4	....	....	....	....	....
1997-98	Edmonton Oilers	29	12	11	23	6	11	1	1	2	0
1998-99	New York Rangers	28	2	4	6	14	....	....	....	....	....
	NHL Totals	**72**	**16**	**15**	**31**	**24**	**11**	**1**	**1**	**2**	**0**

Traded to **Calgary** by **Montreal** for David Ling and Calgary's 6th round choice (Gordie Dwyer) in 1998 Entry Draft, October 24, 1996. Traded to **San Antonio** (IHL) by **Calgary** for Brent Bilodeau, February, 1997. Signed as a free agent by **Edmonton**, July 28, 1997. Signed as a free agent by **NY Rangers**, August 29, 1998.

FRAWLEY, Dan

Right wing. Shoots right. 6'1", 195 lbs. Born, Sturgeon Falls, Ont., June 2, 1962.
(Chicago's 15th choice, 204th overall, in 1980 Entry Draft).

Season	Club	GP	G	A	Pts	PIM	GP	G	A	Pts	PIM
1983-84	Chicago Black Hawks	3	0	0	0	0	....	....	....	....	....
1984-85	Chicago Black Hawks	30	4	3	7	64	1	0	0	0	0
1985-86	Pittsburgh Penguins	69	10	11	21	174	....	....	....	....	....
1986-87	Pittsburgh Penguins	78	14	14	28	218	....	....	....	....	....
1987-88	Pittsburgh Penguins	47	6	8	14	152	....	....	....	....	....

Season	Club	Regular Season GP	G	A	Pts	PIM	Playoffs GP	G	A	Pts	PIM
1988-89	Pittsburgh Penguins	46	3	4	7	66	....	....	....	....	....
	NHL Totals	**273**	**37**	**40**	**77**	**674**	**1**	**0**	**0**	**0**	**0**

Claimed by **Pittsburgh** from **Chicago** in Waiver Draft, October 7, 1985.

FREADRICH, Kyle

Left wing. Shoots left. 6'7", 260 lbs. Born, Edmonton, Alta., December 28, 1978.
(Vancouver's 4th choice, 64th overall, in 1997 Entry Draft).

Season	Club	GP	G	A	Pts	PIM	GP	G	A	Pts	PIM
99-2000	Tampa Bay Lightning	10	0	0	0	39	....	....	....	....	....
2000-01	Tampa Bay Lightning	13	0	1	1	36	....	....	....	....	....
	NHL Totals	**23**	**0**	**1**	**1**	**75**	....	....	....	....	....

Signed as a free agent by **Tampa Bay**, July 16, 1999. Traded to **NY Rangers** by **Tampa Bay** with Nils Ekman for Tim Taylor, June 30, 2001.

FREDRICKSON, Frank

HHOF

Center. Shoots left. 5'11", 180 lbs. Born, Winnipeg, Man., June 11, 1895.

Season	Club	GP	G	A	Pts	PIM	GP	G	A	Pts	PIM
1926-27	Detroit Cougars	16	4	6	10	12	....	....	....	....	....
	Boston Bruins	28	14	7	21	33	8	2	2	4	20
1927-28	Boston Bruins	41	10	4	14	83	2	0	1	1	4
1928-29	Boston Bruins	12	3	1	4	24	....	....	....	....	....
	Pittsburgh Pirates	31	3	7	10	28	....	....	....	....	....
1929-30	Pittsburgh Pirates	9	4	7	11	20	....	....	....	....	....
1930-31	Detroit Falcons	24	1	2	3	6	....	....	....	....	....
	NHL Totals	**161**	**39**	**34**	**73**	**206**	**10**	**2**	**3**	**5**	**24**

NHL rights transferred to **Detroit** after NHL club purchased **Victoria** (WHL) franchise, May 15, 1926. Traded to **Boston** by **Detroit** with Harry Meeking for Duke Keats and Archie Briden, January 7, 1927. Traded to **Pittsburgh** by **Boston** for Mickey MacKay and $12,000, December 21, 1928. • Missed majority of the 1929-30 season after undergoing knee surgery, December 21, 1929. Transferred to **Philadelphia** after **Pittsburgh** franchise relocated. • Released by **Philadelphia**, October 20, 1930. Signed as a free agent by **Detroit**, November 23, 1930. .

FREER, Mark

Center. Shoots left. 5'10", 180 lbs. Born, Peterborough, Ont., July 14, 1968.

Season	Club	GP	G	A	Pts	PIM	GP	G	A	Pts	PIM
1986-87	Philadelphia Flyers	1	0	1	1	0	....	....	....	....	....
1987-88	Philadelphia Flyers	1	0	0	0	0	....	....	....	....	....
1988-89	Philadelphia Flyers	5	0	1	1	0	....	....	....	....	....
1989-90	Philadelphia Flyers	2	0	0	0	0	....	....	....	....	....
1991-92	Philadelphia Flyers	50	6	7	13	18	....	....	....	....	....
1992-93	Ottawa Senators	63	10	14	24	39	....	....	....	....	....
1993-94	Calgary Flames	2	0	0	0	4	....	....	....	....	....
	NHL Totals	**124**	**16**	**23**	**39**	**61**	....	....	....	....	....

Signed as a free agent by **Philadelphia**, October 7, 1986. Claimed by **Ottawa** from **Philadelphia** in Expansion Draft, June 18, 1992. Signed as a free agent by **Calgary**, August 10, 1993.

FREW, Irv

Defense. Shoots right. 5'10", 180 lbs. Born, Kilsyth, Scotland, August 16, 1907.

Season	Club	GP	G	A	Pts	PIM	GP	G	A	Pts	PIM
1933-34	Montreal Maroons	30	2	1	3	41	4	0	0	0	6
1934-35	St. Louis Eagles	48	0	2	2	89	....	....	....	....	....
1935-36	Montreal Canadiens	18	0	2	2	16	....	....	....	....	....
	NHL Totals	**96**	**2**	**5**	**7**	**146**	**4**	**0**	**0**	**0**	**6**

Traded to **Ottawa** by **Mtl. Maroons** with future considerations (Vern Ayres and Normie Smith, October 22, 1934) for Al Shields, September 20, 1934. Transferred to **St. Louis** after **Ottawa** franchise relocated, September 22, 1934. Claimed by **Montreal** from **St. Louis** in Dispersal Draft, October 15, 1935.

FRIDAY, Tim

Defense. Shoots right. 6', 190 lbs. Born, Burbank, CA, March 5, 1961.

Season	Club	GP	G	A	Pts	PIM	GP	G	A	Pts	PIM
1985-86	Detroit Red Wings	23	0	3	3	6	....	....	....	....	....
	NHL Totals	**23**	**0**	**3**	**3**	**6**	....	....	....	....	....

Signed as a free agent by **Detroit**, May 27, 1985. • Suffered eventual career-ending shoulder injury in game vs. Philadelphia, December 3, 1985.

FRIDGEN, Dan

Left wing. Shoots left. 5'11", 175 lbs. Born, Arnprior, Ont., May 18, 1959.

Season	Club	GP	G	A	Pts	PIM	GP	G	A	Pts	PIM
1981-82	Hartford Whalers	2	0	1	1	0	....	....	....	....	....
1982-83	Hartford Whalers	11	2	2	4	2	....	....	....	....	....
	NHL Totals	**13**	**2**	**3**	**5**	**2**	....	....	....	....	....

Signed as a free agent by **Hartford**, April 5, 1982.

FRIEDMAN, Doug

Left wing. Shoots left. 6'1", 200 lbs. Born, Cape Elizabeth, ME, September 1, 1971.
(Quebec's 13th choice, 222nd overall, in 1991 Entry Draft).

Season	Club	GP	G	A	Pts	PIM	GP	G	A	Pts	PIM
1997-98	Edmonton Oilers	16	0	0	0	20	....	....	....	....	....
1998-99	Nashville Predators	2	0	1	1	14	....	....	....	....	....
	NHL Totals	**18**	**0**	**1**	**1**	**34**	....	....	....	....	....

Rights transferred to **Colorado** after **Quebec** franchise relocated, June 21, 1995. Signed as a free agent by **Edmonton**, July 14, 1997. Claimed by **Nashville** from **Edmonton** in Expansion Draft, June 26, 1998. Signed as a free agent by **San Jose**, August 26, 1999.

FRIESEN, Jeff

Left wing. Shoots left. 6', 215 lbs. Born, Meadow Lake, Sask., August 5, 1976.
(San Jose's 1st choice, 11th overall, in 1994 Entry Draft).

Season	Club	GP	G	A	Pts	PIM	GP	G	A	Pts	PIM
1994-95	San Jose Sharks	48	15	10	25	14	11	1	5	6	4
1995-96	San Jose Sharks	79	15	31	46	42	....	....	....	....	....
1996-97	San Jose Sharks	82	28	34	62	75	....	....	....	....	....
1997-98	San Jose Sharks	79	31	32	63	40	6	0	1	1	2
1998-99	San Jose Sharks	78	22	35	57	42	6	2	2	4	14
99-2000	San Jose Sharks	82	26	35	61	47	11	2	2	4	10
2000-01	San Jose Sharks	64	12	24	36	56	....	....	....	....	....
	Mighty Ducks of Anaheim	15	2	10	12	10	....	....	....	....	....
2001-02	Mighty Ducks of Anaheim	81	17	26	43	44	....	....	....	....	....
2002-03 ♦	New Jersey Devils	81	23	28	51	26	24	10	4	14	6
	NHL Totals	**689**	**191**	**265**	**456**	**396**	**58**	**15**	**14**	**29**	**36**

Traded to **Anaheim** by **San Jose** with Steve Shields and San Jose's 2nd round choice (later traded to Dallas – Dallas selected Vojtech Polak) in 2003 Entry Draft for Teemu Selanne, March 5, 2001. Traded to **New Jersey** by **Anaheim** with Oleg Tverdovsky and Maxim Balmochnykh for Petr Sykora, Mike Commodore, Jean-Francois Damphousse and Igor Pohanka, July 6, 2002.

FRIEST, Ron

Left wing. Shoots left. 5'11", 185 lbs. Born, Windsor, Ont., November 4, 1958.

Season	Club	GP	G	A	Pts	PIM	GP	G	A	Pts	PIM
1980-81	Minnesota North Stars	4	1	0	1	10	....	....	....	....	....
1981-82	Minnesota North Stars	10	0	0	0	31	2	0	0	0	5
1982-83	Minnesota North Stars	50	6	7	13	150	4	1	0	1	2
	NHL Totals	**64**	**7**	**7**	**14**	**191**	**6**	**1**	**0**	**1**	**7**

Signed as a free agent by **Minnesota**, June 26, 1980.

FRIG, Len

Defense. Shoots right. 5'11", 190 lbs. Born, Lethbridge, Alta., October 30, 1950.
(Chicago's 3rd choice, 42nd overall, in 1970 Amateur Draft).

Season	Club	GP	G	A	Pts	PIM	GP	G	A	Pts	PIM
1972-73	Chicago Black Hawks	....	....	....	....	....	4	1	1	2	0
1973-74	Chicago Black Hawks	66	4	10	14	35	7	1	0	1	0
1974-75	California Golden Seals	80	3	17	20	127	....	....	....	....	....
1975-76	California Golden Seals	62	3	12	15	55	....	....	....	....	....
1976-77	Cleveland Barons	66	2	7	9	213	....	....	....	....	....
1977-78	St. Louis Blues	30	1	3	4	45	....	....	....	....	....
1979-80	St. Louis Blues	7	0	2	2	4	3	0	0	0	0
	NHL Totals	**311**	**13**	**51**	**64**	**479**	**14**	**2**	**1**	**3**	**0**

Traded to **California** by **Chicago** with Mike Christie for Ivan Boldirev, May 24, 1974. Transferred to **Cleveland** after **California** franchise relocated, August 26, 1976. Traded to **St. Louis** by **Cleveland** for the rights to Mike Eaves, August 17, 1977.

FROLOV, Alexander

Left wing. Shoots right. 6'4", 191 lbs. Born, Moscow, USSR, June 19, 1982.
(Los Angeles' 1st choice, 20th overall, in 2000 Entry Draft).

Season	Club	GP	G	A	Pts	PIM	GP	G	A	Pts	PIM
2002-03	Los Angeles Kings	79	14	17	31	34	....	....	....	....	....
	NHL Totals	**79**	**14**	**17**	**31**	**34**	....	....	....	....	....

FROST, Harry

Right wing. Shoots right. 5'11", 165 lbs. Born, Kerr Lake, Ont., August 17, 1914.

Season	Club	GP	G	A	Pts	PIM	GP	G	A	Pts	PIM
1938-39 ♦	Boston Bruins	4	0	0	0	0	1	0	0	0	0
	NHL Totals	**4**	**0**	**0**	**0**	**0**	**1**	**0**	**0**	**0**	**0**

FRYCER, Miroslav

Right wing. Shoots left. 6', 200 lbs. Born, Ostrava, Czech., September 27, 1959.

Season	Club	GP	G	A	Pts	PIM	GP	G	A	Pts	PIM
1981-82	Quebec Nordiques	49	20	17	37	47	....	....	....	....	....
	Toronto Maple Leafs	10	4	6	10	31	....	....	....	....	....
1982-83	Toronto Maple Leafs	67	25	30	55	90	4	2	5	7	0
1983-84	Toronto Maple Leafs	47	10	16	26	55	....	....	....	....	....
1984-85	Toronto Maple Leafs	65	25	30	55	55	....	....	....	....	....
1985-86	Toronto Maple Leafs	73	32	43	75	74	10	1	3	4	10
1986-87	Toronto Maple Leafs	29	7	8	15	28	....	....	....	....	....
1987-88	Toronto Maple Leafs	38	12	20	32	41	3	0	0	0	6
1988-89	Detroit Red Wings	23	7	8	15	47	....	....	....	....	....
	Edmonton Oilers	14	5	5	10	18	....	....	....	....	....
	NHL Totals	**415**	**147**	**183**	**330**	**486**	**17**	**3**	**8**	**11**	**16**

Played in NHL All-Star Game (1985)

Signed as a free agent by **Quebec**, April 2, 1980. Traded to **Toronto** by **Quebec** with Quebec's 7th round choice (Jeff Triano) in 1982 Entry Draft for Wilf Paiement, March 9, 1982. Traded to **Detroit** by **Toronto** for Darren Veitch, June 10, 1988. Traded to **Edmonton** by **Detroit** for Edmonton's 10th round choice (Rick Judson) in 1989 Entry Draft, January 3, 1989.

FRYDAY, Bob

Right wing. Shoots right. 5'10", 155 lbs. Born, Toronto, Ont., December 5, 1928.

Season	Club	GP	G	A	Pts	PIM	GP	G	A	Pts	PIM
1949-50	Montreal Canadiens	2	1	0	1	0	....	....	....	....	....
1951-52	Montreal Canadiens	3	0	0	0	0	....	....	....	....	....
	NHL Totals	**5**	**1**	**0**	**1**	**0**	....	....	....	....	....

FTOREK, Robbie

USHOF

Center/Left wing. Shoots left. 5'10", 155 lbs. Born, Needham, MA, January 2, 1952.

Season	Club	GP	G	A	Pts	PIM	GP	G	A	Pts	PIM
1972-73	Detroit Red Wings	3	0	0	0	0	....	....	....	....	....
1973-74	Detroit Red Wings	12	2	5	7	4	....	....	....	....	....
1979-80	Quebec Nordiques	52	18	33	51	28	....	....	....	....	....
1980-81	Quebec Nordiques	78	24	49	73	104	5	1	2	3	17
1981-82	Quebec Nordiques	19	1	8	9	4	....	....	....	....	....
	New York Rangers	30	8	24	32	24	10	7	4	11	11
1982-83	New York Rangers	61	12	19	31	41	4	1	0	1	0
1983-84	New York Rangers	31	3	2	5	22	....	....	....	....	....

Season	Club	GP	G	A	Pts	PIM	GP	G	A	Pts	PIM
		REGULAR SEASON					PLAYOFFS				
1984-85	New York Rangers	48	9	10	19	35	....	....	....	....	....
	NHL Totals	**334**	**77**	**150**	**227**	**262**	**19**	**9**	**6**	**15**	**28**

Signed as a free agent by **Detroit**, August 15, 1972. Signed as a free agent by **Quebec**, August 13, 1979. Traded to **NY Rangers** by **Quebec** with Quebec's 8th round choice (Brian Glynn) in 1982 Entry Draft for Jere Gillis and Dean Talafous (later changed to Pat Hickey (March 8, 1982) when Talafous decided to retire), December 30, 1981.

FULLAN, Larry

Left wing. Shoots left. 5'11", 185 lbs. Born, Toronto, Ont., August 11, 1949.

Season	Club	GP	G	A	Pts	PIM	GP	G	A	Pts	PIM
1974-75	Washington Capitals	4	1	0	1	0	....	....	....	....	....
	NHL Totals	**4**	**1**	**0**	**1**	**0**	....	....	....	....	....

Signed as a free agent by **Montreal**, June, 1972. Claimed by **Washington** from **Montreal** in Expansion Draft, June 12, 1974.

FUSCO, Mark

USHOF

Defense. Shoots right. 5'9", 175 lbs. Born, Burlington, MA, March 12, 1961.

Season	Club	GP	G	A	Pts	PIM	GP	G	A	Pts	PIM
1983-84	Hartford Whalers	17	0	4	4	2	....	....	....	....	....
1984-85	Hartford Whalers	63	3	8	11	40	....	....	....	....	....
	NHL Totals	**80**	**3**	**12**	**15**	**42**	....	....	....	....	....

Signed as a free agent by **Hartford**, February 25, 1984.

GABORIK, Marian

Right wing. Shoots left. 6'1", 183 lbs. Born, Trencin, Czech., February 14, 1982.
(Minnesota's 1st choice, 3rd overall, in 2000 Entry Draft).

Season	Club	GP	G	A	Pts	PIM	GP	G	A	Pts	PIM
2000-01	Minnesota Wild	71	18	18	36	32	....	....	....	....	....
2001-02	Minnesota Wild	78	30	37	67	34	....	....	....	....	....
2002-03	Minnesota Wild	81	30	35	65	46	18	9	8	17	6
	NHL Totals	**230**	**78**	**90**	**168**	**112**	**18**	**9**	**8**	**17**	**6**

Played in NHL All-Star Game (2003)

GADSBY, Bill

HHOF

Defense. Shoots left. 6', 180 lbs. Born, Calgary, Alta., August 8, 1927.

Season	Club	GP	G	A	Pts	PIM	GP	G	A	Pts	PIM
1946-47	Chicago Black Hawks	48	8	10	18	31	....	....	....	....	....
1947-48	Chicago Black Hawks	60	6	10	16	66	....	....	....	....	....
1948-49	Chicago Black Hawks	50	3	10	13	85	....	....	....	....	....
1949-50	Chicago Black Hawks	70	10	25	35	138	....	....	....	....	....
1950-51	Chicago Black Hawks	25	3	7	10	32	....	....	....	....	....
1951-52	Chicago Black Hawks	59	7	15	22	87	....	....	....	....	....
1952-53	Chicago Black Hawks	68	2	20	22	84	7	0	1	1	4
1953-54	Chicago Black Hawks	70	12	29	41	108	....	....	....	....	....
1954-55	Chicago Black Hawks	18	3	5	8	17	....	....	....	....	....
	New York Rangers	52	8	8	16	44	....	....	....	....	....
1955-56	New York Rangers	70	9	42	51	84	5	1	3	4	4
1956-57	New York Rangers	70	4	37	41	72	5	1	2	3	2
1957-58	New York Rangers	65	14	32	46	48	6	0	3	3	4
1958-59	New York Rangers	70	5	46	51	56	....	....	....	....	....
1959-60	New York Rangers	65	9	22	31	60	....	....	....	....	....
1960-61	New York Rangers	65	9	26	35	49	....	....	....	....	....
1961-62	Detroit Red Wings	70	7	30	37	88	....	....	....	....	....
1962-63	Detroit Red Wings	70	4	24	28	116	11	1	4	5	*36
1963-64	Detroit Red Wings	64	2	16	18	80	14	0	4	4	22
1964-65	Detroit Red Wings	61	0	12	12	122	7	0	3	3	8
1965-66	Detroit Red Wings	58	5	12	17	72	12	1	3	4	12
	NHL Totals	**1248**	**130**	**438**	**568**	**1539**	**67**	**4**	**23**	**27**	**92**

NHL Second All-Star Team (1953, 1954, 1957, 1965) • NHL First All-Star Team (1956, 1958, 1959)

Played in NHL All-Star Game (1953, 1954, 1956, 1957, 1958, 1959, 1960, 1965)

Signed as a free agent by **Chicago**, July 14, 1946. • Missed majority of 1950-51 season recovering from leg injury suffered in game vs. Toronto, November 22, 1950. Traded to **NY Rangers** by **Chicago** with Pete Conacher for Allan Stanley, Nick Mickoski and Rich Lamoureux, November 23, 1954. Traded to **Detroit** by **NY Rangers** with Eddie Shack for Billy McNeill and Red Kelly, February 5, 1960. • Kelly and McNeill refused to report and transaction was cancelled, February 7, 1960. Traded to **Detroit** by **NY Rangers** for Les Hunt, June 12, 1961.

GAETZ, Link

Defense. Shoots left. 6'3", 215 lbs. Born, Vancouver, B.C., October 2, 1968.
(Minnesota's 2nd choice, 40th overall, in 1988 Entry Draft).

Season	Club	GP	G	A	Pts	PIM	GP	G	A	Pts	PIM
1988-89	Minnesota North Stars	12	0	2	2	53	....	....	....	....	....
1989-90	Minnesota North Stars	5	0	0	0	33	....	....	....	....	....
1991-92	San Jose Sharks	48	6	6	12	326	....	....	....	....	....
	NHL Totals	**65**	**6**	**8**	**14**	**412**	....	....	....	....	....

Claimed by **San Jose** from **Minnesota** in Dispersal Draft, May 30, 1991. Traded to **Edmonton** by **San Jose** for Edmonton's 10th round choice (Tomas Pisa) in 1994 Entry Draft, September 10, 1993.

GAGE, Jody

Right wing. Shoots right. 6', 190 lbs. Born, Toronto, Ont., November 29, 1959.
(Detroit's 2nd choice, 45th overall, in 1979 Entry Draft).

Season	Club	GP	G	A	Pts	PIM	GP	G	A	Pts	PIM
1980-81	Detroit Red Wings	16	2	2	4	22	....	....	....	....	....
1981-82	Detroit Red Wings	31	9	10	19	2	....	....	....	....	....
1983-84	Detroit Red Wings	3	0	0	0	0	....	....	....	....	....
1985-86	Buffalo Sabres	7	3	2	5	0	....	....	....	....	....
1987-88	Buffalo Sabres	2	0	0	0	0	....	....	....	....	....
1991-92	Buffalo Sabres	9	0	1	1	2	....	....	....	....	....
	NHL Totals	**68**	**14**	**15**	**29**	**26**	....	....	....	....	....

Signed as a free agent by **Buffalo**, July 31, 1985.

GAGNE, Art

Right wing. Shoots right. 5'7", 160 lbs. Born, Ottawa, Ont., October 11, 1897.

Season	Club	GP	G	A	Pts	PIM	GP	G	A	Pts	PIM
1926-27	Montreal Canadiens	44	14	3	17	42	4	0	0	0	0
1927-28	Montreal Canadiens	44	20	10	30	75	2	1	1	2	4
1928-29	Montreal Canadiens	44	7	3	10	52	3	0	0	0	12
1929-30	Boston Bruins	6	0	1	1	6	....	....	....	....	....
	Ottawa Senators	33	6	4	10	32	2	1	0	1	4
1930-31	Ottawa Senators	44	19	11	30	50	....	....	....	....	....
1931-32	Detroit Falcons	13	1	1	2	0	....	....	....	....	....
	NHL Totals	**228**	**67**	**33**	**100**	**257**	**11**	**2**	**1**	**3**	**20**

Traded to **Chicago** by **Detroit** with Gord Fraser for the rights to Art Duncan, October 18, 1926. Traded to **Montreal** by **Chicago** for cash, October 18, 1926. Traded to **Boston** by **Montreal** for cash, May 13, 1929. Traded to **Ottawa** by **Boston** for cash, December 21, 1929. Claimed by **Detroit** from **Ottawa** for 1931-32 season in Dispersal Draft, September 26, 1931.

GAGNE, Paul

Left wing. Shoots left. 5'10", 180 lbs. Born, Iroquois Falls, Ont., February 6, 1962.
(Colorado's 1st choice, 19th overall, in 1980 Entry Draft).

Season	Club	GP	G	A	Pts	PIM	GP	G	A	Pts	PIM
1980-81	Colorado Rockies	61	25	16	41	12	....	....	....	....	....
1981-82	Colorado Rockies	59	10	12	22	17	....	....	....	....	....
1982-83	New Jersey Devils	53	14	15	29	13	....	....	....	....	....
1983-84	New Jersey Devils	66	14	18	32	33	....	....	....	....	....
1984-85	New Jersey Devils	79	24	19	43	28	....	....	....	....	....
1985-86	New Jersey Devils	47	19	19	38	14	....	....	....	....	....
1988-89	Toronto Maple Leafs	16	3	2	5	6	....	....	....	....	....
1989-90	New York Islanders	9	1	0	1	4	....	....	....	....	....
	NHL Totals	**390**	**110**	**101**	**211**	**127**	....	....	....	....	....

Transferred to **New Jersey** after **Colorado** franchise relocated, June 30, 1982. • Missed remainder of 1985-86 season and entire 1986-87 and 1987-88 seasons recovering from back injury suffered in game vs. Winnipeg, March 25, 1986. Signed as a free agent by **Toronto**, July 28, 1988. Traded to **NY Islanders** by **Toronto** with Derek Laxdal and Jack Capuano for Gilles Thibaudeau and Mike Stevens, December 20, 1989.

GAGNE, Pierre

Left wing. Shoots left. 6'1", 180 lbs. Born, North Bay, Ont., June 5, 1940.

Season	Club	GP	G	A	Pts	PIM	GP	G	A	Pts	PIM
1959-60	Boston Bruins	2	0	0	0	0	....	....	....	....	....
	NHL Totals	**2**	**0**	**0**	**0**	**0**	....	....	....	....	....

GAGNE, Simon

Left wing. Shoots left. 6', 190 lbs. Born, Ste-Foy, Que., February 29, 1980.
(Philadelphia's 1st choice, 22nd overall, in 1998 Entry Draft).

Season	Club	GP	G	A	Pts	PIM	GP	G	A	Pts	PIM
99-2000	Philadelphia Flyers	80	20	28	48	22	17	5	5	10	2
2000-01	Philadelphia Flyers	69	27	32	59	18	6	3	0	3	0
2001-02	Philadelphia Flyers	79	33	33	66	32	5	0	0	0	2
2002-03	Philadelphia Flyers	46	9	18	27	16	13	4	1	5	6
	NHL Totals	**274**	**89**	**111**	**200**	**88**	**41**	**12**	**6**	**18**	**10**

NHL All-Rookie Team (2000)

Played in NHL ALL-Star Game (2001)

GAGNER, Dave

Center. Shoots left. 5'10", 188 lbs. Born, Chatham, Ont., December 11, 1964.
(NY Rangers' 1st choice, 12th overall, in 1983 Entry Draft).

Season	Club	GP	G	A	Pts	PIM	GP	G	A	Pts	PIM
1984-85	New York Rangers	38	6	6	12	16	....	....	....	....	....
1985-86	New York Rangers	32	4	6	10	19	....	....	....	....	....
1986-87	New York Rangers	10	1	4	5	12	....	....	....	....	....
1987-88	Minnesota North Stars	51	8	11	19	55	....	....	....	....	....
1988-89	Minnesota North Stars	75	35	43	78	104	....	....	....	....	....
1989-90	Minnesota North Stars	79	40	38	78	54	7	2	3	5	16
1990-91	Minnesota North Stars	73	40	42	82	114	23	12	15	27	28
1991-92	Minnesota North Stars	78	31	40	71	107	7	2	4	6	8
1992-93	Minnesota North Stars	84	33	43	76	143	....	....	....	....	....
1993-94	Dallas Stars	76	32	29	61	83	9	5	1	6	2
1994-95	Dallas Stars	48	14	28	42	42	5	1	1	2	4
1995-96	Dallas Stars	45	14	13	27	44	....	....	....	....	....
	Toronto Maple Leafs	28	7	15	22	59	6	0	2	2	6
1996-97	Calgary Flames	82	27	33	60	48	....	....	....	....	....
1997-98	Florida Panthers	78	20	28	48	55	....	....	....	....	....
1998-99	Florida Panthers	36	4	10	14	39	....	....	....	....	....
	Vancouver Canucks	33	2	12	14	24	....	....	....	....	....
	NHL Totals	**946**	**318**	**401**	**719**	**1018**	**57**	**22**	**26**	**48**	**64**

Played in NHL All-Star Game (1991)

Traded to **Minnesota** by **NY Rangers** with Jay Caufield for Jari Gronstrand and Paul Boutilier, October 8, 1987. Transferred to **Dallas** after **Minnesota** franchise relocated, June 9, 1993. Traded to **Toronto** by **Dallas** with Dallas' 6th round choice (Dmitri Yakushin) in 1996 Entry Draft for Benoit Hogue and Randy Wood, January 29, 1996. Traded to **Calgary** by **Toronto** for Calgary's 3rd round choice (Mike Lankshear) in 1996 Entry Draft, June 22, 1996. Signed as a free agent by **Florida**, July 12, 1997. Traded to **Vancouver** by **Florida** with Ed Jovanovski, Mike Brown, Kevin Weekes and Florida's 1st round choice (Nathan Smith) in 2000 Entry Draft for Pavel Bure, Bret Hedican, Brad Ference and Vancouver's 3rd round choice (Robert Fried) in 2000 Entry Draft, January 17, 1999. • Officially announced retirement, September 9, 1999.

GAGNON, Germain

Left wing. Shoots left. 6', 175 lbs. Born, Chicoutimi, Que., December 9, 1942.

Season	Club	GP	G	A	Pts	PIM	GP	G	A	Pts	PIM
		REGULAR SEASON					PLAYOFFS				
1971-72	Montreal Canadiens	4	0	0	0	0					
1972-73	New York Islanders	63	12	29	41	31					
1973-74	New York Islanders	62	8	14	22	8					
	Chicago Black Hawks	14	3	14	17	4	11	2	2	4	2
1974-75	Chicago Black Hawks	80	16	35	51	21	8	0	1	1	0
1975-76	Chicago Black Hawks	5	0	0	0	2					
	Kansas City Scouts	31	1	9	10	6					
	NHL Totals	**259**	**40**	**101**	**141**	**72**	**19**	**2**	**3**	**5**	**2**

Claimed by **Salt Lake** (WHL) from **Montreal** in Reverse Draft, June 12, 1969. Traded to **Vancouver** (WHL) by **Salt Lake** (WHL) with cash for Billy McNeill, August 19, 1969. • Rights transferred to **Vancouver** when NHL club purchased **Vancouver** (WHL) franchise, December 19, 1969. Traded to **Montreal** by **Vancouver** for cash, November 3, 1970. Traded to **NY Islanders** by **Montreal** to complete transaction that sent Denis DeJordy, Glenn Resch and Alex Campbell to NY Islanders for cash and NY Islanders' 2nd round choice (Glenn Goldup) in 1973 Amateur Draft (June 6, 1972) , June 26, 1972. Traded to **Chicago** by **NY Islanders** for cash and future considerations (Walt Ledingham, May 24, 1974), March 7, 1974. Claimed on waivers by **Kansas City** from **Chicago**, October 28, 1975.

GAGNON, Johnny

Right wing. Shoots right. 5'5", 140 lbs. Born, Chicoutimi, Que., June 8, 1905.

Season	Club	GP	G	A	Pts	PIM	GP	G	A	Pts	PIM
1930-31 ♦	Montreal Canadiens	41	18	7	25	43	10	*6	2	8	8
1931-32	Montreal Canadiens	48	19	18	37	40	4	1	1	2	4
1932-33	Montreal Canadiens	48	12	23	35	64	2	0	2	2	0
1933-34	Montreal Canadiens	48	9	15	24	25	2	1	0	1	2
1934-35	Boston Bruins	24	1	1	2	9					
	Montreal Canadiens	23	1	5	6	2	2	0	1	1	2
1935-36	Montreal Canadiens	48	7	9	16	42					
1936-37	Montreal Canadiens	48	20	16	36	38	5	2	1	3	9
1937-38	Montreal Canadiens	47	13	17	30	9	3	1	3	4	2
1938-39	Montreal Canadiens	45	12	22	34	23	3	0	2	2	10
1939-40	Montreal Canadiens	10	4	5	9	0					
	New York Americans	24	4	3	7	0	1	1	0	1	0
	NHL Totals	**454**	**120**	**141**	**261**	**295**	**32**	**12**	**12**	**24**	**37**

Played in NHL All-Star Game (1937, 1939)

Traded to **Montreal** by **Providence** (Can-Am) for Gerry Carson, the loan of Jean Pusie and cash, October 21, 1930. Traded to **Boston** by **Montreal** for Joe Lamb, October 2, 1934. Traded to **Montreal** by **Boston** for cash, January 9, 1935. Traded to **NY Americans** by **Montreal** for cash, January 3, 1940.

GAGNON, Sean

Defense. Shoots left. 6'2", 219 lbs. Born, Sault Ste. Marie, Ont., September 11, 1973.

Season	Club	GP	G	A	Pts	PIM	GP	G	A	Pts	PIM
1997-98	Phoenix Coyotes	5	0	1	1	14					
1998-99	Phoenix Coyotes	2	0	0	0	7					
2000-01	Ottawa Senators	5	0	0	0	13					
	NHL Totals	**12**	**0**	**1**	**1**	**34**					

Signed as a free agent by **Phoenix**, May 14, 1997. Signed as a free agent by **Ottawa**, July 7, 2000. Traded to **NY Rangers** by **Ottawa** for Jason Doig and Jeff Ulmer, June 29, 2001.

GAINEY, Bob

HHOF

Left wing. Shoots left. 6'2", 200 lbs. Born, Peterborough, Ont., December 13, 1953.
(Montreal's 1st choice, 8th overall, in 1973 Amateur Draft).

Season	Club	GP	G	A	Pts	PIM	GP	G	A	Pts	PIM
1973-74	Montreal Canadiens	66	3	7	10	34	6	0	0	0	6
1974-75	Montreal Canadiens	80	17	20	37	49	11	2	4	6	4
1975-76 ♦	Montreal Canadiens	78	15	13	28	57	13	1	3	4	20
1976-77 ♦	Montreal Canadiens	80	14	19	33	41	14	4	1	5	25
1977-78 ♦	Montreal Canadiens	66	15	16	31	57	15	2	7	9	14
1978-79 ♦	Montreal Canadiens	79	20	18	38	44	16	6	10	16	10
1979-80	Montreal Canadiens	64	14	19	33	32	10	1	1	2	4
1980-81	Montreal Canadiens	78	23	24	47	36	3	0	0	0	2
1981-82	Montreal Canadiens	79	21	24	45	24	5	0	1	1	8
1982-83	Montreal Canadiens	80	12	18	30	43	3	0	0	0	4
1983-84	Montreal Canadiens	77	17	22	39	41	15	1	5	6	9
1984-85	Montreal Canadiens	79	19	13	32	40	12	1	3	4	13
1985-86 ♦	Montreal Canadiens	80	20	23	43	20	20	5	5	10	12
1986-87	Montreal Canadiens	47	8	8	16	19	17	1	3	4	6
1987-88	Montreal Canadiens	78	11	11	22	14	6	0	1	1	6
1988-89	Montreal Canadiens	49	10	7	17	34	16	1	4	5	8
	NHL Totals	**1160**	**239**	**262**	**501**	**585**	**182**	**25**	**48**	**73**	**151**

• Father of Steve • Frank J. Selke Trophy (1978, 1979, 1980, 1981) • Conn Smythe Trophy (1979)
Played in NHL All-Star Game (1977, 1978, 1980, 1981)

GAINEY, Steve

Left wing. Shoots left. 6'1", 192 lbs. Born, Montreal, Que., January 26, 1979.
(Dallas' 3rd choice, 77th overall, in 1997 Entry Draft).

Season	Club	GP	G	A	Pts	PIM	GP	G	A	Pts	PIM
2000-01	Dallas Stars	1	0	0	0	0					
2001-02	Dallas Stars	5	0	1	1	7					
	NHL Totals	**6**	**0**	**1**	**1**	**7**					

• Son of Bob

GAINOR, Dutch

Center. Shoots left. 6'1", 170 lbs. Born, Calgary, Alta., April 10, 1904.

Season	Club	GP	G	A	Pts	PIM	GP	G	A	Pts	PIM
1927-28	Boston Bruins	42	8	4	12	35	2	0	0	0	6
1928-29 ♦	Boston Bruins	44	14	5	19	30	5	2	0	2	4
1929-30	Boston Bruins	42	18	31	49	39	3	0	0	0	0
1930-31	Boston Bruins	35	8	3	11	14	5	0	1	1	2
1931-32	New York Rangers	46	3	9	12	9	7	0	0	0	2
1932-33	Ottawa Senators	2	0	0	0	0					
1934-35 ♦	Montreal Maroons	35	0	4	4	2					
	NHL Totals	**246**	**51**	**56**	**107**	**129**	**22**	**2**	**1**	**3**	**14**

Traded to **Boston** by **Minneapolis** (AHA) with Nobby Clark for Red Stuart, cash and future considerations, October 24, 1927. Traded to **NY Rangers** by **Boston** for Joe Jerwa, August 25, 1931. Traded to **Ottawa** by **NY Rangers** for cash after Springfield (Can-Am) franchise folded (December 18, 1932), December 23, 1932. Signed as a free agent by **Mtl. Maroons**, October 22, 1934.

GALANOV, Maxim

Defense. Shoots left. 6'1", 205 lbs. Born, Krasnoyarsk, USSR, March 13, 1974.
(NY Rangers' 3rd choice, 61st overall, in 1993 Entry Draft).

Season	Club	GP	G	A	Pts	PIM	GP	G	A	Pts	PIM
1997-98	New York Rangers	6	0	1	1	2					
1998-99	Pittsburgh Penguins	51	4	3	7	14	1	0	0	0	0
99-2000	Atlanta Thrashers	40	4	3	7	20					
2000-01	Tampa Bay Lightning	25	0	5	5	8					
	NHL Totals	**122**	**8**	**12**	**20**	**44**	**1**	**0**	**0**	**0**	**0**

Claimed by **Pittsburgh** from **NY Rangers** in Waiver Draft, October 5, 1998. Claimed by **Atlanta** from **Pittsburgh** in Expansion Draft, June 25, 1999. • Missed majority of 1999-2000 season recovering from hand injury suffered in game vs. NY Rangers, October 17, 1999. Signed as a free agent by **Florida**, September, 2000. Claimed on waivers by **Tampa Bay** from **Florida**, November 1, 2000. Traded to **Toronto** by **Tampa Bay** for Konstantin Kalmikov, February 20, 2001.

GALARNEAU, Michel

Center. Shoots right. 6'2", 180 lbs. Born, Montreal, Que., March 1, 1961.
(Hartford's 2nd choice, 29th overall, in 1980 Entry Draft).

Season	Club	GP	G	A	Pts	PIM	GP	G	A	Pts	PIM
1980-81	Hartford Whalers	30	2	6	8	9					
1981-82	Hartford Whalers	10	0	0	0	4					
1982-83	Hartford Whalers	38	5	4	9	21					
	NHL Totals	**78**	**7**	**10**	**17**	**34**					

GALBRAITH, Percy

Left wing/Defense. Shoots left. 5'10", 162 lbs. Born, Toronto, Ont., December 5, 1898.

Season	Club	GP	G	A	Pts	PIM	GP	G	A	Pts	PIM
1926-27	Boston Bruins	42	9	8	17	26	8	3	*3	*6	2
1927-28	Boston Bruins	42	6	5	11	26	2	0	1	1	6
1928-29 ♦	Boston Bruins	38	2	1	3	44	5	0	0	0	2
1929-30	Boston Bruins	44	7	9	16	38	6	1	3	4	8
1930-31	Boston Bruins	43	2	3	5	28	5	0	0	0	6
1931-32	Boston Bruins	47	2	1	3	28					
1932-33	Boston Bruins	47	1	2	3	28	5	0	0	0	0
1933-34	Ottawa Senators	2	0	0	0	0					
	Boston Bruins	42	0	2	2	6					
	NHL Totals	**347**	**29**	**31**	**60**	**224**	**31**	**4**	**7**	**11**	**24**

Rights traded to **Boston** by **St. Paul** (AHA) with the rights to Bill Hill for cash, January 3, 1926. Traded to **Ottawa** by **Boston** with Ted Saunders and Bud Cook for Bob Gracie, October 4, 1933. • Released by Ottawa, November 17, 1933. Signed as a free agent by **Boston**, November 21, 1933.

GALLAGHER, John

Defense. Shoots left. 5'11", 188 lbs. Born, Kenora, Ont., January 19, 1909.

Season	Club	GP	G	A	Pts	PIM	GP	G	A	Pts	PIM
1930-31	Montreal Maroons	35	4	2	6	35	2	0	0	0	0
1931-32	Montreal Maroons	19	1	0	1	18					
1932-33	Montreal Maroons	6	1	0	1	0					
	Detroit Red Wings	35	3	6	9	48	4	1	1	2	4
1933-34	Detroit Red Wings	1	0	0	0	0					
1936-37	New York Americans	9	0	0	0	8					
♦	Detroit Red Wings	11	1	0	1	4	10	1	0	1	17
1937-38	New York Americans	46	3	6	9	18	6	0	2	2	6
1938-39	New York Americans	43	1	5	6	22	2	0	0	0	0
	NHL Totals	**205**	**14**	**19**	**33**	**153**	**24**	**2**	**3**	**5**	**27**

Signed as a free agent by **Toronto**, July 30, 1930. • Mtl. Maroons also claimed Gallagher's rights. NHL ruled he was property of Mtl. Maroons, September 27, 1930. Traded to **Detroit** by **Mtl. Maroons** for Reg Noble, December 9, 1932. • Missed majority of 1933-34 season recovering from injuries suffered in an automobile accident, November, 1933. Loaned to **Windsor** (IHL) by **Detroit** and played games in Canada only because he was denied entry into the U.S.A., November 30, 1934. Traded to **NY Americans** by **Detroit** for $6,000, October 7, 1936. Traded to **Detroit** by **NY Americans** for cash, November 29, 1936. Traded to **NY Americans** by **Detroit** for $6,000, October 7, 1937.

GALLANT, Gerard

Left wing. Shoots left. 5'10", 190 lbs. Born, Summerside, P.E.I., September 2, 1963.
(Detroit's 4th choice, 107th overall, in 1981 Entry Draft).

Season	Club	GP	G	A	Pts	PIM	GP	G	A	Pts	PIM
1984-85	Detroit Red Wings	32	6	12	18	66	3	0	0	0	11
1985-86	Detroit Red Wings	52	20	19	39	106					
1986-87	Detroit Red Wings	80	38	34	72	216	16	8	6	14	43
1987-88	Detroit Red Wings	73	34	39	73	242	16	6	9	15	55
1988-89	Detroit Red Wings	76	39	54	93	230	6	1	2	3	40
1989-90	Detroit Red Wings	69	36	44	80	254					
1990-91	Detroit Red Wings	45	10	16	26	111					
1991-92	Detroit Red Wings	69	14	22	36	187	11	2	2	4	25
1992-93	Detroit Red Wings	67	10	20	30	188	6	1	2	3	4
1993-94	Tampa Bay Lightning	51	4	9	13	74					

Season	Club	REGULAR SEASON GP	G	A	Pts	PIM	PLAYOFFS GP	G	A	Pts	PIM
1994-95	Tampa Bay Lightning	1	0	0	0	0	....	....	....	....	....
	NHL Totals	**615**	**211**	**269**	**480**	**1674**	**58**	**18**	**21**	**39**	**178**

NHL Second All-Star Team (1989)

Signed as a free agent by **Tampa Bay**, July 21, 1993.

GALLEY, Garry

Defense. Shoots left. 6', 202 lbs. Born, Montreal, Que., April 16, 1963.
(Los Angeles' 4th choice, 103rd overall, in 1983 Entry Draft).

Season	Club	GP	G	A	Pts	PIM	GP	G	A	Pts	PIM
1984-85	Los Angeles Kings	78	8	30	38	82	3	1	0	1	2
1985-86	Los Angeles Kings	49	9	13	22	46	....	....	....	....	....
1986-87	Los Angeles Kings	30	5	11	16	57	....	....	....	....	....
	Washington Capitals	18	1	10	11	10	2	0	0	0	0
1987-88	Washington Capitals	58	7	23	30	44	13	2	4	6	13
1988-89	Boston Bruins	78	8	22	30	80	9	0	1	1	33
1989-90	Boston Bruins	71	8	27	35	75	21	3	3	6	34
1990-91	Boston Bruins	70	6	21	27	84	16	1	5	6	17
1991-92	Boston Bruins	38	2	12	14	83	....	....	....	....	....
	Philadelphia Flyers	39	3	15	18	34	....	....	....	....	....
1992-93	Philadelphia Flyers	83	13	49	62	115	....	....	....	....	....
1993-94	Philadelphia Flyers	81	10	60	70	91	....	....	....	....	....
1994-95	Philadelphia Flyers	33	2	20	22	20	....	....	....	....	....
	Buffalo Sabres	14	1	9	10	10	5	0	3	3	4
1995-96	Buffalo Sabres	78	10	44	54	81	....	....	....	....	....
1996-97	Buffalo Sabres	71	4	34	38	102	12	0	6	6	14
1997-98	Los Angeles Kings	74	9	28	37	63	4	0	1	1	2
1998-99	Los Angeles Kings	60	4	12	16	30	....	....	....	....	....
99-2000	Los Angeles Kings	70	9	21	30	52	4	0	0	0	0
2000-01	New York Islanders	56	6	14	20	59	....	....	....	....	....
	NHL Totals	**1149**	**125**	**475**	**600**	**1218**	**89**	**7**	**23**	**30**	**119**

Played in NHL All-Star Game (1991, 1994)

Traded to **Washington** by **Los Angeles** for Al Jensen, February 14, 1987. Signed as a free agent by **Boston**, July 8, 1988. Traded to **Philadelphia** by **Boston** with Wes Walz and Boston's 3rd round choice (Milos Holan) in 1993 Entry Draft for Gord Murphy, Brian Dobbin, Philadelphia's 3rd round choice (Sergei Zholtok) in 1992 Entry Draft and 4th round choice (Charles Paquette) in 1993 Entry Draft, January 2, 1992. Traded to **Buffalo** by **Philadelphia** for Petr Svoboda, April 7, 1995. Signed as a free agent by **Los Angeles**, July 15, 1997. Signed as a free agent by **NY Islanders**, September 25, 2000.

GALLIMORE, Jamie

Right wing. Shoots right. 6', 180 lbs. Born, Edmonton, Alta., November 28, 1957.
(Minnesota's 5th choice, 97th overall, in 1977 Amateur Draft).

Season	Club	GP	G	A	Pts	PIM	GP	G	A	Pts	PIM
1977-78	Minnesota North Stars	2	0	0	0	0	....	....	....	....	....
	NHL Totals	**2**	**0**	**0**	**0**	**0**	....	....	....	....	....

GALLINGER, Don

Center. Shoots left. 6', 170 lbs. Born, Port Colborne, Ont., April 16, 1925.

Season	Club	GP	G	A	Pts	PIM	GP	G	A	Pts	PIM
1942-43	Boston Bruins	48	14	20	34	16	9	3	1	4	10
1943-44	Boston Bruins	23	13	5	18	6	....	....	....	....	....
1945-46	Boston Bruins	50	17	23	40	18	10	2	4	6	2
1946-47	Boston Bruins	47	11	19	30	12	4	0	0	0	7
1947-48	Boston Bruins	54	10	21	31	37	....	....	....	....	....
	NHL Totals	**222**	**65**	**88**	**153**	**89**	**23**	**5**	**5**	**10**	**19**

• Suspended for remainder of 1947-48 season by NHL for gambling violations, March 9, 1948. • Suspended for life by NHL for gambling violations, September 27, 1948. • Suspension lifted by NHL, August 28, 1970.

GAMACHE, Simon

Center. Shoots left. 5'9", 185 lbs. Born, Montreal, Que., January 3, 1981.
(Atlanta's 14th choice, 290th overall, in 2000 Entry Draft).

Season	Club	GP	G	A	Pts	PIM	GP	G	A	Pts	PIM
2002-03	Atlanta Thrashers	2	0	0	0	2	....	....	....	....	....
	NHL Totals	**2**	**0**	**0**	**0**	**2**	....	....	....	....	....

GAMBLE, Dick

Left wing. Shoots left. 6', 178 lbs. Born, Moncton, N.B., November 16, 1928.

Season	Club	GP	G	A	Pts	PIM	GP	G	A	Pts	PIM
1950-51	Montreal Canadiens	1	0	0	0	0	....	....	....	....	....
1951-52	Montreal Canadiens	64	23	17	40	8	7	0	2	2	0
1952-53 ♦	Montreal Canadiens	69	11	13	24	26	5	1	0	1	2
1953-54	Montreal Canadiens	32	4	8	12	18	....	....	....	....	....
1954-55	Chicago Black Hawks	14	2	0	2	6	....	....	....	....	....
	Montreal Canadiens	....	....	....	....	....	2	0	0	0	2
1955-56	Montreal Canadiens	12	0	3	3	8	....	....	....	....	....
1965-66	Toronto Maple Leafs	2	1	0	1	0	....	....	....	....	....
1966-67	Toronto Maple Leafs	1	0	0	0	0	....	....	....	....	....
	NHL Totals	**195**	**41**	**41**	**82**	**66**	**14**	**1**	**2**	**3**	**4**

Played in NHL All-Star Game (1953)

Signed as a free agent by **Montreal**, September 24, 1951. • Montreal loaned Murdo MacKay to Quebec (QMHL) as compensation. Traded to **NY Rangers** by **Montreal** with the rights to Eddie Dorohoy for Hy Buller with Montreal holding right of recall if Dorohoy failed to make NY Rangers roster, June 8, 1954. • Transaction cancelled after Buller retired, September, 1954. Traded to **Chicago** by **Montreal** for Bill Shevtz and cash with Montreal holding right of recall, October 9, 1954. Rights returned to **Montreal** by **Chicago**, November 23, 1954. Traded to **Buffalo** (AHL) by **Montreal** for cash, July, 1957. Traded to **Toronto** by **Buffalo** (AHL) for Dave Creighton, July, 1961.

GAMBUCCI, Gary

Center. Shoots left. 5'9", 175 lbs. Born, Hibbing, MN, September 27, 1946.

Season	Club	GP	G	A	Pts	PIM	GP	G	A	Pts	PIM
1971-72	Minnesota North Stars	9	1	0	1	0	....	....	....	....	....
1973-74	Minnesota North Stars	42	1	7	8	9	....	....	....	....	....
	NHL Totals	**51**	**2**	**7**	**9**	**9**	....	....	....	....	....

Signed as a free agent by **Montreal**, May, 1971. Rights traded to **Minnesota** by **Montreal** with Bob Paradise for cash, May, 1971.

GANCHAR, Perry

Right wing. Shoots right. 5'9", 180 lbs. Born, Saskatoon, Sask., October 28, 1963.
(St. Louis' 3rd choice, 113th overall, in 1982 Entry Draft).

Season	Club	GP	G	A	Pts	PIM	GP	G	A	Pts	PIM
1983-84	St. Louis Blues	1	0	0	0	0	7	3	1	4	0
1984-85	St. Louis Blues	7	0	2	2	0	....	....	....	....	....
1987-88	Montreal Canadiens	1	1	0	1	0	....	....	....	....	....
	Pittsburgh Penguins	30	2	5	7	36	....	....	....	....	....
1988-89	Pittsburgh Penguins	3	0	0	0	0	....	....	....	....	....
	NHL Totals	**42**	**3**	**7**	**10**	**36**	**7**	**3**	**1**	**4**	**0**

Traded to **Montreal** by **St. Louis** for Ron Flockhart, August 26, 1985. Traded to **Pittsburgh** by **Montreal** for future considerations, December 17, 1987.

GANS, Dave

Center. Shoots right. 5'10", 180 lbs. Born, Brantford, Ont., June 6, 1964.
(Los Angeles' 3rd choice, 64th overall, in 1982 Entry Draft).

Season	Club	GP	G	A	Pts	PIM	GP	G	A	Pts	PIM
1982-83	Los Angeles Kings	3	0	0	0	0	....	....	....	....	....
1985-86	Los Angeles Kings	3	0	0	0	2	....	....	....	....	....
	NHL Totals	**6**	**0**	**0**	**0**	**2**	....	....	....	....	....

GARDINER, Bruce

Right wing. Shoots right. 6'1", 193 lbs. Born, Barrie, Ont., February 11, 1972.
(St. Louis' 6th choice, 131st overall, in 1991 Entry Draft).

Season	Club	GP	G	A	Pts	PIM	GP	G	A	Pts	PIM
1996-97	Ottawa Senators	67	11	10	21	49	7	0	1	1	2
1997-98	Ottawa Senators	55	7	11	18	50	11	1	3	4	2
1998-99	Ottawa Senators	59	4	8	12	43	3	0	0	0	4
99-2000	Ottawa Senators	10	0	3	3	4	....	....	....	....	....
	Tampa Bay Lightning	41	3	6	9	37	....	....	....	....	....
2000-01	Columbus Blue Jackets	73	7	15	22	78	....	....	....	....	....
2001-02	New Jersey Devils	7	2	1	3	2	....	....	....	....	....
	NHL Totals	**312**	**34**	**54**	**88**	**263**	**21**	**1**	**4**	**5**	**8**

Signed as a free agent by **Ottawa**, June 14, 1994. Traded to **Tampa Bay** by **Ottawa** for Colin Forbes, November 11, 1999. Selected by **Columbus** from **Tampa Bay** in Expansion Draft, June 23, 2000. Signed as a free agent by **New Jersey**, October 21, 2001.

GARDINER, Herb

HHOF

Defense. Shoots left. 5'10", 190 lbs. Born, Winnipeg, Man., May 8, 1891.

Season	Club	GP	G	A	Pts	PIM	GP	G	A	Pts	PIM
1926-27	Montreal Canadiens	44	6	6	12	26	4	0	0	0	10
1927-28	Montreal Canadiens	44	4	3	7	26	2	0	1	1	4
1928-29	Chicago Black Hawks	13	0	0	0	0	....	....	....	....	....
	Montreal Canadiens	7	0	0	0	0	3	0	0	0	2
	NHL Totals	**108**	**10**	**9**	**19**	**52**	**9**	**0**	**1**	**1**	**16**

Hart Trophy (1927)

Rights traded to **Montreal** by **Calgary** (WHL) for cash, October 20, 1926. Loaned to **Chicago** by **Montreal** and named playing coach of Black Hawks, August 27, 1928. • Recalled by Montreal, February 12, 1929. Traded to **Boston** by **Montreal** for cash, May 13, 1929. Traded to **Philadelphia** (Can-Am) by **Boston** for cash, October 4, 1929.

GARDNER, Bill

Center. Shoots left. 5'10", 180 lbs. Born, Toronto, Ont., March 18, 1960.
(Chicago's 3rd choice, 49th overall, in 1979 Entry Draft).

Season	Club	GP	G	A	Pts	PIM	GP	G	A	Pts	PIM
1980-81	Chicago Black Hawks	1	0	0	0	0	....	....	....	....	....
1981-82	Chicago Black Hawks	69	8	15	23	20	15	1	4	5	6
1982-83	Chicago Black Hawks	77	15	25	40	12	13	1	0	1	9
1983-84	Chicago Black Hawks	79	27	21	48	12	5	0	1	1	0
1984-85	Chicago Black Hawks	74	17	34	51	12	12	1	3	4	2
1985-86	Chicago Black Hawks	46	3	10	13	6	....	....	....	....	....
	Hartford Whalers	18	1	8	9	4	....	....	....	....	....
1986-87	Hartford Whalers	8	0	1	1	0	....	....	....	....	....
1987-88	Chicago Blackhawks	2	1	0	1	2	....	....	....	....	....
1988-89	Chicago Blackhawks	6	1	1	2	0	....	....	....	....	....
	NHL Totals	**380**	**73**	**115**	**188**	**68**	**45**	**3**	**8**	**11**	**17**

Traded to **Hartford** by **Chicago** for Hartford's 3rd round choice (Mike Dagenais) in 1987 Entry Draft, February 3, 1986. Signed as a free agent by **Chicago**, September 25, 1987.

GARDNER, Cal

Center. Shoots left. 6'1", 172 lbs. Born, Transcona, Man., October 30, 1924.

Season	Club	GP	G	A	Pts	PIM	GP	G	A	Pts	PIM
1945-46	New York Rangers	16	8	2	10	2	....	....	....	....	....
1946-47	New York Rangers	52	13	16	29	30	....	....	....	....	....
1947-48	New York Rangers	58	7	18	25	71	5	0	0	0	0
1948-49 ♦	Toronto Maple Leafs	53	13	22	35	35	9	2	5	7	0
1949-50	Toronto Maple Leafs	31	7	19	26	12	7	1	0	1	4
1950-51 ♦	Toronto Maple Leafs	66	23	28	51	42	11	1	1	2	4
1951-52	Toronto Maple Leafs	70	15	26	41	40	3	0	0	0	2
1952-53	Chicago Black Hawks	70	11	24	35	60	7	0	2	2	4
1953-54	Boston Bruins	70	14	20	34	62	4	1	1	2	0
1954-55	Boston Bruins	70	16	22	38	40	5	0	0	0	4

Season	Club	REGULAR SEASON GP	G	A	Pts	PIM	PLAYOFFS GP	G	A	Pts	PIM
1955-56	Boston Bruins	70	15	21	36	57	....	....	....	....	....
1956-57	Boston Bruins	70	12	20	32	66	10	2	1	3	2
	NHL Totals	**696**	**154**	**238**	**392**	**517**	**61**	**7**	**10**	**17**	**20**

• Father of Dave and Paul

Played in NHL All-Star Game (1948, 1949)

Traded to **Toronto** by **NY Rangers** with Bill Juzda, Rene Trudell and the rights to Frank Mathers for Wally Stanowski and Moe Morris, April 26, 1948. • Missed majority of 1949-50 season recovering from broken jaw suffered in game vs. Montreal, November 11, 1949. Traded to **Chicago** by **Toronto** with Ray Hannigan, Al Rollins and Gus Mortson for Harry Lumley, September 11, 1952. Traded to **Boston** by **Chicago** for cash, June 26, 1953.

GARDNER, Dave

Center. Shoots right. 6', 185 lbs. Born, Toronto, Ont., August 23, 1952.
(Montreal's 3rd choice, 8th overall, in 1972 Amateur Draft).

Season	Club	GP	G	A	Pts	PIM	GP	G	A	Pts	PIM
1972-73	Montreal Canadiens	5	1	1	2	0	....	....	....	....	....
1973-74	Montreal Canadiens	31	1	10	11	2	....	....	....	....	....
	St. Louis Blues	15	5	2	7	6	....	....	....	....	....
1974-75	St. Louis Blues	8	0	2	2	0	....	....	....	....	....
	California Golden Seals	64	16	20	36	6	....	....	....	....	....
1975-76	California Golden Seals	74	16	32	48	8	....	....	....	....	....
1976-77	Cleveland Barons	76	16	22	38	9	....	....	....	....	....
1977-78	Cleveland Barons	75	19	25	44	10	....	....	....	....	....
1979-80	Philadelphia Flyers	2	1	1	2	0	....	....	....	....	....
	NHL Totals	**350**	**75**	**115**	**190**	**41**	....	....	....	....	....

• Son of Cal • Brother of Paul

Traded to **St. Louis** by **Montreal** for St. Louis' 1st round choice (Doug Risebrough) in 1974 Amateur Draft, March 9, 1974. Traded to **California** by **St. Louis** with Butch Williams for Craig Patrick and Stan Gilbertson, November 11, 1974. Transferred to **Cleveland** after **California** franchise relocated, August 26, 1976. Placed on **Minnesota** Reserve List after **Minnesota-Cleveland** Dispersal Draft, June 15, 1978. Transferred to **Los Angeles** by **Minnesota** with Rick Hampton and Steve Jensen as compensation for Minnesota's signing of free agent Gary Sargent, July 15, 1978. Signed as a free agent by **Philadelphia**, January 21, 1980.

GARDNER, Paul

Center. Shoots left. 6', 195 lbs. Born, Toronto, Ont., March 5, 1956.
(Kansas City's 1st choice, 11th overall, in 1976 Amateur Draft).

Season	Club	GP	G	A	Pts	PIM	GP	G	A	Pts	PIM
1976-77	Colorado Rockies	60	30	29	59	25	....	....	....	....	....
1977-78	Colorado Rockies	46	30	22	52	29	....	....	....	....	....
1978-79	Colorado Rockies	64	23	26	49	32	....	....	....	....	....
	Toronto Maple Leafs	11	7	2	9	0	6	0	1	1	4
1979-80	Toronto Maple Leafs	45	11	13	24	10	....	....	....	....	....
1980-81	Pittsburgh Penguins	62	34	40	74	59	5	1	0	1	8
1981-82	Pittsburgh Penguins	59	36	33	69	28	5	1	5	6	2
1982-83	Pittsburgh Penguins	70	28	27	55	12	....	....	....	....	....
1983-84	Pittsburgh Penguins	16	0	5	5	6	....	....	....	....	....
1984-85	Washington Capitals	12	2	4	6	6	....	....	....	....	....
1985-86	Buffalo Sabres	2	0	0	0	0	....	....	....	....	....
	NHL Totals	**447**	**201**	**201**	**402**	**207**	**16**	**2**	**6**	**8**	**14**

• Son of Cal • Brother of Dave

Rights transferred to **Colorado** after **Kansas City** relocated, July 15, 1976. Traded to **Toronto** by **Colorado** for Don Ashby and Trevor Johansen, March 13, 1979. Traded to **Pittsburgh** by **Toronto** with Dave Burrows for Kim Davis and Paul Marshall, November 18, 1980. Signed as a free agent by **Washington**, July 17, 1984. Signed as a free agent by **Buffalo**, July 31, 1985.

GARE, Danny

Right wing. Shoots right. 5'9", 175 lbs. Born, Nelson, B.C., May 14, 1954.
(Buffalo's 2nd choice, 29th overall, in 1974 Amateur Draft).

Season	Club	GP	G	A	Pts	PIM	GP	G	A	Pts	PIM
1974-75	Buffalo Sabres	78	31	31	62	75	17	7	6	13	19
1975-76	Buffalo Sabres	79	50	23	73	129	9	5	2	7	21
1976-77	Buffalo Sabres	35	11	15	26	73	4	0	0	0	18
1977-78	Buffalo Sabres	69	39	38	77	95	8	4	6	10	37
1978-79	Buffalo Sabres	71	27	40	67	90	3	0	0	0	9
1979-80	Buffalo Sabres	76	*56	33	89	90	14	4	7	11	35
1980-81	Buffalo Sabres	73	46	39	85	109	3	3	0	3	8
1981-82	Buffalo Sabres	22	7	14	21	25	....	....	....	....	....
	Detroit Red Wings	36	13	9	22	74	....	....	....	....	....
1982-83	Detroit Red Wings	79	26	35	61	107	....	....	....	....	....
1983-84	Detroit Red Wings	63	13	13	26	147	4	2	0	2	38
1984-85	Detroit Red Wings	71	27	29	56	163	2	0	0	0	10
1985-86	Detroit Red Wings	57	7	9	16	102	....	....	....	....	....
1986-87	Edmonton Oilers	18	1	3	4	6	....	....	....	....	....
	NHL Totals	**827**	**354**	**331**	**685**	**1285**	**64**	**25**	**21**	**46**	**195**

NHL Second All-Star Team (1980)

Played in NHL All-Star Game (1980, 1981)

Traded to **Detroit** by **Buffalo** with Jim Schoenfeld and Derek Smith for Mike Foligno, Dale McCourt and Brent Peterson, December 2, 1981. Signed as a free agent by **Edmonton**, September, 1986.

GARIEPY, Ray

Defense. Shoots left. 5'9", 180 lbs. Born, Toronto, Ont., September 4, 1928.

Season	Club	GP	G	A	Pts	PIM	GP	G	A	Pts	PIM
1953-54	Boston Bruins	35	1	6	7	39	....	....	....	....	....
1955-56	Toronto Maple Leafs	1	0	0	0	4	....	....	....	....	....
	NHL Totals	**36**	**1**	**6**	**7**	**43**	....	....	....	....	....

Traded to **Boston** by **Hershey** for Dunc Fisher and Ellard O'Brien, June, 1953. Traded to **Toronto** by **Boston** for John Henderson, September 23, 1954. Traded to **Detroit** (Hershey-AHL) by **Toronto** (Pittsburgh-AHL) with Gilles Mayer, Jack Price, Willie Marshall, Bob Hassard and Bob Solinger for cash, July 7, 1956.

GARLAND, Scott

Center. Shoots right. 6'1", 185 lbs. Born, Regina, Sask., May 16, 1952.

Season	Club	GP	G	A	Pts	PIM	GP	G	A	Pts	PIM
1975-76	Toronto Maple Leafs	16	4	3	7	8	7	1	2	3	35
1976-77	Toronto Maple Leafs	69	9	20	29	83	....	....	....	....	....
1978-79	Los Angeles Kings	6	0	1	1	24	....	....	....	....	....
	NHL Totals	**91**	**13**	**24**	**37**	**115**	**7**	**1**	**2**	**3**	**35**

Signed as a free agent by **Toronto**, September 30, 1973. Traded to **Los Angeles** by **Toronto** with Brian Glennie, Kurt Walker and Toronto's 2nd round choice (Mark Hardy) in 1979 Entry Draft for Dave Hutchison and Lorne Stamler, June 14, 1978. • Died of injuries suffered in automobile accident, June 9, 1979.

GARNER, Rob

Center. Shoots left. 5'11", 180 lbs. Born, Weston, Ont., August 17, 1958.
(Pittsburgh's 3rd choice, 75th overall, in 1978 Amateur Draft).

Season	Club	GP	G	A	Pts	PIM	GP	G	A	Pts	PIM
1982-83	Pittsburgh Penguins	1	0	0	0	0	....	....	....	....	....
	NHL Totals	**1**	**0**	**0**	**0**	**0**	....	....	....	....	....

GARPENLOV, Johan

Left wing. Shoots left. 6', 185 lbs. Born, Stockholm, Sweden, March 21, 1968.
(Detroit's 5th choice, 85th overall, in 1986 Entry Draft).

Season	Club	GP	G	A	Pts	PIM	GP	G	A	Pts	PIM
1990-91	Detroit Red Wings	71	18	22	40	18	6	0	1	1	4
1991-92	Detroit Red Wings	16	1	1	2	4	....	....	....	....	....
	San Jose Sharks	12	5	6	11	4	....	....	....	....	....
1992-93	San Jose Sharks	79	22	44	66	56	....	....	....	....	....
1993-94	San Jose Sharks	80	18	35	53	28	14	4	6	10	6
1994-95	San Jose Sharks	13	1	1	2	2	....	....	....	....	....
	Florida Panthers	27	3	9	12	0	....	....	....	....	....
1995-96	Florida Panthers	82	23	28	51	36	20	4	2	6	8
1996-97	Florida Panthers	53	11	25	36	47	4	2	0	2	4
1997-98	Florida Panthers	39	2	3	5	8	....	....	....	....	....
1998-99	Florida Panthers	64	8	9	17	42	....	....	....	....	....
99-2000	Atlanta Thrashers	73	2	14	16	31	....	....	....	....	....
	NHL Totals	**609**	**114**	**197**	**311**	**276**	**44**	**10**	**9**	**19**	**22**

Traded to **San Jose** by **Detroit** for Bob McGill and Vancouver's 8th round choice (previously acquired, Detroit selected C.J. Denomme) in 1992 Entry Draft, March 9, 1992. Traded to **Florida** by **San Jose** for Florida's 5th round choice (previously acquired, Florida selected Jaroslav Spacek) in 1998 Entry Draft, March 3, 1995. Claimed by **Atlanta** from **Florida** in Expansion Draft, June 25, 1999.

GARRETT, Red

Defense. Shoots left. 5'11", 190 lbs. Born, Toronto, Ont., July 24, 1924.

Season	Club	GP	G	A	Pts	PIM	GP	G	A	Pts	PIM
1942-43	New York Rangers	23	1	1	2	18	....	....	....	....	....
	NHL Totals	**23**	**1**	**1**	**2**	**18**	....	....	....	....	....

Traded to **NY Rangers** by **Toronto** with Hank Goldup for Babe Pratt, November 27, 1942. • Killed in action during destroyer escort run off the coast of Port-aux-Basques, Newfoundland, November 24, 1944.

GARTNER, Mike **HHOF**

Right wing. Shoots right. 6', 187 lbs. Born, Ottawa, Ont., October 29, 1959.
(Washington's 1st choice, 4th overall, in 1979 Entry Draft).

Season	Club	GP	G	A	Pts	PIM	GP	G	A	Pts	PIM
1979-80	Washington Capitals	77	36	32	68	66	....	....	....	....	....
1980-81	Washington Capitals	80	48	46	94	100	....	....	....	....	....
1981-82	Washington Capitals	80	35	45	80	121	....	....	....	....	....
1982-83	Washington Capitals	73	38	38	76	54	4	0	0	0	4
1983-84	Washington Capitals	80	40	45	85	90	8	3	7	10	16
1984-85	Washington Capitals	80	50	52	102	71	5	4	3	7	9
1985-86	Washington Capitals	74	35	40	75	63	9	2	10	12	4
1986-87	Washington Capitals	78	41	32	73	61	7	4	3	7	14
1987-88	Washington Capitals	80	48	33	81	73	14	3	4	7	14
1988-89	Washington Capitals	56	26	29	55	71	....	....	....	....	....
	Minnesota North Stars	13	7	7	14	2	5	0	0	0	6
1989-90	Minnesota North Stars	67	34	36	70	32	....	....	....	....	....
	New York Rangers	12	11	5	16	6	10	5	3	8	12
1990-91	New York Rangers	79	49	20	69	53	6	1	1	2	0
1991-92	New York Rangers	76	40	41	81	55	13	8	8	16	4
1992-93	New York Rangers	84	45	23	68	59	....	....	....	....	....
1993-94	New York Rangers	71	28	24	52	58	....	....	....	....	....
	Toronto Maple Leafs	10	6	6	12	4	18	5	6	11	14
1994-95	Toronto Maple Leafs	38	12	8	20	6	5	2	2	4	2
1995-96	Toronto Maple Leafs	82	35	19	54	52	6	4	1	5	4
1996-97	Phoenix Coyotes	82	32	31	63	38	7	1	2	3	4
1997-98	Phoenix Coyotes	60	12	15	27	24	5	1	0	1	18
	NHL Totals	**1432**	**708**	**627**	**1335**	**1159**	**122**	**43**	**50**	**93**	**125**

Played in NHL All-Star Game (1981, 1985, 1986, 1988, 1990, 1993, 1996)

Traded to **Minnesota** by **Washington** with Larry Murphy for Dino Ciccarelli and Bob Rouse, March 7, 1989. Traded to **NY Rangers** by **Minnesota** for Ulf Dahlen, Los Angeles' 4th round choice (previously acquired, Minnesota selected Cal McGowan) in 1990 Entry Draft, March 6, 1990. Traded to **Toronto** by **NY Rangers** for Glenn Anderson, the rights to Scott Malone and Toronto's 4th round choice (Alexander Korobolin) in 1994 Entry Draft, March 21, 1994. Traded to **Phoenix** by **Toronto** for Chicago's 4th round choice (previously acquired, Toronto selected Vladimir Antipov) in 1996 Entry Draft, June 22, 1996.

GASSOFF, Bob

Defense. Shoots left. 5'10", 195 lbs. Born, Quesnel, B.C., April 17, 1953.
(St. Louis' 3rd choice, 48th overall, in 1973 Amateur Draft).

Season	Club	GP	G	A	Pts	PIM	GP	G	A	Pts	PIM
1973-74	St. Louis Blues	28	0	3	3	84	....	....	....	....	....

Season	Club	GP	G	A	Pts	PIM	GP	G	A	Pts	PIM
		REGULAR SEASON					PLAYOFFS				
1974-75	St. Louis Blues	60	4	14	18	222	2	0	0	0	0
1975-76	St. Louis Blues	80	1	12	13	306	3	0	0	0	6
1976-77	St. Louis Blues	77	6	18	24	254	4	0	1	1	10
	NHL Totals	**245**	**11**	**47**	**58**	**866**	**9**	**0**	**1**	**1**	**16**

• Brother of Brad • Died of injuries suffered in motorbike accident, May 27, 1977.

GASSOFF, Brad

Left wing. Shoots left. 5'11", 195 lbs. Born, Quesnel, B.C., November 13, 1955.
(Vancouver's 2nd choice, 28th overall, in 1975 Amateur Draft).

Season	Club	GP	G	A	Pts	PIM	GP	G	A	Pts	PIM
1975-76	Vancouver Canucks	4	0	0	0	5	....	....	....	....	....
1976-77	Vancouver Canucks	37	6	4	10	35	....	....	....	....	....
1977-78	Vancouver Canucks	47	9	6	15	70	....	....	....	....	....
1978-79	Vancouver Canucks	34	4	7	11	53	3	0	0	0	0
	NHL Totals	**122**	**19**	**17**	**36**	**163**	**3**	**0**	**0**	**0**	**0**

• Brother of Bob

GATZOS, Steve

Right wing. Shoots right. 5'11", 185 lbs. Born, Toronto, Ont., June 22, 1961.
(Pittsburgh's 1st choice, 28th overall, in 1981 Entry Draft).

Season	Club	GP	G	A	Pts	PIM	GP	G	A	Pts	PIM
1981-82	Pittsburgh Penguins	16	6	8	14	14	1	0	0	0	0
1982-83	Pittsburgh Penguins	44	6	7	13	52	....	....	....	....	....
1983-84	Pittsburgh Penguins	23	3	3	6	15	....	....	....	....	....
1984-85	Pittsburgh Penguins	6	0	2	2	2	....	....	....	....	....
	NHL Totals	**89**	**15**	**20**	**35**	**83**	**1**	**0**	**0**	**0**	**0**

GAUDREAU, Rob

Right wing. Shoots right. 5'11", 185 lbs. Born, Lincoln, RI, January 20, 1970.
(Pittsburgh's 8th choice, 172nd overall, in 1988 Entry Draft).

Season	Club	GP	G	A	Pts	PIM	GP	G	A	Pts	PIM
1992-93	San Jose Sharks	59	23	20	43	18	....	....	....	....	....
1993-94	San Jose Sharks	84	15	20	35	28	14	2	0	2	0
1994-95	Ottawa Senators	36	5	9	14	8	....	....	....	....	....
1995-96	Ottawa Senators	52	8	5	13	15	....	....	....	....	....
	NHL Totals	**231**	**51**	**54**	**105**	**69**	**14**	**2**	**0**	**2**	**0**

Rights traded to **Minnesota** by **Pittsburgh** for Richard Zemlak, November 1, 1988. Claimed by **San Jose** from **Minnesota** in Dispersal Draft, May 30, 1991. Claimed by **Ottawa** from **San Jose** in Waiver Draft, January 18, 1995.

GAUDREAULT, Armand

Left wing. Shoots left. 5'9", 155 lbs. Born, Lac St-Jean, Que., July 14, 1921.

Season	Club	GP	G	A	Pts	PIM	GP	G	A	Pts	PIM
1944-45	Boston Bruins	44	15	9	24	27	7	0	2	2	8
	NHL Totals	**44**	**15**	**9**	**24**	**27**	**7**	**0**	**2**	**2**	**8**

Signed as a free agent by **Boston**, November 2, 1944.

GAUDREAULT, Leo

Left wing/Center. Shoots left. 5'10", 152 lbs. Born, Chicoutimi, Que., October 19, 1905.

Season	Club	GP	G	A	Pts	PIM	GP	G	A	Pts	PIM
1927-28	Montreal Canadiens	32	6	2	8	24	....	....	....	....	....
1928-29	Montreal Canadiens	11	0	0	0	4	....	....	....	....	....
1932-33	Montreal Canadiens	24	2	2	4	2	....	....	....	....	....
	NHL Totals	**67**	**8**	**4**	**12**	**30**	....	....	....	....	....

Signed as a free agent by **Montreal**, October 7, 1927. Traded to **Providence** (Can-Am) by **Montreal** for Armand Mondou, December 19, 1928. Signed as a free agent by **Montreal**, September, 1932. Traded to **Providence** (Can-Am) by **Montreal** with Armand Mondou for Hago Harrington and Leo Murray with both teams holding right of recall, January, 1933.

GAUL, Mike

Defense. Shoots right. 6'1", 200 lbs. Born, Lachine, Que., April 22, 1973.
(Los Angeles' 10th choice, 262nd overall, in 1991 Entry Draft).

Season	Club	GP	G	A	Pts	PIM	GP	G	A	Pts	PIM
1998-99	Colorado Avalanche	1	0	0	0	0	....	....	....	....	....
2000-01	Columbus Blue Jackets	2	0	0	0	4	....	....	....	....	....
	NHL Totals	**3**	**0**	**0**	**0**	**4**	....	....	....	....	....

Signed as a free agent by **NY Islanders**, July 16, 1998. Traded to **Colorado** by **NY Islanders** for Ted Crowley, December 15, 1998. Signed as a free agent by **Columbus**, July 18, 2000.

GAULIN, Jean-Marc

Right wing. Shoots right. 5'10", 180 lbs. Born, Balve, West Germany, March 3, 1962.
(Quebec's 2nd choice, 53rd overall, in 1981 Entry Draft).

Season	Club	GP	G	A	Pts	PIM	GP	G	A	Pts	PIM
1982-83	Quebec Nordiques	1	0	0	0	0	....	....	....	....	....
1983-84	Quebec Nordiques	2	0	0	0	0	....	....	....	....	....
1984-85	Quebec Nordiques	22	3	3	6	8	1	0	0	0	0
1985-86	Quebec Nordiques	1	1	0	1	0	....	....	....	....	....
	NHL Totals	**26**	**4**	**3**	**7**	**8**	**1**	**0**	**0**	**0**	**0**

GAUME, Dallas

Center. Shoots left. 5'10", 185 lbs. Born, Innisfail, Alta., August 27, 1963.

Season	Club	GP	G	A	Pts	PIM	GP	G	A	Pts	PIM
1988-89	Hartford Whalers	4	1	1	2	0	....	....	....	....	....
	NHL Totals	**4**	**1**	**1**	**2**	**0**	....	....	....	....	....

Signed as a free agent by **Hartford**, July 10, 1986.

GAUSTAD, Paul

Center. Shoots left. 6'4", 217 lbs. Born, Fargo, ND, February 3, 1982.
(Buffalo's 6th choice, 220th overall, in 2000 Entry Draft).

Season	Club	GP	G	A	Pts	PIM	GP	G	A	Pts	PIM
2002-03	Buffalo Sabres	1	0	0	0	0	....	....	....	....	....
	NHL Totals	**1**	**0**	**0**	**0**	**0**	....	....	....	....	....

GAUTHIER, Art

Center. Shoots left. 5'8", 158 lbs. Born, Espanola, Ont., October 10, 1904.

Season	Club	GP	G	A	Pts	PIM	GP	G	A	Pts	PIM
1926-27	Montreal Canadiens	13	0	0	0	0	1	0	0	0	0
	NHL Totals	**13**	**0**	**0**	**0**	**0**	**1**	**0**	**0**	**0**	**0**

Signed as a free agent by **Montreal**, February 9, 1927. Traded to **London** (Can-Pro) by **Montreal** (Providence-Can-Am) for cash, January 10, 1928.

GAUTHIER, Daniel

Left wing. Shoots left. 6'1", 190 lbs. Born, Charlemagne, Que., May 17, 1970.
(Pittsburgh's 3rd choice, 62nd overall, in 1988 Entry Draft).

Season	Club	GP	G	A	Pts	PIM	GP	G	A	Pts	PIM
1994-95	Chicago Blackhawks	5	0	0	0	0	....	....	....	....	....
	NHL Totals	**5**	**0**	**0**	**0**	**0**	....	....	....	....	....

Signed as a free agent by **Florida**, July 14, 1993. Signed as a free agent by **Chicago**, June 14, 1994.

GAUTHIER, Denis

Defense. Shoots left. 6'2", 224 lbs. Born, Montreal, Que., October 1, 1976.
(Calgary's 1st choice, 20th overall, in 1995 Entry Draft).

Season	Club	GP	G	A	Pts	PIM	GP	G	A	Pts	PIM
1997-98	Calgary Flames	10	0	0	0	16	....	....	....	....	....
1998-99	Calgary Flames	55	3	4	7	68	....	....	....	....	....
99-2000	Calgary Flames	39	1	1	2	50	....	....	....	....	....
2000-01	Calgary Flames	62	2	6	8	78	....	....	....	....	....
2001-02	Calgary Flames	66	5	8	13	91	....	....	....	....	....
2002-03	Calgary Flames	72	1	11	12	99	....	....	....	....	....
	NHL Totals	**304**	**12**	**30**	**42**	**402**	....	....	....	....	....

• Missed majority of 1999-2000 season recovering from hip injury suffered in game vs. St. Louis, February 1, 2000.

GAUTHIER, Fern

Right wing. Shoots right. 5'11", 175 lbs. Born, Chicoutimi, Que., August 31, 1919.

Season	Club	GP	G	A	Pts	PIM	GP	G	A	Pts	PIM
1943-44	New York Rangers	33	14	10	24	0	....	....	....	....	....
1944-45	Montreal Canadiens	50	18	13	31	23	4	0	0	0	0
1945-46	Detroit Red Wings	30	9	8	17	6	5	3	0	3	2
1946-47	Detroit Red Wings	40	1	12	13	2	3	1	0	1	0
1947-48	Detroit Red Wings	35	1	5	6	2	10	1	1	2	5
1948-49	Detroit Red Wings	41	3	2	5	2	....	....	....	....	....
	NHL Totals	**229**	**46**	**50**	**96**	**35**	**22**	**5**	**1**	**6**	**7**

Traded to **Montreal** (Buffalo-AHL) by **Washington** (AHL) for cash, February 8, 1943. Loaned to **NY Rangers** by **Montreal** with Dutch Hiller, John Mahaffy, Charlie Sands and future considerations (Tony Demers, December, 1943) for the loan of Phil Watson, October 27, 1943. Traded to **Detroit** by **Montreal** to complete transaction that sent Billy Reay to Montreal (September 11, 1945), October 18, 1945. Traded to **St. Louis** (AHL) by **Detroit** with Cliff Simpson, Ed Nicholson and future considerations for Steve Black and Bill Brennan, August 29, 1949.

GAUTHIER, Jean

Defense. Shoots right. 6'1", 190 lbs. Born, Montreal, Que., April 29, 1937.

Season	Club	GP	G	A	Pts	PIM	GP	G	A	Pts	PIM
1960-61	Montreal Canadiens	4	0	1	1	8	....	....	....	....	....
1961-62	Montreal Canadiens	12	0	1	1	10	....	....	....	....	....
1962-63	Montreal Canadiens	65	1	17	18	46	5	0	0	0	12
1963-64	Montreal Canadiens	1	0	0	0	2	....	....	....	....	....
1964-65 ♦	Montreal Canadiens	....	....	....	....	....	2	0	0	0	4
1965-66	Montreal Canadiens	2	0	0	0	0	....	....	....	....	....
1966-67	Montreal Canadiens	2	0	0	0	2	....	....	....	....	....
1967-68	Philadelphia Flyers	65	5	7	12	74	7	1	3	4	6
1968-69	Boston Bruins	11	0	2	2	8	....	....	....	....	....
1969-70	Montreal Canadiens	4	0	1	1	0	....	....	....	....	....
	NHL Totals	**166**	**6**	**29**	**35**	**150**	**14**	**1**	**3**	**4**	**22**

Claimed by **Philadelphia** from **Montreal** in Expansion Draft, June 6, 1967. Claimed by **Boston** from **Philadelphia** in Intra-League Draft, June 12, 1968. Claimed by **Cleveland** (AHL) from **Boston** (Oklahoma City-CHL) in Reverse Draft, June 12, 1969. Traded to **Montreal** by **Cleveland** (AHL) for cash, October, 1969.

GAUTHIER, Luc

Defense. Shoots right. 5'9", 195 lbs. Born, Longueuil, Que., April 19, 1964.

Season	Club	GP	G	A	Pts	PIM	GP	G	A	Pts	PIM
1990-91	Montreal Canadiens	3	0	0	0	2	....	....	....	....	....
	NHL Totals	**3**	**0**	**0**	**0**	**2**	....	....	....	....	....

Signed as a free agent by **Montreal**, October 7, 1986.

GAUVREAU, Jocelyn

Defense. Shoots left. 5'11", 180 lbs. Born, Masham, Que., March 4, 1964.
(Montreal's 2nd choice, 31st overall, in 1982 Entry Draft).

Season	Club	GP	G	A	Pts	PIM	GP	G	A	Pts	PIM
1983-84	Montreal Canadiens	2	0	0	0	0	....	....	....	....	....
	NHL Totals	**2**	**0**	**0**	**0**	**0**	....	....	....	....	....

GAVEY, Aaron

Center. Shoots left. 6'2", 200 lbs. Born, Sudbury, Ont., February 22, 1974.
(Tampa Bay's 4th choice, 74th overall, in 1992 Entry Draft).

Season	Club	GP	G	A	Pts	PIM	GP	G	A	Pts	PIM
1995-96	Tampa Bay Lightning	73	8	4	12	56	6	0	0	0	4
1996-97	Tampa Bay Lightning	16	1	2	3	12	....	....	....	....	....
	Calgary Flames	41	7	9	16	34	....	....	....	....	....
1997-98	Calgary Flames	26	2	3	5	24	....	....	....	....	....
1998-99	Dallas Stars	7	0	0	0	10	....	....	....	....	....
99-2000	Dallas Stars	41	7	6	13	44	13	1	2	3	10

Season	Club	REGULAR SEASON GP	G	A	Pts	PIM	PLAYOFFS GP	G	A	Pts	PIM
2000-01	Minnesota Wild	75	10	14	24	52	....	....	....	....	....
2001-02	Minnesota Wild	71	6	11	17	38	....	....	....	....	....
2002-03	Toronto Maple Leafs	5	0	1	1	0	....	....	....	....	....
	NHL Totals	**355**	**41**	**50**	**91**	**270**	**19**	**1**	**2**	**3**	**14**

Traded to **Calgary** by **Tampa Bay** for Rick Tabaracci, November 19, 1996. Traded to **Dallas** by **Calgary** for Bob Bassen, July 14, 1998. Traded to **Minnesota** by **Dallas** with Pavel Patera, Dallas' 8th round choice (Eric Johansson) in 2000 Entry Draft and Minnesota's 4th round choice (previously acquired, later traded to Los Angeles – Los Angeles selected Aaron Rome) in 2002 Entry Draft for Brad Lukowich and Minnesota's 3rd (Yared Hagos) and 9th (Dale Sullivan) round choices in 2001 Entry Draft, June 25, 2000. Signed as a free agent by **Toronto**, July 24, 2002.

GAVIN, Stew

Left wing. Shoots left. 6', 190 lbs. Born, Ottawa, Ont., March 15, 1960.
(Toronto's 4th choice, 74th overall, in 1980 Entry Draft).

Season	Club	REGULAR SEASON GP	G	A	Pts	PIM	PLAYOFFS GP	G	A	Pts	PIM
1980-81	Toronto Maple Leafs	14	1	2	3	13	....	....	....	....	....
1981-82	Toronto Maple Leafs	38	5	6	11	29	....	....	....	....	....
1982-83	Toronto Maple Leafs	63	6	5	11	44	4	0	0	0	0
1983-84	Toronto Maple Leafs	80	10	22	32	90	....	....	....	....	....
1984-85	Toronto Maple Leafs	73	12	13	25	38	....	....	....	....	....
1985-86	Hartford Whalers	76	26	29	55	51	10	4	1	5	13
1986-87	Hartford Whalers	79	20	21	41	28	6	2	4	6	10
1987-88	Hartford Whalers	56	11	10	21	59	6	2	2	4	4
1988-89	Minnesota North Stars	73	8	18	26	34	5	3	1	4	10
1989-90	Minnesota North Stars	80	12	13	25	76	7	0	2	2	12
1990-91	Minnesota North Stars	38	4	4	8	36	21	3	10	13	20
1991-92	Minnesota North Stars	35	5	4	9	27	7	0	0	0	6
1992-93	Minnesota North Stars	63	10	8	18	59	....	....	....	....	....
	NHL Totals	**768**	**130**	**155**	**285**	**584**	**66**	**14**	**20**	**34**	**75**

Traded to **Hartford** by **Toronto** for Chris Kotsopoulos, October 7, 1985. Claimed by **Minnesota** from **Hartford** in Waiver Draft, October 3, 1988.

GEALE, Bob

Center. Shoots right. 5'11", 175 lbs. Born, Edmonton, Alta., April 17, 1962.
(Pittsburgh's 6th choice, 156th overall, in 1980 Entry Draft).

Season	Club	REGULAR SEASON GP	G	A	Pts	PIM	PLAYOFFS GP	G	A	Pts	PIM
1984-85	Pittsburgh Penguins	1	0	0	0	2	....	....	....	....	....
	NHL Totals	**1**	**0**	**0**	**0**	**2**	....	....	....	....	....

GEE, George

Center. Shoots left. 5'11", 180 lbs. Born, Stratford, Ont., June 28, 1922.

Season	Club	REGULAR SEASON GP	G	A	Pts	PIM	PLAYOFFS GP	G	A	Pts	PIM
1945-46	Chicago Black Hawks	35	14	15	29	12	4	1	1	2	4
1946-47	Chicago Black Hawks	60	20	20	40	26	....	....	....	....	....
1947-48	Chicago Black Hawks	60	14	25	39	18	....	....	....	....	....
1948-49	Chicago Black Hawks	4	0	2	2	4	....	....	....	....	....
	Detroit Red Wings	47	7	12	19	27	10	1	3	4	22
1949-50 ◆	Detroit Red Wings	69	17	21	38	42	14	3	*6	9	0
1950-51	Detroit Red Wings	70	17	20	37	19	6	0	1	1	0
1951-52	Chicago Black Hawks	70	18	31	49	39	....	....	....	....	....
1952-53	Chicago Black Hawks	67	18	21	39	99	7	1	2	3	6
1953-54	Chicago Black Hawks	69	10	16	26	59	....	....	....	....	....
	NHL Totals	**551**	**135**	**183**	**318**	**345**	**41**	**6**	**13**	**19**	**32**

Played in NHL All-Star Game (1950)

Signed as a free agent by **Chicago**, November 10, 1941. Traded to **Detroit** by **Chicago** with Bud Poile for Jim Conacher, Bep Guidolin and Doug McCaig, October 25, 1948. Traded to **Chicago** by **Detroit** with Jim McFadden, Max McNab, Jimmy Peters Sr., Clare Martin and Rags Raglan for $75,000 and future considerations (Hugh Coflin, October, 1951), August 20, 1951.

GELDART, Gary

Defense. Shoots left. 5'8", 160 lbs. Born, Moncton, N.B., June 14, 1950.
(Minnesota's 7th choice, 89th overall, in 1970 Amateur Draft).

Season	Club	REGULAR SEASON GP	G	A	Pts	PIM	PLAYOFFS GP	G	A	Pts	PIM
1970-71	Minnesota North Stars	4	0	0	0	5	....	....	....	....	....
	NHL Totals	**4**	**0**	**0**	**0**	**5**	....	....	....	....	....

Traded to **Montreal** by **Minnesota** for cash, September, 1973.

GELINAS, Martin

Left wing. Shoots left. 5'11", 195 lbs. Born, Shawinigan, Que., June 5, 1970.
(Los Angeles' 1st choice, 7th overall, in 1988 Entry Draft).

Season	Club	REGULAR SEASON GP	G	A	Pts	PIM	PLAYOFFS GP	G	A	Pts	PIM
1988-89	Edmonton Oilers	6	1	2	3	0	....	....	....	....	....
1989-90 ◆	Edmonton Oilers	46	17	8	25	30	20	2	3	5	6
1990-91	Edmonton Oilers	73	20	20	40	34	18	3	6	9	25
1991-92	Edmonton Oilers	68	11	18	29	62	15	1	3	4	10
1992-93	Edmonton Oilers	65	11	12	23	30	....	....	....	....	....
1993-94	Quebec Nordiques	31	6	6	12	8	....	....	....	....	....
	Vancouver Canucks	33	8	8	16	26	24	5	4	9	14
1994-95	Vancouver Canucks	46	13	10	23	36	3	0	1	1	0
1995-96	Vancouver Canucks	81	30	26	56	59	6	1	1	2	12
1996-97	Vancouver Canucks	74	35	33	68	42	....	....	....	....	....
1997-98	Vancouver Canucks	24	4	4	8	10	....	....	....	....	....
	Carolina Hurricanes	40	12	14	26	30	....	....	....	....	....
1998-99	Carolina Hurricanes	76	13	15	28	67	6	0	3	3	2
99-2000	Carolina Hurricanes	81	14	16	30	40	....	....	....	....	....
2000-01	Carolina Hurricanes	79	23	29	52	59	6	0	1	1	6
2001-02	Carolina Hurricanes	72	13	16	29	30	23	3	4	7	10
2002-03	Calgary Flames	81	21	31	52	51	....	....	....	....	....
	NHL Totals	**976**	**252**	**268**	**520**	**614**	**121**	**15**	**26**	**41**	**85**

Traded to **Edmonton** by **Los Angeles** with Jimmy Carson and Los Angeles' 1st round choices in 1989 (later traded to New Jersey – New Jersey selected Jason Miller), 1991 (Martin Rucinsky) and 1993 (Nick Stajduhar) Entry Drafts and cash for Wayne Gretzky, Mike Krushelnyski and Marty McSorley, August 9, 1988. Traded to **Quebec** by **Edmonton** with Edmonton's 6th round choice (Nicholas Checco) in 1993 Entry Draft for Scott Pearson, June 20, 1993. Claimed on waivers by **Vancouver** from **Quebec**, January 15, 1994. Traded to **Carolina** by **Vancouver** with Kirk McLean for Sean Burke, Geoff Sanderson and Enrico Ciccone, January 3, 1998. Signed as a free agent by **Calgary**, July 2, 2002.

GENDRON, Jean-Guy

Left wing. Shoots left. 5'9", 165 lbs. Born, Montreal, Que., August 30, 1934.

Season	Club	REGULAR SEASON GP	G	A	Pts	PIM	PLAYOFFS GP	G	A	Pts	PIM
1955-56	New York Rangers	63	5	7	12	38	5	2	1	3	2
1956-57	New York Rangers	70	9	6	15	40	5	0	1	1	6
1957-58	New York Rangers	70	10	17	27	68	6	1	0	1	11
1958-59	Boston Bruins	60	15	9	24	57	7	1	0	1	18
1959-60	Boston Bruins	67	24	11	35	64	....	....	....	....	....
1960-61	Boston Bruins	13	1	7	8	24	....	....	....	....	....
	Montreal Canadiens	53	9	12	21	51	5	0	0	0	2
1961-62	New York Rangers	69	14	11	25	71	6	3	1	4	2
1962-63	Boston Bruins	66	21	22	43	42	....	....	....	....	....
1963-64	Boston Bruins	54	5	13	18	43	....	....	....	....	....
1967-68	Philadelphia Flyers	1	0	1	1	2	....	....	....	....	....
1968-69	Philadelphia Flyers	74	20	35	55	65	4	0	0	0	6
1969-70	Philadelphia Flyers	71	23	21	44	54	....	....	....	....	....
1970-71	Philadelphia Flyers	76	20	16	36	46	4	0	1	1	0
1971-72	Philadelphia Flyers	56	6	13	19	36	....	....	....	....	....
	NHL Totals	**863**	**182**	**201**	**383**	**701**	**42**	**7**	**4**	**11**	**47**

Traded to **NY Rangers** by **Providence** (AHL) for Bill Ezinicki and cash, May 8, 1955. Claimed by **Boston** from **NY Rangers** in Intra-League Draft, June 3, 1958. Traded to **Montreal** by **Boston** for Andre Pronovost, November 27, 1960. Claimed by **NY Rangers** from **Montreal** in Intra-League Draft, June 13, 1961. Claimed by **Boston** from **NY Rangers** in Intra-League Draft, June 4, 1962. NHL rights transferred to **Philadelphia** after NHL club purchased **Quebec** (AHL) franchise, May 8, 1967. Claimed by **Montreal** from **Philadelphia** in Intra-League Draft, June 11, 1969. Traded to **Philadelphia** by **Montreal** for cash, June 12, 1969.

GENDRON, Martin

Right wing. Shoots right. 5'9", 190 lbs. Born, Valleyfield, Que., February 15, 1974.
(Washington's 4th choice, 71st overall, in 1992 Entry Draft).

Season	Club	REGULAR SEASON GP	G	A	Pts	PIM	PLAYOFFS GP	G	A	Pts	PIM
1994-95	Washington Capitals	8	2	1	3	2	....	....	....	....	....
1995-96	Washington Capitals	20	2	1	3	8	....	....	....	....	....
1997-98	Chicago Blackhawks	2	0	0	0	0	....	....	....	....	....
	NHL Totals	**30**	**4**	**2**	**6**	**10**	....	....	....	....	....

Traded to **Chicago** by **Washington** with Washington's 6th round choice (Jonathan Pelletier) in 1998 Entry Draft for Chicago's 5th round choice (Erik Wendell) in 1998 Entry Draft, October 10, 1997. Traded to **Montreal** by **Chicago** for David Ling, March 14, 1998. Signed as a free agent **Vancouver**, August 25, 1999.

GEOFFRION, Bernie — HHOF

Right wing. Shoots right. 5'9", 166 lbs. Born, Montreal, Que., February 16, 1931.

Season	Club	REGULAR SEASON GP	G	A	Pts	PIM	PLAYOFFS GP	G	A	Pts	PIM
1950-51	Montreal Canadiens	18	8	6	14	9	11	1	1	2	6
1951-52	Montreal Canadiens	67	30	24	54	66	11	3	1	4	6
1952-53 ◆	Montreal Canadiens	65	22	17	39	37	12	6	4	10	12
1953-54	Montreal Canadiens	54	29	25	54	87	11	*6	5	11	18
1954-55	Montreal Canadiens	70	*38	37	*75	57	12	8	5	13	8
1955-56 ◆	Montreal Canadiens	59	29	33	62	66	10	5	9	14	6
1956-57 ◆	Montreal Canadiens	41	19	21	40	18	10	*11	7	*18	2
1957-58 ◆	Montreal Canadiens	42	27	23	50	51	10	6	5	11	2
1958-59 ◆	Montreal Canadiens	59	22	44	66	30	11	5	8	13	10
1959-60 ◆	Montreal Canadiens	59	30	41	71	36	8	2	*10	*12	4
1960-61	Montreal Canadiens	64	*50	45	*95	29	4	2	1	3	0
1961-62	Montreal Canadiens	62	23	36	59	36	5	0	1	1	6
1962-63	Montreal Canadiens	51	23	18	41	73	5	0	1	1	4
1963-64	Montreal Canadiens	55	21	18	39	41	7	1	1	2	4
1966-67	New York Rangers	58	17	25	42	42	4	2	0	2	0
1967-68	New York Rangers	59	5	16	21	11	1	0	1	1	0
	NHL Totals	**883**	**393**	**429**	**822**	**689**	**132**	**58**	**60**	**118**	**88**

• Father of Danny • Calder Memorial Trophy (1952) • NHL Second All-Star Team (1955, 1960) • Art Ross Trophy (1955, 1961) • NHL First All-Star Team (1961) • Hart Trophy (1961)

Played in NHL All-Star Game (1952, 1953, 1954, 1955, 1956, 1958, 1959, 1960, 1961, 1962, 1963)

Signed as a free agent by **Montreal**, February 14, 1951. Claimed on waivers by **NY Rangers** from **Montreal**, June 9, 1966.

GEOFFRION, Danny

Right wing. Shoots right. 5'10", 185 lbs. Born, Montreal, Que., January 24, 1958.
(Montreal's 1st choice, 8th overall, in 1978 Amateur Draft).

Season	Club	REGULAR SEASON GP	G	A	Pts	PIM	PLAYOFFS GP	G	A	Pts	PIM
1979-80	Montreal Canadiens	32	0	6	6	12	2	0	0	0	7
1980-81	Winnipeg Jets	78	20	26	46	82	....	....	....	....	....
1981-82	Winnipeg Jets	1	0	0	0	5	....	....	....	....	....
	NHL Totals	**111**	**20**	**32**	**52**	**99**	**2**	**0**	**0**	**0**	**7**

• Son of Bernie

Reclaimed by **Montreal** from **Quebec** prior to Expansion Draft, June 9, 1979. Claimed by **Quebec** from **Montreal** in Waiver Draft, October 8, 1980. Traded to **Winnipeg** by **Quebec** for cash, October 8, 1980.

GERAN, Gerry

Center. Shoots right. 5'9", 180 lbs. Born, Holyoke, MA, August 3, 1896.

Season	Club	GP	G	A	Pts	PIM	GP	G	A	Pts	PIM
		REGULAR SEASON					PLAYOFFS				
1917-18	Montreal Wanderers	4	0	0	0	0	....	....	....	....	....
1925-26	Boston Bruins	33	5	1	6	6	....	....	....	....	....
	NHL Totals	**37**	**5**	**1**	**6**	**6**	....	....	....	....	....

Signed as a free agent by **Mtl. Wanderers**, December 3, 1917. Signed as a free agent by **Boston**, November 23, 1925. Traded to **St. Paul** (AHA) by **Boston** for cash, November 4, 1926.

GERARD, Eddie

HHOF

Left wing/Defense. Shoots left. 5'9", 168 lbs. Born, Ottawa, Ont., February 22, 1890.

Season	Club	GP	G	A	Pts	PIM	GP	G	A	Pts	PIM
1917-18	Ottawa Senators	20	13	7	20	26	....	....	....	....	....
1918-19	Ottawa Senators	18	4	*6	10	17	5	3	0	3	3
1919-20 ♦	Ottawa Senators	22	9	7	16	19	....	....	....	....	....
	Ottawa Senators (Cup)	....	....	....	....	....	*5*	*2*	*1*	*3*	*3*
1920-21 ♦	Ottawa Senators	24	11	4	15	18	2	1	0	1	*6
	Ottawa Senators (Cup)	....	....	....	....	....	*5*	*0*	*0*	*0*	*44*
1921-22	Ottawa Senators	21	7	11	18	16	2	0	0	0	8
	♦ *Toronto St. Pats (Cup)*	....	....	....	....	....	*5*	*0*	*2*	*2*	*0*
1922-23 ♦	Ottawa Senators	23	6	13	19	12	2	0	0	0	0
	Ottawa Senators (Cup)	....	....	....	....	....	*6*	*1*	*0*	*1*	*4*
	NHL Totals	**128**	**50**	**48**	**98**	**108**	**11**	**4**	**0**	**4**	**17**

Rights retained by **Ottawa** after NHA folded, November 26, 1917. Loaned to **Toronto** by **Ottawa** as an emergency injury replacement, March 25, 1922. • 1922-23 Stanley Cup totals includes series with Regina (WCHL) and Edmonton (PCHA).

GERMAIN, Eric

Defense. Shoots left. 6'1", 195 lbs. Born, Quebec City, Que., June 26, 1966.

Season	Club	GP	G	A	Pts	PIM	GP	G	A	Pts	PIM
1987-88	Los Angeles Kings	4	0	1	1	13	1	0	0	0	4
	NHL Totals	**4**	**0**	**1**	**1**	**13**	**1**	**0**	**0**	**0**	**4**

Signed as a free agent by **Los Angeles**, July 1, 1986. Signed as a free agent by **NY Rangers**, July 11, 1990.

GERNANDER, Ken

Right wing. Shoots left. 5'10", 175 lbs. Born, Coleraine, MN, June 30, 1969.
(Winnipeg's 4th choice, 96th overall, in 1987 Entry Draft).

Season	Club	GP	G	A	Pts	PIM	GP	G	A	Pts	PIM
1995-96	New York Rangers	10	2	3	5	4	6	0	0	0	0
1996-97	New York Rangers	....	....	....	....	....	9	0	0	0	0
	NHL Totals	**10**	**2**	**3**	**5**	**4**	**15**	**0**	**0**	**0**	**0**

Signed as a free agent by **NY Rangers**, July 4, 1994.

GETLIFFE, Ray

Center/Left wing. Shoots left. 5'11", 175 lbs. Born, Galt, Ont., April 3, 1914.

Season	Club	GP	G	A	Pts	PIM	GP	G	A	Pts	PIM
1935-36	Boston Bruins	1	0	0	0	2	2	0	0	0	0
1936-37	Boston Bruins	48	16	15	31	28	3	2	1	3	2
1937-38	Boston Bruins	36	11	13	24	16	3	0	1	1	2
1938-39 ♦	Boston Bruins	43	10	12	22	11	11	1	1	2	2
1939-40	Montreal Canadiens	46	11	12	23	29	....	....	....	....	....
1940-41	Montreal Canadiens	39	15	10	25	25	3	1	1	2	0
1941-42	Montreal Canadiens	45	11	15	26	35	3	0	0	0	0
1942-43	Montreal Canadiens	50	18	28	46	26	5	0	1	1	8
1943-44 ♦	Montreal Canadiens	44	28	25	53	44	9	5	4	9	16
1944-45	Montreal Canadiens	41	16	7	23	34	6	0	1	1	0
	NHL Totals	**393**	**136**	**137**	**273**	**250**	**45**	**9**	**10**	**19**	**30**

Played in NHL All-Star Game (1939)

Signed as a free agent by **NY Rangers**, November 8, 1935. Traded to **Boston** by **NY Rangers** for cash, December 28, 1935. • Walter Jackson loaned to London (IHL) as compensation, December 31, 1935. Traded to **Montreal** by **Boston** with Charlie Sands for Herb Cain, October 10, 1939. Traded to **Detroit** by **Montreal** with Roly Rossignol for Billy Reay, September 11, 1945. Detroit received Fern Gauthier as compensation when Getliffe decided to retire, October 18, 1945.

GIALLONARDO, Mario

Defense. Shoots left. 5'11", 201 lbs. Born, Toronto, Ont., September 23, 1957.

Season	Club	GP	G	A	Pts	PIM	GP	G	A	Pts	PIM
1979-80	Colorado Rockies	8	0	1	1	2	....	....	....	....	....
1980-81	Colorado Rockies	15	0	2	2	4	....	....	....	....	....
	NHL Totals	**23**	**0**	**3**	**3**	**6**	....	....	....	....	....

Signed as a free agent by **Colorado**, December 21, 1978.

GIBBS, Barry

Defense. Shoots right. 5'11", 195 lbs. Born, Lloydminster, Sask., September 28, 1948.
(Boston's 1st choice, 1st overall, in 1966 Amateur Draft).

Season	Club	GP	G	A	Pts	PIM	GP	G	A	Pts	PIM
1967-68	Boston Bruins	16	0	0	0	2	....	....	....	....	....
1968-69	Boston Bruins	8	0	0	0	2	....	....	....	....	....
1969-70	Minnesota North Stars	56	3	13	16	182	6	1	0	1	7
1970-71	Minnesota North Stars	68	5	15	20	132	12	0	1	1	47
1971-72	Minnesota North Stars	75	4	20	24	128	7	1	1	2	9
1972-73	Minnesota North Stars	63	10	24	34	54	5	1	0	1	0
1973-74	Minnesota North Stars	76	9	29	38	82	....	....	....	....	....
1974-75	Minnesota North Stars	37	4	20	24	22	....	....	....	....	....
	Atlanta Flames	39	3	13	16	39	....	....	....	....	....
1975-76	Atlanta Flames	76	8	21	29	92	2	1	0	1	2
1976-77	Atlanta Flames	66	1	16	17	63	3	0	0	0	2
1977-78	Atlanta Flames	27	1	5	6	24	....	....	....	....	....
	St. Louis Blues	51	6	12	18	45	....	....	....	....	....
1978-79	St. Louis Blues	76	2	27	29	46	....	....	....	....	....
1979-80	Los Angeles Kings	63	2	9	11	32	1	0	0	0	0
	NHL Totals	**797**	**58**	**224**	**282**	**945**	**36**	**4**	**2**	**6**	**67**

Played in NHL All-Star Game (1973)

Traded to **Minnesota** by **Boston** with Tommy Williams for Minnesota's 1st round choice (Don Tannahill) in 1969 Amateur Draft and future considerations (Fred O'Donnell, May 7, 1971), May 7, 1969. Traded to **Atlanta** by **Minnesota** for Dean Talafous and Dwight Bialowas, January 3, 1975. Traded to **St. Louis** by **Atlanta** with Phil Myre and Curt Bennett for Yves Belanger, Dick Redmond, Bob MacMillan and St. Louis' 2nd round choice (Mike Perovich) in 1979 Entry Draft, December 12, 1977. Traded to **NY Islanders** by **St. Louis** with Terry Richardson for future considerations, June 9, 1979. Traded to **Los Angeles** by **NY Islanders** for future considerations (Tom Williams, August 16, 1979), June 9, 1979.

GIBSON, Don

Defense. Shoots right. 6'1", 210 lbs. Born, Deloraine, Man., December 29, 1967.
(Vancouver's 2nd choice, 49th overall, in 1986 Entry Draft).

Season	Club	GP	G	A	Pts	PIM	GP	G	A	Pts	PIM
1990-91	Vancouver Canucks	14	0	3	3	20	....	....	....	....	....
	NHL Totals	**14**	**0**	**3**	**3**	**20**	....	....	....	....	....

GIBSON, Doug

Center. Shoots left. 5'10", 175 lbs. Born, Peterborough, Ont., September 28, 1953.
(Boston's 3rd choice, 36th overall, in 1973 Amateur Draft).

Season	Club	GP	G	A	Pts	PIM	GP	G	A	Pts	PIM
1973-74	Boston Bruins	2	0	0	0	0	1	0	0	0	0
1975-76	Boston Bruins	50	7	18	25	0	....	....	....	....	....
1977-78	Washington Capitals	11	2	1	3	0	....	....	....	....	....
	NHL Totals	**63**	**9**	**19**	**28**	**0**	**1**	**0**	**0**	**0**	**0**

Claimed on waivers by **Washington** from **Boston**, May 29, 1977.

GIBSON, John

Defense. Shoots left. 6'3", 210 lbs. Born, St. Catharines, Ont., June 2, 1959.
(Los Angeles' 5th choice, 71st overall, in 1979 Entry Draft).

Season	Club	GP	G	A	Pts	PIM	GP	G	A	Pts	PIM
1980-81	Los Angeles Kings	4	0	0	0	21	....	....	....	....	....
1981-82	Los Angeles Kings	6	0	0	0	18	....	....	....	....	....
	Toronto Maple Leafs	27	0	2	2	67	....	....	....	....	....
1983-84	Winnipeg Jets	11	0	0	0	14	....	....	....	....	....
	NHL Totals	**48**	**0**	**2**	**2**	**120**	....	....	....	....	....

Traded to **Toronto** by **Los Angeles** with Billy Harris for Ian Turnbull, November 11, 1981. Signed as a free agent by **Winnipeg**, September 19, 1983.

GIESEBRECHT, Gus

Center. Shoots left. 6', 177 lbs. Born, Pembroke, Ont., September 14, 1917.

Season	Club	GP	G	A	Pts	PIM	GP	G	A	Pts	PIM
1938-39	Detroit Red Wings	28	10	10	20	2	6	0	2	2	0
1939-40	Detroit Red Wings	30	4	7	11	2	....	....	....	....	....
1940-41	Detroit Red Wings	43	7	18	25	7	9	2	1	3	0
1941-42	Detroit Red Wings	34	6	16	22	2	2	0	0	0	0
	NHL Totals	**135**	**27**	**51**	**78**	**13**	**17**	**2**	**3**	**5**	**0**

GIFFIN, Lee

Right wing. Shoots right. 6', 188 lbs. Born, Chatham, Ont., April 1, 1967.
(Pittsburgh's 2nd choice, 23rd overall, in 1985 Entry Draft).

Season	Club	GP	G	A	Pts	PIM	GP	G	A	Pts	PIM
1986-87	Pittsburgh Penguins	8	1	1	2	0	....	....	....	....	....
1987-88	Pittsburgh Penguins	19	0	2	2	9	....	....	....	....	....
	NHL Totals	**27**	**1**	**3**	**4**	**9**	....	....	....	....	....

Traded to **NY Rangers** by **Pittsburgh** for future considerations, September 14, 1989.

GILBERT, Ed

Center. Shoots left. 6', 185 lbs. Born, Hamilton, Ont., March 12, 1952.
(Montreal's 5th choice, 46th overall, in 1972 Amateur Draft).

Season	Club	GP	G	A	Pts	PIM	GP	G	A	Pts	PIM
1974-75	Kansas City Scouts	80	16	22	38	14	....	....	....	....	....
1975-76	Kansas City Scouts	41	4	8	12	8	....	....	....	....	....
	Pittsburgh Penguins	38	1	1	2	0	....	....	....	....	....
1976-77	Pittsburgh Penguins	7	0	0	0	0	....	....	....	....	....
	NHL Totals	**166**	**21**	**31**	**52**	**22**	....	....	....	....	....

Claimed by **Kansas City** from **Montreal** in Expansion Draft, June 12, 1974. Traded to **Pittsburgh** by **Kansas City** with Simon Nolet and Kansas City's 1st round choice (Blair Chapman) in 1976 Amateur Draft for Steve Durbano, Chuck Arnason and Pittsburgh's 1st round choice (Greg Carroll) in 1976 Amateur Draft, January 9, 1976.

GILBERT, Greg

Left wing. Shoots left. 6'1", 191 lbs. Born, Mississauga, Ont., January 22, 1962.
(NY Islanders' 5th choice, 80th overall, in 1980 Entry Draft).

Season	Club	GP	G	A	Pts	PIM	GP	G	A	Pts	PIM
1981-82 ♦	New York Islanders	1	1	0	1	0	4	1	1	2	2
1982-83 ♦	New York Islanders	45	8	11	19	30	10	1	0	1	14
1983-84	New York Islanders	79	31	35	66	59	21	5	7	12	39
1984-85	New York Islanders	58	13	25	38	36	....	....	....	....	....
1985-86	New York Islanders	60	9	19	28	82	2	0	0	0	9
1986-87	New York Islanders	51	6	7	13	26	10	2	2	4	6
1987-88	New York Islanders	76	17	28	45	46	4	0	0	0	6
1988-89	New York Islanders	55	8	13	21	45	....	....	....	....	....
	Chicago Blackhawks	4	0	0	0	0	15	1	5	6	20
1989-90	Chicago Blackhawks	70	12	25	37	54	19	5	8	13	34
1990-91	Chicago Blackhawks	72	10	15	25	58	5	0	1	1	2
1991-92	Chicago Blackhawks	50	7	5	12	35	10	1	3	4	16
1992-93	Chicago Blackhawks	77	13	19	32	57	3	0	0	0	0
1993-94 ♦	New York Rangers	76	4	11	15	29	23	1	3	4	8

Season	Club	GP	G	A	Pts	PIM	GP	G	A	Pts	PIM
		REGULAR SEASON					PLAYOFFS				
1994-95	St. Louis Blues	46	11	14	25	11	7	0	3	3	6
1995-96	St. Louis Blues	17	0	1	1	8	....	....	....	....	....
	NHL Totals	**837**	**150**	**228**	**378**	**576**	**133**	**17**	**33**	**50**	**162**

Traded to **Chicago** by **NY Islanders** for Chicago's 5th round choice (Steve Young) in 1989 Entry Draft, March 7, 1989. Signed as a free agent by **NY Rangers**, July 29, 1993. Claimed by **St. Louis** from **NY Rangers** in Waiver Draft, January 19, 1995.

GILBERT, Jeannot

Center. Shoots left. 5'10", 170 lbs. Born, Grande Baie, Que., December 29, 1940.

Season	Club	GP	G	A	Pts	PIM	GP	G	A	Pts	PIM
1962-63	Boston Bruins	5	0	0	0	4	....	....	....	....	....
1964-65	Boston Bruins	4	0	1	1	0	....	....	....	....	....
	NHL Totals	**9**	**0**	**1**	**1**	**4**	....	....	....	....	....

Claimed by **Pittsburgh** from **Boston** in Expansion Draft, June 6, 1967. Traded to **Hershey** (AHL) by **Pittsburgh** for Gene Ubriaco, October, 1967.

GILBERT, Rod

HHOF

Right wing. Shoots right. 5'9", 180 lbs. Born, Montreal, Que., July 1, 1941.

Season	Club	GP	G	A	Pts	PIM	GP	G	A	Pts	PIM
1960-61	New York Rangers	1	0	1	1	2	....	....	....	....	....
1961-62	New York Rangers	1	0	0	0	0	4	2	3	5	4
1962-63	New York Rangers	70	11	20	31	20	....	....	....	....	....
1963-64	New York Rangers	70	24	40	64	62	....	....	....	....	....
1964-65	New York Rangers	70	25	36	61	52	....	....	....	....	....
1965-66	New York Rangers	34	10	15	25	20	....	....	....	....	....
1966-67	New York Rangers	64	28	18	46	12	4	2	2	4	6
1967-68	New York Rangers	73	29	48	77	12	6	5	0	5	4
1968-69	New York Rangers	66	28	49	77	22	4	1	0	1	2
1969-70	New York Rangers	72	16	37	53	22	6	4	5	9	0
1970-71	New York Rangers	78	30	31	61	65	13	4	6	10	8
1971-72	New York Rangers	73	43	54	97	64	16	7	8	15	11
1972-73	New York Rangers	76	25	59	84	25	10	5	1	6	2
1973-74	New York Rangers	75	36	41	77	20	13	3	5	8	4
1974-75	New York Rangers	76	36	61	97	22	3	1	3	4	2
1975-76	New York Rangers	70	36	50	86	32	....	....	....	....	....
1976-77	New York Rangers	77	27	48	75	50	....	....	....	....	....
1977-78	New York Rangers	19	2	7	9	6	....	....	....	....	....
	NHL Totals	**1065**	**406**	**615**	**1021**	**508**	**79**	**34**	**33**	**67**	**43**

NHL Second All-Star Team (1968) • NHL First All-Star Team (1972) • Bill Masterton Trophy (1976) • Lester Patrick Trophy (1991)

Played in NHL All-Star Game (1964, 1965, 1967, 1969, 1970, 1972, 1975, 1977)

GILBERTSON, Stan

Left wing. Shoots left. 6', 175 lbs. Born, Duluth, MN, October 29, 1944.

Season	Club	GP	G	A	Pts	PIM	GP	G	A	Pts	PIM
1971-72	California Golden Seals	78	16	16	32	47	....	....	....	....	....
1972-73	California Golden Seals	66	6	15	21	19	....	....	....	....	....
1973-74	California Golden Seals	76	18	12	30	39	....	....	....	....	....
1974-75	California Golden Seals	15	1	4	5	2	....	....	....	....	....
	St. Louis Blues	22	1	4	5	4	....	....	....	....	....
	Washington Capitals	25	11	7	18	12	....	....	....	....	....
1975-76	Washington Capitals	31	13	14	27	6	....	....	....	....	....
	Pittsburgh Penguins	48	13	8	21	6	3	1	1	2	2
1976-77	Pittsburgh Penguins	67	6	9	15	13	....	....	....	....	....
	NHL Totals	**428**	**85**	**89**	**174**	**148**	**3**	**1**	**1**	**2**	**2**

Signed as a free agent by **Boston** (San Francisco-WHL), January 13, 1966. Traded to **Vancouver** (WHL) by **Boston** for cash, October, 1967. Traded to **Boston** by **Vancouver** (WHL) for cash, June, 1968. Claimed by **California** from **Boston** in Intra-League Draft, June 8, 1971. Traded to **St. Louis** by **California** with Craig Patrick for Dave Gardner and Butch Williams, November 11, 1974. Traded to **Washington** by **St. Louis** with Garnet Bailey for Denis Dupere, February 10, 1975. Traded to **Pittsburgh** by **Washington** for Harvey Bennett Jr., December 16, 1975. • Suffered career-ending leg injury in automobile accident, September 30, 1977.

GILCHRIST, Brent

Left wing. Shoots left. 5'11", 180 lbs. Born, Moose Jaw, Sask., April 3, 1967. (Montreal's 6th choice, 79th overall, in 1985 Entry Draft).

Season	Club	GP	G	A	Pts	PIM	GP	G	A	Pts	PIM
1988-89	Montreal Canadiens	49	8	16	24	16	9	1	1	2	10
1989-90	Montreal Canadiens	57	9	15	24	28	8	2	0	2	2
1990-91	Montreal Canadiens	51	6	9	15	10	13	5	3	8	6
1991-92	Montreal Canadiens	79	23	27	50	57	11	2	4	6	6
1992-93	Edmonton Oilers	60	10	10	20	47	....	....	....	....	....
	Minnesota North Stars	8	0	1	1	2	....	....	....	....	....
1993-94	Dallas Stars	76	17	14	31	31	9	3	1	4	2
1994-95	Dallas Stars	32	9	4	13	16	5	0	1	1	2
1995-96	Dallas Stars	77	20	22	42	36	....	....	....	....	....
1996-97	Dallas Stars	67	10	20	30	24	6	2	2	4	2
1997-98 ♦	Detroit Red Wings	61	13	14	27	40	15	2	1	3	12
1998-99	Detroit Red Wings	5	1	0	1	0	3	0	0	0	0
99-2000	Detroit Red Wings	24	4	2	6	24	6	0	0	0	6
2000-01	Detroit Red Wings	60	1	8	9	41	5	0	1	1	0
2001-02	Detroit Red Wings	19	1	1	2	8	....	....	....	....	....
	Dallas Stars	26	2	5	7	6	....	....	....	....	....
2002-03	Nashville Predators	41	1	2	3	14	....	....	....	....	....
	NHL Totals	**792**	**135**	**170**	**305**	**400**	**90**	**17**	**14**	**31**	**48**

Traded to **Edmonton** by **Montreal** with Shayne Corson and Vladimir Vujtek for Vincent Damphousse and Edmonton's 4th round choice (Adam Wiesel) in 1993 Entry Draft, August 27, 1992. Traded to **Minnesota** by **Edmonton** for Todd Elik, March 5, 1993. Transferred to **Dallas** after **Minnesota** franchise relocated, June 9, 1993. Signed as a free agent by **Detroit**, August 1, 1997. Claimed by **Tampa Bay** from **Detroit** in Waiver Draft, October 5, 1998. Traded to **Detroit** by **Tampa Bay** for future considerations, October 5, 1998. • Missed majority of 1998-99 and 1999-2000 seasons recovering from hernia surgery, September 22, 1998. Claimed on waivers by **Dallas** from **Detroit**, February 13, 2002. Signed as a free agent by **Nashville**, July 11, 2002. • Missed majority of 2002-03 season recovering from back injury suffered in game vs. Edmonton, January 18, 2003.

GILES, Curt

Defense. Shoots left. 5'8", 175 lbs. Born, The Pas, Man., November 30, 1958. (Minnesota's 4th choice, 54th overall, in 1978 Amateur Draft).

Season	Club	GP	G	A	Pts	PIM	GP	G	A	Pts	PIM
1979-80	Minnesota North Stars	37	2	7	9	31	12	2	4	6	10
1980-81	Minnesota North Stars	67	5	22	27	56	19	1	4	5	14
1981-82	Minnesota North Stars	74	3	12	15	87	4	0	0	0	2
1982-83	Minnesota North Stars	76	2	21	23	70	5	0	2	2	6
1983-84	Minnesota North Stars	70	6	22	28	59	16	1	3	4	25
1984-85	Minnesota North Stars	77	5	25	30	49	9	0	0	0	17
1985-86	Minnesota North Stars	69	6	21	27	30	5	0	1	1	10
1986-87	Minnesota North Stars	11	0	3	3	4	....	....	....	....	....
	New York Rangers	61	2	17	19	50	5	0	0	0	6
1987-88	New York Rangers	13	0	0	0	10	....	....	....	....	....
	Minnesota North Stars	59	1	12	13	66	....	....	....	....	....
1988-89	Minnesota North Stars	76	5	10	15	77	5	0	0	0	4
1989-90	Minnesota North Stars	74	1	12	13	48	7	0	1	1	6
1990-91	Minnesota North Stars	70	4	10	14	48	10	1	0	1	16
1991-92	St. Louis Blues	13	1	1	2	8	3	1	1	2	0
1992-93	St. Louis Blues	48	0	4	4	40	3	0	0	0	2
	NHL Totals	**895**	**43**	**199**	**242**	**733**	**103**	**6**	**16**	**22**	**118**

Traded to **NY Rangers** by **Minnesota** with Tony McKegney and Minnesota's 2nd round choice (Troy Mallette) in 1988 Entry Draft for Bob Brooke and Minnesota's 4th round choice (previously acquired, Minnesota selected Jeffrey Stolp) in 1988 Entry Draft, November 13, 1986. Traded to **Minnesota** by **NY Rangers** for Byron Lomow and future considerations, November 20, 1987. Signed as a free agent by **St. Louis**, February 29, 1992.

GILHEN, Randy

Center. Shoots left. 6', 190 lbs. Born, Zweibrucken, West Germany, June 13, 1963. (Hartford's 6th choice, 109th overall, in 1982 Entry Draft).

Season	Club	GP	G	A	Pts	PIM	GP	G	A	Pts	PIM
1982-83	Hartford Whalers	2	0	1	1	0	....	....	....	....	....
1986-87	Winnipeg Jets	2	0	0	0	0	....	....	....	....	....
1987-88	Winnipeg Jets	13	3	2	5	15	4	1	0	1	10
1988-89	Winnipeg Jets	64	5	3	8	38	....	....	....	....	....
1989-90	Pittsburgh Penguins	61	5	11	16	54	....	....	....	....	....
1990-91 ♦	Pittsburgh Penguins	72	15	10	25	51	16	1	0	1	14
1991-92	Los Angeles Kings	33	3	6	9	14	....	....	....	....	....
	New York Rangers	40	7	7	14	14	13	1	2	3	2
1992-93	New York Rangers	33	3	2	5	8	....	....	....	....	....
	Tampa Bay Lightning	11	0	2	2	6	....	....	....	....	....
1993-94	Florida Panthers	20	4	4	8	16	....	....	....	....	....
	Winnipeg Jets	40	3	3	6	34	....	....	....	....	....
1994-95	Winnipeg Jets	44	5	6	11	52	....	....	....	....	....
1995-96	Winnipeg Jets	22	2	3	5	12	....	....	....	....	....
	NHL Totals	**457**	**55**	**60**	**115**	**314**	**33**	**3**	**2**	**5**	**26**

Signed as a free agent by **Winnipeg**, November 8, 1985. Traded to **Pittsburgh** by **Winnipeg** with Jim Kyte and Andrew McBain for Randy Cunneyworth, Rick Tabaracci and Dave McLlwain, June 17, 1989. Claimed by **Minnesota** from **Pittsburgh** in Expansion Draft, May 30, 1991. Traded to **Los Angeles** by **Minnesota** with Charlie Huddy, Jim Thomson and NY Rangers' 4th round choice (previously acquired, Los Angeles selected Alexei Zhitnik) in 1991 Entry Draft for Todd Elik, June 22, 1991. Traded to **NY Rangers** by **Los Angeles** for Corey Millen, December 23, 1991. Traded to **Tampa Bay** by **NY Rangers** for Mike Hartman, March 22, 1993. Claimed by **Florida** from **Tampa Bay** in Expansion Draft, June 24, 1993. Traded to **Winnipeg** by **Florida** for Stu Barnes and St. Louis' 6th round choice (previously acquired, later traded to Edmonton – later traded back to Winnipeg – Winnipeg selected Chris Kibermanis) in 1994 Entry Draft, November 25, 1993.

GILL, Hal

Defense. Shoots left. 6'7", 230 lbs. Born, Concord, MA, April 6, 1975. (Boston's 8th choice, 207th overall, in 1993 Entry Draft).

Season	Club	GP	G	A	Pts	PIM	GP	G	A	Pts	PIM
1997-98	Boston Bruins	68	2	4	6	47	6	0	0	0	4
1998-99	Boston Bruins	80	3	7	10	63	12	0	0	0	14
99-2000	Boston Bruins	81	3	9	12	51	....	....	....	....	....
2000-01	Boston Bruins	80	1	10	11	71	....	....	....	....	....
2001-02	Boston Bruins	79	4	18	22	77	6	0	1	1	2
2002-03	Boston Bruins	76	4	13	17	56	5	0	0	0	4
	NHL Totals	**464**	**17**	**61**	**78**	**365**	**29**	**0**	**1**	**1**	**24**

GILL, Todd

Defense. Shoots left. 6', 180 lbs. Born, Cardinal, Ont., November 9, 1965. (Toronto's 2nd choice, 25th overall, in 1984 Entry Draft).

Season	Club	GP	G	A	Pts	PIM	GP	G	A	Pts	PIM
1984-85	Toronto Maple Leafs	10	1	0	1	13	....	....	....	....	....
1985-86	Toronto Maple Leafs	15	1	2	3	28	1	0	0	0	0
1986-87	Toronto Maple Leafs	61	4	27	31	92	13	2	2	4	42
1987-88	Toronto Maple Leafs	65	8	17	25	131	6	1	3	4	20
1988-89	Toronto Maple Leafs	59	11	14	25	72	....	....	....	....	....
1989-90	Toronto Maple Leafs	48	1	14	15	92	5	0	3	3	16

Season	Club	GP	G	A	Pts	PIM	GP	G	A	Pts	PIM
		REGULAR SEASON					PLAYOFFS				
1990-91	Toronto Maple Leafs	72	2	22	24	113	....	....	....	....	....
1991-92	Toronto Maple Leafs	74	2	15	17	91	....	....	....	....	....
1992-93	Toronto Maple Leafs	69	11	32	43	66	21	1	10	11	26
1993-94	Toronto Maple Leafs	45	4	24	28	44	18	1	5	6	37
1994-95	Toronto Maple Leafs	47	7	25	32	64	7	0	3	3	6
1995-96	Toronto Maple Leafs	74	7	18	25	116	6	0	0	0	24
1996-97	San Jose Sharks	79	0	21	21	101	....	....	....	....	....
1997-98	San Jose Sharks	64	8	13	21	31	....	....	....	....	....
	St. Louis Blues	11	5	4	9	10	10	2	2	4	10
1998-99	St. Louis Blues	28	2	3	5	16	....	....	....	....	....
	Detroit Red Wings	23	2	2	4	11	2	0	1	1	0
99-2000	Phoenix Coyotes	41	1	6	7	30	....	....	....	....	....
	Detroit Red Wings	13	2	0	2	15	9	0	1	1	4
2000-01	Detroit Red Wings	68	3	8	11	53	5	0	0	0	8
2001-02	Colorado Avalanche	36	0	4	4	25	....	....	....	....	....
2002-03	Chicago Blackhawks	5	0	1	1	0	....	....	....	....	....
	NHL Totals	**1007**	**82**	**272**	**354**	**1214**	**103**	**7**	**30**	**37**	**193**

Traded to **San Jose** by **Toronto** for Jamie Baker and San Jose's 5th round choice (Peter Cava) in 1996 Entry Draft, June 14, 1996. Traded to **St. Louis** by **San Jose** for Joe Murphy, March 24, 1998. Claimed on waivers by **Detroit** from **St. Louis**, December 30, 1998. Signed as a free agent by **Phoenix**, July 21, 1999. Traded to **Detroit** by **Phoenix** for Philippe Audet, March 13, 2000. Signed as a free agent by **Colorado**, July 24, 2001. • Released by **Colorado**, February 12, 2002. Signed as a free agent by **Chicago**, March 5, 2003.

GILLEN, Don

Right wing. Shoots right. 6'3", 210 lbs. Born, Dodsland, Sask., December 24, 1960.
(Philadelphia's 5th choice, 77th overall, in 1979 Entry Draft).

Season	Club	GP	G	A	Pts	PIM	GP	G	A	Pts	PIM
1979-80	Philadelphia Flyers	1	1	0	1	0	....	....	....	....	....
1981-82	Hartford Whalers	34	1	4	5	22	....	....	....	....	....
	NHL Totals	**35**	**2**	**4**	**6**	**22**	....	....	....	....	....

Traded to **Hartford** by **Philadelphia** with Rick MacLeish, Blake Wesley and Philadelphia's 1st (Paul Lawless), 2nd (Mark Paterson) and 3rd (Kevin Dineen) round choices in 1982 Entry Draft for Ray Allison, Fred Arthur and Hartford's 1st (Ron Sutter) and 3rd (Miroslav Dvorak) round choices in 1982 Entry Draft, July 3, 1981.

GILLIE, Farrand

Left wing/Defense. Shoots right. 5'10", 150 lbs. Born, Cornwall, Ont., May 11, 1905.

Season	Club	GP	G	A	Pts	PIM	GP	G	A	Pts	PIM
1928-29	Detroit Cougars	1	0	0	0	0	....	....	....	....	....
	NHL Totals	**1**	**0**	**0**	**0**	**0**	....	....	....	....	....

Signed as a free agent by **Detroit**, November 1, 1927. Transferred to **London** (IHL) by **Detroit** as compensation for Detroit's signing of free agent Gord Brydson, October 24, 1932.

GILLIES, Clark

HHOF

Left wing. Shoots left. 6'3", 215 lbs. Born, Moose Jaw, Sask., April 7, 1954.
(NY Islanders' 1st choice, 4th overall, in 1974 Amateur Draft).

Season	Club	GP	G	A	Pts	PIM	GP	G	A	Pts	PIM
1974-75	New York Islanders	80	25	22	47	66	17	4	2	6	36
1975-76	New York Islanders	80	34	27	61	96	13	2	4	6	16
1976-77	New York Islanders	70	33	22	55	93	12	4	4	8	15
1977-78	New York Islanders	80	35	50	85	76	7	2	0	2	15
1978-79	New York Islanders	75	35	56	91	68	10	1	2	3	11
1979-80 ◆	New York Islanders	73	19	35	54	49	21	6	10	16	63
1980-81 ◆	New York Islanders	80	33	45	78	99	18	6	9	15	28
1981-82 ◆	New York Islanders	79	38	39	77	75	19	8	6	14	34
1982-83 ◆	New York Islanders	70	21	20	41	76	8	0	2	2	10
1983-84	New York Islanders	76	12	16	28	65	21	12	7	19	19
1984-85	New York Islanders	54	15	17	32	73	10	1	0	1	9
1985-86	New York Islanders	55	4	10	14	55	3	1	0	1	6
1986-87	Buffalo Sabres	61	10	17	27	81	....	....	....	....	....
1987-88	Buffalo Sabres	25	5	2	7	51	5	0	1	1	25
	NHL Totals	**958**	**319**	**378**	**697**	**1023**	**164**	**47**	**47**	**94**	**287**

NHL First All-Star Team (1978, 1979)

Played in NHL All-Star Game (1978)

Claimed by **Buffalo** from **NY Islanders** in Waiver Draft, October 6, 1986. • Suffered eventual career-ending knee injury in game vs. Edmonton, November 7, 1987.

GILLIS, Jere

Left wing. Shoots left. 6', 194 lbs. Born, Bend, OR, January 18, 1957.
(Vancouver's 1st choice, 4th overall, in 1977 Amateur Draft).

Season	Club	GP	G	A	Pts	PIM	GP	G	A	Pts	PIM
1977-78	Vancouver Canucks	79	23	18	41	35	....	....	....	....	....
1978-79	Vancouver Canucks	78	13	12	25	33	1	0	1	1	0
1979-80	Vancouver Canucks	67	13	17	30	108	....	....	....	....	....
1980-81	Vancouver Canucks	11	0	4	4	4	....	....	....	....	....
	New York Rangers	35	10	10	20	4	14	2	5	7	9
1981-82	New York Rangers	26	3	9	12	16	....	....	....	....	....
	Quebec Nordiques	12	2	1	3	0	....	....	....	....	....
1982-83	Buffalo Sabres	3	0	0	0	0	....	....	....	....	....
1983-84	Vancouver Canucks	37	9	13	22	7	4	2	1	3	0
1984-85	Vancouver Canucks	37	5	11	16	23	....	....	....	....	....
1986-87	Philadelphia Flyers	1	0	0	0	0	....	....	....	....	....
	NHL Totals	**386**	**78**	**95**	**173**	**230**	**19**	**4**	**7**	**11**	**9**

Traded to **NY Rangers** by **Vancouver** with Jeff Bandura for Mario Marois and Jim Mayer, November 11, 1980. Traded to **Quebec** by **NY Rangers** with Dean Talafous (later changed to Pat Hickey (March 8, 1982) when Talafous decided to retire) for Robbie Ftorek and Quebec's 8th round choice (Brian Glynn) in 1982 Entry Draft, December 30, 1981. Signed as a free agent by **Buffalo**, September 11, 1982. Signed as a free agent by **Vancouver**, September 26, 1983. Signed as a free agent by **Philadelphia**, October, 1986.

GILLIS, Mike

Left wing. Shoots left. 6'1", 195 lbs. Born, Sudbury, Ont., December 1, 1958.
(Colorado's 1st choice, 5th overall, in 1978 Amateur Draft).

Season	Club	GP	G	A	Pts	PIM	GP	G	A	Pts	PIM
		REGULAR SEASON					PLAYOFFS				
1978-79	Colorado Rockies	30	1	7	8	6	....	....	....	....	....
1979-80	Colorado Rockies	40	4	5	9	22	....	....	....	....	....
1980-81	Colorado Rockies	51	11	7	18	54	....	....	....	....	....
	Boston Bruins	17	2	4	6	15	1	0	0	0	0
1981-82	Boston Bruins	53	9	8	17	54	11	1	2	3	6
1982-83	Boston Bruins	5	0	1	1	0	12	1	3	4	2
1983-84	Boston Bruins	50	6	11	17	35	3	0	0	0	2
	NHL Totals	**246**	**33**	**43**	**76**	**186**	**27**	**2**	**5**	**7**	**10**

• Brother of Paul

Claimed by **Colorado** as a fill-in during Expansion Draft, June 13, 1979. Traded to **Boston** by **Colorado** for Bob Miller, February 18, 1981.

GILLIS, Paul

Center. Shoots left. 5'11", 198 lbs. Born, Toronto, Ont., December 31, 1963.
(Quebec's 2nd choice, 34th overall, in 1982 Entry Draft).

Season	Club	GP	G	A	Pts	PIM	GP	G	A	Pts	PIM
1982-83	Quebec Nordiques	7	0	2	2	2	....	....	....	....	....
1983-84	Quebec Nordiques	57	8	9	17	59	1	0	0	0	2
1984-85	Quebec Nordiques	77	14	28	42	168	18	1	7	8	73
1985-86	Quebec Nordiques	80	19	24	43	203	3	0	2	2	14
1986-87	Quebec Nordiques	76	13	26	39	267	13	2	4	6	65
1987-88	Quebec Nordiques	80	7	10	17	164	....	....	....	....	....
1988-89	Quebec Nordiques	79	15	25	40	163	....	....	....	....	....
1989-90	Quebec Nordiques	71	8	14	22	234	....	....	....	....	....
1990-91	Quebec Nordiques	49	3	8	11	91	....	....	....	....	....
	Chicago Blackhawks	13	0	5	5	53	2	0	0	0	2
1991-92	Chicago Blackhawks	2	0	0	0	6	....	....	....	....	....
	Hartford Whalers	12	0	2	2	48	5	0	1	1	0
1992-93	Hartford Whalers	21	1	1	2	40	....	....	....	....	....
	NHL Totals	**624**	**88**	**154**	**242**	**1498**	**42**	**3**	**14**	**17**	**156**

• Brother of Mike

Traded to **Chicago** by **Quebec** with Dan Vincelette for Ryan McGill and Mike McNeill, March 5, 1991. Traded to **Hartford** by **Chicago** for future considerations, January 27, 1992.

GILMOUR, Doug

Center. Shoots left. 5'11", 177 lbs. Born, Kingston, Ont., June 25, 1963.
(St. Louis' 4th choice, 134th overall, in 1982 Entry Draft).

Season	Club	GP	G	A	Pts	PIM	GP	G	A	Pts	PIM
1983-84	St. Louis Blues	80	25	28	53	57	11	2	9	11	10
1984-85	St. Louis Blues	78	21	36	57	49	3	1	1	2	2
1985-86	St. Louis Blues	74	25	28	53	41	19	9	12	*21	25
1986-87	St. Louis Blues	80	42	63	105	58	6	2	2	4	16
1987-88	St. Louis Blues	72	36	50	86	59	10	3	14	17	18
1988-89 ◆	Calgary Flames	72	26	59	85	44	22	11	11	22	20
1989-90	Calgary Flames	78	24	67	91	54	6	3	1	4	8
1990-91	Calgary Flames	78	20	61	81	144	7	1	1	2	0
1991-92	Calgary Flames	38	11	27	38	46	....	....	....	....	....
	Toronto Maple Leafs	40	15	34	49	32	....	....	....	....	....
1992-93	Toronto Maple Leafs	83	32	95	127	100	21	10	*25	35	30
1993-94	Toronto Maple Leafs	83	27	84	111	105	18	6	22	28	42
1994-95	Toronto Maple Leafs	44	10	23	33	26	7	0	6	6	6
1995-96	Toronto Maple Leafs	81	32	40	72	77	6	1	7	8	12
1996-97	Toronto Maple Leafs	61	15	45	60	46	....	....	....	....	....
	New Jersey Devils	20	7	15	22	22	10	0	4	4	14
1997-98	New Jersey Devils	63	13	40	53	68	6	5	2	7	4
1998-99	Chicago Blackhawks	72	16	40	56	56	....	....	....	....	....
99-2000	Chicago Blackhawks	63	22	34	56	51	....	....	....	....	....
	Buffalo Sabres	11	3	14	17	12	5	0	1	1	0
2000-01	Buffalo Sabres	71	7	31	38	70	13	2	4	6	12
2001-02	Montreal Canadiens	70	10	31	41	48	12	4	6	10	16
2002-03	Montreal Canadiens	61	11	19	30	36	....	....	....	....	....
	Toronto Maple Leafs	1	0	0	0	0	....	....	....	....	....
	NHL Totals	**1474**	**450**	**964**	**1414**	**1301**	**182**	**60**	**128**	**188**	**235**

Frank J. Selke Trophy (1993)

Played in NHL All-Star Game (1993, 1994)

Traded to **Calgary** by **St. Louis** with Mark Hunter, Steve Bozek and Michael Dark for Mike Bullard, Craig Coxe and Tim Corkery, September 6, 1988. Traded to **Toronto** by **Calgary** with Jamie Macoun, Ric Nattress, Kent Manderville and Rick Wamsley for Gary Leeman, Alexander Godynyuk, Jeff Reese, Michel Petit and Craig Berube, January 2, 1992. Traded to **New Jersey** by **Toronto** with Dave Ellett and New Jersey's 3rd round choice (previously acquired, New Jersey selected Andre Lakos) in 1999 Entry Draft for Jason Smith, Steve Sullivan and the rights to Alyn McCauley, February 25, 1997. Signed as a free agent by **Chicago**, July 28, 1998. Traded to **Buffalo** by **Chicago** with J.P. Dumont for Michal Grosek, March 10, 2000. Signed as a free agent by **Montreal**, October 5, 2001. Traded to **Toronto** by **Montreal** for Toronto's 6th round choice (Mark Flood) in 2003 Entry Draft, March 11, 2003.

GINGRAS, Gaston

Defense. Shoots left. 6'1", 200 lbs. Born, Temiscamingue, Que., February 13, 1959.
(Montreal's 1st choice, 27th overall, in 1979 Entry Draft).

Season	Club	GP	G	A	Pts	PIM	GP	G	A	Pts	PIM
1979-80	Montreal Canadiens	34	3	7	10	18	10	1	6	7	8
1980-81	Montreal Canadiens	55	5	16	21	22	1	1	0	1	0
1981-82	Montreal Canadiens	34	6	18	24	28	5	0	1	1	0
1982-83	Montreal Canadiens	22	1	8	9	8	....	....	....	....	....
	Toronto Maple Leafs	45	10	18	28	10	3	1	2	3	2
1983-84	Toronto Maple Leafs	59	7	20	27	16	....	....	....	....	....
1984-85	Toronto Maple Leafs	5	0	2	2	0	....	....	....	....	....

Season	Club	GP	G	A	Pts	PIM	GP	G	A	Pts	PIM
		REGULAR SEASON					PLAYOFFS				
1985-86 ◆	Montreal Canadiens	34	8	18	26	12	11	2	3	5	4
1986-87	Montreal Canadiens	66	11	34	45	21	5	0	2	2	0
1987-88	Montreal Canadiens	2	0	1	1	2	....	....	....	....	....
	St. Louis Blues	68	7	22	29	18	10	1	3	4	4
1988-89	St. Louis Blues	52	3	10	13	6	7	0	1	1	2
	NHL Totals	**476**	**61**	**174**	**235**	**161**	**52**	**6**	**18**	**24**	**20**

Traded to **Toronto** by **Montreal** for Toronto's 2nd round choice (Benoit Brunet) in 1986 Entry Draft, December 17, 1982. Traded to **Montreal** by **Toronto** for Larry Landon, February 14, 1985. Traded to **St. Louis** by **Montreal** with Montreal's 3rd round choice (later traded to Winnipeg – Winnipeg selected Kris Draper) in 1989 Entry Draft for Larry Trader and St. Louis' 3rd round choice (Pierre Sevigny) in 1989 Entry Draft, October 13, 1987.

GIONTA, Brian

Right wing. Shoots right. 5'7", 175 lbs. Born, Rochester, NY, January 18, 1979.
(New Jersey's 4th choice, 82nd overall, in 1998 Entry Draft).

Season	Club	GP	G	A	Pts	PIM	GP	G	A	Pts	PIM
2001-02	New Jersey Devils	33	4	7	11	8	6	2	2	4	0
2002-03 ◆	New Jersey Devils	58	12	13	25	23	24	1	8	9	6
	NHL Totals	**91**	**16**	**20**	**36**	**31**	**30**	**3**	**10**	**13**	**6**

GIRARD, Bob

Left wing. Shoots left. 6', 180 lbs. Born, Montreal, Que., April 12, 1949.

Season	Club	GP	G	A	Pts	PIM	GP	G	A	Pts	PIM
1975-76	California Golden Seals	80	16	26	42	54	....	....	....	....	....
1976-77	Cleveland Barons	68	11	10	21	33	....	....	....	....	....
1977-78	Cleveland Barons	25	0	4	4	11	....	....	....	....	....
	Washington Capitals	52	9	14	23	6	....	....	....	....	....
1978-79	Washington Capitals	79	9	15	24	36	....	....	....	....	....
1979-80	Washington Capitals	1	0	0	0	0	....	....	....	....	....
	NHL Totals	**305**	**45**	**69**	**114**	**140**	....	....	....	....	....

Signed as a free agent by **California**, September, 1973. Transferred to **Cleveland** after **California** franchise relocated, August 26, 1976. Traded to **Washington** by **Cleveland** with Cleveland's 2nd round choice (Paul MacKinnon) in 1978 Amateur Draft for Walt McKechnie, December 9, 1977. Claimed by **Washington** as a fill-in during Expansion Draft, June 13, 1979.

GIRARD, Jonathan

Defense. Shoots right. 5'11", 192 lbs. Born, Joliette, Que., May 27, 1980.
(Boston's 1st choice, 48th overall, in 1998 Entry Draft).

Season	Club	GP	G	A	Pts	PIM	GP	G	A	Pts	PIM
1998-99	Boston Bruins	3	0	0	0	0	....	....	....	....	....
99-2000	Boston Bruins	23	1	2	3	2	....	....	....	....	....
2000-01	Boston Bruins	31	3	13	16	14	....	....	....	....	....
2001-02	Boston Bruins	20	0	3	3	9	1	0	0	0	2
2002-03	Boston Bruins	73	6	16	22	21	2	0	1	1	0
	NHL Totals	**150**	**10**	**34**	**44**	**46**	**3**	**0**	**1**	**1**	**2**

GIRARD, Kenny

Right wing. Shoots right. 6', 184 lbs. Born, Toronto, Ont., December 8, 1936.

Season	Club	GP	G	A	Pts	PIM	GP	G	A	Pts	PIM
1956-57	Toronto Maple Leafs	3	0	1	1	2	....	....	....	....	....
1957-58	Toronto Maple Leafs	3	0	0	0	0	....	....	....	....	....
1959-60	Toronto Maple Leafs	1	0	0	0	0	....	....	....	....	....
	NHL Totals	**7**	**0**	**1**	**1**	**2**	....	....	....	....	....

GIROUX, Art

Right wing. Shoots right. 5'10", 165 lbs. Born, Winnipeg, Man., June 6, 1908.

Season	Club	GP	G	A	Pts	PIM	GP	G	A	Pts	PIM
1932-33	Montreal Canadiens	40	5	2	7	14	2	0	0	0	0
1934-35	Boston Bruins	10	1	0	1	0	....	....	....	....	....
1935-36	Detroit Red Wings	4	0	2	2	0	....	....	....	....	....
	NHL Totals	**54**	**6**	**4**	**10**	**14**	**2**	**0**	**0**	**0**	**0**

Traded to **Montreal** by **San Francisco** (Cal-Pro) for $5,000, February 13, 1930. Traded to **Boston** by **Montreal** for cash, October 18, 1934. Traded to **Detroit** by **Boston** with Marty Barry for Cooney Weiland and Walt Buswell, July 11, 1935.

GIROUX, Larry

Defense. Shoots right. 6', 190 lbs. Born, Weyburn, Sask., August 28, 1951.

Season	Club	GP	G	A	Pts	PIM	GP	G	A	Pts	PIM
1973-74	St. Louis Blues	74	5	17	22	59	....	....	....	....	....
1974-75	Kansas City Scouts	21	0	6	6	24	....	....	....	....	....
	Detroit Red Wings	39	2	20	22	60	....	....	....	....	....
1975-76	Detroit Red Wings	10	1	1	2	25	....	....	....	....	....
1976-77	Detroit Red Wings	2	0	0	0	2	....	....	....	....	....
1977-78	Detroit Red Wings	5	0	3	3	4	2	0	0	0	2
1978-79	St. Louis Blues	73	5	22	27	111	....	....	....	....	....
1979-80	St. Louis Blues	3	0	0	0	4	....	....	....	....	....
	Hartford Whalers	47	2	5	7	44	3	0	0	0	2
	NHL Totals	**274**	**15**	**74**	**89**	**333**	**5**	**0**	**0**	**0**	**4**

Signed as a free agent by **St. Louis**, October, 1972. Traded to **Kansas City** by **St. Louis** for Chris Evans and Kansas City's 4th round choice (Mike Liut) in 1976 Amateur Draft, October 29, 1974. Traded to **Detroit** by **Kansas City** with Bart Crashley and Ted Snell for Guy Charron and Claude Houde, December 14, 1974. Claimed by **St. Louis** from **Detroit** in Waiver Draft, October 9, 1978. Signed as a free agent by **Hartford**, December 13, 1979.

GIROUX, Pierre

Center. Shoots right. 5'11", 185 lbs. Born, Brownsburg, Que., November 17, 1955.
(Chicago's 4th choice, 61st overall, in 1975 Amateur Draft).

Season	Club	GP	G	A	Pts	PIM	GP	G	A	Pts	PIM
1982-83	Los Angeles Kings	6	1	0	1	17	....	....	....	....	....
	NHL Totals	**6**	**1**	**0**	**1**	**17**	....	....	....	....	....

Signed as a free agent by **Los Angeles**, August 5, 1982.

GIROUX, Raymond

Defense. Shoots left. 6'1", 190 lbs. Born, North Bay, Ont., July 20, 1976.
(Philadelphia's 7th choice, 202nd overall, in 1994 Entry Draft).

Season	Club	GP	G	A	Pts	PIM	GP	G	A	Pts	PIM
99-2000	New York Islanders	14	0	9	9	10	....	....	....	....	....
2001-02	New York Islanders	2	0	0	0	2	....	....	....	....	....
2002-03	New Jersey Devils	11	0	1	1	6	....	....	....	....	....
	NHL Totals	**27**	**0**	**10**	**10**	**18**	....	....	....	....	....

Rights traded to **NY Islanders** by **Philadelphia** for NY Islanders' 6th round choice (later traded to Montreal – Montreal selected Scott Selig) in 2000 Entry Draft, August 25, 1998. Signed as a free agent by **New Jersey**, July 12, 2002.

GLADNEY, Bob

Defense. Shoots left. 5'11", 185 lbs. Born, Come-by-Chance, Nfld., August 27, 1957.
(Toronto's 3rd choice, 24th overall, in 1977 Amateur Draft).

Season	Club	GP	G	A	Pts	PIM	GP	G	A	Pts	PIM
1982-83	Los Angeles Kings	1	0	0	0	2	....	....	....	....	....
1983-84	Pittsburgh Penguins	13	1	5	6	2	....	....	....	....	....
	NHL Totals	**14**	**1**	**5**	**6**	**4**	....	....	....	....	....

Traded to **Los Angeles** by **Toronto** with Toronto's 6th round choice (Kevin Stevens) in 1983 Entry Draft for Don Luce, August 10, 1981. Signed as a free agent by **Pittsburgh**, September 12, 1983.

GLADU, Jean-Paul

Left wing. Shoots left. 5'11", 180 lbs. Born, St-Hyacinthe, Que., June 20, 1921.

Season	Club	GP	G	A	Pts	PIM	GP	G	A	Pts	PIM
1944-45	Boston Bruins	40	6	14	20	2	7	2	2	4	0
	NHL Totals	**40**	**6**	**14**	**20**	**2**	**7**	**2**	**2**	**4**	**0**

Traded to **St. Louis** (AHL) by **Boston** (Hershey-AHL) for cash, December 6, 1945. Traded to **Cleveland** (AHL) by **Chicago** (St. Louis-AHL) for Harry Taylor, August 19, 1951. Traded to **Boston** (Providence-AHL) by **Cleveland** (AHL) with Joe Lund for Buck Davies and Vic Lynn, December 10, 1951.

GLENNIE, Brian

Defense. Shoots left. 6'1", 197 lbs. Born, Toronto, Ont., August 29, 1946.

Season	Club	GP	G	A	Pts	PIM	GP	G	A	Pts	PIM
1969-70	Toronto Maple Leafs	52	1	14	15	50	....	....	....	....	....
1970-71	Toronto Maple Leafs	54	0	8	8	31	3	0	0	0	0
1971-72	Toronto Maple Leafs	61	2	8	10	44	5	0	0	0	25
1972-73	Toronto Maple Leafs	44	1	10	11	54	....	....	....	....	....
1973-74	Toronto Maple Leafs	65	4	18	22	100	3	0	0	0	10
1974-75	Toronto Maple Leafs	63	1	7	8	110	....	....	....	....	....
1975-76	Toronto Maple Leafs	60	0	8	8	75	6	0	1	1	15
1976-77	Toronto Maple Leafs	69	1	10	11	73	2	0	0	0	0
1977-78	Toronto Maple Leafs	77	2	15	17	62	13	0	0	0	16
1978-79	Los Angeles Kings	18	2	2	4	22	....	....	....	....	....
	NHL Totals	**572**	**14**	**100**	**114**	**621**	**32**	**0**	**1**	**1**	**66**

Traded to **Los Angeles** by **Toronto** with Kurt Walker, Scott Garland, Toronto's 2nd round choice (Mark Hardy) in 1979 Entry Draft for Dave Hutchison and Lorne Stamler, June 14, 1978.

GLENNON, Matt

Left wing. Shoots left. 6', 185 lbs. Born, Hull, MA, September 20, 1968.
(Boston's 7th choice, 119th overall, in 1987 Entry Draft).

Season	Club	GP	G	A	Pts	PIM	GP	G	A	Pts	PIM
1991-92	Boston Bruins	3	0	0	0	2	....	....	....	....	....
	NHL Totals	**3**	**0**	**0**	**0**	**2**	....	....	....	....	....

GLOECKNER, Lorry

Defense. Shoots left. 6'2", 210 lbs. Born, Kindersley, Sask., January 25, 1956.
(Boston's 2nd choice, 34th overall, in 1976 Amateur Draft).

Season	Club	GP	G	A	Pts	PIM	GP	G	A	Pts	PIM
1978-79	Detroit Red Wings	13	0	2	2	6	....	....	....	....	....
	NHL Totals	**13**	**0**	**2**	**2**	**6**	....	....	....	....	....

Signed as a free agent by **Detroit**, October 12, 1978.

GLOOR, Dan

Center. Shoots left. 5'9", 170 lbs. Born, Stratford, Ont., December 4, 1952.
(Vancouver's 7th choice, 99th overall, in 1972 Amateur Draft).

Season	Club	GP	G	A	Pts	PIM	GP	G	A	Pts	PIM
1973-74	Vancouver Canucks	2	0	0	0	0	....	....	....	....	....
	NHL Totals	**2**	**0**	**0**	**0**	**0**	....	....	....	....	....

GLOVER, Fred

Center. Shoots right. 5'9", 170 lbs. Born, Toronto, Ont., January 5, 1928.

Season	Club	GP	G	A	Pts	PIM	GP	G	A	Pts	PIM
1948-49	Detroit Red Wings	....	....	....	....	....	2	0	0	0	0
1949-50	Detroit Red Wings	7	0	0	0	0	....	....	....	....	....
1950-51	Detroit Red Wings	....	....	....	....	....	6	0	0	0	0
1951-52 ◆	Detroit Red Wings	54	9	9	18	25	....	....	....	....	....
1952-53	Chicago Black Hawks	31	4	2	6	37	....	....	....	....	....
	NHL Totals	**92**	**13**	**11**	**24**	**62**	**8**	**0**	**0**	**0**	**0**

• Brother of Howie

Traded to **Chicago** by **Detroit** with Enio Sclisizzi for cash, August 14, 1952. Traded to **Cleveland** (AHL) by **Chicago** to complete transaction that sent Vic Lynn to Chicago (January 4, 1953), January 16, 1953.

GLOVER, Howie

Right wing. Shoots right. 5'11", 180 lbs. Born, Toronto, Ont., February 14, 1935.

Season	Club	GP	G	A	Pts	PIM	GP	G	A	Pts	PIM
1958-59	Chicago Black Hawks	13	0	1	1	2	....	....	....	....	....
1960-61	Detroit Red Wings	66	21	8	29	46	11	1	2	3	2
1961-62	Detroit Red Wings	39	7	8	15	44	....	....	....	....	....

Season	Club	GP	G	A	Pts	PIM	GP	G	A	Pts	PIM
		REGULAR SEASON					PLAYOFFS				
1963-64	New York Rangers	25	1	0	1	9	....	....	....	....	....
1968-69	Montreal Canadiens	1	0	0	0	0	....	....	....	....	....
	NHL Totals	**144**	**29**	**17**	**46**	**101**	**11**	**1**	**2**	**3**	**2**

• Brother of Fred

Claimed by **Chicago** from **Winnipeg** (WHL) in Inter-League Draft, June 3, 1958. Traded to **Detroit** by **Chicago** for Jim Morrison, June 5, 1960. Traded to **Portland** (WHL) by **Detroit** for cash, May 27, 1963. Traded to **NY Rangers** by **Portland** (WHL) for Pat Hannigan, September 19, 1963. • Suspended by **NY Rangers** for refusing demotion to **Baltimore** (AHL), January, 1964. Traded to **Montreal** by **NY Rangers** for Ray Brunel and Bev Bell, April 19, 1964. Traded to **Cleveland** (AHL) by **Montreal** for cash, April 19, 1964. Traded to **Montreal** by **Cleveland** (AHL) for Jim Mikol and Bill Staub, August 27, 1968.

GLYNN, Brian

Defense. Shoots left. 6'4", 218 lbs. Born, Iserlohn, West Germany, November 23, 1967.
(Calgary's 2nd choice, 37th overall, in 1986 Entry Draft).

Season	Club	GP	G	A	Pts	PIM	GP	G	A	Pts	PIM
1987-88	Calgary Flames	67	5	14	19	87	1	0	0	0	0
1988-89	Calgary Flames	9	0	1	1	19	....	....	....	....	....
1989-90	Calgary Flames	1	0	0	0	0	....	....	....	....	....
1990-91	Minnesota North Stars	66	8	11	19	83	23	2	6	8	18
1991-92	Minnesota North Stars	37	2	12	14	24	....	....	....	....	....
	Edmonton Oilers	25	2	6	8	6	16	4	1	5	12
1992-93	Edmonton Oilers	64	4	12	16	60	....	....	....	....	....
1993-94	Ottawa Senators	48	2	13	15	41	....	....	....	....	....
	Vancouver Canucks	16	0	0	0	12	17	0	3	3	10
1994-95	Hartford Whalers	43	1	6	7	32	....	....	....	....	....
1995-96	Hartford Whalers	54	0	4	4	44	....	....	....	....	....
1996-97	Hartford Whalers	1	1	0	1	2	....	....	....	....	....
	NHL Totals	**431**	**25**	**79**	**104**	**410**	**57**	**6**	**10**	**16**	**40**

Traded to **Minnesota** by **Calgary** for Frantisek Musil, October 26, 1990. Traded to **Edmonton** by **Minnesota** for David Shaw, January 21, 1992. Traded to **Ottawa** by **Edmonton** for Ottawa's 8th round choice (Rob Guinn) in 1994 Entry Draft, September 15, 1993. Claimed on waivers by **Vancouver** from **Ottawa**, February 5, 1994. Claimed by **Hartford** from **Vancouver** in Waiver Draft, January 18, 1995. Traded to **Detroit** by **Hartford** with Brendan Shanahan for Paul Coffey, Keith Primeau and Detroit's 1st round choice (Nikos Tselios) in 1997 Entry Draft, October 9, 1996.

GOC, Sascha

Defense. Shoots right. 6'2", 225 lbs. Born, Calw, West Germany, April 17, 1979.
(New Jersey's 5th choice, 159th overall, in 1997 Entry Draft).

Season	Club	GP	G	A	Pts	PIM	GP	G	A	Pts	PIM
2000-01	New Jersey Devils	11	0	0	0	4	....	....	....	....	....
2001-02	New Jersey Devils	2	0	0	0	0	....	....	....	....	....
	Tampa Bay Lightning	9	0	0	0	0	....	....	....	....	....
	NHL Totals	**22**	**0**	**0**	**0**	**4**	....	....	....	....	....

Traded to **Tampa Bay** by **New Jersey** with Josef Boumedienne and the rights to Anton But for Andrei Zyuzin, November 9, 2001.

GODARD, Eric

Right wing. Shoots right. 6'4", 227 lbs. Born, Vernon, B.C., March 7, 1980.

Season	Club	GP	G	A	Pts	PIM	GP	G	A	Pts	PIM
2002-03	New York Islanders	19	0	0	0	48	2	0	1	1	4
	NHL Totals	**19**	**0**	**0**	**0**	**48**	**2**	**0**	**1**	**1**	**4**

Signed as a free agent by **Florida**, September 24, 1999. Traded to **NY Islanders** by **Florida** for Florida's 3rd round choice (previously acquired, Florida selected Gregory Campbell) in 2002 Entry Draft, June 22, 2002.

GODDEN, Ernie

Center. Shoots left. 5'8", 160 lbs. Born, Keswick, Ont., March 13, 1961.
(Toronto's 3rd choice, 55th overall, in 1981 Entry Draft).

Season	Club	GP	G	A	Pts	PIM	GP	G	A	Pts	PIM
1981-82	Toronto Maple Leafs	5	1	1	2	6	....	....	....	....	....
	NHL Totals	**5**	**1**	**1**	**2**	**6**	....	....	....	....	....

GODFREY, Warren

Defense. Shoots left. 6'1", 190 lbs. Born, Toronto, Ont., March 23, 1931.

Season	Club	GP	G	A	Pts	PIM	GP	G	A	Pts	PIM
1952-53	Boston Bruins	60	1	13	14	40	11	0	1	1	2
1953-54	Boston Bruins	70	5	9	14	71	4	0	0	0	4
1954-55	Boston Bruins	62	1	17	18	58	3	0	0	0	0
1955-56	Detroit Red Wings	67	2	6	8	86	....	....	....	....	....
1956-57	Detroit Red Wings	69	1	8	9	103	5	0	0	0	6
1957-58	Detroit Red Wings	67	2	16	18	56	4	0	0	0	0
1958-59	Detroit Red Wings	69	6	4	10	44	....	....	....	....	....
1959-60	Detroit Red Wings	69	5	9	14	60	6	1	0	1	10
1960-61	Detroit Red Wings	63	3	16	19	62	11	0	2	2	18
1961-62	Detroit Red Wings	69	4	13	17	84	....	....	....	....	....
1962-63	Boston Bruins	66	2	9	11	56	....	....	....	....	....
1963-64	Detroit Red Wings	4	0	0	0	2	....	....	....	....	....
1964-65	Detroit Red Wings	11	0	0	0	8	4	0	1	1	2
1965-66	Detroit Red Wings	26	0	4	4	22	4	0	0	0	0
1966-67	Detroit Red Wings	2	0	0	0	0	....	....	....	....	....
1967-68	Detroit Red Wings	12	0	1	1	0	....	....	....	....	....
	NHL Totals	**786**	**32**	**125**	**157**	**752**	**52**	**1**	**4**	**5**	**42**

Played in NHL All-Star Game (1955)

Traded to **Detroit** by **Boston** with Gilles Boisvert, Real Chevrefils, Norm Corcoran and Ed Sandford for Marcel Bonin, Lorne Davis, Terry Sawchuk and Vic Stasiuk, June 3, 1955. Claimed by **Boston** from **Detroit** in Intra-League Draft, June 4, 1962. Traded to **Detroit** by **Boston** for Gerry Odrowski, October 10, 1963. Traded to **Vancouver** (WHL) by **Detroit** for cash, August 19, 1968.

GODIN, Eddy

Right wing. Shoots left. 5'10", 190 lbs. Born, Donnacona, Que., March 29, 1957.
(Washington's 3rd choice, 39th overall, in 1977 Amateur Draft).

Season	Club	GP	G	A	Pts	PIM	GP	G	A	Pts	PIM
1977-78	Washington Capitals	18	3	3	6	6	....	....	....	....	....
1978-79	Washington Capitals	9	0	3	3	6	....	....	....	....	....
	NHL Totals	**27**	**3**	**6**	**9**	**12**	....	....	....	....	....

Claimed by **Washington** as a fill-in during Expansion Draft, June 13, 1979.

GODIN, Sam

Right wing. Shoots right. 5'10", 156 lbs. Born, Rockland, Ont., September 20, 1909.

Season	Club	GP	G	A	Pts	PIM	GP	G	A	Pts	PIM
1927-28	Ottawa Senators	24	0	0	0	0	....	....	....	....	....
1928-29	Ottawa Senators	23	2	1	3	21	....	....	....	....	....
1933-34	Montreal Canadiens	36	2	2	4	15	....	....	....	....	....
	NHL Totals	**83**	**4**	**3**	**7**	**36**	....	....	....	....	....

Signed as a free agent by **Ottawa**, January 24, 1928. Traded to **Buffalo** (IHL) by **Ottawa** for cash, November, 1929. Traded to **Montreal** by **Buffalo** (IHL) for cash, October, 1933. Traded to **Springfield** (IAHL) by **Montreal** for Red Conn, September 30, 1937.

GODYNYUK, Alexander

Defense. Shoots left. 6', 207 lbs. Born, Kiev, Ukraine, January 27, 1970.
(Toronto's 5th choice, 115th overall, in 1990 Entry Draft).

Season	Club	GP	G	A	Pts	PIM	GP	G	A	Pts	PIM
1990-91	Toronto Maple Leafs	18	0	3	3	16	....	....	....	....	....
1991-92	Toronto Maple Leafs	31	3	6	9	59	....	....	....	....	....
	Calgary Flames	6	0	1	1	4	....	....	....	....	....
1992-93	Calgary Flames	27	3	4	7	19	....	....	....	....	....
1993-94	Florida Panthers	26	0	10	10	35	....	....	....	....	....
	Hartford Whalers	43	3	9	12	40	....	....	....	....	....
1994-95	Hartford Whalers	14	0	0	0	8	....	....	....	....	....
1995-96	Hartford Whalers	3	0	0	0	2	....	....	....	....	....
1996-97	Hartford Whalers	55	1	6	7	41	....	....	....	....	....
	NHL Totals	**223**	**10**	**39**	**49**	**224**	....	....	....	....	....

Traded to **Calgary** by **Toronto** with Craig Berube, Gary Leeman, Michel Petit and Jeff Reese for Doug Gilmour, Jamie Macoun, Ric Nattress, Rick Wamsley and Kent Manderville, January 2, 1992. Claimed by **Florida** from **Calgary** in Expansion Draft, June 24, 1993. Traded to **Hartford** by **Florida** for Jim McKenzie, December 16, 1993. Transferred to **Carolina** after **Hartford** franchise relocated, June 25, 1997. Traded to **St. Louis** by **Carolina** with Carolina's 6th round choice (Brad Voth) in 1998 Entry Draft for Stephen Leach, June 27, 1997.

GOEGAN, Pete

Defense. Shoots left. 6'1", 195 lbs. Born, Fort William, Ont., March 6, 1934.

Season	Club	GP	G	A	Pts	PIM	GP	G	A	Pts	PIM
1957-58	Detroit Red Wings	14	0	2	2	28	4	0	0	0	18
1958-59	Detroit Red Wings	67	1	11	12	109	....	....	....	....	....
1959-60	Detroit Red Wings	21	3	0	3	6	6	1	0	1	13
1960-61	Detroit Red Wings	67	5	29	34	78	11	0	1	1	18
1961-62	Detroit Red Wings	39	5	5	10	24	....	....	....	....	....
	New York Rangers	7	0	2	2	6	....	....	....	....	....
1962-63	Detroit Red Wings	62	1	8	9	48	11	0	2	2	12
1963-64	Detroit Red Wings	12	0	0	0	8	....	....	....	....	....
1964-65	Detroit Red Wings	4	1	0	1	2	....	....	....	....	....
1965-66	Detroit Red Wings	13	0	2	2	14	1	0	0	0	0
1966-67	Detroit Red Wings	31	2	6	8	12	....	....	....	....	....
1967-68	Minnesota North Stars	46	1	2	3	30	....	....	....	....	....
	NHL Totals	**383**	**19**	**67**	**86**	**365**	**33**	**1**	**3**	**4**	**61**

Traded to **Detroit** by **Cleveland** (AHL) for Gord Hollingworth and cash, February 20, 1958. Traded to **NY Rangers** by **Detroit** for Noel Price, February 16, 1962. Traded to **Detroit** by **NY Rangers** for Noel Price, October 8, 1962. Claimed by **Minnesota** from **Detroit** in Expansion Draft, June 6, 1967.

GOERTZ, Dave

Defense. Shoots right. 5'11", 210 lbs. Born, Edmonton, Alta., March 28, 1965.
(Pittsburgh's 10th choice, 232nd overall, in 1983 Entry Draft).

Season	Club	GP	G	A	Pts	PIM	GP	G	A	Pts	PIM
1987-88	Pittsburgh Penguins	2	0	0	0	2	....	....	....	....	....
	NHL Totals	**2**	**0**	**0**	**0**	**2**	....	....	....	....	....

GOLDHAM, Bob

Defense. Shoots left. 6'2", 195 lbs. Born, Georgetown, Ont., May 12, 1922.

Season	Club	GP	G	A	Pts	PIM	GP	G	A	Pts	PIM
1941-42	◆ Toronto Maple Leafs	19	4	7	11	25	13	2	2	4	31
1945-46	Toronto Maple Leafs	49	7	14	21	44	....	....	....	....	....
1946-47	◆ Toronto Maple Leafs	11	1	1	2	10	....	....	....	....	....
1947-48	Chicago Black Hawks	38	2	9	11	38	....	....	....	....	....
1948-49	Chicago Black Hawks	60	1	10	11	43	....	....	....	....	....
1949-50	Chicago Black Hawks	67	2	10	12	57	....	....	....	....	....
1950-51	Detroit Red Wings	61	5	18	23	31	6	0	1	1	2
1951-52	◆ Detroit Red Wings	69	0	14	14	24	8	0	1	1	8
1952-53	Detroit Red Wings	70	1	13	14	32	6	1	1	2	2
1953-54	◆ Detroit Red Wings	69	1	15	16	50	12	0	2	2	2
1954-55	◆ Detroit Red Wings	69	1	16	17	14	11	0	4	4	4

Season	Club	REGULAR SEASON GP	G	A	Pts	PIM	PLAYOFFS GP	G	A	Pts	PIM
1955-56	Detroit Red Wings	68	3	16	19	32	10	0	3	3	4
	NHL Totals	**650**	**28**	**143**	**171**	**400**	**66**	**3**	**14**	**17**	**53**

NHL Second All-Star Team (1955)

Played in NHL All-Star Game (1947, 1949, 1950, 1952, 1954, 1955)

• Missed remainder of 1946-47 season recovering from arm injury suffered in game vs. Boston, December 4, 1946. Traded to **Chicago** by **Toronto** with Gus Bodnar, Bud Poile, Gaye Stewart and Ernie Dickens for Max Bentley and Cy Thomas, November 2, 1947. Traded to **Detroit** by **Chicago** with Jim Henry, Gaye Stewart and Metro Prystai for Al Dewsbury, Harry Lumley, Jack Stewart, Don Morrison and Pete Babando, July 13, 1950.

GOLDMANN, Erich

Defense. Shoots left. 6'3", 212 lbs. Born, Dingolfing, West Germany, April 7, 1976.
(Ottawa's 5th choice, 212th overall, in 1996 Entry Draft).

Season	Club	GP	G	A	Pts	PIM	GP	G	A	Pts	PIM
99-2000	Ottawa Senators	1	0	0	0	0	....	....	....	....	....
	NHL Totals	**1**	**0**	**0**	**0**	**0**	....	....	....	....	....

GOLDSWORTHY, Bill

Right wing. Shoots right. 6', 190 lbs. Born, Waterloo, Ont., August 24, 1944.

Season	Club	GP	G	A	Pts	PIM	GP	G	A	Pts	PIM
1964-65	Boston Bruins	2	0	0	0	0	....	....	....	....	....
1965-66	Boston Bruins	13	3	1	4	6	....	....	....	....	....
1966-67	Boston Bruins	18	3	5	8	21	....	....	....	....	....
1967-68	Minnesota North Stars	68	14	19	33	68	14	*8	7	*15	12
1968-69	Minnesota North Stars	68	14	10	24	110	....	....	....	....	....
1969-70	Minnesota North Stars	75	36	29	65	89	6	4	3	7	6
1970-71	Minnesota North Stars	77	34	31	65	85	7	2	4	6	6
1971-72	Minnesota North Stars	78	31	31	62	59	7	2	3	5	6
1972-73	Minnesota North Stars	75	27	33	60	97	6	2	2	4	0
1973-74	Minnesota North Stars	74	48	26	74	73	....	....	....	....	....
1974-75	Minnesota North Stars	71	37	35	72	77	....	....	....	....	....
1975-76	Minnesota North Stars	68	24	22	46	47	....	....	....	....	....
1976-77	Minnesota North Stars	16	2	3	5	6	....	....	....	....	....
	New York Rangers	61	10	12	22	43	....	....	....	....	....
1977-78	New York Rangers	7	0	1	1	12	....	....	....	....	....
	NHL Totals	**771**	**283**	**258**	**541**	**793**	**40**	**18**	**19**	**37**	**30**

Played in NHL All-Star Game (1970, 1972, 1974, 1976)

Claimed by **Minnesota** from **Boston** in Expansion Draft, June 6, 1967. Traded to **NY Rangers** by **Minnesota** for Bill Fairbairn and Nick Beverley, November 11, 1976. Traded to **Indianapolis** (WHA) by **NY Rangers** for Frank Spring, December, 1977.

GOLDSWORTHY, Leroy

Right wing. Shoots right. 6', 165 lbs. Born, Two Harbors, MN, October 18, 1906.

Season	Club	GP	G	A	Pts	PIM	GP	G	A	Pts	PIM
1928-29	New York Rangers	....	....	....	....	....	1	0	0	0	0
1929-30	New York Rangers	44	4	1	5	16	4	0	0	0	2
1930-31	Detroit Falcons	12	1	0	1	2	....	....	....	....	....
1932-33	Detroit Red Wings	25	3	6	9	6	2	0	0	0	0
1933-34 ♦	Chicago Black Hawks	27	3	3	6	0	7	0	0	0	0
1934-35	Chicago Black Hawks	7	0	0	0	2	....	....	....	....	....
	Montreal Canadiens	33	20	9	29	13	2	1	0	1	0
1935-36	Montreal Canadiens	47	15	11	26	8	....	....	....	....	....
1936-37	Boston Bruins	47	8	6	14	8	3	0	0	0	0
1937-38	Boston Bruins	46	9	10	19	14	3	0	0	0	2
1938-39	New York Americans	48	3	11	14	10	2	0	0	0	0
	NHL Totals	**336**	**66**	**57**	**123**	**79**	**24**	**1**	**0**	**1**	**4**

Traded to **NY Rangers** by **Edmonton** (WHL) for cash, October 19, 1926. Traded to **London** (IHL) by **NY Rangers** for cash, October 29, 1930. Traded to **Detroit** by **London** (IHL) for Henry Hicks, January 12, 1931. Traded to **Chicago** (London-IHL) by **Detroit** with Frank Waite for Gene Carrigan, October 19, 1933. Traded to **London** (IHL) by **Chicago** for cash, November 22, 1933. Traded to **Chicago** by **London** (IHL) for $3,000 and the loan of Bill Kendall, January 4, 1934. Traded to **Montreal** by **Chicago** with Roger Jenkins and Lionel Conacher for Howie Morenz, Marty Burke and Lorne Chabot, October 3, 1934. Traded to **Chicago** by **Montreal** for cash, October 17, 1934. Traded to **Montreal** by **Chicago** for cash, December 18, 1934. Traded to **Boston** by **Montreal** with Sammy McManus and $10,000 for Babe Siebert and Roger Jenkins, September 10, 1936. Traded to **NY Americans** by **Boston** with the loan of Art Jackson for the 1938-39 season for cash, October 24, 1938. Traded to **Cleveland** (IAHL) by **NY Americans** for cash, October 12, 1939.

GOLDUP, Glenn

Right wing. Shoots left. 6', 190 lbs. Born, St. Catharines, Ont., April 26, 1953.
(Montreal's 2nd choice, 17th overall, in 1973 Amateur Draft).

Season	Club	GP	G	A	Pts	PIM	GP	G	A	Pts	PIM
1973-74	Montreal Canadiens	6	0	0	0	0	....	....	....	....	....
1974-75	Montreal Canadiens	9	0	1	1	2	....	....	....	....	....
1975-76	Montreal Canadiens	3	0	0	0	2	....	....	....	....	....
1976-77	Los Angeles Kings	28	7	6	13	29	8	2	2	4	2
1977-78	Los Angeles Kings	66	14	18	32	66	2	1	0	1	11
1978-79	Los Angeles Kings	73	15	22	37	89	2	0	1	1	9
1979-80	Los Angeles Kings	55	10	11	21	78	4	1	0	1	0
1980-81	Los Angeles Kings	49	6	9	15	35	....	....	....	....	....
1981-82	Los Angeles Kings	2	0	0	0	2	....	....	....	....	....
	NHL Totals	**291**	**52**	**67**	**119**	**303**	**16**	**4**	**3**	**7**	**22**

• Son of Hank

Traded to **Los Angeles** by **Montreal** with Montreal's 3rd round choice (later traded to Detroit – Detroit selected Doug Derkson) in 1978 Amateur Draft for Los Angeles' 3rd round choice (Moe Robinson) in 1977 Amateur Draft and 1st round choice (Danny Geoffrion) in 1978 Amateur Draft, June 12, 1976.

GOLDUP, Hank

Left wing. Shoots left. 5'11", 175 lbs. Born, Kingston, Ont., October 29, 1918.

Season	Club	GP	G	A	Pts	PIM	GP	G	A	Pts	PIM
1939-40	Toronto Maple Leafs	21	6	4	10	2	10	*5	1	6	4
1940-41	Toronto Maple Leafs	26	10	5	15	9	7	0	0	0	0
1941-42 ♦	Toronto Maple Leafs	44	12	18	30	13	9	0	0	0	2
1942-43	Toronto Maple Leafs	8	1	7	8	4	....	....	....	....	....
	New York Rangers	36	11	20	31	33	....	....	....	....	....
1944-45	New York Rangers	48	17	25	42	25	....	....	....	....	....
1945-46	New York Rangers	19	6	1	7	11	....	....	....	....	....
	NHL Totals	**202**	**63**	**80**	**143**	**97**	**26**	**5**	**1**	**6**	**6**

• Father of Glenn

Traded to **NY Rangers** by **Toronto** with Red Garrett for Babe Pratt, November 27, 1942. Traded to **Detroit** by **NY Rangers** with Ab DeMarco for Flash Hollett, June 19, 1946. Transaction voided when Hollett decided to retire, June, 1946. Traded to **Cleveland** (AHL) by **NY Rangers** for cash, October 4, 1946.

GOLUBOVSKY, Yan

Defense. Shoots right. 6'3", 183 lbs. Born, Novosibirsk, USSR, March 9, 1976.
(Detroit's 1st choice, 23rd overall, in 1994 Entry Draft).

Season	Club	GP	G	A	Pts	PIM	GP	G	A	Pts	PIM
1997-98	Detroit Red Wings	12	0	2	2	6	....	....	....	....	....
1998-99	Detroit Red Wings	17	0	1	1	16	....	....	....	....	....
99-2000	Detroit Red Wings	21	1	2	3	8	....	....	....	....	....
2000-01	Florida Panthers	6	0	2	2	2	....	....	....	....	....
	NHL Totals	**56**	**1**	**7**	**8**	**32**	....	....	....	....	....

Traded to **Florida** by **Detroit** for Igor Larionov, December 28, 2000.

GOMEZ, Scott

Center. Shoots left. 5'11", 200 lbs. Born, Anchorage, AK, December 23, 1979.
(New Jersey's 2nd choice, 27th overall, in 1998 Entry Draft).

Season	Club	GP	G	A	Pts	PIM	GP	G	A	Pts	PIM
99-2000 ♦	New Jersey Devils	82	19	51	70	78	23	4	6	10	4
2000-01	New Jersey Devils	76	14	49	63	46	25	5	9	14	24
2001-02	New Jersey Devils	76	10	38	48	36	....	....	....	....	....
2002-03 ♦	New Jersey Devils	80	13	42	55	48	24	3	9	12	2
	NHL Totals	**314**	**56**	**180**	**236**	**208**	**72**	**12**	**24**	**36**	**30**

NHL All-Rookie Team (2000) • Calder Memorial Trophy (2000)

Played in NHL All-Star Game (2000)

GONCHAR, Sergei

Defense. Shoots left. 6'2", 208 lbs. Born, Chelyabinsk, USSR, April 13, 1974.
(Washington's 1st choice, 14th overall, in 1992 Entry Draft).

Season	Club	GP	G	A	Pts	PIM	GP	G	A	Pts	PIM
1994-95	Washington Capitals	31	2	5	7	22	7	2	2	4	2
1995-96	Washington Capitals	78	15	26	41	60	6	2	4	6	4
1996-97	Washington Capitals	57	13	17	30	36	....	....	....	....	....
1997-98	Washington Capitals	72	5	16	21	66	21	7	4	11	30
1998-99	Washington Capitals	53	21	10	31	57	....	....	....	....	....
99-2000	Washington Capitals	73	18	36	54	52	5	1	0	1	6
2000-01	Washington Capitals	76	19	38	57	70	6	1	3	4	2
2001-02	Washington Capitals	76	26	33	59	58	....	....	....	....	....
2002-03	Washington Capitals	82	18	49	67	52	6	0	5	5	4
	NHL Totals	**598**	**137**	**230**	**367**	**473**	**51**	**13**	**18**	**31**	**48**

NHL Second All-Star Team (2002, 2003)

Played in NHL All-Star Game (2001, 2002, 2003)

GONEAU, Daniel

Left wing. Shoots left. 6', 195 lbs. Born, Montreal, Que., January 16, 1976.
(NY Rangers' 2nd choice, 48th overall, in 1996 Entry Draft).

Season	Club	GP	G	A	Pts	PIM	GP	G	A	Pts	PIM
1996-97	New York Rangers	41	10	3	13	10	....	....	....	....	....
1997-98	New York Rangers	11	2	0	2	4	....	....	....	....	....
99-2000	New York Rangers	1	0	0	0	0	....	....	....	....	....
	NHL Totals	**53**	**12**	**3**	**15**	**14**	....	....	....	....	....

• Re-entered NHL Entry Draft. Originally Boston's 2nd choice, 47th overall, in 1994 Entry Draft.

GOODEN, Bill

Left wing. Shoots left. 5'9", 175 lbs. Born, Winnipeg, Man., September 8, 1923.

Season	Club	GP	G	A	Pts	PIM	GP	G	A	Pts	PIM
1942-43	New York Rangers	12	0	3	3	0	....	....	....	....	....
1943-44	New York Rangers	41	9	8	17	15	....	....	....	....	....
	NHL Totals	**53**	**9**	**11**	**20**	**15**	....	....	....	....	....

Signed as a free agent by **NY Rangers**, October 30, 1942.

GOODENOUGH, Larry

Defense. Shoots right. 6', 195 lbs. Born, Toronto, Ont., January 19, 1953.
(Philadelphia's 1st choice, 20th overall, in 1973 Amateur Draft).

Season	Club	GP	G	A	Pts	PIM	GP	G	A	Pts	PIM
1974-75 ♦	Philadelphia Flyers	20	3	9	12	0	5	0	4	4	2
1975-76	Philadelphia Flyers	77	8	34	42	83	16	3	11	14	6
1976-77	Philadelphia Flyers	32	4	13	17	21	....	....	....	....	....
	Vancouver Canucks	30	2	4	6	27	....	....	....	....	....
1977-78	Vancouver Canucks	42	1	6	7	28	....	....	....	....	....
1978-79	Vancouver Canucks	36	4	9	13	18	1	0	0	0	2

Season	Club	REGULAR SEASON GP	G	A	Pts	PIM	PLAYOFFS GP	G	A	Pts	PIM
1979-80	Vancouver Canucks	5	0	2	2	2	....	....	....	....	....
	NHL Totals	**242**	**22**	**77**	**99**	**179**	**22**	**3**	**15**	**18**	**10**

Traded to **Vancouver** by **Philadelphia** with Jack McIlhargey for Bob Dailey, January 20, 1977. Signed as a free agent by **Los Angeles**, August, 1980. Traded to **Chicago** by **Los Angeles** with Los Angeles' 3rd round choice (Trent Yawney) in 1984 Entry Draft for Terry Ruskowski, October 24, 1982.

GOODFELLOW, Ebbie — HHOF

Center/Defense. Shoots left. 6', 175 lbs. Born, Ottawa, Ont., April 9, 1907.

Season	Club	GP	G	A	Pts	PIM	GP	G	A	Pts	PIM
1929-30	Detroit Cougars	44	17	17	34	54	....	....	....	....	....
1930-31	Detroit Falcons	44	25	23	48	32	....	....	....	....	....
1931-32	Detroit Falcons	48	14	16	30	56	2	0	0	0	0
1932-33	Detroit Red Wings	41	12	8	20	47	4	1	0	1	11
1933-34	Detroit Red Wings	48	13	13	26	45	9	4	3	7	12
1934-35	Detroit Red Wings	48	12	24	36	44	....	....	....	....	....
1935-36 ♦	Detroit Red Wings	48	5	18	23	69	7	1	0	1	4
1936-37 ♦	Detroit Red Wings	48	9	16	25	43	9	2	2	4	12
1937-38	Detroit Red Wings	30	0	7	7	13	....	....	....	....	....
1938-39	Detroit Red Wings	48	8	8	16	36	6	0	0	0	8
1939-40	Detroit Red Wings	43	11	17	28	31	5	0	2	2	9
1940-41	Detroit Red Wings	47	5	17	22	35	3	0	1	1	9
1941-42	Detroit Red Wings	9	2	2	4	2	....	....	....	....	....
1942-43 ♦	Detroit Red Wings	11	1	4	5	4	....	....	....	....	....
	NHL Totals	**557**	**134**	**190**	**324**	**511**	**45**	**8**	**8**	**16**	**65**

NHL Second All-Star Team (1936) • NHL First All-Star Team (1937, 1940) • Hart Trophy (1940)
Played in NHL All-Star Game (1937, 1939)

• Barred from playing in the NHL after it was determined he had a valid contract with Saskatoon (PrHL), January 17, 1927. Traded to **Detroit** by **Saskatoon** (PrHL) for $4,000, February 2, 1927. • Missed majority of the 1941-42 and 1942-43 seasons recovering from knee surgery, December 1, 1941.

GORDIOUK, Viktor

Left wing. Shoots right. 5'10", 176 lbs. Born, Odintsovo, USSR, April 11, 1970.
(Buffalo's 6th choice, 142nd overall, in 1990 Entry Draft).

Season	Club	GP	G	A	Pts	PIM	GP	G	A	Pts	PIM
1992-93	Buffalo Sabres	16	3	6	9	0	....	....	....	....	....
1994-95	Buffalo Sabres	10	0	2	2	0	....	....	....	....	....
	NHL Totals	**26**	**3**	**8**	**11**	**0**	....	....	....	....	....

GORDON, Fred

Right wing. Shoots right. 5'10", 185 lbs. Born, Fleming, Sask., May 6, 1900.

Season	Club	GP	G	A	Pts	PIM	GP	G	A	Pts	PIM
1926-27	Detroit Cougars	38	5	5	10	28	....	....	....	....	....
1927-28	Boston Bruins	43	3	2	5	40	2	0	0	0	0
	NHL Totals	**81**	**8**	**7**	**15**	**68**	**2**	**0**	**0**	**0**	**0**

Traded to **Detroit** by **Saskatoon** (WHL) for cash, October 27, 1926. Traded to **Boston** by **Detroit** for Harry Meeking, May 22, 1927.

GORDON, Jack

Center. Shoots right. 5'9", 154 lbs. Born, Winnipeg, Man., March 3, 1928.

Season	Club	GP	G	A	Pts	PIM	GP	G	A	Pts	PIM
1948-49	New York Rangers	31	3	9	12	0	....	....	....	....	....
1949-50	New York Rangers	1	0	0	0	0	9	1	1	2	7
1950-51	New York Rangers	4	0	1	1	0	....	....	....	....	....
	NHL Totals	**36**	**3**	**10**	**13**	**0**	**9**	**1**	**1**	**2**	**7**

Traded to **Cleveland** (AHL) by **NY Rangers** with Ed Reigle, Fred Shero, Fern Perreault and cash for Wally Hergesheimer and Hy Buller, May 14, 1951.

GORDON, Robb

Center. Shoots right. 5'11", 190 lbs. Born, Murrayville, B.C., January 13, 1976.
(Vancouver's 2nd choice, 39th overall, in 1994 Entry Draft).

Season	Club	GP	G	A	Pts	PIM	GP	G	A	Pts	PIM
1998-99	Vancouver Canucks	4	0	0	0	2	....	....	....	....	....
	NHL Totals	**4**	**0**	**0**	**0**	**2**	....	....	....	....	....

GOREN, Lee

Right wing. Shoots right. 6'3", 205 lbs. Born, Winnipeg, Man., December 26, 1977.
(Boston's 5th choice, 63rd overall, in 1997 Entry Draft).

Season	Club	GP	G	A	Pts	PIM	GP	G	A	Pts	PIM
2000-01	Boston Bruins	21	2	0	2	7	....	....	....	....	....
2002-03	Boston Bruins	14	2	1	3	7	5	0	0	0	5
	NHL Totals	**35**	**4**	**1**	**5**	**14**	**5**	**0**	**0**	**0**	**5**

Signed as a free agent by **Florida**, July 24, 2003.

GORENCE, Tom

Right wing. Shoots right. 6', 190 lbs. Born, St. Paul, MN, March 11, 1957.
(Philadelphia's 2nd choice, 35th overall, in 1977 Amateur Draft).

Season	Club	GP	G	A	Pts	PIM	GP	G	A	Pts	PIM
1978-79	Philadelphia Flyers	42	13	6	19	10	7	3	1	4	0
1979-80	Philadelphia Flyers	51	8	13	21	15	15	3	3	6	18
1980-81	Philadelphia Flyers	79	24	18	42	46	12	3	2	5	29
1981-82	Philadelphia Flyers	66	5	8	13	8	3	0	0	0	0
1982-83	Philadelphia Flyers	53	7	7	14	10	....	....	....	....	....
1983-84	Edmonton Oilers	12	1	1	2	0	....	....	....	....	....
	NHL Totals	**303**	**58**	**53**	**111**	**89**	**37**	**9**	**6**	**15**	**47**

Signed as a free agent by **Edmonton**, November 1, 1983. Signed as a free agent by **New Jersey**, March 5, 1985.

GORING, Butch

Center. Shoots left. 5'9", 170 lbs. Born, St. Boniface, Man., October 22, 1949.
(Los Angeles' 4th choice, 51st overall, in 1969 Amateur Draft).

Season	Club	GP	G	A	Pts	PIM	GP	G	A	Pts	PIM
1969-70	Los Angeles Kings	59	13	23	36	8	....	....	....	....	....
1970-71	Los Angeles Kings	19	2	5	7	2	....	....	....	....	....
1971-72	Los Angeles Kings	74	21	29	50	2	....	....	....	....	....
1972-73	Los Angeles Kings	67	28	31	59	2	....	....	....	....	....
1973-74	Los Angeles Kings	70	28	33	61	2	5	0	1	1	0
1974-75	Los Angeles Kings	60	27	33	60	6	3	0	0	0	0
1975-76	Los Angeles Kings	80	33	40	73	8	9	2	3	5	4
1976-77	Los Angeles Kings	78	30	55	85	6	9	7	5	12	0
1977-78	Los Angeles Kings	80	37	36	73	2	2	0	0	0	2
1978-79	Los Angeles Kings	80	36	51	87	16	2	0	0	0	0
1979-80	Los Angeles Kings	69	20	48	68	12	....	....	....	....	....
	♦ New York Islanders	12	6	5	11	2	21	7	12	19	2
1980-81 ♦	New York Islanders	78	23	37	60	0	18	10	10	20	6
1981-82 ♦	New York Islanders	67	15	17	32	10	19	6	5	11	12
1982-83 ♦	New York Islanders	75	19	20	39	8	20	4	8	12	4
1983-84	New York Islanders	71	22	24	46	8	21	1	5	6	2
1984-85	New York Islanders	29	2	5	7	2	....	....	....	....	....
	Boston Bruins	39	13	21	34	6	5	1	1	2	0
	NHL Totals	**1107**	**375**	**513**	**888**	**102**	**134**	**38**	**50**	**88**	**32**

Bill Masterton Trophy (1978) • Lady Byng Trophy (1978) • Conn Smythe Trophy (1981)
Played in NHL All-Star Game (1980)

Traded to **NY Islanders** by **Los Angeles** for Billy Harris and Dave Lewis, March 10, 1980. Claimed on waivers by **Boston** from **NY Islanders**, January 8, 1985.

GORMAN, Dave

Right wing. Shoots right. 5'11", 185 lbs. Born, Oshawa, Ont., April 8, 1955.
(Montreal's 7th choice, 70th overall, in 1975 Amateur Draft).

Season	Club	GP	G	A	Pts	PIM	GP	G	A	Pts	PIM
1979-80	Atlanta Flames	3	0	0	0	0	....	....	....	....	....
	NHL Totals	**3**	**0**	**0**	**0**	**0**	....	....	....	....	....

Signed as a free agent by **Atlanta**, August, 1979. Transferred to **Calgary** after **Atlanta** franchise relocated, June 24, 1980. Traded to **Montreal** by **Calgary** for Tim Burke, September, 1980. Signed as a free agent by **Buffalo**, June 30, 1981.

GORMAN, Ed

Defense. Shoots left. 6', 180 lbs. Born, Buckingham, Que., September 25, 1892.

Season	Club	GP	G	A	Pts	PIM	GP	G	A	Pts	PIM
1924-25	Ottawa Senators	28	11	4	15	49	....	....	....	....	....
1925-26	Ottawa Senators	23	2	1	3	12	2	0	0	0	2
1926-27 ♦	Ottawa Senators	41	1	0	1	17	6	0	0	0	0
1927-28	Toronto Maple Leafs	19	0	1	1	30	....	....	....	....	....
	NHL Totals	**111**	**14**	**6**	**20**	**108**	**8**	**0**	**0**	**0**	**2**

Signed as a free agent by **Ottawa**, November 6, 1924. Traded to **Toronto** by **Ottawa** for cash, October 26, 1927. • Suspended by Toronto for refusing assignment to Toronto Ravinas (Can-Pro), February 10, 1928. Traded to **Kitchener** (Can-Pro) by **Toronto** for cash, February 13, 1928.

GOSSELIN, Benoit

Left wing. Shoots left. 5'11", 190 lbs. Born, Montreal, Que., July 19, 1957.
(NY Rangers' 6th choice, 80th overall, in 1977 Amateur Draft).

Season	Club	GP	G	A	Pts	PIM	GP	G	A	Pts	PIM
1977-78	New York Rangers	7	0	0	0	33	....	....	....	....	....
	NHL Totals	**7**	**0**	**0**	**0**	**33**	....	....	....	....	....

Signed as a free agent by **Winnipeg**, September 25, 1979.

GOSSELIN, David

Right wing. Shoots right. 6'1", 205 lbs. Born, Levis, Que., June 22, 1977.
(New Jersey's 4th choice, 78th overall, in 1995 Entry Draft).

Season	Club	GP	G	A	Pts	PIM	GP	G	A	Pts	PIM
99-2000	Nashville Predators	10	2	1	3	6	....	....	....	....	....
2001-02	Nashville Predators	3	0	0	0	5	....	....	....	....	....
	NHL Totals	**13**	**2**	**1**	**3**	**11**	....	....	....	....	....

Signed as a free agent by **Nashville**, July 1, 1998. Traded to **Dallas** by **Nashville** with Nashville's 5th round choice (Eero Kilpelainen) in 2003 Entry Draft for Ed Belfour and Cameron Mann, June 29, 2002.

GOSSELIN, Guy

Defense. Shoots right. 5'10", 185 lbs. Born, Rochester, MN, January 6, 1964.
(Winnipeg's 6th choice, 159th overall, in 1982 Entry Draft).

Season	Club	GP	G	A	Pts	PIM	GP	G	A	Pts	PIM
1987-88	Winnipeg Jets	5	0	0	0	6	....	....	....	....	....
	NHL Totals	**5**	**0**	**0**	**0**	**6**	....	....	....	....	....

Signed as a free agent by **San Jose**, August 25, 1993.

GOTAAS, Steve

Center. Shoots right. 5'10", 180 lbs. Born, Camrose, Alta., May 10, 1967.
(Pittsburgh's 4th choice, 86th overall, in 1985 Entry Draft).

Season	Club	GP	G	A	Pts	PIM	GP	G	A	Pts	PIM
1987-88	Pittsburgh Penguins	36	5	6	11	45	....	....	....	....	....
1988-89	Minnesota North Stars	12	1	3	4	6	3	0	1	1	5
1990-91	Minnesota North Stars	1	0	0	0	2	....	....	....	....	....
	NHL Totals	**49**	**6**	**9**	**15**	**53**	**3**	**0**	**1**	**1**	**5**

Traded to **Minnesota** by **Pittsburgh** with Ville Siren for Gord Dineen and Scott Bjugstad, December 17, 1988.

GOTTSELIG, Johnny

Left wing. Shoots left. 5'11", 158 lbs. Born, Odessa, Russia, June 24, 1905.

		REGULAR SEASON					PLAYOFFS				
Season	Club	GP	G	A	Pts	PIM	GP	G	A	Pts	PIM
1928-29	Chicago Black Hawks	44	5	3	8	26	....	....	....	....	....
1929-30	Chicago Black Hawks	39	21	4	25	28	2	0	0	0	4
1930-31	Chicago Black Hawks	42	20	12	32	14	9	3	3	6	2
1931-32	Chicago Black Hawks	44	13	15	28	28	2	0	0	0	2
1932-33	Chicago Black Hawks	41	11	11	22	6	....	....	....	....	....
1933-34 ♦	Chicago Black Hawks	48	16	14	30	4	8	4	3	7	4
1934-35	Chicago Black Hawks	48	19	18	37	16	2	0	0	0	0
1935-36	Chicago Black Hawks	40	14	15	29	4	2	0	2	2	0
1936-37	Chicago Black Hawks	47	9	21	30	10	....	....	....	....	....
1937-38 ♦	Chicago Black Hawks	48	13	19	32	22	10	5	3	*8	4
1938-39	Chicago Black Hawks	48	16	23	39	15	....	....	....	....	....
1939-40	Chicago Black Hawks	39	8	15	23	7	2	0	1	1	0
1940-41	Chicago Black Hawks	5	1	4	5	5	....	....	....	....	....
1942-43	Chicago Black Hawks	10	2	6	8	12	....	....	....	....	....
1943-44	Chicago Black Hawks	45	8	15	23	6	6	1	1	2	2
1944-45	Chicago Black Hawks	1	0	0	0	0	....	....	....	....	....
	NHL Totals	**589**	**176**	**195**	**371**	**203**	**43**	**13**	**13**	**26**	**18**

NHL Second All-Star Team (1939)

Played in NHL All-Star Game (1937, 1939)

Claimed by **Chicago** from **Winnipeg** (AHA) in Inter-League Draft, May 14, 1928.

GOULD, Bobby

Right wing. Shoots right. 6', 195 lbs. Born, Petrolia, Ont., September 2, 1957.
(Atlanta's 7th choice, 118th overall, in 1977 Amateur Draft).

Season	Club	GP	G	A	Pts	PIM	GP	G	A	Pts	PIM
1979-80	Atlanta Flames	1	0	0	0	0	....	....	....	....	....
1980-81	Calgary Flames	3	0	0	0	0	11	3	1	4	4
1981-82	Calgary Flames	16	3	0	3	4	....	....	....	....	....
	Washington Capitals	60	18	13	31	69	....	....	....	....	....
1982-83	Washington Capitals	80	22	18	40	43	4	5	0	5	4
1983-84	Washington Capitals	78	21	19	40	74	5	0	2	2	4
1984-85	Washington Capitals	78	14	19	33	69	5	0	1	1	2
1985-86	Washington Capitals	79	19	19	38	26	9	4	3	7	11
1986-87	Washington Capitals	78	23	27	50	74	7	0	3	3	8
1987-88	Washington Capitals	72	12	14	26	56	14	3	1	4	21
1988-89	Washington Capitals	75	5	13	18	65	6	0	2	2	0
1989-90	Boston Bruins	77	8	17	25	92	17	0	0	0	4
	NHL Totals	**697**	**145**	**159**	**304**	**572**	**78**	**15**	**13**	**28**	**58**

Transferred to **Calgary** after **Atlanta** franchise relocated, June 24, 1980. Traded to **Washington** by **Calgary** with Randy Holt for Pat Ribble and Washington's 2nd round choice (later traded to Montreal – Montreal selected Todd Francis) in 1983 Entry Draft, November 25, 1981. Traded to **Boston** by **Washington** for Alain Cote, September 28, 1989.

GOULD, John

Right wing. Shoots left. 5'11", 197 lbs. Born, Beeton, Ont., April 11, 1949.

Season	Club	GP	G	A	Pts	PIM	GP	G	A	Pts	PIM
1971-72	Buffalo Sabres	2	1	0	1	0	....	....	....	....	....
1972-73	Buffalo Sabres	8	0	1	1	0	....	....	....	....	....
1973-74	Buffalo Sabres	30	4	2	6	2	....	....	....	....	....
	Vancouver Canucks	45	9	10	19	8	....	....	....	....	....
1974-75	Vancouver Canucks	78	34	31	65	27	5	2	2	4	0
1975-76	Vancouver Canucks	70	32	27	59	16	2	1	0	1	0
1976-77	Vancouver Canucks	25	7	8	15	2	....	....	....	....	....
	Atlanta Flames	54	8	15	23	8	3	0	0	0	2
1977-78	Atlanta Flames	79	19	28	47	21	2	0	0	0	2
1978-79	Atlanta Flames	61	8	7	15	18	2	0	0	0	0
1979-80	Buffalo Sabres	52	9	9	18	11	....	....	....	....	....
	NHL Totals	**504**	**131**	**138**	**269**	**113**	**14**	**3**	**2**	**5**	**4**

• Brother of Larry

Signed as a free agent by **Buffalo**, August, 1971. Traded to **Vancouver** by **Buffalo** with Tracy Pratt for Jerry Korab, December 27, 1973. Traded to **Atlanta** by **Vancouver** with Los Angeles' 2nd round choice (previously acquired, Atlanta selected Brian Hill) in 1977 Amateur Draft for Hilliard Graves and Larry Carriere, December 2, 1976. Claimed by **Edmonton** from **Atlanta** in Expansion Draft, June 13, 1979. Traded to **Buffalo** by **Edmonton** for Alex Tidey, November 13, 1979.

GOULD, Larry

Left wing. Shoots left. 5'9", 170 lbs. Born, Alliston, Ont., August 16, 1952.

Season	Club	GP	G	A	Pts	PIM	GP	G	A	Pts	PIM
1973-74	Vancouver Canucks	2	0	0	0	0	....	....	....	....	....
	NHL Totals	**2**	**0**	**0**	**0**	**0**	....	....	....	....	....

• Brother of John

Signed as a free agent by **Vancouver**, October, 1973.

GOULET, Michel

HHOF

Left wing. Shoots left. 6'1", 195 lbs. Born, Peribonka, Que., April 21, 1960.
(Quebec's 1st choice, 20th overall, in 1979 Entry Draft).

Season	Club	GP	G	A	Pts	PIM	GP	G	A	Pts	PIM
1979-80	Quebec Nordiques	77	22	32	54	48	....	....	....	....	....
1980-81	Quebec Nordiques	76	32	39	71	45	4	3	4	7	7
1981-82	Quebec Nordiques	80	42	42	84	48	16	8	5	13	6
1982-83	Quebec Nordiques	80	57	48	105	51	4	0	0	0	6
1983-84	Quebec Nordiques	75	56	65	121	76	9	2	4	6	17
1984-85	Quebec Nordiques	69	55	40	95	55	17	11	10	21	17
1985-86	Quebec Nordiques	75	53	51	104	64	3	1	2	3	10
1986-87	Quebec Nordiques	75	49	47	96	61	13	9	5	14	35
1987-88	Quebec Nordiques	80	48	58	106	56	....	....	....	....	....
1988-89	Quebec Nordiques	69	26	38	64	67	....	....	....	....	....
1989-90	Quebec Nordiques	57	16	29	45	42	....	....	....	....	....
	Chicago Blackhawks	8	4	1	5	9	14	2	4	6	6
1990-91	Chicago Blackhawks	74	27	38	65	65	....	....	....	....	....
1991-92	Chicago Blackhawks	75	22	41	63	69	9	3	4	7	6
1992-93	Chicago Blackhawks	63	23	21	44	43	3	0	1	1	0
1993-94	Chicago Blackhawks	56	16	14	30	26	....	....	....	....	....
	NHL Totals	**1089**	**548**	**604**	**1152**	**825**	**92**	**39**	**39**	**78**	**110**

NHL Second All-Star Team (1983, 1988) • NHL First All-Star Team (1984, 1986, 1987)

Played in NHL All-Star Game (1983, 1984, 1985, 1986, 1988)

Traded to **Chicago** by **Quebec** with Greg Millen and Quebec's 6th round choice (Kevin St. Jacques) in 1991 Entry Draft for Mario Doyon, Everett Sanipass and Dan Vincelette, March 5, 1990. • Suffered career-ending head injury in game vs. Montreal, March 16, 1994.

GOUPILLE, Red

Defense. Shoots left. 6', 190 lbs. Born, Trois-Rivieres, Que., September 2, 1915.

Season	Club	GP	G	A	Pts	PIM	GP	G	A	Pts	PIM
1935-36	Montreal Canadiens	4	0	0	0	0	....	....	....	....	....
1936-37	Montreal Canadiens	4	0	0	0	0	....	....	....	....	....
1937-38	Montreal Canadiens	47	4	5	9	44	3	2	0	2	4
1938-39	Montreal Canadiens	18	0	2	2	24	....	....	....	....	....
1939-40	Montreal Canadiens	48	2	10	12	48	....	....	....	....	....
1940-41	Montreal Canadiens	48	3	6	9	81	2	0	0	0	0
1941-42	Montreal Canadiens	47	1	5	6	51	3	0	0	0	2
1942-43	Montreal Canadiens	6	2	0	2	8	....	....	....	....	....
	NHL Totals	**222**	**12**	**28**	**40**	**256**	**8**	**2**	**0**	**2**	**6**

Played in NHL All-Star Game (1939)

GOVEDARIS, Chris

Left wing. Shoots left. 6', 200 lbs. Born, Toronto, Ont., February 2, 1970.
(Hartford's 1st choice, 11th overall, in 1988 Entry Draft).

Season	Club	GP	G	A	Pts	PIM	GP	G	A	Pts	PIM
1989-90	Hartford Whalers	12	0	1	1	6	2	0	0	0	2
1990-91	Hartford Whalers	14	1	3	4	4	....	....	....	....	....
1992-93	Hartford Whalers	7	1	0	1	0	....	....	....	....	....
1993-94	Toronto Maple Leafs	12	2	2	4	14	2	0	0	0	0
	NHL Totals	**45**	**4**	**6**	**10**	**24**	**4**	**0**	**0**	**0**	**2**

Signed as a free agent by **Toronto**, September 16, 1993. Signed as a free agent by **Winnipeg**, August 14, 1995.

GOYER, Gerry

Center. Shoots left. 6'2", 196 lbs. Born, Belleville, Ont., October 20, 1936.

Season	Club	GP	G	A	Pts	PIM	GP	G	A	Pts	PIM
1967-68	Chicago Black Hawks	40	1	2	3	4	3	0	0	0	2
	NHL Totals	**40**	**1**	**2**	**3**	**4**	**3**	**0**	**0**	**0**	**2**

Claimed by **Toronto** from **LA Blades** (WHL) in Inter-League Draft, June 4, 1962. Traded to **Portland** (WHL) by **Toronto** for cash, September, 1962. Traded to **Chicago** by **Portland** (WHL) for cash, October, 1967. Traded to **Portland** (WHL) by **Chicago** for cash, July, 1968. Traded to **Vancouver** (WHL) by **Portland** (WHL) for cash, November 2, 1969. NHL rights transferred to **Vancouver** after NHL club purchased **Vancouver** (WHL) franchise, December 19, 1969.

GOYETTE, Phil

Center. Shoots left. 5'11", 170 lbs. Born, Lachine, Que., October 31, 1933.

Season	Club	GP	G	A	Pts	PIM	GP	G	A	Pts	PIM
1956-57 ♦	Montreal Canadiens	14	3	4	7	0	10	2	1	3	4
1957-58 ♦	Montreal Canadiens	70	9	37	46	8	10	4	1	5	4
1958-59 ♦	Montreal Canadiens	63	10	18	28	8	10	0	4	4	0
1959-60 ♦	Montreal Canadiens	65	21	22	43	4	8	2	1	3	4
1960-61	Montreal Canadiens	62	7	4	11	4	6	3	3	6	0
1961-62	Montreal Canadiens	69	7	27	34	18	6	1	4	5	2
1962-63	Montreal Canadiens	32	5	8	13	2	2	0	0	0	0
1963-64	New York Rangers	67	24	41	65	15	....	....	....	....	....
1964-65	New York Rangers	52	12	34	46	6	....	....	....	....	....
1965-66	New York Rangers	60	11	31	42	6	....	....	....	....	....
1966-67	New York Rangers	70	12	49	61	6	4	1	0	1	0
1967-68	New York Rangers	73	25	40	65	10	6	0	1	1	4
1968-69	New York Rangers	67	13	32	45	8	3	0	0	0	0
1969-70	St. Louis Blues	72	29	49	78	16	16	3	11	14	6
1970-71	Buffalo Sabres	60	15	46	61	6	....	....	....	....	....
1971-72	Buffalo Sabres	37	3	21	24	14	....	....	....	....	....
	New York Rangers	8	1	4	5	0	13	1	3	4	2
	NHL Totals	**941**	**207**	**467**	**674**	**131**	**94**	**17**	**29**	**46**	**26**

Lady Byng Trophy (1970)

Played in NHL All-Star Game (1957, 1958, 1959, 1961)

Claimed by **Montreal** from **Montreal Royals** (QHL) in Inter-League Draft, June 5, 1956. Traded to **NY Rangers** by **Montreal** with Don Marshall and Jacques Plante for Gump Worsley, Dave Balon, Leon Rochefort and Len Ronson, June 4, 1963. Traded to **St. Louis** by **NY Rangers** for St. Louis' 1st round choice (Andre Dupont) in 1969 Amateur Draft, June 10, 1969. Claimed by **Buffalo** from **St. Louis** in Expansion Draft, June 10, 1970. Traded to **NY Rangers** by **Buffalo** for cash, March 5, 1972.

GRABOSKI, Tony

Left wing/Defense. Shoots left. 5'10", 178 lbs. Born, Timmins, Ont., May 9, 1916.

Season	Club	GP	G	A	Pts	PIM	GP	G	A	Pts	PIM
1940-41	Montreal Canadiens	34	4	3	7	12	3	0	0	0	6
1941-42	Montreal Canadiens	23	2	5	7	8	....	....	....	....	....
1942-43	Montreal Canadiens	9	0	2	2	4	....	....	....	....	....
	NHL Totals	**66**	**6**	**10**	**16**	**24**	**3**	**0**	**0**	**0**	**6**

Signed as a free agent by **Montreal**, October 25, 1940. Traded to **Hershey** (AHL) by **Montreal** (Washington-AHL) for cash, January 18, 1943.

GRACIE, Bob

Center/Left wing. Shoots left. 5'9", 155 lbs. Born, North Bay, Ont., November 8, 1910.

Season	Club	REGULAR SEASON GP	G	A	Pts	PIM	PLAYOFFS GP	G	A	Pts	PIM
1930-31	Toronto Maple Leafs	8	4	2	6	4	2	0	0	0	0
1931-32 ♦	Toronto Maple Leafs	48	13	8	21	29	7	3	1	4	0
1932-33	Toronto Maple Leafs	48	9	13	22	27	9	0	1	1	0
1933-34	Boston Bruins	24	2	6	8	8	....	....	....	....	....
	New York Americans	24	4	6	10	10	....	....	....	....	....
1934-35	New York Americans	14	2	1	3	4	....	....	....	....	....
♦	Montreal Maroons	32	10	8	18	11	7	0	2	2	2
1935-36	Montreal Maroons	48	11	14	25	31	3	0	1	1	0
1936-37	Montreal Maroons	47	11	25	36	18	5	1	2	3	2
1937-38	Montreal Maroons	48	12	19	31	32	....	....	....	....	....
1938-39	Montreal Canadiens	7	0	1	1	4	....	....	....	....	....
	Chicago Black Hawks	31	4	6	10	27	....	....	....	....	....
	NHL Totals	**379**	**82**	**109**	**191**	**205**	**33**	**4**	**7**	**11**	**4**

Signed as a free agent by **Toronto**, February 27, 1931. Traded to **Ottawa** by **Toronto** with $10,000 for Hec Kilrea, October 4, 1933. Traded to **Boston** by **Ottawa** for Percy Galbraith, Bud Cook and Ted Saunders, October 4, 1933. Traded to **NY Americans** by **Boston** with Art Chapman for Lloyd Gross and George Patterson, January 11, 1934. Traded to **Mtl. Maroons** by **NY Americans** for cash, December 25, 1934. Traded to **Montreal** by **Mtl. Maroons** for cash, September 14, 1938. Traded to **Chicago** by **Montreal** for cash, November 25, 1938. Traded to **Detroit** (Indianapolis-IAHL) by **Cleveland** (IAHL) with $30,000 for Don Deacon, February 5, 1940. Traded to **Buffalo** (AHL) by **Detroit** for cash, October 20, 1940.

GRADIN, Thomas

Center. Shoots right. 5'11", 176 lbs. Born, Solleftea, Sweden, February 18, 1956.
(Chicago's 3rd choice, 45th overall, in 1976 Amateur Draft).

Season	Club	REGULAR SEASON GP	G	A	Pts	PIM	PLAYOFFS GP	G	A	Pts	PIM
1978-79	Vancouver Canucks	76	20	31	51	22	3	4	1	5	4
1979-80	Vancouver Canucks	80	30	45	75	22	4	0	2	2	0
1980-81	Vancouver Canucks	79	21	48	69	34	3	1	3	4	0
1981-82	Vancouver Canucks	76	37	49	86	32	17	9	10	19	10
1982-83	Vancouver Canucks	80	32	54	86	61	4	1	3	4	2
1983-84	Vancouver Canucks	75	21	57	78	32	4	0	1	1	2
1984-85	Vancouver Canucks	76	22	42	64	43	....	....	....	....	....
1985-86	Vancouver Canucks	71	14	27	41	34	3	2	1	3	2
1986-87	Boston Bruins	64	12	31	43	18	4	0	4	4	0
	NHL Totals	**677**	**209**	**384**	**593**	**298**	**42**	**17**	**25**	**42**	**20**

Played in NHL All-Star Game (1985)

Rights traded to **Vancouver** by **Chicago** for Vancouver's 2nd round choice (Steve Ludzik) in 1980 Entry Draft, June 14, 1978. Signed as a free agent by **Boston**, June 24, 1986.

GRAHAM, Dirk

Right/left wing. Shoots right. 5'11", 198 lbs. Born, Regina, Sask., July 29, 1959.
(Vancouver's 5th choice, 89th overall, in 1979 Entry Draft).

Season	Club	REGULAR SEASON GP	G	A	Pts	PIM	PLAYOFFS GP	G	A	Pts	PIM
1983-84	Minnesota North Stars	6	1	1	2	0	1	0	0	0	2
1984-85	Minnesota North Stars	36	12	11	23	23	9	0	4	4	7
1985-86	Minnesota North Stars	80	22	33	55	87	5	3	1	4	2
1986-87	Minnesota North Stars	76	25	29	54	142	....	....	....	....	....
1987-88	Minnesota North Stars	28	7	5	12	39	....	....	....	....	....
	Chicago Blackhawks	42	17	19	36	32	4	1	2	3	4
1988-89	Chicago Blackhawks	80	33	45	78	89	16	2	4	6	38
1989-90	Chicago Blackhawks	73	22	32	54	102	5	1	5	6	2
1990-91	Chicago Blackhawks	80	24	21	45	88	6	1	2	3	17
1991-92	Chicago Blackhawks	80	17	30	47	89	18	7	5	12	8
1992-93	Chicago Blackhawks	84	20	17	37	139	4	0	0	0	0
1993-94	Chicago Blackhawks	67	15	18	33	45	6	0	1	1	4
1994-95	Chicago Blackhawks	40	4	9	13	42	16	2	3	5	8
	NHL Totals	**772**	**219**	**270**	**489**	**917**	**90**	**17**	**27**	**44**	**92**

Frank J. Selke Trophy (1991)

Signed as a free agent by **Minnesota**, August 17, 1983. Traded to **Chicago** by **Minnesota** for Curt Fraser, January 4, 1988.

GRAHAM, Leth

Left wing. Shoots left. 5'9", 150 lbs. Born, Ottawa, Ont., 1894.

Season	Club	REGULAR SEASON GP	G	A	Pts	PIM	PLAYOFFS GP	G	A	Pts	PIM
1920-21 ♦	Ottawa Senators	14	0	0	0	0	1	0	0	0	0
1921-22	Ottawa Senators	1	2	0	2	0	....	....	....	....	....
1922-23	Hamilton Tigers	5	1	0	1	0	....	....	....	....	....
1923-24	Ottawa Senators	3	0	0	0	0	....	....	....	....	....
1924-25	Ottawa Senators	3	0	0	0	0	....	....	....	....	....
1925-26	Ottawa Senators	1	0	0	0	0	....	....	....	....	....
	NHL Totals	**27**	**3**	**0**	**3**	**0**	**1**	**0**	**0**	**0**	**0**

Signed as a free agent by **Ottawa**, November 10, 1920. Traded to **Saskatoon** (WCHL) by **Ottawa** for cash, December 2, 1921. • Released by Saskatoon (WCHL), December 10, 1921. Signed as a free agent by **Ottawa**, December, 1921. Signed as a free agent by **Hamilton**, November 15, 1922. Traded to **Ottawa** by **Hamilton** for cash, December 18, 1923.

GRAHAM, Pat

Left wing. Shoots left. 6'1", 190 lbs. Born, Toronto, Ont., May 25, 1961.
(Pittsburgh's 5th choice, 114th overall, in 1980 Entry Draft).

Season	Club	REGULAR SEASON GP	G	A	Pts	PIM	PLAYOFFS GP	G	A	Pts	PIM
1981-82	Pittsburgh Penguins	42	6	8	14	55	4	0	0	0	2
1982-83	Pittsburgh Penguins	20	1	5	6	16	....	....	....	....	....
1983-84	Toronto Maple Leafs	41	4	4	8	65	....	....	....	....	....
	NHL Totals	**103**	**11**	**17**	**28**	**136**	**4**	**0**	**0**	**0**	**2**

Traded to **Toronto** by **Pittsburgh** with Nick Ricci for Rocky Saganiuk and Vincent Tremblay, August 15, 1983.

GRAHAM, Rod

Left wing. Shoots left. 6', 185 lbs. Born, London, Ont., August 19, 1946.

Season	Club	REGULAR SEASON GP	G	A	Pts	PIM	PLAYOFFS GP	G	A	Pts	PIM
1974-75	Boston Bruins	14	2	1	3	7	....	....	....	....	....
	NHL Totals	**14**	**2**	**1**	**3**	**7**	....	....	....	....	....

Signed as a free agent by **Rochester** (AHL), September, 1972. Rights transferred to **Boston** after NHL club signed affiliate agreement with **Rochester** (AHL), June 14, 1974.

GRAHAM, Ted

Defense. Shoots left. 5'8", 170 lbs. Born, Owen Sound, Ont., January 30, 1906.

Season	Club	REGULAR SEASON GP	G	A	Pts	PIM	PLAYOFFS GP	G	A	Pts	PIM
1927-28	Chicago Black Hawks	19	1	0	1	8	....	....	....	....	....
1929-30	Chicago Black Hawks	26	1	2	3	23	2	0	0	0	8
1930-31	Chicago Black Hawks	42	0	7	7	38	9	0	0	0	12
1931-32	Chicago Black Hawks	48	0	3	3	40	2	0	0	0	2
1932-33	Chicago Black Hawks	47	3	8	11	57	....	....	....	....	....
1933-34	Montreal Maroons	19	2	1	3	10	....	....	....	....	....
	Detroit Red Wings	28	1	0	1	29	9	3	1	4	8
1934-35	Detroit Red Wings	24	0	2	2	26	....	....	....	....	....
	St. Louis Eagles	13	0	0	0	2	....	....	....	....	....
1935-36	Boston Bruins	48	4	1	5	37	2	0	0	0	0
1936-37	Boston Bruins	1	0	0	0	0	....	....	....	....	....
	New York Americans	31	2	1	3	30	....	....	....	....	....
	NHL Totals	**346**	**14**	**25**	**39**	**300**	**24**	**3**	**1**	**4**	**30**

Signed as a free agent by **Chicago** (Chicago-AHA), October 4, 1926. Traded to **Moose Jaw** (PrHL) by **Chicago** for Amby Moran and future considerations (Vic Hoffinger, January 23, 1928), January 11, 1928. Traded to **Saskatoon** (PrHL) by **Moose Jaw** (PrHL) for cash, January 11, 1928. Signed as a free agent by **Tulsa** (AHA), October 29, 1928. Traded to **Chicago** by **Tulsa** (AHA) for Ralph Taylor and cash, January 4, 1930. • Cash amount in January 4, 1930 transaction was increased after Taylor was returned to Chicago by NHL after they determined that Taylor was not offered on waivers to other NHL clubs. Traded to **Mtl. Maroons** by **Chicago** for Lionel Conacher, October 1, 1933. Traded to **Detroit** by **Mtl. Maroons** for Stewart Evans, January 2, 1934. Traded to **St. Louis** by **Detroit** with $50,000 for Syd Howe and Ralph Bowman, February 11, 1935. Claimed by **Boston** from **St. Louis** in Dispersal Draft, October 15, 1935. Traded to **NY Americans** by **Boston** for Walter Kalbfleish, December 19, 1936.

GRANATO, Tony

Right wing. Shoots right. 5'10", 185 lbs. Born, Downers Grove, IL, July 25, 1964.
(NY Rangers' 5th choice, 120th overall, in 1982 Entry Draft).

Season	Club	REGULAR SEASON GP	G	A	Pts	PIM	PLAYOFFS GP	G	A	Pts	PIM
1988-89	New York Rangers	78	36	27	63	140	4	1	1	2	21
1989-90	New York Rangers	37	7	18	25	77	....	....	....	....	....
	Los Angeles Kings	19	5	6	11	45	10	5	4	9	12
1990-91	Los Angeles Kings	68	30	34	64	154	12	1	4	5	28
1991-92	Los Angeles Kings	80	39	29	68	187	6	1	5	6	10
1992-93	Los Angeles Kings	81	37	45	82	171	24	6	11	17	50
1993-94	Los Angeles Kings	50	7	14	21	150	....	....	....	....	....
1994-95	Los Angeles Kings	33	13	11	24	68	....	....	....	....	....
1995-96	Los Angeles Kings	49	17	18	35	46	....	....	....	....	....
1996-97	San Jose Sharks	76	25	15	40	159	....	....	....	....	....
1997-98	San Jose Sharks	59	16	9	25	70	1	0	0	0	0
1998-99	San Jose Sharks	35	6	6	12	54	6	1	1	2	2
99-2000	San Jose Sharks	48	6	7	13	39	12	0	1	1	14
2000-01	San Jose Sharks	60	4	5	9	65	4	1	0	1	4
	NHL Totals	**773**	**248**	**244**	**492**	**1425**	**79**	**16**	**27**	**43**	**141**

NHL All-Rookie Team (1989) • Bill Masterton Memorial Trophy (1997)

Played in NHL All-Star Game (1997)

Traded to **Los Angeles** by **NY Rangers** with Tomas Sandstrom for Bernie Nicholls, January 20, 1990. Signed as a free agent by **San Jose**, August 15, 1996.

GRAND-PIERRE, Jean-Luc

Defense. Shoots right. 6'3", 223 lbs. Born, Montreal, Que., February 2, 1977.
(St. Louis' 6th choice, 179th overall, in 1995 Entry Draft).

Season	Club	REGULAR SEASON GP	G	A	Pts	PIM	PLAYOFFS GP	G	A	Pts	PIM
1998-99	Buffalo Sabres	16	0	1	1	17	....	....	....	....	....
99-2000	Buffalo Sabres	11	0	0	0	15	4	0	0	0	4
2000-01	Columbus Blue Jackets	64	1	4	5	73	....	....	....	....	....
2001-02	Columbus Blue Jackets	81	2	6	8	90	....	....	....	....	....
2002-03	Columbus Blue Jackets	41	1	0	1	64	....	....	....	....	....
	NHL Totals	**213**	**4**	**11**	**15**	**259**	**4**	**0**	**0**	**0**	**4**

Traded to **Buffalo** by **St. Louis** with Ottawa's 2nd round choice (previously acquired, Buffalo selected Cory Sarich) in 1996 Entry Draft and St. Louis' 3rd round choice (Maxim Afinogenov) in 1997 Entry Draft for Yuri Khmylev and Buffalo's 8th round choice (Andrei Podkonicky) in 1996 Entry Draft, March 20, 1996. Traded to **Columbus** by **Buffalo** with Matt Davidson, San Jose's 5th round choice (previously acquired, Columbus selected Tyler Kolarik) in 2000 Entry Draft and Buffalo's 5th round choice (later traded to Calgary – later traded to Detroit – Detroit selected Andreas Jamtin) in 2001 Entry Draft to complete Expansion Draft agreement which had Columbus select Geoff Sanderson and Dwayne Roloson from Buffalo, June 23, 2000.

GRANT, Danny

Right wing. Shoots left. 5'10", 188 lbs. Born, Fredericton, N.B., February 21, 1946.

Season	Club	REGULAR SEASON GP	G	A	Pts	PIM	PLAYOFFS GP	G	A	Pts	PIM
1965-66	Montreal Canadiens	1	0	0	0	0	....	....	....	....	....
1967-68 ♦	Montreal Canadiens	22	3	4	7	10	10	0	3	3	5
1968-69	Minnesota North Stars	75	34	31	65	46	....	....	....	....	....
1969-70	Minnesota North Stars	76	29	28	57	23	6	0	2	2	4
1970-71	Minnesota North Stars	78	34	23	57	46	12	5	5	10	8
1971-72	Minnesota North Stars	78	18	25	43	18	7	2	1	3	0
1972-73	Minnesota North Stars	78	32	35	67	12	6	3	1	4	0
1973-74	Minnesota North Stars	78	29	35	64	16	....	....	....	....	....
1974-75	Detroit Red Wings	80	50	37	87	28	....	....	....	....	....
1975-76	Detroit Red Wings	39	10	13	23	20	....	....	....	....	....

Season	Club	GP	G	A	Pts	PIM	GP	G	A	Pts	PIM
		REGULAR SEASON					PLAYOFFS				
1976-77	Detroit Red Wings	42	2	10	12	4	....	....	....	....	....
1977-78	Detroit Red Wings	13	2	2	4	6	....	....	....	....	....
	Los Angeles Kings	41	10	19	29	2	2	0	2	2	2
1978-79	Los Angeles Kings	35	10	11	21	8	....	....	....	....	....
	NHL Totals	**736**	**263**	**273**	**536**	**239**	**43**	**10**	**14**	**24**	**19**

Calder Memorial Trophy (1969)

Played in NHL All-Star Game (1969, 1970, 1971)

Traded to **Minnesota** by **Montreal** with Claude Larose and future considerations (Bob Murdoch, May 25, 1971) for Minnesota's 1st round choice (Dave Gardner) in 1972 Amateur Draft, cash and future considerations (Marshall Johnston, May 25, 1971), June 10, 1968. Traded to **Detroit** by **Minnesota** for Henry Boucha, August 27, 1974. • Missed majority of 1975-76 season recovering from ruptured anterior thigh muscle suffered in game vs. Kansas City, December 19, 1975. Consecutive games played streak halted at 566. Traded to **Los Angeles** by **Detroit** for the rights to Barry Long and Montreal's 3rd round choice (previously acquired, Detroit selected Doug Derkson) in 1978 Amateur Draft, January 9, 1978.

GRATTON, Benoit

Center. Shoots left. 5'11", 194 lbs. Born, Montreal, Que., December 28, 1976.
(Washington's 6th choice, 105th overall, in 1995 Entry Draft).

Season	Club	GP	G	A	Pts	PIM	GP	G	A	Pts	PIM
1997-98	Washington Capitals	6	0	1	1	6	....	....	....	....	....
1998-99	Washington Capitals	16	4	3	7	16	....	....	....	....	....
99-2000	Calgary Flames	10	0	2	2	10	....	....	....	....	....
2000-01	Calgary Flames	14	1	3	4	14	....	....	....	....	....
2001-02	Montreal Canadiens	8	1	0	1	8	....	....	....	....	....
	NHL Totals	**54**	**6**	**9**	**15**	**54**	....	....	....	....	....

Traded to **Calgary** by **Washington** for Steve Shirreffs, August 18, 1999. Claimed on waivers by **Montreal** from **Calgary**, April 11, 2001.

GRATTON, Chris

Center. Shoots left. 6'4", 225 lbs. Born, Brantford, Ont., July 5, 1975.
(Tampa Bay's 1st choice, 3rd overall, in 1993 Entry Draft).

Season	Club	GP	G	A	Pts	PIM	GP	G	A	Pts	PIM
1993-94	Tampa Bay Lightning	84	13	29	42	123	....	....	....	....	....
1994-95	Tampa Bay Lightning	46	7	20	27	89	....	....	....	....	....
1995-96	Tampa Bay Lightning	82	17	21	38	105	6	0	2	2	27
1996-97	Tampa Bay Lightning	82	30	32	62	201	....	....	....	....	....
1997-98	Philadelphia Flyers	82	22	40	62	159	5	2	0	2	10
1998-99	Philadelphia Flyers	26	1	7	8	41	....	....	....	....	....
	Tampa Bay Lightning	52	7	19	26	102	....	....	....	....	....
99-2000	Tampa Bay Lightning	58	14	27	41	121	....	....	....	....	....
	Buffalo Sabres	14	1	7	8	15	5	0	1	1	4
2000-01	Buffalo Sabres	82	19	21	40	102	13	6	4	10	14
2001-02	Buffalo Sabres	82	15	24	39	75	....	....	....	....	....
2002-03	Buffalo Sabres	66	15	29	44	86	....	....	....	....	....
	Phoenix Coyotes	14	0	1	1	21	....	....	....	....	....
	NHL Totals	**770**	**161**	**277**	**438**	**1240**	**29**	**8**	**7**	**15**	**55**

Signed as a free agent by **Philadelphia**, August 14, 1997. Traded to **Tampa Bay** by **Philadelphia** with Mike Sillinger for Mikael Renberg and Daymond Langkow, December 12, 1998. Traded to **Buffalo** by **Tampa Bay** with Tampa Bay's 2nd round choice (Derek Roy) in 2001 Entry Draft for Cory Sarich, Wayne Primeau, Brian Holzinger and Buffalo's 3rd round choice (Alexander Kharitonov) in 2000 Entry Draft, March 9, 2000. Traded to **Phoenix** by **Buffalo** with Buffalo's 4th round choice in 2004 Entry Draft for Daniel Briere and Phoenix's 3rd round choice in 2004 Entry Draft, March 10, 2003.

GRATTON, Dan

Center. Shoots left. 6', 185 lbs. Born, Brantford, Ont., December 7, 1966.
(Los Angeles' 2nd choice, 10th overall, in 1985 Entry Draft).

Season	Club	GP	G	A	Pts	PIM	GP	G	A	Pts	PIM
1987-88	Los Angeles Kings	7	1	0	1	5	....	....	....	....	....
	NHL Totals	**7**	**1**	**0**	**1**	**5**	....	....	....	....	....

Signed as a free agent by **Minnesota**, August 22, 1990.

GRATTON, Norm

Left wing. Shoots left. 5'11", 165 lbs. Born, LaSalle, Que., December 22, 1950.
(NY Rangers' 1st choice, 11th overall, in 1970 Amateur Draft).

Season	Club	GP	G	A	Pts	PIM	GP	G	A	Pts	PIM
1971-72	New York Rangers	3	0	1	1	0	....	....	....	....	....
1972-73	Atlanta Flames	29	3	6	9	12	....	....	....	....	....
	Buffalo Sabres	21	6	5	11	12	6	0	1	1	2
1973-74	Buffalo Sabres	57	6	11	17	16	....	....	....	....	....
1974-75	Buffalo Sabres	25	3	6	9	2	....	....	....	....	....
	Minnesota North Stars	34	14	12	26	8	....	....	....	....	....
1975-76	Minnesota North Stars	32	7	3	10	14	....	....	....	....	....
	NHL Totals	**201**	**39**	**44**	**83**	**64**	**6**	**0**	**1**	**1**	**2**

• Brother of Gilles

Claimed by **Atlanta** from **NY Rangers** in Expansion Draft, June 6, 1972. Traded to **Buffalo** by **Atlanta** for Butch Deadmarsh, February 14, 1973. Traded to **Minnesota** by **Buffalo** with Buffalo's 3rd round choice (Ron Zanussi) in 1976 Amateur Draft for Fred Stanfield, January 27, 1975.

GRAVELLE, Leo

Right wing. Shoots right. 5'9", 160 lbs. Born, Aylmer, Que., June 10, 1925.

Season	Club	GP	G	A	Pts	PIM	GP	G	A	Pts	PIM
1946-47	Montreal Canadiens	53	16	14	30	12	6	2	0	2	2
1947-48	Montreal Canadiens	15	0	0	0	0	....	....	....	....	....
1948-49	Montreal Canadiens	36	4	6	10	6	7	2	1	3	0
1949-50	Montreal Canadiens	70	19	10	29	18	4	0	0	0	0
1950-51	Montreal Canadiens	31	4	2	6	0	....	....	....	....	....
	Detroit Red Wings	18	1	2	3	6	....	....	....	....	....
	NHL Totals	**223**	**44**	**34**	**78**	**42**	**17**	**4**	**1**	**5**	**2**

Traded to **Detroit** by **Montreal** for Bert Olmstead, December 19, 1950. Traded to **Ottawa** (QMHL) by **Detroit** for cash, September 5, 1951.

GRAVES, Adam

Left wing. Shoots left. 6', 205 lbs. Born, Toronto, Ont., April 12, 1968.
(Detroit's 2nd choice, 22nd overall, in 1986 Entry Draft).

Season	Club	GP	G	A	Pts	PIM	GP	G	A	Pts	PIM
1987-88	Detroit Red Wings	9	0	1	1	8	....	....	....	....	....
1988-89	Detroit Red Wings	56	7	5	12	60	5	0	0	0	4
1989-90	Detroit Red Wings	13	0	1	1	13	....	....	....	....	....
	◆ Edmonton Oilers	63	9	12	21	123	22	5	6	11	17
1990-91	Edmonton Oilers	76	7	18	25	127	18	2	4	6	22
1991-92	New York Rangers	80	26	33	59	139	10	5	3	8	22
1992-93	New York Rangers	84	36	29	65	148	....	....	....	....	....
1993-94 ◆	New York Rangers	84	52	27	79	127	23	10	7	17	24
1994-95	New York Rangers	47	17	14	31	51	10	4	4	8	8
1995-96	New York Rangers	82	22	36	58	100	10	7	1	8	4
1996-97	New York Rangers	82	33	28	61	66	15	2	1	3	12
1997-98	New York Rangers	72	23	12	35	41	....	....	....	....	....
1998-99	New York Rangers	82	38	15	53	47	....	....	....	....	....
99-2000	New York Rangers	77	23	17	40	14	....	....	....	....	....
2000-01	New York Rangers	82	10	16	26	77	....	....	....	....	....
2001-02	San Jose Sharks	81	17	14	31	51	12	3	1	4	6
2002-03	San Jose Sharks	82	9	9	18	32	....	....	....	....	....
	NHL Totals	**1152**	**329**	**287**	**616**	**1224**	**125**	**38**	**27**	**65**	**119**

NHL Second All-Star Team (1994) • King Clancy Memorial Trophy (1994) • Bill Masterton Memorial Trophy (2001)

Played in NHL All-Star Game (1994)

Traded to **Edmonton** by **Detroit** with Petr Klima, Joe Murphy and Jeff Sharples for Jimmy Carson, Kevin McClelland and Edmonton's 5th round choice (later traded to Montreal – Montreal selected Brad Layzell) in 1991 Entry Draft, November 2, 1989. Signed as a free agent by **NY Rangers**, September 3, 1991. Traded to **San Jose** by **NY Rangers** with future considerations for Mikael Samuelsson and Christian Gosselin, June 24, 2001.

GRAVES, Hilliard

Right wing. Shoots right. 5'11", 175 lbs. Born, Saint John, N.B., October 18, 1950.

Season	Club	GP	G	A	Pts	PIM	GP	G	A	Pts	PIM
1970-71	California Seals	14	0	0	0	0	....	....	....	....	....
1972-73	California Golden Seals	75	27	25	52	34	....	....	....	....	....
1973-74	California Golden Seals	64	11	18	29	48	....	....	....	....	....
1974-75	Atlanta Flames	67	10	19	29	30	....	....	....	....	....
1975-76	Atlanta Flames	80	19	30	49	16	2	0	0	0	0
1976-77	Atlanta Flames	25	8	5	13	17	....	....	....	....	....
	Vancouver Canucks	54	10	20	30	17	....	....	....	....	....
1977-78	Vancouver Canucks	80	21	26	47	18	....	....	....	....	....
1978-79	Vancouver Canucks	62	11	15	26	14	....	....	....	....	....
1979-80	Winnipeg Jets	35	1	5	6	15	....	....	....	....	....
	NHL Totals	**556**	**118**	**163**	**281**	**209**	**2**	**0**	**0**	**0**	**0**

Signed as a free agent by **California**, October, 1970. Traded to **Atlanta** by **California** for John Stewart, July 18, 1974. Traded to **Vancouver** by **Atlanta** with Larry Carriere for John Gould and Los Angeles' 2nd round choice (previously acquired, Atlanta selected Brian Hill) in 1977 Amateur Draft, December 2, 1976. Claimed by **Winnipeg** from **Vancouver** in Expansion Draft, June 13, 1979.

GRAVES, Steve

Left wing. Shoots left. 5'10", 175 lbs. Born, Trenton, Ont., April 7, 1964.
(Edmonton's 2nd choice, 41st overall, in 1982 Entry Draft).

Season	Club	GP	G	A	Pts	PIM	GP	G	A	Pts	PIM
1983-84	Edmonton Oilers	2	0	0	0	0	....	....	....	....	....
1986-87	Edmonton Oilers	12	2	0	2	0	....	....	....	....	....
1987-88	Edmonton Oilers	21	3	4	7	10	....	....	....	....	....
	NHL Totals	**35**	**5**	**4**	**9**	**10**	....	....	....	....	....

Signed as a free agent by **Los Angeles**, July 16, 1990.

GRAY, Alex

Right wing. Shoots right. 5'10", 170 lbs. Born, Glasgow, Scotland, June 21, 1899.

Season	Club	GP	G	A	Pts	PIM	GP	G	A	Pts	PIM
1927-28 ◆	New York Rangers	43	7	0	7	30	9	1	0	1	0
1928-29	Toronto Maple Leafs	7	0	0	0	2	4	0	0	0	0
	NHL Totals	**50**	**7**	**0**	**7**	**32**	**13**	**1**	**0**	**1**	**0**

Signed as a free agent by **NY Rangers**, August 22, 1926. Traded to **Toronto** by **NY Rangers** for Butch Keeling, April 16, 1928. Traded to **Toronto Ravinas** (Can-Pro) by **Toronto** for cash, November 28, 1928.

GRAY, Terry

Right wing. Shoots right. 6', 175 lbs. Born, Montreal, Que., March 21, 1938.

Season	Club	GP	G	A	Pts	PIM	GP	G	A	Pts	PIM
1961-62	Boston Bruins	42	8	7	15	15	....	....	....	....	....
1963-64	Montreal Canadiens	4	0	0	0	6	....	....	....	....	....
1967-68	Los Angeles Kings	65	12	16	28	22	7	0	2	2	10
1968-69	St. Louis Blues	8	4	0	4	4	11	3	2	5	8
1969-70	St. Louis Blues	28	2	5	7	17	16	2	1	3	4

Season	Club	REGULAR SEASON GP	G	A	Pts	PIM	PLAYOFFS GP	G	A	Pts	PIM
1970-71	St. Louis Blues	....	....	....	....	....	1	0	0	0	0
	NHL Totals	**147**	**26**	**28**	**54**	**64**	**35**	**5**	**5**	**10**	**22**

Traded to **Montreal** by **Chicago** with Glen Skov, the rights to Danny Lewicki, Lorne Ferguson and Bob Bailey for Cec Hoekstra, Reggie Fleming, Ab McDonald and Bob Courcy, June 7, 1960. Traded to **Boston** by **Montreal** with Cliff Pennington for Willie O'Ree and Stan Maxwell, June, 1961. Loaned to **Montreal** (Cleveland-AHL) by **Boston** for cash, July, 1962. Traded to **Quebec** (AHL) by **Montreal** (Cleveland-AHL) for Gary Bergman with Boston retaining NHL rights, November 1, 1962. Traded to **Springfield** (AHL) by **Boston** with Don Rolfe, Bruce Gamble and Randy Miller for Bob McCord, June, 1963. Traded to **Montreal** by **Springfield** (AHL) with Ted Harris, Bruce Cline, Wayne Larkin and John Chasczewski for Wayne Boddy, Fred Hilts, Brian Smith, John Rodger, Lorne O'Donnell and the loan of Gary Bergman, June, 1963. Traded to **Detroit** (Pittsburgh-AHL) by **Quebec** (AHL) for Claude Laforge, March 1, 1966. Claimed by **Los Angeles** from **Detroit** in Expansion Draft, June 6, 1967. Traded to **St. Louis** by **Los Angeles** for Myron Stankiewicz, June 11, 1968.

GREEN, Josh

Left wing. Shoots left. 6'4", 212 lbs. Born, Camrose, Alta., November 16, 1977.
(Los Angeles' 1st choice, 30th overall, in 1996 Entry Draft).

Season	Club	GP	G	A	Pts	PIM	GP	G	A	Pts	PIM
1998-99	Los Angeles Kings	27	1	3	4	8	....	....	....	....	....
99-2000	New York Islanders	49	12	14	26	41	....	....	....	....	....
2000-01	Edmonton Oilers	....	....	....	....	....	3	0	0	0	0
2001-02	Edmonton Oilers	61	10	5	15	52	....	....	....	....	....
2002-03	Edmonton Oilers	20	0	2	2	12	....	....	....	....	....
	New York Rangers	4	0	0	0	2	....	....	....	....	....
	Washington Capitals	21	1	2	3	7	....	....	....	....	....
	NHL Totals	**182**	**24**	**26**	**50**	**122**	**3**	**0**	**0**	**0**	**0**

Traded to **NY Islanders** by **Los Angeles** with Olli Jokinen, Mathieu Biron and Los Angeles' 1st round choice (Taylor Pyatt) in 1999 Entry Draft for Ziggy Palffy, Brian Smolinski, Marcel Cousineau and New Jersey's 4th round choice (previously acquired, Los Angeles selected Daniel Johansson) in 1999 Entry Draft, June 20, 1999. Traded to **Edmonton** by **NY Islanders** with Eric Brewer and NY Islanders' 2nd round choice (Brad Winchester) in 2000 Entry Draft for Roman Hamrlik, June 24, 2000. • Missed majority of 2000-01 season recovering from shoulder injury suffered in game vs. Detroit, October 10, 2000. Traded to **NY Rangers** by **Edmonton** for future considerations, December 12, 2002. Claimed on waivers by **Washington** from **NY Rangers**, January 15, 2003. Signed as a free agent by **Calgary**, July 17, 2003.

GREEN, Red

Left wing. Shoots left. 5'8", 148 lbs. Born, Sudbury, Ont., December 12, 1899.

Season	Club	GP	G	A	Pts	PIM	GP	G	A	Pts	PIM
1923-24	Hamilton Tigers	23	11	2	13	31	....	....	....	....	....
1924-25	Hamilton Tigers	30	19	*15	34	81	....	....	....	....	....
1925-26	New York Americans	35	13	4	17	42	....	....	....	....	....
1926-27	New York Americans	43	10	4	14	53	....	....	....	....	....
1927-28	New York Americans	40	6	1	7	67	....	....	....	....	....
1928-29 ♦	Boston Bruins	22	0	0	0	16	1	0	0	0	0
	Detroit Cougars	2	0	0	0	0	....	....	....	....	....
	NHL Totals	**195**	**59**	**26**	**85**	**290**	**1**	**0**	**0**	**0**	**0**

• Brother of Shorty

Signed as a free agent by **Hamilton**, November 13, 1923. Transferred to **NY Americans** after NHL club purchased **Hamilton** franchise, September 25, 1925. Traded to **Boston** by **NY Americans** for Harry Connor, May 18, 1928. Claimed on waivers by **Detroit** from **Boston**, February 16, 1929. Claimed on waivers by **Boston** from **Detroit**, March 4, 1929.

GREEN, Rick

Defense. Shoots left. 6'3", 220 lbs. Born, Belleville, Ont., February 20, 1956.
(Washington's 1st choice, 1st overall, in 1976 Amateur Draft).

Season	Club	GP	G	A	Pts	PIM	GP	G	A	Pts	PIM
1976-77	Washington Capitals	45	3	12	15	16	....	....	....	....	....
1977-78	Washington Capitals	60	5	14	19	67	....	....	....	....	....
1978-79	Washington Capitals	71	8	33	41	62	....	....	....	....	....
1979-80	Washington Capitals	71	4	20	24	52	....	....	....	....	....
1980-81	Washington Capitals	65	8	23	31	91	....	....	....	....	....
1981-82	Washington Capitals	65	3	25	28	93	....	....	....	....	....
1982-83	Montreal Canadiens	66	2	24	26	58	3	0	0	0	2
1983-84	Montreal Canadiens	7	0	1	1	7	15	1	2	3	33
1984-85	Montreal Canadiens	77	1	18	19	30	12	0	3	3	14
1985-86 ♦	Montreal Canadiens	46	3	2	5	20	18	1	4	5	8
1986-87	Montreal Canadiens	72	1	9	10	10	17	0	4	4	8
1987-88	Montreal Canadiens	59	2	11	13	33	11	0	2	2	2
1988-89	Montreal Canadiens	72	1	14	15	25	21	1	1	2	6
1990-91	Detroit Red Wings	65	2	14	16	24	3	0	0	0	0
1991-92	New York Islanders	4	0	0	0	0	....	....	....	....	....
	NHL Totals	**845**	**43**	**220**	**263**	**588**	**100**	**3**	**16**	**19**	**73**

Traded to **Montreal** by **Washington** with Ryan Walter for Brian Engblom, Rod Langway, Doug Jarvis and Craig Laughlin, September 9, 1982. Traded to **Detroit** by **Montreal** for Edmonton's 5th round choice (previously acquired, Montreal selected Brad Layzell) in 1991 Entry Draft, June 15, 1990. Traded to **NY Islanders** by **Detroit** for Alan Kerr and future considerations, May 26, 1991.

GREEN, Shorty

HHOF

Right wing. Shoots right. 5'10", 152 lbs. Born, Sudbury, Ont., July 17, 1896.

Season	Club	GP	G	A	Pts	PIM	GP	G	A	Pts	PIM
1923-24	Hamilton Tigers	22	7	6	13	31	....	....	....	....	....
1924-25	Hamilton Tigers	28	18	9	27	63	....	....	....	....	....
1925-26	New York Americans	32	6	4	10	40	....	....	....	....	....
1926-27	New York Americans	21	2	1	3	17	....	....	....	....	....
	NHL Totals	**103**	**33**	**20**	**53**	**151**	....	....	....	....	....

• Brother of Red

Signed as a free agent by **Hamilton**, November 22, 1923. Transferred to **NY Americans** after NHL club purchased **Hamilton** franchise, September 25, 1925.

GREEN, Ted

Defense. Shoots right. 5'10", 200 lbs. Born, Eriksdale, Man., March 23, 1940.

Season	Club	GP	G	A	Pts	PIM	GP	G	A	Pts	PIM
1960-61	Boston Bruins	1	0	0	0	2	....	....	....	....	....
1961-62	Boston Bruins	66	3	8	11	116	....	....	....	....	....
1962-63	Boston Bruins	70	1	11	12	117	....	....	....	....	....
1963-64	Boston Bruins	70	4	10	14	145	....	....	....	....	....
1964-65	Boston Bruins	70	8	27	35	156	....	....	....	....	....
1965-66	Boston Bruins	27	5	13	18	113	....	....	....	....	....
1966-67	Boston Bruins	47	6	10	16	67	....	....	....	....	....
1967-68	Boston Bruins	72	7	36	43	133	4	1	1	2	11
1968-69	Boston Bruins	65	8	38	46	99	10	2	7	9	18
1970-71	Boston Bruins	78	5	37	42	60	7	1	0	1	25
1971-72 ♦	Boston Bruins	54	1	16	17	21	10	0	0	0	0
	NHL Totals	**620**	**48**	**206**	**254**	**1029**	**31**	**4**	**8**	**12**	**54**

NHL Second All-Star Team (1969)

Played in NHL All-Star Game (1965, 1969)

Claimed by **Montreal** from **Winnipeg** (WHL) in Inter-League Draft, June 7, 1960. Claimed by **Boston** from **Montreal** in Intra-League Draft, June 8, 1960. • Missed entire 1969-70 season recovering from head injury suffered in exhibition game vs. St. Louis, September 21, 1969.

GREEN, Travis

Center. Shoots right. 6'2", 200 lbs. Born, Castlegar, B.C., December 20, 1970.
(NY Islanders' 2nd choice, 23rd overall, in 1989 Entry Draft).

Season	Club	GP	G	A	Pts	PIM	GP	G	A	Pts	PIM
1992-93	New York Islanders	61	7	18	25	43	12	3	1	4	6
1993-94	New York Islanders	83	18	22	40	44	4	0	0	0	2
1994-95	New York Islanders	42	5	7	12	25	....	....	....	....	....
1995-96	New York Islanders	69	25	45	70	42	....	....	....	....	....
1996-97	New York Islanders	79	23	41	64	38	....	....	....	....	....
1997-98	New York Islanders	54	14	12	26	66	....	....	....	....	....
	Mighty Ducks of Anaheim	22	5	11	16	16	....	....	....	....	....
1998-99	Mighty Ducks of Anaheim	79	13	17	30	81	4	0	1	1	4
99-2000	Phoenix Coyotes	78	25	21	46	45	5	2	1	3	2
2000-01	Phoenix Coyotes	69	13	15	28	63	....	....	....	....	....
2001-02	Toronto Maple Leafs	82	11	23	34	61	20	3	6	9	34
2002-03	Toronto Maple Leafs	75	12	12	24	67	4	2	1	3	4
	NHL Totals	**793**	**171**	**244**	**415**	**591**	**49**	**10**	**10**	**20**	**52**

Traded to **Anaheim** by **NY Islanders** with Doug Houda and Tony Tuzzolino for Joe Sacco, J.J. Daigneault and Mark Janssens, February 6, 1998. Traded to **Phoenix** by **Anaheim** with Anaheim's 1st round choice (Scott Kelman) in 1999 Entry Draft for Oleg Tverdovsky, June 26, 1999. Traded to **Toronto** by **Phoenix** with Robert Reichel and Craig Mills for Danny Markov, June 12, 2001.

GREENLAW, Jeff

Left wing. Shoots left. 6'1", 230 lbs. Born, Toronto, Ont., February 28, 1968.
(Washington's 1st choice, 19th overall, in 1986 Entry Draft).

Season	Club	GP	G	A	Pts	PIM	GP	G	A	Pts	PIM
1986-87	Washington Capitals	22	0	3	3	44	....	....	....	....	....
1987-88	Washington Capitals	....	....	....	....	....	1	0	0	0	19
1990-91	Washington Capitals	10	2	0	2	10	1	0	0	0	2
1991-92	Washington Capitals	5	0	1	1	34	....	....	....	....	....
1992-93	Washington Capitals	16	1	1	2	18	....	....	....	....	....
1993-94	Florida Panthers	4	0	1	1	2	....	....	....	....	....
	NHL Totals	**57**	**3**	**6**	**9**	**108**	**2**	**0**	**0**	**0**	**21**

Signed as a free agent by **Florida**, July 14, 1993.

GREGG, Randy

Defense. Shoots left. 6'4", 215 lbs. Born, Edmonton, Alta., February 19, 1956.

Season	Club	GP	G	A	Pts	PIM	GP	G	A	Pts	PIM
1981-82	Edmonton Oilers	....	....	....	....	....	4	0	0	0	0
1982-83	Edmonton Oilers	80	6	22	28	54	16	2	4	6	13
1983-84 ♦	Edmonton Oilers	80	13	27	40	56	19	3	7	10	21
1984-85 ♦	Edmonton Oilers	57	3	20	23	32	17	0	6	6	12
1985-86	Edmonton Oilers	64	2	26	28	47	10	1	0	1	12
1986-87 ♦	Edmonton Oilers	52	8	16	24	42	18	3	6	9	17
1987-88 ♦	Edmonton Oilers	15	1	2	3	8	19	1	8	9	24
1988-89	Edmonton Oilers	57	3	15	18	28	7	1	0	1	4
1989-90 ♦	Edmonton Oilers	48	4	20	24	42	20	2	6	8	16
1991-92	Vancouver Canucks	21	1	4	5	24	7	0	1	1	8
	NHL Totals	**474**	**41**	**152**	**193**	**333**	**137**	**13**	**38**	**51**	**127**

Signed as a free agent by **Edmonton**, October 18, 1982. Claimed by **Vancouver** from **Edmonton** in Waiver Draft, October 1, 1990.

GREIG, Bruce

Left wing. Shoots left. 6'2", 220 lbs. Born, High River, Alta., May 9, 1953.
(California's 6th choice, 114th overall, in 1973 Amateur Draft).

Season	Club	GP	G	A	Pts	PIM	GP	G	A	Pts	PIM
1973-74	California Golden Seals	1	0	0	0	4	....	....	....	....	....
1974-75	California Golden Seals	8	0	1	1	42	....	....	....	....	....
	NHL Totals	**9**	**0**	**1**	**1**	**46**	....	....	....	....	....

• Brother of Mark

GREIG, Mark

Right wing. Shoots right. 5'11", 190 lbs. Born, High River, Alta., January 25, 1970.
(Hartford's 1st choice, 15th overall, in 1990 Entry Draft).

Season	Club	GP	G	A	Pts	PIM	GP	G	A	Pts	PIM
1990-91	Hartford Whalers	4	0	0	0	0	....	....	....	....	....
1991-92	Hartford Whalers	17	0	5	5	6	....	....	....	....	....
1992-93	Hartford Whalers	22	1	7	8	27	....	....	....	....	....

		REGULAR SEASON					PLAYOFFS				
Season	Club	GP	G	A	Pts	PIM	GP	G	A	Pts	PIM
1993-94	Hartford Whalers	31	4	5	9	31	....	....	....	....	....
	Toronto Maple Leafs	13	2	2	4	10	....	....	....	....	....
1994-95	Calgary Flames	8	1	1	2	2	....	....	....	....	....
1998-99	Philadelphia Flyers	7	1	3	4	2	2	0	1	1	0
99-2000	Philadelphia Flyers	11	3	2	5	6	3	0	0	0	0
2000-01	Philadelphia Flyers	7	1	1	2	4	....	....	....	....	....
2002-03	Philadelphia Flyers	5	0	1	1	2	....	....	....	....	....
	NHL Totals	**125**	**13**	**27**	**40**	**90**	**5**	**0**	**1**	**1**	**0**

• Brother of Bruce

Traded to **Toronto** by **Hartford** with Hartford's 6th round choice (Doug Bonner) in 1995 Entry Draft for Ted Crowley, January 25, 1994. Signed as a free agent by **Calgary**, August 9, 1994. Signed as a free agent by **Philadelphia**, July 28, 1998.

GRENIER, Lucien

Right wing. Shoots left. 5'10", 163 lbs. Born, Malartic, Que., November 3, 1946.

Season	Club	GP	G	A	Pts	PIM	GP	G	A	Pts	PIM
1968-69 ♦	Montreal Canadiens	....	....	....	....	....	2	0	0	0	0
1969-70	Montreal Canadiens	23	2	3	5	2	....	....	....	....	....
1970-71	Los Angeles Kings	68	9	7	16	12	....	....	....	....	....
1971-72	Los Angeles Kings	60	3	4	7	4	....	....	....	....	....
	NHL Totals	**151**	**14**	**14**	**28**	**18**	**2**	**0**	**0**	**0**	**0**

Traded to **Los Angeles** by **Montreal** with Larry Mickey and Jack Norris for Leon Rochefort, Gregg Boddy and Wayne Thomas, May 22, 1970. Claimed by **Atlanta** from **Los Angeles** in Expansion Draft, June 6, 1972. • Missed entire 1972-73 season recovering from ankle injury suffered in training camp, September, 1972.

GRENIER, Martin

Defense. Shoots left. 6'5", 245 lbs. Born, Laval, Que., November 2, 1980.
(Colorado's 2nd choice, 45th overall, in 1999 Entry Draft).

Season	Club	GP	G	A	Pts	PIM	GP	G	A	Pts	PIM
2001-02	Phoenix Coyotes	5	0	0	0	5	....	....	....	....	....
2002-03	Phoenix Coyotes	3	0	0	0	0	....	....	....	....	....
	NHL Totals	**8**	**0**	**0**	**0**	**5**	....	....	....	....	....

Traded to **Boston** by **Colorado** with Brian Rolston, Samuel Pahlsson and New Jersey's 1st round choice (previously acquired, Boston selected Martin Samuelsson) in 2000 Entry Draft for Raymond Bourque and Dave Andreychuk, March 6, 2000. Signed as a free agent by **Phoenix**, June 27, 2001. Traded to **Vancouver** by **Phoenix** for Bryan Helmer, July 25, 2003.

GRENIER, Richard

Center. Shoots left. 5'11", 170 lbs. Born, Montreal, Que., September 18, 1952.
(NY Islanders' 5th choice, 65th overall, in 1972 Amateur Draft).

Season	Club	GP	G	A	Pts	PIM	GP	G	A	Pts	PIM
1972-73	New York Islanders	10	1	1	2	2	....	....	....	....	....
	NHL Totals	**10**	**1**	**1**	**2**	**2**	....	....	....	....	....

GRESCHNER, Ron

Defense. Shoots left. 6'2", 205 lbs. Born, Goodsoil, Sask., December 22, 1954.
(NY Rangers' 2nd choice, 32nd overall, in 1974 Amateur Draft).

Season	Club	GP	G	A	Pts	PIM	GP	G	A	Pts	PIM
1974-75	New York Rangers	70	8	37	45	93	3	0	1	1	2
1975-76	New York Rangers	77	6	21	27	93	....	....	....	....	....
1976-77	New York Rangers	80	11	36	47	89	....	....	....	....	....
1977-78	New York Rangers	78	24	48	72	100	3	0	0	0	2
1978-79	New York Rangers	60	17	36	53	66	18	7	5	12	16
1979-80	New York Rangers	76	21	37	58	103	9	0	6	6	10
1980-81	New York Rangers	74	27	41	68	112	14	4	8	12	17
1981-82	New York Rangers	29	5	11	16	16	....	....	....	....	....
1982-83	New York Rangers	10	3	5	8	0	8	2	2	4	12
1983-84	New York Rangers	77	12	44	56	117	2	1	0	1	2
1984-85	New York Rangers	48	16	29	45	42	2	0	3	3	12
1985-86	New York Rangers	78	20	28	48	104	5	3	1	4	11
1986-87	New York Rangers	61	6	34	40	62	6	0	5	5	0
1987-88	New York Rangers	51	1	5	6	82	....	....	....	....	....
1988-89	New York Rangers	58	1	10	11	94	4	0	1	1	6
1989-90	New York Rangers	55	1	9	10	53	10	0	0	0	16
	NHL Totals	**982**	**179**	**431**	**610**	**1226**	**84**	**17**	**32**	**49**	**106**

Played in NHL All-Star Game (1980)

Missed majority of 1981-82 season recovering from back injury suffered in game vs. Philadelphia, November 18, 1981. • Missed majority of 1982-83 season recovering from back injury suffered in training camp, September, 1982.

GRETZKY, Brent

Center. Shoots left. 5'10", 160 lbs. Born, Brantford, Ont., February 20, 1972.
(Tampa Bay's 3rd choice, 49th overall, in 1992 Entry Draft).

Season	Club	GP	G	A	Pts	PIM	GP	G	A	Pts	PIM
1993-94	Tampa Bay Lightning	10	1	2	3	2	....	....	....	....	....
1994-95	Tampa Bay Lightning	3	0	1	1	0	....	....	....	....	....
	NHL Totals	**13**	**1**	**3**	**4**	**2**	....	....	....	....	....

• Brother of Wayne

Signed as a free agent by **Toronto**, September 20, 1995.

GRETZKY, Wayne

HHOF

Center. Shoots left. 6', 185 lbs. Born, Brantford, Ont., January 26, 1961.

Season	Club	GP	G	A	Pts	PIM	GP	G	A	Pts	PIM
1979-80	Edmonton Oilers	79	51	*86	*137	21	3	2	1	3	0
1980-81	Edmonton Oilers	80	55	*109	*164	28	9	7	14	21	4
1981-82	Edmonton Oilers	80	*92	*120	*212	26	5	5	7	12	8
1982-83	Edmonton Oilers	80	*71	*125	*196	59	16	12	*26	*38	4
1983-84 ♦	Edmonton Oilers	74	*87	*118	*205	39	19	13	*22	*35	12
1984-85 ♦	Edmonton Oilers	80	*73	*135	*208	52	18	17	*30	*47	4
1985-86	Edmonton Oilers	80	52	*163	*215	46	10	8	11	19	2
1986-87 ♦	Edmonton Oilers	79	*62	*121	*183	28	21	5	*29	*34	6
1987-88 ♦	Edmonton Oilers	64	40	*109	149	24	19	12	*31	*43	16
1988-89	Los Angeles Kings	78	54	*114	168	26	11	5	17	22	0
1989-90	Los Angeles Kings	73	40	*102	*142	42	7	3	7	10	0
1990-91	Los Angeles Kings	78	41	*122	*163	16	12	4	11	15	2
1991-92	Los Angeles Kings	74	31	*90	121	34	6	2	5	7	2
1992-93	Los Angeles Kings	45	16	49	65	6	24	*15	*25	*40	4
1993-94	Los Angeles Kings	81	38	*92	*130	20	....	....	....	....	....
1994-95	Los Angeles Kings	48	11	37	48	6	....	....	....	....	....
1995-96	Los Angeles Kings	62	15	66	81	32	....	....	....	....	....
	St. Louis Blues	18	8	13	21	2	13	2	14	16	0
1996-97	New York Rangers	82	25	*72	97	28	15	10	10	20	2
1997-98	New York Rangers	82	23	*67	90	28	....	....	....	....	....
1998-99	New York Rangers	70	9	53	62	14	....	....	....	....	....
	NHL Totals	**1487**	**894**	**1963**	**2857**	**577**	**208**	**122**	**260**	**382**	**66**

• Brother of Brent • Hart Trophy (1980, 1981, 1982, 1983, 1984, 1985, 1986, 1987, 1989) • Lady Byng Trophy (1980, 1991, 1992, 1994, 1999) • NHL Second All-Star Team (1980, 1988, 1989, 1990, 1994, 1997, 1998) • NHL First All-Star Team (1981, 1982, 1983, 1984, 1985, 1986, 1987, 1991) • Art Ross Trophy (1981, 1982, 1983, 1984, 1985, 1986, 1987, 1990, 1991, 1994) • NHL record for assists in regular season (1981, 1982, 1983, 1985, 1986) • NHL record for points in regular season (1981, 1982, 1986) • NHL record for goals in regular season (1982) • Lester B. Pearson Award (1982, 1983, 1984, 1985, 1987) • NHL Plus/Minus Leader (1982, 1984, 1985, 1987) • NHL record for assists in one playoff year (1983, 1985, 1988) • NHL record for points in one playoff year (1983, 1985) • Conn Smythe Trophy (1985, 1988) • Selected Chrysler-Dodge/NHL Performer of the Year (1985, 1986, 1987) • Dodge Performance of the Year Award (1989) • Lester Patrick Trophy (1994)

Played in NHL All-Star Game (1980, 1981, 1982, 1983, 1984, 1985, 1986, 1988, 1989, 1990, 1991, 1992, 1993, 1994, 1996, 1997, 1998, 1999)

Reclaimed by **Edmonton** as an under-age junior prior to Expansion Draft, June 9, 1979. Claimed as priority selection by **Edmonton**, June 9, 1979. Traded to **Los Angeles** by **Edmonton** with Mike Krushelnyski and Marty McSorley for Jimmy Carson, Martin Gelinas, Los Angeles' 1st round choices in 1989 (later traded to New Jersey – New Jersey selected Jason Miller), 1991 (Martin Rucinsky) and 1993 (Nick Stajduhar) Entry Drafts and cash, August 9, 1988. Traded to **St. Louis** by **Los Angeles** for Craig Johnson, Patrice Tardif, Roman Vopat, St. Louis 5th round choice (Peter Hogan) in 1996 Entry Draft and 1st round choice (Matt Zultek) in 1997 Entry Draft, February 27, 1996. Signed as a free agent by **NY Rangers**, July 21, 1996. • Officially announced retirement, April 16, 1999.

GRIER, Mike

Right wing. Shoots right. 6'1", 227 lbs. Born, Detroit, MI, January 5, 1975.
(St. Louis' 7th choice, 219th overall, in 1993 Entry Draft).

Season	Club	GP	G	A	Pts	PIM	GP	G	A	Pts	PIM
1996-97	Edmonton Oilers	79	15	17	32	45	12	3	1	4	4
1997-98	Edmonton Oilers	66	9	6	15	73	12	2	2	4	13
1998-99	Edmonton Oilers	82	20	24	44	54	4	1	1	2	6
99-2000	Edmonton Oilers	65	9	22	31	68	....	....	....	....	....
2000-01	Edmonton Oilers	74	20	16	36	20	6	0	0	0	8
2001-02	Edmonton Oilers	82	8	17	25	32	....	....	....	....	....
2002-03	Washington Capitals	82	15	17	32	36	6	1	1	2	2
	NHL Totals	**530**	**96**	**119**	**215**	**328**	**40**	**7**	**5**	**12**	**33**

Rights traded to **Edmonton** by **St. Louis** with Curtis Joseph for St. Louis' 1st round choices in 1996 (previously acquired, St. Louis selected Marty Reasoner) and 1997 (previously acquired, later traded to Los Angeles – Los Angeles selected Matt Zultek) Entry Drafts, August 4, 1995. Traded to **Washington** by **Edmonton** for Washington's 2nd round choice (later traded to NY Islanders – NY Islanders selected Evgeni Tunik) in 2003 Entry Draft and Vancouver's 3rd round choice (previously acquired, Edmonton selected Zachery Stortini) in 2003 Entry Draft, October 7, 2002.

GRIEVE, Brent

Left wing. Shoots left. 6'1", 202 lbs. Born, Oshawa, Ont., May 9, 1969.
(NY Islanders' 4th choice, 65th overall, in 1989 Entry Draft).

Season	Club	GP	G	A	Pts	PIM	GP	G	A	Pts	PIM
1993-94	New York Islanders	3	0	0	0	7	....	....	....	....	....
	Edmonton Oilers	24	13	5	18	14	....	....	....	....	....
1994-95	Chicago Blackhawks	24	1	5	6	23	....	....	....	....	....
1995-96	Chicago Blackhawks	28	2	4	6	28	....	....	....	....	....
1996-97	Los Angeles Kings	18	4	2	6	15	....	....	....	....	....
	NHL Totals	**97**	**20**	**16**	**36**	**87**	....	....	....	....	....

Traded to **Edmonton** by **NY Islanders** for Marc Laforge, December 15, 1993. Signed as a free agent by **Chicago**, July 7, 1994. Signed as a free agent by **Los Angeles**, August 2, 1996.

GRIGOR, George

Center. Shoots right. 5'7", 150 lbs. Born, Edinburgh, Scotland, September 3, 1916.

Season	Club	GP	G	A	Pts	PIM	GP	G	A	Pts	PIM
1943-44	Chicago Black Hawks	2	1	0	1	0	1	0	0	0	0
	NHL Totals	**2**	**1**	**0**	**1**	**0**	**1**	**0**	**0**	**0**	**0**

Signed as a free agent by **Chicago**, October 7, 1943. • Military authorities allowed him to play only part-time with Chicago because of his essential wartime position in Toronto.

GRIMSON, Stu

Left wing. Shoots left. 6'4", 240 lbs. Born, Kamloops, B.C., May 20, 1965.
(Calgary's 8th choice, 143rd overall, in 1985 Entry Draft).

Season	Club	GP	G	A	Pts	PIM	GP	G	A	Pts	PIM
1988-89	Calgary Flames	1	0	0	0	5	....	....	....	....	....
1989-90	Calgary Flames	3	0	0	0	17	....	....	....	....	....
1990-91	Chicago Blackhawks	35	0	1	1	183	5	0	0	0	46
1991-92	Chicago Blackhawks	54	2	2	4	234	14	0	1	1	10
1992-93	Chicago Blackhawks	78	1	1	2	193	2	0	0	0	4
1993-94	Mighty Ducks of Anaheim	77	1	5	6	199	....	....	....	....	....
1994-95	Mighty Ducks of Anaheim	31	0	1	1	110	....	....	....	....	....
	Detroit Red Wings	11	0	0	0	37	11	1	0	1	26
1995-96	Detroit Red Wings	56	0	1	1	128	2	0	0	0	0
1996-97	Detroit Red Wings	1	0	0	0	0	....	....	....	....	....
	Hartford Whalers	75	2	2	4	218	....	....	....	....	....

Season	Club	REGULAR SEASON GP	G	A	Pts	PIM	PLAYOFFS GP	G	A	Pts	PIM
1997-98	Carolina Hurricanes	82	3	4	7	204	....	....	....	....	....
1998-99	Mighty Ducks of Anaheim	73	3	0	3	158	3	0	0	0	30
99-2000	Mighty Ducks of Anaheim	50	1	2	3	116	....	....	....	....	....
2000-01	Los Angeles Kings	72	3	2	5	235	5	0	0	0	4
2001-02	Nashville Predators	30	1	1	2	76	....	....	....	....	....
	NHL Totals	**729**	**17**	**22**	**39**	**2113**	**42**	**1**	**1**	**2**	**120**

• Re-entered NHL Entry Draft. Originally Detroit's 11th choice, 193rd overall, in 1983 Entry Draft.

Claimed on waivers by **Chicago** from **Calgary**, October 1, 1990. Claimed by **Anaheim** from **Chicago** in Expansion Draft, June 24, 1993. Traded to **Detroit** by **Anaheim** with Mark Ferner and Anaheim's 6th round choice (Magnus Nilsson) in 1996 Entry Draft for Mike Sillinger and Jason York, April 4, 1995. Claimed on waivers by **Hartford** from **Detroit**, October 13, 1996. Transferred to **Carolina** after **Hartford** franchise relocated, June 25, 1997. Traded to **Anaheim** by **Carolina** with Kevin Haller for Dave Karpa and Anaheim's 4th round choice (later traded to Atlanta – Atlanta selected Blake Robson) in 2000 Entry Draft, August 11, 1998. Signed as a free agent by **Los Angeles**, July 6, 2000. Signed as a free agent by **Nashville**, July 2, 2001. • Missed majority of 2001-02 season and entire 2002-03 season recovering from head injury suffered in game vs. Anaheim, December 2, 2001. • Officially announced retirement, June 3, 2003.

GRISDALE, John

Defense. Shoots right. 6', 195 lbs. Born, Geraldton, Ont., August 23, 1948.

Season	Club	GP	G	A	Pts	PIM	GP	G	A	Pts	PIM
1972-73	Toronto Maple Leafs	49	1	7	8	76	....	....	....	....	....
1974-75	Toronto Maple Leafs	2	0	0	0	4	....	....	....	....	....
	Vancouver Canucks	58	1	12	13	91	5	0	1	1	13
1975-76	Vancouver Canucks	38	2	6	8	54	2	0	0	0	0
1976-77	Vancouver Canucks	20	0	2	2	20	....	....	....	....	....
1977-78	Vancouver Canucks	42	0	9	9	47	....	....	....	....	....
1978-79	Vancouver Canucks	41	0	3	3	54	3	0	0	0	2
	NHL Totals	**250**	**4**	**39**	**43**	**346**	**10**	**0**	**1**	**1**	**15**

Signed as a free agent by **Toronto** (Tulsa-CHL) to four-game tryout contract, March, 1971. Traded to **Vancouver** by **Toronto** with Garry Monahan for Dave Dunn, October 16, 1974.

GROLEAU, Francois

Defense. Shoots left. 6', 197 lbs. Born, Longueuil, Que., January 23, 1973.
(Calgary's 2nd choice, 41st overall, in 1991 Entry Draft).

Season	Club	GP	G	A	Pts	PIM	GP	G	A	Pts	PIM
1995-96	Montreal Canadiens	2	0	1	1	2	....	....	....	....	....
1996-97	Montreal Canadiens	5	0	0	0	4	....	....	....	....	....
1997-98	Montreal Canadiens	1	0	0	0	0	....	....	....	....	....
	NHL Totals	**8**	**0**	**1**	**1**	**6**	....	....	....	....	....

Traded to **Quebec** by **Calgary** for Ed Ward, March 23, 1995. Signed as a free agent by **Montreal**, June 17, 1995.

GRON, Stanislav

Right wing. Shoots left. 6'2", 205 lbs. Born, Bratislava, Czech., October 28, 1978.
(New Jersey's 2nd choice, 38th overall, in 1997 Entry Draft).

Season	Club	GP	G	A	Pts	PIM	GP	G	A	Pts	PIM
2000-01	New Jersey Devils	1	0	0	0	0	....	....	....	....	....
	NHL Totals	**1**	**0**	**0**	**0**	**0**	....	....	....	....	....

GRONMAN, Tuomas

Defense. Shoots right. 6'3", 219 lbs. Born, Viitasaari, Finland, March 22, 1974.
(Quebec's 3rd choice, 29th overall, in 1992 Entry Draft).

Season	Club	GP	G	A	Pts	PIM	GP	G	A	Pts	PIM
1996-97	Chicago Blackhawks	16	0	1	1	13	....	....	....	....	....
1997-98	Pittsburgh Penguins	22	1	2	3	25	1	0	0	0	0
	NHL Totals	**38**	**1**	**3**	**4**	**38**	**1**	**0**	**0**	**0**	**0**

Transferred to **Colorado** after **Quebec** franchise relocated, June 21, 1995. Rights traded to **Chicago** by **Colorado** for Chicago's 2nd round choice (Phillippe Sauve) in 1998 Entry Draft, July 10, 1996. Traded to **Pittsburgh** by **Chicago** for Greg Johnson, October 27, 1997.

GRONSDAHL, Lloyd

Right wing. Shoots right. 5'9", 170 lbs. Born, Norquay, Sask., May 10, 1921.

Season	Club	GP	G	A	Pts	PIM	GP	G	A	Pts	PIM
1941-42	Boston Bruins	10	1	2	3	0	....	....	....	....	....
	NHL Totals	**10**	**1**	**2**	**3**	**0**	....	....	....	....	....

GRONSTRAND, Jari

Defense. Shoots left. 6'3", 195 lbs. Born, Tampere, Finland, November 14, 1962.
(Minnesota's 8th choice, 96th overall, in 1986 Entry Draft).

Season	Club	GP	G	A	Pts	PIM	GP	G	A	Pts	PIM
1986-87	Minnesota North Stars	47	1	6	7	27	....	....	....	....	....
1987-88	New York Rangers	62	3	11	14	63	....	....	....	....	....
1988-89	Quebec Nordiques	25	1	3	4	14	....	....	....	....	....
1989-90	Quebec Nordiques	7	0	1	1	2	....	....	....	....	....
	New York Islanders	41	3	4	7	27	3	0	0	0	4
1990-91	New York Islanders	3	0	1	1	2	....	....	....	....	....
	NHL Totals	**185**	**8**	**26**	**34**	**135**	**3**	**0**	**0**	**0**	**4**

Traded to **NY Rangers** by **Minnesota** with Paul Boutilier for Jay Caufield and Dave Gagner, October 8, 1987. Traded to **Quebec** by **NY Rangers** with Bruce Bell, Walt Poddubny and NY Rangers 4th round choice (Eric Dubois) in 1989 Entry Draft for Jason Lafreniere and Normand Rochefort, August 1, 1988. Claimed on waivers by **NY Islanders**, November 21, 1989.

GROSEK, Michal

Left wing. Shoots right. 6'2", 207 lbs. Born, Vyskov, Czech., June 1, 1975.
(Winnipeg's 7th choice, 145th overall, in 1993 Entry Draft).

Season	Club	GP	G	A	Pts	PIM	GP	G	A	Pts	PIM
1993-94	Winnipeg Jets	3	1	0	1	0	....	....	....	....	....
1994-95	Winnipeg Jets	24	2	2	4	21	....	....	....	....	....
1995-96	Winnipeg Jets	1	0	0	0	0	....	....	....	....	....
	Buffalo Sabres	22	6	4	10	31	....	....	....	....	....
1996-97	Buffalo Sabres	82	15	21	36	71	12	3	3	6	8
1997-98	Buffalo Sabres	67	10	20	30	60	15	6	4	10	28
1998-99	Buffalo Sabres	76	20	30	50	102	13	0	4	4	28
99-2000	Buffalo Sabres	61	11	23	34	35	....	....	....	....	....
	Chicago Blackhawks	14	2	4	6	12	....	....	....	....	....
2000-01	New York Rangers	65	9	11	20	61	....	....	....	....	....
2001-02	New York Rangers	15	3	2	5	12	....	....	....	....	....
2002-03	Boston Bruins	63	2	18	20	71	5	0	0	0	13
	NHL Totals	**493**	**81**	**135**	**216**	**476**	**45**	**9**	**11**	**20**	**77**

Traded to **Buffalo** by **Winnipeg** with Darryl Shannon for Craig Muni, February 15, 1996. Traded to **Chicago** by **Buffalo** for Doug Gilmour, J.P. Dumont and future considerations, March 10, 2000. Traded to **NY Rangers** by **Chicago** with Brad Brown for future considerations, October 5, 2000. Signed as a free agent by **Boston**, July 16, 2002.

GROSS, Lloyd

Left wing. Shoots left. 5'9", 175 lbs. Born, Berlin, Ont., September 5, 1905.

Season	Club	GP	G	A	Pts	PIM	GP	G	A	Pts	PIM
1926-27	Toronto St. Pats/Maple Leafs	16	1	1	2	0	....	....	....	....	....
1933-34	New York Americans	21	7	3	10	10	....	....	....	....	....
	Boston Bruins	6	1	0	1	6	....	....	....	....	....
	Detroit Red Wings	13	1	1	2	2	1	0	0	0	0
1934-35	Detroit Red Wings	6	1	0	1	2	....	....	....	....	....
	NHL Totals	**62**	**11**	**5**	**16**	**20**	**1**	**0**	**0**	**0**	**0**

Signed as a free agent by **Toronto**, March 7, 1927. Traded to **Niagara Falls** (IHL) by **Toronto** (IHL) with Fred Elliot for Ike Morrison, Harry Lott and Jim Smith, December 15, 1929. Traded to **Buffalo** (IHL) by **Niagara Falls** (IHL) with Gamey Lederman for Wilf McDonald, January 9, 1930. Claimed by **NY Rangers** from **Buffalo** (IHL) in Inter-League Draft, May 13, 1933. Rights returned to **Buffalo** (IHL) by **NY Rangers** when NHL club failed to complete terms of purchase, May 25, 1933. Traded to **NY Americans** by **Buffalo** (IHL) for cash, October 11, 1933. Traded to **Boston** by **NY Americans** with George Patterson for Art Chapman and Bob Gracie, January 11, 1934. Traded to **Detroit** by **Boston** for cash, February 13, 1934. Traded to **Buffalo** (IHL) by **Detroit** with Garney Lederman for Bucko McDonald, January 9, 1935.

GROSSO, Don

Left wing/Center. Shoots left. 5'11", 170 lbs. Born, Sault Ste. Marie, Ont., April 12, 1915.

Season	Club	GP	G	A	Pts	PIM	GP	G	A	Pts	PIM
1938-39	Detroit Red Wings	1	1	1	2	0	3	1	2	3	7
1939-40	Detroit Red Wings	29	2	3	5	11	5	0	0	0	0
1940-41	Detroit Red Wings	45	8	7	15	14	9	1	4	5	0
1941-42	Detroit Red Wings	48	23	30	53	13	12	*8	6	*14	29
1942-43 ♦	Detroit Red Wings	50	15	17	32	10	10	4	2	6	10
1943-44	Detroit Red Wings	42	16	31	47	13	5	1	0	1	0
1944-45	Detroit Red Wings	20	6	10	16	6	....	....	....	....	....
	Chicago Black Hawks	21	9	6	15	4	....	....	....	....	....
1945-46	Chicago Black Hawks	47	7	10	17	17	4	0	0	0	17
1946-47	Boston Bruins	33	0	2	2	2	....	....	....	....	....
	NHL Totals	**336**	**87**	**117**	**204**	**90**	**48**	**15**	**14**	**29**	**63**

Traded to **Chicago** by **Detroit** with Cully Simon and Butch McDonald for Earl Seibert and future considerations (Fido Purpur, January 4, 1945), January 2, 1945. Traded to **Boston** by **Chicago** for cash, June, 1946. Traded to **St. Louis** (AHL) by **Boston** for cash, June 14, 1947.

GROSVENOR, Len

Center/Right wing. Shoots right. 5'9", 172 lbs. Born, Ottawa, Ont., July 21, 1905.

Season	Club	GP	G	A	Pts	PIM	GP	G	A	Pts	PIM
1927-28	Ottawa Senators	43	1	2	3	18	2	0	0	0	2
1928-29	Ottawa Senators	42	3	2	5	16	....	....	....	....	....
1929-30	Ottawa Senators	15	0	3	3	19	....	....	....	....	....
1930-31	Ottawa Senators	33	5	4	9	25	....	....	....	....	....
1931-32	New York Americans	12	0	0	0	0	....	....	....	....	....
1932-33	Montreal Canadiens	4	0	0	0	0	2	0	0	0	0
	NHL Totals	**149**	**9**	**11**	**20**	**78**	**4**	**0**	**0**	**0**	**2**

Signed as a free agent by **Ottawa**, October 24, 1927. Loaned to **London** (IHL) by **Ottawa** for cash, December 26, 1929. Traded to **London** (IHL) by **Ottawa** for cash, October 24, 1930. Traded to **Ottawa** by **London** (IHL) for Harry Connor, December 1, 1930. Claimed by **NY Americans** from **Ottawa** for 1931-32 season in Dispersal Draft, September 26, 1931. Signed as a free agent by **Montreal**, January 7, 1933.

GROULX, Wayne

Center. Shoots right. 6'1", 185 lbs. Born, Welland, Ont., February 2, 1965.
(Quebec's 8th choice, 179th overall, in 1983 Entry Draft).

Season	Club	GP	G	A	Pts	PIM	GP	G	A	Pts	PIM
1984-85	Quebec Nordiques	1	0	0	0	0	....	....	....	....	....
	NHL Totals	**1**	**0**	**0**	**0**	**0**	....	....	....	....	....

GRUDEN, John

Defense. Shoots left. 6', 203 lbs. Born, Virginia, MN, June 4, 1970.
(Boston's 7th choice, 168th overall, in 1990 Entry Draft).

Season	Club	GP	G	A	Pts	PIM	GP	G	A	Pts	PIM
1993-94	Boston Bruins	7	0	1	1	2	....	....	....	....	....
1994-95	Boston Bruins	38	0	6	6	22	....	....	....	....	....
1995-96	Boston Bruins	14	0	0	0	4	3	0	1	1	0
1998-99	Ottawa Senators	13	0	1	1	8	....	....	....	....	....
99-2000	Ottawa Senators	9	0	0	0	4	....	....	....	....	....
	NHL Totals	**81**	**0**	**8**	**8**	**40**	**3**	**0**	**1**	**1**	**0**

Signed as a free agent by **Ottawa**, August 7, 1998.

GRUEN, Danny

Left wing. Shoots left. 5'11", 190 lbs. Born, Thunder Bay, Ont., June 26, 1952.
(Detroit's 3rd choice, 58th overall, in 1972 Amateur Draft).

Season	Club	GP	G	A	Pts	PIM	GP	G	A	Pts	PIM
1972-73	Detroit Red Wings	2	0	0	0	0	....	....	....	....	....
1973-74	Detroit Red Wings	18	1	3	4	7	....	....	....	....	....

Season	Club	GP	G	A	Pts	PIM	GP	G	A	Pts	PIM
		REGULAR SEASON					PLAYOFFS				
1976-77	Colorado Rockies	29	8	10	18	12	....	....	....	....	....
	NHL Totals	**49**	**9**	**13**	**22**	**19**	....	....	....	....	....

Rights traded to **Colorado** by **Detroit** for cash, February 11, 1977. Signed as a free agent by **Detroit**, August 17, 1977.

GRUHL, Scott

Left wing. Shoots left. 5'11", 185 lbs. Born, Port Colborne, Ont., September 13, 1959.

Season	Club	GP	G	A	Pts	PIM	GP	G	A	Pts	PIM
1981-82	Los Angeles Kings	7	2	1	3	2	....	....	....	....	....
1982-83	Los Angeles Kings	7	0	2	2	4	....	....	....	....	....
1987-88	Pittsburgh Penguins	6	1	0	1	0	....	....	....	....	....
	NHL Totals	**20**	**3**	**3**	**6**	**6**	....	....	....	....	....

Signed as a free agent by **Los Angeles**, October 11, 1979. Signed as a free agent by **Pittsburgh**, December 14, 1987.

GRYP, Bob

Left wing. Shoots left. 6'1", 190 lbs. Born, Chatham, Ont., May 6, 1950.
(Toronto's 4th choice, 50th overall, in 1970 Amateur Draft).

Season	Club	GP	G	A	Pts	PIM	GP	G	A	Pts	PIM
1973-74	Boston Bruins	1	0	0	0	0	....	....	....	....	....
1974-75	Washington Capitals	27	5	8	13	21	....	....	....	....	....
1975-76	Washington Capitals	46	6	5	11	12	....	....	....	....	....
	NHL Totals	**74**	**11**	**13**	**24**	**33**	....	....	....	....	....

Claimed by **Boston** from **Tulsa** (CHL) in Reverse Draft, June, 1972. Claimed by **Washington** from **Boston** in Expansion Draft, June 12, 1974. Traded to **New Haven** (AHL) by **Washington** with Ron Anderson for Rich Nantais and Alain Langlais, February 23, 1976.

GUAY, Francois

Center. Shoots left. 6', 190 lbs. Born, Gatineau, Que., June 8, 1968.
(Buffalo's 9th choice, 152nd overall, in 1986 Entry Draft).

Season	Club	GP	G	A	Pts	PIM	GP	G	A	Pts	PIM
1989-90	Buffalo Sabres	1	0	0	0	0	....	....	....	....	....
	NHL Totals	**1**	**0**	**0**	**0**	**0**	....	....	....	....	....

GUAY, Paul

Right wing. Shoots right. 5'11", 185 lbs. Born, Providence, RI, September 2, 1963.
(Minnesota's 10th choice, 118th overall, in 1981 Entry Draft).

Season	Club	GP	G	A	Pts	PIM	GP	G	A	Pts	PIM
1983-84	Philadelphia Flyers	14	2	6	8	14	3	0	0	0	4
1984-85	Philadelphia Flyers	2	0	1	1	0	....	....	....	....	....
1985-86	Los Angeles Kings	23	3	3	6	18	....	....	....	....	....
1986-87	Los Angeles Kings	35	2	5	7	16	2	0	0	0	0
1987-88	Los Angeles Kings	33	4	4	8	40	4	0	1	1	8
1988-89	Los Angeles Kings	2	0	0	0	2	....	....	....	....	....
	Boston Bruins	5	0	2	2	0	....	....	....	....	....
1990-91	New York Islanders	3	0	2	2	2	....	....	....	....	....
	NHL Totals	**117**	**11**	**23**	**34**	**92**	**9**	**0**	**1**	**1**	**12**

Rights traded to **Philadelphia** by **Minnesota** with Minnesota's 3rd round choice (Darryl Gilmour) in 1985 Entry Draft for Paul Holmgren, February 23, 1984. Traded to **Los Angeles** by **Philadelphia** with Philadelphia's 4th round choice (Sylvain Couturier) in 1986 Entry Draft for Steve Seguin and Los Angeles' 2nd round choice (Jukka Seppo) in 1986 Entry Draft, October 11, 1985. Traded to **Boston** by **Los Angeles** for the rights to Dave Pasin, November 3, 1988. Signed as a free agent by **New Jersey**, August 14, 1989. Signed as a free agent by **NY Islanders**, August 13, 1990.

GUERARD, Daniel

Right wing. Shoots right. 6'4", 215 lbs. Born, LaSalle, Que., April 9, 1974.
(Ottawa's 5th choice, 98th overall, in 1992 Entry Draft).

Season	Club	GP	G	A	Pts	PIM	GP	G	A	Pts	PIM
1994-95	Ottawa Senators	2	0	0	0	0	....	....	....	....	....
	NHL Totals	**2**	**0**	**0**	**0**	**0**	....	....	....	....	....

GUERARD, Stephane

Defense. Shoots left. 6'2", 198 lbs. Born, Ste-Elizabeth, Que., April 12, 1968.
(Quebec's 3rd choice, 41st overall, in 1986 Entry Draft).

Season	Club	GP	G	A	Pts	PIM	GP	G	A	Pts	PIM
1987-88	Quebec Nordiques	30	0	0	0	34	....	....	....	....	....
1989-90	Quebec Nordiques	4	0	0	0	6	....	....	....	....	....
	NHL Totals	**34**	**0**	**0**	**0**	**40**	....	....	....	....	....

• Missed majority of 1987-88 season recovering from knee injury suffered in game vs. St. Louis, November 3, 1987. Traded to **NY Rangers** by **Quebec** for Miloslav Horava, May 25, 1991. Traded to **Quebec** by **NY Rangers** for cash, September 3, 1991.

GUERIN, Bill

Right wing. Shoots right. 6'2", 210 lbs. Born, Worcester, MA, November 9, 1970.
(New Jersey's 1st choice, 5th overall, in 1989 Entry Draft).

Season	Club	GP	G	A	Pts	PIM	GP	G	A	Pts	PIM
1991-92	New Jersey Devils	5	0	1	1	9	6	3	0	3	4
1992-93	New Jersey Devils	65	14	20	34	63	5	1	1	2	4
1993-94	New Jersey Devils	81	25	19	44	101	17	2	1	3	35
1994-95 ♦	New Jersey Devils	48	12	13	25	72	20	3	8	11	30
1995-96	New Jersey Devils	80	23	30	53	116	....	....	....	....	....
1996-97	New Jersey Devils	82	29	18	47	95	8	2	1	3	18
1997-98	New Jersey Devils	19	5	5	10	13	....	....	....	....	....
	Edmonton Oilers	40	13	16	29	80	12	7	1	8	17
1998-99	Edmonton Oilers	80	30	34	64	133	3	0	2	2	2
99-2000	Edmonton Oilers	70	24	22	46	123	5	3	2	5	9
2000-01	Edmonton Oilers	21	12	10	22	18	....	....	....	....	....
	Boston Bruins	64	28	35	63	122	....	....	....	....	....
2001-02	Boston Bruins	78	41	25	66	91	6	4	2	6	6
2002-03	Dallas Stars	64	25	25	50	113	4	0	0	0	[illegible]
	NHL Totals	**797**	**281**	**273**	**554**	**1149**	**86**	**25**	**18**	**43**	**129**

NHL Second All-Star Team (2002)

Played in NHL All-Star Game (2001, 2003)

Traded to **Edmonton** by **New Jersey** with Valeri Zelepukin for Jason Arnott and Bryan Muir, January 4, 1998. Traded to **Boston** by **Edmonton** for Anson Carter, Boston's 1st (Ales Hemsky) and 2nd (Doug Lynch) round choices in 2001 Entry Draft and future considerations, November 15, 2000. Signed as a free agent by **Dallas**, July 3, 2002.

GUEVREMONT, Jocelyn

Defense. Shoots right. 6'2", 200 lbs. Born, Montreal, Que., March 1, 1951.
(Vancouver's 1st choice, 3rd overall, in 1971 Amateur Draft).

Season	Club	GP	G	A	Pts	PIM	GP	G	A	Pts	PIM
1971-72	Vancouver Canucks	75	13	38	51	44	....	....	....	....	....
1972-73	Vancouver Canucks	78	16	26	42	46	....	....	....	....	....
1973-74	Vancouver Canucks	72	15	24	39	34	....	....	....	....	....
1974-75	Vancouver Canucks	2	0	0	0	0	....	....	....	....	....
	Buffalo Sabres	64	7	25	32	32	17	0	6	6	14
1975-76	Buffalo Sabres	80	12	40	52	57	9	0	5	5	2
1976-77	Buffalo Sabres	80	9	29	38	46	6	3	4	7	0
1977-78	Buffalo Sabres	66	7	28	35	46	8	1	2	3	2
1978-79	Buffalo Sabres	34	3	8	11	8	....	....	....	....	....
1979-80	New York Rangers	20	2	5	7	6	....	....	....	....	....
	NHL Totals	**571**	**84**	**223**	**307**	**319**	**40**	**4**	**17**	**21**	**18**

Played in NHL All-Star Game (1974)

Traded to **Buffalo** by **Vancouver** with Bryan McSheffrey for Gerry Meehan and Mike Robitaille, October 14, 1974. Traded to **NY Rangers** by **Buffalo** for future considerations, March 12, 1979.

GUIDOLIN, Aldo

Right wing/Defense. Shoots right. 6', 180 lbs. Born, Forks of Credit, Ont., June 6, 1932.

Season	Club	GP	G	A	Pts	PIM	GP	G	A	Pts	PIM
1952-53	New York Rangers	30	4	4	8	24	....	....	....	....	....
1953-54	New York Rangers	68	2	6	8	51	....	....	....	....	....
1954-55	New York Rangers	70	2	5	7	34	....	....	....	....	....
1955-56	New York Rangers	14	1	0	1	8	....	....	....	....	....
	NHL Totals	**182**	**9**	**15**	**24**	**117**	....	....	....	....	....

Traded to **Cleveland** (AHL) by **NY Rangers** with Ed Hoekstra for Art Stratton with NY Rangers holding right of recall, June, 1959. Traded to **Baltimore** (AHL) by **Cleveland** (AHL) for cash, August, 1962. Traded to **Providence** (AHL) by **NY Rangers** (Baltimore-AHL) with Marcel Paille, Jim Mikol and Sandy McGregor for Ed Giacomin, May 18, 1965. • McGregor refused to report and was replaced with Buzz Deschamps.

GUIDOLIN, Bep

Left wing. Shoots left. 5'8", 175 lbs. Born, Thorold, Ont., December 9, 1925.

Season	Club	GP	G	A	Pts	PIM	GP	G	A	Pts	PIM
1942-43	Boston Bruins	42	7	15	22	43	9	0	4	4	12
1943-44	Boston Bruins	47	17	25	42	58	....	....	....	....	....
1945-46	Boston Bruins	50	15	17	32	62	10	5	2	7	13
1946-47	Boston Bruins	56	10	13	23	73	3	0	1	1	6
1947-48	Detroit Red Wings	58	12	10	22	78	2	0	0	0	4
1948-49	Detroit Red Wings	4	0	0	0	0	....	....	....	....	....
	Chicago Black Hawks	56	4	17	21	116	....	....	....	....	....
1949-50	Chicago Black Hawks	70	17	34	51	42	....	....	....	....	....
1950-51	Chicago Black Hawks	69	12	22	34	56	....	....	....	....	....
1951-52	Chicago Black Hawks	67	13	18	31	78	....	....	....	....	....
	NHL Totals	**519**	**107**	**171**	**278**	**606**	**24**	**5**	**7**	**12**	**35**

• Youngest player (16 years, 11 months) to play in a NHL game, November 12, 1942. (Toronto 3, Boston 1). Traded to **Detroit** by **Boston** for Billy Taylor, October 15, 1947. Traded to **Chicago** by **Detroit** with Jim Conacher and Doug McCaig for George Gee and Bud Poile, October 25, 1948.

GUINDON, Bobby

Left wing. Shoots left. 5'9", 175 lbs. Born, Labelle, Que., November 19, 1950.
(Detroit's 2nd choice, 26th overall, in 1970 Amateur Draft).

Season	Club	GP	G	A	Pts	PIM	GP	G	A	Pts	PIM
1979-80	Winnipeg Jets	6	0	1	1	0	....	....	....	....	....
	NHL Totals	**6**	**0**	**1**	**1**	**0**	....	....	....	....	....

Rights retained by **Winnipeg** prior to NHL Expansion Draft, June 9, 1979.

GUOLLA, Stephen

Center. Shoots left. 6', 190 lbs. Born, Scarborough, Ont., March 15, 1973.
(Ottawa's 1st choice, 3rd overall, in 1994 Supplemental Draft).

Season	Club	GP	G	A	Pts	PIM	GP	G	A	Pts	PIM
1996-97	San Jose Sharks	43	13	8	21	14	....	....	....	....	....
1997-98	San Jose Sharks	7	1	1	2	0	....	....	....	....	....
1998-99	San Jose Sharks	14	2	2	4	6	....	....	....	....	....
99-2000	Tampa Bay Lightning	46	6	10	16	11	....	....	....	....	....
	Atlanta Thrashers	20	4	9	13	4	....	....	....	....	....
2000-01	Atlanta Thrashers	63	12	16	28	23	....	....	....	....	....
2002-03	New Jersey Devils	12	2	0	2	2	....	....	....	....	....
	NHL Totals	**205**	**40**	**46**	**86**	**60**	....	....	....	....	....

Signed as a free agent by **San Jose**, August 22, 1996. Traded to **Tampa Bay** by **San Jose** with Bill Houlder, Shawn Burr and Andrei Zyuzin for Niklas Sundstrom and NY Rangers' 3rd round choice (previously acquired, later traded to Chicago – Chicago selected Igor Radulov) in 2000 Entry Draft, August 4, 1999. Claimed on waivers by **Atlanta** from **Tampa Bay**, March 1, 2000. Signed as a free agent by **New Jersey**, October 21, 2001. • Missed majority of 2002-03 seasc recovering from back injury suffered in game vs. NY Islanders, November 27, 2002.

GUREN, Miloslav

Defense. Shoots left. 6'2", 215 lbs. Born, Uherske Hradiste, Czech., September 24
(Montreal's 2nd choice, 60th overall, in 1995 Entry Draft).

Season	Club	GP	G	A	Pts	PIM	GP	G	A	Pts	PIM
1998-99	Montreal Canadiens	12	0	1	1	4	....	...			

		REGULAR SEASON					PLAYOFFS				
Season	Club	GP	G	A	Pts	PIM	GP	G	A	Pts	PIM
9-2000	Montreal Canadiens	24	1	2	3	12	....	....	....	....	....
	NHL Totals	**36**	**1**	**3**	**4**	**16**	....	....	....	....	....

GUSAROV, Alexei

Defense. Shoots left. 6'3", 185 lbs. Born, Leningrad, USSR, July 8, 1964.
(Quebec's 11th choice, 213th overall, in 1988 Entry Draft).

Season	Club	GP	G	A	Pts	PIM	GP	G	A	Pts	PIM
1990-91	Quebec Nordiques	36	3	9	12	12	....	....	....	....	....
1991-92	Quebec Nordiques	68	5	18	23	22	....	....	....	....	....
1992-93	Quebec Nordiques	79	8	22	30	57	5	0	1	1	0
1993-94	Quebec Nordiques	76	5	20	25	38	....	....	....	....	....
1994-95	Quebec Nordiques	14	1	2	3	6	....	....	....	....	....
1995-96 ♦	Colorado Avalanche	65	5	15	20	56	21	0	9	9	12
1996-97	Colorado Avalanche	58	2	12	14	28	17	0	3	3	14
1997-98	Colorado Avalanche	72	4	10	14	42	7	0	1	1	6
1998-99	Colorado Avalanche	54	3	10	13	24	5	0	0	0	2
99-2000	Colorado Avalanche	34	2	2	4	10	....	....	....	....	....
2000-01	Colorado Avalanche	9	0	1	1	6	....	....	....	....	....
	New York Rangers	26	1	3	4	6	....	....	....	....	....
	St. Louis Blues	16	0	4	4	6	13	0	0	0	4
	NHL Totals	**607**	**39**	**128**	**167**	**313**	**68**	**0**	**14**	**14**	**38**

Transferred to **Colorado** after **Quebec** franchise relocated, June 21, 1995. • Missed majority of 1999-2000 season recovering from leg injury suffered in game vs. Dallas, February 27, 2000. Traded to **NY Rangers** by **Colorado** for NY Rangers' 5th round choice (Frantisek Skladany) in 2001 Entry Draft, December 28, 2000. Traded to **St. Louis** by **NY Rangers** for Peter Smrek, March 5, 2001.

GUSEV, Sergey

Defense. Shoots left. 6'1", 205 lbs. Born, Nizhny Tagil, USSR, July 31, 1975.
(Dallas' 4th choice, 69th overall, in 1995 Entry Draft).

Season	Club	GP	G	A	Pts	PIM	GP	G	A	Pts	PIM
1997-98	Dallas Stars	9	0	0	0	2	....	....	....	....	....
1998-99	Dallas Stars	22	1	4	5	6	....	....	....	....	....
	Tampa Bay Lightning	14	0	3	3	10	....	....	....	....	....
99-2000	Tampa Bay Lightning	28	2	3	5	6	....	....	....	....	....
2000-01	Tampa Bay Lightning	16	1	0	1	10	....	....	....	....	....
	NHL Totals	**89**	**4**	**10**	**14**	**34**	....	....	....	....	....

Traded to **Tampa Bay** by **Dallas** for Benoit Hogue and Tampa Bay's 6th round choice (Michal Blazek) in 2001 Entry Draft, March 21, 1999.

GUSMANOV, Ravil

Left wing. Shoots left. 6'3", 185 lbs. Born, Naberezhnye Chelny, USSR, July 25, 1972.
(Winnipeg's 5th choice, 93rd overall, in 1993 Entry Draft).

Season	Club	GP	G	A	Pts	PIM	GP	G	A	Pts	PIM
1995-96	Winnipeg Jets	4	0	0	0	0	....	....	....	....	....
	NHL Totals	**4**	**0**	**0**	**0**	**0**	....	....	....	....	....

Traded to **Chicago** by **Winnipeg** for Chicago's 4th round choice (later traded to Toronto – Toronto selected Vladimir Antipov) in 1996 Entry Draft, March 20, 1996. Traded to **Calgary** by **Chicago** for Marc Hussey, March 18, 1997. Signed as a free agent by **Minnesota**, June 21, 2001.

GUSTAFSSON, Bengt-Ake

Right wing. Shoots left. 6', 185 lbs. Born, Karlskoga, Sweden, March 23, 1958.
(Washington's 7th choice, 55th overall, in 1978 Amateur Draft).

Season	Club	GP	G	A	Pts	PIM	GP	G	A	Pts	PIM
1979-80	Washington Capitals	80	22	38	60	17	....	....	....	....	....
1980-81	Washington Capitals	72	21	34	55	26	....	....	....	....	....
1981-82	Washington Capitals	70	26	34	60	40	....	....	....	....	....
1982-83	Washington Capitals	67	22	42	64	16	4	0	1	1	4
1983-84	Washington Capitals	69	32	43	75	16	5	2	3	5	0
1984-85	Washington Capitals	51	14	29	43	8	5	1	3	4	0
1985-86	Washington Capitals	70	23	52	75	26	....	....	....	....	....
1987-88	Washington Capitals	78	18	36	54	29	14	4	9	13	6
1988-89	Washington Capitals	72	18	51	69	18	4	2	3	5	6
	NHL Totals	**629**	**196**	**359**	**555**	**196**	**32**	**9**	**19**	**28**	**16**

Claimed by **Washington** from **Edmonton** prior to Expansion Draft, June 9, 1979.

GUSTAFSSON, Per

Defense. Shoots left. 6'2", 190 lbs. Born, Osterham, Sweden, June 6, 1970.
(Florida's 10th choice, 261st overall, in 1994 Entry Draft).

Season	Club	GP	G	A	Pts	PIM	GP	G	A	Pts	PIM
1996-97	Florida Panthers	58	7	22	29	22	....	....	....	....	....
1997-98	Toronto Maple Leafs	22	1	4	5	10	....	....	....	....	....
	Ottawa Senators	9	0	1	1	6	1	0	0	0	0
	NHL Totals	**89**	**8**	**27**	**35**	**38**	**1**	**0**	**0**	**0**	**0**

Traded to **Toronto** by **Florida** for Mike Lankshear, June 13, 1997. Traded to **Ottawa** by **Toronto** for Ottawa's 8th round choice (Dwight Wolfe) in 1998 Entry Draft, March 17, 1998.

GUSTAVSSON, Peter

Left wing. Shoots left. 6'1", 188 lbs. Born, Bollebygd, Sweden, March 30, 1958.

Season	Club	GP	G	A	Pts	PIM	GP	G	A	Pts	PIM
-82	Colorado Rockies	2	0	0	0	0	....	....	....	....	....
	NHL Totals	**2**	**0**	**0**	**0**	**0**	....	....	....	....	....

agent by **Colorado**, May 11, 1981.

6'3", 202 lbs. Born, Edmonton, Alta., July 16, 1965.
3rd overall, in 1983 Entry Draft).

Season	Club	GP	G	A	Pts	PIM	GP	G	A	Pts	PIM
		24	0	4	4	19	4	0	1	1	23
		11	0	3	3	8	....	....	....	....	....
	s	45	2	2	4	34	1	0	0	0	0
	s	30	2	5	7	32	....	....	....	....	....

Season	Club	GP	G	A	Pts	PIM	GP	G	A	Pts	PIM
1990-91	Vancouver Canucks	39	1	6	7	39	....	....	....	....	....
	Calgary Flames	4	0	0	0	4	....	....	....	....	....
1991-92	Calgary Flames	3	0	0	0	2	....	....	....	....	....
	NHL Totals	**156**	**5**	**20**	**25**	**138**	**5**	**0**	**1**	**1**	**23**

Traded to **Vancouver** by **Calgary** with Brian Bradley and Peter Bakovic for Craig Coxe, March 6, 1988. Traded to **Calgary** by **Vancouver** with Ron Stern for Dana Murzyn, March 5, 1991. Signed as a free agent by **NY Islanders**, September 18, 1993.

HAAKANA, Kari

Defense. Shoots left. 6'1", 222 lbs. Born, Outokumpu, Finland, November 8, 1973.
(Edmonton's 9th choice, 248th overall, in 2001 Entry Draft).

Season	Club	GP	G	A	Pts	PIM	GP	G	A	Pts	PIM
2002-03	Edmonton Oilers	13	0	0	0	4	....	....	....	....	....
	NHL Totals	**13**	**0**	**0**	**0**	**4**	....	....	....	....	....

HAANPAA, Ari

Right wing. Shoots right. 6'1", 185 lbs. Born, Nokla, Finland, November 28, 1965.
(NY Islanders' 5th choice, 83rd overall, in 1984 Entry Draft).

Season	Club	GP	G	A	Pts	PIM	GP	G	A	Pts	PIM
1985-86	New York Islanders	18	0	7	7	20	....	....	....	....	....
1986-87	New York Islanders	41	6	4	10	17	6	0	0	0	10
1987-88	New York Islanders	1	0	0	0	0	....	....	....	....	....
	NHL Totals	**60**	**6**	**11**	**17**	**37**	**6**	**0**	**0**	**0**	**10**

HAAS, David

Left wing. Shoots left. 6'2", 200 lbs. Born, Toronto, Ont., June 23, 1968.
(Edmonton's 5th choice, 105th overall, in 1986 Entry Draft).

Season	Club	GP	G	A	Pts	PIM	GP	G	A	Pts	PIM
1990-91	Edmonton Oilers	5	1	0	1	0	....	....	....	....	....
1993-94	Calgary Flames	2	1	1	2	7	....	....	....	....	....
	NHL Totals	**7**	**2**	**1**	**3**	**7**	....	....	....	....	....

Signed as a free agent by **Calgary**, August 10, 1993.

HABSCHEID, Marc

Right wing/Center. Shoots right. 6', 185 lbs. Born, Swift Current, Sask., March 1, 1963.
(Edmonton's 6th choice, 113th overall, in 1981 Entry Draft).

Season	Club	GP	G	A	Pts	PIM	GP	G	A	Pts	PIM
1981-82	Edmonton Oilers	7	1	3	4	2	....	....	....	....	....
1982-83	Edmonton Oilers	32	3	10	13	14	....	....	....	....	....
1983-84	Edmonton Oilers	9	1	0	1	6	....	....	....	....	....
1984-85	Edmonton Oilers	26	5	3	8	4	....	....	....	....	....
1985-86	Minnesota North Stars	6	2	3	5	0	2	0	0	0	0
1986-87	Minnesota North Stars	15	2	0	2	2	....	....	....	....	....
1987-88	Minnesota North Stars	16	4	11	15	6	....	....	....	....	....
1988-89	Minnesota North Stars	76	23	31	54	40	5	1	3	4	13
1989-90	Detroit Red Wings	66	15	11	26	33	....	....	....	....	....
1990-91	Detroit Red Wings	46	9	8	17	22	5	0	0	0	0
1991-92	Calgary Flames	46	7	11	18	42	....	....	....	....	....
	NHL Totals	**345**	**72**	**91**	**163**	**171**	**12**	**1**	**3**	**4**	**13**

• Suspended by Edmonton for refusing to report to Nova Scotia (AHL), October, 1985. Traded to **Minnesota** by **Edmonton** with Don Barber and Emanuel Viveiros for Gord Sherven and Don Biggs, December 20, 1985. Signed as a free agent by **Detroit**, June 9, 1989. Traded to **Calgary** by **Detroit** for Brian MacLellan, June 11, 1991.

HACHBORN, Len

Center. Shoots left. 5'10", 175 lbs. Born, Brantford, Ont., September 4, 1961.
(Philadelphia's 12th choice, 184th overall, in 1981 Entry Draft).

Season	Club	GP	G	A	Pts	PIM	GP	G	A	Pts	PIM
1983-84	Philadelphia Flyers	38	11	21	32	4	3	0	0	0	7
1984-85	Philadelphia Flyers	40	5	17	22	23	4	0	3	3	0
1985-86	Los Angeles Kings	24	4	1	5	2	....	....	....	....	....
	NHL Totals	**102**	**20**	**39**	**59**	**29**	**7**	**0**	**3**	**3**	**7**

Traded to **Los Angeles** by **Philadelphia** for cash, December 6, 1985.

HADDON, Lloyd

Defense. Shoots left. 6', 195 lbs. Born, Sarnia, Ont., August 10, 1938.

Season	Club	GP	G	A	Pts	PIM	GP	G	A	Pts	PIM
1959-60	Detroit Red Wings	8	0	0	0	2	1	0	0	0	0
	NHL Totals	**8**	**0**	**0**	**0**	**2**	**1**	**0**	**0**	**0**	**0**

Traded to **LA Blades** (WHL) by **Detroit** for cash, July, 1962. Traded to **Chicago** (St. Louis – AHL) by **LA Blades** (WHL) for Norm Johnson, Ron Leopold and Gord Vejprava, August 12, 1963.

HADFIELD, Vic

Left wing. Shoots left. 6', 190 lbs. Born, Oakville, Ont., October 4, 1940.

Season	Club	GP	G	A	Pts	PIM	GP	G	A	Pts	PIM
1961-62	New York Rangers	44	3	1	4	22	4	0	0	0	2
1962-63	New York Rangers	36	5	6	11	32	....	....	....	....	....
1963-64	New York Rangers	69	14	11	25	*151	....	....	....	....	....
1964-65	New York Rangers	70	18	20	38	102	....	....	....	....	....
1965-66	New York Rangers	67	16	19	35	112	....	....	....	....	....
1966-67	New York Rangers	69	13	20	33	80	4	1	0	1	17
1967-68	New York Rangers	59	20	19	39	45	6	1	2	3	6
1968-69	New York Rangers	73	26	40	66	108	4	2	1	3	2
1969-70	New York Rangers	71	20	34	54	69	....	....	....	....	....
1970-71	New York Rangers	63	22	22	44	38	12	8	5	13	46
1971-72	New York Rangers	78	50	56	106	142	16	7	9	16	22
1972-73	New York Rangers	63	28	34	62	60	9	2	2	4	11
1973-74	New York Rangers	77	27	28	55	75	6	1	0	1	0
1974-75	Pittsburgh Penguins	78	31	42	73	72	9	4	2	6	0
1975-76	Pittsburgh Penguins	76	30	35	65	46	3	1	0	1	11

Season	Club	Regular Season GP	G	A	Pts	PIM	Playoffs GP	G	A	Pts	PIM
1976-77	Pittsburgh Penguins	9	0	2	2	0	....	....	....	....	....
	NHL Totals	**1002**	**323**	**389**	**712**	**1154**	**73**	**27**	**21**	**48**	**117**

NHL Second All-Star Team (1972)
Played in NHL All-Star Game (1965, 1972)

Claimed by **NY Rangers** from **Chicago** in Intra-League Draft, June 13, 1961. Traded to **Pittsburgh** by **NY Rangers** for Nick Beverley, May 27, 1974. • Suffered eventual career-ending knee injury in game vs. Toronto, March 29, 1976.

HAGGARTY, Jim

Left wing. Shoots left. 5'11", 167 lbs. Born, Port Arthur, Ont., April 14, 1914.

Season	Club	GP	G	A	Pts	PIM	GP	G	A	Pts	PIM
1941-42	Montreal Canadiens	5	1	1	2	0	3	2	1	3	0
	NHL Totals	**5**	**1**	**1**	**2**	**0**	**3**	**2**	**1**	**3**	**0**

Signed as a free agent by **Montreal**, March 3, 1942.

HAGGERTY, Sean

Left wing. Shoots left. 6'1", 186 lbs. Born, Rye, NY, February 11, 1976.
(Toronto's 2nd choice, 48th overall, in 1994 Entry Draft).

Season	Club	GP	G	A	Pts	PIM	GP	G	A	Pts	PIM
1995-96	Toronto Maple Leafs	1	0	0	0	0	....	....	....	....	....
1997-98	New York Islanders	5	0	0	0	0	....	....	....	....	....
99-2000	New York Islanders	5	1	1	2	4	....	....	....	....	....
2000-01	Nashville Predators	3	0	1	1	0	....	....	....	....	....
	NHL Totals	**14**	**1**	**2**	**3**	**4**	....	....	....	....	....

Traded to **NY Islanders** by **Toronto** with Darby Hendrickson, Kenny Jonsson and Toronto's 1st round choice (Roberto Luongo) in 1997 Entry Draft for Wendel Clark, Mathieu Schneider and D.J. Smith, March 13, 1996. Claimed on waivers by **Nashville** from **NY Islanders**, May 23, 2000.

HAGGLUND, Roger

Defense. Shoots left. 6'1", 175 lbs. Born, Umea, Sweden, July 2, 1961.
(St. Louis' 6th choice, 138th overall, in 1980 Entry Draft).

Season	Club	GP	G	A	Pts	PIM	GP	G	A	Pts	PIM
1984-85	Quebec Nordiques	3	0	0	0	0	....	....	....	....	....
	NHL Totals	**3**	**0**	**0**	**0**	**0**	....	....	....	....	....

Traded to **Quebec** by **St. Louis** for cash, July, 1984.

HAGMAN, Matti

Center. Shoots left. 6'1", 184 lbs. Born, Helsinki, Finland, September 21, 1955.
(Boston's 6th choice, 104th overall, in 1975 Amateur Draft).

Season	Club	GP	G	A	Pts	PIM	GP	G	A	Pts	PIM
1976-77	Boston Bruins	75	11	17	28	0	8	0	1	1	0
1977-78	Boston Bruins	15	4	1	5	2	....	....	....	....	....
1980-81	Edmonton Oilers	75	20	33	53	16	9	4	1	5	6
1981-82	Edmonton Oilers	72	21	38	59	18	3	1	0	1	0
	NHL Totals	**237**	**56**	**89**	**145**	**36**	**20**	**5**	**2**	**7**	**6**

Traded to **Quebec** (WHA) by **Boston** for cash, December, 1977. Signed as a free agent by **Edmonton**, September 11, 1980.

HAGMAN, Niklas

Left wing. Shoots left. 6', 200 lbs. Born, Espoo, Finland, December 5, 1979.
(Florida's 3rd choice, 70th overall, in 1999 Entry Draft).

Season	Club	GP	G	A	Pts	PIM	GP	G	A	Pts	PIM
2001-02	Florida Panthers	78	10	18	28	8	....	....	....	....	....
2002-03	Florida Panthers	80	8	15	23	20	....	....	....	....	....
	NHL Totals	**158**	**18**	**33**	**51**	**28**	....	....	....	....	....

HAHL, Riku

Center. Shoots left. 6', 190 lbs. Born, Hameenlinna, Finland, November 1, 1980.
(Colorado's 9th choice, 183rd overall, in 1999 Entry Draft).

Season	Club	GP	G	A	Pts	PIM	GP	G	A	Pts	PIM
2001-02	Colorado Avalanche	22	2	3	5	14	21	1	2	3	0
2002-03	Colorado Avalanche	42	3	4	7	12	6	0	2	2	2
	NHL Totals	**64**	**5**	**7**	**12**	**26**	**27**	**1**	**4**	**5**	**2**

HAIDY, Gord

Right wing. Shoots right. 5'11", 185 lbs. Born, Winnipeg, Man., April 11, 1928.

Season	Club	GP	G	A	Pts	PIM	GP	G	A	Pts	PIM
1949-50 ♦	Detroit Red Wings	....	....	....	....	....	1	0	0	0	0
	NHL Totals	....	....	....	....	....	**1**	**0**	**0**	**0**	**0**

HAINSEY, Ron

Defense. Shoots left. 6'3", 200 lbs. Born, Bolton, CT, March 24, 1981.
(Montreal's 1st choice, 13th overall, in 2000 Entry Draft).

Season	Club	GP	G	A	Pts	PIM	GP	G	A	Pts	PIM
2002-03	Montreal Canadiens	21	0	0	0	2	....	....	....	....	....
	NHL Totals	**21**	**0**	**0**	**0**	**2**	....	....	....	....	....

HAJDU, Richard

Left wing. Shoots left. 6'1", 185 lbs. Born, Victoria, B.C., May 10, 1965.
(Buffalo's 5th choice, 34th overall, in 1983 Entry Draft).

Season	Club	GP	G	A	Pts	PIM	GP	G	A	Pts	PIM
1985-86	Buffalo Sabres	3	0	0	0	4	....	....	....	....	....
1986-87	Buffalo Sabres	2	0	0	0	0	....	....	....	....	....
	NHL Totals	**5**	**0**	**0**	**0**	**4**	....	....	....	....	....

HAJT, Bill

Defense. Shoots left. 6'3", 215 lbs. Born, Borden, Sask., November 18, 1951.
(Buffalo's 3rd choice, 33rd overall, in 1971 Amateur Draft).

Season	Club	GP	G	A	Pts	PIM	GP	G	A	Pts	PIM
1973-74	Buffalo Sabres	6	0	2	2	0	....	....	....	....	....
1974-75	Buffalo Sabres	76	3	26	29	68	17	1	4	5	18
1975-76	Buffalo Sabres	80	6	21	27	48	9	0	1	1	15
1976-77	Buffalo Sabres	79	6	20	26	56	6	0	1	1	4
1977-78	Buffalo Sabres	76	4	18	22	30	8	0	0	0	2
1978-79	Buffalo Sabres	40	3	8	11	20	....	....	....	....	....
1979-80	Buffalo Sabres	75	4	12	16	24	14	0	5	5	4
1980-81	Buffalo Sabres	68	2	19	21	42	8	0	2	2	17
1981-82	Buffalo Sabres	65	2	9	11	44	2	0	0	0	0
1982-83	Buffalo Sabres	72	3	12	15	26	10	0	0	0	4
1983-84	Buffalo Sabres	79	3	24	27	32	3	0	0	0	0
1984-85	Buffalo Sabres	57	5	13	18	14	3	1	3	4	6
1985-86	Buffalo Sabres	58	1	16	17	25	....	....	....	....	....
1986-87	Buffalo Sabres	23	0	2	2	4	....	....	....	....	....
	NHL Totals	**854**	**42**	**202**	**244**	**433**	**80**	**2**	**16**	**18**	**70**

• Father of Chris

HAJT, Chris

Defense. Shoots left. 6'3", 206 lbs. Born, Saskatoon, Sask., July 5, 1978.
(Edmonton's 3rd choice, 32nd overall, in 1996 Entry Draft).

Season	Club	GP	G	A	Pts	PIM	GP	G	A	Pts	PIM
2000-01	Edmonton Oilers	1	0	0	0	0	....	....	....	....	....
	NHL Totals	**1**	**0**	**0**	**0**	**0**	....	....	....	....	....

• Son of Bill

Signed as a free agent by **Washington**, July 23, 2002.

HAKANSSON, Anders

Left wing. Shoots left. 6'2", 190 lbs. Born, Munkfors, Sweden, April 27, 1956.
(St. Louis' 15th choice, 134th overall, in 1976 Amateur Draft).

Season	Club	GP	G	A	Pts	PIM	GP	G	A	Pts	PIM
1981-82	Minnesota North Stars	72	12	4	16	29	3	0	0	0	2
1982-83	Minnesota North Stars	5	0	0	0	9	....	....	....	....	....
	Pittsburgh Penguins	62	9	12	21	26	....	....	....	....	....
1983-84	Los Angeles Kings	80	15	17	32	41	....	....	....	....	....
1984-85	Los Angeles Kings	73	12	12	24	28	3	0	0	0	0
1985-86	Los Angeles Kings	38	4	1	5	8	....	....	....	....	....
	NHL Totals	**330**	**52**	**46**	**98**	**141**	**6**	**0**	**0**	**0**	**2**

Signed as a free agent by **Minnesota**, July 22, 1981. Traded to **Pittsburgh** by **Minnesota** with Ron Meighan and Minnesota's 1st round choice (Bob Errey) in 1983 Entry Draft for George Ferguson and Pittsburgh's 1st round choice (Brian Lawton) in 1983 Entry Draft, October 28, 1982. Traded to **Los Angeles** by **Pittsburgh** for the rights to Kevin Stevens, September 9, 1983.

HALDERSON, Harold

Defense. Shoots right. 6'3", 200 lbs. Born, Winnipeg, Man., January 6, 1900.

Season	Club	GP	G	A	Pts	PIM	GP	G	A	Pts	PIM
1926-27	Detroit Cougars	19	2	0	2	29	....	....	....	....	....
	Toronto St. Pats/Maple Leafs	25	1	2	3	36	....	....	....	....	....
	NHL Totals	**44**	**3**	**2**	**5**	**65**	....	....	....	....	....

Transferred to **Detroit** after NHL club purchased **Victoria** (WHL) franchise, May 15, 1926. Traded to **Toronto** by **Detroit** for Pete Bellefeuille, January 7, 1927.

HALE, Larry

Defense. Shoots left. 6'1", 180 lbs. Born, Summerland, B.C., October 9, 1941.

Season	Club	GP	G	A	Pts	PIM	GP	G	A	Pts	PIM
1968-69	Philadelphia Flyers	67	3	16	19	28	4	0	0	0	10
1969-70	Philadelphia Flyers	53	1	9	10	28	....	....	....	....	....
1970-71	Philadelphia Flyers	70	1	11	12	34	4	0	0	0	2
1971-72	Philadelphia Flyers	6	0	1	1	0	....	....	....	....	....
	NHL Totals	**196**	**5**	**37**	**42**	**90**	**8**	**0**	**0**	**0**	**12**

Claimed by **Minnesota** from **Seattle** (WHL) in Inter-League Draft, June 11, 1968. Claimed by **Philadelphia** from **Minnesota** in Intra-League Draft, June 12, 1968. Claimed by **Atlanta** from **Philadelphia** in Expansion Draft, June 6, 1972.

HALEY, Len

Right wing. Shoots right. 5'6", 160 lbs. Born, Edmonton, Alta., September 15, 1931.

Season	Club	GP	G	A	Pts	PIM	GP	G	A	Pts	PIM
1959-60	Detroit Red Wings	27	1	2	3	12	6	1	3	4	6
1960-61	Detroit Red Wings	3	1	0	1	2	....	....	....	....	....
	NHL Totals	**30**	**2**	**2**	**4**	**14**	**6**	**1**	**3**	**4**	**6**

Traded to **Saskatoon** (WHL) by **Detroit** (Edmonton-WHL) for cash, November, 1954. Claimed by **Hershey** (AHL) from **Brandon** (WHL) in Inter-League Draft, June 4, 1957. Traded to **Detroit** (Edmonton-WHL) by **Hershey** (AHL) for Ray Kinasewich, September, 1959. Traded to **Montreal** (Seattle-WHL) by **San Francisco** (WHL) for Gerry Brisson, October 22, 1965. Claimed by **Detroit** (Pittsburgh-AHL) from **Montreal** (Seattle-WHL) in Reverse Draft, June 15, 1966. Traded to **San Diego** (WHL) by **Detroit** (Pittsburgh-AHL) with Ed Ehrenverth and Al Nicholson for $20,000, June 20, 1966. Traded to **NY Rangers** by **San Diego** for Bruce Carmichael, September, 1968. Traded to **Des Moines** (IHL) by **NY Rangers** (New Haven-EHL) for Nelson Tremblay, September, 1970.

HALKIDIS, Bob

Defense. Shoots left. 5'11", 205 lbs. Born, Toronto, Ont., March 5, 1966.
(Buffalo's 4th choice, 81st overall, in 1984 Entry Draft).

Season	Club	GP	G	A	Pts	PIM	GP	G	A	Pts	PIM
1984-85	Buffalo Sabres	....	....	....	....	....	4	0	0	0	19
1985-86	Buffalo Sabres	37	1	9	10	115	....	....	....	....	....
1986-87	Buffalo Sabres	6	1	1	2	19	....	....	....	....	..
1987-88	Buffalo Sabres	30	0	3	3	115	4	0	0	0	
1988-89	Buffalo Sabres	16	0	1	1	66	....	....	....	....	
1989-90	Los Angeles Kings	20	0	4	4	56	8	0	1	1	
1990-91	Los Angeles Kings	34	1	3	4	133	3	0	0		
1991-92	Toronto Maple Leafs	46	3	3	6	145	....	....	....		
1993-94	Detroit Red Wings	28	1	4	5	93	1	0			
1994-95	Detroit Red Wings	4	0	1	1	6	....	....			
	Tampa Bay Lightning	27	1	3	4	40	....	....			

Season	Club	GP	G	A	Pts	PIM	GP	G	A	Pts	PIM
		REGULAR SEASON					PLAYOFFS				
1995-96	Tampa Bay Lightning	3	0	0	0	7	....	....	....	....	....
	New York Islanders	5	0	0	0	30	....	....	....	....	....
	NHL Totals	**256**	**8**	**32**	**40**	**825**	**20**	**0**	**1**	**1**	**51**

Traded to **Los Angeles** by **Buffalo** for Dale DeGray, November 24, 1989. Signed as a free agent by **Toronto**, July 24, 1991. Signed as a free agent by **Detroit**, September 2, 1993. Claimed on waivers by **Tampa Bay** from **Detroit**, February 10, 1995. Claimed on waivers by **Chicago** from **Tampa Bay**, December 6, 1995. Traded to **NY Islanders** by **Chicago** for Danton Cole, February 2, 1996. Signed as a free agent by **Florida**, July 25, 1996.

HALKO, Steven

Defense. Shoots right. 6'1", 200 lbs. Born, Etobicoke, Ont., March 8, 1974.
(Hartford's 10th choice, 225th overall, in 1992 Entry Draft).

Season	Club	GP	G	A	Pts	PIM	GP	G	A	Pts	PIM
1997-98	Carolina Hurricanes	18	0	2	2	10	....	....	....	....	....
1998-99	Carolina Hurricanes	20	0	3	3	24	4	0	0	0	2
99-2000	Carolina Hurricanes	58	0	8	8	25	....	....	....	....	....
2000-01	Carolina Hurricanes	48	0	1	1	6	....	....	....	....	....
2001-02	Carolina Hurricanes	5	0	1	1	6	....	....	....	....	....
2002-03	Carolina Hurricanes	6	0	0	0	0	....	....	....	....	....
	NHL Totals	**155**	**0**	**15**	**15**	**71**	**4**	**0**	**0**	**0**	**2**

Transferred to **Carolina** after **Hartford** franchise relocated, June 25, 1997. Traded to **St. Louis** by **Carolina** with Carolina's 4th round choice (later traded to Atlanta – Atlanta selected Lane Manson) in 2002 Entry Draft for Sean Hill, December 5, 2001. Signed as a free agent by **Carolina**, August 5, 2002.

HALL, Adam

Right wing. Shoots right. 6'3", 205 lbs. Born, Kalamazoo, MI, August 14, 1980.
(Nashville's 3rd choice, 52nd overall, in 1999 Entry Draft).

Season	Club	GP	G	A	Pts	PIM	GP	G	A	Pts	PIM
2001-02	Nashville Predators	1	0	1	1	0	....	....	....	....	....
2002-03	Nashville Predators	79	16	12	28	31	....	....	....	....	....
	NHL Totals	**80**	**16**	**13**	**29**	**31**	....	....	....	....	....

HALL, Bob

Forward. Shoots left. 5'8", 165 lbs. Born, Oak Park, IL, October 13, 1899.

Season	Club	GP	G	A	Pts	PIM	GP	G	A	Pts	PIM
1925-26	New York Americans	8	0	0	0	0	....	....	....	....	....
	NHL Totals	**8**	**0**	**0**	**0**	**0**	....	....	....	....	....

Signed as a free agent **NY Americans**, February 8, 1926.

HALL, Del

Center. Shoots left. 5'10", 170 lbs. Born, Peterborough, Ont., May 7, 1949.

Season	Club	GP	G	A	Pts	PIM	GP	G	A	Pts	PIM
1971-72	California Golden Seals	1	0	0	0	0	....	....	....	....	....
1972-73	California Golden Seals	6	0	0	0	0	....	....	....	....	....
1973-74	California Golden Seals	2	2	0	2	2	....	....	....	....	....
	NHL Totals	**9**	**2**	**0**	**2**	**2**	....	....	....	....	....

HALL, Joe

HHOF

Defense. Shoots right. 5'10", 175 lbs. Born, Staffordshire, England, May 3, 1882.

Season	Club	GP	G	A	Pts	PIM	GP	G	A	Pts	PIM
1917-18	Montreal Canadiens	21	8	7	15	*100	2	0	1	1	12
1918-19	Montreal Canadiens	17	7	1	8	*89	5	0	0	0	*17
	Montreal Canadiens (Cup)	....	....	....	....	....	*5*	*0*	*0*	*0*	*6*
	NHL Totals	**38**	**15**	**8**	**23**	**189**	**7**	**0**	**1**	**1**	**29**

Claimed by **Montreal** from **Quebec** in Dispersal Draft, November 26, 1917. • Died in a Seattle hospital from complications brought on by influenza, April 5, 1919.

HALL, Murray

Right wing. Shoots right. 6', 175 lbs. Born, Kirkland Lake, Ont., November 24, 1940.

Season	Club	GP	G	A	Pts	PIM	GP	G	A	Pts	PIM
1961-62	Chicago Black Hawks	2	0	0	0	0	....	....	....	....	....
1962-63	Chicago Black Hawks	....	....	....	....	....	4	0	0	0	0
1963-64	Chicago Black Hawks	23	2	0	2	4	....	....	....	....	....
1964-65	Detroit Red Wings	....	....	....	....	....	1	0	0	0	0
1965-66	Detroit Red Wings	1	0	0	0	0	1	0	0	0	0
1966-67	Detroit Red Wings	12	4	3	7	4	....	....	....	....	....
1967-68	Minnesota North Stars	17	2	1	3	10	....	....	....	....	....
1970-71	Vancouver Canucks	77	21	38	59	22	....	....	....	....	....
1971-72	Vancouver Canucks	32	6	6	12	6	....	....	....	....	....
	NHL Totals	**164**	**35**	**48**	**83**	**46**	**6**	**0**	**0**	**0**	**0**

Played in NHL All-Star Game (1961)

Claimed by **Detroit** from **Chicago** in Intra-League Draft, June 10, 1964. Loaned to **Chicago** (LA Blades-WHL) by **Detroit** with Al LeBrun for remainder of 1966-67 season and future considerations (Murray Hall, Al LeBrun and Rick Morris, June, 1967) for Howie Young, December 20, 1966. Traded to **Chicago** by **Detroit** with Al LeBrun and Rick Morris to complete transaction that sent Howie Young to Detroit (December 20, 1966), June, 1967. Claimed by **Minnesota** from **Chicago** in Expansion Draft, June 6, 1967. Traded to **Toronto** (Rochester-AHL) by **Minnesota** with Ted Taylor, Len Lunde, Don Johns, Duke Harris and the loan of Carl Wetzel [illegible] P. Parise and Milan Marcetta, December 23, 1967. Traded to **Rochester** (AHL) by **Toronto** [illegible] June, 1968. Rights transferred to **Vancouver** (WHL) after WHL club purchased [illegible] HL) franchise, August 13, 1968. NHL rights transferred to **Vancouver** after NHL club [illegible] **ver** (WHL) franchise, December 19, 1969.

[illegible] '11", 180 lbs. Born, Regina, Sask., February 20, 1964.
[illegible] 116th overall, in 1982 Entry Draft).

Season	Club	GP	G	A	Pts	PIM	GP	G	A	Pts	PIM
[illegible]	[illegible] ks	4	1	0	1	0	....	....	....	....	....
[illegible]	[illegible] s	7	1	4	5	19	....	....	....	....	....
[illegible]	[illegible]	19	5	5	10	6	....	....	....	....	....
[illegible]	[illegible]	4	0	0	0	0	....	....	....	....	....

Season	Club	GP	G	A	Pts	PIM	GP	G	A	Pts	PIM
		REGULAR SEASON					PLAYOFFS				
1987-88	Boston Bruins	7	0	0	0	4	....	....	....	....	....
	NHL Totals	**41**	**7**	**9**	**16**	**29**	....	....	....	....	....

• Missed remainder of 1984-85 season recovering from knee injury suffered in game vs. NY Islanders, October 23, 1984. Signed as a free agent by **Boston**, July, 1987.

HALL, Wayne

Left wing. Shoots left. 5'9", 165 lbs. Born, Melita, Man., May 22, 1939.

Season	Club	GP	G	A	Pts	PIM	GP	G	A	Pts	PIM
1960-61	New York Rangers	4	0	0	0	0	....	....	....	....	....
	NHL Totals	**4**	**0**	**0**	**0**	**0**	....	....	....	....	....

HALLER, Kevin

Defense. Shoots left. 6'2", 199 lbs. Born, Trochu, Alta., December 5, 1970.
(Buffalo's 1st choice, 14th overall, in 1989 Entry Draft).

Season	Club	GP	G	A	Pts	PIM	GP	G	A	Pts	PIM
1989-90	Buffalo Sabres	2	0	0	0	0	....	....	....	....	....
1990-91	Buffalo Sabres	21	1	8	9	20	6	1	4	5	10
1991-92	Buffalo Sabres	58	6	15	21	75	....	....	....	....	....
	Montreal Canadiens	8	2	2	4	17	9	0	0	0	6
1992-93 ♦	Montreal Canadiens	73	11	14	25	117	17	1	6	7	16
1993-94	Montreal Canadiens	68	4	9	13	118	7	1	1	2	19
1994-95	Philadelphia Flyers	36	2	8	10	48	15	4	4	8	10
1995-96	Philadelphia Flyers	69	5	9	14	92	6	0	1	1	8
1996-97	Philadelphia Flyers	27	0	5	5	37	....	....	....	....	....
	Hartford Whalers	35	2	6	8	48	....	....	....	....	....
1997-98	Carolina Hurricanes	65	3	5	8	94	....	....	....	....	....
1998-99	Mighty Ducks of Anaheim	82	1	6	7	122	4	0	0	0	2
99-2000	Mighty Ducks of Anaheim	67	3	5	8	61	....	....	....	....	....
2000-01	New York Islanders	30	1	5	6	56	....	....	....	....	....
2001-02	New York Islanders	1	0	0	0	2	....	....	....	....	....
	NHL Totals	**642**	**41**	**97**	**138**	**907**	**64**	**7**	**16**	**23**	**71**

Traded to **Montreal** by **Buffalo** for Petr Svoboda, March 10, 1992. Traded to **Philadelphia** by **Montreal** for Yves Racine, June 29, 1994. Traded to **Hartford** by **Philadelphia** with Philadelphia's 1st round choice (later traded to San Jose – San Jose selected Scott Hannan) in 1997 Entry Draft and Hartford/Carolina's 7th round choice (previously acquired, Carolina selected Andrew Merrick) in 1997 Entry Draft for Paul Coffey and Hartford/Carolina's 3rd round choice (Kris Mallette) in 1997 Entry Draft, December 15, 1996. Transferred to **Carolina** after **Hartford** franchise relocated, June 25, 1997. Traded to **Anaheim** by **Carolina** with Stu Grimson for Dave Karpa and Anaheim's 4th round choice (later traded to Atlanta – Atlanta selected Blake Robson) in 2000 Entry Draft, August 11, 1998. Signed as a free agent by **NY Islanders**, July 3, 2000. • Missed majority of 2000-01 season recovering from hernia injury suffered in game vs. Ottawa, December 16, 2000. • Missed majority of 2001-02 season recovering from groin injury suffered in game vs. Los Angeles, October 19, 2001.

HALLIDAY, Milt

Left wing. Shoots left. 5'10", 180 lbs. Born, Ottawa, Ont., September 21, 1906.

Season	Club	GP	G	A	Pts	PIM	GP	G	A	Pts	PIM
1926-27 ♦	Ottawa Senators	38	1	0	1	2	6	0	0	0	0
1927-28	Ottawa Senators	13	0	0	0	2	....	....	....	....	....
1928-29	Ottawa Senators	16	0	0	0	0	....	....	....	....	....
	NHL Totals	**67**	**1**	**0**	**1**	**4**	**6**	**0**	**0**	**0**	**0**

Signed as a free agent by **Ottawa**, October 24, 1926. Traded to **Hamilton** (IHL) by **Ottawa** for cash, November 7, 1929.

HALLIN, Mats

Left wing. Shoots left. 6'2", 200 lbs. Born, Eskilstuna, Sweden, March 9, 1958.
(Washington's 10th choice, 105th overall, in 1978 Amateur Draft).

Season	Club	GP	G	A	Pts	PIM	GP	G	A	Pts	PIM
1982-83 ♦	New York Islanders	30	7	7	14	26	7	1	0	1	6
1983-84	New York Islanders	40	2	5	7	27	6	0	0	0	7
1984-85	New York Islanders	38	5	0	5	50	1	0	0	0	0
1985-86	Minnesota North Stars	38	3	2	5	86	1	0	0	0	0
1986-87	Minnesota North Stars	6	0	0	0	4	....	....	....	....	....
	NHL Totals	**152**	**17**	**14**	**31**	**193**	**15**	**1**	**0**	**1**	**13**

Signed as a free agent by **NY Islanders**, June 12, 1981. Traded to **Minnesota** by **NY Islanders** for Minnesota's 7th round choice (Will Anderson) in 1986 Entry Draft, September 9, 1985.

HALPERN, Jeff

Center. Shoots right. 6', 201 lbs. Born, Potomac, MD, May 3, 1976.

Season	Club	GP	G	A	Pts	PIM	GP	G	A	Pts	PIM
99-2000	Washington Capitals	79	18	11	29	39	5	2	1	3	0
2000-01	Washington Capitals	80	21	21	42	60	6	2	3	5	17
2001-02	Washington Capitals	48	5	14	19	29	....	....	....	....	....
2002-03	Washington Capitals	82	13	21	34	88	6	0	1	1	2
	NHL Totals	**289**	**57**	**67**	**124**	**216**	**17**	**4**	**5**	**9**	**19**

Signed as a free agent by **Washington**, March 29, 1999.

HALVERSON, Trevor

Left wing. Shoots left. 6', 200 lbs. Born, White River, Ont., April 6, 1971.
(Washington's 2nd choice, 21st overall, in 1991 Entry Draft).

Season	Club	GP	G	A	Pts	PIM	GP	G	A	Pts	PIM
1998-99	Washington Capitals	17	0	4	4	28	....	....	....	....	....
	NHL Totals	**17**	**0**	**4**	**4**	**28**	....	....	....	....	....

Claimed by **Anaheim** from **Washington** in Expansion Draft, June 24, 1993. Signed as a free agent by **Washington**, September, 1998.

HALWARD, Doug

Defense. Shoots left. 6'1", 200 lbs. Born, Toronto, Ont., November 1, 1955.
(Boston's 1st choice, 14th overall, in 1975 Amateur Draft).

Season	Club	GP	G	A	Pts	PIM	GP	G	A	Pts	PIM
1975-76	Boston Bruins	22	1	5	6	6	1	0	0	0	0
1976-77	Boston Bruins	18	2	2	4	6	6	0	0	0	4

Season	Club	REGULAR SEASON GP	G	A	Pts	PIM	PLAYOFFS GP	G	A	Pts	PIM
1977-78	Boston Bruins	25	0	2	2	2	....	....	....	....	....
1978-79	Los Angeles Kings	27	1	5	6	13	1	0	0	0	12
1979-80	Los Angeles Kings	63	11	45	56	52	1	0	0	0	2
1980-81	Los Angeles Kings	51	4	15	19	96	....	....	....	....	....
	Vancouver Canucks	7	0	1	1	4	2	0	1	1	6
1981-82	Vancouver Canucks	37	4	13	17	40	15	2	4	6	44
1982-83	Vancouver Canucks	75	19	33	52	83	4	1	0	1	21
1983-84	Vancouver Canucks	54	7	16	23	35	4	3	1	4	2
1984-85	Vancouver Canucks	71	7	27	34	82	....	....	....	....	....
1985-86	Vancouver Canucks	70	8	25	33	111	3	0	0	0	4
1986-87	Vancouver Canucks	10	0	3	3	34	....	....	....	....	....
	Detroit Red Wings	11	0	3	3	19	....	....	....	....	....
1987-88	Detroit Red Wings	70	5	21	26	130	8	1	4	5	18
1988-89	Detroit Red Wings	18	0	1	1	36	....	....	....	....	....
	Edmonton Oilers	24	0	7	7	25	2	0	0	0	0
	NHL Totals	**653**	**69**	**224**	**293**	**774**	**47**	**7**	**10**	**17**	**113**

Traded to **Los Angeles** by **Boston** for future considerations, September 18, 1978. Claimed by **Los Angeles** as a fill-in during Expansion Draft, June 13, 1979. Traded to **Vancouver** by **Los Angeles** for Vancouver's 5th round choice (Ulf Isaksson) in 1982 Entry Draft and future considerations (Gary Bromley, May 12, 1981), March 8, 1981. Traded to **Detroit** by **Vancouver** for Detroit's 6th round choice (Phil Von Stefenelli) in 1988 Entry Draft, November 21, 1986. Traded to **Edmonton** by **Detroit** for Edmonton's 12th round choice (Jason Glickman) in 1989 Entry Draft, January 23, 1989.

HAMEL, Denis

Left wing. Shoots left. 6'1", 201 lbs. Born, Lachute, Que., May 10, 1977.
(St. Louis' 5th choice, 153rd overall, in 1995 Entry Draft).

Season	Club	GP	G	A	Pts	PIM	GP	G	A	Pts	PIM
99-2000	Buffalo Sabres	3	1	0	1	0	....	....	....	....	....
2000-01	Buffalo Sabres	41	8	3	11	22	....	....	....	....	....
2001-02	Buffalo Sabres	61	2	6	8	28	....	....	....	....	....
2002-03	Buffalo Sabres	25	2	0	2	17	....	....	....	....	....
	NHL Totals	**130**	**13**	**9**	**22**	**67**	....	....	....	....	....

Traded to **Buffalo** by **St. Louis** for Charlie Huddy and Buffalo's 7th round choice (Daniel Corso) in 1996 Entry Draft, March 19, 1996. Signed as a free agent by **Ottawa**, July 5, 2003.

HAMEL, Gilles

Left wing. Shoots left. 6'3", 183 lbs. Born, Asbestos, Que., March 18, 1960.
(Buffalo's 5th choice, 74th overall, in 1979 Entry Draft).

Season	Club	GP	G	A	Pts	PIM	GP	G	A	Pts	PIM
1980-81	Buffalo Sabres	51	10	9	19	53	5	0	1	1	4
1981-82	Buffalo Sabres	16	2	7	9	2	....	....	....	....	....
1982-83	Buffalo Sabres	66	22	20	42	26	9	2	2	4	2
1983-84	Buffalo Sabres	75	21	23	44	37	3	0	2	2	2
1984-85	Buffalo Sabres	80	18	30	48	36	1	0	0	0	0
1985-86	Buffalo Sabres	77	19	25	44	61	....	....	....	....	....
1986-87	Winnipeg Jets	79	27	21	48	24	8	2	0	2	2
1987-88	Winnipeg Jets	63	8	11	19	35	1	0	0	0	0
1988-89	Winnipeg Jets	1	0	0	0	0	....	....	....	....	....
	Los Angeles Kings	11	0	1	1	2	....	....	....	....	....
	NHL Totals	**519**	**127**	**147**	**274**	**276**	**27**	**4**	**5**	**9**	**10**

• Brother of Jean

Traded to **Winnipeg** by **Buffalo** for Scott Arniel, June 21, 1986. Traded to **Los Angeles** by **Winnipeg** for Paul Fenton, Novemnber 25, 1988

HAMEL, Herb

Right wing. Shoots right. 5'11", 155 lbs. Born, New Hamburg, Ont., June 8, 1904.

Season	Club	GP	G	A	Pts	PIM	GP	G	A	Pts	PIM
1930-31	Toronto Maple Leafs	2	0	0	0	4	....	....	....	....	....
	NHL Totals	**2**	**0**	**0**	**0**	**4**	....	....	....	....	....

Signed as a free agent by **Toronto**, December 8, 1930.

HAMEL, Jean

Defense. Shoots left. 5'11", 195 lbs. Born, Asbestos, Que., June 6, 1952.
(St. Louis' 2nd choice, 41st overall, in 1972 Amateur Draft).

Season	Club	GP	G	A	Pts	PIM	GP	G	A	Pts	PIM
1972-73	St. Louis Blues	55	2	7	9	24	2	0	0	0	0
1973-74	St. Louis Blues	23	1	1	2	6	....	....	....	....	....
	Detroit Red Wings	22	0	3	3	40	....	....	....	....	....
1974-75	Detroit Red Wings	80	5	19	24	136	....	....	....	....	....
1975-76	Detroit Red Wings	77	3	9	12	129	....	....	....	....	....
1976-77	Detroit Red Wings	71	1	10	11	63	....	....	....	....	....
1977-78	Detroit Red Wings	32	2	6	8	34	7	0	0	0	10
1978-79	Detroit Red Wings	52	2	4	6	72	....	....	....	....	....
1979-80	Detroit Red Wings	49	1	4	5	43	....	....	....	....	....
1980-81	Detroit Red Wings	68	5	7	12	57	....	....	....	....	....
1981-82	Quebec Nordiques	40	1	6	7	32	5	0	0	0	16
1982-83	Quebec Nordiques	51	2	7	9	38	4	0	0	0	2
1983-84	Montreal Canadiens	79	1	12	13	92	15	0	2	2	16
	NHL Totals	**699**	**26**	**95**	**121**	**766**	**33**	**0**	**2**	**2**	**44**

• Brother of Gilles

Traded to **Detroit** by **St. Louis** with Chris Evans and Bryan Watson for Ted Harris, Bill Collins and Garnet Bailey, February 14, 1974. Claimed as a fill-in by **Detroit** during Expansion Draft, June 13, 1979. Signed as a free agent by **Quebec**, October 6, 1981. Claimed by **Montreal** from **Quebec** in Waiver Draft, October 3, 1983.

HAMILL, Red

Left wing. Shoots left. 5'11", 180 lbs. Born, Toronto, Ont., January 11, 1917.

Season	Club	GP	G	A	Pts	PIM	GP	G	A	Pts	PIM
1937-38	Boston Bruins	6	0	1	1	2	....	....	....	....	....
1938-39 ♦	Boston Bruins	6	0	1	1	0	12	0	0	0	8
1939-40	Boston Bruins	30	10	8	18	16	5	0	1	1	5
1940-41	Boston Bruins	8	0	1	1	0	....	....	....	....	....
1941-42	Boston Bruins	9	6	3	9	2	....	....	....	....	....
	Chicago Black Hawks	34	18	9	27	21	3	0	1	1	0
1942-43	Chicago Black Hawks	50	28	16	44	44	....	....	....	....	....
1945-46	Chicago Black Hawks	38	20	17	37	23	4	1	0	1	7
1946-47	Chicago Black Hawks	60	21	19	40	12	....	....	....	....	....
1947-48	Chicago Black Hawks	60	11	13	24	18	....	....	....	....	....
1948-49	Chicago Black Hawks	57	8	4	12	16	....	....	....	....	....
1949-50	Chicago Black Hawks	59	6	2	8	6	....	....	....	....	....
1950-51	Chicago Black Hawks	2	0	0	0	0	....	....	....	....	....
	NHL Totals	**419**	**128**	**94**	**222**	**160**	**24**	**1**	**2**	**3**	**20**

Signed as a free agent by **Boston**, October 26, 1937. Traded to **Chicago** by **Boston** for cash, December 18, 1941.

HAMILTON, Al

Defense. Shoots right. 6'1", 195 lbs. Born, Flin Flon, Man., August 20, 1946.

Season	Club	GP	G	A	Pts	PIM	GP	G	A	Pts	PIM
1965-66	New York Rangers	4	0	0	0	0	....	....	....	....	....
1967-68	New York Rangers	2	0	0	0	0	....	....	....	....	....
1968-69	New York Rangers	16	0	0	0	8	1	0	0	0	0
1969-70	New York Rangers	59	0	5	5	54	5	0	0	0	2
1970-71	Buffalo Sabres	69	2	28	30	71	....	....	....	....	....
1971-72	Buffalo Sabres	76	4	30	34	105	....	....	....	....	....
1979-80	Edmonton Oilers	31	4	15	19	20	1	0	0	0	0
	NHL Totals	**257**	**10**	**78**	**88**	**258**	**7**	**0**	**0**	**0**	**2**

Claimed by **Buffalo** from **NY Rangers** in Expansion Draft, June 10, 1970. Rights retained by **Edmonton** prior to Expansion Draft, June 9, 1979.

HAMILTON, Chuck

Left wing. Shoots left. 5'11", 175 lbs. Born, Kirkland Lake, Ont., January 18, 1939.

Season	Club	GP	G	A	Pts	PIM	GP	G	A	Pts	PIM
1961-62	Montreal Canadiens	1	0	0	0	0	....	....	....	....	....
1972-73	St. Louis Blues	3	0	2	2	2	....	....	....	....	....
	NHL Totals	**4**	**0**	**2**	**2**	**2**	....	....	....	....	....

Loaned to **Hershey** (AHL) by **Montreal** with the trade of Ralph Keller for Mark Reaume, June 11, 1963. Traded to **Hershey** (AHL) by **Montreal** for cash, October, 1964. Claimed by **Detroit** from **Hershey** (AHL) in Inter-League Draft, June 10, 1969. Traded to **Montreal** by **Detroit** for cash, June 11, 1969. Traded to **Hershey** (AHL) by **Montreal** for cash, October, 1969. Traded to **St. Louis** (Denver-WHL) by **Hershey** (AHL) for cash, September, 1971.

HAMILTON, Jack

Center. Shoots left. 5'7", 170 lbs. Born, Trenton, Ont., June 2, 1925.

Season	Club	GP	G	A	Pts	PIM	GP	G	A	Pts	PIM
1942-43	Toronto Maple Leafs	13	1	6	7	4	6	1	1	2	0
1943-44	Toronto Maple Leafs	49	20	17	37	4	5	1	0	1	0
1945-46	Toronto Maple Leafs	40	7	9	16	12	....	....	....	....	....
	NHL Totals	**102**	**28**	**32**	**60**	**20**	**11**	**2**	**1**	**3**	**0**

Traded to **Providence** (AHL) by **Toronto** with cash to complete transaction that sent the rights to Danny Lewicki to Toronto (July 27, 1948), October 27, 1948. Traded to **Chicago** (St. Louis-AHL) by **Providence** (AHL) for Barry Sullivan, January 29, 1951.

HAMILTON, Jim

Right wing. Shoots left. 6', 180 lbs. Born, Barrie, Ont., January 18, 1957.
(Pittsburgh's 1st choice, 30th overall, in 1977 Amateur Draft).

Season	Club	GP	G	A	Pts	PIM	GP	G	A	Pts	PIM
1977-78	Pittsburgh Penguins	25	2	4	6	2	....	....	....	....	....
1978-79	Pittsburgh Penguins	2	0	0	0	0	5	3	0	3	0
1979-80	Pittsburgh Penguins	10	2	0	2	0	....	....	....	....	....
1980-81	Pittsburgh Penguins	20	1	6	7	18	1	0	0	0	0
1981-82	Pittsburgh Penguins	11	5	3	8	2	....	....	....	....	....
1982-83	Pittsburgh Penguins	5	0	2	2	2	....	....	....	....	....
1983-84	Pittsburgh Penguins	11	2	2	4	4	....	....	....	....	....
1984-85	Pittsburgh Penguins	11	2	1	3	0	....	....	....	....	....
	NHL Totals	**95**	**14**	**18**	**32**	**28**	**6**	**3**	**0**	**3**	**0**

HAMILTON, Reg

Defense. Shoots left. 5'11", 180 lbs. Born, Toronto, Ont., April 29, 1914.

Season	Club	GP	G	A	Pts	PIM	GP	G	A	Pts	PIM
1935-36	Toronto Maple Leafs	7	0	0	0	0	....	....	....	....	....
1936-37	Toronto Maple Leafs	39	3	7	10	32	2	0	1	1	2
1937-38	Toronto Maple Leafs	45	1	4	5	43	7	0	1	1	2
1938-39	Toronto Maple Leafs	48	0	7	7	54	10	0	2	2	4
1939-40	Toronto Maple Leafs	23	2	2	4	23	10	0	0	0	0
1940-41	Toronto Maple Leafs	45	3	12	15	59	7	1	2	3	13
1941-42 ♦	Toronto Maple Leafs	22	0	4	4	27	....	....	....	....	....
1942-43	Toronto Maple Leafs	48	4	17	21	68	6	1	1	2	9
1943-44	Toronto Maple Leafs	39	4	12	16	32	5	1	0	1	8
1944-45 ♦	Toronto Maple Leafs	50	3	12	15	41	13	0	0	0	6
1945-46	Chicago Black Hawks	48	1	7	8	31	4	0	1	1	2
1946-47	Chicago Black Hawks	10	0	3	3	2	....	....	....	....	....
	NHL Totals	**424**	**21**	**87**	**108**	**412**	**64**	**3**	**8**	**11**	[illegible]

Traded to **Chicago** by **Toronto** for cash and future considerations, July 9, 1945.

HAMMARSTROM, Inge

Left wing. Shoots left. 6', 180 lbs. Born, Sundsvall, Sweden, January 20, 1948.

Season	Club	GP	G	A	Pts	PIM	GP	G	A	Pts	PIM
1973-74	Toronto Maple Leafs	66	20	23	43	14	4	1	[illegible]		
1974-75	Toronto Maple Leafs	69	21	20	41	23	7	1			
1975-76	Toronto Maple Leafs	76	19	21	40	21	....	....			
1976-77	Toronto Maple Leafs	78	24	17	41	16	2				

Season	Club	Regular Season GP	G	A	Pts	PIM	Playoffs GP	G	A	Pts	PIM
1977-78	Toronto Maple Leafs	3	1	1	2	0	....	....	....	....	....
	St. Louis Blues	70	19	19	38	4	....	....	....	....	....
1978-79	St. Louis Blues	65	12	22	34	8	....	....	....	....	....
	NHL Totals	**427**	**116**	**123**	**239**	**86**	**13**	**2**	**3**	**5**	**4**

Signed as a free agent by **Toronto**, May 12, 1973. Traded to **St. Louis** by **Toronto** for Jerry Butler, November 1, 1977.

HAMMOND, Ken

Defense. Shoots left. 6'1", 190 lbs. Born, Port Credit, Ont., August 22, 1963.
(Los Angeles' 8th choice, 152nd overall, in 1983 Entry Draft).

Season	Club	GP	G	A	Pts	PIM	GP	G	A	Pts	PIM
1984-85	Los Angeles Kings	3	1	0	1	0	3	0	0	0	4
1985-86	Los Angeles Kings	3	0	1	1	2	....	....	....	....	....
1986-87	Los Angeles Kings	10	0	2	2	11	....	....	....	....	....
1987-88	Los Angeles Kings	46	7	9	16	69	2	0	0	0	4
1988-89	Edmonton Oilers	5	0	1	1	8	....	....	....	....	....
	New York Rangers	3	0	0	0	0	....	....	....	....	....
	Toronto Maple Leafs	14	0	2	2	12	....	....	....	....	....
1990-91	Boston Bruins	1	1	0	1	2	8	0	0	0	10
1991-92	San Jose Sharks	46	5	10	15	82	....	....	....	....	....
	Vancouver Canucks	....	....	....	....	....	2	0	0	0	6
1992-93	Ottawa Senators	62	4	4	8	104	....	....	....	....	....
	NHL Totals	**193**	**18**	**29**	**47**	**290**	**15**	**0**	**0**	**0**	**24**

Claimed by **Edmonton** from **Los Angeles** in Waiver Draft, October 3, 1988. Claimed on waivers by **NY Rangers** from **Edmonton**, November 1, 1988. Traded to **Toronto** by **NY Rangers** for Chris McRae, February 21, 1989. Traded to **Boston** by **Toronto** for cash, August 20, 1990. Signed as a free agent by **San Jose**, August 9, 1991. Traded to **Vancouver** by **San Jose** for Vancouver's 8th round choice (later traded to Detroit – Detroit selected C.J. Denomme) in 1992 Entry Draft, March 9, 1992. Claimed by **Ottawa** from **Vancouver** in Expansion Draft, June 18, 1992.

HAMPSON, Gord

Left wing. Shoots left. 6'3", 210 lbs. Born, Vancouver, B.C., February 13, 1959.

Season	Club	GP	G	A	Pts	PIM	GP	G	A	Pts	PIM
1982-83	Calgary Flames	4	0	0	0	5	....	....	....	....	....
	NHL Totals	**4**	**0**	**0**	**0**	**5**	....	....	....	....	....

• Son of Ted

Signed as a free agent by **Calgary**, June 8, 1981.

HAMPSON, Ted

Center. Shoots left. 5'8", 173 lbs. Born, Togo, Sask., December 11, 1936.

Season	Club	GP	G	A	Pts	PIM	GP	G	A	Pts	PIM
1959-60	Toronto Maple Leafs	41	2	8	10	17	....	....	....	....	....
1960-61	New York Rangers	69	6	14	20	4	....	....	....	....	....
1961-62	New York Rangers	68	4	24	28	10	6	0	1	1	0
1962-63	New York Rangers	46	4	2	6	2	....	....	....	....	....
1963-64	Detroit Red Wings	7	0	1	1	0	....	....	....	....	....
1964-65	Detroit Red Wings	1	0	0	0	0	....	....	....	....	....
1966-67	Detroit Red Wings	65	13	35	48	4	....	....	....	....	....
1967-68	Detroit Red Wings	37	9	18	27	10	....	....	....	....	....
	Oakland Seals	34	8	19	27	4	....	....	....	....	....
1968-69	Oakland Seals	76	26	49	75	6	7	3	4	7	2
1969-70	Oakland Seals	76	17	35	52	13	4	1	1	2	0
1970-71	California Seals	60	10	20	30	14	....	....	....	....	....
	Minnesota North Stars	18	4	6	10	4	11	3	3	6	0
1971-72	Minnesota North Stars	78	5	14	19	6	7	0	1	1	0
	NHL Totals	**676**	**108**	**245**	**353**	**94**	**35**	**7**	**10**	**17**	**2**

• Father of Gord • Bill Masterton Trophy (1969)

Played in NHL All-Star Game (1969)

Claimed on waivers by **Toronto** from **NY Rangers**, September 18, 1959. Claimed by **NY Rangers** from **Toronto** in Intra-League Draft, June 8, 1960. Claimed by **Detroit** from **NY Rangers** in Intra-League Draft, June 4, 1963. Traded to **Oakland** by **Detroit** with John Brenneman and Bert Marshall for Kent Douglas, January 9, 1968. Traded to **Minnesota** by **California** with Wayne Muloin for Tommy Williams and Dick Redmond, March 7, 1971. Claimed by **NY Islanders** from **Minnesota** in Expansion Draft, June 6, 1972. Signed as a free agent by **Minnesota**, January 1, 1979.

HAMPTON, Rick

Left wing/Defense. Shoots left. 6', 190 lbs. Born, King City, Ont., June 14, 1956.
(California's 1st choice, 3rd overall, in 1974 Amateur Draft).

Season	Club	GP	G	A	Pts	PIM	GP	G	A	Pts	PIM
1974-75	California Golden Seals	78	8	17	25	39	....	....	....	....	....
1975-76	California Golden Seals	73	14	37	51	54	....	....	....	....	....
1976-77	Cleveland Barons	57	16	24	40	13	....	....	....	....	....
1977-78	Cleveland Barons	77	18	18	36	19	....	....	....	....	....
1978-79	Los Angeles Kings	49	3	17	20	22	2	0	0	0	0
1979-80	Los Angeles Kings	3	0	0	0	0	....	....	....	....	....
	NHL Totals	**337**	**59**	**113**	**172**	**147**	**2**	**0**	**0**	**0**	**0**

Transferred to **Cleveland** after **California** franchise relocated, August 26, 1976. Placed on **...esota** Reserve List prior to Minnesota-Cleveland Dispersal Draft, June 14, 1978. Transferred **...geles** by **Minnesota** with Steve Jensen and Dave Gardner as compensation for ...ing of free agent Gary Sargent, July 15, 1978

...'11", 175 lbs. Born, Usti nad Labem, Czech., June 15, 1974.
...rd overall, in 1992 Entry Draft).

Season	Club	GP	G	A	Pts	PIM	GP	G	A	Pts	PIM
	...s	4	0	0	0	0	....	....	....	....	....
	...	7	0	0	0	0	....	....	....	....	....
		11	**0**	**0**	**0**	**0**	....	....	....	....	....

HAMRLIK, Roman

Defense. Shoots left. 6'2", 200 lbs. Born, Zlin, Czech., April 12, 1974.
(Tampa Bay's 1st choice, 1st overall, in 1992 Entry Draft).

Season	Club	GP	G	A	Pts	PIM	GP	G	A	Pts	PIM
1992-93	Tampa Bay Lightning	67	6	15	21	71	....	....	....	....	....
1993-94	Tampa Bay Lightning	64	3	18	21	135	....	....	....	....	....
1994-95	Tampa Bay Lightning	48	12	11	23	86	....	....	....	....	....
1995-96	Tampa Bay Lightning	82	16	49	65	103	5	0	1	1	4
1996-97	Tampa Bay Lightning	79	12	28	40	57	....	....	....	....	....
1997-98	Tampa Bay Lightning	37	3	12	15	22	....	....	....	....	....
	Edmonton Oilers	41	6	20	26	48	12	0	6	6	12
1998-99	Edmonton Oilers	75	8	24	32	70	3	0	0	0	2
99-2000	Edmonton Oilers	80	8	37	45	68	5	0	1	1	4
2000-01	New York Islanders	76	16	30	46	92	....	....	....	....	....
2001-02	New York Islanders	70	11	26	37	78	7	1	6	7	6
2002-03	New York Islanders	73	9	32	41	87	5	0	2	2	2
	NHL Totals	**792**	**110**	**302**	**412**	**917**	**37**	**1**	**16**	**17**	**30**

Played in NHL All-Star Game (1996, 1999, 2003)

Traded to **Edmonton** by **Tampa Bay** with Paul Comrie for Bryan Marchment, Steve Kelly and Jason Bonsignore, December 30, 1997. Traded to **NY Islanders** by **Edmonton** for Eric Brewer, Josh Green and NY Islanders' 2nd round choice (Brad Winchester) in 2000 Entry Draft, June 24, 2000.

HAMWAY, Mark

Right wing. Shoots right. 6', 190 lbs. Born, Detroit, MI, August 9, 1961.
(NY Islanders' 8th choice, 143rd overall, in 1980 Entry Draft).

Season	Club	GP	G	A	Pts	PIM	GP	G	A	Pts	PIM
1984-85	New York Islanders	2	0	0	0	0	....	....	....	....	....
1985-86	New York Islanders	49	5	12	17	9	1	0	0	0	0
1986-87	New York Islanders	2	0	1	1	0	....	....	....	....	....
	NHL Totals	**53**	**5**	**13**	**18**	**9**	**1**	**0**	**0**	**0**	**0**

HANDY, Ron

Left wing. Shoots left. 5'11", 175 lbs. Born, Toronto, Ont., January 15, 1963.
(NY Islanders' 3rd choice, 57th overall, in 1981 Entry Draft).

Season	Club	GP	G	A	Pts	PIM	GP	G	A	Pts	PIM
1984-85	New York Islanders	10	0	2	2	0	....	....	....	....	....
1987-88	St. Louis Blues	4	0	1	1	0	....	....	....	....	....
	NHL Totals	**14**	**0**	**3**	**3**	**0**	....	....	....	....	....

Signed as a free agent by **St. Louis**, September, 1987.

HANDZUS, Michal

Center. Shoots left. 6'5", 210 lbs. Born, Banska Bystrica, Czech., March 11, 1977.
(St. Louis' 3rd choice, 101st overall, in 1995 Entry Draft).

Season	Club	GP	G	A	Pts	PIM	GP	G	A	Pts	PIM
1998-99	St. Louis Blues	66	4	12	16	30	11	0	2	2	8
99-2000	St. Louis Blues	81	25	28	53	44	7	0	3	3	6
2000-01	St. Louis Blues	36	10	14	24	12	....	....	....	....	....
	Phoenix Coyotes	10	4	4	8	21	....	....	....	....	....
2001-02	Phoenix Coyotes	79	15	30	45	34	5	0	0	0	2
2002-03	Philadelphia Flyers	82	23	21	44	46	13	2	6	8	6
	NHL Totals	**354**	**81**	**109**	**190**	**187**	**36**	**2**	**11**	**13**	**22**

Traded to **Phoenix** by **St. Louis** with Ladislav Nagy, the rights to Jeff Taffe and St. Louis' 1st round choice (Ben Eager) in 2002 Entry Draft for Keith Tkachuk, March 13, 2001. Traded to **Philadelphia** by **Phoenix** with Robert Esche for Brian Boucher and Nashville's 3rd round choice (previously acquired, Phoenix selected Joe Callahan) in 2002 Entry Draft, June 12, 2002.

HANGSLEBEN, Al

Defense. Shoots left. 6'1", 195 lbs. Born, Warroad, MN, February 22, 1953.
(Montreal's 6th choice, 56th overall, in 1973 Amateur Draft).

Season	Club	GP	G	A	Pts	PIM	GP	G	A	Pts	PIM
1979-80	Hartford Whalers	37	3	15	18	69	....	....	....	....	....
	Washington Capitals	37	10	7	17	45	....	....	....	....	....
1980-81	Washington Capitals	76	5	19	24	198	....	....	....	....	....
1981-82	Washington Capitals	17	1	1	2	19	....	....	....	....	....
	Los Angeles Kings	18	2	6	8	65	....	....	....	....	....
	NHL Totals	**185**	**21**	**48**	**69**	**396**	....	....	....	....	....

Reclaimed by **Montreal** from **Hartford** prior to Expansion Draft, June 9, 1979. Claimed by **Hartford** from **Montreal** in Expansion Draft, June 13, 1979. Traded to **Washington** by **Hartford** for Tom Rowe, January 17, 1980. Signed as a free agent by **Los Angeles**, January 4, 1982. Traded to **Edmonton** by **Los Angeles** for Rick Blight, December 7, 1982.

HANKINSON, Ben

Right wing. Shoots right. 6'2", 210 lbs. Born, Edina, MN, May 1, 1969.
(New Jersey's 5th choice, 107th overall, in 1987 Entry Draft).

Season	Club	GP	G	A	Pts	PIM	GP	G	A	Pts	PIM
1992-93	New Jersey Devils	4	2	1	3	9	....	....	....	....	....
1993-94	New Jersey Devils	13	1	0	1	23	2	1	0	1	4
1994-95	New Jersey Devils	8	0	0	0	7	....	....	....	....	....
	Tampa Bay Lightning	18	0	2	2	6	....	....	....	....	....
	NHL Totals	**43**	**3**	**3**	**6**	**45**	**2**	**1**	**0**	**1**	**4**

Traded to **Tampa Bay** by **New Jersey** with Alexander Semak for Shawn Chambers and Danton Cole, March 14, 1995. Traded to **Detroit** by **Tampa Bay** with Marc Bergevin for Shawn Burr and Detroit's 3rd round choice (later traded to Boston – Boston selected Jason Doyle) in 1996 Entry Draft, August 17, 1995.

HANKINSON, Casey

Left wing. Shoots left. 6'1", 187 lbs. Born, Edina, MN, May 8, 1976.
(Chicago's 9th choice, 201st overall, in 1995 Entry Draft).

Season	Club	GP	G	A	Pts	PIM	GP	G	A	Pts	PIM
2000-01	Chicago Blackhawks	11	0	1	1	9	....	....	....	....	....

Season	Club	GP	G	A	Pts	PIM	GP	G	A	Pts	PIM
		REGULAR SEASON					PLAYOFFS				
2001-02	Chicago Blackhawks	3	0	0	0	0	....	....	....	....	....
	NHL Totals	**14**	**0**	**1**	**1**	**9**	....	....	....	....	....

Signed as a free agent by **Anaheim**, July 25, 2003.

HANNA, John

Defense. Shoots right. 5'11", 175 lbs. Born, Sydney, N.S., April 5, 1935.

Season	Club	GP	G	A	Pts	PIM	GP	G	A	Pts	PIM
1958-59	New York Rangers	70	1	10	11	83	....	....	....	....	....
1959-60	New York Rangers	61	4	8	12	87	....	....	....	....	....
1960-61	New York Rangers	46	1	8	9	34	....	....	....	....	....
1963-64	Montreal Canadiens	6	0	0	0	2	....	....	....	....	....
1967-68	Philadelphia Flyers	15	0	0	0	0	....	....	....	....	....
	NHL Totals	**198**	**6**	**26**	**32**	**206**	....	....	....	....	....

Claimed by **NY Rangers** from **Montreal** in Intra-League Draft, June 5, 1957. Traded to **Montreal** by **NY Rangers** for Albert Langlois, June 13, 1961. NHL rights transferred to **Philadelphia** after NHL club purchased **Quebec** (AHL) franchise, May 8, 1967. Traded to **Seattle** (WHL) by **Philadelphia** with Art Stratton to complete transaction that sent Earl Heiskala to Philadelphia (May 19, 1968), June, 1968.

HANNAN, Dave

Center. Shoots left. 5'10", 180 lbs. Born, Sudbury, Ont., November 26, 1961.
(Pittsburgh's 9th choice, 196th overall, in 1981 Entry Draft).

Season	Club	GP	G	A	Pts	PIM	GP	G	A	Pts	PIM
1981-82	Pittsburgh Penguins	1	0	0	0	0	....	....	....	....	....
1982-83	Pittsburgh Penguins	74	11	22	33	127	....	....	....	....	....
1983-84	Pittsburgh Penguins	24	2	3	5	33	....	....	....	....	....
1984-85	Pittsburgh Penguins	30	6	7	13	43	....	....	....	....	....
1985-86	Pittsburgh Penguins	75	17	18	35	91	....	....	....	....	....
1986-87	Pittsburgh Penguins	58	10	15	25	56	....	....	....	....	....
1987-88	Pittsburgh Penguins	21	4	3	7	23	....	....	....	....	....
	♦ Edmonton Oilers	51	9	11	20	43	12	1	1	2	8
1988-89	Pittsburgh Penguins	72	10	20	30	157	8	0	1	1	4
1989-90	Toronto Maple Leafs	39	6	9	15	55	3	1	0	1	4
1990-91	Toronto Maple Leafs	74	11	23	34	82	....	....	....	....	....
1991-92	Toronto Maple Leafs	35	2	2	4	16	....	....	....	....	....
	Buffalo Sabres	12	2	4	6	48	7	2	0	2	2
1992-93	Buffalo Sabres	55	5	15	20	43	8	1	1	2	18
1993-94	Buffalo Sabres	83	6	15	21	53	7	1	0	1	6
1994-95	Buffalo Sabres	42	4	12	16	32	5	0	2	2	2
1995-96	Buffalo Sabres	57	6	10	16	30	....	....	....	....	....
	♦ Colorado Avalanche	4	1	0	1	2	13	0	2	2	2
1996-97	Ottawa Senators	34	2	2	4	8	....	....	....	....	....
	NHL Totals	**841**	**114**	**191**	**305**	**942**	**63**	**6**	**7**	**13**	**46**

Traded to **Edmonton** by **Pittsburgh** with Craig Simpson, Moe Mantha and Chris Joseph for Paul Coffey, Dave Hunter and Wayne Van Dorp, November 24, 1987. Claimed by **Pittsburgh** from **Edmonton** in Waiver Draft, October 3, 1988. Claimed by **Toronto** from **Pittsburgh** in Waiver Draft, October 2, 1989. Traded to **Buffalo** by **Toronto** for Minnesota's 5th round choice (previously acquired, Toronto selected Chris Deruiter) in 1992 Entry Draft, March 10, 1992. Traded to **Colorado** by **Buffalo** for Colorado's 6th round choice (Darren Mortier) in 1996 Entry Draft, March 20, 1996. Signed as a free agent by **Ottawa**, September 13, 1996.

HANNAN, Scott

Defense. Shoots left. 6'2", 220 lbs. Born, Richmond, B.C., January 23, 1979.
(San Jose's 2nd choice, 23rd overall, in 1997 Entry Draft).

Season	Club	GP	G	A	Pts	PIM	GP	G	A	Pts	PIM
1998-99	San Jose Sharks	5	0	2	2	6	....	....	....	....	....
99-2000	San Jose Sharks	30	1	2	3	10	1	0	1	1	0
2000-01	San Jose Sharks	75	3	14	17	51	6	0	1	1	6
2001-02	San Jose Sharks	75	2	12	14	57	12	0	2	2	12
2002-03	San Jose Sharks	81	3	19	22	61	....	....	....	....	....
	NHL Totals	**266**	**9**	**49**	**58**	**185**	**19**	**0**	**4**	**4**	**18**

HANNIGAN, Gord

Center. Shoots left. 5'8", 155 lbs. Born, Schumacher, Ont., January 19, 1929.

Season	Club	GP	G	A	Pts	PIM	GP	G	A	Pts	PIM
1952-53	Toronto Maple Leafs	65	17	18	35	51	....	....	....	....	....
1953-54	Toronto Maple Leafs	35	4	4	8	18	5	2	0	2	4
1954-55	Toronto Maple Leafs	13	0	2	2	8	....	....	....	....	....
1955-56	Toronto Maple Leafs	48	8	7	15	40	4	0	0	0	4
	NHL Totals	**161**	**29**	**31**	**60**	**117**	**9**	**2**	**0**	**2**	**8**

• Brother of Pat and Ray

Traded to **Edmonton** (WHL) by **Toronto** for $5,000, February 25, 1958.

HANNIGAN, Pat

Left wing. Shoots right. 5'10", 183 lbs. Born, Timmins, Ont., March 5, 1936.

Season	Club	GP	G	A	Pts	PIM	GP	G	A	Pts	PIM
1959-60	Toronto Maple Leafs	1	0	0	0	0	....	....	....	....	....
1960-61	New York Rangers	53	11	9	20	24	....	....	....	....	....
1961-62	New York Rangers	56	8	14	22	34	4	0	0	0	2
1967-68	Philadelphia Flyers	65	11	15	26	36	7	1	2	3	9
1968-69	Philadelphia Flyers	7	0	1	1	22	....	....	....	....	....
	NHL Totals	**182**	**30**	**39**	**69**	**116**	**11**	**1**	**2**	**3**	**11**

• Brother of Gord and Ray

Traded to **NY Rangers** by **Toronto** with Johnny Wilson for Eddie Shack, November 7, 1960. Traded to **Portland** (WHL) by **NY Rangers** for Howie Glover, September 19, 1963. Traded to **Buffalo** (AHL) by **Portland** (WHL) for Cliff Schmautz, December, 1963. Claimed by **Detroit** from **Chicago** (Buffalo-AHL) in Inter-League Draft, June 8, 1965. Traded to **Chicago** (Buffalo-AHL) by **Detroit** for $15,000, November 15, 1965. Claimed by **Philadelphia** from **Chicago** in Expansion Draft, June 6, 1967. Traded to **Vancouver** (WHL) by **Philadelphia** for cash, March 2, 1969. NHL rights transferred to **Vancouver** after NHL club purchased **Vancouver** (WHL) franchise, December 19, 1969. Traded to **Toronto** (Phoenix-WHL) by **Vancouver** with Ted McCaskill for Andre Hinse, August, 1970.

HANNIGAN, Ray

Right wing. Shoots right. 5'8", 155 lbs. Born, Schumacher, Ont., July 14, 1927.

Season	Club	GP	G	A	Pts	PIM	GP	G	A	Pts	PIM
1948-49	Toronto Maple Leafs	3	0	0	0	2	....	....	....	....	....
	NHL Totals	**3**	**0**	**0**	**0**	**2**	....	....	....	....	....

• Brother of Pat and Gord

Traded to **Chicago** by **Toronto** with Cal Gardner, Gus Mortson and Al Rollins for Harry Lumley, September 11, 1952. Loaned to **Detroit** (Edmonton-WHL) by **Chicago** for 1952-53 season for the loan of Guyle Fielder for 1952-53 season, October 15, 1952. Traded to **Detroit** (Edmonton-WHL) by **Chicago** for Bill Brennan, August 4, 1953.

HANSEN, Richie

Center. Shoots left. 5'10", 185 lbs. Born, Bronx, NY, October 30, 1955.
(NY Islanders' 7th choice, 119th overall, in 1975 Amateur Draft).

Season	Club	GP	G	A	Pts	PIM	GP	G	A	Pts	PIM
1976-77	New York Islanders	4	1	0	1	0	....	....	....	....	....
1977-78	New York Islanders	2	0	0	0	0	....	....	....	....	....
1978-79	New York Islanders	12	1	6	7	4	....	....	....	....	....
1981-82	St. Louis Blues	2	0	2	2	0	....	....	....	....	....
	NHL Totals	**20**	**2**	**8**	**10**	**4**	....	....	....	....	....

Transferred to **Minnesota** by **NY Islanders** as compensation for NY Islander's signing of free agent Jean Potvin, June 10, 1979. Traded to **St. Louis** by **Minnesota** with Bryan Maxwell for St. Louis' 2nd round choice (later traded to Calgary – Calgary selected Dave Reierson) in 1982 Entry Draft, June 10, 1979. Signed as a free agent by **Minnesota**, July 30, 1983.

HANSEN, Tavis

Right wing. Shoots right. 6'1", 205 lbs. Born, Prince Albert, Sask., June 17, 1975.
(Winnipeg's 3rd choice, 58th overall, in 1994 Entry Draft).

Season	Club	GP	G	A	Pts	PIM	GP	G	A	Pts	PIM
1994-95	Winnipeg Jets	1	0	0	0	0	....	....	....	....	....
1996-97	Phoenix Coyotes	1	0	0	0	0	....	....	....	....	....
1998-99	Phoenix Coyotes	20	2	1	3	12	2	0	0	0	0
99-2000	Phoenix Coyotes	5	0	0	0	0	....	....	....	....	....
2000-01	Phoenix Coyotes	7	0	0	0	4	....	....	....	....	....
	NHL Totals	**34**	**2**	**1**	**3**	**16**	**2**	**0**	**0**	**0**	**0**

Transferred to **Phoenix** after **Winnipeg** franchise relocated, July 1, 1996. Signed as a free agent by **San Jose**, September 5, 2002.

HANSON, Dave

Defense. Shoots left. 6', 190 lbs. Born, Cumberland, WI, April 12, 1954.

Season	Club	GP	G	A	Pts	PIM	GP	G	A	Pts	PIM
1978-79	Detroit Red Wings	11	0	0	0	26	....	....	....	....	....
1979-80	Minnesota North Stars	22	1	1	2	39	....	....	....	....	....
	NHL Totals	**33**	**1**	**1**	**2**	**65**	....	....	....	....	....

Signed as a free agent by **Detroit**, October 4, 1977. Loaned to **Birmingham** (WHA) by **Detroit** with the loan of Steve Durbano and future considerations for Vaclav Nedomansky and Tim Sheehy, November 18, 1977. Traded to **Minnesota** by **Detroit** for future considerations, January 3, 1980. Claimed on waivers by **Detroit** from **Minnesota**, June 8, 1980. Signed as a free agent by **NY Islanders**, September 9, 1982.

HANSON, Emil

Right wing/Defense. Shoots left. 5'8", 165 lbs. Born, Camrose, Alta., November 18, 1907.

Season	Club	GP	G	A	Pts	PIM	GP	G	A	Pts	PIM
1932-33	Detroit Red Wings	7	0	0	0	6	....	....	....	....	....
	NHL Totals	**7**	**0**	**0**	**0**	**6**	....	....	....	....	....

• Brother of Oscar

NHL rights transferred to **Detroit** from **Chicago Shamrocks** (AHA) after AHA club owners purchased Detroit (NHL and IHL) franchises, September 2, 1932.

HANSON, Keith

Defense. Shoots right. 6'5", 215 lbs. Born, Ada, MN, April 26, 1957.
(Minnesota's 8th choice, 145th overall, in 1977 Amateur Draft).

Season	Club	GP	G	A	Pts	PIM	GP	G	A	Pts	PIM
1983-84	Calgary Flames	25	0	2	2	77	....	....	....	....	....
	NHL Totals	**25**	**0**	**2**	**2**	**77**	....	....	....	....	....

Traded to **Calgary** by **Minnesota** with Mike Eaves for Steve Christoff and Calgary's 2nd round choice (Frantisek Musil) in 1983 Entry Draft, June 8, 1983.

HANSON, Oscar

Center. Shoots left. 5'10", 175 lbs. Born, Camrose, Alta., December 27, 1909.

Season	Club	GP	G	A	Pts	PIM	GP	G	A	Pts	PIM
1937-38	Chicago Black Hawks	8	0	0	0	0	....	....	....	....	....
	NHL Totals	**8**	**0**	**0**	**0**	**0**	....	....	....	....	....

• Brother of Emil

Traded to **Chicago** by **St. Louis** (AHA) for cash, January 27, 1937. Traded to **St. Louis** (AHA) by **Chicago** with Bill Kendall for cash, December 2, 1937.

HARBARUK, Nick

Right wing. Shoots right. 6', 195 lbs. Born, Drohiczyn, Poland, August 16, 1943.

Season	Club	GP	G	A	Pts	PIM	PO GP	PO G	PO A	PO Pts	PO PIM
1969-70	Pittsburgh Penguins	74	5	17	22	56	10	3	0	3	20
1970-71	Pittsburgh Penguins	78	13	12	25	108	....	....	....	....	....
1971-72	Pittsburgh Penguins	78	12	17	29	46	4	0	1	1	0
1972-73	Pittsburgh Penguins	78	10	15	25	47	....	....	....	....	....
1973-74	St. Louis Blues	56	5	14	19	16	....	....	....	....	....
	NHL Totals	**364**	**45**	**75**	**120**	**273**	**14**	**3**	**1**	**4**	**20**

Claimed by **Pittsburgh** from **Vancouver** (WHL) in Intra-League Draft, June 10, 1969. Traded to **St. Louis** by **Pittsburgh** for Bob Johnson, October 4, 1973.

HARDING, Jeff

Right wing. Shoots right. 6'3", 220 lbs. Born, Toronto, Ont., April 6, 1969.
(Philadelphia's 2nd choice, 30th overall, in 1987 Entry Draft).

Season	Club	GP	G	A	Pts	PIM	PO GP	PO G	PO A	PO Pts	PO PIM
1988-89	Philadelphia Flyers	6	0	0	0	29	....	....	....	....	....
1989-90	Philadelphia Flyers	9	0	0	0	18	....	....	....	....	....
	NHL Totals	**15**	**0**	**0**	**0**	**47**	....	....	....	....	....

HARDY, Joe

Center. Shoots left. 6', 185 lbs. Born, Kenogami, Que., December 5, 1945.

Season	Club	GP	G	A	Pts	PIM	PO GP	PO G	PO A	PO Pts	PO PIM
1969-70	Oakland Seals	23	5	4	9	20	4	0	0	0	0
1970-71	California Seals	40	4	10	14	31	....	....	....	....	....
	NHL Totals	**63**	**9**	**14**	**23**	**51**	**4**	**0**	**0**	**0**	**0**

Signed as a free agent by **Oakland**, September, 1969. Traded to **Montreal** by **Oakland** for cash, October, 1971.

HARDY, Mark

Defense. Shoots left. 5'11", 195 lbs. Born, Semaden, Switz., February 1, 1959.
(Los Angeles' 3rd choice, 30th overall, in 1979 Entry Draft).

Season	Club	GP	G	A	Pts	PIM	PO GP	PO G	PO A	PO Pts	PO PIM
1979-80	Los Angeles Kings	15	0	1	1	10	4	1	1	2	9
1980-81	Los Angeles Kings	77	5	20	25	77	4	1	2	3	4
1981-82	Los Angeles Kings	77	6	39	45	130	10	1	2	3	9
1982-83	Los Angeles Kings	74	5	34	39	101	....	....	....	....	....
1983-84	Los Angeles Kings	79	8	41	49	122	....	....	....	....	....
1984-85	Los Angeles Kings	78	14	39	53	97	3	0	1	1	2
1985-86	Los Angeles Kings	55	6	21	27	71	....	....	....	....	....
1986-87	Los Angeles Kings	73	3	27	30	120	5	1	2	3	10
1987-88	Los Angeles Kings	61	6	22	28	99	....	....	....	....	....
	New York Rangers	19	2	2	4	31	....	....	....	....	....
1988-89	Minnesota North Stars	15	2	4	6	26	....	....	....	....	....
	New York Rangers	45	2	12	14	45	4	0	1	1	31
1989-90	New York Rangers	54	0	15	15	94	3	0	1	1	2
1990-91	New York Rangers	70	1	5	6	89	6	0	1	1	30
1991-92	New York Rangers	52	1	8	9	65	13	0	3	3	31
1992-93	New York Rangers	44	1	10	11	85	....	....	....	....	....
	Los Angeles Kings	11	0	3	3	4	15	1	2	3	30
1993-94	Los Angeles Kings	16	0	3	3	27	....	....	....	....	....
	NHL Totals	**915**	**62**	**306**	**368**	**1293**	**67**	**5**	**16**	**21**	**158**

Traded to **NY Rangers** by **Los Angeles** for Ron Duguay, February 23, 1988. Traded to **Minnesota** by **NY Rangers** for future considerations (Louie Debrusk) June 13, 1988. Traded to **NY Rangers** by **Minnesota** for Larry Bernard and NY Rangers' 5th round choice (Rhys Hollyman) in 1989 Entry Draft, December 9, 1988. Traded to **Los Angeles** by **NY Rangers** with Ottawa's 5th round choice (previously acquired, Los Angeles selected Frederick Beaubien) in 1993 Entry Draft for John McIntyre, March 22, 1993.

HARGREAVES, Jim

Defense. Shoots right. 5'11", 195 lbs. Born, Winnipeg, Man., May 2, 1950.
(Vancouver's 2nd choice, 16th overall, in 1970 Amateur Draft).

Season	Club	GP	G	A	Pts	PIM	PO GP	PO G	PO A	PO Pts	PO PIM
1970-71	Vancouver Canucks	7	0	1	1	33	....	....	....	....	....
1972-73	Vancouver Canucks	59	1	6	7	72	....	....	....	....	....
	NHL Totals	**66**	**1**	**7**	**8**	**105**	....	....	....	....	....

HARKINS, Brett

Left wing. Shoots left. 6'1", 185 lbs. Born, North Ridgeville, OH, July 2, 1970.
(NY Islanders' 9th choice, 133rd overall, in 1989 Entry Draft).

Season	Club	GP	G	A	Pts	PIM	PO GP	PO G	PO A	PO Pts	PO PIM
1994-95	Boston Bruins	1	0	1	1	0	....	....	....	....	....
1995-96	Florida Panthers	8	0	3	3	6	....	....	....	....	....
1996-97	Boston Bruins	44	4	14	18	8	....	....	....	....	....
2001-02	Columbus Blue Jackets	25	2	12	14	8	....	....	....	....	....
	NHL Totals	**78**	**6**	**30**	**36**	**22**	....	....	....	....	....

• Brother of Todd

Signed as a free agent by **Boston**, July 1, 1994. Signed as a free agent by **Florida**, July 24, 1995. Signed as a free agent by **Boston**, September 4, 1996. Signed as a free agent by **Columbus**, May 29, 2001.

HARKINS, Todd

Center. Shoots right. 6'3", 210 lbs. Born, Cleveland, OH, October 8, 1968.
(Calgary's 2nd choice, 42nd overall, in 1988 Entry Draft).

Season	Club	GP	G	A	Pts	PIM	PO GP	PO G	PO A	PO Pts	PO PIM
1991-92	Calgary Flames	5	0	0	0	7	....	....	....	....	....
1992-93	Calgary Flames	15	2	3	5	22	....	....	....	....	....
1993-94	Hartford Whalers	28	1	0	1	49	....	....	....	....	....
	NHL Totals	**48**	**3**	**3**	**6**	**78**	....	....	....	....	....

• Brother of Brett

Traded to **Hartford** by **Calgary** for Scott Morrow, January 24, 1994. Signed as a free agent by **Florida**, June 6, 1995.

HARLOCK, David

Defense. Shoots left. 6'2", 215 lbs. Born, Toronto, Ont., March 16, 1971.
(New Jersey's 2nd choice, 24th overall, in 1990 Entry Draft).

Season	Club	GP	G	A	Pts	PIM	PO GP	PO G	PO A	PO Pts	PO PIM
1993-94	Toronto Maple Leafs	6	0	0	0	0	....	....	....	....	....
1994-95	Toronto Maple Leafs	1	0	0	0	0	....	....	....	....	....
1995-96	Toronto Maple Leafs	1	0	0	0	0	....	....	....	....	....
1997-98	Washington Capitals	6	0	0	0	4	....	....	....	....	....
1998-99	New York Islanders	70	2	6	8	68	....	....	....	....	....
99-2000	Atlanta Thrashers	44	0	6	6	36	....	....	....	....	....
2000-01	Atlanta Thrashers	65	0	1	1	62	....	....	....	....	....
2001-02	Atlanta Thrashers	19	0	1	1	18	....	....	....	....	....
	NHL Totals	**212**	**2**	**14**	**16**	**188**	....	....	....	....	....

Signed as a free agent by **Toronto**, August 20, 1993. Signed as a free agent by **Washington**, August 20, 1997. Signed as a free agent by **NY Islanders**, August 24, 1998. Claimed by **Atlanta** from **NY Islanders** in Expansion Draft, June 25, 1999. Traded to **Philadelphia** by **Atlanta** with Atlanta's 3rd (later traded to Phoenix – Phoenix selected Tyler Redenbach) and 7th (later traded to San Jose – San Jose selected Joe Pavelski) round choices in 2003 Entry Draft for Francis Lessard, March 15, 2002.

HARLOW, Scott

Left wing. Shoots left. 6'1", 185 lbs. Born, East Bridgewater, MA, October 11, 1963.
(Montreal's 6th choice, 61st overall, in 1982 Entry Draft).

Season	Club	GP	G	A	Pts	PIM	PO GP	PO G	PO A	PO Pts	PO PIM
1987-88	St. Louis Blues	1	0	1	1	0	....	....	....	....	....
	NHL Totals	**1**	**0**	**1**	**1**	**0**	....	....	....	....	....

Traded to **St. Louis** by **Montreal** for future considerations, January 21, 1988. Traded to **Boston** by **St. Louis** for Phil DeGaetano, February 3, 1989.

HARMON, Glen

Defense. Shoots left. 5'9", 165 lbs. Born, Holland, Man., January 2, 1921.

Season	Club	GP	G	A	Pts	PIM	PO GP	PO G	PO A	PO Pts	PO PIM
1942-43	Montreal Canadiens	27	5	9	14	25	5	0	1	1	2
1943-44♦	Montreal Canadiens	43	5	16	21	36	9	1	2	3	4
1944-45	Montreal Canadiens	42	5	8	13	41	6	1	0	1	2
1945-46♦	Montreal Canadiens	49	7	10	17	28	9	1	4	5	0
1946-47	Montreal Canadiens	57	5	9	14	53	11	1	1	2	4
1947-48	Montreal Canadiens	56	10	4	14	52	....	....	....	....	....
1948-49	Montreal Canadiens	59	8	12	20	44	7	1	1	2	4
1949-50	Montreal Canadiens	62	3	16	19	28	5	0	1	1	21
1950-51	Montreal Canadiens	57	2	12	14	27	1	0	0	0	0
	NHL Totals	**452**	**50**	**96**	**146**	**334**	**53**	**5**	**10**	**15**	**37**

NHL Second All-Star Team (1945, 1949)
Played in NHL All-Star Game (1949, 1950)

Claimed by **Montreal** from **Tulsa** (AHA) in Inter-League Draft, June, 27. 1941.

HARMS, John

Right wing. Shoots right. 5'8", 160 lbs. Born, Saskatoon, Sask., April 25, 1925.

Season	Club	GP	G	A	Pts	PIM	PO GP	PO G	PO A	PO Pts	PO PIM
1943-44	Chicago Black Hawks	1	0	0	0	0	4	3	0	3	2
1944-45	Chicago Black Hawks	43	5	5	10	21	....	....	....	....	....
	NHL Totals	**44**	**5**	**5**	**10**	**21**	**4**	**3**	**0**	**3**	**2**

HARNOTT, Walter

Left wing. Shoots left. 5'10", 175 lbs. Born, Montreal, Que., September 24, 1909.

Season	Club	GP	G	A	Pts	PIM	PO GP	PO G	PO A	PO Pts	PO PIM
1933-34	Boston Bruins	6	0	0	0	2	....	....	....	....	....
	NHL Totals	**6**	**0**	**0**	**0**	**2**	....	....	....	....	....

Loaned to **Syracuse** (IHL) by **Boston** with Don Smillie for cash, November 27, 1934.

HARPER, Terry

Defense. Shoots right. 6'1", 200 lbs. Born, Regina, Sask., January 27, 1940.

Season	Club	GP	G	A	Pts	PIM	PO GP	PO G	PO A	PO Pts	PO PIM
1962-63	Montreal Canadiens	14	1	1	2	10	5	1	0	1	8
1963-64	Montreal Canadiens	70	2	15	17	149	7	0	0	0	6
1964-65♦	Montreal Canadiens	62	0	7	7	93	13	0	0	0	19
1965-66♦	Montreal Canadiens	69	1	11	12	91	10	2	3	5	18
1966-67	Montreal Canadiens	56	0	16	16	99	10	0	1	1	15
1967-68♦	Montreal Canadiens	57	3	8	11	66	13	0	1	1	8
1968-69♦	Montreal Canadiens	21	0	3	3	37	11	0	0	0	8
1969-70	Montreal Canadiens	75	4	18	22	109	....	....	....	....	....
1970-71♦	Montreal Canadiens	78	1	21	22	116	20	0	6	6	28
1971-72	Montreal Canadiens	52	2	12	14	35	5	1	1	2	6
1972-73	Los Angeles Kings	77	1	8	9	74	....	....	....	....	....
1973-74	Los Angeles Kings	77	0	17	17	119	5	0	0	0	16
1974-75	Los Angeles Kings	80	5	21	26	120	3	0	0	0	2
1975-76	Detroit Red Wings	69	8	25	33	59	....	....	....	....	....
1976-77	Detroit Red Wings	52	4	8	12	28	....	....	....	....	....
1977-78	Detroit Red Wings	80	2	17	19	85	7	0	1	1	4
1978-79	Detroit Red Wings	51	0	6	6	58	....	....	....	....	....
1979-80	St. Louis Blues	11	1	5	6	6	3	0	0	0	2

Season	Club	REGULAR SEASON GP	G	A	Pts	PIM	PLAYOFFS GP	G	A	Pts	PIM
1980-81	Colorado Rockies	15	0	2	2	8	....	....	....	....	....
	NHL Totals	**1066**	**35**	**221**	**256**	**1362**	**112**	**4**	**13**	**17**	**140**

Played in NHL All-Star Game (1965, 1967, 1973, 1975)

Traded to **Los Angeles** by **Montreal** for Los Angeles' 2nd round choice (Gary MacGregor) in 1974 Amateur Draft, 1st (Pierre Mondou) and 3rd (Paul Woods) round choices in 1975 Amateur Draft and 1st round choice (Rod Schutt) in 1976 Amateur Draft, August 22, 1972. Traded to **Detroit** by **Los Angeles** with Dan Maloney and Los Angeles' 2nd round choice (later traded to Minnesota – Minnesota selected Jim Roberts) in 1976 Amateur Draft for Bart Crashley and the rights to Marcel Dionne, June 23, 1975. Signed as a free agent by **St. Louis**, March 10, 1980. Signed as a free agent by **Colorado**, February 12, 1981.

HARRER, Tim

Right wing. Shoots right. 6', 185 lbs. Born, Bloomington, MN, May 10, 1957.
(Atlanta's 9th choice, 148th overall, in 1977 Amateur Draft).

Season	Club	GP	G	A	Pts	PIM	GP	G	A	Pts	PIM
1982-83	Calgary Flames	3	0	0	0	2	....	....	....	....	....
	NHL Totals	**3**	**0**	**0**	**0**	**2**	....	....	....	....	....

Transferred to **Calgary** after **Atlanta** franchise relocated, June 24, 1980. Signed as a free agent by **Minnesota**, August 1, 1983.

HARRINGTON, Hago

Left wing. Shoots left. 5'8", 163 lbs. Born, Melrose, MA, August 13, 1904.

Season	Club	GP	G	A	Pts	PIM	GP	G	A	Pts	PIM
1925-26	Boston Bruins	26	7	2	9	6	....	....	....	....	....
1927-28	Boston Bruins	22	1	0	1	7	2	0	0	0	0
1932-33	Montreal Canadiens	24	1	1	2	2	2	1	0	1	2
	NHL Totals	**72**	**9**	**3**	**12**	**15**	**4**	**1**	**0**	**1**	**2**

Signed as a free agent by **Boston**, January 4, 1926. Traded to **Providence** (Can-Am) by **Boston** for cash, October, 1928. Traded to **Montreal** by **Providence** (Can-Am) with Leo Murray for Leo Gaudreault and Armand Mondou with both teams holding right of recall, January, 1933.

HARRIS, Billy

Center. Shoots left. 6', 155 lbs. Born, Toronto, Ont., July 29, 1935.

Season	Club	GP	G	A	Pts	PIM	GP	G	A	Pts	PIM
1955-56	Toronto Maple Leafs	70	9	13	22	8	5	1	0	1	4
1956-57	Toronto Maple Leafs	23	4	6	10	6	....	....	....	....	....
1957-58	Toronto Maple Leafs	68	16	28	44	32	....	....	....	....	....
1958-59	Toronto Maple Leafs	70	22	30	52	29	12	3	4	7	16
1959-60	Toronto Maple Leafs	70	13	25	38	29	9	0	3	3	4
1960-61	Toronto Maple Leafs	66	12	27	39	30	5	1	0	1	0
1961-62 ◆	Toronto Maple Leafs	67	15	10	25	14	12	2	1	3	2
1962-63 ◆	Toronto Maple Leafs	65	8	24	32	22	10	0	1	1	0
1963-64 ◆	Toronto Maple Leafs	63	6	12	18	17	9	1	1	2	4
1964-65	Toronto Maple Leafs	48	1	6	7	0	....	....	....	....	....
1965-66	Detroit Red Wings	24	1	4	5	6	....	....	....	....	....
1967-68	Oakland Seals	62	12	17	29	2	....	....	....	....	....
1968-69	Oakland Seals	19	0	4	4	2	....	....	....	....	....
	Pittsburgh Penguins	54	7	13	20	8	....	....	....	....	....
	NHL Totals	**769**	**126**	**219**	**345**	**205**	**62**	**8**	**10**	**18**	**30**

Played in NHL All-Star Game (1958, 1962, 1963, 1964)

Traded to **Detroit** by **Toronto** with Andy Bathgate and Gary Jarrett for Marcel Pronovost, Larry Jeffrey, Ed Joyal, Lowell MacDonald and Aut Erickson, May 20, 1965. Claimed by **California** (Oakland) from **Detroit** in Expansion Draft, June 6, 1967. Traded to **Pittsburgh** by **Oakland** for Bob Dillabough, November 29, 1968.

HARRIS, Billy

Right wing. Shoots left. 6'2", 195 lbs. Born, Toronto, Ont., January 29, 1952.
(NY Islanders' 1st choice, 1st overall, in 1972 Amateur Draft).

Season	Club	GP	G	A	Pts	PIM	GP	G	A	Pts	PIM
1972-73	New York Islanders	78	28	22	50	35	....	....	....	....	....
1973-74	New York Islanders	78	23	27	50	34	....	....	....	....	....
1974-75	New York Islanders	80	25	37	62	34	17	3	7	10	12
1975-76	New York Islanders	80	32	38	70	54	13	5	2	7	10
1976-77	New York Islanders	80	24	43	67	44	12	7	7	14	8
1977-78	New York Islanders	80	22	38	60	40	7	0	0	0	4
1978-79	New York Islanders	80	15	39	54	18	10	2	1	3	10
1979-80	New York Islanders	67	15	15	30	37	....	....	....	....	....
	Los Angeles Kings	11	4	3	7	6	4	0	0	0	2
1980-81	Los Angeles Kings	80	20	29	49	36	4	2	1	3	0
1981-82	Los Angeles Kings	16	1	3	4	6	....	....	....	....	....
	Toronto Maple Leafs	20	2	0	2	4	....	....	....	....	....
1982-83	Toronto Maple Leafs	76	11	19	30	26	4	0	1	1	2
1983-84	Toronto Maple Leafs	50	7	10	17	14	....	....	....	....	....
	Los Angeles Kings	21	2	4	6	6	....	....	....	....	....
	NHL Totals	**897**	**231**	**327**	**558**	**394**	**71**	**19**	**19**	**38**	**48**

Played in NHL All-Star Game (1976)

Traded to **Los Angeles** by **NY Islanders** with Dave Lewis for Butch Goring, March 10, 1980. Traded to **Toronto** by **Los Angeles** with John Gibson for Ian Turnbull, November 11, 1981. Traded to **Los Angeles** by **Toronto** for cash, February 15, 1984.

HARRIS, Duke

Right wing. Shoots right. 5'10", 180 lbs. Born, Sarnia, Ont., February 25, 1942.

Season	Club	GP	G	A	Pts	PIM	GP	G	A	Pts	PIM
1967-68	Minnesota North Stars	22	1	4	5	4	....	....	....	....	....
	Toronto Maple Leafs	4	0	0	0	0	....	....	....	....	....
	NHL Totals	**26**	**1**	**4**	**5**	**4**	....	....	....	....	....

Claimed by **Detroit** from **St. Louis** (CHL) in Intra-League Draft, June 10, 1964. Traded to **Minnesota** by **Detroit** with Bob McCord for Jean-Guy Talbot and Dave Richardson, October 19, 1967. Traded to **Toronto** (Rochester-AHL) by **Minnesota** with Murray Hall, Ted Taylor, Len Lunde, Don Johns, and the loan of Carl Wetzel for J.P. Parise and Milan Marcetta, December 23, 1967. Traded to **Rochester** (AHL) by **Toronto** for cash, March, 1968. Rights transferred to **Vancouver** (WHL) after WHL club purchased **Rochester** (AHL) franchise, August 13, 1968. NHL rights transferred to **Vancouver** after NHL club purchased **Vancouver** (WHL) franchise, December 19, 1969.

HARRIS, Henry

Right wing. Shoots left. 5'11", 185 lbs. Born, Kenora, Ont., April 28, 1906.

Season	Club	GP	G	A	Pts	PIM	GP	G	A	Pts	PIM
1930-31	Boston Bruins	32	2	4	6	20	....	....	....	....	....
	NHL Totals	**32**	**2**	**4**	**6**	**20**	....	....	....	....	....

• Brother of Smokey

Traded to **Boston** by **Seattle** (PCHL) for cash, February 4, 1930.

HARRIS, Hugh

Center. Shoots left. 6'1", 195 lbs. Born, Toronto, Ont., June 7, 1948.

Season	Club	GP	G	A	Pts	PIM	GP	G	A	Pts	PIM
1972-73	Buffalo Sabres	60	12	26	38	17	3	0	0	0	0
	NHL Totals	**60**	**12**	**26**	**38**	**17**	**3**	**0**	**0**	**0**	**0**

Claimed by **Buffalo** from **Montreal** in Intra-League Draft, June 8, 1971.

HARRIS, Ron

Defense. Shoots right. 5'10", 190 lbs. Born, Verdun, Que., June 30, 1942.

Season	Club	GP	G	A	Pts	PIM	GP	G	A	Pts	PIM
1962-63	Detroit Red Wings	1	0	1	1	0	....	....	....	....	....
1963-64	Detroit Red Wings	3	0	0	0	7	....	....	....	....	....
1967-68	Oakland Seals	54	4	6	10	60	....	....	....	....	....
1968-69	Detroit Red Wings	73	3	13	16	91	....	....	....	....	....
1969-70	Detroit Red Wings	72	2	19	21	99	4	0	0	0	8
1970-71	Detroit Red Wings	42	2	8	10	65	....	....	....	....	....
1971-72	Detroit Red Wings	61	1	10	11	80	....	....	....	....	....
1972-73	Atlanta Flames	24	2	4	6	8	....	....	....	....	....
	New York Rangers	46	3	10	13	17	10	0	3	3	2
1973-74	New York Rangers	63	2	12	14	25	11	3	0	3	14
1974-75	New York Rangers	34	1	7	8	22	3	1	0	1	9
1975-76	New York Rangers	3	0	1	1	0	....	....	....	....	....
	NHL Totals	**476**	**20**	**91**	**111**	**474**	**28**	**4**	**3**	**7**	**33**

Traded to **Boston** by **Detroit** with Albert Langlois, Parker MacDonald and Bob Dillabough for Ab McDonald, Bob McCord and Ken Stephanson, May 31, 1965. Claimed by **California** (Oakland) from **Boston** in Expansion Draft, June 6, 1967. Traded to **Detroit** by **Oakland** with Bob Baun for Gary Jarrett, Doug Roberts, Howie Young and Chris Worthy, May 27, 1968. Claimed by **Atlanta** from **Detroit** in Expansion Draft, June 6, 1972. Traded to **NY Rangers** by **Atlanta** for Curt Bennett, November 28, 1972. • Suffered career-ending knee injury in game vs. NY Islanders, October 25, 1975.

HARRIS, Smokey

Left wing. Shoots left. 5'11", 165 lbs. Born, Port Arthur, Ont., October 11, 1890.

Season	Club	GP	G	A	Pts	PIM	GP	G	A	Pts	PIM
1924-25	Boston Bruins	6	3	1	4	8	....	....	....	....	....
	NHL Totals	**6**	**3**	**1**	**4**	**8**	....	....	....	....	....

• Brother of Henry

Traded to **Boston** by **Seattle** (PCHA) for cash, November 2, 1924. Traded to **Vancouver** (WCHL) by **Boston** for cash, December 21, 1924.

HARRIS, Ted

Defense. Shoots left. 6'2", 183 lbs. Born, Winnipeg, Man., July 18, 1936.

Season	Club	GP	G	A	Pts	PIM	GP	G	A	Pts	PIM
1963-64	Montreal Canadiens	4	0	1	1	0	....	....	....	....	....
1964-65 ◆	Montreal Canadiens	68	1	14	15	107	13	0	5	5	45
1965-66 ◆	Montreal Canadiens	53	0	13	13	87	10	0	0	0	38
1966-67	Montreal Canadiens	65	2	16	18	86	10	0	1	1	19
1967-68 ◆	Montreal Canadiens	67	5	16	21	78	13	0	4	4	22
1968-69 ◆	Montreal Canadiens	76	7	18	25	102	14	1	2	3	34
1969-70	Montreal Canadiens	74	3	17	20	116	....	....	....	....	....
1970-71	Minnesota North Stars	78	2	13	15	130	12	0	4	4	36
1971-72	Minnesota North Stars	78	2	15	17	77	7	0	1	1	17
1972-73	Minnesota North Stars	78	7	23	30	83	5	0	1	1	15
1973-74	Minnesota North Stars	12	0	1	1	4	....	....	....	....	....
	Detroit Red Wings	41	0	11	11	66	....	....	....	....	....
	St. Louis Blues	24	0	4	4	16	....	....	....	....	....
1974-75 ◆	Philadelphia Flyers	70	1	6	7	48	16	0	4	4	4
	NHL Totals	**788**	**30**	**168**	**198**	**1000**	**100**	**1**	**22**	**23**	**230**

NHL Second All-Star Team (1969)

Played in NHL All-Star Game (1965, 1967, 1969, 1971, 1972)

Traded to **Montreal** by **Springfield** (AHL) with Wayne Larkin, Terry Gray, Bruce Cline and John Chasczewski for Wayne Boddy, Fred Hilts, Brian Smith, John Rodger, Lorne O'Donnell and the loan of Gary Bergman, June, 1963. Claimed by **Minnesota** from **Montreal** in Intra-League Draft, June 9, 1970. Traded to **Detroit** by **Minnesota** for Gary Bergman, November 7, 1973. Traded to **St. Louis** by **Detroit** with Bill Collins and Garnet Bailey for Chris Evans, Bryan Watson and Jean Hamel, February 14, 1974. Traded to **Philadelphia** by **St. Louis** for cash, September 16, 1974

HARRISON, Ed

Center/Left wing. Shoots left. 6', 165 lbs. Born, Mimico, Ont., July 25, 1927.

Season	Club	GP	G	A	Pts	PIM	GP	G	A	Pts	PIM
		REGULAR SEASON					PLAYOFFS				
1947-48	Boston Bruins	52	6	7	13	8	5	1	0	1	2
1948-49	Boston Bruins	59	5	5	10	20	4	0	0	0	0
1949-50	Boston Bruins	70	14	12	26	23	....	....	....	....	....
1950-51	Boston Bruins	9	1	0	1	0	....	....	....	....	....
	New York Rangers	4	1	0	1	2	....	....	....	....	....
	NHL Totals	**194**	**27**	**24**	**51**	**53**	**9**	**1**	**0**	**1**	**2**

Traded to **NY Rangers** by **Boston** with Zellio Toppazzini for Dunc Fisher and future considerations (loan of Alex Kaleta to Hershey-AHL, November 20, 1950), November 16, 1950.

HARRISON, Jim

Center. Shoots right. 5'11", 185 lbs. Born, Bonnyville, Alta., July 9, 1947.

Season	Club	GP	G	A	Pts	PIM	GP	G	A	Pts	PIM
1968-69	Boston Bruins	16	1	2	3	21	....	....	....	....	....
1969-70	Boston Bruins	23	3	1	4	16	....	....	....	....	....
	Toronto Maple Leafs	31	7	10	17	36	....	....	....	....	....
1970-71	Toronto Maple Leafs	78	13	20	33	108	6	0	1	1	33
1971-72	Toronto Maple Leafs	66	19	17	36	104	5	1	0	1	10
1976-77	Chicago Black Hawks	60	18	23	41	97	2	0	0	0	0
1977-78	Chicago Black Hawks	26	2	8	10	31	....	....	....	....	....
1978-79	Chicago Black Hawks	21	4	5	9	22	....	....	....	....	....
1979-80	Edmonton Oilers	3	0	0	0	0	....	....	....	....	....
	NHL Totals	**324**	**67**	**86**	**153**	**435**	**13**	**1**	**1**	**2**	**43**

Traded to **Toronto** by **Boston** for Wayne Carleton, December 10, 1969. Rights traded to **Chicago** by **Toronto** for Chicago's 2nd round choice (Bob Gladney) in 1977 Amateur Draft, September 28, 1976. Traded to **Edmonton** by **Chicago** for future considerations, September 24, 1979.

HART, Gerry

Defense. Shoots left. 5'9", 190 lbs. Born, Flin Flon, Man., January 1, 1948.

Season	Club	GP	G	A	Pts	PIM	GP	G	A	Pts	PIM
1968-69	Detroit Red Wings	1	0	0	0	2	....	....	....	....	....
1969-70	Detroit Red Wings	3	0	0	0	2	....	....	....	....	....
1970-71	Detroit Red Wings	64	2	7	9	148	....	....	....	....	....
1971-72	Detroit Red Wings	3	0	0	0	0	....	....	....	....	....
1972-73	New York Islanders	47	1	11	12	158	....	....	....	....	....
1973-74	New York Islanders	70	1	10	11	61	....	....	....	....	....
1974-75	New York Islanders	71	4	14	18	143	17	2	2	4	42
1975-76	New York Islanders	80	6	18	24	151	13	1	3	4	24
1976-77	New York Islanders	80	4	18	22	98	12	0	2	2	23
1977-78	New York Islanders	78	2	23	25	94	7	0	0	0	16
1978-79	New York Islanders	50	2	14	16	78	9	0	2	2	10
1979-80	Quebec Nordiques	71	3	23	26	59	....	....	....	....	....
1980-81	Quebec Nordiques	6	0	0	0	10	....	....	....	....	....
	St. Louis Blues	63	4	11	15	132	10	0	0	0	27
1981-82	St. Louis Blues	35	0	1	1	102	10	0	3	3	33
1982-83	St. Louis Blues	8	0	0	0	2	....	....	....	....	....
	NHL Totals	**730**	**29**	**150**	**179**	**1240**	**78**	**3**	**12**	**15**	**175**

Claimed by **NY Islanders** from **Detroit** in Expansion Draft, June 6, 1972. Claimed by **Quebec** from **NY Islanders** in Expansion Draft, June 13, 1979. Signed as a free agent by **St. Louis**, November 12, 1980. • Missed majority of 1981-82 season recovering from knee injury suffered in game vs. Detroit, October 15, 1981. • Officially announced retirement, December 1, 1982.

HART, Gizzy

Left wing. Shoots left. 5'9", 171 lbs. Born, Weyburn, Sask., June 1, 1902.

Season	Club	GP	G	A	Pts	PIM	GP	G	A	Pts	PIM
1926-27	Detroit Cougars	2	0	0	0	0	....	....	....	....	....
	Montreal Canadiens	40	3	3	6	8	4	0	0	0	0
1927-28	Montreal Canadiens	44	3	2	5	4	2	0	0	0	0
1932-33	Montreal Canadiens	18	0	3	3	0	2	0	1	1	0
	NHL Totals	**104**	**6**	**8**	**14**	**12**	**8**	**0**	**1**	**1**	**0**

Transferred to **Detroit** after NHL club purchased **Victoria** (WHL) franchise, May 15, 1926. Traded to **Montreal** by **Detroit** for cash, December 12, 1926. Traded to **Providence** (Can-Am) by **Montreal** for cash, October 17, 1928.

HARTIGAN, Mark

Center. Shoots left. 6', 200 lbs. Born, Fort St. John, B.C., October 15, 1977.

Season	Club	GP	G	A	Pts	PIM	GP	G	A	Pts	PIM
2001-02	Atlanta Thrashers	2	0	0	0	2	....	....	....	....	....
2002-03	Atlanta Thrashers	23	5	2	7	6	....	....	....	....	....
	NHL Totals	**25**	**5**	**2**	**7**	**8**	....	....	....	....	....

Signed as a free agent by **Atlanta**, March 27, 2002. Signed as a free agent by **Columbus**, July 15, 2003.

HARTMAN, Mike

Left wing. Shoots left. 6', 190 lbs. Born, Detroit, MI, February 7, 1967.
(Buffalo's 8th choice, 131st overall, in 1986 Entry Draft).

Season	Club	GP	G	A	Pts	PIM	GP	G	A	Pts	PIM
1986-87	Buffalo Sabres	17	3	3	6	69	....	....	....	....	....
1987-88	Buffalo Sabres	18	3	1	4	90	6	0	0	0	35
1988-89	Buffalo Sabres	70	8	9	17	316	5	0	0	0	34
1989-90	Buffalo Sabres	60	11	10	21	211	6	0	0	0	18
1990-91	Buffalo Sabres	60	9	3	12	204	2	0	0	0	17
1991-92	Winnipeg Jets	75	4	4	8	264	2	0	0	0	2
[illegible]-93	Tampa Bay Lightning	58	4	4	8	154	....	....	....	....	....
	New York Rangers	3	0	0	0	6	....	....	....	....	....
[illegible]	New York Rangers	35	1	1	2	70	....	....	....	....	....
1994-95	New York Rangers	1	0	0	0	4	....	....	....	....	....
	NHL Totals	**397**	**43**	**35**	**78**	**1388**	**21**	**0**	**0**	**0**	**106**

Traded to **Winnipeg** by **Buffalo** with Darrin Shannon and Dean Kennedy for Dave McLlwain, Gord Donnelly, Winnipeg's 5th round choice (Yuri Khmylev) in 1992 Entry Draft and future considerations, October 11, 1991. Claimed by **Tampa Bay** from **Winnipeg** in Expansion Draft, June 18, 1992. Traded to **NY Rangers** by **Tampa Bay** for Randy Gilhen, March 22, 1993. Signed as a free agent by **Colorado**, September 26, 1996.

HARTNELL, Scott

Left wing. Shoots left. 6'2", 208 lbs. Born, Regina, Sask., April 18, 1982.
(Nashville's 1st choice, 6th overall, in 2000 Entry Draft).

Season	Club	GP	G	A	Pts	PIM	GP	G	A	Pts	PIM
2000-01	Nashville Predators	75	2	14	16	48	....	....	....	....	....
2001-02	Nashville Predators	75	14	27	41	111	....	....	....	....	....
2002-03	Nashville Predators	82	12	22	34	101	....	....	....	....	....
	NHL Totals	**232**	**28**	**63**	**91**	**260**	....	....	....	....	....

HARTSBURG, Craig

Defense. Shoots left. 6'1", 200 lbs. Born, Stratford, Ont., June 29, 1959.
(Minnesota's 1st choice, 6th overall, in 1979 Entry Draft).

Season	Club	GP	G	A	Pts	PIM	GP	G	A	Pts	PIM
1979-80	Minnesota North Stars	79	14	30	44	81	15	3	1	4	17
1980-81	Minnesota North Stars	74	13	30	43	124	19	3	12	15	16
1981-82	Minnesota North Stars	76	17	60	77	117	4	1	2	3	14
1982-83	Minnesota North Stars	78	12	50	62	109	9	3	8	11	7
1983-84	Minnesota North Stars	26	7	7	14	37	....	....	....	....	....
1984-85	Minnesota North Stars	32	7	11	18	54	9	5	3	8	14
1985-86	Minnesota North Stars	75	10	47	57	127	5	0	1	1	2
1986-87	Minnesota North Stars	73	11	50	61	93	....	....	....	....	....
1987-88	Minnesota North Stars	27	3	16	19	29	....	....	....	....	....
1988-89	Minnesota North Stars	30	4	14	18	47	....	....	....	....	....
	NHL Totals	**570**	**98**	**315**	**413**	**818**	**61**	**15**	**27**	**42**	**70**

Played in NHL All-Star Game (1980, 1982, 1983)

HARVEY, Buster

Right wing. Shoots right. 6', 185 lbs. Born, Fredericton, N.B., April 2, 1950.
(Minnesota's 1st choice, 17th overall, in 1970 Amateur Draft).

Season	Club	GP	G	A	Pts	PIM	GP	G	A	Pts	PIM
1970-71	Minnesota North Stars	59	12	8	20	36	7	0	0	0	4
1971-72	Minnesota North Stars	....	....	....	....	....	1	0	0	0	0
1972-73	Minnesota North Stars	68	21	34	55	16	6	0	2	2	4
1973-74	Minnesota North Stars	72	16	17	33	14	....	....	....	....	....
1974-75	Atlanta Flames	79	17	27	44	16	....	....	....	....	....
1975-76	Atlanta Flames	1	0	0	0	0	....	....	....	....	....
	Kansas City Scouts	39	5	12	17	6	....	....	....	....	....
	Detroit Red Wings	35	8	9	17	25	....	....	....	....	....
1976-77	Detroit Red Wings	54	11	11	22	18	....	....	....	....	....
	NHL Totals	**407**	**90**	**118**	**208**	**131**	**14**	**0**	**2**	**2**	**8**

Traded to **Atlanta** by **Minnesota** with Jerry Byers for John Flesch and Don Martineau, May 27, 1974. Traded to **Kansas City** by **Atlanta** for Rich Lemieux and Kansas City's 2nd round choice (Miles Zaharko) in 1977 Amateur Draft, October 13, 1975. Traded to **Detroit** by **Kansas City** for Phil Roberto, January 14, 1976.

HARVEY, Doug

HHOF

Defense. Shoots left. 5'11", 187 lbs. Born, Montreal, Que., December 19, 1924.

Season	Club	GP	G	A	Pts	PIM	GP	G	A	Pts	PIM
1947-48	Montreal Canadiens	35	4	4	8	32	....	....	....	....	....
1948-49	Montreal Canadiens	55	3	13	16	87	7	0	1	1	10
1949-50	Montreal Canadiens	70	4	20	24	76	5	0	2	2	10
1950-51	Montreal Canadiens	70	5	24	29	93	11	0	5	5	12
1951-52	Montreal Canadiens	68	6	23	29	82	11	0	3	3	8
1952-53◆	Montreal Canadiens	69	4	30	34	67	12	0	5	5	8
1953-54	Montreal Canadiens	68	8	29	37	110	10	0	2	2	12
1954-55	Montreal Canadiens	70	6	43	49	58	12	0	8	8	6
1955-56◆	Montreal Canadiens	62	5	39	44	60	10	2	5	7	10
1956-57◆	Montreal Canadiens	70	6	44	50	92	10	0	7	7	10
1957-58◆	Montreal Canadiens	68	9	32	41	131	10	2	9	11	16
1958-59◆	Montreal Canadiens	61	4	16	20	61	11	1	11	12	22
1959-60◆	Montreal Canadiens	66	6	21	27	45	8	3	0	3	6
1960-61	Montreal Canadiens	58	6	33	39	48	6	0	1	1	8
1961-62	New York Rangers	69	6	24	30	42	6	0	1	1	2
1962-63	New York Rangers	68	4	35	39	92	....	....	....	....	....
1963-64	New York Rangers	14	0	2	2	10	....	....	....	....	....
1966-67	Detroit Red Wings	2	0	0	0	0	....	....	....	....	....
1967-68	St. Louis Blues	....	....	....	....	....	8	0	4	4	12
1968-69	St. Louis Blues	70	2	20	22	30	....	....	....	....	....
	NHL Totals	**1113**	**88**	**452**	**540**	**1216**	**137**	**8**	**64**	**72**	**152**

NHL First All-Star Team (1952, 1953, 1954, 1955, 1956, 1957, 1958, 1960, 1961, 1962) • James Norris Trophy (1955, 1956, 1957, 1958, 1960, 1961, 1962) • NHL Second All-Star Team (1959)

Played in NHL All-Star Game (1951, 1952, 1953, 1954, 1955, 1956, 1957, 1958, 1959, 1960, 1961, 1962, 1969)

Traded to **NY Rangers** by **Montreal** for Lou Fontinato, June 13, 1961. Traded to **Providence** (AHL) by **Baltimore** (AHL) for cash, December 23, 1966. • Activated contract clause that allowed him to become a free agent if traded by Baltimore and signed with **Detroit** (Pittsburgh-AHL), January 6, 1967. Signed as a free agent by **St. Louis** and named playing coach of Kansas City (CPHL), June, 1967.

HARVEY, Hugh

Center/Left wing. Shoots left. 6', 175 lbs. Born, Kingston, Ont., June 25, 1949.

Season	Club	GP	G	A	Pts	PIM	GP	G	A	Pts	PIM
1974-75	Kansas City Scouts	8	0	0	0	2	....	....	....	....	....

Season	Club	REGULAR SEASON					PLAYOFFS				
		GP	G	A	Pts	PIM	GP	G	A	Pts	PIM
1975-76	Kansas City Scouts	10	1	1	2	2	....	....	....	....	....
	NHL Totals	**18**	**1**	**1**	**2**	**4**	....	....	....	....	....

Signed as a free agent by **Philadelphia**, June, 1970. Claimed by **Hershey** (AHL) from **Philadelphia** in Reverse Draft, June 10, 1970. Claimed by **Kansas City** from **Hershey** (AHL) in Inter-League Draft, June 12, 1974.

HARVEY, Todd

Right wing/Center. Shoots right. 6', 200 lbs. Born, Hamilton, Ont., February 17, 1975.
(Dallas' 1st choice, 9th overall, in 1993 Entry Draft).

Season	Club	GP	G	A	Pts	PIM	GP	G	A	Pts	PIM
1994-95	Dallas Stars	40	11	9	20	67	5	0	0	0	8
1995-96	Dallas Stars	69	9	20	29	136	....	....	....	....	....
1996-97	Dallas Stars	71	9	22	31	142	7	0	1	1	10
1997-98	Dallas Stars	59	9	10	19	104	....	....	....	....	....
1998-99	New York Rangers	37	11	17	28	72	....	....	....	....	....
99-2000	New York Rangers	31	3	3	6	62	....	....	....	....	....
	San Jose Sharks	40	8	4	12	78	12	1	0	1	8
2000-01	San Jose Sharks	69	10	11	21	72	6	0	0	0	8
2001-02	San Jose Sharks	69	9	13	22	73	12	0	2	2	12
2002-03	San Jose Sharks	76	3	16	19	74	....	....	....	....	....
	NHL Totals	**561**	**82**	**125**	**207**	**880**	**42**	**1**	**3**	**4**	**46**

Traded to **NY Rangers** by **Dallas** with Bob Errey and Dallas' 4th round choice (Boyd Kane) in 1998 Entry Draft for Brian Skrudland, Mike Keane and NY Rangers' 6th round choice (Pavel Patera) in 1998 Entry Draft, March 24, 1998. Traded to **San Jose** by **NY Rangers** with NY Rangers' 4th round choice (Dimitri Patzold) in 2001 Entry Draft for Radek Dvorak, December 30, 1999.

HASSARD, Bob

Center. Shoots right. 6', 167 lbs. Born, Lloydminster, Sask., March 26, 1929.

Season	Club	GP	G	A	Pts	PIM	GP	G	A	Pts	PIM
1949-50	Toronto Maple Leafs	1	0	0	0	0	....	....	....	....	....
1950-51 ♦	Toronto Maple Leafs	12	0	1	1	0	....	....	....	....	....
1952-53	Toronto Maple Leafs	70	8	23	31	14	....	....	....	....	....
1953-54	Toronto Maple Leafs	26	1	4	5	4	....	....	....	....	....
1954-55	Chicago Black Hawks	17	0	0	0	4	....	....	....	....	....
	NHL Totals	**126**	**9**	**28**	**37**	**22**	....	....	....	....	....

Traded to **Chicago** by **Toronto** for cash, August 10, 1954. Traded to **Toronto** (Pittsburgh-AHL) by **Chicago** for cash, November 16, 1954. Traded to **Detroit** (Hershey-AHL) by **Toronto** (Pittsburgh-AHL) with Gilles Mayer, Jack Price, Willie Marshall, Bob Solinger and Ray Gariepy for cash, July 7, 1956. Traded to **Chicago** (Buffalo-AHL) by **Hershey** (AHL) for Al Dewsbury, February 14, 1957.

HATCHER, Derian

Defense. Shoots left. 6'5", 235 lbs. Born, Sterling Hts., MI, June 4, 1972.
(Minnesota's 1st choice, 8th overall, in 1990 Entry Draft).

Season	Club	GP	G	A	Pts	PIM	GP	G	A	Pts	PIM
1991-92	Minnesota North Stars	43	8	4	12	88	5	0	2	2	8
1992-93	Minnesota North Stars	67	4	15	19	178	....	....	....	....	....
1993-94	Dallas Stars	83	12	19	31	211	9	0	2	2	14
1994-95	Dallas Stars	43	5	11	16	105	....	....	....	....	....
1995-96	Dallas Stars	79	8	23	31	129	....	....	....	....	....
1996-97	Dallas Stars	63	3	19	22	97	7	0	2	2	20
1997-98	Dallas Stars	70	6	25	31	132	17	3	3	6	39
1998-99 ♦	Dallas Stars	80	9	21	30	102	18	1	6	7	24
99-2000	Dallas Stars	57	2	22	24	68	23	1	3	4	29
2000-01	Dallas Stars	80	2	21	23	77	10	0	1	1	16
2001-02	Dallas Stars	80	4	21	25	87	....	....	....	....	....
2002-03	Dallas Stars	82	8	22	30	106	11	1	2	3	33
	NHL Totals	**827**	**71**	**223**	**294**	**1380**	**100**	**6**	**21**	**27**	**183**

• Brother of Kevin • NHL Second All-Star Team (2003)

Played in NHL All-Star Game (1997)

Transferred to **Dallas** after **Minnesota** franchise relocated, June 9, 1993. Signed as a free agent by **Detroit**, July 3, 2003.

HATCHER, Kevin

Defense. Shoots right. 6'3", 230 lbs. Born, Detroit, MI, September 9, 1966.
(Washington's 1st choice, 17th overall, in 1984 Entry Draft).

Season	Club	GP	G	A	Pts	PIM	GP	G	A	Pts	PIM
1984-85	Washington Capitals	2	1	0	1	0	1	0	0	0	0
1985-86	Washington Capitals	79	9	10	19	119	9	1	1	2	19
1986-87	Washington Capitals	78	8	16	24	144	7	1	0	1	20
1987-88	Washington Capitals	71	14	27	41	137	14	5	7	12	55
1988-89	Washington Capitals	62	13	27	40	101	6	1	4	5	20
1989-90	Washington Capitals	80	13	41	54	102	11	0	8	8	32
1990-91	Washington Capitals	79	24	50	74	69	11	3	3	6	8
1991-92	Washington Capitals	79	17	37	54	105	7	2	4	6	19
1992-93	Washington Capitals	83	34	45	79	114	6	0	1	1	14
1993-94	Washington Capitals	72	16	24	40	108	11	3	4	7	37
1994-95	Dallas Stars	47	10	19	29	66	5	2	1	3	2
1995-96	Dallas Stars	74	15	26	41	58	....	....	....	....	....
1996-97	Pittsburgh Penguins	80	15	39	54	103	5	1	1	2	4
1997-98	Pittsburgh Penguins	74	19	29	48	66	6	1	0	1	12
1998-99	Pittsburgh Penguins	66	11	27	38	24	13	2	3	5	4
99-2000	New York Rangers	74	4	19	23	38	....	....	....	....	....
2000-01	Carolina Hurricanes	57	4	14	18	38	6	0	0	0	6
	NHL Totals	**1157**	**227**	**450**	**677**	**1392**	**118**	**22**	**37**	**59**	**252**

• Brother of Derian

Played in NHL All-Star Game (1990, 1991, 1992, 1996, 1997)

Traded to **Dallas** by **Washington** for Mark Tinordi and Rick Mrozik, January 18, 1995. Traded to **Pittsburgh** by **Dallas** for Sergei Zubov, June 22, 1996. Traded to **NY Rangers** by **Pittsburgh** for Peter Popovic, September 30, 1999. Signed as a free agent by **Carolina**, July 31, 2000.

HATOUM, Ed

Right wing. Shoots right. 5'10", 180 lbs. Born, Beirut, Lebanon, December 7, 1947.

Season	Club	GP	G	A	Pts	PIM	GP	G	A	Pts	PIM
1968-69	Detroit Red Wings	16	2	1	3	2	....	....	....	....	....
1969-70	Detroit Red Wings	5	0	2	2	2	....	....	....	....	....
1970-71	Vancouver Canucks	26	1	3	4	21	....	....	....	....	....
	NHL Totals	**47**	**3**	**6**	**9**	**25**	....	....	....	....	....

Claimed by **Vancouver** from **Detroit** in Expansion Draft, June 10, 1970. Loaned to **Seattle** (WHL) by **Vancouver** with Jim Wiste for the remainder of the 1970-71 season for Bobby Schmautz, February 9, 1971.

HAUER, Brett

Defense. Shoots right. 6'2", 210 lbs. Born, Richfield, MN, July 11, 1971.
(Vancouver's 3rd choice, 71st overall, in 1989 Entry Draft).

Season	Club	GP	G	A	Pts	PIM	GP	G	A	Pts	PIM
1995-96	Edmonton Oilers	29	4	2	6	30	....	....	....	....	....
99-2000	Edmonton Oilers	5	0	2	2	2	....	....	....	....	....
2001-02	Nashville Predators	3	0	0	0	6	....	....	....	....	....
	NHL Totals	**37**	**4**	**4**	**8**	**38**	....	....	....	....	....

Traded to **Edmonton** by **Vancouver** for Edmonton's 7th round choice (Larry Shapley) in 1997 Entry Draft, August 24, 1995. Signed as a free agent by **Los Angeles**, July 8, 2001. Traded to **Nashville** by **Los Angeles** for Rich Brennan, December 19, 2001.

HAVELID, Niclas

Defense. Shoots left. 5'11", 196 lbs. Born, Stockholm, Sweden, April 12, 1973.
(Anaheim's 2nd choice, 83rd overall, in 1999 Entry Draft).

Season	Club	GP	G	A	Pts	PIM	GP	G	A	Pts	PIM
99-2000	Mighty Ducks of Anaheim	50	2	7	9	20	....	....	....	....	....
2000-01	Mighty Ducks of Anaheim	47	4	10	14	34	....	....	....	....	....
2001-02	Mighty Ducks of Anaheim	52	1	2	3	40	....	....	....	....	....
2002-03	Mighty Ducks of Anaheim	82	11	22	33	30	21	0	4	4	2
	NHL Totals	**231**	**18**	**41**	**59**	**124**	**21**	**0**	**4**	**4**	**2**

HAVLAT, Martin

Left wing. Shoots left. 6'1", 190 lbs. Born, Mlada Boleslav, Czech., April 19, 1981.
(Ottawa's 1st choice, 26th overall, in 1999 Entry Draft).

Season	Club	GP	G	A	Pts	PIM	GP	G	A	Pts	PIM
2000-01	Ottawa Senators	73	19	23	42	20	4	0	0	0	2
2001-02	Ottawa Senators	72	22	28	50	66	12	2	5	7	14
2002-03	Ottawa Senators	67	24	35	59	30	18	5	6	11	14
	NHL Totals	**212**	**65**	**86**	**151**	**116**	**34**	**7**	**11**	**18**	**30**

NHL All-Rookie Team (2001)

HAWERCHUK, Dale

HHOF

Center. Shoots left. 5'11", 190 lbs. Born, Toronto, Ont., April 4, 1963.
(Winnipeg's 1st choice, 1st overall, in 1981 Entry Draft).

Season	Club	GP	G	A	Pts	PIM	GP	G	A	Pts	PIM
1981-82	Winnipeg Jets	80	45	58	103	47	4	1	7	8	5
1982-83	Winnipeg Jets	79	40	51	91	31	3	1	4	5	8
1983-84	Winnipeg Jets	80	37	65	102	73	3	1	1	2	0
1984-85	Winnipeg Jets	80	53	77	130	74	3	2	1	3	4
1985-86	Winnipeg Jets	80	46	59	105	44	3	0	3	3	0
1986-87	Winnipeg Jets	80	47	53	100	52	10	5	8	13	4
1987-88	Winnipeg Jets	80	44	77	121	59	5	3	4	7	16
1988-89	Winnipeg Jets	75	41	55	96	28	....	....	....	....	....
1989-90	Winnipeg Jets	79	26	55	81	60	7	3	5	8	2
1990-91	Buffalo Sabres	80	31	58	89	32	6	2	4	6	10
1991-92	Buffalo Sabres	77	23	75	98	27	7	2	5	7	0
1992-93	Buffalo Sabres	81	16	80	96	52	8	5	9	14	2
1993-94	Buffalo Sabres	81	35	51	86	91	7	0	7	7	4
1994-95	Buffalo Sabres	23	5	11	16	2	2	0	0	0	0
1995-96	St. Louis Blues	66	13	28	41	22	....	....	....	....	....
	Philadelphia Flyers	16	4	16	20	4	12	3	6	9	12
1996-97	Philadelphia Flyers	51	12	22	34	32	17	2	5	7	0
	NHL Totals	**1188**	**518**	**891**	**1409**	**730**	**97**	**30**	**69**	**99**	**67**

• Calder Memorial Trophy (1982) • NHL Second All-Star Team (1985)

Played in NHL All-Star Game (1982, 1985, 1986, 1988, 1997)

Traded to **Buffalo** by **Winnipeg** with Winnipeg's 1st round choice (Brad May) in 1990 Entry Draft for Phil Housley, Scott Arniel, Jeff Parker and Buffalo's 1st round choice (Keith Tkachuk) in 1990 Entry Draft, June 16, 1990. Signed as a free agent by **St. Louis**, September 8, 1995. Traded to **Philadelphia** by **St. Louis** for Craig MacTavish, March 15, 1996.

HAWGOOD, Greg

Defense. Shoots left. 5'10", 190 lbs. Born, Edmonton, Alta., August 10, 1968.
(Boston's 9th choice, 202nd overall, in 1986 Entry Draft).

Season	Club	GP	G	A	Pts	PIM	GP	G	A	Pts	PIM
1987-88	Boston Bruins	1	0	0	0	0	3	1	0	1	0
1988-89	Boston Bruins	56	16	24	40	84	10	0	2	2	2
1989-90	Boston Bruins	77	11	27	38	76	15	1	3	4	12
1990-91	Edmonton Oilers	6	0	1	1	6	....	....	....	....	....
1991-92	Edmonton Oilers	20	2	11	13	22	13	0	3	3	23
1992-93	Edmonton Oilers	29	5	13	18	35	....	....	....	....	....
	Philadelphia Flyers	40	6	22	28	39	....	....	....	....	....

Season	Club	GP	G	A	Pts	PIM	GP	G	A	Pts	PIM
		REGULAR SEASON					PLAYOFFS				
1993-94	Philadelphia Flyers	19	3	12	15	19	....	....	....	....	....
	Florida Panthers	33	2	14	16	9	....	....	....	....	....
	Pittsburgh Penguins	12	1	2	3	8	1	0	0	0	0
1994-95	Pittsburgh Penguins	21	1	4	5	25	....	....	....	....	....
1996-97	San Jose Sharks	63	6	12	18	69	....	....	....	....	....
99-2000	Vancouver Canucks	79	5	17	22	26	....	....	....	....	....
2000-01	Vancouver Canucks	16	2	5	7	6	....	....	....	....	....
2001-02	Dallas Stars	2	0	0	0	2	....	....	....	....	....
	NHL Totals	**474**	**60**	**164**	**224**	**426**	**42**	**2**	**8**	**10**	**37**

Traded to **Edmonton** by **Boston** for Vladimir Ruzicka, October 22, 1990. Traded to **Philadelphia** by **Edmonton** with Josef Beranek for Brian Benning, January 16, 1993. Traded to **Florida** by **Philadelphia** for cash, November 30, 1993. Traded to **Pittsburgh** by **Florida** for Jeff Daniels, March 19, 1994. Signed as a free agent by **San Jose**, September 25, 1996. Signed as a free agent by **Vancouver**, September 30, 1999. Signed as a free agent by **Dallas**, July 17, 2001.

HAWKINS, Todd

Wing. Shoots right. 6'1", 195 lbs. Born, Kingston, Ont., August 2, 1966.
(Vancouver's 10th choice, 217th overall, in 1986 Entry Draft).

Season	Club	GP	G	A	Pts	PIM	GP	G	A	Pts	PIM
1988-89	Vancouver Canucks	4	0	0	0	9	....	....	....	....	....
1989-90	Vancouver Canucks	4	0	0	0	6	....	....	....	....	....
1991-92	Toronto Maple Leafs	2	0	0	0	0	....	....	....	....	....
	NHL Totals	**10**	**0**	**0**	**0**	**15**	....	....	....	....	....

Traded to **Toronto** by **Vancouver** for Brian Blad, January 22, 1991. Signed as a free agent by **Pittsburgh**, August 20, 1993.

HAWORTH, Alan

Center. Shoots right. 5'10", 190 lbs. Born, Drummondville, Que., September 1, 1960.
(Buffalo's 6th choice, 95th overall, in 1979 Entry Draft).

Season	Club	GP	G	A	Pts	PIM	GP	G	A	Pts	PIM
1980-81	Buffalo Sabres	49	16	20	36	34	7	4	4	8	2
1981-82	Buffalo Sabres	57	21	18	39	30	3	0	1	1	2
1982-83	Washington Capitals	74	23	27	50	34	4	0	0	0	2
1983-84	Washington Capitals	75	24	31	55	52	8	3	2	5	4
1984-85	Washington Capitals	76	23	26	49	48	5	1	0	1	0
1985-86	Washington Capitals	71	34	39	73	72	9	4	6	10	11
1986-87	Washington Capitals	50	25	16	41	43	6	0	3	3	7
1987-88	Quebec Nordiques	72	23	34	57	112	....	....	....	....	....
	NHL Totals	**524**	**189**	**211**	**400**	**425**	**42**	**12**	**16**	**28**	**28**

• Son of Gord

Traded to **Washington** by **Buffalo** with Buffalo's 3rd round choice (Milan Novy) in 1982 Entry Draft for Washington's 2nd round choice (Mike Anderson) and 4th round choice (Timo Jutila) in 1982 Entry Draft, June 9, 1982. Traded to **Quebec** by **Washington** with Gaetan Duchesne and Washington's 1st round choice (Joe Sakic) in 1987 Entry Draft for Clint Malarchuk and Dale Hunter, June 13, 1987.

HAWORTH, Gord

Center. Shoots left. 5'10", 165 lbs. Born, Drummondville, Que., February 20, 1932.

Season	Club	GP	G	A	Pts	PIM	GP	G	A	Pts	PIM
1952-53	New York Rangers	2	0	1	1	0	....	....	....	....	....
	NHL Totals	**2**	**0**	**1**	**1**	**0**	....	....	....	....	....

• Father of Alan

Traded to **Boston** (Victoria-WHL) by **NY Rangers** for cash, September, 1956. Traded to **Detroit** by **Boston** for Gene Achtymichuk, August, 1961. Traded to **LA Blades** (WHL) by **Detroit** for cash, July, 1962.

HAWRYLIW, Neil

Right wing. Shoots left. 5'11", 185 lbs. Born, Fielding, Sask., November 9, 1955.

Season	Club	GP	G	A	Pts	PIM	GP	G	A	Pts	PIM
1981-82	New York Islanders	1	0	0	0	0	....	....	....	....	....
	NHL Totals	**1**	**0**	**0**	**0**	**0**	....	....	....	....	....

Signed as a free agent by **NY Islanders**, October 10, 1978.

HAY, Bill

Center. Shoots left. 6'3", 190 lbs. Born, Lumsden, Sask., December 9, 1935.

Season	Club	GP	G	A	Pts	PIM	GP	G	A	Pts	PIM
1959-60	Chicago Black Hawks	70	18	37	55	31	4	1	2	3	2
1960-61 ◆	Chicago Black Hawks	69	11	48	59	45	12	2	5	7	20
1961-62	Chicago Black Hawks	60	11	52	63	34	12	3	7	10	18
1962-63	Chicago Black Hawks	64	12	33	45	36	6	3	2	5	6
1963-64	Chicago Black Hawks	70	23	33	56	30	7	3	1	4	4
1964-65	Chicago Black Hawks	69	11	26	37	36	14	3	1	4	4
1965-66	Chicago Black Hawks	68	20	31	51	20	6	0	2	2	4
1966-67	Chicago Black Hawks	36	7	13	20	12	6	0	1	1	4
	NHL Totals	**506**	**113**	**273**	**386**	**244**	**67**	**15**	**21**	**36**	**62**

Calder Memorial Trophy (1960)

Played in NHL All-Star Game (1960, 1961)

Traded to **Chicago** by **Montreal** for cash, April, 1959. Claimed by **St. Louis** from **Chicago** in Expansion Draft, June 6, 1967. Claimed by **Chicago** (Providence-AHL) from **St. Louis** in Reverse Draft, June 13, 1968.

HAY, Dwayne

Left wing. Shoots left. 6'1", 203 lbs. Born, London, Ont., February 11, 1977.
(Washington's 3rd choice, 43rd overall, in 1995 Entry Draft).

Season	Club	GP	G	A	Pts	PIM	GP	G	A	Pts	PIM
1997-98	Washington Capitals	2	0	0	0	2	....	....	....	....	....
1998-99	Florida Panthers	9	0	0	0	0	....	....	....	....	....
99-2000	Florida Panthers	6	0	0	0	2	....	....	....	....	....
	Tampa Bay Lightning	13	1	1	2	2	....	....	....	....	....
2000-01	Calgary Flames	49	1	3	4	16	....	....	....	....	....
	NHL Totals	**79**	**2**	**4**	**6**	**22**	....	....	....	....	....

Traded to **Florida** by **Washington** with future considerations for Esa Tikkanen, March 9, 1998. Traded to **Tampa Bay** by **Florida** with Ryan Johnson for Mike Sillinger, March 14, 2000. Claimed on waivers by **Calgary** from **Tampa Bay**, October 3, 2000.

HAY, George

HHOF

Left wing. Shoots left. 5'10", 155 lbs. Born, Listowel, Ont., January 10, 1898.

Season	Club	GP	G	A	Pts	PIM	GP	G	A	Pts	PIM
1926-27	Chicago Black Hawks	35	14	8	22	12	2	1	2	3	2
1927-28	Detroit Cougars	42	22	13	35	20	....	....	....	....	....
1928-29	Detroit Cougars	39	11	8	19	14	2	1	0	1	0
1929-30	Detroit Cougars	44	18	15	33	8	....	....	....	....	....
1930-31	Detroit Falcons	44	8	10	18	24	....	....	....	....	....
1932-33	Detroit Red Wings	34	1	6	7	6	4	0	1	1	0
1933-34	Detroit Red Wings	1	0	0	0	0	....	....	....	....	....
	NHL Totals	**239**	**74**	**60**	**134**	**84**	**8**	**2**	**3**	**5**	**2**

Transferred to **Chicago** after NHL club purchased **Portland** (WHL) franchise, May 15, 1926. Traded to **Detroit** by **Chicago** with Percy Traub for $15,000, April 11, 1927.

HAY, Jim

Defense. Shoots right. 5'11", 185 lbs. Born, Saskatoon, Sask., May 15, 1931.

Season	Club	GP	G	A	Pts	PIM	GP	G	A	Pts	PIM
1952-53	Detroit Red Wings	42	1	4	5	2	4	0	0	0	2
1953-54	Detroit Red Wings	12	0	0	0	0	....	....	....	....	....
1954-55 ◆	Detroit Red Wings	21	0	1	1	20	5	1	0	1	0
	NHL Totals	**75**	**1**	**5**	**6**	**22**	**9**	**1**	**0**	**1**	**2**

HAYDAR, Darren

Right wing. Shoots left. 5'9", 170 lbs. Born, Toronto, Ont., October 22, 1979.
(Nashville's 14th choice, 248th overall, in 1999 Entry Draft).

Season	Club	GP	G	A	Pts	PIM	GP	G	A	Pts	PIM
2002-03	Nashville Predators	2	0	0	0	0	....	....	....	....	....
	NHL Totals	**2**	**0**	**0**	**0**	**0**	....	....	....	....	....

HAYEK, Peter

Defense. Shoots left. 5'10", 200 lbs. Born, Minneapolis, MN, November 16, 1957.

Season	Club	GP	G	A	Pts	PIM	GP	G	A	Pts	PIM
1981-82	Minnesota North Stars	1	0	0	0	0	....	....	....	....	....
	NHL Totals	**1**	**0**	**0**	**0**	**0**	....	....	....	....	....

Signed as a free agent by **Minnesota**, September, 1981.

HAYES, Chris

Left wing. Shoots left. 5'10", 180 lbs. Born, Rouyn, Que., August 24, 1946.

Season	Club	GP	G	A	Pts	PIM	GP	G	A	Pts	PIM
1971-72 ◆	Boston Bruins	....	....	....	....	....	1	0	0	0	0
	NHL Totals	....	....	....	....	....	**1**	**0**	**0**	**0**	**0**

Signed as a free agent by **Boston**, September, 1971.

HAYNES, Paul

Center. Shoots left. 5'10", 160 lbs. Born, Montreal, Que., March 1, 1910.

Season	Club	GP	G	A	Pts	PIM	GP	G	A	Pts	PIM
1930-31	Montreal Maroons	19	1	0	1	0	....	....	....	....	....
1931-32	Montreal Maroons	12	1	0	1	0	4	0	0	0	0
1932-33	Montreal Maroons	48	16	25	41	18	2	0	0	0	2
1933-34	Montreal Maroons	44	5	4	9	18	4	0	1	1	2
1934-35	Montreal Maroons	11	1	2	3	0	....	....	....	....	....
	Boston Bruins	37	4	3	7	8	3	0	0	0	0
1935-36	Montreal Canadiens	48	5	19	24	24	....	....	....	....	....
1936-37	Montreal Canadiens	47	8	18	26	24	5	2	3	5	0
1937-38	Montreal Canadiens	48	13	22	35	25	3	0	4	4	5
1938-39	Montreal Canadiens	47	5	33	38	27	3	0	0	0	4
1939-40	Montreal Canadiens	23	2	8	10	8	....	....	....	....	....
1940-41	Montreal Canadiens	7	0	0	0	12	....	....	....	....	....
	NHL Totals	**391**	**61**	**134**	**195**	**164**	**24**	**2**	**8**	**10**	**13**

Played in NHL All-Star Game (1937, 1939)

Traded to **Boston** by **Mtl. Maroons** for cash, December 28, 1934. Traded to **Montreal** by **Boston** for Jack Riley, September 30, 1935.

HAYWARD, Rick

Defense. Shoots left. 6', 180 lbs. Born, Toledo, OH, February 25, 1966.
(Montreal's 9th choice, 162nd overall, in 1986 Entry Draft).

Season	Club	GP	G	A	Pts	PIM	GP	G	A	Pts	PIM
1990-91	Los Angeles Kings	4	0	0	0	5	....	....	....	....	....
	NHL Totals	**4**	**0**	**0**	**0**	**5**	....	....	....	....	....

Traded to **Calgary** by **Montreal** for Martin Nicoletti, February 20, 1988. Signed as a free agent by **Los Angeles**, July 15, 1990. Signed as a free agent by **Winnipeg**, July 30, 1992. Traded to **NY Islanders** by **Winnipeg** for future considerations, February 22, 1993.

HAZLETT, Steve

Left wing. Shoots left. 5'9", 170 lbs. Born, Sarnia, Ont., December 12, 1957.
(Vancouver's 6th choice, 76th overall, in 1977 Amateur Draft).

Season	Club	GP	G	A	Pts	PIM	GP	G	A	Pts	PIM
1979-80	Vancouver Canucks	1	0	0	0	0	....	....	....	....	....
	NHL Totals	**1**	**0**	**0**	**0**	**0**	....	....	....	....	....

HEAD, Galen

Right wing. Shoots right. 5'9", 160 lbs. Born, Grande Prairie, Alta., April 16, 1947.

Season	Club	Regular Season GP	G	A	Pts	PIM	Playoffs GP	G	A	Pts	PIM
1967-68	Detroit Red Wings	1	0	0	0	0	....	....	....	....	....
	NHL Totals	**1**	**0**	**0**	**0**	**0**	....	....	....	....	....

Claimed by **Salt Lake** (WHL) from **Detroit** in Reverse Draft, June 10, 1969.

HEADLEY, Fern

Defense. Shoots left. 5'11", 175 lbs. Born, Crystal, ND, March 2, 1901.

Season	Club	Regular Season GP	G	A	Pts	PIM	Playoffs GP	G	A	Pts	PIM
1924-25	Boston Bruins	13	1	2	3	4	....	....	....	....	....
	Montreal Canadiens	17	0	1	1	6	1	0	0	0	0
	Montreal Canadiens (Cup)	....	....	....	....	....	*4*	*0*	*0*	*0*	*0*
	NHL Totals	**30**	**1**	**3**	**4**	**10**	**1**	**0**	**0**	**0**	**0**

Traded to **Boston** by **Saskatoon** (WCHL) for cash, November 2, 1924. Loaned to **Montreal** by **Boston** for remainder of the 1924-25 season, January 14, 1925. Traded to **Vancouver** (WHL) by **Boston** for cash, October 29, 1925. Rights transferred to **Detroit** from **Chicago Shamrocks** (AHA) after AHA club owners purchased Detroit (NHL and IHL) franchises, September 2, 1932.

HEALEY, Paul

Left wing. Shoots right. 6'2", 198 lbs. Born, Edmonton, Alta., March 20, 1975.
(Philadelphia's 7th choice, 192nd overall, in 1993 Entry Draft).

Season	Club	Regular Season GP	G	A	Pts	PIM	Playoffs GP	G	A	Pts	PIM
1996-97	Philadelphia Flyers	2	0	0	0	0	....	....	....	....	....
1997-98	Philadelphia Flyers	4	0	0	0	12	....	....	....	....	....
2001-02	Toronto Maple Leafs	21	3	7	10	2	18	0	1	1	2
2002-03	Toronto Maple Leafs	44	3	7	10	16	4	0	1	1	2
	NHL Totals	**71**	**6**	**14**	**20**	**30**	**22**	**0**	**2**	**2**	**4**

Traded to **Nashville** by **Philadelphia** for Matt Henderson, September 27, 1999. Signed as a free agent by **Edmonton**, August 31, 2000. Signed as a free agent by **Toronto**, July 24, 2001. Signed as a free agent by **NY Rangers**, July 28, 2003.

HEALEY, Rich

Defense. Shoots left. 5'10", 170 lbs. Born, Vancouver, B.C., March 12, 1938.

Season	Club	Regular Season GP	G	A	Pts	PIM	Playoffs GP	G	A	Pts	PIM
1960-61	Detroit Red Wings	1	0	0	0	2	....	....	....	....	....
	NHL Totals	**1**	**0**	**0**	**0**	**2**	....	....	....	....	....

HEAPHY, Shawn

Center. Shoots left. 5'8", 180 lbs. Born, Sudbury, Ont., November 27, 1968.
(Calgary's 1st choice, 26th overall, in 1989 Supplemental Draft).

Season	Club	Regular Season GP	G	A	Pts	PIM	Playoffs GP	G	A	Pts	PIM
1992-93	Calgary Flames	1	0	0	0	0	....	....	....	....	....
	NHL Totals	**1**	**0**	**0**	**0**	**0**	....	....	....	....	....

HEASLIP, Mark

Right wing. Shoots right. 5'10", 190 lbs. Born, Duluth, MN, December 26, 1951.

Season	Club	Regular Season GP	G	A	Pts	PIM	Playoffs GP	G	A	Pts	PIM
1976-77	New York Rangers	19	1	0	1	31	....	....	....	....	....
1977-78	New York Rangers	29	5	10	15	34	3	0	0	0	0
1978-79	Los Angeles Kings	69	4	9	13	45	2	0	0	0	2
	NHL Totals	**117**	**10**	**19**	**29**	**110**	**5**	**0**	**0**	**0**	**2**

Signed as a free agent by **Los Angeles**, September, 1973. Traded to **NY Rangers** by **Los Angeles** for John Campbell, May 28, 1976. Signed as a free agent by **Los Angeles**, June 14, 1978. Claimed by **Winnipeg** from **Los Angeles** in Expansion Draft, June 13, 1979.

HEATH, Randy

Left wing. Shoots left. 5'8", 160 lbs. Born, Vancouver, B.C., November 11, 1964.
(NY Rangers' 2nd choice, 33rd overall, in 1983 Entry Draft).

Season	Club	Regular Season GP	G	A	Pts	PIM	Playoffs GP	G	A	Pts	PIM
1984-85	New York Rangers	12	2	3	5	15	....	....	....	....	....
1985-86	New York Rangers	1	0	1	1	0	....	....	....	....	....
	NHL Totals	**13**	**2**	**4**	**6**	**15**	....	....	....	....	....

HEATLEY, Dany

Right wing. Shoots left. 6'3", 210 lbs. Born, Freiburg, West Germany, January 21, 1981.
(Atlanta's 1st choice, 2nd overall, in 2000 Entry Draft).

Season	Club	Regular Season GP	G	A	Pts	PIM	Playoffs GP	G	A	Pts	PIM
2001-02	Atlanta Thrashers	82	26	41	67	56	....	....	....	....	....
2002-03	Atlanta Thrashers	77	41	48	89	58	....	....	....	....	....
	NHL Totals	**159**	**67**	**89**	**156**	**114**	....	....	....	....	....

NHL All-Rookie Team (2002) • Calder Memorial Trophy (2002)
Played in NHL All-Star Game (2003)

HEBENTON, Andy

Right wing. Shoots left. 5'9", 180 lbs. Born, Winnipeg, Man., October 3, 1929.

Season	Club	Regular Season GP	G	A	Pts	PIM	Playoffs GP	G	A	Pts	PIM
1955-56	New York Rangers	70	24	14	38	8	5	1	0	1	2
1956-57	New York Rangers	70	21	23	44	10	5	2	0	2	2
1957-58	New York Rangers	70	21	24	45	17	6	2	3	5	4
1958-59	New York Rangers	70	33	29	62	8	....	....	....	....	....
1959-60	New York Rangers	70	19	27	46	4	....	....	....	....	....
1960-61	New York Rangers	70	26	28	54	10	....	....	....	....	....
1961-62	New York Rangers	70	18	24	42	10	6	1	2	3	0
1962-63	New York Rangers	70	15	22	37	8	....	....	....	....	....
1963-64	Boston Bruins	70	12	11	23	8	....	....	....	....	....
	NHL Totals	**630**	**189**	**202**	**391**	**83**	**22**	**6**	**5**	**11**	**8**

Lady Byng Trophy (1957)
Played in NHL All-Star Game (1960)

Signed as a free agent by **Montreal**, April 30, 1947. Traded to **NY Rangers** by **Victoria** (WHL) for cash, April 28, 1955. Claimed by **Boston** from **NY Rangers** in Intra-League Draft, June 4, 1963. Traded to **Portland** (WHL) by **Boston** for cash, June 5, 1964. Traded to **Toronto** by **Boston** with Orland Kurtenbach and Pat Stapleton for Ron Stewart, June 8, 1965. Traded to **Phoenix** (WHL) by **Toronto** (Victoria-WHL) for cash, September, 1967.

HECHT, Jochen

Left wing. Shoots left. 6'1", 200 lbs. Born, Mannheim, West Germany, June 21, 1977.
(St. Louis' 1st choice, 49th overall, in 1995 Entry Draft).

Season	Club	Regular Season GP	G	A	Pts	PIM	Playoffs GP	G	A	Pts	PIM
1998-99	St. Louis Blues	3	0	0	0	0	5	2	0	2	0
99-2000	St. Louis Blues	63	13	21	34	28	7	4	6	10	2
2000-01	St. Louis Blues	72	19	25	44	48	15	2	4	6	4
2001-02	Edmonton Oilers	82	16	24	40	60	....	....	....	....	....
2002-03	Buffalo Sabres	49	10	16	26	30	....	....	....	....	....
	NHL Totals	**269**	**58**	**86**	**144**	**166**	**27**	**8**	**10**	**18**	**6**

Traded to **Edmonton** by **St. Louis** with Marty Reasoner and Jan Horacek for Doug Weight and Michel Riesen, July 1, 2001. Traded to **Buffalo** by **Edmonton** for Atlanta's 2nd round choice (previously acquired, Edmonton selected Jeff Deslauriers) in 2002 Entry Draft and Nashville's 2nd round choice (previously acquired, Edmonton selected Jarret Stoll) in 2002 Entry Draft, June 22, 2002.

HECL, Radoslav

Defense. Shoots left. 6'1", 196 lbs. Born, Partizanske, Czech., October 11, 1974.
(Buffalo's 8th choice, 208th overall, in 2002 Entry Draft).

Season	Club	Regular Season GP	G	A	Pts	PIM	Playoffs GP	G	A	Pts	PIM
2002-03	Buffalo Sabres	14	0	0	0	2	....	....	....	....	....
	NHL Totals	**14**	**0**	**0**	**0**	**2**	....	....	....	....	....

HEDBERG, Anders

Right wing. Shoots left. 5'11", 175 lbs. Born, Ornskoldsvik, Sweden, February 25, 1951.

Season	Club	Regular Season GP	G	A	Pts	PIM	Playoffs GP	G	A	Pts	PIM
1978-79	New York Rangers	80	33	45	78	33	18	4	5	9	12
1979-80	New York Rangers	80	32	39	71	21	9	3	2	5	7
1980-81	New York Rangers	80	30	40	70	52	14	8	8	16	6
1981-82	New York Rangers	4	0	1	1	0	....	....	....	....	....
1982-83	New York Rangers	78	25	34	59	12	9	4	8	12	4
1983-84	New York Rangers	79	32	35	67	16	5	1	0	1	0
1984-85	New York Rangers	64	20	31	51	10	3	2	1	3	2
	NHL Totals	**465**	**172**	**225**	**397**	**144**	**58**	**22**	**24**	**46**	**31**

Bill Masterton Trophy (1985)
Played in NHL All-Star Game (1985)
Signed as a free agent by **NY Rangers**, June 5, 1978.

HEDICAN, Bret

Defense. Shoots left. 6'2", 205 lbs. Born, St. Paul, MN, August 10, 1970.
(St. Louis' 10th choice, 198th overall, in 1988 Entry Draft).

Season	Club	Regular Season GP	G	A	Pts	PIM	Playoffs GP	G	A	Pts	PIM
1991-92	St. Louis Blues	4	1	0	1	0	5	0	0	0	0
1992-93	St. Louis Blues	42	0	8	8	30	10	0	0	0	14
1993-94	St. Louis Blues	61	0	11	11	64	....	....	....	....	....
	Vancouver Canucks	8	0	1	1	0	24	1	6	7	16
1994-95	Vancouver Canucks	45	2	11	13	34	11	0	2	2	6
1995-96	Vancouver Canucks	77	6	23	29	83	6	0	1	1	10
1996-97	Vancouver Canucks	67	4	15	19	51	....	....	....	....	....
1997-98	Vancouver Canucks	71	3	24	27	79	....	....	....	....	....
1998-99	Vancouver Canucks	42	2	11	13	34	....	....	....	....	....
	Florida Panthers	25	3	7	10	17	....	....	....	....	....
99-2000	Florida Panthers	76	6	19	25	68	4	0	0	0	0
2000-01	Florida Panthers	70	5	15	20	72	....	....	....	....	....
2001-02	Florida Panthers	31	3	7	10	12	....	....	....	....	....
	Carolina Hurricanes	26	2	4	6	10	23	1	4	5	20
2002-03	Carolina Hurricanes	72	3	14	17	75	....	....	....	....	....
	NHL Totals	**717**	**40**	**170**	**210**	**629**	**83**	**2**	**13**	**15**	**66**

Traded to **Vancouver** by **St. Louis** with Jeff Brown and Nathan LaFayette for Craig Janney, March 21, 1994. Traded to **Florida** by **Vancouver** with Pavel Bure, Brad Ference and Vancouver's 3rd round choice (Robert Fried) in 2000 Entry Draft for Ed Jovanovski, Dave Gagner, Mike Brown, Kevin Weekes and Florida's 1st round choice (Nathan Smith) in 2000 Entry Draft, January 17, 1999. Traded to **Carolina** by **Florida** with Kevyn Adams, Tomas Malec and a conditional 2nd round choice in 2003 Entry Draft for Sandis Ozolinsh and Byron Ritchie, January 16, 2002.

HEDSTROM, Jonathan

Right wing. Shoots left. 6', 200 lbs. Born, Skelleftea, Sweden, December 27, 1977.
(Toronto's 8th choice, 221st overall, in 1997 Entry Draft).

Season	Club	Regular Season GP	G	A	Pts	PIM	Playoffs GP	G	A	Pts	PIM
2002-03	Mighty Ducks of Anaheim	4	0	0	0	0	....	....	....	....	....
	NHL Totals	**4**	**0**	**0**	**0**	**0**	....	....	....	....	....

Rights traded to **Anaheim** by **Toronto** for Anaheim's 6th (Vadim Sozinov) and 7th (Markus Seikola) round choices in 2000 Entry Draft, June 25, 2000.

HEEREMA, Jeff

Right wing. Shoots right. 6'1", 190 lbs. Born, Thunder Bay, Ont., January 17, 1980.
(Carolina's 1st choice, 11th overall, in 1998 Entry Draft).

Season	Club	Regular Season GP	G	A	Pts	PIM	Playoffs GP	G	A	Pts	PIM
2002-03	Carolina Hurricanes	10	3	0	3	2	....	....	....	....	....
	NHL Totals	**10**	**3**	**0**	**3**	**2**	....	....	....	....	....

HEFFERNAN, Frank

Defense. Shoots left. 6', 210 lbs. Born, Peterborough, Ont.,

Season	Club	Regular Season GP	G	A	Pts	PIM	Playoffs GP	G	A	Pts	PIM
1919-20	Toronto St. Pats	19	0	1	1	10	....	....	....	....	....
	NHL Totals	**19**	**0**	**1**	**1**	**10**	....	....	....	....	....

Signed as a free agent by **Toronto**, December 8, 1919.

HEFFERNAN, Gerry

Right wing. Shoots right. 5'9", 160 lbs. Born, Montreal, Que., July 24, 1916.

Season	Club	Regular Season GP	G	A	Pts	PIM	Playoffs GP	G	A	Pts	PIM
1941-42	Montreal Canadiens	40	5	15	20	15	2	2	1	3	0
1942-43	Montreal Canadiens	....	....	....	....	....	2	0	0	0	0
1943-44 ♦	Montreal Canadiens	43	28	20	48	12	7	1	2	3	8
	NHL Totals	**83**	**33**	**35**	**68**	**27**	**11**	**3**	**3**	**6**	**8**

Signed as a free agent by **Montreal**, November 28, 1941.

HEIDT, Mike

Defense. Shoots left. 6'1", 190 lbs. Born, Calgary, Alta., November 4, 1963.
(Los Angeles' 1st choice, 27th overall, in 1982 Entry Draft).

Season	Club	Regular Season GP	G	A	Pts	PIM	Playoffs GP	G	A	Pts	PIM
1983-84	Los Angeles Kings	6	0	1	1	7	....	....	....	....	....
	NHL Totals	**6**	**0**	**1**	**1**	**7**	....	....	....	....	....

HEINDL, Bill

Left wing. Shoots left. 5'10", 175 lbs. Born, Sherbrooke, Que., May 13, 1946.

Season	Club	Regular Season GP	G	A	Pts	PIM	Playoffs GP	G	A	Pts	PIM
1970-71	Minnesota North Stars	12	1	1	2	0	....	....	....	....	....
1971-72	Minnesota North Stars	2	0	0	0	0	....	....	....	....	....
1972-73	New York Rangers	4	1	0	1	0	....	....	....	....	....
	NHL Totals	**18**	**2**	**1**	**3**	**0**	....	....	....	....	....

Claimed by **Minnesota** (Cleveland-AHL) from **Boston** in Reverse Draft, June, 1970. Claimed by **Atlanta** from **Minnesota** in Expansion Draft, June, 1972. Traded to **NY Rangers** by **Atlanta** for Bill Hogaboom, June 16, 1972.

HEINRICH, Lionel

Left wing. Shoots left. 5'10", 180 lbs. Born, Churchbridge, Sask., April 20, 1934.

Season	Club	Regular Season GP	G	A	Pts	PIM	Playoffs GP	G	A	Pts	PIM
1955-56	Boston Bruins	35	1	1	2	33	....	....	....	....	....
	NHL Totals	**35**	**1**	**1**	**2**	**33**	....	....	....	....	....

HEINS, Shawn

Defense. Shoots left. 6'4", 210 lbs. Born, Eganville, Ont., December 24, 1973.

Season	Club	Regular Season GP	G	A	Pts	PIM	Playoffs GP	G	A	Pts	PIM
1998-99	San Jose Sharks	5	0	0	0	13	....	....	....	....	....
99-2000	San Jose Sharks	1	0	0	0	2	....	....	....	....	....
2000-01	San Jose Sharks	38	3	4	7	57	2	0	0	0	0
2001-02	San Jose Sharks	17	0	2	2	24	....	....	....	....	....
2002-03	San Jose Sharks	20	0	1	1	9	....	....	....	....	....
	Pittsburgh Penguins	27	1	1	2	33	....	....	....	....	....
	NHL Totals	**108**	**4**	**8**	**12**	**138**	**2**	**0**	**0**	**0**	**0**

Signed as a free agent by **San Jose**, January 5, 1997. • Missed majority of 2000-01 season recovering from head injury suffered in game vs. Chicago, February 14, 2001. • Missed majority of 2001-02 season recovering from knee (December 4, 2001 vs. Calgary) and jaw (January 19, 2002 vs. Colorado) injuries. Traded to **Pittsburgh** by **San Jose** for Pittsburgh's 5th round choice (Patrick Ehelechner) in 2003 Entry Draft, February 9, 2003.

HEINZE, Steve

Right wing. Shoots right. 5'11", 202 lbs. Born, Lawrence, MA, January 30, 1970.
(Boston's 2nd choice, 60th overall, in 1988 Entry Draft).

Season	Club	Regular Season GP	G	A	Pts	PIM	Playoffs GP	G	A	Pts	PIM
1991-92	Boston Bruins	14	3	4	7	6	7	0	3	3	17
1992-93	Boston Bruins	73	18	13	31	24	4	1	1	2	2
1993-94	Boston Bruins	77	10	11	21	32	13	2	3	5	7
1994-95	Boston Bruins	36	7	9	16	23	5	0	0	0	0
1995-96	Boston Bruins	76	16	12	28	43	5	1	1	2	4
1996-97	Boston Bruins	30	17	8	25	27	....	....	....	....	....
1997-98	Boston Bruins	61	26	20	46	54	6	0	0	0	6
1998-99	Boston Bruins	73	22	18	40	30	12	4	3	7	0
99-2000	Boston Bruins	75	12	13	25	36	....	....	....	....	....
2000-01	Columbus Blue Jackets	65	22	20	42	38	....	....	....	....	....
	Buffalo Sabres	14	5	7	12	8	13	3	4	7	10
2001-02	Los Angeles Kings	73	15	16	31	46	4	0	0	0	2
2002-03	Los Angeles Kings	27	5	7	12	12	....	....	....	....	....
	NHL Totals	**694**	**178**	**158**	**336**	**379**	**69**	**11**	**15**	**26**	**48**

Selected by **Columbus** from **Boston** in Expansion Draft, June 23, 2000. Traded to **Buffalo** by **Columbus** for Buffalo's 3rd round choice (Per Mars) in 2001 Entry Draft, March 13, 2001. Signed as a free agent by **Los Angeles**, July 4, 2001.

HEISKALA, Earl

Left wing. Shoots left. 6', 185 lbs. Born, Kirkland Lake, Ont., November 30, 1942.

Season	Club	Regular Season GP	G	A	Pts	PIM	Playoffs GP	G	A	Pts	PIM
1968-69	Philadelphia Flyers	21	3	3	6	51	....	....	....	....	....
1969-70	Philadelphia Flyers	65	8	7	15	171	....	....	....	....	....
1970-71	Philadelphia Flyers	41	2	1	3	72	....	....	....	....	....
	NHL Totals	**127**	**13**	**11**	**24**	**294**	....	....	....	....	....

Traded to **Philadelphia** by **Seattle** (WHL) for the loan of Bob Courcy and Ray Larose and future considerations (the trade of Art Stratton and John Hanna, June, 1968), May 19, 1968. Loaned to **Seattle** (WHL) by **Philadelphia** for cash, December 23, 1968.

HEISTEN, Barrett

Left wing. Shoots left. 6'1", 200 lbs. Born, Anchorage, AK, March 19, 1980.
(Buffalo's 1st choice, 20th overall, in 1999 Entry Draft).

Season	Club	Regular Season GP	G	A	Pts	PIM	Playoffs GP	G	A	Pts	PIM
2001-02	New York Rangers	10	0	0	0	2	....	....	....	....	....
	NHL Totals	**10**	**0**	**0**	**0**	**2**	....	....	....	....	....

Signed as a free agent by **NY Rangers**, June 16, 2001. Traded to **Dallas** by **NY Rangers** with Manny Malhotra for Martin Rucinsky and Roman Lyashenko, March 12, 2002.

HEJDUK, Milan

Right wing. Shoots right. 5'11", 185 lbs. Born, Usti-nad-Labem, Czech., February 14, 1976.
(Quebec's 6th choice, 87th overall, in 1994 Entry Draft).

Season	Club	Regular Season GP	G	A	Pts	PIM	Playoffs GP	G	A	Pts	PIM
1998-99	Colorado Avalanche	82	14	34	48	26	16	6	6	12	4
99-2000	Colorado Avalanche	82	36	36	72	16	17	5	4	9	6
2000-01 ♦	Colorado Avalanche	80	41	38	79	36	23	7	*16	23	6
2001-02	Colorado Avalanche	62	21	23	44	24	16	3	3	6	4
2002-03	Colorado Avalanche	82	*50	48	98	32	7	2	2	4	2
	NHL Totals	**388**	**162**	**179**	**341**	**134**	**79**	**23**	**31**	**54**	**22**

NHL All-Rookie Team (1999) • NHL Second All-Star Team (2003) • Maurice "Rocket" Richard Trophy (2003)

Played in NHL All-Star Game (2000, 2001)

Rights transferred to **Colorado** after **Quebec** franchise relocated, June 21, 1995.

HELANDER, Peter

Defense. Shoots left. 6'1", 185 lbs. Born, Stockholm, Sweden, December 4, 1951.
(Los Angeles' 8th choice, 153rd overall, in 1982 Entry Draft).

Season	Club	Regular Season GP	G	A	Pts	PIM	Playoffs GP	G	A	Pts	PIM
1982-83	Los Angeles Kings	7	0	1	1	0	....	....	....	....	....
	NHL Totals	**7**	**0**	**1**	**1**	**0**	....	....	....	....	....

HELENIUS, Sami

Defense. Shoots left. 6'6", 230 lbs. Born, Helsinki, Finland, January 22, 1974.
(Calgary's 5th choice, 102nd overall, in 1992 Entry Draft).

Season	Club	Regular Season GP	G	A	Pts	PIM	Playoffs GP	G	A	Pts	PIM
1996-97	Calgary Flames	3	0	1	1	0	....	....	....	....	....
1998-99	Calgary Flames	4	0	0	0	8	....	....	....	....	....
	Tampa Bay Lightning	4	1	0	1	15	....	....	....	....	....
99-2000	Colorado Avalanche	33	0	0	0	46	....	....	....	....	....
2000-01	Dallas Stars	57	1	2	3	99	1	0	0	0	0
2001-02	Dallas Stars	39	0	0	0	58	....	....	....	....	....
2002-03	Dallas Stars	5	0	0	0	6	....	....	....	....	....
	Chicago Blackhawks	10	0	1	1	28	....	....	....	....	....
	NHL Totals	**155**	**2**	**4**	**6**	**260**	**1**	**0**	**0**	**0**	**0**

Traded to **Tampa Bay** by **Calgary** for future considerations, January 29, 1999. Traded to **Colorado** by **Tampa Bay** for future considerations, March 23, 1999. Signed as a free agent by **Dallas**, July 12, 2000. Traded to **Chicago** by **Dallas** with Dallas's 7th round choice in 2004 Entry Draft for Lyle Odelein, March 10, 2003.

HELLER, Ott

Defense. Shoots right. 6', 190 lbs. Born, Berlin, Ont., June 2, 1910.

Season	Club	Regular Season GP	G	A	Pts	PIM	Playoffs GP	G	A	Pts	PIM
1931-32	New York Rangers	21	2	2	4	9	7	3	1	4	8
1932-33 ♦	New York Rangers	40	5	7	12	31	8	3	0	3	10
1933-34	New York Rangers	48	2	5	7	29	2	0	0	0	0
1934-35	New York Rangers	47	3	11	14	31	4	0	1	1	4
1935-36	New York Rangers	43	2	11	13	40	....	....	....	....	....
1936-37	New York Rangers	48	5	12	17	42	9	0	0	0	11
1937-38	New York Rangers	48	2	14	16	68	3	0	1	1	2
1938-39	New York Rangers	48	0	23	23	42	7	0	1	1	10
1939-40 ♦	New York Rangers	47	5	14	19	26	12	0	3	3	12
1940-41	New York Rangers	48	2	16	18	42	3	0	1	1	4
1941-42	New York Rangers	35	6	5	11	22	6	0	0	0	0
1942-43	New York Rangers	45	4	14	18	14	....	....	....	....	....
1943-44	New York Rangers	50	8	27	35	29	....	....	....	....	....
1944-45	New York Rangers	45	7	12	19	26	....	....	....	....	....
1945-46	New York Rangers	34	2	3	5	14	....	....	....	....	....
	NHL Totals	**647**	**55**	**176**	**231**	**465**	**61**	**6**	**8**	**14**	**61**

NHL Second All-Star Team (1941)

Traded to **NY Rangers** by **Springfield** (Can-Am) for cash, May 9, 1931.

HELMAN, Harry

Right wing. Shoots right. 5'6", 145 lbs. Born, Ottawa, Ont., August 28, 1894.

Season	Club	Regular Season GP	G	A	Pts	PIM	Playoffs GP	G	A	Pts	PIM
1922-23 ♦	Ottawa Senators	24	0	0	0	5	2	0	0	0	0
	Ottawa Senators (Cup)	....	....	....	....	....	*2*	*0*	*0*	*0*	*0*
1923-24	Ottawa Senators	19	1	0	1	2	....	....	....	....	....
1924-25	Ottawa Senators	1	0	0	0	0	....	....	....	....	....
	NHL Totals	**44**	**1**	**0**	**1**	**7**	**2**	**0**	**0**	**0**	**0**

Signed as a free agent by **Ottawa**, November 16, 1922.

HELMER, Bryan

Defense. Shoots right. 6'1", 200 lbs. Born, Sault Ste. Marie, Ont., July 15, 1972.

Season	Club	Regular Season GP	G	A	Pts	PIM	Playoffs GP	G	A	Pts	PIM
1998-99	Phoenix Coyotes	11	0	0	0	23	....	....	....	....	....
	St. Louis Blues	29	0	4	4	19	....	....	....	....	....
99-2000	St. Louis Blues	15	1	1	2	10	....	....	....	....	....
2000-01	Vancouver Canucks	20	2	4	6	18	....	....	....	....	....
2001-02	Vancouver Canucks	40	5	5	10	53	6	0	0	0	0

Season	Club	GP	G	A	Pts	PIM	GP	G	A	Pts	PIM
		REGULAR SEASON					PLAYOFFS				
2002-03	Vancouver Canucks	2	0	0	0	0	....	....	....	....	....
	NHL Totals	**117**	**8**	**14**	**22**	**123**	**6**	**0**	**0**	**0**	**0**

Signed as a free agent by **New Jersey**, July 10, 1994. Signed as a free agent by **Phoenix**, July 17, 1998. Claimed on waivers by **St. Louis** from **Phoenix**, December 19, 1998. Signed as a free agent by **Vancouver**, August 21, 2000. Traded to **Phoenix** by **Vancouver** for Martin Grenier, July 25, 2003.

HELMINEN, Raimo

Center. Shoots left. 6', 185 lbs. Born, Tampere, Finland, March 11, 1964.
(NY Rangers' 2nd choice, 35th overall, in 1984 Entry Draft).

Season	Club	GP	G	A	Pts	PIM	GP	G	A	Pts	PIM
1985-86	New York Rangers	66	10	30	40	10	2	0	0	0	0
1986-87	New York Rangers	21	2	4	6	2	....	....	....	....	....
	Minnesota North Stars	6	0	1	1	0	....	....	....	....	....
1988-89	New York Islanders	24	1	11	12	4	....	....	....	....	....
	NHL Totals	**117**	**13**	**46**	**59**	**16**	**2**	**0**	**0**	**0**	**0**

Traded to **Minnesota** by **NY Rangers** for future considerations, March 10, 1987. Signed as a free agent by **NY Islanders**, June 1, 1988.

HEMMERLING, Tony

Left wing. Shoots left. 5'11", 178 lbs. Born, Landis, Sask., May 15, 1914.

Season	Club	GP	G	A	Pts	PIM	GP	G	A	Pts	PIM
1935-36	New York Americans	3	0	0	0	0	....	....	....	....	....
1936-37	New York Americans	19	3	3	6	4	....	....	....	....	....
	NHL Totals	**22**	**3**	**3**	**6**	**4**	....	....	....	....	....

Traded to **NY Americans** by **Calgary** (NWHL) for cash, December 2, 1935. Traded to **New Haven** (IAHL) by **NY Americans** for cash, January, 1937.

HEMSKY, Ales

Right wing. Shoots right. 6', 191 lbs. Born, Pardubice, Czech., August 13, 1983.
(Edmonton's 1st choice, 13th overall, in 2001 Entry Draft).

Season	Club	GP	G	A	Pts	PIM	GP	G	A	Pts	PIM
2002-03	Edmonton Oilers	59	6	24	30	14	6	0	0	0	0
	NHL Totals	**59**	**6**	**24**	**30**	**14**	**6**	**0**	**0**	**0**	**0**

HENDERSON, Archie

Right wing. Shoots right. 6'6", 220 lbs. Born, Calgary, Alta., February 17, 1957.
(Washington's 10th choice, 156th overall, in 1977 Amateur Draft).

Season	Club	GP	G	A	Pts	PIM	GP	G	A	Pts	PIM
1980-81	Washington Capitals	7	1	0	1	28	....	....	....	....	....
1981-82	Minnesota North Stars	1	0	0	0	0	....	....	....	....	....
1982-83	Hartford Whalers	15	2	1	3	64	....	....	....	....	....
	NHL Totals	**23**	**3**	**1**	**4**	**92**	....	....	....	....	....

Signed as a free agent by **Minnesota**, July 15, 1981. Signed as a free agent by **Hartford**, August 9, 1982. Signed as a free agent by **Los Angeles**, August 29, 1983. Signed as a free agent by **New Jersey**, September 11, 1985.

HENDERSON, Jay

Left wing. Shoots left. 5'11", 190 lbs. Born, Edmonton, Alta., September 17, 1978.
(Boston's 12th choice, 246th overall, in 1997 Entry Draft).

Season	Club	GP	G	A	Pts	PIM	GP	G	A	Pts	PIM
1998-99	Boston Bruins	4	0	0	0	2	....	....	....	....	....
99-2000	Boston Bruins	16	1	3	4	9	....	....	....	....	....
2000-01	Boston Bruins	13	0	0	0	26	....	....	....	....	....
	NHL Totals	**33**	**1**	**3**	**4**	**37**	....	....	....	....	....

Traded to **NY Rangers** by **Boston** for Boston's 9th round choice in 2004 Entry Draft, January 17, 2003. Traded to **Minnesota** by **NY Rangers** for Cory Larose, February 20, 2003.

HENDERSON, Matt

Right wing. Shoots left. 6'1", 200 lbs. Born, White Bear Lake, MN, June 22, 1974.

Season	Club	GP	G	A	Pts	PIM	GP	G	A	Pts	PIM
1998-99	Nashville Predators	2	0	0	0	2	....	....	....	....	....
2001-02	Chicago Blackhawks	4	0	1	1	0	....	....	....	....	....
	NHL Totals	**6**	**0**	**1**	**1**	**2**	....	....	....	....	....

Signed as a free agent by **Nashville**, July 14, 1998. Traded to **Philadelphia** by **Nashville** for Paul Healey, September 27, 1999. Signed as a free agent by **Chicago**, September 5 2001.

HENDERSON, Murray

Defense. Shoots left. 6', 180 lbs. Born, Toronto, Ont., September 5, 1921.

Season	Club	GP	G	A	Pts	PIM	GP	G	A	Pts	PIM
1944-45	Boston Bruins	5	0	1	1	4	7	0	1	1	2
1945-46	Boston Bruins	48	4	11	15	30	10	1	1	2	4
1946-47	Boston Bruins	57	5	12	17	63	4	0	0	0	4
1947-48	Boston Bruins	49	6	8	14	50	3	1	0	1	5
1948-49	Boston Bruins	60	2	9	11	28	5	0	1	1	2
1949-50	Boston Bruins	64	3	8	11	42	....	....	....	....	....
1950-51	Boston Bruins	66	4	7	11	37	5	0	0	0	2
1951-52	Boston Bruins	56	0	6	6	51	7	0	0	0	4
	NHL Totals	**405**	**24**	**62**	**86**	**305**	**41**	**2**	**3**	**5**	**23**

Signed as a free agent by **Boston**, February 28, 1945.

HENDERSON, Paul

Right wing. Shoots right. 5'11", 180 lbs. Born, Kincardine, Ont., January 28, 1943.

Season	Club	GP	G	A	Pts	PIM	GP	G	A	Pts	PIM
1962-63	Detroit Red Wings	2	0	0	0	9	....	....	....	....	....
1963-64	Detroit Red Wings	32	3	3	6	14	14	2	3	5	6
1964-65	Detroit Red Wings	70	8	13	21	30	7	0	2	2	0
1965-66	Detroit Red Wings	69	22	24	46	34	12	3	3	6	10
1966-67	Detroit Red Wings	46	21	19	40	10	....	....	....	....	....
1967-68	Detroit Red Wings	50	13	20	33	35	....	....	....	....	....
	Toronto Maple Leafs	13	5	6	11	8	....	....	....	....	....
1968-69	Toronto Maple Leafs	74	27	32	59	16	4	0	1	1	0
1969-70	Toronto Maple Leafs	67	20	22	42	18	....	....	....	....	....
1970-71	Toronto Maple Leafs	72	30	30	60	34	6	5	1	6	4
1971-72	Toronto Maple Leafs	73	38	19	57	32	5	1	2	3	6
1972-73	Toronto Maple Leafs	40	18	16	34	18	....	....	....	....	....
1973-74	Toronto Maple Leafs	69	24	31	55	40	4	0	2	2	2
1979-80	Atlanta Flames	30	7	6	13	6	4	0	0	0	0
	NHL Totals	**707**	**236**	**241**	**477**	**304**	**56**	**11**	**14**	**25**	**28**

Played in NHL All-Star Game (1972, 1973)

Traded to **Toronto** by **Detroit** with Norm Ullman, Floyd Smith and Doug Barrie for Frank Mahovlich, Garry Unger, Pete Stemkowski and the rights to Carl Brewer, March 3, 1968. Signed as a free agent by **Atlanta**, September 17, 1979.

HENDRICKSON, Darby

Center. Shoots left. 6'1", 195 lbs. Born, Richfield, MN, August 28, 1972.
(Toronto's 3rd choice, 73rd overall, in 1990 Entry Draft).

Season	Club	GP	G	A	Pts	PIM	GP	G	A	Pts	PIM
1993-94	Toronto Maple Leafs	....	....	....	....	....	2	0	0	0	0
1994-95	Toronto Maple Leafs	8	0	1	1	4	....	....	....	....	....
1995-96	Toronto Maple Leafs	46	6	6	12	47	....	....	....	....	....
	New York Islanders	16	1	4	5	33	....	....	....	....	....
1996-97	Toronto Maple Leafs	64	11	6	17	47	....	....	....	....	....
1997-98	Toronto Maple Leafs	80	8	4	12	67	....	....	....	....	....
1998-99	Toronto Maple Leafs	35	2	3	5	30	....	....	....	....	....
	Vancouver Canucks	27	2	2	4	22	....	....	....	....	....
99-2000	Vancouver Canucks	40	5	4	9	14	....	....	....	....	....
2000-01	Minnesota Wild	72	18	11	29	36	....	....	....	....	....
2001-02	Minnesota Wild	68	9	15	24	50	....	....	....	....	....
2002-03	Minnesota Wild	28	1	5	6	8	17	2	3	5	4
	NHL Totals	**484**	**63**	**61**	**124**	**358**	**19**	**2**	**3**	**5**	**4**

Traded to **NY Islanders** by **Toronto** with Sean Haggerty, Kenny Jonsson and Toronto's 1st round choice (Roberto Luongo) in 1997 Entry Draft for Wendel Clark, Mathieu Schneider and D.J. Smith, March 13, 1996. Traded to **Toronto** by **NY Islanders** for Toronto's 5th round choice (Jiri Dopita) in 1998 Entry Draft, October 11, 1996. Traded to **Vancouver** by **Toronto** for Chris McAllister, February 16, 1999. Selected by **Minnesota** from **Vancouver** in Expansion Draft, June 23, 2000.

HENDRICKSON, John

Defense. Shoots right. 5'11", 175 lbs. Born, Kingston, Ont., December 5, 1936.

Season	Club	GP	G	A	Pts	PIM	GP	G	A	Pts	PIM
1957-58	Detroit Red Wings	1	0	0	0	0	....	....	....	....	....
1958-59	Detroit Red Wings	3	0	0	0	2	....	....	....	....	....
1961-62	Detroit Red Wings	1	0	0	0	2	....	....	....	....	....
	NHL Totals	**5**	**0**	**0**	**0**	**4**	....	....	....	....	....

Traded to **Chicago** by **Detroit** for cash, July, 1962. Traded to **LA Blades** (WHL) by **Chicago** (St. Louis-AHL) for cash, March 1, 1965.

HENNING, Lorne

Center. Shoots left. 5'11", 185 lbs. Born, Melfort, Sask., February 22, 1952.
(NY Islanders' 2nd choice, 17th overall, in 1972 Amateur Draft).

Season	Club	GP	G	A	Pts	PIM	GP	G	A	Pts	PIM
1972-73	New York Islanders	63	7	19	26	14	....	....	....	....	....
1973-74	New York Islanders	60	12	15	27	6	....	....	....	....	....
1974-75	New York Islanders	61	5	6	11	6	17	0	2	2	0
1975-76	New York Islanders	80	7	10	17	16	13	2	0	2	2
1976-77	New York Islanders	80	13	18	31	10	12	0	1	1	0
1977-78	New York Islanders	79	12	15	27	6	7	0	0	0	4
1978-79	New York Islanders	73	13	20	33	14	10	2	0	2	0
1979-80 ♦	New York Islanders	39	3	6	9	6	21	3	4	7	2
1980-81 ♦	New York Islanders	9	1	2	3	24	1	0	0	0	0
	NHL Totals	**544**	**73**	**111**	**184**	**102**	**81**	**7**	**7**	**14**	**8**

HENRY, Alex

Defense. Shoots left. 6'5", 220 lbs. Born, Elliot Lake, Ont., October 18, 1979.
(Edmonton's 2nd choice, 67th overall, in 1998 Entry Draft).

Season	Club	GP	G	A	Pts	PIM	GP	G	A	Pts	PIM
2002-03	Edmonton Oilers	3	0	0	0	0	....	....	....	....	....
	Washington Capitals	38	0	0	0	80	....	....	....	....	....
	NHL Totals	**41**	**0**	**0**	**0**	**80**	....	....	....	....	....

Claimed on waivers by **Washington** from **Edmonton**, October 24, 2002.

HENRY, Burke

Defense. Shoots left. 6'3", 190 lbs. Born, Ste. Rose, Man., January 21, 1979.
(NY Rangers' 3rd choice, 73rd overall, in 1997 Entry Draft).

Season	Club	GP	G	A	Pts	PIM	GP	G	A	Pts	PIM
2002-03	Chicago Blackhawks	16	0	2	2	9	....	....	....	....	....
	NHL Totals	**16**	**0**	**2**	**2**	**9**	....	....	....	....	....

Traded to **Calgary** by **NY Rangers** for Chris St. Croix, June 23, 2001.

HENRY, Camille

Center. Shoots left. 5'9", 152 lbs. Born, Quebec City, Que., January 31, 1933.

Season	Club	GP	G	A	Pts	PIM	GP	G	A	Pts	PIM
1953-54	New York Rangers	66	24	15	39	10	....	....	....	....	....
1954-55	New York Rangers	21	5	2	7	4	....	....	....	....	....
1956-57	New York Rangers	36	14	15	29	2	5	2	3	5	0
1957-58	New York Rangers	70	32	24	56	2	6	1	4	5	5
1958-59	New York Rangers	70	23	35	58	2	....	....	....	....	....
1959-60	New York Rangers	49	12	15	27	6	....	....	....	....	....
1960-61	New York Rangers	53	28	25	53	8	....	....	....	....	....
1961-62	New York Rangers	60	23	15	38	8	5	0	0	0	0
1962-63	New York Rangers	60	37	23	60	8	....	....	....	....	....
1963-64	New York Rangers	68	29	26	55	8	....	....	....	....	....

Season	Club	GP	G	A	Pts	PIM	GP	G	A	Pts	PIM
		REGULAR SEASON					PLAYOFFS				
1964-65	New York Rangers	48	21	15	36	20	....	....	....	....	....
	Chicago Black Hawks	22	5	3	8	2	14	1	0	1	2
1967-68	New York Rangers	36	8	12	20	0	6	0	0	0	0
1968-69	St. Louis Blues	64	17	22	39	8	11	2	5	7	0
1969-70	St. Louis Blues	4	1	2	3	0	....	....	....	....	....
	NHL Totals	**727**	**279**	**249**	**528**	**88**	**47**	**6**	**12**	**18**	**7**

Calder Memorial Trophy (1954) • NHL Second All-Star Team (1958) • Lady Byng Trophy (1958)

Played in NHL All-Star Game (1958, 1963, 1964)

Traded to **Providence** (AHL) by **NY Rangers** for cash and the return of Earl Johnson (on loan), December 5, 1954. Traded to **NY Rangers** by **Providence** (AHL) for cash, October 2, 1955. Traded to **Chicago** by **NY Rangers** with Don Johns, Wally Chevrier and Billy Taylor for Doug Robinson, Wayne Hillman and John Brenneman, February 4, 1965. Traded to **NY Rangers** by **Chicago** for Paul Shmyr, August 17, 1967. Traded to **St. Louis** by **NY Rangers** with Bill Plager and Robbie Irons for Don Caley and Wayne Rivers, June 13, 1968. Claimed by **Buffalo** (AHL) from **St. Louis** in Reverse Draft, June 12, 1969. Traded to **St. Louis** by **NY Rangers** (Buffalo-AHL) with Norm Beaudin for cash, June 27, 1969.

HENRY, Dale

Left wing. Shoots left. 6', 205 lbs. Born, Prince Albert, Sask., September 24, 1964.
(NY Islanders' 10th choice, 163rd overall, in 1983 Entry Draft).

Season	Club	GP	G	A	Pts	PIM	GP	G	A	Pts	PIM
1984-85	New York Islanders	16	2	1	3	19	....	....	....	....	....
1985-86	New York Islanders	7	1	3	4	15	....	....	....	....	....
1986-87	New York Islanders	19	3	3	6	46	8	0	0	0	2
1987-88	New York Islanders	48	5	15	20	115	6	1	0	1	17
1988-89	New York Islanders	22	2	2	4	66	....	....	....	....	....
1989-90	New York Islanders	20	0	2	2	2	....	....	....	....	....
	NHL Totals	**132**	**13**	**26**	**39**	**263**	**14**	**1**	**0**	**1**	**19**

HENTUNEN, Jukka

Right wing. Shoots right. 5'10", 194 lbs. Born, Joroinen, Finland, May 3, 1974.
(Calgary's 7th choice, 176th overall, in 2000 Entry Draft).

Season	Club	GP	G	A	Pts	PIM	GP	G	A	Pts	PIM
2001-02	Calgary Flames	28	2	3	5	4	....	....	....	....	....
	Nashville Predators	10	2	2	4	0	....	....	....	....	....
	NHL Totals	**38**	**4**	**5**	**9**	**4**	....	....	....	....	....

Traded to **Nashville** by **Calgary** for a conditional choice in 2003 Entry Draft, March 17, 2002.

HEPPLE, Alan

Defense. Shoots left. 5'9", 200 lbs. Born, Blaydon-on-Tyne, England, August 16, 1963.
(New Jersey's 9th choice, 169th overall, in 1982 Entry Draft).

Season	Club	GP	G	A	Pts	PIM	GP	G	A	Pts	PIM
1983-84	New Jersey Devils	1	0	0	0	7	....	....	....	....	....
1984-85	New Jersey Devils	1	0	0	0	0	....	....	....	....	....
1985-86	New Jersey Devils	1	0	0	0	0	....	....	....	....	....
	NHL Totals	**3**	**0**	**0**	**0**	**7**	....	....	....	....	....

Signed as a free agent by **Toronto**, June 24, 1988.

HERBERS, Ian

Defense. Shoots left. 6'4", 225 lbs. Born, Jasper, Alta., July 18, 1967.
(Buffalo's 11th choice, 190th overall, in 1987 Entry Draft).

Season	Club	GP	G	A	Pts	PIM	GP	G	A	Pts	PIM
1993-94	Edmonton Oilers	22	0	2	2	32	....	....	....	....	....
99-2000	Tampa Bay Lightning	37	0	0	0	45	....	....	....	....	....
	New York Islanders	6	0	3	3	2	....	....	....	....	....
	NHL Totals	**65**	**0**	**5**	**5**	**79**	....	....	....	....	....

Signed as a free agent by **Edmonton**, September 9, 1992. Signed as a free agent by **Tampa Bay**, September, 1999. Traded to **NY Islanders** by **Tampa Bay** for NY Islanders' 7th round choice (later traded back to NY Islanders – NY Islanders selected Ryan Caldwell) in 2000 Entry Draft, March 9, 2000. Selected by **Minnesota** from **NY Islanders** in Expansion Draft, June 23, 2000.

HERBERT, Jimmy

Center/Right wing. Shoots right. 5'10", 185 lbs. Born, Cayuga, Ont., October 31, 1897.

Season	Club	GP	G	A	Pts	PIM	GP	G	A	Pts	PIM
1924-25	Boston Bruins	30	17	7	24	55	....	....	....	....	....
1925-26	Boston Bruins	36	26	5	31	47	....	....	....	....	....
1926-27	Boston Bruins	34	15	7	22	51	8	3	0	3	8
1927-28	Boston Bruins	12	8	3	11	22	....	....	....	....	....
	Toronto Maple Leafs	31	7	1	8	40	....	....	....	....	....
1928-29	Detroit Cougars	40	9	5	14	34	1	0	0	0	2
1929-30	Detroit Cougars	23	1	3	4	4	....	....	....	....	....
	NHL Totals	**206**	**83**	**31**	**114**	**253**	**9**	**3**	**0**	**3**	**10**

Signed as a free agent by **Boston**, November 2, 1924. Traded to **Toronto** by **Boston** for the rights to Eric Pettinger and $15,000, December 21, 1927. Traded to **Detroit** by **Toronto** for the rights to Jack Arbour and $12,500, April 8, 1928.

HERCHENRATTER, Art

Left wing. Shoots left. 6', 185 lbs. Born, Berlin, Ont., November 24, 1917.

Season	Club	GP	G	A	Pts	PIM	GP	G	A	Pts	PIM
1940-41	Detroit Red Wings	10	1	2	3	2	....	....	....	....	....
	NHL Totals	**10**	**1**	**2**	**3**	**2**	....	....	....	....	....

Signed as a free agent by **Detroit**, October 16, 1940.

HERGERTS, Fred

Center. Shoots right. 6'1", 190 lbs. Born, Calgary, Alta., January 29, 1913.

Season	Club	GP	G	A	Pts	PIM	GP	G	A	Pts	PIM
1934-35	New York Americans	19	2	4	6	2	....	....	....	....	....
1935-36	New York Americans	1	0	0	0	0	....	....	....	....	....
	NHL Totals	**20**	**2**	**4**	**6**	**2**	....	....	....	....	....

Signed as a free agent by **Chicago**, October 15, 1933. Traded to **Detroit** by **NY Americans** with $7,500 for Eddie Wiseman, November 21, 1935.

HERGESHEIMER, Phil

Right wing. Shoots right. 5'10", 175 lbs. Born, Winnipeg, Man., July 9, 1914.

Season	Club	GP	G	A	Pts	PIM	GP	G	A	Pts	PIM
1939-40	Chicago Black Hawks	42	9	11	20	6	1	0	0	0	0
1940-41	Chicago Black Hawks	48	8	16	24	9	5	0	0	0	2
1941-42	Chicago Black Hawks	23	3	11	14	2	....	....	....	....	....
	Boston Bruins	3	0	0	0	2	....	....	....	....	....
1942-43	Chicago Black Hawks	9	1	3	4	0	....	....	....	....	....
	NHL Totals	**125**	**21**	**41**	**62**	**19**	**6**	**0**	**0**	**0**	**2**

• Brother of Wally

Traded to **Chicago** by **Cleveland** (IAHL) for Charley Mason, Harold Jackson and $15,000, May 17, 1939. • Suspended by **Chicago** for refusing assignment to **Kansas City** (AHA), January 16, 1942. Traded to **Boston** by **Chicago** for cash with Chicago holding right of recall, January 26, 1942. • Rights returned to **Chicago** by **Boston**, July 1, 1942.

HERGESHEIMER, Wally

Right wing. Shoots right. 5'8", 155 lbs. Born, Winnipeg, Man., January 8, 1927.

Season	Club	GP	G	A	Pts	PIM	GP	G	A	Pts	PIM
1951-52	New York Rangers	68	26	12	38	6	....	....	....	....	....
1952-53	New York Rangers	70	30	29	59	10	....	....	....	....	....
1953-54	New York Rangers	66	27	16	43	42	....	....	....	....	....
1954-55	New York Rangers	14	4	2	6	4	....	....	....	....	....
1955-56	New York Rangers	70	22	18	40	26	5	1	0	1	0
1956-57	Chicago Black Hawks	41	2	8	10	12	....	....	....	....	....
1958-59	New York Rangers	22	3	0	3	6	....	....	....	....	....
	NHL Totals	**351**	**114**	**85**	**199**	**106**	**5**	**1**	**0**	**1**	**0**

• Brother of Phil

Played in NHL All-Star Game (1953, 1956)

Traded to **Cleveland** (AHL) by **NY Rangers** (Denver-USHL) for Bill Richardson, Neil Strain, Bob Jackson and Joe McArthur, September 5, 1950. Traded to **NY Rangers** by **Cleveland** (AHL) with Hy Buller for Ed Reigle, Jackie Gordon, Fred Shero, Fern Perreault and cash, May 14, 1951. • Missed remainder of 1954-55 season recovering from leg injury suffered in game vs. Toronto, December 18, 1954. Traded to **Chicago** by **NY Rangers** for Red Sullivan, June 19, 1956. Traded to **Buffalo** (AHL) by **Chicago** with Frank Martin for Ken Wharram, May 5, 1958. NHL rights transferred to **NY Rangers** from **Buffalo** after NHL club purchased AHL franchise, June, 1958. Claimed on waivers by **Montreal** from **NY Rangers**, December 10, 1958. Claimed on waivers by **NY Rangers** from **Montreal**, December 17, 1958.

HERON, Red

Center. Shoots left. 5'11", 170 lbs. Born, Toronto, Ont., December 31, 1917.

Season	Club	GP	G	A	Pts	PIM	GP	G	A	Pts	PIM
1938-39	Toronto Maple Leafs	6	0	0	0	0	2	0	0	0	4
1939-40	Toronto Maple Leafs	42	11	12	23	12	9	2	0	2	2
1940-41	Toronto Maple Leafs	35	9	5	14	12	7	0	2	2	0
1941-42	Brooklyn Americans	11	0	1	1	2	....	....	....	....	....
	Montreal Canadiens	12	1	1	2	12	3	0	0	0	0
	NHL Totals	**106**	**21**	**19**	**40**	**38**	**21**	**2**	**2**	**4**	**6**

Loaned to **Brooklyn** by **Toronto** with Nick Knott and Gus Marker and future considerations (cash, February 2, 1942) for Lorne Carr, October 30, 1941. Loaned to **Montreal** by **Brooklyn** for the loan of Murph Chamberlain, February 13, 1942.

HEROUX, Yves

Right wing. Shoots right. 5'11", 185 lbs. Born, Terrebonne, Que., April 27, 1965.
(Quebec's 1st choice, 32nd overall, in 1983 Entry Draft).

Season	Club	GP	G	A	Pts	PIM	GP	G	A	Pts	PIM
1986-87	Quebec Nordiques	1	0	0	0	0	....	....	....	....	....
	NHL Totals	**1**	**0**	**0**	**0**	**0**	....	....	....	....	....

Signed as a free agent by **St. Louis**, March 13, 1990. Signed as a free agent by **Minnesota**, August 10, 1992.

HERPERGER, Chris

Center. Shoots left. 6', 190 lbs. Born, Esterhazy, Sask., February 24, 1974.
(Philadelphia's 9th choice, 223rd overall, in 1992 Entry Draft).

Season	Club	GP	G	A	Pts	PIM	GP	G	A	Pts	PIM
99-2000	Chicago Blackhawks	9	0	0	0	5	....	....	....	....	....
2000-01	Chicago Blackhawks	61	10	15	25	20	....	....	....	....	....
2001-02	Ottawa Senators	72	4	9	13	43	....	....	....	....	....
2002-03	Atlanta Thrashers	27	4	1	5	7	....	....	....	....	....
	NHL Totals	**169**	**18**	**25**	**43**	**75**	....	....	....	....	....

Traded to **Anaheim** by **Philadelphia** with Winnipeg/Phoenix's 7th round choice (previously acquired, Anaheim selected Tony Mohagen) in 1997 Entry Draft for Bob Corkum, February 6, 1996. Signed as a free agent by **Chicago**, September 2, 1998. Signed as a free agent by **Ottawa**, July 13, 2001. Signed as a free agent by **Atlanta**, August 1, 2002. Traded to **Vancouver** by **Atlanta** with Chris Nielsen for Jeff Farkas, January 20, 2003.

HERR, Matt

Center. Shoots left. 6'2", 204 lbs. Born, Hackensack, NJ, May 26, 1976.
(Washington's 4th choice, 93rd overall, in 1994 Entry Draft).

Season	Club	GP	G	A	Pts	PIM	GP	G	A	Pts	PIM
1998-99	Washington Capitals	30	2	2	4	8	....	....	....	....	....
2000-01	Washington Capitals	22	2	3	5	17	....	....	....	....	....
2001-02	Florida Panthers	3	0	0	0	0	....	....	....	....	....
2002-03	Boston Bruins	3	0	0	0	0	....	....	....	....	....
	NHL Totals	**58**	**4**	**5**	**9**	**25**	....	....	....	....	....

Traded to **Philadelphia** by **Washington** for Dean Melanson, March 13, 2001. Signed as a free agent by **Florida**, August 21, 2001. Signed as a free agent by **Boston**, July 18, 2002.

HERTER, Jason

Defense. Shoots right. 6'1", 190 lbs. Born, Hafford, Sask., October 2, 1970.
(Vancouver's 1st choice, 8th overall, in 1989 Entry Draft).

Season	Club	REGULAR SEASON GP	G	A	Pts	PIM	PLAYOFFS GP	G	A	Pts	PIM
1995-96	New York Islanders	1	0	1	1	0	....	....	....	....	....
	NHL Totals	**1**	**0**	**1**	**1**	**0**	....	....	....	....	....

Signed as a free agent by **Dallas**, August 6, 1993. Traded to **NY Islanders** by **Dallas** for cash, September 21, 1995.

HERVEY, Matt

Defense. Shoots right. 5'11", 205 lbs. Born, Whittier, CA, May 16, 1968.

Season	Club	REGULAR SEASON GP	G	A	Pts	PIM	PLAYOFFS GP	G	A	Pts	PIM
1988-89	Winnipeg Jets	2	0	0	0	4	....	....	....	....	....
1991-92	Boston Bruins	16	0	1	1	55	5	0	0	0	6
1992-93	Tampa Bay Lightning	17	0	4	4	38	....	....	....	....	....
	NHL Totals	**35**	**0**	**5**	**5**	**97**	**5**	**0**	**0**	**0**	**6**

Signed as a free agent by **Winnipeg**, September 27, 1988. Signed as a free agent by **Boston**, August 15, 1991. Traded to **Tampa Bay** by **Boston** with Ken Hodge for Darin Kimble and future considerations, September 4, 1992.

HESS, Bob

Defense. Shoots left. 5'11", 180 lbs. Born, Middleton, N.S., May 19, 1955.
(St. Louis' 1st choice, 26th overall, in 1974 Amateur Draft).

Season	Club	REGULAR SEASON GP	G	A	Pts	PIM	PLAYOFFS GP	G	A	Pts	PIM
1974-75	St. Louis Blues	76	9	30	39	58	1	0	0	0	2
1975-76	St. Louis Blues	78	9	23	32	58	1	0	1	1	0
1976-77	St. Louis Blues	53	4	18	22	14	1	0	0	0	0
1977-78	St. Louis Blues	55	2	12	14	16	....	....	....	....	....
1978-79	St. Louis Blues	27	3	4	7	14	....	....	....	....	....
1980-81	St. Louis Blues	4	0	0	0	4	....	....	....	....	....
	Buffalo Sabres	....	....	....	....	....	1	1	0	1	0
1981-82	Buffalo Sabres	33	0	8	8	14	....	....	....	....	....
1983-84	Hartford Whalers	3	0	0	0	0	....	....	....	....	....
	NHL Totals	**329**	**27**	**95**	**122**	**178**	**4**	**1**	**1**	**2**	**2**

Traded to **Buffalo** by **St. Louis** with St. Louis' 4th round choice (Anders Wikberg) in 1981 Entry Draft for Bill Stewart, October 30, 1980. Signed as a free agent by **Hartford**, December, 1984.

HEWARD, Jamie

Defense. Shoots right. 6'2", 207 lbs. Born, Regina, Sask., March 30, 1971.
(Pittsburgh's 1st choice, 16th overall, in 1989 Entry Draft).

Season	Club	REGULAR SEASON GP	G	A	Pts	PIM	PLAYOFFS GP	G	A	Pts	PIM
1995-96	Toronto Maple Leafs	5	0	0	0	0	....	....	....	....	....
1996-97	Toronto Maple Leafs	20	1	4	5	6	....	....	....	....	....
1998-99	Nashville Predators	63	6	12	18	44	....	....	....	....	....
99-2000	New York Islanders	54	6	11	17	26	....	....	....	....	....
2000-01	Columbus Blue Jackets	69	11	16	27	33	....	....	....	....	....
2001-02	Columbus Blue Jackets	28	1	2	3	7	....	....	....	....	....
	NHL Totals	**239**	**25**	**45**	**70**	**116**	....	....	....	....	....

Signed as a free agent by **Toronto**, May 4, 1995. Signed as a free agent by **Philadelphia**, July 31, 1997. Signed as a free agent by **Nashville**, August 10, 1998. Signed as a free agent by **NY Islanders**, July 27, 1999. Claimed on waivers by **Columbus** from **NY Islanders**, May 26, 2000.

HEXIMER, Obs

Left wing/Center. Shoots left. 5'7", 159 lbs. Born, Niagara Falls, Ont., February 16, 1910.

Season	Club	REGULAR SEASON GP	G	A	Pts	PIM	PLAYOFFS GP	G	A	Pts	PIM
1929-30	New York Rangers	19	1	0	1	4	....	....	....	....	....
1932-33	Boston Bruins	48	7	5	12	12	5	0	0	0	2
1934-35	New York Americans	17	5	2	7	0	....	....	....	....	....
	NHL Totals	**84**	**13**	**7**	**20**	**16**	**5**	**0**	**0**	**0**	**2**

Signed as a free agent by **NY Rangers**, December 10, 1929. Traded to **Boston** by **NY Rangers** for $10,000, August 22, 1932. Traded to **NY Americans** by **Boston** with Hap Emms for Walter Jackson, December 14, 1934. Traded to **New Haven** (Can-Am) by **NY Americans** for cash, October 21, 1935.

HEXTALL Jr., Bryan

Center. Shoots left. 5'11", 185 lbs. Born, Winnipeg, Man., May 23, 1941.

Season	Club	REGULAR SEASON GP	G	A	Pts	PIM	PLAYOFFS GP	G	A	Pts	PIM
1962-63	New York Rangers	21	0	2	2	10	....	....	....	....	....
1969-70	Pittsburgh Penguins	66	12	19	31	87	10	0	1	1	34
1970-71	Pittsburgh Penguins	76	16	32	48	133	....	....	....	....	....
1971-72	Pittsburgh Penguins	78	20	24	44	126	4	0	2	2	9
1972-73	Pittsburgh Penguins	78	21	33	54	113	....	....	....	....	....
1973-74	Pittsburgh Penguins	37	2	7	9	39	....	....	....	....	....
	Atlanta Flames	40	2	4	6	55	4	0	1	1	16
1974-75	Atlanta Flames	74	18	16	34	62	....	....	....	....	....
1975-76	Detroit Red Wings	21	0	4	4	29	....	....	....	....	....
	Minnesota North Stars	58	8	20	28	84	....	....	....	....	....
	NHL Totals	**549**	**99**	**161**	**260**	**738**	**18**	**0**	**4**	**4**	**59**

• Son of Bryan • Brother of Dennis • Father of Ron

Claimed by **California** (Oakland) from **NY Rangers** in Expansion Draft, June 6, 1967. Traded to **Toronto** (Rochester-AHL) by **Oakland** with J.P. Parise for Gerry Ehman, October 12, 1967. Rights transferred to **Vancouver** (WHL) after WHL club purchased **Rochester** (AHL) franchise, August 13, 1968. Traded to **Pittsburgh** by **Vancouver** (WHL) for Paul Andrea, John Arbour and the loan of Andy Bathgate for the 1969-70 season, May 20, 1969. Claimed on waivers by **Atlanta** from **Pittsburgh**, January 6, 1974. Traded to **Detroit** by **Atlanta** for Dave Kryskow, June 5, 1975. Traded to **Minnesota** by **Detroit** for Rick Chinnick, November 21, 1975.

HEXTALL, Bryan

HHOF

Right wing. Shoots left. 5'10", 180 lbs. Born, Grenfell, Sask., July 31, 1913.

Season	Club	REGULAR SEASON GP	G	A	Pts	PIM	PLAYOFFS GP	G	A	Pts	PIM
1936-37	New York Rangers	3	0	1	1	0	....	....	....	....	....
1937-38	New York Rangers	48	17	4	21	6	3	2	0	2	0
1938-39	New York Rangers	48	20	15	35	18	7	0	1	1	4
1939-40◆	New York Rangers	48	*24	15	39	52	12	4	3	7	11
1940-41	New York Rangers	48	*26	18	44	16	3	0	1	1	0
1941-42	New York Rangers	48	24	32	*56	30	6	1	1	2	4
1942-43	New York Rangers	50	27	32	59	28	....	....	....	....	....
1943-44	New York Rangers	50	21	33	54	41	....	....	....	....	....
1945-46	New York Rangers	3	0	1	1	0	....	....	....	....	....
1946-47	New York Rangers	60	20	10	30	18	....	....	....	....	....
1947-48	New York Rangers	43	8	14	22	18	6	1	3	4	0
	NHL Totals	**449**	**187**	**175**	**362**	**227**	**37**	**8**	**9**	**17**	**19**

• Father of Bryan Jr. and Dennis • NHL First All-Star Team (1940, 1941, 1942) • NHL Second All-Star Team (1943)

• Missed entire 1944-45 and majority of 1945-46 seasons after being refused permission to enter USA by War Mobilization Command, November 22, 1944. Traded to **Cleveland** (AHL) by **NY Rangers** for cash, September 21, 1948.

HEXTALL, Dennis

Left wing. Shoots left. 5'11", 175 lbs. Born, Poplar Point, Man., April 17, 1943.

Season	Club	REGULAR SEASON GP	G	A	Pts	PIM	PLAYOFFS GP	G	A	Pts	PIM
1967-68	New York Rangers	....	....	....	....	....	2	0	0	0	0
1968-69	New York Rangers	13	1	4	5	25	....	....	....	....	....
1969-70	Los Angeles Kings	28	5	7	12	40	....	....	....	....	....
1970-71	California Seals	78	21	31	52	217	....	....	....	....	....
1971-72	Minnesota North Stars	33	6	10	16	49	7	0	2	2	19
1972-73	Minnesota North Stars	78	30	52	82	140	6	2	0	2	16
1973-74	Minnesota North Stars	78	20	62	82	138	....	....	....	....	....
1974-75	Minnesota North Stars	80	17	57	74	147	....	....	....	....	....
1975-76	Minnesota North Stars	59	11	35	46	93	....	....	....	....	....
	Detroit Red Wings	17	5	9	14	71	....	....	....	....	....
1976-77	Detroit Red Wings	78	14	32	46	158	....	....	....	....	....
1977-78	Detroit Red Wings	78	16	33	49	195	7	1	1	2	10
1978-79	Detroit Red Wings	20	4	8	12	33	....	....	....	....	....
	Washington Capitals	26	2	9	11	43	....	....	....	....	....
1979-80	Washington Capitals	15	1	1	2	49	....	....	....	....	....
	NHL Totals	**681**	**153**	**350**	**503**	**1398**	**22**	**3**	**3**	**6**	**45**

• Son of Bryan • Brother of Bryan Jr.

Played in NHL All-Star Game (1974, 1975)

Traded to **Los Angeles** by **NY Rangers** with Leon Rochefort for Real Lemieux, June 9, 1969. Traded to **Montreal** by **Los Angeles** for Dick Duff, January 23, 1970. Traded to **California** by **Montreal** for cash, May 22, 1970. Traded to **Minnesota** by **California** for Joey Johnston and Walt McKechnie, May 20, 1971. Traded to **Detroit** by **Minnesota** for Bill Hogaboam and Los Angeles' 2nd round choice (previously acquired, Minnesota selected Jim Roberts) in 1976 Amateur Draft, February 27, 1976. Signed as a free agent by **Washington**, February 7, 1979.

HEYLIGER, Vic

USHOF

Center. Shoots left. 5'9", 175 lbs. Born, Boston, MA, September 26, 1919.

Season	Club	REGULAR SEASON GP	G	A	Pts	PIM	PLAYOFFS GP	G	A	Pts	PIM
1937-38	Chicago Black Hawks	7	0	0	0	0	....	....	....	....	....
1943-44	Chicago Black Hawks	26	2	3	5	2	....	....	....	....	....
	NHL Totals	**33**	**2**	**3**	**5**	**2**	....	....	....	....	....

Signed as a free agent by **Chicago**, November 3, 1937. Signed as a free agent by **Chicago**, October 18, 1943.

HICKE, Bill

Right wing. Shoots left. 5'8", 164 lbs. Born, Regina, Sask., March 31, 1938.

Season	Club	REGULAR SEASON GP	G	A	Pts	PIM	PLAYOFFS GP	G	A	Pts	PIM
1958-59◆	Montreal Canadiens	....	....	....	....	....	1	0	0	0	0
1959-60◆	Montreal Canadiens	43	3	10	13	17	7	1	2	3	0
1960-61	Montreal Canadiens	70	18	27	45	31	5	2	0	2	19
1961-62	Montreal Canadiens	70	20	31	51	42	6	0	2	2	14
1962-63	Montreal Canadiens	70	17	22	39	39	5	0	0	0	0
1963-64	Montreal Canadiens	48	11	9	20	41	7	0	2	2	2
1964-65	Montreal Canadiens	17	0	1	1	6	....	....	....	....	....
	New York Rangers	40	6	11	17	26	....	....	....	....	....
1965-66	New York Rangers	49	9	18	27	21	....	....	....	....	....
1966-67	New York Rangers	48	3	4	7	11	....	....	....	....	....
1967-68	Oakland Seals	52	21	19	40	32	....	....	....	....	....
1968-69	Oakland Seals	67	25	36	61	68	7	0	3	3	4
1969-70	Oakland Seals	69	15	29	44	14	4	0	1	1	2
1970-71	California Seals	74	18	17	35	41	....	....	....	....	....
1971-72	Pittsburgh Penguins	12	2	0	2	6	....	....	....	....	....
	NHL Totals	**729**	**168**	**234**	**402**	**395**	**42**	**3**	**10**	**13**	**41**

• Brother of Ernie

Played in NHL All-Star Game (1959, 1960, 1969)

Traded to **NY Rangers** by **Montreal** with the loan of Jean-Guy Morissette for remainder of 1964-65 season for Dick Duff and Dave McComb, December 22, 1964. Claimed by **California** (Oakland) from **NY Rangers** in Expansion Draft, June 6, 1967. Traded to **Pittsburgh** by **California** for cash, September 7, 1971. Traded to **Detroit** by **Pittsburgh** for cash, November 22, 1971.

HICKE, Ernie

Left wing. Shoots left. 5'11", 185 lbs. Born, Regina, Sask., November 7, 1947.

Season	Club	REGULAR SEASON GP	G	A	Pts	PIM	PLAYOFFS GP	G	A	Pts	PIM
1970-71	California Seals	78	22	25	47	62	....	....	....	....	....
1971-72	California Golden Seals	68	11	12	23	55	....	....	....	....	....
1972-73	Atlanta Flames	58	14	23	37	37	....	....	....	....	....
	New York Islanders	1	0	0	0	0	....	....	....	....	....
1973-74	New York Islanders	55	6	7	13	26	....	....	....	....	....

		REGULAR SEASON					PLAYOFFS				
Season	**Club**	**GP**	**G**	**A**	**Pts**	**PIM**	**GP**	**G**	**A**	**Pts**	**PIM**
1974-75	New York Islanders	20	2	6	8	40	....	....	....	....	....
	Minnesota North Stars	42	15	13	28	51	....	....	....	....	....
1975-76	Minnesota North Stars	80	23	19	42	77	....	....	....	....	....
1976-77	Minnesota North Stars	77	30	20	50	41	2	1	0	1	0
1977-78	Los Angeles Kings	41	9	15	24	18	....	....	....	....	....
	NHL Totals	**520**	**132**	**140**	**272**	**407**	**2**	**1**	**0**	**1**	**0**

• Brother of Bill

Traded to **California** by **Montreal** with Montreal's 1st round choice (Chris Oddleifson) in 1970 Amateur Draft for Francois Lacombe with cash and California's 1st round choice (Guy Lafleur) in 1971 Amateur Draft, May 22, 1970. Claimed by **Atlanta** from **California** in Expansion Draft, June 6, 1972. Traded to **NY Islanders** by **Atlanta** with future considerations (Billy MacMillan, May 29, 1973) for Arnie Brown, February 13, 1973. Traded to **Minnesota** by **NY Islanders** with Doug Rombough for Jean-Paul Parise, January 5, 1975. Signed as a free agent by **Los Angeles**, September 16, 1977.

HICKEY, Greg

Left wing. Shoots left. 5'10", 160 lbs. Born, Toronto, Ont., March 8, 1955.
(NY Rangers' 3rd choice, 48th overall, in 1975 Amateur Draft).

Season	Club	GP	G	A	Pts	PIM	GP	G	A	Pts	PIM
1977-78	New York Rangers	1	0	0	0	0	....	....	....	....	....
	NHL Totals	**1**	**0**	**0**	**0**	**0**	....	....	....	....	....

• Brother of Pat

HICKEY, Pat

Left wing. Shoots left. 6'1", 190 lbs. Born, Brantford, Ont., May 15, 1953.
(NY Rangers' 2nd choice, 30th overall, in 1973 Amateur Draft).

Season	Club	GP	G	A	Pts	PIM	GP	G	A	Pts	PIM
1975-76	New York Rangers	70	14	22	36	36	....	....	....	....	....
1976-77	New York Rangers	80	23	17	40	35	....	....	....	....	....
1977-78	New York Rangers	80	40	33	73	47	3	2	0	2	0
1978-79	New York Rangers	80	34	41	75	56	18	1	7	8	6
1979-80	New York Rangers	7	2	2	4	10	....	....	....	....	....
	Colorado Rockies	24	7	9	16	10	....	....	....	....	....
	Toronto Maple Leafs	45	22	16	38	16	3	0	0	0	2
1980-81	Toronto Maple Leafs	72	16	33	49	49	2	0	0	0	0
1981-82	Toronto Maple Leafs	1	0	0	0	0	....	....	....	....	....
	New York Rangers	53	15	14	29	32	....	....	....	....	....
	Quebec Nordiques	7	0	1	1	4	15	1	3	4	21
1982-83	St. Louis Blues	1	0	0	0	0	....	....	....	....	....
1983-84	St. Louis Blues	69	9	11	20	24	11	1	1	2	6
1984-85	St. Louis Blues	57	10	13	23	32	3	0	0	0	2
	NHL Totals	**646**	**192**	**212**	**404**	**351**	**55**	**5**	**11**	**16**	**37**

• Brother of Greg

Traded to **Colorado** by **NY Rangers** with Lucien DeBlois, Mike McEwen, Dean Turner and future considerations (Bobby Crawford, January 15, 1980) for Barry Beck, November 2, 1979. Traded to **Toronto** by **Colorado** with Wilf Paiement for Lanny McDonald and Joel Quenneville, December 29, 1979. Traded to **NY Rangers** by **Toronto** for NY Rangers' 5th round choice (Sylvain Charland) in 1982 Entry Draft, October 16, 1981. Traded to **Quebec** by **NY Rangers** to complete transaction that sent Robbie Ftorek to NY Rangers (December 30, 1981), March 8, 1982. Traded to **St. Louis** by **Quebec** for Rick Lapointe, August 4, 1982.

HICKS, Alex

Left wing. Shoots left. 6', 190 lbs. Born, Calgary, Alta., September 4, 1969.

Season	Club	GP	G	A	Pts	PIM	GP	G	A	Pts	PIM
1995-96	Mighty Ducks of Anaheim	64	10	11	21	37	....	....	....	....	....
1996-97	Mighty Ducks of Anaheim	18	2	6	8	14	....	....	....	....	....
	Pittsburgh Penguins	55	5	15	20	76	5	0	1	1	2
1997-98	Pittsburgh Penguins	58	7	13	20	54	6	0	0	0	2
1998-99	San Jose Sharks	4	0	1	1	4	....	....	....	....	....
	Florida Panthers	51	0	6	6	58	....	....	....	....	....
99-2000	Florida Panthers	8	1	2	3	4	4	0	1	1	4
	NHL Totals	**258**	**25**	**54**	**79**	**247**	**15**	**0**	**2**	**2**	**8**

• Son of Wayne

Signed as a free agent by **Anaheim**, August 17, 1995. Traded to **Pittsburgh** by **Anaheim** with Fredrik Olausson for Shawn Antoski and Dmitri Mironov, November 19, 1996. Signed as a free agent by **San Jose**, October, 1998. Traded to **Florida** by **San Jose** with San Jose's 5th round choice (later traded to NY Islanders – NY Islanders selected Adam Johnson) in 1999 Entry Draft for Jeff Norton, November 11, 1998.

HICKS, Doug

Defense. Shoots left. 6', 185 lbs. Born, Cold Lake, Alta., May 28, 1955.
(Minnesota's 1st choice, 6th overall, in 1974 Amateur Draft).

Season	Club	GP	G	A	Pts	PIM	GP	G	A	Pts	PIM
1974-75	Minnesota North Stars	80	6	12	18	51	....	....	....	....	....
1975-76	Minnesota North Stars	80	5	13	18	54	....	....	....	....	....
1976-77	Minnesota North Stars	79	5	14	19	68	2	0	0	0	7
1977-78	Minnesota North Stars	61	2	9	11	51	....	....	....	....	....
	Chicago Black Hawks	13	1	7	8	2	4	1	0	1	2
1978-79	Chicago Black Hawks	44	1	8	9	15	....	....	....	....	....
1979-80	Edmonton Oilers	78	9	31	40	52	3	0	0	0	2
1980-81	Edmonton Oilers	59	5	16	21	76	9	1	1	2	4
1981-82	Edmonton Oilers	49	3	20	23	55	....	....	....	....	....
	Washington Capitals	12	0	1	1	11	....	....	....	....	....
1982-83	Washington Capitals	6	0	0	0	7	....	....	....	....	....
	NHL Totals	**561**	**37**	**131**	**168**	**442**	**18**	**2**	**1**	**3**	**15**

• Brother of Glenn

Traded to **Chicago** by **Minnesota** with Minnesota's 3rd round choice (Marcel Frere) in 1980 Entry Draft for Eddie Mio and future considerations (Pierre Plante, May 4, 1978), March 14, 1978. Claimed by **Edmonton** from **Chicago** in Expansion Draft, June 13, 1979. Traded to **Washington** by **Edmonton** for Todd Bidner, March 9, 1982.

HICKS, Glenn

Left wing. Shoots left. 5'10", 177 lbs. Born, Red Deer, Alta., August 28, 1958.
(Detroit's 3rd choice, 28th overall, in 1978 Amateur Draft).

		REGULAR SEASON					PLAYOFFS				
Season	**Club**	**GP**	**G**	**A**	**Pts**	**PIM**	**GP**	**G**	**A**	**Pts**	**PIM**
1979-80	Detroit Red Wings	50	1	2	3	43	....	....	....	....	....
1980-81	Detroit Red Wings	58	5	10	15	84	....	....	....	....	....
	NHL Totals	**108**	**6**	**12**	**18**	**127**	....	....	....	....	....

• Brother of Doug

Reclaimed by **Detroit** from **Winnipeg** prior to Expansion Draft, June 9, 1979. Signed as a free agent by **Minnesota**, September 2, 1983.

HICKS, Henry

Defense. Shoots left. 5'7", 170 lbs. Born, Sillery, Que., December 10, 1900.

Season	Club	GP	G	A	Pts	PIM	GP	G	A	Pts	PIM
1928-29	Montreal Maroons	44	2	0	2	27	....	....	....	....	....
1929-30	Detroit Cougars	30	3	2	5	35	....	....	....	....	....
1930-31	Detroit Falcons	22	2	0	2	10	....	....	....	....	....
	NHL Totals	**96**	**7**	**2**	**9**	**72**	....	....	....	....	....

Traded to **Mtl. Maroons** by **Stratford** (Can-Pro) for cash, April 23, 1928. Traded to **Detroit** by **Mtl. Maroons** for $8,000, September 30, 1929. Traded to **London** (IHL) by **Detroit** for Leroy Goldsworthy, January 12, 1931.

HICKS, Wayne

Right wing. Shoots right. 5'11", 185 lbs. Born, Aberdeen, WA, April 9, 1937.

Season	Club	GP	G	A	Pts	PIM	GP	G	A	Pts	PIM
1959-60	Chicago Black Hawks	....	....	....	....	....	1	0	1	1	0
1960-61 ♦	Chicago Black Hawks	1	0	0	0	0	1	0	0	0	2
1962-63	Boston Bruins	65	7	9	16	14	....	....	....	....	....
1963-64	Montreal Canadiens	2	0	0	0	0	....	....	....	....	....
1967-68	Philadelphia Flyers	32	2	7	9	6	....	....	....	....	....
	Pittsburgh Penguins	15	4	7	11	2	....	....	....	....	....
	NHL Totals	**115**	**13**	**23**	**36**	**22**	**2**	**0**	**1**	**1**	**2**

• Father of Alex

Traded to **Montreal** by **Chicago** for Al MacNeil, May 30, 1962. Claimed by **Boston** from **Montreal** in Intra-League Draft, June 5, 1962. Traded to **Montreal** by **Boston** for cash, September 28, 1963. NHL rights transferred to **Philadelphia** after NHL club purchased **Quebec** (AHL) franchise, May 8, 1967. Traded to **Pittsburgh** by **Philadelphia** for Art Stratton, February 27, 1968.

HIDI, Andre

Left wing. Shoots left. 6'2", 205 lbs. Born, Toronto, Ont., June 5, 1960.
(Colorado's 7th choice, 148th overall, in 1980 Entry Draft).

Season	Club	GP	G	A	Pts	PIM	GP	G	A	Pts	PIM
1983-84	Washington Capitals	1	0	0	0	0	2	0	0	0	0
1984-85	Washington Capitals	6	2	1	3	9	....	....	....	....	....
	NHL Totals	**7**	**2**	**1**	**3**	**9**	**2**	**0**	**0**	**0**	**0**

Signed as a free agent by **Washington**, March 29, 1984.

HIEMER, Uli

Defense. Shoots left. 6'1", 190 lbs. Born, Fussen, West Germany, September 21, 1962.
(Colorado's 3rd choice, 48th overall, in 1981 Entry Draft).

Season	Club	GP	G	A	Pts	PIM	GP	G	A	Pts	PIM
1984-85	New Jersey Devils	53	5	24	29	70	....	....	....	....	....
1985-86	New Jersey Devils	50	8	16	24	61	....	....	....	....	....
1986-87	New Jersey Devils	40	6	14	20	45	....	....	....	....	....
	NHL Totals	**143**	**19**	**54**	**73**	**176**	....	....	....	....	....

Transferred to **New Jersey** after **Colorado** franchise relocated, June 30, 1982.

HIGGINS, Matt

Center. Shoots left. 6'2", 190 lbs. Born, Calgary, Alta., October 29, 1977.
(Montreal's 1st choice, 18th overall, in 1996 Entry Draft).

Season	Club	GP	G	A	Pts	PIM	GP	G	A	Pts	PIM
1997-98	Montreal Canadiens	1	0	0	0	0	....	....	....	....	....
1998-99	Montreal Canadiens	25	1	0	1	0	....	....	....	....	....
99-2000	Montreal Canadiens	25	0	2	2	4	....	....	....	....	....
2000-01	Montreal Canadiens	6	0	0	0	2	....	....	....	....	....
	NHL Totals	**57**	**1**	**2**	**3**	**6**	....	....	....	....	....

HIGGINS, Paul

Right wing. Shoots right. 6'1", 195 lbs. Born, St. John, N.B., January 13, 1962.
(Toronto's 10th choice, 200th overall, in 1980 Entry Draft).

Season	Club	GP	G	A	Pts	PIM	GP	G	A	Pts	PIM
1981-82	Toronto Maple Leafs	3	0	0	0	17	....	....	....	....	....
1982-83	Toronto Maple Leafs	22	0	0	0	135	1	0	0	0	0
	NHL Totals	**25**	**0**	**0**	**0**	**152**	**1**	**0**	**0**	**0**	**0**

HIGGINS, Tim

Right wing. 6', 185 lbs. Born, Ottawa, Ont., February 7, 1958.
(Chicago's 1st choice, 10th overall, in 1978 Amateur Draft).

Season	Club	GP	G	A	Pts	PIM	GP	G	A	Pts	PIM
1978-79	Chicago Black Hawks	36	7	16	23	30	4	0	0	0	0
1979-80	Chicago Black Hawks	74	13	12	25	50	7	0	3	3	10
1980-81	Chicago Black Hawks	78	24	35	59	86	3	0	0	0	0
1981-82	Chicago Black Hawks	74	20	30	50	85	12	3	1	4	15
1982-83	Chicago Black Hawks	64	14	9	23	63	13	1	3	4	10
1983-84	Chicago Black Hawks	32	1	4	5	21	....	....	....	....	....
	New Jersey Devils	37	18	10	28	27	....	....	....	....	....
1984-85	New Jersey Devils	71	19	29	48	30	....	....	....	....	....
1985-86	New Jersey Devils	59	9	17	26	47	....	....	....	....	....
1986-87	Detroit Red Wings	77	12	14	26	124	12	0	1	1	16
1987-88	Detroit Red Wings	62	12	13	25	94	13	1	0	1	26

Season	Club	REGULAR SEASON GP	G	A	Pts	PIM	PLAYOFFS GP	G	A	Pts	PIM
1988-89	Detroit Red Wings	42	5	9	14	62	1	0	0	0	0
	NHL Totals	**706**	**154**	**198**	**352**	**719**	**65**	**5**	**8**	**13**	**77**

Traded to **New Jersey** by **Chicago** for Jeff Larmer, January 11, 1984. Traded to **Detroit** by **New Jersey** for Claude Loiselle, June 25, 1986.

HILBERT, Andy

Center/Left wing. Shoots left. 5'11", 190 lbs. Born, Howell, MI, February 6, 1981.
(Boston's 3rd choice, 37th overall, in 2000 Entry Draft).

Season	Club	GP	G	A	Pts	PIM	GP	G	A	Pts	PIM
2001-02	Boston Bruins	6	1	0	1	2	....	....	....	....	....
2002-03	Boston Bruins	14	0	3	3	7	....	....	....	....	....
	NHL Totals	**20**	**1**	**3**	**4**	**9**	....	....	....	....	....

HILDEBRAND, Ike

Right wing. Shoots right. 5'7", 147 lbs. Born, Winnipeg, Man., May 27, 1927.

Season	Club	GP	G	A	Pts	PIM	GP	G	A	Pts	PIM
1953-54	New York Rangers	31	6	7	13	12	....	....	....	....	....
	Chicago Black Hawks	7	1	4	5	4	....	....	....	....	....
1954-55	Chicago Black Hawks	3	0	0	0	0	....	....	....	....	....
	NHL Totals	**41**	**7**	**11**	**18**	**16**	....	....	....	....	....

Traded to **Vancouver** (WHL) by **NY Rangers** for cash, January 7, 1954. Traded to **Chicago** by **Vancouver** (WHL) for cash, January 20, 1954. Traded to **Montreal** by **Chicago** with future considerations for Lorne Davis, October 13, 1954.

HILL, Al

Center. Shoots left. 6'1", 175 lbs. Born, Nanaimo, B.C., April 22, 1955.

Season	Club	GP	G	A	Pts	PIM	GP	G	A	Pts	PIM
1976-77	Philadelphia Flyers	9	2	4	6	27	....	....	....	....	....
1977-78	Philadelphia Flyers	3	0	0	0	2	....	....	....	....	....
1978-79	Philadelphia Flyers	31	5	11	16	28	7	1	0	1	2
1979-80	Philadelphia Flyers	61	16	10	26	53	19	3	5	8	19
1980-81	Philadelphia Flyers	57	10	15	25	45	12	2	4	6	18
1981-82	Philadelphia Flyers	41	6	13	19	58	3	0	0	0	0
1986-87	Philadelphia Flyers	7	0	2	2	4	9	2	1	3	0
1987-88	Philadelphia Flyers	12	1	0	1	10	1	0	1	1	4
	NHL Totals	**221**	**40**	**55**	**95**	**227**	**51**	**8**	**11**	**19**	**43**

Signed as a free agent by **Philadelphia**, October 22, 1976. Signed as a free agent by **Edmonton**, November 10, 1982. Signed as a free agent by **Philadelphia**, October 8, 1984.

HILL, Brian

Right wing. Shoots right. 6', 175 lbs. Born, Regina, Sask., January 12, 1957.
(Atlanta's 3rd choice, 31st overall, in 1977 Amateur Draft).

Season	Club	GP	G	A	Pts	PIM	GP	G	A	Pts	PIM
1979-80	Hartford Whalers	19	1	1	2	4	....	....	....	....	....
	NHL Totals	**19**	**1**	**1**	**2**	**4**	....	....	....	....	....

Claimed by **Hartford** from **Atlanta** in Expansion Draft, June 13, 1979.

HILL, Mel

Right wing. Shoots right. 5'10", 175 lbs. Born, Glenboro, Man., February 15, 1914.

Season	Club	GP	G	A	Pts	PIM	GP	G	A	Pts	PIM
1937-38	Boston Bruins	6	2	0	2	2	1	0	0	0	0
1938-39 ♦	Boston Bruins	46	10	10	20	16	12	6	3	9	12
1939-40	Boston Bruins	38	9	11	20	19	3	0	0	0	0
1940-41 ♦	Boston Bruins	41	5	4	9	4	8	1	1	2	0
1941-42	Brooklyn Americans	47	14	23	37	10	....	....	....	....	....
1942-43	Toronto Maple Leafs	49	17	27	44	47	6	3	0	3	0
1943-44	Toronto Maple Leafs	17	9	10	19	6	....	....	....	....	....
1944-45 ♦	Toronto Maple Leafs	45	18	17	35	14	13	2	3	5	6
1945-46	Toronto Maple Leafs	35	5	7	12	10	....	....	....	....	....
	NHL Totals	**324**	**89**	**109**	**198**	**128**	**43**	**12**	**7**	**19**	**18**

Signed as a free agent by **Boston**, October 26, 1937. Traded to **Brooklyn** by **Boston** for cash, June 27, 1941. Rights transferred to **Toronto** from **Brooklyn** in Special Dispersal Draw, October 9, 1942. • Missed remainder of 1943-44 season recovering from broken ankle suffered in game vs. Detroit, December 16, 1943.

HILL, Sean

Defense. Shoots right. 6', 203 lbs. Born, Duluth, MN, February 14, 1970.
(Montreal's 9th choice, 167th overall, in 1988 Entry Draft).

Season	Club	GP	G	A	Pts	PIM	GP	G	A	Pts	PIM
1990-91	Montreal Canadiens	....	....	....	....	....	1	0	0	0	0
1991-92	Montreal Canadiens	....	....	....	....	....	4	1	0	1	2
1992-93 ♦	Montreal Canadiens	31	2	6	8	54	3	0	0	0	4
1993-94	Mighty Ducks of Anaheim	68	7	20	27	78	....	....	....	....	....
1994-95	Ottawa Senators	45	1	14	15	30	....	....	....	....	....
1995-96	Ottawa Senators	80	7	14	21	94	....	....	....	....	....
1996-97	Ottawa Senators	5	0	0	0	4	....	....	....	....	....
1997-98	Ottawa Senators	13	1	1	2	6	....	....	....	....	....
	Carolina Hurricanes	42	0	5	5	48	....	....	....	....	....
1998-99	Carolina Hurricanes	54	0	10	10	48	....	....	....	....	....
99-2000	Carolina Hurricanes	62	13	31	44	59	....	....	....	....	....
2000-01	St. Louis Blues	48	1	10	11	51	15	0	1	1	12
2001-02	St. Louis Blues	23	0	3	3	28	....	....	....	....	....
	Carolina Hurricanes	49	7	23	30	61	23	4	4	8	20
2002-03	Carolina Hurricanes	82	5	24	29	141	....	....	....	....	....
	NHL Totals	**602**	**44**	**161**	**205**	**702**	**46**	**5**	**5**	**10**	**38**

Claimed by **Anaheim** from **Montreal** in Expansion Draft, June 24, 1993. Traded to **Ottawa** by **Anaheim** with Anaheim's 9th round choice (Frederic Cassivi) in 1994 Entry Draft for Ottawa's 3rd round choice (later traded to Tampa Bay – Tampa Bay selected Vadim Epanchintsev) in 1994 Entry Draft, June 29, 1994. • Missed remainder of 1996-97 season recovering from knee injury suffered in game vs. New Jersey, October 18, 1996. Traded to **Carolina** by **Ottawa** for Chris Murray, November 18, 1997. Signed as a free agent by **St. Louis**, July 1, 2000. Traded to **Carolina** by **St. Louis** for Steve Halko and Carolina's 4th round choice (later traded to Atlanta – Atlanta selected Lane Manson) in 2002 Entry Draft, December 5, 2001.

HILLER, Dutch

Left wing. Shoots left. 5'8", 170 lbs. Born, Berlin, Ont., May 11, 1915.

Season	Club	GP	G	A	Pts	PIM	GP	G	A	Pts	PIM
1937-38	New York Rangers	8	0	1	1	2	1	0	0	0	0
1938-39	New York Rangers	48	10	19	29	22	7	1	0	1	9
1939-40 ♦	New York Rangers	48	13	18	31	57	12	2	4	6	2
1940-41	New York Rangers	44	8	10	18	20	3	0	0	0	0
1941-42	Detroit Red Wings	7	0	0	0	0	....	....	....	....	....
	Boston Bruins	43	7	10	17	19	5	0	1	1	0
1942-43	Boston Bruins	3	0	0	0	0	....	....	....	....	....
	Montreal Canadiens	39	8	6	14	4	5	1	0	1	4
1943-44	New York Rangers	50	18	22	40	15	....	....	....	....	....
1944-45	Montreal Canadiens	48	20	16	36	20	6	1	1	2	4
1945-46 ♦	Montreal Canadiens	45	7	11	18	4	9	4	2	6	2
	NHL Totals	**383**	**91**	**113**	**204**	**163**	**48**	**9**	**8**	**17**	**21**

Signed as a free agent by **NY Rangers**, February 24, 1938. Claimed on waivers by **Detroit** from **NY Rangers**, April 8, 1941. Traded to **Boston** by **Detroit** with $5,000 for Pat McReavy, November 24, 1941. Traded to **Montreal** by **Boston** for cash, August 15, 1942. Loaned to **NY Rangers** by **Montreal** with John Mahaffy, Fern Gauthier, Charlie Sands and future considerations (Tony Demers, December, 1943) for the loan of Phil Watson, October 27, 1943. Traded to **Toronto** (Pittsburgh-AHL) by **Montreal** (Buffalo-AHL) with Vic Lynn for John Mahaffy and Gerry Brown, September 21, 1946.

HILLER, Jim

Right wing. Shoots right. 6', 190 lbs. Born, Port Alberni, B.C., May 15, 1969.
(Los Angeles' 10th choice, 207th overall, in 1989 Entry Draft).

Season	Club	GP	G	A	Pts	PIM	GP	G	A	Pts	PIM
1992-93	Los Angeles Kings	40	6	6	12	90	....	....	....	....	....
	Detroit Red Wings	21	2	6	8	19	2	0	0	0	4
1993-94	New York Rangers	2	0	0	0	7	....	....	....	....	....
	NHL Totals	**63**	**8**	**12**	**20**	**116**	**2**	**0**	**0**	**0**	**4**

Traded to **Detroit** by **Los Angeles** with Paul Coffey and Sylvain Couturier for Jimmy Carson, Marc Potvin and Gary Shuchuk, January 29, 1993. Claimed on waivers by **NY Rangers** from **Detroit**, October 12, 1993.

HILLIER, Randy

Defense. Shoots left. 6'1", 192 lbs. Born, Toronto, Ont., March 30, 1960.
(Boston's 4th choice, 102nd overall, in 1980 Entry Draft).

Season	Club	GP	G	A	Pts	PIM	GP	G	A	Pts	PIM
1981-82	Boston Bruins	25	0	8	8	29	8	0	1	1	16
1982-83	Boston Bruins	70	0	10	10	99	3	0	0	0	4
1983-84	Boston Bruins	69	3	12	15	125	....	....	....	....	....
1984-85	Pittsburgh Penguins	45	2	19	21	56	....	....	....	....	....
1985-86	Pittsburgh Penguins	28	0	3	3	53	....	....	....	....	....
1986-87	Pittsburgh Penguins	55	4	8	12	97	....	....	....	....	....
1987-88	Pittsburgh Penguins	55	1	12	13	144	....	....	....	....	....
1988-89	Pittsburgh Penguins	68	1	23	24	141	9	0	1	1	49
1989-90	Pittsburgh Penguins	61	3	12	15	71	....	....	....	....	....
1990-91 ♦	Pittsburgh Penguins	31	2	2	4	32	8	0	0	0	24
1991-92	New York Islanders	8	0	0	0	11	....	....	....	....	....
	Buffalo Sabres	28	0	1	1	48	....	....	....	....	....
	NHL Totals	**543**	**16**	**110**	**126**	**906**	**28**	**0**	**2**	**2**	**93**

Traded to **Pittsburgh** by **Boston** for Pittsburgh's 4th round choice (later traded to Quebec – Quebec selected Peter Massey) in 1985 Entry Draft, October 15, 1984. Signed as a free agent by **NY Islanders**, June 30, 1984. Traded to **Buffalo** by **NY Islanders** with Pat LaFontaine, Randy Wood and NY Islanders' 4th round choice (Dean Melanson) in 1992 Entry Draft for Pierre Turgeon, Uwe Krupp, Benoit Hogue and Dave McLlwain, October 25, 1991.

HILLMAN, Floyd

Defense. Shoots left. 5'11", 170 lbs. Born, Ruthven, Ont., November 19, 1933.

Season	Club	GP	G	A	Pts	PIM	GP	G	A	Pts	PIM
1956-57	Boston Bruins	6	0	0	0	10	....	....	....	....	....
	NHL Totals	**6**	**0**	**0**	**0**	**10**	....	....	....	....	....

• Brother of Larry and Wayne

Traded to **Boston** by **Victoria** (WHL) for Arnott Whitney, December, 1955.

HILLMAN, Larry

Defense. Shoots left. 6', 185 lbs. Born, Kirkland Lake, Ont., February 5, 1937.

Season	Club	GP	G	A	Pts	PIM	GP	G	A	Pts	PIM
1954-55 ♦	Detroit Red Wings	6	0	0	0	2	3	0	0	0	0
1955-56	Detroit Red Wings	47	0	3	3	53	10	0	1	1	6
1956-57	Detroit Red Wings	16	1	2	3	4	....	....	....	....	....
1957-58	Boston Bruins	70	3	19	22	60	11	0	2	2	6
1958-59	Boston Bruins	55	3	10	13	19	7	0	1	1	0
1959-60	Boston Bruins	2	0	1	1	2	....	....	....	....	....
1960-61	Toronto Maple Leafs	62	3	10	13	59	5	0	0	0	0
1961-62 ♦	Toronto Maple Leafs	5	0	0	0	4	....	....	....	....	....
1962-63 ♦	Toronto Maple Leafs	5	0	0	0	2	....	....	....	....	....
1963-64 ♦	Toronto Maple Leafs	33	0	4	4	31	11	0	0	0	2
1964-65	Toronto Maple Leafs	2	0	0	0	2	....	....	....	....	....
1965-66	Toronto Maple Leafs	48	3	25	28	34	4	1	1	2	6

		REGULAR SEASON					PLAYOFFS				
Season	Club	GP	G	A	Pts	PIM	GP	G	A	Pts	PIM
1966-67 ◆	Toronto Maple Leafs	55	4	19	23	40	12	1	2	3	0
1967-68	Toronto Maple Leafs	55	3	17	20	13	....	....	....	....	....
1968-69	Minnesota North Stars	12	1	5	6	0	....	....	....	....	....
◆	Montreal Canadiens	25	0	5	5	17	1	0	0	0	0
1969-70	Philadelphia Flyers	76	5	26	31	73	....	....	....	....	....
1970-71	Philadelphia Flyers	73	3	13	16	39	4	0	2	2	2
1971-72	Los Angeles Kings	22	1	2	3	11	....	....	....	....	....
	Buffalo Sabres	43	1	11	12	58	....	....	....	....	....
1972-73	Buffalo Sabres	78	5	24	29	56	6	0	0	0	8
	NHL Totals	**790**	**36**	**196**	**232**	**579**	**74**	**2**	**9**	**11**	**30**

• Brother of Floyd and Wayne

Played in NHL All-Star Game (1955, 1962, 1963, 1964, 1968)

Claimed by **Chicago** from **Detroit** in Intra-League Draft, June 5, 1957. Claimed on waivers by **Boston** from **Chicago**, October 14, 1957. Claimed by **Toronto** from **Boston** in Intra-League Draft, June 8, 1960. Claimed by **NY Rangers** from **Toronto** in Intra-League Draft, June 12, 1968. Claimed by **Minnesota** from **NY Rangers** in Intra-League Draft, June 12, 1968. Claimed on waivers by **Pittsburgh** from **Minnesota**, November 22, 1968. Traded to **Montreal** by **Pittsburgh** for Jean-Guy Lagace and cash, November 22, 1968. Claimed by **Philadelphia** from **Montreal** in Intra-League Draft, June 11, 1969. Traded to **Los Angeles** by **Philadelphia** for Larry Mickey, June 13, 1971. Traded to **Buffalo** by **Los Angeles** with Mike Byers for Doug Barrie and Mike Keeler, December 16, 1971.

HILLMAN, Wayne

Defense. Shoots right. 6'1", 205 lbs. Born, Kirkland Lake, Ont., November 13, 1938.

Season	Club	GP	G	A	Pts	PIM	GP	G	A	Pts	PIM
1960-61 ◆	Chicago Black Hawks	....	....	....	....	....	1	0	0	0	0
1961-62	Chicago Black Hawks	19	0	2	2	14	....	....	....	....	....
1962-63	Chicago Black Hawks	67	3	5	8	74	6	0	2	2	2
1963-64	Chicago Black Hawks	59	1	4	5	51	7	0	1	1	15
1964-65	Chicago Black Hawks	19	0	1	1	8	....	....	....	....	....
	New York Rangers	22	1	7	8	26	....	....	....	....	....
1965-66	New York Rangers	68	3	17	20	70	....	....	....	....	....
1966-67	New York Rangers	67	2	12	14	43	4	0	0	0	2
1967-68	New York Rangers	62	0	5	5	46	2	0	0	0	0
1968-69	Minnesota North Stars	50	0	8	8	32	....	....	....	....	....
1969-70	Philadelphia Flyers	68	3	5	8	69	....	....	....	....	....
1970-71	Philadelphia Flyers	69	5	7	12	47	....	....	....	....	....
1971-72	Philadelphia Flyers	47	0	3	3	21	....	....	....	....	....
1972-73	Philadelphia Flyers	74	0	10	10	33	8	0	0	0	0
	NHL Totals	**691**	**18**	**86**	**104**	**534**	**28**	**0**	**3**	**3**	**19**

• Brother of Floyd and Larry

Traded to **NY Rangers** by **Chicago** with Doug Robinson and John Brenneman for Camille Henry, Don Johns, Billy Taylor and Wally Chevrier, February 4, 1965. Traded to **Minnesota** by **NY Rangers** with Dan Seguin and Joey Johnston for Dave Balon, June 12, 1968. Traded to **Philadelphia** by **Minnesota** for John Miszuk, May 14, 1969.

HILWORTH, John

Defense. Shoots right. 6'4", 205 lbs. Born, Jasper, Alta., May 23, 1957.
(Detroit's 3rd choice, 55th overall, in 1977 Amateur Draft).

Season	Club	GP	G	A	Pts	PIM	GP	G	A	Pts	PIM
1977-78	Detroit Red Wings	5	0	0	0	12	....	....	....	....	....
1978-79	Detroit Red Wings	37	1	1	2	66	....	....	....	....	....
1979-80	Detroit Red Wings	15	0	0	0	11	....	....	....	....	....
	NHL Totals	**57**	**1**	**1**	**2**	**89**	....	....	....	....	....

Claimed on waivers by **Edmonton** from **Detroit**, March, 1980.

HIMES, Normie

Center. Shoots right. 5'9", 145 lbs. Born, Galt, Ont., April 13, 1903.

Season	Club	GP	G	A	Pts	PIM	GP	G	A	Pts	PIM
1926-27	New York Americans	42	9	2	11	14	....	....	....	....	....
1927-28	New York Americans	44	14	5	19	22	....	....	....	....	....
1928-29	New York Americans	44	10	0	10	25	2	0	0	0	0
1929-30	New York Americans	44	28	22	50	15	....	....	....	....	....
1930-31	New York Americans	44	15	9	24	18	....	....	....	....	....
1931-32	New York Americans	48	7	21	28	9	....	....	....	....	....
1932-33	New York Americans	48	9	25	34	12	....	....	....	....	....
1933-34	New York Americans	48	9	16	25	10	....	....	....	....	....
1934-35	New York Americans	40	5	13	18	2	....	....	....	....	....
	NHL Totals	**402**	**106**	**113**	**219**	**127**	**2**	**0**	**0**	**0**	**0**

Played in NHL All-Star Game (1934)

Signed as a free agent by **NY Americans**, October 1, 1926.

HINDMARCH, Dave

Right wing. Shoots right. 5'11", 182 lbs. Born, Vancouver, B.C., October 15, 1958.
(Atlanta's 6th choice, 114th overall, in 1978 Amateur Draft).

Season	Club	GP	G	A	Pts	PIM	GP	G	A	Pts	PIM
1980-81	Calgary Flames	1	1	0	1	0	6	0	0	0	2
1981-82	Calgary Flames	9	3	0	3	0	....	....	....	....	....
1982-83	Calgary Flames	60	11	12	23	23	4	0	0	0	4
1983-84	Calgary Flames	29	6	5	11	2	....	....	....	....	....
	NHL Totals	**99**	**21**	**17**	**38**	**25**	**10**	**0**	**0**	**0**	**6**

Transferred to **Calgary** after **Atlanta** franchise relocated, June 24, 1980. • Suffered career-ending knee injury in game vs. Vancouver, December 16, 1983.

HINOTE, Dan

Right wing. Shoots right. 6', 190 lbs. Born, Leesburg, FL, January 30, 1977.
(Colorado's 9th choice, 167th overall, in 1996 Entry Draft).

Season	Club	GP	G	A	Pts	PIM	GP	G	A	Pts	PIM
99-2000	Colorado Avalanche	27	1	3	4	10	....	....	....	....	....
2000-01 ◆	Colorado Avalanche	76	5	10	15	51	23	2	4	6	21
2001-02	Colorado Avalanche	58	6	6	12	39	19	1	2	3	9
2002-03	Colorado Avalanche	60	6	4	10	49	7	1	2	3	2
	NHL Totals	**221**	**18**	**23**	**41**	**149**	**49**	**4**	**8**	**12**	**32**

HINSE, Andre

Left wing. Shoots left. 5'9", 175 lbs. Born, Trois-Rivieres, Que., April 19, 1945.

Season	Club	GP	G	A	Pts	PIM	GP	G	A	Pts	PIM
1967-68	Toronto Maple Leafs	4	0	0	0	0	....	....	....	....	....
	NHL Totals	**4**	**0**	**0**	**0**	**0**	....	....	....	....	....

Signed as a free agent by **Toronto**, September, 1966. Traded to **Vancouver** by **Toronto** (Phoenix-WHL) for Ted McCaskill and Pat Hannigan, August, 1970. Loaned to **Toronto** (Phoenix-WHL) by **Vancouver** for cash, September, 1970. Traded to **Toronto** by **Vancouver** for Doug Brindley, September 27, 1971.

HINTON, Dan

Left wing. Shoots left. 6'1", 180 lbs. Born, Toronto, Ont., May 24, 1953.
(Chicago's 5th choice, 77th overall, in 1973 Amateur Draft).

Season	Club	GP	G	A	Pts	PIM	GP	G	A	Pts	PIM
1976-77	Chicago Black Hawks	14	0	0	0	16	....	....	....	....	....
	NHL Totals	**14**	**0**	**0**	**0**	**16**	....	....	....	....	....

HIRSCH, Tom

Defense. Shoots right. 6'4", 210 lbs. Born, Minneapolis, MN, January 27, 1963.
(Minnesota's 4th choice, 33rd overall, in 1981 Entry Draft).

Season	Club	GP	G	A	Pts	PIM	GP	G	A	Pts	PIM
1983-84	Minnesota North Stars	15	1	3	4	20	12	0	0	0	6
1984-85	Minnesota North Stars	15	0	4	4	10	....	....	....	....	....
1987-88	Minnesota North Stars	1	0	0	0	0	....	....	....	....	....
	NHL Totals	**31**	**1**	**7**	**8**	**30**	**12**	**0**	**0**	**0**	**6**

• Missed entire 1985-86 and 1986-87 seasons recovering from shoulder surgery, October, 1985.

HIRSCHFELD, Bert

Left wing. Shoots left. 5'10", 165 lbs. Born, Halifax, N.S., March 1, 1929.

Season	Club	GP	G	A	Pts	PIM	GP	G	A	Pts	PIM
1949-50	Montreal Canadiens	13	1	2	3	2	5	1	0	1	0
1950-51	Montreal Canadiens	20	0	2	2	0	....	....	....	....	....
	NHL Totals	**33**	**1**	**4**	**5**	**2**	**5**	**1**	**0**	**1**	**0**

Traded to **Detroit** by **Montreal** for Gerry Couture, June 19, 1951.

HISLOP, Jamie

Right wing. Shoots right. 5'10", 180 lbs. Born, Sarnia, Ont., January 20, 1954.
(Montreal's 13th choice, 140th overall, in 1974 Amateur Draft).

Season	Club	GP	G	A	Pts	PIM	GP	G	A	Pts	PIM
1979-80	Quebec Nordiques	80	19	20	39	6	....	....	....	....	....
1980-81	Quebec Nordiques	50	19	22	41	15	....	....	....	....	....
	Calgary Flames	29	6	9	15	11	16	3	0	3	5
1981-82	Calgary Flames	80	16	25	41	35	3	0	0	0	0
1982-83	Calgary Flames	79	14	19	33	17	9	0	2	2	6
1983-84	Calgary Flames	27	1	8	9	2	....	....	....	....	....
	NHL Totals	**345**	**75**	**103**	**178**	**86**	**28**	**3**	**2**	**5**	**11**

Claimed by **Winnipeg** from **Cincinnati** (WHA) in WHA Dispersal Draft, June 22, 1979. Traded to **Quebec** by **Winnipeg** with Barry Legge for Barry Melrose, June 28, 1979. Traded to **Calgary** by **Quebec** for Dan Bouchard, January 30, 1981. • Suffered eventual career-ending eye injury in game vs. NY Islanders, December 1, 1983.

HITCHMAN, Lionel

Defense. Shoots left. 6'1", 167 lbs. Born, Toronto, Ont., November 3, 1901.

Season	Club	GP	G	A	Pts	PIM	GP	G	A	Pts	PIM
1922-23 ◆	Ottawa Senators	3	0	1	1	12	2	0	0	0	0
	Ottawa Senators (Cup)	....	....	....	....	....	*5*	*1*	*0*	*1*	*4*
1923-24	Ottawa Senators	24	2	6	8	24	2	0	0	0	4
1924-25	Ottawa Senators	12	0	0	0	2	....	....	....	....	....
	Boston Bruins	19	3	1	4	22	....	....	....	....	....
1925-26	Boston Bruins	36	7	4	11	70	....	....	....	....	....
1926-27	Boston Bruins	41	3	6	9	70	8	1	0	1	31
1927-28	Boston Bruins	44	5	3	8	87	2	0	0	0	2
1928-29 ◆	Boston Bruins	38	1	0	1	64	5	0	1	1	22
1929-30	Boston Bruins	39	2	7	9	58	6	1	0	1	14
1930-31	Boston Bruins	41	0	2	2	40	5	0	0	0	0
1931-32	Boston Bruins	48	4	3	7	36	....	....	....	....	....
1932-33	Boston Bruins	45	0	1	1	34	5	1	0	1	0
1933-34	Boston Bruins	27	1	0	1	4	....	....	....	....	....
	NHL Totals	**417**	**28**	**34**	**62**	**523**	**35**	**3**	**1**	**4**	**73**

Signed as a free agent by **Ottawa**, February 28, 1923. Traded to **Boston** by **Ottawa** for cash, January 10, 1925.

HLAVAC, Jan

Left wing. Shoots left. 6', 185 lbs. Born, Prague, Czech., September 20, 1976.
(NY Islanders' 2nd choice, 28th overall, in 1995 Entry Draft).

Season	Club	GP	G	A	Pts	PIM	GP	G	A	Pts	PIM
99-2000	New York Rangers	67	19	23	42	16	....	....	....	....	....
2000-01	New York Rangers	79	28	36	64	20	....	....	....	....	....
2001-02	Philadelphia Flyers	31	7	3	10	8	....	....	....	....	....
	Vancouver Canucks	46	9	12	21	10	5	0	1	1	0

Season	Club	REGULAR SEASON GP	G	A	Pts	PIM	PLAYOFFS GP	G	A	Pts	PIM
2002-03	Vancouver Canucks	9	1	1	2	6	....	....	....	....	....
	Carolina Hurricanes	52	9	15	24	22	....	....	....	....	....
	NHL Totals	**284**	**73**	**90**	**163**	**82**	**5**	**0**	**1**	**1**	**0**

Traded to **Calgary** by **NY Islanders** for Jorgen Jonsson, July 14, 1998. Rights traded to **NY Rangers** by **Calgary** with Calgary's 1st (Jamie Lundmark) and 3rd (later traded back to Calgary – Calgary selected Craig Andersson) round choices in 1999 Entry Draft for Marc Savard and NY Rangers' 1st round choice (Oleg Saprykin) in 1999 Entry Draft, June 26, 1999. Traded to **Philadelphia** by **NY Rangers** with Kim Johnsson, Pavel Brendl and NY Rangers' 3rd round choice (Stefan Ruzicka) in 2003 Entry Draft for Eric Lindros, August 20, 2001. Traded to **Vancouver** by **Philadelphia** with Tampa Bay's 3rd round choice (previously acquired, Vancouver selected Brett Skinner) in 2002 Entry Draft for Donald Brashear and Vancouver's 6th round choice (later traded to Columbus – Columbus selected Jaroslav Balastik) in 2002 Entry Draft, December 17, 2001. Traded to **Carolina** by **Vancouver** with Harold Druken for Darren Langdon and Marek Malik, November 1, 2002.

HLINKA, Ivan

Center. Shoots left. 6'2", 220 lbs. Born, Most, Czech., January 26, 1950.

Season	Club	GP	G	A	Pts	PIM	GP	G	A	Pts	PIM
1981-82	Vancouver Canucks	72	23	37	60	16	12	2	6	8	4
1982-83	Vancouver Canucks	65	19	44	63	12	4	1	4	5	4
	NHL Totals	**137**	**42**	**81**	**123**	**28**	**16**	**3**	**10**	**13**	**8**

Claimed in Special Czechoslovakian Entry Draft by **Winnipeg**, May 28, 1981. Rights traded to **Vancouver** by **Winnipeg** for Brent Ashton and Vancouver's 4th round choice (Tom Martin) in 1982 Entry Draft, July 15, 1981.

HLUSHKO, Todd

Center. Shoots left. 5'11", 185 lbs. Born, Toronto, Ont., February 7, 1970.
(Washington's 14th choice, 240th overall, in 1990 Entry Draft).

Season	Club	GP	G	A	Pts	PIM	GP	G	A	Pts	PIM
1993-94	Philadelphia Flyers	2	1	0	1	0	....	....	....	....	....
1994-95	Calgary Flames	2	0	1	1	2	1	0	0	0	2
1995-96	Calgary Flames	4	0	0	0	6	....	....	....	....	....
1996-97	Calgary Flames	58	7	11	18	49	....	....	....	....	....
1997-98	Calgary Flames	13	0	1	1	27	....	....	....	....	....
1998-99	Pittsburgh Penguins	....	....	....	....	....	2	0	0	0	0
	NHL Totals	**79**	**8**	**13**	**21**	**84**	**3**	**0**	**0**	**0**	**2**

Signed as a free agent by **Philadelphia**, March 7, 1994. Signed as a free agent by **Calgary**, June 17, 1994. Traded to **Pittsburgh** by **Calgary** with German Titov for Ken Wregget and Dave Roche, June 17, 1998.

HNIDY, Shane

Defense. Shoots right. 6'2", 204 lbs. Born, Neepawa, Man., November 8, 1975.
(Buffalo's 7th choice, 173rd overall, in 1994 Entry Draft).

Season	Club	GP	G	A	Pts	PIM	GP	G	A	Pts	PIM
2000-01	Ottawa Senators	52	3	2	5	84	1	0	0	0	0
2001-02	Ottawa Senators	33	1	1	2	57	12	1	1	2	12
2002-03	Ottawa Senators	67	0	8	8	130	1	0	0	0	0
	NHL Totals	**152**	**4**	**11**	**15**	**271**	**14**	**1**	**1**	**2**	**12**

Signed as a free agent by **Detroit**, August 6, 1998. Traded to **Ottawa** by **Detroit** for Ottawa's 8th round choice (Todd Jackson) in 2000 Entry Draft, June 25, 2000. • Missed majority of 2001-02 season recovering from ankle injury suffered in game vs. Boston, December 26, 2001.

HOCKING, Justin

Defense. Shoots right. 6'4", 215 lbs. Born, Stettler, Alta., January 9, 1974.
(Los Angeles' 1st choice, 39th overall, in 1992 Entry Draft).

Season	Club	GP	G	A	Pts	PIM	GP	G	A	Pts	PIM
1993-94	Los Angeles Kings	1	0	0	0	0	....	....	....	....	....
	NHL Totals	**1**	**0**	**0**	**0**	**0**	....	....	....	....	....

Claimed by **Ottawa** from **Los Angeles** in Waiver Draft, October 2, 1995. Traded to **Chicago** by **Ottawa** for Brian Felsner, August 21, 1998. Signed as a free agent by **Toronto**, July 23, 1999. Signed as a free agent by **Phoenix**, August 1, 2000.

HODGE Jr., Ken

Center/Right wing. Shoots left. 6'1", 200 lbs. Born, Windsor, Ont., April 13, 1966.
(Minnesota's 2nd choice, 46th overall, in 1984 Entry Draft).

Season	Club	GP	G	A	Pts	PIM	GP	G	A	Pts	PIM
1988-89	Minnesota North Stars	5	1	1	2	0	....	....	....	....	....
1990-91	Boston Bruins	70	30	29	59	20	15	4	6	10	6
1991-92	Boston Bruins	42	6	11	17	10	....	....	....	....	....
1992-93	Tampa Bay Lightning	25	2	7	9	2	....	....	....	....	....
	NHL Totals	**142**	**39**	**48**	**87**	**32**	**15**	**4**	**6**	**10**	**6**

• Son of Ken • NHL All-Rookie Team (1991)

Traded to **Boston** by **Minnesota** for Boston's 4th round choice (Jere Lehtinen) in 1992 Entry Draft, August 21, 1990. Traded to **Tampa Bay** by **Boston** with Matt Hervey for Darin Kimble and future considerations, September 4, 1992. Signed as a free agent by **NY Rangers**, September 2, 1993.

HODGE, Ken

Right wing. Shoots right. 6'2", 210 lbs. Born, Birmingham, England, June 25, 1944.

Season	Club	GP	G	A	Pts	PIM	GP	G	A	Pts	PIM
1964-65	Chicago Black Hawks	1	0	0	0	2	....	....	....	....	....
1965-66	Chicago Black Hawks	63	6	17	23	47	5	0	0	0	8
1966-67	Chicago Black Hawks	69	10	25	35	59	6	0	0	0	4
1967-68	Boston Bruins	74	25	31	56	31	4	3	0	3	2
1968-69	Boston Bruins	75	45	45	90	75	10	5	7	12	4
1969-70◆	Boston Bruins	72	25	29	54	87	14	3	10	13	7
1970-71	Boston Bruins	78	43	62	105	113	7	2	5	7	6
1971-72◆	Boston Bruins	60	16	40	56	81	15	9	8	17	*62
1972-73	Boston Bruins	73	37	44	81	58	5	1	0	1	7
1973-74	Boston Bruins	76	50	55	105	43	16	6	10	16	16
1974-75	Boston Bruins	72	23	43	66	90	3	1	1	2	0
1975-76	Boston Bruins	72	25	36	61	42	12	4	6	10	4
1976-77	New York Rangers	78	21	41	62	43	....	....	....	....	....
1977-78	New York Rangers	18	2	4	6	8	....	....	....	....	....
	NHL Totals	**881**	**328**	**472**	**800**	**779**	**97**	**34**	**47**	**81**	**120**

• Father of Ken • NHL First All-Star Team (1971, 1974)

Played in NHL All-Star Game (1971, 1973, 1974)

Traded to **Boston** by **Chicago** with Phil Esposito and Fred Stanfield for Gilles Marotte, Pit Martin and Jack Norris, May 15, 1967. Traded to **NY Rangers** by **Boston** for Rick Middleton, May 26, 1976.

HODGSON, Dan

Center. Shoots right. 5'10", 175 lbs. Born, Fort Vermillon, Alta., August 29, 1965.
(Toronto's 4th choice, 85th overall, in 1983 Entry Draft).

Season	Club	GP	G	A	Pts	PIM	GP	G	A	Pts	PIM
1985-86	Toronto Maple Leafs	40	13	12	25	12	....	....	....	....	....
1986-87	Vancouver Canucks	43	9	13	22	25	....	....	....	....	....
1987-88	Vancouver Canucks	8	3	7	10	2	....	....	....	....	....
1988-89	Vancouver Canucks	23	4	13	17	25	....	....	....	....	....
	NHL Totals	**114**	**29**	**45**	**74**	**64**	....	....	....	....	....

Traded to **Vancouver** by **Toronto** with Jim Benning for Rick Lanz, December 2, 1986.

HODGSON, Rick

Defense. Shoots right. 6', 175 lbs. Born, Medicine Hat, Alta., May 23, 1956.
(Atlanta's 4th choice, 46th overall, in 1976 Amateur Draft).

Season	Club	GP	G	A	Pts	PIM	GP	G	A	Pts	PIM
1979-80	Hartford Whalers	6	0	0	0	6	1	0	0	0	0
	NHL Totals	**6**	**0**	**0**	**0**	**6**	**1**	**0**	**0**	**0**	**0**

Claimed by **Hartford** from **Atlanta** in Expansion Draft, June 13, 1979.

HODGSON, Ted

Right wing. Shoots right. 5'11", 185 lbs. Born, Hobbema, Alta., June 30, 1945.

Season	Club	GP	G	A	Pts	PIM	GP	G	A	Pts	PIM
1966-67	Boston Bruins	4	0	0	0	0	....	....	....	....	....
	NHL Totals	**4**	**0**	**0**	**0**	**0**	....	....	....	....	....

Traded to **Salt Lake** (WHL) by **Boston** for cash, October 22, 1969. Traded to **NY Rangers** by **Salt Lake** (WHL) for cash, May 22, 1970. Traded to **Buffalo** by **NY Rangers** for cash, June, 1970.

HOEKSTRA, Cec

Center. Shoots left. 6', 175 lbs. Born, Winnipeg, Man., April 2, 1935.

Season	Club	GP	G	A	Pts	PIM	GP	G	A	Pts	PIM
1959-60	Montreal Canadiens	4	0	0	0	0	....	....	....	....	....
	NHL Totals	**4**	**0**	**0**	**0**	**0**	....	....	....	....	....

• Brother of Ed

Traded to **Chicago** by **Montreal** with Reggie Fleming, Ab McDonald and Bob Courcy for Terry Gray, Glen Skov, the rights to Danny Lewicki, Lorne Ferguson and Bob Bailey, June 7, 1960. Traded to **Pittsburgh** (AHL) by **Chicago** for cash, June, 1961. Traded to **Chicago** by **Pittsburgh** (AHL) for cash, September, 1962. Traded to **Boston** (San Francisco-WHL) by **Chicago** (Calgary-WHL) for Al Nicholson, January 22, 1963. • Transaction voided when Nicholson refused to report to club, January, 1963.

HOEKSTRA, Ed

Center. Shoots right. 5'11", 170 lbs. Born, Winnipeg, Man., November 4, 1937.

Season	Club	GP	G	A	Pts	PIM	GP	G	A	Pts	PIM
1967-68	Philadelphia Flyers	70	15	21	36	6	7	0	1	1	0
	NHL Totals	**70**	**15**	**21**	**36**	**6**	**7**	**0**	**1**	**1**	**0**

• Brother of Cec

Claimed by **NY Rangers** from **Chicago** (Calgary-WHL) in Inter-League Draft, June 9, 1959. Traded to **Cleveland** (AHL) by **NY Rangers** with Aldo Guidolin for Art Stratton with NY Rangers holding right of recall, June, 1959. Loaned to **California** (WHL) by **Quebec** (AHL) for the loan of Jean-Guy Morissette, January, 1967. NHL rights transferred to **Philadelphia** after NHL club purchased **Quebec** (AHL) franchise, May 8, 1967. Claimed by **Denver** (WHL) from **Philadelphia** in Reverse Draft, June 13, 1968. Traded to **Los Angeles** by **Denver** (WHL) for Jimmy Peters Jr. with Los Angeles holding right of recall, December, 1970.

HOENE, Phil

Left wing. Shoots left. 5'9", 175 lbs. Born, Duluth, MN, March 15, 1949.

Season	Club	GP	G	A	Pts	PIM	GP	G	A	Pts	PIM
1972-73	Los Angeles Kings	4	0	1	1	0	....	....	....	....	....
1973-74	Los Angeles Kings	31	2	3	5	22	....	....	....	....	....
1974-75	Los Angeles Kings	2	0	0	0	0	....	....	....	....	....
	NHL Totals	**37**	**2**	**4**	**6**	**22**	....	....	....	....	....

Signed as a free agent by **Los Angeles**, June, 1971.

HOFFINGER, Val

Defense. Shoots left. 5'6", 190 lbs. Born, Seltz, Russia, January 1, 1901.

Season	Club	GP	G	A	Pts	PIM	GP	G	A	Pts	PIM
1927-28	Chicago Black Hawks	18	0	1	1	18	....	....	....	....	....
1928-29	Chicago Black Hawks	10	0	0	0	12	....	....	....	....	....
	NHL Totals	**28**	**0**	**1**	**1**	**30**	....	....	....	....	....

Traded to **Chicago** by **Saskatoon** (PrHL) to complete transaction that sent Teddy Graham to Saskatoon (January 11, 1928), January 23, 1928. Traded to **Detroit** by **Syracuse** (IHL) for James Hughes, December 7, 1930.

HOFFMAN, Mike

Left wing. Shoots left. 5'11", 190 lbs. Born, Barrie, Ont., February 26, 1963.
(Hartford's 3rd choice, 67th overall, in 1981 Entry Draft).

Season	Club	GP	G	A	Pts	PIM	GP	G	A	Pts	PIM
1982-83	Hartford Whalers	2	0	1	1	0	....	....	....	....	....
1984-85	Hartford Whalers	1	0	0	0	0	....	....	....	....	....
1985-86	Hartford Whalers	6	1	2	3	2	....	....	....	....	....
	NHL Totals	**9**	**1**	**3**	**4**	**2**	....	....	....	....	....

HOFFMEYER, Bob

Defense. Shoots left. 6', 182 lbs. Born, Dodsland, Sask., July 27, 1955.
(Chicago's 5th choice, 79th overall, in 1975 Amateur Draft).

Season	Club	GP	G	A	Pts	PIM	GP	G	A	Pts	PIM
		REGULAR SEASON					PLAYOFFS				
1977-78	Chicago Black Hawks	5	0	1	1	12	....	....	....	....	....
1978-79	Chicago Black Hawks	6	0	2	2	5	....	....	....	....	....
1981-82	Philadelphia Flyers	57	7	20	27	142	2	0	1	1	25
1982-83	Philadelphia Flyers	35	2	11	13	40	1	0	0	0	0
1983-84	New Jersey Devils	58	4	12	16	61	....	....	....	....	....
1984-85	New Jersey Devils	37	1	6	7	65	....	....	....	....	....
	NHL Totals	**198**	**14**	**52**	**66**	**325**	**3**	**0**	**1**	**1**	**25**

Signed as a free agent by **Philadelphia**, November 22, 1981. Claimed by **Edmonton** from **Philadelphia** in Waiver Draft, October 4, 1982. Traded to **Philadelphia** by **Edmonton** for Peter Dineen, October 22, 1982. Signed as a free agent by **New Jersey**, August 15, 1983.

HOFFORD, Jim

Defense. Shoots right. 6', 190 lbs. Born, Sudbury, Ont., October 4, 1964.
(Buffalo's 8th choice, 118th overall, in 1983 Entry Draft).

Season	Club	GP	G	A	Pts	PIM	GP	G	A	Pts	PIM
1985-86	Buffalo Sabres	5	0	0	0	5	....	....	....	....	....
1986-87	Buffalo Sabres	12	0	0	0	40	....	....	....	....	....
1988-89	Los Angeles Kings	1	0	0	0	2	....	....	....	....	....
	NHL Totals	**18**	**0**	**0**	**0**	**47**	....	....	....	....	....

Claimed by **Los Angeles** from **Buffalo**, in Waiver Draft, October 3, 1988.

HOGABOAM, Bill

Center. Shoots right. 5'11", 170 lbs. Born, Swift Current, Sask., September 5, 1949.

Season	Club	GP	G	A	Pts	PIM	GP	G	A	Pts	PIM
1972-73	Atlanta Flames	2	0	0	0	0	....	....	....	....	....
	Detroit Red Wings	4	1	0	1	2	....	....	....	....	....
1973-74	Detroit Red Wings	47	18	23	41	12	....	....	....	....	....
1974-75	Detroit Red Wings	60	14	27	41	16	....	....	....	....	....
1975-76	Detroit Red Wings	50	21	16	37	30	....	....	....	....	....
	Minnesota North Stars	18	7	7	14	6	....	....	....	....	....
1976-77	Minnesota North Stars	73	10	15	25	16	2	0	0	0	0
1977-78	Minnesota North Stars	8	1	2	3	4	....	....	....	....	....
1978-79	Minnesota North Stars	10	1	1	2	0	....	....	....	....	....
	Detroit Red Wings	18	4	6	10	4	....	....	....	....	....
1979-80	Detroit Red Wings	42	3	12	15	10	....	....	....	....	....
	NHL Totals	**332**	**80**	**109**	**189**	**100**	**2**	**0**	**0**	**0**	**0**

Traded to **Atlanta** by **NY Rangers** for Bill Heindl, June 16, 1972. Traded to **Detroit** by **Atlanta** for Leon Rochefort, November 28, 1972. Traded to **Minnesota** by **Detroit** with Los Angeles' 2nd round choice (previously acquired, Minnesota selected Jim Roberts) in 1976 Amateur Draft for Dennis Hextall, February 27, 1976. Signed as a free agent by **Detroit**, February 12, 1979.

HOGANSON, Dale

Defense. Shoots left. 5'10", 190 lbs. Born, North Battleford, Sask., July 8, 1949.
(Los Angeles' 1st choice, 16th overall, in 1969 Amateur Draft).

Season	Club	GP	G	A	Pts	PIM	GP	G	A	Pts	PIM
1969-70	Los Angeles Kings	49	1	7	8	37	....	....	....	....	....
1970-71	Los Angeles Kings	70	4	10	14	52	....	....	....	....	....
1971-72	Los Angeles Kings	10	1	2	3	14	....	....	....	....	....
	Montreal Canadiens	21	0	0	0	2	....	....	....	....	....
1972-73	Montreal Canadiens	25	0	2	2	2	....	....	....	....	....
1979-80	Quebec Nordiques	77	4	36	40	31	....	....	....	....	....
1980-81	Quebec Nordiques	61	3	14	17	32	5	0	3	3	10
1981-82	Quebec Nordiques	30	0	6	6	16	6	0	0	0	2
	NHL Totals	**343**	**13**	**77**	**90**	**186**	**11**	**0**	**3**	**3**	**12**

Traded to **Montreal** by **Los Angeles** with Denis DeJordy, Noel Price and Doug Robinson for Rogie Vachon, November 4, 1971. Rights traded to **Atlanta** by **Montreal** for cash, May 29, 1973. Rights retained by **Quebec** prior to Expansion Draft, June 9, 1979.

HOGLUND, Jonas

Left wing. Shoots right. 6'3", 215 lbs. Born, Hammaro, Sweden, August 29, 1972.
(Calgary's 11th choice, 222nd overall, in 1992 Entry Draft).

Season	Club	GP	G	A	Pts	PIM	GP	G	A	Pts	PIM
1996-97	Calgary Flames	68	19	16	35	12	....	....	....	....	....
1997-98	Calgary Flames	50	6	8	14	16	....	....	....	....	....
	Montreal Canadiens	28	6	5	11	6	10	2	0	2	0
1998-99	Montreal Canadiens	74	8	10	18	16	....	....	....	....	....
99-2000	Toronto Maple Leafs	82	29	27	56	10	12	2	4	6	2
2000-01	Toronto Maple Leafs	82	23	26	49	14	10	0	0	0	4
2001-02	Toronto Maple Leafs	82	13	34	47	26	20	4	6	10	2
2002-03	Toronto Maple Leafs	79	13	19	32	12	7	0	1	1	0
	NHL Totals	**545**	**117**	**145**	**262**	**112**	**59**	**8**	**11**	**19**	**8**

Traded to **Montreal** by **Calgary** with Zarley Zalapski for Valeri Bure and Montreal's 4th round choice (Shaun Sutter) in 1998 Entry Draft, February 1, 1998. Signed as a free agent by **Toronto**, July 13, 1999.

HOGUE, Benoit

Center. Shoots left. 5'10", 194 lbs. Born, Repentigny, Que., October 28, 1966.
(Buffalo's 2nd choice, 35th overall, in 1985 Entry Draft).

Season	Club	GP	G	A	Pts	PIM	GP	G	A	Pts	PIM
1987-88	Buffalo Sabres	3	1	1	2	0	....	....	....	....	....
1988-89	Buffalo Sabres	69	14	30	44	120	5	0	0	0	17
1989-90	Buffalo Sabres	45	11	7	18	79	3	0	0	0	10
1990-91	Buffalo Sabres	76	19	28	47	76	5	3	1	4	10
1991-92	Buffalo Sabres	3	0	1	1	0	....	....	....	....	....
	New York Islanders	72	30	45	75	67	....	....	....	....	....
1992-93	New York Islanders	70	33	42	75	108	18	6	6	12	31
1993-94	New York Islanders	83	36	33	69	73	4	0	1	1	4
1994-95	New York Islanders	33	6	4	10	34	....	....	....	....	....
	Toronto Maple Leafs	12	3	3	6	0	7	0	0	0	6
1995-96	Toronto Maple Leafs	44	12	25	37	68	....	....	....	....	....
	Dallas Stars	34	7	20	27	36	....	....	....	....	....
1996-97	Dallas Stars	73	19	24	43	54	7	2	2	4	6
1997-98	Dallas Stars	53	6	16	22	35	17	4	2	6	16
1998-99	Tampa Bay Lightning	62	11	14	25	50	....	....	....	....	....
	◆ Dallas Stars	12	1	3	4	4	14	0	2	2	16
99-2000	Phoenix Coyotes	27	3	10	13	10	5	1	2	3	2
2000-01	Dallas Stars	34	3	7	10	26	7	1	0	1	6
2001-02	Dallas Stars	32	3	3	6	24	....	....	....	....	....
	Boston Bruins	17	4	4	8	9	....	....	....	....	....
	Washington Capitals	9	0	1	1	4	....	....	....	....	....
	NHL Totals	**863**	**222**	**321**	**543**	**877**	**92**	**17**	**16**	**33**	**124**

Traded to **NY Islanders** by **Buffalo** with Pierre Turgeon, Uwe Krupp and Dave McLlwain for Pat LaFontaine, Randy Hillier, Randy Wood and NY Islanders' 4th round choice (Dean Melanson) in 1992 Entry Draft, October 25, 1991. Traded to **Toronto** by **NY Islanders** with NY Islanders' 3rd round choice (Ryan Pepperall) in 1995 Entry Draft and 5th round choice (Brandon Sugden) in 1996 Entry Draft for Eric Fichaud, April 6, 1995. Traded to **Dallas** by **Toronto** with Randy Wood for Dave Gagner and Dallas' 6th round choice (Dmitri Yakushin) in 1996 Entry Draft, January 29, 1996. Signed as a free agent by **Tampa Bay**, August 19, 1998. Traded to **Dallas** by **Tampa Bay** with Tampa Bay's 6th round choice (Michal Blazek) in 2001 Entry Draft for Sergey Gusev, March 21, 1999. Signed as a free agent by **Phoenix**, February 3, 2000. Signed as a free agent by **Dallas**, January 5, 2001. Traded to **Boston** by **Dallas** for future considerations, January 12, 2002. Claimed on waivers by **Washington** from **Boston**, March 19, 2002.

HOLAN, Milos

Defense. Shoots left. 5'11", 191 lbs. Born, Bilovec, Czech., April 22, 1971.
(Philadelphia's 3rd choice, 77th overall, in 1993 Entry Draft).

Season	Club	GP	G	A	Pts	PIM	GP	G	A	Pts	PIM
1993-94	Philadelphia Flyers	8	1	1	2	4	....	....	....	....	....
1994-95	Mighty Ducks of Anaheim	25	2	8	10	14	....	....	....	....	....
1995-96	Mighty Ducks of Anaheim	16	2	2	4	24	....	....	....	....	....
	NHL Totals	**49**	**5**	**11**	**16**	**42**	....	....	....	....	....

Traded to **Anaheim** by **Philadelphia** for Anatoli Semenov, March 8, 1995.

HOLBROOK, Terry

Right wing. Shoots right. 6', 185 lbs. Born, Petrolia, Ont., July 11, 1950.
(Los Angeles' 2nd choice, 38th overall, in 1970 Amateur Draft).

Season	Club	GP	G	A	Pts	PIM	GP	G	A	Pts	PIM
1972-73	Minnesota North Stars	21	2	3	5	0	6	0	0	0	0
1973-74	Minnesota North Stars	22	1	3	4	4	....	....	....	....	....
	NHL Totals	**43**	**3**	**6**	**9**	**4**	**6**	**0**	**0**	**0**	**0**

Traded to **Minnesota** by **Los Angeles** for Wayne Schultz and the rights to Steve Sutherland, March, 1971.

HOLDEN, Josh

Center. Shoots left. 6', 190 lbs. Born, Calgary, Alta., January 18, 1978.
(Vancouver's 1st choice, 12th overall, in 1996 Entry Draft).

Season	Club	GP	G	A	Pts	PIM	GP	G	A	Pts	PIM
1998-99	Vancouver Canucks	30	2	4	6	10	....	....	....	....	....
99-2000	Vancouver Canucks	6	1	5	6	2	....	....	....	....	....
2000-01	Vancouver Canucks	10	1	0	1	0	....	....	....	....	....
2001-02	Carolina Hurricanes	8	0	0	0	2	....	....	....	....	....
2002-03	Toronto Maple Leafs	5	1	0	1	2	....	....	....	....	....
	NHL Totals	**59**	**5**	**9**	**14**	**16**	....	....	....	....	....

Claimed by **Carolina** from **Vancouver** in Waiver Draft, September 28, 2001. Claimed on waivers by **Vancouver** from **Carolina**, October 25, 2001. Traded to **Toronto** by **Vancouver** for Jeff Farkas, June 23, 2002.

HOLIK, Bobby

Center. Shoots right. 6'4", 230 lbs. Born, Jihlava, Czech., January 1, 1971.
(Hartford's 1st choice, 10th overall, in 1989 Entry Draft).

Season	Club	GP	G	A	Pts	PIM	GP	G	A	Pts	PIM
1990-91	Hartford Whalers	78	21	22	43	113	6	0	0	0	7
1991-92	Hartford Whalers	76	21	24	45	44	7	0	1	1	6
1992-93	New Jersey Devils	61	20	19	39	76	5	1	1	2	6
1993-94	New Jersey Devils	70	13	20	33	72	20	0	3	3	6
1994-95 ◆	New Jersey Devils	48	10	10	20	18	20	4	4	8	22
1995-96	New Jersey Devils	63	13	17	30	58	....	....	....	....	....
1996-97	New Jersey Devils	82	23	39	62	54	10	2	3	5	4
1997-98	New Jersey Devils	82	29	36	65	100	5	0	0	0	8
1998-99	New Jersey Devils	78	27	37	64	119	7	0	7	7	6
99-2000 ◆	New Jersey Devils	79	23	23	46	106	23	3	7	10	14
2000-01	New Jersey Devils	80	15	35	50	97	25	6	10	16	37
2001-02	New Jersey Devils	81	25	29	54	97	6	4	1	5	2
2002-03	New York Rangers	64	16	19	35	52	....	....	....	....	....
	NHL Totals	**942**	**256**	**330**	**586**	**1006**	**134**	**20**	**37**	**57**	**118**

Played in NHL All-Star Game (1998, 1999)

Traded to **New Jersey** by **Hartford** with Hartford's 2nd round choice (Jay Pandolfo) in 1993 Entry Draft for Sean Burke and Eric Weinrich, August 28, 1992. Signed as a free agent by **NY Rangers**, July 1, 2002.

HOLLAND, Jason

Defense. Shoots right. 6'3", 209 lbs. Born, Morinville, Alta., April 30, 1976.
(NY Islanders' 2nd choice, 38th overall, in 1994 Entry Draft).

Season	Club	GP	G	A	Pts	PIM	GP	G	A	Pts	PIM
1996-97	New York Islanders	4	1	0	1	0	....	....	....	....	....
1997-98	New York Islanders	8	0	0	0	4	....	....	....	....	....
1998-99	Buffalo Sabres	3	0	0	0	8	....	....	....	....	....
99-2000	Buffalo Sabres	9	0	1	1	0	1	0	0	0	0
2001-02	Los Angeles Kings	3	0	0	0	0	....	....	....	....	....

Season	Club	GP	G	A	Pts	PIM	GP	G	A	Pts	PIM
		REGULAR SEASON					PLAYOFFS				
2002-03	Los Angeles Kings	2	0	1	1	0	....	....	....	....	....
	NHL Totals	**29**	**1**	**2**	**3**	**12**	**1**	**0**	**0**	**0**	**0**

Traded to **Buffalo** by **NY Islanders** with Paul Kruse for Jason Dawe, March 24, 1998. Signed as a free agent by **Los Angeles**, August 23, 2001.

HOLLAND, Jerry

Left wing. Shoots left. 5'10", 180 lbs. Born, Beaverlodge, Alta., August 25, 1954.
(NY Rangers' 3rd choice, 50th overall, in 1974 Amateur Draft).

Season	Club	GP	G	A	Pts	PIM	GP	G	A	Pts	PIM
1974-75	New York Rangers	1	1	0	1	0	....	....	....	....	....
1975-76	New York Rangers	36	7	4	11	6	....	....	....	....	....
	NHL Totals	**37**	**8**	**4**	**12**	**6**	....	....	....	....	....

HOLLETT, Flash

Defense. Shoots left. 6', 180 lbs. Born, North Sydney, N.S., April 13, 1912.

Season	Club	GP	G	A	Pts	PIM	GP	G	A	Pts	PIM
1933-34	Toronto Maple Leafs	4	0	0	0	4	....	....	....	....	....
	Ottawa Senators	30	7	4	11	21	....	....	....	....	....
1934-35	Toronto Maple Leafs	48	10	16	26	38	7	0	0	0	6
1935-36	Toronto Maple Leafs	11	1	4	5	8	....	....	....	....	....
	Boston Bruins	6	1	2	3	2	....	....	....	....	....
1936-37	Boston Bruins	48	3	7	10	22	3	0	0	0	2
1937-38	Boston Bruins	48	4	10	14	54	3	0	1	1	0
1938-39 ♦	Boston Bruins	44	10	17	27	35	12	1	3	4	2
1939-40	Boston Bruins	44	10	18	28	18	5	1	2	3	2
1940-41 ♦	Boston Bruins	41	9	15	24	23	11	3	4	7	8
1941-42	Boston Bruins	48	19	14	33	21	5	0	1	1	2
1942-43	Boston Bruins	50	19	25	44	19	9	0	9	9	4
1943-44	Boston Bruins	25	9	7	16	4	....	....	....	....	....
	Detroit Red Wings	27	6	12	18	34	5	0	0	0	6
1944-45	Detroit Red Wings	50	20	21	41	39	14	3	4	7	6
1945-46	Detroit Red Wings	38	4	9	13	16	5	0	2	2	0
	NHL Totals	**562**	**132**	**181**	**313**	**358**	**79**	**8**	**26**	**34**	**38**

NHL Second All-Star Team (1943) • NHL First All-Star Team (1945)

Loaned to **Ottawa** by **Toronto** for remainder of 1933-34 season, January 2, 1934. Traded to **Boston** by **Toronto** for $16,000, January 15 1936. Traded to **Detroit** by **Boston** for Pat Egan, January 5, 1944. Traded to **NY Rangers** by **Detroit** for Ab DeMarco and Hank Goldup, June 19, 1946. Transaction voided when Hollett decided to retire, June, 1946.

HOLLINGER, Terry

Defense. Shoots left. 6'1", 200 lbs. Born, Regina, Sask., February 24, 1971.
(St. Louis' 7th choice, 153rd overall, in 1991 Entry Draft).

Season	Club	GP	G	A	Pts	PIM	GP	G	A	Pts	PIM
1993-94	St. Louis Blues	2	0	0	0	0	....	....	....	....	....
1994-95	St. Louis Blues	5	0	0	0	2	....	....	....	....	....
	NHL Totals	**7**	**0**	**0**	**0**	**2**	....	....	....	....	....

Signed as a free agent by **Buffalo**, August 23, 1995. Signed as a free agent by **St. Louis**, July 28, 1997.

HOLLINGWORTH, Gord

Defense. Shoots left. 5'11", 170 lbs. Born, Montreal, Que., July 24, 1933.

Season	Club	GP	G	A	Pts	PIM	GP	G	A	Pts	PIM
1954-55	Chicago Black Hawks	70	3	9	12	135	....	....	....	....	....
1955-56	Detroit Red Wings	41	0	2	2	28	3	0	0	0	2
1956-57	Detroit Red Wings	25	0	1	1	16	....	....	....	....	....
1957-58	Detroit Red Wings	27	1	2	3	22	....	....	....	....	....
	NHL Totals	**163**	**4**	**14**	**18**	**201**	**3**	**0**	**0**	**0**	**2**

Played in NHL All-Star Game (1955)

Traded to **Chicago** by **Montreal** for $15,000, October 3, 1954. Traded to **Detroit** by **Chicago** with Jerry Toppazzini, John McCormack and Dave Creighton for Tony Leswick, Glen Skov, Johnny Wilson and Benny Woit, May 28, 1955. Traded to **Cleveland** (AHL) by **Detroit** with cash for Pete Goegan, February 20, 1958.

HOLLOWAY, Bruce

Defense. Shoots left. 6', 200 lbs. Born, Revelstoke, B.C., June 27, 1963.
(Vancouver's 6th choice, 136th overall, in 1981 Entry Draft).

Season	Club	GP	G	A	Pts	PIM	GP	G	A	Pts	PIM
1984-85	Vancouver Canucks	2	0	0	0	0	....	....	....	....	....
	NHL Totals	**2**	**0**	**0**	**0**	**0**	....	....	....	....	....

HOLMES, Bill

Center. Shoots right. 6', 200 lbs. Born, Portage la Prairie, Man., March 9, 1899.

Season	Club	GP	G	A	Pts	PIM	GP	G	A	Pts	PIM
1925-26	Montreal Canadiens	9	1	0	1	2	....	....	....	....	....
1926-27	New York Americans	1	0	0	0	0	....	....	....	....	....
1929-30	New York Americans	42	5	4	9	33	....	....	....	....	....
	NHL Totals	**52**	**6**	**4**	**10**	**35**	....	....	....	....	....

Traded to **NY Americans** by **Edmonton** (WCHL) for cash, October 2, 1925. Signed as a free agent by **Montreal** after being released by NY Americans, December 25, 1925. Signed as a free agent by **NY Americans** (Niagara Falls-Can-Pro), November 1, 1926. Traded to **Kitchener** (Can-Pro) by **Niagara Falls** (Can-Pro) for cash, January 13, 1928. Traded to **London** (Can-Pro) by **Kitchener** (Can-Pro) for $1,500 and future considerations (Albert Pudas, March, 1928), January 16, 1928. Traded to **NY Americans** by **London** (Can-Pro) for Mickey Roach, October 29, 1928.

HOLMES, Chuck

Right wing. Shoots right. 6', 185 lbs. Born, Edmonton, Alta., September 21, 1934.

Season	Club	GP	G	A	Pts	PIM	GP	G	A	Pts	PIM
1958-59	Detroit Red Wings	15	0	3	3	6	....	....	....	....	....
1961-62	Detroit Red Wings	8	1	0	1	4	....	....	....	....	....
	NHL Totals	**23**	**1**	**3**	**4**	**10**	....	....	....	....	....

• Son of Lou

Traded to **Montreal** (Seattle-WHL) by **Detroit** (Pittsburgh-AHL) for Billy Carter with Detroit holding right of recall, December, 1964. Traded to **Portland** (WHL) by **Detroit** for cash, July, 1965.

HOLMES, Lou

Center/Left wing. Shoots left. 5'10", 150 lbs. Born, Rushall, England, January 29, 1911.

Season	Club	GP	G	A	Pts	PIM	GP	G	A	Pts	PIM
1931-32	Chicago Black Hawks	41	1	4	5	6	2	0	0	0	2
1932-33	Chicago Black Hawks	18	0	0	0	0	....	....	....	....	....
	NHL Totals	**59**	**1**	**4**	**5**	**6**	**2**	**0**	**0**	**0**	**2**

• Father of Chuck

Signed as a free agent by **Chicago**, October 14, 1931. Traded to **Tulsa** (AHA) by **Chicago** for cash, May, 1932. Traded to **Chicago** by **St. Paul** (AHA) for Gerry Lowrey, November 9, 1932. Traded to **Tulsa** (AHA) by **Chicago** for the rights to Norm Locking, March 7, 1933.

HOLMES, Warren

Center. Shoots left. 6'1", 195 lbs. Born, Beeton, Ont., February 18, 1957.
(Los Angeles' 2nd choice, 85th overall, in 1977 Amateur Draft).

Season	Club	GP	G	A	Pts	PIM	GP	G	A	Pts	PIM
1981-82	Los Angeles Kings	3	0	2	2	0	....	....	....	....	....
1982-83	Los Angeles Kings	39	8	16	24	7	....	....	....	....	....
1983-84	Los Angeles Kings	3	0	0	0	0	....	....	....	....	....
	NHL Totals	**45**	**8**	**18**	**26**	**7**	....	....	....	....	....

HOLMGREN, Paul

Right wing. Shoots right. 6'3", 210 lbs. Born, St. Paul, MN, December 2, 1955.
(Philadelphia's 5th choice, 108th overall, in 1975 Amateur Draft).

Season	Club	GP	G	A	Pts	PIM	GP	G	A	Pts	PIM
1975-76	Philadelphia Flyers	1	0	0	0	2	....	....	....	....	....
1976-77	Philadelphia Flyers	59	14	12	26	201	10	1	1	2	25
1977-78	Philadelphia Flyers	62	16	18	34	190	12	1	4	5	26
1978-79	Philadelphia Flyers	57	19	10	29	168	8	1	5	6	22
1979-80	Philadelphia Flyers	74	30	35	65	267	18	10	10	20	47
1980-81	Philadelphia Flyers	77	22	37	59	306	12	5	9	14	49
1981-82	Philadelphia Flyers	41	9	22	31	183	4	1	2	3	6
1982-83	Philadelphia Flyers	77	19	24	43	178	3	0	0	0	6
1983-84	Philadelphia Flyers	52	9	13	22	105	....	....	....	....	....
	Minnesota North Stars	11	2	5	7	46	12	0	1	1	6
1984-85	Minnesota North Stars	16	4	3	7	38	3	0	0	0	8
	NHL Totals	**527**	**144**	**179**	**323**	**1684**	**82**	**19**	**32**	**51**	**195**

Played in NHL All-Star Game (1981)

Traded to **Minnesota** by **Philadelphia** for the rights to Paul Guay and Minnesota's 3rd round choice (Darryl Gilmour) in 1985 Entry Draft, February 23, 1984.

HOLMSTROM, Tomas

Left wing. Shoots left. 6', 200 lbs. Born, Pitea, Sweden, January 23, 1973.
(Detroit's 9th choice, 257th overall, in 1994 Entry Draft).

Season	Club	GP	G	A	Pts	PIM	GP	G	A	Pts	PIM
1996-97 ♦	Detroit Red Wings	47	6	3	9	33	1	0	0	0	0
1997-98 ♦	Detroit Red Wings	57	5	17	22	44	22	7	12	19	16
1998-99	Detroit Red Wings	82	13	21	34	69	10	4	3	7	4
99-2000	Detroit Red Wings	72	13	22	35	43	9	3	1	4	16
2000-01	Detroit Red Wings	73	16	24	40	40	6	1	3	4	8
2001-02 ♦	Detroit Red Wings	69	8	18	26	58	23	8	3	11	8
2002-03	Detroit Red Wings	74	20	20	40	62	4	1	1	2	4
	NHL Totals	**474**	**81**	**125**	**206**	**349**	**75**	**24**	**23**	**47**	**56**

HOLOTA, John

Center. Shoots left. 5'6", 160 lbs. Born, Hamilton, Ont., February 25, 1921.

Season	Club	GP	G	A	Pts	PIM	GP	G	A	Pts	PIM
1942-43	Detroit Red Wings	12	2	0	2	0	....	....	....	....	....
1945-46	Detroit Red Wings	3	0	0	0	0	....	....	....	....	....
	NHL Totals	**15**	**2**	**0**	**2**	**0**	....	....	....	....	....

Signed as a free agent by **Detroit**, October 14, 1941. Traded to **Chicago** by **Detroit** for Bernie Strongman, September, 1946.

HOLST, Greg

Center. Shoots left. 5'10", 170 lbs. Born, Montreal, Que., February 21, 1954.
(NY Rangers' 8th choice, 139th overall, in 1974 Amateur Draft).

Season	Club	GP	G	A	Pts	PIM	GP	G	A	Pts	PIM
1975-76	New York Rangers	2	0	0	0	0	....	....	....	....	....
1976-77	New York Rangers	5	0	0	0	0	....	....	....	....	....
1977-78	New York Rangers	4	0	0	0	0	....	....	....	....	....
	NHL Totals	**11**	**0**	**0**	**0**	**0**	....	....	....	....	....

HOLT, Gary

Left wing. Shoots left. 5'9", 175 lbs. Born, Sarnia, Ont., January 1, 1952.

Season	Club	GP	G	A	Pts	PIM	GP	G	A	Pts	PIM
1973-74	California Golden Seals	1	0	0	0	0	....	....	....	....	....
1974-75	California Golden Seals	1	0	1	1	0	....	....	....	....	....
1975-76	California Golden Seals	48	6	5	11	50	....	....	....	....	....
1976-77	Cleveland Barons	2	0	1	1	2	....	....	....	....	....
1977-78	St. Louis Blues	49	7	4	11	81	....	....	....	....	....
	NHL Totals	**101**	**13**	**11**	**24**	**133**	....	....	....	....	....

• Brother of Randy

Signed as a free agent by **California**, September, 1973. Signed as a free agent by **St. Louis**, October 20, 1977.

HOLT, Randy

Defense. Shoots right. 5'11", 185 lbs. Born, Pembroke, Ont., January 15, 1953.
(Chicago's 3rd choice, 45th overall, in 1973 Amateur Draft).

Season	Club	GP	G	A	Pts	PIM	GP	G	A	Pts	PIM
		REGULAR SEASON					PLAYOFFS				
1974-75	Chicago Black Hawks	12	0	1	1	13	....	....	....	....	....
1975-76	Chicago Black Hawks	12	0	0	0	13	....	....	....	....	....
1976-77	Chicago Black Hawks	12	0	3	3	14	2	0	0	0	7
1977-78	Chicago Black Hawks	6	0	0	0	20	....	....	....	....	....
	Cleveland Barons	48	1	4	5	229	....	....	....	....	....
1978-79	Vancouver Canucks	22	1	3	4	80	....	....	....	....	....
	Los Angeles Kings	36	0	6	6	202	2	0	0	0	4
1979-80	Los Angeles Kings	42	0	1	1	94	....	....	....	....	....
1980-81	Calgary Flames	48	0	5	5	165	13	2	2	4	52
1981-82	Calgary Flames	8	0	0	0	9	....	....	....	....	....
	Washington Capitals	53	2	6	8	250	....	....	....	....	....
1982-83	Washington Capitals	70	0	8	8	*275	4	0	1	1	20
1983-84	Philadelphia Flyers	26	0	0	0	74	....	....	....	....	....
	NHL Totals	**395**	**4**	**37**	**41**	**1438**	**21**	**2**	**3**	**5**	**83**

• Brother of Gary

Traded to **Cleveland** by **Chicago** for Reg Kerr, November 23, 1977. Claimed by **Vancouver** in **Cleveland-Minnesota** Dispersal Draft, June 15, 1978. Traded to **Los Angeles** by **Vancouver** for Don Kozak, December 31, 1978. Traded to **Calgary** by **Los Angeles** with Bert Wilson for Gary Unger, June 6, 1980. Traded to **Washington** by **Calgary** with Bobby Gould for Pat Ribble and Washington's 2nd round choice (later traded to Montreal – Montreal selected Todd Francis) in 1983 Entry Draft, November 25, 1981. Signed as a free agent by **Philadelphia**, August 30, 1983.

HOLWAY, Albert

Defense. Shoots left. 6'2", 190 lbs. Born, Belleville, Ont., September 24, 1902.

Season	Club	GP	G	A	Pts	PIM	GP	G	A	Pts	PIM
1923-24	Toronto St. Pats	5	1	0	1	0	....	....	....	....	....
1924-25	Toronto St. Pats	25	2	2	4	20	2	0	0	0	0
1925-26	Toronto St. Pats	12	0	0	0	0	....	....	....	....	....
	♦ Montreal Maroons	17	0	0	0	6	4	0	0	0	0
	Montreal Maroons (Cup)	....	....	....	....	....	*2*	*0*	*0*	*0*	*0*
1926-27	Montreal Maroons	13	0	0	0	2	....	....	....	....	....
1928-29	Pittsburgh Pirates	40	4	0	4	20	....	....	....	....	....
	NHL Totals	**112**	**7**	**2**	**9**	**48**	**6**	**0**	**0**	**0**	**0**

Signed as a free agent by **Toronto**, February 15, 1924. Claimed on waivers by **Mtl. Maroons** from **Toronto**, January 12, 1926. • 1925-26 Mtl. Maroons playoff totals includes series against Ottawa and Pittsburgh. Traded to **Stratford** (Can-Pro) by **Mtl. Maroons** for cash with Mtl. Maroons holding right of recall, January, 1927. Traded to **Pittsburgh** by **Mtl. Maroons** for cash, September 30, 1928. Traded to **London** (IHL) by **Pittsburgh** for cash, October 22, 1929.

HOLZINGER, Brian

Center. Shoots right. 5'11", 190 lbs. Born, Parma, OH, October 10, 1972.
(Buffalo's 7th choice, 124th overall, in 1991 Entry Draft).

Season	Club	GP	G	A	Pts	PIM	GP	G	A	Pts	PIM
1994-95	Buffalo Sabres	4	0	3	3	0	4	2	1	3	2
1995-96	Buffalo Sabres	58	10	10	20	37	....	....	....	....	....
1996-97	Buffalo Sabres	81	22	29	51	54	12	2	5	7	8
1997-98	Buffalo Sabres	69	14	21	35	36	15	4	7	11	18
1998-99	Buffalo Sabres	81	17	17	34	45	21	3	5	8	33
99-2000	Buffalo Sabres	59	7	17	24	30	....	....	....	....	....
	Tampa Bay Lightning	14	3	3	6	21	....	....	....	....	....
2000-01	Tampa Bay Lightning	70	11	25	36	64	....	....	....	....	....
2001-02	Tampa Bay Lightning	23	1	2	3	4	....	....	....	....	....
2002-03	Tampa Bay Lightning	5	0	1	1	2	....	....	....	....	....
	Pittsburgh Penguins	9	1	2	3	6	....	....	....	....	....
	NHL Totals	**473**	**86**	**130**	**216**	**299**	**52**	**11**	**18**	**29**	**61**

Traded to **Tampa Bay** by **Buffalo** with Cory Sarich, Wayne Primeau and Buffalo's 3rd round choice (Alexander Kharitonov) in 2000 Entry Draft for Chris Gratton and Tampa Bay's 2nd round choice (Derek Roy) in 2001 Entry Draft, March 9, 2000. • Missed majority of 2001-02 season recovering from shoulder injury suffered in game vs. Florida, October 7, 2001. Traded to **Pittsburgh** by **Tampa Bay** for Marc Bergevin, March 11, 2003.

HOMENUKE, Ron

Right wing. Shoots right. 5'10", 180 lbs. Born, Hazelton, B.C., January 5, 1952.
(Vancouver's 4th choice, 51st overall, in 1972 Amateur Draft).

Season	Club	GP	G	A	Pts	PIM	GP	G	A	Pts	PIM
1972-73	Vancouver Canucks	1	0	0	0	0	....	....	....	....	....
	NHL Totals	**1**	**0**	**0**	**0**	**0**	....	....	....	....	....

HOOVER, Ron

Center. Shoots left. 6'1", 185 lbs. Born, Oakville, Ont., October 28, 1966.
(Hartford's 7th choice, 158th overall, in 1986 Entry Draft).

Season	Club	GP	G	A	Pts	PIM	GP	G	A	Pts	PIM
1989-90	Boston Bruins	2	0	0	0	0	....	....	....	....	....
1990-91	Boston Bruins	15	4	0	4	31	8	0	0	0	18
1991-92	St. Louis Blues	1	0	0	0	0	....	....	....	....	....
	NHL Totals	**18**	**4**	**0**	**4**	**31**	**8**	**0**	**0**	**0**	**18**

Signed as a free agent by **Boston**, September 1, 1989. Signed as a free agent by **St. Louis**, July 23, 1991.

HOPKINS, Dean

Right wing. Shoots right. 6'1", 210 lbs. Born, Cobourg, Ont., June 6, 1959.
(Los Angeles' 2nd choice, 29th overall, in 1979 Entry Draft).

Season	Club	GP	G	A	Pts	PIM	GP	G	A	Pts	PIM
1979-80	Los Angeles Kings	60	8	6	14	39	4	0	1	1	5
1980-81	Los Angeles Kings	67	8	18	26	118	4	1	0	1	9
1981-82	Los Angeles Kings	41	2	13	15	102	10	0	4	4	15
1982-83	Los Angeles Kings	49	5	12	17	43	....	....	....	....	....
1985-86	Edmonton Oilers	1	0	0	0	0	....	....	....	....	....
1988-89	Quebec Nordiques	5	0	2	2	4	....	....	....	....	....
	NHL Totals	**223**	**23**	**51**	**74**	**306**	**18**	**1**	**5**	**6**	**29**

Traded to **Edmonton** by **Los Angeles** for cash, November 27, 1984. Traded to **Los Angeles** by **Edmonton** for future considerations, May 31, 1985. Signed as a free agent by **Edmonton**, September 27, 1985. Signed as a free agent by **Quebec**, July 30, 1988.

HOPKINS, Larry

Left wing. Shoots left. 6'1", 215 lbs. Born, Oshawa, Ont., March 17, 1954.
(Atlanta's 9th choice, 152nd overall, in 1974 Amateur Draft).

Season	Club	GP	G	A	Pts	PIM	GP	G	A	Pts	PIM
1977-78	Toronto Maple Leafs	2	0	0	0	0	....	....	....	....	....
1979-80	Winnipeg Jets	5	0	0	0	0	....	....	....	....	....
1981-82	Winnipeg Jets	41	10	15	25	22	4	0	0	0	2
1982-83	Winnipeg Jets	12	3	1	4	4	2	0	0	0	0
	NHL Totals	**60**	**13**	**16**	**29**	**26**	**6**	**0**	**0**	**0**	**2**

Signed to an amateur try-out contract by **Toronto**, March 8, 1978. Signed as a free agent by **Winnipeg**, August 15, 1979.

HORACEK, Tony

Left wing. Shoots left. 6'4", 210 lbs. Born, Vancouver, B.C., February 3, 1967.
(Philadelphia's 8th choice, 147th overall, in 1985 Entry Draft).

Season	Club	GP	G	A	Pts	PIM	GP	G	A	Pts	PIM
1989-90	Philadelphia Flyers	48	5	5	10	117	....	....	....	....	....
1990-91	Philadelphia Flyers	34	3	6	9	49	....	....	....	....	....
1991-92	Philadelphia Flyers	34	1	3	4	51	....	....	....	....	....
	Chicago Blackhawks	12	1	4	5	21	2	1	0	1	2
1993-94	Chicago Blackhawks	7	0	0	0	53	....	....	....	....	....
1994-95	Chicago Blackhawks	19	0	1	1	25	....	....	....	....	....
	NHL Totals	**154**	**10**	**19**	**29**	**316**	**2**	**1**	**0**	**1**	**2**

Traded to **Chicago** by **Philadelphia** for Ryan McGill, February 7, 1992.

HORAVA, Miloslav

Defense. Shoots left. 6', 193 lbs. Born, Kladno, Czech., August 14, 1961.
(Edmonton's 8th choice, 176th overall, in 1981 Entry Draft).

Season	Club	GP	G	A	Pts	PIM	GP	G	A	Pts	PIM
1988-89	New York Rangers	6	0	1	1	0	....	....	....	....	....
1989-90	New York Rangers	45	4	10	14	26	2	0	1	1	0
1990-91	New York Rangers	29	1	6	7	12	....	....	....	....	....
	NHL Totals	**80**	**5**	**17**	**22**	**38**	**2**	**0**	**1**	**1**	**0**

Traded to **NY Rangers** by **Edmonton** with Don Jackson, Mike Golden and future considerations (Stu Kulak, March 10, 1987) for Reijo Ruotsalainen, Ville Kentala, Clark Donatelli and Jim Wiemer, October 23, 1986. Traded to **Quebec** by **NY Rangers** for Stephane Guerard, May 25, 1991.

HORBUL, Doug

Left wing. Shoots left. 5'9", 170 lbs. Born, Nokomis, Sask., July 27, 1952.
(NY Rangers' 6th choice, 63rd overall, in 1972 Amateur Draft).

Season	Club	GP	G	A	Pts	PIM	GP	G	A	Pts	PIM
1974-75	Kansas City Scouts	4	1	0	1	2	....	....	....	....	....
	NHL Totals	**4**	**1**	**0**	**1**	**2**	....	....	....	....	....

Claimed by **Kansas City** from **NY Rangers** in Expansion Draft, June 12, 1974.

HORCOFF, Shawn

Center. Shoots left. 6'1", 202 lbs. Born, Trail, B.C., September 17, 1978.
(Edmonton's 3rd choice, 99th overall, in 1998 Entry Draft).

Season	Club	GP	G	A	Pts	PIM	GP	G	A	Pts	PIM
2000-01	Edmonton Oilers	49	9	7	16	10	5	0	0	0	0
2001-02	Edmonton Oilers	61	8	14	22	18	....	....	....	....	....
2002-03	Edmonton Oilers	78	12	21	33	55	6	3	1	4	6
	NHL Totals	**188**	**29**	**42**	**71**	**83**	**11**	**3**	**1**	**4**	**6**

HORDICHUK, Darcy

Left wing. Shoots left. 6'1", 215 lbs. Born, Kamsack, Sask., August 10, 1980.
(Atlanta's 9th choice, 180th overall, in 2000 Entry Draft).

Season	Club	GP	G	A	Pts	PIM	GP	G	A	Pts	PIM
2000-01	Atlanta Thrashers	11	0	0	0	38	....	....	....	....	....
2001-02	Atlanta Thrashers	33	1	1	2	127	....	....	....	....	....
	Phoenix Coyotes	1	0	0	0	14	....	....	....	....	....
2002-03	Phoenix Coyotes	25	0	0	0	82	....	....	....	....	....
	Florida Panthers	3	0	0	0	15	....	....	....	....	....
	NHL Totals	**73**	**1**	**1**	**2**	**276**	....	....	....	....	....

Traded to **Phoenix** by **Atlanta** with Atlanta's 4th (Lance Monych) and 5th (John Zeiler) round choices in 2002 Entry Draft for Kiril Safronov, the rights to Ruslan Zainullin and Phoenix's 4th round choice (Patrick Dwyer) in 2002 Entry Draft, March 19, 2002. Traded to **Florida** by **Phoenix** with Phoenix's 2nd round choice (later traded to Tampa Bay – Tampa Bay selected Matt Smaby) in 2003 Entry Draft for Brad Ference, March 8, 2003.

HORDY, Mike

Defense. Shoots right. 5'10", 180 lbs. Born, Thunder Bay, Ont., October 10, 1956.
(NY Islanders' 5th choice, 86th overall, in 1976 Amateur Draft).

Season	Club	GP	G	A	Pts	PIM	GP	G	A	Pts	PIM
1978-79	New York Islanders	2	0	0	0	0	....	....	....	....	....
1979-80	New York Islanders	9	0	0	0	7	....	....	....	....	....
	NHL Totals	**11**	**0**	**0**	**0**	**7**	....	....	....	....	....

Signed as a free agent by **New Jersey**, August 23, 1983.

HORECK, Pete

Left wing. Shoots left. 5'9", 158 lbs. Born, Massey, Ont., June 15, 1923.

Season	Club	GP	G	A	Pts	PIM	GP	G	A	Pts	PIM
1944-45	Chicago Black Hawks	50	20	16	36	44	....	....	....	....	....
1945-46	Chicago Black Hawks	50	20	21	41	34	4	0	0	0	2
1946-47	Chicago Black Hawks	18	4	6	10	12	....	....	....	....	....
	Detroit Red Wings	38	12	13	25	59	5	2	0	2	6

		REGULAR SEASON					PLAYOFFS				
Season	Club	GP	G	A	Pts	PIM	GP	G	A	Pts	PIM
1947-48	Detroit Red Wings	50	12	17	29	44	10	3	*7	10	12
1948-49	Detroit Red Wings	60	14	16	30	46	11	1	1	2	10
1949-50	Boston Bruins	34	5	5	10	22	....	....	....	....	....
1950-51	Boston Bruins	66	10	13	23	57	4	0	0	0	13
1951-52	Chicago Black Hawks	60	9	11	20	22	....	....	....	....	....
	NHL Totals	**426**	**106**	**118**	**224**	**340**	**34**	**6**	**8**	**14**	**43**

Claimed by **Chicago** from **Cleveland** (AHL) in Inter-League Draft, May 12, 1944. Traded to **Detroit** by **Chicago** with Leo Reise for Adam Brown and Ray Powell, December 9, 1946. Traded to **Boston** by **Detroit** with Bill Quackenbush for Pete Babando, Clare Martin, Lloyd Durham and Jimmy Peters, August 16, 1949. Traded to **Chicago** by **Boston** for cash, November 1, 1951.

HORNE, George

Right wing. Shoots right. 5'6", 165 lbs. Born, Sudbury, Ont., June 27, 1904.

Season	Club	GP	G	A	Pts	PIM	GP	G	A	Pts	PIM
1925-26 ♦	Montreal Maroons	13	0	0	0	2	....	....	....	....	....
1926-27	Montreal Maroons	2	0	0	0	0	....	....	....	....	....
1928-29	Toronto Maple Leafs	39	9	3	12	32	4	0	0	0	4
	NHL Totals	**54**	**9**	**3**	**12**	**34**	**4**	**0**	**0**	**0**	**4**

Signed as a free agent by **Mtl. Maroons**, October 8, 1925. Claimed on waivers by **Stratford** (Can-Pro) from **Mtl. Maroons**, February 1, 1927. Traded to **Toronto** by **Mtl. Maroons** for Fred Elliot, October 1, 1928. • Drowned in Sagatoski Lake, Ontario, July 31, 1929.

HORNER, Red

HHOF

Defense. Shoots right. 6', 190 lbs. Born, Lynden, Ont., May 28, 1909.

Season	Club	GP	G	A	Pts	PIM	GP	G	A	Pts	PIM
1928-29	Toronto Maple Leafs	22	0	0	0	30	4	1	0	1	2
1929-30	Toronto Maple Leafs	33	2	7	9	96	....	....	....	....	....
1930-31	Toronto Maple Leafs	42	1	11	12	71	2	0	0	0	4
1931-32 ♦	Toronto Maple Leafs	42	7	9	16	97	7	2	2	4	20
1932-33	Toronto Maple Leafs	48	3	8	11	*144	9	1	0	1	10
1933-34	Toronto Maple Leafs	40	11	10	21	*146	5	1	0	1	6
1934-35	Toronto Maple Leafs	46	4	8	12	*125	7	0	1	1	4
1935-36	Toronto Maple Leafs	43	2	9	11	*167	9	1	2	3	*22
1936-37	Toronto Maple Leafs	48	3	9	12	*124	2	0	0	0	7
1937-38	Toronto Maple Leafs	47	4	20	24	*82	7	0	1	1	14
1938-39	Toronto Maple Leafs	48	4	10	14	*85	10	1	2	3	*26
1939-40	Toronto Maple Leafs	31	1	9	10	*87	9	0	2	2	55
	NHL Totals	**490**	**42**	**110**	**152**	**1254**	**71**	**7**	**10**	**17**	**170**

Played in NHL All-Star Game (1934, 1937)

Signed as a free agent by **Toronto**, January 20, 1929.

HORNUNG, Larry

Defense. Shoots left. 6', 190 lbs. Born, Weyburn, Sask., November 10, 1945.

Season	Club	GP	G	A	Pts	PIM	GP	G	A	Pts	PIM
1970-71	St. Louis Blues	1	0	0	0	0	....	....	....	....	....
1971-72	St. Louis Blues	47	2	9	11	10	11	0	2	2	2
	NHL Totals	**48**	**2**	**9**	**11**	**10**	**11**	**0**	**2**	**2**	**2**

Traded to **St. Louis** by **Detroit** with Craig Cameron and Dan Giesebrecht for John Brenneman, October 9, 1967. Loaned to **NY Rangers** by **St. Louis** for the remainder of the 1969-70 season for the loan of Sheldon Kannegiesser for the remainder of the 1969-70 season, November, 1969. Claimed by **NY Islanders** from **St. Louis** in Expansion Draft, June 6, 1972. Rights traded to **Kansas City** by **NY Islanders** with future considerations (Bart Crashley, September 16, 1974) for Bob Bourne, September 10, 1974.

HORTON, Tim

HHOF

Defense. Shoots right. 5'10", 180 lbs. Born, Cochrane, Ont., January 12, 1930.

Season	Club	GP	G	A	Pts	PIM	GP	G	A	Pts	PIM
1949-50	Toronto Maple Leafs	1	0	0	0	2	1	0	0	0	2
1951-52	Toronto Maple Leafs	4	0	0	0	8	....	....	....	....	....
1952-53	Toronto Maple Leafs	70	2	14	16	85	....	....	....	....	....
1953-54	Toronto Maple Leafs	70	7	24	31	94	5	1	1	2	4
1954-55	Toronto Maple Leafs	67	5	9	14	84	....	....	....	....	....
1955-56	Toronto Maple Leafs	35	0	5	5	36	2	0	0	0	4
1956-57	Toronto Maple Leafs	66	6	19	25	72	....	....	....	....	....
1957-58	Toronto Maple Leafs	53	6	20	26	39	....	....	....	....	....
1958-59	Toronto Maple Leafs	70	5	21	26	76	12	0	3	3	16
1959-60	Toronto Maple Leafs	70	3	29	32	69	10	0	1	1	6
1960-61	Toronto Maple Leafs	57	6	15	21	75	5	0	0	0	0
1961-62 ♦	Toronto Maple Leafs	70	10	28	38	88	12	3	13	16	16
1962-63 ♦	Toronto Maple Leafs	70	6	19	25	69	10	1	3	4	10
1963-64 ♦	Toronto Maple Leafs	70	9	20	29	71	14	0	4	4	20
1964-65	Toronto Maple Leafs	70	12	16	28	95	6	0	2	2	13
1965-66	Toronto Maple Leafs	70	6	22	28	76	4	1	0	1	12
1966-67 ♦	Toronto Maple Leafs	70	8	17	25	70	12	3	5	8	25
1967-68	Toronto Maple Leafs	69	4	23	27	82	....	....	....	....	....
1968-69	Toronto Maple Leafs	74	11	29	40	107	4	0	0	0	7
1969-70	Toronto Maple Leafs	59	3	19	22	91	....	....	....	....	....
	New York Rangers	15	1	5	6	16	6	1	1	2	28
1970-71	New York Rangers	78	2	18	20	57	13	1	4	5	14
1971-72	Pittsburgh Penguins	44	2	9	11	40	4	0	1	1	2
1972-73	Buffalo Sabres	69	1	16	17	56	6	0	1	1	4
1973-74	Buffalo Sabres	55	0	6	6	53	....	....	....	....	....
	NHL Totals	**1446**	**115**	**403**	**518**	**1611**	**126**	**11**	**39**	**50**	**183**

NHL Second All-Star Team (1954, 1963, 1967) • NHL First All-Star Team (1964, 1968, 1969)

Played in NHL All-Star Game (1954, 1961, 1962, 1963, 1964, 1968, 1969)

Traded to **NY Rangers** by **Toronto** for future considerations (Denis Dupere, May 14, 1970), March 3, 1970. Claimed by **Pittsburgh** from **NY Rangers** in Intra-League Draft, June 8, 1971. Claimed by **Buffalo** from **Pittsburgh** in Intra-League Draft, June 5, 1972. • Died from injuries suffered in automobile accident, February 21, 1974.

HORVATH, Bronco

Center. Shoots left. 5'11", 185 lbs. Born, Port Colborne, Ont., March 12, 1930.

Season	Club	GP	G	A	Pts	PIM	GP	G	A	Pts	PIM
1955-56	New York Rangers	66	12	17	29	40	5	1	2	3	4
1956-57	New York Rangers	7	1	2	3	4	....	....	....	....	....
	Montreal Canadiens	1	0	0	0	0	....	....	....	....	....
1957-58	Boston Bruins	67	30	36	66	71	12	5	3	8	8
1958-59	Boston Bruins	45	19	20	39	58	7	2	3	5	0
1959-60	Boston Bruins	68	*39	41	80	60	....	....	....	....	....
1960-61	Boston Bruins	47	15	15	30	15	....	....	....	....	....
1961-62	Chicago Black Hawks	68	17	29	46	21	12	4	1	5	6
1962-63	New York Rangers	41	7	15	22	34	....	....	....	....	....
	Toronto Maple Leafs	10	0	4	4	12	....	....	....	....	....
1967-68	Minnesota North Stars	14	1	6	7	4	....	....	....	....	....
	NHL Totals	**434**	**141**	**185**	**326**	**319**	**36**	**12**	**9**	**21**	**18**

NHL Second All-Star Team (1960)

Played in NHL All-Star Game (1960, 1961)

Traded to **NY Rangers** by **Detroit** with Dave Creighton for Billy Dea, Aggie Kukulowicz and cash, August 18, 1955. Traded to **Montreal** by **NY Rangers** for cash, November 4, 1956. Claimed by **Boston** from **Montreal** in Intra-League Draft, June 5, 1957. Claimed by **Chicago** from **Boston** in Intra-League Draft, June 13, 1961. Claimed by **NY Rangers** from **Chicago** in Intra-League Draft, June 4, 1962. Claimed on waivers by **Toronto** from **NY Rangers**, January 23, 1963. Loaned to **Minnesota** by **Toronto** as injury replacement for Bill Masterton, January 21, 1968. Returned to **Toronto** (Rochester-AHL) by **Minnesota** when trade negotiations failed, February 27, 1968. Rights transferred to **Vancouver** (WHL) after WHL club purchased **Rochester** (AHL) franchise, August 13, 1968.

HOSPODAR, Ed

Defense. Shoots right. 6'2", 210 lbs. Born, Bowling Green, OH, February 9, 1959.
(NY Rangers' 2nd choice, 34th overall, in 1979 Entry Draft).

Season	Club	GP	G	A	Pts	PIM	GP	G	A	Pts	PIM
1979-80	New York Rangers	20	0	1	1	76	7	1	0	1	42
1980-81	New York Rangers	61	5	14	19	214	12	2	0	2	*93
1981-82	New York Rangers	41	3	8	11	152	....	....	....	....	....
1982-83	Hartford Whalers	72	1	9	10	199	....	....	....	....	....
1983-84	Hartford Whalers	59	0	9	9	163	....	....	....	....	....
1984-85	Philadelphia Flyers	50	3	4	7	130	18	1	1	2	69
1985-86	Philadelphia Flyers	17	3	1	4	55	....	....	....	....	....
	Minnesota North Stars	43	0	2	2	91	2	0	0	0	2
1986-87	Philadelphia Flyers	45	2	2	4	136	5	0	0	0	2
1987-88	Buffalo Sabres	42	0	1	1	98	....	....	....	....	....
	NHL Totals	**450**	**17**	**51**	**68**	**1314**	**44**	**4**	**1**	**5**	**208**

Traded to **Hartford** by **NY Rangers** for Kent-Erik Andersson, October 1, 1982. Signed as a free agent by **Philadelphia**, July 25, 1984. Traded to **Minnesota** by **Philadelphia** with Todd Bergen for Bo Berglund and Dave Richter, November 29, 1985. Signed as a free agent by **Philadelphia**, June 12, 1986. Claimed by **Buffalo** from **Philadelphia** in Waiver Draft, October 5, 1987.

HOSSA, Marcel

Left wing. Shoots left. 6'2", 211 lbs. Born, Ilava, Czech., October 12, 1981.
(Montreal's 2nd choice, 16th overall, in 2000 Entry Draft).

Season	Club	GP	G	A	Pts	PIM	GP	G	A	Pts	PIM
2001-02	Montreal Canadiens	10	3	1	4	2	....	....	....	....	....
2002-03	Montreal Canadiens	34	6	7	13	14	....	....	....	....	....
	NHL Totals	**44**	**9**	**8**	**17**	**16**	....	....	....	....	....

HOSSA, Marian

Right wing. Shoots left. 6'1", 199 lbs. Born, Stara Lubovna, Czech., January 12, 1979.
(Ottawa's 1st choice, 12th overall, in 1997 Entry Draft).

Season	Club	GP	G	A	Pts	PIM	GP	G	A	Pts	PIM
1997-98	Ottawa Senators	7	0	1	1	0	....	....	....	....	....
1998-99	Ottawa Senators	60	15	15	30	37	4	0	2	2	4
99-2000	Ottawa Senators	78	29	27	56	32	6	0	0	0	2
2000-01	Ottawa Senators	81	32	43	75	44	4	1	1	2	4
2001-02	Ottawa Senators	80	31	35	66	50	12	4	6	10	2
2002-03	Ottawa Senators	80	45	35	80	34	18	5	11	16	6
	NHL Totals	**386**	**152**	**156**	**308**	**197**	**44**	**10**	**20**	**30**	**18**

NHL All-Rookie Team (1999)

Played in NHL All-Star Game (2001, 2003)

HOSTAK, Martin

Center. Shoots left. 6'3", 198 lbs. Born, Hradec Kralove, Czech., November 11, 1967.
(Philadelphia's 3rd choice, 62nd overall, in 1987 Entry Draft).

Season	Club	GP	G	A	Pts	PIM	GP	G	A	Pts	PIM
1990-91	Philadelphia Flyers	50	3	10	13	22	....	....	....	....	....
1991-92	Philadelphia Flyers	5	0	1	1	2	....	....	....	....	....
	NHL Totals	**55**	**3**	**11**	**14**	**24**	....	....	....	....	....

HOTHAM, Greg

Defense. Shoots right. 5'11", 183 lbs. Born, London, Ont., March 7, 1956.
(Toronto's 5th choice, 84th overall, in 1976 Amateur Draft).

Season	Club	GP	G	A	Pts	PIM	GP	G	A	Pts	PIM
1979-80	Toronto Maple Leafs	46	3	10	13	10	....	....	....	....	....
1980-81	Toronto Maple Leafs	11	1	1	2	11	....	....	....	....	....
1981-82	Toronto Maple Leafs	3	0	0	0	0	....	....	....	....	....
	Pittsburgh Penguins	25	4	6	10	16	5	0	3	3	6
1982-83	Pittsburgh Penguins	58	2	30	32	39	....	....	....	....	....
1983-84	Pittsburgh Penguins	76	5	25	30	59	....	....	....	....	....
1984-85	Pittsburgh Penguins	11	0	2	2	4	....	....	....	....	....
	NHL Totals	**230**	**15**	**74**	**89**	**139**	**5**	**0**	**3**	**3**	**6**

Traded to **Pittsburgh** by **Toronto** for Pittsburgh's 6th round choice (Craig Kales) in 1982 Entry Draft, February 3, 1982.

HOUCK, Paul

Right wing. Shoots right. 5'11", 185 lbs. Born, North Vancouver, B.C., August 12, 1963.
(Edmonton's 3rd choice, 71st overall, in 1981 Amateur Draft).

Season	Club	REGULAR SEASON GP	G	A	Pts	PIM	PLAYOFFS GP	G	A	Pts	PIM
1985-86	Minnesota North Stars	3	1	0	1	0	....	....	....	....	....
1986-87	Minnesota North Stars	12	0	2	2	2	....	....	....	....	....
1987-88	Minnesota North Stars	1	0	0	0	0	....	....	....	....	....
	NHL Totals	**16**	**1**	**2**	**3**	**2**	....	....	....	....	....

Traded to **Minnesota** by **Edmonton** for Gilles Meloche, May 31, 1985.

HOUDA, Doug

Defense. Shoots right. 6'2", 208 lbs. Born, Blairmore, Alta., June 3, 1966.
(Detroit's 2nd choice, 28th overall, in 1984 Entry Draft).

Season	Club	REGULAR SEASON GP	G	A	Pts	PIM	PLAYOFFS GP	G	A	Pts	PIM
1985-86	Detroit Red Wings	6	0	0	0	4	....	....	....	....	....
1987-88	Detroit Red Wings	11	1	1	2	10	....	....	....	....	....
1988-89	Detroit Red Wings	57	2	11	13	67	6	0	1	1	0
1989-90	Detroit Red Wings	73	2	9	11	127	....	....	....	....	....
1990-91	Detroit Red Wings	22	0	4	4	43	....	....	....	....	....
	Hartford Whalers	19	1	2	3	41	6	0	0	0	8
1991-92	Hartford Whalers	56	3	6	9	125	6	0	2	2	13
1992-93	Hartford Whalers	60	2	6	8	167	....	....	....	....	....
1993-94	Hartford Whalers	7	0	0	0	23	....	....	....	....	....
	Los Angeles Kings	54	2	6	8	165	....	....	....	....	....
1994-95	Buffalo Sabres	28	1	2	3	68	....	....	....	....	....
1995-96	Buffalo Sabres	38	1	3	4	52	....	....	....	....	....
1996-97	New York Islanders	70	2	8	10	99	....	....	....	....	....
1997-98	New York Islanders	31	1	2	3	47	....	....	....	....	....
	Mighty Ducks of Anaheim	24	1	2	3	52	....	....	....	....	....
1998-99	Detroit Red Wings	3	0	1	1	0	....	....	....	....	....
99-2000	Buffalo Sabres	1	0	0	0	12	....	....	....	....	....
2002-03	Buffalo Sabres	1	0	0	0	2	....	....	....	....	....
	NHL Totals	**561**	**19**	**63**	**82**	**1104**	**18**	**0**	**3**	**3**	**21**

Traded to **Hartford** by **Detroit** for Doug Crossman, February 20, 1991. Traded to **Los Angeles** by **Hartford** for Marc Potvin, November 3, 1993. Traded to **Buffalo** by **Los Angeles** for Sean O'Donnell, July 26, 1994. Signed as a free agent by **NY Islanders**, October 26, 1996. Traded to **Anaheim** by **NY Islanders** with Travis Green and Tony Tuzzolino for Joe Sacco, J.J. Daigneault and Mark Janssens, February 6, 1998. Traded to **Detroit** by **Anaheim** for future considerations, October 9, 1998. Signed as a free agent by **Buffalo**, July 13, 1999.

HOUDE, Claude

Defense. Shoots left. 6'1", 188 lbs. Born, Drummondville, Que., November 8, 1947.

Season	Club	REGULAR SEASON GP	G	A	Pts	PIM	PLAYOFFS GP	G	A	Pts	PIM
1974-75	Kansas City Scouts	34	3	4	7	20	....	....	....	....	....
1975-76	Kansas City Scouts	25	0	2	2	20	....	....	....	....	....
	NHL Totals	**59**	**3**	**6**	**9**	**40**	....	....	....	....	....

Traded to **Detroit** by **NY Rangers** for Brian Lavender, February 28, 1974. Traded to **Kansas City** by **Detroit** with Guy Charron for Bart Crashley, Ted Snell and Larry Giroux, December 14, 1974.

HOUDE, Eric

Center. Shoots left. 5'11", 191 lbs. Born, Montreal, Que., December 19, 1976.
(Montreal's 9th choice, 216th overall, in 1995 Entry Draft).

Season	Club	REGULAR SEASON GP	G	A	Pts	PIM	PLAYOFFS GP	G	A	Pts	PIM
1996-97	Montreal Canadiens	13	0	2	2	2	....	....	....	....	....
1997-98	Montreal Canadiens	9	1	0	1	0	....	....	....	....	....
1998-99	Montreal Canadiens	8	1	1	2	2	....	....	....	....	....
	NHL Totals	**30**	**2**	**3**	**5**	**4**	....	....	....	....	....

Signed as a free agent by **Edmonton**, August 11, 1999. Traded to **Phoenix** by **Edmonton** for Rob Murray, November 30, 1999. Signed as a free agent by **Dallas**, July 28, 2000.

HOUGH, Mike

Left wing. Shoots left. 6'1", 197 lbs. Born, Montreal, Que., February 6, 1963.
(Quebec's 7th choice, 181st overall, in 1982 Entry Draft).

Season	Club	REGULAR SEASON GP	G	A	Pts	PIM	PLAYOFFS GP	G	A	Pts	PIM
1986-87	Quebec Nordiques	56	6	8	14	79	9	0	3	3	26
1987-88	Quebec Nordiques	17	3	2	5	2	....	....	....	....	....
1988-89	Quebec Nordiques	46	9	10	19	39	....	....	....	....	....
1989-90	Quebec Nordiques	43	13	13	26	84	....	....	....	....	....
1990-91	Quebec Nordiques	63	13	20	33	111	....	....	....	....	....
1991-92	Quebec Nordiques	61	16	22	38	77	....	....	....	....	....
1992-93	Quebec Nordiques	77	8	22	30	69	6	0	1	1	2
1993-94	Florida Panthers	78	6	23	29	62	....	....	....	....	....
1994-95	Florida Panthers	48	6	7	13	38	....	....	....	....	....
1995-96	Florida Panthers	64	7	16	23	37	22	4	1	5	8
1996-97	Florida Panthers	69	8	6	14	48	5	1	0	1	2
1997-98	New York Islanders	74	5	7	12	27	....	....	....	....	....
1998-99	New York Islanders	11	0	0	0	2	....	....	....	....	....
	NHL Totals	**707**	**100**	**156**	**256**	**675**	**42**	**5**	**5**	**10**	**38**

Traded to **Washington** by **Quebec** for Reggie Savage and Paul MacDermid, June 20, 1993. Claimed by **Florida** from **Washington** in Expansion Draft, June 24, 1993. Signed as a free agent by **NY Islanders**, July 21, 1997.

HOULDER, Bill

Defense. Shoots left. 6'2", 217 lbs. Born, Thunder Bay, Ont., March 11, 1967.
(Washington's 4th choice, 82nd overall, in 1985 Entry Draft).

Season	Club	REGULAR SEASON GP	G	A	Pts	PIM	PLAYOFFS GP	G	A	Pts	PIM
1987-88	Washington Capitals	30	1	2	3	10	....	....	....	....	....
1988-89	Washington Capitals	8	0	3	3	4	....	....	....	....	....
1989-90	Washington Capitals	41	1	11	12	28	....	....	....	....	....
1990-91	Buffalo Sabres	7	0	2	2	4	....	....	....	....	....
1991-92	Buffalo Sabres	10	1	0	1	8	....	....	....	....	....
1992-93	Buffalo Sabres	15	3	5	8	6	8	0	2	2	4
1993-94	Mighty Ducks of Anaheim	80	14	25	39	40	....	....	....	....	....
1994-95	St. Louis Blues	41	5	13	18	20	4	1	1	2	0
1995-96	Tampa Bay Lightning	61	5	23	28	22	6	0	1	1	4
1996-97	Tampa Bay Lightning	79	4	21	25	30	....	....	....	....	....
1997-98	San Jose Sharks	82	7	25	32	48	6	1	2	3	2
1998-99	San Jose Sharks	76	9	23	32	40	6	3	0	3	4
99-2000	Tampa Bay Lightning	14	1	2	3	2	....	....	....	....	....
	Nashville Predators	57	2	12	14	24	....	....	....	....	....
2000-01	Nashville Predators	81	4	12	16	40	....	....	....	....	....
2001-02	Nashville Predators	82	0	8	8	40	....	....	....	....	....
2002-03	Nashville Predators	82	2	4	6	46	....	....	....	....	....
	NHL Totals	**846**	**59**	**191**	**250**	**412**	**30**	**5**	**6**	**11**	**14**

Traded to **Buffalo** by **Washington** for Shawn Anderson, September 30, 1990. Claimed by **Anaheim** from **Buffalo** in Expansion Draft, June 24, 1993. Traded to **St. Louis** by **Anaheim** for Jason Marshall, August 29, 1994. Signed as a free agent by **Tampa Bay**, July 26, 1995. Signed as a free agent by **San Jose**, July 16, 1997. Traded to **Tampa Bay** by **San Jose** with Andrei Zyuzin, Shawn Burr and Steve Guolla for Niklas Sundstrom and NY Rangers' 3rd round choice (previously acquired, later traded to Chicago – Chicago selected Igor Radulov) in 2000 Entry Draft, August 4, 1999. Claimed on waivers by **Nashville** from **Tampa Bay**, November 10, 1999.

HOULE, Rejean

Wing. Shoots left. 5'11", 170 lbs. Born, Rouyn, Que., October 25, 1949.
(Montreal's 1st choice, 1st overall, in 1969 Amateur Draft).

Season	Club	REGULAR SEASON GP	G	A	Pts	PIM	PLAYOFFS GP	G	A	Pts	PIM
1969-70	Montreal Canadiens	9	0	1	1	0	....	....	....	....	....
1970-71 ◆	Montreal Canadiens	66	10	9	19	28	20	2	5	7	20
1971-72	Montreal Canadiens	77	11	17	28	21	6	0	0	0	2
1972-73 ◆	Montreal Canadiens	72	13	35	48	36	17	3	6	9	0
1976-77 ◆	Montreal Canadiens	65	22	30	52	24	6	0	1	1	4
1977-78 ◆	Montreal Canadiens	76	30	28	58	50	15	3	8	11	14
1978-79 ◆	Montreal Canadiens	66	17	34	51	43	7	1	5	6	2
1979-80	Montreal Canadiens	60	18	27	45	68	10	4	5	9	12
1980-81	Montreal Canadiens	77	27	31	58	83	3	1	0	1	6
1981-82	Montreal Canadiens	51	11	32	43	34	5	0	4	4	6
1982-83	Montreal Canadiens	16	2	3	5	8	1	0	0	0	0
	NHL Totals	**635**	**161**	**247**	**408**	**395**	**90**	**14**	**34**	**48**	**66**

Signed as a free agent by **Montreal**, June 10, 1976.

HOUSLEY, Phil

Defense. Shoots left. 5'10", 185 lbs. Born, St. Paul, MN, March 9, 1964.
(Buffalo's 1st choice, 6th overall, in 1982 Entry Draft).

Season	Club	REGULAR SEASON GP	G	A	Pts	PIM	PLAYOFFS GP	G	A	Pts	PIM
1982-83	Buffalo Sabres	77	19	47	66	39	10	3	4	7	2
1983-84	Buffalo Sabres	75	31	46	77	33	3	0	0	0	6
1984-85	Buffalo Sabres	73	16	53	69	28	5	3	2	5	2
1985-86	Buffalo Sabres	79	15	47	62	54	....	....	....	....	....
1986-87	Buffalo Sabres	78	21	46	67	57	....	....	....	....	....
1987-88	Buffalo Sabres	74	29	37	66	96	6	2	4	6	6
1988-89	Buffalo Sabres	72	26	44	70	47	5	1	3	4	2
1989-90	Buffalo Sabres	80	21	60	81	32	6	1	4	5	4
1990-91	Winnipeg Jets	78	23	53	76	24	....	....	....	....	....
1991-92	Winnipeg Jets	74	23	63	86	92	7	1	4	5	0
1992-93	Winnipeg Jets	80	18	79	97	52	6	0	7	7	2
1993-94	St. Louis Blues	26	7	15	22	12	4	2	1	3	4
1994-95	Calgary Flames	43	8	35	43	18	7	0	9	9	0
1995-96	Calgary Flames	59	16	36	52	22	....	....	....	....	....
	New Jersey Devils	22	1	15	16	8	....	....	....	....	....
1996-97	Washington Capitals	77	11	29	40	24	....	....	....	....	....
1997-98	Washington Capitals	64	6	25	31	24	18	0	4	4	4
1998-99	Calgary Flames	79	11	43	54	52	....	....	....	....	....
99-2000	Calgary Flames	78	11	44	55	24	....	....	....	....	....
2000-01	Calgary Flames	69	4	30	34	24	....	....	....	....	....
2001-02	Chicago Blackhawks	80	15	24	39	34	5	0	1	1	4
2002-03	Chicago Blackhawks	57	6	23	29	24	....	....	....	....	....
	Toronto Maple Leafs	1	0	0	0	2	3	0	0	0	0
	NHL Totals	**1495**	**338**	**894**	**1232**	**822**	**85**	**13**	**43**	**56**	**36**

NHL All-Rookie Team (1983) • NHL Second All-Star Team (1992)

Played in NHL All-Star Game (1984, 1989, 1990, 1991, 1992, 1993, 2000)

Traded to **Winnipeg** by **Buffalo** with Scott Arniel, Jeff Parker and Buffalo's 1st round choice (Keith Tkachuk) in 1990 Entry Draft for Dale Hawerchuk and Winnipeg's 1st round choice (Brad May) in 1990 Entry Draft, June 16, 1990. Traded to **St. Louis** by **Winnipeg** for Nelson Emerson and Stephane Quintal, September 24, 1993. Traded to **Calgary** by **St. Louis** with St. Louis' 2nd round choices in 1996 (Steve Begin) and 1997 (John Tripp) Entry Drafts for Al MacInnis and Calgary's 4th round choice (Didier Tremblay) in 1997 Entry Draft, July 4, 1994. Traded to **New Jersey** by **Calgary** with Dan Keczmer for Tommy Albelin, Cale Hulse and Jocelyn Lemieux, February 26, 1996. Signed as a free agent by **Washington**, July 22, 1996. Claimed on waivers by **Calgary** from **Washington**, July 21, 1998. Claimed by **Chicago** from **Calgary** in Waiver Draft, September 28, 2001. Traded to **Toronto** by **Chicago** for Toronto's 9th round choice (Chris Porter) in 2003 Entry Draft and Toronto's 4th round choice in 2004 Entry Draft, March 11, 2003.

HOUSTON, Ken

Right wing. Shoots right. 6'2", 210 lbs. Born, Dresden, Ont., September 15, 1953.
(Atlanta's 6th choice, 85th overall, in 1973 Amateur Draft).

Season	Club	REGULAR SEASON GP	G	A	Pts	PIM	PLAYOFFS GP	G	A	Pts	PIM
1975-76	Atlanta Flames	38	5	6	11	11	2	0	0	0	0
1976-77	Atlanta Flames	78	20	24	44	35	3	0	0	0	4
1977-78	Atlanta Flames	74	22	16	38	51	2	0	0	0	0
1978-79	Atlanta Flames	80	21	31	52	135	1	0	0	0	16
1979-80	Atlanta Flames	80	23	31	54	100	4	1	1	2	10
1980-81	Calgary Flames	42	15	15	30	93	16	7	8	15	28

Season	Club	REGULAR SEASON GP	G	A	Pts	PIM	PLAYOFFS GP	G	A	Pts	PIM
1981-82	Calgary Flames	70	22	22	44	91	3	1	0	1	4
1982-83	Washington Capitals	71	25	14	39	93	4	1	0	1	4
1983-84	Washington Capitals	4	0	0	0	4	....	....	....	....	....
	Los Angeles Kings	33	8	8	16	11	....	....	....	....	....
	NHL Totals	**570**	**161**	**167**	**328**	**624**	**35**	**10**	**9**	**19**	**66**

Transferred to **Calgary** after **Atlanta** franchise relocated, June 24, 1980. Traded to **Washington** by **Calgary** with Pat Riggin for Howard Walker, George White, Washington's 6th round choice (Mats Kihlstrom) in 1982 Entry Draft, 3rd round choice (Perry Berezan) in 1983 Entry Draft and 2nd round choice (Paul Ranheim) in 1984 Entry Draft, June 9, 1982. Traded to **Los Angeles** by **Washington** with Brian Engblom for Larry Murphy, October 18, 1983.

HOWARD, Jack

Defense. Shoots left. 6', 190 lbs. Born, London, Ont., October 15, 1911.

Season	Club	GP	G	A	Pts	PIM	GP	G	A	Pts	PIM
1936-37	Toronto Maple Leafs	2	0	0	0	0	....	....	....	....	....
	NHL Totals	**2**	**0**	**0**	**0**	**0**	....	....	....	....	....

Signed as a free agent by **Toronto**, October 22, 1935. Traded to **St. Louis** (AHA) by **Toronto** for cash, October 13, 1939. Traded to **NY Americans** (Springfield-AHL) by **St. Louis** (AHA) for cash, November 29, 1940. Traded to **Toronto** (Pittsburgh-AHL) by **NY Americans** (Springfield-AHL) with the loan of Peanuts O'Flaherty for Clarence Drouillard, January 17, 1941.

HOWATT, Garry

Left wing. Shoots right. 5'9", 175 lbs. Born, Grand Center, Alta., September 26, 1952.
(NY Islanders' 13th choice, 144th overall, in 1972 Amateur Draft).

Season	Club	GP	G	A	Pts	PIM	GP	G	A	Pts	PIM
1972-73	New York Islanders	8	0	1	1	18	....	....	....	....	....
1973-74	New York Islanders	78	6	11	17	204	....	....	....	....	....
1974-75	New York Islanders	77	18	30	48	121	17	3	3	6	59
1975-76	New York Islanders	80	21	13	34	197	13	5	5	10	23
1976-77	New York Islanders	70	13	15	28	182	12	1	1	2	28
1977-78	New York Islanders	61	7	12	19	146	7	0	1	1	62
1978-79	New York Islanders	75	16	12	28	205	9	0	1	1	18
1979-80 ♦	New York Islanders	77	8	11	19	219	21	3	1	4	84
1980-81 ♦	New York Islanders	70	4	15	19	174	8	0	2	2	15
1981-82	Hartford Whalers	80	18	32	50	242	....	....	....	....	....
1982-83	New Jersey Devils	38	1	4	5	114	....	....	....	....	....
1983-84	New Jersey Devils	6	0	0	0	14	....	....	....	....	....
	NHL Totals	**720**	**112**	**156**	**268**	**1836**	**87**	**12**	**14**	**26**	**289**

Traded to **Hartford** by **NY Islanders** for Hartford's 5th round choice (Bob Caulfield) in 1983 Entry Draft, October 2, 1981. Traded to **New Jersey** by **Hartford** with Rick Meagher for Merlin Malinowski and the rights to Scott Fusco, October 15, 1982.

HOWE, Gordie

HHOF

Right wing. Shoots right. 6', 205 lbs. Born, Floral, Sask., March 31, 1928.

Season	Club	GP	G	A	Pts	PIM	GP	G	A	Pts	PIM
1946-47	Detroit Red Wings	58	7	15	22	52	5	0	0	0	18
1947-48	Detroit Red Wings	60	16	28	44	63	10	1	1	2	11
1948-49	Detroit Red Wings	40	12	25	37	57	11	*8	3	*11	19
1949-50 ♦	Detroit Red Wings	70	35	33	68	69	1	0	0	0	7
1950-51	Detroit Red Wings	70	*43	*43	*86	74	6	4	3	7	4
1951-52 ♦	Detroit Red Wings	70	*47	39	*86	78	8	2	*5	*7	2
1952-53	Detroit Red Wings	70	*49	*46	*95	57	6	2	5	7	2
1953-54 ♦	Detroit Red Wings	70	33	*48	*81	109	12	4	5	9	*31
1954-55 ♦	Detroit Red Wings	64	29	33	62	68	11	*9	*11	*20	24
1955-56	Detroit Red Wings	70	38	41	79	100	10	3	9	12	8
1956-57	Detroit Red Wings	70	*44	45	*89	72	5	2	5	7	6
1957-58	Detroit Red Wings	64	33	44	77	40	4	1	1	2	0
1958-59	Detroit Red Wings	70	32	46	78	57	....	....	....	....	....
1959-60	Detroit Red Wings	70	28	45	73	46	6	1	5	6	4
1960-61	Detroit Red Wings	64	23	49	72	30	11	4	11	*15	10
1961-62	Detroit Red Wings	70	33	44	77	54	....	....	....	....	....
1962-63	Detroit Red Wings	70	*38	48	*86	100	11	7	9	*16	22
1963-64	Detroit Red Wings	69	26	47	73	70	14	*9	10	*19	16
1964-65	Detroit Red Wings	70	29	47	76	104	7	4	2	6	20
1965-66	Detroit Red Wings	70	29	46	75	83	12	4	6	10	12
1966-67	Detroit Red Wings	69	25	40	65	53	....	....	....	....	....
1967-68	Detroit Red Wings	74	39	43	82	53	....	....	....	....	....
1968-69	Detroit Red Wings	76	44	59	103	58	....	....	....	....	....
1969-70	Detroit Red Wings	76	31	40	71	58	4	2	0	2	2
1970-71	Detroit Red Wings	63	23	29	52	38	....	....	....	....	....
1979-80	Hartford Whalers	80	15	26	41	42	3	1	1	2	2
	NHL Totals	**1767**	**801**	**1049**	**1850**	**1685**	**157**	**68**	**92**	**160**	**220**

• Brother of Vic • Father of Marty and Mark • NHL Second All-Star Team (1949, 1950, 1956, 1959, 1961, 1962, 1964, 1965, 1967) • NHL First All-Star Team (1951, 1952, 1953, 1954, 1957, 1958, 1960, 1963, 1966, 1968, 1969, 1970) • Art Ross Trophy (1951, 1952, 1953, 1954, 1957, 1963) • Hart Trophy (1952, 1953, 1957, 1958, 1960, 1963) • Lester Patrick Trophy (1967)

Played in NHL All-Star Game (1948, 1949, 1950, 1951, 1952, 1953, 1954, 1955, 1957, 1958, 1959, 1960, 1961, 1962, 1963, 1964, 1965, 1967, 1968, 1969, 1970, 1971, 1980)

Signed as a free agent by **Detroit**, October 8, 1946. Rights retained by **Hartford** prior to Expansion Draft, June 9, 1979. • Oldest player (52 years, 10 days) to play in a NHL game, April 11, 1980. (Montreal 4, Hartford 3).

HOWE, Mark

USHOF

Defense. Shoots left. 5'11", 185 lbs. Born, Detroit, MI, May 28, 1955.
(Boston's 2nd choice, 25th overall, in 1974 Amateur Draft).

Season	Club	GP	G	A	Pts	PIM	GP	G	A	Pts	PIM
1979-80	Hartford Whalers	74	24	56	80	20	3	1	2	3	2
1980-81	Hartford Whalers	63	19	46	65	54	....	....	....	....	....
1981-82	Hartford Whalers	76	8	45	53	18	....	....	....	....	....
1982-83	Philadelphia Flyers	76	20	47	67	18	3	0	2	2	4
1983-84	Philadelphia Flyers	71	19	34	53	44	3	0	0	0	2
1984-85	Philadelphia Flyers	73	18	39	57	31	19	3	8	11	6
1985-86	Philadelphia Flyers	77	24	58	82	36	5	0	4	4	0
1986-87	Philadelphia Flyers	69	15	43	58	37	26	2	10	12	4
1987-88	Philadelphia Flyers	75	19	43	62	62	7	3	6	9	4
1988-89	Philadelphia Flyers	52	9	29	38	45	19	0	15	15	10
1989-90	Philadelphia Flyers	40	7	21	28	24	....	....	....	....	....
1990-91	Philadelphia Flyers	19	0	10	10	8	....	....	....	....	....
1991-92	Philadelphia Flyers	42	7	18	25	18	....	....	....	....	....
1992-93	Detroit Red Wings	60	3	31	34	22	7	1	3	4	2
1993-94	Detroit Red Wings	44	4	20	24	8	6	0	1	1	0
1994-95	Detroit Red Wings	18	1	5	6	10	3	0	0	0	0
	NHL Totals	**929**	**197**	**545**	**742**	**455**	**101**	**10**	**51**	**61**	**34**

• Son of Gordie • Brother of Marty • NHL First All-Star Team (1983, 1986, 1987) • NHL Plus/Minus Leader (1986)

Played in NHL All-Star Game (1981, 1983, 1986, 1988)

Reclaimed by **Boston** from **Hartford** prior to Expansion Draft, June 9, 1979. Claimed as a priority selection by **Hartford**, June 9, 1979. Traded to **Philadelphia** by **Hartford** with Hartford's 3rd round choice (Derrick Smith) in 1983 Entry Draft for Ken Linseman, Greg Adams and Philadelphia's 1st (David Jensen) and 3rd (Leif Karlsson) round choices in 1983 Entry Draft, August 19, 1982. • Missed majority of 1990-91 season recovering from back injury originally suffered in game vs. Chicago, November 3, 1990. Signed as a free agent by **Detroit**, July 7, 1992.

HOWE, Marty

Defense. Shoots left. 6'1", 195 lbs. Born, Detroit, MI, February 18, 1954.
(Montreal's 8th choice, 51st overall, in 1974 Amateur Draft).

Season	Club	GP	G	A	Pts	PIM	GP	G	A	Pts	PIM
1979-80	Hartford Whalers	6	0	1	1	4	3	1	1	2	0
1980-81	Hartford Whalers	12	0	1	1	25	....	....	....	....	....
1981-82	Hartford Whalers	13	0	4	4	2	....	....	....	....	....
1982-83	Boston Bruins	78	1	11	12	24	12	0	1	1	9
1983-84	Hartford Whalers	69	0	11	11	34	....	....	....	....	....
1984-85	Hartford Whalers	19	1	1	2	10	....	....	....	....	....
	NHL Totals	**197**	**2**	**29**	**31**	**99**	**15**	**1**	**2**	**3**	**9**

• Son of Gordie • Brother of Mark

Rights traded to **Detroit** by **Montreal** for cash and future considerations, February 25, 1977. Rights retained by **Hartford** prior to Expansion Draft, June 9, 1979. Traded to **Boston** by **Hartford** for future considerations, October 1, 1982. Traded to **Hartford** by **Boston** for future considerations, September 29, 1983.

HOWE, Syd

HHOF

Center/Left wing. Shoots left. 5'9", 165 lbs. Born, Ottawa, Ont., September 28, 1911.

Season	Club	GP	G	A	Pts	PIM	GP	G	A	Pts	PIM
1929-30	Ottawa Senators	12	1	1	2	0	2	0	0	0	0
1930-31	Philadelphia Quakers	44	9	11	20	20	....	....	....	....	....
1931-32	Toronto Maple Leafs	3	0	0	0	0	....	....	....	....	....
1932-33	Ottawa Senators	48	12	12	24	17	....	....	....	....	....
1933-34	Ottawa Senators	42	13	7	20	18	....	....	....	....	....
1934-35	St. Louis Eagles	36	14	13	27	23	....	....	....	....	....
	Detroit Red Wings	14	8	12	20	11	....	....	....	....	....
1935-36 ♦	Detroit Red Wings	48	16	14	30	26	7	3	3	6	2
1936-37 ♦	Detroit Red Wings	45	17	10	27	10	10	2	5	7	0
1937-38	Detroit Red Wings	48	8	19	27	14	....	....	....	....	....
1938-39	Detroit Red Wings	48	16	20	36	11	6	3	1	4	4
1939-40	Detroit Red Wings	46	14	23	37	17	5	2	2	4	2
1940-41	Detroit Red Wings	48	20	24	44	8	9	1	*7	8	0
1941-42	Detroit Red Wings	48	16	19	35	6	12	3	5	8	0
1942-43 ♦	Detroit Red Wings	50	20	35	55	10	7	1	2	3	0
1943-44	Detroit Red Wings	46	32	28	60	6	5	2	2	4	0
1944-45	Detroit Red Wings	46	17	36	53	6	7	0	0	0	2
1945-46	Detroit Red Wings	26	4	7	11	9	....	....	....	....	....
	NHL Totals	**698**	**237**	**291**	**528**	**212**	**70**	**17**	**27**	**44**	**10**

NHL Second All-Star Team (1945)

Played in NHL All-Star Game (1939)

Signed as a free agent by **Ottawa**, January 16, 1930. Loaned to **Philadelphia** by **Ottawa** for 1930-31 season, November, 1930. Claimed by **Toronto** from **Ottawa** for 1931-32 season in Dispersal Draft, September 26, 1931. Transferred to **St. Louis** after **Ottawa** franchise relocated, September 22, 1934. Traded to **Detroit** by **St. Louis** with Ralph Bowman for Teddy Graham and $50,000, February 11, 1935. Traded to **St. Louis** (AHL) by **Detroit** (Indianapolis-AHL) for cash, August 17, 1946.

HOWE, Vic

Right wing. Shoots right. 6', 172 lbs. Born, Saskatoon, Sask., November 2, 1929.

Season	Club	GP	G	A	Pts	PIM	GP	G	A	Pts	PIM
1950-51	New York Rangers	3	1	0	1	0	....	....	....	....	....
1953-54	New York Rangers	1	0	0	0	0	....	....	....	....	....
1954-55	New York Rangers	29	2	4	6	10	....	....	....	....	....
	NHL Totals	**33**	**3**	**4**	**7**	**10**	....	....	....	....	....

• Brother of Gordie

Traded to **NY Rangers** by **Cleveland** (AHL) with Andy Bathgate for Glen Sonmor and Eric Pogue, November 15, 1954.

HOWELL, Harry

HHOF

Defense. Shoots left. 6'1", 195 lbs. Born, Hamilton, Ont., December 28, 1932.

Season	Club	GP	G	A	Pts	PIM	GP	G	A	Pts	PIM
1952-53	New York Rangers	67	3	8	11	46	....	....	....	....	....
1953-54	New York Rangers	67	7	9	16	58	....	....	....	....	....
1954-55	New York Rangers	70	2	14	16	87	....	....	....	....	....
1955-56	New York Rangers	70	3	15	18	77	5	0	1	1	4
1956-57	New York Rangers	65	2	10	12	70	5	1	0	1	6
1957-58	New York Rangers	70	4	7	11	62	6	1	0	1	8

Season	Club	REGULAR SEASON GP	G	A	Pts	PIM	PLAYOFFS GP	G	A	Pts	PIM
1958-59	New York Rangers	70	4	10	14	101	....	....	....	....	....
1959-60	New York Rangers	67	7	6	13	58	....	....	....	....	....
1960-61	New York Rangers	70	7	10	17	62	....	....	....	....	....
1961-62	New York Rangers	66	6	15	21	89	6	0	1	1	8
1962-63	New York Rangers	70	5	20	25	55	....	....	....	....	....
1963-64	New York Rangers	70	5	31	36	75	....	....	....	....	....
1964-65	New York Rangers	68	2	20	22	63	....	....	....	....	....
1965-66	New York Rangers	70	4	29	33	92	....	....	....	....	....
1966-67	New York Rangers	70	12	28	40	54	4	0	0	0	4
1967-68	New York Rangers	74	5	24	29	62	6	1	0	1	0
1968-69	New York Rangers	56	4	7	11	36	2	0	0	0	0
1969-70	Oakland Seals	55	4	16	20	52	4	0	1	1	2
1970-71	California Seals	28	0	9	9	14	....	....	....	....	....
	Los Angeles Kings	18	3	8	11	4	....	....	....	....	....
1971-72	Los Angeles Kings	77	1	17	18	53	....	....	....	....	....
1972-73	Los Angeles Kings	73	4	11	15	28	....	....	....	....	....
	NHL Totals	**1411**	**94**	**324**	**418**	**1298**	**38**	**3**	**3**	**6**	**32**

• Brother of Ron • NHL First All-Star Team (1967) • James Norris Trophy (1967)

Played in NHL All-Star Game (1954, 1963, 1964, 1965, 1967, 1968, 1970)

Traded to **Oakland** by **NY Rangers** for cash, June 10, 1969. Traded to **Los Angeles** by **California** for cash, February 5, 1971.

HOWELL, Ron

Defense/Left wing. Shoots left. 6', 185 lbs. Born, Hamilton, Ont., December 4, 1935.

Season	Club	GP	G	A	Pts	PIM	GP	G	A	Pts	PIM
1954-55	New York Rangers	3	0	0	0	0	....	....	....	....	....
1955-56	New York Rangers	1	0	0	0	0	....	....	....	....	....
	NHL Totals	**4**	**0**	**0**	**0**	**0**	....	....	....	....	....

• Brother of Harry

Claimed on waivers by **Toronto** from **NY Rangers**, December 4, 1960.

HOWSE, Don

Left wing. Shoots left. 6', 182 lbs. Born, Grand Falls, Nfld., July 28, 1952.

Season	Club	GP	G	A	Pts	PIM	GP	G	A	Pts	PIM
1979-80	Los Angeles Kings	33	2	5	7	6	2	0	0	0	0
	NHL Totals	**33**	**2**	**5**	**7**	**6**	**2**	**0**	**0**	**0**	**0**

Signed as a free agent by **Montreal**, June, 1973. Signed as a free agent by **Los Angeles**, October, 1979.

HOWSON, Scott

Center. Shoots right. 5'11", 160 lbs. Born, Toronto, Ont., April 9, 1960.

Season	Club	GP	G	A	Pts	PIM	GP	G	A	Pts	PIM
1984-85	New York Islanders	8	4	1	5	2	....	....	....	....	....
1985-86	New York Islanders	10	1	2	3	2	....	....	....	....	....
	NHL Totals	**18**	**5**	**3**	**8**	**4**	....	....	....	....	....

Signed as a free agent by **NY Islanders**, August 25, 1981.

HOYDA, Dave

Left wing. Shoots left. 6'1", 205 lbs. Born, Edmonton, Alta., May 20, 1957.
(Philadelphia's 3rd choice, 53rd overall, in 1977 Amateur Draft).

Season	Club	GP	G	A	Pts	PIM	GP	G	A	Pts	PIM
1977-78	Philadelphia Flyers	41	1	3	4	119	9	0	0	0	17
1978-79	Philadelphia Flyers	67	3	13	16	138	3	0	0	0	0
1979-80	Winnipeg Jets	15	1	1	2	35	....	....	....	....	....
1980-81	Winnipeg Jets	9	1	0	1	7	....	....	....	....	....
	NHL Totals	**132**	**6**	**17**	**23**	**299**	**12**	**0**	**0**	**0**	**17**

Claimed by **Winnipeg** from **Philadelphia** in Expansion Draft, June 13, 1979.

HRDINA, Jan

Center. Shoots right. 6', 206 lbs. Born, Hradec Kralove, Czech., February 5, 1976.
(Pittsburgh's 4th choice, 128th overall, in 1995 Entry Draft).

Season	Club	GP	G	A	Pts	PIM	GP	G	A	Pts	PIM
1998-99	Pittsburgh Penguins	82	13	29	42	40	13	4	1	5	12
99-2000	Pittsburgh Penguins	70	13	33	46	43	9	4	8	12	2
2000-01	Pittsburgh Penguins	78	15	28	43	48	18	2	5	7	8
2001-02	Pittsburgh Penguins	79	24	33	57	50	....	....	....	....	....
2002-03	Pittsburgh Penguins	57	14	25	39	34	....	....	....	....	....
	Phoenix Coyotes	4	0	4	4	8	....	....	....	....	....
	NHL Totals	**370**	**79**	**152**	**231**	**223**	**40**	**10**	**14**	**24**	**22**

Traded to **Phoenix** by **Pittsburgh** with Francois Leroux for Ramzi Abid, Dan Focht and Guillaume Lefebvre, March 11, 2003.

HRDINA, Jiri

Center. Shoots left. 6', 195 lbs. Born, Prague, Czech., January 5, 1958.
(Calgary's 8th choice, 159th overall, in 1984 Entry Draft).

Season	Club	GP	G	A	Pts	PIM	GP	G	A	Pts	PIM
1987-88	Calgary Flames	9	2	5	7	2	1	0	0	0	0
1988-89 ♦	Calgary Flames	70	22	32	54	26	4	0	0	0	0
1989-90	Calgary Flames	64	12	18	30	31	6	0	1	1	2
1990-91	Calgary Flames	14	0	3	3	4	....	....	....	....	....
♦	Pittsburgh Penguins	37	6	14	20	13	14	2	2	4	6
1991-92 ♦	Pittsburgh Penguins	56	3	13	16	16	21	0	2	2	16
	NHL Totals	**250**	**45**	**85**	**130**	**92**	**46**	**2**	**5**	**7**	**24**

Traded to **Pittsburgh** by **Calgary** for Jim Kyte, December 13, 1990.

HRECHKOSY, Dave

Left wing. Shoots left. 6'2", 195 lbs. Born, Winnipeg, Man., November 1, 1951.

Season	Club	GP	G	A	Pts	PIM	GP	G	A	Pts	PIM
1973-74	California Golden Seals	2	0	0	0	0	....	....	....	....	....
1974-75	California Golden Seals	72	29	14	43	25	....	....	....	....	....
1975-76	California Golden Seals	38	9	5	14	14	....	....	....	....	....
	St. Louis Blues	13	3	3	6	0	3	1	0	1	2
1976-77	St. Louis Blues	15	1	2	3	2	....	....	....	....	....
	NHL Totals	**140**	**42**	**24**	**66**	**41**	**3**	**1**	**0**	**1**	**2**

Traded to **California** by **NY Rangers** with Gary Coalter to complete transaction that sent Bert Marshall to NY Rangers (March 4, 1973), May 17, 1973. Traded to **St. Louis** by **California** for St. Louis' 5th round choice (Cal Sandbeck) in 1976 Amateur Draft and California's 3rd round choice (previously acquired, California selected Reg Kerr) in 1977 Amateur Draft, March 9, 1976.

HRKAC, Tony

Center. Shoots left. 5'10", 190 lbs. Born, Thunder Bay, Ont., July 7, 1966.
(St. Louis' 2nd choice, 32nd overall, in 1984 Entry Draft).

Season	Club	GP	G	A	Pts	PIM	GP	G	A	Pts	PIM
1986-87	St. Louis Blues	....	....	....	....	....	3	0	0	0	0
1987-88	St. Louis Blues	67	11	37	48	22	10	6	1	7	4
1988-89	St. Louis Blues	70	17	28	45	8	4	1	1	2	0
1989-90	St. Louis Blues	28	5	12	17	8	....	....	....	....	....
	Quebec Nordiques	22	4	8	12	2	....	....	....	....	....
1990-91	Quebec Nordiques	70	16	32	48	16	....	....	....	....	....
1991-92	San Jose Sharks	22	2	10	12	4	....	....	....	....	....
	Chicago Blackhawks	18	1	2	3	6	3	0	0	0	2
1993-94	St. Louis Blues	36	6	5	11	8	4	0	0	0	0
1997-98	Dallas Stars	13	5	3	8	0	....	....	....	....	....
	Edmonton Oilers	36	8	11	19	10	12	0	3	3	2
1998-99 ♦	Dallas Stars	69	13	14	27	26	5	0	2	2	4
99-2000	New York Islanders	7	0	2	2	0	....	....	....	....	....
	Mighty Ducks of Anaheim	60	4	7	11	8	....	....	....	....	....
2000-01	Mighty Ducks of Anaheim	80	13	25	38	29	....	....	....	....	....
2001-02	Atlanta Thrashers	80	18	26	44	12	....	....	....	....	....
2002-03	Atlanta Thrashers	80	9	17	26	14	....	....	....	....	....
	NHL Totals	**758**	**132**	**239**	**371**	**173**	**41**	**7**	**7**	**14**	**12**

Traded to **Quebec** by **St. Louis** with Greg Millen for Jeff Brown, December 13, 1989. Traded to **San Jose** by **Quebec** for Greg Paslawski, May 31, 1991. Traded to **Chicago** by **San Jose** for Chicago's 6th round choice (Fredrik Oduya) in 1993 Entry Draft, February 7, 1992. Signed as a free agent by **St. Louis**, July 30, 1993. Signed as a free agent by **Dallas**, August 12, 1997. Claimed on waivers by **Edmonton** from **Dallas**, January 6, 1998. Traded to **Pittsburgh** by **Edmonton** with Bobby Dollas for Josef Beranek, June 16, 1998. Claimed by **Nashville** from **Pittsburgh** in Expansion Draft, June 26, 1998. Traded to **Dallas** by **Nashville** for future considerations, July 9, 1998. Signed as a free agent by **NY Islanders**, July 29, 1999. Traded to **Anaheim** by **NY Islanders** with Dean Malkoc for Ted Drury, October 29, 1999. Signed as a free agent by **Atlanta**, July 25, 2001.

HRYCUIK, Jim

Center. Shoots left. 5'10", 180 lbs. Born, Rosthern, Sask., October 7, 1949.

Season	Club	GP	G	A	Pts	PIM	GP	G	A	Pts	PIM
1974-75	Washington Capitals	21	5	5	10	12	....	....	....	....	....
	NHL Totals	**21**	**5**	**5**	**10**	**12**	....	....	....	....	....

Claimed by **Washington** from **Hershey** (AHL) in Intra-League Draft, June 12, 1974.

HRYMNAK, Steve

Defense. Shoots left. 5'11", 178 lbs. Born, Port Arthur, Ont., March 3, 1926.

Season	Club	GP	G	A	Pts	PIM	GP	G	A	Pts	PIM
1951-52	Chicago Black Hawks	18	2	1	3	4	....	....	....	....	....
1952-53	Detroit Red Wings	....	....	....	....	....	2	0	0	0	0
	NHL Totals	**18**	**2**	**1**	**3**	**4**	**2**	**0**	**0**	**0**	**0**

Traded to **Chicago** (St. Louis-AHL) by **NY Rangers** for cash, September 19, 1950. Traded to **Detroit** by **Chicago** with Red Almas and Guyle Fielder for cash, September 23, 1952.

HRYNEWICH, Tim

Left wing. Shoots left. 5'11", 190 lbs. Born, Leamington, Ont., October 2, 1963.
(Pittsburgh's 2nd choice, 38th overall, in 1982 Entry Draft).

Season	Club	GP	G	A	Pts	PIM	GP	G	A	Pts	PIM
1982-83	Pittsburgh Penguins	30	2	3	5	48	....	....	....	....	....
1983-84	Pittsburgh Penguins	25	4	5	9	34	....	....	....	....	....
	NHL Totals	**55**	**6**	**8**	**14**	**82**	....	....	....	....	....

Traded to **Edmonton** by **Pittsburgh** with Marty McSorley and future considerations (Craig Muni, October 6, 1986) for Gilles Meloche, September 11, 1985.

HUARD, Bill

Left wing. Shoots left. 6'1", 215 lbs. Born, Welland, Ont., June 24, 1967.

Season	Club	GP	G	A	Pts	PIM	GP	G	A	Pts	PIM
1992-93	Boston Bruins	2	0	0	0	0	....	....	....	....	....
1993-94	Ottawa Senators	63	2	2	4	162	....	....	....	....	....
1994-95	Ottawa Senators	26	1	1	2	64	....	....	....	....	....
	Quebec Nordiques	7	2	2	4	13	1	0	0	0	0
1995-96	Dallas Stars	51	6	6	12	176	....	....	....	....	....
1996-97	Dallas Stars	40	5	6	11	105	....	....	....	....	....
1997-98	Edmonton Oilers	30	0	1	1	72	4	0	0	0	2
1998-99	Edmonton Oilers	3	0	0	0	0	....	....	....	....	....
99-2000	Los Angeles Kings	1	0	0	0	2	....	....	....	....	....
	NHL Totals	**223**	**16**	**18**	**34**	**594**	**5**	**0**	**0**	**0**	**2**

Signed as a free agent by **New Jersey**, October 1, 1989. Signed as a free agent by **Boston**, December 4, 1992. Signed as a free agent by **Ottawa**, June 30, 1993. Traded to **Quebec** by **Ottawa** for the rights to Mika Stromberg and Quebec's 4th round choice (Kevin Boyd) in 1995 Entry Draft, April 7, 1995. Transferred to **Colorado** after **Quebec** franchise relocated, July 1, 1995. Claimed by **Dallas** from **Colorado** in NHL Waiver Draft, October 2, 1995. Signed as a free agent by **Edmonton**, July 22, 1997. Signed as a free agent by **Los Angeles**, July 19, 1999. Traded to **Atlanta** by **Los Angeles** for future considerations, January 25, 2000.

HUARD, Rolly

Center. Shoots left. 5'10", 170 lbs. Born, Ottawa, Ont., September 6, 1902.

Season	Club	REGULAR SEASON GP	G	A	Pts	PIM	PLAYOFFS GP	G	A	Pts	PIM
1930-31	Toronto Maple Leafs	1	1	0	1	0	....	....	....	....	....
	NHL Totals	**1**	**1**	**0**	**1**	**0**	....	....	....	....	....

Traded to **Buffalo** (Can-Pro) by **Mtl. Maroons** (Windsor/Can-Pro) for Mike Neville, November 18, 1928. Loaned to **Toronto** by **Buffalo** (IHL) as an emergency injury replacement, December 14, 1930. • One of only three players (Dean Morton, Matt Stajan) to score a goal in only NHL game. Traded to **Syracuse** (IHL) by **Buffalo** (IHL) for Martin Lauder, January 3, 1931. Traded to **Toronto** (London-IHL) by **Syracuse** (IHL) for Wallace Moore and Jimmy Smith, January 29, 1931.

HUBACEK, Petr

Center. Shoots right. 6'2", 183 lbs. Born, Brno, Czech., September 2, 1979.
(Philadelphia's 11th choice, 243rd overall, in 1998 Entry Draft).

Season	Club	GP	G	A	Pts	PIM	GP	G	A	Pts	PIM
2000-01	Philadelphia Flyers	6	1	0	1	2	....	....	....	....	....
	NHL Totals	**6**	**1**	**0**	**1**	**2**	....	....	....	....	....

Traded to **Nashville** by **Philadelphia** with Jason Beckett for Yves Sarault and a conditional choice in 2003 Entry Draft, January 11, 2002.

HUBER, Willie

Defense. Shoots right. 6'5", 228 lbs. Born, Strasskirchen, West Germany, January 15, 1958.
(Detroit's 1st choice, 9th overall, in 1978 Amateur Draft).

Season	Club	GP	G	A	Pts	PIM	GP	G	A	Pts	PIM
1978-79	Detroit Red Wings	68	7	24	31	114	....	....	....	....	....
1979-80	Detroit Red Wings	76	17	23	40	164	....	....	....	....	....
1980-81	Detroit Red Wings	80	15	34	49	130	....	....	....	....	....
1981-82	Detroit Red Wings	74	15	30	45	98	....	....	....	....	....
1982-83	Detroit Red Wings	74	14	29	43	106	....	....	....	....	....
1983-84	New York Rangers	42	9	14	23	60	4	1	1	2	9
1984-85	New York Rangers	49	3	11	14	55	2	1	0	1	2
1985-86	New York Rangers	70	7	8	15	85	16	3	2	5	16
1986-87	New York Rangers	66	8	22	30	68	6	0	2	2	6
1987-88	New York Rangers	11	1	3	4	14	....	....	....	....	....
	Vancouver Canucks	35	4	10	14	40	....	....	....	....	....
	Philadelphia Flyers	10	4	9	13	16	5	0	0	0	2
	NHL Totals	**655**	**104**	**217**	**321**	**950**	**33**	**5**	**5**	**10**	**35**

Played in NHL All-Star Game (1983)

Traded to **NY Rangers** by **Detroit** with Mike Blaisdell and Mark Osborne for Ron Duguay, Eddie Mio and Eddie Johnstone, June 13, 1983. Traded to **Vancouver** by **NY Rangers** with Larry Melynk for Michel Petit, November 4, 1987. Traded to **Philadelphia** by **Vancouver** for Paul Lawless and Vancouver's 5th round choice (previously acquired, later traded to Edmonton – Edmonton selected Peter White) in 1989 Entry Draft, March 1, 1988.

HUBICK, Greg

Defense. Shoots left. 5'11", 185 lbs. Born, Strasbourg, Sask., November 12, 1951.
(Montreal's 9th choice, 53rd overall, in 1971 Amateur Draft).

Season	Club	GP	G	A	Pts	PIM	GP	G	A	Pts	PIM
1975-76	Toronto Maple Leafs	72	6	8	14	10	....	....	....	....	....
1979-80	Vancouver Canucks	5	0	1	1	0	....	....	....	....	....
	NHL Totals	**77**	**6**	**9**	**15**	**10**	....	....	....	....	....

Traded to **Toronto** by **Montreal** for Doug Jarvis, June 26, 1975. Signed as a free agent by **Vancouver**, September 7, 1979.

HUCK, Fran

Center. Shoots left. 5'7", 165 lbs. Born, Regina, Sask., December 4, 1945.

Season	Club	GP	G	A	Pts	PIM	GP	G	A	Pts	PIM
1969-70	Montreal Canadiens	2	0	0	0	0	....	....	....	....	....
1970-71	Montreal Canadiens	5	1	2	3	0	....	....	....	....	....
	St. Louis Blues	29	7	8	15	18	6	1	2	3	2
1972-73	St. Louis Blues	58	16	20	36	20	5	2	2	4	0
	NHL Totals	**94**	**24**	**30**	**54**	**38**	**11**	**3**	**4**	**7**	**2**

Signed as a free agent by **Montreal**, March, 1970. Traded to **St. Louis** by **Montreal** for St. Louis' 2nd round choice (Michel Deguise) in 1971 Amateur Draft, January 28, 1971.

HUCUL, Fred

Defense. Shoots left. 5'10", 170 lbs. Born, Tubrose, Sask., December 4, 1931.

Season	Club	GP	G	A	Pts	PIM	GP	G	A	Pts	PIM
1950-51	Chicago Black Hawks	3	1	0	1	2	....	....	....	....	....
1951-52	Chicago Black Hawks	34	3	7	10	37	....	....	....	....	....
1952-53	Chicago Black Hawks	57	5	7	12	25	6	1	0	1	10
1953-54	Chicago Black Hawks	27	0	3	3	19	....	....	....	....	....
1967-68	St. Louis Blues	43	2	13	15	30	....	....	....	....	....
	NHL Totals	**164**	**11**	**30**	**41**	**113**	**6**	**1**	**0**	**1**	**10**

Traded to **Calgary** (WHL) by **Chicago** for cash, September, 1954. Traded to **Toronto** by **Calgary** (WHL) for cash, August, 1963. Claimed by **St. Louis** from **Toronto** in Expansion Draft, June 6, 1967.

HUDDY, Charlie

Defense. Shoots left. 6', 210 lbs. Born, Oshawa, Ont., June 2, 1959.

Season	Club	GP	G	A	Pts	PIM	GP	G	A	Pts	PIM
1980-81	Edmonton Oilers	12	2	5	7	6	....	....	....	....	....
1981-82	Edmonton Oilers	41	4	11	15	46	5	1	2	3	14
1982-83	Edmonton Oilers	76	20	37	57	58	15	1	6	7	10
1983-84 ♦	Edmonton Oilers	75	8	34	42	43	12	1	9	10	8
1984-85 ♦	Edmonton Oilers	80	7	44	51	46	18	3	17	20	17
1985-86	Edmonton Oilers	76	6	35	41	55	7	0	2	2	0
1986-87 ♦	Edmonton Oilers	58	4	15	19	35	21	1	7	8	21
1987-88 ♦	Edmonton Oilers	77	13	28	41	71	13	4	5	9	10
1988-89	Edmonton Oilers	76	11	33	44	52	7	2	0	2	4
1989-90 ♦	Edmonton Oilers	70	1	23	24	56	22	0	6	6	11
1990-91	Edmonton Oilers	53	5	22	27	32	18	3	7	10	10
1991-92	Los Angeles Kings	56	4	19	23	43	6	1	1	2	10
1992-93	Los Angeles Kings	82	2	25	27	64	23	1	4	5	12
1993-94	Los Angeles Kings	79	5	13	18	71	....	....	....	....	....
1994-95	Los Angeles Kings	9	0	1	1	6	....	....	....	....	....
	Buffalo Sabres	32	2	4	6	36	3	0	0	0	0
1995-96	Buffalo Sabres	52	5	5	10	59	....	....	....	....	....
	St. Louis Blues	12	0	0	0	6	13	1	0	1	8
1996-97	Buffalo Sabres	1	0	0	0	0	....	....	....	....	....
	NHL Totals	**1017**	**99**	**354**	**453**	**785**	**183**	**19**	**66**	**85**	**135**

NHL Plus/Minus Leader (1983)

Signed as a free agent by **Edmonton**, September 14, 1979. Claimed by **Minnesota** from **Edmonton** in Expansion Draft, May 30, 1991. Traded to **Los Angeles** by **Minnesota** with Randy Gilhen, Jim Thomson and NY Rangers' 4th round choice (previously acquired, Los Angeles selected Alexei Zhitnik) in 1991 Entry Draft for Todd Elik, June 22, 1991. Traded to **Buffalo** by **Los Angeles** with Alexei Zhitnik, Robb Stauber and Los Angeles' 5th round choice (Marian Menhart) in 1995 Entry Draft for Philippe Boucher, Denis Tsygurov and Grant Fuhr, February 14, 1995. Traded to **St. Louis** by **Buffalo** with Buffalo's 7th round choice (Daniel Corso) in 1996 Entry Draft for Denis Hamel, March 19, 1996. Signed as a free agent by **Buffalo**, September 26, 1996.

HUDSON, Dave

Center. Shoots left. 6', 185 lbs. Born, St. Thomas, Ont., December 28, 1949.
(Chicago's 6th choice, 71st overall, in 1969 Amateur Draft).

Season	Club	GP	G	A	Pts	PIM	GP	G	A	Pts	PIM
1972-73	New York Islanders	69	12	19	31	17	....	....	....	....	....
1973-74	New York Islanders	63	2	10	12	7	....	....	....	....	....
1974-75	Kansas City Scouts	70	9	32	41	27	....	....	....	....	....
1975-76	Kansas City Scouts	74	11	20	31	12	....	....	....	....	....
1976-77	Colorado Rockies	73	15	21	36	14	....	....	....	....	....
1977-78	Colorado Rockies	60	10	22	32	12	2	1	1	2	0
	NHL Totals	**409**	**59**	**124**	**183**	**89**	**2**	**1**	**1**	**2**	**0**

Claimed by **Chicago** (Portland-WHL) from **Chicago** in Reverse Draft, June 10, 1970. Claimed by **NY Islanders** from **Chicago** in Expansion Draft, June 6, 1972. Claimed by **Kansas City** from **NY Islanders** in Expansion Draft, June 12, 1974. Transferred to **Colorado** after **Kansas City** franchise relocated, June, 1976.

HUDSON, Lex

Defense. Shoots left. 6'3", 184 lbs. Born, Winnipeg, Man., December 31, 1955.
(Pittsburgh's 12th choice, 196th overall, in 1975 Amateur Draft).

Season	Club	GP	G	A	Pts	PIM	GP	G	A	Pts	PIM
1978-79	Pittsburgh Penguins	2	0	0	0	0	2	0	0	0	0
	NHL Totals	**2**	**0**	**0**	**0**	**0**	**2**	**0**	**0**	**0**	**0**

HUDSON, Mike

Center/Left wing. Shoots left. 6'1", 205 lbs. Born, Guelph, Ont., February 6, 1967.
(Chicago's 6th choice, 140th overall, in 1986 Entry Draft).

Season	Club	GP	G	A	Pts	PIM	GP	G	A	Pts	PIM
1988-89	Chicago Blackhawks	41	7	16	23	20	10	1	2	3	18
1989-90	Chicago Blackhawks	49	9	12	21	56	4	0	0	0	2
1990-91	Chicago Blackhawks	55	7	9	16	62	6	0	2	2	8
1991-92	Chicago Blackhawks	76	14	15	29	92	16	3	5	8	26
1992-93	Chicago Blackhawks	36	1	6	7	44	....	....	....	....	....
	Edmonton Oilers	5	0	1	1	2	....	....	....	....	....
1993-94 ♦	New York Rangers	48	4	7	11	47	....	....	....	....	....
1994-95	Pittsburgh Penguins	40	2	9	11	34	11	0	0	0	6
1995-96	Toronto Maple Leafs	27	2	0	2	29	....	....	....	....	....
	St. Louis Blues	32	3	12	15	26	2	0	1	1	4
1996-97	Phoenix Coyotes	7	0	0	0	2	....	....	....	....	....
	NHL Totals	**416**	**49**	**87**	**136**	**414**	**49**	**4**	**10**	**14**	**64**

Traded to **Edmonton** by **Chicago** for Craig Muni, March 22, 1993. Claimed by **NY Rangers** from **Edmonton** in NHL Waiver Draft, October 3, 1993. Claimed by **Pittsburgh** from **NY Rangers** in NHL Waiver Draft, January 18, 1995. Signed as a free agent by **Toronto**, September 22, 1995. Claimed on waivers by **St. Louis** from **Toronto**, January 4, 1996. Signed as a free agent by **Phoenix**, November 12, 1996.

HUDSON, Ron

Center. Shoots left. 5'8", 148 lbs. Born, Calgary, Alta., July 14, 1911.

Season	Club	GP	G	A	Pts	PIM	GP	G	A	Pts	PIM
1937-38	Detroit Red Wings	32	5	2	7	2	....	....	....	....	....
1939-40	Detroit Red Wings	1	0	0	0	0	....	....	....	....	....
	NHL Totals	**33**	**5**	**2**	**7**	**2**	....	....	....	....	....

Signed as a free agent by **Detroit**, October 15, 1935. Traded to **Providence** (IAHL) by **Detroit** (Pittsburgh-IAHL) for cash, November 1, 1938.

HUFFMAN, Kerry

Defense. Shoots left. 6'2", 200 lbs. Born, Peterborough, Ont., January 3, 1968.
(Philadelphia's 1st choice, 20th overall, in 1986 Entry Draft).

Season	Club	GP	G	A	Pts	PIM	GP	G	A	Pts	PIM
1986-87	Philadelphia Flyers	9	0	0	0	2	....	....	....	....	....
1987-88	Philadelphia Flyers	52	6	17	23	34	2	0	0	0	0
1988-89	Philadelphia Flyers	29	0	11	11	31	....	....	....	....	....
1989-90	Philadelphia Flyers	43	1	12	13	34	....	....	....	....	....
1990-91	Philadelphia Flyers	10	1	2	3	10	....	....	....	....	....
1991-92	Philadelphia Flyers	60	14	18	32	41	....	....	....	....	....
1992-93	Quebec Nordiques	52	4	18	22	54	3	0	0	0	0
1993-94	Quebec Nordiques	28	0	6	6	28	....	....	....	....	....
	Ottawa Senators	34	4	8	12	12	....	....	....	....	....
1994-95	Ottawa Senators	37	2	4	6	46	....	....	....	....	....

Season	Club	REGULAR SEASON GP	G	A	Pts	PIM	PLAYOFFS GP	G	A	Pts	PIM
1995-96	Ottawa Senators	43	4	11	15	63	....	....	....	....	....
	Philadelphia Flyers	4	1	1	2	6	6	0	0	0	2
	NHL Totals	**401**	**37**	**108**	**145**	**361**	**11**	**0**	**0**	**0**	**2**

Traded to **Quebec** by **Philadelphia** with Steve Duchesne, Peter Forsberg, Mike Ricci, Ron Hextall, Philadelphia's 1st round choice (Jocelyn Thibault) in 1993 Entry Draft, $15,000,000 and future considerations (Chris Simon and Philadelphia's 1st round choice (later traded to Toronto – later traded to Washington – Washington selected Nolan Baumgartner) in 1994 Entry Draft, July 21, 1992) for Eric Lindros, June 30, 1992. Claimed on waivers by **Ottawa** from **Quebec**, January 15, 1994. Traded to **Philadelphia** by **Ottawa** for future considerations, March 19, 1996.

HUGGINS, Al

Left wing. Shoots left. 6', 160 lbs. Born, Toronto, Ont., December 21, 1910.

Season	Club	REGULAR SEASON GP	G	A	Pts	PIM	PLAYOFFS GP	G	A	Pts	PIM
1930-31	Montreal Maroons	20	1	1	2	2	....	....	....	....	....
	NHL Totals	**20**	**1**	**1**	**2**	**2**	....	....	....	....	....

Signed as a free agent by **Mtl. Maroons**, September 2, 1930. Traded to **Toronto** (Syracuse-IHL) by **Mtl. Maroons** (Windsor-IHL) for Stew Adams, November 1, 1933.

HUGHES, Albert

Center/Left wing. Shoots right. 5'9", 165 lbs. Born, Guelph, Ont., May 13, 1901.

Season	Club	REGULAR SEASON GP	G	A	Pts	PIM	PLAYOFFS GP	G	A	Pts	PIM
1930-31	New York Americans	42	5	7	12	14	....	....	....	....	....
1931-32	New York Americans	18	1	1	2	8	....	....	....	....	....
	NHL Totals	**60**	**6**	**8**	**14**	**22**	....	....	....	....	....

Signed as a free agent by **NY Americans**, January 18, 1927.

HUGHES, Brent

Defense. Shoots left. 6', 205 lbs. Born, Bowmanville, Ont., June 17, 1943.

Season	Club	REGULAR SEASON GP	G	A	Pts	PIM	PLAYOFFS GP	G	A	Pts	PIM
1967-68	Los Angeles Kings	44	4	10	14	36	7	0	0	0	10
1968-69	Los Angeles Kings	72	2	19	21	73	11	1	3	4	37
1969-70	Los Angeles Kings	52	1	7	8	108	....	....	....	....	....
1970-71	Philadelphia Flyers	30	1	10	11	21	4	0	0	0	6
1971-72	Philadelphia Flyers	63	2	20	22	35	....	....	....	....	....
1972-73	Philadelphia Flyers	29	2	11	13	32	....	....	....	....	....
	St. Louis Blues	8	1	1	2	0	....	....	....	....	....
1973-74	St. Louis Blues	2	0	0	0	0	....	....	....	....	....
	Detroit Red Wings	69	1	21	22	92	....	....	....	....	....
1974-75	Kansas City Scouts	66	1	18	19	43	....	....	....	....	....
	NHL Totals	**435**	**15**	**117**	**132**	**440**	**22**	**1**	**3**	**4**	**53**

Claimed by **Detroit** (Springfield-AHL) from **Boston** in Reverse Draft, June 9, 1965. Claimed by **Los Angeles** from **Detroit** in Expansion Draft, June 6, 1967. Traded to **Philadelphia** by **Los Angeles** for Mike Byers, May 20, 1970. Traded to **St. Louis** by **Philadelphia** with Pierre Plante for Andre Dupont and St. Louis' 3rd round choice (Bob Stumpf) in 1973 Amateur Draft, December 14, 1972. Traded to **Detroit** by **St. Louis** for cash, October 27, 1973. Claimed by **Kansas City** from **Detroit** in Expansion Draft, June 12, 1974.

HUGHES, Brent

Left wing. Shoots left. 5'11", 195 lbs. Born, New Westminster, B.C., April 5, 1966.

Season	Club	REGULAR SEASON GP	G	A	Pts	PIM	PLAYOFFS GP	G	A	Pts	PIM
1988-89	Winnipeg Jets	28	3	2	5	82	....	....	....	....	....
1989-90	Winnipeg Jets	11	1	2	3	33	....	....	....	....	....
1991-92	Boston Bruins	8	1	1	2	38	10	2	0	2	20
1992-93	Boston Bruins	62	5	4	9	191	1	0	0	0	2
1993-94	Boston Bruins	77	13	11	24	143	13	2	1	3	27
1994-95	Boston Bruins	44	6	6	12	139	5	0	0	0	4
1995-96	Buffalo Sabres	76	5	10	15	148	....	....	....	....	....
1996-97	New York Islanders	51	7	3	10	57	....	....	....	....	....
	NHL Totals	**357**	**41**	**39**	**80**	**831**	**29**	**4**	**1**	**5**	**53**

Signed as a free agent by **Winnipeg**, June 13, 1988. Traded to **Washington** by **Winnipeg** with Craig Duncanson and Simon Wheeldon for Bob Joyce, Tyler Larter and Kent Paynter, May 21, 1991. Traded to **Boston** by **Washington** with future considerations for John Byce and Dennis Smith, February 24, 1992. Claimed By **Buffalo** from **Boston** in NHL Waiver Draft, October 2, 1995. Signed as a free agent by **NY Islanders**, August 9, 1996.

HUGHES, Frank

Left wing. Shoots left. 5'10", 180 lbs. Born, Fernie, B.C., October 1, 1949.
(Toronto's 4th choice, 43rd overall, in 1969 Amateur Draft).

Season	Club	REGULAR SEASON GP	G	A	Pts	PIM	PLAYOFFS GP	G	A	Pts	PIM
1971-72	California Golden Seals	5	0	0	0	0	....	....	....	....	....
	NHL Totals	**5**	**0**	**0**	**0**	**0**	....	....	....	....	....

Claimed by **California** from **Toronto** in Intra-League Draft, June 8, 1971. Claimed by **Atlanta** from **California** in Expansion Draft, June 6, 1972.

HUGHES, Howie

Right wing. Shoots left. 5'9", 180 lbs. Born, St. Boniface, Man., April 4, 1939.

Season	Club	REGULAR SEASON GP	G	A	Pts	PIM	PLAYOFFS GP	G	A	Pts	PIM
1967-68	Los Angeles Kings	74	9	14	23	20	7	2	0	2	0
1968-69	Los Angeles Kings	73	16	14	30	10	7	0	0	0	2
1969-70	Los Angeles Kings	21	0	4	4	0	....	....	....	....	....
	NHL Totals	**168**	**25**	**32**	**57**	**30**	**14**	**2**	**0**	**2**	**2**

Claimed by **Los Angeles** from **Montreal** in Expansion Draft, June 6, 1967. Loaned to **Denver** (WHL) by **Los Angeles** for cash, November, 1970. Claimed by **San Diego** (WHL) from **Los Angeles** (Seattle-WHL) in Reverse Draft, June, 1972.

HUGHES, Jack

Defense. Shoots right. 6'1", 205 lbs. Born, Somerville, MA, July 20, 1957.
(Colorado's 8th choice, 142nd overall, in 1977 Amateur Draft).

Season	Club	REGULAR SEASON GP	G	A	Pts	PIM	PLAYOFFS GP	G	A	Pts	PIM
1980-81	Colorado Rockies	38	2	5	7	91	....	....	....	....	....
1981-82	Colorado Rockies	8	0	0	0	13	....	....	....	....	....
	NHL Totals	**46**	**2**	**5**	**7**	**104**	....	....	....	....	....

HUGHES, James

Defense. Shoots right. 5'9", 190 lbs. Born, Webbwood, Ont., May 12, 1906.

Season	Club	REGULAR SEASON GP	G	A	Pts	PIM	PLAYOFFS GP	G	A	Pts	PIM
1929-30	Detroit Cougars	40	0	1	1	48	....	....	....	....	....
	NHL Totals	**40**	**0**	**1**	**1**	**48**	....	....	....	....	....

Claimed by **Detroit** from **Windsor** (Can-Pro) in Inter-League Draft, May 13, 1929. Traded to **Syracuse** (IHL) by **Detroit** for Val Hoffinger, December 7, 1930.

HUGHES, John

Defense. Shoots left. 5'11", 200 lbs. Born, Charlottetown, P.E.I., March 18, 1954.
(Vancouver's 2nd choice, 41st overall, in 1974 Amateur Draft).

Season	Club	REGULAR SEASON GP	G	A	Pts	PIM	PLAYOFFS GP	G	A	Pts	PIM
1979-80	Vancouver Canucks	52	2	11	13	181	4	0	0	0	10
1980-81	Edmonton Oilers	18	0	3	3	30	....	....	....	....	....
	New York Rangers	....	....	....	....	....	3	0	1	1	6
	NHL Totals	**70**	**2**	**14**	**16**	**211**	**7**	**0**	**1**	**1**	**16**

Reclaimed by **Vancouver** from **Edmonton** prior to Expansion Draft, June 9, 1979. Claimed on waivers by **Edmonton** from **Vancouver**, December 15, 1980. Traded to **NY Rangers** by **Edmonton** for Ray Markham, March 10, 1981.

HUGHES, Pat

Right wing. Shoots right. 6'1", 180 lbs. Born, Calgary, Alta., March 25, 1955.
(Montreal's 6th choice, 52nd overall, in 1975 Amateur Draft).

Season	Club	REGULAR SEASON GP	G	A	Pts	PIM	PLAYOFFS GP	G	A	Pts	PIM
1977-78	Montreal Canadiens	3	0	0	0	2	....	....	....	....	....
1978-79♦	Montreal Canadiens	41	9	8	17	22	8	1	2	3	4
1979-80	Pittsburgh Penguins	76	18	14	32	78	5	0	0	0	21
1980-81	Pittsburgh Penguins	58	10	9	19	161	....	....	....	....	....
	Edmonton Oilers	2	0	0	0	0	5	0	5	5	16
1981-82	Edmonton Oilers	68	24	22	46	99	5	2	1	3	6
1982-83	Edmonton Oilers	80	25	20	45	85	16	2	5	7	14
1983-84♦	Edmonton Oilers	77	27	28	55	61	19	2	11	13	12
1984-85♦	Edmonton Oilers	73	12	13	25	85	10	1	1	2	4
1985-86	Buffalo Sabres	50	4	9	13	25	....	....	....	....	....
1986-87	St. Louis Blues	43	1	5	6	26	....	....	....	....	....
	Hartford Whalers	2	0	0	0	2	3	0	0	0	0
	NHL Totals	**573**	**130**	**128**	**258**	**646**	**71**	**8**	**25**	**33**	**77**

Traded to **Pittsburgh** by **Montreal** with Robbie Holland for Denis Herron and Pittsburgh's 2nd round choice (Jocelyn Gauvreau) in 1982 Entry Draft, August 30, 1979. Traded to **Edmonton** by **Pittsburgh** for Pat Price, March 10, 1981. Traded to **Pittsburgh** by **Edmonton** for Mike Moller, October 4, 1985. Traded to **Buffalo** by **Pittsburgh** for Mike Moller and Randy Cunneyworth, October 4, 1985. Claimed by **St. Louis** from **Buffalo** in Waiver Draft, October 6, 1986. Traded to **Hartford** by **St. Louis** for Hartford's 10th round choice (Andy Cesarski) in 1987 Entry Draft, March 10, 1987.

HUGHES, Ryan

Center. Shoots left. 6'2", 196 lbs. Born, Montreal, Que., January 17, 1972.
(Quebec's 2nd choice, 22nd overall, in 1990 Entry Draft).

Season	Club	REGULAR SEASON GP	G	A	Pts	PIM	PLAYOFFS GP	G	A	Pts	PIM
1995-96	Boston Bruins	3	0	0	0	0	....	....	....	....	....
	NHL Totals	**3**	**0**	**0**	**0**	**0**	....	....	....	....	....

Signed as a free agent by **Boston**, October 6, 1995.

HULBIG, Joe

Left wing. Shoots left. 6'3", 215 lbs. Born, Norwood, MA, September 29, 1973.
(Edmonton's 1st choice, 13th overall, in 1992 Entry Draft).

Season	Club	REGULAR SEASON GP	G	A	Pts	PIM	PLAYOFFS GP	G	A	Pts	PIM
1996-97	Edmonton Oilers	6	0	0	0	0	6	0	1	1	2
1997-98	Edmonton Oilers	17	2	2	4	2	....	....	....	....	....
1998-99	Edmonton Oilers	1	0	0	0	2	....	....	....	....	....
99-2000	Boston Bruins	24	2	2	4	8	....	....	....	....	....
2000-01	Boston Bruins	7	0	0	0	4	....	....	....	....	....
	NHL Totals	**55**	**4**	**4**	**8**	**16**	**6**	**0**	**1**	**1**	**2**

Signed as a free agent by **Boston**, July 23, 1999.

HULL, Bobby

HHOF

Left wing. Shoots left. 5'10", 195 lbs. Born, Pointe Anne, Ont., January 3, 1939.

Season	Club	REGULAR SEASON GP	G	A	Pts	PIM	PLAYOFFS GP	G	A	Pts	PIM
1957-58	Chicago Black Hawks	70	13	34	47	62	....	....	....	....	....
1958-59	Chicago Black Hawks	70	18	32	50	50	6	1	1	2	2
1959-60	Chicago Black Hawks	70	*39	42	*81	68	3	1	0	1	2
1960-61♦	Chicago Black Hawks	67	31	25	56	43	12	4	10	14	4
1961-62	Chicago Black Hawks	70	*50	34	*84	35	12	*8	6	14	12
1962-63	Chicago Black Hawks	65	31	31	62	27	5	*8	2	10	4
1963-64	Chicago Black Hawks	70	*43	44	87	50	7	2	5	7	2
1964-65	Chicago Black Hawks	61	39	32	71	32	14	*10	7	*17	27
1965-66	Chicago Black Hawks	65	*54	43	*97	70	6	2	2	4	10
1966-67	Chicago Black Hawks	66	*52	28	80	52	6	4	2	6	0
1967-68	Chicago Black Hawks	71	*44	31	75	39	11	4	6	10	15
1968-69	Chicago Black Hawks	74	*58	49	107	48	....	....	....	....	....
1969-70	Chicago Black Hawks	61	38	29	67	8	8	3	8	11	2
1970-71	Chicago Black Hawks	78	44	52	96	32	18	11	14	25	16
1971-72	Chicago Black Hawks	78	50	43	93	24	8	4	4	8	6

Season	Club	GP	G	A	Pts	PIM	GP	G	A	Pts	PIM
		REGULAR SEASON					PLAYOFFS				
1979-80	Winnipeg Jets	18	4	6	10	0	....	....	....	....	....
	Hartford Whalers	9	2	5	7	0	3	0	0	0	0
	NHL Totals	**1063**	**610**	**560**	**1170**	**640**	**119**	**62**	**67**	**129**	**102**

• Brother of Dennis • Father of Brett • NHL First All-Star Team (1960, 1962, 1964, 1965, 1966, 1967, 1968, 1969, 1970, 1972) • Art Ross Trophy (1960, 1962, 1966) • NHL Second All-Star Team (1963, 1971) • Lady Byng Trophy (1965) • Hart Trophy (1965, 1966) • Lester Patrick Trophy (1969)

Played in NHL All-Star Game (1960, 1961, 1962, 1963, 1964, 1965, 1967, 1968, 1969, 1970, 1971, 1972)

Reclaimed by **Chicago** from **Winnipeg** prior to Expansion Draft, June 9, 1979. Claimed by **Winnipeg** from **Chicago** in Expansion Draft, June 13, 1979. Traded to **Hartford** by **Winnipeg** for future considerations, February 27, 1980.

HULL, Brett

Right wing. Shoots right. 5'11", 203 lbs. Born, Belleville, Ont., August 9, 1964.
(Calgary's 6th choice, 117th overall, in 1984 Entry Draft).

Season	Club	GP	G	A	Pts	PIM	GP	G	A	Pts	PIM
1985-86	Calgary Flames	....	....	....	....	....	2	0	0	0	0
1986-87	Calgary Flames	5	1	0	1	0	4	2	1	3	0
1987-88	Calgary Flames	52	26	24	50	12	....	....	....	....	....
	St. Louis Blues	13	6	8	14	4	10	7	2	9	4
1988-89	St. Louis Blues	78	41	43	84	33	10	5	5	10	6
1989-90	St. Louis Blues	80	*72	41	113	24	12	13	8	21	17
1990-91	St. Louis Blues	78	*86	45	131	22	13	11	8	19	4
1991-92	St. Louis Blues	73	*70	39	109	48	6	4	4	8	4
1992-93	St. Louis Blues	80	54	47	101	41	11	8	5	13	2
1993-94	St. Louis Blues	81	57	40	97	38	4	2	1	3	0
1994-95	St. Louis Blues	48	29	21	50	10	7	6	2	8	0
1995-96	St. Louis Blues	70	43	40	83	30	13	6	5	11	10
1996-97	St. Louis Blues	77	42	40	82	10	6	2	7	9	2
1997-98	St. Louis Blues	66	27	45	72	26	10	3	3	6	2
1998-99 ♦	Dallas Stars	60	32	26	58	30	22	8	7	15	4
99-2000	Dallas Stars	79	24	35	59	43	23	*11	*13	*24	4
2000-01	Dallas Stars	79	39	40	79	18	10	2	5	7	6
2001-02 ♦	Detroit Red Wings	82	30	33	63	35	23	*10	8	18	4
2002-03	Detroit Red Wings	82	37	39	76	22	4	0	1	1	0
	NHL Totals	**1183**	**716**	**606**	**1322**	**446**	**190**	**100**	**85**	**185**	**69**

• Son of Bobby • NHL First All-Star Team (1990, 1991, 1992) • Lady Byng Trophy (1990) • Dodge Ram Tough Award (1990, 1991) • Hart Memorial Trophy (1991) • Lester B. Pearson Award (1991) • ProSet/NHL Player of the Year Award (1991)

Played in NHL All-Star Game (1989, 1990, 1992, 1993, 1994, 1996, 1997, 2001)

Traded to **St. Louis** by **Calgary** with Steve Bozek for Rob Ramage and Rick Wamsley, March 7, 1988. Signed as a free agent by **Dallas**, July 3, 1998. Signed as a free agent by **Detroit**, August 22, 2001.

HULL, Dennis

Left wing. Shoots left. 5'11", 198 lbs. Born, Pointe Anne, Ont., November 19, 1944.

Season	Club	GP	G	A	Pts	PIM	GP	G	A	Pts	PIM
1964-65	Chicago Black Hawks	55	10	4	14	18	6	0	0	0	0
1965-66	Chicago Black Hawks	25	1	5	6	6	3	0	0	0	0
1966-67	Chicago Black Hawks	70	25	17	42	33	6	0	1	1	12
1967-68	Chicago Black Hawks	74	18	15	33	34	11	1	3	4	6
1968-69	Chicago Black Hawks	72	30	34	64	25	....	....	....	....	....
1969-70	Chicago Black Hawks	76	17	35	52	31	8	5	2	7	0
1970-71	Chicago Black Hawks	78	40	26	66	16	18	7	6	13	2
1971-72	Chicago Black Hawks	78	30	39	69	10	8	4	2	6	4
1972-73	Chicago Black Hawks	78	39	51	90	27	16	9	*15	24	4
1973-74	Chicago Black Hawks	74	29	39	68	15	10	6	3	9	0
1974-75	Chicago Black Hawks	69	16	21	37	10	5	0	2	2	0
1975-76	Chicago Black Hawks	80	27	39	66	28	4	0	0	0	0
1976-77	Chicago Black Hawks	75	16	17	33	2	2	1	0	1	0
1977-78	Detroit Red Wings	55	5	9	14	6	7	0	0	0	2
	NHL Totals	**959**	**303**	**351**	**654**	**261**	**104**	**33**	**34**	**67**	**30**

• Brother of Bobby • NHL Second All-Star Team (1973)

Played in NHL All-Star Game (1969, 1971, 1972, 1973, 1974)

Traded to **Detroit** by **Chicago** for Detroit's 4th round choice (Carey Wilson) in 1980 Entry Draft, December 2, 1977.

HULL, Jody

Right wing. Shoots right. 6'2", 200 lbs. Born, Petrolia, Ont., February 2, 1969.
(Hartford's 1st choice, 18th overall, in 1987 Entry Draft).

Season	Club	GP	G	A	Pts	PIM	GP	G	A	Pts	PIM
1988-89	Hartford Whalers	60	16	18	34	10	1	0	0	0	2
1989-90	Hartford Whalers	38	7	10	17	21	5	0	1	1	2
1990-91	New York Rangers	47	5	8	13	10	....	....	....	....	....
1991-92	New York Rangers	3	0	0	0	2	....	....	....	....	....
1992-93	Ottawa Senators	69	13	21	34	14	....	....	....	....	....
1993-94	Florida Panthers	69	13	13	26	8	....	....	....	....	....
1994-95	Florida Panthers	46	11	8	19	8	....	....	....	....	....
1995-96	Florida Panthers	78	20	17	37	25	14	3	2	5	0
1996-97	Florida Panthers	67	10	6	16	4	5	0	0	0	0
1997-98	Florida Panthers	21	2	0	2	4	....	....	....	....	....
	Tampa Bay Lightning	28	2	4	6	4	....	....	....	....	....
1998-99	Philadelphia Flyers	72	3	11	14	12	6	0	0	0	4
99-2000	Philadelphia Flyers	67	10	3	13	4	18	0	1	1	0
2000-01	Philadelphia Flyers	71	7	8	15	10	6	0	0	0	4
2001-02	Ottawa Senators	24	2	2	4	6	12	1	1	2	2
2002-03	Ottawa Senators	70	3	8	11	14	2	0	0	0	0
	NHL Totals	**830**	**124**	**137**	**261**	**156**	**69**	**4**	**5**	**9**	**14**

Traded to **NY Rangers** by **Hartford** for Carey Wilson and NY Rangers' 3rd round choice (Michael Nylander) in the 1991 Entry Draft, July 9, 1990. Traded to **Ottawa** by **NY Rangers** for future considerations, July 28, 1992. Signed as a free agent by **Florida**, August 10, 1993. Traded to **Tampa Bay** by **Florida** with Mark Fitzpatrick for Dino Ciccarelli and Jeff Norton, January 15, 1998. Signed as a free agent by **Philadelphia**, October 7, 1998. Claimed by **Atlanta** from **Philadelphia** in Expansion Draft, June 25, 1999. Traded to **Philadelphia** by **Atlanta** for cash, October 15, 1999. Signed as a free agent by **Ottawa**, January 24, 2002.

HULSE, Cale

Defense. Shoots right. 6'3", 220 lbs. Born, Edmonton, Alta., November 10, 1973.
(New Jersey's 3rd choice, 66th overall, in 1992 Entry Draft).

Season	Club	GP	G	A	Pts	PIM	GP	G	A	Pts	PIM
1995-96	New Jersey Devils	8	0	0	0	15	....	....	....	....	....
	Calgary Flames	3	0	0	0	5	1	0	0	0	0
1996-97	Calgary Flames	63	1	6	7	91	....	....	....	....	....
1997-98	Calgary Flames	79	5	22	27	169	....	....	....	....	....
1998-99	Calgary Flames	73	3	9	12	117	....	....	....	....	....
99-2000	Calgary Flames	47	1	6	7	47	....	....	....	....	....
2000-01	Nashville Predators	82	1	7	8	128	....	....	....	....	....
2001-02	Nashville Predators	63	0	2	2	121	....	....	....	....	....
2002-03	Nashville Predators	80	2	6	8	121	....	....	....	....	....
	NHL Totals	**498**	**13**	**58**	**71**	**814**	**1**	**0**	**0**	**0**	**0**

Traded to **Calgary** by **New Jersey** with Tommy Albelin and Jocelyn Lemieux for Phil Housley and Dan Keczmer, February 26, 1996. Traded to **Nashville** by **Calgary** with Calgary's 3rd round choice (Denis Platonov) in 2001 Entry Draft for Sergei Krivokrasov, March 14, 2000. Signed as a free agent by **Phoenix**, July 10, 2003.

HUML, Ivan

Left wing. Shoots left. 6'2", 195 lbs. Born, Kladno, Czech., September 6, 1981.
(Boston's 4th choice, 59th overall, in 2000 Entry Draft).

Season	Club	GP	G	A	Pts	PIM	GP	G	A	Pts	PIM
2001-02	Boston Bruins	1	0	1	1	0	....	....	....	....	....
2002-03	Boston Bruins	41	6	11	17	30	....	....	....	....	....
	NHL Totals	**42**	**6**	**12**	**18**	**30**	....	....	....	....	....

HUNT, Fred

Right wing. Shoots right. 5'8", 160 lbs. Born, Brantford, Ont., January 17, 1918.

Season	Club	GP	G	A	Pts	PIM	GP	G	A	Pts	PIM
1940-41	New York Americans	15	2	5	7	0	....	....	....	....	....
1944-45	New York Rangers	44	13	9	22	6	....	....	....	....	....
	NHL Totals	**59**	**15**	**14**	**29**	**6**	....	....	....	....	....

Signed as a free agent by **NY Americans**, September 29, 1939. • Team name changed to **Brooklyn Americans** prior to 1941-42 season. Rights transferred to **NY Rangers** from **Brooklyn** in Special Dispersal Draw, September 11, 1943.

HUNTER, Dale

Center. Shoots left. 5'10", 198 lbs. Born, Petrolia, Ont., July 31, 1960.
(Quebec's 2nd choice, 41st overall, in 1979 Entry Draft).

Season	Club	GP	G	A	Pts	PIM	GP	G	A	Pts	PIM
1980-81	Quebec Nordiques	80	19	44	63	226	5	4	2	6	34
1981-82	Quebec Nordiques	80	22	50	72	272	16	3	7	10	52
1982-83	Quebec Nordiques	80	17	46	63	206	4	2	1	3	24
1983-84	Quebec Nordiques	77	24	55	79	232	9	2	3	5	41
1984-85	Quebec Nordiques	80	20	52	72	209	17	4	6	10	*97
1985-86	Quebec Nordiques	80	28	42	70	265	3	0	0	0	15
1986-87	Quebec Nordiques	46	10	29	39	135	13	1	7	8	56
1987-88	Washington Capitals	79	22	37	59	240	14	7	5	12	98
1988-89	Washington Capitals	80	20	37	57	219	6	0	4	4	29
1989-90	Washington Capitals	80	23	39	62	233	15	4	8	12	61
1990-91	Washington Capitals	76	16	30	46	234	11	1	9	10	41
1991-92	Washington Capitals	80	28	50	78	205	7	1	4	5	16
1992-93	Washington Capitals	84	20	59	79	198	6	7	1	8	35
1993-94	Washington Capitals	52	9	29	38	131	7	0	3	3	14
1994-95	Washington Capitals	45	8	15	23	101	7	4	4	8	24
1995-96	Washington Capitals	82	13	24	37	112	6	1	5	6	24
1996-97	Washington Capitals	82	14	32	46	125	....	....	....	....	....
1997-98	Washington Capitals	82	8	18	26	103	21	0	4	4	30
1998-99	Washington Capitals	50	0	5	5	102	....	....	....	....	....
	Colorado Avalanche	12	2	4	6	17	19	1	3	4	38
	NHL Totals	**1407**	**323**	**697**	**1020**	**3565**	**186**	**42**	**76**	**118**	**729**

• Brother of Dave and Mark

Played in NHL All-Star Game (1997)

Traded to **Washington** by **Quebec** with Clint Malarchuk for Gaetan Duchesne, Alan Haworth and Washington's 1st round choice (Joe Sakic) in 1987 Entry Draft, June 13, 1987. Traded to **Colorado** by **Washington** with Washington's 3rd round choice (Sergei Kliazmine) in 2000 Entry Draft for Vancouver's 2nd round choice (previously acquired, Washington selected Charlie Stephens) in 1999 Entry Draft, March 23, 1999.

HUNTER, Dave

Left wing. Shoots left. 5'11", 195 lbs. Born, Petrolia, Ont., January 1, 1958.
(Montreal's 2nd choice, 17th overall, in 1978 Amateur Draft).

Season	Club	GP	G	A	Pts	PIM	GP	G	A	Pts	PIM
1979-80	Edmonton Oilers	80	12	31	43	103	3	0	0	0	7
1980-81	Edmonton Oilers	78	12	16	28	98	9	0	0	0	28
1981-82	Edmonton Oilers	63	16	22	38	63	5	0	1	1	26
1982-83	Edmonton Oilers	80	13	18	31	120	16	4	7	11	60
1983-84 ♦	Edmonton Oilers	80	22	26	48	90	17	5	5	10	14
1984-85 ♦	Edmonton Oilers	80	17	19	36	122	18	2	5	7	33
1985-86	Edmonton Oilers	62	15	22	37	77	10	2	3	5	23
1986-87 ♦	Edmonton Oilers	77	6	9	15	79	21	3	3	6	20

Season	Club	GP	G	A	Pts	PIM	GP	G	A	Pts	PIM
		REGULAR SEASON					PLAYOFFS				
1987-88	Edmonton Oilers	21	3	3	6	6	....	....	....	....	....
	Pittsburgh Penguins	59	11	18	29	77	....	....	....	....	....
1988-89	Winnipeg Jets	34	3	1	4	61	....	....	....	....	....
	Edmonton Oilers	32	3	5	8	22	6	0	0	0	0
	NHL Totals	**746**	**133**	**190**	**323**	**918**	**105**	**16**	**24**	**40**	**211**

• Brother of Dale and Mark

Claimed by **Edmonton** from **Montreal** in Expansion Draft, June 13, 1979. Traded to **Pittsburgh** by **Edmonton** with Paul Coffey and Wayne Van Dorp for Craig Simpson, Dave Hannan, Moe Mantha and Chris Joseph, November 24, 1987. Transferred to **Edmonton** by **Pittsburgh** as compensation for Pittsburgh's claiming Dave Hannan in Waiver Draft, October 3, 1988. Claimed by **Winnipeg** from **Edmonton** in Waiver Draft, October 3, 1988. Claimed on waivers by **Edmonton** from **Winnipeg**, January 14, 1989.

HUNTER, Mark

Right wing. Shoots right. 6', 200 lbs. Born, Petrolia, Ont., November 12, 1962.
(Montreal's 1st choice, 7th overall, in 1981 Entry Draft).

Season	Club	GP	G	A	Pts	PIM	GP	G	A	Pts	PIM
1981-82	Montreal Canadiens	71	18	11	29	143	5	0	0	0	20
1982-83	Montreal Canadiens	31	8	8	16	73	....	....	....	....	....
1983-84	Montreal Canadiens	22	6	4	10	42	14	2	1	3	69
1984-85	Montreal Canadiens	72	21	12	33	123	11	0	3	3	13
1985-86	St. Louis Blues	78	44	30	74	171	19	7	7	14	48
1986-87	St. Louis Blues	74	36	33	69	167	5	0	3	3	10
1987-88	St. Louis Blues	66	32	31	63	136	5	2	3	5	24
1988-89◆	Calgary Flames	66	22	8	30	194	10	2	2	4	23
1989-90	Calgary Flames	10	2	3	5	39	....	....	....	....	....
1990-91	Calgary Flames	57	10	15	25	125	....	....	....	....	....
	Hartford Whalers	11	4	3	7	40	6	5	1	6	17
1991-92	Hartford Whalers	63	10	13	23	159	4	0	0	0	6
1992-93	Washington Capitals	7	0	0	0	14	....	....	....	....	....
	NHL Totals	**628**	**213**	**171**	**384**	**1426**	**79**	**18**	**20**	**38**	**230**

• Brother of Dave and Dale

Played in NHL All-Star Game (1986)

• Missed majority of 1982-83 season recovering from knee injury suffered in game vs. Quebec, December 26, 1982. • Missed majority of 1983-84 season recovering from knee surgery, September, 1983. Traded to **St. Louis** by **Montreal** with Michael Dark and Montreal's 2nd (Herb Raglan), 3rd (Nelson Emerson), 5th (Dan Brooks) and 6th (Rich Burchill) round choices in 1985 Entry Draft for St. Louis' 1st (Jose Charbonneau), 2nd (Todd Richards), 4th (Martin Desjardins), 5th (Tom Sagissor) and 6th (Donald Dufresne) round choices in 1985 Entry Draft, June 15, 1985. Traded to **Calgary** by **St. Louis** with Doug Gilmour, Steve Bozek and Michael Dark for Mike Bullard, Craig Coxe and Tim Corkery, September 6, 1988. • Missed majority of 1989-90 season recovering from knee surgery, December 15, 1989. Traded to **Hartford** by **Calgary** for Carey Wilson, March 5, 1991. Traded to **Washington** by **Hartford** with future considerations (Yvon Corriveau, August 20, 1992) for Nick Kypreos, June 15, 1992.

HUNTER, Tim

Right wing. Shoots right. 6'2", 202 lbs. Born, Calgary, Alta., September 10, 1960.
(Atlanta's 4th choice, 54th overall, in 1979 Entry Draft).

Season	Club	GP	G	A	Pts	PIM	GP	G	A	Pts	PIM
1981-82	Calgary Flames	2	0	0	0	9	....	....	....	....	....
1982-83	Calgary Flames	16	1	0	1	54	9	1	0	1	*70
1983-84	Calgary Flames	43	4	4	8	130	7	0	0	0	21
1984-85	Calgary Flames	71	11	11	22	259	4	0	0	0	24
1985-86	Calgary Flames	66	8	7	15	291	19	0	3	3	108
1986-87	Calgary Flames	73	6	15	21	*361	6	0	0	0	51
1987-88	Calgary Flames	68	8	5	13	337	9	4	0	4	32
1988-89◆	Calgary Flames	75	3	9	12	*375	19	0	4	4	32
1989-90	Calgary Flames	67	2	3	5	279	6	0	0	0	4
1990-91	Calgary Flames	34	5	2	7	143	7	0	0	0	10
1991-92	Calgary Flames	30	1	3	4	167	....	....	....	....	....
1992-93	Quebec Nordiques	48	5	3	8	94	....	....	....	....	....
	Vancouver Canucks	26	0	4	4	99	11	0	0	0	26
1993-94	Vancouver Canucks	56	3	4	7	171	24	0	0	0	26
1994-95	Vancouver Canucks	34	3	2	5	120	11	0	0	0	22
1995-96	Vancouver Canucks	60	2	0	2	122	....	....	....	....	....
1996-97	San Jose Sharks	46	0	4	4	135	....	....	....	....	....
	NHL Totals	**815**	**62**	**76**	**138**	**3146**	**132**	**5**	**7**	**12**	**426**

Claimed by **Tampa Bay** from **Calgary** in Expansion Draft, June 18, 1992. Traded to **Quebec** by **Tampa Bay** for future considerations (Martin Simard, September 14, 1992), June 19, 1992. Claimed on waivers by **Vancouver** from **Quebec**, February 12, 1993. Signed as a free agent by **San Jose**, July 23, 1996.

HUNTER, Trent

Right wing. Shoots right. 6'3", 191 lbs. Born, Red Deer, Alta., July 5, 1980.
(Anaheim's 4th choice, 150th overall, in 1998 Entry Draft).

Season	Club	GP	G	A	Pts	PIM	GP	G	A	Pts	PIM
2001-02	New York Islanders	....	....	....	....	....	4	1	1	2	2
2002-03	New York Islanders	8	0	4	4	4	....	....	....	....	....
	NHL Totals	**8**	**0**	**4**	**4**	**4**	**4**	**1**	**1**	**2**	**2**

Traded to **NY Islanders** by **Anaheim** for Columbus' 4th round choice (previously acquired, Anaheim selected Jonas Ronnqvist) in 2000 Entry Draft, May 23, 2000.

HURAS, Larry

Defense. Shoots left. 6'2", 200 lbs. Born, Listowel, Ont., July 8, 1955.
(NY Rangers' 5th choice, 84th overall, in 1975 Amateur Draft).

Season	Club	GP	G	A	Pts	PIM	GP	G	A	Pts	PIM
1976-77	New York Rangers	2	0	0	0	0	....	....	....	....	....
	NHL Totals	**2**	**0**	**0**	**0**	**0**	....	....	....	....	....

Signed as a free agent by **St. Louis**, October 12, 1977.

HURLBURT, Bob

Left wing. Shoots left. 5'11", 185 lbs. Born, Toronto, Ont., May 1, 1950.

Season	Club	GP	G	A	Pts	PIM	GP	G	A	Pts	PIM
1974-75	Vancouver Canucks	1	0	0	0	2	....	....	....	....	....
	NHL Totals	**1**	**0**	**0**	**0**	**2**	....	....	....	....	....

Traded to **San Diego** (WHL) by **Philadelphia** with Tom Trevelyan, Bob Currier and Jim Stanfield for Bruce Cowick, May 25, 1973. Traded to **Vancouver** by **San Diego** (WHL) for cash, July 23, 1974.

HURLBUT, Mike

Defense. Shoots left. 6'2", 206 lbs. Born, Massena, NY, October 7, 1966.
(NY Rangers' 1st choice, 5th overall, in 1988 Supplemental Draft).

Season	Club	GP	G	A	Pts	PIM	GP	G	A	Pts	PIM
1992-93	New York Rangers	23	1	8	9	16	....	....	....	....	....
1993-94	Quebec Nordiques	1	0	0	0	0	....	....	....	....	....
1997-98	Buffalo Sabres	3	0	0	0	2	....	....	....	....	....
1998-99	Buffalo Sabres	1	0	0	0	0	....	....	....	....	....
99-2000	Buffalo Sabres	1	0	0	0	2	....	....	....	....	....
	NHL Totals	**29**	**1**	**8**	**9**	**20**	....	....	....	....	....

Traded to **Quebec** by **NY Rangers** for Alexander Karpovtsev, September 7, 1993. Signed as a free agent by **Buffalo**, September 9, 1997.

HURLEY, Paul

Defense. Shoots right. 5'11", 185 lbs. Born, Melrose, MA, July 12, 1946.

Season	Club	GP	G	A	Pts	PIM	GP	G	A	Pts	PIM
1968-69	Boston Bruins	1	0	1	1	0	....	....	....	....	....
	NHL Totals	**1**	**0**	**1**	**1**	**0**	....	....	....	....	....

Signed as a free agent by **Boston**, March, 1969.

HURST, Ron

Right wing. Shoots right. 5'9", 175 lbs. Born, Toronto, Ont., May 18, 1931.

Season	Club	GP	G	A	Pts	PIM	GP	G	A	Pts	PIM
1955-56	Toronto Maple Leafs	50	7	5	12	62	3	0	2	2	4
1956-57	Toronto Maple Leafs	14	2	2	4	8	....	....	....	....	....
	NHL Totals	**64**	**9**	**7**	**16**	**70**	**3**	**0**	**2**	**2**	**4**

Traded to **Hershey** (AHL) by **Toronto** with Mike Nykoluk and the loan of Wally Boyer for the 1958-59 and 1959-60 seasons for Willie Marshall, April 29, 1958.

HUSCROFT, Jamie

Defense. Shoots right. 6'3", 210 lbs. Born, Creston, B.C., January 9, 1967.
(New Jersey's 9th choice, 171st overall, in 1985 Entry Draft).

Season	Club	GP	G	A	Pts	PIM	GP	G	A	Pts	PIM
1988-89	New Jersey Devils	15	0	2	2	51	....	....	....	....	....
1989-90	New Jersey Devils	42	2	3	5	149	5	0	0	0	16
1990-91	New Jersey Devils	8	0	1	1	27	3	0	0	0	6
1993-94	Boston Bruins	36	0	1	1	144	4	0	0	0	9
1994-95	Boston Bruins	34	0	6	6	103	5	0	0	0	11
1995-96	Calgary Flames	70	3	9	12	162	4	0	1	1	4
1996-97	Calgary Flames	39	0	4	4	117	....	....	....	....	....
	Tampa Bay Lightning	13	0	1	1	34	....	....	....	....	....
1997-98	Tampa Bay Lightning	44	0	3	3	122	....	....	....	....	....
	Vancouver Canucks	7	0	1	1	55	....	....	....	....	....
1998-99	Vancouver Canucks	26	0	1	1	63	....	....	....	....	....
	Phoenix Coyotes	11	0	1	1	27	....	....	....	....	....
99-2000	Washington Capitals	7	0	0	0	11	....	....	....	....	....
	NHL Totals	**352**	**5**	**33**	**38**	**1065**	**21**	**0**	**1**	**1**	**46**

Signed as a free agent by **Boston**, July 23, 1992. Signed as a free agent by **Calgary**, August 22, 1995. Traded to **Tampa Bay** by **Calgary** for Tyler Moss, March 18, 1997. Traded to **Vancouver** by **Tampa Bay** for Enrico Ciccone, March 14, 1998. Traded to **Phoenix** by **Vancouver** for future considerations, March 8, 1999. Signed as a free agent by **Washington**, August 9, 1999.

HUSELIUS, Kristian

Left wing. Shoots left. 6'1", 190 lbs. Born, Osterhaninge, Sweden, November 10, 1978.
(Florida's 2nd choice, 47th overall, in 1997 Entry Draft).

Season	Club	GP	G	A	Pts	PIM	GP	G	A	Pts	PIM
2001-02	Florida Panthers	79	23	22	45	14	....	....	....	....	....
2002-03	Florida Panthers	78	20	23	43	20	....	....	....	....	....
	NHL Totals	**157**	**43**	**45**	**88**	**34**	....	....	....	....	....

NHL All-Rookie Team (2002)

HUSKA, Ryan

Left wing. Shoots left. 6'2", 194 lbs. Born, Cranbrook, B.C., July 2, 1975.
(Chicago's 4th choice, 76th overall, in 1993 Entry Draft).

Season	Club	GP	G	A	Pts	PIM	GP	G	A	Pts	PIM
1997-98	Chicago Blackhawks	1	0	0	0	0	....	....	....	....	....
	NHL Totals	**1**	**0**	**0**	**0**	**0**	....	....	....	....	....

Signed as a free agent by **NY Islanders**, September 9, 1998. Signed as a free agent by **Phoenix**, August 15, 1999.

HUSTON, Ron

Center. Shoots right. 5'9", 170 lbs. Born, Manitou, Man., April 8, 1945.

Season	Club	GP	G	A	Pts	PIM	GP	G	A	Pts	PIM
1973-74	California Golden Seals	23	3	10	13	0	....	....	....	....	....
1974-75	California Golden Seals	56	12	21	33	8	....	....	....	....	....
	NHL Totals	**79**	**15**	**31**	**46**	**8**	....	....	....	....	....

Signed as a free agent by **California**, September, 1972. Rights traded to **Phoenix** (WHA) by **California** with the rights to Del Hall for the rights to Gary Holt, June, 1975.

HUTCHINSON, Ron

Center. Shoots left. 5'10", 165 lbs. Born, Flin Flon, Man., October 24, 1936.

Season	Club	REGULAR SEASON GP	G	A	Pts	PIM	PLAYOFFS GP	G	A	Pts	PIM
1960-61	New York Rangers	9	0	0	0	0	....	....	....	....	....
	NHL Totals	**9**	**0**	**0**	**0**	**0**	....	....	....	....	....

HUTCHISON, Dave

Defense. Shoots left. 6'3", 205 lbs. Born, London, Ont., May 2, 1952.
(Los Angeles' 2nd choice, 36th overall, in 1972 Amateur Draft).

Season	Club	REGULAR SEASON GP	G	A	Pts	PIM	PLAYOFFS GP	G	A	Pts	PIM
1974-75	Los Angeles Kings	68	0	6	6	133	2	0	0	0	22
1975-76	Los Angeles Kings	50	0	10	10	181	9	0	3	3	29
1976-77	Los Angeles Kings	70	6	11	17	220	9	1	4	5	17
1977-78	Los Angeles Kings	44	0	10	10	71	....	....	....	....	....
1978-79	Toronto Maple Leafs	79	4	15	19	235	6	0	3	3	23
1979-80	Toronto Maple Leafs	31	1	6	7	28	....	....	....	....	....
	Chicago Black Hawks	38	0	5	5	73	6	0	0	0	12
1980-81	Chicago Black Hawks	59	2	9	11	124	2	0	0	0	2
1981-82	Chicago Black Hawks	66	5	18	23	246	14	1	2	3	44
1982-83	New Jersey Devils	32	1	4	5	102	....	....	....	....	....
1983-84	Toronto Maple Leafs	47	0	3	3	137	....	....	....	....	....
	NHL Totals	**584**	**19**	**97**	**116**	**1550**	**48**	**2**	**12**	**14**	**149**

Traded to **Toronto** by **Los Angeles** with Lorne Stamler for Brian Glennie, Kurt Walker, Scott Garland and Toronto's 2nd round choice (Mark Hardy) in 1979 Entry Draft, June 14, 1978. Traded to **Chicago** by **Toronto** for Pat Ribble, January 10, 1980. Traded to **Washington** by **Chicago** with Ted Bulley for Washington's 6th round choice (Jari Torkki) in 1983 Entry Draft and 5th round choice (Darin Sceviour) in 1984 Entry Draft, August 24, 1982. Claimed by **New Jersey** from **Washington** in Waiver Draft, October 4, 1982. Signed as a free agent by **Toronto**, November 15, 1983.

HUTTON, Bill

Defense/Right wing. Shoots right. 5'11", 165 lbs. Born, Calgary, Alta., January 28, 1910.

Season	Club	REGULAR SEASON GP	G	A	Pts	PIM	PLAYOFFS GP	G	A	Pts	PIM
1929-30	Boston Bruins	16	2	0	2	2	....	....	....	....	....
	Ottawa Senators	18	0	1	1	0	2	0	0	0	0
1930-31	Boston Bruins	9	0	0	0	2	....	....	....	....	....
	Philadelphia Quakers	21	1	1	2	4	....	....	....	....	....
	NHL Totals	**64**	**3**	**2**	**5**	**8**	**2**	**0**	**0**	**0**	**0**

Traded to **Ottawa** by **Boston** for Harry Connor, January 30, 1930. Traded to **Boston** by **Ottawa** for Harry Connor, October 16, 1930. Traded to **Philadelphia** by **Boston** with Ron Lyons for Harold Darragh, December 8, 1930. Traded to **Detroit** (IHL) by **Philadelphia** for cash, February 24, 1931.

HYLAND, Harry

Right wing. Shoots right. 5'6", 156 lbs. Born, Montreal, Que., January 2, 1889.

Season	Club	REGULAR SEASON GP	G	A	Pts	PIM	PLAYOFFS GP	G	A	Pts	PIM
1917-18	Montreal Wanderers	4	6	1	7	6	....	....	....	....	....
	Ottawa Senators	13	8	1	9	59	....	....	....	....	....
	NHL Totals	**17**	**14**	**2**	**16**	**65**	....	....	....	....	....

Rights retained by **Mtl. Wanderers** after NHA folded, November 26, 1917. Claimed by **Ottawa** from **Mtl. Wanderers** in Dispersal Draft, January 4, 1918. Rights traded to **Montreal** by **Ottawa** for Skene Ronan, December 9, 1918.

HYNES, Dave

Left wing. Shoots left. 5'9", 182 lbs. Born, Cambridge, MA, April 17, 1951.
(Boston's 5th choice, 56th overall, in 1971 Amateur Draft).

Season	Club	REGULAR SEASON GP	G	A	Pts	PIM	PLAYOFFS GP	G	A	Pts	PIM
1973-74	Boston Bruins	3	0	0	0	0	....	....	....	....	....
1974-75	Boston Bruins	19	4	0	4	2	....	....	....	....	....
	NHL Totals	**22**	**4**	**0**	**4**	**2**	....	....	....	....	....

HYNES, Gord

Defense. Shoots left. 6'1", 170 lbs. Born, Montreal, Que., July 22, 1966.
(Boston's 5th choice, 115th overall, in 1985 Entry Draft).

Season	Club	REGULAR SEASON GP	G	A	Pts	PIM	PLAYOFFS GP	G	A	Pts	PIM
1991-92	Boston Bruins	15	0	5	5	6	12	1	2	3	6
1992-93	Philadelphia Flyers	37	3	4	7	16	....	....	....	....	....
	NHL Totals	**52**	**3**	**9**	**12**	**22**	**12**	**1**	**2**	**3**	**6**

Signed as a free agent by **Philadelphia**, August 25, 1992. Claimed by **Florida** from **Philadelphia** in Expansion Draft, June 24, 1993.

HYVONEN, Hannes

Right wing. Shoots right. 6'2", 200 lbs. Born, Oulu, Finland, August 29, 1975.
(San Jose's 7th choice, 257th overall, in 1999 Entry Draft).

Season	Club	REGULAR SEASON GP	G	A	Pts	PIM	PLAYOFFS GP	G	A	Pts	PIM
2001-02	San Jose Sharks	6	0	0	0	0	....	....	....	....	....
2002-03	Columbus Blue Jackets	36	4	5	9	22	....	....	....	....	....
	NHL Totals	**42**	**4**	**5**	**9**	**22**	....	....	....	....	....

Traded to **Florida** by **San Jose** for Florida's 7th round choice (Jonathon Tremblay) in 2003 Entry Draft, July 16, 2002. Claimed on waivers by **Columbus** from **Florida**, October 5, 2002.

IAFRATE, Al

Defense. Shoots left. 6'3", 235 lbs. Born, Dearborn, MI, March 21, 1966.
(Toronto's 1st choice, 4th overall, in 1984 Entry Draft).

Season	Club	REGULAR SEASON GP	G	A	Pts	PIM	PLAYOFFS GP	G	A	Pts	PIM
1984-85	Toronto Maple Leafs	68	5	16	21	51	....	....	....	....	....
1985-86	Toronto Maple Leafs	65	8	25	33	40	10	0	3	3	4
1986-87	Toronto Maple Leafs	80	9	21	30	55	13	1	3	4	11
1987-88	Toronto Maple Leafs	77	22	30	52	80	6	3	4	7	6
1988-89	Toronto Maple Leafs	65	13	20	33	72	....	....	....	....	....
1989-90	Toronto Maple Leafs	75	21	42	63	135	....	....	....	....	....
1990-91	Toronto Maple Leafs	42	3	15	18	113	....	....	....	....	....
	Washington Capitals	30	6	8	14	124	10	1	3	4	22
1991-92	Washington Capitals	78	17	34	51	180	7	4	2	6	14
1992-93	Washington Capitals	81	25	41	66	169	6	6	0	6	4
1993-94	Washington Capitals	67	10	35	45	143	....	....	....	....	....
	Boston Bruins	12	5	8	13	20	13	3	1	4	6
1996-97	San Jose Sharks	38	6	9	15	91	....	....	....	....	....
1997-98	San Jose Sharks	21	2	7	9	28	6	1	0	1	10
	NHL Totals	**799**	**152**	**311**	**463**	**1301**	**71**	**19**	**16**	**35**	**77**

NHL Second All-Star Team (1993)

Played in NHL All-Star Game (1988, 1990, 1993, 1994)

Traded to **Washington** by **Toronto** for Peter Zezel and Bob Rouse, January 16, 1991. Traded to **Boston** by **Washington** for Joe Juneau, March 21, 1994. • Missed entire 1994-95 and 1995-96 seasons recovering from knee surgery. Traded to **San Jose** by **Boston** for Jeff Odgers and Pittsburgh's 5th round choice (previously acquired, Boston selected Elias Abrahamsson) in 1996 Entry Draft, June 21, 1996. Claimed by **Nashville** from **San Jose** in Expansion Draft, June 26, 1998. Signed as a free agent by **Carolina**, July 14, 1998. • Officially announced retirement, September 1, 1998.

IGINLA, Jarome

Right wing. Shoots right. 6'1", 207 lbs. Born, Edmonton, Alta., July 1, 1977.
(Dallas' 1st choice, 11th overall, in 1995 Entry Draft).

Season	Club	REGULAR SEASON GP	G	A	Pts	PIM	PLAYOFFS GP	G	A	Pts	PIM
1995-96	Calgary Flames	....	....	....	....	....	2	1	1	2	0
1996-97	Calgary Flames	82	21	29	50	37	....	....	....	....	....
1997-98	Calgary Flames	70	13	19	32	29	....	....	....	....	....
1998-99	Calgary Flames	82	28	23	51	58	....	....	....	....	....
99-2000	Calgary Flames	77	29	34	63	26	....	....	....	....	....
2000-01	Calgary Flames	77	31	40	71	62	....	....	....	....	....
2001-02	Calgary Flames	82	*52	44	*96	77	....	....	....	....	....
2002-03	Calgary Flames	75	35	32	67	49	....	....	....	....	....
	NHL Totals	**545**	**209**	**221**	**430**	**338**	**2**	**1**	**1**	**2**	**0**

NHL All-Rookie Team (1997) • NHL First All-Star Team (2002) • Maurice "Rocket" Richard Trophy (2002) • Art Ross Trophy (2002) • Lester B. Pearson Award (2002)

Played in NHL All-Star Game (2002, 2003)

Traded to **Calgary** by **Dallas** with Corey Millen for Joe Nieuwendyk, December 19, 1995.

IGNATJEV, Victor

Defense. Shoots left. 6'4", 215 lbs. Born, Riga, USSR, April 26, 1970.
(San Jose's 11th choice, 243rd overall, in 1992 Entry Draft).

Season	Club	REGULAR SEASON GP	G	A	Pts	PIM	PLAYOFFS GP	G	A	Pts	PIM
1998-99	Pittsburgh Penguins	11	0	1	1	6	1	0	0	0	2
	NHL Totals	**11**	**0**	**1**	**1**	**6**	**1**	**0**	**0**	**0**	**2**

Signed as a free agent by **Pittsburgh**, August 11, 1998.

IHNACAK, Miroslav

Left wing. Shoots left. 5'11", 175 lbs. Born, Poprad, Czech., November 19, 1962.
(Toronto's 12th choice, 171st overall, in 1982 Entry Draft).

Season	Club	REGULAR SEASON GP	G	A	Pts	PIM	PLAYOFFS GP	G	A	Pts	PIM
1985-86	Toronto Maple Leafs	21	2	4	6	27	....	....	....	....	....
1986-87	Toronto Maple Leafs	34	6	5	11	12	1	0	0	0	0
1988-89	Detroit Red Wings	1	0	0	0	0	....	....	....	....	....
	NHL Totals	**56**	**8**	**9**	**17**	**39**	**1**	**0**	**0**	**0**	**0**

• Brother of Peter

Signed as a free agent by **Detroit**, November 18, 1988.

IHNACAK, Peter

Center. Shoots right. 5'11", 180 lbs. Born, Poprad, Czech., May 3, 1957.
(Toronto's 3rd choice, 25th overall, in 1982 Entry Draft).

Season	Club	REGULAR SEASON GP	G	A	Pts	PIM	PLAYOFFS GP	G	A	Pts	PIM
1982-83	Toronto Maple Leafs	80	28	38	66	44	....	....	....	....	....
1983-84	Toronto Maple Leafs	47	10	13	23	24	....	....	....	....	....
1984-85	Toronto Maple Leafs	70	22	22	44	24	....	....	....	....	....
1985-86	Toronto Maple Leafs	63	18	27	45	16	10	2	3	5	12
1986-87	Toronto Maple Leafs	58	12	27	39	16	13	2	4	6	9
1987-88	Toronto Maple Leafs	68	10	20	30	41	5	0	3	3	4
1988-89	Toronto Maple Leafs	26	2	16	18	10	....	....	....	....	....
1989-90	Toronto Maple Leafs	5	0	2	2	0	....	....	....	....	....
	NHL Totals	**417**	**102**	**165**	**267**	**175**	**28**	**4**	**10**	**14**	**25**

• Brother of Miroslav

IMLACH, Brent

Forward. Shoots left. 5'8", 160 lbs. Born, Quebec City, Que., November 16, 1946.

Season	Club	REGULAR SEASON GP	G	A	Pts	PIM	PLAYOFFS GP	G	A	Pts	PIM
1965-66	Toronto Maple Leafs	2	0	0	0	0	....	....	....	....	....
1966-67	Toronto Maple Leafs	1	0	0	0	0	....	....	....	....	....
	NHL Totals	**3**	**0**	**0**	**0**	**0**	....	....	....	....	....

Traded to **Buffalo** by **Toronto** for cash, August 31, 1970.

INGARFIELD Jr., Earl

Center. Shoots left. 5'11", 180 lbs. Born, New York, NY, January 30, 1959.

Season	Club	REGULAR SEASON GP	G	A	Pts	PIM	PLAYOFFS GP	G	A	Pts	PIM
1979-80	Atlanta Flames	1	0	0	0	0	2	0	1	1	0
1980-81	Calgary Flames	16	2	3	5	6	....	....	....	....	....
	Detroit Red Wings	22	2	1	3	16	....	....	....	....	....
	NHL Totals	**39**	**4**	**4**	**8**	**22**	**2**	**0**	**1**	**1**	**0**

• Son of Earl

Signed as a free agent by **Atlanta**, October 9, 1979. Transferred to **Calgary** after **Atlanta** franchise relocated, June 30, 1980. Traded to **Detroit** by **Calgary** for Dan Labraaten, February 3, 1981.

INGARFIELD, Earl

Center. Shoots left. 5'11", 185 lbs. Born, Lethbridge, Alta., October 25, 1934.

Season	Club	Regular Season GP	G	A	Pts	PIM	Playoffs GP	G	A	Pts	PIM
1958-59	New York Rangers	35	1	2	3	10	....	....	....	....	....
1959-60	New York Rangers	20	1	2	3	2	....	....	....	....	....
1960-61	New York Rangers	66	13	21	34	18	....	....	....	....	....
1961-62	New York Rangers	70	26	31	57	18	6	3	2	5	2
1962-63	New York Rangers	69	19	24	43	40	....	....	....	....	....
1963-64	New York Rangers	63	15	11	26	26	....	....	....	....	....
1964-65	New York Rangers	69	15	13	28	40	....	....	....	....	....
1965-66	New York Rangers	68	20	16	36	35	....	....	....	....	....
1966-67	New York Rangers	67	12	22	34	12	4	1	0	1	2
1967-68	Pittsburgh Penguins	50	15	22	37	12	....	....	....	....	....
1968-69	Pittsburgh Penguins	40	8	15	23	4	....	....	....	....	....
	Oakland Seals	26	8	15	23	8	7	4	6	10	2
1969-70	Oakland Seals	54	21	24	45	10	4	1	0	1	4
1970-71	California Seals	49	5	8	13	4	....	....	....	....	....
	NHL Totals	**746**	**179**	**226**	**405**	**239**	**21**	**9**	**8**	**17**	**10**

• Father of Earl Jr.

Traded to **Montreal** by **NY Rangers** with Noel Price, Gord Labossiere, Dave McComb and cash for Cesare Maniago and Garry Peters, June 8, 1965. Claimed by **NY Rangers** from **Montreal** in Intra-League Draft, June 9, 1965. Claimed by **Pittsburgh** from **NY Rangers** in Expansion Draft, June 6, 1967. Traded to **Oakland** by **Pittsburgh** with Gene Ubriaco and Dick Mattiussi for Bryan Watson, George Swarbrick and Tracy Pratt, January 30, 1969.

INGLIS, Billy

Center. Shoots left. 5'9", 160 lbs. Born, Ottawa, Ont., May 11, 1943.

Season	Club	Regular Season GP	G	A	Pts	PIM	Playoffs GP	G	A	Pts	PIM
1967-68	Los Angeles Kings	12	1	1	2	0	....	....	....	....	....
1968-69	Los Angeles Kings	10	0	1	1	0	11	1	2	3	4
1970-71	Buffalo Sabres	14	0	1	1	4	....	....	....	....	....
	NHL Totals	**36**	**1**	**3**	**4**	**4**	**11**	**1**	**2**	**3**	**4**

Claimed by **Los Angeles** from **Montreal** in Expansion Draft, June 6, 1967. Claimed by **Montreal** from **Los Angeles** in Intra-League Draft, June 9, 1970. Claimed by **Buffalo** from **Montreal** in Intra-League Draft, June 9, 1970.

INGOLDSBY, Johnny

Right wing/Defense. Shoots right. 6'2", 210 lbs. Born, Toronto, Ont., June 21, 1924.

Season	Club	Regular Season GP	G	A	Pts	PIM	Playoffs GP	G	A	Pts	PIM
1942-43	Toronto Maple Leafs	8	0	1	1	0	....	....	....	....	....
1943-44	Toronto Maple Leafs	21	5	0	5	15	....	....	....	....	....
	NHL Totals	**29**	**5**	**1**	**6**	**15**	....	....	....	....	....

Signed as a free agent by **Toronto**, November 18, 1942.

INGRAM, Frank

Right wing. Shoots right. 5'8", 185 lbs. Born, Craven, Sask., September 17, 1907.

Season	Club	Regular Season GP	G	A	Pts	PIM	Playoffs GP	G	A	Pts	PIM
1929-30	Chicago Black Hawks	37	6	10	16	28	2	0	0	0	0
1930-31	Chicago Black Hawks	43	17	4	21	37	9	0	1	1	2
1931-32	Chicago Black Hawks	21	1	2	3	4	....	....	....	....	....
	NHL Totals	**101**	**24**	**16**	**40**	**69**	**11**	**0**	**1**	**1**	**2**

Claimed by **Chicago** from **St. Paul** (AHA) in Inter-League Draft, May 13, 1929. Loaned to **Philadelphia** (Can-Am) by **Chicago** with cash for Art Coulter, February, 1932. Traded to **Boston** by **Chicago** for cash, October 17, 1932. Traded to **Cleveland** (IHL) by **Boston** (Boston-Can-Am) for cash, November, 1932.

INGRAM, John

Center. Shoots left. 5'11", 170 lbs. Born, Halifax, N.S., 1894.

Season	Club	Regular Season GP	G	A	Pts	PIM	Playoffs GP	G	A	Pts	PIM
1924-25	Boston Bruins	1	0	0	0	0	....	....	....	....	....
	NHL Totals	**1**	**0**	**0**	**0**	**0**	....	....	....	....	....

Signed as a free agent by **Boston**, January 5, 1925.

INGRAM, Ron

Defense. Shoots right. 5'11", 185 lbs. Born, Toronto, Ont., July 5, 1933.

Season	Club	Regular Season GP	G	A	Pts	PIM	Playoffs GP	G	A	Pts	PIM
1956-57	Chicago Black Hawks	45	1	6	7	21	....	....	....	....	....
1962-63	Chicago Black Hawks	....	....	....	....	....	2	0	0	0	0
1963-64	Detroit Red Wings	50	3	6	9	50	....	....	....	....	....
	New York Rangers	16	1	3	4	8	....	....	....	....	....
1964-65	New York Rangers	3	0	0	0	2	....	....	....	....	....
	NHL Totals	**114**	**5**	**15**	**20**	**81**	**2**	**0**	**0**	**0**	**0**

Traded to **Cleveland** (AHL) by **Chicago** for Ian Cushenan, September 4, 1956. Traded to **Detroit** by **Chicago** with Roger Crozier for Howie Young, June 5, 1963. Traded to **NY Rangers** by **Detroit** for Albert Langlois, February 14, 1964. Traded to **Seattle** (WHL) by **NY Rangers** (Buffalo-AHL) for cash, October, 1969.

INTRANUOVO, Ralph

Center. Shoots left. 5'8", 185 lbs. Born, East York, Ont., December 11, 1973.
(Edmonton's 5th choice, 96th overall, in 1992 Entry Draft).

Season	Club	Regular Season GP	G	A	Pts	PIM	Playoffs GP	G	A	Pts	PIM
1994-95	Edmonton Oilers	1	0	1	1	0	....	....	....	....	....
1995-96	Edmonton Oilers	13	1	2	3	4	....	....	....	....	....
1996-97	Toronto Maple Leafs	3	0	1	1	0	....	....	....	....	....
	Edmonton Oilers	5	1	0	1	0	....	....	....	....	....
	NHL Totals	**22**	**2**	**4**	**6**	**4**	....	....	....	....	....

Claimed by **Toronto** from **Edmonton** in Waiver Draft, September 30, 1996. Claimed on waivers by **Edmonton** from **Toronto**, October 25, 1996.

IRVIN, Dick

HHOF

Center. Shoots left. 5'9", 162 lbs. Born, Hamilton, Ont., July 19, 1892.

Season	Club	Regular Season GP	G	A	Pts	PIM	Playoffs GP	G	A	Pts	PIM
1926-27	Chicago Black Hawks	43	18	*18	36	34	2	2	0	2	4
1927-28	Chicago Black Hawks	12	5	4	9	14	....	....	....	....	....
1928-29	Chicago Black Hawks	39	6	1	7	30	....	....	....	....	....
	NHL Totals	**94**	**29**	**23**	**52**	**78**	**2**	**2**	**0**	**2**	**4**

NHL rights transferred to **Chicago** after NHL club purchased **Portland** (WHL) franchise, May 15, 1926. • Missed remainder of 1927-28 season recovering from head injury suffered in game vs. Mtl. Maroons, December 28, 1927.

IRVINE, Ted

Left wing. Shoots left. 6'2", 195 lbs. Born, Winnipeg, Man., December 8, 1944.

Season	Club	Regular Season GP	G	A	Pts	PIM	Playoffs GP	G	A	Pts	PIM
1963-64	Boston Bruins	1	0	0	0	0	....	....	....	....	....
1967-68	Los Angeles Kings	73	18	22	40	26	6	1	3	4	2
1968-69	Los Angeles Kings	76	15	24	39	47	11	5	1	6	7
1969-70	Los Angeles Kings	58	11	13	24	28	....	....	....	....	....
	New York Rangers	17	0	3	3	10	6	1	2	3	8
1970-71	New York Rangers	76	20	18	38	137	12	1	2	3	28
1971-72	New York Rangers	78	15	21	36	66	16	4	5	9	19
1972-73	New York Rangers	53	8	12	20	54	10	1	3	4	20
1973-74	New York Rangers	75	26	20	46	105	13	3	5	8	16
1974-75	New York Rangers	79	17	17	34	66	3	0	1	1	11
1975-76	St. Louis Blues	69	10	13	23	80	3	0	2	2	2
1976-77	St. Louis Blues	69	14	14	28	38	3	0	0	0	2
	NHL Totals	**724**	**154**	**177**	**331**	**657**	**83**	**16**	**24**	**40**	**115**

Claimed by **Los Angeles** from **Boston** in Expansion Draft, June 6, 1967. Traded to **NY Rangers** by **Los Angeles** for Real Lemieux and Juha Widing, February 28, 1970. Traded to **St. Louis** by **NY Rangers** with Bert Wilson and Jerry Butler for Bill Collins and John Davidson, June 18, 1975.

IRWIN, Ivan

Defense. Shoots left. 6'2", 185 lbs. Born, Chicago, IL, March 13, 1927.

Season	Club	Regular Season GP	G	A	Pts	PIM	Playoffs GP	G	A	Pts	PIM
1952-53	Montreal Canadiens	4	0	1	1	0	....	....	....	....	....
1953-54	New York Rangers	56	2	12	14	109	....	....	....	....	....
1954-55	New York Rangers	60	0	13	13	85	....	....	....	....	....
1955-56	New York Rangers	34	0	1	1	20	5	0	0	0	8
1957-58	New York Rangers	1	0	0	0	0	....	....	....	....	....
	NHL Totals	**155**	**2**	**27**	**29**	**214**	**5**	**0**	**0**	**0**	**8**

Rights traded to **Montreal** by **Cincinnati** (AHL) for cash, October 3, 1951. Traded to **NY Rangers** by **Montreal** for Eddie Slowinski and Pete Babando, August 8, 1953.

ISAKSSON, Ulf

Left wing. Shoots left. 6'1", 185 lbs. Born, Norrsunda, Sweden, March 19, 1954.
(Los Angeles' 6th choice, 95th overall, in 1982 Entry Draft).

Season	Club	Regular Season GP	G	A	Pts	PIM	Playoffs GP	G	A	Pts	PIM
1982-83	Los Angeles Kings	50	7	15	22	10	....	....	....	....	....
	NHL Totals	**50**	**7**	**15**	**22**	**10**	....	....	....	....	....

ISBISTER, Brad

Left wing. Shoots right. 6'4", 227 lbs. Born, Edmonton, Alta., May 7, 1977.
(Winnipeg's 4th choice, 67th overall, in 1995 Entry Draft).

Season	Club	Regular Season GP	G	A	Pts	PIM	Playoffs GP	G	A	Pts	PIM
1997-98	Phoenix Coyotes	66	9	8	17	102	5	0	0	0	2
1998-99	Phoenix Coyotes	32	4	4	8	46	....	....	....	....	....
99-2000	New York Islanders	64	22	20	42	100	....	....	....	....	....
2000-01	New York Islanders	51	18	14	32	59	....	....	....	....	....
2001-02	New York Islanders	79	17	21	38	113	3	1	1	2	17
2002-03	New York Islanders	53	10	13	23	34	....	....	....	....	....
	Edmonton Oilers	13	3	2	5	9	6	0	1	1	12
	NHL Totals	**358**	**83**	**82**	**165**	**463**	**14**	**1**	**2**	**3**	**31**

Rights transferred to **Phoenix** after **Winnipeg** franchise relocated, July 1, 1996. Traded to **NY Islanders** by **Phoenix** with Phoenix's 3rd round choice (Brian Collins) in 1999 Entry Draft for Robert Reichel, NY Islanders' 3rd round choice (Jason Jaspers) in 1999 Entry Draft and Ottawa's 4th round choice (previously acquired, Phoenix selected Preston Mizzi) in 1999 Entry Draft, March 20, 1999. Traded to **Edmonton** by **NY Islanders** with Raffi Torres for Janne Niinimaa and Washington's 2nd round choice (previously acquired, NY Islanders selected Evgeni Tunik) in 2003 Entry Draft , March 11, 2003.

ISSEL, Kim

Right wing. Shoots right. 6'4", 196 lbs. Born, Calgary, Alta., September 25, 1967.
(Edmonton's 1st choice, 21st overall, in 1986 Entry Draft).

Season	Club	Regular Season GP	G	A	Pts	PIM	Playoffs GP	G	A	Pts	PIM
1988-89	Edmonton Oilers	4	0	0	0	0	....	....	....	....	....
	NHL Totals	**4**	**0**	**0**	**0**	**0**	....	....	....	....	....

Traded to **Pittsburgh** by **Edmonton** for Brad Aitken, March 5, 1991. Signed as a free agent by **Vancouver**, August, 1991.

JACKMAN, Barret

Defense. Shoots left. 6'1", 200 lbs. Born, Trail, B.C., March 5, 1981.
(St. Louis' 1st choice, 17th overall, in 1999 Entry Draft).

Season	Club	Regular Season GP	G	A	Pts	PIM	Playoffs GP	G	A	Pts	PIM
2001-02	St. Louis Blues	1	0	0	0	0	1	0	0	0	2
2002-03	St. Louis Blues	82	3	16	19	190	7	0	0	0	14
	NHL Totals	**83**	**3**	**16**	**19**	**190**	**8**	**0**	**0**	**0**	**16**

NHL All-Rookie Team (2003) • Calder Memorial Trophy (2003)

JACKMAN, Richard

Defense. Shoots right. 6'2", 192 lbs. Born, Toronto, Ont., June 28, 1978.
(Dallas' 1st choice, 5th overall, in 1996 Entry Draft).

Season	Club	REGULAR SEASON GP	G	A	Pts	PIM	PLAYOFFS GP	G	A	Pts	PIM
99-2000	Dallas Stars	22	1	2	3	6	....	....	....	....	....
2000-01	Dallas Stars	16	0	0	0	18	....	....	....	....	....
2001-02	Boston Bruins	2	0	0	0	2	....	....	....	....	....
2002-03	Toronto Maple Leafs	42	0	2	2	41	....	....	....	....	....
	NHL Totals	**82**	**1**	**4**	**5**	**67**	....	....	....	....	....

Traded to **Boston** by **Dallas** for Cameron Mann, June 23, 2001. Traded to **Toronto** by **Boston** for the rights to Kris Vernarsky, May 13, 2002.

JACKSON, Art

Center. Shoots left. 5'8", 165 lbs. Born, Toronto, Ont., December 15, 1915.

Season	Club	REGULAR SEASON GP	G	A	Pts	PIM	PLAYOFFS GP	G	A	Pts	PIM
1934-35	Toronto Maple Leafs	20	1	3	4	4	1	0	0	0	2
1935-36	Toronto Maple Leafs	48	5	15	20	14	8	0	3	3	2
1936-37	Toronto Maple Leafs	14	2	0	2	2	....	....	....	....	....
1937-38	Boston Bruins	48	9	3	12	24	3	0	0	0	0
1938-39	New York Americans	48	12	13	25	15	2	0	0	0	2
1939-40	Boston Bruins	46	7	18	25	6	5	1	2	3	0
1940-41 ♦	Boston Bruins	48	17	15	32	10	11	1	3	4	16
1941-42	Boston Bruins	47	6	18	24	25	5	0	1	1	0
1942-43	Boston Bruins	50	22	31	53	20	9	6	3	9	7
1943-44	Boston Bruins	49	28	41	69	8	....	....	....	....	....
1944-45	Boston Bruins	19	5	8	13	10	....	....	....	....	....
	♦ Toronto Maple Leafs	31	9	13	22	6	8	0	0	0	0
	NHL Totals	**468**	**123**	**178**	**301**	**144**	**52**	**8**	**12**	**20**	**29**

• Brother of Busher

Traded to **Boston** by **Toronto** for cash and future considerations, September 23, 1937. Loaned to **NY Americans** by **Boston** for the 1938-39 season with the trade of Leroy Goldsworthy for cash, October 24, 1938. Traded to **Toronto** by **Boston** for $7,500 and future considerations (Bingo Kampman, October 29, 1945), December 24, 1944.

JACKSON, Busher

HHOF

Left wing. Shoots left. 5'11", 195 lbs. Born, Toronto, Ont., January 19, 1911.

Season	Club	REGULAR SEASON GP	G	A	Pts	PIM	PLAYOFFS GP	G	A	Pts	PIM
1929-30	Toronto Maple Leafs	31	12	6	18	29	....	....	....	....	....
1930-31	Toronto Maple Leafs	43	18	13	31	81	2	0	0	0	0
1931-32 ♦	Toronto Maple Leafs	48	28	25	*53	63	7	5	2	7	13
1932-33	Toronto Maple Leafs	48	27	17	44	43	9	3	1	4	2
1933-34	Toronto Maple Leafs	38	20	18	38	38	5	1	0	1	8
1934-35	Toronto Maple Leafs	42	22	22	44	27	7	3	2	*5	2
1935-36	Toronto Maple Leafs	47	11	11	22	19	9	3	2	5	4
1936-37	Toronto Maple Leafs	46	21	19	40	12	2	1	0	1	2
1937-38	Toronto Maple Leafs	48	17	17	34	18	6	1	0	1	8
1938-39	Toronto Maple Leafs	41	10	17	27	12	7	0	1	1	2
1939-40	New York Americans	43	12	8	20	10	3	0	1	1	2
1940-41	New York Americans	46	8	18	26	4	....	....	....	....	....
1941-42	Boston Bruins	26	5	7	12	18	5	0	1	1	0
1942-43	Boston Bruins	44	19	15	34	38	9	1	2	3	10
1943-44	Boston Bruins	42	11	21	32	25	....	....	....	....	....
	NHL Totals	**633**	**241**	**234**	**475**	**437**	**71**	**18**	**12**	**30**	**53**

• Brother of Art • NHL First All-Star Team (1932, 1934, 1935, 1937) • NHL Second All-Star Team (1933)

Played in NHL All-Star Game (1934, 1937, 1939)

Signed as a free agent by **Toronto**, December 6, 1929. Traded to **NY Americans** by **Toronto** with Buzz Boll, Doc Romnes, Jimmy Fowler and Murray Armstrong for Sweeney Schriner, May 18, 1939. • Team name changed to **Brooklyn Americans** prior to 1941-42 season. Traded to **Boston** by **Brooklyn** for $7,500, January 4, 1942.

JACKSON, Dane

Right wing. Shoots right. 6'1", 200 lbs. Born, Castlegar, B.C., May 17, 1970.
(Vancouver's 3rd choice, 44th overall, in 1988 Entry Draft).

Season	Club	REGULAR SEASON GP	G	A	Pts	PIM	PLAYOFFS GP	G	A	Pts	PIM
1993-94	Vancouver Canucks	12	5	1	6	9	....	....	....	....	....
1994-95	Vancouver Canucks	3	1	0	1	4	6	0	0	0	10
1995-96	Buffalo Sabres	22	5	4	9	41	....	....	....	....	....
1997-98	New York Islanders	8	1	1	2	4	....	....	....	....	....
	NHL Totals	**45**	**12**	**6**	**18**	**58**	**6**	**0**	**0**	**0**	**10**

Signed as a free agent by **Buffalo**, September 20, 1995. Signed as a free agent by **NY Islanders**, July 21, 1997.

JACKSON, Don

Defense. Shoots left. 6'3", 210 lbs. Born, Minneapolis, MN, September 2, 1956.
(Minnesota's 3rd choice, 39th overall, in 1976 Amateur Draft).

Season	Club	REGULAR SEASON GP	G	A	Pts	PIM	PLAYOFFS GP	G	A	Pts	PIM
1977-78	Minnesota North Stars	2	0	0	0	2	....	....	....	....	....
1978-79	Minnesota North Stars	5	0	0	0	2	....	....	....	....	....
1979-80	Minnesota North Stars	10	0	4	4	18	1	0	0	0	0
1980-81	Minnesota North Stars	10	0	3	3	19	....	....	....	....	....
1981-82	Edmonton Oilers	8	0	0	0	18	....	....	....	....	....
1982-83	Edmonton Oilers	71	2	8	10	136	16	3	3	6	30
1983-84 ♦	Edmonton Oilers	60	8	12	20	120	19	1	2	3	32
1984-85 ♦	Edmonton Oilers	78	3	17	20	141	9	0	0	0	64
1985-86	Edmonton Oilers	45	2	8	10	93	8	0	0	0	21
1986-87	New York Rangers	22	1	0	1	91	....	....	....	....	....
	NHL Totals	**311**	**16**	**52**	**68**	**640**	**53**	**4**	**5**	**9**	**147**

Traded to **Edmonton** by **Minnesota** with Minnesota's 3rd round choice (later traded back to Minnesota – Minnesota selected Wally Chapman) in 1982 Entry Draft for the rights to Don Murdoch, August 21, 1981. Traded to **NY Rangers** by **Edmonton** with Mike Golden, Miroslav Horava and future considerations (Stu Kulak, March 10, 1987) for Reijo Ruotsalainen, Ville Kentala, Clark Donatelli and Jim Wiemer, October 23, 1986.

JACKSON, Harold

Defense. Shoots right. 6', 195 lbs. Born, Cedar Springs, Ont., August 1, 1918.

Season	Club	REGULAR SEASON GP	G	A	Pts	PIM	PLAYOFFS GP	G	A	Pts	PIM
1936-37	Chicago Black Hawks	38	1	3	4	6	....	....	....	....	....
1937-38 ♦	Chicago Black Hawks	3	0	0	0	0	1	0	0	0	2
1940-41	Detroit Red Wings	1	0	0	0	0	....	....	....	....	....
1942-43 ♦	Detroit Red Wings	4	0	4	4	6	6	0	1	1	4
1943-44	Detroit Red Wings	50	7	12	19	76	5	0	0	0	11
1944-45	Detroit Red Wings	50	5	6	11	45	14	1	1	2	10
1945-46	Detroit Red Wings	36	3	4	7	36	5	0	0	0	6
1946-47	Detroit Red Wings	37	1	5	6	39	....	....	....	....	....
	NHL Totals	**219**	**17**	**34**	**51**	**208**	**31**	**1**	**2**	**3**	**33**

Traded to **Cleveland** (IAHL) by **Chicago** with Charley Mason and $15,000 for Phil Hergesheimer, May 17, 1939. Traded to **Detroit** by **Providence** (AHL) for Cecil Dillon and Eddie Bush, December 15, 1940. Traded to **Buffalo** (AHL) by **Detroit** with Les Douglas for Jim McFadden, June, 1947. Traded to **Boston** (Hershey-AHL) by **Montreal** (Buffalo-AHL) with Gerry Brown for Jack McGill, June 30, 1948.

JACKSON, Jack

Defense. Shoots right. 5'10", 185 lbs. Born, Windsor, Ont., May 3, 1925.

Season	Club	REGULAR SEASON GP	G	A	Pts	PIM	PLAYOFFS GP	G	A	Pts	PIM
1946-47	Chicago Black Hawks	48	2	5	7	38	....	....	....	....	....
	NHL Totals	**48**	**2**	**5**	**7**	**38**	....	....	....	....	....

JACKSON, Jeff

Left wing. Shoots left. 6'1", 195 lbs. Born, Dresden, Ont., April 24, 1965.
(Toronto's 2nd choice, 28th overall, in 1983 Entry Draft).

Season	Club	REGULAR SEASON GP	G	A	Pts	PIM	PLAYOFFS GP	G	A	Pts	PIM
1984-85	Toronto Maple Leafs	17	0	1	1	24	....	....	....	....	....
1985-86	Toronto Maple Leafs	5	1	2	3	2	....	....	....	....	....
1986-87	Toronto Maple Leafs	55	8	7	15	64	....	....	....	....	....
	New York Rangers	9	5	1	6	15	6	1	1	2	16
1987-88	Quebec Nordiques	68	9	18	27	103	....	....	....	....	....
1988-89	Quebec Nordiques	33	4	6	10	28	....	....	....	....	....
1989-90	Quebec Nordiques	65	8	12	20	71	....	....	....	....	....
1990-91	Quebec Nordiques	10	3	1	4	4	....	....	....	....	....
1991-92	Chicago Blackhawks	1	0	0	0	2	....	....	....	....	....
	NHL Totals	**263**	**38**	**48**	**86**	**313**	**6**	**1**	**1**	**2**	**16**

Traded to **NY Rangers** by **Toronto** with Toronto's 3rd round choice (Rob Zamuner) in 1989 Entry Draft for Mark Osborne, March 5, 1987. Traded to **Quebec** by **NY Rangers** with Terry Carkner for John Ogrodnick and David Shaw, September 30, 1987. Signed as a free agent by **Chicago**, February 19, 1992.

JACKSON, Jim

Left wing. Shoots right. 5'9", 190 lbs. Born, Oshawa, Ont., February 1, 1960.

Season	Club	REGULAR SEASON GP	G	A	Pts	PIM	PLAYOFFS GP	G	A	Pts	PIM
1982-83	Calgary Flames	48	8	12	20	7	8	2	1	3	2
1983-84	Calgary Flames	49	6	14	20	13	6	1	1	2	4
1984-85	Calgary Flames	10	1	4	5	0	....	....	....	....	....
1987-88	Buffalo Sabres	5	2	0	2	0	....	....	....	....	....
	NHL Totals	**112**	**17**	**30**	**47**	**20**	**14**	**3**	**2**	**5**	**6**

Signed as a free agent by **Calgary**, October 8, 1982. Signed as a free agent by **Buffalo**, September 26, 1985.

JACKSON, Lloyd

Center. Shoots left. 5'9", 150 lbs. Born, Ottawa, Ont., January 7, 1912.

Season	Club	REGULAR SEASON GP	G	A	Pts	PIM	PLAYOFFS GP	G	A	Pts	PIM
1936-37	New York Americans	14	1	1	2	0	....	....	....	....	....
	NHL Totals	**14**	**1**	**1**	**2**	**0**	....	....	....	....	....

Traded to **New Haven** (AHL) by **NY Americans** with cash for Alfie Moore, November, 1936.

JACKSON, Stan

Left wing. Shoots left. 6', 180 lbs. Born, Parrsboro, N.S., August 27, 1898.

Season	Club	REGULAR SEASON GP	G	A	Pts	PIM	PLAYOFFS GP	G	A	Pts	PIM
1921-22 ♦	Toronto St. Pats	1	0	0	0	0	....	....	....	....	....
1923-24	Toronto St. Pats	22	1	1	2	6	....	....	....	....	....
1924-25	Toronto St. Pats	3	0	0	0	7	....	....	....	....	....
	Boston Bruins	24	5	2	7	30	....	....	....	....	....
1925-26	Boston Bruins	28	3	3	6	30	....	....	....	....	....
1926-27	Ottawa Senators	8	0	0	0	2	....	....	....	....	....
	NHL Totals	**86**	**9**	**6**	**15**	**75**	....	....	....	....	....

Signed as a free agent by **Toronto**, December 23, 1921. Signed as a free agent by **Boston**, December 17, 1924. Traded to **Ottawa** by **Boston** for cash, January 18, 1927. Traded to **London** (Can-Pro) by **Ottawa** for cash, February, 1927.

JACKSON, Walter

Left wing. Shoots left. 5'8", 164 lbs. Born, Ibstock, England, June 3, 1908.

Season	Club	REGULAR SEASON GP	G	A	Pts	PIM	PLAYOFFS GP	G	A	Pts	PIM
1932-33	New York Americans	34	10	2	12	6	....	....	....	....	....
1933-34	New York Americans	47	6	9	15	12	....	....	....	....	....
1934-35	New York Americans	1	0	0	0	0	....	....	....	....	....

Season	Club	GP	G	A	Pts	PIM	GP	G	A	Pts	PIM
		REGULAR SEASON					PLAYOFFS				
1935-36	Boston Bruins	2	0	0	0	0	....	....	....	....	....
	NHL Totals	**84**	**16**	**11**	**27**	**18**	....	....	....	....	....

Traded to **NY Americans** by **St. Louis** (AHA) for George Massecar, October 30, 1932. Loaned to **Syracuse** (IHL) by **NY Americans** with the trade of Ron Martin for Lorne Carr, November 5, 1934. Loan moved to **Cleveland** (IHL) by **NY Americans**, December 2, 1934. Traded to **Boston** by **NY Americans** for Obs Heximer and Hap Emms, December 14, 1934. Transferred to **London** (IHL) by **Boston** as compensation for Boston's trading for Ray Getliffe, December 31, 1935.

JACOBS, Paul

Defense. Shoots Left. 5'8", 160 lbs. Born, Montreal, Que.,

Season	Club	GP	G	A	Pts	PIM	GP	G	A	Pts	PIM
1918-19	Toronto Arenas	1	0	0	0	0	....	....	....	....	....
	NHL Totals	**1**	**0**	**0**	**0**	**0**	....	....	....	....	....

Signed as a free agent by **Toronto**, December 15, 1918.

JACOBS, Tim

Defense. Shoots left. 5'10", 180 lbs. Born, Espanola, Ont., March 28, 1952.
(California's 5th choice, 70th overall, in 1972 Amateur Draft).

Season	Club	GP	G	A	Pts	PIM	GP	G	A	Pts	PIM
1975-76	California Golden Seals	46	0	10	10	35	....	....	....	....	....
	NHL Totals	**46**	**0**	**10**	**10**	**35**	....	....	....	....	....

JAGR, Jaromir

Right wing. Shoots left. 6'2", 234 lbs. Born, Kladno, Czech., February 15, 1972.
(Pittsburgh's 1st choice, 5th overall, in 1990 Entry Draft).

Season	Club	GP	G	A	Pts	PIM	GP	G	A	Pts	PIM
1990-91 ♦	Pittsburgh Penguins	80	27	30	57	42	24	3	10	13	6
1991-92 ♦	Pittsburgh Penguins	70	32	37	69	34	21	11	13	24	6
1992-93	Pittsburgh Penguins	81	34	60	94	61	12	5	4	9	23
1993-94	Pittsburgh Penguins	80	32	67	99	61	6	2	4	6	16
1994-95	Pittsburgh Penguins	48	32	38	*70	37	12	10	5	15	6
1995-96	Pittsburgh Penguins	82	62	87	149	96	18	11	12	23	18
1996-97	Pittsburgh Penguins	63	47	48	95	40	5	4	4	8	4
1997-98	Pittsburgh Penguins	77	35	*67	*102	64	6	4	5	9	2
1998-99	Pittsburgh Penguins	81	44	*83	*127	66	9	5	7	12	16
99-2000	Pittsburgh Penguins	63	42	54	*96	50	11	8	8	16	6
2000-01	Pittsburgh Penguins	81	52	*69	*121	42	16	2	10	12	18
2001-02	Washington Capitals	69	31	48	79	30	....	....	....	....	....
2002-03	Washington Capitals	75	36	41	77	38	6	2	5	7	2
	NHL Totals	**950**	**506**	**729**	**1235**	**661**	**146**	**67**	**87**	**154**	**123**

NHL All-Rookie Team (1991) • NHL First All-Star Team (1995, 1996, 1998, 1999, 2000, 2001) • Art Ross Trophy (1995, 1998, 1999, 2000, 2001) • NHL Second All-Star Team (1997) • Lester B. Pearson Award (1999, 2000) • Hart Trophy (1999)

Played in NHL All-Star Game (1992, 1993, 1996, 1998, 1999, 2000, 2002, 2003)

Traded to **Washington** by **Pittsburgh** with Frantisek Kucera for Kris Beech, Michal Sivek, Ross Lupaschuk and future considerations, July 11, 2001.

JAKOPIN, John

Defense. Shoots right. 6'5", 240 lbs. Born, Toronto, Ont., May 16, 1975.
(Detroit's 4th choice, 97th overall, in 1993 Entry Draft).

Season	Club	GP	G	A	Pts	PIM	GP	G	A	Pts	PIM
1997-98	Florida Panthers	2	0	0	0	4	....	....	....	....	....
1998-99	Florida Panthers	3	0	0	0	0	....	....	....	....	....
99-2000	Florida Panthers	17	0	0	0	26	....	....	....	....	....
2000-01	Florida Panthers	60	1	2	3	62	....	....	....	....	....
2001-02	Pittsburgh Penguins	19	0	4	4	42	....	....	....	....	....
2002-03	San Jose Sharks	12	0	0	0	11	....	....	....	....	....
	NHL Totals	**113**	**1**	**6**	**7**	**145**	....	....	....	....	....

Signed as a free agent by **Florida**, May 14, 1997. Claimed on waivers by **Pittsburgh** from **Florida**, October 3, 2001. Signed as a free agent by **San Jose**, September 5, 2002.

JALO, Risto

Center. Shoots left. 5'11", 185 lbs. Born, Tampere, Finland, July 18, 1962.
(Washington's 7th choice, 131st overall, in 1981 Entry Draft).

Season	Club	GP	G	A	Pts	PIM	GP	G	A	Pts	PIM
1985-86	Edmonton Oilers	3	0	3	3	0	....	....	....	....	....
	NHL Totals	**3**	**0**	**3**	**3**	**0**	....	....	....	....	....

Traded to **Edmonton** by **Washington** for Edmonton's 4th round choice (Larry Shaw) in 1985 Entry Draft, March 6, 1984.

JALONEN, Kari

Center. Shoots right. 6'3", 190 lbs. Born, Oulu, Finland, January 6, 1960.

Season	Club	GP	G	A	Pts	PIM	GP	G	A	Pts	PIM
1982-83	Calgary Flames	25	9	3	12	4	5	1	0	1	0
1983-84	Calgary Flames	9	0	3	3	0	....	....	....	....	....
	Edmonton Oilers	3	0	0	0	0	....	....	....	....	....
	NHL Totals	**37**	**9**	**6**	**15**	**4**	**5**	**1**	**0**	**1**	**0**

Signed as a free agent by **Calgary**, January 21, 1982. Signed as a free agent by **Edmonton**, December, 1983.

JAMES, Gerry

Right wing. Shoots right. 5'11", 185 lbs. Born, Regina, Sask., October 22, 1934.

Season	Club	GP	G	A	Pts	PIM	GP	G	A	Pts	PIM
		REGULAR SEASON					PLAYOFFS				
1954-55	Toronto Maple Leafs	1	0	0	0	0	....	....	....	....	....
1955-56	Toronto Maple Leafs	46	3	3	6	50	5	1	0	1	8
1956-57	Toronto Maple Leafs	53	4	12	16	90	....	....	....	....	....
1957-58	Toronto Maple Leafs	15	3	2	5	61	....	....	....	....	....
1959-60	Toronto Maple Leafs	34	4	9	13	56	10	0	0	0	0
	NHL Totals	**149**	**14**	**26**	**40**	**257**	**15**	**1**	**0**	**1**	**8**

• Missed the entire 1958-59 season recovering from leg injury suffered in football game between Winnipeg Blue Bombers (CFL) and Saskatchewan Roughriders (CFL), September 7, 1958. Loaned to **Winnipeg** (WHL) by **Toronto** (Victoria-WHL) for the remainder of the 1960-61 season for Barrie Ross, January, 1961.

JAMES, Val

Left wing. Shoots left. 6'2", 205 lbs. Born, Ocala, FL, February 14, 1957.
(Detroit's 15th choice, 184th overall, in 1977 Amateur Draft).

Season	Club	GP	G	A	Pts	PIM	GP	G	A	Pts	PIM
1981-82	Buffalo Sabres	7	0	0	0	16	....	....	....	....	....
1986-87	Toronto Maple Leafs	4	0	0	0	14	....	....	....	....	....
	NHL Totals	**11**	**0**	**0**	**0**	**30**	....	....	....	....	....

Signed as a free agent by **Buffalo**, July 22, 1981. Signed as a free agent by **Toronto**, October 3, 1985.

JAMIESON, Jim

Defense. Shoots left. 5'9", 170 lbs. Born, Brantford, Ont., March 21, 1922.

Season	Club	GP	G	A	Pts	PIM	GP	G	A	Pts	PIM
1943-44	New York Rangers	1	0	1	1	0	....	....	....	....	....
	NHL Totals	**1**	**0**	**1**	**1**	**0**	....	....	....	....	....

JANIK, Doug

Defense. Shoots left. 6'2", 209 lbs. Born, Agawam, MA, March 26, 1980.
(Buffalo's 3rd choice, 55th overall, in 1999 Entry Draft).

Season	Club	GP	G	A	Pts	PIM	GP	G	A	Pts	PIM
2002-03	Buffalo Sabres	6	0	0	0	2	....	....	....	....	....
	NHL Totals	**6**	**0**	**0**	**0**	**2**	....	....	....	....	....

JANKOWSKI, Lou

Center/Right wing. Shoots right. 6', 180 lbs. Born, Regina, Sask., June 27, 1931.

Season	Club	GP	G	A	Pts	PIM	GP	G	A	Pts	PIM
1950-51	Detroit Red Wings	1	0	1	1	0	....	....	....	....	....
1952-53	Detroit Red Wings	22	1	2	3	0	1	0	0	0	0
1953-54	Chicago Black Hawks	68	15	13	28	7	....	....	....	....	....
1954-55	Chicago Black Hawks	36	3	2	5	8	....	....	....	....	....
	NHL Totals	**127**	**19**	**18**	**37**	**15**	**1**	**0**	**0**	**0**	**0**

Rights traded to **Detroit** by **Cleveland** (AHL) with the rights to Bill Dineen for Bob Bailey and John Bailey, June, 1951. Traded to **Chicago** by **Detroit** with Larry Zeidel and Larry Wilson for cash, August 12, 1953. Signed as a free agent by **Denver** (WHL), September, 1963. Claimed by **Toronto** from **Toronto** (Denver-WHL) in Reverse Draft, June 8, 1964. Traded to **Phoenix** (WHL) by **Toronto** (Victoria-WHL) for cash, September, 1967.

JANNEY, Craig

Center. Shoots left. 6'1", 190 lbs. Born, Hartford, CT, September 26, 1967.
(Boston's 1st choice, 13th overall, in 1986 Entry Draft).

Season	Club	GP	G	A	Pts	PIM	GP	G	A	Pts	PIM
1987-88	Boston Bruins	15	7	9	16	0	23	6	10	16	11
1988-89	Boston Bruins	62	16	46	62	12	10	4	9	13	21
1989-90	Boston Bruins	55	24	38	62	4	18	3	19	22	2
1990-91	Boston Bruins	77	26	66	92	8	18	4	18	22	11
1991-92	Boston Bruins	53	12	39	51	20	....	....	....	....	....
	St. Louis Blues	25	6	30	36	2	6	0	6	6	0
1992-93	St. Louis Blues	84	24	82	106	12	11	2	9	11	0
1993-94	St. Louis Blues	69	16	68	84	24	4	1	3	4	0
1994-95	St. Louis Blues	8	2	5	7	0	....	....	....	....	....
	San Jose Sharks	27	5	15	20	10	11	3	4	7	4
1995-96	San Jose Sharks	71	13	49	62	26	....	....	....	....	....
	Winnipeg Jets	13	7	13	20	0	6	1	2	3	0
1996-97	Phoenix Coyotes	77	15	38	53	26	7	0	3	3	4
1997-98	Phoenix Coyotes	68	10	43	53	12	6	0	3	3	0
1998-99	Tampa Bay Lightning	38	4	18	22	10	....	....	....	....	....
	New York Islanders	18	1	4	5	4	....	....	....	....	....
	NHL Totals	**760**	**188**	**563**	**751**	**170**	**120**	**24**	**86**	**110**	**53**

Traded to **St. Louis** by **Boston** with Stephane Quintal for Adam Oates, February 7, 1992. Acquired by **Vancouver** from **St. Louis** with St. Louis' 2nd round choice (Dave Scathard) in 1994 Entry Draft as compensation for St. Louis' signing of free agent Petr Nedved, March 14, 1994. Traded to **St. Louis** by **Vancouver** for Jeff Brown, Bret Hedican and Nathan LaFayette, March 21, 1994. Traded to **San Jose** by **St. Louis** with cash for Jeff Norton and future considerations, March 6, 1995. Traded to **Winnipeg** by **San Jose** for Darren Turcotte and Dallas' 2nd round choice (previously acquired, later traded to Chicago – Chicago selected Remi Royer) in 1996 Entry Draft, March 18, 1996. Transferred to **Phoenix** after **Winnipeg** franchise relocated, July 1, 1996. Traded to **Tampa Bay** by **Phoenix** for Louie Debrusk and Tampa Bay's 5th round choice (Jay Leach) in 1998 Entry Draft, June 11, 1998. Traded to **NY Islanders** by **Tampa Bay** for Toronto's 6th round choice (previously acquired, Tampa Bay selected Fedor Fedorov) in 1999 Entry Draft, January 18, 1999.

JANSSENS, Mark

Center. Shoots left. 6'3", 212 lbs. Born, Surrey, B.C., May 19, 1968.
(NY Rangers' 4th choice, 72nd overall, in 1986 Entry Draft).

Season	Club	GP	G	A	Pts	PIM	GP	G	A	Pts	PIM
1987-88	New York Rangers	1	0	0	0	0	....	....	....	....	....
1988-89	New York Rangers	5	0	0	0	0	....	....	....	....	....
1989-90	New York Rangers	80	5	8	13	161	9	2	1	3	10
1990-91	New York Rangers	67	9	7	16	172	6	3	0	3	6
1991-92	New York Rangers	4	0	0	0	5	....	....	....	....	....
	Minnesota North Stars	3	0	0	0	0	....	....	....	....	....
1992-93	Hartford Whalers	76	12	17	29	237	....	....	....	....	....
1993-94	Hartford Whalers	84	2	10	12	137	....	....	....	....	....
1994-95	Hartford Whalers	46	2	5	7	93	....	....	....	....	....
1995-96	Hartford Whalers	81	2	7	9	155	....	....	....	....	....

Season	Club	Regular Season GP	G	A	Pts	PIM	Playoffs GP	G	A	Pts	PIM
1996-97	Hartford Whalers	54	2	4	6	90	....	....	....	....	....
	Mighty Ducks of Anaheim	12	0	2	2	47	11	0	0	0	15
1997-98	Mighty Ducks of Anaheim	55	4	5	9	116	....	....	....	....	....
	New York Islanders	12	0	0	0	34	....	....	....	....	....
	Phoenix Coyotes	7	1	2	3	4	1	0	0	0	2
1998-99	Chicago Blackhawks	60	1	0	1	65	....	....	....	....	....
99-2000	Chicago Blackhawks	36	0	6	6	73	....	....	....	....	....
2000-01	Chicago Blackhawks	28	0	0	0	33	....	....	....	....	....
	NHL Totals	**711**	**40**	**73**	**113**	**1422**	**27**	**5**	**1**	**6**	**33**

Traded to **Minnesota** by **NY Rangers** for Mario Thyer and Minnesota's 3rd round choice (Maxim Galanov) in 1993 Entry Draft, March 10, 1992. Traded to **Hartford** by **Minnesota** for James Black, September 3, 1992. Traded to **Anaheim** by **Hartford** for Bates Battaglia and Anaheim's 4th round choice (Carolina selected Josef Vasicek) in 1998 Entry Draft, March 18, 1997. Traded to **NY Islanders** by **Anaheim** with Joe Sacco and J.J. Daigneault for Travis Green, Doug Houda and Tony Tuzzolino, February 6, 1998. Traded to **Phoenix** by **NY Islanders** for Phoenix's 9th round choice (Jason Doyle) in 1998 Entry Draft, March 24, 1998. Signed as a free agent by **Chicago**, July 28, 1998. • Missed majority of 1999-2000 season recovering from back injury suffered in game vs. Edmonton, December 3, 1999. Traded to **Philadelphia** by **Chicago** for Philadelphia's 9th round choice (Arne Ramholt) in 2000 Entry Draft, June 12, 2000. Claimed on waivers by **Chicago** from **Philadelphia**, July 6, 2000.

JANTUNEN, Marko

Center. Shoots left. 5'10", 185 lbs. Born, Lahti, Finland, February 14, 1971.
(Calgary's 13th choice, 239th overall, in 1991 Entry Draft).

Season	Club	GP	G	A	Pts	PIM	GP	G	A	Pts	PIM
1996-97	Calgary Flames	3	0	0	0	0	....	....	....	....	....
	NHL Totals	**3**	**0**	**0**	**0**	**0**	....	....	....	....	....

JARDINE, Ryan

Left wing. Shoots left. 6', 210 lbs. Born, Ottawa, Ont., March 15, 1980.
(Florida's 4th choice, 89th overall, in 1998 Entry Draft).

Season	Club	GP	G	A	Pts	PIM	GP	G	A	Pts	PIM
2001-02	Florida Panthers	8	0	2	2	2	....	....	....	....	....
	NHL Totals	**8**	**0**	**2**	**2**	**2**	....	....	....	....	....

JARRETT, Doug

Defense. Shoots left. 6'3", 205 lbs. Born, London, Ont., April 22, 1944.

Season	Club	GP	G	A	Pts	PIM	GP	G	A	Pts	PIM
1964-65	Chicago Black Hawks	46	2	15	17	34	11	1	0	1	10
1965-66	Chicago Black Hawks	66	4	12	16	71	5	0	1	1	9
1966-67	Chicago Black Hawks	70	5	21	26	76	6	0	3	3	8
1967-68	Chicago Black Hawks	74	4	19	23	48	11	4	0	4	9
1968-69	Chicago Black Hawks	69	0	13	13	58	....	....	....	....	....
1969-70	Chicago Black Hawks	72	4	20	24	78	8	1	0	1	4
1970-71	Chicago Black Hawks	51	1	12	13	46	18	1	6	7	11
1971-72	Chicago Black Hawks	78	6	23	29	68	8	0	2	2	16
1972-73	Chicago Black Hawks	49	2	11	13	18	15	0	3	3	2
1973-74	Chicago Black Hawks	67	5	11	16	45	10	0	1	1	6
1974-75	Chicago Black Hawks	79	5	21	26	66	7	0	0	0	4
1975-76	New York Rangers	45	0	4	4	19	....	....	....	....	....
1976-77	New York Rangers	9	0	0	0	4	....	....	....	....	....
	NHL Totals	**775**	**38**	**182**	**220**	**631**	**99**	**7**	**16**	**23**	**82**

Played in NHL All-Star Game (1975)

Traded to **NY Rangers** by **Chicago** for Gilles Villemure, October 28, 1975.

JARRETT, Gary

Left wing. Shoots left. 5'8", 170 lbs. Born, Toronto, Ont., September 3, 1942.

Season	Club	GP	G	A	Pts	PIM	GP	G	A	Pts	PIM
1960-61	Toronto Maple Leafs	1	0	0	0	0	....	....	....	....	....
1966-67	Detroit Red Wings	4	0	0	0	0	....	....	....	....	....
1967-68	Detroit Red Wings	68	18	21	39	20	....	....	....	....	....
1968-69	Oakland Seals	63	22	23	45	22	7	2	1	3	4
1969-70	Oakland Seals	75	12	19	31	31	4	1	0	1	5
1970-71	California Seals	75	15	19	34	40	....	....	....	....	....
1971-72	California Golden Seals	55	5	10	15	18	....	....	....	....	....
	NHL Totals	**341**	**72**	**92**	**164**	**131**	**11**	**3**	**1**	**4**	**9**

Traded to **Detroit** by **Toronto** with Billy Harris and Andy Bathgate for Lowell MacDonald, Marcel Pronovost, Eddie Joyal, Larry Jeffrey and Aut Erickson, May 20, 1965. Traded to **Oakland** by **Detroit** with Doug Roberts, Howie Young and Chris Worthy for Bob Baun and Ron Harris, May 27, 1968.

JARRY, Pierre

Left wing. Shoots left. 5'11", 190 lbs. Born, Montreal, Que., March 30, 1949.
(NY Rangers' 2nd choice, 12th overall, in 1969 Amateur Draft).

Season	Club	GP	G	A	Pts	PIM	GP	G	A	Pts	PIM
1971-72	New York Rangers	34	3	3	6	20	....	....	....	....	....
	Toronto Maple Leafs	18	3	4	7	13	5	0	1	1	0
1972-73	Toronto Maple Leafs	74	19	18	37	42	....	....	....	....	....
1973-74	Toronto Maple Leafs	12	2	8	10	10	....	....	....	....	....
	Detroit Red Wings	52	15	23	38	17	....	....	....	....	....
1974-75	Detroit Red Wings	39	8	13	21	4	....	....	....	....	....
1975-76	Minnesota North Stars	59	21	18	39	32	....	....	....	....	....
1976-77	Minnesota North Stars	21	8	13	21	2	....	....	....	....	....
1977-78	Minnesota North Stars	35	9	17	26	2	....	....	....	....	....
	NHL Totals	**344**	**88**	**117**	**205**	**142**	**5**	**0**	**1**	**1**	**0**

Traded to **Toronto** by **NY Rangers** for Jim Dorey, February 20, 1972. Traded to **Detroit** by **Toronto** for Tim Ecclestone, November 29, 1973. Traded to **Minnesota** by **Detroit** for Don Martineau, November 25, 1975. • Missed majority of 1976-77 season recovering from knee injury suffered in game vs. Toronto, November 20, 1976. Traded to **Edmonton** (WHA) by **Minnesota** with Chris Aherns for future considerations, March, 1978.

JARVENPAA, Hannu

Right wing. Shoots left. 6', 195 lbs. Born, Ii, Finland, May 19, 1963.
(Winnipeg's 4th choice, 71st overall, in 1986 Entry Draft).

Season	Club	GP	G	A	Pts	PIM	GP	G	A	Pts	PIM
1986-87	Winnipeg Jets	20	1	8	9	8	....	....	....	....	....
1987-88	Winnipeg Jets	41	6	11	17	34	....	....	....	....	....
1988-89	Winnipeg Jets	53	4	7	11	41	....	....	....	....	....
	NHL Totals	**114**	**11**	**26**	**37**	**83**	....	....	....	....	....

• Re-entered NHL Entry Draft. Originally Montreal's 11th choice, 145th overall, in 1982 Entry Draft.

JARVENTIE, Martti

Defense. Shoots left. 5'11", 196 lbs. Born, Tampere, Finland, April 4, 1976.
(Montreal's 5th choice, 109th overall, in 2001 Entry Draft).

Season	Club	GP	G	A	Pts	PIM	GP	G	A	Pts	PIM
2001-02	Montreal Canadiens	1	0	0	0	0	....	....	....	....	....
	NHL Totals	**1**	**0**	**0**	**0**	**0**	....	....	....	....	....

JARVI, Iiro

Right wing. Shoots left. 6'1", 198 lbs. Born, Helsinki, Finland, March 23, 1965.
(Quebec's 3rd choice, 55th overall, in 1983 Entry Draft).

Season	Club	GP	G	A	Pts	PIM	GP	G	A	Pts	PIM
1988-89	Quebec Nordiques	75	11	30	41	40	....	....	....	....	....
1989-90	Quebec Nordiques	41	7	13	20	18	....	....	....	....	....
	NHL Totals	**116**	**18**	**43**	**61**	**58**	....	....	....	....	....

JARVIS, Doug

Center. Shoots left. 5'9", 170 lbs. Born, Brantford, Ont., March 24, 1955.
(Toronto's 2nd choice, 24th overall, in 1975 Amateur Draft).

Season	Club	GP	G	A	Pts	PIM	GP	G	A	Pts	PIM
1975-76◆	Montreal Canadiens	80	5	30	35	16	13	2	1	3	2
1976-77◆	Montreal Canadiens	80	16	22	38	14	14	0	7	7	2
1977-78◆	Montreal Canadiens	80	11	28	39	23	15	3	5	8	12
1978-79◆	Montreal Canadiens	80	10	13	23	16	12	1	3	4	4
1979-80	Montreal Canadiens	80	13	11	24	28	10	4	4	8	2
1980-81	Montreal Canadiens	80	16	22	38	34	3	0	0	0	0
1981-82	Montreal Canadiens	80	20	28	48	20	5	1	0	1	4
1982-83	Washington Capitals	80	8	22	30	10	4	0	1	1	0
1983-84	Washington Capitals	80	13	29	42	12	8	2	3	5	6
1984-85	Washington Capitals	80	9	28	37	32	5	1	0	1	2
1985-86	Washington Capitals	25	1	2	3	16	....	....	....	....	....
	Hartford Whalers	57	8	16	24	20	10	0	3	3	4
1986-87	Hartford Whalers	80	9	13	22	20	6	0	0	0	4
1987-88	Hartford Whalers	2	0	0	0	2	....	....	....	....	....
	NHL Totals	**964**	**139**	**264**	**403**	**263**	**105**	**14**	**27**	**41**	**42**

Frank J. Selke Trophy (1984) • Bill Masterton Trophy (1987)

Traded to **Montreal** by **Toronto** for Greg Hubick, June 26, 1975. Traded to **Washington** by **Montreal** with Rod Langway, Craig Laughlin and Brian Engblom for Ryan Walter and Rick Green, September 9, 1982. Traded to **Hartford** by **Washington** for Jorgen Pettersson, December 6, 1985.

JARVIS, James

Left wing. Shoots left. 5'6", 165 lbs. Born, Fort William, Ont., December 7, 1907.

Season	Club	GP	G	A	Pts	PIM	GP	G	A	Pts	PIM
1929-30	Pittsburgh Pirates	44	11	8	19	32	....	....	....	....	....
1930-31	Philadelphia Quakers	44	5	7	12	30	....	....	....	....	....
1936-37	Toronto Maple Leafs	24	1	0	1	0	....	....	....	....	....
	NHL Totals	**112**	**17**	**15**	**32**	**62**	....	....	....	....	....

Signed as a free agent by **Pittsburgh**, October 31, 1929. Transferred to **Philadelphia** after **Pittsburgh** franchise relocated, October 18, 1930. Claimed by **NY Rangers** from **Philadelphia** in Dispersal Draft, September 26, 1931. Signed as a free agent by **Toronto** (Syracuse-IAHL) after **Buffalo** (IAHL) franchise folded, December 9, 1936.

JARVIS, Wes

Center. Shoots left. 5'11", 185 lbs. Born, Toronto, Ont., May 30, 1958.
(Washington's 18th choice, 213th overall, in 1978 Amateur Draft).

Season	Club	GP	G	A	Pts	PIM	GP	G	A	Pts	PIM
1979-80	Washington Capitals	63	11	15	26	8	....	....	....	....	....
1980-81	Washington Capitals	55	9	14	23	30	....	....	....	....	....
1981-82	Washington Capitals	26	1	12	13	18	....	....	....	....	....
1982-83	Minnesota North Stars	3	0	0	0	2	....	....	....	....	....
1983-84	Los Angeles Kings	61	9	13	22	36	....	....	....	....	....
1984-85	Toronto Maple Leafs	26	0	1	1	2	....	....	....	....	....
1985-86	Toronto Maple Leafs	2	1	0	1	2	....	....	....	....	....
1986-87	Toronto Maple Leafs	....	....	....	....	....	2	0	0	0	2
1987-88	Toronto Maple Leafs	1	0	0	0	0	....	....	....	....	....
	NHL Totals	**237**	**31**	**55**	**86**	**98**	**2**	**0**	**0**	**0**	**2**

Traded to **Minnesota** by **Washington** with Rollie Boutin for Robbie Moore and Minnesota's 11th round choice (Anders Huss) in 1983 Entry Draft, August 4, 1982. Signed as a free agent by **Los Angeles**, August 10, 1983. Signed as a free agent by **Toronto**, October 2, 1984.

JASPERS, Jason

Center. Shoots left. 5'11", 204 lbs. Born, Thunder Bay, Ont., April 8, 1981.
(Phoenix's 4th choice, 71st overall, in 1999 Entry Draft).

Season	Club	GP	G	A	Pts	PIM	GP	G	A	Pts	PIM
2001-02	Phoenix Coyotes	4	0	1	1	4	....	....	....	....	....
2002-03	Phoenix Coyotes	2	0	0	0	0	....	....	....	....	....
	NHL Totals	**6**	**0**	**1**	**1**	**4**	....	....	....	....	....

JAVANAINEN, Arto

Right wing. Shoots right. 6', 185 lbs. Born, Pori, Finland, April 8, 1959.
(Pittsburgh's 5th choice, 85th overall, in 1984 Entry Draft).

Season	Club	Regular Season GP	G	A	Pts	PIM	Playoffs GP	G	A	Pts	PIM
1984-85	Pittsburgh Penguins	14	4	1	5	2	....	....	....	....	....
	NHL Totals	**14**	**4**	**1**	**5**	**2**	....	....	....	....	....

• Re-entered NHL Entry Draft. Originally Montreal's 8th choice, 122nd overall, in 1983 Entry Draft.

JAY, Bob

Defense. Shoots right. 5'11", 190 lbs. Born, Burlington, MA, November 18, 1965.

Season	Club	Regular Season GP	G	A	Pts	PIM	Playoffs GP	G	A	Pts	PIM
1993-94	Los Angeles Kings	3	0	1	1	0	....	....	....	....	....
	NHL Totals	**3**	**0**	**1**	**1**	**0**	....	....	....	....	....

Signed as a free agent by **Los Angeles**, July 16, 1993.

JEFFREY, Larry

Left wing. Shoots left. 5'11", 189 lbs. Born, Goderich, Ont., October 12, 1940.

Season	Club	Regular Season GP	G	A	Pts	PIM	Playoffs GP	G	A	Pts	PIM
1961-62	Detroit Red Wings	18	5	3	8	20	....	....	....	....	....
1962-63	Detroit Red Wings	53	5	11	16	62	9	3	3	6	8
1963-64	Detroit Red Wings	58	10	18	28	87	14	1	6	7	28
1964-65	Detroit Red Wings	41	4	2	6	48	2	0	0	0	0
1965-66	Toronto Maple Leafs	20	1	1	2	22	....	....	....	....	....
1966-67 ◆	Toronto Maple Leafs	56	11	17	28	27	6	0	1	1	4
1967-68	New York Rangers	47	2	4	6	15	3	0	0	0	0
1968-69	New York Rangers	75	1	6	7	12	4	0	0	0	2
	NHL Totals	**368**	**39**	**62**	**101**	**293**	**38**	**4**	**10**	**14**	**42**

Traded to **Toronto** by **Detroit** with Marcel Pronovost, Eddie Joyal, Aut Erickson and Lowell MacDonald for Andy Bathgate, Billy Harris and Gary Jarrett, May 20, 1965. Claimed by **Pittsburgh** from **Toronto** in Expansion Draft, June 6, 1967. Traded to **NY Rangers** by **Pittsburgh** for George Konik, Paul Andrea, Dunc McCallum and Frank Francis, June 6, 1967. Traded to **Detroit** by **NY Rangers** for Sandy Snow and Terry Sawchuk, June 17, 1969. • Suffered career-ending leg injury in automobile accident, October 5, 1969.

JELINEK, Tomas

Right wing. Shoots left. 5'9", 189 lbs. Born, Prague, Czech., April 29, 1962.
(Ottawa's 11th choice, 242nd overall, in 1992 Entry Draft).

Season	Club	Regular Season GP	G	A	Pts	PIM	Playoffs GP	G	A	Pts	PIM
1992-93	Ottawa Senators	49	7	6	13	52	....	....	....	....	....
	NHL Totals	**49**	**7**	**6**	**13**	**52**	....	....	....	....	....

JENKINS, Dean

Right wing. Shoots right. 6', 190 lbs. Born, Billerica, MA, November 21, 1959.

Season	Club	Regular Season GP	G	A	Pts	PIM	Playoffs GP	G	A	Pts	PIM
1983-84	Los Angeles Kings	5	0	0	0	2	....	....	....	....	....
	NHL Totals	**5**	**0**	**0**	**0**	**2**	....	....	....	....	....

Signed as a free agent by **Los Angeles**, April 30, 1981. Signed as a free agent by **Boston**, October 10, 1984.

JENKINS, Roger

Right wing/Defense. Shoots right. 5'11", 173 lbs. Born, Appleton, WI, November 18, 1911.

Season	Club	Regular Season GP	G	A	Pts	PIM	Playoffs GP	G	A	Pts	PIM
1930-31	Chicago Black Hawks	10	0	1	1	2	3	0	0	0	0
	Toronto Maple Leafs	21	0	0	0	12	....	....	....	....	....
1932-33	Chicago Black Hawks	46	3	10	13	42	....	....	....	....	....
1933-34 ◆	Chicago Black Hawks	48	2	2	4	37	8	0	0	0	0
1934-35	Montreal Canadiens	45	4	6	10	63	2	1	0	1	2
1935-36	Boston Bruins	40	2	6	8	51	2	0	1	1	2
1936-37	Montreal Canadiens	10	0	0	0	8	....	....	....	....	....
	Montreal Maroons	1	0	0	0	0	....	....	....	....	....
	New York Americans	26	1	4	5	6	....	....	....	....	....
1937-38 ◆	Chicago Black Hawks	37	1	8	9	26	10	0	*6	6	8
1938-39	Chicago Black Hawks	14	1	1	2	2	....	....	....	....	....
	New York Americans	27	1	1	2	4	....	....	....	....	....
	NHL Totals	**325**	**15**	**39**	**54**	**253**	**25**	**1**	**7**	**8**	**12**

Signed as a free agent by **Chicago**, October 28, 1930. Loaned to **Toronto** by **Chicago**, December 4, 1930. • Returned to **Chicago** by **Toronto**, February 3, 1931. Traded to **Montreal** by **Chicago** with Leroy Goldsworthy and Lionel Conacher for Lorne Chabot, Howie Morenz and Marty Burke, October 3, 1934. Traded to **Boston** by **Montreal** for Jean Pusie, Walt Buswell and cash, July 13, 1935. Traded to **Montreal** by **Boston** with Babe Siebert for Leroy Goldsworthy, Sammy McManus and $10,000, September 10, 1936. Signed as a free agent by **Mtl. Maroons** after securing release from **Montreal**, December 17, 1936. Loaned to **NY Americans** by **Mtl. Maroons** for cash, January 1, 1937. Signed as a free agent by **Chicago** after securing release from **Mtl. Maroons**, November 20, 1937. Signed as a free agent by **NY Americans**, January 1, 1939. Traded to **Springfield** (IAHL) by **NY Americans** for cash, October 2, 1939.

JENNINGS, Bill

Right wing. Shoots right. 5'10", 165 lbs. Born, Toronto, Ont., June 28, 1917.

Season	Club	Regular Season GP	G	A	Pts	PIM	Playoffs GP	G	A	Pts	PIM
1940-41	Detroit Red Wings	12	1	5	6	2	9	2	2	4	0
1941-42	Detroit Red Wings	16	2	1	3	6	....	....	....	....	....
1942-43	Detroit Red Wings	8	3	3	6	2	....	....	....	....	....
1943-44	Detroit Red Wings	33	6	11	17	10	4	0	0	0	0
1944-45	Boston Bruins	39	20	13	33	25	7	2	2	4	6
	NHL Totals	**108**	**32**	**33**	**65**	**45**	**20**	**4**	**4**	**8**	**6**

Signed as a free agent by **Detroit**, October 16, 1940. Traded to **Boston** by **Detroit** for Pete Leswick, October 30, 1944. Traded to **Chicago** (St. Louis-AHL) by **Boston** (Hershey-AHL) for Norm McAtee, February 5, 1946.

JENNINGS, Grant

Defense. Shoots left. 6'3", 210 lbs. Born, Hudson Bay, Sask., May 5, 1965.

Season	Club	Regular Season GP	G	A	Pts	PIM	Playoffs GP	G	A	Pts	PIM
1987-88	Washington Capitals	....	....	....	....	....	1	0	0	0	0
1988-89	Hartford Whalers	55	3	10	13	159	4	1	0	1	17
1989-90	Hartford Whalers	64	3	6	9	171	7	0	0	0	13
1990-91	Hartford Whalers	44	1	4	5	82	....	....	....	....	....
	◆ Pittsburgh Penguins	13	1	3	4	26	13	1	1	2	16
1991-92 ◆	Pittsburgh Penguins	53	4	5	9	104	10	0	0	0	12
1992-93	Pittsburgh Penguins	58	0	5	5	65	12	0	0	0	8
1993-94	Pittsburgh Penguins	61	2	4	6	126	3	0	0	0	2
1994-95	Pittsburgh Penguins	25	0	4	4	36	....	....	....	....	....
	Toronto Maple Leafs	10	0	2	2	7	4	0	0	0	0
1995-96	Buffalo Sabres	6	0	0	0	28	....	....	....	....	....
	NHL Totals	**389**	**14**	**43**	**57**	**804**	**54**	**2**	**1**	**3**	**68**

Signed as a free agent by **Washington**, June 25, 1985. Traded to **Hartford** by **Washington** with Ed Kastelic for Mike Millar and Neil Sheehy, July 6, 1988. Traded to **Pittsburgh** by **Hartford** with Ron Francis and Ulf Samuelsson for John Cullen, Jeff Parker and Zarley Zalapski, March 4, 1991. Traded to **Toronto** by **Pittsburgh** for Drake Berehowsky, April 7, 1995. Signed as a free agent by **Buffalo**, September 20, 1995.

JENSEN, Chris

Right wing. Shoots right. 5'11", 180 lbs. Born, Fort St. John, B.C., October 28, 1963.
(NY Rangers' 4th choice, 78th overall, in 1982 Entry Draft).

Season	Club	Regular Season GP	G	A	Pts	PIM	Playoffs GP	G	A	Pts	PIM
1985-86	New York Rangers	9	1	3	4	0	....	....	....	....	....
1986-87	New York Rangers	37	6	7	13	21	....	....	....	....	....
1987-88	New York Rangers	7	0	1	1	2	....	....	....	....	....
1989-90	Philadelphia Flyers	1	0	0	0	2	....	....	....	....	....
1990-91	Philadelphia Flyers	18	2	1	3	2	....	....	....	....	....
1991-92	Philadelphia Flyers	2	0	0	0	0	....	....	....	....	....
	NHL Totals	**74**	**9**	**12**	**21**	**27**	....	....	....	....	....

Traded to **Philadelphia** by **NY Rangers** for Michael Boyce, September 28, 1988.

JENSEN, David

Defense. Shoots left. 6'1", 185 lbs. Born, Minneapolis, MN, May 3, 1961.
(Minnesota's 5th choice, 100th overall, in 1980 Entry Draft).

Season	Club	Regular Season GP	G	A	Pts	PIM	Playoffs GP	G	A	Pts	PIM
1983-84	Minnesota North Stars	8	0	1	1	0	....	....	....	....	....
1984-85	Minnesota North Stars	5	0	1	1	4	....	....	....	....	....
1985-86	Minnesota North Stars	5	0	0	0	7	....	....	....	....	....
	NHL Totals	**18**	**0**	**2**	**2**	**11**	....	....	....	....	....

JENSEN, David

Center. Shoots left. 6'1", 195 lbs. Born, Newton, MA, August 19, 1965.
(Hartford's 2nd choice, 20th overall, in 1983 Entry Draft).

Season	Club	Regular Season GP	G	A	Pts	PIM	Playoffs GP	G	A	Pts	PIM
1984-85	Hartford Whalers	13	0	4	4	6	....	....	....	....	....
1985-86	Washington Capitals	5	1	0	1	0	4	0	0	0	0
1986-87	Washington Capitals	46	8	8	16	12	7	0	0	0	2
1987-88	Washington Capitals	5	0	1	1	4	....	....	....	....	....
	NHL Totals	**69**	**9**	**13**	**22**	**22**	**11**	**0**	**0**	**0**	**2**

Traded to **Washington** by **Hartford** for Dean Evason and Peter Sidorkiewicz, March 12, 1985. Signed as a free agent by **Boston**, August 1, 1988.

JENSEN, Steve

Left wing. Shoots left. 6'2", 190 lbs. Born, Minneapolis, MN, April 14, 1955.
(Minnesota's 4th choice, 58th overall, in 1975 Amateur Draft).

Season	Club	Regular Season GP	G	A	Pts	PIM	Playoffs GP	G	A	Pts	PIM
1975-76	Minnesota North Stars	19	7	6	13	6	....	....	....	....	....
1976-77	Minnesota North Stars	78	22	23	45	62	2	0	1	1	0
1977-78	Minnesota North Stars	74	13	17	30	73	....	....	....	....	....
1978-79	Los Angeles Kings	72	23	8	31	57	2	0	0	0	0
1979-80	Los Angeles Kings	76	21	15	36	13	4	0	0	0	2
1980-81	Los Angeles Kings	74	19	19	38	88	4	0	2	2	7
1981-82	Los Angeles Kings	45	8	19	27	19	....	....	....	....	....
	NHL Totals	**438**	**113**	**107**	**220**	**318**	**12**	**0**	**3**	**3**	**9**

Transferred to **Los Angeles** by **Minnesota** with Dave Gardner and Rick Hampton as compensation for Minnesota's signing of free agent Gary Sargent, July 15, 1978.

JEREMIAH, Ed

USHOF

Right wing/Defense. Shoots right. 5'9", 160 lbs. Born, Worcester, MA, November 4, 1905.

Season	Club	Regular Season GP	G	A	Pts	PIM	Playoffs GP	G	A	Pts	PIM
1931-32	New York Americans	9	0	1	1	0	....	....	....	....	....
	Boston Bruins	6	0	0	0	0	....	....	....	....	....
	NHL Totals	**15**	**0**	**1**	**1**	**0**	....	....	....	....	....

Lester Patrick Trophy (1969)

Traded to **Boston** by **NY Americans** for cash, February 1, 1932.

JERRARD, Paul

Defense. Shoots right. 5'10", 185 lbs. Born, Winnipeg, Man., April 20, 1965.
(NY Rangers' 10th choice, 180th overall, in 1983 Entry Draft).

Season	Club	Regular Season GP	G	A	Pts	PIM	Playoffs GP	G	A	Pts	PIM
1988-89	Minnesota North Stars	5	0	0	0	4	....	....	....	....	....
	NHL Totals	**5**	**0**	**0**	**0**	**4**	....	....	....	....	....

Traded to **Minnesota** by **NY Rangers** with Mark Tinordi, the rights to Bret Barnett and Mike Sullivan and Los Angeles' 3rd round choice (previously acquired, Minnesota selected Murray Garbutt) in 1989 Entry Draft for Brian Lawton, Igor Liba and the rights to Rick Bennett, October 11, 1988.

JERWA, Frank

Left wing/Defense. Shoots left. 6'1", 179 lbs. Born, Bankhead, Alta., March 15, 1909.

Season	Club	GP	G	A	Pts	PIM	GP	G	A	Pts	PIM
		REGULAR SEASON					PLAYOFFS				
1931-32	Boston Bruins	24	4	5	9	14	....	....	....	....	....
1932-33	Boston Bruins	31	3	4	7	23	....	....	....	....	....
1933-34	Boston Bruins	5	0	0	0	2	....	....	....	....	....
1934-35	Boston Bruins	5	0	0	0	0	....	....	....	....	....
	St. Louis Eagles	16	4	7	11	14	....	....	....	....	....
	NHL Totals	**81**	**11**	**16**	**27**	**53**	....	....	....	....	....

• Brother of Joe

Traded to **Boston** by **Vancouver** (PCHL) for cash, April 15, 1931. Traded to **St. Louis** by **Boston** for Gerry Shannon, January 10, 1935.

JERWA, Joe

Defense. Shoots left. 6'2", 185 lbs. Born, Bankhead, Alta., January 20, 1907.

Season	Club	GP	G	A	Pts	PIM	GP	G	A	Pts	PIM
1930-31	New York Rangers	33	4	7	11	72	4	0	0	0	4
1931-32	Boston Bruins	11	0	0	0	8	....	....	....	....	....
1933-34	Boston Bruins	2	0	0	0	2	....	....	....	....	....
1935-36	New York Americans	47	9	12	21	65	5	2	3	5	2
1936-37	Boston Bruins	26	3	5	8	30	....	....	....	....	....
	New York Americans	20	6	8	14	27	....	....	....	....	....
1937-38	New York Americans	48	3	14	17	53	6	0	0	0	8
1938-39	New York Americans	47	4	12	16	52	2	0	0	0	2
	NHL Totals	**234**	**29**	**58**	**87**	**309**	**17**	**2**	**3**	**5**	**16**

• Brother of Frank

Traded to **NY Rangers** by **Vancouver** (PCHL) with Red Beattie for $25,000, May 6, 1930. Traded to **Boston** by **NY Rangers** for Norm Gainor, August 25, 1931. Traded to **NY Americans** by **Boston** with Nels Stewart for cash, September 28, 1935. • Rights returned to **Boston** by **NY Americans** after NY Americans failed to complete purchase agreement, May 27, 1936. Traded to **NY Americans** by **Boston** for the loan of Al Shields and future considerations (rights to Terry Reardon and Tom Cooper, October 17, 1937), January 25, 1937. Traded to **Cleveland** (IAHL) by **NY Americans** for cash, October 12, 1939.

JILLSON, Jeff

Defense. Shoots right. 6'3", 220 lbs. Born, North Smithfield, RI, July 24, 1980.
(San Jose's 1st choice, 14th overall, in 1999 Entry Draft).

Season	Club	GP	G	A	Pts	PIM	GP	G	A	Pts	PIM
2001-02	San Jose Sharks	48	5	13	18	29	4	0	0	0	0
2002-03	San Jose Sharks	26	0	6	6	9	....	....	....	....	....
	NHL Totals	**74**	**5**	**19**	**24**	**38**	**4**	**0**	**0**	**0**	**0**

Traded to **Boston** by **San Jose** with Jeff Hackett for Kyle McLaren and Boston's 4th round choice in 2004 Entry Draft, January 23, 2003.

JIRIK, Jaroslav

left wing. Shoots left. 5'11", 170 lbs. Born, Vojnuv Mestec, Czech., December 10, 1939.

Season	Club	GP	G	A	Pts	PIM	GP	G	A	Pts	PIM
1969-70	St. Louis Blues	3	0	0	0	0	....	....	....	....	....
	NHL Totals	**3**	**0**	**0**	**0**	**0**	....	....	....	....	....

Signed as a free agent by **St. Louis**, September 11, 1969. • First player from Iron Curtain country to play in NHL.

JOANETTE, Rosario

Center. Shoots right. 5'8", 165 lbs. Born, Valleyfield, Que., July 27, 1919.

Season	Club	GP	G	A	Pts	PIM	GP	G	A	Pts	PIM
1944-45	Montreal Canadiens	2	0	1	1	4	....	....	....	....	....
	NHL Totals	**2**	**0**	**1**	**1**	**4**	....	....	....	....	....

JODZIO, Rick

Left wing. Shoots left. 6'1", 190 lbs. Born, Edmonton, Alta., June 3, 1954.
(Buffalo's 9th choice, 153rd overall, in 1974 Amateur Draft).

Season	Club	GP	G	A	Pts	PIM	GP	G	A	Pts	PIM
1977-78	Colorado Rockies	32	0	5	5	28	....	....	....	....	....
	Cleveland Barons	38	2	3	5	43	....	....	....	....	....
	NHL Totals	**70**	**2**	**8**	**10**	**71**	....	....	....	....	....

Traded to **Colorado** by **Buffalo** for cash, September 22, 1977. Traded to **Cleveland** by **Colorado** with Chuck Arnason for Ralph Klassen and Fred Ahern, January 9, 1978. Placed on Reserve List by **Minnesota** after **Cleveland-Minnesota** Dispersal Draft, June 15, 1978.

JOHANNESEN, Glenn

Left wing. Shoots right. 6'2", 220 lbs. Born, Lac La Ronge, Sask., February 15, 1962.
(NY Islanders' 11th choice, 206th overall, in 1980 Entry Draft).

Season	Club	GP	G	A	Pts	PIM	GP	G	A	Pts	PIM
1985-86	New York Islanders	2	0	0	0	0	....	....	....	....	....
	NHL Totals	**2**	**0**	**0**	**0**	**0**	....	....	....	....	....

JOHANNSON, John

Center. Shoots left. 6'1", 175 lbs. Born, Rochester, MN, October 18, 1961.
(Colorado's 10th choice, 192nd overall, in 1981 Entry Draft).

Season	Club	GP	G	A	Pts	PIM	GP	G	A	Pts	PIM
1983-84	New Jersey Devils	5	0	0	0	0	....	....	....	....	....
	NHL Totals	**5**	**0**	**0**	**0**	**0**	....	....	....	....	....

Rights transferred to **New Jersey** after **Colorado** franchise relocated, June 30, 1982.

JOHANSEN, Bill

Center/Right wing. Shoots right. 6', 163 lbs. Born, Port Arthur, Ont., July 27, 1928.

Season	Club	GP	G	A	Pts	PIM	GP	G	A	Pts	PIM
1949-50	Toronto Maple Leafs	1	0	0	0	0	....	....	....	....	....
	NHL Totals	**1**	**0**	**0**	**0**	**0**	....	....	....	....	....

• Father of Trevor • Known as "Johnson" during his playing career

Claimed by **Providence** (AHL) from **Toronto** (Ottawa-QHL) in Inter-League Draft, June 10, 1953. Traded to **Toronto** by **Providence** (AHL) for cash, October, 1953. Traded to **Providence** (AHL) by **Toronto** for cash, December 21, 1954. Rights transferred to **Toronto** after NHL club purchased **Spokane** (WHL) franchise, June 4, 1963.

JOHANSEN, Trevor

Defense. Shoots right. 5'9", 200 lbs. Born, Thunder Bay, Ont., March 30, 1957.
(Toronto's 2nd choice, 12th overall, in 1977 Amateur Draft).

Season	Club	GP	G	A	Pts	PIM	GP	G	A	Pts	PIM
1977-78	Toronto Maple Leafs	79	2	14	16	82	13	0	3	3	21
1978-79	Toronto Maple Leafs	40	1	4	5	48	....	....	....	....	....
	Colorado Rockies	11	1	3	4	16	....	....	....	....	....
1979-80	Colorado Rockies	62	3	8	11	45	....	....	....	....	....
1980-81	Colorado Rockies	35	0	7	7	18	....	....	....	....	....
1981-82	Los Angeles Kings	46	3	7	10	69	....	....	....	....	....
	Toronto Maple Leafs	13	1	3	4	4	....	....	....	....	....
	NHL Totals	**286**	**11**	**46**	**57**	**282**	**13**	**0**	**3**	**3**	**21**

• Son of Bill

Traded to **Colorado** by **Toronto** with Don Ashby for Paul Gardner, March 13, 1979. Claimed by **Los Angeles** from **Colorado** in Waiver Draft, October 5, 1981. Claimed on waivers by **Toronto** from **Los Angeles**, February 19, 1982.

JOHANSSON, Andreas

Center. Shoots left. 6', 202 lbs. Born, Hofors, Sweden, May 19, 1973.
(NY Islanders' 7th choice, 136th overall, in 1991 Entry Draft).

Season	Club	GP	G	A	Pts	PIM	GP	G	A	Pts	PIM
1995-96	New York Islanders	3	0	1	1	0	....	....	....	....	....
1996-97	New York Islanders	15	2	2	4	0	....	....	....	....	....
	Pittsburgh Penguins	27	2	7	9	20	....	....	....	....	....
1997-98	Pittsburgh Penguins	50	5	10	15	20	1	0	0	0	0
1998-99	Ottawa Senators	69	21	16	37	34	2	0	0	0	0
99-2000	Tampa Bay Lightning	12	2	3	5	8	....	....	....	....	....
	Calgary Flames	28	3	7	10	14	....	....	....	....	....
2001-02	New York Rangers	70	14	10	24	46	....	....	....	....	....
2002-03	Nashville Predators	56	20	17	37	22	....	....	....	....	....
	NHL Totals	**330**	**69**	**73**	**142**	**164**	**3**	**0**	**0**	**0**	**0**

Traded to **Pittsburgh** by **NY Islanders** with Darius Kasparaitis for Bryan Smolinski, November 17, 1996. Signed as a free agent by **Ottawa**, September 29, 1998. Traded to **Tampa Bay** by **Ottawa** for Rob Zamuner and Tampa Bay's 2nd round choice (later traded to Philadelphia – later traded back to Tampa Bay – later traded to Dallas – Dallas selected Tobias Stephan) in 2002 Entry Draft, June 29, 1999. Traded to **Calgary** by **Tampa Bay** for Nils Ekman and Calgary's 4th round choice (later traded to NY Islanders – NY Islanders selected Vladimir Gorbunov) in 2000 Entry Draft, November 13, 1999. • Missed majority of 1999-2000 season recovering from back injury suffered in game vs. Vancouver, January 7, 2000. Claimed by **NY Rangers** from **Calgary** in Waiver Draft, September 29, 2000. Signed as a free agent by **Nashville**, September 6, 2002.

JOHANSSON, Bjorn

Defense. Shoots left. 6', 195 lbs. Born, Orebro, Sweden, January 15, 1956.
(California's 1st choice, 5th overall, in 1976 Amateur Draft).

Season	Club	GP	G	A	Pts	PIM	GP	G	A	Pts	PIM
1976-77	Cleveland Barons	10	1	1	2	4	....	....	....	....	....
1977-78	Cleveland Barons	5	0	0	0	6	....	....	....	....	....
	NHL Totals	**15**	**1**	**1**	**2**	**10**	....	....	....	....	....

Transferred to **Cleveland** after **California** franchise relocated, August 26, 1976.

JOHANSSON, Calle

Defense. Shoots left. 5'11", 203 lbs. Born, Goteborg, Sweden, February 14, 1967.
(Buffalo's 1st choice, 14th overall, in 1985 Entry Draft).

Season	Club	GP	G	A	Pts	PIM	GP	G	A	Pts	PIM
1987-88	Buffalo Sabres	71	4	38	42	37	6	0	1	1	0
1988-89	Buffalo Sabres	47	2	11	13	33	....	....	....	....	....
	Washington Capitals	12	1	7	8	4	6	1	2	3	0
1989-90	Washington Capitals	70	8	31	39	25	15	1	6	7	4
1990-91	Washington Capitals	80	11	41	52	23	10	2	7	9	8
1991-92	Washington Capitals	80	14	42	56	49	7	0	5	5	4
1992-93	Washington Capitals	77	7	38	45	56	6	0	5	5	4
1993-94	Washington Capitals	84	9	33	42	59	6	1	3	4	4
1994-95	Washington Capitals	46	5	26	31	35	7	3	1	4	0
1995-96	Washington Capitals	78	10	25	35	50	....	....	....	....	....
1996-97	Washington Capitals	65	6	11	17	16	....	....	....	....	....
1997-98	Washington Capitals	73	15	20	35	30	21	2	8	10	16
1998-99	Washington Capitals	67	8	21	29	22	....	....	....	....	....
99-2000	Washington Capitals	82	7	25	32	24	5	1	2	3	0
2000-01	Washington Capitals	76	7	29	36	26	6	1	2	3	2
2001-02	Washington Capitals	11	2	0	2	8	....	....	....	....	....
2002-03	Washington Capitals	82	3	12	15	22	6	0	1	1	0
	NHL Totals	**1101**	**119**	**410**	**529**	**519**	**101**	**12**	**43**	**55**	**42**

NHL All-Rookie Team (1988)

Traded to **Washington** by **Buffalo** with Buffalo's 2nd round choice (Byron Dafoe) in 1989 Entry Draft for Clint Malarchuk, Grant Ledyard and Washington's 6th round choice (Brian Holzinger) in 1991 Entry Draft, March 7, 1989. • Missed majority of 2001-02 season recovering from rotator cuff injury suffered in game vs. Atlanta, November 10, 2001.

JOHANSSON, Mathias

Center. Shoots left. 6'2", 185 lbs. Born, Oskarshamn, Sweden, February 22, 1974.
(Calgary's 3rd choice, 54th overall, in 1992 Entry Draft).

Season	Club	GP	G	A	Pts	PIM	GP	G	A	Pts	PIM
		REGULAR SEASON					PLAYOFFS				
2002-03	Calgary Flames	46	4	5	9	12	....	....	....	....	....
	Pittsburgh Penguins	12	1	5	6	4	....	....	....	....	....
	NHL Totals	**58**	**5**	**10**	**15**	**16**	....	....	....	....	....

Traded to **Pittsburgh** by **Calgary** with Micki Dupont for Shean Donovan, March 11, 2003.

JOHANSSON, Roger

Defense. Shoots left. 6'1", 190 lbs. Born, Ljungby, Sweden, April 17, 1967.
(Calgary's 5th choice, 80th overall, in 1985 Entry Draft).

Season	Club	GP	G	A	Pts	PIM	GP	G	A	Pts	PIM
1989-90	Calgary Flames	35	0	5	5	48	....	....	....	....	....
1990-91	Calgary Flames	38	4	13	17	47	....	....	....	....	....
1992-93	Calgary Flames	77	4	16	20	62	5	0	1	1	2
1994-95	Chicago Blackhawks	11	1	0	1	6	....	....	....	....	....
	NHL Totals	**161**	**9**	**34**	**43**	**163**	**5**	**0**	**1**	**1**	**2**

Claimed by **Chicago** from **Calgary** in Waiver Draft, January 18, 1995.

JOHNS, Don

Defense. Shoots right. 6', 180 lbs. Born, St. George, Ont., December 13, 1937.

Season	Club	GP	G	A	Pts	PIM	GP	G	A	Pts	PIM
1960-61	New York Rangers	63	1	7	8	34	....	....	....	....	....
1962-63	New York Rangers	6	0	4	4	6	....	....	....	....	....
1963-64	New York Rangers	57	1	9	10	26	....	....	....	....	....
1964-65	New York Rangers	22	0	1	1	4	....	....	....	....	....
1965-66	Montreal Canadiens	1	0	0	0	0	....	....	....	....	....
1967-68	Minnesota North Stars	4	0	0	0	6	....	....	....	....	....
	NHL Totals	**153**	**2**	**21**	**23**	**76**	....	....	....	....	....

Claimed by **NY Rangers** from **Winnipeg** (WHL) in Inter-League Draft, June 7, 1960. Traded to **Chicago** by **NY Rangers** with Camille Henry, Billy Taylor and Wally Chevrier for Doug Robinson, Wayne Hillman and John Brenneman, February 4, 1965. Traded to **Montreal** by **Chicago** for Bryan Watson, June 8, 1965. Traded to **Minnesota** by **Montreal** for cash, October 5, 1967. Traded to **Toronto** (Rochester-AHL) by **Minnesota** with Murray Hall, Ted Taylor, Len Lunde, Duke Harris, and the loan of Carl Wetzel for J.P. Parise and Milan Marcetta, December 23, 1967.

JOHNSON, Allan

Right wing/Center. Shoots right. 5'11", 180 lbs. Born, Winnipeg, Man., March 30, 1935.

Season	Club	GP	G	A	Pts	PIM	GP	G	A	Pts	PIM
1956-57	Montreal Canadiens	2	0	1	1	2	....	....	....	....	....
1960-61	Detroit Red Wings	70	16	21	37	14	11	2	2	4	6
1961-62	Detroit Red Wings	31	5	6	11	14	....	....	....	....	....
1962-63	Detroit Red Wings	2	0	0	0	0	....	....	....	....	....
	NHL Totals	**105**	**21**	**28**	**49**	**30**	**11**	**2**	**2**	**4**	**6**

Claimed by **Detroit** from **Montreal** (Spokane-WHL) in Inter-League Draft, June, 1960.

JOHNSON, Brian

Right wing. Shoots right. 6'1", 198 lbs. Born, Montreal, Que., April 1, 1960.
(Hartford's 7th choice, 107th overall, in 1983 Entry Draft).

Season	Club	GP	G	A	Pts	PIM	GP	G	A	Pts	PIM
1983-84	Detroit Red Wings	3	0	0	0	5	....	....	....	....	....
	NHL Totals	**3**	**0**	**0**	**0**	**5**	....	....	....	....	....

Signed as a free agent by **Detroit**, October 30, 1979.

JOHNSON, Ching

HHOF

Defense. Shoots left. 5'11", 210 lbs. Born, Winnipeg, Man., December 7, 1898.

Season	Club	GP	G	A	Pts	PIM	GP	G	A	Pts	PIM
1926-27	New York Rangers	27	3	2	5	66	2	0	0	0	8
1927-28 ♦	New York Rangers	42	10	6	16	146	9	1	1	2	*46
1928-29	New York Rangers	8	0	0	0	14	6	0	0	0	26
1929-30	New York Rangers	30	3	3	6	82	4	0	0	0	14
1930-31	New York Rangers	44	2	6	8	77	4	1	0	1	17
1931-32	New York Rangers	47	3	10	13	106	7	2	0	2	*24
1932-33 ♦	New York Rangers	48	8	9	17	127	8	1	0	1	14
1933-34	New York Rangers	48	2	6	8	86	2	0	0	0	4
1934-35	New York Rangers	29	2	3	5	34	4	0	0	0	2
1935-36	New York Rangers	47	5	3	8	58	....	....	....	....	....
1936-37	New York Rangers	35	0	0	0	2	9	0	1	1	4
1937-38	New York Americans	31	0	0	0	10	6	0	0	0	2
	NHL Totals	**436**	**38**	**48**	**86**	**808**	**61**	**5**	**2**	**7**	**161**

Played in NHL All-Star Game (1934)

Signed as a free agent by **NY Rangers**, September 2, 1926. • Missed majority of 1928-29 season recovering from ankle injury suffered in game vs. Mtl. Maroons, December 1, 1928. Signed as a free agent by **NY Americans**, November 19, 1937.

JOHNSON, Craig

Left wing. Shoots left. 6'2", 200 lbs. Born, St. Paul, MN, March 18, 1972.
(St. Louis' 1st choice, 33rd overall, in 1990 Entry Draft).

Season	Club	GP	G	A	Pts	PIM	GP	G	A	Pts	PIM
1994-95	St. Louis Blues	15	3	3	6	6	1	0	0	0	2
1995-96	St. Louis Blues	49	8	7	15	30	....	....	....	....	....
	Los Angeles Kings	11	5	4	9	6	....	....	....	....	....
1996-97	Los Angeles Kings	31	4	3	7	26	....	....	....	....	....
1997-98	Los Angeles Kings	74	17	21	38	42	4	1	0	1	4
1998-99	Los Angeles Kings	69	7	12	19	32	....	....	....	....	....
99-2000	Los Angeles Kings	76	9	14	23	28	4	1	0	1	2
2000-01	Los Angeles Kings	26	4	5	9	16	....	....	....	....	....
2001-02	Los Angeles Kings	72	13	14	27	24	7	1	2	3	2
2002-03	Los Angeles Kings	70	3	6	9	22	....	....	....	....	....
	NHL Totals	**493**	**73**	**89**	**162**	**232**	**16**	**3**	**2**	**5**	**10**

Traded to **Los Angeles** by **St. Louis** with Patrice Tardif, Roman Vopat, St. Louis' 5th round choice (Peter Hogan) in 1996 Entry Draft and St. Louis' 1st round choice (Matt Zultek) in 1997 Entry Draft for Wayne Gretzky, February 27, 1996. • Missed majority of 2000-01 season recovering from ankle injury suffered in game vs. San Jose, December 26, 2000.

JOHNSON, Danny

Center. Shoots left. 5'11", 170 lbs. Born, Winnipegosis, Man., October 1, 1944.

Season	Club	GP	G	A	Pts	PIM	GP	G	A	Pts	PIM
1969-70	Toronto Maple Leafs	1	0	0	0	0	....	....	....	....	....
1970-71	Vancouver Canucks	66	15	11	26	16	....	....	....	....	....
1971-72	Vancouver Canucks	11	1	3	4	0	....	....	....	....	....
	Detroit Red Wings	43	2	5	7	8	....	....	....	....	....
	NHL Totals	**121**	**18**	**19**	**37**	**24**	....	....	....	....	....

Claimed by **Toronto** from **Tulsa** (CHL) in Inter-League Draft, June, 1966. Claimed by **Toronto** (Rochester-AHL) from **Toronto** in Reverse Draft, June 15, 1966. Claimed by **Vancouver** from **Toronto** in Expansion Draft, June 10, 1970. Claimed on waivers by **Detroit** from **Vancouver**, November 22, 1971.

JOHNSON, Earl

Left wing. Shoots left. 6', 185 lbs. Born, Fort Frances, Ont., June 28, 1931.

Season	Club	GP	G	A	Pts	PIM	GP	G	A	Pts	PIM
1953-54	Detroit Red Wings	1	0	0	0	0	....	....	....	....	....
	NHL Totals	**1**	**0**	**0**	**0**	**0**	....	....	....	....	....

Loaned to **Quebec** (QHL) by **NY Rangers** for cash, October, 1954. Returned to **NY Rangers** from **Quebec** (QHL) with cash for the trade of Camille Henry to Providence (AHL), December 5, 1954.

JOHNSON, Greg

Center. Shoots left. 5'11", 202 lbs. Born, Thunder Bay, Ont., March 16, 1971.
(Philadelphia's 1st choice, 33rd overall, in 1989 Entry Draft).

Season	Club	GP	G	A	Pts	PIM	GP	G	A	Pts	PIM
1993-94	Detroit Red Wings	52	6	11	17	22	7	2	2	4	2
1994-95	Detroit Red Wings	22	3	5	8	14	1	0	0	0	0
1995-96	Detroit Red Wings	60	18	22	40	30	13	3	1	4	8
1996-97	Detroit Red Wings	43	6	10	16	12	....	....	....	....	....
	Pittsburgh Penguins	32	7	9	16	14	5	1	0	1	2
1997-98	Pittsburgh Penguins	5	1	0	1	2	....	....	....	....	....
	Chicago Blackhawks	69	11	22	33	38	....	....	....	....	....
1998-99	Nashville Predators	68	16	34	50	24	....	....	....	....	....
99-2000	Nashville Predators	82	11	33	44	40	....	....	....	....	....
2000-01	Nashville Predators	82	15	17	32	46	....	....	....	....	....
2001-02	Nashville Predators	82	18	26	44	38	....	....	....	....	....
2002-03	Nashville Predators	38	8	9	17	22	....	....	....	....	....
	NHL Totals	**635**	**120**	**198**	**318**	**302**	**26**	**6**	**3**	**9**	**12**

• Brother of Ryan

Traded to **Detroit** by **Philadelphia** with Philadelphia's 5th round choice (Frederic Deschenes) in 1994 Entry Draft for Jim Cummins and Philadelphia's 4th round choice (previously acquired, later traded to Boston – Boston selected Charles Paquette) in 1993 Entry Draft, June 20, 1993. Traded to **Pittsburgh** by **Detroit** for Tomas Sandstrom, January 27, 1997. Traded to **Chicago** by **Pittsburgh** for Tuomas Gronman, October 27, 1997. Claimed by **Nashville** from **Chicago** in Expansion Draft, June 26, 1998.

JOHNSON, Jim

Center. Shoots left. 5'9", 190 lbs. Born, Winnipeg, Man., November 7, 1942.

Season	Club	GP	G	A	Pts	PIM	GP	G	A	Pts	PIM
1964-65	New York Rangers	1	0	0	0	0	....	....	....	....	....
1965-66	New York Rangers	5	1	0	1	0	....	....	....	....	....
1966-67	New York Rangers	2	0	0	0	0	....	....	....	....	....
1967-68	Philadelphia Flyers	13	2	1	3	2	....	....	....	....	....
1968-69	Philadelphia Flyers	69	17	27	44	20	3	0	0	0	2
1969-70	Philadelphia Flyers	72	18	30	48	17	....	....	....	....	....
1970-71	Philadelphia Flyers	66	16	29	45	16	4	0	2	2	0
1971-72	Philadelphia Flyers	46	13	15	28	12	....	....	....	....	....
	Los Angeles Kings	28	8	9	17	6	....	....	....	....	....
	NHL Totals	**302**	**75**	**111**	**186**	**73**	**7**	**0**	**2**	**2**	**2**

Claimed by **NY Rangers** from **Baltimore** (AHL) in Inter-League Draft, June 8, 1964. Claimed by **Philadelphia** from **NY Rangers** in Expansion Draft, June 6, 1967. Traded to **Los Angeles** by **Philadelphia** with Bill Lesuk and Serge Bernier for Bill Flett, Eddie Joyal, Jean Potvin and Ross Lonsberry, January 28, 1972.

JOHNSON, Jim

Defense. Shoots left. 6'1", 190 lbs. Born, New Hope, MN, August 9, 1962.

Season	Club	GP	G	A	Pts	PIM	GP	G	A	Pts	PIM
1985-86	Pittsburgh Penguins	80	3	26	29	115	....	....	....	....	....
1986-87	Pittsburgh Penguins	80	5	25	30	116	....	....	....	....	....
1987-88	Pittsburgh Penguins	55	1	12	13	87	....	....	....	....	....
1988-89	Pittsburgh Penguins	76	2	14	16	163	11	0	5	5	44
1989-90	Pittsburgh Penguins	75	3	13	16	154	....	....	....	....	....
1990-91	Pittsburgh Penguins	24	0	5	5	23	....	....	....	....	....
	Minnesota North Stars	44	1	9	10	100	14	0	1	1	52
1991-92	Minnesota North Stars	71	4	10	14	102	7	1	3	4	18
1992-93	Minnesota North Stars	79	3	20	23	105	....	....	....	....	....
1993-94	Dallas Stars	53	0	7	7	51	....	....	....	....	....
	Washington Capitals	8	0	0	0	12	....	....	....	....	....
1994-95	Washington Capitals	47	0	13	13	43	7	0	2	2	8
1995-96	Washington Capitals	66	2	4	6	34	6	0	0	0	6
1996-97	Phoenix Coyotes	55	3	7	10	74	6	0	0	0	4

Season	Club	REGULAR SEASON GP	G	A	Pts	PIM	PLAYOFFS GP	G	A	Pts	PIM
1997-98	Phoenix Coyotes	16	2	1	3	18	....	....	....	....	....
	NHL Totals	**829**	**29**	**166**	**195**	**1197**	**51**	**1**	**11**	**12**	**132**

Signed as a free agent by **Pittsburgh**, June 9, 1985. Traded to **Minnesota** by **Pittsburgh** with Chris Dahlquist for Larry Murphy and Peter Taglianetti, December 11, 1990. Transferred to **Dallas** after **Minnesota** franchise relocated, June 9, 1993. Traded to **Washington** by **Dallas** for Alan May and Washington's 7th round choice (Jeff Dewar) in 1995 Entry Draft, March 21, 1994. Signed as a free agent by **Phoenix**, July 6, 1996. • Suffered career-ending head injury in game vs. Tampa Bay, November 11, 1997. • Officially announced retirement, July 21, 1998.

JOHNSON, Mark

Center. Shoots left. 5'9", 170 lbs. Born, Madison, WI, September 22, 1957.
(Pittsburgh's 3rd choice, 66th overall, in 1977 Amateur Draft).

Season	Club	GP	G	A	Pts	PIM	GP	G	A	Pts	PIM
1979-80	Pittsburgh Penguins	17	3	5	8	4	5	2	2	4	0
1980-81	Pittsburgh Penguins	73	10	23	33	50	5	2	1	3	6
1981-82	Pittsburgh Penguins	46	10	11	21	30	....	....	....	....	....
	Minnesota North Stars	10	2	2	4	10	4	2	0	2	0
1982-83	Hartford Whalers	73	31	38	69	28	....	....	....	....	....
1983-84	Hartford Whalers	79	35	52	87	27	....	....	....	....	....
1984-85	Hartford Whalers	49	19	28	47	21	....	....	....	....	....
	St. Louis Blues	17	4	6	10	2	3	0	1	1	0
1985-86	New Jersey Devils	80	21	41	62	16	....	....	....	....	....
1986-87	New Jersey Devils	68	25	26	51	22	....	....	....	....	....
1987-88	New Jersey Devils	54	14	19	33	14	18	10	8	18	4
1988-89	New Jersey Devils	40	13	25	38	24	....	....	....	....	....
1989-90	New Jersey Devils	63	16	29	45	12	2	0	0	0	0
	NHL Totals	**669**	**203**	**305**	**508**	**260**	**37**	**16**	**12**	**28**	**10**

Played in NHL All-Star Game (1984)

Traded to **Minnesota** by **Pittsburgh** for Minnesota's 2nd round choice (Tim Hrynewich) in 1982 Entry Draft, March 2, 1982. Traded to **Hartford** by **Minnesota** with Kent-Erik Andersson for Jordy Douglas and Hartford's 5th round choice (Jiri Poner) in 1984 Entry Draft, October 1, 1982. Traded to **St. Louis** by **Hartford** with Greg Millen for Mike Luit and Jorgen Petterson, February 21, 1985. Traded to **New Jersey** by **St. Louis** for Shawn Evans and New Jersey's 5th round choice (Michael Wolak) in 1986 Entry Draft, September 19, 1985.

JOHNSON, Matt

Left wing. Shoots left. 6'5", 232 lbs. Born, Welland, Ont., November 23, 1975.
(Los Angeles' 2nd choice, 33rd overall, in 1994 Entry Draft).

Season	Club	GP	G	A	Pts	PIM	GP	G	A	Pts	PIM
1994-95	Los Angeles Kings	14	1	0	1	102	....	....	....	....	....
1995-96	Los Angeles Kings	1	0	0	0	5	....	....	....	....	....
1996-97	Los Angeles Kings	52	1	3	4	194	....	....	....	....	....
1997-98	Los Angeles Kings	66	2	4	6	249	4	0	0	0	6
1998-99	Los Angeles Kings	49	2	1	3	131	....	....	....	....	....
99-2000	Atlanta Thrashers	64	2	5	7	144	....	....	....	....	....
2000-01	Minnesota Wild	50	1	1	2	137	....	....	....	....	....
2001-02	Minnesota Wild	60	4	0	4	183	....	....	....	....	....
2002-03	Minnesota Wild	60	3	5	8	201	12	0	0	0	25
	NHL Totals	**416**	**16**	**19**	**35**	**1346**	**16**	**0**	**0**	**0**	**31**

Claimed by **Atlanta** from **Los Angeles** in Expansion Draft, June 25, 1999. Traded to **Minnesota** by **Atlanta** for San Jose's 3rd round choice (previously acquired, later traded to Pittsburgh, later traded to Columbus – Columbus selected Aaron Johnson) in 2001 Entry Draft, September 29, 2000.

JOHNSON, Mike

Right wing. Shoots right. 6'2", 201 lbs. Born, Scarborough, Ont., October 3, 1974.

Season	Club	GP	G	A	Pts	PIM	GP	G	A	Pts	PIM
1996-97	Toronto Maple Leafs	13	2	2	4	4	....	....	....	....	....
1997-98	Toronto Maple Leafs	82	15	32	47	24	....	....	....	....	....
1998-99	Toronto Maple Leafs	79	20	24	44	35	17	3	2	5	4
99-2000	Toronto Maple Leafs	52	11	14	25	23	....	....	....	....	....
	Tampa Bay Lightning	28	10	12	22	4	....	....	....	....	....
2000-01	Tampa Bay Lightning	64	11	27	38	38	....	....	....	....	....
	Phoenix Coyotes	12	2	3	5	4	....	....	....	....	....
2001-02	Phoenix Coyotes	57	5	22	27	28	5	1	1	2	6
2002-03	Phoenix Coyotes	82	23	40	63	47	....	....	....	....	....
	NHL Totals	**469**	**99**	**176**	**275**	**207**	**22**	**4**	**3**	**7**	**10**

NHL All-Rookie Team (1998)

Signed as a free agent by **Toronto**, March 16, 1997. Traded to **Tampa Bay** by **Toronto** with Marek Posmyk, Toronto's 5th (Pavel Sedov) and 6th (Aaron Gionet) round choices in 2000 Entry Draft and future considerations for Darcy Tucker, Tampa Bay's 4th round choice (Miguel Delisle) in 2000 Entry Draft and future considerations, February 9, 2000. Traded to **Phoenix** by **Tampa Bay** with Paul Mara, Ruslan Zainullin and NY Islanders' 2nd round choice (previously acquired, Phoenix selected Matthew Spiller) in 2001 Entry Draft for Nikolai Khabibulin and Stan Neckar, March 5, 2001.

JOHNSON, Norm

Center. Shoots left. 5'10", 170 lbs. Born, Moose Jaw, Sask., November 27, 1932.

Season	Club	GP	G	A	Pts	PIM	GP	G	A	Pts	PIM
1957-58	Boston Bruins	15	2	3	5	8	12	4	0	4	6
1958-59	Boston Bruins	39	2	17	19	25	....	....	....	....	....
	Chicago Black Hawks	7	1	0	1	8	....	....	....	....	....
1959-60	Chicago Black Hawks	....	....	....	....	....	2	0	0	0	0
	NHL Totals	**61**	**5**	**20**	**25**	**41**	**14**	**4**	**0**	**4**	**6**

Claimed by **Boston** from **Brandon** (WHL) in Inter-League Draft, June 4, 1957. Claimed on waivers by **Chicago** from **Boston**, January 7, 1959. Loaned to **Montreal** (Rochester-AHL) by **Chicago** to complete transaction that sent Dollard St. Laurent to Chicago (June 3, 1958), February 20, 1959. Traded to **LA Blades** (WHL) by **Chicago** (St. Louis-AHL) with Ron Leopold and Gord Vejprava for Lloyd Haddon, August 12, 1963.

JOHNSON, Ryan

Center. Shoots left. 6'1", 200 lbs. Born, Thunder Bay, Ont., June 14, 1976.
(Florida's 4th choice, 36th overall, in 1994 Entry Draft).

Season	Club	GP	G	A	Pts	PIM	GP	G	A	Pts	PIM
1997-98	Florida Panthers	10	0	2	2	0	....	....	....	....	....
1998-99	Florida Panthers	1	1	0	1	0	....	....	....	....	....
99-2000	Florida Panthers	66	4	12	16	14	....	....	....	....	....
	Tampa Bay Lightning	14	0	2	2	2	....	....	....	....	....
2000-01	Tampa Bay Lightning	80	7	14	21	44	....	....	....	....	....
2001-02	Florida Panthers	29	1	3	4	10	....	....	....	....	....
2002-03	Florida Panthers	58	2	5	7	26	....	....	....	....	....
	St. Louis Blues	17	0	0	0	12	6	0	2	2	6
	NHL Totals	**275**	**15**	**38**	**53**	**108**	**6**	**0**	**2**	**2**	**6**

• Brother of Greg

Traded to **Tampa Bay** by **Florida** with Dwayne Hay for Mike Sillinger, March 14, 2000. Traded to **Florida** by **Tampa Bay** with Tampa Bay's 6th round choice (later traded back to Tampa Bay – Tampa Bay selected Doug O'Brien) in 2003 Entry Draft for Vaclav Prospal, July 10, 2001. • Missed majority of 2001-02 season recovering from head injury suffered in game vs. St. Louis, December 22, 2001. Claimed on waivers by **St. Louis** from **Florida**, February 19, 2003.

JOHNSON, Terry

Defense. Shoots left. 6'3", 210 lbs. Born, Calgary, Alta., November 28, 1958.

Season	Club	GP	G	A	Pts	PIM	GP	G	A	Pts	PIM
1979-80	Quebec Nordiques	3	0	0	0	2	....	....	....	....	....
1980-81	Quebec Nordiques	13	0	1	1	46	2	0	0	0	0
1981-82	Quebec Nordiques	6	0	1	1	5	....	....	....	....	....
1982-83	Quebec Nordiques	3	0	0	0	2	....	....	....	....	....
1983-84	St. Louis Blues	65	2	6	8	143	11	0	1	1	25
1984-85	St. Louis Blues	74	0	7	7	120	3	0	0	0	19
1985-86	St. Louis Blues	49	0	4	4	87	....	....	....	....	....
	Calgary Flames	24	1	4	5	71	17	0	3	3	64
1986-87	Toronto Maple Leafs	48	0	1	1	104	2	0	0	0	0
1987-88	Toronto Maple Leafs	....	....	....	....	....	3	0	0	0	10
	NHL Totals	**285**	**3**	**24**	**27**	**580**	**38**	**0**	**4**	**4**	**118**

Signed as a free agent by **Quebec**, October 1, 1978. Claimed by **St. Louis** from **Quebec** in Waiver Draft, October 3, 1983. Traded to **Calgary** by **St. Louis** with Joe Mullen and Rik Wilson for Eddy Beers, Charlie Bourgeois and Gino Cavallini, February 1, 1986. Traded to **Toronto** by **Calgary** for Jim Korn, October 3, 1986.

JOHNSON, Tom

HHOF

Defense. Shoots left. 6', 180 lbs. Born, Baldur, Man., February 18, 1928.

Season	Club	GP	G	A	Pts	PIM	GP	G	A	Pts	PIM
1947-48	Montreal Canadiens	1	0	0	0	0	....	....	....	....	....
1949-50	Montreal Canadiens	....	....	....	....	....	1	0	0	0	0
1950-51	Montreal Canadiens	70	2	8	10	128	11	0	0	0	6
1951-52	Montreal Canadiens	67	0	7	7	76	11	1	0	1	2
1952-53 ♦	Montreal Canadiens	70	3	8	11	63	12	2	3	5	8
1953-54	Montreal Canadiens	70	7	11	18	85	11	1	2	3	30
1954-55	Montreal Canadiens	70	6	19	25	74	12	2	0	2	22
1955-56 ♦	Montreal Canadiens	64	3	10	13	75	10	0	2	2	8
1956-57 ♦	Montreal Canadiens	70	4	11	15	59	10	0	2	2	13
1957-58 ♦	Montreal Canadiens	66	3	18	21	75	2	0	0	0	0
1958-59 ♦	Montreal Canadiens	70	10	29	39	76	11	2	3	5	8
1959-60 ♦	Montreal Canadiens	64	4	25	29	59	8	0	1	1	4
1960-61	Montreal Canadiens	70	1	15	16	54	6	0	1	1	8
1961-62	Montreal Canadiens	62	1	17	18	45	6	0	1	1	0
1962-63	Montreal Canadiens	43	3	5	8	28	....	....	....	....	....
1963-64	Boston Bruins	70	4	21	25	33	....	....	....	....	....
1964-65	Boston Bruins	51	0	9	9	30	....	....	....	....	....
	NHL Totals	**978**	**51**	**213**	**264**	**960**	**111**	**8**	**15**	**23**	**109**

NHL Second All-Star Team (1956) • NHL First All-Star Team (1959) • James Norris Trophy (1959)

Played in NHL All-Star Game (1952, 1953, 1956, 1957, 1958, 1959, 1960, 1963)

Signed as a free agent by **Montreal**, April 30, 1947. Claimed by **Boston** from **Montreal** in Waiver Draft, June 4, 1963. • Suffered career-ending leg injury in game vs. Chicago, February 28, 1965.

JOHNSON, Virgil

USHOF

Defense. Shoots left. 5'9", 165 lbs. Born, Minneapolis, MN, March 4, 1912.

Season	Club	GP	G	A	Pts	PIM	GP	G	A	Pts	PIM
1937-38 ♦	Chicago Black Hawks	25	0	2	2	2	10	0	0	0	0
1943-44	Chicago Black Hawks	48	1	8	9	23	9	0	3	3	4
1944-45	Chicago Black Hawks	2	0	1	1	2	....	....	....	....	....
	NHL Totals	**75**	**1**	**11**	**12**	**27**	**19**	**0**	**3**	**3**	**4**

Traded to **Chicago** by **St. Paul** (AHA) for cash, January 8, 1938.

JOHNSSON, Kim

Defense. Shoots left. 6'1", 205 lbs. Born, Malmo, Sweden, March 16, 1976.
(NY Rangers' 15th choice, 286th overall, in 1994 Entry Draft).

Season	Club	GP	G	A	Pts	PIM	GP	G	A	Pts	PIM
99-2000	New York Rangers	76	6	15	21	46	....	....	....	....	....
2000-01	New York Rangers	75	5	21	26	40	....	....	....	....	....
2001-02	Philadelphia Flyers	82	11	30	41	42	5	0	0	0	2
2002-03	Philadelphia Flyers	82	10	29	39	38	13	0	3	3	8
	NHL Totals	**315**	**32**	**95**	**127**	**166**	**18**	**0**	**3**	**3**	**10**

Traded to **Philadelphia** by **NY Rangers** with Jan Hlavac, Pavel Brendl and NY Rangers' 3rd round choice (Stefan Ruzicka) in 2003 Entry Draft for Eric Lindros, August 20, 2001.

JOHNSTON, Bernie

Center. Shoots left. 5'11", 185 lbs. Born, Toronto, Ont., September 15, 1956.

Season	Club	GP	G	A	Pts	PIM	GP	G	A	Pts	PIM
		REGULAR SEASON					PLAYOFFS				
1979-80	Hartford Whalers	32	8	13	21	8	3	0	1	1	0
1980-81	Hartford Whalers	25	4	11	15	8	....	....	....	....	....
	NHL Totals	**57**	**12**	**24**	**36**	**16**	**3**	**0**	**1**	**1**	**0**

Signed as a free agent by **Philadelphia**, September 28, 1977. Claimed by **Hartford** from **Philadelphia** in Expansion Draft, June 13, 1979.

JOHNSTON, George

Right wing. Shoots right. 5'8", 160 lbs. Born, St. Charles, Man., July 30, 1920.

Season	Club	GP	G	A	Pts	PIM	GP	G	A	Pts	PIM
1941-42	Chicago Black Hawks	2	2	0	2	0	....	....	....	....	....
1942-43	Chicago Black Hawks	30	10	7	17	0	....	....	....	....	....
1945-46	Chicago Black Hawks	16	5	4	9	2	....	....	....	....	....
1946-47	Chicago Black Hawks	10	3	1	4	0	....	....	....	....	....
	NHL Totals	**58**	**20**	**12**	**32**	**2**	....	....	....	....	....

Traded to **NY Rangers** by **Cleveland** (AHL) for Church Russell, December 18, 1947.

JOHNSTON, Greg

Right wing. Shoots right. 6'1", 205 lbs. Born, Barrie, Ont., January 14, 1965.
(Boston's 2nd choice, 42nd overall, in 1983 Entry Draft).

Season	Club	GP	G	A	Pts	PIM	GP	G	A	Pts	PIM
1983-84	Boston Bruins	15	2	1	3	2	....	....	....	....	....
1984-85	Boston Bruins	6	0	0	0	0	....	....	....	....	....
1985-86	Boston Bruins	20	0	2	2	0	....	....	....	....	....
1986-87	Boston Bruins	76	12	15	27	79	4	0	0	0	0
1987-88	Boston Bruins	....	....	....	....	....	3	0	1	1	2
1988-89	Boston Bruins	57	11	9	20	32	10	1	0	1	6
1989-90	Boston Bruins	9	1	1	2	6	5	1	0	1	4
1990-91	Toronto Maple Leafs	1	0	0	0	0	....	....	....	....	....
1991-92	Toronto Maple Leafs	3	0	1	1	5	....	....	....	....	....
	NHL Totals	**187**	**26**	**29**	**55**	**124**	**22**	**2**	**1**	**3**	**12**

Traded to **NY Rangers** by **Boston** with cash for Chris Nilan, June 28, 1990. Traded to **Toronto** by **NY Rangers** for Tie Domi and Mark LaForest, June 28, 1990.

JOHNSTON, Jay

Defense. Shoots left. 5'11", 195 lbs. Born, Hamilton, Ont., February 28, 1958.
(Washington's 6th choice, 45th overall, in 1978 Amateur Draft).

Season	Club	GP	G	A	Pts	PIM	GP	G	A	Pts	PIM
1980-81	Washington Capitals	2	0	0	0	9	....	....	....	....	....
1981-82	Washington Capitals	6	0	0	0	4	....	....	....	....	....
	NHL Totals	**8**	**0**	**0**	**0**	**13**	....	....	....	....	....

JOHNSTON, Joey

Left wing. Shoots left. 5'10", 180 lbs. Born, Peterborough, Ont., March 3, 1949.
(NY Rangers' 2nd choice, 8th overall, in 1966 Amateur Draft).

Season	Club	GP	G	A	Pts	PIM	GP	G	A	Pts	PIM
1968-69	Minnesota North Stars	11	1	0	1	6	....	....	....	....	....
1971-72	California Golden Seals	77	15	17	32	107	....	....	....	....	....
1972-73	California Golden Seals	71	28	21	49	62	....	....	....	....	....
1973-74	California Golden Seals	78	27	40	67	67	....	....	....	....	....
1974-75	California Golden Seals	62	14	23	37	72	....	....	....	....	....
1975-76	Chicago Black Hawks	32	0	5	5	6	....	....	....	....	....
	NHL Totals	**331**	**85**	**106**	**191**	**320**	....	....	....	....	....

Played in NHL All-Star Game (1973, 1974, 1975)

Traded to **Minnesota** by **NY Rangers** with Wayne Hillman and Dan Seguin for Dave Balon, June 12, 1968. Traded to **California** by **Minnesota** with Walt McKechnie for Dennis Hextall, May 20, 1971. Traded to **Chicago** by **California** for Jim Pappin and Chicago's 3rd round choice (Guy Lash) in 1977 Amateur Draft, June 1, 1975.

JOHNSTON, Larry

Defense. Shoots right. 5'11", 195 lbs. Born, Kitchener, Ont., July 20, 1943.

Season	Club	GP	G	A	Pts	PIM	GP	G	A	Pts	PIM
1967-68	Los Angeles Kings	4	0	0	0	4	....	....	....	....	....
1971-72	Detroit Red Wings	65	4	20	24	111	....	....	....	....	....
1972-73	Detroit Red Wings	73	1	12	13	169	....	....	....	....	....
1973-74	Detroit Red Wings	65	2	12	14	139	....	....	....	....	....
1974-75	Kansas City Scouts	16	0	7	7	10	....	....	....	....	....
1975-76	Kansas City Scouts	72	2	10	12	112	....	....	....	....	....
1976-77	Colorado Rockies	25	0	3	3	35	....	....	....	....	....
	NHL Totals	**320**	**9**	**64**	**73**	**580**	....	....	....	....	....

Claimed by **Toronto** from **Tulsa** (CPHL) in Inter-League Draft, June 8, 1965. Traded to **Springfield** (AHL) by **Toronto** with Bill Smith for Bruce Gamble, September, 1965. NHL rights transferred to **Los Angeles** after NHL club purchased **Springfield** (AHL) franchise, May, 1967. Traded to **Detroit** by **Los Angeles** with Dale Rolfe and Gary Croteau for Garry Monahan, Brian Gibbons and Matt Ravlich, February 20, 1970. Signed as a free agent by **Kansas City**, March 1, 1975. Transferred to **Colorado** after **Kansas City** franchise relocated, June, 1976.

JOHNSTON, Marshall

Defense. Shoots right. 5'11", 175 lbs. Born, Birch Hills, Sask., June 6, 1941.

Season	Club	GP	G	A	Pts	PIM	GP	G	A	Pts	PIM
1967-68	Minnesota North Stars	7	0	0	0	0	....	....	....	....	....
1968-69	Minnesota North Stars	13	0	0	0	2	....	....	....	....	....
1969-70	Minnesota North Stars	28	0	5	5	14	6	0	0	0	2
1970-71	Minnesota North Stars	1	0	0	0	0	....	....	....	....	....
1971-72	California Golden Seals	74	2	11	13	4	....	....	....	....	....
1972-73	California Golden Seals	78	10	20	30	14	....	....	....	....	....
1973-74	California Golden Seals	50	2	16	18	24	....	....	....	....	....
	NHL Totals	**251**	**14**	**52**	**66**	**58**	**6**	**0**	**0**	**0**	**2**

Rights traded to **Minnesota** by **NY Rangers** for cash, June, 1967. Traded to **Montreal** by **Minnesota** for Bob Murdoch to complete transaction that sent Danny Grant and Claude Larose to Minnesota (June 10, 1968), May 25, 1971. Traded to **California** by **Montreal** for cash, August 31, 1971.

JOHNSTON, Randy

Defense. Shoots left. 6', 190 lbs. Born, Brampton, Ont., June 2, 1958.
(NY Islanders' 2nd choice, 34th overall, in 1978 Amateur Draft).

Season	Club	GP	G	A	Pts	PIM	GP	G	A	Pts	PIM
1979-80	New York Islanders	4	0	0	0	4	....	....	....	....	....
	NHL Totals	**4**	**0**	**0**	**0**	**4**	....	....	....	....	....

JOHNSTONE, Eddie

Right wing. Shoots right. 5'9", 175 lbs. Born, Brandon, Man., March 2, 1954.
(NY Rangers' 6th choice, 104th overall, in 1974 Amateur Draft).

Season	Club	GP	G	A	Pts	PIM	GP	G	A	Pts	PIM
1975-76	New York Rangers	10	2	1	3	4	....	....	....	....	....
1977-78	New York Rangers	53	13	13	26	44	....	....	....	....	....
1978-79	New York Rangers	30	5	3	8	27	17	5	0	5	10
1979-80	New York Rangers	78	14	21	35	60	9	0	1	1	25
1980-81	New York Rangers	80	30	38	68	100	8	2	2	4	4
1981-82	New York Rangers	68	30	28	58	57	10	2	6	8	25
1982-83	New York Rangers	52	15	21	36	27	9	4	1	5	19
1983-84	Detroit Red Wings	46	12	11	23	54	2	0	0	0	0
1985-86	Detroit Red Wings	3	1	0	1	2	....	....	....	....	....
1986-87	Detroit Red Wings	6	0	0	0	0	....	....	....	....	....
	NHL Totals	**426**	**122**	**136**	**258**	**375**	**55**	**13**	**10**	**23**	**83**

Played in NHL All-Star Game (1981)

Claimed by **NY Rangers** as a fill-in during Expansion Draft, June 13, 1979. Traded to **Detroit** by **NY Rangers** with Eddie Mio and Ron Duguay for Mike Blaisdell, Mark Osborne and Willie Huber, June 13, 1983.

JOHNSTONE, Ross

Defense. Shoots left. 6', 185 lbs. Born, Montreal, Que., April 7, 1926.

Season	Club	GP	G	A	Pts	PIM	GP	G	A	Pts	PIM
1943-44	Toronto Maple Leafs	18	2	0	2	6	3	0	0	0	0
1944-45 ♦	Toronto Maple Leafs	24	3	4	7	8	....	....	....	....	....
	NHL Totals	**42**	**5**	**4**	**9**	**14**	**3**	**0**	**0**	**0**	**0**

Traded to **Toronto** by **Buffalo** (AHL) for cash, November 7, 1942. • Suspended by **Toronto** for refusing to report to **Tulsa** (USHL), October, 1946. Traded to **Springfield** (AHL) by **Toronto** for cash, December 31, 1946.

JOKELA, Mikko

Defense. Shoots right. 6'1", 210 lbs. Born, Lappeenranta, Finland, March 4, 1980.
(New Jersey's 5th choice, 96th overall, in 1998 Entry Draft).

Season	Club	GP	G	A	Pts	PIM	GP	G	A	Pts	PIM
2002-03	Vancouver Canucks	1	0	0	0	0	....	....	....	....	....
	NHL Totals	**1**	**0**	**0**	**0**	**0**	....	....	....	....	....

Traded to **Vancouver** by **New Jersey** for Steve Kariya, January 24, 2003.

JOKINEN, Olli

Center. Shoots left. 6'3", 205 lbs. Born, Kuopio, Finland, December 5, 1978.
(Los Angeles' 1st choice, 3rd overall, in 1997 Entry Draft).

Season	Club	GP	G	A	Pts	PIM	GP	G	A	Pts	PIM
1997-98	Los Angeles Kings	8	0	0	0	6	....	....	....	....	....
1998-99	Los Angeles Kings	66	9	12	21	44	....	....	....	....	....
99-2000	New York Islanders	82	11	10	21	80	....	....	....	....	....
2000-01	Florida Panthers	78	6	10	16	106	....	....	....	....	....
2001-02	Florida Panthers	80	9	20	29	98	....	....	....	....	....
2002-03	Florida Panthers	81	36	29	65	79	....	....	....	....	....
	NHL Totals	**395**	**71**	**81**	**152**	**413**	....	....	....	....	....

Played in NHL All-Star Game (2003)

Traded to **NY Islanders** by **Los Angeles** with Josh Green, Mathieu Biron and Los Angeles' 1st round choice (Taylor Pyatt) in 1999 Entry Draft for Ziggy Palffy, Brian Smolinski, Marcel Cousineau and New Jersey's 4th round choice (previously acquired, Los Angeles selected Daniel Johansson) in 1999 Entry Draft, June 20, 1999. Traded to **Florida** by **NY Islanders** with Roberto Luongo for Mark Parrish and Oleg Kvasha, June 24, 2000.

JOLIAT, Aurel

HHOF

Left wing. Shoots left. 5'7", 136 lbs. Born, Ottawa, Ont., August 29, 1901.

Season	Club	GP	G	A	Pts	PIM	GP	G	A	Pts	PIM
1922-23	Montreal Canadiens	24	12	9	21	37	2	1	0	1	11
1923-24 ♦	Montreal Canadiens	24	15	5	20	27	2	1	1	2	0
	Montreal Canadiens (Cup)	....	....	....	....	....	*4*	*3*	*1*	*4*	*6*
1924-25	Montreal Canadiens	25	30	11	41	85	1	0	0	0	5
	Montreal Canadiens (Cup)	....	....	....	....	....	*4*	*2*	*0*	*2*	*16*
1925-26	Montreal Canadiens	35	17	9	26	52	....	....	....	....	....
1926-27	Montreal Canadiens	43	14	4	18	79	4	1	0	1	10
1927-28	Montreal Canadiens	44	28	11	39	105	2	0	0	0	4
1928-29	Montreal Canadiens	44	12	5	17	59	3	1	1	2	10
1929-30 ♦	Montreal Canadiens	42	19	12	31	40	6	0	2	2	6
1930-31 ♦	Montreal Canadiens	43	13	22	35	73	10	0	*4	4	12
1931-32	Montreal Canadiens	48	15	24	39	46	4	2	0	2	4
1932-33	Montreal Canadiens	48	18	21	39	53	2	2	1	3	2
1933-34	Montreal Canadiens	48	22	15	37	27	3	0	1	1	0
1934-35	Montreal Canadiens	48	17	12	29	18	2	1	0	1	0
1935-36	Montreal Canadiens	48	15	8	23	16	....	....	....	....	....
1936-37	Montreal Canadiens	47	17	15	32	30	5	0	3	3	2

Season	Club	GP	G	A	Pts	PIM	GP	G	A	Pts	PIM
		REGULAR SEASON					PLAYOFFS				
1937-38	Montreal Canadiens	44	6	7	13	24	....	....	....	....	....
	NHL Totals	**655**	**270**	**190**	**460**	**771**	**46**	**9**	**13**	**22**	**66**

• Brother of Rene • NHL First All-Star Team (1931) • NHL Second All-Star Team (1932, 1934, 1935) • Hart Trophy (1934)

Played in NHL All-Star Game (1934, 1937)

Rights traded to **Montreal** by **Saskatoon** (WCHL) with $3,500 for Newsy Lalonde, September 18, 1922. • 1923-24 Stanley Cup totals includes series with Calgary (WCHL) and Vancouver (PCHA).

JOLIAT, Rene

Right wing/Defense. Shoots left. 5'5", 140 lbs. Born, Ottawa, Ont., April 25, 1898.

Season	Club	GP	G	A	Pts	PIM	GP	G	A	Pts	PIM
1924-25	Montreal Canadiens	1	0	0	0	0	....	....	....	....	....
	NHL Totals	**1**	**0**	**0**	**0**	**0**	....	....	....	....	....

• Brother of Aurel

Signed as a free agent by **Montreal**, November 17, 1924.

JOLY, Greg

Defense. Shoots left. 6'1", 190 lbs. Born, Calgary, Alta., May 30, 1954.
(Washington's 1st choice, 1st overall, in 1974 Amateur Draft).

Season	Club	GP	G	A	Pts	PIM	GP	G	A	Pts	PIM
1974-75	Washington Capitals	44	1	7	8	44	....	....	....	....	....
1975-76	Washington Capitals	54	8	17	25	28	....	....	....	....	....
1976-77	Detroit Red Wings	53	1	11	12	14	....	....	....	....	....
1977-78	Detroit Red Wings	79	7	20	27	73	5	0	0	0	8
1978-79	Detroit Red Wings	20	0	4	4	6	....	....	....	....	....
1979-80	Detroit Red Wings	59	3	10	13	45	....	....	....	....	....
1980-81	Detroit Red Wings	17	0	2	2	10	....	....	....	....	....
1981-82	Detroit Red Wings	37	1	5	6	30	....	....	....	....	....
1982-83	Detroit Red Wings	2	0	0	0	0	....	....	....	....	....
	NHL Totals	**365**	**21**	**76**	**97**	**250**	**5**	**0**	**0**	**0**	**8**

Traded to **Detroit** by **Washington** for Bryan Watson, November 30, 1976.

JOLY, Yvan

Right wing. Shoots right. 5'8", 175 lbs. Born, Hawkesbury, Ont., February 6, 1960.
(Montreal's 7th choice, 100th overall, in 1979 Entry Draft).

Season	Club	GP	G	A	Pts	PIM	GP	G	A	Pts	PIM
1979-80	Montreal Canadiens	....	....	....	....	....	1	0	0	0	0
1980-81	Montreal Canadiens	1	0	0	0	0	....	....	....	....	....
1982-83	Montreal Canadiens	1	0	0	0	0	....	....	....	....	....
	NHL Totals	**2**	**0**	**0**	**0**	**0**	**1**	**0**	**0**	**0**	**0**

JOMPHE, Jean-Francois

Center. Shoots left. 6'1", 195 lbs. Born, Harve St-Pierre, Que., December 28, 1972.

Season	Club	GP	G	A	Pts	PIM	GP	G	A	Pts	PIM
1995-96	Mighty Ducks of Anaheim	31	2	12	14	39	....	....	....	....	....
1996-97	Mighty Ducks of Anaheim	64	7	14	21	53	....	....	....	....	....
1997-98	Mighty Ducks of Anaheim	9	1	3	4	8	....	....	....	....	....
1998-99	Phoenix Coyotes	1	0	0	0	2	....	....	....	....	....
	Montreal Canadiens	6	0	0	0	0	....	....	....	....	....
	NHL Totals	**111**	**10**	**29**	**39**	**102**	....	....	....	....	....

Signed as a free agent by **Anaheim**, September 7, 1993. Traded to **Phoenix** by **Anaheim** for Jim McKenzie, June 18, 1998. Traded to **Montreal** by **Phoenix** for cash, March 23, 1999.

JONATHAN, Stan

Left wing. Shoots left. 5'8", 175 lbs. Born, Ohsweken, Ont., September 5, 1955.
(Boston's 5th choice, 86th overall, in 1975 Amateur Draft).

Season	Club	GP	G	A	Pts	PIM	GP	G	A	Pts	PIM
1975-76	Boston Bruins	1	0	0	0	0	....	....	....	....	....
1976-77	Boston Bruins	69	17	13	30	69	14	4	2	6	24
1977-78	Boston Bruins	68	27	25	52	116	15	0	1	1	36
1978-79	Boston Bruins	33	6	9	15	96	11	4	1	5	12
1979-80	Boston Bruins	79	21	19	40	208	9	0	0	0	29
1980-81	Boston Bruins	74	14	24	38	192	3	0	0	0	30
1981-82	Boston Bruins	67	6	17	23	57	11	0	0	0	6
1982-83	Boston Bruins	1	0	0	0	0	....	....	....	....	....
	Pittsburgh Penguins	19	0	3	3	13	....	....	....	....	....
	NHL Totals	**411**	**91**	**110**	**201**	**751**	**63**	**8**	**4**	**12**	**137**

Traded to **Pittsburgh** by **Boston** for cash, November 8, 1982.

JONES, Bob

Left wing. Shoots left. 6'1", 185 lbs. Born, Espanola, Ont., November 27, 1945.
(Detroit's 9th choice, 179th overall, in 1989 Entry Draft).

Season	Club	GP	G	A	Pts	PIM	GP	G	A	Pts	PIM
1968-69	New York Rangers	2	0	0	0	0	....	....	....	....	....
	NHL Totals	**2**	**0**	**0**	**0**	**0**	....	....	....	....	....

• Brother of Jim

Traded to **Salt Lake** (WHL) by **NY Rangers** for Rick Charron, May, 1971.

JONES, Brad

Left wing. Shoots left. 6', 195 lbs. Born, Sterling Heights, MI, June 26, 1965.
(Winnipeg's 8th choice, 156th overall, in 1984 Entry Draft).

Season	Club	GP	G	A	Pts	PIM	GP	G	A	Pts	PIM
1986-87	Winnipeg Jets	4	1	0	1	0	....	....	....	....	....
1987-88	Winnipeg Jets	19	2	5	7	15	1	0	0	0	0
1988-89	Winnipeg Jets	22	6	5	11	6	....	....	....	....	....
1989-90	Winnipeg Jets	2	0	0	0	0	....	....	....	....	....
1990-91	Los Angeles Kings	53	9	11	20	57	8	1	1	2	2
1991-92	Philadelphia Flyers	48	7	10	17	44	....	....	....	....	....
	NHL Totals	**148**	**25**	**31**	**56**	**122**	**9**	**1**	**1**	**2**	**2**

Traded to **Los Angeles** by **Winnipeg** for Phil Sykes, December 1, 1989. Signed as a free agent by **Philadelphia**, August 6, 1991.

JONES, Buck

Defense. Shoots right. 5'11", 200 lbs. Born, Owen Sound, Ont., August 17, 1918.

Season	Club	GP	G	A	Pts	PIM	GP	G	A	Pts	PIM
1938-39	Detroit Red Wings	11	0	1	1	6	6	0	1	1	10
1939-40	Detroit Red Wings	2	0	0	0	0	....	....	....	....	....
1941-42	Detroit Red Wings	21	2	1	3	8	....	....	....	....	....
1942-43	Toronto Maple Leafs	16	0	0	0	22	6	0	0	0	8
	NHL Totals	**50**	**2**	**2**	**4**	**36**	**12**	**0**	**1**	**1**	**18**

Traded to **Providence** (AHL) by **Detroit** with Bob Whitelaw for Eddie Bush and future considerations, February 3, 1942. Traded to **Toronto** by **Providence** (AHL) with the loan of Ab Demarco for the loan of Jack Forsey and George Boothman, February 3, 1943. Traded to **Tulsa** (USHL) by **Toronto** for cash, May 15, 1947.

JONES, Jim

Defense. Shoots left. 5'10", 185 lbs. Born, Espanola, Ont., July 27, 1949.
(Boston's 8th choice, 69th overall, in 1969 Amateur Draft).

Season	Club	GP	G	A	Pts	PIM	GP	G	A	Pts	PIM
1971-72	California Golden Seals	2	0	0	0	0	....	....	....	....	....
	NHL Totals	**2**	**0**	**0**	**0**	**0**	....	....	....	....	....

• Brother of Bob

Signed as a free agent by **California**, June, 1971.

JONES, Jimmy

Right wing. Shoots right. 5'9", 180 lbs. Born, Woodbridge, Ont., January 2, 1953.
(Boston's 2nd choice, 31st overall, in 1973 Amateur Draft).

Season	Club	GP	G	A	Pts	PIM	GP	G	A	Pts	PIM
1977-78	Toronto Maple Leafs	78	4	9	13	23	13	1	5	6	7
1978-79	Toronto Maple Leafs	69	9	9	18	45	6	0	0	0	4
1979-80	Toronto Maple Leafs	1	0	0	0	0	....	....	....	....	....
	NHL Totals	**148**	**13**	**18**	**31**	**68**	**19**	**1**	**5**	**6**	**11**

Signed as a free agent by **Toronto**, October 25, 1977. Claimed as a fill-in by **Toronto** during Expansion Draft, June 13, 1979.

JONES, Keith

Right wing. Shoots left. 6'2", 200 lbs. Born, Brantford, Ont., November 8, 1968.
(Washington's 7th choice, 141st overall, in 1988 Entry Draft).

Season	Club	GP	G	A	Pts	PIM	GP	G	A	Pts	PIM
1992-93	Washington Capitals	71	12	14	26	124	6	0	0	0	10
1993-94	Washington Capitals	68	16	19	35	149	11	0	1	1	36
1994-95	Washington Capitals	40	14	6	20	65	7	4	4	8	22
1995-96	Washington Capitals	68	18	23	41	103	2	0	0	0	7
1996-97	Washington Capitals	11	2	3	5	13	....	....	....	....	....
	Colorado Avalanche	67	23	20	43	105	6	3	3	6	4
1997-98	Colorado Avalanche	23	3	7	10	22	7	0	0	0	13
1998-99	Colorado Avalanche	12	2	2	4	20	....	....	....	....	....
	Philadelphia Flyers	66	18	31	49	78	6	2	1	3	14
99-2000	Philadelphia Flyers	57	9	16	25	82	18	3	3	6	14
2000-01	Philadelphia Flyers	8	0	0	0	4	....	....	....	....	....
	NHL Totals	**491**	**117**	**141**	**258**	**765**	**63**	**12**	**12**	**24**	**120**

Traded to **Colorado** by **Washington** with Washington's 1st (Scott Parker) and 4th (later traded back to Washington – Washington selected Krys Barch) in 1998 Entry Draft for Curtis Leschyshyn and Chris Simon, November 2, 1996. • Missed remainder of 1996-97 and majority of 1997-98 seasons recovering from knee injury suffered in game vs. Chicago, May 13, 1996. Traded to **Philadelphia** by **Colorado** for Shjon Podein, November 12, 1998. • Officially announced retirement, November 21, 2000.

JONES, Ron

Defense. Shoots left. 6'1", 195 lbs. Born, Vermillion, Alta., April 11, 1951.
(Boston's 1st choice, 6th overall, in 1971 Amateur Draft).

Season	Club	GP	G	A	Pts	PIM	GP	G	A	Pts	PIM
1971-72	Boston Bruins	1	0	0	0	0	....	....	....	....	....
1972-73	Boston Bruins	7	0	0	0	0	....	....	....	....	....
1973-74	Pittsburgh Penguins	25	0	3	3	15	....	....	....	....	....
1974-75	Washington Capitals	19	1	1	2	16	....	....	....	....	....
1975-76	Washington Capitals	2	0	0	0	0	....	....	....	....	....
	NHL Totals	**54**	**1**	**4**	**5**	**31**	....	....	....	....	....

Claimed by **Pittsburgh** from **Boston** in Intra-League Draft, June 12, 1973. Traded to **Washington** by **Pittsburgh** for Pete Laframboise, January 21, 1975.

JONES, Ty

Right wing. Shoots right. 6'3", 218 lbs. Born, Richland, WA, February 22, 1979.
(Chicago's 2nd choice, 16th overall, in 1997 Entry Draft).

Season	Club	GP	G	A	Pts	PIM	GP	G	A	Pts	PIM
1998-99	Chicago Blackhawks	8	0	0	0	12	....	....	....	....	....
	NHL Totals	**8**	**0**	**0**	**0**	**12**	....	....	....	....	....

JONSSON, Hans

Defense. Shoots left. 6'1", 205 lbs. Born, Jarved, Sweden, August 2, 1973.
(Pittsburgh's 11th choice, 286th overall, in 1993 Entry Draft).

Season	Club	GP	G	A	Pts	PIM	GP	G	A	Pts	PIM
99-2000	Pittsburgh Penguins	68	3	11	14	12	11	0	1	1	6
2000-01	Pittsburgh Penguins	58	4	18	22	22	16	0	0	0	8
2001-02	Pittsburgh Penguins	53	2	5	7	22	....	....	....	....	....
2002-03	Pittsburgh Penguins	63	1	4	5	36	....	....	....	....	....
	NHL Totals	**242**	**10**	**38**	**48**	**92**	**27**	**0**	**1**	**1**	**14**

JONSSON, Jorgen

Left wing. Shoots left. 6', 185 lbs. Born, Angelholm, Sweden, September 29, 1972.
(Calgary's 11th choice, 227th overall, in 1994 Entry Draft).

Season	Club	Regular Season GP	G	A	Pts	PIM	Playoffs GP	G	A	Pts	PIM
99-2000	New York Islanders	68	11	17	28	16	....	....	....	....	....
	Mighty Ducks of Anaheim	13	1	2	3	0	....	....	....	....	....
	NHL Totals	**81**	**12**	**19**	**31**	**16**	....	....	....	....	....

• Brother of Kenny.

Traded to **NY Islanders** by **Calgary** for Jan Hlavac, July 14, 1998. Traded to **Anaheim** by **NY Islanders** for Johan Davidsson and future considerations, March 11, 2000.

JONSSON, Kenny

Defense. Shoots left. 6'3", 217 lbs. Born, Angelholm, Sweden, October 6, 1974.
(Toronto's 1st choice, 12th overall, in 1993 Entry Draft).

Season	Club	Regular Season GP	G	A	Pts	PIM	Playoffs GP	G	A	Pts	PIM
1994-95	Toronto Maple Leafs	39	2	7	9	16	4	0	0	0	0
1995-96	Toronto Maple Leafs	50	4	22	26	22	....	....	....	....	....
	New York Islanders	16	0	4	4	10	....	....	....	....	....
1996-97	New York Islanders	81	3	18	21	24	....	....	....	....	....
1997-98	New York Islanders	81	14	26	40	58	....	....	....	....	....
1998-99	New York Islanders	63	8	18	26	34	....	....	....	....	....
99-2000	New York Islanders	65	1	24	25	32	....	....	....	....	....
2000-01	New York Islanders	65	8	21	29	30	....	....	....	....	....
2001-02	New York Islanders	76	10	22	32	26	5	1	2	3	4
2002-03	New York Islanders	71	8	18	26	24	5	0	1	1	0
	NHL Totals	**607**	**58**	**180**	**238**	**276**	**14**	**1**	**3**	**4**	**4**

• Brother of Jorgen • NHL All-Rookie Team (1995)

Traded to **NY Islanders** by **Toronto** with Sean Haggerty, Darby Hendrickson and Toronto's 1st round choice (Roberto Luongo) in 1997 Entry Draft for Wendel Clark, Mathieu Schneider and D.J. Smith, March 13, 1996.

JONSSON, Tomas

Defense. Shoots left. 5'10", 185 lbs. Born, Falun, Sweden, April 12, 1960.
(NY Islanders' 2nd choice, 25th overall, in 1979 Entry Draft).

Season	Club	Regular Season GP	G	A	Pts	PIM	Playoffs GP	G	A	Pts	PIM
1981-82 ♦	New York Islanders	70	9	25	34	51	10	0	2	2	21
1982-83 ♦	New York Islanders	72	13	35	48	50	20	2	10	12	18
1983-84	New York Islanders	72	11	36	47	54	21	3	5	8	22
1984-85	New York Islanders	69	16	34	50	58	7	1	2	3	10
1985-86	New York Islanders	77	14	30	44	62	3	0	1	1	4
1986-87	New York Islanders	47	6	25	31	36	10	1	4	5	6
1987-88	New York Islanders	72	6	41	47	115	5	2	2	4	10
1988-89	New York Islanders	53	9	23	32	34	....	....	....	....	....
	Edmonton Oilers	20	1	10	11	22	4	2	0	2	6
	NHL Totals	**552**	**85**	**259**	**344**	**482**	**80**	**11**	**26**	**37**	**97**

Traded to **Edmonton** by **NY Islanders** for future considerations, February 15, 1989.

JOSEPH, Chris

Defense. Shoots right. 6'3", 212 lbs. Born, Burnaby, B.C., September 10, 1969.
(Pittsburgh's 1st choice, 5th overall, in 1987 Entry Draft).

Season	Club	Regular Season GP	G	A	Pts	PIM	Playoffs GP	G	A	Pts	PIM
1987-88	Pittsburgh Penguins	17	0	4	4	12	....	....	....	....	....
	Edmonton Oilers	7	0	4	4	6	....	....	....	....	....
1988-89	Edmonton Oilers	44	4	5	9	54	....	....	....	....	....
1989-90	Edmonton Oilers	4	0	2	2	2	....	....	....	....	....
1990-91	Edmonton Oilers	49	5	17	22	59	....	....	....	....	....
1991-92	Edmonton Oilers	7	0	0	0	8	5	1	3	4	2
1992-93	Edmonton Oilers	33	2	10	12	48	....	....	....	....	....
1993-94	Edmonton Oilers	10	1	1	2	28	....	....	....	....	....
	Tampa Bay Lightning	66	10	19	29	108	....	....	....	....	....
1994-95	Pittsburgh Penguins	33	5	10	15	46	10	1	1	2	12
1995-96	Pittsburgh Penguins	70	5	14	19	71	15	1	0	1	8
1996-97	Vancouver Canucks	63	3	13	16	62	....	....	....	....	....
1997-98	Philadelphia Flyers	15	1	0	1	19	1	0	0	0	2
1998-99	Philadelphia Flyers	2	0	0	0	2	....	....	....	....	....
99-2000	Vancouver Canucks	38	2	9	11	6	....	....	....	....	....
	Phoenix Coyotes	9	0	0	0	0	....	....	....	....	....
2000-01	Phoenix Coyotes	24	1	1	2	16	....	....	....	....	....
	Atlanta Thrashers	19	0	3	3	20	....	....	....	....	....
	NHL Totals	**510**	**39**	**112**	**151**	**567**	**31**	**3**	**4**	**7**	**24**

Traded to **Edmonton** by **Pittsburgh** with Craig Simpson, Dave Hannan and Moe Mantha for Paul Coffey, Dave Hunter and Wayne Van Dorp, November 24, 1987. Traded to **Tampa Bay** by **Edmonton** for Bob Beers, November 11, 1993. Claimed by **Pittsburgh** from **Tampa Bay** in Waiver Draft, January 18, 1995. Claimed by **Vancouver** from **Pittsburgh** in Waiver Draft, September 30, 1996. Signed as a free agent by **Philadelphia**, September 11, 1997. Signed as a free agent by **Ottawa**, August 18, 1999. Claimed by **Vancouver** from **Ottawa** in Waiver Draft, September 27, 1999. Claimed on waivers by **Phoenix** from **Vancouver**, March 14, 2000. Claimed on waivers by **Atlanta** from **Phoenix**, February 14, 2001.

JOSEPH, Tony

Right wing. Shoots right. 6'4", 203 lbs. Born, Cornwall, Ont., March 1, 1969.
(Winnipeg's 5th choice, 94th overall, in 1988 Entry Draft).

Season	Club	Regular Season GP	G	A	Pts	PIM	Playoffs GP	G	A	Pts	PIM
1988-89	Winnipeg Jets	2	1	0	1	0	....	....	....	....	....
	NHL Totals	**2**	**1**	**0**	**1**	**0**	....	....	....	....	....

Traded to **Minnesota** by **Winnipeg** for Tyler Larter, October 15, 1991. Traded to **Winnipeg** by **Minnesota** for Warren Rychel, December 30, 1991.

JOVANOVSKI, Ed

Defense. Shoots left. 6'2", 210 lbs. Born, Windsor, Ont., June 26, 1976.
(Florida's 1st choice, 1st overall, in 1994 Entry Draft).

Season	Club	Regular Season GP	G	A	Pts	PIM	Playoffs GP	G	A	Pts	PIM
1995-96	Florida Panthers	70	10	11	21	137	22	1	8	9	52
1996-97	Florida Panthers	61	7	16	23	172	5	0	0	0	4
1997-98	Florida Panthers	81	9	14	23	158	....	....	....	....	....
1998-99	Florida Panthers	41	3	13	16	82	....	....	....	....	....
	Vancouver Canucks	31	2	9	11	44	....	....	....	....	....
99-2000	Vancouver Canucks	75	5	21	26	54	....	....	....	....	....
2000-01	Vancouver Canucks	79	12	35	47	102	4	1	1	2	0
2001-02	Vancouver Canucks	82	17	31	48	101	6	1	4	5	8
2002-03	Vancouver Canucks	67	6	40	46	113	14	7	1	8	22
	NHL Totals	**587**	**71**	**190**	**261**	**963**	**51**	**10**	**14**	**24**	**86**

NHL All-Rookie Team (1996)

Played in NHL All-Star Game (2001, 2002, 2003)

Traded to **Vancouver** by **Florida** with Dave Gagner, Mike Brown, Kevin Weekes and Florida's 1st round choice (Nathan Smith) in 2000 Entry Draft for Pavel Bure, Bret Hedican, Brad Ference and Vancouver's 3rd round choice (Robert Fried) in 2000 Entry Draft, January 17, 1999.

JOYAL, Eddie

Center. Shoots left. 6', 178 lbs. Born, Edmonton, Alta., May 8, 1940.

Season	Club	Regular Season GP	G	A	Pts	PIM	Playoffs GP	G	A	Pts	PIM
1962-63	Detroit Red Wings	14	2	8	10	0	11	1	0	1	2
1963-64	Detroit Red Wings	47	10	7	17	6	14	2	3	5	10
1964-65	Detroit Red Wings	46	8	14	22	4	7	1	1	2	4
1965-66	Toronto Maple Leafs	14	0	2	2	2	....	....	....	....	....
1967-68	Los Angeles Kings	74	23	34	57	20	7	4	1	5	2
1968-69	Los Angeles Kings	73	33	19	52	24	11	3	3	6	0
1969-70	Los Angeles Kings	59	18	22	40	8	....	....	....	....	....
1970-71	Los Angeles Kings	69	20	21	41	14	....	....	....	....	....
1971-72	Los Angeles Kings	44	11	3	14	17	....	....	....	....	....
	Philadelphia Flyers	26	3	4	7	8	....	....	....	....	....
	NHL Totals	**466**	**128**	**134**	**262**	**103**	**50**	**11**	**8**	**19**	**18**

Traded to **Toronto** by **Detroit** with Marcel Pronovost, Larry Jeffrey, Lowell MacDonald and Aut Erickson for Andy Bathgate, Billy Harris and Gary Jarrett, May 20, 1965. Claimed by **Los Angeles** from **Toronto** in Expansion Draft, June 6, 1967. Traded to **Philadelphia** by **Los Angeles** with Bill Flett, Jean Potvin and Ross Lonsberry for Bill Lesuk, Jim Johnson and Serge Bernier, January 28, 1972.

JOYCE, Bob

Left wing. Shoots left. 6', 195 lbs. Born, St. John, N.B., July 11, 1966.
(Boston's 4th choice, 82nd overall, in 1984 Entry Draft).

Season	Club	Regular Season GP	G	A	Pts	PIM	Playoffs GP	G	A	Pts	PIM
1987-88	Boston Bruins	15	7	5	12	10	23	8	6	14	18
1988-89	Boston Bruins	77	18	31	49	46	9	5	2	7	2
1989-90	Boston Bruins	23	1	2	3	22	....	....	....	....	....
	Washington Capitals	24	5	8	13	4	14	2	1	3	9
1990-91	Washington Capitals	17	3	3	6	8	....	....	....	....	....
1991-92	Winnipeg Jets	1	0	0	0	0	....	....	....	....	....
1992-93	Winnipeg Jets	1	0	0	0	0	....	....	....	....	....
	NHL Totals	**158**	**34**	**49**	**83**	**90**	**46**	**15**	**9**	**24**	**29**

Traded to **Washington** by **Boston** for Dave Christian, December 13, 1989. Traded to **Winnipeg** by **Washington** with Tyler Larter and Kent Paynter for Craig Duncanson, Brent Hughes and Simon Wheeldon, May 21, 1991.

JOYCE, Duane

Defense. Shoots right. 6'2", 203 lbs. Born, Pembroke, MA, May 5, 1965.

Season	Club	Regular Season GP	G	A	Pts	PIM	Playoffs GP	G	A	Pts	PIM
1993-94	Dallas Stars	3	0	0	0	0	....	....	....	....	....
	NHL Totals	**3**	**0**	**0**	**0**	**0**	....	....	....	....	....

Signed as a free agent by **San Jose**, August 13, 1991. Signed as a free agent by **Dallas**, December 3, 1993.

JUCKES, Bing

Left wing. Shoots left. 5'10", 165 lbs. Born, Hamiota, Man., June 14, 1926.

Season	Club	Regular Season GP	G	A	Pts	PIM	Playoffs GP	G	A	Pts	PIM
1947-48	New York Rangers	2	0	0	0	0	....	....	....	....	....
1949-50	New York Rangers	14	2	1	3	6	....	....	....	....	....
	NHL Totals	**16**	**2**	**1**	**3**	**6**	....	....	....	....	....

Traded to **Denver** (USHL) by **NY Rangers** for cash, October 16, 1950.

JUHLIN, Patrik

Left wing. Shoots left. 6', 194 lbs. Born, Huddinge, Sweden, April 24, 1970.
(Philadelphia's 2nd choice, 34th overall, in 1989 Entry Draft).

Season	Club	Regular Season GP	G	A	Pts	PIM	Playoffs GP	G	A	Pts	PIM
1994-95	Philadelphia Flyers	42	4	3	7	6	13	1	0	1	2
1995-96	Philadelphia Flyers	14	3	3	6	17	....	....	....	....	....
	NHL Totals	**56**	**7**	**6**	**13**	**23**	**13**	**1**	**0**	**1**	**2**

JULIEN, Claude

Defense. Shoots right. 6', 198 lbs. Born, Blind River, Ont., April 23, 1960.

Season	Club	Regular Season GP	G	A	Pts	PIM	Playoffs GP	G	A	Pts	PIM
1984-85	Quebec Nordiques	1	0	0	0	0	....	....	....	....	....
1985-86	Quebec Nordiques	13	0	1	1	25	....	....	....	....	....
	NHL Totals	**14**	**0**	**1**	**1**	**25**	....	....	....	....	....

Signed as a free agent by **St. Louis**, September 28, 1981. Transferred to **Quebec** by **St. Louis** with Gord Donnelly as compensation for St. Louis' signing of Jacques Demers as coach, August 19, 1983.

JUNEAU, Joe

Center. Shoots left. 6', 195 lbs. Born, Pont-Rouge, Que., January 5, 1968.
(Boston's 3rd choice, 81st overall, in 1988 Entry Draft).

		REGULAR SEASON					PLAYOFFS				
Season	**Club**	**GP**	**G**	**A**	**Pts**	**PIM**	**GP**	**G**	**A**	**Pts**	**PIM**
1991-92	Boston Bruins	14	5	14	19	4	15	4	8	12	21
1992-93	Boston Bruins	84	32	70	102	33	4	2	4	6	6
1993-94	Boston Bruins	63	14	58	72	35	....	....	....	....	....
	Washington Capitals	11	5	8	13	6	11	4	5	9	6
1994-95	Washington Capitals	44	5	38	43	8	7	2	6	8	2
1995-96	Washington Capitals	80	14	50	64	30	5	0	7	7	6
1996-97	Washington Capitals	58	15	27	42	8	....	....	....	....	....
1997-98	Washington Capitals	56	9	22	31	26	21	7	10	17	8
1998-99	Washington Capitals	63	14	27	41	20	....	....	....	....	....
	Buffalo Sabres	9	1	1	2	2	20	3	8	11	10
99-2000	Ottawa Senators	65	13	24	37	22	6	2	1	3	0
2000-01	Phoenix Coyotes	69	10	23	33	28	....	....	....	....	....
2001-02	Montreal Canadiens	70	8	28	36	10	12	1	4	5	6
2002-03	Montreal Canadiens	72	6	16	22	20	....	....	....	....	....
	NHL Totals	**758**	**151**	**406**	**557**	**252**	**101**	**25**	**53**	**78**	**65**

NHL All-Rookie Team (1993)

Traded to **Washington** by **Boston** for Al Iafrate, March 21, 1994. Traded to **Buffalo** by **Washington** with Washington's 3rd round choice (Tim Preston) in 1999 Entry Draft for Alexei Tezikov and Buffalo's 4th round compensatory choice (later traded to Calgary – Calgary selected Levente Szuper) in 2000 Entry Draft, March 22, 1999. Signed as a free agent by **Ottawa**, October 25, 1999. Selected by **Minnesota** from **Ottawa** in Expansion Draft, June 23, 2000. Traded to **Phoenix** by **Minnesota** for the rights to Rickard Wallin, June 23, 2000. Traded to **Montreal** by **Phoenix** for future considerations, June 15, 2001.

JUNKER, Steve

Left wing. Shoots left. 6', 184 lbs. Born, Castlegar, B.C., June 26, 1972.
(NY Islanders' 5th choice, 92nd overall, in 1991 Entry Draft).

		REGULAR SEASON					PLAYOFFS				
Season	**Club**	**GP**	**G**	**A**	**Pts**	**PIM**	**GP**	**G**	**A**	**Pts**	**PIM**
1992-93	New York Islanders	....	....	....	....	....	3	0	1	1	0
1993-94	New York Islanders	5	0	0	0	0	....	....	....	....	....
	NHL Totals	**5**	**0**	**0**	**0**	**0**	**3**	**0**	**1**	**1**	**0**

JUTILA, Timo

Defense. Shoots left. 5'7", 175 lbs. Born, Tampere, Finland, December 24, 1963.
(Buffalo's 6th choice, 68th overall, in 1982 Entry Draft).

		REGULAR SEASON					PLAYOFFS				
Season	**Club**	**GP**	**G**	**A**	**Pts**	**PIM**	**GP**	**G**	**A**	**Pts**	**PIM**
1984-85	Buffalo Sabres	10	1	5	6	13	....	....	....	....	....
	NHL Totals	**10**	**1**	**5**	**6**	**13**	....	....	....	....	....

JUZDA, Bill

Defense. Shoots right. 5'9", 190 lbs. Born, Winnipeg, Man., October 29, 1920.

		REGULAR SEASON					PLAYOFFS				
Season	**Club**	**GP**	**G**	**A**	**Pts**	**PIM**	**GP**	**G**	**A**	**Pts**	**PIM**
1940-41	New York Rangers	5	0	0	0	2	....	....	....	....	....
1941-42	New York Rangers	45	4	8	12	29	6	0	1	1	4
1945-46	New York Rangers	32	1	3	4	17	....	....	....	....	....
1946-47	New York Rangers	45	3	5	8	60	....	....	....	....	....
1947-48	New York Rangers	60	3	9	12	70	6	0	0	0	9
1948-49 ◆	Toronto Maple Leafs	38	1	2	3	23	9	0	2	2	8
1949-50	Toronto Maple Leafs	62	1	14	15	68	7	0	0	0	16
1950-51 ◆	Toronto Maple Leafs	65	0	9	9	64	11	0	0	0	7
1951-52	Toronto Maple Leafs	46	1	4	5	65	3	0	0	0	2
	NHL Totals	**398**	**14**	**54**	**68**	**398**	**42**	**0**	**3**	**3**	**46**

Played in NHL All-Star Game (1948, 1949)

Signed as a free agent by **NY Rangers**, October 21, 1940. Traded to **Toronto** by **NY Rangers** with Cal Gardner, Rene Trudell and the rights to Frank Mathers for Wally Stanowski and Moe Morris, April 26, 1948.

KABEL, Bob

Center. Shoots right. 6', 183 lbs. Born, Dauphin, Man., November 11, 1934.

		REGULAR SEASON					PLAYOFFS				
Season	**Club**	**GP**	**G**	**A**	**Pts**	**PIM**	**GP**	**G**	**A**	**Pts**	**PIM**
1959-60	New York Rangers	44	5	11	16	32	....	....	....	....	....
1960-61	New York Rangers	4	0	2	2	2	....	....	....	....	....
	NHL Totals	**48**	**5**	**13**	**18**	**34**	....	....	....	....	....

Traded to **California** (WHL) by **NY Rangers** for Gerry Brisson with NY Rangers holding right of recall, October, 1966.

KABERLE, Frantisek

Defense. Shoots left. 6', 190 lbs. Born, Kladno, Czech., November 8, 1973.
(Los Angeles' 3rd choice, 76th overall, in 1999 Entry Draft).

		REGULAR SEASON					PLAYOFFS				
Season	**Club**	**GP**	**G**	**A**	**Pts**	**PIM**	**GP**	**G**	**A**	**Pts**	**PIM**
99-2000	Los Angeles Kings	37	0	9	9	4	....	....	....	....	....
	Atlanta Thrashers	14	1	6	7	6	....	....	....	....	....
2000-01	Atlanta Thrashers	51	4	11	15	18	....	....	....	....	....
2001-02	Atlanta Thrashers	61	5	20	25	24	....	....	....	....	....
2002-03	Atlanta Thrashers	79	7	19	26	32	....	....	....	....	....
	NHL Totals	**242**	**17**	**65**	**82**	**84**	....	....	....	....	....

• Brother of Tomas

Traded to **Atlanta** by **Los Angeles** with Donald Audette for Kelly Buchberger and Nelson Emerson, March 13, 2000.

KABERLE, Tomas

Defense. Shoots left. 6'2", 200 lbs. Born, Rakovnik, Czech., March 2, 1978.
(Toronto's 13th choice, 204th overall, in 1996 Entry Draft).

		REGULAR SEASON					PLAYOFFS				
Season	**Club**	**GP**	**G**	**A**	**Pts**	**PIM**	**GP**	**G**	**A**	**Pts**	**PIM**
1998-99	Toronto Maple Leafs	57	4	18	22	12	14	0	3	3	2
99-2000	Toronto Maple Leafs	82	7	33	40	24	12	1	4	5	0
2000-01	Toronto Maple Leafs	82	6	39	45	24	11	1	3	4	0
2001-02	Toronto Maple Leafs	69	10	29	39	2	20	2	8	10	16
2002-03	Toronto Maple Leafs	82	11	36	47	30	7	2	1	3	0
	NHL Totals	**372**	**38**	**155**	**193**	**92**	**64**	**6**	**19**	**25**	**18**

• Brother of Frantisek

Played in NHL All-Star Game (2002)

KACHOWSKI, Mark

Left wing. Shoots left. 5'11", 200 lbs. Born, Edmonton, Alta., February 20, 1965.

		REGULAR SEASON					PLAYOFFS				
Season	**Club**	**GP**	**G**	**A**	**Pts**	**PIM**	**GP**	**G**	**A**	**Pts**	**PIM**
1987-88	Pittsburgh Penguins	38	5	3	8	126	....	....	....	....	....
1988-89	Pittsburgh Penguins	12	1	1	2	43	....	....	....	....	....
1989-90	Pittsburgh Penguins	14	0	1	1	40	....	....	....	....	....
	NHL Totals	**64**	**6**	**5**	**11**	**209**	....	....	....	....	....

Signed as a free agent by **Pittsburgh**, August 31, 1987.

KACHUR, Ed

Right wing. Shoots right. 5'8", 170 lbs. Born, Fort William, Ont., April 22, 1934.

		REGULAR SEASON					PLAYOFFS				
Season	**Club**	**GP**	**G**	**A**	**Pts**	**PIM**	**GP**	**G**	**A**	**Pts**	**PIM**
1956-57	Chicago Black Hawks	34	5	7	12	21	....	....	....	....	....
1957-58	Chicago Black Hawks	62	5	7	12	14	....	....	....	....	....
	NHL Totals	**96**	**10**	**14**	**24**	**35**	....	....	....	....	....

Traded to **Chicago** by **Montreal** with Forbes Kennedy for $50,000, May 24, 1956. Traded to **LA Blades** (WHL) by **Chicago** (Buffalo-AHL) for cash, August 30, 1964.

KAESE, Trent

Right wing. Shoots right. 5'11", 225 lbs. Born, Nanaimo, B.C., September 9, 1967.
(Buffalo's 8th choice, 161st overall, in 1985 Entry Draft).

		REGULAR SEASON					PLAYOFFS				
Season	**Club**	**GP**	**G**	**A**	**Pts**	**PIM**	**GP**	**G**	**A**	**Pts**	**PIM**
1988-89	Buffalo Sabres	1	0	0	0	0	....	....	....	....	....
	NHL Totals	**1**	**0**	**0**	**0**	**0**	....	....	....	....	....

KAISER, Vern

Left wing. Shoots left. 6', 180 lbs. Born, Preston, Ont., September 28, 1926.

		REGULAR SEASON					PLAYOFFS				
Season	**Club**	**GP**	**G**	**A**	**Pts**	**PIM**	**GP**	**G**	**A**	**Pts**	**PIM**
1950-51	Montreal Canadiens	50	7	5	12	33	2	0	0	0	0
	NHL Totals	**50**	**7**	**5**	**12**	**33**	**2**	**0**	**0**	**0**	**0**

Traded to **Montreal** by **Springfield** (AHL) for Charles Gagnon and future considerations, April 18, 1950. Traded to **Syracuse** (AHL) by **Montreal** for cash, January 1, 1954.

KALBFLEISH, Walter

Defense. Shoots right. 5'10", 175 lbs. Born, New Hamburg, Ont., December 18, 1911.

		REGULAR SEASON					PLAYOFFS				
Season	**Club**	**GP**	**G**	**A**	**Pts**	**PIM**	**GP**	**G**	**A**	**Pts**	**PIM**
1933-34	Ottawa Senators	22	0	4	4	20	....	....	....	....	....
1934-35	St. Louis Eagles	3	0	0	0	6	....	....	....	....	....
1935-36	New York Americans	4	0	0	0	2	5	0	0	0	2
1936-37	New York Americans	6	0	0	0	4	....	....	....	....	....
	Boston Bruins	1	0	0	0	0	....	....	....	....	....
	NHL Totals	**36**	**0**	**4**	**4**	**32**	**5**	**0**	**0**	**0**	**2**

Signed as a free agent by **Ottawa**, May 10, 1933. Transferred to **St. Louis** after **Ottawa** franchise relocated, September 22, 1934. Claimed by **NY Americans** from **St. Louis** in Dispersal Draft, October 15, 1935. Traded to **Boston** by **NY Americans** for Teddy Graham, December 19, 1936.

KALETA, Alex

Left wing. Shoots left. 6', 175 lbs. Born, Canmore, Alta., November 29, 1919.

		REGULAR SEASON					PLAYOFFS				
Season	**Club**	**GP**	**G**	**A**	**Pts**	**PIM**	**GP**	**G**	**A**	**Pts**	**PIM**
1941-42	Chicago Black Hawks	48	7	21	28	12	3	1	2	3	0
1945-46	Chicago Black Hawks	49	19	27	46	17	4	0	1	1	2
1946-47	Chicago Black Hawks	57	24	20	44	37	....	....	....	....	....
1947-48	Chicago Black Hawks	52	10	16	26	40	....	....	....	....	....
1948-49	New York Rangers	56	12	19	31	18	....	....	....	....	....
1949-50	New York Rangers	67	17	14	31	40	10	0	3	3	0
1950-51	New York Rangers	58	3	4	7	26	....	....	....	....	....
	NHL Totals	**387**	**92**	**121**	**213**	**190**	**17**	**1**	**6**	**7**	**2**

Traded to **NY Rangers** by **Chicago** with Emile Francis for Jim Henry, October 7, 1948. Loaned to **Boston** (Hershey-AHL) by **NY Rangers** to complete transaction that sent Zellio Toppazzini and Ed Harrison to NY Rangers (November 16, 1950), November 20, 1950.

KALININ, Dmitri

Defense. Shoots left. 6'3", 215 lbs. Born, Chelyabinsk, USSR, July 22, 1980.
(Buffalo's 1st choice, 18th overall, in 1998 Entry Draft).

		REGULAR SEASON					PLAYOFFS				
Season	**Club**	**GP**	**G**	**A**	**Pts**	**PIM**	**GP**	**G**	**A**	**Pts**	**PIM**
99-2000	Buffalo Sabres	4	0	0	0	4	....	....	....	....	....
2000-01	Buffalo Sabres	79	4	18	22	38	13	0	2	2	4
2001-02	Buffalo Sabres	58	2	11	13	26	....	....	....	....	....
2002-03	Buffalo Sabres	65	8	13	21	57	....	....	....	....	....
	NHL Totals	**206**	**14**	**42**	**56**	**125**	**13**	**0**	**2**	**2**	**4**

KALLIO, Tomi

Right wing. Shoots left. 6', 190 lbs. Born, Turku, Finland, January 27, 1977.
(Colorado's 4th choice, 81st overall, in 1995 Entry Draft).

		REGULAR SEASON					PLAYOFFS				
Season	**Club**	**GP**	**G**	**A**	**Pts**	**PIM**	**GP**	**G**	**A**	**Pts**	**PIM**
2000-01	Atlanta Thrashers	56	14	13	27	22	....	....	....	....	....
2001-02	Atlanta Thrashers	60	8	14	22	12	....	....	....	....	....
2002-03	Atlanta Thrashers	5	0	2	2	4	....	....	....	....	....
	Columbus Blue Jackets	12	1	2	3	8	....	....	....	....	....
	Philadelphia Flyers	7	1	0	1	2	....	....	....	....	....
	NHL Totals	**140**	**24**	**31**	**55**	**48**	....	....	....	....	....

Claimed by **Atlanta** from **Colorado** in Expansion Draft, June 25, 1999. Traded to **Columbus** by **Atlanta** with Pauli Levokari for Chris Nielsen and Petteri Nummelin, December 2, 2002. Claimed on waivers by **Philadelphia** from **Columbus**, January 1, 2003.

KALLUR, Anders

Right wing. Shoots left. 5'11", 185 lbs. Born, Ludvika, Sweden, July 6, 1952.

Season	Club	Regular Season GP	G	A	Pts	PIM	Playoffs GP	G	A	Pts	PIM
1979-80	♦ New York Islanders	76	22	30	52	16	....	....	....	....	....
1980-81	♦ New York Islanders	78	36	28	64	32	12	4	3	7	10
1981-82	♦ New York Islanders	58	18	22	40	18	19	1	6	7	8
1982-83	♦ New York Islanders	55	6	8	14	33	20	3	12	15	12
1983-84	New York Islanders	65	9	14	23	24	17	2	2	4	2
1984-85	New York Islanders	51	10	8	18	26	10	2	0	2	0
	NHL Totals	**383**	**101**	**110**	**211**	**149**	**78**	**12**	**23**	**35**	**32**

Signed as a free agent by **NY Islanders**, August 15, 1979.

KAMENSKY, Valeri

Left wing. Shoots right. 6'2", 198 lbs. Born, Voskresensk, USSR, April 18, 1966.
(Quebec's 8th choice, 129th overall, in 1988 Entry Draft).

Season	Club	Regular Season GP	G	A	Pts	PIM	Playoffs GP	G	A	Pts	PIM
1991-92	Quebec Nordiques	23	7	14	21	14	....	....	....	....	....
1992-93	Quebec Nordiques	32	15	22	37	14	6	0	1	1	6
1993-94	Quebec Nordiques	76	28	37	65	42	....	....	....	....	....
1994-95	Quebec Nordiques	40	10	20	30	22	2	1	0	1	0
1995-96	♦ Colorado Avalanche	81	38	47	85	85	22	10	12	22	28
1996-97	Colorado Avalanche	68	28	38	66	38	17	8	14	22	16
1997-98	Colorado Avalanche	75	26	40	66	60	7	2	3	5	18
1998-99	Colorado Avalanche	65	14	30	44	28	10	4	5	9	4
99-2000	New York Rangers	58	13	19	32	24	....	....	....	....	....
2000-01	New York Rangers	65	14	20	34	36	....	....	....	....	....
2001-02	Dallas Stars	24	3	6	9	2	....	....	....	....	....
	New Jersey Devils	30	4	8	12	18	2	0	0	0	0
	NHL Totals	**637**	**200**	**301**	**501**	**383**	**66**	**25**	**35**	**60**	**72**

Played in NHL All-Star Game (1998)

• Missed majority of 1991-92 season recovering from ankle injury suffered in game vs. Tampa Bay, October 27, 1991. Transferred to **Colorado** after **Quebec** franchise relocated, June 21, 1995. Signed as a free agent by **NY Rangers**, July 7, 1999. Signed as a free agent by **Dallas**, July 5, 2001. Traded to **New Jersey** by **Dallas** for Andre Lakos and future considerations, January 16, 2002.

KAMINSKI, Kevin

Center. Shoots left. 5'10", 190 lbs. Born, Churchbridge, Sask., March 13, 1969.
(Minnesota's 3rd choice, 48th overall, in 1987 Entry Draft).

Season	Club	Regular Season GP	G	A	Pts	PIM	Playoffs GP	G	A	Pts	PIM
1988-89	Minnesota North Stars	1	0	0	0	0	....	....	....	....	....
1989-90	Quebec Nordiques	1	0	0	0	0	....	....	....	....	....
1991-92	Quebec Nordiques	5	0	0	0	45	....	....	....	....	....
1993-94	Washington Capitals	13	0	5	5	87	....	....	....	....	....
1994-95	Washington Capitals	27	1	1	2	102	5	0	0	0	36
1995-96	Washington Capitals	54	1	2	3	164	3	0	0	0	16
1996-97	Washington Capitals	38	1	2	3	130	....	....	....	....	....
	NHL Totals	**139**	**3**	**10**	**13**	**528**	**8**	**0**	**0**	**0**	**52**

Traded to **Quebec** by **Minnesota** for Gaetan Duchesne, June 19, 1989. Traded to **Washington** by **Quebec** for Mark Matier, June 15, 1993.

KAMINSKY, Max

Center. Shoots left. 5'11", 160 lbs. Born, Niagara Falls, Ont., April 19, 1913.

Season	Club	Regular Season GP	G	A	Pts	PIM	Playoffs GP	G	A	Pts	PIM
1933-34	Ottawa Senators	38	9	17	26	14	....	....	....	....	....
1934-35	Boston Bruins	38	12	15	27	4	4	0	0	0	0
	St. Louis Eagles	12	0	0	0	0	....	....	....	....	....
1935-36	Boston Bruins	36	1	2	3	20	....	....	....	....	....
1936-37	Montreal Maroons	6	0	0	0	0	....	....	....	....	....
	NHL Totals	**130**	**22**	**34**	**56**	**38**	**4**	**0**	**0**	**0**	**0**

Signed as a free agent by **Ottawa**, December 4, 1933. Transferred to **St. Louis** after **Ottawa** franchise relocated, September 22, 1934. Traded to **Boston** by **St. Louis** with Des Roche for Joe Lamb, December 4, 1934. Traded to **Mtl. Maroons** by **Boston** for cash, December 7, 1936.

KAMINSKY, Yan

Right wing. Shoots left. 6'1", 176 lbs. Born, Penza, USSR, July 28, 1971.
(Winnipeg's 4th choice, 99th overall, in 1991 Entry Draft).

Season	Club	Regular Season GP	G	A	Pts	PIM	Playoffs GP	G	A	Pts	PIM
1993-94	Winnipeg Jets	1	0	0	0	0	....	....	....	....	....
	New York Islanders	23	2	1	3	4	2	0	0	0	4
1994-95	New York Islanders	2	1	1	2	0	....	....	....	....	....
	NHL Totals	**26**	**3**	**2**	**5**	**4**	**2**	**0**	**0**	**0**	**4**

Traded to **NY Islanders** by **Winnipeg** for Wayne McBean, February 1, 1994.

KAMPMAN, Bingo

Defense. Shoots right. 5'10", 187 lbs. Born, Berlin, Ont., March 12, 1914.

Season	Club	Regular Season GP	G	A	Pts	PIM	Playoffs GP	G	A	Pts	PIM
1937-38	Toronto Maple Leafs	32	1	2	3	56	7	0	1	1	6
1938-39	Toronto Maple Leafs	41	2	8	10	52	10	1	1	2	20
1939-40	Toronto Maple Leafs	39	6	9	15	59	10	0	0	0	0
1940-41	Toronto Maple Leafs	39	1	4	5	53	7	0	0	0	0
1941-42	♦ Toronto Maple Leafs	38	4	7	11	67	13	0	2	2	12
	NHL Totals	**189**	**14**	**30**	**44**	**287**	**47**	**1**	**4**	**5**	**38**

Traded to **Boston** by **Toronto** to complete transaction that sent Art Jackson to Toronto (December 24, 1944), October 29, 1945.

KANE, Francis

Defense. Shoots left. 5'11", 186 lbs. Born, Stratford, Ont., January 19, 1923.

Season	Club	Regular Season GP	G	A	Pts	PIM	Playoffs GP	G	A	Pts	PIM
1943-44	Detroit Red Wings	2	0	0	0	0	....	....	....	....	....
	NHL Totals	**2**	**0**	**0**	**0**	**0**	....	....	....	....	....

Traded to **Tulsa** (USHL) by **Detroit** for cash, November, 1945.

KANNEGIESSER, Gord

Defense. Shoots left. 6', 190 lbs. Born, North Bay, Ont., December 21, 1945.

Season	Club	Regular Season GP	G	A	Pts	PIM	Playoffs GP	G	A	Pts	PIM
1967-68	St. Louis Blues	19	0	1	1	13	....	....	....	....	....
1971-72	St. Louis Blues	4	0	0	0	2	....	....	....	....	....
	NHL Totals	**23**	**0**	**1**	**1**	**15**	....	....	....	....	....

• Brother of Sheldon

Traded to **St. Louis** by **NY Rangers** with Gary Sabourin, Bob Plager and Tim Ecclestone for Rod Seiling, June 6, 1967.

KANNEGIESSER, Sheldon

Defense. Shoots left. 6', 198 lbs. Born, North Bay, Ont., August 15, 1947.

Season	Club	Regular Season GP	G	A	Pts	PIM	Playoffs GP	G	A	Pts	PIM
1970-71	Pittsburgh Penguins	18	0	2	2	29	....	....	....	....	....
1971-72	Pittsburgh Penguins	54	2	4	6	47	....	....	....	....	....
1972-73	Pittsburgh Penguins	3	0	0	0	0	....	....	....	....	....
	New York Rangers	3	0	1	1	4	1	0	0	0	2
1973-74	New York Rangers	12	1	3	4	6	....	....	....	....	....
	Los Angeles Kings	51	3	17	20	49	5	0	1	1	0
1974-75	Los Angeles Kings	74	2	23	25	57	3	0	1	1	4
1975-76	Los Angeles Kings	70	4	9	13	36	9	0	0	0	4
1976-77	Los Angeles Kings	39	1	1	2	28	....	....	....	....	....
1977-78	Vancouver Canucks	42	1	7	8	36	....	....	....	....	....
	NHL Totals	**366**	**14**	**67**	**81**	**292**	**18**	**0**	**2**	**2**	**10**

• Brother of Gord

Loaned to **St. Louis** by **NY Rangers** for the remainder of the 1969-70 season for the loan of Larry Hornung for the remainder of the 1969-70 season, November, 1969. Traded to **Pittsburgh** by **NY Rangers** with Syl Apps Jr. for Glen Sather, January 26, 1971. Traded to **NY Rangers** by **Pittsburgh** for future considerations (Steve Andrascik, May 16, 1973), March 2, 1973. Traded to **Los Angeles** by **NY Rangers** with Mike Murphy and Tom Williams for Gilles Marotte and Real Lemieux, November 30, 1973. Traded to **Vancouver** by **Los Angeles** for Larry Carriere, November 21, 1977.

KAPANEN, Niko

Center. Shoots left. 5'9", 180 lbs. Born, Hattula, Finland, April 29, 1978.
(Dallas' 5th choice, 173rd overall, in 1998 Entry Draft).

Season	Club	Regular Season GP	G	A	Pts	PIM	Playoffs GP	G	A	Pts	PIM
2001-02	Dallas Stars	9	0	1	1	2	....	....	....	....	....
2002-03	Dallas Stars	82	5	29	34	44	12	4	3	7	12
	NHL Totals	**91**	**5**	**30**	**35**	**46**	**12**	**4**	**3**	**7**	**12**

KAPANEN, Sami

Right wing. Shoots left. 5'10", 195 lbs. Born, Vantaa, Finland, June 14, 1973.
(Hartford's 4th choice, 87th overall, in 1995 Entry Draft).

Season	Club	Regular Season GP	G	A	Pts	PIM	Playoffs GP	G	A	Pts	PIM
1995-96	Hartford Whalers	35	5	4	9	6	....	....	....	....	....
1996-97	Hartford Whalers	45	13	12	25	2	....	....	....	....	....
1997-98	Carolina Hurricanes	81	26	37	63	16	....	....	....	....	....
1998-99	Carolina Hurricanes	81	24	35	59	10	5	1	1	2	0
99-2000	Carolina Hurricanes	76	24	24	48	12	....	....	....	....	....
2000-01	Carolina Hurricanes	82	20	37	57	24	6	2	3	5	0
2001-02	Carolina Hurricanes	77	27	42	69	23	23	1	8	9	6
2002-03	Carolina Hurricanes	43	6	12	18	12	....	....	....	....	....
	Philadelphia Flyers	28	4	9	13	6	13	4	3	7	6
	NHL Totals	**548**	**149**	**212**	**361**	**111**	**47**	**8**	**15**	**23**	**12**

Played in NHL All-Star Game (2000, 2002)

Transferred to **Carolina** after **Hartford** franchise relocated, June 25, 1997. Traded to **Philadelphia** by **Carolina** with Ryan Bast for Pavel Brendl and Bruno St. Jacques, February 7, 2003.

KARABIN, Ladislav

Left wing. Shoots left. 6'1", 189 lbs. Born, Spisska Nova Ves, Czech., February 16, 1970.
(Pittsburgh's 11th choice, 173rd overall, in 1990 Entry Draft).

Season	Club	Regular Season GP	G	A	Pts	PIM	Playoffs GP	G	A	Pts	PIM
1993-94	Pittsburgh Penguins	9	0	0	0	2	....	....	....	....	....
	NHL Totals	**9**	**0**	**0**	**0**	**2**	....	....	....	....	....

Signed as a free agent by **Buffalo**, September 20, 1995.

KARALAHTI, Jere

Defense. Shoots right. 6'2", 210 lbs. Born, Helsinki, Finland, March 25, 1975.
(Los Angeles' 7th choice, 146th overall, in 1993 Entry Draft).

Season	Club	Regular Season GP	G	A	Pts	PIM	Playoffs GP	G	A	Pts	PIM
99-2000	Los Angeles Kings	48	6	10	16	18	4	0	1	1	2
2000-01	Los Angeles Kings	56	2	7	9	38	13	0	0	0	18
2001-02	Los Angeles Kings	30	0	1	1	29	....	....	....	....	....
	Nashville Predators	15	0	1	1	12	....	....	....	....	....
	NHL Totals	**149**	**8**	**19**	**27**	**97**	**17**	**0**	**1**	**1**	**20**

Traded to **Nashville** by **Los Angeles** with Los Angeles' 4th choice (Teemu Lassila) in 2003 Entry Draft for Cliff Ronning, March 16, 2002.

KARAMNOV, Vitali

Left wing. Shoots left. 6'2", 185 lbs. Born, Moscow, USSR, July 6, 1968.
(St. Louis' 2nd choice, 62nd overall, in 1992 Entry Draft).

Season	Club	Regular Season GP	G	A	Pts	PIM	Playoffs GP	G	A	Pts	PIM
1992-93	St. Louis Blues	7	0	1	1	0	....	....	....	....	....

		REGULAR SEASON					PLAYOFFS				
Season	Club	GP	G	A	Pts	PIM	GP	G	A	Pts	PIM
1993-94	St. Louis Blues	59	9	12	21	51	....	....	....	....	....
1994-95	St. Louis Blues	26	3	7	10	14	2	0	0	0	2
	NHL Totals	**92**	**12**	**20**	**32**	**65**	**2**	**0**	**0**	**0**	**2**

KARIYA, Paul

Left wing. Shoots left. 5'10", 176 lbs. Born, Vancouver, B.C., October 16, 1974.
(Anaheim's 1st choice, 4th overall, in 1993 Entry Draft).

Season	Club	GP	G	A	Pts	PIM	GP	G	A	Pts	PIM
1994-95	Mighty Ducks of Anaheim	47	18	21	39	4	....	....	....	....	....
1995-96	Mighty Ducks of Anaheim	82	50	58	108	20	....	....	....	....	....
1996-97	Mighty Ducks of Anaheim	69	44	55	99	6	11	7	6	13	4
1997-98	Mighty Ducks of Anaheim	22	17	14	31	23	....	....	....	....	....
1998-99	Mighty Ducks of Anaheim	82	39	62	101	40	3	1	3	4	0
99-2000	Mighty Ducks of Anaheim	74	42	44	86	24	....	....	....	....	....
2000-01	Mighty Ducks of Anaheim	66	33	34	67	20	....	....	....	....	....
2001-02	Mighty Ducks of Anaheim	82	32	25	57	28	....	....	....	....	....
2002-03	Mighty Ducks of Anaheim	82	25	56	81	48	21	6	6	12	6
	NHL Totals	**606**	**300**	**369**	**669**	**213**	**35**	**14**	**15**	**29**	**10**

• Brother of Steve • NHL All-Rookie Team (1995) • Lady Byng Trophy (1996, 1997) • NHL First All-Star Team (1996, 1997, 1999) • NHL Second All-Star Team (2000, 2003)

Played in NHL All-Star Game (1996, 1997, 1999, 2000, 2001, 2002, 2003)

• Missed majority of 1997-98 season after failing to come to contract terms with **Anaheim** and recovering from head injury suffered in game vs. San Jose, February 1, 1998. Signed as a free agent by **Colorado**, July 3, 2003.

KARIYA, Steve

Left wing. Shoots right. 5'8", 170 lbs. Born, North Vancouver, B.C., December 22, 1977.

Season	Club	GP	G	A	Pts	PIM	GP	G	A	Pts	PIM
99-2000	Vancouver Canucks	45	8	11	19	22	....	....	....	....	....
2000-01	Vancouver Canucks	17	1	6	7	8	....	....	....	....	....
2001-02	Vancouver Canucks	3	0	1	1	2	....	....	....	....	....
	NHL Totals	**65**	**9**	**18**	**27**	**32**	....	....	....	....	....

• Brother of Paul

Signed as a free agent by **Vancouver**, April 21, 1999. Traded to **New Jersey** by **Vancouver** for Mikko Jokela, January 24, 2003.

KARJALAINEN, Kyosti

Right wing. Shoots right. 6'2", 190 lbs. Born, Gavle, Sweden, June 19, 1967.
(Los Angeles' 6th choice, 132nd overall, in 1987 Entry Draft).

Season	Club	GP	G	A	Pts	PIM	GP	G	A	Pts	PIM
1991-92	Los Angeles Kings	28	1	8	9	12	3	0	1	1	2
	NHL Totals	**28**	**1**	**8**	**9**	**12**	**3**	**0**	**1**	**1**	**2**

KARLANDER, Al

Center. Shoots left. 5'8", 170 lbs. Born, Lac La H'ache, B.C., November 5, 1946.
(Detroit's 2nd choice, 17th overall, in 1967 Amateur Draft).

Season	Club	GP	G	A	Pts	PIM	GP	G	A	Pts	PIM
1969-70	Detroit Red Wings	41	5	10	15	6	4	0	1	1	0
1970-71	Detroit Red Wings	23	1	4	5	10	....	....	....	....	....
1971-72	Detroit Red Wings	71	15	20	35	29	....	....	....	....	....
1972-73	Detroit Red Wings	77	15	22	37	25	....	....	....	....	....
	NHL Totals	**212**	**36**	**56**	**92**	**70**	**4**	**0**	**1**	**1**	**0**

KARLSSON, Andreas

Center. Shoots left. 6'4", 205 lbs. Born, Ludvika, Sweden, August 19, 1975.
(Calgary's 8th choice, 148th overall, in 1993 Entry Draft).

Season	Club	GP	G	A	Pts	PIM	GP	G	A	Pts	PIM
99-2000	Atlanta Thrashers	51	5	9	14	14	....	....	....	....	....
2000-01	Atlanta Thrashers	60	5	11	16	16	....	....	....	....	....
2001-02	Atlanta Thrashers	42	1	7	8	20	....	....	....	....	....
	NHL Totals	**153**	**11**	**27**	**38**	**50**	....	....	....	....	....

Traded to **Atlanta** by **Calgary** for future considerations, June 25, 1999.

KARPA, Dave

Defense. Shoots right. 6'1", 210 lbs. Born, Regina, Sask., May 7, 1971.
(Quebec's 4th choice, 68th overall, in 1991 Entry Draft).

Season	Club	GP	G	A	Pts	PIM	GP	G	A	Pts	PIM
1991-92	Quebec Nordiques	4	0	0	0	14	....	....	....	....	....
1992-93	Quebec Nordiques	12	0	1	1	13	3	0	0	0	0
1993-94	Quebec Nordiques	60	5	12	17	148	....	....	....	....	....
1994-95	Quebec Nordiques	2	0	0	0	0	....	....	....	....	....
	Mighty Ducks of Anaheim	26	1	5	6	91	....	....	....	....	....
1995-96	Mighty Ducks of Anaheim	72	3	16	19	270	....	....	....	....	....
1996-97	Mighty Ducks of Anaheim	69	2	11	13	210	8	1	1	2	20
1997-98	Mighty Ducks of Anaheim	78	1	11	12	217	....	....	....	....	....
1998-99	Carolina Hurricanes	33	0	2	2	55	2	0	0	0	2
99-2000	Carolina Hurricanes	27	1	4	5	52	....	....	....	....	....
2000-01	Carolina Hurricanes	80	4	6	10	159	6	0	0	0	17
2001-02	New York Rangers	75	1	10	11	131	....	....	....	....	....
2002-03	New York Rangers	19	0	2	2	14	....	....	....	....	....
	NHL Totals	**557**	**18**	**80**	**98**	**1374**	**19**	**1**	**1**	**2**	**39**

Traded to **Anaheim** by **Quebec** for Anaheim's 4th round choice (later traded to St. Louis – St. Louis selected Jan Horacek) in 1997 Entry Draft, March 9, 1995. Traded to **Carolina** by **Anaheim** with Anaheim's 4th round choice (later traded to Atlanta – Atlanta selected Blake Robson) in 2000 Entry Draft for Stu Grimson and Kevin Haller, August 11, 1998. Signed as a free agent by **NY Rangers**, July 1, 2001.

KARPOV, Valeri

Right wing. Shoots left. 5'10", 176 lbs. Born, Chelyabinsk, USSR, August 5, 1971.
(Anaheim's 3rd choice, 56th overall, in 1993 Entry Draft).

Season	Club	GP	G	A	Pts	PIM	GP	G	A	Pts	PIM
1994-95	Mighty Ducks of Anaheim	30	4	7	11	6	....	....	....	....	....
1995-96	Mighty Ducks of Anaheim	37	9	8	17	10	....	....	....	....	....
1996-97	Mighty Ducks of Anaheim	9	1	0	1	16	....	....	....	....	....
	NHL Totals	**76**	**14**	**15**	**29**	**32**	....	....	....	....	....

Signed as a free agent by **Calgary**, September 3, 1997.

KARPOVTSEV, Alexander

Defense. Shoots right. 6'3", 215 lbs. Born, Moscow, USSR, April 7, 1970.
(Quebec's 7th choice, 158th overall, in 1990 Entry Draft).

Season	Club	GP	G	A	Pts	PIM	GP	G	A	Pts	PIM
1993-94 ◆	New York Rangers	67	3	15	18	58	17	0	4	4	12
1994-95	New York Rangers	47	4	8	12	30	8	1	0	1	0
1995-96	New York Rangers	40	2	16	18	26	6	0	1	1	4
1996-97	New York Rangers	77	9	29	38	59	13	1	3	4	20
1997-98	New York Rangers	47	3	7	10	38	....	....	....	....	....
1998-99	New York Rangers	2	1	0	1	0	....	....	....	....	....
	Toronto Maple Leafs	56	2	25	27	52	14	1	3	4	12
99-2000	Toronto Maple Leafs	69	3	14	17	54	11	0	3	3	4
2000-01	Chicago Blackhawks	53	2	13	15	39	....	....	....	....	....
2001-02	Chicago Blackhawks	65	1	9	10	40	5	1	0	1	0
2002-03	Chicago Blackhawks	40	4	10	14	12	....	....	....	....	....
	NHL Totals	**563**	**34**	**146**	**180**	**408**	**74**	**4**	**14**	**18**	**52**

Traded to **NY Rangers** by **Quebec** for Mike Hurlbut, September 7, 1993. Traded to **Toronto** by **NY Rangers** with NY Rangers' 4th round choice (Mirko Murovic) in 1999 Entry Draft for Mathieu Schneider, October 14, 1998. Traded to **Chicago** by **Toronto** with Toronto's 4th round choice (Vladimir Gusev) in 2001 Entry Draft for Bryan McCabe, October 2, 2000.

KASATONOV, Alexei

Defense. Shoots left. 6'1", 215 lbs. Born, Leningrad, USSR, October 14, 1959.
(New Jersey's 10th choice, 234th overall, in 1983 Entry Draft).

Season	Club	GP	G	A	Pts	PIM	GP	G	A	Pts	PIM
1989-90	New Jersey Devils	39	6	15	21	16	6	0	3	3	14
1990-91	New Jersey Devils	78	10	31	41	76	7	1	3	4	10
1991-92	New Jersey Devils	76	12	28	40	70	7	1	1	2	12
1992-93	New Jersey Devils	64	3	14	17	57	4	0	0	0	0
1993-94	Mighty Ducks of Anaheim	55	4	18	22	43	....	....	....	....	....
	St. Louis Blues	8	0	2	2	19	4	2	0	2	2
1994-95	Boston Bruins	44	2	14	16	33	5	0	0	0	2
1995-96	Boston Bruins	19	1	0	1	12	....	....	....	....	....
	NHL Totals	**383**	**38**	**122**	**160**	**326**	**33**	**4**	**7**	**11**	**40**

Played in NHL All-Star Game (1994)

Claimed by **Anaheim** from **New Jersey** in Expansion Draft, June 24, 1993. Traded to **St. Louis** by **Anaheim** for the rights to Maxim Bets and St. Louis' 6th round choice (later traded back to St. Louis – St. Louis selected Denis Hamel) in 1995 Entry Draft, March 21, 1994. Signed as a free agent by **Boston**, June 22, 1994.

KASPARAITIS, Darius

Defense. Shoots left. 5'11", 212 lbs. Born, Elektrenai, USSR, October 16, 1972.
(NY Islanders' 1st choice, 5th overall, in 1992 Entry Draft).

Season	Club	GP	G	A	Pts	PIM	GP	G	A	Pts	PIM
1992-93	New York Islanders	79	4	17	21	166	18	0	5	5	31
1993-94	New York Islanders	76	1	10	11	142	4	0	0	0	8
1994-95	New York Islanders	13	0	1	1	22	....	....	....	....	....
1995-96	New York Islanders	46	1	7	8	93	....	....	....	....	....
1996-97	New York Islanders	18	0	5	5	16	....	....	....	....	....
	Pittsburgh Penguins	57	2	16	18	84	5	0	0	0	6
1997-98	Pittsburgh Penguins	81	4	8	12	127	5	0	0	0	8
1998-99	Pittsburgh Penguins	48	1	4	5	70	....	....	....	....	....
99-2000	Pittsburgh Penguins	73	3	12	15	146	11	1	1	2	10
2000-01	Pittsburgh Penguins	77	3	16	19	111	17	1	1	2	26
2001-02	Pittsburgh Penguins	69	2	12	14	123	....	....	....	....	....
	Colorado Avalanche	11	0	0	0	19	21	0	3	3	18
2002-03	New York Rangers	80	3	11	14	85	....	....	....	....	....
	NHL Totals	**728**	**24**	**119**	**143**	**1204**	**81**	**2**	**10**	**12**	**107**

Traded to **Pittsburgh** by **NY Islanders** with Andreas Johansson for Bryan Smolinski, November 17, 1996. Traded to **Colorado** by **Pittsburgh** for Ville Niemenen and Rick Berry, March 19, 2002. Signed as a free agent by **NY Rangers**, July 2, 2002.

KASPER, Steve

Center. Shoots left. 5'8", 175 lbs. Born, Montreal, Que., September 28, 1961.
(Boston's 3rd choice, 81st overall, in 1980 Entry Draft).

Season	Club	GP	G	A	Pts	PIM	GP	G	A	Pts	PIM
1980-81	Boston Bruins	76	21	35	56	94	3	0	1	1	0
1981-82	Boston Bruins	73	20	31	51	72	11	3	6	9	22
1982-83	Boston Bruins	24	2	6	8	24	12	2	1	3	10
1983-84	Boston Bruins	27	3	11	14	19	3	0	0	0	7
1984-85	Boston Bruins	77	16	24	40	33	5	1	0	1	9
1985-86	Boston Bruins	80	17	23	40	73	3	1	0	1	4
1986-87	Boston Bruins	79	20	30	50	51	3	0	2	2	0
1987-88	Boston Bruins	79	26	44	70	35	23	7	6	13	10
1988-89	Boston Bruins	49	10	16	26	49	....	....	....	....	....
	Los Angeles Kings	29	9	15	24	14	11	1	5	6	10
1989-90	Los Angeles Kings	77	17	28	45	27	10	1	1	2	2
1990-91	Los Angeles Kings	67	9	19	28	33	10	4	6	10	8
1991-92	Philadelphia Flyers	16	3	2	5	10	....	....	....	....	....

Season	Club	GP	G	A	Pts	PIM	GP	G	A	Pts	PIM
		REGULAR SEASON					PLAYOFFS				
1992-93	Philadelphia Flyers	21	1	3	4	2	....	....	....	....	....
	Tampa Bay Lightning	47	3	4	7	18	....	....	....	....	....
	NHL Totals	**821**	**177**	**291**	**468**	**554**	**94**	**20**	**28**	**48**	**82**

Frank J. Selke Trophy (1982)

Traded to **Los Angeles** by **Boston** for Bob Carpenter to complete transaction that sent Jay Miller to Los Angeles (January 22, 1989), January 23, 1989. Traded to **Philadelphia** by **Los Angeles** with Steve Duchesne and Los Angeles' 4th round choice (Aris Brimanis) in 1991 Entry Draft for Jari Kurri and Jeff Chychrun, May 30, 1991. • Missed remainder of 1991-92 season recovering from knee injury suffered in game vs. Pittsburgh, November 20, 1991. Traded to **Tampa Bay** by **Philadelphia** for Dan Vincelette, December 8, 1992.

KASTELIC, Ed

Wing. Shoots right. 6'4", 215 lbs. Born, Toronto, Ont., January 29, 1964.
(Washington's 4th choice, 110th overall, in 1982 Entry Draft).

Season	Club	GP	G	A	Pts	PIM	GP	G	A	Pts	PIM
1985-86	Washington Capitals	15	0	0	0	73	....	....	....	....	....
1986-87	Washington Capitals	23	1	1	2	83	5	1	0	1	13
1987-88	Washington Capitals	35	1	0	1	78	1	0	0	0	19
1988-89	Hartford Whalers	10	0	2	2	15	....	....	....	....	....
1989-90	Hartford Whalers	67	6	2	8	198	2	0	0	0	0
1990-91	Hartford Whalers	45	2	2	4	211	....	....	....	....	....
1991-92	Hartford Whalers	25	1	3	4	61	....	....	....	....	....
	NHL Totals	**220**	**11**	**10**	**21**	**719**	**8**	**1**	**0**	**1**	**32**

Traded to **Hartford** by **Washington** with Grant Jennings for Mike Millar and Neil Sheehy, July 6, 1988.

KASZYCKI, Mike

Center. Shoots left. 5'9", 190 lbs. Born, Milton, Ont., February 27, 1956.
(NY Islanders' 2nd choice, 32nd overall, in 1976 Amateur Draft).

Season	Club	GP	G	A	Pts	PIM	GP	G	A	Pts	PIM
1977-78	New York Islanders	58	13	29	42	24	7	1	3	4	4
1978-79	New York Islanders	71	16	18	34	37	10	1	3	4	4
1979-80	New York Islanders	16	1	4	5	15	....	....	....	....	....
	Washington Capitals	28	7	10	17	10	....	....	....	....	....
	Toronto Maple Leafs	25	4	4	8	10	2	0	0	0	2
1980-81	Toronto Maple Leafs	6	0	2	2	2	....	....	....	....	....
1982-83	Toronto Maple Leafs	22	1	13	14	10	....	....	....	....	....
	NHL Totals	**226**	**42**	**80**	**122**	**108**	**19**	**2**	**6**	**8**	**10**

Traded to **Washington** by **NY Islanders** for Gord Lane, December 7, 1979. Traded to **Toronto** by **Washington** for Pat Ribble, February 16, 1980.

KAVANAGH, Pat

Right wing. Shoots right. 6'3", 192 lbs. Born, Ottawa, Ont., March 14, 1979.
(Philadelphia's 2nd choice, 50th overall, in 1997 Entry Draft).

Season	Club	GP	G	A	Pts	PIM	GP	G	A	Pts	PIM
2000-01	Vancouver Canucks	....	....	....	....	....	3	0	0	0	2
2002-03	Vancouver Canucks	3	1	0	1	2	....	....	....	....	....
	NHL Totals	**3**	**1**	**0**	**1**	**2**	**3**	**0**	**0**	**0**	**2**

Traded to **Vancouver** by **Philadelphia** for Vancouver's 6th round choice (Konstantin Rudenko) in 1999 Entry Draft, June 1, 1999.

KEA, Ed

Defense. Shoots left. 6'3", 200 lbs. Born, Weesp, Holland, January 19, 1948.

Season	Club	GP	G	A	Pts	PIM	GP	G	A	Pts	PIM
1973-74	Atlanta Flames	3	0	2	2	0	....	....	....	....	....
1974-75	Atlanta Flames	50	1	9	10	39	....	....	....	....	....
1975-76	Atlanta Flames	78	8	19	27	101	2	0	0	0	7
1976-77	Atlanta Flames	72	4	21	25	63	3	0	1	1	2
1977-78	Atlanta Flames	60	3	23	26	40	1	0	0	0	0
1978-79	Atlanta Flames	53	6	18	24	40	2	0	0	0	0
1979-80	St. Louis Blues	69	3	16	19	79	3	0	0	0	2
1980-81	St. Louis Blues	74	3	18	21	60	11	1	2	3	12
1981-82	St. Louis Blues	78	2	14	16	62	10	1	1	2	16
1982-83	St. Louis Blues	46	0	5	5	24	....	....	....	....	....
	NHL Totals	**583**	**30**	**145**	**175**	**508**	**32**	**2**	**4**	**6**	**39**

Signed as a free agent by **Atlanta**, October 6, 1972. Traded to **St. Louis** by **Atlanta** with Don Laurence and Atlanta's 2nd round choice (Hakan Nordin) in 1981 Entry Draft for Garry Unger, October 10, 1979.

KEANE, Mike

Right wing. Shoots right. 5'10", 185 lbs. Born, Winnipeg, Man., May 29, 1967.

Season	Club	GP	G	A	Pts	PIM	GP	G	A	Pts	PIM
1988-89	Montreal Canadiens	69	16	19	35	69	21	4	3	7	17
1989-90	Montreal Canadiens	74	9	15	24	78	11	0	1	1	8
1990-91	Montreal Canadiens	73	13	23	36	50	12	3	2	5	6
1991-92	Montreal Canadiens	67	11	30	41	64	8	1	1	2	16
1992-93 ♦	Montreal Canadiens	77	15	45	60	95	19	2	13	15	6
1993-94	Montreal Canadiens	80	16	30	46	119	6	3	1	4	4
1994-95	Montreal Canadiens	48	10	10	20	15	....	....	....	....	....
1995-96	Montreal Canadiens	18	0	7	7	6	....	....	....	....	....
♦	Colorado Avalanche	55	10	10	20	40	22	3	2	5	16
1996-97	Colorado Avalanche	81	10	17	27	63	17	3	1	4	24
1997-98	New York Rangers	70	8	10	18	47	....	....	....	....	....
	Dallas Stars	13	2	3	5	5	17	4	4	8	0
1998-99 ♦	Dallas Stars	81	6	23	29	62	23	5	2	7	6
99-2000	Dallas Stars	81	13	21	34	41	23	2	4	6	14
2000-01	Dallas Stars	67	10	14	24	35	10	3	2	5	4
2001-02	St. Louis Blues	56	4	6	10	22	....	....	....	....	....
	Colorado Avalanche	22	2	5	7	16	18	1	4	5	8
2002-03	Colorado Avalanche	65	5	5	10	34	6	0	0	0	2
	NHL Totals	**1097**	**160**	**293**	**453**	**861**	**213**	**34**	**40**	**74**	**131**

Signed as a free agent by **Montreal**, September 25, 1985. Traded to **Colorado** by **Montreal** with Patrick Roy for Andrei Kovalenko, Martin Rucinsky and Jocelyn Thibault, December 6, 1995. Signed as a free agent by **NY Rangers**, July 30, 1997. Traded to **Dallas** by **NY Rangers** with Brian Skrudland and NY Rangers' 6th round choice (Pavel Patera) in 1998 Entry Draft for Todd Harvey, Bob Errey and Dallas' 4th round choice (Boyd Kane) in 1998 Entry Draft, March 24, 1998. Signed as a free agent by **St. Louis**, July 10, 2001. Traded to **Colorado** by **St. Louis** for Shjon Podein, February 11, 2002.

KEARNS, Dennis

Defense. Shoots left. 5'9", 185 lbs. Born, Kingston, Ont., September 27, 1945.

Season	Club	GP	G	A	Pts	PIM	GP	G	A	Pts	PIM
1971-72	Vancouver Canucks	73	3	26	29	59	....	....	....	....	....
1972-73	Vancouver Canucks	72	4	33	37	51	....	....	....	....	....
1973-74	Vancouver Canucks	52	4	13	17	30	....	....	....	....	....
1974-75	Vancouver Canucks	49	1	11	12	31	4	0	0	0	4
1975-76	Vancouver Canucks	80	5	46	51	48	2	0	1	1	0
1976-77	Vancouver Canucks	80	5	55	60	60	....	....	....	....	....
1977-78	Vancouver Canucks	80	4	43	47	27	....	....	....	....	....
1978-79	Vancouver Canucks	78	3	31	34	28	3	1	1	2	2
1979-80	Vancouver Canucks	67	1	18	19	24	2	0	0	0	2
1980-81	Vancouver Canucks	46	1	14	15	28	....	....	....	....	....
	NHL Totals	**677**	**31**	**290**	**321**	**386**	**11**	**1**	**2**	**3**	**8**

Traded to **Chicago** (Dallas-CHL) by **Portland** (WHL) for cash, August, 1970. Claimed by **Vancouver** from **Chicago** in Intra-League Draft, June 8, 1971.

KEATING, Jack

Left wing. Shoots left. 6', 180 lbs. Born, Kitchener, Ont., October 9, 1916.

Season	Club	GP	G	A	Pts	PIM	GP	G	A	Pts	PIM
1938-39	Detroit Red Wings	1	1	0	1	2	....	....	....	....	....
1939-40	Detroit Red Wings	10	2	0	2	2	....	....	....	....	....
	NHL Totals	**11**	**3**	**0**	**3**	**4**	....	....	....	....	....

KEATING, John

Left wing. Shoots left. 5'7", 145 lbs. Born, St. John, N.B., February 12, 1908.

Season	Club	GP	G	A	Pts	PIM	GP	G	A	Pts	PIM
1931-32	New York Americans	22	5	3	8	6	....	....	....	....	....
1932-33	New York Americans	13	0	2	2	11	....	....	....	....	....
	NHL Totals	**35**	**5**	**5**	**10**	**17**	....	....	....	....	....

Signed as a free agent by **NY Americans**, October 22, 1930. Traded to **Providence** (Can-Am) by **NY Americans** for cash, November 13, 1934.

KEATING, Mike

Left wing. Shoots left. 6', 185 lbs. Born, Toronto, Ont., January 21, 1957.
(NY Rangers' 3rd choice, 26th overall, in 1977 Amateur Draft).

Season	Club	GP	G	A	Pts	PIM	GP	G	A	Pts	PIM
1977-78	New York Rangers	1	0	0	0	0	....	....	....	....	....
	NHL Totals	**1**	**0**	**0**	**0**	**0**	....	....	....	....	....

KEATS, Duke

HHOF

Center. Shoots right. 5'11", 195 lbs. Born, Montreal, Que., March 21, 1895.

Season	Club	GP	G	A	Pts	PIM	GP	G	A	Pts	PIM
1926-27	Boston Bruins	17	4	7	11	20	....	....	....	....	....
	Detroit Cougars	25	12	1	13	32	....	....	....	....	....
1927-28	Detroit Cougars	5	0	2	2	6	....	....	....	....	....
	Chicago Black Hawks	32	14	8	22	55	....	....	....	....	....
1928-29	Chicago Black Hawks	3	0	1	1	0	....	....	....	....	....
	NHL Totals	**82**	**30**	**19**	**49**	**113**	....	....	....	....	....

Signed as a free agent by **Toronto**, December 9, 1919. Traded to **Boston** by **Edmonton** (WHL) for cash, September 4, 1926. Traded to **Detroit** by **Boston** with Archie Briden for Frank Fredrickson and Harry Meeking, January 7, 1927. Traded to **Chicago** by **Detroit** for Gord Fraser and $5,000, December 16, 1927. Traded to **Tulsa** (AHA) by **Chicago** for cash, November, 1928.

KECZMER, Dan

Defense. Shoots left. 6'1", 190 lbs. Born, Mt. Clemens, MI, May 25, 1968.
(Minnesota's 11th choice, 201st overall, in 1986 Entry Draft).

Season	Club	GP	G	A	Pts	PIM	GP	G	A	Pts	PIM
1990-91	Minnesota North Stars	9	0	1	1	6	....	....	....	....	....
1991-92	Hartford Whalers	1	0	0	0	0	....	....	....	....	....
1992-93	Hartford Whalers	23	4	4	8	28	....	....	....	....	....
1993-94	Hartford Whalers	12	0	1	1	12	....	....	....	....	....
	Calgary Flames	57	1	20	21	48	3	0	0	0	4
1994-95	Calgary Flames	28	2	3	5	10	7	0	1	1	2
1995-96	Calgary Flames	13	0	0	0	14	....	....	....	....	....
1996-97	Dallas Stars	13	0	1	1	6	....	....	....	....	....
1997-98	Dallas Stars	17	1	2	3	26	2	0	0	0	2
1998-99	Dallas Stars	22	0	1	1	22	....	....	....	....	....
	Nashville Predators	16	0	0	0	12	....	....	....	....	....
99-2000	Nashville Predators	24	0	5	5	28	....	....	....	....	....
	NHL Totals	**235**	**8**	**38**	**46**	**212**	**12**	**0**	**1**	**1**	**8**

Claimed by **San Jose** from **Minnesota** in Dispersal Draft, May 30, 1991. Traded to **Hartford** by **San Jose** for Dean Evason, October 2, 1991. Traded to **Calgary** by **Hartford** for Jeff Reese, November 19, 1993. Traded to **New Jersey** by **Calgary** with Phil Housley for Tommy Albelin, Cale Hulse and Jocelyn Lemieux, February 26, 1996. Signed as a free agent by **Dallas**, August 19, 1996. Claimed on waivers by **Nashville** from **Dallas**, March 12, 1999. Traded to **St. Louis** by **Nashville** for Rory Fitzpatrick, February 9, 2000.

KEEFE, Sheldon

Right wing. Shoots right. 5'11", 185 lbs. Born, Brampton, Ont., September 17, 1980.
(Tampa Bay's 1st choice, 47th overall, in 1999 Entry Draft).

Season	Club	GP	G	A	Pts	PIM	GP	G	A	Pts	PIM
2000-01	Tampa Bay Lightning	49	4	0	4	38	....	....	....	....	....

Season	Club	GP	G	A	Pts	PIM	GP	G	A	Pts	PIM
		REGULAR SEASON					PLAYOFFS				
2001-02	Tampa Bay Lightning	39	6	7	13	16	....	....	....	....	....
2002-03	Tampa Bay Lightning	37	2	5	7	24	....	....	....	....	....
	NHL Totals	**125**	**12**	**12**	**24**	**78**	....	....	....	....	....

KEELING, Butch

Left wing. Shoots left. 5'11", 180 lbs. Born, Owen Sound, Ont., August 10, 1905.

Season	Club	GP	G	A	Pts	PIM	GP	G	A	Pts	PIM
1926-27	Toronto St. Pats/Maple Leafs	30	11	2	13	29	....	....	....	....	....
1927-28	Toronto Maple Leafs	43	10	6	16	52	....	....	....	....	....
1928-29	New York Rangers	43	6	3	9	35	6	*3	0	*3	2
1929-30	New York Rangers	43	19	7	26	34	4	0	3	3	8
1930-31	New York Rangers	44	13	9	22	35	4	1	1	2	0
1931-32	New York Rangers	48	17	3	20	38	7	2	1	3	12
1932-33◆	New York Rangers	47	8	6	14	22	8	0	2	2	8
1933-34	New York Rangers	48	15	5	20	20	2	0	0	0	0
1934-35	New York Rangers	47	15	4	19	14	4	2	1	3	0
1935-36	New York Rangers	46	13	5	18	22	....	....	....	....	....
1936-37	New York Rangers	48	22	4	26	18	9	3	2	5	2
1937-38	New York Rangers	38	8	9	17	12	3	0	1	1	2
	NHL Totals	**525**	**157**	**63**	**220**	**331**	**47**	**11**	**11**	**22**	**34**

Signed as a free agent by **Toronto**, September 7, 1926. Traded to **NY Rangers** by **Toronto** for Alex Gray, April 16, 1928.

KEENAN, Larry

Left wing. Shoots left. 5'11", 175 lbs. Born, North Bay, Ont., October 1, 1940.

Season	Club	GP	G	A	Pts	PIM	GP	G	A	Pts	PIM
1961-62	Toronto Maple Leafs	2	0	0	0	0	....	....	....	....	....
1967-68	St. Louis Blues	40	12	8	20	4	18	4	5	9	4
1968-69	St. Louis Blues	46	5	9	14	6	12	4	5	9	8
1969-70	St. Louis Blues	56	10	23	33	8	16	7	6	13	0
1970-71	St. Louis Blues	10	1	3	4	0	....	....	....	....	....
	Buffalo Sabres	51	7	20	27	6	....	....	....	....	....
1971-72	Buffalo Sabres	14	2	0	2	2	....	....	....	....	....
	Philadelphia Flyers	14	1	1	2	2	....	....	....	....	....
	NHL Totals	**233**	**38**	**64**	**102**	**28**	**46**	**15**	**16**	**31**	**12**

Claimed by **St. Louis** from **Toronto** in Expansion Draft, June 6, 1967. Traded to **Buffalo** by **St. Louis** with Jean-Guy Talbot for Bob Baun, November 4, 1970. Traded to **Philadelphia** by **Buffalo** for Larry Mickey, November 16, 1971.

KEHOE, Rick

Right wing. Shoots right. 5'11", 180 lbs. Born, Windsor, Ont., July 15, 1951.
(Toronto's 1st choice, 22nd overall, in 1971 Amateur Draft).

Season	Club	GP	G	A	Pts	PIM	GP	G	A	Pts	PIM
1971-72	Toronto Maple Leafs	38	8	8	16	4	2	0	0	0	2
1972-73	Toronto Maple Leafs	77	33	42	75	20	....	....	....	....	....
1973-74	Toronto Maple Leafs	69	18	22	40	8	....	....	....	....	....
1974-75	Pittsburgh Penguins	76	32	31	63	22	9	0	2	2	0
1975-76	Pittsburgh Penguins	71	29	47	76	6	3	0	0	0	0
1976-77	Pittsburgh Penguins	80	30	27	57	10	3	0	2	2	0
1977-78	Pittsburgh Penguins	70	29	21	50	10	....	....	....	....	....
1978-79	Pittsburgh Penguins	57	27	18	45	2	7	0	2	2	0
1979-80	Pittsburgh Penguins	79	30	30	60	4	5	2	5	7	0
1980-81	Pittsburgh Penguins	80	55	33	88	6	5	0	3	3	0
1981-82	Pittsburgh Penguins	71	33	52	85	8	5	2	3	5	2
1982-83	Pittsburgh Penguins	75	29	36	65	12	....	....	....	....	....
1983-84	Pittsburgh Penguins	57	18	27	45	8	....	....	....	....	....
1984-85	Pittsburgh Penguins	6	0	2	2	0	....	....	....	....	....
	NHL Totals	**906**	**371**	**396**	**767**	**120**	**39**	**4**	**17**	**21**	**4**

Lady Byng Trophy (1981)

Played in NHL All-Star Game (1981, 1983)

Traded to **Pittsburgh** by **Toronto** for Blaine Stoughton and Pittsburgh's 1st round choice (Trevor Johansen) in 1977 Entry Draft, September 13, 1974. • Suffered eventual career-ending neck injury in game vs. Quebec, February 13, 1984.

KEKALAINEN, Jarmo

Left wing. Shoots left. 6', 190 lbs. Born, Tampere, Finland, July 3, 1966.

Season	Club	GP	G	A	Pts	PIM	GP	G	A	Pts	PIM
1989-90	Boston Bruins	11	2	2	4	8	....	....	....	....	....
1990-91	Boston Bruins	16	2	1	3	6	....	....	....	....	....
1993-94	Ottawa Senators	28	1	5	6	14	....	....	....	....	....
	NHL Totals	**55**	**5**	**8**	**13**	**28**	....	....	....	....	....

Signed as a free agent by **Boston**, May 3, 1989. Signed as a free agent by **Ottawa**, August 13, 1993.

KELLEHER, Chris

Defense. Shoots left. 6'1", 210 lbs. Born, Cambridge, MA, March 23, 1975.
(Pittsburgh's 5th choice, 130th overall, in 1993 Entry Draft).

Season	Club	GP	G	A	Pts	PIM	GP	G	A	Pts	PIM
2001-02	Boston Bruins	1	0	0	0	0	....	....	....	....	....
	NHL Totals	**1**	**0**	**0**	**0**	**0**	....	....	....	....	....

Signed as a free agent by **Boston**, July 24, 2001.

KELLER, Ralph

Defense. Shoots right. 5'9", 174 lbs. Born, Wilkie, Sask., February 6, 1936.

Season	Club	GP	G	A	Pts	PIM	GP	G	A	Pts	PIM
1962-63	New York Rangers	3	1	0	1	6	....	....	....	....	....
	NHL Totals	**3**	**1**	**0**	**1**	**6**	....	....	....	....	....

Claimed by **Montreal** from **NY Rangers** (Baltimore-AHL) in Inter-League Draft, June 4, 1963. Traded to **Hershey** (AHL) by **Montreal** with the loan of Chuck Hamilton for Marc Reaume, June 11, 1963.

KELLGREN, Christer

Right wing. Shoots left. 6', 173 lbs. Born, Goteborg, Sweden, August 15, 1958.

Season	Club	GP	G	A	Pts	PIM	GP	G	A	Pts	PIM
1981-82	Colorado Rockies	5	0	0	0	0	....	....	....	....	....
	NHL Totals	**5**	**0**	**0**	**0**	**0**	....	....	....	....	....

Signed as a free agent by **Colorado**, May 11, 1981.

KELLY, Bob

Left wing. Shoots left. 5'10", 200 lbs. Born, Oakville, Ont., November 25, 1950.
(Philadelphia's 2nd choice, 32nd overall, in 1970 Amateur Draft).

Season	Club	GP	G	A	Pts	PIM	GP	G	A	Pts	PIM
1970-71	Philadelphia Flyers	76	14	18	32	70	4	1	0	1	2
1971-72	Philadelphia Flyers	78	14	15	29	157	....	....	....	....	....
1972-73	Philadelphia Flyers	77	10	11	21	238	11	0	1	1	8
1973-74◆	Philadelphia Flyers	65	4	10	14	130	5	0	0	0	11
1974-75◆	Philadelphia Flyers	67	11	18	29	99	16	3	3	6	15
1975-76	Philadelphia Flyers	79	12	8	20	125	16	0	2	2	44
1976-77	Philadelphia Flyers	73	22	24	46	117	10	0	1	1	18
1977-78	Philadelphia Flyers	74	19	13	32	95	12	3	5	8	26
1978-79	Philadelphia Flyers	77	7	31	38	132	8	1	1	2	10
1979-80	Philadelphia Flyers	75	15	20	35	122	19	1	1	2	38
1980-81	Washington Capitals	80	26	36	62	157	....	....	....	....	....
1981-82	Washington Capitals	16	0	4	4	12	....	....	....	....	....
	NHL Totals	**837**	**154**	**208**	**362**	**1454**	**101**	**9**	**14**	**23**	**172**

Traded to **Washington** by **Philadelphia** for Washington's 3rd round choice (Bill Campbell) in 1982 Entry Draft, August 21, 1980.

KELLY, Bob

Left wing. Shoots left. 6'2", 195 lbs. Born, Fort William, Ont., June 6, 1946.
(Toronto's 1st choice, 16th overall, in 1967 Amateur Draft).

Season	Club	GP	G	A	Pts	PIM	GP	G	A	Pts	PIM
1973-74	St. Louis Blues	37	9	8	17	45	....	....	....	....	....
	Pittsburgh Penguins	30	7	10	17	78	....	....	....	....	....
1974-75	Pittsburgh Penguins	69	27	24	51	120	9	5	3	8	17
1975-76	Pittsburgh Penguins	77	25	30	55	149	3	0	0	0	2
1976-77	Pittsburgh Penguins	74	10	21	31	115	3	1	0	1	4
1977-78	Chicago Black Hawks	75	7	11	18	95	4	0	0	0	8
1978-79	Chicago Black Hawks	63	2	5	7	85	4	0	0	0	9
	NHL Totals	**425**	**87**	**109**	**196**	**687**	**23**	**6**	**3**	**9**	**40**

Traded to **NY Rangers** by **Columbus** (IHL) for cash, October, 1970. Traded to **Rochester** (AHL) by **NY Rangers** for $7,500, October, 1972. Traded to **NY Rangers** by **Rochester** (AHL) for Bill Knibbs and $20,000, June, 1973. Traded to **St. Louis** by **NY Rangers** for Norm Dennis and Don Borgeson, September 8, 1973. Traded to **Pittsburgh** by **St. Louis** with Steve Durbano and Ab DeMarco Jr. for Bryan Watson, Greg Polis and Pittsburgh's 2nd round choice (Bob Hess) in 1974 Amateur Draft, January 17, 1974. Signed as a free agent by **Chicago**, August 17, 1977.

KELLY, Dave

Right wing. Shoots right. 6'2", 205 lbs. Born, Chatham, Ont., September 20, 1952.

Season	Club	GP	G	A	Pts	PIM	GP	G	A	Pts	PIM
1976-77	Detroit Red Wings	16	2	0	2	4	....	....	....	....	....
	NHL Totals	**16**	**2**	**0**	**2**	**4**	....	....	....	....	....

Signed as a free agent by **Philadelphia**, August 12, 1975. Traded to **Detroit** by **Philadelphia** with Terry Murray, Bob Ritchie and Steve Coates for Rick Lapointe and Mike Korney, February 17, 1977.

KELLY, John Paul

Left wing. Shoots left. 6'1", 215 lbs. Born, Edmonton, Alta., November 15, 1959.
(Los Angeles' 4th choice, 50th overall, in 1979 Entry Draft).

Season	Club	GP	G	A	Pts	PIM	GP	G	A	Pts	PIM
1979-80	Los Angeles Kings	40	2	5	7	28	3	0	0	0	2
1980-81	Los Angeles Kings	19	3	6	9	8	4	0	1	1	25
1981-82	Los Angeles Kings	70	12	11	23	100	10	1	0	1	14
1982-83	Los Angeles Kings	65	16	15	31	52	....	....	....	....	....
1983-84	Los Angeles Kings	72	7	14	21	73	....	....	....	....	....
1984-85	Los Angeles Kings	73	8	10	18	55	1	0	0	0	0
1985-86	Los Angeles Kings	61	6	9	15	50	....	....	....	....	....
	NHL Totals	**400**	**54**	**70**	**124**	**366**	**18**	**1**	**1**	**2**	**41**

KELLY, Pep

Right wing. Shoots right. 5'7", 152 lbs. Born, North Bay, Ont., January 17, 1914.

Season	Club	GP	G	A	Pts	PIM	GP	G	A	Pts	PIM
1934-35	Toronto Maple Leafs	47	11	8	19	14	7	2	0	2	4
1935-36	Toronto Maple Leafs	42	11	8	19	24	9	2	3	5	4
1936-37	Toronto Maple Leafs	16	2	0	2	8	....	....	....	....	....
	Chicago Black Hawks	29	13	4	17	0	....	....	....	....	....
1937-38	Toronto Maple Leafs	43	9	10	19	25	7	2	2	4	2
1938-39	Toronto Maple Leafs	48	11	11	22	12	9	1	0	1	0
1939-40	Toronto Maple Leafs	34	11	9	20	15	6	0	1	1	0
1940-41	Chicago Black Hawks	21	5	3	8	7	....	....	....	....	....
1941-42	Brooklyn Americans	8	1	0	1	0	....	....	....	....	....
	NHL Totals	**288**	**74**	**53**	**127**	**105**	**38**	**7**	**6**	**13**	**10**

Loaned to **Chicago** by **Toronto** for remainder of the 1936-37 season for the loan of Bill Kendall, December 29, 1936. Traded to **Chicago** by **Toronto** for cash, May 10, 1940. Traded to **Buffalo** (AHL) by **Chicago** for cash, October, 1941. Traded to **Brooklyn** by **Buffalo** (AHL) for cash, October 19, 1941.

KELLY, Pete

Right wing. Shoots right. 5'11", 170 lbs. Born, St. Vital, Man., May 22, 1913.

Season	Club	GP	G	A	Pts	PIM	GP	G	A	Pts	PIM
1934-35	St. Louis Eagles	25	3	10	13	14	....	....	....	....	....
1935-36◆	Detroit Red Wings	46	6	8	14	30	7	1	1	2	2

Season	Club	GP	G	A	Pts	PIM	GP	G	A	Pts	PIM
		REGULAR SEASON					PLAYOFFS				
1936-37 ◆	Detroit Red Wings	47	5	4	9	12	8	2	0	2	0
1937-38	Detroit Red Wings	9	0	1	1	2	....	....	....	....	....
1938-39	Detroit Red Wings	32	4	9	13	4	4	0	0	0	0
1940-41	New York Americans	11	3	5	8	2	....	....	....	....	....
1941-42	Brooklyn Americans	7	0	1	1	4	....	....	....	....	....
	NHL Totals	**177**	**21**	**38**	**59**	**68**	**19**	**3**	**1**	**4**	**2**

Signed as a free agent by **St. Louis**, November, 1934. Claimed by **NY Americans** from **St. Louis** in Dispersal Draft, October 15, 1935. Traded to **Detroit** by **NY Americans** for Carl Voss, October 16, 1935. Traded to **Pittsburgh** (AHL) by **Detroit** for cash, December 2, 1937. Traded to **NY Americans** (Springfield-AHL) by **Pittsburgh** (AHL) for Norm Schultz, December 31, 1940. • Team name changed to **Brooklyn Americans** prior to 1941-42 season.

KELLY, Red HHOF

Defense/Center. Shoots left. 5'11", 180 lbs. Born, Simcoe, Ont., July 9, 1927.

Season	Club	GP	G	A	Pts	PIM	GP	G	A	Pts	PIM
1947-48	Detroit Red Wings	60	6	14	20	13	10	3	2	5	2
1948-49	Detroit Red Wings	59	5	11	16	10	11	1	1	2	10
1949-50 ◆	Detroit Red Wings	70	15	25	40	9	14	1	3	4	2
1950-51	Detroit Red Wings	70	17	37	54	24	6	0	1	1	0
1951-52 ◆	Detroit Red Wings	67	16	31	47	16	5	1	0	1	0
1952-53	Detroit Red Wings	70	19	27	46	8	6	0	4	4	0
1953-54 ◆	Detroit Red Wings	62	16	33	49	18	12	5	1	6	0
1954-55 ◆	Detroit Red Wings	70	15	30	45	28	11	2	4	6	17
1955-56	Detroit Red Wings	70	16	34	50	39	10	2	4	6	2
1956-57	Detroit Red Wings	70	10	25	35	18	5	1	0	1	0
1957-58	Detroit Red Wings	61	13	18	31	26	4	0	1	1	2
1958-59	Detroit Red Wings	67	8	13	21	34	....	....	....	....	....
1959-60	Detroit Red Wings	50	6	12	18	10	....	....	....	....	....
	Toronto Maple Leafs	18	6	5	11	8	10	3	8	11	2
1960-61	Toronto Maple Leafs	64	20	50	70	12	2	1	0	1	0
1961-62 ◆	Toronto Maple Leafs	58	22	27	49	6	12	4	6	10	0
1962-63 ◆	Toronto Maple Leafs	66	20	40	60	8	10	2	6	8	6
1963-64 ◆	Toronto Maple Leafs	70	11	34	45	16	14	4	9	13	4
1964-65	Toronto Maple Leafs	70	18	28	46	8	6	3	2	5	2
1965-66	Toronto Maple Leafs	63	8	24	32	12	4	0	2	2	0
1966-67 ◆	Toronto Maple Leafs	61	14	24	38	4	12	0	5	5	2
	NHL Totals	**1316**	**281**	**542**	**823**	**327**	**164**	**33**	**59**	**92**	**51**

NHL Second All-Star Team (1950, 1956) • NHL First All-Star Team (1951, 1952, 1953, 1954, 1955, 1957) • Lady Byng Trophy (1951, 1953, 1954, 1961) • James Norris Trophy (1954)

Played in NHL All-Star Game (1950, 1951, 1952, 1953, 1954, 1955, 1956, 1957, 1958, 1960, 1961, 1962, 1963)

Traded to **NY Rangers** by **Detroit** with Billy McNeill for Bill Gadsby and Eddie Shack, February 5, 1960. • Kelly and McNeill refused to report and transaction was cancelled, February 7, 1960. Traded to **Toronto** by **Detroit** for Marc Reaume, February 10, 1960. Rights traded to **Los Angeles** by **Toronto** for Ken Block, June 8, 1967.

KELLY, Steve

Center. Shoots left. 6'2", 210 lbs. Born, Vancouver, B.C., October 26, 1976.
(Edmonton's 1st choice, 6th overall, in 1995 Entry Draft).

Season	Club	GP	G	A	Pts	PIM	GP	G	A	Pts	PIM
1996-97	Edmonton Oilers	8	1	0	1	6	6	0	0	0	2
1997-98	Edmonton Oilers	19	0	2	2	8	....	....	....	....	....
	Tampa Bay Lightning	24	2	1	3	15	....	....	....	....	....
1998-99	Tampa Bay Lightning	34	1	3	4	27	....	....	....	....	....
99-2000 ◆	New Jersey Devils	1	0	0	0	0	10	0	0	0	4
2000-01	New Jersey Devils	24	2	2	4	21	....	....	....	....	....
	Los Angeles Kings	11	1	0	1	4	8	0	0	0	2
2001-02	Los Angeles Kings	8	0	1	1	2	1	0	0	0	0
2002-03	Los Angeles Kings	15	2	3	5	0	....	....	....	....	....
	NHL Totals	**144**	**9**	**12**	**21**	**83**	**25**	**0**	**0**	**0**	**8**

Traded to **Tampa Bay** by **Edmonton** with Bryan Marchment and Jason Bonsignore for Roman Hamrlik and Paul Comrie, December 30, 1997. Traded to **New Jersey** by **Tampa Bay** for New Jersey's 7th round choice (Brian Eklund) in 2000 Entry Draft, October 7, 1999. Traded to **Los Angeles** by **New Jersey** to complete transaction that sent Bob Corkum to New Jersey (February 23, 2001), February 27, 2001. • Healthy scratch for majority of 2000-01 season.

KEMP, Kevin

Defense. Shoots left. 6', 188 lbs. Born, Ottawa, Ont., May 3, 1954.
(Toronto's 8th choice, 138th overall, in 1974 Amateur Draft).

Season	Club	GP	G	A	Pts	PIM	GP	G	A	Pts	PIM
1980-81	Hartford Whalers	3	0	0	0	4	....	....	....	....	....
	NHL Totals	**3**	**0**	**0**	**0**	**4**	....	....	....	....	....

Claimed by **Hartford** from **Toronto** in Expansion Draft, June 13, 1979.

KEMP, Stan

Defense. Shoots right. 5'9", 165 lbs. Born, Hamilton, Ont., March 2, 1924.

Season	Club	GP	G	A	Pts	PIM	GP	G	A	Pts	PIM
1948-49	Toronto Maple Leafs	1	0	0	0	2	....	....	....	....	....
	NHL Totals	**1**	**0**	**0**	**0**	**2**	....	....	....	....	....

KENADY, Chris

Right wing. Shoots right. 6'2", 195 lbs. Born, Mound, MN, April 10, 1973.
(St. Louis' 8th choice, 175th overall, in 1991 Entry Draft).

Season	Club	GP	G	A	Pts	PIM	GP	G	A	Pts	PIM
1997-98	St. Louis Blues	5	0	2	2	0	....	....	....	....	....
99-2000	New York Rangers	2	0	0	0	0	....	....	....	....	....
	NHL Totals	**7**	**0**	**2**	**2**	**0**	....	....	....	....	....

Traded to **NY Rangers** by **St. Louis** to complete transaction that sent Jeff Finley and Geoff Smith to St. Louis (February 13, 1999), February 22, 1999.

KENDALL, Bill

Right wing. Shoots right. 5'8", 168 lbs. Born, Winnipeg, Man., April 1, 1910.

Season	Club	GP	G	A	Pts	PIM	GP	G	A	Pts	PIM
1933-34 ◆	Chicago Black Hawks	21	3	0	3	0	2	0	0	0	0
1934-35	Chicago Black Hawks	47	6	4	10	16	2	0	0	0	0
1935-36	Chicago Black Hawks	22	2	1	3	0	2	0	0	0	0
1936-37	Chicago Black Hawks	17	3	0	3	6	....	....	....	....	....
	Toronto Maple Leafs	15	2	4	6	4	....	....	....	....	....
1937-38	Chicago Black Hawks	9	0	1	1	2	....	....	....	....	....
	NHL Totals	**131**	**16**	**10**	**26**	**28**	**6**	**0**	**0**	**0**	**0**

Loaned to **London** (IHL) by **Chicago** with $3,000 for Leroy Goldsworthy, January 4, 1934. Loaned to **London** (IHL) by **Chicago** for cash, October, 1935. Returned to **Chicago** by **London** (IHL) for the loan of Norm Locking, January 23, 1936. Loaned to **Toronto** by **Chicago** for remainder of the 1936-37 season for the loan of Regis Kelly, December 29, 1936. Traded to **St. Louis** (AHA) by **Chicago** with Oscar Hanson for cash, December 2, 1937.

KENNEDY, Dean

Defense. Shoots right. 6'2", 208 lbs. Born, Redvers, Sask., January 18, 1963.
(Los Angeles' 2nd choice, 39th overall, in 1981 Entry Draft).

Season	Club	GP	G	A	Pts	PIM	GP	G	A	Pts	PIM
1982-83	Los Angeles Kings	55	0	12	12	97	....	....	....	....	....
1983-84	Los Angeles Kings	37	1	5	6	50	....	....	....	....	....
1985-86	Los Angeles Kings	78	2	10	12	132	....	....	....	....	....
1986-87	Los Angeles Kings	66	6	14	20	91	5	0	2	2	10
1987-88	Los Angeles Kings	58	1	11	12	158	4	0	1	1	10
1988-89	Los Angeles Kings	25	2	5	7	23	....	....	....	....	....
	New York Rangers	16	0	1	1	40	....	....	....	....	....
	Los Angeles Kings	26	1	3	4	40	11	0	2	2	8
1989-90	Buffalo Sabres	80	2	12	14	53	6	1	1	2	12
1990-91	Buffalo Sabres	64	4	8	12	119	2	0	1	1	17
1991-92	Winnipeg Jets	18	2	4	6	21	2	0	0	0	0
1992-93	Winnipeg Jets	78	1	7	8	105	6	0	0	0	2
1993-94	Winnipeg Jets	76	2	8	10	164	....	....	....	....	....
1994-95	Edmonton Oilers	40	2	8	10	25	....	....	....	....	....
	NHL Totals	**717**	**26**	**108**	**134**	**1118**	**36**	**1**	**7**	**8**	**59**

Traded to **NY Rangers** by **Los Angeles** with Denis Larocque for Igor Liba, Michael Boyce, Todd Elik and future considerations, December 12, 1988. Traded to **Los Angeles** by **NY Rangers** for Los Angeles' 4th round choice (later traded to Minnesota – Minnesota selected Cal McGowan) in 1990 Entry Draft, February 3, 1989. Traded to **Buffalo** by **Los Angeles** for Buffalo's 4th round choice (Keith Redmond) in 1991 Entry Draft, October 4, 1989. Traded to **Winnipeg** by **Buffalo** with Darrin Shannon and Mike Hartman for Dave McLlwain, Gord Donnelly, Winnipeg's 5th round choice (Yuri Khmylev) in 1992 Entry Draft and future considerations, October 11, 1991. • Missed majority of 1991-92 season recovering from knee injury suffered in game vs. NY Islanders, November 20, 1991. Claimed by **Edmonton** from **Winnipeg** in NHL Waiver Draft, January 18, 1995.

KENNEDY, Forbes

Center. Shoots left. 5'8", 150 lbs. Born, Dorchester, N.B., August 18, 1935.

Season	Club	GP	G	A	Pts	PIM	GP	G	A	Pts	PIM
1956-57	Chicago Black Hawks	69	8	13	21	102	....	....	....	....	....
1957-58	Detroit Red Wings	70	11	16	27	135	4	1	0	1	12
1958-59	Detroit Red Wings	67	1	4	5	149	....	....	....	....	....
1959-60	Detroit Red Wings	17	1	2	3	8	....	....	....	....	....
1961-62	Detroit Red Wings	14	1	0	1	8	....	....	....	....	....
1962-63	Boston Bruins	49	12	18	30	46	....	....	....	....	....
1963-64	Boston Bruins	70	8	17	25	95	....	....	....	....	....
1964-65	Boston Bruins	52	6	4	10	41	....	....	....	....	....
1965-66	Boston Bruins	50	4	6	10	55	....	....	....	....	....
1967-68	Philadelphia Flyers	73	10	18	28	130	7	1	4	5	14
1968-69	Philadelphia Flyers	59	8	7	15	*195	....	....	....	....	....
	Toronto Maple Leafs	13	0	3	3	*24	1	0	0	0	38
	NHL Totals	**603**	**70**	**108**	**178**	**988**	**12**	**2**	**4**	**6**	**64**

Traded to **Chicago** by **Montreal** with Ed Kachur for $50,000, May 24, 1956. Traded to **Detroit** by **Chicago** with Johnny Wilson, Hank Bassen and Bill Preston for Ted Lindsay and Glenn Hall, July 23, 1957. Traded to **Boston** by **Detroit** for Andre Pronovost, December 3, 1962. Claimed by **Philadelphia** from **Boston** in Expansion Draft, June 6, 1967. Traded to **Toronto** by **Philadelphia** with Brit Selby for Gerry Meehan, Mike Byers and Bill Sutherland, March 2, 1969. Traded to **Pittsburgh** by **Toronto** for cash, May 30, 1969. Claimed by **NY Rangers** from **Pittsburgh** in Intra-League Draft, June 11, 1969.

KENNEDY, Mike

Center. Shoots right. 6'1", 195 lbs. Born, Vancouver, B.C., April 13, 1972.
(Minnesota's 3rd choice, 97th overall, in 1991 Entry Draft).

Season	Club	GP	G	A	Pts	PIM	GP	G	A	Pts	PIM
1994-95	Dallas Stars	44	6	12	18	33	5	0	0	0	9
1995-96	Dallas Stars	61	9	17	26	48	....	....	....	....	....
1996-97	Dallas Stars	24	1	6	7	13	....	....	....	....	....
1997-98	Toronto Maple Leafs	13	0	1	1	14	....	....	....	....	....
	Dallas Stars	2	0	0	0	2	....	....	....	....	....
1998-99	New York Islanders	1	0	0	0	2	....	....	....	....	....
	NHL Totals	**145**	**16**	**36**	**52**	**112**	**5**	**0**	**0**	**0**	**9**

Rights transferred to **Dallas** after **Minnesota** franchise relocated, June 9, 1993. Signed as a free agent by **Toronto**, July 2, 1997. Traded to **Dallas** by **Toronto** for Dallas' 8th round choice (Michal Travnicek) in 1998 Entry Draft, March 24, 1998. Signed as a free agent by **NY Islanders**, July 1, 1998.

KENNEDY, Sheldon

Right wing. Shoots right. 5'10", 180 lbs. Born, Elkhorn, Man., June 15, 1969.
(Detroit's 5th choice, 80th overall, in 1988 Entry Draft).

Season	Club	GP	G	A	Pts	PIM	GP	G	A	Pts	PIM
1989-90	Detroit Red Wings	20	2	7	9	10	....	....	....	....	....
1990-91	Detroit Red Wings	7	1	0	1	12	....	....	....	....	....
1991-92	Detroit Red Wings	27	3	8	11	24	....	....	....	....	....

Season	Club	REGULAR SEASON GP	G	A	Pts	PIM	PLAYOFFS GP	G	A	Pts	PIM
1992-93	Detroit Red Wings	68	19	11	30	46	7	1	1	2	2
1993-94	Detroit Red Wings	61	6	7	13	30	7	1	2	3	0
1994-95	Calgary Flames	30	7	8	15	45	7	3	1	4	16
1995-96	Calgary Flames	41	3	7	10	36	3	1	0	1	2
1996-97	Boston Bruins	56	8	10	18	30	....	....	....	....	....
	NHL Totals	**310**	**49**	**58**	**107**	**233**	**24**	**6**	**4**	**10**	**20**

Traded to **Winnipeg** by **Detroit** for Winnipeg's 3rd round choice (Darryl Laplante) in 1995 Entry Draft, May 25, 1994. Claimed by **Calgary** from **Winnipeg** in NHL Waiver Draft, January 18, 1995. Signed as free agent by **Boston**, August 7, 1996.

KENNEDY, Ted

HHOF

Center. Shoots right. 5'11", 175 lbs. Born, Humberstone, Ont., December 12, 1925.

Season	Club	GP	G	A	Pts	PIM	GP	G	A	Pts	PIM
1942-43	Toronto Maple Leafs	2	0	1	1	0	....	....	....	....	....
1943-44	Toronto Maple Leafs	49	26	23	49	2	5	1	1	2	4
1944-45 ♦	Toronto Maple Leafs	49	29	25	54	14	13	*7	2	9	2
1945-46	Toronto Maple Leafs	21	3	2	5	4	....	....	....	....	....
1946-47 ♦	Toronto Maple Leafs	60	28	32	60	27	11	4	5	9	4
1947-48 ♦	Toronto Maple Leafs	60	25	21	46	32	9	*8	6	*14	0
1948-49 ♦	Toronto Maple Leafs	59	18	21	39	25	9	2	*6	8	2
1949-50	Toronto Maple Leafs	53	20	24	44	34	7	1	2	3	8
1950-51 ♦	Toronto Maple Leafs	63	18	*43	61	32	11	4	5	9	6
1951-52	Toronto Maple Leafs	70	19	33	52	33	4	0	0	0	4
1952-53	Toronto Maple Leafs	43	14	23	37	42	....	....	....	....	....
1953-54	Toronto Maple Leafs	67	15	23	38	78	5	1	1	2	2
1954-55	Toronto Maple Leafs	70	10	42	52	74	4	1	3	4	0
1956-57	Toronto Maple Leafs	30	6	16	22	35	....	....	....	....	....
	NHL Totals	**696**	**231**	**329**	**560**	**432**	**78**	**29**	**31**	**60**	**32**

NHL Second All-Star Team (1950, 1951, 1954) • Hart Trophy (1955)

Played in NHL All-Star Game (1947, 1948, 1949, 1950, 1951, 1954)

• Rights were held by Montreal at time of first appearance in NHL. Rights traded to **Toronto** by **Montreal** for the rights to Frank Eddolls, September 10, 1943. Missed majority of 1956-57 season while still in retirement but returned as an active player in game vs. Detroit, January 6, 1957.

KENNY, Ernest

Defense. Shoots left. 6'2", 195 lbs. Born, Vermillion, Alta., August 20, 1907.

Season	Club	GP	G	A	Pts	PIM	GP	G	A	Pts	PIM
1930-31	New York Rangers	6	0	0	0	0	....	....	....	....	....
1934-35	Chicago Black Hawks	4	0	0	0	18	....	....	....	....	....
	NHL Totals	**10**	**0**	**0**	**0**	**18**	....	....	....	....	....

Traded to **NY Rangers** by **Tacoma** (PCHL) for cash, January 3, 1931. Traded to **Chicago** by **Edmonton** (NWHL) for cash, October 22, 1934.

KEON, Dave

HHOF

Center. Shoots left. 5'9", 165 lbs. Born, Noranda, Que., March 22, 1940.

Season	Club	GP	G	A	Pts	PIM	GP	G	A	Pts	PIM
1960 61	Toronto Maple Leafs	70	20	25	45	6	5	1	1	2	0
1961-62 ♦	Toronto Maple Leafs	64	26	35	61	2	12	5	3	8	0
1962-63 ♦	Toronto Maple Leafs	68	28	28	56	2	10	7	5	12	0
1963-64 ♦	Toronto Maple Leafs	70	23	37	60	6	14	7	2	9	2
1964-65	Toronto Maple Leafs	65	21	29	50	10	6	2	2	4	2
1965-66	Toronto Maple Leafs	69	24	30	54	4	4	0	2	2	0
1966-67 ♦	Toronto Maple Leafs	66	19	33	52	2	12	3	5	8	0
1967-68	Toronto Maple Leafs	67	11	37	48	4	....	....	....	....	....
1968-69	Toronto Maple Leafs	75	27	34	61	12	4	1	3	4	2
1969-70	Toronto Maple Leafs	72	32	30	62	6	....	....	....	....	....
1970-71	Toronto Maple Leafs	76	38	38	76	4	6	3	2	5	0
1971-72	Toronto Maple Leafs	72	18	30	48	4	5	2	3	5	0
1972-73	Toronto Maple Leafs	76	37	36	73	2	....	....	....	....	....
1973-74	Toronto Maple Leafs	74	25	28	53	7	4	1	2	3	0
1974-75	Toronto Maple Leafs	78	16	43	59	4	7	0	5	5	0
1979-80	Hartford Whalers	76	10	52	62	10	3	0	1	1	0
1980-81	Hartford Whalers	80	13	34	47	26	....	....	....	....	....
1981-82	Hartford Whalers	78	8	11	19	6	....	....	....	....	....
	NHL Totals	**1296**	**396**	**590**	**986**	**117**	**92**	**32**	**36**	**68**	**6**

Calder Memorial Trophy (1961) • NHL Second All-Star Team (1962, 1971) • Lady Byng Trophy (1962, 1963) • Conn Smythe Trophy (1967)

Played in NHL All-Star Game (1962, 1963, 1964, 1967, 1968, 1970, 1971, 1973)

Rights retained by **Hartford** prior to Expansion Draft, June 9, 1979.

KERCH, Alexander

Left wing. Shoots right. 5'10", 190 lbs. Born, Arkhangelsk, USSR, March 16, 1967.
(Edmonton's 5th choice, 60th overall, in 1993 Entry Draft).

Season	Club	GP	G	A	Pts	PIM	GP	G	A	Pts	PIM
1993-94	Edmonton Oilers	5	0	0	0	2	....	....	....	....	....
	NHL Totals	**5**	**0**	**0**	**0**	**2**	....	....	....	....	....

KERR, Alan

Right wing. Shoots right. 5'11", 195 lbs. Born, Hazelton, B.C., March 28, 1964.
(NY Islanders' 4th choice, 84th overall, in 1982 Entry Draft).

Season	Club	GP	G	A	Pts	PIM	GP	G	A	Pts	PIM
1984-85	New York Islanders	19	3	1	4	24	4	1	0	1	4
1985-86	New York Islanders	7	0	1	1	16	1	0	0	0	0
1986-87	New York Islanders	72	7	10	17	175	14	1	4	5	25
1987-88	New York Islanders	80	24	34	58	198	6	1	0	1	14
1988-89	New York Islanders	71	20	18	38	144	....	....	....	....	....
1989-90	New York Islanders	75	15	21	36	129	4	0	0	0	10
1990-91	New York Islanders	2	0	0	0	5	....	....	....	....	....
1991-92	Detroit Red Wings	58	3	8	11	133	9	2	0	2	17
1992-93	Winnipeg Jets	7	0	1	1	2	....	....	....	....	....
	NHL Totals	**391**	**72**	**94**	**166**	**826**	**38**	**5**	**4**	**9**	**70**

Traded to **Detroit** by **NY Islanders** with future considerations for Rick Green, May 26, 1991. Traded to **Winnipeg** by **Detroit** to complete transaction that sent Aaron Ward to Detroit (June 11, 1993), June 19, 1993.

KERR, Reg

Left wing. Shoots left. 5'10", 180 lbs. Born, Oxbow, Sask., October 16, 1957.
(Cleveland's 3rd choice, 41st overall, in 1977 Amateur Draft).

Season	Club	GP	G	A	Pts	PIM	GP	G	A	Pts	PIM
1977-78	Cleveland Barons	7	0	2	2	7	....	....	....	....	....
	Chicago Black Hawks	2	0	2	2	0	....	....	....	....	....
1978-79	Chicago Black Hawks	73	16	24	40	50	4	1	0	1	5
1979-80	Chicago Black Hawks	49	9	8	17	17	....	....	....	....	....
1980-81	Chicago Black Hawks	70	30	30	60	56	3	0	0	0	2
1981-82	Chicago Black Hawks	59	11	28	39	39	....	....	....	....	....
1983-84	Edmonton Oilers	3	0	0	0	0	....	....	....	....	....
	NHL Totals	**263**	**66**	**94**	**160**	**169**	**7**	**1**	**0**	**1**	**7**

Traded to **Chicago** by **Cleveland** for Randy Holt, November 23, 1977. Signed as a free agent by **Edmonton**, November 9, 1983.

KERR, Tim

Center/Right wing. Shoots right. 6'3", 230 lbs. Born, Windsor, Ont., January 5, 1960.

Season	Club	GP	G	A	Pts	PIM	GP	G	A	Pts	PIM
1980-81	Philadelphia Flyers	68	22	23	45	84	10	1	3	4	2
1981-82	Philadelphia Flyers	61	21	30	51	138	4	0	2	2	2
1982-83	Philadelphia Flyers	24	11	8	19	6	2	2	0	2	0
1983-84	Philadelphia Flyers	79	54	39	93	29	3	0	0	0	0
1984-85	Philadelphia Flyers	74	54	44	98	57	12	10	4	14	13
1985-86	Philadelphia Flyers	76	58	26	84	79	5	3	3	6	8
1986-87	Philadelphia Flyers	75	58	37	95	57	12	8	5	13	2
1987-88	Philadelphia Flyers	8	3	2	5	12	6	1	3	4	4
1988-89	Philadelphia Flyers	69	48	40	88	73	19	14	11	25	27
1989-90	Philadelphia Flyers	40	24	24	48	34	....	....	....	....	....
1990-91	Philadelphia Flyers	27	10	14	24	8	....	....	....	....	....
1991-92	New York Rangers	32	7	11	18	12	8	1	0	1	0
1992-93	Hartford Whalers	22	0	6	6	7	....	....	....	....	....
	NHL Totals	**655**	**370**	**304**	**674**	**596**	**81**	**40**	**31**	**71**	**58**

NHL Second All-Star Team (1987) • Bill Masterton Trophy (1989)

Played in NHL All-Star Game (1984, 1985, 1986)

Signed as a free agent by **Philadelphia**, October 25, 1979. • Missed majority of 1982-83 season recovering from knee injury suffered in game vs. Buffalo, November 24, 1982. • Missed majority of 1987-88 season recovering from shoulder surgery, December, 1987. Claimed by **San Jose** from **Philadelphia** in Expansion Draft, May 30, 1991. Traded to **NY Rangers** by **San Jose** for Brian Mullen, May 30, 1991. Traded to **Hartford** by **NY Rangers** for future considerations, July 9, 1992.

KESA, Dan

Right wing. Shoots right. 6', 198 lbs. Born, Vancouver, B.C., November 23, 1971.
(Vancouver's 4th choice, 95th overall, in 1991 Entry Draft).

Season	Club	GP	G	A	Pts	PIM	GP	G	A	Pts	PIM
1993-94	Vancouver Canucks	19	2	4	6	18	....	....	....	....	....
1995-96	Dallas Stars	3	0	0	0	0	....	....	....	....	....
1998-99	Pittsburgh Penguins	67	2	8	10	27	13	1	0	1	0
99-2000	Tampa Bay Lightning	50	4	10	14	21	....	....	....	....	....
	NHL Totals	**139**	**8**	**22**	**30**	**66**	**13**	**1**	**0**	**1**	**0**

Traded to **Dallas** by **Vancouver** with Greg Adams and Vancouver's 5th round choice (later traded to Los Angeles – Los Angeles selected Jason Morgan) in 1995 Entry Draft for Russ Courtnall, April 7, 1995. Traded to **Hartford** by **Dallas** for Robert Petrovicky, November 29, 1995. Signed as a free agent by **Pittsburgh**, August 20, 1998. Signed as a free agent by **Tampa Bay**, September 6, 1999.

KESSELL, Rick

Center. Shoots left. 5'10", 175 lbs. Born, Toronto, Ont., July 27, 1949.
(Pittsburgh's 1st choice, 15th overall, in 1969 Amateur Draft).

Season	Club	GP	G	A	Pts	PIM	GP	G	A	Pts	PIM
1969-70	Pittsburgh Penguins	8	1	2	3	0	....	....	....	....	....
1970-71	Pittsburgh Penguins	6	0	2	2	2	....	....	....	....	....
1971-72	Pittsburgh Penguins	3	0	1	1	0	....	....	....	....	....
1972-73	Pittsburgh Penguins	67	1	13	14	0	....	....	....	....	....
1973-74	California Golden Seals	51	2	6	8	4	....	....	....	....	....
	NHL Totals	**135**	**4**	**24**	**28**	**6**	....	....	....	....	....

Claimed by **California** (Salt Lake-CHL) from **Pittsburgh** in Reverse Draft, June 13, 1973.

KETOLA, Veli-Pekka

Center. Shoots left. 6'3", 220 lbs. Born, Pori, Finland, March 28, 1948.

Season	Club	GP	G	A	Pts	PIM	GP	G	A	Pts	PIM
1981-82	Colorado Rockies	44	9	5	14	4	....	....	....	....	....
	NHL Totals	**44**	**9**	**5**	**14**	**4**	....	....	....	....	....

Signed as a free agent by **Colorado**, July 8, 1981.

KETTER, Kerry

Defense. Shoots left. 6'1", 202 lbs. Born, Prince George, B.C., September 20, 1947.

Season	Club	GP	G	A	Pts	PIM	GP	G	A	Pts	PIM
1972-73	Atlanta Flames	41	0	2	2	58	....	....	....	....	....
	NHL Totals	**41**	**0**	**2**	**2**	**58**	....	....	....	....	....

Traded to **Montreal** by **Detroit** with cash for Leon Rochefort, May 25, 1971. Claimed by **Atlanta** from **Montreal** in Expansion Draft, June 6, 1972. Claimed by **Kansas City** from **Atlanta** in Expansion Draft, June 12, 1974.

KHARIN, Sergei

Right wing. Shoots left. 5'11", 180 lbs. Born, Odintsovo, USSR, February 20, 1963.
(Winnipeg's 15th choice, 240th overall, in 1989 Entry Draft).

Season	Club	Regular Season GP	G	A	Pts	PIM	Playoffs GP	G	A	Pts	PIM
1990-91	Winnipeg Jets	7	2	3	5	2	....	....	....	....	....
	NHL Totals	**7**	**2**	**3**	**5**	**2**	....	....	....	....	....

Traded to **Quebec** by **Winnipeg** for Shawn Anderson, October 22, 1991.

KHARITONOV, Alexander

Left wing. Shoots right. 5'9", 169 lbs. Born, Moscow, USSR, March 30, 1976.
(Tampa Bay's 3rd choice, 81st overall, in 2000 Entry Draft).

Season	Club	Regular Season GP	G	A	Pts	PIM	Playoffs GP	G	A	Pts	PIM
2000-01	Tampa Bay Lightning	66	7	15	22	8	....	....	....	....	....
2001-02	New York Islanders	5	0	0	0	4	....	....	....	....	....
	NHL Totals	**71**	**7**	**15**	**22**	**12**	....	....	....	....	....

Traded to **NY Islanders** by **Tampa Bay** with Adrian Aucoin for Mathieu Biron and NY Islanders' 2nd round choice (later traded to Washington – later traded to Vancouver – Vancouver selected Denis Grot) in 2002 Entry Draft, June 22, 2001.

KHAVANOV, Alexander

Defense. Shoots left. 6', 187 lbs. Born, Ryazan, USSR, January 30, 1972.
(St. Louis' 8th choice, 232nd overall, in 1999 Entry Draft).

Season	Club	Regular Season GP	G	A	Pts	PIM	Playoffs GP	G	A	Pts	PIM
2000-01	St. Louis Blues	74	7	16	23	52	15	3	2	5	14
2001-02	St. Louis Blues	81	3	21	24	55	4	0	0	0	2
2002-03	St. Louis Blues	81	8	25	33	48	7	2	3	5	2
	NHL Totals	**236**	**18**	**62**	**80**	**155**	**26**	**5**	**5**	**10**	**18**

KHMYLEV, Yuri

Left wing. Shoots right. 6'1", 189 lbs. Born, Moscow, USSR, August 9, 1964.
(Buffalo's 7th choice, 108th overall, in 1992 Entry Draft).

Season	Club	Regular Season GP	G	A	Pts	PIM	Playoffs GP	G	A	Pts	PIM
1992-93	Buffalo Sabres	68	20	19	39	28	8	4	3	7	4
1993-94	Buffalo Sabres	72	27	31	58	49	7	3	1	4	8
1994-95	Buffalo Sabres	48	8	17	25	14	5	0	1	1	8
1995-96	Buffalo Sabres	66	8	20	28	40	....	....	....	....	....
	St. Louis Blues	7	0	1	1	0	6	1	1	2	4
1996-97	St. Louis Blues	2	1	0	1	2	....	....	....	....	....
	NHL Totals	**263**	**64**	**88**	**152**	**133**	**26**	**8**	**6**	**14**	**24**

Traded to **St. Louis** by **Buffalo** with Buffalo's 8th round choice (Andrei Podkonicky) in 1996 Entry Draft for Jean-Luc Grand-Pierre, Ottawa's 2nd round choice (previously acquired, Buffalo selected Cory Sarich) in 1996 Entry Draft and St. Louis' 3rd round choice (Maxim Afinogenov) in 1997 Entry Draft, March 20, 1996.

KHRISTICH, Dmitri

Left wing/Center. Shoots right. 6'2", 195 lbs. Born, Kiev, USSR, July 23, 1969.
(Washington's 6th choice, 120th overall, in 1988 Entry Draft).

Season	Club	Regular Season GP	G	A	Pts	PIM	Playoffs GP	G	A	Pts	PIM
1990-91	Washington Capitals	40	13	14	27	21	11	1	3	4	6
1991-92	Washington Capitals	80	36	37	73	35	7	3	2	5	15
1992-93	Washington Capitals	64	31	35	66	28	6	2	5	7	2
1993-94	Washington Capitals	83	29	29	58	73	11	2	3	5	10
1994-95	Washington Capitals	48	12	14	26	41	7	1	4	5	0
1995-96	Los Angeles Kings	76	27	37	64	44	....	....	....	....	....
1996-97	Los Angeles Kings	75	19	37	56	38	....	....	....	....	....
1997-98	Boston Bruins	82	29	37	66	42	6	2	2	4	2
1998-99	Boston Bruins	79	29	42	71	48	12	3	4	7	6
99-2000	Toronto Maple Leafs	53	12	18	30	24	12	1	2	3	0
2000-01	Toronto Maple Leafs	27	3	6	9	8	....	....	....	....	....
	Washington Capitals	43	10	19	29	8	3	0	0	0	0
2001-02	Washington Capitals	61	9	12	21	12	....	....	....	....	....
	NHL Totals	**811**	**259**	**337**	**596**	**422**	**75**	**15**	**25**	**40**	**41**

Played in NHL All-Star Game (1997, 1999)

Traded to **Los Angeles** by **Washington** with Byron Dafoe for Los Angeles' 1st round choice (Alexandre Volchkov) and Dallas' 4th round choice (previously acquired, Washington selected Justin Davis) in 1996 Entry Draft, July 8, 1995. Traded to **Boston** by **Los Angeles** with Byron Dafoe for Jozef Stumpel, Sandy Moger and Boston's 4th round choice (later traded to New Jersey – New Jersey selected Pierre Dagenais) in 1998 Entry Draft, August 29, 1997. Traded to **Toronto** by **Boston** for Toronto's 2nd round choice (Ivan Huml) in 2000 Entry Draft, October 20, 1999. Traded to **Washington** by **Toronto** for Tampa Bay's 3rd round choice (previously acquired, Toronto selected Brendan Bell) in 2001 Entry Draft, December 11, 2000.

KIDD, Ian

Defense. Shoots right. 5'11", 195 lbs. Born, Gresham, OR, May 11, 1964.

Season	Club	Regular Season GP	G	A	Pts	PIM	Playoffs GP	G	A	Pts	PIM
1987-88	Vancouver Canucks	19	4	7	11	25	....	....	....	....	....
1988-89	Vancouver Canucks	1	0	0	0	0	....	....	....	....	....
	NHL Totals	**20**	**4**	**7**	**11**	**25**	....	....	....	....	....

Signed as a free agent by **Vancouver**, July 30, 1987.

KIESSLING, Udo

Defense. Shoots left. 5'10", 180 lbs. Born, Crimmitschau, East Germany, May 21, 1955.

Season	Club	Regular Season GP	G	A	Pts	PIM	Playoffs GP	G	A	Pts	PIM
1981-82	Minnesota North Stars	1	0	0	0	2	....	....	....	....	....
	NHL Totals	**1**	**0**	**0**	**0**	**2**	....	....	....	....	....

Signed as a free agent by **Minnesota**, March 5, 1982.

KILGER, Chad

Center. Shoots left. 6'4", 224 lbs. Born, Cornwall, Ont., November 27, 1976.
(Anaheim's 1st choice, 4th overall, in 1995 Entry Draft).

Season	Club	Regular Season GP	G	A	Pts	PIM	Playoffs GP	G	A	Pts	PIM
1995-96	Mighty Ducks of Anaheim	45	5	7	12	22	....	....	....	....	....
	Winnipeg Jets	29	2	3	5	12	4	1	0	1	0
1996-97	Phoenix Coyotes	24	4	3	7	13	....	....	....	....	....
1997-98	Phoenix Coyotes	10	0	1	1	4	....	....	....	....	....
	Chicago Blackhawks	22	3	8	11	6	....	....	....	....	....
1998-99	Chicago Blackhawks	64	14	11	25	30	....	....	....	....	....
	Edmonton Oilers	13	1	1	2	4	4	0	0	0	4
99-2000	Edmonton Oilers	40	3	2	5	18	3	0	0	0	0
2000-01	Edmonton Oilers	34	5	2	7	17	....	....	....	....	....
	Montreal Canadiens	43	9	16	25	34	....	....	....	....	....
2001-02	Montreal Canadiens	75	8	15	23	27	12	0	1	1	9
2002-03	Montreal Canadiens	60	9	7	16	21	....	....	....	....	....
	NHL Totals	**459**	**63**	**76**	**139**	**208**	**23**	**1**	**1**	**2**	**13**

Traded to **Winnipeg** by **Anaheim** with Oleg Tverdovsky and Anaheim's 3rd round choice (Per-Anton Lundstrom) in 1996 Entry Draft for Teemu Selanne, Marc Chouinard and Winnipeg's 4th round choice (later traded to Toronto – later traded to Montreal – Montreal selected Kim Staal) in 1996 Entry Draft, February 7, 1996. Transferred to **Phoenix** after **Winnipeg** franchise relocated, July 1, 1996. Traded to **Chicago** by **Phoenix** with Jayson More for Keith Carney and Jim Cummins, March 4, 1998. Traded to **Edmonton** by **Chicago** with Daniel Cleary, Ethan Moreau and Christian Laflamme for Boris Mironov, Dean McAmmond and Jonas Elofsson, March 20, 1999. Traded to **Montreal** by **Edmonton** for Sergei Zholtok, December 18, 2000.

KILREA, Brian

Center. Shoots right. 5'11", 175 lbs. Born, Ottawa, Ont., October 21, 1934.

Season	Club	Regular Season GP	G	A	Pts	PIM	Playoffs GP	G	A	Pts	PIM
1957-58	Detroit Red Wings	1	0	0	0	0	....	....	....	....	....
1967-68	Los Angeles Kings	25	3	5	8	12	....	....	....	....	....
	NHL Totals	**26**	**3**	**5**	**8**	**12**	....	....	....	....	....

NHL rights transferred to **Los Angeles** after NHL club purchased **Springfield** (AHL) franchise, May, 1967. Claimed by **Vancouver** (WHL) from **Los Angeles** in Reverse Draft, June 13, 1968.

KILREA, Hec

Left wing. Shoots left. 5'8", 175 lbs. Born, Blackburn, Ont., June 11, 1907.

Season	Club	Regular Season GP	G	A	Pts	PIM	Playoffs GP	G	A	Pts	PIM
1925-26	Ottawa Senators	35	5	0	5	12	2	0	0	0	0
1926-27◆	Ottawa Senators	42	11	7	18	48	6	1	1	2	4
1927-28	Ottawa Senators	43	19	4	23	66	2	1	0	1	0
1928-29	Ottawa Senators	38	5	7	12	36	....	....	....	....	....
1929-30	Ottawa Senators	44	36	22	58	72	2	0	0	0	4
1930-31	Ottawa Senators	44	14	8	22	44	....	....	....	....	....
1931-32	Detroit Falcons	47	13	3	16	28	2	0	0	0	0
1932-33	Ottawa Senators	47	14	8	22	26	....	....	....	....	....
1933-34	Toronto Maple Leafs	43	10	13	23	15	5	2	0	2	2
1934-35	Toronto Maple Leafs	46	11	13	24	16	6	0	0	0	4
1935-36◆	Detroit Red Wings	48	6	17	23	37	7	0	3	3	2
1936-37◆	Detroit Red Wings	48	6	9	15	20	10	3	1	4	2
1937-38	Detroit Red Wings	48	9	9	18	10	....	....	....	....	....
1938-39	Detroit Red Wings	48	8	9	17	8	6	1	2	3	0
1939-40	Detroit Red Wings	12	0	0	0	0	....	....	....	....	....
	NHL Totals	**633**	**167**	**129**	**296**	**438**	**48**	**8**	**7**	**15**	**18**

• Brother of Wally and Ken

Played in NHL All-Star Game (1934)

Signed as a free agent by **Ottawa**, November 12, 1925. Claimed by **Detroit** from **Ottawa** for 1931-32 season in Dispersal Draft, September 26, 1931. Traded to **Toronto** by **Ottawa** for Bob Gracie and $10,000, October 4, 1933. Traded to **Detroit** by **Toronto** for $7,000 and future considerations (Knucker Irvine, October, 1935), September 29, 1935.

KILREA, Ken

Left wing. Shoots left. 6', 170 lbs. Born, Ottawa, Ont., January 16, 1919.

Season	Club	Regular Season GP	G	A	Pts	PIM	Playoffs GP	G	A	Pts	PIM
1938-39	Detroit Red Wings	1	0	0	0	0	3	1	1	2	4
1939-40	Detroit Red Wings	40	10	8	18	4	5	1	1	2	0
1940-41	Detroit Red Wings	15	2	0	2	0	5	0	0	0	0
1941-42	Detroit Red Wings	21	3	12	15	4	....	....	....	....	....
1943-44	Detroit Red Wings	14	1	3	4	0	2	0	0	0	0
	NHL Totals	**91**	**16**	**23**	**39**	**8**	**15**	**2**	**2**	**4**	**4**

• Brother of Wally and Hec

Signed as a free agent by **Detroit**, March 18, 1938.

KILREA, Wally

Right wing/Center. Shoots right. 5'7", 150 lbs. Born, Ottawa, Ont., February 18, 1909.

Season	Club	Regular Season GP	G	A	Pts	PIM	Playoffs GP	G	A	Pts	PIM
1929-30	Ottawa Senators	38	4	2	6	4	2	0	0	0	0
1930-31	Philadelphia Quakers	44	8	12	20	22	....	....	....	....	....
1931-32	New York Americans	48	3	8	11	18	....	....	....	....	....
1932-33	Ottawa Senators	32	4	5	9	14	....	....	....	....	....
	Montreal Maroons	19	1	7	8	2	2	0	0	0	0
1933-34	Montreal Maroons	45	3	1	4	7	4	0	0	0	0
1934-35	Detroit Red Wings	3	0	0	0	0	....	....	....	....	....
1935-36◆	Detroit Red Wings	48	4	10	14	10	7	2	2	4	2
1936-37◆	Detroit Red Wings	47	8	13	21	6	10	0	2	2	4

Season	Club	REGULAR SEASON GP	G	A	Pts	PIM	PLAYOFFS GP	G	A	Pts	PIM
1937-38	Detroit Red Wings	5	0	0	0	4	....	....	....	....	....
	NHL Totals	**329**	**35**	**58**	**93**	**87**	**25**	**2**	**4**	**6**	**6**

• Brother of Hec and Ken

Loaned to **Philadelphia** by **Ottawa** for 1930-31 season, September, 1930. Claimed by **NY Americans** from **Ottawa** for 1931-32 season in Dispersal Draft, September 26, 1931. Traded to **Mtl. Maroons** by **Ottawa** for Des Roche, February 3, 1933. Traded to **Detroit** by **Mtl. Maroons** for Gus Marker, September 23, 1934. Traded to **Hershey** (IAHL) by **Detroit** for cash, June 23, 1938.

KIMBLE, Darin

Right wing. Shoots right. 6'2", 210 lbs. Born, Lucky Lake, Sask., November 22, 1968.
(Quebec's 5th choice, 66th overall, in 1988 Entry Draft).

Season	Club	GP	G	A	Pts	PIM	GP	G	A	Pts	PIM
1988-89	Quebec Nordiques	26	3	1	4	149	....	....	....	....	....
1989-90	Quebec Nordiques	44	5	5	10	185	....	....	....	....	....
1990-91	Quebec Nordiques	35	2	5	7	114	....	....	....	....	....
	St. Louis Blues	26	1	1	2	128	13	0	0	0	38
1991-92	St. Louis Blues	46	1	3	4	166	5	0	0	0	7
1992-93	Boston Bruins	55	7	3	10	177	4	0	0	0	2
1993-94	Chicago Blackhawks	65	4	2	6	133	1	0	0	0	5
1994-95	Chicago Blackhawks	14	0	0	0	30	....	....	....	....	....
	NHL Totals	**311**	**23**	**20**	**43**	**1082**	**23**	**0**	**0**	**0**	**52**

Traded to **St. Louis** by **Quebec** for Herb Raglan, Tony Twist and Andy Rymsha, February 4, 1991. Traded to **Tampa Bay** by **St. Louis** with Pat Jablonski, Steve Tuttle and Rob Robinson for future considerations, June 19, 1992. Traded to **Boston** by **Tampa Bay** with future considerations for Ken Hodge and Matt Hervey, September 4, 1992. Signed as a free agent by **Florida**, July 9, 1993. Traded to **Chicago** by **Florida** for Keith Brown, September 30, 1993. Traded to **New Jersey** by **Chicago** for Michael Vukonich and Bill Armstrong, November 1, 1995. Signed as a free agent by **Phoenix**, July 28, 1997.

KINDRACHUK, Orest

Center. Shoots left. 5'10", 175 lbs. Born, Nanton, Alta., September 14, 1950.

Season	Club	GP	G	A	Pts	PIM	GP	G	A	Pts	PIM
1972-73	Philadelphia Flyers	2	0	0	0	0	....	....	....	....	....
1973-74 ♦	Philadelphia Flyers	71	11	30	41	85	17	5	4	9	17
1974-75 ♦	Philadelphia Flyers	60	10	21	31	72	14	0	2	2	12
1975-76	Philadelphia Flyers	76	26	49	75	101	16	4	7	11	4
1976-77	Philadelphia Flyers	78	15	36	51	79	10	2	1	3	0
1977-78	Philadelphia Flyers	73	17	45	62	128	12	5	5	10	13
1978-79	Pittsburgh Penguins	79	18	42	60	84	7	4	1	5	7
1979-80	Pittsburgh Penguins	52	17	29	46	63	....	....	....	....	....
1980-81	Pittsburgh Penguins	13	3	9	12	34	....	....	....	....	....
1981-82	Washington Capitals	4	1	0	1	2	....	....	....	....	....
	NHL Totals	**508**	**118**	**261**	**379**	**648**	**76**	**20**	**20**	**40**	**53**

Signed as a free agent by **Philadelphia**, July, 1971. Traded to **Pittsburgh** by **Philadelphia** with Tom Bladon and Ross Lonsberry for Pittsburgh's 1st round choice (Behn Wilson) in 1978 Amateur Draft, June 14, 1978. Signed as a free agent by **Washington**, September 4, 1981.

KING, Derek

Left wing. Shoots left. 6'1", 203 lbs. Born, Hamilton, Ont., February 11, 1967.
(NY Islanders' 2nd choice, 13th overall, in 1985 Entry Draft).

Season	Club	GP	G	A	Pts	PIM	GP	G	A	Pts	PIM
1986-87	New York Islanders	2	0	0	0	0	....	....	....	....	....
1987-88	New York Islanders	55	12	24	36	30	5	0	2	2	2
1988-89	New York Islanders	60	14	29	43	14	....	....	....	....	....
1989-90	New York Islanders	46	13	27	40	20	4	0	0	0	4
1990-91	New York Islanders	66	19	26	45	44	....	....	....	....	....
1991-92	New York Islanders	80	40	38	78	46	....	....	....	....	....
1992-93	New York Islanders	77	38	38	76	47	18	3	11	14	14
1993-94	New York Islanders	78	30	40	70	59	4	0	1	1	0
1994-95	New York Islanders	43	10	16	26	41	....	....	....	....	....
1995-96	New York Islanders	61	12	20	32	23	....	....	....	....	....
1996-97	New York Islanders	70	23	30	53	20	....	....	....	....	....
	Hartford Whalers	12	3	3	6	2	....	....	....	....	....
1997-98	Toronto Maple Leafs	77	21	25	46	43	....	....	....	....	....
1998-99	Toronto Maple Leafs	81	24	28	52	20	16	1	3	4	4
99-2000	Toronto Maple Leafs	3	0	0	0	2	....	....	....	....	....
	St. Louis Blues	19	2	7	9	6	....	....	....	....	....
	NHL Totals	**830**	**261**	**351**	**612**	**417**	**47**	**4**	**17**	**21**	**24**

Traded to **Hartford** by **NY Islanders** for Hartford's 5th round choice (Adam Edinger) in 1997 Entry Draft, March 18, 1997. Signed as a free agent by **Toronto**, July 4, 1997. Traded to **St. Louis** by **Toronto** for Tyler Harlton and future considerations, October 20, 1999. Signed as a free agent by **Ottawa**, August 10, 2000. Signed as a free agent by **Detroit**, July 24, 2002.

KING, Frank

Center. Shoots left. 5'11", 185 lbs. Born, Toronto, Ont., March 7, 1929.

Season	Club	GP	G	A	Pts	PIM	GP	G	A	Pts	PIM
1950-51	Montreal Canadiens	10	1	0	1	2	....	....	....	....	....
	NHL Totals	**10**	**1**	**0**	**1**	**2**	....	....	....	....	....

Traded to **Montreal** by **Cleveland** (AHL) for cash, April 12, 1950. Loaned to **Seattle** (PCHL) by **Montreal** for cash, January 9, 1951. Traded to **Providence** (AHL) by **Montreal** (Cincinnati-AHL) for Roger Bedard, January 29, 1951.

KING, Jason

Center. Shoots left. 6'1", 195 lbs. Born, Corner Brook, Nfld., September 14, 1981.
(Vancouver's 5th choice, 212th overall, in 2001 Entry Draft).

Season	Club	GP	G	A	Pts	PIM	GP	G	A	Pts	PIM
2002-03	Vancouver Canucks	8	0	2	2	0	....	....	....	....	....
	NHL Totals	**8**	**0**	**2**	**2**	**0**	....	....	....	....	....

KING, Kris

Left wing. Shoots left. 5'11", 208 lbs. Born, Bracebridge, Ont., February 18, 1966.
(Washington's 4th choice, 80th overall, in 1984 Entry Draft).

Season	Club	GP	G	A	Pts	PIM	GP	G	A	Pts	PIM
1987-88	Detroit Red Wings	3	1	0	1	2	....	....	....	....	....
1988-89	Detroit Red Wings	55	2	3	5	168	2	0	0	0	2
1989-90	New York Rangers	68	6	7	13	286	10	0	1	1	38
1990-91	New York Rangers	72	11	14	25	154	6	2	0	2	36
1991-92	New York Rangers	79	10	9	19	224	13	4	1	5	14
1992-93	New York Rangers	30	0	3	3	67	....	....	....	....	....
	Winnipeg Jets	48	8	8	16	136	6	1	1	2	4
1993-94	Winnipeg Jets	83	4	8	12	205	....	....	....	....	....
1994-95	Winnipeg Jets	48	4	2	6	85	....	....	....	....	....
1995-96	Winnipeg Jets	81	9	11	20	151	5	0	1	1	4
1996-97	Phoenix Coyotes	81	3	11	14	185	7	0	0	0	17
1997-98	Toronto Maple Leafs	82	3	3	6	199	....	....	....	....	....
1998-99	Toronto Maple Leafs	67	2	2	4	105	17	1	1	2	25
99-2000	Toronto Maple Leafs	39	2	4	6	55	1	0	0	0	2
2000-01	Chicago Blackhawks	13	1	0	1	8	....	....	....	....	....
	NHL Totals	**849**	**66**	**85**	**151**	**2030**	**67**	**8**	**5**	**13**	**142**

King Clancy Memorial Trophy (1996)

Signed as a free agent by **Detroit**, March 23, 1987. Traded to **NY Rangers** by **Detroit** for Chris McRae and Detroit's 5th round choice (previously acquired, Detroit selected Tony Burns) in 1990 Entry Draft, September 7, 1989. Traded to **Winnipeg** by **NY Rangers** with Tie Domi for Ed Olczyk, December 28, 1992. Transferred to **Phoenix** after **Winnipeg** franchise relocated, July 1, 1996. Signed as a free agent by **Toronto**, July 23, 1997. Signed as a free agent by **Chicago**, October 9, 2000. • Officially announced retirement, December 3, 2000.

KING, Steven

Right wing. Shoots right. 6', 195 lbs. Born, East Greenwich, RI, July 22, 1969.
(NY Rangers' 1st choice, 21st overall, in 1991 Supplemental Draft).

Season	Club	GP	G	A	Pts	PIM	GP	G	A	Pts	PIM
1992-93	New York Rangers	24	7	5	12	16	....	....	....	....	....
1993-94	Mighty Ducks of Anaheim	36	8	3	11	44	....	....	....	....	....
1995-96	Mighty Ducks of Anaheim	7	2	0	2	15	....	....	....	....	....
	NHL Totals	**67**	**17**	**8**	**25**	**75**	....	....	....	....	....

Claimed by **Anaheim** from **NY Rangers** in Expansion Draft, June 24, 1993. Signed as a free agent by **Philadelphia**, July 31, 1996. Signed as a free agent by **Phoenix**, July 28, 1999.

KING, Wayne

Center. Shoots right. 5'10", 185 lbs. Born, Midland, Ont., September 4, 1951.

Season	Club	GP	G	A	Pts	PIM	GP	G	A	Pts	PIM
1973-74	California Golden Seals	2	0	0	0	0	....	....	....	....	....
1974-75	California Golden Seals	25	4	7	11	8	....	....	....	....	....
1975-76	California Golden Seals	46	1	11	12	26	....	....	....	....	....
	NHL Totals	**73**	**5**	**18**	**23**	**34**	....	....	....	....	....

Signed as a free agent by **California**, October, 1971.

KINNEAR, Geordie

Defense. Shoots left. 6'1", 195 lbs. Born, Simcoe, Ont., July 9, 1973.
(New Jersey's 8th choice, 162nd overall, in 1992 Entry Draft).

Season	Club	GP	G	A	Pts	PIM	GP	G	A	Pts	PIM
99-2000	Atlanta Thrashers	4	0	0	0	13	....	....	....	....	....
	NHL Totals	**4**	**0**	**0**	**0**	**13**	....	....	....	....	....

Signed as a free agent by **Atlanta**, August 12, 1999. Traded to **New Jersey** by **Atlanta** for future considerations, November 6, 2000. • Officially announced retirement, December 20, 2000.

KINSELLA, Brian

Center. Shoots right. 5'11", 180 lbs. Born, Barrie, Ont., February 11, 1954.
(Washington's 6th choice, 91st overall, in 1974 Amateur Draft).

Season	Club	GP	G	A	Pts	PIM	GP	G	A	Pts	PIM
1975-76	Washington Capitals	4	0	1	1	0	....	....	....	....	....
1976-77	Washington Capitals	6	0	0	0	0	....	....	....	....	....
	NHL Totals	**10**	**0**	**1**	**1**	**0**	....	....	....	....	....

KINSELLA, Ray

Left wing. Shoots left. 5'10", 162 lbs. Born, Ottawa, Ont., January 27, 1911.

Season	Club	GP	G	A	Pts	PIM	GP	G	A	Pts	PIM
1930-31	Ottawa Senators	14	0	0	0	0	....	....	....	....	....
	NHL Totals	**14**	**0**	**0**	**0**	**0**	....	....	....	....	....

Signed as a free agent by **Ottawa**, February 3, 1931.

KIPRUSOFF, Marko

Defense. Shoots left. 6'1", 195 lbs. Born, Turku, Finland, June 6, 1972.
(Montreal's 4th choice, 70th overall, in 1994 Entry Draft).

Season	Club	GP	G	A	Pts	PIM	GP	G	A	Pts	PIM
1995-96	Montreal Canadiens	24	0	4	4	8	....	....	....	....	....
2001-02	New York Islanders	27	0	6	6	4	....	....	....	....	....
	NHL Totals	**51**	**0**	**10**	**10**	**12**	....	....	....	....	....

Signed as a free agent by **NY Islanders**, June 15, 2001.

KIRK, Bobby

Right wing. Shoots right. 5'9", 180 lbs. Born, Dough Grange, Ireland, August 8, 1909.

Season	Club	GP	G	A	Pts	PIM	GP	G	A	Pts	PIM
1937-38	New York Rangers	39	4	8	12	14	....	....	....	....	....
	NHL Totals	**39**	**4**	**8**	**12**	**14**	....	....	....	....	....

Claimed by **NY Rangers** from **Vancouver** (NWHL) in Inter-League Draft, May 11, 1935.

KIRKPATRICK, Bob

Center. Shoots left. 5'10", 165 lbs. Born, Regina, Sask., December 1, 1915.

Season	Club	GP	G	A	Pts	PIM	GP	G	A	Pts	PIM
		REGULAR SEASON					PLAYOFFS				
1942-43	New York Rangers	49	12	12	24	6	....	....	....	....	....
	NHL Totals	**49**	**12**	**12**	**24**	**6**	....	....	....	....	....

KIRTON, Mark

Center. Shoots left. 5'10", 170 lbs. Born, Regina, Sask., February 3, 1958.
(Toronto's 2nd choice, 48th overall, in 1978 Amateur Draft).

Season	Club	GP	G	A	Pts	PIM	GP	G	A	Pts	PIM
1979-80	Toronto Maple Leafs	2	1	0	1	2	....	....	....	....	....
1980-81	Toronto Maple Leafs	11	0	0	0	0	....	....	....	....	....
	Detroit Red Wings	50	18	13	31	24	....	....	....	....	....
1981-82	Detroit Red Wings	74	14	28	42	62	....	....	....	....	....
1982-83	Detroit Red Wings	10	1	1	2	6	....	....	....	....	....
	Vancouver Canucks	31	4	6	10	4	4	1	2	3	7
1983-84	Vancouver Canucks	26	2	3	5	2	....	....	....	....	....
1984-85	Vancouver Canucks	62	17	5	22	21	....	....	....	....	....
	NHL Totals	**266**	**57**	**56**	**113**	**121**	**4**	**1**	**2**	**3**	**7**

Traded to **Detroit** by **Toronto** for Jim Rutherford, December 4, 1980. Traded to **Vancouver** by **Detroit** for Ivan Boldirev, January 17, 1983. Signed as a free agent by **Toronto**, August 15, 1987.

KISIO, Kelly

Center. Shoots right. 5'10", 185 lbs. Born, Peace River, Alta., September 18, 1959.

Season	Club	GP	G	A	Pts	PIM	GP	G	A	Pts	PIM
1982-83	Detroit Red Wings	15	4	3	7	0	....	....	....	....	....
1983-84	Detroit Red Wings	70	23	37	60	34	4	1	0	1	4
1984-85	Detroit Red Wings	75	20	41	61	56	3	0	2	2	2
1985-86	Detroit Red Wings	76	21	48	69	85	....	....	....	....	....
1986-87	New York Rangers	70	24	40	64	73	4	0	1	1	2
1987-88	New York Rangers	77	23	55	78	88	....	....	....	....	....
1988-89	New York Rangers	70	26	36	62	91	4	0	0	0	9
1989-90	New York Rangers	68	22	44	66	105	10	2	8	10	8
1990-91	New York Rangers	51	15	20	35	58	....	....	....	....	....
1991-92	San Jose Sharks	48	11	26	37	54	....	....	....	....	....
1992-93	San Jose Sharks	78	26	52	78	90	....	....	....	....	....
1993-94	Calgary Flames	51	7	23	30	28	7	0	2	2	8
1994-95	Calgary Flames	12	7	4	11	6	7	3	2	5	19
	NHL Totals	**761**	**229**	**429**	**658**	**768**	**39**	**6**	**15**	**21**	**52**

Played in NHL All-Star Game (1993)

Signed as a free agent by **Detroit**, March 2, 1983. Traded to **NY Rangers** by **Detroit** with Lane Lambert, Jim Leavins and Detroit's 5th round choice (later traded to Winnipeg – Winnipeg selected Benoit Lebeau) in 1988 Entry Draft for Glen Hanlon and NY Rangers' 3rd round choices in 1987 (Dennis Holland) and 1988 (Guy Dupuis) Entry Drafts, July 29, 1986. Claimed by **Minnesota** from **NY Rangers** in Expansion Draft, May 30, 1991. Traded to **San Jose** by **Minnesota** for Shane Churla, June 3, 1991. Signed as a free agent by **Calgary**, August 18, 1993. • Missed majority of 1994-95 season recovering from shoulder injury suffered in game vs. Washington, January 22, 1995.

KITCHEN, Bill

Defense. Shoots left. 6'1", 200 lbs. Born, Schomberg, Ont., October 2, 1960.

Season	Club	GP	G	A	Pts	PIM	GP	G	A	Pts	PIM
1981-82	Montreal Canadiens	1	0	0	0	7	3	0	1	1	0
1982-83	Montreal Canadiens	8	0	0	0	4	....	....	....	....	....
1983-84	Montreal Canadiens	3	0	0	0	2	....	....	....	....	....
1984-85	Toronto Maple Leafs	29	1	4	5	27	....	....	....	....	....
	NHL Totals	**41**	**1**	**4**	**5**	**40**	**3**	**0**	**1**	**1**	**0**

• Brother of Mike

Signed as a free agent by **Montreal**, October 23, 1979. Signed as a free agent by **Toronto**, August 16, 1984.

KITCHEN, Hobie

Defense. Shoots left. 5'11", 187 lbs. Born, Toronto, Ont., February 8, 1904.

Season	Club	GP	G	A	Pts	PIM	GP	G	A	Pts	PIM
1925-26 ♦	Montreal Maroons	30	5	2	7	16	....	....	....	....	....
1926-27	Detroit Cougars	17	0	2	2	42	....	....	....	....	....
	NHL Totals	**47**	**5**	**4**	**9**	**58**	....	....	....	....	....

Signed as a free agent by **Mtl. Maroons**, April 13, 1925. Signed as a free agent by **Detroit**, October 27, 1926. Traded to **New Haven** (Can-Am) by **Detroit** for cash, January 28, 1927.

KITCHEN, Mike

Defense. Shoots left. 5'10", 185 lbs. Born, Newmarket, Ont., February 1, 1956.
(Kansas City's 2nd choice, 38th overall, in 1976 Amateur Draft).

Season	Club	GP	G	A	Pts	PIM	GP	G	A	Pts	PIM
1976-77	Colorado Rockies	60	1	8	9	36	....	....	....	....	....
1977-78	Colorado Rockies	61	2	17	19	45	2	0	0	0	2
1978-79	Colorado Rockies	53	1	4	5	28	....	....	....	....	....
1979-80	Colorado Rockies	42	1	6	7	25	....	....	....	....	....
1980-81	Colorado Rockies	75	1	7	8	100	....	....	....	....	....
1981-82	Colorado Rockies	63	1	8	9	60	....	....	....	....	....
1982-83	New Jersey Devils	77	4	8	12	52	....	....	....	....	....
1983-84	New Jersey Devils	43	1	4	5	24	....	....	....	....	....
	NHL Totals	**474**	**12**	**62**	**74**	**370**	**2**	**0**	**0**	**0**	**2**

• Brother of Bill

Rights transferred to **Colorado** when **Kansas City** franchise relocated, July 15, 1976. Transferred to **New Jersey** after **Colorado** franchise relocated, June 30, 1982.

KJELLBERG, Patric

Right wing. Shoots left. 6'2", 210 lbs. Born, Trelleborg, Sweden, June 17, 1969.
(Montreal's 4th choice, 83rd overall, in 1988 Entry Draft).

Season	Club	GP	G	A	Pts	PIM	GP	G	A	Pts	PIM
1992-93	Montreal Canadiens	7	0	0	0	2	....	....	....	....	....
1998-99	Nashville Predators	71	11	20	31	24	....	....	....	....	....
99-2000	Nashville Predators	82	23	23	46	14	....	....	....	....	....
2000-01	Nashville Predators	81	14	31	45	12	....	....	....	....	....
2001-02	Nashville Predators	12	1	3	4	6	....	....	....	....	....
	Mighty Ducks of Anaheim	65	7	8	15	10	....	....	....	....	....
2002-03	Mighty Ducks of Anaheim	76	8	11	19	16	10	0	0	0	0
	NHL Totals	**394**	**64**	**96**	**160**	**84**	**10**	**0**	**0**	**0**	**0**

Signed as a free agent by **Nashville**, June 27, 1998. Traded to **Anaheim** by **Nashville** for Petr Tenkrat, November 1, 2001.

KLASSEN, Ralph

Center. Shoots left. 5'11", 175 lbs. Born, Humboldt, Sask., September 15, 1955.
(California's 1st choice, 3rd overall, in 1975 Amateur Draft).

Season	Club	GP	G	A	Pts	PIM	GP	G	A	Pts	PIM
1975-76	California Golden Seals	71	6	15	21	26	....	....	....	....	....
1976-77	Cleveland Barons	80	14	18	32	23	....	....	....	....	....
1977-78	Cleveland Barons	13	2	1	3	6	....	....	....	....	....
	Colorado Rockies	44	6	9	15	8	2	0	0	0	0
1978-79	Colorado Rockies	64	6	13	19	12	....	....	....	....	....
1979-80	St. Louis Blues	80	9	16	25	10	3	0	0	0	0
1980-81	St. Louis Blues	66	6	12	18	23	11	2	0	2	2
1981-82	St. Louis Blues	45	3	7	10	6	10	2	2	4	10
1982-83	St. Louis Blues	29	0	2	2	6	....	....	....	....	....
1983-84	St. Louis Blues	5	0	0	0	0	....	....	....	....	....
	NHL Totals	**497**	**52**	**93**	**145**	**120**	**26**	**4**	**2**	**6**	**12**

Transferred to **Cleveland** after **California** franchise relocated, June, 1976. Traded to **Colorado** by **Cleveland** with Fred Ahern for Rick Jodzio and Chuck Arnason, January 9, 1978. Claimed by **Hartford** from **Colorado** in Expansion Draft, June 13, 1979. Traded to **NY Islanders** by **Hartford** for Terry Richardson, June 14, 1979. Traded to **St. Louis** by **NY Islanders** as part of three-team transaction that sent Barry Gibbs and Tom Williams to NY Islanders (June 9, 1979) and Tom Williams to Los Angeles (August 16, 1979), June 14, 1979.

KLATT, Trent

Right wing. Shoots right. 6'1", 210 lbs. Born, Robbinsdale, MN, January 30, 1971.
(Washington's 5th choice, 82nd overall, in 1989 Entry Draft).

Season	Club	GP	G	A	Pts	PIM	GP	G	A	Pts	PIM
1991-92	Minnesota North Stars	1	0	0	0	0	6	0	0	0	2
1992-93	Minnesota North Stars	47	4	19	23	38	....	....	....	....	....
1993-94	Dallas Stars	61	14	24	38	30	9	2	1	3	4
1994-95	Dallas Stars	47	12	10	22	26	5	1	0	1	0
1995-96	Dallas Stars	22	4	4	8	23	....	....	....	....	....
	Philadelphia Flyers	49	3	8	11	21	12	4	1	5	0
1996-97	Philadelphia Flyers	76	24	21	45	20	19	4	3	7	12
1997-98	Philadelphia Flyers	82	14	28	42	16	5	0	0	0	0
1998-99	Philadelphia Flyers	2	0	0	0	0	....	....	....	....	....
	Vancouver Canucks	73	4	10	14	12	....	....	....	....	....
99-2000	Vancouver Canucks	47	10	10	20	26	....	....	....	....	....
2000-01	Vancouver Canucks	77	13	20	33	31	4	3	0	3	0
2001-02	Vancouver Canucks	34	8	7	15	10	....	....	....	....	....
2002-03	Vancouver Canucks	82	16	13	29	8	14	2	4	6	2
	NHL Totals	**700**	**126**	**174**	**300**	**261**	**74**	**16**	**9**	**25**	**20**

Traded to **Minnesota** by **Washington** with Steve Maltais for Shawn Chambers, June 21, 1991. Transferred to **Dallas** after **Minnesota** franchise relocated, June 9, 1993. Traded to **Philadelphia** by **Dallas** for Brent Fedyk, December 13, 1995. Traded to **Vancouver** by **Philadelphia** for Vancouver's 6th round choice (later traded to Atlanta – Atlanta selected Jeff Dwyer) in 2000 Entry Draft, October 19, 1998. • Missed majority of 2001-02 season recovering from abdominal injury suffered in game vs. Ottawa, November 20, 2001. Signed as a free agent by **Los Angeles**, July 7, 2003.

KLEE, Ken

Defense. Shoots right. 6', 210 lbs. Born, Indianapolis, IN, April 24, 1971.
(Washington's 11th choice, 177th overall, in 1990 Entry Draft).

Season	Club	GP	G	A	Pts	PIM	GP	G	A	Pts	PIM
1994-95	Washington Capitals	23	3	1	4	41	7	0	0	0	4
1995-96	Washington Capitals	66	8	3	11	60	1	0	0	0	0
1996-97	Washington Capitals	80	3	8	11	115	....	....	....	....	....
1997-98	Washington Capitals	51	4	2	6	46	9	1	0	1	10
1998-99	Washington Capitals	78	7	13	20	80	....	....	....	....	....
99-2000	Washington Capitals	80	7	13	20	79	5	0	1	1	10
2000-01	Washington Capitals	54	2	4	6	60	6	0	1	1	8
2001-02	Washington Capitals	68	8	8	16	38	....	....	....	....	....
2002-03	Washington Capitals	70	1	16	17	89	6	0	0	0	6
	NHL Totals	**570**	**43**	**68**	**111**	**608**	**34**	**1**	**2**	**3**	**38**

KLEIN, Lloyd

Left wing. Shoots left. 6', 185 lbs. Born, Saskatoon, Sask., January 13, 1910.

Season	Club	GP	G	A	Pts	PIM	GP	G	A	Pts	PIM
1928-29 ♦	Boston Bruins	8	1	0	1	5	....	....	....	....	....
1931-32	Boston Bruins	5	1	0	1	0	....	....	....	....	....
1932-33	New York Americans	15	2	2	4	4	....	....	....	....	....
1933-34	New York Americans	48	13	9	22	34	....	....	....	....	....
1934-35	New York Americans	29	7	3	10	9	....	....	....	....	....
1935-36	New York Americans	42	4	8	12	14	5	0	0	0	2
1936-37	New York Americans	14	2	1	3	2	....	....	....	....	....

Season	Club	GP	G	A	Pts	PIM	GP	G	A	Pts	PIM
		REGULAR SEASON					PLAYOFFS				
1937-38	New York Americans	3	0	1	1	0	....	....	....	....	....
	NHL Totals	**164**	**30**	**24**	**54**	**68**	**5**	**0**	**0**	**0**	**2**

Traded to **NY Americans** by **Boston** for Tommy Filmore, February 12, 1933. Traded to **Cleveland** (IAHL) by **NY Americans** for Les Cunningham, January 14, 1937.

KLEINENDORST, Scot

Defense. Shoots left. 6'3", 215 lbs. Born, Grand Rapids, MN, January 16, 1960.
(NY Rangers' 4th choice, 98th overall, in 1980 Entry Draft).

Season	Club	GP	G	A	Pts	PIM	GP	G	A	Pts	PIM
1982-83	New York Rangers	30	2	9	11	8	6	0	2	2	2
1983-84	New York Rangers	23	0	2	2	35	....	....	....	....	....
1984-85	Hartford Whalers	35	1	8	9	69	....	....	....	....	....
1985-86	Hartford Whalers	41	2	7	9	62	10	0	1	1	18
1986-87	Hartford Whalers	66	3	9	12	130	4	1	3	4	20
1987-88	Hartford Whalers	44	3	6	9	86	3	1	1	2	0
1988-89	Hartford Whalers	24	0	1	1	36	....	....	....	....	....
	Washington Capitals	3	0	1	1	10	....	....	....	....	....
1989-90	Washington Capitals	15	1	3	4	16	3	0	0	0	0
	NHL Totals	**281**	**12**	**46**	**58**	**452**	**26**	**2**	**7**	**9**	**40**

Traded to **Hartford** by **NY Rangers** for Blaine Stoughton, February 27, 1984. Traded to **Washington** by **Hartford** for Jim Thomson, March 6, 1989.

KLEMM, Jon

Defense. Shoots right. 6'2", 200 lbs. Born, Cranbrook, B.C., January 8, 1970.

Season	Club	GP	G	A	Pts	PIM	GP	G	A	Pts	PIM
1991-92	Quebec Nordiques	4	0	1	1	0	....	....	....	....	....
1993-94	Quebec Nordiques	7	0	0	0	4	....	....	....	....	....
1994-95	Quebec Nordiques	4	1	0	1	2	....	....	....	....	....
1995-96 ◆	Colorado Avalanche	56	3	12	15	20	15	2	1	3	0
1996-97	Colorado Avalanche	80	9	15	24	37	17	1	1	2	6
1997-98	Colorado Avalanche	67	6	8	14	30	4	0	0	0	0
1998-99	Colorado Avalanche	39	1	2	3	31	19	0	1	1	10
99-2000	Colorado Avalanche	73	5	7	12	34	17	2	1	3	9
2000-01 ◆	Colorado Avalanche	78	4	11	15	54	22	1	2	3	16
2001-02	Chicago Blackhawks	82	4	16	20	42	5	0	1	1	4
2002-03	Chicago Blackhawks	70	2	14	16	44	....	....	....	....	....
	NHL Totals	**560**	**35**	**86**	**121**	**298**	**99**	**6**	**7**	**13**	**45**

Signed as a free agent by **Quebec**, May 14, 1991. Transferred to **Colorado** after **Quebec** franchise relocated, June 21, 1995. • Missed majority of 1998-99 season recovering from knee injury suffered in game vs. Phoenix, November 10, 1998. Signed as a free agent by **Chicago**, July 1, 2001.

KLESLA, Rostislav

Defense. Shoots left. 6'3", 206 lbs. Born, Novy Jicin, Czech., March 21, 1982.
(Columbus' 1st choice, 4th overall, in 2000 Entry Draft).

Season	Club	GP	G	A	Pts	PIM	GP	G	A	Pts	PIM
2000-01	Columbus Blue Jackets	8	2	0	2	6	....	....	....	....	....
2001-02	Columbus Blue Jackets	75	8	8	16	74	....	....	....	....	....
2002 03	Columbus Blue Jackets	72	2	14	16	71	....	....	....	....	....
	NHL Totals	**155**	**12**	**22**	**34**	**151**	....	....	....	....	....

KLIMA, Petr

Wing. Shoots right. 6', 190 lbs. Born, Chomutov, Czech., December 23, 1964.
(Detroit's 5th choice, 88th overall, in 1983 Entry Draft).

Season	Club	GP	G	A	Pts	PIM	GP	G	A	Pts	PIM
1985-86	Detroit Red Wings	74	32	24	56	16	....	....	....	....	....
1986-87	Detroit Red Wings	77	30	23	53	42	13	1	2	3	4
1987-88	Detroit Red Wings	78	37	25	62	46	12	10	8	18	10
1988-89	Detroit Red Wings	51	25	16	41	44	6	2	4	6	19
1989-90	Detroit Red Wings	13	5	5	10	6	....	....	....	....	....
◆	Edmonton Oilers	63	25	28	53	66	21	5	0	5	8
1990-91	Edmonton Oilers	70	40	28	68	113	18	7	6	13	16
1991-92	Edmonton Oilers	57	21	13	34	52	15	1	4	5	8
1992-93	Edmonton Oilers	68	32	16	48	100	....	....	....	....	....
1993-94	Tampa Bay Lightning	75	28	27	55	76	....	....	....	....	....
1994-95	Tampa Bay Lightning	47	13	13	26	26	....	....	....	....	....
1995-96	Tampa Bay Lightning	67	22	30	52	68	4	2	0	2	14
1996-97	Los Angeles Kings	8	0	4	4	2	....	....	....	....	....
	Pittsburgh Penguins	9	1	3	4	4	....	....	....	....	....
	Edmonton Oilers	16	1	5	6	6	6	0	0	0	4
1998-99	Detroit Red Wings	13	1	0	1	4	....	....	....	....	....
	NHL Totals	**786**	**313**	**260**	**573**	**671**	**95**	**28**	**24**	**52**	**83**

Traded to **Edmonton** by **Detroit** with Joe Murphy, Adam Graves and Jeff Sharples for Jimmy Carson, Kevin McClelland and Edmonton's 5th round choice (later traded to Montreal – Montreal selected Brad Layzell) in 1991 Entry Draft, November 2, 1989. Traded to **Tampa Bay** by **Edmonton** for Tampa Bay's 3rd round choice (Brad Symes) in 1994 Entry Draft, June 16, 1993. Traded to **Los Angeles** by **Tampa Bay** for Los Angeles' 5th round choice (Jan Sulc) in 1997 Entry Draft, August 22, 1996. Traded to **Pittsburgh** by **Los Angeles** for conditional draft choice, October 25, 1996. • Klima failed to meet conditions specified in the trade agreement and conditional pick was forfeited. Signed as a free agent by **Edmonton**, February 26, 1997. Signed as a free agent by **Detroit**, January 11, 1999.

KLIMOVICH, Sergei

Center. Shoots right. 6'3", 189 lbs. Born, Novosibirsk, USSR, March 8, 1974.
(Chicago's 3rd choice, 41st overall, in 1992 Entry Draft).

Season	Club	GP	G	A	Pts	PIM	GP	G	A	Pts	PIM
1996-97	Chicago Blackhawks	1	0	0	0	2	....	....	....	....	....
	NHL Totals	**1**	**0**	**0**	**0**	**2**	....	....	....	....	....

KLINGBEIL, Ike

Defense. Shoots left. 5'10", 180 lbs. Born, Hancock, MI, November 3, 1908.

Season	Club	GP	G	A	Pts	PIM	GP	G	A	Pts	PIM
1936-37	Chicago Black Hawks	5	1	2	3	2	....	....	....	....	....
	NHL Totals	**5**	**1**	**2**	**3**	**2**	....	....	....	....	....

KLOUCEK, Tomas

Defense. Shoots left. 6'3", 203 lbs. Born, Prague, Czech., March 7, 1980.
(NY Rangers' 6th choice, 131st overall, in 1998 Entry Draft).

Season	Club	GP	G	A	Pts	PIM	GP	G	A	Pts	PIM
2000-01	New York Rangers	43	1	4	5	74	....	....	....	....	....
2001-02	New York Rangers	52	1	3	4	137	....	....	....	....	....
2002-03	Nashville Predators	3	0	0	0	2	....	....	....	....	....
	NHL Totals	**98**	**2**	**7**	**9**	**213**	....	....	....	....	....

Traded to **Nashville** by **NY Rangers** with Rem Murray and Marek Zidlicky for Mike Dunham, December 12, 2002.

KLUKAY, Joe

Left wing. Shoots left. 6', 182 lbs. Born, Sault Ste. Marie, Ont., November 6, 1922.

Season	Club	GP	G	A	Pts	PIM	GP	G	A	Pts	PIM
1942-43	Toronto Maple Leafs	....	....	....	....	....	1	0	0	0	0
1946-47 ◆	Toronto Maple Leafs	55	9	20	29	12	11	1	0	1	0
1947-48 ◆	Toronto Maple Leafs	59	15	15	30	28	9	1	1	2	2
1948-49 ◆	Toronto Maple Leafs	45	11	10	21	11	9	2	3	5	4
1949-50	Toronto Maple Leafs	70	15	16	31	19	7	3	0	3	4
1950-51 ◆	Toronto Maple Leafs	70	14	16	30	16	11	4	3	7	0
1951-52	Toronto Maple Leafs	43	4	8	12	6	4	1	1	2	0
1952-53	Boston Bruins	70	13	16	29	20	11	1	2	3	9
1953-54	Boston Bruins	70	20	17	37	27	4	0	0	0	0
1954-55	Boston Bruins	10	0	0	0	4	....	....	....	....	....
	Toronto Maple Leafs	56	8	8	16	44	4	0	0	0	4
1955-56	Toronto Maple Leafs	18	0	1	1	2	....	....	....	....	....
	NHL Totals	**566**	**109**	**127**	**236**	**189**	**71**	**13**	**10**	**23**	**23**

Played in NHL All-Star Game (1947, 1948, 1949)

Signed as a free agent by **Toronto**, March 15, 1943. Traded to **Boston** by **Toronto** for cash, September 16, 1952. Traded to **Toronto** by **Boston** for Leo Boivin, November 9, 1954.

KLUZAK, Gord

Defense. Shoots left. 6'4", 220 lbs. Born, Climax, Sask., March 4, 1964.
(Boston's 1st choice, 1st overall, in 1982 Entry Draft).

Season	Club	GP	G	A	Pts	PIM	GP	G	A	Pts	PIM
1982-83	Boston Bruins	70	1	6	7	105	17	1	4	5	54
1983-84	Boston Bruins	80	10	27	37	135	3	0	0	0	0
1985-86	Boston Bruins	70	8	31	39	155	3	1	1	2	16
1987-88	Boston Bruins	66	6	31	37	135	23	4	8	12	59
1988-89	Boston Bruins	3	0	1	1	2	....	....	....	....	....
1989-90	Boston Bruins	8	0	2	2	11	....	....	....	....	....
1990-91	Boston Bruins	2	0	0	0	0	....	....	....	....	....
	NHL Totals	**299**	**25**	**98**	**123**	**543**	**46**	**6**	**13**	**19**	**129**

Bill Masterton Trophy (1990)

• Missed entire 1984-85 season recovering from knee injury suffered in pre-season game vs. New Jersey, October 7, 1984. • Missed entire 1986-87 season recovering from knee surgery, September, 1986. • Missed majority of 1988-89 season recovering from 8th knee surgery, September 17, 1988. • Missed majority of 1989-90 season recovering from 10th knee surgery, October 27, 1989.

KNIBBS, Bill

Center. Shoots left. 6'1", 180 lbs. Born, Toronto, Ont., January 24, 1942.

Season	Club	GP	G	A	Pts	PIM	GP	G	A	Pts	PIM
1964-65	Boston Bruins	53	7	10	17	4	....	....	....	....	....
	NHL Totals	**53**	**7**	**10**	**17**	**4**	....	....	....	....	....

Claimed on waivers by **NY Rangers** from **Boston**, June 8, 1965. Traded to **Rochester** (AHL) by **NY Rangers** with $20,000 for Bob Kelly, June, 1973.

KNIPSCHEER, Fred

Center. Shoots left. 5'11", 185 lbs. Born, Ft. Wayne, IN, September 3, 1969.

Season	Club	GP	G	A	Pts	PIM	GP	G	A	Pts	PIM
1993-94	Boston Bruins	11	3	2	5	14	12	2	1	3	6
1994-95	Boston Bruins	16	3	1	4	2	4	0	0	0	0
1995-96	St. Louis Blues	1	0	0	0	2	....	....	....	....	....
	NHL Totals	**28**	**6**	**3**	**9**	**18**	**16**	**2**	**1**	**3**	**6**

Signed as a free agent by **Boston**, April 30, 1993. Traded to **St. Louis** by **Boston** for Rick Zombo, October 2, 1995. Signed as a free agent by **Chicago**, August 16, 1996.

KNOTT, Nick

Defense. Shoots left. 6'2", 200 lbs. Born, Kingston, Ont., July 23, 1920.

Season	Club	GP	G	A	Pts	PIM	GP	G	A	Pts	PIM
1941-42	Brooklyn Americans	14	3	1	4	9	....	....	....	....	....
	NHL Totals	**14**	**3**	**1**	**4**	**9**	....	....	....	....	....

Signed as a free agent by **Toronto**, October 31, 1940. Loaned to **Brooklyn** by **Toronto** with Red Heron and Gus Marker and future considerations (cash, February 2, 1942) for Lorne Carr, October 30, 1941. Traded to **Tulsa** (USHL) by **Toronto** for cash, May 15, 1947.

KNOX, Paul

Right wing. Shoots right. 5'10", 160 lbs. Born, Toronto, Ont., November 23, 1933.

Season	Club	GP	G	A	Pts	PIM	GP	G	A	Pts	PIM
1954-55	Toronto Maple Leafs	1	0	0	0	0	....	....	....	....	....
	NHL Totals	**1**	**0**	**0**	**0**	**0**	....	....	....	....	....

KNUBLE, Mike

Right wing. Shoots right. 6'3", 208 lbs. Born, Toronto, Ont., July 4, 1972.
(Detroit's 4th choice, 76th overall, in 1991 Entry Draft).

Season	Club	Regular Season GP	G	A	Pts	PIM	Playoffs GP	G	A	Pts	PIM
1996-97	Detroit Red Wings	9	1	0	1	0	....	....	....	....	....
1997-98 ♦	Detroit Red Wings	53	7	6	13	16	3	0	1	1	0
1998-99	New York Rangers	82	15	20	35	26	....	....	....	....	....
99-2000	New York Rangers	59	9	5	14	18	....	....	....	....	....
	Boston Bruins	14	3	3	6	8	....	....	....	....	....
2000-01	Boston Bruins	82	7	13	20	37	....	....	....	....	....
2001-02	Boston Bruins	54	8	6	14	42	2	0	0	0	0
2002-03	Boston Bruins	75	30	29	59	45	5	0	2	2	2
	NHL Totals	**428**	**80**	**82**	**162**	**192**	**10**	**0**	**3**	**3**	**2**

Traded to **NY Rangers** by **Detroit** for NY Rangers' 2nd round choice (Tomas Kopecky) in 2000 Entry Draft, October 1, 1998. Traded to **Boston** by **NY Rangers** for Rob DiMaio, March 10, 2000.

KNUTSEN, Espen

Center. Shoots left. 5'11", 188 lbs. Born, Oslo, Norway, January 12, 1972.
(Hartford's 9th choice, 204th overall, in 1990 Entry Draft).

Season	Club	Regular Season GP	G	A	Pts	PIM	Playoffs GP	G	A	Pts	PIM
1997-98	Mighty Ducks of Anaheim	19	3	0	3	6	....	....	....	....	....
2000-01	Columbus Blue Jackets	66	11	42	53	30	....	....	....	....	....
2001-02	Columbus Blue Jackets	77	11	31	42	47	....	....	....	....	....
2002-03	Columbus Blue Jackets	31	5	4	9	20	....	....	....	....	....
	NHL Totals	**193**	**30**	**77**	**107**	**103**	....	....	....	....	....

Played in NHL All-Star Game (2002)

Rights traded to **Anaheim** by **Hartford** for Kevin Brown, October 1, 1996. Traded to **Columbus** by **Anaheim** for Columbus' 4th round choice (Vladmir Korsunov) in 2001 Entry Draft, May 25, 2000.

KOBASEW, Chuck

Center. Shoots left. 5'11", 195 lbs. Born, Osoyoos, B.C., April 17, 1982.
(Calgary's 1st choice, 14th overall, in 2001 Entry Draft).

Season	Club	Regular Season GP	G	A	Pts	PIM	Playoffs GP	G	A	Pts	PIM
2002-03	Calgary Flames	23	4	2	6	8	....	....	....	....	....
	NHL Totals	**23**	**4**	**2**	**6**	**8**	....	....	....	....	....

KOCUR, Joe

Right wing. Shoots right. 6', 205 lbs. Born, Calgary, Alta., December 21, 1964.
(Detroit's 6th choice, 91st overall, in 1983 Entry Draft).

Season	Club	Regular Season GP	G	A	Pts	PIM	Playoffs GP	G	A	Pts	PIM
1984-85	Detroit Red Wings	17	1	0	1	64	3	1	0	1	5
1985-86	Detroit Red Wings	59	9	6	15	*377	....	....	....	....	....
1986-87	Detroit Red Wings	77	9	9	18	276	16	2	3	5	71
1987-88	Detroit Red Wings	63	7	7	14	263	10	0	1	1	13
1988-89	Detroit Red Wings	60	9	9	18	213	3	0	1	1	6
1989-90	Detroit Red Wings	71	16	20	36	268	....	....	....	....	....
1990-91	Detroit Red Wings	52	5	4	9	253	....	....	....	....	....
	New York Rangers	5	0	0	0	36	6	0	2	2	21
1991-92	New York Rangers	51	7	4	11	121	12	1	1	2	38
1992-93	New York Rangers	65	3	6	9	131	....	....	....	....	....
1993-94 ♦	New York Rangers	71	2	1	3	129	20	1	1	2	17
1994-95	New York Rangers	48	1	2	3	71	10	0	0	0	8
1995-96	New York Rangers	38	1	2	3	49	....	....	....	....	....
	Vancouver Canucks	7	0	1	1	19	1	0	0	0	0
1996-97 ♦	Detroit Red Wings	34	2	1	3	70	19	1	3	4	22
1997-98 ♦	Detroit Red Wings	63	6	5	11	92	18	4	0	4	30
1998-99	Detroit Red Wings	39	2	5	7	87	....	....	....	....	....
	NHL Totals	**820**	**80**	**82**	**162**	**2519**	**118**	**10**	**12**	**22**	**231**

Traded to **NY Rangers** by **Detroit** with Per Djoos for Kevin Miller, Jim Cummins and Dennis Vial, March 5, 1991. Traded to **Vancouver** by **NY Rangers** for Kay Whitmore, March 20, 1996. Signed as a free agent by **Detroit**, December 27, 1996. • Missed remainder of 1998-99 and entire 1999-2000 seasons recovering from hernia injury and surgery, May, 1999. • Officially announced retirement, October 10, 2000.

KOEHLER, Greg

Center. Shoots left. 6'2", 195 lbs. Born, Scarborough, Ont., February 27, 1975.

Season	Club	Regular Season GP	G	A	Pts	PIM	Playoffs GP	G	A	Pts	PIM
2000-01	Carolina Hurricanes	1	0	0	0	0	....	....	....	....	....
	NHL Totals	**1**	**0**	**0**	**0**	**0**	....	....	....	....	....

Signed as a free agent by **Carolina**, March 31, 1998. Traded to **Philadelphia** by **Carolina** for Jesse Boulerice, February 13, 2002. Signed as a free agent by **Nashville**, July 15, 2002. Traded to **Los Angeles** by **Nashville** for future considerations, February 4, 2003.

KOHN, Ladislav

Right wing. Shoots left. 5'11", 194 lbs. Born, Uherske Hradiste, Czech., March 4, 1975.
(Calgary's 9th choice, 175th overall, in 1994 Entry Draft).

Season	Club	Regular Season GP	G	A	Pts	PIM	Playoffs GP	G	A	Pts	PIM
1995-96	Calgary Flames	5	1	0	1	2	....	....	....	....	....
1997-98	Calgary Flames	4	0	1	1	0	....	....	....	....	....
1998-99	Toronto Maple Leafs	16	1	3	4	4	2	0	0	0	5
99-2000	Mighty Ducks of Anaheim	77	5	16	21	27	....	....	....	....	....
2000-01	Mighty Ducks of Anaheim	51	4	3	7	42	....	....	....	....	....
	Atlanta Thrashers	26	3	4	7	44	....	....	....	....	....
2001-02	Detroit Red Wings	4	0	0	0	4	....	....	....	....	....
2002-03	Calgary Flames	3	0	1	1	2	....	....	....	....	....
	NHL Totals	**186**	**14**	**28**	**42**	**125**	**2**	**0**	**0**	**0**	**5**

Traded to **Toronto** by **Calgary** for David Cooper, July 2, 1998. Claimed by **Atlanta** from **Toronto** in Waiver Draft, September 27, 1999. Traded to **Anaheim** by **Atlanta** for Anaheim's 8th round choice (Evan Nielsen) in 2000 Entry Draft, September 27, 1999. Traded to **Atlanta** by **Anaheim** for Sergei Vyshedkevich and Scott Langkow, February 9, 2001. Signed as a free agent by **Detroit** with player option to return to Finland, October 22, 2001. Traded to **Calgary** by **Detroit** for future considerations, September 10, 2002.

KOIVISTO, Tom

Defense. Shoots right. 5'10", 194 lbs. Born, Turku, Finland, June 4, 1974.
(St. Louis' 8th choice, 253rd overall, in 2002 Entry Draft).

Season	Club	Regular Season GP	G	A	Pts	PIM	Playoffs GP	G	A	Pts	PIM
2002-03	St. Louis Blues	22	2	4	6	10	....	....	....	....	....
	NHL Totals	**22**	**2**	**4**	**6**	**10**	....	....	....	....	....

KOIVU, Saku

Center. Shoots left. 5'10", 181 lbs. Born, Turku, Finland, November 23, 1974.
(Montreal's 1st choice, 21st overall, in 1993 Entry Draft).

Season	Club	Regular Season GP	G	A	Pts	PIM	Playoffs GP	G	A	Pts	PIM
1995-96	Montreal Canadiens	82	20	25	45	40	6	3	1	4	8
1996-97	Montreal Canadiens	50	17	39	56	38	5	1	3	4	10
1997-98	Montreal Canadiens	69	14	43	57	48	6	2	3	5	2
1998-99	Montreal Canadiens	65	14	30	44	38	....	....	....	....	....
99-2000	Montreal Canadiens	24	3	18	21	14	....	....	....	....	....
2000-01	Montreal Canadiens	54	17	30	47	40	....	....	....	....	....
2001-02	Montreal Canadiens	3	0	2	2	0	12	4	6	10	4
2002-03	Montreal Canadiens	82	21	50	71	72	....	....	....	....	....
	NHL Totals	**429**	**106**	**237**	**343**	**290**	**29**	**10**	**13**	**23**	**24**

Bill Masterton Memorial Trophy (2002)
Played in NHL All-Star Game (1998)

Missed majority of 1999-2000 season recovering from shoulder injury suffered in game vs. NY Rangers, October 30, 1999. • Missed majority of 2001-02 season recovering from non-Hodgkins lymphoma, September 6, 2001.

KOLANOS, Krys

Center. Shoots right. 6'3", 201 lbs. Born, Calgary, Alta., July 27, 1981.
(Phoenix's 1st choice, 19th overall, in 2000 Entry Draft).

Season	Club	Regular Season GP	G	A	Pts	PIM	Playoffs GP	G	A	Pts	PIM
2001-02	Phoenix Coyotes	57	11	11	22	48	2	0	0	0	6
2002-03	Phoenix Coyotes	2	0	0	0	0	....	....	....	....	....
	NHL Totals	**59**	**11**	**11**	**22**	**48**	**2**	**0**	**0**	**0**	**6**

KOLARIK, Pavel

Defense. Shoots left. 6'1", 207 lbs. Born, Vyskov, Czech., October 24, 1972.
(Boston's 11th choice, 268th overall, in 2000 Entry Draft).

Season	Club	Regular Season GP	G	A	Pts	PIM	Playoffs GP	G	A	Pts	PIM
2000-01	Boston Bruins	10	0	0	0	4	....	....	....	....	....
2001-02	Boston Bruins	13	0	0	0	6	....	....	....	....	....
	NHL Totals	**23**	**0**	**0**	**0**	**10**	....	....	....	....	....

KOLESAR, Mark

Left wing. Shoots right. 6'1", 188 lbs. Born, Brampton, Ont., January 23, 1973.

Season	Club	Regular Season GP	G	A	Pts	PIM	Playoffs GP	G	A	Pts	PIM
1995-96	Toronto Maple Leafs	21	2	2	4	14	3	1	0	1	2
1996-97	Toronto Maple Leafs	7	0	0	0	0	....	....	....	....	....
	NHL Totals	**28**	**2**	**2**	**4**	**14**	**3**	**1**	**0**	**1**	**2**

Signed as a free agent by **Toronto**, May 24, 1994.

KOLNIK, Juraj

Right wing. Shoots right. 5'10", 182 lbs. Born, Nitra, Czech., November 13, 1980.
(NY Islanders' 7th choice, 101st overall, in 1999 Entry Draft).

Season	Club	Regular Season GP	G	A	Pts	PIM	Playoffs GP	G	A	Pts	PIM
2000-01	New York Islanders	29	4	3	7	12	....	....	....	....	....
2001-02	New York Islanders	7	2	0	2	0	....	....	....	....	....
2002-03	Florida Panthers	10	0	1	1	0	....	....	....	....	....
	NHL Totals	**46**	**6**	**4**	**10**	**12**	....	....	....	....	....

Traded to **Florida** by **NY Islanders** with NY Islanders' 9th round choice (later traded to San Jose – San Jose selected Carter Lee) in 2003 Entry Draft for Sven Butenschon, October 11, 2002.

KOLSTAD, Dean

Defense. Shoots left. 6'6", 220 lbs. Born, Edmonton, Alta., June 16, 1968.
(Minnesota's 3rd choice, 33rd overall, in 1986 Entry Draft).

Season	Club	Regular Season GP	G	A	Pts	PIM	Playoffs GP	G	A	Pts	PIM
1988-89	Minnesota North Stars	25	1	5	6	42	....	....	....	....	....
1990-91	Minnesota North Stars	5	0	0	0	15	....	....	....	....	....
1992-93	San Jose Sharks	10	0	2	2	12	....	....	....	....	....
	NHL Totals	**40**	**1**	**7**	**8**	**69**	....	....	....	....	....

Claimed by **San Jose** from **Minnesota** in Dispersal Draft, May 30, 1991.

KOLTSOV, Konstantin

Right wing. Shoots left. 6', 190 lbs. Born, Minsk, USSR, April 17, 1981.
(Pittsburgh's 1st choice, 18th overall, in 1999 Entry Draft).

Season	Club	Regular Season GP	G	A	Pts	PIM	Playoffs GP	G	A	Pts	PIM
2002-03	Pittsburgh Penguins	2	0	0	0	0	....	....	....	....	....
	NHL Totals	**2**	**0**	**0**	**0**	**0**	....	....	....	....	....

KOMADOSKI, Neil

Defense. Shoots left. 6'2", 200 lbs. Born, Winnipeg, Man., November 5, 1951.
(Los Angeles' 2nd choice, 48th overall, in 1971 Amateur Draft).

Season	Club	Regular Season GP	G	A	Pts	PIM	Playoffs GP	G	A	Pts	PIM
1972-73	Los Angeles Kings	62	1	8	9	67	....	....	....	....	....
1973-74	Los Angeles Kings	68	2	4	6	43	2	0	0	0	12

Season	Club	REGULAR SEASON GP	G	A	Pts	PIM	PLAYOFFS GP	G	A	Pts	PIM
1974-75	Los Angeles Kings	75	4	12	16	69	3	0	0	0	2
1975-76	Los Angeles Kings	80	3	15	18	165	9	0	0	0	18
1976-77	Los Angeles Kings	68	3	9	12	109	9	0	2	2	15
1977-78	Los Angeles Kings	25	0	6	6	24	....	....	....	....	....
	St. Louis Blues	33	2	8	10	73	....	....	....	....	....
1978-79	St. Louis Blues	42	1	2	3	30	....	....	....	....	....
1979-80	St. Louis Blues	49	0	12	12	52	....	....	....	....	....
	NHL Totals	**502**	**16**	**76**	**92**	**632**	**23**	**0**	**2**	**2**	**47**

Traded to **St. Louis** by **Los Angeles** for St. Louis' 2nd round choice (Greg Terrion) in 1980 Entry Draft, January 14, 1978. Claimed by **St. Louis** as a fill-in during Expansion Draft, June 13, 1979.

KOMARNISKI, Zenith

Defense. Shoots left. 6', 200 lbs. Born, Edmonton, Alta., August 13, 1978.
(Vancouver's 2nd choice, 75th overall, in 1996 Entry Draft).

Season	Club	GP	G	A	Pts	PIM	GP	G	A	Pts	PIM
99-2000	Vancouver Canucks	18	1	1	2	8	....	....	....	....	....
2002-03	Vancouver Canucks	1	0	0	0	2	....	....	....	....	....
	NHL Totals	**19**	**1**	**1**	**2**	**10**	....	....	....	....	....

KOMISAREK, Mike

Defense. Shoots right. 6'4", 240 lbs. Born, Islip Terrace, NY, January 19, 1982.
(Montreal's 1st choice, 7th overall, in 2001 Entry Draft).

Season	Club	GP	G	A	Pts	PIM	GP	G	A	Pts	PIM
2002-03	Montreal Canadiens	21	0	1	1	28	....	....	....	....	....
	NHL Totals	**21**	**0**	**1**	**1**	**28**	....	....	....	....	....

KONIK, George

Defense/Left wing. Shoots left. 5'11", 190 lbs. Born, Flin Flon, Man., May 4, 1937.

Season	Club	GP	G	A	Pts	PIM	GP	G	A	Pts	PIM
1967-68	Pittsburgh Penguins	52	7	8	15	26	....	....	....	....	....
	NHL Totals	**52**	**7**	**8**	**15**	**26**	....	....	....	....	....

Traded to **Pittsburgh** by **NY Rangers** with Paul Andrea, Dunc McCallum and Frank Francis for Larry Jeffrey, June 6, 1967. Traded to **Oakland** by **Pittsburgh** for cash, July 4, 1968.

KONOWALCHUK, Steve

Left wing. Shoots left. 6'1", 207 lbs. Born, Salt Lake City, UT, November 11, 1972.
(Washington's 5th choice, 58th overall, in 1991 Entry Draft).

Season	Club	GP	G	A	Pts	PIM	GP	G	A	Pts	PIM
1991-92	Washington Capitals	1	0	0	0	0	....	....	....	....	....
1992-93	Washington Capitals	36	4	7	11	16	2	0	1	1	0
1993-94	Washington Capitals	62	12	14	26	33	11	0	1	1	10
1994-95	Washington Capitals	46	11	14	25	44	7	2	5	7	12
1995-96	Washington Capitals	70	23	22	45	92	2	0	2	2	0
1996-97	Washington Capitals	78	17	25	42	67	....	....	....	....	....
1997-98	Washington Capitals	80	10	24	34	80	....	....	....	....	....
1998-99	Washington Capitals	45	12	12	24	26	....	....	....	....	....
99-2000	Washington Capitals	82	16	27	43	80	5	1	0	1	2
2000-01	Washington Capitals	82	24	23	47	87	6	2	3	5	14
2001-02	Washington Capitals	28	2	12	14	23	....	....	....	....	....
2002-03	Washington Capitals	77	15	15	30	71	6	0	0	0	6
	NHL Totals	**687**	**146**	**195**	**341**	**619**	**39**	**5**	**12**	**17**	**44**

• Missed majority of 2001-02 season recovering from shoulder injury suffered in game vs. Los Angeles, October 16, 2001.

KONROYD, Steve

Defense. Shoots left. 6'1", 195 lbs. Born, Scarborough, Ont., February 10, 1961.
(Calgary's 4th choice, 39th overall, in 1980 Entry Draft).

Season	Club	GP	G	A	Pts	PIM	GP	G	A	Pts	PIM
1980-81	Calgary Flames	4	0	0	0	4	....	....	....	....	....
1981-82	Calgary Flames	63	3	14	17	78	3	0	0	0	12
1982-83	Calgary Flames	79	4	13	17	73	9	2	1	3	18
1983-84	Calgary Flames	80	1	13	14	94	8	1	2	3	8
1984-85	Calgary Flames	64	3	23	26	73	4	1	4	5	2
1985-86	Calgary Flames	59	7	20	27	64	....	....	....	....	....
	New York Islanders	14	0	5	5	16	3	0	0	0	6
1986-87	New York Islanders	72	5	16	21	70	14	1	4	5	10
1987-88	New York Islanders	62	2	15	17	99	6	1	0	1	4
1988-89	New York Islanders	21	1	5	6	2	....	....	....	....	....
	Chicago Blackhawks	57	5	7	12	40	16	2	0	2	10
1989-90	Chicago Blackhawks	75	3	14	17	34	20	1	3	4	19
1990-91	Chicago Blackhawks	70	0	12	12	40	6	1	0	1	8
1991-92	Chicago Blackhawks	49	2	14	16	65	....	....	....	....	....
	Hartford Whalers	33	2	10	12	32	7	0	1	1	2
1992-93	Hartford Whalers	59	3	11	14	63	....	....	....	....	....
	Detroit Red Wings	6	0	1	1	4	1	0	0	0	0
1993-94	Detroit Red Wings	19	0	0	0	10	....	....	....	....	....
	Ottawa Senators	8	0	2	2	2	....	....	....	....	....
1994-95	Calgary Flames	1	0	0	0	0	....	....	....	....	....
	NHL Totals	**895**	**41**	**195**	**236**	**863**	**97**	**10**	**15**	**25**	**99**

• Original family name was Koniarski

Traded to **NY Islanders** by **Calgary** with Richard Kromm for John Tonelli, March 11, 1986. Traded to **Chicago** by **NY Islanders** with Bob Bassen for Marc Bergevin and Gary Nylund, November 25, 1988. Traded to **Hartford** by **Chicago** for Rob Brown, January 24, 1992. Traded to **Detroit** by **Hartford** for Detroit's 6th round choice (traded back to Detroit – Detroit selected Tim Spitzig) in 1993 Entry Draft, March 22, 1993. Traded to **Ottawa** by **Detroit** for Daniel Berthiaume, March 21, 1994. Signed as a free agent by **Calgary**, April 7, 1995.

KONSTANTINOV, Vladimir

Defense. Shoots right. 5'11", 190 lbs. Born, Murmansk, USSR, March 19, 1967.
(Detroit's 12th choice, 221st overall, in 1989 Entry Draft).

Season	Club	GP	G	A	Pts	PIM	GP	G	A	Pts	PIM
1991-92	Detroit Red Wings	79	8	26	34	172	11	0	1	1	16
1992-93	Detroit Red Wings	82	5	17	22	137	7	0	1	1	8
1993-94	Detroit Red Wings	80	12	21	33	138	7	0	2	2	4
1994-95	Detroit Red Wings	47	3	11	14	101	18	1	1	2	22
1995-96	Detroit Red Wings	81	14	20	34	139	19	4	5	9	28
1996-97 ♦	Detroit Red Wings	77	5	33	38	151	20	0	4	4	29
	NHL Totals	**446**	**47**	**128**	**175**	**838**	**82**	**5**	**14**	**19**	**107**

NHL All-Rookie Team (1992) • NHL Second All-Star Team (1996) • Alka-Seltzer Plus Award (1996)

• Suffered career-ending injuries in automobile accident, July 13, 1997.

KONTOS, Chris

Left wing/Center. Shoots left. 6'1", 195 lbs. Born, Toronto, Ont., December 10, 1963.
(NY Rangers' 1st choice, 15th overall, in 1982 Entry Draft).

Season	Club	GP	G	A	Pts	PIM	GP	G	A	Pts	PIM
1982-83	New York Rangers	44	8	7	15	33	....	....	....	....	....
1983-84	New York Rangers	6	0	1	1	8	....	....	....	....	....
1984-85	New York Rangers	28	4	8	12	24	....	....	....	....	....
1986-87	Pittsburgh Penguins	31	8	9	17	6	....	....	....	....	....
1987-88	Pittsburgh Penguins	36	1	7	8	12	....	....	....	....	....
	Los Angeles Kings	6	2	10	12	2	4	1	0	1	4
1988-89	Los Angeles Kings	7	2	1	3	2	11	9	0	9	8
1989-90	Los Angeles Kings	6	2	2	4	4	5	1	0	1	0
1992-93	Tampa Bay Lightning	66	27	24	51	12	....	....	....	....	....
	NHL Totals	**230**	**54**	**69**	**123**	**103**	**20**	**11**	**0**	**11**	**12**

Traded to **Pittsburgh** by **NY Rangers** for Ron Duguay, January 21, 1987. Traded to **Los Angeles** by **Pittsburgh** with Pittsburgh's 6th round choice (Micah Aivazoff) in 1988 Entry Draft for Bryan Erickson, February 5, 1988. Signed as a free agent by **Tampa Bay**, July 21, 1992. Signed as a free agent by **Florida**, July 7, 1995.

KOPAK, Russ

Center. Shoots left. 5'10", 158 lbs. Born, Edmonton, Alta., April 26, 1924.

Season	Club	GP	G	A	Pts	PIM	GP	G	A	Pts	PIM
1943-44	Boston Bruins	24	7	9	16	0	....	....	....	....	....
	NHL Totals	**24**	**7**	**9**	**16**	**0**	....	....	....	....	....

Signed as a free agent by **Victoria** (PCHL) after being released by **Seattle** (PCHL), November 16, 1949.

KORAB, Jerry

Defense. Shoots left. 6'3", 220 lbs. Born, Sault Ste. Marie, Ont., September 15, 1948.

Season	Club	GP	G	A	Pts	PIM	GP	G	A	Pts	PIM
1970-71	Chicago Black Hawks	46	4	14	18	152	7	1	0	1	20
1971-72	Chicago Black Hawks	73	9	5	14	95	8	0	1	1	20
1972-73	Chicago Black Hawks	77	12	15	27	94	15	0	0	0	22
1973-74	Vancouver Canucks	31	4	7	11	64	....	....	....	....	....
	Buffalo Sabres	45	6	12	18	73	....	....	....	....	....
1974-75	Buffalo Sabres	79	12	44	56	184	16	3	2	5	32
1975-76	Buffalo Sabres	65	13	28	41	85	9	1	3	4	12
1976-77	Buffalo Sabres	77	14	33	47	120	6	2	4	6	8
1977-78	Buffalo Sabres	77	7	34	41	119	8	0	5	5	6
1978-79	Buffalo Sabres	78	11	40	51	104	3	1	0	1	4
1979-80	Buffalo Sabres	43	1	10	11	74	....	....	....	....	....
	Los Angeles Kings	11	1	2	3	34	3	0	1	1	11
1980-81	Los Angeles Kings	78	9	43	52	139	4	0	0	0	33
1981-82	Los Angeles Kings	50	5	13	18	91	10	0	2	2	26
1982-83	Los Angeles Kings	72	3	26	29	90	....	....	....	....	....
1983-84	Buffalo Sabres	48	2	9	11	82	3	0	0	0	5
1984-85	Buffalo Sabres	25	1	6	7	29	1	0	0	0	2
	NHL Totals	**975**	**114**	**341**	**455**	**1629**	**93**	**8**	**18**	**26**	**201**

Played in NHL All-Star Game (1975, 1976)

Traded to **Vancouver** by **Chicago** with Gary Smith for Dale Tallon, May 14, 1973. Traded to **Buffalo** by **Vancouver** for John Gould and Tracy Pratt, December 27, 1973. Traded to **Los Angeles** by **Buffalo** for Los Angeles' 1st round choice (Phil Housley) in 1982 Entry Draft, March 10, 1980. Signed as a free agent by **Minnesota**, October 17, 1983. Claimed on waivers by **Buffalo** from **Minnesota**, October 20, 1983.

KORDIC, Dan

Left wing. Shoots left. 6'5", 234 lbs. Born, Edmonton, Alta., April 18, 1971.
(Philadelphia's 9th choice, 88th overall, in 1990 Entry Draft).

Season	Club	GP	G	A	Pts	PIM	GP	G	A	Pts	PIM
1991-92	Philadelphia Flyers	46	1	3	4	126	....	....	....	....	....
1993-94	Philadelphia Flyers	4	0	0	0	5	....	....	....	....	....
1995-96	Philadelphia Flyers	9	1	0	1	31	....	....	....	....	....
1996-97	Philadelphia Flyers	75	1	4	5	210	12	1	0	1	22
1997-98	Philadelphia Flyers	61	1	1	2	210	....	....	....	....	....
1998-99	Philadelphia Flyers	2	0	0	0	2	....	....	....	....	....
	NHL Totals	**197**	**4**	**8**	**12**	**584**	**12**	**1**	**0**	**1**	**22**

• Brother of John

KORDIC, John

Right wing. Shoots right. 6'2", 210 lbs. Born, Edmonton, Alta., March 22, 1965.
(Montreal's 6th choice, 80th overall, in 1983 Entry Draft).

Season	Club	GP	G	A	Pts	PIM	GP	G	A	Pts	PIM
1985-86 ♦	Montreal Canadiens	5	0	1	1	12	18	0	0	0	53
1986-87	Montreal Canadiens	44	5	3	8	151	11	2	0	2	19
1987-88	Montreal Canadiens	60	2	6	8	159	7	2	2	4	26
1988-89	Montreal Canadiens	6	0	0	0	13	....	....	....	....	....
	Toronto Maple Leafs	46	1	2	3	185	....	....	....	....	....

Season	Club	GP	G	A	Pts	PIM	GP	G	A	Pts	PIM
		REGULAR SEASON					PLAYOFFS				
1989-90	Toronto Maple Leafs	55	9	4	13	252	5	0	1	1	33
1990-91	Toronto Maple Leafs	3	0	0	0	9	....	....	....	....	....
	Washington Capitals	7	0	0	0	101	....	....	....	....	....
1991-92	Quebec Nordiques	18	0	2	2	115	....	....	....	....	....
	NHL Totals	**244**	**17**	**18**	**35**	**997**	**41**	**4**	**3**	**7**	**131**

• Brother of Dan

Traded to **Toronto** by **Montreal** with Montreal's 6th round choice (Michael Doers) in 1989 Entry Draft for Russ Courtnall, November 7, 1988. Traded to **Washington** by **Toronto** with Paul Fenton for Washington's 5th round choice (Alexei Kudashov) in 1991 Entry Draft, January 24, 1991. Signed as a free agent by **Quebec**, October 4, 1991.

KORN, Jim

Defense/Left wing. Shoots left. 6'4", 220 lbs. Born, Hopkins, MN, July 28, 1957.
(Detroit's 4th choice, 73rd overall, in 1977 Amateur Draft).

Season	Club	GP	G	A	Pts	PIM	GP	G	A	Pts	PIM
1979-80	Detroit Red Wings	63	5	13	18	108	....	....	....	....	....
1980-81	Detroit Red Wings	63	5	15	20	246	....	....	....	....	....
1981-82	Detroit Red Wings	59	1	7	8	104	....	....	....	....	....
	Toronto Maple Leafs	11	1	3	4	44	....	....	....	....	....
1982-83	Toronto Maple Leafs	80	8	21	29	236	3	0	0	0	26
1983-84	Toronto Maple Leafs	65	12	14	26	257	....	....	....	....	....
1984-85	Toronto Maple Leafs	41	5	5	10	171	....	....	....	....	....
1986-87	Buffalo Sabres	52	4	10	14	158	....	....	....	....	....
1987-88	New Jersey Devils	52	8	13	21	140	9	0	2	2	71
1988-89	New Jersey Devils	65	15	16	31	212	....	....	....	....	....
1989-90	New Jersey Devils	37	2	3	5	99	....	....	....	....	....
	Calgary Flames	9	0	2	2	26	4	1	0	1	12
	NHL Totals	**597**	**66**	**122**	**188**	**1801**	**16**	**1**	**2**	**3**	**109**

Traded to **Toronto** by **Detroit** for Toronto's 4th round choice (Craig Coxe) in 1982 Entry Draft and Toronto's 5th round choice (Joe Kocur) in 1983 Entry Draft, March 8, 1982. • Missed entire 1985-86 season recovering from knee injury suffered in training camp, September 29, 1985. Traded to **Calgary** by **Toronto** for Terry Johnson, October 3, 1986. Traded to **Buffalo** by **Calgary** for Brian Engblom, October 3, 1986. Traded to **New Jersey** by **Buffalo** for Jan Ludwig, May 22, 1987. Traded to **Calgary** by **New Jersey** for Calgary's 5th round choice (Petr Kuchyna) in 1990 Entry Draft, March 6, 1990.

KORNEY, Mike

Right wing. Shoots right. 6'3", 195 lbs. Born, Dauphin, Man., September 15, 1953.
(Detroit's 4th choice, 59th overall, in 1973 Amateur Draft).

Season	Club	GP	G	A	Pts	PIM	GP	G	A	Pts	PIM
1973-74	Detroit Red Wings	2	0	0	0	0	....	....	....	....	....
1974-75	Detroit Red Wings	30	8	2	10	18	....	....	....	....	....
1975-76	Detroit Red Wings	27	1	7	8	23	....	....	....	....	....
1978-79	New York Rangers	18	0	1	1	18	....	....	....	....	....
	NHL Totals	**77**	**9**	**10**	**19**	**59**	....	....	....	....	....

Traded to **Philadelphia** by **Detroit** with Rick Lapointe for Terry Murray, Bob Ritchie, Steve Coates and Dave Kelly, February 17, 1977. Signed as a free agent by **St. Louis**, July 22, 1978. Traded to **Montreal** by **St. Louis** for Gord McTavish, October 7, 1978. Claimed by **NY Rangers** from **Montreal** in Waiver Draft, October 9, 1978.

KOROLEV, Evgeny

Defense. Shoots left. 6'1", 214 lbs. Born, Moscow, USSR, July 24, 1978.
(NY Islanders' 6th choice, 182nd overall, in 1998 Entry Draft).

Season	Club	GP	G	A	Pts	PIM	GP	G	A	Pts	PIM
99-2000	New York Islanders	17	1	2	3	8	....	....	....	....	....
2000-01	New York Islanders	8	0	0	0	6	....	....	....	....	....
2001-02	New York Islanders	17	0	2	2	6	2	0	0	0	0
	NHL Totals	**42**	**1**	**4**	**5**	**20**	**2**	**0**	**0**	**0**	**0**

• Re-entered NHL Entry Draft. Originally NY Islanders' 9th choice, 192nd overall, in 1996 Entry Draft.

KOROLEV, Igor

Center. Shoots left. 6'1", 190 lbs. Born, Moscow, USSR, September 6, 1970.
(St. Louis' 1st choice, 38th overall, in 1992 Entry Draft).

Season	Club	GP	G	A	Pts	PIM	GP	G	A	Pts	PIM
1992-93	St. Louis Blues	74	4	23	27	20	3	0	0	0	0
1993-94	St. Louis Blues	73	6	10	16	40	2	0	0	0	0
1994-95	Winnipeg Jets	45	8	22	30	10	....	....	....	....	....
1995-96	Winnipeg Jets	73	22	29	51	42	6	0	3	3	0
1996-97	Phoenix Coyotes	41	3	7	10	28	1	0	0	0	0
1997-98	Toronto Maple Leafs	78	17	22	39	22	....	....	....	....	....
1998-99	Toronto Maple Leafs	66	13	34	47	46	1	0	0	0	0
99-2000	Toronto Maple Leafs	80	20	26	46	22	12	0	4	4	6
2000-01	Toronto Maple Leafs	73	10	19	29	28	11	0	0	0	0
2001-02	Chicago Blackhawks	82	9	20	29	20	5	0	1	1	0
2002-03	Chicago Blackhawks	48	4	5	9	30	....	....	....	....	....
	NHL Totals	**733**	**116**	**217**	**333**	**308**	**41**	**0**	**8**	**8**	**6**

Claimed by **Winnipeg** from **St. Louis** in NHL Waiver Draft, January 18, 1995. Transferred to **Phoenix** after **Winnipeg** franchise relocated, July 1, 1996. Signed as a free agent by **Toronto**, September 29, 1997. Traded to **Chicago** by **Toronto** for Philadelphia's 3rd round choice (previously acquired, Toronto selected Nicolas Corbeil) in 2001 Entry Draft, June 23, 2001.

KOROLL, Cliff

Right wing. Shoots right. 6'1", 195 lbs. Born, Canora, Sask., October 1, 1946.

Season	Club	GP	G	A	Pts	PIM	GP	G	A	Pts	PIM
1969-70	Chicago Black Hawks	73	18	19	37	44	8	1	4	5	9
1970-71	Chicago Black Hawks	72	16	34	50	85	18	7	9	16	18
1971-72	Chicago Black Hawks	76	22	23	45	51	8	0	0	0	11
1972-73	Chicago Black Hawks	77	33	24	57	38	16	4	6	10	6
1973-74	Chicago Black Hawks	78	21	25	46	32	11	2	5	7	13
1974-75	Chicago Black Hawks	80	27	32	59	27	8	3	5	8	8
1975-76	Chicago Black Hawks	80	25	33	58	29	4	1	0	1	0
1976-77	Chicago Black Hawks	80	15	26	41	25	2	0	0	0	0
1977-78	Chicago Black Hawks	73	16	15	31	19	4	1	0	1	0
1978-79	Chicago Black Hawks	78	12	19	31	20	4	0	0	0	0
1979-80	Chicago Black Hawks	47	3	4	7	6	2	0	0	0	2
	NHL Totals	**814**	**208**	**254**	**462**	**376**	**85**	**19**	**29**	**48**	**67**

Rights traded to **Chicago** by **LA Blades** (WHL) for cash, August, 1967.

KOROLYUK, Alexander

Left wing. Shoots left. 5'9", 195 lbs. Born, Moscow, USSR, January 15, 1976.
(San Jose's 6th choice, 141st overall, in 1994 Entry Draft).

Season	Club	GP	G	A	Pts	PIM	GP	G	A	Pts	PIM
1997-98	San Jose Sharks	19	2	3	5	6	....	....	....	....	....
1998-99	San Jose Sharks	55	12	18	30	26	6	1	3	4	2
99-2000	San Jose Sharks	57	14	21	35	35	9	0	3	3	6
2000-01	San Jose Sharks	70	12	13	25	41	2	0	0	0	0
2001-02	San Jose Sharks	32	3	7	10	14	....	....	....	....	....
	NHL Totals	**233**	**43**	**62**	**105**	**122**	**17**	**1**	**6**	**7**	**8**

• Spent majority of 2001-02 season on practice roster.

KORTKO, Roger

Center. Shoots left. 5'11", 195 lbs. Born, Hafford, Sask., February 1, 1963.
(NY Islanders' 6th choice, 126th overall, in 1982 Entry Draft).

Season	Club	GP	G	A	Pts	PIM	GP	G	A	Pts	PIM
1984-85	New York Islanders	27	2	9	11	9	10	0	3	3	17
1985-86	New York Islanders	52	5	8	13	19	....	....	....	....	....
	NHL Totals	**79**	**7**	**17**	**24**	**28**	**10**	**0**	**3**	**3**	**17**

Signed as a free agent by **Hartford**, September 15, 1987.

KOSTOPOULOS, Tom

Right wing. Shoots right. 6', 200 lbs. Born, Mississauga, Ont., January 24, 1979.
(Pittsburgh's 9th choice, 204th overall, in 1999 Entry Draft).

Season	Club	GP	G	A	Pts	PIM	GP	G	A	Pts	PIM
2001-02	Pittsburgh Penguins	11	1	2	3	9	....	....	....	....	....
2002-03	Pittsburgh Penguins	8	0	1	1	0	....	....	....	....	....
	NHL Totals	**19**	**1**	**3**	**4**	**9**	....	....	....	....	....

KOSTYNSKI, Doug

Center. Shoots right. 6'1", 170 lbs. Born, Castlegar, B.C., February 23, 1963.
(Boston's 9th choice, 186th overall, in 1982 Entry Draft).

Season	Club	GP	G	A	Pts	PIM	GP	G	A	Pts	PIM
1983-84	Boston Bruins	9	3	1	4	2	....	....	....	....	....
1984-85	Boston Bruins	6	0	0	0	2	....	....	....	....	....
	NHL Totals	**15**	**3**	**1**	**4**	**4**	....	....	....	....	....

KOTALIK, Ales

Right wing. Shoots right. 6'1", 217 lbs. Born, Jindrichuv Hradec, Czech., December 23, 1978.
(Buffalo's 7th choice, 164th overall, in 1998 Entry Draft).

Season	Club	GP	G	A	Pts	PIM	GP	G	A	Pts	PIM
2001-02	Buffalo Sabres	13	1	3	4	2	....	....	....	....	....
2002-03	Buffalo Sabres	68	21	14	35	30	....	....	....	....	....
	NHL Totals	**81**	**22**	**17**	**39**	**32**	....	....	....	....	....

KOTANEN, Dick

Defense. Shoots right. 5'11", 190 lbs. Born, Port Arthur, Ont., November 18, 1925.

Season	Club	GP	G	A	Pts	PIM	GP	G	A	Pts	PIM
1950-51	New York Rangers	1	0	0	0	0	....	....	....	....	....
	NHL Totals	**1**	**0**	**0**	**0**	**0**	....	....	....	....	....

KOTSOPOULOS, Chris

Defense. Shoots right. 6'3", 215 lbs. Born, Scarborough, Ont., November 27, 1958.

Season	Club	GP	G	A	Pts	PIM	GP	G	A	Pts	PIM
1980-81	New York Rangers	54	4	12	16	153	14	0	3	3	63
1981-82	Hartford Whalers	68	13	20	33	147	....	....	....	....	....
1982-83	Hartford Whalers	68	6	24	30	125	....	....	....	....	....
1983-84	Hartford Whalers	72	5	13	18	118	....	....	....	....	....
1984-85	Hartford Whalers	33	5	3	8	53	....	....	....	....	....
1985-86	Toronto Maple Leafs	61	6	11	17	83	10	1	0	1	14
1986-87	Toronto Maple Leafs	43	2	10	12	75	7	0	0	0	14
1987-88	Toronto Maple Leafs	21	2	2	4	19	....	....	....	....	....
1988-89	Toronto Maple Leafs	57	1	14	15	44	....	....	....	....	....
1989-90	Detroit Red Wings	2	0	0	0	10	....	....	....	....	....
	NHL Totals	**479**	**44**	**109**	**153**	**827**	**31**	**1**	**3**	**4**	**91**

Signed as a free agent by **NY Rangers**, July 10, 1980. Traded to **Hartford** by **NY Rangers** with Gerry McDonald and Doug Sulliman for Mike Rogers and Hartford's 10th round choice (Simo Saarinen) in 1982 Entry Draft, October 2, 1981. Traded to **Toronto** by **Hartford** for Stew Gavin, October 7, 1985. Signed as a free agent by **Detroit**, June 23, 1989.

KOVALCHUK, Ilya

Left wing. Shoots right. 6'1", 220 lbs. Born, Tver, USSR, April 15, 1983.
(Atlanta's 1st choice, 1st overall, in 2001 Entry Draft).

Season	Club	GP	G	A	Pts	PIM	GP	G	A	Pts	PIM
2001-02	Atlanta Thrashers	65	29	22	51	28	....	....	....	....	....
2002-03	Atlanta Thrashers	81	38	29	67	57	....	....	....	....	....
	NHL Totals	**146**	**67**	**51**	**118**	**85**	....	....	....	....	....

NHL All-Rookie Team (2002)

KOVALENKO, Andrei

Right wing. Shoots left. 5'10", 200 lbs. Born, Balakovo, USSR, June 7, 1970.
(Quebec's 6th choice, 148th overall, in 1990 Entry Draft).

Season	Club	GP	G	A	Pts	PIM	GP	G	A	Pts	PIM
1992-93	Quebec Nordiques	81	27	41	68	57	4	1	0	1	2

Season	Club	GP	G	A	Pts	PIM	GP	G	A	Pts	PIM
		REGULAR SEASON					PLAYOFFS				
1993-94	Quebec Nordiques	58	16	17	33	46	....	....	....	....	....
1994-95	Quebec Nordiques	45	14	10	24	31	6	0	1	1	2
1995-96	Colorado Avalanche	26	11	11	22	16	....	....	....	....	....
	Montreal Canadiens	51	17	17	34	33	6	0	0	0	6
1996-97	Edmonton Oilers	74	32	27	59	81	12	4	3	7	6
1997-98	Edmonton Oilers	59	6	17	23	28	1	0	0	0	2
1998-99	Edmonton Oilers	43	13	14	27	30	....	....	....	....	....
	Philadelphia Flyers	13	0	1	1	2	....	....	....	....	....
	Carolina Hurricanes	18	6	6	12	0	4	0	2	2	2
99-2000	Carolina Hurricanes	76	15	24	39	38	....	....	....	....	....
2000-01	Boston Bruins	76	16	21	37	27	....	....	....	....	....
	NHL Totals	**620**	**173**	**206**	**379**	**389**	**33**	**5**	**6**	**11**	**20**

Transferred to **Colorado** after **Quebec** franchise relocated, June 21, 1995. Traded to **Montreal** by **Colorado** with Martin Rucinsky and Jocelyn Thibault for Patrick Roy and Mike Keane, December 6, 1995. Traded to **Edmonton** by **Montreal** for Scott Thornton, September 6, 1996. Traded to **Philadelphia** by **Edmonton** for Alexandre Daigle, January 29, 1999. Traded to **Carolina** by **Philadelphia** for Adam Burt, March 6, 1999. Signed as a free agent by **Boston**, July 25, 2000.

KOVALEV, Alexei

Right wing. Shoots left. 6'1", 220 lbs. Born, Togliatti, USSR, February 24, 1973.
(NY Rangers' 1st choice, 15th overall, in 1991 Entry Draft).

Season	Club	GP	G	A	Pts	PIM	GP	G	A	Pts	PIM
1992-93	New York Rangers	65	20	18	38	79	....	....	....	....	....
1993-94◆	New York Rangers	76	23	33	56	154	23	9	12	21	18
1994-95	New York Rangers	48	13	15	28	30	10	4	7	11	10
1995-96	New York Rangers	81	24	34	58	98	11	3	4	7	14
1996-97	New York Rangers	45	13	22	35	42	....	....	....	....	....
1997-98	New York Rangers	73	23	30	53	44	....	....	....	....	....
1998-99	New York Rangers	14	3	4	7	12	....	....	....	....	....
	Pittsburgh Penguins	63	20	26	46	37	10	5	7	12	14
99-2000	Pittsburgh Penguins	82	26	40	66	94	11	1	5	6	10
2000-01	Pittsburgh Penguins	79	44	51	95	96	18	5	5	10	16
2001-02	Pittsburgh Penguins	67	32	44	76	80	....	....	....	....	....
2002-03	Pittsburgh Penguins	54	27	37	64	50	....	....	....	....	....
	New York Rangers	24	10	3	13	20	....	....	....	....	....
	NHL Totals	**771**	**278**	**357**	**635**	**836**	**83**	**27**	**40**	**67**	**82**

Played in NHL All-Star Game (2001, 2003)

Traded to **Pittsburgh** by **NY Rangers** with Harry York for Petr Nedved, Chris Tamer and Sean Pronger, November 25, 1998. Traded to **NY Rangers** by **Pittsburgh** with Mike Wilson, Janne Laukkanen and Dan LaCouture for Joel Bouchard, Richard Lintner, Rico Fata, Mikael Samuelsson and future considerations, February 10, 2003.

KOWAL, Joe

Left wing. Shoots left. 6'5", 212 lbs. Born, Toronto, Ont., February 3, 1956.
(Buffalo's 1st choice, 33rd overall, in 1976 Amateur Draft).

Season	Club	GP	G	A	Pts	PIM	GP	G	A	Pts	PIM
1976-77	Buffalo Sabres	16	0	5	5	6	....	....	....	....	....
1977-78	Buffalo Sabres	6	0	0	0	7	2	0	0	0	0
	NHL Totals	**22**	**0**	**5**	**5**	**13**	**2**	**0**	**0**	**0**	**0**

KOZAK, Don

Right wing. Shoots right. 5'11", 190 lbs. Born, Saskatoon, Sask., February 2, 1952.
(Los Angeles' 1st choice, 20th overall, in 1972 Amateur Draft).

Season	Club	GP	G	A	Pts	PIM	GP	G	A	Pts	PIM
1972-73	Los Angeles Kings	72	14	6	20	104	....	....	....	....	....
1973-74	Los Angeles Kings	76	21	14	35	54	5	0	0	0	33
1974-75	Los Angeles Kings	77	16	15	31	64	3	1	1	2	7
1975-76	Los Angeles Kings	62	20	24	44	94	9	1	0	1	12
1976-77	Los Angeles Kings	79	15	17	32	89	9	4	1	5	17
1977-78	Los Angeles Kings	43	8	5	13	45	....	....	....	....	....
1978-79	Vancouver Canucks	28	2	5	7	30	3	1	0	1	0
	NHL Totals	**437**	**96**	**86**	**182**	**480**	**29**	**7**	**2**	**9**	**69**

Traded to **Vancouver** by **Los Angeles** for Randy Holt, December 31, 1978. Claimed by **Hartford** from **Vancouver** in Expansion Draft, June 13, 1979.

KOZAK, Les

Left wing. Shoots left. 6', 185 lbs. Born, Dauphin, Man., October 28, 1940.

Season	Club	GP	G	A	Pts	PIM	GP	G	A	Pts	PIM
1961-62	Toronto Maple Leafs	12	1	0	1	2	....	....	....	....	....
	NHL Totals	**12**	**1**	**0**	**1**	**2**	....	....	....	....	....

KOZLOV, Viktor

Center. Shoots right. 6'5", 225 lbs. Born, Togliatti, USSR, February 14, 1975.
(San Jose's 1st choice, 6th overall, in 1993 Entry Draft).

Season	Club	GP	G	A	Pts	PIM	GP	G	A	Pts	PIM
1994-95	San Jose Sharks	16	2	0	2	2	....	....	....	....	....
1995-96	San Jose Sharks	62	6	13	19	6	....	....	....	....	....
1996-97	San Jose Sharks	78	16	25	41	40	....	....	....	....	....
1997-98	San Jose Sharks	18	5	2	7	2	....	....	....	....	....
	Florida Panthers	46	12	11	23	14	....	....	....	....	....
1998-99	Florida Panthers	65	16	35	51	24	....	....	....	....	....
99-2000	Florida Panthers	80	17	53	70	16	4	0	1	1	0
2000-01	Florida Panthers	51	14	23	37	10	....	....	....	....	....
2001-02	Florida Panthers	50	9	18	27	20	....	....	....	....	....
2002-03	Florida Panthers	74	22	34	56	18	....	....	....	....	....
	NHL Totals	**540**	**119**	**214**	**333**	**152**	**4**	**0**	**1**	**1**	**0**

Played in NHL All-Star Game (2000)

Traded to **Florida** by **San Jose** with Florida's 5th round choice (previously acquired, Florida selected Jaroslav Spacek) in 1998 Entry Draft for Dave Lowry and Florida's 1st round choice (later traded to Tampa Bay – Tampa Bay selected Vincent Lecavalier) in 1998 Entry Draft, November 13, 1997.

KOZLOV, Vyacheslav

Right wing. Shoots left. 5'10", 185 lbs. Born, Voskresensk, USSR, May 3, 1972.
(Detroit's 2nd choice, 45th overall, in 1990 Entry Draft).

Season	Club	GP	G	A	Pts	PIM	GP	G	A	Pts	PIM
1991-92	Detroit Red Wings	7	0	2	2	2	....	....	....	....	....
1992-93	Detroit Red Wings	17	4	1	5	14	4	0	2	2	2
1993-94	Detroit Red Wings	77	34	39	73	50	7	2	5	7	12
1994-95	Detroit Red Wings	46	13	20	33	45	18	9	7	16	10
1995-96	Detroit Red Wings	82	36	37	73	70	19	5	7	12	10
1996-97◆	Detroit Red Wings	75	23	22	45	46	20	8	5	13	14
1997-98◆	Detroit Red Wings	80	25	27	52	46	22	6	8	14	10
1998-99	Detroit Red Wings	79	29	29	58	45	10	6	1	7	4
99-2000	Detroit Red Wings	72	18	18	36	28	8	2	1	3	12
2000-01	Detroit Red Wings	72	20	18	38	30	6	4	1	5	2
2001-02	Buffalo Sabres	38	9	13	22	16	....	....	....	....	....
2002-03	Atlanta Thrashers	79	21	49	70	66	....	....	....	....	....
	NHL Totals	**724**	**232**	**275**	**507**	**458**	**114**	**42**	**37**	**79**	**76**

Traded to **Buffalo** by **Detroit** with Detroit's 1st round choice (later traded to Columbus – later traded to Atlanta – Atlanta selected Jim Slater) in 2002 Entry Draft and future considerations for Dominik Hasek, July 1, 2001. • Missed majority of 2001-02 season recovering from Achilles tendon injury suffered in game vs. Columbus, December 31, 2001. Traded to **Atlanta** by **Buffalo** with Buffalo's 2nd round choice (later traded to Nashville – Nashville selected Konstantin Glazachev) in 2003 Entry Draft for Atlanta's 2nd (later traded to Florida – Florida selected Kamil Kreps) and 3rd (later traded to Phoenix – Phoenix selected Tyler Redenbach) round choices in 2003 Entry Draft, June 22, 2002.

KRAFT, Milan

Center. Shoots right. 6'3", 211 lbs. Born, Plzen, Czech., January 7, 1980.
(Pittsburgh's 1st choice, 23rd overall, in 1998 Entry Draft).

Season	Club	GP	G	A	Pts	PIM	GP	G	A	Pts	PIM
2000-01	Pittsburgh Penguins	42	7	7	14	8	8	0	0	0	2
2001-02	Pittsburgh Penguins	68	8	8	16	16	....	....	....	....	....
2002-03	Pittsburgh Penguins	31	7	5	12	10	....	....	....	....	....
	NHL Totals	**141**	**22**	**20**	**42**	**34**	**8**	**0**	**0**	**0**	**2**

KRAFT, Ryan

Center. Shoots left. 5'9", 190 lbs. Born, Bottineau, ND, November 7, 1975.
(San Jose's 11th choice, 194th overall, in 1995 Entry Draft).

Season	Club	GP	G	A	Pts	PIM	GP	G	A	Pts	PIM
2002-03	San Jose Sharks	7	0	1	1	0	....	....	....	....	....
	NHL Totals	**7**	**0**	**1**	**1**	**0**	....	....	....	....	....

KRAFTCHECK, Stephen

Defense. Shoots right. 5'11", 190 lbs. Born, Tinturn, Ont., March 3, 1929.

Season	Club	GP	G	A	Pts	PIM	GP	G	A	Pts	PIM
1950-51	Boston Bruins	22	0	0	0	8	6	0	0	0	7
1951-52	New York Rangers	58	8	9	17	30	....	....	....	....	....
1952-53	New York Rangers	69	2	9	11	45	....	....	....	....	....
1958-59	Toronto Maple Leafs	8	1	0	1	0	....	....	....	....	....
	NHL Totals	**157**	**11**	**18**	**29**	**83**	**6**	**0**	**0**	**0**	**7**

Traded to **Boston** by **Cleveland** (AHL) for cash, April 17, 1950. Traded to **Detroit** (Indianapolis-AHL) by **Boston** for loan of Max Quackenbush for remainder of 1950-51 season, December 5, 1950. Traded to **NY Rangers** by **Detroit** with Ed Reigle for $30,000, May 14, 1951. Traded to **Cleveland** (AHL) by **NY Rangers** with cash for Bob Chrystal, June, 1953. Traded to **Toronto** by **Cleveland** (AHL) for Ian Anderson, April 30, 1958. Traded to **Providence** (AHL) by **Toronto** (Rochester-AHL) for cash, June, 1962.

KRAJICEK, Lukas

Defense. Shoots left. 6'2", 182 lbs. Born, Prostejov, Czech., March 11, 1983.
(Florida's 2nd choice, 24th overall, in 2001 Entry Draft).

Season	Club	GP	G	A	Pts	PIM	GP	G	A	Pts	PIM
2001-02	Florida Panthers	5	0	0	0	0	....	....	....	....	....
	NHL Totals	**5**	**0**	**0**	**0**	**0**	....	....	....	....	....

KRAKE, Skip

Center. Shoots right. 5'11", 170 lbs. Born, North Battleford, Sask., October 14, 1943.

Season	Club	GP	G	A	Pts	PIM	GP	G	A	Pts	PIM
1963-64	Boston Bruins	2	0	0	0	0	....	....	....	....	....
1965-66	Boston Bruins	2	0	0	0	0	....	....	....	....	....
1966-67	Boston Bruins	15	6	2	8	4	....	....	....	....	....
1967-68	Boston Bruins	68	5	7	12	13	4	0	0	0	2
1968-69	Los Angeles Kings	30	3	9	12	11	6	1	0	1	15
1969-70	Los Angeles Kings	58	5	17	22	86	....	....	....	....	....
1970-71	Buffalo Sabres	74	4	5	9	68	....	....	....	....	....
	NHL Totals	**249**	**23**	**40**	**63**	**182**	**10**	**1**	**0**	**1**	**17**

Traded to **Los Angeles** by **Boston** for Los Angeles' 1st round choice (Reggie Leach) in 1970 Amateur Draft, May 20, 1968. Claimed by **Buffalo** from **Los Angeles** in Expansion Draft, June 10, 1970.

KRAVCHUK, Igor

Defense. Shoots left. 6'1", 218 lbs. Born, Ufa, USSR, September 13, 1966.
(Chicago's 5th choice, 71st overall, in 1991 Entry Draft).

Season	Club	GP	G	A	Pts	PIM	GP	G	A	Pts	PIM
1991-92	Chicago Blackhawks	18	1	8	9	4	18	2	6	8	8

Season	Club	REGULAR SEASON GP	G	A	Pts	PIM	PLAYOFFS GP	G	A	Pts	PIM
1992-93	Chicago Blackhawks	38	6	9	15	30	....	....	....	....	....
	Edmonton Oilers	17	4	8	12	2	....	....	....	....	....
1993-94	Edmonton Oilers	81	12	38	50	16	....	....	....	....	....
1994-95	Edmonton Oilers	36	7	11	18	29	....	....	....	....	....
1995-96	Edmonton Oilers	26	4	4	8	10	....	....	....	....	....
	St. Louis Blues	40	3	12	15	24	10	1	5	6	4
1996-97	St. Louis Blues	82	4	24	28	35	2	0	0	0	2
1997-98	Ottawa Senators	81	8	27	35	8	11	2	3	5	4
1998-99	Ottawa Senators	79	4	21	25	32	4	0	0	0	0
99-2000	Ottawa Senators	64	6	12	18	20	6	1	1	2	0
2000-01	Ottawa Senators	15	1	5	6	14	....	....	....	....	....
	Calgary Flames	37	0	8	8	4	....	....	....	....	....
2001-02	Calgary Flames	78	4	22	26	19	....	....	....	....	....
2002-03	Florida Panthers	7	0	1	1	4	....	....	....	....	....
	NHL Totals	**699**	**64**	**210**	**274**	**251**	**51**	**6**	**15**	**21**	**18**

Played in NHL All-Star Game (1999)

Traded to **Edmonton** by **Chicago** with Dean McAmmond for Joe Murphy, February 24, 1993. Traded to **St. Louis** by **Edmonton** with Ken Sutton for Jeff Norton and Donald Dufresne, January 4, 1996. Traded to **Ottawa** by **St. Louis** for Steve Duchesne, August 25, 1997. Claimed on waivers by **Calgary** from **Ottawa**, November 10, 2000.

KRAVETS, Mikhail

Right wing. Shoots left. 5'10", 195 lbs. Born, Leningrad, USSR, November 12, 1963.
(San Jose's 13th choice, 243rd overall, in 1991 Entry Draft).

Season	Club	GP	G	A	Pts	PIM	GP	G	A	Pts	PIM
1991-92	San Jose Sharks	1	0	0	0	0	....	....	....	....	....
1992-93	San Jose Sharks	1	0	0	0	0	....	....	....	....	....
	NHL Totals	**2**	**0**	**0**	**0**	**0**	....	....	....	....	....

KRENTZ, Dale

Left wing. Shoots left. 5'11", 190 lbs. Born, Steinbach, Man., December 19, 1961.

Season	Club	GP	G	A	Pts	PIM	GP	G	A	Pts	PIM
1986-87	Detroit Red Wings	8	0	0	0	0	....	....	....	....	....
1987-88	Detroit Red Wings	6	2	0	2	5	2	0	0	0	0
1988-89	Detroit Red Wings	16	3	3	6	4	....	....	....	....	....
	NHL Totals	**30**	**5**	**3**	**8**	**9**	**2**	**0**	**0**	**0**	**0**

Signed as a free agent by **Detroit**, June 5, 1985.

KRESTANOVICH, Jordan

Left wing. Shoots left. 6'1", 170 lbs. Born, Langley, B.C., June 14, 1981.
(Colorado's 7th choice, 152nd overall, in 1999 Entry Draft).

Season	Club	GP	G	A	Pts	PIM	GP	G	A	Pts	PIM
2001-02	Colorado Avalanche	8	0	2	2	0	....	....	....	....	....
	NHL Totals	**8**	**0**	**2**	**2**	**0**	....	....	....	....	....

KRISTEK, Jaroslav

Right wing. Shoots left. 6'1", 188 lbs. Born, Zlin, Czech., March 16, 1980.
(Buffalo's 4th choice, 50th overall, in 1998 Entry Draft).

Season	Club	GP	G	A	Pts	PIM	GP	G	A	Pts	PIM
2002-03	Buffalo Sabres	6	0	0	0	4	....	....	....	....	....
	NHL Totals	**6**	**0**	**0**	**0**	**4**	....	....	....	....	....

KRIVOKRASOV, Sergei

Right wing. Shoots left. 5'11", 185 lbs. Born, Angarsk, USSR, April 15, 1974.
(Chicago's 1st choice, 12th overall, in 1992 Entry Draft).

Season	Club	GP	G	A	Pts	PIM	GP	G	A	Pts	PIM
1992-93	Chicago Blackhawks	4	0	0	0	2	....	....	....	....	....
1993-94	Chicago Blackhawks	9	1	0	1	4	....	....	....	....	....
1994-95	Chicago Blackhawks	41	12	7	19	33	10	0	0	0	8
1995-96	Chicago Blackhawks	46	6	10	16	32	5	1	0	1	2
1996-97	Chicago Blackhawks	67	13	11	24	42	6	1	0	1	4
1997-98	Chicago Blackhawks	58	10	13	23	33	....	....	....	....	....
1998-99	Nashville Predators	70	25	23	48	42	....	....	....	....	....
99-2000	Nashville Predators	63	9	17	26	40	....	....	....	....	....
	Calgary Flames	12	1	10	11	4	....	....	....	....	....
2000-01	Minnesota Wild	54	7	15	22	20	....	....	....	....	....
2001-02	Minnesota Wild	9	1	1	2	17	....	....	....	....	....
	Mighty Ducks of Anaheim	17	1	2	3	19	....	....	....	....	....
	NHL Totals	**450**	**86**	**109**	**195**	**288**	**21**	**2**	**0**	**2**	**14**

Played in NHL All-Star Game (1999)

Traded to **Nashville** by **Chicago** for future considerations, June 26, 1998. Traded to **Calgary** by **Nashville** for Cale Hulse and Calgary's 3rd round choice (Denis Platonov) in 2001 Entry Draft, March 14, 2000. Selected by **Minnesota** from **Calgary** in Expansion Draft, June 23, 2000. Traded to **Anaheim** by **Minnesota** for Anaheim's 7th round choice (Niklas Eckerblom) in 2002 Entry Draft and a conditional choice in 2003 Entry Draft, November 1, 2001.

KROG, Jason

Center. Shoots right. 5'11", 191 lbs. Born, Fernie, B.C., October 9, 1975.

Season	Club	GP	G	A	Pts	PIM	GP	G	A	Pts	PIM
99-2000	New York Islanders	17	2	4	6	6	....	....	....	....	....
2000-01	New York Islanders	9	0	3	3	0	....	....	....	....	....
2001-02	New York Islanders	2	0	0	0	0	....	....	....	....	....
2002-03	Mighty Ducks of Anaheim	67	10	15	25	12	21	3	1	4	4
	NHL Totals	**95**	**12**	**22**	**34**	**18**	**21**	**3**	**1**	**4**	**4**

Signed as a free agent by **NY Islanders**, May 14, 1999. Loaned to **Providence** (AHL) by **NY Islanders**, March 1, 2000. Signed as a free agent by **Anaheim**, July 17, 2002.

KROL, Joe

Left wing. Shoots left. 5'11", 173 lbs. Born, Winnipeg, Man., August 13, 1915.

Season	Club	GP	G	A	Pts	PIM	GP	G	A	Pts	PIM
1936-37	New York Rangers	1	0	0	0	0	....	....	....	....	....
1938-39	New York Rangers	1	1	1	2	0	....	....	....	....	....
1941-42	Brooklyn Americans	24	9	3	12	8	....	....	....	....	....
	NHL Totals	**26**	**10**	**4**	**14**	**8**	....	....	....	....	....

Signed as a free agent by **NY Rangers**, November, 1936. Traded to **Hershey** (IAHL) by **NY Rangers** for cash, April 4, 1940. Traded to **NY Americans** (Springfield-AHL) by **Hershey** for John Sorrell, February 14, 1941.

KROMM, Richard

Left wing. Shoots left. 5'11", 180 lbs. Born, Trail, B.C., March 29, 1964.
(Calgary's 2nd choice, 37th overall, in 1982 Entry Draft).

Season	Club	GP	G	A	Pts	PIM	GP	G	A	Pts	PIM
1983-84	Calgary Flames	53	11	12	23	27	11	1	1	2	9
1984-85	Calgary Flames	73	20	32	52	32	3	0	1	1	4
1985-86	Calgary Flames	63	12	17	29	31	....	....	....	....	....
	New York Islanders	14	7	7	14	4	3	0	1	1	0
1986-87	New York Islanders	70	12	17	29	20	14	1	3	4	4
1987-88	New York Islanders	71	5	10	15	20	5	0	0	0	5
1988-89	New York Islanders	20	1	6	7	4	....	....	....	....	....
1990-91	New York Islanders	6	1	0	1	0	....	....	....	....	....
1991-92	New York Islanders	1	0	0	0	0	....	....	....	....	....
1992-93	New York Islanders	1	1	2	3	0	....	....	....	....	....
	NHL Totals	**372**	**70**	**103**	**173**	**138**	**36**	**2**	**6**	**8**	**22**

Traded to **NY Islanders** by **Calgary** with Steve Konroyd for John Tonelli, March 11, 1986.

KRON, Robert

Left wing. Shoots left. 5'11", 185 lbs. Born, Brno, Czech., February 27, 1967.
(Vancouver's 5th choice, 88th overall, in 1985 Entry Draft).

Season	Club	GP	G	A	Pts	PIM	GP	G	A	Pts	PIM
1990-91	Vancouver Canucks	76	12	20	32	21	....	....	....	....	....
1991-92	Vancouver Canucks	36	2	2	4	2	11	1	2	3	2
1992-93	Vancouver Canucks	32	10	11	21	14	....	....	....	....	....
	Hartford Whalers	13	4	2	6	4	....	....	....	....	....
1993-94	Hartford Whalers	77	24	26	50	8	....	....	....	....	....
1994-95	Hartford Whalers	37	10	8	18	10	....	....	....	....	....
1995-96	Hartford Whalers	77	22	28	50	6	....	....	....	....	....
1996-97	Hartford Whalers	68	10	12	22	10	....	....	....	....	....
1997-98	Carolina Hurricanes	81	16	20	36	12	....	....	....	....	....
1998-99	Carolina Hurricanes	75	9	16	25	10	5	2	0	2	0
99-2000	Carolina Hurricanes	81	13	27	40	8	....	....	....	....	....
2000-01	Columbus Blue Jackets	59	8	11	19	10	....	....	....	....	....
2001-02	Columbus Blue Jackets	59	4	11	15	4	....	....	....	....	....
	NHL Totals	**771**	**144**	**194**	**338**	**119**	**16**	**3**	**2**	**5**	**2**

Traded to **Hartford** by **Vancouver** with Vancouver's 3rd round choice (Marek Malik) in 1993 Entry Draft and future considerations (Jim Sandlak, May 17, 1993) for Murray Craven and Vancouver's 5th round choice (previously acquired, Vancouver selected Scott Walker) in 1993 Entry Draft, March 22, 1993. Transferred to **Carolina** after **Hartford** franchise relocated, June 25, 1997. Selected by **Columbus** from **Carolina** in Expansion Draft, June 23, 2000.

KROOK, Kevin

Defense. Shoots left. 5'11", 187 lbs. Born, Cold Lake, Alta., April 5, 1958.
(Colorado's 10th choice, 142nd overall, in 1978 Amateur Draft).

Season	Club	GP	G	A	Pts	PIM	GP	G	A	Pts	PIM
1978-79	Colorado Rockies	3	0	0	0	2	....	....	....	....	....
	NHL Totals	**3**	**0**	**0**	**0**	**2**	....	....	....	....	....

KROUPA, Vlastimil

Defense. Shoots left. 6'3", 215 lbs. Born, Most, Czech., April 27, 1975.
(San Jose's 3rd choice, 45th overall, in 1993 Entry Draft).

Season	Club	GP	G	A	Pts	PIM	GP	G	A	Pts	PIM
1993-94	San Jose Sharks	27	1	3	4	20	14	1	2	3	21
1994-95	San Jose Sharks	14	0	2	2	16	6	0	0	0	4
1995-96	San Jose Sharks	27	1	7	8	18	....	....	....	....	....
1996-97	San Jose Sharks	35	2	6	8	12	....	....	....	....	....
1997-98	New Jersey Devils	2	0	1	1	0	....	....	....	....	....
	NHL Totals	**105**	**4**	**19**	**23**	**66**	**20**	**1**	**2**	**3**	**25**

Traded to **New Jersey** by **San Jose** for New Jersey's 3rd round choice (later traded to Nashville – Nashville selected Geoff Koch) in 1998 Entry Draft, August 22, 1997.

KRULICKI, Jim

Left wing. Shoots left. 5'11", 180 lbs. Born, Kitchener, Ont., March 9, 1948.

Season	Club	GP	G	A	Pts	PIM	GP	G	A	Pts	PIM
1970-71	New York Rangers	27	0	2	2	6	....	....	....	....	....
	Detroit Red Wings	14	0	1	1	0	....	....	....	....	....
	NHL Totals	**41**	**0**	**3**	**3**	**6**	....	....	....	....	....

Traded to **Detroit** by **NY Rangers** for Dale Rolfe, March 2, 1971.

KRUPP, Uwe

Defense. Shoots right. 6'6", 235 lbs. Born, Cologne, West Germany, June 24, 1965.
(Buffalo's 13th choice, 223rd overall, in 1983 Entry Draft).

Season	Club	GP	G	A	Pts	PIM	GP	G	A	Pts	PIM
1986-87	Buffalo Sabres	26	1	4	5	23	....	....	....	....	....
1987-88	Buffalo Sabres	75	2	9	11	151	6	0	0	0	15
1988-89	Buffalo Sabres	70	5	13	18	55	5	0	1	1	4
1989-90	Buffalo Sabres	74	3	20	23	85	6	0	0	0	4
1990-91	Buffalo Sabres	74	12	32	44	66	6	1	1	2	6
1991-92	Buffalo Sabres	8	2	0	2	6	....	....	....	....	....
	New York Islanders	59	6	29	35	43	....	....	....	....	....
1992-93	New York Islanders	80	9	29	38	67	18	1	5	6	12
1993-94	New York Islanders	41	7	14	21	30	4	0	1	1	4
1994-95	Quebec Nordiques	44	6	17	23	20	5	0	2	2	2
1995-96 ◆	Colorado Avalanche	6	0	3	3	4	22	4	12	16	33

Season	Club	GP	G	A	Pts	PIM	GP	G	A	Pts	PIM
		REGULAR SEASON					PLAYOFFS				
1996-97	Colorado Avalanche	60	4	17	21	48	....	....	....	....	....
1997-98	Colorado Avalanche	78	9	22	31	38	7	0	1	1	4
1998-99	Detroit Red Wings	22	3	2	5	6	....	....	....	....	....
2001-02	Detroit Red Wings	8	0	1	1	8	2	0	0	0	2
2002-03	Atlanta Thrashers	4	0	0	0	10	....	....	....	....	....
	NHL Totals	**729**	**69**	**212**	**281**	**660**	**81**	**6**	**23**	**29**	**86**

Played in NHL All-Star Game (1991)

Traded to **NY Islanders** by **Buffalo** with Pierre Turgeon, Benoit Hogue and Dave McLlwain for Pat LaFontaine, Randy Hillier, Randy Wood and NY Islanders' 4th round choice (Dean Melanson) in 1992 Entry Draft, October 25, 1991. Traded to **Quebec** by **NY Islanders** with NY Islanders' 1st round choice (Wade Belak) in 1994 Entry Draft for Ron Sutter and Quebec's 1st round choice (Brett Lindros) in 1994 Entry Draft, June 28, 1994. Transferred to **Colorado** after **Quebec** franchise relocated, June 21, 1995. Claimed by **Nashville** from **Colorado** in Expansion Draft, June 26, 1998. Signed as a free agent by **Detroit**, July 7, 1998. • Missed remainder of 1998-99 season and entire 1999-2000 and 2000-01 seasons recovering from back injury suffered prior to game vs. Phoenix, December 19, 1998. Signed as a free agent by **Atlanta**, July 19, 2002.

KRUPPKE, Gord

Defense. Shoots right. 6'1", 215 lbs. Born, Slave Lake, Alta., April 2, 1969.
(Detroit's 2nd choice, 32nd overall, in 1987 Entry Draft).

Season	Club	GP	G	A	Pts	PIM	GP	G	A	Pts	PIM
1990-91	Detroit Red Wings	4	0	0	0	0	....	....	....	....	....
1992-93	Detroit Red Wings	10	0	0	0	20	....	....	....	....	....
1993-94	Detroit Red Wings	9	0	0	0	12	....	....	....	....	....
	NHL Totals	**23**	**0**	**0**	**0**	**32**	....	....	....	....	....

Traded to **Toronto** by **Detroit** for future considerations, April 7, 1995.

KRUSE, Paul

Left wing. Shoots left. 6'1", 215 lbs. Born, Merritt, B.C., March 15, 1970.
(Calgary's 6th choice, 83rd overall, in 1990 Entry Draft).

Season	Club	GP	G	A	Pts	PIM	GP	G	A	Pts	PIM
1990-91	Calgary Flames	1	0	0	0	7	....	....	....	....	....
1991-92	Calgary Flames	16	3	1	4	65	....	....	....	....	....
1992-93	Calgary Flames	27	2	3	5	41	....	....	....	....	....
1993-94	Calgary Flames	68	3	8	11	185	7	0	0	0	14
1994-95	Calgary Flames	45	11	5	16	141	7	4	2	6	10
1995-96	Calgary Flames	75	3	12	15	145	3	0	0	0	4
1996-97	Calgary Flames	14	2	0	2	30	....	....	....	....	....
	New York Islanders	48	4	2	6	111	....	....	....	....	....
1997-98	New York Islanders	62	6	1	7	138	....	....	....	....	....
	Buffalo Sabres	12	1	1	2	49	1	1	0	1	4
1998-99	Buffalo Sabres	43	3	0	3	114	10	0	0	0	4
99-2000	Buffalo Sabres	11	0	0	0	43	....	....	....	....	....
2000-01	San Jose Sharks	1	0	0	0	5	....	....	....	....	....
	NHL Totals	**423**	**38**	**33**	**71**	**1074**	**28**	**5**	**2**	**7**	**36**

Traded to **NY Islanders** by **Calgary** for Colorado's 3rd round choice (previously acquired by NY Islanders – later traded to Hartford – Hartford selected Francis Lessard) in 1997 Entry Draft, November 27, 1996. Traded to **Buffalo** by **NY Islanders** with Jason Holland for Jason Dawe, March 24, 1998. Signed as a free agent by **San Jose**, September 10, 2000.

KRUSHELNYSKI, Mike

Left wing/Center. Shoots left. 6'2", 200 lbs. Born, Montreal, Que., April 27, 1960.
(Boston's 7th choice, 120th overall, in 1979 Entry Draft).

Season	Club	GP	G	A	Pts	PIM	GP	G	A	Pts	PIM
1981-82	Boston Bruins	17	3	3	6	2	1	0	0	0	2
1982-83	Boston Bruins	79	23	42	65	43	17	8	6	14	12
1983-84	Boston Bruins	66	25	20	45	55	2	0	0	0	0
1984-85 ♦	Edmonton Oilers	80	43	45	88	60	18	5	8	13	22
1985-86	Edmonton Oilers	54	16	24	40	22	10	4	5	9	16
1986-87 ♦	Edmonton Oilers	80	16	35	51	67	21	3	4	7	18
1987-88 ♦	Edmonton Oilers	76	20	27	47	64	19	4	6	10	12
1988-89	Los Angeles Kings	78	26	36	62	110	11	1	4	5	4
1989-90	Los Angeles Kings	63	16	25	41	50	10	1	3	4	12
1990-91	Los Angeles Kings	15	1	5	6	10	....	....	....	....	....
	Toronto Maple Leafs	59	17	22	39	48	....	....	....	....	....
1991-92	Toronto Maple Leafs	72	9	15	24	72	....	....	....	....	....
1992-93	Toronto Maple Leafs	84	19	20	39	62	16	3	7	10	8
1993-94	Toronto Maple Leafs	54	5	6	11	28	6	0	0	0	0
1994-95	Detroit Red Wings	20	2	3	5	6	8	0	0	0	0
	NHL Totals	**897**	**241**	**328**	**569**	**699**	**139**	**29**	**43**	**72**	**106**

Played in NHL All-Star Game (1985)

Traded to **Edmonton** by **Boston** for Ken Linseman, June 21, 1984. Traded to **Los Angeles** by **Edmonton** with Wayne Gretzky and Marty McSorley for Jimmy Carson, Martin Gelinas, Los Angeles' 1st round choices in 1989 (later traded to New Jersey – New Jersey selected Jason Miller), 1991 (Martin Rucinsky) and 1993 (Nick Stajduhar) Entry Drafts and cash, August 9, 1988. Traded to **Toronto** by **Los Angeles** for John McIntyre, November 9, 1990. Signed as a free agent by **Detroit**, August 1, 1994.

KRUTOV, Vladimir

Left wing. Shoots left. 5'9", 195 lbs. Born, Moscow, Soviet Union, June 1, 1960.
(Vancouver's 11th choice, 238th overall, in 1986 Entry Draft).

Season	Club	GP	G	A	Pts	PIM	GP	G	A	Pts	PIM
1989-90	Vancouver Canucks	61	11	23	34	20	....	....	....	....	....
	NHL Totals	**61**	**11**	**23**	**34**	**20**	....	....	....	....	....

KRYGIER, Todd

Left wing. Shoots left. 6', 185 lbs. Born, Chicago Heights, IL, October 12, 1965.
(Hartford's 1st choice, 16th overall, in 1988 Supplemental Draft).

Season	Club	GP	G	A	Pts	PIM	GP	G	A	Pts	PIM
1989-90	Hartford Whalers	58	18	12	30	52	7	2	1	3	4
1990-91	Hartford Whalers	72	13	17	30	95	6	0	2	2	0
1991-92	Washington Capitals	67	13	17	30	107	5	2	1	3	4
1992-93	Washington Capitals	77	11	12	23	60	6	1	1	2	4
1993-94	Washington Capitals	66	12	18	30	60	5	2	0	2	10
1994-95	Mighty Ducks of Anaheim	35	11	11	22	10	....	....	....	....	....
1995-96	Mighty Ducks of Anaheim	60	9	28	37	70	....	....	....	....	....
	Washington Capitals	16	6	5	11	12	6	2	0	2	12
1996-97	Washington Capitals	47	5	11	16	37	....	....	....	....	....
1997-98	Washington Capitals	45	2	12	14	30	13	1	2	3	6
	NHL Totals	**543**	**100**	**143**	**243**	**533**	**48**	**10**	**7**	**17**	**40**

Traded to **Washington** by **Hartford** for Washington's 4th round choice (later traded to Calgary – Calgary selected Jason Smith) in 1993 Entry Draft, October 3, 1991. Traded to **Anaheim** by **Washington** for Anaheim's 4th round choice (later traded to Dallas – Dallas selected Mike Hurley) in 1996 Entry Draft, February 2, 1995. Traded to **Washington** by **Anaheim** for Mike Torchia, March 8, 1996.

KRYSKOW, Dave

Left wing. Shoots left. 5'10", 175 lbs. Born, Edmonton, Alta., December 25, 1957.
(Chicago's 2nd choice, 26th overall, in 1971 Amateur Draft).

Season	Club	GP	G	A	Pts	PIM	GP	G	A	Pts	PIM
1972-73	Chicago Black Hawks	11	1	0	1	0	3	2	0	2	0
1973-74	Chicago Black Hawks	72	7	12	19	22	7	0	0	0	2
1974-75	Washington Capitals	51	9	15	24	83	....	....	....	....	....
	Detroit Red Wings	18	1	4	5	4	....	....	....	....	....
1975-76	Atlanta Flames	79	15	25	40	65	2	0	0	0	2
	NHL Totals	**231**	**33**	**56**	**89**	**174**	**12**	**2**	**0**	**2**	**4**

Claimed by **Washington** from **Chicago** in Expansion Draft, June 12, 1974. Traded to **Detroit** by **Washington** for Jack Lynch, February 8, 1975. Traded to **Atlanta** by **Detroit** for Bryan Hextall Jr., June 5, 1975.

KRYZANOWSKI, Ed

Defense. Shoots right. 5'11", 175 lbs. Born, Fort Frances, Ont., November 14, 1925.

Season	Club	GP	G	A	Pts	PIM	GP	G	A	Pts	PIM
1948-49	Boston Bruins	36	1	3	4	10	5	0	1	1	2
1949-50	Boston Bruins	57	6	10	16	12	....	....	....	....	....
1950-51	Boston Bruins	69	3	6	9	10	6	0	0	0	2
1951-52	Boston Bruins	70	5	3	8	33	7	0	0	0	0
1952-53	Chicago Black Hawks	5	0	0	0	0	....	....	....	....	....
	NHL Totals	**237**	**15**	**22**	**37**	**65**	**18**	**0**	**1**	**1**	**4**

Signed as a free agent by **Boston**, October 8, 1948. Traded to **Chicago** by **Boston** for cash, August 14, 1952. Traded to **Boston** by **Chicago** for cash, October 31, 1952. Traded to **Providence** (AHL) by **Boston** for cash, November 8, 1952.

KUBA, Filip

Defense. Shoots left. 6'3", 205 lbs. Born, Ostrava, Czech., December 29, 1976.
(Florida's 8th choice, 192nd overall, in 1995 Entry Draft).

Season	Club	GP	G	A	Pts	PIM	GP	G	A	Pts	PIM
1998-99	Florida Panthers	5	0	1	1	0	....	....	....	....	....
99-2000	Florida Panthers	13	1	5	6	2	....	....	....	....	....
2000-01	Minnesota Wild	75	9	21	30	28	....	....	....	....	....
2001-02	Minnesota Wild	62	5	19	24	32	....	....	....	....	....
2002-03	Minnesota Wild	78	8	21	29	29	18	3	5	8	24
	NHL Totals	**233**	**23**	**67**	**90**	**91**	**18**	**3**	**5**	**8**	**24**

Traded to **Calgary** by **Florida** for Rocky Thompson, March 16, 2000. Selected by **Minnesota** from **Calgary** in Expansion Draft, June 23, 2000.

KUBINA, Pavel

Defense. Shoots right. 6'4", 230 lbs. Born, Celadna, Czech., April 15, 1977.
(Tampa Bay's 6th choice, 179th overall, in 1996 Entry Draft).

Season	Club	GP	G	A	Pts	PIM	GP	G	A	Pts	PIM
1997-98	Tampa Bay Lightning	10	1	2	3	22	....	....	....	....	....
1998-99	Tampa Bay Lightning	68	9	12	21	80	....	....	....	....	....
99-2000	Tampa Bay Lightning	69	8	18	26	93	....	....	....	....	....
2000-01	Tampa Bay Lightning	70	11	19	30	103	....	....	....	....	....
2001-02	Tampa Bay Lightning	82	11	23	34	106	....	....	....	....	....
2002-03	Tampa Bay Lightning	75	3	19	22	78	11	0	0	0	12
	NHL Totals	**374**	**43**	**93**	**136**	**482**	**11**	**0**	**0**	**0**	**12**

KUCERA, Frantisek

Defense. Shoots right. 6'2", 205 lbs. Born, Prague, Czech., February 3, 1968.
(Chicago's 3rd choice, 77th overall, in 1986 Entry Draft).

Season	Club	GP	G	A	Pts	PIM	GP	G	A	Pts	PIM
1990-91	Chicago Blackhawks	40	2	12	14	32	....	....	....	....	....
1991-92	Chicago Blackhawks	61	3	10	13	36	6	0	0	0	0
1992-93	Chicago Blackhawks	71	5	14	19	59	....	....	....	....	....
1993-94	Chicago Blackhawks	60	4	13	17	34	....	....	....	....	....
	Hartford Whalers	16	1	3	4	14	....	....	....	....	....
1994-95	Hartford Whalers	48	3	17	20	30	....	....	....	....	....
1995-96	Hartford Whalers	30	2	6	8	10	....	....	....	....	....
	Vancouver Canucks	24	1	0	1	10	6	0	1	1	0
1996-97	Vancouver Canucks	2	0	0	0	0	....	....	....	....	....
	Philadelphia Flyers	2	0	0	0	2	....	....	....	....	....
2000-01	Columbus Blue Jackets	48	2	5	7	12	....	....	....	....	....
	Pittsburgh Penguins	7	0	2	2	0	....	....	....	....	....

Season	Club	REGULAR SEASON GP	G	A	Pts	PIM	PLAYOFFS GP	G	A	Pts	PIM
2001-02	Washington Capitals	56	1	13	14	12					
	NHL Totals	**465**	**24**	**95**	**119**	**251**	**12**	**0**	**1**	**1**	**0**

Traded to **Hartford** by **Chicago** with Jocelyn Lemieux for Gary Suter, Randy Cunneyworth and Hartford's 3rd round choice (later traded to Vancouver – Vancouver selected Larry Courville) in 1995 Entry Draft, March 11, 1994. Traded to **Vancouver** by **Hartford** with Jim Dowd and Hartford's 2nd round choice (Ryan Bonni) in 1997 Entry Draft for Jeff Brown and Vancouver's 3rd round choice (later traded to Calgary – Calgary selected Paul Manning) in 1998 Entry Draft, December 19, 1995. Traded to **Philadelphia** by **Vancouver** for future considerations, March 18, 1997. Signed as a free agent by **Columbus**, July 7, 2000. Traded to **Pittsburgh** by **Columbus** for Pittsburgh's 6th round choice (Scott Horvath) in 2001 Entry Draft, March 13, 2001. Traded to **Washington** by **Pittsburgh** with Jaromir Jagr for Kris Beech, Michal Sivek, Ross Lupaschuk and future considerations, July 11, 2001.

KUDASHOV, Alexei

Center. Shoots right. 6', 183 lbs. Born, Elektrostal, USSR, July 21, 1971.
(Toronto's 3rd choice, 102nd overall, in 1991 Entry Draft).

Season	Club	GP	G	A	Pts	PIM	GP	G	A	Pts	PIM
1993-94	Toronto Maple Leafs	25	1	0	1	4					
	NHL Totals	**25**	**1**	**0**	**1**	**4**					

Signed as a free agent by **Florida**, September 10, 1995.

KUDELSKI, Bob

Right wing. Shoots right. 6'1", 205 lbs. Born, Springfield, MA, March 3, 1964.
(Los Angeles' 1st choice, 2nd overall, in 1986 Supplemental Draft).

Season	Club	GP	G	A	Pts	PIM	GP	G	A	Pts	PIM
1987-88	Los Angeles Kings	26	0	1	1	8					
1988-89	Los Angeles Kings	14	1	3	4	17					
1989-90	Los Angeles Kings	62	23	13	36	49	8	1	2	3	2
1990-91	Los Angeles Kings	72	23	13	36	46	8	3	2	5	2
1991-92	Los Angeles Kings	80	22	21	43	42	6	0	0	0	0
1992-93	Los Angeles Kings	15	3	3	6	8					
	Ottawa Senators	48	21	14	35	22					
1993-94	Ottawa Senators	42	26	15	41	14					
	Florida Panthers	44	14	15	29	10					
1994-95	Florida Panthers	26	6	3	9	2					
1995-96	Florida Panthers	13	0	1	1	0					
	NHL Totals	**442**	**139**	**102**	**241**	**218**	**22**	**4**	**4**	**8**	**4**

Played in NHL All-Star Game (1994)

Traded to **Ottawa** by **Los Angeles** with Shawn McCosh for Marc Fortier and Jim Thomson, December 19, 1992. Traded to **Florida** by **Ottawa** for Evgeny Davydov, Scott Levins, Florida's 6th round choice (Mike Gaffney) in 1994 Entry Draft and Dallas' 4th round choice (previously acquired, Ottawa selected Kevin Bolibruck) in 1995 Entry Draft, January 6, 1994.

KUDROC, Kristian

Defense. Shoots right. 6'6", 255 lbs. Born, Michalovce, Czech., May 21, 1981.
(NY Islanders' 4th choice, 28th overall, in 1999 Entry Draft).

Season	Club	GP	G	A	Pts	PIM	GP	G	A	Pts	PIM
2000-01	Tampa Bay Lightning	22	2	2	4	36					
2001-02	Tampa Bay Lightning	2	0	0	0	0					
	NHL Totals	**24**	**2**	**2**	**4**	**36**					

Traded to **Tampa Bay** by **NY Islanders** with Kevin Weekes and NY Islanders' 2nd round choice (later traded to Phoenix – Phoenix selected Matthew Spiller) in 2001 Entry Draft for Tampa Bay's 1st round choice (Raffi Torres) in 2000 Entry Draft, Calgary's 4th round choice (previously acquired, NY Islanders selected Vladimir Gorbunov) in 2000 Entry Draft and NY Islanders' 7th round choice (previously acquired, NY Islanders selected Ryan Caldwell) in 2000 Entry Draft, June 24, 2000. Signed as a free agent by **Florida**, July 3, 2003.

KUHN, Gord

Right wing. Shoots right. 5'7", 145 lbs. Born, Truro, N.S., November 19, 1905.

Season	Club	GP	G	A	Pts	PIM	GP	G	A	Pts	PIM
1932-33	New York Americans	12	1	1	2	4					
	NHL Totals	**12**	**1**	**1**	**2**	**4**					

Signed as a free agent by **NY Americans**, October 27, 1930. Traded to **Buffalo** (IHL) by **NY Americans** for cash, January 9, 1934.

KUKULOWICZ, Aggie

Center. Shoots left. 6'3", 175 lbs. Born, Winnipeg, Man., April 2, 1933.

Season	Club	GP	G	A	Pts	PIM	GP	G	A	Pts	PIM
1952-53	New York Rangers	3	1	0	1	0					
1953-54	New York Rangers	1	0	0	0	0					
	NHL Totals	**4**	**1**	**0**	**1**	**0**					

Traded to **Detroit** by **NY Rangers** with Billy Dea and cash for Dave Creighton and Bronco Horvath, August 18, 1955.

KULAK, Stu

Right wing. Shoots right. 5'10", 180 lbs. Born, Edmonton, Alta., March 10, 1963.
(Vancouver's 5th choice, 115th overall, in 1981 Entry Draft).

Season	Club	GP	G	A	Pts	PIM	GP	G	A	Pts	PIM
1982-83	Vancouver Canucks	4	1	1	2	0					
1986-87	Vancouver Canucks	28	1	1	2	37					
	Edmonton Oilers	23	3	1	4	41					
	New York Rangers	3	0	0	0	0	3	0	0	0	2
1987-88	Quebec Nordiques	14	1	1	2	28					
1988-89	Winnipeg Jets	18	2	0	2	24					
	NHL Totals	**90**	**8**	**4**	**12**	**130**	**3**	**0**	**0**	**0**	**2**

Traded to **Edmonton** by **Vancouver** for cash December 11, 1986. Traded to **NY Rangers** by **Edmonton** to complete transaction that sent Reijo Ruotsalanien, Clark Donatelli, Velle Kentala and Jim Wiemer to Edmonton (October 23, 1986), March 10, 1987. Claimed by **Quebec** from **NY Rangers** in Waiver Draft, October 5, 1987. Traded to **Winnipeg** by **Quebec** for Bobby Dollas, December 17,1987.

KULLMAN, Arnie

Center. Shoots left. 5'7", 170 lbs. Born, Winnipeg, Man., October 9, 1927.

Season	Club	GP	G	A	Pts	PIM	GP	G	A	Pts	PIM
1947-48	Boston Bruins	1	0	0	0	0					
1949-50	Boston Bruins	12	0	1	1	11					
	NHL Totals	**13**	**0**	**1**	**1**	**11**					

KULLMAN, Eddie

Right wing. Shoots right. 5'7", 165 lbs. Born, Winnipeg, Man., December 12, 1923.

Season	Club	GP	G	A	Pts	PIM	GP	G	A	Pts	PIM
1947-48	New York Rangers	51	15	17	32	32	6	1	0	1	2
1948-49	New York Rangers	18	4	5	9	14					
1950-51	New York Rangers	70	14	18	32	88					
1951-52	New York Rangers	64	11	10	21	59					
1952-53	New York Rangers	70	8	10	18	61					
1953-54	New York Rangers	70	4	10	14	44					
	NHL Totals	**343**	**56**	**70**	**126**	**298**	**6**	**1**	**0**	**1**	**2**

Traded to **Providence** (AHL) by **NY Rangers** with Moe Morris, cash and future considerations (Buck Davies, June, 1949) for Allan Stanley, December 9, 1948. Traded to **NY Rangers** by **Providence** (AHL) for Orville LaValle and Sheldon Bloomer, August 16, 1950.

KULTANEN, Jarno

Defense. Shoots left. 6'2", 198 lbs. Born, Luumaki, Finland, January 8, 1973.
(Boston's 8th choice, 174th overall, in 2000 Entry Draft).

Season	Club	GP	G	A	Pts	PIM	GP	G	A	Pts	PIM
2000-01	Boston Bruins	62	2	8	10	26					
2001-02	Boston Bruins	38	0	3	3	33					
2002-03	Boston Bruins	2	0	0	0	0					
	NHL Totals	**102**	**2**	**11**	**13**	**59**					

• Missed majority of 2001-02 season recovering from knee injury suffered in game vs. Minnesota, October 8, 2001.

KUMPEL, Mark

Right wing. Shoots right. 6', 190 lbs. Born, Wakefield, MA, March 7, 1961.
(Quebec's 4th choice, 108th overall, in 1980 Entry Draft).

Season	Club	GP	G	A	Pts	PIM	GP	G	A	Pts	PIM
1984-85	Quebec Nordiques	42	8	7	15	26	18	3	4	7	4
1985-86	Quebec Nordiques	47	10	12	22	17	2	1	0	1	0
1986-87	Quebec Nordiques	40	1	8	9	16					
	Detroit Red Wings	5	0	1	1	0	8	0	0	0	4
1987-88	Detroit Red Wings	13	0	2	2	4					
	Winnipeg Jets	32	4	4	8	19	4	0	0	0	4
1989-90	Winnipeg Jets	56	8	9	17	21	7	2	0	2	2
1990-91	Winnipeg Jets	53	7	3	10	10					
	NHL Totals	**288**	**38**	**46**	**84**	**113**	**39**	**6**	**4**	**10**	**14**

Traded to **Detroit** by **Quebec** with Brent Ashton and Gilbert Delorme for Basil McRae, John Ogrodnick and Doug Sheddon, January 17, 1987. Traded to **Winnipeg** by **Detroit** for Jim Nill, January 11, 1988.

KUNTZ, Alan

Left wing. Shoots left. 5'11", 165 lbs. Born, Toronto, Ont., June 4, 1919.

Season	Club	GP	G	A	Pts	PIM	GP	G	A	Pts	PIM
1941-42	New York Rangers	31	10	11	21	10	6	1	0	1	2
1945-46	New York Rangers	14	0	1	1	2					
	NHL Totals	**45**	**10**	**12**	**22**	**12**	**6**	**1**	**0**	**1**	**2**

Traded to **Springfield** (AHL) by **NY Rangers** for $5,000, August, 1948.

KUNTZ, Murray

Left wing. Shoots left. 5'10", 180 lbs. Born, Ottawa, Ont., December 19, 1945.

Season	Club	GP	G	A	Pts	PIM	GP	G	A	Pts	PIM
1974-75	St. Louis Blues	7	1	2	3	0					
	NHL Totals	**7**	**1**	**2**	**3**	**0**					

Signed as a free agent by **Buffalo**, September, 1970. Claimed by **Rochester** (AHL) from **Buffalo** in Reverse Draft, June 12, 1973. Traded to **St. Louis** by **Rochester** (AHL) for cash, June, 1974.

KURKA, Tomas

Left wing. Shoots left. 5'11", 190 lbs. Born, Most, Czech., December 14, 1981.
(Carolina's 1st choice, 32nd overall, in 2000 Entry Draft).

Season	Club	GP	G	A	Pts	PIM	GP	G	A	Pts	PIM
2002-03	Carolina Hurricanes	14	3	2	5	2					
	NHL Totals	**14**	**3**	**2**	**5**	**2**					

KURRI, Jari

HHOF

Right wing. Shoots right. 6'1", 195 lbs. Born, Helsinki, Finland, May 18, 1960.
(Edmonton's 3rd choice, 69th overall, in 1980 Entry Draft).

Season	Club	GP	G	A	Pts	PIM	GP	G	A	Pts	PIM
1980-81	Edmonton Oilers	75	32	43	75	40	9	5	7	12	4
1981-82	Edmonton Oilers	71	32	54	86	32	5	2	5	7	10
1982-83	Edmonton Oilers	80	45	59	104	22	16	8	15	23	8
1983-84 ♦	Edmonton Oilers	64	52	61	113	14	19	*14	14	28	13
1984-85 ♦	Edmonton Oilers	73	71	64	135	30	18	*19	12	31	6
1985-86	Edmonton Oilers	78	*68	63	131	22	10	2	10	12	4
1986-87 ♦	Edmonton Oilers	79	54	54	108	41	21	*15	10	25	20
1987-88 ♦	Edmonton Oilers	80	43	53	96	30	19	*14	17	31	12
1988-89	Edmonton Oilers	76	44	58	102	69	7	3	5	8	6
1989-90 ♦	Edmonton Oilers	78	33	60	93	48	22	10	15	25	18
1991-92	Los Angeles Kings	73	23	37	60	24	4	1	2	3	4
1992-93	Los Angeles Kings	82	27	60	87	38	24	9	8	17	12
1993-94	Los Angeles Kings	81	31	46	77	48					
1994-95	Los Angeles Kings	38	10	19	29	24					

		REGULAR SEASON					PLAYOFFS				
Season	Club	GP	G	A	Pts	PIM	GP	G	A	Pts	PIM
1995-96	Los Angeles Kings	57	17	23	40	37	....	....	....	....	....
	New York Rangers	14	1	4	5	2	11	3	5	8	2
1996-97	Mighty Ducks of Anaheim	82	13	22	35	12	11	1	2	3	4
1997-98	Colorado Avalanche	70	5	17	22	12	4	0	0	0	0
	NHL Totals	**1251**	**601**	**797**	**1398**	**545**	**200**	**106**	**127**	**233**	**123**

NHL Second All-Star Team (1984, 1986, 1989) • Lady Byng Memorial Trophy (1985) • NHL First All-Star Team (1985, 1987)

Played in NHL All-Star Game (1983, 1985, 1986, 1988, 1989, 1990, 1993, 1998)

Traded to **Philadelphia** by **Edmonton** with Dave Brown and Corey Foster for Craig Fisher, Scott Mellanby and Craig Berube, May 30, 1991. Traded to **Los Angeles** by **Philadelphia** with Jeff Chychrun for Steve Duchesne, Steve Kasper and Los Angeles' 4th round choice (Aris Brimanis) in 1991 Entry Draft, May 30, 1991. Traded to **NY Rangers** by **Los Angeles** with Marty McSorley and Shane Churla for Ray Ferraro, Ian Laperriere, Mattias Norstrom, Nathan LaFayette and NY Rangers' 4th round choice (Sean Blanchard) in 1997 Entry Draft, March 14, 1996. Signed as a free agent by **Anaheim**, September 10, 1996. Signed as a free agent by **Colorado**, September 15, 1997.

KURTENBACH, Orland

Center. Shoots left. 6'2", 180 lbs. Born, Cudworth, Sask., September 7, 1936.

Season	Club	GP	G	A	Pts	PIM	GP	G	A	Pts	PIM
1960-61	New York Rangers	10	0	6	6	2	....	....	....	....	....
1961-62	Boston Bruins	8	0	0	0	6	....	....	....	....	....
1963-64	Boston Bruins	70	12	25	37	91	....	....	....	....	....
1964-65	Boston Bruins	64	6	20	26	86	....	....	....	....	....
1965-66	Toronto Maple Leafs	70	9	6	15	54	4	0	0	0	20
1966-67	New York Rangers	60	11	25	36	58	3	0	2	2	0
1967-68	New York Rangers	73	15	20	35	82	6	1	0	1	26
1968-69	New York Rangers	2	0	0	0	2	....	....	....	....	....
1969-70	New York Rangers	53	4	10	14	47	6	1	2	3	24
1970-71	Vancouver Canucks	52	21	32	53	84	....	....	....	....	....
1971-72	Vancouver Canucks	78	24	37	61	48	....	....	....	....	....
1972-73	Vancouver Canucks	47	9	19	28	38	....	....	....	....	....
1973-74	Vancouver Canucks	52	8	13	21	30	....	....	....	....	....
	NHL Totals	**639**	**119**	**213**	**332**	**628**	**19**	**2**	**4**	**6**	**70**

Claimed by **Boston** from **NY Rangers** in Intra-League Draft, June 13, 1961. Traded to **San Francisco** (WHL) by **Boston** with Ed Panagabko and future considerations (Gerry Ouellette, July 7, 1963) for Larry McNabb and cash, July 26, 1962. Traded to **Boston** by **San Francisco** (WHL) for cash, October, 1963. Traded to **Toronto** by **Boston** with Pat Stapleton and Andy Hebenton for Ron Stewart, June 8, 1965. Claimed by **NY Rangers** from **Toronto** in Intra-league Draft, June 15, 1966. Claimed by **Vancouver** from **NY Rangers** in Expansion Draft, June 10, 1970.

KURTZ, Justin

Defense. Shoots left. 6', 188 lbs. Born, Winnipeg, Man., January 14, 1977.
(Winnipeg's 5th choice, 84th overall, in 1995 Entry Draft).

Season	Club	GP	G	A	Pts	PIM	GP	G	A	Pts	PIM
2001-02	Vancouver Canucks	27	3	5	8	14	....	....	....	....	....
	NHL Totals	**27**	**3**	**5**	**8**	**14**	....	....	....	....	....

Signed as a free agent by **Vancouver**, October 15, 2001.

KURVERS, Tom

Defense. Shoots left. 6'2", 195 lbs. Born, Minneapolis, MN, September 14, 1962.
(Montreal's 10th choice, 145th overall, in 1981 Entry Draft).

Season	Club	GP	G	A	Pts	PIM	GP	G	A	Pts	PIM
1984-85	Montreal Canadiens	75	10	35	45	30	12	0	6	6	6
1985-86♦	Montreal Canadiens	62	7	23	30	36	....	....	....	....	....
1986-87	Montreal Canadiens	1	0	0	0	0	....	....	....	....	....
	Buffalo Sabres	55	6	17	23	22	....	....	....	....	....
1987-88	New Jersey Devils	56	5	29	34	46	19	6	9	15	38
1988-89	New Jersey Devils	74	16	50	66	38	....	....	....	....	....
1989-90	New Jersey Devils	1	0	0	0	0	....	....	....	....	....
	Toronto Maple Leafs	70	15	37	52	29	5	0	3	3	4
1990-91	Toronto Maple Leafs	19	0	3	3	8	....	....	....	....	....
	Vancouver Canucks	32	4	23	27	20	6	2	2	4	12
1991-92	New York Islanders	74	9	47	56	30	....	....	....	....	....
1992-93	New York Islanders	52	8	30	38	38	12	0	2	2	6
1993-94	New York Islanders	66	9	31	40	47	3	0	0	0	2
1994-95	Mighty Ducks of Anaheim	22	4	3	7	6	....	....	....	....	....
	NHL Totals	**659**	**93**	**328**	**421**	**350**	**57**	**8**	**22**	**30**	**68**

Traded to **Buffalo** by **Montreal** for Buffalo's 2nd round choice (Martin St. Amour) in 1988 Entry Draft, November 18, 1986. Traded to **New Jersey** by **Buffalo** for Detroit's 3rd round choice (previously acquired, Buffalo selected Andrew MacVicar) in 1987 Entry Draft, June 13, 1987. Traded to **Toronto** by **New Jersey** for Toronto's 1st round choice (Scott Niedermayer) in 1991 Entry Draft, October 16, 1989. Traded to **Vancouver** by **Toronto** for Brian Bradley, January 12, 1991. Traded to **Minnesota** by **Vancouver** for Dave Babych, June 22, 1991. Traded to **NY Islanders** by **Minnesota** for Craig Ludwig, June 22, 1991. Traded to **Anaheim** by **NY Islanders** for Troy Loney, June 29, 1994.

KURYLUK, Merv

Left wing. Shoots left. 5'11", 185 lbs. Born, Yorkton, Sask., August 10, 1937.

Season	Club	GP	G	A	Pts	PIM	GP	G	A	Pts	PIM
1961-62	Chicago Black Hawks	....	....	....	....	....	2	0	0	0	0
	NHL Totals	....	....	....	....	....	**2**	**0**	**0**	**0**	**0**

KUSHNER, Dale

Right wing. Shoots left. 6'1", 195 lbs. Born, Terrace, B.C., June 13, 1966.

Season	Club	GP	G	A	Pts	PIM	GP	G	A	Pts	PIM
1989-90	New York Islanders	2	0	0	0	2	....	....	....	....	....
1990-91	Philadelphia Flyers	63	7	11	18	195	....	....	....	....	....
1991-92	Philadelphia Flyers	19	3	2	5	18	....	....	....	....	....
	NHL Totals	**84**	**10**	**13**	**23**	**215**	....	....	....	....	....

Signed as a free agent by **NY Islanders**, April 7, 1987. Signed as a free agent by **Philadelphia**, July 31, 1990.

KUTLAK, Zdenek

Defense. Shoots left. 6'3", 207 lbs. Born, Budejovice, Czech., February 13, 1980.
(Boston's 10th choice, 237th overall, in 2000 Entry Draft).

Season	Club	GP	G	A	Pts	PIM	GP	G	A	Pts	PIM
2000-01	Boston Bruins	10	0	2	2	4	....	....	....	....	....
2002-03	Boston Bruins	4	1	0	1	0	....	....	....	....	....
	NHL Totals	**14**	**1**	**2**	**3**	**4**	....	....	....	....	....

KUZNETSOV, Maxim

Defense. Shoots left. 6'5", 198 lbs. Born, Pavlodar, USSR, March 24, 1977.
(Detroit's 1st choice, 26th overall, in 1995 Entry Draft).

Season	Club	GP	G	A	Pts	PIM	GP	G	A	Pts	PIM
2000-01	Detroit Red Wings	25	1	2	3	23	....	....	....	....	....
2001-02	Detroit Red Wings	39	1	2	3	40	....	....	....	....	....
2002-03	Detroit Red Wings	53	0	3	3	54	....	....	....	....	....
	Los Angeles Kings	3	0	0	0	0	....	....	....	....	....
	NHL Totals	**120**	**2**	**7**	**9**	**117**	....	....	....	....	....

• Missed majority of 2000-01 season recovering from knee injury suffered in game vs. Vancouver, November 24, 2000. Traded to **Los Angeles** by **Detroit** with Sean Avery, Detroit's 1st round choice (Jeff Tambellini) in 2003 Entry Draft and Detroit's 2nd round choice in 2004 Entry Draft for Mathieu Schneider, March 11, 2003.

KUZNIK, Greg

Defense. Shoots left. 6', 185 lbs. Born, Prince George, B.C., June 12, 1978.
(Hartford's 7th choice, 171st overall, in 1996 Entry Draft).

Season	Club	GP	G	A	Pts	PIM	GP	G	A	Pts	PIM
2000-01	Carolina Hurricanes	1	0	0	0	0	....	....	....	....	....
	NHL Totals	**1**	**0**	**0**	**0**	**0**	....	....	....	....	....

Transferred to **Carolina** after **Hartford** franchise relocated, June 25, 1997.

KUZYK, Ken

Right wing. Shoots right. 6'1", 195 lbs. Born, Toronto, Ont., August 11, 1953.

Season	Club	GP	G	A	Pts	PIM	GP	G	A	Pts	PIM
1976-77	Cleveland Barons	13	0	5	5	2	....	....	....	....	....
1977-78	Cleveland Barons	28	5	4	9	6	....	....	....	....	....
	NHL Totals	**41**	**5**	**9**	**14**	**8**	....	....	....	....	....

Signed as a free agent by **Cleveland**, September, 1976. Placed on **Minnesota** Reserve List after **Cleveland-Minnesota** Dispersal Draft, June 15, 1978. Claimed by **Quebec** from **Minnesota** in Expansion Draft, June 13, 1979. Signed as a free agent by **Minnesota**, February 1, 1980.

KVARTALNOV, Dmitri

Left wing. Shoots left. 5'11", 180 lbs. Born, Voskresensk, USSR, March 25, 1966.
(Boston's 1st choice, 16th overall, in 1992 Entry Draft).

Season	Club	GP	G	A	Pts	PIM	GP	G	A	Pts	PIM
1992-93	Boston Bruins	73	30	42	72	16	4	0	0	0	0
1993-94	Boston Bruins	39	12	7	19	10	....	....	....	....	....
	NHL Totals	**112**	**42**	**49**	**91**	**26**	**4**	**0**	**0**	**0**	**0**

KVASHA, Oleg

Left wing/Center. Shoots right. 6'5", 230 lbs. Born, Moscow, USSR, July 26, 1978.
(Florida's 3rd choice, 65th overall, in 1996 Entry Draft).

Season	Club	GP	G	A	Pts	PIM	GP	G	A	Pts	PIM
1998-99	Florida Panthers	68	12	13	25	45	....	....	....	....	....
99-2000	Florida Panthers	78	5	20	25	34	4	0	0	0	0
2000-01	New York Islanders	62	11	9	20	46	....	....	....	....	....
2001-02	New York Islanders	71	13	25	38	80	7	0	1	1	6
2002-03	New York Islanders	69	12	14	26	44	5	0	1	1	2
	NHL Totals	**348**	**53**	**81**	**134**	**249**	**16**	**0**	**2**	**2**	**8**

Traded to **NY Islanders** by **Florida** with Mark Parrish for Roberto Luongo and Olli Jokinen, June 24, 2000.

KWIATKOWSKI, Joel

Defense. Shoots left. 6'2", 210 lbs. Born, Kindersley, Sask., March 22, 1977.
(Dallas' 7th choice, 194th overall, in 1996 Entry Draft).

Season	Club	GP	G	A	Pts	PIM	GP	G	A	Pts	PIM
2000-01	Ottawa Senators	4	1	0	1	0	....	....	....	....	....
2001-02	Ottawa Senators	11	0	0	0	12	....	....	....	....	....
2002-03	Ottawa Senators	20	0	2	2	6	....	....	....	....	....
	Washington Capitals	34	0	3	3	12	6	0	0	0	2
	NHL Totals	**69**	**1**	**5**	**6**	**30**	**6**	**0**	**0**	**0**	**2**

Signed as a free agent by **Anaheim**, June 18, 1998. Traded to **Ottawa** by **Anaheim** for Patrick Traverse, June 12, 2000. Traded to **Washington** by **Ottawa** for Washington's 9th round choice (later traded back to Washington – Washington selected Mark Olafson) in 2003 Entry Draft, January 15, 2003.

KWONG, Larry

Right wing. Shoots right. 5'6", 150 lbs. Born, Vernon, B.C., June 17, 1923.

Season	Club	GP	G	A	Pts	PIM	GP	G	A	Pts	PIM
1947-48	New York Rangers	1	0	0	0	0	....	....	....	....	....
	NHL Totals	**1**	**0**	**0**	**0**	**0**	....	....	....	....	....

KYLE, Bill

Center. Shoots right. 6'1", 210 lbs. Born, Dysart, Sask., December 23, 1924.

Season	Club	GP	G	A	Pts	PIM	GP	G	A	Pts	PIM
1949-50	New York Rangers	2	0	0	0	0	....	....	....	....	....
1950-51	New York Rangers	1	0	3	3	0	....	....	....	....	....
	NHL Totals	**3**	**0**	**3**	**3**	**0**	....	....	....	....	....

• Brother of Gus

KYLE, Gus

Defense. Shoots left. 6'1", 202 lbs. Born, Dysart, Sask., September 11, 1923.

Season	Club	GP	G	A	Pts	PIM	GP	G	A	Pts	PIM
1949-50	New York Rangers	70	3	5	8	143	12	1	2	3	30

Season	Club	GP	G	A	Pts	PIM	GP	G	A	Pts	PIM
		REGULAR SEASON					PLAYOFFS				
1950-51	New York Rangers	64	2	3	5	92	....	....	....	....	....
1951-52	Boston Bruins	69	1	12	13	*127	2	0	0	0	4
	NHL Totals	**203**	**6**	**20**	**26**	**362**	**14**	**1**	**2**	**3**	**34**

• Brother of Bill

Signed as a free agent by **NY Rangers**, October 7, 1949. Traded to **Boston** by **NY Rangers** with the rights to Penti Lund and cash for Paul Ronty, September 20, 1951.

KYLLONEN, Markku

Left wing. Shoots left. 6'2", 200 lbs. Born, Joensuu, Finland, February 15, 1962.
(Winnipeg's 8th choice, 163rd overall, in 1987 Entry Draft).

Season	Club	GP	G	A	Pts	PIM	GP	G	A	Pts	PIM
1988-89	Winnipeg Jets	9	0	2	2	2	....	....	....	....	....
	NHL Totals	**9**	**0**	**2**	**2**	**2**	....	....	....	....	....

KYPREOS, Nick

Left wing. Shoots left. 6', 205 lbs. Born, Toronto, Ont., June 4, 1966.

Season	Club	GP	G	A	Pts	PIM	GP	G	A	Pts	PIM
1989-90	Washington Capitals	31	5	4	9	82	7	1	0	1	15
1990-91	Washington Capitals	79	9	9	18	196	9	0	1	1	38
1991-92	Washington Capitals	65	4	6	10	206	....	....	....	....	....
1992-93	Hartford Whalers	75	17	10	27	325	....	....	....	....	....
1993-94	Hartford Whalers	10	0	0	0	37	....	....	....	....	....
	♦ New York Rangers	46	3	5	8	102	3	0	0	0	2
1994-95	New York Rangers	40	1	3	4	93	10	0	2	2	6
1995-96	New York Rangers	42	3	4	7	77	....	....	....	....	....
	Toronto Maple Leafs	19	1	1	2	30	5	0	0	0	4
1996-97	Toronto Maple Leafs	35	3	2	5	62	....	....	....	....	....
	NHL Totals	**442**	**46**	**44**	**90**	**1210**	**34**	**1**	**3**	**4**	**65**

Signed as a free agent by **Philadelphia,** September 30, 1984. Claimed by **Washington** from **Philadelphia** in NHL Waiver Draft, October 2, 1989. Traded to **Hartford** by **Washington** for Mark Hunter and future considerations (Yvon Corriveau, August 20, 1992), June 15, 1992. Traded to **NY Rangers** by **Hartford** with Steve Larmer, Barry Richter and Hartford's 6th round choice (Yuri Litvinov) in 1994 Entry Draft for Darren Turcotte and James Patrick, November 2, 1993. Traded to **Toronto** by **NY Rangers** for Bill Berg, February 29, 1996. • Suffered career-ending head injury in exhibition game vs. NY Rangers, September 17, 1997.

KYTE, Jim

Defense. Shoots left. 6'5", 210 lbs. Born, Ottawa, Ont., March 21, 1964.
(Winnipeg's 1st choice, 12th overall, in 1982 Entry Draft).

Season	Club	GP	G	A	Pts	PIM	GP	G	A	Pts	PIM
1982-83	Winnipeg Jets	2	0	0	0	0	....	....	....	....	....
1983-84	Winnipeg Jets	58	1	2	3	55	3	0	0	0	11
1984-85	Winnipeg Jets	71	0	3	3	111	8	0	0	0	14
1985-86	Winnipeg Jets	71	1	3	4	126	3	0	0	0	12
1986-87	Winnipeg Jets	72	5	5	10	162	10	0	4	4	36
1987-88	Winnipeg Jets	51	1	3	4	128	....	....	....	....	....
1988-89	Winnipeg Jets	74	3	9	12	190	....	....	....	....	....
1989-90	Pittsburgh Penguins	56	3	1	4	125	....	....	....	....	....
1990-91	Pittsburgh Penguins	1	0	0	0	2	....	....	....	....	....
	Calgary Flames	42	0	9	9	153	7	0	0	0	7
1991-92	Calgary Flames	21	0	1	1	107	....	....	....	....	....
1992-93	Ottawa Senators	4	0	1	1	4	....	....	....	....	....
1994-95	San Jose Sharks	18	2	5	7	33	11	0	2	2	14
1995-96	San Jose Sharks	57	1	7	8	146	....	....	....	....	....
	NHL Totals	**598**	**17**	**49**	**66**	**1342**	**42**	**0**	**6**	**6**	**94**

Traded to **Pittsburgh** by **Winnipeg** with Andrew McBain and Randy Gilhen for Randy Cunneyworth, Rick Tabaracci and Dave McLlwain, June 17, 1989. Traded to **Calgary** by **Pittsburgh** for Jiri Hrdina, December 13, 1990. Signed as a free agent by **Ottawa**, September 10, 1992. Signed as a free agent by **San Jose**, March 31, 1995.

LAAKSONEN, Antti

Left wing. Shoots left. 6', 180 lbs. Born, Tammela, Finland, October 3, 1973.
(Boston's 10th choice, 191st overall, in 1997 Entry Draft).

Season	Club	GP	G	A	Pts	PIM	GP	G	A	Pts	PIM
1998-99	Boston Bruins	11	1	2	3	2	....	....	....	....	....
99-2000	Boston Bruins	27	6	3	9	2	....	....	....	....	....
2000-01	Minnesota Wild	82	12	16	28	24	....	....	....	....	....
2001-02	Minnesota Wild	82	16	17	33	22	....	....	....	....	....
2002-03	Minnesota Wild	82	15	16	31	26	16	1	3	4	4
	NHL Totals	**284**	**50**	**54**	**104**	**76**	**16**	**1**	**3**	**4**	**4**

Signed as a free agent by **Minnesota**, July 14, 2000.

LABADIE, Mike

Right wing. Shoots right. 5'11", 170 lbs. Born, St-Francis D'Assisi, Que., August 17, 1932.

Season	Club	GP	G	A	Pts	PIM	GP	G	A	Pts	PIM
1952-53	New York Rangers	3	0	0	0	0	....	....	....	....	....
	NHL Totals	**3**	**0**	**0**	**0**	**0**	....	....	....	....	....

LABATTE, Neil

Center/Defense. Shoots left. 6'2", 178 lbs. Born, Toronto, Ont., April 24, 1957.
(St. Louis' 2nd choice, 27th overall, in 1977 Amateur Draft).

Season	Club	GP	G	A	Pts	PIM	GP	G	A	Pts	PIM
1978-79	St. Louis Blues	22	0	2	2	13	....	....	....	....	....
1981-82	St. Louis Blues	4	0	0	0	6	....	....	....	....	....
	NHL Totals	**26**	**0**	**2**	**2**	**19**	....	....	....	....	....

L'ABBE, Moe

Right wing. Shoots left. 5'9", 170 lbs. Born, Montreal, Que., August 12, 1947.
(Chicago's 4th choice, 22nd overall, in 1964 Amateur Draft).

Season	Club	GP	G	A	Pts	PIM	GP	G	A	Pts	PIM
1972-73	Chicago Black Hawks	5	0	1	1	0	....	....	....	....	....
	NHL Totals	**5**	**0**	**1**	**1**	**0**	....	....	....	....	....

LABELLE, Marc

Left wing. Shoots left. 6'1", 215 lbs. Born, Maniwaki, Que., December 20, 1969.

Season	Club	GP	G	A	Pts	PIM	GP	G	A	Pts	PIM
1996-97	Dallas Stars	9	0	0	0	46	....	....	....	....	....
	NHL Totals	**9**	**0**	**0**	**0**	**46**	....	....	....	....	....

Signed as a free agent by **Montreal**, January 21, 1991. Signed as a free agent by **Ottawa**, July 30, 1992. Claimed by **Florida** from **Ottawa** in Expansion Draft, June 24, 1993. Signed as a free agent by **Dallas**, April 15, 1996. Signed as a free agent by **Ottawa**, July 14, 1997.

LABINE, Leo

Right wing. Shoots right. 5'10", 170 lbs. Born, Haileybury, Ont., July 22, 1931.

Season	Club	GP	G	A	Pts	PIM	GP	G	A	Pts	PIM
1951-52	Boston Bruins	15	2	4	6	9	5	0	1	1	4
1952-53	Boston Bruins	51	8	15	23	69	7	2	1	3	*19
1953-54	Boston Bruins	68	16	19	35	57	4	0	1	1	8
1954-55	Boston Bruins	67	24	18	42	75	5	2	1	3	11
1955-56	Boston Bruins	68	16	18	34	104	....	....	....	....	....
1956-57	Boston Bruins	67	18	29	47	128	10	3	2	5	*14
1957-58	Boston Bruins	62	7	14	21	60	11	0	2	2	10
1958-59	Boston Bruins	70	9	23	32	74	7	2	1	3	12
1959-60	Boston Bruins	63	16	28	44	58	....	....	....	....	....
1960-61	Boston Bruins	40	7	12	19	34	....	....	....	....	....
	Detroit Red Wings	24	2	9	11	32	11	3	2	5	4
1961-62	Detroit Red Wings	48	3	4	7	30	....	....	....	....	....
	NHL Totals	**643**	**128**	**193**	**321**	**730**	**60**	**12**	**11**	**23**	**82**

Played in NHL All-Star Game (1955, 1956)

Traded to **Detroit** by **Boston** with Vic Stasiuk for Gary Aldcorn, Murray Oliver and Tom McCarthy, January 23, 1961. Traded to **LA Blades** (WHL) by **Detroit** for cash, July, 1962.

LABOSSIERE, Gord

Center. Shoots right. 6'1", 190 lbs. Born, St. Boniface, Man., January 2, 1940.

Season	Club	GP	G	A	Pts	PIM	GP	G	A	Pts	PIM
1963-64	New York Rangers	15	0	0	0	12	....	....	....	....	....
1964-65	New York Rangers	1	0	0	0	0	....	....	....	....	....
1967-68	Los Angeles Kings	68	13	27	40	31	7	2	3	5	24
1968-69	Los Angeles Kings	48	10	18	28	12	....	....	....	....	....
1970-71	Los Angeles Kings	45	11	10	21	16	....	....	....	....	....
	Minnesota North Stars	29	8	4	12	4	3	0	0	0	4
1971-72	Minnesota North Stars	9	2	3	5	0	....	....	....	....	....
	NHL Totals	**215**	**44**	**62**	**106**	**75**	**10**	**2**	**3**	**5**	**28**

Claimed by **Detroit** from **NY Rangers** (Saskatoon-WHL) in Inter-League Draft, June 9, 1959. Loaned to **Winnipeg** (WHL) by **Detroit** (Edmonton-WHL) for the loan of Ray Brunel, December, 1960. Claimed by **NY Rangers** from **Detroit** (Sudbury-EPHL) in Inter-League Draft, June 4, 1963. Traded to **Montreal** by **NY Rangers** with Earl Ingarfield, Noel Price, Dave McComb and cash for Garry Peters and Cesare Maniago, June 8, 1965. Claimed by **Los Angeles** from **Montreal** in Expansion Draft, June 6, 1967. Traded to **Montreal** by **Los Angeles** with Ray Fortin for Ralph Backstrom, January 26, 1971. Traded to **Minnesota** by **Montreal** for Rey Comeau, January 26, 1971. Traded to **NY Islanders** by **Minnesota** for future considerations for cash, June 6, 1972.

LABOVITCH, Max

Right wing. Shoots right. 5'11", 165 lbs. Born, Winnipeg, Man., January 18, 1924.

Season	Club	GP	G	A	Pts	PIM	GP	G	A	Pts	PIM
1943-44	New York Rangers	5	0	0	0	4	....	....	....	....	....
	NHL Totals	**5**	**0**	**0**	**0**	**4**	....	....	....	....	....

LABRAATEN, Dan

Left wing. Shoots right. 6', 190 lbs. Born, Leksand, Sweden, June 9, 1951.

Season	Club	GP	G	A	Pts	PIM	GP	G	A	Pts	PIM
1978-79	Detroit Red Wings	78	19	19	38	8	....	....	....	....	....
1979-80	Detroit Red Wings	76	30	27	57	8	....	....	....	....	....
1980-81	Detroit Red Wings	44	3	8	11	12	....	....	....	....	....
	Calgary Flames	27	9	7	16	13	5	1	0	1	4
1981-82	Calgary Flames	43	10	12	22	6	3	0	0	0	0
	NHL Totals	**268**	**71**	**73**	**144**	**47**	**8**	**1**	**0**	**1**	**4**

Signed as a free agent by **Detroit**, October 12, 1978. Traded to **Calgary** by **Detroit** for Earl Ingarfield Jr., February 3, 1981.

LABRE, Yvon

Defense. Shoots left. 5'11", 190 lbs. Born, Sudbury, Ont., November 29, 1949.
(Pittsburgh's 3rd choice, 38th overall, in 1969 Amateur Draft).

Season	Club	GP	G	A	Pts	PIM	GP	G	A	Pts	PIM
1970-71	Pittsburgh Penguins	21	1	1	2	19	....	....	....	....	....
1973-74	Pittsburgh Penguins	16	1	2	3	13	....	....	....	....	....
1974-75	Washington Capitals	76	4	23	27	182	....	....	....	....	....
1975-76	Washington Capitals	80	2	20	22	146	....	....	....	....	....
1976-77	Washington Capitals	62	3	11	14	169	....	....	....	....	....
1977-78	Washington Capitals	22	0	8	8	41	....	....	....	....	....
1978-79	Washington Capitals	51	1	13	14	80	....	....	....	....	....
1979-80	Washington Capitals	18	0	5	5	38	....	....	....	....	....
1980-81	Washington Capitals	25	2	4	6	100	....	....	....	....	....
	NHL Totals	**371**	**14**	**87**	**101**	**788**	....	....	....	....	....

Claimed by **Washington** from **Pittsburgh** in Expansion Draft, June 12, 1974.

LABRIE, Guy

Defense. Shoots left. 6', 185 lbs. Born, St-Charles Bellechasse, Que., August 11, 1920.

Season	Club	GP	G	A	Pts	PIM	GP	G	A	Pts	PIM
1943-44	Boston Bruins	15	2	7	9	2	....	....	....	....	....

Season	Club	REGULAR SEASON GP	G	A	Pts	PIM	PLAYOFFS GP	G	A	Pts	PIM
1944-45	New York Rangers	27	2	2	4	14	....	....	....	....	....
	NHL Totals	**42**	**4**	**9**	**13**	**16**	....	....	....	....	....

Traded to **NY Rangers** by **Boston** for $12,000, November 27, 1944. Traded to **New Haven** (AHL) by **NY Rangers** (Providence-AHL) with Paul Courteau and Roland Forget for George Boothman and cash, November 19, 1945.

LACH, Elmer

HHOF

Center. Shoots left. 5'10", 165 lbs. Born, Nokomis, Sask., January 22, 1918.

Season	Club	GP	G	A	Pts	PIM	GP	G	A	Pts	PIM
1940-41	Montreal Canadiens	43	7	14	21	16	3	1	0	1	0
1941-42	Montreal Canadiens	1	0	1	1	0	....	....	....	....	....
1942-43	Montreal Canadiens	45	18	40	58	14	5	2	4	6	6
1943-44♦	Montreal Canadiens	48	24	48	72	23	9	2	*11	13	4
1944-45	Montreal Canadiens	50	26	*54	*80	37	6	4	4	8	2
1945-46♦	Montreal Canadiens	50	13	*34	47	34	9	5	*12	*17	4
1946-47	Montreal Canadiens	31	14	16	30	22	....	....	....	....	....
1947-48	Montreal Canadiens	60	30	31	*61	72	....	....	....	....	....
1948-49	Montreal Canadiens	36	11	18	29	59	1	0	0	0	4
1949-50	Montreal Canadiens	64	15	33	48	33	5	1	2	3	4
1950-51	Montreal Canadiens	65	21	24	45	48	11	2	2	4	2
1951-52	Montreal Canadiens	70	15	*50	65	36	11	1	2	3	4
1952-53♦	Montreal Canadiens	53	16	25	41	56	12	1	6	7	6
1953-54	Montreal Canadiens	48	5	20	25	28	4	0	2	2	0
	NHL Totals	**664**	**215**	**408**	**623**	**478**	**76**	**19**	**45**	**64**	**36**

NHL Second All-Star Team (1944, 1946) • NHL First All-Star Team (1945, 1948, 1952) • Hart Trophy (1945) • Art Ross Trophy (1948)

Played in NHL All-Star Game (1948, 1952, 1953)

Signed as a free agent by **Montreal**, October 24, 1940. • Missed remainder of 1941-42 season after suffering elbow injury in game vs. Detroit, November 1, 1941.

LACHANCE, Michel

Defense. Shoots right. 6', 190 lbs. Born, Quebec City, Que., April 11, 1955.
(Montreal's 9th choice, 106th overall, in 1975 Amateur Draft).

Season	Club	GP	G	A	Pts	PIM	GP	G	A	Pts	PIM
1978-79	Colorado Rockies	21	0	4	4	22	....	....	....	....	....
	NHL Totals	**21**	**0**	**4**	**4**	**22**	....	....	....	....	....

Signed as a free agent by **Colorado**, October 13, 1978.

LACHANCE, Scott

Defense. Shoots left. 6'1", 215 lbs. Born, Charlottesville, VA, October 22, 1972.
(NY Islanders' 1st choice, 4th overall, in 1991 Entry Draft).

Season	Club	GP	G	A	Pts	PIM	GP	G	A	Pts	PIM
1991-92	New York Islanders	17	1	4	5	9	....	....	....	....	....
1992-93	New York Islanders	75	7	17	24	67	....	....	....	....	....
1993-94	New York Islanders	74	3	11	14	70	3	0	0	0	0
1994-95	New York Islanders	26	6	7	13	26	....	....	....	....	....
1995-96	New York Islanders	55	3	10	13	54	....	....	....	....	....
1996-97	New York Islanders	81	3	11	14	47	....	....	....	....	....
1997-98	New York Islanders	63	2	11	13	45	....	....	....	....	....
1998-99	New York Islanders	59	1	8	9	30	....	....	....	....	....
	Montreal Canadiens	17	1	1	2	11	....	....	....	....	....
99-2000	Montreal Canadiens	57	0	6	6	22	....	....	....	....	....
2000-01	Vancouver Canucks	76	3	11	14	46	2	0	1	1	2
2001-02	Vancouver Canucks	81	1	10	11	50	6	1	1	2	4
2002-03	Columbus Blue Jackets	61	0	1	1	46	....	....	....	....	....
	NHL Totals	**742**	**31**	**108**	**139**	**523**	**11**	**1**	**2**	**3**	**6**

Played in NHL All-Star Game (1997)

Traded to **Montreal** by **NY Islanders** for Montreal's 3rd round choice (Mattias Weinhandl) in 1999 Entry Draft, March 9, 1999. Signed as a free agent by **Vancouver**, August 13, 2000. Signed as a free agent by **Columbus**, July 4, 2002.

LACOMBE, Francois

Defense. Shoots left. 5'10", 185 lbs. Born, Montreal, Que., February 24, 1948.

Season	Club	GP	G	A	Pts	PIM	GP	G	A	Pts	PIM
1968-69	Oakland Seals	72	2	16	18	50	3	1	0	1	0
1969-70	Oakland Seals	2	0	0	0	0	....	....	....	....	....
1970-71	Buffalo Sabres	1	0	1	1	2	....	....	....	....	....
1979-80	Quebec Nordiques	3	0	0	0	2	....	....	....	....	....
	NHL Totals	**78**	**2**	**17**	**19**	**54**	**3**	**1**	**0**	**1**	**0**

Traded to **Oakland** by **Montreal** with Michel Jacques to complete transaction that sent Wally Boyer to Montreal (May 21, 1968), June, 1968. Traded to **Montreal** by **California** with cash and California's 1st round choice (Guy Lafleur) in 1971 Amateur Draft for Ernie Hicke and Montreal's 1st round choice (Chris Oddleifson) in 1970 Amateur Draft, May 22, 1970. Claimed by **Buffalo** from **Montreal** in Expansion Draft, June 10, 1970. Rights retained by **Quebec** prior to Expansion Draft, June 9, 1979.

LACOMBE, Normand

Right wing. Shoots right. 6', 205 lbs. Born, Pierrefonds, Que., October 18, 1964.
(Buffalo's 2nd choice, 10th overall, in 1983 Entry Draft).

Season	Club	GP	G	A	Pts	PIM	GP	G	A	Pts	PIM
1984-85	Buffalo Sabres	30	2	4	6	25	....	....	....	....	....
1985-86	Buffalo Sabres	25	6	7	13	13	....	....	....	....	....
1986-87	Buffalo Sabres	39	4	7	11	8	....	....	....	....	....
	Edmonton Oilers	1	0	0	0	2	....	....	....	....	....
1987-88♦	Edmonton Oilers	53	8	9	17	36	19	3	0	3	28
1988-89	Edmonton Oilers	64	17	11	28	57	7	2	1	3	21
1989-90	Edmonton Oilers	15	5	2	7	21	....	....	....	....	....
	Philadelphia Flyers	18	0	2	2	7	....	....	....	....	....
1990-91	Philadelphia Flyers	74	11	20	31	27	....	....	....	....	....
	NHL Totals	**319**	**53**	**62**	**115**	**196**	**26**	**5**	**1**	**6**	**49**

Traded to **Edmonton** by **Buffalo** with Wayne Van Dorp and Buffalo's 4th round choice (Peter Eriksson) in 1987 Entry Draft for Lee Fogolin, Mark Napier and Edmonton's 4th round choice (John Bradley) in 1987 Entry Draft, March 6, 1987. Traded to **Philadelphia** by **Edmonton** for future considerations, January 5, 1990.

LaCOUTURE, Dan

Left wing. Shoots left. 6'2", 208 lbs. Born, Hyannis, MA, April 18, 1977.
(NY Islanders' 2nd choice, 29th overall, in 1996 Entry Draft).

Season	Club	GP	G	A	Pts	PIM	GP	G	A	Pts	PIM
1998-99	Edmonton Oilers	3	0	0	0	0	....	....	....	....	....
99-2000	Edmonton Oilers	5	0	0	0	10	1	0	0	0	0
2000-01	Edmonton Oilers	37	2	4	6	29	....	....	....	....	....
	Pittsburgh Penguins	11	0	0	0	14	5	0	0	0	2
2001-02	Pittsburgh Penguins	82	6	11	17	71	....	....	....	....	....
2002-03	Pittsburgh Penguins	44	2	2	4	72	....	....	....	....	....
	New York Rangers	24	1	4	5	0	....	....	....	....	....
	NHL Totals	**206**	**11**	**21**	**32**	**196**	**6**	**0**	**0**	**0**	**2**

Traded to **Edmonton** by **NY Islanders** for Mariusz Czerkawski, August 25, 1997. Traded to **Pittsburgh** by **Edmonton** for Sven Butenschon, March 13, 2001. Traded to **NY Rangers** by **Pittsburgh** with Mike Wilson, Alexei Kovalev and Janne Laukkanen for Joel Bouchard, Richard Lintner, Rico Fata, Mikael Samuelsson and future considerations, February 10, 2003.

LACROIX, Andre

Center. Shoots left. 5'8", 175 lbs. Born, Lauzon, Que., June 5, 1945.

Season	Club	GP	G	A	Pts	PIM	GP	G	A	Pts	PIM
1967-68	Philadelphia Flyers	18	6	8	14	6	7	2	3	5	0
1968-69	Philadelphia Flyers	75	24	32	56	4	4	0	0	0	0
1969-70	Philadelphia Flyers	74	22	36	58	14	....	....	....	....	....
1970-71	Philadelphia Flyers	78	20	22	42	12	4	0	2	2	0
1971-72	Chicago Black Hawks	51	4	7	11	6	1	0	0	0	0
1979-80	Hartford Whalers	29	3	14	17	2	....	....	....	....	....
	NHL Totals	**325**	**79**	**119**	**198**	**44**	**16**	**2**	**5**	**7**	**0**

NHL rights transferred to **Philadelphia** after NHL club purchased **Quebec** (AHL) franchise, May 8, 1967. Traded to **Chicago** by **Philadelphia** for Rick Foley, October 15, 1971. Rights retained by **Hartford** prior to Expansion Draft, June 9, 1979.

LACROIX, Daniel

Left wing. Shoots left. 6'2", 205 lbs. Born, Montreal, Que., March 11, 1969.
(NY Rangers' 2nd choice, 31st overall, in 1987 Entry Draft).

Season	Club	GP	G	A	Pts	PIM	GP	G	A	Pts	PIM
1993-94	New York Rangers	4	0	0	0	0	....	....	....	....	....
1994-95	Boston Bruins	23	1	0	1	38	....	....	....	....	....
	New York Rangers	1	0	0	0	0	....	....	....	....	....
1995-96	New York Rangers	25	2	2	4	30	....	....	....	....	....
1996-97	Philadelphia Flyers	74	7	1	8	163	12	0	1	1	22
1997-98	Philadelphia Flyers	56	1	4	5	135	4	0	0	0	4
1998-99	Edmonton Oilers	4	0	0	0	13	....	....	....	....	....
99-2000	New York Islanders	1	0	0	0	0	....	....	....	....	....
	NHL Totals	**188**	**11**	**7**	**18**	**379**	**16**	**0**	**1**	**1**	**26**

Traded to **Boston** by **NY Rangers** for Glen Featherstone, August 19, 1994. Claimed on waivers by **NY Rangers** from **Boston**, March 23, 1995. Signed as a free agent by **Philadelphia**, July 18, 1996. Traded to **Edmonton** by **Philadelphia** for Valeri Zelepukin, October 5, 1998. Signed as a free agent by **NY Islanders**, August 11, 1999.

LACROIX, Eric

Left wing. Shoots left. 6'1", 210 lbs. Born, Montreal, Que., July 15, 1971.
(Toronto's 6th choice, 136th overall, in 1990 Entry Draft).

Season	Club	GP	G	A	Pts	PIM	GP	G	A	Pts	PIM
1993-94	Toronto Maple Leafs	3	0	0	0	2	2	0	0	0	0
1994-95	Los Angeles Kings	45	9	7	16	54	....	....	....	....	....
1995-96	Los Angeles Kings	72	16	16	32	110	....	....	....	....	....
1996-97	Colorado Avalanche	81	18	18	36	26	17	1	4	5	19
1997-98	Colorado Avalanche	82	16	15	31	84	7	0	0	0	6
1998-99	Colorado Avalanche	7	0	0	0	2	....	....	....	....	....
	Los Angeles Kings	27	0	1	1	12	....	....	....	....	....
	New York Rangers	30	2	1	3	4	....	....	....	....	....
99-2000	New York Rangers	70	4	8	12	24	....	....	....	....	....
2000-01	New York Rangers	46	2	3	5	39	....	....	....	....	....
	Ottawa Senators	9	0	1	1	4	4	0	1	1	0
	NHL Totals	**472**	**67**	**70**	**137**	**361**	**30**	**1**	**5**	**6**	**25**

Traded to **Los Angeles** by **Toronto** with Chris Snell and Toronto's 4th round choice (Eric Belanger) in 1996 Entry Draft for Dixon Ward, Guy Leveque, Kelly Fairchild and Shayne Toporowski, October 3, 1994. Traded to **Colorado** by **Los Angeles** with Los Angeles' 1st round choice (Martin Skoula) in 1998 Entry Draft for Stephane Fiset and Colorado's 1st round choice (Mathieu Biron) in 1998 Entry Draft, June 20, 1996. Traded to **Los Angeles** by **Colorado** for Roman Vopat and Los Angeles' 6th round choice (later traded to Ottawa – Ottawa selected Martin Prusek) in 1999 Entry Draft, October 29, 1998. Traded to **NY Rangers** by **Los Angeles** for Sean Pronger, February 12, 1999. Traded to **Ottawa** by **NY Rangers** for Colin Forbes, March 1, 2001.

LACROIX, Pierre

Defense. Shoots left. 5'11", 185 lbs. Born, Quebec City, Que., April 11, 1959.
(Quebec's 5th choice, 104th overall, in 1979 Entry Draft).

Season	Club	GP	G	A	Pts	PIM	GP	G	A	Pts	PIM
1979-80	Quebec Nordiques	76	9	21	30	45	....	....	....	....	....
1980-81	Quebec Nordiques	61	5	34	39	54	5	0	2	2	10
1981-82	Quebec Nordiques	68	4	23	27	74	3	0	0	0	0

		REGULAR SEASON					PLAYOFFS				
Season	Club	GP	G	A	Pts	PIM	GP	G	A	Pts	PIM
1982-83	Quebec Nordiques	13	0	5	5	6	....	....	....	....	....
	Hartford Whalers	56	6	25	31	18	....	....	....	....	....
	NHL Totals	**274**	**24**	**108**	**132**	**197**	**8**	**0**	**2**	**2**	**10**

Traded to **Hartford** by **Quebec** for Blake Wesley, December 3, 1982.

LADOUCEUR, Randy

Defense. Shoots left. 6'2", 220 lbs. Born, Brockville, Ont., June 30, 1960.

Season	Club	GP	G	A	Pts	PIM	GP	G	A	Pts	PIM
1982-83	Detroit Red Wings	27	0	4	4	16	....	....	....	....	....
1983-84	Detroit Red Wings	71	3	17	20	58	4	1	0	1	6
1984-85	Detroit Red Wings	80	3	27	30	108	3	1	0	1	0
1985-86	Detroit Red Wings	78	5	13	18	196	....	....	....	....	....
1986-87	Detroit Red Wings	34	3	6	9	70	....	....	....	....	....
	Hartford Whalers	36	2	3	5	51	6	0	2	2	12
1987-88	Hartford Whalers	67	1	7	8	91	6	1	1	2	4
1988-89	Hartford Whalers	75	2	5	7	95	1	0	0	0	10
1989-90	Hartford Whalers	71	3	12	15	126	7	1	0	1	10
1990-91	Hartford Whalers	67	1	3	4	118	6	1	4	5	6
1991-92	Hartford Whalers	74	1	9	10	127	7	0	1	1	11
1992-93	Hartford Whalers	62	2	4	6	109	....	....	....	....	....
1993-94	Mighty Ducks of Anaheim	81	1	9	10	74	....	....	....	....	....
1994-95	Mighty Ducks of Anaheim	44	2	4	6	36	....	....	....	....	....
1995-96	Mighty Ducks of Anaheim	63	1	3	4	47	....	....	....	....	....
	NHL Totals	**930**	**30**	**126**	**156**	**1322**	**40**	**5**	**8**	**13**	**59**

Signed as a free agent by **Detroit**, November 1, 1979. Traded to **Hartford** by **Detroit** for Dave Barr, January 12, 1987. Claimed by **Anaheim** from **Hartford** in Expansion Draft, June 24, 1993.

LaFAYETTE, Nathan

Center. Shoots right. 6'1", 205 lbs. Born, New Westminster, B.C., February 17, 1973.
(St. Louis' 3rd choice, 65th overall, in 1991 Entry Draft).

Season	Club	GP	G	A	Pts	PIM	GP	G	A	Pts	PIM
1993-94	St. Louis Blues	38	2	3	5	14	....	....	....	....	....
	Vancouver Canucks	11	1	1	2	4	20	2	7	9	4
1994-95	Vancouver Canucks	27	4	4	8	2	....	....	....	....	....
	New York Rangers	12	0	0	0	0	8	0	0	0	2
1995-96	New York Rangers	5	0	0	0	2	....	....	....	....	....
	Los Angeles Kings	12	2	4	6	6	....	....	....	....	....
1996-97	Los Angeles Kings	15	1	3	4	8	....	....	....	....	....
1997-98	Los Angeles Kings	34	5	3	8	32	4	0	0	0	2
1998-99	Los Angeles Kings	33	2	2	4	35	....	....	....	....	....
	NHL Totals	**187**	**17**	**20**	**37**	**103**	**32**	**2**	**7**	**9**	**8**

Traded to **Vancouver** by **St. Louis** with Jeff Brown and Bret Hedican for Craig Janney, March 21, 1994. Traded to **NY Rangers** by **Vancouver** for Corey Hirsch, April 7, 1995. Traded to **Los Angeles** by **NY Rangers** with Ray Ferraro, Mattias Norstrom, Ian Laperriere and NY Rangers' 4th round choice (Sean Blanchard) in 1997 Entry Draft for Marty McSorley, Jari Kurri and Shane Churla, March 14, 1996.

LAFLAMME, Christian

Defense. Shoots right. 6'1", 210 lbs. Born, St-Charles, Que., November 24, 1976.
(Chicago's 2nd choice, 45th overall, in 1995 Entry Draft).

Season	Club	GP	G	A	Pts	PIM	GP	G	A	Pts	PIM
1996-97	Chicago Blackhawks	4	0	1	1	2	....	....	....	....	....
1997-98	Chicago Blackhawks	72	0	11	11	59	....	....	....	....	....
1998-99	Chicago Blackhawks	62	2	11	13	70	....	....	....	....	....
	Edmonton Oilers	11	0	1	1	0	4	0	1	1	2
99-2000	Edmonton Oilers	50	0	5	5	32	....	....	....	....	....
	Montreal Canadiens	15	0	2	2	8	....	....	....	....	....
2000-01	Montreal Canadiens	39	0	3	3	42	....	....	....	....	....
2001-02	St. Louis Blues	8	0	1	1	4	....	....	....	....	....
2002-03	St. Louis Blues	47	0	9	9	45	5	0	0	0	4
	NHL Totals	**308**	**2**	**44**	**46**	**262**	**9**	**0**	**1**	**1**	**6**

Traded to **Edmonton** by **Chicago** with Daniel Cleary, Ethan Moreau and Chad Kilger for Boris Mironov, Dean McAmmond and Jonas Elofsson, March 20, 1999. Traded to **Montreal** by **Edmonton** with Matthieu Descoteaux for Igor Ulanov and Alain Nasreddine, March 9, 2000.
• Missed majority of 2000-01 season recovering from groin injury suffered in game vs. Calgary, December 13, 2000. Signed as a free agent by **St. Louis**, August 21, 2001.

LAFLEUR, Guy

HHOF

Right wing. Shoots right. 6', 185 lbs. Born, Thurso, Que., September 20, 1951.
(Montreal's 1st choice, 1st overall, in 1971 Amateur Draft).

Season	Club	GP	G	A	Pts	PIM	GP	G	A	Pts	PIM
1971-72	Montreal Canadiens	73	29	35	64	48	6	1	4	5	2
1972-73 ♦	Montreal Canadiens	69	28	27	55	51	17	3	5	8	9
1973-74	Montreal Canadiens	73	21	35	56	29	6	0	1	1	4
1974-75	Montreal Canadiens	70	53	66	119	37	11	*12	7	19	15
1975-76 ♦	Montreal Canadiens	80	56	69	*125	36	13	7	10	17	2
1976-77 ♦	Montreal Canadiens	80	56	*80	*136	20	14	9	*17	*26	6
1977-78 ♦	Montreal Canadiens	78	*60	72	*132	26	15	*10	11	*21	16
1978-79 ♦	Montreal Canadiens	80	52	77	129	28	16	10	*13	*23	0
1979-80	Montreal Canadiens	74	50	75	125	12	3	3	1	4	0
1980-81	Montreal Canadiens	51	27	43	70	29	3	0	1	1	2
1981-82	Montreal Canadiens	66	27	57	84	24	5	2	1	3	4
1982-83	Montreal Canadiens	68	27	49	76	12	3	0	2	2	2
1983-84	Montreal Canadiens	80	30	40	70	19	12	0	3	3	5
1984-85	Montreal Canadiens	19	2	3	5	10	....	....	....	....	....
1988-89	New York Rangers	67	18	27	45	12	4	1	0	1	0
1989-90	Quebec Nordiques	39	12	22	34	4	....	....	....	....	....
1990-91	Quebec Nordiques	59	12	16	28	2	....	....	....	....	....
	NHL Totals	**1126**	**560**	**793**	**1353**	**399**	**128**	**58**	**76**	**134**	**67**

• NHL First All-Star Team (1975, 1976, 1977, 1978, 1979, 1980) • Art Ross Trophy (1976, 1977, 1978) • Lester B. Pearson Award (1976, 1977, 1978) • Hart Trophy (1977, 1978) • Conn Smythe Trophy (1977) • NHL Plus/Minus Leader (1978)

Played in NHL All-Star Game (1975, 1976, 1977, 1978, 1980, 1991)

Signed as a free agent by **NY Rangers**, September 26, 1988. Signed as a free agent by **Quebec**, July 14, 1989. NY Rangers received Quebec's 5th round choice (Sergei Zubov) in 1990 Entry Draft as compensation. Claimed by **Minnesota** from **Quebec** in Expansion Draft, May 30, 1991. Traded to **Quebec** by **Minnesota** for Alan Haworth, May 31, 1991.

LAFLEUR, Roland

Left wing. Shoots left. 5'6", 145 lbs. Born, Ottawa, Ont., 1899.

Season	Club	GP	G	A	Pts	PIM	GP	G	A	Pts	PIM
1924-25	Montreal Canadiens	1	0	0	0	0	....	....	....	....	....
	NHL Totals	**1**	**0**	**0**	**0**	**0**	....	....	....	....	....

Signed as a free agent by **Montreal**, November 17, 1924.

LaFONTAINE, Pat

USHOF HHOF

Center. Shoots right. 5'10", 182 lbs. Born, St. Louis, MO, February 22, 1965.
(NY Islanders' 1st choice, 3rd overall, in 1983 Entry Draft).

Season	Club	GP	G	A	Pts	PIM	GP	G	A	Pts	PIM
1983-84	New York Islanders	15	13	6	19	6	16	3	6	9	8
1984-85	New York Islanders	67	19	35	54	32	9	1	2	3	4
1985-86	New York Islanders	65	30	23	53	43	3	1	0	1	0
1986-87	New York Islanders	80	38	32	70	70	14	5	7	12	10
1987-88	New York Islanders	75	47	45	92	52	6	4	5	9	8
1988-89	New York Islanders	79	45	43	88	26	....	....	....	....	....
1989-90	New York Islanders	74	54	51	105	38	2	0	1	1	0
1990-91	New York Islanders	75	41	44	85	42	....	....	....	....	....
1991-92	Buffalo Sabres	57	46	47	93	98	7	8	3	11	4
1992-93	Buffalo Sabres	84	53	95	148	63	7	2	10	12	0
1993-94	Buffalo Sabres	16	5	13	18	2	....	....	....	....	....
1994-95	Buffalo Sabres	22	12	15	27	4	5	2	2	4	2
1995-96	Buffalo Sabres	76	40	51	91	36	....	....	....	....	....
1996-97	Buffalo Sabres	13	2	6	8	4	....	....	....	....	....
1997-98	New York Rangers	67	23	39	62	36	....	....	....	....	....
	NHL Totals	**865**	**468**	**545**	**1013**	**552**	**69**	**26**	**36**	**62**	**36**

Dodge Performer of the Year Award (1990) • NHL Second All-Star Team (1993) • Bill Masterton Memorial Trophy (1995)

• Played in NHL All-Star Game (1988, 1989, 1990, 1991, 1993)

Traded to **Buffalo** by **NY Islanders** with Randy Hillier, Randy Wood and NY Islanders' 4th round choice (Dean Melanson) in 1992 Entry Draft for Pierre Turgeon, Uwe Krupp, Benoit Hogue and Dave McLlwain, October 25, 1991. Traded to **NY Rangers** by **Buffalo** for NY Rangers' 2nd round choice (Andrew Peters) in 1998 Entry Draft and future considerations, September 29, 1997.
• Suffered career-ending head injury in game vs. Ottawa, March 16, 1998. • Officially announced retirement, October 12, 1999.

LAFORCE, Ernie

Defense. Shoots left. 5'11", 175 lbs. Born, Montreal, Que., June 23, 1916.

Season	Club	GP	G	A	Pts	PIM	GP	G	A	Pts	PIM
1942-43	Montreal Canadiens	1	0	0	0	0	....	....	....	....	....
	NHL Totals	**1**	**0**	**0**	**0**	**0**	....	....	....	....	....

LaFOREST, Bob

Right wing. Shoots right. 5'10", 195 lbs. Born, Sault Ste. Marie, Ont., May 19, 1963.
(Los Angeles' 3rd choice, 89th overall, in 1983 Entry Draft).

Season	Club	GP	G	A	Pts	PIM	GP	G	A	Pts	PIM
1983-84	Los Angeles Kings	5	1	0	1	2	....	....	....	....	....
	NHL Totals	**5**	**1**	**0**	**1**	**2**	....	....	....	....	....

• Brother of Mark

Traded to **Boston** by **Los Angeles** for Marco Baron, January 3, 1984.

LAFORGE, Claude

Left wing. Shoots left. 5'9", 172 lbs. Born, Sorel, Que., July 1, 1936.

Season	Club	GP	G	A	Pts	PIM	GP	G	A	Pts	PIM
1957-58	Montreal Canadiens	5	0	0	0	0	....	....	....	....	....
1958-59	Detroit Red Wings	57	2	5	7	18	....	....	....	....	....
1960-61	Detroit Red Wings	10	1	0	1	2	....	....	....	....	....
1961-62	Detroit Red Wings	38	10	9	19	20	....	....	....	....	....
1963-64	Detroit Red Wings	17	2	3	5	4	....	....	....	....	....
1964-65	Detroit Red Wings	1	0	0	0	2	....	....	....	....	....
1967-68	Philadelphia Flyers	63	9	16	25	36	5	1	2	3	15
1968-69	Philadelphia Flyers	2	0	0	0	0	....	....	....	....	....
	NHL Totals	**193**	**24**	**33**	**57**	**82**	**5**	**1**	**2**	**3**	**15**

Traded to **Detroit** by **Montreal** with Gene Achtymichuk and Bud MacPherson for cash, June 3, 1958. Traded to **Quebec** (AHL) by **Detroit** (Pittsburgh-AHL) for Terry Gray, March 1, 1966. NHL rights transferred to **Philadelphia** after NHL club purchased **Quebec** (AHL) franchise, May 8, 1967. Traded to **Denver** (WHL) by **Philadelphia** for cash, August, 1970.

LAFORGE, Marc

Left wing. Shoots left. 6'2", 210 lbs. Born, Sudbury, Ont., January 3, 1968.
(Hartford's 2nd choice, 32nd overall, in 1986 Entry Draft).

Season	Club	GP	G	A	Pts	PIM	GP	G	A	Pts	PIM
1989-90	Hartford Whalers	9	0	0	0	43	....	....	....	....	....
1993-94	Edmonton Oilers	5	0	0	0	21	....	....	....	....	....
	NHL Totals	**14**	**0**	**0**	**0**	**64**	....	....	....	....	....

Traded to **Edmonton** by **Hartford** for the rights to Cam Brauer, March 6, 1990. Traded to **NY Islanders** by **Edmonton** for Brent Grieve, December 15, 1993.

LAFRAMBOISE, Pete

Left wing/Center. Shoots left. 6'2", 185 lbs. Born, Ottawa, Ont., January 18, 1950.
(California's 2nd choice, 19th overall, in 1970 Amateur Draft).

Season	Club	Regular Season GP	G	A	Pts	PIM	Playoffs GP	G	A	Pts	PIM
1971-72	California Golden Seals	5	0	0	0	0	....	....	....	....	....
1972-73	California Golden Seals	77	16	25	41	26	....	....	....	....	....
1973-74	California Golden Seals	65	7	7	14	14	....	....	....	....	....
1974-75	Washington Capitals	45	5	10	15	22	....	....	....	....	....
	Pittsburgh Penguins	35	5	13	18	8	9	1	0	1	0
	NHL Totals	**227**	**33**	**55**	**88**	**70**	**9**	**1**	**0**	**1**	**0**

Claimed by **Washington** from **California** in Expansion Draft, June 12, 1974. Traded to **Pittsburgh** by **Washington** for Ron Jones, January 21, 1975.

LAFRANCE, Adie

Left wing. Shoots left. 5'10", 165 lbs. Born, Chapleau, Ont., January 13, 1912.

Season	Club	Regular Season GP	G	A	Pts	PIM	Playoffs GP	G	A	Pts	PIM
1933-34	Montreal Canadiens	3	0	0	0	2	2	0	0	0	0
	NHL Totals	**3**	**0**	**0**	**0**	**2**	**2**	**0**	**0**	**0**	**0**

Signed as a free agent by **Montreal**, March 9, 1934.

LAFRANCE, Leo

Left wing. Shoots left. 5'8", 160 lbs. Born, Allomette, Que., November 3, 1902.

Season	Club	Regular Season GP	G	A	Pts	PIM	Playoffs GP	G	A	Pts	PIM
1926-27	Montreal Canadiens	4	0	0	0	0	....	....	....	....	....
1927-28	Montreal Canadiens	15	1	0	1	2	....	....	....	....	....
	Chicago Black Hawks	14	1	0	1	4	....	....	....	....	....
	NHL Totals	**33**	**2**	**0**	**2**	**6**	....	....	....	....	....

Traded to **Montreal** by **Duluth** (AHA) for cash, November 10, 1926. • Suspended by Montreal for leaving the team, November, 24, 1926. Loaned to **Chicago** by **Montreal** for cash, December 30, 1927. Traded to **Seattle** (NWHL) by **Montreal** for cash, January 1, 1936.

LAFRENIERE, Jason

Center. Shoots right. 5'11", 185 lbs. Born, St. Catharines, Ont., December 6, 1966.
(Quebec's 2nd choice, 36th overall, in 1985 Entry Draft).

Season	Club	Regular Season GP	G	A	Pts	PIM	Playoffs GP	G	A	Pts	PIM
1986-87	Quebec Nordiques	56	13	15	28	8	12	1	5	6	2
1987-88	Quebec Nordiques	40	10	19	29	4	....	....	....	....	....
1988-89	New York Rangers	38	8	16	24	6	3	0	0	0	17
1992-93	Tampa Bay Lightning	11	3	3	6	4	....	....	....	....	....
1993-94	Tampa Bay Lightning	1	0	0	0	0	....	....	....	....	....
	NHL Totals	**146**	**34**	**53**	**87**	**22**	**15**	**1**	**5**	**6**	**19**

• Son of Roger

Traded to **NY Rangers** by **Quebec** with Normand Rochefort for Bruce Bell, Jari Gronstrand, Walt Poddubny and NY Rangers' 4th round choice (Eric Dubois) in 1989 Entry Draft, August 1, 1988. Signed as a free agent by **Tampa Bay**, July 29, 1992.

LAFRENIERE, Roger

Left wing. Shoots left. 6', 190 lbs. Born, Montreal, Que., July 24, 1942.

Season	Club	Regular Season GP	G	A	Pts	PIM	Playoffs GP	G	A	Pts	PIM
1962-63	Detroit Red Wings	3	0	0	0	4	....	....	....	....	....
1972-73	St. Louis Blues	10	0	0	0	0	....	....	....	....	....
	NHL Totals	**13**	**0**	**0**	**0**	**4**	....	....	....	....	....

• Father of Jason

Claimed by **Buffalo** (AHL) from **Detroit** in Reverse Draft, June 9, 1965. Traded to **St. Louis** (Denver-WHL) by **Buffalo** for cash, October, 1969. Traded to **San Diego** (WHL) by **St. Louis** for cash, September, 1973.

LAGACE, Jean-Guy

Defense. Shoots right. 5'10", 185 lbs. Born, L'Abord-a-Plouffe, Que., February 5, 1945.

Season	Club	Regular Season GP	G	A	Pts	PIM	Playoffs GP	G	A	Pts	PIM
1968-69	Pittsburgh Penguins	17	0	1	1	14	....	....	....	....	....
1970-71	Buffalo Sabres	3	0	0	0	2	....	....	....	....	....
1972-73	Pittsburgh Penguins	31	1	5	6	32	....	....	....	....	....
1973-74	Pittsburgh Penguins	31	2	6	8	34	....	....	....	....	....
1974-75	Pittsburgh Penguins	27	1	8	9	39	....	....	....	....	....
	Kansas City Scouts	19	2	9	11	22	....	....	....	....	....
1975-76	Kansas City Scouts	69	3	10	13	108	....	....	....	....	....
	NHL Totals	**197**	**9**	**39**	**48**	**251**	....	....	....	....	....

Traded to **Pittsburgh** by **Montreal** with cash for Larry Hillman, November 22, 1968. Claimed by **Minnesota** from **Pittsburgh** in Intra-League Draft, June 9, 1970. Claimed by **Buffalo** from **Minnesota** in Expansion Draft, June 10, 1970. Traded to **Pittsburgh** by **Buffalo** for Terry Ball, January 24, 1971. Traded to **Kansas City** by **Pittsburgh** with Denis Herron for Michel Plasse, January 10, 1975.

LAIDLAW, Tom

Defense. Shoots left. 6'2", 215 lbs. Born, Brampton, Ont., April 15, 1958.
(NY Rangers' 7th choice, 93rd overall, in 1978 Amateur Draft).

Season	Club	Regular Season GP	G	A	Pts	PIM	Playoffs GP	G	A	Pts	PIM
1980-81	New York Rangers	80	6	23	29	100	14	1	4	5	18
1981-82	New York Rangers	79	3	18	21	104	10	0	3	3	14
1982-83	New York Rangers	80	0	10	10	75	9	1	1	2	10
1983-84	New York Rangers	79	3	15	18	62	5	0	0	0	8
1984-85	New York Rangers	61	1	11	12	52	3	0	2	2	4
1985-86	New York Rangers	68	6	12	18	103	7	0	2	2	12
1986-87	New York Rangers	63	1	10	11	65	....	....	....	....	....
	Los Angeles Kings	11	0	3	3	4	5	0	0	0	2
1987-88	Los Angeles Kings	57	1	12	13	47	5	0	2	2	4
1988-89	Los Angeles Kings	70	3	17	20	63	11	2	3	5	6
1989-90	Los Angeles Kings	57	1	8	9	42	....	....	....	....	....
	NHL Totals	**705**	**25**	**139**	**164**	**717**	**69**	**4**	**17**	**21**	**78**

Traded to **Los Angeles** by **NY Rangers** with Bob Carpenter for Jeff Crossman, Marcel Dionne and Los Angeles' 3rd round choice (later traded to Minnesota – Minnesota selected Murray Garbutt) in 1989 Entry Draft, March 10, 1987.

LAIRD, Robbie

Left wing. Shoots left. 5'9", 165 lbs. Born, Regina, Sask., December 29, 1954.
(Pittsburgh's 6th choice, 116th overall, in 1974 Amateur Draft).

Season	Club	Regular Season GP	G	A	Pts	PIM	Playoffs GP	G	A	Pts	PIM
1979-80	Minnesota North Stars	1	0	0	0	0	....	....	....	....	....
	NHL Totals	**1**	**0**	**0**	**0**	**0**	....	....	....	....	....

Signed as a free agent by **Minnesota**, September 15, 1979.

LAJEUNESSE, Serge

Defense/Right wing. Shoots left. 5'10", 185 lbs. Born, Montreal, Que., June 11, 1950.
(Detroit's 1st choice, 12th overall, in 1970 Amateur Draft).

Season	Club	Regular Season GP	G	A	Pts	PIM	Playoffs GP	G	A	Pts	PIM
1970-71	Detroit Red Wings	62	1	3	4	55	....	....	....	....	....
1971-72	Detroit Red Wings	7	0	0	0	20	....	....	....	....	....
1972-73	Detroit Red Wings	28	0	1	1	26	....	....	....	....	....
1973-74	Philadelphia Flyers	1	0	0	0	0	....	....	....	....	....
1974-75	Philadelphia Flyers	5	0	0	0	2	....	....	....	....	....
	NHL Totals	**103**	**1**	**4**	**5**	**103**	....	....	....	....	....

Traded to **Philadelphia** by **Detroit** for Rick Foley, May 15, 1973.

LAKOVIC, Sasha

Right wing. Shoots left. 6', 220 lbs. Born, Vancouver, B.C., September 7, 1971.

Season	Club	Regular Season GP	G	A	Pts	PIM	Playoffs GP	G	A	Pts	PIM
1996-97	Calgary Flames	19	0	1	1	54	....	....	....	....	....
1997-98	New Jersey Devils	2	0	0	0	5	....	....	....	....	....
1998-99	New Jersey Devils	16	0	3	3	59	....	....	....	....	....
	NHL Totals	**37**	**0**	**4**	**4**	**118**	....	....	....	....	....

Signed as a free agent by **Calgary**, October 10, 1996. Signed as a free agent by **New Jersey**, September 24, 1997.

LALANDE, Hec

Center. Shoots left. 5'9", 150 lbs. Born, North Bay, Ont., November 24, 1934.

Season	Club	Regular Season GP	G	A	Pts	PIM	Playoffs GP	G	A	Pts	PIM
1953-54	Chicago Black Hawks	2	0	0	0	0	....	....	....	....	....
1955-56	Chicago Black Hawks	65	8	18	26	70	....	....	....	....	....
1956-57	Chicago Black Hawks	50	11	17	28	38	....	....	....	....	....
1957-58	Chicago Black Hawks	22	2	2	4	10	....	....	....	....	....
	Detroit Red Wings	12	0	2	2	2	....	....	....	....	....
	NHL Totals	**151**	**21**	**39**	**60**	**120**	....	....	....	....	....

Traded to **Detroit** by **Chicago** with Nick Mickoski, Bob Bailey and Jack McIntyre for Bill Dineen, Billy Dea, Lorne Ferguson and Earl Reibel, December 17, 1957. Traded to **Hershey** (AHL) by **Detroit** with Don Poile and cash for Dunc Fisher, April 23, 1958.

LALONDE, Bobby

Center. Shoots left. 5'5", 155 lbs. Born, Montreal, Que., March 27, 1951.
(Vancouver's 2nd choice, 17th overall, in 1971 Amateur Draft).

Season	Club	Regular Season GP	G	A	Pts	PIM	Playoffs GP	G	A	Pts	PIM
1971-72	Vancouver Canucks	27	1	5	6	2	....	....	....	....	....
1972-73	Vancouver Canucks	77	20	27	47	32	....	....	....	....	....
1973-74	Vancouver Canucks	36	3	4	7	18	....	....	....	....	....
1974-75	Vancouver Canucks	74	17	30	47	48	5	0	0	0	0
1975-76	Vancouver Canucks	71	14	36	50	46	1	0	0	0	2
1976-77	Vancouver Canucks	68	17	15	32	39	....	....	....	....	....
1977-78	Atlanta Flames	73	14	23	37	28	1	1	0	1	0
1978-79	Atlanta Flames	78	24	32	56	24	2	1	0	1	0
1979-80	Atlanta Flames	3	0	1	1	2	....	....	....	....	....
	Boston Bruins	71	10	25	35	28	4	0	1	1	2
1980-81	Boston Bruins	62	4	12	16	31	3	2	1	3	2
1981-82	Calgary Flames	1	0	0	0	0	....	....	....	....	....
	NHL Totals	**641**	**124**	**210**	**334**	**298**	**16**	**4**	**2**	**6**	**6**

Signed as a free agent by **Atlanta**, September 20, 1977. Claimed by **Atlanta** as a fill-in during Expansion Draft, June 13, 1979. Traded to **Boston** by **Atlanta** for future considerations, October 23, 1979. Signed as a free agent by **Calgary**, October 25, 1981.

LALONDE, Newsy

HHOF

Center. Shoots right. 5'9", 168 lbs. Born, Cornwall, Ont., October 31, 1888.

Season	Club	Regular Season GP	G	A	Pts	PIM	Playoffs GP	G	A	Pts	PIM
1917-18	Montreal Canadiens	14	23	7	30	51	2	4	2	6	17
1918-19	Montreal Canadiens	17	*22	*10	*32	40	5	*11	2	*13	6
	Montreal Canadiens (Cup)	....	....	....	....	....	*5*	*6*	*0*	*6*	*3*
1919-20	Montreal Canadiens	23	37	9	46	34	....	....	....	....	....
1920-21	Montreal Canadiens	24	33	10	*43	36	....	....	....	....	....
1921-22	Montreal Canadiens	20	9	5	14	20	....	....	....	....	....
1926-27	New York Americans	1	0	0	0	2	....	....	....	....	....
	NHL Totals	**99**	**124**	**41**	**165**	**183**	**7**	**15**	**4**	**19**	**23**

Rights retained by **Montreal** after NHA folded, November 26, 1917. Traded to **Saskatoon** (WCHL) by **Montreal** for $3,500 and the rights to Aurel Joliat, September 18, 1922. Traded to **NY Americans** by **Saskatoon** (WHL) for cash, September 27, 1926.

LALONDE, Ron

Center. Shoots left. 5'10", 170 lbs. Born, Toronto, Ont., October 30, 1952.
(Pittsburgh's 4th choice, 56th overall, in 1972 Amateur Draft).

Season	Club	Regular Season GP	G	A	Pts	PIM	Playoffs GP	G	A	Pts	PIM
1972-73	Pittsburgh Penguins	9	0	0	0	2	....	....	....	....	....
1973-74	Pittsburgh Penguins	73	10	17	27	14	....	....	....	....	....

Season	Club	GP	G	A	Pts	PIM	GP	G	A	Pts	PIM
		REGULAR SEASON					PLAYOFFS				
1974-75	Pittsburgh Penguins	24	0	3	3	0					
	Washington Capitals	50	12	14	26	27					
1975-76	Washington Capitals	80	9	19	28	19					
1976-77	Washington Capitals	76	12	17	29	24					
1977-78	Washington Capitals	67	1	5	6	16					
1978-79	Washington Capitals	18	1	3	4	4					
	NHL Totals	**397**	**45**	**78**	**123**	**106**					

Traded to **Washington** by **Pittsburgh** for Lew Morrison, December 14, 1974.

LALOR, Mike

Defense. Shoots left. 6', 200 lbs. Born, Buffalo, NY, March 8, 1963.

Season	Club	GP	G	A	Pts	PIM	GP	G	A	Pts	PIM
1985-86 ♦	Montreal Canadiens	62	3	5	8	56	17	1	2	3	29
1986-87	Montreal Canadiens	57	0	10	10	47	13	2	1	3	29
1987-88	Montreal Canadiens	66	1	10	11	113	11	0	0	0	11
1988-89	Montreal Canadiens	12	1	4	5	15					
	St. Louis Blues	36	1	14	15	54	10	1	1	2	14
1989-90	St. Louis Blues	78	0	16	16	81	12	0	2	2	31
1990-91	Washington Capitals	68	1	5	6	61	10	1	2	3	22
1991-92	Washington Capitals	64	5	7	12	64					
	Winnipeg Jets	15	2	3	5	14	7	0	0	0	19
1992-93	Winnipeg Jets	64	1	8	9	76	4	0	2	2	4
1993-94	San Jose Sharks	23	0	2	2	8					
	Dallas Stars	12	0	1	1	6	5	0	0	0	6
1994-95	Dallas Stars	12	0	0	0	9	3	0	0	0	2
1995-96	Dallas Stars	63	1	2	3	31					
1996-97	Dallas Stars	55	1	1	2	42					
	NHL Totals	**687**	**17**	**88**	**105**	**677**	**92**	**5**	**10**	**15**	**167**

Signed as a free agent by **Montreal**, September, 1983. Traded to **St. Louis** by **Montreal** with Montreal's 1st round choice (later traded to Vancouver – Vancouver selected Shawn Antoski) in 1990 Entry Draft for St. Louis' 1st round choice (Turner Stevenson) in 1990 Entry Draft and St. Louis' 3rd round choice (later traded back to St. Louis, St. Louis selected Nathan LaFayette) in 1991 Entry Draft, January 16, 1989. Traded to **Washington** by **St. Louis** with Peter Zezel for Geoff Courtnall, July 13, 1990. Traded to **Winnipeg** by **Washington** for Paul MacDermid, March 2, 1992. Signed as a free agent by **San Jose**, August 13, 1993. Traded to **Dallas** by **San Jose** with Doug Zmolek for Ulf Dahlen and Dallas' 7th round choice (Brad Mehalko) in 1995 Entry Draft, March 19, 1994.

LAMB, Joe

Right wing. Shoots right. 5'10", 170 lbs. Born, Sussex, N.B., June 18, 1906.

Season	Club	GP	G	A	Pts	PIM	GP	G	A	Pts	PIM
1927-28	Montreal Maroons	21	8	5	13	39	8	1	0	1	32
1928-29	Montreal Maroons	30	4	1	5	44					
	Ottawa Senators	6	0	0	0	8					
1929-30	Ottawa Senators	44	29	20	49	*119	2	0	0	0	11
1930-31	Ottawa Senators	44	11	14	25	91					
1931-32	New York Americans	48	14	11	25	71					
1932-33	Boston Bruins	42	11	8	19	68	5	0	1	1	6
1933-34	Boston Bruins	48	10	15	25	47					
1934-35	Montreal Canadiens	7	3	2	5	4					
	St. Louis Eagles	31	11	12	23	19					
1935-36	Montreal Maroons	35	0	3	3	12	3	0	0	0	2
1936-37	New York Americans	48	3	9	12	53					
1937-38	New York Americans	25	1	0	1	20					
	Detroit Red Wings	14	3	1	4	6					
	NHL Totals	**443**	**108**	**101**	**209**	**601**	**18**	**1**	**1**	**2**	**51**

Signed as a free agent by **Mtl. Maroons**, January 29, 1928. Traded to **Ottawa** by **Mtl. Maroons** for Georges Boucher, February 14, 1929. Claimed by **NY Americans** from **Ottawa** for 1931-32 season in Dispersal Draft, September 26, 1931. Traded to **Boston** by **Ottawa** with $7,000 for Cooney Weiland, July 25, 1932. Traded to **Montreal** by **Boston** for Johnny Gagnon, October 2, 1934. Traded to **Boston** by **Montreal** for cash, December 4, 1934. Traded to **St. Louis** by **Boston** for Max Kaminsky and Des Roche, December 4, 1934. Claimed by **Mtl. Maroons** from **St. Louis** in Dispersal Draft, October 15, 1935. Traded to **NY Americans** by **Mtl. Maroons** with $10,000 for Carl Voss, September 6, 1936. Traded to **Detroit** by **NY Americans** for Red Beattie with NY Americans holding right of recall, January 24, 1938. • Recalled by NY Americans, October 9, 1938.

LAMB, Mark

Center. Shoots left. 5'9", 180 lbs. Born, Ponteix, Sask., August 3, 1964.
(Calgary's 5th choice, 72nd overall, in 1982 Entry Draft).

Season	Club	GP	G	A	Pts	PIM	GP	G	A	Pts	PIM
1985-86	Calgary Flames	1	0	0	0	0					
1986-87	Detroit Red Wings	22	2	1	3	8	11	0	0	0	11
1987-88	Edmonton Oilers	2	0	0	0	0					
1988-89	Edmonton Oilers	20	2	8	10	14	6	0	2	2	8
1989-90 ♦	Edmonton Oilers	58	12	16	28	42	22	6	11	17	2
1990-91	Edmonton Oilers	37	4	8	12	25	15	0	5	5	20
1991-92	Edmonton Oilers	59	6	22	28	46	16	1	1	2	10
1992-93	Ottawa Senators	71	7	19	26	64					
1993-94	Ottawa Senators	66	11	18	29	56					
	Philadelphia Flyers	19	1	6	7	16					
1994-95	Philadelphia Flyers	8	0	2	2	2					
	Montreal Canadiens	39	1	0	1	18					
1995-96	Montreal Canadiens	1	0	0	0	0					
	NHL Totals	**403**	**46**	**100**	**146**	**291**	**70**	**7**	**19**	**26**	**51**

Signed as a free agent by **Detroit**, July 28, 1986. Claimed by **Edmonton** from **Detroit** in Waiver Draft, October 5, 1987. Claimed by **Ottawa** from **Edmonton** in Expansion Draft, June 18, 1992. Traded to **Philadelphia** by **Ottawa** for Claude Boivin and Kirk Daubenspeck, March 5, 1994. Traded to **Montreal** by **Philadelphia** for cash, February 10, 1995.

LAMBERT, Dan

Defense. Shoots left. 5'8", 177 lbs. Born, St. Boniface, Man., January 12, 1970.
(Quebec's 8th choice, 106th overall, in 1989 Entry Draft).

Season	Club	GP	G	A	Pts	PIM	GP	G	A	Pts	PIM
1990-91	Quebec Nordiques	1	0	0	0	0					
1991-92	Quebec Nordiques	28	6	9	15	22					
	NHL Totals	**29**	**6**	**9**	**15**	**22**					

Traded to **Winnipeg** by **Quebec** for Shawn Cronin, August 25, 1992.

LAMBERT, Denny

Left wing. Shoots left. 5'11", 211 lbs. Born, Wawa, Ont., January 7, 1970.

Season	Club	GP	G	A	Pts	PIM	GP	G	A	Pts	PIM
1994-95	Mighty Ducks of Anaheim	13	1	3	4	4					
1995-96	Mighty Ducks of Anaheim	33	0	8	8	55					
1996-97	Ottawa Senators	80	4	16	20	217	6	0	1	1	9
1997-98	Ottawa Senators	72	9	10	19	250	11	0	0	0	19
1998-99	Nashville Predators	76	5	11	16	218					
99-2000	Atlanta Thrashers	73	5	6	11	*219					
2000-01	Atlanta Thrashers	67	1	7	8	215					
2001-02	Mighty Ducks of Anaheim	73	2	5	7	213					
	NHL Totals	**487**	**27**	**66**	**93**	**1391**	**17**	**0**	**1**	**1**	**28**

Signed as a free agent by **Anaheim**, August 16, 1993. Signed as a free agent by **Ottawa**, July 29, 1996. Claimed by **Nashville** from **Ottawa** in Expansion Draft, June 26, 1998. Traded to **Atlanta** by **Nashville** for the rights to Randy Robitaille, August 16, 1999. Traded to **Anaheim** by **Atlanta** with Atlanta's 9th round choice (Francois Caron) in 2002 Entry Draft for Anaheim's 8th round choice (Tyler Boldt) in 2002 Entry Draft, July 2, 2001.

LAMBERT, Lane

Right wing. Shoots right. 6', 185 lbs. Born, Melfort, Sask., November 18, 1964.
(Detroit's 2nd choice, 25th overall, in 1983 Entry Draft).

Season	Club	GP	G	A	Pts	PIM	GP	G	A	Pts	PIM
1983-84	Detroit Red Wings	73	20	15	35	115	4	0	0	0	10
1984-85	Detroit Red Wings	69	14	11	25	104					
1985-86	Detroit Red Wings	34	2	3	5	130					
1986-87	New York Rangers	18	2	2	4	33					
	Quebec Nordiques	15	5	5	10	18	13	2	4	6	30
1987-88	Quebec Nordiques	61	13	28	41	98					
1988-89	Quebec Nordiques	13	2	2	4	23					
	NHL Totals	**283**	**58**	**66**	**124**	**521**	**17**	**2**	**4**	**6**	**40**

Traded to **NY Rangers** by **Detroit** with Kelly Kisio, Jim Leavins and Detroit's 5th round choice (later traded to Winnipeg – Winnipeg selected Benoit Lebeau) in 1988 Entry Draft for Glen Hanlon and NY Rangers' 3rd round choices in 1987 (Dennis Holland) and 1988 (Guy Dupuis) Entry Drafts, July 29, 1986. Traded to **Quebec** by **NY Rangers** for Pat Price, March 5, 1987.

LAMBERT, Yvon

Left wing. Shoots left. 6'2", 200 lbs. Born, Drummondville, Que., May 20, 1950.
(Detroit's 3rd choice, 40th overall, in 1970 Amateur Draft).

Season	Club	GP	G	A	Pts	PIM	GP	G	A	Pts	PIM
1972-73	Montreal Canadiens	1	0	0	0	0					
1973-74	Montreal Canadiens	60	6	10	16	42	5	0	0	0	7
1974-75	Montreal Canadiens	80	32	35	67	74	11	4	2	6	0
1975-76 ♦	Montreal Canadiens	80	32	35	67	28	12	2	3	5	18
1976-77 ♦	Montreal Canadiens	79	24	28	52	50	14	3	3	6	12
1977-78 ♦	Montreal Canadiens	77	18	22	40	20	15	2	4	6	6
1978-79 ♦	Montreal Canadiens	79	26	40	66	26	16	5	6	11	16
1979-80	Montreal Canadiens	77	21	32	53	23	10	8	4	12	4
1980-81	Montreal Canadiens	73	22	32	54	39	3	0	0	0	2
1981-82	Buffalo Sabres	77	25	39	64	38	4	3	0	3	2
	NHL Totals	**683**	**206**	**273**	**479**	**340**	**90**	**27**	**22**	**49**	**67**

Claimed by **Montreal** from **Detroit** (Port Huron-IHL) in Reverse Draft, June 9, 1971. Claimed by **Buffalo** from **Montreal** in Waiver Draft, October 5, 1981.

LAMBY, Dick

Defense. Shoots right. 6'1", 200 lbs. Born, Auburn, MA, May 3, 1955.
(St. Louis' 7th choice, 135th overall, in 1975 Amateur Draft).

Season	Club	GP	G	A	Pts	PIM	GP	G	A	Pts	PIM
1978-79	St. Louis Blues	9	0	4	4	12					
1979-80	St. Louis Blues	12	0	1	1	10					
1980-81	St. Louis Blues	1	0	0	0	0					
	NHL Totals	**22**	**0**	**5**	**5**	**22**					

Traded to **Colorado** by **St. Louis** with Joe Micheletti for Bill Baker, December 4, 1981.

LAMIRANDE, Jean-Paul

Left wing/Defense. Shoots right. 5'8", 170 lbs. Born, Shawinigan Falls, Que., August 21, 1924.

Season	Club	GP	G	A	Pts	PIM	GP	G	A	Pts	PIM
1946-47	New York Rangers	14	1	1	2	14					
1947-48	New York Rangers	18	0	1	1	6	6	0	0	0	4
1949-50	New York Rangers	16	4	3	7	6	2	0	0	0	0
1954-55	Montreal Canadiens	1	0	0	0	0					
	NHL Totals	**49**	**5**	**5**	**10**	**26**	**8**	**0**	**0**	**0**	**4**

Traded to **Chicago** (St. Louis-AHL) by **NY Rangers** for cash, September 19, 1950. Traded to **Montreal** by **Chicago** for cash, October 25, 1954.

LAMMENS, Hank

Defense. Shoots left. 6'2", 210 lbs. Born, Brockville, Ont., February 21, 1966.
(NY Islanders' 10th choice, 160th overall, in 1985 Entry Draft).

Season	Club	GP	G	A	Pts	PIM	GP	G	A	Pts	PIM
1993-94	Ottawa Senators	27	1	2	3	22					
	NHL Totals	**27**	**1**	**2**	**3**	**22**					

Signed as a free agent by **Ottawa**, June 25, 1993.

LAMOUREUX, Leo

Center/Defense. Shoots left. 5'11", 175 lbs. Born, Espanola, Ont., October 1, 1916.

Season	Club	Regular Season GP	G	A	Pts	PIM	Playoffs GP	G	A	Pts	PIM
1941-42	Montreal Canadiens	1	0	0	0	0	....	....	....	....	....
1942-43	Montreal Canadiens	46	2	16	18	53	....	....	....	....	....
1943-44 ♦	Montreal Canadiens	44	8	23	31	32	9	0	3	3	8
1944-45	Montreal Canadiens	49	2	22	24	58	6	1	1	2	2
1945-46 ♦	Montreal Canadiens	45	5	7	12	18	9	0	2	2	2
1946-47	Montreal Canadiens	50	2	11	13	14	4	0	0	0	4
	NHL Totals	**235**	**19**	**79**	**98**	**175**	**28**	**1**	**6**	**7**	**16**

Signed as a free agent by **Montreal**, October 16, 1941. Traded to **Springfield** (AHL) by **Montreal** for cash, December 17, 1947.

LAMOUREUX, Mitch

Center. Shoots left. 5'6", 175 lbs. Born, Ottawa, Ont., August 22, 1962.
(Pittsburgh's 7th choice, 154th overall, in 1981 Entry Draft).

Season	Club	Regular Season GP	G	A	Pts	PIM	Playoffs GP	G	A	Pts	PIM
1983-84	Pittsburgh Penguins	8	1	1	2	6	....	....	....	....	....
1984-85	Pittsburgh Penguins	62	10	8	18	53	....	....	....	....	....
1987-88	Philadelphia Flyers	3	0	0	0	0	....	....	....	....	....
	NHL Totals	**73**	**11**	**9**	**20**	**59**	....	....	....	....	....

Signed as a free agent by **Philadelphia**, June 30, 1986.

LAMPMAN, Mike

Left wing. Shoots left. 6'2", 195 lbs. Born, Lakewood, CA, April 20, 1950.
(St. Louis' 10th choice, 111th overall, in 1970 Amateur Draft).

Season	Club	Regular Season GP	G	A	Pts	PIM	Playoffs GP	G	A	Pts	PIM
1972-73	St. Louis Blues	18	2	3	5	2	....	....	....	....	....
1973-74	St. Louis Blues	15	1	0	1	0	....	....	....	....	....
	Vancouver Canucks	14	1	0	1	0	....	....	....	....	....
1975-76	Washington Capitals	27	7	12	19	28	....	....	....	....	....
1976-77	Washington Capitals	22	6	5	11	4	....	....	....	....	....
	NHL Totals	**96**	**17**	**20**	**37**	**34**	....	....	....	....	....

Traded to **Vancouver** by **St. Louis** for John Wright, December 10, 1973. Claimed by **Washington** from **Vancouver** in Expansion Draft, June 12, 1974.

LANCIEN, Jack

Defense. Shoots left. 6', 188 lbs. Born, Regina, Sask., June 14, 1923.

Season	Club	Regular Season GP	G	A	Pts	PIM	Playoffs GP	G	A	Pts	PIM
1946-47	New York Rangers	1	0	0	0	0	....	....	....	....	....
1947-48	New York Rangers	....	....	....	....	....	2	0	0	0	2
1949-50	New York Rangers	43	1	4	5	27	4	0	1	1	0
1950-51	New York Rangers	19	0	1	1	0	....	....	....	....	....
	NHL Totals	**63**	**1**	**5**	**6**	**35**	**6**	**0**	**1**	**1**	**2**

LANDON, Larry

Right wing. Shoots right. 6', 191 lbs. Born, Niagara Falls, Ont., May 4, 1958.
(Montreal's 10th choice, 137th overall, in 1978 Amateur Draft).

Season	Club	Regular Season GP	G	A	Pts	PIM	Playoffs GP	G	A	Pts	PIM
1983-84	Montreal Canadiens	2	0	0	0	0	....	....	....	....	....
1984-85	Toronto Maple Leafs	7	0	0	0	2	....	....	....	....	....
	NHL Totals	**9**	**0**	**0**	**0**	**2**	....	....	....	....	....

Traded to **Toronto** by **Montreal** for Gaston Gingras, February 14, 1985.

LANDRY, Eric

Center. Shoots left. 5'10", 184 lbs. Born, Gatineau, Que., January 20, 1975.

Season	Club	Regular Season GP	G	A	Pts	PIM	Playoffs GP	G	A	Pts	PIM
1997-98	Calgary Flames	12	1	0	1	4	....	....	....	....	....
1998-99	Calgary Flames	3	0	1	1	0	....	....	....	....	....
2000-01	Montreal Canadiens	51	4	7	11	43	....	....	....	....	....
2001-02	Montreal Canadiens	2	0	1	1	0	....	....	....	....	....
	NHL Totals	**68**	**5**	**9**	**14**	**47**	....	....	....	....	....

Signed as a free agent by **Calgary**, August 20, 1997. Traded to **San Jose** by **Calgary** for Fredrik Oduya, July 12, 1999. Signed as a free agent by **Montreal**, July 7, 2000.

LANE, Gord

Defense. Shoots left. 6'1", 190 lbs. Born, Brandon, Man., March 31, 1953.
(Pittsburgh's 9th choice, 134th overall, in 1973 Amateur Draft).

Season	Club	Regular Season GP	G	A	Pts	PIM	Playoffs GP	G	A	Pts	PIM
1975-76	Washington Capitals	3	1	0	1	12	....	....	....	....	....
1976-77	Washington Capitals	80	2	15	17	207	....	....	....	....	....
1977-78	Washington Capitals	69	2	9	11	195	....	....	....	....	....
1978-79	Washington Capitals	64	3	15	18	147	....	....	....	....	....
1979-80	Washington Capitals	19	2	4	6	53	....	....	....	....	....
	♦ New York Islanders	55	2	14	16	152	21	1	3	4	*85
1980-81 ♦	New York Islanders	60	3	9	12	124	12	1	5	6	32
1981-82 ♦	New York Islanders	51	0	13	13	98	19	0	4	4	61
1982-83 ♦	New York Islanders	44	3	4	7	87	18	1	2	3	32
1983-84	New York Islanders	37	0	3	3	70	4	0	0	0	2
1984-85	New York Islanders	57	1	8	9	83	1	0	0	0	2
	NHL Totals	**539**	**19**	**94**	**113**	**1228**	**75**	**3**	**14**	**17**	**214**

Signed as a free agent by **Washington**, October 5, 1976. Traded to **NY Islanders** by **Washington** for Mike Kaszycki, December 7, 1979.

LANE, Myles

USHOF

Defense. Shoots left. 6', 180 lbs. Born, Melrose, MA, October 2, 1905.

Season	Club	Regular Season GP	G	A	Pts	PIM	Playoffs GP	G	A	Pts	PIM
1928-29	New York Rangers	24	1	0	1	22	....	....	....	....	....
	♦ Boston Bruins	19	1	0	1	2	5	0	0	0	0
1929-30	Boston Bruins	3	0	0	0	0	6	0	0	0	0
1933-34	Boston Bruins	25	2	1	3	17	....	....	....	....	....
	NHL Totals	**71**	**4**	**1**	**5**	**41**	**11**	**0**	**0**	**0**	**0**

Signed as a free agent by **NY Rangers**, October 1, 1928. Traded to **Boston** by **NY Rangers** for $7,500, January 21, 1929.

LANG, Robert

Center. Shoots right. 6'2", 216 lbs. Born, Teplice, Czech., December 19, 1970.
(Los Angeles' 6th choice, 133rd overall, in 1990 Entry Draft).

Season	Club	Regular Season GP	G	A	Pts	PIM	Playoffs GP	G	A	Pts	PIM
1992-93	Los Angeles Kings	11	0	5	5	2	....	....	....	....	....
1993-94	Los Angeles Kings	32	9	10	19	10	....	....	....	....	....
1994-95	Los Angeles Kings	36	4	8	12	4	....	....	....	....	....
1995-96	Los Angeles Kings	68	6	16	22	10	....	....	....	....	....
1997-98	Boston Bruins	3	0	0	0	2	....	....	....	....	....
	Pittsburgh Penguins	51	9	13	22	14	6	0	3	3	2
1998-99	Pittsburgh Penguins	72	21	23	44	24	12	0	2	2	0
99-2000	Pittsburgh Penguins	78	23	42	65	14	11	3	3	6	0
2000-01	Pittsburgh Penguins	82	32	48	80	28	16	4	4	8	4
2001-02	Pittsburgh Penguins	62	18	32	50	16	....	....	....	....	....
2002-03	Washington Capitals	82	22	47	69	22	6	2	1	3	2
	NHL Totals	**577**	**144**	**244**	**388**	**146**	**51**	**9**	**13**	**22**	**8**

Signed as a free agent by **Pittsburgh**, September 2, 1997. Claimed by **Boston** from **Pittsburgh** in Waiver Draft, September 28, 1997. Claimed on waivers by **Pittsburgh** from **Boston**, October 25, 1997. Signed as a free agent by **Washington**, July 1, 2002.

LANGDON, Darren

Left wing. Shoots left. 6'1", 205 lbs. Born, Deer Lake, Nfld., January 8, 1971.

Season	Club	Regular Season GP	G	A	Pts	PIM	Playoffs GP	G	A	Pts	PIM
1994-95	New York Rangers	18	1	1	2	62	....	....	....	....	....
1995-96	New York Rangers	64	7	4	11	175	2	0	0	0	0
1996-97	New York Rangers	60	3	6	9	195	10	0	0	0	2
1997-98	New York Rangers	70	3	3	6	197	....	....	....	....	....
1998-99	New York Rangers	44	0	0	0	80	....	....	....	....	....
99-2000	New York Rangers	21	0	1	1	26	....	....	....	....	....
2000-01	Carolina Hurricanes	54	0	2	2	94	4	0	0	0	12
2001-02	Carolina Hurricanes	58	2	1	3	106	....	....	....	....	....
2002-03	Carolina Hurricanes	9	0	0	0	16	....	....	....	....	....
	Vancouver Canucks	45	0	1	1	143	....	....	....	....	....
	NHL Totals	**443**	**16**	**19**	**35**	**1094**	**16**	**0**	**0**	**0**	**14**

Signed as a free agent by **NY Rangers**, August 16, 1993. • Missed majority of 1999-2000 season recovering from hernia injury suffered in game vs. New Jersey, December 1, 1999. Traded to **Carolina** by **NY Rangers** with Rob DiMaio for Sandy McCarthy and Carolina's 4th round choice (Bryce Lampman) in 2001 Entry Draft, August 4, 2000. Traded to **Vancouver** by **Carolina** with Marek Malik for Jan Hlavac and Harold Druken, November 1, 2002.

LANGDON, Steve

Left wing. Shoots left. 5'11", 175 lbs. Born, Toronto, Ont., December 23, 1953.
(Boston's 5th choice, 63rd overall, in 1973 Amateur Draft).

Season	Club	Regular Season GP	G	A	Pts	PIM	Playoffs GP	G	A	Pts	PIM
1974-75	Boston Bruins	1	0	1	1	0	....	....	....	....	....
1975-76	Boston Bruins	4	0	0	0	2	4	0	0	0	0
1977-78	Boston Bruins	2	0	0	0	0	....	....	....	....	....
	NHL Totals	**7**	**0**	**1**	**1**	**2**	**4**	**0**	**0**	**0**	**0**

LANGELLE, Pete

Center. Shoots left. 5'11", 170 lbs. Born, Winnipeg, Man., November 4, 1917.

Season	Club	Regular Season GP	G	A	Pts	PIM	Playoffs GP	G	A	Pts	PIM
1938-39	Toronto Maple Leafs	2	1	0	1	0	11	1	2	3	2
1939-40	Toronto Maple Leafs	39	7	14	21	2	10	0	3	3	0
1940-41	Toronto Maple Leafs	47	4	15	19	0	7	1	1	2	0
1941-42 ♦	Toronto Maple Leafs	48	10	22	32	9	13	3	3	6	2
	NHL Totals	**136**	**22**	**51**	**73**	**11**	**41**	**5**	**9**	**14**	**4**

Signed as a free agent by **Toronto**, October 27, 1937.

LANGENBRUNNER, Jamie

Right wing. Shoots right. 6'1", 200 lbs. Born, Duluth, MN, July 24, 1975.
(Dallas' 2nd choice, 35th overall, in 1993 Entry Draft).

Season	Club	Regular Season GP	G	A	Pts	PIM	Playoffs GP	G	A	Pts	PIM
1994-95	Dallas Stars	2	0	0	0	2	....	....	....	....	....
1995-96	Dallas Stars	12	2	2	4	6	....	....	....	....	....
1996-97	Dallas Stars	76	13	26	39	51	5	1	1	2	14
1997-98	Dallas Stars	81	23	29	52	61	16	1	4	5	14
1998-99 ♦	Dallas Stars	75	12	33	45	62	23	10	7	17	16
99-2000	Dallas Stars	65	18	21	39	68	15	1	7	8	18
2000-01	Dallas Stars	53	12	18	30	57	10	2	2	4	6
2001-02	Dallas Stars	68	10	16	26	54	....	....	....	....	....
	New Jersey Devils	14	3	3	6	23	5	0	1	1	8
2002-03 ♦	New Jersey Devils	78	22	33	55	65	24	*11	7	*18	16
	NHL Totals	**524**	**115**	**181**	**296**	**449**	**98**	**26**	**29**	**55**	**92**

Traded to **New Jersey** by **Dallas** with Joe Nieuwendyk for Jason Arnott, Randy McKay and New Jersey's 1st round choice (later traded to Columbus – later traded to Buffalo – Buffalo selected Dan Paille) in 2002 Entry Draft, March 19, 2002.

LANGEVIN, Chris

Left wing. Shoots left. 6', 190 lbs. Born, Montreal, Que., November 27, 1959.

Season	Club	Regular Season GP	G	A	Pts	PIM	Playoffs GP	G	A	Pts	PIM
1983-84	Buffalo Sabres	6	1	0	1	2	....	....	....	....	....
1985-86	Buffalo Sabres	16	2	1	3	20	....	....	....	....	....
	NHL Totals	**22**	**3**	**1**	**4**	**22**	....	....	....	....	....

Signed as a free agent by **Buffalo**, October 14, 1983. • Suffered career-ending knee injury in game vs. Quebec, November 22, 1985.

LANGEVIN, Dave — USHOF

Defense. Shoots left. 6'2", 200 lbs. Born, St. Paul, MN, May 15, 1954.
(NY Islanders' 6th choice, 112th overall, in 1974 Amateur Draft).

Season	Club	Regular Season GP	G	A	Pts	PIM	Playoffs GP	G	A	Pts	PIM
1979-80 ◆	New York Islanders	76	3	13	16	109	21	0	3	3	32
1980-81 ◆	New York Islanders	75	1	16	17	122	18	0	3	3	25
1981-82 ◆	New York Islanders	73	1	20	21	82	19	2	4	6	16
1982-83 ◆	New York Islanders	73	4	17	21	64	8	0	2	2	2
1983-84	New York Islanders	69	3	16	19	53	12	0	4	4	18
1984-85	New York Islanders	56	0	13	13	35	4	0	0	0	4
1985-86	Minnesota North Stars	80	0	8	8	58	5	0	1	1	9
1986-87	Los Angeles Kings	11	0	4	4	7	....	....	....	....	....
	NHL Totals	**513**	**12**	**107**	**119**	**530**	**87**	**2**	**17**	**19**	**106**

Played in NHL All-Star Game (1983)

Reclaimed by **NY Islanders** from **Edmonton** prior to Expansion Draft, June 9, 1979. Claimed by **Minnesota** from **NY Islanders** in Waiver Draft, October 7, 1985. Signed as a free agent by **Los Angeles**, February 4, 1987.

LANGFELD, Josh

Right wing. Shoots right. 6'3", 216 lbs. Born, Fridley, MN, July 17, 1977.
(Ottawa's 3rd choice, 66th overall, in 1997 Entry Draft).

Season	Club	Regular Season GP	G	A	Pts	PIM	Playoffs GP	G	A	Pts	PIM
2001-02	Ottawa Senators	1	0	0	0	2	....	....	....	....	....
2002-03	Ottawa Senators	12	0	1	1	4	....	....	....	....	....
	NHL Totals	**13**	**0**	**1**	**1**	**6**	....	....	....	....	....

LANGKOW, Daymond

Center. Shoots left. 5'11", 183 lbs. Born, Edmonton, Alta., September 27, 1976.
(Tampa Bay's 1st choice, 5th overall, in 1995 Entry Draft).

Season	Club	Regular Season GP	G	A	Pts	PIM	Playoffs GP	G	A	Pts	PIM
1995-96	Tampa Bay Lightning	4	0	1	1	0	....	....	....	....	....
1996-97	Tampa Bay Lightning	79	15	13	28	35	....	....	....	....	....
1997-98	Tampa Bay Lightning	68	8	14	22	62	....	....	....	....	....
1998-99	Tampa Bay Lightning	22	4	6	10	15	....	....	....	....	....
	Philadelphia Flyers	56	10	13	23	24	6	0	2	2	2
99-2000	Philadelphia Flyers	82	18	32	50	56	16	5	5	10	23
2000-01	Philadelphia Flyers	71	13	41	54	50	6	2	4	6	2
2001-02	Phoenix Coyotes	80	27	35	62	36	5	1	0	1	0
2002-03	Phoenix Coyotes	82	20	32	52	56	....	....	....	....	....
	NHL Totals	**544**	**115**	**187**	**302**	**334**	**33**	**8**	**11**	**19**	**27**

• Brother of Scott

Traded to **Philadelphia** by **Tampa Bay** with Mikael Renberg for Chris Gratton and Mike Sillinger, December 12, 1998. Traded to **Phoenix** by **Philadelphia** for Phoenix's 2nd round choice (later traded to Tampa Bay – later traded to San Jose – San Jose selected Dan Spang) in 2002 Entry Draft and Phoenix's 1st round choice (Jeff Carter) in 2003 Entry Draft, July 2, 2001.

LANGLAIS, Alain

Left wing. Shoots left. 5'10", 175 lbs. Born, Chicoutimi, Que., October 9, 1950.

Season	Club	Regular Season GP	G	A	Pts	PIM	Playoffs GP	G	A	Pts	PIM
1973-74	Minnesota North Stars	14	3	3	6	8	....	....	....	....	....
1974-75	Minnesota North Stars	11	1	1	2	2	....	....	....	....	....
	NHL Totals	**25**	**4**	**4**	**8**	**10**	....	....	....	....	....

Signed as a free agent by **Minnesota**, September, 1973. Traded to **Washington** by **New Haven** (AHL) with Rich Nantais for Ron Anderson and Bob Gryp, February 23, 1976.

LANGLOIS, Albert

Defense. Shoots left. 6', 205 lbs. Born, Magog, Que., November 6, 1934.

Season	Club	Regular Season GP	G	A	Pts	PIM	Playoffs GP	G	A	Pts	PIM
1957-58 ◆	Montreal Canadiens	1	0	0	0	0	7	0	1	1	4
1958-59 ◆	Montreal Canadiens	48	0	3	3	26	7	0	0	0	4
1959-60 ◆	Montreal Canadiens	67	1	14	15	48	8	0	3	3	18
1960-61	Montreal Canadiens	61	1	12	13	56	5	0	0	0	6
1961-62	New York Rangers	69	7	18	25	90	6	0	1	1	2
1962-63	New York Rangers	60	2	14	16	62	....	....	....	....	....
1963-64	New York Rangers	44	4	2	6	32	....	....	....	....	....
	Detroit Red Wings	17	1	6	7	13	14	0	0	0	12
1964-65	Detroit Red Wings	65	1	12	13	107	6	1	0	1	4
1965-66	Boston Bruins	65	4	10	14	54	....	....	....	....	....
	NHL Totals	**497**	**21**	**91**	**112**	**488**	**53**	**1**	**5**	**6**	**50**

Played in NHL All-Star Game (1959, 1960)

Traded to **NY Rangers** by **Montreal** for John Hanna, June 13, 1961. Traded to **Detroit** by **NY Rangers** for Ron Ingram, February 14, 1964. Traded to **Boston** by **Detroit** with Ron Harris, Parker MacDonald and Bob Dillabough for Ab McDonald, Bob McCord and Ken Stephanson, May 31, 1965.

LANGLOIS, Charlie

Right wing/Defense. Shoots right. 6', 210 lbs. Born, Lotbiniere, Que., August 25, 1894.

Season	Club	Regular Season GP	G	A	Pts	PIM	Playoffs GP	G	A	Pts	PIM
1924-25	Hamilton Tigers	30	6	3	9	47	....	....	....	....	....
1925-26	New York Americans	36	9	1	10	76	....	....	....	....	....
1926-27	New York Americans	9	2	0	2	8	....	....	....	....	....
	Pittsburgh Pirates	36	5	1	6	36	....	....	....	....	....
1927-28	Pittsburgh Pirates	8	0	0	0	8	....	....	....	....	....
	Montreal Canadiens	32	0	0	0	14	2	0	0	0	0
	NHL Totals	**151**	**22**	**5**	**27**	**189**	**2**	**0**	**0**	**0**	**0**

Signed as a free agent by **Hamilton**, October 16, 1924. Transferred to **NY Americans** after NHL club purchased **Hamilton** franchise, September 26, 1925. Traded to **Pittsburgh** by **NY Americans** with $2,000 for Lionel Conacher, December 16, 1926. Loaned to **Montreal** by **Pittsburgh** for remainder of 1927-28 season for the loan of Marty Burke, December 16, 1927.

LANGWAY, Rod — USHOF HHOF

Defense. Shoots left. 6'3", 218 lbs. Born, Maag, Formosa, May 3, 1957.
(Montreal's 3rd choice, 36th overall, in 1977 Amateur Draft).

Season	Club	Regular Season GP	G	A	Pts	PIM	Playoffs GP	G	A	Pts	PIM
1978-79 ◆	Montreal Canadiens	45	3	4	7	30	8	0	0	0	16
1979-80	Montreal Canadiens	77	7	29	36	81	10	3	3	6	2
1980-81	Montreal Canadiens	80	11	34	45	120	3	0	0	0	6
1981-82	Montreal Canadiens	66	5	34	39	116	5	0	3	3	18
1982-83	Washington Capitals	80	3	29	32	75	4	0	0	0	0
1983-84	Washington Capitals	80	9	24	33	61	8	0	5	5	7
1984-85	Washington Capitals	79	4	22	26	54	5	0	1	1	6
1985-86	Washington Capitals	71	1	17	18	61	9	1	2	3	6
1986-87	Washington Capitals	78	2	25	27	53	7	0	1	1	2
1987-88	Washington Capitals	63	3	13	16	28	6	0	0	0	8
1988-89	Washington Capitals	76	2	19	21	65	6	0	0	0	6
1989-90	Washington Capitals	58	0	8	8	39	15	1	4	5	12
1990-91	Washington Capitals	56	1	7	8	24	11	0	2	2	6
1991-92	Washington Capitals	64	0	13	13	22	7	0	1	1	2
1992-93	Washington Capitals	21	0	0	0	20	....	....	....	....	....
	NHL Totals	**994**	**51**	**278**	**329**	**849**	**104**	**5**	**22**	**27**	**97**

NHL First All-Star Team (1983, 1984) • James Norris Trophy (1983, 1984) • NHL Second All-Star Team (1985)

Played in NHL All-Star Game (1981, 1982, 1983, 1984, 1985, 1986)

Claimed by **Montreal** as a fill-in during Expansion Draft, June 13, 1979. Traded to **Washington** by **Montreal** with Doug Jarvis, Craig Laughlin and Brian Engblom for Ryan Walter and Rick Green, September 9, 1982.

LANK, Jeff

Defense. Shoots left. 6'3", 205 lbs. Born, Indian Head, Sask., March 1, 1975.
(Philadelphia's 9th choice, 230th overall, in 1995 Entry Draft).

Season	Club	Regular Season GP	G	A	Pts	PIM	Playoffs GP	G	A	Pts	PIM
99-2000	Philadelphia Flyers	2	0	0	0	2	....	....	....	....	....
	NHL Totals	**2**	**0**	**0**	**0**	**2**	....	....	....	....	....

• Re-entered NHL Entry Draft. Originally Montreal's 6th choice, 113th overall, in 1993 Entry Draft.

LANTHIER, Jean-Marc

Right wing. Shoots right. 6'2", 195 lbs. Born, Montreal, Que., March 27, 1963.
(Vancouver's 2nd choice, 52nd overall, in 1981 Entry Draft).

Season	Club	Regular Season GP	G	A	Pts	PIM	Playoffs GP	G	A	Pts	PIM
1983-84	Vancouver Canucks	11	2	1	3	2	....	....	....	....	....
1984-85	Vancouver Canucks	27	6	4	10	13	....	....	....	....	....
1985-86	Vancouver Canucks	62	7	10	17	12	....	....	....	....	....
1987-88	Vancouver Canucks	5	1	1	2	2	....	....	....	....	....
	NHL Totals	**105**	**16**	**16**	**32**	**29**	....	....	....	....	....

Signed as a free agent by **Boston**, July 1, 1988. Traded to **New Jersey** by **Boston** for Dan Dorion, December 9, 1988.

LANYON, Ted

Defense. Shoots right. 5'11", 175 lbs. Born, Winnipeg, Man., June 11, 1939.

Season	Club	Regular Season GP	G	A	Pts	PIM	Playoffs GP	G	A	Pts	PIM
1967-68	Pittsburgh Penguins	5	0	0	0	4	....	....	....	....	....
	NHL Totals	**5**	**0**	**0**	**0**	**4**	....	....	....	....	....

Traded to **Pittsburgh** by **Cleveland** (AHL) for cash, August 11, 1966. Loaned to **Buffalo** (AHL) by **Pittsburgh** for 1966-67 season, October, 1966.

LANZ, Rick

Defense. Shoots right. 6'2", 203 lbs. Born, Karlovy Vary, Czech., September 16, 1961.
(Vancouver's 1st choice, 7th overall, in 1980 Entry Draft).

Season	Club	Regular Season GP	G	A	Pts	PIM	Playoffs GP	G	A	Pts	PIM
1980-81	Vancouver Canucks	76	7	22	29	40	3	0	0	0	4
1981-82	Vancouver Canucks	39	3	11	14	48	....	....	....	....	....
1982-83	Vancouver Canucks	74	10	38	48	46	4	2	1	3	0
1983-84	Vancouver Canucks	79	18	39	57	45	4	0	4	4	2
1984-85	Vancouver Canucks	57	2	17	19	69	....	....	....	....	....
1985-86	Vancouver Canucks	75	15	38	53	73	3	0	0	0	0
1986-87	Vancouver Canucks	17	1	6	7	10	....	....	....	....	....
	Toronto Maple Leafs	44	2	19	21	32	13	1	3	4	27
1987-88	Toronto Maple Leafs	75	6	22	28	65	1	0	0	0	2
1988-89	Toronto Maple Leafs	32	1	9	10	18	....	....	....	....	....
1991-92	Chicago Blackhawks	1	0	0	0	2	....	....	....	....	....
	NHL Totals	**569**	**65**	**221**	**286**	**448**	**28**	**3**	**8**	**11**	**35**

Traded to **Toronto** by **Vancouver** for Jim Benning and Dan Hodgson, December 2, 1986. Signed as a free agent by **Chicago**, August 13, 1990. Traded to **Los Angeles** by **Chicago** for cash, November 29, 1991.

LAPERRIERE, Daniel

Defense. Shoots left. 6'1", 195 lbs. Born, Laval, Que., March 28, 1969.
(St. Louis' 4th choice, 93rd overall, in 1989 Entry Draft).

Season	Club	Regular Season GP	G	A	Pts	PIM	Playoffs GP	G	A	Pts	PIM
1992-93	St. Louis Blues	5	0	1	1	0	....	....	....	....	....
1993-94	St. Louis Blues	20	1	3	4	8	....	....	....	....	....
1994-95	St. Louis Blues	4	0	0	0	15	....	....	....	....	....
	Ottawa Senators	13	1	1	2	0	....	....	....	....	....
1995-96	Ottawa Senators	6	0	0	0	4	....	....	....	....	....
	NHL Totals	**48**	**2**	**5**	**7**	**27**	....	....	....	....	....

• Son of Jacques

Traded to **Ottawa** by **St. Louis** with St. Louis' 9th round choice (Erik Kaminski) in 1995 Entry Draft for Ottawa's 9th round choice (Libor Zabransky) in 1995 Entry Draft, April 7, 1995. Signed as a free agent by **Washington**, July 12, 1996.

LAPERRIERE, Ian

Center/Right wing. Shoots right. 6'1", 201 lbs. Born, Montreal, Que., January 19, 1974.
(St. Louis' 6th choice, 158th overall, in 1992 Entry Draft).

Season	Club	Regular Season GP	G	A	Pts	PIM	Playoffs GP	G	A	Pts	PIM
1993-94	St. Louis Blues	1	0	0	0	0	....	....	....	....	....
1994-95	St. Louis Blues	37	13	14	27	85	7	0	4	4	21
1995-96	St. Louis Blues	33	3	6	9	87	....	....	....	....	....
	New York Rangers	28	1	2	3	53	....	....	....	....	....
	Los Angeles Kings	10	2	3	5	15	....	....	....	....	....
1996-97	Los Angeles Kings	62	8	15	23	102	....	....	....	....	....
1997-98	Los Angeles Kings	77	6	15	21	131	4	1	0	1	6
1998-99	Los Angeles Kings	72	3	10	13	138	....	....	....	....	....
99-2000	Los Angeles Kings	79	9	13	22	185	4	0	0	0	2
2000-01	Los Angeles Kings	79	8	10	18	141	13	1	2	3	12
2001-02	Los Angeles Kings	81	8	14	22	125	7	0	1	1	9
2002-03	Los Angeles Kings	73	7	12	19	122	....	....	....	....	....
	NHL Totals	**632**	**68**	**114**	**182**	**1184**	**35**	**2**	**7**	**9**	**50**

Traded to **NY Rangers** by **St. Louis** for Stephane Matteau, December 28, 1995. Traded to **Los Angeles** by **NY Rangers** with Ray Ferraro, Mattias Norstrom, Nathan LaFayette and NY Rangers' 4th round choice (Sean Blanchard) in 1997 Entry Draft for Marty McSorley, Jari Kurri and Shane Churla, March 14, 1996.

LAPERRIERE, Jacques

HHOF

Defense. Shoots left. 6'2", 180 lbs. Born, Rouyn, Que., November 22, 1941.

Season	Club	Regular Season GP	G	A	Pts	PIM	Playoffs GP	G	A	Pts	PIM
1962-63	Montreal Canadiens	6	0	2	2	2	5	0	1	1	4
1963-64	Montreal Canadiens	65	2	28	30	102	7	1	1	2	8
1964-65♦	Montreal Canadiens	67	5	22	27	92	6	1	1	2	16
1965-66♦	Montreal Canadiens	57	6	25	31	85	....	....	....	....	....
1966-67	Montreal Canadiens	61	0	20	20	48	9	0	1	1	9
1967-68♦	Montreal Canadiens	72	4	21	25	84	13	1	3	4	20
1968-69♦	Montreal Canadiens	69	5	26	31	45	14	1	3	4	28
1969-70	Montreal Canadiens	73	6	31	37	98	....	....	....	....	....
1970-71♦	Montreal Canadiens	49	0	16	16	20	20	4	9	13	12
1971-72	Montreal Canadiens	73	3	25	28	50	4	0	0	0	2
1972-73♦	Montreal Canadiens	57	7	16	23	34	10	1	3	4	2
1973-74	Montreal Canadiens	42	2	10	12	14	....	....	....	....	....
	NHL Totals	**691**	**40**	**242**	**282**	**674**	**88**	**9**	**22**	**31**	**101**

• Father of Daniel • NHL Second All-Star Team (1964, 1970) • Calder Memorial Trophy (1964) • NHL First All-Star Team (1965, 1966) • James Norris Trophy (1966) • NHL Plus/Minus Leader (1973)

Played in NHL All-Star Game (1964, 1965, 1967, 1968, 1970)

• Suffered career-ending knee injury in game vs. Boston, January 19, 1974.

LAPLANTE, Darryl

Center. Shoots left. 6', 198 lbs. Born, Calgary, Alta., March 28, 1977.
(Detroit's 3rd choice, 58th overall, in 1995 Entry Draft).

Season	Club	Regular Season GP	G	A	Pts	PIM	Playoffs GP	G	A	Pts	PIM
1997-98	Detroit Red Wings	2	0	0	0	0	....	....	....	....	....
1998-99	Detroit Red Wings	3	0	0	0	0	....	....	....	....	....
99-2000	Detroit Red Wings	30	0	6	6	10	....	....	....	....	....
	NHL Totals	**35**	**0**	**6**	**6**	**10**	....	....	....	....	....

Selected by **Minnesota** from **Detroit** in Expansion Draft, June 23, 2000. Traded to **Boston** by **Minnesota** for Greg Crozier, March 19, 2002.

LAPOINTE, Claude

Left wing/Center. Shoots left. 5'9", 188 lbs. Born, Lachine, Que., October 11, 1968.
(Quebec's 12th choice, 234th overall, in 1988 Entry Draft).

Season	Club	Regular Season GP	G	A	Pts	PIM	Playoffs GP	G	A	Pts	PIM
1990-91	Quebec Nordiques	13	2	2	4	4	....	....	....	....	....
1991-92	Quebec Nordiques	78	13	20	33	86	....	....	....	....	....
1992-93	Quebec Nordiques	74	10	26	36	98	6	2	4	6	8
1993-94	Quebec Nordiques	59	11	17	28	70	....	....	....	....	....
1994-95	Quebec Nordiques	29	4	8	12	41	5	0	0	0	8
1995-96	Colorado Avalanche	3	0	0	0	0	....	....	....	....	....
	Calgary Flames	32	4	5	9	20	2	0	0	0	0
1996-97	New York Islanders	73	13	5	18	49	....	....	....	....	....
1997-98	New York Islanders	78	10	10	20	47	....	....	....	....	....
1998-99	New York Islanders	82	14	23	37	62	....	....	....	....	....
99-2000	New York Islanders	76	15	16	31	60	....	....	....	....	....
2000-01	New York Islanders	80	9	23	32	56	....	....	....	....	....
2001-02	New York Islanders	80	9	12	21	60	7	0	0	0	14
2002-03	New York Islanders	66	6	6	12	20	....	....	....	....	....
	Philadelphia Flyers	14	2	2	4	16	13	2	3	5	14
	NHL Totals	**837**	**122**	**175**	**297**	**689**	**33**	**4**	**7**	**11**	**44**

Transferred to **Colorado** after **Quebec** franchise relocated, June 21, 1995. Traded to **Calgary** by **Colorado** for Calgary's 7th round choice (Sami Pahlsson) in 1996 Entry Draft, November 1, 1995. Signed as a free agent by **NY Islanders**, August 14, 1996. Traded to **Philadelphia** by **NY Islanders** for Philadelphia's 5th round choice (later traded to Pittsburgh – Pittsburgh selected Evgeni Isakov) in 2003 Entry Draft, March 9, 2003.

LAPOINTE, Guy

HHOF

Defense. Shoots left. 6', 205 lbs. Born, Montreal, Que., March 18, 1948.

Season	Club	Regular Season GP	G	A	Pts	PIM	Playoffs GP	G	A	Pts	PIM
1968-69	Montreal Canadiens	1	0	0	0	2	....	....	....	....	....
1969-70	Montreal Canadiens	5	0	0	0	4	....	....	....	....	....
1970-71♦	Montreal Canadiens	78	15	29	44	107	20	4	5	9	34
1971-72	Montreal Canadiens	69	11	38	49	58	6	0	1	1	0
1972-73♦	Montreal Canadiens	76	19	35	54	117	17	6	7	13	20
1973-74	Montreal Canadiens	71	13	40	53	63	6	0	2	2	4
1974-75	Montreal Canadiens	80	28	47	75	88	11	6	4	10	4
1975-76♦	Montreal Canadiens	77	21	47	68	78	13	3	3	6	12
1976-77♦	Montreal Canadiens	77	25	51	76	53	12	3	9	12	4
1977-78♦	Montreal Canadiens	49	13	29	42	19	14	1	6	7	16
1978-79♦	Montreal Canadiens	69	13	42	55	43	10	2	6	8	10
1979-80	Montreal Canadiens	45	6	20	26	29	2	0	0	0	0
1980-81	Montreal Canadiens	33	1	9	10	79	1	0	0	0	17
1981-82	Montreal Canadiens	47	1	19	20	72	....	....	....	....	....
	St. Louis Blues	8	0	6	6	4	7	1	0	1	8
1982-83	St. Louis Blues	54	3	23	26	43	4	0	1	1	9
1983-84	Boston Bruins	45	2	16	18	34	....	....	....	....	....
	NHL Totals	**884**	**171**	**451**	**622**	**893**	**123**	**26**	**44**	**70**	**138**

NHL Second All-Star Team (1975, 1976, 1977)

Played in NHL All-Star Game (1973, 1975, 1976, 1977)

Traded to **St. Louis** by **Montreal** for St. Louis' 2nd round choice (Sergio Momesso) in 1983 Entry Draft, March 9, 1982. Signed as a free agent by **Boston**, August 15, 1983.

LAPOINTE, Martin

Right wing. Shoots right. 5'11", 200 lbs. Born, Ville St-Pierre, Que., September 12, 1973.
(Detroit's 1st choice, 10th overall, in 1991 Entry Draft).

Season	Club	Regular Season GP	G	A	Pts	PIM	Playoffs GP	G	A	Pts	PIM
1991-92	Detroit Red Wings	4	0	1	1	5	3	0	1	1	4
1992-93	Detroit Red Wings	3	0	0	0	0	....	....	....	....	....
1993-94	Detroit Red Wings	50	8	8	16	55	4	0	0	0	6
1994-95	Detroit Red Wings	39	4	6	10	73	2	0	1	1	8
1995-96	Detroit Red Wings	58	6	3	9	93	11	1	2	3	12
1996-97♦	Detroit Red Wings	78	16	17	33	167	20	4	8	12	60
1997-98♦	Detroit Red Wings	79	15	19	34	106	21	9	6	15	20
1998-99	Detroit Red Wings	77	16	13	29	141	10	0	2	2	20
99-2000	Detroit Red Wings	82	16	25	41	121	9	3	1	4	20
2000-01	Detroit Red Wings	82	27	30	57	127	6	0	1	1	8
2001-02	Boston Bruins	68	17	23	40	101	6	1	2	3	12
2002-03	Boston Bruins	59	8	10	18	87	5	1	0	1	14
	NHL Totals	**679**	**133**	**155**	**288**	**1076**	**97**	**19**	**24**	**43**	**184**

Signed as a free agent by **Boston**, July 2, 2001.

LAPOINTE, Rick

Defense. Shoots left. 6'2", 200 lbs. Born, Victoria, B.C., August 2, 1955.
(Detroit's 1st choice, 5th overall, in 1975 Amateur Draft).

Season	Club	Regular Season GP	G	A	Pts	PIM	Playoffs GP	G	A	Pts	PIM
1975-76	Detroit Red Wings	80	10	23	33	95					
1976-77	Detroit Red Wings	49	2	11	13	80	....	....	....	....	....
	Philadelphia Flyers	22	1	8	9	39	10	0	0	0	7
1977-78	Philadelphia Flyers	47	4	16	20	91	12	0	3	3	19
1978-79	Philadelphia Flyers	77	3	18	21	53	7	0	1	1	14
1979-80	St. Louis Blues	80	6	19	25	87	3	0	1	1	6
1980-81	St. Louis Blues	80	8	25	33	124	8	2	2	4	12
1981-82	St. Louis Blues	71	2	20	22	127	3	0	0	0	6
1982-83	Quebec Nordiques	43	2	9	11	59	....	....	....	....	....
1983-84	Quebec Nordiques	22	2	10	12	12	3	0	0	0	0
1984-85	Los Angeles Kings	73	4	13	17	46	....	....	....	....	....
1985-86	Los Angeles Kings	20	0	4	4	18	....	....	....	....	....
	NHL Totals	**664**	**44**	**176**	**220**	**831**	**46**	**2**	**7**	**9**	**64**

Traded to **Philadelphia** by **Detroit** with Mike Korney for Terry Murray, Bob Ritchie, Steve Coates and Dave Kelly, February 17, 1977. Traded to **St. Louis** by **Philadelphia** with Blake Dunlop for Phil Myre, June 7, 1979. Traded to **Quebec** by **St. Louis** for Pat Hickey, August 4, 1982. Signed as a free agent by **Los Angeles**, October 10, 1984.

LAPPIN, Peter

Right wing. Shoots right. 5'11", 180 lbs. Born, St. Charles, IL, December 31, 1965.
(Calgary's 1st choice, 24th overall, in 1987 Supplemental Draft).

Season	Club	Regular Season GP	G	A	Pts	PIM	Playoffs GP	G	A	Pts	PIM
1989-90	Minnesota North Stars	6	0	0	0	2	....	....	....	....	....
1991-92	San Jose Sharks	1	0	0	0	0	....	....	....	....	....
	NHL Totals	**7**	**0**	**0**	**0**	**2**	....	....	....	....	....

Traded to **Minnesota** by **Calgary** for Minnesota's 2nd round choice (later traded to New Jersey – New Jersey selected Chris Gotziaman) in 1990 Entry Draft, September 5, 1989. Claimed by **San Jose** from **Minnesota** in Dispersal Draft, May 30, 1991.

LAPRADE, Edgar

HHOF

Center. Shoots right. 5'8", 160 lbs. Born, Port Arthur, Ont., October 10, 1919.

Season	Club	Regular Season GP	G	A	Pts	PIM	Playoffs GP	G	A	Pts	PIM
1945-46	New York Rangers	49	15	19	34	0	....	....	....	....	....
1946-47	New York Rangers	58	15	25	40	9	....	....	....	....	....
1947-48	New York Rangers	59	13	34	47	7	6	1	4	5	0
1948-49	New York Rangers	56	18	12	30	12	....	....	....	....	....
1949-50	New York Rangers	60	22	22	44	2	12	3	5	8	4
1950-51	New York Rangers	42	10	13	23	0	....	....	....	....	....
1951-52	New York Rangers	70	9	29	38	8	....	....	....	....	....
1952-53	New York Rangers	11	2	1	3	2	....	....	....	....	....
1953-54	New York Rangers	35	1	6	7	2	....	....	....	....	....
1954-55	New York Rangers	60	3	11	14	0	....	....	....	....	....
	NHL Totals	**500**	**108**	**172**	**280**	**42**	**18**	**4**	**9**	**13**	**4**

Calder Memorial Trophy (1946) • Lady Byng Trophy (1950)

Played in NHL All-Star Game (1947, 1948, 1949, 1950)

Signed as a free agent by **NY Rangers**, October 15, 1945.

LaPRAIRIE, Benjamin

Defense. Shoots right. 5'10", 160 lbs. Born, Sault Ste. Marie, MI,

Season	Club	GP	G	A	Pts	PIM	GP	G	A	Pts	PIM
		REGULAR SEASON					PLAYOFFS				
1936-37	Chicago Black Hawks	7	0	0	0	0	....	....	....	....	....
	NHL Totals	**7**	**0**	**0**	**0**	**0**	....	....	....	....	....

LARAQUE, Georges

Right wing. Shoots right. 6'3", 240 lbs. Born, Montreal, Que., December 7, 1976.
(Edmonton's 2nd choice, 31st overall, in 1995 Entry Draft).

Season	Club	GP	G	A	Pts	PIM	GP	G	A	Pts	PIM
1997-98	Edmonton Oilers	11	0	0	0	59	....	....	....	....	....
1998-99	Edmonton Oilers	39	3	2	5	57	4	0	0	0	2
99-2000	Edmonton Oilers	76	8	8	16	123	5	0	1	1	6
2000-01	Edmonton Oilers	82	13	16	29	148	6	1	1	2	8
2001-02	Edmonton Oilers	80	5	14	19	157	....	....	....	....	....
2002-03	Edmonton Oilers	64	6	7	13	110	6	1	3	4	4
	NHL Totals	**352**	**35**	**47**	**82**	**654**	**21**	**2**	**5**	**7**	**20**

LARIONOV, Igor

Center. Shoots left. 5'9", 170 lbs. Born, Voskresensk, USSR, December 3, 1960.
(Vancouver's 11th choice, 214th overall, in 1985 Entry Draft).

Season	Club	GP	G	A	Pts	PIM	GP	G	A	Pts	PIM
1989-90	Vancouver Canucks	74	17	27	44	20	....	....	....	....	....
1990-91	Vancouver Canucks	64	13	21	34	14	6	1	0	1	6
1991-92	Vancouver Canucks	72	21	44	65	54	13	3	7	10	4
1993-94	San Jose Sharks	60	18	38	56	40	14	5	13	18	10
1994-95	San Jose Sharks	33	4	20	24	14	11	1	8	9	2
1995-96	San Jose Sharks	4	1	1	2	0	....	....	....	....	....
	Detroit Red Wings	69	21	50	71	34	19	6	7	13	6
1996-97◆	Detroit Red Wings	64	12	42	54	26	20	4	8	12	8
1997-98◆	Detroit Red Wings	69	8	39	47	40	22	3	10	13	12
1998-99	Detroit Red Wings	75	14	49	63	48	7	0	2	2	0
99-2000	Detroit Red Wings	79	9	38	47	28	9	1	2	3	6
2000-01	Florida Panthers	26	5	6	11	10	....	....	....	....	....
	Detroit Red Wings	39	4	25	29	28	6	1	3	4	2
2001-02◆	Detroit Red Wings	70	11	32	43	50	18	5	6	11	4
2002-03	Detroit Red Wings	74	10	33	43	48	4	0	1	1	0
	NHL Totals	**872**	**168**	**465**	**633**	**454**	**149**	**30**	**67**	**97**	**60**

Played in NHL All-Star Game (1998)

Claimed by **San Jose** from **Vancouver** in Waiver Draft, October 4, 1992. Traded to **Detroit** by **San Jose** for Ray Sheppard, October 24, 1995. Signed as a free agent by **Florida**, July 1, 2000. Traded to **Detroit** by **Florida** for Yan Golubovsky, December 28, 2000.

LARIVIERE, Garry

Defense. Shoots right. 6', 190 lbs. Born, St. Catharines, Ont., December 6, 1954.
(Buffalo's 5th choice, 83rd overall, in 1974 Amateur Draft).

Season	Club	GP	G	A	Pts	PIM	GP	G	A	Pts	PIM
1979-80	Quebec Nordiques	75	2	19	21	56	....	....	....	....	....
1980-81	Quebec Nordiques	52	3	13	16	50	....	....	....	....	....
	Edmonton Oilers	13	0	2	2	6	9	0	3	3	8
1981-82	Edmonton Oilers	62	1	21	22	41	4	0	1	1	0
1982-83	Edmonton Oilers	17	0	2	2	14	1	0	1	1	0
	NHL Totals	**219**	**6**	**57**	**63**	**167**	**14**	**0**	**5**	**5**	**8**

Rights traded to **NY Islanders** by **Buffalo** for the rights to Gerry Desjardins, February 19, 1975. Reclaimed by **NY Islanders** from **Quebec** prior to Expansion Draft, June 9, 1979. Claimed as a priority selection by **Quebec**, June 9, 1979. Traded to **Vancouver** by **Quebec** for Mario Marois, March 10, 1981. Traded to **Edmonton** by **Vancouver** with Ken Berry for Blair MacDonald and the rights to Lars-Gunnar Pettersson, March 10, 1981.

LARMER, Jeff

Left wing. Shoots left. 5'10", 175 lbs. Born, Peterborough, Ont., November 10, 1962.
(Colorado's 7th choice, 129th overall, in 1981 Entry Draft).

Season	Club	GP	G	A	Pts	PIM	GP	G	A	Pts	PIM
1981-82	Colorado Rockies	8	1	1	2	8	....	....	....	....	....
1982-83	New Jersey Devils	65	21	24	45	21	....	....	....	....	....
1983-84	New Jersey Devils	40	6	13	19	8	....	....	....	....	....
	Chicago Black Hawks	36	9	13	22	20	5	1	0	1	2
1984-85	Chicago Black Hawks	7	0	0	0	0	....	....	....	....	....
1985-86	Chicago Black Hawks	2	0	0	0	0	....	....	....	....	....
	NHL Totals	**158**	**37**	**51**	**88**	**57**	**5**	**1**	**0**	**1**	**2**

• Brother of Steve

Transferred to **New Jersey** after **Colorado** franchise relocated, June 30, 1982. Traded to **Chicago** by **New Jersey** for Tim Higgins, January 11, 1984.

LARMER, Steve

Right wing. Shoots left. 5'11", 195 lbs. Born, Peterborough, Ont., June 16, 1961.
(Chicago's 11th choice, 120th overall, in 1980 Entry Draft).

Season	Club	GP	G	A	Pts	PIM	GP	G	A	Pts	PIM
1980-81	Chicago Black Hawks	4	0	1	1	0	....	....	....	....	....
1981-82	Chicago Black Hawks	3	0	0	0	0	....	....	....	....	....
1982-83	Chicago Black Hawks	80	43	47	90	28	11	5	7	12	8
1983-84	Chicago Black Hawks	80	35	40	75	34	5	2	2	4	7
1984-85	Chicago Black Hawks	80	46	40	86	16	15	9	13	22	14
1985-86	Chicago Black Hawks	80	31	45	76	47	3	0	3	3	4
1986-87	Chicago Blackhawks	80	28	56	84	22	4	0	0	0	2
1987-88	Chicago Blackhawks	80	41	48	89	42	5	1	6	7	0
1988-89	Chicago Blackhawks	80	43	44	87	54	16	8	9	17	22
1989-90	Chicago Blackhawks	80	31	59	90	40	20	7	15	22	2
1990-91	Chicago Blackhawks	80	44	57	101	79	6	5	1	6	4
1991-92	Chicago Blackhawks	80	29	45	74	65	18	8	7	15	6
1992-93	Chicago Blackhawks	84	35	35	70	48	4	0	3	3	0
1993-94◆	New York Rangers	68	21	39	60	41	23	9	7	16	14
1994-95	New York Rangers	47	14	15	29	16	10	2	2	4	6
	NHL Totals	**1006**	**441**	**571**	**1012**	**532**	**140**	**56**	**75**	**131**	**89**

• Brother of Jeff • NHL All-Rookie Team (1983) • Calder Memorial Trophy (1983)
Played in NHL All-Star Game (1990, 1991)

Traded to **Hartford** by **Chicago** with Bryan Marchment for Eric Weinrich and Patrick Poulin, November 2, 1993. Traded to **NY Rangers** by **Hartford** with Nick Kypreos, Barry Richter and Hartford's 6th round choice (Yuri Litvinov) in 1994 Entry Draft for Darren Turcotte and James Patrick, November 2, 1993.

LAROCHELLE, Wildor

Right wing. Shoots right. 5'8", 158 lbs. Born, Sorel, Que., September 23, 1906.

Season	Club	GP	G	A	Pts	PIM	GP	G	A	Pts	PIM
1925-26	Montreal Canadiens	33	2	1	3	10	....	....	....	....	....
1926-27	Montreal Canadiens	41	0	1	1	6	4	0	0	0	0
1927-28	Montreal Canadiens	40	3	1	4	30	2	0	0	0	0
1928-29	Montreal Canadiens	2	0	0	0	0	....	....	....	....	....
1929-30◆	Montreal Canadiens	44	14	11	25	28	6	1	0	1	12
1930-31◆	Montreal Canadiens	40	8	5	13	35	10	1	2	3	8
1931-32	Montreal Canadiens	48	18	8	26	16	4	2	1	3	4
1932-33	Montreal Canadiens	47	11	4	15	27	2	1	0	1	0
1933-34	Montreal Canadiens	48	16	11	27	27	2	1	1	2	0
1934-35	Montreal Canadiens	48	9	19	28	12	2	0	0	0	0
1935-36	Montreal Canadiens	13	0	2	2	6	....	....	....	....	....
	Chicago Black Hawks	27	2	1	3	8	2	0	0	0	0
1936-37	Chicago Black Hawks	43	9	10	19	6	....	....	....	....	....
	NHL Totals	**474**	**92**	**74**	**166**	**211**	**34**	**6**	**4**	**10**	**24**

Signed as a free agent by **Montreal**, November 23, 1925. Traded to **Chicago** by **Montreal** for cash, December 21, 1935. Traded to **St. Louis** (AHA) by **Chicago** for cash, September 24, 1937.
• Larochelle opted to retire rather than report to St. Louis.

LAROCQUE, Denis

Defense. Shoots left. 6'1", 195 lbs. Born, Hawkesbury, Ont., October 5, 1967.
(Los Angeles' 2nd choice, 44th overall, in 1986 Entry Draft).

Season	Club	GP	G	A	Pts	PIM	GP	G	A	Pts	PIM
1987-88	Los Angeles Kings	8	0	1	1	18	....	....	....	....	....
	NHL Totals	**8**	**0**	**1**	**1**	**18**	....	....	....	....	....

Traded to **NY Rangers** by **Los Angeles** with Dean Kennedy for Igor Liba, Michael Boyce, Todd Elik and future considerations, December 12, 1988.

LAROCQUE, Mario

Defense. Shoots left. 6'2", 182 lbs. Born, Montreal, Que., April 24, 1978.
(Tampa Bay's 1st choice, 16th overall, in 1996 Entry Draft).

Season	Club	GP	G	A	Pts	PIM	GP	G	A	Pts	PIM
1998-99	Tampa Bay Lightning	5	0	0	0	16	....	....	....	....	....
	NHL Totals	**5**	**0**	**0**	**0**	**16**	....	....	....	....	....

Signed as a free agent by **Buffalo**, August 7, 2001.

LAROSE, Bonner

Left wing. Shoots right. 5'8", 170 lbs. Born, Ottawa, Ont., February 14, 1901.

Season	Club	GP	G	A	Pts	PIM	GP	G	A	Pts	PIM
1925-26	Boston Bruins	6	0	0	0	0	....	....	....	....	....
	NHL Totals	**6**	**0**	**0**	**0**	**0**	....	....	....	....	....

Signed as a free agent by **Boston**, February 19, 1926. Traded to **New Haven** (Can-Am) by **Boston** (Boston-Can-Am) for Reg McLlwain, January 31, 1927.

LAROSE, Claude

Right wing. Shoots right. 6', 180 lbs. Born, Hearst, Ont., March 2, 1942.

Season	Club	GP	G	A	Pts	PIM	GP	G	A	Pts	PIM
1962-63	Montreal Canadiens	4	0	0	0	0	....	....	....	....	....
1963-64	Montreal Canadiens	21	1	1	2	43	2	1	0	1	0
1964-65◆	Montreal Canadiens	68	21	16	37	82	13	0	1	1	14
1965-66◆	Montreal Canadiens	64	15	18	33	67	6	0	1	1	31
1966-67	Montreal Canadiens	69	19	16	35	82	10	1	5	6	15
1967-68◆	Montreal Canadiens	42	2	9	11	28	12	3	2	5	8
1968-69	Minnesota North Stars	67	25	37	62	106	....	....	....	....	....
1969-70	Minnesota North Stars	75	24	23	47	109	6	1	1	2	25
1970-71◆	Montreal Canadiens	64	10	13	23	90	11	1	0	1	10
1971-72	Montreal Canadiens	77	20	18	38	64	6	2	1	3	23
1972-73◆	Montreal Canadiens	73	11	23	34	30	17	3	4	7	6
1973-74	Montreal Canadiens	39	17	7	24	52	5	0	2	2	11
1974-75	Montreal Canadiens	8	1	2	3	6	....	....	....	....	....
	St. Louis Blues	56	10	17	27	38	2	1	1	2	0
1975-76	St. Louis Blues	67	13	25	38	48	3	0	0	0	0
1976-77	St. Louis Blues	80	29	19	48	22	4	1	0	1	0
1977-78	St. Louis Blues	69	8	13	21	20	....	....	....	....	....
	NHL Totals	**943**	**226**	**257**	**483**	**887**	**97**	**14**	**18**	**32**	**143**

• Father of Guy
Played in NHL All-Star Game (1965, 1967, 1969, 1970)

Traded to **Minnesota** by **Montreal** with Danny Grant and future considerations (Bob Murdoch, May 25, 1971) for Minnesota's 1st round choice (Dave Gardner) in 1972 Amateur Draft, cash and future considerations (Marshall Johnston, May 25, 1971), June 10, 1968. Traded to **Montreal** by **Minnesota** for Bobby Rousseau, June 10, 1970. Traded to **St. Louis** by **Montreal** for cash, December 5, 1974.

LAROSE, Claude

Left wing. Shoots left. 5'10", 175 lbs. Born, St-Jean, Que., May 17, 1955.
(NY Rangers' 7th choice, 120th overall, in 1975 Amateur Draft).

Season	Club	GP	G	A	Pts	PIM	GP	G	A	Pts	PIM
1979-80	New York Rangers	25	4	7	11	2	....	....	....	....	....

Season	Club	GP	G	A	Pts	PIM	GP	G	A	Pts	PIM
		REGULAR SEASON					PLAYOFFS				
1981-82	New York Rangers	....	....	....	....	....	2	0	0	0	0
	NHL Totals	**25**	**4**	**7**	**11**	**2**	**2**	**0**	**0**	**0**	**0**

Rights reclaimed by **NY Rangers** after **Indianapolis** (WHA) franchise folded, December 15, 1978.

LAROSE, Guy

Center. Shoots left. 5'9", 180 lbs. Born, Hull, Que., August 31, 1967.
(Buffalo's 11th choice, 224th overall, in 1985 Entry Draft).

Season	Club	GP	G	A	Pts	PIM	GP	G	A	Pts	PIM
1988-89	Winnipeg Jets	3	0	1	1	6	....	....	....	....	....
1990-91	Winnipeg Jets	7	0	0	0	8	....	....	....	....	....
1991-92	Toronto Maple Leafs	34	9	5	14	27	....	....	....	....	....
1992-93	Toronto Maple Leafs	9	0	0	0	8	....	....	....	....	....
1993-94	Toronto Maple Leafs	10	1	2	3	10	....	....	....	....	....
	Calgary Flames	7	0	1	1	4	....	....	....	....	....
1994-95	Boston Bruins	....	....	....	....	....	4	0	0	0	0
	NHL Totals	**70**	**10**	**9**	**19**	**63**	**4**	**0**	**0**	**0**	**0**

• Son of Claude

Signed as a free agent by **Winnipeg**, July 16, 1987. Traded to **NY Rangers** by **Winnipeg** for Rudy Poeschek, January 22, 1991. Traded to **Toronto** by **NY Rangers** for Mike Stevens, December 26, 1991. Claimed on waivers by **Calgary** from **Toronto**, January 1, 1994. Signed as a free agent by **Boston**, July 11, 1994.

LAROUCHE, Pierre

Center. Shoots right. 5'11", 175 lbs. Born, Taschereau, Que., November 16, 1955.
(Pittsburgh's 1st choice, 8th overall, in 1974 Amateur Draft).

Season	Club	GP	G	A	Pts	PIM	GP	G	A	Pts	PIM
1974-75	Pittsburgh Penguins	79	31	37	68	52	9	2	5	7	2
1975-76	Pittsburgh Penguins	76	53	58	111	33	3	0	1	1	0
1976-77	Pittsburgh Penguins	65	29	34	63	14	3	0	3	3	0
1977-78	Pittsburgh Penguins	20	6	5	11	0	....	....	....	....	....
	♦ Montreal Canadiens	44	17	32	49	11	5	2	1	3	4
1978-79	♦ Montreal Canadiens	36	9	13	22	4	6	1	3	4	0
1979-80	Montreal Canadiens	73	50	41	91	16	9	1	7	8	2
1980-81	Montreal Canadiens	61	25	28	53	28	2	0	2	2	0
1981-82	Montreal Canadiens	22	9	12	21	0	....	....	....	....	....
	Hartford Whalers	45	25	25	50	12	....	....	....	....	....
1982-83	Hartford Whalers	38	18	22	40	8	....	....	....	....	....
1983-84	New York Rangers	77	48	33	81	22	5	3	1	4	2
1984-85	New York Rangers	65	24	36	60	8	....	....	....	....	....
1985-86	New York Rangers	28	20	7	27	4	16	8	9	17	2
1986-87	New York Rangers	73	28	35	63	12	6	3	2	5	4
1987-88	New York Rangers	10	3	9	12	13	....	....	....	....	....
	NHL Totals	**812**	**395**	**427**	**822**	**237**	**64**	**20**	**34**	**54**	**16**

Played in NHL All-Star Game (1976, 1984)

Traded to **Montreal** by **Pittsburgh** with future considerations (rights to Peter Marsh, December 15, 1977) for Pete Mahovlich and Peter Lee, November 29, 1977. Traded to **Hartford** by **Montreal** with Montreal's 1st round choice (Sylvain Cote) in 1984 Entry Draft and 3rd round choice (later traded to Pittsburgh – Pittsburgh selected Bruce Racine) in 1985 Entry Draft for Hartford's 1st (Petr Svoboda) and 2nd (later traded to St. Louis – St. Louis selected Brian Benning) round choices in 1984 Entry Draft and 3rd round choice (Rocky Dundas) in 1985 Entry Draft, December 21, 1981. Signed as a free agent by **NY Rangers**, September 12, 1983.

LAROUCHE, Steve

Center. Shoots right. 6', 180 lbs. Born, Rouyn, Que., April 14, 1971.
(Montreal's 3rd choice, 41st overall, in 1989 Entry Draft).

Season	Club	GP	G	A	Pts	PIM	GP	G	A	Pts	PIM
1994-95	Ottawa Senators	18	8	7	15	6	....	....	....	....	....
1995-96	New York Rangers	1	0	0	0	0	....	....	....	....	....
	Los Angeles Kings	7	1	2	3	4	....	....	....	....	....
	NHL Totals	**26**	**9**	**9**	**18**	**10**	....	....	....	....	....

Signed as a free agent by **Ottawa**, September 11, 1994. Traded to **NY Rangers** by **Ottawa** for Jean-Yves Roy, October 5, 1995. Traded to **Los Angeles** by **NY Rangers** for Chris Snell, January 14, 1996.

LARSEN, Brad

Left wing. Shoots left. 6', 200 lbs. Born, Nakusp, B.C., June 28, 1977.
(Colorado's 5th choice, 87th overall, in 1997 Entry Draft).

Season	Club	GP	G	A	Pts	PIM	GP	G	A	Pts	PIM
1997-98	Colorado Avalanche	1	0	0	0	0	....	....	....	....	....
2000-01	Colorado Avalanche	9	0	0	0	0	....	....	....	....	....
2001-02	Colorado Avalanche	50	2	7	9	47	21	1	1	2	13
2002-03	Colorado Avalanche	6	0	3	3	2	....	....	....	....	....
	NHL Totals	**66**	**2**	**10**	**12**	**49**	**21**	**1**	**1**	**2**	**13**

• Re-entered NHL Entry Draft. Originally Ottawa's 3rd choice, 53rd overall, in 1995 Entry Draft.
Rights traded to **Colorado** by **Ottawa** for Janne Laukkanen, January 26, 1996.

LARSON, Norm

Right wing. Shoots right. 6', 175 lbs. Born, Moose Jaw, Sask., October 13, 1920.

Season	Club	GP	G	A	Pts	PIM	GP	G	A	Pts	PIM
1940-41	New York Americans	48	9	9	18	6	....	....	....	....	....
1941-42	Brooklyn Americans	40	16	9	25	6	....	....	....	....	....
1946-47	New York Rangers	1	0	0	0	0	....	....	....	....	....
	NHL Totals	**89**	**25**	**18**	**43**	**12**	....	....	....	....	....

Signed as a free agent by **NY Americans**, October 23, 1940. • Team name changed to **Brooklyn Americans** prior to 1941-42 season.

LARSON, Reed

USHOF

Defense. Shoots right. 6', 195 lbs. Born, Minneapolis, MN, July 30, 1956.
(Detroit's 2nd choice, 22nd overall, in 1976 Amateur Draft).

Season	Club	GP	G	A	Pts	PIM	GP	G	A	Pts	PIM
1976-77	Detroit Red Wings	14	0	1	1	23	....	....	....	....	....
1977-78	Detroit Red Wings	75	19	41	60	95	7	0	2	2	4
1978-79	Detroit Red Wings	79	18	49	67	169	....	....	....	....	....
1979-80	Detroit Red Wings	80	22	44	66	101	....	....	....	....	....
1980-81	Detroit Red Wings	78	27	31	58	153	....	....	....	....	....
1981-82	Detroit Red Wings	80	21	39	60	112	....	....	....	....	....
1982-83	Detroit Red Wings	80	22	52	74	104	....	....	....	....	....
1983-84	Detroit Red Wings	78	23	39	62	122	4	2	0	2	21
1984-85	Detroit Red Wings	77	17	45	62	139	3	1	2	3	20
1985-86	Detroit Red Wings	67	19	41	60	109	....	....	....	....	....
	Boston Bruins	13	3	4	7	8	3	1	0	1	6
1986-87	Boston Bruins	66	12	24	36	95	4	0	2	2	2
1987-88	Boston Bruins	62	10	24	34	93	8	0	1	1	6
1988-89	Edmonton Oilers	10	2	7	9	15	....	....	....	....	....
	New York Islanders	33	7	13	20	35	....	....	....	....	....
	Minnesota North Stars	11	0	9	9	18	3	0	0	0	4
1989-90	Buffalo Sabres	1	0	0	0	0	....	....	....	....	....
	NHL Totals	**904**	**222**	**463**	**685**	**1391**	**32**	**4**	**7**	**11**	**63**

Played in NHL All-Star Game (1978, 1980, 1981)

Traded to **Boston** by **Detroit** for Mike O'Connell, March 10, 1986. Signed as a free agent by **Edmonton**, September 30, 1988. Signed as a free agent by **NY Islanders**, December 5, 1988. Traded to **Minnesota** by **NY Islanders** for Minnesota's 7th round choice (Brett Harkins) in 1989 Entry Draft and future considerations (Mike Kelfer, May 12, 1989), March 7, 1989. Signed as a free agent by **Buffalo**, March 6, 1990.

LARTER, Tyler

Center. Shoots left. 5'10", 185 lbs. Born, Charlottetown, P.E.I., March 12, 1968.
(Washington's 3rd choice, 78th overall, in 1987 Entry Draft).

Season	Club	GP	G	A	Pts	PIM	GP	G	A	Pts	PIM
1989-90	Washington Capitals	1	0	0	0	0	....	....	....	....	....
	NHL Totals	**1**	**0**	**0**	**0**	**0**	....	....	....	....	....

Traded to **Winnipeg** by **Washington** with Bob Joyce and Kent Paynter for Craig Duncanson, Brent Hughes and Simon Wheeldon, May 21, 1991. Claimed by **Minnesota** from **Winnipeg** in Expansion Draft, May 30, 1991. Traded to **Winnipeg** by **Minnesota** for Tony Joseph, October 15, 1991.

LATAL, Jiri

Defense. Shoots left. 6', 190 lbs. Born, Olomouc, Czech., February 2, 1967.
(Toronto's 6th choice, 106th overall, in 1985 Entry Draft).

Season	Club	GP	G	A	Pts	PIM	GP	G	A	Pts	PIM
1989-90	Philadelphia Flyers	32	6	13	19	6	....	....	....	....	....
1990-91	Philadelphia Flyers	50	5	21	26	14	....	....	....	....	....
1991-92	Philadelphia Flyers	10	1	2	3	4	....	....	....	....	....
	NHL Totals	**92**	**12**	**36**	**48**	**24**	....	....	....	....	....

Rights traded to **Philadelphia** by **Toronto** for Philadelphia's 7th round choice (later traded back to Philadelphia – Philadelphia selected Andrei Lomakin) in 1991 Entry Draft, August 28, 1989.

LATOS, James

Right wing. Shoots right. 6'1", 200 lbs. Born, Wakaw, Sask., January 4, 1966.

Season	Club	GP	G	A	Pts	PIM	GP	G	A	Pts	PIM
1988-89	New York Rangers	1	0	0	0	0	....	....	....	....	....
	NHL Totals	**1**	**0**	**0**	**0**	**0**	....	....	....	....	....

Signed as a free agent by **NY Rangers**, June 5, 1987.

LATREILLE, Phil

Center/Right wing. Shoots right. 5'10", 185 lbs. Born, Montreal, Que., April 22, 1938.

Season	Club	GP	G	A	Pts	PIM	GP	G	A	Pts	PIM
1960-61	New York Rangers	4	0	0	0	2	....	....	....	....	....
	NHL Totals	**4**	**0**	**0**	**0**	**2**	....	....	....	....	....

Signed as a free agent by **NY Rangers** to a five-game amateur tryout contract, March 10, 1961.

LATTA, David

Left wing. Shoots left. 6'1", 190 lbs. Born, Thunder Bay, Ont., January 3, 1967.
(Quebec's 1st choice, 15th overall, in 1985 Entry Draft).

Season	Club	GP	G	A	Pts	PIM	GP	G	A	Pts	PIM
1985-86	Quebec Nordiques	1	0	0	0	0	....	....	....	....	....
1987-88	Quebec Nordiques	10	0	0	0	0	....	....	....	....	....
1988-89	Quebec Nordiques	24	4	8	12	4	....	....	....	....	....
1990-91	Quebec Nordiques	1	0	0	0	0	....	....	....	....	....
	NHL Totals	**36**	**4**	**8**	**12**	**4**	....	....	....	....	....

LAUDER, Martin

Defense/Center. Shoots left. 5'6", 165 lbs. Born, Durham, Ont., January 26, 1907.

Season	Club	GP	G	A	Pts	PIM	GP	G	A	Pts	PIM
1927-28	Boston Bruins	3	0	0	0	2	....	....	....	....	....
	NHL Totals	**3**	**0**	**0**	**0**	**2**	....	....	....	....	....

Signed as a free agent by **Boston**, October 2, 1927.

LAUEN, Mike

Right wing. Shoots right. 6'1", 185 lbs. Born, Edina, MN, February 9, 1961.
(Winnipeg's 8th choice, 135th overall, in 1980 Entry Draft).

Season	Club	GP	G	A	Pts	PIM	GP	G	A	Pts	PIM
1983-84	Winnipeg Jets	4	0	1	1	0	....	....	....	....	....
	NHL Totals	**4**	**0**	**1**	**1**	**0**	....	....	....	....	....

LAUER, Brad

Left wing. Shoots left. 6', 195 lbs. Born, Humboldt, Sask., October 27, 1966.
(NY Islanders' 3rd choice, 34th overall, in 1985 Entry Draft).

Season	Club	GP	G	A	Pts	PIM	GP	G	A	Pts	PIM
1986-87	New York Islanders	61	7	14	21	65	6	2	0	2	4
1987-88	New York Islanders	69	17	18	35	67	5	3	1	4	4
1988-89	New York Islanders	14	3	2	5	2	....	....	....	....	....
1989-90	New York Islanders	63	6	18	24	19	4	0	2	2	10

		REGULAR SEASON					PLAYOFFS				
Season	Club	GP	G	A	Pts	PIM	GP	G	A	Pts	PIM
1990-91	New York Islanders	44	4	8	12	45	....	....	....	....	....
1991-92	New York Islanders	8	1	0	1	2	....	....	....	....	....
	Chicago Blackhawks	6	0	0	0	4	7	1	1	2	2
1992-93	Chicago Blackhawks	7	0	1	1	2	....	....	....	....	....
1993-94	Ottawa Senators	30	2	5	7	6	....	....	....	....	....
1995-96	Pittsburgh Penguins	21	4	1	5	6	12	1	1	2	4
	NHL Totals	**323**	**44**	**67**	**111**	**218**	**34**	**7**	**5**	**12**	**24**

• Missed majority of 1988-89 season recovering from knee injury suffered in training camp, October, 1988. Traded to **Chicago** by **NY Islanders** with Brent Sutter for Adam Creighton and Steve Thomas, October 25, 1991. Signed as a free agent by **Ottawa**, January 3, 1994. Signed as a free agent by **Pittsburgh**, August 10, 1995.

LAUGHLIN, Craig

Right wing. Shoots right. 6', 190 lbs. Born, Toronto, Ont., September 19, 1957.
(Montreal's 17th choice, 162nd overall, in 1977 Amateur Draft).

Season	Club	GP	G	A	Pts	PIM	GP	G	A	Pts	PIM
1981-82	Montreal Canadiens	36	12	11	23	33	3	0	1	1	0
1982-83	Washington Capitals	75	17	27	44	41	4	1	0	1	0
1983-84	Washington Capitals	80	20	32	52	69	8	4	2	6	6
1984-85	Washington Capitals	78	16	34	50	38	5	0	0	0	2
1985-86	Washington Capitals	75	30	45	75	43	9	1	2	3	10
1986-87	Washington Capitals	80	22	30	52	67	1	0	0	0	0
1987-88	Washington Capitals	40	5	5	10	26	....	....	....	....	....
	Los Angeles Kings	19	4	8	12	6	3	0	1	1	2
1988-89	Toronto Maple Leafs	66	10	13	23	41	....	....	....	....	....
	NHL Totals	**549**	**136**	**205**	**341**	**364**	**33**	**6**	**6**	**12**	**20**

Traded to **Washington** by **Montreal** with Doug Jarvis, Rod Langway and Brian Engblom for Ryan Walter and Rick Green, September 9, 1982. Traded to **Los Angeles** by **Washington** for Grant Ledyard, February 9, 1988. Signed as a free agent by **Toronto**, June 10, 1988.

LAUGHTON, Mike

Center. Shoots left. 6'2", 185 lbs. Born, Nelson, B.C., February 21, 1944.

Season	Club	GP	G	A	Pts	PIM	GP	G	A	Pts	PIM
1967-68	Oakland Seals	35	2	6	8	38	....	....	....	....	....
1968-69	Oakland Seals	53	20	23	43	22	7	2	3	5	0
1969-70	Oakland Seals	76	16	19	35	39	4	0	1	1	0
1970-71	California Seals	25	1	0	1	2	....	....	....	....	....
	NHL Totals	**189**	**39**	**48**	**87**	**101**	**11**	**2**	**4**	**6**	**0**

Claimed by **California** (Oakland) from **Toronto** in Expansion Draft, June 6, 1967. Traded to **Montreal** by **California** for cash, October, 1971.

LAUKKANEN, Janne

Defense. Shoots left. 6'1", 196 lbs. Born, Lahti, Finland, March 19, 1970.
(Quebec's 8th choice, 156th overall, in 1991 Entry Draft).

Season	Club	GP	G	A	Pts	PIM	GP	G	A	Pts	PIM
1994-95	Quebec Nordiques	11	0	3	3	4	6	1	0	1	2
1995-96	Colorado Avalanche	3	1	0	1	0	....	....	....	....	....
	Ottawa Senators	20	0	2	2	14	....	....	....	....	....
1996-97	Ottawa Senators	76	3	18	21	76	7	0	1	1	6
1997-98	Ottawa Senators	60	4	17	21	64	11	2	2	4	8
1998-99	Ottawa Senators	50	1	11	12	40	4	0	0	0	4
99-2000	Ottawa Senators	60	1	11	12	55	....	....	....	....	....
	Pittsburgh Penguins	11	1	7	8	12	11	2	4	6	10
2000-01	Pittsburgh Penguins	50	3	17	20	34	18	2	2	4	14
2001-02	Pittsburgh Penguins	47	6	7	13	28	....	....	....	....	....
2002-03	Pittsburgh Penguins	17	1	6	7	8	....	....	....	....	....
	Tampa Bay Lightning	2	1	0	1	0	2	0	0	0	2
	NHL Totals	**407**	**22**	**99**	**121**	**335**	**59**	**7**	**9**	**16**	**46**

Transferred to **Colorado** after **Quebec** franchise relocated, June 21, 1995. Traded to **Ottawa** by **Colorado** for the rights to Brad Larsen, January 26, 1996. Traded to **Pittsburgh** by **Ottawa** with Ron Tugnutt for Tom Barrasso, March 14, 2000. Traded to **NY Rangers** by **Pittsburgh** with Mike Wilson, Alexei Kovalev and Dan LaCouture for Joel Bouchard, Richard Lintner, Rico Fata, Mikael Samuelsson and future considerations, February 10, 2003. Claimed on waivers by **Tampa Bay** from **NY Rangers**, March 11, 2003.

LAURENCE, Don

Center. Shoots right. 5'9", 175 lbs. Born, Galt, Ont., June 27, 1957.
(Atlanta's 2nd choice, 28th overall, in 1977 Amateur Draft).

Season	Club	GP	G	A	Pts	PIM	GP	G	A	Pts	PIM
1978-79	Atlanta Flames	59	14	20	34	6	....	....	....	....	....
1979-80	St. Louis Blues	20	1	2	3	8	....	....	....	....	....
	NHL Totals	**79**	**15**	**22**	**37**	**14**	....	....	....	....	....

Traded to **St. Louis** by **Atlanta** with Ed Kea and Atlanta's 2nd round choice (Hakan Nordin) in 1981 Entry Draft for Garry Unger, October 10, 1979. Signed as a free agent by **NY Islanders**, October 16, 1981.

LAUS, Paul

Defense. Shoots right. 6'1", 215 lbs. Born, Beamsville, Ont., September 26, 1970.
(Pittsburgh's 2nd choice, 37th overall, in 1989 Entry Draft).

Season	Club	GP	G	A	Pts	PIM	GP	G	A	Pts	PIM
1993-94	Florida Panthers	39	2	0	2	109	....	....	....	....	....
1994-95	Florida Panthers	37	0	7	7	138	....	....	....	....	....
1995-96	Florida Panthers	78	3	6	9	236	21	2	6	8	*62
1996-97	Florida Panthers	77	0	12	12	313	5	0	1	1	4
1997-98	Florida Panthers	77	0	11	11	293	....	....	....	....	....
1998-99	Florida Panthers	75	1	9	10	218	....	....	....	....	....
99-2000	Florida Panthers	77	3	8	11	172	4	0	0	0	8
2000-01	Florida Panthers	25	1	2	3	66	....	....	....	....	....
2001-02	Florida Panthers	45	4	3	7	157	....	....	....	....	....
	NHL Totals	**530**	**14**	**58**	**72**	**1702**	**30**	**2**	**7**	**9**	**74**

Claimed by **Florida** from **Pittsburgh** in Expansion Draft, June 24, 1993. • Missed majority of 2000-01 season recovering from hernia injury suffered in game vs. Carolina, November 15, 2000.

LaVALLEE, Kevin

Left wing. Shoots left. 5'8", 180 lbs. Born, Sudbury, Ont., September 16, 1961.
(Calgary's 3rd choice, 32nd overall, in 1980 Entry Draft).

Season	Club	GP	G	A	Pts	PIM	GP	G	A	Pts	PIM
1980-81	Calgary Flames	77	15	20	35	16	8	2	3	5	4
1981-82	Calgary Flames	75	32	29	61	30	3	0	0	0	7
1982-83	Calgary Flames	60	19	16	35	17	8	1	3	4	4
1983-84	Los Angeles Kings	19	3	3	6	2	....	....	....	....	....
1984-85	St. Louis Blues	38	15	17	32	8	....	....	....	....	....
1985-86	St. Louis Blues	64	18	20	38	8	13	2	2	4	6
1986-87	Pittsburgh Penguins	33	8	20	28	4	....	....	....	....	....
	NHL Totals	**366**	**110**	**125**	**235**	**85**	**32**	**5**	**8**	**13**	**21**

Traded to **Los Angeles** by **Calgary** with Carl Mokosak for Steve Bozek, June 20, 1983. Signed as a free agent by **St. Louis**, September 13, 1984. Signed as a free agent by **Pittsburgh**, September 13, 1986.

LaVARRE, Mark

Right wing. Shoots right. 5'11", 170 lbs. Born, Evanston, IL, February 21, 1965.
(Chicago's 7th choice, 123rd overall, in 1983 Entry Draft).

Season	Club	GP	G	A	Pts	PIM	GP	G	A	Pts	PIM
1985-86	Chicago Black Hawks	2	0	0	0	0	....	....	....	....	....
1986-87	Chicago Blackhawks	58	8	15	23	33	....	....	....	....	....
1987-88	Chicago Blackhawks	18	1	1	2	25	1	0	0	0	2
	NHL Totals	**78**	**9**	**16**	**25**	**58**	**1**	**0**	**0**	**0**	**2**

Traded to **Hartford** by **Chicago** for future considerations, October 6, 1988.

LAVENDER, Brian

Left wing. Shoots left. 6', 174 lbs. Born, Edmonton, Alta., April 20, 1947.

Season	Club	GP	G	A	Pts	PIM	GP	G	A	Pts	PIM
1971-72	St. Louis Blues	46	5	11	16	54	3	0	0	0	2
1972-73	New York Islanders	43	6	6	12	47	....	....	....	....	....
	Detroit Red Wings	26	2	2	4	14	....	....	....	....	....
1973-74	Detroit Red Wings	4	0	0	0	11	....	....	....	....	....
1974-75	California Golden Seals	65	3	7	10	48	....	....	....	....	....
	NHL Totals	**184**	**16**	**26**	**42**	**174**	**3**	**0**	**0**	**0**	**2**

Claimed by **Minnesota** from **Montreal** in Intra-League Draft, June 8, 1971. Claimed by **St. Louis** (Denver-WHL) from **Minnesota** in Reverse Draft, June 8, 1971. Traded to **NY Islanders** by **St. Louis** for cash, September 1, 1972. Traded to **Detroit** by **NY Islanders** with Ken Murray for Ralph Stewart and Bob Cook, January 17, 1973. Traded to **NY Rangers** by **Detroit** for Claude Houde, February 28, 1974. Traded to **California** by **NY Rangers** for Hartland Monahan, September 23, 1974.

LAVIGNE, Eric

Defense. Shoots left. 6'3", 195 lbs. Born, Victoriaville, Que., November 4, 1972.
(Washington's 3rd choice, 25th overall, in 1991 Entry Draft).

Season	Club	GP	G	A	Pts	PIM	GP	G	A	Pts	PIM
1994-95	Los Angeles Kings	1	0	0	0	0	....	....	....	....	....
	NHL Totals	**1**	**0**	**0**	**0**	**0**	....	....	....	....	....

Signed as a free agent by **Los Angeles**, October 13, 1993.

LAVIOLETTE, Jack

HHOF

Defense/Right wing. Shoots right. 5'11", 170 lbs. Born, Belleville, Ont., July 27, 1879.

Season	Club	GP	G	A	Pts	PIM	GP	G	A	Pts	PIM
1917-18	Montreal Canadiens	18	2	1	3	6	2	0	0	0	0
	NHL Totals	**18**	**2**	**1**	**3**	**6**	**2**	**0**	**0**	**0**	**0**

Rights retained by **Montreal** after NHA folded, November 26, 1917.

LAVIOLETTE, Peter

Defense. Shoots left. 6'2", 200 lbs. Born, Norwood, MA, December 7, 1964.

Season	Club	GP	G	A	Pts	PIM	GP	G	A	Pts	PIM
1988-89	New York Rangers	12	0	0	0	6	....	....	....	....	....
	NHL Totals	**12**	**0**	**0**	**0**	**6**	....	....	....	....	....

Signed as a free agent by **NY Rangers**, August 12, 1987. Signed as a free agent by **Boston**, September 8, 1992.

LAVOIE, Dominic

Defense. Shoots right. 6'2", 205 lbs. Born, Montreal, Que., November 21, 1967.

Season	Club	GP	G	A	Pts	PIM	GP	G	A	Pts	PIM
1988-89	St. Louis Blues	1	0	0	0	0	....	....	....	....	....
1989-90	St. Louis Blues	13	1	1	2	16	....	....	....	....	....
1990-91	St. Louis Blues	6	1	2	3	2	....	....	....	....	....
1991-92	St. Louis Blues	6	0	1	1	10	....	....	....	....	....
1992-93	Ottawa Senators	2	0	1	1	0	....	....	....	....	....
	Boston Bruins	2	0	0	0	2	....	....	....	....	....
1993-94	Los Angeles Kings	8	3	3	6	2	....	....	....	....	....
	NHL Totals	**38**	**5**	**8**	**13**	**32**	....	....	....	....	....

Signed as a free agent by **St. Louis**, September 22, 1986. Claimed by **Ottawa** from **St. Louis** in Expansion Draft, June 18, 1992. Claimed on waivers by **Boston** from **Ottawa**, November 20, 1992. Signed as a free agent by **Los Angeles**, July 16, 1993.

LAW, Kirby

Right wing. Shoots right. 6'1", 185 lbs. Born, McCreary, Man., March 11, 1977.

Season	Club	GP	G	A	Pts	PIM	GP	G	A	Pts	PIM
2000-01	Philadelphia Flyers	1	0	0	0	0	....	....	....	....	....

		REGULAR SEASON					PLAYOFFS				
Season	Club	GP	G	A	Pts	PIM	GP	G	A	Pts	PIM
2002-03	Philadelphia Flyers	2	0	0	0	2	....	....	....	....	....
	NHL Totals	**3**	**0**	**0**	**0**	**2**	....	....	....	....	....

Signed as a free agent by **Atlanta**, July 27, 1999. Traded to **Philadelphia** by **Atlanta** for Vancouver's 6th round choice (previously acquired, Atlanta selected Jeff Dwyer) in 2000 Entry Draft and Philadelphia's 6th round choice (Pasi Nurminen) in 2001 Entry Draft, March 14, 2000.

LAWLESS, Paul

Left wing. Shoots left. 5'11", 185 lbs. Born, Scarborough, Ont., July 2, 1964.
(Hartford's 1st choice, 14th overall, in 1982 Entry Draft).

Season	Club	GP	G	A	Pts	PIM	GP	G	A	Pts	PIM
1982-83	Hartford Whalers	47	6	9	15	4	....	....	....	....	....
1983-84	Hartford Whalers	6	0	3	3	0	....	....	....	....	....
1985-86	Hartford Whalers	64	17	21	38	20	1	0	0	0	0
1986-87	Hartford Whalers	60	22	32	54	14	2	0	2	2	2
1987-88	Hartford Whalers	28	4	5	9	16	....	....	....	....	....
	Philadelphia Flyers	8	0	5	5	0	....	....	....	....	....
	Vancouver Canucks	13	0	1	1	0	....	....	....	....	....
1988-89	Toronto Maple Leafs	7	0	0	0	0	....	....	....	....	....
1989-90	Toronto Maple Leafs	6	0	1	1	0	....	....	....	....	....
	NHL Totals	**239**	**49**	**77**	**126**	**54**	**3**	**0**	**2**	**2**	**2**

Traded to **Philadelphia** by **Hartford** for Lindsay Carson, January 22, 1988. Traded to **Vancouver** by **Philadelphia** with Vancouver's 5th round choice (previously acquired, later traded to Edmonton – Edmonton selected Peter White) in 1989 Entry Draft for Willie Huber, March 1, 1988. Traded to **Toronto** by **Vancouver** for the rights to Peter Deboer, February 27, 1989.

LAWRENCE, Mark

Right wing. Shoots right. 6'4", 215 lbs. Born, Burlington, Ont., January 27, 1972.
(Minnesota's 4th choice, 118th overall, in 1991 Entry Draft).

Season	Club	GP	G	A	Pts	PIM	GP	G	A	Pts	PIM
1994-95	Dallas Stars	2	0	0	0	0	....	....	....	....	....
1995-96	Dallas Stars	13	0	1	1	17	....	....	....	....	....
1997-98	New York Islanders	2	0	0	0	2	....	....	....	....	....
1998-99	New York Islanders	60	14	16	30	38	....	....	....	....	....
99-2000	New York Islanders	29	1	5	6	26	....	....	....	....	....
2000-01	New York Islanders	36	3	4	7	32	....	....	....	....	....
	NHL Totals	**142**	**18**	**26**	**44**	**115**	....	....	....	....	....

Rights transferred to **Dallas** after **Minnesota** franchise relocated, June 9, 1993. Signed as a free agent by **NY Islanders**, August 25, 1997.

LAWSON, Danny

Right wing. Shoots right. 5'11", 180 lbs. Born, Toronto, Ont., October 30, 1947.

Season	Club	GP	G	A	Pts	PIM	GP	G	A	Pts	PIM
1967-68	Detroit Red Wings	1	0	0	0	0					
1968-69	Detroit Red Wings	44	5	7	12	21	....	....	....	....	....
	Minnesota North Stars	18	3	3	6	4	....	....	....	....	....
1969-70	Minnesota North Stars	45	9	8	17	19	6	0	1	1	2
1970-71	Minnesota North Stars	33	1	5	6	2	10	0	0	0	0
1971-72	Buffalo Sabres	78	10	6	16	15	....	....	....	....	....
	NHL Totals	**219**	**28**	**29**	**57**	**61**	**16**	**0**	**1**	**1**	**2**

Traded to **Minnesota** by **Detroit** with the rights to Brian Conacher for Wayne Connelly, February 15, 1969. Claimed by **Buffalo** from **Minnesota** in Intra-League Draft, June 8, 1971.

LAWTON, Brian

Left wing. Shoots left. 6', 180 lbs. Born, New Brunswick, NJ, June 29, 1965.
(Minnesota's 1st choice, 1st overall, in 1983 Entry Draft).

Season	Club	GP	G	A	Pts	PIM	GP	G	A	Pts	PIM
1983-84	Minnesota North Stars	58	10	21	31	33	5	0	0	0	10
1984-85	Minnesota North Stars	40	5	6	11	24	....	....	....	....	....
1985-86	Minnesota North Stars	65	18	17	35	36	3	0	1	1	2
1986-87	Minnesota North Stars	66	21	23	44	86	....	....	....	....	....
1987-88	Minnesota North Stars	74	17	24	41	71	....	....	....	....	....
1988-89	New York Rangers	30	7	10	17	39	....	....	....	....	....
	Hartford Whalers	35	10	16	26	28	3	1	0	1	0
1989-90	Hartford Whalers	13	2	1	3	6	....	....	....	....	....
	Quebec Nordiques	14	5	6	11	10	....	....	....	....	....
	Boston Bruins	8	0	0	0	14	....	....	....	....	....
1991-92	San Jose Sharks	59	15	22	37	42	....	....	....	....	....
1992-93	San Jose Sharks	21	2	8	10	12	....	....	....	....	....
	NHL Totals	**483**	**112**	**154**	**266**	**401**	**11**	**1**	**1**	**2**	**12**

Traded to **NY Rangers** by **Minnesota** with Igor Liba and the rights to Rick Bennett for Paul Jerrard, Mark Tinordi, the rights to Bret Barnett and Mike Sullivan and Los Angeles' 3rd round choice (previously acquired, Minnesota selected Murray Garbutt) in 1989 Entry Draft, October 11, 1988. Traded to **Hartford** by **NY Rangers** with Norm MacIver and Don Maloney for Carey Wilson and Hartford's 5th round choice (Lubos Rob) in 1990 Entry Draft, December 26, 1988. Claimed on waivers by **Quebec** from **Hartford**, December 1, 1989. Signed as a free agent by **Boston**, February 7, 1990. Signed as a free agent by **Los Angeles**, July 27, 1990. Signed as a free agent by **San Jose**, August 9, 1991. Traded to **New Jersey** by **San Jose** for future considerations, January 22, 1993.

LAXDAL, Derek

Right wing. Shoots right. 6'1", 175 lbs. Born, St. Boniface, Man., February 21, 1966.
(Toronto's 7th choice, 151st overall, in 1984 Entry Draft).

Season	Club	GP	G	A	Pts	PIM	GP	G	A	Pts	PIM
1984-85	Toronto Maple Leafs	3	0	0	0	6	....	....	....	....	....
1986-87	Toronto Maple Leafs	2	0	0	0	7	....	....	....	....	....
1987-88	Toronto Maple Leafs	5	0	0	0	6	....	....	....	....	....
1988-89	Toronto Maple Leafs	41	9	6	15	65	....	....	....	....	....
1989-90	New York Islanders	12	3	1	4	4	1	0	2	2	2
1990-91	New York Islanders	4	0	0	0	0	....	....	....	....	....
	NHL Totals	**67**	**12**	**7**	**19**	**88**	**1**	**0**	**2**	**2**	**2**

Traded to **NY Islanders** by **Toronto** with Jack Capuano and Paul Gagne for Mike Stevens and Gilles Thibaudeau, December 20, 1989.

LAYCOE, Hal

Defense. Shoots left. 6'2", 185 lbs. Born, Sutherland, Sask., June 23, 1922.

Season	Club	GP	G	A	Pts	PIM	GP	G	A	Pts	PIM
1945-46	New York Rangers	17	0	2	2	6	....	....	....	....	....
1946-47	New York Rangers	58	1	12	13	25	....	....	....	....	....
1947-48	Montreal Canadiens	14	1	2	3	4	....	....	....	....	....
1948-49	Montreal Canadiens	51	3	5	8	31	7	0	1	1	13
1949-50	Montreal Canadiens	30	0	2	2	21	2	0	0	0	0
1950-51	Montreal Canadiens	38	0	2	2	25	....	....	....	....	....
	Boston Bruins	6	1	1	2	4	6	0	1	1	5
1951-52	Boston Bruins	70	5	7	12	61	7	1	1	2	11
1952-53	Boston Bruins	54	2	10	12	36	11	0	2	2	10
1953-54	Boston Bruins	58	3	16	19	29	2	0	0	0	0
1954-55	Boston Bruins	70	4	13	17	34	5	1	0	1	0
1955-56	Boston Bruins	65	5	5	10	16	....	....	....	....	....
	NHL Totals	**531**	**25**	**77**	**102**	**292**	**40**	**2**	**5**	**7**	**39**

Traded to **Montreal** by **NY Rangers** with Joe Bell and George Robertson for Buddy O'Connor and Frank Eddolls, August 19, 1947. Traded to **Boston** by **Montreal** for Ross Lowe, February 14, 1951.

LAZARO, Jeff

Left wing. Shoots left. 5'10", 180 lbs. Born, Waltham, MA, March 21, 1968.

Season	Club	GP	G	A	Pts	PIM	GP	G	A	Pts	PIM
1990-91	Boston Bruins	49	5	13	18	67	19	3	2	5	30
1991-92	Boston Bruins	27	3	6	9	31	9	0	1	1	2
1992-93	Ottawa Senators	26	6	4	10	16	....	....	....	....	....
	NHL Totals	**102**	**14**	**23**	**37**	**114**	**28**	**3**	**3**	**6**	**32**

Signed as a free agent by **Boston**, September 26, 1990. Claimed by **Ottawa** from **Boston** in Expansion Draft, June 18, 1992.

LEACH, Jamie

Right wing. Shoots right. 6'1", 205 lbs. Born, Winnipeg, Man., August 25, 1969.
(Pittsburgh's 3rd choice, 47th overall, in 1987 Entry Draft).

Season	Club	GP	G	A	Pts	PIM	GP	G	A	Pts	PIM
1989-90	Pittsburgh Penguins	10	0	3	3	0	....	....	....	....	....
1990-91	Pittsburgh Penguins	7	2	0	2	0	....	....	....	....	....
1991-92 ◆	Pittsburgh Penguins	38	5	4	9	8	....	....	....	....	....
1992-93	Pittsburgh Penguins	5	0	0	0	2	....	....	....	....	....
	Hartford Whalers	19	3	2	5	2	....	....	....	....	....
1993-94	Florida Panthers	2	1	0	1	0	....	....	....	....	....
	NHL Totals	**81**	**11**	**9**	**20**	**12**	....	....	....	....	....

• Son of Reggie

Claimed on waivers by **Hartford** from **Pittsburgh**, November 21, 1992. Signed as a free agent by **Florida**, August 31, 1993.

LEACH, Larry

Center. Shoots left. 6'2", 175 lbs. Born, Lloydminster, Sask., June 18, 1936.

Season	Club	GP	G	A	Pts	PIM	GP	G	A	Pts	PIM
1958-59	Boston Bruins	29	4	12	16	26	7	1	1	2	8
1959-60	Boston Bruins	69	7	12	19	47	....	....	....	....	....
1961-62	Boston Bruins	28	2	5	7	18	....	....	....	....	....
	NHL Totals	**126**	**13**	**29**	**42**	**91**	**7**	**1**	**1**	**2**	**8**

Traded to **Portland** (WHL) by **Boston** for cash, May 1964. Claimed by **Chicago** from **Portland** (WHL) in Inter-League Draft, June, 1968. Traded to **Portland** (WHL) by **Chicago** for cash, October, 1968.

LEACH, Reggie

Right wing. Shoots right. 6', 180 lbs. Born, Riverton, Man., April 23, 1950.
(Boston's 1st choice, 3rd overall, in 1970 Amateur Draft).

Season	Club	GP	G	A	Pts	PIM	GP	G	A	Pts	PIM
1970-71	Boston Bruins	23	2	4	6	0	3	0	0	0	0
1971-72	Boston Bruins	56	7	13	20	12	....	....	....	....	....
	California Golden Seals	17	6	7	13	7	....	....	....	....	....
1972-73	California Golden Seals	76	23	12	35	45	....	....	....	....	....
1973-74	California Golden Seals	78	22	24	46	34	....	....	....	....	....
1974-75 ◆	Philadelphia Flyers	80	45	33	78	63	17	8	2	10	6
1975-76	Philadelphia Flyers	80	*61	30	91	41	16	*19	5	*24	8
1976-77	Philadelphia Flyers	77	32	14	46	23	10	4	5	9	0
1977-78	Philadelphia Flyers	72	24	28	52	24	12	2	2	4	0
1978-79	Philadelphia Flyers	76	34	20	54	20	8	5	1	6	0
1979-80	Philadelphia Flyers	76	50	26	76	28	19	9	7	16	6
1980-81	Philadelphia Flyers	79	34	36	70	59	9	0	0	0	2
1981-82	Philadelphia Flyers	66	26	21	47	18	....	....	....	....	....
1982-83	Detroit Red Wings	78	15	17	32	13	....	....	....	....	....
	NHL Totals	**934**	**381**	**285**	**666**	**387**	**94**	**47**	**22**	**69**	**22**

• Father of Jamie • NHL Second All-Star Team (1976) • Conn Smythe Trophy (1976)
Played in NHL All-Star Game (1976, 1980)

Traded to **California** by **Boston** with Rick Smith and Bob Stewart for Carol Vadnais and Don O'Donoghue, February 23, 1972. Traded to **Philadelphia** by **California** for Larry Wright, Al MacAdam and Philadelphia's 1st round choice (Ron Chipperfield) in 1974 Amateur Draft, May 24, 1974. Signed as a free agent by **Detroit**, August 25, 1982.

LEACH, Stephen

Right wing. Shoots right. 5'11", 197 lbs. Born, Cambridge, MA, January 16, 1966.
(Washington's 2nd choice, 34th overall, in 1984 Entry Draft).

Season	Club	GP	G	A	Pts	PIM	GP	G	A	Pts	PIM
1985-86	Washington Capitals	11	1	1	2	2	6	0	1	1	0
1986-87	Washington Capitals	15	1	0	1	6	....	....	....	....	....
1987-88	Washington Capitals	8	1	1	2	17	9	2	1	3	0
1988-89	Washington Capitals	74	11	19	30	94	6	1	0	1	12
1989-90	Washington Capitals	70	18	14	32	104	14	2	2	4	8

Season	Club	Regular Season GP	G	A	Pts	PIM	Playoffs GP	G	A	Pts	PIM
1990-91	Washington Capitals	68	11	19	30	99	9	1	2	3	8
1991-92	Boston Bruins	78	31	29	60	147	15	4	0	4	10
1992-93	Boston Bruins	79	26	25	51	126	4	1	1	2	2
1993-94	Boston Bruins	42	5	10	15	74	5	0	1	1	2
1994-95	Boston Bruins	35	5	6	11	68	....	....	....	....	....
1995-96	Boston Bruins	59	9	13	22	86	....	....	....	....	....
	St. Louis Blues	14	2	4	6	22	11	3	2	5	10
1996-97	St. Louis Blues	17	2	1	3	24	6	0	0	0	33
1997-98	Carolina Hurricanes	45	4	5	9	42	....	....	....	....	....
1998-99	Ottawa Senators	9	0	2	2	6	....	....	....	....	....
	Phoenix Coyotes	22	1	1	2	37	7	1	1	2	2
99-2000	Pittsburgh Penguins	56	2	3	5	24	....	....	....	....	....
	NHL Totals	**702**	**130**	**153**	**283**	**978**	**92**	**15**	**11**	**26**	**87**

Traded to **Boston** by **Washington** for Randy Burridge, June 21, 1991. Traded to **St. Louis** by **Boston** for Kevin Sawyer and Steve Staios, March 8, 1996. Traded to **Carolina** by **St. Louis** for Alexander Godynyuk and Carolina's 6th round choice (Brad Voth) in 1998 Entry Draft, June 27, 1997. Signed as a free agent by **Ottawa**, October 4, 1998. Signed as a free agent by **Phoenix**, December 3, 1998. Signed as a free agent by **Pittsburgh**, October 19, 1999.

LEAVINS, Jim

Defense. Shoots left. 5'11", 185 lbs. Born, Dinsmore, Sask., July 28, 1960.

Season	Club	GP	G	A	Pts	PIM	GP	G	A	Pts	PIM
1985-86	Detroit Red Wings	37	2	11	13	26	....	....	....	....	....
1986-87	New York Rangers	4	0	1	1	4	....	....	....	....	....
	NHL Totals	**41**	**2**	**12**	**14**	**30**	....	....	....	....	....

Signed as a free agent by **Detroit**, November 9, 1985. Traded to **NY Rangers** by **Detroit** with Kelly Kisio, Lane Lambert and Detroit's 5th round choice (later traded to Winnipeg – Winnipeg selected Benoit Lebeau) in 1988 Entry Draft for Glen Hanlon and NY Rangers' 3rd round choices in 1987 (Dennis Holland) and 1988 (Guy Dupuis) Entry Drafts, July 29, 1986. Traded to **Calgary** by **NY Rangers** for Don Mercier, November 6, 1987.

LEBEAU, Patrick

Left wing. Shoots left. 5'10", 172 lbs. Born, St-Jerome, Que., March 17, 1970.
(Montreal's 8th choice, 167th overall, in 1989 Entry Draft).

Season	Club	GP	G	A	Pts	PIM	GP	G	A	Pts	PIM
1990-91	Montreal Canadiens	2	1	1	2	0	....	....	....	....	....
1992-93	Calgary Flames	1	0	0	0	0	....	....	....	....	....
1993-94	Florida Panthers	4	1	1	2	4	....	....	....	....	....
1998-99	Pittsburgh Penguins	8	1	0	1	2	....	....	....	....	....
	NHL Totals	**15**	**3**	**2**	**5**	**6**	....	....	....	....	....

• Brother of Stephan

Traded to **Calgary** by **Montreal** for future considerations, September 27, 1986. Signed as a free agent by **Florida**, July 26, 1993. Signed as a free agent by **Pittsburgh**, October 18, 1998.

LEBEAU, Stephan

Center. Shoots right. 5'10", 173 lbs. Born, St-Jerome, Que., February 28, 1968.

Season	Club	GP	G	A	Pts	PIM	GP	G	A	Pts	PIM
1988-89	Montreal Canadiens	1	0	1	1	2	....	....	....	....	....
1989-90	Montreal Canadiens	57	15	20	35	11	2	3	0	3	0
1990-91	Montreal Canadiens	73	22	31	53	24	7	2	1	3	2
1991-92	Montreal Canadiens	77	27	31	58	14	8	1	3	4	4
1992-93 ◆	Montreal Canadiens	71	31	49	80	20	13	3	3	6	6
1993-94	Montreal Canadiens	34	9	7	16	8	....	....	....	....	....
	Mighty Ducks of Anaheim	22	6	4	10	14	....	....	....	....	....
1994-95	Mighty Ducks of Anaheim	38	8	16	24	12	....	....	....	....	....
	NHL Totals	**373**	**118**	**159**	**277**	**105**	**30**	**9**	**7**	**16**	**12**

• Brother of Patrick

Signed as a free agent by **Montreal**, September 27, 1986. Traded to **Anaheim** by **Montreal** for Ron Tugnutt, February 20, 1994.

LeBLANC, Fern

Center. Shoots left. 5'9", 170 lbs. Born, Gaspesie, Que., January 12, 1956.
(Detroit's 7th choice, 111th overall, in 1976 Amateur Draft).

Season	Club	GP	G	A	Pts	PIM	GP	G	A	Pts	PIM
1976-77	Detroit Red Wings	3	0	0	0	0	....	....	....	....	....
1977-78	Detroit Red Wings	2	0	0	0	0	....	....	....	....	....
1978-79	Detroit Red Wings	29	5	6	11	0	....	....	....	....	....
	NHL Totals	**34**	**5**	**6**	**11**	**0**	....	....	....	....	....

LeBLANC, J.P.

Center. Shoots left. 5'10", 170 lbs. Born, South Durham, Que., October 20, 1946.

Season	Club	GP	G	A	Pts	PIM	GP	G	A	Pts	PIM
1968-69	Chicago Black Hawks	6	1	2	3	0	....	....	....	....	....
1975-76	Detroit Red Wings	46	4	9	13	39	....	....	....	....	....
1976-77	Detroit Red Wings	74	7	11	18	40	....	....	....	....	....
1977-78	Detroit Red Wings	3	0	2	2	4	2	0	0	0	0
1978-79	Detroit Red Wings	24	2	6	8	4	....	....	....	....	....
	NHL Totals	**153**	**14**	**30**	**44**	**87**	**2**	**0**	**0**	**0**	**0**

Traded to **Detroit** by **Chicago** for Detroit's 2nd round choice (Jean Savard) in 1977 Amateur Draft, November 20, 1975.

LeBLANC, John

Right wing. Shoots left. 6'1", 190 lbs. Born, Campbellton, N.B., January 21, 1964.

Season	Club	GP	G	A	Pts	PIM	GP	G	A	Pts	PIM
1986-87	Vancouver Canucks	2	1	0	1	0	....	....	....	....	....
1987-88	Vancouver Canucks	41	12	10	22	18	....	....	....	....	....
1988-89	Edmonton Oilers	2	1	0	1	0	1	0	0	0	0
1991-92	Winnipeg Jets	16	6	1	7	6	....	....	....	....	....
1992-93	Winnipeg Jets	3	0	0	0	2	....	....	....	....	....
1993-94	Winnipeg Jets	17	6	2	8	2	....	....	....	....	....
1994-95	Winnipeg Jets	2	0	0	0	0	....	....	....	....	....
	NHL Totals	**83**	**26**	**13**	**39**	**28**	**1**	**0**	**0**	**0**	**0**

Signed as a free agent by **Vancouver**, April 12, 1986. Traded to **Edmonton** by **Vancouver** with Vancouver's 5th round choice (Peter White) in 1989 Entry Draft for Doug Smith and Greg Adams, March 7, 1989. • Sat out entire 1990-91 season after failing to come to contract terms with Edmonton. Traded to **Winnipeg** by **Edmonton** with Edmonton's 10th round choice (Teemu Numminen) in 1992 Entry Draft for Winnipeg's 5th round choice (Ryan Haggerty) in 1991 Entry Draft, June 12, 1991.

LeBOUTILLIER, Peter

Right wing. Shoots right. 6'1", 190 lbs. Born, Minnedosa, Man., January 11, 1975.
(Anaheim's 5th choice, 133rd overall, in 1995 Entry Draft).

Season	Club	GP	G	A	Pts	PIM	GP	G	A	Pts	PIM
1996-97	Mighty Ducks of Anaheim	23	1	0	1	121	....	....	....	....	....
1997-98	Mighty Ducks of Anaheim	12	1	1	2	55	....	....	....	....	....
	NHL Totals	**35**	**2**	**1**	**3**	**176**	....	....	....	....	....

• Re-entered NHL Entry Draft. Originally NY Islanders' 6th choice, 144th overall, in 1993 Entry Draft.

Signed as a free agent by **Los Angeles**, August 11, 2000.

LeBRUN, Al

Defense. Shoots right. 6', 185 lbs. Born, Timmins, Ont., December 1, 1940.

Season	Club	GP	G	A	Pts	PIM	GP	G	A	Pts	PIM
1960-61	New York Rangers	4	0	2	2	4	....	....	....	....	....
1965-66	New York Rangers	2	0	0	0	0	....	....	....	....	....
	NHL Totals	**6**	**0**	**2**	**2**	**4**	....	....	....	....	....

Claimed by **Detroit** from **NY Rangers** in Intra-League Draft, June 15, 1966. Loaned to **Chicago** (LA Blades-WHL) by **Detroit** with Murray Hall for remainder of 1966-67 season and future considerations (Murray Hall, Al Lebrun and Rick Morris, June, 1967) for Howie Young, December 20, 1966. Traded to **Chicago** by **Detroit** with Murray Hall and Rick Morris to complete transaction that sent Howie Yound to Detroit (December 20, 1966), June, 1967. Claimed by **San Diego** (WHL) from **Chicago** in Reverse Draft, June 13, 1968.

LECAINE, Bill

Left wing. Shoots right. 6', 172 lbs. Born, Moose Jaw, Sask., March 11, 1940.

Season	Club	GP	G	A	Pts	PIM	GP	G	A	Pts	PIM
1968-69	Pittsburgh Penguins	4	0	0	0	0	....	....	....	....	....
	NHL Totals	**4**	**0**	**0**	**0**	**0**	....	....	....	....	....

Signed as a free agent by **Pittsburgh**, August, 1967.

LECAVALIER, Vincent

Center. Shoots left. 6'4", 205 lbs. Born, Ile Bizard, Que., April 21, 1980.
(Tampa Bay's 1st choice, 1st overall, in 1998 Entry Draft).

Season	Club	GP	G	A	Pts	PIM	GP	G	A	Pts	PIM
1998-99	Tampa Bay Lightning	82	13	15	28	23	....	....	....	....	....
99-2000	Tampa Bay Lightning	80	25	42	67	43	....	....	....	....	....
2000-01	Tampa Bay Lightning	68	23	28	51	66	....	....	....	....	....
2001-02	Tampa Bay Lightning	76	20	17	37	61	....	....	....	....	....
2002-03	Tampa Bay Lightning	80	33	45	78	39	11	3	3	6	22
	NHL Totals	**386**	**114**	**147**	**261**	**232**	**11**	**3**	**3**	**6**	**22**

Played in NHL All-Star Game (2003)

LECLAIR, Jack

Center. Shoots left. 5'10", 150 lbs. Born, Quebec City, Que., May 30, 1929.

Season	Club	GP	G	A	Pts	PIM	GP	G	A	Pts	PIM
1954-55	Montreal Canadiens	59	11	22	33	12	12	5	0	5	2
1955-56 ◆	Montreal Canadiens	54	6	8	14	30	8	1	1	2	4
1956-57 ◆	Montreal Canadiens	47	3	10	13	14	....	....	....	....	....
	NHL Totals	**160**	**20**	**40**	**60**	**56**	**20**	**6**	**1**	**7**	**6**

Played in NHL All-Star Game (1956)

Traded to **Ottawa** (QHL) by **Toronto** for cash, October, 1952. Claimed by **Toronto** from **Ottawa** (QHL) in Inter-League Draft, June 10, 1953. Traded to **Chicago** (Buffalo-AHL) by **Toronto** with Dusty Blair and Frank Sullivan for Brian Cullen, May 4, 1954. Traded to **Montreal** by **Buffalo** (AHL) with cash for Gaye Stewart, Eddie Slowinski and Pete Babando, August 17, 1954. Traded to **Chicoutimi** (QHL) by **Montreal** with Guy Rousseau and Jacques Deslauriers for Stan Smrke, October 27, 1957.

LeCLAIR, John

Left wing. Shoots left. 6'3", 226 lbs. Born, St. Albans, VT, July 5, 1969.
(Montreal's 2nd choice, 33rd overall, in 1987 Entry Draft).

Season	Club	GP	G	A	Pts	PIM	GP	G	A	Pts	PIM
1990-91	Montreal Canadiens	10	2	5	7	2	3	0	0	0	0
1991-92	Montreal Canadiens	59	8	11	19	14	8	1	1	2	4
1992-93 ◆	Montreal Canadiens	72	19	25	44	33	20	4	6	10	14
1993-94	Montreal Canadiens	74	19	24	43	32	7	2	1	3	8
1994-95	Montreal Canadiens	9	1	4	5	10	....	....	....	....	....
	Philadelphia Flyers	37	25	24	49	20	15	5	7	12	4
1995-96	Philadelphia Flyers	82	51	46	97	64	11	6	5	11	6
1996-97	Philadelphia Flyers	82	50	47	97	58	19	9	12	21	10
1997-98	Philadelphia Flyers	82	51	36	87	32	5	1	1	2	8
1998-99	Philadelphia Flyers	76	43	47	90	30	6	3	0	3	12
99-2000	Philadelphia Flyers	82	40	37	77	36	18	6	7	13	6
2000-01	Philadelphia Flyers	16	7	5	12	0	6	1	2	3	2
2001-02	Philadelphia Flyers	82	25	26	51	30	5	0	0	0	2

Season	Club	GP	G	A	Pts	PIM	GP	G	A	Pts	PIM
		REGULAR SEASON					PLAYOFFS				
2002-03	Philadelphia Flyers	35	18	10	28	16	13	2	3	5	10
	NHL Totals	**798**	**359**	**347**	**706**	**377**	**136**	**40**	**45**	**85**	**86**

NHL First All-Star Team (1995, 1998) • NHL Second All-Star Team (1996, 1997, 1999) • Bud Light Plus/Minus Award (1997) • Bud Ice Plus/Minus Award (1999)

Played in NHL All-Star Game (1996, 1997, 1998, 1999, 2000)

Traded to **Philadelphia** by **Montreal** with Eric Desjardins and Gilbert Dionne for Mark Recchi and Philadelphia's 3rd round choice (Martin Hohenberger) in 1995 Entry Draft, February 9, 1995. • Missed majority of 2000-01 season recovering from back injury suffered in game vs. Boston, October 7, 2000.

LECLERC, Mike

Left wing. Shoots left. 6'2", 208 lbs. Born, Winnipeg, Man., November 10, 1976. (Anaheim's 3rd choice, 55th overall, in 1995 Entry Draft).

Season	Club	GP	G	A	Pts	PIM	GP	G	A	Pts	PIM
1996-97	Mighty Ducks of Anaheim	5	1	1	2	0	1	0	0	0	0
1997-98	Mighty Ducks of Anaheim	7	0	0	0	6	....	....	....	....	....
1998-99	Mighty Ducks of Anaheim	7	0	0	0	4	1	0	0	0	0
99-2000	Mighty Ducks of Anaheim	69	8	11	19	70	....	....	....	....	....
2000-01	Mighty Ducks of Anaheim	54	15	20	35	26	....	....	....	....	....
2001-02	Mighty Ducks of Anaheim	82	20	24	44	107	....	....	....	....	....
2002-03	Mighty Ducks of Anaheim	57	9	19	28	34	21	2	9	11	12
	NHL Totals	**281**	**53**	**75**	**128**	**247**	**23**	**2**	**9**	**11**	**12**

LECLERC, Rene

Right wing. Shoots right. 5'11", 165 lbs. Born, Vanier, Que., November 12, 1947. (Detroit's 4th choice, 19th overall, in 1964 Amateur Draft).

Season	Club	GP	G	A	Pts	PIM	GP	G	A	Pts	PIM
1968-69	Detroit Red Wings	43	2	3	5	62	....	....	....	....	....
1970-71	Detroit Red Wings	44	8	8	16	43	....	....	....	....	....
	NHL Totals	**87**	**10**	**11**	**21**	**105**	....	....	....	....	....

LECUYER, Doug

Left wing. Shoots left. 5'9", 180 lbs. Born, Wainwright, Alta., March 10, 1958. (Chicago's 2nd choice, 29th overall, in 1978 Amateur Draft).

Season	Club	GP	G	A	Pts	PIM	GP	G	A	Pts	PIM
1978-79	Chicago Black Hawks	2	1	0	1	0	....	....	....	....	....
1979-80	Chicago Black Hawks	53	3	10	13	59	7	4	0	4	15
1980-81	Chicago Black Hawks	14	0	0	0	41	....	....	....	....	....
	Winnipeg Jets	45	6	17	23	66	....	....	....	....	....
1982-83	Pittsburgh Penguins	12	1	4	5	12	....	....	....	....	....
	NHL Totals	**126**	**11**	**31**	**42**	**178**	**7**	**4**	**0**	**4**	**15**

Traded to **Winnipeg** by **Chicago** with Tim Trimper for Peter Marsh, December 1, 1980. Claimed by **Pittsburgh** from **Winnipeg** in Waiver Draft, October 4, 1982.

LEDINGHAM, Walt

Left wing. Shoots left. 5'11", 180 lbs. Born, Weyburn, Sask., October 26, 1950. (Chicago's 4th choice, 56th overall, in 1970 Amateur Draft).

Season	Club	GP	G	A	Pts	PIM	GP	G	A	Pts	PIM
1972-73	Chicago Black Hawks	9	0	1	1	4	....	....	....	....	....
1974-75	New York Islanders	2	0	1	1	0	....	....	....	....	....
1976-77	New York Islanders	4	0	0	0	0	....	....	....	....	....
	NHL Totals	**15**	**0**	**2**	**2**	**4**	....	....	....	....	....

Traded to **NY Islanders** by **Chicago** to complete transaction that sent Germain Gagnon to Chicago (March 7, 1974), May 24, 1974.

LEDUC, Albert

Defense. Shoots right. 5'9", 180 lbs. Born, Valleyfield, Que., November 22, 1902.

Season	Club	GP	G	A	Pts	PIM	GP	G	A	Pts	PIM
1925-26	Montreal Canadiens	32	10	3	13	62	....	....	....	....	....
1926-27	Montreal Canadiens	43	5	2	7	62	4	0	0	0	2
1927-28	Montreal Canadiens	42	8	5	13	73	2	1	0	1	5
1928-29	Montreal Canadiens	43	9	2	11	79	3	1	0	1	4
1929-30♦	Montreal Canadiens	44	6	8	14	90	6	1	3	4	8
1930-31♦	Montreal Canadiens	44	8	6	14	82	7	0	2	2	9
1931-32	Montreal Canadiens	41	5	3	8	60	4	1	1	2	2
1932-33	Montreal Canadiens	48	5	3	8	62	2	1	0	1	2
1933-34	Ottawa Senators	32	1	3	4	34	....	....	....	....	....
	New York Rangers	10	0	0	0	6	....	....	....	....	....
1934-35	Montreal Canadiens	4	0	0	0	4	....	....	....	....	....
	NHL Totals	**383**	**57**	**35**	**92**	**614**	**28**	**5**	**6**	**11**	**32**

Signed as a free agent by **Montreal**, April 16, 1925. Traded to **Ottawa** by **Montreal** for cash with Montreal retaining the right of repurchase, October 22, 1933. Loaned to **NY Rangers** by **Ottawa** for remainder of 1933-34 season, February 15, 1934. Traded to **Montreal** by **Ottawa** for cash, April 9, 1934.

LEDUC, Rich

Center. Shoots left. 5'11", 170 lbs. Born, Ile Perrot, Que., August 24, 1951. (California's 2nd choice, 29th overall, in 1971 Amateur Draft).

Season	Club	GP	G	A	Pts	PIM	GP	G	A	Pts	PIM
1972-73	Boston Bruins	5	1	1	2	2	....	....	....	....	....
1973-74	Boston Bruins	28	3	3	6	12	5	0	0	0	9
1979-80	Quebec Nordiques	75	21	27	48	49	....	....	....	....	....
1980-81	Quebec Nordiques	22	3	7	10	6	....	....	....	....	....
	NHL Totals	**130**	**28**	**38**	**66**	**69**	**5**	**0**	**0**	**0**	**9**

Traded to **Boston** by **California** with Chris Oddleifson for Ivan Boldirev, November 17, 1971. Rights retained by **Quebec** prior to Expansion Draft, June 9, 1979. Signed as a free agent by **Minnesota**, February, 1981.

LEDYARD, Grant

Defense. Shoots left. 6'2", 195 lbs. Born, Winnipeg, Man., November 19, 1961.

Season	Club	GP	G	A	Pts	PIM	GP	G	A	Pts	PIM
		REGULAR SEASON					PLAYOFFS				
1984-85	New York Rangers	42	8	12	20	53	3	0	2	2	4
1985-86	New York Rangers	27	2	9	11	20	....	....	....	....	....
	Los Angeles Kings	52	7	18	25	78	....	....	....	....	....
1986-87	Los Angeles Kings	67	14	23	37	93	5	0	0	0	10
1987-88	Los Angeles Kings	23	1	7	8	52	....	....	....	....	....
	Washington Capitals	21	4	3	7	14	14	1	0	1	30
1988-89	Washington Capitals	61	3	11	14	43	....	....	....	....	....
	Buffalo Sabres	13	1	5	6	8	5	1	2	3	2
1989-90	Buffalo Sabres	67	2	13	15	37	....	....	....	....	....
1990-91	Buffalo Sabres	60	8	23	31	46	6	3	3	6	10
1991-92	Buffalo Sabres	50	5	16	21	45	....	....	....	....	....
1992-93	Buffalo Sabres	50	2	14	16	45	8	0	0	0	8
1993-94	Dallas Stars	84	9	37	46	42	9	1	2	3	6
1994-95	Dallas Stars	38	5	13	18	20	3	0	0	0	2
1995-96	Dallas Stars	73	5	19	24	20	....	....	....	....	....
1996-97	Dallas Stars	67	1	15	16	61	7	0	2	2	0
1997-98	Vancouver Canucks	49	2	13	15	14	....	....	....	....	....
	Boston Bruins	22	2	7	9	6	6	0	0	0	2
1998-99	Boston Bruins	47	4	8	12	33	2	0	0	0	2
99-2000	Ottawa Senators	40	2	4	6	8	6	0	0	0	16
2000-01	Tampa Bay Lightning	14	2	2	4	12	....	....	....	....	....
	Dallas Stars	8	0	1	1	4	9	0	1	1	4
2001-02	Tampa Bay Lightning	53	1	3	4	12	....	....	....	....	....
	NHL Totals	**1028**	**90**	**276**	**366**	**766**	**83**	**6**	**12**	**18**	**96**

Signed as a free agent by **NY Rangers**, July 7, 1982. Traded to **Los Angeles** by **NY Rangers** with Roland Melanson for Los Angeles' 4th round choice (Mike Sullivan) in 1987 Entry Draft and Brian MacLellan, December 9, 1985. Traded to **Washington** by **Los Angeles** for Craig Laughlin, February 9, 1988. Traded to **Buffalo** by **Washington** with Clint Malarchuk and Washington's 6th round choice (Brian Holzinger) in 1991 Entry Draft for Calle Johansson and Buffalo's 2nd round choice (Byron Dafoe) in 1989 Entry Draft, March 7, 1989. Signed as a free agent by **Dallas**, August 12, 1993. Signed as a free agent by **Vancouver**, July 17, 1997. Traded to **Boston** by **Vancouver** for Boston's 8th round choice (Curtis Valentine) in 1998 Entry Draft, March 3, 1998. Signed as a free agent by **Ottawa**, November 16, 1999. Signed as a free agent by **Tampa Bay**, January 31, 2001. Traded to **Dallas** by **Tampa Bay** for Dallas' 7th round choice (Jeremy Van Hoof) in 2001 Entry Draft, March 13, 2001. Signed as a free agent by **Tampa Bay**, July 13, 2001.

LEE, Bobby

Center. Shoots left. 5'10", 165 lbs. Born, Verdun, Que., December 28, 1911.

Season	Club	GP	G	A	Pts	PIM	GP	G	A	Pts	PIM
1942-43	Montreal Canadiens	1	0	0	0	0	....	....	....	....	....
	NHL Totals	**1**	**0**	**0**	**0**	**0**	....	....	....	....	....

LEE, Edward

Right wing. Shoots right. 6'2", 180 lbs. Born, Rochester, NY, December 17, 1961. (Quebec's 4th choice, 95th overall, in 1981 Entry Draft).

Season	Club	GP	G	A	Pts	PIM	GP	G	A	Pts	PIM
1984-85	Quebec Nordiques	2	0	0	0	5	....	....	....	....	....
	NHL Totals	**2**	**0**	**0**	**0**	**5**	....	....	....	....	....

Traded to **Minnesota** by **Quebec** for Minnesota's 6th round choice (Scott White) in 1986 Entry Draft, November 15, 1985.

LEE, Peter

Right wing. Shoots right. 5'9", 180 lbs. Born, Ellesmere, England, January 2, 1956. (Montreal's 1st choice, 12th overall, in 1976 Amateur Draft).

Season	Club	GP	G	A	Pts	PIM	GP	G	A	Pts	PIM
1977-78	Pittsburgh Penguins	60	5	13	18	19	....	....	....	....	....
1978-79	Pittsburgh Penguins	80	32	26	58	24	7	0	3	3	0
1979-80	Pittsburgh Penguins	74	16	29	45	20	4	0	1	1	0
1980-81	Pittsburgh Penguins	80	30	34	64	86	5	0	4	4	4
1981-82	Pittsburgh Penguins	74	18	16	34	98	3	0	0	0	0
1982-83	Pittsburgh Penguins	63	13	13	26	10	....	....	....	....	....
	NHL Totals	**431**	**114**	**131**	**245**	**257**	**19**	**0**	**8**	**8**	**4**

Traded to **Pittsburgh** by **Montreal** with Pete Mahovlich for Pierre Larouche and future considerations (rights to Peter Marsh, December 15, 1977), November 29, 1977.

LEEB, Brad

Right wing. Shoots right. 5'11", 180 lbs. Born, Red Deer, Alta., August 27, 1979.

Season	Club	GP	G	A	Pts	PIM	GP	G	A	Pts	PIM
99-2000	Vancouver Canucks	2	0	0	0	2	....	....	....	....	....
2001-02	Vancouver Canucks	2	0	0	0	0	....	....	....	....	....
	NHL Totals	**4**	**0**	**0**	**0**	**2**	....	....	....	....	....

Signed as a free agent by **Vancouver**, October 8, 1999. Traded to **Toronto** by **Vancouver** for Tomas Mojzis, September 4, 2002.

LEEB, Greg

Center. Shoots left. 5'9", 165 lbs. Born, Red Deer, Alta., May 31, 1977.

Season	Club	GP	G	A	Pts	PIM	GP	G	A	Pts	PIM
2000-01	Dallas Stars	2	0	0	0	0	....	....	....	....	....
	NHL Totals	**2**	**0**	**0**	**0**	**0**	....	....	....	....	....

Signed as a free agent by **Dallas**, July 24, 1998. Signed as a free agent by **Edmonton**, July 17, 2001.

LEEMAN, Gary

Right wing. Shoots right. 5'11", 175 lbs. Born, Toronto, Ont., February 19, 1964. (Toronto's 2nd choice, 24th overall, in 1982 Entry Draft).

Season	Club	GP	G	A	Pts	PIM	GP	G	A	Pts	PIM
1982-83	Toronto Maple Leafs	....	....	....	....	....	2	0	0	0	0
1983-84	Toronto Maple Leafs	52	4	8	12	31	....	....	....	....	....
1984-85	Toronto Maple Leafs	53	5	26	31	72	....	....	....	....	....
1985-86	Toronto Maple Leafs	53	9	23	32	20	10	2	10	12	2
1986-87	Toronto Maple Leafs	80	21	31	52	66	5	0	1	1	14
1987-88	Toronto Maple Leafs	80	30	31	61	62	2	2	0	2	2
1988-89	Toronto Maple Leafs	61	32	43	75	66	....	....	....	....	....

Season	Club	Regular Season GP	G	A	Pts	PIM	Playoffs GP	G	A	Pts	PIM
1989-90	Toronto Maple Leafs	80	51	44	95	63	5	3	3	6	16
1990-91	Toronto Maple Leafs	52	17	12	29	39	....	....	....	....	....
1991-92	Toronto Maple Leafs	34	7	13	20	44	....	....	....	....	....
	Calgary Flames	29	2	7	9	27	....	....	....	....	....
1992-93	Calgary Flames	30	9	5	14	10	....	....	....	....	....
	♦ Montreal Canadiens	20	6	12	18	14	11	1	2	3	2
1993-94	Montreal Canadiens	31	4	11	15	17	1	0	0	0	0
1994-95	Vancouver Canucks	10	2	0	2	0	....	....	....	....	....
1996-97	St. Louis Blues	2	0	1	1	0	....	....	....	....	....
	NHL Totals	**667**	**199**	**267**	**466**	**531**	**36**	**8**	**16**	**24**	**36**

Played in NHL All-Star Game (1989)

Traded to **Calgary** by **Toronto** with Craig Berube, Alexander Godynyuk, Michel Petit and Jeff Reese for Doug Gilmour, Jamie Macoun, Ric Nattress, Rick Wamsley and Kent Manderville, January 2, 1992. Traded to **Montreal** by **Calgary** for Brian Skrudland, January 28, 1993. Signed as a free agent by **Vancouver**, January 18, 1995. Signed as a free agent by **St. Louis**, September 26, 1996.

LEETCH, Brian

Defense. Shoots left. 6'1", 190 lbs. Born, Corpus Christi, TX, March 3, 1968.
(NY Rangers' 1st choice, 9th overall, in 1986 Entry Draft).

Season	Club	Regular Season GP	G	A	Pts	PIM	Playoffs GP	G	A	Pts	PIM
1987-88	New York Rangers	17	2	12	14	0	....	....	....	....	....
1988-89	New York Rangers	68	23	48	71	50	4	3	2	5	2
1989-90	New York Rangers	72	11	45	56	26	....	....	....	....	....
1990-91	New York Rangers	80	16	72	88	42	6	1	3	4	0
1991-92	New York Rangers	80	22	80	102	26	13	4	11	15	4
1992-93	New York Rangers	36	6	30	36	26	....	....	....	....	....
1993-94 ♦	New York Rangers	84	23	56	79	67	23	11	*23	*34	6
1994-95	New York Rangers	48	9	32	41	18	10	6	8	14	8
1995-96	New York Rangers	82	15	70	85	30	11	1	6	7	4
1996-97	New York Rangers	82	20	58	78	40	15	2	8	10	6
1997-98	New York Rangers	76	17	33	50	32	....	....	....	....	....
1998-99	New York Rangers	82	13	42	55	42	....	....	....	....	....
99-2000	New York Rangers	50	7	19	26	20	....	....	....	....	....
2000-01	New York Rangers	82	21	58	79	34	....	....	....	....	....
2001-02	New York Rangers	82	10	45	55	28	....	....	....	....	....
2002-03	New York Rangers	51	12	18	30	20	....	....	....	....	....
	NHL Totals	**1072**	**227**	**718**	**945**	**501**	**82**	**28**	**61**	**89**	**30**

NHL All-Rookie Team (1989) • Calder Memorial Trophy (1989) • NHL Second All-Star Team (1991, 1994, 1996) • James Norris Memorial Trophy (1992, 1997) • NHL First All-Star Team (1992, 1997) • Conn Smythe Trophy (1994)

Played in NHL All-Star Game (1990, 1991, 1992, 1994, 1996, 1997, 1998, 2001, 2002)

Rights traded to **Edmonton** by **NY Rangers** for Jussi Markkanen and future considerations, June 30, 2003.

LEFEBVRE, Guillaume

Left wing. Shoots left. 6'1", 195 lbs. Born, Amos, Que., May 7, 1981.
(Philadelphia's 6th choice, 227th overall, in 2000 Entry Draft).

Season	Club	Regular Season GP	G	A	Pts	PIM	Playoffs GP	G	A	Pts	PIM
2001-02	Philadelphia Flyers	3	0	0	0	0	....	....	....	....	....
2002-03	Philadelphia Flyers	14	0	0	0	4	....	....	....	....	....
	Pittsburgh Penguins	12	2	4	6	0	....	....	....	....	....
	NHL Totals	**29**	**2**	**4**	**6**	**4**	....	....	....	....	....

Traded to **Phoenix** by **Philadelphia** with Atlanta's 3rd round choice (previously acquired, Phoenix selected Tyler Redenbach) in 2003 Entry Draft and Philadelphia's 2nd round choice in 2004 Entry Draft for Tony Amonte, March 10, 2003. Traded to **Pittsburgh** by **Phoenix** with Ramzi Abid and Dan Focht for Jan Hrdina and Francois Leroux, March 11, 2003.

LEFEBVRE, Patrice

Right wing. Shoots left. 5'6", 160 lbs. Born, Montreal, Que., June 28, 1967.

Season	Club	Regular Season GP	G	A	Pts	PIM	Playoffs GP	G	A	Pts	PIM
1998-99	Washington Capitals	3	0	0	0	2	....	....	....	....	....
	NHL Totals	**3**	**0**	**0**	**0**	**2**	....	....	....	....	....

Signed as a free agent by **Washington**, December 18, 1998.

LEFEBVRE, Sylvain

Defense. Shoots left. 6'2", 205 lbs. Born, Richmond, Que., October 14, 1967.

Season	Club	Regular Season GP	G	A	Pts	PIM	Playoffs GP	G	A	Pts	PIM
1989-90	Montreal Canadiens	68	3	10	13	61	6	0	0	0	2
1990-91	Montreal Canadiens	63	5	18	23	30	11	1	0	1	6
1991-92	Montreal Canadiens	69	3	14	17	91	2	0	0	0	2
1992-93	Toronto Maple Leafs	81	2	12	14	90	21	3	3	6	20
1993-94	Toronto Maple Leafs	84	2	9	11	79	18	0	3	3	16
1994-95	Quebec Nordiques	48	2	11	13	17	6	0	2	2	2
1995-96 ♦	Colorado Avalanche	75	5	11	16	49	22	0	5	5	12
1996-97	Colorado Avalanche	71	2	11	13	30	17	0	0	0	25
1997-98	Colorado Avalanche	81	0	10	10	48	7	0	0	0	4
1998-99	Colorado Avalanche	76	2	18	20	48	19	0	1	1	12
99-2000	New York Rangers	82	2	10	12	43	....	....	....	....	....
2000-01	New York Rangers	71	2	13	15	55	....	....	....	....	....
2001-02	New York Rangers	41	0	5	5	23	....	....	....	....	....
2002-03	New York Rangers	35	0	2	2	10	....	....	....	....	....
	NHL Totals	**945**	**30**	**154**	**184**	**674**	**129**	**4**	**14**	**18**	**101**

Signed as a free agent by **Montreal**, September 24, 1986. Traded to **Toronto** by **Montreal** for Toronto's 3rd round choice (Martin Belanger) in 1994 Entry Draft, August 20, 1992. Traded to **Quebec** by **Toronto** with Wendel Clark, Landon Wilson and Toronto's 1st round choice (Jeffrey Kealty) in 1994 Entry Draft for Mats Sundin, Garth Butcher, Todd Warriner and Philadelphia's 1st round choice (previously acquired, later traded to Washington – Washington selected Nolan Baumgartner) in 1994 Entry Draft, June 28, 1994. Transferred to **Colorado** after **Quebec** franchise relocated, June 21, 1995. Signed as a free agent by **NY Rangers**, July 22, 1999.

LEFLEY, Bryan

Defense/Left wing. Shoots left. 6', 195 lbs. Born, Grosse Isle, Man., October 18, 1948.

Season	Club	Regular Season GP	G	A	Pts	PIM	Playoffs GP	G	A	Pts	PIM
1972-73	New York Islanders	63	3	7	10	56	....	....	....	....	....
1973-74	New York Islanders	7	0	0	0	0	....	....	....	....	....
1974-75	Kansas City Scouts	29	0	3	3	6	....	....	....	....	....
1976-77	Colorado Rockies	58	0	6	6	27	....	....	....	....	....
1977-78	Colorado Rockies	71	4	13	17	12	2	0	0	0	0
	NHL Totals	**228**	**7**	**29**	**36**	**101**	**2**	**0**	**0**	**0**	**0**

• Brother of Chuck

Claimed by **NY Islanders** from **NY Rangers** in Expansion Draft, June 6, 1972. Claimed by **Kansas City** from **NY Islanders** in Expansion Draft, June 12, 1974. Transferred to **Colorado** after **Kansas City** franchise relocated, July 15, 1976.

LEFLEY, Chuck

Left wing. Shoots left. 6'2", 185 lbs. Born, Winnipeg, Man., January 20, 1950.
(Montreal's 2nd choice, 6th overall, in 1970 Amateur Draft).

Season	Club	Regular Season GP	G	A	Pts	PIM	Playoffs GP	G	A	Pts	PIM
1970-71 ♦	Montreal Canadiens	1	0	0	0	0	1	0	0	0	0
1971-72	Montreal Canadiens	16	0	2	2	0	....	....	....	....	....
1972-73 ♦	Montreal Canadiens	65	21	25	46	22	17	3	5	8	6
1973-74	Montreal Canadiens	74	23	31	54	34	6	0	1	1	0
1974-75	Montreal Canadiens	18	1	2	3	4	....	....	....	....	....
	St. Louis Blues	57	23	26	49	24	2	0	0	0	2
1975-76	St. Louis Blues	75	43	42	85	41	2	2	1	3	0
1976-77	St. Louis Blues	71	11	30	41	12	1	0	1	1	2
1979-80	St. Louis Blues	28	6	6	12	0	....	....	....	....	....
1980-81	St. Louis Blues	2	0	0	0	0	....	....	....	....	....
	NHL Totals	**407**	**128**	**164**	**292**	**137**	**29**	**5**	**8**	**13**	**10**

• Brother of Bryan

Traded to **St. Louis** by **Montreal** for Don Awrey, November 28, 1974.

LEGER, Roger

Defense. Shoots right. 5'11", 200 lbs. Born, L'Annonciation, Que., March 26, 1919.

Season	Club	Regular Season GP	G	A	Pts	PIM	Playoffs GP	G	A	Pts	PIM
1943-44	New York Rangers	7	1	2	3	2	....	....	....	....	....
1946-47	Montreal Canadiens	49	4	18	22	12	11	0	6	6	10
1947-48	Montreal Canadiens	48	4	14	18	26	....	....	....	....	....
1948-49	Montreal Canadiens	28	6	7	13	10	5	0	1	1	2
1949-50	Montreal Canadiens	55	3	12	15	21	4	0	0	0	2
	NHL Totals	**187**	**18**	**53**	**71**	**71**	**20**	**0**	**7**	**7**	**14**

Signed as a free agent by **NY Rangers**, November 23, 1943. Traded to **Montreal** (Buffalo-AHL) by **NY Rangers** with the loan of Gord Davidson for Bob Dill, January 4, 1944. Traded to **Victoria** (WHL) by **Montreal** for cash and named playing-coach, September 16, 1950.

LEGGE, Barry

Defense. Shoots left. 6', 186 lbs. Born, Winnipeg, Man., October 22, 1954.
(Montreal's 9th choice, 61st overall, in 1974 Amateur Draft).

Season	Club	Regular Season GP	G	A	Pts	PIM	Playoffs GP	G	A	Pts	PIM
1979-80	Quebec Nordiques	31	0	3	3	18	....	....	....	....	....
1980-81	Winnipeg Jets	38	0	6	6	69	....	....	....	....	....
1981-82	Winnipeg Jets	38	1	2	3	57	....	....	....	....	....
	NHL Totals	**107**	**1**	**11**	**12**	**144**	....	....	....	....	....

Claimed by **Winnipeg** from **Cincinnati** (WHA) in WHA Dispersal Draft, June 8, 1979. Traded to **Quebec** by **Winnipeg** with Jamie Hislop for Barry Melrose, June 28, 1979. Traded to **Winnipeg** by **Quebec** for cash, May 26, 1980.

LEGGE, Randy

Defense. Shoots right. 5'11", 184 lbs. Born, Newmarket, Ont., December 16, 1945.

Season	Club	Regular Season GP	G	A	Pts	PIM	Playoffs GP	G	A	Pts	PIM
1972-73	New York Rangers	12	0	2	2	2	....	....	....	....	....
	NHL Totals	**12**	**0**	**2**	**2**	**2**	....	....	....	....	....

LEGWAND, David

Center. Shoots left. 6'2", 190 lbs. Born, Detroit, MI, August 17, 1980.
(Nashville's 1st choice, 2nd overall, in 1998 Entry Draft).

Season	Club	Regular Season GP	G	A	Pts	PIM	Playoffs GP	G	A	Pts	PIM
1998-99	Nashville Predators	1	0	0	0	0	....	....	....	....	....
99-2000	Nashville Predators	71	13	15	28	30	....	....	....	....	....
2000-01	Nashville Predators	81	13	28	41	38	....	....	....	....	....
2001-02	Nashville Predators	63	11	19	30	54	....	....	....	....	....
2002-03	Nashville Predators	64	17	31	48	34	....	....	....	....	....
	NHL Totals	**280**	**54**	**93**	**147**	**156**	....	....	....	....	....

LEHMAN, Tommy

Center. Shoots left. 6'1", 185 lbs. Born, Stockholm, Sweden, February 3, 1964.
(Boston's 11th choice, 228th overall, in 1982 Entry Draft).

Season	Club	Regular Season GP	G	A	Pts	PIM	Playoffs GP	G	A	Pts	PIM
1987-88	Boston Bruins	9	1	3	4	6	....	....	....	....	....
1988-89	Boston Bruins	26	4	2	6	10	....	....	....	....	....
1989-90	Edmonton Oilers	1	0	0	0	0	....	....	....	....	....
	NHL Totals	**36**	**5**	**5**	**10**	**16**	....	....	....	....	....

Traded to **Edmonton** by **Boston** for Edmonton's 3rd round choice (Wes Walz) in 1989 Entry Draft, June 17, 1989.

LEHTINEN, Jere

Right wing. Shoots right. 6', 200 lbs. Born, Espoo, Finland, June 24, 1973.
(Minnesota's 3rd choice, 88th overall, in 1992 Entry Draft).

Season	Club	Regular Season GP	G	A	Pts	PIM	Playoffs GP	G	A	Pts	PIM
1995-96	Dallas Stars	57	6	22	28	16	....	....	....	....	....
1996-97	Dallas Stars	63	16	27	43	2	7	2	2	4	0

Season	Club	GP	G	A	Pts	PIM	GP	G	A	Pts	PIM
		REGULAR SEASON					PLAYOFFS				
1997-98	Dallas Stars	72	23	19	42	20	12	3	5	8	2
1998-99 ♦	Dallas Stars	74	20	32	52	18	23	10	3	13	2
99-2000	Dallas Stars	17	3	5	8	0	13	1	5	6	2
2000-01	Dallas Stars	74	20	25	45	24	10	1	0	1	2
2001-02	Dallas Stars	73	25	24	49	14	....	....	....	....	....
2002-03	Dallas Stars	80	31	17	48	20	12	3	2	5	0
	NHL Totals	**510**	**144**	**171**	**315**	**114**	**77**	**20**	**17**	**37**	**8**

Frank J. Selke Trophy (1998, 1999, 2003)
Played in NHL All-Star Game (1998)

Rights transferred to **Dallas** after **Minnesota** franchise relocated, June 9, 1993. • Missed majority of 1999-2000 season recovering from leg injury suffered in game vs. Nashville, October 16, 1999.

LEHTO, Petteri

Defense. Shoots left. 5'11", 195 lbs. Born, Turku, Finland, March 13, 1961.

Season	Club	GP	G	A	Pts	PIM	GP	G	A	Pts	PIM
1984-85	Pittsburgh Penguins	6	0	0	0	4	....	....	....	....	....
	NHL Totals	**6**	**0**	**0**	**0**	**4**	....	....	....	....	....

Signed as a free agent by **Pittsburgh**, July, 1984.

LEHTONEN, Antero

Left wing. Shoots left. 6', 185 lbs. Born, Tampere, Finland, April 12, 1954.

Season	Club	GP	G	A	Pts	PIM	GP	G	A	Pts	PIM
1979-80	Washington Capitals	65	9	12	21	14	....	....	....	....	....
	NHL Totals	**65**	**9**	**12**	**21**	**14**	....	....	....	....	....

Signed as a free agent by **Washington**, September 16, 1979.

LEHVONEN, Henri

Defense. Shoots left. 5'11", 200 lbs. Born, Sarnia, Ont., August 26, 1950.
(Minnesota's 5th choice, 62nd overall, in 1970 Amateur Draft).

Season	Club	GP	G	A	Pts	PIM	GP	G	A	Pts	PIM
1974-75	Kansas City Scouts	4	0	0	0	0	....	....	....	....	....
	NHL Totals	**4**	**0**	**0**	**0**	**0**	....	....	....	....	....

Traded to **Detroit** (Kalamazoo-IHL) by **Kansas City** (IHL) for Frank Bathe, November, 1975. Traded to **Toledo** (IHL) by **Detroit** (Kalamazoo-IHL) for Reg Meserve, Jim Mitchell and Tony Piroski, November, 1975.

LEIER, Edward

Center. Shoots right. 5'11", 175 lbs. Born, November 3, 1927.

Season	Club	GP	G	A	Pts	PIM	GP	G	A	Pts	PIM
1949-50	Chicago Black Hawks	5	0	1	1	0	....	....	....	....	....
1950-51	Chicago Black Hawks	11	2	0	2	2	....	....	....	....	....
	NHL Totals	**16**	**2**	**1**	**3**	**2**					

LEINONEN, Mikko

Center. Shoots left. 6', 175 lbs. Born, Tampere, Finland, July 15, 1955.

Season	Club	GP	G	A	Pts	PIM	GP	G	A	Pts	PIM
1981-82	New York Rangers	53	11	20	31	18	7	1	6	7	20
1982-83	New York Rangers	78	17	34	51	23	7	1	3	4	4
1983-84	New York Rangers	28	3	23	26	28	5	0	2	2	4
1984-85	Washington Capitals	3	0	1	1	2	1	0	0	0	0
	NHL Totals	**162**	**31**	**78**	**109**	**71**	**20**	**2**	**11**	**13**	**28**

Signed as a free agent by **NY Rangers**, September 8, 1981. Signed as a free agent by **Washington**, March 13, 1985.

LEITER, Bobby

Center. Shoots left. 5'9", 175 lbs. Born, Winnipeg, Man., March 22, 1941.

Season	Club	GP	G	A	Pts	PIM	GP	G	A	Pts	PIM
1962-63	Boston Bruins	51	9	13	22	34	....	....	....	....	....
1963-64	Boston Bruins	56	6	13	19	43	....	....	....	....	....
1964-65	Boston Bruins	18	3	1	4	6	....	....	....	....	....
1965-66	Boston Bruins	9	2	1	3	2	....	....	....	....	....
1968-69	Boston Bruins	1	0	0	0	0	....	....	....	....	....
1971-72	Pittsburgh Penguins	78	14	17	31	18	4	3	0	3	0
1972-73	Atlanta Flames	78	26	34	60	19	....	....	....	....	....
1973-74	Atlanta Flames	78	26	26	52	10	4	0	0	0	2
1974-75	Atlanta Flames	52	10	18	28	8	....	....	....	....	....
1975-76	Atlanta Flames	26	2	3	5	4	....	....	....	....	....
	NHL Totals	**447**	**98**	**126**	**224**	**144**	**8**	**3**	**0**	**3**	**2**

Traded to **Pittsburgh** by **Boston** for cash, May, 1971. Claimed by **Atlanta** from **Pittsburgh** in Expansion Draft, June 6, 1972.

LEITER, Ken

Defense. Shoots left. 6'1", 195 lbs. Born, Detroit, MI, April 19, 1961.
(NY Islanders' 6th choice, 101st overall, in 1980 Entry Draft).

Season	Club	GP	G	A	Pts	PIM	GP	G	A	Pts	PIM
1984-85	New York Islanders	5	0	2	2	2	....	....	....	....	....
1985-86	New York Islanders	9	1	1	2	6	....	....	....	....	....
1986-87	New York Islanders	74	9	20	29	30	11	0	5	5	6
1987-88	New York Islanders	51	4	13	17	24	4	0	1	1	2
1989-90	Minnesota North Stars	4	0	0	0	0	....	....	....	....	....
	NHL Totals	**143**	**14**	**36**	**50**	**62**	**15**	**0**	**6**	**6**	**8**

Claimed by **Minnesota** from **NY Islanders** in Waiver Draft, October 2, 1989.

LEMAIRE, Jacques

HHOF

Center. Shoots left. 5'10", 180 lbs. Born, LaSalle, Que., September 7, 1945.

Season	Club	GP	G	A	Pts	PIM	GP	G	A	Pts	PIM
1967-68 ♦	Montreal Canadiens	69	22	20	42	16	13	7	6	13	6
1968-69 ♦	Montreal Canadiens	75	29	34	63	29	14	4	2	6	6
1969-70	Montreal Canadiens	69	32	28	60	16	....	....	....	....	....
1970-71 ♦	Montreal Canadiens	78	28	28	56	18	20	9	10	19	17
1971-72	Montreal Canadiens	77	32	49	81	26	6	2	1	3	2
1972-73 ♦	Montreal Canadiens	77	44	51	95	16	17	7	13	20	2
1973-74	Montreal Canadiens	66	29	38	67	10	6	0	4	4	2
1974-75	Montreal Canadiens	80	36	56	92	20	11	5	7	12	4
1975-76 ♦	Montreal Canadiens	61	20	32	52	20	13	3	3	6	2
1976-77 ♦	Montreal Canadiens	75	34	41	75	22	14	7	12	19	6
1977-78 ♦	Montreal Canadiens	76	36	61	97	14	15	6	8	14	10
1978-79 ♦	Montreal Canadiens	50	24	31	55	10	16	*11	12	*23	6
	NHL Totals	**853**	**366**	**469**	**835**	**217**	**145**	**61**	**78**	**139**	**63**

Played in NHL All-Star Game (1970, 1973)

LEMAY, Moe

Left wing. Shoots left. 5'11", 185 lbs. Born, Saskatoon, Sask., February 18, 1962.
(Vancouver's 4th choice, 105th overall, in 1981 Entry Draft).

Season	Club	GP	G	A	Pts	PIM	GP	G	A	Pts	PIM
1981-82	Vancouver Canucks	5	1	2	3	0	....	....	....	....	....
1982-83	Vancouver Canucks	44	11	9	20	41	....	....	....	....	....
1983-84	Vancouver Canucks	56	12	18	30	38	4	0	0	0	12
1984-85	Vancouver Canucks	74	21	31	52	68	....	....	....	....	....
1985-86	Vancouver Canucks	48	16	15	31	92	....	....	....	....	....
1986-87	Vancouver Canucks	52	9	17	26	128	....	....	....	....	....
	♦ Edmonton Oilers	10	1	2	3	36	9	2	1	3	11
1987-88	Edmonton Oilers	4	0	0	0	2	....	....	....	....	....
	Boston Bruins	2	0	0	0	0	15	4	2	6	32
1988-89	Boston Bruins	12	0	0	0	23	....	....	....	....	....
	Winnipeg Jets	10	1	0	1	14	....	....	....	....	....
	NHL Totals	**317**	**72**	**94**	**166**	**442**	**28**	**6**	**3**	**9**	**55**

Traded to **Edmonton** by **Vancouver** for Raimo Summanen, March 10, 1987. Traded to **Boston** by **Edmonton** for Alan May, March 8, 1988. Traded to **Winnipeg** by **Boston** for Ray Neufeld, December 30, 1988.

LEMELIN, Roger

Defense. Shoots right. 6'3", 215 lbs. Born, Iroquois Falls, Ont., February 6, 1954.
(Kansas City's 4th choice, 56th overall, in 1974 Amateur Draft).

Season	Club	GP	G	A	Pts	PIM	GP	G	A	Pts	PIM
1974-75	Kansas City Scouts	8	0	1	1	6	....	....	....	....	....
1975-76	Kansas City Scouts	11	0	0	0	0	....	....	....	....	....
1976-77	Colorado Rockies	14	1	1	2	21	....	....	....	....	....
1977-78	Colorado Rockies	3	0	0	0	0	....	....	....	....	....
	NHL Totals	**36**	**1**	**2**	**3**	**27**	....	....	....	....	....

Transferred to **Colorado** after **Kansas City** franchise relocated, July 15, 1976.

LEMIEUX, Alain

Center. Shoots left. 6', 185 lbs. Born, Montreal, Que., May 24, 1961.
(St. Louis' 4th choice, 96th overall, in 1980 Entry Draft).

Season	Club	GP	G	A	Pts	PIM	GP	G	A	Pts	PIM
1981-82	St. Louis Blues	3	0	1	1	0	....	....	....	....	....
1982-83	St. Louis Blues	42	9	25	34	18	4	0	1	1	0
1983-84	St. Louis Blues	17	4	5	9	6	....	....	....	....	....
1984-85	St. Louis Blues	19	4	2	6	0	....	....	....	....	....
	Quebec Nordiques	30	11	11	22	12	14	3	3	6	0
1985-86	Quebec Nordiques	7	0	0	0	2	1	1	2	3	0
1986-87	Pittsburgh Penguins	1	0	0	0	0	....	....	....	....	....
	NHL Totals	**119**	**28**	**44**	**72**	**38**	**19**	**4**	**6**	**10**	**0**

• Brother of Mario

Traded to **Quebec** by **St. Louis** for Luc Dufour, January 29, 1985. Signed as a free agent by **Pittsburgh**, December, 1986.

LEMIEUX, Bob

Defense. Shoots left. 6'1", 195 lbs. Born, Montreal, Que., December 16, 1944.

Season	Club	GP	G	A	Pts	PIM	GP	G	A	Pts	PIM
1967-68	Oakland Seals	19	0	1	1	12	....	....	....	....	....
	NHL Totals	**19**	**0**	**1**	**1**	**12**	....	....	....	....	....

Claimed by **California** (Oakland) from **Montreal** in Expansion Draft, June 6, 1967.

LEMIEUX, Claude

Right wing. Shoots right. 6'1", 227 lbs. Born, Buckingham, Que., July 16, 1965.
(Montreal's 2nd choice, 26th overall, in 1983 Entry Draft).

Season	Club	GP	G	A	Pts	PIM	GP	G	A	Pts	PIM
1983-84	Montreal Canadiens	8	1	1	2	12	....	....	....	....	....
1984-85	Montreal Canadiens	1	0	1	1	7	....	....	....	....	....
1985-86 ♦	Montreal Canadiens	10	1	2	3	22	20	10	6	16	68
1986-87	Montreal Canadiens	76	27	26	53	156	17	4	9	13	41
1987-88	Montreal Canadiens	78	31	30	61	137	11	3	2	5	20
1988-89	Montreal Canadiens	69	29	22	51	136	18	4	3	7	58
1989-90	Montreal Canadiens	39	8	10	18	106	11	1	3	4	38
1990-91	New Jersey Devils	78	30	17	47	105	7	4	0	4	34
1991-92	New Jersey Devils	74	41	27	68	109	7	4	3	7	26
1992-93	New Jersey Devils	77	30	51	81	155	5	2	0	2	19
1993-94	New Jersey Devils	79	18	26	44	86	20	7	11	18	44
1994-95 ♦	New Jersey Devils	45	6	13	19	86	20	*13	3	16	20
1995-96 ♦	Colorado Avalanche	79	39	32	71	117	19	5	7	12	55
1996-97	Colorado Avalanche	45	11	17	28	43	17	*13	10	23	32
1997-98	Colorado Avalanche	78	26	27	53	115	7	3	3	6	8
1998-99	Colorado Avalanche	82	27	24	51	102	19	3	11	14	26
99-2000	Colorado Avalanche	13	3	6	9	4	....	....	....	....	....
	♦ New Jersey Devils	70	17	21	38	86	23	4	6	10	28
2000-01	Phoenix Coyotes	46	10	16	26	58	....	....	....	....	....
2001-02	Phoenix Coyotes	82	16	25	41	70	5	0	0	0	2

Season	Club	Regular Season GP	G	A	Pts	PIM	Playoffs GP	G	A	Pts	PIM
2002-03	Phoenix Coyotes	36	6	8	14	30	....	....	....	....	....
	Dallas Stars	32	2	4	6	14	7	0	1	1	10
	NHL Totals	**1197**	**379**	**406**	**785**	**1756**	**233**	**80**	**78**	**158**	**529**

• Brother of Jocelyn • Conn Smythe Trophy (1995)

• Missed majority of 1989-90 season recovering from abdominal injury suffered in game vs. Boston, October 9, 1989. Traded to **New Jersey** by **Montreal** for Sylvain Turgeon, September 4, 1990. Traded to **NY Islanders** by **New Jersey** for Steve Thomas, October 3, 1995. Traded to **Colorado** by **NY Islanders** for Wendel Clark, October 3, 1995. Traded to **New Jersey** by **Colorado** with Colorado's 1st (David Hale) and 2nd (Matt DeMarchi) round choices in 2000 Entry Draft for Brian Rolston and New Jersey's 1st round choice (later traded to Boston – Boston selected Martin Samuelsson) in 2000 Entry Draft, November 3, 1999. Signed as a free agent by **Phoenix**, December 5, 2000. Traded to **Dallas** by **Phoenix** for Scott Pellerin and future considerations, January 16, 2003.

LEMIEUX, Jacques

Defense. Shoots right. 6'2", 190 lbs. Born, Matane, Que., April 8, 1943.

Season	Club	GP	G	A	Pts	PIM	GP	G	A	Pts	PIM
1967-68	Los Angeles Kings	16	0	3	3	8	....	....	....	....	....
1968-69	Los Angeles Kings	....	....	....	....	....	1	0	0	0	0
1969-70	Los Angeles Kings	3	0	1	1	0	....	....	....	....	....
	NHL Totals	**19**	**0**	**4**	**4**	**8**	**1**	**0**	**0**	**0**	**0**

Claimed by **Los Angeles** from **Montreal** in Expansion Draft, June 6, 1967. Traded to **Toronto** (Phoenix-WHL) by **Los Angeles** for Gary Marsh, February, 1970. • Suspended for remainder of 1969-70 season by **Toronto** for refusing to report to **Phoenix** (WHL), February, 1970.

LEMIEUX, Jean

Defense. Shoots right. 6'1", 180 lbs. Born, Noranda, Que., May 31, 1952.
(Atlanta's 3rd choice, 34th overall, in 1972 Amateur Draft).

Season	Club	GP	G	A	Pts	PIM	GP	G	A	Pts	PIM
1973-74	Atlanta Flames	32	3	5	8	6	3	1	1	2	0
1974-75	Atlanta Flames	75	3	24	27	19	....	....	....	....	....
1975-76	Atlanta Flames	33	4	9	13	10	....	....	....	....	....
	Washington Capitals	33	6	14	20	2	....	....	....	....	....
1976-77	Washington Capitals	15	4	4	8	2	....	....	....	....	....
1977-78	Washington Capitals	16	3	7	10	0	....	....	....	....	....
	NHL Totals	**204**	**23**	**63**	**86**	**39**	**3**	**1**	**1**	**2**	**0**

Traded to **Washington** by **Atlanta** with Gerry Meehan and Buffalo's 1st round choice (previously acquired, Washington selected Greg Carroll) in 1976 Amateur Draft for Bill Clement, January 22, 1976.

LEMIEUX, Jocelyn

Right wing. Shoots left. 5'11", 220 lbs. Born, Mont-Laurier, Que., November 18, 1967.
(St. Louis' 1st choice, 10th overall, in 1986 Entry Draft).

Season	Club	GP	G	A	Pts	PIM	GP	G	A	Pts	PIM
1986-87	St. Louis Blues	53	10	8	18	94	5	0	1	1	6
1987-88	St. Louis Blues	23	1	0	1	42	5	0	0	0	15
1988-89	Montreal Canadiens	1	0	1	1	0	....	....	....	....	....
1989-90	Montreal Canadiens	34	4	2	6	61	....	....	....	....	....
	Chicago Blackhawks	39	10	11	21	47	18	1	8	9	28
1990-91	Chicago Blackhawks	67	6	7	13	119	4	0	0	0	0
1991-92	Chicago Blackhawks	78	6	10	16	80	18	3	1	4	33
1992-93	Chicago Blackhawks	81	10	21	31	111	4	1	0	1	2
1993-94	Chicago Blackhawks	66	12	8	20	63	....	....	....	....	....
	Hartford Whalers	16	6	1	7	19	....	....	....	....	....
1994-95	Hartford Whalers	41	6	5	11	32	....	....	....	....	....
1995-96	Hartford Whalers	29	1	2	3	31	....	....	....	....	....
	New Jersey Devils	18	0	1	1	4	....	....	....	....	....
	Calgary Flames	20	4	4	8	10	4	0	0	0	0
1996-97	Phoenix Coyotes	2	1	0	1	0	2	0	0	0	4
1997-98	Phoenix Coyotes	30	3	3	6	27	....	....	....	....	....
	NHL Totals	**598**	**80**	**84**	**164**	**740**	**60**	**5**	**10**	**15**	**88**

• Brother of Claude

Traded to **Montreal** by **St. Louis** with Darrell May and St. Louis' 2nd round choice (Patrice Brisebois) in 1989 Entry Draft for Sergio Momesso and Vincent Riendeau, August 9, 1988. Traded to **Chicago** by **Montreal** for Chicago's 3rd round choice (Charles Poulin) in 1990 Entry Draft, January 5, 1990. Traded to **Hartford** by **Chicago** with Frantisek Kucera for Gary Suter, Randy Cunneyworth and Hartford's 3rd round choice (later traded to Vancouver – Vancouver selected Larry Courville) in 1995 Entry Draft, March 11, 1994. Traded to **New Jersey** by **Hartford** with Hartford/Carolina's 2nd round choice (later traded to Dallas – Dallas selected John Erskine) in 1998 Entry Draft for Jim Dowd and New Jersey's 2nd round choice (later traded to Calgary – Calgary selected Dmitri Kokorev) in 1997 Entry Draft, December 19, 1995. Traded to **Calgary** by **New Jersey** with Tommy Albelin and Cale Hulse for Phil Housley and Dan Keczmer, February 26, 1996. Signed as a free agent by **Phoenix**, March 18, 1997.

LEMIEUX, Mario

HHOF

Center. Shoots right. 6'4", 230 lbs. Born, Montreal, Que., October 5, 1965.
(Pittsburgh's 1st choice, 1st overall, in 1984 Entry Draft).

Season	Club	GP	G	A	Pts	PIM	GP	G	A	Pts	PIM
1984-85	Pittsburgh Penguins	73	43	57	100	54	....	....	....	....	....
1985-86	Pittsburgh Penguins	79	48	93	141	43	....	....	....	....	....
1986-87	Pittsburgh Penguins	63	54	53	107	57	....	....	....	....	....
1987-88	Pittsburgh Penguins	77	*70	98	*168	92	....	....	....	....	....
1988-89	Pittsburgh Penguins	76	*85	*114	*199	100	11	12	7	19	16
1989-90	Pittsburgh Penguins	59	45	78	123	78	....	....	....	....	....
1990-91 ♦	Pittsburgh Penguins	26	19	26	45	30	23	16	*28	*44	16
1991-92 ♦	Pittsburgh Penguins	64	44	87	*131	94	15	*16	18	*34	2
1992-93	Pittsburgh Penguins	60	69	91	*160	38	11	8	10	18	10
1993-94	Pittsburgh Penguins	22	17	20	37	32	6	4	3	7	2
1994-95	Pittsburgh Penguins	DID NOT PLAY									
1995-96	Pittsburgh Penguins	70	*69	*92	*161	54	18	11	16	27	33
1996-97	Pittsburgh Penguins	76	50	*72	*122	65	5	3	3	6	4
2000-01	Pittsburgh Penguins	43	35	41	76	18	18	6	11	17	4
2001-02	Pittsburgh Penguins	24	6	25	31	14	....	....	....	....	....
2002-03	Pittsburgh Penguins	67	28	63	91	43	....	....	....	....	....
	NHL Totals	**879**	**682**	**1010**	**1692**	**812**	**107**	**76**	**96**	**172**	**87**

• Brother of Alain • NHL All-Rookie Team (1985) • Calder Memorial Trophy (1985) • NHL Second All-Star Team (1986, 1987, 1992, 2001) • Lester B. Pearson Award (1986, 1988, 1993, 1996) • • NHL First All-Star Team (1988, 1989, 1993, 1996, 1997) • Dodge Performance of the Year Award (1988) • Dodge Performer of the Year Award (1988, 1989) • Art Ross Trophy (1988, 1989, 1992, 1993, 1996, 1997) • Hart Trophy (1988, 1993, 1996) • Dodge Ram Tough Award (1989) • Conn Smythe Trophy (1991, 1992) • ProSet/NHL Player of the Year Award (1992) • Alka-Seltzer Plus Award (1993) • Bill Masterton Memorial Trophy (1993) • Lester Patrick Trophy (2000)

Played in NHL All-Star Game (1985, 1986, 1988, 1989, 1990, 1992, 1996, 1997, 2001, 2002)

• Missed remainder of 1989-90 and majority of 1990-91 seasons recovering from back injury suffered in game vs. NY Rangers, February 14, 1989. • Missed remainder of 1992-93 season after being diagnosed with Hodgkin's Disease, January 12, 1993. • Missed majority of 1993-94 season recovering from back injury suffered in game vs. Chicago, November 11, 1993. • Missed entire 1994-95 season recovering from effects of treatment for Hodgkin's Disease and back injury suffered in game vs. NY Rangers, March 12, 1994. • Became third player (Gordie Howe, Guy Lafleur) to appear in NHL game after being inducted into Hockey Hall of Fame, December 27, 2000. • Missed majority of 2001-02 season recovering from hip injury suffered in game vs. Anaheim, October 6, 2001.

LEMIEUX, Real

Left wing. Shoots left. 5'11", 180 lbs. Born, Victoriaville, Que., January 3, 1945.

Season	Club	GP	G	A	Pts	PIM	GP	G	A	Pts	PIM
1966-67	Detroit Red Wings	1	0	0	0	0	....	....	....	....	....
1967-68	Los Angeles Kings	74	12	23	35	60	7	1	1	2	0
1968-69	Los Angeles Kings	75	11	29	40	68	11	1	3	4	10
1969-70	New York Rangers	55	4	6	10	51	....	....	....	....	....
	Los Angeles Kings	18	2	4	6	10	....	....	....	....	....
1970-71	Los Angeles Kings	43	3	6	9	22	....	....	....	....	....
1971-72	Los Angeles Kings	78	13	25	38	28	....	....	....	....	....
1972-73	Los Angeles Kings	74	5	10	15	19	....	....	....	....	....
1973-74	Los Angeles Kings	20	0	0	0	0	....	....	....	....	....
	New York Rangers	7	0	0	0	0	....	....	....	....	....
	Buffalo Sabres	11	1	1	2	4	....	....	....	....	....
	NHL Totals	**456**	**51**	**104**	**155**	**262**	**18**	**2**	**4**	**6**	**10**

Claimed by **Los Angeles** from **Detroit** in Expansion Draft, June 6, 1967. Traded to **NY Rangers** by **Los Angeles** for Leon Rochefort and Dennis Hextall, June 9, 1969. Traded to **Los Angeles** by **NY Rangers** with Juha Widing for Ted Irvine, February 28, 1970. Traded to **NY Rangers** by **Los Angeles** with Gilles Marotte for Sheldon Kannegiesser, Mike Murphy and Tom Williams, November 30, 1973. Traded to **Buffalo** by **NY Rangers** for Paul Curtis, January 21, 1974.

LEMIEUX, Rich

Center. Shoots left. 5'8", 155 lbs. Born, Temiscamingue, Que., April 19, 1951.
(Vancouver's 3rd choice, 39th overall, in 1971 Amateur Draft).

Season	Club	GP	G	A	Pts	PIM	GP	G	A	Pts	PIM
1971-72	Vancouver Canucks	42	7	9	16	4	....	....	....	....	....
1972-73	Vancouver Canucks	78	17	35	52	41	....	....	....	....	....
1973-74	Vancouver Canucks	72	5	17	22	23	....	....	....	....	....
1974-75	Kansas City Scouts	79	10	20	30	64	....	....	....	....	....
1975-76	Kansas City Scouts	2	0	0	0	0	....	....	....	....	....
	Atlanta Flames	1	0	1	1	0	2	0	0	0	0
	NHL Totals	**274**	**39**	**82**	**121**	**132**	**2**	**0**	**0**	**0**	**0**

Claimed by **Kansas City** from **Vancouver** in Expansion Draft, June 12, 1974. Traded to **Atlanta** by **Kansas City** with Kansas City's 2nd round choice (Miles Zaharko) in 1977 Amateur Draft for Buster Harvey, October 13, 1975.

LENARDON, Tim

Center. Shoots left. 6'2", 185 lbs. Born, Trail, B.C., May 11, 1962.

Season	Club	GP	G	A	Pts	PIM	GP	G	A	Pts	PIM
1986-87	New Jersey Devils	7	1	1	2	0	....	....	....	....	....
1989-90	Vancouver Canucks	8	1	0	1	4	....	....	....	....	....
	NHL Totals	**15**	**2**	**1**	**3**	**4**	....	....	....	....	....

Signed as a free agent by **New Jersey**, August 6, 1986. Traded to **Vancouver** by **New Jersey** for Claude Vilgrain, March 7, 1989. Signed as a free agent by **Minnesota**, July 25, 1991.

LEOPOLD, Jordan

Defense. Shoots left. 6', 193 lbs. Born, Golden Valley, MN, August 3, 1980.
(Anaheim's 1st choice, 44th overall, in 1999 Entry Draft).

Season	Club	GP	G	A	Pts	PIM	GP	G	A	Pts	PIM
2002-03	Calgary Flames	58	4	10	14	12	....	....	....	....	....
	NHL Totals	**58**	**4**	**10**	**14**	**12**	....	....	....	....	....

Traded to **Calgary** by **Anaheim** for Andrei Nazarov and Calgary's 2nd round choice (later traded to Phoenix – later traded back to Calgary – Calgary selected Andrei Taratukhin) in 2001 Entry Draft, September 26, 2000.

LEPINE, Hec

Center. Shoots right. 5'11", 185 lbs. Born, Ste-Anne-de-Bellevue, Que., December 7, 1897.

Season	Club	GP	G	A	Pts	PIM	GP	G	A	Pts	PIM
1925-26	Montreal Canadiens	33	5	2	7	2	....	....	....	....	....
	NHL Totals	**33**	**5**	**2**	**7**	**2**	....	....	....	....	....

• Brother of Pit

Signed as a free agent by **Montreal**, December 29, 1925.

LEPINE, Pit

Center. Shoots left. 5'11", 168 lbs. Born, Ste-Anne-de-Bellevue, Que., July 30, 1901.

Season	Club	GP	G	A	Pts	PIM	GP	G	A	Pts	PIM
1925-26	Montreal Canadiens	27	9	1	10	18	....	....	....	....	....
1926-27	Montreal Canadiens	44	16	1	17	20	4	0	0	0	4
1927-28	Montreal Canadiens	20	4	1	5	6	1	0	0	0	0
1928-29	Montreal Canadiens	44	6	1	7	48	3	0	0	0	2
1929-30 ♦	Montreal Canadiens	44	24	9	33	47	6	2	2	4	6
1930-31 ♦	Montreal Canadiens	44	17	7	24	63	10	4	2	6	6

Season	Club	REGULAR SEASON GP	G	A	Pts	PIM	PLAYOFFS GP	G	A	Pts	PIM
1931-32	Montreal Canadiens	48	19	11	30	42	3	1	0	1	4
1932-33	Montreal Canadiens	46	8	8	16	45	2	0	0	0	2
1933-34	Montreal Canadiens	48	10	8	18	44	2	0	0	0	0
1934-35	Montreal Canadiens	48	12	19	31	16	2	0	0	0	2
1935-36	Montreal Canadiens	32	6	10	16	4	....	....	....	....	....
1936-37	Montreal Canadiens	34	7	8	15	15	5	0	1	1	0
1937-38	Montreal Canadiens	47	5	14	19	24	3	0	0	0	0
	NHL Totals	**526**	**143**	**98**	**241**	**392**	**41**	**7**	**5**	**12**	**26**

• Brother of Hec

Played in NHL All-Star Game (1937)

Signed as a free agent by **Montreal**, November 13, 1925.

LEROUX, Francois

Defense. Shoots left. 6'6", 247 lbs. Born, Ste-Adele, Que., April 18, 1970.
(Edmonton's 1st choice, 19th overall, in 1988 Entry Draft).

Season	Club	GP	G	A	Pts	PIM	GP	G	A	Pts	PIM
1988-89	Edmonton Oilers	2	0	0	0	0	....	....	....	....	....
1989-90	Edmonton Oilers	3	0	1	1	0	....	....	....	....	....
1990-91	Edmonton Oilers	1	0	2	2	0	....	....	....	....	....
1991-92	Edmonton Oilers	4	0	0	0	7	....	....	....	....	....
1992-93	Edmonton Oilers	1	0	0	0	4	....	....	....	....	....
1993-94	Ottawa Senators	23	0	1	1	70	....	....	....	....	....
1994-95	Pittsburgh Penguins	40	0	2	2	114	12	0	2	2	14
1995-96	Pittsburgh Penguins	66	2	9	11	161	18	1	1	2	20
1996-97	Pittsburgh Penguins	59	0	3	3	81	3	0	0	0	0
1997-98	Colorado Avalanche	50	1	2	3	140	....	....	....	....	....
	NHL Totals	**249**	**3**	**20**	**23**	**577**	**33**	**1**	**3**	**4**	**34**

Claimed on waivers by **Ottawa** from **Edmonton**, October 6, 1993. Claimed by **Pittsburgh** from **Ottawa** in Waiver Draft, January 18, 1995. Traded to **Colorado** by **Pittsburgh** for Colorado's 3rd round choice (David Cameron) in 1998 Entry Draft, September 28, 1997. Signed as a free agent by **Phoenix**, July 20, 1999.Signed as a free agent by **Pittsburgh**, July 16, 2002. Traded to **Phoenix** by **Pittsburgh** with Jan Hrdina for Ramzi Abid, Dan Focht and Guillaume Lefebvre, March 11, 2003.

LEROUX, Gaston

Defense. Shoots right. 6', 195 lbs. Born, Montreal, Que., January 9, 1913.

Season	Club	GP	G	A	Pts	PIM	GP	G	A	Pts	PIM
1935-36	Montreal Canadiens	2	0	0	0	0	....	....	....	....	....
	NHL Totals	**2**	**0**	**0**	**0**	**0**	....	....	....	....	....

Signed as a free agent by **Montreal**, October 24, 1935.

LEROUX, Jean-Yves

Left wing. Shoots left. 6'2", 211 lbs. Born, Montreal, Que., June 24, 1976.
(Chicago's 2nd choice, 40th overall, in 1994 Entry Draft).

Season	Club	GP	G	A	Pts	PIM	GP	G	A	Pts	PIM
1996-97	Chicago Blackhawks	1	0	1	1	5	....	....	....	....	....
1997-98	Chicago Blackhawks	66	6	7	13	55	....	....	....	....	....
1998-99	Chicago Blackhawks	40	3	5	8	21	....	....	....	....	....
99-2000	Chicago Blackhawks	54	3	5	8	43	....	....	....	....	....
2000-01	Chicago Blackhawks	59	4	4	8	22	....	....	....	....	....
	NHL Totals	**220**	**16**	**22**	**38**	**146**	....	....	....	....	....

LESCHYSHYN, Curtis

Defense. Shoots left. 6'1", 220 lbs. Born, Thompson, Man., September 21, 1969.
(Quebec's 1st choice, 3rd overall, in 1988 Entry Draft).

Season	Club	GP	G	A	Pts	PIM	GP	G	A	Pts	PIM
1988-89	Quebec Nordiques	71	4	9	13	71	....	....	....	....	....
1989-90	Quebec Nordiques	68	2	6	8	44	....	....	....	....	....
1990-91	Quebec Nordiques	55	3	7	10	49	....	....	....	....	....
1991-92	Quebec Nordiques	42	5	12	17	42	....	....	....	....	....
1992-93	Quebec Nordiques	82	9	23	32	61	6	1	1	2	6
1993-94	Quebec Nordiques	72	5	17	22	65	....	....	....	....	....
1994-95	Quebec Nordiques	44	2	13	15	20	3	0	1	1	4
1995-96 ◆	Colorado Avalanche	77	4	15	19	73	17	1	2	3	8
1996-97	Colorado Avalanche	11	0	5	5	6	....	....	....	....	....
	Washington Capitals	2	0	0	0	2	....	....	....	....	....
	Hartford Whalers	64	4	13	17	30	....	....	....	....	....
1997-98	Carolina Hurricanes	73	2	10	12	45	....	....	....	....	....
1998-99	Carolina Hurricanes	65	2	7	9	50	6	0	0	0	6
99-2000	Carolina Hurricanes	53	0	2	2	14	....	....	....	....	....
2000-01	Minnesota Wild	54	2	3	5	19	....	....	....	....	....
	Ottawa Senators	11	0	4	4	0	4	0	0	0	0
2001-02	Ottawa Senators	79	1	9	10	44	12	0	1	1	0
2002-03	Ottawa Senators	54	1	6	7	18	18	0	1	1	10
	NHL Totals	**977**	**46**	**161**	**207**	**653**	**66**	**2**	**6**	**8**	**34**

Transferred to **Colorado** after **Quebec** franchise relcoated, June 21, 1995. Traded to **Washington** by **Colorado** with Chris Simon for Keith Jones, Washington's 1st (Scott Parker) and 4th (later traded back to Washington – Washington selected Krys Barch) round choices in 1998 Entry Draft, November 2, 1996. Traded to **Hartford** by **Washington** for Andrei Nikolishin, November 9, 1996. Transferred to **Carolina** after **Hartford** franchise relocated, June 25, 1997. Selected by **Minnesota** from **Carolina** in Expansion Draft, June 23, 2000. Traded to **Ottawa** by **Minnesota** for Ottawa's 3rd round choice (Stephane Veilleux) in 2001 Entry Draft and future considerations, March 13, 2001.

LESIEUR, Art

Defense. Shoots right. 5'11", 191 lbs. Born, Fall River, MA, September 13, 1907.

Season	Club	GP	G	A	Pts	PIM	GP	G	A	Pts	PIM
1928-29	Montreal Canadiens	15	0	0	0	0	....	....	....	....	....
	Chicago Black Hawks	2	0	0	0	0	....	....	....	....	....
1930-31 ◆	Montreal Canadiens	21	2	0	2	14	10	0	0	0	4
1931-32	Montreal Canadiens	24	1	2	3	12	4	0	0	0	0
1935-36	Montreal Canadiens	38	1	0	1	24	....	....	....	....	....
	NHL Totals	**100**	**4**	**2**	**6**	**50**	**14**	**0**	**0**	**0**	**4**

Signed as a free agent by **Montreal**, October 30, 1928. Loaned to **Chicago** by **Montreal** for the remainder of the 1928-29 season for the loan of Herb Gardiner, January 9, 1929. Traded to **Montreal** by **Providence** (Can-Am) for cash and future considerations, September 30, 1935. Traded to **Pittsburgh** (AHL) by **Montreal** (Providence-AHL) for Babe Tapin, October 15, 1940.

LESSARD, Francis

Defense/Right wing. Shoots right. 6'2", 220 lbs. Born, Montreal, Que., May 30, 1979.
(Carolina's 3rd choice, 80th overall, in 1997 Entry Draft).

Season	Club	GP	G	A	Pts	PIM	GP	G	A	Pts	PIM
2001-02	Atlanta Thrashers	5	0	0	0	26	....	....	....	....	....
2002-03	Atlanta Thrashers	18	0	2	2	61	....	....	....	....	....
	NHL Totals	**23**	**0**	**2**	**2**	**87**	....	....	....	....	....

Traded to **Philadelphia** by **Carolina** for Philadelphia's 8th round choice (Antti Jokella) in 1999 Entry Draft, May 25, 1999. Traded to **Atlanta** by **Philadelphia** for David Harlock and Atlanta's 3rd (later traded to Phoenix – Phoenix selected Tyler Redenbach) and 7th (later traded to San Jose – San Jose selected Joe Pavelski) round choices in 2003 Entry Draft, March 15, 2002.

LESSARD, Rick

Defense. Shoots left. 6'2", 206 lbs. Born, Timmins, Ont., January 9, 1968.
(Calgary's 6th choice, 142nd overall, in 1986 Entry Draft).

Season	Club	GP	G	A	Pts	PIM	GP	G	A	Pts	PIM
1988-89	Calgary Flames	6	0	1	1	2	....	....	....	....	....
1990-91	Calgary Flames	1	0	1	1	0	....	....	....	....	....
1991-92	San Jose Sharks	8	0	2	2	16	....	....	....	....	....
	NHL Totals	**15**	**0**	**4**	**4**	**18**	....	....	....	....	....

Claimed by **San Jose** from **Calgary** in Expansion Draft, May 30, 1991. Traded to **Vancouver** by **San Jose** for Robin Bawa, December 15, 1992.

LESUK, Bill

Left wing. Shoots left. 5'9", 187 lbs. Born, Moose Jaw, Sask., November 1, 1946.

Season	Club	GP	G	A	Pts	PIM	GP	G	A	Pts	PIM
1968-69	Boston Bruins	5	0	1	1	0	1	0	0	0	0
1969-70 ◆	Boston Bruins	3	0	0	0	0	2	0	0	0	0
1970-71	Philadelphia Flyers	78	17	19	36	81	4	1	0	1	8
1971-72	Philadelphia Flyers	45	7	6	13	31	....	....	....	....	....
	Los Angeles Kings	27	4	10	14	14	....	....	....	....	....
1972-73	Los Angeles Kings	67	6	14	20	90	....	....	....	....	....
1973-74	Los Angeles Kings	35	2	1	3	32	2	0	0	0	4
1974-75	Washington Capitals	79	8	11	19	77	....	....	....	....	....
1979-80	Winnipeg Jets	49	0	1	1	43	....	....	....	....	....
	NHL Totals	**388**	**44**	**63**	**107**	**368**	**9**	**1**	**0**	**1**	**12**

Traded to **Boston** by **Detroit** with Gary Doak, Ron Murphy and future considerations (Steve Atkinson, June 6, 1966) for Leo Boivin and Dean Prentice, February 16, 1966. Claimed by **Philadelphia** from **Boston** in Intra-League Draft, June 9, 1970. Traded to **Los Angeles** by **Philadelphia** with Jim Johnson and Serge Bernier for Bill Flett, Eddie Joyal, Jean Potvin, and Ross Lonsberry, January 28, 1972. Traded to **Washington** by **Los Angeles** for cash, July 28, 1974.

LESWICK, Jack

Center. Shoots right. 5'6", 155 lbs. Born, Saskatoon, Sask., January 1, 1910.

Season	Club	GP	G	A	Pts	PIM	GP	G	A	Pts	PIM
1933-34 ◆	Chicago Black Hawks	37	1	7	8	16	....	....	....	....	....
	NHL Totals	**37**	**1**	**7**	**8**	**16**	....	....	....	....	....

• Brother of Pete and Tony

Signed as a free agent by **Chicago** (Duluth-AHA), January, 1930.

LESWICK, Pete

Wing. Shoots right. 5'7", 163 lbs. Born, Saskatoon, Sask., July 12, 1918.

Season	Club	GP	G	A	Pts	PIM	GP	G	A	Pts	PIM
1936-37	New York Americans	1	1	0	1	0	....	....	....	....	....
1944-45	Boston Bruins	2	0	0	0	0	....	....	....	....	....
	NHL Totals	**3**	**1**	**0**	**1**	**0**	....	....	....	....	....

• Brother of Jack and Tony

Signed as a free agent by **NY Americans**, October 15, 1935. Signed as a free agent by **Boston**, October 12, 1944. Traded to **Detroit** by **Boston** for Bill Jennings, October 30, 1944. Traded to **Cleveland** (AHL) by **Detroit** for cash, September 10, 1946. Traded to **Montreal** (Buffalo-AHL) by **Cleveland** (AHL) for Murdo MacKay, August 4, 1950.

LESWICK, Tony

Wing. Shoots right. 5'7", 160 lbs. Born, Humboldt, Sask., March 17, 1923.

Season	Club	GP	G	A	Pts	PIM	GP	G	A	Pts	PIM
1945-46	New York Rangers	50	15	9	24	26	....	....	....	....	....
1946-47	New York Rangers	59	27	14	41	51	....	....	....	....	....
1947-48	New York Rangers	60	24	16	40	76	6	3	2	5	8
1948-49	New York Rangers	60	13	14	27	70	....	....	....	....	....
1949-50	New York Rangers	69	19	25	44	85	12	2	4	6	12
1950-51	New York Rangers	70	15	11	26	112	....	....	....	....	....
1951-52 ◆	Detroit Red Wings	70	9	10	19	93	8	3	1	4	22
1952-53	Detroit Red Wings	70	15	12	27	87	6	1	0	1	11
1953-54 ◆	Detroit Red Wings	70	6	18	24	90	12	3	1	4	18
1954-55 ◆	Detroit Red Wings	70	10	17	27	137	11	1	2	3	20
1955-56	Chicago Black Hawks	70	11	11	22	71	....	....	....	....	....
1957-58	Detroit Red Wings	22	1	2	3	2	4	0	0	0	0
	NHL Totals	**740**	**165**	**159**	**324**	**900**	**59**	**13**	**10**	**23**	**91**

• Brother of Jack and Pete • NHL Second All-Star Team (1950)

Played in NHL All-Star Game (1947, 1948, 1949, 1950, 1952, 1954)

Claimed by **NY Rangers** from **Buffalo** (AHL) in Inter-League Draft, June 14, 1945. Traded to **Detroit** by **NY Rangers** for Gaye Stewart, June 8, 1951. Traded to **Chicago** by **Detroit** with Glen Skov, Johnny Wilson and Benny Woit for Jerry Toppazzini, John McCormack, Dave Creighton and Gord Hollingworth, May 27, 1955. Traded to **Detroit** by **Chicago** for cash, August 1, 1956.

LETANG, Alan

Defense. Shoots left. 6'1", 205 lbs. Born, Renfrew, Ont., September 4, 1975.
(Montreal's 10th choice, 203rd overall, in 1993 Entry Draft).

Season	Club	Regular Season GP	G	A	Pts	PIM	Playoffs GP	G	A	Pts	PIM
99-2000	Dallas Stars	8	0	0	0	2	....	....	....	....	....
2001-02	Calgary Flames	2	0	0	0	0	....	....	....	....	....
2002-03	New York Islanders	4	0	0	0	0	....	....	....	....	....
	NHL Totals	**14**	**0**	**0**	**0**	**2**	....	....	....	....	....

Signed as a free agent by **Dallas**, March 22, 1999. Signed as a free agent by **Calgary**, August 22, 2001. Signed as a free agent by **NY Islanders**, July 18, 2002.

LETOWSKI, Trevor

Right wing. Shoots right. 5'10", 176 lbs. Born, Thunder Bay, Ont., April 5, 1977.
(Phoenix's 6th choice, 174th overall, in 1996 Entry Draft).

Season	Club	Regular Season GP	G	A	Pts	PIM	Playoffs GP	G	A	Pts	PIM
1998-99	Phoenix Coyotes	14	2	2	4	2	....	....	....	....	....
99-2000	Phoenix Coyotes	82	19	20	39	20	5	1	1	2	4
2000-01	Phoenix Coyotes	77	7	15	22	32	....	....	....	....	....
2001-02	Phoenix Coyotes	33	2	6	8	4	....	....	....	....	....
	Vancouver Canucks	42	7	10	17	15	6	0	1	1	8
2002-03	Vancouver Canucks	78	11	14	25	36	6	0	1	1	0
	NHL Totals	**326**	**48**	**67**	**115**	**109**	**17**	**1**	**3**	**4**	**12**

Traded to **Vancouver** by **Phoenix** with Todd Warriner, Tyler Bouck and Phoenix's 3rd round choice (later traded back to Phoenix – Phoenix selected Dimitri Pestunov) in 2003 Entry Draft for Drake Berehowsky and Denis Pederson, December 28, 2001. Signed as a free agent by **Columbus**, July 3, 2003.

LEVANDOSKI, Joe

Right wing. Shoots right. 5'11", 185 lbs. Born, Cobalt, Ont., March 17, 1921.

Season	Club	Regular Season GP	G	A	Pts	PIM	Playoffs GP	G	A	Pts	PIM
1946-47	New York Rangers	8	1	1	2	0	....	....	....	....	....
	NHL Totals	**8**	**1**	**1**	**2**	**0**	....	....	....	....	....

Traded to **Calgary** (WHL) by **NY Rangers** for cash, September 22, 1952.

LEVEILLE, Normand

Left wing. Shoots left. 5'10", 175 lbs. Born, Montreal, Que., January 10, 1963.
(Boston's 1st choice, 14th overall, in 1981 Entry Draft).

Season	Club	Regular Season GP	G	A	Pts	PIM	Playoffs GP	G	A	Pts	PIM
1981-82	Boston Bruins	66	14	19	33	49	....	....	....	....	....
1982-83	Boston Bruins	9	3	6	9	0	....	....	....	....	....
	NHL Totals	**75**	**17**	**25**	**42**	**49**	....	....	....	....	....

Suffered career-ending brain aneurysm during game vs. Vancouver, October 23, 1982.

LEVEQUE, Guy

Center. Shoots right. 5'11", 180 lbs. Born, Kingston, Ont., December 28, 1972.
(Los Angeles' 1st choice, 42nd overall, in 1991 Entry Draft).

Season	Club	Regular Season GP	G	A	Pts	PIM	Playoffs GP	G	A	Pts	PIM
1992-93	Los Angeles Kings	12	2	1	3	19	....	....	....	....	....
1993-94	Los Angeles Kings	5	0	1	1	2	....	....	....	....	....
	NHL Totals	**17**	**2**	**2**	**4**	**21**	....	....	....	....	....

Traded to **Toronto** by **Los Angeles** with Dixon Ward, Kelly Fairchild and Shayne Toporowski for Eric Lacroix, Chris Snell and Toronto's 4th round choice (Eric Belanger) in 1996 Entry Draft, October 3, 1994.

LEVER, Don

Left wing. Shoots left. 5'11", 185 lbs. Born, South Porcupine, Ont., November 14, 1952.
(Vancouver's 1st choice, 3rd overall, in 1972 Amateur Draft).

Season	Club	Regular Season GP	G	A	Pts	PIM	Playoffs GP	G	A	Pts	PIM
1972-73	Vancouver Canucks	78	12	26	38	49	....	....	....	....	....
1973-74	Vancouver Canucks	78	23	25	48	28	....	....	....	....	....
1974-75	Vancouver Canucks	80	38	30	68	49	5	0	1	1	4
1975-76	Vancouver Canucks	80	25	40	65	93	2	0	0	0	0
1976-77	Vancouver Canucks	80	27	30	57	28	....	....	....	....	....
1977-78	Vancouver Canucks	75	17	32	49	58	....	....	....	....	....
1978-79	Vancouver Canucks	71	23	21	44	17	3	2	1	3	2
1979-80	Vancouver Canucks	51	21	17	38	32	....	....	....	....	....
	Atlanta Flames	28	14	16	30	4	4	1	1	2	0
1980-81	Calgary Flames	62	26	31	57	56	16	4	7	11	20
1981-82	Calgary Flames	23	8	11	19	6	....	....	....	....	....
	Colorado Rockies	59	22	28	50	20	....	....	....	....	....
1982-83	New Jersey Devils	79	23	30	53	68	....	....	....	....	....
1983-84	New Jersey Devils	70	14	19	33	44	....	....	....	....	....
1984-85	New Jersey Devils	67	10	8	18	31	....	....	....	....	....
1985-86	Buffalo Sabres	29	7	1	8	6	....	....	....	....	....
1986-87	Buffalo Sabres	10	3	2	5	4	....	....	....	....	....
	NHL Totals	**1020**	**313**	**367**	**680**	**593**	**30**	**7**	**10**	**17**	**26**

Played in NHL All-Star Game (1982)

Traded to **Atlanta** by **Vancouver** with Brad Smith for Ivan Boldirev and Darcy Rota, February 8, 1980. Transferred to **Calgary** after **Colorado** franchise relocated, June 24, 1980. Traded to **Colorado** by **Calgary** with Bob MacMillan for Lanny McDonald and Colorado's 4th round choice (later traded to NY Islanders – NY Islanders selected Mikko Makela) in 1983 Entry Draft, November 25, 1981. Transferred to **New Jersey** after **Colorado** franchise relocated, June 30, 1982. Rights traded to **Buffalo** by **New Jersey** for cash, September 9, 1985.

LEVIE, Craig

Defense. Shoots right. 5'11", 190 lbs. Born, Calgary, Alta., August 17, 1959.
(Montreal's 3rd choice, 43rd overall, in 1979 Entry Draft).

Season	Club	Regular Season GP	G	A	Pts	PIM	Playoffs GP	G	A	Pts	PIM
1981-82	Winnipeg Jets	40	4	9	13	48	....	....	....	....	....
1982-83	Winnipeg Jets	22	4	5	9	31	....	....	....	....	....
1983-84	Minnesota North Stars	37	6	13	19	44	15	2	3	5	32
1984-85	St. Louis Blues	61	6	23	29	33	1	0	0	0	0
1985-86	Minnesota North Stars	14	2	2	4	8	....	....	....	....	....
1986-87	Vancouver Canucks	9	0	1	1	13	....	....	....	....	....
	NHL Totals	**183**	**22**	**53**	**75**	**177**	**16**	**2**	**3**	**5**	**32**

Claimed by **Winnipeg** from **Montreal** in Waiver Draft, October 5, 1981. Traded to **Minnesota** by **Winnipeg** with the rights to Tom Ward for Tim Young, August 3, 1983. Claimed by **St. Louis** from **Minnesota** in Waiver Draft, October 9, 1984. Claimed by **Calgary** from **St. Louis** in Waiver Draft, October 7, 1985. Claimed on waivers by **Minnesota** from **Calgary**, October 7, 1985. Signed as a free agent by **Vancouver**, March 1, 1987.

LEVINS, Scott

Center/Right wing. Shoots right. 6'4", 210 lbs. Born, Spokane, WA, January 30, 1970.
(Winnipeg's 4th choice, 75th overall, in 1990 Entry Draft).

Season	Club	Regular Season GP	G	A	Pts	PIM	Playoffs GP	G	A	Pts	PIM
1992-93	Winnipeg Jets	9	0	1	1	18	....	....	....	....	....
1993-94	Florida Panthers	29	5	6	11	69	....	....	....	....	....
	Ottawa Senators	33	3	5	8	93	....	....	....	....	....
1994-95	Ottawa Senators	24	5	6	11	51	....	....	....	....	....
1995-96	Ottawa Senators	27	0	2	2	80	....	....	....	....	....
1997-98	Phoenix Coyotes	2	0	0	0	5	....	....	....	....	....
	NHL Totals	**124**	**13**	**20**	**33**	**316**	....	....	....	....	....

Claimed by **Florida** from **Winnipeg** in Expansion Draft, June 24, 1993. Traded to **Ottawa** by **Florida** with Evgeny Davydov, Florida's 6th round choice (Mike Gaffney) in 1994 Entry Draft and Dallas' 4th round choice (previously acquired, Ottawa selected Kevin Bolibruck) in 1995 Entry Draft for Bob Kudelski, January 6, 1994. Signed as a free agent by **Phoenix**, October 3, 1996. Signed as a free agent by **Carolina**, August 18, 1998.

LEVINSKY, Alex

Defense. Shoots right. 5'10", 184 lbs. Born, Syracuse, NY, February 2, 1910.

Season	Club	Regular Season GP	G	A	Pts	PIM	Playoffs GP	G	A	Pts	PIM
1930-31	Toronto Maple Leafs	8	0	1	1	2	2	0	0	0	0
1931-32 ♦	Toronto Maple Leafs	47	5	5	10	29	7	0	0	0	6
1932-33	Toronto Maple Leafs	48	1	4	5	61	9	1	0	1	14
1933-34	Toronto Maple Leafs	47	5	11	16	38	5	0	0	0	6
1934-35	New York Rangers	20	0	4	4	6	....	....	....	....	....
	Chicago Black Hawks	23	3	4	7	16	2	0	0	0	0
1935-36	Chicago Black Hawks	48	1	7	8	69	2	0	1	1	0
1936-37	Chicago Black Hawks	48	0	8	8	32	....	....	....	....	....
1937-38 ♦	Chicago Black Hawks	48	3	2	5	18	10	1	0	1	0
1938-39	Chicago Black Hawks	30	1	3	4	36	....	....	....	....	....
	NHL Totals	**367**	**19**	**49**	**68**	**307**	**37**	**2**	**1**	**3**	**26**

Played in NHL All-Star Game (1934)

Signed as a free agent by **Toronto**, March 2, 1931. Traded to **NY Rangers** by **Toronto** for cash, April 11, 1934. Traded to **Chicago** by **NY Rangers** for cash, January 16, 1935. Traded to **NY Rangers** by **Chicago** with $5,000 for Joe Cooper, January 16, 1939.

LEVO, Tapio

Defense. Shoots left. 6'2", 200 lbs. Born, Pori, Finland, September 24, 1955.
(Pittsburgh's 8th choice, 139th overall, in 1975 Amateur Draft).

Season	Club	Regular Season GP	G	A	Pts	PIM	Playoffs GP	G	A	Pts	PIM
1981-82	Colorado Rockies	34	9	13	22	14	....	....	....	....	....
1982-83	New Jersey Devils	73	7	40	47	22	....	....	....	....	....
	NHL Totals	**107**	**16**	**53**	**69**	**36**	....	....	....	....	....

Signed as a free agent by **New Jersey**, July 8, 1981. Transferred to **New Jersey** after **Colorado** franchise relocated, June 30, 1982.

LEWICKI, Danny

Left wing. Shoots left. 5'8", 147 lbs. Born, Fort William, Ont., March 12, 1931.

Season	Club	Regular Season GP	G	A	Pts	PIM	Playoffs GP	G	A	Pts	PIM
1950-51 ♦	Toronto Maple Leafs	61	16	18	34	26	9	0	0	0	0
1951-52	Toronto Maple Leafs	51	4	9	13	26	....	....	....	....	....
1952-53	Toronto Maple Leafs	4	1	3	4	2	....	....	....	....	....
1953-54	Toronto Maple Leafs	7	0	1	1	12	....	....	....	....	....
1954-55	New York Rangers	70	29	24	53	8	....	....	....	....	....
1955-56	New York Rangers	70	18	27	45	26	5	0	3	3	0
1956-57	New York Rangers	70	18	20	38	47	5	0	1	1	2
1957-58	New York Rangers	70	11	19	30	26	6	0	0	0	6
1958-59	Chicago Black Hawks	58	8	14	22	4	3	0	0	0	0
	NHL Totals	**461**	**105**	**135**	**240**	**177**	**28**	**0**	**4**	**4**	**8**

NHL Second All-Star Team (1955)

Played in NHL All-Star Game (1955)

Rights traded to **Toronto** by **Providence** (AHL) for cash and future considerations (Jack Hamilton, October 27, 1948), July 27, 1948. Traded to **NY Rangers** by **Toronto** for cash, July 20, 1954. Claimed by **Montreal** from **NY Rangers** in Intra-League Draft, June 3, 1958. Claimed on waivers by **Chicago** from **Montreal**, September 23, 1958. Rights traded to **Montreal** by **Chicago** with Glen Skov, Bob Bailey, Terry Gray and Lorne Ferguson for Cec Hoekstra, Reggie Fleming, Ab McDonald and Bob Courcy, June 7, 1960.

LEWIS, Dale

Left wing. Shoots left. 6', 190 lbs. Born, Edmonton, Alta., July 28, 1952.

Season	Club	Regular Season GP	G	A	Pts	PIM	Playoffs GP	G	A	Pts	PIM
1975-76	New York Rangers	8	0	0	0	0	....	....	....	....	....
	NHL Totals	**8**	**0**	**0**	**0**	**0**	....	....	....	....	....

Signed as a free agent by **Los Angeles**, September, 1973. Claimed by **NY Rangers** from **Los Angeles** (Springfield-AHL) in Intra-League Draft, June 17, 1975. Signed as a free agent by **Atlanta**, September 11, 1979. Transferred to **Calgary** after **Atlanta** franchise relocated, June 24, 1980. Traded to **NY Rangers** by **Calgary** for Frank Beaton, November 18, 1980.

LEWIS, Dave

Defense. Shoots left. 6'2", 205 lbs. Born, Kindersley, Sask., July 3, 1953.
(NY Islanders' 2nd choice, 33rd overall, in 1973 Amateur Draft).

Season	Club	Regular Season GP	G	A	Pts	PIM	Playoffs GP	G	A	Pts	PIM
1973-74	New York Islanders	66	2	15	17	58	....	....	....	....	....

Season	Club	GP	G	A	Pts	PIM	GP	G	A	Pts	PIM
		REGULAR SEASON					PLAYOFFS				
1974-75	New York Islanders	78	5	14	19	98	17	0	1	1	28
1975-76	New York Islanders	73	0	19	19	54	13	0	1	1	44
1976-77	New York Islanders	79	4	24	28	44	12	1	6	7	4
1977-78	New York Islanders	77	3	11	14	58	7	0	1	1	11
1978-79	New York Islanders	79	5	18	23	43	10	0	0	0	4
1979-80	New York Islanders	62	5	16	21	54	....	....	....	....	....
	Los Angeles Kings	11	1	1	2	12	4	0	1	1	2
1980-81	Los Angeles Kings	67	1	12	13	98	4	0	2	2	4
1981-82	Los Angeles Kings	64	1	13	14	75	10	0	4	4	36
1982-83	Los Angeles Kings	79	2	10	12	53	....	....	....	....	....
1983-84	New Jersey Devils	66	2	5	7	63	....	....	....	....	....
1984-85	New Jersey Devils	74	3	9	12	78	....	....	....	....	....
1985-86	New Jersey Devils	69	0	15	15	81	....	....	....	....	....
1986-87	Detroit Red Wings	58	2	5	7	66	14	0	4	4	10
1987-88	Detroit Red Wings	6	0	0	0	18	....	....	....	....	....
	NHL Totals	**1008**	**36**	**187**	**223**	**953**	**91**	**1**	**20**	**21**	**143**

Traded to **Los Angeles** by **NY Islanders** with Billy Harris for Butch Goring, March 10, 1980. Traded to **Minnesota** by **Los Angeles** for Steve Christoff and Fred Barrett, October 3, 1983. Traded to **New Jersey** by **Minnesota** for Brent Ashton, October 3, 1983. Signed as a free agent by **Detroit**, July 27, 1986.

LEWIS, Doug

Left wing. Shoots left. 5'8", 155 lbs. Born, Winnipeg, Man., March 3, 1921.

Season	Club	GP	G	A	Pts	PIM	GP	G	A	Pts	PIM
1946-47	Montreal Canadiens	3	0	0	0	0	....	....	....	....	....
	NHL Totals	**3**	**0**	**0**	**0**	**0**	....	....	....	....	....

LEWIS, Herbie

HHOF

Left wing. Shoots left. 5'9", 163 lbs. Born, Calgary, Alta., April 17, 1906.

Season	Club	GP	G	A	Pts	PIM	GP	G	A	Pts	PIM
1928-29	Detroit Cougars	36	9	5	14	33	....	....	....	....	....
1929-30	Detroit Cougars	44	20	11	31	36	....	....	....	....	....
1930-31	Detroit Falcons	43	15	6	21	38	....	....	....	....	....
1931-32	Detroit Falcons	48	5	14	19	21	2	0	0	0	0
1932-33	Detroit Red Wings	48	20	14	34	20	4	1	0	1	0
1933-34	Detroit Red Wings	43	16	15	31	15	9	*5	2	7	2
1934-35	Detroit Red Wings	47	16	27	43	26	....	....	....	....	....
1935-36 ◆	Detroit Red Wings	45	14	23	37	25	7	2	3	5	0
1936-37 ◆	Detroit Red Wings	45	14	18	32	14	10	*4	3	7	4
1937-38	Detroit Red Wings	42	13	18	31	12	....	....	....	....	....
1938-39	Detroit Red Wings	42	6	10	16	8	6	1	2	3	0
	NHL Totals	**483**	**148**	**161**	**309**	**248**	**38**	**13**	**10**	**23**	**6**

Played in NHL All-Star Game (1934)

Claimed by **Detroit** from **Duluth** (AHA) in Inter-League Draft, May 14, 1928.

LEY, Rick

Defense. Shoots left. 5'9", 190 lbs. Born, Orillia, Ont., November 2, 1948.
(Toronto's 3rd choice, 16th overall, in 1966 Amateur Draft).

Season	Club	GP	G	A	Pts	PIM	GP	G	A	Pts	PIM
1968-69	Toronto Maple Leafs	38	1	11	12	39	3	0	0	0	9
1969-70	Toronto Maple Leafs	48	2	13	15	102	....	....	....	....	....
1970-71	Toronto Maple Leafs	76	4	16	20	151	6	0	2	2	4
1971-72	Toronto Maple Leafs	67	1	14	15	124	5	0	0	0	7
1979-80	Hartford Whalers	65	4	16	20	92	....	....	....	....	....
1980-81	Hartford Whalers	16	0	2	2	20	....	....	....	....	....
	NHL Totals	**310**	**12**	**72**	**84**	**528**	**14**	**0**	**2**	**2**	**20**

Reclaimed by **Toronto** from **Hartford** prior to Expansion Draft, June 9, 1979. Claimed by **Hartford** from **Toronto** in Expansion Draft, June 13, 1979.

LIBA, Igor

Left wing. Shoots right. 6', 192 lbs. Born, Kosice, Czech., November 4, 1960.
(Calgary's 7th choice, 94th overall, in 1983 Entry Draft).

Season	Club	GP	G	A	Pts	PIM	GP	G	A	Pts	PIM
1988-89	New York Rangers	10	2	5	7	15	....	....	....	....	....
	Los Angeles Kings	27	5	13	18	21	2	0	0	0	2
	NHL Totals	**37**	**7**	**18**	**25**	**36**	**2**	**0**	**0**	**0**	**2**

Rights traded to **Minnesota** by **Calgary** for Minnesota's 5th round choice (Tomas Forslund) in 1988 Entry Draft, May 20, 1988. Traded to **NY Rangers** by **Minnesota** with Brian Lawton and the rights to Rick Bennett for Paul Jerrard, Mark Tinordi the rights to Bret Barnett and Mike Sullivan and Los Angeles' 3rd round choice (previously acquired, Minnesota selected Murray Garbutt) in 1989 Entry Draft, October 11, 1988. Traded to **Los Angeles** by **NY Rangers** with Todd Elik, Michael Boyce and future considerations for Dean Kennedy and Denis Larocque, December 12, 1988.

LIBBY, Jeff

Defense. Shoots left. 6'3", 215 lbs. Born, Waterville, ME, March 1, 1974.

Season	Club	GP	G	A	Pts	PIM	GP	G	A	Pts	PIM
1997-98	New York Islanders	1	0	0	0	0	....	....	....	....	....
	NHL Totals	**1**	**0**	**0**	**0**	**0**	....	....	....	....	....

Signed as a free agent by **NY Islanders**, May 12, 1997.

LIBETT, Nick

Left wing. Shoots left. 6'1", 195 lbs. Born, Stratford, Ont., December 9, 1945.

Season	Club	GP	G	A	Pts	PIM	GP	G	A	Pts	PIM
		REGULAR SEASON					PLAYOFFS				
1967-68	Detroit Red Wings	22	2	1	3	12	....	....	....	....	....
1968-69	Detroit Red Wings	75	10	14	24	34	....	....	....	....	....
1969-70	Detroit Red Wings	76	20	20	40	39	4	2	0	2	2
1970-71	Detroit Red Wings	78	16	13	29	25	....	....	....	....	....
1971-72	Detroit Red Wings	77	31	22	53	50	....	....	....	....	....
1972-73	Detroit Red Wings	78	19	34	53	56	....	....	....	....	....
1973-74	Detroit Red Wings	67	24	24	48	37	....	....	....	....	....
1974-75	Detroit Red Wings	80	23	28	51	39	....	....	....	....	....
1975-76	Detroit Red Wings	80	20	26	46	71	....	....	....	....	....
1976-77	Detroit Red Wings	80	14	27	41	25	....	....	....	....	....
1977-78	Detroit Red Wings	80	23	22	45	46	7	3	1	4	0
1978-79	Detroit Red Wings	68	15	19	34	20	....	....	....	....	....
1979-80	Pittsburgh Penguins	78	14	12	26	14	5	1	1	2	0
1980-81	Pittsburgh Penguins	43	6	6	12	4	....	....	....	....	....
	NHL Totals	**982**	**237**	**268**	**505**	**472**	**16**	**6**	**2**	**8**	**2**

Played in NHL All-Star Game (1977)

Traded to **Pittsburgh** by **Detroit** for Pete Mahovlich, August 3, 1979.

LICARI, Tony

Right wing. Shoots right. 5'7", 147 lbs. Born, Ottawa, Ont., April 9, 1921.

Season	Club	GP	G	A	Pts	PIM	GP	G	A	Pts	PIM
1946-47	Detroit Red Wings	9	0	1	1	0	....	....	....	....	....
	NHL Totals	**9**	**0**	**1**	**1**	**0**	....	....	....	....	....

Traded to **Chicago** (St. Louis-AHL) by **Detroit** with Red Almas, Lloyd Doran, Barry Sullivan and Thain Simon for Joe Lund and Hec Highton, September 9, 1948.

LIDDINGTON, Bob

Left wing. Shoots left. 6', 175 lbs. Born, Calgary, Alta., September 15, 1948.

Season	Club	GP	G	A	Pts	PIM	GP	G	A	Pts	PIM
1970-71	Toronto Maple Leafs	11	0	1	1	2	....	....	....	....	....
	NHL Totals	**11**	**0**	**1**	**1**	**2**	....	....	....	....	....

Signed as a free agent by **Toronto**, October, 1969.

LIDSTER, Doug

Defense. Shoots right. 6'1", 190 lbs. Born, Kamloops, B.C., October 18, 1960.
(Vancouver's 6th choice, 133rd overall, in 1980 Entry Draft).

Season	Club	GP	G	A	Pts	PIM	GP	G	A	Pts	PIM
1983-84	Vancouver Canucks	8	0	0	0	4	2	0	1	1	0
1984-85	Vancouver Canucks	78	6	24	30	55	....	....	....	....	....
1985-86	Vancouver Canucks	78	12	16	28	56	3	0	1	1	2
1986-87	Vancouver Canucks	80	12	51	63	40	....	....	....	....	....
1987-88	Vancouver Canucks	64	4	32	36	105	....	....	....	....	....
1988-89	Vancouver Canucks	63	5	17	22	78	7	1	1	2	9
1989-90	Vancouver Canucks	80	8	28	36	36	....	....	....	....	....
1990-91	Vancouver Canucks	78	6	32	38	77	6	0	2	2	6
1991-92	Vancouver Canucks	66	6	23	29	39	11	1	2	3	11
1992-93	Vancouver Canucks	71	6	19	25	36	12	0	3	3	8
1993-94 ◆	New York Rangers	34	0	2	2	33	9	2	0	2	10
1994-95	St. Louis Blues	37	2	7	9	12	4	0	0	0	2
1995-96	New York Rangers	59	5	9	14	50	7	1	0	1	6
1996-97	New York Rangers	48	3	4	7	24	15	1	5	6	8
1997-98	New York Rangers	36	0	4	4	24	....	....	....	....	....
1998-99	Dallas Stars	17	0	0	0	10	4	0	0	0	2
	NHL Totals	**897**	**75**	**268**	**343**	**679**	**80**	**6**	**15**	**21**	**64**

Traded to **NY Rangers** by **Vancouver** to complete transaction that sent John Vanbiesbrouck to Vancouver (June 20, 1993), June 25, 1993. Traded to **St. Louis** by **NY Rangers** with Esa Tikkanen for Petr Nedved, July 24, 1994. Traded to **NY Rangers** by **St. Louis** for Jay Wells, July 28, 1995. Signed as a free agent by **Dallas**, February 26, 1999.

LIDSTROM, Nicklas

Defense. Shoots left. 6'2", 185 lbs. Born, Vasteras, Sweden, April 28, 1970.
(Detroit's 3rd choice, 53rd overall, in 1989 Entry Draft).

Season	Club	GP	G	A	Pts	PIM	GP	G	A	Pts	PIM
1991-92	Detroit Red Wings	80	11	49	60	22	11	1	2	3	0
1992-93	Detroit Red Wings	84	7	34	41	28	7	1	0	1	0
1993-94	Detroit Red Wings	84	10	46	56	26	7	3	2	5	0
1994-95	Detroit Red Wings	43	10	16	26	6	18	4	12	16	8
1995-96	Detroit Red Wings	81	17	50	67	20	19	5	9	14	10
1996-97 ◆	Detroit Red Wings	79	15	42	57	30	20	2	6	8	2
1997-98 ◆	Detroit Red Wings	80	17	42	59	18	22	6	13	19	8
1998-99	Detroit Red Wings	81	14	43	57	14	10	2	9	11	4
99-2000	Detroit Red Wings	81	20	53	73	18	9	2	4	6	4
2000-01	Detroit Red Wings	82	15	56	71	18	6	1	7	8	0
2001-02 ◆	Detroit Red Wings	78	9	50	59	20	23	5	11	16	2
2002-03	Detroit Red Wings	82	18	44	62	38	4	0	2	2	0
	NHL Totals	**935**	**163**	**525**	**688**	**258**	**156**	**32**	**77**	**109**	**38**

NHL All-Rookie Team (1992) • NHL First All-Star Team (1998, 1999, 2000, 2001, 2002, 2003) • James Norris Memorial Trophy (2001, 2002, 2003) • Conn Smythe Trophy (2002)

Played in NHL All-Star Game (1996, 1998, 1999, 2000, 2001, 2002, 2003)

LILJA, Andreas

Defense. Shoots left. 6'3", 222 lbs. Born, Landskrona, Sweden, July 13, 1975.
(Los Angeles' 2nd choice, 54th overall, in 2000 Entry Draft).

Season	Club	GP	G	A	Pts	PIM	GP	G	A	Pts	PIM
2000-01	Los Angeles Kings	2	0	0	0	4	1	0	0	0	0
2001-02	Los Angeles Kings	26	1	4	5	22	5	0	0	0	6
2002-03	Los Angeles Kings	17	0	3	3	14	....	....	....	....	....
	Florida Panthers	56	4	8	12	56	....	....	....	....	....
	NHL Totals	**101**	**5**	**15**	**20**	**96**	**6**	**0**	**0**	**0**	**6**

• Spent majority of 2001-02 season on practice roster. Traded to **Florida** by **Los Angeles** with Jaroslav Bednar for Dmitry Yushkevich and Florida's 5th round choice (previously acquired, Los Angeles selected Brady Murray) in 2003 Entry Draft, November 26, 2002.

LILLEY, John

Right wing. Shoots right. 5'9", 170 lbs. Born, Wakefield, MA, August 3, 1972.
(Winnipeg's 8th choice, 140th overall, in 1990 Entry Draft).

Season	Club	Regular Season GP	G	A	Pts	PIM	Playoffs GP	G	A	Pts	PIM
1993-94	Mighty Ducks of Anaheim	13	1	6	7	8	....	....	....	....	....
1994-95	Mighty Ducks of Anaheim	9	2	2	4	5	....	....	....	....	....
1995-96	Mighty Ducks of Anaheim	1	0	0	0	0	....	....	....	....	....
	NHL Totals	**23**	**3**	**8**	**11**	**13**	....	....	....	....	....

Signed as a free agent by **Anaheim**, March 9, 1994.

LIND, Juha

Center. Shoots left. 5'11", 185 lbs. Born, Helsinki, Finland, January 2, 1974.
(Minnesota's 6th choice, 178th overall, in 1992 Entry Draft).

Season	Club	Regular Season GP	G	A	Pts	PIM	Playoffs GP	G	A	Pts	PIM
1997-98	Dallas Stars	39	2	3	5	6	15	2	2	4	8
99-2000	Dallas Stars	34	3	4	7	6	....	....	....	....	....
	Montreal Canadiens	13	1	2	3	4	....	....	....	....	....
2000-01	Montreal Canadiens	47	3	4	7	4	....	....	....	....	....
	NHL Totals	**133**	**9**	**13**	**22**	**20**	**15**	**2**	**2**	**4**	**8**

Rights transferred to **Dallas** after **Minnesota** franchise relocated, June 9, 1993. Traded to **Montreal** by **Dallas** for Scott Thornton, January 22, 2000.

LINDBERG, Chris

Left wing. Shoots left. 6'1", 190 lbs. Born, Fort Frances, Ont., April 16, 1967.

Season	Club	Regular Season GP	G	A	Pts	PIM	Playoffs GP	G	A	Pts	PIM
1991-92	Calgary Flames	17	2	5	7	17	....	....	....	....	....
1992-93	Calgary Flames	62	9	12	21	18	2	0	1	1	2
1993-94	Quebec Nordiques	37	6	8	14	12	....	....	....	....	....
	NHL Totals	**116**	**17**	**25**	**42**	**47**	**2**	**0**	**1**	**1**	**2**

Signed as a free agent by **Hartford**, March 17, 1989. Signed as a free agent by **Calgary**, August 2, 1991. Claimed by **Ottawa** from **Calgary** in Expansion Draft, June 18, 1992. Traded to **Calgary** by **Ottawa** for Mark Osiecki, June 22, 1992. Signed as a free agent by **Quebec**, September 9, 1993.

LINDBOM, Johan

Left wing. Shoots left. 6'2", 216 lbs. Born, Alvesta, Sweden, July 8, 1971.
(NY Rangers' 6th choice, 134th overall, in 1997 Entry Draft).

Season	Club	Regular Season GP	G	A	Pts	PIM	Playoffs GP	G	A	Pts	PIM
1997-98	New York Rangers	38	1	3	4	28	....	....	....	....	....
	NHL Totals	**38**	**1**	**3**	**4**	**28**	....	....	....	....	....

LINDEN, Jamie

Right wing. Shoots right. 6'3", 185 lbs. Born, Medicine Hat, Alta., July 19, 1972.

Season	Club	Regular Season GP	G	A	Pts	PIM	Playoffs GP	G	A	Pts	PIM
1994-95	Florida Panthers	4	0	0	0	17	....	....	....	....	....
	NHL Totals	**4**	**0**	**0**	**0**	**17**	....	....	....	....	....

• Family name was originally Van der Linden • Brother of Trevor

Signed as a free agent by **Florida**, October 4, 1993.

LINDEN, Trevor

Right wing. Shoots right. 6'4", 215 lbs. Born, Medicine Hat, Alta., April 11, 1970.
(Vancouver's 1st choice, 2nd overall, in 1988 Entry Draft).

Season	Club	Regular Season GP	G	A	Pts	PIM	Playoffs GP	G	A	Pts	PIM
1988-89	Vancouver Canucks	80	30	29	59	41	7	3	4	7	8
1989-90	Vancouver Canucks	73	21	30	51	43	....	....	....	....	....
1990-91	Vancouver Canucks	80	33	37	70	65	6	0	7	7	2
1991-92	Vancouver Canucks	80	31	44	75	101	13	4	8	12	6
1992-93	Vancouver Canucks	84	33	39	72	64	12	5	8	13	16
1993-94	Vancouver Canucks	84	32	29	61	73	24	12	13	25	18
1994-95	Vancouver Canucks	48	18	22	40	40	11	2	6	8	12
1995-96	Vancouver Canucks	82	33	47	80	42	6	4	4	8	6
1996-97	Vancouver Canucks	49	9	31	40	27	....	....	....	....	....
1997-98	Vancouver Canucks	42	7	14	21	49	....	....	....	....	....
	New York Islanders	25	10	7	17	33	....	....	....	....	....
1998-99	New York Islanders	82	18	29	47	32	....	....	....	....	....
99-2000	Montreal Canadiens	50	13	17	30	34	....	....	....	....	....
2000-01	Montreal Canadiens	57	12	21	33	52	....	....	....	....	....
	Washington Capitals	12	3	1	4	8	6	0	4	4	14
2001-02	Washington Capitals	16	1	2	3	6	....	....	....	....	....
	Vancouver Canucks	64	12	22	34	65	6	1	4	5	0
2002-03	Vancouver Canucks	71	19	22	41	30	14	1	2	3	10
	NHL Totals	**1079**	**335**	**443**	**778**	**805**	**105**	**32**	**60**	**92**	**92**

• Family name was originally Van der Linden • Brother of Jamie • NHL All-Rookie Team (1989)
• King Clancy Memorial Trophy (1997)

Played in NHL All-Star Game (1991, 1992)

Traded to **NY Islanders** by **Vancouver** for Todd Bertuzzi, Bryan McCabe and NY Islanders' 3rd round choice (Jarkko Ruutu) in 1998 Entry Draft, February 6, 1998. Traded to **Montreal** by **NY Islanders** for Montreal's 1st round choice (Branislav Mezei) in 1999 Entry Draft, May 29, 1999. Traded to **Washington** by **Montreal** with Dainius Zubrus and New Jersey's 2nd round choice (previously acquired, later traded to Tampa Bay – Tampa Bay selected Andreas Holmqvist) in 2001 Entry Draft for Richard Zednik, Jan Bulis and Washington's 1st round choice (Alexander Perezhogin) in 2001 Entry Draft, March 13, 2001. Traded to **Vancouver** by **Washington** with NY Islanders' 2nd round choice (previously acquired, Vancouver selected Denis Grot) in 2002 Entry Draft for Vancouver's 1st round choice (Boyd Gordon) in 2002 Entry Draft and Vancouver's 3rd round choice (later traded to Edmonton – Edmonton selected Zachery Stortini) in 2003 Entry Draft, November 10, 2001.

LINDGREN, Lars

Defense. Shoots left. 6'1", 200 lbs. Born, Pitea, Sweden, October 12, 1952.

Season	Club	Regular Season GP	G	A	Pts	PIM	Playoffs GP	G	A	Pts	PIM
1978-79	Vancouver Canucks	64	2	19	21	68	3	0	0	0	6
1979-80	Vancouver Canucks	73	5	30	35	66	2	0	1	1	0
1980-81	Vancouver Canucks	52	4	18	22	32	....	....	....	....	....
1981-82	Vancouver Canucks	75	5	16	21	74	16	2	4	6	6
1982-83	Vancouver Canucks	64	6	14	20	48	4	1	1	2	2
1983-84	Vancouver Canucks	7	1	2	3	4	....	....	....	....	....
	Minnesota North Stars	59	2	14	16	33	15	2	0	2	6
	NHL Totals	**394**	**25**	**113**	**138**	**325**	**40**	**5**	**6**	**11**	**20**

Played in NHL All-Star Game (1980)

Signed as a free agent by **Vancouver**, June 5, 1978. Traded to **Minnesota** by **Vancouver** for Minnesota's 3rd round choice (Landis Chaulk) in 1984 Entry Draft, October 20, 1983.

LINDGREN, Mats

Center/Left wing. Shoots left. 6'2", 202 lbs. Born, Skelleftea, Sweden, October 1, 1974.
(Winnipeg's 1st choice, 15th overall, in 1993 Entry Draft).

Season	Club	Regular Season GP	G	A	Pts	PIM	Playoffs GP	G	A	Pts	PIM
1996-97	Edmonton Oilers	69	11	14	25	12	12	0	4	4	0
1997-98	Edmonton Oilers	82	13	13	26	42	12	1	1	2	10
1998-99	Edmonton Oilers	48	5	12	17	22	....	....	....	....	....
	New York Islanders	12	5	3	8	2	....	....	....	....	....
99-2000	New York Islanders	43	9	7	16	24	....	....	....	....	....
2000-01	New York Islanders	20	3	4	7	10	....	....	....	....	....
2001-02	New York Islanders	59	3	12	15	16	....	....	....	....	....
2002-03	Vancouver Canucks	54	5	9	14	18	....	....	....	....	....
	NHL Totals	**387**	**54**	**74**	**128**	**146**	**24**	**1**	**5**	**6**	**10**

Traded to **Edmonton** by **Winnipeg** with Boris Mironov, Winnipeg's 1st round choice (Jason Bonsignore) in 1994 Entry Draft and Florida's 4th round choice (previously acquired, Edmonton selected Adam Copeland) in 1994 Entry Draft for Dave Manson and St. Louis' 6th round choice (previously acquired, Winnipeg selected Chris Kibermanis) in 1994 Entry Draft, March 15, 1994. Traded to **NY Islanders** by **Edmonton** with Edmonton's 8th round choice (Radek Martinek) in 1999 Entry Draft for Tommy Salo, March 20, 1999. • Missed majority of 2000-01 season recovering from shoulder injury suffered in game vs. Anaheim, November 25, 2000. Signed as a free agent by **Vancouver**, November 3, 2002.

LINDHOLM, Mikael

Center. Shoots left. 6'1", 194 lbs. Born, Gavle, Sweden, December 19, 1964.
(Los Angeles' 10th choice, 237th overall, in 1987 Entry Draft).

Season	Club	Regular Season GP	G	A	Pts	PIM	Playoffs GP	G	A	Pts	PIM
1989-90	Los Angeles Kings	18	2	2	4	2	....	....	....	....	....
	NHL Totals	**18**	**2**	**2**	**4**	**2**	....	....	....	....	....

LINDQUIST, Fredrik

Center. Shoots left. 6', 190 lbs. Born, Stockholm, Sweden, June 21, 1973.
(New Jersey's 4th choice, 55th overall, in 1991 Entry Draft).

Season	Club	Regular Season GP	G	A	Pts	PIM	Playoffs GP	G	A	Pts	PIM
1998-99	Edmonton Oilers	8	0	0	0	2	....	....	....	....	....
	NHL Totals	**8**	**0**	**0**	**0**	**2**	....	....	....	....	....

Traded to **Edmonton** by **New Jersey** with New Jersey's 4th (Kristian Antila) and 5th (Oleg Smirnov) round choices in 1998 Entry Draft for Pittsburgh's 3rd round choice (previously acquired, New Jersey selected Brian Gionta) in 1998 Entry Draft, June 27, 1998.

LINDROS, Brett

Right wing. Shoots right. 6'4", 215 lbs. Born, London, Ont., December 2, 1975.
(NY Islanders' 1st choice, 9th overall, in 1994 Entry Draft).

Season	Club	Regular Season GP	G	A	Pts	PIM	Playoffs GP	G	A	Pts	PIM
1994-95	New York Islanders	33	1	3	4	100	....	....	....	....	....
1995-96	New York Islanders	18	1	2	3	47	....	....	....	....	....
	NHL Totals	**51**	**2**	**5**	**7**	**147**	....	....	....	....	....

• Brother of Eric
• Suffered eventual career-ending head injury in game vs. Los Angeles, November 2, 1995.
• Officially announced retirement, May 1, 1996.

LINDROS, Eric

Center. Shoots right. 6'4", 240 lbs. Born, London, Ont., February 28, 1973.
(Quebec's 1st choice, 1st overall, in 1991 Entry Draft).

Season	Club	Regular Season GP	G	A	Pts	PIM	Playoffs GP	G	A	Pts	PIM
1992-93	Philadelphia Flyers	61	41	34	75	147	....	....	....	....	....
1993-94	Philadelphia Flyers	65	44	53	97	103	....	....	....	....	....
1994-95	Philadelphia Flyers	46	29	41	*70	60	12	4	11	15	18
1995-96	Philadelphia Flyers	73	47	68	115	163	12	6	6	12	43
1996-97	Philadelphia Flyers	52	32	47	79	136	19	12	14	*26	40
1997-98	Philadelphia Flyers	63	30	41	71	134	5	1	2	3	17
1998-99	Philadelphia Flyers	71	40	53	93	120	....	....	....	....	....
99-2000	Philadelphia Flyers	55	27	32	59	83	2	1	0	1	0
2001-02	New York Rangers	72	37	36	73	138	....	....	....	....	....
2002-03	New York Rangers	81	19	34	53	141	....	....	....	....	....
	NHL Totals	**639**	**346**	**439**	**785**	**1225**	**50**	**24**	**33**	**57**	**118**

• Brother of Brett • NHL All-Rookie Team (1993) • NHL First All-Star Team (1995) • Lester B. Pearson Award (1995) • Hart Trophy (1995) • NHL Second All-Star Team (1996)

Played in NHL All-Star Game (1994, 1996, 1997, 1998, 1999, 2000)

Traded to **Philadelphia** by **Quebec** for Peter Forsberg, Steve Duchesne, Kerry Huffman, Mike Ricci, Ron Hextall, Philadelphia's 1st round choice (Jocelyn Thibault) in 1993 Entry Draft, $15,000,000 and future considerations (Chris Simon and Philadelphia's 1st round choice (later traded to Toronto – later traded to Washington – Washington selected Nolan Baumgartner) in 1994 Entry Draft, July 21, 1992), June 30, 1992. • Missed entire 2000-01 season recovering from head injury suffered in game vs. New Jersey, May 26, 2000 and contract dispute with Philadelphia Flyers management. Traded to **NY Rangers** by **Philadelphia** for Kim Johnsson, Jan Havac, Pavel Brendl and NY Rangers' 3rd round choice (Stefan Ruzicka) in 2003 Entry Draft, August 20, 2001.

LINDSAY, Bill

Right wing. Shoots left. 6', 195 lbs. Born, Fernie, B.C., May 17, 1971.
(Quebec's 6th choice, 103rd overall, in 1991 Entry Draft).

Season	Club	Regular Season GP	G	A	Pts	PIM	Playoffs GP	G	A	Pts	PIM
1991-92	Quebec Nordiques	23	2	4	6	14	....	....	....	....	....
1992-93	Quebec Nordiques	44	4	9	13	16	....	....	....	....	....

Season	Club	Regular Season GP	G	A	Pts	PIM	Playoffs GP	G	A	Pts	PIM
1993-94	Florida Panthers	84	6	6	12	97	....	....	....	....	....
1994-95	Florida Panthers	48	10	9	19	46	....	....	....	....	....
1995-96	Florida Panthers	73	12	22	34	57	22	5	5	10	18
1996-97	Florida Panthers	81	11	23	34	120	3	0	1	1	8
1997-98	Florida Panthers	82	12	16	28	80	....	....	....	....	....
1998-99	Florida Panthers	75	12	15	27	92	....	....	....	....	....
99-2000	Calgary Flames	80	8	12	20	86	....	....	....	....	....
2000-01	Calgary Flames	52	1	9	10	97	....	....	....	....	....
	San Jose Sharks	16	0	4	4	29	6	0	0	0	16
2001-02	Florida Panthers	63	4	7	11	117	....	....	....	....	....
	Montreal Canadiens	13	1	3	4	23	11	2	2	4	2
2002-03	Montreal Canadiens	19	0	2	2	23	....	....	....	....	....
	NHL Totals	**753**	**83**	**141**	**224**	**897**	**42**	**7**	**8**	**15**	**44**

Claimed by **Florida** from **Quebec** in Expansion Draft, June 24, 1993. Traded to **Calgary** by **Florida** for Todd Simpson, September 30, 1999. Traded to **San Jose** by **Calgary** for Minnesota's 8th round choice (previously acquired, Calgary selected Joe Campbell) in 2001 Entry Draft, March 6, 2001. Signed as a free agent by **Florida**, August 23, 2001. Claimed on waivers by **Montreal** from **Florida**, March 19, 2002.

LINDSAY, Ted

HHOF

Left wing. Shoots left. 5'8", 163 lbs. Born, Renfrew, Ont., July 29, 1925.

Season	Club	GP	G	A	Pts	PIM	GP	G	A	Pts	PIM
1944-45	Detroit Red Wings	45	17	6	23	43	14	2	0	2	6
1945-46	Detroit Red Wings	47	7	10	17	14	5	0	1	1	0
1946-47	Detroit Red Wings	59	27	15	42	57	5	2	2	4	10
1947-48	Detroit Red Wings	60	*33	19	52	95	10	3	1	4	6
1948-49	Detroit Red Wings	50	26	28	54	97	11	2	*6	8	31
1949-50 ♦	Detroit Red Wings	69	23	*55	*78	141	13	4	4	8	16
1950-51	Detroit Red Wings	67	24	35	59	110	6	0	1	1	8
1951-52 ♦	Detroit Red Wings	70	30	39	69	123	8	*5	2	*7	8
1952-53	Detroit Red Wings	70	32	39	71	111	6	4	4	8	6
1953-54 ♦	Detroit Red Wings	70	26	36	62	110	12	4	4	8	14
1954-55 ♦	Detroit Red Wings	49	19	19	38	85	11	7	12	19	12
1955-56	Detroit Red Wings	67	27	23	50	161	10	6	3	9	22
1956-57	Detroit Red Wings	70	30	*55	85	103	5	2	4	6	8
1957-58	Chicago Black Hawks	68	15	24	39	110	....	....	....	....	....
1958-59	Chicago Black Hawks	70	22	36	58	*184	6	2	4	6	13
1959-60	Chicago Black Hawks	68	7	19	26	91	4	1	1	2	0
1964-65	Detroit Red Wings	69	14	14	28	173	7	3	0	3	34
	NHL Totals	**1068**	**379**	**472**	**851**	**1808**	**133**	**47**	**49**	**96**	**194**

• Son of Bert • NHL First All-Star Team (1948, 1950, 1951, 1952, 1953, 1954, 1956, 1957) • NHL Second All-Star Team (1949) • Art Ross Trophy (1950)

Played in NHL All-Star Game (1947, 1948, 1949, 1950, 1951, 1952, 1953, 1954, 1955, 1956, 1957)

Signed as a free agent by **Detroit**, October 18, 1944. Traded to **Chicago** by **Detroit** with Glenn Hall for Johnny Wilson, Forbes Kennedy, Hank Bassen and Bill Preston, July 23, 1957. Traded to **Detroit** by **Chicago** for cash, October 14, 1964.

LINDSTROM, Willy

Right wing. Shoots left. 6', 180 lbs. Born, Grums, Sweden, May 5, 1951.

Season	Club	GP	G	A	Pts	PIM	GP	G	A	Pts	PIM
1979-80	Winnipeg Jets	79	23	26	49	20	....	....	....	....	....
1980-81	Winnipeg Jets	72	22	13	35	45	....	....	....	....	....
1981-82	Winnipeg Jets	74	32	27	59	33	4	2	1	3	2
1982-83	Winnipeg Jets	63	20	25	45	8	....	....	....	....	....
	Edmonton Oilers	10	6	5	11	2	16	2	11	13	4
1983-84 ♦	Edmonton Oilers	73	22	16	38	38	19	5	5	10	10
1984-85 ♦	Edmonton Oilers	80	12	20	32	18	18	5	1	6	8
1985-86	Pittsburgh Penguins	71	14	17	31	30	....	....	....	....	....
1986-87	Pittsburgh Penguins	60	10	13	23	6	....	....	....	....	....
	NHL Totals	**582**	**161**	**162**	**323**	**200**	**57**	**14**	**18**	**32**	**24**

Signed as a free agent by **Winnipeg**, July 25, 1979. Traded to **Edmonton** by **Winnipeg** for Laurie Boschman, March 7, 1983. Claimed by **Pittsburgh** from **Edmonton** in Waiver Draft, October 7, 1985.

LING, David

Right wing. Shoots right. 5'10", 204 lbs. Born, Halifax, N.S., January 9, 1975.
(Quebec's 9th choice, 179th overall, in 1993 Entry Draft).

Season	Club	GP	G	A	Pts	PIM	GP	G	A	Pts	PIM
1996-97	Montreal Canadiens	2	0	0	0	0	....	....	....	....	....
1997-98	Montreal Canadiens	1	0	0	0	0	....	....	....	....	....
2001-02	Columbus Blue Jackets	5	0	0	0	7	....	....	....	....	....
2002-03	Columbus Blue Jackets	35	3	2	5	86	....	....	....	....	....
	NHL Totals	**43**	**3**	**2**	**5**	**93**	....	....	....	....	....

Rights transferred to **Colorado** after **Quebec** franchise relocated, June 21, 1995. Traded to **Calgary** by **Colorado** with Colorado's 9th round choice (Steve Shirreffs) in 1995 Entry Draft for Calgary's 9th round choice (Chris George) in 1995 Entry Draft, July 7, 1995. Traded to **Montreal** by **Calgary** with Calgary's 6th round choice (Gordie Dwyer) in 1998 Entry Draft for Scott Fraser, October 24, 1996. Traded to **Chicago** by **Montreal** for Martin Gendron, March 14, 1998. Traded to **Dallas** by **Chicago** for future considerations, August 11, 2000. Signed as a free agent by **Columbus**, July 7, 2001.

LINSEMAN, Ken

Center. Shoots left. 5'11", 180 lbs. Born, Kingston, Ont., August 11, 1958.
(Philadelphia's 2nd choice, 7th overall, in 1978 Amateur Draft).

Season	Club	GP	G	A	Pts	PIM	GP	G	A	Pts	PIM
1978-79	Philadelphia Flyers	30	5	20	25	23	8	2	6	8	22
1979-80	Philadelphia Flyers	80	22	57	79	107	17	4	*18	22	40
1980-81	Philadelphia Flyers	51	17	30	47	150	12	4	16	20	67
1981-82	Philadelphia Flyers	79	24	68	92	275	4	1	2	3	6
1982-83	Edmonton Oilers	72	33	42	75	181	16	6	8	14	22
1983-84 ♦	Edmonton Oilers	72	18	49	67	119	19	10	4	14	65
1984-85	Boston Bruins	74	25	49	74	126	5	4	6	10	8
1985-86	Boston Bruins	64	23	58	81	97	3	0	1	1	17
1986-87	Boston Bruins	64	15	34	49	126	4	1	1	2	22
1987-88	Boston Bruins	77	29	45	74	167	23	11	14	25	56
1988-89	Boston Bruins	78	27	45	72	164	....	....	....	....	....
1989-90	Boston Bruins	32	6	16	22	66	....	....	....	....	....
	Philadelphia Flyers	29	5	9	14	30	....	....	....	....	....
1990-91	Edmonton Oilers	56	7	29	36	94	2	0	1	1	0
1991-92	Toronto Maple Leafs	2	0	0	0	2	....	....	....	....	....
	NHL Totals	**860**	**256**	**551**	**807**	**1727**	**113**	**43**	**77**	**120**	**325**

Traded to **Hartford** by **Philadelphia** with Greg Adams and Philadelphia's 1st (David Jensen) and 3rd (Leif Karlsson) round choices in 1983 Entry Draft for Mark Howe and Hartford's 3rd round choice (Derrick Smith) in 1983 Entry Draft, August 19, 1982. Traded to **Edmonton** by **Harford** with Dan Nachbaur for Risto Siltanen and the rights to Brent Loney, August 19, 1982. Traded to **Boston** by **Edmonton** for Mike Krushelnyski, June 21, 1984. Traded to **Philadelphia** by **Boston** for Dave Poulin, January 16, 1990. Signed as a free agent by **Edmonton**, August 31, 1990. Traded to **Toronto** by **Edmonton** for cash, October 7, 1991.

LINTNER, Richard

Defense. Shoots right. 6'3", 212 lbs. Born, Trencin, Czech., November 15, 1977.
(Phoenix's 4th choice, 119th overall, in 1996 Entry Draft).

Season	Club	GP	G	A	Pts	PIM	GP	G	A	Pts	PIM
99-2000	Nashville Predators	33	1	5	6	22	....	....	....	....	....
2000-01	Nashville Predators	50	3	5	8	22	....	....	....	....	....
2002-03	New York Rangers	10	1	0	1	0	....	....	....	....	....
	Pittsburgh Penguins	19	3	2	5	10	....	....	....	....	....
	NHL Totals	**112**	**8**	**12**	**20**	**54**	....	....	....	....	....

Traded to **Nashville** by **Phoenix** with Cliff Ronning for future considerations, October 31, 1998. Traded to **NY Rangers** by **Nashville** for Peter Smrek, March 19, 2002. Traded to **Pittsburgh** by **NY Rangers** with Joel Bouchard, Rico Fata, Mikael Samuelsson and future considerations for Mike Wilson, Alexei Kovalev, Janne Laukkanen and Dan LaCouture, February 10, 2003.

LIPUMA, Chris

Defense. Shoots left. 6', 183 lbs. Born, Bridgeview, IL, March 23, 1971.

Season	Club	GP	G	A	Pts	PIM	GP	G	A	Pts	PIM
1992-93	Tampa Bay Lightning	15	0	5	5	34	....	....	....	....	....
1993-94	Tampa Bay Lightning	27	0	4	4	77	....	....	....	....	....
1994-95	Tampa Bay Lightning	1	0	0	0	0	....	....	....	....	....
1995-96	Tampa Bay Lightning	21	0	0	0	13	....	....	....	....	....
1996-97	San Jose Sharks	8	0	0	0	22	....	....	....	....	....
	NHL Totals	**72**	**0**	**9**	**9**	**146**	....	....	....	....	....

Signed as a free agent by **Tampa Bay**, June 30, 1992. Signed as a free agent by **San Jose**, August 23, 1996. Claimed on waivers by **New Jersey** from **San Jose**, March 18, 1997.

LISCOMBE, Carl

Left wing. Shoots left. 5'7", 162 lbs. Born, Perth, Ont., May 17, 1915.

Season	Club	GP	G	A	Pts	PIM	GP	G	A	Pts	PIM
1937-38	Detroit Red Wings	41	14	10	24	30	....	....	....	....	....
1938-39	Detroit Red Wings	41	8	18	26	13	6	0	0	0	2
1939-40	Detroit Red Wings	25	2	7	9	4	....	....	....	....	....
1940-41	Detroit Red Wings	33	10	10	20	0	8	4	3	7	12
1941-42	Detroit Red Wings	47	13	17	30	14	12	6	6	12	2
1942-43 ♦	Detroit Red Wings	50	19	23	42	19	10	*6	8	*14	2
1943-44	Detroit Red Wings	50	36	37	73	17	5	1	0	1	2
1944-45	Detroit Red Wings	42	23	9	32	18	14	4	2	6	0
1945-46	Detroit Red Wings	44	12	9	21	2	4	1	0	1	0
	NHL Totals	**373**	**137**	**140**	**277**	**117**	**59**	**22**	**19**	**41**	**20**

Signed as a free agent by **Detroit**, September 24, 1935. Traded to **St. Louis** (AHL) by **Detroit** for cash, August 17, 1946.

LITZENBERGER, Ed

Center/Right wing. Shoots right. 6'1", 174 lbs. Born, Neudorf, Sask., July 15, 1932.

Season	Club	GP	G	A	Pts	PIM	GP	G	A	Pts	PIM
1952-53	Montreal Canadiens	2	1	0	1	2	....	....	....	....	....
1953-54	Montreal Canadiens	3	0	0	0	0	....	....	....	....	....
1954-55	Montreal Canadiens	29	7	4	11	12	....	....	....	....	....
	Chicago Black Hawks	44	16	24	40	28	....	....	....	....	....
1955-56	Chicago Black Hawks	70	10	29	39	36	....	....	....	....	....
1956-57	Chicago Black Hawks	70	32	32	64	48	....	....	....	....	....
1957-58	Chicago Black Hawks	70	32	30	62	63	....	....	....	....	....
1958-59	Chicago Black Hawks	70	33	44	77	37	6	3	5	8	8
1959-60	Chicago Black Hawks	52	12	18	30	15	4	0	1	1	4
1960-61 ♦	Chicago Black Hawks	62	10	22	32	14	10	1	3	4	2
1961-62	Detroit Red Wings	32	8	12	20	4	....	....	....	....	....
	♦ Toronto Maple Leafs	37	10	10	20	14	10	0	2	2	4
1962-63 ♦	Toronto Maple Leafs	58	5	13	18	10	9	1	2	3	6
1963-64 ♦	Toronto Maple Leafs	19	2	0	2	0	1	0	0	0	10
	NHL Totals	**618**	**178**	**238**	**416**	**283**	**40**	**5**	**13**	**18**	**34**

Calder Memorial Trophy (1955) • NHL Second All-Star Team (1957)

Played in NHL All-Star Game (1955, 1957, 1958, 1959, 1962, 1963)

Traded to **Chicago** by **Montreal** for cash, December 10, 1954. Traded to **Detroit** by **Chicago** for Gerry Melnyk and Brian Smith, June 12, 1961. Claimed on waivers by **Toronto** from **Detroit**, December 29, 1961.

LOACH, Lonnie

Left wing. Shoots left. 5'10", 181 lbs. Born, New Liskeard, Ont., April 14, 1968.
(Chicago's 4th choice, 98th overall, in 1986 Entry Draft).

Season	Club	GP	G	A	Pts	PIM	GP	G	A	Pts	PIM
1992-93	Ottawa Senators	3	0	0	0	0	....	....	....	....	....
	Los Angeles Kings	50	10	13	23	27	1	0	0	0	0

Season	Club	GP	G	A	Pts	PIM	GP	G	A	Pts	PIM
		REGULAR SEASON					PLAYOFFS				
1993-94	Mighty Ducks of Anaheim	3	0	0	0	2	....	....	....	....	....
	NHL Totals	**56**	**10**	**13**	**23**	**29**	**1**	**0**	**0**	**0**	**0**

Signed as a free agent by **Detroit**, June 7, 1991. Claimed by **Ottawa** from **Detroit** in Expansion Draft, June 18, 1992. Claimed on waivers by **Los Angeles** from **Ottawa**, October 21, 1992. Claimed by **Anaheim** from **Los Angeles** in Expansion Draft, June 24, 1993.

LOCAS, Jacques

Right wing. Shoots right. 5'11", 175 lbs. Born, Pointe aux Trembles, Que., February 12, 1926.

Season	Club	GP	G	A	Pts	PIM	GP	G	A	Pts	PIM
1947-48	Montreal Canadiens	56	7	8	15	66	....	....	....	....	....
1948-49	Montreal Canadiens	3	0	0	0	0	....	....	....	....	....
	NHL Totals	**59**	**7**	**8**	**15**	**66**	....	....	....	....	....

LOCHEAD, Bill

Left wing. Shoots right. 6'1", 195 lbs. Born, Forest, Ont., October 13, 1954. (Detroit's 1st choice, 9th overall, in 1974 Amateur Draft).

Season	Club	GP	G	A	Pts	PIM	GP	G	A	Pts	PIM
1974-75	Detroit Red Wings	65	16	12	28	34	....	....	....	....	....
1975-76	Detroit Red Wings	53	9	11	20	22	....	....	....	....	....
1976-77	Detroit Red Wings	61	16	14	30	39	....	....	....	....	....
1977-78	Detroit Red Wings	77	20	16	36	47	7	3	0	3	6
1978-79	Detroit Red Wings	40	4	7	11	20	....	....	....	....	....
	Colorado Rockies	27	4	2	6	14	....	....	....	....	....
1979-80	New York Rangers	7	0	0	0	4	....	....	....	....	....
	NHL Totals	**330**	**69**	**62**	**131**	**180**	**7**	**3**	**0**	**3**	**6**

Claimed on waivers by **Colorado** from **Detroit**, February 9, 1979. Traded to **NY Rangers** by **Colorado** for the rights to Hardy Astrom, July 2, 1979.

LOCKING, Norm

Left wing/Center. Shoots left. 6', 165 lbs. Born, Owen Sound, Ont., May 24, 1911.

Season	Club	GP	G	A	Pts	PIM	GP	G	A	Pts	PIM
1934-35	Chicago Black Hawks	35	2	5	7	19	....	....	....	....	....
1935-36	Chicago Black Hawks	13	0	1	1	7	....	....	....	....	....
	NHL Totals	**48**	**2**	**6**	**8**	**26**	....	....	....	....	....

Rights traded to **Chicago** by **Tulsa** (AHA) for Lou Holmes, March 7, 1933. Traded to **Cleveland** (IHL) by **Chicago** for cash, November, 1933. Traded to **Chicago** by **Cleveland** (IHL) for cash, November 1, 1934. Loaned to **London** (IHL) by **Chicago** for the return from loan of Bill Kendall, January 23, 1936.

LOEWEN, Darcy

Left wing. Shoots left. 5'10", 185 lbs. Born, Calgary, Alta., February 26, 1969. (Buffalo's 2nd choice, 55th overall, in 1988 Entry Draft).

Season	Club	GP	G	A	Pts	PIM	GP	G	A	Pts	PIM
1989-90	Buffalo Sabres	4	0	0	0	4	....	....	....	....	....
1990-91	Buffalo Sabres	6	0	0	0	8	....	....	....	....	....
1991-92	Buffalo Sabres	2	0	0	0	2	....	....	....	....	....
1992-93	Ottawa Senators	79	4	5	9	145	....	....	....	....	....
1993-94	Ottawa Senators	44	0	3	3	52	....	....	....	....	....
	NHL Totals	**135**	**4**	**8**	**12**	**211**	....	....	....	....	....

Claimed by **Ottawa** from **Buffalo** in Expansion Draft, June 18, 1992.

LOFTHOUSE, Mark

Right wing/Center. Shoots right. 6'2", 195 lbs. Born, New Westminster, B.C., April 21, 1957. (Washington's 2nd choice, 21st overall, in 1977 Amateur Draft).

Season	Club	GP	G	A	Pts	PIM	GP	G	A	Pts	PIM
1977-78	Washington Capitals	18	2	1	3	8	....	....	....	....	....
1978-79	Washington Capitals	52	13	10	23	10	....	....	....	....	....
1979-80	Washington Capitals	68	15	18	33	20	....	....	....	....	....
1980-81	Washington Capitals	3	1	1	2	4	....	....	....	....	....
1981-82	Detroit Red Wings	12	3	4	7	13	....	....	....	....	....
1982-83	Detroit Red Wings	28	8	4	12	18	....	....	....	....	....
	NHL Totals	**181**	**42**	**38**	**80**	**73**	....	....	....	....	....

Traded to **Detroit** by **Washington** for Al Jensen, July 23, 1981. Signed as a free agent by **Los Angeles**, August 10, 1983. Signed as a free agent by **Philadelphia**, August 15, 1987.

LOGAN, Dave

Defense. Shoots left. 5'10", 190 lbs. Born, Montreal, Que., July 2, 1954. (Chicago's 5th choice, 88th overall, in 1974 Amateur Draft).

Season	Club	GP	G	A	Pts	PIM	GP	G	A	Pts	PIM
1975-76	Chicago Black Hawks	2	0	0	0	0	....	....	....	....	....
1976-77	Chicago Black Hawks	34	0	2	2	61	....	....	....	....	....
1977-78	Chicago Black Hawks	54	1	5	6	77	4	0	0	0	8
1978-79	Chicago Black Hawks	76	1	14	15	176	4	0	0	0	2
1979-80	Chicago Black Hawks	12	2	3	5	34	....	....	....	....	....
	Vancouver Canucks	33	1	5	6	109	4	0	0	0	0
1980-81	Vancouver Canucks	7	0	0	0	13	....	....	....	....	....
	NHL Totals	**218**	**5**	**29**	**34**	**470**	**12**	**0**	**0**	**0**	**10**

Traded to **Vancouver** by **Chicago** with Harold Phillipoff for Ron Sedlbauer, December 21, 1979. Signed as a free agent by **Philadelphia**, March 6, 1981. Signed as a free agent by **Toronto**, August 11, 1981. Traded to **Minnesota** by **Toronto** for cash, January 10, 1983.

LOGAN, Robert

Right wing. Shoots left. 6', 190 lbs. Born, Montreal, Que., February 22, 1964. (Buffalo's 8th choice, 100th overall, in 1982 Entry Draft).

Season	Club	GP	G	A	Pts	PIM	GP	G	A	Pts	PIM
1986-87	Buffalo Sabres	22	7	3	10	0	....	....	....	....	....
1987-88	Buffalo Sabres	16	3	2	5	0	....	....	....	....	....
1988-89	Los Angeles Kings	4	0	0	0	0	....	....	....	....	....
	NHL Totals	**42**	**10**	**5**	**15**	**0**	....	....	....	....	....

Traded to **Los Angeles** by **Buffalo** with Buffalo's 9th round choice (Jim Giacin) in 1989 Entry Draft, October 21, 1988.

LOISELLE, Claude

Center. Shoots left. 5'11", 195 lbs. Born, Ottawa, Ont., May 29, 1963. (Detroit's 1st choice, 23rd overall, in 1981 Entry Draft).

Season	Club	GP	G	A	Pts	PIM	GP	G	A	Pts	PIM
1981-82	Detroit Red Wings	4	1	0	1	2	....	....	....	....	....
1982-83	Detroit Red Wings	18	2	0	2	15	....	....	....	....	....
1983-84	Detroit Red Wings	28	4	6	10	32	....	....	....	....	....
1984-85	Detroit Red Wings	30	8	1	9	45	3	0	2	2	0
1985-86	Detroit Red Wings	48	7	15	22	142	....	....	....	....	....
1986-87	New Jersey Devils	75	16	24	40	137	....	....	....	....	....
1987-88	New Jersey Devils	68	17	18	35	121	20	4	6	10	48
1988-89	New Jersey Devils	74	7	14	21	209	....	....	....	....	....
1989-90	Quebec Nordiques	72	11	14	25	104	....	....	....	....	....
1990-91	Quebec Nordiques	59	5	10	15	86	....	....	....	....	....
	Toronto Maple Leafs	7	1	1	2	2	....	....	....	....	....
1991-92	Toronto Maple Leafs	64	6	9	15	102	....	....	....	....	....
	New York Islanders	11	1	1	2	13	....	....	....	....	....
1992-93	New York Islanders	41	5	3	8	90	18	0	3	3	10
1993-94	New York Islanders	17	1	1	2	49	....	....	....	....	....
	NHL Totals	**616**	**92**	**117**	**209**	**1149**	**41**	**4**	**11**	**15**	**58**

Traded to **New Jersey** by **Detroit** for Tim Higgins, June 25, 1986. Traded to **Quebec** by **New Jersey** with Joe Cirella and New Jersey's 8th round choice (Alexander Karpovtsev) in 1990 Entry Draft for Walt Poddubny and Quebec's 4th round choice (Mike Bodnarchuk) in 1990 Entry Draft, June 17, 1989. Claimed on waivers by **Toronto** from **Quebec**, March 5, 1991. Traded to **NY Islanders** by **Toronto** with Daniel Marois for Ken Baumgartner and Dave McLlwain, March 10, 1992. • Suffered career-ending knee injury in game vs. Dallas, November 24, 1993.

LOMAKIN, Andrei

Right wing. Shoots left. 5'10", 175 lbs. Born, Voskresensk, USSR, April 3, 1964. (Philadelphia's 7th choice, 138th overall, in 1991 Entry Draft).

Season	Club	GP	G	A	Pts	PIM	GP	G	A	Pts	PIM
1991-92	Philadelphia Flyers	57	14	16	30	26	....	....	....	....	....
1992-93	Philadelphia Flyers	51	8	12	20	34	....	....	....	....	....
1993-94	Florida Panthers	76	19	28	47	26	....	....	....	....	....
1994-95	Florida Panthers	31	1	6	7	6	....	....	....	....	....
	NHL Totals	**215**	**42**	**62**	**104**	**92**	....	....	....	....	....

Claimed by **Florida** from **Philadelphia** in Expansion Draft, June 24, 1993.

LONEY, Brian

Right wing. Shoots right. 6'2", 200 lbs. Born, Winnipeg, Man., August 9, 1972. (Vancouver's 6th choice, 110th overall, in 1992 Entry Draft).

Season	Club	GP	G	A	Pts	PIM	GP	G	A	Pts	PIM
1995-96	Vancouver Canucks	12	2	3	5	6	....	....	....	....	....
	NHL Totals	**12**	**2**	**3**	**5**	**6**	....	....	....	....	....

LONEY, Troy

Left wing. Shoots left. 6'3", 209 lbs. Born, Bow Island, Alta., September 21, 1963. (Pittsburgh's 3rd choice, 52nd overall, in 1982 Entry Draft).

Season	Club	GP	G	A	Pts	PIM	GP	G	A	Pts	PIM
1983-84	Pittsburgh Penguins	13	0	0	0	9	....	....	....	....	....
1984-85	Pittsburgh Penguins	46	10	8	18	59	....	....	....	....	....
1985-86	Pittsburgh Penguins	47	3	9	12	95	....	....	....	....	....
1986-87	Pittsburgh Penguins	23	8	7	15	22	....	....	....	....	....
1987-88	Pittsburgh Penguins	65	5	13	18	151	....	....	....	....	....
1988-89	Pittsburgh Penguins	69	10	6	16	165	11	1	3	4	24
1989-90	Pittsburgh Penguins	67	11	16	27	168	....	....	....	....	....
1990-91 ♦	Pittsburgh Penguins	44	7	9	16	85	24	2	2	4	41
1991-92 ♦	Pittsburgh Penguins	76	10	16	26	127	21	4	5	9	32
1992-93	Pittsburgh Penguins	82	5	16	21	99	10	1	4	5	0
1993-94	Mighty Ducks of Anaheim	62	13	6	19	88	....	....	....	....	....
1994-95	New York Islanders	26	5	4	9	23	....	....	....	....	....
	New York Rangers	4	0	0	0	0	1	0	0	0	0
	NHL Totals	**624**	**87**	**110**	**197**	**1091**	**67**	**8**	**14**	**22**	**97**

Claimed by **Anaheim** from **Pittsburgh** in Expansion Draft, June 24, 1993. Traded to **NY Islanders** by **Anaheim** for Tom Kurvers, June 29, 1994. Claimed on waivers by **NY Rangers** from **NY Islanders**, April 10, 1995.

LONG, Barry

Defense. Shoots left. 6'2", 210 lbs. Born, Brantford, Ont., January 3, 1949.

Season	Club	GP	G	A	Pts	PIM	GP	G	A	Pts	PIM
1972-73	Los Angeles Kings	70	2	13	15	48	....	....	....	....	....
1973-74	Los Angeles Kings	60	3	19	22	118	5	0	1	1	18
1979-80	Detroit Red Wings	80	0	17	17	38	....	....	....	....	....
1980-81	Winnipeg Jets	65	6	17	23	42	....	....	....	....	....
1981-82	Winnipeg Jets	5	0	2	2	4	....	....	....	....	....
	NHL Totals	**280**	**11**	**68**	**79**	**250**	**5**	**0**	**1**	**1**	**18**

Claimed by **Los Angeles** from **Chicago** in Intra-League Draft, June 5, 1972. Rights traded to **Detroit** by **Los Angeles** with Montreal's 3rd round choice (previously acquired, Detroit selected Doug Derkson) in 1978 Amateur Draft for Danny Grant, January 9, 1978. Reclaimed by **Detroit** from **Winnipeg** prior to Expansion Draft, June 9, 1979. Traded to **Winnipeg** by **Detroit** for cash, October 31, 1980.

LONG, Stan

Defense. Shoots left. 5'11", 190 lbs. Born, Owen Sound, Ont., November 6, 1929.

Season	Club	GP	G	A	Pts	PIM	GP	G	A	Pts	PIM
1951-52	Montreal Canadiens	....	....	....	....	....	3	0	0	0	0
	NHL Totals	....	....	....	....	....	**3**	**0**	**0**	**0**	**0**

Traded to **Buffalo** (AHL) by **Montreal** for cash, October 15, 1953.

LONSBERRY, Ross

Left wing. Shoots left. 5'11", 195 lbs. Born, Humboldt, Sask., February 7, 1947.

Season	Club	REGULAR SEASON GP	G	A	Pts	PIM	PLAYOFFS GP	G	A	Pts	PIM
1966-67	Boston Bruins	8	0	1	1	2	....	....	....	....	....
1967-68	Boston Bruins	19	2	2	4	12	....	....	....	....	....
1968-69	Boston Bruins	6	0	0	0	2	....	....	....	....	....
1969-70	Los Angeles Kings	76	20	22	42	118	....	....	....	....	....
1970-71	Los Angeles Kings	76	25	28	53	80	....	....	....	....	....
1971-72	Los Angeles Kings	50	9	14	23	39	....	....	....	....	....
	Philadelphia Flyers	32	7	7	14	22	....	....	....	....	....
1972-73	Philadelphia Flyers	77	21	29	50	59	11	4	3	7	9
1973-74 ♦	Philadelphia Flyers	75	32	19	51	48	17	4	9	13	18
1974-75 ♦	Philadelphia Flyers	80	24	25	49	99	17	4	3	7	10
1975-76	Philadelphia Flyers	80	19	28	47	87	16	4	3	7	2
1976-77	Philadelphia Flyers	75	23	32	55	43	10	1	2	3	29
1977-78	Philadelphia Flyers	78	18	30	48	45	12	2	2	4	6
1978-79	Pittsburgh Penguins	80	24	22	46	38	7	0	2	2	9
1979-80	Pittsburgh Penguins	76	15	18	33	36	5	2	1	3	2
1980-81	Pittsburgh Penguins	80	17	33	50	76	5	0	0	0	2
	NHL Totals	**968**	**256**	**310**	**566**	**806**	**100**	**21**	**25**	**46**	**87**

Played in NHL All-Star Game (1972)

Traded to **Los Angeles** by **Boston** with Eddie Shack for Ken Turlik and Los Angeles' 1st round choice in the 1971 (Ron Jones) and 1973 (Andre Savard) Amateur Drafts, May 14, 1969. Traded to **Philadelphia** by **Los Angeles** with Bill Flett, Eddie Joyal and Jean Potvin for Bill Lesuk, Jim Johnson and Serge Bernier, January 28, 1972. Traded to **Pittsburgh** by **Philadelphia** with Tom Bladon and Orest Kindrachuk for Pittsburgh's 1st round choice (Behn Wilson) in 1978 Amateur Draft, June 14, 1978.

LOOB, Hakan

Right wing. Shoots right. 5'9", 170 lbs. Born, Karlstad, Sweden, July 3, 1960.
(Calgary's 10th choice, 181st overall, in 1980 Entry Draft).

Season	Club	REGULAR SEASON GP	G	A	Pts	PIM	PLAYOFFS GP	G	A	Pts	PIM
1983-84	Calgary Flames	77	30	25	55	22	11	2	3	5	2
1984-85	Calgary Flames	78	37	35	72	14	4	3	3	6	0
1985-86	Calgary Flames	68	31	36	67	36	22	4	10	14	6
1986-87	Calgary Flames	68	18	26	44	26	5	1	2	3	0
1987-88	Calgary Flames	80	50	56	106	47	9	8	1	9	4
1988-89 ♦	Calgary Flames	79	27	58	85	44	22	8	9	17	4
	NHL Totals	**450**	**193**	**236**	**429**	**189**	**73**	**26**	**28**	**54**	**16**

• Brother of Peter • NHL All-Rookie Team (1984) • NHL First All-Star Team (1988)

LOOB, Peter

Defense. Shoots right. 6'3", 190 lbs. Born, Karlstad, Sweden, July 23, 1957.
(Quebec's 10th choice, 244th overall, in 1984 Entry Draft).

Season	Club	REGULAR SEASON GP	G	A	Pts	PIM	PLAYOFFS GP	G	A	Pts	PIM
1984-85	Quebec Nordiques	8	1	2	3	0	....	....	....	....	....
	NHL Totals	**8**	**1**	**2**	**3**	**0**	....	....	....	....	....

• Brother of Hakan

LORENTZ, Jim

Center/Right wing. Shoots left. 6', 190 lbs. Born, Waterloo, Ont., May 1, 1947.

Season	Club	REGULAR SEASON GP	G	A	Pts	PIM	PLAYOFFS GP	G	A	Pts	PIM
1968-69	Boston Bruins	11	1	3	4	6	....	....	....	....	....
1969-70 ♦	Boston Bruins	68	7	16	23	30	11	1	0	1	4
1970-71	St. Louis Blues	76	19	21	40	34	6	0	1	1	4
1971-72	St. Louis Blues	12	0	1	1	12	....	....	....	....	....
	New York Rangers	7	0	0	0	0	....	....	....	....	....
	Buffalo Sabres	33	10	14	24	12	....	....	....	....	....
1972-73	Buffalo Sabres	78	27	35	62	30	6	0	3	3	2
1973-74	Buffalo Sabres	78	23	31	54	28	....	....	....	....	....
1974-75	Buffalo Sabres	72	25	45	70	18	16	6	4	10	6
1975-76	Buffalo Sabres	75	17	24	41	18	9	1	2	3	6
1976-77	Buffalo Sabres	79	23	33	56	8	6	4	0	4	8
1977-78	Buffalo Sabres	70	9	15	24	12	....	....	....	....	....
	NHL Totals	**659**	**161**	**238**	**399**	**208**	**54**	**12**	**10**	**22**	**30**

Traded to **St. Louis** by **Boston** for St. Louis' 1st round choice (Ron Plumb) in 1970 Amateur Draft, May 26, 1970. Traded to **NY Rangers** by **St. Louis** with Gene Carr and Wayne Connelly for Jack Egers, Andre Dupont and Mike Murphy, November 15, 1971. Traded to **Buffalo** by **NY Rangers** for Buffalo's 2nd round choice (Larry Sacharuk) in 1972 Amateur Draft, January 14, 1972.

LORIMER, Bob

Defense. Shoots right. 6'1", 200 lbs. Born, Toronto, Ont., August 25, 1953.
(NY Islanders' 10th choice, 129th overall, in 1973 Amateur Draft).

Season	Club	REGULAR SEASON GP	G	A	Pts	PIM	PLAYOFFS GP	G	A	Pts	PIM
1976-77	New York Islanders	1	0	1	1	0	....	....	....	....	....
1977-78	New York Islanders	5	1	0	1	0	....	....	....	....	....
1978-79	New York Islanders	67	3	18	21	42	10	1	3	4	15
1979-80 ♦	New York Islanders	74	3	16	19	53	21	1	3	4	41
1980-81 ♦	New York Islanders	73	1	12	13	77	18	1	4	5	27
1981-82	Colorado Rockies	79	5	15	20	68	....	....	....	....	....
1982-83	New Jersey Devils	66	3	10	13	42	....	....	....	....	....
1983-84	New Jersey Devils	72	2	10	12	62	....	....	....	....	....
1984-85	New Jersey Devils	46	2	6	8	35	....	....	....	....	....
1985-86	New Jersey Devils	46	2	2	4	52	....	....	....	....	....
	NHL Totals	**529**	**22**	**90**	**112**	**431**	**49**	**3**	**10**	**13**	**83**

Traded to **Colorado** by **NY Islanders** with Dave Cameron for Colorado's 1st round choice (Pat LaFontaine) in 1983 Entry Draft, October 1, 1981. Transferred to **New Jersey** after **Colorado** franchise relocated, June 30, 1982.

LORRAIN, Rod

Right wing. Shoots right. 5'5", 156 lbs. Born, Buckingham, Que., July 26, 1914.

Season	Club	REGULAR SEASON GP	G	A	Pts	PIM	PLAYOFFS GP	G	A	Pts	PIM
1935-36	Montreal Canadiens	1	0	0	0	2	....	....	....	....	....
1936-37	Montreal Canadiens	47	3	6	9	8	5	0	0	0	0
1937-38	Montreal Canadiens	48	13	19	32	14	3	0	0	0	0
1938-39	Montreal Canadiens	38	10	9	19	0	3	0	3	3	0
1939-40	Montreal Canadiens	41	1	5	6	6	....	....	....	....	....
1941-42	Montreal Canadiens	4	1	0	1	0	....	....	....	....	....
	NHL Totals	**179**	**28**	**39**	**67**	**30**	**11**	**0**	**3**	**3**	**0**

Played in NHL All-Star Game (1939)

Signed as a free agent by **Montreal**, October 11, 1935.

LOUGHLIN, Clem

Defense. Shoots left. 6', 180 lbs. Born, Carroll, Man., November 15, 1894.

Season	Club	REGULAR SEASON GP	G	A	Pts	PIM	PLAYOFFS GP	G	A	Pts	PIM
1926-27	Detroit Cougars	34	7	3	10	40	....	....	....	....	....
1927-28	Detroit Cougars	43	1	2	3	21	....	....	....	....	....
1928-29	Chicago Black Hawks	24	0	1	1	16	....	....	....	....	....
	NHL Totals	**101**	**8**	**6**	**14**	**77**	....	....	....	....	....

• Brother of Wilf

Transferred to **Detroit** after NHL club purchased **Victoria** (WHL) franchise, May 15, 1926. Traded to **Chicago** by **Detroit** for cash, October 18, 1928. Signed as a free agent by **Toronto**, November 12, 1929. Traded to **London** (IAHL) by **Toronto** for cash, November 12, 1929.

LOUGHLIN, Wilf

Defense/Left wing. Shoots left. 6'2", 200 lbs. Born, Carroll, Man., February 28, 1896.

Season	Club	REGULAR SEASON GP	G	A	Pts	PIM	PLAYOFFS GP	G	A	Pts	PIM
1923-24	Toronto St. Pats	14	0	0	0	2	....	....	....	....	....
	NHL Totals	**14**	**0**	**0**	**0**	**2**	....	....	....	....	....

• Brother of Clem

Traded to **Toronto** by **Victoria** (PCHA) for cash, October 24, 1923.

LOVSIN, Ken

Defense. Shoots right. 6', 195 lbs. Born, Peace River, Alta., December 3, 1966.
(Hartford's 1st choice, 22nd overall, in 1987 Supplemental Draft).

Season	Club	REGULAR SEASON GP	G	A	Pts	PIM	PLAYOFFS GP	G	A	Pts	PIM
1990-91	Washington Capitals	1	0	0	0	0	....	....	....	....	....
	NHL Totals	**1**	**0**	**0**	**0**	**0**	....	....	....	....	....

Signed as a free agent by **Washington**, July 3, 1990.

LOW, Reed

Right wing. Shoots right. 6'3", 222 lbs. Born, Moose Jaw, Sask., June 21, 1976.
(St. Louis' 7th choice, 177th overall, in 1996 Entry Draft).

Season	Club	REGULAR SEASON GP	G	A	Pts	PIM	PLAYOFFS GP	G	A	Pts	PIM
2000-01	St. Louis Blues	56	1	5	6	159	....	....	....	....	....
2001-02	St. Louis Blues	58	0	5	5	160	....	....	....	....	....
2002-03	St. Louis Blues	79	2	4	6	234	....	....	....	....	....
	NHL Totals	**193**	**3**	**14**	**17**	**553**	....	....	....	....	....

LOWDERMILK, Dwayne

Defense. Shoots right. 6', 201 lbs. Born, Burnaby, B.C., January 9, 1958.
(NY Islanders' 3rd choice, 51st overall, in 1978 Amateur Draft).

Season	Club	REGULAR SEASON GP	G	A	Pts	PIM	PLAYOFFS GP	G	A	Pts	PIM
1980-81	Washington Capitals	2	0	1	1	2	....	....	....	....	....
	NHL Totals	**2**	**0**	**1**	**1**	**2**	....	....	....	....	....

Traded to **Washington** by **NY Islanders** for future considerations, December 26, 1980.

LOWE, Darren

Right wing. Shoots right. 5'10", 185 lbs. Born, Toronto, Ont., October 13, 1960.

Season	Club	REGULAR SEASON GP	G	A	Pts	PIM	PLAYOFFS GP	G	A	Pts	PIM
1983-84	Pittsburgh Penguins	8	1	2	3	0	....	....	....	....	....
	NHL Totals	**8**	**1**	**2**	**3**	**0**	....	....	....	....	....

Signed as a free agent by **Pittsburgh**, February, 1984.

LOWE, Kevin

Defense. Shoots left. 6'2", 200 lbs. Born, Lachute, Que., April 15, 1959.
(Edmonton's 1st choice, 21st overall, in 1979 Entry Draft).

Season	Club	REGULAR SEASON GP	G	A	Pts	PIM	PLAYOFFS GP	G	A	Pts	PIM
1979-80	Edmonton Oilers	64	2	19	21	70	3	0	1	1	0
1980-81	Edmonton Oilers	79	10	24	34	94	9	0	2	2	11
1981-82	Edmonton Oilers	80	9	31	40	63	5	0	3	3	0
1982-83	Edmonton Oilers	80	6	34	40	43	16	1	8	9	10
1983-84 ♦	Edmonton Oilers	80	4	42	46	59	19	3	7	10	16
1984-85 ♦	Edmonton Oilers	80	4	21	25	104	16	0	5	5	8
1985-86	Edmonton Oilers	74	2	16	18	90	10	1	3	4	15
1986-87 ♦	Edmonton Oilers	77	8	29	37	94	21	2	4	6	22
1987-88 ♦	Edmonton Oilers	70	9	15	24	89	19	0	2	2	26
1988-89	Edmonton Oilers	76	7	18	25	98	7	1	2	3	4
1989-90 ♦	Edmonton Oilers	78	7	26	33	140	20	0	2	2	10
1990-91	Edmonton Oilers	73	3	13	16	113	14	1	1	2	14
1991-92	Edmonton Oilers	55	2	8	10	107	11	0	3	3	16
1992-93	New York Rangers	49	3	12	15	58	....	....	....	....	....
1993-94 ♦	New York Rangers	71	5	14	19	70	22	1	0	1	20
1994-95	New York Rangers	44	1	7	8	58	10	0	1	1	12
1995-96	New York Rangers	53	1	5	6	76	10	0	4	4	4
1996-97	Edmonton Oilers	64	1	13	14	50	1	0	0	0	0

Season	Club	Regular Season GP	G	A	Pts	PIM	Playoffs GP	G	A	Pts	PIM
1997-98	Edmonton Oilers	7	0	0	0	22	1	0	0	0	4
	NHL Totals	**1254**	**84**	**347**	**431**	**1498**	**214**	**10**	**48**	**58**	**192**

Bud Man of the Year Award (1990) • King Clancy Memorial Trophy (1990)

Played in NHL All-Star Game (1984, 1985, 1986, 1988, 1989, 1990, 1993)

Traded to **NY Rangers** by **Edmonton** for Roman Oksiuta and NY Rangers' 3rd round choice (Alexander Kerch) in 1993 Entry Draft, December 11, 1992. Signed as a free agent by **Edmonton**, September 28, 1996.

LOWE, Odie

Center. Shoots right. 5'8", 140 lbs. Born, Winnipeg, Man., April 15, 1928.

Season	Club	GP	G	A	Pts	PIM	GP	G	A	Pts	PIM
1949-50	New York Rangers	4	1	1	2	0	....	....	....	....	....
	NHL Totals	**4**	**1**	**1**	**2**	**0**	....	....	....	....	....

LOWE, Ross

Defense/Left wing. Shoots right. 6'2", 180 lbs. Born, Oshawa, Ont., September 21, 1928.

Season	Club	GP	G	A	Pts	PIM	GP	G	A	Pts	PIM
1949-50	Boston Bruins	3	0	0	0	0	....	....	....	....	....
1950-51	Boston Bruins	43	5	3	8	40	....	....	....	....	....
	Montreal Canadiens	....	....	....	....	....	2	0	0	0	0
1951-52	Montreal Canadiens	31	1	5	6	42	....	....	....	....	....
	NHL Totals	**77**	**6**	**8**	**14**	**82**	**2**	**0**	**0**	**0**	**0**

Traded to **Montreal** by **Boston** for Hal Laycoe, February 14, 1951. Claimed by **Syracuse** (AHL) from **Montreal** (Victoria-WHL) in Inter-League Draft, June 14, 1954. Transferred to **Springfield** (AHL) after **Syracuse** (AHL) franchise relocated, September, 1954. Claimed by **NY Rangers** from **Springfield** (AHL) in Inter-League Draft, May 31, 1955.

LOWREY, Ed

Center. Shoots right. 5'6", 160 lbs. Born, Manotick, Ont., August 13, 1891.

Season	Club	GP	G	A	Pts	PIM	GP	G	A	Pts	PIM
1917-18	Ottawa Senators	12	2	1	3	3	....	....	....	....	....
1918-19	Ottawa Senators	10	0	1	1	3	....	....	....	....	....
1920-21	Hamilton Tigers	5	0	0	0	0	....	....	....	....	....
	NHL Totals	**27**	**2**	**2**	**4**	**6**	....	....	....	....	....

Rights retained by **Ottawa** after NHA folded, November 26, 1917. Signed as a free agent by **Hamilton**, December 12, 1920.

LOWREY, Fred

Right wing. Shoots right. 5'9", 155 lbs. Born, Ottawa, Ont., August 12, 1902.

Season	Club	GP	G	A	Pts	PIM	GP	G	A	Pts	PIM
1924-25	Montreal Maroons	27	0	1	1	6	....	....	....	....	....
1925-26	Montreal Maroons	10	1	0	1	2	....	....	....	....	....
	Pittsburgh Pirates	16	0	0	0	2	2	0	0	0	....
	NHL Totals	**53**	**1**	**1**	**2**	**10**	**2**	**0**	**0**	**0**	....

• Brother of Gerry

Signed as a free agent by **Mtl. Maroons**, November 3, 1924. Claimed on waivers by **Pittsburgh** from **Mtl. Maroons**, January 12, 1926.

LOWREY, Gerry

Left wing. Shoots left. 5'8", 150 lbs. Born, Ottawa, Ont., February 14, 1906.

Season	Club	GP	G	A	Pts	PIM	GP	G	A	Pts	PIM
1927-28	Toronto Maple Leafs	25	6	5	11	29	....	....	....	....	....
1928-29	Toronto Maple Leafs	32	3	11	14	24	....	....	....	....	....
	Pittsburgh Pirates	12	2	1	3	6	....	....	....	....	....
1929-30	Pittsburgh Pirates	44	16	14	30	30	....	....	....	....	....
1930-31	Philadelphia Quakers	43	13	14	27	27	....	....	....	....	....
1931-32	Chicago Black Hawks	48	8	3	11	32	2	1	0	1	2
1932-33	Ottawa Senators	7	0	0	0	0	....	....	....	....	....
	NHL Totals	**211**	**48**	**48**	**96**	**148**	**2**	**1**	**0**	**1**	**2**

• Brother of Fred

Traded to **Toronto** by **London** (Can-Pro) for Al Pudas, October 20, 1927. Traded to **Pittsburgh** by **Toronto** with $9,500 for Baldy Cotton, February 12, 1929. Transferred to **Philadelphia** after **Pittsburgh** franchise relocated, September 27, 1930. Claimed by **Chicago** from **Philadelphia** in Dispersal Draft, September 21, 1931. Traded to **St. Paul** (AHA) by **Chicago** for Lou Holmes, November 9, 1932. Signed as a free agent by **Ottawa** after securing release from **St. Paul** (AHA), January 4, 1933. Signed as a free agent by **Quebec** (Can-Am) after being released by **Ottawa**, January 19, 1933.

LOWRY, Dave

Left wing. Shoots left. 6'1", 195 lbs. Born, Sudbury, Ont., February 14, 1965.
(Vancouver's 6th choice, 114th overall, in 1983 Entry Draft).

Season	Club	GP	G	A	Pts	PIM	GP	G	A	Pts	PIM
1985-86	Vancouver Canucks	73	10	8	18	143	3	0	0	0	0
1986-87	Vancouver Canucks	70	8	10	18	176	....	....	....	....	....
1987-88	Vancouver Canucks	22	1	3	4	38	....	....	....	....	....
1988-89	St. Louis Blues	21	3	3	6	11	10	0	5	5	4
1989-90	St. Louis Blues	78	19	6	25	75	12	2	1	3	39
1990-91	St. Louis Blues	79	19	21	40	168	13	1	4	5	35
1991-92	St. Louis Blues	75	7	13	20	77	6	0	1	1	20
1992-93	St. Louis Blues	58	5	8	13	101	11	2	0	2	14
1993-94	Florida Panthers	80	15	22	37	64	....	....	....	....	....
1994-95	Florida Panthers	45	10	10	20	25	....	....	....	....	....
1995-96	Florida Panthers	63	10	14	24	36	22	10	7	17	39
1996-97	Florida Panthers	77	15	14	29	51	5	0	0	0	0
1997-98	Florida Panthers	7	0	0	0	2	....	....	....	....	....
	San Jose Sharks	50	4	4	8	51	6	0	0	0	18
1998-99	San Jose Sharks	61	6	9	15	24	1	0	0	0	0
99-2000	San Jose Sharks	32	1	4	5	18	12	1	2	3	6
2000-01	Calgary Flames	79	18	17	35	47	....	....	....	....	....
2001-02	Calgary Flames	62	7	6	13	51	....	....	....	....	....
2002-03	Calgary Flames	34	5	14	19	22	....	....	....	....	....
	NHL Totals	**1066**	**163**	**186**	**349**	**1180**	**101**	**16**	**20**	**36**	**175**

Traded to **St. Louis** by **Vancouver** for Ernie Vargas, September 29, 1988. Claimed by **Florida** from **St. Louis** in Expansion Draft, June 24, 1993. Traded to **San Jose** by **Florida** with Florida's 1st round choice (later traded to Tampa Bay – Tampa Bay selected Vincent Lecavalier) in 1998 Entry Draft for Viktor Kozlov and Florida's 5th round choice (previously acquired, Florida selected Jaroslav Spacek) in 1998 Entry Draft, November 13, 1997. • Missed majority of 1999-2000 season recovering from shoulder injury suffered in game vs. Montreal, November 23, 1999. Signed as a free agent by **Calgary**, July 24, 2000.

LOYNS, Lynn

Left wing. Shoots left. 5'11", 200 lbs. Born, Naicam, Sask., February 21, 1981.

Season	Club	GP	G	A	Pts	PIM	GP	G	A	Pts	PIM
2002-03	San Jose Sharks	19	3	0	3	19	....	....	....	....	....
	NHL Totals	**19**	**3**	**0**	**3**	**19**	....	....	....	....	....

Signed as a free agent by **San Jose**, October 3, 2001.

LUCAS, Danny

Right wing. Shoots left. 6'1", 197 lbs. Born, Powell River, B.C., February 28, 1958.
(Philadelphia's 3rd choice, 14th overall, in 1978 Amateur Draft).

Season	Club	GP	G	A	Pts	PIM	GP	G	A	Pts	PIM
1978-79	Philadelphia Flyers	6	1	0	1	0	....	....	....	....	....
	NHL Totals	**6**	**1**	**0**	**1**	**0**	....	....	....	....	....

Signed as a free agent by **Colorado**, October, 1980.

LUCAS, Dave

Defense. Shoots left. 6', 205 lbs. Born, Downeyville, Ont., March 22, 1932.

Season	Club	GP	G	A	Pts	PIM	GP	G	A	Pts	PIM
1962-63	Detroit Red Wings	1	0	0	0	0	....	....	....	....	....
	NHL Totals	**1**	**0**	**0**	**0**	**0**	....	....	....	....	....

LUCE, Don

Center. Shoots left. 6'2", 185 lbs. Born, London, Ont., October 2, 1948.
(NY Rangers' 3rd choice, 14th overall, in 1966 Amateur Draft).

Season	Club	GP	G	A	Pts	PIM	GP	G	A	Pts	PIM
1969-70	New York Rangers	12	1	2	3	8	5	0	1	1	4
1970-71	New York Rangers	9	0	1	1	0	....	....	....	....	....
	Detroit Red Wings	58	3	11	14	18	....	....	....	....	....
1971-72	Buffalo Sabres	78	11	8	19	38	....	....	....	....	....
1972-73	Buffalo Sabres	78	18	25	43	32	6	1	1	2	2
1973-74	Buffalo Sabres	75	26	31	57	44	....	....	....	....	....
1974-75	Buffalo Sabres	80	33	43	76	45	16	5	8	13	19
1975-76	Buffalo Sabres	77	21	49	70	42	9	4	3	7	6
1976-77	Buffalo Sabres	80	26	43	69	16	6	3	1	4	2
1977-78	Buffalo Sabres	78	26	35	61	24	8	0	2	2	6
1978-79	Buffalo Sabres	79	26	35	61	14	3	1	1	2	0
1979-80	Buffalo Sabres	80	14	29	43	30	14	3	3	6	11
1980-81	Buffalo Sabres	61	15	13	28	19	....	....	....	....	....
	Los Angeles Kings	10	1	0	1	2	4	0	2	2	2
1981-82	Toronto Maple Leafs	39	4	4	8	32	....	....	....	....	....
	NHL Totals	**894**	**225**	**329**	**554**	**364**	**71**	**17**	**22**	**39**	**52**

Bill Masterton Trophy (1975)

Played in NHL All-Star Game (1975)

Traded to **Detroit** by **NY Rangers** for Steve Andrascik, November 2, 1970. Traded to **Buffalo** by **Detroit** with Mike Robitaille for Joe Daley, May 25, 1971. Traded to **Los Angeles** by **Buffalo** for Los Angeles' 6th round choice (Jacob Gustavsson) in 1982 Entry Draft, March 10, 1981. Traded to **Toronto** by **Los Angeles** for Bob Gladney and Toronto's 6th round choice (Kevin Stevens) in 1983 Entry Draft, August 10, 1981.

LUDVIG, Jan

Right wing. Shoots right. 5'10", 190 lbs. Born, Liberec, Czech., September 17, 1961.

Season	Club	GP	G	A	Pts	PIM	GP	G	A	Pts	PIM
1982-83	New Jersey Devils	51	7	10	17	30	....	....	....	....	....
1983-84	New Jersey Devils	74	22	32	54	70	....	....	....	....	....
1984-85	New Jersey Devils	74	12	19	31	53	....	....	....	....	....
1985-86	New Jersey Devils	42	5	9	14	63	....	....	....	....	....
1986-87	New Jersey Devils	47	7	9	16	98	....	....	....	....	....
1987-88	Buffalo Sabres	13	1	6	7	65	....	....	....	....	....
1988-89	Buffalo Sabres	13	0	2	2	39	....	....	....	....	....
	NHL Totals	**314**	**54**	**87**	**141**	**418**	....	....	....	....	....

Signed as a free agent by **New Jersey**, October 28, 1982. Traded to **Buffalo** by **New Jersey** for Jim Korn, May 22, 1987.

LUDWIG, Craig

Defense. Shoots left. 6'3", 220 lbs. Born, Rhinelander, WI, March 15, 1961.
(Montreal's 5th choice, 61st overall, in 1980 Entry Draft).

Season	Club	GP	G	A	Pts	PIM	GP	G	A	Pts	PIM
1982-83	Montreal Canadiens	80	0	25	25	59	3	0	0	0	2
1983-84	Montreal Canadiens	80	7	18	25	52	15	0	3	3	23
1984-85	Montreal Canadiens	72	5	14	19	90	12	0	2	2	6
1985-86 ♦	Montreal Canadiens	69	2	4	6	63	20	0	1	1	48
1986-87	Montreal Canadiens	75	4	12	16	105	17	2	3	5	30
1987-88	Montreal Canadiens	74	4	10	14	69	11	1	1	2	6
1988-89	Montreal Canadiens	74	3	13	16	73	21	0	2	2	24
1989-90	Montreal Canadiens	73	1	15	16	108	11	0	1	1	16
1990-91	New York Islanders	75	1	8	9	77	....	....	....	....	....
1991-92	Minnesota North Stars	73	2	9	11	54	7	0	1	1	19
1992-93	Minnesota North Stars	78	1	10	11	153	....	....	....	....	....
1993-94	Dallas Stars	84	1	13	14	123	9	0	3	3	8
1994-95	Dallas Stars	47	2	7	9	61	4	0	1	1	2
1995-96	Dallas Stars	65	1	2	3	70	....	....	....	....	....

Season	Club	REGULAR SEASON GP	G	A	Pts	PIM	PLAYOFFS GP	G	A	Pts	PIM
1996-97	Dallas Stars	77	2	11	13	62	7	0	2	2	18
1997-98	Dallas Stars	80	0	7	7	131	17	0	1	1	22
1998-99 ◆	Dallas Stars	80	2	6	8	87	23	1	4	5	20
	NHL Totals	**1256**	**38**	**184**	**222**	**1437**	**177**	**4**	**25**	**29**	**244**

Traded to **NY Islanders** by **Montreal** for Gerald Diduck, September 4, 1990. Traded to **Minnesota** by **NY Islanders** for Tom Kurvers, June 22, 1991. Transferred to **Dallas** after **Minnesota** franchise relocated, June 9, 1993.

LUDZIK, Steve

Center. Shoots left. 5'11", 185 lbs. Born, Toronto, Ont., April 3, 1962.
(Chicago's 3rd choice, 28th overall, in 1980 Entry Draft).

Season	Club	GP	G	A	Pts	PIM	GP	G	A	Pts	PIM
1981-82	Chicago Black Hawks	8	2	1	3	2	....	....	....	....	....
1982-83	Chicago Black Hawks	66	6	19	25	63	13	3	5	8	20
1983-84	Chicago Black Hawks	80	9	20	29	73	4	0	1	1	9
1984-85	Chicago Black Hawks	79	11	20	31	86	15	1	1	2	16
1985-86	Chicago Black Hawks	49	6	5	11	21	3	0	0	0	12
1986-87	Chicago Blackhawks	52	5	12	17	34	4	0	0	0	0
1987-88	Chicago Blackhawks	73	6	15	21	40	5	0	1	1	13
1988-89	Chicago Blackhawks	6	1	0	1	8	....	....	....	....	....
1989-90	Buffalo Sabres	11	0	1	1	6	....	....	....	....	....
	NHL Totals	**424**	**46**	**93**	**139**	**333**	**44**	**4**	**8**	**12**	**70**

Traded to **Buffalo** by **Chicago** with Buffalo's 6th round choice (Derek Edgerly) in 1990 Entry Draft for Jacques Cloutier and Chicago's 5th round choice (Todd Bojcun) in 1990 Entry Draft, September 28, 1989.

LUHNING, Warren

Right wing. Shoots right. 6'2", 185 lbs. Born, Edmonton, Alta., July 3, 1975.
(NY Islanders' 4th choice, 92nd overall, in 1993 Entry Draft).

Season	Club	GP	G	A	Pts	PIM	GP	G	A	Pts	PIM
1997-98	New York Islanders	8	0	0	0	0	....	....	....	....	....
1998-99	New York Islanders	11	0	0	0	8	....	....	....	....	....
99-2000	Dallas Stars	10	0	1	1	13	....	....	....	....	....
	NHL Totals	**29**	**0**	**1**	**1**	**21**	....	....	....	....	....

Traded to **Dallas** by **NY Islanders** for Dallas' 3rd round choice (previously acquired, Dallas selected Mathias Tjarnqvist) in 1999 Entry Draft, June 25, 1999.

LUKOWICH, Bernie

Right wing. Shoots right. 6', 190 lbs. Born, North Battleford, Sask., March 18, 1952.
(Pittsburgh's 2nd choice, 30th overall, in 1972 Amateur Draft).

Season	Club	GP	G	A	Pts	PIM	GP	G	A	Pts	PIM
1973-74	Pittsburgh Penguins	53	9	10	19	32	....	....	....	....	....
1974-75	St. Louis Blues	26	4	5	9	2	2	0	0	0	0
	NHL Totals	**79**	**13**	**15**	**28**	**34**	**2**	**0**	**0**	**0**	**0**

Traded to **St. Louis** by **Pittsburgh** for Bob Stumpf, January 20, 1975.

LUKOWICH, Brad

Defense. Shoots left. 6'1", 200 lbs. Born, Cranbrook, B.C., August 12, 1976.
(NY Islanders' 4th choice, 90th overall, in 1994 Entry Draft).

Season	Club	GP	G	A	Pts	PIM	GP	G	A	Pts	PIM
1997-98	Dallas Stars	4	0	1	1	2	....	....	....	....	....
1998-99	Dallas Stars	14	1	2	3	19	8	0	1	1	4
99-2000	Dallas Stars	60	3	1	4	50	....	....	....	....	....
2000-01	Dallas Stars	80	4	10	14	76	10	1	0	1	4
2001-02	Dallas Stars	66	1	6	7	40	....	....	....	....	....
2002-03	Tampa Bay Lightning	70	1	14	15	46	9	0	1	1	2
	NHL Totals	**294**	**10**	**34**	**44**	**233**	**27**	**1**	**2**	**3**	**10**

Traded to **Dallas** by **NY Islanders** for Dallas' 3rd round choice (Robert Schnabel) in 1997 Entry Draft, June 1, 1996. Traded to **Minnesota** by **Dallas** with Manny Fernandez for Minnesota's 3rd round choice (Joel Lundqvist) in 2000 Entry Draft and 4th round choice (later traded back to Minnesota – later traded to Los Angeles – Los Angeles selected Aaron Rome) in 2002 Entry Draft, June 12, 2000. Traded to **Dallas** by **Minnesota** with Minnesota's 3rd (Yared Hagos) and 9th (Dale Sullivan) round choices in 2001 Entry Draft for Aaron Gavey, Pavel Patera, Dallas' 8th round choice (Eric Johansson) in 2000 Entry Draft and Minnesota's 4th round choice (previously acquired, later traded to Los Angeles – Los Angeles selected Aaron Rome) in 2002 Entry Draft, June 25, 2000. Traded to **Tampa Bay** by **Dallas** with Dallas' 7th round choice (Jay Rosehill) in 2003 Entry Draft for Tampa Bay's 2nd round choice (previously acquired, later traded back to Tampa Bay – later traded to Dallas – Dallas selected Tobias Stephan) in 2002 Entry Draft, June 22, 2002.

LUKOWICH, Morris

Left wing. Shoots left. 5'9", 170 lbs. Born, Speers, Sask., June 1, 1956.
(Pittsburgh's 4th choice, 47th overall, in 1976 Amateur Draft).

Season	Club	GP	G	A	Pts	PIM	GP	G	A	Pts	PIM
1979-80	Winnipeg Jets	78	35	39	74	77	....	....	....	....	....
1980-81	Winnipeg Jets	80	33	34	67	90	....	....	....	....	....
1981-82	Winnipeg Jets	77	43	49	92	102	4	0	2	2	16
1982-83	Winnipeg Jets	69	22	21	43	67	....	....	....	....	....
1983-84	Winnipeg Jets	80	30	25	55	71	3	0	0	0	0
1984-85	Winnipeg Jets	47	5	9	14	31	....	....	....	....	....
	Boston Bruins	22	5	8	13	21	1	0	0	0	0
1985-86	Boston Bruins	14	1	4	5	10	....	....	....	....	....
	Los Angeles Kings	55	11	9	20	51	....	....	....	....	....
1986-87	Los Angeles Kings	60	14	21	35	64	3	0	0	0	8
	NHL Totals	**582**	**199**	**219**	**418**	**584**	**11**	**0**	**2**	**2**	**24**

Played in NHL All-Star Game (1980, 1981)

Reclaimed by **Pittsburgh** from **Winnipeg** prior to Expansion Draft, June 9, 1979. Claimed as a priority selection by **Winnipeg**, June 9, 1979. Traded to **Boston** by **Winnipeg** for Jim Nill, February 4, 1985. Claimed on waivers by **Los Angeles** from **Boston**, November 15, 1985.

LUKSA, Charlie

Defense. Shoots left. 6'1", 190 lbs. Born, Toronto, Ont., February 19, 1954.
(Montreal's 15th choice, 172nd overall, in 1974 Amateur Draft).

Season	Club	GP	G	A	Pts	PIM	GP	G	A	Pts	PIM
1979-80	Hartford Whalers	8	0	1	1	4	....	....	....	....	....
	NHL Totals	**8**	**0**	**1**	**1**	**4**	....	....	....	....	....

Claimed by **Hartford** from **Cincinnati** (WHA) in WHA Dispersal Draft, June 9, 1979.

LUMLEY, Dave

Right wing. Shoots right. 6', 185 lbs. Born, Toronto, Ont., September 1, 1954.
(Montreal's 17th choice, 199th overall, in 1974 Amateur Draft).

Season	Club	GP	G	A	Pts	PIM	GP	G	A	Pts	PIM
1978-79	Montreal Canadiens	3	0	0	0	0	....	....	....	....	....
1979-80	Edmonton Oilers	80	20	38	58	138	3	1	0	1	12
1980-81	Edmonton Oilers	53	7	9	16	74	7	1	0	1	4
1981-82	Edmonton Oilers	66	32	42	74	96	5	2	1	3	21
1982-83	Edmonton Oilers	72	13	24	37	158	16	0	0	0	19
1983-84 ◆	Edmonton Oilers	56	6	15	21	68	19	2	5	7	44
1984-85	Hartford Whalers	48	8	20	28	98	....	....	....	....	....
◆	Edmonton Oilers	12	1	3	4	13	8	0	0	0	29
1985-86	Edmonton Oilers	46	11	9	20	35	3	0	2	2	2
1986-87	Edmonton Oilers	1	0	0	0	0	....	....	....	....	....
	NHL Totals	**437**	**98**	**160**	**258**	**680**	**61**	**6**	**8**	**14**	**131**

Traded to **Edmonton** by **Montreal** with Dan Newman for Edmonton's 2nd round choice (Ric Nattress) in 1980 Entry Draft, June 13, 1979. Claimed by **Hartford** from **Edmonton** in Waiver Draft, October 9, 1984. Claimed on waivers by **Edmonton** from **Hartford**, February 6, 1985.
• Officially announced retirement, November 5, 1986.

LUMME, Jyrki

Defense. Shoots left. 6'1", 209 lbs. Born, Tampere, Finland, July 16, 1966.
(Montreal's 3rd choice, 57th overall, in 1986 Entry Draft).

Season	Club	GP	G	A	Pts	PIM	GP	G	A	Pts	PIM
1988-89	Montreal Canadiens	21	1	3	4	10	....	....	....	....	....
1989-90	Montreal Canadiens	54	1	19	20	41	....	....	....	....	....
	Vancouver Canucks	11	3	7	10	8	....	....	....	....	....
1990-91	Vancouver Canucks	80	5	27	32	59	6	2	3	5	0
1991-92	Vancouver Canucks	75	12	32	44	65	13	2	3	5	4
1992-93	Vancouver Canucks	74	8	36	44	55	12	0	5	5	6
1993-94	Vancouver Canucks	83	13	42	55	50	24	2	11	13	16
1994-95	Vancouver Canucks	36	5	12	17	26	11	2	6	8	8
1995-96	Vancouver Canucks	80	17	37	54	50	6	1	3	4	2
1996-97	Vancouver Canucks	66	11	24	35	32	....	....	....	....	....
1997-98	Vancouver Canucks	74	9	21	30	34	....	....	....	....	....
1998-99	Phoenix Coyotes	60	7	21	28	34	7	0	1	1	6
99-2000	Phoenix Coyotes	74	8	32	40	44	5	0	1	1	2
2000-01	Phoenix Coyotes	58	4	21	25	44	....	....	....	....	....
2001-02	Dallas Stars	15	0	1	1	4	....	....	....	....	....
	Toronto Maple Leafs	51	4	8	12	18	14	0	0	0	4
2002-03	Toronto Maple Leafs	73	6	11	17	46	7	0	2	2	4
	NHL Totals	**985**	**114**	**354**	**468**	**620**	**105**	**9**	**35**	**44**	**52**

Traded to **Vancouver** by **Montreal** for St. Louis' 2nd round choice (previously acquired, Montreal selected Craig Darby) in 1991 Entry Draft, March 6, 1990. Signed as a free agent by **Phoenix**, July 3, 1998. Traded to **Dallas** by **Phoenix** for Tyler Bouck, June 23, 2001. Traded to **Toronto** by **Dallas** for Dave Manson, November 21, 2001.

LUND, Pentti

Right wing. Shoots right. 6', 185 lbs. Born, Karijoki, Finland, December 6, 1925.

Season	Club	GP	G	A	Pts	PIM	GP	G	A	Pts	PIM
1946-47	Boston Bruins	....	....	....	....	....	1	0	0	0	0
1947-48	Boston Bruins	....	....	....	....	....	2	0	0	0	0
1948-49	New York Rangers	59	14	16	30	16	....	....	....	....	....
1949-50	New York Rangers	64	18	9	27	16	12	*6	5	*11	0
1950-51	New York Rangers	59	4	16	20	6	....	....	....	....	....
1951-52	Boston Bruins	23	0	5	5	0	2	1	0	1	0
1952-53	Boston Bruins	54	8	9	17	2	2	0	0	0	0
	NHL Totals	**259**	**44**	**55**	**99**	**40**	**19**	**7**	**5**	**12**	**0**

Calder Memorial Trophy (1949)

Traded to **NY Rangers** by **Boston** with Ray Manson to complete transaction that sent Grant Warwick to Boston (February 6, 1948), June, 1948. Rights traded to **Boston** by **NY Rangers** with Gus Kyle and cash for Paul Ronty, September 20, 1951. Traded to **Victoria** (WHL) by **Boston** with Sam Bettio for cash, July 1, 1953.

LUNDBERG, Brian

Defense. Shoots right. 5'10", 190 lbs. Born, Burnaby, B.C., June 5, 1960.
(Pittsburgh's 7th choice, 177th overall, in 1980 Entry Draft).

Season	Club	GP	G	A	Pts	PIM	GP	G	A	Pts	PIM
1982-83	Pittsburgh Penguins	1	0	0	0	2	....	....	....	....	....
	NHL Totals	**1**	**0**	**0**	**0**	**2**	....	....	....	....	....

LUNDE, Len

Center. Shoots right. 6'1", 194 lbs. Born, Campbell River, B.C., November 13, 1936.

Season	Club	GP	G	A	Pts	PIM	GP	G	A	Pts	PIM
1958-59	Detroit Red Wings	68	14	12	26	15	....	....	....	....	....
1959-60	Detroit Red Wings	66	6	17	23	10	6	1	2	3	0
1960-61	Detroit Red Wings	53	6	12	18	10	10	2	0	2	0
1961-62	Detroit Red Wings	23	2	9	11	4	....	....	....	....	....
1962-63	Chicago Black Hawks	60	6	22	28	30	4	0	0	0	2
1965-66	Chicago Black Hawks	24	4	7	11	4	....	....	....	....	....
1967-68	Minnesota North Stars	7	0	1	1	0	....	....	....	....	....

Season	Club	GP	G	A	Pts	PIM	GP	G	A	Pts	PIM
		REGULAR SEASON					PLAYOFFS				
1970-71	Vancouver Canucks	20	1	3	4	2	....	....	....	....	....
	NHL Totals	**321**	**39**	**83**	**122**	**75**	**20**	**3**	**2**	**5**	**2**

Traded to **Chicago** by **Detroit** with John McKenzie for Doug Barkley, June 5, 1962. Claimed by **Minnesota** from **Chicago** in Expansion Draft, June 6, 1967. Traded to **Toronto** (Rochester-AHL) by **Minnesota** with Murray Hall, Ted Taylor, Don Johns, Duke Harris, and the loan of Carl Wetzel for J.P. Parise and Milan Marcetta, December 23, 1967. Rights transferred to **Vancouver** (WHL) after WHL club purchased **Rochester** (AHL) franchise, August 13, 1968. NHL rights transferred to **Vancouver** after NHL club purchased **Vancouver** (WHL) franchise, December 13, 1969.

LUNDHOLM, Bengt

Left wing. Shoots left. 6', 180 lbs. Born, Falun, Sweden, August 4, 1955.

Season	Club	GP	G	A	Pts	PIM	GP	G	A	Pts	PIM
1981-82	Winnipeg Jets	66	14	30	44	10	4	1	1	2	2
1982-83	Winnipeg Jets	58	14	28	42	16	3	0	1	1	2
1983-84	Winnipeg Jets	57	5	14	19	20	....	....	....	....	....
1984-85	Winnipeg Jets	78	12	18	30	20	5	2	2	4	8
1985-86	Winnipeg Jets	16	3	5	8	6	2	0	0	0	2
	NHL Totals	**275**	**48**	**95**	**143**	**72**	**14**	**3**	**4**	**7**	**14**

Signed as a free agent by **Winnipeg**, June 19, 1981.

LUNDMARK, Jamie

Center. Shoots right. 6', 174 lbs. Born, Edmonton, Alta., January 16, 1981.
(NY Rangers' 2nd choice, 9th overall, in 1999 Entry Draft).

Season	Club	GP	G	A	Pts	PIM	GP	G	A	Pts	PIM
2002-03	New York Rangers	55	8	11	19	16	....	....	....	....	....
	NHL Totals	**55**	**8**	**11**	**19**	**16**	....	....	....	....	....

LUNDRIGAN, Joe

Defense. Shoots left. 5'11", 180 lbs. Born, Corner Brook, Nfld., September 12, 1948.

Season	Club	GP	G	A	Pts	PIM	GP	G	A	Pts	PIM
1972-73	Toronto Maple Leafs	49	2	8	10	20	....	....	....	....	....
1974-75	Washington Capitals	3	0	0	0	2	....	....	....	....	....
	NHL Totals	**52**	**2**	**8**	**10**	**22**	....	....	....	....	....

Signed as a free agent by **Toronto**, October 1, 1971. Claimed by **Washington** from **Toronto** in Expansion Draft, June 12, 1974.

LUNDSTROM, Tord

Left wing. Shoots left. 5'11", 176 lbs. Born, Kiruna, Sweden, March 4, 1945.

Season	Club	GP	G	A	Pts	PIM	GP	G	A	Pts	PIM
1973-74	Detroit Red Wings	11	1	1	2	0	....	....	....	....	....
	NHL Totals	**11**	**1**	**1**	**2**	**0**	....	....	....	....	....

Signed as a free agent by **Detroit**, June, 1973.

LUNDY, Pat

Center. Shoots right. 5'11", 170 lbs. Born, Saskatoon, Sask., July 31, 1924.

Season	Club	GP	G	A	Pts	PIM	GP	G	A	Pts	PIM
1945-46	Detroit Red Wings	4	3	2	5	2	2	1	0	1	0
1946-47	Detroit Red Wings	59	17	17	34	10	5	0	1	1	2
1947-48	Detroit Red Wings	11	4	1	5	6	5	1	1	2	0
1948-49	Detroit Red Wings	15	4	3	7	4	4	0	0	0	0
1950-51	Chicago Black Hawks	61	9	9	18	9	....	....	....	....	....
	NHL Totals	**150**	**37**	**32**	**69**	**31**	**16**	**2**	**2**	**4**	**2**

Traded to **Chicago** by **Detroit** for cash, October 1, 1950.

LUONGO, Chris

Defense. Shoots right. 5'10", 206 lbs. Born, Detroit, MI, March 17, 1967.
(Detroit's 5th choice, 92nd overall, in 1985 Entry Draft).

Season	Club	GP	G	A	Pts	PIM	GP	G	A	Pts	PIM
1990-91	Detroit Red Wings	4	0	1	1	4	....	....	....	....	....
1992-93	Ottawa Senators	76	3	9	12	68	....	....	....	....	....
1993-94	New York Islanders	17	1	3	4	13	....	....	....	....	....
1994-95	New York Islanders	47	1	3	4	36	....	....	....	....	....
1995-96	New York Islanders	74	3	7	10	55	....	....	....	....	....
	NHL Totals	**218**	**8**	**23**	**31**	**176**	....	....	....	....	....

Signed as a free agent by **Ottawa**, September 9, 1992. Traded to **NY Islanders** by **Ottawa** for Jeff Finley, June 30, 1993. Traded to **Ottawa** by **NY Islanders** for cash, March 19, 1999.

LUPASCHUK, Ross

Defense. Shoots right. 6'1", 217 lbs. Born, Edmonton, Alta., January 19, 1981.
(Washington's 4th choice, 34th overall, in 1999 Entry Draft).

Season	Club	GP	G	A	Pts	PIM	GP	G	A	Pts	PIM
2002-03	Pittsburgh Penguins	3	0	0	0	4	....	....	....	....	....
	NHL Totals	**3**	**0**	**0**	**0**	**4**	....	....	....	....	....

Traded to **Pittsburgh** by **Washington** with Kris Beech, Michal Sivek and future considerations for Jaromir Jagr and Frantisek Kucera, July 11, 2001.

LUPIEN, Gilles

Defense. Shoots left. 6'6", 210 lbs. Born, Lachute, Que., April 20, 1954.
(Montreal's 7th choice, 33rd overall, in 1974 Amateur Draft).

Season	Club	GP	G	A	Pts	PIM	GP	G	A	Pts	PIM
1977-78 ♦	Montreal Canadiens	46	1	3	4	108	8	0	0	0	17
1978-79 ♦	Montreal Canadiens	72	1	9	10	124	13	0	0	0	2
1979-80	Montreal Canadiens	56	1	7	8	109	4	0	0	0	2
1980-81	Pittsburgh Penguins	31	0	1	1	34	....	....	....	....	....
	Hartford Whalers	20	2	4	6	39	....	....	....	....	....
1981-82	Hartford Whalers	1	0	1	1	2	....	....	....	....	....
	NHL Totals	**226**	**5**	**25**	**30**	**416**	**25**	**0**	**0**	**0**	**21**

Claimed by **Montreal** as a fill-in during Expansion Draft, June 13, 1979. Traded to **Pittsburgh** by **Montreal** for Pittsburgh's 3rd round choice (later traded to Winnipeg – Winnipeg selected Peter Taglianetti) in 1983 Entry Draft, September 26, 1980. Traded to **Hartford** by **Pittsburgh** for Hartford's 6th round choice (Paul Edwards) in 1981 Entry Draft, February 20, 1981.

LUPUL, Gary

Center/Left wing. Shoots left. 5'9", 172 lbs. Born, Powell River, B.C., April 4, 1959.

Season	Club	GP	G	A	Pts	PIM	GP	G	A	Pts	PIM
1979-80	Vancouver Canucks	51	9	11	20	24	4	1	0	1	0
1980-81	Vancouver Canucks	7	0	2	2	2	....	....	....	....	....
1981-82	Vancouver Canucks	41	10	7	17	26	10	2	3	5	4
1982-83	Vancouver Canucks	40	18	10	28	46	4	1	3	4	0
1983-84	Vancouver Canucks	69	17	27	44	51	4	0	1	1	7
1984-85	Vancouver Canucks	66	12	17	29	82	....	....	....	....	....
1985-86	Vancouver Canucks	19	4	1	5	12	3	0	0	0	0
	NHL Totals	**293**	**70**	**75**	**145**	**243**	**25**	**4**	**7**	**11**	**11**

Signed as a free agent by **Vancouver**, September 14, 1979.

LYASHENKO, Roman

Center. Shoots right. 6', 189 lbs. Born, Murmansk, Russia, May 2, 1979.
(Dallas' 2nd choice, 52nd overall, in 1997 Entry Draft).

Season	Club	GP	G	A	Pts	PIM	GP	G	A	Pts	PIM
99-2000	Dallas Stars	58	6	6	12	10	16	2	1	3	0
2000-01	Dallas Stars	60	6	3	9	45	1	0	0	0	0
2001-02	Dallas Stars	4	0	0	0	0	....	....	....	....	....
	New York Rangers	15	2	0	2	0	....	....	....	....	....
2002-03	New York Rangers	2	0	0	0	0	....	....	....	....	....
	NHL Totals	**139**	**14**	**9**	**23**	**55**	**17**	**2**	**1**	**3**	**0**

Traded to **NY Rangers** by **Dallas** with Martin Rucinsky for Manny Malhotra and Barrett Heisten, March 12, 2002.

LYDMAN, Toni

Defense. Shoots left. 6'1", 202 lbs. Born, Lahti, Finland, September 25, 1977.
(Calgary's 5th choice, 89th overall, in 1996 Entry Draft).

Season	Club	GP	G	A	Pts	PIM	GP	G	A	Pts	PIM
2000-01	Calgary Flames	62	3	16	19	30	....	....	....	....	....
2001-02	Calgary Flames	79	6	22	28	52	....	....	....	....	....
2002-03	Calgary Flames	81	6	20	26	28	....	....	....	....	....
	NHL Totals	**222**	**15**	**58**	**73**	**110**	....	....	....	....	....

LYLE, George

Left wing. Shoots left. 6'2", 205 lbs. Born, North Vancouver, B.C., November 24, 1953.
(Detroit's 9th choice, 123rd overall, in 1973 Amateur Draft).

Season	Club	GP	G	A	Pts	PIM	GP	G	A	Pts	PIM
1979-80	Detroit Red Wings	27	7	4	11	2	....	....	....	....	....
1980-81	Detroit Red Wings	31	10	14	24	28	....	....	....	....	....
1981-82	Detroit Red Wings	11	1	2	3	4	....	....	....	....	....
	Hartford Whalers	14	2	12	14	9	....	....	....	....	....
1982-83	Hartford Whalers	16	4	6	10	8	....	....	....	....	....
	NHL Totals	**99**	**24**	**38**	**62**	**51**	....	....	....	....	....

Reclaimed by **Detroit** from **Hartford** prior to Expansion Draft, June 9, 1979. Claimed on waivers by **Hartford** from **Detroit**, November 13, 1981.

LYNCH, Jack

Defense. Shoots right. 6'2", 180 lbs. Born, Toronto, Ont., May 28, 1952.
(Pittsburgh's 1st choice, 24th overall, in 1972 Amateur Draft).

Season	Club	GP	G	A	Pts	PIM	GP	G	A	Pts	PIM
1972-73	Pittsburgh Penguins	47	1	18	19	40	....	....	....	....	....
1973-74	Pittsburgh Penguins	17	0	7	7	21	....	....	....	....	....
	Detroit Red Wings	35	3	9	12	27	....	....	....	....	....
1974-75	Detroit Red Wings	50	2	15	17	46	....	....	....	....	....
	Washington Capitals	20	1	5	6	16	....	....	....	....	....
1975-76	Washington Capitals	79	9	13	22	78	....	....	....	....	....
1976-77	Washington Capitals	75	5	25	30	90	....	....	....	....	....
1977-78	Washington Capitals	29	1	8	9	4	....	....	....	....	....
1978-79	Washington Capitals	30	2	6	8	14	....	....	....	....	....
	NHL Totals	**382**	**24**	**106**	**130**	**336**	....	....	....	....	....

Traded to **Detroit** by **Pittsburgh** with Jim Rutherford for Ron Stackhouse, January 17, 1974. Traded to **Washington** by **Detroit** for Dave Kryskow, February 8, 1975.

LYNN, Vic

Left wing/Defense. Shoots left. 5'10", 175 lbs. Born, Saskatoon, Sask., January 26, 1925.

Season	Club	GP	G	A	Pts	PIM	GP	G	A	Pts	PIM
1942-43	New York Rangers	1	0	0	0	0	....	....	....	....	....
1943-44	Detroit Red Wings	3	0	0	0	4	....	....	....	....	....
1945-46	Montreal Canadiens	2	0	0	0	0	....	....	....	....	....
1946-47 ♦	Toronto Maple Leafs	31	6	14	20	44	11	4	1	5	16
1947-48 ♦	Toronto Maple Leafs	60	12	22	34	53	9	2	5	7	*20
1948-49 ♦	Toronto Maple Leafs	52	7	9	16	36	8	0	1	1	2
1949-50	Toronto Maple Leafs	70	7	13	20	39	7	0	2	2	2
1950-51	Boston Bruins	56	14	6	20	69	5	0	0	0	2
1951-52	Boston Bruins	12	2	2	4	4	....	....	....	....	....
1952-53	Chicago Black Hawks	29	0	10	10	23	7	1	1	2	4
1953-54	Chicago Black Hawks	11	1	0	1	2	....	....	....	....	....
	NHL Totals	**327**	**49**	**76**	**125**	**274**	**47**	**7**	**10**	**17**	**46**

Played in NHL All-Star Game (1947, 1948, 1949)

Traded to **Montreal** (Buffalo-AHL) by **Detroit** for cash, October 14,1945. Traded to **Toronto** (Pittsburgh-AHL) by **Montreal** (Buffalo-AHL) with Dutch Hiller for John Mahaffy and Gerry Brown, September 21, 1946. Traded to **Boston** by **Toronto** with Bill Ezinicki for Fern Flaman, Leo Boivin, Ken Smith and Phil Maloney, November 16, 1950. Traded to **Cleveland** (AHL) by **Boston** (Providence-AHL) with Buck Davies for Joe Lund and Jean-Paul Gladu, December 10, 1951. Traded to **Chicago** by **Cleveland** (AHL) for future considerations (Fred Glover, January 16, 1953), January 4, 1953.

LYON, Steve

Defense/Right wing. Shoots right. 5'10", 169 lbs. Born, Toronto, Ont., May 16, 1952.
(Minnesota's 10th choice, 145th overall, in 1972 Amateur Draft).

		REGULAR SEASON					PLAYOFFS				
Season	Club	GP	G	A	Pts	PIM	GP	G	A	Pts	PIM
1976-77	Pittsburgh Penguins	3	0	0	0	2	....	....	....	....	....
	NHL Totals	**3**	**0**	**0**	**0**	**2**	....	....	....	....	....

Signed as a free agent by **Pittsburgh**, November, 1976.

LYONS, Ron

Left wing. Shoots left. 5'11", 170 lbs. Born, Portage la Prairie, Man., February 15, 1909.

Season	Club	GP	G	A	Pts	PIM	GP	G	A	Pts	PIM
1930-31	Boston Bruins	14	0	0	0	19	5	0	0	0	0
	Philadelphia Quakers	22	2	4	6	8	....	....	....	....	....
	NHL Totals	**36**	**2**	**4**	**6**	**27**	**5**	**0**	**0**	**0**	**0**

Rights sold to **Boston** by **Portland** (PCHL) for $5,000, April 17, 1930. Traded to **Philadelphia** by **Boston** with Bill Hutton for Harold Darragh, December 8, 1930. Traded to **Boston** by **Philadelphia** for cash, February, 1931.

LYSIAK, Tom

Center. Shoots left. 6'1", 185 lbs. Born, High Prairie, Alta., April 22, 1953.
(Atlanta's 1st choice, 2nd overall, in 1973 Amateur Draft).

Season	Club	GP	G	A	Pts	PIM	GP	G	A	Pts	PIM
1973-74	Atlanta Flames	77	19	45	64	54	4	0	2	2	0
1974-75	Atlanta Flames	77	25	52	77	73	....	....	....	....	....
1975-76	Atlanta Flames	80	31	51	82	60	2	0	0	0	2
1976-77	Atlanta Flames	79	30	51	81	52	3	1	3	4	8
1977-78	Atlanta Flames	80	27	42	69	54	2	1	0	1	2
1978-79	Atlanta Flames	52	23	35	58	36	....	....	....	....	....
	Chicago Black Hawks	14	0	10	10	14	4	0	0	0	2
1979-80	Chicago Black Hawks	77	26	43	69	31	7	4	4	8	0
1980-81	Chicago Black Hawks	72	21	55	76	20	3	0	3	3	0
1981-82	Chicago Black Hawks	71	32	50	82	84	15	6	9	15	13
1982-83	Chicago Black Hawks	61	23	38	61	27	13	6	7	13	8
1983-84	Chicago Black Hawks	54	17	30	47	35	5	1	1	2	2
1984-85	Chicago Black Hawks	74	16	30	46	13	15	4	8	12	10
1985-86	Chicago Black Hawks	51	2	19	21	14	3	2	1	3	2
	NHL Totals	**919**	**292**	**551**	**843**	**567**	**76**	**25**	**38**	**63**	**49**

Played in NHL All-Star Game (1975, 1976, 1977)

Traded to **Chicago** by **Atlanta** with Pat Ribble, Greg Fox, Harold Phillipoff and Miles Zaharko for Ivan Boldirev, Phil Russell and Darcy Rota, March 13, 1979. • Suspended for 20 games for abusing linesman Ron Foyt, October 30, 1983.

MacADAM, Al

Right wing. Shoots left. 6', 180 lbs. Born, Charlottetown, P.E.I., March 16, 1952.
(Philadelphia's 4th choice, 55th overall, in 1972 Amateur Draft).

Season	Club	GP	G	A	Pts	PIM	GP	G	A	Pts	PIM
1973-74♦	Philadelphia Flyers	5	0	0	0	0	1	0	0	0	0
1974-75	California Golden Seals	80	18	25	43	55	....	....	....	....	....
1975-76	California Golden Seals	80	32	31	63	49	....	....	....	....	....
1976-77	Cleveland Barons	80	22	41	63	68	....	....	....	....	....
1977-78	Cleveland Barons	80	16	32	48	42	....	....	....	....	....
1978-79	Minnesota North Stars	69	24	34	58	30	....	....	....	....	....
1979-80	Minnesota North Stars	80	42	51	93	24	15	7	9	16	4
1980-81	Minnesota North Stars	78	21	39	60	94	19	9	10	19	4
1981-82	Minnesota North Stars	79	18	43	61	37	4	1	0	1	4
1982-83	Minnesota North Stars	73	11	22	33	60	9	2	1	3	2
1983-84	Minnesota North Stars	80	22	13	35	23	16	1	4	5	7
1984-85	Vancouver Canucks	80	14	20	34	27	....	....	....	....	....
	NHL Totals	**864**	**240**	**351**	**591**	**509**	**64**	**20**	**24**	**44**	**21**

Bill Masterton Trophy (1980)

Played in NHL All-Star Game (1976, 1977)

Traded to **California** by **Philadelphia** with Larry Wright and Philadelphia's 1st round choice (Rob Chipperfield) in 1974 Amateur Draft for Reggie Leach, May 24, 1974. Transferred to **Cleveland** after **California** franchise relocated, August 26, 1976. Protected by **Minnesota** prior to **Minnesota-Cleveland** Dispersal Draft, June 15, 1978. Traded to **Vancouver** by **Minnesota** for Harold Snepsts, June 21, 1984.

MacDERMID, Paul

Right wing. Shoots right. 6'1", 205 lbs. Born, Chesley, Ont., April 14, 1963.
(Hartford's 2nd choice, 61st overall, in 1981 Entry Draft).

		REGULAR SEASON					PLAYOFFS				
Season	Club	GP	G	A	Pts	PIM	GP	G	A	Pts	PIM
1981-82	Hartford Whalers	3	1	0	1	2	....	....	....	....	....
1982-83	Hartford Whalers	7	0	0	0	2	....	....	....	....	....
1983-84	Hartford Whalers	3	0	1	1	0	....	....	....	....	....
1984-85	Hartford Whalers	31	4	7	11	29	....	....	....	....	....
1985-86	Hartford Whalers	74	13	10	23	160	10	2	1	3	20
1986-87	Hartford Whalers	72	7	11	18	202	6	2	1	3	34
1987-88	Hartford Whalers	80	20	15	35	139	6	0	5	5	14
1988-89	Hartford Whalers	74	17	27	44	141	4	1	1	2	16
1989-90	Hartford Whalers	29	6	12	18	69	....	....	....	....	....
	Winnipeg Jets	44	7	10	17	100	7	0	2	2	8
1990-91	Winnipeg Jets	69	15	21	36	128	....	....	....	....	....
1991-92	Winnipeg Jets	59	10	11	21	151	....	....	....	....	....
	Washington Capitals	15	2	5	7	43	7	0	1	1	22
1992-93	Washington Capitals	72	9	8	17	80	....	....	....	....	....
1993-94	Quebec Nordiques	44	2	3	5	35	....	....	....	....	....
1994-95	Quebec Nordiques	14	3	1	4	22	3	0	0	0	2
	NHL Totals	**690**	**116**	**142**	**258**	**1303**	**43**	**5**	**11**	**16**	**116**

Traded to **Winnipeg** by **Hartford** for Randy Cunneyworth, December 13, 1989. Traded to **Washington** by **Winnipeg** for Mike Lalor, March 2, 1992. Traded to **Quebec** by **Washington** with Reggie Savage for Mike Hough, June 20, 1993. • Suffered eventual career-ending back injury in game vs. Vancouver, November 23, 1993.

MacDONALD, Blair

Right wing. Shoots right. 5'10", 180 lbs. Born, Cornwall, Ont., November 17, 1953.
(Los Angeles' 4th choice, 86th overall, in 1973 Amateur Draft).

Season	Club	GP	G	A	Pts	PIM	GP	G	A	Pts	PIM
1979-80	Edmonton Oilers	80	46	48	94	6	3	0	3	3	0
1980-81	Edmonton Oilers	51	19	24	43	27	....	....	....	....	....
	Vancouver Canucks	12	5	9	14	10	3	0	1	1	2
1981-82	Vancouver Canucks	59	18	15	33	20	3	0	0	0	0
1982-83	Vancouver Canucks	17	3	4	7	2	2	0	2	2	0
	NHL Totals	**219**	**91**	**100**	**191**	**65**	**11**	**0**	**6**	**6**	**2**

Played in NHL All-Star Game (1980)

Rights retained by **Edmonton** prior to Expansion Draft, June 9, 1979. Traded to **Vancouver** by **Edmonton** with the rights to Lars-Gunnar Petterson for Garry Lariviere and Ken Berry, March 10, 1981.

MacDONALD, Brett

Defense. Shoots left. 6'1", 205 lbs. Born, Bothwell, Ont., January 5, 1966.
(Vancouver's 7th choice, 94th overall, in 1984 Entry Draft).

Season	Club	GP	G	A	Pts	PIM	GP	G	A	Pts	PIM
1987-88	Vancouver Canucks	1	0	0	0	0	....	....	....	....	....
	NHL Totals	**1**	**0**	**0**	**0**	**0**	....	....	....	....	....

MacDONALD, Craig

Left wing. Shoots left. 6'2", 195 lbs. Born, Antigonish, N.S., April 7, 1977.
(Hartford's 3rd choice, 88th overall, in 1996 Entry Draft).

Season	Club	GP	G	A	Pts	PIM	GP	G	A	Pts	PIM
1998-99	Carolina Hurricanes	11	0	0	0	0	1	0	0	0	0
2001-02	Carolina Hurricanes	12	1	1	2	0	4	0	0	0	2
2002-03	Carolina Hurricanes	35	1	3	4	20	....	....	....	....	....
	NHL Totals	**58**	**2**	**4**	**6**	**20**	**5**	**0**	**0**	**0**	**2**

Rights transferred to **Carolina** after **Hartford** franchise relocated, June 25, 1997

MacDONALD, Doug

Left wing. Shoots left. 6', 192 lbs. Born, Assiniboia, Sask., February 8, 1969.
(Buffalo's 3rd choice, 77th overall, in 1989 Entry Draft).

Season	Club	GP	G	A	Pts	PIM	GP	G	A	Pts	PIM
1992-93	Buffalo Sabres	5	1	0	1	2	....	....	....	....	....
1993-94	Buffalo Sabres	4	0	0	0	0	....	....	....	....	....
1994-95	Buffalo Sabres	2	0	0	0	0	....	....	....	....	....
	NHL Totals	**11**	**1**	**0**	**1**	**2**	....	....	....	....	....

MacDONALD, Kevin

Defense. Shoots right. 6', 200 lbs. Born, Prescott, Ont., February 24, 1966.

Season	Club	GP	G	A	Pts	PIM	GP	G	A	Pts	PIM
1993-94	Ottawa Senators	1	0	0	0	2	....	....	....	....	....
	NHL Totals	**1**	**0**	**0**	**0**	**2**	....	....	....	....	....

Signed as a free agent by **Edmonton**, July, 1990. Signed as a free agent by **Ottawa**, December 22, 1993.

MacDONALD, Kilby

Left wing. Shoots left. 5'11", 178 lbs. Born, Ottawa, Ont., September 6, 1914.

Season	Club	GP	G	A	Pts	PIM	GP	G	A	Pts	PIM
1939-40♦	New York Rangers	44	15	13	28	19	12	0	2	2	4
1940-41	New York Rangers	47	5	6	11	12	3	1	0	1	0
1943-44	New York Rangers	24	7	9	16	4	....	....	....	....	....
1944-45	New York Rangers	36	9	6	15	12	....	....	....	....	....
	NHL Totals	**151**	**36**	**34**	**70**	**47**	**15**	**1**	**2**	**3**	**4**

Calder Trophy (1940)

Traded to **Hershey** (AHL) by **NY Rangers** for cash, September 11, 1941. Traded to **Buffalo** (AHL) by **Hershey** (AHL) for Bob Gracie, February 2, 1942. Traded to **NY Rangers** by **Montreal** (Buffalo-AHL) for Hub Macey, Nestor Lubeck and Spence Tatchell, January 12, 1944.

MacDONALD, Lowell

Left wing. Shoots right. 5'11", 185 lbs. Born, New Glasgow, N.S., August 30, 1941.

Season	Club	GP	G	A	Pts	PIM	GP	G	A	Pts	PIM
1961-62	Detroit Red Wings	1	0	0	0	2	....	....	....	....	....
1962-63	Detroit Red Wings	26	2	1	3	8	1	0	0	0	2
1963-64	Detroit Red Wings	10	1	4	5	0	....	....	....	....	....
1964-65	Detroit Red Wings	9	2	1	3	0	....	....	....	....	....
1967-68	Los Angeles Kings	74	21	24	45	12	7	3	4	7	2
1968-69	Los Angeles Kings	58	14	14	28	10	7	2	3	5	0
1970-71	Pittsburgh Penguins	10	0	1	1	0	....	....	....	....	....
1972-73	Pittsburgh Penguins	78	34	41	75	8	....	....	....	....	....
1973-74	Pittsburgh Penguins	78	43	39	82	14	....	....	....	....	....
1974-75	Pittsburgh Penguins	71	27	33	60	24	9	4	2	6	4
1975-76	Pittsburgh Penguins	69	30	43	73	12	3	1	0	1	0
1976-77	Pittsburgh Penguins	3	1	1	2	0	3	1	2	3	4

Season	Club	GP	G	A	Pts	PIM	GP	G	A	Pts	PIM
		REGULAR SEASON					PLAYOFFS				
1977-78	Pittsburgh Penguins	19	5	8	13	2	....	....	....	....	....
	NHL Totals	**506**	**180**	**210**	**390**	**92**	**30**	**11**	**11**	**22**	**12**

Bill Masterton Trophy (1973)

Played in NHL All-Star Game (1973, 1974)

Traded to **Toronto** by **Detroit** with Marcel Pronovost, Eddie Joyal, Larry Jeffrey and Aut Erickson for Andy Bathgate, Billy Harris and Gary Jarrett, May 20, 1965. Claimed by **Los Angeles** from **Toronto** in Expansion Draft, June 6, 1967. Claimed by **Pittsburgh** from **Los Angeles** in Intra-League Draft, June 9, 1970. • Missed majority of 1970-71 and entire 1971-72 seasons recovering from knee injury suffered in game vs. Los Angeles, October 21, 1970. • Missed majority of 1976-77 and 1977-78 seasons recovering from shoulder injury originally suffered in game vs. Detroit, December 10, 1975.

MacDONALD, Parker

Center. Shoots left. 5'11", 160 lbs. Born, Sydney, N.S., June 14, 1933.

Season	Club	GP	G	A	Pts	PIM	GP	G	A	Pts	PIM
1952-53	Toronto Maple Leafs	1	0	0	0	0	....	....	....	....	....
1954-55	Toronto Maple Leafs	62	8	3	11	36	4	0	0	0	4
1956-57	New York Rangers	45	7	8	15	24	1	1	1	2	0
1957-58	New York Rangers	70	8	10	18	30	6	1	2	3	2
1959-60	New York Rangers	4	0	0	0	0	....	....	....	....	....
1960-61	Detroit Red Wings	70	14	12	26	6	9	1	0	1	0
1961-62	Detroit Red Wings	32	5	7	12	8	....	....	....	....	....
1962-63	Detroit Red Wings	69	33	28	61	32	11	3	2	5	2
1963-64	Detroit Red Wings	68	21	25	46	25	14	3	3	6	2
1964-65	Detroit Red Wings	69	13	33	46	38	7	1	1	2	6
1965-66	Boston Bruins	29	6	4	10	6	....	....	....	....	....
	Detroit Red Wings	37	5	12	17	24	9	0	0	0	2
1966-67	Detroit Red Wings	16	3	5	8	2	....	....	....	....	....
1967-68	Minnesota North Stars	69	19	23	42	22	14	4	5	9	2
1968-69	Minnesota North Stars	35	2	9	11	0	....	....	....	....	....
	NHL Totals	**676**	**144**	**179**	**323**	**253**	**75**	**14**	**14**	**28**	**20**

Signed as a free agent by **Toronto** (Pittsburgh-AHL), September 28, 1953. Claimed by **NY Rangers** from **Toronto** in Intra-League Draft, June 5, 1956. Claimed by **Detroit** from **NY Rangers** in Intra-League Draft, June 8, 1960. Traded to **Boston** by **Detroit** with Albert Langlois, Ron Harris and Bob Dillabough for Ab McDonald, Bob McCord and Ken Stephanson, May 31, 1965. Traded to **Detroit** by **Boston** for Pit Martin, December 30, 1965. Claimed by **Minnesota** from **Detroit** in Expansion Draft, June 6, 1967.

MacDOUGALL, Kim

Defense. Shoots left. 5'11", 180 lbs. Born, Regina, Sask., August 29, 1954.
(Minnesota's 4th choice, 60th overall, in 1974 Amateur Draft).

Season	Club	GP	G	A	Pts	PIM	GP	G	A	Pts	PIM
1974-75	Minnesota North Stars	1	0	0	0	0	....	....	....	....	....
	NHL Totals	**1**	**0**	**0**	**0**	**0**	....	....	....	....	....

MacEACHERN, Shane

Center. Shoots left. 5'11", 180 lbs. Born, Charlottetown, P.E.I., December 14, 1967.

Season	Club	GP	G	A	Pts	PIM	GP	G	A	Pts	PIM
1987-88	St. Louis Blues	1	0	0	0	0	....	....	....	....	....
	NHL Totals	**1**	**0**	**0**	**0**	**0**	....	....	....	....	....

Signed as a free agent by **St. Louis**, September 22, 1986.

MACEY, Hub

Left wing. Shoots left. 5'8", 178 lbs. Born, Big River, Sask., April 13, 1921.

Season	Club	GP	G	A	Pts	PIM	GP	G	A	Pts	PIM
1941-42	New York Rangers	9	3	5	8	0	1	0	0	0	0
1942-43	New York Rangers	9	3	3	6	0	....	....	....	....	....
1946-47	Montreal Canadiens	12	0	1	1	0	7	0	0	0	0
	NHL Totals	**30**	**6**	**9**	**15**	**0**	**8**	**0**	**0**	**0**	**0**

Traded to **Montreal** (Buffalo-AHL) by **NY Rangers** with Nestor Lubeck and Spence Tatchell for Kilby MacDonald, January 12, 1944. Traded to **Springfield** (AHL) by **Montreal** (Buffalo-AHL) for Gordie Bell and the rights to Sid McNabney, December 21, 1948.

MacGREGOR, Bruce

Center. Shoots right. 5'10", 180 lbs. Born, Edmonton, Alta., April 26, 1941.

Season	Club	GP	G	A	Pts	PIM	GP	G	A	Pts	PIM
1960-61	Detroit Red Wings	12	0	1	1	0	8	1	2	3	6
1961-62	Detroit Red Wings	65	6	12	18	16	....	....	....	....	....
1962-63	Detroit Red Wings	67	11	11	22	12	10	1	4	5	10
1963-64	Detroit Red Wings	63	11	21	32	15	14	5	2	7	12
1964-65	Detroit Red Wings	66	21	20	41	19	7	0	2	2	2
1965-66	Detroit Red Wings	70	20	14	34	28	12	1	4	5	2
1966-67	Detroit Red Wings	70	28	19	47	14	....	....	....	....	....
1967-68	Detroit Red Wings	71	15	24	39	13	....	....	....	....	....
1968-69	Detroit Red Wings	69	18	23	41	14	....	....	....	....	....
1969-70	Detroit Red Wings	73	15	23	38	24	4	1	0	1	2
1970-71	Detroit Red Wings	47	6	16	22	18	....	....	....	....	....
	New York Rangers	27	12	13	25	4	13	0	4	4	2
1971-72	New York Rangers	75	19	21	40	22	16	2	6	8	4
1972-73	New York Rangers	52	14	12	26	12	10	2	2	4	2
1973-74	New York Rangers	66	17	27	44	6	13	6	2	8	2
	NHL Totals	**893**	**213**	**257**	**470**	**217**	**107**	**19**	**28**	**47**	**44**

Traded to **NY Rangers** by **Detroit** with Larry Brown for Arnie Brown, Mike Robitaille and Tom Miller, February 2, 1971.

MacGREGOR, Randy

Right wing. Shoots left. 5'9", 175 lbs. Born, Cobourg, Ont., July 9, 1953.

Season	Club	GP	G	A	Pts	PIM	GP	G	A	Pts	PIM
1981-82	Hartford Whalers	2	1	1	2	2	....	....	....	....	....
	NHL Totals	**2**	**1**	**1**	**2**	**2**	....	....	....	....	....

Signed as a free agent by **Hartford**, February, 1981.

MacGUIGAN, Garth

Center. Shoots left. 6', 190 lbs. Born, Charlottetown, P.E.I., February 16, 1956.
(NY Islanders' 3rd choice, 50th overall, in 1976 Amateur Draft).

Season	Club	GP	G	A	Pts	PIM	GP	G	A	Pts	PIM
		REGULAR SEASON					PLAYOFFS				
1979-80	New York Islanders	2	0	0	0	2	....	....	....	....	....
1983-84	New York Islanders	3	0	1	1	0	....	....	....	....	....
	NHL Totals	**5**	**0**	**1**	**1**	**2**	....	....	....	....	....

MacINNIS, Al

Defense. Shoots right. 6'2", 209 lbs. Born, Inverness, N.S., July 11, 1963.
(Calgary's 1st choice, 15th overall, in 1981 Entry Draft).

Season	Club	GP	G	A	Pts	PIM	GP	G	A	Pts	PIM
1981-82	Calgary Flames	2	0	0	0	0	....	....	....	....	....
1982-83	Calgary Flames	14	1	3	4	9	....	....	....	....	....
1983-84	Calgary Flames	51	11	34	45	42	11	2	12	14	13
1984-85	Calgary Flames	67	14	52	66	75	4	1	2	3	8
1985-86	Calgary Flames	77	11	57	68	76	21	4	*15	19	30
1986-87	Calgary Flames	79	20	56	76	97	4	1	0	1	0
1987-88	Calgary Flames	80	25	58	83	114	7	3	6	9	18
1988-89♦	Calgary Flames	79	16	58	74	136	22	7	*24	*31	46
1989-90	Calgary Flames	79	28	62	90	82	6	2	3	5	8
1990-91	Calgary Flames	78	28	75	103	90	7	2	3	5	8
1991-92	Calgary Flames	72	20	57	77	83	....	....	....	....	....
1992-93	Calgary Flames	50	11	43	54	61	6	1	6	7	10
1993-94	Calgary Flames	75	28	54	82	95	7	2	6	8	12
1994-95	St. Louis Blues	32	8	20	28	43	7	1	5	6	10
1995-96	St. Louis Blues	82	17	44	61	88	13	3	4	7	20
1996-97	St. Louis Blues	72	13	30	43	65	6	1	2	3	4
1997-98	St. Louis Blues	71	19	30	49	80	8	2	6	8	12
1998-99	St. Louis Blues	82	20	42	62	70	13	4	8	12	20
99-2000	St. Louis Blues	61	11	28	39	34	7	1	3	4	14
2000-01	St. Louis Blues	59	12	42	54	52	15	2	8	10	18
2001-02	St. Louis Blues	71	11	35	46	52	10	0	7	7	4
2002-03	St. Louis Blues	80	16	52	68	61	3	0	1	1	0
	NHL Totals	**1413**	**340**	**932**	**1272**	**1505**	**177**	**39**	**121**	**160**	**255**

NHL Second All-Star Team (1987, 1989, 1994) • Conn Smythe Trophy (1989) • NHL First All-Star Team (1990, 1991, 1999, 2003) • James Norris Memorial Trophy (1999)

Played in NHL All-Star Game (1985, 1988, 1990, 1991, 1992, 1994, 1996, 1997, 1998, 1999, 2000, 2003)

Traded to **St. Louis** by **Calgary** with Calgary's 4th round choice (Didier Tremblay) in 1997 Entry Draft for Phil Housley and St. Louis' 2nd round choices in 1996 (Steve Begin) and 1997 (John Tripp) Entry Drafts, July 4, 1994.

MacINTOSH, Ian

Right wing. Shoots right. 5'11", 175 lbs. Born, Selkirk, Man., June 10, 1927.

Season	Club	GP	G	A	Pts	PIM	GP	G	A	Pts	PIM
1952-53	New York Rangers	4	0	0	0	4	....	....	....	....	....
	NHL Totals	**4**	**0**	**0**	**0**	**4**	....	....	....	....	....

MacIVER, Don

Defense. Shoots left. 6', 200 lbs. Born, Montreal, Que., May 3, 1955.

Season	Club	GP	G	A	Pts	PIM	GP	G	A	Pts	PIM
1979-80	Winnipeg Jets	6	0	0	0	2	....	....	....	....	....
	NHL Totals	**6**	**0**	**0**	**0**	**2**	....	....	....	....	....

Signed as a free agent by **Winnipeg**, October 16, 1979.

MACIVER, Norm

Defense. Shoots left. 5'11", 180 lbs. Born, Thunder Bay, Ont., September 8, 1964.

Season	Club	GP	G	A	Pts	PIM	GP	G	A	Pts	PIM
1986-87	New York Rangers	3	0	1	1	0	....	....	....	....	....
1987-88	New York Rangers	37	9	15	24	14	....	....	....	....	....
1988-89	New York Rangers	26	0	10	10	14	....	....	....	....	....
	Hartford Whalers	37	1	22	23	24	1	0	0	0	2
1989-90	Edmonton Oilers	1	0	0	0	0	....	....	....	....	....
1990-91	Edmonton Oilers	21	2	5	7	14	18	0	4	4	8
1991-92	Edmonton Oilers	57	6	34	40	38	13	1	2	3	10
1992-93	Ottawa Senators	80	17	46	63	84	....	....	....	....	....
1993-94	Ottawa Senators	53	3	20	23	26	....	....	....	....	....
1994-95	Ottawa Senators	28	4	7	11	10	....	....	....	....	....
	Pittsburgh Penguins	13	0	9	9	6	12	1	4	5	8
1995-96	Pittsburgh Penguins	32	2	21	23	32	....	....	....	....	....
	Winnipeg Jets	39	5	25	30	26	6	1	0	1	2
1996-97	Phoenix Coyotes	32	4	9	13	24	....	....	....	....	....
1997-98	Phoenix Coyotes	41	2	6	8	38	6	0	1	1	2
	NHL Totals	**500**	**55**	**230**	**285**	**350**	**56**	**3**	**11**	**14**	**32**

Signed as a free agent by **NY Rangers**, September 8, 1986. Traded to **Hartford** by **NY Rangers** with Brian Lawton and Don Maloney for Carey Wilson and Hartford's 5th round choice (Lubos Rob) in 1990 Entry Draft, December 26, 1988. Traded to **Edmonton** by **Hartford** for Jim Ennis, October 10, 1989. Claimed by **Ottawa** from **Edmonton** in NHL Waiver Draft, October 4, 1992. Traded to **Pittsburgh** by **Ottawa** with Troy Murray for Martin Straka, April 7, 1995. Traded to **Winnipeg** by **Pittsburgh** for Neil Wilkinson, December 28, 1995. Transferred to **Phoenix** after **Winnipeg** franchise relocated, July 1, 1996.

MacKASEY, Blair

Defense. Shoots right. 6'2", 200 lbs. Born, Hamilton, Ont., December 13, 1955.
(Washington's 3rd choice, 55th overall, in 1975 Amateur Draft).

Season	Club	GP	G	A	Pts	PIM	GP	G	A	Pts	PIM
1976-77	Toronto Maple Leafs	1	0	0	0	2	....	....	....	....	....
	NHL Totals	**1**	**0**	**0**	**0**	**2**	....	....	....	....	....

Traded to **Toronto** by **Washington** for cash, September 27, 1976.

MacKAY, Calum

Left wing. Shoots left. 5'10", 178 lbs. Born, Toronto, Ont., January 1, 1927.

Season	Club	GP	G	A	Pts	PIM	GP	G	A	Pts	PIM
		REGULAR SEASON					PLAYOFFS				
1946-47	Detroit Red Wings	5	0	0	0	0	....	....	....	....	....
1948-49	Detroit Red Wings	1	0	0	0	0	....	....	....	....	....
1949-50	Montreal Canadiens	52	8	10	18	44	5	0	1	1	2
1950-51	Montreal Canadiens	70	18	10	28	69	11	1	0	1	0
1951-52	Montreal Canadiens	12	0	1	1	8	....	....	....	....	....
1952-53 ◆	Montreal Canadiens	....	....	....	....	....	7	1	3	4	10
1953-54	Montreal Canadiens	47	10	13	23	54	3	0	1	1	0
1954-55	Montreal Canadiens	50	14	21	35	39	12	3	8	11	8
	NHL Totals	**237**	**50**	**55**	**105**	**214**	**38**	**5**	**13**	**18**	**20**

Played in NHL All-Star Game (1953)

Traded to **Montreal** by **Detroit** for Joe Carveth, November 11, 1949.

MacKAY, Dave

Defense. Shoots right. 6', 210 lbs. Born, Edmonton, Alta., January 14, 1919.

Season	Club	GP	G	A	Pts	PIM	GP	G	A	Pts	PIM
1940-41	Chicago Black Hawks	29	3	0	3	26	5	0	1	1	2
	NHL Totals	**29**	**3**	**0**	**3**	**26**	**5**	**0**	**1**	**1**	**2**

• Alberta Military Authority rejected his request to go to Chicago, October 10, 1941.

MacKAY, Mickey

HHOF

Center. Shoots left. 5'9", 162 lbs. Born, Chelsey, Ont., May 25, 1894.

Season	Club	GP	G	A	Pts	PIM	GP	G	A	Pts	PIM
1926-27	Chicago Black Hawks	34	14	8	22	23	2	0	0	0	0
1927-28	Chicago Black Hawks	36	17	4	21	23	....	....	....	....	....
1928-29	Pittsburgh Pirates	10	1	0	1	2	....	....	....	....	....
	◆ Boston Bruins	30	8	2	10	18	3	0	0	0	2
1929-30	Boston Bruins	37	4	5	9	13	6	0	0	0	4
	NHL Totals	**147**	**44**	**19**	**63**	**79**	**11**	**0**	**0**	**0**	**6**

Traded to **Chicago** by **Vancouver** (WHL) for cash, October 4, 1926. Traded to **Pittsburgh** by **Chicago** for cash, September, 1928. Traded to **Boston** by **Pittsburgh** with $12,000 for Frank Fredrickson, December 21, 1928.

MacKAY, Murdo

Right wing/Center. Shoots right. 5'11", 175 lbs. Born, Fort William, Ont., August 8, 1917.

Season	Club	GP	G	A	Pts	PIM	GP	G	A	Pts	PIM
1945-46	Montreal Canadiens	5	0	1	1	0	....	....	....	....	....
1946-47	Montreal Canadiens	....	....	....	....	....	9	0	1	1	0
1947-48	Montreal Canadiens	14	0	2	2	0	....	....	....	....	....
1948-49	Montreal Canadiens						6	1	1	2	0
	NHL Totals	**19**	**0**	**3**	**3**	**0**	**15**	**1**	**2**	**3**	**0**

Signed as a free agent by **NY Rangers**, October 21, 1940. Traded to **Buffalo** (AHL) by **NY Rangers** for cash, September 11, 1941. Traded to **Montreal** by **Buffalo** (AHL) for John Adams and Moe White with Montreal holding right of recall, January 14, 1946. Traded to **Cleveland** (AHL) by **Montreal** (Buffalo-AHL) for Pete Leswick, August 4, 1950. Signed as a free agent by **Montreal**, September, 1951. Transferred to **Quebec** (QSHL) from **Montreal** as compensation for Montreal's signing of free agent Dick Gamble, September 24, 1951.

MacKELL, Fleming

Center. Shoots left. 5'7", 156 lbs. Born, Montreal, Que., April 30, 1929.

Season	Club	GP	G	A	Pts	PIM	GP	G	A	Pts	PIM
1947-48	Toronto Maple Leafs	3	0	0	0	2	....	....	....	....	....
1948-49 ◆	Toronto Maple Leafs	11	1	1	2	6	9	2	4	6	4
1949-50	Toronto Maple Leafs	36	7	13	20	24	7	1	1	2	11
1950-51 ◆	Toronto Maple Leafs	70	12	13	25	40	11	2	3	5	9
1951-52	Toronto Maple Leafs	32	2	8	10	16	....	....	....	....	....
	Boston Bruins	30	1	8	9	24	5	2	1	3	12
1952-53	Boston Bruins	65	27	17	44	63	11	2	*7	9	7
1953-54	Boston Bruins	67	15	32	47	60	4	1	1	2	8
1954-55	Boston Bruins	60	11	24	35	76	4	0	1	1	0
1955-56	Boston Bruins	52	7	9	16	59	....	....	....	....	....
1956-57	Boston Bruins	65	22	17	39	73	10	5	3	8	4
1957-58	Boston Bruins	70	20	40	60	72	12	5	14	*19	12
1958-59	Boston Bruins	57	17	23	40	28	7	2	6	8	8
1959-60	Boston Bruins	47	7	15	22	19	....	....	....	....	....
	NHL Totals	**665**	**149**	**220**	**369**	**562**	**80**	**22**	**41**	**63**	**75**

• Son of Jack • NHL First All-Star Team (1953)

Played in NHL All-Star Game (1947, 1948, 1949, 1954)

Traded to **Boston** by **Toronto** for Jim Morrison, January 9, 1952.

MacKELL, Jack

Right wing/Defense. Shoots right. 5'7", 150 lbs. Born, Ottawa, Ont., April 12, 1896.

Season	Club	GP	G	A	Pts	PIM	GP	G	A	Pts	PIM
1919-20 ◆	Ottawa Senators	23	2	1	3	33	....	....	....	....	....
	Ottawa Senators (Cup)	....	....	....	....	....	*5*	*0*	*0*	*0*	*0*
1920-21 ◆	Ottawa Senators	22	2	1	3	26	2	0	0	0	0
	NHL Totals	**45**	**4**	**2**	**6**	**59**	**2**	**0**	**0**	**0**	**0**

• Father of Fleming

Signed as a free agent by **Ottawa**, December 19, 1919.

MacKENZIE, Barry

Defense. Shoots left. 6', 190 lbs. Born, Toronto, Ont., August 16, 1941.

Season	Club	GP	G	A	Pts	PIM	GP	G	A	Pts	PIM
1968-69	Minnesota North Stars	6	0	1	1	6	....	....	....	....	....
	NHL Totals	**6**	**0**	**1**	**1**	**6**	....	....	....	....	....

Traded to **Minnesota** by **Toronto** for cash, June 6, 1967.

MacKENZIE, Bill

Defense. Shoots right. 5'11", 175 lbs. Born, Winnipeg, Man., December 12, 1911.

Season	Club	GP	G	A	Pts	PIM	GP	G	A	Pts	PIM
1932-33	Chicago Black Hawks	36	4	4	8	13	....	....	....	....	....
1933-34	Montreal Maroons	47	4	3	7	20	4	0	0	0	0
1934-35	Montreal Maroons	5	0	0	0	0	....	....	....	....	....
	New York Rangers	15	1	0	1	10	3	0	0	0	0
1936-37	Montreal Maroons	10	0	1	1	6	....	....	....	....	....
	Montreal Canadiens	39	4	3	7	22	5	1	0	1	0
1937-38	Montreal Canadiens	11	0	0	0	4	....	....	....	....	....
	◆ Chicago Black Hawks	35	1	2	3	20	9	0	1	1	11
1938-39	Chicago Black Hawks	47	1	0	1	36	....	....	....	....	....
1939-40	Chicago Black Hawks	19	0	1	1	14	....	....	....	....	....
	NHL Totals	**264**	**15**	**14**	**29**	**145**	**21**	**1**	**1**	**2**	**11**

Signed as a free agent by **Mtl. Maroons** after securing release from **Chicago**, June 25, 1933. Loaned to **NY Rangers** by **Mtl. Maroons** for the remainder of the 1934-35 season, January 29, 1935. Traded to **Montreal** by **Mtl. Maroons** for Paul Runge, December 3, 1936. Traded to **Chicago** by **Montreal** for Marty Burke, December 10, 1937. Traded to **Montreal** by **Chicago** for cash, May 11, 1940. Traded to **Cleveland** (IAHL) by **Montreal** with Bill Summerhill for Jim O'Neil, May 17, 1940.

MacKENZIE, Derek

Center. Shoots left. 5'11", 175 lbs. Born, Sudbury, Ont., June 11, 1981.
(Atlanta's 6th choice, 128th overall, in 1999 Entry Draft).

Season	Club	GP	G	A	Pts	PIM	GP	G	A	Pts	PIM
2001-02	Atlanta Thrashers	1	0	0	0	2	....	....	....	....	....
	NHL Totals	**1**	**0**	**0**	**0**	**2**	....	....	....	....	....

MACKEY, David

Left wing. Shoots left. 6'4", 205 lbs. Born, Richmond, B.C., July 24, 1966.
(Chicago's 12th choice, 224th overall, in 1984 Entry Draft).

Season	Club	GP	G	A	Pts	PIM	GP	G	A	Pts	PIM
1987-88	Chicago Blackhawks	23	1	3	4	71	....	....	....	....	....
1988-89	Chicago Blackhawks	23	1	2	3	78	....	....	....	....	....
1989-90	Minnesota North Stars	16	2	0	2	28	....	....	....	....	....
1991-92	St. Louis Blues	19	1	0	1	49	1	0	0	0	0
1992-93	St. Louis Blues	15	1	4	5	23	....	....	....	....	....
1993-94	St. Louis Blues	30	2	3	5	56	2	0	0	0	2
	NHL Totals	**126**	**8**	**12**	**20**	**305**	**3**	**0**	**0**	**0**	**2**

Claimed by **Minnesota** from **Chicago** in Waiver Draft, October 2, 1989. Traded to **Vancouver** by **Minnesota** for future considerations, September 7, 1990. Signed as a free agent by **St. Louis**, August 7, 1991.

MACKEY, Reg

Defense. Shoots left. 5'7", 155 lbs. Born, Ottawa, Ont., May 7, 1900.

Season	Club	GP	G	A	Pts	PIM	GP	G	A	Pts	PIM
1926-27	New York Rangers	34	0	0	0	16	1	0	0	0	0
	NHL Totals	**34**	**0**	**0**	**0**	**16**	**1**	**0**	**0**	**0**	**0**

Traded to **NY Rangers** by **Vancouver** (WHL) for cash, October 9, 1926. Traded to **Boston** (Can-Am) by **NY Rangers** for cash, November 8, 1927.

MACKIE, Howie

Right wing/Defense. Shoots left. 5'10", 190 lbs. Born, Berlin, Ont., August 30, 1913.

Season	Club	GP	G	A	Pts	PIM	GP	G	A	Pts	PIM
1936-37 ◆	Detroit Red Wings	13	1	0	1	4	8	0	0	0	0
1937-38	Detroit Red Wings	7	0	0	0	0	....	....	....	....	....
	NHL Totals	**20**	**1**	**0**	**1**	**4**	**8**	**0**	**0**	**0**	**0**

Signed as a free agent by **Detroit**, September 20, 1936.

MacKINNON, Paul

Defense. Shoots right. 6', 195 lbs. Born, Brantford, Ont., November 6, 1958.
(Washington's 4th choice, 23rd overall, in 1978 Amateur Draft).

Season	Club	GP	G	A	Pts	PIM	GP	G	A	Pts	PIM
1979-80	Washington Capitals	63	1	11	12	22	....	....	....	....	....
1980-81	Washington Capitals	14	0	0	0	22	....	....	....	....	....
1981-82	Washington Capitals	39	2	9	11	35	....	....	....	....	....
1982-83	Washington Capitals	19	2	2	4	8	....	....	....	....	....
1983-84	Washington Capitals	12	0	1	1	4	....	....	....	....	....
	NHL Totals	**147**	**5**	**23**	**28**	**91**	....	....	....	....	....

Reclaimed by **Washington** from **Winnipeg** prior to Expansion Draft, June 9, 1979.

MacLEAN, Don

Center. Shoots left. 6'2", 199 lbs. Born, Sydney, N.S., January 14, 1977.
(Los Angeles' 2nd choice, 33rd overall, in 1995 Entry Draft).

Season	Club	GP	G	A	Pts	PIM	GP	G	A	Pts	PIM
1997-98	Los Angeles Kings	22	5	2	7	4	....	....	....	....	....
2000-01	Toronto Maple Leafs	3	0	1	1	2	....	....	....	....	....
2001-02	Toronto Maple Leafs	....	....	....	....	....	3	0	0	0	0
	NHL Totals	**25**	**5**	**3**	**8**	**6**	**3**	**0**	**0**	**0**	**0**

Traded to **Toronto** by **Los Angeles** for Craig Charron, February 23, 2000. Signed as a free agent by **Columbus**, July 17, 2002.

MacLEAN, John

Right wing. Shoots right. 6', 200 lbs. Born, Oshawa, Ont., November 20, 1964.
(New Jersey's 1st choice, 6th overall, in 1983 Entry Draft).

Season	Club	GP	G	A	Pts	PIM	GP	G	A	Pts	PIM
1983-84	New Jersey Devils	23	1	0	1	10	....	....	....	....	....
1984-85	New Jersey Devils	61	13	20	33	44	....	....	....	....	....
1985-86	New Jersey Devils	74	21	36	57	112	....	....	....	....	....
1986-87	New Jersey Devils	80	31	36	67	120	....	....	....	....	....
1987-88	New Jersey Devils	76	23	16	39	147	20	7	11	18	60
1988-89	New Jersey Devils	74	42	45	87	122	....	....	....	....	....

Season	Club	GP	G	A	Pts	PIM	GP	G	A	Pts	PIM
		REGULAR SEASON					PLAYOFFS				
1989-90	New Jersey Devils	80	41	38	79	80	6	4	1	5	12
1990-91	New Jersey Devils	78	45	33	78	150	7	5	3	8	20
1992-93	New Jersey Devils	80	24	24	48	102	5	0	1	1	10
1993-94	New Jersey Devils	80	37	33	70	95	20	6	10	16	22
1994-95 ♦	New Jersey Devils	46	17	12	29	32	20	5	13	18	14
1995-96	New Jersey Devils	76	20	28	48	91	....	....	....	....	....
1996-97	New Jersey Devils	80	29	25	54	49	10	4	5	9	4
1997-98	New Jersey Devils	26	3	8	11	14	....	....	....	....	....
	San Jose Sharks	51	13	19	32	28	6	2	3	5	4
1998-99	New York Rangers	82	28	27	55	46	....	....	....	....	....
99-2000	New York Rangers	77	18	24	42	52	....	....	....	....	....
2000-01	New York Rangers	2	0	0	0	0	....	....	....	....	....
	Dallas Stars	28	4	2	6	17	10	2	1	3	6
2001-02	Dallas Stars	20	3	3	6	17	....	....	....	....	....
	NHL Totals	**1194**	**413**	**429**	**842**	**1328**	**104**	**35**	**48**	**83**	**152**

Played in NHL All-Star Game (1989, 1991)

• Missed entire 1991-92 season recovering from knee surgery, June, 1991. Traded to **San Jose** by **New Jersey** with Ken Sutton for Doug Bodger and Dody Wood, December 7, 1997. Signed as a free agent by **NY Rangers**, July 22, 1998. Traded to **Dallas** by **NY Rangers** for future considerations, February 5, 2001. Signed as a free agent by **Dallas**, February 26, 2002. • Officially announced retirement, June 7, 2002.

MacLEAN, Paul

Right wing. Shoots right. 6'2", 218 lbs. Born, Grostenquin, France, March 9, 1958.
(St. Louis' 6th choice, 109th overall, in 1978 Amateur Draft).

Season	Club	GP	G	A	Pts	PIM	GP	G	A	Pts	PIM
1980-81	St. Louis Blues	1	0	0	0	0	1	0	0	0	0
1981-82	Winnipeg Jets	74	36	25	61	106	4	3	2	5	26
1982-83	Winnipeg Jets	80	32	44	76	121	3	1	2	3	6
1983-84	Winnipeg Jets	76	40	31	71	155	3	1	0	1	0
1984-85	Winnipeg Jets	79	41	60	101	119	8	3	4	7	4
1985-86	Winnipeg Jets	69	27	29	56	74	2	1	0	1	7
1986-87	Winnipeg Jets	72	32	42	74	75	10	5	2	7	16
1987-88	Winnipeg Jets	77	40	39	79	76	5	2	0	2	23
1988-89	Detroit Red Wings	76	36	35	71	118	5	1	1	2	8
1989-90	St. Louis Blues	78	34	33	67	100	12	4	3	7	20
1990-91	St. Louis Blues	37	6	11	17	24	....	....	....	....	....
	NHL Totals	**719**	**324**	**349**	**673**	**968**	**53**	**21**	**14**	**35**	**110**

Played in NHL All-Star Game (1985)

Traded to **Winnipeg** by **St. Louis** with Bryan Maxwell and Ed Staniowski for Scott Campbell and John Markell, July 3, 1981. Traded to **Detroit** by **Winnipeg** for Brent Ashton, June 13, 1988. Traded to **St. Louis** by **Detroit** with Adam Oates for Bernie Federko and Tony McKegney, June 15, 1989.

MacLEISH, Rick

Center. Shoots left. 5'11", 185 lbs. Born, Lindsay, Ont., January 3, 1950.
(Boston's 2nd choice, 4th overall, in 1970 Amateur Draft).

Season	Club	GP	G	A	Pts	PIM	GP	G	A	Pts	PIM
1970-71	Philadelphia Flyers	26	2	4	6	19	4	1	0	1	0
1971-72	Philadelphia Flyers	17	1	2	3	9	....	....	....	....	....
1972-73	Philadelphia Flyers	78	50	50	100	69	10	3	4	7	2
1973-74 ♦	Philadelphia Flyers	78	32	45	77	42	17	*13	9	*22	20
1974-75 ♦	Philadelphia Flyers	80	38	41	79	50	17	11	9	*20	8
1975-76	Philadelphia Flyers	51	22	23	45	16	....	....	....	....	....
1976-77	Philadelphia Flyers	79	49	48	97	42	10	4	9	13	2
1977-78	Philadelphia Flyers	76	31	39	70	33	12	7	9	16	4
1978-79	Philadelphia Flyers	71	26	32	58	47	7	0	1	1	0
1979-80	Philadelphia Flyers	78	31	35	66	28	19	9	6	15	2
1980-81	Philadelphia Flyers	78	38	36	74	25	12	5	5	10	0
1981-82	Hartford Whalers	34	6	16	22	16	....	....	....	....	....
	Pittsburgh Penguins	40	13	12	25	28	5	1	1	2	0
1982-83	Pittsburgh Penguins	6	0	5	5	2	....	....	....	....	....
1983-84	Philadelphia Flyers	29	8	14	22	4	....	....	....	....	....
	Detroit Red Wings	25	2	8	10	4	1	0	0	0	0
	NHL Totals	**846**	**349**	**410**	**759**	**434**	**114**	**54**	**53**	**107**	**38**

Played in NHL All-Star Game (1976, 1977, 1980)

Traded to **Philadelphia** by **Boston** with Danny Schock for Mike Walton, February 1, 1971. Traded to **Hartford** by **Philadelphia** with Blake Wesley, Don Gillen and Philadelphia's 1st (Paul Lawless), 2nd (Mark Paterson) and 3rd (Kevin Dineen) round choices in 1982 Entry Draft for Ray Allison, Fred Arthur and Hartford's 1st (Ron Sutter), and 3rd (Miroslav Dvorak) round choices in 1983 Entry Draft, July 3, 1981. Traded to **Pittsburgh** by **Hartford** for Russ Anderson and Pittsburgh's 8th round choice (Chris Duperron) in 1983 Entry Draft, December 29, 1981. Signed as a free agent by **Philadelphia**, October 6, 1983. Traded to **Detroit** by **Philadelphia** for future considerations, January 8, 1984.

MacLELLAN, Brian

Left wing. Shoots left. 6'3", 220 lbs. Born, Guelph, Ont., October 27, 1958.

Season	Club	GP	G	A	Pts	PIM	GP	G	A	Pts	PIM
1982-83	Los Angeles Kings	8	0	3	3	7	....	....	....	....	....
1983-84	Los Angeles Kings	72	25	29	54	45	....	....	....	....	....
1984-85	Los Angeles Kings	80	31	54	85	53	3	0	1	1	0
1985-86	Los Angeles Kings	27	5	8	13	19	....	....	....	....	....
	New York Rangers	51	11	21	32	47	16	2	4	6	15
1986-87	Minnesota North Stars	76	32	31	63	69	....	....	....	....	....
1987-88	Minnesota North Stars	75	16	32	48	74	....	....	....	....	....
1988-89	Minnesota North Stars	60	16	23	39	104	....	....	....	....	....
♦	Calgary Flames	12	2	3	5	14	21	3	2	5	19
1989-90	Calgary Flames	65	20	18	38	26	6	0	2	2	8
1990-91	Calgary Flames	57	13	14	27	55	1	0	0	0	0
1991-92	Detroit Red Wings	23	1	5	6	38	....	....	....	....	....
	NHL Totals	**606**	**172**	**241**	**413**	**551**	**47**	**5**	**9**	**14**	**42**

Signed as a free agent by **Los Angeles**, May 12, 1982. Traded to **NY Rangers** by **Los Angeles** with Los Angeles' 4th round choice (Mike Sullivan) in 1987 Entry Draft for Roland Melanson and Grant Ledyard, December 9, 1985. Traded to **Minnesota** by **NY Rangers** for Minnesota's 3rd round choice (Simon Gagne) in 1987 Entry Draft, September 8, 1986. Traded to **Calgary** by **Minnesota** with Minnesota's 4th round choice (Robert Reichel) in 1989 Entry Draft for Shane Churla and Perry Berezan, March 4, 1989. Traded to **Detroit** by **Calgary** for Marc Habscheid, June 11, 1991.

MacLEOD, Pat

Defense. Shoots left. 5'11", 190 lbs. Born, Melfort, Sask., June 15, 1969.
(Minnesota's 5th choice, 87th overall, in 1989 Entry Draft).

Season	Club	GP	G	A	Pts	PIM	GP	G	A	Pts	PIM
1990-91	Minnesota North Stars	1	0	1	1	0	....	....	....	....	....
1991-92	San Jose Sharks	37	5	11	16	4	....	....	....	....	....
1992-93	San Jose Sharks	13	0	1	1	10	....	....	....	....	....
1995-96	Dallas Stars	2	0	0	0	0	....	....	....	....	....
	NHL Totals	**53**	**5**	**13**	**18**	**14**	....	....	....	....	....

Claimed by **San Jose** from **Minnesota** in Dispersal Draft, May 30, 1991. Signed as a free agent by **Dallas**, July 31, 1995.

MacMILLAN, Billy

Right wing. Shoots left. 5'10", 185 lbs. Born, Charlottetown, P.E.I., March 7, 1943.

Season	Club	GP	G	A	Pts	PIM	GP	G	A	Pts	PIM
1970-71	Toronto Maple Leafs	76	22	19	41	42	6	0	3	3	2
1971-72	Toronto Maple Leafs	61	10	7	17	39	5	0	0	0	0
1972-73	Atlanta Flames	78	10	15	25	52	....	....	....	....	....
1973-74	New York Islanders	55	4	9	13	16	....	....	....	....	....
1974-75	New York Islanders	69	13	12	25	12	17	0	1	1	23
1975-76	New York Islanders	64	9	7	16	10	13	4	2	6	8
1976-77	New York Islanders	43	6	8	14	13	12	2	0	2	7
	NHL Totals	**446**	**74**	**77**	**151**	**184**	**53**	**6**	**6**	**12**	**40**

• Brother of Bob

Claimed by **Atlanta** from **Toronto** in Expansion Draft, June 6, 1972. Traded to **NY Islanders** by **Atlanta** to complete transaction that sent Arnie Brown to Atlanta (February 13, 1973), May 29, 1973.

MacMILLAN, Bob

Right wing. Shoots left. 5'11", 185 lbs. Born, Charlottetown, P.E.I., December 3, 1952.
(NY Rangers' 2nd choice, 15th overall, in 1972 Amateur Draft).

Season	Club	GP	G	A	Pts	PIM	GP	G	A	Pts	PIM
1974-75	New York Rangers	22	1	2	3	4	....	....	....	....	....
1975-76	St. Louis Blues	80	20	32	52	41	3	0	1	1	0
1976-77	St. Louis Blues	80	19	39	58	11	4	0	1	1	0
1977-78	St. Louis Blues	28	7	12	19	23	....	....	....	....	....
	Atlanta Flames	52	31	21	52	26	2	0	2	2	0
1978-79	Atlanta Flames	79	37	71	108	14	2	0	1	1	0
1979-80	Atlanta Flames	77	22	39	61	10	4	0	0	0	9
1980-81	Calgary Flames	77	28	35	63	47	16	8	6	14	7
1981-82	Calgary Flames	23	4	7	11	14	....	....	....	....	....
	Colorado Rockies	57	18	32	50	27	....	....	....	....	....
1982-83	New Jersey Devils	71	19	29	48	8	....	....	....	....	....
1983-84	New Jersey Devils	71	17	23	40	23	....	....	....	....	....
1984-85	Chicago Black Hawks	36	5	7	12	12	....	....	....	....	....
	NHL Totals	**753**	**228**	**349**	**577**	**260**	**31**	**8**	**11**	**19**	**16**

• Brother of Billy • Lady Byng Trophy (1979)

Traded to **St. Louis** by **NY Rangers** for Larry Sacharuk, September 20, 1975. Traded to **Atlanta** by **St. Louis** with Yves Belanger, Dick Redmond and St. Louis' 2nd round choice (Mike Perovich) in 1979 Entry Draft for Phil Myre, Barry Gibbs and Curt Bennett, December 12, 1977. Transferred to **Calgary** after **Atlanta** franchise relocated, June 24, 1980. Traded to **Colorado** by **Calgary** with Don Lever for Lanny McDonald and Colorado's 4th round choice (later traded to NY Islanders – NY Islanders selected Mikko Makela) in 1983 Entry Draft, November 25, 1981. Transferred to **New Jersey** after **Colorado** franchise relocated, June 30, 1982. Traded to **Chicago** by **New Jersey** with New Jersey's 5th round choice (Rick Herbert) in 1985 Entry Draft for Don Dietrich, Rich Preston and Chicago's 2nd round choice (Eric Weinrich) in 1985 Entry Draft, June 19, 1984.

MacMILLAN, John

Right wing. Shoots left. 5'10", 185 lbs. Born, Lethbridge, Alta., October 25, 1935.

Season	Club	GP	G	A	Pts	PIM	GP	G	A	Pts	PIM
1960-61	Toronto Maple Leafs	31	3	5	8	8	4	0	0	0	0
1961-62 ♦	Toronto Maple Leafs	31	1	0	1	8	3	0	0	0	0
1962-63 ♦	Toronto Maple Leafs	6	1	1	2	6	1	0	0	0	0
1963-64	Toronto Maple Leafs	13	0	0	0	4	....	....	....	....	....
	Detroit Red Wings	20	0	3	3	6	4	0	1	1	2
1964-65	Detroit Red Wings	3	0	1	1	0	....	....	....	....	....
	NHL Totals	**104**	**5**	**10**	**15**	**32**	**12**	**0**	**1**	**1**	**2**

Played in NHL All-Star Game (1962, 1963)

Claimed on waivers by **Detroit** from **Toronto**, December 3, 1963. Traded to **San Diego** (WHL) by **Detroit** for cash, June, 1966.

MacNEIL, Al

Defense. Shoots left. 5'10", 183 lbs. Born, Sydney, N.S., September 27, 1935.

Season	Club	GP	G	A	Pts	PIM	GP	G	A	Pts	PIM
1955-56	Toronto Maple Leafs	1	0	0	0	2	....	....	....	....	....
1956-57	Toronto Maple Leafs	53	4	8	12	84	....	....	....	....	....
1957-58	Toronto Maple Leafs	13	0	0	0	9	....	....	....	....	....
1959-60	Toronto Maple Leafs	4	0	0	0	2	....	....	....	....	....
1961-62	Montreal Canadiens	61	1	7	8	74	5	0	0	0	2
1962-63	Chicago Black Hawks	70	2	19	21	100	4	0	1	1	4
1963-64	Chicago Black Hawks	70	5	19	24	91	7	0	2	2	25

Season	Club	REGULAR SEASON GP	G	A	Pts	PIM	PLAYOFFS GP	G	A	Pts	PIM
1964-65	Chicago Black Hawks	69	3	7	10	119	14	0	1	1	34
1965-66	Chicago Black Hawks	51	0	1	1	34	3	0	0	0	0
1966-67	New York Rangers	58	0	4	4	44	4	0	0	0	2
1967-68	Pittsburgh Penguins	74	2	10	12	58	....	....	....	....	....
	NHL Totals	**524**	**17**	**75**	**92**	**617**	**37**	**0**	**4**	**4**	**67**

Traded to **Montreal** by **Toronto** for Stan Smrke, June 7, 1960. Traded to **Chicago** by **Montreal** for Wayne Hicks, May 30, 1962. Claimed by **Montreal** from **Chicago** in Intra-League Draft, June 15, 1966. Claimed by **NY Rangers** from **Montreal** in Intra-League Draft, June 15, 1966. Claimed by **Pittsburgh** from **NY Rangers** in Expansion Draft, June 6, 1967. Traded to **Montreal** by **Pittsburgh** for Wally Boyer, June 12, 1968.

MacNEIL, Bernie

Left wing. Shoots left. 5'11", 190 lbs. Born, Sudbury, Ont., March 7, 1950.
(Detroit's 6th choice, 82nd overall, in 1970 Amateur Draft).

Season	Club	GP	G	A	Pts	PIM	GP	G	A	Pts	PIM
1973-74	St. Louis Blues	4	0	0	0	0	....	....	....	....	....
	NHL Totals	**4**	**0**	**0**	**0**	**0**	....	....	....	....	....

Traded to **San Diego** (WHL) by **St. Louis** (Denver-WHL) for Jim Stanfield, January 16, 1974. Signed as a free agent by **St. Louis**, September, 1975.

MacNEIL, Ian

Center. Shoots left. 6'2", 190 lbs. Born, Halifax, N.S., April 27, 1977.
(Hartford's 3rd choice, 85th overall, in 1995 Entry Draft).

Season	Club	GP	G	A	Pts	PIM	GP	G	A	Pts	PIM
2002-03	Philadelphia Flyers	2	0	0	0	0	....	....	....	....	....
	NHL Totals	**2**	**0**	**0**	**0**	**0**	....	....	....	....	....

Rights transferred to **Carolina** after **Hartford** franchise relocated, June 25, 1997. Signed as a free agent by **Philadelphia**, July 2, 2002.

MACOUN, Jamie

Defense. Shoots left. 6'2", 200 lbs. Born, Newmarket, Ont., August 17, 1961.

Season	Club	GP	G	A	Pts	PIM	GP	G	A	Pts	PIM
1982-83	Calgary Flames	22	1	4	5	25	9	0	2	2	8
1983-84	Calgary Flames	72	9	23	32	97	11	1	0	1	0
1984-85	Calgary Flames	70	9	30	39	67	4	1	0	1	4
1985-86	Calgary Flames	77	11	21	32	81	22	1	6	7	23
1986-87	Calgary Flames	79	7	33	40	111	3	0	1	1	8
1988-89 ♦	Calgary Flames	72	8	19	27	76	22	3	6	9	30
1989-90	Calgary Flames	78	8	27	35	70	6	0	3	3	10
1990-91	Calgary Flames	79	7	15	22	84	7	0	1	1	4
1991-92	Calgary Flames	37	2	12	14	53	....	....	....	....	....
	Toronto Maple Leafs	39	3	13	16	18	....	....	....	....	....
1992-93	Toronto Maple Leafs	77	4	15	19	55	21	0	6	6	36
1993-94	Toronto Maple Leafs	82	3	27	30	115	18	1	1	2	12
1994-95	Toronto Maple Leafs	46	2	8	10	75	7	1	2	3	8
1995-96	Toronto Maple Leafs	82	0	8	8	87	6	0	2	2	8
1996-97	Toronto Maple Leafs	73	1	10	11	93	....	....	....	....	....
1997-98	Toronto Maple Leafs	67	0	7	7	63	....	....	....	....	....
♦	Detroit Red Wings	7	0	0	0	2	22	2	2	4	18
1998-99	Detroit Red Wings	69	1	10	11	36	1	0	0	0	0
	NHL Totals	**1128**	**76**	**282**	**358**	**1208**	**159**	**10**	**32**	**42**	**169**

NHL All-Rookie Team (1984)

Signed as a free agent by **Calgary**, January 30, 1983. • Missed entire 1987-88 season recovering from arm injury suffered in automobile accident, May, 1987. Traded to **Toronto** by **Calgary** with Doug Gilmour, Ric Natress, Kent Manderville and Rick Wamsley for Gary Leeman, Alexander Godynyuk, Jeff Reese, Michel Petit and Craig Berube, January 2, 1992. Traded to **Detroit** by **Toronto** for Tampa Bay's 4th round choice (previously acquired, Toronto selected Alexei Ponikarovsky) in 1998 Entry Draft, March 24, 1998.

MacPHERSON, Bud

Defense. Shoots left. 6'4", 200 lbs. Born, Edmonton, Alta., March 31, 1927.

Season	Club	GP	G	A	Pts	PIM	GP	G	A	Pts	PIM
1948-49	Montreal Canadiens	3	0	0	0	2	....	....	....	....	....
1950-51	Montreal Canadiens	62	0	16	16	40	11	0	2	2	8
1951-52	Montreal Canadiens	54	2	1	3	24	11	0	0	0	0
1952-53 ♦	Montreal Canadiens	59	2	3	5	67	4	0	1	1	9
1953-54	Montreal Canadiens	41	0	5	5	41	3	0	0	0	4
1954-55	Montreal Canadiens	30	1	8	9	55	....	....	....	....	....
1956-57	Montreal Canadiens	10	0	0	0	4	....	....	....	....	....
	NHL Totals	**259**	**5**	**33**	**38**	**233**	**29**	**0**	**3**	**3**	**21**

Played in NHL All-Star Game (1953)

Traded to **Chicago** by **Montreal** with Kenny Mosdell for $30,000 with Montreal holding right of recall, May 17, 1956. • Returned to **Montreal** by **Chicago** after training camp, October 10, 1956. Traded to **Detroit** by **Montreal** with Gene Achtymichuk and Claude Laforge for cash, June 3, 1958.

MacSWEYN, Ralph

Defense. Shoots right. 5'11", 190 lbs. Born, Hawkesbury, Ont., September 8, 1942.

Season	Club	GP	G	A	Pts	PIM	GP	G	A	Pts	PIM
1967-68	Philadelphia Flyers	4	0	0	0	0	....	....	....	....	....
1968-69	Philadelphia Flyers	24	0	4	4	6	4	0	0	0	4
1969-70	Philadelphia Flyers	17	0	0	0	4	....	....	....	....	....
1970-71	Philadelphia Flyers	....	....	....	....	....	4	0	0	0	2
1971-72	Philadelphia Flyers	2	0	1	1	0	....	....	....	....	....
	NHL Totals	**47**	**0**	**5**	**5**	**10**	**8**	**0**	**0**	**0**	**6**

NHL rights transferred to **Philadelphia** after NHL club purchased **Quebec** (AHL) franchise, May 8, 1967.

MacTAVISH, Craig

Center. Shoots left. 6'1", 195 lbs. Born, London, Ont., August 15, 1958.
(Boston's 8th choice, 153rd overall, in 1978 Amateur Draft).

Season	Club	GP	G	A	Pts	PIM	GP	G	A	Pts	PIM
1979-80	Boston Bruins	46	11	17	28	8	10	2	3	5	7
1980-81	Boston Bruins	24	3	5	8	13	....	....	....	....	....
1981-82	Boston Bruins	2	0	1	1	0	....	....	....	....	....
1982-83	Boston Bruins	75	10	20	30	18	17	3	1	4	18
1983-84	Boston Bruins	70	20	23	43	35	1	0	0	0	0
1985-86	Edmonton Oilers	74	23	24	47	70	10	4	4	8	11
1986-87 ♦	Edmonton Oilers	79	20	19	39	55	21	1	9	10	16
1987-88 ♦	Edmonton Oilers	80	15	17	32	47	19	0	1	1	31
1988-89	Edmonton Oilers	80	21	31	52	55	7	0	1	1	8
1989-90 ♦	Edmonton Oilers	80	21	22	43	89	22	2	6	8	29
1990-91	Edmonton Oilers	80	17	15	32	76	18	3	3	6	20
1991-92	Edmonton Oilers	80	12	18	30	98	16	3	0	3	28
1992-93	Edmonton Oilers	82	10	20	30	110	....	....	....	....	....
1993-94	Edmonton Oilers	66	16	10	26	80	....	....	....	....	....
♦	New York Rangers	12	4	2	6	11	23	1	4	5	22
1994-95	Philadelphia Flyers	45	3	9	12	23	15	1	4	5	20
1995-96	Philadelphia Flyers	55	5	8	13	62	....	....	....	....	....
	St. Louis Blues	13	0	1	1	8	13	0	2	2	6
1996-97	St. Louis Blues	50	2	5	7	33	1	0	0	0	2
	NHL Totals	**1093**	**213**	**267**	**480**	**891**	**193**	**20**	**38**	**58**	**218**

Played in NHL All-Star Game (1996)

• Suspended for entire 1984-85 season after being convicted of vehicular homicide, May, 1984. Signed as a free agent by **Edmonton,** February 1, 1985. Traded to **NY Rangers** by **Edmonton** for Todd Marchant, March 21, 1994. Signed as a free agent by **Philadelphia**, July 6, 1994. Traded to **St. Louis** by **Philadelphia** for Dale Hawerchuk, March 15, 1996.

MacWILLIAM, Mike

Left wing. Shoots left. 6'4", 230 lbs. Born, Burnaby, B.C., February 14, 1967.

Season	Club	GP	G	A	Pts	PIM	GP	G	A	Pts	PIM
1995-96	New York Islanders	6	0	0	0	14	....	....	....	....	....
	NHL Totals	**6**	**0**	**0**	**0**	**14**	....	....	....	....	....

Signed as a free agent by **Philadelphia**, October 7, 1986. Signed as a free agent by **Toronto**, July 30, 1991. Signed as a free agent by **NY Islanders**, July 25, 1995.

MADDEN, John

Center. Shoots left. 5'11", 190 lbs. Born, Barrie, Ont., May 4, 1973.

Season	Club	GP	G	A	Pts	PIM	GP	G	A	Pts	PIM
1998-99	New Jersey Devils	4	0	1	1	0					
99-2000 ♦	New Jersey Devils	74	16	9	25	6	20	3	4	7	0
2000-01	New Jersey Devils	80	23	15	38	12	25	4	3	7	6
2001-02	New Jersey Devils	82	15	8	23	25	6	0	0	0	0
2002-03 ♦	New Jersey Devils	80	19	22	41	26	24	6	10	16	2
	NHL Totals	**320**	**73**	**55**	**128**	**69**	**75**	**13**	**17**	**30**	**8**

Frank J. Selke Trophy (2001)

Signed as a free agent by **New Jersey**, June 26, 1997.

MADIGAN, Connie

Defense. Shoots left. 5'10", 185 lbs. Born, Port Arthur, Ont., October 4, 1934.

Season	Club	GP	G	A	Pts	PIM	GP	G	A	Pts	PIM
1972-73	St. Louis Blues	20	0	3	3	25	5	0	0	0	4
	NHL Totals	**20**	**0**	**3**	**3**	**25**	**5**	**0**	**0**	**0**	**4**

Rights transferred to **Toronto** after NHL club purchased **Spokane** (WHL) franchise, June 4, 1963. Traded to **LA Blades** (WHL) by **Toronto** (Denver-WHL) for cash, October, 1963. Traded to **Providence** (AHL) by **LA Blades** (WHL) for cash, September, 1964. Traded to **Portland** (WHL) by **Providence** (AHL) for cash, October, 1964. Traded to **St. Louis** by **Portland** (WHL) for cash and the loan of Andre Aubry for the remainder of the 1972-73 season, January 31, 1973. • Oldest rookie in NHL history. Traded to **San Diego** (WHL) by **St. Louis** for cash, September, 1973.

MADILL, Jeff

Right wing. Shoots left. 5'11", 195 lbs. Born, Oshawa, Ont., June 21, 1965.
(New Jersey's 2nd choice, 7th overall, in 1987 Supplemental Draft).

Season	Club	GP	G	A	Pts	PIM	GP	G	A	Pts	PIM
1990-91	New Jersey Devils	14	4	0	4	46	7	0	2	2	8
	NHL Totals	**14**	**4**	**0**	**4**	**46**	**7**	**0**	**2**	**2**	**8**

Claimed by **San Jose** from **New Jersey** in Expansion Draft, May 30, 1991.

MAGEE, Dean

Left wing. Shoots left. 6'2", 210 lbs. Born, Rocky Mountain House, Alta., April 29, 1955.
(Minnesota's 8th choice, 130th overall, in 1975 Amateur Draft).

Season	Club	GP	G	A	Pts	PIM	GP	G	A	Pts	PIM
1977-78	Minnesota North Stars	7	0	0	0	4	....	....	....	....	....
	NHL Totals	**7**	**0**	**0**	**0**	**4**	....	....	....	....	....

MAGGS, Daryl

Defense. Shoots right. 6'2", 195 lbs. Born, Victoria, B.C., April 6, 1949.
(Chicago's 4th choice, 48th overall, in 1969 Amateur Draft).

Season	Club	GP	G	A	Pts	PIM	GP	G	A	Pts	PIM
1971-72	Chicago Black Hawks	59	7	4	11	4	4	0	0	0	0
1972-73	Chicago Black Hawks	17	0	0	0	4	....	....	....	....	....
	California Golden Seals	54	7	15	22	46	....	....	....	....	....
1979-80	Toronto Maple Leafs	5	0	0	0	0	....	....	....	....	....
	NHL Totals	**135**	**14**	**19**	**33**	**54**	**4**	**0**	**0**	**0**	**0**

Traded to **California** by **Chicago** for Dick Redmond and the rights to Bobby Sheehan, December 5, 1972. Signed to 5-game free agent try-out contract by **Toronto**, December, 1979.

MAGNAN, Marc

Left wing. Shoots left. 5'11", 195 lbs. Born, Beaumont, Alta., February 17, 1962.
(Toronto's 9th choice, 195th overall, in 1981 Entry Draft).

Season	Club	Regular Season GP	G	A	Pts	PIM	Playoffs GP	G	A	Pts	PIM
1982-83	Toronto Maple Leafs	4	0	1	1	5	....	....	....	....	....
	NHL Totals	**4**	**0**	**1**	**1**	**5**	....	....	....	....	....

MAGNUSON, Keith

Defense. Shoots right. 6', 185 lbs. Born, Saskatoon, Sask., April 27, 1947.

Season	Club	Regular Season GP	G	A	Pts	PIM	Playoffs GP	G	A	Pts	PIM
1969-70	Chicago Black Hawks	76	0	24	24	*213	8	1	2	3	17
1970-71	Chicago Black Hawks	76	3	20	23	*291	18	0	2	2	*63
1971-72	Chicago Black Hawks	74	2	19	21	201	8	0	1	1	29
1972-73	Chicago Black Hawks	77	0	19	19	140	7	0	2	2	4
1973-74	Chicago Black Hawks	57	2	11	13	105	11	1	0	1	17
1974-75	Chicago Black Hawks	48	2	12	14	117	8	1	2	3	15
1975-76	Chicago Black Hawks	48	1	6	7	99	4	0	0	0	12
1976-77	Chicago Black Hawks	37	1	6	7	86	....	....	....	....	....
1977-78	Chicago Black Hawks	67	2	4	6	145	4	0	0	0	7
1978-79	Chicago Black Hawks	26	1	4	5	41	....	....	....	....	....
1979-80	Chicago Black Hawks	3	0	0	0	4	....	....	....	....	....
	NHL Totals	**589**	**14**	**125**	**139**	**1442**	**68**	**3**	**9**	**12**	**164**

Played in NHL All-Star Game (1971, 1972)

Signed as a free agent by **Chicago**, September, 1969. • Missed majority of 1978-79 season recovering from knee injury suffered in game vs. St. Louis, December 27, 1978. Claimed by **Chicago** as a fill-in during Expansion Draft, June 13, 1979.

MAGUIRE, Kevin

Right wing. Shoots right. 6'2", 200 lbs. Born, Toronto, Ont., January 5, 1963.

Season	Club	Regular Season GP	G	A	Pts	PIM	Playoffs GP	G	A	Pts	PIM
1986-87	Toronto Maple Leafs	17	0	0	0	74	1	0	0	0	0
1987-88	Buffalo Sabres	46	4	6	10	162	5	0	0	0	50
1988-89	Buffalo Sabres	60	8	10	18	241	5	0	0	0	36
1989-90	Buffalo Sabres	61	6	9	15	115	....	....	....	....	....
	Philadelphia Flyers	5	1	0	1	6	....	....	....	....	....
1990-91	Toronto Maple Leafs	63	9	5	14	180	....	....	....	....	....
1991-92	Toronto Maple Leafs	8	1	0	1	4	....	....	....	....	....
	NHL Totals	**260**	**29**	**30**	**59**	**782**	**11**	**0**	**0**	**0**	**86**

Signed as a free agent by **Toronto**, October 10, 1984. Claimed by **Buffalo** from **Toronto** in Waiver Draft, October 5, 1987. Traded to **Philadelphia** by **Buffalo** with Buffalo's 2nd round choice (Mikael Renberg) in 1990 Entry Draft for Jay Wells and Philadelphia's 4th round choice (Peter Ambroziak) in 1991 Entry Draft, March 5, 1990. Traded to **Toronto** by **Philadelphia** with Philadelphia's 8th round choice (Dmitri Mironov) in 1991 Entry Draft for Toronto's 3rd round choice (Al Kinisky) in 1990 Entry Draft, June 16, 1990.

MAHAFFY, John

Center. Shoots left. 5'7", 165 lbs. Born, Montreal, Que., July 18, 1919.

Season	Club	Regular Season GP	G	A	Pts	PIM	Playoffs GP	G	A	Pts	PIM
1942-43	Montreal Canadiens	9	2	5	7	4	....	....	....	....	....
1943-44	New York Rangers	28	9	20	29	0	....	....	....	....	....
1944-45	Montreal Canadiens	....	....	....	....	....	1	0	1	1	0
	NHL Totals	**37**	**11**	**25**	**36**	**4**	**1**	**0**	**1**	**1**	**0**

Loaned to **NY Rangers** by **Montreal** with Dutch Hiller, Fern Gauthier, Charlie Sands and future considerations (Tony Demers, December, 1943) for the loan of Phil Watson, October 27, 1943. Traded to **Pittsburgh** (AHL) by **Montreal** for cash, November 24, 1944. • Played for Montreal in playoff game on March 24, 1945 though he was subsequently ruled ineligible to play in any further playoff games as his rights were still owned by Pittsburgh (AHL). Traded to **Montreal** (Buffalo-AHL) by **Toronto** (Pittsburgh-AHL) with Gerry Brown for Dutch Hiller and Vic Lynn, September 21, 1946.

MAHOVLICH, Frank

HHOF

Left wing. Shoots left. 6', 205 lbs. Born, Timmins, Ont., January 10, 1938.

Season	Club	Regular Season GP	G	A	Pts	PIM	Playoffs GP	G	A	Pts	PIM
1956-57	Toronto Maple Leafs	3	1	0	1	2	....	....	....	....	....
1957-58	Toronto Maple Leafs	67	20	16	36	67	....	....	....	....	....
1958-59	Toronto Maple Leafs	63	22	27	49	94	12	6	5	11	18
1959-60	Toronto Maple Leafs	70	18	21	39	61	10	3	1	4	27
1960-61	Toronto Maple Leafs	70	48	36	84	131	5	1	1	2	6
1961-62 ♦	Toronto Maple Leafs	70	33	38	71	87	12	6	6	12	*29
1962-63 ♦	Toronto Maple Leafs	67	36	37	73	56	9	0	2	2	8
1963-64 ♦	Toronto Maple Leafs	70	26	29	55	66	14	4	*11	15	20
1964-65	Toronto Maple Leafs	59	23	28	51	76	6	0	3	3	9
1965-66	Toronto Maple Leafs	68	32	24	56	68	4	1	0	1	10
1966-67 ♦	Toronto Maple Leafs	63	18	28	46	44	12	3	7	10	8
1967-68	Toronto Maple Leafs	50	19	17	36	30	....	....	....	....	....
	Detroit Red Wings	13	7	9	16	2	....	....	....	....	....
1968-69	Detroit Red Wings	76	49	29	78	38	....	....	....	....	....
1969-70	Detroit Red Wings	74	38	32	70	59	4	0	0	0	2
1970-71	Detroit Red Wings	35	14	18	32	30	....	....	....	....	....
	♦ Montreal Canadiens	38	17	24	41	11	20	*14	13	*27	18
1971-72	Montreal Canadiens	76	43	53	96	36	6	3	2	5	2
1972-73 ♦	Montreal Canadiens	78	38	55	93	51	17	9	14	23	6
1973-74	Montreal Canadiens	71	31	49	80	47	6	1	2	3	0
	NHL Totals	**1181**	**533**	**570**	**1103**	**1056**	**137**	**51**	**67**	**118**	**163**

• Brother of Peter • Calder Memorial Trophy (1958) • NHL First All-Star Team (1961, 1963, 1973) • NHL Second All-Star Team (1962, 1964, 1965, 1966, 1969, 1970)

Played in NHL All-Star Game (1959, 1960, 1961, 1962, 1963, 1964, 1965, 1967, 1968, 1969, 1970, 1971, 1972, 1973, 1974)

Traded to **Detroit** by **Toronto** with Pete Stemkowski, Garry Unger and the rights to Carl Brewer for Norm Ullman, Paul Henderson, Floyd Smith and Doug Barrie, March 3, 1968. Traded to **Montreal** by **Detroit** for Guy Charron, Bill Collins and Mickey Redmond, January 13, 1971.

MAHOVLICH, Pete

Center. Shoots left. 6'5", 210 lbs. Born, Timmins, Ont., October 10, 1946.
(Detroit's 1st choice, 2nd overall, in 1963 Amateur Draft).

Season	Club	Regular Season GP	G	A	Pts	PIM	Playoffs GP	G	A	Pts	PIM
1965-66	Detroit Red Wings	3	0	1	1	0	....	....	....	....	....
1966-67	Detroit Red Wings	34	1	3	4	16	....	....	....	....	....
1967-68	Detroit Red Wings	15	6	4	10	13	....	....	....	....	....
1968-69	Detroit Red Wings	30	2	2	4	21	....	....	....	....	....
1969-70	Montreal Canadiens	36	9	8	17	51	....	....	....	....	....
1970-71 ♦	Montreal Canadiens	78	35	26	61	181	20	10	6	16	43
1971-72	Montreal Canadiens	75	35	32	67	103	6	0	2	2	12
1972-73 ♦	Montreal Canadiens	61	21	38	59	49	17	4	9	13	22
1973-74	Montreal Canadiens	78	36	37	73	122	6	2	1	3	4
1974-75	Montreal Canadiens	80	35	82	117	64	11	6	10	16	10
1975-76 ♦	Montreal Canadiens	80	34	71	105	76	13	4	8	12	24
1976-77 ♦	Montreal Canadiens	76	15	47	62	45	13	4	5	9	19
1977-78	Montreal Canadiens	17	3	5	8	4	....	....	....	....	....
	Pittsburgh Penguins	57	25	36	61	37	....	....	....	....	....
1978-79	Pittsburgh Penguins	60	14	39	53	39	2	0	1	1	0
1979-80	Detroit Red Wings	80	16	50	66	69	....	....	....	....	....
1980-81	Detroit Red Wings	24	1	4	5	26	....	....	....	....	....
	NHL Totals	**884**	**288**	**485**	**773**	**916**	**88**	**30**	**42**	**72**	**134**

• Brother of Frank

Played in NHL All-Star Game (1971, 1976)

Traded to **Montreal** by **Detroit** with Bart Crashley for Garry Monahan and Doug Piper, June 6, 1969. Traded to **Pittsburgh** by **Montreal** with Peter Lee for Pierre Larouche and future considerations (rights to Peter Marsh, December 15, 1977), November 29, 1977. Traded to **Detroit** by **Pittsburgh** for Nick Libett, August 3, 1979.

MAILHOT, Jacques

Left wing. Shoots left. 6'2", 208 lbs. Born, Shawinigan, Que., December 5, 1961.

Season	Club	Regular Season GP	G	A	Pts	PIM	Playoffs GP	G	A	Pts	PIM
1988-89	Quebec Nordiques	5	0	0	0	33	....	....	....	....	....
	NHL Totals	**5**	**0**	**0**	**0**	**33**	....	....	....	....	....

Signed as a free agent by **Quebec**, August 15, 1988.

MAILLEY, Frank

Defense. Shoots left. 5'9", 182 lbs. Born, Lachine, Que., August 1, 1916.

Season	Club	Regular Season GP	G	A	Pts	PIM	Playoffs GP	G	A	Pts	PIM
1942-43	Montreal Canadiens	1	0	0	0	0	....	....	....	....	....
	NHL Totals	**1**	**0**	**0**	**0**	**0**	....	....	....	....	....

MAIR, Adam

Center. Shoots right. 6'2", 215 lbs. Born, Hamilton, Ont., February 15, 1979.
(Toronto's 2nd choice, 84th overall, in 1997 Entry Draft).

Season	Club	Regular Season GP	G	A	Pts	PIM	Playoffs GP	G	A	Pts	PIM
1998-99	Toronto Maple Leafs	....	....	....	....	....	5	1	0	1	14
99-2000	Toronto Maple Leafs	8	1	0	1	6	5	0	0	0	8
2000-01	Toronto Maple Leafs	16	0	2	2	14	....	....	....	....	....
	Los Angeles Kings	10	0	0	0	6	....	....	....	....	....
2001-02	Los Angeles Kings	18	1	1	2	57	....	....	....	....	....
2002-03	Buffalo Sabres	79	6	11	17	146	....	....	....	....	....
	NHL Totals	**131**	**8**	**14**	**22**	**229**	**10**	**1**	**0**	**1**	**22**

Traded to **Los Angeles** by **Toronto** with Toronto's 2nd round choice (Mike Cammalleri) in 2001 Entry Draft for Aki Berg, March 13, 2001. Traded to **Buffalo** by **Los Angeles** with Los Angeles' 5th round choice (Thomas Morrow) in 2003 Entry Draft for Erik Rasmussen, July 24, 2002.

MAIR, Jim

Defense. Shoots right. 5'9", 170 lbs. Born, Schumacher, Ont., May 15, 1946.

Season	Club	Regular Season GP	G	A	Pts	PIM	Playoffs GP	G	A	Pts	PIM
1970-71	Philadelphia Flyers	2	0	0	0	0	3	1	2	3	4
1971-72	Philadelphia Flyers	2	0	0	0	0	....	....	....	....	....
1972-73	New York Islanders	49	2	11	13	41	....	....	....	....	....
	Vancouver Canucks	15	1	0	1	8	....	....	....	....	....
1973-74	Vancouver Canucks	6	1	3	4	0	....	....	....	....	....
1974-75	Vancouver Canucks	2	0	1	1	0	....	....	....	....	....
	NHL Totals	**76**	**4**	**15**	**19**	**49**	**3**	**1**	**2**	**3**	**4**

Signed as a free agent by **Philadelphia**, September 29, 1969. Claimed by **NY Islanders** from **Philadelphia** in Expansion Draft, June 6, 1972. Claimed by **Vancouver** from **NY Islanders** in Waiver Draft, February 19, 1973.

MAJEAU, Fern

Center/Left wing. Shoots left. 5'9", 155 lbs. Born, Verdun, Que., May 3, 1916.

Season	Club	Regular Season GP	G	A	Pts	PIM	Playoffs GP	G	A	Pts	PIM
1943-44 ♦	Montreal Canadiens	44	20	18	38	39	1	0	0	0	0
1944-45	Montreal Canadiens	12	2	6	8	4	....	....	....	....	....
	NHL Totals	**56**	**22**	**24**	**46**	**43**	**1**	**0**	**0**	**0**	**0**

Signed as a free agent by **Montreal**, October 28, 1943.

MAJESKY, Ivan

Defense. Shoots right. 6'5", 224 lbs. Born, Banska Bystrica, Czech., September 2, 1976.
(Florida's 12th choice, 267th overall, in 2001 Entry Draft).

Season	Club	Regular Season GP	G	A	Pts	PIM	Playoffs GP	G	A	Pts	PIM
2002-03	Florida Panthers	82	4	8	12	92	....	....	....	....	....
	NHL Totals	**82**	**4**	**8**	**12**	**92**	....	....	....	....	....

Traded to **Atlanta** by **Florida** for Atlanta's 2nd round choice (Kamil Kreps) in 2003 Entry Draft, June 21, 2003.

MAJOR, Bruce

Center. Shoots left. 6'3", 180 lbs. Born, Vernon, B.C., January 3, 1967.
(Quebec's 6th choice, 99th overall, in 1985 Entry Draft).

		REGULAR SEASON					PLAYOFFS				
Season	Club	GP	G	A	Pts	PIM	GP	G	A	Pts	PIM
1990-91	Quebec Nordiques	4	0	0	0	0	....	....	....	....	....
	NHL Totals	**4**	**0**	**0**	**0**	**0**	....	....	....	....	....

MAJOR, Mark

Left wing. Shoots left. 6'3", 223 lbs. Born, Toronto, Ont., March 20, 1970.
(Pittsburgh's 2nd choice, 25th overall, in 1988 Entry Draft).

		REGULAR SEASON					PLAYOFFS				
Season	Club	GP	G	A	Pts	PIM	GP	G	A	Pts	PIM
1996-97	Detroit Red Wings	2	0	0	0	5	....	....	....	....	....
	NHL Totals	**2**	**0**	**0**	**0**	**5**	....	....	....	....	....

Signed as a free agent by **Boston**, July 22, 1993. Signed as a free agent by **Detroit**, June 26, 1995. Signed as a free agent by **Washington**, August 20, 1997.

MAKAROV, Sergei

Right wing. Shoots left. 5'11", 185 lbs. Born, Chelyabinsk, USSR, June 19, 1958.
(Calgary's 14th choice, 241st overall, in 1983 Entry Draft).

		REGULAR SEASON					PLAYOFFS				
Season	Club	GP	G	A	Pts	PIM	GP	G	A	Pts	PIM
1989-90	Calgary Flames	80	24	62	86	55	6	0	6	6	0
1990-91	Calgary Flames	78	30	49	79	44	3	1	0	1	0
1991-92	Calgary Flames	68	22	48	70	60	....	....	....	....	....
1992-93	Calgary Flames	71	18	39	57	40	....	....	....	....	....
1993-94	San Jose Sharks	80	30	38	68	78	14	8	2	10	4
1994-95	San Jose Sharks	43	10	14	24	40	11	3	3	6	4
1996-97	Dallas Stars	4	0	0	0	0	....	....	....	....	....
	NHL Totals	**424**	**134**	**250**	**384**	**317**	**34**	**12**	**11**	**23**	**8**

NHL All-Rookie Team (1990) • Calder Memorial Trophy (1990)

Traded to **Hartford** by **Calgary** for future considerations (Washington's 4th round choice – previously acquired, Calgary selected Jason Smith – in 1993 Entry Draft, June 26, 1993), June 20, 1993. Traded to **San Jose** by **Hartford** with Hartford's 1st (Viktor Kozlov) and 3rd (Ville Peltonen) round choices in 1993 Entry Draft and Toronto's 2nd round choice (previously acquired, San Jose selected Vlastimil Kroupa) in 1993 Entry Draft for San Jose's 1st round choice (Chris Pronger) in 1993 Entry Draft, June 26, 1993. Signed as a free agent by **Dallas**, November 1, 1996.

MAKELA, Mikko

Left wing. Shoots left. 6'1", 194 lbs. Born, Tampere, Finland, February 28, 1965.
(NY Islanders' 5th choice, 66th overall, in 1983 Entry Draft).

		REGULAR SEASON					PLAYOFFS				
Season	Club	GP	G	A	Pts	PIM	GP	G	A	Pts	PIM
1985-86	New York Islanders	58	16	20	36	28	....	....	....	....	....
1986-87	New York Islanders	80	24	33	57	24	11	2	4	6	8
1987-88	New York Islanders	73	36	40	76	22	6	1	4	5	6
1988-89	New York Islanders	76	17	28	45	22	....	....	....	....	....
1989-90	New York Islanders	20	2	3	5	2	....	....	....	....	....
	Los Angeles Kings	45	7	14	21	16	1	0	0	0	0
1990-91	Buffalo Sabres	60	15	7	22	25	....	....	....	....	....
1994-95	Boston Bruins	11	1	2	3	0	....	....	....	....	....
	NHL Totals	**423**	**118**	**147**	**265**	**139**	**18**	**3**	**8**	**11**	**14**

Traded to **Los Angeles** by **NY Islanders** for Ken Baumgartner and Hubie McDonough, November 29, 1989. Traded to **Buffalo** by **Los Angeles** for Mike Donnelly, September 30, 1990. Signed as a free agent by **Boston**, July 18, 1994.

MAKI, Chico

Right wing. Shoots right. 5'10", 170 lbs. Born, Sault Ste. Marie, Ont., August 17, 1939.

		REGULAR SEASON					PLAYOFFS				
Season	Club	GP	G	A	Pts	PIM	GP	G	A	Pts	PIM
1960-61 ♦	Chicago Black Hawks	....	....	....	....	....	1	0	0	0	0
1961-62	Chicago Black Hawks	16	4	6	10	2	....	....	....	....	....
1962-63	Chicago Black Hawks	65	7	17	24	35	6	0	1	1	2
1963-64	Chicago Black Hawks	68	8	14	22	70	7	0	0	0	15
1964-65	Chicago Black Hawks	65	16	24	40	58	14	3	9	12	8
1965-66	Chicago Black Hawks	68	17	31	48	41	3	1	1	2	0
1966-67	Chicago Black Hawks	56	9	29	38	14	6	0	0	0	0
1967-68	Chicago Black Hawks	60	8	16	24	4	11	2	5	7	4
1968-69	Chicago Black Hawks	66	7	21	28	30	....	....	....	....	....
1969-70	Chicago Black Hawks	75	10	24	34	27	8	2	2	4	2
1970-71	Chicago Black Hawks	72	22	26	48	18	18	6	5	11	6
1971-72	Chicago Black Hawks	62	13	34	47	22	8	1	4	5	4
1972-73	Chicago Black Hawks	77	13	19	32	10	16	2	8	10	0
1973-74	Chicago Black Hawks	69	9	25	34	12	11	0	1	1	2
1975-76	Chicago Black Hawks	22	0	6	6	2	4	0	0	0	0
	NHL Totals	**841**	**143**	**292**	**435**	**345**	**113**	**17**	**36**	**53**	**43**

• Brother of Wayne

Played in NHL All-Star Game (1961, 1971, 1972)

MAKI, Wayne

Left wing. Shoots left. 6', 185 lbs. Born, Sault Ste. Marie, Ont., November 10, 1944.

		REGULAR SEASON					PLAYOFFS				
Season	Club	GP	G	A	Pts	PIM	GP	G	A	Pts	PIM
1967-68	Chicago Black Hawks	49	5	5	10	32	2	1	0	1	2
1968-69	Chicago Black Hawks	1	0	0	0	0	....	....	....	....	....
1969-70	St. Louis Blues	16	2	1	3	4	....	....	....	....	....
1970-71	Vancouver Canucks	78	25	38	63	99	....	....	....	....	....
1971-72	Vancouver Canucks	76	22	25	47	43	....	....	....	....	....
1972-73	Vancouver Canucks	26	3	10	13	6	....	....	....	....	....
	NHL Totals	**246**	**57**	**79**	**136**	**184**	**2**	**1**	**0**	**1**	**2**

• Brother of Chico

Claimed by **St. Louis** from **Chicago** in Intra-League Draft, June 11, 1969. Claimed by **Vancouver** from **St. Louis** in Expansion Draft, June 10, 1970. • Missed remainder of 1972-73 season after being diagnosed with brain cancer, December 14, 1972.

MAKKONEN, Kari

Right wing. Shoots right. 6', 190 lbs. Born, Pori, Finland, January 20, 1955.
(NY Islanders' 12th choice, 194th overall, in 1975 Amateur Draft).

		REGULAR SEASON					PLAYOFFS				
Season	Club	GP	G	A	Pts	PIM	GP	G	A	Pts	PIM
1979-80	Edmonton Oilers	9	2	2	4	0	....	....	....	....	....
	NHL Totals	**9**	**2**	**2**	**4**	**0**	....	....	....	....	....

Signed as a free agent by **Edmonton**, July 22, 1979.

MALAKHOV, Vladimir

Defense. Shoots left. 6'4", 230 lbs. Born, Sverdlovsk, USSR, August 30, 1968.
(NY Islanders' 12th choice, 191st overall, in 1989 Entry Draft).

		REGULAR SEASON					PLAYOFFS				
Season	Club	GP	G	A	Pts	PIM	GP	G	A	Pts	PIM
1992-93	New York Islanders	64	14	38	52	59	17	3	6	9	12
1993-94	New York Islanders	76	10	47	57	80	4	0	0	0	6
1994-95	New York Islanders	26	3	13	16	32	....	....	....	....	....
	Montreal Canadiens	14	1	4	5	14	....	....	....	....	....
1995-96	Montreal Canadiens	61	5	23	28	79	....	....	....	....	....
1996-97	Montreal Canadiens	65	10	20	30	43	5	0	0	0	6
1997-98	Montreal Canadiens	74	13	31	44	70	9	3	4	7	10
1998-99	Montreal Canadiens	62	13	21	34	77	....	....	....	....	....
99-2000	Montreal Canadiens	7	0	0	0	4	....	....	....	....	....
	♦ New Jersey Devils	17	1	4	5	19	23	1	4	5	18
2000-01	New York Rangers	3	0	2	2	4	....	....	....	....	....
2001-02	New York Rangers	81	6	22	28	83	....	....	....	....	....
2002-03	New York Rangers	71	3	14	17	52	....	....	....	....	....
	NHL Totals	**621**	**79**	**239**	**318**	**616**	**58**	**7**	**14**	**21**	**52**

NHL All-Rookie Team (1993)

Traded to **Montreal** by **NY Islanders** with Pierre Turgeon for Kirk Muller, Mathieu Schneider and Craig Darby, April 5, 1995. • Missed majority of 1999-2000 season recovering from knee injury suffered in exhibition game vs. Boston, September 27, 1999. Traded to **New Jersey** by **Montreal** for Sheldon Souray, Josh DeWolf and New Jersey's 2nd round choice (later traded to Washington – later traded to Tampa Bay – Tampa Bay selected Andreas Holmqvist) in 2001 Entry Draft, March 1, 2000. Signed as a free agent by **NY Rangers**, July 10, 2000. • Missed majority of 2000-01 season recovering from knee injury suffered in game vs. Montreal, November 11, 2000.

MALEC, Tomas

Defense. Shoots left. 6'2", 193 lbs. Born, Skalica, Czech., May 13, 1982.
(Florida's 4th choice, 64th overall, in 2001 Entry Draft).

		REGULAR SEASON					PLAYOFFS				
Season	Club	GP	G	A	Pts	PIM	GP	G	A	Pts	PIM
2002-03	Carolina Hurricanes	41	0	2	2	43	....	....	....	....	....
	NHL Totals	**41**	**0**	**2**	**2**	**43**	....	....	....	....	....

Traded to **Carolina** by **Florida** with Bret Hedican, Kevyn Adams and a conditional 2nd round choice in 2002 Entry Draft for Sandis Ozolinsh and Byron Ritchie, January 16, 2002.

MALEY, David

Left wing. Shoots left. 6'2", 195 lbs. Born, Beaver Dam, WI, April 24, 1963.
(Montreal's 4th choice, 33rd overall, in 1982 Entry Draft).

		REGULAR SEASON					PLAYOFFS				
Season	Club	GP	G	A	Pts	PIM	GP	G	A	Pts	PIM
1985-86 ♦	Montreal Canadiens	3	0	0	0	0	7	1	3	4	2
1986-87	Montreal Canadiens	48	6	12	18	55	....	....	....	....	....
1987-88	New Jersey Devils	44	4	2	6	65	20	3	1	4	80
1988-89	New Jersey Devils	68	5	6	11	249	....	....	....	....	....
1989-90	New Jersey Devils	67	8	17	25	160	6	0	0	0	25
1990-91	New Jersey Devils	64	8	14	22	151	....	....	....	....	....
1991-92	New Jersey Devils	37	7	11	18	58	....	....	....	....	....
	Edmonton Oilers	23	3	6	9	46	10	1	1	2	4
1992-93	Edmonton Oilers	13	1	1	2	29	....	....	....	....	....
	San Jose Sharks	43	1	6	7	126	....	....	....	....	....
1993-94	San Jose Sharks	19	0	0	0	30	....	....	....	....	....
	New York Islanders	37	0	6	6	74	3	0	0	0	0
	NHL Totals	**466**	**43**	**81**	**124**	**1043**	**46**	**5**	**5**	**10**	**111**

Traded to **New Jersey** by **Montreal** for New Jersey's 3rd round choice (Mathieu Schneider) in 1987 Entry Draft, June 13, 1987. Traded to **Edmonton** by **New Jersey** for Troy Mallette, January 12, 1992. Claimed on waivers by **San Jose** from **Edmonton**, January 1, 1993. Traded to **NY Islanders** by **San Jose** for cash, January 23, 1994. Signed as a free agent by **New Jersey**, October 1, 1999.

MALGUNAS, Stewart

Defense. Shoots left. 6', 200 lbs. Born, Prince George, B.C., April 21, 1970.
(Detroit's 3rd choice, 66th overall, in 1990 Entry Draft).

		REGULAR SEASON					PLAYOFFS				
Season	Club	GP	G	A	Pts	PIM	GP	G	A	Pts	PIM
1993-94	Philadelphia Flyers	67	1	3	4	86	....	....	....	....	....
1994-95	Philadelphia Flyers	4	0	0	0	4	....	....	....	....	....
1995-96	Winnipeg Jets	29	0	1	1	32	....	....	....	....	....
	Washington Capitals	1	0	0	0	0	....	....	....	....	....
1996-97	Washington Capitals	6	0	0	0	2	....	....	....	....	....
1997-98	Washington Capitals	8	0	0	0	12	....	....	....	....	....
1998-99	Washington Capitals	10	0	0	0	6	....	....	....	....	....
99-2000	Calgary Flames	4	0	1	1	2	....	....	....	....	....
	NHL Totals	**129**	**1**	**5**	**6**	**144**	....	....	....	....	....

Traded to **Philadelphia** by **Detroit** for Philadelphia's 5th round choice (David Arsenault) in 1995 Entry Draft, September 9, 1993. Signed as a free agent by **Winnipeg**, August 9, 1995. Traded to **Washington** by **Winnipeg** for Denis Chasse, February 15, 1996. Traded to **Nashville** by **Washington** for future considerations, February 2, 2000. Claimed on waivers by **Calgary** from **Nashville**, February 3, 2000. Signed as a free agent by **Colorado**, August 29, 2000.

MALHOTRA, Manny

Center. Shoots left. 6'2", 215 lbs. Born, Mississauga, Ont., May 18, 1980.
(NY Rangers' 1st choice, 7th overall, in 1998 Entry Draft).

		REGULAR SEASON					PLAYOFFS				
Season	Club	GP	G	A	Pts	PIM	GP	G	A	Pts	PIM
1998-99	New York Rangers	73	8	8	16	13	....	....	....	....	....
99-2000	New York Rangers	27	0	0	0	4	....	....	....	....	....

Season	Club	GP	G	A	Pts	PIM	GP	G	A	Pts	PIM
		REGULAR SEASON					PLAYOFFS				
2000-01	New York Rangers	50	4	8	12	31	....	....	....	....	....
2001-02	New York Rangers	56	7	6	13	42	....	....	....	....	....
	Dallas Stars	16	1	0	1	5	....	....	....	....	....
2002-03	Dallas Stars	59	3	7	10	42	5	1	0	1	0
	NHL Totals	**281**	**23**	**29**	**52**	**137**	**5**	**1**	**0**	**1**	**0**

Traded to **Dallas** by **NY Rangers** with Barrett Heisten for Martin Rucinsky and Roman Lyashenko, March 12, 2002.

MALIK, Marek

Defense. Shoots left. 6'5", 215 lbs. Born, Ostrava, Czech., June 24, 1975.
(Hartford's 2nd choice, 72nd overall, in 1993 Entry Draft).

Season	Club	GP	G	A	Pts	PIM	GP	G	A	Pts	PIM
1994-95	Hartford Whalers	1	0	1	1	0	....	....	....	....	....
1995-96	Hartford Whalers	7	0	0	0	4	....	....	....	....	....
1996-97	Hartford Whalers	47	1	5	6	50	....	....	....	....	....
1998-99	Carolina Hurricanes	52	2	9	11	36	4	0	0	0	4
99-2000	Carolina Hurricanes	57	4	10	14	63	....	....	....	....	....
2000-01	Carolina Hurricanes	61	6	14	20	34	3	0	0	0	6
2001-02	Carolina Hurricanes	82	4	19	23	88	23	0	3	3	18
2002-03	Carolina Hurricanes	10	0	2	2	16	....	....	....	....	....
	Vancouver Canucks	69	7	11	18	52	14	1	1	2	10
	NHL Totals	**386**	**24**	**71**	**95**	**343**	**44**	**1**	**4**	**5**	**38**

Transferred to **Carolina** after **Hartford** franchise relocated, June 25, 1997. Traded to **Vancouver** by **Carolina** with Darren Langdon for Jan Hlavac and Harold Druken, November 1, 2002.

MALINOWSKI, Merlin

Center. Shoots left. 6', 190 lbs. Born, North Battleford, Sask., September 27, 1958.
(Colorado's 2nd choice, 27th overall, in 1978 Amateur Draft).

Season	Club	GP	G	A	Pts	PIM	GP	G	A	Pts	PIM
1978-79	Colorado Rockies	54	6	17	23	10	....	....	....	....	....
1979-80	Colorado Rockies	10	2	4	6	2	....	....	....	....	....
1980-81	Colorado Rockies	69	25	37	62	61	....	....	....	....	....
1981-82	Colorado Rockies	69	13	28	41	32	....	....	....	....	....
1982-83	New Jersey Devils	5	3	2	5	0	....	....	....	....	....
	Hartford Whalers	75	5	23	28	16	....	....	....	....	....
	NHL Totals	**282**	**54**	**111**	**165**	**121**	....	....	....	....	....

Transferred to **New Jersey** after **Colorado** franchise relocated, June 30, 1982. Traded to **Hartford** by **New Jersey** with the rights to Scott Fusco for Garry Howatt and Rick Meagher, October 15, 1982.

MALKOC, Dean

Defense. Shoots left. 6'3", 215 lbs. Born, Vancouver, B.C., January 26, 1970.
(New Jersey's 7th choice, 95th overall, in 1990 Entry Draft).

Season	Club	GP	G	A	Pts	PIM	GP	G	A	Pts	PIM
1995-96	Vancouver Canucks	41	0	2	2	136	....	....	....	....	....
1996-97	Boston Bruins	33	0	0	0	70	....	....	....	....	....
1997-98	Boston Bruins	40	1	0	1	86	....	....	....	....	....
1998-99	New York Islanders	2	0	1	1	7	....	....	....	....	....
	NHL Totals	**116**	**1**	**3**	**4**	**299**	....	....	....	....	....

Traded to **Chicago** by **New Jersey** for Rob Conn, January 30, 1995. Signed as a free agent by **Vancouver**, September 8, 1995. Claimed by **Boston** from **Vancouver** in NHL Waiver Draft, September 30, 1996. Signed as a free agent by **NY Islanders**, August 19, 1998. Traded to **Anaheim** by **NY Islanders** with Tony Hrkac for Ted Drury, October 29, 1999.

MALLETTE, Troy

Left wing. Shoots left. 6'2", 210 lbs. Born, Sudbury, Ont., February 25, 1970.
(NY Rangers' 1st choice, 22nd overall, in 1988 Entry Draft).

Season	Club	GP	G	A	Pts	PIM	GP	G	A	Pts	PIM
1989-90	New York Rangers	79	13	16	29	305	10	2	2	4	81
1990-91	New York Rangers	71	12	10	22	252	5	0	0	0	18
1991-92	Edmonton Oilers	15	1	3	4	36	....	....	....	....	....
	New Jersey Devils	17	3	4	7	43	....	....	....	....	....
1992-93	New Jersey Devils	34	4	3	7	56	....	....	....	....	....
1993-94	Ottawa Senators	82	7	16	23	166	....	....	....	....	....
1994-95	Ottawa Senators	23	3	5	8	35	....	....	....	....	....
1995-96	Ottawa Senators	64	2	3	5	171	....	....	....	....	....
1996-97	Boston Bruins	68	6	8	14	155	....	....	....	....	....
1997-98	Tampa Bay Lightning	3	0	0	0	7	....	....	....	....	....
	NHL Totals	**456**	**51**	**68**	**119**	**1226**	**15**	**2**	**2**	**4**	**99**

Transferred to **Edmonton** by **NY Rangers** as compensation for NY Rangers' signing of free agent Adam Graves, September 12, 1991. Traded to **New Jersey** by **Edmonton** for David Maley, January 12, 1992. Traded to **Ottawa** by **New Jersey** with Craig Billington and New Jersey's 4th round choice (Cosmo Dupaul) in 1993 Entry Draft for Peter Sidorkiewicz and future considerations (Mike Peluso, June 26, 1993), June 20, 1993. Signed as a free agent by **Boston**, July 24, 1996. Signed as a free agent by **Tampa Bay**, October 2, 1997. • Suffered eventual career-ending back injury in game vs. Chicago, October 25, 1997.

MALONE, Cliff

Right wing. Shoots right. 5'10", 155 lbs. Born, Quebec City, Que., September 4, 1925.

Season	Club	GP	G	A	Pts	PIM	GP	G	A	Pts	PIM
1951-52	Montreal Canadiens	3	0	0	0	0	....	....	....	....	....
	NHL Totals	**3**	**0**	**0**	**0**	**0**	....	....	....	....	....

MALONE, Greg

Center. Shoots left. 6', 190 lbs. Born, Fredericton, N.B., March 8, 1956.
(Pittsburgh's 2nd choice, 19th overall, in 1976 Amateur Draft).

Season	Club	GP	G	A	Pts	PIM	GP	G	A	Pts	PIM
1976-77	Pittsburgh Penguins	66	18	19	37	43	3	1	1	2	2
1977-78	Pittsburgh Penguins	78	18	43	61	80	....	....	....	....	....
1978-79	Pittsburgh Penguins	80	35	30	65	52	7	0	1	1	10
1979-80	Pittsburgh Penguins	51	19	32	51	46	....	....	....	....	....
1980-81	Pittsburgh Penguins	62	21	29	50	68	5	2	3	5	16
1981-82	Pittsburgh Penguins	78	15	24	39	125	3	0	0	0	4
1982-83	Pittsburgh Penguins	80	17	44	61	82	....	....	....	....	....
1983-84	Hartford Whalers	78	17	37	54	56	....	....	....	....	....
1984-85	Hartford Whalers	76	22	39	61	67	....	....	....	....	....
1985-86	Hartford Whalers	22	6	7	13	24	....	....	....	....	....
	Quebec Nordiques	27	3	5	8	18	1	0	0	0	0
1986-87	Quebec Nordiques	6	0	1	1	0	1	0	0	0	0
	NHL Totals	**704**	**191**	**310**	**501**	**661**	**20**	**3**	**5**	**8**	**32**

Traded to **Hartford** by **Pittsburgh** for Hartford's 5th round choice (Bruce Racine) in 1985 Entry Draft, September 30, 1983. Traded to **Quebec** by **Hartford** for Wayne Babych, January 17, 1986.

MALONE, Joe

HHOF

Center/Left wing. Shoots left. 5'10", 150 lbs. Born, Quebec City, Que., February 28, 1890.

Season	Club	GP	G	A	Pts	PIM	GP	G	A	Pts	PIM
1917-18	Montreal Canadiens	20	*44	4	*48	30	2	1	0	1	3
1918-19	Montreal Canadiens	8	7	2	9	3	5	5	0	5	0
1919-20	Quebec Bulldogs	24	*39	10	*49	12	....	....	....	....	....
1920-21	Hamilton Tigers	20	28	9	37	6	....	....	....	....	....
1921-22	Hamilton Tigers	24	24	7	31	4	....	....	....	....	....
1922-23	Montreal Canadiens	20	1	0	1	2	2	0	0	0	0
1923-24 ♦	Montreal Canadiens	10	0	0	0	0	....	....	....	....	....
	NHL Totals	**126**	**143**	**32**	**175**	**57**	**9**	**6**	**0**	**6**	**3**

Claimed by **Montreal** from **Quebec** in Dispersal Draft, November 26, 1917. Transferred to **Quebec** by **Montreal** when Quebec franchise returned to NHL, November 25, 1919. Transferred to **Hamilton** after **Quebec** franchise relocated, November 2, 1920. • Suspended by **Hamilton** for refusing to report to training camp, December 6, 1922. Traded to **Montreal** by **Hamilton** for Edmond Bouchard, December 22, 1922.

MALONEY, Dan

Left wing. Shoots left. 6'2", 195 lbs. Born, Barrie, Ont., September 24, 1950.
(Chicago's 1st choice, 14th overall, in 1970 Amateur Draft).

Season	Club	GP	G	A	Pts	PIM	GP	G	A	Pts	PIM
1970-71	Chicago Black Hawks	74	12	14	26	174	10	0	1	1	8
1972-73	Chicago Black Hawks	57	13	17	30	63	....	....	....	....	....
	Los Angeles Kings	14	4	7	11	18	....	....	....	....	....
1973-74	Los Angeles Kings	65	15	17	32	113	5	0	0	0	2
1974-75	Los Angeles Kings	80	27	39	66	165	3	0	0	0	2
1975-76	Detroit Red Wings	77	27	39	66	203	....	....	....	....	....
1976-77	Detroit Red Wings	34	13	13	26	64	....	....	....	....	....
1977-78	Detroit Red Wings	66	16	29	45	151	....	....	....	....	....
	Toronto Maple Leafs	13	3	4	7	25	13	1	3	4	17
1978-79	Toronto Maple Leafs	77	17	36	53	157	6	3	3	6	2
1979-80	Toronto Maple Leafs	71	17	16	33	102	....	....	....	....	....
1980-81	Toronto Maple Leafs	65	20	21	41	183	3	0	0	0	4
1981-82	Toronto Maple Leafs	44	8	7	15	71	....	....	....	....	....
	NHL Totals	**737**	**192**	**259**	**451**	**1489**	**40**	**4**	**7**	**11**	**35**

Played in NHL All-Star Game (1976)

Traded to **Los Angeles** by **Chicago** for Ralph Backstrom, February 26, 1973. Traded to **Detroit** by **Los Angeles** with Terry Harper and Los Angeles' 2nd round choice (later traded to Minnesota – Minnesota selected Jim Roberts) in 1976 Amateur Draft for Bart Crashley and the rights to Marcel Dionne, June 23, 1975. Traded to **Toronto** by **Detroit** with Detroit's 2nd round choice (Craig Muni) in 1980 Entry Draft for Errol Thompson and Toronto's 1st (Brent Peterson) and 2nd (Al Jensen) round choices in 1978 Amateur Draft and Toronto's 1st round choice (Mike Blaisdell) in 1980 Entry Draft, March 13, 1978.

MALONEY, Dave

Defense. Shoots left. 6'1", 195 lbs. Born, Kitchener, Ont., July 31, 1956.
(NY Rangers' 1st choice, 14th overall, in 1974 Amateur Draft).

Season	Club	GP	G	A	Pts	PIM	GP	G	A	Pts	PIM
1974-75	New York Rangers	4	0	2	2	0	....	....	....	....	....
1975-76	New York Rangers	21	1	3	4	66	....	....	....	....	....
1976-77	New York Rangers	66	3	18	21	100	....	....	....	....	....
1977-78	New York Rangers	56	2	19	21	63	3	0	0	0	11
1978-79	New York Rangers	76	11	17	28	151	17	3	4	7	45
1979-80	New York Rangers	77	12	25	37	186	8	2	1	3	8
1980-81	New York Rangers	79	11	36	47	132	2	0	2	2	9
1981-82	New York Rangers	64	13	36	49	105	10	1	4	5	6
1982-83	New York Rangers	78	8	42	50	132	7	1	6	7	10
1983-84	New York Rangers	68	7	26	33	168	1	0	0	0	2
1984-85	New York Rangers	16	2	1	3	10	....	....	....	....	....
	Buffalo Sabres	52	1	21	22	41	1	0	0	0	0
	NHL Totals	**657**	**71**	**246**	**317**	**1154**	**49**	**7**	**17**	**24**	**91**

• Brother of Don

Traded to **Buffalo** by **NY Rangers** with Chris Renaud for Steve Patrick and Jim Wiemer, December 6, 1984.

MALONEY, Don

Left wing. Shoots left. 6'1", 190 lbs. Born, Lindsay, Ont., September 5, 1958.
(NY Rangers' 1st choice, 26th overall, in 1978 Amateur Draft).

Season	Club	GP	G	A	Pts	PIM	GP	G	A	Pts	PIM
1978-79	New York Rangers	28	9	17	26	39	18	7	*13	20	19
1979-80	New York Rangers	79	25	48	73	97	9	0	4	4	10
1980-81	New York Rangers	61	29	23	52	99	13	1	6	7	13
1981-82	New York Rangers	54	22	36	58	73	10	5	5	10	10
1982-83	New York Rangers	78	29	40	69	88	5	0	1	1	0
1983-84	New York Rangers	79	24	42	66	62	5	1	4	5	0
1984-85	New York Rangers	37	11	16	27	32	3	4	0	4	2
1985-86	New York Rangers	68	11	17	28	56	16	2	1	3	31
1986-87	New York Rangers	72	19	38	57	117	6	2	1	3	6
1987-88	New York Rangers	66	12	21	33	60	....	....	....	....	....

Season	Club	GP	G	A	Pts	PIM	GP	G	A	Pts	PIM
		REGULAR SEASON					PLAYOFFS				
1988-89	New York Rangers	31	4	9	13	16	....	....	....	....	....
	Hartford Whalers	21	3	11	14	23	4	0	0	0	8
1989-90	New York Islanders	79	16	27	43	47	5	0	0	0	2
1990-91	New York Islanders	12	0	5	5	6	....	....	....	....	....
	NHL Totals	**765**	**214**	**350**	**564**	**815**	**94**	**22**	**35**	**57**	**101**

• Brother of Dave

Played in NHL All-Star Game (1983, 1984)

• Missed majority of 1984-85 season recovering from leg injury suffered in game vs. New Jersey, November 18, 1984. Traded to **Hartford** by **NY Rangers** with Brian Lawton and Norm Maciver for Carey Wilson and Hartford's 5th round choice (Lubos Rob) in 1990 Entry Draft, December 26, 1988. Signed as a free agent by **NY Islanders**, August 25, 1989.

MALONEY, Phil

Center. Shoots left. 5'8", 165 lbs. Born, Ottawa, Ont., October 6, 1927.

Season	Club	GP	G	A	Pts	PIM	GP	G	A	Pts	PIM
1949-50	Boston Bruins	70	15	31	46	6	....	....	....	....	....
1950-51	Boston Bruins	13	2	0	2	2	....	....	....	....	....
	Toronto Maple Leafs	1	1	0	1	0	....	....	....	....	....
1952-53	Toronto Maple Leafs	29	2	6	8	2	....	....	....	....	....
1958-59	Chicago Black Hawks	24	2	2	4	6	6	0	0	0	0
1959-60	Chicago Black Hawks	21	6	4	10	0	....	....	....	....	....
	NHL Totals	**158**	**28**	**43**	**71**	**16**	**6**	**0**	**0**	**0**	**0**

Signed as a free agent by **Boston**, October 5, 1948. Traded to **Toronto** by **Boston** with Fern Flaman, Ken Smith and Leo Boivin for Bill Ezinicki and Vic Lynn, November 16, 1950. Traded to **Vancouver** (WHL) by **Toronto** with Bill Ezinicki and Hugh Barlow for $10,000, December 21, 1954. Claimed by **NY Rangers** from **Vancouver** (WHL) in Inter-League Draft, June 4, 1957. Traded to **Chicago** by **NY Rangers** (Vancouver-WHL) for $7,500, the loan of Ray Cyr and future considerations, December 21, 1958. Traded to **Vancouver** (WHL) by **Chicago** (Buffalo-AHL) for cash, September, 1961.

MALTAIS, Steve

Left wing. Shoots left. 6'2", 205 lbs. Born, Arvida, Que., January 25, 1969.
(Washington's 2nd choice, 57th overall, in 1987 Entry Draft).

Season	Club	GP	G	A	Pts	PIM	GP	G	A	Pts	PIM
1989-90	Washington Capitals	8	0	0	0	2	1	0	0	0	0
1990-91	Washington Capitals	7	0	0	0	2	....	....	....	....	....
1991-92	Minnesota North Stars	12	2	1	3	2	....	....	....	....	....
1992-93	Tampa Bay Lightning	63	7	13	20	35	....	....	....	....	....
1993-94	Detroit Red Wings	4	0	1	1	0	....	....	....	....	....
2000-01	Columbus Blue Jackets	26	0	3	3	12	....	....	....	....	....
	NHL Totals	**120**	**9**	**18**	**27**	**53**	**1**	**0**	**0**	**0**	**0**

Traded to **Minnesota** by **Washington** with Trent Klatt for Shawn Chambers, June 21, 1991. Traded to **Quebec** by **Minnesota** for Kip Miller, March 8, 1992. Claimed by **Tampa Bay** from **Quebec** in Expansion Draft, June 18, 1992. Traded to **Detroit** by **Tampa Bay** for Dennis Vial, June 8, 1993. Signed as a free agent by **Columbus**, October 6, 2000.

MALTBY, Kirk

Right wing. Shoots right. 6', 180 lbs. Born, Guelph, Ont., December 22, 1972.
(Edmonton's 4th choice, 65th overall, in 1992 Entry Draft).

Season	Club	GP	G	A	Pts	PIM	GP	G	A	Pts	PIM
1993-94	Edmonton Oilers	68	11	8	19	74	....	....	....	....	....
1994-95	Edmonton Oilers	47	8	3	11	49	....	....	....	....	....
1995-96	Edmonton Oilers	49	2	6	8	61	....	....	....	....	....
	Detroit Red Wings	6	1	0	1	6	8	0	1	1	4
1996-97 ♦	Detroit Red Wings	66	3	5	8	75	20	5	2	7	24
1997-98 ♦	Detroit Red Wings	65	14	9	23	89	22	3	1	4	30
1998-99	Detroit Red Wings	53	8	6	14	34	10	1	0	1	8
99-2000	Detroit Red Wings	41	6	8	14	24	8	0	1	1	4
2000-01	Detroit Red Wings	79	12	7	19	22	6	0	0	0	6
2001-02 ♦	Detroit Red Wings	82	9	15	24	40	23	3	3	6	32
2002-03	Detroit Red Wings	82	14	23	37	91	4	0	0	0	4
	NHL Totals	**638**	**88**	**90**	**178**	**565**	**101**	**12**	**8**	**20**	**112**

Traded to **Detroit** by **Edmonton** for Dan McGillis, March 20, 1996. • Missed majority of 1999-2000 season recovering from hernia injury suffered in game vs. Dallas, October 5, 1999.

MALUTA, Ray

Defense. Shoots left. 5'8", 173 lbs. Born, Flin Flon, Man., July 24, 1954.
(Boston's 8th choice, 126th overall, in 1974 Amateur Draft).

Season	Club	GP	G	A	Pts	PIM	GP	G	A	Pts	PIM
1975-76	Boston Bruins	2	0	0	0	2	2	0	0	0	0
1976-77	Boston Bruins	23	2	3	5	4	....	....	....	....	....
	NHL Totals	**25**	**2**	**3**	**5**	**6**	**2**	**0**	**0**	**0**	**0**

MANASTERSKY, Tom

Defense. Shoots right. 5'9", 185 lbs. Born, Montreal, Que., March 7, 1929.

Season	Club	GP	G	A	Pts	PIM	GP	G	A	Pts	PIM
1950-51	Montreal Canadiens	6	0	0	0	11	....	....	....	....	....
	NHL Totals	**6**	**0**	**0**	**0**	**11**	....	....	....	....	....

Signed as a free agent by **Montreal**, November 30, 1949.

MANCUSO, Gus

Right wing. Shoots left. 5'7", 160 lbs. Born, Niagara Falls, Ont., April 11, 1914.

Season	Club	GP	G	A	Pts	PIM	GP	G	A	Pts	PIM
1937-38	Montreal Canadiens	17	1	1	2	4	....	....	....	....	....
1938-39	Montreal Canadiens	2	0	0	0	0	....	....	....	....	....
1939-40	Montreal Canadiens	2	0	0	0	0	....	....	....	....	....
1942-43	New York Rangers	21	6	8	14	13	....	....	....	....	....
	NHL Totals	**42**	**7**	**9**	**16**	**17**	....	....	....	....	....

Signed as a free agent by **Montreal**, October 30, 1937. Traded to **NY Rangers** by **Montreal** for cash, November 4, 1942.

MANDERVILLE, Kent

Center. Shoots left. 6'3", 200 lbs. Born, Edmonton, Alta., April 12, 1971.
(Calgary's 1st choice, 24th overall, in 1989 Entry Draft).

Season	Club	GP	G	A	Pts	PIM	GP	G	A	Pts	PIM
		REGULAR SEASON					PLAYOFFS				
1991-92	Toronto Maple Leafs	15	0	4	4	0	....	....	....	....	....
1992-93	Toronto Maple Leafs	18	1	1	2	17	18	1	0	1	8
1993-94	Toronto Maple Leafs	67	7	9	16	63	12	1	0	1	4
1994-95	Toronto Maple Leafs	36	0	1	1	22	7	0	0	0	6
1995-96	Edmonton Oilers	37	3	5	8	38	....	....	....	....	....
1996-97	Hartford Whalers	44	6	5	11	18	....	....	....	....	....
1997-98	Carolina Hurricanes	77	4	4	8	31	....	....	....	....	....
1998-99	Carolina Hurricanes	81	5	11	16	38	6	0	0	0	2
99-2000	Carolina Hurricanes	56	1	4	5	12	....	....	....	....	....
	Philadelphia Flyers	13	0	3	3	4	18	0	1	1	22
2000-01	Philadelphia Flyers	82	5	10	15	47	6	1	2	3	2
2001-02	Philadelphia Flyers	34	2	5	7	8	....	....	....	....	....
	Pittsburgh Penguins	4	1	0	1	4	....	....	....	....	....
2002-03	Pittsburgh Penguins	82	2	5	7	46	....	....	....	....	....
	NHL Totals	**646**	**37**	**67**	**104**	**348**	**67**	**3**	**3**	**6**	**44**

Traded to **Toronto** by **Calgary** with Doug Gilmour, Jamie Macoun, Rick Wamsley and Ric Nattress for Gary Leeman, Alexander Godynyuk, Jeff Reese, Michel Petit and Craig Berube, January 2, 1992. Traded to **Edmonton** by **Toronto** for Peter White and Edmonton's 4th round choice (Jason Sessa) in 1996 Entry Draft, December 4, 1995. Signed as a free agent by **Hartford**, October 2, 1996. Transferred to **Carolina** after **Hartford** franchise relocated, June 25, 1997. Traded to **Philadelphia** by **Carolina** for Sandy McCarthy, March 14, 2000. • Missed majority of 2001-02 season recovering from ankle injury suffered in game vs. Montreal, October 27, 2001. Traded to **Pittsburgh** by **Philadelphia** for Billy Tibbetts, March 17, 2002.

MANDICH, Dan

Defense. Shoots right. 6'3", 205 lbs. Born, Brantford, Ont., June 12, 1960.

Season	Club	GP	G	A	Pts	PIM	GP	G	A	Pts	PIM
1982-83	Minnesota North Stars	67	3	4	7	169	7	0	0	0	2
1983-84	Minnesota North Stars	31	2	7	9	77	....	....	....	....	....
1984-85	Minnesota North Stars	10	0	0	0	32	....	....	....	....	....
1985-86	Minnesota North Stars	3	0	0	0	25	....	....	....	....	....
	NHL Totals	**111**	**5**	**11**	**16**	**303**	**7**	**0**	**0**	**0**	**2**

Signed as a free agent by **Minnesota**, July 19, 1982. • Suffered eventual career-ending knee injury in game vs. Los Angeles, January 16, 1984.

MANELUK, Mike

Left wing. Shoots right. 5'11", 190 lbs. Born, Winnipeg, Man., October 1, 1973.

Season	Club	GP	G	A	Pts	PIM	GP	G	A	Pts	PIM
1998-99	Philadelphia Flyers	13	2	6	8	8	....	....	....	....	....
	Chicago Blackhawks	28	4	3	7	8	....	....	....	....	....
	New York Rangers	4	0	0	0	4	....	....	....	....	....
99-2000	Philadelphia Flyers	1	0	0	0	4	....	....	....	....	....
2000-01	Columbus Blue Jackets	39	5	1	6	33	....	....	....	....	....
	NHL Totals	**85**	**11**	**10**	**21**	**57**	....	....	....	....	....

Signed as a free agent by **Anaheim**, January 28, 1994. Traded to **Ottawa** by **Anaheim** for Kevin Brown, July 1, 1996. Traded to **Philadelphia** by **Ottawa** for future considerations, October 21, 1997. Traded to **Chicago** by **Philadelphia** for Roman Vopat, November 17, 1998. Claimed on waivers by **NY Rangers** from **Chicago**, March 4, 1999. Signed as a free agent by **Philadelphia**, August 2, 1999. Signed as a free agent by **Columbus**, August 24, 2000.

MANERY, Kris

Center/Right wing. Shoots right. 6', 185 lbs. Born, Leamington, Ont., September 24, 1954.

Season	Club	GP	G	A	Pts	PIM	GP	G	A	Pts	PIM
1977-78	Cleveland Barons	78	22	27	49	14	....	....	....	....	....
1978-79	Minnesota North Stars	60	17	19	36	16	....	....	....	....	....
1979-80	Minnesota North Stars	28	3	4	7	16	....	....	....	....	....
	Vancouver Canucks	21	2	1	3	15	....	....	....	....	....
	Winnipeg Jets	16	6	4	10	6	....	....	....	....	....
1980-81	Winnipeg Jets	47	13	9	22	24	....	....	....	....	....
	NHL Totals	**250**	**63**	**64**	**127**	**91**	....	....	....	....	....

• Brother of Randy

Signed as a free agent by **Cleveland**, October, 1977. Placed on **Minnesota** Reserve List after **Minnesota-Cleveland** Dispersal Draft, June 15, 1978. Traded to **Vancouver** by **Minnesota** for Vancouver's 2nd round choice (later traded to Montreal – Montreal selected Kent Carlson) in 1982 Entry Draft, January 4, 1980. Claimed on waivers by **Winnipeg** from **Vancouver**, February 27, 1980.

MANERY, Randy

Defense. Shoots right. 6', 185 lbs. Born, Leamington, Ont., January 10, 1949.

Season	Club	GP	G	A	Pts	PIM	GP	G	A	Pts	PIM
1970-71	Detroit Red Wings	2	0	0	0	0	....	....	....	....	....
1971-72	Detroit Red Wings	1	0	0	0	0	....	....	....	....	....
1972-73	Atlanta Flames	78	5	30	35	44	....	....	....	....	....
1973-74	Atlanta Flames	78	8	29	37	75	4	0	2	2	4
1974-75	Atlanta Flames	68	5	27	32	48	....	....	....	....	....
1975-76	Atlanta Flames	80	7	32	39	42	2	0	0	0	0
1976-77	Atlanta Flames	73	5	24	29	33	3	0	0	0	0
1977-78	Los Angeles Kings	79	6	27	33	61	2	0	0	0	2
1978-79	Los Angeles Kings	71	8	27	35	64	2	0	0	0	6
1979-80	Los Angeles Kings	52	6	10	16	48	....	....	....	....	....
	NHL Totals	**582**	**50**	**206**	**256**	**415**	**13**	**0**	**2**	**2**	**12**

• Brother of Kris

Played in NHL All-Star Game (1973)

Claimed by **Atlanta** from **Detroit** in Expansion Draft, June 6, 1972. Traded to **Los Angeles** by **Atlanta** for Ab DeMarco Jr., May 23, 1977.

MANLOW, Eric

Center. Shoots left. 6', 180 lbs. Born, Belleville, Ont., April 7, 1975.
(Chicago's 2nd choice, 50th overall, in 1993 Entry Draft).

Season	Club	Regular Season GP	G	A	Pts	PIM	Playoffs GP	G	A	Pts	PIM
2000-01	Boston Bruins	8	0	1	1	2	....	....	....	....	....
2001-02	Boston Bruins	3	0	0	0	0	....	....	....	....	....
2002-03	New York Islanders	8	2	1	3	4	....	....	....	....	....
	NHL Totals	**19**	**2**	**2**	**4**	**6**	....	....	....	....	....

Signed as a free agent by **Boston**, July 11, 2000. Signed as a free agent by **NY Islanders**, July 21, 2002.

MANN, Cameron

Right wing. Shoots right. 6', 195 lbs. Born, Thompson, Man., April 20, 1977.
(Boston's 5th choice, 99th overall, in 1995 Entry Draft).

Season	Club	Regular Season GP	G	A	Pts	PIM	Playoffs GP	G	A	Pts	PIM
1997-98	Boston Bruins	9	0	1	1	4	....	....	....	....	....
1998-99	Boston Bruins	33	5	2	7	17	1	0	0	0	0
99-2000	Boston Bruins	32	8	4	12	13	....	....	....	....	....
2000-01	Boston Bruins	15	1	3	4	6	....	....	....	....	....
2002-03	Nashville Predators	4	0	0	0	0	....	....	....	....	....
	NHL Totals	**93**	**14**	**10**	**24**	**40**	**1**	**0**	**0**	**0**	**0**

Traded to **Dallas** by **Boston** for Richard Jackman, June 23, 2001. Traded to **Nashville** by **Dallas** with Ed Belfour for David Gosselin and Nashville's 5th round choice (Eero Kilpelainen) in 2003 Entry Draft, June 29, 2002.

MANN, Jack

Center. Shoots left. 5'7", 160 lbs. Born, Winnipeg, Man., July 27, 1919.

Season	Club	Regular Season GP	G	A	Pts	PIM	Playoffs GP	G	A	Pts	PIM
1943-44	New York Rangers	3	0	0	0	0	....	....	....	....	....
1944-45	New York Rangers	6	3	4	7	0	....	....	....	....	....
	NHL Totals	**9**	**3**	**4**	**7**	**0**	....	....	....	....	....

MANN, Jimmy

Right wing. Shoots right. 6', 205 lbs. Born, Montreal, Que., April 17, 1959.
(Winnipeg's 1st choice, 19th overall, in 1979 Entry Draft).

Season	Club	Regular Season GP	G	A	Pts	PIM	Playoffs GP	G	A	Pts	PIM
1979-80	Winnipeg Jets	72	3	5	8	*287	....	....	....	....	....
1980-81	Winnipeg Jets	37	3	3	6	105	....	....	....	....	....
1981-82	Winnipeg Jets	37	3	2	5	79	3	0	0	0	7
1982-83	Winnipeg Jets	40	0	1	1	73	1	0	0	0	0
1983-84	Winnipeg Jets	16	0	1	1	54	....	....	....	....	....
	Quebec Nordiques	22	1	1	2	42	3	0	0	0	22
1984-85	Quebec Nordiques	25	0	4	4	54	13	0	0	0	41
1985-86	Quebec Nordiques	35	0	3	3	148	2	0	0	0	19
1987-88	Pittsburgh Penguins	9	0	0	0	53	....	....	....	....	....
	NHL Totals	**293**	**10**	**20**	**30**	**895**	**22**	**0**	**0**	**0**	**89**

Traded to **Quebec** by **Winnipeg** for Quebec's 5th round choice (Brent Severyn) in 1984 Entry Draft, February 6, 1984. • Missed entire 1986-87 season recovering from abdominal injury originally suffered in December, 1984. Signed as a free agent by **Pittsburgh**, June 16, 1987.

MANN, Ken

Right wing. Shoots right. 5'11", 200 lbs. Born, Hamilton, Ont., September 5, 1953.

Season	Club	Regular Season GP	G	A	Pts	PIM	Playoffs GP	G	A	Pts	PIM
1975-76	Detroit Red Wings	1	0	0	0	0	....	....	....	....	....
	NHL Totals	**1**	**0**	**0**	**0**	**0**	....	....	....	....	....

Signed as a free agent by **Detroit**, October 2, 1974.

MANN, Norm

Right wing/Center. Shoots right. 5'10", 155 lbs. Born, Bradford, England, March 3, 1914.

Season	Club	Regular Season GP	G	A	Pts	PIM	Playoffs GP	G	A	Pts	PIM
1935-36	Toronto Maple Leafs	....	....	....	....	....	1	0	0	0	0
1938-39	Toronto Maple Leafs	16	0	0	0	2	....	....	....	....	....
1940-41	Toronto Maple Leafs	15	0	3	3	2	1	0	0	0	0
	NHL Totals	**31**	**0**	**3**	**3**	**4**	**2**	**0**	**0**	**0**	**0**

Signed as a free agent by **Toronto**, October 7, 1935. Claimed by **NY Rangers** from **Syracuse** (IAHL) in Inter-League Draft, May 9, 1937. Traded to **Toronto** by **NY Rangers** for $4,000, November 15, 1938. Traded to **Pittsburgh** (AHL) by **Toronto** for cash, October 30, 1941.

MANNERS, Rennison

Center. Shoots left. 5'11", 160 lbs. Born, Ottawa, Ont., February 5, 1904.

Season	Club	Regular Season GP	G	A	Pts	PIM	Playoffs GP	G	A	Pts	PIM
1929-30	Pittsburgh Pirates	33	3	2	5	14	....	....	....	....	....
1930-31	Philadelphia Quakers	4	0	0	0	0	....	....	....	....	....
	NHL Totals	**37**	**3**	**2**	**5**	**14**	....	....	....	....	....

Transferred to **Philadelphia** after **Pittsburgh** franchise relocated, September 26, 1930.

MANNING, Paul

Defense. Shoots left. 6'4", 205 lbs. Born, Red Deer, Alta., April 15, 1979.
(Calgary's 3rd choice, 62nd overall, in 1998 Entry Draft).

Season	Club	Regular Season GP	G	A	Pts	PIM	Playoffs GP	G	A	Pts	PIM
2002-03	Columbus Blue Jackets	8	0	0	0	2	....	....	....	....	....
	NHL Totals	**8**	**0**	**0**	**0**	**2**	....	....	....	....	....

Rights traded to **Columbus** by **Calgary** for Buffalo's 5th round choice (previously acquired, later traded to Detroit – Detroit selected Andreas Jamtin) in 2001 Entry Draft, June 24, 2001.

MANNO, Bob

Defense. Shoots left. 6', 185 lbs. Born, Niagara Falls, Ont., October 31, 1956.
(Vancouver's 1st choice, 26th overall, in 1976 Amateur Draft).

Season	Club	Regular Season GP	G	A	Pts	PIM	Playoffs GP	G	A	Pts	PIM
1976-77	Vancouver Canucks	2	0	0	0	0	....	....	....	....	....
1977-78	Vancouver Canucks	49	5	14	19	29	....	....	....	....	....
1978-79	Vancouver Canucks	52	5	16	21	42	3	0	1	1	4
1979-80	Vancouver Canucks	40	3	14	17	14	4	1	0	1	6
1980-81	Vancouver Canucks	20	0	11	11	30	3	0	0	0	2
1981-82	Toronto Maple Leafs	72	9	41	50	67	....	....	....	....	....
1983-84	Detroit Red Wings	62	9	13	22	60	4	0	3	3	0
1984-85	Detroit Red Wings	74	10	22	32	32	3	1	0	1	0
	NHL Totals	**371**	**41**	**131**	**172**	**274**	**17**	**2**	**4**	**6**	**12**

Played in NHL All-Star Game (1982)

Signed as a free agent by **Toronto**, September 30, 1981. Signed as a free agent by **Detroit**, August 2, 1983.

MANSON, Dave

Defense. Shoots left. 6'2", 200 lbs. Born, Prince Albert, Sask., January 27, 1967.
(Chicago's 1st choice, 11th overall, in 1985 Entry Draft).

Season	Club	Regular Season GP	G	A	Pts	PIM	Playoffs GP	G	A	Pts	PIM
1986-87	Chicago Blackhawks	63	1	8	9	146	3	0	0	0	10
1987-88	Chicago Blackhawks	54	1	6	7	185	5	0	0	0	27
1988-89	Chicago Blackhawks	79	18	36	54	352	16	0	8	8	84
1989-90	Chicago Blackhawks	59	5	23	28	301	20	2	4	6	46
1990-91	Chicago Blackhawks	75	14	15	29	191	6	0	1	1	36
1991-92	Edmonton Oilers	79	15	32	47	220	16	3	9	12	44
1992-93	Edmonton Oilers	83	15	30	45	210	....	....	....	....	....
1993-94	Edmonton Oilers	57	3	13	16	140	....	....	....	....	....
	Winnipeg Jets	13	1	4	5	51	....	....	....	....	....
1994-95	Winnipeg Jets	44	3	15	18	139	....	....	....	....	....
1995-96	Winnipeg Jets	82	7	23	30	205	6	2	1	3	30
1996-97	Phoenix Coyotes	66	3	17	20	164	....	....	....	....	....
	Montreal Canadiens	9	1	1	2	23	5	0	0	0	17
1997-98	Montreal Canadiens	81	4	30	34	122	10	0	1	1	14
1998-99	Montreal Canadiens	11	0	2	2	48	....	....	....	....	....
	Chicago Blackhawks	64	6	15	21	107	....	....	....	....	....
99-2000	Chicago Blackhawks	37	0	7	7	40	....	....	....	....	....
	Dallas Stars	26	1	2	3	22	23	0	0	0	33
2000-01	Toronto Maple Leafs	74	4	7	11	93	2	0	0	0	2
2001-02	Toronto Maple Leafs	13	0	1	1	10	....	....	....	....	....
	Dallas Stars	34	0	1	1	23	....	....	....	....	....
	NHL Totals	**1103**	**102**	**288**	**390**	**2792**	**112**	**7**	**24**	**31**	**343**

Played in NHL All-Star Game (1989, 1993)

Traded to **Edmonton** by **Chicago** with Chicago's 3rd round choice (Kirk Maltby) in 1992 Entry Draft for Steve Smith, October 2, 1991. Traded to **Winnipeg** by **Edmonton** with St. Louis' 6th round choice (previously acquired, Winnipeg selected Chris Kibermanis) in 1994 Entry Draft for Boris Mironov, Mats Lindgren, Winnipeg's 1st round choice (Jason Bonsignore) in 1994 Entry Draft and Florida's 4th round choice (previously acquired, Edmonton selected Adam Copeland) in 1994 Entry Draft, March 15, 1994. Transferred to **Phoenix** after **Winnipeg** franchise relocated, July 1, 1996. Traded to **Montreal** by **Phoenix** for Murray Baron and Chris Murray, March 18, 1997. Traded to **Chicago** by **Montreal** with Jocelyn Thibault and Brad Brown for Jeff Hackett, Eric Weinrich, Alain Nasreddine and Tampa Bay's 4th round choice (previously acquired, Montreal selected Chris Dyment) in 1999 Entry Draft, November 16, 1998. Traded to **Dallas** by **Chicago** with Sylvain Cote for Kevin Dean, Derek Plante and Dallas' 2nd round choice (Matt Keith) in 2001 Entry Draft, February 8, 2000. Signed as a free agent by **Toronto**, August 16, 2000. Traded to **Dallas** by **Toronto** for Jyrki Lumme, November 21, 2001.

MANSON, Ray

Left wing. Shoots left. 5'11", 180 lbs. Born, St. Boniface, Man., December 3, 1926.

Season	Club	Regular Season GP	G	A	Pts	PIM	Playoffs GP	G	A	Pts	PIM
1947-48	Boston Bruins	1	0	0	0	0	....	....	....	....	....
1948-49	New York Rangers	1	0	1	1	0	....	....	....	....	....
	NHL Totals	**2**	**0**	**1**	**1**	**0**	....	....	....	....	....

Traded to **NY Rangers** by **Boston** with Pentti Lund to complete transaction that sent Grant Warwick to Boston (February 6, 1948), June, 1948.

MANTHA, Georges

Defense/Left wing. Shoots left. 5'8", 165 lbs. Born, Lachine, Que., November 29, 1908.

Season	Club	Regular Season GP	G	A	Pts	PIM	Playoffs GP	G	A	Pts	PIM
1928-29	Montreal Canadiens	21	0	0	0	8	3	0	0	0	0
1929-30 ♦	Montreal Canadiens	44	5	2	7	16	6	0	0	0	8
1930-31 ♦	Montreal Canadiens	44	11	6	17	25	10	5	1	6	4
1931-32	Montreal Canadiens	48	1	7	8	8	4	0	1	1	8
1932-33	Montreal Canadiens	43	3	6	9	10	....	....	....	....	....
1933-34	Montreal Canadiens	44	6	9	15	12	....	....	....	....	....
1934-35	Montreal Canadiens	42	12	10	22	14	2	0	0	0	4
1935-36	Montreal Canadiens	35	1	12	13	14	....	....	....	....	....
1936-37	Montreal Canadiens	47	13	14	27	17	5	0	0	0	0
1937-38	Montreal Canadiens	47	23	19	42	12	3	1	0	1	0
1938-39	Montreal Canadiens	25	5	5	10	6	3	0	0	0	0
1939-40	Montreal Canadiens	42	9	11	20	6	....	....	....	....	....
1940-41	Montreal Canadiens	6	0	1	1	0	....	....	....	....	....
	NHL Totals	**488**	**89**	**102**	**191**	**148**	**36**	**6**	**2**	**8**	**24**

• Brother of Sylvio

Played in NHL All-Star Game (1937, 1939)

Traded to **Washington** (AHL) by **Montreal** for cash, October 9, 1941.

MANTHA, Moe

Defense. Shoots right. 6'2", 210 lbs. Born, Lakewood, OH, January 21, 1961.
(Winnipeg's 2nd choice, 23rd overall, in 1980 Entry Draft).

Season	Club	Regular Season GP	G	A	Pts	PIM	Playoffs GP	G	A	Pts	PIM
1980-81	Winnipeg Jets	58	2	23	25	35	....	....	....	....	....
1981-82	Winnipeg Jets	25	0	12	12	28	4	1	3	4	16
1982-83	Winnipeg Jets	21	2	7	9	6	2	2	2	4	0
1983-84	Winnipeg Jets	72	16	38	54	67	3	1	0	1	0
1984-85	Pittsburgh Penguins	71	11	40	51	54	....	....	....	....	....
1985-86	Pittsburgh Penguins	78	15	52	67	102	....	....	....	....	....

Season	Club	REGULAR SEASON GP	G	A	Pts	PIM	PLAYOFFS GP	G	A	Pts	PIM
1986-87	Pittsburgh Penguins	62	9	31	40	44	....	....	....	....	....
1987-88	Pittsburgh Penguins	21	2	8	10	23	....	....	....	....	....
	Edmonton Oilers	25	0	6	6	26	....	....	....	....	....
	Minnesota North Stars	30	9	13	22	4	....	....	....	....	....
1988-89	Minnesota North Stars	16	1	6	7	10	....	....	....	....	....
	Philadelphia Flyers	30	3	8	11	33	1	0	0	0	0
1989-90	Winnipeg Jets	73	2	26	28	28	7	1	5	6	2
1990-91	Winnipeg Jets	57	9	15	24	33	....	....	....	....	....
1991-92	Winnipeg Jets	12	0	4	4	6	....	....	....	....	....
	Philadelphia Flyers	5	0	0	0	2	....	....	....	....	....
	NHL Totals	**656**	**81**	**289**	**370**	**501**	**17**	**5**	**10**	**15**	**18**

Traded to **Pittsburgh** by **Winnipeg** to complete transaction that sent Randy Carlyle to Winnipeg (March 5, 1984), May 1, 1984. Traded to **Edmonton** by **Pittsburgh** with Craig Simpson, Dave Hanna and Chris Joseph for Paul Coffey, Dave Hunter and Wayne Van Dorp, November 24, 1987. Traded to **Minnesota** by **Edmonton** for Keith Acton, January 22, 1988. Traded to **Philadelphia** by **Minnesota** for Toronto's 5th round choice (previously acquired, Minnesota selected Pat MacLeod) in 1989 Entry Draft, December 8, 1988. Claimed by **Winnipeg** from **Philadelphia** in Waiver Draft, October 2, 1989. Traded to **Philadelphia** by **Winnipeg** for future considerations, February 27, 1992.

MANTHA, Sylvio

HHOF

Defense. Shoots right. 5'10", 178 lbs. Born, Montreal, Que., April 14, 1902.

Season	Club	GP	G	A	Pts	PIM	GP	G	A	Pts	PIM
1923-24 ♦	Montreal Canadiens	24	1	3	4	11	2	0	0	0	0
	Montreal Canadiens (Cup)	....	....	....	....	....	*4*	*0*	*0*	*0*	*0*
1924-25	Montreal Canadiens	30	2	3	5	18	2	0	1	1	0
	Montreal Canadiens (Cup)	....	....	....	....	....	*4*	*0*	*0*	*0*	*2*
1925-26	Montreal Canadiens	34	2	1	3	66	....	....	....	....	....
1926-27	Montreal Canadiens	43	10	5	15	77	4	1	0	1	0
1927-28	Montreal Canadiens	43	4	11	15	61	2	0	0	0	6
1928-29	Montreal Canadiens	44	9	4	13	56	3	0	0	0	0
1929-30 ♦	Montreal Canadiens	44	13	11	24	108	6	2	1	3	18
1930-31 ♦	Montreal Canadiens	44	4	7	11	75	10	2	1	3	*26
1931-32	Montreal Canadiens	47	5	5	10	62	4	0	1	1	8
1932-33	Montreal Canadiens	48	4	7	11	50	2	0	1	1	2
1933-34	Montreal Canadiens	48	4	6	10	24	2	0	0	0	2
1934-35	Montreal Canadiens	47	3	11	14	36	2	0	0	0	2
1935-36	Montreal Canadiens	42	2	4	6	25	....	....	....	....	....
1936-37	Boston Bruins	4	0	0	0	2	....	....	....	....	....
	NHL Totals	**542**	**63**	**78**	**141**	**671**	**39**	**5**	**5**	**10**	**64**

• Brother of Georges • NHL Second All-Star Team (1931, 1932)

Signed as a free agent by **Montreal**, December 3, 1923. • 1923-24 Stanley Cup totals includes series with Calgary (WCHL) and Vancouver (PCHA). Signed as a free agent by **Boston**, February 11, 1937.

MAPLETOFT, Justin

Center. Shoots left. 6'1", 180 lbs. Born, Lloydminster, Sask., January 11, 1981. (NY Islanders' 9th choice, 130th overall, in 1999 Entry Draft).

Season	Club	GP	G	A	Pts	PIM	GP	G	A	Pts	PIM
2002-03	New York Islanders	11	2	2	4	2	2	0	0	0	0
	NHL Totals	**11**	**2**	**2**	**4**	**2**	**2**	**0**	**0**	**0**	**0**

MARA, Paul

Defense. Shoots left. 6'4", 217 lbs. Born, Ridgewood, NJ, September 7, 1979. (Tampa Bay's 1st choice, 7th overall, in 1997 Entry Draft).

Season	Club	GP	G	A	Pts	PIM	GP	G	A	Pts	PIM
1998-99	Tampa Bay Lightning	1	1	1	2	0	....	....	....	....	....
99-2000	Tampa Bay Lightning	54	7	11	18	73	....	....	....	....	....
2000-01	Tampa Bay Lightning	46	6	10	16	40	....	....	....	....	....
	Phoenix Coyotes	16	0	4	4	14	....	....	....	....	....
2001-02	Phoenix Coyotes	75	7	17	24	58	5	0	0	0	4
2002-03	Phoenix Coyotes	73	10	15	25	78	....	....	....	....	....
	NHL Totals	**265**	**31**	**58**	**89**	**263**	**5**	**0**	**0**	**0**	**4**

Traded to **Phoenix** by **Tampa Bay** with Mike Johnson, Ruslan Zainullin and NY Islanders' 2nd round choice (previously acquired, Phoenix selected Matthew Spiller) in 2001 Entry Draft for Nikolai Khabibulin and Stan Neckar, March 5, 2001.

MARACLE, Bud

Left wing. Shoots left. 5'11", 195 lbs. Born, Ayr, Ont., September 8, 1904.

Season	Club	GP	G	A	Pts	PIM	GP	G	A	Pts	PIM
1930-31	New York Rangers	11	1	3	4	4	4	0	0	0	0
	NHL Totals	**11**	**1**	**3**	**4**	**4**	**4**	**0**	**0**	**0**	**0**

Traded to **Bronx** (Can-Am) by **NY Rangers** for cash, November 1, 1931.

MARCETTA, Milan

Center. Shoots left. 6', 195 lbs. Born, Cadomin, Alta., September 19, 1936.

Season	Club	GP	G	A	Pts	PIM	GP	G	A	Pts	PIM
1966-67 ♦	Toronto Maple Leafs	....	....	....	....	....	3	0	0	0	0
1967-68	Minnesota North Stars	36	4	13	17	6	14	7	7	14	4
1968-69	Minnesota North Stars	18	3	2	5	4	....	....	....	....	....
	NHL Totals	**54**	**7**	**15**	**22**	**10**	**17**	**7**	**7**	**14**	**4**

Signed as a free agent by **NY Rangers**, September, 1958. Loaned to **Vancouver** (WHL) by **NY Rangers** (Springfield-AHL) for the loan of Larry Cahan, January 10, 1959. Traded to **Saskatoon** (WHL) by **NY Rangers** with Alex Kuzma for Bob Robinson and Les Lilley, February 3, 1959. Signed as a free agent by **Chicago**, September, 1959. Traded to **Calgary** (WHL) by **Chicago** for Jack Turner and cash, December, 1962. Signed as a free agent by **Toronto** (Denver-WHL), August, 1963. Traded to **Minnesota** by **Toronto** (Rochester-AHL) with J.P. Parise for Murray Hall, Ted Taylor, Duke Harris, Len Lunde, Don Johns and the loan of Carl Wetzel, December 23, 1967. Traded to **Phoenix** (WHL) by **Minnesota** with Brian D. Smith for Tom Polanic, February 11, 1969.

MARCH, Mush

Right wing. Shoots right. 5'5", 154 lbs. Born, Silton, Sask., October 18, 1908.

Season	Club	REGULAR SEASON GP	G	A	Pts	PIM	PLAYOFFS GP	G	A	Pts	PIM
1928-29	Chicago Black Hawks	35	3	3	6	6	....	....	....	....	....
1929-30	Chicago Black Hawks	43	8	7	15	48	....	....	....	....	....
1930-31	Chicago Black Hawks	44	11	6	17	36	9	3	1	4	11
1931-32	Chicago Black Hawks	48	12	10	22	59	2	0	0	0	2
1932-33	Chicago Black Hawks	48	9	11	20	38	....	....	....	....	....
1933-34 ♦	Chicago Black Hawks	48	4	13	17	26	8	2	2	4	6
1934-35	Chicago Black Hawks	48	13	17	30	48	2	0	0	0	0
1935-36	Chicago Black Hawks	48	16	19	35	42	2	2	3	5	0
1936-37	Chicago Black Hawks	37	11	6	17	31	....	....	....	....	....
1937-38 ♦	Chicago Black Hawks	41	11	17	28	16	9	2	4	6	12
1938-39	Chicago Black Hawks	46	10	11	21	29	....	....	....	....	....
1939-40	Chicago Black Hawks	45	9	14	23	49	2	1	0	1	2
1940-41	Chicago Black Hawks	44	8	9	17	16	4	2	3	5	0
1941-42	Chicago Black Hawks	48	6	26	32	22	3	0	2	2	4
1942-43	Chicago Black Hawks	50	7	29	36	46	....	....	....	....	....
1943-44	Chicago Black Hawks	48	10	27	37	16	4	0	0	0	4
1944-45	Chicago Black Hawks	38	5	5	10	12	....	....	....	....	....
	NHL Totals	**759**	**153**	**230**	**383**	**540**	**45**	**12**	**15**	**27**	**41**

Played in NHL All-Star Game (1937)

Signed as a free agent by **Chicago**, November 29, 1928.

MARCHANT, Todd

Center. Shoots left. 5'10", 178 lbs. Born, Buffalo, NY, August 12, 1973. (NY Rangers' 8th choice, 164th overall, in 1993 Entry Draft).

Season	Club	GP	G	A	Pts	PIM	GP	G	A	Pts	PIM
1993-94	New York Rangers	1	0	0	0	0	....	....	....	....	....
	Edmonton Oilers	3	0	1	1	2	....	....	....	....	....
1994-95	Edmonton Oilers	45	13	14	27	32	....	....	....	....	....
1995-96	Edmonton Oilers	81	19	19	38	66	....	....	....	....	....
1996-97	Edmonton Oilers	79	14	19	33	44	12	4	2	6	12
1997-98	Edmonton Oilers	76	14	21	35	71	12	1	1	2	10
1998-99	Edmonton Oilers	82	14	22	36	65	4	1	1	2	12
99-2000	Edmonton Oilers	82	17	23	40	70	3	1	0	1	2
2000-01	Edmonton Oilers	71	13	26	39	51	6	0	0	0	4
2001-02	Edmonton Oilers	82	12	22	34	41	....	....	....	....	....
2002-03	Edmonton Oilers	77	20	40	60	48	6	0	2	2	2
	NHL Totals	**679**	**136**	**207**	**343**	**490**	**43**	**7**	**6**	**13**	**42**

Traded to **Edmonton** by **NY Rangers** for Craig MacTavish, March 21, 1994. Signed as a free agent by **Columbus**, July 3, 2003.

MARCHINKO, Brian

Center. Shoots right. 6', 180 lbs. Born, Weyburn, Sask., August 2, 1948.

Season	Club	GP	G	A	Pts	PIM	GP	G	A	Pts	PIM
1970-71	Toronto Maple Leafs	2	0	0	0	0	....	....	....	....	....
1971-72	Toronto Maple Leafs	3	0	0	0	0	....	....	....	....	....
1972-73	New York Islanders	36	2	6	8	0	....	....	....	....	....
1973-74	New York Islanders	6	0	0	0	0	....	....	....	....	....
	NHL Totals	**47**	**2**	**6**	**8**	**0**	....	....	....	....	....

Signed as a free agent by **Toronto**, October 1, 1969. Claimed by **NY Islanders** from **Toronto** in Expansion Draft, June 6, 1972.

MARCHMENT, Bryan

Defense. Shoots left. 6'1", 200 lbs. Born, Scarborough, Ont., May 1, 1969. (Winnipeg's 1st choice, 16th overall, in 1987 Entry Draft).

Season	Club	GP	G	A	Pts	PIM	GP	G	A	Pts	PIM
1988-89	Winnipeg Jets	2	0	0	0	2	....	....	....	....	....
1989-90	Winnipeg Jets	7	0	2	2	28	....	....	....	....	....
1990-91	Winnipeg Jets	28	2	2	4	91	....	....	....	....	....
1991-92	Chicago Blackhawks	58	5	10	15	168	16	1	0	1	36
1992-93	Chicago Blackhawks	78	5	15	20	313	4	0	0	0	12
1993-94	Chicago Blackhawks	13	1	4	5	42	....	....	....	....	....
	Hartford Whalers	42	3	7	10	124	....	....	....	....	....
1994-95	Edmonton Oilers	40	1	5	6	184	....	....	....	....	....
1995-96	Edmonton Oilers	78	3	15	18	202	....	....	....	....	....
1996-97	Edmonton Oilers	71	3	13	16	132	3	0	0	0	4
1997-98	Edmonton Oilers	27	0	4	4	58	....	....	....	....	....
	Tampa Bay Lightning	22	2	4	6	43	....	....	....	....	....
	San Jose Sharks	12	0	3	3	43	6	0	0	0	10
1998-99	San Jose Sharks	59	2	6	8	101	6	0	0	0	4
99-2000	San Jose Sharks	49	0	4	4	72	11	2	1	3	12
2000-01	San Jose Sharks	75	7	11	18	204	5	0	1	1	2
2001-02	San Jose Sharks	72	2	20	22	178	12	1	1	2	10
2002-03	San Jose Sharks	67	2	9	11	108	....	....	....	....	....
	Colorado Avalanche	14	0	3	3	33	7	0	0	0	4
	NHL Totals	**814**	**38**	**137**	**175**	**2126**	**70**	**4**	**3**	**7**	**94**

Traded to **Chicago** by **Winnipeg** with Chris Norton for Troy Murray and Warren Rychel, July 22, 1991. Traded to **Hartford** by **Chicago** with Steve Larmer for Eric Weinrich and Patrick Poulin, November 2, 1993. Transferred to **Edmonton** from **Hartford** as compensation for Hartford's signing of free agent Steven Rice, August 30, 1994. Traded to **Tampa Bay** by **Edmonton** with Steve Kelly and Jason Bonsignore for Roman Hamrlik and Paul Comrie, December 30, 1997. Traded to **San Jose** by **Tampa Bay** with David Shaw and Tampa Bay's 1st round choice (later traded to Nashville – Nashville selected David Legwand) in 1998 Entry Draft for Andrei Nazarov and Florida's 1st round choice (previously acquired, Tampa Bay selected Vincent Lecavallier) in 1998 Entry Draft, March 24, 1998. Traded to **Colorado** by **San Jose** for Colorado's 3rd (later traded to Calgary – Calgary selected Ryan Donally) and 5th (later traded back to Colorado – Colorado selected Brad Richardson) round choices in 2003 Entry Draft, March 8, 2003. Signed as a free agent by **Toronto**, July 11, 2003.

MARCINYSHYN, Dave

Defense. Shoots left. 6'3", 210 lbs. Born, Edmonton, Alta., February 4, 1967.

		REGULAR SEASON					PLAYOFFS				
Season	Club	GP	G	A	Pts	PIM	GP	G	A	Pts	PIM
1990-91	New Jersey Devils	9	0	1	1	21	....	....	....	....	....
1991-92	Quebec Nordiques	5	0	0	0	26	....	....	....	....	....
1992-93	New York Rangers	2	0	0	0	2	....	....	....	....	....
	NHL Totals	**16**	**0**	**1**	**1**	**49**	....	....	....	....	....

Signed as a free agent by **New Jersey**, September 26, 1986. Traded to **Quebec** by **New Jersey** for Brent Severyn, June 3, 1991. Signed as a free agent by **NY Rangers**, August 5, 1992.

MARCON, Lou

Defense. Shoots right. 5'9", 168 lbs. Born, Fort William, Ont., May 28, 1935.

		REGULAR SEASON					PLAYOFFS				
Season	Club	GP	G	A	Pts	PIM	GP	G	A	Pts	PIM
1958-59	Detroit Red Wings	21	0	1	1	12	....	....	....	....	....
1959-60	Detroit Red Wings	38	0	3	3	30	....	....	....	....	....
1962-63	Detroit Red Wings	1	0	0	0	0	....	....	....	....	....
	NHL Totals	**60**	**0**	**4**	**4**	**42**	....	....	....	....	....

Claimed by **Detroit** from **Montreal** in Intra-League Draft, June 3, 1958.

MARCOTTE, Don

Left wing. Shoots left. 5'11", 183 lbs. Born, Asbestos, Que., April 15, 1947.

		REGULAR SEASON					PLAYOFFS				
Season	Club	GP	G	A	Pts	PIM	GP	G	A	Pts	PIM
1965-66	Boston Bruins	1	0	0	0	0	....	....	....	....	....
1968-69	Boston Bruins	7	1	0	1	2	....	....	....	....	....
1969-70 ♦	Boston Bruins	35	9	3	12	14	14	2	0	2	11
1970-71	Boston Bruins	75	15	13	28	30	4	0	0	0	0
1971-72 ♦	Boston Bruins	47	6	4	10	12	14	3	0	3	6
1972-73	Boston Bruins	78	24	31	55	49	5	1	1	2	0
1973-74	Boston Bruins	78	24	26	50	18	16	4	2	6	8
1974-75	Boston Bruins	80	31	33	64	76	3	1	0	1	0
1975-76	Boston Bruins	58	16	20	36	24	12	4	2	6	8
1976-77	Boston Bruins	80	27	18	45	20	14	5	6	11	10
1977-78	Boston Bruins	77	20	34	54	16	15	5	4	9	8
1978-79	Boston Bruins	79	20	27	47	10	11	5	3	8	10
1979-80	Boston Bruins	32	4	11	15	0	10	2	3	5	4
1980-81	Boston Bruins	72	20	13	33	32	3	2	2	4	6
1981-82	Boston Bruins	69	13	21	34	14	11	0	4	4	10
	NHL Totals	**868**	**230**	**254**	**484**	**317**	**132**	**34**	**27**	**61**	**81**

MARHA, Josef

Center. Shoots left. 6', 176 lbs. Born, Havlickuv Brod, Czech., June 2, 1976.
(Quebec's 3rd choice, 35th overall, in 1994 Entry Draft).

		REGULAR SEASON					PLAYOFFS				
Season	Club	GP	G	A	Pts	PIM	GP	G	A	Pts	PIM
1995-96	Colorado Avalanche	2	0	1	1	0	....	....	....	....	....
1996-97	Colorado Avalanche	6	0	1	1	0	....	....	....	....	....
1997-98	Colorado Avalanche	11	2	5	7	4	....	....	....	....	....
	Mighty Ducks of Anaheim	12	7	4	11	0	....	....	....	....	....
1998-99	Mighty Ducks of Anaheim	10	0	1	1	0	....	....	....	....	....
	Chicago Blackhawks	22	2	5	7	4	....	....	....	....	....
99-2000	Chicago Blackhawks	81	10	12	22	18	....	....	....	....	....
2000-01	Chicago Blackhawks	15	0	3	3	6	....	....	....	....	....
	NHL Totals	**159**	**21**	**32**	**53**	**32**	....	....	....	....	....

Rights transferred to **Colorado** after **Quebec** franchise relocated, June 21, 1995. Traded to **Anaheim** by **Colorado** for Warren Rychel and Anaheim's 4th round choice (Sanny Lindstrom) in 1999 Entry Draft, March 24, 1998. Traded to **Chicago** by **Anaheim** for Chicago's 4th round choice (Alexandr Chagodayev) in 1999 Entry Draft, January 28, 1999.

MARINI, Hector

Right wing. Shoots right. 6'1", 204 lbs. Born, Timmins, Ont., January 27, 1957.
(NY Islanders' 3rd choice, 50th overall, in 1977 Amateur Draft).

		REGULAR SEASON					PLAYOFFS				
Season	Club	GP	G	A	Pts	PIM	GP	G	A	Pts	PIM
1978-79	New York Islanders	1	0	0	0	2	1	0	0	0	0
1980-81 ♦	New York Islanders	14	4	7	11	39	9	3	6	9	14
1981-82 ♦	New York Islanders	30	4	9	13	53	....	....	....	....	....
1982-83	New Jersey Devils	77	17	28	45	105	....	....	....	....	....
1983-84	New Jersey Devils	32	2	2	4	47	....	....	....	....	....
	NHL Totals	**154**	**27**	**46**	**73**	**246**	**10**	**3**	**6**	**9**	**14**

Played in NHL All-Star Game (1983)

Traded to **New Jersey** by **NY Islanders** with NY Islanders' 4th round choice (later traded to Calgary – Calgary selected Bill Claviter) in 1983 Entry Draft for New Jersey's 4th round choice (Mikko Makela) in 1983 Entry Draft, October 1, 1982.

MARINUCCI, Chris

Center. Shoots left. 6', 188 lbs. Born, Grand Rapids, MN, December 29, 1971.
(NY Islanders' 4th choice, 90th overall, in 1990 Entry Draft).

		REGULAR SEASON					PLAYOFFS				
Season	Club	GP	G	A	Pts	PIM	GP	G	A	Pts	PIM
1994-95	New York Islanders	12	1	4	5	2	....	....	....	....	....
1996-97	Los Angeles Kings	1	0	0	0	0	....	....	....	....	....
	NHL Totals	**13**	**1**	**4**	**5**	**2**	....	....	....	....	....

Traded to **Los Angeles** by **NY Islanders** for Nick Vachon, November 19, 1996.

MARIO, Frank

Center. Shoots left. 5'8", 170 lbs. Born, Esterhazy, Sask., February 25, 1921.

		REGULAR SEASON					PLAYOFFS				
Season	Club	GP	G	A	Pts	PIM	GP	G	A	Pts	PIM
1941-42	Boston Bruins	9	1	1	2	0	....	....	....	....	....
1944-45	Boston Bruins	44	8	18	26	24	....	....	....	....	....
	NHL Totals	**53**	**9**	**19**	**28**	**24**	....	....	....	....	....

Signed as a free agent by **Boston**, October 21, 1941.

MARIUCCI, John

USHOF HHOF

Defense. Shoots left. 5'10", 200 lbs. Born, Eveleth, MN, May 8, 1916.

		REGULAR SEASON					PLAYOFFS				
Season	Club	GP	G	A	Pts	PIM	GP	G	A	Pts	PIM
1940-41	Chicago Black Hawks	23	0	5	5	33	5	0	2	2	16
1941-42	Chicago Black Hawks	47	5	8	13	44	3	0	0	0	0
1945-46	Chicago Black Hawks	50	3	8	11	58	4	0	1	1	10
1946-47	Chicago Black Hawks	52	2	9	11	110	....	....	....	....	....
1947-48	Chicago Black Hawks	51	1	4	5	63	....	....	....	....	....
	NHL Totals	**223**	**11**	**34**	**45**	**308**	**12**	**0**	**3**	**3**	**26**

Lester Patrick Trophy (1977)

Traded to **St. Louis** (AHL) by **Chicago** for cash, October 28, 1948.

MARK, Gordon

Defense. Shoots right. 6'4", 218 lbs. Born, Edmonton, Alta., September 10, 1964.
(New Jersey's 4th choice, 108th overall, in 1983 Entry Draft).

		REGULAR SEASON					PLAYOFFS				
Season	Club	GP	G	A	Pts	PIM	GP	G	A	Pts	PIM
1986-87	New Jersey Devils	36	3	5	8	82	....	....	....	....	....
1987-88	New Jersey Devils	19	0	2	2	27	....	....	....	....	....
1993-94	Edmonton Oilers	12	0	1	1	43	....	....	....	....	....
1994-95	Edmonton Oilers	18	0	2	2	35	....	....	....	....	....
	NHL Totals	**85**	**3**	**10**	**13**	**187**	....	....	....	....	....

Signed as a free agent by **Edmonton**, February 1, 1994.

MARKELL, John

Left wing. Shoots left. 5'11", 185 lbs. Born, Cornwall, Ont., March 10, 1956.

		REGULAR SEASON					PLAYOFFS				
Season	Club	GP	G	A	Pts	PIM	GP	G	A	Pts	PIM
1979-80	Winnipeg Jets	38	10	7	17	21	....	....	....	....	....
1980-81	Winnipeg Jets	14	1	3	4	15	....	....	....	....	....
1983-84	St. Louis Blues	2	0	0	0	0	....	....	....	....	....
1984-85	Minnesota North Stars	1	0	0	0	0	....	....	....	....	....
	NHL Totals	**55**	**11**	**10**	**21**	**36**	....	....	....	....	....

Signed as a free agent by **Winnipeg**, April 16, 1979. Traded to **St. Louis** by **Winnipeg** with Scott Campbell for Ed Staniowski, Bryan Maxwell and Paul MacLean, July 3, 1981. Signed as a free agent by **Minnesota**, December 17, 1984.

MARKER, Gus

Right wing. Shoots right. 5'9", 162 lbs. Born, Wetaskiwin, Alta., August 1, 1907.

		REGULAR SEASON					PLAYOFFS				
Season	Club	GP	G	A	Pts	PIM	GP	G	A	Pts	PIM
1932-33	Detroit Red Wings	13	1	1	2	8	....	....	....	....	....
1933-34	Detroit Red Wings	7	1	0	1	2	4	0	0	0	2
1934-35 ♦	Montreal Maroons	44	11	4	15	18	7	1	1	2	4
1935-36	Montreal Maroons	48	7	12	19	10	3	1	0	1	2
1936-37	Montreal Maroons	47	10	12	22	22	5	0	1	1	0
1937-38	Montreal Maroons	48	9	15	24	35	....	....	....	....	....
1938-39	Toronto Maple Leafs	29	9	6	15	11	10	2	2	4	0
1939-40	Toronto Maple Leafs	42	10	9	19	15	10	1	3	4	23
1940-41	Toronto Maple Leafs	27	4	5	9	10	7	0	0	0	5
1941-42	Brooklyn Americans	17	2	5	7	2	....	....	....	....	....
	NHL Totals	**322**	**64**	**69**	**133**	**133**	**46**	**5**	**7**	**12**	**36**

NHL rights transferred to **Detroit** from **Chicago Shamrocks** (AHA) after AHA club owners purchased Detroit (NHL and IAHL) franchises, September 2, 1932. Traded to **Mtl. Maroons** by **Detroit** for Wally Kilrea, September 23, 1934. Traded to **Toronto** by **Mtl. Maroons** for $4,000, November 3, 1938. Loaned to **Brooklyn** by **Toronto** with Red Heron and Nick Knott and future considerations (cash, February 2, 1942) for Lorne Carr, October 30, 1941.

MARKHAM, Ray

Center. Shoots right. 6'3", 220 lbs. Born, Windsor, Ont., January 23, 1958.
(NY Rangers' 2nd choice, 43rd overall, in 1978 Amateur Draft).

		REGULAR SEASON					PLAYOFFS				
Season	Club	GP	G	A	Pts	PIM	GP	G	A	Pts	PIM
1979-80	New York Rangers	14	1	1	2	21	7	1	0	1	24
	NHL Totals	**14**	**1**	**1**	**2**	**21**	**7**	**1**	**0**	**1**	**24**

Traded to **Edmonton** by **NY Rangers** for John Hughes, March 10, 1981.

MARKLE, Jack

Right wing. Shoots right. 5'9", 155 lbs. Born, Thessalon, Ont., May 15, 1907.

		REGULAR SEASON					PLAYOFFS				
Season	Club	GP	G	A	Pts	PIM	GP	G	A	Pts	PIM
1935-36	Toronto Maple Leafs	8	0	1	1	0	....	....	....	....	....
	NHL Totals	**8**	**0**	**1**	**1**	**0**	....	....	....	....	....

Loaned to **Toronto** by **Syracuse** (IHL), January 20, 1936.

MARKOV, Andrei

Defense. Shoots left. 6', 208 lbs. Born, Voskresensk, USSR, December 20, 1978.
(Montreal's 6th choice, 162nd overall, in 1998 Entry Draft).

		REGULAR SEASON					PLAYOFFS				
Season	Club	GP	G	A	Pts	PIM	GP	G	A	Pts	PIM
2000-01	Montreal Canadiens	63	6	17	23	18	....	....	....	....	....
2001-02	Montreal Canadiens	56	5	19	24	24	12	1	3	4	8
2002-03	Montreal Canadiens	79	13	24	37	34	....	....	....	....	....
	NHL Totals	**198**	**24**	**60**	**84**	**76**	**12**	**1**	**3**	**4**	**8**

MARKOV, Danny

Defense. Shoots left. 6'1", 190 lbs. Born, Moscow, USSR, July 30, 1976.
(Toronto's 7th choice, 223rd overall, in 1995 Entry Draft).

		REGULAR SEASON					PLAYOFFS				
Season	Club	GP	G	A	Pts	PIM	GP	G	A	Pts	PIM
1997-98	Toronto Maple Leafs	25	2	5	7	28	....	....	....	....	....
1998-99	Toronto Maple Leafs	57	4	8	12	47	17	0	6	6	18
99-2000	Toronto Maple Leafs	59	0	10	10	28	12	0	3	3	10
2000-01	Toronto Maple Leafs	59	3	13	16	34	11	1	1	2	12
2001-02	Phoenix Coyotes	72	6	30	36	67	....	....	....	....	....

Season	Club	REGULAR SEASON GP	G	A	Pts	PIM	PLAYOFFS GP	G	A	Pts	PIM
2002-03	Phoenix Coyotes	64	4	16	20	36	....	....	....	....	....
	NHL Totals	**336**	**19**	**82**	**101**	**240**	**40**	**1**	**10**	**11**	**40**

Traded to **Phoenix** by **Toronto** for Robert Reichel, Travis Green and Craig Mills, June 12, 2001. Traded to **Carolina** by **Phoenix** for David Tanabe and Igor Knyazev, June 21, 2003.

MARKS, Jack

Left wing/Defense. Shoots left. 6', 180 lbs. Born, Brantford, Ont., June 11, 1885.

Season	Club	GP	G	A	Pts	PIM	GP	G	A	Pts	PIM
1917-18	Montreal Wanderers	1	0	0	0	0	....	....	....	....	....
	♦ Toronto Arenas	5	0	0	0	0	....	....	....	....	....
1919-20	Quebec Bulldogs	1	0	0	0	4	....	....	....	....	....
	NHL Totals	**7**	**0**	**0**	**0**	**4**	....	....	....	....	....

Claimed by **Mtl. Wanderers** from **Quebec** in Dispersal Draft, November 26, 1917. Claimed by **Montreal** from **Mtl. Wanderers** in Dispersal Draft, January 4, 1918. Loaned to **Toronto** by **Montreal**, January 4, 1918. NHL rights transferred to **Quebec** from **Montreal** when Quebec franchise returned to NHL, November 25, 1919.

MARKS, John

Left wing. Shoots left. 6'2", 200 lbs. Born, Hamiota, Man., March 22, 1948.
(Chicago's 1st choice, 9th overall, in 1968 Amateur Draft).

Season	Club	GP	G	A	Pts	PIM	GP	G	A	Pts	PIM
1972-73	Chicago Black Hawks	55	3	10	13	21	16	1	2	3	2
1973-74	Chicago Black Hawks	76	13	18	31	22	11	2	0	2	8
1974-75	Chicago Black Hawks	80	17	30	47	56	8	2	6	8	34
1975-76	Chicago Black Hawks	80	21	23	44	43	4	0	0	0	10
1976-77	Chicago Black Hawks	80	7	15	22	41	2	0	0	0	4
1977-78	Chicago Black Hawks	80	15	22	37	26	4	0	1	1	0
1978-79	Chicago Black Hawks	80	21	24	45	35	4	0	0	0	2
1979-80	Chicago Black Hawks	74	6	15	21	51	4	0	0	0	0
1980-81	Chicago Black Hawks	39	8	6	14	28	3	0	0	0	0
1981-82	Chicago Black Hawks	13	1	0	1	7	1	0	0	0	0
	NHL Totals	**657**	**112**	**163**	**275**	**330**	**57**	**5**	**9**	**14**	**60**

Played in NHL All-Star Game (1976)

MARKWART, Nevin

Left wing. Shoots left. 5'10", 180 lbs. Born, Toronto, Ont., December 9, 1964.
(Boston's 1st choice, 21st overall, in 1983 Entry Draft).

Season	Club	GP	G	A	Pts	PIM	GP	G	A	Pts	PIM
1983-84	Boston Bruins	70	14	16	30	121	....	....	....	....	....
1984-85	Boston Bruins	26	0	4	4	36	1	0	0	0	0
1985-86	Boston Bruins	65	7	15	22	207	....	....	....	....	....
1986-87	Boston Bruins	64	10	9	19	225	4	0	0	0	9
1987-88	Boston Bruins	25	1	12	13	85	2	0	0	0	2
1989-90	Boston Bruins	8	1	2	3	15	....	....	....	....	....
1990-91	Boston Bruins	23	3	3	6	36	12	1	0	1	22
1991-92	Boston Bruins	18	3	6	9	44	....	....	....	....	....
	Calgary Flames	10	2	1	3	25	....	....	....	....	....
	NHL Totals	**309**	**41**	**68**	**109**	**794**	**19**	**1**	**0**	**1**	**33**

Claimed on waivers by **Calgary** from **Boston**, February 14, 1992.

MARLEAU, Patrick

Center. Shoots left. 6'2", 210 lbs. Born, Aneroid, Sask., September 15, 1979.
(San Jose's 1st choice, 2nd overall, in 1997 Entry Draft).

Season	Club	GP	G	A	Pts	PIM	GP	G	A	Pts	PIM
1997-98	San Jose Sharks	74	13	19	32	14	5	0	1	1	0
1998-99	San Jose Sharks	81	21	24	45	24	6	2	1	3	4
99-2000	San Jose Sharks	81	17	23	40	36	5	1	1	2	2
2000-01	San Jose Sharks	81	25	27	52	22	6	2	0	2	4
2001-02	San Jose Sharks	79	21	23	44	40	12	6	5	11	6
2002-03	San Jose Sharks	82	28	29	57	33	....	....	....	....	....
	NHL Totals	**478**	**125**	**145**	**270**	**169**	**34**	**11**	**8**	**19**	**16**

MAROIS, Daniel

Right wing. Shoots right. 6', 190 lbs. Born, Montreal, Que., October 3, 1968.
(Toronto's 2nd choice, 28th overall, in 1987 Entry Draft).

Season	Club	GP	G	A	Pts	PIM	GP	G	A	Pts	PIM
1987-88	Toronto Maple Leafs	....	....	....	....	....	3	1	0	1	0
1988-89	Toronto Maple Leafs	76	31	23	54	76	....	....	....	....	....
1989-90	Toronto Maple Leafs	68	39	37	76	82	5	2	2	4	12
1990-91	Toronto Maple Leafs	78	21	9	30	112	....	....	....	....	....
1991-92	Toronto Maple Leafs	63	15	11	26	76	....	....	....	....	....
	New York Islanders	12	2	5	7	18	....	....	....	....	....
1992-93	New York Islanders	28	2	5	7	35	....	....	....	....	....
1993-94	Boston Bruins	22	7	3	10	18	11	0	1	1	16
1995-96	Dallas Stars	3	0	0	0	2	....	....	....	....	....
	NHL Totals	**350**	**117**	**93**	**210**	**419**	**19**	**3**	**3**	**6**	**28**

Traded to **NY Islanders** by **Toronto** with Claude Loiselle for Ken Baumgartner and Dave McLlwain, March 10, 1992. Traded to **Boston** by **NY Islanders** for Boston's 8th round choice (Peter Hogardh) in 1994 Entry Draft, March 18, 1993. • Missed entire 1994-95 season recovering from back surgery. Signed as a free agent by **Dallas**, January 26, 1995. Signed as a free agent by **Toronto**, August 22, 1996.

MAROIS, Mario

Defense. Shoots right. 5'11", 190 lbs. Born, Quebec City, Que., December 15, 1957.
(NY Rangers' 5th choice, 62nd overall, in 1977 Amateur Draft).

Season	Club	GP	G	A	Pts	PIM	GP	G	A	Pts	PIM
1977-78	New York Rangers	8	1	1	2	15	1	0	0	0	5
1978-79	New York Rangers	71	5	26	31	153	18	0	6	6	29
1979-80	New York Rangers	79	8	23	31	142	9	0	2	2	8
1980-81	New York Rangers	8	1	2	3	46	....	....	....	....	....
	Vancouver Canucks	50	4	12	16	115	....	....	....	....	....
	Quebec Nordiques	11	0	7	7	20	5	0	1	1	6
1981-82	Quebec Nordiques	71	11	32	43	161	13	1	2	3	44
1982-83	Quebec Nordiques	36	2	12	14	108	....	....	....	....	....
1983-84	Quebec Nordiques	80	13	36	49	151	9	1	4	5	6
1984-85	Quebec Nordiques	76	6	37	43	91	18	0	8	8	12
1985-86	Quebec Nordiques	20	1	12	13	42	....	....	....	....	....
	Winnipeg Jets	56	4	28	32	110	3	1	4	5	6
1986-87	Winnipeg Jets	79	4	40	44	106	10	1	3	4	23
1987-88	Winnipeg Jets	79	7	44	51	111	5	0	4	4	6
1988-89	Winnipeg Jets	7	1	1	2	17	....	....	....	....	....
	Quebec Nordiques	42	2	11	13	101	....	....	....	....	....
1989-90	Quebec Nordiques	67	3	15	18	104	....	....	....	....	....
1990-91	St. Louis Blues	64	2	14	16	81	9	0	0	0	37
1991-92	St. Louis Blues	17	0	1	1	38	....	....	....	....	....
	Winnipeg Jets	34	1	3	4	34	....	....	....	....	....
	NHL Totals	**955**	**76**	**357**	**433**	**1746**	**100**	**4**	**34**	**38**	**182**

Traded to **Vancouver** by **NY Rangers** with Jim Mayer for Jere Gillis and Jeff Bandura, November 11, 1980. Traded to **Quebec** by **Vancouver** for Garry Lariviere, March 10, 1981. • Missed majority of 1982-83 season recovering from leg injury suffered in exhibition game vs. USSR, December 30, 1982. Traded to **Winnipeg** by **Quebec** for Robert Picard, November 27, 1985. Traded to **Quebec** by **Winnipeg** for Gord Donnelly, December 6, 1988. Claimed by **St. Louis** from **Quebec** in Waiver Draft, October 3, 1990. Traded to **Winnipeg** by **St. Louis** for Winnipeg's 8th round choice (Igor Boldin) in 1992 Entry Draft, November 26, 1991.

MAROTTE, Gilles

Defense. Shoots left. 5'9", 205 lbs. Born, Montreal, Que., June 7, 1945.

Season	Club	GP	G	A	Pts	PIM	GP	G	A	Pts	PIM
1965-66	Boston Bruins	51	3	17	20	52	....	....	....	....	....
1966-67	Boston Bruins	67	7	8	15	112	....	....	....	....	....
1967-68	Chicago Black Hawks	73	0	21	21	122	11	3	1	4	14
1968-69	Chicago Black Hawks	68	5	29	34	120	....	....	....	....	....
1969-70	Chicago Black Hawks	51	5	13	18	52	....	....	....	....	....
	Los Angeles Kings	21	0	6	6	32	....	....	....	....	....
1970-71	Los Angeles Kings	78	6	27	33	96	....	....	....	....	....
1971-72	Los Angeles Kings	72	10	24	34	83	....	....	....	....	....
1972-73	Los Angeles Kings	78	6	39	45	70	....	....	....	....	....
1973-74	Los Angeles Kings	22	1	11	12	23	....	....	....	....	....
	New York Rangers	46	2	17	19	28	12	0	1	1	6
1974-75	New York Rangers	77	4	32	36	69	3	0	1	1	4
1975-76	New York Rangers	57	4	17	21	34					
1976-77	St. Louis Blues	47	3	4	7	26	3	0	0	0	2
	NHL Totals	**808**	**56**	**265**	**321**	**919**	**29**	**3**	**3**	**6**	**26**

Played in NHL All-Star Game (1973)

Traded to **Chicago** by **Boston** with Jack Norris and Pit Martin for Phil Esposito, Ken Hodge and Fred Stanfield, May 15, 1967. Traded to **Los Angeles** by **Chicago** with Jim Stanfield and Denis DeJordy for Bryan Campbell, Bill White and Gerry Desjardins, February 20, 1970. Traded to **NY Rangers** by **Los Angeles** with Real Lemieux for Sheldon Kannegiesser, Mike Murphy and Tom Williams, November 30, 1973. Claimed on waivers by **St. Louis** from **NY Rangers**, October 12, 1976.

MARQUESS, Mark

Right wing. Shoots right. 5'8", 160 lbs. Born, Bassano, Alta., March 26, 1925.

Season	Club	GP	G	A	Pts	PIM	GP	G	A	Pts	PIM
1946-47	Boston Bruins	27	5	4	9	6	4	0	0	0	0
	NHL Totals	**27**	**5**	**4**	**9**	**6**	**4**	**0**	**0**	**0**	**0**

MARSH, Brad

Defense. Shoots left. 6'3", 220 lbs. Born, London, Ont., March 31, 1958.
(Atlanta's 1st choice, 11th overall, in 1978 Amateur Draft).

Season	Club	GP	G	A	Pts	PIM	GP	G	A	Pts	PIM
1978-79	Atlanta Flames	80	0	19	19	101	2	0	0	0	17
1979-80	Atlanta Flames	80	2	9	11	119	4	0	1	1	2
1980-81	Calgary Flames	80	1	12	13	87	16	0	5	5	8
1981-82	Calgary Flames	17	0	1	1	10	....	....	....	....	....
	Philadelphia Flyers	66	2	22	24	106	4	0	0	0	2
1982-83	Philadelphia Flyers	68	2	11	13	52	2	0	1	1	0
1983-84	Philadelphia Flyers	77	3	14	17	83	3	1	1	2	2
1984-85	Philadelphia Flyers	77	2	18	20	91	19	0	6	6	65
1985-86	Philadelphia Flyers	79	0	13	13	123	5	0	0	0	2
1986-87	Philadelphia Flyers	77	2	9	11	124	26	3	4	7	16
1987-88	Philadelphia Flyers	70	3	9	12	57	7	1	0	1	8
1988-89	Toronto Maple Leafs	80	1	15	16	79	....	....	....	....	....
1989-90	Toronto Maple Leafs	79	1	13	14	95	5	1	0	1	2
1990-91	Toronto Maple Leafs	22	0	0	0	15	....	....	....	....	....
	Detroit Red Wings	20	1	3	4	16	1	0	0	0	0
1991-92	Detroit Red Wings	55	3	4	7	53	3	0	0	0	0
1992-93	Ottawa Senators	59	0	3	3	30	....	....	....	....	....
	NHL Totals	**1086**	**23**	**175**	**198**	**1241**	**97**	**6**	**18**	**24**	**124**

Played in NHL All-Star Game (1993)

Claimed by **Atlanta** as a fill-in during Expansion Draft, June 13, 1979. Transferred to **Calgary** after **Atlanta** franchise relocated, June 21, 1982. Traded to **Philadelphia** by **Calgary** for Mel Bridgman, November 11, 1981. Claimed by **Toronto** from **Philadelphia** in Waiver Draft, October 3, 1988. Traded to **Detroit** by **Toronto** for Detroit's 8th round choice (Robb McIntyre) in 1991 Entry Draft, February 4, 1991. Traded to **Toronto** by **Detroit** for cash, June 10, 1992. Traded to **Ottawa** by **Toronto** for future considerations, July 20, 1992.

MARSH, Gary

Left wing. Shoots left. 5'10", 172 lbs. Born, Toronto, Ont., March 9, 1946.

Season	Club	Regular Season GP	G	A	Pts	PIM	Playoffs GP	G	A	Pts	PIM
1967-68	Detroit Red Wings	6	1	3	4	4	....	....	....	....	....
1968-69	Toronto Maple Leafs	1	0	0	0	0	....	....	....	....	....
	NHL Totals	**7**	**1**	**3**	**4**	**4**	....	....	....	....	....

Claimed by **Toronto** from **Detroit** in Intra-League Draft, June 12, 1968. Traded to **Los Angeles** by **Toronto** (Phoenix-WHL) for Jacques Lemieux, February, 1970.

MARSH, Peter

Right wing. Shoots left. 6'1", 180 lbs. Born, Halifax, N.S., December 21, 1956.
(Pittsburgh's 3rd choice, 29th overall, in 1976 Amateur Draft).

Season	Club	Regular Season GP	G	A	Pts	PIM	Playoffs GP	G	A	Pts	PIM
1979-80	Winnipeg Jets	57	18	20	38	59	....	....	....	....	....
1980-81	Winnipeg Jets	24	6	7	13	9	....	....	....	....	....
	Chicago Black Hawks	29	4	6	10	10	2	1	1	2	2
1981-82	Chicago Black Hawks	57	10	18	28	47	12	0	2	2	31
1982-83	Chicago Black Hawks	68	6	14	20	55	12	0	2	2	0
1983-84	Chicago Black Hawks	43	4	6	10	44	....	....	....	....	....
	NHL Totals	**278**	**48**	**71**	**119**	**224**	**26**	**1**	**5**	**6**	**33**

Rights traded to **Montreal** by **Pittsburgh** to complete transaction that sent Pete Mahovlich to Pittsburgh (November 29, 1977), December 15, 1977. Reclaimed by **Montreal** from **Cincinnati** (WHA) prior to Expansion Draft, June 9, 1979. Claimed by **Winnipeg** from **Montreal** in Expansion Draft, June 13, 1979. Traded to **Chicago** by **Winnipeg** for Doug Lecuyer and Tim Trimper, December 1, 1980.

MARSHALL, Bert

Defense. Shoots left. 6'3", 205 lbs. Born, Kamloops, B.C., November 22, 1943.

Season	Club	Regular Season GP	G	A	Pts	PIM	Playoffs GP	G	A	Pts	PIM
1965-66	Detroit Red Wings	61	0	19	19	45	12	1	3	4	16
1966-67	Detroit Red Wings	57	0	10	10	68	....	....	....	....	....
1967-68	Detroit Red Wings	37	1	5	6	56	....	....	....	....	....
	Oakland Seals	20	0	4	4	18	....	....	....	....	....
1968-69	Oakland Seals	68	3	15	18	81	7	0	7	7	20
1969-70	Oakland Seals	72	1	15	16	109	4	0	1	1	12
1970-71	California Seals	32	2	6	8	48	....	....	....	....	....
1971-72	California Golden Seals	66	0	14	14	68	....	....	....	....	....
1972-73	California Golden Seals	55	2	6	8	71	....	....	....	....	....
	New York Rangers	8	0	0	0	14	6	0	1	1	8
1973-74	New York Islanders	69	1	7	8	84	....	....	....	....	....
1974-75	New York Islanders	77	2	28	30	58	17	2	5	7	16
1975-76	New York Islanders	71	0	16	16	72	13	1	3	4	12
1976-77	New York Islanders	72	4	21	25	61	6	0	0	0	6
1977-78	New York Islanders	58	0	7	7	44	7	0	2	2	9
1978-79	New York Islanders	45	1	8	9	29	....	....	....	....	....
	NHL Totals	**868**	**17**	**181**	**198**	**926**	**72**	**4**	**22**	**26**	**99**

Traded to **Oakland** by **Detroit** with John Brenneman and Ted Hampson for Kent Douglas, January 9, 1968. Traded to **NY Rangers** by **California** for cash and future considerations (Dave Hrechkosy and Gary Coalter, May 17, 1973), March 4, 1973. Claimed by **NY Islanders** from **NY Rangers** in Intra-League Draft, June 12, 1973.

MARSHALL, Don

Left wing. Shoots left. 5'10", 160 lbs. Born, Montreal, Que., March 23, 1932.

Season	Club	Regular Season GP	G	A	Pts	PIM	Playoffs GP	G	A	Pts	PIM
1951-52	Montreal Canadiens	1	0	0	0	0	....	....	....	....	....
1954-55	Montreal Canadiens	39	5	3	8	9	12	1	1	2	2
1955-56 ♦	Montreal Canadiens	66	4	1	5	10	10	1	0	1	0
1956-57 ♦	Montreal Canadiens	70	12	8	20	6	10	1	3	4	2
1957-58 ♦	Montreal Canadiens	68	22	19	41	14	10	0	2	2	4
1958-59 ♦	Montreal Canadiens	70	10	22	32	12	11	0	2	2	2
1959-60 ♦	Montreal Canadiens	70	16	22	38	4	8	2	2	4	0
1960-61	Montreal Canadiens	70	14	17	31	8	6	0	2	2	0
1961-62	Montreal Canadiens	66	18	28	46	12	6	0	1	1	2
1962-63	Montreal Canadiens	65	13	20	33	6	5	0	0	0	0
1963-64	New York Rangers	70	11	12	23	8	....	....	....	....	....
1964-65	New York Rangers	69	20	15	35	2	....	....	....	....	....
1965-66	New York Rangers	69	26	28	54	6	....	....	....	....	....
1966-67	New York Rangers	70	24	22	46	4	4	0	1	1	2
1967-68	New York Rangers	70	19	30	49	2	6	2	1	3	0
1968-69	New York Rangers	74	20	19	39	12	4	1	0	1	0
1969-70	New York Rangers	57	9	15	24	6	1	0	0	0	0
1970-71	Buffalo Sabres	62	20	29	49	6	....	....	....	....	....
1971-72	Toronto Maple Leafs	50	2	14	16	0	1	0	0	0	0
	NHL Totals	**1176**	**265**	**324**	**589**	**127**	**94**	**8**	**15**	**23**	**14**

NHL Second All-Star Team (1967)

Played in NHL All-Star Game (1956, 1957, 1958, 1959, 1960, 1961, 1968)

Traded to **NY Rangers** by **Montreal** with Jacques Plante and Phil Goyette for Dave Balon, Leon Rochefort, Len Ronson and Gump Worsley, June 4, 1963. Claimed by **Buffalo** from **NY Rangers** in Expansion Draft, June 10, 1970. Claimed by **Toronto** from **Buffalo** in Intra-League Draft, June 8, 1971.

MARSHALL, Grant

Right wing. Shoots right. 6'1", 200 lbs. Born, Mississauga, Ont., June 9, 1973.
(Toronto's 2nd choice, 23rd overall, in 1992 Entry Draft).

Season	Club	Regular Season GP	G	A	Pts	PIM	Playoffs GP	G	A	Pts	PIM
1994-95	Dallas Stars	2	0	1	1	0	....	....	....	....	....
1995-96	Dallas Stars	70	9	19	28	111	....	....	....	....	....
1996-97	Dallas Stars	56	6	4	10	98	5	0	2	2	8
1997-98	Dallas Stars	72	9	10	19	96	17	0	2	2	*47
1998-99 ♦	Dallas Stars	82	13	18	31	85	14	0	3	3	20
99-2000	Dallas Stars	45	2	6	8	38	14	0	1	1	4
2000-01	Dallas Stars	75	13	24	37	64	9	0	0	0	0
2001-02	Columbus Blue Jackets	81	15	18	33	86	....	....	....	....	....
2002-03	Columbus Blue Jackets	66	8	20	28	71	....	....	....	....	....
	♦ New Jersey Devils	10	1	3	4	7	24	6	2	8	8
	NHL Totals	**559**	**76**	**123**	**199**	**656**	**83**	**6**	**10**	**16**	**87**

Transferred to **Dallas** from **Toronto** with Peter Zezel as compensation for Toronto's signing of free agent Mike Craig, August 10, 1994. Traded to **Columbus** by **Dallas** for Columbus' 2nd round choice (Loui Eriksson) in 2003 Entry Draft, August 29, 2001. Traded to **New Jersey** by **Columbus** for future considerations, March 10, 2003.

MARSHALL, Jason

Defense. Shoots right. 6'2", 200 lbs. Born, Cranbrook, B.C., February 22, 1971.
(St. Louis' 1st choice, 9th overall, in 1989 Entry Draft).

Season	Club	Regular Season GP	G	A	Pts	PIM	Playoffs GP	G	A	Pts	PIM
1991-92	St. Louis Blues	2	1	0	1	4	....	....	....	....	....
1994-95	Mighty Ducks of Anaheim	1	0	0	0	0	....	....	....	....	....
1995-96	Mighty Ducks of Anaheim	24	0	1	1	42	....	....	....	....	....
1996-97	Mighty Ducks of Anaheim	73	1	9	10	140	7	0	1	1	4
1997-98	Mighty Ducks of Anaheim	72	3	6	9	189	....	....	....	....	....
1998-99	Mighty Ducks of Anaheim	72	1	7	8	142	4	1	0	1	10
99-2000	Mighty Ducks of Anaheim	55	0	3	3	88	....	....	....	....	....
2000-01	Mighty Ducks of Anaheim	50	3	4	7	105	....	....	....	....	....
	Washington Capitals	5	0	0	0	17	....	....	....	....	....
2001-02	Minnesota Wild	80	5	6	11	148	....	....	....	....	....
2002-03	Minnesota Wild	45	1	5	6	69	15	1	1	2	16
	NHL Totals	**479**	**15**	**41**	**56**	**944**	**26**	**2**	**2**	**4**	**30**

Traded to **Anaheim** by **St. Louis** for Bill Houlder, August 29, 1994. Traded to **Washington** by **Anaheim** for Alexei Tezikov and Edmonton's 4th round choice (previously acquired, Anaheim selected Brandon Rogers) in 2001 Entry Draft, March 13, 2001. Signed as a free agent by **Minnesota**, July 2, 2001.

MARSHALL, Paul

Left wing. Shoots left. 6'2", 180 lbs. Born, Toronto, Ont., September 7, 1960.
(Pittsburgh's 1st choice, 31st overall, in 1979 Entry Draft).

Season	Club	Regular Season GP	G	A	Pts	PIM	Playoffs GP	G	A	Pts	PIM
1979-80	Pittsburgh Penguins	46	9	12	21	9	1	0	0	0	0
1980-81	Pittsburgh Penguins	13	3	0	3	4	....	....	....	....	....
	Toronto Maple Leafs	13	0	2	2	2	....	....	....	....	....
1981-82	Toronto Maple Leafs	10	2	2	4	2	....	....	....	....	....
1982-83	Hartford Whalers	13	1	2	3	0	....	....	....	....	....
	NHL Totals	**95**	**15**	**18**	**33**	**17**	**1**	**0**	**0**	**0**	**0**

Traded to **Toronto** by **Pittsburgh** with Kim Davis for Dave Burrows and Paul Gardner, November 18, 1980. Traded to **Hartford** by **Toronto** for Hartford's 10th round choice (Greg Rolston) in 1983 Entry Draft, October 5, 1982.

MARSHALL, Willie

Center. Shoots left. 5'10", 165 lbs. Born, Kirkland Lake, Ont., December 1, 1931.

Season	Club	Regular Season GP	G	A	Pts	PIM	Playoffs GP	G	A	Pts	PIM
1952-53	Toronto Maple Leafs	2	0	0	0	0	....	....	....	....	....
1954-55	Toronto Maple Leafs	16	1	4	5	0	....	....	....	....	....
1955-56	Toronto Maple Leafs	6	0	0	0	0	....	....	....	....	....
1958-59	Toronto Maple Leafs	9	0	1	1	2	....	....	....	....	....
	NHL Totals	**33**	**1**	**5**	**6**	**2**	....	....	....	....	....

Traded to **Detroit** (Hershey-AHL) by **Toronto** (Pittsburgh-AHL) with Gilles Mayer, Jack Price, Bob Hassard, Bob Solinger and Ray Gariepy for cash, July 7, 1956. Traded to **Toronto** by **Hershey** (AHL) for Mike Nykoluk, Ron Hurst and the loan of Wally Boyer for the 1958-59 and 1959-60 seasons, April 29, 1958. Loaned to **Detroit** (Hershey-AHL) by **Toronto** with cash for Gerry Ehman, December 23, 1958. Traded to **Boston** (Providence-AHL) by **Hershey** (AHL) for Dan Poliziani, June, 1963.

MARSON, Mike

Left wing. Shoots left. 5'9", 200 lbs. Born, Scarborough, Ont., July 24, 1955.
(Washington's 2nd choice, 19th overall, in 1974 Amateur Draft).

Season	Club	Regular Season GP	G	A	Pts	PIM	Playoffs GP	G	A	Pts	PIM
1974-75	Washington Capitals	76	16	12	28	59	....	....	....	....	....
1975-76	Washington Capitals	57	4	7	11	50	....	....	....	....	....
1976-77	Washington Capitals	10	0	1	1	18	....	....	....	....	....
1977-78	Washington Capitals	46	4	4	8	101	....	....	....	....	....
1978-79	Washington Capitals	4	0	0	0	0	....	....	....	....	....
1979-80	Los Angeles Kings	3	0	0	0	5	....	....	....	....	....
	NHL Totals	**196**	**24**	**24**	**48**	**233**	....	....	....	....	....

Traded to **Los Angeles** by **Washington** for Steve Clippingdale, June 11, 1979.

MARTIN, Clare

Defense. Shoots right. 5'11", 180 lbs. Born, Waterloo, Ont., February 25, 1922.

Season	Club	Regular Season GP	G	A	Pts	PIM	Playoffs GP	G	A	Pts	PIM
1941-42	Boston Bruins	13	0	1	1	4	5	0	0	0	0
1946-47	Boston Bruins	6	3	0	3	0	5	0	1	1	0
1947-48	Boston Bruins	59	5	13	18	34	5	0	0	0	6
1949-50 ♦	Detroit Red Wings	64	2	5	7	14	10	0	1	1	0
1950-51	Detroit Red Wings	50	1	6	7	12	2	0	0	0	0
1951-52	Chicago Black Hawks	31	1	2	3	8	....	....	....	....	....
	New York Rangers	14	0	1	1	6	....	....	....	....	....
	NHL Totals	**237**	**12**	**28**	**40**	**78**	**27**	**0**	**2**	**2**	**6**

Traded to **Detroit** by **Boston** with Pete Babando, Lloyd Durham and Jimmy Peters for Bill Quackenbush and Pete Horeck, August 16, 1949. Traded to **Chicago** by **Detroit** with George Gee, Jimmy Peters Sr., Rags Raglan, Max McNab and Jim McFadden for $75,000 and future considerations (Hugh Coflin, October, 1951), August 20, 1951. Traded to **NY Rangers** by **Chicago** for cash, December 28, 1951.

MARTIN, Craig

Right wing. Shoots right. 6'2", 215 lbs. Born, Amherst, N.S., January 21, 1971.
(Winnipeg's 6th choice, 98th overall, in 1990 Entry Draft).

Season	Club	GP	G	A	Pts	PIM	GP	G	A	Pts	PIM
		REGULAR SEASON					PLAYOFFS				
1994-95	Winnipeg Jets	20	0	1	1	19	....	....	....	....	....
1996-97	Florida Panthers	1	0	0	0	5	....	....	....	....	....
	NHL Totals	**21**	**0**	**1**	**1**	**24**	....	....	....	....	....

Signed as a free agent by **Detroit**, July 28, 1993. Claimed on waivers by **Winnipeg** from **Detroit**, January 20, 1995. Signed as a free agent by **Florida**, August 1, 1996.

MARTIN, Frank

Defense. Shoots left. 6'2", 190 lbs. Born, Cayuga, Ont., May 1, 1933.

Season	Club	GP	G	A	Pts	PIM	GP	G	A	Pts	PIM
1952-53	Boston Bruins	14	0	2	2	6	6	0	1	1	2
1953-54	Boston Bruins	68	3	17	20	38	4	0	1	1	0
1954-55	Chicago Black Hawks	66	4	8	12	35	....	....	....	....	....
1955-56	Chicago Black Hawks	61	3	11	14	21	....	....	....	....	....
1956-57	Chicago Black Hawks	70	1	8	9	12	....	....	....	....	....
1957-58	Chicago Black Hawks	3	0	0	0	10	....	....	....	....	....
	NHL Totals	**282**	**11**	**46**	**57**	**122**	**10**	**0**	**2**	**2**	**2**

Played in NHL All-Star Game (1955)

Traded to **Chicago** by **Boston** for Murray Costello, October 4, 1954. Traded to **Buffalo** (AHL) by **Chicago** with Wally Hergesheimer for Ken Wharram, May 5, 1958. Claimed by **Providence** (AHL) from **Montreal** in Reverse Draft, June 9, 1965.

MARTIN, Grant

Left wing. Shoots left. 5'10", 190 lbs. Born, Smooth Rock Falls, Ont., March 13, 1962.
(Vancouver's 9th choice, 196th overall, in 1980 Entry Draft).

Season	Club	GP	G	A	Pts	PIM	GP	G	A	Pts	PIM
1983-84	Vancouver Canucks	12	0	2	2	6	....	....	....	....	....
1984-85	Vancouver Canucks	12	0	1	1	39	....	....	....	....	....
1985-86	Washington Capitals	11	0	1	1	6	....	....	....	....	....
1986-87	Washington Capitals	9	0	0	0	4	1	1	0	1	2
	NHL Totals	**44**	**0**	**4**	**4**	**55**	**1**	**1**	**0**	**1**	**2**

Signed as a free agent by **Washington**, August 6, 1985.

MARTIN, Jack

Center. Shoots left. 5'11", 184 lbs. Born, St. Catharines, Ont., November 29, 1940.

Season	Club	GP	G	A	Pts	PIM	GP	G	A	Pts	PIM
1960-61	Toronto Maple Leafs	1	0	0	0	0	....	....	....	....	....
	NHL Totals	**1**	**0**	**0**	**0**	**0**	....	....	....	....	....

MARTIN, Matt

Defense. Shoots left. 6'3", 230 lbs. Born, Hamden, CT, April 30, 1971.
(Toronto's 4th choice, 66th overall, in 1989 Entry Draft).

Season	Club	GP	G	A	Pts	PIM	GP	G	A	Pts	PIM
1993-94	Toronto Maple Leafs	12	0	1	1	6	....	....	....	....	....
1994-95	Toronto Maple Leafs	15	0	0	0	13	....	....	....	....	....
1995-96	Toronto Maple Leafs	13	0	0	0	14	....	....	....	....	....
1996-97	Toronto Maple Leafs	36	0	4	4	38	....	....	....	....	....
	NHL Totals	**76**	**0**	**5**	**5**	**71**	....	....	....	....	....

Signed as a free agent by **Dallas**, July 24, 1998.

MARTIN, Pit

Center. Shoots right. 5'9", 170 lbs. Born, Noranda, Que., December 9, 1943.

Season	Club	GP	G	A	Pts	PIM	GP	G	A	Pts	PIM
1961-62	Detroit Red Wings	1	0	1	1	0	....	....	....	....	....
1963-64	Detroit Red Wings	50	9	12	21	28	14	1	4	5	14
1964-65	Detroit Red Wings	58	8	9	17	32	3	0	1	1	2
1965-66	Detroit Red Wings	10	1	1	2	0	....	....	....	....	....
	Boston Bruins	41	16	11	27	10	....	....	....	....	....
1966-67	Boston Bruins	70	20	22	42	40	....	....	....	....	....
1967-68	Chicago Black Hawks	63	16	19	35	36	11	3	6	9	2
1968-69	Chicago Black Hawks	76	23	38	61	73	....	....	....	....	....
1969-70	Chicago Black Hawks	73	30	33	63	61	8	3	3	6	4
1970-71	Chicago Black Hawks	62	22	33	55	40	17	2	7	9	12
1971-72	Chicago Black Hawks	78	24	51	75	56	8	4	2	6	4
1972-73	Chicago Black Hawks	78	29	61	90	30	15	10	6	16	6
1973-74	Chicago Black Hawks	78	30	47	77	43	7	2	0	2	4
1974-75	Chicago Black Hawks	70	19	26	45	34	8	1	1	2	2
1975-76	Chicago Black Hawks	80	32	39	71	44	4	1	0	1	4
1976-77	Chicago Black Hawks	75	17	36	53	22	2	0	0	0	0
1977-78	Chicago Black Hawks	7	1	1	2	0	....	....	....	....	....
	Vancouver Canucks	67	15	31	46	36	....	....	....	....	....
1978-79	Vancouver Canucks	64	12	14	26	24	3	0	1	1	2
	NHL Totals	**1101**	**324**	**485**	**809**	**609**	**100**	**27**	**31**	**58**	**56**

Played in NHL All-Star Game (1971, 1972, 1973, 1974)

Traded to **Boston** by **Detroit** for Parker MacDonald, December 30, 1965. Traded to **Chicago** by **Boston** with Jack Norris and Gilles Marotte for Phil Esposito, Ken Hodge and Fred Stanfield, May 15, 1967. Traded to **Vancouver** by **Chicago** for future considerations (Murray Bannerman, May 27, 1978), November 4, 1977.

MARTIN, Rick

Left wing. Shoots left. 5'11", 179 lbs. Born, Verdun, Que., July 26, 1951.
(Buffalo's 1st choice, 5th overall, in 1971 Amateur Draft).

Season	Club	GP	G	A	Pts	PIM	GP	G	A	Pts	PIM
1971-72	Buffalo Sabres	73	44	30	74	36	....	....	....	....	....
1972-73	Buffalo Sabres	75	37	36	73	79	6	3	2	5	12
1973-74	Buffalo Sabres	78	52	34	86	38	....	....	....	....	....
1974-75	Buffalo Sabres	68	52	43	95	72	17	7	8	15	20
1975-76	Buffalo Sabres	80	49	37	86	67	9	4	7	11	12
1976-77	Buffalo Sabres	66	36	29	65	58	6	2	1	3	9
1977-78	Buffalo Sabres	65	28	35	63	16	7	2	4	6	13
1978-79	Buffalo Sabres	73	32	21	53	35	3	0	3	3	0
1979-80	Buffalo Sabres	80	45	34	79	54	14	6	4	10	8
1980-81	Buffalo Sabres	23	7	14	21	20	....	....	....	....	....
	Los Angeles Kings	1	1	1	2	0	1	0	0	0	0
1981-82	Los Angeles Kings	3	1	3	4	2	....	....	....	....	....
	NHL Totals	**685**	**384**	**317**	**701**	**477**	**63**	**24**	**29**	**53**	**74**

NHL First All-Star Team (1974, 1975) • NHL Second All-Star Team (1976, 1977)
Played in NHL All-Star Game (1972, 1973, 1974, 1975, 1976, 1977, 1978)

• Suffered eventual career-ending knee injury in game vs. Washington, November 8, 1980.
Traded to **Los Angeles** by **Buffalo** for Los Angeles' 3rd round choice (Colin Chisholm) in 1981 Entry Draft and 1st round choice (Tom Barrasso) in 1983 Entry Draft, March 10, 1981.

MARTIN, Ron

Right wing. Shoots right. 5'6", 130 lbs. Born, Calgary, Alta., August 22, 1909.

Season	Club	GP	G	A	Pts	PIM	GP	G	A	Pts	PIM
1932-33	New York Americans	47	5	7	12	6	....	....	....	....	....
1933-34	New York Americans	47	8	9	17	30	....	....	....	....	....
	NHL Totals	**94**	**13**	**16**	**29**	**36**	....	....	....	....	....

Claimed by **Detroit** from **Buffalo** (IHL) in Inter-League Draft, May 9, 1931. Traded to **NY Americans** by **Detroit** for Doug Young, October 18, 1931. Traded to **Syracuse** (IHL) by **NY Americans** with the loan of Walter Jackson for Lorne Carr, November 5, 1934.

MARTIN, Terry

Left wing. Shoots left. 5'11", 195 lbs. Born, Barrie, Ont., October 25, 1955.
(Buffalo's 3rd choice, 44th overall, in 1975 Amateur Draft).

Season	Club	GP	G	A	Pts	PIM	GP	G	A	Pts	PIM
1975-76	Buffalo Sabres	1	0	0	0	0	....	....	....	....	....
1976-77	Buffalo Sabres	62	11	12	23	8	3	0	2	2	5
1977-78	Buffalo Sabres	21	3	2	5	9	8	2	0	2	5
1978-79	Buffalo Sabres	64	6	8	14	33	....	....	....	....	....
1979-80	Quebec Nordiques	3	0	0	0	0	....	....	....	....	....
	Toronto Maple Leafs	37	6	15	21	2	3	2	0	2	7
1980-81	Toronto Maple Leafs	69	23	14	37	32	3	0	0	0	0
1981-82	Toronto Maple Leafs	72	25	24	49	39	....	....	....	....	....
1982-83	Toronto Maple Leafs	76	14	13	27	28	4	0	0	0	9
1983-84	Toronto Maple Leafs	63	15	10	25	51	....	....	....	....	....
1984-85	Edmonton Oilers	4	0	2	2	0	....	....	....	....	....
	Minnesota North Stars	7	1	1	2	0	....	....	....	....	....
	NHL Totals	**479**	**104**	**101**	**205**	**202**	**21**	**4**	**2**	**6**	**26**

Claimed by **Quebec** from **Buffalo** in Expansion Draft, June 13, 1979. Traded to **Toronto** by **Quebec** with Dave Farrish for Reg Thomas, December 13, 1979. Claimed by **Edmonton** from **Toronto** in Waiver Draft, October 9, 1984. Traded to **Minnesota** by **Edmonton** with Gord Sherven for Mark Napier, January 24, 1985.

MARTIN, Tom

Right wing. Shoots right. 5'9", 170 lbs. Born, Toronto, Ont., October 16, 1947.
(Toronto's 1st choice, 5th overall, in 1964 Amateur Draft).

Season	Club	GP	G	A	Pts	PIM	GP	G	A	Pts	PIM
1967-68	Toronto Maple Leafs	3	1	0	1	0	....	....	....	....	....
	NHL Totals	**3**	**1**	**0**	**1**	**0**	....	....	....	....	....

Traded to **Phoenix** (WHL) by **Toronto** for cash, May 22, 1970. Claimed by **Detroit** from **Phoenix** (WHL) in Intra-League Draft, June 9, 1970.

MARTIN, Tom

Left wing. Shoots left. 6'2", 200 lbs. Born, Kelowna, B.C., May 11, 1965.
(Winnipeg's 2nd choice, 74th overall, in 1982 Entry Draft).

Season	Club	GP	G	A	Pts	PIM	GP	G	A	Pts	PIM
1984-85	Winnipeg Jets	8	1	0	1	42	3	0	0	0	2
1985-86	Winnipeg Jets	5	0	0	0	0	....	....	....	....	....
1986-87	Winnipeg Jets	11	1	0	1	49	....	....	....	....	....
1987-88	Hartford Whalers	5	1	2	3	14	....	....	....	....	....
1988-89	Minnesota North Stars	4	1	1	2	4	....	....	....	....	....
	Hartford Whalers	38	7	6	13	113	1	0	0	0	4
1989-90	Hartford Whalers	21	1	2	3	27	....	....	....	....	....
	NHL Totals	**92**	**12**	**11**	**23**	**249**	**4**	**0**	**0**	**0**	**6**

Signed as a free agent by **Hartford**, July 29, 1987. Claimed by **Minnesota** from **Hartford** in Waiver Draft, October 3, 1988. Claimed on waivers by **Hartford** from **Minnesota**, December, 1988. Signed as a free agent by **Los Angeles**, July, 1990.

MARTINEAU, Don

Right wing. Shoots right. 6', 190 lbs. Born, Kimberley, B.C., April 25, 1952.
(Atlanta's 4th choice, 50th overall, in 1972 Amateur Draft).

Season	Club	GP	G	A	Pts	PIM	GP	G	A	Pts	PIM
1973-74	Atlanta Flames	4	0	0	0	2	....	....	....	....	....
1974-75	Minnesota North Stars	76	6	9	15	61	....	....	....	....	....
1975-76	Detroit Red Wings	9	0	1	1	0	....	....	....	....	....
1976-77	Detroit Red Wings	1	0	0	0	0	....	....	....	....	....
	NHL Totals	**90**	**6**	**10**	**16**	**63**	....	....	....	....	....

Traded to **Minnesota** by **Atlanta** with John Flesch for Buster Harvey and Jerry Byers, May 27, 1974. Traded to **Detroit** by **Minnesota** for Pierre Jarry, November 25, 1975.

MARTINEK, Radek

Defense. Shoots right. 6'1", 200 lbs. Born, Havlickuv Brod, Czech., August 31, 1976.
(NY Islanders' 12th choice, 228th overall, in 1999 Entry Draft).

Season	Club	GP	G	A	Pts	PIM	GP	G	A	Pts	PIM
2001-02	New York Islanders	23	1	4	5	16	....	....	....	....	....

Season	Club	GP	G	A	Pts	PIM	GP	G	A	Pts	PIM
		REGULAR SEASON					PLAYOFFS				
2002-03	New York Islanders	66	2	11	13	26	4	0	0	0	4
	NHL Totals	**89**	**3**	**15**	**18**	**42**	**4**	**0**	**0**	**0**	**4**

• Missed majority of 2001-02 season recovering from knee injury suffered in game vs. NY Rangers, November 11, 2001.

MARTINI, Darcy

Defense. Shoots left. 6'4", 220 lbs. Born, Castlegar, B.C., January 30, 1969.
(Edmonton's 8th choice, 162nd overall, in 1989 Entry Draft).

Season	Club	GP	G	A	Pts	PIM	GP	G	A	Pts	PIM
1993-94	Edmonton Oilers	2	0	0	0	0					
	NHL Totals	**2**	**0**	**0**	**0**	**0**					

MARTINS, Steve

Center. Shoots left. 5'9", 175 lbs. Born, Gatineau, Que., April 13, 1972.
(Hartford's 1st choice, 5th overall, in 1994 Supplemental Draft).

Season	Club	GP	G	A	Pts	PIM	GP	G	A	Pts	PIM
1995-96	Hartford Whalers	23	1	3	4	8					
1996-97	Hartford Whalers	2	0	1	1	0					
1997-98	Carolina Hurricanes	3	0	0	0	0					
1998-99	Ottawa Senators	36	4	3	7	10					
99-2000	Ottawa Senators	2	1	0	1	0					
	Tampa Bay Lightning	57	5	7	12	37					
2000-01	Tampa Bay Lightning	20	1	1	2	13					
	New York Islanders	39	1	3	4	20					
2001-02	Ottawa Senators	14	1	0	1	4	2	0	0	0	0
2002-03	Ottawa Senators	14	2	3	5	10					
	St. Louis Blues	28	3	3	6	18	2	0	1	1	0
	NHL Totals	**238**	**19**	**24**	**43**	**120**	**4**	**0**	**1**	**1**	**0**

Transferred to **Carolina** after **Hartford** franchise relocated, June 25, 1997. Signed as a free agent by **Ottawa**, July 20, 1998. Claimed on waivers by **Tampa Bay** from **Ottawa**, October 29, 1999. Traded to **NY Islanders** by **Tampa Bay** for future considerations, January 3, 2001. Signed as a free agent by **Ottawa**, August 30, 2001. Claimed on waivers by **St. Louis** from **Ottawa**, January 15, 2003.

MARTINSON, Steve

Left wing. Shoots left. 6'1", 205 lbs. Born, Minnetonka, MN, June 21, 1959.

Season	Club	GP	G	A	Pts	PIM	GP	G	A	Pts	PIM
1987-88	Detroit Red Wings	10	1	1	2	84					
1988-89	Montreal Canadiens	25	1	0	1	87	1	0	0	0	10
1989-90	Montreal Canadiens	13	0	0	0	64					
1991-92	Minnesota North Stars	1	0	0	0	9					
	NHL Totals	**49**	**2**	**1**	**3**	**244**	**1**	**0**	**0**	**0**	**10**

Signed as a free agent by **Philadelphia**, September 30, 1985. Signed as a free agent by **Detroit**, October 3, 1987. Signed as a free agent by **Montreal**, August 2, 1988. Signed as a free agent by **Winnipeg**, August 28, 1990. Signed as a free agent by **Minnesota**, October 1, 1991.

MARUK, Dennis

Center. Shoots left. 5'8", 175 lbs. Born, Toronto, Ont., November 17, 1955.
(California's 2nd choice, 21st overall, in 1975 Amateur Draft).

Season	Club	GP	G	A	Pts	PIM	GP	G	A	Pts	PIM
1975-76	California Golden Seals	80	30	32	62	44					
1976-77	Cleveland Barons	80	28	50	78	68					
1977-78	Cleveland Barons	76	36	35	71	50					
1978-79	Minnesota North Stars	2	0	0	0	0					
	Washington Capitals	76	31	59	90	71					
1979-80	Washington Capitals	27	10	17	27	8					
1980-81	Washington Capitals	80	50	47	97	87					
1981-82	Washington Capitals	80	60	76	136	128					
1982-83	Washington Capitals	80	31	50	81	71	4	1	1	2	2
1983-84	Minnesota North Stars	71	17	43	60	42	16	5	5	10	8
1984-85	Minnesota North Stars	71	19	41	60	56	9	4	7	11	12
1985-86	Minnesota North Stars	70	21	37	58	67	5	4	9	13	4
1986-87	Minnesota North Stars	67	16	30	46	52					
1987-88	Minnesota North Stars	22	7	4	11	15					
1988-89	Minnesota North Stars	6	0	1	1	2					
	NHL Totals	**888**	**356**	**522**	**878**	**761**	**34**	**14**	**22**	**36**	**26**

Played in NHL All-Star Game (1978, 1982)

Transferred to **Cleveland** after **California** franchise relocated, August 26, 1976. Protected by **Minnesota** prior to **Minnesota-Cleveland** Dispersal Draft, June 15, 1978. Traded to **Washington** by **Minnesota** for Pittsburgh's 1st round choice (previously acquired, Minnesota selected Tom McCarthy) in 1979 Entry Draft, October 18, 1978. Traded to **Minnesota** by **Washington** for Minnesota's 2nd round choice (Stephen Leach) in 1984 Entry Draft, July 5, 1983.

MASNICK, Paul

Center. Shoots right. 5'9", 165 lbs. Born, Regina, Sask., April 14, 1931.

Season	Club	GP	G	A	Pts	PIM	GP	G	A	Pts	PIM
1950-51	Montreal Canadiens	43	4	1	5	14	11	2	1	3	4
1951-52	Montreal Canadiens	15	1	2	3	2	6	1	0	1	12
1952-53 ♦	Montreal Canadiens	53	5	7	12	44	6	1	0	1	7
1953-54	Montreal Canadiens	50	5	21	26	57	10	0	4	4	4
1954-55	Montreal Canadiens	11	0	0	0	0					
	Chicago Black Hawks	11	1	0	1	8					
	Montreal Canadiens	8	0	1	1	0					
1957-58	Toronto Maple Leafs	41	2	9	11	14					
	NHL Totals	**232**	**18**	**41**	**59**	**139**	**33**	**4**	**5**	**9**	**27**

Signed as a free agent by **Montreal**, October 10, 1950. Traded to **Cincinnati** (AHL) by **Montreal** for Bobby Dawes, February 13, 1951. Loaned to **Chicago** by **Montreal** for cash and the loan of Al Dewsbury, November 9, 1954. Returned to **Montreal** by **Chicago**, December 10, 1954. Traded to **Toronto** by **Montreal** for cash, September 30, 1957.

MASON, Charley

Right wing. Shoots right. 5'10", 160 lbs. Born, Seaforth, Ont., February 1, 1912.

Season	Club	GP	G	A	Pts	PIM	GP	G	A	Pts	PIM
1934-35	New York Rangers	46	5	9	14	14	4	0	1	1	0
1935-36	New York Rangers	28	1	5	6	30					
1937-38	New York Americans	2	0	0	0	0					
1938-39	Detroit Red Wings	6	0	1	1	0					
	Chicago Black Hawks	13	1	3	4	0					
	NHL Totals	**95**	**7**	**18**	**25**	**44**	**4**	**0**	**1**	**1**	**0**

Traded to **NY Rangers** by **Vancouver** (NWHL) for cash, September 27, 1934. Traded to **NY Americans** by **NY Rangers** (Philadelphia-IAHL) for cash with NY Rangers holding right of recall, October 7, 1937. Traded to **Detroit** by **NY Rangers** for cash, October 21, 1938. Traded to **Chicago** by **Detroit** for Phil Besler, January 27, 1939. Traded to **Cleveland** (IAHL) by **Chicago** with Harold Jackson and $15,000 for Phil Hergesheimer, May 17, 1939.

MASSECAR, George

Left wing. Shoots left. 5'9", 165 lbs. Born, Waterford, Ont., July 10, 1904.

Season	Club	GP	G	A	Pts	PIM	GP	G	A	Pts	PIM
1929-30	New York Americans	43	7	3	10	18					
1930-31	New York Americans	43	4	7	11	16					
1931-32	New York Americans	14	1	1	2	12					
	NHL Totals	**100**	**12**	**11**	**23**	**46**					

Traded to **NY Americans** by **New Haven** (Can-Am) for Babe Dye, November 13, 1929. Traded to **St. Louis** (AHA) by **NY Americans** for Walter Jackson, October 30, 1932. Traded to **Detroit** by **St. Louis** (AHA) for cash, April 25, 1933. Traded to **Buffalo** (IHL) by **Detroit** (Detroit-IHL) for cash, October 31, 1934.

MASTERS, Jamie

Defense. Shoots right. 6'1", 190 lbs. Born, Toronto, Ont., April 14, 1955.
(St. Louis' 2nd choice, 36th overall, in 1975 Amateur Draft).

Season	Club	GP	G	A	Pts	PIM	GP	G	A	Pts	PIM
1975-76	St. Louis Blues	7	0	0	0	0	1	0	0	0	0
1976-77	St. Louis Blues	16	1	7	8	2	1	0	0	0	0
1978-79	St. Louis Blues	10	0	6	6	0					
	NHL Totals	**33**	**1**	**13**	**14**	**2**	**2**	**0**	**0**	**0**	**0**

Claimed by **Quebec** from **St. Louis** in Expansion Draft, June 13, 1979.

MASTERTON, Bill

Center. Shoots right. 6', 189 lbs. Born, Winnipeg, Man., August 13, 1938.

Season	Club	GP	G	A	Pts	PIM	GP	G	A	Pts	PIM
1967-68	Minnesota North Stars	38	4	8	12	4					
	NHL Totals	**38**	**4**	**8**	**12**	**4**					

Rights traded to **Minnesota** by **Montreal** for cash, June 14, 1967. • Died of head injury suffered in game vs. California (January 13, 1968), January 15, 1968.

MATHERS, Frank

HHOF

Defense. Shoots left. 6'1", 182 lbs. Born, Winnipeg, Man., March 29, 1924.

Season	Club	GP	G	A	Pts	PIM	GP	G	A	Pts	PIM
1948-49	Toronto Maple Leafs	15	1	2	3	2					
1949-50	Toronto Maple Leafs	6	0	1	1	2					
1951-52	Toronto Maple Leafs	2	0	0	0	0					
	NHL Totals	**23**	**1**	**3**	**4**	**4**					

Lester Patrick Trophy (1987)

Played in NHL All-Star Game (1948)

Rights traded to **Toronto** by **NY Rangers** with Cal Gardner, Bill Juzda and Rene Trudell for Wally Stanowski and Moe Morris, April 26, 1948.

MATHIASEN, Dwight

Right wing. Shoots right. 6'1", 190 lbs. Born, Brandon, Man., May 12, 1963.

Season	Club	GP	G	A	Pts	PIM	GP	G	A	Pts	PIM
1985-86	Pittsburgh Penguins	4	1	0	1	2					
1986-87	Pittsburgh Penguins	6	0	1	1	2					
1987-88	Pittsburgh Penguins	23	0	6	6	14					
	NHL Totals	**33**	**1**	**7**	**8**	**18**					

Signed as a free agent by **Pittsburgh**, March 31, 1986.

MATHIESON, Jim

Defense. Shoots left. 6'1", 209 lbs. Born, Kindersley, Sask., January 24, 1970.
(Washington's 3rd choice, 59th overall, in 1989 Entry Draft).

Season	Club	GP	G	A	Pts	PIM	GP	G	A	Pts	PIM
1989-90	Washington Capitals	2	0	0	0	4					
	NHL Totals	**2**	**0**	**0**	**0**	**4**					

MATHIEU, Marquis

Center. Shoots right. 5'11", 190 lbs. Born, Hartford, CT, May 31, 1973.

Season	Club	GP	G	A	Pts	PIM	GP	G	A	Pts	PIM
1998-99	Boston Bruins	9	0	0	0	8					
99-2000	Boston Bruins	6	0	2	2	4					
2000-01	Boston Bruins	1	0	0	0	2					
	NHL Totals	**16**	**0**	**2**	**2**	**14**					

Signed as a free agent by **Boston**, October 26, 1998.

MATTE, Christian

Right wing. Shoots right. 6', 190 lbs. Born, Hull, Que., January 20, 1975.
(Quebec's 8th choice, 153rd overall, in 1993 Entry Draft).

Season	Club	GP	G	A	Pts	PIM	GP	G	A	Pts	PIM
1996-97	Colorado Avalanche	5	1	1	2	0					
1997-98	Colorado Avalanche	5	0	0	0	6					
1998-99	Colorado Avalanche	7	1	1	2	0					
99-2000	Colorado Avalanche	5	0	1	1	4					

Season	Club	GP	G	A	Pts	PIM	GP	G	A	Pts	PIM
		REGULAR SEASON					PLAYOFFS				
2000-01	Minnesota Wild	3	0	0	0	2	....	....	....	....	....
	NHL Totals	**25**	**2**	**3**	**5**	**12**	....	....	....	....	....

Rights transferred to **Colorado** after **Quebec** franchise relocated, June 21, 1995. Signed as a free agent by **Minnesota**, July 11, 2000. Signed as a free agent by **Buffalo**, August 2, 2001.

MATTE, Joe

Defense. Shoots right. 5'11", 165 lbs. Born, Bourget, Ont., March 6, 1893.

Season	Club	GP	G	A	Pts	PIM	GP	G	A	Pts	PIM
1919-20	Toronto St. Pats	17	8	3	11	19	....	....	....	....	....
1920-21	Hamilton Tigers	21	6	9	15	29	....	....	....	....	....
1921-22	Hamilton Tigers	21	3	3	6	6	....	....	....	....	....
1925-26	Boston Bruins	3	0	0	0	0	....	....	....	....	....
	Montreal Canadiens	6	0	0	0	0	....	....	....	....	....
	NHL Totals	**68**	**17**	**15**	**32**	**54**	....	....	....	....	....

Signed as a free agent by **Toronto**, January 16, 1920. Traded to **Montreal** by **Toronto** with Goldie Prodgers for Harry Cameron, November 27, 1920. Traded to **Hamilton** by **Montreal** with Jack Coughlin, Goldie Prodgers and loan of Billy Coutu for 1920-21 season for Harry Mummery, Jack McDonald and Dave Ritchie, November 27, 1920. Traded to **Saskatoon** (WCHL) by **Hamilton** for cash, October 1, 1922. Signed as a free agent by **Boston**, December 5, 1925. Claimed on waivers by **Montreal** from **Boston**, January 15, 1926.

MATTE, Joe

Defense. Shoots right. 5'11", 178 lbs. Born, Bourget, Ont., March 15, 1909.

Season	Club	GP	G	A	Pts	PIM	GP	G	A	Pts	PIM
1929-30	Detroit Cougars	12	0	1	1	0	....	....	....	....	....
1942-43	Chicago Black Hawks	12	0	2	2	8	....	....	....	....	....
	NHL Totals	**24**	**0**	**3**	**3**	**8**	....	....	....	....	....

• Father of NFL player Tom Matte (Baltimore Colts 1961-1972). • Signed as a free agent by **Detroit**, September 12, 1929. Signed as a free agent by **Chicago**, September, 1942.

MATTEAU, Stephane

Left wing. Shoots left. 6'4", 215 lbs. Born, Rouyn-Noranda, Que., September 2, 1969.
(Calgary's 2nd choice, 25th overall, in 1987 Entry Draft).

Season	Club	GP	G	A	Pts	PIM	GP	G	A	Pts	PIM
1990-91	Calgary Flames	78	15	19	34	93	5	0	1	1	0
1991-92	Calgary Flames	4	1	0	1	19	....	....	....	....	....
	Chicago Blackhawks	20	5	8	13	45	18	4	6	10	24
1992-93	Chicago Blackhawks	79	15	18	33	98	3	0	1	1	2
1993-94	Chicago Blackhawks	65	15	16	31	55	....	....	....	....	....
	♦ New York Rangers	12	4	3	7	2	23	6	3	9	20
1994-95	New York Rangers	41	3	5	8	25	9	0	1	1	10
1995-96	New York Rangers	32	4	2	6	22	....	....	....	....	....
	St. Louis Blues	46	7	13	20	65	11	0	2	2	8
1996-97	St. Louis Blues	74	16	20	36	50	5	0	0	0	0
1997-98	San Jose Sharks	73	15	14	29	60	4	0	1	1	0
1998-99	San Jose Sharks	68	8	15	23	73	5	0	0	0	6
99-2000	San Jose Sharks	69	12	12	24	61	10	0	2	2	8
2000-01	San Jose Sharks	80	13	19	32	32	6	1	3	4	0
2001-02	San Jose Sharks	55	7	4	11	15	10	1	2	3	2
2002-03	Florida Panthers	52	4	4	8	27	....	....	....	....	....
	NHL Totals	**848**	**144**	**172**	**316**	**742**	**109**	**12**	**22**	**34**	**80**

• Missed majority of 1991-92 season recovering from thigh injury suffered in game vs. Los Angeles, October 10, 1991. Traded to **Chicago** by **Calgary** for Trent Yawney, December 16, 1991. Traded to **NY Rangers** by **Chicago** with Brian Noonan for Tony Amonte and the rights to Matt Oates, March 21, 1994. Traded to **St. Louis** by **NY Rangers** for Ian Laperriere, December 28, 1995. Traded to **San Jose** by **St. Louis** for Darren Turcotte, July 24, 1997. Signed as a free agent by **Florida**, August 2, 2002.

MATTEUCCI, Mike

Defense. Shoots left. 6'2", 210 lbs. Born, Trail, B.C., December 27, 1971.

Season	Club	GP	G	A	Pts	PIM	GP	G	A	Pts	PIM
2000-01	Minnesota Wild	3	0	0	0	2	....	....	....	....	....
2001-02	Minnesota Wild	3	0	0	0	2	....	....	....	....	....
	NHL Totals	**6**	**0**	**0**	**0**	**4**	....	....	....	....	....

Signed as a free agent by **Edmonton**, September 10, 1998. Traded to **Boston** by **Edmonton** for Kay Whitmore, December 29, 1999. Signed as a free agent by **Minnesota**, July 20, 2000. Signed as a free agent by **New Jersey**, July 12, 2002.

MATTIUSSI, Dick

Left wing. Shoots left. 5'10", 185 lbs. Born, Smooth Rock Falls, Ont., May 1, 1938.

Season	Club	GP	G	A	Pts	PIM	GP	G	A	Pts	PIM
1967-68	Pittsburgh Penguins	32	0	2	2	18	....	....	....	....	....
1968-69	Pittsburgh Penguins	12	0	2	2	14	....	....	....	....	....
	Oakland Seals	24	1	9	10	16	7	0	1	1	6
1969-70	Oakland Seals	65	4	10	14	38	1	0	0	0	0
1970-71	California Seals	67	3	8	11	38	....	....	....	....	....
	NHL Totals	**200**	**8**	**31**	**39**	**124**	**8**	**0**	**1**	**1**	**6**

Traded to **Springfield** (AHL) by **Toronto** (Rochester-AHL) with Jim Wilcox, Bill White, Roger Cote and the loan of Wally Boyer for Kent Douglas, June 7, 1962. Traded to **Cleveland** (AHL) by **Springfield** (AHL) for Wayne Larkin and Murray Davison, October 16, 1962. Traded to **Pittsburgh** by **Cleveland** (AHL) for cash, August 11, 1966. Loaned to **Cleveland** (AHL) by **Pittsburgh** for the 1966-67 season for cash, October, 1966. Traded to **Oakland** by **Pittsburgh** with Earl Ingarfield and Gene Ubriaco for Bryan Watson, George Swarbrick and Tracy Pratt, January 30, 1969.

MATVICHUK, Richard

Defense. Shoots left. 6'2", 215 lbs. Born, Edmonton, Alta., February 5, 1973.
(Minnesota's 1st choice, 8th overall, in 1991 Entry Draft).

Season	Club	GP	G	A	Pts	PIM	GP	G	A	Pts	PIM
1992-93	Minnesota North Stars	53	2	3	5	26	....	....	....	....	....
1993-94	Dallas Stars	25	0	3	3	22	7	1	1	2	12
1994-95	Dallas Stars	14	0	2	2	14	5	0	2	2	4
1995-96	Dallas Stars	73	6	16	22	71	....	....	....	....	....
1996-97	Dallas Stars	57	5	7	12	87	7	0	1	1	20
1997-98	Dallas Stars	74	3	15	18	63	16	1	1	2	14
1998-99 ♦	Dallas Stars	64	3	9	12	51	22	1	5	6	20
99-2000	Dallas Stars	70	4	21	25	42	23	2	5	7	14
2000-01	Dallas Stars	78	4	16	20	62	10	0	0	0	14
2001-02	Dallas Stars	82	9	12	21	52	....	....	....	....	....
2002-03	Dallas Stars	68	1	5	6	58	12	0	3	3	8
	NHL Totals	**658**	**37**	**109**	**146**	**548**	**102**	**5**	**18**	**23**	**106**

Transferred to **Dallas** after **Minnesota** franchise relocated, June 9, 1993.

MATZ, Johnny

Center. Shoots right. , Born, Omaha, NB, June 1, 1891.

Season	Club	GP	G	A	Pts	PIM	GP	G	A	Pts	PIM
1924-25	Montreal Canadiens	30	2	3	5	0	1	0	0	0	0
	Montreal Canadiens (Cup)	....	....	....	....	....	*4*	*0*	*0*	*0*	*2*
	NHL Totals	**30**	**2**	**3**	**5**	**0**	**1**	**0**	**0**	**0**	**0**

Traded to **Montreal** by **Saskatoon** (WCHL) for cash, November 25, 1924.

MAXNER, Wayne

Left wing. Shoots left. 5'11", 180 lbs. Born, Halifax, N.S., September 27, 1942.

Season	Club	GP	G	A	Pts	PIM	GP	G	A	Pts	PIM
1964-65	Boston Bruins	54	7	6	13	42	....	....	....	....	....
1965-66	Boston Bruins	8	1	3	4	6	....	....	....	....	....
	NHL Totals	**62**	**8**	**9**	**17**	**48**	....	....	....	....	....

Traded to **Hershey** (AHL) by **Boston** for cash, June, 1968.

MAXWELL, Brad

Defense. Shoots right. 6'2", 195 lbs. Born, Brandon, Man., July 8, 1957.
(Minnesota's 1st choice, 7th overall, in 1977 Amateur Draft).

Season	Club	GP	G	A	Pts	PIM	GP	G	A	Pts	PIM
1977-78	Minnesota North Stars	75	18	29	47	100	....	....	....	....	....
1978-79	Minnesota North Stars	70	9	28	37	145	....	....	....	....	....
1979-80	Minnesota North Stars	58	7	30	37	126	11	0	8	8	20
1980-81	Minnesota North Stars	27	3	13	16	98	18	3	11	14	35
1981-82	Minnesota North Stars	51	10	21	31	96	4	0	3	3	13
1982-83	Minnesota North Stars	77	11	28	39	157	9	5	6	11	23
1983-84	Minnesota North Stars	78	19	54	73	225	16	2	11	13	40
1984-85	Minnesota North Stars	18	3	7	10	53	....	....	....	....	....
	Quebec Nordiques	50	7	24	31	119	18	2	9	11	35
1985-86	Toronto Maple Leafs	52	8	18	26	108	3	0	1	1	12
1986-87	Vancouver Canucks	30	1	7	8	28	....	....	....	....	....
	New York Rangers	9	0	1	1	6	....	....	....	....	....
	Minnesota North Stars	17	2	7	9	31	....	....	....	....	....
	NHL Totals	**612**	**98**	**270**	**368**	**1292**	**79**	**12**	**49**	**61**	**178**

Played in NHL All-Star Game (1984)

Traded to **Quebec** by **Minnesota** with Brent Ashton for Tony McKegney and Bo Berglund, December 14, 1984. Traded to **Toronto** by **Quebec** for John Anderson, August 21, 1985. Traded to **Vancouver** by **Toronto** for Vancouver's 5th round choice (Len Esau) in 1988 Entry Draft, October 3, 1986. Claimed on waivers by **NY Rangers** from **Vancouver**, January 20, 1987. Traded to **Minnesota** by **NY Rangers** for future considerations, February 21, 1987.

MAXWELL, Bryan

Defense. Shoots left. 6'2", 200 lbs. Born, North Bay, Ont., September 7, 1955.
(Minnesota's 1st choice, 4th overall, in 1975 Amateur Draft).

Season	Club	GP	G	A	Pts	PIM	GP	G	A	Pts	PIM
1977-78	Minnesota North Stars	18	2	5	7	41	....	....	....	....	....
1978-79	Minnesota North Stars	25	1	6	7	46	....	....	....	....	....
1979-80	St. Louis Blues	57	1	11	12	112	1	0	0	0	9
1980-81	St. Louis Blues	40	3	10	13	137	11	0	1	1	54
1981-82	Winnipeg Jets	45	1	9	10	110	....	....	....	....	....
1982-83	Winnipeg Jets	54	7	13	20	131	3	1	0	1	23
1983-84	Winnipeg Jets	3	0	3	3	27	....	....	....	....	....
	Pittsburgh Penguins	45	3	12	15	84	....	....	....	....	....
1984-85	Pittsburgh Penguins	44	0	8	8	57	....	....	....	....	....
	NHL Totals	**331**	**18**	**77**	**95**	**745**	**15**	**1**	**1**	**2**	**86**

Signed as a free agent by **Minnesota** after securing release from **New England** (WHA), February, 1978. Traded to **St. Louis** by **Minnesota** with Richie Hansen for St. Louis' 2nd round choice (later traded to Calgary – Calgary selected Dave Reierson) in 1982 Entry Draft, June 10, 1979. Traded to **Winnipeg** by **St. Louis** with Paul MacLean and Ed Staniowski for Scott Campbell and John Markell, July 3, 1981. Claimed on waivers by **Pittsburgh** from **Winnipeg**, October 13, 1983.

MAXWELL, Kevin

Center. Shoots right. 5'9", 165 lbs. Born, Edmonton, Alta., March 30, 1960.
(Minnesota's 4th choice, 63rd overall, in 1979 Entry Draft).

Season	Club	GP	G	A	Pts	PIM	GP	G	A	Pts	PIM
1980-81	Minnesota North Stars	6	0	3	3	7	16	3	4	7	24
1981-82	Minnesota North Stars	12	1	4	5	8	....	....	....	....	....
	Colorado Rockies	34	5	5	10	44	....	....	....	....	....
1983-84	New Jersey Devils	14	0	3	3	2	....	....	....	....	....
	NHL Totals	**66**	**6**	**15**	**21**	**61**	**16**	**3**	**4**	**7**	**24**

Traded to **Colorado** by **Minnesota** with the rights to Jim Dobson for cash, December 31, 1981. Transferred to **New Jersey** after **Colorado** franchise relocated, June 30, 1982.

MAXWELL, Wally

Center. Shoots left. 5'10", 158 lbs. Born, Ottawa, Ont., August 24, 1933.

Season	Club	GP	G	A	Pts	PIM	GP	G	A	Pts	PIM
1952-53	Toronto Maple Leafs	2	0	0	0	0	....	....	....	....	....
	NHL Totals	**2**	**0**	**0**	**0**	**0**	....	....	....	....	....

MAY, Alan

Right wing. Shoots right. 6'1", 200 lbs. Born, Swan Hills, Alta., January 14, 1965.

Season	Club	Regular Season GP	G	A	Pts	PIM	Playoffs GP	G	A	Pts	PIM
1987-88	Boston Bruins	3	0	0	0	15	....	....	....	....	....
1988-89	Edmonton Oilers	3	1	0	1	7	....	....	....	....	....
1989-90	Washington Capitals	77	7	10	17	339	15	0	0	0	37
1990-91	Washington Capitals	67	4	6	10	264	11	1	1	2	37
1991-92	Washington Capitals	75	6	9	15	221	7	0	0	0	0
1992-93	Washington Capitals	83	6	10	16	268	6	0	1	1	6
1993-94	Washington Capitals	43	4	7	11	97	....	....	....	....	....
	Dallas Stars	8	1	0	1	18	1	0	0	0	0
1994-95	Dallas Stars	27	1	1	2	106	....	....	....	....	....
	Calgary Flames	7	1	2	3	13	....	....	....	....	....
	NHL Totals	**393**	**31**	**45**	**76**	**1348**	**40**	**1**	**2**	**3**	**80**

Signed as a free agent by **Boston**, October 30, 1987. Traded to **Edmonton** by **Boston** for Moe Lemay, March 8, 1988. Traded to **Los Angeles** by **Edmonton** with Jim Wiemer for Brian Wilks and John English, March 7, 1989. Traded to **Washington** by **Los Angeles** for Washington's 5th round choice (Thomas Newman) in 1989 Entry Draft, June 17, 1989. Traded to **Dallas** by **Washington** with Washington's 7th round choice (Jeff Dewar) in 1995 Entry Draft for Jim Johnson, March 21, 1994. Traded to **Calgary** by **Dallas** for Calgary's 8th round choice (Sergei Luchinkin) in 1995 Entry Draft, April 7, 1995.

MAY, Brad

Left wing. Shoots left. 6'1", 217 lbs. Born, Toronto, Ont., November 29, 1971.
(Buffalo's 1st choice, 14th overall, in 1990 Entry Draft).

Season	Club	Regular Season GP	G	A	Pts	PIM	Playoffs GP	G	A	Pts	PIM
1991-92	Buffalo Sabres	69	11	6	17	309	7	1	4	5	2
1992-93	Buffalo Sabres	82	13	13	26	242	8	1	1	2	14
1993-94	Buffalo Sabres	84	18	27	45	171	7	0	2	2	9
1994-95	Buffalo Sabres	33	3	3	6	87	4	0	0	0	2
1995-96	Buffalo Sabres	79	15	29	44	295	....	....	....	....	....
1996-97	Buffalo Sabres	42	3	4	7	106	10	1	1	2	32
1997-98	Buffalo Sabres	36	4	7	11	113	....	....	....	....	....
	Vancouver Canucks	27	9	3	12	41	....	....	....	....	....
1998-99	Vancouver Canucks	66	6	11	17	102	....	....	....	....	....
99-2000	Vancouver Canucks	59	9	7	16	90	....	....	....	....	....
2000-01	Phoenix Coyotes	62	11	14	25	107	....	....	....	....	....
2001-02	Phoenix Coyotes	72	10	12	22	95	5	0	0	0	0
2002-03	Phoenix Coyotes	20	3	4	7	32	....	....	....	....	....
	Vancouver Canucks	3	0	0	0	10	14	0	0	0	15
	NHL Totals	**734**	**115**	**140**	**255**	**1800**	**55**	**3**	**8**	**11**	**74**

Traded to **Vancouver** by **Buffalo** with Buffalo's 3rd round choice (later traded to Tampa Bay – Tampa Bay selected Jimmie Olvestad) in 1999 Entry Draft for Geoff Sanderson, February 4, 1998. Traded to **Phoenix** by **Vancouver** for future considerations, June 24, 2000. Traded to **Vancouver** by **Phoenix** for Phoenix's 3rd round choice (previously acquired, Phoenix selected Dimitri Pestunov), March 11, 2003.

MAYER, Derek

Defense. Shoots right. 6', 200 lbs. Born, Rossland, B.C., May 21, 1967.
(Detroit's 3rd choice, 43rd overall, in 1986 Entry Draft).

Season	Club	Regular Season GP	G	A	Pts	PIM	Playoffs GP	G	A	Pts	PIM
1993-94	Ottawa Senators	17	2	2	4	8	....	....	....	....	....
	NHL Totals	**17**	**2**	**2**	**4**	**8**	....	....	....	....	....

Signed as a free agent by **Ottawa**, March 4, 1994.

MAYER, Jim

Right wing. Shoots right. 6', 190 lbs. Born, Capreol, Ont., October 30, 1954.
(NY Rangers' 20th choice, 239th overall, in 1974 Amateur Draft).

Season	Club	Regular Season GP	G	A	Pts	PIM	Playoffs GP	G	A	Pts	PIM
1979-80	New York Rangers	4	0	0	0	0	....	....	....	....	....
	NHL Totals	**4**	**0**	**0**	**0**	**0**	....	....	....	....	....

Reclaimed by **NY Rangers** from **Edmonton** prior to Expansion Draft, June 9, 1979. Traded to **Vancouver** by **NY Rangers** with Mario Marois for Jeff Bandura and Jere Gillis, November 11, 1980. Traded to **Colorado** by **Vancouver** for Mike Christie, December, 1980.

MAYER, Pat

Defense. Shoots left. 6'3", 225 lbs. Born, Royal Oak, MI, July 24, 1961.

Season	Club	Regular Season GP	G	A	Pts	PIM	Playoffs GP	G	A	Pts	PIM
1987-88	Pittsburgh Penguins	1	0	0	0	4	....	....	....	....	....
	NHL Totals	**1**	**0**	**0**	**0**	**4**	....	....	....	....	....

Signed as a free agent by **Pittsburgh**, July 10, 1987. Traded to **Los Angeles** by **Pittsburgh** for Tim Tookey, March 7, 1989.

MAYER, Shep

Right wing. Shoots right. 5'8", 180 lbs. Born, Sturgeon Falls, Ont., September 11, 1923.

Season	Club	Regular Season GP	G	A	Pts	PIM	Playoffs GP	G	A	Pts	PIM
1942-43	Toronto Maple Leafs	12	1	2	3	4	....	....	....	....	....
	NHL Totals	**12**	**1**	**2**	**3**	**4**	....	....	....	....	....

MAYERS, Jamal

Right wing. Shoots right. 6'1", 212 lbs. Born, Toronto, Ont., October 24, 1974.
(St. Louis' 3rd choice, 89th overall, in 1993 Entry Draft).

Season	Club	Regular Season GP	G	A	Pts	PIM	Playoffs GP	G	A	Pts	PIM
1996-97	St. Louis Blues	6	0	1	1	2	....	....	....	....	....
1998-99	St. Louis Blues	34	4	5	9	40	11	0	1	1	8
99-2000	St. Louis Blues	79	7	10	17	90	7	0	4	4	2
2000-01	St. Louis Blues	77	8	13	21	117	15	2	3	5	8
2001-02	St. Louis Blues	77	9	8	17	99	10	3	0	3	2
2002-03	St. Louis Blues	15	2	5	7	8	....	....	....	....	....
	NHL Totals	**288**	**30**	**42**	**72**	**356**	**43**	**5**	**8**	**13**	**20**

MAZUR, Eddie

Defense/Left wing. Shoots left. 6'2", 186 lbs. Born, Winnipeg, Man., July 25, 1929.

Season	Club	Regular Season GP	G	A	Pts	PIM	Playoffs GP	G	A	Pts	PIM
1950-51	Montreal Canadiens	....	....	....	....	....	2	0	0	0	0
1951-52	Montreal Canadiens	....	....	....	....	....	5	2	0	2	4
1952-53 ♦	Montreal Canadiens	....	....	....	....	....	7	2	2	4	11
1953-54	Montreal Canadiens	67	7	14	21	95	11	0	3	3	7
1954-55	Montreal Canadiens	25	1	5	6	21	....	....	....	....	....
1956-57	Chicago Black Hawks	15	0	1	1	4	....	....	....	....	....
	NHL Totals	**107**	**8**	**20**	**28**	**120**	**25**	**4**	**5**	**9**	**22**

Played in NHL All-Star Game (1953)

Signed as a free agent by **Montreal**, September 27, 1948. Traded to **Chicago** by **Montreal** for $5,000 with Montreal holding right of recall, May 24, 1956. Returned to **Montreal** (Rochester-AHL) by **Chicago**, November, 1956. Signed as a free agent by **Toronto** (Victoria-WHL), September, 1964. Traded to **Baltimore** (AHL) by **Toronto** for cash, September, 1965.

MAZUR, Jay

Center/Right wing. Shoots right. 6'2", 205 lbs. Born, Hamilton, Ont., January 22, 1965.
(Vancouver's 12th choice, 240th overall, in 1983 Entry Draft).

Season	Club	Regular Season GP	G	A	Pts	PIM	Playoffs GP	G	A	Pts	PIM
1988-89	Vancouver Canucks	1	0	0	0	0	....	....	....	....	....
1989-90	Vancouver Canucks	5	0	0	0	4	....	....	....	....	....
1990-91	Vancouver Canucks	36	11	7	18	14	6	0	1	1	8
1991-92	Vancouver Canucks	5	0	0	0	2	....	....	....	....	....
	NHL Totals	**47**	**11**	**7**	**18**	**20**	**6**	**0**	**1**	**1**	**8**

McADAM, Gary

Left wing. Shoots left. 5'11", 175 lbs. Born, Smiths Falls, Ont., December 31, 1955.
(Buffalo's 4th choice, 53rd overall, in 1975 Amateur Draft).

Season	Club	Regular Season GP	G	A	Pts	PIM	Playoffs GP	G	A	Pts	PIM
1975-76	Buffalo Sabres	31	1	2	3	2	1	0	0	0	0
1976-77	Buffalo Sabres	73	13	16	29	17	6	1	0	1	0
1977-78	Buffalo Sabres	79	19	22	41	44	8	2	2	4	7
1978-79	Buffalo Sabres	40	6	5	11	13	....	....	....	....	....
	Pittsburgh Penguins	28	5	9	14	2	7	2	1	3	0
1979-80	Pittsburgh Penguins	78	19	22	41	63	5	1	2	3	9
1980-81	Pittsburgh Penguins	34	3	9	12	30	....	....	....	....	....
	Detroit Red Wings	40	5	14	19	27	....	....	....	....	....
1981-82	Calgary Flames	46	12	15	27	18	3	0	0	0	0
1982-83	Buffalo Sabres	4	1	0	1	0	....	....	....	....	....
1983-84	Washington Capitals	24	1	5	6	12	....	....	....	....	....
	New Jersey Devils	38	9	6	15	15	....	....	....	....	....
1984-85	New Jersey Devils	4	1	1	2	0	....	....	....	....	....
1985-86	Toronto Maple Leafs	15	1	6	7	0	....	....	....	....	....
	NHL Totals	**534**	**96**	**132**	**228**	**243**	**30**	**6**	**5**	**11**	**16**

Traded to **Pittsburgh** by **Buffalo** for Dave Schultz, February 6, 1979. Traded to **Detroit** by **Pittsburgh** for Errol Thompson, January 8, 1981. Traded to **Calgary** by **Detroit** with Detroit's 4th round choice (John Bekkers) in 1983 Entry Draft for Eric Vail, November 10, 1981. Signed as a free agent by **Buffalo**, September 17, 1982. Signed as a free agent by **New Jersey**, August 4, 1983. Claimed on waivers by **Washington** from **New Jersey**, November 17, 1983. Rights traded to **New Jersey** by **Washington** for cash, January 18, 1984. Signed as a free agent by **Toronto**, July 31, 1985.

McADAM, Sam

Center/Left wing. Shoots left. 5'8", 175 lbs. Born, Sterling, Scotland, May 31, 1908.

Season	Club	Regular Season GP	G	A	Pts	PIM	Playoffs GP	G	A	Pts	PIM
1930-31	New York Rangers	5	0	0	0	0	....	....	....	....	....
	NHL Totals	**5**	**0**	**0**	**0**	**0**	....	....	....	....	....

Traded to **NY Rangers** by **Vancouver** (PCHL) for $7,000, January 3, 1931.

McALLISTER, Chris

Defense. Shoots left. 6'8", 240 lbs. Born, Saskatoon, Sask., June 16, 1975.
(Vancouver's 1st choice, 40th overall, in 1995 Entry Draft).

Season	Club	Regular Season GP	G	A	Pts	PIM	Playoffs GP	G	A	Pts	PIM
1997-98	Vancouver Canucks	36	1	2	3	106	....	....	....	....	....
1998-99	Vancouver Canucks	28	1	1	2	63	....	....	....	....	....
	Toronto Maple Leafs	20	0	2	2	39	6	0	1	1	4
99-2000	Toronto Maple Leafs	36	0	3	3	68	....	....	....	....	....
2000-01	Philadelphia Flyers	60	2	2	4	124	2	0	0	0	0
2001-02	Philadelphia Flyers	42	0	5	5	113	....	....	....	....	....
2002-03	Philadelphia Flyers	19	0	0	0	21	....	....	....	....	....
	Colorado Avalanche	14	0	1	1	26	1	0	0	0	0
	NHL Totals	**255**	**4**	**16**	**20**	**560**	**9**	**0**	**1**	**1**	**4**

Traded to **Toronto** by **Vancouver** for Darby Hendrickson, February 16, 1999. Traded to **Philadelphia** by **Toronto** for the rights to Regan Kelly, September 26, 2000. Traded to **Colorado** by **Philadelphia** for Colorado's 6th round choice (Ville Hostikka) in 2003 Entry Draft, February 5, 2003.

McALPINE, Chris

Defense. Shoots right. 6', 210 lbs. Born, Roseville, MN, December 1, 1971.
(New Jersey's 10th choice, 137th overall, in 1990 Entry Draft).

Season	Club	Regular Season GP	G	A	Pts	PIM	Playoffs GP	G	A	Pts	PIM
1994-95 ♦	New Jersey Devils	24	0	3	3	17	....	....	....	....	....
1996-97	St. Louis Blues	15	0	0	0	24	4	0	1	1	0
1997-98	St. Louis Blues	54	3	7	10	36	10	0	0	0	16
1998-99	St. Louis Blues	51	1	1	2	50	13	0	0	0	2
99-2000	St. Louis Blues	21	1	1	2	14	....	....	....	....	....
	Tampa Bay Lightning	10	1	1	2	10	....	....	....	....	....
	Atlanta Thrashers	3	0	0	0	2	....	....	....	....	....
2000-01	Chicago Blackhawks	50	0	6	6	32	....	....	....	....	....
2001-02	Chicago Blackhawks	40	0	3	3	36	1	0	0	0	0

Season	Club	GP	G	A	Pts	PIM	GP	G	A	Pts	PIM
		REGULAR SEASON					PLAYOFFS				
2002-03	Los Angeles Kings	21	0	2	2	24	....	....	....	....	....
	NHL Totals	**289**	**6**	**24**	**30**	**245**	**28**	**0**	**1**	**1**	**18**

Traded to **St. Louis** by **New Jersey** with New Jersey's 9th round choice (James Desmarais) in 1999 Entry Draft for Peter Zezel, February 11, 1997. Traded to **Tampa Bay** by **St. Louis** with Rich Parent for Stephane Richer, January 13, 2000. Traded to **Atlanta** by **Tampa Bay** for Mikko Kuparinen, March 11, 2000. Signed as a free agent by **Chicago**, July 27, 2000. Signed as a free agent by **Los Angeles**, August 27, 2002.

McAMMOND, Dean

Left wing. Shoots left. 5'11", 193 lbs. Born, Grand Cache, Alta., June 15, 1973.
(Chicago's 1st choice, 22nd overall, in 1991 Entry Draft).

Season	Club	GP	G	A	Pts	PIM	GP	G	A	Pts	PIM
1991-92	Chicago Blackhawks	5	0	2	2	0	3	0	0	0	2
1993-94	Edmonton Oilers	45	6	21	27	16	....	....	....	....	....
1994-95	Edmonton Oilers	6	0	0	0	0	....	....	....	....	....
1995-96	Edmonton Oilers	53	15	15	30	23	....	....	....	....	....
1996-97	Edmonton Oilers	57	12	17	29	28	....	....	....	....	....
1997-98	Edmonton Oilers	77	19	31	50	46	12	1	4	5	12
1998-99	Edmonton Oilers	65	9	16	25	36	....	....	....	....	....
	Chicago Blackhawks	12	1	4	5	2	....	....	....	....	....
99-2000	Chicago Blackhawks	76	14	18	32	72	....	....	....	....	....
2000-01	Chicago Blackhawks	61	10	16	26	43	....	....	....	....	....
	Philadelphia Flyers	10	1	1	2	0	4	0	0	0	2
2001-02	Calgary Flames	73	21	30	51	60	....	....	....	....	....
2002-03	Colorado Avalanche	41	10	8	18	10	....	....	....	....	....
	NHL Totals	**581**	**118**	**179**	**297**	**336**	**19**	**1**	**4**	**5**	**16**

Traded to **Edmonton** by **Chicago** with Igor Kravchuk for Joe Murphy, February 24, 1993. Traded to **Chicago** by **Edmonton** with Boris Mironov and Jonas Elofsson for Chad Kilger, Daniel Cleary, Ethan Moreau and Christian Laflamme, March 20, 1999. Traded to **Philadelphia** by **Chicago** for Philadelphia's 3rd round choice (later traded to Toronto – Toronto selected Nicolas Corbeil) in 2001 Entry Draft, March 13, 2001. Traded to **Calgary** by **Philadelphia** for Calgary's 4th round choice (Rosario Ruggeri) in 2002 Entry Draft, June 24, 2001. Traded to **Colorado** by **Calgary** with Derek Morris and Jeff Shantz for Chris Drury and Stephane Yelle, October 1, 2002. Traded to **Calgary** by **Colorado** for Calgary's 5th round choice (Mark McCutcheon) in 2003 Entry Draft, March 11, 2003.

McANDREW, Hazen

Defense. Shoots left. 5'10", 175 lbs. Born, Mayo, Yukon, August 7, 1917.

Season	Club	GP	G	A	Pts	PIM	GP	G	A	Pts	PIM
1941-42	Brooklyn Americans	7	0	1	1	6	....	....	....	....	....
	NHL Totals	**7**	**0**	**1**	**1**	**6**	....	....	....	....	....

Signed as a free agent by **NY Americans** (Springfield-AHL), February 21, 1941.

McANEELEY, Ted

Defense. Shoots left. 5'9", 185 lbs. Born, Cranbrook, B.C., November 7, 1950.
(California's 4th choice, 47th overall, in 1970 Amateur Draft).

Season	Club	GP	G	A	Pts	PIM	GP	G	A	Pts	PIM
1972-73	California Golden Seals	77	4	13	17	75	....	....	....	....	....
1973-74	California Golden Seals	72	4	20	24	62	....	....	....	....	....
1974-75	California Golden Seals	9	0	2	2	4	....	....	....	....	....
	NHL Totals	**158**	**8**	**35**	**43**	**141**	....	....	....	....	....

McATEE, Jud

Left wing. Shoots left. 5'9", 170 lbs. Born, Stratford, Ont., February 5, 1920.

Season	Club	GP	G	A	Pts	PIM	GP	G	A	Pts	PIM
1942-43	Detroit Red Wings	1	0	0	0	0	....	....	....	....	....
1943-44	Detroit Red Wings	1	0	2	2	0	....	....	....	....	....
1944-45	Detroit Red Wings	44	15	11	26	6	14	2	1	3	0
	NHL Totals	**46**	**15**	**13**	**28**	**6**	**14**	**2**	**1**	**3**	**0**

• Brother of Norm

Signed as a free agent by **Detroit**, October 16, 1940. Traded to **Chicago** (St. Louis-AHL) by **Detroit** (Indianapolis-AHL) with Norm McAtee, George Ritchie and Roy Sawyer for Doug McCaig, George Blake and cash, December 26, 1945.

McATEE, Norm

Center. Shoots left. 5'8", 165 lbs. Born, Stratford, Ont., June 28, 1921.

Season	Club	GP	G	A	Pts	PIM	GP	G	A	Pts	PIM
1946-47	Boston Bruins	13	0	1	1	0	....	....	....	....	....
	NHL Totals	**13**	**0**	**1**	**1**	**0**	....	....	....	....	....

• Brother of Jud

Traded to **Chicago** (St. Louis-AHL) by **Detroit** (Indianapolis-AHL) with Jud McAtee, George Ritchie and Roy Sawyer for Doug McCaig, George Blake and cash, December 26, 1945. Traded to **Boston** (Hershey-AHL) by **Chicago** (St. Louis-AHL) for Bill Jennings, February 5, 1946.

McAVOY, George

Defense. Shoots left. 6', 185 lbs. Born, Edmonton, Alta., June 21, 1931.

Season	Club	GP	G	A	Pts	PIM	GP	G	A	Pts	PIM
1954-55	Montreal Canadiens	....	....	....	....	....	4	0	0	0	0
	NHL Totals	....	....	....	....	....	**4**	**0**	**0**	**0**	**0**

McBAIN, Andrew

Right wing. Shoots right. 6'1", 205 lbs. Born, Scarborough, Ont., January 18, 1965.
(Winnipeg's 1st choice, 8th overall, in 1983 Entry Draft).

Season	Club	GP	G	A	Pts	PIM	GP	G	A	Pts	PIM
1983-84	Winnipeg Jets	78	11	19	30	37	3	2	0	2	0
1984-85	Winnipeg Jets	77	7	15	22	45	7	1	0	1	0
1985-86	Winnipeg Jets	28	3	3	6	17	....	....	....	....	....
1986-87	Winnipeg Jets	71	11	21	32	106	9	0	2	2	10
1987-88	Winnipeg Jets	74	32	31	63	145	5	2	5	7	29
1988-89	Winnipeg Jets	80	37	40	77	71	....	....	....	....	....
1989-90	Pittsburgh Penguins	41	5	9	14	51	....	....	....	....	....
	Vancouver Canucks	26	4	5	9	22	....	....	....	....	....
1990-91	Vancouver Canucks	13	0	5	5	32	....	....	....	....	....
1991-92	Vancouver Canucks	6	1	0	1	0	....	....	....	....	....
1992-93	Ottawa Senators	59	7	16	23	43	....	....	....	....	....
1993-94	Ottawa Senators	55	11	8	19	64	....	....	....	....	....
	NHL Totals	**608**	**129**	**172**	**301**	**633**	**24**	**5**	**7**	**12**	**39**

• Missed majority of 1985-86 season recovering from knee injury suffered in game vs. Los Angeles, December 8, 1985. Traded to **Pittsburgh** by **Winnipeg** with Jim Kyte and Randy Gilhen for Randy Cunneyworth, Rick Tabaracci and Dave McLlwain, June 17, 1989. Traded to **Vancouver** by **Pittsburgh** with Dave Capuano and Dan Quinn for Rod Buskas, Barry Pederson and Tony Tanti, January 8, 1990. Signed as a free agent by **Ottawa**, July 30, 1992.

McBAIN, Jason

Defense. Shoots left. 6'2", 180 lbs. Born, Ilion, NY, April 12, 1974.
(Hartford's 5th choice, 81st overall, in 1992 Entry Draft).

Season	Club	GP	G	A	Pts	PIM	GP	G	A	Pts	PIM
1995-96	Hartford Whalers	3	0	0	0	0	....	....	....	....	....
1996-97	Hartford Whalers	6	0	0	0	0	....	....	....	....	....
	NHL Totals	**9**	**0**	**0**	**0**	**0**	....	....	....	....	....

Transferred to **Carolina** after **Hartford** franchise relocated, June 25, 1997. Signed as a free agent by **Montreal**, August 23, 1999.

McBAIN, Mike

Defense. Shoots left. 6'2", 195 lbs. Born, Kimberley, B.C., January 12, 1977.
(Tampa Bay's 2nd choice, 30th overall, in 1995 Entry Draft).

Season	Club	GP	G	A	Pts	PIM	GP	G	A	Pts	PIM
1997-98	Tampa Bay Lightning	27	0	1	1	8	....	....	....	....	....
1998-99	Tampa Bay Lightning	37	0	6	6	14	....	....	....	....	....
	NHL Totals	**64**	**0**	**7**	**7**	**22**	....	....	....	....	....

Traded to **Montreal** by **Tampa Bay** for Gordie Dwyer, November 26, 1999.

McBEAN, Wayne

Defense. Shoots left. 6'2", 185 lbs. Born, Calgary, Alta., February 21, 1969.
(Los Angeles' 1st choice, 4th overall, in 1987 Entry Draft).

Season	Club	GP	G	A	Pts	PIM	GP	G	A	Pts	PIM
1987-88	Los Angeles Kings	27	0	1	1	26	....	....	....	....	....
1988-89	Los Angeles Kings	33	0	5	5	23	....	....	....	....	....
	New York Islanders	19	0	1	1	12	....	....	....	....	....
1989-90	New York Islanders	5	0	1	1	2	2	1	1	2	0
1990-91	New York Islanders	52	5	14	19	47	....	....	....	....	....
1991-92	New York Islanders	25	2	4	6	18	....	....	....	....	....
1993-94	New York Islanders	19	1	4	5	16	....	....	....	....	....
	Winnipeg Jets	31	2	9	11	24	....	....	....	....	....
	NHL Totals	**211**	**10**	**39**	**49**	**100**	**2**	**1**	**1**	**2**	**0**

Traded to **NY Islanders** by **Los Angeles** with Mark Fitzpatrick and future considerations (Doug Crossman, May 23, 1989) for Kelly Hrudey, February 22, 1989. • Missed remainder of 1991-92 season recovering from knee injury suffered in game vs. Pittsburgh, December 23, 1991. Traded to **Winnipeg** by **NY Islanders** for Yan Kaminsky, February 1, 1994. Claimed by **Pittsburgh** from **Winnipeg** in Waiver Draft, January 18, 1995.

McBRIDE, Cliff

Right wing/Defense. Shoots right. 5'10", 180 lbs. Born, Toronto, Ont., January 10, 1909.

Season	Club	GP	G	A	Pts	PIM	GP	G	A	Pts	PIM
1928-29	Montreal Maroons	1	0	0	0	0	....	....	....	....	....
1929-30	Toronto Maple Leafs	1	0	0	0	0	....	....	....	....	....
	NHL Totals	**2**	**0**	**0**	**0**	**0**	....	....	....	....	....

Traded to **Toronto** by **Mtl. Maroons** for cash, October 23, 1929. Loaned to **London** (IHL) by **Toronto**, November 12, 1929. Traded to **Toronto Millionaires** (IHL) by **Toronto** for cash, February 6, 1930.

McBURNEY, Jim

Left wing. Shoots left. 5'7", 150 lbs. Born, Sault Ste. Marie, Ont., June 3, 1933.

Season	Club	GP	G	A	Pts	PIM	GP	G	A	Pts	PIM
1952-53	Chicago Black Hawks	1	0	1	1	0	....	....	....	....	....
	NHL Totals	**1**	**0**	**1**	**1**	**0**	....	....	....	....	....

McCABE, Bryan

Defense. Shoots left. 6'2", 213 lbs. Born, St. Catharines, Ont., June 8, 1975.
(NY Islanders' 2nd choice, 40th overall, in 1993 Entry Draft).

Season	Club	GP	G	A	Pts	PIM	GP	G	A	Pts	PIM
1995-96	New York Islanders	82	7	16	23	156	....	....	....	....	....
1996-97	New York Islanders	82	8	20	28	165	....	....	....	....	....
1997-98	New York Islanders	56	3	9	12	145	....	....	....	....	....
	Vancouver Canucks	26	1	11	12	64	....	....	....	....	....
1998-99	Vancouver Canucks	69	7	14	21	120	....	....	....	....	....
99-2000	Chicago Blackhawks	79	6	19	25	139	....	....	....	....	....
2000-01	Toronto Maple Leafs	82	5	24	29	123	11	2	3	5	16
2001-02	Toronto Maple Leafs	82	17	26	43	129	20	5	5	10	30
2002-03	Toronto Maple Leafs	75	6	18	24	135	7	0	3	3	10
	NHL Totals	**633**	**60**	**157**	**217**	**1176**	**38**	**7**	**11**	**18**	**56**

Traded to **Vancouver** by **NY Islanders** with Todd Bertuzzi and NY Islanders' 3rd round choice (Jarkko Ruutu) in 1998 Entry Draft for Trevor Linden, February 6, 1998. Traded to **Chicago** by **Vancouver** with Vancouver's 1st round choice (Pavel Vorobiev) in 2000 Entry Draft for Chicago's 1st round choice (later traded to Tampa Bay – later traded to NY Rangers – NY Rangers selected Pavel Brendl) in 1999 Entry Draft, June 25, 1999. Traded to **Toronto** by **Chicago** for Alexander Karpovtsev and Toronto's 4th round choice (Vladimir Gusev) in 2001 Entry Draft, October 2, 2000.

McCABE, Stan

Left wing. Shoots left. 5'6", 165 lbs. Born, Ottawa, Ont., June 16, 1908.

Season	Club	GP	G	A	Pts	PIM	GP	G	A	Pts	PIM
1929-30	Detroit Cougars	25	7	3	10	23	....	....	....	....	....
1930-31	Detroit Falcons	44	2	1	3	22	....	....	....	....	....
1932-33	Montreal Maroons	1	0	0	0	0	....	....	....	....	....

Season	Club	Regular Season GP	G	A	Pts	PIM	Playoffs GP	G	A	Pts	PIM
1933-34	Montreal Maroons	8	0	0	0	4	....	....	....	....	....
	NHL Totals	**78**	**9**	**4**	**13**	**49**	....	....	....	....	....

Signed as a free agent by **Detroit**, November 1, 1927. Claimed on waivers by **Mtl. Maroons** from **Detroit**, November 14, 1932. Traded to **Quebec** (Can-Am) by **Mtl. Maroons** for cash, November 27, 1932. Traded to **Mtl. Maroons** by **Montreal** (Quebec-Can-Am) for Paul Runge, December 6, 1933.

McCAFFREY, Bert

Right wing/Defense. Shoots right. 5'10", 180 lbs. Born, Chesley, Ont.,

Season	Club	GP	G	A	Pts	PIM	GP	G	A	Pts	PIM
1924-25	Toronto St. Pats	30	10	6	16	12	2	1	0	1	4
1925-26	Toronto St. Pats	36	14	7	21	42	....	....	....	....	....
1926-27	Toronto St. Pats/Maple Leafs	43	5	5	10	43	....	....	....	....	....
1927-28	Toronto Maple Leafs	9	1	1	2	9	....	....	....	....	....
	Pittsburgh Pirates	35	6	3	9	14	....	....	....	....	....
1928-29	Pittsburgh Pirates	42	1	0	1	34	....	....	....	....	....
1929-30	Pittsburgh Pirates	15	3	4	7	12	....	....	....	....	....
	♦ Montreal Canadiens	28	1	3	4	26	6	1	1	2	6
1930-31	Montreal Canadiens	22	2	1	3	10	....	....	....	....	....
	NHL Totals	**260**	**43**	**30**	**73**	**202**	**8**	**2**	**1**	**3**	**10**

Signed as a free agent by **Toronto**, October 16, 1924. Traded to **Pittsburgh** by **Toronto** to complete three team transaction that sent Ty Arbour to Chicago and Eddie Rodden to Toronto, December, 1927. Traded to **Montreal** by **Pittsburgh** for Gord Fraser, December 23, 1929.

McCAHILL, John

Defense. Shoots right. 6'1", 215 lbs. Born, Sarnia, Ont., December 2, 1955.

Season	Club	GP	G	A	Pts	PIM	GP	G	A	Pts	PIM
1977-78	Colorado Rockies	1	0	0	0	0	....	....	....	....	....
	NHL Totals	**1**	**0**	**0**	**0**	**0**	....	....	....	....	....

Signed as a free agent by **Colorado**, March 17, 1978.

McCAIG, Doug

Defense. Shoots right. 6', 190 lbs. Born, Guelph, Ont., February 24, 1919.

Season	Club	GP	G	A	Pts	PIM	GP	G	A	Pts	PIM
1941-42	Detroit Red Wings	9	0	1	1	6	2	0	0	0	6
1945-46	Detroit Red Wings	6	0	1	1	12	....	....	....	....	....
1946-47	Detroit Red Wings	47	2	4	6	62	5	0	1	1	4
1947-48	Detroit Red Wings	29	3	3	6	37	....	....	....	....	....
1948-49	Detroit Red Wings	1	0	0	0	0	....	....	....	....	....
	Chicago Black Hawks	55	1	3	4	60	....	....	....	....	....
1949-50	Chicago Black Hawks	63	0	4	4	49	....	....	....	....	....
1950-51	Chicago Black Hawks	53	2	5	7	29	....	....	....	....	....
	NHL Totals	**263**	**8**	**21**	**29**	**255**	**7**	**0**	**1**	**1**	**10**

Signed as a free agent by **Detroit**, December 31, 1940. Signed as a free agent by **St. Louis** (AHL), October, 1945. Traded to **Detroit** (Indianapolis-AHL) by **Chicago** (St. Louis-AHL) with George Blake and cash for Norm McAtee, Jud McAtee, George Ritchie and Roy Sawyer, December 26, 1945. Traded to **Chicago** by **Detroit** with Jim Conacher and Bep Guidolin for George Gee and Bud Poile, October 25, 1948. Traded to **Detroit** by **Chicago** for Max Quackenbush, September 18, 1951.

McCALLUM, Dunc

Defense. Shoots right. 6'1", 193 lbs. Born, Flin Flon, Man., March 29, 1940.

Season	Club	GP	G	A	Pts	PIM	GP	G	A	Pts	PIM
1965-66	New York Rangers	2	0	0	0	2	....	....	....	....	....
1967-68	Pittsburgh Penguins	32	0	2	2	36	....	....	....	....	....
1968-69	Pittsburgh Penguins	62	5	13	18	81	....	....	....	....	....
1969-70	Pittsburgh Penguins	14	0	0	0	16	10	1	2	3	12
1970-71	Pittsburgh Penguins	77	9	20	29	95	....	....	....	....	....
	NHL Totals	**187**	**14**	**35**	**49**	**230**	**10**	**1**	**2**	**3**	**12**

Claimed by **Detroit** from **Vancouver** (WHL) in Inter-League Draft, June 8, 1965. Traded to **NY Rangers** by **Detroit** (Pittsburgh-AHL) for Bob Cunningham, June, 1965. Traded to **Pittsburgh** by **NY Rangers** with George Konik, Paul Andrea and Frank Francis for Larry Jeffrey, June 6, 1967. Selected by **Providence** (AHL) from **Pittsburgh** in Reverse Draft, June 12, 1969. Suspended by **Providence** (AHL) for refusing to report to club, October, 1969. Traded to **Pittsburgh** by **Providence** (AHL) for cash, January, 1970.

McCALMON, Eddie

Right wing. Shoots right. 5'8", 170 lbs. Born, Varney, Ont., May 30, 1902.

Season	Club	GP	G	A	Pts	PIM	GP	G	A	Pts	PIM
1927-28	Chicago Black Hawks	23	2	0	2	8	....	....	....	....	....
1930-31	Philadelphia Quakers	16	3	0	3	6	....	....	....	....	....
	NHL Totals	**39**	**5**	**0**	**5**	**14**	....	....	....	....	....

Traded to **Chicago** by **Saskatoon** (PrHL) with Earl Miller for Nick Wasnie and Corb Denneny, January 11, 1928. Signed as a free agent by **Philadelphia**, December 15, 1930.

McCANN, Rick

Center. Shoots left. 5'9", 178 lbs. Born, Hamilton, Ont., May 27, 1944.

Season	Club	GP	G	A	Pts	PIM	GP	G	A	Pts	PIM
1967-68	Detroit Red Wings	3	0	0	0	0	....	....	....	....	....
1968-69	Detroit Red Wings	3	0	0	0	0	....	....	....	....	....
1969-70	Detroit Red Wings	18	0	1	1	4	....	....	....	....	....
1970-71	Detroit Red Wings	5	0	0	0	0	....	....	....	....	....
1971-72	Detroit Red Wings	1	0	0	0	0	....	....	....	....	....
1974-75	Detroit Red Wings	13	1	3	4	2	....	....	....	....	....
	NHL Totals	**43**	**1**	**4**	**5**	**6**	....	....	....	....	....

Signed as a free agent by **Detroit** (Memphis-CPHL), September, 1967.

McCARTHY, Dan

Center. Shoots left. 5'9", 185 lbs. Born, St. Marys, Ont., April 7, 1958.
(NY Rangers' 16th choice, 223rd overall, in 1978 Amateur Draft).

Season	Club	GP	G	A	Pts	PIM	GP	G	A	Pts	PIM
1980-81	New York Rangers	5	4	0	4	4	....	....	....	....	....
	NHL Totals	**5**	**4**	**0**	**4**	**4**	....	....	....	....	....

Traded to **Minnesota** by **NY Rangers** for Shawn Dineen, August 23, 1982.

McCARTHY, Kevin

Defense. Shoots right. 5'11", 195 lbs. Born, Winnipeg, Man., July 14, 1957.
(Philadelphia's 1st choice, 17th overall, in 1977 Amateur Draft).

Season	Club	GP	G	A	Pts	PIM	GP	G	A	Pts	PIM
1977-78	Philadelphia Flyers	62	2	15	17	32	10	0	1	1	8
1978-79	Philadelphia Flyers	22	1	2	3	21	....	....	....	....	....
	Vancouver Canucks	1	0	0	0	0	....	....	....	....	....
1979-80	Vancouver Canucks	79	15	30	45	70	4	1	0	1	0
1980-81	Vancouver Canucks	80	16	37	53	85	3	0	1	1	0
1981-82	Vancouver Canucks	71	6	39	45	84	....	....	....	....	....
1982-83	Vancouver Canucks	74	12	28	40	88	4	1	1	2	12
1983-84	Vancouver Canucks	47	2	14	16	61	....	....	....	....	....
	Pittsburgh Penguins	31	4	16	20	52	....	....	....	....	....
1984-85	Pittsburgh Penguins	64	9	10	19	30	....	....	....	....	....
1985-86	Philadelphia Flyers	4	0	0	0	4	....	....	....	....	....
1986-87	Philadelphia Flyers	2	0	0	0	0	....	....	....	....	....
	NHL Totals	**537**	**67**	**191**	**258**	**527**	**21**	**2**	**3**	**5**	**20**

Played in NHL All-Star Game (1981)

Traded to **Vancouver** by **Philadelphia** with Drew Callander for Dennis Ververgaert, December 29, 1978. Traded to **Pittsburgh** by **Vancouver** for Philadelphia's 3rd round choice (previously acquired, later traded back to Philadelphia – Philadelphia selected David McClay) in 1984 Entry Draft, January 26, 1984. Signed as a free agent by **Philadelphia**, July 19, 1985.

McCARTHY, Sandy

Right wing. Shoots right. 6'3", 225 lbs. Born, Toronto, Ont., June 15, 1972.
(Calgary's 3rd choice, 52nd overall, in 1991 Entry Draft).

Season	Club	GP	G	A	Pts	PIM	GP	G	A	Pts	PIM
1993-94	Calgary Flames	79	5	5	10	173	7	0	0	0	34
1994-95	Calgary Flames	37	5	3	8	101	6	0	1	1	17
1995-96	Calgary Flames	75	9	7	16	173	4	0	0	0	10
1996-97	Calgary Flames	33	3	5	8	113	....	....	....	....	....
1997-98	Calgary Flames	52	8	5	13	170	....	....	....	....	....
	Tampa Bay Lightning	14	0	5	5	71	....	....	....	....	....
1998-99	Tampa Bay Lightning	67	5	7	12	135	....	....	....	....	....
	Philadelphia Flyers	13	0	1	1	25	6	0	1	1	0
99-2000	Philadelphia Flyers	58	6	5	11	111	....	....	....	....	....
	Carolina Hurricanes	13	0	0	0	9	....	....	....	....	....
2000-01	New York Rangers	81	11	10	21	171	....	....	....	....	....
2001-02	New York Rangers	82	10	13	23	171	....	....	....	....	....
2002-03	New York Rangers	82	6	9	15	81	....	....	....	....	....
	NHL Totals	**686**	**68**	**75**	**143**	**1504**	**23**	**0**	**2**	**2**	**61**

Traded to **Tampa Bay** by **Calgary** with Calgary's 3rd (Brad Richards) and 5th (Curtis Rich) round choices in 1998 Entry Draft for Jason Wiemer, March 24, 1998. Traded to **Philadelphia** by **Tampa Bay** with Mikael Andersson for Colin Forbes and Philadelphia's 4th round choice (Michal Lanicek) in 1999 Entry Draft, March 20, 1999. Traded to **Carolina** by **Philadelphia** for Kent Manderville, March 14, 2000. Traded to **NY Rangers** by **Carolina** with Carolina's' 4th round choice (Bryce Lampman) in 2001 Entry Draft for Darren Langdon and Rob DiMaio, August 4, 2000.

McCARTHY, Steve

Defense. Shoots left. 6'1", 197 lbs. Born, Trail, B.C., February 3, 1981.
(Chicago's 1st choice, 23rd overall, in 1999 Entry Draft).

Season	Club	GP	G	A	Pts	PIM	GP	G	A	Pts	PIM
99-2000	Chicago Blackhawks	5	1	1	2	4	....	....	....	....	....
2000-01	Chicago Blackhawks	44	0	5	5	8	....	....	....	....	....
2001-02	Chicago Blackhawks	3	0	0	0	2	....	....	....	....	....
2002-03	Chicago Blackhawks	57	1	4	5	23	....	....	....	....	....
	NHL Totals	**109**	**2**	**10**	**12**	**37**	....	....	....	....	....

McCARTHY, Thomas

Right wing. Shoots right. 5'11", 165 lbs. Born, Hamilton, Ont.,

Season	Club	GP	G	A	Pts	PIM	GP	G	A	Pts	PIM
1919-20	Quebec Bulldogs	12	12	6	18	0	....	....	....	....	....
1920-21	Hamilton Tigers	23	10	1	11	10	....	....	....	....	....
	NHL Totals	**35**	**22**	**7**	**29**	**10**	....	....	....	....	....

Signed as a free agent by **Quebec**, February 2, 1920. Transferred to **Hamilton** after **Quebec** franchise relocated, November 2, 1920.

McCARTHY, Tom

Left wing. Shoots left. 6'2", 200 lbs. Born, Toronto, Ont., July 31, 1960.
(Minnesota's 2nd choice, 10th overall, in 1979 Entry Draft).

Season	Club	GP	G	A	Pts	PIM	GP	G	A	Pts	PIM
1979-80	Minnesota North Stars	68	16	20	36	39	15	5	6	11	20
1980-81	Minnesota North Stars	62	23	25	48	62	8	0	3	3	6
1981-82	Minnesota North Stars	40	12	30	42	36	4	0	2	2	4
1982-83	Minnesota North Stars	80	28	48	76	59	9	2	4	6	9
1983-84	Minnesota North Stars	66	39	31	70	49	8	1	4	5	6
1984-85	Minnesota North Stars	44	16	21	37	36	7	0	2	2	0
1985-86	Minnesota North Stars	25	12	12	24	12	....	....	....	....	....
1986-87	Boston Bruins	68	30	29	59	31	4	1	1	2	4

Season	Club	REGULAR SEASON GP	G	A	Pts	PIM	PLAYOFFS GP	G	A	Pts	PIM
1987-88	Boston Bruins	7	2	5	7	6	13	3	4	7	18
	NHL Totals	**460**	**178**	**221**	**399**	**330**	**68**	**12**	**26**	**38**	**67**

Played in NHL All-Star Game (1983)

• Missed majority of 1985-86 season recovering from Bells Palsy, November 23, 1985. Traded to **Boston** by **Minnesota** for Boston's 3rd round choice (Rob Zettler) in 1986 Entry Draft and 2nd round choice (Scott McGrady) in 1987 Entry Draft, May 16, 1986.

McCARTHY, Tom

Left wing. Shoots left. 6'1", 191 lbs. Born, Toronto, Ont., September 15, 1934.

Season	Club	GP	G	A	Pts	PIM	GP	G	A	Pts	PIM
1956-57	Detroit Red Wings	3	0	0	0	0	....	....	....	....	....
1957-58	Detroit Red Wings	18	2	1	3	4	....	....	....	....	....
1958-59	Detroit Red Wings	15	2	3	5	4	....	....	....	....	....
1960-61	Boston Bruins	24	4	5	9	0	....	....	....	....	....
	NHL Totals	**60**	**8**	**9**	**17**	**8**	....	....	....	....	....

Traded to **NY Rangers** by **Toronto** for $2,000, August 29, 1955. Claimed by **Detroit** from **NY Rangers** in Intra-League Draft, September, 1956. Traded to **Boston** by **Detroit** with Murray Oliver and Gary Aldcorn for Vic Stasiuk and Leo Labine, January 23, 1961. Traded to **Toronto** by **Boston** for cash, August, 1964. Claimed by **Montreal** from **Toronto** (Tulsa-CPHL) in Inter-League Draft, June 8, 1965. Rights transferred to **Vancouver** (WHL) after WHL club purchased **Rochester** (AHL) franchise, August 13, 1968. NHL rights transferred to **Vancouver** after NHL club purchased **Vancouver** (WHL) franchise, December 19, 1969.

McCARTNEY, Walt

Left wing. Shoots left. 5'10", 160 lbs. Born, Regina, Sask., April 26, 1911.

Season	Club	GP	G	A	Pts	PIM	GP	G	A	Pts	PIM
1932-33	Montreal Canadiens	2	0	0	0	0	....	....	....	....	....
	NHL Totals	**2**	**0**	**0**	**0**	**0**	....	....	....	....	....

McCARTY, Darren

Right wing. Shoots right. 6'1", 210 lbs. Born, Burnaby, B.C., April 1, 1972.
(Detroit's 2nd choice, 46th overall, in 1992 Entry Draft).

Season	Club	GP	G	A	Pts	PIM	GP	G	A	Pts	PIM
1993-94	Detroit Red Wings	67	9	17	26	181	7	2	2	4	8
1994-95	Detroit Red Wings	31	5	8	13	88	18	3	2	5	14
1995-96	Detroit Red Wings	63	15	14	29	158	19	3	2	5	20
1996-97 ♦	Detroit Red Wings	68	19	30	49	126	20	3	4	7	34
1997-98 ♦	Detroit Red Wings	71	15	22	37	157	22	3	8	11	34
1998-99	Detroit Red Wings	69	14	26	40	108	10	1	1	2	23
99-2000	Detroit Red Wings	24	6	6	12	48	9	0	1	1	12
2000-01	Detroit Red Wings	72	12	10	22	123	6	1	0	1	2
2001-02 ♦	Detroit Red Wings	62	5	7	12	98	23	4	4	8	34
2002-03	Detroit Red Wings	73	13	9	22	138	4	0	0	0	6
	NHL Totals	**600**	**113**	**149**	**262**	**1225**	**138**	**20**	**24**	**44**	**187**

• Missed majority of 1999-2000 season recovering from hernia injury suffered in game vs. Dallas, November 10, 1999.

McCASKILL, Ted

Center. Shoots left. 6'1", 195 lbs. Born, Kapuskasing, Ont., October 29, 1936.

Season	Club	GP	G	A	Pts	PIM	GP	G	A	Pts	PIM
1967-68	Minnesota North Stars	4	0	2	2	0	....	....	....	....	....
	NHL Totals	**4**	**0**	**2**	**2**	**0**	....	....	....	....	....

• Father of major league pitcher Kirk McCaskill. Signed as a free agent by **Minnesota** (Memphis-CPHL), September, 1967. Claimed on waivers by **Vancouver** (WHL) from **Minnesota**, November, 1968. NHL rights transferred to **Vancouver** after NHL club purchased **Vancouver** (WHL) franchise, December 19, 1969. Traded to **Toronto** (Phoenix-WHL) by **Vancouver** with Pat Hannigan for Andre Hinse, August, 1970.

McCAULEY, Alyn

Center. Shoots left. 5'11", 190 lbs. Born, Brockville, Ont., May 29, 1977.
(New Jersey's 5th choice, 79th overall, in 1995 Entry Draft).

Season	Club	GP	G	A	Pts	PIM	GP	G	A	Pts	PIM
1997-98	Toronto Maple Leafs	60	6	10	16	6	....	....	....	....	....
1998-99	Toronto Maple Leafs	39	9	15	24	2	....	....	....	....	....
99-2000	Toronto Maple Leafs	45	5	5	10	10	5	0	0	0	6
2000-01	Toronto Maple Leafs	14	1	0	1	0	10	0	0	0	2
2001-02	Toronto Maple Leafs	82	6	10	16	18	20	5	10	15	4
2002-03	Toronto Maple Leafs	64	6	9	15	16	....	....	....	....	....
	San Jose Sharks	16	3	7	10	4	....	....	....	....	....
	NHL Totals	**320**	**36**	**56**	**92**	**56**	**35**	**5**	**10**	**15**	**12**

Rights traded to **Toronto** by **New Jersey** with Jason Smith and Steve Sullivan for Doug Gilmour, Dave Ellett and New Jersey's 3rd round choice (previously acquired, New Jersey selected Andre Lakos) in 1999 Entry Draft, February 25, 1997. Traded to **San Jose** by **Toronto** with Brad Boyes and Toronto's 1st round choice (later traded to Boston – Boston selected Mark Stuart) in 2003 Entry Draft for Owen Nolan, March 5, 2003.

McCLANAHAN, Rob

Center. Shoots right. 5'10", 180 lbs. Born, St. Paul, MN, January 9, 1958.
(Buffalo's 3rd choice, 49th overall, in 1978 Amateur Draft).

Season	Club	GP	G	A	Pts	PIM	GP	G	A	Pts	PIM
1979-80	Buffalo Sabres	13	2	5	7	0	10	0	1	1	4
1980-81	Buffalo Sabres	53	3	12	15	38	5	0	1	1	13
1981-82	Hartford Whalers	17	0	3	3	11	....	....	....	....	....
	New York Rangers	22	5	9	14	10	10	2	5	7	2
1982-83	New York Rangers	78	22	26	48	46	9	2	5	7	12
1983-84	New York Rangers	41	6	8	14	21	....	....	....	....	....
	NHL Totals	**224**	**38**	**63**	**101**	**126**	**34**	**4**	**12**	**16**	**31**

Claimed by **Hartford** from **Buffalo** in Waiver Draft, October 6, 1981. Traded to **NY Rangers** by **Hartford** for NY Rangers' 10th round choice (Reine Karlsson) in 1983 Entry Draft, February 2, 1982. Traded to **Detroit** by **NY Rangers** for future considerations, May 23, 1984. Traded to **Vancouver** by **Detroit** for Tiger Williams, August 8, 1984.

McCLEARY, Trent

Right wing. Shoots right. 6', 182 lbs. Born, Swift Current, Sask., September 8, 1972.

Season	Club	GP	G	A	Pts	PIM	GP	G	A	Pts	PIM
1995-96	Ottawa Senators	75	4	10	14	68	....	....	....	....	....
1996-97	Boston Bruins	59	3	5	8	33	....	....	....	....	....
1998-99	Montreal Canadiens	46	0	0	0	29	....	....	....	....	....
99-2000	Montreal Canadiens	12	1	0	1	4	....	....	....	....	....
	NHL Totals	**192**	**8**	**15**	**23**	**134**	....	....	....	....	....

Signed as a free agent by **Ottawa**, October 9, 1992. Traded to **Boston** by **Ottawa** with Ottawa's 3rd round choice (Eric Naud) in 1996 Entry Draft for Shawn McEachern, June 22, 1996. Signed as a free agent by **Montreal**, October 9, 1998. • Suffered career-ending throat injury in game vs. Philadelphia, January 29, 2000. • Officially announced retirement, September 20, 2000.

McCLELLAND, Kevin

Right wing. Shoots right. 6'2", 205 lbs. Born, Oshawa, Ont., July 4, 1962.
(Hartford's 4th choice, 71st overall, in 1980 Entry Draft).

Season	Club	GP	G	A	Pts	PIM	GP	G	A	Pts	PIM
1981-82	Pittsburgh Penguins	10	1	4	5	4	5	1	1	2	5
1982-83	Pittsburgh Penguins	38	5	4	9	73	....	....	....	....	....
1983-84	Pittsburgh Penguins	24	2	4	6	62	....	....	....	....	....
♦	Edmonton Oilers	52	8	20	28	127	18	4	6	10	42
1984-85 ♦	Edmonton Oilers	62	8	15	23	205	18	1	3	4	75
1985-86	Edmonton Oilers	79	11	25	36	266	10	1	0	1	32
1986-87 ♦	Edmonton Oilers	72	12	13	25	238	21	2	3	5	43
1987-88 ♦	Edmonton Oilers	74	10	6	16	281	19	2	3	5	68
1988-89	Edmonton Oilers	79	6	14	20	161	7	0	2	2	16
1989-90	Edmonton Oilers	10	1	1	2	13	....	....	....	....	....
	Detroit Red Wings	61	4	5	9	183	....	....	....	....	....
1990-91	Detroit Red Wings	3	0	0	0	7	....	....	....	....	....
1991-92	Toronto Maple Leafs	18	0	1	1	33	....	....	....	....	....
1993-94	Winnipeg Jets	6	0	0	0	19	....	....	....	....	....
	NHL Totals	**588**	**68**	**112**	**180**	**1672**	**98**	**11**	**18**	**29**	**281**

Transferred to **Pittsburgh** by **Hartford** with Pat Boutette as compensation for Hartford's signing of free agent Greg Millen, June 29, 1981. • Missed majority of 1982-83 season recovering from a shoulder injury suffered in game vs. Toronto, January 24, 1983. Traded to **Edmonton** by **Pittsburgh** with Pittsburgh's 6th round choice (Emanuel Viveiros) in 1984 Entry Draft for Tom Roulston, December 5, 1983. Traded to **Detroit** by **Edmonton** with Jimmy Carson and Edmonton's 5th round choice (later traded to Montreal – Montreal selected Brad Layzell) in 1991 Entry Draft for Petr Klima, Joe Murphy, Adam Graves and Jeff Sharples, November 2, 1989. Signed as a free agent by **Toronto**, September 2, 1991. Traded to **Winnipeg** by **Toronto** for cash, August 12, 1993. Traded to **Buffalo** by **Winnipeg** for future considerations, July 8, 1994.

McCORD, Bob

Defense. Shoots right. 6'1", 202 lbs. Born, Matheson, Ont., March 30, 1934.

Season	Club	GP	G	A	Pts	PIM	GP	G	A	Pts	PIM
1963-64	Boston Bruins	65	1	9	10	49	....	....	....	....	....
1964-65	Boston Bruins	43	0	6	6	26	....	....	....	....	....
1965-66	Detroit Red Wings	9	0	2	2	16	....	....	....	....	....
1966-67	Detroit Red Wings	14	1	2	3	27	....	....	....	....	....
1967-68	Detroit Red Wings	3	0	0	0	2	....	....	....	....	....
	Minnesota North Stars	70	3	9	12	39	14	2	5	7	10
1968-69	Minnesota North Stars	69	4	17	21	70	....	....	....	....	....
1972-73	St. Louis Blues	43	1	13	14	33	....	....	....	....	....
	NHL Totals	**316**	**10**	**58**	**68**	**262**	**14**	**2**	**5**	**7**	**10**

Traded to **Springfield** (AHL) by **Montreal** for Kelly Burnett, September 12, 1954. Traded to **Boston** by **Springfield** (AHL) for Bruce Gamble, Dale Rolfe, Terry Gray and Randy Miller, June, 1963. Traded to **Detroit** by **Boston** with Ab McDonald and Ken Stephanson for Albert Langlois, Ron Harris, Parker MacDonald and Bob Dillabough, May 31, 1965. Traded to **Minnesota** by **Detroit** with Duke Harris for Jean-Guy Talbot and Dave Richardson, October 19, 1967. Claimed by **Montreal** from **Minnesota** in Intra-League Draft, June 9, 1970. Traded to **Minnesota** by **Montreal** for cash, August, 1970. Traded to **St. Louis** (Denver-WHL) by **Minnesota** for cash, August, 1970.

McCORD, Dennis

Defense. Shoots left. 5'10", 190 lbs. Born, Chatham, Ont., July 28, 1951.
(Vancouver's 8th choice, 115th overall, in 1972 Amateur Draft).

Season	Club	GP	G	A	Pts	PIM	GP	G	A	Pts	PIM
1973-74	Vancouver Canucks	3	0	0	0	6	....	....	....	....	....
	NHL Totals	**3**	**0**	**0**	**0**	**6**	....	....	....	....	....

McCORMACK, John

Center. Shoots left. 6', 185 lbs. Born, Edmonton, Alta., August 2, 1925.

Season	Club	GP	G	A	Pts	PIM	GP	G	A	Pts	PIM
1947-48	Toronto Maple Leafs	3	0	1	1	0	....	....	....	....	....
1948-49	Toronto Maple Leafs	1	0	0	0	0	....	....	....	....	....
1949-50	Toronto Maple Leafs	34	6	5	11	0	6	1	0	1	0
1950-51 ♦	Toronto Maple Leafs	46	6	7	13	2	....	....	....	....	....
1951-52	Montreal Canadiens	54	2	10	12	4	....	....	....	....	....
1952-53 ♦	Montreal Canadiens	59	1	9	10	9	9	0	0	0	0
1953-54	Montreal Canadiens	51	5	10	15	12	7	0	1	1	0
1954-55	Chicago Black Hawks	63	5	7	12	8	....	....	....	....	....
	NHL Totals	**311**	**25**	**49**	**74**	**35**	**22**	**1**	**1**	**2**	**0**

Played in NHL All-Star Game (1953)

Signed as a free agent by **Toronto**, January 11, 1950. Traded to **Montreal** by **Toronto** for cash, September 23, 1951. Claimed by **Chicago** from **Montreal** in Intra-League Draft, September 15, 1954. Traded to **Detroit** by **Chicago** with Dave Creighton, Gord Hollingworth and Jerry Toppazzini for Tony Leswick, Glen Skov, Johnny Wilson and Benny Woit, May 27, 1955.

McCOSH, Shawn

Center. Shoots right. 6', 197 lbs. Born, Oshawa, Ont., June 5, 1969.
(Detroit's 5th choice, 95th overall, in 1989 Entry Draft).

Season	Club	GP	G	A	Pts	PIM	GP	G	A	Pts	PIM
1991-92	Los Angeles Kings	4	0	0	0	4	....	....	....	....	....

		REGULAR SEASON					PLAYOFFS				
Season	Club	GP	G	A	Pts	PIM	GP	G	A	Pts	PIM
1994-95	New York Rangers	5	1	0	1	2	....	....	....	....	....
	NHL Totals	**9**	**1**	**0**	**1**	**6**	....	....	....	....	....

Traded to **Los Angeles** by **Detroit** for Los Angeles' 8th round choice (Justin Krall) in 1992 Entry Draft, August 15, 1990. Traded to **Ottawa** by **Los Angeles** with Bob Kudelski for Marc Fortier and Jim Thomson, December 19, 1992. Signed as a free agent by **NY Rangers**, July 30, 1993. Signed as a free agent by **Philadelphia**, July 31, 1995.

McCOURT, Dale

Center. Shoots right. 5'10", 180 lbs. Born, Falconbridge, Ont., January 26, 1957.
(Detroit's 1st choice, 1st overall, in 1977 Amateur Draft).

Season	Club	GP	G	A	Pts	PIM	GP	G	A	Pts	PIM
1977-78	Detroit Red Wings	76	33	39	72	10	7	4	2	6	2
1978-79	Detroit Red Wings	79	28	43	71	14	....	....	....	....	....
1979-80	Detroit Red Wings	80	30	51	81	12	....	....	....	....	....
1980-81	Detroit Red Wings	80	30	56	86	50	....	....	....	....	....
1981-82	Detroit Red Wings	26	13	14	27	6	....	....	....	....	....
	Buffalo Sabres	52	20	22	42	12	4	2	3	5	0
1982-83	Buffalo Sabres	62	20	32	52	10	10	3	2	5	4
1983-84	Buffalo Sabres	5	1	3	4	0	....	....	....	....	....
	Toronto Maple Leafs	72	19	24	43	10	....	....	....	....	....
	NHL Totals	**532**	**194**	**284**	**478**	**124**	**21**	**9**	**7**	**16**	**6**

Rights transferred to **Los Angeles** by **Detroit** as compensation for Detroit's signing of free agent Rogie Vachon, August 8, 1978. McCourt remained property of Detroit pending result of litigation hearing. Rights traded to **Detroit** by **Los Angeles** for Andre St. Laurent and Detroit's 1st round choices in 1980 (Larry Murphy) and 1981 (Doug Smith) Entry Drafts, August 22, 1979. Traded to **Buffalo** by **Detroit** with Mike Foligno and Brent Peterson for Danny Gare, Jim Schoenfeld and Derek Smith, December 2, 1981. Signed as a free agent by **Toronto**, October 22, 1983.

McCREARY, Bill

Left wing. Shoots left. 5'10", 172 lbs. Born, Sundridge, Ont., December 2, 1934.

Season	Club	GP	G	A	Pts	PIM	GP	G	A	Pts	PIM
1953-54	New York Rangers	2	0	0	0	2	....	....	....	....	....
1954-55	New York Rangers	8	0	2	2	0	....	....	....	....	....
1957-58	Detroit Red Wings	3	1	0	1	2	....	....	....	....	....
1962-63	Montreal Canadiens	14	2	3	5	0	....	....	....	....	....
1967-68	St. Louis Blues	70	13	13	26	22	15	3	2	5	0
1968-69	St. Louis Blues	71	13	17	30	50	12	1	5	6	14
1969-70	St. Louis Blues	73	15	17	32	16	15	1	7	8	0
1970-71	St. Louis Blues	68	9	10	19	16	6	1	2	3	0
	NHL Totals	**309**	**53**	**62**	**115**	**108**	**48**	**6**	**16**	**22**	**14**

• Brother of Keith • Father of Bill Jr.

Claimed by **Detroit** from **NY Rangers** in Intra-League Draft, June 5, 1956. Traded to **Springfield** (AHL) by **Detroit** with Dennis Olson and Hank Bassen for Gerry Ehman, May 1, 1958. Traded to **Montreal** by **Springfield** (AHL) for Bob McCammon, Andre Tardiff and Norm Waslowski, October 25, 1962. Traded to **St. Louis** by **Montreal** for Claude Cardin and Phil Obendorf, June 14, 1967.

McCREARY Jr., Bill

Right wing. Shoots right. 6', 190 lbs. Born, Springfield, MA, April 15, 1960.
(Toronto's 5th choice, 114th overall, in 1979 Entry Draft).

Season	Club	GP	G	A	Pts	PIM	GP	G	A	Pts	PIM
1980-81	Toronto Maple Leafs	12	1	0	1	4	....	....	....	....	....
	NHL Totals	**12**	**1**	**0**	**1**	**4**	....	....	....	....	....

• Son of Bill

McCREARY, Keith

Right wing. Shoots left. 5'10", 180 lbs. Born, Sundridge, Ont., June 19, 1940.

Season	Club	GP	G	A	Pts	PIM	GP	G	A	Pts	PIM
1961-62	Montreal Canadiens	....	....	....	....	....	1	0	0	0	0
1964-65	Montreal Canadiens	9	0	3	3	4	....	....	....	....	....
1967-68	Pittsburgh Penguins	70	14	12	26	44	....	....	....	....	....
1968-69	Pittsburgh Penguins	70	25	23	48	42	....	....	....	....	....
1969-70	Pittsburgh Penguins	60	18	8	26	67	10	0	4	4	4
1970-71	Pittsburgh Penguins	59	21	12	33	24	....	....	....	....	....
1971-72	Pittsburgh Penguins	33	4	4	8	22	1	0	0	0	2
1972-73	Atlanta Flames	77	20	21	41	21	....	....	....	....	....
1973-74	Atlanta Flames	76	18	19	37	62	4	0	0	0	0
1974-75	Atlanta Flames	78	11	10	21	8	....	....	....	....	....
	NHL Totals	**532**	**131**	**112**	**243**	**294**	**16**	**0**	**4**	**4**	**6**

• Brother of Bill

Claimed by **Pittsburgh** from **Montreal** in Expansion Draft, June 6, 1967. Claimed by **Atlanta** from **Pittsburgh** in Expansion Draft, June 6, 1972.

McCREEDY, John

Right wing. Shoots right. 5'9", 160 lbs. Born, Winnipeg, Man., March 23, 1911.

Season	Club	GP	G	A	Pts	PIM	GP	G	A	Pts	PIM
1941-42 ◆	Toronto Maple Leafs	47	15	8	23	14	13	4	3	7	6
1944-45 ◆	Toronto Maple Leafs	17	2	4	6	11	8	0	0	0	10
	NHL Totals	**64**	**17**	**12**	**29**	**25**	**21**	**4**	**3**	**7**	**16**

McCRIMMON, Brad

Defense. Shoots left. 5'11", 197 lbs. Born, Dodsland, Sask., March 29, 1959.
(Boston's 2nd choice, 15th overall, in 1979 Entry Draft).

Season	Club	GP	G	A	Pts	PIM	GP	G	A	Pts	PIM
1979-80	Boston Bruins	72	5	11	16	94	10	1	1	2	28
1980-81	Boston Bruins	78	11	18	29	148	3	0	1	1	2
1981-82	Boston Bruins	78	1	8	9	83	2	0	0	0	2
1982-83	Philadelphia Flyers	79	4	21	25	61	3	0	0	0	4
1983-84	Philadelphia Flyers	71	0	24	24	76	1	0	0	0	4
1984-85	Philadelphia Flyers	66	8	35	43	81	11	2	1	3	15
1985-86	Philadelphia Flyers	80	13	43	56	85	5	2	0	2	2
1986-87	Philadelphia Flyers	71	10	29	39	52	26	3	5	8	30
1987-88	Calgary Flames	80	7	35	42	98	9	2	3	5	22
1988-89 ◆	Calgary Flames	72	5	17	22	96	22	0	3	3	30
1989-90	Calgary Flames	79	4	15	19	78	6	0	2	2	8
1990-91	Detroit Red Wings	64	0	13	13	81	7	1	1	2	21
1991-92	Detroit Red Wings	79	7	22	29	118	11	0	1	1	8
1992-93	Detroit Red Wings	60	1	14	15	71	....	....	....	....	....
1993-94	Hartford Whalers	65	1	5	6	72	....	....	....	....	....
1994-95	Hartford Whalers	33	0	1	1	42	....	....	....	....	....
1995-96	Hartford Whalers	58	3	6	9	62	....	....	....	....	....
1996-97	Phoenix Coyotes	37	1	5	6	18	....	....	....	....	....
	NHL Totals	**1222**	**81**	**322**	**403**	**1416**	**116**	**11**	**18**	**29**	**176**

NHL Second All-Star Team (1988) • NHL Plus/Minus Leader (1988)

Played in NHL All-Star Game (1988)

Traded to **Philadelphia** by **Boston** for Pete Peeters, June 9, 1982. Traded to **Calgary** by **Philadelphia** for Calgary's 3rd round choice (Dominic Roussel) in 1988 Entry Draft and 1st round choice (later traded to Toronto – Toronto selected Steve Bancroft) in 1989 Entry Draft, August 26, 1987. Traded to **Detroit** by **Calgary** for Detroit's 2nd round choice (later traded to New Jersey – New Jersey selected David Harlock) in 1990 Entry Draft, June 15, 1990. Traded to **Hartford** by **Detroit** for Detroit's 6th round choice (previously acquired, Detroit selected Tim Spitzig) in 1993 Entry Draft, June 1, 1993. Signed as a free agent by **Phoenix**, July 16, 1996.

McCRIMMON, Jim

Defense. Shoots right. 6'1", 210 lbs. Born, Ponoka, Alta., May 29, 1953.
(Los Angeles' 2nd choice, 54th overall, in 1973 Amateur Draft).

Season	Club	GP	G	A	Pts	PIM	GP	G	A	Pts	PIM
1974-75	St. Louis Blues	2	0	0	0	0	....	....	....	....	....
	NHL Totals	**2**	**0**	**0**	**0**	**0**	....	....	....	....	....

Traded to **St. Louis** by **Los Angeles** for cash, March 10, 1975.

McCULLEY, Bob

Right wing/Defense. Shoots right. 6'2", 210 lbs. Born, Stratford, Ont., February 8, 1914.

Season	Club	GP	G	A	Pts	PIM	GP	G	A	Pts	PIM
1934-35	Montreal Canadiens	1	0	0	0	0	....	....	....	....	....
	NHL Totals	**1**	**0**	**0**	**0**	**0**	....	....	....	....	....

Signed as a free agent by **Montreal**, October 23, 1932. Traded to **Boston** (Can-Am) by **Montreal** for Sheldon Buckles, December 2, 1934. Traded to **Providence** (AHL) by **Boston** for cash, October 7, 1936.

McCURRY, Duke

Left wing. Shoots left. 5'8", 160 lbs. Born, Toronto, Ont., June 13, 1900.

Season	Club	GP	G	A	Pts	PIM	GP	G	A	Pts	PIM
1925-26	Pittsburgh Pirates	36	13	4	17	32	2	0	2	2	4
1926-27	Pittsburgh Pirates	33	3	3	6	23	....	....	....	....	....
1927-28	Pittsburgh Pirates	44	5	3	8	60	2	0	0	0	0
1928-29	Pittsburgh Pirates	35	0	1	1	4	....	....	....	....	....
	NHL Totals	**148**	**21**	**11**	**32**	**119**	**4**	**0**	**2**	**2**	**4**

Signed as a free agent by **Pittsburgh**, September 26, 1925. Traded to **Mtl. Maroons** by **Pittsburgh** for cash, September, 1929. • Refused to report and sat out entire season.

McCUTCHEON, Brian

Left wing. Shoots left. 5'10", 180 lbs. Born, Toronto, Ont., August 3, 1949.

Season	Club	GP	G	A	Pts	PIM	GP	G	A	Pts	PIM
1974-75	Detroit Red Wings	17	3	1	4	2	....	....	....	....	....
1975-76	Detroit Red Wings	8	0	0	0	5	....	....	....	....	....
1976-77	Detroit Red Wings	12	0	0	0	0	....	....	....	....	....
	NHL Totals	**37**	**3**	**1**	**4**	**7**	....	....	....	....	....

Signed as a free agent by **Detroit**, September 29, 1971.

McCUTCHEON, Darwin

Defense. Shoots left. 6'4", 190 lbs. Born, Listowel, Ont., April 19, 1962.
(Toronto's 9th choice, 179th overall, in 1980 Entry Draft).

Season	Club	GP	G	A	Pts	PIM	GP	G	A	Pts	PIM
1981-82	Toronto Maple Leafs	1	0	0	0	2	....	....	....	....	....
	NHL Totals	**1**	**0**	**0**	**0**	**2**	....	....	....	....	....

Signed as a free agent by **Calgary**, March 10, 1986.

McDILL, Jeff

Right wing. Shoots right. 5'11", 190 lbs. Born, Thunder Bay, Ont., March 16, 1956.
(Chicago's 2nd choice, 27th overall, in 1976 Amateur Draft).

Season	Club	GP	G	A	Pts	PIM	GP	G	A	Pts	PIM
1976-77	Chicago Black Hawks	1	0	0	0	0	....	....	....	....	....
	NHL Totals	**1**	**0**	**0**	**0**	**0**	....	....	....	....	....

Signed as a free agent by **NY Rangers**, October 13, 1978.

McDONAGH, Bill

Left wing. Shoots left. 5'9", 150 lbs. Born, Rouyn, Que., April 30, 1928.

Season	Club	GP	G	A	Pts	PIM	GP	G	A	Pts	PIM
1949-50	New York Rangers	4	0	0	0	2	....	....	....	....	....
	NHL Totals	**4**	**0**	**0**	**0**	**2**	....	....	....	....	....

Traded to **NY Rangers** by **Detroit** for cash, June, 1949.

McDONALD, Ab

Left wing. Shoots left. 6'3", 192 lbs. Born, Winnipeg, Man., February 18, 1936.

Season	Club	GP	G	A	Pts	PIM	GP	G	A	Pts	PIM
1957-58 ◆	Montreal Canadiens	....	....	....	....	....	2	0	0	0	2
1958-59 ◆	Montreal Canadiens	69	13	23	36	35	11	1	1	2	6
1959-60 ◆	Montreal Canadiens	68	9	13	22	26	....	....	....	....	....
1960-61 ◆	Chicago Black Hawks	61	17	16	33	22	8	2	2	4	0
1961-62	Chicago Black Hawks	65	22	18	40	8	12	6	6	12	0
1962-63	Chicago Black Hawks	69	20	41	61	12	6	2	3	5	9

		REGULAR SEASON					PLAYOFFS				
Season	Club	GP	G	A	Pts	PIM	GP	G	A	Pts	PIM
1963-64	Chicago Black Hawks	70	14	32	46	19	7	2	2	4	0
1964-65	Boston Bruins	60	9	9	18	6	....	....	....	....	....
1965-66	Detroit Red Wings	43	6	16	22	6	10	1	4	5	2
1966-67	Detroit Red Wings	12	2	0	2	2	....	....	....	....	....
1967-68	Pittsburgh Penguins	74	22	21	43	38	....	....	....	....	....
1968-69	St. Louis Blues	68	21	21	42	12	12	2	1	3	10
1969-70	St. Louis Blues	64	25	30	55	8	16	5	10	15	13
1970-71	St. Louis Blues	20	0	5	5	6	....	....	....	....	....
1971-72	Detroit Red Wings	19	2	3	5	0	....	....	....	....	....
	NHL Totals	**762**	**182**	**248**	**430**	**200**	**84**	**21**	**29**	**50**	**42**

Played in NHL All-Star Game (1958, 1959, 1961, 1969, 1970)

Traded to **Chicago** by **Montreal** with Reggie Fleming, Bob Courcy and Cec Hoekstra for Terry Gray, Glen Skov, the rights to Danny Lewicki, Lorne Ferguson and Bob Bailey, June 7, 1960. Traded to **Boston** by **Chicago** with Reggie Fleming for Doug Mohns, June 8, 1964. Traded to **Detroit** by **Boston** with Bob McCord and Ken Stephanson for Albert Langlois, Ron Harris, Parker MacDonald and Bob Dillabough, May 31, 1965. Claimed by **Pittsburgh** from **Detroit** in Expansion Draft, June 6, 1967. Traded to **St. Louis** by **Pittsburgh** for Lou Angotti, June 11, 1968. Traded to **Detroit** by **St. Louis** with Bob Wall and Mike Lowe to complete transaction that sent Carl Brewer to St. Louis (February 22, 1971), May 12, 1971.

McDONALD, Andy

Center. Shoots left. 5'10", 186 lbs. Born, Strathroy, Ont., August 25, 1977.

Season	Club	GP	G	A	Pts	PIM	GP	G	A	Pts	PIM
2000-01	Mighty Ducks of Anaheim	16	1	0	1	6	....	....	....	....	....
2001-02	Mighty Ducks of Anaheim	53	7	21	28	10	....	....	....	....	....
2002-03	Mighty Ducks of Anaheim	46	10	11	21	14	....	....	....	....	....
	NHL Totals	**115**	**18**	**32**	**50**	**30**	....	....	....	....	....

Signed as a free agent by **Anaheim**, April 3, 2000.

McDONALD, Brian

Center. Shoots right. 5'11", 190 lbs. Born, Toronto, Ont., March 23, 1945.

Season	Club	GP	G	A	Pts	PIM	GP	G	A	Pts	PIM
1967-68	Chicago Black Hawks	....	....	....	....	....	8	0	0	0	2
1970-71	Buffalo Sabres	12	0	0	0	29	....	....	....	....	....
	NHL Totals	**12**	**0**	**0**	**0**	**29**	**8**	**0**	**0**	**0**	**2**

Traded to **Denver** (WHL) by **Chicago** for cash, September, 1970. Claimed by **Buffalo** from **Denver** (WHL) in Inter-League Draft, June 9, 1970. Claimed by **San Diego** (WHL) from **Buffalo** (Salt Lake-CHL) in Reverse Draft, June, 1971.

McDONALD, Bucko

Defense. Shoots left. 5'10", 205 lbs. Born, Fergus, Ont., October 31, 1914.

Season	Club	GP	G	A	Pts	PIM	GP	G	A	Pts	PIM
1934-35	Detroit Red Wings	15	1	2	3	8					
1935-36 ♦	Detroit Red Wings	47	4	6	10	32	7	3	0	3	10
1936-37 ♦	Detroit Red Wings	47	3	5	8	20	10	0	0	0	2
1937-38	Detroit Red Wings	47	3	7	10	14	....	....	....	....	....
1938-39	Detroit Red Wings	14	0	0	0	2	....	....	....	....	....
	Toronto Maple Leafs	33	3	3	6	20	10	0	0	0	4
1939-40	Toronto Maple Leafs	34	2	5	7	13	1	0	0	0	0
1940-41	Toronto Maple Leafs	31	6	11	17	12	7	2	0	2	2
1941-42 ♦	Toronto Maple Leafs	48	2	19	21	24	9	0	1	1	2
1942-43	Toronto Maple Leafs	40	2	11	13	39	6	1	0	1	4
1943-44	Toronto Maple Leafs	9	2	4	6	8	....	....	....	....	....
	New York Rangers	41	5	6	11	14	....	....	....	....	....
1944-45	New York Rangers	40	2	9	11	0	....	....	....	....	....
	NHL Totals	**446**	**35**	**88**	**123**	**206**	**50**	**6**	**1**	**7**	**24**

NHL Second All-Star Team (1942)

Traded to **Detroit** by **Buffalo** (IHL) for Gamey Lederman and Lloyd Gross, January 9, 1935. Traded to **Toronto** by **Detroit** for Bill Thomson and $10,000, December 19, 1938. Traded to **NY Rangers** by **Toronto** for cash, November, 1943.

McDONALD, Butch

Left wing/Center. Shoots left. 6', 185 lbs. Born, Moose Jaw, Sask., November 21, 1916.

Season	Club	GP	G	A	Pts	PIM	GP	G	A	Pts	PIM
1939-40	Detroit Red Wings	37	1	6	7	2	5	0	2	2	10
1944-45	Detroit Red Wings	3	1	1	2	0	....	....	....	....	....
	Chicago Black Hawks	26	6	13	19	0	....	....	....	....	....
	NHL Totals	**66**	**8**	**20**	**28**	**2**	**5**	**0**	**2**	**2**	**10**

Signed as a free agent by **Detroit** (Pittsburgh-IAHL), October 30, 1937. Traded to **Chicago** by **Detroit** with Don Grosso and Cully Simon for Earl Seibert and future considerations (Fido Purpur, January 4, 1945), January 2, 1945.

McDONALD, Gerry

Defense. Shoots right. 6'3", 190 lbs. Born, Weymouth, MA, March 18, 1958.

Season	Club	GP	G	A	Pts	PIM	GP	G	A	Pts	PIM
1981-82	Hartford Whalers	3	0	0	0	0	....	....	....	....	....
1983-84	Hartford Whalers	5	0	0	0	4	....	....	....	....	....
	NHL Totals	**8**	**0**	**0**	**0**	**4**	....	....	....	....	....

Signed as a free agent by **NY Rangers**, December 12, 1980. Traded to **Hartford** by **NY Rangers** with Doug Sulliman and Chris Kotsopoulos for Mike Rogers and Hartford's 10th round choice (Simo Saarinen) in 1982 Entry Draft, October 2, 1981.

McDONALD, Jack

Left wing. Born,

Season	Club	GP	G	A	Pts	PIM	GP	G	A	Pts	PIM
1917-18	Montreal Wanderers	4	3	1	4	3	....	....	....	....	....
	Montreal Canadiens	8	9	1	10	12	2	1	0	1	0
1918-19	Montreal Canadiens	18	8	4	12	9	5	0	1	1	3
	Montreal Canadiens (Cup)	....	....	....	....	....	*5*	*1*	*1*	*2*	*3*
1919-20	Quebec Bulldogs	24	6	7	13	4	....	....	....	....	....
1920-21	Montreal Canadiens	6	0	1	1	0	....	....	....	....	....
	Toronto St. Pats	6	0	0	0	2	....	....	....	....	....
1921-22	Montreal Canadiens	3	0	0	0	0	....	....	....	....	....
	NHL Totals	**69**	**26**	**14**	**40**	**30**	**7**	**1**	**1**	**2**	**3**

Claimed by **Mtl. Wanderers** from **Quebec** in Dispersal Draft, November 26, 1917. Claimed by **Montreal** from **Mtl. Wanderers** in Dispersal Draft, January 4, 1918. Transferred to **Quebec** by **Montreal** when Quebec franchise returned to NHL, November 25, 1919. Transferred to **Hamilton** after **Quebec** franchise relocated, November 2, 1920. Traded to **Montreal** by **Hamilton** with Harry Mummery and Dave Ritchie for Goldie Prodgers, Joe Matte, Jack Coughlin and loan of Billy Coutu for 1920-21 season, November 27, 1920. Loaned to **Toronto** by **Montreal** for the remainder of the 1920-21 season, February 11, 1921.

McDONALD, Jack

Right wing. Shoots right. 5'11", 205 lbs. Born, Swan River, Man., November 24, 1921.

Season	Club	GP	G	A	Pts	PIM	GP	G	A	Pts	PIM
1943-44	New York Rangers	43	10	9	19	6	....	....	....	....	....
	NHL Totals	**43**	**10**	**9**	**19**	**6**	....	....	....	....	....

McDONALD, Lanny

HHOF

Right wing. Shoots right. 6', 185 lbs. Born, Hanna, Alta., February 16, 1953.
(Toronto's 1st choice, 4th overall, in 1973 Amateur Draft).

Season	Club	GP	G	A	Pts	PIM	GP	G	A	Pts	PIM
1973-74	Toronto Maple Leafs	70	14	16	30	43	....	....	....	....	....
1974-75	Toronto Maple Leafs	64	17	27	44	86	7	0	0	0	2
1975-76	Toronto Maple Leafs	75	37	56	93	70	10	4	4	8	4
1976-77	Toronto Maple Leafs	80	46	44	90	77	9	10	7	17	6
1977-78	Toronto Maple Leafs	74	47	40	87	54	13	3	4	7	10
1978-79	Toronto Maple Leafs	79	43	42	85	32	6	3	2	5	0
1979-80	Toronto Maple Leafs	35	15	15	30	10	....	....	....	....	....
	Colorado Rockies	46	25	20	45	43	....	....	....	....	....
1980-81	Colorado Rockies	80	35	46	81	56	....	....	....	....	....
1981-82	Colorado Rockies	16	6	9	15	20	....	....	....	....	....
	Calgary Flames	55	34	33	67	37	3	0	1	1	6
1982-83	Calgary Flames	80	66	32	98	90	7	3	4	7	19
1983-84	Calgary Flames	65	33	33	66	64	11	6	7	13	6
1984-85	Calgary Flames	43	19	18	37	36	1	0	0	0	0
1985-86	Calgary Flames	80	28	43	71	44	22	11	7	18	30
1986-87	Calgary Flames	58	14	12	26	54	5	0	0	0	2
1987-88	Calgary Flames	60	10	13	23	57	9	3	1	4	6
1988-89 ♦	Calgary Flames	51	11	7	18	26	14	1	3	4	29
	NHL Totals	**1111**	**500**	**506**	**1006**	**899**	**117**	**44**	**40**	**84**	**120**

NHL Second All-Star Team (1977, 1983) • Bill Masterton Trophy (1983) • King Clancy Memorial Trophy (1988) • Bud Man of the Year Award (1989)

Played in NHL All-Star Game (1977, 1978, 1983, 1984)

Traded to **Colorado** by **Toronto** with Joel Quenneville for Pat Hickey and Wilf Paiement, December 29, 1979. Traded to **Calgary** by **Colorado** with Colorado's 4th round choice (later traded to NY Islanders – NY Islanders selected Mikko Makela) in 1983 Entry Draft for Bob MacMillan and Don Lever, November 25, 1981.

McDONALD, Robert

Right wing. Shoots left. 5'10", 170 lbs. Born, Toronto, Ont., January 4, 1923.

Season	Club	GP	G	A	Pts	PIM	GP	G	A	Pts	PIM
1943-44	New York Rangers	1	0	0	0	0	....	....	....	....	....
	NHL Totals	**1**	**0**	**0**	**0**	**0**	....	....	....	....	....

McDONALD, Terry

Defense. Shoots left. 6'1", 180 lbs. Born, Coquitlam, B.C., January 1, 1956.
(Kansas City's 5th choice, 74th overall, in 1975 Amateur Draft).

Season	Club	GP	G	A	Pts	PIM	GP	G	A	Pts	PIM
1975-76	Kansas City Scouts	8	0	1	1	6	....	....	....	....	....
	NHL Totals	**8**	**0**	**1**	**1**	**6**	....	....	....	....	....

McDONELL, Kent

Right wing. Shoots right. 6'2", 205 lbs. Born, Williamstown, Ont., March 1, 1979.
(Detroit's 3rd choice, 181st overall, in 1999 Entry Draft).

Season	Club	GP	G	A	Pts	PIM	GP	G	A	Pts	PIM
2002-03	Columbus Blue Jackets	3	0	0	0	0	....	....	....	....	....
	NHL Totals	**3**	**0**	**0**	**0**	**0**	....	....	....	....	....

• Re-entered NHL Entry Draft. Originally Carolina's 9th choice, 225th overall, in 1997 Entry Draft.

Traded to **Columbus** by **Detroit** for Columbus's 6th round choice (Andreas Sundin) in 2003 Entry Draft, August 14, 2000.

McDONNELL, Joe

Defense. Shoots right. 6'2", 200 lbs. Born, Kitchener, Ont., May 11, 1961.

Season	Club	GP	G	A	Pts	PIM	GP	G	A	Pts	PIM
1981-82	Vancouver Canucks	7	0	1	1	12	....	....	....	....	....
1984-85	Pittsburgh Penguins	40	2	9	11	20	....	....	....	....	....
1985-86	Pittsburgh Penguins	3	0	0	0	2	....	....	....	....	....
	NHL Totals	**50**	**2**	**10**	**12**	**34**	....	....	....	....	....

Signed as a free agent by **Vancouver**, September 22, 1980. Signed as a free agent by **Edmonton**, August 16, 1982. Signed as a free agent by **Pittsburgh**, December 30, 1984.

McDONNELL, Moylan

Defense. Shoots right. 5'9", 145 lbs. Born, Stony Mountain, Man., August 27, 1889.

Season	Club	GP	G	A	Pts	PIM	GP	G	A	Pts	PIM
1920-21	Hamilton Tigers	22	1	2	3	2	....	....	....	....	....
	NHL Totals	**22**	**1**	**2**	**3**	**2**	....	....	....	....	....

Signed as a free agent by **Hamilton**, December 21, 1920.

McDONOUGH, Al

Right wing. Shoots right. 6'1", 175 lbs. Born, Hamilton, Ont., June 6, 1950.
(Los Angeles' 1st choice, 24th overall, in 1970 Amateur Draft).

Season	Club	Regular Season GP	G	A	Pts	PIM	Playoffs GP	G	A	Pts	PIM
1970-71	Los Angeles Kings	6	2	1	3	0	....	....	....	....	....
1971-72	Los Angeles Kings	31	3	2	5	8	....	....	....	....	....
	Pittsburgh Penguins	37	7	11	18	8	4	0	1	1	0
1972-73	Pittsburgh Penguins	78	35	41	76	26	....	....	....	....	....
1973-74	Pittsburgh Penguins	37	14	22	36	12	....	....	....	....	....
	Atlanta Flames	35	10	9	19	15	4	0	0	0	2
1977-78	Detroit Red Wings	13	2	2	4	4	....	....	....	....	....
	NHL Totals	**237**	**73**	**88**	**161**	**73**	**8**	**0**	**1**	**1**	**2**

Played in NHL All-Star Game (1974)

Traded to **Pittsburgh** by **Los Angeles** for Bob Woytowich, January 11, 1972. Traded to **Atlanta** by **Pittsburgh** for Chuck Arnason and Bob Paradise, January 4, 1974. Traded to **Detroit** by **Atlanta** for future considerations, August, 1977.

McDONOUGH, Hubie

Center. Shoots left. 5'9", 180 lbs. Born, Manchester, NH, July 8, 1963.

Season	Club	Regular Season GP	G	A	Pts	PIM	Playoffs GP	G	A	Pts	PIM
1988-89	Los Angeles Kings	4	0	1	1	0	....	....	....	....	....
1989-90	Los Angeles Kings	22	3	4	7	10	....	....	....	....	....
	New York Islanders	54	18	11	29	26	5	1	0	1	4
1990-91	New York Islanders	52	6	6	12	10	....	....	....	....	....
1991-92	New York Islanders	33	7	2	9	15	....	....	....	....	....
1992-93	San Jose Sharks	30	6	2	8	6	....	....	....	....	....
	NHL Totals	**195**	**40**	**26**	**66**	**67**	**5**	**1**	**0**	**1**	**4**

Signed as a free agent by **Los Angeles**, April 18, 1988. Traded to **NY Islanders** by **Los Angeles** with Ken Baumgartner for Mikko Makela, November 29, 1989. Traded to **San Jose** by **NY Islanders** for cash, August 28, 1992.

McDOUGAL, Mike

Right wing. Shoots left. 6'2", 200 lbs. Born, Port Huron, MI, April 30, 1958.
(NY Rangers' 6th choice, 76th overall, in 1978 Amateur Draft).

Season	Club	Regular Season GP	G	A	Pts	PIM	Playoffs GP	G	A	Pts	PIM
1978-79	New York Rangers	1	0	0	0	0	....	....	....	....	....
1980-81	New York Rangers	2	0	0	0	0	....	....	....	....	....
1981-82	Hartford Whalers	3	0	0	0	0	....	....	....	....	....
1982-83	Hartford Whalers	55	8	10	18	43	....	....	....	....	....
	NHL Totals	**61**	**8**	**10**	**18**	**43**	....	....	....	....	....

Claimed by **Hartford** from **NY Rangers** in Waiver Draft, October 6, 1981.

McDOUGALL, Bill

Center. Shoots right. 6', 185 lbs. Born, Mississauga, Ont., August 10, 1966.

Season	Club	Regular Season GP	G	A	Pts	PIM	Playoffs GP	G	A	Pts	PIM
1990-91	Detroit Red Wings	2	0	1	1	0	1	0	0	0	0
1992-93	Edmonton Oilers	4	2	1	3	4	....	....	....	....	....
1993-94	Tampa Bay Lightning	22	3	3	6	8	....	....	....	....	....
	NHL Totals	**28**	**5**	**5**	**10**	**12**	**1**	**0**	**0**	**0**	**0**

Signed as a free agent by **Detroit**, January 9, 1990. Traded to **Edmonton** by **Detroit** for Max Middendorf, February 22, 1992. Signed as a free agent by **Tampa Bay**, August 13, 1993.

McEACHERN, Shawn

Right wing. Shoots left. 5'11", 200 lbs. Born, Waltham, MA, February 28, 1969.
(Pittsburgh's 6th choice, 110th overall, in 1987 Entry Draft).

Season	Club	Regular Season GP	G	A	Pts	PIM	Playoffs GP	G	A	Pts	PIM
1991-92 ♦	Pittsburgh Penguins	15	0	4	4	0	19	2	7	9	4
1992-93	Pittsburgh Penguins	84	28	33	61	46	12	3	2	5	10
1993-94	Los Angeles Kings	49	8	13	21	24	....	....	....	....	....
	Pittsburgh Penguins	27	12	9	21	10	6	1	0	1	2
1994-95	Pittsburgh Penguins	44	13	13	26	22	11	0	2	2	8
1995-96	Boston Bruins	82	24	29	53	34	5	2	1	3	8
1996-97	Ottawa Senators	65	11	20	31	18	7	2	0	2	8
1997-98	Ottawa Senators	81	24	24	48	42	11	0	4	4	8
1998-99	Ottawa Senators	77	31	25	56	46	4	2	0	2	6
99-2000	Ottawa Senators	69	29	22	51	24	6	0	3	3	4
2000-01	Ottawa Senators	82	32	40	72	62	4	0	2	2	2
2001-02	Ottawa Senators	80	15	31	46	52	12	0	4	4	2
2002-03	Atlanta Thrashers	46	10	16	26	28	....	....	....	....	....
	NHL Totals	**801**	**237**	**279**	**516**	**408**	**97**	**12**	**25**	**37**	**62**

Traded to **Los Angeles** by **Pittsburgh** for Marty McSorley, August 27, 1993. Traded to **Pittsburgh** by **Los Angeles** with Tomas Sandstrom for Marty McSorley and Jim Paek, February 16, 1994. Traded to **Boston** by **Pittsburgh** with Kevin Stevens for Glen Murray, Bryan Smolinski and Boston's 3rd round choice (Boyd Kane) in 1996 Entry Draft, August 2, 1995. Traded to **Ottawa** by **Boston** for Trent McCleary and Ottawa's 3rd round choice (Eric Naud) in 1996 Entry Draft, June 22, 1996. Traded to **Atlanta** by **Ottawa** with Ottawa's 6th round choice in 2004 Entry Draft for Brian Pothier, June 29, 2002.

McELMURY, Jim

Defense. Shoots left. 6'1", 190 lbs. Born, St. Paul, MN, October 3, 1949.

Season	Club	Regular Season GP	G	A	Pts	PIM	Playoffs GP	G	A	Pts	PIM
1972-73	Minnesota North Stars	7	0	1	1	2	....	....	....	....	....
1974-75	Kansas City Scouts	78	5	17	22	25	....	....	....	....	....
1975-76	Kansas City Scouts	38	2	6	8	6	....	....	....	....	....
1976-77	Colorado Rockies	55	7	23	30	16	....	....	....	....	....
1977-78	Colorado Rockies	2	0	0	0	0	....	....	....	....	....
	NHL Totals	**180**	**14**	**47**	**61**	**49**	....	....	....	....	....

Signed as a free agent by **Minnesota**, February 29, 1972. Traded to **Los Angeles** by **Minnesota** for cash, March 1, 1974. Signed as a free agent by **Kansas City**, June 27, 1974. Transferred to **Colorado** after **Kansas City** franchise relocated, July 15, 1976.

McEWEN, Mike

Defense. Shoots left. 6'1", 185 lbs. Born, Hornepayne, Ont., August 10, 1956.
(NY Rangers' 3rd choice, 42nd overall, in 1976 Amateur Draft).

Season	Club	Regular Season GP	G	A	Pts	PIM	Playoffs GP	G	A	Pts	PIM
1976-77	New York Rangers	80	14	29	43	38	....	....	....	....	....
1977-78	New York Rangers	57	5	13	18	52	....	....	....	....	....
1978-79	New York Rangers	80	20	38	58	35	18	2	11	13	8
1979-80	New York Rangers	9	1	7	8	8	....	....	....	....	....
	Colorado Rockies	67	11	40	51	33	....	....	....	....	....
1980-81	Colorado Rockies	65	11	35	46	84	....	....	....	....	....
♦	New York Islanders	13	0	3	3	10	17	6	8	14	6
1981-82 ♦	New York Islanders	73	10	39	49	50	15	3	7	10	18
1982-83 ♦	New York Islanders	42	2	11	13	16	12	0	2	2	4
1983-84	New York Islanders	15	0	2	2	6	....	....	....	....	....
	Los Angeles Kings	47	10	24	34	14	....	....	....	....	....
1984-85	Washington Capitals	56	11	27	38	42	5	0	1	1	4
1985-86	Detroit Red Wings	29	0	10	10	16	....	....	....	....	....
	New York Rangers	16	2	5	7	8	....	....	....	....	....
	Hartford Whalers	10	3	2	5	6	8	0	4	4	6
1986-87	Hartford Whalers	48	8	8	16	32	1	1	1	2	0
1987-88	Hartford Whalers	9	0	3	3	10	2	0	2	2	2
	NHL Totals	**716**	**108**	**296**	**404**	**460**	**78**	**12**	**36**	**48**	**48**

Played in NHL All-Star Game (1980)

Traded to **Colorado** by **NY Rangers** with Lucien DeBlois, Pat Hickey, Dean Turner and future considerations (Bobby Crawford, January 15, 1980) for Barry Beck, November 2, 1979. Traded to **NY Islanders** by **Colorado** with Jari Kaarela for Glenn Resch and Steve Tambellini, March 10, 1981. Traded to **Los Angeles** by **NY Islanders** for Detroit's 4th round choice (previously acquired, NY Islanders selected Doug Wieck) in 1984 Entry Draft, November 17, 1983. Signed as a free agent by **Washington**, August 7, 1984. Signed as a free agent by **Detroit**, August 12, 1985. Traded to **NY Rangers** by **Detroit** for Steve Richmond, December 26, 1985. Traded to **Hartford** by **NY Rangers** for Bob Crawford, March 11, 1986.

McFADDEN, Jim

Center. Shoots left. 5'7", 178 lbs. Born, Belfast, Ireland, April 15, 1920.

Season	Club	Regular Season GP	G	A	Pts	PIM	Playoffs GP	G	A	Pts	PIM
1946-47	Detroit Red Wings	....	....	....	....	....	4	0	2	2	0
1947-48	Detroit Red Wings	60	24	24	48	12	10	5	3	8	10
1948-49	Detroit Red Wings	55	12	20	32	10	8	0	1	1	6
1949-50 ♦	Detroit Red Wings	68	14	16	30	8	14	2	3	5	8
1950-51	Detroit Red Wings	70	14	18	32	10	6	0	0	0	2
1951-52	Chicago Black Hawks	70	10	24	34	14	....	....	....	....	....
1952-53	Chicago Black Hawks	70	23	21	44	29	7	3	0	3	4
1953-54	Chicago Black Hawks	19	3	3	6	6	....	....	....	....	....
	NHL Totals	**412**	**100**	**126**	**226**	**89**	**49**	**10**	**9**	**19**	**30**

Calder Memorial Trophy (1948)
Played in NHL All-Star Game (1950)

Traded to **Montreal** by **Portland** (PCHL) for cash, December 25, 1940. Loaned to **Ottawa** (QSHL) by **Montreal** with Lude Check as compensation for Montreal's signing of Mike McMahon, October 24, 1945. Traded to **Buffalo** (AHL) by **Montreal** with Butch Stahan for Tom Rockey and cash, October 8, 1946. Traded to **Detroit** by **Buffalo** (AHL) for Les Douglas and Harold Jackson, June, 1947. Traded to **Chicago** by **Detroit** with George Gee, Max McNab, Jimmy Peters Sr., Clare Martin and Rags Raglan for $75,000 and future considerations (Hugh Coflin, October, 1951), August 20, 1951.

McFADYEN, Don

Center/Left wing. Shoots left. 5'9", 163 lbs. Born, Crossfield, Alta., March 24, 1907.

Season	Club	Regular Season GP	G	A	Pts	PIM	Playoffs GP	G	A	Pts	PIM
1932-33	Chicago Black Hawks	48	5	9	14	20	....	....	....	....	....
1933-34 ♦	Chicago Black Hawks	46	1	3	4	20	8	2	2	4	5
1934-35	Chicago Black Hawks	37	2	5	7	4	2	0	0	0	0
1935-36	Chicago Black Hawks	48	4	16	20	33	1	0	0	0	0
	NHL Totals	**179**	**12**	**33**	**45**	**77**	**11**	**2**	**2**	**4**	**5**

Traded to **Chicago** by **Chicago** (AHA) for cash, September 2, 1932.

McFALL, Dan

Defense. Shoots right. 6', 180 lbs. Born, Kenmore, NY, April 8, 1963.
(Winnipeg's 8th choice, 148th overall, in 1981 Entry Draft).

Season	Club	Regular Season GP	G	A	Pts	PIM	Playoffs GP	G	A	Pts	PIM
1984-85	Winnipeg Jets	2	0	0	0	0	....	....	....	....	....
1985-86	Winnipeg Jets	7	0	1	1	0	....	....	....	....	....
	NHL Totals	**9**	**0**	**1**	**1**	**0**	....	....	....	....	....

McFARLANE, Gord

Right wing/Defense. Shoots right. 6'2", 180 lbs. Born, Snow Lake, Man., July 18, 1901.

Season	Club	Regular Season GP	G	A	Pts	PIM	Playoffs GP	G	A	Pts	PIM
1926-27	Chicago Black Hawks	2	0	0	0	0	....	....	....	....	....
	NHL Totals	**2**	**0**	**0**	**0**	**0**	....	....	....	....	....

Traded to **Chicago** by **Calgary** (WHL) for cash, November 16, 1926.

McGEOUGH, Jim

Center. Shoots left. 5'8", 170 lbs. Born, Regina, Sask., April 13, 1963.
(Washington's 6th choice, 110th overall, in 1981 Entry Draft).

Season	Club	Regular Season GP	G	A	Pts	PIM	Playoffs GP	G	A	Pts	PIM
1981-82	Washington Capitals	4	0	0	0	0	....	....	....	....	....
1984-85	Washington Capitals	11	3	0	3	12	....	....	....	....	....
	Pittsburgh Penguins	14	0	4	4	4	....	....	....	....	....
1985-86	Pittsburgh Penguins	17	3	2	5	8	....	....	....	....	....
1986-87	Pittsburgh Penguins	11	1	4	5	8	....	....	....	....	....
	NHL Totals	**57**	**7**	**10**	**17**	**32**	....	....	....	....	....

Traded to **Pittsburgh** by **Washington** for Mark Taylor, March 12, 1985.

McGIBBON, Irv

Right wing. Shoots right. 6', 180 lbs. Born, Antigonish, N.S., October 11, 1914.

Season	Club	GP	G	A	Pts	PIM	GP	G	A	Pts	PIM
		REGULAR SEASON					PLAYOFFS				
1942-43	Montreal Canadiens	1	0	0	0	2	....	....	....	....	....
	NHL Totals	**1**	**0**	**0**	**0**	**2**	....	....	....	....	....

Signed as a free agent by **Montreal**, October 16, 1941.

McGILL, Bob

Defense. Shoots right. 6'1", 193 lbs. Born, Edmonton, Alta., April 27, 1962.
(Toronto's 2nd choice, 26th overall, in 1980 Entry Draft).

Season	Club	GP	G	A	Pts	PIM	GP	G	A	Pts	PIM
1981-82	Toronto Maple Leafs	68	1	10	11	263	....	....	....	....	....
1982-83	Toronto Maple Leafs	30	0	0	0	146	....	....	....	....	....
1983-84	Toronto Maple Leafs	11	0	2	2	51	....	....	....	....	....
1984-85	Toronto Maple Leafs	72	0	5	5	250	....	....	....	....	....
1985-86	Toronto Maple Leafs	61	1	4	5	141	9	0	0	0	35
1986-87	Toronto Maple Leafs	56	1	4	5	103	3	0	0	0	0
1987-88	Chicago Blackhawks	67	4	7	11	131	3	0	0	0	2
1988-89	Chicago Blackhawks	68	0	4	4	155	16	0	0	0	33
1989-90	Chicago Blackhawks	69	2	10	12	204	5	0	0	0	2
1990-91	Chicago Blackhawks	77	4	5	9	151	5	0	0	0	2
1991-92	San Jose Sharks	62	3	1	4	70	....	....	....	....	....
	Detroit Red Wings	12	0	0	0	21	8	0	0	0	14
1992-93	Toronto Maple Leafs	19	1	0	1	34	....	....	....	....	....
1993-94	New York Islanders	3	0	0	0	5	....	....	....	....	....
	Hartford Whalers	30	0	3	3	41	....	....	....	....	....
	NHL Totals	**705**	**17**	**55**	**72**	**1766**	**49**	**0**	**0**	**0**	**88**

Traded to **Chicago** by **Toronto** with Steve Thomas and Rick Vaive for Ed Olczyk and Al Secord, September 3, 1987. Claimed by **San Jose** from **Chicago** in Expansion Draft, May 30, 1991. Traded to **Detroit** by **San Jose** with Vancouver's 8th round choice (previously acquired, Detroit selected C.J. Denomme) in 1992 Entry Draft for Johan Garpenlov, March 9, 1992. Claimed by **Tampa Bay** from **Detroit** in Expansion Draft, June 18, 1992. Claimed on waivers by **Toronto** from **Tampa Bay**, September 9, 1992. Signed as a free agent by **NY Islanders**, September 7, 1993. Claimed on waivers by **Hartford** from **NY Islanders**, November 3, 1993.

McGILL, Jack

Left wing. Shoots left. 5'10", 150 lbs. Born, Ottawa, Ont., November 3, 1910.

Season	Club	GP	G	A	Pts	PIM	GP	G	A	Pts	PIM
1934-35	Montreal Canadiens	44	9	1	10	34	2	2	0	2	0
1935-36	Montreal Canadiens	46	13	7	20	28	....	....	....	....	....
1936-37	Montreal Canadiens	44	5	2	7	9	1	0	0	0	0
	NHL Totals	**134**	**27**	**10**	**37**	**71**	**3**	**2**	**0**	**2**	**0**

McGILL, Jack

Center. Shoots left. 6'1", 180 lbs. Born, Edmonton, Alta., September 19, 1920.

Season	Club	GP	G	A	Pts	PIM	GP	G	A	Pts	PIM
1941-42	Boston Bruins	13	8	11	19	2	5	4	1	5	6
1944-45	Boston Bruins	14	4	2	6	0	7	3	3	6	0
1945-46	Boston Bruins	46	6	14	20	21	10	0	0	0	0
1946-47	Boston Bruins	24	5	9	14	19	5	0	0	0	11
	NHL Totals	**97**	**23**	**36**	**59**	**42**	**27**	**7**	**4**	**11**	**17**

Traded to **Montreal** (Buffalo-AHL) by **Boston** (Hershey-AHL) for Gerry Brown and Hal Jackson, June 30, 1948.

McGILL, Ryan

Defense. Shoots right. 6'2", 210 lbs. Born, Prince Albert, Sask., February 28, 1969.
(Chicago's 2nd choice, 29th overall, in 1987 Entry Draft).

Season	Club	GP	G	A	Pts	PIM	GP	G	A	Pts	PIM
1991-92	Chicago Blackhawks	9	0	2	2	20	....	....	....	....	....
1992-93	Philadelphia Flyers	72	3	10	13	238	....	....	....	....	....
1993-94	Philadelphia Flyers	50	1	3	4	112	....	....	....	....	....
1994-95	Philadelphia Flyers	12	0	0	0	13	....	....	....	....	....
	Edmonton Oilers	8	0	0	0	8	....	....	....	....	....
	NHL Totals	**151**	**4**	**15**	**19**	**391**	....	....	....	....	....

Traded to **Quebec** by **Chicago** with Mike McNeill for Paul Gillis and Dan Vincelette, March 5, 1991. Traded to **Chicago** by **Quebec** for Mike Dagenais, September 27, 1991. Traded to **Philadelphia** by **Chicago** for Tony Horacek, February 7, 1992. Traded to **Edmonton** by **Philadelphia** for Brad Zavisha and Edmonton's 6th round choice (Jamie Sokolsky) in 1995 Entry Draft, March 13, 1995. • Suffered career-ending eye injury in game vs. Anaheim, April 5, 1995.

McGILLIS, Dan

Defense. Shoots left. 6'2", 230 lbs. Born, Hawkesbury, Ont., July 1, 1972.
(Detroit's 10th choice, 238th overall, in 1992 Entry Draft).

Season	Club	GP	G	A	Pts	PIM	GP	G	A	Pts	PIM
1996-97	Edmonton Oilers	73	6	16	22	52	12	0	5	5	24
1997-98	Edmonton Oilers	67	10	15	25	74	....	....	....	....	....
	Philadelphia Flyers	13	1	5	6	35	5	1	2	3	10
1998-99	Philadelphia Flyers	78	8	37	45	61	6	0	1	1	12
99-2000	Philadelphia Flyers	68	4	14	18	55	18	2	6	8	12
2000-01	Philadelphia Flyers	82	14	35	49	86	6	1	0	1	6
2001-02	Philadelphia Flyers	75	5	14	19	46	5	1	0	1	8
2002-03	Philadelphia Flyers	24	0	3	3	20	....	....	....	....	....
	San Jose Sharks	37	3	13	16	30	....	....	....	....	....
	Boston Bruins	10	0	1	1	10	5	3	0	3	2
	NHL Totals	**527**	**51**	**153**	**204**	**469**	**57**	**8**	**14**	**22**	**74**

Traded to **Edmonton** by **Detroit** for Kirk Maltby, March 20, 1996. Traded to **Philadelphia** by **Edmonton** with Edmonton's 2nd round choice (Jason Beckett) in 1998 Entry Draft for Janne Niinimaa, March 24, 1998. Traded to **San Jose** by **Philadelphia** for Marcus Ragnarsson, December 6, 2002. Traded to **Boston** by **San Jose** for Boston's 2nd round choice (later traded to NY Rangers – NY Rangers selected Ivan Baranka) in 2003 Entry Draft, March 11, 2003.

McGREGOR, Sandy

Right wing. Shoots right. 5'11", 165 lbs. Born, Toronto, Ont., March 30, 1939.

Season	Club	GP	G	A	Pts	PIM	GP	G	A	Pts	PIM
1963-64	New York Rangers	2	0	0	0	2	....	....	....	....	....
	NHL Totals	**2**	**0**	**0**	**0**	**2**	....	....	....	....	....

Traded to **Providence** (AHL) by **NY Rangers** with Jim Mikol, Marcel Paille and Aldo Guidolin for Ed Giacomin, May 18, 1965.

McGUIRE, Mickey

Left wing. Shoots left. 5'10", 158 lbs. Born, Gravenhurst, Ont., July 7, 1898.

Season	Club	GP	G	A	Pts	PIM	GP	G	A	Pts	PIM
1926-27	Pittsburgh Pirates	32	3	0	3	6	....	....	....	....	....
1927-28	Pittsburgh Pirates	4	0	0	0	0	....	....	....	....	....
	NHL Totals	**36**	**3**	**0**	**3**	**6**	....	....	....	....	....

Signed as a free agent by **Pittsburgh**, October 7, 1926. Traded to **Windsor** (Can-Pro) by **Pittsburgh** for cash, December 1, 1927. Traded to **Toronto** (London-Can-Pro) by **Windsor** (Can-Pro) with cash for Jack Arbour, January 15, 1929.

McHUGH, Mike

Left wing. Shoots left. 5'10", 190 lbs. Born, Bowdoin, MA, August 16, 1965.
(Minnesota's 1st choice, 1st overall, in 1988 Supplemental Draft).

Season	Club	GP	G	A	Pts	PIM	GP	G	A	Pts	PIM
1988-89	Minnesota North Stars	3	0	0	0	2	....	....	....	....	....
1989-90	Minnesota North Stars	3	0	0	0	0	....	....	....	....	....
1990-91	Minnesota North Stars	6	0	0	0	0	....	....	....	....	....
1991-92	San Jose Sharks	8	1	0	1	14	....	....	....	....	....
	NHL Totals	**20**	**1**	**0**	**1**	**16**	....	....	....	....	....

Claimed by **San Jose** from **Minnesota** in Dispersal Draft, May 30, 1991. Traded to **Hartford** by **San Jose** for Paul Fenton, October 18, 1991.

McILHARGEY, Jack

Defense. Shoots left. 6', 190 lbs. Born, Edmonton, Alta., March 7, 1952.

Season	Club	GP	G	A	Pts	PIM	GP	G	A	Pts	PIM
1974-75	Philadelphia Flyers	2	0	0	0	11	....	....	....	....	....
1975-76	Philadelphia Flyers	57	1	2	3	205	15	0	3	3	41
1976-77	Philadelphia Flyers	40	2	1	3	164	....	....	....	....	....
	Vancouver Canucks	21	1	7	8	61	....	....	....	....	....
1977-78	Vancouver Canucks	69	3	5	8	172	....	....	....	....	....
1978-79	Vancouver Canucks	53	2	4	6	129	3	0	0	0	2
1979-80	Vancouver Canucks	24	0	2	2	41	....	....	....	....	....
	Philadelphia Flyers	26	0	4	4	95	9	0	0	0	25
1980-81	Philadelphia Flyers	3	0	0	0	22	....	....	....	....	....
	Hartford Whalers	48	1	6	7	142	....	....	....	....	....
1981-82	Hartford Whalers	50	1	5	6	60	....	....	....	....	....
	NHL Totals	**393**	**11**	**36**	**47**	**1102**	**27**	**0**	**3**	**3**	**68**

Signed as a free agent by **Philadelphia** (Jersey-EHL), September, 1972. Traded to **Vancouver** by **Philadelphia** with Larry Goodenough for Bob Dailey, January 20, 1977. Traded to **Philadelphia** by **Vancouver** for cash, January 2, 1980. Traded to **Hartford** by **Philadelphia** with Norm Barnes for Hartford's 2nd round choice (later traded to Toronto – Toronto selected Peter Ihnacak) in 1982 Entry Draft, November 21, 1980.

McINENLY, Bert

Left wing/Defense. Shoots left. 5'9", 160 lbs. Born, Quebec City, Que., May 6, 1906.

Season	Club	GP	G	A	Pts	PIM	GP	G	A	Pts	PIM
1930-31	Detroit Falcons	44	3	5	8	48	....	....	....	....	....
1931-32	Detroit Falcons	17	0	1	1	16	....	....	....	....	....
	New York Americans	30	12	6	18	44	....	....	....	....	....
1932-33	Ottawa Senators	30	2	2	4	8	....	....	....	....	....
1933-34	Ottawa Senators	2	0	0	0	0	....	....	....	....	....
	Boston Bruins	7	0	0	0	4	....	....	....	....	....
1934-35	Boston Bruins	33	2	1	3	24	4	0	0	0	2
1935-36	Boston Bruins	3	0	0	0	0	....	....	....	....	....
	NHL Totals	**166**	**19**	**15**	**34**	**144**	**4**	**0**	**0**	**0**	**2**

Signed as a free agent by **Detroit**, October 20, 1928. Traded to **NY Americans** by **Detroit** with Tommy Filmore for Hap Emms and Frank Carson, December 29, 1931. Traded to **Ottawa** by **NY Americans** for cash, October 19, 1932. Traded to **Boston** by **Ottawa** for cash, November, 1933. Traded to **Providence** (IAHL) by **Boston** for cash, October 7, 1936.

McINNIS, Marty

Right wing. Shoots right. 5'11", 187 lbs. Born, Hingham, MA, June 2, 1970.
(NY Islanders' 10th choice, 163rd overall, in 1988 Entry Draft).

Season	Club	GP	G	A	Pts	PIM	GP	G	A	Pts	PIM
1991-92	New York Islanders	15	3	5	8	0	....	....	....	....	....
1992-93	New York Islanders	56	10	20	30	24	3	0	1	1	0
1993-94	New York Islanders	81	25	31	56	24	4	0	0	0	0
1994-95	New York Islanders	41	9	7	16	8	....	....	....	....	....
1995-96	New York Islanders	74	12	34	46	39	....	....	....	....	....
1996-97	New York Islanders	70	20	22	42	20	....	....	....	....	....
	Calgary Flames	10	3	4	7	2	....	....	....	....	....
1997-98	Calgary Flames	75	19	25	44	34	....	....	....	....	....
1998-99	Calgary Flames	6	1	1	2	6	....	....	....	....	....
	Mighty Ducks of Anaheim	75	18	34	52	36	4	2	0	2	2
99-2000	Mighty Ducks of Anaheim	62	10	18	28	26	....	....	....	....	....
2000-01	Mighty Ducks of Anaheim	75	20	22	42	40	....	....	....	....	....
2001-02	Mighty Ducks of Anaheim	60	9	14	23	25	....	....	....	....	....
	Boston Bruins	19	2	3	5	8	6	0	1	1	0

		REGULAR SEASON					PLAYOFFS				
Season	Club	GP	G	A	Pts	PIM	GP	G	A	Pts	PIM
2002-03	Boston Bruins	77	9	10	19	38	5	1	0	1	2
	NHL Totals	**796**	**170**	**250**	**420**	**330**	**22**	**3**	**2**	**5**	**4**

Traded to **Calgary** by **NY Islanders** with Tyrone Garner and Calgary's 6th round choice (previously acquired, Calgary selected Ilja Demidov) in 1997 Entry Draft for Robert Reichel, March 18, 1997. Traded to **Chicago** by **Calgary** with Eric Andersson and Jamie Allison for Jeff Shantz and Steve Dubinsky, October 27, 1998. Traded to **Anaheim** by **Chicago** for Toronto's 4th round choice (previously acquired, later traded to Washington – Washington selected Ryan Vanbuskirk) in 2000 Entry Draft, October 27, 1998. Traded to **Boston by Anaheim** for Boston's 3rd round choice (later traded to Nashville – later traded to Detroit – Detroit selected Valtteri Filppula) in 2002 Entry Draft, March 6, 2002.

McINTOSH, Bruce

Defense. Shoots left. 6', 178 lbs. Born, Minneapolis, MN, March 17, 1949.

Season	Club	GP	G	A	Pts	PIM	GP	G	A	Pts	PIM
1972-73	Minnesota North Stars	2	0	0	0	0	....	....	....	....	....
	NHL Totals	**2**	**0**	**0**	**0**	**0**	....	....	....	....	....

Signed as a free agent by **Minnesota**, September 30, 1972.

McINTOSH, Paul

Defense. Shoots right. 5'10", 177 lbs. Born, Listowel, Ont., March 13, 1954.
(Buffalo's 4th choice, 65th overall, in 1974 Amateur Draft).

Season	Club	GP	G	A	Pts	PIM	GP	G	A	Pts	PIM
1974-75	Buffalo Sabres	6	0	1	1	5	1	0	0	0	0
1975-76	Buffalo Sabres	42	0	1	1	61	1	0	0	0	7
	NHL Totals	**48**	**0**	**2**	**2**	**66**	**2**	**0**	**0**	**0**	**7**

McINTYRE, Jack

Defense. Shoots left. 5'11", 170 lbs. Born, Brussels, Ont., September 8, 1930.

Season	Club	GP	G	A	Pts	PIM	GP	G	A	Pts	PIM
1949-50	Boston Bruins	1	0	1	1	0	....	....	....	....	....
1950-51	Boston Bruins	....	....	....	....	....	2	0	0	0	0
1951-52	Boston Bruins	52	12	19	31	18	7	1	2	3	2
1952-53	Boston Bruins	70	7	15	22	31	10	4	2	6	2
1953-54	Chicago Black Hawks	23	8	3	11	4	....	....	....	....	....
1954-55	Chicago Black Hawks	65	16	13	29	40	....	....	....	....	....
1955-56	Chicago Black Hawks	46	10	5	15	14	....	....	....	....	....
1956-57	Chicago Black Hawks	70	18	14	32	32	....	....	....	....	....
1957-58	Chicago Black Hawks	27	0	4	4	10	....	....	....	....	....
	Detroit Red Wings	41	15	7	22	4	4	1	1	2	0
1958-59	Detroit Red Wings	55	15	14	29	14	....	....	....	....	....
1959-60	Detroit Red Wings	49	8	7	15	6	6	1	1	2	0
	NHL Totals	**499**	**109**	**102**	**211**	**173**	**29**	**7**	**6**	**13**	**4**

Signed as a free agent by **Boston**, March 23, 1949. Traded to **Chicago** by **Boston** for cash, January 21, 1954. Traded to **Detroit** by **Chicago** with Bob Bailey, Nick Mickoski and Hec Lalonde for Earl Reibel, Billy Dea, Lorne Ferguson and Bill Dineen, December 17, 1957. Traded to **Hershey** (AHL) by **Detroit** with Pete Conacher and Marc Reaume for Howie Young, January, 1961.

McINTYRE, John

Center. Shoots left. 6'1", 190 lbs. Born, Ravenswood, Ont., April 29, 1969.
(Toronto's 3rd choice, 49th overall, in 1987 Entry Draft).

Season	Club	GP	G	A	Pts	PIM	GP	G	A	Pts	PIM
1989-90	Toronto Maple Leafs	59	5	12	17	117	2	0	0	0	2
1990-91	Toronto Maple Leafs	13	0	3	3	25	....	....	....	....	....
	Los Angeles Kings	56	8	5	13	115	12	0	1	1	24
1991-92	Los Angeles Kings	73	5	19	24	100	6	0	4	4	12
1992-93	Los Angeles Kings	49	2	5	7	80	....	....	....	....	....
	New York Rangers	11	1	0	1	4	....	....	....	....	....
1993-94	Vancouver Canucks	62	3	6	9	38	24	0	1	1	16
1994-95	Vancouver Canucks	28	0	4	4	37	....	....	....	....	....
	NHL Totals	**351**	**24**	**54**	**78**	**516**	**44**	**0**	**6**	**6**	**54**

Traded to **Los Angeles** by **Toronto** for Mike Krushelnyski, November 9, 1990. Traded to **NY Rangers** by **Los Angeles** for Mark Hardy and Ottawa's 5th round choice (previously acquired, Los Angeles selected Frederick Beaubien) in 1993 Entry Draft, March 22, 1993. Claimed by **Vancouver** from **NY Rangers** in Waiver Draft, October 3, 1993.

McINTYRE, Larry

Defense. Shoots left. 6'1", 190 lbs. Born, Moose Jaw, Sask., July 13, 1949.
(Toronto's 3rd choice, 31st overall, in 1969 Amateur Draft).

Season	Club	GP	G	A	Pts	PIM	GP	G	A	Pts	PIM
1969-70	Toronto Maple Leafs	1	0	0	0	0	....	....	....	....	....
1972-73	Toronto Maple Leafs	40	0	3	3	26	....	....	....	....	....
	NHL Totals	**41**	**0**	**3**	**3**	**26**	....	....	....	....	....

Traded to **Vancouver** by **Toronto** with Murray Heatley for Dunc Wilson, May 29, 1973.

McKAY, Doug

Left wing. Shoots left. 5'9", 165 lbs. Born, Hamilton, Ont., May 28, 1929.

Season	Club	GP	G	A	Pts	PIM	GP	G	A	Pts	PIM
1949-50 ♦	Detroit Red Wings	....	....	....	....	....	1	0	0	0	0
	NHL Totals	....	....	....	....	....	**1**	**0**	**0**	**0**	**0**

McKAY, Randy

Right wing. Shoots right. 6'2", 210 lbs. Born, Montreal, Que., January 25, 1967.
(Detroit's 6th choice, 113th overall, in 1985 Entry Draft).

Season	Club	GP	G	A	Pts	PIM	GP	G	A	Pts	PIM
1988-89	Detroit Red Wings	3	0	0	0	0	2	0	0	0	2
1989-90	Detroit Red Wings	33	3	6	9	51	....	....	....	....	....
1990-91	Detroit Red Wings	47	1	7	8	183	5	0	1	1	41
1991-92	New Jersey Devils	80	17	16	33	246	7	1	3	4	10
1992-93	New Jersey Devils	73	11	11	22	206	5	0	0	0	16
1993-94	New Jersey Devils	78	12	15	27	244	20	1	2	3	24
1994-95 ♦	New Jersey Devils	33	5	7	12	44	19	8	4	12	11
1995-96	New Jersey Devils	76	11	10	21	145	....	....	....	....	....
1996-97	New Jersey Devils	77	9	18	27	109	10	1	1	2	0
1997-98	New Jersey Devils	74	24	24	48	86	6	0	1	1	0
1998-99	New Jersey Devils	70	17	20	37	143	7	3	2	5	2
99-2000 ♦	New Jersey Devils	67	16	23	39	80	23	0	6	6	9
2000-01	New Jersey Devils	77	23	20	43	50	19	6	3	9	8
2001-02	New Jersey Devils	55	6	7	13	65	....	....	....	....	....
	Dallas Stars	14	1	4	5	7	....	....	....	....	....
2002-03	Montreal Canadiens	75	6	13	19	72	....	....	....	....	....
	NHL Totals	**932**	**162**	**201**	**363**	**1731**	**123**	**20**	**23**	**43**	**123**

Transferred to **New Jersey** by **Detroit** with Dave Barr as compensation for Detroit's signing of free agent Troy Crowder, September 9, 1991. Traded to **Dallas** by **New Jersey** with Jason Arnott and New Jersey's 1st round choice (later traded to Columbus – later traded to Buffalo – Buffalo selected Dan Paille) in 2002 Entry Draft for Joe Nieuwendyk and Jamie Langenbrunner, March 19, 2002. Signed as a free agent by **Montreal**, July 4, 2002.

McKAY, Ray

Defense. Shoots left. 6'4", 183 lbs. Born, Edmonton, Alta., August 22, 1946.

Season	Club	GP	G	A	Pts	PIM	GP	G	A	Pts	PIM
1968-69	Chicago Black Hawks	9	0	1	1	12	....	....	....	....	....
1969-70	Chicago Black Hawks	17	0	0	0	23	....	....	....	....	....
1970-71	Chicago Black Hawks	2	0	0	0	0	....	....	....	....	....
1971-72	Buffalo Sabres	39	0	3	3	18	....	....	....	....	....
1972-73	Buffalo Sabres	1	0	0	0	0	....	....	....	....	....
1973-74	California Golden Seals	72	2	12	14	49	....	....	....	....	....
	NHL Totals	**140**	**2**	**16**	**18**	**102**	....	....	....	....	....

Claimed by **Buffalo** from **Chicago** in Intra-League Draft, June 8, 1971. Claimed by **California** from **Buffalo** in Intra-League Draft, June 12, 1973.

McKAY, Scott

Center. Shoots right. 5'11", 200 lbs. Born, Burlington, Ont., January 26, 1972.

Season	Club	GP	G	A	Pts	PIM	GP	G	A	Pts	PIM
1993-94	Mighty Ducks of Anaheim	1	0	0	0	0	....	....	....	....	....
	NHL Totals	**1**	**0**	**0**	**0**	**0**	....	....	....	....	....

Signed as a free agent by **Anaheim**, August 2, 1993.

McKECHNIE, Walt

Center. Shoots left. 6'2", 195 lbs. Born, London, Ont., June 19, 1947.
(Toronto's 1st choice, 6th overall, in 1963 Amateur Draft).

Season	Club	GP	G	A	Pts	PIM	GP	G	A	Pts	PIM
1967-68	Minnesota North Stars	4	0	0	0	0	9	3	2	5	0
1968-69	Minnesota North Stars	58	5	9	14	22	....	....	....	....	....
1969-70	Minnesota North Stars	20	1	3	4	21	....	....	....	....	....
1970-71	Minnesota North Stars	30	3	1	4	34	....	....	....	....	....
1971-72	California Golden Seals	56	11	20	31	40	....	....	....	....	....
1972-73	California Golden Seals	78	16	38	54	58	....	....	....	....	....
1973-74	California Golden Seals	63	23	29	52	14	....	....	....	....	....
1974-75	Boston Bruins	53	3	3	6	8	....	....	....	....	....
	Detroit Red Wings	23	6	11	17	6	....	....	....	....	....
1975-76	Detroit Red Wings	80	26	56	82	85	....	....	....	....	....
1976-77	Detroit Red Wings	80	25	34	59	50	....	....	....	....	....
1977-78	Washington Capitals	16	4	1	5	0	....	....	....	....	....
	Cleveland Barons	53	12	22	34	12	....	....	....	....	....
1978-79	Toronto Maple Leafs	79	25	36	61	18	6	4	3	7	7
1979-80	Toronto Maple Leafs	54	7	36	43	4	....	....	....	....	....
	Colorado Rockies	17	0	4	4	2	....	....	....	....	....
1980-81	Colorado Rockies	53	15	23	38	18	....	....	....	....	....
1981-82	Detroit Red Wings	74	18	37	55	35	....	....	....	....	....
1982-83	Detroit Red Wings	64	14	29	43	42	....	....	....	....	....
	NHL Totals	**955**	**214**	**392**	**606**	**469**	**15**	**7**	**5**	**12**	**7**

Traded to **Phoenix** (WHL) by **Toronto** for Steve Witiuk, October 15, 1967. Traded to **Minnesota** by **Phoenix** (WHL) for future considerations (Leo Thiffault and Bob Charlebois, June, 1968), February 17, 1968. Traded to **California** by **Minnesota** with Joey Johnson for Dennis Hextall, May 20, 1971. Claimed by **NY Rangers** from **California** in Intra-League Draft, June 10, 1974. Traded to **Boston** by **NY Rangers** for Derek Sanderson, June 12, 1974. Traded to **Detroit** by **Boston** with Boston's 3rd round choice (Clarke Hamilton) in 1975 Amateur Draft for Hank Nowak and Earl Anderson, February 18, 1975. Traded to **Washington** by **Detroit** with Detroit's 3rd round choice (Jay Johnston) in 1978 Amateur Draft and 2nd round choice (Errol Rausse) in 1979 Amateur Draft for the rights to Ron Low and Washington's 3rd round choice (Boris Fistric) in 1979 Amateur Draft, August 17, 1977. Traded to **Cleveland** by **Washington** for Bob Girard and Cleveland's 2nd round choice (Paul MacKinnon) in 1978 Amateur Draft, December 9, 1977. Placed on **Minnesota** Reserve List after **Cleveland-Minnesota** Dispersal Draft, June 15, 1978. Traded to **Toronto** by **Minnesota** for Toronto's 3rd round choice (Randy Velischek) in 1980 Entry Draft, October 5, 1978. Traded to **Colorado** by **Toronto** for Colorado's 3rd round choice (Fred Boimistruck) in 1980 Entry Draft, March 3, 1980. Signed as a free agent by **Detroit**, October 1, 1981.

McKEE, Jay

Defense. Shoots left. 6'4", 212 lbs. Born, Kingston, Ont., September 8, 1977.
(Buffalo's 1st choice, 14th overall, in 1995 Entry Draft).

Season	Club	GP	G	A	Pts	PIM	GP	G	A	Pts	PIM
1995-96	Buffalo Sabres	1	0	1	1	2	....	....	....	....	....
1996-97	Buffalo Sabres	43	1	9	10	35	3	0	0	0	0
1997-98	Buffalo Sabres	56	1	13	14	42	1	0	0	0	0
1998-99	Buffalo Sabres	72	0	6	6	75	21	0	3	3	24
99-2000	Buffalo Sabres	78	5	12	17	50	1	0	0	0	0
2000-01	Buffalo Sabres	74	1	10	11	76	8	1	0	1	6
2001-02	Buffalo Sabres	81	2	11	13	43	....	....	....	....	....
2002-03	Buffalo Sabres	59	0	5	5	49	....	....	....	....	....
	NHL Totals	**464**	**10**	**67**	**77**	**372**	**34**	**1**	**3**	**4**	**30**

McKEE, Mike

Left wing. Shoots right. 6'3", 203 lbs. Born, Toronto, Ont., June 18, 1969.
(Quebec's 1st choice, 1st overall, in 1990 Supplemental Draft).

Season	Club	REGULAR SEASON GP	G	A	Pts	PIM	PLAYOFFS GP	G	A	Pts	PIM
1993-94	Quebec Nordiques	48	3	12	15	41	....	....	....	....	....
	NHL Totals	**48**	**3**	**12**	**15**	**41**	....	....	....	....	....

McKEGNEY, Ian

Defense. Shoots left. 5'11", 165 lbs. Born, Sarnia, Ont., May 7, 1947.

Season	Club	REGULAR SEASON GP	G	A	Pts	PIM	PLAYOFFS GP	G	A	Pts	PIM
1976-77	Chicago Black Hawks	3	0	0	0	2	....	....	....	....	....
	NHL Totals	**3**	**0**	**0**	**0**	**2**	....	....	....	....	....

Signed as a free agent by **Chicago**, September 30, 1972.

McKEGNEY, Tony

Left wing. Shoots left. 6'th", 200 lbs. Born, Montreal, Que., February 15, 1958.
(Buffalo's 2nd choice, 32nd overall, in 1978 Amateur Draft).

Season	Club	REGULAR SEASON GP	G	A	Pts	PIM	PLAYOFFS GP	G	A	Pts	PIM
1978-79	Buffalo Sabres	52	8	14	22	10	2	0	1	1	0
1979-80	Buffalo Sabres	80	23	29	52	24	14	3	4	7	2
1980-81	Buffalo Sabres	80	37	32	69	24	8	5	3	8	2
1981-82	Buffalo Sabres	73	23	29	52	41	4	0	0	0	2
1982-83	Buffalo Sabres	78	36	37	73	18	10	3	1	4	4
1983-84	Quebec Nordiques	75	24	27	51	23	7	0	0	0	0
1984-85	Quebec Nordiques	30	12	9	21	12	....	....	....	....	....
	Minnesota North Stars	27	11	13	24	4	9	8	6	14	0
1985-86	Minnesota North Stars	70	15	25	40	48	5	2	1	3	22
1986-87	Minnesota North Stars	11	2	3	5	16	....	....	....	....	....
	New York Rangers	64	29	17	46	56	6	0	0	0	12
1987-88	St. Louis Blues	80	40	38	78	82	9	3	6	9	8
1988-89	St. Louis Blues	71	25	17	42	58	3	0	1	1	0
1989-90	Detroit Red Wings	14	2	1	3	8	....	....	....	....	....
	Quebec Nordiques	48	16	11	27	45	....	....	....	....	....
1990-91	Quebec Nordiques	50	17	16	33	44	....	....	....	....	....
	Chicago Blackhawks	9	0	1	1	4	2	0	0	0	4
	NHL Totals	**912**	**320**	**319**	**639**	**517**	**79**	**24**	**23**	**47**	**56**

Traded to **Quebec** by **Buffalo** with Andre Savard, Jean-Francois Sauve and Buffalo's 3rd round choice (Iiro Jarvi) in 1983 Entry Draft for Real Cloutier and Quebec's 1st round choice (Adam Creighton) in 1983 Entry Draft, June 8, 1983. Traded to **Minnesota** by **Quebec** with Bo Berglund for Brad Maxwell and Brent Ashton, December 14, 1984. Traded to **NY Rangers** by **Minnesota** with Curt Giles and Minnesota's 2nd round choice (Troy Mallette) in 1988 Entry Draft for Bob Brooke and Minnesota's 4th round choice (previously acquired. Minnesota selected Jeffrey Stolp) in 1988 Entry Draft, November 13, 1986. Traded to **St. Louis** by **NY Rangers** with Rob Whistle for Bruce Bell and future considerations, May 28, 1987. Traded to **Detroit** by **St. Louis** with Bernie Federko for Adam Oates and Paul MacLean, June 15, 1989. Traded to **Quebec** by **Detroit** for Robert Picard and Greg Adams, December 4, 1989. Traded to **Chicago** by **Quebec** for Jacques Cloutier, January 29, 1991.

McKENDRY, Alex

Wing. Shoots left. 6'4", 200 lbs. Born, Midland, Ont., November 21, 1956.
(NY Islanders' 1st choice, 14th overall, in 1976 Amateur Draft).

Season	Club	REGULAR SEASON GP	G	A	Pts	PIM	PLAYOFFS GP	G	A	Pts	PIM
1977-78	New York Islanders	4	0	0	0	2	....	....	....	....	....
1978-79	New York Islanders	4	0	0	0	0	....	....	....	....	....
1979-80 ♦	New York Islanders	2	0	0	0	0	6	2	2	4	0
1980-81	Calgary Flames	36	3	6	9	19	....	....	....	....	....
	NHL Totals	**46**	**3**	**6**	**9**	**21**	**6**	**2**	**2**	**4**	**0**

Traded to **Calgary** by **NY Islanders** for Calgary's 3rd round choice (Ron Handy) in 1981 Entry Draft, October 9, 1980.

McKENNA, Sean

Right wing. Shoots right. 6', 190 lbs. Born, Asbestos, Que., March 7, 1962.
(Buffalo's 3rd choice, 56th overall, in 1980 Entry Draft).

Season	Club	REGULAR SEASON GP	G	A	Pts	PIM	PLAYOFFS GP	G	A	Pts	PIM
1981-82	Buffalo Sabres	3	0	1	1	2	....	....	....	....	....
1982-83	Buffalo Sabres	46	10	14	24	4	....	....	....	....	....
1983-84	Buffalo Sabres	78	20	10	30	45	3	1	0	1	2
1984-85	Buffalo Sabres	65	20	16	36	41	5	0	1	1	0
1985-86	Buffalo Sabres	45	6	12	18	28	....	....	....	....	....
	Los Angeles Kings	30	4	0	4	7	....	....	....	....	....
1986-87	Los Angeles Kings	69	14	19	33	10	5	0	1	1	0
1987-88	Los Angeles Kings	30	3	2	5	12	....	....	....	....	....
	Toronto Maple Leafs	40	5	5	10	12	2	0	0	0	0
1988-89	Toronto Maple Leafs	3	0	1	1	0	....	....	....	....	....
1989-90	Toronto Maple Leafs	5	0	0	0	20	....	....	....	....	....
	NHL Totals	**414**	**82**	**80**	**162**	**181**	**15**	**1**	**2**	**3**	**2**

Traded to **Los Angeles** by **Buffalo** with Larry Playfair and Ken Baumgartner for Brian Engblom and Doug Smith, Janurary 30, 1986. Traded to **Toronto** by **Los Angeles** for Mike Allison, December 14, 1987.

McKENNA, Steve

Left wing. Shoots left. 6'8", 255 lbs. Born, Toronto, Ont., August 21, 1973.

Season	Club	REGULAR SEASON GP	G	A	Pts	PIM	PLAYOFFS GP	G	A	Pts	PIM
1996-97	Los Angeles Kings	9	0	0	0	37	....	....	....	....	....
1997-98	Los Angeles Kings	62	4	4	8	150	3	0	1	1	8
1998-99	Los Angeles Kings	20	1	0	1	36	....	....	....	....	....
99-2000	Los Angeles Kings	46	0	5	5	125	....	....	....	....	....
2000-01	Minnesota Wild	20	1	1	2	19	....	....	....	....	....
	Pittsburgh Penguins	34	0	0	0	100	....	....	....	....	....
2001-02	New York Rangers	54	2	1	3	144	....	....	....	....	....
2002-03	Pittsburgh Penguins	79	9	1	10	128	....	....	....	....	....
	NHL Totals	**324**	**17**	**12**	**29**	**739**	**3**	**0**	**1**	**1**	**8**

Signed as a free agent by **Los Angeles**, May 23, 1996. Selected by **Minnesota** from **Los Angeles** in Expansion Draft, June 23, 2000. Traded to **Pittsburgh** by **Minnesota** for Roman Simicek, January 13, 2001. Signed as a free agent by **NY Rangers**, August 28, 2001. Signed as a free agent by **Pittsburgh**, July 12, 2002.

McKENNEY, Don

Center. Shoots left. 5'11", 160 lbs. Born, Smiths Falls, Ont., April 30, 1934.

Season	Club	REGULAR SEASON GP	G	A	Pts	PIM	PLAYOFFS GP	G	A	Pts	PIM
1954-55	Boston Bruins	69	22	20	42	34	5	1	2	3	4
1955-56	Boston Bruins	65	10	24	34	20	....	....	....	....	....
1956-57	Boston Bruins	69	21	39	60	31	10	1	5	6	4
1957-58	Boston Bruins	70	28	30	58	22	12	9	8	17	0
1958-59	Boston Bruins	70	32	30	62	20	7	2	5	7	0
1959-60	Boston Bruins	70	20	*49	69	28	....	....	....	....	....
1960-61	Boston Bruins	68	26	23	49	22	....	....	....	....	....
1961-62	Boston Bruins	70	22	33	55	10	....	....	....	....	....
1962-63	Boston Bruins	41	14	19	33	2	....	....	....	....	....
	New York Rangers	21	8	16	24	4	....	....	....	....	....
1963-64	New York Rangers	55	9	17	26	6	....	....	....	....	....
	♦ Toronto Maple Leafs	15	9	6	15	2	12	4	8	12	0
1964-65	Toronto Maple Leafs	52	6	13	19	6	6	0	0	0	0
1965-66	Detroit Red Wings	24	1	6	7	0	....	....	....	....	....
1967-68	St. Louis Blues	39	9	20	29	4	6	1	1	2	2
	NHL Totals	**798**	**237**	**345**	**582**	**211**	**58**	**18**	**29**	**47**	**10**

Lady Byng Trophy (1960)

Played in NHL All-Star Game (1957, 1958, 1959, 1960, 1961, 1962, 1964)

Traded to **NY Rangers** by **Boston** with Dick Meissner for Dean Prentice, February 4, 1963.
• Terms of transaction stipulated that Meissner would report to the NY Rangers following the 1962-63 season. Traded to **Toronto** by **NY Rangers** with Andy Bathgate for Dick Duff, Rod Seiling, Bill Collins, Bob Nevin and Arnie Brown, February 22, 1964. Claimed on waivers by **Detroit** from **Toronto**, June 8, 1965. Claimed by **St. Louis** from **Detroit** in Expansion Draft, June 6, 1967.

McKENNY, Jim

Defense. Shoots right. 5'11", 192 lbs. Born, Ottawa, Ont., December 1, 1946.
(Toronto's 3rd choice, 17th overall, in 1963 Amateur Draft).

Season	Club	REGULAR SEASON GP	G	A	Pts	PIM	PLAYOFFS GP	G	A	Pts	PIM
1965-66	Toronto Maple Leafs	2	0	0	0	2	....	....	....	....	....
1966-67	Toronto Maple Leafs	6	1	0	1	0	....	....	....	....	....
1967-68	Toronto Maple Leafs	5	1	0	1	0	....	....	....	....	....
1968-69	Toronto Maple Leafs	7	0	0	0	2	....	....	....	....	....
1969-70	Toronto Maple Leafs	73	11	33	44	34	....	....	....	....	....
1970-71	Toronto Maple Leafs	68	4	26	30	42	6	2	1	3	2
1971-72	Toronto Maple Leafs	76	5	31	36	27	5	3	0	3	2
1972-73	Toronto Maple Leafs	77	11	41	52	55	....	....	....	....	....
1973-74	Toronto Maple Leafs	77	14	28	42	36	4	0	2	2	0
1974-75	Toronto Maple Leafs	66	8	35	43	31	7	0	1	1	2
1975-76	Toronto Maple Leafs	46	10	19	29	19	6	2	3	5	2
1976-77	Toronto Maple Leafs	76	14	31	45	36	9	0	2	2	2
1977-78	Toronto Maple Leafs	15	2	2	4	8	....	....	....	....	....
1978-79	Minnesota North Stars	10	1	1	2	2	....	....	....	....	....
	NHL Totals	**604**	**82**	**247**	**329**	**294**	**37**	**7**	**9**	**16**	**10**

Played in NHL All-Star Game (1974)

Traded to **Minnesota** by **Toronto** for cash and future considerations (the rights to Owen Lloyd, October 25, 1978), May 15, 1978.

McKENZIE, Brian

Left wing. Shoots left. 5'10", 165 lbs. Born, St. Catharines, Ont., March 16, 1951.
(Pittsburgh's 1st choice, 18th overall, in 1971 Amateur Draft).

Season	Club	REGULAR SEASON GP	G	A	Pts	PIM	PLAYOFFS GP	G	A	Pts	PIM
1971-72	Pittsburgh Penguins	6	1	1	2	4	....	....	....	....	....
	NHL Totals	**6**	**1**	**1**	**2**	**4**	....	....	....	....	....

Traded to **Atlanta** by **Pittsburgh** for cash, October, 1972.

McKENZIE, Jim

Left wing. Shoots left. 6'4", 230 lbs. Born, Gull Lake, Sask., November 3, 1969.
(Hartford's 3rd choice, 73rd overall, in 1989 Entry Draft).

Season	Club	REGULAR SEASON GP	G	A	Pts	PIM	PLAYOFFS GP	G	A	Pts	PIM
1989-90	Hartford Whalers	5	0	0	0	4	....	....	....	....	....
1990-91	Hartford Whalers	41	4	3	7	108	6	0	0	0	8
1991-92	Hartford Whalers	67	5	1	6	87	....	....	....	....	....
1992-93	Hartford Whalers	64	3	6	9	202	....	....	....	....	....
1993-94	Hartford Whalers	26	1	2	3	67	....	....	....	....	....
	Dallas Stars	34	2	3	5	63	....	....	....	....	....
	Pittsburgh Penguins	11	0	0	0	16	3	0	0	0	0
1994-95	Pittsburgh Penguins	39	2	1	3	63	5	0	0	0	4
1995-96	Winnipeg Jets	73	4	2	6	202	1	0	0	0	2
1996-97	Phoenix Coyotes	65	5	3	8	200	7	0	0	0	2
1997-98	Phoenix Coyotes	64	3	4	7	146	1	0	0	0	0
1998-99	Mighty Ducks of Anaheim	73	5	4	9	99	4	0	0	0	4
99-2000	Mighty Ducks of Anaheim	31	3	3	6	48	....	....	....	....	....
	Washington Capitals	30	1	2	3	16	1	0	0	0	0
2000-01	New Jersey Devils	53	2	2	4	119	3	0	0	0	2
2001-02	New Jersey Devils	67	3	5	8	123	6	0	0	0	2

Season	Club	GP	G	A	Pts	PIM	GP	G	A	Pts	PIM
		REGULAR SEASON					PLAYOFFS				
2002-03 ◆	New Jersey Devils	76	4	8	12	88	13	0	0	0	14
	NHL Totals	**819**	**47**	**49**	**96**	**1651**	**50**	**0**	**0**	**0**	**38**

Traded to **Florida** by **Hartford** for Alexander Godynyuk, December 16, 1993. Traded to **Dallas** by **Florida** for Dallas' 4th round choice (later traded to Ottawa – Ottawa selected Kevin Bolibruck) in 1995 Entry Draft, December 16, 1993. Traded to **Pittsburgh** by **Dallas** for Mike Needham, March 21, 1994. Signed as a free agent by **NY Islanders**, August 2, 1995. Claimed by **Winnipeg** from **NY Islanders** in Waiver Draft, October 2, 1995. Transferred to **Phoenix** after **Winnipeg** franchise relocated, July 1, 1996. Traded to **Anaheim** by **Phoenix** for Jean-Francois Jomphe, June 18, 1998. Claimed on waivers by **Washington** from **Anaheim**, January 20, 2000. Signed as a free agent by **New Jersey**, July 3, 2000. Signed as a free agent by **Nashville**, July 22, 2003.

McKENZIE, John

Right wing. Shoots right. 5'9", 175 lbs. Born, High River, Alta., December 12, 1937.

Season	Club	GP	G	A	Pts	PIM	GP	G	A	Pts	PIM
1958-59	Chicago Black Hawks	32	3	4	7	22	2	0	0	0	2
1959-60	Detroit Red Wings	59	8	12	20	50	2	0	0	0	0
1960-61	Detroit Red Wings	16	3	1	4	13	....	....	....	....	....
1963-64	Chicago Black Hawks	45	9	9	18	50	4	0	1	1	6
1964-65	Chicago Black Hawks	51	8	10	18	46	11	0	1	1	6
1965-66	New York Rangers	35	6	5	11	36	....	....	....	....	....
	Boston Bruins	36	13	9	22	36	....	....	....	....	....
1966-67	Boston Bruins	69	17	19	36	98	....	....	....	....	....
1967-68	Boston Bruins	74	28	38	66	107	4	1	1	2	8
1968-69	Boston Bruins	60	29	27	56	99	10	2	2	4	17
1969-70 ◆	Boston Bruins	72	29	41	70	114	14	5	12	17	35
1970-71	Boston Bruins	65	31	46	77	120	7	2	3	5	22
1971-72 ◆	Boston Bruins	77	22	47	69	126	15	5	12	17	37
	NHL Totals	**691**	**206**	**268**	**474**	**917**	**69**	**15**	**32**	**47**	**133**

NHL Second All-Star Team (1970)

Played in NHL All-Star Game (1970, 1972)

Claimed by **Detroit** from **Chicago** in Intra-League Draft, June 10, 1959. Traded to **Chicago** by **Detroit** with Len Lunde for Doug Barkley, June 5, 1962. Traded to **NY Rangers** by **Chicago** with Ray Cullen for Tracy Pratt, Dick Meissner, Dave Richardson and Mel Pearson, June 4, 1965. Traded to **Boston** by **NY Rangers** for Reggie Fleming, January 10, 1966. Traded to **Philadelphia** by **Boston** for cash, August 3, 1972.

McKIM, Andrew

Center. Shoots right. 5'8", 175 lbs. Born, St. John, N.B., July 6, 1970.

Season	Club	GP	G	A	Pts	PIM	GP	G	A	Pts	PIM
1992-93	Boston Bruins	7	1	3	4	0	....	....	....	....	....
1993-94	Boston Bruins	29	0	1	1	4	....	....	....	....	....
1994-95	Detroit Red Wings	2	0	0	0	2	....	....	....	....	....
	NHL Totals	**38**	**1**	**4**	**5**	**6**	....	....	....	....	....

Signed as a free agent by **Calgary**, October 5, 1990. Signed as a free agent by **Toronto**, October, 1991. Signed as a free agent by **Boston**, July 23, 1992. Signed as a free agent by **Detroit**, August 31, 1994.

McKINNON, Alex

Right wing. Shoots right. 5'8", 175 lbs. Born, Sault Ste. Marie, Ont., April 17, 1895.

Season	Club	GP	G	A	Pts	PIM	GP	G	A	Pts	PIM
1924-25	Hamilton Tigers	29	8	3	11	47	....	....	....	....	....
1925-26	New York Americans	35	5	3	8	34	....	....	....	....	....
1926-27	New York Americans	42	2	1	3	29	....	....	....	....	....
1927-28	New York Americans	43	3	3	6	71	....	....	....	....	....
1928-29	Chicago Black Hawks	44	1	1	2	56	....	....	....	....	....
	NHL Totals	**193**	**19**	**11**	**30**	**237**	....	....	....	....	....

Signed as a free agent by **Hamilton**, October 16, 1924. Transferred to **NY Americans** after NHL club purchased **Hamilton** franchise, September 26, 1925. Traded to **Chicago** by **NY Americans** for Charley McVeigh, October 15, 1928.

McKINNON, John

Defense. Shoots right. 5'8", 170 lbs. Born, Guysborough, N.S., July 15, 1902.

Season	Club	GP	G	A	Pts	PIM	GP	G	A	Pts	PIM
1925-26	Montreal Canadiens	2	0	0	0	0	....	....	....	....	....
1926-27	Pittsburgh Pirates	44	13	0	13	21	....	....	....	....	....
1927-28	Pittsburgh Pirates	43	3	3	6	71	2	0	0	0	4
1928-29	Pittsburgh Pirates	39	1	0	1	44	....	....	....	....	....
1929-30	Pittsburgh Pirates	41	10	7	17	42	....	....	....	....	....
1930-31	Philadelphia Quakers	39	1	1	2	46	....	....	....	....	....
	NHL Totals	**208**	**28**	**11**	**39**	**224**	**2**	**0**	**0**	**0**	**4**

Signed as a free agent by **Montreal**, November 23, 1925. Traded to **Pittsburgh** by **Montreal** for cash, October 28, 1926. Transferred to **Philadelphia** after **Pittsburgh** franchise relocated, October 18, 1930.

McLAREN, Kyle

Defense. Shoots left. 6'4", 230 lbs. Born, Humboldt, Sask., June 18, 1977.
(Boston's 1st choice, 9th overall, in 1995 Entry Draft).

Season	Club	GP	G	A	Pts	PIM	GP	G	A	Pts	PIM
1995-96	Boston Bruins	74	5	12	17	73	5	0	0	0	14
1996-97	Boston Bruins	58	5	9	14	54	....	....	....	....	....
1997-98	Boston Bruins	66	5	20	25	56	6	1	0	1	4
1998-99	Boston Bruins	52	6	18	24	48	12	0	3	3	10
99-2000	Boston Bruins	71	8	11	19	67	....	....	....	....	....
2000-01	Boston Bruins	58	5	12	17	53	....	....	....	....	....
2001-02	Boston Bruins	38	0	8	8	19	4	0	0	0	20
2002-03	San Jose Sharks	33	0	8	8	30	....	....	....	....	....
	NHL Totals	**450**	**34**	**98**	**132**	**400**	**27**	**1**	**3**	**4**	**48**

NHL All-Rookie Team (1996)

• Missed majority of 2001-02 season recovering from chest (October 10, 2001 vs. Minnesota) and wrist (December 26, 2001 vs. Ottawa) injuries. Traded to **San Jose** by **Boston** with Boston's 4th round choice in 2004 Entry Draft for Jeff Hackett and Jeff Jillson, January 23, 2003.

McLEAN, Brett

Center. Shoots left. 5'11", 194 lbs. Born, Comox, B.C., August 14, 1978.
(Dallas' 9th choice, 242nd overall, in 1997 Entry Draft).

Season	Club	GP	G	A	Pts	PIM	GP	G	A	Pts	PIM
2002-03	Chicago Blackhawks	2	0	0	0	0	....	....	....	....	....
	NHL Totals	**2**	**0**	**0**	**0**	**0**	....	....	....	....	....

Signed as a free agent by **Calgary**, September, 1999. Signed as a free agent by **Minnesota**, July 13, 2000. Signed as a free agent by **Chicago**, July 23, 2002.

McLEAN, Don

Defense. Shoots right. 6'1", 200 lbs. Born, Niagara Falls, Ont., January 19, 1954.
(Philadelphia's 1st choice, 35th overall, in 1974 Amateur Draft).

Season	Club	GP	G	A	Pts	PIM	GP	G	A	Pts	PIM
1975-76	Washington Capitals	9	0	0	0	6	....	....	....	....	....
	NHL Totals	**9**	**0**	**0**	**0**	**6**	....	....	....	....	....

Traded to **Washington** by **Philadelphia** with Bill Clement and Philadelphia's 1st round choice (Alex Forsyth) in 1975 Amateur Draft for Washington's 1st round choice (Mel Bridgman) in 1975 Amateur Draft, June 4, 1975.

McLEAN, Fred

Defense. Shoots left. 6'2", 200 lbs. Born, Lakeville Corner, N.B., March 16, 1893.

Season	Club	GP	G	A	Pts	PIM	GP	G	A	Pts	PIM
1919-20	Quebec Bulldogs	7	0	0	0	2	....	....	....	....	....
1920-21	Hamilton Tigers	1	0	0	0	0	....	....	....	....	....
	NHL Totals	**8**	**0**	**0**	**0**	**2**	....	....	....	....	....

Signed as a free agent by **Quebec**, February 16, 1920. Transferred to **Hamilton** after **Quebec** franchise relocated, November 2, 1920.

McLEAN, Jack

Center/Right wing. Shoots right. 5'8", 165 lbs. Born, Winnipeg, Man., January 31, 1923.

Season	Club	GP	G	A	Pts	PIM	GP	G	A	Pts	PIM
1942-43	Toronto Maple Leafs	27	9	8	17	33	6	2	2	4	2
1943-44	Toronto Maple Leafs	32	3	15	18	30	3	0	0	0	6
1944-45 ◆	Toronto Maple Leafs	8	2	1	3	13	4	0	0	0	0
	NHL Totals	**67**	**14**	**24**	**38**	**76**	**13**	**2**	**2**	**4**	**8**

• Missed majority of 1944-45 season recovering from ankle injury suffered in game vs. Detroit, December 15, 1944.

McLEAN, Jeff

Center. Shoots left. 5'10", 190 lbs. Born, Port Moody, B.C., October 6, 1969.
(San Jose's 1st choice, 1st overall, in 1991 Supplemental Draft).

Season	Club	GP	G	A	Pts	PIM	GP	G	A	Pts	PIM
1993-94	San Jose Sharks	6	1	0	1	0	....	....	....	....	....
	NHL Totals	**6**	**1**	**0**	**1**	**0**	....	....	....	....	....

McLELLAN, John

Center. Shoots left. 5'11", 150 lbs. Born, South Porcupine, Ont., August 6, 1928.

Season	Club	GP	G	A	Pts	PIM	GP	G	A	Pts	PIM
1951-52	Toronto Maple Leafs	2	0	0	0	0	....	....	....	....	....
	NHL Totals	**2**	**0**	**0**	**0**	**0**	....	....	....	....	....

Traded to **Cleveland** (AHL) by **Toronto** with cash for Hugh Barlow, September 15, 1954.

McLELLAN, Scott

Right wing. Shoots right. 6'1", 175 lbs. Born, Toronto, Ont., February 10, 1963.
(Boston's 3rd choice, 77th overall, in 1981 Entry Draft).

Season	Club	GP	G	A	Pts	PIM	GP	G	A	Pts	PIM
1982-83	Boston Bruins	2	0	0	0	0	....	....	....	....	....
	NHL Totals	**2**	**0**	**0**	**0**	**0**	....	....	....	....	....

McLELLAN, Todd

Center. Shoots left. 5'11", 185 lbs. Born, Melville, Sask., October 3, 1967.
(NY Islanders' 6th choice, 104th overall, in 1986 Entry Draft).

Season	Club	GP	G	A	Pts	PIM	GP	G	A	Pts	PIM
1987-88	New York Islanders	5	1	1	2	0	....	....	....	....	....
	NHL Totals	**5**	**1**	**1**	**2**	**0**	....	....	....	....	....

McLENAHAN, Rollie

Defense. Shoots left. 5'7", 169 lbs. Born, Fredericton, N.B., October 26, 1921.

Season	Club	GP	G	A	Pts	PIM	GP	G	A	Pts	PIM
1945-46	Detroit Red Wings	9	2	1	3	10	2	0	0	0	0
	NHL Totals	**9**	**2**	**1**	**3**	**10**	**2**	**0**	**0**	**0**	**0**

Traded to **Chicago** by **Detroit** for cash, April, 1946.

McLEOD, Al

Defense. Shoots left. 5'11", 200 lbs. Born, Medicine Hat, Alta., June 17, 1949.

Season	Club	GP	G	A	Pts	PIM	GP	G	A	Pts	PIM
1973-74	Detroit Red Wings	26	2	2	4	24	....	....	....	....	....
	NHL Totals	**26**	**2**	**2**	**4**	**24**	....	....	....	....	....

Signed as a free agent by **Detroit** (Fort Worth-CHL), October 1, 1971.

McLEOD, Jackie

Right wing. Shoots right. 5'9", 150 lbs. Born, Regina, Sask., April 30, 1930.

Season	Club	GP	G	A	Pts	PIM	GP	G	A	Pts	PIM
1949-50	New York Rangers	38	6	9	15	2	7	0	0	0	0
1950-51	New York Rangers	41	5	10	15	2	....	....	....	....	....
1951-52	New York Rangers	13	2	3	5	2	....	....	....	....	....
1952-53	New York Rangers	3	0	0	0	2	....	....	....	....	....
1954-55	New York Rangers	11	1	1	2	4	....	....	....	....	....
	NHL Totals	**106**	**14**	**23**	**37**	**12**	**7**	**0**	**0**	**0**	**0**

Signed as a free agent by **NY Rangers**, December 9, 1949. Traded to **Vancouver** (WHL) by **NY Rangers** with cash for Bill Ezinicki, February 12, 1955. Claimed by **NY Rangers** (Providence-AHL) from **NY Rangers** (Vancouver-WHL) in Inter-League Draft, June 4, 1957.

McLLWAIN, Dave

Center/Right wing. Shoots left. 6', 185 lbs. Born, Seaforth, Ont., January 9, 1967.
(Pittsburgh's 9th choice, 172nd overall, in 1986 Entry Draft).

Season	Club	Regular Season GP	G	A	Pts	PIM	Playoffs GP	G	A	Pts	PIM
1987-88	Pittsburgh Penguins	66	11	8	19	40	....	....	....	....	....
1988-89	Pittsburgh Penguins	24	1	2	3	4	3	0	1	1	0
1989-90	Winnipeg Jets	80	25	26	51	60	7	0	1	1	2
1990-91	Winnipeg Jets	60	14	11	25	46	....	....	....	....	....
1991-92	Winnipeg Jets	3	1	1	2	2	....	....	....	....	....
	Buffalo Sabres	5	0	0	0	2	....	....	....	....	....
	New York Islanders	54	8	15	23	28	....	....	....	....	....
	Toronto Maple Leafs	11	1	2	3	4	....	....	....	....	....
1992-93	Toronto Maple Leafs	66	14	4	18	30	4	0	0	0	0
1993-94	Ottawa Senators	66	17	26	43	48	....	....	....	....	....
1994-95	Ottawa Senators	43	5	6	11	22	....	....	....	....	....
1995-96	Ottawa Senators	1	0	1	1	2	....	....	....	....	....
	Pittsburgh Penguins	18	2	4	6	4	6	0	0	0	0
1996-97	New York Islanders	4	1	1	2	0	....	....	....	....	....
	NHL Totals	**501**	**100**	**107**	**207**	**292**	**20**	**0**	**2**	**2**	**2**

Traded to **Winnipeg** by **Pittsburgh** with Randy Cunneyworth and Rick Tabaracci for Jim Kyte, Andrew McBain and Randy Gilhen, June 17, 1989. Traded to **Buffalo** by **Winnipeg** with Gord Donnelly, Winnipeg's 5th round choice (Yuri Khmylev) in 1992 Entry Draft and cash for Darrin Shannon, Mike Hartman and Dean Kennedy, October 11, 1991. Traded to **NY Islanders** by **Buffalo** with Pierre Turgeon, Uwe Krupp and Benoit Hogue for Pat LaFontaine, Randy Hillier, Randy Wood and NY Islanders' 4th round choice (Dean Melanson) in 1992 Entry Draft, October 25, 1991. Traded to **Toronto** by **NY Islanders** with Ken Baumgartner for Daniel Marois and Claude Loiselle, March 10, 1992. Claimed by **Ottawa** from **Toronto** in NHL Waiver Draft, October 3, 1993. Traded to **Pittsburgh** by **Ottawa** for Pittsburgh's 8th round choice (Erich Goldmann) in 1996 Entry Draft, March 1, 1996. Signed as a free agent by **NY Islanders**, July 29, 1996.

McMAHON, Mike

Defense. Shoots left. 5'8", 215 lbs. Born, Brockville, Ont., February 1, 1915.

Season	Club	Regular Season GP	G	A	Pts	PIM	Playoffs GP	G	A	Pts	PIM
1942-43	Montreal Canadiens	....	....	....	....	....	5	0	0	0	14
1943-44 ♦	Montreal Canadiens	42	7	17	24	*98	8	1	2	3	16
1945-46	Montreal Canadiens	13	0	1	1	2	....	....	....	....	....
	Boston Bruins	2	0	0	0	2	....	....	....	....	....
	NHL Totals	**57**	**7**	**18**	**25**	**102**	**13**	**1**	**2**	**3**	**30**

• Father of Mike Jr.

Signed as a free agent by **Montreal**, October 24, 1945. Loaned to **Boston** by **Montreal** as compensation for Montreal's recall of Paul Bibeault, January 8, 1946. Returned to **Montreal** by **Boston**, January 17, 1946.

McMAHON Jr., Mike

Defense. Shoots left. 5'11", 180 lbs. Born, Quebec City, Que., August 30, 1941.

Season	Club	Regular Season GP	G	A	Pts	PIM	Playoffs GP	G	A	Pts	PIM
1963-64	New York Rangers	18	0	1	1	16	....	....	....	....	....
1964-65	New York Rangers	1	0	0	0	0	....	....	....	....	....
1965-66	New York Rangers	41	0	12	12	31	....	....	....	....	....
1967-68	Minnesota North Stars	74	14	33	47	71	14	3	7	10	4
1968-69	Minnesota North Stars	43	0	11	11	21	....	....	....	....	....
	Chicago Black Hawks	20	0	8	8	6	....	....	....	....	....
1969-70	Detroit Red Wings	2	0	0	0	0	....	....	....	....	....
	Pittsburgh Penguins	12	1	3	4	19	....	....	....	....	....
1970-71	Buffalo Sabres	12	0	0	0	4	....	....	....	....	....
1971-72	New York Rangers	1	0	0	0	0	....	....	....	....	....
	NHL Totals	**224**	**15**	**68**	**83**	**171**	**14**	**3**	**7**	**10**	**4**

• Son of Mike

Claimed by **Montreal** from **NY Rangers** in Intra-League Draft, June 15, 1966. Traded to **Minnesota** by **Montreal** for cash, June 14, 1967. Traded to **Chicago** by **Minnesota** with Andre Boudrias for Tom Reid and Bill Orban, February 14, 1969. Claimed on waivers by **Detroit** from **Chicago**, October 14, 1969. Traded to **Pittsburgh** by **Detroit** for Billy Dea, October 28, 1969. Claimed by **Buffalo** from **Pittsburgh** in Expansion Draft, June 10, 1970. Traded to **Los Angeles** by **Buffalo** with future considerations for Eddie Shack and Dick Duff, November 24, 1970. Traded to **NY Rangers** (Baltimore-AHL) by **Los Angeles** (Springfield-AHL) for Wayne Rivers, October, 1971. Loaned to **Vancouver** (Rochester-AHL) by **NY Rangers** (Providence-AHL) for the remainder of the 1971-72 season for Ron Stewart, March 5, 1972.

McMANAMA, Bob

Center. Shoots left. 6', 180 lbs. Born, Belmont, MA, October 7, 1951.

Season	Club	Regular Season GP	G	A	Pts	PIM	Playoffs GP	G	A	Pts	PIM
1973-74	Pittsburgh Penguins	47	5	14	19	18	....	....	....	....	....
1974-75	Pittsburgh Penguins	40	5	9	14	6	8	0	1	1	6
1975-76	Pittsburgh Penguins	12	1	2	3	4	....	....	....	....	....
	NHL Totals	**99**	**11**	**25**	**36**	**28**	**8**	**0**	**1**	**1**	**6**

Signed as a free agent by **Pittsburgh**, August, 1973.

McMANUS, Sammy

Left wing. Shoots left. 5'9", 160 lbs. Born, Belfast, Ireland, October 22, 1911.

Season	Club	Regular Season GP	G	A	Pts	PIM	Playoffs GP	G	A	Pts	PIM
1934-35 ♦	Montreal Maroons	25	0	1	1	8	1	0	0	0	0
1936-37	Boston Bruins	1	0	0	0	0	....	....	....	....	....
	NHL Totals	**26**	**0**	**1**	**1**	**8**	**1**	**0**	**0**	**0**	**0**

Signed as a free agent by **Mtl. Maroons**, October 31, 1934. Loaned to **New Haven** (Can-Am) by **Mtl. Maroons** (Windsor-IHL) for cash, January 6, 1935. Traded to **NY Rangers** by **Mtl. Maroons** for $10,000, October 26, 1935. Traded to **Mtl. Maroons** by **NY Rangers** for cash, September, 1936. Traded to **Montreal** by **Mtl. Maroons** for the rights to Buddy O'Connor, September 10, 1936. Traded to **Boston** by **Montreal** with Leroy Goldsworthy and $10,000 for Babe Siebert and Roger Jenkins, September 10, 1936. Signed as a free agent by **Chicago**, October, 1940. Traded to **St. Louis** (AHA) by **Chicago** with cash for Fido Purpur, May 3, 1941.

McMORROW, Sean

Left wing. Shoots right. 6'4", 214 lbs. Born, Vancouver, B.C., January 19, 1982.
(Buffalo's 7th choice, 258th overall, in 2000 Entry Draft).

Season	Club	Regular Season GP	G	A	Pts	PIM	Playoffs GP	G	A	Pts	PIM
2002-03	Buffalo Sabres	1	0	0	0	0	....	....	....	....	....
	NHL Totals	**1**	**0**	**0**	**0**	**0**	....	....	....	....	....

McMURCHY, Tom

Right wing. Shoots left. 5'9", 165 lbs. Born, New Westminster, B.C., December 2, 1963.
(Chicago's 3rd choice, 49th overall, in 1982 Entry Draft).

Season	Club	Regular Season GP	G	A	Pts	PIM	Playoffs GP	G	A	Pts	PIM
1983-84	Chicago Black Hawks	27	3	1	4	42	....	....	....	....	....
1984-85	Chicago Black Hawks	15	1	2	3	13	....	....	....	....	....
1985-86	Chicago Black Hawks	4	0	0	0	2	....	....	....	....	....
1987-88	Edmonton Oilers	9	4	1	5	8	....	....	....	....	....
	NHL Totals	**55**	**8**	**4**	**12**	**65**	....	....	....	....	....

Traded to **Calgary** by **Chicago** for Rik Wilson, March 11, 1986. Signed as a free agent by **Edmonton**, August 18, 1986.

McNAB, Max

Center. Shoots left. 6'2", 179 lbs. Born, Watson, Sask., June 21, 1924.

Season	Club	Regular Season GP	G	A	Pts	PIM	Playoffs GP	G	A	Pts	PIM
1947-48	Detroit Red Wings	12	2	2	4	2	3	0	0	0	2
1948-49	Detroit Red Wings	51	10	13	23	14	10	1	0	1	2
1949-50 ♦	Detroit Red Wings	65	4	4	8	8	10	0	0	0	0
1950-51	Detroit Red Wings	....	....	....	....	....	2	0	0	0	0
	NHL Totals	**128**	**16**	**19**	**35**	**24**	**25**	**1**	**0**	**1**	**4**

• Father of Peter

Traded to **Chicago** by **Detroit** with George Gee, Jimmy Peters, Clare Martin, Rags Raglan and Jim McFadden for $75,000 and future considerations (Hugh Coflin, October, 1951), August 20, 1951.

McNAB, Peter

Center. Shoots left. 6'3", 210 lbs. Born, Vancouver, B.C., May 8, 1952.
(Buffalo's 6th choice, 85th overall, in 1972 Amateur Draft).

Season	Club	Regular Season GP	G	A	Pts	PIM	Playoffs GP	G	A	Pts	PIM
1973-74	Buffalo Sabres	22	3	6	9	2	....	....	....	....	....
1974-75	Buffalo Sabres	53	22	21	43	8	17	2	6	8	4
1975-76	Buffalo Sabres	79	24	32	56	16	8	0	0	0	0
1976-77	Boston Bruins	80	38	48	86	11	14	5	3	8	2
1977-78	Boston Bruins	79	41	39	80	4	15	8	11	19	2
1978-79	Boston Bruins	76	35	45	80	10	11	5	3	8	0
1979-80	Boston Bruins	74	40	30	70	10	10	0	6	11	2
1980-81	Boston Bruins	80	37	46	83	24	3	3	0	3	0
1981-82	Boston Bruins	80	36	40	76	19	11	6	8	14	6
1982-83	Boston Bruins	74	22	52	74	23	15	3	5	8	4
1983-84	Boston Bruins	52	14	16	30	10	....	....	....	....	....
	Vancouver Canucks	13	1	6	7	10	3	0	0	0	0
1984-85	Vancouver Canucks	75	23	25	48	10	....	....	....	....	....
1985-86	New Jersey Devils	71	19	24	43	14	....	....	....	....	....
1986-87	New Jersey Devils	46	8	12	20	8	....	....	....	....	....
	NHL Totals	**954**	**363**	**450**	**813**	**179**	**107**	**40**	**42**	**82**	**20**

• Son of Max

Played in NHL All-Star Game (1977)

Transferred to **Boston** by **Buffalo** as compensation for Buffalo's signing of free agent Andre Savard, June 11, 1976. Traded to **Vancouver** by **Boston** for Jim Nill, February 3, 1984. Signed as a free agent by **New Jersey**, August 20, 1985.

McNABNEY, Sid

Center. Shoots left. 5'7", 150 lbs. Born, Toronto, Ont., January 15, 1929.

Season	Club	Regular Season GP	G	A	Pts	PIM	Playoffs GP	G	A	Pts	PIM
1950-51	Montreal Canadiens	....	....	....	....	....	5	0	1	1	2
	NHL Totals	....	....	....	....	....	**5**	**0**	**1**	**1**	**2**

Rights traded to **Montreal** (Buffalo-AHL) by **Springfield** (AHL) with Gordie Bell for Hub Macey, December 21, 1948.

McNAMARA, Howard

Defense. Shoots left. 6', 240 lbs. Born, Randolph, Ont., August 3, 1893.

Season	Club	Regular Season GP	G	A	Pts	PIM	Playoffs GP	G	A	Pts	PIM
1919-20	Montreal Canadiens	10	1	0	1	4	....	....	....	....	....
	NHL Totals	**10**	**1**	**0**	**1**	**4**	....	....	....	....	....

Signed as a free agent by **Montreal**, December 7, 1919.

McNAUGHTON, George

Right wing/Center. Shoots right. 5'9", 150 lbs. Born, Gaspe, Que., April 4, 1897.

Season	Club	Regular Season GP	G	A	Pts	PIM	Playoffs GP	G	A	Pts	PIM
1919-20	Quebec Bulldogs	1	0	0	0	0	....	....	....	....	....
	NHL Totals	**1**	**0**	**0**	**0**	**0**	....	....	....	....	....

Signed as a free agent by **Quebec**, December 21, 1919.

McNEILL, Billy

Right wing. Shoots right. 5'10", 175 lbs. Born, Edmonton, Alta., January 26, 1936.

Season	Club	Regular Season GP	G	A	Pts	PIM	Playoffs GP	G	A	Pts	PIM
1956-57	Detroit Red Wings	64	5	10	15	34	....	....	....	....	....
1957-58	Detroit Red Wings	35	5	10	15	29	4	1	1	2	4
1958-59	Detroit Red Wings	54	2	5	7	32	....	....	....	....	....
1959-60	Detroit Red Wings	47	5	13	18	33	....	....	....	....	....
1962-63	Detroit Red Wings	42	3	7	10	12	....	....	....	....	....

		REGULAR SEASON					PLAYOFFS				
Season	Club	GP	G	A	Pts	PIM	GP	G	A	Pts	PIM
1963-64	Detroit Red Wings	15	1	1	2	2	....	....	....	....	....
	NHL Totals	**257**	**21**	**46**	**67**	**142**	**4**	**1**	**1**	**2**	**4**

Traded to **NY Rangers** by **Detroit** with Red Kelly for Eddie Shack and Bill Gadsby, February 5, 1960. • Kelly and McNeill refused to report and transaction was cancelled, February 7, 1960. • Suspended by Detroit for remainder of 1959-60 season for failing to report to NY Rangers, February 7, 1960. Claimed by **NY Rangers** from **Detroit** in Intra-League Draft, June 7, 1960. • Retired from hockey in order to pursue business interests in Edmonton, Summer, 1960. Rights traded to **Detroit** (Edmonton-WHL) by **NY Rangers** for cash, January, 1961. Traded to **Vancouver** (WHL) by **Detroit** for Barrie Ross and future considerations, January, 1964.

McNEILL, Mike

Right wing. Shoots left. 6'1", 195 lbs. Born, Winona, MN, July 22, 1966.
(St. Louis' 1st choice, 14th overall, in 1988 Supplemental Draft).

1990-91	Chicago Blackhawks	23	2	2	4	6	....	....	....	....	....
	Quebec Nordiques	14	2	5	7	4	....	....	....	....	....
1991-92	Quebec Nordiques	26	1	4	5	8	....	....	....	....	....
	NHL Totals	**63**	**5**	**11**	**16**	**18**	....	....	....	....	....

Signed as a free agent by **Chicago**, September, 1989. Traded to **Quebec** by **Chicago** with Ryan McGill for Paul Gillis and Dan Vincelette, March 5, 1991.

McNEILL, Stu

Center. Shoots right. 5'10", 170 lbs. Born, Port Arthur, Ont., September 25, 1938.

1957-58	Detroit Red Wings	2	0	0	0	0	....	....	....	....	....
1958-59	Detroit Red Wings	3	1	1	2	2	....	....	....	....	....
1959-60	Detroit Red Wings	5	0	0	0	0	....	....	....	....	....
	NHL Totals	**10**	**1**	**1**	**2**	**2**	....	....	....	....	....

McPHEE, George

Left wing. Shoots left. 5'9", 170 lbs. Born, Guelph, Ont., July 2, 1958.

1982-83	New York Rangers	....	....	....	....	....	9	3	3	6	2
1983-84	New York Rangers	9	1	1	2	11	....	....	....	....	....
1984-85	New York Rangers	49	12	15	27	139	3	1	0	1	7
1985-86	New York Rangers	30	4	4	8	63	11	0	0	0	32
1986-87	New York Rangers	21	4	4	8	34	6	1	0	1	28
1987-88	New Jersey Devils	5	3	0	3	8	....	....	....	....	....
1988-89	New Jersey Devils	1	0	1	1	2	....	....	....	....	....
	NHL Totals	**115**	**24**	**25**	**49**	**257**	**29**	**5**	**3**	**8**	**69**

Signed as a free agent by **NY Rangers**, July 1, 1982. • Suffered eventual career-ending back injury in game vs. Pittsburgh, November 4, 1985. Traded to **Winnipeg** by **NY Rangers** for Winnipeg's 4th round choice (Jim Cummins) in 1989 Entry Draft, September 30, 1987. • Missed majority of 1986-87 season recovering from shoulder injury suffered in exhibition game vs. Pittsburgh, October 5, 1986. Traded to **New Jersey** by **Winnipeg** for New Jersey's 7th round choice (Doug Evans) in 1989 Entry Draft, October 7, 1987.

McPHEE, Mike

Left wing. Shoots left. 6'1", 203 lbs. Born, Sydney, N.S., July 14, 1960.
(Montreal's 8th choice, 124th overall, in 1980 Entry Draft).

1983-84	Montreal Canadiens	14	5	2	7	41	15	1	0	1	31
1984-85	Montreal Canadiens	70	17	22	39	120	12	4	1	5	32
1985-86◆	Montreal Canadiens	70	19	21	40	69	20	3	4	7	45
1986-87	Montreal Canadiens	79	18	21	39	58	17	7	2	9	13
1987-88	Montreal Canadiens	77	23	20	43	53	11	4	3	7	8
1988-89	Montreal Canadiens	73	19	22	41	74	20	4	7	11	30
1989-90	Montreal Canadiens	56	23	18	41	47	9	1	1	2	16
1990-91	Montreal Canadiens	64	22	21	43	56	13	1	7	8	12
1991-92	Montreal Canadiens	78	16	15	31	63	8	1	1	2	4
1992-93	Minnesota North Stars	84	18	22	40	44	....	....	....	....	....
1993-94	Dallas Stars	79	20	15	35	36	9	2	1	3	2
	NHL Totals	**744**	**200**	**199**	**399**	**661**	**134**	**28**	**27**	**55**	**193**

Played in NHL All-Star Game (1989)

Traded to **Minnesota** by **Montreal** for Minnesota/Dallas' 5th round choice (Jeff Lank) in 1993 Entry Draft, August 14, 1992. Transferred to **Dallas** after **Minnesota** franchise relocated, June 9, 1993.

McRAE, Basil

Left wing. Shoots left. 6'2", 210 lbs. Born, Beaverton, Ont., January 5, 1961.
(Quebec's 3rd choice, 87th overall, in 1980 Entry Draft).

1981-82	Quebec Nordiques	20	4	3	7	69	9	1	0	1	34
1982-83	Quebec Nordiques	22	1	1	2	59	....	....	....	....	....
1983-84	Toronto Maple Leafs	3	0	0	0	19	....	....	....	....	....
1984-85	Toronto Maple Leafs	1	0	0	0	0	....	....	....	....	....
1985-86	Detroit Red Wings	4	0	0	0	5	....	....	....	....	....
1986-87	Detroit Red Wings	36	2	2	4	193	....	....	....	....	....
	Quebec Nordiques	33	9	5	14	149	13	3	1	4	*99
1987-88	Minnesota North Stars	80	5	11	16	382	....	....	....	....	....
1988-89	Minnesota North Stars	78	12	19	31	365	5	0	0	0	58
1989-90	Minnesota North Stars	66	9	17	26	*351	7	1	0	1	24
1990-91	Minnesota North Stars	40	1	3	4	224	22	1	1	2	*94
1991-92	Minnesota North Stars	59	5	8	13	245	....	....	....	....	....
1992-93	Tampa Bay Lightning	14	2	3	5	71	....	....	....	....	....
	St. Louis Blues	33	1	3	4	98	11	0	1	1	24
1993-94	St. Louis Blues	40	1	2	3	103	2	0	0	0	12
1994-95	St. Louis Blues	21	0	5	5	72	7	2	1	3	4
1995-96	St. Louis Blues	18	1	1	2	40	2	0	0	0	0

		REGULAR SEASON					PLAYOFFS				
Season	Club	GP	G	A	Pts	PIM	GP	G	A	Pts	PIM
1996-97	Chicago Blackhawks	8	0	0	0	12	....	....	....	....	....
	NHL Totals	**576**	**53**	**83**	**136**	**2457**	**78**	**8**	**4**	**12**	**349**

• Brother of Chris

Traded to **Toronto** by **Quebec** for Richard Turmel, August 12, 1983. Signed as a free agent by **Detroit**, July 17, 1985. Traded to **Quebec** by **Detroit** with John Ogrodnick and Doug Shedden for Brent Ashton, Gilbert Delorme and Mark Kumpel, January 17, 1987. Signed as a free agent by **Minnesota**, June 29, 1987. Claimed by **Tampa Bay** from **Minnesota** in Expansion Draft, June 18, 1992. Traded to **St. Louis** by **Tampa Bay** with Doug Crossman and Tampa Bay's 4th round choice (Andrei Petrakov) in 1996 Entry Draft for Jason Ruff, January 28, 1993. Signed as a free agent by **Chicago**, October 9, 1996.

McRAE, Chris

Left wing. Shoots left. 6', 200 lbs. Born, Beaverton, Ont., August 26, 1965.

1987-88	Toronto Maple Leafs	11	0	0	0	65	....	....	....	....	....
1988-89	Toronto Maple Leafs	3	0	0	0	12	....	....	....	....	....
1989-90	Detroit Red Wings	7	1	0	1	45	....	....	....	....	....
	NHL Totals	**21**	**1**	**0**	**1**	**122**	....	....	....	....	....

• Brother of Basil

Signed as a free agent by **Toronto**, October 16, 1985. Traded to **NY Rangers** by **Toronto** for Ken Hammond, February 21, 1989. Traded to **Detroit** by **NY Rangers** with Detroit's 5th round choice (previously acquired, Detroit selected Tony Burns) in 1990 Entry Draft for Kris King, September 7, 1989.

McRAE, Ken

Center. Shoots right. 6'1", 195 lbs. Born, Winchester, Ont., April 23, 1968.
(Quebec's 1st choice, 18th overall, in 1986 Entry Draft).

1987-88	Quebec Nordiques	1	0	0	0	0	....	....	....	....	....
1988-89	Quebec Nordiques	37	6	11	17	68	....	....	....	....	....
1989-90	Quebec Nordiques	66	7	8	15	191	....	....	....	....	....
1990-91	Quebec Nordiques	12	0	0	0	36	....	....	....	....	....
1991-92	Quebec Nordiques	10	0	1	1	31	....	....	....	....	....
1992-93	Toronto Maple Leafs	2	0	0	0	2	....	....	....	....	....
1993-94	Toronto Maple Leafs	9	1	1	2	36	6	0	0	0	4
	NHL Totals	**137**	**14**	**21**	**35**	**364**	**6**	**0**	**0**	**0**	**4**

Traded to **Toronto** by **Quebec** for Len Esau, July 21, 1992.

McREAVY, Pat

Center. Shoots right. 5'11", 165 lbs. Born, Owen Sound, Ont., January 16, 1918.

1938-39	Boston Bruins	6	0	0	0	0	....	....	....	....	....
1939-40	Boston Bruins	2	0	0	0	2	....	....	....	....	....
1940-41◆	Boston Bruins	7	0	1	1	2	11	2	2	4	5
1941-42	Boston Bruins	6	0	1	1	0	....	....	....	....	....
	Detroit Red Wings	34	5	8	13	0	11	1	1	2	4
	NHL Totals	**55**	**5**	**10**	**15**	**4**	**22**	**3**	**3**	**6**	**9**

Traded to **Detroit** by **Boston** for Dutch Hiller and $5,000, November 24, 1941. Traded to **St. Louis** (AHL) by **Detroit** for cash, November 5, 1945.

McREYNOLDS, Brian

Center. Shoots left. 6'1", 192 lbs. Born, Penetanguishene, Ont., January 5, 1965.
(NY Rangers' 6th choice, 112th overall, in 1985 Entry Draft).

1989-90	Winnipeg Jets	9	0	2	2	4	....	....	....	....	....
1990-91	New York Rangers	1	0	0	0	0	....	....	....	....	....
1993-94	Los Angeles Kings	20	1	3	4	4	....	....	....	....	....
	NHL Totals	**30**	**1**	**5**	**6**	**8**	....	....	....	....	....

Signed as a free agent by **Winnipeg**, June 20, 1989. Traded to **NY Rangers** by **Winnipeg** for Simon Wheeldon, July 9, 1990. Signed as a free agent by **Los Angeles**, July 29, 1993.

McSHEFFREY, Bryan

Right wing. Shoots right. 6'2", 205 lbs. Born, Ottawa, Ont., September 25, 1952.
(Vancouver's 2nd choice, 19th overall, in 1972 Amateur Draft).

1972-73	Vancouver Canucks	33	4	4	8	10	....	....	....	....	....
1973-74	Vancouver Canucks	54	9	3	12	34	....	....	....	....	....
1974-75	Buffalo Sabres	3	0	0	0	0	....	....	....	....	....
	NHL Totals	**90**	**13**	**7**	**20**	**44**	....	....	....	....	....

Traded to **Buffalo** by **Vancouver** with Jocelyn Guevremont for Gerry Meehan and Mike Robitaille, October 14, 1974.

McSORLEY, Marty

Defense. Shoots right. 6'1", 235 lbs. Born, Hamilton, Ont., May 18, 1963.

1983-84	Pittsburgh Penguins	72	2	7	9	224	....	....	....	....	....
1984-85	Pittsburgh Penguins	15	0	0	0	15	....	....	....	....	....
1985-86	Edmonton Oilers	59	11	12	23	265	8	0	2	2	50
1986-87◆	Edmonton Oilers	41	2	4	6	159	21	4	3	7	65
1987-88◆	Edmonton Oilers	60	9	17	26	223	16	0	3	3	67
1988-89	Los Angeles Kings	66	10	17	27	350	11	0	2	2	33
1989-90	Los Angeles Kings	75	15	21	36	322	10	1	3	4	18
1990-91	Los Angeles Kings	61	7	32	39	221	12	0	0	0	58
1991-92	Los Angeles Kings	71	7	22	29	268	6	1	0	1	21
1992-93	Los Angeles Kings	81	15	26	41	*399	24	4	6	10	*60
1993-94	Pittsburgh Penguins	47	3	18	21	139	....	....	....	....	....
	Los Angeles Kings	18	4	6	10	55	....	....	....	....	....
1994-95	Los Angeles Kings	41	3	18	21	83	....	....	....	....	....
1995-96	Los Angeles Kings	59	10	21	31	148	....	....	....	....	....
	New York Rangers	9	0	2	2	21	4	0	0	0	0
1996-97	San Jose Sharks	57	4	12	16	186	....	....	....	....	....

		REGULAR SEASON					PLAYOFFS				
Season	Club	GP	G	A	Pts	PIM	GP	G	A	Pts	PIM
1997-98	San Jose Sharks	56	2	10	12	140	....	....	....	....	....
1998-99	Edmonton Oilers	46	2	3	5	101	3	0	0	0	2
99-2000	Boston Bruins	27	2	3	5	62	....	....	....	....	....
	NHL Totals	**961**	**108**	**251**	**359**	**3381**	**115**	**10**	**19**	**29**	**374**

Shared Alka-Seltzer Plus Award with Theoren Fleury (1991)

Signed as a free agent by **Pittsburgh**, July 30, 1982. Traded to **Edmonton** by **Pittsburgh** with Tim Hrynewich and future considerations (Craig Muni, October 6, 1986) for Gilles Meloche, September 11, 1985. Traded to **Los Angeles** by **Edmonton** with Wayne Gretzky and Mike Krushelnyski for Jimmy Carson, Martin Gelinas, Los Angeles' 1st round choices in 1989 (later traded to New Jersey – New Jersey selected Jason Miller), 1991 (Martin Rucinsky) and 1993 (Nick Stajduhar) Entry Drafts and cash, August 9, 1988. Traded to **Pittsburgh** by **Los Angeles**, for Shawn McEachern, August 27, 1993. Traded to **Los Angeles** by **Pittsburgh** with Jim Paek for Tomas Sandstrom and Shawn McEachern, February 16, 1994. Traded to **NY Rangers** by **Los Angeles** with Jari Kurri and Shane Churla for Ray Ferraro, Ian Laperriere, Mattias Norstrom, Nathan LaFayette and NY Rangers' 4th round choice (Sean Blanchard) in 1997 Entry Draft, March 14, 1996. Traded to **San Jose** by **NY Rangers** for Jayson More, Brian Swanson and San Jose's 4th round choice (later traded back to San Jose – San Jose selected Adam Colagiacomo) in 1997 Entry Draft, August 20, 1996. Signed as a free agent by **Edmonton**, October 1, 1998. Signed as a free agent by **Boston**, December 9, 1999. • Suspended by NHL until February 21, 2001 for stick assault on Donald Brashear in game vs. Vancouver, February 21, 2000.

McSWEEN, Don

Defense. Shoots left. 5'11", 197 lbs. Born, Detroit, MI, June 9, 1964.
(Buffalo's 10th choice, 160th overall, in 1983 Entry Draft).

Season	Club	GP	G	A	Pts	PIM	GP	G	A	Pts	PIM
1987-88	Buffalo Sabres	5	0	1	1	6	....	....	....	....	....
1989-90	Buffalo Sabres	4	0	0	0	6	....	....	....	....	....
1993-94	Mighty Ducks of Anaheim	32	3	9	12	39	....	....	....	....	....
1994-95	Mighty Ducks of Anaheim	2	0	0	0	0	....	....	....	....	....
1995-96	Mighty Ducks of Anaheim	4	0	0	0	4	....	....	....	....	....
	NHL Totals	**47**	**3**	**10**	**13**	**55**	....	....	....	....	....

Signed as a free agent by **Anaheim**, January 12, 1994. • Missed majority of 1994-95 season recovering from arm injury suffered in game vs. Winnipeg, January 21, 1995.

McTAGGART, Jim

Defense. Shoots left. 5'11", 200 lbs. Born, Weyburn, Sask., March 31, 1960.

Season	Club	GP	G	A	Pts	PIM	GP	G	A	Pts	PIM
1980-81	Washington Capitals	52	1	6	7	185	....	....	....	....	....
1981-82	Washington Capitals	19	2	4	6	20	....	....	....	....	....
	NHL Totals	**71**	**3**	**10**	**13**	**205**	....	....	....	....	....

Signed as a free agent by **Washington**, November 9, 1979. Signed as a free agent by **Edmonton**, October 27, 1982. Traded to **New Jersey** by **Edmonton** with Ron Low for Lindsay Middlebrook and Paul Miller, February 19, 1983.

McTAVISH, Dale

Center. Shoots left. 6'1", 200 lbs. Born, Eganville, Ont., February 28, 1972.

Season	Club	GP	G	A	Pts	PIM	GP	G	A	Pts	PIM
1996-97	Calgary Flames	9	1	2	3	2	....	....	....	....	....
	NHL Totals	**9**	**1**	**2**	**3**	**2**	....	....	....	....	....

Signed as a free agent by **Calgary**, August 1, 1996.

McTAVISH, Gord

Center. Shoots right. 6'4", 200 lbs. Born, Guelph, Ont., June 3, 1954.
(Montreal's 5th choice, 15th overall, in 1974 Amateur Draft).

Season	Club	GP	G	A	Pts	PIM	GP	G	A	Pts	PIM
1978-79	St. Louis Blues	1	0	0	0	0	....	....	....	....	....
1979-80	Winnipeg Jets	10	1	3	4	2	....	....	....	....	....
	NHL Totals	**11**	**1**	**3**	**4**	**2**	....	....	....	....	....

Traded to **St. Louis** by **Montreal** for Mike Korney, October 7, 1978. Selected by **Winnipeg** from **St. Louis** in Expansion Draft, June 13, 1979.

McVEIGH, Charley

Center/Left wing. Shoots left. 5'6", 145 lbs. Born, Kenora, Ont., March 29, 1898.

Season	Club	GP	G	A	Pts	PIM	GP	G	A	Pts	PIM
1926-27	Chicago Black Hawks	43	12	4	16	23	2	0	0	0	0
1927-28	Chicago Black Hawks	43	6	7	13	10	....	....	....	....	....
1928-29	New York Americans	44	6	2	8	16	2	0	0	0	2
1929-30	New York Americans	40	14	14	28	32	....	....	....	....	....
1930-31	New York Americans	44	5	11	16	23	....	....	....	....	....
1931-32	New York Americans	48	12	15	27	16	....	....	....	....	....
1932-33	New York Americans	40	7	12	19	10	....	....	....	....	....
1933-34	New York Americans	48	15	12	27	4	....	....	....	....	....
1934-35	New York Americans	47	7	11	18	4	....	....	....	....	....
	NHL Totals	**397**	**84**	**88**	**172**	**138**	**4**	**0**	**0**	**0**	**2**

Rights transferred to **Chicago** after NHL club purchased **Portland** (WHL) franchise, May 15, 1926. Traded to **NY Americans** by **Chicago** for Alex McKinnon, October 15, 1928.

McVICAR, Jack

Defense. Shoots right. 6', 160 lbs. Born, Renfrew, Ont., June 4, 1904.

Season	Club	GP	G	A	Pts	PIM	GP	G	A	Pts	PIM
1930-31	Montreal Maroons	40	2	4	6	35	2	0	0	0	2
1931-32	Montreal Maroons	48	0	0	0	28	4	0	0	0	0
	NHL Totals	**88**	**2**	**4**	**6**	**63**	**6**	**0**	**0**	**0**	**2**

Traded to **Mtl. Maroons** by **Providence** (Can-Am) for cash, August, 1930. Traded to **Providence** (Can-Am) by **Mtl. Maroons** (Windsor-IHL) for Harvey Rockburn, December 13, 1932.

MEAGHER, Rick

Center. Shoots left. 5'9", 192 lbs. Born, Belleville, Ont., November 2, 1953.

Season	Club	GP	G	A	Pts	PIM	GP	G	A	Pts	PIM
1979-80	Montreal Canadiens	2	0	0	0	0	....	....	....	....	....
1980-81	Hartford Whalers	27	7	10	17	19	....	....	....	....	....
1981-82	Hartford Whalers	65	24	19	43	51	....	....	....	....	....
1982-83	Hartford Whalers	4	0	0	0	0	....	....	....	....	....
	New Jersey Devils	57	15	14	29	11	....	....	....	....	....
1983-84	New Jersey Devils	52	14	14	28	16	....	....	....	....	....
1984-85	New Jersey Devils	71	11	20	31	22	....	....	....	....	....
1985-86	St. Louis Blues	79	11	19	30	28	19	4	4	8	12
1986-87	St. Louis Blues	80	18	21	39	54	6	0	0	0	11
1987-88	St. Louis Blues	76	18	16	34	76	10	0	0	0	8
1988-89	St. Louis Blues	78	15	14	29	53	10	3	2	5	6
1989-90	St. Louis Blues	76	8	17	25	47	8	1	0	1	2
1990-91	St. Louis Blues	24	3	1	4	6	9	0	1	1	2
	NHL Totals	**691**	**144**	**165**	**309**	**383**	**62**	**8**	**7**	**15**	**41**

Frank J. Selke Trophy (1990)

Signed as a free agent by **Montreal**, June 27, 1977. Traded to **Hartford** by **Montreal** with Montreal's 3rd (Paul MacDermid) and 5th (Dan Bourbonnais) round choices in 1981 Entry Draft for Hartford's 3rd (Dieter Hegen) and 5th (Steve Rooney) round choices in 1981 Entry Draft, June 5, 1980. Traded to **New Jersey** by **Hartford** with Garry Howatt for Merlin Malinowski and the rights to Scott Fusco, October 15, 1982. Traded to **St. Louis** by **New Jersey** with New Jersey's 12th round choice (Bill Butler) in 1986 Entry Draft for Perry Anderson, August 29, 1985.

MEEHAN, Gerry

Center. Shoots left. 6'2", 200 lbs. Born, Toronto, Ont., September 3, 1946.
(Toronto's 4th choice, 21st overall, in 1963 Amateur Draft).

Season	Club	GP	G	A	Pts	PIM	GP	G	A	Pts	PIM
1968-69	Toronto Maple Leafs	25	0	2	2	2	....	....	....	....	....
	Philadelphia Flyers	12	0	3	3	4	4	0	0	0	0
1970-71	Buffalo Sabres	77	24	31	55	8	....	....	....	....	....
1971-72	Buffalo Sabres	77	19	27	46	12	....	....	....	....	....
1972-73	Buffalo Sabres	77	31	29	60	21	6	0	1	1	0
1973-74	Buffalo Sabres	72	20	26	46	17	....	....	....	....	....
1974-75	Buffalo Sabres	3	0	1	1	2	....	....	....	....	....
	Vancouver Canucks	57	10	15	25	4	....	....	....	....	....
	Atlanta Flames	14	4	10	14	0	....	....	....	....	....
1975-76	Atlanta Flames	48	7	20	27	8	....	....	....	....	....
	Washington Capitals	32	16	15	31	10	....	....	....	....	....
1976-77	Washington Capitals	80	28	36	64	13	....	....	....	....	....
1977-78	Washington Capitals	78	19	24	43	10	....	....	....	....	....
1978-79	Washington Capitals	18	2	4	6	0	....	....	....	....	....
	NHL Totals	**670**	**180**	**243**	**423**	**111**	**10**	**0**	**1**	**1**	**0**

Traded to **Philadelphia** by **Toronto** with Mike Byers and Bill Sutherland for Brit Selby and Forbes Kennedy, March 3, 1969. Claimed by **Buffalo** from **Philadelphia** in Expansion Draft, June 10, 1970. Traded to **Vancouver** by **Buffalo** with Mike Robitaille for Jocelyn Guevremont and Bryan McSheffrey, October 14, 1974. Traded to **Atlanta** by **Vancouver** for Bob J. Murray, March 9, 1975. Traded to **Washington** by **Atlanta** with Jean Lemieux and Buffalo's 1st round choice (previously acquired, Washington selected Greg Carroll) in 1976 Amateur Draft for Bill Clement, January 22, 1976.

MEEKE, Brent

Defense. Shoots left. 5'11", 175 lbs. Born, Toronto, Ont., April 10, 1952.
(California's 8th choice, 118th overall, in 1972 Amateur Draft).

Season	Club	GP	G	A	Pts	PIM	GP	G	A	Pts	PIM
1972-73	California Golden Seals	3	0	0	0	0	....	....	....	....	....
1973-74	California Golden Seals	18	1	9	10	4	....	....	....	....	....
1974-75	California Golden Seals	4	0	0	0	0	....	....	....	....	....
1975-76	California Golden Seals	1	0	0	0	0	....	....	....	....	....
1976-77	Cleveland Barons	49	8	13	21	4	....	....	....	....	....
	NHL Totals	**75**	**9**	**22**	**31**	**8**	....	....	....	....	....

Transferred to **Cleveland** after **California** franchise relocated, August 26, 1976.

MEEKER, Howie

Right wing. Shoots right. 5'9", 165 lbs. Born, Kitchener, Ont., November 4, 1924.

Season	Club	GP	G	A	Pts	PIM	GP	G	A	Pts	PIM
1946-47 ♦	Toronto Maple Leafs	55	27	18	45	76	11	3	3	6	6
1947-48 ♦	Toronto Maple Leafs	58	14	20	34	62	9	2	4	6	15
1948-49 ♦	Toronto Maple Leafs	30	7	7	14	56	....	....	....	....	....
1949-50	Toronto Maple Leafs	70	18	22	40	35	7	0	1	1	4
1950-51 ♦	Toronto Maple Leafs	49	6	14	20	24	11	1	1	2	14
1951-52	Toronto Maple Leafs	54	9	14	23	50	4	0	0	0	11
1952-53	Toronto Maple Leafs	25	1	7	8	26	....	....	....	....	....
1953-54	Toronto Maple Leafs	5	1	0	1	0	....	....	....	....	....
	NHL Totals	**346**	**83**	**102**	**185**	**329**	**42**	**6**	**9**	**15**	**50**

Calder Memorial Trophy (1947)

Played in NHL All-Star Game (1947, 1948, 1949)

Signed as a free agent by **Toronto**, April 13, 1946. • Missed majority of 1948-49 season recovering from collarbone injury suffered in practice, December 27, 1948.

MEEKER, Mike

Right wing. Shoots right. 5'11", 195 lbs. Born, Kingston, Ont., February 23, 1958.
(Pittsburgh's 1st choice, 25th overall, in 1978 Amateur Draft).

Season	Club	GP	G	A	Pts	PIM	GP	G	A	Pts	PIM
1978-79	Pittsburgh Penguins	4	0	0	0	5	....	....	....	....	....
	NHL Totals	**4**	**0**	**0**	**0**	**5**	....	....	....	....	....

MEEKING, Harry

Left wing. Shoots left. 5'7", 160 lbs. Born, Berlin, Ont., November 4, 1894.

Season	Club	GP	G	A	Pts	PIM	GP	G	A	Pts	PIM
1917-18	Toronto Arenas	21	10	9	19	28	2	3	0	3	6
	♦ *Toronto Arenas (Cup)*	....	....	....	....	....	*5*	*1*	*2*	*3*	*0*
1918-19	Toronto Arenas	14	7	3	10	32	....	....	....	....	....

Season	Club	GP	G	A	Pts	PIM	GP	G	A	Pts	PIM
		REGULAR SEASON					PLAYOFFS				
1926-27	Detroit Cougars	6	0	0	0	4	....	....	....	....	....
	Boston Bruins	23	1	0	1	2	7	0	0	0	0
	NHL Totals	**64**	**18**	**12**	**30**	**66**	**9**	**3**	**0**	**3**	**6**

Signed as a free agent by **Toronto**, December 5, 1917. • Suspended by Toronto for jumping contract to sign with Cape Breton (CBHL), February 19, 1919. Traded to **Victoria** (PCHA) by **Toronto** for cash, December 7, 1919. Rights transferred to **Detroit** after NHL club purchased **Victoria** (WHL) franchise, May 15, 1926. Traded to **Boston** by **Detroit** with Frank Frederickson for Duke Keats and Archie Briden, January 7, 1927. Traded to **Detroit** by **Boston** for Fred Gordon, May 22, 1927. Traded to **NY Rangers** by **Detroit** with Archie Briden for Stan Brown, October 10, 1927.

MEGER, Paul

Left wing. Shoots left. 5'7", 160 lbs. Born, Watrous, Sask., February 17, 1929.

Season	Club	GP	G	A	Pts	PIM	GP	G	A	Pts	PIM
1949-50	Montreal Canadiens	....	....	....	....	....	2	0	0	0	2
1950-51	Montreal Canadiens	17	2	4	6	6	11	1	3	4	4
1951-52	Montreal Canadiens	69	24	18	42	44	11	0	3	3	2
1952-53 ♦	Montreal Canadiens	69	9	17	26	38	5	1	2	3	4
1953-54	Montreal Canadiens	44	4	9	13	24	6	1	0	1	4
1954-55	Montreal Canadiens	13	0	4	4	6	....	....	....	....	....
	NHL Totals	**212**	**39**	**52**	**91**	**118**	**35**	**3**	**8**	**11**	**16**

Played in NHL All-Star Game (1951, 1952, 1953)

• Suffered career-ending head injury in game vs. Chicago, November 25, 1954.

MEIGHAN, Ron

Defense. Shoots right. 6'3", 195 lbs. Born, Montreal, Que., May 26, 1963.
(Minnesota's 1st choice, 13th overall, in 1981 Entry Draft).

Season	Club	GP	G	A	Pts	PIM	GP	G	A	Pts	PIM
1981-82	Minnesota North Stars	7	1	1	2	2	....	....	....	....	....
1982-83	Pittsburgh Penguins	41	2	6	8	16	....	....	....	....	....
	NHL Totals	**48**	**3**	**7**	**10**	**18**	....	....	....	....	....

Traded to **Pittsburgh** by **Minnesota** with Anders Hakansson and Minnesota's 1st round choice (Bob Errey) in 1983 Entry Draft for George Ferguson and Pittsburgh's 1st round choice (Brian Lawton) in 1983 Entry Draft, October 28, 1982.

MEISSNER, Barrie

Left wing. Shoots left. 5'9", 165 lbs. Born, Kindersley, Sask., July 26, 1946.

Season	Club	GP	G	A	Pts	PIM	GP	G	A	Pts	PIM
1967-68	Minnesota North Stars	1	0	0	0	2	....	....	....	....	....
1968-69	Minnesota North Stars	5	0	1	1	2	....	....	....	....	....
	NHL Totals	**6**	**0**	**1**	**1**	**4**	....	....	....	....	....

• Brother of Dick

Rights traded to **Minnesota** by **Montreal** with Bill Plager and the rights to Leo Thiffault for Bryan Watson, June 6, 1967.

MEISSNER, Dick

Right wing. Shoots right. 5'11", 200 lbs. Born, Kindersley, Sask., January 6, 1940.

Season	Club	GP	G	A	Pts	PIM	GP	G	A	Pts	PIM
1959-60	Boston Bruins	60	5	6	11	22	....	....	....	....	....
1960-61	Boston Bruins	9	0	1	1	2	....	....	....	....	....
1961-62	Boston Bruins	66	3	3	6	13	....	....	....	....	....
1963-64	New York Rangers	35	3	5	8	0	....	....	....	....	....
1964-65	New York Rangers	1	0	0	0	0	....	....	....	....	....
	NHL Totals	**171**	**11**	**15**	**26**	**37**	....	....	....	....	....

• Brother of Barrie

Traded to **NY Rangers** by **Boston** with Don McKenney for Dean Prentice, February 4, 1963. • Terms of transaction stipulated that Meissner would report to the NY Rangers following the 1962-63 season. Traded to **Chicago** by **NY Rangers** with Dave Richardson, Tracy Pratt and Mel Pearson for John McKenzie and Ray Cullen, June 4, 1965. Selected by **Providence** (AHL) from **Chicago** in Reverse Draft, June 13, 1968.

MELAMETSA, Anssi

Left wing. Shoots left. 6', 190 lbs. Born, Jyvaskyla, Finland, June 21, 1961.
(Winnipeg's 12th choice, 249th overall, in 1985 Entry Draft).

Season	Club	GP	G	A	Pts	PIM	GP	G	A	Pts	PIM
1985-86	Winnipeg Jets	27	0	3	3	2	....	....	....	....	....
	NHL Totals	**27**	**0**	**3**	**3**	**2**	....	....	....	....	....

MELANSON, Dean

Defense. Shoots right. 5'11", 190 lbs. Born, Antigonish, N.S., November 19, 1973.
(Buffalo's 4th choice, 80th overall, in 1992 Entry Draft).

Season	Club	GP	G	A	Pts	PIM	GP	G	A	Pts	PIM
1994-95	Buffalo Sabres	5	0	0	0	4	....	....	....	....	....
2001-02	Washington Capitals	4	0	0	0	4	....	....	....	....	....
	NHL Totals	**9**	**0**	**0**	**0**	**8**	....	....	....	....	....

Signed as a free agent by **Philadelphia**, July 22, 1999. Traded to **Washington** by **Philadelphia** for Matt Herr, March 13, 2001. Traded to **Ottawa** by **Washington** for Josef Boumedienne, December 16, 2002.

MELICHAR, Josef

Defense. Shoots left. 6'2", 221 lbs. Born, Ceske Budejovice, Czech., January 20, 1979.
(Pittsburgh's 3rd choice, 71st overall, in 1997 Entry Draft).

Season	Club	GP	G	A	Pts	PIM	GP	G	A	Pts	PIM
2000-01	Pittsburgh Penguins	18	0	2	2	21	....	....	....	....	....
2001-02	Pittsburgh Penguins	60	0	3	3	68	....	....	....	....	....
2002-03	Pittsburgh Penguins	8	0	0	0	2	....	....	....	....	....
	NHL Totals	**86**	**0**	**5**	**5**	**91**	....	....	....	....	....

MELIN, Roger

Left wing. Shoots left. 6'4", 195 lbs. Born, Enkoping, Sweden, April 25, 1956.

Season	Club	GP	G	A	Pts	PIM	GP	G	A	Pts	PIM
1980-81	Minnesota North Stars	1	0	0	0	0	....	....	....	....	....
1981-82	Minnesota North Stars	2	0	0	0	0	....	....	....	....	....
	NHL Totals	**3**	**0**	**0**	**0**	**0**	....	....	....	....	....

Signed as a free agent by **Minnesota**, March 23, 1981.

MELLANBY, Scott

Right wing. Shoots right. 6'1", 205 lbs. Born, Montreal, Que., June 11, 1966.
(Philadelphia's 2nd choice, 27th overall, in 1984 Entry Draft).

Season	Club	GP	G	A	Pts	PIM	GP	G	A	Pts	PIM
1985-86	Philadelphia Flyers	2	0	0	0	0	....	....	....	....	....
1986-87	Philadelphia Flyers	71	11	21	32	94	24	5	5	10	46
1987-88	Philadelphia Flyers	75	25	26	51	185	7	0	1	1	16
1988-89	Philadelphia Flyers	76	21	29	50	183	19	4	5	9	28
1989-90	Philadelphia Flyers	57	6	17	23	77	....	....	....	....	....
1990-91	Philadelphia Flyers	74	20	21	41	155	....	....	....	....	....
1991-92	Edmonton Oilers	80	23	27	50	197	16	2	1	3	29
1992-93	Edmonton Oilers	69	15	17	32	147	....	....	....	....	....
1993-94	Florida Panthers	80	30	30	60	149	....	....	....	....	....
1994-95	Florida Panthers	48	13	12	25	90	....	....	....	....	....
1995-96	Florida Panthers	79	32	38	70	160	22	3	6	9	44
1996-97	Florida Panthers	82	27	29	56	170	5	0	2	2	4
1997-98	Florida Panthers	79	15	24	39	127	....	....	....	....	....
1998-99	Florida Panthers	67	18	27	45	85	....	....	....	....	....
99-2000	Florida Panthers	77	18	28	46	126	4	0	1	1	2
2000-01	Florida Panthers	40	4	9	13	46	....	....	....	....	....
	St. Louis Blues	23	7	1	8	25	15	3	3	6	17
2001-02	St. Louis Blues	64	15	26	41	93	10	7	3	10	18
2002-03	St. Louis Blues	80	26	31	57	176	6	0	1	1	10
	NHL Totals	**1223**	**326**	**413**	**739**	**2285**	**128**	**24**	**28**	**52**	**214**

Played in NHL All-Star Game (1996)

Traded to **Edmonton** by **Philadelphia** with Craig Fisher and Craig Berube for Dave Brown, Corey Foster and Jari Kurri, May 30, 1991. Claimed by **Florida** from **Edmonton** in Expansion Draft, June 24, 1993. Traded to **St. Louis** by **Florida** for rights to Dave Morisset and St. Louis' 5th round choice (Vince Bellissimo) in 2002 Entry Draft, February 9, 2001.

MELLOR, Tom

Defense. Shoots right. 6'1", 185 lbs. Born, Cranston, RI, January 27, 1950.
(Detroit's 5th choice, 68th overall, in 1970 Amateur Draft).

Season	Club	GP	G	A	Pts	PIM	GP	G	A	Pts	PIM
1973-74	Detroit Red Wings	25	2	4	6	25	....	....	....	....	....
1974-75	Detroit Red Wings	1	0	0	0	0	....	....	....	....	....
	NHL Totals	**26**	**2**	**4**	**6**	**25**	....	....	....	....	....

MELNYK, Gerry

Center. Shoots right. 5'10", 165 lbs. Born, Edmonton, Alta., September 16, 1934.

Season	Club	GP	G	A	Pts	PIM	GP	G	A	Pts	PIM
1955-56	Detroit Red Wings	....	....	....	....	....	6	0	0	0	0
1959-60	Detroit Red Wings	63	10	10	20	12	6	3	0	3	0
1960-61	Detroit Red Wings	70	9	16	25	2	11	1	0	1	2
1961-62	Chicago Black Hawks	63	5	16	21	6	7	0	0	0	2
1964-65	Chicago Black Hawks	....	....	....	....	....	6	0	0	0	0
1967-68	St. Louis Blues	73	15	35	50	14	17	2	6	8	2
	NHL Totals	**269**	**39**	**77**	**116**	**34**	**53**	**6**	**6**	**12**	**6**

Played in NHL All-Star Game (1961)

Traded to **Chicago** by **Detroit** with Brian Smith for Eddie Litzenberger, June 12, 1961. Claimed by **St. Louis** from **Chicago** in Expansion Draft, June 6, 1967. Traded to **Philadelphia** by **St. Louis** with Darryl Edestrand for Lou Angotti and Ian Campbell, June 11, 1968.

MELNYK, Larry

Defense. Shoots left. 6', 195 lbs. Born, Saskatoon, Sask., February 21, 1960.
(Boston's 5th choice, 78th overall, in 1979 Entry Draft).

Season	Club	GP	G	A	Pts	PIM	GP	G	A	Pts	PIM
1980-81	Boston Bruins	26	0	4	4	39	....	....	....	....	....
1981-82	Boston Bruins	48	0	8	8	84	11	0	3	3	40
1982-83	Boston Bruins	1	0	0	0	0	11	0	0	0	9
1983-84 ♦	Edmonton Oilers	....	....	....	....	....	6	0	1	1	0
1984-85 ♦	Edmonton Oilers	28	0	11	11	25	12	1	3	4	26
1985-86	Edmonton Oilers	6	2	3	5	11	....	....	....	....	....
	New York Rangers	46	1	8	9	65	16	1	2	3	46
1986-87	New York Rangers	73	3	12	15	182	6	0	0	0	4
1987-88	New York Rangers	14	0	1	1	34	....	....	....	....	....
	Vancouver Canucks	49	2	3	5	73	....	....	....	....	....
1988-89	Vancouver Canucks	74	3	11	14	82	4	0	0	0	2
1989-90	Vancouver Canucks	67	0	2	2	91	....	....	....	....	....
	NHL Totals	**432**	**11**	**63**	**74**	**686**	**66**	**2**	**9**	**11**	**127**

Traded to **Edmonton** by **Boston** for John Blum, March 6, 1984. Traded to **NY Rangers** by **Edmonton** with Todd Strueby for Mike Rogers, December 20, 1985. Traded to **Vancouver** by **NY Rangers** with Willie Huber for Michel Petit, November 4, 1987.

MELOCHE, Eric

Right wing. Shoots right. 5'10", 195 lbs. Born, Montreal, Que., May 1, 1976.
(Pittsburgh's 7th choice, 186th overall, in 1996 Entry Draft).

Season	Club	GP	G	A	Pts	PIM	GP	G	A	Pts	PIM
2001-02	Pittsburgh Penguins	23	0	1	1	8	....	....	....	....	....
	NHL Totals	**23**	**0**	**1**	**1**	**8**	....	....	....	....	....

MELROSE, Barry

Defense. Shoots right. 6', 205 lbs. Born, Kelvington, Sask., July 15, 1956.
(Montreal's 4th choice, 36th overall, in 1976 Amateur Draft).

Season	Club	GP	G	A	Pts	PIM	GP	G	A	Pts	PIM
1979-80	Winnipeg Jets	74	4	6	10	124	....	....	....	....	....

Season	Club	REGULAR SEASON GP	G	A	Pts	PIM	PLAYOFFS GP	G	A	Pts	PIM
1980-81	Winnipeg Jets	18	1	1	2	40	....	....	....	....	....
	Toronto Maple Leafs	57	2	5	7	166	3	0	1	1	15
1981-82	Toronto Maple Leafs	64	1	5	6	186	....	....	....	....	....
1982-83	Toronto Maple Leafs	52	2	5	7	68	4	0	1	1	23
1983-84	Detroit Red Wings	21	0	1	1	74	....	....	....	....	....
1985-86	Detroit Red Wings	14	0	0	0	70	....	....	....	....	....
	NHL Totals	**300**	**10**	**23**	**33**	**728**	**7**	**0**	**2**	**2**	**38**

Claimed by **Quebec** from **Cincinnati** (WHA) in WHA Dispersal Draft, June 8, 1979. Traded to **Winnipeg** by **Quebec** for Jamie Hislop and Barry Legge, June 28, 1979. Claimed on waivers by **Toronto** from **Winnipeg**, November 30, 1980. Signed as a free agent by **Detroit**, July 5, 1983.

MENARD, Hillary

Left wing. Shoots left. 5'8", 165 lbs. Born, Timmins, Ont., January 15, 1934.

Season	Club	GP	G	A	Pts	PIM	GP	G	A	Pts	PIM
1953-54	Chicago Black Hawks	1	0	0	0	0	....	....	....	....	....
	NHL Totals	**1**	**0**	**0**	**0**	**0**	....	....	....	....	....

• Brother of Howie

MENARD, Howie

Center. Shoots right. 5'8", 160 lbs. Born, Timmins, Ont., April 28, 1942.

Season	Club	GP	G	A	Pts	PIM	GP	G	A	Pts	PIM
1963-64	Detroit Red Wings	3	0	0	0	0	....	....	....	....	....
1967-68	Los Angeles Kings	35	9	15	24	32	7	0	5	5	24
1968-69	Los Angeles Kings	56	10	17	27	31	11	3	2	5	12
1969-70	Chicago Black Hawks	19	2	3	5	8	....	....	....	....	....
	Oakland Seals	38	2	7	9	16	1	0	0	0	0
	NHL Totals	**151**	**23**	**42**	**65**	**87**	**19**	**3**	**7**	**10**	**36**

• Brother of Hillary

Claimed by **Springfield** (AHL) from **Detroit** in Reverse Draft, June, 1965. NHL rights transferred to **Los Angeles** after NHL club purchased **Springfield** (AHL) franchise, May, 1967. Claimed by **Chicago** from **Los Angeles** in Intra-League Draft, June 11, 1969. Traded to **Oakland** by **Chicago** for Gene Ubriaco, December 15, 1969. Claimed by **Buffalo** from **Oakland** in Expansion Draft, June 10, 1970. Traded to **California** by **Buffalo** for cash, October, 1970.

MERCREDI, Vic

Center. Shoots right. 5'11", 185 lbs. Born, Yellowknife, N.W.T., March 31, 1953.
(Atlanta's 2nd choice, 16th overall, in 1973 Amateur Draft).

Season	Club	GP	G	A	Pts	PIM	GP	G	A	Pts	PIM
1974-75	Atlanta Flames	2	0	0	0	0	....	....	....	....	....
	NHL Totals	**2**	**0**	**0**	**0**	**0**	....	....	....	....	....

MEREDITH, Greg

Right wing. Shoots right. 6'1", 210 lbs. Born, Toronto, Ont., February 23, 1958.
(Atlanta's 5th choice, 97th overall, in 1978 Amateur Draft).

Season	Club	GP	G	A	Pts	PIM	GP	G	A	Pts	PIM
1980-81	Calgary Flames	3	1	0	1	0	....	....	....	....	....
1982-83	Calgary Flames	35	5	4	9	8	5	3	1	4	4
	NHL Totals	**38**	**6**	**4**	**10**	**8**	**5**	**3**	**1**	**4**	**4**

Transferred to **Calgary** after **Atlanta** franchise relocated, June 24, 1980.

MERKOSKY, Glenn

Center. Shoots left. 5'10", 185 lbs. Born, Edmonton, Alta., April 8, 1959.

Season	Club	GP	G	A	Pts	PIM	GP	G	A	Pts	PIM
1981-82	Hartford Whalers	7	0	0	0	2	....	....	....	....	....
1982-83	New Jersey Devils	34	4	10	14	20	....	....	....	....	....
1983-84	New Jersey Devils	5	1	0	1	0	....	....	....	....	....
1985-86	Detroit Red Wings	17	0	2	2	0	....	....	....	....	....
1989-90	Detroit Red Wings	3	0	0	0	0	....	....	....	....	....
	NHL Totals	**66**	**5**	**12**	**17**	**22**	....	....	....	....	....

Signed as a free agent by **Hartford**, August 10, 1980. Signed as a free agent by **New Jersey**, September 14, 1982. Signed as a free agent by **Detroit**, July 15, 1985.

MERONEK, Bill

Center. Shoots left. 5'9", 155 lbs. Born, Stony Mountain, Man., April 15, 1917.

Season	Club	GP	G	A	Pts	PIM	GP	G	A	Pts	PIM
1939-40	Montreal Canadiens	7	2	2	4	0	....	....	....	....	....
1942-43	Montreal Canadiens	12	3	6	9	0	1	0	0	0	0
	NHL Totals	**19**	**5**	**8**	**13**	**0**	**1**	**0**	**0**	**0**	**0**

Signed as a free agent by **Montreal**, February 1, 1943. • Played home games only in 1942-43 because of work commitments.

MERRICK, Wayne

Center. Shoots left. 6'1", 195 lbs. Born, Sarnia, Ont., April 23, 1952.
(St. Louis' 1st choice, 9th overall, in 1972 Amateur Draft).

Season	Club	GP	G	A	Pts	PIM	GP	G	A	Pts	PIM
1972-73	St. Louis Blues	50	10	11	21	10	5	0	1	1	2
1973-74	St. Louis Blues	64	20	23	43	32	....	....	....	....	....
1974-75	St. Louis Blues	76	28	37	65	57	2	1	1	2	0
1975-76	St. Louis Blues	19	7	8	15	0	....	....	....	....	....
	California Golden Seals	56	25	27	52	36	....	....	....	....	....
1976-77	Cleveland Barons	80	18	38	56	25	....	....	....	....	....
1977-78	Cleveland Barons	18	2	5	7	8	....	....	....	....	....
	New York Islanders	37	10	14	24	8	7	1	0	1	0
1978-79	New York Islanders	75	20	21	41	24	10	2	3	5	2
1979-80 ◆	New York Islanders	70	13	22	35	16	21	2	4	6	2
1980-81 ◆	New York Islanders	71	16	15	31	30	18	6	12	18	8
1981-82 ◆	New York Islanders	68	12	27	39	20	19	6	6	12	6
1982-83 ◆	New York Islanders	59	4	12	16	27	19	1	3	4	10
1983-84	New York Islanders	31	6	5	11	10	1	0	0	0	0
	NHL Totals	**774**	**191**	**265**	**456**	**303**	**102**	**19**	**30**	**49**	**30**

Traded to **California** by **St. Louis** for Larry Patey and California's 3rd round choice (later traded back to California – California/Cleveland selected Reg Kerr) in 1977 Amateur Draft, November 24, 1975. Transferred to **Cleveland** after **California** franchise relocated, August 26, 1976. Traded to **NY Islanders** by **Cleveland** with Darcy Regier and Cleveland's 4th round choice (draft choice cancelled by the Cleveland-Minnesota merger) in 1978 Amateur Draft for Jean-Paul Parise and Jean Potvin, January 10, 1978.

MERRILL, Horace

Defense. Shoots left. 5'9", 176 lbs. Born, Ottawa, Ont., November 30, 1885.

Season	Club	GP	G	A	Pts	PIM	GP	G	A	Pts	PIM
1917-18	Ottawa Senators	3	0	0	0	3	....	....	....	....	....
1919-20 ◆	Ottawa Senators	5	0	0	0	0	....	....	....	....	....
	NHL Totals	**8**	**0**	**0**	**0**	**3**	....	....	....	....	....

Signed as a free agent by **Ottawa**, February 20, 1918. Signed as a free agent by **Ottawa**, November 28, 1919.

MERTZIG, Jan

Defense. Shoots left. 6'4", 218 lbs. Born, Huddinge, Sweden, July 18, 1970.
(NY Rangers' 9th choice, 235th overall, in 1998 Entry Draft).

Season	Club	GP	G	A	Pts	PIM	GP	G	A	Pts	PIM
1998-99	New York Rangers	23	0	2	2	8	....	....	....	....	....
	NHL Totals	**23**	**0**	**2**	**2**	**8**	....	....	....	....	....

MESSIER, Eric

Left wing. Shoots left. 6'2", 200 lbs. Born, Drummondville, Que., October 29, 1973.

Season	Club	GP	G	A	Pts	PIM	GP	G	A	Pts	PIM
1996-97	Colorado Avalanche	21	0	0	0	4	6	0	0	0	4
1997-98	Colorado Avalanche	62	4	12	16	20	....	....	....	....	....
1998-99	Colorado Avalanche	31	4	2	6	14	3	0	0	0	0
99-2000	Colorado Avalanche	61	3	6	9	24	14	0	1	1	4
2000-01 ◆	Colorado Avalanche	64	5	7	12	26	23	2	2	4	14
2001-02	Colorado Avalanche	74	5	10	15	26	21	1	2	3	0
2002-03	Colorado Avalanche	72	4	10	14	16	5	0	0	0	0
	NHL Totals	**385**	**25**	**47**	**72**	**130**	**72**	**3**	**5**	**8**	**22**

Signed as a free agent by **Colorado**, June 14, 1995. • Missed majority of 1998-99 season recovering from elbow injury suffered in game vs. Ottawa, October 10, 1998. Traded to **Florida** by **Colorado** with Vaclav Nedorost for Peter Worrell and Florida's 2nd round choice in 2004 Entry Draft, July 19, 2003.

MESSIER, Joby

Defense. Shoots right. 6', 200 lbs. Born, Regina, Sask., March 2, 1970.
(NY Rangers' 7th choice, 118th overall, in 1989 Entry Draft).

Season	Club	GP	G	A	Pts	PIM	GP	G	A	Pts	PIM
1992-93	New York Rangers	11	0	0	0	6	....	....	....	....	....
1993-94	New York Rangers	4	0	2	2	0	....	....	....	....	....
1994-95	New York Rangers	10	0	2	2	18	....	....	....	....	....
	NHL Totals	**25**	**0**	**4**	**4**	**24**	....	....	....	....	....

• Brother of Mitch

Signed as a free agent by **NY Islanders**, September 5, 1995.

MESSIER, Mark

Center. Shoots left. 6'1", 210 lbs. Born, Edmonton, Alta., January 18, 1961.
(Edmonton's 2nd choice, 48th overall, in 1979 Entry Draft).

Season	Club	GP	G	A	Pts	PIM	GP	G	A	Pts	PIM
1979-80	Edmonton Oilers	75	12	21	33	120	3	1	2	3	2
1980-81	Edmonton Oilers	72	23	40	63	102	9	2	5	7	13
1981-82	Edmonton Oilers	78	50	38	88	119	5	1	2	3	8
1982-83	Edmonton Oilers	77	48	58	106	72	15	15	6	21	14
1983-84 ◆	Edmonton Oilers	73	37	64	101	165	19	8	18	26	19
1984-85 ◆	Edmonton Oilers	55	23	31	54	57	18	12	13	25	12
1985-86	Edmonton Oilers	63	35	49	84	68	10	4	6	10	18
1986-87 ◆	Edmonton Oilers	77	37	70	107	73	21	12	16	28	16
1987-88 ◆	Edmonton Oilers	77	37	74	111	103	19	11	23	34	29
1988-89	Edmonton Oilers	72	33	61	94	130	7	1	11	12	8
1989-90 ◆	Edmonton Oilers	79	45	84	129	79	22	9	*22	*31	20
1990-91	Edmonton Oilers	53	12	52	64	34	18	4	11	15	16
1991-92	New York Rangers	79	35	72	107	76	11	7	7	14	6
1992-93	New York Rangers	75	25	66	91	72	....	....	....	....	....
1993-94 ◆	New York Rangers	76	26	58	84	76	23	12	18	30	33
1994-95	New York Rangers	46	14	39	53	40	10	3	10	13	8
1995-96	New York Rangers	74	47	52	99	122	11	4	7	11	16
1996-97	New York Rangers	71	36	48	84	88	15	3	9	12	6
1997-98	Vancouver Canucks	82	22	38	60	58	....	....	....	....	....
1998-99	Vancouver Canucks	59	13	35	48	33	....	....	....	....	....
99-2000	Vancouver Canucks	66	17	37	54	30	....	....	....	....	....
2000-01	New York Rangers	82	24	43	67	89	....	....	....	....	....
2001-02	New York Rangers	41	7	16	23	32	....	....	....	....	....

		REGULAR SEASON					PLAYOFFS				
Season	Club	GP	G	A	Pts	PIM	GP	G	A	Pts	PIM
2002-03	New York Rangers	78	18	22	40	30	....	....	....	....	....
	NHL Totals	**1680**	**676**	**1168**	**1844**	**1868**	**236**	**109**	**186**	**295**	**244**

• Brother of Paul • NHL First All-Star Team (1982, 1983, 1990, 1992) • NHL Second All-Star Team (1984) • Conn Smythe Trophy (1984) • Lester B. Pearson Award (1990, 1992) • Hart Trophy (1990, 1992)

Played in NHL All-Star Game (1982, 1983, 1984, 1986, 1988, 1989, 1990, 1991, 1992, 1994, 1996, 1997, 1998, 2000)

Traded to **NY Rangers** by **Edmonton** with future considerations (Jeff Beukeboom for David Shaw, November 12, 1991) for Bernie Nicholls, Steven Rice and Louie DeBrusk, October 4, 1991. Signed as a free agent by **Vancouver**, July 30, 1997. Signed as a free agent by **NY Rangers**, July 13, 2000. • Missed majority of 2001-02 season recovering from back injury suffered in game vs. Toronto, December 8, 2001. Rights traded to **San Jose** by **NY Rangers** for future considerations, June 30, 2003.

MESSIER, Mitch

Center. Shoots right. 6'2", 200 lbs. Born, Regina, Sask., August 21, 1965.
(Minnesota's 4th choice, 57th overall, in 1983 Entry Draft).

Season	Club	GP	G	A	Pts	PIM	GP	G	A	Pts	PIM
1987-88	Minnesota North Stars	13	0	1	1	11	....	....	....	....	....
1988-89	Minnesota North Stars	3	0	1	1	0	....	....	....	....	....
1989-90	Minnesota North Stars	2	0	0	0	0	....	....	....	....	....
1990-91	Minnesota North Stars	2	0	0	0	0	....	....	....	....	....
	NHL Totals	**20**	**0**	**2**	**2**	**11**	....	....	....	....	....

• Brother of Joby

MESSIER, Paul

Center. Shoots right. 6'1", 185 lbs. Born, Nottingham, England, January 27, 1958.
(Colorado's 3rd choice, 41st overall, in 1978 Amateur Draft).

Season	Club	GP	G	A	Pts	PIM	GP	G	A	Pts	PIM
1978-79	Colorado Rockies	9	0	0	0	4	....	....	....	....	....
	NHL Totals	**9**	**0**	**0**	**0**	**4**	....	....	....	....	....

• Brother of Mark

METCALFE, Scott

Left wing. Shoots left. 6', 195 lbs. Born, Toronto, Ont., January 6, 1967.
(Edmonton's 1st choice, 20th overall, in 1985 Entry Draft).

Season	Club	GP	G	A	Pts	PIM	GP	G	A	Pts	PIM
1987-88	Edmonton Oilers	2	0	0	0	0	....	....	....	....	....
	Buffalo Sabres	1	0	1	1	0	....	....	....	....	....
1988-89	Buffalo Sabres	9	1	1	2	13	....	....	....	....	....
1989-90	Buffalo Sabres	7	0	0	0	5	....	....	....	....	....
	NHL Totals	**19**	**1**	**2**	**3**	**18**	....	....	....	....	....

Traded to **Buffalo** by **Edmonton** with Edmonton's 9th round choice (Donald Audette) in 1989 Entry Draft for Steve Dykstra and Buffalo's 7th round choice (Davis Payne) in 1989 Entry Draft, February 11, 1988.

METROPOLIT, Glen

Center. Shoots right. 5'10", 200 lbs. Born, Toronto, Ont., June 25, 1974.

Season	Club	GP	G	A	Pts	PIM	GP	G	A	Pts	PIM
99-2000	Washington Capitals	30	6	13	19	4	2	0	0	0	2
2000-01	Washington Capitals	15	1	5	6	10	1	0	0	0	0
2001-02	Tampa Bay Lightning	2	0	0	0	0	....	....	....	....	....
	Washington Capitals	33	1	16	17	6	....	....	....	....	....
2002-03	Washington Capitals	23	2	3	5	6	....	....	....	....	....
	NHL Totals	**103**	**10**	**37**	**47**	**26**	**3**	**0**	**0**	**0**	**2**

Signed as a free agent by **Washington**, July 19, 1999. Claimed by **Tampa Bay** from **Washington** in Waiver Draft, September 28, 2001. Claimed on waivers by **Washington** from **Tampa Bay**, October 20, 2001.

METZ, Don

Right wing. Shoots right. 5'10", 165 lbs. Born, Wilcox, Sask., January 10, 1916.

Season	Club	GP	G	A	Pts	PIM	GP	G	A	Pts	PIM
1938-39	Toronto Maple Leafs	....	....	....	....	....	2	0	0	0	0
1939-40	Toronto Maple Leafs	10	1	1	2	4	2	0	0	0	0
1940-41	Toronto Maple Leafs	31	4	10	14	6	7	1	1	2	2
1941-42 ◆	Toronto Maple Leafs	25	2	3	5	8	4	4	3	7	0
1944-45 ◆	Toronto Maple Leafs	....	....	....	....	....	11	0	1	1	4
1945-46	Toronto Maple Leafs	7	1	0	1	0	....	....	....	....	....
1946-47 ◆	Toronto Maple Leafs	40	4	9	13	10	11	2	3	5	4
1947-48 ◆	Toronto Maple Leafs	26	4	6	10	2	2	0	0	0	2
1948-49 ◆	Toronto Maple Leafs	33	4	6	10	12	3	0	0	0	0
	NHL Totals	**172**	**20**	**35**	**55**	**42**	**42**	**7**	**8**	**15**	**12**

• Brother of Nick

Played in NHL All-Star Game (1947)

METZ, Nick

Left wing. Shoots left. 5'11", 160 lbs. Born, Wilcox, Sask., February 16, 1914.

Season	Club	GP	G	A	Pts	PIM	GP	G	A	Pts	PIM
1934-35	Toronto Maple Leafs	18	2	2	4	4	6	1	1	2	0
1935-36	Toronto Maple Leafs	38	14	6	20	14	....	....	....	....	....
1936-37	Toronto Maple Leafs	48	9	11	20	19	2	0	0	0	0
1937-38	Toronto Maple Leafs	48	15	7	22	12	7	0	2	2	0
1938-39	Toronto Maple Leafs	47	11	10	21	15	10	3	3	6	6
1939-40	Toronto Maple Leafs	31	6	5	11	2	9	1	3	4	9
1940-41	Toronto Maple Leafs	47	14	21	35	10	7	3	4	7	0
1941-42 ◆	Toronto Maple Leafs	30	11	9	20	20	13	4	4	8	12
1944-45 ◆	Toronto Maple Leafs	50	22	13	35	26	7	1	1	2	2
1945-46	Toronto Maple Leafs	41	11	11	22	4	....	....	....	....	....
1946-47 ◆	Toronto Maple Leafs	60	12	16	28	15	6	4	2	6	0
1947-48 ◆	Toronto Maple Leafs	60	4	8	12	8	9	2	0	2	2
	NHL Totals	**518**	**131**	**119**	**250**	**149**	**76**	**19**	**20**	**39**	**31**

• Brother of Don

MEZEI, Branislav

Defense. Shoots left. 6'5", 236 lbs. Born, Nitra, Czech., October 8, 1980.
(NY Islanders' 3rd choice, 10th overall, in 1999 Entry Draft).

Season	Club	GP	G	A	Pts	PIM	GP	G	A	Pts	PIM
2000-01	New York Islanders	42	1	4	5	53	....	....	....	....	....
2001-02	New York Islanders	24	0	2	2	12	....	....	....	....	....
2002-03	Florida Panthers	11	2	0	2	10	....	....	....	....	....
	NHL Totals	**77**	**3**	**6**	**9**	**75**	....	....	....	....	....

Traded to **Florida** by **NY Islanders** for Jason Wiemer, July 3, 2002.

MICHALUK, Art

Defense. Shoots right. 6', 180 lbs. Born, Canmore, Alta., May 4, 1923.

Season	Club	GP	G	A	Pts	PIM	GP	G	A	Pts	PIM
1947-48	Chicago Black Hawks	5	0	0	0	0	....	....	....	....	....
	NHL Totals	**5**	**0**	**0**	**0**	**0**	....	....	....	....	....

• Brother of John

Signed as a free agent by **Chicago**, September 14, 1947.

MICHALUK, John

Left wing. Shoots left. 5'10", 155 lbs. Born, Canmore, Alta., November 2, 1928.

Season	Club	GP	G	A	Pts	PIM	GP	G	A	Pts	PIM
1950-51	Chicago Black Hawks	1	0	0	0	0	....	....	....	....	....
	NHL Totals	**1**	**0**	**0**	**0**	**0**	....	....	....	....	....

• Brother of Art

MICHAYLUK, Dave

Left wing. Shoots left. 5'10", 189 lbs. Born, Wakaw, Sask., May 18, 1962.
(Philadelphia's 5th choice, 65th overall, in 1981 Entry Draft).

Season	Club	GP	G	A	Pts	PIM	GP	G	A	Pts	PIM
1981-82	Philadelphia Flyers	1	0	0	0	0	....	....	....	....	....
1982-83	Philadelphia Flyers	13	2	6	8	8	....	....	....	....	....
1991-92 ◆	Pittsburgh Penguins	....	....	....	....	....	7	1	1	2	0
	NHL Totals	**14**	**2**	**6**	**8**	**8**	**7**	**1**	**1**	**2**	**0**

Signed as a free agent by **Pittsburgh**, May 24, 1989.

MICHELETTI, Joe

Defense. Shoots left. 6', 185 lbs. Born, Hibbing, MN, October 24, 1954.
(Montreal's 12th choice, 123rd overall, in 1974 Amateur Draft).

Season	Club	GP	G	A	Pts	PIM	GP	G	A	Pts	PIM
1979-80	St. Louis Blues	54	2	16	18	29	....	....	....	....	....
1980-81	St. Louis Blues	63	4	27	31	53	11	1	11	12	10
1981-82	St. Louis Blues	20	3	11	14	28	....	....	....	....	....
	Colorado Rockies	21	2	6	8	4	....	....	....	....	....
	NHL Totals	**158**	**11**	**60**	**71**	**114**	**11**	**1**	**11**	**12**	**10**

• Brother of Pat

Rights retained by **Edmonton** prior to Expansion Draft, June 9, 1979. Traded to **St. Louis** by **Edmonton** for Tom Roulston and Risto Siltanen, August 7, 1979. Traded to **Colorado** by **St. Louis** with Dick Lamby for Bill Baker, December 4, 1981.

MICHELETTI, Pat

Center. Shoots left. 5'10", 175 lbs. Born, Hibbing, MN, December 11, 1963.
(Minnesota's 9th choice, 185th overall, in 1982 Entry Draft).

Season	Club	GP	G	A	Pts	PIM	GP	G	A	Pts	PIM
1987-88	Minnesota North Stars	12	2	0	2	8	....	....	....	....	....
	NHL Totals	**12**	**2**	**0**	**2**	**8**	....	....	....	....	....

• Brother of Joe

MICKEY, Larry

Right wing. Shoots right. 5'11", 175 lbs. Born, Lacombe, Alta., October 21, 1943.

Season	Club	GP	G	A	Pts	PIM	GP	G	A	Pts	PIM
1964-65	Chicago Black Hawks	1	0	0	0	0	....	....	....	....	....
1965-66	New York Rangers	7	0	0	0	2	....	....	....	....	....
1966-67	New York Rangers	8	0	0	0	0	....	....	....	....	....
1967-68	New York Rangers	4	0	2	2	0	....	....	....	....	....
1968-69	Toronto Maple Leafs	55	8	19	27	43	3	0	0	0	5
1969-70	Montreal Canadiens	21	4	4	8	4	....	....	....	....	....
1970-71	Los Angeles Kings	65	6	12	18	46	....	....	....	....	....
1971-72	Philadelphia Flyers	14	1	2	3	8	....	....	....	....	....
	Buffalo Sabres	4	0	1	1	0	....	....	....	....	....
1972-73	Buffalo Sabres	77	15	9	24	47	6	1	0	1	5
1973-74	Buffalo Sabres	13	3	4	7	8	....	....	....	....	....
1974-75	Buffalo Sabres	23	2	0	2	2	....	....	....	....	....
	NHL Totals	**292**	**39**	**53**	**92**	**160**	**9**	**1**	**0**	**1**	**10**

Claimed by **NY Rangers** from **Chicago** (St. Louis-CHL) in Inter-League Draft, June 8, 1965. Claimed by **Toronto** from **NY Rangers** in Intra-League Draft, June 12, 1968. Claimed by **Montreal** from **Toronto** in Intra-League Draft, June 11, 1969. Traded to **Los Angeles** by **Montreal** with Lucien Grenier and Jack Norris for Leon Rochefort, Wayne Thomas and Gregg Boddy, May 22, 1970. Traded to **Philadelphia** by **Los Angeles** for Larry Hillman, June 13, 1971. Traded to **Buffalo** by **Philadelphia** for Larry Keenan, November 16, 1971.

MICKOSKI, Nick

Left wing. Shoots left. 6'1", 183 lbs. Born, Winnipeg, Man., December 7, 1927.

Season	Club	GP	G	A	Pts	PIM	GP	G	A	Pts	PIM
1947-48	New York Rangers	....	....	....	....	....	2	0	1	1	0
1948-49	New York Rangers	54	13	9	22	20	....	....	....	....	....
1949-50	New York Rangers	45	10	10	20	10	12	1	5	6	2
1950-51	New York Rangers	64	20	15	35	12	....	....	....	....	....

		REGULAR SEASON					PLAYOFFS				
Season	Club	GP	G	A	Pts	PIM	GP	G	A	Pts	PIM
1951-52	New York Rangers	43	7	13	20	20	....	....	....	....	....
1952-53	New York Rangers	70	19	16	35	39	....	....	....	....	....
1953-54	New York Rangers	68	19	16	35	22	....	....	....	....	....
1954-55	New York Rangers	18	0	14	14	6	....	....	....	....	....
	Chicago Black Hawks	52	10	19	29	42	....	....	....	....	....
1955-56	Chicago Black Hawks	70	19	20	39	52	....	....	....	....	....
1956-57	Chicago Black Hawks	70	16	20	36	24	....	....	....	....	....
1957-58	Chicago Black Hawks	28	5	6	11	20	....	....	....	....	....
	Detroit Red Wings	37	8	12	20	30	4	0	0	0	4
1958-59	Detroit Red Wings	66	11	15	26	20	....	....	....	....	....
1959-60	Boston Bruins	18	1	0	1	2	....	....	....	....	....
	NHL Totals	**703**	**158**	**185**	**343**	**319**	**18**	**1**	**6**	**7**	**6**

Played in NHL All-Star Game (1956)

Traded to **Chicago** by **NY Rangers** with Allan Stanley and Rich Lamoureux for Bill Gadsby and Pete Conacher, November 23, 1954. Traded to **Detroit** by **Chicago** with Hec Lalonde, Bob Bailey and Jack McIntyre for Bill Dineen, Billy Dea, Lorne Ferguson and Earl Reibel, December 17, 1957. Traded to **Boston** by **Detroit** for Jim Morrison, August 25, 1959.

MIDDENDORF, Max

Right wing. Shoots right. 6'4", 210 lbs. Born, Syracuse, NY, August 18, 1967.
(Quebec's 3rd choice, 57th overall, in 1985 Entry Draft).

Season	Club	GP	G	A	Pts	PIM	GP	G	A	Pts	PIM
1986-87	Quebec Nordiques	6	1	4	5	4	....	....	....	....	....
1987-88	Quebec Nordiques	1	0	0	0	0	....	....	....	....	....
1989-90	Quebec Nordiques	3	0	0	0	0	....	....	....	....	....
1990-91	Edmonton Oilers	3	1	0	1	2	....	....	....	....	....
	NHL Totals	**13**	**2**	**4**	**6**	**6**	....	....	....	....	....

Traded to **Edmonton** by **Quebec** for Edmonton's 9th round choice (Brent Brekke) in 1991 Entry Draft, November 10, 1990. Traded to **Detroit** by **Edmonton** for Bill McDougall, February 22, 1992.

MIDDLETON, Rick

Right wing. Shoots right. 5'11", 170 lbs. Born, Toronto, Ont., December 4, 1953.
(NY Rangers' 1st choice, 14th overall, in 1973 Amateur Draft).

Season	Club	GP	G	A	Pts	PIM	GP	G	A	Pts	PIM
1974-75	New York Rangers	47	22	18	40	19	3	0	0	0	2
1975-76	New York Rangers	77	24	26	50	14	....	....	....	....	....
1976-77	Boston Bruins	72	20	22	42	2	13	5	4	9	0
1977-78	Boston Bruins	79	25	35	60	8	15	5	2	7	0
1978-79	Boston Bruins	71	38	48	86	7	11	4	8	12	0
1979-80	Boston Bruins	80	40	52	92	24	10	4	2	6	5
1980-81	Boston Bruins	80	44	59	103	16	3	0	1	1	2
1981-82	Boston Bruins	75	51	43	94	12	11	6	9	15	0
1982-83	Boston Bruins	80	49	47	96	8	17	11	22	33	6
1983-84	Boston Bruins	80	47	58	105	14	3	0	0	0	0
1984-85	Boston Bruins	80	30	46	76	6	5	3	0	3	0
1985-86	Boston Bruins	49	14	30	44	10	....	....	....	....	....
1986-87	Boston Bruins	76	31	37	68	6	4	2	2	4	0
1987-88	Boston Bruins	59	13	19	32	11	19	5	5	10	4
	NHL Totals	**1005**	**448**	**540**	**988**	**157**	**114**	**45**	**55**	**100**	**19**

NHL Second All-Star Team (1982) • Lady Byng Trophy (1982)

Played in NHL All-Star Game (1981, 1982, 1984)

Traded to **Boston** by **NY Rangers** for Ken Hodge, May 26, 1976.

MIEHM, Kevin

Center. Shoots left. 6'2", 200 lbs. Born, Kitchener, Ont., September 10, 1969.
(St. Louis' 2nd choice, 54th overall, in 1987 Entry Draft).

Season	Club	GP	G	A	Pts	PIM	GP	G	A	Pts	PIM
1992-93	St. Louis Blues	8	1	3	4	4	2	0	1	1	0
1993-94	St. Louis Blues	14	0	1	1	4	....	....	....	....	....
	NHL Totals	**22**	**1**	**4**	**5**	**8**	**2**	**0**	**1**	**1**	**0**

MIGAY, Rudy

Center. Shoots left. 5'6", 150 lbs. Born, Fort William, Ont., November 18, 1928.

Season	Club	GP	G	A	Pts	PIM	GP	G	A	Pts	PIM
1949-50	Toronto Maple Leafs	18	1	5	6	8	....	....	....	....	....
1951-52	Toronto Maple Leafs	19	2	1	3	12	....	....	....	....	....
1952-53	Toronto Maple Leafs	40	5	4	9	22	....	....	....	....	....
1953-54	Toronto Maple Leafs	70	8	15	23	60	5	1	0	1	4
1954-55	Toronto Maple Leafs	67	8	16	24	66	3	0	0	0	10
1955-56	Toronto Maple Leafs	70	12	16	28	52	5	0	0	0	6
1956-57	Toronto Maple Leafs	66	15	20	35	51	....	....	....	....	....
1957-58	Toronto Maple Leafs	48	7	14	21	18	....	....	....	....	....
1958-59	Toronto Maple Leafs	19	1	1	2	4	2	0	0	0	0
1959-60	Toronto Maple Leafs	1	0	0	0	0	....	....	....	....	....
	NHL Totals	**418**	**59**	**92**	**151**	**293**	**15**	**1**	**0**	**1**	**20**

Played in NHL All-Star Game (1957)

MIKA, Petr

Left wing. Shoots right. 6'4", 194 lbs. Born, Prague, Czech., February 12, 1979.
(NY Islanders' 6th choice, 85th overall, in 1997 Entry Draft).

Season	Club	GP	G	A	Pts	PIM	GP	G	A	Pts	PIM
99-2000	New York Islanders	3	0	0	0	0	....	....	....	....	....
	NHL Totals	**3**	**0**	**0**	**0**	**0**	....	....	....	....	....

MIKITA, Stan

HHOF

Center/Right wing. Shoots right. 5'9", 169 lbs. Born, Sokolce, Czech., May 20, 1940.

Season	Club	GP	G	A	Pts	PIM	GP	G	A	Pts	PIM
1958-59	Chicago Black Hawks	3	0	1	1	4	....	....	....	....	....
1959-60	Chicago Black Hawks	67	8	18	26	119	3	0	1	1	2
1960-61 ◆	Chicago Black Hawks	66	19	34	53	100	12	*6	5	11	21
1961-62	Chicago Black Hawks	70	25	52	77	97	12	6	*15	*21	19
1962-63	Chicago Black Hawks	65	31	45	76	69	6	3	2	5	2
1963-64	Chicago Black Hawks	70	39	50	*89	146	7	3	6	9	8
1964-65	Chicago Black Hawks	70	28	*59	*87	154	14	3	7	10	*53
1965-66	Chicago Black Hawks	68	30	*48	78	58	6	1	2	3	2
1966-67	Chicago Black Hawks	70	35	*62	*97	12	6	2	2	4	2
1967-68	Chicago Black Hawks	72	40	47	*87	14	11	5	7	12	6
1968-69	Chicago Black Hawks	74	30	67	97	52	....	....	....	....	....
1969-70	Chicago Black Hawks	76	39	47	86	50	8	4	6	10	2
1970-71	Chicago Black Hawks	74	24	48	72	85	18	5	13	18	16
1971-72	Chicago Black Hawks	74	26	39	65	46	8	3	1	4	4
1972-73	Chicago Black Hawks	57	27	56	83	32	15	7	13	20	8
1973-74	Chicago Black Hawks	76	30	50	80	46	11	5	6	11	8
1974-75	Chicago Black Hawks	79	36	50	86	48	8	3	4	7	12
1975-76	Chicago Black Hawks	48	16	41	57	37	4	0	0	0	4
1976-77	Chicago Black Hawks	57	19	30	49	20	2	0	1	1	0
1977-78	Chicago Black Hawks	76	18	41	59	35	4	3	0	3	0
1978-79	Chicago Black Hawks	65	19	36	55	34	....	....	....	....	....
1979-80	Chicago Black Hawks	17	2	5	7	12	....	....	....	....	....
	NHL Totals	**1394**	**541**	**926**	**1467**	**1270**	**155**	**59**	**91**	**150**	**169**

NHL First All-Star Team (1962, 1963, 1964, 1966, 1967, 1968) • Art Ross Trophy (1964, 1965, 1967, 1968) • NHL Second All-Star Team (1965, 1970) • Lady Byng Trophy (1967, 1968) • Hart Trophy (1967, 1968) • Lester Patrick Trophy (1976

Played in NHL All-Star Game (1964, 1967, 1968, 1969, 1971, 1972, 1973, 1974, 1975)

• Missed remainder of 1979-80 season recovering from back surgery, November, 1979.

MIKKELSON, Bill

Defense. Shoots left. 6', 185 lbs. Born, Neepouna, Man., May 21, 1948.

Season	Club	GP	G	A	Pts	PIM	GP	G	A	Pts	PIM
1971-72	Los Angeles Kings	15	0	1	1	6	....	....	....	....	....
1972-73	New York Islanders	72	1	10	11	45	....	....	....	....	....
1974-75	Washington Capitals	59	3	7	10	52	....	....	....	....	....
1976-77	Washington Capitals	1	0	0	0	2	....	....	....	....	....
	NHL Totals	**147**	**4**	**18**	**22**	**105**	....	....	....	....	....

Signed as a free agent by **Los Angeles** (Springfield-AHL), September, 1970. Claimed by **NY Islanders** from **Los Angeles** in Expansion Draft, June 6, 1972. Claimed by **Washington** from **NY Islanders** in Expansion Draft, June 12, 1974.

MIKOL, Jim

Left wing/Defense. Shoots right. 6', 175 lbs. Born, Kitchener, Ont., June 11, 1938.

Season	Club	GP	G	A	Pts	PIM	GP	G	A	Pts	PIM
1962-63	Toronto Maple Leafs	4	0	1	1	2	....	....	....	....	....
1964-65	New York Rangers	30	1	3	4	6	....	....	....	....	....
	NHL Totals	**34**	**1**	**4**	**5**	**8**	....	....	....	....	....

Claimed by **Boston** from **Cleveland** (AHL) in Inter-League Draft, June 10, 1964. Claimed by **NY Rangers** from **Boston** in Intra-League Draft, June 10, 1964. Traded to **Providence** (AHL) by **NY Rangers** with Sandy McGregor, Marcel Paille and Aldo Guidolin for Ed Giacomin, May 18, 1965. • McGregor refused to report and was replaced with Buzz Deschamps. Traded to **Montreal** by **Providence** (AHL) for Yves Locas, July 1, 1968. Traded to **Cleveland** (AHL) by **Montreal** with Bill Staub for Howie Glover, August 27, 1968.

MIKULCHIK, Oleg

Defense. Shoots right. 6'2", 200 lbs. Born, Minsk, USSR, June 27, 1964.

Season	Club	GP	G	A	Pts	PIM	GP	G	A	Pts	PIM
1993-94	Winnipeg Jets	4	0	1	1	17	....	....	....	....	....
1994-95	Winnipeg Jets	25	0	2	2	12	....	....	....	....	....
1995-96	Mighty Ducks of Anaheim	8	0	0	0	4	....	....	....	....	....
	NHL Totals	**37**	**0**	**3**	**3**	**33**	....	....	....	....	....

Signed as a free agent by **Winnipeg**, July 26, 1993. Signed as a free agent by **Anaheim**, August 8, 1995.

MILBURY, Mike

Defense. Shoots left. 6'1", 200 lbs. Born, Brighton, MA, June 17, 1952.

Season	Club	GP	G	A	Pts	PIM	GP	G	A	Pts	PIM
1975-76	Boston Bruins	3	0	0	0	9	11	0	0	0	29
1976-77	Boston Bruins	77	6	18	24	166	13	2	2	4	*47
1977-78	Boston Bruins	80	8	30	38	151	15	1	8	9	27
1978-79	Boston Bruins	74	1	34	35	149	11	1	7	8	7
1979-80	Boston Bruins	72	10	13	23	59	10	0	2	2	50
1980-81	Boston Bruins	77	0	18	18	222	2	0	1	1	10
1981-82	Boston Bruins	51	2	10	12	71	11	0	4	4	6
1982-83	Boston Bruins	78	9	15	24	216	....	....	....	....	....
1983-84	Boston Bruins	74	2	17	19	159	3	0	0	0	12
1984-85	Boston Bruins	78	3	13	16	152	5	0	0	0	10
1985-86	Boston Bruins	22	2	5	7	102	1	0	0	0	17
1986-87	Boston Bruins	68	6	16	22	96	4	0	0	0	4
	NHL Totals	**754**	**49**	**189**	**238**	**1552**	**86**	**4**	**24**	**28**	**219**

Signed as a free agent by **Boston**, November 5, 1974.

MILKS, Hib

Left wing/Center. Shoots left. 5'11", 165 lbs. Born, Eardley, Que., April 1, 1899.

Season	Club	GP	G	A	Pts	PIM	GP	G	A	Pts	PIM
1925-26	Pittsburgh Pirates	36	14	5	19	17	2	0	0	0	0
1926-27	Pittsburgh Pirates	44	16	6	22	18	....	....	....	....	....
1927-28	Pittsburgh Pirates	44	18	3	21	32	2	0	0	0	2
1928-29	Pittsburgh Pirates	44	9	3	12	22	....	....	....	....	....
1929-30	Pittsburgh Pirates	41	13	11	24	36	....	....	....	....	....
1930-31	Philadelphia Quakers	44	17	6	23	42	....	....	....	....	....
1931-32	New York Rangers	48	0	4	4	12	7	0	0	0	0

Season	Club	REGULAR SEASON					PLAYOFFS				
		GP	G	A	Pts	PIM	GP	G	A	Pts	PIM
1932-33	Ottawa Senators	16	0	3	3	0	....	....	....	....	....
	NHL Totals	**317**	**87**	**41**	**128**	**179**	**11**	**0**	**0**	**0**	**2**

Signed as a free agent by **Pittsburgh**, September 26, 1925. Transferred to **Philadelphia** after **Pittsburgh** franchise relocated, October 18, 1930. Claimed by **NY Rangers** from **Philadelphia** in Dispersal Draft, September 26, 1931. Signed as a free agent by **Ottawa**, October 2, 1932.
• Suffered eventual career-ending knee injury prior to game vs. Montreal, December 28, 1932..

MILLAR, Craig

Defense. Shoots left. 6'2", 212 lbs. Born, Winnipeg, Man., July 12, 1976.
(Buffalo's 10th choice, 225th overall, in 1994 Entry Draft).

Season	Club	GP	G	A	Pts	PIM	GP	G	A	Pts	PIM
1996-97	Edmonton Oilers	1	0	0	0	2	....	....	....	....	....
1997-98	Edmonton Oilers	11	4	0	4	8	....	....	....	....	....
1998-99	Edmonton Oilers	24	0	2	2	19	....	....	....	....	....
99-2000	Nashville Predators	57	3	11	14	28	....	....	....	....	....
2000-01	Nashville Predators	5	0	0	0	6	....	....	....	....	....
	Tampa Bay Lightning	16	1	1	2	10	....	....	....	....	....
	NHL Totals	**114**	**8**	**14**	**22**	**73**	....	....	....	....	....

Traded to **Edmonton** by **Buffalo** with Barrie Moore for Miroslav Satan, March 18, 1997. Traded to **Nashville** by **Edmonton** for Detroit's 3rd round choice (previously acquired, Edmonton selected Mike Comrie) in 1999 Entry Draft, June 26, 1999. Claimed on waivers by **Tampa Bay** from **Nashville**, October 25, 2000. Traded to **Ottawa** by **Tampa Bay** for John Emmons, March 13, 2001.

MILLAR, Hugh

Defense. Shoots left. 5'9", 200 lbs. Born, Edmonton, Alta., April 3, 1921.

Season	Club	GP	G	A	Pts	PIM	GP	G	A	Pts	PIM
1946-47	Detroit Red Wings	4	0	0	0	0	1	0	0	0	0
	NHL Totals	**4**	**0**	**0**	**0**	**0**	**1**	**0**	**0**	**0**	**0**

• Suspended for entire 1948-49 season by **Detroit** for refusing to sign contract.

MILLAR, Mike

Right wing. Shoots left. 5'10", 170 lbs. Born, St. Catharines, Ont., April 28, 1965.
(Hartford's 2nd choice, 110th overall, in 1984 Entry Draft).

Season	Club	GP	G	A	Pts	PIM	GP	G	A	Pts	PIM
1986-87	Hartford Whalers	10	2	2	4	0	....	....	....	....	....
1987-88	Hartford Whalers	28	7	7	14	6	....	....	....	....	....
1988-89	Washington Capitals	18	6	3	9	4	....	....	....	....	....
1989-90	Boston Bruins	15	1	4	5	0	....	....	....	....	....
1990-91	Toronto Maple Leafs	7	2	2	4	2	....	....	....	....	....
	NHL Totals	**78**	**18**	**18**	**36**	**12**	....	....	....	....	....

Traded to **Washington** by **Hartford** with Neil Sheehy for Grant Jennings and Ed Kastelic, July 6, 1988. Traded to **Boston** by **Washington** for Alfie Turcotte, October 2, 1989. Signed as a free agent by **Toronto**, July 19, 1990.

MILLEN, Corey

Center. Shoots right. 5'7", 170 lbs. Born, Cloquet, MN, March 30, 1964.
(NY Rangers' 3rd choice, 57th overall, in 1982 Entry Draft).

Season	Club	GP	G	A	Pts	PIM	GP	G	A	Pts	PIM
1989-90	New York Rangers	4	0	0	0	2	....	....	....	....	....
1990-91	New York Rangers	4	3	1	4	0	6	1	2	3	0
1991-92	New York Rangers	11	1	4	5	10	....	....	....	....	....
	Los Angeles Kings	46	20	21	41	44	6	0	1	1	6
1992-93	Los Angeles Kings	42	23	16	39	42	23	2	4	6	12
1993-94	New Jersey Devils	78	20	30	50	52	7	1	0	1	2
1994-95	New Jersey Devils	17	2	3	5	8	....	....	....	....	....
	Dallas Stars	28	3	15	18	28	5	1	0	1	2
1995-96	Dallas Stars	13	3	4	7	8	....	....	....	....	....
	Calgary Flames	31	4	10	14	10	....	....	....	....	....
1996-97	Calgary Flames	61	11	15	26	32	....	....	....	....	....
	NHL Totals	**335**	**90**	**119**	**209**	**236**	**47**	**5**	**7**	**12**	**22**

Traded to **Los Angeles** by **NY Rangers** for Randy Gilhen, December 23, 1991. Traded to **New Jersey** by **Los Angeles** for New Jersey's 5th round choice (Jason Saal) in 1993 Entry Draft, June 26, 1993. Traded to **Dallas** by **New Jersey** for Neal Broten, February 27, 1995. Traded to **Calgary** by **Dallas** with Jarome Iginla for Joe Nieuwendyk, December 19, 1995.

MILLER, Aaron

Defense. Shoots right. 6'3", 200 lbs. Born, Buffalo, NY, August 11, 1971.
(NY Rangers' 6th choice, 88th overall, in 1989 Entry Draft).

Season	Club	GP	G	A	Pts	PIM	GP	G	A	Pts	PIM
1993-94	Quebec Nordiques	1	0	0	0	0	....	....	....	....	....
1994-95	Quebec Nordiques	9	0	3	3	6	....	....	....	....	....
1995-96	Colorado Avalanche	5	0	0	0	0	....	....	....	....	....
1996-97	Colorado Avalanche	56	5	12	17	15	17	1	2	3	10
1997-98	Colorado Avalanche	55	2	2	4	51	7	0	0	0	8
1998-99	Colorado Avalanche	76	5	13	18	42	19	1	5	6	10
99-2000	Colorado Avalanche	53	1	7	8	36	17	1	1	2	6
2000-01	Colorado Avalanche	56	4	9	13	29	....	....	....	....	....
	Los Angeles Kings	13	0	5	5	14	13	0	1	1	6
2001-02	Los Angeles Kings	74	5	12	17	54	7	0	0	0	0
2002-03	Los Angeles Kings	49	1	5	6	24	....	....	....	....	....
	NHL Totals	**447**	**23**	**68**	**91**	**271**	**80**	**3**	**9**	**12**	**40**

Traded to **Quebec** by **NY Rangers** with NY Rangers' 5th round choice (Bill Lindsay) in 1991 Entry Draft for Joe Cirella, January 17, 1991. Transferred to **Colorado** after **Quebec** franchise relocated, June 21, 1995. Traded to **Los Angeles** by **Colorado** with Adam Deadmarsh, a player to be named later (Jared Aulin, March 22, 2001), Colorado's 1st round choice (Dave Steckel) in 2001 Entry Draft and Colorado's 1st round choice (Brian Boyle) in 2003 Entry Draft for Rob Blake and Steve Reinprecht, February 21, 2001.

MILLER, Bill

Center/Defense. Shoots right. 6', 160 lbs. Born, Campbellton, N.B., August 1, 1908.

Season	Club	GP	G	A	Pts	PIM	GP	G	A	Pts	PIM
1934-35◆	Montreal Maroons	22	3	0	3	2	7	0	0	0	0
1935-36	Montreal Maroons	8	0	0	0	0	....	....	....	....	....
	Montreal Canadiens	17	1	2	3	2	....	....	....	....	....
1936-37	Montreal Canadiens	48	3	1	4	12	5	0	0	0	0
	NHL Totals	**95**	**7**	**3**	**10**	**16**	**12**	**0**	**0**	**0**	**0**

• Recalled from **New Haven** (Can-Am) by **Mtl. Maroons** to coach in Tommy Gorman's absence, January 3, 1936. Traded to **Montreal** by **Mtl. Maroons** with Toe Blake and the rights to Ken Grivel for Lorne Chabot, February, 1936.

MILLER, Bob

Center. Shoots left. 5'11", 180 lbs. Born, Medford, MA, September 28, 1956.
(Boston's 3rd choice, 70th overall, in 1976 Amateur Draft).

Season	Club	GP	G	A	Pts	PIM	GP	G	A	Pts	PIM
1977-78	Boston Bruins	76	20	20	40	41	13	0	3	3	15
1978-79	Boston Bruins	77	15	33	48	30	11	1	1	2	8
1979-80	Boston Bruins	80	16	25	41	53	10	3	2	5	4
1980-81	Boston Bruins	30	4	4	8	19	....	....	....	....	....
	Colorado Rockies	22	5	1	6	15	....	....	....	....	....
1981-82	Colorado Rockies	56	11	20	31	27	....	....	....	....	....
1984-85	Los Angeles Kings	63	4	16	20	35	2	0	1	1	0
	NHL Totals	**404**	**75**	**119**	**194**	**220**	**36**	**4**	**7**	**11**	**27**

• Brother of Paul

Traded to **Colorado** by **Boston** for Mike Gillis, February 18, 1981. Signed as a free agent by **Los Angeles**, October 9, 1984.

MILLER, Brad

Defense. Shoots left. 6'4", 220 lbs. Born, Edmonton, Alta., July 23, 1969.
(Buffalo's 2nd choice, 22nd overall, in 1987 Entry Draft).

Season	Club	GP	G	A	Pts	PIM	GP	G	A	Pts	PIM
1988-89	Buffalo Sabres	7	0	0	0	6	....	....	....	....	....
1989-90	Buffalo Sabres	1	0	0	0	0	....	....	....	....	....
1990-91	Buffalo Sabres	13	0	0	0	67	....	....	....	....	....
1991-92	Buffalo Sabres	42	1	4	5	192	....	....	....	....	....
1992-93	Ottawa Senators	11	0	0	0	42	....	....	....	....	....
1993-94	Calgary Flames	8	0	1	1	14	....	....	....	....	....
	NHL Totals	**82**	**1**	**5**	**6**	**321**	....	....	....	....	....

Claimed by **Ottawa** from **Buffalo** in Expansion Draft, June 18, 1992. Traded to **Toronto** by **Ottawa** for Toronto's 9th round choice (Pavol Demitra) in 1993 Entry Draft, February 25, 1993. Traded to **Calgary** by **Toronto** with Jeff Perry for Todd Gillingham and Paul Holden, September 2, 1993.

MILLER, Earl

Left wing. Shoots left. 5'11", 180 lbs. Born, Lumsden, Sask., September 12, 1905.

Season	Club	GP	G	A	Pts	PIM	GP	G	A	Pts	PIM
1927-28	Chicago Black Hawks	21	1	1	2	32	....	....	....	....	....
1928-29	Chicago Black Hawks	17	1	1	2	24	....	....	....	....	....
1929-30	Chicago Black Hawks	28	11	5	16	50	2	1	0	1	6
1930-31	Chicago Black Hawks	19	3	4	7	8	1	0	0	0	0
1931-32	Chicago Black Hawks	9	0	0	0	0	....	....	....	....	....
	◆ Toronto Maple Leafs	15	3	3	6	10	7	0	0	0	0
	NHL Totals	**109**	**19**	**14**	**33**	**124**	**10**	**1**	**0**	**1**	**6**

Traded to **Chicago** by **Saskatoon** (PrHL) with Eddie McCalmon for Corb Denneny and Nick Wasnie, January 11, 1928. Traded to **Toronto** by **Chicago** for cash, February 8, 1932.

MILLER, Jack

Center. Shoots left. 5'8", 155 lbs. Born, Delisle, Sask., September 16, 1925.

Season	Club	GP	G	A	Pts	PIM	GP	G	A	Pts	PIM
1949-50	Chicago Black Hawks	6	0	0	0	0	....	....	....	....	....
1950-51	Chicago Black Hawks	11	0	0	0	4	....	....	....	....	....
	NHL Totals	**17**	**0**	**0**	**0**	**4**	....	....	....	....	....

MILLER, Jason

Left wing. Shoots left. 6'1", 190 lbs. Born, Edmonton, Alta., March 1, 1971.
(New Jersey's 2nd choice, 18th overall, in 1989 Entry Draft).

Season	Club	GP	G	A	Pts	PIM	GP	G	A	Pts	PIM
1990-91	New Jersey Devils	1	0	0	0	0	....	....	....	....	....
1991-92	New Jersey Devils	3	0	0	0	0	....	....	....	....	....
1992-93	New Jersey Devils	2	0	0	0	0	....	....	....	....	....
	NHL Totals	**6**	**0**	**0**	**0**	**0**	....	....	....	....	....

Signed as a free agent by **Detroit**, August 26, 1994.

MILLER, Jay

Left wing. Shoots left. 6'2", 210 lbs. Born, Wellesley, MA, July 16, 1960.
(Quebec's 2nd choice, 66th overall, in 1980 Entry Draft).

Season	Club	GP	G	A	Pts	PIM	GP	G	A	Pts	PIM
1985-86	Boston Bruins	46	3	0	3	178	2	0	0	0	17
1986-87	Boston Bruins	55	1	4	5	208	....	....	....	....	....
1987-88	Boston Bruins	78	7	12	19	304	12	0	0	0	*124
1988-89	Boston Bruins	37	2	4	6	168	....	....	....	....	....
	Los Angeles Kings	29	5	3	8	133	11	0	1	1	63
1989-90	Los Angeles Kings	68	10	2	12	224	10	1	1	2	10
1990-91	Los Angeles Kings	66	8	12	20	259	8	0	0	0	17
1991-92	Los Angeles Kings	67	4	7	11	249	5	1	1	2	12
	NHL Totals	**446**	**40**	**44**	**84**	**1723**	**48**	**2**	**3**	**5**	**243**

Traded to **Minnesota** by **Quebec** for Jim Dobson, June 29, 1983. Signed as a free agent by **Boston**, October 1, 1985. Traded to **Los Angeles** by **Boston** for future considerations (Steve Kasper traded to Los Angeles by Boston for Bob Carpenter, January 23, 1989), January 22, 1989.

MILLER, Kelly

Left wing. Shoots left. 5'11", 197 lbs. Born, Lansing, MI, March 3, 1963.
(NY Rangers' 9th choice, 183rd overall, in 1982 Entry Draft).

Season	Club	GP	G	A	Pts	PIM	GP	G	A	Pts	PIM
		REGULAR SEASON					PLAYOFFS				
1984-85	New York Rangers	5	0	2	2	2	3	0	0	0	2
1985-86	New York Rangers	74	13	20	33	52	16	3	4	7	4
1986-87	New York Rangers	38	6	14	20	22	....	....	....	....	....
	Washington Capitals	39	10	12	22	26	7	2	2	4	0
1987-88	Washington Capitals	80	9	23	32	35	14	4	4	8	10
1988-89	Washington Capitals	78	19	21	40	45	6	1	0	1	2
1989-90	Washington Capitals	80	18	22	40	49	15	3	5	8	23
1990-91	Washington Capitals	80	24	26	50	29	11	4	2	6	6
1991-92	Washington Capitals	78	14	38	52	49	7	1	2	3	4
1992-93	Washington Capitals	84	18	27	45	32	6	0	3	3	2
1993-94	Washington Capitals	84	14	25	39	32	11	2	7	9	0
1994-95	Washington Capitals	48	10	13	23	6	7	0	3	3	4
1995-96	Washington Capitals	74	7	13	20	30	6	0	1	1	4
1996-97	Washington Capitals	77	10	14	24	33	....	....	....	....	....
1997-98	Washington Capitals	76	7	7	14	41	10	0	1	1	4
1998-99	Washington Capitals	62	2	5	7	29	....	....	....	....	....
	NHL Totals	**1057**	**181**	**282**	**463**	**512**	**119**	**20**	**34**	**54**	**65**

• Brother of Kevin and Kip

Traded to **Washington** by **NY Rangers** with Bob Crawford and Mike Ridley for Bob Carpenter and Washington's 2nd round choice (Jason Prosofsky) in 1989 Entry Draft, January 1, 1987.

MILLER, Kevin

Center. Shoots right. 5'11", 184 lbs. Born, Lansing, MI, September 2, 1965.
(NY Rangers' 10th choice, 202nd overall, in 1984 Entry Draft).

Season	Club	GP	G	A	Pts	PIM	GP	G	A	Pts	PIM
		REGULAR SEASON					PLAYOFFS				
1988-89	New York Rangers	24	3	5	8	2	....	....	....	....	....
1989-90	New York Rangers	16	0	5	5	2	1	0	0	0	0
1990-91	New York Rangers	63	17	27	44	63	....	....	....	....	....
	Detroit Red Wings	11	5	2	7	4	7	3	2	5	20
1991-92	Detroit Red Wings	80	20	26	46	53	9	0	2	2	4
1992-93	Washington Capitals	10	0	3	3	35	....	....	....	....	....
	St. Louis Blues	72	24	22	46	65	10	0	3	3	11
1993-94	St. Louis Blues	75	23	25	48	83	3	1	0	1	4
1994-95	St. Louis Blues	15	2	5	7	0	....	....	....	....	....
	San Jose Sharks	21	6	7	13	13	6	0	0	0	2
1995-96	San Jose Sharks	68	22	20	42	41	....	....	....	....	....
	Pittsburgh Penguins	13	6	5	11	4	18	3	2	5	8
1996-97	Chicago Blackhawks	69	14	17	31	41	6	0	1	1	0
1997-98	Chicago Blackhawks	37	4	7	11	8	....	....	....	....	....
1998-99	New York Islanders	33	1	5	6	13	....	....	....	....	....
99-2000	Ottawa Senators	9	3	2	5	2	1	0	0	0	0
	NHL Totals	**616**	**150**	**183**	**333**	**429**	**61**	**7**	**10**	**17**	**49**

• Brother of Kelly and Kip

Traded to **Detroit** by **NY Rangers** with Jim Cummins and Dennis Vial for Joe Kocur and Per Djoos, March 5, 1991. Traded to **Washington** by **Detroit** for Dino Ciccarelli, June 20, 1992. Traded to **St. Louis** by **Washington** for Paul Cavallini, November 2, 1992. Traded to **San Jose** by **St. Louis** for Todd Elik, March 23, 1995. Traded to **Pittsburgh** by **San Jose** for Pittsburgh's 5th round choice (later traded to Boston – Boston selected Elias Abrahamsson) in 1996 Entry Draft , March 20, 1996. Signed as a free agent by **Chicago**, July 18, 1996. Signed as a free agent by **NY Islanders**, October 9, 1998. Signed as a free agent by **Ottawa**, August 24, 1999.

MILLER, Kip

Center. Shoots left. 5'10", 190 lbs. Born, Lansing, MI, June 11, 1969.
(Quebec's 4th choice, 72nd overall, in 1987 Entry Draft).

Season	Club	GP	G	A	Pts	PIM	GP	G	A	Pts	PIM
		REGULAR SEASON					PLAYOFFS				
1990-91	Quebec Nordiques	13	4	3	7	7	....	....	....	....	....
1991-92	Quebec Nordiques	36	5	10	15	12	....	....	....	....	....
	Minnesota North Stars	3	1	2	3	2	....	....	....	....	....
1993-94	San Jose Sharks	11	2	2	4	6	....	....	....	....	....
1994-95	New York Islanders	8	0	1	1	0	....	....	....	....	....
1995-96	Chicago Blackhawks	10	1	4	5	2	....	....	....	....	....
1997-98	New York Islanders	9	1	3	4	2	....	....	....	....	....
1998-99	Pittsburgh Penguins	77	19	23	42	22	13	2	7	9	19
99-2000	Pittsburgh Penguins	44	4	15	19	10	....	....	....	....	....
	Mighty Ducks of Anaheim	30	6	17	23	4	....	....	....	....	....
2000-01	Pittsburgh Penguins	33	3	8	11	6	....	....	....	....	....
2001-02	New York Islanders	37	7	17	24	6	7	4	2	6	2
2002-03	Washington Capitals	72	12	38	50	18	5	0	2	2	2
	NHL Totals	**383**	**65**	**143**	**208**	**97**	**25**	**6**	**11**	**17**	**23**

• Brother of Kelly and Kevin

Traded to **Minnesota** by **Quebec** for Steve Maltais, March 8, 1992. Signed as a free agent by **San Jose**, August 10, 1993. Signed as a free agent by **NY Islanders**, July 7, 1994. Signed as a free agent by **Chicago**, July 21, 1995. Signed as a free agent by **NY Islanders**, November 26, 1997. Claimed by **Pittsburgh** from **NY Islanders** in Waiver Draft, October 5, 1998. Traded to **Anaheim** by **Pittsburgh** for Anaheim's 9th round choice (Roman Simicek) in 2000 Entry Draft, January 29, 2000. Signed as a free agent by **Pittsburgh**, September 24, 2000. Signed as a free agent by **NY Islanders**, January 16, 2002. Signed as a free agent by **Washington**, July 9, 2002.

MILLER, Paul

Center. Shoots left. 5'10", 170 lbs. Born, Billerica, MA, August 21, 1959.

Season	Club	GP	G	A	Pts	PIM	GP	G	A	Pts	PIM
		REGULAR SEASON					PLAYOFFS				
1981-82	Colorado Rockies	3	0	3	3	0	....	....	....	....	....
	NHL Totals	**3**	**0**	**3**	**3**	**0**	....	....	....	....	....

• Brother of Bob

Signed as a free agent by **Colorado**, November 20, 1981. Transferred to **New Jersey** after **Colorado** franchise relocated, June 30, 1982. Traded to **Edmonton** by **New Jersey** with Lindsay Middlebrook for Ron Low and Jim McTaggart, February 19, 1983.

MILLER, Perry

Defense. Shoots left. 6'1", 194 lbs. Born, Winnipeg, Man., June 24, 1952.

Season	Club	GP	G	A	Pts	PIM	GP	G	A	Pts	PIM
		REGULAR SEASON					PLAYOFFS				
1977-78	Detroit Red Wings	62	4	17	21	120	....	....	....	....	....
1978-79	Detroit Red Wings	75	5	23	28	156	....	....	....	....	....
1979-80	Detroit Red Wings	16	0	3	3	41	....	....	....	....	....
1980-81	Detroit Red Wings	64	1	8	9	70	....	....	....	....	....
	NHL Totals	**217**	**10**	**51**	**61**	**387**	....	....	....	....	....

Signed as a free agent by **Detroit**, July 8, 1977.

MILLER, Tom

Center. Shoots left. 6', 187 lbs. Born, Kitchener, Ont., March 31, 1947.

Season	Club	GP	G	A	Pts	PIM	GP	G	A	Pts	PIM
		REGULAR SEASON					PLAYOFFS				
1970-71	Detroit Red Wings	29	1	7	8	9	....	....	....	....	....
1972-73	New York Islanders	69	13	17	30	21	....	....	....	....	....
1973-74	New York Islanders	19	2	1	3	4	....	....	....	....	....
1974-75	New York Islanders	1	0	0	0	0	....	....	....	....	....
	NHL Totals	**118**	**16**	**25**	**41**	**34**	....	....	....	....	....

Traded to **Detroit** by **NY Rangers** with Arnie Brown and Mike Robitaille for Bruce MacGregor and Larry Brown, February 2, 1971. Claimed by **Buffalo** from **Detroit** in Intra-League Draft, June 8, 1971. Claimed by **NY Islanders** from **Buffalo** in Expansion Draft, June 6, 1972.

MILLER, Warren

Right wing. Shoots right. 6', 180 lbs. Born, South St. Paul, MN, January 1, 1954.
(NY Rangers' 21st choice, 241st overall, in 1974 Amateur Draft).

Season	Club	GP	G	A	Pts	PIM	GP	G	A	Pts	PIM
		REGULAR SEASON					PLAYOFFS				
1979-80	New York Rangers	55	7	6	13	17	6	1	0	1	0
1980-81	Hartford Whalers	77	22	22	44	37	....	....	....	....	....
1981-82	Hartford Whalers	74	10	12	22	68	....	....	....	....	....
1982-83	Hartford Whalers	56	1	10	11	15	....	....	....	....	....
	NHL Totals	**262**	**40**	**50**	**90**	**137**	**6**	**1**	**0**	**1**	**0**

Reclaimed by **NY Rangers** from **Hartford** prior to Expansion Draft, June 9, 1979. Traded to **Hartford** by **NY Rangers** for cash, August 7, 1980.

MILLEY, Norm

Right wing. Shoots right. 6', 200 lbs. Born, Toronto, Ont., February 14, 1980.
(Buffalo's 3rd choice, 47th overall, in 1998 Entry Draft).

Season	Club	GP	G	A	Pts	PIM	GP	G	A	Pts	PIM
		REGULAR SEASON					PLAYOFFS				
2001-02	Buffalo Sabres	5	0	1	1	0	....	....	....	....	....
2002-03	Buffalo Sabres	8	0	2	2	6	....	....	....	....	....
	NHL Totals	**13**	**0**	**3**	**3**	**6**	....	....	....	....	....

MILLS, Craig

Right wing. Shoots right. 6', 190 lbs. Born, Toronto, Ont., August 27, 1976.
(Winnipeg's 5th choice, 108th overall, in 1994 Entry Draft).

Season	Club	GP	G	A	Pts	PIM	GP	G	A	Pts	PIM
		REGULAR SEASON					PLAYOFFS				
1995-96	Winnipeg Jets	4	0	2	2	0	1	0	0	0	0
1997-98	Chicago Blackhawks	20	0	3	3	34	....	....	....	....	....
1998-99	Chicago Blackhawks	7	0	0	0	2	....	....	....	....	....
	NHL Totals	**31**	**0**	**5**	**5**	**36**	**1**	**0**	**0**	**0**	**0**

Rights transferred to **Phoenix** after **Winnipeg** franchise relocated, July 1, 1996. Traded to **Chicago** by **Phoenix** with Alexei Zhamnov and Phoenix's 1st round choice (Ty Jones) in 1997 Entry Draft for Jeremy Roenick, August 16, 1996. Traded to **Phoenix** by **Chicago** for cash, September 11, 1999. Traded to **Toronto** by **Phoenix** with Robert Reichel and Travis Green for Danny Markov, June 12, 2001.

MINER, John

Defense. Shoots right. 5'10", 180 lbs. Born, Moose Jaw, Sask., August 28, 1965.
(Edmonton's 10th choice, 229th overall, in 1983 Entry Draft).

Season	Club	GP	G	A	Pts	PIM	GP	G	A	Pts	PIM
		REGULAR SEASON					PLAYOFFS				
1987-88	Edmonton Oilers	14	2	3	5	16	....	....	....	....	....
	NHL Totals	**14**	**2**	**3**	**5**	**16**	....	....	....	....	....

Traded to **Los Angeles** by **Edmonton** for Craig Redmond, August 10, 1988.

MINOR, Gerry

Center. Shoots left. 5'8", 178 lbs. Born, Regina, Sask., October 27, 1958.
(Vancouver's 6th choice, 90th overall, in 1978 Amateur Draft).

Season	Club	GP	G	A	Pts	PIM	GP	G	A	Pts	PIM
		REGULAR SEASON					PLAYOFFS				
1979-80	Vancouver Canucks	5	0	1	1	2	....	....	....	....	....
1980-81	Vancouver Canucks	74	10	14	24	108	3	0	0	0	8
1981-82	Vancouver Canucks	13	0	1	1	6	9	1	3	4	17
1982-83	Vancouver Canucks	39	1	5	6	57	....	....	....	....	....
1983-84	Vancouver Canucks	9	0	0	0	0	....	....	....	....	....
	NHL Totals	**140**	**11**	**21**	**32**	**173**	**12**	**1**	**3**	**4**	**25**

MIRONOV, Boris

Defense. Shoots right. 6'3", 223 lbs. Born, Moscow, USSR, March 21, 1972.
(Winnipeg's 2nd choice, 27th overall, in 1992 Entry Draft).

Season	Club	GP	G	A	Pts	PIM	GP	G	A	Pts	PIM
		REGULAR SEASON					PLAYOFFS				
1993-94	Winnipeg Jets	65	7	22	29	96	....	....	....	....	....
	Edmonton Oilers	14	0	2	2	14	....	....	....	....	....
1994-95	Edmonton Oilers	29	1	7	8	40	....	....	....	....	....
1995-96	Edmonton Oilers	78	8	24	32	101	....	....	....	....	....
1996-97	Edmonton Oilers	55	6	26	32	85	12	2	8	10	16
1997-98	Edmonton Oilers	81	16	30	46	100	12	3	3	6	27
1998-99	Edmonton Oilers	63	11	29	40	104	....	....	....	....	....
	Chicago Blackhawks	12	0	9	9	27	....	....	....	....	....
99-2000	Chicago Blackhawks	58	9	28	37	72	....	....	....	....	....
2000-01	Chicago Blackhawks	66	5	17	22	42	....	....	....	....	....
2001-02	Chicago Blackhawks	64	4	14	18	68	1	0	0	0	2

		REGULAR SEASON					PLAYOFFS				
Season	Club	GP	G	A	Pts	PIM	GP	G	A	Pts	PIM
2002-03	Chicago Blackhawks	20	3	1	4	22	....	....	....	....	....
	New York Rangers	36	3	9	12	34	....	....	....	....	....
	NHL Totals	**641**	**73**	**218**	**291**	**805**	**25**	**5**	**11**	**16**	**45**

• Brother of Dmitri • NHL All-Rookie Team (1994)

Traded to **Edmonton** by **Winnipeg** with Mats Lindgren, Winnipeg's 1st round choice (Jason Bonsignore) in 1994 Entry Draft and Florida's 4th round choice (previously acquired, Edmonton selected Adam Copeland) in 1994 Entry Draft for Dave Manson and St. Louis' 6th round choice (previously acquired, Winnipeg selected Chris Kibermanis) in 1994 Entry Draft, March 15, 1994. Traded to **Chicago** by **Edmonton** with Dean McAmmond and Jonas Elofsson for Chad Kilger, Daniel Cleary, Ethan Moreau and Christian Laflamme, March 20, 1999. Traded to **NY Rangers** by **Chicago** for future considerations, January 8, 2003.

MIRONOV, Dmitri

Defense. Shoots right. 6'4", 224 lbs. Born, Moscow, USSR, December 25, 1965.
(Toronto's 7th choice, 160th overall, in 1991 Entry Draft).

Season	Club	GP	G	A	Pts	PIM	GP	G	A	Pts	PIM
1991-92	Toronto Maple Leafs	7	1	0	1	0	....	....	....	....	....
1992-93	Toronto Maple Leafs	59	7	24	31	40	14	1	2	3	2
1993-94	Toronto Maple Leafs	76	9	27	36	78	18	6	9	15	6
1994-95	Toronto Maple Leafs	33	5	12	17	28	6	2	1	3	2
1995-96	Pittsburgh Penguins	72	3	31	34	88	15	0	1	1	10
1996-97	Pittsburgh Penguins	15	1	5	6	24	....	....	....	....	....
	Mighty Ducks of Anaheim	62	12	34	46	77	11	1	10	11	10
1997-98	Mighty Ducks of Anaheim	66	6	30	36	115	....	....	....	....	....
	◆ Detroit Red Wings	11	2	5	7	4	7	0	3	3	14
1998-99	Washington Capitals	46	2	14	16	80	....	....	....	....	....
99-2000	Washington Capitals	73	3	19	22	28	4	0	0	0	4
2000-01	Washington Capitals	36	3	5	8	6	....	....	....	....	....
2001-02	Washington Capitals	DID NOT PLAY – INJURED									
	NHL Totals	**556**	**54**	**206**	**260**	**568**	**75**	**10**	**26**	**36**	**48**

• Brother of Boris

Played in NHL All-Star Game (1998)

Traded to **Pittsburgh** by **Toronto** with Toronto's 2nd round choice (later traded to New Jersey – New Jersey selected Josh DeWolf) in 1996 Entry Draft for Larry Murphy, July 8, 1995. Traded to **Anaheim** by **Pittsburgh** with Shawn Antoski for Alex Hicks and Fredrik Olausson, November 19, 1996. Traded to **Detroit** by **Anaheim** for Jamie Pushor and Detroit's 4th round choice (Viktor Wallin) in 1998 Entry Draft, March 24, 1998. Signed as a free agent by **Washington**, July 29, 1998. • Missed majority of 2000-01 season and entire 2001-02 season recovering from back injury suffered in game vs. Tampa Bay, January 23, 2001.

MISZUK, John

Defense. Shoots left. 6'1", 192 lbs. Born, Naliboki, Poland, September 29, 1940.

Season	Club	GP	G	A	Pts	PIM	GP	G	A	Pts	PIM
1963-64	Detroit Red Wings	42	0	2	2	30	3	0	0	0	2
1965-66	Chicago Black Hawks	2	1	1	2	2	3	0	0	0	4
1966-67	Chicago Black Hawks	3	0	0	0	0	2	0	0	0	2
1967-68	Philadelphia Flyers	74	5	17	22	79	7	0	3	3	11
1968-69	Philadelphia Flyers	66	1	13	14	70	4	0	0	0	0
1969-70	Minnesota North Stars	50	0	6	6	51	....	....	....	....	....
	NHL Totals	**237**	**7**	**39**	**46**	**232**	**19**	**0**	**3**	**3**	**19**

Traded to **Chicago** by **Detroit** with Art Stratton and Ian Cushenan for Ron Murphy and Aut Erickson, June 9, 1964. Claimed by **Philadelphia** from **Chicago** in Expansion Draft, June 6, 1967. Traded to **Minnesota** by **Philadelphia** for Wayne Hillman, May 14, 1969. Traded to **San Diego** (WHL) by **Minnesota** for cash, July, 1970.

MITCHELL, Bill

Defense. Shoots left. 5'11", 180 lbs. Born, Port Dalhousie, Ont., February 22, 1930.

Season	Club	GP	G	A	Pts	PIM	GP	G	A	Pts	PIM
1963-64	Detroit Red Wings	1	0	0	0	0	....	....	....	....	....
	NHL Totals	**1**	**0**	**0**	**0**	**0**	....	....	....	....	....

Signed as a free agent by **Detroit**, February 22, 1964.

MITCHELL, Herb

Left wing. Shoots left. 5'10", 190 lbs. Born, Meaford, Ont., January 4, 1896.

Season	Club	GP	G	A	Pts	PIM	GP	G	A	Pts	PIM
1924-25	Boston Bruins	18	3	0	3	22	....	....	....	....	....
1925-26	Boston Bruins	26	3	0	3	14	....	....	....	....	....
	NHL Totals	**44**	**6**	**0**	**6**	**36**	....	....	....	....	....

Signed as a free agent by **Boston**, November 2, 1924. • First player signed in Boston franchise history.

MITCHELL, Jeff

Center/Right wing. Shoots right. 6'1", 190 lbs. Born, Wayne, MI, May 16, 1975.
(Los Angeles' 2nd choice, 68th overall, in 1993 Entry Draft).

Season	Club	GP	G	A	Pts	PIM	GP	G	A	Pts	PIM
1997-98	Dallas Stars	7	0	0	0	7	....	....	....	....	....
	NHL Totals	**7**	**0**	**0**	**0**	**7**	....	....	....	....	....

Rights traded to **Dallas** by **Los Angeles** for Vancouver's 5th round choice (previously acquired, Los Angeles selected Jason Morgan) in 1995 Entry Draft, June 7, 1995.

MITCHELL, Red

Defense. Shoots right. 5'10", 185 lbs. Born, Toronto, Ont., September 6, 1912.

Season	Club	GP	G	A	Pts	PIM	GP	G	A	Pts	PIM
1941-42	Chicago Black Hawks	1	0	0	0	4	....	....	....	....	....
1942-43	Chicago Black Hawks	42	1	1	2	47	....	....	....	....	....
1944-45	Chicago Black Hawks	40	3	4	7	16	....	....	....	....	....
	NHL Totals	**83**	**4**	**5**	**9**	**67**	....	....	....	....	....

Signed as a free agent by **Detroit**, December 29, 1932.

MITCHELL, Roy

Defense. Shoots right. 6'1", 199 lbs. Born, Edmonton, Alta., March 14, 1969.
(Montreal's 9th choice, 188th overall, in 1989 Entry Draft).

Season	Club	GP	G	A	Pts	PIM	GP	G	A	Pts	PIM
1992-93	Minnesota North Stars	3	0	0	0	0	....	....	....	....	....
	NHL Totals	**3**	**0**	**0**	**0**	**0**	....	....	....	....	....

Signed as a free agent by **Minnesota**, July 25, 1991. Transferred to **Dallas** after **Minnesota** franchise relocated, June 9, 1993. Traded to **New Jersey** by **Dallas** with Reid Simpson for future considerations, March 21, 1994.

MITCHELL, Willie

Defense. Shoots left. 6'3", 205 lbs. Born, Port McNeill, B.C., April 23, 1977.
(New Jersey's 12th choice, 199th overall, in 1996 Entry Draft).

Season	Club	GP	G	A	Pts	PIM	GP	G	A	Pts	PIM
99-2000	New Jersey Devils	2	0	0	0	0	....	....	....	....	....
2000-01	New Jersey Devils	16	0	2	2	29	....	....	....	....	....
	Minnesota Wild	17	1	7	8	11	....	....	....	....	....
2001-02	Minnesota Wild	68	3	10	13	68	....	....	....	....	....
2002-03	Minnesota Wild	69	2	12	14	84	18	1	3	4	14
	NHL Totals	**172**	**6**	**31**	**37**	**192**	**18**	**1**	**3**	**4**	**14**

Traded to **Minnesota** by **New Jersey** for Sean O'Donnell, March 4, 2001.

MODANO, Mike

Center. Shoots left. 6'3", 205 lbs. Born, Livonia, MI, June 7, 1970.
(Minnesota's 1st choice, 1st overall, in 1988 Entry Draft).

Season	Club	GP	G	A	Pts	PIM	GP	G	A	Pts	PIM
1988-89	Minnesota North Stars	....	....	....	....	....	2	0	0	0	0
1989-90	Minnesota North Stars	80	29	46	75	63	7	1	1	2	12
1990-91	Minnesota North Stars	79	28	36	64	65	23	8	12	20	16
1991-92	Minnesota North Stars	76	33	44	77	46	7	3	2	5	4
1992-93	Minnesota North Stars	82	33	60	93	83	....	....	....	....	....
1993-94	Dallas Stars	76	50	43	93	54	9	7	3	10	16
1994-95	Dallas Stars	30	12	17	29	8	....	....	....	....	....
1995-96	Dallas Stars	78	36	45	81	63	....	....	....	....	....
1996-97	Dallas Stars	80	35	48	83	42	7	4	1	5	0
1997-98	Dallas Stars	52	21	38	59	32	17	4	10	14	12
1998-99◆	Dallas Stars	77	34	47	81	44	23	5	*18	23	16
99-2000	Dallas Stars	77	38	43	81	48	23	10	*13	23	10
2000-01	Dallas Stars	81	33	51	84	52	9	3	4	7	0
2001-02	Dallas Stars	78	34	43	77	38	....	....	....	....	....
2002-03	Dallas Stars	79	28	57	85	30	12	5	10	15	4
	NHL Totals	**1025**	**444**	**618**	**1062**	**668**	**139**	**50**	**74**	**124**	**90**

NHL All-Rookie Team (1990) • NHL Second All-Star Team (2000)

Played in NHL All-Star Game (1993, 1998, 1999, 2000, 2003)

Transferred to **Dallas** after **Minnesota** franchise relocated, June 9, 1993.

MODIN, Fredrik

Left wing. Shoots left. 6'4", 225 lbs. Born, Sundsvall, Sweden, October 8, 1974.
(Toronto's 3rd choice, 64th overall, in 1994 Entry Draft).

Season	Club	GP	G	A	Pts	PIM	GP	G	A	Pts	PIM
1996-97	Toronto Maple Leafs	76	6	7	13	24	....	....	....	....	....
1997-98	Toronto Maple Leafs	74	16	16	32	32	....	....	....	....	....
1998-99	Toronto Maple Leafs	67	16	15	31	35	8	0	0	0	6
99-2000	Tampa Bay Lightning	80	22	26	48	18	....	....	....	....	....
2000-01	Tampa Bay Lightning	76	32	24	56	48	....	....	....	....	....
2001-02	Tampa Bay Lightning	54	14	17	31	27	....	....	....	....	....
2002-03	Tampa Bay Lightning	76	17	23	40	43	11	2	0	2	18
	NHL Totals	**503**	**123**	**128**	**251**	**227**	**19**	**2**	**0**	**2**	**24**

Played in NHL All-Star Game (2001)

Traded to **Tampa Bay** by **Toronto** for Cory Cross and Tampa Bay's 7th round choice (Ivan Kolozvary) in 2001 Entry Draft, October 1, 1999.

MODRY, Jaroslav

Defense. Shoots left. 6'2", 220 lbs. Born, Ceske Budejovice, Czech., February 27, 1971.
(New Jersey's 11th choice, 179th overall, in 1990 Entry Draft).

Season	Club	GP	G	A	Pts	PIM	GP	G	A	Pts	PIM
1993-94	New Jersey Devils	41	2	15	17	18	....	....	....	....	....
1994-95	New Jersey Devils	11	0	0	0	0	....	....	....	....	....
1995-96	Ottawa Senators	64	4	14	18	38	....	....	....	....	....
	Los Angeles Kings	9	0	3	3	6	....	....	....	....	....
1996-97	Los Angeles Kings	30	3	3	6	25	....	....	....	....	....
1998-99	Los Angeles Kings	5	0	1	1	0	....	....	....	....	....
99-2000	Los Angeles Kings	26	5	4	9	18	2	0	0	0	2
2000-01	Los Angeles Kings	63	4	15	19	48	10	1	0	1	4
2001-02	Los Angeles Kings	80	4	38	42	65	7	0	2	2	0
2002-03	Los Angeles Kings	82	13	25	38	68	....	....	....	....	....
	NHL Totals	**411**	**35**	**118**	**153**	**286**	**19**	**1**	**2**	**3**	**6**

Played in NHL All-Star Game (2002)

Traded to **Ottawa** by **New Jersey** for Ottawa's 4th round choice (Alyn McCauley) in 1995 Entry Draft, July 8, 1995. Traded to **Los Angeles** by **Ottawa** with Ottawa's 8th round choice (Stephen Valiquette) in 1996 Entry Draft for Kevin Brown, March 20, 1996.

MOE, Bill

USHOF

Defense. Shoots left. 5'11", 170 lbs. Born, Danvers, MA, October 2, 1916.

Season	Club	GP	G	A	Pts	PIM	GP	G	A	Pts	PIM
1944-45	New York Rangers	35	2	4	6	14	....	....	....	....	....
1945-46	New York Rangers	48	4	4	8	14	....	....	....	....	....
1946-47	New York Rangers	59	4	10	14	44	....	....	....	....	....
1947-48	New York Rangers	59	1	15	16	31	1	0	0	0	0

		REGULAR SEASON					PLAYOFFS				
Season	Club	GP	G	A	Pts	PIM	GP	G	A	Pts	PIM
1948-49	New York Rangers	60	0	9	9	60	....	....	....	....	....
	NHL Totals	**261**	**11**	**42**	**53**	**163**	**1**	**0**	**0**	**0**	**0**

Traded to **Boston** by **NY Rangers** with the rights to Lorne Ferguson and future considerations for Pat Egan, October 7, 1949.

MOFFAT, Lyle

Left wing. 5'10", 180 lbs. Born, Calgary, Alta., March 19, 1948.

Season	Club	GP	G	A	Pts	PIM	GP	G	A	Pts	PIM
1972-73	Toronto Maple Leafs	1	0	0	0	0	....	....	....	....	....
1974-75	Toronto Maple Leafs	22	2	7	9	13	....	....	....	....	....
1979-80	Winnipeg Jets	74	10	9	19	38	....	....	....	....	....
	NHL Totals	**97**	**12**	**16**	**28**	**51**	....	....	....	....	....

Signed as a free agent by **Toronto**, September, 1971. Rights retained by **Winnipeg** prior to Expansion Draft, June 9, 1979.

MOFFAT, Ron

Left wing. Shoots left. 5'11", 180 lbs. Born, West Hope, ND, August 21, 1905.

Season	Club	GP	G	A	Pts	PIM	GP	G	A	Pts	PIM
1932-33	Detroit Red Wings	24	1	1	2	6	4	0	0	0	0
1933-34	Detroit Red Wings	5	0	0	0	2	3	0	0	0	0
1934-35	Detroit Red Wings	8	0	0	0	0	....	....	....	....	....
	NHL Totals	**37**	**1**	**1**	**2**	**8**	**7**	**0**	**0**	**0**	**0**

Signed as a free agent by **Detroit**, August 1, 1932. Traded to **Windsor** (IHL) by **Detroit** for cash, October 18, 1935.

MOGER, Sandy

Center. Shoots right. 6'4", 220 lbs. Born, 100 Mile House, B.C., March 21, 1969.
(Vancouver's 7th choice, 176th overall, in 1989 Entry Draft).

Season	Club	GP	G	A	Pts	PIM	GP	G	A	Pts	PIM
1994-95	Boston Bruins	18	2	6	8	6	....	....	....	....	....
1995-96	Boston Bruins	80	15	14	29	65	5	2	2	4	12
1996-97	Boston Bruins	34	10	3	13	45	....	....	....	....	....
1997-98	Los Angeles Kings	62	11	13	24	70	....	....	....	....	....
1998-99	Los Angeles Kings	42	3	2	5	26	....	....	....	....	....
	NHL Totals	**236**	**41**	**38**	**79**	**212**	**5**	**2**	**2**	**4**	**12**

Signed as a free agent by **Boston**, June 22, 1994. • Missed majority of 1996-97 season recovering from elbow injury suffered in game vs. Buffalo, December 14, 1996. Traded to **Los Angeles** by **Boston** with Jozef Stumpel and Boston's 4th round choice (later traded to New Jersey – New Jersey selected Pierre Dagenais) in 1998 Entry Draft for Dmitri Khristich and Byron Dafoe, August 29, 1997.

MOGILNY, Alexander

Right wing. Shoots left. 6', 200 lbs. Born, Khabarovsk, USSR, February 18, 1969.
(Buffalo's 4th choice, 89th overall, in 1988 Entry Draft).

Season	Club	GP	G	A	Pts	PIM	GP	G	A	Pts	PIM
1989-90	Buffalo Sabres	65	15	28	43	16	4	0	1	1	2
1990-91	Buffalo Sabres	62	30	34	64	16	6	0	6	6	2
1991-92	Buffalo Sabres	67	39	45	84	73	2	0	2	2	0
1992-93	Buffalo Sabres	77	*76	51	127	40	7	7	3	10	6
1993-94	Buffalo Sabres	66	32	47	79	22	7	4	2	6	6
1994-95	Buffalo Sabres	44	19	28	47	36	5	3	2	5	2
1995-96	Vancouver Canucks	79	55	52	107	16	6	1	8	9	8
1996-97	Vancouver Canucks	76	31	42	73	18	....	....	....	....	....
1997-98	Vancouver Canucks	51	18	27	45	36	....	....	....	....	....
1998-99	Vancouver Canucks	59	14	31	45	58	....	....	....	....	....
99-2000	Vancouver Canucks	47	21	17	38	16	....	....	....	....	....
	♦ New Jersey Devils	12	3	3	6	4	23	4	3	7	4
2000-01	New Jersey Devils	75	43	40	83	43	25	5	11	16	8
2001-02	Toronto Maple Leafs	66	24	33	57	8	20	8	3	11	8
2002-03	Toronto Maple Leafs	73	33	46	79	12	6	5	2	7	4
	NHL Totals	**919**	**453**	**524**	**977**	**414**	**111**	**37**	**43**	**80**	**50**

NHL Second All-Star Team (1993, 1996) • Lady Byng Trophy (2003)

Played in NHL All-Star Game (1992, 1993, 1994, 1996)

Traded to **Vancouver** by **Buffalo** with Buffalo's 5th round choice (Todd Norman) in 1995 Entry Draft for Michael Peca, Mike Wilson and Vancouver's 1st round choice (Jay McKee) in 1995 Entry Draft, July 8, 1995. Traded to **New Jersey** by **Vancouver** for Brendan Morrison and Denis Pederson, March 14, 2000. Signed as a free agent by **Toronto**, July 3, 2001.

MOHER, Mike

Right wing. Shoots right. 5'10", 180 lbs. Born, Manitouwadge, Ont., March 26, 1962.
(New Jersey's 6th choice, 106th overall, in 1982 Entry Draft).

Season	Club	GP	G	A	Pts	PIM	GP	G	A	Pts	PIM
1982-83	New Jersey Devils	9	0	1	1	28	....	....	....	....	....
	NHL Totals	**9**	**0**	**1**	**1**	**28**	....	....	....	....	....

MOHNS, Doug

Left wing/Defense. Shoots left. 6', 185 lbs. Born, Capreol, Ont., December 13, 1933.

Season	Club	GP	G	A	Pts	PIM	GP	G	A	Pts	PIM
1953-54	Boston Bruins	70	13	14	27	27	4	1	0	1	4
1954-55	Boston Bruins	70	14	18	32	82	5	0	0	0	4
1955-56	Boston Bruins	64	10	8	18	48	....	....	....	....	....
1956-57	Boston Bruins	68	6	34	40	89	10	2	3	5	2
1957-58	Boston Bruins	54	5	16	21	28	12	3	10	13	18
1958-59	Boston Bruins	47	6	24	30	40	4	0	2	2	12
1959-60	Boston Bruins	65	20	25	45	62	....	....	....	....	....
1960-61	Boston Bruins	65	12	21	33	63	....	....	....	....	....
1961-62	Boston Bruins	69	16	29	45	74	....	....	....	....	....
1962-63	Boston Bruins	68	7	23	30	63	....	....	....	....	....
1963-64	Boston Bruins	70	9	17	26	95	....	....	....	....	....
1964-65	Chicago Black Hawks	49	13	20	33	84	14	3	4	7	21
1965-66	Chicago Black Hawks	70	22	27	49	63	5	1	0	1	4
1966-67	Chicago Black Hawks	61	25	35	60	58	5	0	5	5	8
1967-68	Chicago Black Hawks	65	24	29	53	53	11	1	5	6	12
1968-69	Chicago Black Hawks	65	22	19	41	47	....	....	....	....	....
1969-70	Chicago Black Hawks	66	6	27	33	46	8	0	2	2	15
1970-71	Chicago Black Hawks	39	4	6	10	16	....	....	....	....	....
	Minnesota North Stars	17	2	5	7	14	6	2	2	4	10
1971-72	Minnesota North Stars	78	6	30	36	82	4	1	2	3	10
1972-73	Minnesota North Stars	67	4	13	17	52	6	0	1	1	2
1973-74	Atlanta Flames	28	0	3	3	10	....	....	....	....	....
1974-75	Washington Capitals	75	2	19	21	54	....	....	....	....	....
	NHL Totals	**1390**	**248**	**462**	**710**	**1250**	**94**	**14**	**36**	**50**	**122**

Played in NHL All-Star Game (1954, 1958, 1959, 1961, 1962, 1965, 1972)

Traded to **Chicago** by **Boston** for Reggie Fleming and Ab McDonald, June 8, 1964. Traded to **Minnesota** by **Chicago** with Terry Caffery for Danny O'Shea, February 22, 1971. Claimed by **Atlanta** from **Minnesota** in Intra-League Draft, June 12, 1973. Traded to **Washington** by **Atlanta** for cash, June 20, 1974.

MOHNS, Lloyd

Defense. Shoots right. 5'9", 185 lbs. Born, Petawawa, Ont., July 31, 1921.

Season	Club	GP	G	A	Pts	PIM	GP	G	A	Pts	PIM
1943-44	New York Rangers	1	0	0	0	0	....	....	....	....	....
	NHL Totals	**1**	**0**	**0**	**0**	**0**	....	....	....	....	....

MOKOSAK, Carl

Left wing. Shoots left. 6'1", 180 lbs. Born, Fort Saskatchewan, Alta., September 22, 1962.

Season	Club	GP	G	A	Pts	PIM	GP	G	A	Pts	PIM
1981-82	Calgary Flames	1	0	1	1	0	....	....	....	....	....
1982-83	Calgary Flames	41	7	6	13	87	....	....	....	....	....
1984-85	Los Angeles Kings	30	4	8	12	43	....	....	....	....	....
1985-86	Philadelphia Flyers	1	0	0	0	5	....	....	....	....	....
1986-87	Pittsburgh Penguins	3	0	0	0	4	....	....	....	....	....
1988-89	Boston Bruins	7	0	0	0	31	1	0	0	0	0
	NHL Totals	**83**	**11**	**15**	**26**	**170**	**1**	**0**	**0**	**0**	**0**

• Brother of John

Signed as a free agent by **Calgary**, July 21, 1981. Traded to **Los Angeles** by **Calgary** with Kevin LaVallee for Steve Bozek, June 20, 1983. Signed as a free agent by **Philadelphia**, July 23, 1985. Signed as a free agent by **Pittsburgh**, July 23, 1986. Signed as a free agent by **Boston**, October 4, 1988.

MOKOSAK, John

Defense. Shoots left. 5'11", 200 lbs. Born, Edmonton, Alta., September 7, 1963.
(Hartford's 6th choice, 130th overall, in 1981 Entry Draft).

Season	Club	GP	G	A	Pts	PIM	GP	G	A	Pts	PIM
1988-89	Detroit Red Wings	8	0	1	1	14	....	....	....	....	....
1989-90	Detroit Red Wings	33	0	1	1	82	....	....	....	....	....
	NHL Totals	**41**	**0**	**2**	**2**	**96**	....	....	....	....	....

• Brother of Carl

Signed as a free agent by **Detroit**, August 29, 1988. Signed as a free agent by **Boston**, July 16, 1990. Signed as a free agent by **NY Rangers**, August 28, 1991.

MOLIN, Lars

Left wing. Shoots left. 6', 180 lbs. Born, Ornskoldsvik, Sweden, May 7, 1956.

Season	Club	GP	G	A	Pts	PIM	GP	G	A	Pts	PIM
1981-82	Vancouver Canucks	72	15	31	46	10	17	2	9	11	7
1982-83	Vancouver Canucks	58	12	27	39	23	....	....	....	....	....
1983-84	Vancouver Canucks	42	6	7	13	4	2	0	0	0	0
	NHL Totals	**172**	**33**	**65**	**98**	**37**	**19**	**2**	**9**	**11**	**7**

Signed as a free agent by **Vancouver**, May 18, 1981.

MOLLER, Mike

Right wing. Shoots right. 6', 194 lbs. Born, Calgary, Alta., June 16, 1962.
(Buffalo's 2nd choice, 41st overall, in 1980 Entry Draft).

Season	Club	GP	G	A	Pts	PIM	GP	G	A	Pts	PIM
1980-81	Buffalo Sabres	5	2	2	4	0	3	0	1	1	0
1981-82	Buffalo Sabres	9	0	0	0	0	....	....	....	....	....
1982-83	Buffalo Sabres	49	6	12	18	14	....	....	....	....	....
1983-84	Buffalo Sabres	59	5	11	16	27	....	....	....	....	....
1984-85	Buffalo Sabres	5	0	2	2	0	....	....	....	....	....
1985-86	Edmonton Oilers	1	0	0	0	0	....	....	....	....	....
1986-87	Edmonton Oilers	6	2	1	3	0	....	....	....	....	....
	NHL Totals	**134**	**15**	**28**	**43**	**41**	**3**	**0**	**1**	**1**	**0**

• Brother of Randy

Traded to **Pittsburgh** by **Buffalo** with Randy Cunneyworth for Pat Hughes, October 4, 1985. Traded to **Edmonton** by **Pittsburgh** for Pat Hughes, October 4, 1985.

MOLLER, Randy

Defense. Shoots right. 6'2", 210 lbs. Born, Red Deer, Alta., August 23, 1963.
(Quebec's 1st choice, 11th overall, in 1981 Entry Draft).

Season	Club	GP	G	A	Pts	PIM	GP	G	A	Pts	PIM
1981-82	Quebec Nordiques	....	....	....	....	....	1	0	0	0	0
1982-83	Quebec Nordiques	75	2	12	14	145	4	1	0	1	4
1983-84	Quebec Nordiques	74	4	14	18	147	9	1	0	1	45
1984-85	Quebec Nordiques	79	7	22	29	120	18	2	2	4	40
1985-86	Quebec Nordiques	69	5	18	23	141	3	0	0	0	26
1986-87	Quebec Nordiques	71	5	9	14	144	13	1	4	5	23
1987-88	Quebec Nordiques	66	3	22	25	169	....	....	....	....	....
1988-89	Quebec Nordiques	74	7	22	29	136	....	....	....	....	....
1989-90	New York Rangers	60	1	12	13	139	10	1	6	7	32
1990-91	New York Rangers	61	4	19	23	161	6	0	2	2	11
1991-92	New York Rangers	43	2	7	9	78	....	....	....	....	....
	Buffalo Sabres	13	1	2	3	59	7	0	0	0	8

Season	Club	GP	G	A	Pts	PIM	GP	G	A	Pts	PIM
		REGULAR SEASON					PLAYOFFS				
1992-93	Buffalo Sabres	35	2	7	9	83	....	....	....	....	....
1993-94	Buffalo Sabres	78	2	11	13	154	7	0	2	2	8
1994-95	Florida Panthers	17	0	3	3	16	....	....	....	....	....
	NHL Totals	**815**	**45**	**180**	**225**	**1692**	**78**	**6**	**16**	**22**	**197**

• Brother of Mike

Traded to **NY Rangers** by **Quebec** for Michel Petit, October 5, 1989. Traded to **Buffalo** by **NY Rangers** for Jay Wells, March 9, 1992. Signed as a free agent by **Florida**, July 11, 1994.

MOLLOY, Mitch

Left wing. Shoots left. 6'3", 212 lbs. Born, Red Lake, Ont., October 10, 1966.

Season	Club	GP	G	A	Pts	PIM	GP	G	A	Pts	PIM
1989-90	Buffalo Sabres	2	0	0	0	10	....	....	....	....	....
	NHL Totals	**2**	**0**	**0**	**0**	**10**	....	....	....	....	....

Signed as a free agent by **Buffalo**, Februrary, 1990.

MOLYNEAUX, Larry

Defense. Shoots right. 5'11", 208 lbs. Born, Sutton West, Ont., July 9, 1912.

Season	Club	GP	G	A	Pts	PIM	GP	G	A	Pts	PIM
1937-38	New York Rangers	2	0	0	0	2	3	0	0	0	8
1938-39	New York Rangers	43	0	1	1	18	7	0	0	0	0
	NHL Totals	**45**	**0**	**1**	**1**	**20**	**10**	**0**	**0**	**0**	**8**

MOMESSO, Sergio

Left wing. Shoots left. 6'3", 215 lbs. Born, Montreal, Que., September 4, 1965.
(Montreal's 3rd choice, 27th overall, in 1983 Entry Draft).

Season	Club	GP	G	A	Pts	PIM	GP	G	A	Pts	PIM
1983-84	Montreal Canadiens	1	0	0	0	0	....	....	....	....	....
1985-86	Montreal Canadiens	24	8	7	15	46	....	....	....	....	....
1986-87	Montreal Canadiens	59	14	17	31	96	11	1	3	4	31
1987-88	Montreal Canadiens	53	7	14	21	101	6	0	2	2	16
1988-89	St. Louis Blues	53	9	17	26	139	10	2	5	7	24
1989-90	St. Louis Blues	79	24	32	56	199	12	3	2	5	63
1990-91	St. Louis Blues	59	10	18	28	131	....	....	....	....	....
	Vancouver Canucks	11	6	2	8	43	6	0	3	3	25
1991-92	Vancouver Canucks	58	20	23	43	198	13	0	5	5	30
1992-93	Vancouver Canucks	84	18	20	38	200	12	3	0	3	30
1993-94	Vancouver Canucks	68	14	13	27	149	24	3	4	7	56
1994-95	Vancouver Canucks	48	10	15	25	65	11	3	1	4	16
1995-96	Toronto Maple Leafs	54	7	8	15	112	....	....	....	....	....
	New York Rangers	19	4	4	8	30	11	3	1	4	14
1996-97	New York Rangers	9	0	0	0	11	....	....	....	....	....
	St. Louis Blues	31	1	3	4	37	3	0	0	0	6
	NHL Totals	**710**	**152**	**193**	**345**	**1557**	**119**	**18**	**26**	**44**	**311**

• Missed remainder of 1985-86 season recovering from knee injury, suffered in game vs. Boston, December 5, 1985. Traded to **St. Louis** by **Montreal** with Vincent Riendeau for Jocelyn Lemieux, Darrell May and St. Louis' 2nd round choice (Patrice Brisebois) in 1989 Entry Draft, August 9, 1988. Traded to **Vancouver** by **St. Louis** with Geoff Courtnall, Robert Dirk, Cliff Ronning and St. Louis' 5th round choice (Brian Loney) in 1992 Entry Draft for Dan Quinn and Garth Butcher, March 5, 1991. Traded to **Toronto** by **Vancouver** for Mike Ridley, July 8, 1995. Traded to **NY Rangers** by **Toronto** for Wayne Presley, February 29, 1996. Traded to **St. Louis** by **NY Rangers** for Brian Noonan, November 13, 1996.

MONAHAN, Garry

Left wing. Shoots left. 6', 199 lbs. Born, Barrie, Ont., October 20, 1946.
(Montreal's 1st choice, 1st overall, in 1963 Amateur Draft).

Season	Club	GP	G	A	Pts	PIM	GP	G	A	Pts	PIM
1967-68	Montreal Canadiens	11	0	0	0	8	....	....	....	....	....
1968-69	Montreal Canadiens	3	0	0	0	0	....	....	....	....	....
1969-70	Detroit Red Wings	51	3	4	7	24	....	....	....	....	....
	Los Angeles Kings	21	0	3	3	12	....	....	....	....	....
1970-71	Toronto Maple Leafs	78	15	22	37	79	6	2	0	2	2
1971-72	Toronto Maple Leafs	78	14	17	31	47	5	0	0	0	0
1972-73	Toronto Maple Leafs	78	13	18	31	53	....	....	....	....	....
1973-74	Toronto Maple Leafs	78	9	16	25	70	4	0	1	1	7
1974-75	Toronto Maple Leafs	1	0	0	0	0	....	....	....	....	....
	Vancouver Canucks	78	14	20	34	51	5	1	0	1	2
1975-76	Vancouver Canucks	66	16	17	33	39	2	0	0	0	2
1976-77	Vancouver Canucks	76	18	26	44	48	....	....	....	....	....
1977-78	Vancouver Canucks	67	10	19	29	28	....	....	....	....	....
1978-79	Toronto Maple Leafs	62	4	7	11	25	....	....	....	....	....
	NHL Totals	**748**	**116**	**169**	**285**	**484**	**22**	**3**	**1**	**4**	**13**

Traded to **Detroit** by **Montreal** with Doug Piper for Pete Mahovlich and Bart Crashley, June 6, 1969. Traded to **Los Angeles** by **Detroit** with Matt Ravlich and Brian Gibbons for Dale Rolfe, Gary Croteau and Larry Johnston, February 20, 1970. Traded to **Toronto** by **Los Angeles** with Brian Murphy for Bob Pulford, September 3, 1970. Traded to **Vancouver** by **Toronto** with John Grisdale for Dave Dunn, October 16, 1974. Traded to **Toronto** by **Vancouver** for cash, September 13, 1978.

MONAHAN, Hartland

Right wing. Shoots right. 5'11", 197 lbs. Born, Montreal, Que., March 29, 1951.
(California's 3rd choice, 43rd overall, in 1971 Amateur Draft).

Season	Club	GP	G	A	Pts	PIM	GP	G	A	Pts	PIM
1973-74	California Golden Seals	1	0	0	0	0	....	....	....	....	....
1974-75	New York Rangers	6	0	1	1	4	....	....	....	....	....
1975-76	Washington Capitals	80	17	29	46	35	....	....	....	....	....
1976-77	Washington Capitals	79	23	27	50	37	....	....	....	....	....
1977-78	Pittsburgh Penguins	7	2	0	2	2	....	....	....	....	....
	Los Angeles Kings	64	10	9	19	45	2	0	0	0	0
1979-80	St. Louis Blues	72	5	12	17	36	3	0	0	0	0
1980-81	St. Louis Blues	25	4	2	6	4	1	0	0	0	4
	NHL Totals	**334**	**61**	**80**	**141**	**163**	**6**	**0**	**0**	**0**	**4**

Traded to **NY Rangers** by **California** for Brian Lavender, September 23, 1974. Claimed by **Washington** from **NY Rangers** in Intra-League Draft, June 17, 1975. Traded to **Pittsburgh** by **Washington** for Pittsburgh's 1st round choice (later traded to Minnesota – Minnesota selected Tom McCarthy) in 1979 Entry Draft, October 17, 1977. Traded to **Los Angeles** by **Pittsburgh** with Syl Apps Jr. for Dave Schultz, Gene Carr and Los Angeles' 4th round choice (Shane Pearsall) in 1978 Amateur Draft, November 2, 1977. Claimed by **Quebec** from **Los Angeles** in Expansion Draft, June 13, 1979. Traded to **St. Louis** by **Quebec** for cash, June 13, 1979.

MONDOU, Armand

Left wing. Shoots left. 5'10", 175 lbs. Born, Yamaska, Que., June 27, 1905.

Season	Club	GP	G	A	Pts	PIM	GP	G	A	Pts	PIM
1928-29	Montreal Canadiens	32	3	4	7	6	3	0	0	0	2
1929-30♦	Montreal Canadiens	44	3	5	8	24	6	1	1	2	6
1930-31♦	Montreal Canadiens	40	5	4	9	10	8	0	0	0	0
1931-32	Montreal Canadiens	47	6	12	18	22	4	1	2	3	2
1932-33	Montreal Canadiens	24	1	3	4	15	....	....	....	....	....
1933-34	Montreal Canadiens	48	5	3	8	4	1	0	1	1	0
1934-35	Montreal Canadiens	46	9	15	24	6	2	0	1	1	0
1935-36	Montreal Canadiens	36	7	11	18	10	....	....	....	....	....
1936-37	Montreal Canadiens	7	1	1	2	0	5	0	0	0	0
1937-38	Montreal Canadiens	7	2	4	6	0	....	....	....	....	....
1938-39	Montreal Canadiens	34	3	7	10	2	3	1	0	1	2
1939-40	Montreal Canadiens	21	2	2	4	0	....	....	....	....	....
	NHL Totals	**386**	**47**	**71**	**118**	**99**	**32**	**3**	**5**	**8**	**12**

Played in NHL All-Star Game (1939)

Traded to **Montreal** by **Providence** (Can-Am) for Leo Gaudreault, December 19, 1928. Traded to **Providence** (Can-Am) by **Montreal** with Leo Gaudreault for Hago Harrington and Leo Murray with both teams holding right of recall, January, 1933.

MONDOU, Pierre

Center. Shoots right. 5'10", 185 lbs. Born, Sorel, Que., November 27, 1955.
(Montreal's 2nd choice, 15th overall, in 1975 Amateur Draft).

Season	Club	GP	G	A	Pts	PIM	GP	G	A	Pts	PIM
1976-77♦	Montreal Canadiens	....	....	....	....	....	4	0	0	0	0
1977-78♦	Montreal Canadiens	71	19	30	49	8	15	3	7	10	4
1978-79♦	Montreal Canadiens	77	31	41	72	26	16	3	6	9	4
1979-80	Montreal Canadiens	75	30	36	66	12	4	1	4	5	4
1980-81	Montreal Canadiens	57	17	24	41	16	3	0	1	1	0
1981-82	Montreal Canadiens	73	35	33	68	57	5	2	5	7	8
1982-83	Montreal Canadiens	76	29	37	66	31	3	0	1	1	2
1983-84	Montreal Canadiens	52	15	22	37	8	14	6	3	9	2
1984-85	Montreal Canadiens	67	18	39	57	21	5	2	1	3	2
	NHL Totals	**548**	**194**	**262**	**456**	**179**	**69**	**17**	**28**	**45**	**26**

• Suffered eventual career-ending eye injury in game vs. Hartford, March 9, 1985.

MONGEAU, Michel

Center. Shoots left. 5'9", 190 lbs. Born, Montreal, Que., February 9, 1965.

Season	Club	GP	G	A	Pts	PIM	GP	G	A	Pts	PIM
1989-90	St. Louis Blues	7	1	5	6	2	2	0	1	1	0
1990-91	St. Louis Blues	7	1	1	2	0	....	....	....	....	....
1991-92	St. Louis Blues	36	3	12	15	6	....	....	....	....	....
1992-93	Tampa Bay Lightning	4	1	1	2	2	....	....	....	....	....
	NHL Totals	**54**	**6**	**19**	**25**	**10**	**2**	**0**	**1**	**1**	**0**

Signed as a free agent by **St. Louis**, August 21, 1989. Claimed by **Tampa Bay** from **St. Louis** in Expansion Draft, June 18, 1992. Traded to **Quebec** by **Tampa Bay** with Martin Simard and Steve Tuttle for Herb Raglan, February 12, 1993.

MONGRAIN, Bob

Center. Shoots left. 5'10", 165 lbs. Born, La Sarre, Que., August 31, 1959.

Season	Club	GP	G	A	Pts	PIM	GP	G	A	Pts	PIM
1979-80	Buffalo Sabres	34	4	6	10	4	9	1	2	3	2
1980-81	Buffalo Sabres	4	0	0	0	2	....	....	....	....	....
1981-82	Buffalo Sabres	24	6	4	10	6	1	0	0	0	0
1983-84	Buffalo Sabres	....	....	....	....	....	1	0	0	0	0
1984-85	Buffalo Sabres	8	1	1	2	0	....	....	....	....	....
1985-86	Los Angeles Kings	11	2	3	5	2	....	....	....	....	....
	NHL Totals	**81**	**13**	**14**	**27**	**14**	**11**	**1**	**2**	**3**	**2**

Signed as a free agent by **Buffalo**, September 16, 1979. Signed as a free agent by **Los Angeles**, Macrch 6, 1986.

MONTADOR, Steve

Defense. Shoots right. 6', 210 lbs. Born, Vancouver, B.C., December 21, 1979.

Season	Club	GP	G	A	Pts	PIM	GP	G	A	Pts	PIM
2001-02	Calgary Flames	11	1	2	3	26	....	....	....	....	....
2002-03	Calgary Flames	50	1	1	2	114	....	....	....	....	....
	NHL Totals	**61**	**2**	**3**	**5**	**140**	....	....	....	....	....

Signed as a free agent by **Calgary**, April 10, 2000.

MONTEITH, Hank

Left wing. Shoots left. 5'10", 170 lbs. Born, Stratford, Ont., October 2, 1945.

Season	Club	GP	G	A	Pts	PIM	GP	G	A	Pts	PIM
1968-69	Detroit Red Wings	34	1	9	10	6	....	....	....	....	....
1969-70	Detroit Red Wings	9	0	0	0	0	4	0	0	0	0
1970-71	Detroit Red Wings	34	4	3	7	0	....	....	....	....	....
	NHL Totals	**77**	**5**	**12**	**17**	**6**	**4**	**0**	**0**	**0**	**0**

Signed as a free agent by **Detroit**, September, 1967.

MONTGOMERY, Jim

Center. Shoots right. 5'10", 180 lbs. Born, Montreal, Que., June 30, 1969.

Season	Club	Regular Season GP	G	A	Pts	PIM	Playoffs GP	G	A	Pts	PIM
1993-94	St. Louis Blues	67	6	14	20	44	....	....	....	....	....
1994-95	Montreal Canadiens	5	0	0	0	2	....	....	....	....	....
	Philadelphia Flyers	8	1	1	2	6	7	1	0	1	2
1995-96	Philadelphia Flyers	5	1	2	3	9	1	0	0	0	0
2000-01	San Jose Sharks	28	1	6	7	19	....	....	....	....	....
2001-02	Dallas Stars	8	0	2	2	0	....	....	....	....	....
	NHL Totals	**121**	**9**	**25**	**34**	**80**	**8**	**1**	**0**	**1**	**2**

Signed as a free agent by **St. Louis**, June 2, 1993. Traded to **Montreal** by **St. Louis** for Guy Carbonneau, August 19, 1994. Claimed on waivers by **Philadelphia** from **Montreal**, February 10, 1995. Signed as a free agent by **San Jose**, August 15, 2000. Signed as a free agent by **Dallas**, July 10, 2001.

MOORE, Barrie

Left wing. Shoots left. 5'11", 198 lbs. Born, London, Ont., May 22, 1975.
(Buffalo's 7th choice, 220th overall, in 1993 Entry Draft).

Season	Club	Regular Season GP	G	A	Pts	PIM	Playoffs GP	G	A	Pts	PIM
1995-96	Buffalo Sabres	3	0	0	0	0	....	....	....	....	....
1996-97	Buffalo Sabres	31	2	6	8	18	....	....	....	....	....
	Edmonton Oilers	4	0	0	0	0	....	....	....	....	....
99-2000	Washington Capitals	1	0	0	0	0	....	....	....	....	....
	NHL Totals	**39**	**2**	**6**	**8**	**18**	....	....	....	....	....

Traded to **Edmonton** by **Buffalo** with Craig Millar for Miroslav Satan, March 18, 1997. Rights traded to **Washington** by **Edmonton** for Brad Church, February 3, 1999. Selected by **Columbus** from **Washington** in Expansion Draft, June 23, 2000.

MOORE, Dickie

HHOF

Left wing. Shoots left. 5'10", 168 lbs. Born, Montreal, Que., January 6, 1931.

Season	Club	Regular Season GP	G	A	Pts	PIM	Playoffs GP	G	A	Pts	PIM
1951-52	Montreal Canadiens	33	18	15	33	44	11	1	1	2	12
1952-53 ♦	Montreal Canadiens	18	2	6	8	19	12	3	2	5	13
1953-54	Montreal Canadiens	13	1	4	5	12	11	5	*8	*13	8
1954-55	Montreal Canadiens	67	16	20	36	32	12	1	5	6	22
1955-56 ♦	Montreal Canadiens	70	11	39	50	55	10	3	6	9	12
1956-57 ♦	Montreal Canadiens	70	29	29	58	56	10	3	7	10	4
1957-58 ♦	Montreal Canadiens	70	*36	48	*84	65	10	4	7	11	4
1958-59 ♦	Montreal Canadiens	70	41	*55	*96	61	11	5	*12	*17	8
1959-60 ♦	Montreal Canadiens	62	22	42	64	54	8	*6	4	10	4
1960-61	Montreal Canadiens	57	35	34	69	62	6	3	1	4	4
1961-62	Montreal Canadiens	57	19	22	41	54	6	4	2	6	8
1962-63	Montreal Canadiens	67	24	26	50	61	5	0	1	1	2
1964-65	Toronto Maple Leafs	38	2	4	6	68	5	1	1	2	6
1967-68	St. Louis Blues	27	5	3	8	9	18	7	7	14	15
	NHL Totals	**719**	**261**	**347**	**608**	**652**	**135**	**46**	**64**	**110**	**122**

NHL First All-Star Team (1958, 1959) • Art Ross Trophy (1958, 1959) • NHL Second All-Star Team (1961)

Played in NHL All-Star Game (1953, 1956, 1957, 1958, 1959, 1960)

• Missed majority of 1953-54 season recovering from collarbone injury suffered in game vs. Boston, October 10, 1953. Claimed by **Toronto** from **Montreal** in Intra-League Draft, June 10, 1964. Signed as a free agent by **St. Louis**, December 3, 1967.

MOORE, Steve

Center. Shoots right. 6'2", 205 lbs. Born, Windsor, Ont., September 22, 1978.
(Colorado's 7th choice, 53rd overall, in 1998 Entry Draft).

Season	Club	Regular Season GP	G	A	Pts	PIM	Playoffs GP	G	A	Pts	PIM
2001-02	Colorado Avalanche	8	0	0	0	4	....	....	....	....	....
2002-03	Colorado Avalanche	4	0	0	0	0	....	....	....	....	....
	NHL Totals	**12**	**0**	**0**	**0**	**4**	....	....	....	....	....

MORAN, Amby

Defense. Shoots left. 6', 200 lbs. Born, Winnipeg, Man., April 3, 1895.

Season	Club	Regular Season GP	G	A	Pts	PIM	Playoffs GP	G	A	Pts	PIM
1926-27	Montreal Canadiens	12	0	0	0	10	....	....	....	....	....
1927-28	Chicago Black Hawks	23	1	1	2	14	....	....	....	....	....
	NHL Totals	**35**	**1**	**1**	**2**	**24**	....	....	....	....	....

Traded to **Boston** by **Vancouver** (WHL) for cash, September 4, 1926. Traded to **Montreal** by **Boston** for Billy Coutu, October 22, 1926. Traded to **Boston** (Can-Am) by **Montreal** for cash, December 23, 1926. Signed as a free agent by **Moose Jaw** (PrHL) following release by Boston, January 29, 1927. Traded to **Chicago** by **Moose Jaw** (PrHL) with future considerations (Vic Hoffinger, January 23, 1928) for Teddy Graham, January 11, 1928.

MORAN, Brad

Center. Shoots left. 5'11", 187 lbs. Born, Abbotsford, B.C., March 20, 1979.
(Buffalo's 8th choice, 191st overall, in 1998 Entry Draft).

Season	Club	Regular Season GP	G	A	Pts	PIM	Playoffs GP	G	A	Pts	PIM
2001-02	Columbus Blue Jackets	3	0	0	0	0	....	....	....	....	....
	NHL Totals	**3**	**0**	**0**	**0**	**0**	....	....	....	....	....

Signed as a free agent by **Columbus**, June 5, 2000.

MORAN, Ian

Defense. Shoots right. 6', 200 lbs. Born, Cleveland, OH, August 24, 1972.
(Pittsburgh's 5th choice, 107th overall, in 1990 Entry Draft).

Season	Club	Regular Season GP	G	A	Pts	PIM	Playoffs GP	G	A	Pts	PIM
1994-95	Pittsburgh Penguins	....	....	....	....	....	8	0	0	0	0
1995-96	Pittsburgh Penguins	51	1	1	2	47	....	....	....	....	....
1996-97	Pittsburgh Penguins	36	4	5	9	22	5	1	2	3	4
1997-98	Pittsburgh Penguins	37	1	6	7	19	6	0	0	0	2
1998-99	Pittsburgh Penguins	62	4	5	9	37	13	0	2	2	8
99-2000	Pittsburgh Penguins	73	4	8	12	28	11	0	1	1	2
2000-01	Pittsburgh Penguins	40	3	4	7	28	18	0	1	1	4
2001-02	Pittsburgh Penguins	64	2	8	10	54	....	....	....	....	....
2002-03	Pittsburgh Penguins	70	0	7	7	46	....	....	....	....	....
	Boston Bruins	8	0	1	1	2	5	0	1	1	4
	NHL Totals	**441**	**19**	**45**	**64**	**283**	**66**	**1**	**7**	**8**	**24**

• Missed majority of 1997-98 season recovering from knee injury suffered in training camp, September 30, 1997. • Missed majority of 2000-01 season recovering from hand injury originally suffered in game vs. Edmonton, November 11, 2000. Traded to **Boston** by **Pittsburgh** for Boston's 4th round choice (Paul Bissonnette) in 2003 Entry Draft, March 11, 2003.

MORAVEC, David

Right wing. Shoots left. 6', 180 lbs. Born, Vitkovice, Czech., March 24, 1973.
(Buffalo's 9th choice, 218th overall, in 1998 Entry Draft).

Season	Club	Regular Season GP	G	A	Pts	PIM	Playoffs GP	G	A	Pts	PIM
99-2000	Buffalo Sabres	1	0	0	0	0	....	....	....	....	....
	NHL Totals	**1**	**0**	**0**	**0**	**0**	....	....	....	....	....

MORE, Jay

Defense. Shoots right. 6'1", 210 lbs. Born, Souris, Man., January 12, 1969.
(NY Rangers' 1st choice, 10th overall, in 1987 Entry Draft).

Season	Club	Regular Season GP	G	A	Pts	PIM	Playoffs GP	G	A	Pts	PIM
1988-89	New York Rangers	1	0	0	0	0	....	....	....	....	....
1989-90	Minnesota North Stars	5	0	0	0	16	....	....	....	....	....
1991-92	San Jose Sharks	46	4	13	17	85	....	....	....	....	....
1992-93	San Jose Sharks	73	5	6	11	179	....	....	....	....	....
1993-94	San Jose Sharks	49	1	6	7	63	13	0	2	2	32
1994-95	San Jose Sharks	45	0	6	6	71	11	0	4	4	6
1995-96	San Jose Sharks	74	2	7	9	147	....	....	....	....	....
1996-97	New York Rangers	14	0	1	1	25	....	....	....	....	....
	Phoenix Coyotes	23	1	6	7	37	7	0	0	0	7
1997-98	Phoenix Coyotes	41	5	5	10	53	....	....	....	....	....
	Chicago Blackhawks	17	0	2	2	8	....	....	....	....	....
1998-99	Nashville Predators	18	0	2	2	18	....	....	....	....	....
	NHL Totals	**406**	**18**	**54**	**72**	**702**	**31**	**0**	**6**	**6**	**45**

Traded to **Minnesota** by **NY Rangers** for Dave Archibald, November 1, 1989. Traded to **Montreal** by **Minnesota** for Brian Hayward, November 7, 1990. Claimed by **San Jose** from **Montreal** in Expansion Draft, May 30, 1991. Traded to **NY Rangers** by **San Jose** with Brian Swanson and San Jose's 4th round choice (later traded back to San Jose – San Jose selected Adam Colagiacomo) in 1997 Entry Draft for Marty McSorley, August 20, 1996. Traded to **Phoenix** by **NY Rangers** for Mike Eastwood and Dallas Eakins, February 6, 1997. Traded to **Chicago** by **Phoenix** with Chad Kilger for Keith Carney and Jim Cummins, March 4, 1998. Signed as a free agent by **Nashville**, June 4, 1998. • Suffered career-ending head injury in game vs. Florida, December 10, 1998.

MOREAU, Ethan

Left wing. Shoots left. 6'2", 211 lbs. Born, Huntsville, Ont., September 22, 1975.
(Chicago's 1st choice, 14th overall, in 1994 Entry Draft).

Season	Club	Regular Season GP	G	A	Pts	PIM	Playoffs GP	G	A	Pts	PIM
1995-96	Chicago Blackhawks	8	0	1	1	4	....	....	....	....	....
1996-97	Chicago Blackhawks	82	15	16	31	123	6	1	0	1	9
1997-98	Chicago Blackhawks	54	9	9	18	73	....	....	....	....	....
1998-99	Chicago Blackhawks	66	9	6	15	84	....	....	....	....	....
	Edmonton Oilers	14	1	5	6	8	4	0	3	3	6
99-2000	Edmonton Oilers	73	17	10	27	62	5	0	1	1	0
2000-01	Edmonton Oilers	68	9	10	19	90	4	0	0	0	2
2001-02	Edmonton Oilers	80	11	5	16	81	....	....	....	....	....
2002-03	Edmonton Oilers	78	14	17	31	112	6	0	1	1	16
	NHL Totals	**523**	**85**	**79**	**164**	**637**	**25**	**1**	**5**	**6**	**33**

Traded to **Edmonton** by **Chicago** with Daniel Cleary, Chad Kilger and Christian Laflamme for Boris Mironov, Dean McAmmond and Jonas Elofsson, March 20, 1999.

MORENZ, Howie

HHOF

Center. Shoots left. 5'9", 165 lbs. Born, Mitchell, Ont., June 21, 1902.

Season	Club	Regular Season GP	G	A	Pts	PIM	Playoffs GP	G	A	Pts	PIM
1923-24 ♦	Montreal Canadiens	24	13	3	16	20	2	3	1	4	6
	Montreal Canadiens (Cup)	....	....	....	....	....	*4*	*4*	*2*	*6*	*4*
1924-25	Montreal Canadiens	30	28	11	39	46	2	3	0	3	4
	Montreal Canadiens (Cup)	....	....	....	....	....	*4*	*4*	*0*	*4*	*4*
1925-26	Montreal Canadiens	31	23	3	26	39	....	....	....	....	....
1926-27	Montreal Canadiens	44	25	7	32	49	4	1	0	1	4
1927-28	Montreal Canadiens	43	*33	*18	*51	66	2	0	0	0	12
1928-29	Montreal Canadiens	42	17	10	27	47	3	0	0	0	6
1929-30 ♦	Montreal Canadiens	44	40	10	50	72	6	3	0	3	10
1930-31 ♦	Montreal Canadiens	39	28	23	*51	49	10	1	*4	5	10
1931-32	Montreal Canadiens	48	24	25	49	46	4	1	0	1	4
1932-33	Montreal Canadiens	46	14	21	35	32	2	0	3	3	2
1933-34	Montreal Canadiens	39	8	13	21	21	2	1	1	2	0
1934-35	Chicago Black Hawks	48	8	26	34	21	2	0	0	0	0
1935-36	Chicago Black Hawks	23	4	11	15	20	....	....	....	....	....
	New York Rangers	19	2	4	6	6	....	....	....	....	....
1936-37	Montreal Canadiens	30	4	16	20	12	....	....	....	....	....
	NHL Totals	**550**	**271**	**201**	**472**	**546**	**39**	**13**	**9**	**22**	**58**

Hart Trophy (1928, 1931, 1932) • NHL First All-Star Team (1931, 1932) • NHL Second All-Star Team (1933)

Played in NHL All-Star Game (1934)

Signed as a free agent by **Montreal**, September 30, 1923. • 1923-24 Stanley Cup totals includes series with Calgary (WCHL) and Vancouver (PCHA). Traded to **Chicago** by **Montreal** with Lorne Chabot and Marty Burke for Leroy Goldsworthy, Lionel Conacher and Roger Jenkins, October 3, 1934. Traded to **NY Rangers** by **Chicago** for Glenn Brydson, January 26, 1936. Traded to **Montreal** by **NY Rangers** for cash, September 1, 1936. • Suffered career-ending leg injury in game vs. Chicago, January 28, 1937.

MORETTO, Angelo

Center. Shoots left. 6'3", 212 lbs. Born, Toronto, Ont., September 18, 1953.
(California's 9th choice, 160th overall, in 1973 Amateur Draft).

Season	Club	GP	G	A	Pts	PIM	GP	G	A	Pts	PIM
		REGULAR SEASON					**PLAYOFFS**				
1976-77	Cleveland Barons	5	1	2	3	2	....	....	....	....	....
	NHL Totals	**5**	**1**	**2**	**3**	**2**	....	....	....	....	....

Transferred to **Cleveland** after **California** franchise relocated, August 26, 1976.

MORGAN, Jason

Center. Shoots left. 6'1", 200 lbs. Born, St. John's, Nfld., October 9, 1976.
(Los Angeles' 5th choice, 118th overall, in 1995 Entry Draft).

Season	Club	GP	G	A	Pts	PIM	GP	G	A	Pts	PIM
1996-97	Los Angeles Kings	3	0	0	0	0	....	....	....	....	....
1997-98	Los Angeles Kings	11	1	0	1	4	....	....	....	....	....
	NHL Totals	**14**	**1**	**0**	**1**	**4**	....	....	....	....	....

Signed as a free agent by **Calgary**, July 11, 2002.

MORIN, Pete

Left wing. Shoots left. 5'6", 150 lbs. Born, Lachine, Que., December 8, 1915.

Season	Club	GP	G	A	Pts	PIM	GP	G	A	Pts	PIM
1941-42	Montreal Canadiens	31	10	12	22	7	1	0	0	0	0
	NHL Totals	**31**	**10**	**12**	**22**	**7**	**1**	**0**	**0**	**0**	**0**

Signed as a free agent by **Montreal**, November 28, 1941.

MORIN, Stephane

Center. Shoots left. 6', 174 lbs. Born, Montreal, Que., March 27, 1969.
(Quebec's 3rd choice, 43rd overall, in 1989 Entry Draft).

Season	Club	GP	G	A	Pts	PIM	GP	G	A	Pts	PIM
1989-90	Quebec Nordiques	6	0	2	2	2	....	....	....	....	....
1990-91	Quebec Nordiques	48	13	27	40	30	....	....	....	....	....
1991-92	Quebec Nordiques	30	2	8	10	14	....	....	....	....	....
1992-93	Vancouver Canucks	1	0	1	1	0	....	....	....	....	....
1993-94	Vancouver Canucks	5	1	1	2	6	....	....	....	....	....
	NHL Totals	**90**	**16**	**39**	**55**	**52**	....	....	....	....	....

Signed as a free agent by **Vancouver**, October 5, 1992.

MORISSET, Dave

Right wing. Shoots right. 6'2", 195 lbs. Born, Langley, B.C., April 6, 1981.
(St. Louis' 2nd choice, 65th overall, in 2000 Entry Draft).

Season	Club	GP	G	A	Pts	PIM	GP	G	A	Pts	PIM
2001-02	Florida Panthers	4	0	0	0	5	....	....	....	....	....
	NHL Totals	**4**	**0**	**0**	**0**	**5**	....	....	....	....	....

Rights traded to **Florida** by **St. Louis** with St. Louis' 5th round choice (Vince Bellissimo) in 2002 Entry Draft for Scott Mellanby, February 9, 2001.

MORISSETTE, Dave

Left wing. Shoots left. 6'1", 224 lbs. Born, Baie Comeau, Que., December 24, 1971.
(Washington's 7th choice, 146th overall, in 1991 Entry Draft).

Season	Club	GP	G	A	Pts	PIM	GP	G	A	Pts	PIM
1998-99	Montreal Canadiens	10	0	0	0	52	....	....	....	....	....
99-2000	Montreal Canadiens	1	0	0	0	5	....	....	....	....	....
	NHL Totals	**11**	**0**	**0**	**0**	**57**	....	....	....	....	....

Signed as a free agent by **Montreal**, June 10, 1998.

MORO, Marc

Defense. Shoots left. 6'1", 220 lbs. Born, Toronto, Ont., July 17, 1977.
(Ottawa's 2nd choice, 27th overall, in 1995 Entry Draft).

Season	Club	GP	G	A	Pts	PIM	GP	G	A	Pts	PIM
1997-98	Mighty Ducks of Anaheim	1	0	0	0	0	....	....	....	....	....
99-2000	Nashville Predators	8	0	0	0	40	....	....	....	....	....
2000-01	Nashville Predators	6	0	0	0	12	....	....	....	....	....
2001-02	Nashville Predators	13	0	0	0	23	....	....	....	....	....
	Toronto Maple Leafs	2	0	0	0	2	....	....	....	....	....
	NHL Totals	**30**	**0**	**0**	**0**	**77**	....	....	....	....	....

Rights traded to **Anaheim** by **Ottawa** with Ted Drury for Jason York and Shaun Van Allen, October 1, 1996. Traded to **Nashville** by **Anaheim** with Chris Mason for Dominic Roussel, October 5, 1998. Traded to **Toronto** by **Nashville** for D.J. Smith and Marty Wilford, March 1, 2002.

MOROZOV, Aleksey

Right wing. Shoots left. 6'1", 202 lbs. Born, Moscow, USSR, February 16, 1977.
(Pittsburgh's 1st choice, 24th overall, in 1995 Entry Draft).

Season	Club	GP	G	A	Pts	PIM	GP	G	A	Pts	PIM
1997-98	Pittsburgh Penguins	76	13	13	26	8	6	0	1	1	2
1998-99	Pittsburgh Penguins	67	9	10	19	14	10	1	1	2	0
99-2000	Pittsburgh Penguins	68	12	19	31	14	5	0	0	0	0
2000-01	Pittsburgh Penguins	66	5	14	19	6	18	3	3	6	6
2001-02	Pittsburgh Penguins	72	20	29	49	16	....	....	....	....	....
2002-03	Pittsburgh Penguins	27	9	16	25	16	....	....	....	....	....
	NHL Totals	**376**	**68**	**101**	**169**	**74**	**39**	**4**	**5**	**9**	**8**

MORRIS, Bernie

Center/Right wing. Shoots right. 5'7", 145 lbs. Born, Regina, Sask.,

Season	Club	GP	G	A	Pts	PIM	GP	G	A	Pts	PIM
1924-25	Boston Bruins	6	1	0	1	0	....	....	....	....	....
	NHL Totals	**6**	**1**	**0**	**1**	**0**	....	....	....	....	....

Traded to **Boston** by **Mtl. Maroons** with Bobby Benson for Alf Skinner, January 3, 1925.

MORRIS, Derek

Defense. Shoots right. 5'11", 210 lbs. Born, Edmonton, Alta., August 24, 1978.
(Calgary's 1st choice, 13th overall, in 1996 Entry Draft).

Season	Club	GP	G	A	Pts	PIM	GP	G	A	Pts	PIM
1997-98	Calgary Flames	82	9	20	29	88	....	....	....	....	....
1998-99	Calgary Flames	71	7	27	34	73	....	....	....	....	....
99-2000	Calgary Flames	78	9	29	38	80	....	....	....	....	....
2000-01	Calgary Flames	51	5	23	28	56	....	....	....	....	....
2001-02	Calgary Flames	61	4	30	34	88	....	....	....	....	....
2002-03	Colorado Avalanche	75	11	37	48	68	7	0	3	3	6
	NHL Totals	**418**	**45**	**166**	**211**	**453**	**7**	**0**	**3**	**3**	**6**

NHL All-Rookie Team (1998)

Traded to **Colorado** by **Calgary** with Jeff Shantz and Dean McAmmond for Chris Drury and Stephane Yelle, October 1, 2002.

MORRIS, Jon

Center. Shoots right. 6', 175 lbs. Born, Lowell, MA, May 6, 1966.
(New Jersey's 5th choice, 86th overall, in 1984 Entry Draft).

Season	Club	GP	G	A	Pts	PIM	GP	G	A	Pts	PIM
1988-89	New Jersey Devils	4	0	2	2	0	....	....	....	....	....
1989-90	New Jersey Devils	20	6	7	13	8	6	1	3	4	23
1990-91	New Jersey Devils	53	9	19	28	27	5	0	4	4	2
1991-92	New Jersey Devils	7	1	2	3	6	....	....	....	....	....
1992-93	New Jersey Devils	2	0	0	0	0	....	....	....	....	....
	San Jose Sharks	13	0	3	3	6	....	....	....	....	....
1993-94	Boston Bruins	4	0	0	0	0	....	....	....	....	....
	NHL Totals	**103**	**16**	**33**	**49**	**47**	**11**	**1**	**7**	**8**	**25**

Claimed on waivers by **San Jose** from **New Jersey**, March 13, 1993. Traded to **Boston** by **San Jose** for cash, October 28, 1993.

MORRIS, Moe

Defense. Shoots left. 5'8", 187 lbs. Born, Toronto, Ont., January 3, 1921.

Season	Club	GP	G	A	Pts	PIM	GP	G	A	Pts	PIM
1943-44	Toronto Maple Leafs	50	12	21	33	22	5	1	2	3	2
1944-45 ♦	Toronto Maple Leafs	29	0	2	2	18	13	3	0	3	*14
1945-46	Toronto Maple Leafs	38	1	5	6	10	....	....	....	....	....
1948-49	New York Rangers	18	0	1	1	8	....	....	....	....	....
	NHL Totals	**135**	**13**	**29**	**42**	**58**	**18**	**4**	**2**	**6**	**16**

Traded to **NY Rangers** by **Toronto** with Wally Stanowski for Cal Gardner, Bill Juzda, Rene Trudell and the rights to Frank Mathers, April 26, 1948. Traded to **Providence** (AHL) by **NY Rangers** with Eddie Kullman, cash and future considerations (Buck Davies, June, 1949) for Allan Stanley, December 9, 1948.

MORRISON, Brendan

Center. Shoots left. 5'11", 190 lbs. Born, Pitt Meadows, B.C., August 15, 1975.
(New Jersey's 3rd choice, 39th overall, in 1993 Entry Draft).

Season	Club	GP	G	A	Pts	PIM	GP	G	A	Pts	PIM
1997-98	New Jersey Devils	11	5	4	9	0	3	0	1	1	0
1998-99	New Jersey Devils	76	13	33	46	18	7	0	2	2	0
99-2000	New Jersey Devils	44	5	21	26	8	....	....	....	....	....
	Vancouver Canucks	12	2	7	9	10	....	....	....	....	....
2000-01	Vancouver Canucks	82	16	38	54	42	4	1	2	3	0
2001-02	Vancouver Canucks	82	23	44	67	26	6	0	2	2	6
2002-03	Vancouver Canucks	82	25	46	71	36	14	4	7	11	18
	NHL Totals	**389**	**89**	**193**	**282**	**140**	**34**	**5**	**14**	**19**	**24**

Traded to **Vancouver** by **New Jersey** with Denis Pederson for Alexander Mogilny, March 14, 2000.

MORRISON, Dave

Right wing. Shoots right. 6', 190 lbs. Born, Toronto, Ont., June 12, 1962.
(Los Angeles' 4th choice, 34th overall, in 1980 Entry Draft).

Season	Club	GP	G	A	Pts	PIM	GP	G	A	Pts	PIM
1980-81	Los Angeles Kings	3	0	0	0	0	....	....	....	....	....
1981-82	Los Angeles Kings	4	0	0	0	0	....	....	....	....	....
1982-83	Los Angeles Kings	24	3	3	6	4	....	....	....	....	....
1984-85	Vancouver Canucks	8	0	0	0	0	....	....	....	....	....
	NHL Totals	**39**	**3**	**3**	**6**	**4**	....	....	....	....	....

• Son of Jim

Signed as a free agent by **Vancouver**, October 28, 1983.

MORRISON, Don

Center. Shoots right. 5'10", 165 lbs. Born, Saskatoon, Sask., July 14, 1923.

Season	Club	GP	G	A	Pts	PIM	GP	G	A	Pts	PIM
1947-48	Detroit Red Wings	40	10	15	25	6	3	0	1	1	0
1948-49	Detroit Red Wings	13	0	1	1	0	....	....	....	....	....
1950-51	Chicago Black Hawks	59	8	12	20	6	....	....	....	....	....
	NHL Totals	**112**	**18**	**28**	**46**	**12**	**3**	**0**	**1**	**1**	**0**

• Brother of Rod

Traded to **Chicago** by **Detroit** with Harry Lumley, Jack Stewart, Al Dewsbury and Pete Babando for Jim Henry, Bob Goldham, Gaye Stewart and Metro Prystai, July 13, 1950.

MORRISON, Doug

Right wing. Shoots right. 5'11", 184 lbs. Born, Vancouver, B.C., February 1, 1960.
(Boston's 3rd choice, 36th overall, in 1979 Entry Draft).

Season	Club	GP	G	A	Pts	PIM	GP	G	A	Pts	PIM
1979-80	Boston Bruins	1	0	0	0	0	....	....	....	....	....
1980-81	Boston Bruins	18	7	3	10	13	....	....	....	....	....
1981-82	Boston Bruins	3	0	0	0	0	....	....	....	....	....

Season	Club	REGULAR SEASON GP	G	A	Pts	PIM	PLAYOFFS GP	G	A	Pts	PIM
1984-85	Boston Bruins	1	0	0	0	2	....	....	....	....	....
	NHL Totals	**23**	**7**	**3**	**10**	**15**	....	....	....	....	....

• Brother of Mark

MORRISON, Gary

Right wing. Shoots right. 6'2", 200 lbs. Born, Detroit, MI, November 8, 1955.
(Philadelphia's 4th choice, 90th overall, in 1975 Amateur Draft).

Season	Club	GP	G	A	Pts	PIM	GP	G	A	Pts	PIM
1979-80	Philadelphia Flyers	3	0	2	2	0	5	0	1	1	2
1980-81	Philadelphia Flyers	33	1	13	14	68	....	....	....	....	....
1981-82	Philadelphia Flyers	7	0	0	0	2	....	....	....	....	....
	NHL Totals	**43**	**1**	**15**	**16**	**70**	**5**	**0**	**1**	**1**	**2**

MORRISON, George

Left wing. Shoots left. 6'1", 170 lbs. Born, Toronto, Ont., December 24, 1948.

Season	Club	GP	G	A	Pts	PIM	GP	G	A	Pts	PIM
1970-71	St. Louis Blues	73	15	10	25	6	3	0	0	0	0
1971-72	St. Louis Blues	42	2	11	13	7	....	....	....	....	....
	NHL Totals	**115**	**17**	**21**	**38**	**13**	**3**	**0**	**0**	**0**	**0**

Signed as a free agent by **St. Louis**, September 30, 1970. Traded to **Buffalo** by **St. Louis** with St. Louis' 2nd round choice (Larry Carriere) in 1972 Amateur Draft for Chris Evans, March 5, 1972. • Suspended by **Buffalo** for refusing to report to **Rochester** (AHL), March 8, 1972.

MORRISON, Jim

Defense. Shoots left. 5'10", 183 lbs. Born, Montreal, Que., October 11, 1931.

Season	Club	GP	G	A	Pts	PIM	GP	G	A	Pts	PIM
1951-52	Boston Bruins	14	0	2	2	2	....	....	....	....	....
	Toronto Maple Leafs	17	0	1	1	4	2	0	0	0	0
1952-53	Toronto Maple Leafs	56	1	8	9	36	....	....	....	....	....
1953-54	Toronto Maple Leafs	60	9	11	20	51	5	0	0	0	4
1954-55	Toronto Maple Leafs	70	5	12	17	84	4	0	1	1	4
1955-56	Toronto Maple Leafs	63	2	17	19	77	5	0	0	0	4
1956-57	Toronto Maple Leafs	63	3	17	20	44	....	....	....	....	....
1957-58	Toronto Maple Leafs	70	3	21	24	62	....	....	....	....	....
1958-59	Boston Bruins	70	8	17	25	42	6	0	6	6	16
1959-60	Detroit Red Wings	70	3	23	26	62	6	0	2	2	0
1960-61	New York Rangers	19	1	6	7	6	....	....	....	....	....
1969-70	Pittsburgh Penguins	59	5	15	20	40	8	0	3	3	10
1970-71	Pittsburgh Penguins	73	0	10	10	32	....	....	....	....	....
	NHL Totals	**704**	**40**	**160**	**200**	**542**	**36**	**0**	**12**	**12**	**38**

• Father of Dave

Played in NHL All-Star Game (1955, 1956, 1957)

Traded to **Toronto** by **Boston** for Fleming MacKell, January 9, 1952. Traded to **Boston** by **Toronto** for Allan Stanley, October 8, 1958. Traded to **Detroit** by **Boston** for Nick Mickoski, August 25, 1959. Traded to **Chicago** by **Detroit** for Howie Glover, June 5, 1960. Claimed by **NY Rangers** from **Chicago** in Intra-League Draft, June 8, 1960. Traded to **Quebec** (AHL) by **NY Rangers** for cash, November 28, 1960. NHL rights transferred to **Philadelphia** after NHL club purchased **Quebec** (AHL) franchise, May 8, 1967. Claimed by **Baltimore** (AHL) from **Philadelphia** (Quebec-AHL) in Reverse Draft, June 13, 1968. Traded to **Pittsburgh** by **Baltimore** (AHL) for cash and future considerations (Bob Rivard, November, 1969), October, 1969.

MORRISON, John

Left wing. Shoots right. 5'8", 163 lbs. Born, Selkirk, Man., March 4, 1895.

Season	Club	GP	G	A	Pts	PIM	GP	G	A	Pts	PIM
1925-26	New York Americans	18	0	0	0	0	....	....	....	....	....
	NHL Totals	**18**	**0**	**0**	**0**	**0**	....	....	....	....	....

Traded to **NY Americans** by **Edmonton** (WHL) with Joe Simpson and Roy Rickey for $10,000, September 18, 1925.

MORRISON, Kevin

Defense. Shoots left. 6', 202 lbs. Born, Sydney, N.S., October 28, 1949.
(NY Rangers' 4th choice, 35th overall, in 1969 Amateur Draft).

Season	Club	GP	G	A	Pts	PIM	GP	G	A	Pts	PIM
1979-80	Colorado Rockies	41	4	11	15	23	....	....	....	....	....
	NHL Totals	**41**	**4**	**11**	**15**	**23**	....	....	....	....	....

Claimed by **Detroit** from **NY Rangers** in Intra-League Draft, June, 1970. Signed as a free agent by **Colorado**, June, 1979.

MORRISON, Lew

Right wing. Shoots right. 6', 185 lbs. Born, Gainsborough, Sask., February 11, 1948.
(Philadelphia's 1st choice, 8th overall, in 1968 Amateur Draft).

Season	Club	GP	G	A	Pts	PIM	GP	G	A	Pts	PIM
1969-70	Philadelphia Flyers	66	9	10	19	19	....	....	....	....	....
1970-71	Philadelphia Flyers	78	5	7	12	25	4	0	0	0	2
1971-72	Philadelphia Flyers	58	5	5	10	26	....	....	....	....	....
1972-73	Atlanta Flames	78	6	9	15	19	....	....	....	....	....
1973-74	Atlanta Flames	52	1	4	5	0	....	....	....	....	....
1974-75	Washington Capitals	18	0	4	4	6	....	....	....	....	....
	Pittsburgh Penguins	52	7	5	12	4	9	0	0	0	0
1975-76	Pittsburgh Penguins	78	4	5	9	8	3	0	0	0	0
1976-77	Pittsburgh Penguins	76	2	1	3	0	1	0	0	0	0
1977-78	Pittsburgh Penguins	8	0	2	2	0	....	....	....	....	....
	NHL Totals	**564**	**39**	**52**	**91**	**107**	**17**	**0**	**0**	**0**	**2**

Claimed by **Atlanta** from **Philadelphia** in Expansion Draft, June 6, 1972. Claimed by **Washington** from **Atlanta** in Expansion Draft, June 12, 1974. Traded to **Pittsburgh** by **Washington** for Ron Lalonde, December 14, 1974.

MORRISON, Mark

Center. Shoots right. 5'8", 150 lbs. Born, Prince George, B.C., March 11, 1963.
(NY Rangers' 4th choice, 51st overall, in 1981 Entry Draft).

Season	Club	GP	G	A	Pts	PIM	GP	G	A	Pts	PIM
1981-82	New York Rangers	9	1	1	2	0	....	....	....	....	....
1983-84	New York Rangers	1	0	0	0	0	....	....	....	....	....
	NHL Totals	**10**	**1**	**1**	**2**	**0**	....	....	....	....	....

• Brother of Doug

Traded to **Edmonton** by **NY Rangers** for cash, November 27, 1984.

MORRISON, Rod

Right wing. Shoots right. 5'9", 160 lbs. Born, Saskatoon, Sask., October 7, 1925.

Season	Club	GP	G	A	Pts	PIM	GP	G	A	Pts	PIM
1947-48	Detroit Red Wings	34	8	7	15	4	3	0	0	0	0
	NHL Totals	**34**	**8**	**7**	**15**	**4**	**3**	**0**	**0**	**0**	**0**

• Brother of Don

MORRISONN, Shaone

Defense. Shoots left. 6'3", 205 lbs. Born, Vancouver, B.C., December 23, 1982.
(Boston's 1st choice, 19th overall, in 2001 Entry Draft).

Season	Club	GP	G	A	Pts	PIM	GP	G	A	Pts	PIM
2002-03	Boston Bruins	11	0	0	0	8	....	....	....	....	....
	NHL Totals	**11**	**0**	**0**	**0**	**8**	....	....	....	....	....

MORROW, Brenden

Left wing. Shoots left. 5'11", 200 lbs. Born, Carlyle, Sask., January 16, 1979.
(Dallas' 1st choice, 25th overall, in 1997 Entry Draft).

Season	Club	GP	G	A	Pts	PIM	GP	G	A	Pts	PIM
99-2000	Dallas Stars	64	14	19	33	81	21	2	4	6	22
2000-01	Dallas Stars	82	20	24	44	128	10	0	3	3	12
2001-02	Dallas Stars	72	17	18	35	109	....	....	....	....	....
2002-03	Dallas Stars	71	21	22	43	134	12	3	5	8	16
	NHL Totals	**289**	**72**	**83**	**155**	**452**	**43**	**5**	**12**	**17**	**50**

MORROW, Ken

USHOF

Defense. Shoots right. 6'4", 210 lbs. Born, Flint, MI, October 17, 1956.
(NY Islanders' 4th choice, 68th overall, in 1976 Amateur Draft).

Season	Club	GP	G	A	Pts	PIM	GP	G	A	Pts	PIM
1979-80 ♦	New York Islanders	18	0	3	3	4	20	1	2	3	12
1980-81 ♦	New York Islanders	80	2	11	13	20	18	3	4	7	8
1981-82 ♦	New York Islanders	75	1	18	19	56	19	0	4	4	8
1982-83 ♦	New York Islanders	79	5	11	16	44	19	5	7	12	18
1983-84	New York Islanders	63	3	11	14	45	20	1	2	3	20
1984-85	New York Islanders	15	1	7	8	14	10	0	0	0	17
1985-86	New York Islanders	69	0	12	12	22	2	0	0	0	4
1986-87	New York Islanders	64	3	8	11	32	13	1	3	4	2
1987-88	New York Islanders	53	1	4	5	40	6	0	0	0	8
1988-89	New York Islanders	34	1	3	4	32	....	....	....	....	....
	NHL Totals	**550**	**17**	**88**	**105**	**309**	**127**	**11**	**22**	**33**	**97**

Lester Patrick Trophy (1996)

MORROW, Scott

Left wing. Shoots left. 6'1", 185 lbs. Born, Chicago, IL, June 18, 1969.
(Hartford's 4th choice, 95th overall, in 1988 Entry Draft).

Season	Club	GP	G	A	Pts	PIM	GP	G	A	Pts	PIM
1994-95	Calgary Flames	4	0	0	0	0	....	....	....	....	....
	NHL Totals	**4**	**0**	**0**	**0**	**0**	....	....	....	....	....

Traded to **Calgary** by **Hartford** for Todd Harkins, January 24, 1994. Signed as a free agent by **Philadelphia**, July 31, 1995.

MORTON, Dean

Defense. Shoots right. 6'1", 196 lbs. Born, Peterborough, Ont., February 27, 1968.
(Detroit's 8th choice, 148th overall, in 1986 Entry Draft).

Season	Club	GP	G	A	Pts	PIM	GP	G	A	Pts	PIM
1989-90	Detroit Red Wings	1	1	0	1	2	....	....	....	....	....
	NHL Totals	**1**	**1**	**0**	**1**	**2**	....	....	....	....	....

• One of only three players (Rolly Huard, Matt Stajan) to score a goal in only NHL game.

MORTSON, Gus

Defense. Shoots left. 5'11", 190 lbs. Born, New Liskeard, Ont., January 24, 1925.

Season	Club	GP	G	A	Pts	PIM	GP	G	A	Pts	PIM
1946-47 ♦	Toronto Maple Leafs	60	5	13	18	*133	11	1	3	4	22
1947-48 ♦	Toronto Maple Leafs	58	7	11	18	118	5	1	2	3	2
1948-49 ♦	Toronto Maple Leafs	60	2	13	15	85	9	2	1	3	8
1949-50	Toronto Maple Leafs	68	3	14	17	125	7	0	0	0	18
1950-51 ♦	Toronto Maple Leafs	60	3	10	13	*142	11	0	1	1	4
1951-52	Toronto Maple Leafs	65	1	10	11	106	4	0	0	0	8
1952-53	Chicago Black Hawks	68	5	18	23	88	7	1	1	2	6
1953-54	Chicago Black Hawks	68	5	13	18	*132	....	....	....	....	....
1954-55	Chicago Black Hawks	65	2	11	13	133	....	....	....	....	....
1955-56	Chicago Black Hawks	52	5	10	15	87	....	....	....	....	....
1956-57	Chicago Black Hawks	70	5	18	23	*147	....	....	....	....	....
1957-58	Chicago Black Hawks	67	3	10	13	62	....	....	....	....	....
1958-59	Detroit Red Wings	36	0	1	1	22	....	....	....	....	....
	NHL Totals	**797**	**46**	**152**	**198**	**1380**	**54**	**5**	**8**	**13**	**68**

NHL First All-Star Team (1950)

Played in NHL All-Star Game (1947, 1948, 1950, 1951, 1952, 1953, 1954, 1956)

Traded to **Chicago** by **Toronto** with Ray Hannigan, Al Rollins and Cal Gardner for Harry Lumley, September 11, 1952. Traded to **Detroit** by **Chicago** for future considerations, September 3, 1958. Claimed on waivers by **NY Rangers** (Buffalo-AHL) from **Detroit**, January 17, 1959.

MOSDELL, Ken

Center. Shoots left. 6'1", 170 lbs. Born, Montreal, Que., July 13, 1922.

Season	Club	GP	G	A	Pts	PIM	GP	G	A	Pts	PIM
1941-42	Brooklyn Americans	41	7	9	16	16	....	....	....	....	....

Season	Club	REGULAR SEASON GP	G	A	Pts	PIM	PLAYOFFS GP	G	A	Pts	PIM
1944-45	Montreal Canadiens	31	12	6	18	16	....	....	....	....	....
1945-46♦	Montreal Canadiens	13	2	1	3	8	9	4	1	5	6
1946-47	Montreal Canadiens	54	5	10	15	50	4	2	0	2	4
1947-48	Montreal Canadiens	23	1	0	1	19	....	....	....	....	....
1948-49	Montreal Canadiens	60	17	9	26	50	7	1	1	2	4
1949-50	Montreal Canadiens	67	15	12	27	42	5	0	0	0	12
1950-51	Montreal Canadiens	66	13	18	31	24	11	1	1	2	4
1951-52	Montreal Canadiens	44	5	11	16	19	2	1	0	1	0
1952-53♦	Montreal Canadiens	63	5	14	19	27	7	3	2	5	4
1953-54	Montreal Canadiens	67	22	24	46	64	11	1	0	1	4
1954-55	Montreal Canadiens	70	22	32	54	82	12	2	7	9	8
1955-56♦	Montreal Canadiens	67	13	17	30	48	9	1	1	2	2
1956-57	Chicago Black Hawks	25	2	4	6	10	....	....	....	....	....
1957-58	Montreal Canadiens	2	0	1	1	0	....	....	....	....	....
1958-59♦	Montreal Canadiens	....	....	....	....	....	3	0	0	0	0
	NHL Totals	**693**	**141**	**168**	**309**	**475**	**80**	**16**	**13**	**29**	**48**

NHL First All-Star Team (1954) • NHL Second All-Star Team (1955)

Played in NHL All-Star Game (1951, 1952, 1953, 1954, 1955)

Signed as a free agent by **Brooklyn**, October 28, 1941. Rights transferred to **Montreal** from **Brooklyn** in Special Dispersal Draw, September 11, 1943. Loaned to **Buffalo** (AHL) by **Montreal** with Frank Eddolls, Wilf Field and cash for the loan of Lorrain Thibeault, October 24, 1945. • Missed majority of 1947-48 season recovering from knee injury suffered during softball game, August 15, 1947. Traded to **Chicago** by **Montreal** with Bud MacPherson for $30,000 with Montreal holding right of recall, May 17, 1956. • Returned to **Montreal** by **Chicago**, September 20, 1957.

MOSIENKO, Bill

HHOF

Right wing. Shoots right. 5'8", 160 lbs. Born, Winnipeg, Man., November 2, 1921.

Season	Club	GP	G	A	Pts	PIM	GP	G	A	Pts	PIM
1941-42	Chicago Black Hawks	12	6	8	14	4	3	2	0	2	0
1942-43	Chicago Black Hawks	2	2	0	2	0	....	....	....	....	....
1943-44	Chicago Black Hawks	50	32	38	70	10	8	2	2	4	6
1944-45	Chicago Black Hawks	50	28	26	54	0	....	....	....	....	....
1945-46	Chicago Black Hawks	40	18	30	48	12	4	2	0	2	2
1946-47	Chicago Black Hawks	59	25	27	52	2	....	....	....	....	....
1947-48	Chicago Black Hawks	40	16	9	25	0	....	....	....	....	....
1948-49	Chicago Black Hawks	60	17	25	42	6	....	....	....	....	....
1949-50	Chicago Black Hawks	69	18	28	46	10	....	....	....	....	....
1950-51	Chicago Black Hawks	65	21	15	36	18	....	....	....	....	....
1951-52	Chicago Black Hawks	70	31	22	53	10	....	....	....	....	....
1952-53	Chicago Black Hawks	65	17	20	37	8	7	4	2	6	7
1953-54	Chicago Black Hawks	65	15	19	34	17	....	....	....	....	....
1954-55	Chicago Black Hawks	64	12	15	27	24	....	....	....	....	....
	NHL Totals	**711**	**258**	**282**	**540**	**121**	**22**	**10**	**4**	**14**	**15**

NHL Second All-Star Team (1945, 1946) • Lady Byng Trophy (1945)

Played in NHL All-Star Game (1947, 1949, 1950, 1952, 1953)

Signed as a free agent by **Chicago**, October 27, 1940.

MOTT, Morris

Right wing. Shoots left. 5'8", 165 lbs. Born, Creelman, Sask., May 25, 1946.

Season	Club	GP	G	A	Pts	PIM	GP	G	A	Pts	PIM
1972-73	California Golden Seals	70	6	7	13	8	....	....	....	....	....
1973-74	California Golden Seals	77	9	17	26	33	....	....	....	....	....
1974-75	California Golden Seals	52	3	8	11	8	....	....	....	....	....
	NHL Totals	**199**	**18**	**32**	**50**	**49**	....	....	....	....	....

Signed as a free agent by **California**, October 1, 1972.

MOTTAU, Mike

Defense. Shoots left. 6', 192 lbs. Born, Quincy, MA, March 19, 1978.
(NY Rangers' 10th choice, 182nd overall, in 1997 Entry Draft).

Season	Club	GP	G	A	Pts	PIM	GP	G	A	Pts	PIM
2000-01	New York Rangers	18	0	3	3	13	....	....	....	....	....
2001-02	New York Rangers	1	0	0	0	0	....	....	....	....	....
2002-03	Calgary Flames	4	0	0	0	0	....	....	....	....	....
	NHL Totals	**23**	**0**	**3**	**3**	**13**	....	....	....	....	....

Traded to **Calgary** by **NY Rangers** for Calgary's 6th round choice (Ivan Dornic) in 2003 Entry Draft and future considerations, January 22, 2003. Signed as a free agent by **Anaheim**, July 25, 2003.

MOTTER, Alex

Center. Shoots left. 6', 175 lbs. Born, Melville, Sask., June 20, 1913.

Season	Club	GP	G	A	Pts	PIM	GP	G	A	Pts	PIM
1934-35	Boston Bruins	3	0	0	0	0	4	0	0	0	0
1935-36	Boston Bruins	23	1	4	5	4	2	0	0	0	0
1937-38	Detroit Red Wings	32	5	17	22	6	....	....	....	....	....
1938-39	Detroit Red Wings	44	5	11	16	17	4	0	1	1	0
1939-40	Detroit Red Wings	37	7	12	19	28	5	1	1	2	15
1940-41	Detroit Red Wings	47	13	12	25	18	9	1	3	4	4
1941-42	Detroit Red Wings	19	2	4	6	20	12	1	3	4	20
1942-43♦	Detroit Red Wings	50	6	4	10	42	5	0	1	1	2
	NHL Totals	**255**	**39**	**64**	**103**	**135**	**41**	**3**	**9**	**12**	**41**

Traded to **Detroit** by **Boston** for Clarence Drouillard and cash, December 22, 1937. Loaned to **Cleveland** (AHL) by **Detroit** as an injury replacement for Dick Adolph, October 23, 1942. Traded to **Cleveland** (AHL) by **Detroit** for cash, October 25, 1945.

MOWERS, Mark

Center. Shoots right. 5'11", 187 lbs. Born, Whitesboro, NY, February 16, 1974.

Season	Club	GP	G	A	Pts	PIM	GP	G	A	Pts	PIM
1998-99	Nashville Predators	30	0	6	6	4	....	....	....	....	....
99-2000	Nashville Predators	41	4	5	9	10	....	....	....	....	....
2001-02	Nashville Predators	14	1	2	3	2	....	....	....	....	....
	NHL Totals	**85**	**5**	**13**	**18**	**16**	....	....	....	....	....

Signed as a free agent by **Nashville**, June 11, 1998. Signed as a free agent by **Detroit**, August 5, 2002.

MOXEY, Jim

Right wing. Shoots left. 6'1", 190 lbs. Born, Toronto, Ont., May 28, 1953.
(California's 3rd choice, 66th overall, in 1973 Amateur Draft).

Season	Club	GP	G	A	Pts	PIM	GP	G	A	Pts	PIM
1974-75	California Golden Seals	47	5	4	9	4	....	....	....	....	....
1975-76	California Golden Seals	44	10	16	26	33	....	....	....	....	....
1976-77	Cleveland Barons	35	7	7	14	20	....	....	....	....	....
	Los Angeles Kings	1	0	0	0	2	....	....	....	....	....
	NHL Totals	**127**	**22**	**27**	**49**	**59**	....	....	....	....	....

Transferred to **Cleveland** after **California** franchise relocated, August 26, 1976. Traded to **Los Angeles** by **Cleveland** with Gary Simmons for Juha Widing and Gary Edwards, January 22, 1977.

MROZIK, Rick

Center. Shoots left. 6'2", 214 lbs. Born, Duluth, MN, January 2, 1975.
(Dallas' 4th choice, 136th overall, in 1993 Entry Draft).

Season	Club	GP	G	A	Pts	PIM	GP	G	A	Pts	PIM
2002-03	Calgary Flames	2	0	0	0	0	....	....	....	....	....
	NHL Totals	**2**	**0**	**0**	**0**	**0**	....	....	....	....	....

Traded to **Washington** by **Dallas** with Mark Tinordi for Kevin Hatcher, January 18, 1995. Signed as a free agent by **Calgary**, August 6, 2001.

MUCKALT, Bill

Right wing. Shoots right. 6'1", 200 lbs. Born, Surrey, B.C., July 15, 1974.
(Vancouver's 9th choice, 221st overall, in 1994 Entry Draft).

Season	Club	GP	G	A	Pts	PIM	GP	G	A	Pts	PIM
1998-99	Vancouver Canucks	73	16	20	36	98	....	....	....	....	....
99-2000	Vancouver Canucks	33	4	8	12	17	....	....	....	....	....
	New York Islanders	12	4	3	7	4	....	....	....	....	....
2000-01	New York Islanders	60	11	15	26	33	....	....	....	....	....
2001-02	Ottawa Senators	70	0	8	8	46	....	....	....	....	....
2002-03	Minnesota Wild	8	5	3	8	6	5	0	0	0	0
	NHL Totals	**256**	**40**	**57**	**97**	**204**	**5**	**0**	**0**	**0**	**0**

Traded to **NY Islanders** by **Vancouver** with Kevin Weekes and Dave Scatchard for Felix Potvin, NY Islanders' compensatory 2nd round choice (later traded to New Jersey – New Jersey selected Teemu Laine) in 2000 Entry Draft and NY Islanders' 3rd round choice (Thatcher Bell) in 2000 Entry Draft, December 19, 1999. • Missed majority of 1999-2000 season recovering from shoulder injury suffered in game vs. Tampa Bay, January 13, 2000. Traded to **Ottawa** by **NY Islanders** with Zdeno Chara and NY Islanders' 1st round choice (Jason Spezza) in 2001 Entry Draft for Alexei Yashin, June 23, 2001. Signed as a free agent by **Minnesota**, July 3, 2002.

MUIR, Bryan

Defense. Shoots left. 6'4", 220 lbs. Born, Winnipeg, Man., June 8, 1973.

Season	Club	GP	G	A	Pts	PIM	GP	G	A	Pts	PIM
1995-96	Edmonton Oilers	5	0	0	0	6	....	....	....	....	....
1996-97	Edmonton Oilers	....	....	....	....	....	5	0	0	0	4
1997-98	Edmonton Oilers	7	0	0	0	17	....	....	....	....	....
1998-99	New Jersey Devils	1	0	0	0	0	....	....	....	....	....
	Chicago Blackhawks	53	1	4	5	50	....	....	....	....	....
99-2000	Chicago Blackhawks	11	2	3	5	13	....	....	....	....	....
	Tampa Bay Lightning	30	1	1	2	32	....	....	....	....	....
2000-01	Tampa Bay Lightning	10	0	3	3	15	....	....	....	....	....
	Colorado Avalanche	8	0	0	0	4	3	0	0	0	0
2001-02	Colorado Avalanche	22	1	1	2	9	21	0	0	0	2
2002-03	Colorado Avalanche	32	0	2	2	19	....	....	....	....	....
	NHL Totals	**179**	**5**	**14**	**19**	**165**	**29**	**0**	**0**	**0**	**6**

Signed to five-game amateur tryout contract by **Edmonton**, February 29, 1996. Signed as a free agent by **Edmonton**, April 30, 1996. Traded to **New Jersey** by **Edmonton** with Jason Arnott for Valeri Zelepukin and Bill Guerin, January 4, 1998. Traded to **Chicago** by **New Jersey** for Chicago's 3rd round choice (Michael Rupp) in 2000 Entry Draft. November 13, 1998. Traded to **Tampa Bay** by **Chicago** with Reid Simpson for Michael Nylander, November 12, 1999. • Missed majority of 1999-2000 season recovering from leg injury suffered in game vs. Atlanta, November 17, 1999. Traded to **Colorado** by **Tampa Bay** for Colorado's 8th round choice (Dmitri Bezrukov) in 2001 Entry Draft, January 23, 2001.

MULHERN, Richard

Defense. Shoots left. 6'1", 188 lbs. Born, Edmonton, Alta., March 1, 1955.
(Atlanta's 1st choice, 8th overall, in 1975 Amateur Draft).

Season	Club	GP	G	A	Pts	PIM	GP	G	A	Pts	PIM
1975-76	Atlanta Flames	12	1	0	1	4	....	....	....	....	....
1976-77	Atlanta Flames	79	12	32	44	80	3	0	2	2	5
1977-78	Atlanta Flames	79	9	23	32	47	2	0	1	1	0
1978-79	Atlanta Flames	37	3	12	15	22	....	....	....	....	....
	Los Angeles Kings	36	2	9	11	23	1	0	0	0	0
1979-80	Los Angeles Kings	15	0	3	3	16	....	....	....	....	....
	Toronto Maple Leafs	26	0	10	10	11	1	0	0	0	0
1980-81	Winnipeg Jets	19	0	4	4	14	....	....	....	....	....
	NHL Totals	**303**	**27**	**93**	**120**	**217**	**7**	**0**	**3**	**3**	**5**

Traded to **Los Angeles** by **Atlanta** with Atlanta's 2nd round choice (Dave Morrison) in 1980 Entry Draft for Bob Murdoch and Los Angeles' 2nd round choice (Tony Curtale) in 1980 Entry Draft, January 16, 1979. Claimed on waivers by **Toronto** from **Los Angeles**, February 10, 1980. Traded to **Winnipeg** by **Toronto** for cash, December 2, 1980.

MULHERN, Ryan

Center. Shoots right. 6'1", 202 lbs. Born, Philadelphia, PA, January 11, 1973.
(Calgary's 9th choice, 174th overall, in 1992 Entry Draft).

Season	Club	Regular Season GP	G	A	Pts	PIM	Playoffs GP	G	A	Pts	PIM
1997-98	Washington Capitals	3	0	0	0	0	....	....	....	....	....
	NHL Totals	**3**	**0**	**0**	**0**	**0**	....	....	....	....	....

Signed as a free agent by **Washington**, March 17, 1997.

MULLEN, Brian

Right wing. Shoots left. 5'10", 180 lbs. Born, New York, NY, March 16, 1962.
(Winnipeg's 7th choice, 128th overall, in 1980 Entry Draft).

Season	Club	Regular Season GP	G	A	Pts	PIM	Playoffs GP	G	A	Pts	PIM
1982-83	Winnipeg Jets	80	24	26	50	14	3	1	0	1	0
1983-84	Winnipeg Jets	75	21	41	62	28	3	0	3	3	6
1984-85	Winnipeg Jets	69	32	39	71	32	8	1	2	3	4
1985-86	Winnipeg Jets	79	28	34	62	38	3	1	2	3	6
1986-87	Winnipeg Jets	69	19	32	51	20	9	4	2	6	0
1987-88	New York Rangers	74	25	29	54	42	....	....	....	....	....
1988-89	New York Rangers	78	29	35	64	60	3	0	1	1	4
1989-90	New York Rangers	76	27	41	68	42	10	2	2	4	8
1990-91	New York Rangers	79	19	43	62	44	5	0	2	2	0
1991-92	San Jose Sharks	72	18	28	46	66	....	....	....	....	....
1992-93	New York Islanders	81	18	14	32	28	18	3	4	7	2
	NHL Totals	**832**	**260**	**362**	**622**	**414**	**62**	**12**	**18**	**30**	**30**

• Brother of Joe • Lester Patrick Trophy (1995)

Played in NHL All-Star Game (1989)

Traded to **NY Rangers** by **Winnipeg** with Winnipeg's 10th round choice (Brett Barnett) in 1987 Entry Draft for Detroit's 5th round choice (previously acquired, Winnipeg selected Benoit Lebeau) in 1988 Entry Draft and NY Rangers' 3rd round choice (later traded to St. Louis – St. Louis selected Denny Felsner) in 1989 Entry Draft, June 8, 1987. Traded to **San Jose** by **NY Rangers** for Tim Kerr, May 30, 1991. Traded to **NY Islanders** by **San Jose** for the rights to Marcus Thuresson, August 24, 1992. • Suffered career-ending stroke during training, August 8, 1993.

MULLEN, Joe

USHOF HHOF

Right wing. Shoots right. 5'9", 180 lbs. Born, New York, NY, February 26, 1957.

Season	Club	Regular Season GP	G	A	Pts	PIM	Playoffs GP	G	A	Pts	PIM
1979-80	St. Louis Blues	....	....	....	....	....	1	0	0	0	0
1981-82	St. Louis Blues	45	25	34	59	4	10	7	11	18	4
1982-83	St. Louis Blues	49	17	30	47	6	....	....	....	....	....
1983-84	St. Louis Blues	80	41	44	85	19	6	2	0	2	0
1984-85	St. Louis Blues	79	40	52	92	6	3	0	0	0	0
1985-86	St. Louis Blues	48	28	24	52	10	....	....	....	....	....
	Calgary Flames	29	16	22	38	11	21	*12	7	19	4
1986-87	Calgary Flames	79	47	40	87	14	6	2	1	3	0
1987-88	Calgary Flames	80	40	44	84	30	7	2	4	6	10
1988-89 ♦	Calgary Flames	79	51	59	110	16	21	*16	8	24	4
1989-90	Calgary Flames	78	36	33	69	24	6	3	0	3	0
1990-91 ♦	Pittsburgh Penguins	47	17	22	39	6	22	8	9	17	4
1991-92 ♦	Pittsburgh Penguins	77	42	45	87	30	9	3	1	4	4
1992-93	Pittsburgh Penguins	72	33	37	70	14	12	4	2	6	6
1993-94	Pittsburgh Penguins	84	38	32	70	41	6	1	0	1	2
1994-95	Pittsburgh Penguins	45	16	21	37	6	12	0	3	3	4
1995-96	Boston Bruins	37	8	7	15	0	....	....	....	....	....
1996-97	Pittsburgh Penguins	54	7	15	22	4	1	0	0	0	0
	NHL Totals	**1062**	**502**	**561**	**1063**	**241**	**143**	**60**	**46**	**106**	**42**

• Brother of Brian • Lady Byng Trophy (1987, 1989) • NHL First All-Star Team (1989) • NHL Plus/Minus Leader (1989) • Lester Patrick Trophy (1995)

Played in NHL All-Star Game (1989, 1990, 1994)

Signed as a free agent by **St. Louis,** August 16, 1979. Traded to **Calgary** by **St. Louis** with Terry Johnson and Rik Wilson for Eddy Beers, Charles Bourgeois and Gino Cavallini, February 1, 1986. Traded to **Pittsburgh** by **Calgary** for Pittsburgh's 2nd round choice (Nicolas Perreault) in 1990 Entry Draft, June 16, 1990. Signed as a free agent by **Boston**, September 13, 1995. Signed as a free agent by **Pittsburgh**, September 5, 1996.

MULLER, Kirk

Left wing. Shoots left. 6', 205 lbs. Born, Kingston, Ont., February 8, 1966.
(New Jersey's 1st choice, 2nd overall, in 1984 Entry Draft).

Season	Club	Regular Season GP	G	A	Pts	PIM	Playoffs GP	G	A	Pts	PIM
1984-85	New Jersey Devils	80	17	37	54	69	....	....	....	....	....
1985-86	New Jersey Devils	77	25	41	66	45	....	....	....	....	....
1986-87	New Jersey Devils	79	26	50	76	75	....	....	....	....	....
1987-88	New Jersey Devils	80	37	57	94	114	20	4	8	12	37
1988-89	New Jersey Devils	80	31	43	74	119	....	....	....	....	....
1989-90	New Jersey Devils	80	30	56	86	74	6	1	3	4	11
1990-91	New Jersey Devils	80	19	51	70	76	7	0	2	2	10
1991-92	Montreal Canadiens	78	36	41	77	86	11	4	3	7	31
1992-93 ♦	Montreal Canadiens	80	37	57	94	77	20	10	7	17	18
1993-94	Montreal Canadiens	76	23	34	57	96	7	6	2	8	4
1994-95	Montreal Canadiens	33	8	11	19	33	....	....	....	....	....
	New York Islanders	12	3	5	8	14	....	....	....	....	....
1995-96	New York Islanders	15	4	3	7	15	....	....	....	....	....
	Toronto Maple Leafs	36	9	16	25	42	6	3	2	5	0
1996-97	Toronto Maple Leafs	66	20	17	37	85	....	....	....	....	....
	Florida Panthers	10	1	2	3	4	5	1	2	3	4
1997-98	Florida Panthers	70	8	21	29	54	....	....	....	....	....
1998-99	Florida Panthers	82	4	11	15	49	....	....	....	....	....
99-2000	Dallas Stars	47	7	15	22	24	23	2	3	5	18
2000-01	Dallas Stars	55	1	9	10	26	10	1	3	4	12
2001-02	Dallas Stars	78	10	20	30	28	....	....	....	....	....
2002-03	Dallas Stars	55	1	5	6	18	12	1	1	2	8
	NHL Totals	**1349**	**357**	**602**	**959**	**1223**	**127**	**33**	**36**	**69**	**153**

Played in NHL All-Star Game (1985, 1986, 1988, 1990, 1992, 1993)

Traded to **Montreal** by **New Jersey** with Roland Melanson for Stephane Richer and Tom Chorske, September 20, 1991. Traded to **NY Islanders** by **Montreal** with Mathieu Schneider and Craig Darby for Pierre Turgeon and Vladimir Malakhov, April 5, 1995. Traded to **Toronto** by **NY Islanders** with Don Beaupre to complete transaction that sent Damian Rhodes and Ken Belanger to NY Islanders (January 23, 1996), January 23, 1996. Traded to **Florida** by **Toronto** for Jason Podollan, March 18, 1997. Signed as a free agent by **Dallas**, December 15, 1999. Claimed by **Columbus** from **Dallas** in Waiver Draft, September 28, 2001. Traded to **Dallas** by **Columbus** for the rights to Evgeny Petrochinin, September 28, 2001.

MULOIN, Wayne

Defense. Shoots left. 5'8", 175 lbs. Born, Dryden, Ont., December 24, 1941.

Season	Club	Regular Season GP	G	A	Pts	PIM	Playoffs GP	G	A	Pts	PIM
1963-64	Detroit Red Wings	3	0	1	1	2	....	....	....	....	....
1969-70	Oakland Seals	71	3	6	9	53	4	0	0	0	0
1970-71	California Seals	66	0	14	14	32	....	....	....	....	....
	Minnesota North Stars	7	0	0	0	6	7	0	0	0	2
	NHL Totals	**147**	**3**	**21**	**24**	**93**	**11**	**0**	**0**	**0**	**2**

Claimed by **NY Rangers** from **Detroit** in Intra-League Draft, June, 1964. Traded to **Providence** (AHL) by **Vancouver** (WHL) with Ron Hutchinson for Bob Blackburn, February 3, 1966. • Hutchinson failed to report to Providence (AHL). NHL rights transferred to **Oakland** when NHL club signed affiliation agreement with **Providence** (AHL), June, 1968. Traded to **Minnesota** by **California** with Ted Hampson for Tommy Williams and Dick Redmond, March 7, 1971.

MULVENNA, Glenn

Center. Shoots left. 5'11", 187 lbs. Born, Calgary, Alta., February 18, 1967.

Season	Club	Regular Season GP	G	A	Pts	PIM	Playoffs GP	G	A	Pts	PIM
1991-92	Pittsburgh Penguins	1	0	0	0	2	....	....	....	....	....
1992-93	Philadelphia Flyers	1	0	0	0	2	....	....	....	....	....
	NHL Totals	**2**	**0**	**0**	**0**	**4**	....	....	....	....	....

Signed as a free agent by **Pittsburgh**, December 3, 1987. Signed as a free agent by **Philadelphia**, July 11, 1992.

MULVEY, Grant

Right wing. Shoots right. 6'4", 200 lbs. Born, Sudbury, Ont., September 17, 1956.
(Chicago's 1st choice, 16th overall, in 1974 Amateur Draft).

Season	Club	Regular Season GP	G	A	Pts	PIM	Playoffs GP	G	A	Pts	PIM
1974-75	Chicago Black Hawks	74	7	4	11	36	6	2	0	2	6
1975-76	Chicago Black Hawks	64	11	17	28	72	4	0	0	0	2
1976-77	Chicago Black Hawks	80	10	14	24	111	2	1	0	1	2
1977-78	Chicago Black Hawks	78	14	24	38	135	4	2	2	4	0
1978-79	Chicago Black Hawks	80	19	15	34	99	1	0	0	0	2
1979-80	Chicago Black Hawks	80	39	26	65	122	7	1	1	2	8
1980-81	Chicago Black Hawks	42	18	14	32	81	3	0	0	0	0
1981-82	Chicago Black Hawks	73	30	19	49	141	15	4	2	6	50
1982-83	Chicago Black Hawks	3	0	0	0	0	....	....	....	....	....
1983-84	New Jersey Devils	12	1	2	3	19	....	....	....	....	....
	NHL Totals	**586**	**149**	**135**	**284**	**816**	**42**	**10**	**5**	**15**	**70**

• Brother of Paul

• Missed majority of 1982-83 season recovering from knee inury suffered in game vs. Detroit, October 18, 1982. Claimed by **Pittsburgh** from **Chicago** in Waiver Draft, October 3, 1983. Claimed on waivers by **New Jersey** from **Pittsburgh**, October 8, 1983.

MULVEY, Paul

Left wing. Shoots left. 6'4", 220 lbs. Born, Sudbury, Ont., September 27, 1958.
(Washington's 3rd choice, 20th overall, in 1978 Amateur Draft).

Season	Club	Regular Season GP	G	A	Pts	PIM	Playoffs GP	G	A	Pts	PIM
1978-79	Washington Capitals	55	7	4	11	81	....	....	....	....	....
1979-80	Washington Capitals	77	15	19	34	240	....	....	....	....	....
1980-81	Washington Capitals	55	7	14	21	166	....	....	....	....	....
1981-82	Pittsburgh Penguins	27	1	7	8	76	....	....	....	....	....
	Los Angeles Kings	11	0	7	7	50	....	....	....	....	....
	NHL Totals	**225**	**30**	**51**	**81**	**613**	....	....	....	....	....

• Brother of Grant

Transferred to **Pittsburgh** by **Washington** as compensation for Washington's signing of free agent Orest Kindrachuk, September 4, 1981. Claimed on waivers by **Los Angeles** from **Pittsburgh**, December 30, 1981. Traded to **Edmonton** by **Los Angeles** for Blair Barnes, June 22, 1982.

MUMMERY, Harry

Defense. Shoots left. 5'11", 220 lbs. Born, Chicago, IL, August 25, 1889.

Season	Club	Regular Season GP	G	A	Pts	PIM	Playoffs GP	G	A	Pts	PIM
1917-18 ♦	Toronto Arenas	18	3	3	6	41	2	1	*1	2	17
	Toronto Arenas (Cup)	....	....	....	....	....	*5*	*0*	*6*	*6*	*0*
1918-19	Toronto Arenas	13	2	0	2	30	....	....	....	....	....
1919-20	Quebec Bulldogs	24	9	9	18	42	....	....	....	....	....
1920-21	Montreal Canadiens	24	15	5	20	69	....	....	....	....	....
1921-22	Hamilton Tigers	20	4	2	6	40	....	....	....	....	....
1922-23	Hamilton Tigers	7	0	0	0	4	....	....	....	....	....
	NHL Totals	**106**	**33**	**19**	**52**	**226**	**2**	**1**	**1**	**2**	**17**

NHL rights returned to **Quebec** (NHA) by **Montreal** (NHA) prior to formation of NHL, November, 1917. Claimed by **Toronto** from **Quebec** in Dispersal Draft, November 26, 1917. Transferred to **Quebec** by **Toronto** when Quebec franchise returned to NHL, November 25, 1919. Transferred to **Hamilton** after **Quebec** franchise relocated, November 2, 1920. Traded to **Montreal** by **Hamilton** with Jack McDonald and Dave Ritchie for Goldie Prodgers, Joe Matte, Jack Coughlin and loan of Billy Coutu for 1920-21 season, November 27, 1920. Traded to **Hamilton** by **Montreal** with Amos Arbour for Sprague Cleghorn, November 26, 1921. Traded to **Saskatoon** (WCHL) by **Hamilton** for cash, February 8, 1923.

MUNI, Craig

Defense. Shoots left. 6'3", 208 lbs. Born, Toronto, Ont., July 19, 1962.
(Toronto's 1st choice, 25th overall, in 1980 Entry Draft).

Season	Club	GP	G	A	Pts	PIM	GP	G	A	Pts	PIM
		REGULAR SEASON					PLAYOFFS				
1981-82	Toronto Maple Leafs	3	0	0	0	2	....	....	....	....	....
1982-83	Toronto Maple Leafs	2	0	1	1	0	....	....	....	....	....
1984-85	Toronto Maple Leafs	8	0	0	0	0	....	....	....	....	....
1985-86	Toronto Maple Leafs	6	0	1	1	4	....	....	....	....	....
1986-87 ♦	Edmonton Oilers	79	7	22	29	85	14	0	2	2	17
1987-88 ♦	Edmonton Oilers	72	4	15	19	77	19	0	4	4	31
1988-89	Edmonton Oilers	69	5	13	18	71	7	0	3	3	8
1989-90 ♦	Edmonton Oilers	71	5	12	17	81	22	0	3	3	16
1990-91	Edmonton Oilers	76	1	9	10	77	18	0	3	3	20
1991-92	Edmonton Oilers	54	2	5	7	34	3	0	0	0	2
1992-93	Edmonton Oilers	72	0	11	11	67	....	....	....	....	....
	Chicago Blackhawks	9	0	0	0	8	4	0	0	0	2
1993-94	Chicago Blackhawks	9	0	4	4	4	....	....	....	....	....
	Buffalo Sabres	73	2	8	10	62	7	0	0	0	4
1994-95	Buffalo Sabres	40	0	6	6	36	5	0	1	1	2
1995-96	Buffalo Sabres	47	0	4	4	69	....	....	....	....	....
	Winnipeg Jets	25	1	3	4	37	6	0	1	1	2
1996-97	Pittsburgh Penguins	64	0	4	4	36	3	0	0	0	0
1997-98	Dallas Stars	40	1	1	2	25	5	0	0	0	4
	NHL Totals	**819**	**28**	**119**	**147**	**775**	**113**	**0**	**17**	**17**	**108**

Signed as a free agent by **Edmonton,** August 18, 1986. Traded to **Buffalo** by **Edmonton** for cash, October 2, 1986. Traded to **Pittsburgh** by **Buffalo** for cash, October 3, 1986. Traded to **Edmonton** by **Pittsburgh** to complete September 11, 1985 transaction which sent Gilles Meloche to Pittsburgh, October 6, 1986. Traded to **Chicago** by **Edmonton** for Mike Hudson, March 22, 1993. Traded to **Buffalo** by **Chicago** with Chicago's 5th round choice (Daniel Bienvenue) in 1995 Entry Draft for Keith Carney and Buffalo's 6th round choice (Marc Magliarditi) in 1995 Entry Draft, October 26, 1993. Traded to **Winnipeg** by **Buffalo** for Darryl Shannon and Michal Grosek, February 15, 1996. Signed as a free agent by **Pittsburgh**, October 2, 1996. Signed as a free agent by **Dallas**, October 2, 1997.

MUNRO, Dunc

Defense. Shoots left. 5'8", 190 lbs. Born, Moray, Scotland, January 19, 1901.

Season	Club	GP	G	A	Pts	PIM	GP	G	A	Pts	PIM
1924-25	Montreal Maroons	27	5	1	6	16	....	....	....	....	....
1925-26 ♦	Montreal Maroons	33	4	6	10	55	2	0	0	0	0
	Montreal Maroons (Cup)	....	....	....	....	....	*4*	*1*	*0*	*1*	*6*
1926-27	Montreal Maroons	43	6	5	11	42	2	0	0	0	4
1927-28	Montreal Maroons	43	5	2	7	35	9	0	2	2	8
1928-29	Montreal Maroons	1	0	0	0	0	....	....	....	....	....
1929-30	Montreal Maroons	40	7	2	9	10	4	2	0	2	4
1930-31	Montreal Maroons	4	0	1	1	0	....	....	....	....	....
1931-32	Montreal Canadiens	48	1	1	2	14	4	0	0	0	2
	NHL Totals	**239**	**28**	**18**	**46**	**172**	**21**	**2**	**2**	**4**	**18**

Signed as a free agent by **Mtl. Maroons**, October 30, 1924. • Missed remainder of 1928-29 season recovering from minor heart attack, November 15, 1928. • Named playing coach/manager by **Mtl. Maroons**, September 23, 1929. Signed as a free agent by **Montreal**, November 6, 1931.

MUNRO, Gerry

Defense. Shoots left. 5'10", 175 lbs. Born, Sault Ste. Marie, Ont., November 28, 1897.

Season	Club	GP	G	A	Pts	PIM	GP	G	A	Pts	PIM
1924-25	Montreal Maroons	30	1	0	1	37	....	....	....	....	....
1925-26	Toronto St. Pats	4	0	0	0	0	....	....	....	....	....
	NHL Totals	**34**	**1**	**0**	**1**	**37**	....	....	....	....	....

Signed as a free agent by **Mtl. Maroons**, October 31, 1924. Traded to **Toronto** by **Mtl. Maroons** for cash, October 23, 1925.

MURDOCH, Bob

Right wing. Shoots right. 5'11", 191 lbs. Born, Cranbrook, B.C., January 29, 1954.

Season	Club	GP	G	A	Pts	PIM	GP	G	A	Pts	PIM
1975-76	California Golden Seals	78	22	27	49	53	....	....	....	....	....
1976-77	Cleveland Barons	57	23	19	42	30	....	....	....	....	....
1977-78	Cleveland Barons	71	14	26	40	27	....	....	....	....	....
1978-79	St. Louis Blues	54	13	13	26	17	....	....	....	....	....
	NHL Totals	**260**	**72**	**85**	**157**	**127**	....	....	....	....	....

• Brother of Don

Played in NHL All-Star Game (1975)

Signed as a free agent by **California**, October, 1974. Transferred to **Cleveland** after **California** franchise relocated, August 26, 1976. Placed on **Minnesota** Reserve List after **Cleveland-Minnesota** Dispersal Draft, June 15, 1978. Traded to **St. Louis** by **Minnesota** for cash, August 8, 1978. Claimed by **St. Louis** as a fill-in during Expansion Draft, June 13, 1979.

MURDOCH, Bob

Defense. Shoots right. 6', 200 lbs. Born, Kirkland Lake, Ont., November 20, 1946.

Season	Club	GP	G	A	Pts	PIM	GP	G	A	Pts	PIM
1970-71 ♦	Montreal Canadiens	1	0	2	2	2	2	0	0	0	0
1971-72	Montreal Canadiens	11	1	1	2	8	1	0	0	0	0
1972-73 ♦	Montreal Canadiens	69	2	22	24	55	13	0	3	3	10
1973-74	Los Angeles Kings	76	8	20	28	85	5	0	0	0	2
1974-75	Los Angeles Kings	80	13	29	42	116	3	0	1	1	4
1975-76	Los Angeles Kings	80	6	29	35	103	9	0	5	5	15
1976-77	Los Angeles Kings	70	9	23	32	79	9	2	3	5	14
1977-78	Los Angeles Kings	76	2	17	19	68	2	0	1	1	5
1978-79	Los Angeles Kings	32	3	12	15	46	....	....	....	....	....
	Atlanta Flames	35	5	11	16	24	2	0	0	0	4
1979-80	Atlanta Flames	80	5	16	21	48	4	1	1	2	2
1980-81	Calgary Flames	74	3	19	22	54	16	1	4	5	36
1981-82	Calgary Flames	73	3	17	20	76	3	0	0	0	0
	NHL Totals	**757**	**60**	**218**	**278**	**764**	**69**	**4**	**18**	**22**	**92**

Signed as a free agent by **Montreal**, March 2, 1970. Traded to **Minnesota** by **Montreal** for Marshall Johnston to complete transaction that sent Danny Grant and Claude Larose to Minnesota (June 10, 1968), May 25, 1971. Claimed by **Montreal** from **Minnesota** in Intra-League Draft, June 8, 1971. Traded to **Los Angeles** by **Montreal** with Randy Rota for Los Angeles' 1st round choice (Mario Tremblay) in 1974 Amateur Draft and cash, May 29, 1973. Traded to **Atlanta** by **Los Angeles** with Los Angeles' 2nd round choice (Tony Curtale) in 1980 Entry Draft for Richard Mulhern and Atlanta's 2nd round choice (Dave Morrison) in 1980 Entry Draft, January 16, 1979. Transferred to **Calgary** after **Atlanta** franchise relocated, June 24, 1980.

MURDOCH, Don

Right wing. Shoots right. 5'11", 180 lbs. Born, Cranbrook, B.C., October 25, 1956.
(NY Rangers' 1st choice, 6th overall, in 1976 Amateur Draft).

Season	Club	GP	G	A	Pts	PIM	GP	G	A	Pts	PIM
1976-77	New York Rangers	59	32	24	56	47	....	....	....	....	....
1977-78	New York Rangers	66	27	28	55	41	3	1	3	4	4
1978-79	New York Rangers	40	15	22	37	6	18	7	5	12	12
1979-80	New York Rangers	56	23	19	42	16	....	....	....	....	....
	Edmonton Oilers	10	5	2	7	4	3	2	0	2	0
1980-81	Edmonton Oilers	40	10	9	19	18	....	....	....	....	....
1981-82	Detroit Red Wings	49	9	13	22	23	....	....	....	....	....
	NHL Totals	**320**	**121**	**117**	**238**	**155**	**24**	**10**	**8**	**18**	**16**

• Brother of Bob

Played in NHL All-Star Game (1977)

• Suspended for entire 1978-79 season by NHL for substance abuse violation, July 6, 1978.
• Suspension lifted by NHL after 40 games, January 3, 1979. Traded to **Edmonton** by **NY Rangers** for Cam Connor and Edmonton's 3rd round choice (Peter Sundstrom) in 1981 Entry Draft, March 11, 1980. Rights traded to **Minnesota** by **Edmonton** for Don Jackson and Minnesota's 3rd round choice (later traded back to Minnesota – Minnesota selected Wally Chapman) in 1982 Entry Draft, August 21, 1981. Rights traded to **Detroit** by **Minnesota** with Greg Smith and Minnesota's 1st round choice (Murray Craven) in 1982 Entry Draft for Detroit's 1st round choice (Brian Bellows) in 1982 Entry Draft, August 21, 1981.

MURDOCH, Murray

Left wing. Shoots left. 5'10", 180 lbs. Born, Lucknow, Ont., May 19, 1904.

Season	Club	GP	G	A	Pts	PIM	GP	G	A	Pts	PIM
1926-27	New York Rangers	44	6	4	10	12	2	0	0	0	0
1927-28 ♦	New York Rangers	44	7	3	10	14	9	2	1	3	12
1928-29	New York Rangers	44	8	6	14	18	6	0	0	0	2
1929-30	New York Rangers	44	13	13	26	22	4	3	0	3	6
1930-31	New York Rangers	44	7	7	14	8	4	0	2	2	0
1931-32	New York Rangers	48	5	16	21	32	7	0	2	2	2
1932-33 ♦	New York Rangers	48	5	11	16	23	8	3	*4	7	2
1933-34	New York Rangers	48	17	10	27	29	2	0	0	0	0
1934-35	New York Rangers	48	14	15	29	14	4	0	2	2	4
1935-36	New York Rangers	48	2	9	11	9	....	....	....	....	....
1936-37	New York Rangers	48	0	14	14	16	9	1	1	2	0
	NHL Totals	**508**	**84**	**108**	**192**	**197**	**55**	**9**	**12**	**21**	**28**

Lester Patrick Trophy (1974)

Signed as a free agent by **NY Rangers**, September 2, 1926.

MURPHY, Brian

Center/Left wing. Shoots left. 6'3", 200 lbs. Born, Toronto, Ont., August 20, 1947.

Season	Club	GP	G	A	Pts	PIM	GP	G	A	Pts	PIM
1974-75	Detroit Red Wings	1	0	0	0	0	....	....	....	....	....
	NHL Totals	**1**	**0**	**0**	**0**	**0**	....	....	....	....	....

Traded to **Los Angeles** by **Toronto** with Gary Croteau and Wayne Thomas for Grant Moore and Lou Deveault, October 15, 1968. Traded to **Toronto** by **Los Angeles** with Garry Monahan for Bob Pulford, September 3, 1970. Signed as a free agent by **Springfield** (AHL), November, 1970. Traded to **Baltimore** (AHL) by **Springfield** (AHL) for cash, June, 1971. Traded to **Detroit** by **Baltimore** (AHL) for cash, November, 1974.

MURPHY, Curtis

Defense. Shoots right. 5'8", 185 lbs. Born, Kerrobert, Sask., December 3, 1975.

Season	Club	GP	G	A	Pts	PIM	GP	G	A	Pts	PIM
2002-03	Minnesota Wild	1	0	0	0	0	....	....	....	....	....
	NHL Totals	**1**	**0**	**0**	**0**	**0**	....	....	....	....	....

Signed as a free agent by **Minnesota**, June 18, 2001. Signed as a free agent by **Nashville**, July 8, 2003.

MURPHY, Gord

Defense. Shoots right. 6'2", 195 lbs. Born, Willowdale, Ont., March 23, 1967.
(Philadelphia's 10th choice, 189th overall, in 1985 Entry Draft).

Season	Club	GP	G	A	Pts	PIM	GP	G	A	Pts	PIM
1988-89	Philadelphia Flyers	75	4	31	35	68	19	2	7	9	13
1989-90	Philadelphia Flyers	75	14	27	41	95	....	....	....	....	....
1990-91	Philadelphia Flyers	80	11	31	42	58	....	....	....	....	....
1991-92	Philadelphia Flyers	31	2	8	10	33	....	....	....	....	....
	Boston Bruins	42	3	6	9	51	15	1	0	1	12
1992-93	Boston Bruins	49	5	12	17	62	....	....	....	....	....
1993-94	Florida Panthers	84	14	29	43	71	....	....	....	....	....
1994-95	Florida Panthers	46	6	16	22	24	....	....	....	....	....
1995-96	Florida Panthers	70	8	22	30	30	14	0	4	4	6
1996-97	Florida Panthers	80	8	15	23	51	5	0	5	5	4
1997-98	Florida Panthers	79	6	11	17	46	....	....	....	....	....
1998-99	Florida Panthers	51	0	7	7	16	....	....	....	....	....
99-2000	Atlanta Thrashers	58	1	10	11	38	....	....	....	....	....
2000-01	Atlanta Thrashers	27	3	11	14	12	....	....	....	....	....

Season	Club	REGULAR SEASON GP	G	A	Pts	PIM	PLAYOFFS GP	G	A	Pts	PIM
2001-02	Boston Bruins	15	0	2	2	13	....	....	....	....	....
	NHL Totals	**862**	**85**	**238**	**323**	**668**	**53**	**3**	**16**	**19**	**35**

Traded to **Boston** by **Philadelphia** with Brian Dobbin, Philadelphia's 3rd round choice (Sergei Zholtok) in 1992 Entry Draft and 4th round choice (Charles Paquette) in 1993 Entry Draft, for Garry Galley, Wes Walz and Boston's 3rd round choice (Milos Holan) in 1993 Entry Draft, January 2, 1992. Traded to **Dallas** by **Boston** for future considerations (Jon Casey to Boston for Andy Moog, June 25, 1993), June 20, 1993. Claimed by **Florida** from **Dallas** in Expansion Draft, June 24, 1993. Traded to **Atlanta** by **Florida** with Herbert Vasiljevs, Daniel Tjarnqvist and Ottawa's 6th round choice (previously acquired, later traded to Dallas – Dallas selected Justin Cox) in 1999 Entry Draft for Trevor Kidd, June 25, 1999. • Missed majority of 2000-01 season recovering from shoulder injury suffered in game vs. NY Rangers, October 7, 2000. Signed as a free agent by **Boston**, January 29, 2002. • Officially announced retirement, March 19, 2002.

MURPHY, Joe

Right wing. Shoots left. 6', 190 lbs. Born, London, Ont., October 16, 1967.
(Detroit's 1st choice, 1st overall, in 1986 Entry Draft).

Season	Club	REGULAR SEASON GP	G	A	Pts	PIM	PLAYOFFS GP	G	A	Pts	PIM
1986-87	Detroit Red Wings	5	0	1	1	2	....	....	....	....	....
1987-88	Detroit Red Wings	50	10	9	19	37	8	0	1	1	6
1988-89	Detroit Red Wings	26	1	7	8	28	....	....	....	....	....
1989-90	Detroit Red Wings	9	3	1	4	4	....	....	....	....	....
	◆ Edmonton Oilers	62	7	18	25	56	22	6	8	14	16
1990-91	Edmonton Oilers	80	27	35	62	35	15	2	5	7	14
1991-92	Edmonton Oilers	80	35	47	82	52	16	8	16	24	12
1992-93	Chicago Blackhawks	19	7	10	17	18	4	0	0	0	8
1993-94	Chicago Blackhawks	81	31	39	70	111	6	1	3	4	25
1994-95	Chicago Blackhawks	40	23	18	41	89	16	9	3	12	29
1995-96	Chicago Blackhawks	70	22	29	51	86	10	6	2	8	33
1996-97	St. Louis Blues	75	20	25	45	69	6	1	1	2	10
1997-98	St. Louis Blues	27	4	9	13	22	....	....	....	....	....
	San Jose Sharks	10	5	4	9	14	6	1	1	2	20
1998-99	San Jose Sharks	76	25	23	48	73	6	0	3	3	4
99-2000	Boston Bruins	26	7	7	14	41	....	....	....	....	....
	Washington Capitals	29	5	8	13	53	5	0	0	0	8
2000-01	Washington Capitals	14	1	5	6	20	....	....	....	....	....
	NHL Totals	**779**	**233**	**295**	**528**	**810**	**120**	**34**	**43**	**77**	**185**

Traded to **Edmonton** by **Detroit** with Petr Klima, Adam Graves and Jeff Sharples for Jimmy Carson, Kevin McClelland and Edmonton's 5th round choice (later traded to Montreal – Montreal selected Brad Layzell) in 1991 Entry Draft, November 2, 1989. • Missed majority of 1992-93 season after failing to come to contract terms with **Edmonton**. Traded to **Chicago** by **Edmonton** for Igor Kravchuk and Dean McAmmond, February 24, 1993. Signed as a free agent by **St. Louis**, July 8, 1996. Traded to **San Jose** by **St. Louis** for Todd Gill, March 24, 1998. Signed as a free agent by **Boston**, November 12, 1999. Claimed on waivers by **Washington** from **Boston**, February 10, 2000.

MURPHY, Larry

Defense. Shoots right. 6'2", 210 lbs. Born, Scarborough, Ont., March 8, 1961.
(Los Angeles' 1st choice, 4th overall, in 1980 Entry Draft).

Season	Club	REGULAR SEASON GP	G	A	Pts	PIM	PLAYOFFS GP	G	A	Pts	PIM
1980-81	Los Angeles Kings	80	16	60	76	79	4	3	0	3	2
1981-82	Los Angeles Kings	79	22	44	66	95	10	2	8	10	12
1982-83	Los Angeles Kings	77	14	48	62	81	....	....	....	....	....
1983-84	Los Angeles Kings	6	0	3	3	0	....	....	....	....	....
	Washington Capitals	72	13	33	46	50	8	0	3	3	6
1984-85	Washington Capitals	79	13	42	55	51	5	2	3	5	0
1985-86	Washington Capitals	78	21	44	65	50	9	1	5	6	6
1986-87	Washington Capitals	80	23	58	81	39	7	2	2	4	6
1987-88	Washington Capitals	79	8	53	61	72	13	4	4	8	33
1988-89	Washington Capitals	65	7	29	36	70	....	....	....	....	....
	Minnesota North Stars	13	4	6	10	12	5	0	2	2	8
1989-90	Minnesota North Stars	77	10	58	68	44	7	1	2	3	31
1990-91	Minnesota North Stars	31	4	11	15	38	....	....	....	....	....
	◆ Pittsburgh Penguins	44	5	23	28	30	23	5	18	23	44
1991-92	◆ Pittsburgh Penguins	77	21	56	77	48	21	6	10	16	19
1992-93	Pittsburgh Penguins	83	22	63	85	73	12	2	11	13	10
1993-94	Pittsburgh Penguins	84	17	56	73	44	6	0	5	5	0
1994-95	Pittsburgh Penguins	48	13	25	38	18	12	2	13	15	0
1995-96	Toronto Maple Leafs	82	12	49	61	34	6	0	2	2	4
1996-97	Toronto Maple Leafs	69	7	32	39	20	....	....	....	....	....
	◆ Detroit Red Wings	12	2	4	6	0	20	2	9	11	8
1997-98	◆ Detroit Red Wings	82	11	41	52	37	22	3	12	15	2
1998-99	Detroit Red Wings	80	10	42	52	42	10	0	2	2	8
99-2000	Detroit Red Wings	81	10	30	40	45	9	2	3	5	2
2000-01	Detroit Red Wings	57	2	19	21	12	6	0	1	1	0
	NHL Totals	**1615**	**287**	**929**	**1216**	**1084**	**215**	**37**	**115**	**152**	**201**

NHL Second All-Star Team (1987, 1993, 1995)
Played in NHL All-Star Game (1994, 1996, 1999)

Traded to **Washington** by **Los Angeles** for Ken Houston and Brian Engblom, October 18, 1983. Traded to **Minnesota** by **Washington** with Mike Gartner for Dino Ciccarelli and Bob Rouse, March 7, 1989. Traded to **Pittsburgh** by **Minnesota** with Peter Taglianetti for Chris Dahlquist and Jim Johnson, December 11, 1990. Traded to **Toronto** by **Pittsburgh** for Dmitri Mironov and Toronto's 2nd round choice (later traded to New Jersey – New Jersey selected Josh DeWolf) in 1996 Entry Draft, July 8, 1995. Traded to **Detroit** by **Toronto** for future considerations, March 18, 1997.

MURPHY, Mike

Right wing. Shoots right. 6', 190 lbs. Born, Toronto, Ont., September 12, 1950.
(NY Rangers' 2nd choice, 25th overall, in 1970 Amateur Draft).

Season	Club	REGULAR SEASON GP	G	A	Pts	PIM	PLAYOFFS GP	G	A	Pts	PIM
1971-72	St. Louis Blues	63	20	23	43	19	11	2	3	5	6
1972-73	St. Louis Blues	64	18	27	45	48	....	....	....	....	....
	New York Rangers	15	4	4	8	5	10	0	0	0	0
1973-74	New York Rangers	16	2	1	3	0	....	....	....	....	....
	Los Angeles Kings	53	13	16	29	38	5	0	4	4	0
1974-75	Los Angeles Kings	78	30	38	68	44	3	3	0	3	4
1975-76	Los Angeles Kings	80	26	42	68	61	9	1	4	5	6
1976-77	Los Angeles Kings	76	25	36	61	58	9	4	9	13	4
1977-78	Los Angeles Kings	72	20	36	56	48	2	0	0	0	0
1978-79	Los Angeles Kings	64	16	29	45	38	2	0	1	1	0
1979-80	Los Angeles Kings	80	27	22	49	29	4	1	0	1	2
1980-81	Los Angeles Kings	68	16	23	39	54	1	0	1	1	0
1981-82	Los Angeles Kings	28	5	10	15	20	10	2	1	3	32
1982-83	Los Angeles Kings	74	16	11	27	52	....	....	....	....	....
	NHL Totals	**831**	**238**	**318**	**556**	**514**	**66**	**13**	**23**	**36**	**54**

Played in NHL All-Star Game (1980)

Traded to **St. Louis** by **NY Rangers** with Jack Egers and Andre Dupont for Gene Carr, Jim Lorentz and Wayne Connelly, November 15, 1971. Traded to **NY Rangers** by **St. Louis** for Ab DeMarco Jr., March 2, 1973. Traded to **Los Angeles** by **NY Rangers** with Sheldon Kannegiesser and Tom Williams for Gilles Marcotte and Real Lemieux, November 30, 1973.

MURPHY, Rob

Center. Shoots left. 6'3", 205 lbs. Born, Hull, Que., April 7, 1969.
(Vancouver's 1st choice, 24th overall, in 1987 Entry Draft).

Season	Club	REGULAR SEASON GP	G	A	Pts	PIM	PLAYOFFS GP	G	A	Pts	PIM
1987-88	Vancouver Canucks	5	0	0	0	2	....	....	....	....	....
1988-89	Vancouver Canucks	8	0	1	1	2	....	....	....	....	....
1989-90	Vancouver Canucks	12	1	1	2	0	....	....	....	....	....
1990-91	Vancouver Canucks	42	5	1	6	90	4	0	0	0	2
1991-92	Vancouver Canucks	6	0	1	1	6	....	....	....	....	....
1992-93	Ottawa Senators	44	3	7	10	30	....	....	....	....	....
1993-94	Los Angeles Kings	8	0	1	1	22	....	....	....	....	....
	NHL Totals	**125**	**9**	**12**	**21**	**152**	**4**	**0**	**0**	**0**	**2**

Claimed by **Ottawa** from **Vancouver** in Expansion Draft, June 18, 1992. Signed as a free agent by **Los Angeles**, August 2, 1993.

MURPHY, Ron

Left wing. Shoots left. 5'11", 185 lbs. Born, Hamilton, Ont., April 10, 1933.

Season	Club	REGULAR SEASON GP	G	A	Pts	PIM	PLAYOFFS GP	G	A	Pts	PIM
1952-53	New York Rangers	15	3	1	4	0	....	....	....	....	....
1953-54	New York Rangers	27	1	3	4	20	....	....	....	....	....
1954-55	New York Rangers	66	14	16	30	36	....	....	....	....	....
1955-56	New York Rangers	66	16	28	44	71	5	0	1	1	2
1956-57	New York Rangers	33	7	12	19	14	5	0	0	0	0
1957-58	Chicago Black Hawks	69	11	17	28	32	....	....	....	....	....
1958-59	Chicago Black Hawks	59	17	30	47	52	....	....	....	....	....
1959-60	Chicago Black Hawks	63	15	21	36	18	4	1	0	1	0
1960-61	◆ Chicago Black Hawks	70	21	19	40	30	12	2	1	3	0
1961-62	Chicago Black Hawks	60	12	16	28	41	....	....	....	....	....
1962-63	Chicago Black Hawks	68	18	16	34	28	1	0	0	0	0
1963-64	Chicago Black Hawks	70	11	8	19	32	7	0	1	1	8
1964-65	Detroit Red Wings	58	20	19	39	32	5	0	1	1	4
1965-66	Detroit Red Wings	32	10	7	17	10	....	....	....	....	....
	Boston Bruins	2	0	1	1	0	....	....	....	....	....
1966-67	Boston Bruins	39	11	16	27	6	....	....	....	....	....
1967-68	Boston Bruins	12	0	1	1	4	4	0	0	0	0
1968-69	Boston Bruins	60	16	38	54	26	10	4	4	8	12
1969-70	Boston Bruins	20	2	5	7	8	....	....	....	....	....
	NHL Totals	**889**	**205**	**274**	**479**	**460**	**53**	**7**	**8**	**15**	**26**

Played in NHL All-Star Game (1961)

Traded to **Chicago** by **NY Rangers** for Hank Ciesla, June, 1957. Traded to **Detroit** by **Chicago** with Aut Erickson for Art Stratton, John Miszuk and Ian Cushenan, June 9, 1964. Traded to **Boston** by **Detroit** with Bill Lesuk, Gary Doak and future considerations (Steve Atkinson, June 6, 1966) for Dean Prentice and Leo Boivin, February 16, 1966. • Missed majority of 1967-68 season recovering from shoulder and bicep muscle operations.

MURRAY, Allan

Defense. Shoots left. 5'7", 165 lbs. Born, Stratford, Ont., November 10, 1908.

Season	Club	REGULAR SEASON GP	G	A	Pts	PIM	PLAYOFFS GP	G	A	Pts	PIM
1933-34	New York Americans	39	1	1	2	20	....	....	....	....	....
1934-35	New York Americans	43	2	1	3	36	....	....	....	....	....
1935-36	New York Americans	48	1	0	1	33	5	0	0	0	2
1936-37	New York Americans	40	0	2	2	22	....	....	....	....	....
1937-38	New York Americans	47	0	1	1	34	6	0	0	0	6
1938-39	New York Americans	18	0	0	0	8	....	....	....	....	....
1939-40	New York Americans	36	1	4	5	10	3	0	0	0	2
	NHL Totals	**271**	**5**	**9**	**14**	**163**	**14**	**0**	**0**	**0**	**10**

Signed as a free agent by **NY Americans**, February 20, 1933. • Missed majority of 1938-39 season recovering from shoulder injury suffered in game vs. Boston, December 29, 1938.

MURRAY, Bob

Defense. Shoots right. 6'1", 195 lbs. Born, Peterborough, Ont., July 16, 1948.

Season	Club	REGULAR SEASON GP	G	A	Pts	PIM	PLAYOFFS GP	G	A	Pts	PIM
1973-74	Atlanta Flames	62	0	3	3	34	4	1	0	1	2
1974-75	Atlanta Flames	42	3	3	6	22	....	....	....	....	....
	Vancouver Canucks	13	1	5	6	8	5	0	1	1	13
1975-76	Vancouver Canucks	65	2	5	7	28	1	0	0	0	0
1976-77	Vancouver Canucks	12	0	0	0	6	....	....	....	....	....
	NHL Totals	**194**	**6**	**16**	**22**	**98**	**10**	**1**	**1**	**2**	**15**

Signed as a territoral exemption by **Montreal** from **Peterborough** (OHA), September, 1971. Traded to **Atlanta** by **Montreal** for Atlanta's 3rd round choice (Pierre Lagace) in 1977 Amateur Draft, May 29, 1973. Traded to **Vancouver** by **Atlanta** for Gerry Meehan, March 9, 1975.

MURRAY, Bob

Defense. 5'10", 183 lbs. Born, Kingston, Ont., November 26, 1954.
(Chicago's 3rd choice, 52nd overall, in 1974 Amateur Draft).

Season	Club	Regular Season					Playoffs				
		GP	G	A	Pts	PIM	GP	G	A	Pts	PIM
1975-76	Chicago Black Hawks	64	1	2	3	44	....	....	....	....	....
1976-77	Chicago Black Hawks	77	10	11	21	71	2	0	1	1	2
1977-78	Chicago Black Hawks	70	14	17	31	41	4	1	4	5	2
1978-79	Chicago Black Hawks	79	19	32	51	38	4	1	0	1	6
1979-80	Chicago Black Hawks	74	16	34	50	60	7	2	4	6	6
1980-81	Chicago Black Hawks	77	13	47	60	93	3	0	0	0	2
1981-82	Chicago Black Hawks	45	8	22	30	48	15	1	6	7	16
1982-83	Chicago Black Hawks	79	7	32	39	73	13	2	3	5	10
1983-84	Chicago Black Hawks	78	11	37	48	78	5	3	1	4	6
1984-85	Chicago Black Hawks	80	5	38	43	56	15	3	6	9	20
1985-86	Chicago Black Hawks	80	9	29	38	75	3	0	2	2	0
1986-87	Chicago Blackhawks	79	6	38	44	80	4	1	0	1	4
1987-88	Chicago Blackhawks	62	6	20	26	44	5	1	3	4	2
1988-89	Chicago Blackhawks	15	2	4	6	27	16	2	3	5	22
1989-90	Chicago Blackhawks	49	5	19	24	45	16	2	4	6	8
	NHL Totals	**1008**	**132**	**382**	**514**	**873**	**112**	**19**	**37**	**56**	**106**

Played in NHL All-Star Game (1981, 1983)

MURRAY, Chris

Right wing. Shoots right. 6'2", 213 lbs. Born, Port Hardy, B.C., October 25, 1974.
(Montreal's 3rd choice, 54th overall, in 1994 Entry Draft).

Season	Club	Regular Season					Playoffs				
		GP	G	A	Pts	PIM	GP	G	A	Pts	PIM
1994-95	Montreal Canadiens	3	0	0	0	4	....	....	....	....	....
1995-96	Montreal Canadiens	48	3	4	7	163	4	0	0	0	4
1996-97	Montreal Canadiens	56	4	2	6	114	....	....	....	....	....
	Hartford Whalers	8	1	1	2	10	....	....	....	....	....
1997-98	Carolina Hurricanes	7	0	1	1	22	....	....	....	....	....
	Ottawa Senators	46	5	3	8	96	11	1	0	1	8
1998-99	Ottawa Senators	38	1	6	7	65	....	....	....	....	....
	Chicago Blackhawks	4	0	0	0	14	....	....	....	....	....
99-2000	Dallas Stars	32	2	1	3	62	....	....	....	....	....
	NHL Totals	**242**	**16**	**18**	**34**	**550**	**15**	**1**	**0**	**1**	**12**

Traded to **Phoenix** by **Montreal** with Murray Baron for Dave Manson, March 18, 1997. Traded to **Hartford** by **Phoenix** for Gerald Diduck, March 18, 1997. Transferred to **Carolina** after **Hartford** franchise relocated, June 25, 1997. Traded to **Ottawa** by **Carolina** for Sean Hill, November 18, 1997. Traded to **Chicago** by **Ottawa** for Nelson Emerson, March 23, 1999. Claimed by **Dallas** from **Chicago** in Waiver Draft, September 30, 1999. Signed as a free agent by **St. Louis**, July 27, 2000. Signed as a free agent by **Toronto**, August 7, 2001.

MURRAY, Glen

Right wing. Shoots right. 6'3", 225 lbs. Born, Halifax, N.S., November 1, 1972.
(Boston's 1st choice, 18th overall, in 1991 Entry Draft).

Season	Club	Regular Season					Playoffs				
		GP	G	A	Pts	PIM	GP	G	A	Pts	PIM
1991-92	Boston Bruins	5	3	1	4	0	15	4	2	6	10
1992-93	Boston Bruins	27	3	4	7	8	....	....	....	....	....
1993-94	Boston Bruins	81	18	13	31	48	13	4	5	9	14
1994-95	Boston Bruins	35	5	2	7	46	2	0	0	0	2
1995-96	Pittsburgh Penguins	69	14	15	29	57	18	2	6	8	10
1996-97	Pittsburgh Penguins	66	11	11	22	24	....	....	....	....	....
	Los Angeles Kings	11	5	3	8	8	....	....	....	....	....
1997-98	Los Angeles Kings	81	29	31	60	54	4	2	0	2	6
1998-99	Los Angeles Kings	61	16	15	31	36	....	....	....	....	....
99-2000	Los Angeles Kings	78	29	33	62	60	4	0	0	0	2
2000-01	Los Angeles Kings	64	18	21	39	32	13	4	3	7	4
2001-02	Los Angeles Kings	9	6	5	11	0	....	....	....	....	....
	Boston Bruins	73	35	25	60	40	6	1	4	5	4
2002-03	Boston Bruins	82	44	48	92	64	5	1	1	2	4
	NHL Totals	**742**	**236**	**227**	**463**	**477**	**80**	**18**	**21**	**39**	**56**

Played in NHL All-Star Game (2003)

Traded to **Pittsburgh** by **Boston** with Bryan Smolinski and Boston's 3rd round choice (Boyd Kane) in 1996 Entry Draft for Kevin Stevens and Shawn McEachern, August 2, 1995. Traded to **Los Angeles** by **Pittsburgh** for Ed Olczyk, March 18, 1997. Traded to **Boston** by **Los Angeles** with Jozef Stumpel for Jason Allison and Mikko Eloranta, October 24, 2001.

MURRAY, Jim

Defense. Shoots left. 6'1", 165 lbs. Born, Virden, Man., November 25, 1943.

Season	Club	Regular Season					Playoffs				
		GP	G	A	Pts	PIM	GP	G	A	Pts	PIM
1967-68	Los Angeles Kings	30	0	2	2	14	....	....	....	....	....
	NHL Totals	**30**	**0**	**2**	**2**	**14**	....	....	....	....	....

Traded to **Los Angeles** by **NY Rangers** with Trevor Fahey and Ken Turlik for Barclay Plager, June 16, 1967. Traded to **Phoenix** (WHL) by **Los Angeles** for Roger Cote, September, 1969.

MURRAY, Ken

Defense. Shoots right. 6', 180 lbs. Born, Toronto, Ont., January 22, 1948.

Season	Club	Regular Season					Playoffs				
		GP	G	A	Pts	PIM	GP	G	A	Pts	PIM
1969-70	Toronto Maple Leafs	1	0	1	1	2	....	....	....	....	....
1970-71	Toronto Maple Leafs	4	0	0	0	0	....	....	....	....	....
1972-73	New York Islanders	39	0	4	4	59	....	....	....	....	....
	Detroit Red Wings	31	1	1	2	36	....	....	....	....	....
1974-75	Kansas City Scouts	8	0	2	2	14	....	....	....	....	....
1975-76	Kansas City Scouts	23	0	2	2	24	....	....	....	....	....
	NHL Totals	**106**	**1**	**10**	**11**	**135**	....	....	....	....	....

Signed as a free agent by **Toronto**, April 5, 1970. Claimed by **Buffalo** from **Toronto** in Intra-League Draft, June 8, 1971. Claimed by **NY Islanders** from **Buffalo** in Expansion Draft, June 6, 1972. Traded to **Detroit** by **NY Islanders** with Brian Lavender for Ralph Stewart and Bob Cook, January 17, 1973. Loaned to **Seattle** (WHL) by **Detroit** (Virginia-AHL) for Gene Sobchuk, February 18, 1974. Claimed by **Kansas City** from **Detroit** in Expansion Draft, June 12, 1974. Traded to **Los Angeles** by **Kansas City** for cash, February 10, 1975.

MURRAY, Leo

Center/Left wing. Shoots left. 5'9", 165 lbs. Born, Portage la Prairie, Man., February 15, 1906.

Season	Club	Regular Season					Playoffs				
		GP	G	A	Pts	PIM	GP	G	A	Pts	PIM
1932-33	Montreal Canadiens	6	0	0	0	2	....	....	....	....	....
	NHL Totals	**6**	**0**	**0**	**0**	**2**	....	....	....	....	....

Signed as a free agent by **NY Americans**, October 22, 1930. Signed as a free agent **Providence** (Can-Am), October, 1931. Traded to **Montreal** by **Providence** (Can-Am) with Hago Harrington for Leo Gaudreault and Armand Mondou with both teams holding right of recall, January, 1933.

MURRAY, Marty

Center. Shoots left. 5'9", 180 lbs. Born, Deloraine, Man., February 16, 1975.
(Calgary's 5th choice, 96th overall, in 1993 Entry Draft).

Season	Club	Regular Season					Playoffs				
		GP	G	A	Pts	PIM	GP	G	A	Pts	PIM
1995-96	Calgary Flames	15	3	3	6	0	....	....	....	....	....
1996-97	Calgary Flames	2	0	0	0	4	....	....	....	....	....
1997-98	Calgary Flames	2	0	0	0	2	....	....	....	....	....
2000-01	Calgary Flames	7	0	0	0	0	....	....	....	....	....
2001-02	Philadelphia Flyers	74	12	15	27	10	5	0	1	1	0
2002-03	Philadelphia Flyers	76	11	15	26	13	4	0	0	0	4
	NHL Totals	**176**	**26**	**33**	**59**	**29**	**9**	**0**	**1**	**1**	**4**

Signed as a free agent by **Philadelphia**, July 9, 2001. Traded to **Carolina** by **Philadelphia** for Carolina's 6th round choice in 2004 Entry Draft, June 22, 2003.

MURRAY, Mike

Center. Shoots left. 6', 195 lbs. Born, Kingston, Ont., August 29, 1966.
(NY Islanders' 6th choice, 104th overall, in 1984 Entry Draft).

Season	Club	Regular Season					Playoffs				
		GP	G	A	Pts	PIM	GP	G	A	Pts	PIM
1987-88	Philadelphia Flyers	1	0	0	0	0	....	....	....	....	....
	NHL Totals	**1**	**0**	**0**	**0**	**0**	....	....	....	....	....

Traded to **Philadelphia** by **NY Islanders** for Philadelphia's 5th round choice (Todd McLellan) in 1986 Entry Draft, June 21, 1986.

MURRAY, Pat

Left wing. Shoots left. 6'2", 185 lbs. Born, Stratford, Ont., August 20, 1969.
(Philadelphia's 2nd choice, 35th overall, in 1988 Entry Draft).

Season	Club	Regular Season					Playoffs				
		GP	G	A	Pts	PIM	GP	G	A	Pts	PIM
1990-91	Philadelphia Flyers	16	2	1	3	15	....	....	....	....	....
1991-92	Philadelphia Flyers	9	1	0	1	0	....	....	....	....	....
	NHL Totals	**25**	**3**	**1**	**4**	**15**	....	....	....	....	....

MURRAY, Randy

Defense. Shoots right. 6'1", 195 lbs. Born, Chatham, Ont., August 24, 1945.

Season	Club	Regular Season					Playoffs				
		GP	G	A	Pts	PIM	GP	G	A	Pts	PIM
1969-70	Toronto Maple Leafs	3	0	0	0	2	....	....	....	....	....
	NHL Totals	**3**	**0**	**0**	**0**	**2**	....	....	....	....	....

MURRAY, Rem

Left wing. Shoots left. 6'2", 195 lbs. Born, Stratford, Ont., October 9, 1972.
(Los Angeles' 5th choice, 135th overall, in 1992 Entry Draft).

Season	Club	Regular Season					Playoffs				
		GP	G	A	Pts	PIM	GP	G	A	Pts	PIM
1996-97	Edmonton Oilers	82	11	20	31	16	12	1	2	3	4
1997-98	Edmonton Oilers	61	9	9	18	39	11	1	4	5	2
1998-99	Edmonton Oilers	78	21	18	39	20	4	1	1	2	2
99-2000	Edmonton Oilers	44	9	5	14	8	5	0	1	1	2
2000-01	Edmonton Oilers	82	15	21	36	24	6	2	0	2	6
2001-02	Edmonton Oilers	69	7	17	24	14	....	....	....	....	....
	New York Rangers	11	1	2	3	4	....	....	....	....	....
2002-03	New York Rangers	32	6	6	12	4	....	....	....	....	....
	Nashville Predators	53	6	13	19	18	....	....	....	....	....
	NHL Totals	**512**	**85**	**111**	**196**	**147**	**38**	**5**	**8**	**13**	**16**

Signed as a free agent by **Edmonton**, September 19, 1995. Traded to **NY Rangers** by **Edmonton** with Tom Poti for Mike York and NY Rangers' 4th round choice (Ivan Koltsov) in 2002 Entry Draft, March 19, 2002. Traded to **Nashville** by **NY Rangers** with Tomas Kloucek and Marek Zidlicky for Mike Dunham, December 12, 2002.

MURRAY, Rob

Center. Shoots right. 6'1", 180 lbs. Born, Toronto, Ont., April 4, 1967.
(Washington's 3rd choice, 61st overall, in 1985 Entry Draft).

Season	Club	Regular Season					Playoffs				
		GP	G	A	Pts	PIM	GP	G	A	Pts	PIM
1989-90	Washington Capitals	41	2	7	9	58	9	0	0	0	18
1990-91	Washington Capitals	17	0	3	3	19	....	....	....	....	....
1991-92	Winnipeg Jets	9	0	1	1	18	....	....	....	....	....
1992-93	Winnipeg Jets	10	1	0	1	6	....	....	....	....	....
1993-94	Winnipeg Jets	6	0	0	0	2	....	....	....	....	....
1994-95	Winnipeg Jets	10	0	2	2	2	....	....	....	....	....
1995-96	Winnipeg Jets	1	0	0	0	2	....	....	....	....	....

Season	Club	GP	G	A	Pts	PIM	GP	G	A	Pts	PIM
		REGULAR SEASON					PLAYOFFS				
1998-99	Phoenix Coyotes	13	1	2	3	4	....	....	....	....	....
	NHL Totals	**107**	**4**	**15**	**19**	**111**	**9**	**0**	**0**	**0**	**18**

Claimed by **Minnesota** from **Washington** in Expansion Draft, May 30, 1991. Traded to **Winnipeg** by **Minnesota** with future considerations for Winnipeg's 7th round choice (Geoff Finch) in 1991 Entry Draft and future considerations, May 31, 1991. Transferred to **Phoenix** after **Winnipeg** franchise relocated, July 1, 1996. Traded to **Edmonton** by **Phoenix** for Eric Houde, November 30, 1999. Signed as a free agent by **Philadelphia**, July 24, 2000. Signed as a free agent by **Calgary**, August 2, 2001.

MURRAY, Terry

Defense. Shoots right. 6'2", 190 lbs. Born, Shawville, Que., July 20, 1950.
(Oakland's 3rd choice, 88th overall, in 1970 Amateur Draft).

Season	Club	GP	G	A	Pts	PIM	GP	G	A	Pts	PIM
1972-73	California Golden Seals	23	0	3	3	4	....	....	....	....	....
1973-74	California Golden Seals	58	0	12	12	48	....	....	....	....	....
1974-75	California Golden Seals	9	0	2	2	8	....	....	....	....	....
1975-76	Philadelphia Flyers	3	0	0	0	2	6	0	1	1	0
1976-77	Philadelphia Flyers	36	0	13	13	14	....	....	....	....	....
	Detroit Red Wings	23	0	7	7	10	....	....	....	....	....
1978-79	Philadelphia Flyers	5	0	0	0	0	....	....	....	....	....
1980-81	Philadelphia Flyers	71	1	17	18	53	12	2	1	3	10
1981-82	Washington Capitals	74	3	22	25	60	....	....	....	....	....
	NHL Totals	**302**	**4**	**76**	**80**	**199**	**18**	**2**	**2**	**4**	**10**

Signed as a free agent by **Philadelphia**, September 23, 1975. Traded to **Detroit** by **Philadelphia** with Steve Coates, Bob Ritchie and Dave Kelly for Rick Lapointe and Mike Korney, February 17, 1977. Traded to **Philadelphia** by **Detroit** for cash, November 1, 1977. Claimed by **Washington** from **Philadelphia** in Waiver Draft, October 5, 1981.

MURRAY, Troy

Center. Shoots right. 6'1", 195 lbs. Born, Calgary, Alta., July 31, 1962.
(Chicago's 6th choice, 57th overall, in 1980 Entry Draft).

Season	Club	GP	G	A	Pts	PIM	GP	G	A	Pts	PIM
1981-82	Chicago Black Hawks	1	0	0	0	0	7	1	0	1	5
1982-83	Chicago Black Hawks	54	8	8	16	27	2	0	0	0	0
1983-84	Chicago Black Hawks	61	15	15	30	45	5	1	0	1	7
1984-85	Chicago Black Hawks	80	26	40	66	82	15	5	14	19	24
1985-86	Chicago Black Hawks	80	45	54	99	94	2	0	0	0	2
1986-87	Chicago Blackhawks	77	28	43	71	59	4	0	0	0	5
1987-88	Chicago Blackhawks	79	22	36	58	96	5	1	0	1	8
1988-89	Chicago Blackhawks	79	21	30	51	113	16	3	6	9	25
1989-90	Chicago Blackhawks	68	17	38	55	86	20	4	4	8	22
1990-91	Chicago Blackhawks	75	14	23	37	74	6	0	1	1	12
1991-92	Winnipeg Jets	74	17	30	47	69	7	0	0	0	2
1992-93	Winnipeg Jets	29	3	4	7	34	....	....	....	....	....
	Chicago Blackhawks	22	1	3	4	25	4	0	0	0	2
1993-94	Chicago Blackhawks	12	0	1	1	6	....	....	....	....	....
	Ottawa Senators	15	2	3	5	4	....	....	....	....	....
1994-95	Ottawa Senators	33	4	10	14	16	....	....	....	....	....
	Pittsburgh Penguins	13	0	2	2	23	12	2	1	3	12
1995-96◆	Colorado Avalanche	63	7	14	21	22	8	0	0	0	19
	NHL Totals	**915**	**230**	**354**	**584**	**875**	**113**	**17**	**26**	**43**	**145**

Frank J. Selke Trophy (1986)

Traded to **Winnipeg** by **Chicago** with Warren Rychel for Bryan Marchment and Chris Norton, July 22, 1991. Traded to **Chicago** by **Winnipeg** for Steve Bancroft and future considerations, February 21, 1993. Traded to **Ottawa** by **Chicago** with Chicago's 11th round choice (Antti Tormanen) in 1994 Entry Draft for Ottawa's 11th round choice (Rob Mara) in 1994 Entry Draft, March 11, 1994. Traded to **Pittsburgh** by **Ottawa** with Norm Maciver for Martin Straka, April 7, 1995. Signed as a free agent by **Colorado**, August 7, 1995.

MURZYN, Dana

Defense. Shoots left. 6'2", 200 lbs. Born, Calgary, Alta., December 9, 1966.
(Hartford's 1st choice, 5th overall, in 1985 Entry Draft).

Season	Club	GP	G	A	Pts	PIM	GP	G	A	Pts	PIM
1985-86	Hartford Whalers	78	3	23	26	125	4	0	0	0	10
1986-87	Hartford Whalers	74	9	19	28	95	6	2	1	3	29
1987-88	Hartford Whalers	33	1	6	7	45	....	....	....	....	....
	Calgary Flames	41	6	5	11	94	5	2	0	2	13
1988-89◆	Calgary Flames	63	3	19	22	142	21	0	3	3	20
1989-90	Calgary Flames	78	7	13	20	140	6	2	2	4	2
1990-91	Calgary Flames	19	0	2	2	30	....	....	....	....	....
	Vancouver Canucks	10	1	0	1	8	6	0	1	1	8
1991-92	Vancouver Canucks	70	3	11	14	147	1	0	0	0	15
1992-93	Vancouver Canucks	79	5	11	16	196	12	3	2	5	18
1993-94	Vancouver Canucks	80	6	14	20	109	7	0	0	0	4
1994-95	Vancouver Canucks	40	0	8	8	129	8	0	1	1	22
1995-96	Vancouver Canucks	69	2	10	12	130	6	0	0	0	25
1996-97	Vancouver Canucks	61	1	7	8	118	....	....	....	....	....
1997-98	Vancouver Canucks	31	5	2	7	42	....	....	....	....	....
1998-99	Vancouver Canucks	12	0	2	2	21	....	....	....	....	....
	NHL Totals	**838**	**52**	**152**	**204**	**1571**	**82**	**9**	**10**	**19**	**166**

NHL All-Rookie Team (1986)

Traded to **Calgary** by **Hartford** with Shane Churla for Neil Sheehy, Carey Wilson and the rights to Lane MacDonald, January 3, 1988. Traded to **Vancouver** by **Calgary** for Ron Stern and Kevan Guy, March 5, 1991. • Missed majority of 1997-98 season recovering from knee injury suffered in game vs. Dallas, December 27, 1997.

MUSIL, Frantisek

Defense. Shoots left. 6'3", 215 lbs. Born, Pardubice, Czech., December 17, 1964.
(Minnesota's 3rd choice, 38th overall, in 1983 Entry Draft).

Season	Club	GP	G	A	Pts	PIM	GP	G	A	Pts	PIM
1986-87	Minnesota North Stars	72	2	9	11	148	....	....	....	....	....
1987-88	Minnesota North Stars	80	9	8	17	213	....	....	....	....	....
1988-89	Minnesota North Stars	55	1	19	20	54	5	1	1	2	4
1989-90	Minnesota North Stars	56	2	8	10	109	4	0	0	0	14
1990-91	Minnesota North Stars	8	0	2	2	23	....	....	....	....	....
	Calgary Flames	67	7	14	21	160	7	0	0	0	10
1991-92	Calgary Flames	78	4	8	12	103	....	....	....	....	....
1992-93	Calgary Flames	80	6	10	16	131	6	1	1	2	7
1993-94	Calgary Flames	75	1	8	9	50	7	0	1	1	4
1994-95	Calgary Flames	35	0	5	5	61	5	0	1	1	0
1995-96	Ottawa Senators	65	1	3	4	85	....	....	....	....	....
1996-97	Ottawa Senators	57	0	5	5	58	....	....	....	....	....
1997-98	Edmonton Oilers	17	1	2	3	8	7	0	0	0	6
1998-99	Edmonton Oilers	39	0	3	3	34	1	0	0	0	2
99-2000	Edmonton Oilers	DID NOT PLAY – INJURED									
2000-01	Edmonton Oilers	13	0	2	2	4	....	....	....	....	....
	NHL Totals	**797**	**34**	**106**	**140**	**1241**	**42**	**2**	**4**	**6**	**47**

Traded to **Calgary** by **Minnesota** for Brian Glynn, October 26, 1990. Traded to **Ottawa** by **Calgary** for Ottawa's 4th round choice (Chris St. Croix) in 1997 Entry Draft, October 7, 1995. Traded to **Edmonton** by **Ottawa** for Scott Ferguson, March 9, 1998. • Missed entire 1999-2000 season and start of 2000-01 season recovering from spinal cord injury suffered in practice, October 2, 1999. • Missed majority of 2000-01 season recovering from neck injury suffered in game vs. Columbus, January 7, 2001.

MYERS, Hap

Defense. Shoots left. 5'11", 195 lbs. Born, Edmonton, Alta., July 28, 1947.

Season	Club	GP	G	A	Pts	PIM	GP	G	A	Pts	PIM
1970-71	Buffalo Sabres	13	0	0	0	6	....	....	....	....	....
	NHL Totals	**13**	**0**	**0**	**0**	**6**	....	....	....	....	....

Claimed by **Buffalo** (Salt Lake-CHL) from **Detroit** in Reverse Draft, June 10, 1970.

MYHRES, Brantt

Right wing. Shoots right. 6'3", 220 lbs. Born, Edmonton, Alta., March 18, 1974.
(Tampa Bay's 5th choice, 97th overall, in 1992 Entry Draft).

Season	Club	GP	G	A	Pts	PIM	GP	G	A	Pts	PIM
1994-95	Tampa Bay Lightning	15	2	0	2	81	....	....	....	....	....
1996-97	Tampa Bay Lightning	47	3	1	4	136	....	....	....	....	....
1997-98	Philadelphia Flyers	23	0	0	0	169	....	....	....	....	....
1998-99	San Jose Sharks	30	1	0	1	116	....	....	....	....	....
99-2000	San Jose Sharks	13	0	1	1	97	....	....	....	....	....
2000-01	Nashville Predators	20	0	0	0	28	....	....	....	....	....
	Washington Capitals	5	0	0	0	29	....	....	....	....	....
2002-03	Boston Bruins	1	0	0	0	31	....	....	....	....	....
	NHL Totals	**154**	**6**	**2**	**8**	**687**					

Traded to **Edmonton** by **Tampa Bay** with Toronto's 3rd round choice (previously acquired, Edmonton selected Alex Henry) in 1998 Entry Draft for Vladimir Vujtek and Edmonton's 3rd round choice (Dmitry Afanasenkov) in 1998 Entry Draft, July 16, 1997. Traded to **Philadelphia** by **Edmonton** for Jason Bowen, October 15, 1997. Signed as a free agent by **San Jose**, September 11, 1998. Signed as a free agent by **Nashville**, August 15, 2000. Traded to **Washington** by **Nashville** for future considerations, February 1, 2001.

MYLES, Vic

Defense. Shoots right. 6'1", 208 lbs. Born, Fairlight, Sask., November 12, 1915.

Season	Club	GP	G	A	Pts	PIM	GP	G	A	Pts	PIM
1942-43	New York Rangers	45	6	9	15	57	....	....	....	....	....
	NHL Totals	**45**	**6**	**9**	**15**	**57**	....	....	....	....	....

Traded to **NY Rangers** by **New Haven** (AHL) for cash, November 17, 1942.

MYRVOLD, Anders

Defense. Shoots left. 6'2", 200 lbs. Born, Lorenskog, Norway, August 12, 1975.
(Quebec's 6th choice, 127th overall, in 1993 Entry Draft).

Season	Club	GP	G	A	Pts	PIM	GP	G	A	Pts	PIM
1995-96	Colorado Avalanche	4	0	1	1	6	....	....	....	....	....
1996-97	Boston Bruins	9	0	2	2	4	....	....	....	....	....
2000-01	New York Islanders	12	0	1	1	0	....	....	....	....	....
	NHL Totals	**25**	**0**	**4**	**4**	**10**	....	....	....	....	....

Rights transferred to **Colorado** after **Quebec** franchise relocated, June 21, 1995. Traded to **Boston** by **Colorado** with Landon Wilson for Boston's 1st round choice (Robyn Regehr) in 1998 Entry Draft, November 22, 1996. Signed as a free agent by **NY Islanders**, August 28, 2000. Signed as a free agent by **Florida**, July 28, 2002.

NABOKOV, Dmitri

Center/Left wing. Shoots right. 6'2", 209 lbs. Born, Novosibirsk, USSR, January 4, 1977.
(Chicago's 1st choice, 19th overall, in 1995 Entry Draft).

Season	Club	GP	G	A	Pts	PIM	GP	G	A	Pts	PIM
1997-98	Chicago Blackhawks	25	7	4	11	10	....	....	....	....	....
1998-99	New York Islanders	4	0	2	2	2	....	....	....	....	....
99-2000	New York Islanders	26	4	7	11	16	....	....	....	....	....
	NHL Totals	**55**	**11**	**13**	**24**	**28**	....	....	....	....	....

Traded to **NY Islanders** by **Chicago** for J.P. Dumont and Chicago's 5th round choice (later traded to Philadelphia – Philadelphia selected Francis Belanger) in 1998 Entry Draft, June 1, 1998.

NACHBAUR, Don

Center. Shoots left. 6'2", 200 lbs. Born, Kitimat, B.C., January 30, 1959.
(Hartford's 3rd choice, 60th overall, in 1979 Entry Draft).

Season	Club	GP	G	A	Pts	PIM	GP	G	A	Pts	PIM
1980-81	Hartford Whalers	77	16	17	33	139	....	....	....	....	....
1981-82	Hartford Whalers	77	5	21	26	117	....	....	....	....	....
1982-83	Edmonton Oilers	4	0	0	0	17	2	0	0	0	7
1985-86	Philadelphia Flyers	5	1	1	2	7	....	....	....	....	....
1986-87	Philadelphia Flyers	23	0	2	2	87	7	1	1	2	15
1987-88	Philadelphia Flyers	20	0	4	4	61	2	0	0	0	2
1988-89	Philadelphia Flyers	15	1	0	1	37	....	....	....	....	....

Season	Club	GP	G	A	Pts	PIM	GP	G	A	Pts	PIM
		REGULAR SEASON					PLAYOFFS				
1989-90	Philadelphia Flyers	2	0	1	1	0	....	....	....	....	....
	NHL Totals	**223**	**23**	**46**	**69**	**465**	**11**	**1**	**1**	**2**	**24**

Traded to **Edmonton** by **Hartford** with Ken Linseman for Risto Siltanen and the rights to Brent Loney, August 19, 1982. Claimed by **Los Angeles** from **Edmonton** in Waiver Draft, October 3, 1983. Signed as a free agent by **Philadelphia**, October 4, 1984.

NAGY, Ladislav

Left wing. Shoots left. 5'11", 186 lbs. Born, Saca, Czech., June 1, 1979.
(St. Louis' 6th choice, 177th overall, in 1997 Entry Draft).

Season	Club	GP	G	A	Pts	PIM	GP	G	A	Pts	PIM
99-2000	St. Louis Blues	11	2	4	6	2	6	1	1	2	0
2000-01	St. Louis Blues	40	8	8	16	20	....	....	....	....	....
	Phoenix Coyotes	6	0	1	1	2	....	....	....	....	....
2001-02	Phoenix Coyotes	74	23	19	42	50	5	0	0	0	21
2002-03	Phoenix Coyotes	80	22	35	57	92	....	....	....	....	....
	NHL Totals	**211**	**55**	**67**	**122**	**166**	**11**	**1**	**1**	**2**	**21**

Traded to **Phoenix** by **St. Louis** with Michal Handzus, the rights to Jeff Taffe and St. Louis' 1st round choice (Ben Eager) in 2002 Entry Draft for Keith Tkachuk, March 13, 2001.

NAHRGANG, Jim

Defense. Shoots right. 6', 185 lbs. Born, Millbank, Ont., April 17, 1951.
(Detroit's 7th choice, 86th overall, in 1971 Amateur Draft).

Season	Club	GP	G	A	Pts	PIM	GP	G	A	Pts	PIM
1974-75	Detroit Red Wings	1	0	0	0	0	....	....	....	....	....
1975-76	Detroit Red Wings	3	0	1	1	0	....	....	....	....	....
1976-77	Detroit Red Wings	53	5	11	16	34	....	....	....	....	....
	NHL Totals	**57**	**5**	**12**	**17**	**34**	....	....	....	....	....

NAMESTNIKOV, John

Defense. Shoots right. 5'11", 190 lbs. Born, Arzamis-Ig, USSR, October 9, 1971.
(Vancouver's 5th choice, 117th overall, in 1991 Entry Draft).

Season	Club	GP	G	A	Pts	PIM	GP	G	A	Pts	PIM
1993-94	Vancouver Canucks	17	0	5	5	10	....	....	....	....	....
1994-95	Vancouver Canucks	16	0	3	3	4	1	0	0	0	2
1995-96	Vancouver Canucks	....	....	....	....	....	1	0	0	0	0
1996-97	Vancouver Canucks	2	0	0	0	4	....	....	....	....	....
1997-98	New York Islanders	6	0	1	1	4	....	....	....	....	....
99-2000	Nashville Predators	2	0	0	0	2	....	....	....	....	....
	NHL Totals	**43**	**0**	**9**	**9**	**24**	**2**	**0**	**0**	**0**	**2**

Signed as a free agent by **NY Islanders**, July 21, 1997. Signed as a free agent by **NY Rangers**, August 9, 1999. Claimed by **Vancouver** from **NY Rangers** in Waiver Draft, September 27, 1999. Claimed on waivers by **NY Rangers** from **Vancouver**, October 5, 1999. Traded to **Nashville** by **NY Rangers** for Jason Dawe, February 3, 2000.

NANNE, Lou

Defense/Right wing. Shoots right. 6'1", 185 lbs. Born, Sault Ste. Marie, Ont., June 2, 1941.

Season	Club	GP	G	A	Pts	PIM	GP	G	A	Pts	PIM
1967-68	Minnesota North Stars	2	0	1	1	0	....	....	....	....	....
1968-69	Minnesota North Stars	41	2	12	14	47	....	....	....	....	....
1969-70	Minnesota North Stars	74	3	20	23	75	5	0	2	2	2
1970-71	Minnesota North Stars	68	5	11	16	22	12	3	6	9	4
1971-72	Minnesota North Stars	78	21	28	49	27	7	0	0	0	0
1972-73	Minnesota North Stars	74	15	20	35	39	6	1	2	3	0
1973-74	Minnesota North Stars	76	11	21	32	46	....	....	....	....	....
1974-75	Minnesota North Stars	49	6	9	15	35	....	....	....	....	....
1975-76	Minnesota North Stars	79	3	14	17	45	....	....	....	....	....
1976-77	Minnesota North Stars	68	2	20	22	12	2	0	0	0	2
1977-78	Minnesota North Stars	26	0	1	1	8	....	....	....	....	....
	NHL Totals	**635**	**68**	**157**	**225**	**356**	**32**	**4**	**10**	**14**	**8**

Lester Patrick Trophy (1989)

Signed as a free agent by **Minnesota**, March, 1968.

NANTAIS, Rich

Left wing. Shoots left. 5'11", 188 lbs. Born, Repentigny, Que., October 27, 1954.
(Minnesota's 2nd choice, 24th overall, in 1974 Amateur Draft).

Season	Club	GP	G	A	Pts	PIM	GP	G	A	Pts	PIM
1974-75	Minnesota North Stars	18	4	1	5	9	....	....	....	....	....
1975-76	Minnesota North Stars	5	0	0	0	17	....	....	....	....	....
1976-77	Minnesota North Stars	40	1	3	4	53	....	....	....	....	....
	NHL Totals	**63**	**5**	**4**	**9**	**79**	....	....	....	....	....

Traded to **Washington** by **New Haven** (AHL) with Alain Langlais for Ron Anderson and Bob Gryp, February 23, 1976. Signed as a free agent by **Minnesota**, September, 1976.

NAPIER, Mark

Right wing. Shoots left. 5'10", 182 lbs. Born, Toronto, Ont., January 28, 1957.
(Montreal's 1st choice, 10th overall, in 1977 Amateur Draft).

Season	Club	GP	G	A	Pts	PIM	GP	G	A	Pts	PIM
1978-79 ♦	Montreal Canadiens	54	11	20	31	11	12	3	2	5	2
1979-80	Montreal Canadiens	76	16	33	49	7	10	2	6	8	0
1980-81	Montreal Canadiens	79	35	36	71	24	3	0	0	0	2
1981-82	Montreal Canadiens	80	40	41	81	14	5	3	2	5	0
1982-83	Montreal Canadiens	73	40	27	67	6	3	0	0	0	0
1983-84	Montreal Canadiens	5	3	2	5	0	....	....	....	....	....
	Minnesota North Stars	58	13	28	41	17	12	3	2	5	0
1984-85	Minnesota North Stars	39	10	18	28	2	....	....	....	....	....
♦	Edmonton Oilers	33	9	26	35	19	18	5	5	10	7
1985-86	Edmonton Oilers	80	24	32	56	14	10	1	4	5	0
1986-87	Edmonton Oilers	62	8	13	21	2	....	....	....	....	....
	Buffalo Sabres	15	5	5	10	0	....	....	....	....	....
1987-88	Buffalo Sabres	47	10	8	18	8	6	0	3	3	0
1988-89	Buffalo Sabres	66	11	17	28	33	3	1	0	1	0
	NHL Totals	**767**	**235**	**306**	**541**	**157**	**82**	**18**	**24**	**42**	**11**

Traded to **Minnesota** by **Montreal** with Keith Acton and Toronto's 3rd round choice (previously acquired, Minnesota selected Ken Hodge Jr.) in 1984 Entry Draft for Bobby Smith, October 28, 1983. Traded to **Edmonton** by **Minnesota** for Gord Sherven and Terry Martin, January 24, 1985. Traded to **Buffalo** by **Edmonton** with Lee Fogolin Jr. and Edmonton's 4th round choice (John Bradley) in 1987 Entry Draft for Normand Lacombe, Wayne Van Dorp and Buffalo's 4th round choice (Peter Eriksson) in 1987 Entry Draft, March 6, 1987.

NASH, Rick

Left wing. Shoots left. 6'3", 188 lbs. Born, Brampton, Ont., June 16, 1984.
(Columbus' 1st choice, 1st overall, in 2002 Entry Draft).

Season	Club	GP	G	A	Pts	PIM	GP	G	A	Pts	PIM
2002-03	Columbus Blue Jackets	74	17	22	39	78	....	....	....	....	....
	NHL Totals	**74**	**17**	**22**	**39**	**78**	....	....	....	....	....

NHL All-Rookie Team (2003)

NASH, Tyson

Left wing. Shoots left. 6', 185 lbs. Born, Edmonton, Alta., March 11, 1975.
(Vancouver's 10th choice, 247th overall, in 1994 Entry Draft).

Season	Club	GP	G	A	Pts	PIM	GP	G	A	Pts	PIM
1998-99	St. Louis Blues	2	0	0	0	5	1	0	0	0	2
99-2000	St. Louis Blues	66	4	9	13	150	6	1	0	1	24
2000-01	St. Louis Blues	57	8	7	15	110	....	....	....	....	....
2001-02	St. Louis Blues	64	6	7	13	100	9	0	1	1	20
2002-03	St. Louis Blues	66	6	3	9	114	7	2	1	3	6
	NHL Totals	**255**	**24**	**26**	**50**	**479**	**23**	**3**	**2**	**5**	**52**

Signed as a free agent by **St. Louis**, July 14, 1998. Traded to **Phoenix** by **St. Louis** for Phoenix's 5th round choice (Lee Stempniak) in 2003 Enrey Draft, June 21, 2003.

NASLUND, Markus

Left wing. Shoots left. 5'11", 195 lbs. Born, Ornskoldsvik, Sweden, July 30, 1973.
(Pittsburgh's 1st choice, 16th overall, in 1991 Entry Draft).

Season	Club	GP	G	A	Pts	PIM	GP	G	A	Pts	PIM
1993-94	Pittsburgh Penguins	71	4	7	11	27	....	....	....	....	....
1994-95	Pittsburgh Penguins	14	2	2	4	2	....	....	....	....	....
1995-96	Pittsburgh Penguins	66	19	33	52	36	....	....	....	....	....
	Vancouver Canucks	10	3	0	3	6	6	1	2	3	8
1996-97	Vancouver Canucks	78	21	20	41	30	....	....	....	....	....
1997-98	Vancouver Canucks	76	14	20	34	56	....	....	....	....	....
1998-99	Vancouver Canucks	80	36	30	66	74	....	....	....	....	....
99-2000	Vancouver Canucks	82	27	38	65	64	....	....	....	....	....
2000-01	Vancouver Canucks	72	41	34	75	58	....	....	....	....	....
2001-02	Vancouver Canucks	81	40	50	90	50	6	1	1	2	2
2002-03	Vancouver Canucks	82	48	56	104	52	14	5	9	14	18
	NHL Totals	**712**	**255**	**290**	**545**	**455**	**26**	**7**	**12**	**19**	**28**

NHL First All-Star Team (2002, 2003) • Lester B. Pearson Award (2003)

Played in NHL All-Star Game (1999, 2001, 2002, 2003)

Traded to **Vancouver** by **Pittsburgh** for Alek Stojanov, March 20, 1996.

NASLUND, Mats

Left wing. Shoots left. 5'7", 160 lbs. Born, Timra, Sweden, October 31, 1959.
(Montreal's 2nd choice, 37th overall, in 1979 Entry Draft).

Season	Club	GP	G	A	Pts	PIM	GP	G	A	Pts	PIM
1982-83	Montreal Canadiens	74	26	45	71	10	3	1	0	1	0
1983-84	Montreal Canadiens	77	29	35	64	4	15	6	8	14	4
1984-85	Montreal Canadiens	80	42	37	79	14	12	7	4	11	6
1985-86 ♦	Montreal Canadiens	80	43	67	110	16	20	8	11	19	4
1986-87	Montreal Canadiens	79	25	55	80	16	17	7	15	22	11
1987-88	Montreal Canadiens	78	24	59	83	14	6	0	7	7	2
1988-89	Montreal Canadiens	77	33	51	84	14	21	4	11	15	6
1989-90	Montreal Canadiens	72	21	20	41	19	3	1	1	2	0
1994-95	Boston Bruins	34	8	14	22	4	5	1	0	1	0
	NHL Totals	**651**	**251**	**383**	**634**	**111**	**102**	**35**	**57**	**92**	**33**

NHL All-Rookie Team (1983) • NHL Second All-Star Team (1986) • Lady Byng Trophy (1988)

Played in NHL All-Star Game (1984, 1986, 1988)

Signed as a free agent by **Boston**, February 21, 1994.

NASREDDINE, Alain

Defense. Shoots left. 6'1", 201 lbs. Born, Montreal, Que., July 10, 1975.
(Florida's 8th choice, 135th overall, in 1993 Entry Draft).

Season	Club	GP	G	A	Pts	PIM	GP	G	A	Pts	PIM
1998-99	Chicago Blackhawks	7	0	0	0	19	....	....	....	....	....
	Montreal Canadiens	8	0	0	0	33	....	....	....	....	....
2002-03	New York Islanders	3	0	0	0	2	....	....	....	....	....
	NHL Totals	**18**	**0**	**0**	**0**	**54**	....	....	....	....	....

Traded to **Chicago** by **Florida** for Ivan Droppa, December 18, 1996. Traded to **Montreal** by **Chicago** with Jeff Hackett, Eric Weinrich and Tampa Bay's 4th round choice (previously acquired, Montreal selected Chris Dyment) in 1999 Entry Draft for Jocelyn Thibault, Dave Manson and Brad Brown, November 16, 1998. Traded to **Edmonton** by **Montreal** with Igor Ulanov for Christian Laflamme and Matthieu Descoteaux, March 9, 2000. Signed as a free agent by **NY Islanders**, September 6, 2002.

NATTRASS, Ralph

Defense. Shoots right. 6', 185 lbs. Born, Gainsboro, Sask., May 26, 1925.

Season	Club	GP	G	A	Pts	PIM	GP	G	A	Pts	PIM
1946-47	Chicago Black Hawks	35	4	5	9	34	....	....	....	....	....
1947-48	Chicago Black Hawks	60	5	12	17	79	....	....	....	....	....
1948-49	Chicago Black Hawks	60	4	10	14	99	....	....	....	....	....

		REGULAR SEASON					PLAYOFFS				
Season	Club	GP	G	A	Pts	PIM	GP	G	A	Pts	PIM
1949-50	Chicago Black Hawks	68	5	11	16	96	....	....	....	....	....
	NHL Totals	**223**	**18**	**38**	**56**	**308**	....	....	....	....	....

Traded to **Montreal** by **Chicago** for cash, October 4, 1950.

NATTRESS, Ric

Defense. Shoots right. 6'2", 210 lbs. Born, Hamilton, Ont., May 25, 1962.
(Montreal's 2nd choice, 27th overall, in 1980 Entry Draft).

Season	Club	GP	G	A	Pts	PIM	GP	G	A	Pts	PIM
1982-83	Montreal Canadiens	40	1	3	4	19	3	0	0	0	10
1983-84	Montreal Canadiens	34	0	12	12	15	....	....	....	....	....
1984-85	Montreal Canadiens	5	0	1	1	2	2	0	0	0	2
1985-86	St. Louis Blues	78	4	20	24	52	18	1	4	5	24
1986-87	St. Louis Blues	73	6	22	28	24	6	0	0	0	2
1987-88	Calgary Flames	63	2	13	15	37	6	1	3	4	0
1988-89◆	Calgary Flames	38	1	8	9	47	19	0	3	3	20
1989-90	Calgary Flames	49	1	14	15	26	6	2	0	2	0
1990-91	Calgary Flames	58	5	13	18	63	7	1	0	1	2
1991-92	Calgary Flames	18	0	5	5	31	....	....	....	....	....
	Toronto Maple Leafs	36	2	14	16	32	....	....	....	....	....
1992-93	Philadelphia Flyers	44	7	10	17	29	....	....	....	....	....
	NHL Totals	**536**	**29**	**135**	**164**	**377**	**67**	**5**	**10**	**15**	**60**

Rights traded to **St. Louis** by **Montreal** for cash, October 7, 1985. Traded to **Calgary** by **St. Louis** for Calgary's 4th round choice (Andy Rymsha) in 1987 Entry Draft and 5th round choice (Dave Lacouture) in 1988 Entry Draft, June 13, 1987. Traded to **Toronto** by **Calgary** with Doug Gilmour, Jamie Macoun, Kent Manderville and Rick Wamsley for Gary Leeman, Alexander Godynyuk, Jeff Resse, Michel Petit and Craig Berube, January 2, 1992. Signed as a free agent by **Philadelphia**, August 21, 1992. • Officially announced retirement, October 8, 1993.

NATYSHAK, Mike

Right wing. Shoots right. 6'2", 201 lbs. Born, Belle River, Ont., November 29, 1963.
(Quebec's 1st choice, 23rd overall, in 1986 Supplemental Draft).

Season	Club	GP	G	A	Pts	PIM	GP	G	A	Pts	PIM
1987-88	Quebec Nordiques	4	0	0	0	0	....	....	....	....	....
	NHL Totals	**4**	**0**	**0**	**0**	**0**	....	....	....	....	....

NAZAROV, Andrei

Left wing. Shoots right. 6'5", 241 lbs. Born, Chelyabinsk, USSR, May 22, 1974.
(San Jose's 2nd choice, 10th overall, in 1992 Entry Draft).

Season	Club	GP	G	A	Pts	PIM	GP	G	A	Pts	PIM
1993-94	San Jose Sharks	1	0	0	0	0	....	....	....	....	....
1994-95	San Jose Sharks	26	3	5	8	94	6	0	0	0	9
1995-96	San Jose Sharks	42	7	7	14	62	....	....	....	....	....
1996-97	San Jose Sharks	60	12	15	27	222	....	....	....	....	....
1997-98	San Jose Sharks	40	1	1	2	112					
	Tampa Bay Lightning	14	1	1	2	58	....	....	....	....	....
1998-99	Tampa Bay Lightning	26	2	0	2	43	....	....	....	....	....
	Calgary Flames	36	5	9	14	30	....	....	....	....	....
99-2000	Calgary Flames	76	10	22	32	78	....	....	....	....	....
2000-01	Mighty Ducks of Anaheim	16	1	0	1	29	....	....	....	....	....
	Boston Bruins	63	1	4	5	200	....	....	....	....	....
2001-02	Boston Bruins	47	0	2	2	164	....	....	....	....	....
	Phoenix Coyotes	30	6	3	9	51	3	0	0	0	2
2002-03	Phoenix Coyotes	59	3	0	3	135	....	....	....	....	....
	NHL Totals	**536**	**52**	**69**	**121**	**1278**	**9**	**0**	**0**	**0**	**11**

Traded to **Tampa Bay** by **San Jose** with Florida's 1st round choice (previously acquired, Tampa Bay selected Vincent Lecavalier) in 1998 Entry Draft for Bryan Marchment, David Shaw and Tampa Bay's 1st round choice (later traded to Nashville – Nashville selected David Legwand) in 1998 Entry Draft, March 24, 1998. Traded to **Calgary** by **Tampa Bay** for Michael Nylander, January 19, 1999. Traded to **Anaheim** by **Calgary** with Calgary's 2nd round choice (later traded to Phoenix – later traded back to Calgary – Calgary selected Andrei Taratukhin) in 2001 Entry Draft for Jordan Leopold, September 26, 2000. Traded to **Boston** by **Anaheim** with Patrick Traverse for Samuel Pahlsson, November 18, 2000. Traded to **Phoenix** by **Boston** for Phoenix's 5th round choice (Peter Hamerlik) in 2002 Entry Draft, January 25, 2002.

NDUR, Rumun

Defense. Shoots left. 6'2", 222 lbs. Born, Zaria, Nigeria, July 7, 1975.
(Buffalo's 3rd choice, 69th overall, in 1994 Entry Draft).

Season	Club	GP	G	A	Pts	PIM	GP	G	A	Pts	PIM
1996-97	Buffalo Sabres	2	0	0	0	2	....	....	....	....	....
1997-98	Buffalo Sabres	1	0	0	0	2	....	....	....	....	....
1998-99	Buffalo Sabres	8	0	0	0	16	....	....	....	....	....
	New York Rangers	31	1	3	4	46	....	....	....	....	....
99-2000	Atlanta Thrashers	27	1	0	1	71	....	....	....	....	....
	NHL Totals	**69**	**2**	**3**	**5**	**137**	....	....	....	....	....

Claimed on waivers by **NY Rangers** from **Buffalo**, December 18, 1998. Claimed on waivers by **Atlanta** from **NY Rangers**, December 11, 1999. Signed as a free agent by **Chicago**, August 7, 2001.

NEATON, Pat

Defense. Shoots left. 6', 180 lbs. Born, Redford, MI, May 21, 1971.
(Pittsburgh's 9th choice, 145th overall, in 1990 Entry Draft).

Season	Club	GP	G	A	Pts	PIM	GP	G	A	Pts	PIM
1993-94	Pittsburgh Penguins	9	1	1	2	12	....	....	....	....	....
	NHL Totals	**9**	**1**	**1**	**2**	**12**	....	....	....	....	....

NECHAEV, Viktor

Center. Shoots left. 6'1", 183 lbs. Born, Vostochnaya, USSR, January 28, 1955.
(Los Angeles' 7th choice, 132nd overall, in 1982 Entry Draft).

Season	Club	GP	G	A	Pts	PIM	GP	G	A	Pts	PIM
1982-83	Los Angeles Kings	3	1	0	1	0	....	....	....	....	....
	NHL Totals	**3**	**1**	**0**	**1**	**0**	....	....	....	....	....

NECKAR, Stan

Defense. Shoots left. 6'1", 214 lbs. Born, Ceske Budejovice, Czech., December 22, 1975.
(Ottawa's 2nd choice, 29th overall, in 1994 Entry Draft).

Season	Club	GP	G	A	Pts	PIM	GP	G	A	Pts	PIM
1994-95	Ottawa Senators	48	1	3	4	37	....	....	....	....	....
1995-96	Ottawa Senators	82	3	9	12	54	....	....	....	....	....
1996-97	Ottawa Senators	5	0	0	0	2	....	....	....	....	....
1997-98	Ottawa Senators	60	2	2	4	31	9	0	0	0	2
1998-99	Ottawa Senators	3	0	2	2	0	....	....	....	....	....
	New York Rangers	18	0	0	0	8	....	....	....	....	....
	Phoenix Coyotes	11	0	1	1	10	6	0	1	1	4
99-2000	Phoenix Coyotes	66	2	8	10	36	5	0	0	0	0
2000-01	Phoenix Coyotes	53	2	2	4	63	....	....	....	....	....
	Tampa Bay Lightning	16	0	2	2	8	....	....	....	....	....
2001-02	Tampa Bay Lightning	77	1	7	8	24	....	....	....	....	....
2002-03	Tampa Bay Lightning	70	1	4	5	43	7	0	2	2	2
	NHL Totals	**509**	**12**	**40**	**52**	**316**	**27**	**0**	**3**	**3**	**8**

Traded to **NY Rangers** by **Ottawa** for Bill Berg and NY Rangers' 2nd round choice (later traded to Anaheim – Anaheim selected Jordan Leopold) in 1999 Entry Draft, November 27, 1998. Traded to **Phoenix** by **NY Rangers** for Jason Doig and Phoenix's 6th round choice (Jay Dardis) in 1999 Entry Draft, March 23, 1999. Traded to **Tampa Bay** by **Phoenix** with Nikolai Khabibulin for Mike Johnson, Paul Mara, Ruslan Zainullin and NY Islanders' 2nd round choice (previously acquired, Phoenix selected Matthew Spiller) in 2001 Entry Draft, March 5, 2001.

NEDOMANSKY, Vaclav

Right wing. Shoots left. 6'2", 205 lbs. Born, Hodonin, Czech., March 14, 1944.

Season	Club	GP	G	A	Pts	PIM	GP	G	A	Pts	PIM
1977-78	Detroit Red Wings	63	11	17	28	2	7	3	5	8	0
1978-79	Detroit Red Wings	80	38	35	73	19	....	....	....	....	....
1979-80	Detroit Red Wings	79	35	39	74	13	....	....	....	....	....
1980-81	Detroit Red Wings	74	12	20	32	30	....	....	....	....	....
1981-82	Detroit Red Wings	68	12	28	40	22	....	....	....	....	....
1982-83	New York Rangers	1	1	0	1	0	....	....	....	....	....
	St. Louis Blues	22	2	9	11	2	....	....	....	....	....
	New York Rangers	34	11	8	19	0	....	....	....	....	....
	NHL Totals	**421**	**122**	**156**	**278**	**88**	**7**	**3**	**5**	**8**	**0**

Traded to **Detroit** by **Birmingham** (WHA) with Tim Sheehy for the loan of Steve Durbano and Dave Hanson and future considerations, November 18, 1977. Signed as a free agent by **NY Rangers** on September 30, 1982. Claimed on waivers by **St. Louis** from **NY Rangers**, October 6, 1982. Traded to **NY Rangers** by **St. Louis** with Glen Hanlon for Andre Dore, January 4, 1983.

NEDOROST, Andrej

Left wing. Shoots left. 6', 192 lbs. Born, Trencin, Czech., April 30, 1980.
(Columbus' 10th choice, 286th overall, in 2000 Entry Draft).

Season	Club	GP	G	A	Pts	PIM	GP	G	A	Pts	PIM
2001-02	Columbus Blue Jackets	7	0	2	2	2	....	....	....	....	....
2002-03	Columbus Blue Jackets	12	0	1	1	4	....	....	....	....	....
	NHL Totals	**19**	**0**	**3**	**3**	**6**	....	....	....	....	....

NEDOROST, Vaclav

Center. Shoots left. 6'1", 190 lbs. Born, Budejovice, Czech., March 16, 1982.
(Colorado's 1st choice, 14th overall, in 2000 Entry Draft).

Season	Club	GP	G	A	Pts	PIM	GP	G	A	Pts	PIM
2001-02	Colorado Avalanche	25	2	2	4	2	....	....	....	....	....
2002-03	Colorado Avalanche	42	4	5	9	20	....	....	....	....	....
	NHL Totals	**67**	**6**	**7**	**13**	**22**	....	....	....	....	....

Traded to **Florida** by **Colorado** with Eric Messier for Peter Worrell and Florida's 2nd round choice in 2004 Entry Draft, July 19, 2003.

NEDVED, Petr

Center. Shoots left. 6'3", 195 lbs. Born, Liberec, Czech., December 9, 1971.
(Vancouver's 1st choice, 2nd overall, in 1990 Entry Draft).

Season	Club	GP	G	A	Pts	PIM	GP	G	A	Pts	PIM
1990-91	Vancouver Canucks	61	10	6	16	20	6	0	1	1	0
1991-92	Vancouver Canucks	77	15	22	37	36	10	1	4	5	16
1992-93	Vancouver Canucks	84	38	33	71	96	12	2	3	5	2
1993-94	St. Louis Blues	19	6	14	20	8	4	0	1	1	4
1994-95	New York Rangers	46	11	12	23	26	10	3	2	5	6
1995-96	Pittsburgh Penguins	80	45	54	99	68	18	10	10	20	16
1996-97	Pittsburgh Penguins	74	33	38	71	66	5	1	2	3	12
1998-99	New York Rangers	56	20	27	47	50	....	....	....	....	....
99-2000	New York Rangers	76	24	44	68	40	....	....	....	....	....
2000-01	New York Rangers	79	32	46	78	54	....	....	....	....	....
2001-02	New York Rangers	78	21	25	46	36	....	....	....	....	....
2002-03	New York Rangers	78	27	31	58	64	....	....	....	....	....
	NHL Totals	**808**	**282**	**352**	**634**	**564**	**65**	**17**	**23**	**40**	**56**

Signed as a free agent by **St. Louis**, March 5, 1994. Traded to **NY Rangers** by **St. Louis** for Esa Tikkanen and Doug Lidster, July 24, 1994. Traded to **Pittsburgh** by **NY Rangers** with Sergei Zubov for Luc Robitaille and Ulf Samuelsson, August 31, 1995. Traded to **NY Rangers** by **Pittsburgh** with Chris Tamer and Sean Pronger for Alexei Kovalev and Harry York, November 25, 1998.

NEDVED, Zdenek

Right wing. Shoots left. 6', 180 lbs. Born, Lany, Czech., March 3, 1975.
(Toronto's 3rd choice, 123rd overall, in 1993 Entry Draft).

Season	Club	GP	G	A	Pts	PIM	GP	G	A	Pts	PIM
1994-95	Toronto Maple Leafs	1	0	0	0	2	....	....	....	....	....
1995-96	Toronto Maple Leafs	7	1	1	2	6	....	....	....	....	....
1996-97	Toronto Maple Leafs	23	3	5	8	6	....	....	....	....	....
	NHL Totals	**31**	**4**	**6**	**10**	**14**	....	....	....	....	....

NEEDHAM, Mike

Right wing. Shoots right. 5'10", 185 lbs. Born, Calgary, Alta., April 4, 1970.
(Pittsburgh's 7th choice, 126th overall, in 1989 Entry Draft).

Season	Club	Regular Season GP	G	A	Pts	PIM	Playoffs GP	G	A	Pts	PIM
1991-92 ◆	Pittsburgh Penguins	....	....	....	....	....	5	1	0	1	2
1992-93	Pittsburgh Penguins	56	8	5	13	14	9	1	0	1	2
1993-94	Pittsburgh Penguins	25	1	0	1	2	....	....	....	....	....
	Dallas Stars	5	0	0	0	0	....	....	....	....	....
	NHL Totals	**86**	**9**	**5**	**14**	**16**	**14**	**2**	**0**	**2**	**4**

Traded to **Dallas** by **Pittsburgh** for Jim McKenzie, March 21, 1994.

NEELY, Bob

Left wing. Shoots left. 6'1", 210 lbs. Born, Sarnia, Ont., November 9, 1953.
(Toronto's 2nd choice, 10th overall, in 1973 Amateur Draft).

Season	Club	Regular Season GP	G	A	Pts	PIM	Playoffs GP	G	A	Pts	PIM
1973-74	Toronto Maple Leafs	54	5	7	12	98	4	1	3	4	0
1974-75	Toronto Maple Leafs	57	5	16	21	61	3	0	0	0	2
1975-76	Toronto Maple Leafs	69	9	13	22	89	10	3	1	4	7
1976-77	Toronto Maple Leafs	70	17	16	33	16	9	1	3	4	6
1977-78	Toronto Maple Leafs	11	0	1	1	0	....	....	....	....	....
	Colorado Rockies	22	3	6	9	2	....	....	....	....	....
	NHL Totals	**283**	**39**	**59**	**98**	**266**	**26**	**5**	**7**	**12**	**15**

Traded to **Colorado** by **Toronto** for cash, January 9, 1978. Traded to **Toronto** by **Colorado** for cash, May 30, 1978.

NEELY, Cam

Right wing. Shoots right. 6'1", 218 lbs. Born, Comox, B.C., June 6, 1965.
(Vancouver's 1st choice, 9th overall, in 1983 Entry Draft).

Season	Club	Regular Season GP	G	A	Pts	PIM	Playoffs GP	G	A	Pts	PIM
1983-84	Vancouver Canucks	56	16	15	31	57	4	2	0	2	2
1984-85	Vancouver Canucks	72	21	18	39	137	....	....	....	....	....
1985-86	Vancouver Canucks	73	14	20	34	126	3	0	0	0	6
1986-87	Boston Bruins	75	36	36	72	143	4	5	1	6	8
1987-88	Boston Bruins	69	42	27	69	175	23	9	8	17	51
1988-89	Boston Bruins	74	37	38	75	190	10	7	2	9	8
1989-90	Boston Bruins	76	55	37	92	117	21	12	16	28	51
1990-91	Boston Bruins	69	51	40	91	98	19	16	4	20	36
1991-92	Boston Bruins	9	9	3	12	16	....	....	....	....	....
1992-93	Boston Bruins	13	11	7	18	25	4	4	1	5	4
1993-94	Boston Bruins	49	50	24	74	54	....	....	....	....	....
1994-95	Boston Bruins	42	27	14	41	72	5	2	0	2	2
1995-96	Boston Bruins	49	26	20	46	31	....	....	....	....	....
	NHL Totals	**726**	**395**	**299**	**694**	**1241**	**93**	**57**	**32**	**89**	**168**

NHL Second All-Star Team (1988, 1990, 1991, 1994) • Bill Masterton Trophy (1994)

Played in NHL All-Star Game (1988, 1989, 1990, 1991, 1996)

Traded to **Boston** by **Vancouver** with Vancouver's 1st round choice (Glen Wesley) in 1987 Entry Draft for Barry Pederson, June 6, 1986. • Missed majority of 1991-92 season recovering from thigh (October 15, 1991) and knee (January, 1992) injuries. • Missed majority of 1992-93 season recovering from knee surgery, September 17, 1992.

NEIL, Chris

Right wing. Shoots right. 6', 213 lbs. Born, Markdale, Ont., June 18, 1979.
(Ottawa's 7th choice, 161st overall, in 1998 Entry Draft).

Season	Club	Regular Season GP	G	A	Pts	PIM	Playoffs GP	G	A	Pts	PIM
2001-02	Ottawa Senators	72	10	7	17	231	12	0	0	0	12
2002-03	Ottawa Senators	68	6	4	10	147	15	1	0	1	24
	NHL Totals	**140**	**16**	**11**	**27**	**378**	**27**	**1**	**0**	**1**	**36**

NEILSON, Jim

Defense. Shoots left. 6'2", 205 lbs. Born, Big River, Sask., November 28, 1940.

Season	Club	Regular Season GP	G	A	Pts	PIM	Playoffs GP	G	A	Pts	PIM
1962-63	New York Rangers	69	5	11	16	38	....	....	....	....	....
1963-64	New York Rangers	69	5	24	29	93	....	....	....	....	....
1964-65	New York Rangers	62	0	13	13	58	....	....	....	....	....
1965-66	New York Rangers	65	4	19	23	84	....	....	....	....	....
1966-67	New York Rangers	61	4	11	15	65	4	1	0	1	0
1967-68	New York Rangers	67	6	29	35	60	6	0	2	2	4
1968-69	New York Rangers	76	10	34	44	95	4	0	3	3	5
1969-70	New York Rangers	62	3	20	23	75	6	0	1	1	8
1970-71	New York Rangers	77	8	24	32	69	13	0	3	3	30
1971-72	New York Rangers	78	7	30	37	56	10	0	3	3	8
1972-73	New York Rangers	52	4	16	20	35	10	0	4	4	2
1973-74	New York Rangers	72	4	7	11	38	12	0	1	1	4
1974-75	California Golden Seals	72	3	17	20	56	....	....	....	....	....
1975-76	California Golden Seals	26	1	6	7	20	....	....	....	....	....
1976-77	Cleveland Barons	47	3	17	20	42	....	....	....	....	....
1977-78	Cleveland Barons	68	2	21	23	20	....	....	....	....	....
	NHL Totals	**1023**	**69**	**299**	**368**	**904**	**65**	**1**	**17**	**18**	**61**

NHL Second All-Star Team (1968)

Played in NHL All-Star Game (1967, 1971)

Claimed by **California** from **NY Rangers** in Intra-League Draft, June 10, 1974. Transferred to **Cleveland** after **California** franchise relocated, August 26, 1976. Placed on **Minnesota** Reserve List after **Cleveland-Minnesota** Dispersal Draft, June 15, 1978.

NELSON, Gordie

Defense. Shoots left. 5'8", 180 lbs. Born, Kinistino, Sask., May 10, 1947.

Season	Club	Regular Season GP	G	A	Pts	PIM	Playoffs GP	G	A	Pts	PIM
1969-70	Toronto Maple Leafs	3	0	0	0	11	....	....	....	....	....
	NHL Totals	**3**	**0**	**0**	**0**	**11**	....	....	....	....	....

Signed as a free agent by **Toronto**, December 10, 1969.

NELSON, Jeff

Center. Shoots left. 5'11", 190 lbs. Born, Prince Albert, Sask., December 18, 1972.
(Washington's 4th choice, 36th overall, in 1991 Entry Draft).

Season	Club	Regular Season GP	G	A	Pts	PIM	Playoffs GP	G	A	Pts	PIM
1994-95	Washington Capitals	10	1	0	1	2	....	....	....	....	....
1995-96	Washington Capitals	33	0	7	7	16	3	0	0	0	4
1998-99	Nashville Predators	9	2	1	3	2	....	....	....	....	....
	NHL Totals	**52**	**3**	**8**	**11**	**20**	**3**	**0**	**0**	**0**	**4**

• Brother of Todd

Signed as a free agent by **Nashville**, August 19, 1998. Traded to **Washington** by **Nashville** for cash, June 21, 1999. Signed as a free agent by **San Jose**, September 5, 2002.

NELSON, Todd

Defense. Shoots left. 6', 201 lbs. Born, Prince Albert, Sask., May 11, 1969.
(Pittsburgh's 4th choice, 79th overall, in 1989 Entry Draft).

Season	Club	Regular Season GP	G	A	Pts	PIM	Playoffs GP	G	A	Pts	PIM
1991-92	Pittsburgh Penguins	1	0	0	0	0	....	....	....	....	....
1993-94	Washington Capitals	2	1	0	1	2	4	0	0	0	0
	NHL Totals	**3**	**1**	**0**	**1**	**2**	**4**	**0**	**0**	**0**	**0**

• Brother of Jeff

Signed as a free agent by **Washington**, August 15, 1993.

NEMCHINOV, Sergei

Left wing. Shoots left. 6'1", 205 lbs. Born, Moscow, USSR, January 14, 1964.
(NY Rangers' 14th choice, 244th overall, in 1990 Entry Draft).

Season	Club	Regular Season GP	G	A	Pts	PIM	Playoffs GP	G	A	Pts	PIM
1991-92	New York Rangers	73	30	28	58	15	13	1	4	5	8
1992-93	New York Rangers	81	23	31	54	34	....	....	....	....	....
1993-94 ◆	New York Rangers	76	22	27	49	36	23	2	5	7	6
1994-95	New York Rangers	47	7	6	13	16	10	4	5	9	2
1995-96	New York Rangers	78	17	15	32	38	6	0	1	1	2
1996-97	New York Rangers	63	6	13	19	12	....	....	....	....	....
	Vancouver Canucks	6	2	3	5	4	....	....	....	....	....
1997-98	New York Islanders	74	10	19	29	24	....	....	....	....	....
1998-99	New York Islanders	67	8	8	16	22	....	....	....	....	....
	New Jersey Devils	10	4	0	4	6	4	0	0	0	0
99-2000 ◆	New Jersey Devils	53	10	16	26	18	21	3	2	5	2
2000-01	New Jersey Devils	65	8	22	30	16	25	1	3	4	4
2001-02	New Jersey Devils	68	5	5	10	10	3	0	0	0	0
	NHL Totals	**761**	**152**	**193**	**345**	**251**	**105**	**11**	**20**	**31**	**24**

Traded to **Vancouver** by **NY Rangers** with Brian Noonan for Esa Tikkanen and Russ Courtnall, March 8, 1997. Signed as a free agent by **NY Islanders**, July 10, 1997. Traded to **New Jersey** by **NY Islanders** for New Jersey's 4th round choice (later traded to Los Angeles – Los Angeles selected Daniel Johansson) in 1999 Entry Draft, March 22, 1999.

NEMECEK, Jan

Defense. Shoots Left. 6'1", 220 lbs. Born, Pisek, Czech., February 14, 1976.
(Los Angeles' 7th choice, 215th overall, in 1994 Entry Draft).

Season	Club	Regular Season GP	G	A	Pts	PIM	Playoffs GP	G	A	Pts	PIM
1998-99	Los Angeles Kings	6	1	0	1	4	....	....	....	....	....
99-2000	Los Angeles Kings	1	0	0	0	0	....	....	....	....	....
	NHL Totals	**7**	**1**	**0**	**1**	**4**	....	....	....	....	....

NEMETH, Steve

Center. Shoots left. 5'8", 170 lbs. Born, Calgary, Alta., February 11, 1967.
(NY Rangers' 10th choice, 196th overall, in 1985 Entry Draft).

Season	Club	Regular Season GP	G	A	Pts	PIM	Playoffs GP	G	A	Pts	PIM
1987-88	New York Rangers	12	2	0	2	2	....	....	....	....	....
	NHL Totals	**12**	**2**	**0**	**2**	**2**	....	....	....	....	....

NEMIROVSKY, David

Right wing. Shoots right. 6'2", 205 lbs. Born, Toronto, Ont., August 1, 1976.
(Florida's 5th choice, 84th overall, in 1994 Entry Draft).

Season	Club	Regular Season GP	G	A	Pts	PIM	Playoffs GP	G	A	Pts	PIM
1995-96	Florida Panthers	9	0	2	2	2	....	....	....	....	....
1996-97	Florida Panthers	39	7	7	14	32	3	1	0	1	0
1997-98	Florida Panthers	41	9	12	21	8	....	....	....	....	....
1998-99	Florida Panthers	2	0	1	1	0	....	....	....	....	....
	NHL Totals	**91**	**16**	**22**	**38**	**42**	**3**	**1**	**0**	**1**	**0**

Traded to **Toronto** by **Florida** for Jeff Ware, February 17, 1999.

NESTERENKO, Eric

Right wing. Shoots right. 6'2", 197 lbs. Born, Flin Flon, Man., October 31, 1933.

Season	Club	Regular Season GP	G	A	Pts	PIM	Playoffs GP	G	A	Pts	PIM
1951-52	Toronto Maple Leafs	1	0	0	0	0	....	....	....	....	....
1952-53	Toronto Maple Leafs	35	10	6	16	27	....	....	....	....	....
1953-54	Toronto Maple Leafs	68	14	9	23	70	5	0	1	1	9
1954-55	Toronto Maple Leafs	62	15	15	30	99	4	0	1	1	6
1955-56	Toronto Maple Leafs	40	4	6	10	65	....	....	....	....	....
1956-57	Chicago Black Hawks	24	8	15	23	32	....	....	....	....	....
1957-58	Chicago Black Hawks	70	20	18	38	104	....	....	....	....	....
1958-59	Chicago Black Hawks	70	16	18	34	81	6	2	2	4	8
1959-60	Chicago Black Hawks	61	13	23	36	71	4	0	0	0	2
1960-61 ◆	Chicago Black Hawks	68	19	19	38	125	11	2	3	5	6
1961-62	Chicago Black Hawks	68	15	14	29	97	12	0	5	5	22
1962-63	Chicago Black Hawks	67	12	15	27	103	6	2	3	5	8
1963-64	Chicago Black Hawks	70	7	19	26	93	7	2	1	3	8
1964-65	Chicago Black Hawks	56	14	16	30	63	14	2	2	4	16
1965-66	Chicago Black Hawks	67	15	25	40	58	6	1	0	1	4
1966-67	Chicago Black Hawks	68	14	23	37	38	6	1	2	3	2
1967-68	Chicago Black Hawks	71	11	25	36	37	10	0	1	1	2

Season	Club	GP	G	A	Pts	PIM	GP	G	A	Pts	PIM
		REGULAR SEASON					PLAYOFFS				
1968-69	Chicago Black Hawks	72	15	17	32	29	....	....	....	....	....
1969-70	Chicago Black Hawks	67	16	18	34	26	7	1	2	3	4
1970-71	Chicago Black Hawks	76	8	15	23	28	18	0	1	1	19
1971-72	Chicago Black Hawks	38	4	8	12	27	8	0	0	0	11
	NHL Totals	**1219**	**250**	**324**	**574**	**1273**	**124**	**13**	**24**	**37**	**127**

Played in NHL All-Star Game (1961, 1965)

Signed as a free agent by **Toronto**, January 8, 1953. Traded to **Chicago** by **Toronto** with Harry Lumley for $40,000, May 21, 1956. • Played weekend games only during 1956-57 season while attending University of Toronto.

NETHERY, Lance

Center. Shoots left. 6'1", 185 lbs. Born, Toronto, Ont., June 28, 1957.
(NY Rangers' 9th choice, 131st overall, in 1977 Amateur Draft).

Season	Club	GP	G	A	Pts	PIM	GP	G	A	Pts	PIM
1980-81	New York Rangers	33	11	12	23	12	14	5	3	8	9
1981-82	New York Rangers	5	0	0	0	0	....	....	....	....	....
	Edmonton Oilers	3	0	2	2	2	....	....	....	....	....
	NHL Totals	**41**	**11**	**14**	**25**	**14**	**14**	**5**	**3**	**8**	**9**

Traded to **Edmonton** by **NY Rangers** for Eddie Mio, December 11, 1981.

NEUFELD, Ray

Right wing. Shoots right. 6'3", 210 lbs. Born, St. Boniface, Man., April 15, 1959.
(Hartford's 4th choice, 81st overall, in 1979 Entry Draft).

Season	Club	GP	G	A	Pts	PIM	GP	G	A	Pts	PIM
1979-80	Hartford Whalers	8	1	0	1	0	2	1	0	1	0
1980-81	Hartford Whalers	52	5	10	15	44	....	....	....	....	....
1981-82	Hartford Whalers	19	4	3	7	4	....	....	....	....	....
1982-83	Hartford Whalers	80	26	31	57	86	....	....	....	....	....
1983-84	Hartford Whalers	80	27	42	69	97	....	....	....	....	....
1984-85	Hartford Whalers	76	27	35	62	129	....	....	....	....	....
1985-86	Hartford Whalers	16	5	10	15	40	....	....	....	....	....
	Winnipeg Jets	60	20	28	48	62	3	2	0	2	10
1986-87	Winnipeg Jets	80	18	18	36	105	8	1	1	2	30
1987-88	Winnipeg Jets	78	18	18	36	169	5	2	2	4	6
1988-89	Winnipeg Jets	31	5	2	7	52	....	....	....	....	....
	Boston Bruins	14	1	3	4	28	10	2	3	5	9
1989-90	Boston Bruins	1	0	0	0	0	....	....	....	....	....
	NHL Totals	**595**	**157**	**200**	**357**	**816**	**28**	**8**	**6**	**14**	**55**

Traded to **Winnipeg** by **Hartford** for Dave Babych, November 21, 1985. Traded to **Boston** by **Winnipeg** for Moe Lemay, December 30, 1988.

NEVILLE, Mike

Center. Shoots right. 5'9", 168 lbs. Born, Toronto, Ont., October 11, 1904.

Season	Club	GP	G	A	Pts	PIM	GP	G	A	Pts	PIM
1924-25	Toronto St. Pats	13	1	2	3	4	2	0	0	0	0
1925-26	Toronto St. Pats	33	3	3	6	8	....	....	....	....	....
1930-31	New York Americans	19	1	0	1	2	....	....	....	....	....
	NHL Totals	**65**	**5**	**5**	**10**	**14**	**2**	**0**	**0**	**0**	**0**

Signed as a free agent by **Toronto**, January 14, 1925. Claimed on waivers by **Hamilton** (Can-Pro) from **Toronto**, October 16, 1926. Traded to **Mtl. Maroons** (Windsor-Can-Pro) by **Buffalo** (Can-Pro) for Rolly Huard, November 18, 1928. Traded to **NY Americans** by **Mtl. Maroons** (Windsor-IHL) with Frank Carson, Red Dutton and Hap Emms for $35,000, May 14, 1930. Traded to **London** (IHL) by **NY Americans** for cash, January 28, 1931.

NEVIN, Bob

Right wing. Shoots right. 6', 185 lbs. Born, South Porcupine, Ont., March 18, 1938.

Season	Club	GP	G	A	Pts	PIM	GP	G	A	Pts	PIM
1957-58	Toronto Maple Leafs	4	0	0	0	0	....	....	....	....	....
1958-59	Toronto Maple Leafs	2	0	0	0	2	....	....	....	....	....
1960-61	Toronto Maple Leafs	68	21	37	58	13	5	1	0	1	2
1961-62 ◆	Toronto Maple Leafs	69	15	30	45	10	12	2	4	6	6
1962-63 ◆	Toronto Maple Leafs	58	12	21	33	4	10	3	0	3	2
1963-64	Toronto Maple Leafs	49	7	12	19	26	....	....	....	....	....
	New York Rangers	14	5	4	9	9	....	....	....	....	....
1964-65	New York Rangers	64	16	14	30	28	....	....	....	....	....
1965-66	New York Rangers	69	29	33	62	10	....	....	....	....	....
1966-67	New York Rangers	67	20	24	44	6	4	0	3	3	2
1967-68	New York Rangers	74	28	30	58	20	6	0	3	3	4
1968-69	New York Rangers	71	31	25	56	14	4	0	2	2	0
1969-70	New York Rangers	68	18	19	37	8	6	1	1	2	2
1970-71	New York Rangers	78	21	25	46	10	13	5	3	8	0
1971-72	Minnesota North Stars	72	15	19	34	6	7	1	1	2	0
1972-73	Minnesota North Stars	66	5	13	18	0	....	....	....	....	....
1973-74	Los Angeles Kings	78	20	30	50	12	5	1	0	1	2
1974-75	Los Angeles Kings	80	31	41	72	19	3	0	0	0	0
1975-76	Los Angeles Kings	77	13	42	55	14	9	2	1	3	4
	NHL Totals	**1128**	**307**	**419**	**726**	**211**	**84**	**16**	**18**	**34**	**24**

Played in NHL All-Star Game (1962, 1963, 1967, 1969)

Traded to **NY Rangers** by **Toronto** with Rod Seiling, Dick Duff, Arnie Brown and Bill Collins for Andy Bathgate and Don McKenney, February 22, 1964. Traded to **Minnesota** by **NY Rangers** for future considerations (Bobby Rousseau, June 8, 1971), May 25, 1971. Claimed by **Los Angeles** (Springfield-AHL) from **Minnesota** in Reverse Draft, June 13, 1973.

NEWBERRY, John

Center. Shoots left. 6', 190 lbs. Born, Port Alberni, B.C., April 8, 1962.
(Montreal's 4th choice, 45th overall, in 1980 Entry Draft).

Season	Club	GP	G	A	Pts	PIM	GP	G	A	Pts	PIM
1982-83	Montreal Canadiens	....	....	....	....	....	2	0	0	0	0
1983-84	Montreal Canadiens	3	0	0	0	0	....	....	....	....	....
1984-85	Montreal Canadiens	16	0	4	4	6	....	....	....	....	....
1985-86	Hartford Whalers	3	0	0	0	0	....	....	....	....	....
	NHL Totals	**22**	**0**	**4**	**4**	**6**	**2**	**0**	**0**	**0**	**0**

Signed as a free agent by **Hartford**, September 19, 1985.

NEWELL, Rick

Defense. Shoots left. 5'11", 180 lbs. Born, Winnipeg, Man., February 18, 1948.

Season	Club	GP	G	A	Pts	PIM	GP	G	A	Pts	PIM
1972-73	Detroit Red Wings	3	0	0	0	0	....	....	....	....	....
1973-74	Detroit Red Wings	3	0	0	0	0	....	....	....	....	....
	NHL Totals	**6**	**0**	**0**	**0**	**0**	....	....	....	....	....

Traded to **Detroit** by **NY Rangers** with Gary Doak for Joe Zanussi and Detroit's 1st round choice (Albert Blanchard) in 1972 Amateur Draft, May 24, 1972.

NEWMAN, Dan

Left wing. Shoots left. 6'1", 195 lbs. Born, Windsor, Ont., January 26, 1952.

Season	Club	GP	G	A	Pts	PIM	GP	G	A	Pts	PIM
1976-77	New York Rangers	41	9	8	17	37	....	....	....	....	....
1977-78	New York Rangers	59	5	13	18	22	3	0	0	0	4
1978-79	Montreal Canadiens	16	0	2	2	4	....	....	....	....	....
1979-80	Edmonton Oilers	10	3	1	4	0	....	....	....	....	....
	NHL Totals	**126**	**17**	**24**	**41**	**63**	**3**	**0**	**0**	**0**	**4**

NHL rights transferred to **NY Rangers** after NHL club signed affiliation agreement with **Port Huron** (IHL), June, 1974. Claimed by **Montreal** from **NY Rangers** in Waiver Draft, October 9, 1978. Traded to **Edmonton** by **Montreal** with Dave Lumley for Edmonton's 2nd round choice (Ric Nattress) in 1980 Entry Draft, June 13, 1979. Traded to **Boston** by **Edmonton** for Bobby Schmautz, December 10, 1979.

NEWMAN, John

Center/Left wing. Shoots left. 5'8", 155 lbs. Born, Ottawa, Ont., April 24, 1910.

Season	Club	GP	G	A	Pts	PIM	GP	G	A	Pts	PIM
1930-31	Detroit Falcons	8	1	1	2	0	....	....	....	....	....
	NHL Totals	**8**	**1**	**1**	**2**	**0**	....	....	....	....	....

Signed as a free agent by **Detroit**, September 12, 1929. Traded to **Buffalo** (IAHL) by **Detroit** with Bob Davis and Tip O'Neill for Gamey Lederman, September 24, 1933.

NICHOL, Scott

Center. Shoots right. 5'8", 173 lbs. Born, Edmonton, Alta., December 31, 1974.
(Buffalo's 9th choice, 272nd overall, in 1993 Entry Draft).

Season	Club	GP	G	A	Pts	PIM	GP	G	A	Pts	PIM
1995-96	Buffalo Sabres	2	0	0	0	10	....	....	....	....	....
1997-98	Buffalo Sabres	3	0	0	0	4	....	....	....	....	....
2001-02	Calgary Flames	60	8	9	17	107	....	....	....	....	....
2002-03	Calgary Flames	68	5	5	10	149	....	....	....	....	....
	NHL Totals	**133**	**13**	**14**	**27**	**270**	....	....	....	....	....

Signed as a free agent by **Calgary**, July 1, 2001. Signed as a free agent by **Chicago**, July 1, 2003.

NICHOLLS, Bernie

Center. Shoots right. 6', 185 lbs. Born, Haliburton, Ont., June 24, 1961.
(Los Angeles' 6th choice, 73rd overall, in 1980 Entry Draft).

Season	Club	GP	G	A	Pts	PIM	GP	G	A	Pts	PIM
1981-82	Los Angeles Kings	22	14	18	32	27	10	4	0	4	23
1982-83	Los Angeles Kings	71	28	22	50	124	....	....	....	....	....
1983-84	Los Angeles Kings	78	41	54	95	83	....	....	....	....	....
1984-85	Los Angeles Kings	80	46	54	100	76	3	1	1	2	9
1985-86	Los Angeles Kings	80	36	61	97	78	....	....	....	....	....
1986-87	Los Angeles Kings	80	33	48	81	101	5	2	5	7	6
1987-88	Los Angeles Kings	65	32	46	78	114	5	2	6	8	11
1988-89	Los Angeles Kings	79	70	80	150	96	11	7	9	16	12
1989-90	Los Angeles Kings	47	27	48	75	66	....	....	....	....	....
	New York Rangers	32	12	25	37	20	10	7	5	12	16
1990-91	New York Rangers	71	25	48	73	96	5	4	3	7	8
1991-92	New York Rangers	1	0	0	0	0	....	....	....	....	....
	Edmonton Oilers	49	20	29	49	60	16	8	11	19	25
1992-93	Edmonton Oilers	46	8	32	40	40	....	....	....	....	....
	New Jersey Devils	23	5	15	20	40	5	0	0	0	6
1993-94	New Jersey Devils	61	19	27	46	86	16	4	9	13	28
1994-95	Chicago Blackhawks	48	22	29	51	32	16	1	11	12	8
1995-96	Chicago Blackhawks	59	19	41	60	60	10	2	7	9	4
1996-97	San Jose Sharks	65	12	33	45	63	....	....	....	....	....
1997-98	San Jose Sharks	60	6	22	28	26	6	0	5	5	8
1998-99	San Jose Sharks	10	0	2	2	4	....	....	....	....	....
	NHL Totals	**1127**	**475**	**734**	**1209**	**1292**	**118**	**42**	**72**	**114**	**164**

Played in NHL All-Star Game (1984, 1989, 1990)

Traded to **NY Rangers** by **Los Angeles** for Tomas Sandstrom and Tony Granato, January 20, 1990. Traded to **Edmonton** by **NY Rangers** with Steven Rice and Louie DeBrusk for Mark Messier and future considerations (Jeff Beukeboom for David Shaw, November 12, 1991), October 4, 1991. Traded to **New Jersey** by **Edmonton** for Zdeno Ciger and Kevin Todd, January 13, 1993. Signed as a free agent by **Chicago**, July 14, 1994. Signed as a free agent by **San Jose**, August 5, 1996.

NICHOLSON, Al

Left wing. Shoots left. 6'1", 180 lbs. Born, Estevan, Sask., April 26, 1936.

Season	Club	GP	G	A	Pts	PIM	GP	G	A	Pts	PIM
1955-56	Boston Bruins	14	0	0	0	4	....	....	....	....	....
1956-57	Boston Bruins	5	0	1	1	0	....	....	....	....	....
	NHL Totals	**19**	**0**	**1**	**1**	**4**	....	....	....	....	....

Signed as a free agent by **Boston**, August 23, 1955. Traded to **Chicago** (Calgary-WHL) by **Boston** (San Francisco-WHL) for Cec Hoekstra, January 22, 1963. • Transaction voided when Nicholson refused to report to club, January, 1963. Claimed by **Detroit** (Pittsburgh-AHL) from **Boston** in Reverse Draft, June 12, 1966. Traded to **San Diego** (WHL) by **Detroit** (Pittsburgh-AHL) with Len Haley and Ed Ehrenverth for $20,000, June 20, 1966.

NICHOLSON, Ed

Defense. Shoots left. 5'8", 180 lbs. Born, Portsmouth, Ont., September 9, 1923.

Season	Club	Regular Season GP	G	A	Pts	PIM	Playoffs GP	G	A	Pts	PIM
1947-48	Detroit Red Wings	1	0	0	0	0	....	....	....	....	....
	NHL Totals	**1**	**0**	**0**	**0**	**0**	....	....	....	....	....

Signed as a free agent by **Detroit**, March 20, 1948. Traded to **St. Louis** (AHL) by **Detroit** with Fern Gauthier, Cliff Simpson and future considerations for Steve Black and Bill Brennan, August 29, 1949.

NICHOLSON, Hickey

Left wing. Shoots left. 5'10", 170 lbs. Born, Charlottetown, P.E.I., September 9, 1911.

Season	Club	Regular Season GP	G	A	Pts	PIM	Playoffs GP	G	A	Pts	PIM
1937-38	Chicago Black Hawks	2	1	0	1	0	....	....	....	....	....
	NHL Totals	**2**	**1**	**0**	**1**	**0**	....	....	....	....	....

NICHOLSON, Neil

Defense. Shoots right. 5'11", 180 lbs. Born, Saint John, N.B., September 12, 1949.
(Oakland's 6th choice, 65th overall, in 1969 Amateur Draft).

Season	Club	Regular Season GP	G	A	Pts	PIM	Playoffs GP	G	A	Pts	PIM
1969-70	Oakland Seals	....	....	....	....	....	2	0	0	0	0
1972-73	New York Islanders	30	3	1	4	23	....	....	....	....	....
1973-74	New York Islanders	8	0	0	0	0	....	....	....	....	....
1977-78	New York Islanders	1	0	0	0	0	....	....	....	....	....
	NHL Totals	**39**	**3**	**1**	**4**	**23**	**2**	**0**	**0**	**0**	**0**

Claimed by **NY Islanders** from **California** (Salt Lake-CHL) in Inter-League Draft, June 6, 1972.

NICHOLSON, Paul

Left wing. Shoots left. 6', 190 lbs. Born, London, Ont., February 16, 1954.
(Washington's 4th choice, 55th overall, in 1974 Amateur Draft).

Season	Club	Regular Season GP	G	A	Pts	PIM	Playoffs GP	G	A	Pts	PIM
1974-75	Washington Capitals	39	4	5	9	7	....	....	....	....	....
1975-76	Washington Capitals	14	0	2	2	9	....	....	....	....	....
1976-77	Washington Capitals	9	0	1	1	2	....	....	....	....	....
	NHL Totals	**62**	**4**	**8**	**12**	**18**	....	....	....	....	....

NICKULAS, Eric

Right wing. Shoots right. 5'11", 200 lbs. Born, Hyannis, MA, March 25, 1975.
(Boston's 3rd choice, 99th overall, in 1994 Entry Draft).

Season	Club	Regular Season GP	G	A	Pts	PIM	Playoffs GP	G	A	Pts	PIM
1998-99	Boston Bruins	2	0	0	0	0	1	0	0	0	2
99-2000	Boston Bruins	20	5	6	11	12	....	....	....	....	....
2000-01	Boston Bruins	7	0	0	0	4	....	....	....	....	....
2002-03	St. Louis Blues	8	0	1	1	6	....	....	....	....	....
	NHL Totals	**37**	**5**	**7**	**12**	**22**	**1**	**0**	**0**	**0**	**2**

Signed as a free agent by **St. Louis**, July 16, 2002.

NICOLSON, Graeme

Defense. Shoots right. 6', 185 lbs. Born, North Bay, Ont., January 13, 1958.
(Boston's 2nd choice, 35th overall, in 1978 Amateur Draft).

Season	Club	Regular Season GP	G	A	Pts	PIM	Playoffs GP	G	A	Pts	PIM
1978-79	Boston Bruins	1	0	0	0	0	....	....	....	....	....
1981-82	Colorado Rockies	41	2	7	9	51	....	....	....	....	....
1982-83	New York Rangers	10	0	0	0	9	....	....	....	....	....
	NHL Totals	**52**	**2**	**7**	**9**	**60**	....	....	....	....	....

• Sat out entire 1980-81 season to become unrestricted free agent. Signed as a free agent by **Colorado**, September 2, 1981. Transferred to **New Jersey** after **Colorado** franchise relocated, June 30, 1982. Claimed by **NY Rangers** from **New Jersey** in Waiver Draft, October 4, 1982. Signed as a free agent by **Washington**, August 17, 1984.

NIECKAR, Barry

Left wing. Shoots left. 6'3", 205 lbs. Born, Rama, Sask., December 16, 1967.

Season	Club	Regular Season GP	G	A	Pts	PIM	Playoffs GP	G	A	Pts	PIM
1992-93	Hartford Whalers	2	0	0	0	2	....	....	....	....	....
1994-95	Calgary Flames	3	0	0	0	12	....	....	....	....	....
1996-97	Mighty Ducks of Anaheim	2	0	0	0	5	....	....	....	....	....
1997-98	Mighty Ducks of Anaheim	1	0	0	0	2	....	....	....	....	....
	NHL Totals	**8**	**0**	**0**	**0**	**21**	....	....	....	....	....

Signed as a free agent by **Hartford**, September 25, 1992. Signed as a free agent by **Calgary**, February 11, 1995. Signed as a free agent by **NY Islanders**, August 8, 1995. Signed as a free agent by **Anaheim**, October 2, 1996. Signed as a free agent by **Phoenix**, August 27, 1998.

NIEDERMAYER, Rob

Center. Shoots left. 6'2", 204 lbs. Born, Cassiar, B.C., December 28, 1974.
(Florida's 1st choice, 5th overall, in 1993 Entry Draft).

Season	Club	Regular Season GP	G	A	Pts	PIM	Playoffs GP	G	A	Pts	PIM
1993-94	Florida Panthers	65	9	17	26	51	....	....	....	....	....
1994-95	Florida Panthers	48	4	6	10	36	....	....	....	....	....
1995-96	Florida Panthers	82	26	35	61	107	22	5	3	8	12
1996-97	Florida Panthers	60	14	24	38	54	5	2	1	3	6
1997-98	Florida Panthers	33	8	7	15	41	....	....	....	....	....
1998-99	Florida Panthers	82	18	33	51	50	....	....	....	....	....
99-2000	Florida Panthers	81	10	23	33	46	4	1	0	1	6
2000-01	Florida Panthers	67	12	20	32	50	....	....	....	....	....
2001-02	Calgary Flames	57	6	14	20	49	....	....	....	....	....
2002-03	Calgary Flames	54	8	10	18	42	....	....	....	....	....
	Mighty Ducks of Anaheim	12	2	2	4	15	21	3	7	10	18
	NHL Totals	**641**	**117**	**191**	**308**	**541**	**52**	**11**	**11**	**22**	**42**

• Brother of Scott

• Missed majority of 1997-98 season recovering from thumb (November 26, 1997 vs. Boston) and head (March 19, 1998 vs. Buffalo) injuries. Traded to **Calgary** by **Florida** with Philadelphia's 2nd round choice (previously acquired, Calgary selected Andrei Medvedev) in 2001 Entry Draft for Valeri Bure and Jason Wiemer, June 23, 2001. Traded to **Anaheim** by **Calgary** for Mike Commodore and Jean-Francois Damphousse, March 11, 2003.

NIEDERMAYER, Scott

Defense. Shoots left. 6'1", 205 lbs. Born, Edmonton, Alta., August 31, 1973.
(New Jersey's 1st choice, 3rd overall, in 1991 Entry Draft).

Season	Club	Regular Season GP	G	A	Pts	PIM	Playoffs GP	G	A	Pts	PIM
1991-92	New Jersey Devils	4	0	1	1	2	....	....	....	....	....
1992-93	New Jersey Devils	80	11	29	40	47	5	0	3	3	2
1993-94	New Jersey Devils	81	10	36	46	42	20	2	2	4	8
1994-95 ♦	New Jersey Devils	48	4	15	19	18	20	4	7	11	10
1995-96	New Jersey Devils	79	8	25	33	46	....	....	....	....	....
1996-97	New Jersey Devils	81	5	30	35	64	10	2	4	6	6
1997-98	New Jersey Devils	81	14	43	57	27	6	0	2	2	4
1998-99	New Jersey Devils	72	11	35	46	26	7	1	3	4	18
99-2000 ♦	New Jersey Devils	71	7	31	38	48	22	5	2	7	10
2000-01	New Jersey Devils	57	6	29	35	22	21	0	6	6	14
2001-02	New Jersey Devils	76	11	22	33	30	6	0	2	2	6
2002-03 ♦	New Jersey Devils	81	11	28	39	62	24	2	*16	*18	16
	NHL Totals	**811**	**98**	**324**	**422**	**434**	**141**	**16**	**47**	**63**	**94**

• Brother of Rob • NHL All-Rookie Team (1993) • NHL Second All-Star Team (1998)
Played in NHL All-Star Game (1998, 2001)

NIEKAMP, Jim

Defense. Shoots right. 6'1", 185 lbs. Born, Detroit, MI, March 11, 1946.

Season	Club	Regular Season GP	G	A	Pts	PIM	Playoffs GP	G	A	Pts	PIM
1970-71	Detroit Red Wings	24	0	2	2	27	....	....	....	....	....
1971-72	Detroit Red Wings	5	0	0	0	10	....	....	....	....	....
	NHL Totals	**29**	**0**	**2**	**2**	**37**	....	....	....	....	....

Traded to **Vancouver** by **Detroit** for Ralph Stewart, March 6, 1972.

NIELSEN, Chris

Right wing. Shoots right. 6'2", 204 lbs. Born, Moshi, Tanzania, February 16, 1980.
(NY Islanders' 2nd choice, 36th overall, in 1998 Entry Draft).

Season	Club	Regular Season GP	G	A	Pts	PIM	Playoffs GP	G	A	Pts	PIM
2000-01	Columbus Blue Jackets	29	4	5	9	4	....	....	....	....	....
2001-02	Columbus Blue Jackets	23	2	3	5	4	....	....	....	....	....
	NHL Totals	**52**	**6**	**8**	**14**	**8**	....	....	....	....	....

Traded to **Columbus** by **NY Islanders** for Columbus' 4th (later traded to Anaheim – Anaheim selected Jonas Ronnqvist) and 9th (Dmitri Altarev) round choices in 2000 Entry Draft, May 11, 2000. Traded to **Atlanta** by **Columbus** with Petteri Nummelin for Tomi Kallio and Pauli Levokari, December 2, 2002. Traded to **Vancouver** by **Atlanta** with Chris Herperger for Jeff Farkas, January 20, 2003.

NIELSEN, Jeff

Right wing. Shoots left. 6', 200 lbs. Born, Grand Rapids, MN, September 20, 1971.
(NY Rangers' 4th choice, 69th overall, in 1990 Entry Draft).

Season	Club	Regular Season GP	G	A	Pts	PIM	Playoffs GP	G	A	Pts	PIM
1996-97	New York Rangers	2	0	0	0	2	....	....	....	....	....
1997-98	Mighty Ducks of Anaheim	32	4	5	9	16	....	....	....	....	....
1998-99	Mighty Ducks of Anaheim	80	5	4	9	34	4	0	0	0	2
99-2000	Mighty Ducks of Anaheim	79	8	10	18	14	....	....	....	....	....
2000-01	Minnesota Wild	59	3	8	11	4	....	....	....	....	....
	NHL Totals	**252**	**20**	**27**	**47**	**70**	**4**	**0**	**0**	**0**	**2**

• Brother of Kirk

Signed as a free agent by **Anaheim**, August 18, 1997. Selected by **Minnesota** from **Anaheim** in Expansion Draft, June 23, 2000.

NIELSEN, Kirk

Right wing. Shoots right. 6'1", 205 lbs. Born, Grand Rapids, MN, October 19, 1973.
(Philadelphia's 1st choice, 10th overall, in 1994 Supplemental Draft).

Season	Club	Regular Season GP	G	A	Pts	PIM	Playoffs GP	G	A	Pts	PIM
1997-98	Boston Bruins	6	0	0	0	0	....	....	....	....	....
	NHL Totals	**6**	**0**	**0**	**0**	**0**	....	....	....	....	....

• Brother of Jeff

Signed as a free agent by **Boston**, June 7, 1996.

NIEMI, Antti-Jussi

Defense. Shoots left. 6'1", 195 lbs. Born, Vantaa, Finland, September 22, 1977.
(Ottawa's 2nd choice, 81st overall, in 1996 Entry Draft).

Season	Club	Regular Season GP	G	A	Pts	PIM	Playoffs GP	G	A	Pts	PIM
2000-01	Mighty Ducks of Anaheim	28	1	1	2	22	....	....	....	....	....
2001-02	Mighty Ducks of Anaheim	1	0	0	0	0	....	....	....	....	....
	NHL Totals	**29**	**1**	**1**	**2**	**22**	....	....	....	....	....

Rights traded to **Anaheim** by **Ottawa** with Ted Donato for Patrick Lalime, June 18, 1999.

NIEMINEN, Ville

Left wing. Shoots left. 6', 200 lbs. Born, Tampere, Finland, April 6, 1977.
(Colorado's 4th choice, 78th overall, in 1997 Entry Draft).

Season	Club	Regular Season GP	G	A	Pts	PIM	Playoffs GP	G	A	Pts	PIM
99-2000	Colorado Avalanche	1	0	0	0	0	....	....	....	....	....
2000-01 ♦	Colorado Avalanche	50	14	8	22	38	23	4	6	10	20
2001-02	Colorado Avalanche	53	10	14	24	30	....	....	....	....	....
	Pittsburgh Penguins	13	1	2	3	8	....	....	....	....	....

Season	Club	GP	G	A	Pts	PIM	GP	G	A	Pts	PIM
		REGULAR SEASON					PLAYOFFS				
2002-03	Pittsburgh Penguins	75	9	12	21	93	....	....	....	....	....
	NHL Totals	**192**	**34**	**36**	**70**	**169**	**23**	**4**	**6**	**10**	**20**

Traded to **Pittsburgh** by **Colorado** with Rick Berry for Darius Kasparaitis, March 19, 2002. Signed as a free agent by **Chicago**, July 29, 2003.

NIENHUIS, Kraig

Left wing. Shoots left. 6'2", 205 lbs. Born, Sarnia, Ont., May 9, 1961.

Season	Club	GP	G	A	Pts	PIM	GP	G	A	Pts	PIM
1985-86	Boston Bruins	70	16	14	30	37	2	0	0	0	14
1986-87	Boston Bruins	16	4	2	6	2	....	....	....	....	....
1987-88	Boston Bruins	1	0	0	0	0	....	....	....	....	....
	NHL Totals	**87**	**20**	**16**	**36**	**39**	**2**	**0**	**0**	**0**	**14**

Signed as a free agent by **Boston**, May 28, 1985.

NIEUWENDYK, Joe

Center. Shoots left. 6'1", 205 lbs. Born, Oshawa, Ont., September 10, 1966.
(Calgary's 2nd choice, 27th overall, in 1985 Entry Draft).

Season	Club	GP	G	A	Pts	PIM	GP	G	A	Pts	PIM
1986-87	Calgary Flames	9	5	1	6	0	6	2	2	4	0
1987-88	Calgary Flames	75	51	41	92	23	8	3	4	7	2
1988-89 ♦	Calgary Flames	77	51	31	82	40	22	10	4	14	10
1989-90	Calgary Flames	79	45	50	95	40	6	4	6	10	4
1990-91	Calgary Flames	79	45	40	85	36	7	4	1	5	10
1991-92	Calgary Flames	69	22	34	56	55	....	....	....	....	....
1992-93	Calgary Flames	79	38	37	75	52	6	3	6	9	10
1993-94	Calgary Flames	64	36	39	75	51	6	2	2	4	0
1994-95	Calgary Flames	46	21	29	50	33	5	4	3	7	0
1995-96	Dallas Stars	52	14	18	32	41	....	....	....	....	....
1996-97	Dallas Stars	66	30	21	51	32	7	2	2	4	6
1997-98	Dallas Stars	73	39	30	69	30	1	1	0	1	0
1998-99 ♦	Dallas Stars	67	28	27	55	34	23	*11	10	21	19
99-2000	Dallas Stars	48	15	19	34	26	23	7	3	10	18
2000-01	Dallas Stars	69	29	23	52	30	7	4	0	4	4
2001-02	Dallas Stars	67	23	24	47	18	....	....	....	....	....
	New Jersey Devils	14	2	9	11	4	5	0	1	1	0
2002-03 ♦	New Jersey Devils	80	17	28	45	56	17	3	6	9	4
	NHL Totals	**1113**	**511**	**501**	**1012**	**601**	**149**	**60**	**50**	**110**	**87**

Calder Memorial Trophy (1988) • NHL All-Rookie Team (1988) • Dodge Ram Tough Award (1988) • King Clancy Memorial Trophy (1995) • Conn Smythe Trophy (1999)

Played in NHL All-Star Game (1988, 1989, 1990, 1994)

Traded to **Dallas** by **Calgary** for Corey Millen and Jarome Iginla, December 19, 1995. Traded to **New Jersey** by **Dallas** with Jamie Langenbrunner for Jason Arnott, Randy McKay and New Jersey's 1st round choice (later traded to Columbus – later traded to Buffalo – Buffalo selected Dan Paille) in 2002 Entry Draft, March 19, 2002.

NIGHBOR, Frank

HHOF

Center. Shoots right. 5'9", 160 lbs. Born, Pembroke, Ont., January 26, 1893.

Season	Club	GP	G	A	Pts	PIM	GP	G	A	Pts	PIM
1917-18	Ottawa Senators	10	11	8	19	6	....	....	....	....	....
1918-19	Ottawa Senators	18	19	9	28	27	2	0	2	2	3
1919-20 ♦	Ottawa Senators	23	26	*15	41	18	....	....	....	....	....
	Ottawa Senators (Cup)	....	....	....	....	....	*5*	*6*	*1*	*7*	*2*
1920-21 ♦	Ottawa Senators	24	19	10	29	10	2	1	3	4	2
	Ottawa Senators (Cup)	....	....	....	....	....	*5*	*0*	*1*	*1*	*0*
1921-22	Ottawa Senators	20	8	10	18	4	2	2	1	3	4
1922-23 ♦	Ottawa Senators	22	11	7	18	14	2	0	1	1	0
	Ottawa Senators (Cup)	....	....	....	....	....	*6*	*1*	*1*	*2*	*10*
1923-24	Ottawa Senators	20	11	6	17	16	2	0	1	1	0
1924-25	Ottawa Senators	26	5	5	10	18	....	....	....	....	....
1925-26	Ottawa Senators	35	12	*13	25	40	2	0	0	0	2
1926-27 ♦	Ottawa Senators	38	6	6	12	26	6	1	1	2	0
1927-28	Ottawa Senators	42	8	5	13	46	2	0	0	0	2
1928-29	Ottawa Senators	30	1	4	5	22	....	....	....	....	....
1929-30	Ottawa Senators	19	0	0	0	0	....	....	....	....	....
	Toronto Maple Leafs	22	2	0	2	2	....	....	....	....	....
	NHL Totals	**349**	**139**	**98**	**237**	**249**	**20**	**4**	**9**	**13**	**13**

Hart Trophy (1924) • Lady Byng Trophy (1925, 1926)

Signed as a free agent by **Ottawa**, December 22, 1917. • 1922-23 Stanley Cup totals includes series with Regina (WCHL) and Edmonton (PCHA). Traded to **Toronto** by **Ottawa** for Danny Cox and cash, January 31, 1930.

NIGRO, Frank

Center. Shoots right. 5'9", 182 lbs. Born, Richmond Hill, Ont., February 11, 1960.
(Toronto's 4th choice, 93rd overall, in 1979 Entry Draft).

Season	Club	GP	G	A	Pts	PIM	GP	G	A	Pts	PIM
1982-83	Toronto Maple Leafs	51	6	15	21	23	3	0	0	0	2
1983-84	Toronto Maple Leafs	17	2	3	5	16	....	....	....	....	....
	NHL Totals	**68**	**8**	**18**	**26**	**39**	**3**	**0**	**0**	**0**	**2**

NIINIMAA, Janne

Defense. Shoots left. 6'1", 220 lbs. Born, Raahe, Finland, May 22, 1975.
(Philadelphia's 1st choice, 36th overall, in 1993 Entry Draft).

Season	Club	GP	G	A	Pts	PIM	GP	G	A	Pts	PIM
1996-97	Philadelphia Flyers	77	4	40	44	58	19	1	12	13	16
1997-98	Philadelphia Flyers	66	3	31	34	56	....	....	....	....	....
	Edmonton Oilers	11	1	8	9	6	11	1	1	2	12
1998-99	Edmonton Oilers	81	4	24	28	88	4	0	0	0	2
99-2000	Edmonton Oilers	81	8	25	33	89	5	0	2	2	2
2000-01	Edmonton Oilers	82	12	34	46	90	6	0	2	2	6
2001-02	Edmonton Oilers	81	5	39	44	80	....	....	....	....	....
2002-03	Edmonton Oilers	63	4	24	28	66	....	....	....	....	....
	New York Islanders	13	1	5	6	14	5	0	1	1	12
	NHL Totals	**555**	**42**	**230**	**272**	**547**	**50**	**2**	**18**	**20**	**50**

NHL All-Rookie Team (1997)

Played in NHL All-Star Game (2001)

Traded to **Edmonton** by **Philadelphia** for Dan McGillis and Edmonton's 2nd round choice (Jason Beckett) in 1998 Entry Draft, March 24, 1998. Traded to **NY Islanders** by **Edmonton** with Washington's 2nd round choice (previously acquired, NY Islanders selected Evgeni Tunik) in 2003 Entry Draft for Brad Isbister and Raffi Torres, March 11, 2003.

NIKOLISHIN, Andrei

Center. Shoots left. 6', 213 lbs. Born, Vorkuta, USSR, March 25, 1973.
(Hartford's 2nd choice, 47th overall, in 1992 Entry Draft).

Season	Club	GP	G	A	Pts	PIM	GP	G	A	Pts	PIM
1994-95	Hartford Whalers	39	8	10	18	10	....	....	....	....	....
1995-96	Hartford Whalers	61	14	37	51	34	....	....	....	....	....
1996-97	Hartford Whalers	12	2	5	7	2	....	....	....	....	....
	Washington Capitals	59	7	14	21	30	....	....	....	....	....
1997-98	Washington Capitals	38	6	10	16	14	21	1	13	14	12
1998-99	Washington Capitals	73	8	27	35	28	....	....	....	....	....
99-2000	Washington Capitals	76	11	14	25	28	5	0	2	2	4
2000-01	Washington Capitals	81	13	25	38	34	6	0	0	0	2
2001-02	Washington Capitals	80	13	23	36	40	....	....	....	....	....
2002-03	Chicago Blackhawks	60	6	15	21	26	....	....	....	....	....
	NHL Totals	**579**	**88**	**180**	**268**	**246**	**32**	**1**	**15**	**16**	**18**

Traded to **Washington** by **Hartford** for Curtis Leschyshyn, November 9, 1996. Traded to **Chicago** by **Washington** with Chris Simon for Michael Nylander, Chicago's 3rd round choice (Stephen Werner) in 2003 Entry Draft and future considerations, November 1, 2002. Traded to **Colorado** by **Chicago** for future considerations, June 21, 2003.

NIKULIN, Igor

Right wing. Shoots left. 6'1", 200 lbs. Born, Cherepovets, USSR, August 26, 1972.
(Anaheim's 4th choice, 107th overall, in 1995 Entry Draft).

Season	Club	GP	G	A	Pts	PIM	GP	G	A	Pts	PIM
1996-97	Mighty Ducks of Anaheim	....	....	....	....	....	1	0	0	0	0
	NHL Totals	....	....	....	....	....	**1**	**0**	**0**	**0**	**0**

NILAN, Chris

Right wing. Shoots right. 6', 205 lbs. Born, Boston, MA, February 9, 1958.
(Montreal's 22nd choice, 231st overall, in 1978 Amateur Draft).

Season	Club	GP	G	A	Pts	PIM	GP	G	A	Pts	PIM
1979-80	Montreal Canadiens	15	0	2	2	50	5	0	0	0	2
1980-81	Montreal Canadiens	57	7	8	15	262	2	0	0	0	0
1981-82	Montreal Canadiens	49	7	4	11	204	5	1	1	2	22
1982-83	Montreal Canadiens	66	6	8	14	213	3	0	0	0	5
1983-84	Montreal Canadiens	76	16	10	26	*338	15	1	0	1	*81
1984-85	Montreal Canadiens	77	21	16	37	*358	12	2	1	3	81
1985-86 ♦	Montreal Canadiens	72	19	15	34	274	18	1	2	3	*141
1986-87	Montreal Canadiens	44	4	16	20	266	17	3	0	3	75
1987-88	Montreal Canadiens	50	7	5	12	209	....	....	....	....	....
	New York Rangers	22	3	5	8	96	....	....	....	....	....
1988-89	New York Rangers	38	7	7	14	177	4	0	1	1	38
1989-90	New York Rangers	25	1	2	3	59	4	0	1	1	19
1990-91	Boston Bruins	41	6	9	15	277	19	0	2	2	62
1991-92	Boston Bruins	39	5	5	10	186	....	....	....	....	....
	Montreal Canadiens	17	1	3	4	74	7	0	1	1	15
	NHL Totals	**688**	**110**	**115**	**225**	**3043**	**111**	**8**	**9**	**17**	**541**

Traded to **NY Rangers** by **Montreal** with Montreal's 1st round choice (Steven Rice) in 1989 Entry Draft for NY Rangers' 1st round choice (Lindsay Vallis) in 1989 Entry Draft, January 27, 1988. • Missed majority of 1989-90 season recovering from arm injury suffered in game vs. Montreal, November 4, 1989. Traded to **Boston** by **NY Rangers** for Greg Johnston and cash, June 28, 1990. Claimed on waivers by **Montreal** from **Boston**, February 12, 1992.

NILL, Jim

Right wing. Shoots right. 6', 185 lbs. Born, Hanna, Alta., April 11, 1958.
(St. Louis' 4th choice, 89th overall, in 1978 Amateur Draft).

Season	Club	GP	G	A	Pts	PIM	GP	G	A	Pts	PIM
1981-82	St. Louis Blues	61	9	12	21	127	....	....	....	....	....
	Vancouver Canucks	8	1	2	3	5	16	4	3	7	67
1982-83	Vancouver Canucks	65	7	15	22	136	4	0	0	0	6
1983-84	Vancouver Canucks	51	9	6	15	78	....	....	....	....	....
	Boston Bruins	27	3	2	5	81	3	0	0	0	4
1984-85	Boston Bruins	49	1	9	10	62	....	....	....	....	....
	Winnipeg Jets	20	8	8	16	38	8	0	1	1	28
1985-86	Winnipeg Jets	61	6	8	14	75	3	0	0	0	4
1986-87	Winnipeg Jets	36	3	4	7	52	3	0	0	0	7
1987-88	Winnipeg Jets	24	0	1	1	44	....	....	....	....	....
	Detroit Red Wings	36	3	11	14	55	16	6	1	7	62
1988-89	Detroit Red Wings	71	8	7	15	83	6	0	0	0	25
1989-90	Detroit Red Wings	15	0	2	2	18	....	....	....	....	....
	NHL Totals	**524**	**58**	**87**	**145**	**854**	**59**	**10**	**5**	**15**	**203**

Traded to **Vancouver** by **St. Louis** with Tony Currie, Rick Heinz and St. Louis' 4th round choice (Shawn Kilroy) in 1982 Entry Draft for Glen Hanlon, March 9, 1982. Traded to **Boston** by **Vancouver** for Peter McNab, February 3, 1984. Traded to **Winnipeg** by **Boston** for Morris Lukowich, February 4, 1985. Traded to **Detroit** by **Winnipeg** for Mark Kumpel, January 11, 1988.

NILSON, Marcus

Left wing. Shoots right. 6'2", 195 lbs. Born, Balsta, Sweden, March 1, 1978.
(Florida's 1st choice, 20th overall, in 1996 Entry Draft).

Season	Club	GP	G	A	Pts	PIM	GP	G	A	Pts	PIM
1998-99	Florida Panthers	8	1	1	2	5	....	....	....	....	....

Season	Club	REGULAR SEASON					PLAYOFFS				
		GP	G	A	Pts	PIM	GP	G	A	Pts	PIM
99-2000	Florida Panthers	9	0	2	2	2					
2000-01	Florida Panthers	78	12	24	36	74					
2001-02	Florida Panthers	81	14	19	33	55					
2002-03	Florida Panthers	82	15	19	34	31					
	NHL Totals	**258**	**42**	**65**	**107**	**167**					

NILSSON, Kent

Center. Shoots left. 6'1", 195 lbs. Born, Nynashamn, Sweden, August 31, 1956.
(Atlanta's 5th choice, 64th overall, in 1976 Amateur Draft).

Season	Club	GP	G	A	Pts	PIM	GP	G	A	Pts	PIM
1979-80	Atlanta Flames	80	40	53	93	10	4	0	0	0	2
1980-81	Calgary Flames	80	49	82	131	26	14	3	9	12	2
1981-82	Calgary Flames	41	26	29	55	8	3	0	3	3	2
1982-83	Calgary Flames	80	46	58	104	10	9	1	11	12	2
1983-84	Calgary Flames	67	31	49	80	22					
1984-85	Calgary Flames	77	37	62	99	14	3	0	1	1	0
1985-86	Minnesota North Stars	61	16	44	60	10	5	1	4	5	0
1986-87	Minnesota North Stars	44	13	33	46	12					
	♦ Edmonton Oilers	17	5	12	17	4	21	6	13	19	6
1994-95	Edmonton Oilers	6	1	0	1	0					
	NHL Totals	**553**	**264**	**422**	**686**	**116**	**59**	**11**	**41**	**52**	**14**

Played in NHL All-Star Game (1980, 1981)

Reclaimed by **Atlanta** from **Winnipeg** prior to Expansion Draft, June 9, 1979. Transferred to **Calgary** after **Atlanta** franchise relocated, June 24, 1980. Traded to **Minnesota** by **Calgary** with Calgary's 3rd round choice (Brad Turner) in 1986 Entry Draft for Minnesota's 2nd round choice (Joe Nieuwendyk) in 1985 Entry Draft and 2nd round choice (Stephane Matteau) in 1987 Entry Draft, June 15, 1985. Traded to **Edmonton** by **Minnesota** for cash, March 2, 1987. Signed as a free agent by **Edmonton**, January 26, 1995.

NILSSON, Ulf

Center. Shoots right. 5'11", 175 lbs. Born, Nynashamn, Sweden, May 11, 1950.
(NY Rangers' 12th choice, 243rd overall, in 1983 Entry Draft).

Season	Club	GP	G	A	Pts	PIM	GP	G	A	Pts	PIM
1978-79	New York Rangers	59	27	39	66	21	2	0	0	0	2
1979-80	New York Rangers	50	14	44	58	20	9	0	6	6	2
1980-81	New York Rangers	51	14	25	39	42	14	8	8	16	23
1982-83	New York Rangers	10	2	4	6	2					
	NHL Totals	**170**	**57**	**112**	**169**	**85**	**25**	**8**	**14**	**22**	**27**

Signed as a free agent by **NY Rangers**, June 5, 1978.

NISTICO, Lou

Center. Shoots left. 5'7", 170 lbs. Born, Thunder Bay, Ont., January 25, 1953.
(Minnesota's 7th choice, 105th overall, in 1973 Amateur Draft).

Season	Club	GP	G	A	Pts	PIM	GP	G	A	Pts	PIM
1977-78	Colorado Rockies	3	0	0	0	0					
	NHL Totals	**3**	**0**	**0**	**0**	**0**					

Signed as a free agent by **Colorado** to a five-game tryout contract, November 6, 1977.

NOBLE, Reg — HHOF

Center/Defense. Shoots left. 5'8", 180 lbs. Born, Collingwood, Ont., June 23, 1896.

Season	Club	GP	G	A	Pts	PIM	GP	G	A	Pts	PIM
1917-18 ♦	Toronto Arenas	20	30	*10	40	35	2	1	1	2	9
	Toronto Arenas (Cup)						*5*	*2*	*1*	*3*	*0*
1918-19	Toronto Arenas	17	10	5	15	35					
1919-20	Toronto St. Pats	24	24	9	33	52					
1920-21	Toronto St. Pats	24	19	8	27	54	2	0	0	0	0
1921-22 ♦	Toronto St. Pats	24	17	11	28	19	2	0	0	0	12
	Toronto St. Pats (Cup)						*5*	*0*	*1*	*1*	*9*
1922-23	Toronto St. Pats	24	12	11	23	47					
1923-24	Toronto St. Pats	24	12	5	17	79					
1924-25	Toronto St. Pats	3	1	0	1	8					
	Montreal Maroons	27	8	11	19	56					
1925-26 ♦	Montreal Maroons	33	9	9	18	96	4	1	1	2	6
	Montreal Maroons (Cup)						*4*	*0*	*0*	*0*	*4*
1926-27	Montreal Maroons	43	3	3	6	112	2	0	0	0	2
1927-28	Detroit Cougars	44	6	8	14	63					
1928-29	Detroit Cougars	43	6	4	10	52	2	0	0	0	2
1929-30	Detroit Cougars	43	6	4	10	72					
1930-31	Detroit Falcons	44	2	5	7	42					
1931-32	Detroit Falcons	48	3	3	6	72	2	0	0	0	0
1932-33	Detroit Red Wings	5	0	0	0	6					
	Montreal Maroons	20	0	0	0	16	2	0	0	0	2
	NHL Totals	**510**	**168**	**106**	**274**	**916**	**18**	**2**	**2**	**4**	**33**

Signed as a free agent by **Toronto**, December 5, 1917. • Named player coach of Toronto, November 1, 1921. • Resigned as coach and captain of Toronto, November 1, 1922. Traded to **Mtl. Maroons** by **Toronto** for $8,000, December 9, 1924. Traded to **Detroit** by **Mtl. Maroons** for $7,500, October 4, 1927. Traded to **Mtl. Maroons** by **Detroit** for John Gallagher, December 9, 1932.

NOEL, Claude

Center. Shoots left. 5'11", 165 lbs. Born, Kirkland Lake, Ont., October 31, 1955.

Season	Club	GP	G	A	Pts	PIM	GP	G	A	Pts	PIM
1979-80	Washington Capitals	7	0	0	0	0					
	NHL Totals	**7**	**0**	**0**	**0**	**0**					

Signed as a free agent by **Washington**, October 9, 1979.

NOLAN, Owen

Right wing. Shoots right. 6'1", 210 lbs. Born, Belfast, Ireland, February 12, 1972.
(Quebec's 1st choice, 1st overall, in 1990 Entry Draft).

Season	Club	GP	G	A	Pts	PIM	GP	G	A	Pts	PIM
1990-91	Quebec Nordiques	59	3	10	13	109					
1991-92	Quebec Nordiques	75	42	31	73	183					
1992-93	Quebec Nordiques	73	36	41	77	185	5	1	0	1	2
1993-94	Quebec Nordiques	6	2	2	4	8					
1994-95	Quebec Nordiques	46	30	19	49	46	6	2	3	5	6
1995-96	Colorado Avalanche	9	4	4	8	9					
	San Jose Sharks	72	29	32	61	137					
1996-97	San Jose Sharks	72	31	32	63	155					
1997-98	San Jose Sharks	75	14	27	41	144	6	2	2	4	26
1998-99	San Jose Sharks	78	19	26	45	129	6	1	1	2	6
99-2000	San Jose Sharks	78	44	40	84	110	10	8	2	10	6
2000-01	San Jose Sharks	57	24	25	49	75	6	1	1	2	8
2001-02	San Jose Sharks	75	23	43	66	93	12	3	6	9	8
2002-03	San Jose Sharks	61	22	20	42	91					
	Toronto Maple Leafs	14	7	5	12	16	7	0	2	2	2
	NHL Totals	**850**	**330**	**357**	**687**	**1490**	**58**	**18**	**17**	**35**	**64**

Played in NHL All-Star Game (1992, 1996, 1997, 2000, 2002)

• Missed majority of 1993-94 season recovering from shoulder injury suffered in game vs. Tampa Bay, November 13, 1993. Transferred to **Colorado** after **Quebec** franchise relocated, June 21, 1995. Traded to **San Jose** by **Colorado** for Sandis Ozolinsh, October 26, 1995. Traded to **Toronto** by **San Jose** for Alyn McCauley, Brad Boyes and Toronto's 1st round choice (later traded to Boston – Boston selected Mark Stuart) in 2003 Entry Draft, March 5, 2003.

NOLAN, Paddy

Left wing/Defense. Shoots left. 5'8", 170 lbs. Born, Charlottetown, P.E.I., December 1, 1897.

Season	Club	GP	G	A	Pts	PIM	GP	G	A	Pts	PIM
1921-22	Toronto St. Pats	2	0	0	0	0					
	NHL Totals	**2**	**0**	**0**	**0**	**0**					

Signed as a free agent by **Toronto**, December 23, 1921.

NOLAN, Ted

Center. Shoots left. 6', 185 lbs. Born, Sault Ste. Marie, Ont., April 7, 1958.
(Detroit's 7th choice, 78th overall, in 1978 Amateur Draft).

Season	Club	GP	G	A	Pts	PIM	GP	G	A	Pts	PIM
1981-82	Detroit Red Wings	41	4	13	17	45					
1983-84	Detroit Red Wings	19	1	2	3	26					
1985-86	Pittsburgh Penguins	18	1	1	2	34					
	NHL Totals	**78**	**6**	**16**	**22**	**105**					

Signed as a free agent by **Buffalo**, March 7, 1985. Rights traded to **Pittsburgh** by **Buffalo** for cash, September 16, 1985.

NOLET, Simon

Right wing. Shoots right. 5'9", 185 lbs. Born, St-Odilon, Que., November 23, 1941.

Season	Club	GP	G	A	Pts	PIM	GP	G	A	Pts	PIM
1967-68	Philadelphia Flyers	4	0	0	0	2	1	0	0	0	0
1968-69	Philadelphia Flyers	35	4	10	14	8					
1969-70	Philadelphia Flyers	56	22	22	44	36					
1970-71	Philadelphia Flyers	74	9	19	28	42	4	2	1	3	0
1971-72	Philadelphia Flyers	67	23	20	43	22					
1972-73	Philadelphia Flyers	70	16	20	36	6	11	3	1	4	4
1973-74 ♦	Philadelphia Flyers	52	19	17	36	13	15	1	1	2	4
1974-75	Kansas City Scouts	72	26	32	58	30					
1975-76	Kansas City Scouts	41	10	15	25	16					
	Pittsburgh Penguins	39	9	8	17	2	3	0	0	0	0
1976-77	Colorado Rockies	52	12	19	31	10					
	NHL Totals	**562**	**150**	**182**	**332**	**187**	**34**	**6**	**3**	**9**	**8**

Played in NHL All-Star Game (1972, 1975)

NHL rights transferred to **Philadelphia** after NHL club purchased **Quebec** (AHL) franchise, May 8, 1967. Claimed by **Kansas City** from **Philadelphia** in Expansion Draft, June 12, 1974. Traded to **Pittsburgh** by **Kansas City** with Ed Gilbert and Kansas City's 1st round choice (Blair Chapman) in 1976 Amateur Draft for Steve Durbano, Chuck Arnason and Pittsburgh's 1st round choice (Paul Gardner) in 1976 Amateur Draft, January 9, 1976. Transferred to **Colorado** by **Pittsburgh** with Michel Plasse and the loan of Colin Campbell for the 1976-77 season (September 1, 1976) as compensation for Pittsburgh's signing of free agent Denis Herron, August 7, 1976.

NOONAN, Brian

Right wing. Shoots right. 6'1", 200 lbs. Born, Boston, MA, May 29, 1965.
(Chicago's 10th choice, 186th overall, in 1983 Entry Draft).

Season	Club	GP	G	A	Pts	PIM	GP	G	A	Pts	PIM
1987-88	Chicago Blackhawks	77	10	20	30	44	3	0	0	0	4
1988-89	Chicago Blackhawks	45	4	12	16	28	1	0	0	0	0
1989-90	Chicago Blackhawks	8	0	2	2	6					
1990-91	Chicago Blackhawks	7	0	4	4	2					
1991-92	Chicago Blackhawks	65	19	12	31	81	18	6	9	15	30
1992-93	Chicago Blackhawks	63	16	14	30	82	4	3	0	3	4
1993-94	Chicago Blackhawks	64	14	21	35	57					
	♦ New York Rangers	12	4	2	6	12	22	4	7	11	17
1994-95	New York Rangers	45	14	13	27	26	5	0	0	0	8
1995-96	St. Louis Blues	81	13	22	35	84	13	4	1	5	10
1996-97	St. Louis Blues	13	2	5	7	0					
	New York Rangers	44	6	9	15	28					
	Vancouver Canucks	16	4	8	12	6					
1997-98	Vancouver Canucks	82	10	15	25	62					
1998-99	Phoenix Coyotes	7	0	0	0	0	5	0	2	2	4
	NHL Totals	**629**	**116**	**159**	**275**	**518**	**71**	**17**	**19**	**36**	**77**

Traded to **NY Rangers** by **Chicago** with Stephane Matteau for Tony Amonte and the rights to Matt Oates, March 21, 1994. Signed as a free agent by **St. Louis**, July 24, 1995. Traded to **NY Rangers** by **St. Louis** for Sergio Momesso, November 13, 1996. Traded to **Vancouver** by **NY Rangers** with Sergei Nemchinov for Esa Tikkanen and Russ Courtnall, March 8, 1997. Signed as a free agent by **Phoenix**, March 17, 1999.

NORDMARK, Robert

Defense. Shoots right. 6', 209 lbs. Born, Lulea, Sweden, August 20, 1962.
(St. Louis' 3rd choice, 59th overall, in 1987 Entry Draft).

Season	Club	REGULAR SEASON GP	G	A	Pts	PIM	PLAYOFFS GP	G	A	Pts	PIM
1987-88	St. Louis Blues	67	3	18	21	60	....	....	....	....	....
1988-89	Vancouver Canucks	80	6	35	41	97	7	3	2	5	8
1989-90	Vancouver Canucks	44	2	11	13	34	....	....	....	....	....
1990-91	Vancouver Canucks	45	2	6	8	63	....	....	....	....	....
	NHL Totals	**236**	**13**	**70**	**83**	**254**	**7**	**3**	**2**	**5**	**8**

Traded to **Vancouver** by **St. Louis** with St. Louis's 2nd round choice (later traded to Montreal – Montreal selected Craig Darby) in 1991 Entry Draft for Dave Richter, September 6, 1988.

NORDSTROM, Peter

Center. Shoots left. 6'1", 200 lbs. Born, Munkfors, Sweden, July 26, 1974.
(Boston's 3rd choice, 78th overall, in 1998 Entry Draft).

Season	Club	REGULAR SEASON GP	G	A	Pts	PIM	PLAYOFFS GP	G	A	Pts	PIM
1998-99	Boston Bruins	2	0	0	0	0	....	....	....	....	....
	NHL Totals	**2**	**0**	**0**	**0**	**0**	....	....	....	....	....

NORIS, Joe

Center/Defense. Shoots right. 6', 185 lbs. Born, Denver, CO, October 26, 1951.
(Pittsburgh's 2nd choice, 32nd overall, in 1971 Amateur Draft).

Season	Club	REGULAR SEASON GP	G	A	Pts	PIM	PLAYOFFS GP	G	A	Pts	PIM
1971-72	Pittsburgh Penguins	35	2	5	7	20	....	....	....	....	....
1972-73	St. Louis Blues	2	0	0	0	0	....	....	....	....	....
1973-74	Buffalo Sabres	18	0	0	0	2	....	....	....	....	....
	NHL Totals	**55**	**2**	**5**	**7**	**22**	....	....	....	....	....

Traded to **St. Louis** by **Pittsburgh** for Jim Shires, January 8, 1973. Claimed by **Buffalo** from **St. Louis** in Intra-League Draft, June 12, 1973.

NORRIS, Dwayne

Right wing. Shoots right. 5'10", 175 lbs. Born, St. John's, Nfld., January 8, 1970.
(Quebec's 5th choice, 127th overall, in 1990 Entry Draft).

Season	Club	REGULAR SEASON GP	G	A	Pts	PIM	PLAYOFFS GP	G	A	Pts	PIM
1993-94	Quebec Nordiques	4	1	1	2	4	....	....	....	....	....
1994-95	Quebec Nordiques	13	1	2	3	2	....	....	....	....	....
1995-96	Mighty Ducks of Anaheim	3	0	1	1	2	....	....	....	....	....
	NHL Totals	**20**	**2**	**4**	**6**	**8**	....	....	....	....	....

Signed as a free agent by **Anaheim**, November 3, 1995.

NORRISH, Rod

Left wing. Shoots left. 5'10", 185 lbs. Born, Saskatoon, Sask., November 27, 1951.
(Minnesota's 1st choice, 21st overall, in 1971 Amateur Draft).

Season	Club	REGULAR SEASON GP	G	A	Pts	PIM	PLAYOFFS GP	G	A	Pts	PIM
1973-74	Minnesota North Stars	9	2	1	3	0	....	....	....	....	....
1974-75	Minnesota North Stars	12	1	2	3	2	....	....	....	....	....
	NHL Totals	**21**	**3**	**3**	**6**	**2**	....	....	....	....	....

NORSTROM, Mattias

Defense. Shoots left. 6'2", 211 lbs. Born, Stockholm, Sweden, January 2, 1972.
(NY Rangers' 2nd choice, 48th overall, in 1992 Entry Draft).

Season	Club	REGULAR SEASON GP	G	A	Pts	PIM	PLAYOFFS GP	G	A	Pts	PIM
1993-94	New York Rangers	9	0	2	2	6	....	....	....	....	....
1994-95	New York Rangers	9	0	3	3	2	3	0	0	0	0
1995-96	New York Rangers	25	2	1	3	22	....	....	....	....	....
	Los Angeles Kings	11	0	1	1	18	....	....	....	....	....
1996-97	Los Angeles Kings	80	1	21	22	84	....	....	....	....	....
1997-98	Los Angeles Kings	73	1	12	13	90	4	0	0	0	2
1998-99	Los Angeles Kings	78	2	5	7	36	....	....	....	....	....
99-2000	Los Angeles Kings	82	1	13	14	66	4	0	0	0	6
2000-01	Los Angeles Kings	82	0	18	18	60	13	0	2	2	18
2001-02	Los Angeles Kings	79	2	9	11	38	7	0	0	0	4
2002-03	Los Angeles Kings	82	0	6	6	49	....	....	....	....	....
	NHL Totals	**610**	**9**	**91**	**100**	**471**	**31**	**0**	**2**	**2**	**30**

Played in NHL All-Star Game (1999)

Traded to **Los Angeles** by **NY Rangers** with Ray Ferraro, Ian Laperriere, Nathan Lafayette and NY Rangers' 4th round choice (Sean Blanchard) in 1997 Entry Draft for Marty McSorley, Jari Kurri and Shane Churla, March 14, 1996.

NORTHCOTT, Baldy

Defense/Left wing. Shoots left. 6', 184 lbs. Born, Calgary, Alta., September 7, 1908.

Season	Club	REGULAR SEASON GP	G	A	Pts	PIM	PLAYOFFS GP	G	A	Pts	PIM
1928-29	Montreal Maroons	5	0	0	0	0	....	....	....	....	....
1929-30	Montreal Maroons	43	10	1	11	6	4	0	0	0	4
1930-31	Montreal Maroons	22	7	3	10	15	2	0	1	1	0
1931-32	Montreal Maroons	48	19	6	25	33	4	1	2	3	4
1932-33	Montreal Maroons	48	22	21	43	30	2	0	0	0	4
1933-34	Montreal Maroons	47	20	13	33	27	4	2	0	2	0
1934-35◆	Montreal Maroons	47	9	14	23	44	7	*4	1	*5	0
1935-36	Montreal Maroons	48	15	21	36	41	3	0	0	0	0
1936-37	Montreal Maroons	46	15	14	29	18	5	1	1	2	2
1937-38	Montreal Maroons	46	11	12	23	50	....	....	....	....	....
1938-39	Chicago Black Hawks	46	5	7	12	9	....	....	....	....	....
	NHL Totals	**446**	**133**	**112**	**245**	**273**	**31**	**8**	**5**	**13**	**14**

NHL First All-Star Team (1933)

Played in NHL All-Star Game (1937)

Traded to **Chicago** by **Mtl. Maroons** with Earl Robinson and Russ Blinco for $30,000, September 15, 1938.

NORTON, Brad

Defense. Shoots left. 6'4", 225 lbs. Born, Cambridge, MA, February 13, 1975.
(Edmonton's 9th choice, 215th overall, in 1993 Entry Draft).

Season	Club	REGULAR SEASON GP	G	A	Pts	PIM	PLAYOFFS GP	G	A	Pts	PIM
2001-02	Florida Panthers	22	0	2	2	45	....	....	....	....	....
2002-03	Los Angeles Kings	53	3	3	6	97	....	....	....	....	....
	NHL Totals	**75**	**3**	**5**	**8**	**142**	....	....	....	....	....

Signed as a free agent by **Florida**, July 27, 2001. Signed as a free agent by **Los Angeles**, October, 8, 2002.

NORTON, Jeff

Defense. Shoots left. 6'2", 195 lbs. Born, Acton, MA, November 25, 1965.
(NY Islanders' 3rd choice, 62nd overall, in 1984 Entry Draft).

Season	Club	REGULAR SEASON GP	G	A	Pts	PIM	PLAYOFFS GP	G	A	Pts	PIM
1987-88	New York Islanders	15	1	6	7	14	3	0	2	2	13
1988-89	New York Islanders	69	1	30	31	74	....	....	....	....	....
1989-90	New York Islanders	60	4	49	53	65	4	1	3	4	17
1990-91	New York Islanders	44	3	25	28	16	....	....	....	....	....
1991-92	New York Islanders	28	1	18	19	18	....	....	....	....	....
1992-93	New York Islanders	66	12	38	50	45	10	1	1	2	4
1993-94	San Jose Sharks	64	7	33	40	36	14	1	5	6	20
1994-95	San Jose Sharks	20	1	9	10	39	....	....	....	....	....
	St. Louis Blues	28	2	18	20	33	7	1	1	2	11
1995-96	St. Louis Blues	36	4	7	11	26	....	....	....	....	....
	Edmonton Oilers	30	4	16	20	16	....	....	....	....	....
1996-97	Edmonton Oilers	62	2	11	13	42	....	....	....	....	....
	Tampa Bay Lightning	13	0	5	5	16	....	....	....	....	....
1997-98	Tampa Bay Lightning	37	4	6	10	26	....	....	....	....	....
	Florida Panthers	19	0	7	7	18	....	....	....	....	....
1998-99	Florida Panthers	3	0	0	0	2	....	....	....	....	....
	San Jose Sharks	69	4	18	22	42	6	0	7	7	10
99-2000	San Jose Sharks	62	0	20	20	49	12	0	1	1	7
2000-01	Pittsburgh Penguins	32	2	10	12	20	....	....	....	....	....
	San Jose Sharks	10	0	1	1	8	6	0	1	1	2
2001-02	Florida Panthers	29	0	4	4	8	....	....	....	....	....
	Boston Bruins	3	0	1	1	2	3	0	0	0	5
	NHL Totals	**799**	**52**	**332**	**384**	**615**	**65**	**4**	**21**	**25**	**89**

• Missed majority of 1991-92 season recovering from wrist injury suffered in game vs. Buffalo, January 3, 1992. Traded to **San Jose** by **NY Islanders** for San Jose's 3rd round choice (Jason Strudwick) in 1994 Entry Draft, June 20, 1993. Traded to **St. Louis** by **San Jose** with San Jose's 3rd round choice (later traded to Colorado – Colorado selected Rick Berry) in 1997 Entry Draft for Craig Janney and cash, March 6, 1995. Traded to **Edmonton** by **St. Louis** with Donald Dufresne for Igor Kravchuk and Ken Sutton, January 4, 1996. Traded to **Tampa Bay** by **Edmonton** for Drew Bannister and Tampa Bay's 6th round choice (Peter Sarno) in 1997 Entry Draft, March 18, 1997. Traded to **Florida** by **Tampa Bay** with Dino Ciccarelli for Mark Fitzpatrick and Jody Hull, January 15, 1998. Traded to **San Jose** by **Florida** for Alex Hicks and San Jose's 5th round choice (later traded to NY Islanders – NY Islanders selected Adam Johnson) in 1999 Entry Draft, November 11, 1998. Signed as a free agent by **Pittsburgh**, November 14, 2000. Traded to **San Jose** by **Pittsburgh** for Bobby Dollas and Johan Hedberg, March 12, 2001. Signed as a free agent by **Florida**, July 18, 2001. • Missed majority of 2001-02 season recovering from knee injury suffered in game vs. Toronto, December 28, 2001. Traded to **Boston** by **Florida** for Boston's 6th round choice (Mikael Vuorio) in 2002 Entry Draft, March 19, 2002.

NORWICH, Craig

Defense. Shoots left. 5'11", 175 lbs. Born, Edina, MN, December 15, 1955.
(Montreal's 11th choice, 142nd overall, in 1975 Amateur Draft).

Season	Club	REGULAR SEASON GP	G	A	Pts	PIM	PLAYOFFS GP	G	A	Pts	PIM
1979-80	Winnipeg Jets	70	10	35	45	36	....	....	....	....	....
1980-81	St. Louis Blues	23	4	12	16	14	....	....	....	....	....
	Colorado Rockies	11	3	11	14	10	....	....	....	....	....
	NHL Totals	**104**	**17**	**58**	**75**	**60**	....	....	....	....	....

Claimed by **Winnipeg** from **Cincinnati** (WHA) in WHA Dispersal Draft, June 9, 1979. Traded to **St. Louis** by **Winnipeg** for Rick Bowness, June 19, 1980. Claimed on waivers by **Colorado** from **St. Louis**, February 2, 1981. Signed as a free agent by **NY Rangers**, December, 1981.

NORWOOD, Lee

Defense. Shoots left. 6'1", 198 lbs. Born, Oakland, CA, February 2, 1960.
(Quebec's 3rd choice, 62nd overall, in 1979 Entry Draft).

Season	Club	REGULAR SEASON GP	G	A	Pts	PIM	PLAYOFFS GP	G	A	Pts	PIM
1980-81	Quebec Nordiques	11	1	1	2	9	3	0	0	0	2
1981-82	Quebec Nordiques	2	0	0	0	2	....	....	....	....	....
	Washington Capitals	26	7	10	17	125	....	....	....	....	....
1982-83	Washington Capitals	8	0	1	1	14	....	....	....	....	....
1985-86	St. Louis Blues	71	5	24	29	134	19	2	7	9	64
1986-87	Detroit Red Wings	57	6	21	27	163	16	1	6	7	31
1987-88	Detroit Red Wings	51	9	22	31	131	16	2	6	8	40
1988-89	Detroit Red Wings	66	10	32	42	100	6	1	2	3	16
1989-90	Detroit Red Wings	64	8	14	22	95	....	....	....	....	....
1990-91	Detroit Red Wings	21	3	7	10	50	....	....	....	....	....
	New Jersey Devils	28	3	2	5	87	4	0	0	0	18
1991-92	Hartford Whalers	6	0	0	0	16	....	....	....	....	....
	St. Louis Blues	44	3	11	14	94	1	0	1	1	0
1992-93	St. Louis Blues	32	3	7	10	63	....	....	....	....	....

Season	Club	GP	G	A	Pts	PIM	GP	G	A	Pts	PIM
		REGULAR SEASON					PLAYOFFS				
1993-94	Calgary Flames	16	0	1	1	16	....	....	....	....	....
	NHL Totals	**503**	**58**	**153**	**211**	**1099**	**65**	**6**	**22**	**28**	**171**

Traded to **Washington** by **Quebec** with Quebec's 6th round choice (later traded to Calgary – Calgary selected Mats Kihlstrom) in 1982 Entry Draft for Tim Tookey and Washington's 7th round choice (Daniel Poudrier) in 1982 Entry Draft, February 1, 1982. Traded to **Toronto** by **Washington** for Dave Shand, October 6, 1983. Signed as a free agent by **St. Louis**, August 13, 1985. Traded to **Detroit** by **St. Louis** for Larry Trader, August 7, 1986. Traded to **New Jersey** by **Detroit** with Detroit's 4th round choice (Scott McCabe) in 1992 Entry Draft for Paul Ysebaert, November 27, 1990. Traded to **Hartford** by **New Jersey** for Hartford's 5th round choice (John Guirestante) in 1993 Entry Draft, October 3, 1991. Traded to **St. Louis** by **Hartford** for St. Louis' 5th round choice (Nolan Pratt) in 1993 Entry Draft, November 13, 1991. • Missed remainder of 1992-93 season and majority of 1993-94 season recovering from ankle injury suffered in game vs. Detroit, January 21, 1993. Signed as a free agent by **Calgary**, October 22, 1993.

NOVOSELTSEV, Ivan

Right wing. Shoots left. 6'1", 210 lbs. Born, Golitsino, USSR, January 23, 1979.
(Florida's 5th choice, 95th overall, in 1997 Entry Draft).

Season	Club	GP	G	A	Pts	PIM	GP	G	A	Pts	PIM
99-2000	Florida Panthers	14	2	1	3	8	....	....	....	....	....
2000-01	Florida Panthers	38	3	6	9	16	....	....	....	....	....
2001-02	Florida Panthers	70	13	16	29	44	....	....	....	....	....
2002-03	Florida Panthers	78	10	17	27	30	....	....	....	....	....
	NHL Totals	**200**	**28**	**40**	**68**	**98**	....	....	....	....	....

NOVY, Milan

Center. Shoots left. 5'10", 196 lbs. Born, Kladno, Czech., September 23, 1951.
(Washington's 2nd choice, 58th overall, in 1982 Entry Draft).

Season	Club	GP	G	A	Pts	PIM	GP	G	A	Pts	PIM
1982-83	Washington Capitals	73	18	30	48	16	2	0	0	0	0
	NHL Totals	**73**	**18**	**30**	**48**	**16**	**2**	**0**	**0**	**0**	**0**

NOWAK, Hank

Left wing. Shoots left. 6'1", 195 lbs. Born, Oshawa, Ont., November 24, 1950.
(Philadelphia's 6th choice, 87th overall, in 1970 Amateur Draft).

Season	Club	GP	G	A	Pts	PIM	GP	G	A	Pts	PIM
1973-74	Pittsburgh Penguins	13	0	0	0	11	....	....	....	....	....
1974-75	Detroit Red Wings	56	8	14	22	69	....	....	....	....	....
	Boston Bruins	21	4	7	11	26	3	1	0	1	0
1975-76	Boston Bruins	66	7	3	10	41	10	0	0	0	8
1976-77	Boston Bruins	24	7	5	12	14	....	....	....	....	....
	NHL Totals	**180**	**26**	**29**	**55**	**161**	**13**	**1**	**0**	**1**	**8**

Claimed by **Hershey** (AHL) from **Philadelphia** in Reverse Draft, June 8, 1972. Traded to **Pittsburgh** by **Hershey** (AHL) for cash, May 22, 1973. Traded to **Detroit** by **Pittsburgh** with Pittsburgh's 3rd round choice (Dan Mandryk) in 1974 Amateur Draft for Nelson Debenedet, May 27, 1974. Traded to **Boston** by **Detroit** with Earl Anderson for Walt McKechnie and Boston's 3rd round choice (Clarke Hamilton) in 1975 Amateur Draft, February 18, 1975.

NUMMELIN, Petteri

Defense. Shoots left. 5'10", 196 lbs. Born, Turku, Finland, November 25, 1972.
(Columbus' 3rd choice, 133rd overall, in 2000 Entry Draft).

Season	Club	GP	G	A	Pts	PIM	GP	G	A	Pts	PIM
2000-01	Columbus Blue Jackets	61	4	12	16	10	....	....	....	....	....
	NHL Totals	**61**	**4**	**12**	**16**	**10**	....	....	....	....	....

Traded to **Atlanta** by **Columbus** with Chris Nielsen for Tomi Kallio and Pauli Levokari, December 2, 2002.

NUMMINEN, Teppo

Defense. Shoots right. 6'2", 197 lbs. Born, Tampere, Finland, July 3, 1968.
(Winnipeg's 2nd choice, 29th overall, in 1986 Entry Draft).

Season	Club	GP	G	A	Pts	PIM	GP	G	A	Pts	PIM
1988-89	Winnipeg Jets	69	1	14	15	36	....	....	....	....	....
1989-90	Winnipeg Jets	79	11	32	43	20	7	1	2	3	10
1990-91	Winnipeg Jets	80	8	25	33	28	....	....	....	....	....
1991-92	Winnipeg Jets	80	5	34	39	32	7	0	0	0	0
1992-93	Winnipeg Jets	66	7	30	37	33	6	1	1	2	2
1993-94	Winnipeg Jets	57	5	18	23	28	....	....	....	....	....
1994-95	Winnipeg Jets	42	5	16	21	16	....	....	....	....	....
1995-96	Winnipeg Jets	74	11	43	54	22	6	0	0	0	2
1996-97	Phoenix Coyotes	82	2	25	27	28	7	3	3	6	0
1997-98	Phoenix Coyotes	82	11	40	51	30	1	0	0	0	0
1998-99	Phoenix Coyotes	82	10	30	40	30	7	2	1	3	4
99-2000	Phoenix Coyotes	79	8	34	42	16	5	1	1	2	0
2000-01	Phoenix Coyotes	72	5	26	31	36	....	....	....	....	....
2001-02	Phoenix Coyotes	76	13	35	48	20	4	0	0	0	2
2002-03	Phoenix Coyotes	78	6	24	30	30	....	....	....	....	....
	NHL Totals	**1098**	**108**	**426**	**534**	**405**	**50**	**8**	**8**	**16**	**20**

Played in NHL All-Star Game (1999, 2000, 2001)

Transferred to **Phoenix** after **Winnipeg** franchise relocated, July 1, 1996. Traded to **Dallas** by **Phoenix** for Mike Sillinger, July 22, 2003.

NURMINEN, Kai

Left wing. Shoots left. 6'1", 190 lbs. Born, Turku, Finland, March 29, 1969.
(Los Angeles' 9th choice, 193rd overall, in 1996 Entry Draft).

Season	Club	GP	G	A	Pts	PIM	GP	G	A	Pts	PIM
1996-97	Los Angeles Kings	67	16	11	27	22	....	....	....	....	....
2000-01	Minnesota Wild	2	1	0	1	2	....	....	....	....	....
	NHL Totals	**69**	**17**	**11**	**28**	**24**	....	....	....	....	....

Signed as a free agent by **Minnesota**, May 24, 2000.

NYKOLUK, Mike

Right wing. Shoots right. 5'11", 212 lbs. Born, Toronto, Ont., December 11, 1934.

Season	Club	GP	G	A	Pts	PIM	GP	G	A	Pts	PIM
1956-57	Toronto Maple Leafs	32	3	1	4	20	....	....	....	....	....
	NHL Totals	**32**	**3**	**1**	**4**	**20**	....	....	....	....	....

Traded to **Hershey** (AHL) by **Toronto** with Ron Hurst and the loan of Wally Boyer for the 1958-59 and 1959-60 seasons for Willie Marshall, April 29, 1958

NYLANDER, Michael

Center. Shoots left. 6'1", 195 lbs. Born, Stockholm, Sweden, October 3, 1972.
(Hartford's 4th choice, 59th overall, in 1991 Entry Draft).

Season	Club	GP	G	A	Pts	PIM	GP	G	A	Pts	PIM
1992-93	Hartford Whalers	59	11	22	33	36	....	....	....	....	....
1993-94	Hartford Whalers	58	11	33	44	24	....	....	....	....	....
	Calgary Flames	15	2	9	11	6	3	0	0	0	0
1994-95	Calgary Flames	6	0	1	1	2	6	0	6	6	2
1995-96	Calgary Flames	73	17	38	55	20	4	0	0	0	0
1997-98	Calgary Flames	65	13	23	36	24	....	....	....	....	....
1998-99	Calgary Flames	9	2	3	5	2	....	....	....	....	....
	Tampa Bay Lightning	24	2	7	9	6	....	....	....	....	....
99-2000	Tampa Bay Lightning	11	1	2	3	4	....	....	....	....	....
	Chicago Blackhawks	66	23	28	51	26	....	....	....	....	....
2000-01	Chicago Blackhawks	82	25	39	64	32	....	....	....	....	....
2001-02	Chicago Blackhawks	82	15	46	61	50	5	0	3	3	2
2002-03	Chicago Blackhawks	9	0	4	4	4	....	....	....	....	....
	Washington Capitals	71	17	39	56	36	6	3	2	5	8
	NHL Totals	**630**	**139**	**294**	**433**	**272**	**24**	**3**	**11**	**14**	**12**

Traded to **Calgary** by **Hartford** with James Patrick and Zarley Zalapski for Gary Suter, Paul Ranheim and Ted Drury, March 10, 1994. • Missed majority of 1994-95 season recovering from wrist injury suffered in game vs. St. Louis, January 24, 1995. Traded to **Tampa Bay** by **Calgary** for Andrei Nazarov, January 19, 1999. Traded to **Chicago** by **Tampa Bay** for Bryan Muir and Reid Simpson, November 12, 1999. Traded to **Washington** by **Chicago** with Chicago's 3rd round choice (Stephen Werner) in 2003 Entry Draft and future considerations for Chris Simon and Andrei Nikolishin, November 1, 2002.

NYLUND, Gary

Defense. Shoots left. 6'4", 210 lbs. Born, Surrey, B.C., October 28, 1963.
(Toronto's 1st choice, 3rd overall, in 1982 Entry Draft).

Season	Club	GP	G	A	Pts	PIM	GP	G	A	Pts	PIM
1982-83	Toronto Maple Leafs	16	0	3	3	16	....	....	....	....	....
1983-84	Toronto Maple Leafs	47	2	14	16	103	....	....	....	....	....
1984-85	Toronto Maple Leafs	76	3	17	20	99	....	....	....	....	....
1985-86	Toronto Maple Leafs	79	2	16	18	180	10	0	2	2	25
1986-87	Chicago Blackhawks	80	7	20	27	190	4	0	2	2	11
1987-88	Chicago Blackhawks	76	4	15	19	208	5	0	0	0	10
1988-89	Chicago Blackhawks	23	3	2	5	63	....	....	....	....	....
	New York Islanders	46	4	8	12	74	....	....	....	....	....
1989-90	New York Islanders	64	4	21	25	144	5	0	2	2	17
1990-91	New York Islanders	72	2	21	23	105	....	....	....	....	....
1991-92	New York Islanders	7	0	1	1	10	....	....	....	....	....
1992-93	New York Islanders	22	1	1	2	43	....	....	....	....	....
	NHL Totals	**608**	**32**	**139**	**171**	**1235**	**24**	**0**	**6**	**6**	**63**

Signed as a free agent by **Chicago**, August 27, 1986. Traded to **NY Islanders** by **Chicago** with Marc Bergevin for Steve Konroyd and Bob Bassen, November 25, 1988.

NYROP, Bill

USHOF

Defense. Shoots left. 6'2", 205 lbs. Born, Washington, DC, July 23, 1952.
(Montreal's 7th choice, 66th overall, in 1972 Amateur Draft).

Season	Club	GP	G	A	Pts	PIM	GP	G	A	Pts	PIM
1975-76 ♦	Montreal Canadiens	19	0	3	3	8	13	0	3	3	12
1976-77 ♦	Montreal Canadiens	74	3	19	22	21	8	1	0	1	4
1977-78 ♦	Montreal Canadiens	72	5	21	26	37	12	0	4	4	6
1981-82	Minnesota North Stars	42	4	8	12	35	2	0	0	0	0
	NHL Totals	**207**	**12**	**51**	**63**	**101**	**35**	**1**	**7**	**8**	**22**

Traded to **Minnesota** by **Montreal** for Minnesota's 2nd round choice (Gaston Gingras) in 1979 Entry Draft, August 8, 1979. Traded to **Calgary** by **Minnesota** with Steve Christoff and St. Louis' 2nd round choice (previously acquired, Calgary selected Dave Reierson) in 1982 Entry Draft for Willi Plett and Calgary's 4th round choice (Dusan Pasek) in 1982 Entry Draft, June 7, 1982

NYSTROM, Bob

Right wing. Shoots right. 6'1", 200 lbs. Born, Stockholm, Sweden, October 10, 1952.
(NY Islanders' 3rd choice, 33rd overall, in 1972 Amateur Draft).

Season	Club	GP	G	A	Pts	PIM	GP	G	A	Pts	PIM
1972-73	New York Islanders	11	1	1	2	10	....	....	....	....	....
1973-74	New York Islanders	77	21	20	41	118	....	....	....	....	....
1974-75	New York Islanders	76	27	28	55	122	17	1	3	4	27
1975-76	New York Islanders	80	23	25	48	106	13	3	6	9	30
1976-77	New York Islanders	80	29	27	56	91	12	0	2	2	7
1977-78	New York Islanders	80	30	29	59	94	7	3	1	4	14
1978-79	New York Islanders	78	19	20	39	113	10	3	2	5	4
1979-80 ♦	New York Islanders	67	21	18	39	94	20	9	9	18	50
1980-81 ♦	New York Islanders	79	14	30	44	145	18	6	6	12	20
1981-82 ♦	New York Islanders	74	22	25	47	103	15	5	5	10	32
1982-83 ♦	New York Islanders	74	10	20	30	98	20	7	6	13	15
1983-84	New York Islanders	74	15	29	44	80	15	0	2	2	8
1984-85	New York Islanders	36	2	5	7	58	10	2	2	4	29
1985-86	New York Islanders	14	1	1	2	16	....	....	....	....	....
	NHL Totals	**900**	**235**	**278**	**513**	**1248**	**157**	**39**	**44**	**83**	**236**

Played in NHL All-Star Game (1977)

OATES, Adam

Center. Shoots right. 5'11", 190 lbs. Born, Weston, Ont., August 27, 1962.

		REGULAR SEASON					PLAYOFFS				
Season	Club	GP	G	A	Pts	PIM	GP	G	A	Pts	PIM
1985-86	Detroit Red Wings	38	9	11	20	10	....	....	....	....	....
1986-87	Detroit Red Wings	76	15	32	47	21	16	4	7	11	6
1987-88	Detroit Red Wings	63	14	40	54	20	16	8	12	20	6
1988-89	Detroit Red Wings	69	16	62	78	14	6	0	8	8	2
1989-90	St. Louis Blues	80	23	79	102	30	12	2	12	14	4
1990-91	St. Louis Blues	61	25	90	115	29	13	7	13	20	10
1991-92	St. Louis Blues	54	10	59	69	12	....	....	....	....	....
	Boston Bruins	26	10	20	30	10	15	5	14	19	4
1992-93	Boston Bruins	84	45	*97	142	32	4	0	9	9	4
1993-94	Boston Bruins	77	32	80	112	45	13	3	9	12	8
1994-95	Boston Bruins	48	12	41	53	8	5	1	0	1	2
1995-96	Boston Bruins	70	25	67	92	18	5	2	5	7	2
1996-97	Boston Bruins	63	18	52	70	10	....	....	....	....	....
	Washington Capitals	17	4	8	12	4	....	....	....	....	....
1997-98	Washington Capitals	82	18	58	76	36	21	6	11	17	8
1998-99	Washington Capitals	59	12	42	54	22	....	....	....	....	....
99-2000	Washington Capitals	82	15	56	71	14	5	0	3	3	4
2000-01	Washington Capitals	81	13	*69	82	28	6	0	0	0	0
2001-02	Washington Capitals	66	11	*57	68	22	....	....	....	....	....
	Philadelphia Flyers	14	3	*7	10	6	5	0	2	2	0
2002-03	Mighty Ducks of Anaheim	67	9	36	45	16	21	4	9	13	6
	NHL Totals	**1277**	**339**	**1063**	**1402**	**407**	**163**	**42**	**114**	**156**	**66**

NHL Second All-Star Team (1991)

Played in NHL All-Star Game (1991, 1992, 1993, 1994, 1997)

Signed as a free agent by **Detroit,** June 28, 1985. Traded to **St. Louis** by **Detroit** with Paul MacLean for Bernie Federko and Tony McKegney, June 15, 1989. Traded to **Boston** by **St. Louis** for Craig Janney and Stephane Quintal, February 7, 1992. Traded to **Washington** by **Boston** with Bill Ranford and Rick Tocchet for Jim Carey, Anson Carter, Jason Allison and Washington's 3rd round choice (Lee Goren) in 1997 Entry Draft, March 1, 1997. Traded to **Philadelphia** by **Washington** for Maxime Ouellet and Philadelphia's 1st (later traded to Dallas – Dallas selected Martin Vagner), 2nd (Maxime Daigneault) and 3rd (Derek Krestanovich) round choices in 2002 Entry Draft, March 19, 2002. Signed as a free agent by **Anaheim**, July 1, 2002.

OATMAN, Russell

Left wing. Shoots left. 5'10", 195 lbs. Born, Tillsonburg, Ont., February 19, 1905.

		REGULAR SEASON					PLAYOFFS				
Season	Club	GP	G	A	Pts	PIM	GP	G	A	Pts	PIM
1926-27	Detroit Cougars	14	3	0	3	12	....	....	....	....	....
	Montreal Maroons	25	8	4	12	30	2	0	0	0	0
1927-28	Montreal Maroons	43	7	4	11	36	9	1	0	1	18
1928-29	Montreal Maroons	11	1	0	1	12	....	....	....	....	....
	New York Rangers	27	1	1	2	10	4	0	0	0	0
	NHL Totals	**120**	**20**	**9**	**29**	**100**	**15**	**1**	**0**	**1**	**18**

Rights transferred to **Detroit** after NHL club purchased **Victoria** (WHL) franchise, May 15, 1926. • Suspended by Detroit for insubordination, January 4, 1927. Traded to **Mtl. Maroons** by **Detroit** for cash, January 6, 1927. Traded to **NY Rangers** by **Mtl. Maroons** for cash, December 12, 1928. Traded to **Hamilton** (IHL) by **NY Rangers** for cash, October 30, 1929.

O'BRIEN, Dennis

Defense. Shoots left. 6', 195 lbs. Born, Port Hope, Ont., June 10, 1949.
(Minnesota's 2nd choice, 14th overall, in 1969 Amateur Draft).

		REGULAR SEASON					PLAYOFFS				
Season	Club	GP	G	A	Pts	PIM	GP	G	A	Pts	PIM
1970-71	Minnesota North Stars	27	3	2	5	29	9	0	0	0	20
1971-72	Minnesota North Stars	70	3	6	9	108	3	0	1	1	11
1972-73	Minnesota North Stars	74	3	11	14	75	6	1	0	1	38
1973-74	Minnesota North Stars	77	5	12	17	166	....	....	....	....	....
1974-75	Minnesota North Stars	56	6	10	16	125	....	....	....	....	....
1975-76	Minnesota North Stars	78	1	14	15	187	....	....	....	....	....
1976-77	Minnesota North Stars	75	6	18	24	114	2	0	0	0	4
1977-78	Minnesota North Stars	13	0	2	2	32	....	....	....	....	....
	Colorado Rockies	16	0	2	2	12	....	....	....	....	....
	Cleveland Barons	23	0	3	3	31	....	....	....	....	....
	Boston Bruins	16	2	3	5	29	14	0	1	1	28
1978-79	Boston Bruins	64	2	8	10	107	....	....	....	....	....
1979-80	Boston Bruins	3	0	0	0	2	....	....	....	....	....
	NHL Totals	**592**	**31**	**91**	**122**	**1017**	**34**	**1**	**2**	**3**	**101**

Claimed on waivers by **Colorado** from **Minnesota**, December 2, 1977. Traded to **Cleveland** by **Colorado** for Mike Christie, January 12, 1978. Claimed on waivers by **Boston** from **Cleveland**, March 10, 1978.

O'BRIEN, Ellard

Defense. Shoots left. 6'3", 183 lbs. Born, St. Catharines, Ont., May 27, 1930.

		REGULAR SEASON					PLAYOFFS				
Season	Club	GP	G	A	Pts	PIM	GP	G	A	Pts	PIM
1955-56	Boston Bruins	2	0	0	0	0	....	....	....	....	....
	NHL Totals	**2**	**0**	**0**	**0**	**0**	....	....	....	....	....

Signed as a free agent by **Boston**, October 3, 1950. Traded to **Hershey** (AHL) by **Boston** with Dunc Fisher for Ray Gariepy, June, 1953.

OBSUT, Jaroslav

Defense. Shoots left. 6'1", 200 lbs. Born, Presov, Czech., September 3, 1976.
(Winnipeg's 9th choice, 188th overall, in 1995 Entry Draft).

		REGULAR SEASON					PLAYOFFS				
Season	Club	GP	G	A	Pts	PIM	GP	G	A	Pts	PIM
2000-01	St. Louis Blues	4	0	0	0	2	....	....	....	....	....
2001-02	Colorado Avalanche	3	0	0	0	0	....	....	....	....	....
	NHL Totals	**7**	**0**	**0**	**0**	**2**	....	....	....	....	....

Signed as a free agent by **St. Louis**, April 26, 1999. Signed as a free agent by **Colorado**, August 11, 2001. Signed as a free agent by **Vancouver**, July 10, 2002.

O'CALLAHAN, Jack

Defense. Shoots right. 6'1", 190 lbs. Born, Charleston, MA, July 24, 1957.
(Chicago's 5th choice, 96th overall, in 1977 Amateur Draft).

		REGULAR SEASON					PLAYOFFS				
Season	Club	GP	G	A	Pts	PIM	GP	G	A	Pts	PIM
1982-83	Chicago Black Hawks	39	0	11	11	46	5	0	2	2	2
1983-84	Chicago Black Hawks	70	4	13	17	67	2	0	0	0	2
1984-85	Chicago Black Hawks	66	6	8	14	105	15	3	5	8	25
1985-86	Chicago Black Hawks	80	4	19	23	116	3	0	1	1	4
1986-87	Chicago Blackhawks	48	1	13	14	59	2	0	0	0	2
1987-88	New Jersey Devils	50	7	19	26	97	5	1	3	4	6
1988-89	New Jersey Devils	36	5	21	26	51	....	....	....	....	....
	NHL Totals	**389**	**27**	**104**	**131**	**541**	**32**	**4**	**11**	**15**	**41**

Claimed by **New Jersey** from **Chicago** in Waiver Draft, October 5, 1987.

O'CONNELL, Mike

Defense. Shoots right. 5'9", 180 lbs. Born, Chicago, IL, November 25, 1955.
(Chicago's 3rd choice, 43rd overall, in 1975 Amateur Draft).

		REGULAR SEASON					PLAYOFFS				
Season	Club	GP	G	A	Pts	PIM	GP	G	A	Pts	PIM
1977-78	Chicago Black Hawks	6	1	1	2	2	....	....	....	....	....
1978-79	Chicago Black Hawks	48	4	22	26	20	4	0	0	0	4
1979-80	Chicago Black Hawks	78	8	22	30	52	7	0	1	1	0
1980-81	Chicago Black Hawks	34	5	16	21	32	....	....	....	....	....
	Boston Bruins	48	10	22	32	42	3	1	3	4	2
1981-82	Boston Bruins	80	5	34	39	75	11	2	2	4	20
1982-83	Boston Bruins	80	14	39	53	42	17	3	5	8	12
1983-84	Boston Bruins	75	18	42	60	42	3	0	0	0	0
1984-85	Boston Bruins	78	15	40	55	64	5	1	5	6	0
1985-86	Boston Bruins	63	8	21	29	47	....	....	....	....	....
	Detroit Red Wings	13	1	7	8	16	....	....	....	....	....
1986-87	Detroit Red Wings	77	5	26	31	70	16	1	4	5	14
1987-88	Detroit Red Wings	48	6	13	19	38	10	0	4	4	8
1988-89	Detroit Red Wings	66	1	15	16	41	6	0	0	0	4
1989-90	Detroit Red Wings	66	4	14	18	22	....	....	....	....	....
	NHL Totals	**860**	**105**	**334**	**439**	**605**	**82**	**8**	**24**	**32**	**64**

Played in NHL All-Star Game (1984)

Traded to **Boston** by **Chicago** for Al Secord, December 18, 1980. Traded to **Detroit** by **Boston** for Reed Larson, March 10, 1986.

O'CONNOR, Buddy

HHOF

Center. Shoots right. 5'8", 142 lbs. Born, Montreal, Que., June 21, 1916.

		REGULAR SEASON					PLAYOFFS				
Season	Club	GP	G	A	Pts	PIM	GP	G	A	Pts	PIM
1941-42	Montreal Canadiens	36	9	16	25	4	3	0	1	1	0
1942-43	Montreal Canadiens	50	15	43	58	2	5	4	5	9	0
1943-44 ♦	Montreal Canadiens	44	12	42	54	6	8	1	2	3	2
1944-45	Montreal Canadiens	50	21	23	44	2	2	0	0	0	0
1945-46 ♦	Montreal Canadiens	45	11	11	22	2	9	2	3	5	0
1946-47	Montreal Canadiens	46	10	20	30	6	8	3	4	7	0
1947-48	New York Rangers	60	24	36	60	8	6	1	4	5	0
1948-49	New York Rangers	46	11	24	35	0	....	....	....	....	....
1949-50	New York Rangers	66	11	22	33	4	12	4	2	6	4
1950-51	New York Rangers	66	16	20	36	0	....	....	....	....	....
	NHL Totals	**509**	**140**	**257**	**397**	**34**	**53**	**15**	**21**	**36**	**6**

NHL Second All-Star Team (1948) • Lady Byng Trophy (1948) • Hart Trophy (1948)

Played in NHL All-Star Game (1949)

Rights traded to **Mtl. Maroons** by **Montreal** for Sammy McManus, September 10, 1936. Traded to **Montreal** by **Mtl. Maroons** for cash, September 24, 1938. Traded to **NY Rangers** by **Montreal** with Frank Eddolls for Hal Laycoe, Joe Bell and George Robertson, August 19, 1947.

O'CONNOR, Myles

Defense. Shoots left. 5'11", 190 lbs. Born, Calgary, Alta., April 2, 1967.
(New Jersey's 4th choice, 45th overall, in 1985 Entry Draft).

		REGULAR SEASON					PLAYOFFS				
Season	Club	GP	G	A	Pts	PIM	GP	G	A	Pts	PIM
1990-91	New Jersey Devils	22	3	1	4	41	....	....	....	....	....
1991-92	New Jersey Devils	9	0	2	2	13	....	....	....	....	....
1992-93	New Jersey Devils	7	0	0	0	9	....	....	....	....	....
1993-94	Mighty Ducks of Anaheim	5	0	1	1	6	....	....	....	....	....
	NHL Totals	**43**	**3**	**4**	**7**	**69**	....	....	....	....	....

Signed as a free agent by **Anaheim**, July 22, 1993.

ODDLEIFSON, Chris

Center. Shoots right. 6'2", 185 lbs. Born, Brandon, Man., September 7, 1950.
(California's 1st choice, 10th overall, in 1970 Amateur Draft).

		REGULAR SEASON					PLAYOFFS				
Season	Club	GP	G	A	Pts	PIM	GP	G	A	Pts	PIM
1972-73	Boston Bruins	6	0	0	0	0	....	....	....	....	....
1973-74	Boston Bruins	49	10	11	21	25	....	....	....	....	....
	Vancouver Canucks	21	3	5	8	19	....	....	....	....	....
1974-75	Vancouver Canucks	60	16	35	51	54	5	0	3	3	2
1975-76	Vancouver Canucks	80	16	46	62	88	2	1	2	3	0
1976-77	Vancouver Canucks	80	14	26	40	81	....	....	....	....	....
1977-78	Vancouver Canucks	78	17	22	39	64	....	....	....	....	....
1978-79	Vancouver Canucks	67	11	26	37	51	3	0	1	1	2
1979-80	Vancouver Canucks	75	8	20	28	76	4	0	0	0	4
1980-81	Vancouver Canucks	8	0	0	0	6	....	....	....	....	....
	NHL Totals	**524**	**95**	**191**	**286**	**464**	**14**	**1**	**6**	**7**	**8**

Traded to **Boston** by **California** with Rich Leduc for Ivan Boldirev, November 17, 1971. Traded to **Vancouver** by **Boston** with Fred O'Donnell and the NHL rights to Mike Walton for Bobby Schmautz, February 7, 1974.

ODELEIN, Lyle

Defense. Shoots right. 6', 210 lbs. Born, Quill Lake, Sask., July 21, 1968.
(Montreal's 8th choice, 141st overall, in 1986 Entry Draft).

Season	Club	GP	G	A	Pts	PIM	GP	G	A	Pts	PIM
		REGULAR SEASON					PLAYOFFS				
1989-90	Montreal Canadiens	8	0	2	2	33	....	....	....	....	....
1990-91	Montreal Canadiens	52	0	2	2	259	12	0	0	0	54
1991-92	Montreal Canadiens	71	1	7	8	212	7	0	0	0	11
1992-93 ◆	Montreal Canadiens	83	2	14	16	205	20	1	5	6	30
1993-94	Montreal Canadiens	79	11	29	40	276	7	0	0	0	17
1994-95	Montreal Canadiens	48	3	7	10	152	....	....	....	....	....
1995-96	Montreal Canadiens	79	3	14	17	230	6	1	1	2	6
1996-97	New Jersey Devils	79	3	13	16	110	10	2	2	4	19
1997-98	New Jersey Devils	79	4	19	23	171	6	1	1	2	21
1998-99	New Jersey Devils	70	5	26	31	114	7	0	3	3	10
99-2000	New Jersey Devils	57	1	15	16	104	....	....	....	....	....
	Phoenix Coyotes	16	1	7	8	19	5	0	0	0	16
2000-01	Columbus Blue Jackets	81	3	14	17	118	....	....	....	....	....
2001-02	Columbus Blue Jackets	65	2	14	16	89	....	....	....	....	....
	Chicago Blackhawks	12	0	2	2	4	4	0	1	1	25
2002-03	Chicago Blackhawks	65	7	4	11	76	....	....	....	....	....
	Dallas Stars	3	0	0	0	6	2	0	0	0	0
	NHL Totals	**947**	**46**	**189**	**235**	**2178**	**86**	**5**	**13**	**18**	**209**

• Brother of Selmar

Traded to **New Jersey** by **Montreal** for Stephane Richer, August 22, 1996. Traded to **Phoenix** by **New Jersey** for Deron Quint and Phoenix's 3rd round choice (later traded back to Phoenix – Phoenix selected Beat Forster) in 2001 Entry Draft, March 7, 2000. Selected by **Columbus** from **Phoenix** in Expansion Draft, June 23, 2000. Traded to **Chicago** by **Columbus** for Jaroslav Spacek and Chicago's 2nd round choice (Dan Fritsche) in 2003 Entry Draft, March 19, 2002. Traded to **Dallas** by **Chicago** for Sami Helenius and Dallas's 7th round choice in 2004 Entry Draft, March 10, 2003.

ODELEIN, Selmar

Defense. Shoots right. 6', 195 lbs. Born, Quill Lake, Sask., April 11, 1966.
(Edmonton's 1st choice, 21st overall, in 1984 Entry Draft).

Season	Club	GP	G	A	Pts	PIM	GP	G	A	Pts	PIM
1985-86	Edmonton Oilers	4	0	0	0	0	....	....	....	....	....
1987-88	Edmonton Oilers	12	0	2	2	33	....	....	....	....	....
1988-89	Edmonton Oilers	2	0	0	0	2	....	....	....	....	....
	NHL Totals	**18**	**0**	**2**	**2**	**35**	....	....	....	....	....

• Brother of Lyle

ODGERS, Jeff

Right wing. Shoots right. 5'11", 200 lbs. Born, Spy Hill, Sask., May 31, 1969.

Season	Club	GP	G	A	Pts	PIM	GP	G	A	Pts	PIM
1991-92	San Jose Sharks	61	7	4	11	217	....	....	....	....	....
1992-93	San Jose Sharks	66	12	15	27	253	....	....	....	....	....
1993-94	San Jose Sharks	81	13	8	21	222	11	0	0	0	11
1994-95	San Jose Sharks	48	4	3	7	117	11	1	1	2	23
1995-96	San Jose Sharks	78	12	4	16	192	....	....	....	....	....
1996-97	Boston Bruins	80	7	8	15	197	....	....	....	....	....
1997-98	Colorado Avalanche	68	5	8	13	213	6	0	0	0	25
1998-99	Colorado Avalanche	75	2	3	5	259	15	1	0	1	14
99-2000	Colorado Avalanche	62	1	2	3	162	4	0	0	0	0
2000-01	Atlanta Thrashers	82	6	7	13	226	....	....	....	....	....
2001-02	Atlanta Thrashers	46	4	4	8	135	....	....	....	....	....
2002-03	Atlanta Thrashers	74	2	4	6	171	....	....	....	....	....
	NHL Totals	**821**	**75**	**70**	**145**	**2364**	**47**	**2**	**1**	**3**	**73**

Signed as a free agent by **San Jose**, September 3, 1991. Traded to **Boston** by **San Jose** with Pittsburgh's 5th round choice (previously acquired, Boston selected Elias Abrahamsson) in 1996 Entry Draft for Al Iafrate, June 21, 1996. Signed as a free agent by **Colorado**, October 24, 1997. Selected by **Minnesota** from **Colorado** in Expansion Draft, June 23, 2000. Claimed by **Atlanta** from **Minnesota** in Waiver Draft, September 29, 2000.

ODJICK, Gino

Right wing. Shoots left. 6'3", 224 lbs. Born, Maniwaki, Que., September 7, 1970.
(Vancouver's 5th choice, 86th overall, in 1990 Entry Draft).

Season	Club	GP	G	A	Pts	PIM	GP	G	A	Pts	PIM
1990-91	Vancouver Canucks	45	7	1	8	296	6	0	0	0	18
1991-92	Vancouver Canucks	65	4	6	10	348	4	0	0	0	6
1992-93	Vancouver Canucks	75	4	13	17	370	1	0	0	0	0
1993-94	Vancouver Canucks	76	16	13	29	271	10	0	0	0	18
1994-95	Vancouver Canucks	23	4	5	9	109	5	0	0	0	47
1995-96	Vancouver Canucks	55	3	4	7	181	6	3	1	4	6
1996-97	Vancouver Canucks	70	5	8	13	*371	....	....	....	....	....
1997-98	Vancouver Canucks	35	3	2	5	181	....	....	....	....	....
	New York Islanders	13	0	0	0	31	....	....	....	....	....
1998-99	New York Islanders	23	4	3	7	133	....	....	....	....	....
99-2000	New York Islanders	46	5	10	15	90	....	....	....	....	....
	Philadelphia Flyers	13	3	1	4	10	....	....	....	....	....
2000-01	Philadelphia Flyers	17	1	3	4	28	....	....	....	....	....
	Montreal Canadiens	13	1	0	1	44	....	....	....	....	....
2001-02	Montreal Canadiens	36	4	4	8	104	12	1	0	1	47
	NHL Totals	**605**	**64**	**73**	**137**	**2567**	**44**	**4**	**1**	**5**	**142**

Traded to **NY Islanders** by **Vancouver** for Jason Strudwick, March 23, 1998. Traded to **Philadelphia** by **NY Islanders** for Mikael Andersson and Carolina's 5th round choice (previously acquired, NY Islanders selected Kristofer Ottosson) in 2000 Entry Draft, February 15, 2000. Traded to **Montreal** by **Philadelphia** for P.J. Stock and Montreal's 6th round choice (Dennis Seidenberg) in 2001 Entry Draft, December 7, 2000. • Missed majority of 2000-01 season recovering from wrist injury suffered in game vs. Carolina, January 16, 2001.

O'DONNELL, Fred

Right wing. Shoots right. 5'10", 175 lbs. Born, Kingston, Ont., December 6, 1949.
(Minnesota's 4th choice, 37th overall, in 1969 Amateur Draft).

Season	Club	GP	G	A	Pts	PIM	GP	G	A	Pts	PIM
1972-73	Boston Bruins	72	10	4	14	55	5	0	1	1	5
1973-74	Boston Bruins	43	5	7	12	43	....	....	....	....	....
	NHL Totals	**115**	**15**	**11**	**26**	**98**	**5**	**0**	**1**	**1**	**5**

Traded to **Boston** by **Minnesota** to complete transaction that sent Barry Gibbs and Tommy Williams to Boston (May 7, 1969), May 7, 1971. Traded to **Vancouver** by **Boston** with Chris Oddleifson and the NHL rights to Mike Walton for Bobby Schmautz, February 7, 1974. • Suspended by **Vancouver** for refusing to report to NHL club, February 9, 1974.

O'DONNELL, Sean

Defense. Shoots left. 6'3", 230 lbs. Born, Ottawa, Ont., October 13, 1971.
(Buffalo's 6th choice, 123rd overall, in 1991 Entry Draft).

Season	Club	GP	G	A	Pts	PIM	GP	G	A	Pts	PIM
1994-95	Los Angeles Kings	15	0	2	2	49	....	....	....	....	....
1995-96	Los Angeles Kings	71	2	5	7	127	....	....	....	....	....
1996-97	Los Angeles Kings	55	5	12	17	144	....	....	....	....	....
1997-98	Los Angeles Kings	80	2	15	17	179	4	1	0	1	36
1998-99	Los Angeles Kings	80	1	13	14	186	....	....	....	....	....
99-2000	Los Angeles Kings	80	2	12	14	114	4	1	0	1	4
2000-01	Minnesota Wild	63	4	12	16	128	....	....	....	....	....
	New Jersey Devils	17	0	1	1	33	23	1	2	3	41
2001-02	Boston Bruins	80	3	22	25	89	6	0	2	2	4
2002-03	Boston Bruins	70	1	15	16	76	....	....	....	....	....
	NHL Totals	**611**	**20**	**109**	**129**	**1125**	**37**	**3**	**4**	**7**	**85**

Traded to **Los Angeles** by **Buffalo** for Doug Houda, July 26, 1994. Selected by **Minnesota** from **Los Angeles** in Expansion Draft, June 23, 2000. Traded to **New Jersey** by **Minnesota** for Willie Mitchell, March 4, 2001. Signed as a free agent by **Boston**, July 2, 2001.

O'DONOGHUE, Don

Right wing. Shoots right. 5'10", 180 lbs. Born, Kingston, Ont., August 27, 1949.
(Oakland's 3rd choice, 29th overall, in 1969 Amateur Draft).

Season	Club	GP	G	A	Pts	PIM	GP	G	A	Pts	PIM
1969-70	Oakland Seals	68	5	6	11	21	3	0	0	0	0
1970-71	California Seals	43	11	9	20	10	....	....	....	....	....
1971-72	California Golden Seals	14	2	2	4	4	....	....	....	....	....
	NHL Totals	**125**	**18**	**17**	**35**	**35**	**3**	**0**	**0**	**0**	**0**

Traded to **Boston** by **California** with Carol Vadnais for Reggie Leach, Rick Smith and Bob Stewart, February 23, 1972. Claimed by **Rochester** (AHL) from **Boston** in Reverse Draft, June 12, 1972.

ODROWSKI, Gerry

Defense. Shoots left. 5'10", 185 lbs. Born, Trout Creek, Ont., October 4, 1938.

Season	Club	GP	G	A	Pts	PIM	GP	G	A	Pts	PIM
1960-61	Detroit Red Wings	68	1	4	5	45	10	0	0	0	4
1961-62	Detroit Red Wings	69	1	6	7	24	....	....	....	....	....
1962-63	Detroit Red Wings	1	0	0	0	0	2	0	0	0	2
1967-68	Oakland Seals	42	4	6	10	10	....	....	....	....	....
1968-69	Oakland Seals	74	5	1	6	24	7	0	1	1	2
1971-72	St. Louis Blues	55	1	2	3	8	11	0	0	0	8
	NHL Totals	**309**	**12**	**19**	**31**	**111**	**30**	**0**	**1**	**1**	**16**

Traded to **Boston** by **Detroit** for Warren Godfrey, October 10, 1963. Traded to **San Francisco** (WHL) by **Boston** with future considerations (loan of Dallas Smith for the 1964-65 season, July 8, 1964) for Cliff Pennington, December 17, 1963. NHL rights transferred to **California** after owners of **San Francisco** (WHL) franchise awarded NHL expansion franchise, April 5, 1966. Traded to **San Diego** (WHL) by **Oakland** for cash, October 1, 1969. Traded to **Phoenix** (WHL) by **San Diego** (WHL) for cash, October, 1970. Traded to **St. Louis** by **Phoenix** (WHL) for cash, November 28, 1971.

O'DWYER, Bill

Center. Shoots left. 6', 190 lbs. Born, Boston, MA, January 25, 1960.
(Los Angeles' 10th choice, 157th overall, in 1980 Entry Draft).

Season	Club	GP	G	A	Pts	PIM	GP	G	A	Pts	PIM
1983-84	Los Angeles Kings	5	0	0	0	0	....	....	....	....	....
1984-85	Los Angeles Kings	13	1	0	1	15	....	....	....	....	....
1987-88	Boston Bruins	77	7	10	17	83	9	0	0	0	0
1988-89	Boston Bruins	19	1	2	3	8	....	....	....	....	....
1989-90	Boston Bruins	6	0	1	1	2	1	0	0	0	2
	NHL Totals	**120**	**9**	**13**	**22**	**108**	**10**	**0**	**0**	**0**	**2**

Signed as a free agent by **NY Rangers**, July 13, 1985. Signed as a free agent by **Boston**, August 13, 1987. Signed as a free agent by **Los Angeles**, July 11, 1990.

O'FLAHERTY, Gerry

Left wing. Shoots left. 5'10", 182 lbs. Born, Pittsburgh, PA, August 31, 1950.
(Toronto's 3rd choice, 36th overall, in 1970 Amateur Draft).

Season	Club	GP	G	A	Pts	PIM	GP	G	A	Pts	PIM
1971-72	Toronto Maple Leafs	2	0	0	0	0	....	....	....	....	....
1972-73	Vancouver Canucks	78	13	17	30	29	....	....	....	....	....
1973-74	Vancouver Canucks	78	22	20	42	18	....	....	....	....	....
1974-75	Vancouver Canucks	80	25	17	42	37	5	2	2	4	6
1975-76	Vancouver Canucks	68	20	18	38	47	2	0	0	0	0
1976-77	Vancouver Canucks	72	12	12	24	20	....	....	....	....	....
1977-78	Vancouver Canucks	59	6	11	17	15	....	....	....	....	....
1978-79	Atlanta Flames	1	1	0	1	2	....	....	....	....	....
	NHL Totals	**438**	**99**	**95**	**194**	**168**	**7**	**2**	**2**	**4**	**6**

• Son of Peanuts

Claimed by **Vancouver** from **Toronto** in Intra-League Draft, June 5, 1972. Signed as a free agent by **Minnesota**, July 15, 1978. Traded to **Atlanta** by **Minnesota** for cash, October 10, 1978.

O'FLAHERTY, Peanuts

Right wing. Shoots right. 5'7", 154 lbs. Born, Toronto, Ont., April 10, 1918.

Season	Club	GP	G	A	Pts	PIM	GP	G	A	Pts	PIM
		REGULAR SEASON					PLAYOFFS				
1940-41	New York Americans	10	4	0	4	0	....	....	....	....	....
1941-42	Brooklyn Americans	11	1	1	2	0	....	....	....	....	....
	NHL Totals	**21**	**5**	**1**	**6**	**0**	....	....	....	....	....

• Father of Gerry

Signed as a free agent by **NY Americans**, October 17, 1940. Loaned to **Toronto** (Pittsburgh-AHL) by **NY Americans** (Springfield-AHL) with the trade of Jack Howard for Clarence Drouillard, January 17, 1941. • Team name changed to **Brooklyn Americans** prior to 1941-42 season. Returned to **Brooklyn** by **Toronto** (Pittsburgh-AHL) with the trade of Phil McAtee for Viv Allen and Glenn Brydson, October 8, 1941.

OGILVIE, Brian

Center. Shoots right. 5'11", 186 lbs. Born, Stettler, Alta., January 30, 1952.
(Chicago's 2nd choice, 29th overall, in 1972 Amateur Draft).

Season	Club	GP	G	A	Pts	PIM	GP	G	A	Pts	PIM
1972-73	Chicago Black Hawks	12	1	2	3	4	....	....	....	....	....
1974-75	St. Louis Blues	20	5	5	10	4	....	....	....	....	....
1975-76	St. Louis Blues	9	2	1	3	2	....	....	....	....	....
1976-77	St. Louis Blues	3	0	0	0	0	....	....	....	....	....
1977-78	St. Louis Blues	32	6	8	14	12	....	....	....	....	....
1978-79	St. Louis Blues	14	1	5	6	7	....	....	....	....	....
	NHL Totals	**90**	**15**	**21**	**36**	**29**	....	....	....	....	....

Claimed by **St. Louis** from **Chicago** in Intra-League Draft, June 10, 1974.

O'GRADY, George

Defense. Shoots left. 5'8", 175 lbs. Born, Montreal, Que.,

Season	Club	GP	G	A	Pts	PIM	GP	G	A	Pts	PIM
1917-18	Montreal Wanderers	4	0	0	0	0	....	....	....	....	....
	NHL Totals	**4**	**0**	**0**	**0**	**0**	....	....	....	....	....

Rights retained by **Mtl. Wanderers** after NHA folded, November 26, 1917.

OGRODNICK, John

Left wing. Shoots left. 6', 204 lbs. Born, Ottawa, Ont., June 20, 1959.
(Detroit's 4th choice, 66th overall, in 1979 Entry Draft).

Season	Club	GP	G	A	Pts	PIM	GP	G	A	Pts	PIM
1979-80	Detroit Red Wings	41	8	24	32	8	....	....	....	....	....
1980-81	Detroit Red Wings	80	35	35	70	14	....	....	....	....	....
1981-82	Detroit Red Wings	80	28	26	54	28	....	....	....	....	....
1982-83	Detroit Red Wings	80	41	44	85	30	....	....	....	....	....
1983-84	Detroit Red Wings	64	42	36	78	14	4	0	0	0	0
1984-85	Detroit Red Wings	79	55	50	105	30	3	1	1	2	0
1985-86	Detroit Red Wings	76	38	32	70	18	....	....	....	....	....
1986-87	Detroit Red Wings	39	12	28	40	6	....	....	....	....	....
	Quebec Nordiques	32	11	16	27	4	13	9	4	13	6
1987-88	New York Rangers	64	22	32	54	16	....	....	....	....	....
1988-89	New York Rangers	60	13	29	42	14	3	2	0	2	0
1989-90	New York Rangers	80	43	31	74	44	10	6	3	9	0
1990-91	New York Rangers	79	31	23	54	10	4	0	0	0	0
1991-92	New York Rangers	55	17	13	30	22	3	0	0	0	0
1992-93	Detroit Red Wings	19	6	6	12	2	1	0	0	0	0
	NHL Totals	**928**	**402**	**425**	**827**	**260**	**41**	**18**	**8**	**26**	**6**

NHL First All-Star Team (1985)

Played in NHL All-Star Game (1981, 1982, 1984, 1985, 1986)

Traded to **Quebec** by **Detroit** with Basil McRae and Doug Shedden for Brent Ashton, Gilbert Delorme and Mark Kumpel, January 17, 1987. Traded to **NY Rangers** by **Quebec** with David Shaw for Jeff Jackson and Terry Carkner, September 30, 1987. Signed as a free agent by **Detroit**, September 29, 1992.

OHLUND, Mattias

Defense. Shoots left. 6'2", 220 lbs. Born, Pitea, Sweden, September 9, 1976.
(Vancouver's 1st choice, 13th overall, in 1994 Entry Draft).

Season	Club	GP	G	A	Pts	PIM	GP	G	A	Pts	PIM
1997-98	Vancouver Canucks	77	7	23	30	76	....	....	....	....	....
1998-99	Vancouver Canucks	74	9	26	35	83	....	....	....	....	....
99-2000	Vancouver Canucks	42	4	16	20	24	....	....	....	....	....
2000-01	Vancouver Canucks	65	8	20	28	46	4	1	3	4	6
2001-02	Vancouver Canucks	81	10	26	36	56	6	1	1	2	6
2002-03	Vancouver Canucks	59	2	27	29	42	13	3	4	7	12
	NHL Totals	**398**	**40**	**138**	**178**	**327**	**23**	**5**	**8**	**13**	**24**

NHL All-Rookie Team (1998)

Played in NHL All-Star Game (1999)

OJANEN, Janne

Center. Shoots left. 6'2", 200 lbs. Born, Tampere, Finland, April 9, 1968.
(New Jersey's 3rd choice, 45th overall, in 1986 Entry Draft).

Season	Club	GP	G	A	Pts	PIM	GP	G	A	Pts	PIM
1988-89	New Jersey Devils	3	0	1	1	2	....	....	....	....	....
1989-90	New Jersey Devils	64	17	13	30	12	....	....	....	....	....
1991-92	New Jersey Devils	....	....	....	....	....	3	0	2	2	0
1992-93	New Jersey Devils	31	4	9	13	14	....	....	....	....	....
	NHL Totals	**98**	**21**	**23**	**44**	**28**	**3**	**0**	**2**	**2**	**0**

OKERLUND, Todd

Right wing. Shoots right. 5'11", 200 lbs. Born, Burnsville, MN, September 6, 1964.
(NY Islanders' 8th choice, 168th overall, in 1982 Entry Draft).

Season	Club	GP	G	A	Pts	PIM	GP	G	A	Pts	PIM
1987-88	New York Islanders	4	0	0	0	2	....	....	....	....	....
	NHL Totals	**4**	**0**	**0**	**0**	**2**	....	....	....	....	....

OKSIUTA, Roman

Right wing. Shoots left. 6'3", 230 lbs. Born, Murmansk, USSR, August 21, 1970.
(NY Rangers' 11th choice, 202nd overall, in 1989 Entry Draft).

Season	Club	GP	G	A	Pts	PIM	GP	G	A	Pts	PIM
1993-94	Edmonton Oilers	10	1	2	3	4	....	....	....	....	....
1994-95	Edmonton Oilers	26	11	2	13	8	....	....	....	....	....
	Vancouver Canucks	12	5	2	7	2	10	2	3	5	0
1995-96	Vancouver Canucks	56	16	23	39	42	....	....	....	....	....
	Mighty Ducks of Anaheim	14	7	5	12	18	....	....	....	....	....
1996-97	Mighty Ducks of Anaheim	28	6	7	13	22	....	....	....	....	....
	Pittsburgh Penguins	7	0	0	0	4	....	....	....	....	....
	NHL Totals	**153**	**46**	**41**	**87**	**100**	**10**	**2**	**3**	**5**	**0**

Traded to **Edmonton** by **NY Rangers** with NY Rangers' 3rd round choice (Alexander Kerch) in 1993 Entry Draft for Kevin Lowe, December 11, 1992. Traded to **Vancouver** by **Edmonton** for Jiri Slegr, April 7, 1995. Traded to **Anaheim** by **Vancouver** for Mike Sillinger, March 15, 1996. Traded to **Pittsburgh** by **Anaheim** for Richard Park, March 18, 1997.

OLAUSSON, Fredrik

Defense. Shoots right. 6'2", 198 lbs. Born, Dadesjo, Sweden, October 5, 1966.
(Winnipeg's 4th choice, 81st overall, in 1985 Entry Draft).

Season	Club	GP	G	A	Pts	PIM	GP	G	A	Pts	PIM
1986-87	Winnipeg Jets	72	7	29	36	24	10	2	3	5	4
1987-88	Winnipeg Jets	38	5	10	15	18	5	1	1	2	0
1988-89	Winnipeg Jets	75	15	47	62	32	....	....	....	....	....
1989-90	Winnipeg Jets	77	9	46	55	32	7	0	2	2	2
1990-91	Winnipeg Jets	71	12	29	41	24	....	....	....	....	....
1991-92	Winnipeg Jets	77	20	42	62	34	7	1	5	6	4
1992-93	Winnipeg Jets	68	16	41	57	22	6	0	2	2	2
1993-94	Winnipeg Jets	18	2	5	7	10	....	....	....	....	....
	Edmonton Oilers	55	9	19	28	20	....	....	....	....	....
1994-95	Edmonton Oilers	33	0	10	10	20	....	....	....	....	....
1995-96	Edmonton Oilers	20	0	6	6	14	....	....	....	....	....
	Mighty Ducks of Anaheim	36	2	16	18	24	....	....	....	....	....
1996-97	Mighty Ducks of Anaheim	20	2	9	11	8	....	....	....	....	....
	Pittsburgh Penguins	51	7	20	27	24	4	0	1	1	0
1997-98	Pittsburgh Penguins	76	6	27	33	42	6	0	3	3	2
1998-99	Mighty Ducks of Anaheim	74	16	40	56	30	4	0	2	2	4
99-2000	Mighty Ducks of Anaheim	70	15	19	34	28	....	....	....	....	....
2001-02 ◆	Detroit Red Wings	47	2	13	15	22	21	2	4	6	10
2002-03	Mighty Ducks of Anaheim	44	2	6	8	22	1	0	0	0	0
	NHL Totals	**1022**	**147**	**434**	**581**	**450**	**71**	**6**	**23**	**29**	**28**

Traded to **Edmonton** by **Winnipeg** with Winnipeg's 7th round choice (Curtis Sheptak) in 1994 Entry Draft for Edmonton's 3rd round choice (Tavis Hansen) in 1994 Entry Draft, December 6, 1993. Claimed on waivers by **Anaheim** from **Edmonton**, January 16, 1996. Traded to **Pittsburgh** by **Anaheim** with Alex Hicks for Shawn Antoski and Dmitri Mironov, November 19, 1996. Signed as a free agent by **Anaheim**, August 28, 1998. Signed as a free agent by **Detroit**, May 24, 2001. Signed as a free agent by **Anaheim**, July 12, 2002.

OLCZYK, Ed

Center. Shoots left. 6'1", 207 lbs. Born, Chicago, IL, August 16, 1966.
(Chicago's 1st choice, 3rd overall, in 1984 Entry Draft).

Season	Club	GP	G	A	Pts	PIM	GP	G	A	Pts	PIM
1984-85	Chicago Black Hawks	70	20	30	50	67	15	6	5	11	11
1985-86	Chicago Black Hawks	79	29	50	79	47	3	0	0	0	0
1986-87	Chicago Blackhawks	79	16	35	51	119	4	1	1	2	4
1987-88	Toronto Maple Leafs	80	42	33	75	55	6	5	4	9	2
1988-89	Toronto Maple Leafs	80	38	52	90	75	....	....	....	....	....
1989-90	Toronto Maple Leafs	79	32	56	88	78	5	1	2	3	14
1990-91	Toronto Maple Leafs	18	4	10	14	13	....	....	....	....	....
	Winnipeg Jets	61	26	31	57	69	....	....	....	....	....
1991-92	Winnipeg Jets	64	32	33	65	67	6	2	1	3	4
1992-93	Winnipeg Jets	25	8	12	20	26	....	....	....	....	....
	New York Rangers	46	13	16	29	26	....	....	....	....	....
1993-94 ◆	New York Rangers	37	3	5	8	28	1	0	0	0	0
1994-95	New York Rangers	20	2	1	3	4	....	....	....	....	....
	Winnipeg Jets	13	2	8	10	8	....	....	....	....	....
1995-96	Winnipeg Jets	51	27	22	49	65	6	1	2	3	6
1996-97	Los Angeles Kings	67	21	23	44	45	....	....	....	....	....
	Pittsburgh Penguins	12	4	7	11	6	5	1	0	1	12
1997-98	Pittsburgh Penguins	56	11	11	22	35	6	2	0	2	4
1998-99	Chicago Blackhawks	61	10	15	25	29	....	....	....	....	....
99-2000	Chicago Blackhawks	33	2	2	4	12	....	....	....	....	....
	NHL Totals	**1031**	**342**	**452**	**794**	**874**	**57**	**19**	**15**	**34**	**57**

Traded to **Toronto** by **Chicago** with Al Secord for Rick Vaive, Steve Thomas and Bob McGill, September 3, 1987. Traded to **Winnipeg** by **Toronto** with Mark Osborne for Dave Ellett and Paul Fenton, November 10, 1990. Traded to **NY Rangers** by **Winnipeg** for Kris King and Tie Domi, December 28, 1992. • Missed majority of 1993-94 season recovering from thumb injury suffered in game vs. Florida, January 3, 1994. Traded to **Winnipeg** by **NY Rangers** for Winnipeg's 5th round choice (Alexei Vasiliev) in 1995 Entry Draft, April 7, 1995. Signed as a free agent by **Los Angeles**, July 8, 1996. Traded to **Pittsburgh** by **Los Angeles** for Glen Murray, March 18, 1997. Signed as a free agent by **Chicago**, August 26, 1998. • Missed majority of 1999-2000 season recovering from hernia injury suffered in game vs. Pittsburgh, Oct. 16, 1999.

OLIVER, David

Right wing. Shoots right. 6', 190 lbs. Born, Sechelt, B.C., April 17, 1971.
(Edmonton's 7th choice, 144th overall, in 1991 Entry Draft).

Season	Club	GP	G	A	Pts	PIM	GP	G	A	Pts	PIM
1994-95	Edmonton Oilers	44	16	14	30	20	....	....	....	....	....
1995-96	Edmonton Oilers	80	20	19	39	34	....	....	....	....	....
1996-97	Edmonton Oilers	17	1	2	3	4	....	....	....	....	....
	New York Rangers	14	2	1	3	4	3	0	0	0	0
1998-99	Ottawa Senators	17	2	5	7	4	....	....	....	....	....

Season	Club	GP	G	A	Pts	PIM	GP	G	A	Pts	PIM
		REGULAR SEASON					PLAYOFFS				
99-2000	Phoenix Coyotes	9	1	0	1	2	....	....	....	....	....
2000-01	Ottawa Senators	7	0	0	0	2	....	....	....	....	....
2002-03	Dallas Stars	6	0	3	3	2	6	0	0	0	2
	NHL Totals	**194**	**42**	**44**	**86**	**72**	**9**	**0**	**0**	**0**	**2**

Claimed on waivers by **NY Rangers** from **Edmonton**, February 21, 1997. Signed as a free agent by **Ottawa**, July 2, 1998. Signed as a free agent by **Phoenix**, July 20, 1999. Signed as a free agent by **Ottawa**, August 2, 2000. Signed as a free agent by **Dallas**, July 30, 2002.

OLIVER, Harry — HHOF

Right wing. Shoots right. 5'8", 155 lbs. Born, Selkirk, Man., October 26, 1898.

Season	Club	GP	G	A	Pts	PIM	GP	G	A	Pts	PIM
1926-27	Boston Bruins	42	18	6	24	17	8	4	2	*6	4
1927-28	Boston Bruins	43	13	5	18	20	2	2	0	2	4
1928-29 ◆	Boston Bruins	43	17	6	23	24	5	1	1	2	8
1929-30	Boston Bruins	40	16	5	21	12	6	2	1	3	6
1930-31	Boston Bruins	44	16	14	30	18	4	0	0	0	2
1931-32	Boston Bruins	44	13	7	20	22	....	....	....	....	....
1932-33	Boston Bruins	47	11	7	18	10	5	0	0	0	0
1933-34	Boston Bruins	48	5	9	14	6	....	....	....	....	....
1934-35	New York Americans	47	7	9	16	4	....	....	....	....	....
1935-36	New York Americans	45	9	16	25	12	5	1	2	3	0
1936-37	New York Americans	20	2	1	3	2	....	....	....	....	....
	NHL Totals	**463**	**127**	**85**	**212**	**147**	**35**	**10**	**6**	**16**	**24**

Traded to **Boston** by **Calgary** (WHL) for cash, September 4, 1926. Traded to **NY Americans** by **Boston** for cash, November 2, 1934.

OLIVER, Murray

Center. Shoots left. 5'10", 170 lbs. Born, Hamilton, Ont., November 14, 1937.

Season	Club	GP	G	A	Pts	PIM	GP	G	A	Pts	PIM
1957-58	Detroit Red Wings	1	0	1	1	0	....	....	....	....	....
1959-60	Detroit Red Wings	54	20	19	39	16	6	1	0	1	4
1960-61	Detroit Red Wings	49	11	12	23	8	....	....	....	....	....
	Boston Bruins	21	6	10	16	8	....	....	....	....	....
1961-62	Boston Bruins	70	17	29	46	21	....	....	....	....	....
1962-63	Boston Bruins	65	22	40	62	38	....	....	....	....	....
1963-64	Boston Bruins	70	24	44	68	41	....	....	....	....	....
1964-65	Boston Bruins	65	20	23	43	30	....	....	....	....	....
1965-66	Boston Bruins	70	18	42	60	30	....	....	....	....	....
1966-67	Boston Bruins	65	9	26	35	16	....	....	....	....	....
1967-68	Toronto Maple Leafs	74	16	21	37	18	....	....	....	....	....
1968-69	Toronto Maple Leafs	76	14	36	50	16	4	1	2	3	0
1969-70	Toronto Maple Leafs	76	14	33	47	16	....	....	....	....	....
1970-71	Minnesota North Stars	61	9	23	32	8	12	7	4	11	0
1971-72	Minnesota North Stars	77	27	29	56	16	7	0	6	6	4
1972-73	Minnesota North Stars	75	11	31	42	10	6	0	4	4	2
1973-74	Minnesota North Stars	78	17	20	37	4	....	....	....	....	....
1974-75	Minnesota North Stars	80	19	15	34	24	....	....	....	....	....
	NHL Totals	**1127**	**274**	**454**	**728**	**320**	**35**	**9**	**16**	**25**	**10**

Played in NHL All-Star Game (1963, 1964, 1965, 1967, 1968)

Traded to **Boston** by **Detroit** with Gary Aldcorn and Tom McCarthy for Vic Stasiuk and Leo Labine, January 23, 1961. Traded to **Toronto** by **Boston** with cash for Eddie Shack, May 15, 1967. Traded to **Minnesota** by **Toronto** for Terry O'Malley, the rights to Brian Conacher and cash, May 22, 1970.

OLIWA, Krzysztof

Left wing. Shoots left. 6'5", 235 lbs. Born, Tychy, Poland, April 12, 1973.
(New Jersey's 4th choice, 65th overall, in 1993 Entry Draft).

Season	Club	GP	G	A	Pts	PIM	GP	G	A	Pts	PIM
1996-97	New Jersey Devils	1	0	0	0	5	....	....	....	....	....
1997-98	New Jersey Devils	73	2	3	5	295	6	0	0	0	23
1998-99	New Jersey Devils	64	5	7	12	240	1	0	0	0	2
99-2000 ◆	New Jersey Devils	69	6	10	16	184	....	....	....	....	....
2000-01	Columbus Blue Jackets	10	0	2	2	34	....	....	....	....	....
	Pittsburgh Penguins	26	1	2	3	131	5	0	0	0	16
2001-02	Pittsburgh Penguins	57	0	2	2	150	....	....	....	....	....
2002-03	New York Rangers	9	0	0	0	51	....	....	....	....	....
	Boston Bruins	33	0	0	0	110	....	....	....	....	....
	NHL Totals	**342**	**14**	**26**	**40**	**1200**	**12**	**0**	**0**	**0**	**41**

• Born Krzystof Graboski

Traded to **Columbus** by **New Jersey** with future considerations (Deron Quint, June 23, 2000) for Columbus' 3rd round choice (Brandon Nolan) in 2001 Entry Draft and future considerations (Turner Stevenson, June 23, 2000), June 12, 2000. • Missed majority of 2000-2001 season recovering from arm injury suffered in game vs. Detroit, October 28, 2000. Traded to **Pittsburgh** by **Columbus** for San Jose's 3rd round choice (previously acquired, Columbus selected Aaron Johnson) in 2001 Entry Draft, January 14, 2001. Traded to **NY Rangers** by **Pittsburgh** for NY Rangers' 9th round choice (later traded to Tampa Bay – Tampa Bay selected Albert Vishnyakov) in 2003 Entry Draft, June 23, 2002. Traded to **Boston** by **NY Rangers** for Boston's 9th round choice in 2004 Entry Draft, January 6, 2003.

OLMSTEAD, Bert — HHOF

Left wing. Shoots left. 6'1", 180 lbs. Born, Sceptre, Sask., September 4, 1926.

Season	Club	GP	G	A	Pts	PIM	GP	G	A	Pts	PIM
1948-49	Chicago Black Hawks	9	0	2	2	4	....	....	....	....	....
1949-50	Chicago Black Hawks	70	20	29	49	40	....	....	....	....	....
1950-51	Chicago Black Hawks	15	2	1	3	0	....	....	....	....	....
	Montreal Canadiens	39	16	22	38	50	11	2	4	6	9
1951-52	Montreal Canadiens	69	7	28	35	49	11	0	1	1	4
1952-53 ◆	Montreal Canadiens	69	17	28	45	83	12	2	2	4	4
1953-54	Montreal Canadiens	70	15	37	52	85	11	0	1	1	19
1954-55	Montreal Canadiens	70	10	*48	58	103	12	0	4	4	21
1955-56 ◆	Montreal Canadiens	70	14	*56	70	94	10	4	*10	14	8
1956-57 ◆	Montreal Canadiens	64	15	33	48	74	10	0	*9	9	13
1957-58 ◆	Montreal Canadiens	57	9	28	37	71	9	0	3	3	0
1958-59	Toronto Maple Leafs	70	10	31	41	74	12	4	2	6	13
1959-60	Toronto Maple Leafs	53	15	21	36	63	10	3	4	7	0
1960-61	Toronto Maple Leafs	67	18	34	52	84	3	1	2	3	10
1961-62 ◆	Toronto Maple Leafs	56	13	23	36	10	4	0	1	1	0
	NHL Totals	**848**	**181**	**421**	**602**	**884**	**115**	**16**	**43**	**59**	**101**

NHL Second All-Star Team (1953, 1956)

Played in NHL All-Star Game (1953, 1956, 1957, 1959)

Traded to **Detroit** by **Chicago** with Vic Stasiuk for Lee Fogolin and Steve Black, December 2, 1950. Traded to **Montreal** by **Detroit** for Leo Gravelle, December 19, 1950. Claimed by **Toronto** from **Montreal** in Intra-League Draft, June 3, 1958. Claimed by **NY Rangers** from **Toronto** in Intra-League Draft, June 4, 1962.

OLSEN, Darryl

Defense. Shoots left. 6', 180 lbs. Born, Calgary, Alta., October 7, 1966.
(Calgary's 10th choice, 185th overall, in 1985 Entry Draft).

Season	Club	GP	G	A	Pts	PIM	GP	G	A	Pts	PIM
1991-92	Calgary Flames	1	0	0	0	0	....	....	....	....	....
	NHL Totals	**1**	**0**	**0**	**0**	**0**	....	....	....	....	....

Signed as a free agent by **Boston**, July 23, 1992.

OLSON, Dennis

Center. Shoots right. 6', 182 lbs. Born, Kenora, Ont., November 9, 1934.

Season	Club	GP	G	A	Pts	PIM	GP	G	A	Pts	PIM
1957-58	Detroit Red Wings	4	0	0	0	0	....	....	....	....	....
	NHL Totals	**4**	**0**	**0**	**0**	**0**	....	....	....	....	....

Traded to **Springfield** (AHL) by **Detroit** with Bill McCreary and Hank Bassen for Gerry Ehman, May 1, 1958. Claimed by **NY Rangers** from **Springfield** (AHL) in Inter-League Draft, June, 1961.

OLSSON, Christer

Defense. Shoots left. 5'11", 190 lbs. Born, Arboga, Sweden, July 24, 1970.
(St. Louis' 10th choice, 275th overall, in 1993 Entry Draft).

Season	Club	GP	G	A	Pts	PIM	GP	G	A	Pts	PIM
1995-96	St. Louis Blues	26	2	8	10	14	3	0	0	0	0
1996-97	St. Louis Blues	5	0	1	1	0	....	....	....	....	....
	Ottawa Senators	25	2	3	5	10	....	....	....	....	....
	NHL Totals	**56**	**4**	**12**	**16**	**24**	**3**	**0**	**0**	**0**	**0**

Traded to **Ottawa** by **St. Louis** for Pavol Demitra, November 27, 1996.

OLVESTAD, Jimmie

Left wing. Shoots left. 6'1", 189 lbs. Born, Stockholm, Sweden, February 16, 1980.
(Tampa Bay's 4th choice, 88th overall, in 1999 Entry Draft).

Season	Club	GP	G	A	Pts	PIM	GP	G	A	Pts	PIM
2001-02	Tampa Bay Lightning	74	3	11	14	24	....	....	....	....	....
2002-03	Tampa Bay Lightning	37	0	3	3	16	....	....	....	....	....
	NHL Totals	**111**	**3**	**14**	**17**	**40**	....	....	....	....	....

O'NEIL, Jim

Center/Right wing. Shoots right. 5'8", 160 lbs. Born, Semans, Sask., April 3, 1913.

Season	Club	GP	G	A	Pts	PIM	GP	G	A	Pts	PIM
1933-34	Boston Bruins	23	2	2	4	15	....	....	....	....	....
1934-35	Boston Bruins	48	2	11	13	35	4	0	0	0	9
1935-36	Boston Bruins	48	2	11	13	49	2	1	1	2	4
1936-37	Boston Bruins	21	0	2	2	6	....	....	....	....	....
1940-41	Montreal Canadiens	12	0	3	3	0	3	0	0	0	0
1941-42	Montreal Canadiens	4	0	1	1	4	....	....	....	....	....
	NHL Totals	**156**	**6**	**30**	**36**	**109**	**9**	**1**	**1**	**2**	**13**

Traded to **Montreal** by **Cleveland** (IAHL) for Bill Summerhill and Bill MacKenzie, May 17, 1940.

O'NEIL, Paul

Center/Right wing. Shoots right. 6'1", 185 lbs. Born, Charlestown, MA, August 24, 1953.
(Vancouver's 6th choice, 67th overall, in 1973 Amateur Draft).

Season	Club	GP	G	A	Pts	PIM	GP	G	A	Pts	PIM
1973-74	Vancouver Canucks	5	0	0	0	0	....	....	....	....	....
1975-76	Boston Bruins	1	0	0	0	0	....	....	....	....	....
	NHL Totals	**6**	**0**	**0**	**0**	**0**	....	....	....	....	....

Signed as a free agent by **Boston**, October 10, 1975.

O'NEILL, Jeff

Right wing. Shoots right. 6'1", 190 lbs. Born, Richmond Hill, Ont., February 23, 1976.
(Hartford's 1st choice, 5th overall, in 1994 Entry Draft).

Season	Club	GP	G	A	Pts	PIM	GP	G	A	Pts	PIM
1995-96	Hartford Whalers	65	8	19	27	40	....	....	....	....	....
1996-97	Hartford Whalers	72	14	16	30	40	....	....	....	....	....
1997-98	Carolina Hurricanes	74	19	20	39	67	....	....	....	....	....
1998-99	Carolina Hurricanes	75	16	15	31	66	6	0	1	1	0
99-2000	Carolina Hurricanes	80	25	38	63	72	....	....	....	....	....
2000-01	Carolina Hurricanes	82	41	26	67	106	6	1	2	3	10
2001-02	Carolina Hurricanes	76	31	33	64	63	22	8	5	13	27
2002-03	Carolina Hurricanes	82	30	31	61	38	....	....	....	....	....
	NHL Totals	**606**	**184**	**198**	**382**	**492**	**34**	**9**	**8**	**17**	**37**

Transferred to **Carolina** after **Hartford** franchise relocated, June 25, 1997.

O'NEILL, Tom

Right wing. Shoots right. 5'10", 155 lbs. Born, Deseronto, Ont., September 28, 1923.

Season	Club	GP	G	A	Pts	PIM	GP	G	A	Pts	PIM
1943-44	Toronto Maple Leafs	33	8	7	15	29	4	0	0	0	6
1944-45 ◆	Toronto Maple Leafs	33	2	5	7	24	....	....	....	....	....
	NHL Totals	**66**	**10**	**12**	**22**	**53**	**4**	**0**	**0**	**0**	**6**

ORBAN, Bill

Center/Left wing. Shoots left. 6', 185 lbs. Born, Regina, Sask., February 20, 1944.

Season	Club	GP	G	A	Pts	PIM	GP	G	A	Pts	PIM
		REGULAR SEASON					PLAYOFFS				
1967-68	Chicago Black Hawks	39	3	2	5	17	3	0	0	0	0
1968-69	Chicago Black Hawks	45	4	6	10	33	....	....	....	....	....
	Minnesota North Stars	21	1	5	6	10	....	....	....	....	....
1969-70	Minnesota North Stars	9	0	2	2	7	....	....	....	....	....
	NHL Totals	**114**	**8**	**15**	**23**	**67**	**3**	**0**	**0**	**0**	**0**

Traded to **Chicago** by **LA Blades** (WHL) for cash, July, 1967. Traded to **Minnesota** by **Chicago** with Tom Reid for Andre Boudrias and Mike McMahon Jr., February 14, 1969. Traded to **Los Angeles** (Springfield-AHL) by **Cleveland** (AHL) for Roger Cote, March, 1971. Claimed by **Chicago** from **Los Angeles** in Intra-League Draft, June 5, 1972.

O'REE, Willie

Wing. Shoots left. 5'10", 175 lbs. Born, Fredericton, N.B., October 15, 1935.

Season	Club	GP	G	A	Pts	PIM	GP	G	A	Pts	PIM
1957-58	Boston Bruins	2	0	0	0	0	....	....	....	....	....
1960-61	Boston Bruins	43	4	10	14	26	....	....	....	....	....
	NHL Totals	**45**	**4**	**10**	**14**	**26**	....	....	....	....	....

Traded to **Montreal** by **Boston** with Stan Maxwell for Cliff Pennington and Terry Gray, June, 1961. Traded to **LA Blades** (WHL) by **Montreal** for cash, November 10, 1961.

O'REGAN, Tom

Center/Defense. Shoots left. 5'10", 180 lbs. Born, Cambridge, MA, December 29, 1961.

Season	Club	GP	G	A	Pts	PIM	GP	G	A	Pts	PIM
1983-84	Pittsburgh Penguins	51	4	10	14	8	....	....	....	....	....
1984-85	Pittsburgh Penguins	1	0	0	0	0	....	....	....	....	....
1985-86	Pittsburgh Penguins	9	1	2	3	2	....	....	....	....	....
	NHL Totals	**61**	**5**	**12**	**17**	**10**	....	....	....	....	....

Signed as a free agent by **Pittsburgh**, September 4, 1983. Signed as a free agent by **Detroit**, September 29, 1986.

O'REILLY, Terry

Right wing. Shoots right. 6'1", 200 lbs. Born, Niagara Falls, Ont., June 7, 1951.
(Boston's 2nd choice, 14th overall, in 1971 Amateur Draft).

Season	Club	GP	G	A	Pts	PIM	GP	G	A	Pts	PIM
1971-72	Boston Bruins	1	1	0	1	0	....	....	....	....	....
1972-73	Boston Bruins	72	5	22	27	109	5	0	0	0	2
1973-74	Boston Bruins	76	11	24	35	94	16	2	5	7	38
1974-75	Boston Bruins	68	15	20	35	146	3	0	0	0	17
1975-76	Boston Bruins	80	23	27	50	150	12	3	1	4	25
1976-77	Boston Bruins	79	14	41	55	117	14	5	6	11	28
1977-78	Boston Bruins	77	29	61	90	211	15	5	10	15	40
1978-79	Boston Bruins	80	26	51	77	205	11	0	6	6	25
1979-80	Boston Bruins	71	19	42	61	265	10	3	6	9	69
1980-81	Boston Bruins	77	8	35	43	223	3	1	2	3	12
1981-82	Boston Bruins	70	22	30	52	213	11	5	4	9	56
1982-83	Boston Bruins	19	6	14	20	40	....	....	....	....	....
1983-84	Boston Bruins	58	12	18	30	124	3	0	0	0	14
1984-85	Boston Bruins	63	13	17	30	168	5	1	2	3	9
	NHL Totals	**891**	**204**	**402**	**606**	**2095**	**108**	**25**	**42**	**67**	**335**

Played in NHL All-Star Game (1975, 1978)

• Suspended by NHL for first 10 games of 1982-83 season for assault on referee Andy Van Hellemond, April 25, 1982. • Missed majority of 1982-83 season recovering from finger injury suffered in game vs. NY Islanders (November 18, 1982) and knee injury suffered in game vs. Vancouver, December 31, 1982.

ORLANDO, Gates

Center. Shoots right. 5'8", 180 lbs. Born, Montreal, Que., November 13, 1962.
(Buffalo's 10th choice, 164th overall, in 1981 Entry Draft).

Season	Club	GP	G	A	Pts	PIM	GP	G	A	Pts	PIM
1984-85	Buffalo Sabres	11	3	6	9	6	5	0	4	4	14
1985-86	Buffalo Sabres	60	13	12	25	29	....	....	....	....	....
1986-87	Buffalo Sabres	27	2	8	10	16	....	....	....	....	....
	NHL Totals	**98**	**18**	**26**	**44**	**51**	**5**	**0**	**4**	**4**	**14**

ORLANDO, Jimmy

Defense. Shoots left. 5'11", 185 lbs. Born, Montreal, Que., February 27, 1916.

Season	Club	GP	G	A	Pts	PIM	GP	G	A	Pts	PIM
1936-37	Detroit Red Wings	9	0	1	1	8	....	....	....	....	....
1937-38	Detroit Red Wings	6	0	0	0	4	....	....	....	....	....
1939-40	Detroit Red Wings	48	1	3	4	54	5	0	0	0	15
1940-41	Detroit Red Wings	48	1	10	11	99	9	0	2	2	31
1941-42	Detroit Red Wings	48	1	7	8	111	12	0	4	4	45
1942-43 ♦	Detroit Red Wings	40	3	4	7	99	10	0	3	3	14
	NHL Totals	**199**	**6**	**25**	**31**	**375**	**36**	**0**	**9**	**9**	**105**

Traded to **Springfield** (IAHL) by **Detroit** for cash, September 27, 1938. Traded to **Detroit** by **Springfield** (IAHL) for cash, October, 1939.

ORLESKI, Dave

Left wing. Shoots left. 6'4", 210 lbs. Born, Edmonton, Alta., December 26, 1959.
(Montreal's 6th choice, 79th overall, in 1979 Entry Draft).

Season	Club	GP	G	A	Pts	PIM	GP	G	A	Pts	PIM
1980-81	Montreal Canadiens	1	0	0	0	0	....	....	....	....	....
1981-82	Montreal Canadiens	1	0	0	0	0	....	....	....	....	....
	NHL Totals	**2**	**0**	**0**	**0**	**0**	....	....	....	....	....

ORPIK, Brooks

Defense. Shoots left. 6'2", 222 lbs. Born, San Francisco, CA, September 26, 1980.
(Pittsburgh's 1st choice, 18th overall, in 2000 Entry Draft).

Season	Club	GP	G	A	Pts	PIM	GP	G	A	Pts	PIM
2002-03	Pittsburgh Penguins	6	0	0	0	2	....	....	....	....	....
	NHL Totals	**6**	**0**	**0**	**0**	**2**	....	....	....	....	....

ORR, Bobby

HHOF

Defense. Shoots left. 6', 197 lbs. Born, Parry Sound, Ont., March 20, 1948.

Season	Club	GP	G	A	Pts	PIM	GP	G	A	Pts	PIM
1966-67	Boston Bruins	61	13	28	41	102	....	....	....	....	....
1967-68	Boston Bruins	46	11	20	31	63	4	0	2	2	2
1968-69	Boston Bruins	67	21	43	64	133	10	1	7	8	10
1969-70 ♦	Boston Bruins	76	33	*87	*120	125	14	9	11	20	14
1970-71	Boston Bruins	78	37	*102	139	91	7	5	7	12	25
1971-72 ♦	Boston Bruins	76	37	*80	117	106	15	5	*19	*24	19
1972-73	Boston Bruins	63	29	72	101	99	5	1	1	2	7
1973-74	Boston Bruins	74	32	*90	122	82	16	4	*14	18	28
1974-75	Boston Bruins	80	46	*89	*135	101	3	1	5	6	2
1975-76	Boston Bruins	10	5	13	18	22	....	....	....	....	....
1976-77	Chicago Black Hawks	20	4	19	23	25	....	....	....	....	....
1978-79	Chicago Black Hawks	6	2	2	4	4	....	....	....	....	....
	NHL Totals	**657**	**270**	**645**	**915**	**953**	**74**	**26**	**66**	**92**	**107**

NHL Second All-Star Team (1967) • Calder Memorial Trophy (1967) • NHL First All-Star Team (1968, 1969, 1970, 1971, 1972, 1973, 1974, 1975) • James Norris Trophy (1968, 1969, 1970, 1971, 1972, 1973, 1974,1975) • NHL Plus/Minus Leader (1969, 1970, 1971, 1972, 1974, 1975) • Art Ross Trophy (1970, 1975) • Hart Trophy (1970, 1971, 1972) • Conn Smythe Trophy (1970, 1972) • Lester B. Pearson Award (1975) • Lester Patrick Trophy (1979)

Played in NHL All-Star Game (1968, 1969, 1970, 1971, 1972, 1973, 1975)

• Missed majority of 1975-76 season recovering from knee injury suffered in training camp, September 22, 1975. • Missed majority of 1976-77 season and entire 1977-78 season recovering from knee surgery, April 19, 1976. Signed as a free agent by **Chicago**, June 24, 1976.

ORSZAGH, Vladimir

Right wing. Shoots left. 5'11", 193 lbs. Born, Banska Bystrica, Czech., May 24, 1977.
(NY Islanders' 4th choice, 106th overall, in 1995 Entry Draft).

Season	Club	GP	G	A	Pts	PIM	GP	G	A	Pts	PIM
1997-98	New York Islanders	11	0	1	1	2	....	....	....	....	....
1998-99	New York Islanders	12	1	0	1	6	....	....	....	....	....
99-2000	New York Islanders	11	2	1	3	4	....	....	....	....	....
2001-02	Nashville Predators	79	15	21	36	56	....	....	....	....	....
2002-03	Nashville Predators	78	16	16	32	38	....	....	....	....	....
	NHL Totals	**191**	**34**	**39**	**73**	**106**	....	....	....	....	....

Signed as a free agent by **Nashville**, May 30, 2001.

OSBORNE, Keith

Right wing. Shoots right. 6'1", 180 lbs. Born, Toronto, Ont., April 2, 1969.
(St. Louis' 1st choice, 12th overall, in 1987 Entry Draft).

Season	Club	GP	G	A	Pts	PIM	GP	G	A	Pts	PIM
1989-90	St. Louis Blues	5	0	2	2	8	....	....	....	....	....
1992-93	Tampa Bay Lightning	11	1	1	2	8	....	....	....	....	....
	NHL Totals	**16**	**1**	**3**	**4**	**16**	....	....	....	....	....

Traded to **Toronto** by **St. Louis** for Darren Veitch, March 5, 1991. Claimed by **Tampa Bay** from **Toronto** in Expansion Draft, June 18, 1992.

OSBORNE, Mark

Left wing. Shoots left. 6'2", 205 lbs. Born, Toronto, Ont., August 13, 1961.
(Detroit's 2nd choice, 46th overall, in 1980 Entry Draft).

Season	Club	GP	G	A	Pts	PIM	GP	G	A	Pts	PIM
1981-82	Detroit Red Wings	80	26	41	67	61	....	....	....	....	....
1982-83	Detroit Red Wings	80	19	24	43	83	....	....	....	....	....
1983-84	New York Rangers	73	23	28	51	88	5	0	1	1	7
1984-85	New York Rangers	23	4	4	8	33	3	0	0	0	4
1985-86	New York Rangers	62	16	24	40	80	15	2	3	5	26
1986-87	New York Rangers	58	17	15	32	101	....	....	....	....	....
	Toronto Maple Leafs	16	5	10	15	12	9	1	3	4	6
1987-88	Toronto Maple Leafs	79	23	37	60	102	6	1	3	4	16
1988-89	Toronto Maple Leafs	75	16	30	46	112	....	....	....	....	....
1989-90	Toronto Maple Leafs	78	23	50	73	91	5	2	3	5	12
1990-91	Toronto Maple Leafs	18	3	3	6	4	....	....	....	....	....
	Winnipeg Jets	37	8	8	16	59	....	....	....	....	....
1991-92	Winnipeg Jets	43	4	12	16	65	....	....	....	....	....
	Toronto Maple Leafs	11	3	1	4	8	....	....	....	....	....
1992-93	Toronto Maple Leafs	76	12	14	26	89	19	1	1	2	16
1993-94	Toronto Maple Leafs	73	9	15	24	145	18	4	2	6	52
1994-95	New York Rangers	37	1	3	4	19	7	1	0	1	2
	NHL Totals	**919**	**212**	**319**	**531**	**1152**	**87**	**12**	**16**	**28**	**141**

Traded to **NY Rangers** by **Detroit** with Mike Blaisdell and Willie Huber for Ron Duguay, Eddie Mio and Eddie Johnstone, June 13, 1983. Traded to **Toronto** by **NY Rangers** for Jeff Jackson and Toronto's 3rd round choice (Rob Zamuner) in 1989 Entry Draft, March 5, 1987. Traded to **Winnipeg** by **Toronto** with Ed Olczyk for Dave Ellett and Paul Fenton, November 10, 1989. Traded to **Toronto** by **Winnipeg** for Lucien DeBlois, March 10, 1992. Signed as a free agent by **NY Rangers**, January 25, 1995.

OSBURN, Randy

Left wing. Shoots left. 6', 190 lbs. Born, Collingwood, Ont., November 26, 1952.
(Toronto's 2nd choice, 27th overall, in 1972 Amateur Draft).

Season	Club	GP	G	A	Pts	PIM	GP	G	A	Pts	PIM
1972-73	Toronto Maple Leafs	26	0	2	2	0	....	....	....	....	....

		Regular Season					Playoffs				
Season	Club	GP	G	A	Pts	PIM	GP	G	A	Pts	PIM
1974-75	Philadelphia Flyers	1	0	0	0	0	....	....	....	....	....
	NHL Totals	**27**	**0**	**2**	**2**	**0**	....	....	....	....	....

Traded to **Philadelphia** by **Toronto** with Dave Fortier for Bill Flett, May 27, 1974.

O'SHEA, Danny

Center. Shoots left. 6'1", 190 lbs. Born, Toronto, Ont., June 15, 1945.

Season	Club	GP	G	A	Pts	PIM	GP	G	A	Pts	PIM
1968-69	Minnesota North Stars	74	15	34	49	88	....	....	....	....	....
1969-70	Minnesota North Stars	75	10	24	34	82	6	1	0	1	8
1970-71	Minnesota North Stars	59	14	12	26	16	....	....	....	....	....
	Chicago Black Hawks	18	4	7	11	10	18	2	5	7	15
1971-72	Chicago Black Hawks	48	6	9	15	28	....	....	....	....	....
	St. Louis Blues	20	3	3	6	11	10	0	2	2	36
1972-73	St. Louis Blues	75	12	26	38	30	5	0	0	0	2
	NHL Totals	**369**	**64**	**115**	**179**	**265**	**39**	**3**	**7**	**10**	**61**

• Brother of Kevin

Played in NHL All-Star Game (1969, 1970)

Traded to **Minnesota** by **Montreal** for Minnesota's 1st round choices in 1970 (Chuck Lefley) and 1971 (Chuck Arnason) Amateur Drafts, June 14, 1967. Traded to **Chicago** by **Minnesota** for Doug Mohns and Terry Caffery, February 22, 1971. Traded to **St. Louis** by **Chicago** for Christian Bordeleau and future considerations (John Garrett, September 19, 1972), February 8, 1972. • Missed entire 1973-74 season recovering from heart attack suffered in July of 1973 and could not receive medical clearance to play in the NHL.

O'SHEA, Kevin

Right wing. Shoots right. 6'2", 205 lbs. Born, Toronto, Ont., May 28, 1947.

Season	Club	GP	G	A	Pts	PIM	GP	G	A	Pts	PIM
1970-71	Buffalo Sabres	41	4	4	8	8	....	....	....	....	....
1971-72	Buffalo Sabres	52	6	9	15	44	....	....	....	....	....
	St. Louis Blues	4	0	0	0	2	11	2	1	3	10
1972-73	St. Louis Blues	37	3	5	8	31	1	0	0	0	0
	NHL Totals	**134**	**13**	**18**	**31**	**85**	**12**	**2**	**1**	**3**	**10**

• Brother of Danny

Claimed by **San Diego** (WHL) from **NY Rangers** in Reverse Draft, June 12, 1969. Claimed by **Buffalo** from **San Diego** (WHL) in Inter-League Draft, June 9, 1970. Claimed on waivers by **St. Louis** from **Buffalo**, March 3, 1972.

OSIECKI, Mark

Defense. Shoots right. 6'2", 200 lbs. Born, St. Paul, MN, July 23, 1968.
(Calgary's 10th choice, 187th overall, in 1987 Entry Draft).

Season	Club	GP	G	A	Pts	PIM	GP	G	A	Pts	PIM
1991-92	Calgary Flames	50	2	7	9	24	....	....	....	....	....
1992-93	Ottawa Senators	34	0	4	4	12	....	....	....	....	....
	Winnipeg Jets	4	1	0	1	2	....	....	....	....	....
	Minnesota North Stars	5	0	0	0	5	....	....	....	....	....
	NHL Totals	**93**	**3**	**11**	**14**	**43**	....	....	....	....	....

Traded to **Ottawa** by **Calgary** for Chris Lindberg, June 22, 1992. Claimed on waivers by **Winnipeg** from **Ottawa**, February 20, 1993. Traded to **Minnesota** by **Winnipeg** with Winnipeg's 10th round choice (Bill Lang) in 1993 Entry Draft for Minnesota's 9th round choice (Vladimir Potapov) in 1993 Entry Draft, March 20, 1993. Transferred to **Dallas** after **Minnesota** franchise relocated, June 9, 1993.

O'SULLIVAN, Chris

Defense. Shoots left. 6'2", 205 lbs. Born, Dorchester, MA, May 15, 1974.
(Calgary's 2nd choice, 30th overall, in 1992 Entry Draft).

Season	Club	GP	G	A	Pts	PIM	GP	G	A	Pts	PIM
1996-97	Calgary Flames	27	2	8	10	2	....	....	....	....	....
1997-98	Calgary Flames	12	0	2	2	10	....	....	....	....	....
1998-99	Calgary Flames	10	0	1	1	2	....	....	....	....	....
99-2000	Vancouver Canucks	11	0	5	5	2	....	....	....	....	....
2002-03	Mighty Ducks of Anaheim	2	0	1	1	0	....	....	....	....	....
	NHL Totals	**62**	**2**	**17**	**19**	**16**	....	....	....	....	....

Traded to **NY Rangers** by **Calgary** for Lee Sorochan, March 23, 1999. Signed as a free agent by **Vancouver**, August 20, 1999. Signed as a free agent by **Anaheim**, July 20, 2000. Signed as a free agent by **Anaheim**, July 22, 2002.

OTEVREL, Jaroslav

Left wing. Shoots left. 6'3", 215 lbs. Born, Gottwaldov, Czech., September 16, 1968.
(San Jose's 8th choice, 133rd overall, in 1991 Entry Draft).

Season	Club	GP	G	A	Pts	PIM	GP	G	A	Pts	PIM
1992-93	San Jose Sharks	7	0	2	2	0	....	....	....	....	....
1993-94	San Jose Sharks	9	3	2	5	2	....	....	....	....	....
	NHL Totals	**16**	**3**	**4**	**7**	**2**	....	....	....	....	....

OTT, Steve

Center. Shoots left. 6', 160 lbs. Born, Summerside, P.E.I., August 19, 1982.
(Dallas' 1st choice, 25th overall, in 2000 Entry Draft).

Season	Club	GP	G	A	Pts	PIM	GP	G	A	Pts	PIM
2002-03	Dallas Stars	26	3	4	7	31	1	0	0	0	0
	NHL Totals	**26**	**3**	**4**	**7**	**31**	**1**	**0**	**0**	**0**	**0**

OTTO, Joel

Center. Shoots right. 6'4", 220 lbs. Born, Elk River, MN, October 29, 1961.

Season	Club	GP	G	A	Pts	PIM	GP	G	A	Pts	PIM
1984-85	Calgary Flames	17	4	8	12	30	3	2	1	3	10
1985-86	Calgary Flames	79	25	34	59	188	22	5	10	15	80
1986-87	Calgary Flames	68	19	31	50	185	2	0	2	2	6
1987-88	Calgary Flames	62	13	39	52	194	9	3	2	5	26
1988-89 ♦	Calgary Flames	72	23	30	53	213	22	6	13	19	46
1989-90	Calgary Flames	75	13	20	33	116	6	2	2	4	2
1990-91	Calgary Flames	76	19	20	39	183	7	1	2	3	8
1991-92	Calgary Flames	78	13	21	34	161	....	....	....	....	....
1992-93	Calgary Flames	75	19	33	52	150	6	4	2	6	4
1993-94	Calgary Flames	81	11	12	23	92	3	0	1	1	4
1994-95	Calgary Flames	47	8	13	21	130	7	0	3	3	2
1995-96	Philadelphia Flyers	67	12	29	41	115	12	3	4	7	11
1996-97	Philadelphia Flyers	78	13	19	32	99	18	1	5	6	8
1997-98	Philadelphia Flyers	68	3	4	7	78	5	0	0	0	0
	NHL Totals	**943**	**195**	**313**	**508**	**1934**	**122**	**27**	**47**	**74**	**207**

Signed as a free agent by **Calgary,** September 11, 1984. Signed as a free agent by **Philadelphia**, July 31, 1995.

OUELLETTE, Eddie

Center. Shoots left. 5'9", 181 lbs. Born, Ottawa, Ont., March 9, 1911.

Season	Club	GP	G	A	Pts	PIM	GP	G	A	Pts	PIM
1935-36	Chicago Black Hawks	43	3	2	5	11	1	0	0	0	0
	NHL Totals	**43**	**3**	**2**	**5**	**11**	**1**	**0**	**0**	**0**	**0**

Traded to **Montreal** by **London** (IHL) for cash, April 1, 1935. Signed as a free agent by **Chicago**, October 27, 1935.

OUELLETTE, Gerry

Right wing. Shoots right. 5'9", 170 lbs. Born, Grand Falls, N.B., November 1, 1938.

Season	Club	GP	G	A	Pts	PIM	GP	G	A	Pts	PIM
1960-61	Boston Bruins	34	5	4	9	0	....	....	....	....	....
	NHL Totals	**34**	**5**	**4**	**9**	**0**	....	....	....	....	....

Traded to **San Francisco** (WHL) by **Boston** to complete transaction that sent Orland Kurtenbach and Ed Panagabko to San Francisco (July 26, 1962), July 7, 1963. Claimed by **Buffalo** (AHL) from **Boston** in Reverse Draft, June 9, 1965.

OWCHAR, Dennis

Defense. Shoots right. 5'11", 190 lbs. Born, Dryden, Ont., March 28, 1953.
(Pittsburgh's 4th choice, 55th overall, in 1973 Amateur Draft).

Season	Club	GP	G	A	Pts	PIM	GP	G	A	Pts	PIM
1974-75	Pittsburgh Penguins	46	6	11	17	67	6	0	1	1	4
1975-76	Pittsburgh Penguins	54	5	12	17	19	2	0	0	0	2
1976-77	Pittsburgh Penguins	46	5	18	23	37	....	....	....	....	....
1977-78	Pittsburgh Penguins	22	2	8	10	23	....	....	....	....	....
	Colorado Rockies	60	8	23	31	25	2	1	0	1	2
1978-79	Colorado Rockies	50	3	13	16	27	....	....	....	....	....
1979-80	Colorado Rockies	10	1	0	1	2	....	....	....	....	....
	NHL Totals	**288**	**30**	**85**	**115**	**200**	**10**	**1**	**1**	**2**	**8**

Traded to **Colorado** by **Pittsburgh** for Tom Edur, December 2, 1977. Traded to **New Haven** (AHL) by **Colorado** with Larry Skinner for Bobby Sheehan, May 12, 1979.

OWEN, George

USHOF

Defense. Shoots left. 5'11", 190 lbs. Born, Hamilton, Ont., February 12, 1901.

Season	Club	GP	G	A	Pts	PIM	GP	G	A	Pts	PIM
1928-29 ♦	Boston Bruins	27	5	4	9	48	5	0	0	0	0
1929-30	Boston Bruins	42	9	4	13	31	6	0	2	2	6
1930-31	Boston Bruins	38	12	13	25	33	5	2	3	5	13
1931-32	Boston Bruins	42	12	10	22	29	....	....	....	....	....
1932-33	Boston Bruins	34	6	2	8	10	5	0	0	0	6
	NHL Totals	**183**	**44**	**33**	**77**	**151**	**21**	**2**	**5**	**7**	**25**

Rights traded to **Boston** by **Toronto** for Eric Pettinger and the rights to Hugh Plaxton, January 10, 1929.

OZOLINSH, Sandis

Defense. Shoots left. 6'3", 215 lbs. Born, Riga, Latvia, August 3, 1972.
(San Jose's 3rd choice, 30th overall, in 1991 Entry Draft).

Season	Club	GP	G	A	Pts	PIM	GP	G	A	Pts	PIM
1992-93	San Jose Sharks	37	7	16	23	40	....	....	....	....	....
1993-94	San Jose Sharks	81	26	38	64	24	14	0	10	10	8
1994-95	San Jose Sharks	48	9	16	25	30	11	3	2	5	6
1995-96	San Jose Sharks	7	1	3	4	4	....	....	....	....	....
	♦ Colorado Avalanche	66	13	37	50	50	22	5	14	19	16
1996-97	Colorado Avalanche	80	23	45	68	88	17	4	13	17	24
1997-98	Colorado Avalanche	66	13	38	51	65	7	0	7	7	14
1998-99	Colorado Avalanche	39	7	25	32	22	19	4	8	12	22
99-2000	Colorado Avalanche	82	16	36	52	46	17	5	5	10	20
2000-01	Carolina Hurricanes	72	12	32	44	71	6	0	2	2	5
2001-02	Carolina Hurricanes	46	4	19	23	34	....	....	....	....	....
	Florida Panthers	37	10	19	29	24	....	....	....	....	....
2002-03	Florida Panthers	51	7	19	26	40	....	....	....	....	....
	Mighty Ducks of Anaheim	31	5	13	18	16	21	2	6	8	10
	NHL Totals	**743**	**153**	**356**	**509**	**554**	**134**	**23**	**67**	**90**	**125**

NHL First All-Star Team (1997)

Played in NHL All-Star Game (1994, 1997, 1998, 2000, 2001, 2002, 2003)

• Missed majority of 1992-93 season recovering from knee injury suffered in game vs. Philadelphia, December 30, 1992. Traded to **Colorado** by **San Jose** for Owen Nolan, October 26, 1995. Traded to **Carolina** by **Colorado** with Columbus' 2nd round choice (previously acquired, Carolina selected Tomas Kurka) in 2000 Entry Draft for Nolan Pratt, Carolina's 1st (Vaclav Nedorost) and 2nd (Jared Aulin) round choices in 2000 Entry Draft and Philadelphia's 2nd round choice (previously acquired, Colorado selected Agris Saviels) in 2000 Entry Draft, June 24, 2000. Traded to **Florida** by **Carolina** with Byron Ritchie for Bret Hedican, Kevyn Adams, Tomas Malec and a conditional 2nd round choice in 2003 Entry Draft, January 16, 2002. Traded to **Anaheim** by **Florida** with Lance Ward for Pavel Trnka, Matt Cullen and Anaheim's 4th round choice (James Pemberton) in 2003 Entry Draft, January 30, 2003.

PACHAL, Clayton

Center/Left wing. Shoots left. 5'10", 185 lbs. Born, Yorkton, Sask., April 21, 1956.
(Boston's 1st choice, 16th overall, in 1976 Amateur Draft).

Season	Club	GP	G	A	Pts	PIM	GP	G	A	Pts	PIM
1976-77	Boston Bruins	1	0	0	0	12	....	....	....	....	....
1977-78	Boston Bruins	10	0	0	0	14	....	....	....	....	....

Season	Club	GP	G	A	Pts	PIM	GP	G	A	Pts	PIM
		REGULAR SEASON					PLAYOFFS				
1978-79	Colorado Rockies	24	2	3	5	69	....	....	....	....	....
	NHL Totals	**35**	**2**	**3**	**5**	**95**	....	....	....	....	....

Traded to **Colorado** by **Boston** for Mark Suzor, October 11, 1978. Signed as a free agent by **Edmonton**, July, 1979.

PADDOCK, John

Right wing. Shoots right. 6'3", 190 lbs. Born, Brandon, Man., June 9, 1954.
(Washington's 3rd choice, 37th overall, in 1974 Amateur Draft).

Season	Club	GP	G	A	Pts	PIM	GP	G	A	Pts	PIM
1975-76	Washington Capitals	8	1	1	2	12	....	....	....	....	....
1976-77	Philadelphia Flyers	5	0	0	0	9	....	....	....	....	....
1979-80	Philadelphia Flyers	32	3	7	10	36	3	2	0	2	0
1980-81	Quebec Nordiques	32	2	5	7	25	2	0	0	0	0
1982-83	Philadelphia Flyers	10	2	1	3	4	....	....	....	....	....
	NHL Totals	**87**	**8**	**14**	**22**	**86**	**5**	**2**	**0**	**2**	**0**

Traded to **Philadelphia** by **Washington** to complete transaction that sent Bob Sirois to Washington (December 15, 1975), September 1, 1976. Traded to **Quebec** by **Philadelphia** for cash, August 11, 1980. Signed as a free agent by **Philadelphia**, January 4, 1983. Signed as a free agent by **New Jersey**, August 1, 1983.

PAEK, Jim

Defense. Shoots left. 6'1", 195 lbs. Born, Seoul, South Korea, April 7, 1967.
(Pittsburgh's 9th choice, 170th overall, in 1985 Entry Draft).

Season	Club	GP	G	A	Pts	PIM	GP	G	A	Pts	PIM
1990-91 ♦	Pittsburgh Penguins	3	0	0	0	9	8	1	0	1	2
1991-92 ♦	Pittsburgh Penguins	49	1	7	8	36	19	0	4	4	6
1992-93	Pittsburgh Penguins	77	3	15	18	64	....	....	....	....	....
1993-94	Pittsburgh Penguins	41	0	4	4	8	....	....	....	....	....
	Los Angeles Kings	18	1	1	2	10	....	....	....	....	....
1994-95	Ottawa Senators	29	0	2	2	28	....	....	....	....	....
	NHL Totals	**217**	**5**	**29**	**34**	**155**	**27**	**1**	**4**	**5**	**8**

Traded to **Los Angeles** by **Pittsburgh** with Marty McSorley for Tomas Sandstrom and Shawn McEachern, February 16, 1994. Traded to **Ottawa** by **Los Angeles** for Ottawa's 7th round choice (Benoit Larose) in 1995 Entry Draft, June 25, 1994.

PAHLSSON, Samuel

Center. Shoots left. 5'11", 212 lbs. Born, Ornskoldsvik, Sweden, December 17, 1977.
(Colorado's 10th choice, 176th overall, in 1996 Entry Draft).

Season	Club	GP	G	A	Pts	PIM	GP	G	A	Pts	PIM
2000-01	Boston Bruins	17	1	1	2	6	....	....	....	....	....
	Mighty Ducks of Anaheim	59	3	4	7	14	....	....	....	....	....
2001-02	Mighty Ducks of Anaheim	80	6	14	20	26	....	....	....	....	....
2002-03	Mighty Ducks of Anaheim	34	4	11	15	10	21	2	4	6	12
	NHL Totals	**190**	**14**	**30**	**44**	**64**	**21**	**2**	**4**	**6**	**12**

Traded to **Boston** by **Colorado** with Brian Rolston, Martin Grenier and New Jersey's 1st round choice (previously acquired, Boston selected Martin Samuelsson) in 2000 Entry Draft for Raymond Bourque and Dave Andreychuk, March 6, 2000. Traded to **Anaheim** by **Boston** for Patrick Traverse and Andrei Nazarov, November 18, 2000.

PAIEMENT, Rosaire

Center. Shoots right. 5'11", 170 lbs. Born, Earlton, Ont., August 12, 1945.

Season	Club	GP	G	A	Pts	PIM	GP	G	A	Pts	PIM
1967-68	Philadelphia Flyers	7	1	0	1	11	3	3	0	3	0
1968-69	Philadelphia Flyers	27	2	4	6	52	....	....	....	....	....
1969-70	Philadelphia Flyers	9	1	1	2	11	....	....	....	....	....
1970-71	Vancouver Canucks	78	34	28	62	152	....	....	....	....	....
1971-72	Vancouver Canucks	69	10	19	29	117	....	....	....	....	....
	NHL Totals	**190**	**48**	**52**	**100**	**343**	**3**	**3**	**0**	**3**	**0**

• Brother of Wilf

Traded to **Philadelphia** by **Boston** for Philadelphia's 1st round choice (Rick MacLeish) in 1970 Amateur Draft, October 18, 1967. Claimed by **Vancouver** from **Philadelphia** in Expansion Draft, June 10, 1970.

PAIEMENT, Wilf

Right wing. Shoots right. 6'1", 210 lbs. Born, Earlton, Ont., October 16, 1955.
(Kansas City's 1st choice, 2nd overall, in 1974 Amateur Draft).

Season	Club	GP	G	A	Pts	PIM	GP	G	A	Pts	PIM
1974-75	Kansas City Scouts	78	26	13	39	101	....	....	....	....	....
1975-76	Kansas City Scouts	57	21	22	43	121	....	....	....	....	....
1976-77	Colorado Rockies	78	41	40	81	101	....	....	....	....	....
1977-78	Colorado Rockies	80	31	56	87	114	2	0	0	0	7
1978-79	Colorado Rockies	65	24	36	60	80	....	....	....	....	....
1979-80	Colorado Rockies	34	10	16	26	41	....	....	....	....	....
	Toronto Maple Leafs	41	20	28	48	72	3	0	2	2	17
1980-81	Toronto Maple Leafs	77	40	57	97	145	3	0	0	0	2
1981-82	Toronto Maple Leafs	69	18	40	58	203	....	....	....	....	....
	Quebec Nordiques	8	7	6	13	18	14	6	6	12	28
1982-83	Quebec Nordiques	80	26	38	64	170	4	0	1	1	4
1983-84	Quebec Nordiques	80	39	37	76	121	9	3	1	4	24
1984-85	Quebec Nordiques	68	23	28	51	165	18	4	2	6	58
1985-86	Quebec Nordiques	44	7	12	19	145	....	....	....	....	....
	New York Rangers	8	1	6	7	13	16	5	5	10	45
1986-87	Buffalo Sabres	56	20	17	37	108	....	....	....	....	....
1987-88	Pittsburgh Penguins	23	2	6	8	39	....	....	....	....	....
	NHL Totals	**946**	**356**	**458**	**814**	**1757**	**69**	**18**	**17**	**35**	**185**

• Brother of Rosaire

Played in NHL All-Star Game (1976, 1977, 1978)

Transferred to **Colorado** after **Kansas City** franchise relocated, July 15, 1976. Traded to **Toronto** by **Colorado** with Pat Hickey for Lanny McDonald and Joel Quenneville, December 29, 1979. Traded to **Quebec** by **Toronto** for Miroslav Frycer and Quebec's 7th round choice (Jeff Triano) in 1982 Entry Draft, March 9, 1982. Traded to **NY Rangers** by **Quebec** for Steve Patrick, February 6, 1986. Claimed by **Buffalo** from **NY Rangers** in Waiver Draft, October 6, 1986. Signed as a free agent by **Pittsburgh**, September 10, 1987.

PALANGIO, Pete

Left wing. Shoots left. 5'11", 175 lbs. Born, North Bay, Ont., September 10, 1908.

Season	Club	GP	G	A	Pts	PIM	GP	G	A	Pts	PIM
1926-27	Montreal Canadiens	6	0	0	0	0	4	0	0	0	0
1927-28	Detroit Cougars	14	3	0	3	8	....	....	....	....	....
1928-29	Montreal Canadiens	2	0	0	0	0	....	....	....	....	....
1936-37	Chicago Black Hawks	30	8	9	17	16	....	....	....	....	....
1937-38 ♦	Chicago Black Hawks	19	2	1	3	4	3	0	0	0	0
	NHL Totals	**71**	**13**	**10**	**23**	**28**	**7**	**0**	**0**	**0**	**0**

Signed as a free agent by **Montreal**, February, 1927. Loaned to **Detroit** by **Montreal** (Windsor-Can-Pro) with cash for Stan Brown, February 13, 1928. Loaned to **Kitchener** (Can-Pro) by **Montreal** for cash, November 26, 1928. Traded to **London** (IHL) by **Montreal** for cash, November 11, 1929. Traded to **Syracuse** (IHL) by **London** (IHL) for cash, November 28, 1930. Traded to **St. Louis** (AHA) by **Syracuse** (IHL) for cash, October 19, 1932. Traded to **Chicago** by **St. Louis** (AHA) for $25,000, December 19, 1936. Traded to **Tulsa** (AHA) by **Chicago** for cash, October 24, 1938.

PALAZZARI, Aldo

Right wing. Shoots left. 5'7", 168 lbs. Born, Eveleth, MN, July 25, 1918.

Season	Club	GP	G	A	Pts	PIM	GP	G	A	Pts	PIM
1943-44	Boston Bruins	24	6	3	9	4	....	....	....	....	....
	New York Rangers	11	2	0	2	0	....	....	....	....	....
	NHL Totals	**35**	**8**	**3**	**11**	**4**	....	....	....	....	....

• Father of Doug

Traded to **NY Rangers** by **Boston** for $3,000, February 22, 1944. • Suffered eventual career-ending eye injury in NY Rangers training camp, October 18, 1944.

PALAZZARI, Doug

USHOF

Center. Shoots left. 5'5", 170 lbs. Born, Eveleth, MN, November 3, 1952.

Season	Club	GP	G	A	Pts	PIM	GP	G	A	Pts	PIM
1974-75	St. Louis Blues	73	14	17	31	19	2	0	0	0	0
1976-77	St. Louis Blues	12	1	0	1	0	....	....	....	....	....
1977-78	St. Louis Blues	3	1	0	1	0	....	....	....	....	....
1978-79	St. Louis Blues	20	2	3	5	4	....	....	....	....	....
	NHL Totals	**108**	**18**	**20**	**38**	**23**	**2**	**0**	**0**	**0**	**0**

• Son of Aldo

Signed as a free agent by **St. Louis**, August, 1974.

PALFFY, Ziggy

Right wing. Shoots left. 5'10", 183 lbs. Born, Skalica, Czech., May 5, 1972.
(NY Islanders' 2nd choice, 26th overall, in 1991 Entry Draft).

Season	Club	GP	G	A	Pts	PIM	GP	G	A	Pts	PIM
1993-94	New York Islanders	5	0	0	0	0	....	....	....	....	....
1994-95	New York Islanders	33	10	7	17	6	....	....	....	....	....
1995-96	New York Islanders	81	43	44	87	56	....	....	....	....	....
1996-97	New York Islanders	80	48	42	90	43	....	....	....	....	....
1997-98	New York Islanders	82	45	42	87	34	....	....	....	....	....
1998-99	New York Islanders	50	22	28	50	34	....	....	....	....	....
99-2000	Los Angeles Kings	64	27	39	66	32	4	2	0	2	0
2000-01	Los Angeles Kings	73	38	51	89	20	13	3	5	8	8
2001-02	Los Angeles Kings	63	32	27	59	26	7	4	5	9	0
2002-03	Los Angeles Kings	76	37	48	85	47	....	....	....	....	....
	NHL Totals	**607**	**302**	**328**	**630**	**298**	**24**	**9**	**10**	**19**	**8**

Played in NHL All-Star Game (1998, 2001, 2002)

Traded to **Los Angeles** by **NY Islanders** with Brian Smolinski, Marcel Cousineau and New Jersey's 4th round choice (previously acquired, Los Angeles selected Daniel Johansson) in 1999 Entry Draft for Olli Jokinen, Josh Green, Mathieu Biron and Los Angeles' 1st round choice (Taylor Pyatt) in 1999 Entry Draft, June 20, 1999.

PALMER, Brad

Left wing. Shoots left. 6', 185 lbs. Born, Duncan, B.C., September 14, 1961.
(Minnesota's 1st choice, 16th overall, in 1980 Entry Draft).

Season	Club	GP	G	A	Pts	PIM	GP	G	A	Pts	PIM
1980-81	Minnesota North Stars	23	4	4	8	22	19	8	5	13	4
1981-82	Minnesota North Stars	72	22	23	45	18	3	0	0	0	12
1982-83	Boston Bruins	73	6	11	17	18	7	1	0	1	0
	NHL Totals	**168**	**32**	**38**	**70**	**58**	**29**	**9**	**5**	**14**	**16**

Traded to **Boston** by **Minnesota** with the rights to Dave Donnelly for Boston agreeing not to select Brian Bellows in 1982 Entry Draft, June 9, 1982.

PALMER, Rob

Center. Shoots left. 6', 190 lbs. Born, Detroit, MI, October 2, 1952.
(Chicago's 6th choice, 93rd overall, in 1972 Amateur Draft).

Season	Club	GP	G	A	Pts	PIM	GP	G	A	Pts	PIM
1973-74	Chicago Black Hawks	1	0	0	0	0	....	....	....	....	....
1974-75	Chicago Black Hawks	13	0	2	2	2	....	....	....	....	....
1975-76	Chicago Black Hawks	2	0	1	1	0	....	....	....	....	....
	NHL Totals	**16**	**0**	**3**	**3**	**2**	....	....	....	....	....

PALMER, Robert

Defense. Shoots right. 5'11", 190 lbs. Born, Sarnia, Ont., September 10, 1956.
(Los Angeles' 4th choice, 85th overall, in 1976 Amateur Draft).

Season	Club	GP	G	A	Pts	PIM	GP	G	A	Pts	PIM
		REGULAR SEASON					PLAYOFFS				
1977-78	Los Angeles Kings	48	0	3	3	27	2	0	0	0	0
1978-79	Los Angeles Kings	78	4	41	45	26	2	0	0	0	2
1979-80	Los Angeles Kings	78	4	36	40	18	4	1	2	3	4
1980-81	Los Angeles Kings	13	0	4	4	13	....	....	....	....	....
1981-82	Los Angeles Kings	5	0	2	2	0	....	....	....	....	....
1982-83	New Jersey Devils	60	1	10	11	21	....	....	....	....	....
1983-84	New Jersey Devils	38	0	5	5	10	....	....	....	....	....
	NHL Totals	**320**	**9**	**101**	**110**	**115**	**8**	**1**	**2**	**3**	**6**

Signed as a free agent by **New Jersey**, September 9, 1982.

PANAGABKO, Ed

Center. Shoots left. 5'8", 170 lbs. Born, Norquay, Sask., May 17, 1934.

Season	Club	GP	G	A	Pts	PIM	GP	G	A	Pts	PIM
1955-56	Boston Bruins	28	0	3	3	38	....	....	....	....	....
1956-57	Boston Bruins	1	0	0	0	0	....	....	....	....	....
	NHL Totals	**29**	**0**	**3**	**3**	**38**	....	....	....	....	....

Traded to **San Francisco** (WHL) by **Boston** with Orland Kurtenbach and future considerations (Gerry Ouellette, July 7, 1963) for Larry McNabb and cash, July 26, 1962.

PANDOLFO, Jay

Left wing. Shoots left. 6'1", 190 lbs. Born, Winchester, MA, December 27, 1974.
(New Jersey's 2nd choice, 32nd overall, in 1993 Entry Draft).

Season	Club	GP	G	A	Pts	PIM	GP	G	A	Pts	PIM
1996-97	New Jersey Devils	46	6	8	14	6	6	0	1	1	0
1997-98	New Jersey Devils	23	1	3	4	4	3	0	2	2	0
1998-99	New Jersey Devils	70	14	13	27	10	7	1	0	1	0
99-2000 ♦	New Jersey Devils	71	7	8	15	4	23	0	5	5	0
2000-01	New Jersey Devils	63	4	12	16	16	25	1	4	5	4
2001-02	New Jersey Devils	65	4	10	14	15	6	0	0	0	0
2002-03 ♦	New Jersey Devils	68	6	11	17	23	24	6	6	12	2
	NHL Totals	**406**	**42**	**65**	**107**	**78**	**94**	**8**	**18**	**26**	**6**

PANKEWICZ, Greg

Right wing. Shoots right. 6', 185 lbs. Born, Drayton Valley, Alta., November 6, 1970.

Season	Club	GP	G	A	Pts	PIM	GP	G	A	Pts	PIM
1993-94	Ottawa Senators	3	0	0	0	2	....	....	....	....	....
1998-99	Calgary Flames	18	0	3	3	20	....	....	....	....	....
	NHL Totals	**21**	**0**	**3**	**3**	**22**	....	....	....	....	....

Signed as a free agent by **Ottawa**, May 27, 1993. Signed as a free agent by **Calgary**, September 1, 1998. Traded to **San Jose** by **Calgary** for cash, March 23, 1999.

PANTELEEV, Grigori

Left wing. Shoots left. 5'9", 190 lbs. Born, Gastello, USSR, November 13, 1972.
(Boston's 5th choice, 136th overall, in 1992 Entry Draft).

Season	Club	GP	G	A	Pts	PIM	GP	G	A	Pts	PIM
1992-93	Boston Bruins	39	8	6	14	12	....	....	....	....	....
1993-94	Boston Bruins	10	0	0	0	0	....	....	....	....	....
1994-95	Boston Bruins	1	0	0	0	0	....	....	....	....	....
1995-96	New York Islanders	4	0	0	0	0	....	....	....	....	....
	NHL Totals	**54**	**8**	**6**	**14**	**12**	....	....	....	....	....

Signed as a free agent by **NY Islanders**, September 20, 1995.

PAPIKE, Joe

Right wing. Shoots right. 6', 175 lbs. Born, Eveleth, MN, March 28, 1915.

Season	Club	GP	G	A	Pts	PIM	GP	G	A	Pts	PIM
1940-41	Chicago Black Hawks	9	2	2	4	2	5	0	2	2	0
1941-42	Chicago Black Hawks	9	1	0	1	0	....	....	....	....	....
1944-45	Chicago Black Hawks	2	0	1	1	2	....	....	....	....	....
	NHL Totals	**20**	**3**	**3**	**6**	**4**	**5**	**0**	**2**	**2**	**0**

PAPINEAU, Justin

Center. Shoots left. 5'10", 178 lbs. Born, Ottawa, Ont., January 15, 1980.
(St. Louis' 3rd choice, 75th overall, in 2000 Entry Draft).

Season	Club	GP	G	A	Pts	PIM	GP	G	A	Pts	PIM
2001-02	St. Louis Blues	1	0	0	0	0	....	....	....	....	....
2002-03	St. Louis Blues	11	2	1	3	0	....	....	....	....	....
	New York Islanders	5	1	2	3	4	1	0	0	0	0
	NHL Totals	**17**	**3**	**3**	**6**	**4**	**1**	**0**	**0**	**0**	**0**

• Re-entered NHL Entry Draft. Originally Los Angeles' 2nd choice, 46th overall, in 1998 Entry Draft.

Traded to **NY Islanders** by **St. Louis** with St. Louis' 2nd round choice (Jeremy Colliton) in 2003 Entry Draft for Chris Osgood and NY Islanders' 3rd round choice (Konstantin Barulin) in 2003 Entry Draft, March 11, 2003.

PAPPIN, Jim

Right wing. Shoots right. 6', 190 lbs. Born, Sudbury, Ont., September 10, 1939.

Season	Club	GP	G	A	Pts	PIM	GP	G	A	Pts	PIM
1963-64 ♦	Toronto Maple Leafs	50	11	8	19	33	11	0	0	0	0
1964-65	Toronto Maple Leafs	44	9	9	18	33	....	....	....	....	....
1965-66	Toronto Maple Leafs	7	0	3	3	8	....	....	....	....	....
1966-67 ♦	Toronto Maple Leafs	64	21	11	32	89	12	*7	8	*15	12
1967-68	Toronto Maple Leafs	58	13	15	28	37	....	....	....	....	....
1968-69	Chicago Black Hawks	75	30	40	70	49	....	....	....	....	....
1969-70	Chicago Black Hawks	66	28	25	53	68	8	3	2	5	6
1970-71	Chicago Black Hawks	58	22	23	45	40	18	10	4	14	24
1971-72	Chicago Black Hawks	64	27	21	48	38	8	2	5	7	4
1972-73	Chicago Black Hawks	76	41	51	92	82	16	8	7	15	24
1973-74	Chicago Black Hawks	78	32	41	73	76	11	3	6	9	29
1974-75	Chicago Black Hawks	71	36	27	63	94	8	0	2	2	2
1975-76	California Golden Seals	32	6	13	19	12	....	....	....	....	....
1976-77	Cleveland Barons	24	2	8	10	8	....	....	....	....	....
	NHL Totals	**767**	**278**	**295**	**573**	**667**	**92**	**33**	**34**	**67**	**101**

Played in NHL All-Star Game (1964, 1968, 1973, 1974, 1975)

Traded to **Chicago** by **Toronto** for Pierre Pilote, May 23, 1968. Traded to **California** by **Chicago** with Chicago's 3rd round choice (Guy Lash) in 1977 Amateur Draft for Joey Johnston, June 1, 1975. Transferred to **Cleveland** after **California** franchise relocated, August 26, 1976.

PARADISE, Bob

USHOF

Defense. Shoots left. 6'1", 205 lbs. Born, St. Paul, MN, April 22, 1944.

Season	Club	GP	G	A	Pts	PIM	GP	G	A	Pts	PIM
1971-72	Minnesota North Stars	6	0	0	0	6	4	0	0	0	2
1972-73	Atlanta Flames	71	1	7	8	103	....	....	....	....	....
1973-74	Atlanta Flames	18	0	1	1	13	....	....	....	....	....
	Pittsburgh Penguins	38	2	7	9	39	....	....	....	....	....
1974-75	Pittsburgh Penguins	78	3	15	18	109	6	0	1	1	17
1975-76	Pittsburgh Penguins	9	0	0	0	4	....	....	....	....	....
	Washington Capitals	48	0	8	8	42	....	....	....	....	....
1976-77	Washington Capitals	22	0	5	5	20	....	....	....	....	....
1977-78	Pittsburgh Penguins	64	2	10	12	53	....	....	....	....	....
1978-79	Pittsburgh Penguins	14	0	1	1	4	2	0	0	0	0
	NHL Totals	**368**	**8**	**54**	**62**	**393**	**12**	**0**	**1**	**1**	**19**

Signed as a free agent by **Montreal**, June, 1970. Traded to **Minnesota** by **Montreal** with the rights to Gary Gambucci for cash, May, 1971. Traded to **Atlanta** by **Minnesota** for cash, June 6, 1972. Traded to **Pittsburgh** by **Atlanta** with Chuck Arnason for Al McDonough, January 4, 1974. Traded to **Washington** by **Pittsburgh** for Washington's 2nd round choice (Greg Malone) in 1976 Amateur Draft, November 26, 1975. Traded to **Pittsburgh** by **Washington** for the rights to Don Awrey, October 1, 1977.

PARGETER, George

Left wing. Shoots left. 5'7", 168 lbs. Born, Calgary, Alta., February 24, 1923.

Season	Club	GP	G	A	Pts	PIM	GP	G	A	Pts	PIM
1946-47	Montreal Canadiens	4	0	0	0	0	....	....	....	....	....
	NHL Totals	**4**	**0**	**0**	**0**	**0**	....	....	....	....	....

Traded to **Montreal** (Buffalo-AHL) by **Springfield** (AHL) for John Quilty, November 19, 1946.

PARISE, J.P.

Left wing. Shoots left. 5'9", 175 lbs. Born, Smooth Rock Falls, Ont., December 11, 1941.

Season	Club	GP	G	A	Pts	PIM	GP	G	A	Pts	PIM
1965-66	Boston Bruins	3	0	0	0	0	....	....	....	....	....
1966-67	Boston Bruins	18	2	2	4	10	....	....	....	....	....
1967-68	Toronto Maple Leafs	1	0	1	1	0	....	....	....	....	....
	Minnesota North Stars	43	11	16	27	27	14	2	5	7	10
1968-69	Minnesota North Stars	76	22	27	49	57	....	....	....	....	....
1969-70	Minnesota North Stars	74	24	48	72	72	6	3	2	5	2
1970-71	Minnesota North Stars	73	11	23	34	60	12	3	3	6	22
1971-72	Minnesota North Stars	71	19	18	37	70	7	3	3	6	6
1972-73	Minnesota North Stars	78	27	48	75	96	6	0	0	0	9
1973-74	Minnesota North Stars	78	18	37	55	42	....	....	....	....	....
1974-75	Minnesota North Stars	38	9	16	25	40	....	....	....	....	....
	New York Islanders	41	14	16	30	22	17	8	8	16	22
1975-76	New York Islanders	80	22	35	57	80	13	4	6	10	10
1976-77	New York Islanders	80	25	31	56	46	11	4	4	8	6
1977-78	New York Islanders	39	12	16	28	12	....	....	....	....	....
	Cleveland Barons	40	9	13	22	27	....	....	....	....	....
1978-79	Minnesota North Stars	57	13	9	22	45	....	....	....	....	....
	NHL Totals	**890**	**238**	**356**	**594**	**706**	**86**	**27**	**31**	**58**	**87**

Played in NHL All-Star Game (1970, 1973)

Claimed by **California** (Oakland) from **Boston** in Expansion Draft, June 6, 1967. Traded to **Toronto** (Rochester-AHL) by **Oakland** with Bryan Hextall Jr. for Gerry Ehman, October 12, 1967. Traded to **Minnesota** by **Toronto** (Rochester-AHL) with Milan Marcetta for Murray Hall, Ted Taylor, Len Lunde, Don Johns, Duke Harris and the loan of Carl Wetzel, December 23, 1967. Traded to **NY Islanders** by **Minnesota** for Doug Rombough and Ernie Hicke, January 5, 1975. Traded to **Cleveland** by **NY Islanders** with Jean Potvin for Wayne Merrick, Darcy Regier and Cleveland's 4th round choice (draft choice cancelled by the Cleveland-Minnesota merger) in 1978 Amateur Draft, January 10, 1978. Placed on **Minnesota** Reserve List after **Cleveland-Minnesota** Dispersal Draft, June 5, 1978.

PARIZEAU, Michel

Center. Shoots left. 5'10", 165 lbs. Born, Montreal, Que., April 9, 1948.
(NY Rangers' 3rd choice, 10th overall, in 1965 Amateur Draft).

Season	Club	GP	G	A	Pts	PIM	GP	G	A	Pts	PIM
1971-72	St. Louis Blues	21	1	2	3	8	....	....	....	....	....
	Philadelphia Flyers	37	2	12	14	10	....	....	....	....	....
	NHL Totals	**58**	**3**	**14**	**17**	**18**	....	....	....	....	....

Claimed by **St. Louis** from **NY Rangers** in Intra-League Draft, June 8, 1971. Claimed on waivers by **Philadelphia** from **St. Louis**, December 8, 1971.

PARK, Brad

HHOF

Defense. Shoots left. 6', 200 lbs. Born, Toronto, Ont., July 6, 1948.
(NY Rangers' 1st choice, 2nd overall, in 1966 Amateur Draft).

Season	Club	GP	G	A	Pts	PIM	GP	G	A	Pts	PIM
1968-69	New York Rangers	54	3	23	26	70	4	0	2	2	7
1969-70	New York Rangers	60	11	26	37	98	5	1	2	3	11
1970-71	New York Rangers	68	7	37	44	114	13	0	4	4	42
1971-72	New York Rangers	75	24	49	73	130	16	4	7	11	21
1972-73	New York Rangers	52	10	43	53	51	10	2	5	7	8
1973-74	New York Rangers	78	25	57	82	148	13	4	8	12	38
1974-75	New York Rangers	65	13	44	57	104	3	1	4	5	2

Season	Club	REGULAR SEASON GP	G	A	Pts	PIM	PLAYOFFS GP	G	A	Pts	PIM
1975-76	New York Rangers	13	2	4	6	23	....	....	....	....	....
	Boston Bruins	43	16	37	53	95	11	3	8	11	14
1976-77	Boston Bruins	77	12	55	67	67	14	2	10	12	4
1977-78	Boston Bruins	80	22	57	79	79	15	9	11	20	14
1978-79	Boston Bruins	40	7	32	39	10	11	1	4	5	8
1979-80	Boston Bruins	32	5	16	21	27	10	3	6	9	4
1980-81	Boston Bruins	78	14	52	66	111	3	1	3	4	11
1981-82	Boston Bruins	75	14	42	56	82	11	1	4	5	4
1982-83	Boston Bruins	76	10	26	36	82	16	3	9	12	18
1983-84	Detroit Red Wings	80	5	53	58	85	3	0	3	3	0
1984-85	Detroit Red Wings	67	13	30	43	53	3	0	0	0	11
	NHL Totals	**1113**	**213**	**683**	**896**	**1429**	**161**	**35**	**90**	**125**	**217**

NHL First All-Star Team (1970, 1972, 1974, 1976, 1978) • NHL Second All-Star Team (1971, 1973) • Bill Masterton Trophy (1984)

Played in NHL All-Star Game (1970, 1971, 1972, 1973, 1974, 1975, 1976, 1977, 1978)

Traded to **Boston** by **NY Rangers** with Jean Ratelle and Joe Zanussi for Phil Esposito and Carol Vadnais, November 7, 1975. Signed as a free agent by **Detroit**, August 9, 1983.

PARK, Richard

Right wing. Shoots right. 5'11", 190 lbs. Born, Seoul, South Korea, May 27, 1976.
(Pittsburgh's 2nd choice, 50th overall, in 1994 Entry Draft).

Season	Club	GP	G	A	Pts	PIM	GP	G	A	Pts	PIM
1994-95	Pittsburgh Penguins	1	0	1	1	2	3	0	0	0	2
1995-96	Pittsburgh Penguins	56	4	6	10	36	1	0	0	0	0
1996-97	Pittsburgh Penguins	1	0	0	0	0	....	....	....	....	....
	Mighty Ducks of Anaheim	11	1	1	2	10	11	0	1	1	2
1997-98	Mighty Ducks of Anaheim	15	0	2	2	8	....	....	....	....	....
1998-99	Philadelphia Flyers	7	0	0	0	0	....	....	....	....	....
2001-02	Minnesota Wild	63	10	15	25	10	....	....	....	....	....
2002-03	Minnesota Wild	81	14	10	24	16	18	3	3	6	4
	NHL Totals	**235**	**29**	**35**	**64**	**82**	**33**	**3**	**4**	**7**	**8**

Traded to **Anaheim** by **Pittsburgh** for Roman Oksiuta, March 18, 1997. Signed as a free agent by **Philadelphia**, August 24, 1998. Signed as a free agent by **Utah** (IHL), September 22, 1999. Signed as a free agent by **Minnesota**, June 6, 2000.

PARKER, Jeff

Right wing. Shoots right. 6'3", 194 lbs. Born, St. Paul, MN, September 7, 1964.
(Buffalo's 9th choice, 111th overall, in 1982 Entry Draft).

Season	Club	GP	G	A	Pts	PIM	GP	G	A	Pts	PIM
1986-87	Buffalo Sabres	15	3	3	6	7	....	....	....	....	....
1987-88	Buffalo Sabres	4	0	2	2	2	....	....	....	....	....
1988-89	Buffalo Sabres	57	9	9	18	82	5	0	0	0	26
1989-90	Buffalo Sabres	61	4	5	9	70	....	....	....	....	....
1990-91	Hartford Whalers	4	0	0	0	2	....	....	....	....	....
	NHL Totals	**141**	**16**	**19**	**35**	**163**	**5**	**0**	**0**	**0**	**26**

Traded to **Winnipeg** by **Buffalo** with Phil Housley, Scott Arneil and Buffalo's 1st round choice (Keith Tkachuk) in 1990 Entry Draft for Dale Hawerchuk and Winnipeg's 1st round choice (Brad May) in 1990 Entry Draft, June 16, 1990. Signed as a free agent by **Pittsburgh**, February 5, 1991. Traded to **Harford** by **Pittsburgh** with John Cullen and Zarley Zalapski for Ron Francis, Grant Jennings and Ulf Samuelsson, March 4, 1991.

PARKER, Scott

Right wing. Shoots right. 6'5", 230 lbs. Born, Hanford, CA, January 29, 1978.
(Colorado's 4th choice, 20th overall, in 1998 Entry Draft).

Season	Club	GP	G	A	Pts	PIM	GP	G	A	Pts	PIM
1998-99	Colorado Avalanche	27	0	0	0	71	....	....	....	....	....
2000-01 ♦	Colorado Avalanche	69	2	3	5	155	4	0	0	0	2
2001-02	Colorado Avalanche	63	1	4	5	154	....	....	....	....	....
2002-03	Colorado Avalanche	43	1	3	4	82	1	0	0	0	2
	NHL Totals	**202**	**4**	**10**	**14**	**462**	**5**	**0**	**0**	**0**	**4**

• Re-entered NHL Entry Draft. Originally New Jersey's 6th choice, 63rd overall, in 1996 Entry Draft.

Traded to **San Jose** by **Colorado** for Colorado's 5th round choice (previously acquired, Colorado selected Brad Richardson) in 2003 Entry Draft, June 21, 2003.

PARKES, Ernie

Right wing. Shoots right. 5'10", 150 lbs. Born, Dunnville, Ont., November 4, 1898.

Season	Club	GP	G	A	Pts	PIM	GP	G	A	Pts	PIM
1924-25	Montreal Maroons	17	0	0	0	2	....	....	....	....	....
	NHL Totals	**17**	**0**	**0**	**0**	**2**					

Signed as a free agent by **Toronto**, December 8, 1924. Traded to **Boston** by **Toronto** for cash, December 8, 1924. Rights traded to **Mtl. Maroons** by **Boston** for George Carroll, December 19, 1924.

PARKS, Greg

Center. Shoots right. 5'9", 180 lbs. Born, Edmonton, Alta., March 25, 1967.

Season	Club	GP	G	A	Pts	PIM	GP	G	A	Pts	PIM
1990-91	New York Islanders	20	1	2	3	4	....	....	....	....	....
1991-92	New York Islanders	1	0	0	0	2	....	....	....	....	....
1992-93	New York Islanders	2	0	0	0	0	2	0	0	0	0
	NHL Totals	**23**	**1**	**2**	**3**	**6**	**2**	**0**	**0**	**0**	**0**

Signed as a free agent by **NY Islanders**, August 13, 1990.

PARRISH, Mark

Right wing. Shoots right. 5'11", 200 lbs. Born, Edina, MN, February 2, 1977.
(Colorado's 3rd choice, 79th overall, in 1996 Entry Draft).

Season	Club	GP	G	A	Pts	PIM	GP	G	A	Pts	PIM
1998-99	Florida Panthers	73	24	13	37	25	....	....	....	....	....
99-2000	Florida Panthers	81	26	18	44	39	4	0	1	1	0
2000-01	New York Islanders	70	17	13	30	28	....	....	....	....	....
2001-02	New York Islanders	78	30	30	60	32	7	2	1	3	6
2002-03	New York Islanders	81	23	25	48	28	5	1	0	1	4
	NHL Totals	**383**	**120**	**99**	**219**	**152**	**16**	**3**	**2**	**5**	**10**

Played in NHL All-Star Game (2002)

Rights traded to **Florida** by **Colorado** with Anaheim's 3rd round choice (previously acquired, Florida selected Lance Ward) in 1998 Entry Draft for Tom Fitzgerald, March 24, 1998. Traded to **NY Islanders** by **Florida** with Oleg Kvasha for Roberto Luongo and Olli Jokinen, June 24, 2000.

PARSONS, George

Left wing. Shoots left. 5'11", 174 lbs. Born, Toronto, Ont., June 28, 1914.

Season	Club	GP	G	A	Pts	PIM	GP	G	A	Pts	PIM
1936-37	Toronto Maple Leafs	5	0	0	0	0	....	....	....	....	....
1937-38	Toronto Maple Leafs	30	5	6	11	6	7	3	2	5	11
1938-39	Toronto Maple Leafs	43	7	7	14	14	....	....	....	....	....
	NHL Totals	**78**	**12**	**13**	**25**	**20**	**7**	**3**	**2**	**5**	**11**

Signed as a free agent by **Toronto**, October 22, 1935. • Suffered career-ending eye injury in game vs. Chicago, March 4, 1939.

PARSSINEN, Timo

Left wing. Shoots left. 5'10", 176 lbs. Born, Lohjan mlk., Finland, January 19, 1977.
(Anaheim's 4th choice, 102nd overall, in 2001 Entry Draft).

Season	Club	GP	G	A	Pts	PIM	GP	G	A	Pts	PIM
2001-02	Mighty Ducks of Anaheim	17	0	3	3	2	....	....	....	....	....
	NHL Totals	**17**	**0**	**3**	**3**	**2**	....	....	....	....	....

PASEK, Dusan

Center. Shoots left. 6'1", 200 lbs. Born, Bratislava, Czech., September 7, 1960.
(Minnesota's 4th choice, 81st overall, in 1982 Entry Draft).

Season	Club	GP	G	A	Pts	PIM	GP	G	A	Pts	PIM
1988-89	Minnesota North Stars	48	4	10	14	30	2	1	0	1	0
	NHL Totals	**48**	**4**	**10**	**14**	**30**	**2**	**1**	**0**	**1**	**0**

PASIN, Dave

Right wing. Shoots right. 6'1", 205 lbs. Born, Edmonton, Alta., July 8, 1966.
(Boston's 1st choice, 19th overall, in 1984 Entry Draft).

Season	Club	GP	G	A	Pts	PIM	GP	G	A	Pts	PIM
1985-86	Boston Bruins	71	18	19	37	50	3	0	1	1	0
1988-89	Los Angeles Kings	5	0	0	0	0	....	....	....	....	....
	NHL Totals	**76**	**18**	**19**	**37**	**50**	**3**	**0**	**1**	**1**	**0**

Rights traded to **Los Angeles** by **Boston** for Paul Guay, November 3, 1988. Claimed on waivers by **NY Islanders** from **Los Angeles**, March 6, 1990.

PASLAWSKI, Greg

Right wing. Shoots right. 5'11", 190 lbs. Born, Kindersley, Sask., August 25, 1961.

Season	Club	GP	G	A	Pts	PIM	GP	G	A	Pts	PIM
1983-84	Montreal Canadiens	26	1	4	5	4	....	....	....	....	....
	St. Louis Blues	34	8	6	14	17	9	1	0	1	2
1984-85	St. Louis Blues	72	22	20	42	21	3	0	0	0	2
1985-86	St. Louis Blues	56	22	11	33	18	17	10	7	17	13
1986-87	St. Louis Blues	76	29	35	64	27	6	1	1	2	4
1987-88	St. Louis Blues	17	2	1	3	4	3	1	1	2	2
1988-89	St. Louis Blues	75	26	26	52	18	9	2	1	3	2
1989-90	Winnipeg Jets	71	18	30	48	14	7	1	3	4	0
1990-91	Winnipeg Jets	43	9	10	19	10	....	....	....	....	....
	Buffalo Sabres	12	2	1	3	4	....	....	....	....	....
1991-92	Quebec Nordiques	80	28	17	45	18	....	....	....	....	....
1992-93	Philadelphia Flyers	60	14	19	33	12	....	....	....	....	....
	Calgary Flames	13	4	5	9	0	6	3	0	3	0
1993-94	Calgary Flames	15	2	0	2	2	....	....	....	....	....
	NHL Totals	**650**	**187**	**185**	**372**	**169**	**60**	**19**	**13**	**32**	**25**

Signed as a free agent by **Montreal**, October 5, 1981. Traded to **St. Louis** by **Montreal** with Gilbert Delorme and Doug Wickenheiser for Perry Turnbull, December 21, 1983. • Missed remainder of 1987-88 season recovering from back surgery, November, 1987. Traded to **Winnipeg** by **St. Louis** with Montreal's 3rd round choice (previously acquired, Winnipeg selected Kris Draper) in 1989 Entry Draft for NY Rangers' 3rd round choice (previously acquired, St. Louis selected Denny Felsner) in 1989 Entry Draft and Winnipeg's 2nd round choice (Steve Staios) in 1991 Entry Draft, June 17, 1989. Traded to **Buffalo** by **Winnipeg** for cash, February 4, 1991. Claimed by **San Jose** from **Buffalo** in Expansion Draft, May 30, 1991. Traded to **Quebec** by **San Jose** for Tony Hrkac, May 31, 1991. Signed as a free agent by **Philadelphia**, August 25, 1992. Traded to **Calgary** by **Philadelphia** for Calgary's 9th round choice (E.J. Bradley) in 1993 Entry Draft, March 18, 1993.

PATERA, Pavel

Center. Shoots left. 6'1", 172 lbs. Born, Kladno, Czech., September 6, 1971.
(Dallas' 4th choice, 153rd overall, in 1998 Entry Draft).

Season	Club	GP	G	A	Pts	PIM	GP	G	A	Pts	PIM
99-2000	Dallas Stars	12	1	4	5	4	....	....	....	....	....
2000-01	Minnesota Wild	20	1	3	4	4	....	....	....	....	....
	NHL Totals	**32**	**2**	**7**	**9**	**8**	....	....	....	....	....

Traded to **Minnesota** by **Dallas** with Aaron Gavey, Dallas' 8th round choice (Eric Johansson) in 2000 Entry Draft and Minnesota's 4th round choice (previously acquired, later traded to Los Angeles – Los Angeles selected Aaron Rome) in 2002 Entry Draft for Brad Lukowich and Minnesota's 3rd (Yared Hagos) and 9th (Dale Sullivan) round choices in 2001 Entry Draft, June 25, 2000.

PATERSON, Joe

Left wing. Shoots left. 6'2", 207 lbs. Born, Toronto, Ont., June 25, 1960.
(Detroit's 5th choice, 87th overall, in 1979 Entry Draft).

Season	Club	GP	G	A	Pts	PIM	GP	G	A	Pts	PIM
1980-81	Detroit Red Wings	38	2	5	7	53	....	....	....	....	....
1981-82	Detroit Red Wings	3	0	0	0	0	....	....	....	....	....
1982-83	Detroit Red Wings	33	2	1	3	14	....	....	....	....	....
1983-84	Detroit Red Wings	41	2	5	7	148	3	0	0	0	7
1984-85	Philadelphia Flyers	6	0	0	0	31	17	3	4	7	70

Season	Club	GP	G	A	Pts	PIM	GP	G	A	Pts	PIM
		REGULAR SEASON					PLAYOFFS				
1985-86	Philadelphia Flyers	5	0	0	0	12	....	....	....	....	....
	Los Angeles Kings	47	9	18	27	153	....	....	....	....	....
1986-87	Los Angeles Kings	45	2	1	3	158	2	0	0	0	0
1987-88	Los Angeles Kings	32	1	3	4	113	....	....	....	....	....
	New York Rangers	21	1	3	4	63	....	....	....	....	....
1988-89	New York Rangers	20	0	1	1	84	....	....	....	....	....
	NHL Totals	**291**	**19**	**37**	**56**	**829**	**22**	**3**	**4**	**7**	**77**

Traded to **Philadelphia** by **Detroit** with Murray Craven for Darryl Sittler, October 10, 1984. Trade to **Los Angeles** by **Philadelphia** for Philadelphia's 4th round choice (previously acquired, Philadelphia selected Mark Bar) in 1986 Entry Draft, December 18, 1985. Traded to **NY Rangers** by **Los Angeles** for Gord Walker and Mike Siltala, January 21, 1988.

PATERSON, Mark

Defense. Shoots left. 5'11", 180 lbs. Born, Ottawa, Ont., February 22, 1964.
(Hartford's 2nd choice, 35th overall, in 1982 Entry Draft).

Season	Club	GP	G	A	Pts	PIM	GP	G	A	Pts	PIM
1982-83	Hartford Whalers	2	0	0	0	0	....	....	....	....	....
1983-84	Hartford Whalers	9	2	0	2	4	....	....	....	....	....
1984-85	Hartford Whalers	13	1	3	4	24	....	....	....	....	....
1985-86	Hartford Whalers	5	0	0	0	5	....	....	....	....	....
	NHL Totals	**29**	**3**	**3**	**6**	**33**	....	....	....	....	....

Traded to **Calgary** by **Hartford** for Yves Courteau, October 7, 1986.

PATERSON, Rick

Center. Shoots right. 5'9", 187 lbs. Born, Kingston, Ont., February 10, 1958.
(Chicago's 3rd choice, 46th overall, in 1978 Amateur Draft).

Season	Club	GP	G	A	Pts	PIM	GP	G	A	Pts	PIM
1978-79	Chicago Black Hawks	....	....	....	....	....	1	0	1	1	0
1979-80	Chicago Black Hawks	11	0	2	2	0	7	0	0	0	5
1980-81	Chicago Black Hawks	49	8	2	10	18	2	1	0	1	0
1981-82	Chicago Black Hawks	48	4	7	11	8	15	3	2	5	21
1982-83	Chicago Black Hawks	79	14	9	23	14	13	1	1	2	4
1983-84	Chicago Black Hawks	72	7	6	13	41	5	1	1	2	6
1984-85	Chicago Black Hawks	79	7	12	19	25	15	1	5	6	15
1985-86	Chicago Black Hawks	70	9	3	12	24	3	0	0	0	0
1986-87	Chicago Blackhawks	22	1	2	3	6	....	....	....	....	....
	NHL Totals	**430**	**50**	**43**	**93**	**136**	**61**	**7**	**10**	**17**	**51**

PATEY, Doug

Right wing. Shoots right. 5'11", 180 lbs. Born, Toronto, Ont., December 28, 1956.
(Washington's 5th choice, 73rd overall, in 1976 Amateur Draft).

Season	Club	GP	G	A	Pts	PIM	GP	G	A	Pts	PIM
1976-77	Washington Capitals	37	3	1	4	6	....	....	....	....	....
1977-78	Washington Capitals	2	0	1	1	0	....	....	....	....	....
1978-79	Washington Capitals	6	1	0	1	2	....	....	....	....	....
	NHL Totals	**45**	**4**	**2**	**6**	**8**	....	....	....	....	....

• Brother of Larry

Claimed by **Edmonton** from **Washington** in Expansion Draft, June 13, 1979.

PATEY, Larry

Center. Shoots left. 6'1", 185 lbs. Born, Toronto, Ont., March 19, 1953.
(California's 7th choice, 130th overall, in 1973 Amateur Draft).

Season	Club	GP	G	A	Pts	PIM	GP	G	A	Pts	PIM
1973-74	California Golden Seals	1	0	0	0	0	....	....	....	....	....
1974-75	California Golden Seals	79	25	20	45	68	....	....	....	....	....
1975-76	California Golden Seals	18	4	4	8	23	....	....	....	....	....
	St. Louis Blues	53	8	6	14	26	3	1	1	2	2
1976-77	St. Louis Blues	80	21	29	50	41	4	1	0	1	0
1977-78	St. Louis Blues	80	17	17	34	29	....	....	....	....	....
1978-79	St. Louis Blues	78	15	19	34	60	....	....	....	....	....
1979-80	St. Louis Blues	78	17	17	34	76	3	1	0	1	2
1980-81	St. Louis Blues	80	22	23	45	107	11	2	4	6	30
1981-82	St. Louis Blues	70	14	12	26	97	10	2	4	6	13
1982-83	St. Louis Blues	67	9	12	21	80	4	1	0	1	4
1983-84	St. Louis Blues	17	0	1	1	8	....	....	....	....	....
	New York Rangers	9	1	2	3	4	4	0	1	1	6
1984-85	New York Rangers	7	0	1	1	12	1	0	0	0	0
	NHL Totals	**717**	**153**	**163**	**316**	**631**	**40**	**8**	**10**	**18**	**57**

• Brother of Doug

Traded to **St. Louis** by **California** with California's 3rd round choice (later traded back to California – California/Cleveland selected Reg Kerr) in 1977 Amateur Draft for Wayne Merrick, November 24, 1975. Traded to **NY Rangers** by **St. Louis** with the rights to Bob Brooke for Dave Barr, NY Rangers' 3rd round choice (Alan Perry) in 1984 Entry Draft and cash, March 5, 1984.

PATRICK, Craig

USHOF

Right wing. Shoots left. 6', 190 lbs. Born, Detroit, MI, May 20, 1946.

Season	Club	GP	G	A	Pts	PIM	GP	G	A	Pts	PIM
1971-72	California Golden Seals	59	8	3	11	12	....	....	....	....	....
1972-73	California Golden Seals	71	20	22	42	6	....	....	....	....	....
1973-74	California Golden Seals	59	10	20	30	17	....	....	....	....	....
1974-75	California Golden Seals	14	2	1	3	0	....	....	....	....	....
	St. Louis Blues	43	6	9	15	6	2	0	1	1	0
1975-76	Kansas City Scouts	80	17	18	35	14	....	....	....	....	....
1976-77	Washington Capitals	28	7	10	17	2	....	....	....	....	....
1977-78	Washington Capitals	44	1	7	8	4	....	....	....	....	....
1978-79	Washington Capitals	3	1	1	2	0	....	....	....	....	....
	NHL Totals	**401**	**72**	**91**	**163**	**61**	**2**	**0**	**1**	**1**	**0**

• Son of Lynn • Brother of Glenn • Lester Patrick Trophy (2000)

Signed as a free agent by **California**, October 6, 1971. Traded to **St. Louis** by **California** with Stan Gilbertson for Warren Williams and Dave Gardner, November 11, 1974. Traded to **Kansas City** by **St. Louis** with Denis Dupere and cash for Lynn Powis and Kansas City's 2nd round choice (Brian Sutter) in 1976 Amateur Draft, June 18, 1975. Signed as a free agent by **Washington** after **Minnesota** (WHA) franchise folded, February 1, 1977.

PATRICK, Glenn

Defense. Shoots left. 6'2", 190 lbs. Born, New York, NY, April 26, 1950.

Season	Club	GP	G	A	Pts	PIM	GP	G	A	Pts	PIM
1973-74	St. Louis Blues	1	0	0	0	2	....	....	....	....	....
1974-75	California Golden Seals	2	0	0	0	0	....	....	....	....	....
1976-77	Cleveland Barons	35	2	3	5	70	....	....	....	....	....
	NHL Totals	**38**	**2**	**3**	**5**	**72**	....	....	....	....	....

• Son of Lynn • Brother of Craig

Signed as a free agent by **St. Louis**, March 10, 1970. Traded to **California** by **St. Louis** for Ron Serafini, July 18, 1974. Transferred to **Cleveland** after **California** franchise relocated, August 26, 1976.

PATRICK, James

Defense. Shoots right. 6'2", 202 lbs. Born, Winnipeg, Man., June 14, 1963.
(NY Rangers' 1st choice, 9th overall, in 1981 Entry Draft).

Season	Club	GP	G	A	Pts	PIM	GP	G	A	Pts	PIM
1983-84	New York Rangers	12	1	7	8	2	5	0	3	3	2
1984-85	New York Rangers	75	8	28	36	71	3	0	0	0	4
1985-86	New York Rangers	75	14	29	43	88	16	1	5	6	34
1986-87	New York Rangers	78	10	45	55	62	6	1	2	3	2
1987-88	New York Rangers	70	17	45	62	52	....	....	....	....	....
1988-89	New York Rangers	68	11	36	47	41	4	0	1	1	2
1989-90	New York Rangers	73	14	43	57	50	10	3	8	11	0
1990-91	New York Rangers	74	10	49	59	58	6	0	0	0	6
1991-92	New York Rangers	80	14	57	71	54	13	0	7	7	12
1992-93	New York Rangers	60	5	21	26	61	....	....	....	....	....
1993-94	New York Rangers	6	0	3	3	2	....	....	....	....	....
	Hartford Whalers	47	8	20	28	32	....	....	....	....	....
	Calgary Flames	15	2	2	4	6	7	0	1	1	6
1994-95	Calgary Flames	43	0	10	10	14	5	0	1	1	0
1995-96	Calgary Flames	80	3	32	35	30	4	0	0	0	2
1996-97	Calgary Flames	19	3	1	4	6	....	....	....	....	....
1997-98	Calgary Flames	60	6	11	17	26	....	....	....	....	....
1998-99	Buffalo Sabres	45	1	7	8	16	20	0	1	1	12
99-2000	Buffalo Sabres	66	5	8	13	22	5	0	1	1	2
2000-01	Buffalo Sabres	54	4	9	13	12	13	1	2	3	2
2001-02	Buffalo Sabres	56	5	8	13	16	....	....	....	....	....
2002-03	Buffalo Sabres	69	4	12	16	26	....	....	....	....	....
	NHL Totals	**1225**	**145**	**483**	**628**	**747**	**117**	**6**	**32**	**38**	**86**

• Brother of Steve

Traded to **Hartford** by **NY Rangers** with Darren Turcotte for Steve Larmer, Nick Kypreos, Barry Richter and Hartford's 6th round choice (Yuri Litvinov) in 1994 Entry Draft, November 2, 1993. Traded to **Calgary** by **Hartford** with Zarley Zalapski and Michael Nylander for Gary Suter, Paul Ranheim and Ted Drury, March 10, 1994. • Missed majority of 1996-97 season recovering from knee injury originally suffered in game vs. Pittsburgh, October 24, 1996. Signed as a free agent by **Buffalo**, October 7, 1998.

PATRICK, Lester

HHOF

Defense. Shoots left. 6'1", 180 lbs. Born, Drummondville, Que., December 30, 1883.

Season	Club	GP	G	A	Pts	PIM	GP	G	A	Pts	PIM
1926-27	New York Rangers	1	0	0	0	2	....	....	....	....	....
	NHL Totals	**1**	**0**	**0**	**0**	**2**	....	....	....	....	....

• Father of Muzz and Lynn

PATRICK, Lynn

HHOF

Center/Left wing. Shoots left. 6'1", 192 lbs. Born, Victoria, B.C., February 3, 1912.

Season	Club	GP	G	A	Pts	PIM	GP	G	A	Pts	PIM
1934-35	New York Rangers	48	9	13	22	17	4	2	2	4	0
1935-36	New York Rangers	48	11	14	25	29	....	....	....	....	....
1936-37	New York Rangers	45	8	16	24	23	9	3	0	3	2
1937-38	New York Rangers	48	15	19	34	24	3	0	1	1	2
1938-39	New York Rangers	35	8	21	29	25	7	1	1	2	0
1939-40♦	New York Rangers	48	12	16	28	34	12	2	2	4	4
1940-41	New York Rangers	48	20	24	44	12	3	1	0	1	14
1941-42	New York Rangers	47	*32	22	54	18	6	1	0	1	0
1942-43	New York Rangers	50	22	39	61	28	....	....	....	....	....
1945-46	New York Rangers	38	8	6	14	30	....	....	....	....	....
	NHL Totals	**455**	**145**	**190**	**335**	**240**	**44**	**10**	**6**	**16**	**22**

• Son of Lester • Brother of Muzz • Father of Craig and Glenn • NHL First All-Star Team (1942)
• NHL Second All-Star Team (1943) • Lester Patrick Trophy (1989)

PATRICK, Muzz

Defense. Shoots left. 6'2", 200 lbs. Born, Victoria, B.C., June 28, 1915.

Season	Club	GP	G	A	Pts	PIM	GP	G	A	Pts	PIM
1937-38	New York Rangers	1	0	2	2	0	3	0	0	0	2
1938-39	New York Rangers	48	1	10	11	64	7	1	0	1	17
1939-40♦	New York Rangers	46	2	4	6	44	12	3	0	3	13
1940-41	New York Rangers	47	2	8	10	21	3	0	0	0	2
1945-46	New York Rangers	24	0	2	2	4	....	....	....	....	....
	NHL Totals	**166**	**5**	**26**	**31**	**133**	**25**	**4**	**0**	**4**	**34**

• Son of Lester • Brother of Lynn

PATRICK, Steve

Right wing. Shoots right. 6'4", 206 lbs. Born, Winnipeg, Man., February 4, 1961.
(Buffalo's 1st choice, 20th overall, in 1980 Entry Draft).

Season	Club	GP	G	A	Pts	PIM	GP	G	A	Pts	PIM
		REGULAR SEASON					PLAYOFFS				
1980-81	Buffalo Sabres	30	1	7	8	25	5	0	1	1	6
1981-82	Buffalo Sabres	41	8	8	16	64	....	....	....	....	....
1982-83	Buffalo Sabres	56	9	13	22	26	2	0	0	0	0
1983-84	Buffalo Sabres	11	1	4	5	6	1	0	0	0	0
1984-85	Buffalo Sabres	14	2	2	4	4	....	....	....	....	....
	New York Rangers	43	11	18	29	63	1	0	0	0	0
1985-86	New York Rangers	28	4	3	7	37	....	....	....	....	....
	Quebec Nordiques	27	4	13	17	17	3	0	0	0	6
	NHL Totals	**250**	**40**	**68**	**108**	**242**	**12**	**0**	**1**	**1**	**12**

• Brother of James

Traded to **NY Rangers** by **Buffalo** with Jim Wiemer for Dave Maloney and Chris Renaud, December 6, 1984. Traded to **Quebec** by **NY Rangers** for Wilf Paiement, February 6, 1986.

PATTERSON, Colin

Wing. Shoots right. 6'2", 195 lbs. Born, Rexdale, Ont., May 11, 1960.

Season	Club	GP	G	A	Pts	PIM	GP	G	A	Pts	PIM
1983-84	Calgary Flames	56	13	14	27	15	11	1	1	2	6
1984-85	Calgary Flames	57	22	21	43	5	4	0	0	0	5
1985-86	Calgary Flames	61	14	13	27	22	19	6	3	9	10
1986-87	Calgary Flames	68	13	13	26	41	6	0	2	2	2
1987-88	Calgary Flames	39	7	11	18	28	9	1	0	1	8
1988-89 ♦	Calgary Flames	74	14	24	38	56	22	3	10	13	24
1989-90	Calgary Flames	61	5	3	8	20	....	....	....	....	....
1990-91	Calgary Flames	....	....	....	....	....	1	0	0	0	0
1991-92	Buffalo Sabres	52	4	8	12	30	5	1	0	1	0
1992-93	Buffalo Sabres	36	4	2	6	22	8	0	1	1	2
	NHL Totals	**504**	**96**	**109**	**205**	**239**	**85**	**12**	**17**	**29**	**57**

Signed as a free agent by **Calgary**, March 24, 1983. • Missed entire 1990-91 regular season recovering from knee surgery, October 12, 1990. Traded to **Buffalo** by **Calgary** for future considerations, October 24, 1991.

PATTERSON, Dennis

Defense. Shoots left. 5'8", 175 lbs. Born, Peterborough, Ont., January 9, 1950.
(Minnesota's 3rd choice, 34th overall, in 1970 Amateur Draft).

Season	Club	GP	G	A	Pts	PIM	GP	G	A	Pts	PIM
1974-75	Kansas City Scouts	66	1	5	6	39	....	....	....	....	....
1975-76	Kansas City Scouts	69	5	16	21	28	....	....	....	....	....
1979-80	Philadelphia Flyers	3	0	1	1	0					
	NHL Totals	**138**	**6**	**22**	**28**	**67**	....	....	....	....	....

Claimed by **Kansas City** from **Minnesota** in Expansion Draft, June 12, 1974. Signed as a free agent by **Philadelphia**, August 8, 1979.

PATTERSON, Ed

Right wing. Shoots right. 6'2", 213 lbs. Born, Delta, B.C., November 14, 1972.
(Pittsburgh's 7th choice, 148th overall, in 1991 Entry Draft).

Season	Club	GP	G	A	Pts	PIM	GP	G	A	Pts	PIM
1993-94	Pittsburgh Penguins	27	3	1	4	10	....	....	....	....	....
1995-96	Pittsburgh Penguins	35	0	2	2	38	....	....	....	....	....
1996-97	Pittsburgh Penguins	6	0	0	0	8	....	....	....	....	....
	NHL Totals	**68**	**3**	**3**	**6**	**56**	....	....	....	....	....

PATTERSON, George

Wing. Shoots right. 6'1", 176 lbs. Born, Kingston, Ont., May 22, 1906.

Season	Club	GP	G	A	Pts	PIM	GP	G	A	Pts	PIM
1926-27	Toronto St. Pats/Maple Leafs	17	4	2	6	17	....	....	....	....	....
1927-28	Toronto Maple Leafs	12	1	0	1	14	....	....	....	....	....
	Montreal Canadiens	16	0	1	1	0	....	....	....	....	....
1928-29	Montreal Canadiens	44	4	5	9	34	3	0	0	0	2
1929-30	New York Americans	39	13	4	17	24	....	....	....	....	....
1930-31	New York Americans	44	8	6	14	67	....	....	....	....	....
1931-32	New York Americans	20	6	0	6	26	....	....	....	....	....
1932-33	New York Americans	41	12	7	19	26	....	....	....	....	....
1933-34	New York Americans	13	3	0	3	6	....	....	....	....	....
	Boston Bruins	10	0	1	1	2	....	....	....	....	....
1934-35	Detroit Red Wings	7	0	0	0	0	....	....	....	....	....
	St. Louis Eagles	21	0	1	1	2	....	....	....	....	....
	NHL Totals	**284**	**51**	**27**	**78**	**218**	**3**	**0**	**0**	**0**	**2**

Traded to **Toronto** by **Hamilton** (Can-Pro) for $5,000 and the loan of Al Pudas, February 1, 1927. Traded to **Montreal** by **Toronto** for cash, February 8, 1928. Traded to **Boston** by **Montreal** for cash, May 13, 1929. Claimed on waivers by **NY Americans** from **Boston**, October 23, 1929. Traded to **Boston** by **NY Americans** with Lloyd Gross for Art Chapman and Bob Gracie, January 11, 1934. Traded to **Detroit** by **Boston** for Gene Carrigan, October 10, 1934. Traded to **St. Louis** by **Detroit** for Mickey Blake and $3,500 with Detroit holding right of recall, November 28, 1934. • Returned to **Detroit**, December 24, 1934. Traded to **Buffalo** (IHL) by **Detroit** for cash, January 4, 1935.

PAUL, Butch

Center. Shoots right. 5'11", 160 lbs. Born, Rocky Mountain House, Alta., September 11, 1943.

Season	Club	GP	G	A	Pts	PIM	GP	G	A	Pts	PIM
1964-65	Detroit Red Wings	3	0	0	0	0	....	....	....	....	....
	NHL Totals	**3**	**0**	**0**	**0**	**0**	....	....	....	....	....

PAUL, Jeff

Defense. Shoots right. 6'3", 200 lbs. Born, London, Ont., March 1, 1978.
(Chicago's 2nd choice, 42nd overall, in 1996 Entry Draft).

Season	Club	GP	G	A	Pts	PIM	GP	G	A	Pts	PIM
		REGULAR SEASON					PLAYOFFS				
2002-03	Colorado Avalanche	2	0	0	0	7	....	....	....	....	....
	NHL Totals	**2**	**0**	**0**	**0**	**7**	....	....	....	....	....

Signed as a free agent by **Colorado**, August 8, 2001.

PAULHUS, Rollie

Defense. Shoots left. 5'8", 185 lbs. Born, Montreal, Que., September 1, 1902.

Season	Club	GP	G	A	Pts	PIM	GP	G	A	Pts	PIM
1925-26	Montreal Canadiens	33	0	0	0	0	....	....	....	....	....
	NHL Totals	**33**	**0**	**0**	**0**	**0**	....	....	....	....	....

Signed as a free agent by **Montreal**, November 16, 1925.

PAVELICH, Mark

Center. Shoots right. 5'8", 170 lbs. Born, Eveleth, MN, February 28, 1958.

Season	Club	GP	G	A	Pts	PIM	GP	G	A	Pts	PIM
1981-82	New York Rangers	79	33	43	76	67	6	1	5	6	0
1982-83	New York Rangers	78	37	38	75	52	9	4	5	9	12
1983-84	New York Rangers	77	29	53	82	96	5	2	4	6	0
1984-85	New York Rangers	48	14	31	45	29	3	0	3	3	2
1985-86	New York Rangers	59	20	20	40	82	....	....	....	....	....
1986-87	Minnesota North Stars	12	4	6	10	10	....	....	....	....	....
1991-92	San Jose Sharks	2	0	1	1	4	....	....	....	....	....
	NHL Totals	**355**	**137**	**192**	**329**	**340**	**23**	**7**	**17**	**24**	**14**

Signed as a free agent by **NY Rangers**, June 5, 1981. Traded to **Minnesota** by **NY Rangers** for Minnesota's 2nd round choice (Troy Mallette) in 1988 Entry Draft, October 24, 1986. Signed as a free agent by **San Jose**, August 9, 1991.

PAVELICH, Marty

Left wing. Shoots left. 5'11", 168 lbs. Born, Sault Ste. Marie, Ont., November 6, 1927.

Season	Club	GP	G	A	Pts	PIM	GP	G	A	Pts	PIM
1947-48	Detroit Red Wings	41	4	8	12	10	10	2	2	4	6
1948-49	Detroit Red Wings	60	10	16	26	40	9	0	1	1	8
1949-50 ♦	Detroit Red Wings	65	8	15	23	58	14	4	2	6	13
1950-51	Detroit Red Wings	67	9	20	29	41	6	0	1	1	2
1951-52 ♦	Detroit Red Wings	68	17	19	36	54	8	2	2	4	2
1952-53	Detroit Red Wings	64	13	20	33	49	6	2	1	3	7
1953-54 ♦	Detroit Red Wings	65	9	20	29	57	12	2	2	4	4
1954-55 ♦	Detroit Red Wings	70	15	15	30	59	11	1	3	4	12
1955-56	Detroit Red Wings	70	5	13	18	38	10	0	1	1	14
1956-57	Detroit Red Wings	64	3	13	16	48	5	0	0	0	6
	NHL Totals	**634**	**93**	**159**	**252**	**454**	**91**	**13**	**15**	**28**	**74**

Played in NHL All-Star Game (1950, 1952, 1954, 1955)

PAVESE, Jim

Defense. Shoots left. 6'2", 205 lbs. Born, New York, NY, May 8, 1962.
(St. Louis' 2nd choice, 54th overall, in 1980 Entry Draft).

Season	Club	GP	G	A	Pts	PIM	GP	G	A	Pts	PIM
1981-82	St. Louis Blues	42	2	9	11	101	3	0	3	3	2
1982-83	St. Louis Blues	24	0	2	2	45	4	0	0	0	6
1983-84	St. Louis Blues	4	0	1	1	19	....	....	....	....	....
1984-85	St. Louis Blues	51	2	5	7	69	1	0	0	0	5
1985-86	St. Louis Blues	69	4	7	11	116	19	0	2	2	51
1986-87	St. Louis Blues	69	2	9	11	127	2	0	0	0	2
1987-88	St. Louis Blues	4	0	1	1	8	....	....	....	....	....
	New York Rangers	14	0	1	1	48	....	....	....	....	....
	Detroit Red Wings	7	0	3	3	21	4	0	1	1	15
1988-89	Detroit Red Wings	39	3	6	9	130	....	....	....	....	....
	Hartford Whalers	5	0	0	0	5	1	0	0	0	0
	NHL Totals	**328**	**13**	**44**	**57**	**689**	**34**	**0**	**6**	**6**	**81**

Traded to **NY Rangers** by **St. Louis** for future considerations, October 23, 1987. Traded to **Detroit** by **NY Rangers** for future considerations, March 8, 1988. Traded to **Hartford** by **Detroit** for Torrie Robertson, March 7, 1989.

PAYER, Evariste

Center/Left wing. Shoots left. 5'6", 150 lbs. Born, Rockland, Ont., December 12, 1887.

Season	Club	GP	G	A	Pts	PIM	GP	G	A	Pts	PIM
1917-18	Montreal Canadiens	1	0	0	0	0	....	....	....	....	....
	NHL Totals	**1**	**0**	**0**	**0**	**0**	....	....	....	....	....

Signed as a free agent by **Montreal**, January 29, 1918.

PAYER, Serge

Center. Shoots left. 6', 203 lbs. Born, Rockland, Ont., May 7, 1979.

Season	Club	GP	G	A	Pts	PIM	GP	G	A	Pts	PIM
2000-01	Florida Panthers	43	5	1	6	21	....	....	....	....	....
	NHL Totals	**43**	**5**	**1**	**6**	**21**	....	....	....	....	....

Signed as a free agent by **Florida**, September 30, 1997.

PAYNE, Davis

Left wing. Shoots left. 6'2", 205 lbs. Born, Port Alberni, B.C., September 24, 1970.
(Edmonton's 6th choice, 140th overall, in 1989 Entry Draft).

Season	Club	GP	G	A	Pts	PIM	GP	G	A	Pts	PIM
1995-96	Boston Bruins	7	0	0	0	7	....	....	....	....	....
1996-97	Boston Bruins	15	0	1	1	7	....	....	....	....	....
	NHL Totals	**22**	**0**	**1**	**1**	**14**	....	....	....	....	....

Signed as a free agent by **Boston**, September 6, 1995.

PAYNE, Steve

Left wing. Shoots left. 6'2", 210 lbs. Born, Toronto, Ont., August 16, 1958.
(Minnesota's 2nd choice, 19th overall, in 1978 Amateur Draft).

Season	Club	GP	G	A	Pts	PIM	GP	G	A	Pts	PIM
		REGULAR SEASON					PLAYOFFS				
1978-79	Minnesota North Stars	70	23	17	40	29	....	....	....	....	....
1979-80	Minnesota North Stars	80	42	43	85	40	15	7	7	14	9
1980-81	Minnesota North Stars	76	30	28	58	88	19	17	12	29	6
1981-82	Minnesota North Stars	74	33	45	78	76	4	4	2	6	2
1982-83	Minnesota North Stars	80	30	39	69	53	9	3	6	9	19
1983-84	Minnesota North Stars	78	28	31	59	49	15	3	6	9	18
1984-85	Minnesota North Stars	76	29	22	51	61	9	1	2	3	6
1985-86	Minnesota North Stars	22	8	4	12	8	....	....	....	....	....
1986-87	Minnesota North Stars	48	4	6	10	19	....	....	....	....	....
1987-88	Minnesota North Stars	9	1	3	4	12	....	....	....	....	....
	NHL Totals	**613**	**228**	**238**	**466**	**435**	**71**	**35**	**35**	**70**	**60**

Played in NHL All-Star Game (1980, 1985)

PAYNTER, Kent

Defense. Shoots left. 6', 183 lbs. Born, Summerside, P.E.I., April 17, 1965.
(Chicago's 9th choice, 165th overall, in 1983 Entry Draft).

Season	Club	GP	G	A	Pts	PIM	GP	G	A	Pts	PIM
1987-88	Chicago Blackhawks	2	0	0	0	2	....	....	....	....	....
1988-89	Chicago Blackhawks	1	0	0	0	2	....	....	....	....	....
1989-90	Washington Capitals	13	1	2	3	18	3	0	0	0	10
1990-91	Washington Capitals	1	0	0	0	15	1	0	0	0	0
1991-92	Winnipeg Jets	5	0	0	0	4	....	....	....	....	....
1992-93	Ottawa Senators	6	0	0	0	20	....	....	....	....	....
1993-94	Ottawa Senators	9	0	1	1	8	....	....	....	....	....
	NHL Totals	**37**	**1**	**3**	**4**	**69**	**4**	**0**	**0**	**0**	**10**

Signed as a free agent by **Washington**, August 21, 1989. Traded to **Winnipeg** by **Washington** with Tyler Larter and Bob Joyce for Craig Duncanson, Brent Hughes, and Simon Wheeldon, May 21, 1991. Claimed by **Ottawa** from **Winnipeg** in Expansion Draft, June 18, 1992.

PEAKE, Pat

Center. Shoots right. 6'1", 195 lbs. Born, Rochester, MI, May 28, 1973.
(Washington's 1st choice, 14th overall, in 1991 Entry Draft).

Season	Club	GP	G	A	Pts	PIM	GP	G	A	Pts	PIM
1993-94	Washington Capitals	49	11	18	29	39	8	0	1	1	8
1994-95	Washington Capitals	18	0	4	4	12	....	....	....	....	....
1995-96	Washington Capitals	62	17	19	36	46	5	2	1	3	12
1996-97	Washington Capitals	4	0	0	0	4	....	....	....	....	....
1997-98	Washington Capitals	1	0	0	0	4	....	....	....	....	....
	NHL Totals	**134**	**28**	**41**	**69**	**105**	**13**	**2**	**2**	**4**	**20**

• Suffered eventual career-ending heel injury in game vs Pittsburgh, April 26, 1996.

PEARSON, Mel

Left wing. Shoots left. 5'10", 175 lbs. Born, Flin Flon, Man., April 29, 1938.

Season	Club	GP	G	A	Pts	PIM	GP	G	A	Pts	PIM
1959-60	New York Rangers	23	1	5	6	13	....	....	....	....	....
1961-62	New York Rangers	3	0	0	0	2	....	....	....	....	....
1962-63	New York Rangers	5	1	0	1	6	....	....	....	....	....
1964-65	New York Rangers	5	0	0	0	4	....	....	....	....	....
1967-68	Pittsburgh Penguins	2	0	1	1	0	....	....	....	....	....
	NHL Totals	**38**	**2**	**6**	**8**	**25**	....	....	....	....	....

Traded to **Chicago** by **NY Rangers** with Dave Richardson, Tracy Pratt and Dick Meissner for John McKenzie and Ray Cullen, June 4, 1965. Claimed by **Pittsburgh** from **Chicago** in Expansion Draft, June 6, 1967. Traded to **Portland** (WHL) by **Pittsburgh** for cash, August, 1969.

PEARSON, Rob

Right wing. Shoots right. 6'3", 198 lbs. Born, Oshawa, Ont., March 8, 1971.
(Toronto's 2nd choice, 12th overall, in 1989 Entry Draft).

Season	Club	GP	G	A	Pts	PIM	GP	G	A	Pts	PIM
1991-92	Toronto Maple Leafs	47	14	10	24	58	....	....	....	....	....
1992-93	Toronto Maple Leafs	78	23	14	37	211	14	2	2	4	31
1993-94	Toronto Maple Leafs	67	12	18	30	189	14	1	0	1	32
1994-95	Washington Capitals	32	0	6	6	96	3	1	0	1	17
1995-96	St. Louis Blues	27	6	4	10	54	2	0	0	0	14
1996-97	St. Louis Blues	18	1	2	3	37	....	....	....	....	....
	NHL Totals	**269**	**56**	**54**	**110**	**645**	**33**	**4**	**2**	**6**	**94**

Traded to **Washington** by **Toronto** with Philadelphia's 1st round choice (previously acquired, Washington selected Nolan Baumgartner) in 1994 Entry Draft for Mike Ridley and St. Louis' 1st round choice (previously acquired, Toronto selected Eric Fichaud) in 1994 Entry Draft, June 28, 1994. Traded to **St. Louis** by **Washington** for Denis Chasse, January 29, 1996.

PEARSON, Scott

Left wing. Shoots left. 6'1", 205 lbs. Born, Cornwall, Ont., December 19, 1969.
(Toronto's 1st choice, 6th overall, in 1988 Entry Draft).

Season	Club	GP	G	A	Pts	PIM	GP	G	A	Pts	PIM
1988-89	Toronto Maple Leafs	9	0	1	1	2	....	....	....	....	....
1989-90	Toronto Maple Leafs	41	5	10	15	90	2	2	0	2	10
1990-91	Toronto Maple Leafs	12	0	0	0	20	....	....	....	....	....
	Quebec Nordiques	35	11	4	15	86	....	....	....	....	....
1991-92	Quebec Nordiques	10	1	2	3	14	....	....	....	....	....
1992-93	Quebec Nordiques	41	13	1	14	95	3	0	0	0	0
1993-94	Edmonton Oilers	72	19	18	37	165	....	....	....	....	....
1994-95	Edmonton Oilers	28	1	4	5	54	....	....	....	....	....
	Buffalo Sabres	14	2	1	3	20	5	0	0	0	4
1995-96	Buffalo Sabres	27	4	0	4	67	....	....	....	....	....
1996-97	Toronto Maple Leafs	1	0	0	0	2	....	....	....	....	....
99-2000	New York Islanders	2	0	1	1	0	....	....	....	....	....
	NHL Totals	**292**	**56**	**42**	**98**	**615**	**10**	**2**	**0**	**2**	**14**

Traded to **Quebec** by **Toronto** with Toronto's 2nd round choices in 1991 (later traded to Washington – Washington selected Eric Lavigne) and 1992 (Tuomas Gronman) Entry Drafts for Aaron Broten, Lucien Deblois and Michel Petit, November 17, 1990. Traded to **Edmonton** by **Quebec** for Martin Gelinas and Edmonton's 6th round choice (Nicholas Checco) in 1993 Entry Draft, June 20, 1993. Traded to **Buffalo** by **Edmonton** for Ken Sutton, April 7, 1995. Signed as a free agent by **Toronto**, July 24, 1996. • Missed majority of 1996-97 season recovering from abdominal surgery, November, 1996. Signed as a free agent by **NY Islanders**, August 9, 1999.

PEAT, Stephen

Defense. Shoots right. 6'3", 210 lbs. Born, Princeton, B.C., March 10, 1980.
(Anaheim's 2nd choice, 32nd overall, in 1998 Entry Draft).

Season	Club	GP	G	A	Pts	PIM	GP	G	A	Pts	PIM
2001-02	Washington Capitals	38	2	2	4	85	....	....	....	....	....
2002-03	Washington Capitals	27	1	0	1	57	....	....	....	....	....
	NHL Totals	**65**	**3**	**2**	**5**	**142**	....	....	....	....	....

Rights traded to **Washington** by **Anaheim** for Washington's 4th round choice (later traded to Montreal – later traded to Pittsburgh – Pittsburgh selected Michel Ouellet) in 2000 Entry Draft, June 1, 2000.

PECA, Michael

Center. Shoots right. 5'11", 190 lbs. Born, Toronto, Ont., March 26, 1974.
(Vancouver's 2nd choice, 40th overall, in 1992 Entry Draft).

Season	Club	GP	G	A	Pts	PIM	GP	G	A	Pts	PIM
1993-94	Vancouver Canucks	4	0	0	0	2	....	....	....	....	....
1994-95	Vancouver Canucks	33	6	6	12	30	5	0	1	1	8
1995-96	Buffalo Sabres	68	11	20	31	67	....	....	....	....	....
1996-97	Buffalo Sabres	79	20	29	49	80	10	0	2	2	8
1997-98	Buffalo Sabres	61	18	22	40	57	13	3	2	5	8
1998-99	Buffalo Sabres	82	27	29	56	81	21	5	8	13	18
99-2000	Buffalo Sabres	73	20	21	41	67	5	0	1	1	4
2000-01	Buffalo Sabres	DID NOT PLAY									
2001-02	New York Islanders	80	25	35	60	62	5	1	0	1	2
2002-03	New York Islanders	66	13	29	42	43	5	0	0	0	4
	NHL Totals	**546**	**140**	**191**	**331**	**489**	**64**	**9**	**14**	**23**	**52**

Frank J. Selke Trophy (1997, 2002)

Traded to **Buffalo** by **Vancouver** with Mike Wilson and Vancouver's 1st round choice (Jay McKee) in 1995 Entry Draft for Alexander Mogilny and Buffalo's 5th round choice (Todd Norman) in 1995 Entry Draft, July 8, 1995. • Missed entire 2000-01 season after failing to come to contract terms with **Buffalo**. Rights traded to **NY Islanders** by **Buffalo** for Tim Connolly and Taylor Pyatt, June 24, 2001.

PEDERSEN, Allen

Defense. Shoots left. 6'3", 210 lbs. Born, Fort Saskatchewan, Alta., January 13, 1965.
(Boston's 5th choice, 105th overall, in 1983 Entry Draft).

Season	Club	GP	G	A	Pts	PIM	GP	G	A	Pts	PIM
1986-87	Boston Bruins	79	1	11	12	71	4	0	0	0	4
1987-88	Boston Bruins	78	0	6	6	90	21	0	0	0	34
1988-89	Boston Bruins	51	0	6	6	69	10	0	0	0	2
1989-90	Boston Bruins	68	1	2	3	71	21	0	0	0	41
1990-91	Boston Bruins	57	2	6	8	107	8	0	0	0	10
1991-92	Minnesota North Stars	29	0	1	1	10	....	....	....	....	....
1992-93	Hartford Whalers	59	1	4	5	60	....	....	....	....	....
1993-94	Hartford Whalers	7	0	0	0	9	....	....	....	....	....
	NHL Totals	**428**	**5**	**36**	**41**	**487**	**64**	**0**	**0**	**0**	**91**

Claimed by **Minnesota** from **Boston** in Expansion Draft, May 30, 1991. Traded to **Hartford** by **Minnesota** for Hartford's 6th round choice (Rick Mrozik) in 1993 Entry Draft, June 15, 1992.

PEDERSON, Barry

Center. Shoots right. 5'11", 185 lbs. Born, Big River, Sask., March 13, 1961.
(Boston's 1st choice, 18th overall, in 1980 Entry Draft).

Season	Club	GP	G	A	Pts	PIM	GP	G	A	Pts	PIM
1980-81	Boston Bruins	9	1	4	5	6	....	....	....	....	....
1981-82	Boston Bruins	80	44	48	92	53	11	7	11	18	2
1982-83	Boston Bruins	77	46	61	107	47	17	14	18	32	21
1983-84	Boston Bruins	80	39	77	116	64	3	0	1	1	2
1984-85	Boston Bruins	22	4	8	12	10	....	....	....	....	....
1985-86	Boston Bruins	79	29	47	76	60	3	1	0	1	0
1986-87	Vancouver Canucks	79	24	52	76	50	....	....	....	....	....
1987-88	Vancouver Canucks	76	19	52	71	92	....	....	....	....	....
1988-89	Vancouver Canucks	62	15	26	41	22	....	....	....	....	....
1989-90	Vancouver Canucks	16	2	7	9	10	....	....	....	....	....
	Pittsburgh Penguins	38	4	18	22	29	....	....	....	....	....
1990-91 ♦	Pittsburgh Penguins	46	6	8	14	21	....	....	....	....	....
1991-92	Hartford Whalers	5	2	2	4	0	....	....	....	....	....
	Boston Bruins	32	3	6	9	8	....	....	....	....	....
	NHL Totals	**701**	**238**	**416**	**654**	**472**	**34**	**22**	**30**	**52**	**25**

Played in NHL All-Star Game (1983, 1984)

• Missed majority of 1984-85 season recovering from surgery to remove benign tumour from shoulder, December, 1985. Traded to **Vancouver** by **Boston** for Cam Neely and Vancouver's 1st round choice (Glen Wesley) in 1987 Entry Draft, June 6, 1986. Traded to **Pittsburgh** by **Vancouver** with Rod Buskas and Tony Tanti for Dave Capuano, Andrew McBain and Dan Quinn, January 8, 1990. Signed as a free agent by **Hartford**, September 5, 1991. Traded to **Boston** by **Hartford** for future considerations, November 14, 1991.

PEDERSON, Denis

Center/Right wing. Shoots right. 6'2", 205 lbs. Born, Prince Albert, Sask., September 10, 1975.
(New Jersey's 1st choice, 13th overall, in 1993 Entry Draft).

Season	Club	GP	G	A	Pts	PIM	GP	G	A	Pts	PIM
1995-96	New Jersey Devils	10	3	1	4	0	....	....	....	....	....
1996-97	New Jersey Devils	70	12	20	32	62	9	0	0	0	2

		REGULAR SEASON					PLAYOFFS				
Season	Club	GP	G	A	Pts	PIM	GP	G	A	Pts	PIM
1997-98	New Jersey Devils	80	15	13	28	97	6	1	1	2	2
1998-99	New Jersey Devils	76	11	12	23	66	3	0	1	1	0
99-2000	New Jersey Devils	35	3	3	6	16	....	....	....	....	....
	Vancouver Canucks	12	3	2	5	2	....	....	....	....	....
2000-01	Vancouver Canucks	61	4	8	12	65	4	0	1	1	4
2001-02	Vancouver Canucks	29	1	5	6	31	....	....	....	....	....
	Phoenix Coyotes	19	1	1	2	20	5	0	2	2	0
2002-03	Nashville Predators	43	4	6	10	39	....	....	....	....	....
	NHL Totals	**435**	**57**	**71**	**128**	**398**	**27**	**1**	**5**	**6**	**8**

Traded to **Vancouver** by **New Jersey** with Brendan Morrison for Alexander Mogilny, March 14, 2000. Traded to **Phoenix** by **Vancouver** with Drake Berehowsky for Todd Warriner, Trevor Letowski, Tyler Bouck and Phoenix's 3rd round choice (later traded back to Phoenix – Phoenix selected Dimitri Pestunov) in 2003 Entry Draft, December 28, 2001. Signed as a free agent by **Nashville**, July 24, 2002.

PEDERSON, Mark

Left wing. Shoots left. 6'2", 196 lbs. Born, Prelate, Sask., January 14, 1968.
(Montreal's 1st choice, 15th overall, in 1986 Entry Draft).

Season	Club	GP	G	A	Pts	PIM	GP	G	A	Pts	PIM
1989-90	Montreal Canadiens	9	0	2	2	2	2	0	0	0	0
1990-91	Philadelphia Flyers	12	2	1	3	5	....	....	....	....	....
	Montreal Canadiens	47	8	15	23	18	....	....	....	....	....
1991-92	Philadelphia Flyers	58	15	25	40	22	....	....	....	....	....
1992-93	Philadelphia Flyers	14	3	4	7	6	....	....	....	....	....
	San Jose Sharks	27	7	3	10	22	....	....	....	....	....
1993-94	Detroit Red Wings	2	0	0	0	2	....	....	....	....	....
	NHL Totals	**169**	**35**	**50**	**85**	**77**	**2**	**0**	**0**	**0**	**0**

Traded to **Philadelphia** by **Montreal** for Philadelphia's 2nd round choice (Jim Campbell) in 1991 Entry Draft, March 15, 1991. Traded to **San Jose** by **Philadelphia** with future considerations for Dave Snuggerud, December 19, 1992. Signed as a free agent by **Detroit**, August 23, 1993.

PEDERSON, Tom

Defense. Shoots right. 5'9", 175 lbs. Born, Bloomington, MN, January 14, 1970.
(Minnesota's 12th choice, 217th overall, in 1989 Entry Draft).

Season	Club	GP	G	A	Pts	PIM	GP	G	A	Pts	PIM
1992-93	San Jose Sharks	44	7	13	20	31	....	....	....	....	....
1993-94	San Jose Sharks	74	6	19	25	31	14	1	6	7	2
1994-95	San Jose Sharks	47	5	11	16	31	10	0	5	5	8
1995-96	San Jose Sharks	60	1	4	5	40	....	....	....	....	....
1996-97	Toronto Maple Leafs	15	1	2	3	9	....	....	....	....	....
	NHL Totals	**240**	**20**	**49**	**69**	**142**	**24**	**1**	**11**	**12**	**10**

Claimed by **San Jose** from **Minnesota** in Dispersal Draft, May 30, 1991. Signed as a free agent by **Toronto**, December 11, 1996.

PEER, Bert

Right wing. Shoots right. 5'11", 175 lbs. Born, Port Credit, Ont., November 12, 1910.

Season	Club	GP	G	A	Pts	PIM	GP	G	A	Pts	PIM
1939-40	Detroit Red Wings	1	0	0	0	0	....	....	....	....	....
	NHL Totals	**1**	**0**	**0**	**0**	**0**	....	....	....	....	....

PEIRSON, Johnny

Right wing. Shoots right. 5'11", 170 lbs. Born, Winnipeg, Man., July 21, 1925.

Season	Club	GP	G	A	Pts	PIM	GP	G	A	Pts	PIM
1946-47	Boston Bruins	5	0	0	0	0	....	....	....	....	....
1947-48	Boston Bruins	15	4	2	6	0	5	3	2	5	0
1948-49	Boston Bruins	59	22	21	43	45	5	3	1	4	4
1949-50	Boston Bruins	57	27	25	52	49	....	....	....	....	....
1950-51	Boston Bruins	70	19	19	38	43	2	1	1	2	2
1951-52	Boston Bruins	68	20	30	50	30	7	0	2	2	4
1952-53	Boston Bruins	49	14	15	29	32	11	3	6	9	2
1953-54	Boston Bruins	68	21	19	40	55	4	0	0	0	2
1955-56	Boston Bruins	33	11	14	25	10	....	....	....	....	....
1956-57	Boston Bruins	68	13	26	39	41	10	0	3	3	12
1957-58	Boston Bruins	53	2	2	4	10	5	0	1	1	0
	NHL Totals	**545**	**153**	**173**	**326**	**315**	**49**	**10**	**16**	**26**	**26**

Played in NHL All-Star Game (1950, 1951)

• Missed majority of 1955-56 season while still in retirement but returned as an active player in game vs. Chicago, December 15, 1955.

PELENSKY, Perry

Right wing. Shoots right. 5'11", 180 lbs. Born, Edmonton, Alta., May 22, 1962.
(Chicago's 4th choice, 75th overall, in 1981 Entry Draft).

Season	Club	GP	G	A	Pts	PIM	GP	G	A	Pts	PIM
1983-84	Chicago Black Hawks	4	0	0	0	5	....	....	....	....	....
	NHL Totals	**4**	**0**	**0**	**0**	**5**	....	....	....	....	....

PELLERIN, Scott

Left wing. Shoots left. 5'11", 190 lbs. Born, Shediac, N.B., January 9, 1970.
(New Jersey's 4th choice, 47th overall, in 1989 Entry Draft).

Season	Club	GP	G	A	Pts	PIM	GP	G	A	Pts	PIM
1992-93	New Jersey Devils	45	10	11	21	41	....	....	....	....	....
1993-94	New Jersey Devils	1	0	0	0	2	....	....	....	....	....
1995-96	New Jersey Devils	6	2	1	3	0	....	....	....	....	....
1996-97	St. Louis Blues	54	8	10	18	35	6	0	0	0	6
1997-98	St. Louis Blues	80	8	21	29	62	10	0	2	2	10
1998-99	St. Louis Blues	80	20	21	41	42	8	1	0	1	4
99-2000	St. Louis Blues	80	8	15	23	48	7	0	0	0	2
2000-01	Minnesota Wild	58	11	28	39	45	....	....	....	....	....
	Carolina Hurricanes	19	0	5	5	6	6	0	0	0	4
2001-02	Boston Bruins	35	1	5	6	6	....	....	....	....	....
	Dallas Stars	33	3	5	8	15	....	....	....	....	....
2002-03	Dallas Stars	20	1	3	4	8	....	....	....	....	....
	Phoenix Coyotes	23	0	1	1	8	....	....	....	....	....
	NHL Totals	**534**	**72**	**126**	**198**	**318**	**37**	**1**	**2**	**3**	**26**

• Grandson of Sammy McManus

Signed as a free agent by **St. Louis**, July 10, 1996. Selected by **Minnesota** from **St. Louis** in Expansion Draft, June 23, 2000. Traded to **Carolina** by **Minnesota** for Askhat Rakhmatullin, Carolina's 3rd round choice (later traded to NY Rangers – NY Rangers selected Garth Murray) in 2001 Entry Draft and Carolina's compensatory 5th round choice (Armands Berzins) in 2002 Entry Draft, March 1, 2001. Signed as a free agent by **Boston**, July 26, 2001. Claimed on waivers by **Dallas** from **Boston**, January 12, 2002. Traded to **Phoenix** by **Dallas** with future considerations for Claude Lemieux, January 16, 2003.

PELLETIER, Roger

Defense. Shoots right. 5'11", 195 lbs. Born, Montreal, Que., June 22, 1945.

Season	Club	GP	G	A	Pts	PIM	GP	G	A	Pts	PIM
1967-68	Philadelphia Flyers	1	0	0	0	0	....	....	....	....	....
	NHL Totals	**1**	**0**	**0**	**0**	**0**	....	....	....	....	....

NHL rights transferred to **Philadelphia** after NHL club purchased **Quebec** (AHL) franchise, May 8, 1967. Claimed by **Quebec** (AHL) from **Philadelphia** in Reverse Draft, June 12, 1969.

PELOFFY, Andre

Center. Shoots left. 5'8", 160 lbs. Born, Sote, France, February 25, 1951.
(NY Rangers' 12th choice, 111th overall, in 1971 Amateur Draft).

Season	Club	GP	G	A	Pts	PIM	GP	G	A	Pts	PIM
1974-75	Washington Capitals	9	0	0	0	0	....	....	....	....	....
	NHL Totals	**9**	**0**	**0**	**0**	**0**	....	....	....	....	....

Traded to **Washington** by **NY Rangers** for cash, July 29, 1974.

PELTONEN, Ville

Left wing. Shoots left. 5'11", 188 lbs. Born, Vantaa, Finland, May 24, 1973.
(San Jose's 4th choice, 58th overall, in 1993 Entry Draft).

Season	Club	GP	G	A	Pts	PIM	GP	G	A	Pts	PIM
1995-96	San Jose Sharks	31	2	11	13	14	....	....	....	....	....
1996-97	San Jose Sharks	28	2	3	5	0	....	....	....	....	....
1998-99	Nashville Predators	14	5	5	10	2	....	....	....	....	....
99-2000	Nashville Predators	79	6	22	28	22	....	....	....	....	....
2000-01	Nashville Predators	23	3	1	4	2	....	....	....	....	....
	NHL Totals	**175**	**18**	**42**	**60**	**40**	....	....	....	....	....

Traded to **Nashville** by **San Jose** for Nashville's 5th round choice (later traded to Phoenix – Phoenix selected Josh Blackburn) in 1998 Entry Draft, June 26, 1998.

PELUSO, Mike

Left wing. Shoots left. 6'4", 225 lbs. Born, Pengilly, MN, November 8, 1965.
(New Jersey's 10th choice, 190th overall, in 1984 Entry Draft).

Season	Club	GP	G	A	Pts	PIM	GP	G	A	Pts	PIM
1989-90	Chicago Blackhawks	2	0	0	0	15	....	....	....	....	....
1990-91	Chicago Blackhawks	53	6	1	7	320	3	0	0	0	2
1991-92	Chicago Blackhawks	63	6	3	9	*408	17	1	2	3	8
1992-93	Ottawa Senators	81	15	10	25	318	....	....	....	....	....
1993-94	New Jersey Devils	69	4	16	20	238	17	1	0	1	*64
1994-95 ♦	New Jersey Devils	46	2	9	11	167	20	1	2	3	8
1995-96	New Jersey Devils	57	3	8	11	146	....	....	....	....	....
1996-97	New Jersey Devils	20	0	2	2	68	....	....	....	....	....
	St. Louis Blues	44	2	3	5	158	5	0	0	0	25
1997-98	Calgary Flames	23	0	0	0	113	....	....	....	....	....
	NHL Totals	**458**	**38**	**52**	**90**	**1951**	**62**	**3**	**4**	**7**	**107**

Signed as a free agent by **Chicago**, September 7, 1989. Claimed by **Ottawa** frozm **Chicago** in Expansion Draft, June 18, 1992. Traded to **New Jersey** by **Ottawa** to complete transaction that sent Craig Billington, Troy Mallette and New Jersey's 4th round choice (Cosmo Dupaul) in 1993 Entry Draft to Ottawa (June 20, 1993), June 26, 1993. Traded to **St. Louis** by **New Jersey** with Ricard Persson for Ken Sutton and St. Louis' 2nd round choice (Brett Clouthier) in 1999 Entry Draft, November 26, 1996. Transferred to **NY Rangers** from **St. Louis** as compensation for St. Louis' signing of Larry Pleau as head coach, June 21, 1997. Claimed by **Calgary** from **NY Rangers** in NHL Waiver Draft, September 28, 1997. • Suffered eventual career-ending neck injury suffered in game vs. Phoenix, December 22, 1997. • Officially announced retirement, December 30, 1997.

PELUSO, Mike

Right wing. Shoots right. 6'1", 208 lbs. Born, Bismark, ND, September 2, 1974.
(Calgary's 12th choice, 253rd overall, in 1994 Entry Draft).

Season	Club	GP	G	A	Pts	PIM	GP	G	A	Pts	PIM
2001-02	Chicago Blackhawks	37	4	2	6	19	....	....	....	....	....
	NHL Totals	**37**	**4**	**2**	**6**	**19**	....	....	....	....	....

Signed as a free agent by **Washington**, October 9, 1998. Traded to **St. Louis** by **Washington** for Derek Bekar, November 29, 2000. Signed as a free agent by **Chicago**, August 1, 2001. Signed as a free agent by **Philadelphia**, July 24, 2003.

PELYK, Mike

Defense. Shoots left. 6'1", 190 lbs. Born, Toronto, Ont., September 29, 1947.
(Toronto's 3rd choice, 17th overall, in 1964 Amateur Draft).

Season	Club	GP	G	A	Pts	PIM	GP	G	A	Pts	PIM
1967-68	Toronto Maple Leafs	24	0	3	3	55	....	....	....	....	....
1968-69	Toronto Maple Leafs	65	3	9	12	146	4	0	0	0	8
1969-70	Toronto Maple Leafs	36	1	3	4	37	....	....	....	....	....
1970-71	Toronto Maple Leafs	73	5	21	26	54	6	0	0	0	10
1971-72	Toronto Maple Leafs	46	1	4	5	44	5	0	0	0	8
1972-73	Toronto Maple Leafs	72	3	16	19	118	....	....	....	....	....
1973-74	Toronto Maple Leafs	71	12	19	31	94	4	0	0	0	4
1976-77	Toronto Maple Leafs	13	0	2	2	4	9	0	2	2	4
1977-78	Toronto Maple Leafs	41	1	11	12	14	12	0	1	1	7
	NHL Totals	**441**	**26**	**88**	**114**	**566**	**40**	**0**	**3**	**3**	**41**

Rights traded to **Toronto** by **Cincinnati** (WHA) with the rights to Randy Carlyle for cash, June, 1976.

PENNEY, Chad

Left wing. Shoots left. 6', 195 lbs. Born, Labrador City, Nfld., September 18, 1973.
(Ottawa's 2nd choice, 25th overall, in 1992 Entry Draft).

Season	Club	Regular Season GP	G	A	Pts	PIM	Playoffs GP	G	A	Pts	PIM
1993-94	Ottawa Senators	3	0	0	0	2	....	....	....	....	....
	NHL Totals	**3**	**0**	**0**	**0**	**2**	....	....	....	....	....

PENNINGTON, Cliff

Center. Shoots right. 6', 170 lbs. Born, Winnipeg, Man., April 18, 1940.

Season	Club	Regular Season GP	G	A	Pts	PIM	Playoffs GP	G	A	Pts	PIM
1960-61	Montreal Canadiens	4	1	0	1	0	....	....	....	....	....
1961-62	Boston Bruins	70	9	32	41	2	....	....	....	....	....
1962-63	Boston Bruins	27	7	10	17	4	....	....	....	....	....
	NHL Totals	**101**	**17**	**42**	**59**	**6**	....	....	....	....	....

Traded to **Boston** by **Montreal** with Terry Gray for Willie O'Ree and Stan Maxwell, June, 1961. Traded to **San Francisco** (WHL) by **Boston** for cash, June, 1963. Traded to **Boston** by **San Francisco** (WHL) for Gerry Odrowski and future considerations (loan of Dallas Smith for 1964-65 season, July 8, 1964), December 17, 1963.

PEPLINSKI, Jim

Right wing. Shoots right. 6'3", 210 lbs. Born, Renfrew, Ont., October 24, 1960.
(Atlanta's 5th choice, 75th overall, in 1979 Entry Draft).

Season	Club	Regular Season GP	G	A	Pts	PIM	Playoffs GP	G	A	Pts	PIM
1980-81	Calgary Flames	80	13	25	38	108	16	2	3	5	41
1981-82	Calgary Flames	74	30	37	67	115	3	1	0	1	13
1982-83	Calgary Flames	80	15	26	41	134	8	1	1	2	45
1983-84	Calgary Flames	74	11	22	33	114	11	3	4	7	21
1984-85	Calgary Flames	80	16	29	45	111	4	1	3	4	11
1985-86	Calgary Flames	77	24	35	59	214	22	5	9	14	107
1986-87	Calgary Flames	80	18	32	50	181	6	1	0	1	24
1987-88	Calgary Flames	75	20	31	51	234	9	0	5	5	45
1988-89♦	Calgary Flames	79	13	25	38	241	20	1	6	7	75
1989-90	Calgary Flames	6	1	0	1	4	....	....	....	....	....
1994-95	Calgary Flames	6	0	1	1	11	....	....	....	....	....
	NHL Totals	**711**	**161**	**263**	**424**	**1467**	**99**	**15**	**31**	**46**	**382**

Transferred to **Calgary** after **Atlanta** franchise relocated, June 24, 1980. Signed as a free agent by **Calgary**, April 6, 1995.

PERLINI, Fred

Center. Shoots left. 6'2", 175 lbs. Born, Sault Ste. Marie, Ont., April 12, 1962.
(Toronto's 8th choice, 158th overall, in 1980 Entry Draft).

Season	Club	Regular Season GP	G	A	Pts	PIM	Playoffs GP	G	A	Pts	PIM
1981-82	Toronto Maple Leafs	7	2	3	5	0	....	....	....	....	....
1983-84	Toronto Maple Leafs	1	0	0	0	0	....	....	....	....	....
	NHL Totals	**8**	**2**	**3**	**5**	**0**	....	....	....	....	....

PERREAULT, Fern

Left wing. Shoots left. 5'11", 174 lbs. Born, Chambly, Que., March 31, 1927.

Season	Club	Regular Season GP	G	A	Pts	PIM	Playoffs GP	G	A	Pts	PIM
1947-48	New York Rangers	2	0	0	0	0	....	....	....	....	....
1949-50	New York Rangers	1	0	0	0	0	....	....	....	....	....
	NHL Totals	**3**	**0**	**0**	**0**	**0**	....	....	....	....	....

Traded to **Cleveland** (AHL) by **NY Rangers** with Ed Reigle, Jackie Gordon, Fred Shero and cash for Hy Buller and Wally Hergesheimer, May 14, 1951.

PERREAULT, Gilbert

HHOF

Center. Shoots left. 6'1", 180 lbs. Born, Victoriaville, Que., November 13, 1950.
(Buffalo's 1st choice, 1st overall, in 1970 Amateur Draft).

Season	Club	Regular Season GP	G	A	Pts	PIM	Playoffs GP	G	A	Pts	PIM
1970-71	Buffalo Sabres	78	38	34	72	19	....	....	....	....	....
1971-72	Buffalo Sabres	76	26	48	74	24	....	....	....	....	....
1972-73	Buffalo Sabres	78	28	60	88	10	6	3	7	10	2
1973-74	Buffalo Sabres	55	18	33	51	10	....	....	....	....	....
1974-75	Buffalo Sabres	68	39	57	96	36	17	6	9	15	10
1975-76	Buffalo Sabres	80	44	69	113	36	9	4	4	8	4
1976-77	Buffalo Sabres	80	39	56	95	30	6	1	8	9	4
1977-78	Buffalo Sabres	79	41	48	89	20	8	3	2	5	0
1978-79	Buffalo Sabres	79	27	58	85	20	3	1	0	1	2
1979-80	Buffalo Sabres	80	40	66	106	57	14	10	11	21	8
1980-81	Buffalo Sabres	56	20	39	59	56	8	2	10	12	2
1981-82	Buffalo Sabres	62	31	42	73	40	4	0	7	7	0
1982-83	Buffalo Sabres	77	30	46	76	34	10	0	7	7	8
1983-84	Buffalo Sabres	73	31	59	90	32	....	....	....	....	....
1984-85	Buffalo Sabres	78	30	53	83	42	5	3	5	8	4
1985-86	Buffalo Sabres	72	21	39	60	28	....	....	....	....	....
1986-87	Buffalo Sabres	20	9	7	16	6	....	....	....	....	....
	NHL Totals	**1191**	**512**	**814**	**1326**	**500**	**90**	**33**	**70**	**103**	**44**

Calder Memorial Trophy (1971) • Lady Byng Trophy (1973) • NHL Second All-Star Team (1976, 1977)

Played in NHL All-Star Game (1971, 1977, 1978, 1980, 1984)

Officially announced retirement, November 24, 1986.

PERREAULT, Yanic

Center. Shoots left. 5'11", 185 lbs. Born, Sherbrooke, Que., April 4, 1971.
(Toronto's 1st choice, 47th overall, in 1991 Entry Draft).

Season	Club	Regular Season GP	G	A	Pts	PIM	Playoffs GP	G	A	Pts	PIM
1993-94	Toronto Maple Leafs	13	3	3	6	0	....	....	....	....	....
1994-95	Los Angeles Kings	26	2	5	7	20	....	....	....	....	....
1995-96	Los Angeles Kings	78	25	24	49	16	....	....	....	....	....
1996-97	Los Angeles Kings	41	11	14	25	20	....	....	....	....	....
1997-98	Los Angeles Kings	79	28	20	48	32	4	1	2	3	6
1998-99	Los Angeles Kings	64	10	17	27	30	....	....	....	....	....
	Toronto Maple Leafs	12	7	8	15	12	17	3	6	9	6
99-2000	Toronto Maple Leafs	58	18	27	45	22	1	0	1	1	0
2000-01	Toronto Maple Leafs	76	24	28	52	52	11	2	3	5	4
2001-02	Montreal Canadiens	82	27	29	56	40	11	3	5	8	0
2002-03	Montreal Canadiens	73	24	22	46	30	....	....	....	....	....
	NHL Totals	**602**	**179**	**197**	**376**	**274**	**44**	**9**	**17**	**26**	**16**

Traded to **Los Angeles** by **Toronto** for Los Angeles' 4th round choice (later traded to Philadelphia – later traded to Los Angeles – Los Angeles selected Mikael Simons) in 1996 Entry Draft, July 11, 1994. Traded to **Toronto** by **Los Angeles** for Jason Podollan and Toronto's 3rd round choice (Cory Campbell) in 1999 Entry Draft, March 23, 1999. Signed as a free agent by **Montreal**, July 4, 2001.

PERROTT, Nathan

Right wing. Shoots right. 6', 225 lbs. Born, Owen Sound, Ont., December 8, 1976.
(New Jersey's 2nd choice, 44th overall, in 1995 Entry Draft).

Season	Club	Regular Season GP	G	A	Pts	PIM	Playoffs GP	G	A	Pts	PIM
2001-02	Nashville Predators	22	1	2	3	74	....	....	....	....	....
2002-03	Nashville Predators	1	0	0	0	5	....	....	....	....	....
	NHL Totals	**23**	**1**	**2**	**3**	**79**	....	....	....	....	....

Signed as a free agent by **Chicago**, August 27, 1997. Traded to **Nashville** by **Chicago** for future considerations, October 9, 2001. Traded to **Toronto** by **Nashville** for Bob Wren, Deceber 31, 2002.

PERRY, Brian

Center. Shoots left. 5'11", 180 lbs. Born, Aldershot, England, April 6, 1944.

Season	Club	Regular Season GP	G	A	Pts	PIM	Playoffs GP	G	A	Pts	PIM
1968-69	Oakland Seals	61	10	21	31	10	6	1	1	2	4
1969-70	Oakland Seals	34	6	8	14	14	2	0	0	0	0
1970-71	Buffalo Sabres	1	0	0	0	0	....	....	....	....	....
	NHL Totals	**96**	**16**	**29**	**45**	**24**	**8**	**1**	**1**	**2**	**4**

Claimed by **Oakland** from **Providence** (AHL) in Inter-League Draft, June 6, 1968. Claimed by **Buffalo** from **Oakland** in Expansion Draft, June 10, 1970. Claimed by **Providence** (AHL) from **Buffalo** in Reverse Draft, June, 1971.

PERSSON, Ricard

Defense. Shoots left. 6'1", 201 lbs. Born, Ostersund, Sweden, August 24, 1969.
(New Jersey's 2nd choice, 23rd overall, in 1987 Entry Draft).

Season	Club	Regular Season GP	G	A	Pts	PIM	Playoffs GP	G	A	Pts	PIM
1995-96	New Jersey Devils	12	2	1	3	8	....	....	....	....	....
1996-97	New Jersey Devils	1	0	0	0	0	....	....	....	....	....
	St. Louis Blues	53	4	8	12	45	6	0	0	0	27
1997-98	St. Louis Blues	1	0	0	0	0	....	....	....	....	....
1998-99	St. Louis Blues	54	1	12	13	94	13	0	3	3	17
99-2000	St. Louis Blues	41	0	8	8	38	3	1	0	1	0
2000-01	Ottawa Senators	33	1	8	9	35	2	0	0	0	0
2001-02	Ottawa Senators	34	2	7	9	42	2	0	0	0	15
	NHL Totals	**229**	**10**	**44**	**54**	**262**	**26**	**1**	**3**	**4**	**59**

Traded to **St. Louis** by **New Jersey** with Mike Peluso for Ken Sutton and St. Louis' 2nd round choice (Brett Clouthier) in 1999 Entry Draft, November 26, 1996. Signed as a free agent by **Ottawa**, July 12, 2000. • Missed majority of 2000-01 season recovering from ankle injury suffered in game vs. Pittsburgh, October 25, 2001. • Spent majority of 2001-02 season on **Ottawa** practice roster.

PERSSON, Stefan

Defense. Shoots left. 6'1", 189 lbs. Born, Umea, Sweden, December 22, 1954.
(NY Islanders' 13th choice, 214th overall, in 1974 Amateur Draft).

Season	Club	Regular Season GP	G	A	Pts	PIM	Playoffs GP	G	A	Pts	PIM
1977-78	New York Islanders	66	6	50	56	54	7	0	2	2	6
1978-79	New York Islanders	78	10	56	66	57	10	0	4	4	8
1979-80♦	New York Islanders	73	4	35	39	76	21	5	10	15	16
1980-81♦	New York Islanders	80	9	52	61	82	7	0	5	5	6
1981-82♦	New York Islanders	70	6	37	43	99	13	1	14	15	9
1982-83♦	New York Islanders	70	4	25	29	71	18	1	5	6	18
1983-84	New York Islanders	75	9	24	33	65	16	0	6	6	2
1984-85	New York Islanders	54	3	19	22	30	10	0	4	4	4
1985-86	New York Islanders	56	1	19	20	40	....	....	....	....	....
	NHL Totals	**622**	**52**	**317**	**369**	**574**	**102**	**7**	**50**	**57**	**69**

PESUT, George

Defense. Shoots left. 6'1", 205 lbs. Born, Saskatoon, Sask., June 17, 1953.
(St. Louis' 2nd choice, 24th overall, in 1973 Amateur Draft).

Season	Club	Regular Season GP	G	A	Pts	PIM	Playoffs GP	G	A	Pts	PIM
1974-75	California Golden Seals	47	0	13	13	73	....	....	....	....	....
1975-76	California Golden Seals	45	3	9	12	57	....	....	....	....	....
	NHL Totals	**92**	**3**	**22**	**25**	**130**	....	....	....	....	....

Traded to **Philadelphia** by **St. Louis** for Bob Stumpf, November, 1973. Traded to **California** by **Philadelphia** for the rights to Ron Chipperfield, December 11, 1974.

PETERS, Frank

Defense. Shoots right. 5'11", 160 lbs. Born, Rouses Point, NY, June 5, 1905.

Season	Club	Regular Season GP	G	A	Pts	PIM	Playoffs GP	G	A	Pts	PIM
1930-31	New York Rangers	43	0	0	0	59	4	0	0	0	2
	NHL Totals	**43**	**0**	**0**	**0**	**59**	**4**	**0**	**0**	**0**	**2**

Traded to **NY Rangers** by **Philadelphia** (Can-Am) for cash, February 18, 1930. Traded to **Detroit** by **NY Rangers** for cash, October 19, 1931. Traded to **NY Rangers** by **Detroit** (Detroit-IHL) for Sparky Vail, October 30, 1933. Traded to **Philadelphia** (Can-Am) by **NY Rangers** for George Nichols, October 31, 1933.

PETERS, Garry

Center. Shoots left. 5'10", 185 lbs. Born, Regina, Sask., October 9, 1942.

		REGULAR SEASON					PLAYOFFS				
Season	Club	GP	G	A	Pts	PIM	GP	G	A	Pts	PIM
1964-65	Montreal Canadiens	13	0	2	2	6	....	....	....	....	....
1965-66	New York Rangers	63	7	3	10	42	....	....	....	....	....
1966-67	Montreal Canadiens	4	0	1	1	2	....	....	....	....	....
1967-68	Philadelphia Flyers	31	7	5	12	22	....	....	....	....	....
1968-69	Philadelphia Flyers	66	8	6	14	49	4	1	1	2	16
1969-70	Philadelphia Flyers	59	6	10	16	69	....	....	....	....	....
1970-71	Philadelphia Flyers	73	6	7	13	69	4	1	1	2	15
1971-72 ♦	Boston Bruins	2	0	0	0	2	1	0	0	0	0
	NHL Totals	**311**	**34**	**34**	**68**	**261**	**9**	**2**	**2**	**4**	**31**

Traded to **NY Rangers** by **Montreal** with Cesare Maniago for Earl Ingarfield, Noel Price, Gord Labossiere, Dave McComb and cash, June 8, 1965. Traded to **Montreal** by **NY Rangers** with Ted Taylor for Red Berenson, June 13, 1966. Claimed by **Philadelphia** from **Montreal** in Expansion Draft, June 6, 1967. • Missed majority of 1967-68 season recovering from eye injury suffered in game vs. NY Rangers, December 25, 1967. Claimed by **Boston** from **Philadelphia** in Intra-League Draft, June 8, 1971. Claimed by **NY Islanders** from **Boston** in Expansion Draft, June 6, 1972.

PETERS, Jimmy

Right wing. Shoots right. 5'11", 165 lbs. Born, Montreal, Que., October 2, 1922.

		REGULAR SEASON					PLAYOFFS				
Season	Club	GP	G	A	Pts	PIM	GP	G	A	Pts	PIM
1945-46 ♦	Montreal Canadiens	47	11	19	30	10	9	3	1	4	6
1946-47	Montreal Canadiens	60	11	13	24	27	11	1	2	3	10
1947-48	Montreal Canadiens	22	1	3	4	6	....	....	....	....	....
	Boston Bruins	37	12	15	27	38	5	1	2	3	2
1948-49	Boston Bruins	60	16	15	31	8	4	0	1	1	0
1949-50 ♦	Detroit Red Wings	70	14	16	30	20	8	0	2	2	0
1950-51	Detroit Red Wings	68	17	21	38	14	6	0	0	0	0
1951-52	Chicago Black Hawks	70	15	21	36	16	....	....	....	....	....
1952-53	Chicago Black Hawks	69	22	19	41	16	7	0	1	1	4
1953-54	Chicago Black Hawks	46	6	4	10	21	....	....	....	....	....
♦	Detroit Red Wings	25	0	4	4	10	10	0	0	0	0
	NHL Totals	**574**	**125**	**150**	**275**	**186**	**60**	**5**	**9**	**14**	**22**

• Father of Jimmy Jr.

Played in NHL All-Star Game (1950)

Signed as a free agent by **Brooklyn**, October 28, 1941. Rights transferred to **Buffalo** (AHL) from **Brooklyn** in Special Dispersal Draft, October 9, 1942. Claimed by **Montreal** from **Buffalo** (AHL) in Inter-League Draft, June 14, 1945. Traded to **Boston** by **Montreal** with John Quilty for Joe Carveth, December 16, 1947. Traded to **Detroit** by **Boston** with Pete Babando, Clare Martin and Lloyd Durham for Bill Quakenbush and Pete Horeck, August 16, 1949. Traded to **Chicago** by **Detroit** with George Gee, Clare Martin, Rags Raglan, Max McNab and Jim McFadden for $75,000 and future considerations (Hugh Coflin, October, 1951), August 20, 1951. Traded to **Detroit** by **Chicago** for future considerations, January 25, 1954.

PETERS Jr., Jimmy

Center. Shoots left. 6'2", 185 lbs. Born, Montreal, Que., June 20, 1944.

		REGULAR SEASON					PLAYOFFS				
Season	Club	GP	G	A	Pts	PIM	GP	G	A	Pts	PIM
1964-65	Detroit Red Wings	1	0	0	0	0	....	....	....	....	....
1965-66	Detroit Red Wings	6	1	1	2	2	....	....	....	....	....
1966-67	Detroit Red Wings	2	0	0	0	0	....	....	....	....	....
1967-68	Detroit Red Wings	45	5	6	11	8	....	....	....	....	....
1968-69	Los Angeles Kings	76	10	15	25	28	11	0	2	2	2
1969-70	Los Angeles Kings	74	15	9	24	10	....	....	....	....	....
1972-73	Los Angeles Kings	77	4	5	9	0	....	....	....	....	....
1973-74	Los Angeles Kings	25	2	0	2	0	....	....	....	....	....
1974-75	Los Angeles Kings	3	0	0	0	0	....	....	....	....	....
	NHL Totals	**309**	**37**	**36**	**73**	**48**	**11**	**0**	**2**	**2**	**2**

• Son of Jimmy

Traded to **Los Angeles** by **Detroit** for Terry Sawchuk, October 10, 1968. Traded to **Denver** (WHL) by **Los Angeles** for Ed Hoekstra with Los Angeles holding right of recall, December, 1970.

PETERS, Steve

Center. Shoots left. 5'11", 186 lbs. Born, Peterborough, Ont., January 23, 1960.
(Colorado's 2nd choice, 64th overall, in 1979 Entry Draft).

		REGULAR SEASON					PLAYOFFS				
Season	Club	GP	G	A	Pts	PIM	GP	G	A	Pts	PIM
1979-80	Colorado Rockies	2	0	1	1	0	....	....	....	....	....
	NHL Totals	**2**	**0**	**1**	**1**	**0**	....	....	....	....	....

PETERSEN, Toby

Center. Shoots left. 5'9", 197 lbs. Born, Minneapolis, MN, October 27, 1978.
(Pittsburgh's 9th choice, 244th overall, in 1998 Entry Draft).

		REGULAR SEASON					PLAYOFFS				
Season	Club	GP	G	A	Pts	PIM	GP	G	A	Pts	PIM
2000-01	Pittsburgh Penguins	12	2	6	8	4	....	....	....	....	....
2001-02	Pittsburgh Penguins	79	8	10	18	4	....	....	....	....	....
	NHL Totals	**91**	**10**	**16**	**26**	**8**	....	....	....	....	....

PETERSON, Brent

Left wing. Shoots left. 6'3", 200 lbs. Born, Calgary, Alta., July 20, 1972.
(Tampa Bay's 1st choice, 3rd overall, in 1993 Supplemental Draft).

		REGULAR SEASON					PLAYOFFS				
Season	Club	GP	G	A	Pts	PIM	GP	G	A	Pts	PIM
1996-97	Tampa Bay Lightning	17	2	0	2	4	....	....	....	....	....
1997-98	Tampa Bay Lightning	19	5	0	5	2	....	....	....	....	....
1998-99	Tampa Bay Lightning	20	2	1	3	0	....	....	....	....	....
	NHL Totals	**56**	**9**	**1**	**10**	**6**	....	....	....	....	....

Traded to **Pittsburgh** by **Tampa Bay** for cash, March 18, 1999. Signed as a free agent by **Nashville**, July 24, 1999.

PETERSON, Brent

Center. Shoots right. 6', 190 lbs. Born, Calgary, Alta., February 15, 1958.
(Detroit's 2nd choice, 12th overall, in 1978 Amateur Draft).

		REGULAR SEASON					PLAYOFFS				
Season	Club	GP	G	A	Pts	PIM	GP	G	A	Pts	PIM
1978-79	Detroit Red Wings	5	0	0	0	0	....	....	....	....	....
1979-80	Detroit Red Wings	18	1	2	3	2	....	....	....	....	....
1980-81	Detroit Red Wings	53	6	18	24	24	....	....	....	....	....
1981-82	Detroit Red Wings	15	1	0	1	6	....	....	....	....	....
	Buffalo Sabres	46	9	5	14	43	4	1	0	1	12
1982-83	Buffalo Sabres	75	13	24	37	38	10	1	2	3	28
1983-84	Buffalo Sabres	70	9	12	21	52	3	0	1	1	4
1984-85	Buffalo Sabres	74	12	22	34	47	5	0	0	0	6
1985-86	Vancouver Canucks	77	8	23	31	94	3	2	0	2	9
1986-87	Vancouver Canucks	69	7	15	22	77	....	....	....	....	....
1987-88	Hartford Whalers	52	2	7	9	40	4	0	0	0	2
1988-89	Hartford Whalers	66	4	13	17	61	2	0	1	1	4
	NHL Totals	**620**	**72**	**141**	**213**	**484**	**31**	**4**	**4**	**8**	**65**

Traded to **Buffalo** by **Detroit** with Mike Foligno and Dale McCourt for Danny Gare, Jim Schoenfeld and Derek Smith, December 2, 1981. Claimed by **Vancouver** from **Buffalo** in Waiver Draft, October 7, 1985. Claimed by **Hartford** from **Vancouver** in Waiver Draft, October 5, 1987.

PETIT, Michel

Defense. Shoots right. 6'1", 205 lbs. Born, St-Malo, Que., February 12, 1964.
(Vancouver's 1st choice, 11th overall, in 1982 Entry Draft).

		REGULAR SEASON					PLAYOFFS				
Season	Club	GP	G	A	Pts	PIM	GP	G	A	Pts	PIM
1982-83	Vancouver Canucks	2	0	0	0	0	....	....	....	....	....
1983-84	Vancouver Canucks	44	6	9	15	53	1	0	0	0	0
1984-85	Vancouver Canucks	69	5	26	31	127	....	....	....	....	....
1985-86	Vancouver Canucks	32	1	6	7	27	....	....	....	....	....
1986-87	Vancouver Canucks	69	12	13	25	131	....	....	....	....	....
1987-88	Vancouver Canucks	10	0	3	3	35	....	....	....	....	....
	New York Rangers	64	9	24	33	223	....	....	....	....	....
1988-89	New York Rangers	69	8	25	33	154	4	0	2	2	27
1989-90	Quebec Nordiques	63	12	24	36	215	....	....	....	....	....
1990-91	Quebec Nordiques	19	4	7	11	47	....	....	....	....	....
	Toronto Maple Leafs	54	9	19	28	132	....	....	....	....	....
1991-92	Toronto Maple Leafs	34	1	13	14	85	....	....	....	....	....
	Calgary Flames	36	3	10	13	79	....	....	....	....	....
1992-93	Calgary Flames	35	3	9	12	54	....	....	....	....	....
1993-94	Calgary Flames	63	2	21	23	110	....	....	....	....	....
1994-95	Los Angeles Kings	40	5	12	17	84	....	....	....	....	....
1995-96	Los Angeles Kings	9	0	1	1	27	....	....	....	....	....
	Tampa Bay Lightning	45	4	7	11	108	6	0	0	0	20
1996-97	Edmonton Oilers	18	2	4	6	20	....	....	....	....	....
	Philadelphia Flyers	20	0	3	3	51	3	0	0	0	6
1997-98	Phoenix Coyotes	32	4	2	6	77	5	0	0	0	8
	NHL Totals	**827**	**90**	**238**	**328**	**1839**	**19**	**0**	**2**	**2**	**61**

Traded to **NY Rangers** by **Vancouver** for Willie Huber and Larry Melnyk, November 4, 1987. Traded to **Quebec** by **NY Rangers** for Randy Moller, October 5, 1989. Traded to **Toronto** by **Quebec** with Aaron Broten and Lucien Deblois for Scott Pearson and Toronto's 2nd round choices in 1991 (later traded to Washington – Washington selected Eric Lavigne) and 1992 (Tuomas Gronman) Entry Drafts, November 17, 1990. Traded to **Calgary** by **Toronto** with Craig Berube, Alexander Godynyuk, Gary Leeman and Jeff Reese for Doug Gilmour, Jamie Macoun, Ric Nattress, Rick Wamsley and Kent Manderville, January 2, 1992. Signed as a free agent by **Los Angeles**, June 16, 1994. Traded to **Tampa Bay** by **Los Angeles** for Steven Finn, November 13, 1995. Signed as a free agent by **Edmonton**, October 24, 1996. Claimed on waivers by **Philadelphia** from **Edmonton**, January 17, 1997. Signed as a free agent by **Phoenix**, November 25, 1997.

PETRENKO, Sergei

Left wing. Shoots left. 6', 176 lbs. Born, Kharkov, USSR, September 10, 1968.
(Buffalo's 5th choice, 168th overall, in 1993 Entry Draft).

		REGULAR SEASON					PLAYOFFS				
Season	Club	GP	G	A	Pts	PIM	GP	G	A	Pts	PIM
1993-94	Buffalo Sabres	14	0	4	4	0	....	....	....	....	....
	NHL Totals	**14**	**0**	**4**	**4**	**0**	....	....	....	....	....

PETROV, Oleg

Right wing. Shoots left. 5'9", 172 lbs. Born, Moscow, USSR, April 18, 1971.
(Montreal's 9th choice, 127th overall, in 1991 Entry Draft).

		REGULAR SEASON					PLAYOFFS				
Season	Club	GP	G	A	Pts	PIM	GP	G	A	Pts	PIM
1992-93	Montreal Canadiens	9	2	1	3	10	1	0	0	0	0
1993-94	Montreal Canadiens	55	12	15	27	2	2	0	0	0	0
1994-95	Montreal Canadiens	12	2	3	5	4	....	....	....	....	....
1995-96	Montreal Canadiens	36	4	7	11	23	5	0	1	1	0
99-2000	Montreal Canadiens	44	2	24	26	8	....	....	....	....	....
2000-01	Montreal Canadiens	81	17	30	47	24	....	....	....	....	....
2001-02	Montreal Canadiens	75	24	17	41	12	12	1	5	6	2
2002-03	Montreal Canadiens	53	7	16	23	16	....	....	....	....	....
	Nashville Predators	17	2	2	4	2	....	....	....	....	....
	NHL Totals	**382**	**72**	**115**	**187**	**101**	**20**	**1**	**6**	**7**	**2**

NHL All-Rookie Team (1994)

Signed as a free agent by **Montreal**, July 15, 1999. Traded to **Nashville** by **Montreal** for Nashville's 4th round choice (later traded to Washington – Washington selected Andreas Valdix) in 2003 Entry Draft, March 3, 2003.

PETROVICKY, Robert

Center. Shoots left. 5'11", 172 lbs. Born, Kosice, Czech., October 26, 1973.
(Hartford's 1st choice, 9th overall, in 1992 Entry Draft).

		REGULAR SEASON					PLAYOFFS				
Season	Club	GP	G	A	Pts	PIM	GP	G	A	Pts	PIM
1992-93	Hartford Whalers	42	3	6	9	45	....	....	....	....	....
1993-94	Hartford Whalers	33	6	5	11	39	....	....	....	....	....
1994-95	Hartford Whalers	2	0	0	0	0	....	....	....	....	....
1995-96	Dallas Stars	5	1	1	2	0	....	....	....	....	....

Season	Club	GP	G	A	Pts	PIM	GP	G	A	Pts	PIM
		REGULAR SEASON					PLAYOFFS				
1996-97	St. Louis Blues	44	7	12	19	10	2	0	0	0	0
1998-99	Tampa Bay Lightning	28	3	4	7	6	....	....	....	....	....
99-2000	Tampa Bay Lightning	43	7	10	17	14	....	....	....	....	....
2000-01	New York Islanders	11	0	0	0	4	....	....	....	....	....
	NHL Totals	**208**	**27**	**38**	**65**	**118**	**2**	**0**	**0**	**0**	**0**

Traded to **Dallas** by **Hartford** for Dan Kesa, November 29, 1995. Signed as a free agent by **St. Louis**, September 6, 1996. Signed as a free agent by **Tampa Bay**, February 15, 1999. Signed as a free agent by **NY Islanders**, July 28, 2000.

PETROVICKY, Ronald

Right wing. Shoots right. 5'11", 190 lbs. Born, Zilina, Czech., February 15, 1977.
(Calgary's 9th choice, 228th overall, in 1996 Entry Draft).

Season	Club	GP	G	A	Pts	PIM	GP	G	A	Pts	PIM
2000-01	Calgary Flames	30	4	5	9	54	....	....	....	....	....
2001-02	Calgary Flames	77	5	7	12	85	....	....	....	....	....
2002-03	New York Rangers	66	5	9	14	77	....	....	....	....	....
	NHL Totals	**173**	**14**	**21**	**35**	**216**	....	....	....	....	....

• Missed majority of 2000-01 season recovering from wrist injury suffered in game vs. Detroit, October 5, 2000. Claimed by **NY Rangers** from **Calgary** in Waiver Draft, October 4, 2002.

PETTERSSON, Jorgen

Left wing. Shoots left. 6'2", 185 lbs. Born, Goteborg, Sweden, July 11, 1956.

Season	Club	GP	G	A	Pts	PIM	GP	G	A	Pts	PIM
1980-81	St. Louis Blues	62	37	36	73	24	11	4	3	7	0
1981-82	St. Louis Blues	77	38	31	69	28	7	1	2	3	0
1982-83	St. Louis Blues	74	35	38	73	4	4	1	1	2	0
1983-84	St. Louis Blues	77	28	34	62	29	11	7	3	10	2
1984-85	St. Louis Blues	75	23	32	55	20	3	1	1	2	0
1985-86	Hartford Whalers	23	5	5	10	2	....	....	....	....	....
	Washington Capitals	47	8	16	24	10	8	1	2	3	2
	NHL Totals	**435**	**174**	**192**	**366**	**117**	**44**	**15**	**12**	**27**	**4**

Signed as a free agent by **St. Louis**, May 8, 1980. Traded to **Hartford** by **St. Louis** with Mike Luit for Mark Johnson and Greg Millen, February 21, 1985. Traded to **Washington** by **Hartford** for Doug Jarvis, December 6, 1985.

PETTINEN, Tomi

Defense. Shoots left. 6'3", 220 lbs. Born, Ylojarvi, Finland, June 17, 1977.
(NY Islanders' 9th choice, 267th overall, in 2000 Entry Draft).

Season	Club	GP	G	A	Pts	PIM	GP	G	A	Pts	PIM
2002-03	New York Islanders	2	0	0	0	0	....	....	....	....	....
	NHL Totals	**2**	**0**	**0**	**0**	**0**	....	....	....	....	....

PETTINGER, Eric

Left wing/Center. Shoots left. 6', 175 lbs. Born, North Bierley, England, December 14, 1904.

Season	Club	GP	G	A	Pts	PIM	GP	G	A	Pts	PIM
1928-29	Boston Bruins	17	0	0	0	17	....	....	....	....	....
	Toronto Maple Leafs	25	3	3	6	24	4	1	0	1	8
1929-30	Toronto Maple Leafs	43	4	9	13	40	....	....	....	....	....
1930-31	Ottawa Senators	13	0	0	0	2	....	....	....	....	....
	NHL Totals	**98**	**7**	**12**	**19**	**83**	**4**	**1**	**0**	**1**	**8**

• Brother of Gord

Signed as a free agent by **NY Rangers**, September, 1927. Rights traded to **Toronto** by **NY Rangers** for the rights to Yip Foster, October, 1927. Rights traded to **Boston** by **Toronto** with $15,000 for Jimmy Herberts, December 21, 1927. Traded to **Toronto** by **Boston** with the rights to Hugh Plaxton for the rights to George Owen, January 10, 1929. Traded to **Ottawa** by **Toronto** with Art Smith and $35,000 for King Clancy, October 11, 1930. Traded to **London** (IHL) by **Ottawa** for cash, October 31, 1932.

PETTINGER, Gord

Center. Shoots left. 6', 175 lbs. Born, Harrogate, England, November 11, 1911.

Season	Club	GP	G	A	Pts	PIM	GP	G	A	Pts	PIM
1932-33 ♦	New York Rangers	34	1	2	3	18	8	0	0	0	0
1933-34	Detroit Red Wings	48	3	14	17	14	7	1	0	1	2
1934-35	Detroit Red Wings	13	2	3	5	2	....	....	....	....	....
1935-36 ♦	Detroit Red Wings	30	8	7	15	6	7	2	2	4	0
1936-37 ♦	Detroit Red Wings	48	7	15	22	13	10	0	2	2	2
1937-38	Detroit Red Wings	12	1	3	4	4	....	....	....	....	....
	Boston Bruins	35	7	10	17	10	3	0	0	0	0
1938-39 ♦	Boston Bruins	48	11	14	25	8	12	1	1	2	7
1939-40	Boston Bruins	24	2	6	8	2	....	....	....	....	....
	NHL Totals	**292**	**42**	**74**	**116**	**77**	**47**	**4**	**5**	**9**	**11**

• Brother of Eric

Signed as a free agent by **NY Rangers**, October 29, 1930. Traded to **Detroit** by **NY Rangers** for cash, October 23, 1933. Traded to **Boston** by **Detroit** for Red Beattie, December 19, 1937.

PETTINGER, Matt

Left wing. Shoots left. 6'1", 205 lbs. Born, Edmonton, Alta., October 22, 1980.
(Washington's 2nd choice, 43rd overall, in 2000 Entry Draft).

Season	Club	GP	G	A	Pts	PIM	GP	G	A	Pts	PIM
2000-01	Washington Capitals	10	0	0	0	2	....	....	....	....	....
2001-02	Washington Capitals	61	7	3	10	44	....	....	....	....	....
2002-03	Washington Capitals	1	0	0	0	0	....	....	....	....	....
	NHL Totals	**72**	**7**	**3**	**10**	**46**	....	....	....	....	....

PHAIR, Lyle

Left wing. Shoots left. 6'1", 190 lbs. Born, Pilot Mound, Man., August 31, 1961.

Season	Club	GP	G	A	Pts	PIM	GP	G	A	Pts	PIM
1985-86	Los Angeles Kings	15	0	1	1	2	....	....	....	....	....
1986-87	Los Angeles Kings	5	2	0	2	2	....	....	....	....	....
1987-88	Los Angeles Kings	28	4	6	10	8	1	0	0	0	0
	NHL Totals	**48**	**6**	**7**	**13**	**12**	**1**	**0**	**0**	**0**	**0**

Signed as a free agent by **Los Angeles**, June 7, 1985. Traded to **New Jersey** by **Los Angeles** for cash, December 13, 1988.

PHILLIPOFF, Harold

Left wing. Shoots left. 6'3", 220 lbs. Born, Kamsack, Sask., July 14, 1956.
(Atlanta's 2nd choice, 10th overall, in 1976 Amateur Draft).

Season	Club	GP	G	A	Pts	PIM	GP	G	A	Pts	PIM
1977-78	Atlanta Flames	67	17	36	53	128	2	0	1	1	2
1978-79	Atlanta Flames	51	9	17	26	113	....	....	....	....	....
	Chicago Black Hawks	14	0	4	4	6	4	0	1	1	7
1979-80	Chicago Black Hawks	9	0	0	0	20	....	....	....	....	....
	NHL Totals	**141**	**26**	**57**	**83**	**267**	**6**	**0**	**2**	**2**	**9**

Traded to **Chicago** by **Atlanta** with Pat Ribble, Greg Fox, Tom Lysiak and Miles Zaharko for Ivan Boldirev, Phil Russell and Darcy Rota, March 13, 1979. Traded to **Vancouver** by **Chicago** with Dave Logan for Ron Sedlbauer, December 21, 1979.

PHILLIPS, Bill

Center. Shoots left. 5'10", 163 lbs. Born, Carleton Place, Ont., September 23, 1902.

Season	Club	GP	G	A	Pts	PIM	GP	G	A	Pts	PIM
1929-30	Montreal Maroons	27	1	1	2	6	4	0	0	0	2
	NHL Totals	**27**	**1**	**1**	**2**	**6**	**4**	**0**	**0**	**0**	**2**

Traded to **Mtl. Maroons** by **Vancouver** (PCHL) for $10,000, December 17, 1929. Traded to **Philadelphia** (Can-Am) by **Mtl. Maroons** for cash, October 22, 1932.

PHILLIPS, Charlie

Defense. Shoots left. 5'11", 200 lbs. Born, Toronto, Ont., May 10, 1917.

Season	Club	GP	G	A	Pts	PIM	GP	G	A	Pts	PIM
1942-43	Montreal Canadiens	17	0	0	0	6	....	....	....	....	....
	NHL Totals	**17**	**0**	**0**	**0**	**6**	....	....	....	....	....

PHILLIPS, Chris

Defense. Shoots left. 6'3", 215 lbs. Born, Calgary, Alta., March 9, 1978.
(Ottawa's 1st choice, 1st overall, in 1996 Entry Draft).

Season	Club	GP	G	A	Pts	PIM	GP	G	A	Pts	PIM
1997-98	Ottawa Senators	72	5	11	16	38	11	0	2	2	2
1998-99	Ottawa Senators	34	3	3	6	32	3	0	0	0	0
99-2000	Ottawa Senators	65	5	14	19	39	6	0	1	1	4
2000-01	Ottawa Senators	73	2	12	14	31	1	1	0	1	0
2001-02	Ottawa Senators	63	6	16	22	29	12	0	0	0	12
2002-03	Ottawa Senators	78	3	16	19	71	18	2	4	6	12
	NHL Totals	**385**	**24**	**72**	**96**	**240**	**51**	**3**	**7**	**10**	**30**

• Missed majority of 1998-99 season recovering from ankle injury suffered in game vs. Buffalo, December 30, 1998.

PHILLIPS, Merlyn

Center. Shoots right. 5'7", 160 lbs. Born, Richmond Hill, Ont., May 24, 1899.

Season	Club	GP	G	A	Pts	PIM	GP	G	A	Pts	PIM
1925-26 ♦	Montreal Maroons	12	3	1	4	6	4	3	0	3	4
	Montreal Maroons (Cup)	....	....	....	....	....	*4*	*1*	*1*	*2*	*0*
1926-27	Montreal Maroons	43	15	1	16	45	2	0	0	0	0
1927-28	Montreal Maroons	40	7	5	12	33	9	2	1	3	9
1928-29	Montreal Maroons	42	6	5	11	41	....	....	....	....	....
1929-30	Montreal Maroons	44	13	10	23	48	4	0	0	0	2
1930-31	Montreal Maroons	43	6	1	7	38	1	0	0	0	2
1931-32	Montreal Maroons	46	1	1	2	11	4	0	0	0	2
1932-33	Montreal Maroons	2	0	0	0	0	....	....	....	....	....
	New York Americans	30	1	7	8	10	....	....	....	....	....
	NHL Totals	**302**	**52**	**31**	**83**	**232**	**24**	**5**	**1**	**6**	**19**

Signed as a free agent by **Mtl. Maroons**, February 17, 1926. Signed as a free agent by **NY Americans**, November 21, 1932.

PICARD, Michel

Left wing. Shoots left. 5'11", 190 lbs. Born, Beauport, Que., November 7, 1969.
(Hartford's 8th choice, 178th overall, in 1989 Entry Draft).

Season	Club	GP	G	A	Pts	PIM	GP	G	A	Pts	PIM
1990-91	Hartford Whalers	5	1	0	1	2	....	....	....	....	....
1991-92	Hartford Whalers	25	3	5	8	6	....	....	....	....	....
1992-93	San Jose Sharks	25	4	0	4	24	....	....	....	....	....
1994-95	Ottawa Senators	24	5	8	13	14	....	....	....	....	....
1995-96	Ottawa Senators	17	2	6	8	10	....	....	....	....	....
1997-98	St. Louis Blues	16	1	8	9	29	....	....	....	....	....
1998-99	St. Louis Blues	45	11	11	22	16	5	0	0	0	2
99-2000	Edmonton Oilers	2	0	0	0	2	....	....	....	....	....
2000-01	Philadelphia Flyers	7	1	4	5	0	....	....	....	....	....
	NHL Totals	**166**	**28**	**42**	**70**	**103**	**5**	**0**	**0**	**0**	**2**

Traded to **San Jose** by **Hartford** for future considerations (Yvon Corriveau, January 21, 1993), October 9, 1992. Signed as a free agent by **Ottawa**, June 16, 1994. Traded to **Washington** by **Ottawa** for cash, May 21, 1996. Signed as a free agent by **St. Louis**, January 5, 1998. Signed as a free agent by **Edmonton**, December 2, 1999. Signed as a free agent by **Philadelphia**, August 14, 2000. Signed as a free agent by **Detroit**, July 15, 2002.

PICARD, Noel

Defense. Shoots right. 6'1", 185 lbs. Born, Montreal, Que., December 25, 1938.

Season	Club	GP	G	A	Pts	PIM	GP	G	A	Pts	PIM
1964-65 ♦	Montreal Canadiens	16	0	7	7	33	3	0	1	1	0
1967-68	St. Louis Blues	66	1	10	11	142	13	0	3	3	46
1968-69	St. Louis Blues	67	5	19	24	131	12	1	4	5	30
1969-70	St. Louis Blues	39	1	4	5	88	16	0	2	2	65
1970-71	St. Louis Blues	75	3	8	11	119	6	1	1	2	26

		REGULAR SEASON					PLAYOFFS				
Season	Club	GP	G	A	Pts	PIM	GP	G	A	Pts	PIM
1971-72	St. Louis Blues	15	1	5	6	50	....	....	....	....	....
1972-73	St. Louis Blues	16	1	0	1	10	....	....	....	....	....
	Atlanta Flames	41	0	10	10	43	....	....	....	....	....
	NHL Totals	**335**	**12**	**63**	**75**	**616**	**50**	**2**	**11**	**13**	**167**

• Brother of Roger

Played in NHL All-Star Game (1969)

Claimed by **St. Louis** from **Montreal** in Expansion Draft, June 6, 1967. Claimed on waivers by **Atlanta** from **St. Louis**, November 25, 1972.

PICARD, Robert

Defense. Shoots left. 6'2", 207 lbs. Born, Montreal, Que., May 25, 1957.
(Washington's 1st choice, 3rd overall, in 1977 Amateur Draft).

Season	Club	GP	G	A	Pts	PIM	GP	G	A	Pts	PIM
1977-78	Washington Capitals	75	10	27	37	101	....	....	....	....	....
1978-79	Washington Capitals	77	21	44	65	85	....	....	....	....	....
1979-80	Washington Capitals	78	11	43	54	122	....	....	....	....	....
1980-81	Toronto Maple Leafs	59	6	19	25	68	....	....	....	....	....
	Montreal Canadiens	8	2	2	4	6	1	0	0	0	0
1981-82	Montreal Canadiens	62	2	26	28	106	5	1	1	2	7
1982-83	Montreal Canadiens	64	7	31	38	60	3	0	0	0	0
1983-84	Montreal Canadiens	7	0	2	2	0	....	....	....	....	....
	Winnipeg Jets	62	6	16	22	34	3	0	0	0	12
1984-85	Winnipeg Jets	78	12	22	34	107	8	2	2	4	8
1985-86	Winnipeg Jets	20	2	5	7	17	....	....	....	....	....
	Quebec Nordiques	48	7	27	34	36	3	0	2	2	2
1986-87	Quebec Nordiques	78	8	20	28	71	13	2	10	12	10
1987-88	Quebec Nordiques	65	3	13	16	103	....	....	....	....	....
1988-89	Quebec Nordiques	74	7	14	21	61	....	....	....	....	....
1989-90	Quebec Nordiques	24	0	5	5	28	....	....	....	....	....
	Detroit Red Wings	20	0	3	3	20	....	....	....	....	....
	NHL Totals	**899**	**104**	**319**	**423**	**1025**	**36**	**5**	**15**	**20**	**39**

Played in NHL All-Star Game (1980, 1981)

Traded to **Toronto** by **Washington** with Tim Coulis and Washington's 2nd round choice (Bob McGill) in 1980 Entry Draft for Mike Palmateer and Toronto's 3rd round choice (Torrie Robertson) in 1980 Entry Draft, June 11, 1980. Traded to **Montreal** by **Toronto** for Michel Larocque, March 10, 1981. Traded to **Winnipeg** by **Montreal** for Winnipeg's 3rd round choice (Patrick Roy) in 1984 Entry Draft, November 4, 1983. Traded to **Quebec** by **Winnipeg** for Mario Marois, November 27, 1985. Traded to **Detroit** by **Quebec** with Greg Adams for Tony McKegney, December 4, 1989.

PICARD, Roger

Right wing. Shoots right. 6', 200 lbs. Born, Montreal, Que., January 13, 1935.

Season	Club	GP	G	A	Pts	PIM	GP	G	A	Pts	PIM
1967-68	St. Louis Blues	15	2	2	4	21	....	....	....	....	....
	NHL Totals	**15**	**2**	**2**	**4**	**21**	....	....	....	....	....

• Brother of Noel

Signed as a free agent by **St. Louis**, June 6, 1967.

PICHETTE, Dave

Defense. Shoots left. 6'3", 190 lbs. Born, Grand Falls, Nfld., February 4, 1960.

Season	Club	GP	G	A	Pts	PIM	GP	G	A	Pts	PIM
1980-81	Quebec Nordiques	46	4	16	20	62	1	0	0	0	14
1981-82	Quebec Nordiques	67	7	30	37	152	16	2	4	6	22
1982-83	Quebec Nordiques	53	3	21	24	49	2	0	1	1	0
1983-84	Quebec Nordiques	23	2	7	9	12	....	....	....	....	....
	St. Louis Blues	23	0	11	11	6	9	1	2	3	18
1984-85	New Jersey Devils	71	17	40	57	41	....	....	....	....	....
1985-86	New Jersey Devils	33	7	12	19	22	....	....	....	....	....
1987-88	New York Rangers	6	1	3	4	4	....	....	....	....	....
	NHL Totals	**322**	**41**	**140**	**181**	**348**	**28**	**3**	**7**	**10**	**54**

Signed as a free agent by **Quebec**, October 31, 1979. Traded to **St. Louis** by **Quebec** for Andre Dore, February 10, 1984. Claimed by **New Jersey** from **St. Louis** in Waiver Draft, October 9, 1984.

PICKETTS, Hal

Right wing. Shoots right. 6', 183 lbs. Born, Asquith, Sask., April 22, 1909.

Season	Club	GP	G	A	Pts	PIM	GP	G	A	Pts	PIM
1933-34	New York Americans	48	3	1	4	32	....	....	....	....	....
	NHL Totals	**48**	**3**	**1**	**4**	**32**	....	....	....	....	....

Loaned to **Rochester** (IHL) by **NY Americans** for cash, November 8, 1935. Traded to **London** (IHL) by **NY Americans** for cash, January 3, 1936.

PIDHIRNY, Harry

Center. Shoots left. 5'11", 155 lbs. Born, Toronto, Ont., March 5, 1928.

Season	Club	GP	G	A	Pts	PIM	GP	G	A	Pts	PIM
1957-58	Boston Bruins	2	0	0	0	0	....	....	....	....	....
	NHL Totals	**2**	**0**	**0**	**0**	**0**	....	....	....	....	....

Traded to **San Francisco** (WHL) by **Boston** (Springfield-AHL) for cash, September, 1961. Traded to **Montreal** by **San Francisco** (WHL) for Moe Mantha and the loan of Camille Bedard, Gary Mork and Norm Waslowski, September 12, 1962. Traded to **Providence** (AHL) by **Montreal** for cash, October, 1962.

PIERCE, Randy

Right wing. Shoots right. 5'11", 187 lbs. Born, Arnprior, Ont., November 23, 1957.
(Colorado's 3rd choice, 47th overall, in 1977 Amateur Draft).

Season	Club	GP	G	A	Pts	PIM	GP	G	A	Pts	PIM
1977-78	Colorado Rockies	35	9	10	19	15	2	0	0	0	0
1978-79	Colorado Rockies	70	19	17	36	35	....	....	....	....	....
1979-80	Colorado Rockies	75	16	23	39	100	....	....	....	....	....
1980-81	Colorado Rockies	55	9	21	30	52	....	....	....	....	....
1981-82	Colorado Rockies	5	0	0	0	4	....	....	....	....	....
1982-83	New Jersey Devils	3	0	0	0	0	....	....	....	....	....
1983-84	Hartford Whalers	17	6	3	9	9	....	....	....	....	....
1984-85	Hartford Whalers	17	3	2	5	8	....	....	....	....	....
	NHL Totals	**277**	**62**	**76**	**138**	**223**	**2**	**0**	**0**	**0**	**0**

Transferred to **New Jersey** after **Colorado** franchise relocated, June 30, 1982. Signed as a free agent by **Hartford**, October 6, 1983.

PIKE, Alf

Left wing/Center. Shoots left. 6', 187 lbs. Born, Winnipeg, Man., September 15, 1917.

Season	Club	GP	G	A	Pts	PIM	GP	G	A	Pts	PIM
1939-40 ♦	New York Rangers	47	8	9	17	38	12	3	1	4	6
1940-41	New York Rangers	48	6	13	19	23	3	0	1	1	2
1941-42	New York Rangers	34	8	19	27	16	6	1	0	1	4
1942-43	New York Rangers	41	6	16	22	48	....	....	....	....	....
1945-46	New York Rangers	33	7	9	16	18	....	....	....	....	....
1946-47	New York Rangers	31	7	11	18	2	....	....	....	....	....
	NHL Totals	**234**	**42**	**77**	**119**	**145**	**21**	**4**	**2**	**6**	**12**

PILAR, Karel

Defense. Shoots right. 6'3", 210 lbs. Born, Prague, Czech., December 23, 1977.
(Toronto's 2nd choice, 39th overall, in 2001 Entry Draft).

Season	Club	GP	G	A	Pts	PIM	GP	G	A	Pts	PIM
2001-02	Toronto Maple Leafs	23	1	3	4	8	11	0	4	4	12
2002-03	Toronto Maple Leafs	17	3	4	7	12	....	....	....	....	....
	NHL Totals	**40**	**4**	**7**	**11**	**20**	**11**	**0**	**4**	**4**	**12**

PILON, Rich

Defense. Shoots left. 6'2", 220 lbs. Born, Saskatoon, Sask., April 30, 1968.
(NY Islanders' 9th choice, 143rd overall, in 1986 Entry Draft).

Season	Club	GP	G	A	Pts	PIM	GP	G	A	Pts	PIM
1988-89	New York Islanders	62	0	14	14	242	....	....	....	....	....
1989-90	New York Islanders	14	0	2	2	31	....	....	....	....	....
1990-91	New York Islanders	60	1	4	5	126	....	....	....	....	....
1991-92	New York Islanders	65	1	6	7	183	....	....	....	....	....
1992-93	New York Islanders	44	1	3	4	164	15	0	0	0	50
1993-94	New York Islanders	28	1	4	5	75	....	....	....	....	....
1994-95	New York Islanders	20	1	1	2	40	....	....	....	....	....
1995-96	New York Islanders	27	0	3	3	72	....	....	....	....	....
1996-97	New York Islanders	52	1	4	5	179	....	....	....	....	....
1997-98	New York Islanders	76	0	7	7	291	....	....	....	....	....
1998-99	New York Islanders	52	0	4	4	88	....	....	....	....	....
1999-2000	New York Islanders	9	0	2	2	34	....	....	....	....	....
	New York Rangers	45	0	4	4	36	....	....	....	....	....
2000-01	New York Rangers	69	2	9	11	175	....	....	....	....	....
2001-02	St. Louis Blues	8	0	2	2	9	....	....	....	....	....
	NHL Totals	**631**	**8**	**69**	**77**	**1745**	**15**	**0**	**0**	**0**	**50**

• Missed majority of 1989-90 season recovering from eye injury suffered in game vs. Detroit, November 4, 1989. • Missed majority of 1993-94 season recovering from shoulder injury suffered in game vs. Boston, November 13, 1993. • Missed majority of 1994-95 and 1995-96 seasons recovering from wrist injury suffered in game vs. Quebec, April 18, 1995. Claimed on waivers by **NY Rangers** from **NY Islanders**, December 1, 1999. Traded to **San Jose** by **NY Rangers** for San Jose's 7th round choice (Joseph Crabb) in 2002 Entry Draft, June 29, 2001. Signed as a free agent by **St. Louis**, July 10, 2001. • Missed majority of 2001-02 season recovering from wrist injury suffered in game vs. NY Rangers, October 25, 2001.

PILOTE, Pierre

HHOF

Defense. Shoots left. 5'10", 178 lbs. Born, Kenogami, Que., December 11, 1931.

Season	Club	GP	G	A	Pts	PIM	GP	G	A	Pts	PIM
1955-56	Chicago Black Hawks	20	3	5	8	34	....	....	....	....	....
1956-57	Chicago Black Hawks	70	3	14	17	117	....	....	....	....	....
1957-58	Chicago Black Hawks	70	6	24	30	91	....	....	....	....	....
1958-59	Chicago Black Hawks	70	7	30	37	79	6	0	2	2	10
1959-60	Chicago Black Hawks	70	7	38	45	100	4	0	1	1	8
1960-61 ♦	Chicago Black Hawks	70	6	29	35	*165	12	3	*12	*15	8
1961-62	Chicago Black Hawks	59	7	35	42	97	12	0	7	7	8
1962-63	Chicago Black Hawks	59	8	18	26	57	6	0	8	8	8
1963-64	Chicago Black Hawks	70	7	46	53	84	7	2	6	8	6
1964-65	Chicago Black Hawks	68	14	45	59	162	12	0	7	7	22
1965-66	Chicago Black Hawks	51	2	34	36	60	6	0	2	2	10
1966-67	Chicago Black Hawks	70	6	46	52	90	6	2	4	6	6
1967-68	Chicago Black Hawks	74	1	36	37	69	11	1	3	4	12
1968-69	Toronto Maple Leafs	69	3	18	21	46	4	0	1	1	4
	NHL Totals	**890**	**80**	**418**	**498**	**1251**	**86**	**8**	**53**	**61**	**102**

NHL Second All-Star Team (1960, 1961, 1962) • NHL First All-Star Team (1963, 1964, 1965, 1966, 1967) • James Norris Trophy (1963, 1964, 1965)

Played in NHL All-Star Game (1960, 1961, 1962, 1963, 1964, 1965, 1967, 1968)

Traded to **Toronto** by **Chicago** for Jim Pappin, May 23, 1968.

PINDER, Gerry

Left wing. Shoots right. 5'8", 165 lbs. Born, Saskatoon, Sask., September 15, 1948.

Season	Club	GP	G	A	Pts	PIM	GP	G	A	Pts	PIM
1969-70	Chicago Black Hawks	75	19	20	39	41	8	0	4	4	4
1970-71	Chicago Black Hawks	74	13	18	31	35	9	0	0	0	2
1971-72	California Golden Seals	74	23	31	54	59	....	....	....	....	....
	NHL Totals	**223**	**55**	**69**	**124**	**135**	**17**	**0**	**4**	**4**	**6**

Traded to **California** by **Chicago** with Gerry Desjardins and Kerry Bond for Gary Smith, September 9, 1971.

PIRJETA, Lasse

Left wing. Shoots left. 6'3", 222 lbs. Born, Oulu, Finland, April 4, 1974.
(Columbus' 7th choice, 133rd overall, in 2002 Entry Draft).

Season	Club	REGULAR SEASON GP	G	A	Pts	PIM	PLAYOFFS GP	G	A	Pts	PIM
2002-03	Columbus Blue Jackets	51	11	10	21	12	....	....	....	....	....
	NHL Totals	**51**	**11**	**10**	**21**	**12**	....	....	....	....	....

PIROS, Kamil

Center. Shoots left. 6', 200 lbs. Born, Most, Czech., November 20, 1978.
(Buffalo's 9th choice, 212th overall, in 1997 Entry Draft).

Season	Club	REGULAR SEASON GP	G	A	Pts	PIM	PLAYOFFS GP	G	A	Pts	PIM
2001-02	Atlanta Thrashers	8	0	1	1	4	....	....	....	....	....
2002-03	Atlanta Thrashers	3	3	2	5	2	....	....	....	....	....
	NHL Totals	**11**	**3**	**3**	**6**	**6**	....	....	....	....	....

Rights traded to **Atlanta** by **Buffalo** with Buffalo's 4th round choice (later traded to St. Louis – St. Louis selected Igor Valeyev) in 2001 Entry Draft for Donald Audette, March 13, 2001.

PIRUS, Alex

Right wing. Shoots right. 6'1", 205 lbs. Born, Toronto, Ont., January 12, 1955.
(Minnesota's 3rd choice, 41st overall, in 1975 Amateur Draft).

Season	Club	REGULAR SEASON GP	G	A	Pts	PIM	PLAYOFFS GP	G	A	Pts	PIM
1976-77	Minnesota North Stars	79	20	17	37	47	2	0	1	1	2
1977-78	Minnesota North Stars	61	9	6	15	38	....	....	....	....	....
1978-79	Minnesota North Stars	15	1	3	4	9	....	....	....	....	....
1979-80	Detroit Red Wings	4	0	2	2	0	....	....	....	....	....
	NHL Totals	**159**	**30**	**28**	**58**	**94**	**2**	**0**	**1**	**1**	**2**

Traded to **Detroit** by **Minnesota** for cash, January 3, 1980. Traded to **Minnesota** by **Detroit** for cash, June 6, 1980. Traded to **NY Islanders** by **Minnesota** for future considerations, July 4, 1980.

PISA, Ales

Defense. Shoots left. 6', 195 lbs. Born, Pardibuce, Czech., January 2, 1977.
(Edmonton's 10th choice, 272nd overall, in 2001 Entry Draft).

Season	Club	REGULAR SEASON GP	G	A	Pts	PIM	PLAYOFFS GP	G	A	Pts	PIM
2001-02	Edmonton Oilers	2	0	0	0	2	....	....	....	....	....
2002-03	Edmonton Oilers	48	1	3	4	24	....	....	....	....	....
	New York Rangers	3	0	0	0	0	....	....	....	....	....
	NHL Totals	**53**	**1**	**3**	**4**	**26**	....	....	....	....	....

Traded to **NY Rangers** by **Edmonton** with Anson Carter for Radek Dvorak and Cory Cross, March 11, 2003.

PISANI, Fernando

Right wing. Shoots left. 6'1", 185 lbs. Born, Edmonton, Alta., December 27, 1976.
(Edmonton's 9th choice, 195th overall, in 1996 Entry Draft).

Season	Club	REGULAR SEASON GP	G	A	Pts	PIM	PLAYOFFS GP	G	A	Pts	PIM
2002-03	Edmonton Oilers	35	8	5	13	10	6	1	0	1	2
	NHL Totals	**35**	**8**	**5**	**13**	**10**	**6**	**1**	**0**	**1**	**2**

PITLICK, Lance

Defense. Shoots right. 6', 205 lbs. Born, Minneapolis, MN, November 5, 1967.
(Minnesota's 10th choice, 180th overall, in 1986 Entry Draft).

Season	Club	REGULAR SEASON GP	G	A	Pts	PIM	PLAYOFFS GP	G	A	Pts	PIM
1994-95	Ottawa Senators	15	0	1	1	6	....	....	....	....	....
1995-96	Ottawa Senators	28	1	6	7	20	....	....	....	....	....
1996-97	Ottawa Senators	66	5	5	10	91	7	0	0	0	4
1997-98	Ottawa Senators	69	2	7	9	50	11	0	1	1	17
1998-99	Ottawa Senators	50	3	6	9	33	2	0	0	0	0
99-2000	Florida Panthers	62	3	5	8	44	4	0	1	1	0
2000-01	Florida Panthers	68	1	2	3	42	....	....	....	....	....
2001-02	Florida Panthers	35	1	1	2	12	....	....	....	....	....
	NHL Totals	**393**	**16**	**33**	**49**	**298**	**24**	**0**	**2**	**2**	**21**

Signed as a free agent by **Philadelphia**, September 5, 1990. Signed as a free agent by **Ottawa**, June 22, 1994. Signed as a free agent by **Florida**, July 21, 1999. • Spent majority of 2001-02 season on practice roster, October 4, 2001.

PITRE, Didier

HHOF

Right wing/Defense. Shoots right. 5'11", 185 lbs. Born, Valleyfield, Que., September 1, 1883.

Season	Club	REGULAR SEASON GP	G	A	Pts	PIM	PLAYOFFS GP	G	A	Pts	PIM
1917-18	Montreal Canadiens	20	17	6	23	29	2	0	1	1	13
1918-19	Montreal Canadiens	17	14	5	19	12	5	2	*3	5	3
	Montreal Canadiens (Cup)	....	....	....	....	....	*5*	*0*	*3*	*3*	*0*
1919-20	Montreal Canadiens	22	14	12	26	6	....	....	....	....	....
1920-21	Montreal Canadiens	23	16	5	21	25	....	....	....	....	....
1921-22	Montreal Canadiens	23	2	4	6	12	....	....	....	....	....
1922-23	Montreal Canadiens	22	1	2	3	0	2	0	0	0	0
	NHL Totals	**127**	**64**	**34**	**98**	**84**	**9**	**2**	**4**	**6**	**16**

Rights retained by **Montreal** after NHA folded, November 26, 1917.

PITTIS, Domenic

Center. Shoots left. 5'11", 190 lbs. Born, Calgary, Alta., October 1, 1974.
(Pittsburgh's 2nd choice, 52nd overall, in 1993 Entry Draft).

Season	Club	REGULAR SEASON GP	G	A	Pts	PIM	PLAYOFFS GP	G	A	Pts	PIM
1996-97	Pittsburgh Penguins	1	0	0	0	0	....	....	....	....	....
1998-99	Buffalo Sabres	3	0	0	0	2	....	....	....	....	....
99-2000	Buffalo Sabres	7	1	0	1	6	....	....	....	....	....
2000-01	Edmonton Oilers	47	4	5	9	49	3	0	0	0	2
2001-02	Edmonton Oilers	22	0	6	6	8	....	....	....	....	....
2002-03	Nashville Predators	2	0	0	0	2	....	....	....	....	....
	NHL Totals	**82**	**5**	**11**	**16**	**67**	**3**	**0**	**0**	**0**	**2**

Signed as a free agent by **Buffalo**, August 10, 1998. Signed as a free agent by **Edmonton**, July 25, 2000. • Missed majority of 2001-02 season recovering from head injury suffered in game vs. Nashville, February 28, 2002. Signed as a free agent by **Nashville**, July 24, 2002.

PIVONKA, Michal

Center. Shoots left. 6'2", 200 lbs. Born, Kladno, Czech., January 28, 1966.
(Washington's 3rd choice, 59th overall, in 1984 Entry Draft).

Season	Club	REGULAR SEASON GP	G	A	Pts	PIM	PLAYOFFS GP	G	A	Pts	PIM
1986-87	Washington Capitals	73	18	25	43	41	7	1	1	2	2
1987-88	Washington Capitals	71	11	23	34	28	14	4	9	13	4
1988-89	Washington Capitals	52	8	19	27	30	6	3	1	4	10
1989-90	Washington Capitals	77	25	39	64	54	11	0	2	2	6
1990-91	Washington Capitals	79	20	50	70	34	11	2	3	5	8
1991-92	Washington Capitals	80	23	57	80	47	7	1	5	6	13
1992-93	Washington Capitals	69	21	53	74	66	6	0	2	2	0
1993-94	Washington Capitals	82	14	36	50	38	7	4	4	8	4
1994-95	Washington Capitals	46	10	23	33	50	7	1	4	5	21
1995-96	Washington Capitals	73	16	65	81	36	6	3	2	5	18
1996-97	Washington Capitals	54	7	16	23	22	....	....	....	....	....
1997-98	Washington Capitals	33	3	6	9	20	13	0	3	3	0
1998-99	Washington Capitals	36	5	6	11	12	....	....	....	....	....
	NHL Totals	**825**	**181**	**418**	**599**	**478**	**95**	**19**	**36**	**55**	**86**

Missed majority of 1997-98 season recovering from wrist injury suffered in game vs. Pittsburgh, November 12, 1997. • Missed majority of 1998-99 season recovering from groin injury suffered in game vs. Buffalo, February 7, 1998.

PLAGER, Barclay

Defense. Shoots left. 5'11", 175 lbs. Born, Kirkland Lake, Ont., March 26, 1941.

Season	Club	REGULAR SEASON GP	G	A	Pts	PIM	PLAYOFFS GP	G	A	Pts	PIM
1967-68	St. Louis Blues	49	5	15	20	*153	18	2	5	7	*73
1968-69	St. Louis Blues	61	4	26	30	120	12	0	4	4	31
1969-70	St. Louis Blues	75	6	26	32	128	13	0	2	2	20
1970-71	St. Louis Blues	69	4	20	24	172	6	0	3	3	10
1971-72	St. Louis Blues	78	7	22	29	176	11	1	4	5	21
1972-73	St. Louis Blues	68	8	25	33	102	5	0	1	1	0
1973-74	St. Louis Blues	72	6	20	26	99	....	....	....	....	....
1974-75	St. Louis Blues	76	4	24	28	96	2	0	1	1	14
1975-76	St. Louis Blues	64	0	8	8	67	1	0	0	0	13
1976-77	St. Louis Blues	2	0	1	1	2	....	....	....	....	....
	NHL Totals	**614**	**44**	**187**	**231**	**1115**	**68**	**3**	**20**	**23**	**182**

• Brother of Bill and Bob

Played in NHL All-Star Game (1970, 1971, 1973, 1974)

Claimed by **Detroit** from **Montreal** in Intra-League Draft, June 4, 1962. Traded to **Springfield** (AHL) by **Detroit** for cash, August, 1964. NHL rights transferred to **Los Angeles** after NHL club purchased **Springfield** (AHL) franchise, May, 1967. Traded to **NY Rangers** by **Los Angeles** for Trevor Fahey, Ken Turlick and Jim Murray, June 16, 1967. Traded to **St. Louis** by **NY Rangers** with Red Berenson for Ron Stewart and Ron Attwell, November 29, 1967.

PLAGER, Bill

Defense. Shoots right. 5'9", 175 lbs. Born, Kirkland Lake, Ont., July 6, 1945.

Season	Club	REGULAR SEASON GP	G	A	Pts	PIM	PLAYOFFS GP	G	A	Pts	PIM
1967-68	Minnesota North Stars	32	0	2	2	30	12	0	2	2	8
1968-69	St. Louis Blues	2	0	0	0	2	4	0	0	0	4
1969-70	St. Louis Blues	24	1	4	5	30	3	0	0	0	0
1970-71	St. Louis Blues	36	0	3	3	45	1	0	0	0	2
1971-72	St. Louis Blues	65	1	11	12	64	11	0	0	0	12
1972-73	Atlanta Flames	76	2	11	13	92	....	....	....	....	....
1973-74	Minnesota North Stars	1	0	0	0	2	....	....	....	....	....
1974-75	Minnesota North Stars	7	0	0	0	8	....	....	....	....	....
1975-76	Minnesota North Stars	20	0	3	3	21	....	....	....	....	....
	NHL Totals	**263**	**4**	**34**	**38**	**294**	**31**	**0**	**2**	**2**	**26**

• Brother of Barclay and Bob

Traded to **Minnesota** by **Montreal** with the rights to Barrie Meissner and Leo Thiffault for Bryan Watson, June 6, 1967. Claimed by **NY Rangers** from **Minnesota** in Intra-League Draft, June 12, 1968. Traded to **St. Louis** by **NY Rangers** with Camille Henry and Robbie Irons for Don Caley and Wayne Rivers, June 13, 1968. Claimed by **Atlanta** from **St. Louis** in Expansion Draft, June 6, 1972. Claimed by **Minnesota** from **Atlanta** in Intra-League Draft, June 12, 1973.

PLAGER, Bob

Defense. Shoots left. 5'11", 195 lbs. Born, Kirkland Lake, Ont., March 11, 1943.

Season	Club	REGULAR SEASON GP	G	A	Pts	PIM	PLAYOFFS GP	G	A	Pts	PIM
1964-65	New York Rangers	10	0	0	0	18	....	....	....	....	....
1965-66	New York Rangers	18	0	5	5	22	....	....	....	....	....
1966-67	New York Rangers	1	0	0	0	0	....	....	....	....	....
1967-68	St. Louis Blues	53	2	5	7	86	18	1	2	3	69
1968-69	St. Louis Blues	32	0	7	7	43	9	0	4	4	47
1969-70	St. Louis Blues	64	3	11	14	113	16	0	3	3	46
1970-71	St. Louis Blues	70	1	19	20	114	6	0	2	2	4
1971-72	St. Louis Blues	50	4	7	11	81	11	1	4	5	5
1972-73	St. Louis Blues	77	2	31	33	107	5	0	2	2	2
1973-74	St. Louis Blues	61	3	10	13	48	....	....	....	....	....
1974-75	St. Louis Blues	73	1	14	15	53	2	0	0	0	20
1975-76	St. Louis Blues	63	3	8	11	90	3	0	0	0	2
1976-77	St. Louis Blues	54	1	9	10	23	4	0	0	0	0

Season	Club	GP	G	A	Pts	PIM	GP	G	A	Pts	PIM
		REGULAR SEASON					PLAYOFFS				
1977-78	St. Louis Blues	18	0	0	0	4	....	....	....	....	....
	NHL Totals	**644**	**20**	**126**	**146**	**802**	**74**	**2**	**17**	**19**	**195**

• Brother of Barclay and Bill

Traded to **St. Louis** by **NY Rangers** with Gary Sabourin, Tim Ecclestone and Gord Kannegiesser for Rod Seiling, June 6, 1967.

PLAMONDON, Gerry

Left wing. Shoots left. 5'8", 170 lbs. Born, Sherbrooke, Que., January 5, 1925.

Season	Club	GP	G	A	Pts	PIM	GP	G	A	Pts	PIM
1945-46 ◆	Montreal Canadiens	6	0	2	2	2	1	0	0	0	0
1947-48	Montreal Canadiens	3	1	1	2	0	....	....	....	....	....
1948-49	Montreal Canadiens	27	5	5	10	8	7	5	1	6	0
1949-50	Montreal Canadiens	37	1	5	6	0	3	0	1	1	2
1950-51	Montreal Canadiens	1	0	0	0	0	....	....	....	....	....
	NHL Totals	**74**	**7**	**13**	**20**	**10**	**11**	**5**	**2**	**7**	**2**

Traded to **Pittsburgh** (AHL) by **Montreal** for cash, November 24, 1944.

PLANTE, Cam

Defense. Shoots left. 6'1", 195 lbs. Born, Brandon, Man., March 12, 1964.
(Toronto's 5th choice, 133rd overall, in 1983 Entry Draft).

Season	Club	GP	G	A	Pts	PIM	GP	G	A	Pts	PIM
1984-85	Toronto Maple Leafs	2	0	0	0	0	....	....	....	....	....
	NHL Totals	**2**	**0**	**0**	**0**	**0**	....	....	....	....	....

PLANTE, Dan

Right wing. Shoots right. 5'11", 202 lbs. Born, Hayward, WI, October 5, 1971.
(NY Islanders' 3rd choice, 48th overall, in 1990 Entry Draft).

Season	Club	GP	G	A	Pts	PIM	GP	G	A	Pts	PIM
1993-94	New York Islanders	12	0	1	1	4	1	1	0	1	2
1995-96	New York Islanders	73	5	3	8	50	....	....	....	....	....
1996-97	New York Islanders	67	4	9	13	75	....	....	....	....	....
1997-98	New York Islanders	7	0	1	1	6	....	....	....	....	....
	NHL Totals	**159**	**9**	**14**	**23**	**135**	**1**	**1**	**0**	**1**	**2**

PLANTE, Derek

Center. Shoots left. 5'11", 181 lbs. Born, Cloquet, MN, January 17, 1971.
(Buffalo's 7th choice, 161st overall, in 1989 Entry Draft).

Season	Club	GP	G	A	Pts	PIM	GP	G	A	Pts	PIM
1993-94	Buffalo Sabres	77	21	35	56	24	7	1	0	1	0
1994-95	Buffalo Sabres	47	3	19	22	12	....	....	....	....	....
1995-96	Buffalo Sabres	76	23	33	56	28	....	....	....	....	....
1996-97	Buffalo Sabres	82	27	26	53	24	12	4	6	10	4
1997-98	Buffalo Sabres	72	13	21	34	26	11	0	3	3	10
1998-99	Buffalo Sabres	41	4	11	15	12	....	....	....	....	....
◆	Dallas Stars	10	2	3	5	4	6	1	0	1	4
99-2000	Dallas Stars	16	1	1	2	2	....	....	....	....	....
	Chicago Blackhawks	17	1	1	2	2	....	....	....	....	....
2000-01	Philadelphia Flyers	12	1	2	3	4	5	0	1	1	0
	NHL Totals	**450**	**96**	**152**	**248**	**138**	**41**	**6**	**10**	**16**	**18**

Traded to **Dallas** by **Buffalo** for Dallas' 2nd round choice (Michael Zigomanis) in 1999 Entry Draft, March 23, 1999. Traded to **Chicago** by **Dallas** with Kevin Dean and Dallas' 2nd round choice (Matt Keith) in 2001 Entry Draft for Sylvain Cote and Dave Manson, February 8, 2000. Signed as a free agent by **Philadelphia**, July 26, 2000.

PLANTE, Pierre

Right wing. Shoots right. 6'1", 190 lbs. Born, Valleyfield, Que., May 14, 1951.
(Philadelphia's 2nd choice, 9th overall, in 1971 Amateur Draft).

Season	Club	GP	G	A	Pts	PIM	GP	G	A	Pts	PIM
1971-72	Philadelphia Flyers	24	1	0	1	15	....	....	....	....	....
1972-73	Philadelphia Flyers	2	0	3	3	0	....	....	....	....	....
	St. Louis Blues	49	12	13	25	56	5	2	0	2	15
1973-74	St. Louis Blues	78	26	28	54	85	....	....	....	....	....
1974-75	St. Louis Blues	80	34	32	66	125	2	0	0	0	8
1975-76	St. Louis Blues	74	14	19	33	77	3	0	0	0	6
1976-77	St. Louis Blues	76	18	20	38	77	4	0	0	0	2
1977-78	Chicago Black Hawks	77	10	18	28	59	1	0	0	0	0
1978-79	New York Rangers	70	6	25	31	37	18	0	6	6	20
1979-80	Quebec Nordiques	69	4	14	18	68	....	....	....	....	....
	NHL Totals	**599**	**125**	**172**	**297**	**599**	**33**	**2**	**6**	**8**	**51**

Traded to **St. Louis** by **Philadelphia** with Brent Hughes for Andre Dupont and St. Louis' 3rd round choice (Bob Stumpf) in 1973 Amateur Draft, December 14, 1972. Traded to **Chicago** by **St. Louis** for Dick Redmond, August 9, 1977. Traded to **Minnesota** by **Chicago** to complete transaction that sent Doug Hicks to Chicago (March 14, 1978), May 4, 1978. Claimed on waivers by **Detroit** from **Minnesota**, September 13, 1978. Claimed by **NY Rangers** from **Detroit** in Waiver Draft, October 2, 1978. Claimed by **Quebec** from **NY Rangers** in Expansion Draft, June 13, 1979.

PLANTERY, Mark

Defense. Shoots left. 6'1", 185 lbs. Born, St. Catharines, Ont., August 14, 1959.

Season	Club	GP	G	A	Pts	PIM	GP	G	A	Pts	PIM
1980-81	Winnipeg Jets	25	1	5	6	14	....	....	....	....	....
	NHL Totals	**25**	**1**	**5**	**6**	**14**	....	....	....	....	....

Signed as a free agent by **Winnipeg**, October 5, 1979.

PLAVSIC, Adrien

Defense. Shoots left. 6'1", 200 lbs. Born, Montreal, Que., January 13, 1970.
(St. Louis' 2nd choice, 30th overall, in 1988 Entry Draft).

Season	Club	GP	G	A	Pts	PIM	GP	G	A	Pts	PIM
1989-90	St. Louis Blues	4	0	1	1	2	....	....	....	....	....
	Vancouver Canucks	11	3	2	5	8	....	....	....	....	....
1990-91	Vancouver Canucks	48	2	10	12	62	....	....	....	....	....
1991-92	Vancouver Canucks	16	1	9	10	14	13	1	7	8	4
1992-93	Vancouver Canucks	57	6	21	27	53	....	....	....	....	....
1993-94	Vancouver Canucks	47	1	9	10	6	....	....	....	....	....
1994-95	Vancouver Canucks	3	0	1	1	4	....	....	....	....	....
	Tampa Bay Lightning	15	2	1	3	4	....	....	....	....	....
1995-96	Tampa Bay Lightning	7	1	2	3	6	....	....	....	....	....
1996-97	Mighty Ducks of Anaheim	6	0	0	0	2	....	....	....	....	....
	NHL Totals	**214**	**16**	**56**	**72**	**161**	**13**	**1**	**7**	**8**	**4**

Traded to **Vancouver** by **St. Louis** with Montreal's 1st round choice (previously acquired, Vancouver selected Shawn Antoski) in 1990 Entry Draft and St. Louis' 2nd round choice (later traded to Montreal – Montreal selected Craig Darby) in 1991 Entry Draft for Rich Sutter, Harold Snepsts and St. Louis' 2nd round choice (previously acquired, St. Louis selected Craig Johnson) in 1990 Entry Draft, March 6, 1990. Traded to **Tampa Bay** by **Vancouver** for Tampa Bay's 5th round choice (David Darguzas) in 1997 Entry Draft, March 23, 1995. Signed as a free agent by **Anaheim**, September 6, 1996.

PLAXTON, Hugh

Left wing. Shoots left. 5'10", 184 lbs. Born, Barrie, Ont., May 16, 1904.

Season	Club	GP	G	A	Pts	PIM	GP	G	A	Pts	PIM
1932-33	Montreal Maroons	15	1	2	3	4	....	....	....	....	....
	NHL Totals	**15**	**1**	**2**	**3**	**4**	....	....	....	....	....

Rights traded to **Toronto** by **Boston** with Eric Pettinger for the rights to George Owen, January 10, 1929. Signed as a free agent by **Mtl. Maroons**, October, 1932.

PLAYFAIR, Jim

Defense. Shoots left. 6'4", 200 lbs. Born, Fort St. James, B.C., May 22, 1964.
(Edmonton's 1st choice, 20th overall, in 1982 Entry Draft).

Season	Club	GP	G	A	Pts	PIM	GP	G	A	Pts	PIM
1983-84	Edmonton Oilers	2	1	1	2	2	....	....	....	....	....
1987-88	Chicago Blackhawks	12	1	3	4	21	....	....	....	....	....
1988-89	Chicago Blackhawks	7	0	0	0	28	....	....	....	....	....
	NHL Totals	**21**	**2**	**4**	**6**	**51**	....	....	....	....	....

• Brother of Larry

Signed as a free agent by **Chicago**, July 31, 1987.

PLAYFAIR, Larry

Defense. Shoots left. 6'4", 205 lbs. Born, Fort St. James, B.C., June 23, 1958.
(Buffalo's 1st choice, 13th overall, in 1978 Amateur Draft).

Season	Club	GP	G	A	Pts	PIM	GP	G	A	Pts	PIM
1978-79	Buffalo Sabres	26	0	3	3	60	....	....	....	....	....
1979-80	Buffalo Sabres	79	2	10	12	145	14	0	2	2	29
1980-81	Buffalo Sabres	75	3	9	12	169	8	0	0	0	26
1981-82	Buffalo Sabres	77	6	10	16	258	4	0	0	0	22
1982-83	Buffalo Sabres	79	4	13	17	180	5	0	1	1	11
1983-84	Buffalo Sabres	76	5	11	16	211	3	0	0	0	0
1984-85	Buffalo Sabres	72	3	14	17	157	5	0	3	3	9
1985-86	Buffalo Sabres	47	1	2	3	100	....	....	....	....	....
	Los Angeles Kings	14	0	1	1	26	....	....	....	....	....
1986-87	Los Angeles Kings	37	2	7	9	181	....	....	....	....	....
1987-88	Los Angeles Kings	54	0	7	7	197	3	0	0	0	14
1988-89	Los Angeles Kings	6	0	3	3	16	....	....	....	....	....
	Buffalo Sabres	42	0	3	3	110	1	0	0	0	0
1989-90	Buffalo Sabres	4	0	1	1	2	....	....	....	....	....
	NHL Totals	**688**	**26**	**94**	**120**	**1812**	**43**	**0**	**6**	**6**	**111**

• Brother of Jim

Traded to **Los Angeles** by **Buffalo** with Sean McKenna and Ken Baumgartner for Brian Engblom and Doug Smith, Januray 30, 1986. Traded to **Buffalo** by **Los Angeles** for Bob Logan and Buffalo's 9th round choice (Jim Giacin) in 1989 Entry Draft, Ocotber 21, 1988.

PLEAU, Larry

USHOF

Center. Shoots left. 6'1", 190 lbs. Born, Lynn, MA, January 29, 1947.

Season	Club	GP	G	A	Pts	PIM	GP	G	A	Pts	PIM
1969-70	Montreal Canadiens	20	1	0	1	0	....	....	....	....	....
1970-71	Montreal Canadiens	19	1	5	6	8	....	....	....	....	....
1971-72	Montreal Canadiens	55	7	10	17	19	4	0	0	0	0
	NHL Totals	**94**	**9**	**15**	**24**	**27**	**4**	**0**	**0**	**0**	**0**

Claimed by **Toronto** from **Montreal** in Intra-League Draft, June 5, 1972.

PLETKA, Vaclav

Right wing. Shoots left. 5'11", 182 lbs. Born, Mlada Boleslav, Czech., June 8, 1979.
(Philadelphia's 5th choice, 208th overall, in 1999 Entry Draft).

Season	Club	GP	G	A	Pts	PIM	GP	G	A	Pts	PIM
2001-02	Philadelphia Flyers	1	0	0	0	0	....	....	....	....	....
	NHL Totals	**1**	**0**	**0**	**0**	**0**	....	....	....	....	....

PLETSCH, Charles

Defense. Born, Chesley, Ont., 1893.

Season	Club	GP	G	A	Pts	PIM	GP	G	A	Pts	PIM
1920-21	Hamilton Tigers	1	0	0	0	0	....	....	....	....	....
	NHL Totals	**1**	**0**	**0**	**0**	**0**	....	....	....	....	....

Signed as a free agent by **Hamilton**, December 31, 1920.

PLETT, Willi

Right wing. Shoots right. 6'3", 205 lbs. Born, Asuncion, Paraguay, June 7, 1955.
(Atlanta's 4th choice, 80th overall, in 1975 Amateur Draft).

Season	Club	GP	G	A	Pts	PIM	GP	G	A	Pts	PIM
1975-76	Atlanta Flames	4	0	0	0	0	....	....	....	....	....
1976-77	Atlanta Flames	64	33	23	56	123	3	1	0	1	19
1977-78	Atlanta Flames	78	22	21	43	171	....	....	....	....	....
1978-79	Atlanta Flames	74	23	20	43	213	2	1	0	1	29
1979-80	Atlanta Flames	76	13	19	32	231	4	1	0	1	15
1980-81	Calgary Flames	78	38	30	68	239	15	8	4	12	89

Season	Club	GP	G	A	Pts	PIM	GP	G	A	Pts	PIM
		REGULAR SEASON					PLAYOFFS				
1981-82	Calgary Flames	78	21	36	57	288	3	1	2	3	39
1982-83	Minnesota North Stars	71	25	14	39	170	9	1	3	4	38
1983-84	Minnesota North Stars	73	15	23	38	316	16	6	2	8	51
1984-85	Minnesota North Stars	47	14	14	28	157	9	3	6	9	67
1985-86	Minnesota North Stars	59	10	7	17	231	5	0	1	1	45
1986-87	Minnesota North Stars	67	6	5	11	263	....	....	....	....	....
1987-88	Boston Bruins	65	2	3	5	170	17	2	4	6	74
	NHL Totals	**834**	**222**	**215**	**437**	**2572**	**83**	**24**	**22**	**46**	**466**

Calder Memorial Trophy (1977)

Transferred to **Calgary** after **Atlanta** franchise relocated, June 24, 1980. Traded to **Minnesota** by **Calgary** with Calgary's 4th round choice (Dusan Pasek) in 1982 Entry Draft for Steve Christoff, Bill Nyrop and St. Louis' 2nd round choice (previously acquired, Calgary selected Dave Reierson) in 1982 Entry Draft, June 7, 1982. Traded to **NY Rangers** by **Minnesota** for Pat Price, September 8, 1987. Claimed by **Boston** from **NY Rangers** in Waiver Draft, October 5, 1987.

PLUMB, Rob

Left wing. Shoots left. 5'8", 166 lbs. Born, Kingston, Ont., August 29, 1957.
(Detroit's 10th choice, 163rd overall, in 1977 Amateur Draft).

Season	Club	GP	G	A	Pts	PIM	GP	G	A	Pts	PIM
1977-78	Detroit Red Wings	7	2	1	3	0	....	....	....	....	....
1978-79	Detroit Red Wings	7	1	1	2	2	....	....	....	....	....
	NHL Totals	**14**	**3**	**2**	**5**	**2**	....	....	....	....	....

• Brother of Ron

PLUMB, Ron

Defense. Shoots left. 5'10", 175 lbs. Born, Kingston, Ont., July 17, 1950.
(Boston's 3rd choice, 9th overall, in 1970 Amateur Draft).

Season	Club	GP	G	A	Pts	PIM	GP	G	A	Pts	PIM
1979-80	Hartford Whalers	26	3	4	7	14	....	....	....	....	....
	NHL Totals	**26**	**3**	**4**	**7**	**14**	....	....	....	....	....

• Brother of Rob

Rights retained by **Hartford** prior to Expansion Draft, June 9, 1979.

POAPST, Steve

Defense. Shoots left. 6', 200 lbs. Born, Cornwall, Ont., January 3, 1969.

Season	Club	GP	G	A	Pts	PIM	GP	G	A	Pts	PIM
1995-96	Washington Capitals	3	1	0	1	0	6	0	0	0	0
1998-99	Washington Capitals	22	0	0	0	8	....	....	....	....	....
2000-01	Chicago Blackhawks	36	2	3	5	12	....	....	....	....	....
2001-02	Chicago Blackhawks	56	1	7	8	30	5	0	0	0	0
2002-03	Chicago Blackhawks	75	2	11	13	50	....	....	....	....	....
	NHL Totals	**192**	**6**	**21**	**27**	**100**	**11**	**0**	**0**	**0**	**0**

Signed as a free agent by **Washington**, February 4, 1995. Signed as a free agent by **Chicago**, July 27, 2000.

POCZA, Harvie

Left wing. Shoots left. 6'2", 200 lbs. Born, Lethbridge, Alta., September 22, 1959.
(Washington's 3rd choice, 67th overall, in 1979 Entry Draft).

Season	Club	GP	G	A	Pts	PIM	GP	G	A	Pts	PIM
1979-80	Washington Capitals	1	0	0	0	0	....	....	....	....	....
1981-82	Washington Capitals	2	0	0	0	2	....	....	....	....	....
	NHL Totals	**3**	**0**	**0**	**0**	**2**	....	....	....	....	....

PODDUBNY, Walt

Left wing. Shoots left. 6'1", 210 lbs. Born, Thunder Bay, Ont., February 14, 1960.
(Edmonton's 4th choice, 90th overall, in 1980 Entry Draft).

Season	Club	GP	G	A	Pts	PIM	GP	G	A	Pts	PIM
1981-82	Edmonton Oilers	4	0	0	0	0	....	....	....	....	....
	Toronto Maple Leafs	11	3	4	7	8	....	....	....	....	....
1982-83	Toronto Maple Leafs	72	28	31	59	71	4	3	1	4	0
1983-84	Toronto Maple Leafs	38	11	14	25	48	....	....	....	....	....
1984-85	Toronto Maple Leafs	32	5	15	20	26	....	....	....	....	....
1985-86	Toronto Maple Leafs	33	12	22	34	25	9	4	1	5	4
1986-87	New York Rangers	75	40	47	87	49	6	0	0	0	8
1987-88	New York Rangers	77	38	50	88	76	....	....	....	....	....
1988-89	Quebec Nordiques	72	38	37	75	107	....	....	....	....	....
1989-90	New Jersey Devils	33	4	10	14	28	....	....	....	....	....
1990-91	New Jersey Devils	14	4	6	10	10	....	....	....	....	....
1991-92	New Jersey Devils	7	1	2	3	6	....	....	....	....	....
	NHL Totals	**468**	**184**	**238**	**422**	**454**	**19**	**7**	**2**	**9**	**12**

Played in NHL All-Star Game (1989)

Traded to **Toronto** by **Edmonton** with Phil Drouillard for Laurie Boschman, March 9, 1982. Traded to **NY Rangers** by **Toronto** for Mike Allison, August 18, 1986. Traded to **Quebec** by **NY Rangers** with Jari Gronstad, Bruce Bell and the NY Rangers' 4th round choice (Eric Dubois) in 1989 Entry Draft for Jason Lafreniere and Normand Rochefort, August 1, 1988. Traded to **New Jersey** by **Quebec** with Quebec's 4th round choice (Mike Bodnarchuk) in 1990 Entry Draft for Joe Cirella, Claude Loiselle and New Jersey's 8th round choice (Alexander Karpovtsev) in 1990 Entry Draft, June 17, 1989.

PODEIN, Shjon

Left wing. Shoots left. 6'2", 200 lbs. Born, Rochester, MN, March 5, 1968.
(Edmonton's 9th choice, 166th overall, in 1988 Entry Draft).

Season	Club	GP	G	A	Pts	PIM	GP	G	A	Pts	PIM
1992-93	Edmonton Oilers	40	13	6	19	25	....	....	....	....	....
1993-94	Edmonton Oilers	28	3	5	8	8	....	....	....	....	....
1994-95	Philadelphia Flyers	44	3	7	10	33	15	1	3	4	10
1995-96	Philadelphia Flyers	79	15	10	25	89	12	1	2	3	50
1996-97	Philadelphia Flyers	82	14	18	32	41	19	4	3	7	16
1997-98	Philadelphia Flyers	82	11	13	24	53	5	0	0	0	10
1998-99	Philadelphia Flyers	14	1	0	1	0	....	....	....	....	....
	Colorado Avalanche	41	2	6	8	24	19	1	1	2	12
99-2000	Colorado Avalanche	75	11	8	19	29	17	5	0	5	8
2000-01 ♦	Colorado Avalanche	82	15	17	32	68	23	2	3	5	14
2001-02	Colorado Avalanche	41	6	6	12	39	....	....	....	....	....
	St. Louis Blues	23	2	4	6	2	10	0	0	0	6
2002-03	St. Louis Blues	68	4	6	10	28	7	0	1	1	6
	NHL Totals	**699**	**100**	**106**	**206**	**439**	**127**	**14**	**13**	**27**	**132**

King Clancy Memorial Trophy (2001)

Signed as a free agent by **Philadelphia**, July 27, 1994. Traded to **Colorado** by **Philadelphia** for Keith Jones, November 12, 1998. Traded to **St. Louis** by **Colorado** for Mike Keane, February 11, 2002.

PODKONICKY, Andrej

Center. Shoots left. 6'2", 202 lbs. Born, Zvolen, Czech., May 9, 1978.
(St. Louis' 8th choice, 196th overall, in 1996 Entry Draft).

Season	Club	GP	G	A	Pts	PIM	GP	G	A	Pts	PIM
2000-01	Florida Panthers	6	1	0	1	2	....	....	....	....	....
	NHL Totals	**6**	**1**	**0**	**1**	**2**	....	....	....	....	....

Traded to **Florida** by **St. Louis** for Eric Boguniecki, December 17, 2000. Signed as a free agent by **Washington**, July 14, 2003.

PODLOSKI, Ray

Center. Shoots left. 6'2", 210 lbs. Born, Edmonton, Alta., January 5, 1966.
(Boston's 2nd choice, 40th overall, in 1984 Entry Draft).

Season	Club	GP	G	A	Pts	PIM	GP	G	A	Pts	PIM
1988-89	Boston Bruins	8	0	1	1	17	....	....	....	....	....
	NHL Totals	**8**	**0**	**1**	**1**	**17**	....	....	....	....	....

PODOLLAN, Jason

Right wing. Shoots right. 6'1", 198 lbs. Born, Vernon, B.C., February 18, 1976.
(Florida's 3rd choice, 31st overall, in 1994 Entry Draft).

Season	Club	GP	G	A	Pts	PIM	GP	G	A	Pts	PIM
1996-97	Florida Panthers	19	1	1	2	4	....	....	....	....	....
	Toronto Maple Leafs	10	0	3	3	6	....	....	....	....	....
1998-99	Toronto Maple Leafs	4	0	0	0	0	....	....	....	....	....
	Los Angeles Kings	6	0	0	0	5	....	....	....	....	....
99-2000	Los Angeles Kings	1	0	1	1	2	....	....	....	....	....
2001-02	New York Islanders	1	0	0	0	2	....	....	....	....	....
	NHL Totals	**41**	**1**	**5**	**6**	**19**	....	....	....	....	....

Traded to **Toronto** by **Florida** for Kirk Muller, March 18, 1997. Traded to **Los Angeles** by **Toronto** with Toronto's 3rd round choice (Cory Campbell) in 1999 Entry Draft for Yanic Perreault, March 23, 1999. Claimed by **Tampa Bay** from **Los Angeles** in Waiver Draft, September 29, 2000. Signed as a free agent by **NY Islanders**, August 24, 2001.

PODOLSKY, Nels

Left wing. Shoots left. 5'10", 170 lbs. Born, Winnipeg, Man., December 19, 1925.

Season	Club	GP	G	A	Pts	PIM	GP	G	A	Pts	PIM
1948-49	Detroit Red Wings	1	0	0	0	0	7	0	0	0	4
	NHL Totals	**1**	**0**	**0**	**0**	**0**	**7**	**0**	**0**	**0**	**4**

POESCHEK, Rudy

Right wing/Defense. Shoots right. 6'2", 218 lbs. Born, Kamloops, B.C., September 29, 1966.
(NY Rangers' 12th choice, 238th overall, in 1985 Entry Draft).

Season	Club	GP	G	A	Pts	PIM	GP	G	A	Pts	PIM
1987-88	New York Rangers	1	0	0	0	2	....	....	....	....	....
1988-89	New York Rangers	52	0	2	2	199	....	....	....	....	....
1989-90	New York Rangers	15	0	0	0	55	....	....	....	....	....
1990-91	Winnipeg Jets	1	0	0	0	5	....	....	....	....	....
1991-92	Winnipeg Jets	4	0	0	0	17	....	....	....	....	....
1993-94	Tampa Bay Lightning	71	3	6	9	118	....	....	....	....	....
1994-95	Tampa Bay Lightning	25	1	1	2	92	....	....	....	....	....
1995-96	Tampa Bay Lightning	57	1	3	4	88	3	0	0	0	12
1996-97	Tampa Bay Lightning	60	0	6	6	120	....	....	....	....	....
1997-98	St. Louis Blues	50	1	7	8	64	2	0	0	0	6
1998-99	St. Louis Blues	16	0	0	0	33	....	....	....	....	....
99-2000	St. Louis Blues	12	0	0	0	24	....	....	....	....	....
	NHL Totals	**364**	**6**	**25**	**31**	**817**	**5**	**0**	**0**	**0**	**18**

Traded to **Winnipeg** by **NY Rangers** for Guy Larose, January 22, 1991. Signed as a free agent by **Toronto**, July 8, 1992. Signed as a free agent by **Tampa Bay**, August 10, 1993. Signed as a free agent by **St. Louis**, July 31, 1997.

POETA, Tony

Right wing. Shoots left. 5'5", 168 lbs. Born, North Bay, Ont., March 4, 1933.

Season	Club	GP	G	A	Pts	PIM	GP	G	A	Pts	PIM
1951-52	Chicago Black Hawks	1	0	0	0	0	....	....	....	....	....
	NHL Totals	**1**	**0**	**0**	**0**	**0**	....	....	....	....	....

POILE, Bud

HHOF

Right wing. Shoots right. 6', 189 lbs. Born, Fort William, Ont., February 10, 1924.

Season	Club	GP	G	A	Pts	PIM	GP	G	A	Pts	PIM
1942-43	Toronto Maple Leafs	48	16	19	35	24	6	2	4	6	4
1943-44	Toronto Maple Leafs	11	6	8	14	9	....	....	....	....	....
1945-46	Toronto Maple Leafs	9	1	8	9	0	....	....	....	....	....
1946-47 ♦	Toronto Maple Leafs	59	19	17	36	19	7	2	0	2	2
1947-48	Toronto Maple Leafs	4	2	0	2	0	....	....	....	....	....
	Chicago Black Hawks	54	23	29	52	17	....	....	....	....	....
1948-49	Chicago Black Hawks	4	0	0	0	2	....	....	....	....	....
	Detroit Red Wings	56	21	21	42	6	10	0	1	1	2

Season	Club	GP	G	A	Pts	PIM	GP	G	A	Pts	PIM
		REGULAR SEASON					PLAYOFFS				
1949-50	New York Rangers	27	3	6	9	8	....	....	....	....	....
	Boston Bruins	39	16	14	30	6	....	....	....	....	....
	NHL Totals	**311**	**107**	**122**	**229**	**91**	**23**	**4**	**5**	**9**	**8**

• Brother of Don • NHL Second All-Star Team (1948) • Lester Patrick Trophy (1989)

Played in NHL All-Star Game (1947, 1948)

Traded to **Chicago** by **Toronto** with Gus Bodnar, Gaye Stewart, Ernie Dickens and Bob Goldham for Max Bentley and Cy Thomas, November 2, 1947. Traded to **Detroit** by **Chicago** with George Gee for Jim Conacher, Bep Guidolin and Doug McCaig, October 25, 1948. Traded to **NY Rangers** by **Detroit** for cash, August 16, 1949. Traded to **Boston** by **NY Rangers** for cash, December 22, 1949.

POILE, Don

Center. Shoots left. 5'11", 160 lbs. Born, Fort William, Ont., June 1, 1932.

Season	Club	GP	G	A	Pts	PIM	GP	G	A	Pts	PIM
1954-55	Detroit Red Wings	4	0	0	0	0	....	....	....	....	....
1957-58	Detroit Red Wings	62	7	9	16	12	4	0	0	0	0
	NHL Totals	**66**	**7**	**9**	**16**	**12**	**4**	**0**	**0**	**0**	**0**

• Brother of Bud

Played in NHL All-Star Game (1954)

Traded to **Hershey** (AHL) by **Detroit** with Hec Lalande and cash for Dunc Fisher, April 23, 1958.

POIRIER, Gordie

Center. Shoots left. 5'6", 150 lbs. Born, Maple Creek, Sask., October 27, 1914.

Season	Club	GP	G	A	Pts	PIM	GP	G	A	Pts	PIM
1939-40	Montreal Canadiens	10	0	0	0	0	....	....	....	....	....
	NHL Totals	**10**	**0**	**0**	**0**	**0**	....	....	....	....	....

Signed as a free agent by **Montreal**, February 14, 1940.

POLANIC, Tom

Defense. Shoots left. 6'3", 205 lbs. Born, Toronto, Ont., April 2, 1943.

Season	Club	GP	G	A	Pts	PIM	GP	G	A	Pts	PIM
1969-70	Minnesota North Stars	16	0	2	2	53	5	1	1	2	4
1970-71	Minnesota North Stars	3	0	0	0	0	....	....	....	....	....
	NHL Totals	**19**	**0**	**2**	**2**	**53**	**5**	**1**	**1**	**2**	**4**

Traded to **Phoenix** (WHL) by **Toronto** for cash, September 12, 1967. Traded to **Minnesota** by **Phoenix** (WHL) for Brian D. Smith and Milan Marcetta, February 11, 1969.

POLICH, John

Right wing. Shoots right. 6'2", 200 lbs. Born, Hibbing, MN, July 8, 1916.

Season	Club	GP	G	A	Pts	PIM	GP	G	A	Pts	PIM
1939-40	New York Rangers	1	0	0	0	0	....	....	....	....	....
1940-41	New York Rangers	2	0	1	1	0	....	....	....	....	....
	NHL Totals	**3**	**0**	**1**	**1**	**0**	....	....	....	....	....

Signed as a free agent by **NY Rangers**, October 13, 1939. Traded to **Pittsburgh** (AHL) by **NY Rangers** for cash, September 11, 1941. • Refused to report and retired from professional play, October 10, 1941.

POLICH, Mike

Center/Left wing. Shoots left. 5'8", 170 lbs. Born, Hibbing, MN, December 19, 1952.

Season	Club	GP	G	A	Pts	PIM	GP	G	A	Pts	PIM
1976-77 ♦	Montreal Canadiens	....	....	....	....	....	5	0	0	0	0
1977-78	Montreal Canadiens	1	0	0	0	0	....	....	....	....	....
1978-79	Minnesota North Stars	73	6	10	16	18	....	....	....	....	....
1979-80	Minnesota North Stars	78	10	14	24	20	15	2	1	3	2
1980-81	Minnesota North Stars	74	8	5	13	19	3	0	0	0	0
	NHL Totals	**226**	**24**	**29**	**53**	**57**	**23**	**2**	**1**	**3**	**2**

Signed as a free agent by **Montreal**, September 27, 1975. Signed as a free agent by **Minnesota**, September 6, 1978.

POLIS, Greg

Left wing. Shoots left. 6', 195 lbs. Born, Westlock, Alta., August 8, 1950.
(Pittsburgh's 1st choice, 7th overall, in 1970 Amateur Draft).

Season	Club	GP	G	A	Pts	PIM	GP	G	A	Pts	PIM
1970-71	Pittsburgh Penguins	61	18	15	33	40	....	....	....	....	....
1971-72	Pittsburgh Penguins	76	30	19	49	38	4	0	2	2	0
1972-73	Pittsburgh Penguins	78	26	23	49	36	....	....	....	....	....
1973-74	Pittsburgh Penguins	41	14	13	27	32	....	....	....	....	....
	St. Louis Blues	37	8	12	20	24	....	....	....	....	....
1974-75	New York Rangers	76	26	15	41	55	3	0	0	0	6
1975-76	New York Rangers	79	15	21	36	77	....	....	....	....	....
1976-77	New York Rangers	77	16	23	39	44	....	....	....	....	....
1977-78	New York Rangers	37	7	16	23	12	....	....	....	....	....
1978-79	New York Rangers	6	1	1	2	8	....	....	....	....	....
	Washington Capitals	19	12	6	18	6	....	....	....	....	....
1979-80	Washington Capitals	28	1	5	6	19	....	....	....	....	....
	NHL Totals	**615**	**174**	**169**	**343**	**391**	**7**	**0**	**2**	**2**	**6**

Played in NHL All-Star Game (1971, 1972, 1973)

Traded to **St. Louis** by **Pittsburgh** with Bryan Watson and Pittsburgh's 2nd round choice (Bob Hess) in 1974 Amateur Draft for Steve Durbano, Ab DeMarco Jr. and Bob Kelly, January 17, 1974. Traded to **NY Rangers** by **St. Louis** for Larry Sacharuk and NY Rangers' 1st round choice (later traded back to NY Rangers – NY Rangers selected Lucien DeBlois) in 1977 Entry Draft, August 29, 1974. Claimed on waivers by **Washington** from **NY Rangers**, January 15, 1979.

POLIZIANI, Dan

Right wing. Shoots right. 5'11", 158 lbs. Born, Sydney, N.S., January 8, 1935.

Season	Club	GP	G	A	Pts	PIM	GP	G	A	Pts	PIM
1958-59	Boston Bruins	1	0	0	0	0	3	0	0	0	0
	NHL Totals	**1**	**0**	**0**	**0**	**0**	**3**	**0**	**0**	**0**	**0**

Claimed by **Boston** from **Cleveland** (AHL) in Inter-League Draft, June 3, 1958. Traded to **Hershey** by **Boston** (Providence-AHL) for Willie Marshall, June, 1963.

POLONICH, Dennis

Center/Right wing. Shoots right. 5'6", 166 lbs. Born, Foam Lake, Sask., December 4, 1953.
(Detroit's 8th choice, 118th overall, in 1973 Amateur Draft).

Season	Club	GP	G	A	Pts	PIM	GP	G	A	Pts	PIM
		REGULAR SEASON					PLAYOFFS				
1974-75	Detroit Red Wings	4	0	0	0	0	....	....	....	....	....
1975-76	Detroit Red Wings	57	11	12	23	302	....	....	....	....	....
1976-77	Detroit Red Wings	79	18	28	46	274	....	....	....	....	....
1977-78	Detroit Red Wings	79	16	19	35	254	7	1	0	1	19
1978-79	Detroit Red Wings	62	10	12	22	208	....	....	....	....	....
1979-80	Detroit Red Wings	66	2	8	10	127	....	....	....	....	....
1980-81	Detroit Red Wings	32	2	2	4	77	....	....	....	....	....
1982-83	Detroit Red Wings	11	0	1	1	0	....	....	....	....	....
	NHL Totals	**390**	**59**	**82**	**141**	**1242**	**7**	**1**	**0**	**1**	**19**

PONIKAROVSKY, Alexei

Left wing. Shoots left. 6'4", 196 lbs. Born, Kiev, USSR, April 9, 1980.
(Toronto's 4th choice, 87th overall, in 1998 Entry Draft).

Season	Club	GP	G	A	Pts	PIM	GP	G	A	Pts	PIM
2000-01	Toronto Maple Leafs	22	1	3	4	14	....	....	....	....	....
2001-02	Toronto Maple Leafs	8	2	0	2	0	10	0	0	0	4
2002-03	Toronto Maple Leafs	13	0	3	3	11	....	....	....	....	....
	NHL Totals	**43**	**3**	**6**	**9**	**25**	**10**	**0**	**0**	**0**	**4**

POOLEY, Paul

Center. Shoots right. 6', 175 lbs. Born, Exeter, Ont., August 2, 1960.

Season	Club	GP	G	A	Pts	PIM	GP	G	A	Pts	PIM
1984-85	Winnipeg Jets	12	0	2	2	0	....	....	....	....	....
1985-86	Winnipeg Jets	3	0	1	1	0	....	....	....	....	....
	NHL Totals	**15**	**0**	**3**	**3**	**0**	....	....	....	....	....

Signed as a free agent by **Winnipeg**, May 24, 1984.

POPEIN, Larry

Center. Shoots left. 5'10", 165 lbs. Born, Yorkton, Sask., August 11, 1930.

Season	Club	GP	G	A	Pts	PIM	GP	G	A	Pts	PIM
1954-55	New York Rangers	70	11	17	28	27	....	....	....	....	....
1955-56	New York Rangers	64	14	25	39	37	5	0	1	1	2
1956-57	New York Rangers	67	11	19	30	20	5	0	3	3	0
1957-58	New York Rangers	70	12	22	34	22	6	1	0	1	4
1958-59	New York Rangers	61	13	21	34	28	....	....	....	....	....
1959-60	New York Rangers	66	14	22	36	16	....	....	....	....	....
1960-61	New York Rangers	4	0	1	1	0	....	....	....	....	....
1967-68	Oakland Seals	47	5	14	19	12	....	....	....	....	....
	NHL Totals	**449**	**80**	**141**	**221**	**162**	**16**	**1**	**4**	**5**	**6**

Claimed by **NY Rangers** (Baltimore-AHL) from **NY Rangers** in Reverse Draft, June 13, 1966. Traded to **Oakland** by **NY Rangers** for cash, December, 1967. Traded to **NY Rangers** by **Oakland** for cash, May 14, 1968.

POPIEL, Poul

Defense. Shoots left. 5'10", 175 lbs. Born, Sollested, Denmark, February 28, 1943.

Season	Club	GP	G	A	Pts	PIM	GP	G	A	Pts	PIM
1965-66	Boston Bruins	3	0	1	1	2	....	....	....	....	....
1967-68	Los Angeles Kings	1	0	0	0	0	3	1	0	1	4
1968-69	Detroit Red Wings	62	2	13	15	82	....	....	....	....	....
1969-70	Detroit Red Wings	32	0	4	4	29	1	0	0	0	0
1970-71	Vancouver Canucks	78	10	22	32	61	....	....	....	....	....
1971-72	Vancouver Canucks	38	1	1	2	36	....	....	....	....	....
1979-80	Edmonton Oilers	10	0	0	0	0	....	....	....	....	....
	NHL Totals	**224**	**13**	**41**	**54**	**210**	**4**	**1**	**0**	**1**	**4**

Claimed by **Boston** from **Chicago** in Intra-League Draft, June 9, 1965. Claimed by **Los Angeles** from **Boston** in Expansion Draft, June 6, 1967. Traded to **Detroit** by **Los Angeles** for Ron Anderson, November 12, 1968. Claimed by **Vancouver** from **Detroit** in Expansion Draft, June 10, 1970. Signed as a free agent by **Edmonton**, November 2, 1979.

POPOVIC, Peter

Defense. Shoots left. 6'6", 243 lbs. Born, Koping, Sweden, February 10, 1968.
(Montreal's 5th choice, 93rd overall, in 1988 Entry Draft).

Season	Club	GP	G	A	Pts	PIM	GP	G	A	Pts	PIM
1993-94	Montreal Canadiens	47	2	12	14	26	6	0	1	1	0
1994-95	Montreal Canadiens	33	0	5	5	8	....	....	....	....	....
1995-96	Montreal Canadiens	76	2	12	14	69	6	0	2	2	4
1996-97	Montreal Canadiens	78	1	13	14	32	3	0	0	0	2
1997-98	Montreal Canadiens	69	2	6	8	38	10	1	1	2	2
1998-99	New York Rangers	68	1	4	5	40	....	....	....	....	....
99-2000	Pittsburgh Penguins	54	1	5	6	30	10	0	0	0	10
2000-01	Boston Bruins	60	1	6	7	48	....	....	....	....	....
	NHL Totals	**485**	**10**	**63**	**73**	**291**	**35**	**1**	**4**	**5**	**18**

Traded to **NY Rangers** by **Montreal** for Sylvain Blouin and NY Rangers' 6th round choice (later traded to Phoenix – Phoenix selected Erik Lewerstrom) in 1999 Entry Draft, June 30, 1998. Traded to **Pittsburgh** by **NY Rangers** for Kevin Hatcher, September 30, 1999. Signed as a free agent by **Boston**, July 2, 2000.

PORTLAND, Jack

Defense. Shoots left. 6'2", 185 lbs. Born, Waubaushene, Ont., July 30, 1912.

Season	Club	GP	G	A	Pts	PIM	GP	G	A	Pts	PIM
1933-34	Montreal Canadiens	31	0	2	2	10	2	0	0	0	0
1934-35	Montreal Canadiens	5	0	0	0	2	....	....	....	....	....
	Boston Bruins	15	1	1	2	2	....	....	....	....	....
1935-36	Boston Bruins	2	0	0	0	0	....	....	....	....	....
1936-37	Boston Bruins	46	2	4	6	58	3	0	0	0	4
1937-38	Boston Bruins	48	0	5	5	26	3	0	0	0	4
1938-39 ♦	Boston Bruins	48	4	5	9	46	12	0	0	0	11

Season	Club	GP	G	A	Pts	PIM	GP	G	A	Pts	PIM
		REGULAR SEASON					PLAYOFFS				
1939-40	Boston Bruins	28	0	5	5	16	....	....	....	....	....
	Chicago Black Hawks	16	1	4	5	20	2	0	0	0	2
1940-41	Chicago Black Hawks	5	0	0	0	4	....	....	....	....	....
	Montreal Canadiens	42	2	7	9	34	3	0	1	1	2
1941-42	Montreal Canadiens	46	2	9	11	53	3	0	0	0	0
1942-43	Montreal Canadiens	49	3	14	17	52	5	1	2	3	2
	NHL Totals	**381**	**15**	**56**	**71**	**323**	**33**	**1**	**3**	**4**	**25**

Traded to **Boston** by **Montreal** for Tony Savage and $7,500, December 3, 1934. Traded to **Chicago** by **Boston** for Des Smith, January 27, 1940. Traded to **Montreal** by **Chicago** for $12,500, November 19, 1940.

PORVARI, Jukka

Right wing. Shoots left. 5'11", 175 lbs. Born, Tampere, Finland, January 19, 1954.

Season	Club	GP	G	A	Pts	PIM	GP	G	A	Pts	PIM
1981-82	Colorado Rockies	31	2	6	8	0	....	....	....	....	....
1982-83	New Jersey Devils	8	1	3	4	4	....	....	....	....	....
	NHL Totals	**39**	**3**	**9**	**12**	**4**	....	....	....	....	....

Signed as a free agent by **Colorado**, July 8, 1981. Transferred to **New Jersey** after **Colorado** franchise relocated, June 30, 1982.

POSA, Victor

Left wing/Defense. Shoots left. 6', 195 lbs. Born, Bari, Italy, November 5, 1966.
(Chicago's 7th choice, 137th overall, in 1985 Entry Draft).

Season	Club	GP	G	A	Pts	PIM	GP	G	A	Pts	PIM
1985-86	Chicago Black Hawks	2	0	0	0	2	....	....	....	....	....
	NHL Totals	**2**	**0**	**0**	**0**	**2**	....	....	....	....	....

POSAVAD, Mike

Defense. Shoots right. 5'11", 195 lbs. Born, Brantford, Ont., January 3, 1964.
(St. Louis' 1st choice, 50th overall, in 1982 Entry Draft).

Season	Club	GP	G	A	Pts	PIM	GP	G	A	Pts	PIM
1985-86	St. Louis Blues	6	0	0	0	0	....	....	....	....	....
1986-87	St. Louis Blues	2	0	0	0	0	....	....	....	....	....
	NHL Totals	**8**	**0**	**0**	**0**	**0**	....	....	....	....	....

POSMYK, Marek

Defense. Shoots right. 6'5", 228 lbs. Born, Jihlava, Czech., September 15, 1978.
(Toronto's 1st choice, 36th overall, in 1996 Entry Draft).

Season	Club	GP	G	A	Pts	PIM	GP	G	A	Pts	PIM
99-2000	Tampa Bay Lightning	18	1	2	3	20	....	....	....	....	....
2000-01	Tampa Bay Lightning	1	0	0	0	0	....	....	....	....	....
	NHL Totals	**19**	**1**	**2**	**3**	**20**	....	....	....	....	....

Traded to **Tampa Bay** by **Toronto** with Mike Johnson, Toronto's 5th (Pavel Sedov) and 6th (Aaron Gionet) round choices in 2000 Entry Draft and future considerations for Darcy Tucker, Tampa Bay's 4th round choice (Miguel Delisle) in 2000 Entry Draft and future considerations, February 9, 2000.

POTHIER, Brian

Defense. Shoots right. 6', 195 lbs. Born, New Bedford, MA, April 15, 1977.

Season	Club	GP	G	A	Pts	PIM	GP	G	A	Pts	PIM
2000-01	Atlanta Thrashers	3	0	0	0	2	....	....	....	....	....
2001-02	Atlanta Thrashers	33	3	6	9	22	....	....	....	....	....
2002-03	Ottawa Senators	14	2	4	6	6	1	0	0	0	2
	NHL Totals	**50**	**5**	**10**	**15**	**30**	**1**	**0**	**0**	**0**	**2**

Signed as a free agent by **Atlanta**, March 27, 2000. Traded to **Ottawa** by **Atlanta** for Shawn McEachern and Ottawa's 6th round choice in 2004 Entry Draft, June 29, 2002.

POTI, Tom

Defense. Shoots left. 6'3", 215 lbs. Born, Worcester, MA, March 22, 1977.
(Edmonton's 4th choice, 59th overall, in 1996 Entry Draft).

Season	Club	GP	G	A	Pts	PIM	GP	G	A	Pts	PIM
1998-99	Edmonton Oilers	73	5	16	21	42	4	0	1	1	2
99-2000	Edmonton Oilers	76	9	26	35	65	5	0	1	1	0
2000-01	Edmonton Oilers	81	12	20	32	60	6	0	2	2	2
2001-02	Edmonton Oilers	55	1	16	17	42	....	....	....	....	....
	New York Rangers	11	1	7	8	2	....	....	....	....	....
2002-03	New York Rangers	80	11	37	48	58	....	....	....	....	....
	NHL Totals	**376**	**39**	**122**	**161**	**269**	**15**	**0**	**4**	**4**	**4**

NHL All-Rookie Team (1999)

Played in NHL All-Star Game (2003)

Traded to **NY Rangers** by **Edmonton** with Rem Murray for Mike York and NY Rangers' 4th round choice (Ivan Koltsov) in 2002 Entry Draft, March 19, 2002.

POTOMSKI, Barry

Left wing. Shoots left. 6'2", 215 lbs. Born, Windsor, Ont., November 24, 1972.

Season	Club	GP	G	A	Pts	PIM	GP	G	A	Pts	PIM
1995-96	Los Angeles Kings	33	3	2	5	104	....	....	....	....	....
1996-97	Los Angeles Kings	26	3	2	5	93	....	....	....	....	....
1997-98	San Jose Sharks	9	0	1	1	30	....	....	....	....	....
	NHL Totals	**68**	**6**	**5**	**11**	**227**	....	....	....	....	....

Signed as a free agent by **Los Angeles**, July 7, 1994. Signed as a free agent by **San Jose**, August 15, 1997. Signed as a free agent by **Detroit**, August 13, 1998.

POTVIN, Denis

HHOF

Defense. Shoots left. 6', 205 lbs. Born, Ottawa, Ont., October 29, 1953.
(NY Islanders' 1st choice, 1st overall, in 1973 Amateur Draft).

Season	Club	GP	G	A	Pts	PIM	GP	G	A	Pts	PIM
1973-74	New York Islanders	77	17	37	54	175	....	....	....	....	....
1974-75	New York Islanders	79	21	55	76	105	17	5	9	14	30
1975-76	New York Islanders	78	31	67	98	100	13	5	*14	19	32
1976-77	New York Islanders	80	25	55	80	103	12	6	4	10	20
1977-78	New York Islanders	80	30	64	94	81	7	2	2	4	6
1978-79	New York Islanders	73	31	70	101	58	10	4	7	11	8
1979-80 ◆	New York Islanders	31	8	33	41	44	21	6	13	19	24
1980-81 ◆	New York Islanders	74	20	56	76	104	18	8	17	25	16
1981-82 ◆	New York Islanders	60	24	37	61	83	19	5	16	21	30
1982-83 ◆	New York Islanders	69	12	54	66	60	20	8	12	20	22
1983-84	New York Islanders	78	22	63	85	87	20	1	5	6	28
1984-85	New York Islanders	77	17	51	68	96	10	3	2	5	10
1985-86	New York Islanders	74	21	38	59	78	3	0	1	1	0
1986-87	New York Islanders	58	12	30	42	70	10	2	2	4	21
1987-88	New York Islanders	72	19	32	51	112	5	1	4	5	6
	NHL Totals	**1060**	**310**	**742**	**1052**	**1356**	**185**	**56**	**108**	**164**	**253**

• Brother of Jean • Calder Memorial Trophy (1974) • NHL First All-Star Team (1975, 1976, 1978, 1979, 1981) • James Norris Trophy (1976, 1978, 1979) • NHL Second All-Star Team (1977, 1984)

Played in NHL All-Star Game (1974, 1975, 1976, 1977, 1978, 1981, 1983, 1984, 1988)

• Missed majority of 1979-80 season recovering from thumb injury suffered in game vs. Edmonton, November 30, 1979.

POTVIN, Jean

Defense. Shoots right. 5'11", 188 lbs. Born, Ottawa, Ont., March 25, 1949.

Season	Club	GP	G	A	Pts	PIM	GP	G	A	Pts	PIM
1970-71	Los Angeles Kings	4	1	3	4	2	....	....	....	....	....
1971-72	Los Angeles Kings	39	2	3	5	35	....	....	....	....	....
	Philadelphia Flyers	29	3	12	15	6	....	....	....	....	....
1972-73	Philadelphia Flyers	35	3	9	12	10	....	....	....	....	....
	New York Islanders	10	0	3	3	12	....	....	....	....	....
1973-74	New York Islanders	78	5	23	28	100	....	....	....	....	....
1974-75	New York Islanders	73	9	24	33	59	15	2	4	6	9
1975-76	New York Islanders	78	17	55	72	74	13	0	1	1	2
1976-77	New York Islanders	79	10	36	46	26	11	0	4	4	6
1977-78	New York Islanders	34	1	10	11	8	....	....	....	....	....
	Cleveland Barons	40	3	14	17	30	....	....	....	....	....
1978-79	Minnesota North Stars	64	5	16	21	65	....	....	....	....	....
1979-80 ◆	New York Islanders	32	2	13	15	26	....	....	....	....	....
1980-81	New York Islanders	18	2	3	5	25	....	....	....	....	....
	NHL Totals	**613**	**63**	**224**	**287**	**478**	**39**	**2**	**9**	**11**	**17**

• Brother of Denis

Signed as a free agent by **Los Angeles** (Springfield-AHL), November 15, 1969. Traded to **Philadelphia** by **Los Angeles** with Eddie Joyal, Bill Flett and Ross Lonsberry for Bill Lesuk, Jim Johnson and Serge Bernier, January 28, 1972. Traded to **NY Islanders** by **Philadelphia** with future considerations (Glen Irwin, May 18, 1973) for Terry Crisp, March 5, 1973. Traded to **Cleveland** by **NY Islanders** with Jean-Paul Parise for Wayne Merrick, Darcy Regier and Cleveland's 4th round choice (draft choice cancelled by the Cleveland-Minnesota merger) in the 1978 Amateur Draft, January 10, 1978. Placed on **Minnesota** Reserve List after **Cleveland-Minnesota** Dispersal Draft, June 15, 1978. Signed as a free agent by **NY Islanders**, June 10, 1979.

POTVIN, Marc

Right wing. Shoots right. 6'1", 200 lbs. Born, Ottawa, Ont., January 29, 1967.
(Detroit's 9th choice, 169th overall, in 1986 Entry Draft).

Season	Club	GP	G	A	Pts	PIM	GP	G	A	Pts	PIM
1990-91	Detroit Red Wings	9	0	0	0	55	6	0	0	0	32
1991-92	Detroit Red Wings	5	1	0	1	52	1	0	0	0	0
1992-93	Los Angeles Kings	20	0	1	1	61	1	0	0	0	0
1993-94	Los Angeles Kings	3	0	0	0	26	....	....	....	....	....
	Hartford Whalers	51	2	3	5	246	....	....	....	....	....
1994-95	Boston Bruins	6	0	1	1	4	....	....	....	....	....
1995-96	Boston Bruins	27	0	0	0	12	5	0	1	1	18
	NHL Totals	**121**	**3**	**5**	**8**	**456**	**13**	**0**	**1**	**1**	**50**

Traded to **Los Angeles** by **Detroit** with Jimmy Carson and Gary Shuchuk for Paul Coffey, Sylvain Couturier and Jim Hiller, January 29, 1993. Traded to **Hartford** by **Los Angeles** for Doug Houda, November 3, 1993. Signed as a free agent by **Boston**, June 29, 1994.

POUDRIER, Daniel

Defense. Shoots left. 6'2", 175 lbs. Born, Thetford Mines, Que., February 15, 1964.
(Quebec's 6th choice, 131st overall, in 1982 Entry Draft).

Season	Club	GP	G	A	Pts	PIM	GP	G	A	Pts	PIM
1985-86	Quebec Nordiques	13	1	5	6	10	....	....	....	....	....
1986-87	Quebec Nordiques	6	0	0	0	0	....	....	....	....	....
1987-88	Quebec Nordiques	6	0	0	0	0	....	....	....	....	....
	NHL Totals	**25**	**1**	**5**	**6**	**10**	....	....	....	....	....

POULIN, Daniel

Defense. Shoots right. 5'11", 185 lbs. Born, Robertsville, Que., September 19, 1957.
(Montreal's 18th choice, 167th overall, in 1977 Amateur Draft).

Season	Club	GP	G	A	Pts	PIM	GP	G	A	Pts	PIM
1981-82	Minnesota North Stars	3	1	1	2	2	....	....	....	....	....
	NHL Totals	**3**	**1**	**1**	**2**	**2**	....	....	....	....	....

Signed as a free agent by **Minnesota**, June 16, 1980.

POULIN, Dave

Center. Shoots left. 5'11", 190 lbs. Born, Timmins, Ont., December 17, 1958.

Season	Club	GP	G	A	Pts	PIM	GP	G	A	Pts	PIM
1982-83	Philadelphia Flyers	2	2	0	2	2	3	1	3	4	9
1983-84	Philadelphia Flyers	73	31	45	76	47	3	0	0	0	2
1984-85	Philadelphia Flyers	73	30	44	74	59	11	3	5	8	6
1985-86	Philadelphia Flyers	79	27	42	69	49	5	2	0	2	2
1986-87	Philadelphia Flyers	75	25	45	70	53	15	3	3	6	14
1987-88	Philadelphia Flyers	68	19	32	51	32	7	2	6	8	4
1988-89	Philadelphia Flyers	69	18	17	35	49	19	6	5	11	16
1989-90	Philadelphia Flyers	28	9	8	17	12	....	....	....	....	....
	Boston Bruins	32	6	19	25	12	18	8	5	13	8

Season	Club	GP	G	A	Pts	PIM	GP	G	A	Pts	PIM
		REGULAR SEASON					PLAYOFFS				
1990-91	Boston Bruins	31	8	12	20	25	16	0	9	9	20
1991-92	Boston Bruins	18	4	4	8	18	15	3	3	6	22
1992-93	Boston Bruins	84	16	33	49	62	4	1	1	2	10
1993-94	Washington Capitals	63	6	19	25	52	11	2	2	4	19
1994-95	Washington Capitals	29	4	5	9	10	2	0	0	0	0
	NHL Totals	**724**	**205**	**325**	**530**	**482**	**129**	**31**	**42**	**73**	**132**

Frank J. Selke Trophy (1987) • King Clancy Memorial Trophy (1993)

Played in NHL All-Star Game (1986, 1988)

Signed as a free agent by **Philadelphia**, March 8, 1983. Traded to **Boston** by **Philadelphia** for Ken Linseman, January 16, 1990. • Missed majority of 1991-92 season recovering from groin injury suffered in training camp that required surgery, December 6, 1991. Signed as a free agent by **Washington**, August 3, 1993.

POULIN, Patrick

Center. Shoots left. 6'1", 216 lbs. Born, Vanier, Que., April 23, 1973.
(Hartford's 1st choice, 9th overall, in 1991 Entry Draft).

Season	Club	GP	G	A	Pts	PIM	GP	G	A	Pts	PIM
1991-92	Hartford Whalers	1	0	0	0	2	7	2	1	3	0
1992-93	Hartford Whalers	81	20	31	51	37	....	....	....	....	....
1993-94	Hartford Whalers	9	2	1	3	11	....	....	....	....	....
	Chicago Blackhawks	58	12	13	25	40	4	0	0	0	0
1994-95	Chicago Blackhawks	45	15	15	30	53	16	4	1	5	8
1995-96	Chicago Blackhawks	38	7	8	15	16	....	....	....	....	....
	Tampa Bay Lightning	8	0	1	1	0	2	0	0	0	0
1996-97	Tampa Bay Lightning	73	12	14	26	56	....	....	....	....	....
1997-98	Tampa Bay Lightning	44	2	7	9	19	....	....	....	....	....
	Montreal Canadiens	34	4	6	10	8	3	0	0	0	0
1998-99	Montreal Canadiens	81	8	17	25	21	....	....	....	....	....
99-2000	Montreal Canadiens	82	10	5	15	17	....	....	....	....	....
2000-01	Montreal Canadiens	52	9	11	20	13	....	....	....	....	....
2001-02	Montreal Canadiens	28	0	5	5	6	....	....	....	....	....
	NHL Totals	**634**	**101**	**134**	**235**	**299**	**32**	**6**	**2**	**8**	**8**

Traded to **Chicago** by **Hartford** with Eric Weinrich for Steve Larmer and Bryan Marchment, November 2, 1993. Traded to **Tampa Bay** by **Chicago** with Igor Ulanov and Chicago's 2nd round choice (later traded to New Jersey – New Jersey selected Pierre Dagenais) in 1996 Entry Draft for Enrico Ciccone and Tampa Bay's 2nd round choice (Jeff Paul) in 1996 Entry Draft, March 20, 1996. Traded to **Montreal** by **Tampa Bay** with Mick Vukota and Igor Ulanov for Stephane Richer, Darcy Tucker and David Wilkie, January 15, 1998.

POUZAR, Jaroslav

Left wing. Shoots left. 5'11", 200 lbs. Born, Cakovec, Czech., January 23, 1952.
(Edmonton's 4th choice, 83rd overall, in 1982 Entry Draft).

Season	Club	GP	G	A	Pts	PIM	GP	G	A	Pts	PIM
1982-83	Edmonton Oilers	74	15	18	33	57	1	2	0	2	0
1983-84♦	Edmonton Oilers	67	13	19	32	44	14	1	2	3	12
1984-85♦	Edmonton Oilers	33	4	8	12	28	9	2	1	3	2
1986-87♦	Edmonton Oilers	12	2	3	5	6	5	1	1	2	2
	NHL Totals	**186**	**34**	**48**	**82**	**135**	**29**	**6**	**4**	**10**	**16**

POWELL, Ray

Center. Shoots left. 6', 170 lbs. Born, Timmins, Ont., November 16, 1925.

Season	Club	GP	G	A	Pts	PIM	GP	G	A	Pts	PIM
1950-51	Chicago Black Hawks	31	7	15	22	2	....	....	....	....	....
	NHL Totals	**31**	**7**	**15**	**22**	**2**	....	....	....	....	....

Claimed by **Toronto** from **Fort Worth** (USHL) in Inter-League Draft, June, 1946. Traded to **Detroit** by **Toronto** with Doug Baldwin for Gerry Brown, September 21, 1946. Traded to **Chicago** by **Detroit** with Adam Brown for Leo Reise and Pete Horeck, December 9, 1946. Traded to **Providence** (AHL) by **Chicago** for cash, August 30, 1951.

POWIS, Geoff

Center. Shoots left. 6'1", 170 lbs. Born, Winnipeg, Man., June 14, 1945.

Season	Club	GP	G	A	Pts	PIM	GP	G	A	Pts	PIM
1967-68	Chicago Black Hawks	2	0	0	0	0	....	....	....	....	....
	NHL Totals	**2**	**0**	**0**	**0**	**0**	....	....	....	....	....

POWIS, Lynn

Center. Shoots left. 6', 175 lbs. Born, Maryfield, Sask., July 7, 1949.
(Montreal's 7th choice, 68th overall, in 1969 Amateur Draft).

Season	Club	GP	G	A	Pts	PIM	GP	G	A	Pts	PIM
1973-74	Chicago Black Hawks	57	8	13	21	6	1	0	0	0	0
1974-75	Kansas City Scouts	73	11	20	31	19	....	....	....	....	....
	NHL Totals	**130**	**19**	**33**	**52**	**25**	**1**	**0**	**0**	**0**	**0**

Traded to **Atlanta** by **Montreal** for cash, June 9, 1972. Traded to **Chicago** by **Atlanta** for Mike Baumgartner, August 30, 1973. Claimed by **Kansas City** from **Chicago** in Expansion Draft, June 12, 1974. Traded to **St. Louis** by **Kansas City** with Kansas City's 2nd round choice (Brian Sutter) in 1976 Amateur Draft for Craig Patrick and Denis Dupere, June 18, 1975.

PRAJSLER, Petr

Defense. Shoots left. 6'2", 200 lbs. Born, Hradec Kralove, Czech., September 21, 1965.
(Los Angeles' 5th choice, 93rd overall, in 1985 Entry Draft).

Season	Club	GP	G	A	Pts	PIM	GP	G	A	Pts	PIM
1987-88	Los Angeles Kings	7	0	0	0	2	....	....	....	....	....
1988-89	Los Angeles Kings	2	0	3	3	0	1	0	0	0	0
1989-90	Los Angeles Kings	34	3	7	10	47	3	0	0	0	0
1991-92	Boston Bruins	3	0	0	0	2	....	....	....	....	....
	NHL Totals	**46**	**3**	**10**	**13**	**51**	**4**	**0**	**0**	**0**	**0**

Signed as a free agent by **Boston**, August 1, 1991.

PRATT, Babe

HHOF

Defense. Shoots left. 6'3", 212 lbs. Born, Stony Mountain, Man., January 7, 1916.

Season	Club	GP	G	A	Pts	PIM	GP	G	A	Pts	PIM
1935-36	New York Rangers	17	1	1	2	16	....	....	....	....	....
1936-37	New York Rangers	47	8	7	15	23	9	3	1	4	11
1937-38	New York Rangers	47	5	14	19	56	2	0	0	0	2
1938-39	New York Rangers	48	2	19	21	20	7	1	2	3	9
1939-40♦	New York Rangers	48	4	13	17	61	12	3	1	4	18
1940-41	New York Rangers	47	3	17	20	52	3	1	1	2	6
1941-42	New York Rangers	47	4	24	28	55	6	1	3	4	24
1942-43	New York Rangers	4	0	2	2	6	....	....	....	....	....
	Toronto Maple Leafs	40	12	25	37	44	6	1	2	3	8
1943-44	Toronto Maple Leafs	50	17	40	57	30	5	0	3	3	4
1944-45♦	Toronto Maple Leafs	50	18	23	41	39	13	2	4	6	8
1945-46	Toronto Maple Leafs	41	5	20	25	36	....	....	....	....	....
1946-47	Boston Bruins	31	4	4	8	25	....	....	....	....	....
	NHL Totals	**517**	**83**	**209**	**292**	**463**	**63**	**12**	**17**	**29**	**90**

• Father of Tracy • NHL First All-Star Team (1944) • Hart Trophy (1944) • NHL Second All-Star Team (1945)

Signed as a free agent by **NY Rangers**, October 18, 1935. Traded to **Toronto** by **NY Rangers** for Hank Goldup and Red Garrett, November 27, 1942. • Suspended by NHL President Red Dutton for gambling violations, January 29, 1946. • Suspension lifted by NHL President Red Dutton, February 15, 1946. Traded to **Boston** by **Toronto** for the rights to Eric Pogue and cash, June 19, 1946. Traded to **Cleveland** (AHL) by **Boston** for cash, May 15, 1947.

PRATT, Jack

Center/Defense. Shoots right. 6', 190 lbs. Born, Edinburgh, Scotland, April 13, 1906.

Season	Club	GP	G	A	Pts	PIM	GP	G	A	Pts	PIM
1930-31	Boston Bruins	32	2	0	2	36	4	0	0	0	0
1931-32	Boston Bruins	5	0	0	0	6	....	....	....	....	....
	NHL Totals	**37**	**2**	**0**	**2**	**42**	**4**	**0**	**0**	**0**	**0**

Signed as a free agent by **Boston**, November 5, 1930.

PRATT, Kelly

Right wing. Shoots right. 5'9", 170 lbs. Born, High Prairie, Alta., February 8, 1953.

Season	Club	GP	G	A	Pts	PIM	GP	G	A	Pts	PIM
1974-75	Pittsburgh Penguins	22	0	6	6	15	....	....	....	....	....
	NHL Totals	**22**	**0**	**6**	**6**	**15**	....	....	....	....	....

Traded to **Hershey** (AHL) by **Pittsburgh** for cash, August 28, 1975.

PRATT, Nolan

Defense. Shoots left. 6'3", 200 lbs. Born, Fort McMurray, Alta., August 14, 1975.
(Hartford's 4th choice, 115th overall, in 1993 Entry Draft).

Season	Club	GP	G	A	Pts	PIM	GP	G	A	Pts	PIM
1996-97	Hartford Whalers	9	0	2	2	6	....	....	....	....	....
1997-98	Carolina Hurricanes	23	0	2	2	44	....	....	....	....	....
1998-99	Carolina Hurricanes	61	1	14	15	95	3	0	0	0	2
99-2000	Carolina Hurricanes	64	3	1	4	90	....	....	....	....	....
2000-01	Colorado Avalanche	46	1	2	3	40	....	....	....	....	....
2001-02	Tampa Bay Lightning	46	0	3	3	51	....	....	....	....	....
2002-03	Tampa Bay Lightning	67	1	7	8	35	4	0	1	1	0
	NHL Totals	**316**	**6**	**31**	**37**	**361**	**7**	**0**	**1**	**1**	**2**

Transferred to **Carolina** after **Hartford** franchise relocated, June 25, 1997. Traded to **Colorado** by **Carolina** with Carolina's 1st (Vaclav Nedorost) and 2nd (Jared Aulin) round choices in 2000 Entry Draft and Philadelphia's 2nd round choice (previously acquired, Colorado selected Agris Saviels) in 2000 Entry Draft for Sandis Ozolinsh and Columbus' 2nd round choice (previously acquired, Carolina selected Tomas Kurka) in 2000 Entry Draft, June 24, 2000. Traded to **Tampa Bay** by **Colorado** for Los Angeles' 6th round choice (previously acquired, Colorado selected Scott Horvath) in 2001 Entry Draft, June 24, 2001.

PRATT, Tracy

Defense. Shoots left. 6'2", 195 lbs. Born, New York, NY, March 8, 1943.

Season	Club	GP	G	A	Pts	PIM	GP	G	A	Pts	PIM
1967-68	Oakland Seals	34	0	5	5	90	....	....	....	....	....
1968-69	Pittsburgh Penguins	18	0	5	5	34	....	....	....	....	....
1969-70	Pittsburgh Penguins	65	5	7	12	124	10	0	1	1	51
1970-71	Buffalo Sabres	76	1	7	8	179	....	....	....	....	....
1971-72	Buffalo Sabres	27	0	10	10	52	....	....	....	....	....
1972-73	Buffalo Sabres	74	1	15	16	116	6	0	0	0	6
1973-74	Buffalo Sabres	33	0	7	7	52	....	....	....	....	....
	Vancouver Canucks	45	3	8	11	44	....	....	....	....	....
1974-75	Vancouver Canucks	79	5	17	22	145	3	0	0	0	5
1975-76	Vancouver Canucks	52	1	5	6	72	2	0	0	0	0
1976-77	Colorado Rockies	66	1	10	11	110	....	....	....	....	....
	Toronto Maple Leafs	11	0	1	1	8	4	0	0	0	0
	NHL Totals	**580**	**17**	**97**	**114**	**1026**	**25**	**0**	**1**	**1**	**62**

• Son of Babe

Played in NHL All-Star Game (1975)

Traded to **Chicago** by **NY Rangers** with Dave Richardson, Dick Meissner and Mel Pearson for John McKenzie and Ray Cullen, June 4, 1965. Claimed by **California** (Oakland) from **Chicago** in Expansion Draft, June 6, 1967. Traded to **Pittsburgh** by **Oakland** with George Swarbrick and Bryan Watson for Earl Ingarfield, Gene Ubriaco and Dick Mattiussi, January 30, 1969. Claimed by **Buffalo** from **Pittsburgh** in Expansion Draft, June 10, 1970. Traded to **Vancouver** by **Buffalo** with John Gould for Jerry Korab, December 27, 1973. Signed as a free agent by **Colorado**, September 12, 1976. Traded to **Toronto** by **Colorado** for Toronto's 3rd round choice (Randy Pierce) in 1977 Amateur Draft, March 8, 1977.

PRENTICE, Dean

Left wing. Shoots left. 5'11", 180 lbs. Born, Schumacher, Ont., October 5, 1932.

Season	Club	GP	G	A	Pts	PIM	GP	G	A	Pts	PIM
1952-53	New York Rangers	55	6	3	9	20	....	....	....	....	....
1953-54	New York Rangers	52	4	13	17	18	....	....	....	....	....
1954-55	New York Rangers	70	16	15	31	20	....	....	....	....	....
1955-56	New York Rangers	70	24	18	42	44	5	1	0	1	2
1956-57	New York Rangers	68	19	23	42	38	5	0	2	2	4
1957-58	New York Rangers	38	13	9	22	14	6	1	3	4	4

		Regular Season					Playoffs				
Season	Club	GP	G	A	Pts	PIM	GP	G	A	Pts	PIM
1958-59	New York Rangers	70	17	33	50	11	....	....	....	....	....
1959-60	New York Rangers	70	32	34	66	43	....	....	....	....	....
1960-61	New York Rangers	56	20	25	45	17	....	....	....	....	....
1961-62	New York Rangers	68	22	38	60	20	3	0	2	2	0
1962-63	New York Rangers	49	13	25	38	18	....	....	....	....	....
	Boston Bruins	19	6	9	15	4	....	....	....	....	....
1963-64	Boston Bruins	70	23	16	39	37	....	....	....	....	....
1964-65	Boston Bruins	31	14	9	23	12	....	....	....	....	....
1965-66	Boston Bruins	50	7	22	29	10	....	....	....	....	....
	Detroit Red Wings	19	6	9	15	8	12	5	5	10	4
1966-67	Detroit Red Wings	68	23	22	45	18	....	....	....	....	....
1967-68	Detroit Red Wings	69	17	38	55	42	....	....	....	....	....
1968-69	Detroit Red Wings	74	14	20	34	18	....	....	....	....	....
1969-70	Pittsburgh Penguins	75	26	25	51	14	10	2	5	7	8
1970-71	Pittsburgh Penguins	69	21	17	38	18	....	....	....	....	....
1971-72	Minnesota North Stars	71	20	27	47	14	7	3	0	3	0
1972-73	Minnesota North Stars	73	26	16	42	22	6	1	0	1	16
1973-74	Minnesota North Stars	24	2	3	5	4	....	....	....	....	....
	NHL Totals	**1378**	**391**	**469**	**860**	**484**	**54**	**13**	**17**	**30**	**38**

• Brother of Eric • NHL Second All-Star Team (1960)

Played in NHL All-Star Game (1957, 1961, 1963, 1970)

Traded to **Boston** by **NY Rangers** for Don McKenney and Dick Meissner, February 4, 1963. • Terms of transaction stipulated that Meissner would report to the NY Rangers following the 1962-63 season. • Missed remainder of 1964-65 season recovering from back injury suffered in game vs. Chicago, December 27, 1964. Traded to **Detroit** by **Boston** with Leo Boivin for Gary Doak, Ron Murphy, Bill Lesuk and future considerations (Steve Atkinson June 6, 1966), February 16, 1966. Claimed by **Pittsburgh** from **Detroit** in Intra-League Draft, June 11, 1969. Traded to **Minnesota** by **Pittsburgh** for cash, October 6, 1971.

PRENTICE, Eric

Left wing. Shoots left. 5'11", 150 lbs. Born, Schumacher, Ont., August 22, 1926.

Season	Club	GP	G	A	Pts	PIM	GP	G	A	Pts	PIM
1943-44	Toronto Maple Leafs	5	0	0	0	4	....	....	....	....	....
	NHL Totals	**5**	**0**	**0**	**0**	**4**	....	....	....	....	....

• Brother of Dean

PRESLEY, Wayne

Right wing. Shoots right. 5'11", 195 lbs. Born, Dearborn, MI, March 23, 1965.
(Chicago's 2nd choice, 39th overall, in 1983 Entry Draft).

Season	Club	GP	G	A	Pts	PIM	GP	G	A	Pts	PIM
1984-85	Chicago Black Hawks	3	0	1	1	0	....	....	....	....	....
1985-86	Chicago Black Hawks	38	7	8	15	38	3	0	0	0	0
1986-87	Chicago Blackhawks	80	32	29	61	114	4	1	0	1	9
1987-88	Chicago Blackhawks	42	12	10	22	52	5	0	0	0	4
1988-89	Chicago Blackhawks	72	21	19	40	100	14	7	5	12	18
1989-90	Chicago Blackhawks	49	6	7	13	69	19	9	6	15	29
1990-91	Chicago Blackhawks	71	15	19	34	122	6	0	1	1	38
1991-92	San Jose Sharks	47	8	14	22	76	....	....	....	....	....
	Buffalo Sabres	12	2	2	4	57	7	3	3	6	14
1992-93	Buffalo Sabres	79	15	17	32	96	8	1	0	1	6
1993-94	Buffalo Sabres	65	17	8	25	103	7	2	1	3	14
1994-95	Buffalo Sabres	46	14	5	19	41	5	3	1	4	8
1995-96	New York Rangers	61	4	6	10	71	....	....	....	....	....
	Toronto Maple Leafs	19	2	2	4	14	5	0	0	0	2
	NHL Totals	**684**	**155**	**147**	**302**	**953**	**83**	**26**	**17**	**43**	**142**

Traded to **San Jose** by **Chicago** for San Jose's 3rd round choice (Bogdan Savenko) in 1993 Entry Draft, September 20, 1991. Traded to **Buffalo** by **San Jose** for Dave Snuggerud, March 9, 1992. Signed as a free agent by **NY Rangers**, August 31, 1995. Traded to **Toronto** by **NY Rangers** for Sergio Momesso, February 29, 1996.

PRESTON, Rich

Right wing. Shoots right. 6', 185 lbs. Born, Regina, Sask., May 22, 1952.

Season	Club	GP	G	A	Pts	PIM	GP	G	A	Pts	PIM
1979-80	Chicago Black Hawks	80	31	30	61	70	7	0	3	3	2
1980-81	Chicago Black Hawks	47	7	14	21	24	3	0	1	1	0
1981-82	Chicago Black Hawks	75	15	28	43	30	15	2	4	6	21
1982-83	Chicago Black Hawks	79	25	28	53	64	13	2	7	9	25
1983-84	Chicago Black Hawks	75	10	18	28	50	5	0	1	1	4
1984-85	New Jersey Devils	75	12	15	27	26	....	....	....	....	....
1985-86	New Jersey Devils	76	19	22	41	65	....	....	....	....	....
1986-87	Chicago Blackhawks	73	8	9	17	19	4	0	2	2	4
	NHL Totals	**580**	**127**	**164**	**291**	**348**	**47**	**4**	**18**	**22**	**56**

Claimed by **Chicago** from **Winnipeg** in Expansion Draft, June 13, 1979. Traded to **New Jersey** by **Chicago** with Don Dietrich and Chicago's 2nd round choice (Eric Weinrich) in 1985 Entry Draft for Bob MacMillan and New Jersey's 5th round choice (Rick Herbert) in 1985 Entry Draft, June 19, 1984. Signed as a free agent by **Chicago**, July 14, 1986.

PRESTON, Yves

Left wing. Shoots left. 5'11", 180 lbs. Born, Montreal, Que., June 14, 1956.

Season	Club	GP	G	A	Pts	PIM	GP	G	A	Pts	PIM
1978-79	Philadelphia Flyers	9	3	1	4	0	....	....	....	....	....
1980-81	Philadelphia Flyers	19	4	2	6	4	....	....	....	....	....
	NHL Totals	**28**	**7**	**3**	**10**	**4**	....	....	....	....	....

Signed as a free agent by **Philadelphia**, October 9, 1978.

PRIAKIN, Sergei

Right wing. Shoots left. 6'3", 210 lbs. Born, Moscow, Soviet Union, December 7, 1963.
(Calgary's 12th choice, 252nd overall, in 1988 Entry Draft).

Season	Club	GP	G	A	Pts	PIM	GP	G	A	Pts	PIM
1988-89	Calgary Flames	2	0	0	0	2	1	0	0	0	0
1989-90	Calgary Flames	20	2	2	4	0	....	....	....	....	....
1990-91	Calgary Flames	24	1	6	7	0	....	....	....	....	....
	NHL Totals	**46**	**3**	**8**	**11**	**2**	**1**	**0**	**0**	**0**	**0**

PRICE, Jack

Defense. Shoots left. 5'9", 180 lbs. Born, Goderich, Ont., May 8, 1932.

Season	Club	GP	G	A	Pts	PIM	GP	G	A	Pts	PIM
1951-52	Chicago Black Hawks	1	0	0	0	0	....	....	....	....	....
1952-53	Chicago Black Hawks	10	0	0	0	2	4	0	0	0	0
1953-54	Chicago Black Hawks	46	4	6	10	22	....	....	....	....	....
	NHL Totals	**57**	**4**	**6**	**10**	**24**	**4**	**0**	**0**	**0**	**0**

Traded to **Toronto** by **Chicago** for Ray Timgren, October 4, 1954. Traded to **Detroit** (Hershey – AHL) by **Toronto** (Pittsburgh – AHL) with Gilles Mayer, Willie Marshall, Bob Hassard, Bob Solinger and Ray Gariepy for cash, July 7, 1956.

PRICE, Noel

Defense. Shoots left. 6', 190 lbs. Born, Brockville, Ont., December 9, 1935.

Season	Club	GP	G	A	Pts	PIM	GP	G	A	Pts	PIM
1957-58	Toronto Maple Leafs	1	0	0	0	5	....	....	....	....	....
1958-59	Toronto Maple Leafs	28	0	0	0	4	5	0	0	0	2
1959-60	New York Rangers	6	0	0	0	2	....	....	....	....	....
1960-61	New York Rangers	1	0	0	0	2	....	....	....	....	....
1961-62	Detroit Red Wings	20	0	1	1	6	....	....	....	....	....
1965-66 ♦	Montreal Canadiens	15	0	6	6	8	3	0	1	1	0
1966-67	Montreal Canadiens	24	0	3	3	8	....	....	....	....	....
1967-68	Pittsburgh Penguins	70	6	27	33	48	....	....	....	....	....
1968-69	Pittsburgh Penguins	73	2	18	20	61	....	....	....	....	....
1970-71	Los Angeles Kings	62	1	19	20	29	....	....	....	....	....
1972-73	Atlanta Flames	54	1	13	14	38	....	....	....	....	....
1973-74	Atlanta Flames	62	0	13	13	38	4	0	0	0	6
1974-75	Atlanta Flames	80	4	14	18	82	....	....	....	....	....
1975-76	Atlanta Flames	3	0	0	0	2	....	....	....	....	....
	NHL Totals	**499**	**14**	**114**	**128**	**333**	**12**	**0**	**1**	**1**	**8**

Played in NHL All-Star Game (1967)

Traded to **NY Rangers** by **Toronto** for Hank Ciesla, Bill Kennedy and future considerations, October 3, 1959. Traded to **Detroit** by **NY Rangers** for Pete Goegan, February 16, 1962. Traded to **NY Rangers** by **Detroit** for Pete Goegan, October 8, 1962. Traded to **Montreal** by **NY Rangers** with Earl Ingarfield, Gord Labossiere, Dave McComb and cash for Cesare Maniago and Garry Peters, June 8, 1965. Claimed by **Pittsburgh** from **Montreal** in Expansion Draft, June 6, 1967. Claimed by **Los Angeles** (Springfield-AHL) from **Pittsburgh** in Reverse Draft, June 12, 1969. Traded to **Montreal** by **Los Angeles** with Denis DeJordy, Dale Hoganson and Doug Robinson for Rogie Vachon, November 4, 1971. Traded to **Atlanta** by **Montreal** for cash and future considerations, August 14, 1972.

PRICE, Pat

Defense. Shoots left. 6'2", 200 lbs. Born, Nelson, B.C., March 24, 1955.
(NY Islanders' 1st choice, 11th overall, in 1975 Amateur Draft).

Season	Club	GP	G	A	Pts	PIM	GP	G	A	Pts	PIM
1975-76	New York Islanders	4	0	2	2	2	....	....	....	....	....
1976-77	New York Islanders	71	3	22	25	25	10	0	1	1	2
1977-78	New York Islanders	52	2	10	12	27	5	0	1	1	2
1978-79	New York Islanders	55	3	11	14	50	7	0	1	1	25
1979-80	Edmonton Oilers	75	11	21	32	134	3	0	0	0	11
1980-81	Edmonton Oilers	59	8	24	32	193	....	....	....	....	....
	Pittsburgh Penguins	13	0	10	10	33	5	1	1	2	21
1981-82	Pittsburgh Penguins	77	7	31	38	322	5	0	0	0	28
1982-83	Pittsburgh Penguins	38	1	11	12	104	....	....	....	....	....
	Quebec Nordiques	14	1	2	3	28	4	0	0	0	14
1983-84	Quebec Nordiques	72	3	25	28	188	9	1	0	1	10
1984-85	Quebec Nordiques	68	1	26	27	118	17	0	4	4	51
1985-86	Quebec Nordiques	54	3	13	16	82	3	0	1	1	4
1986-87	Quebec Nordiques	47	0	6	6	81	....	....	....	....	....
	New York Rangers	13	0	2	2	49	6	0	1	1	27
1987-88	Minnesota North Stars	14	0	2	2	20	....	....	....	....	....
	NHL Totals	**726**	**43**	**218**	**261**	**1456**	**74**	**2**	**10**	**12**	**195**

Claimed by **Edmonton** from **NY Islanders** in Expansion Draft, June 13, 1979. Traded to **Pittsburgh** by **Edmonton** for Pat Hughes, March 10, 1981. Claimed on waivers by **Quebec** from **Pittsburgh**, December 31, 1982. Traded to **NY Rangers** by **Quebec** for Lane Lambert, March 5, 1987. Traded to **Minnesota** by **NY Rangers** for Willi Plett, September 8, 1987.

PRICE, Tom

Defense. Shoots left. 6'1", 190 lbs. Born, Toronto, Ont., July 12, 1954.
(California's 5th choice, 57th overall, in 1974 Amateur Draft).

Season	Club	GP	G	A	Pts	PIM	GP	G	A	Pts	PIM
1974-75	California Golden Seals	3	0	0	0	4	....	....	....	....	....
1975-76	California Golden Seals	5	0	0	0	0	....	....	....	....	....
1976-77	Cleveland Barons	2	0	0	0	0	....	....	....	....	....
	Pittsburgh Penguins	7	0	2	2	4	....	....	....	....	....
1977-78	Pittsburgh Penguins	10	0	0	0	0	....	....	....	....	....
1978-79	Pittsburgh Penguins	2	0	0	0	4	....	....	....	....	....
	NHL Totals	**29**	**0**	**2**	**2**	**12**	....	....	....	....	....

Transferred to **Cleveland** after **California** franchise relocated, August 26, 1976. Signed as a free agent by **Pittsburgh** following release by **Cleveland**, Februray 28, 1977.

PRIESTLAY, Ken

Center. Shoots left. 5'10", 190 lbs. Born, Richmond, B.C., August 24, 1967.
(Buffalo's 5th choice, 98th overall, in 1985 Entry Draft).

Season	Club	GP	G	A	Pts	PIM	GP	G	A	Pts	PIM
1986-87	Buffalo Sabres	34	11	6	17	8	....	....	....	....	....
1987-88	Buffalo Sabres	33	5	12	17	35	6	0	0	0	11
1988-89	Buffalo Sabres	15	2	0	2	2	3	0	0	0	2
1989-90	Buffalo Sabres	35	7	7	14	14	5	0	0	0	8
1990-91	Pittsburgh Penguins	2	0	1	1	0	....	....	....	....	....

Season	Club	GP	G	A	Pts	PIM	GP	G	A	Pts	PIM
		REGULAR SEASON					PLAYOFFS				
1991-92 ◆	Pittsburgh Penguins	49	2	8	10	4	....	....	....	....	....
	NHL Totals	**168**	**27**	**34**	**61**	**63**	**14**	**0**	**0**	**0**	**21**

Traded to **Pittsburgh** by **Buffalo** for Tony Tanti, March 5, 1991.

PRIMEAU, Joe

HHOF

Center. Shoots left. 5'11", 153 lbs. Born, Lindsay, Ont., January 29, 1906.

Season	Club	GP	G	A	Pts	PIM	GP	G	A	Pts	PIM
1927-28	Toronto Maple Leafs	2	0	0	0	0	....	....	....	....	....
1928-29	Toronto Maple Leafs	6	0	1	1	2	....	....	....	....	....
1929-30	Toronto Maple Leafs	43	5	21	26	22	....	....	....	....	....
1930-31	Toronto Maple Leafs	38	9	*32	41	18	2	0	0	0	0
1931-32 ◆	Toronto Maple Leafs	46	13	*37	50	25	7	0	*6	6	2
1932-33	Toronto Maple Leafs	48	11	21	32	4	8	0	1	1	4
1933-34	Toronto Maple Leafs	45	14	*32	46	8	5	2	4	6	6
1934-35	Toronto Maple Leafs	37	10	20	30	16	7	0	3	3	0
1935-36	Toronto Maple Leafs	45	4	13	17	10	9	3	4	7	0
	NHL Totals	**310**	**66**	**177**	**243**	**105**	**38**	**5**	**18**	**23**	**12**

Lady Byng Trophy (1932) • NHL Second All-Star Team (1934)
Played in NHL All-Star Game (1934)

Signed as a free agent by **Toronto**, July 17, 1928.

PRIMEAU, Keith

Center. Shoots left. 6'5", 220 lbs. Born, Toronto, Ont., November 24, 1971.
(Detroit's 1st choice, 3rd overall, in 1990 Entry Draft).

Season	Club	GP	G	A	Pts	PIM	GP	G	A	Pts	PIM
1990-91	Detroit Red Wings	58	3	12	15	106	5	1	1	2	25
1991-92	Detroit Red Wings	35	6	10	16	83	11	0	0	0	14
1992-93	Detroit Red Wings	73	15	17	32	152	7	0	2	2	26
1993-94	Detroit Red Wings	78	31	42	73	173	7	0	2	2	6
1994-95	Detroit Red Wings	45	15	27	42	99	17	4	5	9	45
1995-96	Detroit Red Wings	74	27	25	52	168	17	1	4	5	28
1996-97	Hartford Whalers	75	26	25	51	161	....	....	....	....	....
1997-98	Carolina Hurricanes	81	26	37	63	110	....	....	....	....	....
1998-99	Carolina Hurricanes	78	30	32	62	75	6	0	3	3	6
99-2000	Philadelphia Flyers	23	7	10	17	31	18	2	11	13	13
2000-01	Philadelphia Flyers	71	34	39	73	76	4	0	3	3	8
2001-02	Philadelphia Flyers	75	19	29	48	128	5	0	0	0	6
2002-03	Philadelphia Flyers	80	19	27	46	93	13	1	1	2	14
	NHL Totals	**846**	**258**	**332**	**590**	**1455**	**110**	**9**	**32**	**41**	**191**

• Brother of Wayne
Played in NHL All-Star Game (1999)

Traded to **Hartford** by **Detroit** with Paul Coffey and Detroit's 1st round choice (Nikos Tselios) in 1997 Entry Draft for Brendan Shanahan and Brian Glynn, October 9, 1996. Transferred to **Carolina** after **Hartford** franchise relocated, June 25, 1997. • Missed majority of 1999-2000 season after failing to come to contract terms with **Carolina**. Traded to **Philadelphia** by **Carolina** with Carolina's 5th round choice (later traded to NY Islanders – NY Islanders selected Kristofer Ottosson) in 2000 Entry Draft for Rod Brind'Amour, Jean-Marc Pelletier and Philadelphia's 2nd round choice (later traded to Colorado – Colorado selected Agris Saviels) in 2000 Entry Draft, January 23, 2000.

PRIMEAU, Kevin

Right wing. Shoots right. 6', 180 lbs. Born, Edmonton, Alta., January 3, 1956.

Season	Club	GP	G	A	Pts	PIM	GP	G	A	Pts	PIM
1980-81	Vancouver Canucks	2	0	0	0	4	....	....	....	....	....
	NHL Totals	**2**	**0**	**0**	**0**	**4**	....	....	....	....	....

Signed as a free agent by **Vancouver**, 1980.

PRIMEAU, Wayne

Center. Shoots left. 6'3", 220 lbs. Born, Scarborough, Ont., June 4, 1976.
(Buffalo's 1st choice, 17th overall, in 1994 Entry Draft).

Season	Club	GP	G	A	Pts	PIM	GP	G	A	Pts	PIM
1994-95	Buffalo Sabres	1	1	0	1	0	....	....	....	....	....
1995-96	Buffalo Sabres	2	0	0	0	0	....	....	....	....	....
1996-97	Buffalo Sabres	45	2	4	6	64	9	0	0	0	6
1997-98	Buffalo Sabres	69	6	6	12	87	14	1	3	4	6
1998-99	Buffalo Sabres	67	5	8	13	38	19	3	4	7	6
99-2000	Buffalo Sabres	41	5	7	12	38	....	....	....	....	....
	Tampa Bay Lightning	17	2	3	5	25	....	....	....	....	....
2000-01	Tampa Bay Lightning	47	2	13	15	77	....	....	....	....	....
	Pittsburgh Penguins	28	1	6	7	54	18	1	3	4	2
2001-02	Pittsburgh Penguins	33	3	7	10	18	....	....	....	....	....
2002-03	Pittsburgh Penguins	70	5	11	16	55	....	....	....	....	....
	San Jose Sharks	7	1	1	2	0	....	....	....	....	....
	NHL Totals	**427**	**33**	**66**	**99**	**456**	**60**	**5**	**10**	**15**	**20**

• Brother of Keith

Traded to **Tampa Bay** by **Buffalo** with Cory Sarich, Brian Holzinger and Buffalo's 3rd round choice (Alexander Kharitonov) in 2000 Entry Draft for Chris Gratton and Tampa Bay's 2nd round choice (Derek Roy) in 2001 Entry Draft, March 9, 2000. Traded to **Pittsburgh** by **Tampa Bay** for Matthew Barnaby, February 1, 2001. • Missed majority of 2001-02 season recovering from knee injury suffered in game vs. Buffalo, January 8, 2002. Traded to **San Jose** by **Pittsburgh** for Matt Bradley, March 11, 2003.

PRINGLE, Ellie

Defense. Shoots left. 6'2", 205 lbs. Born, Toronto, Ont., August 31, 1911.

Season	Club	GP	G	A	Pts	PIM	GP	G	A	Pts	PIM
1930-31	New York Americans	6	0	0	0	0	....	....	....	....	....
	NHL Totals	**6**	**0**	**0**	**0**	**0**	....	....	....	....	....

Signed as a free agent by **NY Americans**, October 22, 1930.

PROBERT, Bob

Left wing. Shoots left. 6'3", 225 lbs. Born, Windsor, Ont., June 5, 1965.
(Detroit's 3rd choice, 46th overall, in 1983 Entry Draft).

Season	Club	GP	G	A	Pts	PIM	GP	G	A	Pts	PIM
1985-86	Detroit Red Wings	44	8	13	21	186	....	....	....	....	....
1986-87	Detroit Red Wings	63	13	11	24	221	16	3	4	7	63
1987-88	Detroit Red Wings	74	29	33	62	*398	16	8	13	21	51
1988-89	Detroit Red Wings	25	4	2	6	106	....	....	....	....	....
1989-90	Detroit Red Wings	4	3	0	3	21	....	....	....	....	....
1990-91	Detroit Red Wings	55	16	23	39	315	6	1	2	3	50
1991-92	Detroit Red Wings	63	20	24	44	276	11	1	6	7	28
1992-93	Detroit Red Wings	80	14	29	43	292	7	0	3	3	10
1993-94	Detroit Red Wings	66	7	10	17	275	7	1	1	2	8
1995-96	Chicago Blackhawks	78	19	21	40	237	10	0	2	2	23
1996-97	Chicago Blackhawks	82	9	14	23	326	6	2	1	3	41
1997-98	Chicago Blackhawks	14	2	1	3	48	....	....	....	....	....
1998-99	Chicago Blackhawks	78	7	14	21	206	....	....	....	....	....
99-2000	Chicago Blackhawks	69	4	11	15	114	....	....	....	....	....
2000-01	Chicago Blackhawks	79	7	12	19	103	....	....	....	....	....
2001-02	Chicago Blackhawks	61	1	3	4	176	2	0	0	0	0
	NHL Totals	**935**	**163**	**221**	**384**	**3300**	**81**	**16**	**32**	**48**	**274**

Played in NHL All-Star Game (1988)

Signed as a free agent by **Chicago**, July 23, 1994. • Suspended for entire 1994-95 season for violating NHL substance abuse policy, September 2, 1994. • Missed majority of 1997-98 season recovering from rotator cuff injury suffered in game vs. Detroit, November 16, 1997.

PROCHAZKA, Martin

Right wing. Shoots right. 5'11", 180 lbs. Born, Slany, Czech., March 3, 1972.
(Toronto's 6th choice, 135th overall, in 1991 Entry Draft).

Season	Club	GP	G	A	Pts	PIM	GP	G	A	Pts	PIM
1997-98	Toronto Maple Leafs	29	2	4	6	8	....	....	....	....	....
99-2000	Atlanta Thrashers	3	0	1	1	0	....	....	....	....	....
	NHL Totals	**32**	**2**	**5**	**7**	**8**	....	....	....	....	....

Traded to **Atlanta** by **Toronto** for Atlanta's 6th round choice (Maxim Kondratjev) in 2001 Entry Draft, July 15, 1999.

PRODGERS, Goldie

Forward/defense. Shoots right. 5'10", 180 lbs. Born, London, Ont., October 18, 1891.

Season	Club	GP	G	A	Pts	PIM	GP	G	A	Pts	PIM
1919-20	Toronto St. Pats	16	8	6	14	4	....	....	....	....	....
1920-21	Hamilton Tigers	24	18	9	27	8	....	....	....	....	....
1921-22	Hamilton Tigers	24	15	6	21	4	....	....	....	....	....
1922-23	Hamilton Tigers	23	13	4	17	17	....	....	....	....	....
1923-24	Hamilton Tigers	23	9	4	13	6	....	....	....	....	....
1924-25	Hamilton Tigers	1	0	0	0	0	....	....	....	....	....
	NHL Totals	**111**	**63**	**29**	**92**	**39**	....	....	....	....	....

NHL rights transferred to **Quebec** by **NHL** when Quebec franchise returned to NHL, November 25, 1919. • Suspended by **Quebec** after refusing to report to training camp, November 27, 1919. Traded to **Montreal** by **Quebec** for Ed Carpenter, December 21, 1919. Traded to **Toronto** by **Montreal** for Harry Cameron, January 14, 1920. Traded to **Montreal** by **Toronto** with Joe Matte for Harry Cameron, November 27, 1920. Traded to **Hamilton** by **Montreal** with Jack Coughlin, Joe Matte and loan of Billy Coutu for 1920-21 season for Harry Mummery, Jack McDonald and Dave Ritchie, November 27, 1920.

PROKHOROV, Vitali

Left wing. Shoots left. 5'9", 185 lbs. Born, Moscow, USSR, December 25, 1966.
(St. Louis' 3rd choice, 64th overall, in 1992 Entry Draft).

Season	Club	GP	G	A	Pts	PIM	GP	G	A	Pts	PIM
1992-93	St. Louis Blues	26	4	1	5	15	....	....	....	....	....
1993-94	St. Louis Blues	55	15	10	25	20	4	0	0	0	0
1994-95	St. Louis Blues	2	0	0	0	0	....	....	....	....	....
	NHL Totals	**83**	**19**	**11**	**30**	**35**	**4**	**0**	**0**	**0**	**0**

PROKOPEC, Mike

Right wing. Shoots right. 6'2", 190 lbs. Born, Toronto, Ont., May 17, 1974.
(Chicago's 7th choice, 161st overall, in 1992 Entry Draft).

Season	Club	GP	G	A	Pts	PIM	GP	G	A	Pts	PIM
1995-96	Chicago Blackhawks	9	0	0	0	5	....	....	....	....	....
1996-97	Chicago Blackhawks	6	0	0	0	6	....	....	....	....	....
	NHL Totals	**15**	**0**	**0**	**0**	**11**	....	....	....	....	....

Traded to **Ottawa** by **Chicago** for Denis Chasse, the rights to Kevin Bolibruck and Ottawa's 6th round choice (traded back to Ottawa – Ottawa selected Chris Neil) in 1998 Entry Draft, March 18, 1997.

PRONGER, Chris

Defense. Shoots left. 6'6", 220 lbs. Born, Dryden, Ont., October 10, 1974.
(Hartford's 1st choice, 2nd overall, in 1993 Entry Draft).

Season	Club	GP	G	A	Pts	PIM	GP	G	A	Pts	PIM
1993-94	Hartford Whalers	81	5	25	30	113	....	....	....	....	....
1994-95	Hartford Whalers	43	5	9	14	54	....	....	....	....	....
1995-96	St. Louis Blues	78	7	18	25	110	13	1	5	6	16
1996-97	St. Louis Blues	79	11	24	35	143	6	1	1	2	22
1997-98	St. Louis Blues	81	9	27	36	180	10	1	9	10	26
1998-99	St. Louis Blues	67	13	33	46	113	13	1	4	5	28
99-2000	St. Louis Blues	79	14	48	62	92	7	3	4	7	32
2000-01	St. Louis Blues	51	8	39	47	75	15	1	7	8	32
2001-02	St. Louis Blues	78	7	40	47	120	9	1	7	8	24

Season	Club	GP	G	A	Pts	PIM	GP	G	A	Pts	PIM
		REGULAR SEASON					PLAYOFFS				
2002-03	St. Louis Blues	5	1	3	4	10	7	1	3	4	14
	NHL Totals	**642**	**80**	**266**	**346**	**1010**	**80**	**10**	**40**	**50**	**194**

• Brother of Sean • NHL All-Rookie Team (1994) • NHL Second All-Star Team (1998) • Bud Ice Plus/Minus Award (1998) • NHL First All-Star Team (2000) • Bud Light Plus/Minus Award (2000) • James Norris Memorial Trophy (2000) • Hart Trophy (2000)

Played in NHL All-Star Game (1999, 2000, 2002)

Traded to **St. Louis** by **Hartford** for Brendan Shanahan, July 27, 1995.

PRONGER, Sean

Center. Shoots left. 6'3", 209 lbs. Born, Thunder Bay, Ont., November 30, 1972.
(Vancouver's 3rd choice, 51st overall, in 1991 Entry Draft).

Season	Club	GP	G	A	Pts	PIM	GP	G	A	Pts	PIM
1995-96	Mighty Ducks of Anaheim	7	0	1	1	6	....	....	....	....	....
1996-97	Mighty Ducks of Anaheim	39	7	7	14	20	9	0	2	2	4
1997-98	Mighty Ducks of Anaheim	62	5	15	20	30	....	....	....	....	....
	Pittsburgh Penguins	5	1	0	1	2	5	0	0	0	4
1998-99	Pittsburgh Penguins	2	0	0	0	0	....	....	....	....	....
	New York Rangers	14	0	3	3	4	....	....	....	....	....
	Los Angeles Kings	13	0	1	1	4	....	....	....	....	....
99-2000	Boston Bruins	11	0	1	1	13	....	....	....	....	....
2001-02	Columbus Blue Jackets	26	3	1	4	4	....	....	....	....	....
2002-03	Columbus Blue Jackets	78	7	6	13	72	....	....	....	....	....
	NHL Totals	**257**	**23**	**35**	**58**	**155**	**14**	**0**	**2**	**2**	**8**

• Brother of Chris

Signed as a free agent by **Anaheim**, February 14, 1995. Traded to **Pittsburgh** by **Anaheim** for the rights to Patrick Lalime, March 24, 1998. Traded to **NY Rangers** by **Pittsburgh** with Chris Tamer and Petr Nedved for Alexei Kovalev and Harry York, November 25, 1998. Traded to **Los Angeles** by **NY Rangers** for Eric Lacroix, February 12, 1999. Signed as a free agent by **Boston**, August 25, 1999. Traded to **NY Islanders** by **Boston** for future considerations, December 5, 2000. Claimed on waivers by **Columbus** from **NY Islanders**, May 18, 2001.

PRONOVOST, Andre

Left wing. Shoots left. 5'10", 188 lbs. Born, Shawinigan Falls, Que., July 9, 1936.

Season	Club	GP	G	A	Pts	PIM	GP	G	A	Pts	PIM
1956-57♦	Montreal Canadiens	64	10	11	21	58	8	1	0	1	4
1957-58♦	Montreal Canadiens	66	16	12	28	55	10	2	0	2	16
1958-59♦	Montreal Canadiens	70	9	14	23	48	11	2	1	3	6
1959-60♦	Montreal Canadiens	69	12	19	31	61	8	1	2	3	0
1960-61	Montreal Canadiens	21	1	5	6	4	....	....	....	....	....
	Boston Bruins	47	11	11	22	30	....	....	....	....	....
1961-62	Boston Bruins	70	15	8	23	74	....	....	....	....	....
1962-63	Boston Bruins	21	0	2	2	6	....	....	....	....	....
	Detroit Red Wings	47	13	5	18	18	11	1	4	5	6
1963-64	Detroit Red Wings	70	7	16	23	54	14	4	3	7	26
1964-65	Detroit Red Wings	3	0	1	1	0	....	....	....	....	....
1967-68	Minnesota North Stars	8	0	0	0	0	8	0	1	1	0
	NHL Totals	**556**	**94**	**104**	**198**	**408**	**70**	**11**	**11**	**22**	**58**

Played in NHL All-Star Game (1957, 1958, 1959, 1960)

Traded to **Boston** by **Montreal** for Jean-Guy Gendron, November 27, 1960. Traded to **Detroit** by **Boston** for Forbes Kennedy, December 3, 1962. Claimed by **Minnesota** from **Detroit** in Expansion Draft, June 6, 1967.

PRONOVOST, Jean

Right wing. Shoots right. 6', 185 lbs. Born, Shawinigan Falls, Que., December 18, 1945.

Season	Club	GP	G	A	Pts	PIM	GP	G	A	Pts	PIM
1968-69	Pittsburgh Penguins	76	16	25	41	41	....	....	....	....	....
1969-70	Pittsburgh Penguins	72	20	21	41	45	10	3	4	7	2
1970-71	Pittsburgh Penguins	78	21	24	45	35	....	....	....	....	....
1971-72	Pittsburgh Penguins	68	30	23	53	12	4	1	1	2	0
1972-73	Pittsburgh Penguins	66	21	22	43	16	....	....	....	....	....
1973-74	Pittsburgh Penguins	77	40	32	72	22	....	....	....	....	....
1974-75	Pittsburgh Penguins	78	43	32	75	37	9	3	3	6	6
1975-76	Pittsburgh Penguins	80	52	52	104	24	3	0	0	0	2
1976-77	Pittsburgh Penguins	79	33	31	64	24	3	2	1	3	2
1977-78	Pittsburgh Penguins	79	40	25	65	50	....	....	....	....	....
1978-79	Atlanta Flames	75	28	39	67	30	2	2	0	2	0
1979-80	Atlanta Flames	80	24	19	43	12	4	0	0	0	2
1980-81	Washington Capitals	80	22	36	58	61	....	....	....	....	....
1981-82	Washington Capitals	10	1	2	3	4	....	....	....	....	....
	NHL Totals	**998**	**391**	**383**	**774**	**413**	**35**	**11**	**9**	**20**	**14**

• Brother of Marcel and Claude

Played in NHL All-Star Game (1975, 1976, 1977, 1978)

Traded to **Pittsburgh** by **Boston** with John Arbour for cash, May 21, 1968. Traded to **Atlanta** by **Pittsburgh** for Gregg Sheppard, September 6, 1978. Transferred to **Calgary** after **Atlanta** franchise relocated, June 23, 1980. Traded to **Washington** by **Calgary** for cash, July 1, 1980.

PRONOVOST, Marcel

HHOF

Defense. Shoots left. 6', 190 lbs. Born, Lac-de-Tortue, Que., June 15, 1930.

Season	Club	GP	G	A	Pts	PIM	GP	G	A	Pts	PIM
1949-50♦	Detroit Red Wings	....	....	....	....	....	9	0	1	1	10
1950-51	Detroit Red Wings	37	1	6	7	20	6	0	0	0	0
1951-52♦	Detroit Red Wings	69	7	11	18	50	8	0	1	1	10
1952-53	Detroit Red Wings	68	8	19	27	72	6	0	0	0	6
1953-54♦	Detroit Red Wings	57	6	12	18	50	12	2	3	5	12
1954-55♦	Detroit Red Wings	70	9	25	34	90	11	1	2	3	6
1955-56	Detroit Red Wings	68	4	13	17	46	10	0	2	2	8
1956-57	Detroit Red Wings	70	7	9	16	38	5	0	0	0	6
1957-58	Detroit Red Wings	62	2	18	20	52	4	0	1	1	4
1958-59	Detroit Red Wings	69	11	21	32	44	....	....	....	....	....
1959-60	Detroit Red Wings	69	7	17	24	38	6	1	1	2	2
1960-61	Detroit Red Wings	70	6	11	17	44	9	2	3	5	0
1961-62	Detroit Red Wings	70	4	14	18	38	....	....	....	....	....
1962-63	Detroit Red Wings	69	4	9	13	48	11	1	4	5	8
1963-64	Detroit Red Wings	67	3	17	20	42	14	0	2	2	14
1964-65	Detroit Red Wings	68	1	15	16	45	7	0	3	3	4
1965-66	Toronto Maple Leafs	54	2	8	10	34	4	0	0	0	6
1966-67♦	Toronto Maple Leafs	58	2	12	14	28	12	1	0	1	8
1967-68	Toronto Maple Leafs	70	3	17	20	48	....	....	....	....	....
1968-69	Toronto Maple Leafs	34	1	2	3	20	....	....	....	....	....
1969-70	Toronto Maple Leafs	7	0	1	1	4	....	....	....	....	....
	NHL Totals	**1206**	**88**	**257**	**345**	**851**	**134**	**8**	**23**	**31**	**104**

• Brother of Claude and Jean • NHL Second All-Star Team (1958, 1959) • NHL First All-Star Team (1960, 1961)

Played in NHL All-Star Game (1950, 1954, 1955, 1957, 1958, 1959, 1960, 1961, 1963, 1965, 1968)

Traded to **Toronto** by **Detroit** with Aut Erickson, Larry Jeffrey, Eddie Joyal and Lowell MacDonald for Billy Harris, Gary Jarrett and Andy Bathgate, May 20, 1965.

PROPP, Brian

Left wing. Shoots left. 5'10", 195 lbs. Born, Lanigan, Sask., February 15, 1959.
(Philadelphia's 1st choice, 14th overall, in 1979 Entry Draft).

Season	Club	GP	G	A	Pts	PIM	GP	G	A	Pts	PIM
1979-80	Philadelphia Flyers	80	34	41	75	54	19	5	10	15	29
1980-81	Philadelphia Flyers	79	26	40	66	110	12	6	6	12	32
1981-82	Philadelphia Flyers	80	44	47	91	117	4	2	2	4	4
1982-83	Philadelphia Flyers	80	40	42	82	72	3	1	2	3	8
1983-84	Philadelphia Flyers	79	39	53	92	37	3	0	1	1	6
1984-85	Philadelphia Flyers	76	43	54	97	43	19	8	10	18	6
1985-86	Philadelphia Flyers	72	40	57	97	47	5	0	2	2	4
1986-87	Philadelphia Flyers	53	31	36	67	45	26	12	16	28	10
1987-88	Philadelphia Flyers	74	27	49	76	76	7	4	2	6	8
1988-89	Philadelphia Flyers	77	32	46	78	37	18	14	9	23	14
1989-90	Philadelphia Flyers	40	13	15	28	31	....	....	....	....	....
	Boston Bruins	14	3	9	12	10	20	4	9	13	2
1990-91	Minnesota North Stars	79	26	47	73	58	23	8	15	23	28
1991-92	Minnesota North Stars	51	12	23	35	49	1	0	0	0	0
1992-93	Minnesota North Stars	17	3	3	6	0	....	....	....	....	....
1993-94	Hartford Whalers	65	12	17	29	44	....	....	....	....	....
	NHL Totals	**1016**	**425**	**579**	**1004**	**830**	**160**	**64**	**84**	**148**	**151**

Played in NHL All-Star Game (1980, 1982, 1984, 1986, 1990)

Traded to **Boston** by **Philadelphia** for Boston's 2nd round choice (Terran Sandwith) in 1990 Entry Draft, March 2, 1990. Signed as a free agent by **Minnesota**, July 25, 1990. Signed as a free agent by **Hartford**, October 4, 1993.

PROSPAL, Vaclav

Center. Shoots left. 6'2", 195 lbs. Born, Ceske Budejovice, Czech., February 17, 1975.
(Philadelphia's 2nd choice, 71st overall, in 1993 Entry Draft).

Season	Club	GP	G	A	Pts	PIM	GP	G	A	Pts	PIM
1996-97	Philadelphia Flyers	18	5	10	15	4	5	1	3	4	4
1997-98	Philadelphia Flyers	41	5	13	18	17	....	....	....	....	....
	Ottawa Senators	15	1	6	7	4	6	0	0	0	0
1998-99	Ottawa Senators	79	10	26	36	58	4	0	0	0	0
99-2000	Ottawa Senators	79	22	33	55	40	6	0	4	4	4
2000-01	Ottawa Senators	40	1	12	13	12	....	....	....	....	....
	Florida Panthers	34	4	12	16	10	....	....	....	....	....
2001-02	Tampa Bay Lightning	81	18	37	55	38	....	....	....	....	....
2002-03	Tampa Bay Lightning	80	22	57	79	53	11	4	2	6	8
	NHL Totals	**467**	**88**	**206**	**294**	**236**	**32**	**5**	**9**	**14**	**16**

Traded to **Ottawa** by **Philadelphia** with Pat Falloon and Dallas' 2nd round choice (previously acquired, Ottawa selected Chris Bala) in 1998 Entry Draft for Alexandre Daigle, January 17, 1998. Traded to **Florida** by **Ottawa** for future considerations, January 20, 2001. Traded to **Tampa Bay** by **Florida** for Ryan Johnson and Tampa Bay's 6th round choice (later traded back to Tampa Bay – Tampa Bay selected Doug O'Brien) in 2003 Entry Draft, July 10, 2001. Signed as a free agent by **Anaheim**, July 17, 2003.

PROULX, Christian

Defense. Shoots left. 6', 185 lbs. Born, Sherbrooke, Que., December 10, 1973.
(Montreal's 9th choice, 164th overall, in 1992 Entry Draft).

Season	Club	GP	G	A	Pts	PIM	GP	G	A	Pts	PIM
1993-94	Montreal Canadiens	7	1	2	3	20	....	....	....	....	....
	NHL Totals	**7**	**1**	**2**	**3**	**20**	....	....	....	....	....

PROVOST, Claude

Right wing. Shoots right. 5'9", 168 lbs. Born, Montreal, Que., September 17, 1933.

Season	Club	GP	G	A	Pts	PIM	GP	G	A	Pts	PIM
1955-56♦	Montreal Canadiens	60	13	16	29	30	10	3	3	6	12
1956-57♦	Montreal Canadiens	67	16	14	30	24	10	0	1	1	8
1957-58♦	Montreal Canadiens	70	19	32	51	71	10	1	3	4	8
1958-59♦	Montreal Canadiens	69	16	22	38	37	11	6	2	8	2
1959-60♦	Montreal Canadiens	70	17	29	46	42	8	1	1	2	0
1960-61	Montreal Canadiens	49	11	4	15	32	6	1	3	4	4
1961-62	Montreal Canadiens	70	33	29	62	22	6	2	2	4	2
1962-63	Montreal Canadiens	67	20	30	50	26	5	0	1	1	2
1963-64	Montreal Canadiens	68	15	17	32	37	7	2	2	4	22
1964-65♦	Montreal Canadiens	70	27	37	64	28	13	2	6	8	12
1965-66♦	Montreal Canadiens	70	19	36	55	38	10	2	3	5	2
1966-67	Montreal Canadiens	64	11	13	24	16	7	1	1	2	0
1967-68♦	Montreal Canadiens	73	14	30	44	26	13	2	8	10	10
1968-69♦	Montreal Canadiens	73	13	15	28	18	10	2	2	4	2

Season	Club	REGULAR SEASON GP	G	A	Pts	PIM	PLAYOFFS GP	G	A	Pts	PIM
1969-70	Montreal Canadiens	65	10	11	21	22	....	....	....	....	....
	NHL Totals	**1005**	**254**	**335**	**589**	**469**	**126**	**25**	**38**	**63**	**86**

NHL First All-Star Team (1965) • Bill Masterton Trophy (1968)

Played in NHL All-Star Game (1956, 1957, 1958, 1959, 1960, 1961, 1962, 1963, 1964, 1965, 1967)

Traded to **Los Angeles** by **Montreal** for cash, June 8, 1971.

PRPIC, Joel

Center. Shoots left. 6'6", 225 lbs. Born, Sudbury, Ont., September 25, 1974.
(Boston's 9th choice, 233rd overall, in 1993 Entry Draft).

Season	Club	GP	G	A	Pts	PIM	GP	G	A	Pts	PIM
1997-98	Boston Bruins	1	0	0	0	2	....	....	....	....	....
99-2000	Boston Bruins	14	0	3	3	0	....	....	....	....	....
2000-01	Colorado Avalanche	3	0	0	0	2	....	....	....	....	....
	NHL Totals	**18**	**0**	**3**	**3**	**4**	....	....	....	....	....

Signed as a free agent by **Colorado**, August, 2000. Signed as a free agent by **San Jose**, August 15, 2001.

PRYOR, Chris

Defense. Shoots right. 5'11", 210 lbs. Born, St. Paul, MN, January 23, 1961.

Season	Club	GP	G	A	Pts	PIM	GP	G	A	Pts	PIM
1984-85	Minnesota North Stars	4	0	0	0	16	....	....	....	....	....
1985-86	Minnesota North Stars	7	0	1	1	0	....	....	....	....	....
1986-87	Minnesota North Stars	50	1	3	4	49	....	....	....	....	....
1987-88	Minnesota North Stars	3	0	0	0	6	....	....	....	....	....
	New York Islanders	1	0	0	0	2	....	....	....	....	....
1988-89	New York Islanders	7	0	0	0	25	....	....	....	....	....
1989-90	New York Islanders	10	0	0	0	24	....	....	....	....	....
	NHL Totals	**82**	**1**	**4**	**5**	**122**	....	....	....	....	....

Signed as a free agent by **Minnesota**, January 10, 1985. Traded to **NY Islanders** by **Minnesota** with Minnesota's 7th round choice (Brett Harkins) in 1989 Entry Draft for Gord Dineen, March 8, 1988.

PRYSTAI, Metro

Center. Shoots left. 5'8", 155 lbs. Born, Yorkton, Sask., November 7, 1927.

Season	Club	GP	G	A	Pts	PIM	GP	G	A	Pts	PIM
1947-48	Chicago Black Hawks	54	7	11	18	25	....	....	....	....	....
1948-49	Chicago Black Hawks	59	12	7	19	19	....	....	....	....	....
1949-50	Chicago Black Hawks	65	29	22	51	31	....	....	....	....	....
1950-51	Detroit Red Wings	62	20	17	37	27	3	1	0	1	0
1951-52 ♦	Detroit Red Wings	69	21	22	43	16	8	2	*5	*7	0
1952-53	Detroit Red Wings	70	16	34	50	12	6	4	4	8	2
1953-54 ♦	Detroit Red Wings	70	12	15	27	26	12	2	3	5	0
1954-55	Detroit Red Wings	12	2	3	5	9	....	....	....	....	....
	Chicago Black Hawks	57	11	13	24	28	....	....	....	....	....
1955-56	Chicago Black Hawks	8	1	3	4	8	....	....	....	....	....
	Detroit Red Wings	63	12	16	28	10	9	1	2	3	6
1956-57	Detroit Red Wings	70	7	15	22	16	5	2	0	2	0
1957-58	Detroit Red Wings	15	1	1	2	4	....	....	....	....	....
	NHL Totals	**674**	**151**	**179**	**330**	**231**	**43**	**12**	**14**	**26**	**8**

Played in NHL All-Star Game (1950, 1953, 1954)

Traded to **Detroit** by **Chicago** with Jim Henry, Gaye Stewart and Bob Goldham for Al Dewsbury, Harry Lumley, Jack Stewart, Don Morrison and Pete Babando, July 13, 1950. Traded to **Chicago** by **Detroit** for Lorne Davis, November 9, 1954. Traded to **Detroit** by **Chicago** for Ed Sandford, October 24, 1955.

PUDAS, Al

Wing. Shoots right. 5'10", 160 lbs. Born, Siikajoki, Finland, February 17, 1899.

Season	Club	GP	G	A	Pts	PIM	GP	G	A	Pts	PIM
1926-27	Toronto St. Pats/Maple Leafs	4	0	0	0	0	....	....	....	....	....
	NHL Totals	**4**	**0**	**0**	**0**	**0**	....	....	....	....	....

Signed as a free agent by **Toronto**, October 28, 1926. Loaned to **Windsor** by **Toronto** for cash, November 10, 1926. Loaned to **Hamilton** (Can-Pro) by **Toronto** with $5,000 for George Patterson, February 1, 1927. Traded to **London** (Can-Pro) by **Toronto** for Gerry Lowrey, October 20, 1927.

PULFORD, Bob

HHOF

Left wing. Shoots left. 5'11", 188 lbs. Born, Newton Robinson, Ont., March 31, 1936.

Season	Club	GP	G	A	Pts	PIM	GP	G	A	Pts	PIM
1956-57	Toronto Maple Leafs	65	11	11	22	32	....	....	....	....	....
1957-58	Toronto Maple Leafs	70	14	17	31	48	....	....	....	....	....
1958-59	Toronto Maple Leafs	70	23	14	37	53	12	4	4	8	8
1959-60	Toronto Maple Leafs	70	24	28	52	81	10	4	1	5	10
1960-61	Toronto Maple Leafs	40	11	18	29	41	5	0	0	0	8
1961-62 ♦	Toronto Maple Leafs	70	18	21	39	98	12	7	1	8	24
1962-63 ♦	Toronto Maple Leafs	70	19	25	44	49	10	2	5	7	14
1963-64 ♦	Toronto Maple Leafs	70	18	30	48	73	14	5	3	8	20
1964-65	Toronto Maple Leafs	65	19	20	39	46	6	1	1	2	16
1965-66	Toronto Maple Leafs	70	28	28	56	51	4	1	1	2	12
1966-67 ♦	Toronto Maple Leafs	67	17	28	45	28	12	1	*10	11	12
1967-68	Toronto Maple Leafs	74	20	30	50	40	....	....	....	....	....
1968-69	Toronto Maple Leafs	72	11	23	34	20	4	0	0	0	2
1969-70	Toronto Maple Leafs	74	18	19	37	31	....	....	....	....	....
1970-71	Los Angeles Kings	59	17	26	43	53	....	....	....	....	....
1971-72	Los Angeles Kings	73	13	24	37	48	....	....	....	....	....
	NHL Totals	**1079**	**281**	**362**	**643**	**792**	**89**	**25**	**26**	**51**	**126**

Played in NHL All-Star Game (1960, 1962, 1963, 1964, 1968)

Traded to **Los Angeles** by **Toronto** for Garry Monahan and Brian Murphy, September 3, 1970.

PULKKINEN, Dave

Left wing/Defense. Shoots right. 6', 195 lbs. Born, Kapuskasing, Ont., May 18, 1949.
(St. Louis' 8th choice, 77th overall, in 1969 Amateur Draft).

Season	Club	GP	G	A	Pts	PIM	GP	G	A	Pts	PIM
1972-73	New York Islanders	2	0	0	0	0	....	....	....	....	....
	NHL Totals	**2**	**0**	**0**	**0**	**0**	....	....	....	....	....

Traded to **NY Islanders** by **St. Louis** for cash, August, 1972.

PURINTON, Dale

Defense. Shoots left. 6'3", 214 lbs. Born, Fort Wayne, IN, October 11, 1976.
(NY Rangers' 5th choice, 117th overall, in 1995 Entry Draft).

Season	Club	GP	G	A	Pts	PIM	GP	G	A	Pts	PIM
99-2000	New York Rangers	1	0	0	0	7	....	....	....	....	....
2000-01	New York Rangers	42	0	2	2	180	....	....	....	....	....
2001-02	New York Rangers	40	0	4	4	113	....	....	....	....	....
2002-03	New York Rangers	58	3	9	12	161	....	....	....	....	....
	NHL Totals	**141**	**3**	**15**	**18**	**461**	....	....	....	....	....

PURPUR, Fido

USHOF

Right wing. Shoots right. 5'6", 155 lbs. Born, Grand Forks, ND, September 26, 1914.

Season	Club	GP	G	A	Pts	PIM	GP	G	A	Pts	PIM
1934-35	St. Louis Eagles	25	1	2	3	8	....	....	....	....	....
1941-42	Chicago Black Hawks	8	0	0	0	0	....	....	....	....	....
1942-43	Chicago Black Hawks	50	13	16	29	14	....	....	....	....	....
1943-44	Chicago Black Hawks	40	9	10	19	13	9	1	1	2	0
1944-45	Chicago Black Hawks	21	2	7	9	11	....	....	....	....	....
	Detroit Red Wings	....	....	....	....	....	7	0	1	1	4
	NHL Totals	**144**	**25**	**35**	**60**	**46**	**16**	**1**	**2**	**3**	**4**

Traded to **St. Louis** by **Minneapolis** (CHL) for Nick Wasnie and $1,600, December 28, 1934. Claimed by **Toronto** from **St. Louis** in Dispersal Draft, October 15, 1935. Traded to **St. Louis** (AHA) by **Toronto** for cash, November 6, 1935. Traded to **Chicago** by **St. Louis** (AHA) for Sammy McManus and cash, May 3, 1941. Traded to **Detroit** by **Chicago** to complete transaction that sent Earl Seibert to Detroit (January 2, 1945), January 4, 1945. Traded to **St. Louis** (AHL) by **Detroit** for cash, August 24, 1945.

PURVES, John

Right wing. Shoots right. 6'1", 201 lbs. Born, Toronto, Ont., February 12, 1968.
(Washington's 6th choice, 103rd overall, in 1986 Entry Draft).

Season	Club	GP	G	A	Pts	PIM	GP	G	A	Pts	PIM
1990-91	Washington Capitals	7	1	0	1	0	....	....	....	....	....
	NHL Totals	**7**	**1**	**0**	**1**	**0**	....	....	....	....	....

PUSHOR, Jamie

Defense. Shoots right. 6'3", 218 lbs. Born, Lethbridge, Alta., February 11, 1973.
(Detroit's 2nd choice, 32nd overall, in 1991 Entry Draft).

Season	Club	GP	G	A	Pts	PIM	GP	G	A	Pts	PIM
1995-96	Detroit Red Wings	5	0	1	1	17	....	....	....	....	....
1996-97 ♦	Detroit Red Wings	75	4	7	11	129	5	0	1	1	5
1997-98	Detroit Red Wings	54	2	5	7	71	....	....	....	....	....
	Mighty Ducks of Anaheim	10	0	2	2	10	....	....	....	....	....
1998-99	Mighty Ducks of Anaheim	70	1	2	3	112	4	0	0	0	6
99-2000	Dallas Stars	62	0	8	8	53	5	0	0	0	5
2000-01	Columbus Blue Jackets	75	3	10	13	94	....	....	....	....	....
2001-02	Columbus Blue Jackets	61	0	6	6	54	....	....	....	....	....
	Pittsburgh Penguins	15	0	2	2	30	....	....	....	....	....
2002-03	Pittsburgh Penguins	76	3	1	4	76	....	....	....	....	....
	NHL Totals	**503**	**13**	**44**	**57**	**646**	**14**	**0**	**1**	**1**	**16**

Traded to **Anaheim** by **Detroit** with Detroit's 4th round choice (Viktor Wallin) in 1998 Entry Draft for Dmitri Mironov, March 24, 1998. Claimed by **Atlanta** from **Anaheim** in Expansion Draft, June 25, 1999. Traded to **Dallas** by **Atlanta** for Jason Botterill, July 15, 1999. Selected by **Columbus** from **Dallas** in Expansion Draft, June 23, 2000. Traded to **Pittsburgh** by **Columbus** for Pittsburgh's 4th round choice (Kevin Jarman) in 2003 Entry Draft, March 15, 2002.

PUSIE, Jean

Defense. Shoots left. 6', 205 lbs. Born, Montreal, Que., October 15, 1910.

Season	Club	GP	G	A	Pts	PIM	GP	G	A	Pts	PIM
1930-31 ♦	Montreal Canadiens	6	0	0	0	0	3	0	0	0	0
1931-32	Montreal Canadiens	1	0	0	0	0	....	....	....	....	....
1933-34	New York Rangers	19	0	2	2	17	....	....	....	....	....
1934-35	Boston Bruins	4	1	0	1	0	4	0	0	0	0
1935-36	Montreal Canadiens	31	0	2	2	11	....	....	....	....	....
	NHL Totals	**61**	**1**	**4**	**5**	**28**	**7**	**0**	**0**	**0**	**0**

Signed as a free agent by **Montreal**, February 4, 1930. Loaned to **Providence** (Can-Am) by **Montreal** with the trade of Gerry Carson and cash for Johnny Gagnon, October 21, 1930. Loan transferred to **Galt** (OPHL) by **Montreal** for cash, October 30, 1930. Traded to **NY Rangers** by **Vancouver** (WCHL) for cash, March 11, 1933. Traded to **Boston** by **NY Rangers** for Percy Jackson, November 1, 1934. Traded to **Montreal** by **Boston** with Walt Buswell and cash for Roger Jenkins, July 13, 1935. Traded to **Boston** (Can-Am) by **Montreal** for cash, February 9, 1936.

PYATT, Nelson

Center. Shoots left. 6', 175 lbs. Born, Port Arthur, Ont., September 9, 1953.
(Detroit's 2nd choice, 39th overall, in 1973 Amateur Draft).

Season	Club	GP	G	A	Pts	PIM	GP	G	A	Pts	PIM
1973-74	Detroit Red Wings	5	0	0	0	0	....	....	....	....	....
1974-75	Detroit Red Wings	9	0	0	0	2	....	....	....	....	....
	Washington Capitals	16	6	4	10	21	....	....	....	....	....
1975-76	Washington Capitals	77	26	23	49	14	....	....	....	....	....
1976-77	Colorado Rockies	77	23	22	45	20	....	....	....	....	....
1977-78	Colorado Rockies	71	9	12	21	8	....	....	....	....	....
1978-79	Colorado Rockies	28	2	2	4	2	....	....	....	....	....

Season	Club	GP	G	A	Pts	PIM	GP	G	A	Pts	PIM
		REGULAR SEASON					PLAYOFFS				
1979-80	Colorado Rockies	13	5	0	5	2	....	....	....	....	....
	NHL Totals	**296**	**71**	**63**	**134**	**69**	....	....	....	....	....

Traded to **Washington** by **Detroit** for Washington's 3rd round choice (Al Cameron) in 1975 Amateur Draft, February 28, 1975. Signed as a free agent by **Colorado**, September 1, 1976.

PYATT, Taylor

Left wing. Shoots left. 6'4", 222 lbs. Born, Thunder Bay, Ont., August 19, 1981.
(NY Islanders' 2nd choice, 8th overall, in 1999 Entry Draft).

Season	Club	GP	G	A	Pts	PIM	GP	G	A	Pts	PIM
2000-01	New York Islanders	78	4	14	18	39	....	....	....	....	....
2001-02	Buffalo Sabres	48	10	10	20	35	....	....	....	....	....
2002-03	Buffalo Sabres	78	14	14	28	38	....	....	....	....	....
	NHL Totals	**204**	**28**	**38**	**66**	**112**	....	....	....	....	....

Traded to **Buffalo** by **NY Islanders** with Tim Connolly for Michael Peca, June 24, 2001.

QUACKENBUSH, Bill

HHOF

Defense. Shoots left. 5'11", 190 lbs. Born, Toronto, Ont., March 2, 1922.

Season	Club	GP	G	A	Pts	PIM	GP	G	A	Pts	PIM
1942-43	Detroit Red Wings	10	1	1	2	4	....	....	....	....	....
1943-44	Detroit Red Wings	43	4	14	18	6	2	1	0	1	0
1944-45	Detroit Red Wings	50	7	14	21	10	14	0	2	2	2
1945-46	Detroit Red Wings	48	11	10	21	6	5	0	1	1	0
1946-47	Detroit Red Wings	44	5	17	22	6	5	0	0	0	2
1947-48	Detroit Red Wings	58	6	16	22	17	10	0	2	2	0
1948-49	Detroit Red Wings	60	6	17	23	0	11	1	1	2	0
1949-50	Boston Bruins	70	8	17	25	4	....	....	....	....	....
1950-51	Boston Bruins	70	5	24	29	12	6	0	1	1	0
1951-52	Boston Bruins	69	2	17	19	6	7	0	3	3	0
1952-53	Boston Bruins	69	2	16	18	6	11	0	4	4	4
1953-54	Boston Bruins	45	0	17	17	6	4	0	0	0	0
1954-55	Boston Bruins	68	2	20	22	8	5	0	5	5	0
1955-56	Boston Bruins	70	3	22	25	4	....	....	....	....	....
	NHL Totals	**774**	**62**	**222**	**284**	**95**	**80**	**2**	**19**	**21**	**8**

• Brother of Max • NHL Second All-Star Team (1947, 1953) • NHL First All-Star Team (1948, 1949, 1951) • Lady Byng Trophy (1949)

Played in NHL All-Star Game (1947, 1948, 1949, 1950, 1951, 1952, 1953, 1954)

Signed as a free agent by **Detroit**, October 19, 1942. Traded to **Boston** by **Detroit** with Pete Horeck for Pete Babando, Lloyd Durham, Clare Martin and Jimmy Peters, August 16, 1949.

QUACKENBUSH, Max

Defense. Shoots left. 6'2", 180 lbs. Born, Toronto, Ont., August 29, 1928.

Season	Club	GP	G	A	Pts	PIM	GP	G	A	Pts	PIM
1950-51	Boston Bruins	47	4	6	10	26	6	0	0	0	4
1951-52	Chicago Black Hawks	14	0	1	1	4	....	....	....	....	....
	NHL Totals	**61**	**4**	**7**	**11**	**30**	**6**	**0**	**0**	**0**	**4**

• Brother of Bill

Loaned to **Boston** by **Detroit** (Indianapolis-AHL) for remainder of 1950-51 season for Steve Kraftcheck, December 5, 1950. Traded to **Chicago** by **Detroit** for Doug McCaig, September 18, 1951. Claimed by **Chicago** from **Calgary-WHL** (Chicago) in Inter-League Draft, June 14, 1954. Traded to **Montreal** by **Chicago** for Fred Burchell, July 3, 1955. • Transaction voided when Quackenbush officially announced retirement, July 15, 1955.

QUENNEVILLE, Joel

Defense. Shoots left. 6'1", 200 lbs. Born, Windsor, Ont., September 15, 1958.
(Toronto's 1st choice, 21st overall, in 1978 Amateur Draft).

Season	Club	GP	G	A	Pts	PIM	GP	G	A	Pts	PIM
1978-79	Toronto Maple Leafs	61	2	9	11	60	6	0	1	1	4
1979-80	Toronto Maple Leafs	32	1	4	5	24	....	....	....	....	....
	Colorado Rockies	35	5	7	12	26	....	....	....	....	....
1980-81	Colorado Rockies	71	10	24	34	86	....	....	....	....	....
1981-82	Colorado Rockies	64	5	10	15	55	....	....	....	....	....
1982-83	New Jersey Devils	74	5	12	17	46	....	....	....	....	....
1983-84	Hartford Whalers	80	5	8	13	95	....	....	....	....	....
1984-85	Hartford Whalers	79	6	16	22	96	....	....	....	....	....
1985-86	Hartford Whalers	71	5	20	25	83	10	0	2	2	12
1986-87	Hartford Whalers	37	3	7	10	24	6	0	0	0	0
1987-88	Hartford Whalers	77	1	8	9	44	6	0	2	2	2
1988-89	Hartford Whalers	69	4	7	11	32	4	0	3	3	4
1989-90	Hartford Whalers	44	1	4	5	34	....	....	....	....	....
1990-91	Washington Capitals	9	1	0	1	0	....	....	....	....	....
	NHL Totals	**803**	**54**	**136**	**190**	**705**	**32**	**0**	**8**	**8**	**22**

Traded to **Colorado** by **Toronto** with Lanny McDonald for Pat Hickey and Wilf Paiement, December 29, 1979. Transferred to **New Jersey** after **Colorado** franchise relocated, June 30, 1982. Traded to **Calgary** by **New Jersey** with Steve Tambellini for Phil Russell and Mel Bridgman, June 20, 1983. Traded to **Hartford** by **Calgary** with Richie Dunn for Mickey Volcan, July 5, 1983. • Missed majority of the 1986-87 season recovering from shoulder injury suffered in game vs. Boston, December 18, 1986. Traded to **Washington** by **Hartford** for cash, October 3, 1990. Signed as a free agent by **Toronto**, July 30, 1991.

QUENNEVILLE, Leo

Left wing/Center. Shoots left. 5'10", 170 lbs. Born, St-Anicet, Que., June 15, 1900.

Season	Club	GP	G	A	Pts	PIM	GP	G	A	Pts	PIM
1929-30	New York Rangers	25	0	3	3	10	3	0	0	0	0
	NHL Totals	**25**	**0**	**3**	**3**	**10**	**3**	**0**	**0**	**0**	**0**

Claimed by **NY Rangers** from **Newark** (Can-Am) in Inter-League Draft, May 13, 1929. Traded to **London** (IHL) by **NY Rangers** for cash, October 14, 1930.

QUILTY, John

Center. Shoots left. 5'10", 175 lbs. Born, Ottawa, Ont., January 21, 1921.

Season	Club	GP	G	A	Pts	PIM	GP	G	A	Pts	PIM
1940-41	Montreal Canadiens	48	18	16	34	31	3	0	2	2	0
1941-42	Montreal Canadiens	48	12	12	24	44	3	0	1	1	0
1946-47	Montreal Canadiens	3	1	1	2	0	7	3	2	5	9
1947-48	Montreal Canadiens	20	2	3	5	4	....	....	....	....	....
	Boston Bruins	6	3	2	5	2	....	....	....	....	....
	NHL Totals	**125**	**36**	**34**	**70**	**81**	**13**	**3**	**5**	**8**	**9**

Calder Trophy (1941)

Signed as a free agent by **Montreal**, October 29, 1940. Traded to **Springfield** (AHL) by **Montreal** (Buffalo-AHL) for George Pargeter, November 19, 1946. Traded to **Montreal** by **Springfield** (AHL) for cash, March 3, 1947. Traded to **Boston** by **Montreal** with Jimmy Peters for Joe Carveth, December 16, 1947.

QUINN, Dan

Center. Shoots left. 5'11", 182 lbs. Born, Ottawa, Ont., June 1, 1965.
(Calgary's 1st choice, 13th overall, in 1983 Entry Draft).

Season	Club	GP	G	A	Pts	PIM	GP	G	A	Pts	PIM
1983-84	Calgary Flames	54	19	33	52	20	8	3	5	8	4
1984-85	Calgary Flames	74	20	38	58	22	3	0	0	0	0
1985-86	Calgary Flames	78	30	42	72	44	18	8	7	15	10
1986-87	Calgary Flames	16	3	6	9	14	....	....	....	....	....
	Pittsburgh Penguins	64	28	43	71	40	....	....	....	....	....
1987-88	Pittsburgh Penguins	70	40	39	79	50	....	....	....	....	....
1988-89	Pittsburgh Penguins	79	34	60	94	102	11	6	3	9	10
1989-90	Pittsburgh Penguins	41	9	20	29	22	....	....	....	....	....
	Vancouver Canucks	37	16	18	34	27	....	....	....	....	....
1990-91	Vancouver Canucks	64	18	31	49	46	....	....	....	....	....
	St. Louis Blues	14	4	7	11	20	13	4	7	11	32
1991-92	Philadelphia Flyers	67	11	26	37	26	....	....	....	....	....
1992-93	Minnesota North Stars	11	0	4	4	6	....	....	....	....	....
1993-94	Ottawa Senators	13	7	0	7	6	....	....	....	....	....
1994-95	Los Angeles Kings	44	14	17	31	32	....	....	....	....	....
1995-96	Ottawa Senators	28	6	18	24	24	....	....	....	....	....
	Philadelphia Flyers	35	7	14	21	22	12	1	4	5	6
1996-97	Pittsburgh Penguins	16	0	3	3	10	....	....	....	....	....
	NHL Totals	**805**	**266**	**419**	**685**	**533**	**65**	**22**	**26**	**48**	**62**

Traded to **Pittsburgh** by **Calgary** for Mike Bullard, November 12, 1986. Traded to **Vancouver** by **Pittsburgh** with Dave Capuano and Andrew McBain for Rod Buskas, Barry Pederson and Tony Tanti, January 8, 1990. Traded to **St. Louis** by **Vancouver** with Garth Butcher for Geoff Courtnall, Robert Dirk, Sergio Momesso, Cliff Ronning and St. Louis' 5th round choice (Brian Loney) in 1992 Entry Draft, March 5, 1991. Traded to **Philadelphia** by **St. Louis** with Rod Brind'Amour for Ron Sutter and Murray Baron, September 22, 1991. Signed as a free agent by **Minnesota**, October 4, 1992. Signed as a free agent by **Ottawa**, March 15, 1994. Signed as a free agent by **Los Angeles**, September 3, 1994. Signed as a free agent by **Ottawa**, August 1, 1995. Traded to **Philadelphia** by **Ottawa** for cash, January 23, 1996. Signed as a free agent by **Pittsburgh**, July 17, 1996.

QUINN, Pat

Defense. Shoots left. 6'3", 205 lbs. Born, Hamilton, Ont., January 29, 1943.

Season	Club	GP	G	A	Pts	PIM	GP	G	A	Pts	PIM
1968-69	Toronto Maple Leafs	40	2	7	9	95	4	0	0	0	13
1969-70	Toronto Maple Leafs	59	0	5	5	88	....	....	....	....	....
1970-71	Vancouver Canucks	76	2	11	13	149	....	....	....	....	....
1971-72	Vancouver Canucks	57	2	3	5	63	....	....	....	....	....
1972-73	Atlanta Flames	78	2	18	20	113	....	....	....	....	....
1973-74	Atlanta Flames	77	5	27	32	94	4	0	0	0	6
1974-75	Atlanta Flames	80	2	19	21	156	....	....	....	....	....
1975-76	Atlanta Flames	80	2	11	13	134	2	0	1	1	2
1976-77	Atlanta Flames	59	1	12	13	58	1	0	0	0	0
	NHL Totals	**606**	**18**	**113**	**131**	**950**	**11**	**0**	**1**	**1**	**21**

Claimed by **Montreal** from **Detroit** in Intra-League Draft, June 15, 1966. Traded to **St. Louis** by **Montreal** with Ron Attwell for cash, June 14, 1967. Traded to **Toronto** by **St. Louis** for cash, March 25, 1968. Claimed by **Vancouver** from **Toronto** in Expansion Draft, June 10, 1970. Claimed by **Atlanta** from **Vancouver** in Expansion Draft, June 6, 1972.

QUINNEY, Ken

Right wing. Shoots right. 5'10", 186 lbs. Born, New Westminster, B.C., May 23, 1965.
(Quebec's 9th choice, 203rd overall, in 1984 Entry Draft).

Season	Club	GP	G	A	Pts	PIM	GP	G	A	Pts	PIM
1986-87	Quebec Nordiques	25	2	7	9	16	....	....	....	....	....
1987-88	Quebec Nordiques	15	2	2	4	5	....	....	....	....	....
1990-91	Quebec Nordiques	19	3	4	7	2	....	....	....	....	....
	NHL Totals	**59**	**7**	**13**	**20**	**23**	....	....	....	....	....

Signed as a free agent by **Detroit**, August 12, 1991.

QUINT, Deron

Defense. Shoots left. 6'2", 219 lbs. Born, Durham, NH, March 12, 1976.
(Winnipeg's 1st choice, 30th overall, in 1994 Entry Draft).

Season	Club	GP	G	A	Pts	PIM	GP	G	A	Pts	PIM
1995-96	Winnipeg Jets	51	5	13	18	22	....	....	....	....	....
1996-97	Phoenix Coyotes	27	3	11	14	4	7	0	2	2	0
1997-98	Phoenix Coyotes	32	4	7	11	16	....	....	....	....	....
1998-99	Phoenix Coyotes	60	5	8	13	20	....	....	....	....	....
99-2000	Phoenix Coyotes	50	3	7	10	22	....	....	....	....	....
	New Jersey Devils	4	1	0	1	2	....	....	....	....	....
2000-01	Columbus Blue Jackets	57	7	16	23	16	....	....	....	....	....
2001-02	Columbus Blue Jackets	75	7	18	25	26	....	....	....	....	....

Season	Club	GP	G	A	Pts	PIM	GP	G	A	Pts	PIM
		REGULAR SEASON					PLAYOFFS				
2002-03	Phoenix Coyotes	51	7	10	17	20	....	....	....	....	....
	NHL Totals	**407**	**42**	**90**	**132**	**148**	**7**	**0**	**2**	**2**	**0**

Transferred to **Phoenix** after **Winnipeg** franchise relocated, July 1, 1996. Traded to **New Jersey** by **Phoenix** with Phoenix's 3rd round choice (later traded back to Phoenix – Phoenix selected Beat Forster) in 2001 Entry Draft for Lyle Odelein, March 7, 2000. Traded to **Columbus** by **New Jersey** to complete transaction that sent Krzysztof Oliwa to Columbus (June 12, 2000) and Turner Stevenson to New Jersey (June 23, 2000), June 23, 2000. Signed as a free agent by **Phoenix**, October 26, 2002.

QUINTAL, Stephane

Defense. Shoots right. 6'3", 231 lbs. Born, Boucherville, Que., October 22, 1968.
(Boston's 2nd choice, 14th overall, in 1987 Entry Draft).

Season	Club	GP	G	A	Pts	PIM	GP	G	A	Pts	PIM
1988-89	Boston Bruins	26	0	1	1	29	....	....	....	....	....
1989-90	Boston Bruins	38	2	2	4	22	....	....	....	....	....
1990-91	Boston Bruins	45	2	6	8	89	3	0	1	1	7
1991-92	Boston Bruins	49	4	10	14	77	....	....	....	....	....
	St. Louis Blues	26	0	6	6	32	4	1	2	3	6
1992-93	St. Louis Blues	75	1	10	11	100	9	0	0	0	8
1993-94	Winnipeg Jets	81	8	18	26	119	....	....	....	....	....
1994-95	Winnipeg Jets	43	6	17	23	78	....	....	....	....	....
1995-96	Montreal Canadiens	68	2	14	16	117	6	0	1	1	6
1996-97	Montreal Canadiens	71	7	15	22	100	5	0	1	1	6
1997-98	Montreal Canadiens	71	6	10	16	97	9	0	2	2	4
1998-99	Montreal Canadiens	82	8	19	27	84	....	....	....	....	....
99-2000	New York Rangers	75	2	14	16	77	....	....	....	....	....
2000-01	Chicago Blackhawks	72	1	18	19	60	....	....	....	....	....
2001-02	Montreal Canadiens	75	6	10	16	87	12	1	3	4	12
2002-03	Montreal Canadiens	67	5	5	10	70	....	....	....	....	....
	NHL Totals	**964**	**60**	**175**	**235**	**1238**	**48**	**2**	**10**	**12**	**49**

Traded to **St. Louis** by **Boston** with Craig Janney for Adam Oates, February 7, 1992. Traded to **Winnipeg** by **St. Louis** with Nelson Emerson for Phil Housley, September 24, 1993. Traded to **Montreal** by **Winnipeg** for Montreal's 2nd round choice (Jason Doig) in 1995 Entry Draft, July 8, 1995. Signed as a free agent by **NY Rangers**, July 13, 1999. Claimed on waivers by **Chicago** from **NY Rangers**, October 5, 2000. Traded to **Montreal** by **Chicago** for Montreal's 4th round choice (Brent MacLellan) in 2001 Entry Draft, June 23, 2001.

QUINTIN, Jean-Francois

Left wing. Shoots left. 6', 187 lbs. Born, St-Jean, Que., May 28, 1969.
(Minnesota's 4th choice, 75th overall, in 1989 Entry Draft).

Season	Club	GP	G	A	Pts	PIM	GP	G	A	Pts	PIM
1991-92	San Jose Sharks	8	3	0	3	0	....	....	....	....	....
1992-93	San Jose Sharks	14	2	5	7	4	....	....	....	....	....
	NHL Totals	**22**	**5**	**5**	**10**	**4**	....	....	....	....	....

Claimed by **San Jose** from **Minnesota** in Dispersal Draft, May 30, 1991.

RACHUNEK, Karel

Defense. Shoots right. 6'2", 202 lbs. Born, Gottwaldov, Czech., August 27, 1979.
(Ottawa's 8th choice, 229th overall, in 1997 Entry Draft).

Season	Club	GP	G	A	Pts	PIM	GP	G	A	Pts	PIM
99-2000	Ottawa Senators	6	0	0	0	2	....	....	....	....	....
2000-01	Ottawa Senators	71	3	30	33	60	3	0	0	0	0
2001-02	Ottawa Senators	51	3	15	18	24	....	....	....	....	....
2002-03	Ottawa Senators	58	4	25	29	30	17	1	3	4	14
	NHL Totals	**186**	**10**	**70**	**80**	**116**	**20**	**1**	**3**	**4**	**14**

RACINE, Yves

Defense. Shoots left. 6', 205 lbs. Born, Matane, Que., February 7, 1969.
(Detroit's 1st choice, 11th overall, in 1987 Entry Draft).

Season	Club	GP	G	A	Pts	PIM	GP	G	A	Pts	PIM
1989-90	Detroit Red Wings	28	4	9	13	23	....	....	....	....	....
1990-91	Detroit Red Wings	62	7	40	47	33	7	2	0	2	0
1991-92	Detroit Red Wings	61	2	22	24	94	11	2	1	3	10
1992-93	Detroit Red Wings	80	9	31	40	80	7	1	3	4	27
1993-94	Philadelphia Flyers	67	9	43	52	48	....	....	....	....	....
1994-95	Montreal Canadiens	47	4	7	11	42	....	....	....	....	....
1995-96	Montreal Canadiens	25	0	3	3	26	....	....	....	....	....
	San Jose Sharks	32	1	16	17	28	....	....	....	....	....
1996-97	Calgary Flames	46	1	15	16	24	....	....	....	....	....
1997-98	Tampa Bay Lightning	60	0	8	8	41	....	....	....	....	....
	NHL Totals	**508**	**37**	**194**	**231**	**439**	**25**	**5**	**4**	**9**	**37**

Traded to **Philadelphia** by **Detroit** with Detroit's 4th round choice (Sebastien Vallee) in 1994 Entry Draft for Terry Carkner, October 5, 1993. Traded to **Montreal** by **Philadelphia** for Kevin Haller, June 29, 1994. Claimed on waivers by **San Jose** from **Montreal**, January 23, 1996. Traded to **Calgary** by **San Jose** for cash, December 17, 1996. Signed as a free agent by **Tampa Bay**, July 16, 1997.

RADIVOJEVIC, Branko

Right wing. Shoots right. 6'1", 209 lbs. Born, Piestany, Czech., November 24, 1980.
(Colorado's 3rd choice, 93rd overall, in 1999 Entry Draft).

Season	Club	GP	G	A	Pts	PIM	GP	G	A	Pts	PIM
2001-02	Phoenix Coyotes	18	4	2	6	4	1	0	0	0	2
2002-03	Phoenix Coyotes	79	12	15	27	63	....	....	....	....	....
	NHL Totals	**97**	**16**	**17**	**33**	**67**	**1**	**0**	**0**	**0**	**2**

Signed as a free agent by **Phoenix**, June 19, 2001.

RADLEY, Yip

Defense. Shoots left. 6'00", 198 lbs. Born, Ottawa, Ont., June 27, 1908.

Season	Club	GP	G	A	Pts	PIM	GP	G	A	Pts	PIM
1930-31	New York Americans	1	0	0	0	0	....	....	....	....	....
1936-37	Montreal Maroons	17	0	1	1	13	....	....	....	....	....
	NHL Totals	**18**	**0**	**1**	**1**	**13**	....	....	....	....	....

Signed as a free agent by **NY Americans**, October 22, 1930. Signed as a free agent by **Mtl. Maroons**, October 16, 1936 .

RADULOV, Igor

Left wing. Shoots left. 6'1", 194 lbs. Born, Nizhny Tagil, USSR, August 23, 1982.
(Chicago's 4th choice, 74th overall, in 2000 Entry Draft).

Season	Club	GP	G	A	Pts	PIM	GP	G	A	Pts	PIM
2002-03	Chicago Blackhawks	7	5	0	5	4	....	....	....	....	....
	NHL Totals	**7**	**5**	**0**	**5**	**4**	....	....	....	....	....

RAFALSKI, Brian

Defense. Shoots right. 5'9", 190 lbs. Born, Dearborn, MI, September 28, 1973.

Season	Club	GP	G	A	Pts	PIM	GP	G	A	Pts	PIM
99-2000♦	New Jersey Devils	75	5	27	32	28	23	2	6	8	8
2000-01	New Jersey Devils	78	9	43	52	26	25	7	11	18	7
2001-02	New Jersey Devils	76	7	40	47	18	6	3	2	5	4
2002-03♦	New Jersey Devils	79	3	37	40	14	23	2	9	11	8
	NHL Totals	**308**	**24**	**147**	**171**	**86**	**77**	**14**	**28**	**42**	**27**

NHL All-Rookie Team (2000)

Signed as a free agent by **New Jersey**, May 7, 1999.

RAGLAN, Herb

Right wing. Shoots right. 6', 205 lbs. Born, Peterborough, Ont., August 5, 1967.
(St. Louis' 1st choice, 37th overall, in 1985 Entry Draft).

Season	Club	GP	G	A	Pts	PIM	GP	G	A	Pts	PIM
1985-86	St. Louis Blues	7	0	0	0	5	10	1	1	2	24
1986-87	St. Louis Blues	62	6	10	16	159	4	0	0	0	2
1987-88	St. Louis Blues	73	10	15	25	190	10	1	3	4	11
1988-89	St. Louis Blues	50	7	10	17	144	8	1	2	3	13
1989-90	St. Louis Blues	11	0	1	1	21	....	....	....	....	....
1990-91	St. Louis Blues	32	3	3	6	52	....	....	....	....	....
	Quebec Nordiques	15	1	3	4	30	....	....	....	....	....
1991-92	Quebec Nordiques	62	6	14	20	120	....	....	....	....	....
1992-93	Tampa Bay Lightning	2	0	0	0	2	....	....	....	....	....
1993-94	Ottawa Senators	29	0	0	0	52	....	....	....	....	....
	NHL Totals	**343**	**33**	**56**	**89**	**775**	**32**	**3**	**6**	**9**	**50**

• Son of Rags

• Missed remainder of 1989-90 season recovering from wrist injury suffered in game vs. Quebec, November 4, 1989. Traded to **Quebec** by **St. Louis** with Tony Twist and Andy Rymsha for Darin Kimble, February 4, 1991. Traded to **Tampa Bay** by **Quebec** for Martin Simard, Steve Tuttle and Michel Mongeau, February 12, 1993. Signed as a free agent by **Ottawa**, January 1, 1994.

RAGLAN, Rags

Defense. Shoots left. 6'1", 193 lbs. Born, Pembroke, Ont., September 4, 1927.

Season	Club	GP	G	A	Pts	PIM	GP	G	A	Pts	PIM
1950-51	Detroit Red Wings	33	3	1	4	14	....	....	....	....	....
1951-52	Chicago Black Hawks	35	0	5	5	28	....	....	....	....	....
1952-53	Chicago Black Hawks	32	1	3	4	10	3	0	0	0	0
	NHL Totals	**100**	**4**	**9**	**13**	**52**	**3**	**0**	**0**	**0**	**0**

• Father of Herb

Traded to **Chicago** by **Detroit** with George Gee, Jimmy Peters Sr., Clare Martin, Max McNab and Jim McFadden for $75,000 and future considerations (Hugh Coflin, October, 1951), August 20, 1951.

RAGNARSSON, Marcus

Defense. Shoots left. 6'1", 215 lbs. Born, Ostervala, Sweden, August 13, 1971.
(San Jose's 5th choice, 99th overall, in 1992 Entry Draft).

Season	Club	GP	G	A	Pts	PIM	GP	G	A	Pts	PIM
1995-96	San Jose Sharks	71	8	31	39	42	....	....	....	....	....
1996-97	San Jose Sharks	69	3	14	17	63	....	....	....	....	....
1997-98	San Jose Sharks	79	5	20	25	65	6	0	0	0	4
1998-99	San Jose Sharks	74	0	13	13	66	6	0	1	1	6
99-2000	San Jose Sharks	63	3	13	16	38	12	0	3	3	10
2000-01	San Jose Sharks	68	3	12	15	44	5	0	1	1	8
2001-02	San Jose Sharks	70	5	15	20	44	12	1	3	4	12
2002-03	San Jose Sharks	25	1	7	8	30	....	....	....	....	....
	Philadelphia Flyers	43	2	6	8	32	13	0	1	1	6
	NHL Totals	**562**	**30**	**131**	**161**	**424**	**54**	**1**	**9**	**10**	**46**

Played in NHL All-Star Game (2001)

Traded to **Philadelphia** by **San Jose** for Dan McGillis, December 6, 2002.

RALEIGH, Don

Center. Shoots left. 5'11", 150 lbs. Born, Kenora, Ont., June 27, 1926.

Season	Club	GP	G	A	Pts	PIM	GP	G	A	Pts	PIM
1943-44	New York Rangers	15	2	2	4	2	....	....	....	....	....
1947-48	New York Rangers	52	15	18	33	2	6	2	0	2	2
1948-49	New York Rangers	41	10	16	26	8	....	....	....	....	....
1949-50	New York Rangers	70	12	25	37	11	12	4	5	9	4
1950-51	New York Rangers	64	15	24	39	18	....	....	....	....	....
1951-52	New York Rangers	70	19	42	61	14	....	....	....	....	....
1952-53	New York Rangers	55	4	18	22	2	....	....	....	....	....
1953-54	New York Rangers	70	15	30	45	16	....	....	....	....	....
1954-55	New York Rangers	69	8	32	40	19	....	....	....	....	....
1955-56	New York Rangers	29	1	12	13	4	....	....	....	....	....
	NHL Totals	**535**	**101**	**219**	**320**	**96**	**18**	**6**	**5**	**11**	**6**

Played in NHL All-Star Game (1951, 1954)

RALPH, Brad

Left wing. Shoots left. 6'2", 206 lbs. Born, Ottawa, Ont., October 17, 1980.
(Phoenix's 3rd choice, 53rd overall, in 1999 Entry Draft).

		Regular Season					Playoffs				
Season	Club	GP	G	A	Pts	PIM	GP	G	A	Pts	PIM
2000-01	Phoenix Coyotes	1	0	0	0	0	....	....	....	....	....
	NHL Totals	**1**	**0**	**0**	**0**	**0**	....	....	....	....	....

RAMAGE, Rob

Defense. Shoots right. 6'2", 200 lbs. Born, Byron, Ont., January 11, 1959.
(Colorado's 1st choice, 1st overall, in 1979 Entry Draft).

		Regular Season					Playoffs				
Season	Club	GP	G	A	Pts	PIM	GP	G	A	Pts	PIM
1979-80	Colorado Rockies	75	8	20	28	135	....	....	....	....	....
1980-81	Colorado Rockies	79	20	42	62	193	....	....	....	....	....
1981-82	Colorado Rockies	80	13	29	42	201	....	....	....	....	....
1982-83	St. Louis Blues	78	16	35	51	193	4	0	3	3	22
1983-84	St. Louis Blues	80	15	45	60	121	11	1	8	9	32
1984-85	St. Louis Blues	80	7	31	38	178	3	1	3	4	6
1985-86	St. Louis Blues	77	10	56	66	171	19	1	10	11	66
1986-87	St. Louis Blues	59	11	28	39	108	6	2	2	4	21
1987-88	St. Louis Blues	67	8	34	42	127	....	....	....	....	....
	Calgary Flames	12	1	6	7	37	9	1	3	4	21
1988-89 ◆	Calgary Flames	68	3	13	16	156	20	1	11	12	26
1989-90	Toronto Maple Leafs	80	8	41	49	202	5	1	2	3	20
1990-91	Toronto Maple Leafs	80	10	25	35	173	....	....	....	....	....
1991-92	Minnesota North Stars	34	4	5	9	69	....	....	....	....	....
1992-93	Tampa Bay Lightning	66	5	12	17	138	....	....	....	....	....
	◆ Montreal Canadiens	8	0	1	1	8	7	0	0	0	4
1993-94	Montreal Canadiens	6	0	1	1	2	....	....	....	....	....
	Philadelphia Flyers	15	0	1	1	14	....	....	....	....	....
	NHL Totals	**1044**	**139**	**425**	**564**	**2226**	**84**	**8**	**42**	**50**	**218**

Played in NHL All-Star Game (1981, 1984, 1986, 1988)

Traded to **St. Louis** by **New Jersey** for St. Louis' 1st round choice (John MacLean) in 1983 Entry Draft, June 9, 1982. Traded to **Calgary** by **St. Louis** with Rick Wamsley for Brett Hull and Steve Bozek, March 7, 1988. Traded to **Toronto** by **Calgary** for Toronto's 2nd round choice (Kent Manderville) in 1989 Entry Draft June 16, 1989. Claimed by **Minnesota** from **Toronto** in Expansion Draft, May 30, 1991. Claimed by **Tampa Bay** from **Minnesota** in Expansion Draft, June 18, 1992. Traded to **Montreal** by **Tampa Bay** for Eric Charron, Alain Cote and future considerations (Donald Dufresne, June 18, 1993), March 20, 1993. Traded to **Philadelphia** by **Montreal** for cash, November 28, 1993.

RAMSAY, Beattie

Defense. Shoots left. 5'7", 143 lbs. Born, Lumsden, Sask., December 12, 1895.

		Regular Season					Playoffs				
Season	Club	GP	G	A	Pts	PIM	GP	G	A	Pts	PIM
1927-28	Toronto Maple Leafs	43	0	2	2	10	....	....	....	....	....
	NHL Totals	**43**	**0**	**2**	**2**	**10**	....	....	....	....	....

Signed as a free agent by **Toronto**, March 17, 1927.

RAMSAY, Craig

Left wing. Shoots left. 5'10", 175 lbs. Born, Weston, Ont., March 17, 1951.
(Buffalo's 2nd choice, 19th overall, in 1971 Amateur Draft).

		Regular Season					Playoffs				
Season	Club	GP	G	A	Pts	PIM	GP	G	A	Pts	PIM
1971-72	Buffalo Sabres	57	6	10	16	0	....	....	....	....	....
1972-73	Buffalo Sabres	76	11	17	28	15	6	1	1	2	0
1973-74	Buffalo Sabres	78	20	26	46	0	....	....	....	....	....
1974-75	Buffalo Sabres	80	26	38	64	26	17	5	7	12	2
1975-76	Buffalo Sabres	80	22	49	71	34	9	1	2	3	2
1976-77	Buffalo Sabres	80	20	41	61	20	6	0	4	4	0
1977-78	Buffalo Sabres	80	28	43	71	18	8	3	1	4	9
1978-79	Buffalo Sabres	80	26	31	57	10	3	1	0	1	2
1979-80	Buffalo Sabres	80	21	39	60	18	10	0	6	6	4
1980-81	Buffalo Sabres	80	24	35	59	12	8	2	4	6	4
1981-82	Buffalo Sabres	80	16	35	51	8	4	1	1	2	0
1982-83	Buffalo Sabres	64	11	18	29	7	10	2	3	5	4
1983-84	Buffalo Sabres	76	9	17	26	17	3	0	1	1	0
1984-85	Buffalo Sabres	79	12	21	33	16	5	1	1	2	0
	NHL Totals	**1070**	**252**	**420**	**672**	**201**	**89**	**17**	**31**	**48**	**27**

Frank J. Selke Trophy (1985)
Played in NHL All-Star Game (1976)

RAMSAY, Les

Left wing. Shoots left. 5'9", 155 lbs. Born, Verdun, Que., July 1, 1920.

		Regular Season					Playoffs				
Season	Club	GP	G	A	Pts	PIM	GP	G	A	Pts	PIM
1944-45	Chicago Black Hawks	11	2	2	4	2	....	....	....	....	....
	NHL Totals	**11**	**2**	**2**	**4**	**2**	....	....	....	....	....

RAMSEY, Mike

USHOF

Defense. Shoots left. 6'3", 195 lbs. Born, Minneapolis, MN, December 3, 1960.
(Buffalo's 1st choice, 11th overall, in 1979 Entry Draft).

		Regular Season					Playoffs				
Season	Club	GP	G	A	Pts	PIM	GP	G	A	Pts	PIM
1979-80	Buffalo Sabres	13	1	6	7	6	13	1	2	3	12
1980-81	Buffalo Sabres	72	3	14	17	56	8	0	3	3	20
1981-82	Buffalo Sabres	80	7	23	30	56	4	1	1	2	14
1982-83	Buffalo Sabres	77	8	30	38	55	10	4	4	8	15
1983-84	Buffalo Sabres	72	9	22	31	82	3	0	1	1	6
1984-85	Buffalo Sabres	79	8	22	30	102	5	0	1	1	23
1985-86	Buffalo Sabres	76	7	21	28	117	....	....	....	....	....
1986-87	Buffalo Sabres	80	8	31	39	109	....	....	....	....	....
1987-88	Buffalo Sabres	63	5	16	21	77	6	0	3	3	29
1988-89	Buffalo Sabres	56	2	14	16	84	5	1	0	1	11
1989-90	Buffalo Sabres	73	4	21	25	47	6	0	1	1	8
1990-91	Buffalo Sabres	71	6	14	20	46	5	1	0	1	12
1991-92	Buffalo Sabres	66	3	14	17	67	7	0	2	2	8
1992-93	Buffalo Sabres	33	2	8	10	20	....	....	....	....	....
	Pittsburgh Penguins	12	1	2	3	8	12	0	6	6	4
1993-94	Pittsburgh Penguins	65	2	2	4	22	1	0	0	0	0
1994-95	Detroit Red Wings	33	1	2	3	23	15	0	1	1	4
1995-96	Detroit Red Wings	47	2	4	6	35	15	0	4	4	10
1996-97	Detroit Red Wings	2	0	0	0	0	....	....	....	....	....
	NHL Totals	**1070**	**79**	**266**	**345**	**1012**	**115**	**8**	**29**	**37**	**176**

Played in NHL All-Star Game (1982, 1983, 1985, 1986)

Traded to **Pittsburgh** by **Buffalo** for Bob Errey, March 22, 1993. Signed as a free agent by **Detroit**, August 3, 1994.

RAMSEY, Wayne

Defense. Shoots left. 6', 185 lbs. Born, Hamiota, Man., January 31, 1957.
(Buffalo's 5th choice, 104th overall, in 1977 Amateur Draft).

		Regular Season					Playoffs				
Season	Club	GP	G	A	Pts	PIM	GP	G	A	Pts	PIM
1977-78	Buffalo Sabres	2	0	0	0	0	....	....	....	....	....
	NHL Totals	**2**	**0**	**0**	**0**	**0**	....	....	....	....	....

RANDALL, Ken

Right wing/Defense. Shoots right. 5'10", 180 lbs. Born, Kingston, Ont.,

		Regular Season					Playoffs				
Season	Club	GP	G	A	Pts	PIM	GP	G	A	Pts	PIM
1917-18 ◆	Toronto Arenas	21	12	2	14	96	2	1	1	2	*12
	Toronto Arenas (Cup)	....	....	....	....	....	*5*	*1*	*0*	*1*	*0*
1918-19	Toronto Arenas	14	8	6	14	27	....	....	....	....	....
1919-20	Toronto St. Pats	22	10	8	18	42	....	....	....	....	....
1920-21	Toronto St. Pats	22	6	5	11	74	2	0	0	0	11
1921-22 ◆	Toronto St. Pats	24	10	6	16	32	2	1	0	1	4
	Toronto St. Pats (Cup)	....	....	....	....	....	*4*	*1*	*0*	*1*	*19*
1922-23	Toronto St. Pats	24	3	5	8	58	....	....	....	....	....
1923-24	Hamilton Tigers	24	7	6	13	58	....	....	....	....	....
1924-25	Hamilton Tigers	30	8	10	18	52	....	....	....	....	....
1925-26	New York Americans	34	4	2	6	94	....	....	....	....	....
1926-27	New York Americans	3	0	0	0	0	....	....	....	....	....
	NHL Totals	**218**	**68**	**50**	**118**	**533**	**6**	**2**	**1**	**3**	**27**

Signed as a free agent by **Toronto**, December 9, 1917. Traded to **Hamilton** by **Toronto** with the NHL rights to Corb Denneny and cash for Amos Arbour, George Carey and Bert Corbeau, December 14, 1923. Transferred to **NY Americans** after NHL club purchased **Hamilton** franchise, September 26, 1925. Claimed on waivers by **Niagara Falls** (Can-Pro) from **NY Americans** for cash, November 22, 1926.

RANHEIM, Paul

Left wing. Shoots right. 6'1", 210 lbs. Born, St. Louis, MO, January 25, 1966.
(Calgary's 3rd choice, 38th overall, in 1984 Entry Draft).

		Regular Season					Playoffs				
Season	Club	GP	G	A	Pts	PIM	GP	G	A	Pts	PIM
1988-89	Calgary Flames	5	0	0	0	0	....	....	....	....	....
1989-90	Calgary Flames	80	26	28	54	23	6	1	3	4	2
1990-91	Calgary Flames	39	14	16	30	4	7	2	2	4	0
1991-92	Calgary Flames	80	23	20	43	32	....	....	....	....	....
1992-93	Calgary Flames	83	21	22	43	26	6	0	1	1	0
1993-94	Calgary Flames	67	10	14	24	20	....	....	....	....	....
	Hartford Whalers	15	0	3	3	2	....	....	....	....	....
1994-95	Hartford Whalers	47	6	14	20	10	....	....	....	....	....
1995-96	Hartford Whalers	73	10	20	30	14	....	....	....	....	....
1996-97	Hartford Whalers	67	10	11	21	18	....	....	....	....	....
1997-98	Carolina Hurricanes	73	5	9	14	28	....	....	....	....	....
1998-99	Carolina Hurricanes	78	9	10	19	39	6	0	0	0	2
99-2000	Carolina Hurricanes	79	9	13	22	6	....	....	....	....	....
2000-01	Philadelphia Flyers	80	10	7	17	14	6	0	2	2	2
2001-02	Philadelphia Flyers	79	5	4	9	36	5	0	0	0	0
2002-03	Philadelphia Flyers	28	0	4	4	6	....	....	....	....	....
	Phoenix Coyotes	40	3	4	7	10	....	....	....	....	....
	NHL Totals	**1013**	**161**	**199**	**360**	**288**	**36**	**3**	**8**	**11**	**6**

• Missed majority of 1990-91 season recovering from ankle injury suffered in game vs. Minnesota, December 11, 1990. Traded to **Hartford** by **Calgary** with Gary Suter and Ted Drury for James Patrick, Zarley Zalapski and Michael Nylander, March 10, 1994. Transferred to **Carolina** after **Hartford** franchise relocated, June 25, 1997. Traded to **Philadelphia** by **Carolina** for Philadelphia's 8th round choice (later traded to Tampa Bay – Tampa Bay selected Darren Reid) in 2002 Entry Draft, May 31, 2000. Traded to **Phoenix** by **Philadelphia** for future consiserations, December 19, 2002.

RANIERI, George

Left wing. Shoots left. 5'8", 190 lbs. Born, Toronto, Ont., January 14, 1936.

		Regular Season					Playoffs				
Season	Club	GP	G	A	Pts	PIM	GP	G	A	Pts	PIM
1956-57	Boston Bruins	2	0	0	0	0	....	....	....	....	....
	NHL Totals	**2**	**0**	**0**	**0**	**0**	....	....	....	....	....

RASMUSSEN, Erik

Left wing/Center. Shoots left. 6'3", 208 lbs. Born, Minneapolis, MN, March 28, 1977.
(Buffalo's 1st choice, 7th overall, in 1996 Entry Draft).

		Regular Season					Playoffs				
Season	Club	GP	G	A	Pts	PIM	GP	G	A	Pts	PIM
1997-98	Buffalo Sabres	21	2	3	5	14	....	....	....	....	....
1998-99	Buffalo Sabres	42	3	7	10	37	21	2	4	6	18
99-2000	Buffalo Sabres	67	8	6	14	43	3	0	0	0	4
2000-01	Buffalo Sabres	82	12	19	31	51	3	0	1	1	0
2001-02	Buffalo Sabres	69	8	11	19	34	....	....	....	....	....
2002-03	Los Angeles Kings	57	4	12	16	28	....	....	....	....	....
	NHL Totals	**338**	**37**	**58**	**95**	**207**	**27**	**2**	**5**	**7**	**22**

Traded to **Los Angeles** by **Buffalo** for Adam Mair and Los Angeles' 5th round choice (Thomas Morrow) in 2003 Entry Draft, July 24, 2002. Signed as a free agent by **New Jersey**, July 25, 2003.

RATCHUK, Peter

Defense. Shoots left. 6'1", 185 lbs. Born, Buffalo, NY, September 10, 1977.
(Colorado's 1st choice, 25th overall, in 1996 Entry Draft).

Season	Club	GP	G	A	Pts	PIM	GP	G	A	Pts	PIM
		Regular Season					Playoffs				
1998-99	Florida Panthers	24	1	1	2	10	....	....	....	....	....
2000-01	Florida Panthers	8	0	0	0	0	....	....	....	....	....
	NHL Totals	**32**	**1**	**1**	**2**	**10**	....	....	....	....	....

Signed as a free agent by **Florida**, June 15, 1998. Signed as a free agent by **Pittsburgh**, August 14, 2001. Signed as a free agent by **Buffalo**, August 7, 2002.

RATELLE, Jean — HHOF

Center. Shoots left. 6'1", 180 lbs. Born, Lac St-Jean, Que., October 3, 1940.

Season	Club	GP	G	A	Pts	PIM	GP	G	A	Pts	PIM
		Regular Season					Playoffs				
1960-61	New York Rangers	3	2	1	3	0	....	....	....	....	....
1961-62	New York Rangers	31	4	8	12	4	....	....	....	....	....
1962-63	New York Rangers	48	11	9	20	8	....	....	....	....	....
1963-64	New York Rangers	15	0	7	7	6	....	....	....	....	....
1964-65	New York Rangers	54	14	21	35	14	....	....	....	....	....
1965-66	New York Rangers	67	21	30	51	10	....	....	....	....	....
1966-67	New York Rangers	41	6	5	11	4	4	0	0	0	2
1967-68	New York Rangers	74	32	46	78	18	6	0	4	4	2
1968-69	New York Rangers	75	32	46	78	26	4	1	0	1	0
1969-70	New York Rangers	75	32	42	74	28	6	1	3	4	0
1970-71	New York Rangers	78	26	46	72	14	13	2	9	11	8
1971-72	New York Rangers	63	46	63	109	4	6	0	1	1	0
1972-73	New York Rangers	78	41	53	94	12	10	2	7	9	0
1973-74	New York Rangers	68	28	39	67	16	13	2	4	6	0
1974-75	New York Rangers	79	36	55	91	26	3	1	5	6	2
1975-76	New York Rangers	13	5	10	15	2	....	....	....	....	....
	Boston Bruins	67	31	59	90	16	12	8	8	16	4
1976-77	Boston Bruins	78	33	61	94	22	14	5	12	17	4
1977-78	Boston Bruins	80	25	59	84	10	15	3	7	10	0
1978-79	Boston Bruins	80	27	45	72	12	11	7	6	13	2
1979-80	Boston Bruins	67	28	45	73	8	3	0	0	0	0
1980-81	Boston Bruins	47	11	26	37	16	3	0	0	0	0
	NHL Totals	**1281**	**491**	**776**	**1267**	**276**	**123**	**32**	**66**	**98**	**24**

Bill Masterton Trophy (1971) • NHL Second All-Star Team (1972) • Lady Byng Trophy (1972, 1976) • Lester B. Pearson Award (1972)

Played in NHL All-Star Game (1970, 1971, 1972, 1973, 1980)

Traded to **Boston** by **NY Rangers** with Brad Park and Joe Zanussi for Phil Esposito and Carol Vadnais, November 7, 1975.

RATHJE, Mike

Defense. Shoots left. 6'5", 245 lbs. Born, Mannville, Alta., May 11, 1974.
(San Jose's 1st choice, 3rd overall, in 1992 Entry Draft).

Season	Club	GP	G	A	Pts	PIM	GP	G	A	Pts	PIM
		Regular Season					Playoffs				
1993-94	San Jose Sharks	47	1	9	10	59	1	0	0	0	0
1994-95	San Jose Sharks	42	2	7	9	29	11	5	2	7	4
1995-96	San Jose Sharks	27	0	7	7	14	....	....	....	....	....
1996-97	San Jose Sharks	31	0	8	8	21	....	....	....	....	....
1997-98	San Jose Sharks	81	3	12	15	59	6	1	0	1	6
1998-99	San Jose Sharks	82	5	9	14	36	6	0	0	0	4
99-2000	San Jose Sharks	66	2	14	16	31	12	1	3	4	8
2000-01	San Jose Sharks	81	0	11	11	48	6	0	1	1	4
2001-02	San Jose Sharks	52	5	12	17	48	12	1	3	4	6
2002-03	San Jose Sharks	82	7	22	29	48	....	....	....	....	....
	NHL Totals	**591**	**25**	**111**	**136**	**393**	**54**	**8**	**9**	**17**	**32**

• Missed majority of 1996-97 season recovering from groin injury suffered in game vs. Dallas, November 8, 1996.

RATHWELL, Jake

Right wing. Shoots left. 6', 190 lbs. Born, Temiscamingue, Que., August 12, 1947.

Season	Club	GP	G	A	Pts	PIM	GP	G	A	Pts	PIM
		Regular Season					Playoffs				
1974-75	Boston Bruins	1	0	0	0	0	....	....	....	....	....
	NHL Totals	**1**	**0**	**0**	**0**	**0**	....	....	....	....	....

Traded to **Minnesota** by **Montreal** for cash, June, 1968. Claimed by **Salt Lake** (CHL) from **Minnesota** in Reverse Draft, June 10, 1970. Traded to **Portland** (WHL) by **California** (Salt Lake-WHL) with Guyle Fielder for Lyle Bradley and Fred Hilts, January, 1972. Traded to **Buffalo** (Cincinnati-AHL) by **Portland** (WHL) for cash, March, 1972. Traded to **St. Louis** by **Buffalo** for Paul Curtis, June 14, 1973. Traded to **Boston** by **St. Louis** with St. Louis' 2nd round choice (Mark Howe) in 1974 Amateur Draft and cash for Don Awrey, October 5, 1973.

RATUSHNY, Dan

Defense. Shoots right. 6'1", 205 lbs. Born, Nepean, Ont., October 29, 1970.
(Winnipeg's 2nd choice, 25th overall, in 1989 Entry Draft).

Season	Club	GP	G	A	Pts	PIM	GP	G	A	Pts	PIM
		Regular Season					Playoffs				
1992-93	Vancouver Canucks	1	0	1	1	2	....	....	....	....	....
	NHL Totals	**1**	**0**	**1**	**1**	**2**	....	....	....	....	....

Traded to **Vancouver** by **Winnipeg** for Vancouver's 9th round choice (Harijs Vitolinsh) in 1993 Entry Draft, March 22, 1993.

RAUSSE, Errol

Left wing. Shoots left. 5'10", 180 lbs. Born, Quesnel, B.C., May 18, 1959.
(Washington's 2nd choice, 24th overall, in 1979 Entry Draft).

Season	Club	GP	G	A	Pts	PIM	GP	G	A	Pts	PIM
		Regular Season					Playoffs				
1979-80	Washington Capitals	24	6	2	8	0	....	....	....	....	....
1980-81	Washington Capitals	5	1	1	2	0	....	....	....	....	....
1981-82	Washington Capitals	2	0	0	0	0	....	....	....	....	....
	NHL Totals	**31**	**7**	**3**	**10**	**0**	....	....	....	....	....

RAUTAKALLIO, Pekka

Defense. Shoots left. 5'11", 185 lbs. Born, Pori, Finland, July 25, 1953.

Season	Club	GP	G	A	Pts	PIM	GP	G	A	Pts	PIM
		Regular Season					Playoffs				
1979-80	Atlanta Flames	79	5	25	30	18	4	0	1	1	2
1980-81	Calgary Flames	76	11	45	56	64	16	2	4	6	6
1981-82	Calgary Flames	80	17	51	68	40	3	0	0	0	0
	NHL Totals	**235**	**33**	**121**	**154**	**122**	**23**	**2**	**5**	**7**	**8**

Played in NHL All-Star Game (1982)

Signed as a free agent by **Atlanta**, June 5, 1979. Transferred to **Calgary** after **Atlanta** franchise relocated, June 24, 1980.

RAVLICH, Matt

Defense. Shoots left. 5'10", 185 lbs. Born, Sault Ste. Marie, Ont., July 12, 1938.

Season	Club	GP	G	A	Pts	PIM	GP	G	A	Pts	PIM
		Regular Season					Playoffs				
1962-63	Boston Bruins	2	1	0	1	0	....	....	....	....	....
1964-65	Chicago Black Hawks	61	3	16	19	80	14	1	4	5	14
1965-66	Chicago Black Hawks	62	0	16	16	78	6	0	1	1	2
1966-67	Chicago Black Hawks	62	0	3	3	39	....	....	....	....	....
1967-68	Chicago Black Hawks	....	....	....	....	....	4	0	0	0	0
1968-69	Chicago Black Hawks	60	2	12	14	57	....	....	....	....	....
1969-70	Detroit Red Wings	46	0	6	6	33	....	....	....	....	....
	Los Angeles Kings	21	3	7	10	34	....	....	....	....	....
1970-71	Los Angeles Kings	66	3	16	19	41	....	....	....	....	....
1971-72	Boston Bruins	25	0	1	1	2	....	....	....	....	....
1972-73	Boston Bruins	5	0	1	1	0	....	....	....	....	....
	NHL Totals	**410**	**12**	**78**	**90**	**364**	**24**	**1**	**5**	**6**	**16**

Claimed by **Boston** from **Chicago** (Sault Ste. Marie-EPHL) in Inter-League Draft, June 12, 1961. Traded to **Chicago** by **Boston** with Jerry Toppazzini for Murray Balfour and Mike Draper, June 9, 1964. • Missed remainder of 1966-67 season and majority of 1967-68 season recovering from leg injury suffered in game vs. Detroit, March 28, 1967. Claimed by **Detroit** from **Chicago** in Intra-League Draft, June 11, 1969. Traded to **Los Angeles** by **Detroit** with Gary Monahan and Brian Gibbons for Dale Rolfe, Gary Croteau and Larry Johnston, February 20, 1970. Claimed on waivers by **Boston** from **Los Angeles**, November 3, 1971.

RAY, Rob

Right wing. Shoots left. 6', 217 lbs. Born, Stirling, Ont., June 8, 1968.
(Buffalo's 5th choice, 97th overall, in 1988 Entry Draft).

Season	Club	GP	G	A	Pts	PIM	GP	G	A	Pts	PIM
		Regular Season					Playoffs				
1989-90	Buffalo Sabres	27	2	1	3	99	....	....	....	....	....
1990-91	Buffalo Sabres	66	8	8	16	*350	6	1	1	2	56
1991-92	Buffalo Sabres	63	5	3	8	354	7	0	0	0	2
1992-93	Buffalo Sabres	68	3	2	5	211	....	....	....	....	....
1993-94	Buffalo Sabres	82	3	4	7	274	7	1	0	1	43
1994-95	Buffalo Sabres	47	0	3	3	173	5	0	0	0	14
1995-96	Buffalo Sabres	71	3	6	9	287	....	....	....	....	....
1996-97	Buffalo Sabres	82	7	3	10	286	12	0	1	1	28
1997-98	Buffalo Sabres	63	2	4	6	234	10	0	0	0	24
1998-99	Buffalo Sabres	76	0	4	4	*261	5	1	0	1	0
99-2000	Buffalo Sabres	69	1	3	4	158	....	....	....	....	....
2000-01	Buffalo Sabres	63	4	6	10	210	3	0	0	0	2
2001-02	Buffalo Sabres	71	2	3	5	200	....	....	....	....	....
2002-03	Buffalo Sabres	41	0	0	0	92	....	....	....	....	....
	Ottawa Senators	5	0	0	0	4	....	....	....	....	....
	NHL Totals	**894**	**40**	**50**	**90**	**3193**	**55**	**3**	**2**	**5**	**169**

King Clancy Memorial Trophy (1999)

Traded to **Ottawa** by **Buffalo** for future considerations, March 10, 2003.

RAYMOND, Armand

Defense. Shoots left. 5'9", 185 lbs. Born, Mechanicsville, NY, January 12, 1913.

Season	Club	GP	G	A	Pts	PIM	GP	G	A	Pts	PIM
		Regular Season					Playoffs				
1937-38	Montreal Canadiens	11	0	1	1	10	....	....	....	....	....
1939-40	Montreal Canadiens	11	0	1	1	0	....	....	....	....	....
	NHL Totals	**22**	**0**	**2**	**2**	**10**	....	....	....	....	....

RAYMOND, Paul

Right wing. Shoots right. 5'8", 150 lbs. Born, Montreal, Que., February 27, 1913.

Season	Club	GP	G	A	Pts	PIM	GP	G	A	Pts	PIM
		Regular Season					Playoffs				
1932-33	Montreal Canadiens	16	0	0	0	0	....	....	....	....	....
1933-34	Montreal Canadiens	29	1	0	1	2	2	0	0	0	0
1934-35	Montreal Canadiens	20	1	1	2	0	....	....	....	....	....
1938-39	Montreal Canadiens	11	0	2	2	4	3	0	0	0	2
	NHL Totals	**76**	**2**	**3**	**5**	**6**	**5**	**0**	**0**	**0**	**2**

Signed as a free agent by **Montreal**, October 28, 1932.

READ, Mel

Center. Shoots left. 5'8", 165 lbs. Born, Montreal, Que., April 10, 1924.

Season	Club	GP	G	A	Pts	PIM	GP	G	A	Pts	PIM
		Regular Season					Playoffs				
1946-47	New York Rangers	1	0	0	0	0	....	....	....	....	....
	NHL Totals	**1**	**0**	**0**	**0**	**0**	....	....	....	....	....

Loaned to **Tacoma** (PCHL) by **NY Rangers** for cash, September 30, 1948.

REARDON, Ken — HHOF

Defense. Shoots left. 5'10", 180 lbs. Born, Winnipeg, Man., April 1, 1921.

Season	Club	GP	G	A	Pts	PIM	GP	G	A	Pts	PIM
		Regular Season					Playoffs				
1940-41	Montreal Canadiens	34	2	8	10	41	3	0	0	0	4
1941-42	Montreal Canadiens	41	3	12	15	93	3	0	0	0	4
1945-46◆	Montreal Canadiens	43	5	4	9	45	9	1	1	2	4
1946-47	Montreal Canadiens	52	5	17	22	84	7	1	2	3	20
1947-48	Montreal Canadiens	58	7	15	22	129	....	....	....	....	....
1948-49	Montreal Canadiens	46	3	13	16	103	7	0	0	0	18

Season	Club	REGULAR SEASON GP	G	A	Pts	PIM	PLAYOFFS GP	G	A	Pts	PIM
1949-50	Montreal Canadiens	67	1	27	28	109	2	0	2	2	12
	NHL Totals	**341**	**26**	**96**	**122**	**604**	**31**	**2**	**5**	**7**	**62**

• Brother of Terry • NHL Second All-Star Team (1946, 1948, 1949) • NHL First All-Star Team (1947, 1950)

Played in NHL All-Star Game (1947, 1948, 1949)

Signed as a free agent by **Montreal**, October 26, 1940.

REARDON, Terry

Center/Right wing. Shoots right. 5'10", 170 lbs. Born, Winnipeg, Man., April 6, 1919.

Season	Club	GP	G	A	Pts	PIM	GP	G	A	Pts	PIM
1938-39	Boston Bruins	4	0	0	0	0	....	....	....	....	....
1939-40	Boston Bruins	....	....	....	....	....	1	0	1	1	0
1940-41 ♦	Boston Bruins	34	6	5	11	19	11	2	4	6	6
1941-42	Montreal Canadiens	33	17	17	34	14	3	2	2	4	2
1942-43	Montreal Canadiens	13	6	6	12	2	....	....	....	....	....
1945-46	Boston Bruins	49	12	11	23	21	10	4	0	4	2
1946-47	Boston Bruins	60	6	14	20	17	5	0	3	3	2
	NHL Totals	**193**	**47**	**53**	**100**	**73**	**30**	**8**	**10**	**18**	**12**

• Brother of Ken

Rights traded to **Boston** by **NY Americans** with the rights to Tom Cooper to complete transaction that sent Joe Jerwa to NY Americans (January 25, 1937), October 17, 1937. Loaned to **Montreal** by **Boston** for the loan of Paul Gauthier's NHL rights, November 5, 1941.

REASONER, Marty

Center. Shoots left. 6'1", 190 lbs. Born, Rochester, NY, February 26, 1977.
(St. Louis' 1st choice, 14th overall, in 1996 Entry Draft).

Season	Club	GP	G	A	Pts	PIM	GP	G	A	Pts	PIM
1998-99	St. Louis Blues	22	3	7	10	8	....	....	....	....	....
99-2000	St. Louis Blues	32	10	14	24	20	7	2	1	3	4
2000-01	St. Louis Blues	41	4	9	13	14	10	3	1	4	0
2001-02	Edmonton Oilers	52	6	5	11	41	....	....	....	....	....
2002-03	Edmonton Oilers	70	11	20	31	28	6	1	0	1	2
	NHL Totals	**217**	**34**	**55**	**89**	**111**	**23**	**6**	**2**	**8**	**6**

Traded to **Edmonton** by **St. Louis** with Jochen Hecht and Jan Horacek for Doug Weight and Michel Riesen, July 1, 2001.

REAUME, Marc

Defense. Shoots left. 6'1", 185 lbs. Born, La Salle, Ont., February 7, 1934.

Season	Club	GP	G	A	Pts	PIM	GP	G	A	Pts	PIM
1954-55	Toronto Maple Leafs	1	0	0	0	4	4	0	0	0	2
1955-56	Toronto Maple Leafs	48	0	12	12	50	5	0	2	2	6
1956-57	Toronto Maple Leafs	63	6	14	20	81	....	....	....	....	....
1957-58	Toronto Maple Leafs	68	1	7	8	49	....	....	....	....	....
1958-59	Toronto Maple Leafs	51	1	5	6	67	10	0	0	0	0
1959-60	Toronto Maple Leafs	36	0	1	1	6	....	....	....	....	....
	Detroit Red Wings	9	0	1	1	2	2	0	0	0	0
1960-61	Detroit Red Wings	38	0	1	1	8	....	....	....	....	....
1963-64	Montreal Canadiens	3	0	0	0	2	....	....	....	....	....
1970-71	Vancouver Canucks	27	0	2	2	4	....	....	....	....	....
	NHL Totals	**344**	**8**	**43**	**51**	**273**	**21**	**0**	**2**	**2**	**8**

Traded to **Detroit** by **Toronto** for Red Kelly, February 10, 1960. Traded to **Hershey** (AHL) by **Detroit** with Pete Conacher and Jack McIntyre for Howie Young, January, 1961. Traded to **Montreal** by **Hershey** (AHL) for Ralph Keller and the loan of Chuck Hamilton, June 11, 1963. Claimed by **Toronto** (Tulsa-CHL) from **Montreal** in Inter-League Draft, June 9, 1964. Rights transferred to **Vancouver** (WHL) after WHL club purchased **Rochester** (AHL) franchise, August 13, 1968. NHL rights transferred to **Vancouver** after NHL club purchased **Vancouver** (WHL) franchise, December 19, 1969. • Suffered career-ending leg injury in automobile accident, January 24, 1971.

REAY, Billy

Center. Shoots left. 5'7", 155 lbs. Born, Winnipeg, Man., August 21, 1918.

Season	Club	GP	G	A	Pts	PIM	GP	G	A	Pts	PIM
1943-44	Detroit Red Wings	2	2	0	2	0	....	....	....	....	....
1944-45	Detroit Red Wings	2	0	0	0	0	....	....	....	....	....
1945-46 ♦	Montreal Canadiens	44	17	12	29	10	9	1	2	3	4
1946-47	Montreal Canadiens	59	22	20	42	17	11	6	1	7	14
1947-48	Montreal Canadiens	60	6	14	20	24	....	....	....	....	....
1948-49	Montreal Canadiens	60	22	23	45	33	7	1	5	6	4
1949-50	Montreal Canadiens	68	19	26	45	48	4	0	1	1	0
1950-51	Montreal Canadiens	60	6	18	24	24	11	3	3	6	10
1951-52	Montreal Canadiens	68	7	34	41	20	10	2	2	4	7
1952-53 ♦	Montreal Canadiens	56	4	15	19	26	11	0	2	2	4
	NHL Totals	**479**	**105**	**162**	**267**	**202**	**63**	**13**	**16**	**29**	**43**

Played in NHL All-Star Game (1952)

Signed as a free agent by **Detroit**, October 2, 1939. Traded to **Montreal** by **Detroit** for Ray Getliffe and Roly Rossignol, September 11, 1945. • Detroit received Fern Gauthier (October 18, 1945) as compensation after Getliffe decided to retire.

RECCHI, Mark

Right wing. Shoots left. 5'10", 185 lbs. Born, Kamloops, B.C., February 1, 1968.
(Pittsburgh's 4th choice, 67th overall, in 1988 Entry Draft).

Season	Club	GP	G	A	Pts	PIM	GP	G	A	Pts	PIM
1988-89	Pittsburgh Penguins	15	1	1	2	0	....	....	....	....	....
1989-90	Pittsburgh Penguins	74	30	37	67	44	....	....	....	....	....
1990-91 ♦	Pittsburgh Penguins	78	40	73	113	48	24	10	24	34	33
1991-92	Pittsburgh Penguins	58	33	37	70	78	....	....	....	....	....
	Philadelphia Flyers	22	10	17	27	18	....	....	....	....	....
1992-93	Philadelphia Flyers	84	53	70	123	95	....	....	....	....	....
1993-94	Philadelphia Flyers	84	40	67	107	46	....	....	....	....	....
1994-95	Philadelphia Flyers	10	2	3	5	12	....	....	....	....	....
	Montreal Canadiens	39	14	29	43	16	....	....	....	....	....
1995-96	Montreal Canadiens	82	28	50	78	69	6	3	3	6	0
1996-97	Montreal Canadiens	82	34	46	80	58	5	4	2	6	2
1997-98	Montreal Canadiens	82	32	42	74	51	10	4	8	12	6
1998-99	Montreal Canadiens	61	12	35	47	28	....	....	....	....	....
	Philadelphia Flyers	10	4	2	6	6	6	0	1	1	2
99-2000	Philadelphia Flyers	82	28	*63	91	50	18	6	12	18	6
2000-01	Philadelphia Flyers	69	27	50	77	33	6	2	2	4	2
2001-02	Philadelphia Flyers	80	22	42	64	46	4	0	0	0	2
2002-03	Philadelphia Flyers	79	20	32	52	35	13	7	3	10	2
	NHL Totals	**1091**	**430**	**696**	**1126**	**733**	**92**	**36**	**55**	**91**	**55**

NHL Second All-Star Team (1992)

Played in NHL All-Star Game (1991, 1993, 1994, 1997, 1998, 1999, 2000)

Traded to **Philadelphia** by **Pittsburgh** with Brian Benning and Los Angeles' 1st round choice (previously acquired, Philadelphia selected Jason Bowen) in 1992 Entry Draft for Rick Tocchet, Kjell Samuelsson, Ken Wregget and Philadelphia's 3rd round choice (Dave Roche) in 1993 Entry Draft, February 19, 1992. Traded to **Montreal** by **Philadelphia** with Philadelphia's 3rd round choice (Martin Hohenberger) in 1995 Entry Draft for Eric Desjardins, Gilbert Dionne and John LeClair, February 9, 1995. Traded to **Philadelphia** by **Montreal** for Danius Zubrus, Philadelphia's 2nd round choice (Matt Carkner) in 1999 Entry Draft and NY Islanders' 6th round choice (previously acquired, Montreal selected Scott Selig) in 2000 Entry Draft, March 10, 1999.

REDAHL, Gord

Right wing. Shoots left. 5'11", 170 lbs. Born, Kinistino, Sask., August 28, 1935.

Season	Club	GP	G	A	Pts	PIM	GP	G	A	Pts	PIM
1958-59	Boston Bruins	18	0	1	1	2	....	....	....	....	....
	NHL Totals	**18**	**0**	**1**	**1**	**2**	....	....	....	....	....

Claimed by **Boston** from **NY Rangers** in Intra-League Draft, June 3, 1958. Traded to **Toronto** (Rochester-AHL) by **Boston** (Providence-AHL) for Bo Elik, November 21, 1958. Claimed by **Toronto** from **Denver** (WHL) in Inter-League Draft, June 8, 1964. Traded to **Denver** (WHL) by **Toronto** for cash, July, 1968.

REDDEN, Wade

Defense. Shoots left. 6'2", 205 lbs. Born, Lloydminster, Sask., June 12, 1977.
(NY Islanders' 1st choice, 2nd overall, in 1995 Entry Draft).

Season	Club	GP	G	A	Pts	PIM	GP	G	A	Pts	PIM
1996-97	Ottawa Senators	82	6	24	30	41	7	1	3	4	2
1997-98	Ottawa Senators	80	8	14	22	27	9	0	2	2	2
1998-99	Ottawa Senators	72	8	21	29	54	4	1	2	3	2
99-2000	Ottawa Senators	81	10	26	36	49	....	....	....	....	....
2000-01	Ottawa Senators	78	10	37	47	49	4	0	0	0	0
2001-02	Ottawa Senators	79	9	25	34	48	12	3	2	5	6
2002-03	Ottawa Senators	76	10	35	45	70	18	1	8	9	10
	NHL Totals	**548**	**61**	**182**	**243**	**338**	**54**	**6**	**17**	**23**	**22**

Played in NHL All-Star Game (2002)

Traded to **Ottawa** by **NY Islanders** with Damian Rhodes for Don Beaupre, Martin Straka and Bryan Berard, January 23, 1996.

REDDING, George

Left wing/Defense. Shoots left. 5'7", 145 lbs. Born, Peterborough, Ont., March 6, 1903.

Season	Club	GP	G	A	Pts	PIM	GP	G	A	Pts	PIM
1924-25	Boston Bruins	27	3	2	5	10	....	....	....	....	....
1925-26	Boston Bruins	28	0	0	0	13	....	....	....	....	....
	NHL Totals	**55**	**3**	**2**	**5**	**23**	....	....	....	....	....

Signed as a free agent by **Boston**, October 16, 1924.

REDMOND, Craig

Defense. Shoots left. 5'11", 190 lbs. Born, Dawson Creek, B.C., September 22, 1965.
(Los Angeles' 1st choice, 6th overall, in 1984 Entry Draft).

Season	Club	GP	G	A	Pts	PIM	GP	G	A	Pts	PIM
1984-85	Los Angeles Kings	79	6	33	39	57	3	1	0	1	2
1985-86	Los Angeles Kings	73	6	18	24	57	....	....	....	....	....
1986-87	Los Angeles Kings	16	1	7	8	8	....	....	....	....	....
1987-88	Los Angeles Kings	2	0	0	0	0	....	....	....	....	....
1988-89	Edmonton Oilers	21	3	10	13	12	....	....	....	....	....
	NHL Totals	**191**	**16**	**68**	**84**	**134**	**3**	**1**	**0**	**1**	**2**

• Suspended by **Los Angeles** for refusing to report to **New Haven** (AHL), October 15, 1987. Traded to **Edmonton** by **Los Angeles** for John Miner, August 10, 1988. Claimed by **NY Rangers** from **Edmonton** in Waiver Draft, October 3, 1988. Claimed on waivers by **Edmonton** from **NY Rangers**, November 1, 1988.

REDMOND, Dick

Defense. Shoots left. 5'11", 178 lbs. Born, Kirkland Lake, Ont., August 14, 1949.
(Minnesota's 1st choice, 5th overall, in 1969 Amateur Draft).

Season	Club	GP	G	A	Pts	PIM	GP	G	A	Pts	PIM
1969-70	Minnesota North Stars	7	0	1	1	4	....	....	....	....	....
1970-71	Minnesota North Stars	9	0	2	2	16	....	....	....	....	....
	California Seals	11	2	4	6	12	....	....	....	....	....
1971-72	California Golden Seals	74	10	35	45	76	....	....	....	....	....
1972-73	California Golden Seals	24	3	13	16	22	....	....	....	....	....
	Chicago Black Hawks	52	9	19	28	4	13	4	2	6	2
1973-74	Chicago Black Hawks	76	17	42	59	69	11	1	7	8	8
1974-75	Chicago Black Hawks	80	14	43	57	90	8	2	3	5	0
1975-76	Chicago Black Hawks	53	9	27	36	25	4	0	2	2	4
1976-77	Chicago Black Hawks	80	22	25	47	30	2	0	1	1	0
1977-78	St. Louis Blues	28	4	11	15	16	....	....	....	....	....
	Atlanta Flames	42	7	11	18	16	2	1	0	1	0
1978-79	Boston Bruins	64	7	26	33	21	11	1	3	4	2
1979-80	Boston Bruins	76	14	33	47	39	10	0	3	3	9
1980-81	Boston Bruins	78	15	20	35	60	3	0	1	1	2

Season	Club	Regular Season GP	G	A	Pts	PIM	Playoffs GP	G	A	Pts	PIM
1981-82	Boston Bruins	17	0	0	0	4	2	0	0	0	0
	NHL Totals	**771**	**133**	**312**	**445**	**504**	**66**	**9**	**22**	**31**	**27**

• Brother of Mickey

Traded to **California** by **Minnesota** with Tommy Williams for Ted Hampson and Wayne Muloin, March 7, 1971. Traded to **Chicago** by **California** with the rights to Bobby Sheehan for Darryl Maggs, December 5, 1972. Traded to **St. Louis** by **Chicago** for Pierre Plante, August 9, 1977. Traded to **Atlanta** by **St. Louis** with Yves Belanger, Bob MacMillan and St. Louis' 2nd round choice (Mike Perovich) in 1979 Entry Draft for Phil Myre, Curt Bennett and Barry Gibbs, December 12, 1977. Traded to **Boston** by **Atlanta** for Gregg Sheppard, September 6, 1978.

REDMOND, Keith

Left wing. Shoots left. 6'3", 208 lbs. Born, Richmond Hill, Ont., October 25, 1972.
(Los Angeles' 2nd choice, 79th overall, in 1991 Entry Draft).

Season	Club	GP	G	A	Pts	PIM	GP	G	A	Pts	PIM
1993-94	Los Angeles Kings	12	1	0	1	20	....	....	....	....	....
	NHL Totals	**12**	**1**	**0**	**1**	**20**	....	....	....	....	....

REDMOND, Mickey

Right wing. Shoots right. 5'11", 185 lbs. Born, Kirkland Lake, Ont., December 27, 1947.

Season	Club	GP	G	A	Pts	PIM	GP	G	A	Pts	PIM
1967-68 ♦	Montreal Canadiens	41	6	5	11	4	2	0	0	0	0
1968-69 ♦	Montreal Canadiens	65	9	15	24	12	14	2	3	5	2
1969-70	Montreal Canadiens	75	27	27	54	61	....	....	....	....	....
1970-71	Montreal Canadiens	40	14	15	29	35	....	....	....	....	....
	Detroit Red Wings	21	6	8	14	7	....	....	....	....	....
1971-72	Detroit Red Wings	78	42	29	71	34	....	....	....	....	....
1972-73	Detroit Red Wings	76	52	41	93	24	....	....	....	....	....
1973-74	Detroit Red Wings	76	51	26	77	14	....	....	....	....	....
1974-75	Detroit Red Wings	29	15	12	27	18	....	....	....	....	....
1975-76	Detroit Red Wings	37	11	17	28	10	....	....	....	....	....
	NHL Totals	**538**	**233**	**195**	**428**	**219**	**16**	**2**	**3**	**5**	**2**

• Brother of Dick • NHL First All-Star Team (1973) • NHL Second All-Star Team (1974)

Played in NHL All-Star Game (1974)

Traded to **Detroit** by **Montreal** with Guy Charron and Bill Collins for Frank Mahovlich, January 13, 1971.

REEDS, Mark

Right wing. Shoots right. 5'10", 190 lbs. Born, Burlington, Ont., January 24, 1960.
(St. Louis' 3rd choice, 86th overall, in 1979 Entry Draft).

Season	Club	GP	G	A	Pts	PIM	GP	G	A	Pts	PIM
1981-82	St. Louis Blues	9	1	3	4	0	10	0	1	1	2
1982-83	St. Louis Blues	20	5	14	19	6	4	1	0	1	2
1983-84	St. Louis Blues	65	11	14	25	23	11	3	3	6	15
1984-85	St. Louis Blues	80	9	30	39	25	3	0	0	0	0
1985-86	St. Louis Blues	78	10	28	38	28	19	4	4	8	2
1986-87	St. Louis Blues	68	9	16	25	16	6	0	1	1	2
1987-88	Hartford Whalers	38	0	7	7	31	....	....	....	....	....
1988-89	Hartford Whalers	7	0	2	2	6	....	....	....	....	....
	NHL Totals	**365**	**45**	**114**	**159**	**135**	**53**	**8**	**9**	**17**	**23**

Traded to **Hartford** by **St. Louis** for Hartford's 3rd round choice (later traded back to Hartford – Hartford selected Blair Atcheynum) in 1989 Entry Draft, October 5, 1987.

REEKIE, Joe

Defense. Shoots left. 6'3", 220 lbs. Born, Victoria, B.C., February 22, 1965.
(Buffalo's 6th choice, 119th overall, in 1985 Entry Draft).

Season	Club	GP	G	A	Pts	PIM	GP	G	A	Pts	PIM
1985-86	Buffalo Sabres	3	0	0	0	14	....	....	....	....	....
1986-87	Buffalo Sabres	56	1	8	9	82	....	....	....	....	....
1987-88	Buffalo Sabres	30	1	4	5	68	2	0	0	0	4
1988-89	Buffalo Sabres	15	1	3	4	26	....	....	....	....	....
1989-90	New York Islanders	31	1	8	9	43	....	....	....	....	....
1990-91	New York Islanders	66	3	16	19	96	....	....	....	....	....
1991-92	New York Islanders	54	4	12	16	85	....	....	....	....	....
1992-93	Tampa Bay Lightning	42	2	11	13	69	....	....	....	....	....
1993-94	Tampa Bay Lightning	73	1	11	12	127	....	....	....	....	....
	Washington Capitals	12	0	5	5	29	11	2	1	3	29
1994-95	Washington Capitals	48	1	6	7	97	7	0	0	0	2
1995-96	Washington Capitals	78	3	7	10	149	....	....	....	....	....
1996-97	Washington Capitals	65	1	8	9	107	....	....	....	....	....
1997-98	Washington Capitals	68	2	8	10	70	21	1	2	3	20
1998-99	Washington Capitals	73	0	10	10	68	....	....	....	....	....
99-2000	Washington Capitals	59	0	7	7	50	5	0	1	1	2
2000-01	Washington Capitals	74	2	9	11	77	4	0	0	0	4
2001-02	Washington Capitals	38	2	4	6	41	....	....	....	....	....
	Chicago Blackhawks	17	0	2	2	28	1	0	0	0	2
	NHL Totals	**902**	**25**	**139**	**164**	**1326**	**51**	**3**	**4**	**7**	**63**

• Re-entered NHL Entry Draft. Originally Hartford's 8th choice, 128th overall, in 1983 Entry Draft.

• Missed majority of 1987-88 and 1988-89 seasons recovering from knee injury suffered in game vs. Toronto, November 11, 1987. Traded to **NY Islanders** by **Buffalo** for NY Islanders' 6th round choice (Bill Pye) in 1989 Entry Draft, June 17, 1989. Claimed by **Tampa Bay** from **NY Islanders** in Expansion Draft, June 18, 1992. Traded to **Washington** by **Tampa Bay** for Enrico Ciccone, Washington's 3rd round choice (later traded to Anaheim – Anaheim selected Craig Reichert) in 1994 Entry Draft and the return of conditional draft choice transferred in the Pat Elynuik trade (October 22, 1993), March 21, 1994. Traded to **Chicago** by **Washington** for Chicago's 4th round choice (Petr Dvorak) in 2002 Entry Draft, January 17, 2002.

REGAN, Bill

Defense. Shoots left. 6'1", 190 lbs. Born, Creighton Mines, Ont., December 11, 1908.

Season	Club	GP	G	A	Pts	PIM	GP	G	A	Pts	PIM
1929-30	New York Rangers	10	0	0	0	4	4	0	0	0	0
1930-31	New York Rangers	42	2	1	3	49	4	0	0	0	2
1932-33	New York Americans	15	1	1	2	14	....	....	....	....	....
	NHL Totals	**67**	**3**	**2**	**5**	**67**	**8**	**0**	**0**	**0**	**2**

Traded to **NY Rangers** by **Boston** for Yip Foster and $15,000, February 17, 1930. Loaned to **Bronx** (Can-Am) by **NY Rangers** for cash, November 1, 1931. Loaned to **NY Americans** by **NY Rangers** for the remainder of 1932-33 season for cash, December 27, 1932.

REGAN, Larry

Right wing. Shoots right. 5'9", 162 lbs. Born, North Bay, Ont., August 9, 1930.

Season	Club	GP	G	A	Pts	PIM	GP	G	A	Pts	PIM
1956-57	Boston Bruins	69	14	19	33	29	8	0	2	2	10
1957-58	Boston Bruins	59	11	28	39	22	12	3	8	11	6
1958-59	Boston Bruins	36	5	6	11	10	....	....	....	....	....
	Toronto Maple Leafs	32	4	21	25	2	8	1	1	2	2
1959-60	Toronto Maple Leafs	47	4	16	20	6	10	3	3	6	0
1960-61	Toronto Maple Leafs	37	3	5	8	2	4	0	0	0	0
	NHL Totals	**280**	**41**	**95**	**136**	**71**	**42**	**7**	**14**	**21**	**18**

Calder Memorial Trophy (1957)

Claimed by **Boston** from **Quebec** (QHL) in Inter-League Draft, June 5, 1956. Claimed on waivers by **Toronto** from **Boston**, January 7, 1959. Named playing-coach of **Pittsburgh** (AHL), June 12, 1961.

REGEHR, Robyn

Defense. Shoots left. 6'2", 226 lbs. Born, Recife, Brazil, April 19, 1980.
(Colorado's 3rd choice, 19th overall, in 1998 Entry Draft).

Season	Club	GP	G	A	Pts	PIM	GP	G	A	Pts	PIM
99-2000	Calgary Flames	57	5	7	12	46	....	....	....	....	....
2000-01	Calgary Flames	71	1	3	4	70	....	....	....	....	....
2001-02	Calgary Flames	77	2	6	8	93	....	....	....	....	....
2002-03	Calgary Flames	76	0	12	12	87	....	....	....	....	....
	NHL Totals	**281**	**8**	**28**	**36**	**296**	....	....	....	....	....

Traded to **Calgary** by **Colorado** with Rene Corbet, Wade Belak and Colorado's 2nd round compensatory choice (Jarret Stoll) in 2000 Entry Draft for Theoren Fleury and Chris Dingman, February 28, 1999.

REGIER, Darcy

Defense. Shoots left. 5'11", 190 lbs. Born, Swift Current, Sask., November 27, 1956.
(California's 5th choice, 77th overall, in 1976 Amateur Draft).

Season	Club	GP	G	A	Pts	PIM	GP	G	A	Pts	PIM
1977-78	Cleveland Barons	15	0	1	1	28	....	....	....	....	....
1982-83	New York Islanders	6	0	0	0	7	....	....	....	....	....
1983-84	New York Islanders	5	0	1	1	0	....	....	....	....	....
	NHL Totals	**26**	**0**	**2**	**2**	**35**	....	....	....	....	....

Rights transferred to **Cleveland** after **California** franchise relocated, August 26, 1976. Traded to **NY Islanders** by **Cleveland** with Wayne Merrick and Cleveland's 4th round choice (draft choice cancelled by the Cleveland-Minnesota merger) in 1978 Entry Draft for Jean-Paul Parise and Jean Potvin, January 10, 1978.

REIBEL, Dutch

Center. Shoots right. 5'8", 160 lbs. Born, Kitchener, Ont., July 21, 1930.

Season	Club	GP	G	A	Pts	PIM	GP	G	A	Pts	PIM
1953-54 ♦	Detroit Red Wings	69	15	33	48	18	9	1	3	4	0
1954-55 ♦	Detroit Red Wings	70	25	41	66	15	11	5	7	12	2
1955-56	Detroit Red Wings	68	17	39	56	10	10	0	2	2	2
1956-57	Detroit Red Wings	70	13	23	36	6	5	0	2	2	0
1957-58	Detroit Red Wings	29	4	5	9	4	....	....	....	....	....
	Chicago Black Hawks	40	4	12	16	6	....	....	....	....	....
1958-59	Boston Bruins	63	6	8	14	16	4	0	0	0	0
	NHL Totals	**409**	**84**	**161**	**245**	**75**	**39**	**6**	**14**	**20**	**4**

Lady Byng Trophy (1956)

Played in NHL All-Star Game (1954, 1955)

Traded to **Chicago** by **Detroit** with Billy Dea, Bill Dineen and Lorne Ferguson for Hec Lalande, Nick Mickoski, Bob Bailey and Jack McIntyre, December 17, 1957. Claimed by **Boston** from **Chicago** in Intra-League Draft, June 3, 1958.

REICHEL, Robert

Center. Shoots left. 5'10", 185 lbs. Born, Litvinov, Czech., June 25, 1971.
(Calgary's 5th choice, 70th overall, in 1989 Entry Draft).

Season	Club	GP	G	A	Pts	PIM	GP	G	A	Pts	PIM
1990-91	Calgary Flames	66	19	22	41	22	6	1	1	2	0
1991-92	Calgary Flames	77	20	34	54	32	....	....	....	....	....
1992-93	Calgary Flames	80	40	48	88	54	6	2	4	6	2
1993-94	Calgary Flames	84	40	53	93	58	7	0	5	5	0
1994-95	Calgary Flames	48	18	17	35	28	7	2	4	6	4
1996-97	Calgary Flames	70	16	27	43	22	....	....	....	....	....
	New York Islanders	12	5	14	19	4	....	....	....	....	....
1997-98	New York Islanders	82	25	40	65	32	....	....	....	....	....
1998-99	New York Islanders	70	19	37	56	50	....	....	....	....	....
	Phoenix Coyotes	13	7	6	13	4	7	1	3	4	2
2001-02	Toronto Maple Leafs	78	20	31	51	26	18	0	3	3	4
2002-03	Toronto Maple Leafs	81	12	30	42	26	7	2	1	3	0
	NHL Totals	**761**	**241**	**359**	**600**	**358**	**58**	**8**	**21**	**29**	**12**

Traded to **NY Islanders** by **Calgary** for Marty McInnis, Tyrone Garner and Calgary's 6th round choice (previously acquired, Calgary selected Ilja Demidov) in 1997 Entry Draft, March 18, 1997. Traded to **Phoenix** by **NY Islanders** with NY Islanders' 3rd round choice (Jason Jaspers) in 1999 Entry Draft and Ottawa's 4th round choice (previously acquired, Phoenix selected Preston Mizzi) in 1999 Entry Draft for Brad Isbister and Phoenix's 3rd round choice (Brian Collins) in 1999 Entry Draft, March 20, 1999. Traded to **Toronto** by **Phoenix** with Travis Green and Craig Mills for Danny Markov, June 12, 2001.

REICHERT, Craig

Right wing. Shoots right. 6'1", 200 lbs. Born, Winnipeg, Man., May 11, 1974.
(Anaheim's 3rd choice, 67th overall, in 1994 Entry Draft).

Season	Club	Regular Season GP	G	A	Pts	PIM	Playoffs GP	G	A	Pts	PIM
1996-97	Mighty Ducks of Anaheim	3	0	0	0	0	....	....	....	....	....
	NHL Totals	**3**	**0**	**0**	**0**	**0**	....	....	....	....	....

Signed as a free agent by **Florida**, July 21, 1999. Signed as a free agent by **Edmonton**, June 11, 2001.

REID, Brandon

Center. Shoots right. 5'8", 165 lbs. Born, Kirkland, Que., March 9, 1981.
(Vancouver's 5th choice, 208th overall, in 2000 Entry Draft).

Season	Club	Regular Season GP	G	A	Pts	PIM	Playoffs GP	G	A	Pts	PIM
2002-03	Vancouver Canucks	7	2	3	5	0	9	0	1	1	0
	NHL Totals	**7**	**2**	**3**	**5**	**0**	**9**	**0**	**1**	**1**	**0**

REID, Dave

Center. Shoots left. 6'2", 180 lbs. Born, Toronto, Ont., January 11, 1934.

Season	Club	Regular Season GP	G	A	Pts	PIM	Playoffs GP	G	A	Pts	PIM
1952-53	Toronto Maple Leafs	2	0	0	0	0	....	....	....	....	....
1954-55	Toronto Maple Leafs	1	0	0	0	0	....	....	....	....	....
1955-56	Toronto Maple Leafs	4	0	0	0	0	....	....	....	....	....
	NHL Totals	**7**	**0**	**0**	**0**	**0**	....	....	....	....	....

REID, Dave

Left wing. Shoots left. 6'1", 217 lbs. Born, Toronto, Ont., May 15, 1964.
(Boston's 4th choice, 60th overall, in 1982 Entry Draft).

Season	Club	Regular Season GP	G	A	Pts	PIM	Playoffs GP	G	A	Pts	PIM
1983-84	Boston Bruins	8	1	0	1	2	....	....	....	....	....
1984-85	Boston Bruins	35	14	13	27	27	5	1	0	1	0
1985-86	Boston Bruins	37	10	10	20	10	....	....	....	....	....
1986-87	Boston Bruins	12	3	3	6	0	2	0	0	0	0
1987-88	Boston Bruins	3	0	0	0	0	....	....	....	....	....
1988-89	Toronto Maple Leafs	77	9	21	30	22	....	....	....	....	....
1989-90	Toronto Maple Leafs	70	9	19	28	9	3	0	0	0	0
1990-91	Toronto Maple Leafs	69	15	13	28	18	....	....	....	....	....
1991-92	Boston Bruins	43	7	7	14	27	15	2	5	7	4
1992-93	Boston Bruins	65	20	16	36	10	....	....	....	....	....
1993-94	Boston Bruins	83	6	17	23	25	13	2	1	3	2
1994-95	Boston Bruins	38	5	5	10	10	5	0	0	0	0
1995-96	Boston Bruins	63	23	21	44	4	5	0	2	2	2
1996-97	Dallas Stars	82	19	20	39	10	7	1	0	1	4
1997-98	Dallas Stars	65	6	12	18	14	5	0	3	3	2
1998-99 ◆	Dallas Stars	73	6	11	17	16	23	2	8	10	14
99-2000	Colorado Avalanche	65	11	7	18	28	17	1	3	4	0
2000-01 ◆	Colorado Avalanche	73	1	9	10	21	18	0	4	4	6
	NHL Totals	**961**	**165**	**204**	**369**	**253**	**118**	**9**	**26**	**35**	**34**

Signed as a free agent by **Toronto**, June 23, 1988. Signed as a free agent by **Boston**, December 1, 1991. Signed as a free agent by **Dallas**, July 11, 1996. Signed as a free agent by **Colorado**, October 6, 1999.

REID, Gerry

Center. Shoots right. 6'1", 180 lbs. Born, Owen Sound, Ont., October 13, 1928.

Season	Club	Regular Season GP	G	A	Pts	PIM	Playoffs GP	G	A	Pts	PIM
1948-49	Detroit Red Wings	....	....	....	....	....	2	0	0	0	2
	NHL Totals	....	....	....	....	....	**2**	**0**	**0**	**0**	**2**

REID, Gord

Defense. Shoots left. 5'10", 195 lbs. Born, Mount Albert, Ont., February 19, 1912.

Season	Club	Regular Season GP	G	A	Pts	PIM	Playoffs GP	G	A	Pts	PIM
1936-37	New York Americans	1	0	0	0	2	....	....	....	....	....
	NHL Totals	**1**	**0**	**0**	**0**	**2**	....	....	....	....	....

REID, Reg

Left wing. Shoots left. 5'8", 138 lbs. Born, Seaforth, Ont., February 17, 1899.

Season	Club	Regular Season GP	G	A	Pts	PIM	Playoffs GP	G	A	Pts	PIM
1924-25	Toronto St. Pats	27	1	0	1	2	2	0	0	0	0
1925-26	Toronto St. Pats	12	0	0	0	2	....	....	....	....	....
	NHL Totals	**39**	**1**	**0**	**1**	**4**	**2**	**0**	**0**	**0**	**0**

Signed as a free agent by **Toronto**, November 12, 1924.

REID, Tom

Defense. Shoots left. 6'1", 200 lbs. Born, Fort Erie, Ont., June 24, 1946.

Season	Club	Regular Season GP	G	A	Pts	PIM	Playoffs GP	G	A	Pts	PIM
1967-68	Chicago Black Hawks	56	0	4	4	25	9	0	0	0	2
1968-69	Chicago Black Hawks	30	0	3	3	12	....	....	....	....	....
	Minnesota North Stars	18	0	4	4	38	....	....	....	....	....
1969-70	Minnesota North Stars	66	1	7	8	51	6	0	1	1	4
1970-71	Minnesota North Stars	73	3	14	17	62	12	0	6	6	20
1971-72	Minnesota North Stars	78	6	15	21	107	7	1	4	5	17
1972-73	Minnesota North Stars	60	1	13	14	50	6	0	2	2	4
1973-74	Minnesota North Stars	76	4	19	23	81	....	....	....	....	....
1974-75	Minnesota North Stars	74	1	5	6	103	....	....	....	....	....
1975-76	Minnesota North Stars	69	0	15	15	52	....	....	....	....	....
1976-77	Minnesota North Stars	65	0	8	8	52	2	0	0	0	2
1977-78	Minnesota North Stars	36	1	6	7	21	....	....	....	....	....
	NHL Totals	**701**	**17**	**113**	**130**	**654**	**42**	**1**	**13**	**14**	**49**

Traded to **Minnesota** by **Chicago** with Bill Orban for Andre Boudrias and Mike McMahon Jr., February 14, 1969.

REIERSON, Dave

Defense. Shoots right. 6', 185 lbs. Born, Bashaw, Alta., August 30, 1964.
(Calgary's 1st choice, 29th overall, in 1982 Entry Draft).

Season	Club	Regular Season GP	G	A	Pts	PIM	Playoffs GP	G	A	Pts	PIM
1988-89	Calgary Flames	2	0	0	0	2	....	....	....	....	....
	NHL Totals	**2**	**0**	**0**	**0**	**2**	....	....	....	....	....

REIGLE, Ed

Defense. Shoots left. 5'9", 180 lbs. Born, Winnipeg, Man., June 19, 1924.

Season	Club	Regular Season GP	G	A	Pts	PIM	Playoffs GP	G	A	Pts	PIM
1950-51	Boston Bruins	17	0	2	2	25	....	....	....	....	....
	NHL Totals	**17**	**0**	**2**	**2**	**25**	....	....	....	....	....

Traded to **Boston** by **Cleveland** (AHL) for cash, April 17, 1950. Traded to **Detroit** by **Boston** for cash, May, 1951. Traded to **NY Rangers** by **Detroit** with Steve Kraftcheck for $30,000, May 14, 1951. Traded to **Cleveland** (AHL) by **NY Rangers** with Jackie Gordon, Fred Shero, Fern Perreault and cash for Wally Hergesheimer and Hy Buller, May 14, 1951.

REINHART, Paul

Defense. Shoots left. 5'11", 205 lbs. Born, Kitchener, Ont., January 6, 1960.
(Atlanta's 1st choice, 12th overall, in 1979 Entry Draft).

Season	Club	Regular Season GP	G	A	Pts	PIM	Playoffs GP	G	A	Pts	PIM
1979-80	Atlanta Flames	79	9	38	47	31	....	....	....	....	....
1980-81	Calgary Flames	74	18	49	67	52	16	1	14	15	16
1981-82	Calgary Flames	62	13	48	61	17	3	0	1	1	2
1982-83	Calgary Flames	78	17	58	75	28	9	6	3	9	2
1983-84	Calgary Flames	27	6	15	21	10	11	6	11	17	2
1984-85	Calgary Flames	75	23	46	69	18	4	1	1	2	0
1985-86	Calgary Flames	32	8	25	33	15	21	5	13	18	4
1986-87	Calgary Flames	76	15	53	68	22	4	0	1	1	6
1987-88	Calgary Flames	14	0	4	4	10	8	2	7	9	6
1988-89	Vancouver Canucks	64	7	50	57	44	7	2	3	5	4
1989-90	Vancouver Canucks	67	17	40	57	30	....	....	....	....	....
	NHL Totals	**648**	**133**	**426**	**559**	**277**	**83**	**23**	**54**	**77**	**42**

Played in NHL All-Star Game (1985, 1989)

Transferred to **Calgary** after **Atlanta** franchise relocated, June 24, 1980. Traded to **Vancouver** by **Calgary** with Steve Bozek for Vancouver's 3rd round choice (Veli-Pekka Kautonen) in 1989 Entry Draft, September 6, 1988.

REINIKKA, Ollie

Center/Right wing. Shoots right. 5'10", 160 lbs. Born, Shuswap, B.C., August 2, 1901.

Season	Club	Regular Season GP	G	A	Pts	PIM	Playoffs GP	G	A	Pts	PIM
1926-27	New York Rangers	16	0	0	0	0	....	....	....	....	....
	NHL Totals	**16**	**0**	**0**	**0**	**0**	....	....	....	....	....

Traded to **NY Rangers** by **Vancouver** (WHL) for cash, October 25, 1926. Traded to **Stratford** (Can-Pro) by **NY Rangers** for cash, November 11, 1927.

REINPRECHT, Steve

Center. Shoots left. 6', 190 lbs. Born, Edmonton, Alta., May 7, 1976.

Season	Club	Regular Season GP	G	A	Pts	PIM	Playoffs GP	G	A	Pts	PIM
99-2000	Los Angeles Kings	1	0	0	0	2	....	....	....	....	....
2000-01	Los Angeles Kings	59	12	17	29	12	....	....	....	....	....
◆	Colorado Avalanche	21	3	4	7	2	22	2	3	5	2
2001-02	Colorado Avalanche	67	19	27	46	18	21	7	5	12	8
2002-03	Colorado Avalanche	77	18	33	51	18	7	1	2	3	0
	NHL Totals	**225**	**52**	**81**	**133**	**52**	**50**	**10**	**10**	**20**	**10**

Signed as a free agent by **Los Angeles**, March 31, 2000. Traded to **Colorado** by **Los Angeles** with Rob Blake for Adam Deadmarsh, Aaron Miller, a player to be named later (Jared Aulin, March 22, 2001), and Colorado's 1st round choices in 2001 (Dave Steckel) and 2003 (Brian Boyle) Entry Drafts, February 21, 2001. Traded to **Buffalo** by **Colorado** for Keith Ballard, July 3, 2003. Traded to **Calgary** by **Buffalo** with Rhett Warrener for Chris Drury and Steve Begin, July 3, 2003.

REIRDEN, Todd

Defense. Shoots left. 6'5", 225 lbs. Born, Deerfield, IL, June 25, 1971.
(New Jersey's 14th choice, 242nd overall, in 1990 Entry Draft).

Season	Club	Regular Season GP	G	A	Pts	PIM	Playoffs GP	G	A	Pts	PIM
1998-99	Edmonton Oilers	17	2	3	5	20	....	....	....	....	....
99-2000	St. Louis Blues	56	4	21	25	32	4	0	1	1	0
2000-01	St. Louis Blues	38	2	4	6	43	1	0	0	0	0
2001-02	Atlanta Thrashers	65	3	5	8	82	....	....	....	....	....
	NHL Totals	**176**	**11**	**33**	**44**	**177**	**5**	**0**	**1**	**1**	**0**

Signed as a free agent by **Edmonton**, September 17, 1998. Claimed on waivers by **St. Louis** from **Edmonton**, September 30, 1999. Signed as a free agent by **Atlanta**, July 16, 2001. Signed as a free agent by **Anaheim**, July 17, 2002.

REISE, Leo

Defense. Shoots right. 5'11", 175 lbs. Born, Pembroke, Ont., June 1, 1892.

Season	Club	Regular Season GP	G	A	Pts	PIM	Playoffs GP	G	A	Pts	PIM
1920-21	Hamilton Tigers	24	9	14	23	11	....	....	....	....	....
1921-22	Hamilton Tigers	24	9	14	23	11	....	....	....	....	....
1922-23	Hamilton Tigers	24	6	6	12	35	....	....	....	....	....
1923-24	Hamilton Tigers	4	0	0	0	4	....	....	....	....	....
1926-27	New York Americans	40	7	6	13	24	....	....	....	....	....
1927-28	New York Americans	43	8	1	9	62	....	....	....	....	....
1928-29	New York Americans	44	4	1	5	32	2	0	0	0	0

Season	Club	GP	G	A	Pts	PIM	GP	G	A	Pts	PIM
		REGULAR SEASON					PLAYOFFS				
1929-30	New York Americans	24	0	0	0	0	....	....	....	....	....
	New York Rangers	14	0	1	1	8	4	0	0	0	16
	NHL Totals	**241**	**43**	**43**	**86**	**187**	**6**	**0**	**0**	**0**	**16**

• Father of Leo Jr.

Signed as a free agent by **Hamilton**, February 23, 1921. Traded to **Saskatoon** (WCHL) by **Hamilton** for cash, December 29, 1923. Signed as a free agent by **Niagara Falls** (Can-Pro), November 1, 1926. Traded to **NY Americans** by **Niagara Falls** (Can-Pro) for cash, November 22, 1926. Traded to **NY Rangers** by **NY Americans** for cash, February 6, 1930. Traded to **London** (IHL) by **NY Rangers** for cash, October 22, 1930.

REISE Jr., Leo

Defense. Shoots left. 6', 205 lbs. Born, Stoney Creek, Ont., June 7, 1922.

Season	Club	GP	G	A	Pts	PIM	GP	G	A	Pts	PIM
1945-46	Chicago Black Hawks	6	0	0	0	6	....	....	....	....	....
1946-47	Chicago Black Hawks	17	0	0	0	18	....	....	....	....	....
	Detroit Red Wings	31	4	6	10	14	5	0	1	1	4
1947-48	Detroit Red Wings	58	5	4	9	30	10	2	1	3	12
1948-49	Detroit Red Wings	59	3	7	10	60	11	1	0	1	4
1949-50◆	Detroit Red Wings	70	4	17	21	46	14	2	0	2	19
1950-51	Detroit Red Wings	68	5	16	21	67	6	2	3	5	2
1951-52◆	Detroit Red Wings	54	0	11	11	34	6	1	0	1	*27
1952-53	New York Rangers	61	4	15	19	53	....	....	....	....	....
1953-54	New York Rangers	70	3	5	8	71	....	....	....	....	....
	NHL Totals	**494**	**28**	**81**	**109**	**399**	**52**	**8**	**5**	**13**	**68**

• Son of Leo • NHL Second All-Star Team (1950, 1951)

Played in NHL All-Star Game (1950, 1951, 1952, 1953)

Traded to **Detroit** by **Chicago** with Pete Horeck for Adam Brown and Ray Powell, December 9, 1946. Traded to **NY Rangers** by **Detroit** for Reg Sinclair and John Morrison, August 18, 1952.

RENAUD, Mark

Defense. Shoots left. 6', 185 lbs. Born, Windsor, Ont., February 21, 1959.
(Hartford's 5th choice, 102nd overall, in 1979 Entry Draft).

Season	Club	GP	G	A	Pts	PIM	GP	G	A	Pts	PIM
1979-80	Hartford Whalers	13	0	2	2	4	....	....	....	....	....
1980-81	Hartford Whalers	4	1	0	1	0	....	....	....	....	....
1981-82	Hartford Whalers	48	1	17	18	39	....	....	....	....	....
1982-83	Hartford Whalers	77	3	28	31	37	....	....	....	....	....
1983-84	Buffalo Sabres	10	1	3	4	6	....	....	....	....	....
	NHL Totals	**152**	**6**	**50**	**56**	**86**	....	....	....	....	....

Claimed by **Buffalo** from **Hartford** in Waiver Draft, October 3, 1983.

RENBERG, Mikael

Right wing. Shoots left. 6'2", 218 lbs. Born, Pitea, Sweden, May 5, 1972.
(Philadelphia's 3rd choice, 40th overall, in 1990 Entry Draft).

Season	Club	GP	G	A	Pts	PIM	GP	G	A	Pts	PIM
1993-94	Philadelphia Flyers	83	38	44	82	36	....	....	....	....	....
1994-95	Philadelphia Flyers	47	26	31	57	20	15	6	7	13	6
1995-96	Philadelphia Flyers	51	23	20	43	45	11	3	6	9	14
1996-97	Philadelphia Flyers	77	22	37	59	65	18	5	6	11	4
1997-98	Tampa Bay Lightning	68	16	22	38	34	....	....	....	....	....
1998-99	Tampa Bay Lightning	20	4	8	12	4	....	....	....	....	....
	Philadelphia Flyers	46	11	15	26	14	6	0	1	1	0
99-2000	Philadelphia Flyers	62	8	21	29	30	....	....	....	....	....
	Phoenix Coyotes	10	2	4	6	2	5	1	2	3	4
2001-02	Toronto Maple Leafs	71	14	38	52	36	3	0	0	0	2
2002-03	Toronto Maple Leafs	67	14	21	35	36	7	1	0	1	8
	NHL Totals	**602**	**178**	**261**	**439**	**322**	**65**	**16**	**22**	**38**	**38**

NHL All-Rookie Team (1994)

Traded to **Tampa Bay** by **Philadelphia** with Karl Dykhuis for Philadelphia's 1st round choices (previously acquired) in 1998 (Philadelphia selected Simon Gagne), 1999 (Philadelphia selected Maxime Ouellet), 2000 (Philadelphia selected Justin Williams) and 2001 (later traded to Ottawa – Ottawa selected Tim Gleason) Entry Drafts, August 20, 1997. Traded to **Philadelphia** by **Tampa Bay** with Daymond Langkow for Chris Gratton and Mike Sillinger, December 12, 1998. Traded to **Phoenix** by **Philadelphia** for Rick Tocchet, March 8, 2000. Traded to **Toronto** by **Phoenix** for Sergei Berezin, June 23, 2001.

REYNOLDS, Bobby

Left wing. Shoots left. 5'11", 175 lbs. Born, Flint, MI, July 14, 1967.
(Toronto's 10th choice, 190th overall, in 1985 Entry Draft).

Season	Club	GP	G	A	Pts	PIM	GP	G	A	Pts	PIM
1989-90	Toronto Maple Leafs	7	1	1	2	0	....	....	....	....	....
	NHL Totals	**7**	**1**	**1**	**2**	**0**	....	....	....	....	....

Traded to **Washington** by **Toronto** for Rob Mendel, March 5, 1991.

RHEAUME, Pascal

Center. Shoots left. 6'1", 210 lbs. Born, Quebec City, Que., June 21, 1973.

Season	Club	GP	G	A	Pts	PIM	GP	G	A	Pts	PIM
1996-97	New Jersey Devils	2	1	0	1	0	....	....	....	....	....
1997-98	St. Louis Blues	48	6	9	15	35	10	1	3	4	8
1998-99	St. Louis Blues	60	9	18	27	24	5	1	0	1	4
99-2000	St. Louis Blues	7	1	1	2	6	....	....	....	....	....
2000-01	St. Louis Blues	8	2	0	2	5	3	0	1	1	0
2001-02	Chicago Blackhawks	19	0	2	2	4	....	....	....	....	....
	Atlanta Thrashers	42	11	9	20	25	....	....	....	....	....
2002-03	Atlanta Thrashers	56	4	9	13	24	....	....	....	....	....
	◆ New Jersey Devils	21	4	1	5	8	24	1	2	3	13
	NHL Totals	**263**	**38**	**49**	**87**	**131**	**42**	**3**	**6**	**9**	**25**

Signed as a free agent by **New Jersey**, October 1, 1993. Claimed by **St. Louis** from **New Jersey** in Waiver Draft, September 28, 1997. • Missed majority of 1999-2000 season recovering from shoulder surgery, August, 1999. Signed as a free agent by **Chicago**, July 31, 2001. Claimed on waivers by **Atlanta** from **Chicago**, November 14, 2001. Traded to **New Jersey** by **Atlanta** for future considerations, February 24, 2003.

RIBBLE, Pat

Defense. Shoots left. 6'4", 210 lbs. Born, Leamington, Ont., April 26, 1954.
(Atlanta's 3rd choice, 58th overall, in 1974 Amateur Draft).

Season	Club	GP	G	A	Pts	PIM	GP	G	A	Pts	PIM
1975-76	Atlanta Flames	3	0	0	0	0	....	....	....	....	....
1976-77	Atlanta Flames	23	2	2	4	31	2	0	0	0	6
1977-78	Atlanta Flames	80	5	12	17	68	2	0	1	1	2
1978-79	Atlanta Flames	66	5	16	21	69	....	....	....	....	....
	Chicago Black Hawks	12	1	3	4	8	4	0	0	0	4
1979-80	Chicago Black Hawks	23	1	2	3	14	....	....	....	....	....
	Toronto Maple Leafs	13	0	2	2	8	....	....	....	....	....
	Washington Capitals	19	1	5	6	30	....	....	....	....	....
1980-81	Washington Capitals	67	3	15	18	103	....	....	....	....	....
1981-82	Washington Capitals	12	1	2	3	14	....	....	....	....	....
	Calgary Flames	3	0	0	0	2	....	....	....	....	....
1982-83	Calgary Flames	28	0	1	1	18	....	....	....	....	....
	NHL Totals	**349**	**19**	**60**	**79**	**365**	**8**	**0**	**1**	**1**	**12**

Traded to **Chicago** by **Atlanta** with Tom Lysiak, Harold Phillipoff, Greg Fox and Miles Zaharko for Ivan Boldirev, Phil Russell and Darcy Rota, March 13, 1979. Traded to **Toronto** by **Chicago** for Dave Hutchison, January 10, 1980. Traded to **Washington** by **Toronto** for Mike Kaszycki, February 16, 1980. Traded to **Calgary** by **Washington** with Washington's 2nd round choice (later traded to Montreal – Montreal selected Todd Francis) in 1983 Entry Draft for Randy Holt and Bobby Gould, November 25, 1981.

RIBEIRO, Mike

Center. Shoots left. 6', 177 lbs. Born, Montreal, Que., February 10, 1980.
(Montreal's 2nd choice, 45th overall, in 1998 Entry Draft).

Season	Club	GP	G	A	Pts	PIM	GP	G	A	Pts	PIM
99-2000	Montreal Canadiens	19	1	1	2	2	....	....	....	....	....
2000-01	Montreal Canadiens	2	0	0	0	2	....	....	....	....	....
2001-02	Montreal Canadiens	43	8	10	18	12	....	....	....	....	....
2002-03	Montreal Canadiens	52	5	12	17	6	....	....	....	....	....
	NHL Totals	**116**	**14**	**23**	**37**	**22**	....	....	....	....	....

RICCI, Mike

Center. Shoots left. 6', 185 lbs. Born, Scarborough, Ont., October 27, 1971.
(Philadelphia's 1st choice, 4th overall, in 1990 Entry Draft).

Season	Club	GP	G	A	Pts	PIM	GP	G	A	Pts	PIM
1990-91	Philadelphia Flyers	68	21	20	41	64	....	....	....	....	....
1991-92	Philadelphia Flyers	78	20	36	56	93	....	....	....	....	....
1992-93	Quebec Nordiques	77	27	51	78	123	6	0	6	6	8
1993-94	Quebec Nordiques	83	30	21	51	113	....	....	....	....	....
1994-95	Quebec Nordiques	48	15	21	36	40	6	1	3	4	8
1995-96◆	Colorado Avalanche	62	6	21	27	52	22	6	11	17	18
1996-97	Colorado Avalanche	63	13	19	32	59	17	2	4	6	17
1997-98	Colorado Avalanche	6	0	4	4	2	....	....	....	....	....
	San Jose Sharks	59	9	14	23	30	6	1	3	4	6
1998-99	San Jose Sharks	82	13	26	39	68	6	2	3	5	10
99-2000	San Jose Sharks	82	20	24	44	60	12	5	1	6	2
2000-01	San Jose Sharks	81	22	22	44	60	6	0	3	3	0
2001-02	San Jose Sharks	79	19	34	53	44	12	4	6	10	4
2002-03	San Jose Sharks	75	11	23	34	53	....	....	....	....	....
	NHL Totals	**943**	**226**	**336**	**562**	**861**	**93**	**21**	**40**	**61**	**73**

Traded to **Quebec** by **Philadelphia** with Steve Duchesne, Peter Forsberg, Kerry Huffman, Ron Hextall, Philadelphia's 1st round choice (Jocelyn Thibault) in 1993 Entry Draft, $15,000,000 and future considerations (Chris Simon and Philadelphia's 1st round choice (later traded to Toronto – later traded to Washington – Washington selected Nolan Baumgartner) in 1994 Entry Draft, July 21, 1992) for Eric Lindros, June 30, 1992. Transferred to **Colorado** after **Quebec** franchise relocated, June 21, 1995. Traded to **San Jose** by **Colorado** with Colorado's 2nd round choice (later traded to Buffalo – Buffalo selected Jaroslav Kristek) in 1998 Entry Draft for Shean Donovan and San Jose's 1st round choice (Alex Tanguay) in 1998 Entry Draft, November 21, 1997.

RICE, Steven

Right wing. Shoots right. 6', 217 lbs. Born, Kitchener, Ont., May 26, 1971.
(NY Rangers' 1st choice, 20th overall, in 1989 Entry Draft).

Season	Club	GP	G	A	Pts	PIM	GP	G	A	Pts	PIM
1990-91	New York Rangers	11	1	1	2	4	2	2	1	3	6
1991-92	Edmonton Oilers	3	0	0	0	2	....	....	....	....	....
1992-93	Edmonton Oilers	28	2	5	7	28	....	....	....	....	....
1993-94	Edmonton Oilers	63	17	15	32	36	....	....	....	....	....
1994-95	Hartford Whalers	40	11	10	21	61	....	....	....	....	....
1995-96	Hartford Whalers	59	10	12	22	47	....	....	....	....	....
1996-97	Hartford Whalers	78	21	14	35	59	....	....	....	....	....
1997-98	Carolina Hurricanes	47	2	4	6	38	....	....	....	....	....
	NHL Totals	**329**	**64**	**61**	**125**	**275**	**2**	**2**	**1**	**3**	**6**

Traded to **Edmonton** by **NY Rangers** with Bernie Nicholls and Louie DeBrusk for Mark Messier and future considerations (Jeff Beukeboom for David Shaw, November 12, 1991), October 4, 1991. Signed as a free agent by **Hartford**, August 18, 1994. Transferred to **Carolina** after **Hartford** franchise relocated, June 25, 1997.

RICHARD, Henri

HHOF

Center. Shoots right. 5'7", 160 lbs. Born, Montreal, Que., February 29, 1936.

Season	Club	GP	G	A	Pts	PIM	GP	G	A	Pts	PIM
1955-56◆	Montreal Canadiens	64	19	21	40	46	10	4	4	8	21

Season	Club	GP	G	A	Pts	PIM	GP	G	A	Pts	PIM
		REGULAR SEASON					PLAYOFFS				
1956-57 ♦	Montreal Canadiens	63	18	36	54	71	10	2	6	8	10
1957-58 ♦	Montreal Canadiens	67	28	*52	80	56	10	1	7	8	11
1958-59 ♦	Montreal Canadiens	63	21	30	51	33	11	3	8	11	13
1959-60 ♦	Montreal Canadiens	70	30	43	73	66	8	3	9	*12	9
1960-61	Montreal Canadiens	70	24	44	68	91	6	2	4	6	22
1961-62	Montreal Canadiens	54	21	29	50	48	....	....	....	....	....
1962-63	Montreal Canadiens	67	23	*50	73	57	5	1	1	2	2
1963-64	Montreal Canadiens	66	14	39	53	73	7	1	1	2	9
1964-65 ♦	Montreal Canadiens	53	23	29	52	43	13	7	4	11	24
1965-66 ♦	Montreal Canadiens	62	22	39	61	47	8	1	4	5	2
1966-67	Montreal Canadiens	65	21	34	55	28	10	4	6	10	2
1967-68 ♦	Montreal Canadiens	54	9	19	28	16	13	4	4	8	4
1968-69 ♦	Montreal Canadiens	64	15	37	52	45	14	2	4	6	8
1969-70	Montreal Canadiens	62	16	36	52	61	....	....	....	....	....
1970-71 ♦	Montreal Canadiens	75	12	37	49	46	20	5	7	12	20
1971-72	Montreal Canadiens	75	12	32	44	48	6	0	3	3	4
1972-73 ♦	Montreal Canadiens	71	8	35	43	21	17	6	4	10	14
1973-74	Montreal Canadiens	75	19	36	55	28	6	2	2	4	2
1974-75	Montreal Canadiens	16	3	10	13	4	6	1	2	3	4
	NHL Totals	**1256**	**358**	**688**	**1046**	**928**	**180**	**49**	**80**	**129**	**181**

• Brother of Maurice • NHL First All-Star Team (1958) • NHL Second All-Star Team (1959, 1961, 1963) • Bill Masterton Trophy (1974)

Played in NHL All-Star Game (1956, 1957, 1958, 1959, 1960, 1961, 1963, 1965, 1967, 1974)

Signed as a free agent by **Montreal**, October 13, 1955.

RICHARD, Jacques

Left wing. Shoots left. 5'11", 180 lbs. Born, Quebec City, Que., October 7, 1952.
(Atlanta's 1st choice, 2nd overall, in 1972 Amateur Draft).

Season	Club	GP	G	A	Pts	PIM	GP	G	A	Pts	PIM
1972-73	Atlanta Flames	74	13	18	31	32	....	....	....	....	....
1973-74	Atlanta Flames	78	27	16	43	45	4	0	0	0	2
1974-75	Atlanta Flames	63	17	12	29	31	....	....	....	....	....
1975-76	Buffalo Sabres	73	12	23	35	31	9	1	1	2	7
1976-77	Buffalo Sabres	21	2	0	2	16	....	....	....	....	....
1978-79	Buffalo Sabres	61	10	15	25	26	3	1	0	1	0
1979-80	Quebec Nordiques	14	3	12	15	4	....	....	....	....	....
1980-81	Quebec Nordiques	78	52	51	103	39	5	2	4	6	14
1981-82	Quebec Nordiques	59	15	26	41	77	10	1	0	1	9
1982-83	Quebec Nordiques	35	9	14	23	6	4	0	0	0	2
	NHL Totals	**556**	**160**	**187**	**347**	**307**	**35**	**5**	**5**	**10**	**34**

Traded to **Buffalo** by **Atlanta** for Larry Carriere and Buffalo's 1st round choice (later traded to Washington – Washington selected Greg Carroll) in 1976 Amateur Draft and cash, October 1, 1975. Signed as a free agent by **Quebec**, February 12, 1980.

RICHARD, Jean-Marc

Defense. Shoots left. 5'11", 178 lbs. Born, St-Raymond, Que., October 8, 1966.

Season	Club	GP	G	A	Pts	PIM	GP	G	A	Pts	PIM
1987-88	Quebec Nordiques	4	2	1	3	2	....	....	....	....	....
1989-90	Quebec Nordiques	1	0	0	0	0	....	....	....	....	....
	NHL Totals	**5**	**2**	**1**	**3**	**2**	....	....	....	....	....

Signed as a free agent by **Quebec**, April 13, 1987.

RICHARD, Maurice

HHOF

Right wing. Shoots left. 5'10", 170 lbs. Born, Montreal, Que., August 4, 1921.

Season	Club	GP	G	A	Pts	PIM	GP	G	A	Pts	PIM
1942-43	Montreal Canadiens	16	5	6	11	4	....	....	....	....	....
1943-44 ♦	Montreal Canadiens	46	32	22	54	45	9	*12	5	17	10
1944-45	Montreal Canadiens	50	*50	23	73	46	6	6	2	8	10
1945-46 ♦	Montreal Canadiens	50	27	21	48	50	9	*7	4	11	15
1946-47	Montreal Canadiens	60	*45	26	71	69	10	*6	5	*11	*44
1947-48	Montreal Canadiens	53	28	25	53	89	....	....	....	....	....
1948-49	Montreal Canadiens	59	20	18	38	110	7	2	1	3	14
1949-50	Montreal Canadiens	70	*43	22	65	114	5	1	1	2	6
1950-51	Montreal Canadiens	65	42	24	66	97	11	*9	4	*13	13
1951-52	Montreal Canadiens	48	27	17	44	44	11	4	2	6	6
1952-53 ♦	Montreal Canadiens	70	28	33	61	*112	12	7	1	8	2
1953-54	Montreal Canadiens	70	*37	30	67	112	11	3	0	3	22
1954-55	Montreal Canadiens	67	*38	36	74	125	....	....	....	....	....
1955-56 ♦	Montreal Canadiens	70	38	33	71	89	10	5	9	14	*24
1956-57 ♦	Montreal Canadiens	63	33	29	62	74	10	8	3	11	8
1957-58 ♦	Montreal Canadiens	28	15	19	34	28	10	*11	4	15	10
1958-59 ♦	Montreal Canadiens	42	17	21	38	27	4	0	0	0	2
1959-60 ♦	Montreal Canadiens	51	19	16	35	50	8	1	3	4	2
	NHL Totals	**978**	**544**	**421**	**965**	**1285**	**133**	**82**	**44**	**126**	**188**

• Brother of Henri • NHL Second All-Star Team (1944, 1951, 1952, 1953, 1954, 1957) • NHL First All-Star Team (1945, 1946, 1947, 1948, 1949, 1950, 1955, 1956) • Hart Trophy (1947)

Played in NHL All-Star Game (1947, 1948, 1949, 1950, 1951, 1952, 1953, 1954, 1955, 1956, 1957, 1958, 1959)

Signed as a free agent by **Montreal**, October 29, 1942. • Missed remainder of 1942-43 season recovering from leg injury suffered in game vs. Boston, December 27, 1942. • Missed majority of 1957-58 season recovering from achilles tendon injury suffered in game vs. Toronto, November 13, 1957.

RICHARD, Mike

Center. Shoots left. 5'10", 190 lbs. Born, Scarborough, Ont., July 9, 1966.

Season	Club	GP	G	A	Pts	PIM	GP	G	A	Pts	PIM
1987-88	Washington Capitals	4	0	0	0	0	....	....	....	....	....
1989-90	Washington Capitals	3	0	2	2	0	....	....	....	....	....
	NHL Totals	**7**	**0**	**2**	**2**	**0**	....	....	....	....	....

Signed as a free agent by **Washington**, October 9, 1987.

RICHARDS, Brad

Center. Shoots left. 6'1", 198 lbs. Born, Montague, P.E.I., May 2, 1980.
(Tampa Bay's 2nd choice, 64th overall, in 1998 Entry Draft).

Season	Club	GP	G	A	Pts	PIM	GP	G	A	Pts	PIM
2000-01	Tampa Bay Lightning	82	21	41	62	14	....	....	....	....	....
2001-02	Tampa Bay Lightning	82	20	42	62	13	....	....	....	....	....
2002-03	Tampa Bay Lightning	80	17	57	74	24	11	0	5	5	12
	NHL Totals	**244**	**58**	**140**	**198**	**51**	**11**	**0**	**5**	**5**	**12**

NHL All-Rookie Team (2001)

RICHARDS, Todd

Defense. Shoots right. 6', 194 lbs. Born, Robindale, MN, October 20, 1966.
(Montreal's 3rd choice, 33rd overall, in 1985 Entry Draft).

Season	Club	GP	G	A	Pts	PIM	GP	G	A	Pts	PIM
1990-91	Hartford Whalers	2	0	4	4	2	6	0	0	0	2
1991-92	Hartford Whalers	6	0	0	0	2	5	0	3	3	4
	NHL Totals	**8**	**0**	**4**	**4**	**4**	**11**	**0**	**3**	**3**	**6**

Traded to **Hartford** by **Montreal** for future considerations, October 11, 1990.

RICHARDS, Travis

Defense. Shoots left. 6'1", 195 lbs. Born, Crystal, MN, March 22, 1970.
(Minnesota's 6th choice, 169th overall, in 1988 Entry Draft).

Season	Club	GP	G	A	Pts	PIM	GP	G	A	Pts	PIM
1994-95	Dallas Stars	2	0	0	0	0	....	....	....	....	....
1995-96	Dallas Stars	1	0	0	0	2	....	....	....	....	....
	NHL Totals	**3**	**0**	**0**	**0**	**2**	....	....	....	....	....

Rights transferred to **Dallas** after **Minnesota** franchise relocated, June 9, 1993. Signed as a free agent by **Ottawa**, July 13, 2001.

RICHARDSON, Dave

Left wing. Shoots left. 5'9", 175 lbs. Born, St. Boniface, Man., December 11, 1940.

Season	Club	GP	G	A	Pts	PIM	GP	G	A	Pts	PIM
1963-64	New York Rangers	34	3	1	4	21	....	....	....	....	....
1964-65	New York Rangers	7	0	1	1	4	....	....	....	....	....
1965-66	Chicago Black Hawks	3	0	0	0	2	....	....	....	....	....
1967-68	Detroit Red Wings	1	0	0	0	0	....	....	....	....	....
	NHL Totals	**45**	**3**	**2**	**5**	**27**	....	....	....	....	....

Traded to **Chicago** by **NY Rangers** with Tracy Pratt, Mel Pearson and Dick Meissner for Ray Cullen and John McKenzie, June 4, 1965. Claimed by **Minnesota** from **Chicago** in Expansion Draft, June 6, 1967. Traded to **Detroit** by **Minnesota** with Jean-Guy Talbot for Duke Harris and Bob McCord, October 19, 1967.

RICHARDSON, Glen

Left wing. Shoots left. 6'2", 200 lbs. Born, Barrie, Ont., September 20, 1955.
(Vancouver's 4th choice, 64th overall, in 1975 Amateur Draft).

Season	Club	GP	G	A	Pts	PIM	GP	G	A	Pts	PIM
1975-76	Vancouver Canucks	24	3	6	9	19	....	....	....	....	....
	NHL Totals	**24**	**3**	**6**	**9**	**19**	....	....	....	....	....

RICHARDSON, Ken

Center. Shoots left. 6', 190 lbs. Born, North Bay, Ont., April 12, 1951.

Season	Club	GP	G	A	Pts	PIM	GP	G	A	Pts	PIM
1974-75	St. Louis Blues	21	5	7	12	12	....	....	....	....	....
1977-78	St. Louis Blues	12	2	5	7	2	....	....	....	....	....
1978-79	St. Louis Blues	16	1	1	2	2	....	....	....	....	....
	NHL Totals	**49**	**8**	**13**	**21**	**16**	....	....	....	....	....

Signed as a free agent by **St. Louis** (Columbus-IHL), September, 1973.

RICHARDSON, Luke

Defense. Shoots left. 6'4", 210 lbs. Born, Ottawa, Ont., March 26, 1969.
(Toronto's 1st choice, 7th overall, in 1987 Entry Draft).

Season	Club	GP	G	A	Pts	PIM	GP	G	A	Pts	PIM
1987-88	Toronto Maple Leafs	78	4	6	10	90	2	0	0	0	0
1988-89	Toronto Maple Leafs	55	2	7	9	106	....	....	....	....	....
1989-90	Toronto Maple Leafs	67	4	14	18	122	5	0	0	0	22
1990-91	Toronto Maple Leafs	78	1	9	10	238	....	....	....	....	....
1991-92	Edmonton Oilers	75	2	19	21	118	16	0	5	5	45
1992-93	Edmonton Oilers	82	3	10	13	142	....	....	....	....	....
1993-94	Edmonton Oilers	69	2	6	8	131	....	....	....	....	....
1994-95	Edmonton Oilers	46	3	10	13	40	....	....	....	....	....
1995-96	Edmonton Oilers	82	2	9	11	108	....	....	....	....	....
1996-97	Edmonton Oilers	82	1	11	12	91	12	0	2	2	14
1997-98	Philadelphia Flyers	81	2	3	5	139	5	0	0	0	0
1998-99	Philadelphia Flyers	78	0	6	6	106	....	....	....	....	....
99-2000	Philadelphia Flyers	74	2	5	7	140	18	0	1	1	41
2000-01	Philadelphia Flyers	82	2	6	8	131	6	0	0	0	4
2001-02	Philadelphia Flyers	72	1	8	9	102	5	0	0	0	4
2002-03	Columbus Blue Jackets	82	0	13	13	73	....	....	....	....	....
	NHL Totals	**1183**	**31**	**142**	**173**	**1877**	**69**	**0**	**8**	**8**	**130**

Traded to **Edmonton** by **Toronto** with Vincent Damphousse, Peter Ing and Scott Thornton for Grant Fuhr, Glenn Anderson and Craig Berube, September 19, 1991. Signed as a free agent by **Philadelphia**, July 23, 1997. Signed as a free agent by **Columbus**, July 4, 2002.

RICHER, Bob

Center. Shoots left. 5'10", 175 lbs. Born, Cowansville, Que., March 5, 1951.
(Buffalo's 4th choice, 47th overall, in 1971 Amateur Draft).

Season	Club	Regular Season GP	G	A	Pts	PIM	Playoffs GP	G	A	Pts	PIM
1972-73	Buffalo Sabres	3	0	0	0	0	....	....	....	....	....
	NHL Totals	**3**	**0**	**0**	**0**	**0**	....	....	....	....	....

RICHER, Stephane

Right wing. Shoots right. 6'2", 215 lbs. Born, Ripon, Que., June 7, 1966.
(Montreal's 3rd choice, 29th overall, in 1984 Entry Draft).

Season	Club	Regular Season GP	G	A	Pts	PIM	Playoffs GP	G	A	Pts	PIM
1984-85	Montreal Canadiens	1	0	0	0	0	....	....	....	....	....
1985-86♦	Montreal Canadiens	65	21	16	37	50	16	4	1	5	23
1986-87	Montreal Canadiens	57	20	19	39	80	5	3	2	5	0
1987-88	Montreal Canadiens	72	50	28	78	72	8	7	5	12	6
1988-89	Montreal Canadiens	68	25	35	60	61	21	6	5	11	14
1989-90	Montreal Canadiens	75	51	40	91	46	9	7	3	10	2
1990-91	Montreal Canadiens	75	31	30	61	53	13	9	5	14	6
1991-92	New Jersey Devils	74	29	35	64	25	7	1	2	3	0
1992-93	New Jersey Devils	78	38	35	73	44	5	2	2	4	2
1993-94	New Jersey Devils	80	36	36	72	16	20	7	5	12	6
1994-95♦	New Jersey Devils	45	23	16	39	10	19	6	15	21	2
1995-96	New Jersey Devils	73	20	12	32	30	....	....	....	....	....
1996-97	Montreal Canadiens	63	22	24	46	32	5	0	0	0	0
1997-98	Montreal Canadiens	14	5	4	9	5	....	....	....	....	....
	Tampa Bay Lightning	26	9	11	20	36	....	....	....	....	....
1998-99	Tampa Bay Lightning	64	12	21	33	22	....	....	....	....	....
99-2000	Tampa Bay Lightning	20	7	5	12	4	....	....	....	....	....
	St. Louis Blues	36	8	17	25	14	3	1	0	1	0
2001-02	Pittsburgh Penguins	58	13	12	25	14	....	....	....	....	....
	New Jersey Devils	10	1	2	3	0	3	0	0	0	0
	NHL Totals	**1054**	**421**	**398**	**819**	**614**	**134**	**53**	**45**	**98**	**61**

Played in NHL All-Star Game (1990)

Traded to **New Jersey** by **Montreal** with Tom Chorske for Kirk Muller and Roland Melanson, September 20, 1991. Traded to **Montreal** by **New Jersey** for Lyle Odelein, August 22, 1996. Traded to **Tampa Bay** by **Montreal** with Darcy Tucker and David Wilkie for Patrick Poulin, Mick Vukota and Igor Ulanov, January 15, 1998. Traded to **St. Louis** by **Tampa Bay** for Rich Parent and Chris McAlpine, January 13, 2000. Signed as a free agent by **Washington**, August 25, 2000. Signed as a free agent by **Pittsburgh**, October 2, 2001. Traded to **New Jersey** by **Pittsburgh** for New Jersey's 7th round choice (Stephen Dixon) in 2003 Entry Draft, March 19, 2002.

RICHER, Stephane

Defense. Shoots right. 5'11", 190 lbs. Born, Hull, Que., April 28, 1966.

Season	Club	Regular Season GP	G	A	Pts	PIM	Playoffs GP	G	A	Pts	PIM
1992-93	Tampa Bay Lightning	3	0	0	0	0	....	....	....	....	....
	Boston Bruins	21	1	4	5	18	3	0	0	0	0
1993-94	Florida Panthers	2	0	1	1	0	....	....	....	....	....
1994-95	Florida Panthers	1	0	0	0	2	....	....	....	....	....
	NHL Totals	**27**	**1**	**5**	**6**	**20**	**3**	**0**	**0**	**0**	**0**

Signed as a free agent by **Montreal**, January 9, 1988. Signed as a free agent by **Los Angeles**, July 11, 1990. Signed as a free agent by **Montreal**, September 17, 1991. Signed as a free agent by **Tampa Bay**, July 29, 1992. Traded to **Boston** by **Tampa Bay** for Bob Beers, October 28, 1992. Claimed by **Florida** from **Boston** in Expansion Draft, June 24, 1993.

RICHMOND, Steve

Defense. Shoots left. 6'1", 205 lbs. Born, Chicago, IL, December 11, 1959.

Season	Club	Regular Season GP	G	A	Pts	PIM	Playoffs GP	G	A	Pts	PIM
1983-84	New York Rangers	26	2	5	7	110	4	0	0	0	12
1984-85	New York Rangers	34	0	5	5	90	....	....	....	....	....
1985-86	New York Rangers	17	0	2	2	63	....	....	....	....	....
	Detroit Red Wings	29	1	2	3	82	....	....	....	....	....
1986-87	New Jersey Devils	44	1	7	8	143	....	....	....	....	....
1988-89	Los Angeles Kings	9	0	2	2	26	....	....	....	....	....
	NHL Totals	**159**	**4**	**23**	**27**	**514**	**4**	**0**	**0**	**0**	**12**

Signed as a free agent by **NY Rangers**, June 22, 1982. Traded to **Detroit** by **NY Rangers** for Mike McEwen, December 26, 1985. Traded to **New Jersey** by **Detroit** for Sam St. Laurent, August 18, 1986. Signed as a free agent by **Los Angeles**, July, 1988.

RICHTER, Barry

Defense. Shoots left. 6'2", 200 lbs. Born, Madison, WI, September 11, 1970.
(Hartford's 2nd choice, 32nd overall, in 1988 Entry Draft).

Season	Club	Regular Season GP	G	A	Pts	PIM	Playoffs GP	G	A	Pts	PIM
1995-96	New York Rangers	4	0	1	1	0	....	....	....	....	....
1996-97	Boston Bruins	50	5	13	18	32	....	....	....	....	....
1998-99	New York Islanders	72	6	18	24	34	....	....	....	....	....
99-2000	Montreal Canadiens	23	0	2	2	8	....	....	....	....	....
2000-01	Montreal Canadiens	2	0	0	0	2	....	....	....	....	....
	NHL Totals	**151**	**11**	**34**	**45**	**76**	....	....	....	....	....

Traded to **NY Rangers** by **Hartford** with Steve Larmer, Nick Kypreos and Hartford's 6th round choice (Yuri Litvinov) in 1994 Entry Draft for Darren Turcotte and James Patrick, November 2, 1993. Signed as a free agent by **Boston**, July 19, 1996. Signed as a free agent by **NY Islanders**, August 17, 1998. Signed as a free agent by **Montreal**, August 20, 1999. Loaned to **Manitoba** (IHL) by **Montreal** for loan of Patrice Tardif to **Quebec** (AHL), March 3, 2000.

RICHTER, Dave

Defense. Shoots right. 6'5", 225 lbs. Born, St. Boniface, Man., April 8, 1960.
(Minnesota's 10th choice, 205th overall, in 1980 Entry Draft).

Season	Club	Regular Season GP	G	A	Pts	PIM	Playoffs GP	G	A	Pts	PIM
1981-82	Minnesota North Stars	3	0	0	0	11	....	....	....	....	....
1982-83	Minnesota North Stars	6	0	0	0	4	....	....	....	....	....
1983-84	Minnesota North Stars	42	2	3	5	132	8	0	0	0	20
1984-85	Minnesota North Stars	55	2	8	10	221	9	1	0	1	39
1985-86	Minnesota North Stars	14	0	3	3	29	....	....	....	....	....
	Philadelphia Flyers	50	0	2	2	138	5	0	0	0	21
1986-87	Vancouver Canucks	78	2	15	17	172	....	....	....	....	....
1987-88	Vancouver Canucks	49	2	4	6	224	....	....	....	....	....
1988-89	St. Louis Blues	66	1	5	6	99	....	....	....	....	....
1989-90	St. Louis Blues	2	0	0	0	0	....	....	....	....	....
	NHL Totals	**365**	**9**	**40**	**49**	**1030**	**22**	**1**	**0**	**1**	**80**

Traded to **Philadelphia** by **Minnesota** with Bo Berglund for Ed Hospodar and Todd Bergen, November 29, 1985. Traded to **Vancouver** by **Philadelphia** with Rich Sutter and Vancouver's 3rd round choice (previously acquired, Vancouver selected Don Gibson) in 1986 Entry Draft for J.J. Daigneault, Vancouver's 2nd round choice (Kent Hawley) in 1986 Entry Draft and Vancouver's 5th round choice (later traded back to Vancouver – Vancouver selected Sean Fabian) in 1987 Entry Draft, June 6, 1986. Traded to **St. Louis** by **Vancouver** for Robert Nordmark and St. Louis's 2nd round choice (later traded to Montreal – Montreal selected Craig Darby) in 1991 Entry Draft, September 6, 1988.

RIDLEY, Mike

Center. Shoots left. 6', 195 lbs. Born, Winnipeg, Man., July 8, 1963.

Season	Club	Regular Season GP	G	A	Pts	PIM	Playoffs GP	G	A	Pts	PIM
1985-86	New York Rangers	80	22	43	65	69	16	6	8	14	26
1986-87	New York Rangers	38	16	20	36	20	....	....	....	....	....
	Washington Capitals	40	15	19	34	20	7	2	1	3	6
1987-88	Washington Capitals	70	28	31	59	22	14	6	5	11	10
1988-89	Washington Capitals	80	41	48	89	49	6	0	5	5	2
1989-90	Washington Capitals	74	30	43	73	27	14	3	4	7	8
1990-91	Washington Capitals	79	23	48	71	26	11	3	4	7	8
1991-92	Washington Capitals	80	29	40	69	38	7	0	11	11	0
1992-93	Washington Capitals	84	26	56	82	44	6	1	5	6	0
1993-94	Washington Capitals	81	26	44	70	24	11	4	6	10	6
1994-95	Toronto Maple Leafs	48	10	27	37	14	7	3	1	4	2
1995-96	Vancouver Canucks	37	6	15	21	29	5	0	0	0	2
1996-97	Vancouver Canucks	75	20	32	52	42	....	....	....	....	....
	NHL Totals	**866**	**292**	**466**	**758**	**424**	**104**	**28**	**50**	**78**	**70**

NHL All-Rookie Team (1986)

Played in NHL All-Star Game (1989)

Signed as a free agent by **NY Rangers**, September 26, 1985. Traded to **Washington** by **NY Rangers** with Bob Crawford and Kelly Miller for Bob Carpenter and Washington's 2nd round choice (Jason Prosofsky) in 1989 Entry Draft, January 1, 1987. Traded to **Toronto** by **Washington** with St. Louis' 1st round choice (previously acquired, Toronto selected Eric Fichaud) in 1994 Entry Draft for Rob Pearson and Philadelphia's 1st round choice (previously acquired, Washington selected Nolan Baumgartner) in 1994 Entry Draft, June 28, 1994. Traded to **Vancouver** by **Toronto** for Sergio Momesso, July 8, 1995.

RIESEN, Michel

Right wing. Shoots right. 6'2", 190 lbs. Born, Oberbalm, Switz., April 11, 1979.
(Edmonton's 1st choice, 14th overall, in 1997 Entry Draft).

Season	Club	Regular Season GP	G	A	Pts	PIM	Playoffs GP	G	A	Pts	PIM
2000-01	Edmonton Oilers	12	0	1	1	4	....	....	....	....	....
	NHL Totals	**12**	**0**	**1**	**1**	**4**	....	....	....	....	....

Traded to **St. Louis** by **Edmonton** with Doug Weight for Marty Reasoner, Jochen Hecht and Jan Horacek, July 1, 2001.

RILEY, Bill

Right wing. Shoots right. 5'11", 195 lbs. Born, Amherst, N.S., September 20, 1950.

Season	Club	Regular Season GP	G	A	Pts	PIM	Playoffs GP	G	A	Pts	PIM
1974-75	Washington Capitals	1	0	0	0	0	....	....	....	....	....
1976-77	Washington Capitals	43	13	14	27	124	....	....	....	....	....
1977-78	Washington Capitals	57	13	12	25	125	....	....	....	....	....
1978-79	Washington Capitals	24	2	2	4	64	....	....	....	....	....
1979-80	Winnipeg Jets	14	3	2	5	7	....	....	....	....	....
	NHL Totals	**139**	**31**	**30**	**61**	**320**	....	....	....	....	....

Signed as a free agent by **Washington** to a five-game tryout contract, December 20, 1974. Signed as a free agent by **Washington**, January 19, 1977. Claimed by **Winnipeg** from **Washington** in Expansion Draft, June 3, 1979. Signed as a free agent by **Toronto**, February 25, 1981.

RILEY, Jack

Center. Shoots left. 5'11", 160 lbs. Born, Berckenla, Ireland, December 29, 1910.

Season	Club	Regular Season GP	G	A	Pts	PIM	Playoffs GP	G	A	Pts	PIM
1932-33	Detroit Red Wings	1	0	0	0	0	....	....	....	....	....
1933-34	Montreal Canadiens	48	6	11	17	4	2	0	1	1	0
1934-35	Montreal Canadiens	47	4	11	15	4	2	0	2	2	0
1935-36	Boston Bruins	8	0	0	0	0	....	....	....	....	....
	NHL Totals	**104**	**10**	**22**	**32**	**8**	**4**	**0**	**3**	**3**	**0**

NHL rights transferred to **Detroit** from **Chicago** (AHA) after AHA club owners purchased Detroit (NHL and IHL) franchises, September 2, 1932. Traded to **Cleveland** (IHL) by **Detroit** with Tony Prelesnik for Frank Waite, December 2, 1932. Traded to **Montreal** by **Cleveland** (IHL) for cash, June, 1933. Traded to **Boston** by **Montreal** for Paul Haynes, September 30, 1935.

RILEY, Jim

Left wing. Shoots left. 5'11", 180 lbs. Born, Bayfield, N.B., May 25, 1897.

Season	Club	Regular Season GP	G	A	Pts	PIM	Playoffs GP	G	A	Pts	PIM
1926-27	Chicago Black Hawks	3	0	0	0	0	....	....	....	....	....
	Detroit Cougars	6	0	2	2	14	....	....	....	....	....
	NHL Totals	**9**	**0**	**2**	**2**	**14**	....	....	....	....	....

• Only athlete to play both major league baseball (St. Louis – AL, Washington) and NHL hockey.
Signed as a free agent by **Chicago**, January 19, 1927. Traded to **Detroit** by **Chicago** for cash, January 31, 1927. Traded to **Detroit Olympics** (Can-Pro) by **Detroit** for cash, October 11, 1927.

RIOPELLE, Rip

Left wing. Shoots left. 5'11", 165 lbs. Born, Ottawa, Ont., January 30, 1922.

Season	Club	GP	G	A	Pts	PIM	GP	G	A	Pts	PIM
		REGULAR SEASON					PLAYOFFS				
1947-48	Montreal Canadiens	55	5	2	7	12	....	....	....	....	....
1948-49	Montreal Canadiens	48	10	6	16	34	7	1	1	2	2
1949-50	Montreal Canadiens	66	12	8	20	27	1	0	0	0	0
	NHL Totals	**169**	**27**	**16**	**43**	**73**	**8**	**1**	**1**	**2**	**2**

Traded to **Ottawa** (QMHL) by **Montreal** for cash, October 4, 1951.

RIOUX, Gerry

Right wing. Shoots right. 5'11", 195 lbs. Born, Iroquois Falls, Ont., February 17, 1959.

Season	Club	GP	G	A	Pts	PIM	GP	G	A	Pts	PIM
1979-80	Winnipeg Jets	8	0	0	0	6	....	....	....	....	....
	NHL Totals	**8**	**0**	**0**	**0**	**6**	....	....	....	....	....

Signed as a free agent by **Winnipeg**, October, 1979.

RIOUX, Pierre

Right wing. Shoots right. 5'9", 165 lbs. Born, Quebec City, Que., February 1, 1962.

Season	Club	GP	G	A	Pts	PIM	GP	G	A	Pts	PIM
1982-83	Calgary Flames	14	1	2	3	4	....	....	....	....	....
	NHL Totals	**14**	**1**	**2**	**3**	**4**	....	....	....	....	....

Signed as a free agent by **Calgary**, August 24, 1982.

RIPLEY, Vic

Left wing. Shoots left. 5'8", 170 lbs. Born, Elgin, Ont., May 30, 1906.

Season	Club	GP	G	A	Pts	PIM	GP	G	A	Pts	PIM
1928-29	Chicago Black Hawks	34	11	2	13	31	....	....	....	....	....
1929-30	Chicago Black Hawks	40	8	8	16	33	2	0	0	0	2
1930-31	Chicago Black Hawks	37	8	4	12	9	9	2	1	3	4
1931-32	Chicago Black Hawks	46	12	6	18	47	2	0	0	0	0
1932-33	Chicago Black Hawks	15	2	4	6	6	....	....	....	....	....
	Boston Bruins	23	2	5	7	21	5	1	0	1	0
1933-34	Boston Bruins	14	2	1	3	6	....	....	....	....	....
	New York Rangers	34	5	12	17	10	2	1	0	1	4
1934-35	New York Rangers	4	0	2	2	0	....	....	....	....	....
	St. Louis Eagles	31	1	5	6	10	....	....	....	....	....
	NHL Totals	**278**	**51**	**49**	**100**	**173**	**20**	**4**	**1**	**5**	**10**

Claimed by **Chicago** from **Kitchener** (Can-Pro) in Inter-League Draft, May 14, 1928. Traded to **Boston** by **Chicago** for Billy Burch, January 17, 1933. Traded to **NY Rangers** by **Boston** with Roy Burmeister for Babe Siebert, December 18, 1933. Traded to **St. Louis** by **NY Rangers** for cash, November 29, 1934.

RISEBROUGH, Doug

Center. Shoots left. 5'11", 180 lbs. Born, Guelph, Ont., January 29, 1954.
(Montreal's 2nd choice, 7th overall, in 1974 Amateur Draft).

Season	Club	GP	G	A	Pts	PIM	GP	G	A	Pts	PIM
1974-75	Montreal Canadiens	64	15	32	47	198	11	3	5	8	37
1975-76♦	Montreal Canadiens	80	16	28	44	180	13	0	3	3	30
1976-77♦	Montreal Canadiens	78	22	38	60	132	12	2	3	5	16
1977-78♦	Montreal Canadiens	72	18	23	41	97	15	2	2	4	17
1978-79♦	Montreal Canadiens	48	10	15	25	62	15	1	6	7	32
1979-80	Montreal Canadiens	44	8	10	18	81	....	....	....	....	....
1980-81	Montreal Canadiens	48	13	21	34	93	3	1	0	1	0
1981-82	Montreal Canadiens	59	15	18	33	116	5	2	1	3	11
1982-83	Calgary Flames	71	21	37	58	138	9	1	3	4	18
1983-84	Calgary Flames	77	23	28	51	161	11	2	1	3	25
1984-85	Calgary Flames	15	7	5	12	49	4	0	3	3	12
1985-86	Calgary Flames	62	15	28	43	169	22	7	9	16	38
1986-87	Calgary Flames	22	2	3	5	66	4	0	1	1	2
	NHL Totals	**740**	**185**	**286**	**471**	**1542**	**124**	**21**	**37**	**58**	**238**

Traded to **Calgary** by **Montreal** with Montreal's 2nd round choice (later traded to Minnesota – Minnesota selected Frantisek Musil) in 1983 Entry Draft for Washington's 2nd round choice (previously acquired, Montreal selected Todd Francis) in 1983 Entry Draft and Calgary's 3rd round choice (Graeme Bonar) in 1984 Entry Draft, September 11, 1982.

RISSLING, Gary

Left wing. Shoots left. 5'9", 175 lbs. Born, Saskatoon, Sask., August 8, 1956.

Season	Club	GP	G	A	Pts	PIM	GP	G	A	Pts	PIM
1978-79	Washington Capitals	26	3	3	6	127	....	....	....	....	....
1979-80	Washington Capitals	11	0	1	1	49	....	....	....	....	....
1980-81	Pittsburgh Penguins	25	1	0	1	143	5	0	1	1	4
1981-82	Pittsburgh Penguins	16	0	0	0	55	....	....	....	....	....
1982-83	Pittsburgh Penguins	40	5	4	9	128	....	....	....	....	....
1983-84	Pittsburgh Penguins	47	4	13	17	297	....	....	....	....	....
1984-85	Pittsburgh Penguins	56	10	9	19	209	....	....	....	....	....
	NHL Totals	**221**	**23**	**30**	**53**	**1008**	**5**	**0**	**1**	**1**	**4**

Signed as a free agent by **Washington**, December 4, 1978. Traded to **Pittsburgh** by **Washington** for Pittsburgh's 5th round choice (Peter Sidorkiewicz) in 1981 Entry Draft, January 2, 1981.

RITA, Jani

Left wing. Shoots left. 6'1", 206 lbs. Born, Helsinki, Finland, July 25, 1981.
(Edmonton's 1st choice, 13th overall, in 1999 Entry Draft).

Season	Club	GP	G	A	Pts	PIM	GP	G	A	Pts	PIM
2001-02	Edmonton Oilers	1	0	0	0	0	....	....	....	....	....
2002-03	Edmonton Oilers	12	3	1	4	0	....	....	....	....	....
	NHL Totals	**13**	**3**	**1**	**4**	**0**	....	....	....	....	....

RITCHIE, Bob

Left wing. Shoots left. 5'10", 170 lbs. Born, Laverlochere, Que., February 20, 1955.
(Philadelphia's 2nd choice, 54th overall, in 1975 Amateur Draft).

Season	Club	GP	G	A	Pts	PIM	GP	G	A	Pts	PIM
1976-77	Philadelphia Flyers	1	0	0	0	0	....	....	....	....	....
	Detroit Red Wings	17	6	2	8	10	....	....	....	....	....
1977-78	Detroit Red Wings	11	2	2	4	0	....	....	....	....	....
	NHL Totals	**29**	**8**	**4**	**12**	**10**	....	....	....	....	....

Traded to **Detroit** by **Philadelphia** with Terry Murray, Steve Coates and Dave Kelly for Rick Lapointe and Mike Korney, February 17, 1977.

RITCHIE, Byron

Center. Shoots left. 5'10", 195 lbs. Born, Burnaby, B.C., April 24, 1977.
(Hartford's 6th choice, 165th overall, in 1995 Entry Draft).

Season	Club	GP	G	A	Pts	PIM	GP	G	A	Pts	PIM
1998-99	Carolina Hurricanes	3	0	0	0	0	....	....	....	....	....
99-2000	Carolina Hurricanes	26	0	2	2	17	....	....	....	....	....
2001-02	Carolina Hurricanes	4	0	0	0	2	....	....	....	....	....
	Florida Panthers	31	5	6	11	34	....	....	....	....	....
2002-03	Florida Panthers	30	0	3	3	19	....	....	....	....	....
	NHL Totals	**94**	**5**	**11**	**16**	**72**	....	....	....	....	....

Rights transferred to **Carolina** after **Hartford** franchise relocated, June 25, 1997. Traded to **Florida** by **Carolina** with Sandis Ozolinsh for Bret Hedican, Kevyn Adams, Tomas Malec and a conditional 2nd round choice in 2003 Entry Draft, January 16, 2002.

RITCHIE, Dave

Defense. Shoots right. 5'7", 180 lbs. Born, Montreal, Que., January 12, 1892.

Season	Club	GP	G	A	Pts	PIM	GP	G	A	Pts	PIM
1917-18	Montreal Wanderers	4	5	2	7	3	....	....	....	....	....
	Ottawa Senators	14	4	1	5	18	....	....	....	....	....
1918-19	Toronto Arenas	4	0	0	0	9	....	....	....	....	....
1919-20	Quebec Bulldogs	23	6	3	9	18	....	....	....	....	....
1920-21	Montreal Canadiens	6	0	0	0	2	....	....	....	....	....
1924-25	Montreal Canadiens	5	0	0	0	0	1	0	0	0	0
1925-26	Montreal Canadiens	2	0	0	0	0	....	....	....	....	....
	NHL Totals	**58**	**15**	**6**	**21**	**50**	**1**	**0**	**0**	**0**	**0**

Claimed by **Mtl. Wanderers** from **Quebec** in Dispersal Draft, November 26, 1917. Claimed by **Ottawa** from **Mtl. Wanderers** in Dispersal Draft, January 4, 1918. Signed as a free agent by **Toronto**, January 17, 1919. Transferred to **Quebec** by **Toronto** when Quebec franchise returned to NHL, November 25, 1919. Transferred to **Hamilton** after **Quebec** franchise relocated, November 2, 1920. Traded to **Montreal** by **Hamilton** with Harry Mummery and Jack McDonald for Goldie Prodgers, Joe Matte, Jack Coughlin and loan of Billy Coutu for 1920-21 season, November 27, 1920. Signed as a free agent by **Montreal**, January 28, 1925. Signed as a free agent by **Montreal**, January 13, 1926.

RITSON, Alex

Center. Shoots left. 5'11", 172 lbs. Born, Peace River, Alta., March 7, 1922.

Season	Club	GP	G	A	Pts	PIM	GP	G	A	Pts	PIM
1944-45	New York Rangers	1	0	0	0	0	....	....	....	....	....
	NHL Totals	**1**	**0**	**0**	**0**	**0**	....	....	....	....	....

Claimed by **NY Rangers** from **Indianapolis** (AHL) in Inter-League Draft, May 12, 1944.

RITTINGER, Alan

Wing. Shoots right. 5'9", 155 lbs. Born, Regina, Sask., January 28, 1925.

Season	Club	GP	G	A	Pts	PIM	GP	G	A	Pts	PIM
1943-44	Boston Bruins	19	3	7	10	0	....	....	....	....	....
	NHL Totals	**19**	**3**	**7**	**10**	**0**	....	....	....	....	....

RIVARD, Bob

Center/Left wing. Shoots left. 5'8", 155 lbs. Born, Sherbrooke, Que., August 1, 1939.

Season	Club	GP	G	A	Pts	PIM	GP	G	A	Pts	PIM
1967-68	Pittsburgh Penguins	27	5	12	17	4	....	....	....	....	....
	NHL Totals	**27**	**5**	**12**	**17**	**4**	....	....	....	....	....

Claimed by **Pittsburgh** from **Montreal** in Expansion Draft, June 6, 1967. Loaned to **Philadelphia** by **Pittsburgh** for cash, September, 1968. Traded to **Baltimore** (AHL) by **Pittsburgh** to complete transaction that sent Jim Morrison to Pittsburgh (October, 1969), November, 1969.

RIVERS, Gus

Right wing. Shoots right. 5'11", 180 lbs. Born, Winnipeg, Man., November 19, 1909.

Season	Club	GP	G	A	Pts	PIM	GP	G	A	Pts	PIM
1929-30♦	Montreal Canadiens	19	1	0	1	2	6	1	0	1	2
1930-31♦	Montreal Canadiens	44	2	5	7	6	10	1	0	1	0
1931-32	Montreal Canadiens	25	1	0	1	4	....	....	....	....	....
	NHL Totals	**88**	**4**	**5**	**9**	**12**	**16**	**2**	**0**	**2**	**2**

Signed as a free agent by **Montreal**, January 22, 1930.

RIVERS, Jamie

Defense. Shoots left. 6'1", 200 lbs. Born, Ottawa, Ont., March 16, 1975.
(St. Louis' 2nd choice, 63rd overall, in 1993 Entry Draft).

Season	Club	GP	G	A	Pts	PIM	GP	G	A	Pts	PIM
1995-96	St. Louis Blues	3	0	0	0	2	....	....	....	....	....
1996-97	St. Louis Blues	15	2	5	7	6	....	....	....	....	....
1997-98	St. Louis Blues	59	2	4	6	36	....	....	....	....	....
1998-99	St. Louis Blues	76	2	5	7	47	9	1	1	2	2
99-2000	New York Islanders	75	1	16	17	84	....	....	....	....	....
2000-01	Ottawa Senators	45	2	4	6	44	1	0	0	0	4
2001-02	Ottawa Senators	2	0	0	0	4	....	....	....	....	....
	Boston Bruins	64	4	2	6	45	3	0	0	0	0

		REGULAR SEASON					PLAYOFFS				
Season	Club	GP	G	A	Pts	PIM	GP	G	A	Pts	PIM
2002-03	Florida Panthers	1	0	0	0	2					
	NHL Totals	**340**	**13**	**36**	**49**	**270**	**13**	**1**	**1**	**2**	**6**

• Brother of Shawn

Claimed by **NY Islanders** from **St. Louis** in Waiver Draft, September 27, 1999. Signed as a free agent by **Ottawa**, November 30, 2000. Claimed on waivers by **Boston** from **Ottawa**, October 13, 2001. Signed as a free agent by **Florida**, December 16, 2002. Signed as a free agent by **Detroit**, July 29, 2003.

RIVERS, Shawn

Defense. Shoots left. 5'10", 185 lbs. Born, Ottawa, Ont., January 30, 1971.

Season	Club	GP	G	A	Pts	PIM	GP	G	A	Pts	PIM
1992-93	Tampa Bay Lightning	4	0	2	2	2					
	NHL Totals	**4**	**0**	**2**	**2**	**2**					

• Brother of Jamie

Signed as a free agent by **Tampa Bay**, June 29, 1992.

RIVERS, Wayne

Right wing. Shoots right. 5'9", 177 lbs. Born, Hamilton, Ont., February 1, 1942.

Season	Club	GP	G	A	Pts	PIM	GP	G	A	Pts	PIM
1961-62	Detroit Red Wings	2	0	0	0	0					
1963-64	Boston Bruins	12	2	7	9	6					
1964-65	Boston Bruins	58	6	17	23	72					
1965-66	Boston Bruins	2	1	1	2	2					
1966-67	Boston Bruins	8	2	1	3	6					
1967-68	St. Louis Blues	22	4	4	8	8					
1968-69	New York Rangers	4	0	0	0	0					
	NHL Totals	**108**	**15**	**30**	**45**	**94**					

Claimed by **Boston** from **Detroit** (Hershey-AHL) in Inter-League Draft, June 4, 1963. Claimed by **St. Louis** from **Boston** in Expansion Draft, June 6, 1967. Traded to **NY Rangers** by **St. Louis** with Don Caley for Camille Henry, Bill Plager and Robbie Irons, June 13, 1968. Traded to **Los Angeles** (Springfield-AHL) by **NY Rangers** (Baltimore-AHL) for Mike McMahon, October, 1971.

RIVET, Craig

Defense. Shoots right. 6'2", 207 lbs. Born, North Bay, Ont., September 13, 1974.
(Montreal's 4th choice, 68th overall, in 1992 Entry Draft).

Season	Club	GP	G	A	Pts	PIM	GP	G	A	Pts	PIM
1994-95	Montreal Canadiens	5	0	1	1	5					
1995-96	Montreal Canadiens	19	1	4	5	54					
1996-97	Montreal Canadiens	35	0	4	4	54	5	0	1	1	14
1997-98	Montreal Canadiens	61	0	2	2	93	5	0	0	0	2
1998-99	Montreal Canadiens	66	2	8	10	66					
99-2000	Montreal Canadiens	61	3	14	17	76					
2000-01	Montreal Canadiens	26	1	2	3	36					
2001-02	Montreal Canadiens	82	8	17	25	76	12	0	3	3	4
2002-03	Montreal Canadiens	82	7	15	22	71					
	NHL Totals	**437**	**22**	**67**	**89**	**531**	**22**	**0**	**4**	**4**	**20**

• Missed majority of 2000-01 season recovering from shoulder injury suffered in game vs. Vancouver, October 30, 2000.

RIZZUTO, Garth

Center. Shoots left. 5'10", 175 lbs. Born, Trail, B.C., September 11, 1947.

Season	Club	GP	G	A	Pts	PIM	GP	G	A	Pts	PIM
1970-71	Vancouver Canucks	37	3	4	7	16					
	NHL Totals	**37**	**3**	**4**	**7**	**16**					

Claimed by **Vancouver** from **Chicago** in Expansion Draft, June 10, 1970.

ROACH, Mickey

Center. Shoots left. 5'6", 158 lbs. Born, Boston, MA, May 1, 1895.

Season	Club	GP	G	A	Pts	PIM	GP	G	A	Pts	PIM
1919-20	Toronto St. Pats	21	11	2	13	4					
1920-21	Toronto St. Pats	9	1	1	2	2					
	Hamilton Tigers	14	9	8	17	0					
1921-22	Hamilton Tigers	24	14	6	20	7					
1922-23	Hamilton Tigers	24	17	10	27	8					
1923-24	Hamilton Tigers	20	5	3	8	7					
1924-25	Hamilton Tigers	30	6	4	10	8					
1925-26	New York Americans	25	3	0	3	4					
1926-27	New York Americans	44	11	0	11	14					
	NHL Totals	**211**	**77**	**34**	**111**	**54**					

Signed as a free agent by **Toronto**, December 16, 1919. Traded to **Hamilton** by **Toronto** for cash, January 21, 1921. Transferred to **NY Americans** after NHL club purchased **Hamilton** franchise, September 26, 1925. Traded to **Niagara Falls** (Can-Pro) by **NY Americans** and named playing coach for future considerations (Bill Holmes, October 29, 1928), October 5, 1927.

ROBERGE, Mario

Left wing. Shoots left. 5'11", 193 lbs. Born, Quebec City, Que., January 25, 1964.

Season	Club	GP	G	A	Pts	PIM	GP	G	A	Pts	PIM
1990-91	Montreal Canadiens	5	0	0	0	21	12	0	0	0	24
1991-92	Montreal Canadiens	20	2	1	3	62					
1992-93 ♦	Montreal Canadiens	50	4	4	8	142	3	0	0	0	0
1993-94	Montreal Canadiens	28	1	2	3	55					
1994-95	Montreal Canadiens	9	0	0	0	34					
	NHL Totals	**112**	**7**	**7**	**14**	**314**	**15**	**0**	**0**	**0**	**24**

• Brother of Serge

Signed as a free agent by **Montreal**, October 5, 1988.

ROBERGE, Serge

Right wing. Shoots right. 6'1", 195 lbs. Born, Quebec City, Que., March 31, 1965.

Season	Club	GP	G	A	Pts	PIM	GP	G	A	Pts	PIM
1990-91	Quebec Nordiques	9	0	0	0	24					
	NHL Totals	**9**	**0**	**0**	**0**	**24**					

• Brother of Mario

Signed as a free agent by **Montreal**, January 25, 1988. Signed as a free agent by **Quebec**, December 28, 1990.

ROBERT, Claude

Left wing. Shoots left. 5'11", 175 lbs. Born, Montreal, Que., August 10, 1928.

Season	Club	GP	G	A	Pts	PIM	GP	G	A	Pts	PIM
1950-51	Montreal Canadiens	23	1	0	1	9					
	NHL Totals	**23**	**1**	**0**	**1**	**9**					

ROBERT, Rene

Right wing. Shoots right. 5'10", 184 lbs. Born, Trois-Rivieres, Que., December 31, 1948.

Season	Club	GP	G	A	Pts	PIM	GP	G	A	Pts	PIM
1970-71	Toronto Maple Leafs	5	0	0	0	0					
1971-72	Pittsburgh Penguins	49	7	11	18	42					
	Buffalo Sabres	12	6	3	9	2					
1972-73	Buffalo Sabres	75	40	43	83	83	6	5	3	8	2
1973-74	Buffalo Sabres	76	21	44	65	71					
1974-75	Buffalo Sabres	74	40	60	100	75	16	5	8	13	16
1975-76	Buffalo Sabres	72	35	52	87	53	9	3	2	5	6
1976-77	Buffalo Sabres	80	33	40	73	46	6	5	2	7	20
1977-78	Buffalo Sabres	67	25	48	73	25	7	2	0	2	23
1978-79	Buffalo Sabres	68	22	40	62	46	3	2	2	4	4
1979-80	Colorado Rockies	69	28	35	63	79					
1980-81	Colorado Rockies	28	8	11	19	30					
	Toronto Maple Leafs	14	6	7	13	8	3	0	2	2	2
1981-82	Toronto Maple Leafs	55	13	24	37	37					
	NHL Totals	**744**	**284**	**418**	**702**	**597**	**50**	**22**	**19**	**41**	**73**

NHL Second All-Star Team (1975)

Played in NHL All-Star Game (1973, 1975)

Signed as a free agent by **Toronto** (Tulsa-CHL) to a five-game tryout contract, March 20, 1968. Traded to **Vancouver** (WHL) by **Toronto** with Brad Selwood for Ron Ward, May, 1969. Traded to **Toronto** by **Vancouver** (WHL) for cash, May 15, 1970. Claimed by **Buffalo** from **Toronto** in Intra-League Draft, June 8, 1971. Claimed by **Pittsburgh** from **Buffalo** in Intra-League Draft, June 8, 1971. Traded to **Buffalo** by **Pittsburgh** for Eddie Shack, March 4, 1972. Traded to **Colorado** by **Buffalo** for John Van Boxmeer, October 5, 1979. Traded to **Toronto** by **Colorado** for Toronto's 3rd round choice (Ulf Hiemer) in the 1981 Entry Draft, January 30, 1981.

ROBERTO, Phil

Right wing. Shoots right. 6'1", 190 lbs. Born, Niagara Falls, Ont., January 1, 1949.

Season	Club	GP	G	A	Pts	PIM	GP	G	A	Pts	PIM
1969-70	Montreal Canadiens	8	0	1	1	8					
1970-71 ♦	Montreal Canadiens	39	14	7	21	76	15	0	1	1	36
1971-72	Montreal Canadiens	27	3	2	5	22					
	St. Louis Blues	49	12	13	25	76	11	7	6	13	29
1972-73	St. Louis Blues	77	20	22	42	99	5	2	1	3	4
1973-74	St. Louis Blues	15	1	1	2	10					
1974-75	St. Louis Blues	7	0	2	2	2					
	Detroit Red Wings	46	13	27	40	30					
1975-76	Detroit Red Wings	37	1	7	8	68					
	Kansas City Scouts	37	7	15	22	42					
1976-77	Colorado Rockies	22	1	5	6	23					
	Cleveland Barons	21	3	4	7	8					
	NHL Totals	**385**	**75**	**106**	**181**	**464**	**31**	**9**	**8**	**17**	**69**

Traded to **St. Louis** by **Montreal** for Jimmy Roberts, December 13, 1971. Traded to **Detroit** by **St. Louis** with St. Louis's 3rd round choice (Blair Davidson) in 1975 Amateur Draft for Red Berenson, December 30, 1974. Traded to **Kansas City** by **Detroit** for Buster Harvey, January 14, 1976. Transferred to **Colorado** after **Kansas City** franchise relocated, July 15, 1976. Signed as a free agent by **Cleveland** after securing release from **Colorado**, December 24, 1976.

ROBERTS, David

Left wing. Shoots left. 6', 185 lbs. Born, Alameda, CA, May 28, 1970.
(St. Louis' 5th choice, 114th overall, in 1989 Entry Draft).

Season	Club	GP	G	A	Pts	PIM	GP	G	A	Pts	PIM
1993-94	St. Louis Blues	1	0	0	0	2	3	0	0	0	12
1994-95	St. Louis Blues	19	6	5	11	10	6	0	0	0	4
1995-96	St. Louis Blues	28	1	6	7	12					
	Edmonton Oilers	6	2	4	6	6					
1996-97	Vancouver Canucks	58	10	17	27	51					
1997-98	Vancouver Canucks	13	1	1	2	4					
	NHL Totals	**125**	**20**	**33**	**53**	**85**	**9**	**0**	**0**	**0**	**16**

• Son of Doug

Traded to **Edmonton** by **St. Louis** for future considerations, March 12, 1996. Signed as a free agent by **Vancouver**, July 31, 1996. Signed as a free agent by **Dallas**, July 31, 1998.

ROBERTS, Doug

Right wing. Shoots right. 6'2", 212 lbs. Born, Detroit, MI, October 28, 1942.

Season	Club	GP	G	A	Pts	PIM	GP	G	A	Pts	PIM
1965-66	Detroit Red Wings	1	0	0	0	0					
1966-67	Detroit Red Wings	13	3	1	4	0					
1967-68	Detroit Red Wings	37	8	9	17	12					
1968-69	Oakland Seals	76	1	19	20	79	7	0	1	1	34
1969-70	Oakland Seals	76	6	25	31	107	4	0	2	2	6
1970-71	California Seals	78	4	13	17	94					
1971-72	Boston Bruins	3	1	0	1	0					
1972-73	Boston Bruins	45	4	7	11	7	5	2	0	2	6

Season	Club	GP	G	A	Pts	PIM	GP	G	A	Pts	PIM
		REGULAR SEASON					PLAYOFFS				
1973-74	Boston Bruins	7	0	1	1	2	....	....	....	....	....
	Detroit Red Wings	57	12	25	37	33	....	....	....	....	....
1974-75	Detroit Red Wings	26	4	4	8	8	....	....	....	....	....
	NHL Totals	**419**	**43**	**104**	**147**	**342**	**16**	**2**	**3**	**5**	**46**

• Brother of Gordie • Father of David

Played in NHL All-Star Game (1971)

Signed as a free agent by **Detroit**, June 12, 1965. Traded to **Oakland** by **Detroit** with Gary Jarrett, Howie Young and Chris Worthy for Bob Baun and Ron Harris, May 27, 1968. Traded to **Boston** by **California** for cash, September 4, 1971. Traded to **Detroit** by **Boston** for cash, November 23, 1973.

ROBERTS, Gary

Left wing. Shoots left. 6'1", 190 lbs. Born, North York, Ont., May 23, 1966.
(Calgary's 1st choice, 12th overall, in 1984 Entry Draft).

Season	Club	GP	G	A	Pts	PIM	GP	G	A	Pts	PIM
1986-87	Calgary Flames	32	5	10	15	85	2	0	0	0	4
1987-88	Calgary Flames	74	13	15	28	282	9	2	3	5	29
1988-89◆	Calgary Flames	71	22	16	38	250	22	5	7	12	57
1989-90	Calgary Flames	78	39	33	72	222	6	2	5	7	41
1990-91	Calgary Flames	80	22	31	53	252	7	1	3	4	18
1991-92	Calgary Flames	76	53	37	90	207	....	....	....	....	....
1992-93	Calgary Flames	58	38	41	79	172	5	1	6	7	43
1993-94	Calgary Flames	73	41	43	84	145	7	2	6	8	24
1994-95	Calgary Flames	8	2	2	4	43	....	....	....	....	....
1995-96	Calgary Flames	35	22	20	42	78	....	....	....	....	....
1996-97	Calgary Flames	DID NOT PLAY – INJURED									
1997-98	Carolina Hurricanes	61	20	29	49	103	....	....	....	....	....
1998-99	Carolina Hurricanes	77	14	28	42	178	6	1	1	2	8
99-2000	Carolina Hurricanes	69	23	30	53	62	....	....	....	....	....
2000-01	Toronto Maple Leafs	82	29	24	53	109	11	2	9	11	0
2001-02	Toronto Maple Leafs	69	21	27	48	63	19	7	12	19	56
2002-03	Toronto Maple Leafs	14	5	3	8	10	7	1	1	2	8
	NHL Totals	**957**	**369**	**389**	**758**	**2261**	**101**	**24**	**53**	**77**	**288**

Bill Masterton Memorial Trophy (1996)

Played in NHL All-Star Game (1992, 1993)

• Missed remainder of 1994-95 and majority of 1995-96 seasons recovering from neck injury suffered in game vs. Toronto, February 4, 1995. • Missed remainder of 1995-96 and entire 1996-97 seasons recovering from neck injury suffered in game vs. Vancouver, April 3, 1996. Traded to **Carolina** by **Calgary** with Trevor Kidd for Andrew Cassels and Jean-Sebastien Giguere, August 25, 1997. Signed as a free agent by **Toronto**, July 4, 2000.

ROBERTS, Gordie

USHOF

Defense. Shoots left. 6'1", 195 lbs. Born, Detroit, MI, October 2, 1957.
(Montreal's 7th choice, 54th overall, in 1977 Amateur Draft).

Season	Club	GP	G	A	Pts	PIM	GP	G	A	Pts	PIM
1979-80	Hartford Whalers	80	8	28	36	89	3	1	1	2	2
1980-81	Hartford Whalers	27	2	11	13	81	....	....	....	....	....
	Minnesota North Stars	50	6	31	37	94	19	1	5	6	17
1981-82	Minnesota North Stars	79	4	30	34	119	4	0	3	3	27
1982-83	Minnesota North Stars	80	3	41	44	103	9	1	5	6	14
1983-84	Minnesota North Stars	77	8	45	53	132	15	3	7	10	23
1984-85	Minnesota North Stars	78	6	36	42	112	9	1	6	7	6
1985-86	Minnesota North Stars	76	2	21	23	101	5	0	4	4	8
1986-87	Minnesota North Stars	67	3	10	13	68	....	....	....	....	....
1987-88	Minnesota North Stars	48	1	10	11	103	....	....	....	....	....
	Philadelphia Flyers	11	1	2	3	15	....	....	....	....	....
	St. Louis Blues	11	1	3	4	25	10	1	2	3	33
1988-89	St. Louis Blues	77	2	24	26	90	10	1	7	8	8
1989-90	St. Louis Blues	75	3	14	17	140	10	0	2	2	26
1990-91	St. Louis Blues	3	0	1	1	8	....	....	....	....	....
◆	Pittsburgh Penguins	61	3	12	15	70	24	1	2	3	63
1991-92◆	Pittsburgh Penguins	73	2	22	24	87	19	0	2	2	32
1992-93	Boston Bruins	65	5	12	17	105	4	0	0	0	6
1993-94	Boston Bruins	59	1	6	7	40	12	0	1	1	8
	NHL Totals	**1097**	**61**	**359**	**420**	**1582**	**153**	**10**	**47**	**57**	**273**

• Brother of Doug

Claimed by **Hartford** from **Montreal** in Expansion Draft, June 22, 1979. Traded to **Minnesota** by **Hartford** for Mike Fidler, December 16, 1980. Traded to **Philadelphia** by **Minnesota** for future considerations, February 8, 1988. Traded to **St. Louis** by **Philadelphia** for future considerations, March 8, 1988. Traded to **Pittsburgh** by **St. Louis** for Pittsburgh's 11th round choice (Wade Salzman) in 1992 Entry Draft, October 2, 1990. Signed as a free agent by **Boston**, July 23, 1992.

ROBERTS, Jim

Left wing. Shoots left. 6'1", 198 lbs. Born, Toronto, Ont., June 8, 1956.
(Minnesota's 2nd choice, 31st overall, in 1976 Amateur Draft).

Season	Club	GP	G	A	Pts	PIM	GP	G	A	Pts	PIM
1976-77	Minnesota North Stars	53	11	8	19	14	2	0	0	0	0
1977-78	Minnesota North Stars	42	4	14	18	19	....	....	....	....	....
1978-79	Minnesota North Stars	11	2	1	3	0	....	....	....	....	....
	NHL Totals	**106**	**17**	**23**	**40**	**33**	**2**	**0**	**0**	**0**	**0**

Claimed by **Winnipeg** from **Minnesota** in Expansion Draft, June 13, 1979.

ROBERTS, Jimmy

Defense/Right wing. Shoots right. 5'10", 185 lbs. Born, Toronto, Ont., April 9, 1940.

Season	Club	GP	G	A	Pts	PIM	GP	G	A	Pts	PIM
1963-64	Montreal Canadiens	15	0	1	1	2	7	0	1	1	14
1964-65◆	Montreal Canadiens	70	3	10	13	40	13	0	0	0	30
1965-66◆	Montreal Canadiens	70	5	5	10	20	10	1	1	2	10
1966-67	Montreal Canadiens	63	3	0	3	16	4	1	0	1	0
1967-68	St. Louis Blues	74	14	23	37	66	18	4	1	5	20
1968-69	St. Louis Blues	72	14	19	33	81	12	1	4	5	10
1969-70	St. Louis Blues	76	13	17	30	51	16	2	3	5	29
1970-71	St. Louis Blues	72	13	18	31	77	6	2	1	3	11
1971-72	St. Louis Blues	26	5	7	12	4	....	....	....	....	....
	Montreal Canadiens	51	7	15	22	53	6	1	0	1	0
1972-73◆	Montreal Canadiens	77	14	18	32	28	17	0	2	2	22
1973-74	Montreal Canadiens	67	8	16	24	39	6	0	0	0	4
1974-75	Montreal Canadiens	79	5	13	18	52	11	2	2	4	2
1975-76◆	Montreal Canadiens	74	13	8	21	35	13	3	1	4	2
1976-77◆	Montreal Canadiens	45	5	14	19	18	14	3	0	3	6
1977-78	St. Louis Blues	75	4	10	14	39	....	....	....	....	....
	NHL Totals	**1006**	**126**	**194**	**320**	**621**	**153**	**20**	**16**	**36**	**160**

Played in NHL All-Star Game (1965, 1969, 1970)

Claimed by **St. Louis** from **Montreal** in Expansion Draft, June 6, 1967. Traded to **Montreal** by **St. Louis** for Phil Roberto, December 13, 1971. Traded to **St. Louis** by **Montreal** for St. Louis' 3rd round choice (Guy Carbonneau) in 1979 Amateur Draft, August 18, 1977.

ROBERTSON, Fred

Defense. Shoots left. 5'10", 198 lbs. Born, Carlisle, England, October 22, 1911.

Season	Club	GP	G	A	Pts	PIM	GP	G	A	Pts	PIM
1931-32◆	Toronto Maple Leafs	8	0	0	0	23	7	0	0	0	0
1933-34	Toronto Maple Leafs	2	0	0	0	0	....	....	....	....	....
	Detroit Red Wings	24	1	0	1	12	....	....	....	....	....
	NHL Totals	**34**	**1**	**0**	**1**	**35**	**7**	**0**	**0**	**0**	**0**

Signed as a free agent by **Toronto**, February 14, 1932. Traded to **Detroit** by **Toronto** for $6,500, November 13, 1933.

ROBERTSON, Geordie

Right wing. Shoots right. 6', 165 lbs. Born, Victoria, B.C., August 1, 1959.

Season	Club	GP	G	A	Pts	PIM	GP	G	A	Pts	PIM
1982-83	Buffalo Sabres	5	1	2	3	7	....	....	....	....	....
	NHL Totals	**5**	**1**	**2**	**3**	**7**	....	....	....	....	....

• Brother of Torrie

Signed as a free agent by **Buffalo**, September 5, 1979. Signed as a free agent by **Detroit**, July 9, 1985.

ROBERTSON, George

Left wing/Center. Shoots left. 6'1", 172 lbs. Born, Winnipeg, Man., May 11, 1928.

Season	Club	GP	G	A	Pts	PIM	GP	G	A	Pts	PIM
1947-48	Montreal Canadiens	1	0	0	0	0	....	....	....	....	....
1948-49	Montreal Canadiens	30	2	5	7	6	....	....	....	....	....
	NHL Totals	**31**	**2**	**5**	**7**	**6**	....	....	....	....	....

Traded to **Montreal** by **NY Rangers** with Hal Laycoe and Joe Bell for Buddy O'Connor and Frank Eddolls, August 19, 1947. Traded to **Washington** (AHL) by **Montreal** (Buffalo-AHL) for Ab DeMarco with Montreal retaining right of recall, January 28, 1949. Traded to **Victoria** (PCHL) by **Montreal** for cash, December 11, 1949.

ROBERTSON, Torrie

Left wing. Shoots left. 5'11", 200 lbs. Born, Victoria, B.C., August 2, 1961.
(Washington's 3rd choice, 55th overall, in 1980 Entry Draft).

Season	Club	GP	G	A	Pts	PIM	GP	G	A	Pts	PIM
1980-81	Washington Capitals	3	0	0	0	0	....	....	....	....	....
1981-82	Washington Capitals	54	8	13	21	204	....	....	....	....	....
1982-83	Washington Capitals	5	2	0	2	4	....	....	....	....	....
1983-84	Hartford Whalers	66	7	13	20	198	....	....	....	....	....
1984-85	Hartford Whalers	74	11	30	41	337	....	....	....	....	....
1985-86	Hartford Whalers	76	13	24	37	358	10	1	0	1	67
1986-87	Hartford Whalers	20	1	0	1	98	....	....	....	....	....
1987-88	Hartford Whalers	63	2	8	10	293	6	0	1	1	6
1988-89	Hartford Whalers	27	2	4	6	84	....	....	....	....	....
	Detroit Red Wings	12	2	2	4	63	6	1	0	1	17
1989-90	Detroit Red Wings	42	1	5	6	112	....	....	....	....	....
	NHL Totals	**442**	**49**	**99**	**148**	**1751**	**22**	**2**	**1**	**3**	**90**

• Brother of Geordie

Traded to **Hartford** by **Washington** for Greg Adams, October 3, 1983. Traded to **Detroit** by **Hartford** for Jim Pavese, March 7, 1989.

ROBERTSSON, Bert

Defense. Shoots left. 6'3", 205 lbs. Born, Sodertalje, Sweden, June 30, 1974.
(Vancouver's 8th choice, 254th overall, in 1993 Entry Draft).

Season	Club	GP	G	A	Pts	PIM	GP	G	A	Pts	PIM
1997-98	Vancouver Canucks	30	2	4	6	24	....	....	....	....	....
1998-99	Vancouver Canucks	39	2	2	4	13	....	....	....	....	....
99-2000	Edmonton Oilers	52	0	4	4	34	5	0	0	0	0
2000-01	New York Rangers	2	0	0	0	4	....	....	....	....	....
	NHL Totals	**123**	**4**	**10**	**14**	**75**	**5**	**0**	**0**	**0**	**0**

Signed as a free agent by **Edmonton**, August 19, 1999. Selected by **Columbus** from **Edmonton** in Expansion Draft, June 23, 2000. Traded to **NY Rangers** by **Columbus** for Jean-Francois Labbe, November 9, 2000. Traded to **Nashville** by **NY Rangers** for Ryan Tobler, March 7, 2001. Traded to **Anaheim** by **Nashville** for Jay Legault, December 4, 2001. Traded to **Pittsburgh** by **Anaheim** for Mark Moore, March 8, 2002.

ROBIDAS, Stephane

Defense. Shoots right. 5'11", 189 lbs. Born, Sherbrooke, Que., March 3, 1977.
(Montreal's 7th choice, 164th overall, in 1995 Entry Draft).

Season	Club	GP	G	A	Pts	PIM	GP	G	A	Pts	PIM
99-2000	Montreal Canadiens	1	0	0	0	0	....	....	....	....	....
2000-01	Montreal Canadiens	65	6	6	12	14	....	....	....	....	....
2001-02	Montreal Canadiens	56	1	10	11	14	2	0	0	0	4

Season	Club	Regular Season GP	G	A	Pts	PIM	Playoffs GP	G	A	Pts	PIM
2002-03	Dallas Stars	76	3	7	10	35	12	0	1	1	20
	NHL Totals	**198**	**10**	**23**	**33**	**63**	**14**	**0**	**1**	**1**	**24**

Claimed by **Atlanta** from **Montreal** in Waiver Draft, October 4, 2002. Traded to **Dallas** by **Atlanta** for Atlanta's 6th round choice in 2003 Entry Draft, October 4, 2002.

ROBIDOUX, Florent

Left wing. Shoots left. 6'2", 190 lbs. Born, Treheme, Man., May 5, 1960.

Season	Club	Regular Season GP	G	A	Pts	PIM	Playoffs GP	G	A	Pts	PIM
1980-81	Chicago Black Hawks	39	6	2	8	75	....	....	....	....	....
1981-82	Chicago Black Hawks	4	1	2	3	0	....	....	....	....	....
1983-84	Chicago Black Hawks	9	0	0	0	0	....	....	....	....	....
	NHL Totals	**52**	**7**	**4**	**11**	**75**	....	....	....	....	....

Signed as a free agent by **Chicago**, October 20, 1979. • Missed entire 1982-83 season recovering from injuries suffered in automobile accident, July, 1982. Signed as a free agent by **Philadelphia**, October 8, 1985.

ROBINSON, Doug

Left wing. Shoots left. 6'2", 197 lbs. Born, St. Catharines, Ont., August 27, 1940.

Season	Club	Regular Season GP	G	A	Pts	PIM	Playoffs GP	G	A	Pts	PIM
1963-64	Chicago Black Hawks	....	....	....	....	....	4	0	0	0	0
1964-65	Chicago Black Hawks	40	2	9	11	8	....	....	....	....	....
	New York Rangers	21	8	14	22	2	....	....	....	....	....
1965-66	New York Rangers	51	8	12	20	8	....	....	....	....	....
1966-67	New York Rangers	1	0	0	0	0	....	....	....	....	....
1967-68	Los Angeles Kings	34	9	9	18	6	7	4	3	7	0
1968-69	Los Angeles Kings	31	2	10	12	2	....	....	....	....	....
1970-71	Los Angeles Kings	61	15	13	28	8	....	....	....	....	....
	NHL Totals	**239**	**44**	**67**	**111**	**34**	**11**	**4**	**3**	**7**	**0**

• Father of Rob

Traded to **NY Rangers** by **Chicago** with Wayne Hillman and John Brenneman for Camille Henry, Don Johns, Billy Taylor and Wally Chevrier, February 4, 1965. Claimed by **Los Angeles** from **NY Rangers** in Expansion Draft, June 6, 1967. Traded to **Montreal** by **Los Angeles** with Denis DeJordy, Dale Hoganson and Noel Price for Rogie Vachon, November 4, 1971.

ROBINSON, Earl

Right wing/Center. Shoots right. 5'10", 160 lbs. Born, Montreal, Que., March 11, 1907.

Season	Club	Regular Season GP	G	A	Pts	PIM	Playoffs GP	G	A	Pts	PIM
1928-29	Montreal Maroons	38	2	1	3	2	....	....	....	....	....
1929-30	Montreal Maroons	31	1	2	3	10	4	0	0	0	0
1931-32	Montreal Maroons	26	0	3	3	2	....	....	....	....	....
1932-33	Montreal Maroons	44	15	9	24	6	2	0	0	0	0
1933-34	Montreal Maroons	47	12	16	28	14	4	2	0	2	0
1934-35 ♦	Montreal Maroons	48	17	18	35	23	7	2	2	4	0
1935-36	Montreal Maroons	39	6	14	20	27	3	0	0	0	0
1936-37	Montreal Maroons	47	16	18	34	19	5	1	2	3	0
1937-38	Montreal Maroons	39	4	7	11	13	....	....	....	....	....
1938-39	Chicago Black Hawks	47	9	6	15	13	....	....	....	....	....
1939-40	Montreal Canadiens	11	1	4	5	4	....	....	....	....	....
	NHL Totals	**417**	**83**	**98**	**181**	**133**	**25**	**5**	**4**	**9**	**0**

Played in NHL All-Star Game (1937, 1939)

Traded to **Chicago** by **Mtl. Maroons** with Russ Blinco and Baldy Northcott for $30,000, September 15, 1938. Traded to **Montreal** by **Chicago** for cash, October 11, 1939.

ROBINSON, Larry

HHOF

Defense. Shoots left. 6'4", 225 lbs. Born, Winchester, Ont., June 2, 1951.
(Montreal's 4th choice, 20th overall, in 1971 Amateur Draft).

Season	Club	Regular Season GP	G	A	Pts	PIM	Playoffs GP	G	A	Pts	PIM
1972-73 ♦	Montreal Canadiens	36	2	4	6	20	11	1	4	5	9
1973-74	Montreal Canadiens	78	6	20	26	66	6	0	1	1	26
1974-75	Montreal Canadiens	80	14	47	61	76	11	0	4	4	27
1975-76 ♦	Montreal Canadiens	80	10	30	40	59	13	3	3	6	10
1976-77 ♦	Montreal Canadiens	77	19	66	85	45	14	2	10	12	12
1977-78 ♦	Montreal Canadiens	80	13	52	65	39	15	4	*17	*21	6
1978-79 ♦	Montreal Canadiens	67	16	45	61	33	16	6	9	15	8
1979-80	Montreal Canadiens	72	14	61	75	39	10	0	4	4	2
1980-81	Montreal Canadiens	65	12	38	50	37	3	0	1	1	2
1981-82	Montreal Canadiens	71	12	47	59	41	5	0	1	1	8
1982-83	Montreal Canadiens	71	14	49	63	33	3	0	0	0	2
1983-84	Montreal Canadiens	74	9	34	43	39	15	0	5	5	22
1984-85	Montreal Canadiens	76	14	33	47	44	12	3	8	11	8
1985-86 ♦	Montreal Canadiens	78	19	63	82	39	20	0	13	13	22
1986-87	Montreal Canadiens	70	13	37	50	44	17	3	17	20	6
1987-88	Montreal Canadiens	53	6	34	40	30	11	1	4	5	4
1988-89	Montreal Canadiens	74	4	26	30	22	21	2	8	10	12
1989-90	Los Angeles Kings	64	7	32	39	34	10	2	3	5	10
1990-91	Los Angeles Kings	62	1	22	23	16	12	1	4	5	15
1991-92	Los Angeles Kings	56	3	10	13	37	2	0	0	0	0
	NHL Totals	**1384**	**208**	**750**	**958**	**793**	**227**	**28**	**116**	**144**	**211**

• Brother of Moe • NHL First All-Star Team (1977, 1979, 1980) • James Norris Trophy (1977, 1980) • NHL Plus/Minus Leader (1977) • NHL Second All-Star Team (1978, 1981, 1986) • Conn Smythe Trophy (1978)

Played in NHL All-Star Game (1974, 1976, 1977, 1978, 1980, 1982, 1986, 1988, 1989, 1992)

Signed as a free agent by **Los Angeles**, July 26, 1989.

ROBINSON, Moe

Defense. Shoots left. 6'4", 175 lbs. Born, Winchester, Ont., May 29, 1957.
(Montreal's 6th choice, 49th overall, in 1977 Amateur Draft).

Season	Club	Regular Season GP	G	A	Pts	PIM	Playoffs GP	G	A	Pts	PIM
1979-80	Montreal Canadiens	1	0	0	0	0	....	....	....	....	....
	NHL Totals	**1**	**0**	**0**	**0**	**0**	....	....	....	....	....

• Brother of Larry

ROBINSON, Rob

Defense. Shoots left. 6'1", 214 lbs. Born, St. Catharines, Ont., April 19, 1967.
(St. Louis' 6th choice, 117th overall, in 1987 Entry Draft).

Season	Club	Regular Season GP	G	A	Pts	PIM	Playoffs GP	G	A	Pts	PIM
1991-92	St. Louis Blues	22	0	1	1	8	....	....	....	....	....
	NHL Totals	**22**	**0**	**1**	**1**	**8**	....	....	....	....	....

• Son of Doug

Traded to **Tampa Bay** by **St. Louis** with Pat Jablonski, Darin Kimble and Steve Tuttle for future considerations, June 19, 1992.

ROBINSON, Scott

Right wing. Shoots right. 6'2", 180 lbs. Born, 100 Mile House, B.C., March 29, 1964.

Season	Club	Regular Season GP	G	A	Pts	PIM	Playoffs GP	G	A	Pts	PIM
1989-90	Minnesota North Stars	1	0	0	0	2	....	....	....	....	....
	NHL Totals	**1**	**0**	**0**	**0**	**2**	....	....	....	....	....

Signed as a free agent by **Minnesota**, September 27, 1988.

ROBITAILLE, Luc

Left wing. Shoots left. 6'1", 215 lbs. Born, Montreal, Que., February 17, 1966.
(Los Angeles' 9th choice, 171st overall, in 1984 Entry Draft).

Season	Club	Regular Season GP	G	A	Pts	PIM	Playoffs GP	G	A	Pts	PIM
1986-87	Los Angeles Kings	79	45	39	84	28	5	1	4	5	2
1987-88	Los Angeles Kings	80	53	58	111	82	5	2	5	7	18
1988-89	Los Angeles Kings	78	46	52	98	65	11	2	6	8	10
1989-90	Los Angeles Kings	80	52	49	101	38	10	5	5	10	12
1990-91	Los Angeles Kings	76	45	46	91	68	12	12	4	16	22
1991-92	Los Angeles Kings	80	44	63	107	95	6	3	4	7	12
1992-93	Los Angeles Kings	84	63	62	125	100	24	9	13	22	28
1993-94	Los Angeles Kings	83	44	42	86	86	....	....	....	....	....
1994-95	Pittsburgh Penguins	46	23	19	42	37	12	7	4	11	26
1995-96	New York Rangers	77	23	46	69	80	11	1	5	6	8
1996-97	New York Rangers	69	24	24	48	48	15	4	7	11	4
1997-98	Los Angeles Kings	57	16	24	40	66	4	1	2	3	6
1998-99	Los Angeles Kings	82	39	35	74	54					
99-2000	Los Angeles Kings	71	36	38	74	68	4	2	2	4	6
2000-01	Los Angeles Kings	82	37	51	88	66	13	4	3	7	10
2001-02 ♦	Detroit Red Wings	81	30	20	50	38	23	4	5	9	10
2002-03	Detroit Red Wings	81	11	20	31	50	4	1	0	1	0
	NHL Totals	**1286**	**631**	**688**	**1319**	**1069**	**159**	**58**	**69**	**127**	**174**

NHL All-Rookie Team (1987) • NHL Second All-Star Team (1987, 1992, 2001) • Calder Memorial Trophy (1987) • NHL First All-Star Team (1988, 1989, 1990, 1991, 1993)

Played in NHL All-Star Game (1988, 1989, 1990, 1991, 1992, 1993, 1999, 2001)

Traded to **Pittsburgh** by **Los Angeles** for Rick Tocchet and Pittsburgh's 2nd round choice (Pavel Rosa) in 1995 Entry Draft, July 29, 1994. Traded to **NY Rangers** by **Pittsburgh** with Ulf Samuelsson for Petr Nedved and Sergei Zubov, August 31, 1995. Traded to **Los Angeles** by **NY Rangers** for Kevin Stevens, August 28, 1997. Signed as a free agent by **Detroit**, July 5, 2001. Signed as a free agent by **Los Angeles**, July 25, 2003.

ROBITAILLE, Mike

Defense. Shoots right. 5'11", 195 lbs. Born, Midland, Ont., February 12, 1948.

Season	Club	Regular Season GP	G	A	Pts	PIM	Playoffs GP	G	A	Pts	PIM
1969-70	New York Rangers	4	0	0	0	8	....	....	....	....	....
1970-71	New York Rangers	11	1	1	2	7	....	....	....	....	....
	Detroit Red Wings	23	4	8	12	22	....	....	....	....	....
1971-72	Buffalo Sabres	31	2	10	12	22	....	....	....	....	....
1972-73	Buffalo Sabres	65	4	17	21	40	6	0	0	0	0
1973-74	Buffalo Sabres	71	2	18	20	60	....	....	....	....	....
1974-75	Buffalo Sabres	3	0	1	1	0	....	....	....	....	....
	Vancouver Canucks	63	2	22	24	31	5	0	1	1	2
1975-76	Vancouver Canucks	71	8	19	27	69	2	0	0	0	2
1976-77	Vancouver Canucks	40	0	9	9	21	....	....	....	....	....
	NHL Totals	**382**	**23**	**105**	**128**	**280**	**13**	**0**	**1**	**1**	**4**

Traded to **Detroit** by **NY Rangers** with Arnie Brown and Tom Miller for Bruce MacGregor and Larry Brown, February 2, 1971. Traded to **Buffalo** by **Detroit** with Don Luce for Joe Daley, May 25, 1971. Traded to **Vancouver** by **Buffalo** with Gerry Meehan for Jocelyn Guevremont and Bryan McSheffrey, October 14, 1974. • Suffered career-ending neck injury in game vs. Pittsburgh, February 11, 1977.

ROBITAILLE, Randy

Center. Shoots left. 5'11", 196 lbs. Born, Ottawa, Ont., October 12, 1975.

Season	Club	Regular Season GP	G	A	Pts	PIM	Playoffs GP	G	A	Pts	PIM
1996-97	Boston Bruins	1	0	0	0	0	....	....	....	....	....
1997-98	Boston Bruins	4	0	0	0	0	....	....	....	....	....
1998-99	Boston Bruins	4	0	2	2	0	1	0	0	0	0
99-2000	Nashville Predators	69	11	14	25	10	....	....	....	....	....
2000-01	Nashville Predators	62	9	17	26	12	....	....	....	....	....
2001-02	Los Angeles Kings	18	4	3	7	17	....	....	....	....	....
	Pittsburgh Penguins	40	10	20	30	16	....	....	....	....	....

Season	Club	GP	G	A	Pts	PIM	GP	G	A	Pts	PIM
		REGULAR SEASON					PLAYOFFS				
2002-03	Pittsburgh Penguins	41	5	12	17	8	....	....	....	....	....
	New York Islanders	10	1	2	3	2	5	1	1	2	0
	NHL Totals	**249**	**40**	**70**	**110**	**65**	**6**	**1**	**1**	**2**	**0**

Signed as a free agent by **Boston**, March 27, 1997. Traded to **Atlanta** by **Boston** for Peter Ferraro, June 25, 1999. Traded to **Nashville** by **Atlanta** for Denny Lambert, August 16, 1999. Signed as a free agent by **Los Angeles**, July 6, 2001. Claimed on waivers by **Pittsburgh** from **Los Angeles**, January 4, 2002. Traded to **NY Islanders** by **Pittsburgh** for Philadelphia's 5th round choice (previously acquired, Pittsburgh selected Evgeni Isakov) in 2003 Entry Draft, March 9, 2003.

ROCHE, Dave

Left wing. Shoots left. 6'4", 230 lbs. Born, Lindsay, Ont., June 13, 1975.
(Pittsburgh's 3rd choice, 62nd overall, in 1993 Entry Draft).

Season	Club	GP	G	A	Pts	PIM	GP	G	A	Pts	PIM
1995-96	Pittsburgh Penguins	71	7	7	14	130	16	2	7	9	26
1996-97	Pittsburgh Penguins	61	5	5	10	155	....	....	....	....	....
1998-99	Calgary Flames	36	3	3	6	44	....	....	....	....	....
99-2000	Calgary Flames	2	0	0	0	5	....	....	....	....	....
2001-02	New York Islanders	1	0	0	0	0	....	....	....	....	....
	NHL Totals	**171**	**15**	**15**	**30**	**334**	**16**	**2**	**7**	**9**	**26**

Traded to **Calgary** by **Pittsburgh** with Ken Wregget for German Titov and Todd Hlushko, June 17, 1998. Signed as a free agent by **NY Islanders**, August 17, 2001. Traded to **Anaheim** by **NY Islanders** for Jim Cummins, January 14, 2002. Traded to **NY Islanders** by **Anaheim** for Ben Guite and the rights to Bjorn Mellin, March 19, 2002. Signed as a free agent by **New Jersey**, August 27, 2002.

ROCHE, Des

Right wing. Shoots right. 5'7", 165 lbs. Born, Kemptville, Ont., February 1, 1909.

Season	Club	GP	G	A	Pts	PIM	GP	G	A	Pts	PIM
1930-31	Montreal Maroons	19	0	1	1	6	....	....	....	....	....
1932-33	Montreal Maroons	5	0	0	0	0	....	....	....	....	....
	Ottawa Senators	16	3	6	9	6	....	....	....	....	....
1933-34	Ottawa Senators	46	14	10	24	22	....	....	....	....	....
1934-35	St. Louis Eagles	7	0	0	0	0	....	....	....	....	....
	Montreal Canadiens	5	0	1	1	0	....	....	....	....	....
	Detroit Red Wings	15	3	0	3	10	....	....	....	....	....
	NHL Totals	**113**	**20**	**18**	**38**	**44**	....	....	....	....	....

• Brother of Earl

Signed as a free agent by **Mtl. Maroons**, September 2, 1930. Traded to **Ottawa** by **Mtl. Maroons** for Wally Kilrea, February 3, 1933. Transferred to **St. Louis** after **Ottawa** franchise relocated, September 22, 1934. Traded to **Boston** by **St. Louis** with Max Kaminsky for Joe Lamb, December 4, 1934. Traded to **Montreal** by **Boston** for cash, December 8, 1934. Traded to **Buffalo** (IHL) by **Montreal** for cash, December 26, 1934. Traded to **Detroit** by **Buffalo** (IHL) for cash, January 1, 1935. Traded to **Pittsburgh** (IHL) by **Detroit** for cash, October 17, 1935.

ROCHE, Earl

Left wing. Shoots left. 5'11", 175 lbs. Born, Prescott, Ont., February 22, 1910.

Season	Club	GP	G	A	Pts	PIM	GP	G	A	Pts	PIM
1930-31	Montreal Maroons	42	2	0	2	18	2	0	0	0	0
1932-33	Montreal Maroons	5	0	0	0	0	....	....	....	....	....
	Boston Bruins	3	0	0	0	0	....	....	....	....	....
	Ottawa Senators	20	4	5	9	6	....	....	....	....	....
1933-34	Ottawa Senators	45	13	16	29	22	....	....	....	....	....
1934-35	St. Louis Eagles	19	3	3	6	2	....	....	....	....	....
	Detroit Red Wings	13	3	3	6	0	....	....	....	....	....
	NHL Totals	**147**	**25**	**27**	**52**	**48**	**2**	**0**	**0**	**0**	**0**

• Brother of Des

Signed as a free agent by **Mtl. Maroons**, September 2, 1930. Signed as a free agent by **Boston**, January 14, 1933. Traded to **Ottawa** by **Boston** to complete transaction that sent Alex Smith to Boston, January 25, 1933. Transferred to **St. Louis** after **Ottawa** franchise relocated, September 22, 1934. Traded to **Buffalo** (IHL) by **St. Louis** for cash, December 20, 1934. Traded to **Detroit** by **Buffalo** (IHL) for cash, January 1, 1935.

ROCHE, Ernie

Defense. Shoots left. 6'1", 170 lbs. Born, Montreal, Que., February 4, 1930.

Season	Club	GP	G	A	Pts	PIM	GP	G	A	Pts	PIM
1950-51	Montreal Canadiens	4	0	0	0	2	....	....	....	....	....
	NHL Totals	**4**	**0**	**0**	**0**	**2**	....	....	....	....	....

Claimed by **Springfield** (AHL) from **Montreal** (Montreal Royals-QHL) in Inter-League Draft, June 1, 1955.

ROCHE, Travis

Defense. Shoots right. 6'1", 190 lbs. Born, Grand Cache, Alta, June 17, 1978.

Season	Club	GP	G	A	Pts	PIM	GP	G	A	Pts	PIM
2000-01	Minnesota Wild	1	0	0	0	0	....	....	....	....	....
2001-02	Minnesota Wild	4	0	0	0	2	....	....	....	....	....
	NHL Totals	**5**	**0**	**0**	**0**	**2**	....	....	....	....	....

Signed as a free agent by **Minnesota**, April 8, 2001.

ROCHEFORT, Dave

Center. Shoots left. 6', 180 lbs. Born, Red Deer, Alta., July 22, 1946.

Season	Club	GP	G	A	Pts	PIM	GP	G	A	Pts	PIM
1966-67	Detroit Red Wings	1	0	0	0	0	....	....	....	....	....
	NHL Totals	**1**	**0**	**0**	**0**	**0**	....	....	....	....	....

ROCHEFORT, Leon

Right wing. Shoots right. 6', 185 lbs. Born, Cap-de-la-Madeleine, Que., May 4, 1939.

Season	Club	GP	G	A	Pts	PIM	GP	G	A	Pts	PIM
1960-61	New York Rangers	1	0	0	0	0	....	....	....	....	....
1962-63	New York Rangers	23	5	4	9	6	....	....	....	....	....
1963-64	Montreal Canadiens	3	0	0	0	0	....	....	....	....	....
1964-65	Montreal Canadiens	9	2	0	2	0	....	....	....	....	....
1965-66 ♦	Montreal Canadiens	1	0	1	1	0	4	1	1	2	4
1966-67	Montreal Canadiens	27	9	7	16	6	10	1	1	2	4
1967-68	Philadelphia Flyers	74	21	21	42	16	7	2	0	2	2
1968-69	Philadelphia Flyers	65	14	21	35	10	3	0	0	0	0
1969-70	Los Angeles Kings	76	9	23	32	14	....	....	....	....	....
1970-71 ♦	Montreal Canadiens	57	5	10	15	4	10	0	0	0	6
1971-72	Detroit Red Wings	64	17	12	29	10	....	....	....	....	....
1972-73	Detroit Red Wings	20	2	4	6	2	....	....	....	....	....
	Atlanta Flames	54	9	18	27	10	....	....	....	....	....
1973-74	Atlanta Flames	56	10	12	22	13	....	....	....	....	....
1974-75	Vancouver Canucks	76	18	11	29	2	5	0	2	2	0
1975-76	Vancouver Canucks	11	0	3	3	0	....	....	....	....	....
	NHL Totals	**617**	**121**	**147**	**268**	**93**	**39**	**4**	**4**	**8**	**16**

Played in NHL All-Star Game (1968)

Traded to **Montreal** by **NY Rangers** with Dave Balon, Len Ronson and Gump Worsley for Phil Goyette, Don Marshall and Jacques Plante, June 4, 1963. Claimed by **Philadelphia** from **Montreal** in Expansion Draft, June 6, 1967. Traded to **NY Rangers** by **Philadelphia** with Don Blackburn for Reggie Fleming, June 6, 1969. Traded to **Los Angeles** by **NY Rangers** with Dennis Hextall for Real Lemieux, June 9, 1969. Traded to **Montreal** by **Los Angeles** with Wayne Thomas and Gregg Boddy for Larry Mickey, Lucien Grenier and Jack Norris, May 22, 1970. Traded to **Detroit** by **Montreal** for Kerry Ketter and cash, May 25, 1971. Traded to **Atlanta** by **Detroit** for Bill Hogaboam, November 28, 1972. Traded to **Vancouver** by **Atlanta** for cash, October 4, 1974.

ROCHEFORT, Normand

Defense. Shoots left. 6'1", 214 lbs. Born, Trois-Rivieres, Que., January 28, 1961.
(Quebec's 1st choice, 24th overall, in 1980 Entry Draft).

Season	Club	GP	G	A	Pts	PIM	GP	G	A	Pts	PIM
1980-81	Quebec Nordiques	56	3	7	10	51	5	0	0	0	4
1981-82	Quebec Nordiques	72	4	14	18	115	16	0	2	2	10
1982-83	Quebec Nordiques	62	6	17	23	40	1	0	0	0	2
1983-84	Quebec Nordiques	75	2	22	24	47	6	1	0	1	6
1984-85	Quebec Nordiques	73	3	21	24	74	18	2	1	3	8
1985-86	Quebec Nordiques	26	5	4	9	30	....	....	....	....	....
1986-87	Quebec Nordiques	70	6	9	15	46	13	2	1	3	26
1987-88	Quebec Nordiques	46	3	10	13	49	....	....	....	....	....
1988-89	New York Rangers	11	1	5	6	18	....	....	....	....	....
1989-90	New York Rangers	31	3	1	4	24	10	2	1	3	26
1990-91	New York Rangers	44	3	7	10	35	....	....	....	....	....
1991-92	New York Rangers	26	0	2	2	31	....	....	....	....	....
1993-94	Tampa Bay Lightning	6	0	0	0	10	....	....	....	....	....
	NHL Totals	**598**	**39**	**119**	**158**	**570**	**69**	**7**	**5**	**12**	**82**

Traded to **NY Rangers** by **Quebec** with Jason Lafreniere for Bruce Bell, Jari Gronstrand, Walt Poddubny and NY Rangers' 4th round choice (Eric Dubois) in 1989 Entry Draft, August 1, 1988. Signed as a free agent by **Tampa Bay**, September 27, 1993.

ROCKBURN, Harvey

Defense. Shoots left. 5'10", 180 lbs. Born, Ottawa, Ont., August 20, 1908.

Season	Club	GP	G	A	Pts	PIM	GP	G	A	Pts	PIM
1929-30	Detroit Cougars	36	4	0	4	97	....	....	....	....	....
1930-31	Detroit Falcons	42	0	1	1	*118	....	....	....	....	....
1932-33	Ottawa Senators	16	0	1	1	39	....	....	....	....	....
	NHL Totals	**94**	**4**	**2**	**6**	**254**	....	....	....	....	....

Traded to **Detroit** by **Stratford** (Can-Pro) for cash, October 31, 1927. Traded to **Providence** (Can-Am) by **Detroit** for cash, September, 1932. Traded to **Mtl. Maroons** (Windsor-IHL) by **Providence** (Can-Am) for Jack McVicar, December 13, 1932. Traded to **Ottawa** by **Mtl. Maroons** (Windsor-IHL) for cash, February 2, 1933.

RODDEN, Eddie

Center. Shoots right. 5'7", 150 lbs. Born, Mattawa, Ont., March 22, 1901.

Season	Club	GP	G	A	Pts	PIM	GP	G	A	Pts	PIM
1926-27	Chicago Black Hawks	19	3	3	6	0	2	0	1	1	0
1927-28	Chicago Black Hawks	9	0	2	2	6	....	....	....	....	....
	Toronto Maple Leafs	25	3	6	9	36	....	....	....	....	....
1928-29	Boston Bruins	20	0	0	0	10	....	....	....	....	....
1930-31	New York Rangers	24	0	3	3	8	....	....	....	....	....
	NHL Totals	**97**	**6**	**14**	**20**	**60**	**2**	**0**	**1**	**1**	**0**

Traded to **Chicago** by **Minneapolis** (AHA) for cash, January, 1927. Traded to **Toronto** by **Chicago** to complete three team transaction that sent Bert McCaffrey to Pittsburgh and Ty Arbour to Chicago, December, 1927. Traded to **Boston** by **Toronto** for cash, June 20, 1928. Loaned to **Windsor** (Can-Pro) by **Boston** for cash, January 30, 1929. Traded to **London** (IHL) by **Boston** for cash, October 16, 1929. Traded to **NY Rangers** by **London** (IHL) for $8,500, September 11, 1930. Traded to **Pittsburgh** (IHL) by **NY Rangers** for cash, January 3, 1931.

RODGERS, Marc

Right wing. Shoots right. 5'9", 185 lbs. Born, Shawville, Que., March 16, 1972.

Season	Club	GP	G	A	Pts	PIM	GP	G	A	Pts	PIM
99-2000	Detroit Red Wings	21	1	1	2	10	....	....	....	....	....
	NHL Totals	**21**	**1**	**1**	**2**	**10**	....	....	....	....	....

Signed as a free agent by **Detroit**, August 3, 1998.

ROENICK, Jeremy

Center. Shoots right. 6'1", 207 lbs. Born, Boston, MA, January 17, 1970.
(Chicago's 1st choice, 8th overall, in 1988 Entry Draft).

Season	Club	GP	G	A	Pts	PIM	GP	G	A	Pts	PIM
1988-89	Chicago Blackhawks	20	9	9	18	4	10	1	3	4	7
1989-90	Chicago Blackhawks	78	26	40	66	54	20	11	7	18	8
1990-91	Chicago Blackhawks	79	41	53	94	80	6	3	5	8	4
1991-92	Chicago Blackhawks	80	53	50	103	98	18	12	10	22	12
1992-93	Chicago Blackhawks	84	50	57	107	86	4	1	2	3	2
1993-94	Chicago Blackhawks	84	46	61	107	125	6	1	6	7	2
1994-95	Chicago Blackhawks	33	10	24	34	14	8	1	2	3	16
1995-96	Chicago Blackhawks	66	32	35	67	109	10	5	7	12	2

Season	Club	GP	G	A	Pts	PIM	GP	G	A	Pts	PIM
		REGULAR SEASON					PLAYOFFS				
1996-97	Phoenix Coyotes	72	29	40	69	115	6	2	4	6	4
1997-98	Phoenix Coyotes	79	24	32	56	103	6	5	3	8	4
1998-99	Phoenix Coyotes	78	24	48	72	130	1	0	0	0	0
99-2000	Phoenix Coyotes	75	34	44	78	102	5	2	2	4	10
2000-01	Phoenix Coyotes	80	30	46	76	114	....	....	....	....	....
2001-02	Philadelphia Flyers	75	21	46	67	74	5	0	0	0	14
2002-03	Philadelphia Flyers	79	27	32	59	75	13	3	5	8	8
	NHL Totals	**1062**	**456**	**617**	**1073**	**1283**	**118**	**47**	**56**	**103**	**93**

Played in NHL All-Star Game (1991, 1992, 1993, 1994, 1999, 2000, 2002, 2003)

Traded to **Phoenix** by **Chicago** for Alexei Zhamnov, Craig Mills and Phoenix's 1st round choice (Ty Jones) in 1997 Entry Draft, August 16, 1996. Signed as a free agent by **Philadelphia**, July 2, 2001.

ROEST, Stacy

Right wing. Shoots right. 5'9", 185 lbs. Born, Lethbridge, Alta., March 15, 1974.

Season	Club	GP	G	A	Pts	PIM	GP	G	A	Pts	PIM
1998-99	Detroit Red Wings	59	4	8	12	14	....	....	....	....	....
99-2000	Detroit Red Wings	49	7	9	16	12	3	0	0	0	0
2000-01	Minnesota Wild	76	7	20	27	20	....	....	....	....	....
2001-02	Minnesota Wild	58	10	11	21	8	....	....	....	....	....
2002-03	Detroit Red Wings	2	0	0	0	0	....	....	....	....	....
	NHL Totals	**244**	**28**	**48**	**76**	**54**	**3**	**0**	**0**	**0**	**0**

Signed as a free agent by **Detroit**, June 9, 1997. Selected by **Minnesota** from **Detroit** in Expansion Draft, June 23, 2000. Signed as a free agent by **Detroit**, August 27, 2002.

ROGERS, John

Right wing. Shoots right. 5'11", 175 lbs. Born, Paradise Hills, Sask., April 10, 1953.
(Minnesota's 2nd choice, 25th overall, in 1973 Amateur Draft).

Season	Club	GP	G	A	Pts	PIM	GP	G	A	Pts	PIM
1973-74	Minnesota North Stars	10	2	4	6	0	....	....	....	....	....
1974-75	Minnesota North Stars	4	0	0	0	0	....	....	....	....	....
	NHL Totals	**14**	**2**	**4**	**6**	**0**	....	....	....	....	....

ROGERS, Mike

Center. Shoots left. 5'9", 170 lbs. Born, Calgary, Alta., October 24, 1954.
(Vancouver's 4th choice, 77th overall, in 1974 Amateur Draft).

Season	Club	GP	G	A	Pts	PIM	GP	G	A	Pts	PIM
1979-80	Hartford Whalers	80	44	61	105	10	3	0	3	3	0
1980-81	Hartford Whalers	80	40	65	105	32	....	....	....	....	....
1981-82	New York Rangers	80	38	65	103	43	9	1	6	7	2
1982-83	New York Rangers	71	29	47	76	28	1	0	0	0	0
1983-84	New York Rangers	78	23	38	61	45	1	0	0	0	0
1984-85	New York Rangers	78	26	38	64	24	3	0	4	4	4
1985-86	New York Rangers	9	1	3	4	2	....	....	....	....	....
	Edmonton Oilers	8	1	0	1	0	....	....	....	....	....
	NHL Totals	**484**	**202**	**317**	**519**	**184**	**17**	**1**	**13**	**14**	**6**

Played in NHL All Star Game (1981)

Rights retained by **Hartford** prior to Expansion Draft, June 9, 1979. Traded to **NY Rangers** by **Hartford** with Hartford's 10th round choice (Simo Saarinen) in 1982 Entry Draft for Chris Kotsopoulos, Gerry McDonald and Doug Sulliman, October 2, 1981. Traded to **Edmonton** by **NY Rangers** for Larry Melnyk and Todd Strueby, December 20, 1985.

ROHLICEK, Jeff

Center. Shoots left. 6', 180 lbs. Born, Park Ridge, IL, January 27, 1966.
(Vancouver's 2nd choice, 31st overall, in 1984 Entry Draft).

Season	Club	GP	G	A	Pts	PIM	GP	G	A	Pts	PIM
1987-88	Vancouver Canucks	7	0	0	0	4	....	....	....	....	....
1988-89	Vancouver Canucks	2	0	0	0	4	....	....	....	....	....
	NHL Totals	**9**	**0**	**0**	**0**	**8**	....	....	....	....	....

Traded to **NY Islanders** by **Vancouver** for Jack Capuano, March 6, 1990.

ROHLIN, Leif

Defense. Shoots left. 6'1", 198 lbs. Born, Vasteras, Sweden, February 26, 1968.
(Vancouver's 2nd choice, 33rd overall, in 1988 Entry Draft).

Season	Club	GP	G	A	Pts	PIM	GP	G	A	Pts	PIM
1995-96	Vancouver Canucks	56	6	16	22	32	5	0	0	0	0
1996-97	Vancouver Canucks	40	2	8	10	8	....	....	....	....	....
	NHL Totals	**96**	**8**	**24**	**32**	**40**	**5**	**0**	**0**	**0**	**0**

ROHLOFF, Jon

Defense. Shoots right. 5'11", 220 lbs. Born, Mankato, MN, October 3, 1969.
(Boston's 7th choice, 186th overall, in 1988 Entry Draft).

Season	Club	GP	G	A	Pts	PIM	GP	G	A	Pts	PIM
1994-95	Boston Bruins	34	3	8	11	39	5	0	0	0	6
1995-96	Boston Bruins	79	1	12	13	59	5	1	2	3	2
1996-97	Boston Bruins	37	3	5	8	31	....	....	....	....	....
	NHL Totals	**150**	**7**	**25**	**32**	**129**	**10**	**1**	**2**	**3**	**8**

Signed as a free agent by **San Jose**, July 23, 1998. Signed as a free agent by **Carolina**, August 1, 2000.

ROHLOFF, Todd

Defense. Shoots left. 6'3", 213 lbs. Born, Grand Rapids, IL, January 16, 1974.

Season	Club	GP	G	A	Pts	PIM	GP	G	A	Pts	PIM
2001-02	Washington Capitals	16	0	1	1	14	....	....	....	....	....
	NHL Totals	**16**	**0**	**1**	**1**	**14**	....	....	....	....	....

Signed as a free agent by **Chicago**, March 24, 1998. Signed as a free agent by **Washington**, July 21, 2000.

ROLFE, Dale

Defense. Shoots left. 6'4", 210 lbs. Born, Timmins, Ont., April 30, 1940.

Season	Club	GP	G	A	Pts	PIM	GP	G	A	Pts	PIM
1959-60	Boston Bruins	3	0	0	0	0	....	....	....	....	....
1967-68	Los Angeles Kings	68	3	13	16	84	7	0	1	1	14
1968-69	Los Angeles Kings	75	3	19	22	85	10	0	4	4	8
1969-70	Los Angeles Kings	55	1	9	10	77	....	....	....	....	....
	Detroit Red Wings	20	2	9	11	12	4	0	2	2	8
1970-71	Detroit Red Wings	44	3	9	12	48	....	....	....	....	....
	New York Rangers	14	0	7	7	23	13	0	1	1	14
1971-72	New York Rangers	68	2	14	16	67	16	4	3	7	16
1972-73	New York Rangers	72	7	25	32	74	8	0	5	5	6
1973-74	New York Rangers	48	3	12	15	56	13	1	8	9	23
1974-75	New York Rangers	42	1	8	9	30	....	....	....	....	....
	NHL Totals	**509**	**25**	**125**	**150**	**556**	**71**	**5**	**24**	**29**	**89**

Traded to **Springfield** (AHL) by **Boston** with Bruce Gamble, Terry Gray and Randy Miller for Bob McCord, June, 1963. NHL rights transferred to **Los Angeles** after NHL club purchased **Springfield** (AHL) franchise, May, 1967. Traded to **Detroit** by **Los Angeles** with Gary Croteau and Larry Johnston for Garry Monahan, Matt Ravlich and Brian Gibbons, February 20, 1970. Traded to **NY Rangers** by **Detroit** for Jim Krulicki, March 2, 1971.

ROLSTON, Brian

Center/Right wing. Shoots left. 6'2", 205 lbs. Born, Flint, MI, February 21, 1973.
(New Jersey's 2nd choice, 11th overall, in 1991 Entry Draft).

Season	Club	GP	G	A	Pts	PIM	GP	G	A	Pts	PIM
1994-95 ♦	New Jersey Devils	40	7	11	18	17	6	2	1	3	4
1995-96	New Jersey Devils	58	13	11	24	8	....	....	....	....	....
1996-97	New Jersey Devils	81	18	27	45	20	10	4	1	5	6
1997-98	New Jersey Devils	76	16	14	30	16	6	1	0	1	2
1998-99	New Jersey Devils	82	24	33	57	14	7	1	0	1	2
99-2000	New Jersey Devils	11	3	1	4	0	....	....	....	....	....
	Colorado Avalanche	50	8	10	18	12	....	....	....	....	....
	Boston Bruins	16	5	4	9	6	....	....	....	....	....
2000-01	Boston Bruins	77	19	39	58	28	....	....	....	....	....
2001-02	Boston Bruins	82	31	31	62	30	6	4	1	5	0
2002-03	Boston Bruins	81	27	32	59	32	5	0	2	2	0
	NHL Totals	**654**	**171**	**213**	**384**	**183**	**40**	**12**	**5**	**17**	**14**

Traded to **Colorado** by **New Jersey** with New Jersey's 1st round choice (later traded to Boston – Boston selected Martin Samuelsson) in 2000 Entry Draft for Claude Lemieux and Colorado's 1st (David Hale) and 2nd (Matt DeMarchi) round choices in 2000 Entry Draft, November 3, 1999. Traded to **Boston** by **Colorado** with Martin Grenier, Samuel Pahlsson and New Jersey's 1st round choice (previously acquired, Boston selected Martin Samuelsson) in 2000 Entry Draft for Raymond Bourque and Dave Andreychuk, March 6, 2000.

ROMANCHYCH, Larry

Right wing. Shoots right. 6'1", 180 lbs. Born, Vancouver, B.C., September 7, 1949.
(Chicago's 2nd choice, 24th overall, in 1969 Amateur Draft).

Season	Club	GP	G	A	Pts	PIM	GP	G	A	Pts	PIM
1970-71	Chicago Black Hawks	10	0	2	2	2	....	....	....	....	....
1972-73	Atlanta Flames	70	18	30	48	39	....	....	....	....	....
1973-74	Atlanta Flames	73	22	29	51	33	4	2	2	4	4
1974-75	Atlanta Flames	53	8	12	20	16	....	....	....	....	....
1975-76	Atlanta Flames	67	16	19	35	8	2	0	0	0	0
1976-77	Atlanta Flames	25	4	5	9	4	1	0	0	0	0
	NHL Totals	**298**	**68**	**97**	**165**	**102**	**7**	**2**	**2**	**4**	**4**

Claimed by **Atlanta** from **Chicago** in Expansion Draft, June 6, 1972.

ROMANIUK, Russell

Left wing. Shoots left. 6', 195 lbs. Born, Winnipeg, Man., June 9, 1970.
(Winnipeg's 2nd choice, 31st overall, in 1988 Entry Draft).

Season	Club	GP	G	A	Pts	PIM	GP	G	A	Pts	PIM
1991-92	Winnipeg Jets	27	3	5	8	18	....	....	....	....	....
1992-93	Winnipeg Jets	28	3	1	4	22	1	0	0	0	0
1993-94	Winnipeg Jets	24	4	8	12	6	....	....	....	....	....
1994-95	Winnipeg Jets	6	0	0	0	0	....	....	....	....	....
1995-96	Philadelphia Flyers	17	3	0	3	17	1	0	0	0	0
	NHL Totals	**102**	**13**	**14**	**27**	**63**	**2**	**0**	**0**	**0**	**0**

Traded to **Philadelphia** by **Winnipeg** for Jeff Finley, June 27, 1995.

ROMBOUGH, Doug

Center. Shoots left. 6'3", 215 lbs. Born, Fergus, Ont., July 8, 1950.
(Buffalo's 8th choice, 97th overall, in 1970 Amateur Draft).

Season	Club	GP	G	A	Pts	PIM	GP	G	A	Pts	PIM
1972-73	Buffalo Sabres	5	2	0	2	0	....	....	....	....	....
1973-74	Buffalo Sabres	46	6	9	15	27	....	....	....	....	....
	New York Islanders	12	3	1	4	8	....	....	....	....	....
1974-75	New York Islanders	28	5	6	11	6	....	....	....	....	....
	Minnesota North Stars	40	6	9	15	33	....	....	....	....	....
1975-76	Minnesota North Stars	19	2	2	4	6	....	....	....	....	....
	NHL Totals	**150**	**24**	**27**	**51**	**80**	....	....	....	....	....

Traded to **NY Islanders** by **Buffalo** for Brian Spencer, March 10, 1974. Traded to **Minnesota** by **NY Islanders** with Ernie Hicke for Jean-Paul Parise, January 5, 1975.

ROMINSKI, Dale

Right wing. Shoots right. 6'2", 200 lbs. Born, Farmington Hills, MI, October 1, 1975.

Season	Club	GP	G	A	Pts	PIM	GP	G	A	Pts	PIM
99-2000	Tampa Bay Lightning	3	0	1	1	2	....	....	....	....	....
	NHL Totals	**3**	**0**	**1**	**1**	**2**	....	....	....	....	....

Signed as a free agent by **Tampa Bay**, August 31, 1999.

ROMNES, Doc

USHOF

Left wing/Center. Shoots left. 5'11", 156 lbs. Born, White Bear Lake, MN, January 1, 1909.

Season	Club	GP	G	A	Pts	PIM	GP	G	A	Pts	PIM
1930-31	Chicago Black Hawks	30	5	7	12	8	9	1	1	2	2
1931-32	Chicago Black Hawks	18	1	0	1	6	2	0	0	0	0

Season	Club	GP	G	A	Pts	PIM	GP	G	A	Pts	PIM
		REGULAR SEASON					PLAYOFFS				
1932-33	Chicago Black Hawks	47	10	12	22	2	....	....	....	....	....
1933-34 ♦	Chicago Black Hawks	47	8	21	29	6	8	2	*7	9	0
1934-35	Chicago Black Hawks	35	10	14	24	8	2	0	0	0	0
1935-36	Chicago Black Hawks	48	13	25	38	6	2	1	2	3	0
1936-37	Chicago Black Hawks	28	4	14	18	2	....	....	....	....	....
1937-38 ♦	Chicago Black Hawks	44	10	22	32	4	12	2	4	6	2
1938-39	Chicago Black Hawks	12	0	4	4	0	....	....	....	....	....
	Toronto Maple Leafs	36	7	16	23	0	10	1	4	5	0
1939-40	New York Americans	15	0	1	1	0	....	....	....	....	....
	NHL Totals	**360**	**68**	**136**	**204**	**42**	**45**	**7**	**18**	**25**	**4**

Lady Byng Trophy (1936)

Traded to **Chicago** by **St. Paul** (AHA) for cash, October 28, 1930. Traded to **Toronto** by **Chicago** for Bill Thoms, December 8, 1938. Traded to **NY Americans** by **Toronto** with Buzz Boll, Busher Jackson, Murray Armstrong and Jimmy Fowler for Sweeney Schriner, May 18, 1939. Traded to **Omaha** (AHA) by **NY Americans** for cash, February 7, 1940.

RONAN, Ed

Right wing. Shoots right. 6', 197 lbs. Born, Quincy, MA, March 21, 1968.
(Montreal's 13th choice, 227th overall, in 1987 Entry Draft).

Season	Club	GP	G	A	Pts	PIM	GP	G	A	Pts	PIM
1991-92	Montreal Canadiens	3	0	0	0	0	....	....	....	....	....
1992-93 ♦	Montreal Canadiens	53	5	7	12	20	14	2	3	5	10
1993-94	Montreal Canadiens	61	6	8	14	42	7	1	0	1	0
1994-95	Montreal Canadiens	30	1	4	5	12	....	....	....	....	....
1995-96	Winnipeg Jets	17	0	0	0	16	....	....	....	....	....
1996-97	Buffalo Sabres	18	1	4	5	11	6	1	0	1	6
	NHL Totals	**182**	**13**	**23**	**36**	**101**	**27**	**4**	**3**	**7**	**16**

Signed as a free agent by **Winnipeg**, October 13, 1995. Signed as a free agent by **Buffalo**, September 5, 1996.

RONAN, Skene

Defense/Center. Shoots left. 5'6", 150 lbs. Born, Ottawa, Ont.,

Season	Club	GP	G	A	Pts	PIM	GP	G	A	Pts	PIM
1918-19	Ottawa Senators	11	0	0	0	6	....	....	....	....	....
	NHL Totals	**11**	**0**	**0**	**0**	**6**	....	....	....	....	....

Traded to **Ottawa** by **Montreal** for rights to Harry Hyland, December 9, 1918. Released by **Ottawa**, January 26, 1919. Re-signed as a free agent by **Ottawa**, February 17, 1919.

RONNING, Cliff

Center. Shoots left. 5'8", 165 lbs. Born, Burnaby, B.C., October 1, 1965.
(St. Louis' 9th choice, 134th overall, in 1984 Entry Draft).

Season	Club	GP	G	A	Pts	PIM	GP	G	A	Pts	PIM
1985-86	St. Louis Blues	....	....	....	....	....	5	1	1	2	2
1986-87	St. Louis Blues	42	11	14	25	6	4	0	1	1	0
1987-88	St. Louis Blues	26	5	8	13	12	....	....	....	....	....
1988-89	St. Louis Blues	64	24	31	55	18	7	1	3	4	0
1990-91	St. Louis Blues	48	14	18	32	10	....	....	....	....	....
	Vancouver Canucks	11	6	6	12	0	6	6	3	9	12
1991-92	Vancouver Canucks	80	24	47	71	42	13	8	5	13	6
1992-93	Vancouver Canucks	79	29	56	85	30	12	2	9	11	6
1993-94	Vancouver Canucks	76	25	43	68	42	24	5	10	15	16
1994-95	Vancouver Canucks	41	6	19	25	27	11	3	5	8	2
1995-96	Vancouver Canucks	79	22	45	67	42	6	0	2	2	6
1996-97	Phoenix Coyotes	69	19	32	51	26	7	0	7	7	12
1997-98	Phoenix Coyotes	80	11	44	55	36	6	1	3	4	4
1998-99	Phoenix Coyotes	7	2	5	7	2	....	....	....	....	....
	Nashville Predators	72	18	35	53	40	....	....	....	....	....
99-2000	Nashville Predators	82	26	36	62	34	....	....	....	....	....
2000-01	Nashville Predators	80	19	43	62	28	....	....	....	....	....
2001-02	Nashville Predators	67	18	31	49	24	....	....	....	....	....
	Los Angeles Kings	14	1	4	5	8	4	0	1	1	2
2002-03	Minnesota Wild	80	17	31	48	24	17	2	7	9	4
	NHL Totals	**1097**	**297**	**548**	**845**	**451**	**122**	**29**	**57**	**86**	**72**

Traded to **Vancouver** by **St. Louis** with Geoff Courtnall, Robert Dirk, Sergio Momesso and St. Louis' 5th round choice (Brian Loney) in 1992 Entry Draft for Dan Quinn and Garth Butcher, March 5, 1991. Signed as a free agent by **Phoenix**, July 1, 1996. Traded to **Nashville** by **Phoenix** with Richard Lintner for future considerations, October 31, 1998. Traded to **Los Angeles** by **Nashville** for Jere Karalahti and Los Angeles' 4th round choice (Teemu Lassila) in 2003 Entry Draft, March 16, 2002. Traded to **Minnesota** by **Los Angeles** for Minnesota's 4th round choice (Aaron Rome) in 2002 Entry Draft, June 22, 2002.

RONNQVIST, Jonas

Right wing. Shoots right. 6'2", 200 lbs. Born, Kalix, Sweden, August 22, 1973.
(Anaheim's 3rd choice, 98th overall, in 2000 Entry Draft).

Season	Club	GP	G	A	Pts	PIM	GP	G	A	Pts	PIM
2000-01	Mighty Ducks of Anaheim	38	0	4	4	14	....	....	....	....	....
	NHL Totals	**38**	**0**	**4**	**4**	**14**	....	....	....	....	....

RONSON, Len

Left wing. Shoots left. 5'9", 175 lbs. Born, Brantford, Ont., July 8, 1936.

Season	Club	GP	G	A	Pts	PIM	GP	G	A	Pts	PIM
1960-61	New York Rangers	13	2	1	3	10	....	....	....	....	....
1968-69	Oakland Seals	5	0	0	0	0	....	....	....	....	....
	NHL Totals	**18**	**2**	**1**	**3**	**10**	....	....	....	....	....

Traded to **Montreal** by **NY Rangers** with Dave Balon, Leon Rochefort and Gump Worsley for Phil Goyette, Don Marshall and Jacques Plante, June 4, 1963. Traded to **Portland** (WHL) by **Montreal** for cash, July, 1965. Traded to **San Diego** (WHL) by **Portland** (WHL), August, 1966. Claimed by **Montreal** from **San Diego** (WHL) in Reverse Draft, June, 1968. Traded to **Oakland** by **Montreal** for cash, August, 1968. Traded to **San Diego** (WHL) by **Oakland** for cash, November, 1968.

RONTY, Paul

Center. Shoots left. 6', 160 lbs. Born, Toronto, Ont., June 12, 1928.

Season	Club	GP	G	A	Pts	PIM	GP	G	A	Pts	PIM
1947-48	Boston Bruins	24	3	11	14	0	5	0	4	4	0
1948-49	Boston Bruins	60	20	29	49	11	5	1	2	3	2
1949-50	Boston Bruins	70	23	36	59	8	....	....	....	....	....
1950-51	Boston Bruins	70	10	22	32	20	6	0	1	1	2
1951-52	New York Rangers	65	12	31	43	16	....	....	....	....	....
1952-53	New York Rangers	70	16	38	54	20	....	....	....	....	....
1953-54	New York Rangers	70	13	33	46	18	....	....	....	....	....
1954-55	New York Rangers	55	4	11	15	8	....	....	....	....	....
	Montreal Canadiens	4	0	0	0	2	5	0	0	0	2
	NHL Totals	**488**	**101**	**211**	**312**	**103**	**21**	**1**	**7**	**8**	**6**

Played in NHL All-Star Game (1949, 1950, 1953, 1954)

Traded to **NY Rangers** by **Boston** for Gus Kyle, cash and the rights to Pentti Lund, September 20, 1951. Claimed on waivers by **Montreal** from **NY Rangers**, February 20, 1955.

ROONEY, Steve

Left wing. Shoots left. 6'2", 205 lbs. Born, Canton, MA, June 28, 1962.
(Montreal's 8th choice, 88th overall, in 1981 Entry Draft).

Season	Club	GP	G	A	Pts	PIM	GP	G	A	Pts	PIM
1984-85	Montreal Canadiens	3	1	0	1	7	11	2	2	4	19
1985-86 ♦	Montreal Canadiens	38	2	3	5	114	1	0	0	0	0
1986-87	Montreal Canadiens	2	0	0	0	22	....	....	....	....	....
	Winnipeg Jets	30	2	3	5	57	8	0	0	0	34
1987-88	Winnipeg Jets	56	7	6	13	217	5	1	0	1	33
1988-89	New Jersey Devils	25	3	1	4	79	....	....	....	....	....
	NHL Totals	**154**	**15**	**13**	**28**	**496**	**25**	**3**	**2**	**5**	**86**

• Missed majority of 1985-86 season recovering from shoulder injury suffered in game vs. Calgary, Novemmber 23, 1985. Traded to **Winnipeg** by **Montreal** for Winnipeg's 3rd round choice (Francois Gravel) in 1987 Entry Draft, January 8, 1987. Traded to **New Jersey** by **Winnipeg** with Winnipeg's 3rd round choice (Brad Bombardir) in 1990 Entry Draft for Alain Chevrier and New Jersey's 7th round choice (Doug Evans) in 1989 Entry Draft, July 19, 1988.

ROOT, Bill

Defense. Shoots right. 6', 210 lbs. Born, Toronto, Ont., September 6, 1959.

Season	Club	GP	G	A	Pts	PIM	GP	G	A	Pts	PIM
1982-83	Montreal Canadiens	46	2	3	5	24	....	....	....	....	....
1983-84	Montreal Canadiens	72	4	13	17	45	....	....	....	....	....
1984-85	Toronto Maple Leafs	35	1	1	2	23	....	....	....	....	....
1985-86	Toronto Maple Leafs	27	0	1	1	29	7	0	2	2	13
1986-87	Toronto Maple Leafs	34	3	3	6	37	13	1	0	1	12
1987-88	St. Louis Blues	9	0	0	0	6	....	....	....	....	....
	Philadelphia Flyers	24	1	2	3	16	2	0	0	0	0
	NHL Totals	**247**	**11**	**23**	**34**	**180**	**22**	**1**	**2**	**3**	**25**

Signed as a free agent by **Montreal**, October 4, 1979. Traded to **Toronto** by **Montreal** with Montreal's 2nd round choice (Darryl Shannon) in 1986 Entry Draft for Dom Campedelli, August 21, 1984. Traded to **Hartford** by **Toronto** for Dave Semenko, September 8, 1987. Claimed by **St. Louis** from **Hartford** in Waiver Draft, October 5, 1987. Claimed on waivers by **Philadelphia** from **St. Louis**, November 26, 1987. Traded to **Toronto** by **Philadelphia** for Mike Stothers, June 21, 1988.

ROSA, Pavel

Right wing. Shoots right. 6', 195 lbs. Born, Most, Czech., June 7, 1977.
(Los Angeles' 3rd choice, 50th overall, in 1995 Entry Draft).

Season	Club	GP	G	A	Pts	PIM	GP	G	A	Pts	PIM
1998-99	Los Angeles Kings	29	4	12	16	6	....	....	....	....	....
99-2000	Los Angeles Kings	3	0	0	0	0	....	....	....	....	....
2002-03	Los Angeles Kings	2	0	0	0	0	....	....	....	....	....
	NHL Totals	**34**	**4**	**12**	**16**	**6**					

ROSS, Art

HHOF

Defense. Shoots left. 5'11", 190 lbs. Born, Naughton, Ont., January 13, 1886.

Season	Club	GP	G	A	Pts	PIM	GP	G	A	Pts	PIM
1917-18	Montreal Wanderers	3	1	0	1	12	....	....	....	....	....
	NHL Totals	**3**	**1**	**0**	**1**	**12**	....	....	....	....	....

Lester Patrick Trophy (1984)

Rights retained by **Mtl. Wanderers** after NHA folded, November 26, 1917.

ROSS, Jim

Defense. Shoots right. 6'3", 185 lbs. Born, Edinburgh, Scotland, May 20, 1926.

Season	Club	GP	G	A	Pts	PIM	GP	G	A	Pts	PIM
1951-52	New York Rangers	51	2	9	11	25	....	....	....	....	....
1952-53	New York Rangers	11	0	2	2	4	....	....	....	....	....
	NHL Totals	**62**	**2**	**11**	**13**	**29**	....	....	....	....	....

ROSSIGNOL, Roly

Right wing. Shoots right. 5'9", 168 lbs. Born, Edmundston, N.B., October 18, 1921.

Season	Club	GP	G	A	Pts	PIM	GP	G	A	Pts	PIM
1943-44	Detroit Red Wings	1	0	1	1	0	....	....	....	....	....
1944-45	Montreal Canadiens	5	2	2	4	2	1	0	0	0	2
1945-46	Detroit Red Wings	8	1	2	3	4	....	....	....	....	....
	NHL Totals	**14**	**3**	**5**	**8**	**6**	**1**	**0**	**0**	**0**	**2**

Loaned to **Detroit** by **Montreal** (Quebec-QSHL) as an emergency injury replacement, March 11, 1944. Traded to **Detroit** (Pittsburgh-AHL) by **Montreal** for cash, November 24, 1944. Traded to **Montreal** by **Detroit** (Pittsburgh-AHL) for cash, February, 1945. Traded to **Detroit** by **Montreal** with Ray Getliffe for Billy Reay, September 11, 1945. Getliffe decided to retire and Detroit was awarded the rights to Fern Gauthier as compensation, October 18, 1945.

ROSSITER, Kyle

Defense. Shoots left. 6'3", 217 lbs. Born, Edmonton, Alta., June 9, 1980.
(Florida's 1st choice, 30th overall, in 1998 Entry Draft).

Season	Club	Regular Season GP	G	A	Pts	PIM	Playoffs GP	G	A	Pts	PIM
2001-02	Florida Panthers	2	0	0	0	2	....	....	....	....	....
2002-03	Florida Panthers	3	0	0	0	0	....	....	....	....	....
	NHL Totals	**5**	**0**	**0**	**0**	**2**	....	....	....	....	....

ROTA, Darcy

Left wing. Shoots left. 5'11", 180 lbs. Born, Vancouver, B.C., February 16, 1953.
(Chicago's 1st choice, 13th overall, in 1973 Amateur Draft).

Season	Club	Regular Season GP	G	A	Pts	PIM	Playoffs GP	G	A	Pts	PIM
1973-74	Chicago Black Hawks	74	21	12	33	58	11	3	0	3	11
1974-75	Chicago Black Hawks	78	22	22	44	93	7	0	1	1	24
1975-76	Chicago Black Hawks	79	20	17	37	73	4	1	0	1	2
1976-77	Chicago Black Hawks	76	24	22	46	82	2	0	0	0	0
1977-78	Chicago Black Hawks	78	17	20	37	67	4	0	0	0	2
1978-79	Chicago Black Hawks	63	13	17	30	77	....	....	....	....	....
	Atlanta Flames	13	9	5	14	21	2	0	1	1	26
1979-80	Atlanta Flames	44	10	8	18	49	....	....	....	....	....
	Vancouver Canucks	26	5	6	11	29	4	2	0	2	8
1980-81	Vancouver Canucks	80	25	31	56	124	3	2	1	3	14
1981-82	Vancouver Canucks	51	20	20	40	139	17	6	3	9	54
1982-83	Vancouver Canucks	73	42	39	81	88	3	0	0	0	6
1983-84	Vancouver Canucks	59	28	20	48	73	3	0	1	1	0
	NHL Totals	**794**	**256**	**239**	**495**	**973**	**60**	**14**	**7**	**21**	**147**

Played in NHL All-Star Game (1984)

Traded to **Atlanta** by **Chicago** with Ivan Boldirev and Phil Russell for Tom Lysiak, Pat Ribble, Harold Phillipoff, Greg Fox and Miles Zaharko, March 13, 1979. Traded to **Vancouver** by **Atlanta** with Ivan Boldirev for Don Lever and Brad Smith, February 8, 1980. • Missed entire 1984-85 season recovering from neck injury originally suffered in game vs. Los Angeles, February 2, 1984. Officially announced retirement, December 4, 1984.

ROTA, Randy

Center/Left wing. Shoots left. 5'8", 170 lbs. Born, Creston, B.C., August 16, 1950.
(California's 3rd choice, 33rd overall, in 1970 Amateur Draft).

Season	Club	Regular Season GP	G	A	Pts	PIM	Playoffs GP	G	A	Pts	PIM
1972-73	Montreal Canadiens	2	1	1	2	0	....	....	....	....	....
1973-74	Los Angeles Kings	58	10	6	16	16	5	0	1	1	0
1974-75	Kansas City Scouts	80	15	18	33	30	....	....	....	....	....
1975-76	Kansas City Scouts	71	12	14	26	14	....	....	....	....	....
1976-77	Colorado Rockies	1	0	0	0	0	....	....	....	....	....
	NHL Totals	**212**	**38**	**39**	**77**	**60**	**5**	**0**	**1**	**1**	**0**

Traded to **Montreal** by **California** for Lyle Carter and John French, October 8, 1971. Traded to **Los Angeles** by **Montreal** with Bob Murdoch for Los Angeles' 1st round choice (Mario Tremblay) in 1974 Amateur Draft and cash, May 29, 1973. Claimed by **Kansas City** from **Los Angeles** in Expansion Draft, June 12, 1974. Transferred to **Colorado** after **Kansas City** franchise relocated, July 15, 1976. Traded to **Edmonton** (WHA) by **Colorado** for cash, November, 1976.

ROTHSCHILD, Sam

Left wing. Shoots left. 5'6", 145 lbs. Born, Sudbury, Ont., October 16, 1899.

Season	Club	Regular Season GP	G	A	Pts	PIM	Playoffs GP	G	A	Pts	PIM
1924-25	Montreal Maroons	28	5	4	9	5	....	....	....	....	....
1925-26 ♦	Montreal Maroons	33	2	1	3	8	4	0	0	0	0
	Montreal Maroons (Cup)	....	....	....	....	....	*4*	*0*	*0*	*0*	*0*
1926-27	Montreal Maroons	22	1	1	2	8	2	0	0	0	0
1927-28	Pittsburgh Pirates	12	0	0	0	0	....	....	....	....	....
	New York Americans	5	0	0	0	4	....	....	....	....	....
	NHL Totals	**100**	**8**	**6**	**14**	**25**	**6**	**0**	**0**	**0**	**0**

Signed as a free agent by **Mtl. Maroons**, October 20, 1924. Signed as a free agent by **Pittsburgh**, November, 1927. • Suspended by Pittsburgh for breaking training rules, December 26, 1927. Signed as a free agent by **NY Americans**, January 5, 1928.

ROULSTON, Rolly

Left wing/Defense. Shoots left. 6'1", 195 lbs. Born, Toronto, Ont., April 12, 1911.

Season	Club	Regular Season GP	G	A	Pts	PIM	Playoffs GP	G	A	Pts	PIM
1935-36	Detroit Red Wings	1	0	0	0	0	....	....	....	....	....
1936-37 ♦	Detroit Red Wings	21	0	5	5	10	....	....	....	....	....
1937-38	Detroit Red Wings	2	0	1	1	0	....	....	....	....	....
	NHL Totals	**24**	**0**	**6**	**6**	**10**	....	....	....	....	....

Traded to **Detroit** by **Tulsa** (AHA) for cash, September, 1934. Traded to **Hershey** (IAHL) by **Detroit** for cash, June 23, 1938.

ROULSTON, Tom

Center/Right wing. Shoots right. 6'1", 184 lbs. Born, Winnipeg, Man., November 20, 1957.
(St. Louis' 3rd choice, 45th overall, in 1977 Amateur Draft).

Season	Club	Regular Season GP	G	A	Pts	PIM	Playoffs GP	G	A	Pts	PIM
1980-81	Edmonton Oilers	11	1	1	2	2	....	....	....	....	....
1981-82	Edmonton Oilers	35	11	3	14	22	5	1	0	1	2
1982-83	Edmonton Oilers	67	19	21	40	24	16	1	2	3	0
1983-84	Edmonton Oilers	24	5	7	12	16	....	....	....	....	....
	Pittsburgh Penguins	53	11	17	28	8	....	....	....	....	....
1985-86	Pittsburgh Penguins	5	0	0	0	2	....	....	....	....	....
	NHL Totals	**195**	**47**	**49**	**96**	**74**	**21**	**2**	**2**	**4**	**2**

Traded to **Edmonton** by **St. Louis** with Risto Siltanen for Joe Micheletti, August 7, 1979. Traded to **Pittsburgh** by **Edmonton** for Kevin McClelland and Pittsburgh's 6th round choice (Emanuel Viveiros) in 1984 Entry Draft, December 5, 1983.

ROUPE, Magnus

Left wing. Shoots left. 6', 189 lbs. Born, Stockholm, Sweden, March 23, 1963.
(Philadelphia's 9th choice, 182nd overall, in 1982 Entry Draft).

Season	Club	Regular Season GP	G	A	Pts	PIM	Playoffs GP	G	A	Pts	PIM
1987-88	Philadelphia Flyers	33	2	4	6	32	....	....	....	....	....
1988-89	Philadelphia Flyers	7	1	1	2	10	....	....	....	....	....
	NHL Totals	**40**	**3**	**5**	**8**	**42**	....	....	....	....	....

ROUSE, Bob

Defense. Shoots right. 6'2", 215 lbs. Born, Surrey, B.C., June 18, 1964.
(Minnesota's 3rd choice, 80th overall, in 1982 Entry Draft).

Season	Club	Regular Season GP	G	A	Pts	PIM	Playoffs GP	G	A	Pts	PIM
1983-84	Minnesota North Stars	1	0	0	0	0	....	....	....	....	....
1984-85	Minnesota North Stars	63	2	9	11	113	....	....	....	....	....
1985-86	Minnesota North Stars	75	1	14	15	151	3	0	0	0	0
1986-87	Minnesota North Stars	72	2	10	12	179	....	....	....	....	....
1987-88	Minnesota North Stars	74	0	12	12	168	....	....	....	....	....
1988-89	Minnesota North Stars	66	4	13	17	124	....	....	....	....	....
	Washington Capitals	13	0	2	2	36	6	2	0	2	4
1989-90	Washington Capitals	70	4	16	20	123	15	2	3	5	47
1990-91	Washington Capitals	47	5	15	20	65	....	....	....	....	....
	Toronto Maple Leafs	13	2	4	6	10	....	....	....	....	....
1991-92	Toronto Maple Leafs	79	3	19	22	97	....	....	....	....	....
1992-93	Toronto Maple Leafs	82	3	11	14	130	21	3	8	11	29
1993-94	Toronto Maple Leafs	63	5	11	16	101	18	0	3	3	29
1994-95	Detroit Red Wings	48	1	7	8	36	18	0	3	3	8
1995-96	Detroit Red Wings	58	0	6	6	48	7	0	1	1	4
1996-97 ♦	Detroit Red Wings	70	4	9	13	58	20	0	0	0	55
1997-98 ♦	Detroit Red Wings	71	1	11	12	57	22	0	3	3	16
1998-99	San Jose Sharks	70	0	11	11	44	6	0	0	0	6
99-2000	San Jose Sharks	26	0	1	1	19	....	....	....	....	....
	NHL Totals	**1061**	**37**	**181**	**218**	**1559**	**136**	**7**	**21**	**28**	**198**

Traded to **Washington** by **Minnesota** with Dino Ciccarelli for Mike Gartner and Larry Murphy, March 7, 1989. Traded to **Toronto** by **Washington** with Peter Zezel for Al Iafrate, January 16, 1991. Signed as a free agent by **Detroit**, August 5, 1994. Signed as a free agent by **San Jose**, July 13, 1998.

ROUSSEAU, Bobby

Right wing. Shoots right. 5'10", 178 lbs. Born, Montreal, Que., July 26, 1940.

Season	Club	Regular Season GP	G	A	Pts	PIM	Playoffs GP	G	A	Pts	PIM
1960-61	Montreal Canadiens	15	1	2	3	4	....	....	....	....	....
1961-62	Montreal Canadiens	70	21	24	45	26	6	0	2	2	0
1962-63	Montreal Canadiens	62	19	18	37	15	5	0	1	1	2
1963-64	Montreal Canadiens	70	25	31	56	32	7	1	1	2	2
1964-65 ♦	Montreal Canadiens	66	12	35	47	26	13	5	8	13	24
1965-66 ♦	Montreal Canadiens	70	30	*48	78	20	10	4	4	8	6
1966-67	Montreal Canadiens	68	19	44	63	58	10	1	7	8	4
1967-68 ♦	Montreal Canadiens	74	19	46	65	47	13	2	4	6	8
1968-69 ♦	Montreal Canadiens	76	30	40	70	59	14	3	2	5	8
1969-70	Montreal Canadiens	72	24	34	58	30	....	....	....	....	....
1970-71	Minnesota North Stars	63	4	20	24	12	12	2	6	8	0
1971-72	New York Rangers	78	21	36	57	12	16	6	11	17	7
1972-73	New York Rangers	78	8	37	45	14	10	2	3	5	4
1973-74	New York Rangers	72	10	41	51	4	12	1	8	9	4
1974-75	New York Rangers	8	2	2	4	0	....	....	....	....	....
	NHL Totals	**942**	**245**	**458**	**703**	**359**	**128**	**27**	**57**	**84**	**69**

• Brother of Roland and Guy • Calder Memorial Trophy (1962) • NHL Second All-Star Team (1966)

Played in NHL All-Star Game (1965, 1967, 1969)

Traded to **Minnesota** by **Montreal** for Claude Larose, June 10, 1970. Traded to **NY Rangers** by **Minnesota** to complete transaction that sent Bob Nevin to Minnesota (May 25, 1971), June 8, 1971.

ROUSSEAU, Guy

Left wing. Shoots left. 5'6", 140 lbs. Born, Montreal, Que., December 21, 1934.

Season	Club	Regular Season GP	G	A	Pts	PIM	Playoffs GP	G	A	Pts	PIM
1954-55	Montreal Canadiens	2	0	1	1	0	....	....	....	....	....
1956-57	Montreal Canadiens	2	0	0	0	0	....	....	....	....	....
	NHL Totals	**4**	**0**	**1**	**1**	**0**	....	....	....	....	....

• Brother of Bobby and Roland

Traded to **Chicoutimi** (QHL) by **Montreal** with Jack Leclair and Jacques Deslauriers for Stan Smrke, October 27, 1957. Traded to **Toronto** by **Montreal** for cash, June 7, 1960. Traded to **Montreal** (Quebec-AHL) by **Toronto** (Rochester-AHL) for Norm Corcoran, June 1, 1961.

ROUSSEAU, Roland

Defense. Shoots left. 5'8", 160 lbs. Born, Montreal, Que., December 1, 1929.

Season	Club	Regular Season GP	G	A	Pts	PIM	Playoffs GP	G	A	Pts	PIM
1952-53	Montreal Canadiens	2	0	0	0	0	....	....	....	....	....
	NHL Totals	**2**	**0**	**0**	**0**	**0**	....	....	....	....	....

• Brother of Bobby and Guy

Claimed by **Montreal** from **Montreal** (Montreal-QHL) in Inter-League Draft, June 10, 1953.

ROUTHIER, Jean-Marc

Right wing. Shoots right. 6'2", 190 lbs. Born, Quebec City, Que., February 2, 1968.
(Quebec's 2nd choice, 39th overall, in 1986 Entry Draft).

Season	Club	Regular Season GP	G	A	Pts	PIM	Playoffs GP	G	A	Pts	PIM
1989-90	Quebec Nordiques	8	0	0	0	9	....	....	....	....	....
	NHL Totals	**8**	**0**	**0**	**0**	**9**	....	....	....	....	....

ROWE, Bobby

Right wing/Defense. Shoots left. 5'6", 160 lbs. Born, Heathcote, Ont.,

Season	Club	GP	G	A	Pts	PIM	GP	G	A	Pts	PIM
		REGULAR SEASON					PLAYOFFS				
1924-25	Boston Bruins	4	1	0	1	0	....	....	....	....	....
	NHL Totals	**4**	**1**	**0**	**1**	**0**	....	....	....	....	....

Traded to **Boston** by **Seattle** (WCHL) for cash, November 2, 1924.

ROWE, Mike

Defense. Shoots left. 6'1", 208 lbs. Born, Kingston, Ont., March 8, 1965.
(Pittsburgh's 3rd choice, 59th overall, in 1983 Entry Draft).

Season	Club	GP	G	A	Pts	PIM	GP	G	A	Pts	PIM
1984-85	Pittsburgh Penguins	6	0	0	0	7	....	....	....	....	....
1985-86	Pittsburgh Penguins	3	0	0	0	4	....	....	....	....	....
1986-87	Pittsburgh Penguins	2	0	0	0	0	....	....	....	....	....
	NHL Totals	**11**	**0**	**0**	**0**	**11**	....	....	....	....	....

ROWE, Ron

Center/Left wing. Shoots left. 5'8", 170 lbs. Born, Toronto, Ont., November 30, 1923.

Season	Club	GP	G	A	Pts	PIM	GP	G	A	Pts	PIM
1947-48	New York Rangers	5	1	0	1	0	....	....	....	....	....
	NHL Totals	**5**	**1**	**0**	**1**	**0**	....	....	....	....	....

Loaned to **Tacoma** (PCHL) by **NY Rangers** for cash, September 30, 1948. Traded to **Sydney** (MMHL) by **NY Rangers** for cash, November 6, 1951.

ROWE, Tom

Right wing. Shoots right. 6', 190 lbs. Born, Lynn, MA, May 23, 1956.
(Washington's 3rd choice, 37th overall, in 1976 Amateur Draft).

Season	Club	GP	G	A	Pts	PIM	GP	G	A	Pts	PIM
1976-77	Washington Capitals	12	1	2	3	2	....	....	....	....	....
1977-78	Washington Capitals	63	13	8	21	82	....	....	....	....	....
1978-79	Washington Capitals	69	31	30	61	137	....	....	....	....	....
1979-80	Washington Capitals	41	10	17	27	76	....	....	....	....	....
	Hartford Whalers	20	6	4	10	30	3	2	0	2	0
1980-81	Hartford Whalers	74	13	28	41	190	....	....	....	....	....
1981-82	Hartford Whalers	21	4	0	4	36	....	....	....	....	....
	Washington Capitals	6	1	1	2	18	....	....	....	....	....
1982-83	Detroit Red Wings	51	6	10	16	44	....	....	....	....	....
	NHL Totals	**357**	**85**	**100**	**185**	**615**	**3**	**2**	**0**	**2**	**0**

Traded to **Hartford** by **Washington** for Al Hangsleben, January 17, 1980. Signed as a free agent by **Washington**, January 31, 1982. Signed as a free agent by **Detroit**, August 9, 1982. Signed as a free agent by **Edmonton**, September 29, 1983.

ROY, Andre

Right wing. Shoots left. 6'4", 213 lbs. Born, Port Chester, NY, February 8, 1975.
(Boston's 5th choice, 151st overall, in 1994 Entry Draft).

Season	Club	GP	G	A	Pts	PIM	GP	G	A	Pts	PIM
1995-96	Boston Bruins	3	0	0	0	0	....	....	....	....	....
1996-97	Boston Bruins	10	0	2	2	12	....	....	....	....	....
99-2000	Ottawa Senators	73	4	3	7	145	5	0	0	0	2
2000-01	Ottawa Senators	64	3	5	8	169	2	0	0	0	16
2001-02	Ottawa Senators	56	6	8	14	148	....	....	....	....	....
	Tampa Bay Lightning	9	1	1	2	63	....	....	....	....	....
2002-03	Tampa Bay Lightning	62	10	7	17	119	5	0	1	1	2
	NHL Totals	**277**	**24**	**26**	**50**	**656**	**12**	**0**	**1**	**1**	**20**

Signed as a free agent by **Ottawa**, April 28, 1999. Traded to **Tampa Bay** by **Ottawa** with Ottawa's 6th round choice (Paul Ranger) in 2002 Entry Draft for Juha Ylonen, March 15, 2002.

ROY, Jean-Yves

Right wing. Shoots left. 5'10", 180 lbs. Born, Rosemere, Que., February 17, 1969.

Season	Club	GP	G	A	Pts	PIM	GP	G	A	Pts	PIM
1994-95	New York Rangers	3	1	0	1	2	....	....	....	....	....
1995-96	Ottawa Senators	4	1	1	2	2	....	....	....	....	....
1996-97	Boston Bruins	52	10	15	25	22	....	....	....	....	....
1997-98	Boston Bruins	2	0	0	0	0	....	....	....	....	....
	NHL Totals	**61**	**12**	**16**	**28**	**26**	....	....	....	....	....

Signed as a free agent by **NY Rangers**, July 20, 1992. Traded to **Ottawa** by **NY Rangers** for Steve Larouche, October 5, 1995. Signed as a free agent by **Boston**, July 15, 1996.

ROY, Stephane

Center. Shoots left. 6', 190 lbs. Born, Ste-Foy, Que., June 29, 1967.
(Minnesota's 1st choice, 51st overall, in 1985 Entry Draft).

Season	Club	GP	G	A	Pts	PIM	GP	G	A	Pts	PIM
1987-88	Minnesota North Stars	12	1	0	1	0	....	....	....	....	....
	NHL Totals	**12**	**1**	**0**	**1**	**0**	....	....	....	....	....

• Brother of Patrick

Traded to **Quebec** by **Minnesota** for future considerations, December 15, 1988.

ROYER, Gaetan

Right wing. Shoots right. 6'3", 210 lbs. Born, Donnacona, Que., March 13, 1976.

Season	Club	GP	G	A	Pts	PIM	GP	G	A	Pts	PIM
2001-02	Tampa Bay Lightning	3	0	0	0	2	....	....	....	....	....
	NHL Totals	**3**	**0**	**0**	**0**	**2**	....	....	....	....	....

Signed as a free agent by **Calgary**, September 12, 2000. Signed as a free agent by **Tampa Bay**, October 23, 2001.

ROYER, Remi

Defense. Shoots right. 6'2", 200 lbs. Born, Donnacona, Que., February 12, 1978.
(Chicago's 1st choice, 31st overall, in 1996 Entry Draft).

Season	Club	GP	G	A	Pts	PIM	GP	G	A	Pts	PIM
1998-99	Chicago Blackhawks	18	0	0	0	67	....	....	....	....	....
	NHL Totals	**18**	**0**	**0**	**0**	**67**	....	....	....	....	....

Traded to **Washington** by **Chicago** for Nolan Baumgartner, July 20, 2000. Traded to **Florida** by **Washington** for David Emma, March 3, 2001.

ROZSIVAL, Michal

Defense. Shoots right. 6'1", 208 lbs. Born, Vlasim, Czech., September 3, 1978.
(Pittsburgh's 5th choice, 105th overall, in 1996 Entry Draft).

Season	Club	GP	G	A	Pts	PIM	GP	G	A	Pts	PIM
99-2000	Pittsburgh Penguins	75	4	17	21	48	2	0	0	0	4
2000-01	Pittsburgh Penguins	30	1	4	5	26	....	....	....	....	....
2001-02	Pittsburgh Penguins	79	9	20	29	47	....	....	....	....	....
2002-03	Pittsburgh Penguins	53	4	6	10	40	....	....	....	....	....
	NHL Totals	**237**	**18**	**47**	**65**	**161**	**2**	**0**	**0**	**0**	**4**

ROZZINI, Gino

Center. Shoots left. 5'8", 150 lbs. Born, Shawinigan Falls, Que., October 24, 1918.

Season	Club	GP	G	A	Pts	PIM	GP	G	A	Pts	PIM
1944-45	Boston Bruins	31	5	10	15	20	6	1	2	3	6
	NHL Totals	**31**	**5**	**10**	**15**	**20**	**6**	**1**	**2**	**3**	**6**

Signed as a free agent by **Boston**, November 2, 1944.

RUCCHIN, Steve

Center. Shoots left. 6'2", 211 lbs. Born, Thunder Bay, Ont., July 4, 1971.
(Anaheim's 1st choice, 2nd overall, in 1994 Supplemental Draft).

Season	Club	GP	G	A	Pts	PIM	GP	G	A	Pts	PIM
1994-95	Mighty Ducks of Anaheim	43	6	11	17	23	....	....	....	....	....
1995-96	Mighty Ducks of Anaheim	64	19	25	44	12	....	....	....	....	....
1996-97	Mighty Ducks of Anaheim	79	19	48	67	24	8	1	2	3	10
1997-98	Mighty Ducks of Anaheim	72	17	36	53	13	....	....	....	....	....
1998-99	Mighty Ducks of Anaheim	69	23	39	62	22	4	0	3	3	0
99-2000	Mighty Ducks of Anaheim	71	19	38	57	16	....	....	....	....	....
2000-01	Mighty Ducks of Anaheim	16	3	5	8	0	....	....	....	....	....
2001-02	Mighty Ducks of Anaheim	38	7	16	23	6	....	....	....	....	....
2002-03	Mighty Ducks of Anaheim	82	20	38	58	12	21	7	3	10	2
	NHL Totals	**534**	**133**	**256**	**389**	**128**	**33**	**8**	**8**	**16**	**12**

• Missed majority of 2000-01 season recovering from jaw injury suffered in game vs. Colorado, November 15, 2000. • Missed majority of 2001-02 season recovering from leg injury suffered in game vs. San Jose, November 16, 2001.

RUCINSKI, Mike

Center. Shoots left. 5'11", 190 lbs. Born, Wheeling, IL, December 12, 1963.

Season	Club	GP	G	A	Pts	PIM	GP	G	A	Pts	PIM
1987-88	Chicago Blackhawks	....	....	....	....	....	2	0	0	0	0
1988-89	Chicago Blackhawks	1	0	0	0	0	....	....	....	....	....
	NHL Totals	**1**	**0**	**0**	**0**	**0**	**2**	**0**	**0**	**0**	**0**

Signed as a free agent by **Calgary**, August 10, 1986. Signed as a free agent by **Chicago**, July 8, 1987.

RUCINSKI, Mike

Defense. Shoots left. 5'11", 179 lbs. Born, Trenton, MI, March 30, 1975.
(Hartford's 8th choice, 217th overall, in 1995 Entry Draft).

Season	Club	GP	G	A	Pts	PIM	GP	G	A	Pts	PIM
1997-98	Carolina Hurricanes	9	0	1	1	2	....	....	....	....	....
1998-99	Carolina Hurricanes	15	0	1	1	8	....	....	....	....	....
2000-01	Carolina Hurricanes	2	0	0	0	0	....	....	....	....	....
	NHL Totals	**26**	**0**	**2**	**2**	**10**	....	....	....	....	....

Rights transferred to **Carolina** after **Hartford** franchise relocated, June 25, 1997. Traded to **New Jersey** by **Carolina** for Ted Drury, March 4, 2002.

RUCINSKY, Martin

Left wing. Shoots left. 6'1", 205 lbs. Born, Most, Czech., March 11, 1971.
(Edmonton's 2nd choice, 20th overall, in 1991 Entry Draft).

Season	Club	GP	G	A	Pts	PIM	GP	G	A	Pts	PIM
1991-92	Edmonton Oilers	2	0	0	0	0	....	....	....	....	....
	Quebec Nordiques	4	1	1	2	2	....	....	....	....	....
1992-93	Quebec Nordiques	77	18	30	48	51	6	1	1	2	4
1993-94	Quebec Nordiques	60	9	23	32	58	....	....	....	....	....
1994-95	Quebec Nordiques	20	3	6	9	14	....	....	....	....	....
1995-96	Colorado Avalanche	22	4	11	15	14	....	....	....	....	....
	Montreal Canadiens	56	25	35	60	54	....	....	....	....	....
1996-97	Montreal Canadiens	70	28	27	55	62	5	0	0	0	4
1997-98	Montreal Canadiens	78	21	32	53	84	10	3	0	3	4
1998-99	Montreal Canadiens	73	17	17	34	50	....	....	....	....	....
99-2000	Montreal Canadiens	80	25	24	49	70	....	....	....	....	....
2000-01	Montreal Canadiens	57	16	22	38	66	....	....	....	....	....
2001-02	Montreal Canadiens	18	2	6	8	12	....	....	....	....	....
	Dallas Stars	42	6	11	17	24	....	....	....	....	....
	New York Rangers	15	3	10	13	6	....	....	....	....	....

Season	Club	GP	G	A	Pts	PIM	GP	G	A	Pts	PIM
		REGULAR SEASON					PLAYOFFS				
2002-03	St. Louis Blues	61	16	14	30	38	7	4	2	6	4
	NHL Totals	**735**	**194**	**269**	**463**	**605**	**28**	**8**	**3**	**11**	**16**

Played in NHL All-Star Game (2000)

Traded to **Quebec** by **Edmonton** for Ron Tugnutt and Brad Zavisha, March 10, 1992. Transferred to **Colorado** after **Quebec** franchise relocated, June 21, 1995. Traded to **Montreal** by **Colorado** with Andrei Kovalenko and Jocelyn Thibault for Patrick Roy and Mike Keane, December 6, 1995. Traded to **Dallas** by **Montreal** with Benoit Brunet for Donald Audette and Shaun Van Allen, November 21, 2001. Traded to **NY Rangers** by **Dallas** with Roman Lyashenko for Manny Malhotra and Barrett Heisten, March 12, 2002. Signed as a free agent by **St. Louis**, October 30, 2002.

RUELLE, Bernie

Left wing. Shoots left. 5'9", 165 lbs. Born, Houghton, MI, November 23, 1920.

Season	Club	GP	G	A	Pts	PIM	GP	G	A	Pts	PIM
1943-44	Detroit Red Wings	2	1	0	1	0	....	....	....	....	....
	NHL Totals	**2**	**1**	**0**	**1**	**0**	....	....	....	....	....

RUFF, Jason

Left wing. Shoots left. 6'2", 192 lbs. Born, Kelowna, B.C., January 27, 1970.
(St. Louis' 3rd choice, 96th overall, in 1990 Entry Draft).

Season	Club	GP	G	A	Pts	PIM	GP	G	A	Pts	PIM
1992-93	St. Louis Blues	7	2	1	3	8	....	....	....	....	....
	Tampa Bay Lightning	1	0	0	0	0	....	....	....	....	....
1993-94	Tampa Bay Lightning	6	1	2	3	2	....	....	....	....	....
	NHL Totals	**14**	**3**	**3**	**6**	**10**	....	....	....	....	....

Traded to **Tampa Bay** by **St. Louis** for Doug Crossman, Basil McRae and Tampa Bay's 4th round choice (Andrei Petrakov) in 1996 Entry Draft, January 28, 1993.

RUFF, Lindy

Defense/Left wing. Shoots left. 6'2", 201 lbs. Born, Warburg, Alta., February 17, 1960.
(Buffalo's 2nd choice, 32nd overall, in 1979 Entry Draft).

Season	Club	GP	G	A	Pts	PIM	GP	G	A	Pts	PIM
1979-80	Buffalo Sabres	63	5	14	19	38	8	1	1	2	19
1980-81	Buffalo Sabres	65	8	18	26	121	6	3	1	4	23
1981-82	Buffalo Sabres	79	16	32	48	194	4	0	0	0	28
1982-83	Buffalo Sabres	60	12	17	29	130	10	4	2	6	47
1983-84	Buffalo Sabres	58	14	31	45	101	3	1	0	1	9
1984-85	Buffalo Sabres	39	13	11	24	45	5	2	4	6	15
1985-86	Buffalo Sabres	54	20	12	32	158	....	....	....	....	....
1986-87	Buffalo Sabres	50	6	14	20	74	....	....	....	....	....
1987-88	Buffalo Sabres	77	2	23	25	179	6	0	2	2	23
1988-89	Buffalo Sabres	63	6	11	17	86	....	....	....	....	....
	New York Rangers	13	0	5	5	31	2	0	0	0	17
1989-90	New York Rangers	56	3	6	9	80	8	0	3	3	12
1990-91	New York Rangers	14	0	1	1	27	....	....	....	....	....
	NHL Totals	**691**	**105**	**195**	**300**	**1264**	**52**	**11**	**13**	**24**	**193**

Traded to **NY Rangers** by **Buffalo** for NY Rangers' 5th round choice (Richard Smehlik) in 1990 Entry Draft, March 7, 1989.

RUHNKE, Kent

Right wing. Shoots right. 6'1", 190 lbs. Born, Toronto, Ont., September 18, 1952.

Season	Club	GP	G	A	Pts	PIM	GP	G	A	Pts	PIM
1975-76	Boston Bruins	2	0	1	1	0	....	....	....	....	....
	NHL Totals	**2**	**0**	**1**	**1**	**0**	....	....	....	....	....

Signed to five-game try-out contract by **Boston**, March, 1976.

RUMBLE, Darren

Defense. Shoots left. 6'1", 200 lbs. Born, Barrie, Ont., January 23, 1969.
(Philadelphia's 1st choice, 20th overall, in 1987 Entry Draft).

Season	Club	GP	G	A	Pts	PIM	GP	G	A	Pts	PIM
1990-91	Philadelphia Flyers	3	1	0	1	0	....	....	....	....	....
1992-93	Ottawa Senators	69	3	13	16	61	....	....	....	....	....
1993-94	Ottawa Senators	70	6	9	15	116	....	....	....	....	....
1995-96	Philadelphia Flyers	5	0	0	0	4	....	....	....	....	....
1996-97	Philadelphia Flyers	10	0	0	0	0	....	....	....	....	....
2000-01	St. Louis Blues	12	0	4	4	27	....	....	....	....	....
2002-03	Tampa Bay Lightning	19	0	0	0	6	....	....	....	....	....
	NHL Totals	**188**	**10**	**26**	**36**	**214**	....	....	....	....	....

Claimed by **Ottawa** from **Philadelphia** in Expansion Draft, June 18, 1992. Signed as a free agent by **Philadelphia**, July 31, 1995. Signed as a free agent by **St. Louis**, February 1, 2000. Signed as a free agent by **Tampa Bay**, September 11, 2002.

RUNDQVIST, Thomas

Center. Shoots left. 6'3", 195 lbs. Born, Vimmerby, Sweden, May 4, 1960.
(Montreal's 12th choice, 206th overall, in 1983 Entry Draft).

Season	Club	GP	G	A	Pts	PIM	GP	G	A	Pts	PIM
1984-85	Montreal Canadiens	2	0	1	1	0	....	....	....	....	....
	NHL Totals	**2**	**0**	**1**	**1**	**0**	....	....	....	....	....

RUNGE, Paul

Center/Left wing. Shoots left. 5'11", 167 lbs. Born, Edmonton, Alta., September 10, 1908.

Season	Club	GP	G	A	Pts	PIM	GP	G	A	Pts	PIM
1930-31	Boston Bruins	1	0	0	0	0	....	....	....	....	....
1931-32	Boston Bruins	14	0	1	1	8	....	....	....	....	....
1933-34	Montreal Maroons	4	0	0	0	0	....	....	....	....	....
1934-35	Montreal Canadiens	3	0	0	0	2	....	....	....	....	....
1935-36	Montreal Canadiens	12	0	2	2	4	....	....	....	....	....
	Boston Bruins	33	8	2	10	14	2	0	0	0	2
1936-37	Montreal Canadiens	4	1	0	1	2	....	....	....	....	....
	Montreal Maroons	30	4	10	14	6	5	0	0	0	4
1937-38	Montreal Maroons	39	5	7	12	21	....	....	....	....	....
	NHL Totals	**140**	**18**	**22**	**40**	**57**	**7**	**0**	**0**	**0**	**6**

Signed as a free agent by **Boston**, November 5, 1930. Traded to **Philadelphia** (Can-Am) by **Boston** for cash, September, 1932. Traded to **Mtl. Maroons** by **Philadelphia** (Can-Am) for cash, November 25, 1933. Traded to **Montreal** (Quebec-Can-Am) by **Mtl. Maroons** for Stan McCabe, December 6, 1933. Traded to **Boston** by **Montreal** for cash, December 24, 1935. Traded to **Montreal** by **Boston** for cash, April, 1936. Traded to **Mtl. Maroons** by **Montreal** for Bill MacKenzie, December 3, 1936. Traded to **Cleveland** (IAHL) by **Mtl. Maroons** for cash, October 3, 1938.

RUOTSALAINEN, Reijo

Defense. Shoots right. 5'8", 170 lbs. Born, Oulu, Finland, April 1, 1960.
(NY Rangers' 5th choice, 119th overall, in 1980 Entry Draft).

Season	Club	GP	G	A	Pts	PIM	GP	G	A	Pts	PIM
1981-82	New York Rangers	78	18	38	56	27	10	4	5	9	2
1982-83	New York Rangers	77	16	53	69	22	9	4	2	6	6
1983-84	New York Rangers	74	20	39	59	26	5	1	1	2	2
1984-85	New York Rangers	80	28	45	73	32	3	2	0	2	6
1985-86	New York Rangers	80	17	42	59	47	16	0	8	8	6
1986-87 ♦	Edmonton Oilers	16	5	8	13	6	21	2	5	7	10
1989-90	New Jersey Devils	31	2	5	7	14	....	....	....	....	....
♦	Edmonton Oilers	10	1	7	8	6	22	2	11	13	12
	NHL Totals	**446**	**107**	**237**	**344**	**180**	**86**	**15**	**32**	**47**	**44**

Played in NHL All-Star Game (1986)

Traded to **Edmonton** by **NY Rangers** with Clark Donatelli, Ville Kentala and Jim Wiemer for Mike Golden, Don Jackson, Miloslav Horava and future considerations (Stu Kulak, March 10, 1987), October 23, 1986. Claimed by **New Jersey** from **Edmonton** in Waiver Draft, October 5, 1987. Traded to **Edmonton** by **New Jersey** for Jeff Sharples, March 6, 1990.

RUPP, Duane

Defense. Shoots left. 6'1", 195 lbs. Born, MacNutt, Sask., March 29, 1938.

Season	Club	GP	G	A	Pts	PIM	GP	G	A	Pts	PIM
1962-63	New York Rangers	2	0	0	0	0	....	....	....	....	....
1964-65	Toronto Maple Leafs	2	0	0	0	0	....	....	....	....	....
1965-66	Toronto Maple Leafs	2	0	1	1	0	....	....	....	....	....
1966-67	Toronto Maple Leafs	3	0	0	0	0	....	....	....	....	....
1967-68	Toronto Maple Leafs	71	1	8	9	42	....	....	....	....	....
1968-69	Minnesota North Stars	29	2	1	3	8	....	....	....	....	....
	Pittsburgh Penguins	30	3	10	13	24	....	....	....	....	....
1969-70	Pittsburgh Penguins	64	2	14	16	18	6	2	2	4	2
1970-71	Pittsburgh Penguins	59	5	28	33	34	....	....	....	....	....
1971-72	Pittsburgh Penguins	34	4	18	22	32	4	0	0	0	6
1972-73	Pittsburgh Penguins	78	7	13	20	62	....	....	....	....	....
	NHL Totals	**374**	**24**	**93**	**117**	**220**	**10**	**2**	**2**	**4**	**8**

Played in NHL All-Star Game (1968)

Loaned to **Toronto** (Rochester-AHL) by **NY Rangers** (Baltimore-AHL) for cash, February 23, 1964. Traded to **Toronto** (Rochester-AHL) by **NY Rangers** with Ed Ehrenverth for Lou Angotti and Ed Lawson, June 25, 1964. Claimed by **Minnesota** from **Toronto** in Intra-League Draft, June 12, 1968. Traded to **Pittsburgh** by **Minnesota** for Leo Boivin, January 24, 1969.

RUPP, Mike

Right wing. Shoots left. 6'5", 235 lbs. Born, Cleveland, OH, January 13, 1980.
(New Jersey's 7th choice, 76th overall, in 2000 Entry Draft).

Season	Club	GP	G	A	Pts	PIM	GP	G	A	Pts	PIM
2002-03 ♦	New Jersey Devils	26	5	3	8	21	4	1	3	4	0
	NHL Totals	**26**	**5**	**3**	**8**	**21**	**4**	**1**	**3**	**4**	**0**

• Re-entered NHL Entry Draft. Originally NY Islanders' 1st choice, 9th overall, in 1998 Entry Draft.

RUSKOWSKI, Terry

Center. Shoots left. 5'10", 178 lbs. Born, Prince Albert, Sask., December 31, 1954.
(Chicago's 4th choice, 70th overall, in 1974 Amateur Draft).

Season	Club	GP	G	A	Pts	PIM	GP	G	A	Pts	PIM
1979-80	Chicago Black Hawks	74	15	55	70	252	4	0	0	0	22
1980-81	Chicago Black Hawks	72	8	51	59	225	3	0	2	2	11
1981-82	Chicago Black Hawks	60	7	30	37	120	11	1	2	3	53
1982-83	Chicago Black Hawks	5	0	2	2	12	....	....	....	....	....
	Los Angeles Kings	71	14	30	44	127	....	....	....	....	....
1983-84	Los Angeles Kings	77	7	25	32	89	....	....	....	....	....
1984-85	Los Angeles Kings	78	16	33	49	144	3	0	2	2	0
1985-86	Pittsburgh Penguins	73	26	37	63	162	....	....	....	....	....
1986-87	Pittsburgh Penguins	70	14	37	51	145	....	....	....	....	....
1987-88	Minnesota North Stars	47	5	12	17	76	....	....	....	....	....
1988-89	Minnesota North Stars	3	1	1	2	2	....	....	....	....	....
	NHL Totals	**630**	**113**	**313**	**426**	**1354**	**21**	**1**	**6**	**7**	**86**

Reclaimed by **Chicago** from **Winnipeg** prior to Expansion Draft, June 9, 1979. Traded to **Los Angeles** by **Chicago** for Larry Goodenough and Los Angeles's 3rd round choice (Trent Yawney) in 1984 Entry Draft, October 24, 1982. Signed as a free agent by **Pittsburgh**, October 3, 1985. Signed as a free agent by **Minnesota**, July, 1987.

RUSSELL, Cam

Defense. Shoots left. 6'4", 200 lbs. Born, Halifax, N.S., January 12, 1969.
(Chicago's 3rd choice, 50th overall, in 1987 Entry Draft).

Season	Club	GP	G	A	Pts	PIM	GP	G	A	Pts	PIM
1989-90	Chicago Blackhawks	19	0	1	1	27	1	0	0	0	0
1990-91	Chicago Blackhawks	3	0	0	0	5	1	0	0	0	0
1991-92	Chicago Blackhawks	19	0	0	0	34	12	0	2	2	2
1992-93	Chicago Blackhawks	67	2	4	6	151	4	0	0	0	0
1993-94	Chicago Blackhawks	67	1	7	8	200	....	....	....	....	....
1994-95	Chicago Blackhawks	33	1	3	4	88	16	0	3	3	8
1995-96	Chicago Blackhawks	61	2	2	4	129	6	0	0	0	2
1996-97	Chicago Blackhawks	44	1	1	2	65	4	0	0	0	4
1997-98	Chicago Blackhawks	41	1	1	2	79	....	....	....	....	....

Season	Club	GP	G	A	Pts	PIM	GP	G	A	Pts	PIM
		REGULAR SEASON					**PLAYOFFS**				
1998-99	Chicago Blackhawks	7	0	0	0	10	....	....	....	....	....
	Colorado Avalanche	35	1	2	3	84	....	....	....	....	....
	NHL Totals	**396**	**9**	**21**	**30**	**872**	**44**	**0**	**5**	**5**	**16**

Traded to **Colorado** by **Chicago** for Roman Vopat and Los Angeles' 6th round choice (previously acquired, later traded to Ottawa – Ottawa selected Martin Prusek) in 1999 Entry Draft, November 10, 1998. • Suffered career-ending torn rotator cuff injury in game vs. Philadelphia, February 14, 1999.

RUSSELL, Church

Left wing/Center. Shoots left. 5'11", 175 lbs. Born, Winnipeg, Man., March 16, 1923.

Season	Club	GP	G	A	Pts	PIM	GP	G	A	Pts	PIM
1945-46	New York Rangers	17	0	5	5	2	....	....	....	....	....
1946-47	New York Rangers	54	20	8	28	8	....	....	....	....	....
1947-48	New York Rangers	19	0	3	3	2	....	....	....	....	....
	NHL Totals	**90**	**20**	**16**	**36**	**12**	....	....	....	....	....

Traded to **Cleveland** (AHL) by **NY Rangers** for George Johnston, December 18, 1947.

RUSSELL, Phil

Defense. Shoots right. 6'2", 205 lbs. Born, Edmonton, Alta., July 21, 1952.
(Chicago's 1st choice, 13th overall, in 1972 Amateur Draft).

Season	Club	GP	G	A	Pts	PIM	GP	G	A	Pts	PIM
1972-73	Chicago Black Hawks	76	6	19	25	156	16	0	3	3	49
1973-74	Chicago Black Hawks	75	10	25	35	184	9	0	1	1	41
1974-75	Chicago Black Hawks	80	5	24	29	260	8	1	3	4	23
1975-76	Chicago Black Hawks	74	9	29	38	194	4	0	1	1	17
1976-77	Chicago Black Hawks	76	9	36	45	233	2	0	1	1	2
1977-78	Chicago Black Hawks	57	6	20	26	139	....	....	....	....	....
1978-79	Chicago Black Hawks	66	8	23	31	122	....	....	....	....	....
	Atlanta Flames	13	1	6	7	28	2	0	0	0	9
1979-80	Atlanta Flames	80	5	31	36	115	4	0	1	1	6
1980-81	Calgary Flames	80	6	23	29	104	16	2	7	9	29
1981-82	Calgary Flames	71	4	25	29	110	3	0	1	1	2
1982-83	Calgary Flames	78	13	18	31	112	9	1	4	5	24
1983-84	New Jersey Devils	76	9	22	31	96	....	....	....	....	....
1984-85	New Jersey Devils	66	4	16	20	110	....	....	....	....	....
1985-86	New Jersey Devils	30	2	3	5	51	....	....	....	....	....
	Buffalo Sabres	12	2	3	5	12	....	....	....	....	....
1986-87	Buffalo Sabres	6	0	2	2	12	....	....	....	....	....
	NHL Totals	**1016**	**99**	**325**	**424**	**2038**	**73**	**4**	**22**	**26**	**202**

Played in NHL All-Star Game (1976, 1977, 1985)

Traded to **Atlanta** by **Chicago** with Ivan Boldirev and Darcy Rota for Tom Lysiak, Pat Ribble, Harold Phillipoff, Greg Fox and Miles Zaharko, March 13, 1979. Transferred to **Calgary** after **Atlanta** franchise relocated, June 24, 1980. Traded to **New Jersey** by **Calgary** with Mel Bridgman for Steve Tambellini and Joel Quenneville, June 20, 1983. Traded to **Buffalo** by **New Jersey** for Buffalo's 12th round choice (Doug Kirton) in 1986 Entry Draft, March 11, 1986.

RUUTTU, Christian

Center. Shoots left. 5'11", 194 lbs. Born, Lappeenranta, Finland, February 20, 1964.
(Buffalo's 9th choice, 139th overall, in 1983 Entry Draft).

Season	Club	GP	G	A	Pts	PIM	GP	G	A	Pts	PIM
1986-87	Buffalo Sabres	76	22	43	65	62	....	....	....	....	....
1987-88	Buffalo Sabres	73	26	45	71	85	6	2	5	7	4
1988-89	Buffalo Sabres	67	14	46	60	98	2	0	0	0	2
1989-90	Buffalo Sabres	75	19	41	60	66	6	0	0	0	4
1990-91	Buffalo Sabres	77	16	34	50	96	6	1	3	4	29
1991-92	Buffalo Sabres	70	4	21	25	76	3	0	0	0	6
1992-93	Chicago Blackhawks	84	17	37	54	134	4	0	0	0	2
1993-94	Chicago Blackhawks	54	9	20	29	68	6	0	0	0	2
1994-95	Chicago Blackhawks	20	2	5	7	6	....	....	....	....	....
	Vancouver Canucks	25	5	6	11	23	9	1	1	2	0
	NHL Totals	**621**	**134**	**298**	**432**	**714**	**42**	**4**	**9**	**13**	**49**

Played in NHL All-Star Game (1988)

Traded to **Winnipeg** by **Buffalo** with future considerations for Stephane Beauregard, June 15, 1992. Traded to **Chicago** by **Winnipeg** for Stephane Beauregard, August 10, 1992. Traded to **Vancouver** by **Chicago** for Murray Craven, March 10, 1995.

RUUTU, Jarkko

Right wing. Shoots left. 6'2", 194 lbs. Born, Vantaa, Finland, August 23, 1975.
(Vancouver's 3rd choice, 68th overall, in 1998 Entry Draft).

Season	Club	GP	G	A	Pts	PIM	GP	G	A	Pts	PIM
99-2000	Vancouver Canucks	8	0	1	1	6	....	....	....	....	....
2000-01	Vancouver Canucks	21	3	3	6	32	4	0	1	1	8
2001-02	Vancouver Canucks	49	2	7	9	74	1	0	0	0	0
2002-03	Vancouver Canucks	36	2	2	4	66	13	0	2	2	14
	NHL Totals	**114**	**7**	**13**	**20**	**178**	**18**	**0**	**3**	**3**	**22**

RUZICKA, Vladimir

Center. Shoots left. 6'3", 215 lbs. Born, Most, Czech., June 6, 1963.
(Toronto's 5th choice, 73rd overall, in 1982 Entry Draft).

Season	Club	GP	G	A	Pts	PIM	GP	G	A	Pts	PIM
1989-90	Edmonton Oilers	25	11	6	17	10	....	....	....	....	....
1990-91	Boston Bruins	29	8	8	16	19	17	2	11	13	0
1991-92	Boston Bruins	77	39	36	75	48	13	2	3	5	2
1992-93	Boston Bruins	60	19	22	41	38	....	....	....	....	....
1993-94	Ottawa Senators	42	5	13	18	14	....	....	....	....	....
	NHL Totals	**233**	**82**	**85**	**167**	**129**	**30**	**4**	**14**	**18**	**2**

Traded to **Edmonton** by **Toronto** for Edmonton's 4th round choice (Greg Walters) in 1990 Entry Draft, December 21, 1989. Traded to **Boston** by **Edmonton** for Greg Hawgood, October 22, 1990. Signed as a free agent by **Ottawa**, August 12, 1993.

RYAN, Terry

Left wing. Shoots left. 6'1", 202 lbs. Born, St. John's, Nfld., January 14, 1977.
(Montreal's 1st choice, 8th overall, in 1995 Entry Draft).

Season	Club	GP	G	A	Pts	PIM	GP	G	A	Pts	PIM
1996-97	Montreal Canadiens	3	0	0	0	0	....	....	....	....	....
1997-98	Montreal Canadiens	4	0	0	0	31	....	....	....	....	....
1998-99	Montreal Canadiens	1	0	0	0	5	....	....	....	....	....
	NHL Totals	**8**	**0**	**0**	**0**	**36**	....	....	....	....	....

RYCHEL, Warren

Left wing. Shoots left. 6', 205 lbs. Born, Tecumseh, Ont., May 12, 1967.

Season	Club	GP	G	A	Pts	PIM	GP	G	A	Pts	PIM
1988-89	Chicago Blackhawks	2	0	0	0	17	....	....	....	....	....
1990-91	Chicago Blackhawks	....	....	....	....	....	3	1	3	4	2
1992-93	Los Angeles Kings	70	6	7	13	314	23	6	7	13	39
1993-94	Los Angeles Kings	80	10	9	19	322	....	....	....	....	....
1994-95	Los Angeles Kings	7	0	0	0	19	....	....	....	....	....
	Toronto Maple Leafs	26	1	6	7	101	3	0	0	0	0
1995-96♦	Colorado Avalanche	52	6	2	8	147	12	1	0	1	23
1996-97	Mighty Ducks of Anaheim	70	10	7	17	218	11	0	2	2	19
1997-98	Mighty Ducks of Anaheim	63	5	6	11	198	....	....	....	....	....
	Colorado Avalanche	8	0	0	0	23	6	0	0	0	24
1998-99	Colorado Avalanche	28	0	2	2	63	12	0	1	1	14
	NHL Totals	**406**	**38**	**39**	**77**	**1422**	**70**	**8**	**13**	**21**	**121**

Signed as a free agent by **Chicago**, September 19, 1986. Traded to **Winnipeg** by **Chicago** with Troy Murray for Bryan Marchment and Chris Norton, July 22, 1991. Traded to **Minnesota** by **Winnipeg** for Tony Joseph, December 30, 1991. Signed as a free agent by **Los Angeles**, October 1, 1992. Traded to **Washington** by **Los Angeles** for Randy Burridge, February 10, 1995. Traded to **Toronto** by **Washington** for Toronto's 4th round choice (Sebastien Charpentier) in 1995 Entry Draft, February 10, 1995. Traded to **Colorado** by **Toronto** for cash, October 2, 1995. Signed as a free agent by **Anaheim**, August 21, 1996. Traded to **Colorado** by **Anaheim** with future considerations for Josef Marha, March 24, 1998.

RYCROFT, Mark

Right wing. Shoots right. 5'11", 197 lbs. Born, Nanaimo, B.C., July 12, 1978.

Season	Club	GP	G	A	Pts	PIM	GP	G	A	Pts	PIM
2001-02	St. Louis Blues	9	0	3	3	4	....	....	....	....	....
	NHL Totals	**9**	**0**	**3**	**3**	**4**	....	....	....	....	....

Signed as a free agent by **St. Louis**, May 15, 2000.

RYMSHA, Andy

Defense. Shoots left. 6'3", 210 lbs. Born, St. Catharines, Ont., December 10, 1968.
(St. Louis' 5th choice, 82nd overall, in 1987 Entry Draft).

Season	Club	GP	G	A	Pts	PIM	GP	G	A	Pts	PIM
1991-92	Quebec Nordiques	6	0	0	0	23	....	....	....	....	....
	NHL Totals	**6**	**0**	**0**	**0**	**23**	....	....	....	....	....

Traded to **Quebec** by **St. Louis** with Tony Twist and Herb Raglan for Darin Kimble, February 4, 1991.

SAARINEN, Simo

Defense. Shoots left. 5'8", 185 lbs. Born, Helsinki, Finland, February 14, 1963.
(NY Rangers' 10th choice, 193rd overall, in 1982 Entry Draft).

Season	Club	GP	G	A	Pts	PIM	GP	G	A	Pts	PIM
1984-85	New York Rangers	8	0	0	0	0	....	....	....	....	....
	NHL Totals	**8**	**0**	**0**	**0**	**0**	....	....	....	....	....

SABOL, Shaun

Defense. Shoots left. 6'3", 230 lbs. Born, Minneapolis, MN, July 13, 1966.
(Philadelphia's 9th choice, 209th overall, in 1986 Entry Draft).

Season	Club	GP	G	A	Pts	PIM	GP	G	A	Pts	PIM
1989-90	Philadelphia Flyers	2	0	0	0	0	....	....	....	....	....
	NHL Totals	**2**	**0**	**0**	**0**	**0**	....	....	....	....	....

Traded to **NY Rangers** by **Philadelphia** for future considerations, August 5, 1991.

SABOURIN, Bob

Left wing. Shoots left. 5'9", 177 lbs. Born, Sudbury, Ont., March 17, 1933.

Season	Club	GP	G	A	Pts	PIM	GP	G	A	Pts	PIM
1951-52	Toronto Maple Leafs	1	0	0	0	2	....	....	....	....	....
	NHL Totals	**1**	**0**	**0**	**0**	**2**	....	....	....	....	....

Loaned to **Toronto** by **St. Michael's** (OHA-Jr.) as an emergency injury replacement, March 13, 1952. Traded to **Springfield** (AHL) by **Toronto** (Pittsburgh-AHL) with Bob Bailey for $11,000, May 28, 1956.

SABOURIN, Gary

Right wing. Shoots right. 5'11", 180 lbs. Born, Parry Sound, Ont., December 4, 1943.

Season	Club	GP	G	A	Pts	PIM	GP	G	A	Pts	PIM
1967-68	St. Louis Blues	50	13	10	23	50	18	4	2	6	30
1968-69	St. Louis Blues	75	25	23	48	58	12	6	5	11	12
1969-70	St. Louis Blues	72	28	14	42	61	16	5	0	5	10
1970-71	St. Louis Blues	59	14	17	31	56	....	....	....	....	....
1971-72	St. Louis Blues	77	28	17	45	52	11	3	3	6	6
1972-73	St. Louis Blues	76	21	27	48	30	5	1	1	2	0
1973-74	St. Louis Blues	54	7	23	30	27	....	....	....	....	....
1974-75	Toronto Maple Leafs	55	5	18	23	26	....	....	....	....	....
1975-76	California Golden Seals	76	21	28	49	33	....	....	....	....	....
1976-77	Cleveland Barons	33	7	11	18	4	....	....	....	....	....
	NHL Totals	**627**	**169**	**188**	**357**	**397**	**62**	**19**	**11**	**30**	**58**

Played in NHL All-Star Game (1970, 1971)

Traded to **St. Louis** by **NY Rangers** with Bob Plager, Gord Kannegiesser and Tim Ecclestone for Rod Seiling, June 6, 1967. Traded to **Toronto** by **St. Louis** for Eddie Johnston, May 27, 1974. Traded to **California** by **Toronto** for Stan Weir, June 20, 1975. Transferred to **Cleveland** after **California** franchise relocated, August 26, 1976.

SABOURIN, Ken

Defense. Shoots left. 6'3", 205 lbs. Born, Scarborough, Ont., April 28, 1966.
(Calgary's 2nd choice, 33rd overall, in 1984 Entry Draft).

Season	Club	Regular Season GP	G	A	Pts	PIM	Playoffs GP	G	A	Pts	PIM
1988-89	Calgary Flames	6	0	1	1	26	1	0	0	0	0
1989-90	Calgary Flames	5	0	0	0	10	....	....	....	....	....
1990-91	Calgary Flames	16	1	3	4	36	....	....	....	....	....
	Washington Capitals	28	1	4	5	81	11	0	0	0	34
1991-92	Washington Capitals	19	0	0	0	48	....	....	....	....	....
	NHL Totals	**74**	**2**	**8**	**10**	**201**	**12**	**0**	**0**	**0**	**34**

Traded to **Washington** by **Calgary** for Paul Fenton, January 24, 1991. Traded to **Calgary** by **Washington** for future considerations, December 16, 1992. Traded to **Quebec** by **Washington** with Paul MacDermid for Mike Hough, January 20, 1993.

SACCO, David

Right wing. Shoots right. 6', 180 lbs. Born, Malden, MA, July 31, 1970.
(Toronto's 9th choice, 195th overall, in 1988 Entry Draft).

Season	Club	Regular Season GP	G	A	Pts	PIM	Playoffs GP	G	A	Pts	PIM
1993-94	Toronto Maple Leafs	4	1	1	2	4	....	....	....	....	....
1994-95	Mighty Ducks of Anaheim	8	0	2	2	0	....	....	....	....	....
1995-96	Mighty Ducks of Anaheim	23	4	10	14	18	....	....	....	....	....
	NHL Totals	**35**	**5**	**13**	**18**	**22**	....	....	....	....	....

• Brother of Joe

Traded to **Anaheim** by **Toronto** for Terry Yake, September 28, 1994. Signed as a free agent by **NY Islanders**, September 6, 1996.

SACCO, Joe

Right wing. Shoots left. 6'1", 190 lbs. Born, Medford, MA, February 4, 1969.
(Toronto's 4th choice, 71st overall, in 1987 Entry Draft).

Season	Club	Regular Season GP	G	A	Pts	PIM	Playoffs GP	G	A	Pts	PIM
1990-91	Toronto Maple Leafs	20	0	5	5	2	....	....	....	....	....
1991-92	Toronto Maple Leafs	17	7	4	11	4	....	....	....	....	....
1992-93	Toronto Maple Leafs	23	4	4	8	8	....	....	....	....	....
1993-94	Mighty Ducks of Anaheim	84	19	18	37	61	....	....	....	....	....
1994-95	Mighty Ducks of Anaheim	41	10	8	18	23	....	....	....	....	....
1995-96	Mighty Ducks of Anaheim	76	13	14	27	40	....	....	....	....	....
1996-97	Mighty Ducks of Anaheim	77	12	17	29	35	11	2	0	2	2
1997-98	Mighty Ducks of Anaheim	55	8	11	19	24	....	....	....	....	....
	New York Islanders	25	3	3	6	10	....	....	....	....	....
1998-99	New York Islanders	73	3	0	3	45	....	....	....	....	....
99-2000	Washington Capitals	79	7	16	23	50	5	0	0	0	4
2000-01	Washington Capitals	69	7	7	14	48	6	0	0	0	2
2001-02	Washington Capitals	65	0	7	7	51	....	....	....	....	....
2002-03	Philadelphia Flyers	34	1	5	6	20	4	0	0	0	0
	NHL Totals	**738**	**94**	**119**	**213**	**421**	**26**	**2**	**0**	**2**	**8**

• Brother of David

Claimed by **Anaheim** from **Toronto** in Expansion Draft, June 24, 1993. Traded to **NY Islanders** by **Anaheim** with J.J. Daigneault and Mark Janssens for Travis Green, Doug Houda and Tony Tuzzolino, February 6, 1998. Signed as a free agent by **Washington**, August 9, 1999. Signed as a free agent by **Philadelphia**, January 15, 2003.

SACHARUK, Larry

Defense. Shoots right. 6', 200 lbs. Born, Saskatoon, Sask., September 16, 1952.
(NY Rangers' 3rd choice, 21st overall, in 1972 Amateur Draft).

Season	Club	Regular Season GP	G	A	Pts	PIM	Playoffs GP	G	A	Pts	PIM
1972-73	New York Rangers	8	1	0	1	0	....	....	....	....	....
1973-74	New York Rangers	23	2	4	6	4	....	....	....	....	....
1974-75	St. Louis Blues	76	20	22	42	24	2	1	1	2	2
1975-76	New York Rangers	42	6	7	13	14	....	....	....	....	....
1976-77	New York Rangers	2	0	0	0	0	....	....	....	....	....
	NHL Totals	**151**	**29**	**33**	**62**	**42**	**2**	**1**	**1**	**2**	**2**

Traded to **NY Rangers** by **St. Louis** for Bob MacMillan, September 20, 1975. Traded to **St. Louis** by **NY Rangers** with NY Rangers' 1st round choice (later traded back to NY Rangers – NY Rangers selected Lucien DeBlois) in 1977 Amateur Draft for Greg Polis, August 29, 1974.

SAFRONOV, Kirill

Defense. Shoots left. 6'1", 210 lbs. Born, Leningrad, USSR, February 26, 1981.
(Phoenix's 2nd choice, 19th overall, in 1999 Entry Draft).

Season	Club	Regular Season GP	G	A	Pts	PIM	Playoffs GP	G	A	Pts	PIM
2001-02	Phoenix Coyotes	1	0	0	0	0	....	....	....	....	....
	Atlanta Thrashers	2	0	0	0	2	....	....	....	....	....
2002-03	Atlanta Thrashers	32	2	2	4	14	....	....	....	....	....
	NHL Totals	**35**	**2**	**2**	**4**	**16**	....	....	....	....	....

Traded to **Atlanta** by **Phoenix** with the rights to Ruslan Zainullin and Phoenix's 5th round choice (Patrick Dwyer) in 2002 Entry Draft for Darcy Hordichuk and Atlanta's 4th (Lance Monych) and 5th (John Zeiler) round choices in 2002 Entry Draft, March 19, 2002.

SAGANIUK, Rocky

Right wing/Center. Shoots right. 5'8", 185 lbs. Born, Myrnam, Alta., October 15, 1957.
(Toronto's 4th choice, 29th overall, in 1977 Amateur Draft).

Season	Club	Regular Season GP	G	A	Pts	PIM	Playoffs GP	G	A	Pts	PIM
1978-79	Toronto Maple Leafs	16	3	5	8	9	3	1	0	1	5
1979-80	Toronto Maple Leafs	75	24	23	47	52	3	0	0	0	10
1980-81	Toronto Maple Leafs	71	12	18	30	52	....	....	....	....	....
1981-82	Toronto Maple Leafs	65	17	16	33	49	....	....	....	....	....
1982-83	Toronto Maple Leafs	3	0	0	0	2	....	....	....	....	....
1983-84	Pittsburgh Penguins	29	1	3	4	37	....	....	....	....	....
	NHL Totals	**259**	**57**	**65**	**122**	**201**	**6**	**1**	**0**	**1**	**15**

Traded to **Pittsburgh** by **Toronto** with Vincent Tremblay for Pat Graham and Nick Ricci, August 15, 1983. Signed as a free agent by **Toronto**, August 21, 1984.

ST. AMOUR, Martin

Left wing. Shoots left. 6'3", 194 lbs. Born, Montreal, Que., January 30, 1970.
(Montreal's 2nd choice, 34th overall, in 1988 Entry Draft).

Season	Club	Regular Season GP	G	A	Pts	PIM	Playoffs GP	G	A	Pts	PIM
1992-93	Ottawa Senators	1	0	0	0	2	....	....	....	....	....
	NHL Totals	**1**	**0**	**0**	**0**	**2**	....	....	....	....	....

Signed as a free agent by **Ottawa**, July 16, 1992.

ST. JACQUES, Bruno

Defense. Shoots left. 6'2", 210 lbs. Born, Montreal, Que., August 22, 1980.
(Philadelphia's 12th choice, 253rd overall, in 1998 Entry Draft).

Season	Club	Regular Season GP	G	A	Pts	PIM	Playoffs GP	G	A	Pts	PIM
2001-02	Philadelphia Flyers	7	0	0	0	2	....	....	....	....	....
2002-03	Philadelphia Flyers	6	0	0	0	2	....	....	....	....	....
	Carolina Hurricanes	18	2	5	7	12	....	....	....	....	....
	NHL Totals	**31**	**2**	**5**	**7**	**16**	....	....	....	....	....

Traded to **Carolina** by **Philadelphia** with Pavel Brendl for Sami Kapanen and Ryan Bast, February 7, 2003.

ST. LAURENT, Andre

Center. Shoots right. 5'10", 180 lbs. Born, Rouyn, Que., February 16, 1953.
(NY Islanders' 3rd choice, 49th overall, in 1973 Amateur Draft).

Season	Club	Regular Season GP	G	A	Pts	PIM	Playoffs GP	G	A	Pts	PIM
1973-74	New York Islanders	42	5	9	14	18	....	....	....	....	....
1974-75	New York Islanders	78	14	27	41	60	15	2	2	4	6
1975-76	New York Islanders	67	9	17	26	56	13	1	5	6	15
1976-77	New York Islanders	72	10	13	23	55	12	1	2	3	6
1977-78	New York Islanders	2	0	0	0	2	....	....	....	....	....
	Detroit Red Wings	77	31	39	70	108	7	1	1	2	4
1978-79	Detroit Red Wings	76	18	31	49	124	....	....	....	....	....
1979-80	Los Angeles Kings	77	6	24	30	88	4	1	0	1	0
1980-81	Los Angeles Kings	22	10	6	16	63	3	0	1	1	9
1981-82	Los Angeles Kings	16	2	4	6	28	....	....	....	....	....
	Pittsburgh Penguins	18	8	5	13	4	5	2	1	3	8
1982-83	Pittsburgh Penguins	70	13	9	22	105	....	....	....	....	....
1983-84	Pittsburgh Penguins	8	2	0	2	21	....	....	....	....	....
	Detroit Red Wings	19	1	3	4	17	....	....	....	....	....
	NHL Totals	**644**	**129**	**187**	**316**	**749**	**59**	**8**	**12**	**20**	**48**

Traded to **Detroit** by **NY Islanders** for Michel Bergeron, October 20, 1977. Traded to **Los Angeles** by **Detroit** with Detroit's 1st round choices in 1980 (Larry Murphy) and 1981 (Doug Smith) Entry Drafts for Dale McCourt, August 22, 1979. Claimed on waivers by **Pittsburgh** from **Los Angeles**, February 23, 1982. Traded to **Detroit** by **Pittsburgh** for future considerations October 24, 1983.

ST. LAURENT, Dollard

Defense. Shoots left. 5'11", 175 lbs. Born, Verdun, Que., May 12, 1929.

Season	Club	Regular Season GP	G	A	Pts	PIM	Playoffs GP	G	A	Pts	PIM
1950-51	Montreal Canadiens	3	0	0	0	0	....	....	....	....	....
1951-52	Montreal Canadiens	40	3	10	13	30	9	0	3	3	6
1952-53 ♦	Montreal Canadiens	54	2	6	8	34	12	0	3	3	4
1953-54	Montreal Canadiens	53	3	12	15	43	10	1	2	3	8
1954-55	Montreal Canadiens	58	3	14	17	24	12	0	5	5	12
1955-56 ♦	Montreal Canadiens	46	4	9	13	58	4	0	0	0	2
1956-57 ♦	Montreal Canadiens	64	1	11	12	49	7	0	1	1	13
1957-58 ♦	Montreal Canadiens	65	3	20	23	68	5	0	0	0	10
1958-59	Chicago Black Hawks	70	4	8	12	28	6	0	1	1	2
1959-60	Chicago Black Hawks	68	4	13	17	60	4	0	1	1	0
1960-61 ♦	Chicago Black Hawks	67	2	17	19	58	11	1	2	3	12
1961-62	Chicago Black Hawks	64	0	13	13	44	12	0	4	4	18
	NHL Totals	**652**	**29**	**133**	**162**	**496**	**92**	**2**	**22**	**24**	**87**

Played in NHL All-Star Game (1953, 1956, 1957, 1958, 1961)

Traded to **Chicago** by **Montreal** for cash and future considerations (the loan of Norm Johnson, February 20, 1959), June 3, 1958. Traded to **Quebec** (AHL) by **Chicago** for cash, September 6, 1962.

ST. LOUIS, Martin

Right wing. Shoots left. 5'9", 185 lbs. Born, Laval, Que., June 18, 1975.

Season	Club	Regular Season GP	G	A	Pts	PIM	Playoffs GP	G	A	Pts	PIM
1998-99	Calgary Flames	13	1	1	2	10	....	....	....	....	....
99-2000	Calgary Flames	56	3	15	18	22	....	....	....	....	....
2000-01	Tampa Bay Lightning	78	18	22	40	12	....	....	....	....	....
2001-02	Tampa Bay Lightning	53	16	19	35	20	....	....	....	....	....
2002-03	Tampa Bay Lightning	82	33	37	70	32	11	7	5	12	0
	NHL Totals	**282**	**71**	**94**	**165**	**96**	**11**	**7**	**5**	**12**	**0**

Played in NHL All-Star Game (2003)

Signed as a free agent by **Calgary**, February 19, 1998. Signed as a free agent by **Tampa Bay**, July 31, 2000.

ST. MARSEILLE, Frank

Right wing. Shoots right. 5'11", 180 lbs. Born, Levack, Ont., December 14, 1939.

Season	Club	Regular Season GP	G	A	Pts	PIM	Playoffs GP	G	A	Pts	PIM
1967-68	St. Louis Blues	57	16	16	32	12	18	5	8	13	0
1968-69	St. Louis Blues	72	12	26	38	22	12	3	3	6	2
1969-70	St. Louis Blues	74	16	43	59	18	15	6	7	13	4
1970-71	St. Louis Blues	77	19	32	51	26	6	2	1	3	4
1971-72	St. Louis Blues	78	16	36	52	32	11	3	5	8	6
1972-73	St. Louis Blues	45	7	18	25	8	....	....	....	....	....
	Los Angeles Kings	29	7	4	11	2	....	....	....	....	....
1973-74	Los Angeles Kings	78	14	36	50	40	5	0	0	0	0
1974-75	Los Angeles Kings	80	17	36	53	46	3	0	1	1	0

Season	Club	Regular Season GP	G	A	Pts	PIM	Playoffs GP	G	A	Pts	PIM
1975-76	Los Angeles Kings	68	10	16	26	20	9	0	0	0	0
1976-77	Los Angeles Kings	49	6	22	28	16	9	1	0	1	2
	NHL Totals	**707**	**140**	**285**	**425**	**242**	**88**	**20**	**25**	**45**	**18**

Played in NHL All-Star Game (1970)

Signed as a free agent by **St. Louis**, November 23, 1967. Traded to **Los Angeles** by **St. Louis** for Paul Curtis, January 22, 1973.

ST. SAUVEUR, Claude

Center. Shoots left. 6'1", 185 lbs. Born, Sherbrooke, Que., January 2, 1952.
(California's 4th choice, 54th overall, in 1972 Amateur Draft).

Season	Club	Regular Season GP	G	A	Pts	PIM	Playoffs GP	G	A	Pts	PIM
1975-76	Atlanta Flames	79	24	24	48	23	2	0	0	0	0
	NHL Totals	**79**	**24**	**24**	**48**	**23**	**2**	**0**	**0**	**0**	**0**

Traded to **Atlanta** by **California** for cash, September 23, 1975.

SAKIC, Joe

Center. Shoots left. 5'11", 195 lbs. Born, Burnaby, B.C., July 7, 1969.
(Quebec's 2nd choice, 15th overall, in 1987 Entry Draft).

Season	Club	Regular Season GP	G	A	Pts	PIM	Playoffs GP	G	A	Pts	PIM
1988-89	Quebec Nordiques	70	23	39	62	24	....	....	....	....	....
1989-90	Quebec Nordiques	80	39	63	102	27	....	....	....	....	....
1990-91	Quebec Nordiques	80	48	61	109	24	....	....	....	....	....
1991-92	Quebec Nordiques	69	29	65	94	20	....	....	....	....	....
1992-93	Quebec Nordiques	78	48	57	105	40	6	3	3	6	2
1993-94	Quebec Nordiques	84	28	64	92	18	....	....	....	....	....
1994-95	Quebec Nordiques	47	19	43	62	30	6	4	1	5	0
1995-96 ♦	Colorado Avalanche	82	51	69	120	44	22	*18	16	*34	14
1996-97	Colorado Avalanche	65	22	52	74	34	17	8	*17	25	14
1997-98	Colorado Avalanche	64	27	36	63	50	6	2	3	5	6
1998-99	Colorado Avalanche	73	41	55	96	29	19	6	13	19	8
99-2000	Colorado Avalanche	60	28	53	81	28	17	2	7	9	8
2000-01 ♦	Colorado Avalanche	82	54	64	118	30	21	*13	13	*26	6
2001-02	Colorado Avalanche	82	26	53	79	18	21	9	10	19	4
2002-03	Colorado Avalanche	58	26	32	58	24	7	6	3	9	2
	NHL Totals	**1074**	**509**	**806**	**1315**	**440**	**142**	**71**	**86**	**157**	**64**

Conn Smythe Trophy (1996) • NHL First All-Star Team (2001, 2002) • Lady Byng Trophy (2001) • Hart Trophy (2001) • Lester B. Pearson Award (2001)

Played in NHL All-Star Game (1990, 1991, 1992, 1993, 1994, 1996, 1998, 2000, 2001, 2002)

Transferred to **Colorado** after **Quebec** franchise relocated, June 21, 1995.

SALEI, Ruslan

Defense. Shoots left. 6'1", 205 lbs. Born, Minsk, USSR, November 2, 1974.
(Anaheim's 1st choice, 9th overall, in 1996 Entry Draft).

Season	Club	Regular Season GP	G	A	Pts	PIM	Playoffs GP	G	A	Pts	PIM
1996-97	Mighty Ducks of Anaheim	30	0	1	1	37	....	....	....	....	....
1997-98	Mighty Ducks of Anaheim	66	5	10	15	70	....	....	....	....	....
1998-99	Mighty Ducks of Anaheim	74	2	14	16	65	3	0	0	0	4
99-2000	Mighty Ducks of Anaheim	71	5	5	10	94	....	....	....	....	....
2000-01	Mighty Ducks of Anaheim	50	1	5	6	70	....	....	....	....	....
2001-02	Mighty Ducks of Anaheim	82	4	7	11	97	....	....	....	....	....
2002-03	Mighty Ducks of Anaheim	61	4	8	12	78	21	2	3	5	26
	NHL Totals	**434**	**21**	**50**	**71**	**511**	**24**	**2**	**3**	**5**	**30**

SALESKI, Don

Right wing. Shoots right. 6'3", 205 lbs. Born, Moose Jaw, Sask., November 10, 1949.
(Philadelphia's 6th choice, 64th overall, in 1969 Amateur Draft).

Season	Club	Regular Season GP	G	A	Pts	PIM	Playoffs GP	G	A	Pts	PIM
1971-72	Philadelphia Flyers	1	0	0	0	0	....	....	....	....	....
1972-73	Philadelphia Flyers	78	12	9	21	205	11	1	2	3	4
1973-74 ♦	Philadelphia Flyers	77	15	25	40	131	17	2	7	9	24
1974-75 ♦	Philadelphia Flyers	63	10	18	28	107	17	2	3	5	25
1975-76	Philadelphia Flyers	78	21	26	47	68	16	6	5	11	47
1976-77	Philadelphia Flyers	74	22	16	38	33	10	0	0	0	12
1977-78	Philadelphia Flyers	70	27	18	45	44	11	2	0	2	19
1978-79	Philadelphia Flyers	35	11	5	16	14	....	....	....	....	....
	Colorado Rockies	16	2	0	2	4	....	....	....	....	....
1979-80	Colorado Rockies	51	8	8	16	23	....	....	....	....	....
	NHL Totals	**543**	**128**	**125**	**253**	**629**	**82**	**13**	**17**	**30**	**131**

Traded to **Colorado** by **Philadelphia** for future considerations, March 3, 1979.

SALMING, Borje

HHOF

Defense. Shoots left. 6'1", 193 lbs. Born, Kiruna, Sweden, April 17, 1951.

Season	Club	Regular Season GP	G	A	Pts	PIM	Playoffs GP	G	A	Pts	PIM
1973-74	Toronto Maple Leafs	76	5	34	39	48	4	0	1	1	4
1974-75	Toronto Maple Leafs	60	12	25	37	34	7	0	4	4	6
1975-76	Toronto Maple Leafs	78	16	41	57	70	10	3	4	7	9
1976-77	Toronto Maple Leafs	76	12	66	78	46	9	3	6	9	6
1977-78	Toronto Maple Leafs	80	16	60	76	70	6	2	2	4	6
1978-79	Toronto Maple Leafs	78	17	56	73	76	6	0	1	1	8
1979-80	Toronto Maple Leafs	74	19	52	71	94	3	1	1	2	2
1980-81	Toronto Maple Leafs	72	5	61	66	154	3	0	2	2	4
1981-82	Toronto Maple Leafs	69	12	44	56	170	....	....	....	....	....
1982-83	Toronto Maple Leafs	69	7	38	45	104	4	1	4	5	10
1983-84	Toronto Maple Leafs	68	5	38	43	92	....	....	....	....	....
1984-85	Toronto Maple Leafs	73	6	33	39	76	....	....	....	....	....
1985-86	Toronto Maple Leafs	41	7	15	22	48	10	1	6	7	14
1986-87	Toronto Maple Leafs	56	4	16	20	42	13	0	3	3	14
1987-88	Toronto Maple Leafs	66	2	24	26	82	6	1	3	4	8
1988-89	Toronto Maple Leafs	63	3	17	20	86	....	....	....	....	....

Season	Club	Regular Season GP	G	A	Pts	PIM	Playoffs GP	G	A	Pts	PIM
1989-90	Detroit Red Wings	49	2	17	19	52	....	....	....	....	....
	NHL Totals	**1148**	**150**	**637**	**787**	**1344**	**81**	**12**	**37**	**49**	**91**

NHL Second All-Star Team (1975, 1976, 1978, 1979, 1980) • NHL First All-Star Team (1977)

Played in NHL All-Star Game (1976, 1977, 1978)

Signed as a free agent by **Toronto**, May 12, 1973. Signed as a free agent by **Detroit**, June 12, 1989.

SALO, Sami

Defense. Shoots right. 6'3", 215 lbs. Born, Turku, Finland, September 2, 1974.
(Ottawa's 7th choice, 239th overall, in 1996 Entry Draft).

Season	Club	Regular Season GP	G	A	Pts	PIM	Playoffs GP	G	A	Pts	PIM
1998-99	Ottawa Senators	61	7	12	19	24	4	0	0	0	0
99-2000	Ottawa Senators	37	6	8	14	2	6	1	1	2	0
2000-01	Ottawa Senators	31	2	16	18	10	4	0	0	0	0
2001-02	Ottawa Senators	66	4	14	18	14	12	2	1	3	4
2002-03	Vancouver Canucks	79	9	21	30	10	12	1	3	4	0
	NHL Totals	**274**	**28**	**71**	**99**	**60**	**38**	**4**	**5**	**9**	**4**

NHL All-Rookie Team (1999)

• Missed majority of 1999-2000 season recovering from wrist injury suffered in game vs. Philadelphia, November 28, 1999. • Missed majority of 2000-01 season recovering from shoulder injury suffered in game vs. Atlanta, December 14, 2000. Traded to **Vancouver** by **Ottawa** for Peter Schaefer, September 21, 2002.

SALOMONSSON, Andreas

Right wing. Shoots left. 6'1", 200 lbs. Born, Ornskoldsvik, Sweden, December 19, 1973.
(New Jersey's 8th choice, 163rd overall, in 2001 Entry Draft).

Season	Club	Regular Season GP	G	A	Pts	PIM	Playoffs GP	G	A	Pts	PIM
2001-02	New Jersey Devils	39	4	5	9	22	4	0	1	1	0
2002-03	Washington Capitals	32	1	4	5	14	....	....	....	....	....
	NHL Totals	**71**	**5**	**9**	**14**	**36**	**4**	**0**	**1**	**1**	**0**

Claimed on waivers by **Washington** from **New Jersey**, October 15, 2002.

SALOVAARA, Barry

Defense. Shoots right. 5'10", 180 lbs. Born, Cooksville, Ont., January 7, 1948.

Season	Club	Regular Season GP	G	A	Pts	PIM	Playoffs GP	G	A	Pts	PIM
1974-75	Detroit Red Wings	27	0	2	2	18	....	....	....	....	....
1975-76	Detroit Red Wings	63	2	11	13	52	....	....	....	....	....
	NHL Totals	**90**	**2**	**13**	**15**	**70**	....	....	....	....	....

Traded to **Detroit** (Tidewater-AHL) by **Chicago** (Greensboro-EHL) for cash, June 15, 1971.

SALVADOR, Bryce

Defense. Shoots left. 6'2", 215 lbs. Born, Brandon, Man., February 11, 1976.
(Tampa Bay's 6th choice, 138th overall, in 1994 Entry Draft).

Season	Club	Regular Season GP	G	A	Pts	PIM	Playoffs GP	G	A	Pts	PIM
2000-01	St. Louis Blues	75	2	8	10	69	14	2	0	2	18
2001-02	St. Louis Blues	66	5	7	12	78	10	0	1	1	4
2002-03	St. Louis Blues	71	2	8	10	95	7	0	0	0	2
	NHL Totals	**212**	**9**	**23**	**32**	**242**	**31**	**2**	**1**	**3**	**24**

Signed as a free agent by **St. Louis**, December 16, 1996.

SALVIAN, Dave

Right wing. Shoots left. 5'10", 170 lbs. Born, Toronto, Ont., September 9, 1955.
(NY Islanders' 2nd choice, 29th overall, in 1975 Amateur Draft).

Season	Club	Regular Season GP	G	A	Pts	PIM	Playoffs GP	G	A	Pts	PIM
1976-77	New York Islanders	....	....	....	....	....	1	0	1	1	2
	NHL Totals	....	....	....	....	....	**1**	**0**	**1**	**1**	**2**

SAMIS, Phil

Defense. Shoots right. 5'9", 180 lbs. Born, Edmonton, Alta., December 28, 1927.

Season	Club	Regular Season GP	G	A	Pts	PIM	Playoffs GP	G	A	Pts	PIM
1947-48 ♦	Toronto Maple Leafs	....	....	....	....	....	5	0	1	1	2
1949-50	Toronto Maple Leafs	2	0	0	0	0	....	....	....	....	....
	NHL Totals	**2**	**0**	**0**	**0**	**0**	**5**	**0**	**1**	**1**	**2**

Traded to **Cleveland** (AHL) by **Toronto** with Eric Pogue and the rights to Bob Shropshire to complete transaction that sent Al Rollins to Toronto (November 29, 1949), April 6, 1950

SAMPSON, Gary

Left wing. Shoots left. 6', 190 lbs. Born, Atikokan, Ont., August 24, 1959.

Season	Club	Regular Season GP	G	A	Pts	PIM	Playoffs GP	G	A	Pts	PIM
1983-84	Washington Capitals	15	1	1	2	6	8	1	0	1	0
1984-85	Washington Capitals	46	10	15	25	13	4	0	0	0	0
1985-86	Washington Capitals	19	1	4	5	2	....	....	....	....	....
1986-87	Washington Capitals	25	1	2	3	4	....	....	....	....	....
	NHL Totals	**105**	**13**	**22**	**35**	**25**	**12**	**1**	**0**	**1**	**0**

Signed as a free agent by **Washington**, February 21, 1984.

SAMSONOV, Sergei

Left wing. Shoots right. 5'8", 180 lbs. Born, Moscow, USSR, October 27, 1978.
(Boston's 2nd choice, 8th overall, in 1997 Entry Draft).

Season	Club	Regular Season GP	G	A	Pts	PIM	Playoffs GP	G	A	Pts	PIM
1997-98	Boston Bruins	81	22	25	47	8	6	2	5	7	0
1998-99	Boston Bruins	79	25	26	51	18	11	3	1	4	0
99-2000	Boston Bruins	77	19	26	45	4	....	....	....	....	....
2000-01	Boston Bruins	82	29	46	75	18	....	....	....	....	....
2001-02	Boston Bruins	74	29	41	70	27	6	2	2	4	0
2002-03	Boston Bruins	8	5	6	11	2	5	0	2	2	0
	NHL Totals	**401**	**129**	**170**	**299**	**77**	**28**	**7**	**10**	**17**	**0**

NHL All-Rookie Team (1998) • Calder Memorial Trophy (1998)

Played in NHL All-Star Game (2001)

SAMUELSSON, Kjell

Defense. Shoots right. 6'6", 235 lbs. Born, Tingsryd, Sweden, October 18, 1958.
(NY Rangers' 5th choice, 119th overall, in 1984 Entry Draft).

Season	Club	GP	G	A	Pts	PIM	GP	G	A	Pts	PIM
		REGULAR SEASON					PLAYOFFS				
1985-86	New York Rangers	9	0	0	0	10	9	0	1	1	8
1986-87	New York Rangers	30	2	6	8	50	....	....	....	....	....
	Philadelphia Flyers	46	1	6	7	86	26	0	4	4	25
1987-88	Philadelphia Flyers	74	6	24	30	184	7	2	5	7	23
1988-89	Philadelphia Flyers	69	3	14	17	140	19	1	3	4	24
1989-90	Philadelphia Flyers	66	5	17	22	91	....	....	....	....	....
1990-91	Philadelphia Flyers	78	9	19	28	82	....	....	....	....	....
1991-92	Philadelphia Flyers	54	4	9	13	76	....	....	....	....	....
	◆ Pittsburgh Penguins	20	1	2	3	34	15	0	3	3	12
1992-93	Pittsburgh Penguins	63	3	6	9	106	12	0	3	3	2
1993-94	Pittsburgh Penguins	59	5	8	13	118	6	0	0	0	26
1994-95	Pittsburgh Penguins	41	1	6	7	54	11	0	1	1	32
1995-96	Philadelphia Flyers	75	3	11	14	81	12	1	0	1	24
1996-97	Philadelphia Flyers	34	4	3	7	47	5	0	0	0	2
1997-98	Philadelphia Flyers	49	0	3	3	28	1	0	0	0	0
1998-99	Tampa Bay Lightning	46	1	4	5	38	....	....	....	....	....
	NHL Totals	**813**	**48**	**138**	**186**	**1225**	**123**	**4**	**20**	**24**	**178**

Played in NHL All-Star Game (1988)

Traded to **Philadelphia** by **NY Rangers** with NY Rangers' 2nd round choice (Patrik Juhlin) in 1989 Entry Draft for Bob Froese, December 18, 1986. Traded to **Pittsburgh** by **Philadelphia** with Rick Tocchet, Ken Wregget and Philadelphia's 3rd round choice (Dave Roche) in 1993 Entry Draft for Mark Recchi, Brian Benning and Los Angeles' 1st round choice (previously acquired, Philadelphia selected Jason Bowen) in 1992 Entry Draft, February 19, 1992. Signed as a free agent by **Philadelphia**, August 31, 1995. Signed as a free agent by **Tampa Bay**, October 14, 1998.
• Officially announced retirement, April 18, 1999.

SAMUELSSON, Martin

Right wing. Shoots left. 6'2", 194 lbs. Born, Upplands Vasby, Sweden, January 25, 1982.
(Boston's 2nd choice, 27th overall, in 2000 Entry Draft).

Season	Club	GP	G	A	Pts	PIM	GP	G	A	Pts	PIM
2002-03	Boston Bruins	8	0	1	1	2	....	....	....	....	....
	NHL Totals	**8**	**0**	**1**	**1**	**2**	....	....	....	....	....

SAMUELSSON, Mikael

Right wing. Shoots left. 6'1", 195 lbs. Born, Mariefred, Sweden, December 23, 1976.
(San Jose's 7th choice, 145th overall, in 1998 Entry Draft).

Season	Club	GP	G	A	Pts	PIM	GP	G	A	Pts	PIM
2000-01	San Jose Sharks	4	0	0	0	0	....	....	....	....	....
2001-02	New York Rangers	67	6	10	16	23	....	....	....	....	....
2002-03	New York Rangers	58	8	14	22	32	....	....	....	....	....
	Pittsburgh Penguins	22	2	0	2	8	....	....	....	....	....
	NHL Totals	**151**	**16**	**24**	**40**	**63**	....	....	....	....	....

Traded to **NY Rangers** by **San Jose** with Christian Gosselin for Adam Graves and future considerations, June 24, 2001. Traded to **Pittsburgh** by **NY Rangers** with Joel Bouchard, Richard Lintner and Rico Fata for Mike Wilson, Alexei Kovalev, Janne Laukkanen and Dan LaCouture, February 10, 2003. Traded to **Florida** by **Pittsburgh** with Pittsburgh's 1st round choice (Nathan Horton) and 2nd round compensatory choice (Stefan Meyer) in 2003 Entry Draft for Florida's 1st (Marc-Andre Fleury) and 3rd (Daniel Carcillo) round choices in 2003 Entry Draft, June 21, 2003.

SAMUELSSON, Ulf

Defense. Shoots left. 6'1", 205 lbs. Born, Fagersta, Sweden, March 26, 1964.
(Hartford's 4th choice, 67th overall, in 1982 Entry Draft).

Season	Club	GP	G	A	Pts	PIM	GP	G	A	Pts	PIM
1984-85	Hartford Whalers	41	2	6	8	83	....	....	....	....	....
1985-86	Hartford Whalers	80	5	19	24	174	10	1	2	3	38
1986-87	Hartford Whalers	78	2	31	33	162	5	0	1	1	41
1987-88	Hartford Whalers	76	8	33	41	159	5	0	0	0	8
1988-89	Hartford Whalers	71	9	26	35	181	4	0	2	2	4
1989-90	Hartford Whalers	55	2	11	13	177	7	1	0	1	2
1990-91	Hartford Whalers	62	3	18	21	174	....	....	....	....	....
	◆ Pittsburgh Penguins	14	1	4	5	37	20	3	2	5	34
1991-92 ◆	Pittsburgh Penguins	62	1	14	15	206	21	0	2	2	39
1992-93	Pittsburgh Penguins	77	3	26	29	249	12	1	5	6	24
1993-94	Pittsburgh Penguins	80	5	24	29	199	6	0	1	1	18
1994-95	Pittsburgh Penguins	44	1	15	16	113	7	0	2	2	8
1995-96	New York Rangers	74	1	18	19	122	11	1	5	6	16
1996-97	New York Rangers	73	6	11	17	138	15	0	2	2	30
1997-98	New York Rangers	73	3	9	12	122	....	....	....	....	....
1998-99	New York Rangers	67	4	8	12	93	....	....	....	....	....
	Detroit Red Wings	4	0	0	0	6	9	0	3	3	10
99-2000	Philadelphia Flyers	49	1	2	3	58	....	....	....	....	....
	NHL Totals	**1080**	**57**	**275**	**332**	**2453**	**132**	**7**	**27**	**34**	**272**

Traded to **Pittsburgh** by **Hartford** with Ron Francis and Grant Jennings for John Cullen, Jeff Parker and Zarley Zalapski, March 4, 1991. Traded to **NY Rangers** by **Pittsburgh** with Luc Robitaille for Petr Nedved and Sergei Zubov, August 31, 1995. Traded to **Detroit** by **NY Rangers** for Detroit's 2nd round choice (David Inman) in 1999 Entry Draft and NY Rangers' 3rd round choice (previously acquired, NY Rangers' selected Johan Asplund) in 1999 Entry Draft, March 23, 1999. Traded to **Atlanta** by **Detroit** for future considerations, June 25, 1999. Signed as a free agent by **Philadelphia**, October 19, 1999.

SANDELIN, Scott

Defense. Shoots right. 6', 200 lbs. Born, Hibbing, MN, August 8, 1964.
(Montreal's 5th choice, 40th overall, in 1982 Entry Draft).

Season	Club	GP	G	A	Pts	PIM	GP	G	A	Pts	PIM
1986-87	Montreal Canadiens	1	0	0	0	0	....	....	....	....	....
1987-88	Montreal Canadiens	8	0	1	1	2	....	....	....	....	....
1990-91	Philadelphia Flyers	15	0	3	3	0	....	....	....	....	....
1991-92	Minnesota North Stars	1	0	0	0	0	....	....	....	....	....
	NHL Totals	**25**	**0**	**4**	**4**	**2**	....	....	....	....	....

Traded to **Philadelphia** by **Montreal** for J.J. Daigneault, November 7, 1988. Signed as a free agent by **Minnesota**, August 21, 1991.

SANDERSON, Derek

Center. Shoots left. 6', 185 lbs. Born, Niagara Falls, Ont., June 16, 1946.

Season	Club	GP	G	A	Pts	PIM	GP	G	A	Pts	PIM
1965-66	Boston Bruins	2	0	0	0	0	....	....	....	....	....
1966-67	Boston Bruins	2	0	0	0	0	....	....	....	....	....
1967-68	Boston Bruins	71	24	25	49	98	4	0	2	2	9
1968-69	Boston Bruins	61	26	22	48	146	9	*8	2	10	36
1969-70 ◆	Boston Bruins	50	18	23	41	118	14	5	4	9	*72
1970-71	Boston Bruins	71	29	34	63	130	7	2	1	3	13
1971-72 ◆	Boston Bruins	78	25	33	58	108	11	1	1	2	44
1972-73	Boston Bruins	25	5	10	15	38	5	1	2	3	13
1973-74	Boston Bruins	29	8	12	20	48	....	....	....	....	....
1974-75	New York Rangers	75	25	25	50	106	3	0	0	0	0
1975-76	New York Rangers	8	0	0	0	4	....	....	....	....	....
	St. Louis Blues	65	24	43	67	59	3	1	0	1	0
1976-77	St. Louis Blues	32	8	13	21	26	....	....	....	....	....
	Vancouver Canucks	16	7	9	16	30	....	....	....	....	....
1977-78	Pittsburgh Penguins	13	3	1	4	0	....	....	....	....	....
	NHL Totals	**598**	**202**	**250**	**452**	**911**	**56**	**18**	**12**	**30**	**187**

Calder Memorial Trophy (1968)

Signed as a free agent by **Boston** after securing release from **Philadelphia** (WHA), February, 1973. Traded to **NY Rangers** by **Boston** for Walt McKechnie, June 12, 1974. Traded to **St. Louis** by **NY Rangers** for NY Rangers' 1st round choice (previously acquired, NY Rangers selected Lucien DeBlois) in 1975 Amateur Draft, October 30, 1975. Traded to **Vancouver** by **St. Louis** for cash, February 18, 1977. Signed as a free agent by **Pittsburgh**, March 14, 1978.

SANDERSON, Geoff

Left wing. Shoots left. 6', 190 lbs. Born, Hay River, N.W.T., February 1, 1972.
(Hartford's 2nd choice, 36th overall, in 1990 Entry Draft).

Season	Club	GP	G	A	Pts	PIM	GP	G	A	Pts	PIM
1990-91	Hartford Whalers	2	1	0	1	0	3	0	0	0	0
1991-92	Hartford Whalers	64	13	18	31	18	7	1	0	1	2
1992-93	Hartford Whalers	82	46	43	89	28	....	....	....	....	....
1993-94	Hartford Whalers	82	41	26	67	42	....	....	....	....	....
1994-95	Hartford Whalers	46	18	14	32	24	....	....	....	....	....
1995-96	Hartford Whalers	81	34	31	65	40	....	....	....	....	....
1996-97	Hartford Whalers	82	36	31	67	29	....	....	....	....	....
1997-98	Carolina Hurricanes	40	7	10	17	14	....	....	....	....	....
	Vancouver Canucks	9	0	3	3	4	....	....	....	....	....
	Buffalo Sabres	26	4	5	9	20	14	3	1	4	4
1998-99	Buffalo Sabres	75	12	18	30	22	19	4	6	10	14
99-2000	Buffalo Sabres	67	13	13	26	22	5	0	2	2	8
2000-01	Columbus Blue Jackets	68	30	26	56	46	....	....	....	....	....
2001-02	Columbus Blue Jackets	42	11	5	16	12	....	....	....	....	....
2002-03	Columbus Blue Jackets	82	34	33	67	34	....	....	....	....	....
	NHL Totals	**848**	**300**	**276**	**576**	**355**	**48**	**8**	**9**	**17**	**28**

Played in NHL All-Star Game (1994, 1997)

Transferred to **Carolina** after **Hartford** franchise relocated, June 25, 1997. Traded to **Vancouver** by **Carolina** with Sean Burke and Enrico Ciccone for Kirk McLean and Martin Gelinas, January 3, 1998. Traded to **Buffalo** by **Vancouver** for Brad May and Buffalo's 3rd round choice (later traded to Tampa Bay – Tampa Bay selected Jimmie Olvestad) in 1999 Entry Draft, February 4, 1998. Selected by **Columbus** from **Buffalo** in Expansion Draft, June 23, 2000.

SANDFORD, Ed

Left wing. Shoots right. 6'1", 180 lbs. Born, New Toronto, Ont., August 20, 1928.

Season	Club	GP	G	A	Pts	PIM	GP	G	A	Pts	PIM
1947-48	Boston Bruins	59	10	15	25	25	5	1	0	1	0
1948-49	Boston Bruins	56	16	20	36	57	5	1	3	4	2
1949-50	Boston Bruins	19	1	4	5	6	....	....	....	....	....
1950-51	Boston Bruins	51	10	13	23	33	6	0	1	1	4
1951-52	Boston Bruins	65	13	12	25	54	7	2	2	4	0
1952-53	Boston Bruins	61	14	21	35	44	11	*8	3	*11	11
1953-54	Boston Bruins	70	16	31	47	42	3	0	1	1	4
1954-55	Boston Bruins	60	14	20	34	38	5	1	1	2	6
1955-56	Detroit Red Wings	4	0	0	0	0	....	....	....	....	....
	Chicago Black Hawks	57	12	9	21	56	....	....	....	....	....
	NHL Totals	**502**	**106**	**145**	**251**	**355**	**42**	**13**	**11**	**24**	**27**

NHL Second All-Star Team (1954)
Played in NHL All-Star Game (1951, 1952, 1953, 1954, 1955)

• Missed remainder of 1949-50 season recovering from ankle injury suffered in game vs. Toronto, November 13, 1949. Traded to **Detroit** by **Boston** with Gilles Boisvert, Real Chevrefils, Warren Godfrey and Norm Corcoran for Marcel Bonin, Vic Stasiuk, Terry Sawchuk and Lorne Davis, June 3, 1955. Traded to **Chicago** by **Detroit** for Metro Prystai, October 24, 1955.

SANDLAK, Jim

Right wing. Shoots right. 6'4", 219 lbs. Born, Kitchener, Ont., December 12, 1966.
(Vancouver's 1st choice, 4th overall, in 1985 Entry Draft).

Season	Club	GP	G	A	Pts	PIM	GP	G	A	Pts	PIM
1985-86	Vancouver Canucks	23	1	3	4	10	3	0	1	1	0
1986-87	Vancouver Canucks	78	15	21	36	66	....	....	....	....	....
1987-88	Vancouver Canucks	49	16	15	31	81	....	....	....	....	....
1988-89	Vancouver Canucks	72	20	20	40	99	6	1	1	2	2
1989-90	Vancouver Canucks	70	15	8	23	104	....	....	....	....	....
1990-91	Vancouver Canucks	59	7	6	13	125	....	....	....	....	....
1991-92	Vancouver Canucks	66	16	24	40	176	13	4	6	10	22

Season	Club	GP	G	A	Pts	PIM	GP	G	A	Pts	PIM
		REGULAR SEASON					PLAYOFFS				
1992-93	Vancouver Canucks	59	10	18	28	122	6	2	2	4	4
1993-94	Hartford Whalers	27	6	2	8	32	....	....	....	....	....
1994-95	Hartford Whalers	13	0	0	0	0	....	....	....	....	....
1995-96	Vancouver Canucks	33	4	2	6	6	5	0	0	0	2
	NHL Totals	**549**	**110**	**119**	**229**	**821**	**33**	**7**	**10**	**17**	**30**

NHL All-Rookie Team (1987)

Traded to **Hartford** by **Vancouver** to complete transaction that sent Murray Craven to Vancouver (March 22, 1993), May 17, 1993. Signed as a free agent by **Vancouver**, October 1, 1995.

SANDS, Charlie

Center/Right wing. Shoots right. 5'9", 160 lbs. Born, Fort William, Ont., March 23, 1911.

Season	Club	GP	G	A	Pts	PIM	GP	G	A	Pts	PIM
1932-33	Toronto Maple Leafs	3	0	3	3	0	9	2	2	4	2
1933-34	Toronto Maple Leafs	45	8	8	16	2	5	1	0	1	0
1934-35	Boston Bruins	41	15	12	27	0	4	0	0	0	0
1935-36	Boston Bruins	40	6	4	10	8	2	0	0	0	0
1936-37	Boston Bruins	47	18	5	23	6	3	1	2	3	0
1937-38	Boston Bruins	46	17	12	29	12	3	1	1	2	0
1938-39 ♦	Boston Bruins	37	7	5	12	10	1	0	0	0	0
1939-40	Montreal Canadiens	47	9	20	29	10	....	....	....	....	....
1940-41	Montreal Canadiens	43	5	13	18	4	2	1	0	1	0
1941-42	Montreal Canadiens	38	11	16	27	6	3	0	1	1	2
1942-43	Montreal Canadiens	31	3	9	12	0	2	0	0	0	0
1943-44	New York Rangers	9	0	2	2	0	....	....	....	....	....
	NHL Totals	**427**	**99**	**109**	**208**	**58**	**34**	**6**	**6**	**12**	**4**

Played in NHL All-Star Game (1934)

Traded to **Boston** by **Toronto** for cash, May 12, 1934. Traded to **Montreal** by **Boston** with Ray Getliffe for Herb Cain, October 10, 1939. Loaned to **NY Rangers** by **Montreal** with John Mahaffy, Dutch Hiller, Fern Gauthier and future considerations (Tony Demers, December, 1943) for the loan of Phil Watson, October 27, 1943.

SANDSTROM, Tomas

Right wing. Shoots left. 6'2", 205 lbs. Born, Jakobstad, Finland, September 4, 1964.
(NY Rangers' 2nd choice, 36th overall, in 1982 Entry Draft).

Season	Club	GP	G	A	Pts	PIM	GP	G	A	Pts	PIM
1984-85	New York Rangers	74	29	29	58	51	3	0	2	2	0
1985-86	New York Rangers	73	25	29	54	109	16	4	6	10	20
1986-87	New York Rangers	64	40	34	74	60	6	1	2	3	20
1987-88	New York Rangers	69	28	40	68	95	....	....	....	....	....
1988-89	New York Rangers	79	32	56	88	148	4	3	2	5	12
1989-90	New York Rangers	48	19	19	38	100	....	....	....	....	....
	Los Angeles Kings	28	13	20	33	28	10	5	4	9	19
1990-91	Los Angeles Kings	68	45	44	89	106	10	4	4	8	14
1991-92	Los Angeles Kings	49	17	22	39	70	6	0	3	3	8
1992-93	Los Angeles Kings	39	25	27	52	57	24	8	17	25	12
1993-94	Los Angeles Kings	51	17	24	41	59	....	....	....	....	....
	Pittsburgh Penguins	27	6	11	17	24	6	0	0	0	4
1994-95	Pittsburgh Penguins	47	21	23	44	42	12	3	3	6	16
1995-96	Pittsburgh Penguins	58	35	35	70	69	18	4	2	6	30
1996-97	Pittsburgh Penguins	40	9	15	24	33	....	....	....	....	....
	♦ Detroit Red Wings	34	9	9	18	36	20	0	4	4	24
1997-98	Mighty Ducks of Anaheim	77	9	8	17	64	....	....	....	....	....
1998-99	Mighty Ducks of Anaheim	58	15	17	32	42	4	0	0	0	4
	NHL Totals	**983**	**394**	**462**	**856**	**1193**	**139**	**32**	**49**	**81**	**183**

NHL All-Rookie Team (1985)

Played in NHL All-Star Game (1988, 1991)

Traded to **Los Angeles** by **NY Rangers** with Tony Granato for Bernie Nicholls, January 20, 1990. Traded to **Pittsburgh** by **Los Angeles** with Shawn McEachern for Marty McSorley and Jim Paek, February 16, 1994. Traded to **Detroit** by **Pittsburgh** for Greg Johnson, January 27, 1997. Signed as a free agent by **Anaheim**, October 20, 1997.

SANDWITH, Terran

Defense. Shoots left. 6'4", 210 lbs. Born, Edmonton, Alta., April 17, 1972.
(Philadelphia's 4th choice, 42nd overall, in 1990 Entry Draft).

Season	Club	GP	G	A	Pts	PIM	GP	G	A	Pts	PIM
1997-98	Edmonton Oilers	8	0	0	0	6	....	....	....	....	....
	NHL Totals	**8**	**0**	**0**	**0**	**6**	....	....	....	....	....

Signed as a free agent by **Edmonton**, April 10, 1996. Signed as a free agent by **Anaheim**, July 13, 1998. Signed as a free agent by **Toronto**, July 2, 1999. Signed as a free agent by **Edmonton**, July 19, 2000.

SANIPASS, Everett

Left wing. Shoots left. 6'2", 204 lbs. Born, Big Cove, N.B., February 13, 1968.
(Chicago's 1st choice, 14th overall, in 1986 Entry Draft).

Season	Club	GP	G	A	Pts	PIM	GP	G	A	Pts	PIM
1986-87	Chicago Blackhawks	7	1	3	4	2	....	....	....	....	....
1987-88	Chicago Blackhawks	57	8	12	20	126	2	2	0	2	2
1988-89	Chicago Blackhawks	50	6	9	15	164	3	0	0	0	2
1989-90	Chicago Blackhawks	12	2	2	4	17	....	....	....	....	....
	Quebec Nordiques	9	3	3	6	8	....	....	....	....	....
1990-91	Quebec Nordiques	29	5	5	10	41	....	....	....	....	....
	NHL Totals	**164**	**25**	**34**	**59**	**358**	**5**	**2**	**0**	**2**	**4**

Traded to **Quebec** by **Chicago** with Mario Doyon and Dan Vincelette for Greg Millen, Michel Goulet and Quebec's 6th round choice (Kevin St. Jacques) in 1991 Entry Draft, March 5, 1990.
• Suffered eventual career-ending back injury in game vs. Philadelphia, January 17, 1991.

SAPRYKIN, Oleg

Left wing. Shoots left. 6', 195 lbs. Born, Moscow, USSR, February 12, 1981.
(Calgary's 1st choice, 11th overall, in 1999 Entry Draft).

Season	Club	GP	G	A	Pts	PIM	GP	G	A	Pts	PIM
99-2000	Calgary Flames	4	0	1	1	2	....	....	....	....	....
2000-01	Calgary Flames	59	9	14	23	43	....	....	....	....	....
2001-02	Calgary Flames	3	0	0	0	0	....	....	....	....	....
2002-03	Calgary Flames	52	8	15	23	46	....	....	....	....	....
	NHL Totals	**118**	**17**	**30**	**47**	**91**	....	....	....	....	....

SARAULT, Yves

Left wing. Shoots left. 6'1", 190 lbs. Born, Valleyfield, Que., December 23, 1972.
(Montreal's 4th choice, 61st overall, in 1991 Entry Draft).

Season	Club	GP	G	A	Pts	PIM	GP	G	A	Pts	PIM
1994-95	Montreal Canadiens	8	0	1	1	0	....	....	....	....	....
1995-96	Montreal Canadiens	14	0	0	0	4	....	....	....	....	....
	Calgary Flames	11	2	1	3	4	....	....	....	....	....
1996-97	Colorado Avalanche	28	2	1	3	6	5	0	0	0	2
1997-98	Colorado Avalanche	2	1	0	1	0	....	....	....	....	....
1998-99	Ottawa Senators	11	0	1	1	4	....	....	....	....	....
99-2000	Ottawa Senators	11	0	2	2	7	....	....	....	....	....
2000-01	Atlanta Thrashers	20	5	4	9	26	....	....	....	....	....
2001-02	Nashville Predators	1	0	0	0	0	....	....	....	....	....
	NHL Totals	**106**	**10**	**10**	**20**	**51**	**5**	**0**	**0**	**0**	**2**

Traded to **Calgary** by **Montreal** with Craig Ferguson for Calgary's 8th round choice (Petr Kubos) in 1997 Entry Draft, November 26, 1995. Signed as a free agent by **Colorado**, September 13, 1996. Signed as a free agent by **Ottawa**, August 7, 1998. Signed as a free agent by **Atlanta**, July 20, 2000. Claimed on waivers by **Nashville** from **Atlanta**, June 19, 2001. Traded to **Philadelphia** by **Nashville** with a conditional choice in 2003 Entry Draft for Petr Hubacek and Jason Beckett, January 11, 2002.

SARGENT, Gary

Defense. Shoots left. 5'10", 210 lbs. Born, Red Lake, MN, February 8, 1954.
(Los Angeles' 1st choice, 48th overall, in 1974 Amateur Draft).

Season	Club	GP	G	A	Pts	PIM	GP	G	A	Pts	PIM
1975-76	Los Angeles Kings	63	8	16	24	36	....	....	....	....	....
1976-77	Los Angeles Kings	80	14	40	54	65	9	3	4	7	6
1977-78	Los Angeles Kings	72	7	34	41	52	2	0	0	0	0
1978-79	Minnesota North Stars	79	12	32	44	39	....	....	....	....	....
1979-80	Minnesota North Stars	52	13	21	34	22	4	2	1	3	2
1980-81	Minnesota North Stars	23	4	7	11	36	....	....	....	....	....
1981-82	Minnesota North Stars	15	0	5	5	18	....	....	....	....	....
1982-83	Minnesota North Stars	18	3	6	9	5	5	0	2	2	0
	NHL Totals	**402**	**61**	**161**	**222**	**273**	**20**	**5**	**7**	**12**	**8**

Signed as a free agent by **Minnesota**, June 30, 1978. Los Angeles received Rick Hampton, Steve Jensen and Dave Gardner as compensation.

SARICH, Cory

Defense. Shoots right. 6'3", 204 lbs. Born, Saskatoon, Sask., August 16, 1978.
(Buffalo's 2nd choice, 27th overall, in 1996 Entry Draft).

Season	Club	GP	G	A	Pts	PIM	GP	G	A	Pts	PIM
1998-99	Buffalo Sabres	4	0	0	0	0	....	....	....	....	....
99-2000	Buffalo Sabres	42	0	4	4	35	....	....	....	....	....
	Tampa Bay Lightning	17	0	2	2	42	....	....	....	....	....
2000-01	Tampa Bay Lightning	73	1	8	9	106	....	....	....	....	....
2001-02	Tampa Bay Lightning	72	0	11	11	105	....	....	....	....	....
2002-03	Tampa Bay Lightning	82	5	9	14	63	11	0	2	2	6
	NHL Totals	**290**	**6**	**34**	**40**	**351**	**11**	**0**	**2**	**2**	**6**

Traded to **Tampa Bay** by **Buffalo** with Wayne Primeau, Brian Holzinger and Buffalo's 3rd round choice (Alexander Kharitonov) in 2000 Entry Draft for Chris Gratton and Tampa Bay's 2nd round choice (Derek Roy) in 2001 Entry Draft, March 9, 2000.

SARNER, Craig

Right wing. Shoots left. 5'11", 185 lbs. Born, St. Paul, MN, June 20, 1949.

Season	Club	GP	G	A	Pts	PIM	GP	G	A	Pts	PIM
1974-75	Boston Bruins	7	0	0	0	0	....	....	....	....	....
	NHL Totals	**7**	**0**	**0**	**0**	**0**	....	....	....	....	....

Signed as a free agent by **Boston**, March, 1972.

SARRAZIN, Dick

Right wing. Shoots right. 6', 185 lbs. Born, St-Gabriel-de-Brandon, Que., January 22, 1946.

Season	Club	GP	G	A	Pts	PIM	GP	G	A	Pts	PIM
1968-69	Philadelphia Flyers	54	16	30	46	14	4	0	0	0	0
1969-70	Philadelphia Flyers	18	1	1	2	4	....	....	....	....	....
1971-72	Philadelphia Flyers	28	3	4	7	4	....	....	....	....	....
	NHL Totals	**100**	**20**	**35**	**55**	**22**	**4**	**0**	**0**	**0**	**0**

Traded to **Philadelphia** (Quebec-AHL) by **Detroit** for cash, October, 1967.

SASAKAMOOSE, Fred

Center. Shoots right. 5'8", 165 lbs. Born, Sandy Lake Reserve, Sask., December 25, 1933.

Season	Club	GP	G	A	Pts	PIM	GP	G	A	Pts	PIM
1953-54	Chicago Black Hawks	11	0	0	0	6	....	....	....	....	....
	NHL Totals	**11**	**0**	**0**	**0**	**6**	....	....	....	....	....

SASSER, Grant

Center. Shoots right. 5'10", 175 lbs. Born, Portland, OR, February 13, 1964.
(Pittsburgh's 4th choice, 94th overall, in 1982 Entry Draft).

Season	Club	GP	G	A	Pts	PIM	GP	G	A	Pts	PIM
1983-84	Pittsburgh Penguins	3	0	0	0	0	....	....	....	....	....
	NHL Totals	**3**	**0**	**0**	**0**	**0**	....	....	....	....	....

SATAN, Miroslav

Left wing. Shoots left. 6'3", 190 lbs. Born, Topolcany, Czech., October 22, 1974.
(Edmonton's 6th choice, 111th overall, in 1993 Entry Draft).

Season	Club	Reg. GP	G	A	Pts	PIM	Playoffs GP	G	A	Pts	PIM
1995-96	Edmonton Oilers	62	18	17	35	22	....	....	....	....	....
1996-97	Edmonton Oilers	64	17	11	28	22	....	....	....	....	....
	Buffalo Sabres	12	8	2	10	4	7	0	0	0	0
1997-98	Buffalo Sabres	79	22	24	46	34	14	5	4	9	4
1998-99	Buffalo Sabres	81	40	26	66	44	12	3	5	8	2
99-2000	Buffalo Sabres	81	33	34	67	32	5	3	2	5	0
2000-01	Buffalo Sabres	82	29	33	62	36	13	3	10	13	8
2001-02	Buffalo Sabres	82	37	36	73	33	....	....	....	....	....
2002-03	Buffalo Sabres	79	26	49	75	20	....	....	....	....	....
	NHL Totals	**622**	**230**	**232**	**462**	**247**	**51**	**14**	**21**	**35**	**14**

Played in NHL All-Star Game (2000, 2003)

Traded to **Buffalo** by **Edmonton** for Barrie Moore and Craig Millar, March 18, 1997.

SATHER, Glen — HHOF

Left wing. Shoots left. 5'11", 180 lbs. Born, High River, Alta., September 2, 1943.

Season	Club	Reg. GP	G	A	Pts	PIM	Playoffs GP	G	A	Pts	PIM
1966-67	Boston Bruins	5	0	0	0	0	....	....	....	....	....
1967-68	Boston Bruins	65	8	12	20	34	3	0	0	0	0
1968-69	Boston Bruins	76	4	11	15	67	10	0	0	0	18
1969-70	Pittsburgh Penguins	76	12	14	26	114	10	0	2	2	17
1970-71	Pittsburgh Penguins	46	8	3	11	96	....	....	....	....	....
	New York Rangers	31	2	0	2	52	13	0	1	1	18
1971-72	New York Rangers	76	5	9	14	77	16	0	1	1	22
1972-73	New York Rangers	77	11	15	26	64	9	0	0	0	7
1973-74	New York Rangers	2	0	0	0	0	....	....	....	....	....
	St. Louis Blues	69	15	29	44	82	....	....	....	....	....
1974-75	Montreal Canadiens	63	6	10	16	44	11	1	1	2	4
1975-76	Minnesota North Stars	72	9	10	19	94	....	....	....	....	....
	NHL Totals	**658**	**80**	**113**	**193**	**724**	**72**	**1**	**5**	**6**	**86**

Claimed by **Boston** from **Memphis** (CHL) in Inter-League Draft, June 8, 1965. Selected by **Pittsburgh** from **Boston** in Intra-League Draft, June 11, 1969. Traded to **NY Rangers** by **Pittsburgh** for Syl Apps Jr. and Sheldon Kannegiesser, January 26, 1971. Traded to **St. Louis** by **NY Rangers** with Rene Villemure for Jack Egers, October 28, 1973. Traded to **Montreal** by **St. Louis** to complete transaction that sent Rik Wilson to St. Louis (May 27, 1974), June 14, 1974. Traded to **Minnesota** by **Montreal** for Minnesota's 3rd round choice (Alain Cote) in 1977 Amateur Draft and cash, July 9, 1975

SAUER, Kurt

Defense. Shoots left. 6'4", 225 lbs. Born, St. Cloud, MN, January 16, 1981.
(Colorado's 5th choice, 88th overall, in 2000 Entry Draft).

Season	Club	Reg. GP	G	A	Pts	PIM	Playoffs GP	G	A	Pts	PIM
2002-03	Mighty Ducks of Anaheim	80	1	2	3	74	21	1	1	2	6
	NHL Totals	**80**	**1**	**2**	**3**	**74**	**21**	**1**	**1**	**2**	**6**

Signed as a free agent by **Anaheim**, June 6, 2002.

SAUNDERS, Bernie

Left wing. Shoots right. 6', 190 lbs. Born, Montreal, Que., June 21, 1956.

Season	Club	Reg. GP	G	A	Pts	PIM	Playoffs GP	G	A	Pts	PIM
1979-80	Quebec Nordiques	4	0	0	0	0	....	....	....	....	....
1980-81	Quebec Nordiques	6	0	1	1	8	....	....	....	....	....
	NHL Totals	**10**	**0**	**1**	**1**	**8**	....	....	....	....	....

Signed as a free agent by **Quebec**, May 29, 1979.

SAUNDERS, David

Left wing. Shoots left. 6'1", 195 lbs. Born, Ottawa, Ont., May 20, 1966.
(Vancouver's 3rd choice, 52nd overall, in 1984 Entry Draft).

Season	Club	Reg. GP	G	A	Pts	PIM	Playoffs GP	G	A	Pts	PIM
1987-88	Vancouver Canucks	56	7	13	20	10	....	....	....	....	....
	NHL Totals	**56**	**7**	**13**	**20**	**10**	....	....	....	....	....

SAUNDERS, Ted

Right wing. Shoots right. 5'8", 165 lbs. Born, Ottawa, Ont., August 29, 1911.

Season	Club	Reg. GP	G	A	Pts	PIM	Playoffs GP	G	A	Pts	PIM
1933-34	Ottawa Senators	18	1	3	4	4	....	....	....	....	....
	NHL Totals	**18**	**1**	**3**	**4**	**4**	....	....	....	....	....

Traded to **Ottawa** by **Boston** with Percy Galbraith and Bud Cook for Bob Gracie, October 4, 1933. Traded to **Detroit** (IHL) by **Ottawa** for cash, December, 1933.

SAUVE, Jean-Francois

Center. Shoots left. 5'6", 175 lbs. Born, Ste-Genevieve, Que., January 23, 1960.

Season	Club	Reg. GP	G	A	Pts	PIM	Playoffs GP	G	A	Pts	PIM
1980-81	Buffalo Sabres	20	5	9	14	12	5	2	0	2	0
1981-82	Buffalo Sabres	69	19	36	55	46	2	0	2	2	0
1982-83	Buffalo Sabres	9	0	4	4	9	....	....	....	....	....
1983-84	Quebec Nordiques	39	10	17	27	2	9	2	5	7	2
1984-85	Quebec Nordiques	64	13	29	42	21	18	5	5	10	8
1985-86	Quebec Nordiques	75	16	40	56	20	2	0	0	0	0
1986-87	Quebec Nordiques	14	2	3	5	4	....	....	....	....	....
	NHL Totals	**290**	**65**	**138**	**203**	**114**	**36**	**9**	**12**	**21**	**10**

• Brother of Bob

Signed as a free agent by **Buffalo**, November 1, 1979. Traded to **Quebec** by **Buffalo** with Tony McKegney, Andre Savard and Buffalo's 3rd round choice (Iiro Jarvi) in 1983 Entry Draft for Real Cloutier and Quebec's 1st round choice (Adam Creighton) in 1983 Entry Draft, June 8, 1983.

SAVAGE, Andre

Center. Shoots right. 6', 195 lbs. Born, Ottawa, Ont., May 27, 1975.

Season	Club	Reg. GP	G	A	Pts	PIM	Playoffs GP	G	A	Pts	PIM
1998-99	Boston Bruins	6	1	0	1	0	....	....	....	....	....
99-2000	Boston Bruins	43	7	13	20	10	....	....	....	....	....
2000-01	Boston Bruins	1	0	0	0	0	....	....	....	....	....
2002-03	Philadelphia Flyers	16	2	1	3	4	....	....	....	....	....
	NHL Totals	**66**	**10**	**14**	**24**	**14**	....	....	....	....	....

Signed as a free agent by **Boston**, June 18, 1998. Signed as a free agent by **Vancouver**, August 2, 2001. Signed as a free agent by **Philadelphia**, August 20, 2002.

SAVAGE, Brian

Left wing. Shoots left. 6'1", 205 lbs. Born, Sudbury, Ont., February 24, 1971.
(Montreal's 11th choice, 171st overall, in 1991 Entry Draft).

Season	Club	Reg. GP	G	A	Pts	PIM	Playoffs GP	G	A	Pts	PIM
1993-94	Montreal Canadiens	3	1	0	1	0	3	0	2	2	0
1994-95	Montreal Canadiens	37	12	7	19	27	....	....	....	....	....
1995-96	Montreal Canadiens	75	25	8	33	28	6	0	2	2	2
1996-97	Montreal Canadiens	81	23	37	60	39	5	1	1	2	0
1997-98	Montreal Canadiens	64	26	17	43	36	9	0	2	2	6
1998-99	Montreal Canadiens	54	16	10	26	20	....	....	....	....	....
99-2000	Montreal Canadiens	38	17	12	29	19	....	....	....	....	....
2000-01	Montreal Canadiens	62	21	24	45	26	....	....	....	....	....
2001-02	Montreal Canadiens	47	14	15	29	30	....	....	....	....	....
	Phoenix Coyotes	30	6	6	12	8	5	0	0	0	0
2002-03	Phoenix Coyotes	43	6	10	16	22	....	....	....	....	....
	NHL Totals	**534**	**167**	**146**	**313**	**255**	**28**	**1**	**7**	**8**	**8**

• Missed majority of 1999-2000 season recovering from neck injury suffered in game vs. Los Angeles, November 20, 1999. Traded to **Phoenix** by **Montreal** with Montreal's 3rd round choice (Matt Jones) in 2002 Entry Draft and future considerations for Sergei Berezin, January 25, 2002.

SAVAGE, Joel

Right wing. Shoots right. 5'11", 205 lbs. Born, Surrey, B.C., December 25, 1969.
(Buffalo's 1st choice, 13th overall, in 1988 Entry Draft).

Season	Club	Reg. GP	G	A	Pts	PIM	Playoffs GP	G	A	Pts	PIM
1990-91	Buffalo Sabres	3	0	1	1	0	....	....	....	....	....
	NHL Totals	**3**	**0**	**1**	**1**	**0**	....	....	....	....	....

Signed as a free agent by **Anaheim**, September 19, 1993.

SAVAGE, Reggie

Center. Shoots left. 5'10", 187 lbs. Born, Montreal, Que., May 1, 1970.
(Washington's 1st choice, 15th overall, in 1988 Entry Draft).

Season	Club	Reg. GP	G	A	Pts	PIM	Playoffs GP	G	A	Pts	PIM
1990-91	Washington Capitals	1	0	0	0	0	....	....	....	....	....
1992-93	Washington Capitals	16	2	3	5	12	....	....	....	....	....
1993-94	Quebec Nordiques	17	3	4	7	16	....	....	....	....	....
	NHL Totals	**34**	**5**	**7**	**12**	**28**	....	....	....	....	....

Traded to **Quebec** by **Washington** with Paul MacDermid for Mike Hough, June 20, 1993. Signed as a free agent by **Phoenix**, August 28, 1996. Signed as a free agent by **Vancouver**, June 17, 1999. Signed as a free agent by **Columbus**, June 2, 2000.

SAVAGE, Tony

Defense. Shoots left. 6', 175 lbs. Born, Calgary, Alta., July 18, 1906.

Season	Club	Reg. GP	G	A	Pts	PIM	Playoffs GP	G	A	Pts	PIM
1934-35	Boston Bruins	8	0	0	0	2	....	....	....	....	....
	Montreal Canadiens	41	1	5	6	4	2	0	0	0	0
	NHL Totals	**49**	**1**	**5**	**6**	**6**	**2**	**0**	**0**	**0**	**0**

Traded to **Montreal** by **Calgary** (NWHL) for cash, October, 1934. Traded to **Boston** by **Montreal** for Tommy Filmore and cash, November 5, 1934. Traded to **Montreal** by **Boston** with $7,500 for Jack Portland, December 3, 1934.

SAVARD, Andre

Center. Shoots left. 6'1", 185 lbs. Born, Temiscamingue, Que., February 9, 1953.
(Boston's 1st choice, 6th overall, in 1973 Amateur Draft).

Season	Club	Reg. GP	G	A	Pts	PIM	Playoffs GP	G	A	Pts	PIM
1973-74	Boston Bruins	72	16	14	30	39	16	3	2	5	24
1974-75	Boston Bruins	77	19	25	44	45	3	1	1	2	2
1975-76	Boston Bruins	79	17	23	40	60	12	1	4	5	9
1976-77	Buffalo Sabres	80	25	35	60	30	6	0	1	1	2
1977-78	Buffalo Sabres	80	19	20	39	40	6	0	0	0	4
1978-79	Buffalo Sabres	65	18	22	40	20	3	0	2	2	2
1979-80	Buffalo Sabres	33	3	10	13	16	8	1	1	2	2
1980-81	Buffalo Sabres	79	31	43	74	63	8	4	2	6	17
1981-82	Buffalo Sabres	62	18	20	38	24	4	0	1	1	5
1982-83	Buffalo Sabres	68	16	25	41	28	10	0	4	4	8
1983-84	Quebec Nordiques	60	20	24	44	38	9	3	0	3	2
1984-85	Quebec Nordiques	35	9	10	19	8	....	....	....	....	....
	NHL Totals	**790**	**211**	**271**	**482**	**411**	**85**	**13**	**18**	**31**	**77**

Signed as a free agent by **Buffalo**, June 11, 1976. Traded to **Quebec** by **Buffalo** with Tony McKegney, Jean-Francois Sauve and Buffalo's 3rd round choice (Iiro Jarvi) in 1983 Entry Draft for Real Cloutier and Quebec's 1st round choice (Adam Creighton) in 1983 Entry Draft, June 8, 1983.

SAVARD, Denis — HHOF

Center. Shoots right. 5'10", 175 lbs. Born, Pointe Gatineau, Que., February 4, 1961.
(Chicago's 1st choice, 3rd overall, in 1980 Entry Draft).

Season	Club	Reg. GP	G	A	Pts	PIM	Playoffs GP	G	A	Pts	PIM
1980-81	Chicago Black Hawks	76	28	47	75	47	3	0	0	0	0
1981-82	Chicago Black Hawks	80	32	87	119	82	15	11	7	18	52
1982-83	Chicago Black Hawks	78	35	86	121	99	13	8	9	17	22
1983-84	Chicago Black Hawks	75	37	57	94	71	5	1	3	4	9
1984-85	Chicago Black Hawks	79	38	67	105	56	15	9	20	29	20

Season	Club	REGULAR SEASON GP	G	A	Pts	PIM	PLAYOFFS GP	G	A	Pts	PIM
1985-86	Chicago Black Hawks	80	47	69	116	111	3	4	1	5	6
1986-87	Chicago Blackhawks	70	40	50	90	108	4	1	0	1	12
1987-88	Chicago Blackhawks	80	44	87	131	95	5	4	3	7	17
1988-89	Chicago Blackhawks	58	23	59	82	110	16	8	11	19	10
1989-90	Chicago Blackhawks	60	27	53	80	56	20	7	15	22	41
1990-91	Montreal Canadiens	70	28	31	59	52	13	2	11	13	35
1991-92	Montreal Canadiens	77	28	42	70	73	11	3	9	12	8
1992-93♦	Montreal Canadiens	63	16	34	50	90	14	0	5	5	4
1993-94	Tampa Bay Lightning	74	18	28	46	106	....	....	....	....	....
1994-95	Tampa Bay Lightning	31	6	11	17	10	....	....	....	....	....
	Chicago Blackhawks	12	4	4	8	8	16	7	11	18	10
1995-96	Chicago Blackhawks	69	13	35	48	102	10	1	2	3	8
1996-97	Chicago Blackhawks	64	9	18	27	60	6	0	2	2	2
	NHL Totals	**1196**	**473**	**865**	**1338**	**1336**	**169**	**66**	**109**	**175**	**256**

NHL Second All-Star Team (1983)

Played in NHL All-Star Game (1982, 1983, 1984, 1986, 1988, 1991, 1996)

Traded to **Montreal** by **Chicago** for Chris Chelios and Montreal's 2nd round choice (Michael Pomichter) in 1991 Entry Draft, June 29, 1990. Signed as a free agent by **Tampa Bay**, July 29, 1993. Traded to **Chicago** by **Tampa Bay** for Chicago's 6th round choice (Xavier Delisle) in 1996 Entry Draft, April 6, 1995.

SAVARD, Jean

Center. Shoots right. 5'11", 172 lbs. Born, Verdun, Que., April 26, 1957.
(Chicago's 2nd choice, 19th overall, in 1977 Amateur Draft).

Season	Club	GP	G	A	Pts	PIM	GP	G	A	Pts	PIM
1977-78	Chicago Black Hawks	31	7	11	18	20	....	....	....	....	....
1978-79	Chicago Black Hawks	11	0	1	1	9	....	....	....	....	....
1979-80	Hartford Whalers	1	0	0	0	0	....	....	....	....	....
	NHL Totals	**43**	**7**	**12**	**19**	**29**	....	....	....	....	....

Claimed by **Hartford** from **Chicago** in Expansion Draft, June 13, 1979.

SAVARD, Marc

Center. Shoots left. 5'10", 188 lbs. Born, Ottawa, Ont., July 17, 1977.
(NY Rangers' 3rd choice, 91st overall, in 1995 Entry Draft).

Season	Club	GP	G	A	Pts	PIM	GP	G	A	Pts	PIM
1997-98	New York Rangers	28	1	5	6	4	....	....	....	....	....
1998-99	New York Rangers	70	9	36	45	38	....	....	....	....	....
99-2000	Calgary Flames	78	22	31	53	56	....	....	....	....	....
2000-01	Calgary Flames	77	23	42	65	46	....	....	....	....	....
2001-02	Calgary Flames	56	14	19	33	48	....	....	....	....	....
2002-03	Calgary Flames	10	1	2	3	8	....	....	....	....	....
	Atlanta Thrashers	57	16	31	47	77	....	....	....	....	....
	NHL Totals	**376**	**86**	**166**	**252**	**277**	....	....	....	....	....

Traded to **Calgary** by **NY Rangers** with NY Rangers 1st round choice (Oleg Saprykin) in 1999 Entry Draft for the rights to Jan Hlavac and Calgary's 1st (Jamie Lundmark) and 3rd (later traded back to Calgary – Calgary selected Craig Andersson) round choices in 1999 Entry Draft, June 26, 1999. Traded to **Atlanta** by **Calgary** for Ruslan Zainullin, November 15, 2002.

SAVARD, Serge

HHOF

Defense. Shoots left. 6'3", 210 lbs. Born, Montreal, Que., January 22, 1946.

Season	Club	GP	G	A	Pts	PIM	GP	G	A	Pts	PIM
1966-67	Montreal Canadiens	2	0	0	0	0	....	....	....	....	....
1967-68♦	Montreal Canadiens	67	2	13	15	34	6	2	0	2	0
1968-69♦	Montreal Canadiens	74	8	23	31	73	14	4	6	10	24
1969-70	Montreal Canadiens	64	12	19	31	38	....	....	....	....	....
1970-71♦	Montreal Canadiens	37	5	10	15	30	....	....	....	....	....
1971-72	Montreal Canadiens	23	1	8	9	16	6	0	0	0	10
1972-73♦	Montreal Canadiens	74	7	32	39	58	17	3	8	11	22
1973-74	Montreal Canadiens	67	4	14	18	49	6	1	1	2	4
1974-75	Montreal Canadiens	80	20	40	60	64	11	1	7	8	2
1975-76♦	Montreal Canadiens	71	8	39	47	38	13	3	6	9	6
1976-77♦	Montreal Canadiens	78	9	33	42	35	14	2	7	9	2
1977-78♦	Montreal Canadiens	77	8	34	42	24	15	1	7	8	8
1978-79♦	Montreal Canadiens	80	7	26	33	30	16	2	7	9	6
1979-80	Montreal Canadiens	46	5	8	13	18	2	0	0	0	0
1980-81	Montreal Canadiens	77	4	13	17	30	3	0	0	0	0
1981-82	Winnipeg Jets	47	2	5	7	26	4	0	0	0	2
1982-83	Winnipeg Jets	76	4	16	20	29	3	0	0	0	2
	NHL Totals	**1040**	**106**	**333**	**439**	**592**	**130**	**19**	**49**	**68**	**88**

Conn Smythe Trophy (1969) • NHL Second All-Star Team (1979) • Bill Masterton Trophy (1979)

Played in NHL All-Star Game (1970, 1973, 1977, 1978)

• Missed remainder of 1969-70 season and majority of 1970-71 season recovering from leg injury suffered in game vs. NY Rangers, March 11, 1970. • Missed remainder of 1970-71 season and majority of 1971-72 season recovering from leg injury suffered in game vs. Toronto, January 30, 1971. Claimed by **Winnipeg** from **Montreal** in Waiver Draft, October 5, 1981.

SAVOIA, Ryan

Center. Shoots right. 6'1", 204 lbs. Born, Thorold, Ont., May 6, 1973.

Season	Club	GP	G	A	Pts	PIM	GP	G	A	Pts	PIM
1998-99	Pittsburgh Penguins	3	0	0	0	0	....	....	....	....	....
	NHL Totals	**3**	**0**	**0**	**0**	**0**	....	....	....	....	....

Signed as a free agent by **Pittsburgh**, April 7, 1995.

SAWYER, Kevin

Left wing. Shoots left. 6'2", 212 lbs. Born, Christina Lake, B.C., February 21, 1974.

Season	Club	REGULAR SEASON GP	G	A	Pts	PIM	PLAYOFFS GP	G	A	Pts	PIM
1995-96	St. Louis Blues	6	0	0	0	23	....	....	....	....	....
	Boston Bruins	2	0	0	0	5	....	....	....	....	....
1996-97	Boston Bruins	2	0	0	0	0	....	....	....	....	....
99-2000	Phoenix Coyotes	3	0	0	0	12	....	....	....	....	....
2000-01	Mighty Ducks of Anaheim	9	0	1	1	27	....	....	....	....	....
2001-02	Mighty Ducks of Anaheim	57	1	1	2	221	....	....	....	....	....
2002-03	Mighty Ducks of Anaheim	31	2	1	3	115	....	....	....	....	....
	NHL Totals	**110**	**3**	**3**	**6**	**403**	....	....	....	....	....

Signed as a free agent by **St. Louis**, February 28, 1995. Traded to **Boston** by **St. Louis** with Steve Staios for Steve Leach, March 8, 1996. Signed as a free agent by **Dallas**, August 19, 1997. Signed as a free agent by **St. Louis**, September 4, 1998. Signed as a free agent by **Phoenix**, August 15, 1999. Signed as a free agent by **Anaheim**, July 13, 2000.

SCAMURRA, Peter

Defense. Shoots left. 6'3", 185 lbs. Born, Buffalo, NY, February 23, 1955.
(Washington's 2nd choice, 19th overall, in 1975 Amateur Draft).

Season	Club	GP	G	A	Pts	PIM	GP	G	A	Pts	PIM
1975-76	Washington Capitals	58	2	13	15	33	....	....	....	....	....
1976-77	Washington Capitals	21	0	2	2	8	....	....	....	....	....
1978-79	Washington Capitals	30	3	5	8	12	....	....	....	....	....
1979-80	Washington Capitals	23	3	5	8	6	....	....	....	....	....
	NHL Totals	**132**	**8**	**25**	**33**	**59**	....	....	....	....	....

SCATCHARD, Dave

Center. Shoots right. 6'2", 224 lbs. Born, Hinton, Alta., February 20, 1976.
(Vancouver's 3rd choice, 42nd overall, in 1994 Entry Draft).

Season	Club	GP	G	A	Pts	PIM	GP	G	A	Pts	PIM
1997-98	Vancouver Canucks	76	13	11	24	165	....	....	....	....	....
1998-99	Vancouver Canucks	82	13	13	26	140	....	....	....	....	....
99-2000	Vancouver Canucks	21	0	4	4	24	....	....	....	....	....
	New York Islanders	44	12	14	26	93	....	....	....	....	....
2000-01	New York Islanders	81	21	24	45	114	....	....	....	....	....
2001-02	New York Islanders	80	12	15	27	111	7	1	1	2	22
2002-03	New York Islanders	81	27	18	45	108	5	1	0	1	6
	NHL Totals	**465**	**98**	**99**	**197**	**755**	**12**	**2**	**1**	**3**	**28**

Traded to **NY Islanders** by **Vancouver** with Kevin Weekes and Bill Muckalt for Felix Potvin, NY Islanders' compensatory 2nd round choice (later traded to New Jersey – New Jersey selected Teemu Laine) in 2000 Entry Draft and NY Islanders' 3rd round choice (Thatcher Bell) in 2000 Entry Draft, December 19, 1999.

SCEVIOUR, Darin

Right wing. Shoots right. 5'10", 185 lbs. Born, Lacombe, Alta., November 30, 1965.
(Chicago's 5th choice, 101st overall, in 1984 Entry Draft).

Season	Club	GP	G	A	Pts	PIM	GP	G	A	Pts	PIM
1986-87	Chicago Blackhawks	1	0	0	0	0	....	....	....	....	....
	NHL Totals	**1**	**0**	**0**	**0**	**0**	....	....	....	....	....

SCHAEFER, Peter

Left wing. Shoots left. 5'11", 195 lbs. Born, Yellow Grass, Sask., July 12, 1977.
(Vancouver's 3rd choice, 66th overall, in 1995 Entry Draft).

Season	Club	GP	G	A	Pts	PIM	GP	G	A	Pts	PIM
1998-99	Vancouver Canucks	25	4	4	8	8	....	....	....	....	....
99-2000	Vancouver Canucks	71	16	15	31	20	....	....	....	....	....
2000-01	Vancouver Canucks	82	16	20	36	22	3	0	0	0	0
2002-03	Ottawa Senators	75	6	17	23	32	16	2	3	5	6
	NHL Totals	**253**	**42**	**56**	**98**	**82**	**19**	**2**	**3**	**5**	**6**

Traded to **Ottawa** by **Vancouver** for Sami Salo, September 21, 2002.

SCHAEFFER, Butch

Defense. Shoots right. 5'10", 190 lbs. Born, Hinkley, MN, November 7, 1911.

Season	Club	GP	G	A	Pts	PIM	GP	G	A	Pts	PIM
1936-37	Chicago Black Hawks	5	0	0	0	6	....	....	....	....	....
	NHL Totals	**5**	**0**	**0**	**0**	**6**	....	....	....	....	....

SCHAMEHORN, Kevin

Right wing. Shoots right. 5'9", 185 lbs. Born, Calgary, Alta., July 28, 1956.
(Detroit's 4th choice, 58th overall, in 1976 Amateur Draft).

Season	Club	GP	G	A	Pts	PIM	GP	G	A	Pts	PIM
1976-77	Detroit Red Wings	3	0	0	0	9	....	....	....	....	....
1979-80	Detroit Red Wings	2	0	0	0	4	....	....	....	....	....
1980-81	Los Angeles Kings	5	0	0	0	4	....	....	....	....	....
	NHL Totals	**10**	**0**	**0**	**0**	**17**	....	....	....	....	....

Signed as a free agent by **Los Angeles**, October 18, 1980.

SCHASTLIVY, Petr

Left wing. Shoots left. 6'1", 204 lbs. Born, Angarsk, USSR, April 18, 1979.
(Ottawa's 5th choice, 101st overall, in 1998 Entry Draft).

Season	Club	GP	G	A	Pts	PIM	GP	G	A	Pts	PIM
99-2000	Ottawa Senators	13	2	5	7	2	1	0	0	0	0
2000-01	Ottawa Senators	17	3	2	5	6	....	....	....	....	....
2001-02	Ottawa Senators	1	0	1	1	0	....	....	....	....	....
2002-03	Ottawa Senators	33	9	10	19	4	....	....	....	....	....
	NHL Totals	**64**	**14**	**18**	**32**	**12**	**1**	**0**	**0**	**0**	**0**

SCHELLA, John

Defense. Shoots right. 6', 180 lbs. Born, Port Arthur, Ont., May 9, 1947.

Season	Club	GP	G	A	Pts	PIM	GP	G	A	Pts	PIM
1970-71	Vancouver Canucks	38	0	5	5	58	....	....	....	....	....
1971-72	Vancouver Canucks	77	2	13	15	166	....	....	....	....	....
	NHL Totals	**115**	**2**	**18**	**20**	**224**	....	....	....	....	....

Claimed by **Vancouver** from **Montreal** in Expansion Draft, June 10, 1970. Claimed by **NY Islanders** from **Vancouver** in Expansion Draft, June 6, 1972.

SCHERZA, Chuck

Left wing/Center. Shoots left. 5'10", 190 lbs. Born, Brandon, Man., February 15, 1923.

Season	Club	GP	G	A	Pts	PIM	GP	G	A	Pts	PIM
		Regular Season					Playoffs				
1943-44	Boston Bruins	9	1	1	2	6	....	....	....	....	....
	New York Rangers	5	3	2	5	11	....	....	....	....	....
1944-45	New York Rangers	22	2	3	5	18	....	....	....	....	....
	NHL Totals	**36**	**6**	**6**	**12**	**35**	....	....	....	....	....

Traded to **NY Rangers** by **Boston** for cash, November, 1943.

SCHINKEL, Ken

Right wing. Shoots right. 5'10", 172 lbs. Born, Jansen, Sask., November 27, 1932.

Season	Club	GP	G	A	Pts	PIM	GP	G	A	Pts	PIM
1959-60	New York Rangers	69	13	16	29	27	....	....	....	....	....
1960-61	New York Rangers	38	2	6	8	18	....	....	....	....	....
1961-62	New York Rangers	65	7	21	28	17	2	1	0	1	0
1962-63	New York Rangers	69	6	9	15	15	....	....	....	....	....
1963-64	New York Rangers	4	0	0	0	0	....	....	....	....	....
1966-67	New York Rangers	20	6	3	9	0	4	0	1	1	0
1967-68	Pittsburgh Penguins	57	14	25	39	19	....	....	....	....	....
1968-69	Pittsburgh Penguins	76	18	34	52	18	....	....	....	....	....
1969-70	Pittsburgh Penguins	72	20	25	45	19	10	4	1	5	4
1970-71	Pittsburgh Penguins	50	15	19	34	6	....	....	....	....	....
1971-72	Pittsburgh Penguins	74	15	30	45	8	3	2	0	2	0
1972-73	Pittsburgh Penguins	42	11	10	21	16	....	....	....	....	....
	NHL Totals	**636**	**127**	**198**	**325**	**163**	**19**	**7**	**2**	**9**	**4**

Played in NHL All-Star Game (1968, 1969)

Traded to **NY Rangers** by **Springfield** (AHL) for future considerations, June, 1959. Claimed by **Pittsburgh** from **NY Rangers** in Expansion Draft, June 6, 1967.

SCHLEGEL, Brad

Defense. Shoots right. 5'10", 188 lbs. Born, Kitchener, Ont., July 22, 1968.
(Washington's 8th choice, 144th overall, in 1988 Entry Draft).

Season	Club	GP	G	A	Pts	PIM	GP	G	A	Pts	PIM
1991-92	Washington Capitals	15	0	1	1	0	7	0	1	1	2
1992-93	Washington Capitals	7	0	1	1	6	....	....	....	....	....
1993-94	Calgary Flames	26	1	6	7	4	....	....	....	....	....
	NHL Totals	**48**	**1**	**8**	**9**	**10**	**7**	**0**	**1**	**1**	**2**

Traded to **Calgary** by **Washington** for Calgary's 7th round choice (Andrew Brunette) in 1993 Entry Draft, June 26, 1993.

SCHLIEBENER, Andy

Defense. Shoots left. 6', 200 lbs. Born, Ottawa, Ont., August 16, 1962.
(Vancouver's 2nd choice, 49th overall, in 1980 Entry Draft).

Season	Club	GP	G	A	Pts	PIM	GP	G	A	Pts	PIM
1981-82	Vancouver Canucks	22	0	1	1	10	3	0	0	0	0
1983-84	Vancouver Canucks	51	2	10	12	48	3	0	0	0	0
1984-85	Vancouver Canucks	11	0	0	0	16	....	....	....	....	....
	NHL Totals	**84**	**2**	**11**	**13**	**74**	**6**	**0**	**0**	**0**	**0**

SCHMAUTZ, Bobby

Right wing. Shoots right. 5'9", 172 lbs. Born, Saskatoon, Sask., March 28, 1945.

Season	Club	GP	G	A	Pts	PIM	GP	G	A	Pts	PIM
1967-68	Chicago Black Hawks	13	3	2	5	6	11	2	3	5	2
1968-69	Chicago Black Hawks	63	9	7	16	37	....	....	....	....	....
1970-71	Vancouver Canucks	26	5	5	10	14	....	....	....	....	....
1971-72	Vancouver Canucks	60	12	13	25	82	....	....	....	....	....
1972-73	Vancouver Canucks	77	38	33	71	137	....	....	....	....	....
1973-74	Vancouver Canucks	49	26	19	45	58	....	....	....	....	....
	Boston Bruins	27	7	13	20	31	16	3	6	9	44
1974-75	Boston Bruins	56	21	30	51	63	3	1	5	6	6
1975-76	Boston Bruins	75	28	34	62	116	11	2	8	10	13
1976-77	Boston Bruins	57	23	29	52	62	14	*11	1	12	10
1977-78	Boston Bruins	54	27	27	54	87	15	7	8	15	11
1978-79	Boston Bruins	65	20	22	42	77	11	2	2	4	6
1979-80	Boston Bruins	20	8	6	14	8	....	....	....	....	....
	Edmonton Oilers	29	8	8	16	20	....	....	....	....	....
	Colorado Rockies	20	9	4	13	53	....	....	....	....	....
1980-81	Vancouver Canucks	73	27	34	61	137	3	0	0	0	0
	NHL Totals	**764**	**271**	**286**	**557**	**988**	**84**	**28**	**33**	**61**	**92**

• Brother of Cliff

Played in NHL All-Star Game (1973, 1974)

Traded to **Seattle** (WHL) by **Chicago** (LA Blades-WHL) with Marc Boileau for cash with Chicago retaining NHL rights, August 10, 1967. Claimed by **St. Louis** from **Chicago** in Intra-League Draft, June 11, 1969. Traded to **Montreal** by **St. Louis** with Norm Beaudin for Ernie Wakely, June 27, 1969. Traded to **Salt Lake** (WHL) by **Montreal** for cash, August, 1969. Traded to **Seattle** (WHL) by **Salt Lake** (WHL) for Guyle Fielder, November 15, 1969. Traded to **Vancouver** by **Seattle** (WHL) for the loan of Jim Wiste and Ed Hatoum for the remainder of the 1970-71 season, February 9, 1971. Traded to **Boston** by **Vancouver** for Fred O'Donnell, Chris Oddleifson and the NHL rights to Mike Walton, February 7, 1974. Traded to **Edmonton** by **Boston** for Dan Newman, December 10, 1979. Traded to **Colorado** by **Edmonton** for Don Ashby, February 25, 1980. Signed as a free agent by **Vancouver**, October 2, 1980.

SCHMAUTZ, Cliff

Right wing. Shoots right. 5'10", 165 lbs. Born, Saskatoon, Sask., March 17, 1939.

Season	Club	GP	G	A	Pts	PIM	GP	G	A	Pts	PIM
1970-71	Buffalo Sabres	26	5	7	12	10	....	....	....	....	....
	Philadelphia Flyers	30	8	12	20	23	....	....	....	....	....
	NHL Totals	**56**	**13**	**19**	**32**	**33**	....	....	....	....	....

• Brother of Bobby

Claimed by **Buffalo** from **Portland** (WHL) in Inter-League Draft, June 9, 1970. Claimed on waivers by **Philadelphia** from **Buffalo**, December 28, 1970. Traded to **Portland** (WHL) by **Philadelphia** for cash, September, 1971.

SCHMIDT, Chris

Center. Shoots left. 6'3", 212 lbs. Born, Beaverlodge, Alta., March 1, 1976.
(Los Angeles' 4th choice, 111th overall, in 1994 Entry Draft).

Season	Club	GP	G	A	Pts	PIM	GP	G	A	Pts	PIM
2002-03	Los Angeles Kings	10	0	2	2	5	....	....	....	....	....
	NHL Totals	**10**	**0**	**2**	**2**	**5**	....	....	....	....	....

SCHMIDT, Clarence

Right wing. Shoots right. 5'11", 165 lbs. Born, Williams, MN, September 17, 1925.

Season	Club	GP	G	A	Pts	PIM	GP	G	A	Pts	PIM
1943-44	Boston Bruins	7	1	0	1	2	....	....	....	....	....
	NHL Totals	**7**	**1**	**0**	**1**	**2**	....	....	....	....	....

SCHMIDT, Jackie

Left wing. Shoots left. 5'10", 155 lbs. Born, Odessa, Sask., November 11, 1924.

Season	Club	GP	G	A	Pts	PIM	GP	G	A	Pts	PIM
1942-43	Boston Bruins	45	6	7	13	6	5	0	0	0	0
	NHL Totals	**45**	**6**	**7**	**13**	**6**	**5**	**0**	**0**	**0**	**0**

• Brother of Otto

SCHMIDT, Milt

HHOF

Center/Defense. Shoots left. 6', 185 lbs. Born, Kitchener, Ont., March 5, 1918.

Season	Club	GP	G	A	Pts	PIM	GP	G	A	Pts	PIM
1936-37	Boston Bruins	26	2	8	10	15	3	0	0	0	0
1937-38	Boston Bruins	44	13	14	27	15	3	0	0	0	0
1938-39 ♦	Boston Bruins	41	15	17	32	13	12	3	3	6	2
1939-40	Boston Bruins	48	22	*30	*52	37	6	0	0	0	0
1940-41 ♦	Boston Bruins	45	13	25	38	23	11	5	6	*11	9
1941-42	Boston Bruins	36	14	21	35	34	....	....	....	....	....
1945-46	Boston Bruins	48	13	18	31	21	10	3	5	8	2
1946-47	Boston Bruins	59	27	35	62	40	5	3	1	4	4
1947-48	Boston Bruins	33	9	17	26	28	5	2	5	7	2
1948-49	Boston Bruins	44	10	22	32	25	4	0	2	2	8
1949-50	Boston Bruins	68	19	22	41	41	....	....	....	....	....
1950-51	Boston Bruins	62	22	39	61	33	6	0	1	1	7
1951-52	Boston Bruins	69	21	29	50	57	7	2	1	3	0
1952-53	Boston Bruins	68	11	23	34	30	10	5	1	6	6
1953-54	Boston Bruins	62	14	18	32	28	4	1	0	1	20
1954-55	Boston Bruins	23	4	8	12	26	....	....	....	....	....
	NHL Totals	**776**	**229**	**346**	**575**	**466**	**86**	**24**	**25**	**49**	**60**

NHL First All-Star Team (1940, 1947, 1951) • Hart Trophy (1951) • NHL Second All-Star Team (1952) • Lester Patrick Trophy (1996)

Played in NHL All-Star Game (1947, 1948, 1951, 1952)

Signed as a free agent by **Boston**, October 9, 1935.

SCHMIDT, Norm

Defense. Shoots right. 5'11", 190 lbs. Born, Sault Ste. Marie, Ont., January 24, 1963.
(Pittsburgh's 3rd choice, 70th overall, in 1981 Entry Draft).

Season	Club	GP	G	A	Pts	PIM	GP	G	A	Pts	PIM
1983-84	Pittsburgh Penguins	34	6	12	18	12	....	....	....	....	....
1985-86	Pittsburgh Penguins	66	15	14	29	57	....	....	....	....	....
1986-87	Pittsburgh Penguins	20	1	5	6	4	....	....	....	....	....
1987-88	Pittsburgh Penguins	5	1	2	3	0	....	....	....	....	....
	NHL Totals	**125**	**23**	**33**	**56**	**73**	....	....	....	....	....

• Suffered career-ending back injury in game vs. Philadelphia, October 18, 1987.

SCHMIDT, Otto

Defense. Shoots right. 5'10", 157 lbs. Born, Odessa, Sask., November 5, 1926.

Season	Club	GP	G	A	Pts	PIM	GP	G	A	Pts	PIM
1943-44	Boston Bruins	2	0	0	0	0	....	....	....	....	....
	NHL Totals	**2**	**0**	**0**	**0**	**0**	....	....	....	....	....

• Brother of Jackie

Signed as a free agent by **Boston**, December 7, 1943.

SCHNABEL, Robert

Defense. Shoots left. 6'5", 230 lbs. Born, Prague, Czech., November 10, 1978.
(Phoenix's 7th choice, 129th overall, in 1998 Entry Draft).

Season	Club	GP	G	A	Pts	PIM	GP	G	A	Pts	PIM
2001-02	Nashville Predators	1	0	0	0	0	....	....	....	....	....
2002-03	Nashville Predators	1	0	0	0	0	....	....	....	....	....
	NHL Totals	**2**	**0**	**0**	**0**	**0**	....	....	....	....	....

• Re-entered NHL Entry Draft. Originally NY Islanders' 5th choice, 79th overall, in 1997 Entry Draft.

Claimed on waivers by **Nashville** from **Phoenix**, January 2, 2001.

SCHNARR, Werner

Center. Shoots left. 5'7", 145 lbs. Born, Berlin, Ont., March 23, 1903.

Season	Club	GP	G	A	Pts	PIM	GP	G	A	Pts	PIM
1924-25	Boston Bruins	25	0	0	0	0	....	....	....	....	....

		Regular Season					Playoffs				
Season	Club	GP	G	A	Pts	PIM	GP	G	A	Pts	PIM
1925-26	Boston Bruins	1	0	0	0	0	....	....	....	....	....
	NHL Totals	**26**	**0**	**0**	**0**	**0**	....	....	....	....	....

Signed as a free agent by **Boston**, October 29, 1924.

SCHNEIDER, Andy

Left wing. Shoots left. 5'9", 170 lbs. Born, Edmonton, Alta., March 29, 1972.

Season	Club	GP	G	A	Pts	PIM	GP	G	A	Pts	PIM
1993-94	Ottawa Senators	10	0	0	0	15	....	....	....	....	....
	NHL Totals	**10**	**0**	**0**	**0**	**15**	....	....	....	....	....

Signed as a free agent by **Ottawa**, October 9, 1992.

SCHNEIDER, Mathieu

Defense. Shoots left. 5'10", 192 lbs. Born, New York, NY, June 12, 1969.
(Montreal's 4th choice, 44th overall, in 1987 Entry Draft).

Season	Club	GP	G	A	Pts	PIM	GP	G	A	Pts	PIM
1987-88	Montreal Canadiens	4	0	0	0	2	....	....	....	....	....
1989-90	Montreal Canadiens	44	7	14	21	25	9	1	3	4	31
1990-91	Montreal Canadiens	69	10	20	30	63	13	2	7	9	18
1991-92	Montreal Canadiens	78	8	24	32	72	10	1	4	5	6
1992-93 ♦	Montreal Canadiens	60	13	31	44	91	11	1	2	3	16
1993-94	Montreal Canadiens	75	20	32	52	62	1	0	0	0	0
1994-95	Montreal Canadiens	30	5	15	20	49	....	....	....	....	....
	New York Islanders	13	3	6	9	30	....	....	....	....	....
1995-96	New York Islanders	65	11	36	47	93	....	....	....	....	....
	Toronto Maple Leafs	13	2	5	7	10	6	0	4	4	8
1996-97	Toronto Maple Leafs	26	5	7	12	20	....	....	....	....	....
1997-98	Toronto Maple Leafs	76	11	26	37	44	....	....	....	....	....
1998-99	New York Rangers	75	10	24	34	71	....	....	....	....	....
99-2000	New York Rangers	80	10	20	30	78	....	....	....	....	....
2000-01	Los Angeles Kings	73	16	35	51	56	13	0	9	9	10
2001-02	Los Angeles Kings	55	7	23	30	68	7	0	1	1	18
2002-03	Los Angeles Kings	65	14	29	43	57	....	....	....	....	....
	Detroit Red Wings	13	2	5	7	16	4	0	0	0	6
	NHL Totals	**914**	**154**	**352**	**506**	**907**	**74**	**5**	**30**	**35**	**113**

Played in NHL All-Star Game (1996, 2003)

Traded to **NY Islanders** by **Montreal** with Kirk Muller and Craig Darby for Pierre Turgeon and Vladimir Malakhov, April 5, 1995. Traded to **Toronto** by **NY Islanders** with Wendel Clark and D.J. Smith for Darby Hendrickson, Sean Haggerty, Kenny Jonsson and Toronto's 1st round choice (Roberto Luongo) in 1997 Entry Draft, March 13, 1996. • Missed majority of 1996-97 season recovering from groin injury suffered in game vs. St. Louis, December 27, 1996. Rights traded to **NY Rangers** by **Toronto** for Alexander Karpovtsev and NY Rangers' 4th round choice (Mirko Murovic) in 1999 Entry Draft, October 14, 1998. Selected by **Columbus** from **NY Rangers** in Expansion Draft, June 23, 2000. Signed as a free agent by **Los Angeles**, August 14, 2000. Traded to **Detroit** by **Los Angeles** for Sean Avery, Maxim Kuznetsov, Detroit's 1st round choice (Jeff Tambellini) in 2003 Entry Draft and Detroit's 2nd round choice in 2004 Entry Draft, March 11, 2003.

SCHOCK, Danny

Left wing. Shoots left. 5'11", 180 lbs. Born, Terrace Bay, Ont., December 30, 1948.
(Boston's 1st choice, 12th overall, in 1968 Amateur Draft).

Season	Club	GP	G	A	Pts	PIM	GP	G	A	Pts	PIM
1969-70 ♦	Boston Bruins	....	....	....	....	....	1	0	0	0	0
1970-71	Boston Bruins	6	0	0	0	0	....	....	....	....	....
	Philadelphia Flyers	14	1	2	3	0	....	....	....	....	....
	NHL Totals	**20**	**1**	**2**	**3**	**0**	**1**	**0**	**0**	**0**	**0**

• Brother of Ron

Traded to **Philadelphia** by **Boston** with Rick MacLeish for Mike Walton, February 1, 1971.

SCHOCK, Ron

Center. Shoots left. 5'11", 180 lbs. Born, Chapleau, Ont., December 19, 1943.

Season	Club	GP	G	A	Pts	PIM	GP	G	A	Pts	PIM
1963-64	Boston Bruins	5	1	2	3	0	....	....	....	....	....
1964-65	Boston Bruins	33	4	7	11	14	....	....	....	....	....
1965-66	Boston Bruins	24	2	2	4	6	....	....	....	....	....
1966-67	Boston Bruins	66	10	20	30	8	....	....	....	....	....
1967-68	St. Louis Blues	55	9	9	18	17	12	1	2	3	0
1968-69	St. Louis Blues	67	12	27	39	14	12	1	2	3	6
1969-70	Pittsburgh Penguins	76	8	21	29	40	10	1	6	7	7
1970-71	Pittsburgh Penguins	71	14	26	40	20	....	....	....	....	....
1971-72	Pittsburgh Penguins	77	17	29	46	22	4	1	0	1	6
1972-73	Pittsburgh Penguins	78	13	36	49	23	....	....	....	....	....
1973-74	Pittsburgh Penguins	77	14	29	43	22	....	....	....	....	....
1974-75	Pittsburgh Penguins	80	23	63	86	36	9	0	4	4	10
1975-76	Pittsburgh Penguins	80	18	44	62	28	3	0	1	1	0
1976-77	Pittsburgh Penguins	80	17	32	49	10	3	0	1	1	0
1977-78	Buffalo Sabres	40	4	4	8	0	2	0	0	0	0
	NHL Totals	**909**	**166**	**351**	**517**	**260**	**55**	**4**	**16**	**20**	**29**

• Brother of Danny

Claimed by **St. Louis** from **Boston** in Expansion Draft, June 6, 1967. Traded to **Pittsburgh** by **St. Louis** with Craig Cameron and St. Louis' 2nd round choice (Brian McKenzie) for Lou Angotti and Pittsburgh's 1st round choice (Gene Carr) in 1971 Amateur Draft, June 6, 1969. Traded to **Buffalo** by **Pittsburgh** for Brian Spencer, September 20, 1977.

SCHOENFELD, Jim

Defense. Shoots left. 6'2", 200 lbs. Born, Galt, Ont., September 4, 1952.
(Buffalo's 1st choice, 5th overall, in 1972 Amateur Draft).

Season	Club	GP	G	A	Pts	PIM	GP	G	A	Pts	PIM
1972-73	Buffalo Sabres	66	4	15	19	178	6	2	1	3	4
1973-74	Buffalo Sabres	28	1	8	9	56	....	....	....	....	....
1974-75	Buffalo Sabres	68	1	19	20	184	17	1	4	5	38
1975-76	Buffalo Sabres	56	2	22	24	114	8	0	3	3	33
1976-77	Buffalo Sabres	65	7	25	32	97	6	0	0	0	12
1977-78	Buffalo Sabres	60	2	20	22	89	8	0	1	1	28
1978-79	Buffalo Sabres	46	8	17	25	67	3	0	1	1	0
1979-80	Buffalo Sabres	77	9	27	36	72	14	0	3	3	18
1980-81	Buffalo Sabres	71	8	25	33	110	8	0	0	0	14
1981-82	Buffalo Sabres	13	3	2	5	30	....	....	....	....	....
	Detroit Red Wings	39	5	9	14	69	....	....	....	....	....
1982-83	Detroit Red Wings	57	1	10	11	18	....	....	....	....	....
1983-84	Boston Bruins	39	0	2	2	20	....	....	....	....	....
1984-85	Buffalo Sabres	34	0	3	3	28	5	0	0	0	4
	NHL Totals	**719**	**51**	**204**	**255**	**1132**	**75**	**3**	**13**	**16**	**151**

NHL Second All-Star Team (1980)

Played in NHL All-Star Game (1977, 1980)

• Missed majority of 1973-74 season recovering from neck surgery, November 10, 1973. Traded to **Detroit** by **Buffalo** with Danny Gare and Derek Smith for Mike Foligno, Dale McCourt and Brent Peterson, December 2, 1981. Signed as a free agent by **Boston**, August 19, 1983. Signed as a free agent by **Buffalo**, December 6, 1984.

SCHOFIELD, Dwight

Defense. Shoots left. 6'3", 195 lbs. Born, Waltham, MA, March 25, 1956.
(Detroit's 5th choice, 76th overall, in 1976 Amateur Draft).

Season	Club	GP	G	A	Pts	PIM	GP	G	A	Pts	PIM
1976-77	Detroit Red Wings	3	1	0	1	2	....	....	....	....	....
1982-83	Montreal Canadiens	2	0	0	0	7	....	....	....	....	....
1983-84	St. Louis Blues	70	4	10	14	219	4	0	0	0	26
1984-85	St. Louis Blues	43	1	4	5	184	2	0	0	0	15
1985-86	Washington Capitals	50	1	2	3	127	3	0	0	0	14
1986-87	Pittsburgh Penguins	25	1	6	7	59	....	....	....	....	....
1987-88	Winnipeg Jets	18	0	0	0	33	....	....	....	....	....
	NHL Totals	**211**	**8**	**22**	**30**	**631**	**9**	**0**	**0**	**0**	**55**

Signed as a free agent by **Montreal**, September 20, 1982. Claimed by **St. Louis** from **Montreal** in Waiver Draft, October 3, 1983. Claimed by **Washington** from **St. Louis** in Waiver Draft, October 7, 1985. Traded to **Pittsburgh** by **Washington** for cash, October 8, 1986. Signed as a free agent by **Winnipeg**, July, 1987.

SCHREIBER, Wally

Right wing. Shoots right. 5'11", 180 lbs. Born, Edmonton, Alta., April 15, 1962.
(Washington's 5th choice, 152nd overall, in 1982 Entry Draft).

Season	Club	GP	G	A	Pts	PIM	GP	G	A	Pts	PIM
1987-88	Minnesota North Stars	16	6	5	11	2	....	....	....	....	....
1988-89	Minnesota North Stars	25	2	5	7	10	....	....	....	....	....
	NHL Totals	**41**	**8**	**10**	**18**	**12**	....	....	....	....	....

Signed as a free agent by **Minnesota**, May 26, 1987.

SCHRINER, Sweeney — HHOF

Left wing. Shoots left. 6', 185 lbs. Born, Saratov, Russia, November 30, 1911.

Season	Club	GP	G	A	Pts	PIM	GP	G	A	Pts	PIM
1934-35	New York Americans	48	18	22	40	6	....	....	....	....	....
1935-36	New York Americans	48	19	26	*45	8	5	3	1	4	2
1936-37	New York Americans	48	21	25	*46	17	....	....	....	....	....
1937-38	New York Americans	48	21	17	38	22	6	1	0	1	0
1938-39	New York Americans	48	13	31	44	20	2	0	0	0	30
1939-40	Toronto Maple Leafs	39	11	15	26	10	9	1	3	4	4
1940-41	Toronto Maple Leafs	48	24	14	38	6	7	2	1	3	4
1941-42 ♦	Toronto Maple Leafs	47	20	16	36	21	13	6	3	9	10
1942-43	Toronto Maple Leafs	37	19	17	36	13	4	2	2	4	0
1944-45 ♦	Toronto Maple Leafs	26	22	15	37	10	13	3	1	4	4
1945-46	Toronto Maple Leafs	47	13	6	19	15	....	....	....	....	....
	NHL Totals	**484**	**201**	**204**	**405**	**148**	**59**	**18**	**11**	**29**	**54**

NHL Rookie of the Year (1935) • NHL First All-Star Team (1936, 1941) • NHL Second All-Star Team (1937)

Played in NHL All-Star Game (1937)

Traded to **Toronto** by **NY Americans** for Busher Jackson, Buzz Boll, Doc Romnes, Jimmy Fowler and Murray Armstrong, May 18, 1939.

SCHULTE, Paxton

Left wing. Shoots left. 6'2", 217 lbs. Born, Onaway, Alta., July 16, 1972.
(Quebec's 7th choice, 124th overall, in 1992 Entry Draft).

Season	Club	GP	G	A	Pts	PIM	GP	G	A	Pts	PIM
1993-94	Quebec Nordiques	1	0	0	0	2	....	....	....	....	....
1996-97	Calgary Flames	1	0	0	0	2	....	....	....	....	....
	NHL Totals	**2**	**0**	**0**	**0**	**4**	....	....	....	....	....

Transferred to **Colorado** after **Quebec** franchise relocated, July 1, 1995. Traded to **Calgary** by **Colorado** for Vesa Viitakoski, March 19, 1996.

SCHULTZ, Dave

Left wing. Shoots left. 6'1", 190 lbs. Born, Waldheim, Sask., October 14, 1949.
(Philadelphia's 5th choice, 52nd overall, in 1969 Amateur Draft).

Season	Club	GP	G	A	Pts	PIM	GP	G	A	Pts	PIM
1971-72	Philadelphia Flyers	1	0	0	0	0	....	....	....	....	....
1972-73	Philadelphia Flyers	76	9	12	21	*259	11	1	0	1	*51
1973-74 ♦	Philadelphia Flyers	73	20	16	36	*348	17	2	4	6	*139
1974-75 ♦	Philadelphia Flyers	76	9	17	26	*472	17	2	3	5	*83
1975-76	Philadelphia Flyers	71	13	19	32	307	16	2	2	4	*90
1976-77	Los Angeles Kings	76	10	20	30	232	9	1	1	2	45
1977-78	Los Angeles Kings	8	2	0	2	*27	....	....	....	....	....
	Pittsburgh Penguins	66	9	25	34	*378	....	....	....	....	....
1978-79	Pittsburgh Penguins	47	4	9	13	157	....	....	....	....	....
	Buffalo Sabres	28	2	3	5	86	3	0	2	2	4

Season	Club	GP	G	A	Pts	PIM	GP	G	A	Pts	PIM
		REGULAR SEASON					PLAYOFFS				
1979-80	Buffalo Sabres	13	1	0	1	28	....	....	....	....	....
	NHL Totals	**535**	**79**	**121**	**200**	**2294**	**73**	**8**	**12**	**20**	**412**

Traded to **Los Angeles** by **Philadelphia** for Los Angeles' 4th round pick (Yves Guillemette) in 1977 Amateur Draft and 2nd choice (later traded to Colorado – Colorado selected Merlin Malinowski) in 1978 Amateur Draft, September 29, 1976. Traded to **Pittsburgh** by **Los Angeles** with Gene Carr and Los Angeles' 4th round choice (Shane Pearsall) in 1978 Amateur Draft for Hartland Monahan and Syl Apps Jr., November 2, 1977. Traded to **Buffalo** by **Pittsburgh** for Gary McAdam, February 6, 1979.

SCHULTZ, Nick

Defense. Shoots left. 6', 187 lbs. Born, Regina, Sask., August 25, 1982.
(Minnesota's 2nd choice, 33rd overall, in 2000 Entry Draft).

Season	Club	GP	G	A	Pts	PIM	GP	G	A	Pts	PIM
2001-02	Minnesota Wild	52	4	6	10	14	....	....	....	....	....
2002-03	Minnesota Wild	75	3	7	10	23	18	0	1	1	10
	NHL Totals	**127**	**7**	**13**	**20**	**37**	**18**	**0**	**1**	**1**	**10**

SCHULTZ, Ray

Defense. Shoots left. 6'2", 215 lbs. Born, Red Deer, Alta., November 14, 1976.
(Ottawa's 8th choice, 184th overall, in 1995 Entry Draft).

Season	Club	GP	G	A	Pts	PIM	GP	G	A	Pts	PIM
1997-98	New York Islanders	13	0	1	1	45	....	....	....	....	....
1998-99	New York Islanders	4	0	0	0	7	....	....	....	....	....
99-2000	New York Islanders	9	0	1	1	30	....	....	....	....	....
2000-01	New York Islanders	13	0	2	2	40	....	....	....	....	....
2001-02	New York Islanders	2	0	0	0	5	2	0	0	0	2
2002-03	New York Islanders	4	0	0	0	28	....	....	....	....	....
	NHL Totals	**45**	**0**	**4**	**4**	**155**	**2**	**0**	**0**	**0**	**2**

Signed as a free agent by **NY Islanders**, June 9, 1997. Signed as a free agent by **Nashville**, July 17, 2003.

SCHURMAN, Maynard

Left wing. Shoots left. 6'3", 205 lbs. Born, Summerdale, P.E.I., July 16, 1957.

Season	Club	GP	G	A	Pts	PIM	GP	G	A	Pts	PIM
1979-80	Hartford Whalers	7	0	0	0	0					
	NHL Totals	**7**	**0**	**0**	**0**	**0**					

Signed as a free agent by **Philadelphia**, September, 1978. Claimed by **Hartford** from **Philadelphia** in Expansion Draft, June 13, 1979.

SCHUTT, Rod

Left wing. Shoots left. 5'10", 185 lbs. Born, Bancroft, Ont., October 13, 1956.
(Montreal's 2nd choice, 13th overall, in 1976 Amateur Draft).

Season	Club	GP	G	A	Pts	PIM	GP	G	A	Pts	PIM
1977-78	Montreal Canadiens	2	0	0	0	0	....	....	....	....	....
1978-79	Pittsburgh Penguins	74	24	21	45	33	7	2	0	2	4
1979-80	Pittsburgh Penguins	73	18	21	39	43	5	2	1	3	6
1980-81	Pittsburgh Penguins	80	25	35	60	55	5	3	3	6	16
1981-82	Pittsburgh Penguins	35	9	12	21	42	5	1	2	3	0
1982-83	Pittsburgh Penguins	5	0	0	0	0	....	....	....	....	....
1983-84	Pittsburgh Penguins	11	1	3	4	4	....	....	....	....	....
1985-86	Toronto Maple Leafs	6	0	0	0	0	....	....	....	....	....
	NHL Totals	**286**	**77**	**92**	**169**	**177**	**22**	**8**	**6**	**14**	**26**

Traded to **Pittsburgh** by **Montreal** for Pittsburgh's 1st round choice (Mark Hunter) in 1981 Entry Draft, October 18, 1978. Signed as a free agent by **Toronto**, October 3, 1985.

SCISSONS, Scott

Center. Shoots left. 6'1", 201 lbs. Born, Saskatoon, Sask., October 29, 1971.
(NY Islanders' 1st choice, 6th overall, in 1990 Entry Draft).

Season	Club	GP	G	A	Pts	PIM	GP	G	A	Pts	PIM
1990-91	New York Islanders	1	0	0	0	0	....	....	....	....	....
1992-93	New York Islanders	....	....	....	....	....	1	0	0	0	0
1993-94	New York Islanders	1	0	0	0	0	....	....	....	....	....
	NHL Totals	**2**	**0**	**0**	**0**	**0**	**1**	**0**	**0**	**0**	**0**

SCLISIZZI, Enio

Left wing. Shoots left. 5'10", 170 lbs. Born, Milton, Ont., August 1, 1925.

Season	Club	GP	G	A	Pts	PIM	GP	G	A	Pts	PIM
1946-47	Detroit Red Wings	....	....	....	....	....	1	0	0	0	0
1947-48	Detroit Red Wings	4	1	0	1	0	6	0	0	0	4
1948-49	Detroit Red Wings	50	9	8	17	24	6	0	0	0	2
1949-50	Detroit Red Wings	4	0	0	0	2	....	....	....	....	....
1951-52	Detroit Red Wings	9	2	1	3	0	....	....	....	....	....
1952-53	Chicago Black Hawks	14	0	2	2	0	....	....	....	....	....
	NHL Totals	**81**	**12**	**11**	**23**	**26**	**13**	**0**	**0**	**0**	**6**

Traded to **Chicago** by **Detroit** with Fred Glover for cash, August 14, 1952.

SCOTT, Ganton

Right wing. Shoots right. 5'9", 165 lbs. Born, Preston, Ont., March 23, 1903.

Season	Club	GP	G	A	Pts	PIM	GP	G	A	Pts	PIM
1922-23	Toronto St. Pats	17	0	0	0	0	....	....	....	....	....
1923-24	Toronto St. Pats	4	0	0	0	0	....	....	....	....	....
	Hamilton Tigers	8	0	0	0	0	....	....	....	....	....
1924-25	Montreal Maroons	28	1	1	2	0	....	....	....	....	....
	NHL Totals	**57**	**1**	**1**	**2**	**0**	....	....	....	....	....

Signed as a free agent by **Toronto**, October 9, 1922. Traded to **Hamilton** by **Toronto** for cash, January 16, 1924. Signed as a free agent by **Mtl. Maroons**, October 31, 1924.

SCOTT, Laurie

Left wing/Center. Shoots left. 5'6", 155 lbs. Born, South River, Ont., June 19, 1900.

Season	Club	GP	G	A	Pts	PIM	GP	G	A	Pts	PIM
1926-27	New York Americans	39	6	2	8	22	....	....	....	....	....
1927-28	New York Rangers	23	0	1	1	6	....	....	....	....	....
	NHL Totals	**62**	**6**	**3**	**9**	**28**	....	....	....	....	....

Traded to **Toronto** by **Saskatoon** (PrHL) with Corb Denneny and Leo Bourgeault for cash, September 27, 1926. • Ruled to be property of **Toronto** by NHL President Frank Calder after **NY Americans** claimed his rights, November 4, 1926. Traded to **NY Americans** by **Toronto** for Jesse Spring, November 15, 1926. Traded to **NY Rangers** by **NY Americans** for cash, October 14, 1927. Traded to **Duluth** (AHA) by **NY Rangers** for cash, October 18, 1929.

SCOTT, Richard

Left wing. Shoots left. 6'2", 195 lbs. Born, Orillia, Ont., August 1, 1978.

Season	Club	GP	G	A	Pts	PIM	GP	G	A	Pts	PIM
2001-02	New York Rangers	5	0	0	0	5	....	....	....	....	....
	NHL Totals	**5**	**0**	**0**	**0**	**5**	....	....	....	....	....

Signed as a free agent by **NY Rangers**, May 8, 2001.

SCOVILLE, Darrel

Defense. Shoots left. 6'3", 215 lbs. Born, Swift Current, Sask., October 13, 1975.

Season	Club	GP	G	A	Pts	PIM	GP	G	A	Pts	PIM
99-2000	Calgary Flames	6	0	0	0	2	....	....	....	....	....
2002-03	Columbus Blue Jackets	2	0	0	0	4	....	....	....	....	....
	NHL Totals	**8**	**0**	**0**	**0**	**6**	....	....	....	....	....

Signed as a free agent by **Calgary**, June 12, 1998. Signed as a free agent by **Columbus**, July 10, 2001.

SCREMIN, Claudio

Defense. Shoots right. 6'2", 205 lbs. Born, Burnaby, B.C., May 28, 1968.
(Washington's 12th choice, 204th overall, in 1988 Entry Draft).

Season	Club	GP	G	A	Pts	PIM	GP	G	A	Pts	PIM
1991-92	San Jose Sharks	13	0	0	0	25	....	....	....	....	....
1992-93	San Jose Sharks	4	0	1	1	4	....	....	....	....	....
	NHL Totals	**17**	**0**	**1**	**1**	**29**	....	....	....	....	....

Rights traded to **Minnesota** by **Washington** for Don Beaupre, November 1, 1988. Signed as a free agent by **San Jose**, September 3, 1991.

SCRUTON, Howard

Defense. Shoots left. 6'3", 190 lbs. Born, Toronto, Ont., October 6, 1962.

Season	Club	GP	G	A	Pts	PIM	GP	G	A	Pts	PIM
1982-83	Los Angeles Kings	4	0	4	4	9	....	....	....	....	....
	NHL Totals	**4**	**0**	**4**	**4**	**9**	....	....	....	....	....

Signed as a free agent by **Los Angeles**, August 5, 1981.

SEABROOKE, Glen

Center. Shoots left. 6', 190 lbs. Born, Peterborough, Ont., September 11, 1967.
(Philadelphia's 1st choice, 21st overall, in 1985 Entry Draft).

Season	Club	GP	G	A	Pts	PIM	GP	G	A	Pts	PIM
1986-87	Philadelphia Flyers	10	1	4	5	2	....	....	....	....	....
1987-88	Philadelphia Flyers	6	0	1	1	2	....	....	....	....	....
1988-89	Philadelphia Flyers	3	0	1	1	0	....	....	....	....	....
	NHL Totals	**19**	**1**	**6**	**7**	**4**	....	....	....	....	....

SECORD, Al

Left wing. Shoots left. 6'1", 205 lbs. Born, Sudbury, Ont., March 3, 1958.
(Boston's 1st choice, 16th overall, in 1978 Amateur Draft).

Season	Club	GP	G	A	Pts	PIM	GP	G	A	Pts	PIM
1978-79	Boston Bruins	71	16	7	23	125	4	0	0	0	4
1979-80	Boston Bruins	77	23	16	39	170	10	0	3	3	65
1980-81	Boston Bruins	18	0	3	3	42	....	....	....	....	....
	Chicago Black Hawks	41	13	9	22	145	3	4	0	4	14
1981-82	Chicago Black Hawks	80	44	31	75	303	15	2	5	7	61
1982-83	Chicago Black Hawks	80	54	32	86	180	12	4	7	11	66
1983-84	Chicago Black Hawks	14	4	4	8	77	5	3	4	7	28
1984-85	Chicago Black Hawks	51	15	11	26	193	15	7	9	16	42
1985-86	Chicago Black Hawks	80	40	36	76	201	2	0	2	2	26
1986-87	Chicago Blackhawks	77	29	29	58	196	4	0	0	0	21
1987-88	Toronto Maple Leafs	74	15	27	42	221	6	1	0	1	16
1988-89	Toronto Maple Leafs	40	5	10	15	71	....	....	....	....	....
	Philadelphia Flyers	20	1	0	1	38	14	0	4	4	31
1989-90	Chicago Blackhawks	43	14	7	21	131	12	0	0	0	8
	NHL Totals	**766**	**273**	**222**	**495**	**2093**	**102**	**21**	**34**	**55**	**382**

Played in NHL All-Star Game (1982, 1983)

Traded to **Chicago** by **Boston** for Mike O'Connell, December 18, 1980. Traded to **Toronto** by **Chicago** with Ed Olczyk for Rick Vaive, Steve Thomas and Bob McGill, September 3, 1987. Traded to **Philadelphia** by **Toronto** for Philadelphia's 5th round choice (Keith Carney) in 1989 Entry Draft, February 7, 1989. Signed as a free agent by **Chicago**, August 7, 1989.

SEDIN, Daniel

Left wing. Shoots left. 6'1", 200 lbs. Born, Ornskoldsvik, Sweden, September 26, 1980.
(Vancouver's 1st choice, 2nd overall, in 1999 Entry Draft).

Season	Club	GP	G	A	Pts	PIM	GP	G	A	Pts	PIM
2000-01	Vancouver Canucks	75	20	14	34	24	4	1	2	3	0
2001-02	Vancouver Canucks	79	9	23	32	32	6	0	1	1	0
2002-03	Vancouver Canucks	79	14	17	31	34	14	1	5	6	8
	NHL Totals	**233**	**43**	**54**	**97**	**90**	**24**	**2**	**8**	**10**	**8**

SEDIN, Henrik

Center. Shoots left. 6'2", 200 lbs. Born, Ornskoldsvik, Sweden, September 26, 1980.
(Vancouver's 2nd choice, 3rd overall, in 1999 Entry Draft).

Season	Club	GP	G	A	Pts	PIM	GP	G	A	Pts	PIM
2000-01	Vancouver Canucks	82	9	20	29	38	4	0	4	4	0
2001-02	Vancouver Canucks	82	16	20	36	36	6	3	0	3	0
2002-03	Vancouver Canucks	78	8	31	39	38	14	3	2	5	8
	NHL Totals	**242**	**33**	**71**	**104**	**112**	**24**	**6**	**6**	**12**	**8**

SEDLBAUER, Ron

Left wing. Shoots left. 6'3", 195 lbs. Born, Burlington, Ont., October 22, 1954.
(Vancouver's 1st choice, 23rd overall, in 1974 Amateur Draft).

Season	Club	Regular Season GP	G	A	Pts	PIM	Playoffs GP	G	A	Pts	PIM
1974-75	Vancouver Canucks	26	3	4	7	17	5	0	0	0	10
1975-76	Vancouver Canucks	56	19	13	32	66	2	0	0	0	0
1976-77	Vancouver Canucks	70	18	20	38	29	....	....	....	....	....
1977-78	Vancouver Canucks	62	18	12	30	25	....	....	....	....	....
1978-79	Vancouver Canucks	79	40	16	56	26	3	0	1	1	9
1979-80	Vancouver Canucks	32	10	4	14	7	....	....	....	....	....
	Chicago Black Hawks	45	13	10	23	14	7	1	1	2	6
1980-81	Chicago Black Hawks	39	12	3	15	12	....	....	....	....	....
	Toronto Maple Leafs	21	10	4	14	14	2	0	1	1	2
	NHL Totals	**430**	**143**	**86**	**229**	**210**	**19**	**1**	**3**	**4**	**27**

Traded to **Chicago** by **Vancouver** for Dave Logan and Harold Phillipoff, December 21, 1979. Traded to **Toronto** by **Chicago** for cash, February 18, 1981.

SEFTEL, Steve

Left wing. Shoots left. 6'3", 200 lbs. Born, Kitchener, Ont., May 14, 1968.
(Washington's 2nd choice, 40th overall, in 1986 Entry Draft).

Season	Club	Regular Season GP	G	A	Pts	PIM	Playoffs GP	G	A	Pts	PIM
1990-91	Washington Capitals	4	0	0	0	2	....	....	....	....	....
	NHL Totals	**4**	**0**	**0**	**0**	**2**	....	....	....	....	....

SEGUIN, Dan

Left wing. Shoots left. 5'8", 165 lbs. Born, Sudbury, Ont., June 7, 1948.

Season	Club	Regular Season GP	G	A	Pts	PIM	Playoffs GP	G	A	Pts	PIM
1970-71	Minnesota North Stars	11	1	1	2	4	....	....	....	....	....
	Vancouver Canucks	25	0	5	5	46	....	....	....	....	....
1973-74	Vancouver Canucks	1	1	0	1	0	....	....	....	....	....
	NHL Totals	**37**	**2**	**6**	**8**	**50**	....	....	....	....	....

Traded to **Minnesota** by **NY Rangers** with Wayne Hillman and Joey Johnston for Dave Balon, June 12, 1968. Claimed on waivers by **Vancouver** from **Minnesota**, November 23, 1970. Traded to **Rhode Island** (AHL) by **Vancouver** for cash, October, 1976.

SEGUIN, Steve

Wing. Shoots left. 6'2", 200 lbs. Born, Cornwall, Ont., April 10, 1964.
(Los Angeles' 2nd choice, 48th overall, in 1982 Entry Draft).

Season	Club	Regular Season GP	G	A	Pts	PIM	Playoffs GP	G	A	Pts	PIM
1984-85	Los Angeles Kings	5	0	0	0	9	....	....	....	....	....
	NHL Totals	**5**	**0**	**0**	**0**	**9**	....	....	....	....	....

Traded to **Philadelphia** by **Los Angeles** with Los Angeles' 2nd round choice (Jukka Seppo) in 1986 Entry Draft for Paul Guay and Philadelphia's 4th round choice (Sylvain Couturier) in 1986 Entry Draft, October 11, 1985.

SEIBERT, Earl

HHOF

Defense. Shoots right. 6'2", 198 lbs. Born, Berlin, Ont., December 7, 1911.

Season	Club	Regular Season GP	G	A	Pts	PIM	Playoffs GP	G	A	Pts	PIM
1931-32	New York Rangers	46	4	6	10	88	7	1	2	3	14
1932-33♦	New York Rangers	45	2	3	5	92	8	1	0	1	14
1933-34	New York Rangers	48	13	10	23	66	2	0	0	0	4
1934-35	New York Rangers	48	6	19	25	86	4	0	0	0	6
1935-36	New York Rangers	17	2	3	5	6	....	....	....	....	....
	Chicago Black Hawks	15	3	6	9	19	2	2	0	2	0
1936-37	Chicago Black Hawks	43	9	6	15	46	....	....	....	....	....
1937-38♦	Chicago Black Hawks	48	8	13	21	38	10	5	2	7	12
1938-39	Chicago Black Hawks	48	4	11	15	57	....	....	....	....	....
1939-40	Chicago Black Hawks	36	3	7	10	35	2	0	1	1	8
1940-41	Chicago Black Hawks	46	3	17	20	52	5	0	0	0	12
1941-42	Chicago Black Hawks	46	7	14	21	52	3	0	0	0	0
1942-43	Chicago Black Hawks	44	5	27	32	48	....	....	....	....	....
1943-44	Chicago Black Hawks	50	8	25	33	20	9	0	2	2	2
1944-45	Chicago Black Hawks	22	7	8	15	13	....	....	....	....	....
	Detroit Red Wings	25	5	9	14	10	14	2	1	3	4
1945-46	Detroit Red Wings	18	0	3	3	18	....	....	....	....	....
	NHL Totals	**645**	**89**	**187**	**276**	**746**	**66**	**11**	**8**	**19**	**76**

NHL First All-Star Team (1935, 1942, 1943, 1944) • NHL Second All-Star Team (1936, 1937, 1938, 1939, 1940, 1941)

Played in NHL All-Star Game (1939)

Traded to **NY Rangers** by **Springfield** (Can-Am) for cash, May 9, 1931. Traded to **Chicago** by **NY Rangers** for Art Coulter, January 15, 1936. Traded to **Detroit** by **Chicago** with future considerations (Fido Purpur, January 4, 1945) for Cully Simon, Don Grosso and Butch McDonald, January 2, 1945.

SEIDENBERG, Dennis

Defense. Shoots left. 6', 180 lbs. Born, Schwenningen, West Germany, July 18, 1981.
(Philadelphia's 6th choice, 172nd overall, in 2001 Entry Draft).

Season	Club	Regular Season GP	G	A	Pts	PIM	Playoffs GP	G	A	Pts	PIM
2002-03	Philadelphia Flyers	58	4	9	13	20	....	....	....	....	....
	NHL Totals	**58**	**4**	**9**	**13**	**20**	....	....	....	....	....

SEILING, Ric

Right wing/Center. Shoots right. 6'1", 180 lbs. Born, Elmira, Ont., December 15, 1957.
(Buffalo's 1st choice, 14th overall, in 1977 Amateur Draft).

Season	Club	Regular Season GP	G	A	Pts	PIM	Playoffs GP	G	A	Pts	PIM
1977-78	Buffalo Sabres	80	19	19	38	33	8	0	2	2	7
1978-79	Buffalo Sabres	78	20	22	42	56	3	0	1	1	2
1979-80	Buffalo Sabres	80	25	35	60	54	14	5	4	9	6
1980-81	Buffalo Sabres	74	30	27	57	80	8	2	2	4	2
1981-82	Buffalo Sabres	57	22	25	47	58	4	1	1	2	2
1982-83	Buffalo Sabres	75	19	22	41	41	10	2	3	5	6
1983-84	Buffalo Sabres	78	13	22	35	42	3	0	0	0	2
1984-85	Buffalo Sabres	73	16	15	31	86	5	4	1	5	4
1985-86	Buffalo Sabres	69	12	13	25	74	....	....	....	....	....
1986-87	Detroit Red Wings	74	3	8	11	49	7	0	0	0	5
	NHL Totals	**738**	**179**	**208**	**387**	**573**	**62**	**14**	**14**	**28**	**36**

• Brother of Rod

Traded to **Detroit** by **Buffalo** for future considerations, October 7, 1986.

SEILING, Rod

Defense. Shoots left. 6', 195 lbs. Born, Kitchener, Ont., November 14, 1944.

Season	Club	Regular Season GP	G	A	Pts	PIM	Playoffs GP	G	A	Pts	PIM
1962-63	Toronto Maple Leafs	1	0	1	1	0	....	....	....	....	....
1963-64	New York Rangers	2	0	1	1	0	....	....	....	....	....
1964-65	New York Rangers	68	4	22	26	44	....	....	....	....	....
1965-66	New York Rangers	52	5	10	15	24	....	....	....	....	....
1966-67	New York Rangers	12	1	1	2	6	....	....	....	....	....
1967-68	New York Rangers	71	5	11	16	44	6	1	1	2	4
1968-69	New York Rangers	73	4	17	21	73	4	1	0	1	2
1969-70	New York Rangers	76	5	21	26	68	2	0	0	0	0
1970-71	New York Rangers	68	5	22	27	34	13	1	0	1	12
1971-72	New York Rangers	78	5	36	41	62	16	1	4	5	10
1972-73	New York Rangers	72	9	33	42	36	....	....	....	....	....
1973-74	New York Rangers	68	7	23	30	32	13	0	2	2	19
1974-75	New York Rangers	4	0	1	1	0	....	....	....	....	....
	Washington Capitals	1	0	0	0	0	....	....	....	....	....
	Toronto Maple Leafs	60	5	12	17	40	7	0	0	0	0
1975-76	Toronto Maple Leafs	77	3	16	19	46	10	0	1	1	6
1976-77	St. Louis Blues	79	3	26	29	36	4	0	0	0	2
1977-78	St. Louis Blues	78	1	11	12	40	....	....	....	....	....
1978-79	St. Louis Blues	3	0	1	1	4	....	....	....	....	....
	Atlanta Flames	36	0	4	4	12	2	0	0	0	0
	NHL Totals	**979**	**62**	**269**	**331**	**601**	**77**	**4**	**8**	**12**	**55**

• Brother of Ric

Played in NHL All-Star Game (1972)

Traded to **NY Rangers** by **Toronto** with Dick Duff, Bob Nevin, Arnie Brown and Bill Collins for Andy Bathgate and Don McKenney, February 22, 1964. Claimed by **St. Louis** from **NY Rangers** in Expansion Draft, June 6, 1967. Traded to **NY Rangers** by **St. Louis** for Gary Sabourin, Bob Plager, Gord Kannegiesser and Tim Ecclestone, June 6, 1967. Claimed on waivers by **Washington** from **NY Rangers**, October 29, 1974. Traded to **Toronto** by **Washington** for Tim Ecclestone and Willie Brossart, November 2, 1974. Signed as a free agent by **St. Louis**, September 9, 1976. Traded to **Atlanta** by **St. Louis** for cash, November 4, 1978.

SEJBA, Jiri

Left wing. Shoots left. 5'10", 185 lbs. Born, Pardubice, Czech., July 22, 1962.
(Buffalo's 9th choice, 182nd overall, in 1985 Entry Draft).

Season	Club	Regular Season GP	G	A	Pts	PIM	Playoffs GP	G	A	Pts	PIM
1990-91	Buffalo Sabres	11	0	2	2	8	....	....	....	....	....
	NHL Totals	**11**	**0**	**2**	**2**	**8**	....	....	....	....	....

SEJNA, Peter

Left wing. Shoots left. 5'11", 198 lbs. Born, Liptovski Mikulas, Czech., October 5, 1979.

Season	Club	Regular Season GP	G	A	Pts	PIM	Playoffs GP	G	A	Pts	PIM
2002-03	St. Louis Blues	1	1	0	1	0	....	....	....	....	....
	NHL Totals	**1**	**1**	**0**	**1**	**0**	....	....	....	....	....

Signed as a free agent by **St. Louis**, April 6, 2003.

SEKERAS, Lubomir

Defense. Shoots left. 6', 183 lbs. Born, Trencin, Czech., November 18, 1968.
(Minnesota's 8th choice, 232nd overall, in 2000 Entry Draft).

Season	Club	Regular Season GP	G	A	Pts	PIM	Playoffs GP	G	A	Pts	PIM
2000-01	Minnesota Wild	80	11	23	34	52	....	....	....	....	....
2001-02	Minnesota Wild	69	4	20	24	38	....	....	....	....	....
2002-03	Minnesota Wild	60	2	9	11	30	15	1	1	2	6
	NHL Totals	**209**	**17**	**52**	**69**	**120**	**15**	**1**	**1**	**2**	**6**

SELANNE, Teemu

Right wing. Shoots right. 6', 204 lbs. Born, Helsinki, Finland, July 3, 1970.
(Winnipeg's 1st choice, 10th overall, in 1988 Entry Draft).

Season	Club	Regular Season GP	G	A	Pts	PIM	Playoffs GP	G	A	Pts	PIM
1992-93	Winnipeg Jets	84	*76	56	132	45	6	4	2	6	2
1993-94	Winnipeg Jets	51	25	29	54	22	....	....	....	....	....
1994-95	Winnipeg Jets	45	22	26	48	2	....	....	....	....	....
1995-96	Winnipeg Jets	51	24	48	72	18	....	....	....	....	....
	Mighty Ducks of Anaheim	28	16	20	36	4	....	....	....	....	....
1996-97	Mighty Ducks of Anaheim	78	51	58	109	34	11	7	3	10	4
1997-98	Mighty Ducks of Anaheim	73	*52	34	86	30	....	....	....	....	....
1998-99	Mighty Ducks of Anaheim	75	*47	60	107	30	4	2	2	4	2
99-2000	Mighty Ducks of Anaheim	79	33	52	85	12	....	....	....	....	....
2000-01	Mighty Ducks of Anaheim	61	26	33	59	36	....	....	....	....	....
	San Jose Sharks	12	7	6	13	0	6	0	2	2	2
2001-02	San Jose Sharks	82	29	25	54	40	12	5	3	8	2

Season	Club	REGULAR SEASON GP	G	A	Pts	PIM	PLAYOFFS GP	G	A	Pts	PIM
2002-03	San Jose Sharks	82	28	36	64	30	....	....	....	....	....
	NHL Totals	**801**	**436**	**483**	**919**	**303**	**39**	**18**	**12**	**30**	**12**

Calder Memorial Trophy (1993) • NHL First All-Star Team (1993, 1997) • NHL All-Rookie Team (1993) • NHL Second All-Star Team (1998, 1999) • Maurice "Rocket" Richard Trophy (1999)

Played in NHL All-Star Game (1993, 1994, 1996, 1997, 1998, 1999, 2000, 2002, 2003)

Traded to **Anaheim** by **Winnipeg** with Marc Chouinard and Winnipeg's 4th round choice (later traded to Toronto – later traded to Montreal – Montreal selected Kim Staal) in 1996 Entry Draft for Chad Kilger, Oleg Tverdovsky and Anaheim's 3rd round choice (Per-Anton Lundstrom) in 1996 Entry Draft, February 7, 1996. Traded to **San Jose** by **Anaheim** for Jeff Friesen, Steve Shields and San Jose's 2nd round choice (later traded to Dallas – Dallas selected Vojtech Polak) in 2003 Entry Draft, March 5, 2001. Signed as a free agent by **Colorado**, July 3, 2003.

SELBY, Brit

Left wing. Shoots left. 5'10", 175 lbs. Born, Kingston, Ont., March 27, 1945.

Season	Club	GP	G	A	Pts	PIM	GP	G	A	Pts	PIM
1964-65	Toronto Maple Leafs	3	2	0	2	2	....	....	....	....	....
1965-66	Toronto Maple Leafs	61	14	13	27	26	4	0	0	0	0
1966-67	Toronto Maple Leafs	6	1	1	2	0	....	....	....	....	....
1967-68	Philadelphia Flyers	56	15	15	30	24	7	1	1	2	4
1968-69	Philadelphia Flyers	63	10	13	23	23	....	....	....	....	....
	Toronto Maple Leafs	14	2	2	4	19	4	0	0	0	4
1969-70	Toronto Maple Leafs	74	10	13	23	40	....	....	....	....	....
1970-71	Toronto Maple Leafs	11	0	1	1	6	....	....	....	....	....
	St. Louis Blues	56	1	4	5	23	1	0	0	0	0
1971-72	St. Louis Blues	6	0	0	0	0	....	....	....	....	....
	NHL Totals	**350**	**55**	**62**	**117**	**163**	**16**	**1**	**1**	**2**	**8**

Calder Memorial Trophy (1966)

Claimed by **Philadelphia** from **Toronto** in Expansion Draft, June 6, 1967. Traded to **Toronto** by **Philadelphia** with Forbes Kennedy for Gerry Meehan, Bill Sutherland and Mike Byers, March 2, 1969. Traded to **St. Louis** by **Toronto** for Bob Baun, November 13, 1970.

SELF, Steve

Center. Shoots left. 5'9", 170 lbs. Born, Peterborough, Ont., May 9, 1950.

Season	Club	GP	G	A	Pts	PIM	GP	G	A	Pts	PIM
1976-77	Washington Capitals	3	0	0	0	0	....	....	....	....	....
	NHL Totals	**3**	**0**	**0**	**0**	**0**	....	....	....	....	....

Signed as a free agent by **Washington** to a three-game tryout contract, October 10, 1976.

SELIVANOV, Alex

Right wing. Shoots left. 6', 208 lbs. Born, Moscow, USSR, March 23, 1971.
(Philadelphia's 4th choice, 140th overall, in 1994 Entry Draft).

Season	Club	GP	G	A	Pts	PIM	GP	G	A	Pts	PIM
1994-95	Tampa Bay Lightning	43	10	6	16	14	....	....	....	....	....
1995-96	Tampa Bay Lightning	79	31	21	52	93	6	2	2	4	6
1996-97	Tampa Bay Lightning	69	15	18	33	61	....	....	....	....	....
1997-98	Tampa Bay Lightning	70	16	19	35	85	....	....	....	....	....
1998-99	Tampa Bay Lightning	43	6	13	19	18	....	....	....	....	....
	Edmonton Oilers	29	8	6	14	24	2	0	1	1	2
99-2000	Edmonton Oilers	67	27	20	47	46	5	0	0	0	8
2000-01	Columbus Blue Jackets	59	8	11	19	38	....	....	....	....	....
	NHL Totals	**459**	**121**	**114**	**235**	**379**	**13**	**2**	**3**	**5**	**16**

Traded to **Tampa Bay** by **Philadelphia** for Philadelphia's 4th round choice (previously acquired, Philadelphia selected Radovan Somik) in 1995 Entry Draft, September 6, 1994. Traded to **Edmonton** by **Tampa Bay** for Alexandre Daigle, January 29, 1999. Signed as a free agent by **Columbus**, November 27, 2000.

SELLARS, Luke

Defense. Shoots left. 6'1", 205 lbs. Born, Toronto, Ont., May 21, 1981.
(Atlanta's 2nd choice, 30th overall, in 1999 Entry Draft).

Season	Club	GP	G	A	Pts	PIM	GP	G	A	Pts	PIM
2001-02	Atlanta Thrashers	1	0	0	0	2	....	....	....	....	....
	NHL Totals	**1**	**0**	**0**	**0**	**2**	....	....	....	....	....

SELMSER, Sean

Left wing. Shoots left. 6'1", 195 lbs. Born, Calgary, Alta., November 10, 1974.
(Pittsburgh's 7th choice, 182nd overall, in 1993 Entry Draft).

Season	Club	GP	G	A	Pts	PIM	GP	G	A	Pts	PIM
2000-01	Columbus Blue Jackets	1	0	0	0	5	....	....	....	....	....
	NHL Totals	**1**	**0**	**0**	**0**	**5**	....	....	....	....	....

Signed as a free agent by **Columbus**, August 3, 2000. Signed as a free agent by **Edmonton**, August 15, 2001.

SELWOOD, Brad

Defense. Shoots left. 6'1", 200 lbs. Born, Leamington, Ont., March 18, 1948.
(Toronto's 1st choice, 10th overall, in 1968 Amateur Draft).

Season	Club	GP	G	A	Pts	PIM	GP	G	A	Pts	PIM
1970-71	Toronto Maple Leafs	28	2	10	12	13	....	....	....	....	....
1971-72	Toronto Maple Leafs	72	4	17	21	58	5	0	0	0	4
1979-80	Los Angeles Kings	63	1	13	14	82	1	0	0	0	0
	NHL Totals	**163**	**7**	**40**	**47**	**153**	**6**	**0**	**0**	**0**	**4**

Traded to **Vancouver** (WHL) by **Toronto** with Rene Robert for Ron Ward, May, 1969. Traded to **Toronto** by **Vancouver** (WHL) for cash, May, 1970. Claimed by **Montreal** from **Toronto** in Intra-League Draft, June 5, 1972. Reclaimed by **Montreal** from **Hartford** prior to Expansion Draft, June 9, 1979. Traded to **Los Angeles** by **Montreal** with Montreal's 4th round choice (Dave Gans) in 1982 Entry Draft for Los Angeles' 4th round choice (John Devoe) in 1982 Entry Draft, September 14, 1979.

SEMAK, Alexander

Center. Shoots right. 5'10", 185 lbs. Born, Ufa, USSR, February 11, 1966.
(New Jersey's 12th choice, 207th overall, in 1988 Entry Draft).

Season	Club	GP	G	A	Pts	PIM	GP	G	A	Pts	PIM
1991-92	New Jersey Devils	25	5	6	11	0	1	0	0	0	0
1992-93	New Jersey Devils	82	37	42	79	70	5	1	1	2	0
1993-94	New Jersey Devils	54	12	17	29	22	2	0	0	0	0
1994-95	New Jersey Devils	19	2	6	8	13	....	....	....	....	....
	Tampa Bay Lightning	22	5	5	10	12	....	....	....	....	....
1995-96	New York Islanders	69	20	14	34	68	....	....	....	....	....
1996-97	Vancouver Canucks	18	2	1	3	2	....	....	....	....	....
	NHL Totals	**289**	**83**	**91**	**174**	**187**	**8**	**1**	**1**	**2**	**0**

Traded to **Tampa Bay** by **New Jersey** with Ben Hankinson for Shawn Chambers and Danton Cole, March 14, 1995. Traded to **NY Islanders** by **Tampa Bay** for NY Islanders' 5th round choice (Karel Betik) in 1997 Entry Draft, September 14, 1995. Claimed by **Vancouver** from **NY Islanders** in NHL Waiver Draft, September 30, 1996.

SEMCHUK, Brandy

Right wing. Shoots right. 6'1", 185 lbs. Born, Calgary, Alta., September 22, 1971.
(Los Angeles' 2nd choice, 28th overall, in 1990 Entry Draft).

Season	Club	GP	G	A	Pts	PIM	GP	G	A	Pts	PIM
1992-93	Los Angeles Kings	1	0	0	0	2	....	....	....	....	....
	NHL Totals	**1**	**0**	**0**	**0**	**2**	....	....	....	....	....

SEMENKO, Dave

Left wing. Shoots left. 6'3", 200 lbs. Born, Winnipeg, Man., July 12, 1957.
(Minnesota's 2nd choice, 25th overall, in 1977 Amateur Draft).

Season	Club	GP	G	A	Pts	PIM	GP	G	A	Pts	PIM
1979-80	Edmonton Oilers	67	6	7	13	135	3	0	0	0	2
1980-81	Edmonton Oilers	58	11	8	19	80	8	0	0	0	5
1981-82	Edmonton Oilers	59	12	12	24	194	4	0	0	0	2
1982-83	Edmonton Oilers	75	12	15	27	141	15	1	1	2	69
1983-84◆	Edmonton Oilers	52	6	11	17	118	19	5	5	10	44
1984-85◆	Edmonton Oilers	69	6	12	18	172	14	0	0	0	39
1985-86	Edmonton Oilers	69	6	12	18	141	6	0	0	0	32
1986-87	Edmonton Oilers	5	0	0	0	0	....	....	....	....	....
	Hartford Whalers	51	4	8	12	87	4	0	0	0	15
1987-88	Toronto Maple Leafs	70	2	3	5	107	....	....	....	....	....
	NHL Totals	**575**	**65**	**88**	**153**	**1175**	**73**	**6**	**6**	**12**	**208**

Reclaimed by **Minnesota** from **Edmonton** prior to Expansion Draft, June 9, 1979. Traded to **Edmonton** by **Minnesota** for Edmonton's 2nd (Neal Broten) and 3rd (Kevin Maxwell) round choices in 1979 Entry Draft, August 9, 1979. Traded to **Hartford** by **Edmonton** for Hartford's 3rd round choice (Trevor Sim) in 1988 Entry Draft, December 12, 1986. Traded to **Toronto** by **Hartford** for Bill Root, September 8, 1987.

SEMENOV, Alexei

Defense. Shoots left. 6'6", 210 lbs. Born, Murmansk, USSR, April 10, 1981.
(Edmonton's 2nd choice, 36th overall, in 1999 Entry Draft).

Season	Club	GP	G	A	Pts	PIM	GP	G	A	Pts	PIM
2002-03	Edmonton Oilers	46	1	6	7	58	6	0	0	0	0
	NHL Totals	**46**	**1**	**6**	**7**	**58**	**6**	**0**	**0**	**0**	**0**

SEMENOV, Anatoli

Center/Left wing. Shoots left. 6'2", 190 lbs. Born, Moscow, USSR, March 5, 1962.
(Edmonton's 5th choice, 120th overall, in 1989 Entry Draft)

Season	Club	GP	G	A	Pts	PIM	GP	G	A	Pts	PIM
1989-90	Edmonton Oilers	....	....	....	....	....	2	0	0	0	0
1990-91	Edmonton Oilers	57	15	16	31	26	12	5	5	10	6
1991-92	Edmonton Oilers	59	20	22	42	16	8	1	1	2	6
1992-93	Tampa Bay Lightning	13	2	3	5	4	....	....	....	....	....
	Vancouver Canucks	62	10	34	44	28	12	1	3	4	0
1993-94	Mighty Ducks of Anaheim	49	11	19	30	12	....	....	....	....	....
1994-95	Mighty Ducks of Anaheim	15	3	4	7	4	....	....	....	....	....
	Philadelphia Flyers	26	1	2	3	6	15	2	4	6	0
1995-96	Philadelphia Flyers	44	3	13	16	14	....	....	....	....	....
	Mighty Ducks of Anaheim	12	1	9	10	10	....	....	....	....	....
1996-97	Buffalo Sabres	25	2	4	6	2	....	....	....	....	....
	NHL Totals	**362**	**68**	**126**	**194**	**122**	**49**	**9**	**13**	**22**	**12**

Claimed by **Tampa Bay** from **Edmonton** in Expansion Draft, June 18, 1992. Traded to **Vancouver** by **Tampa Bay** for Dave Capuano and Vancouver's 4th round choice (later traded to New Jersey – later traded to Calgary – Calgary selected Ryan Duthie) in 1994 Entry Draft, November 3, 1992. Claimed by **Anaheim** from **Vancouver** in Expansion Draft, June 24, 1993. Traded to **Philadelphia** by **Anaheim** for Milos Holan, March 8, 1995. Traded to **Anaheim** by **Philadelphia** with Mike Crowley for Brian Wesenberg, March 19, 1996. Signed as a free agent by **Buffalo**, September 17, 1996.

SENICK, George

Left wing. Shoots left. 5'11", 195 lbs. Born, Saskatoon, Sask., September 16, 1929.

Season	Club	GP	G	A	Pts	PIM	GP	G	A	Pts	PIM
1952-53	New York Rangers	13	2	3	5	8	....	....	....	....	....
	NHL Totals	**13**	**2**	**3**	**5**	**8**	....	....	....	....	....

SEPPA, Jyrki

Defense. Shoots left. 6'1", 190 lbs. Born, Tampere, Finland, November 14, 1961.
(Winnipeg's 3rd choice, 43rd overall, in 1981 Entry Draft).

Season	Club	GP	G	A	Pts	PIM	GP	G	A	Pts	PIM
1983-84	Winnipeg Jets	13	0	2	2	6	....	....	....	....	....
	NHL Totals	**13**	**0**	**2**	**2**	**6**	....	....	....	....	....

SERAFINI, Ron

Defense. Shoots right. 5'11", 180 lbs. Born, Highland Park, MI, October 31, 1953.
(California's 2nd choice, 50th overall, in 1973 Amateur Draft).

Season	Club	GP	G	A	Pts	PIM	GP	G	A	Pts	PIM
1973-74	California Golden Seals	2	0	0	0	2	....	....	....	....	....
	NHL Totals	**2**	**0**	**0**	**0**	**2**	....	....	....	....	....

Traded to **St. Louis** by **California** for Glenn Patrick, July 18, 1974.

SEROWIK, Jeff

Defense. Shoots right. 6'1", 210 lbs. Born, Manchester, NH, January 10, 1967.
(Toronto's 5th choice, 85th overall, in 1985 Entry Draft).

Season	Club	GP	G	A	Pts	PIM	GP	G	A	Pts	PIM
		REGULAR SEASON					PLAYOFFS				
1990-91	Toronto Maple Leafs	1	0	0	0	0	....	....	....	....	....
1994-95	Boston Bruins	1	0	0	0	0	....	....	....	....	....
1998-99	Pittsburgh Penguins	26	0	6	6	16	....	....	....	....	....
99-2000	Pittsburgh Penguins	DID NOT PLAY – INJURED									
	NHL Totals	**28**	**0**	**6**	**6**	**16**	....	....	....	....	....

Signed as a free agent by **Florida**, July 20, 1993. Signed as a free agent by **Boston**, June 29, 1994. Signed as a free agent by **Chicago**, August 10, 1995. Signed as a free agent by **Pittsburgh**, October 8, 1998. • Missed remainder of 1998-99 season and entire 1999-2000 season recovering from head injury suffered in game vs. Florida, December 30, 1998.

SERVINIS, George

Left wing. Shoots left. 5'11", 180 lbs. Born, Toronto, Ont., April 29, 1962.

Season	Club	GP	G	A	Pts	PIM	GP	G	A	Pts	PIM
1987-88	Minnesota North Stars	5	0	0	0	0	....	....	....	....	....
	NHL Totals	**5**	**0**	**0**	**0**	**0**	....	....	....	....	....

Signed as a free agent by **Minnesota**, August 13, 1985.

SEVCIK, Jaroslav

Left wing. Shoots right. 5'9", 170 lbs. Born, Brno, Czech., May 15, 1965.
(Quebec's 9th choice, 177th overall, in 1987 Entry Draft).

Season	Club	GP	G	A	Pts	PIM	GP	G	A	Pts	PIM
1989-90	Quebec Nordiques	13	0	2	2	2	....	....	....	....	....
	NHL Totals	**13**	**0**	**2**	**2**	**2**	....	....	....	....	....

SEVERSON, Cam

Left wing. Shoots left. 6'1", 215 lbs. Born, Canora, Sask., January 15, 1978.
(San Jose's 6th choice, 192nd overall, in 1997 Entry Draft).

Season	Club	GP	G	A	Pts	PIM	GP	G	A	Pts	PIM
2002-03	Mighty Ducks of Anaheim	2	0	0	0	8	1	0	0	0	0
	NHL Totals	**2**	**0**	**0**	**0**	**8**	**1**	**0**	**0**	**0**	**0**

Signed as a free agent by **Anaheim**, August 22, 2002.

SEVERYN, Brent

Left wing. Shoots left. 6'2", 211 lbs. Born, Vegreville, Alta., February 22, 1966.
(Winnipeg's 5th choice, 99th overall, in 1984 Entry Draft).

Season	Club	GP	G	A	Pts	PIM	GP	G	A	Pts	PIM
1989-90	Quebec Nordiques	35	0	2	2	42	....	....	....	....	....
1993-94	Florida Panthers	67	4	7	11	156	....	....	....	....	....
1994-95	Florida Panthers	9	1	1	2	37	....	....	....	....	....
	New York Islanders	19	1	3	4	34	....	....	....	....	....
1995-96	New York Islanders	65	1	8	9	180	....	....	....	....	....
1996-97	Colorado Avalanche	66	1	4	5	193	8	0	0	0	12
1997-98	Mighty Ducks of Anaheim	37	1	3	4	133	....	....	....	....	....
1998-99	Dallas Stars	30	1	2	3	50	....	....	....	....	....
	NHL Totals	**328**	**10**	**30**	**40**	**825**	**8**	**0**	**0**	**0**	**12**

Signed as a free agent by **Quebec**, July 15, 1988. Traded to **New Jersey** by **Quebec** for Dave Marcinyshyn, June 3, 1991. Traded to **Winnipeg** by **New Jersey** for Winnipeg's 6th round choice (Ryan Smart) in 1994 Entry Draft, September 30, 1993. Traded to **Florida** by **Winnipeg** for Milan Tichy, October 3, 1993. Traded to **NY Islanders** by **Florida** for NY Islanders' 4th round choice (Dave Duerden) in 1995 Entry Draft, March 3, 1995. Traded to **Colorado** by **NY Islanders** for Colorado's 3rd round choice (later traded to Calgary – later traded to Hartford/Carolina – Carolina selected Francis Lessard) in 1997 Entry Draft, September 4, 1996. Claimed by **Anaheim** from **Colorado** in NHL Waiver Draft, September 28, 1997. • Missed majority of 1997-98 season recovering from back injury suffered in game vs. Detroit, October 22, 1997. Signed as a free agent by **Dallas**, August 26, 1998.

SEVIGNY, Pierre

Left wing. Shoots left. 6', 195 lbs. Born, Trois-Rivieres, Que., September 8, 1971.
(Montreal's 4th choice, 51st overall, in 1989 Entry Draft).

Season	Club	GP	G	A	Pts	PIM	GP	G	A	Pts	PIM
1993-94	Montreal Canadiens	43	4	5	9	42	3	0	1	1	0
1994-95	Montreal Canadiens	19	0	0	0	15	....	....	....	....	....
1996-97	Montreal Canadiens	13	0	0	0	5	....	....	....	....	....
1997-98	New York Rangers	3	0	0	0	2	....	....	....	....	....
	NHL Totals	**78**	**4**	**5**	**9**	**64**	**3**	**0**	**1**	**1**	**0**

Signed as a free agent by **NY Rangers**, August 26, 1997.

SHACK, Eddie

Left wing. Shoots left. 6'1", 200 lbs. Born, Sudbury, Ont., February 11, 1937.

Season	Club	GP	G	A	Pts	PIM	GP	G	A	Pts	PIM
1958-59	New York Rangers	67	7	14	21	109	....	....	....	....	....
1959-60	New York Rangers	62	8	10	18	110	....	....	....	....	....
1960-61	New York Rangers	12	1	2	3	17	....	....	....	....	....
	Toronto Maple Leafs	55	14	14	28	90	4	0	0	0	2
1961-62 ♦	Toronto Maple Leafs	44	7	14	21	62	9	0	0	0	18
1962-63 ♦	Toronto Maple Leafs	63	16	9	25	97	10	2	1	3	11
1963-64 ♦	Toronto Maple Leafs	64	11	10	21	128	13	0	1	1	25
1964-65	Toronto Maple Leafs	67	5	9	14	68	5	1	0	1	8
1965-66	Toronto Maple Leafs	63	26	17	43	88	4	2	1	3	33
1966-67 ♦	Toronto Maple Leafs	63	11	14	25	58	8	0	0	0	8
1967-68	Boston Bruins	70	23	19	42	107	4	0	1	1	6
1968-69	Boston Bruins	50	11	11	22	74	9	0	2	2	23
1969-70	Los Angeles Kings	73	22	12	34	113	....	....	....	....	....
1970-71	Los Angeles Kings	11	2	2	4	8	....	....	....	....	....
	Buffalo Sabres	56	25	17	42	93	....	....	....	....	....
1971-72	Buffalo Sabres	50	11	14	25	34	....	....	....	....	....
	Pittsburgh Penguins	18	5	9	14	12	4	0	1	1	15
1972-73	Pittsburgh Penguins	74	25	20	45	84	....	....	....	....	....
1973-74	Toronto Maple Leafs	59	7	8	15	74	4	1	0	1	2
1974-75	Toronto Maple Leafs	26	2	1	3	11	....	....	....	....	....
	NHL Totals	**1047**	**239**	**226**	**465**	**1437**	**74**	**6**	**7**	**13**	**151**

Played in NHL All-Star Game (1962, 1963, 1964)

Traded to **Detroit** by **NY Rangers** with Bill Gadsby for Red Kelly and Billy McNeill, February 5, 1960. • Kelly and McNeill refused to report and transaction was cancelled, February 7, 1960. Traded to **Toronto** by **NY Rangers** for Pat Hannigan and Johnny Wilson, November 7, 1960. Traded to **Boston** by **Toronto** for Murray Oliver and cash, May 15, 1967. Traded to **Los Angeles** by **Boston** with Ross Lonsberry for Ken Turlik and Los Angeles' 1st round choices in 1971 (Ron Jones) and 1973 (Andre Savard) Amateur Drafts, May 14, 1969. Traded to **Buffalo** by **Los Angeles** with Dick Duff for Mike McMahon Jr. and future considerations, November 24, 1970. Traded to **Pittsburgh** by **Buffalo** for Rene Robert, March 4, 1972. Traded to **Toronto** by **Pittsburgh** for cash, July 3, 1973.

SHACK, Joe

Left wing. Shoots left. 5'10", 170 lbs. Born, Winnipeg, Man., December 8, 1915.

Season	Club	GP	G	A	Pts	PIM	GP	G	A	Pts	PIM
1942-43	New York Rangers	20	5	9	14	6	....	....	....	....	....
1944-45	New York Rangers	50	4	18	22	14	....	....	....	....	....
	NHL Totals	**70**	**9**	**27**	**36**	**20**	....	....	....	....	....

Traded to **NY Rangers** by **New Haven** (AHL) for cash after New Haven (AHL) franchise folded, January 18, 1943.

SHAFRANOV, Konstantin

Right wing. Shoots left. 5'11", 176 lbs. Born, Kamengorsk, USSR, September 11, 1968.
(St. Louis' 10th choice, 229th overall, in 1996 Entry Draft).

Season	Club	GP	G	A	Pts	PIM	GP	G	A	Pts	PIM
1996-97	St. Louis Blues	5	2	1	3	0	....	....	....	....	....
	NHL Totals	**5**	**2**	**1**	**3**	**0**	....	....	....	....	....

SHAKES, Paul

Defense. Shoots right. 5'10", 175 lbs. Born, Collingwood, Ont., September 4, 1952.
(California's 3rd choice, 38th overall, in 1972 Amateur Draft).

Season	Club	GP	G	A	Pts	PIM	GP	G	A	Pts	PIM
1973-74	California Golden Seals	21	0	4	4	12	....	....	....	....	....
	NHL Totals	**21**	**0**	**4**	**4**	**12**	....	....	....	....	....

SHALDYBIN, Yevgeny

Defense. Shoots left. 6'2", 198 lbs. Born, Novosibirsk, USSR, July 29, 1975.
(Boston's 6th choice, 151st overall, in 1995 Entry Draft).

Season	Club	GP	G	A	Pts	PIM	GP	G	A	Pts	PIM
1996-97	Boston Bruins	3	1	0	1	0	....	....	....	....	....
	NHL Totals	**3**	**1**	**0**	**1**	**0**	....	....	....	....	....

SHANAHAN, Brendan

Left wing. Shoots right. 6'3", 218 lbs. Born, Mimico, Ont., January 23, 1969.
(New Jersey's 1st choice, 2nd overall, in 1987 Entry Draft).

Season	Club	GP	G	A	Pts	PIM	GP	G	A	Pts	PIM
1987-88	New Jersey Devils	65	7	19	26	131	12	2	1	3	44
1988-89	New Jersey Devils	68	22	28	50	115	....	....	....	....	....
1989-90	New Jersey Devils	73	30	42	72	137	6	3	3	6	20
1990-91	New Jersey Devils	75	29	37	66	141	7	3	5	8	12
1991-92	St. Louis Blues	80	33	36	69	171	6	2	3	5	14
1992-93	St. Louis Blues	71	51	43	94	174	11	4	3	7	18
1993-94	St. Louis Blues	81	52	50	102	211	4	2	5	7	4
1994-95	St. Louis Blues	45	20	21	41	136	5	4	5	9	14
1995-96	Hartford Whalers	74	44	34	78	125	....	....	....	....	....
1996-97	Hartford Whalers	2	1	0	1	0	....	....	....	....	....
	♦ Detroit Red Wings	79	46	41	87	131	20	9	8	17	43
1997-98 ♦	Detroit Red Wings	75	28	29	57	154	20	5	4	9	22
1998-99	Detroit Red Wings	81	31	27	58	123	10	3	7	10	6
99-2000	Detroit Red Wings	78	41	37	78	105	9	3	2	5	10
2000-01	Detroit Red Wings	81	31	45	76	81	2	2	2	4	0
2001-02 ♦	Detroit Red Wings	80	37	38	75	118	23	8	11	19	20
2002-03	Detroit Red Wings	78	30	38	68	103	4	1	1	2	4
	NHL Totals	**1186**	**533**	**565**	**1098**	**2156**	**139**	**51**	**60**	**111**	**231**

NHL First All-Star Team (1994, 2000) • NHL Second All-Star Team (2002) • King Clancy Memorial Trophy (2003)

Played in NHL All-Star Game (1994, 1996, 1997, 1998, 1999, 2000, 2002)

Signed as a free agent by **St. Louis**, July 25, 1991. Traded to **Hartford** by **St. Louis** for Chris Pronger, July 27, 1995. Traded to **Detroit** by **Hartford** with Brian Glynn for Paul Coffey, Keith Primeau and Detroit's 1st round choice (Nikos Tselios) in 1997 Entry Draft, October 9, 1996.

SHANAHAN, Sean

Center/Right wing. Shoots right. 6'3", 205 lbs. Born, Toronto, Ont., February 8, 1951.

Season	Club	GP	G	A	Pts	PIM	GP	G	A	Pts	PIM
1975-76	Montreal Canadiens	4	0	0	0	0	....	....	....	....	....
1976-77	Colorado Rockies	30	1	3	4	40	....	....	....	....	....
1977-78	Boston Bruins	6	0	0	0	7	....	....	....	....	....
	NHL Totals	**40**	**1**	**3**	**4**	**47**	....	....	....	....	....

Signed as a free agent by **Montreal**, September, 1973. Traded to **Colorado** by **Montreal** with Ron Andruff for cash, September 13, 1976. Signed as a free agent by **Boston**, October 13, 1977. Signed as a free agent by **Detroit**, June 6, 1978.

SHAND, Dave

Defense. Shoots right. 6'2", 200 lbs. Born, Cold Lake, Alta., August 11, 1956.
(Atlanta's 1st choice, 8th overall, in 1976 Amateur Draft).

Season	Club	GP	G	A	Pts	PIM	GP	G	A	Pts	PIM
1976-77	Atlanta Flames	55	5	11	16	62	3	0	0	0	33
1977-78	Atlanta Flames	80	2	23	25	94	2	0	0	0	4
1978-79	Atlanta Flames	79	4	22	26	64	2	0	0	0	20
1979-80	Atlanta Flames	74	3	7	10	104	4	0	1	1	0

Season	Club	REGULAR SEASON GP	G	A	Pts	PIM	PLAYOFFS GP	G	A	Pts	PIM
1980-81	Toronto Maple Leafs	47	0	4	4	60	3	0	0	0	0
1982-83	Toronto Maple Leafs	1	0	1	1	2	4	1	0	1	13
1983-84	Washington Capitals	72	4	15	19	124	8	0	1	1	13
1984-85	Washington Capitals	13	1	1	2	34	....	....	....	....	....
	NHL Totals	**421**	**19**	**84**	**103**	**544**	**26**	**1**	**2**	**3**	**83**

Transferred to **Calgary** after **Atlanta** franchise relocated, June 24, 1980. Traded to **Toronto** by **Calgary** with Calgary's 3rd round choice (later traded to Washington – Washington selected Torrie Robertson) in 1980 Entry Draft for Toronto's 2nd round choice (Kevin LaVallee) in 1980 Entry Draft, June 10, 1980. Traded to **Washington** by **Toronto** for Lee Norwood, October 6, 1983.

SHANK, Daniel

Right wing. Shoots right. 5'10", 190 lbs. Born, Montreal, Que., May 12, 1967.

Season	Club	GP	G	A	Pts	PIM	GP	G	A	Pts	PIM
1989-90	Detroit Red Wings	57	11	13	24	143	....	....	....	....	....
1990-91	Detroit Red Wings	7	0	1	1	14	....	....	....	....	....
1991-92	Hartford Whalers	13	2	0	2	18	5	0	0	0	22
	NHL Totals	**77**	**13**	**14**	**27**	**175**	**5**	**0**	**0**	**0**	**22**

Signed as a free agent by **Detroit**, May 26, 1989. Traded to **Hartford** by **Detroit** for Chris Tancill, December 18, 1991.

SHANNON, Chuck

Defense. Shoots left. 5'11", 192 lbs. Born, Campbellford, Ont., March 22, 1916.

Season	Club	GP	G	A	Pts	PIM	GP	G	A	Pts	PIM
1939-40	New York Americans	4	0	0	0	2	....	....	....	....	....
	NHL Totals	**4**	**0**	**0**	**0**	**2**	....	....	....	....	....

• Brother of Gerry

Traded to **NY Americans** by **Toronto** for cash, October 13, 1939. • Rights returned to **Toronto** when **NY Americans** failed to complete the transaction, July 1, 1940. Traded to **Buffalo** (IAHL) by **Toronto** for cash, October 20, 1940.

SHANNON, Darrin

Left wing. Shoots left. 6'2", 210 lbs. Born, Barrie, Ont., December 8, 1969.
(Pittsburgh's 1st choice, 4th overall, in 1988 Entry Draft).

Season	Club	GP	G	A	Pts	PIM	GP	G	A	Pts	PIM
1988-89	Buffalo Sabres	3	0	0	0	0	2	0	0	0	0
1989-90	Buffalo Sabres	17	2	7	9	4	6	0	1	1	4
1990-91	Buffalo Sabres	34	8	6	14	12	6	1	2	3	4
1991-92	Buffalo Sabres	1	0	1	1	0	....	....	....	....	....
	Winnipeg Jets	68	13	26	39	41	7	0	1	1	10
1992-93	Winnipeg Jets	84	20	40	60	91	6	2	4	6	6
1993-94	Winnipeg Jets	77	21	37	58	87	....	....	....	....	....
1994-95	Winnipeg Jets	19	5	3	8	14	....	....	....	....	....
1995-96	Winnipeg Jets	63	5	18	23	28	6	1	0	1	6
1996-97	Phoenix Coyotes	82	11	13	24	41	7	3	1	4	4
1997-98	Phoenix Coyotes	58	2	12	14	26	5	0	1	1	4
	NHL Totals	**506**	**87**	**163**	**250**	**344**	**45**	**7**	**10**	**17**	**38**

• Brother of Darryl

Traded to **Buffalo** by **Pittsburgh** with Doug Bodger for Tom Barrasso and Buffalo's 3rd round choice (Joe Dziedzic) in 1990 Entry Draft, November 12, 1988. Traded to **Winnipeg** by **Buffalo** with Mike Hartman and Dean Kennedy for Dave McLlwain, Gord Donnelly, Winnipeg's 5th round choice (Yuri Khmylev) in 1992 Entry Draft and future considerations, October 11, 1991. Transferred to **Phoenix** after **Winnipeg** franchise relocated, July 1, 1996.

SHANNON, Darryl

Defense. Shoots left. 6'2", 208 lbs. Born, Barrie, Ont., June 21, 1968.
(Toronto's 2nd choice, 36th overall, in 1986 Entry Draft).

Season	Club	GP	G	A	Pts	PIM	GP	G	A	Pts	PIM
1988-89	Toronto Maple Leafs	14	1	3	4	6	....	....	....	....	....
1989-90	Toronto Maple Leafs	10	0	1	1	12	....	....	....	....	....
1990-91	Toronto Maple Leafs	10	0	1	1	0	....	....	....	....	....
1991-92	Toronto Maple Leafs	48	2	8	10	23	....	....	....	....	....
1992-93	Toronto Maple Leafs	16	0	0	0	11	....	....	....	....	....
1993-94	Winnipeg Jets	20	0	4	4	18	....	....	....	....	....
1994-95	Winnipeg Jets	40	5	9	14	48	....	....	....	....	....
1995-96	Winnipeg Jets	48	2	7	9	72	....	....	....	....	....
	Buffalo Sabres	26	2	6	8	20	....	....	....	....	....
1996-97	Buffalo Sabres	82	4	19	23	112	12	2	3	5	8
1997-98	Buffalo Sabres	76	3	19	22	56	15	2	4	6	8
1998-99	Buffalo Sabres	71	3	12	15	52	2	0	0	0	0
99-2000	Atlanta Thrashers	49	5	13	18	65	....	....	....	....	....
	Calgary Flames	27	1	8	9	22	....	....	....	....	....
2000-01	Montreal Canadiens	7	0	1	1	6	....	....	....	....	....
	NHL Totals	**544**	**28**	**111**	**139**	**523**	**29**	**4**	**7**	**11**	**16**

• Brother of Darrin

Signed as a free agent by **Winnipeg**, June 30, 1993. Traded to **Buffalo** by **Winnipeg** with Michal Grosek for Craig Muni, February 15, 1996. Claimed by **Atlanta** from **Buffalo** in Expansion Draft, June 25, 1999. Traded to **Calgary** by **Atlanta** with Jason Botterill for Hnat Domenichelli and Dmitri Vlasenkov, February 11, 2000. Signed as a free agent by **Montreal**, September 25, 2000.

SHANNON, Gerry

Left wing. Shoots left. 5'11", 170 lbs. Born, Campbellford, Ont., October 25, 1910.

Season	Club	GP	G	A	Pts	PIM	GP	G	A	Pts	PIM
1933-34	Ottawa Senators	48	11	15	26	26	....	....	....	....	....
1934-35	St. Louis Eagles	25	2	2	4	11	....	....	....	....	....
	Boston Bruins	17	1	1	2	4	4	0	0	0	2
1935-36	Boston Bruins	23	0	1	1	6	....	....	....	....	....
1936-37	Montreal Maroons	31	9	7	16	13	5	0	1	1	0
1937-38	Montreal Maroons	36	0	3	3	20	....	....	....	....	....
	NHL Totals	**180**	**23**	**29**	**52**	**80**	**9**	**0**	**1**	**1**	**2**

• Brother of Chuck

Signed as a free agent by **Ottawa**, May 10, 1933. Transferred to **St. Louis** after **Ottawa** franchise relocated, September 22, 1934. Traded to **Boston** by **St. Louis** for Frank Jerwa, January 10, 1935. Traded to **Mtl. Maroons** by **Boston** to complete transaction that sent Hooley Smith to Boston (October 26, 1936), December 4, 1936. Traded to **Cleveland** (IAHL) by **Mtl. Maroons** for cash, October 6, 1938.

SHANTZ, Jeff

Center. Shoots right. 6', 195 lbs. Born, Duchess, Alta., October 10, 1973.
(Chicago's 2nd choice, 36th overall, in 1992 Entry Draft).

Season	Club	GP	G	A	Pts	PIM	GP	G	A	Pts	PIM
1993-94	Chicago Blackhawks	52	3	13	16	30	6	0	0	0	6
1994-95	Chicago Blackhawks	45	6	12	18	33	16	3	1	4	2
1995-96	Chicago Blackhawks	78	6	14	20	24	10	2	3	5	6
1996-97	Chicago Blackhawks	69	9	21	30	28	6	0	4	4	6
1997-98	Chicago Blackhawks	61	11	20	31	36	....	....	....	....	....
1998-99	Chicago Blackhawks	7	1	0	1	4	....	....	....	....	....
	Calgary Flames	69	12	17	29	40	....	....	....	....	....
99-2000	Calgary Flames	74	13	18	31	30	....	....	....	....	....
2000-01	Calgary Flames	73	5	15	20	58	....	....	....	....	....
2001-02	Calgary Flames	40	3	3	6	23	....	....	....	....	....
2002-03	Colorado Avalanche	74	3	6	9	35	6	0	0	0	4
	NHL Totals	**642**	**72**	**139**	**211**	**341**	**44**	**5**	**8**	**13**	**24**

Traded to **Calgary** by **Chicago** with Steve Dubinsky for Marty McInnis, Jamie Allison and Eric Andersson, October 27, 1998. Traded to **Colorado** by **Calgary** with Derek Morris and Dean McAmmond for Chris Drury and Stephane Yelle, October 1, 2002.

SHARIFIJANOV, Vadim

Left wing. Shoots left. 6', 205 lbs. Born, Ufa, USSR, December 23, 1975.
(New Jersey's 1st choice, 25th overall, in 1994 Entry Draft).

Season	Club	GP	G	A	Pts	PIM	GP	G	A	Pts	PIM
1996-97	New Jersey Devils	2	0	0	0	0	....	....	....	....	....
1998-99	New Jersey Devils	53	11	16	27	28	4	0	0	0	0
99-2000	New Jersey Devils	20	3	4	7	8	....	....	....	....	....
	Vancouver Canucks	17	2	1	3	14	....	....	....	....	....
	NHL Totals	**92**	**16**	**21**	**37**	**50**	**4**	**0**	**0**	**0**	**0**

Traded to **Vancouver** by **New Jersey** with New Jersey's 3rd round choice (Tim Branham) in 2000 Entry Draft for NY Islanders' compensatory 2nd round choice (previously acquired, New Jersey selected Teemu Laine) in 2000 Entry Draft and Atlanta's 3rd round choice (previously acquired, New Jersey selected Max Birbraer) in 2000 Entry Draft, January 14, 2000.

SHARP, Patrick

Center. Shoots right. 6', 188 lbs. Born, Thunder Bay, Ont., December 27, 1981.
(Philadelphia's 2nd choice, 95th overall, in 2001 Entry Draft).

Season	Club	GP	G	A	Pts	PIM	GP	G	A	Pts	PIM
2002-03	Philadelphia Flyers	3	0	0	0	2	....	....	....	....	....
	NHL Totals	**3**	**0**	**0**	**0**	**2**	....	....	....	....	....

SHARPLES, Jeff

Defense. Shoots left. 6'1", 195 lbs. Born, Terrace, B.C., July 28, 1967.
(Detroit's 2nd choice, 29th overall, in 1985 Entry Draft).

Season	Club	GP	G	A	Pts	PIM	GP	G	A	Pts	PIM
1986-87	Detroit Red Wings	3	0	1	1	2	2	0	0	0	2
1987-88	Detroit Red Wings	56	10	25	35	42	4	0	3	3	4
1988-89	Detroit Red Wings	46	4	9	13	26	1	0	0	0	0
	NHL Totals	**105**	**14**	**35**	**49**	**70**	**7**	**0**	**3**	**3**	**6**

Traded to **Edmonton** by **Detroit** with Petr Klima, Joe Murphy and Adam Graves for Jimmy Carson, Kevin McClelland and Edmonton's 5th round choice (later traded to Montreal – Montreal selected Brad Layzell) in 1991 Entry Draft, November 2, 1989. Traded to **New Jersey** by **Edmonton** for Reijo Ruotsalainen, March 6, 1990.

SHARPLEY, Glen

Center. Shoots right. 6', 190 lbs. Born, York, Ont., September 6, 1956.
(Minnesota's 1st choice, 3rd overall, in 1976 Amateur Draft).

Season	Club	GP	G	A	Pts	PIM	GP	G	A	Pts	PIM
1976-77	Minnesota North Stars	80	25	32	57	48	2	0	0	0	4
1977-78	Minnesota North Stars	79	22	33	55	42	....	....	....	....	....
1978-79	Minnesota North Stars	80	19	34	53	30	....	....	....	....	....
1979-80	Minnesota North Stars	51	20	27	47	38	9	1	6	7	4
1980-81	Minnesota North Stars	28	12	12	24	18	....	....	....	....	....
	Chicago Black Hawks	35	10	16	26	12	1	0	2	2	0
1981-82	Chicago Black Hawks	36	9	7	16	11	15	6	3	9	16
	NHL Totals	**389**	**117**	**161**	**278**	**199**	**27**	**7**	**11**	**18**	**24**

Traded to **Chicago** by **Minnesota** for Ken Solheim and Chicago's 2nd round choice (Tom Hirsch) in 1981 Entry Draft, December 29, 1980. • Suffered eventual NHL career-ending eye injury in game vs. Washington, December 17, 1981. Doctors refused to grant permission to return to active playing duty in the NHL.

SHAUNESSY, Scott

Defense/Left wing. Shoots left. 6'4", 220 lbs. Born, Newport, RI, January 22, 1964.
(Quebec's 9th choice, 200th overall, in 1983 Entry Draft).

Season	Club	GP	G	A	Pts	PIM	GP	G	A	Pts	PIM
1986-87	Quebec Nordiques	3	0	0	0	7	....	....	....	....	....
1988-89	Quebec Nordiques	4	0	0	0	16	....	....	....	....	....
	NHL Totals	**7**	**0**	**0**	**0**	**23**	....	....	....	....	....

SHAW, Brad

Defense. Shoots right. 6', 190 lbs. Born, Cambridge, Ont., April 28, 1964.
(Detroit's 5th choice, 86th overall, in 1982 Entry Draft).

Season	Club	GP	G	A	Pts	PIM	GP	G	A	Pts	PIM
1985-86	Hartford Whalers	8	0	2	2	4	....	....	....	....	....

Season	Club	GP	G	A	Pts	PIM	GP	G	A	Pts	PIM
		REGULAR SEASON					PLAYOFFS				
1986-87	Hartford Whalers	2	0	0	0	0	....	....	....	....	....
1987-88	Hartford Whalers	1	0	0	0	0	....	....	....	....	....
1988-89	Hartford Whalers	3	1	0	1	0	3	1	0	1	0
1989-90	Hartford Whalers	64	3	32	35	30	7	2	5	7	0
1990-91	Hartford Whalers	72	4	28	32	29	6	1	2	3	2
1991-92	Hartford Whalers	62	3	22	25	44	3	0	1	1	4
1992-93	Ottawa Senators	81	7	34	41	34	....	....	....	....	....
1993-94	Ottawa Senators	66	4	19	23	59	....	....	....	....	....
1994-95	Ottawa Senators	2	0	0	0	0	....	....	....	....	....
1998-99	Washington Capitals	4	0	0	0	4	....	....	....	....	....
	St. Louis Blues	12	0	0	0	4	4	0	0	0	0
	NHL Totals	**377**	**22**	**137**	**159**	**208**	**23**	**4**	**8**	**12**	**6**

NHL All-Rookie Team (1990)

Traded to **Hartford** by **Detroit** for Hartford's 8th round choice (Urban Nordin) in 1984 Entry Draft, May 29, 1984. Traded to **New Jersey** by **Hartford** for cash, June 13, 1992. Claimed by **Ottawa** from **New Jersey** in Expansion Draft, June 18, 1992. Signed as a free agent by **Ottawa**, March 8, 1999. Claimed on waivers by **Washington** from **Ottawa**, March 10, 1999. Traded to **St. Louis** by **Washington** with Washington's 8th round choice (Colin Hemingway) in 1999 Entry Draft for St. Louis' 6th round choice (Kyle Clark) in 1999 Entry Draft, March 18, 1999.

SHAW, David

Defense. Shoots right. 6'2", 205 lbs. Born, St. Thomas, Ont., May 25, 1964.
(Quebec's 1st choice, 13th overall, in 1982 Entry Draft).

Season	Club	GP	G	A	Pts	PIM	GP	G	A	Pts	PIM
1982-83	Quebec Nordiques	2	0	0	0	0	....	....	....	....	....
1983-84	Quebec Nordiques	3	0	0	0	0	....	....	....	....	....
1984-85	Quebec Nordiques	14	0	0	0	11	....	....	....	....	....
1985-86	Quebec Nordiques	73	7	19	26	78	....	....	....	....	....
1986-87	Quebec Nordiques	75	0	19	19	69	....	....	....	....	....
1987-88	New York Rangers	68	7	25	32	100	....	....	....	....	....
1988-89	New York Rangers	63	6	11	17	88	4	0	2	2	30
1989-90	New York Rangers	22	2	10	12	22	....	....	....	....	....
1990-91	New York Rangers	77	2	10	12	89	6	0	0	0	11
1991-92	New York Rangers	10	0	1	1	15	....	....	....	....	....
	Edmonton Oilers	12	1	1	2	8	....	....	....	....	....
	Minnesota North Stars	37	0	7	7	49	7	2	2	4	10
1992-93	Boston Bruins	77	10	14	24	108	4	0	1	1	6
1993-94	Boston Bruins	55	1	9	10	85	13	1	2	3	16
1994-95	Boston Bruins	44	3	4	7	36	5	0	1	1	4
1995-96	Tampa Bay Lightning	66	1	11	12	64	6	0	1	1	4
1996-97	Tampa Bay Lightning	57	1	10	11	72	....	....	....	....	....
1997-98	Tampa Bay Lightning	14	0	2	2	12	....	....	....	....	....
	NHL Totals	**769**	**41**	**153**	**194**	**906**	**45**	**3**	**9**	**12**	**81**

Traded to **NY Rangers** by **Quebec** with John Ogrodnick for Jeff Jackson and Terry Carkner, September 30, 1987. • Missed majority of 1989-90 season recovering from shoulder injury suffered in game vs. Quebec, November 2, 1989. Traded to **Edmonton** by **NY Rangers** for Jeff Beukeboom to complete transaction that sent Mark Messier to NY Rangers for Bernie Nicholls, Steven Rice and Louie De Brusk (October 4, 1991), November 12, 1991. Traded to **Minnesota** by **Edmonton** for Brian Glynn, January 21, 1992. Traded to **Boston** by **Minnesota** for future considerations, September 2, 1992. Traded to **Tampa Bay** by **Boston** for Detroit's 3rd round choice (previously acquired, Boston selected Jason Doyle) in 1996 Entry Draft, August 17, 1995. Traded to **San Jose** by **Tampa Bay** with Bryan Marchment and Tampa Bay's 1st round choice (later traded to Nashville – Nashville selected David Legwand) in 1998 Entry Draft for Andrei Nazarov and Florida's 1st round choice (previously acquired, Tampa Bay selected Vincent Lecavalier) in 1998 Entry Draft, March 24, 1998.

SHAY, Norm

Defense/Right wing. Shoots left. 5'9", 158 lbs. Born, Huntsville, Ont., February 3, 1899.

Season	Club	GP	G	A	Pts	PIM	GP	G	A	Pts	PIM
1924-25	Boston Bruins	18	1	2	3	14	....	....	....	....	....
1925-26	Boston Bruins	13	1	0	1	2	....	....	....	....	....
	Toronto St. Pats	22	3	1	4	18	....	....	....	....	....
	NHL Totals	**53**	**5**	**3**	**8**	**34**	....	....	....	....	....

Signed as a free agent by **Boston**, January 9, 1925. Traded to **Toronto** by **Boston** for cash, January 14, 1926. Claimed on waivers by **New Haven** (Can-Am) from **Toronto**, October 18, 1926.

SHEA, Pat

Defense. Shoots left. 5'10", 190 lbs. Born, Potlatch, ID, October 29, 1912.

Season	Club	GP	G	A	Pts	PIM	GP	G	A	Pts	PIM
1931-32	Chicago Black Hawks	10	1	0	1	0	....	....	....	....	....
	NHL Totals	**10**	**1**	**0**	**1**	**0**	....	....	....	....	....

Signed as a free agent by **Chicago**, October 14, 1931. Traded to **St. Paul** (AHA) by **Chicago** for cash, October 26, 1932.

SHEARER, Rob

Center. Shoots right. 5'10", 190 lbs. Born, Kitchener, Ont., October 19, 1976.

Season	Club	GP	G	A	Pts	PIM	GP	G	A	Pts	PIM
2000-01	Colorado Avalanche	2	0	0	0	0	....	....	....	....	....
	NHL Totals	**2**	**0**	**0**	**0**	**0**	....	....	....	....	....

Signed as a free agent by **Colorado**, October 5, 1995.

SHEDDEN, Doug

Center. Shoots right. 6', 185 lbs. Born, Wallaceburg, Ont., April 29, 1961.
(Pittsburgh's 4th choice, 93rd overall, in 1980 Entry Draft).

Season	Club	GP	G	A	Pts	PIM	GP	G	A	Pts	PIM
1981-82	Pittsburgh Penguins	38	10	15	25	12	....	....	....	....	....
1982-83	Pittsburgh Penguins	80	24	43	67	54	....	....	....	....	....
1983-84	Pittsburgh Penguins	67	22	35	57	20	....	....	....	....	....
1984-85	Pittsburgh Penguins	80	35	32	67	30	....	....	....	....	....
1985-86	Pittsburgh Penguins	67	32	34	66	32	....	....	....	....	....
	Detroit Red Wings	11	2	3	5	2	....	....	....	....	....
1986-87	Detroit Red Wings	33	6	12	18	6	....	....	....	....	....
	Quebec Nordiques	16	0	2	2	8	....	....	....	....	....
1988-89	Toronto Maple Leafs	1	0	0	0	2	....	....	....	....	....
1990-91	Toronto Maple Leafs	23	8	10	18	10	....	....	....	....	....
	NHL Totals	**416**	**139**	**186**	**325**	**176**	....	....	....	....	....

Traded to **Detroit** by **Pittsburgh** for Ron Duguay, March 11, 1986. Traded to **Quebec** by **Detroit** with Basil McRae and John Ogrodnick for Brent Ashton, Gilbert Delorme and Mark Kumpel, January 17, 1987. Signed as a free agent by **Toronto**, August 4, 1988.

SHEEHAN, Bobby

Center. Shoots left. 5'7", 155 lbs. Born, Weymouth, MA, January 11, 1949.
(Montreal's 3rd choice, 32nd overall, in 1969 Amateur Draft).

Season	Club	GP	G	A	Pts	PIM	GP	G	A	Pts	PIM
1969-70	Montreal Canadiens	16	2	1	3	2	....	....	....	....	....
1970-71 ♦	Montreal Canadiens	29	6	5	11	2	6	0	0	0	0
1971-72	California Golden Seals	78	20	26	46	12	....	....	....	....	....
1975-76	Chicago Black Hawks	78	11	20	31	8	4	0	0	0	0
1976-77	Detroit Red Wings	34	5	4	9	2	....	....	....	....	....
1978-79	New York Rangers	....	....	....	....	....	15	4	3	7	8
1979-80	Colorado Rockies	30	3	4	7	2	....	....	....	....	....
1980-81	Colorado Rockies	41	1	3	4	10	....	....	....	....	....
1981-82	Los Angeles Kings	4	0	0	0	2	....	....	....	....	....
	NHL Totals	**310**	**48**	**63**	**111**	**40**	**25**	**4**	**3**	**7**	**8**

Traded to **California** by **Montreal** for cash, May 25, 1971. Rights traded to **Chicago** by **California** with the trade of Dick Redmond for Darryl Maggs, December 5, 1972. Signed as a free agent by **Detroit**, October 8, 1976. Signed as a free agent by **NY Rangers**, October 1, 1978. Traded to **Colorado** by **New Haven** (AHL) for Dennis Owchar and Larry Skinner, May 12, 1979. Signed as a free agent by **Los Angeles**, July 8, 1981.

SHEEHY, Neil

Defense. Shoots right. 6'2", 214 lbs. Born, International Falls, MN, February 9, 1960.

Season	Club	GP	G	A	Pts	PIM	GP	G	A	Pts	PIM
1983-84	Calgary Flames	1	1	0	1	2	4	0	0	0	4
1984-85	Calgary Flames	31	3	4	7	109	....	....	....	....	....
1985-86	Calgary Flames	65	2	16	18	271	22	0	2	2	79
1986-87	Calgary Flames	54	4	6	10	151	6	0	0	0	21
1987-88	Calgary Flames	36	2	6	8	73	....	....	....	....	....
	Hartford Whalers	26	1	4	5	116	1	0	0	0	7
1988-89	Washington Capitals	72	3	4	7	179	6	0	0	0	19
1989-90	Washington Capitals	59	1	5	6	291	13	0	1	1	92
1990-91	Washington Capitals	....	....	....	....	....	2	0	0	0	19
1991-92	Calgary Flames	35	1	2	3	119	....	....	....	....	....
	NHL Totals	**379**	**18**	**47**	**65**	**1311**	**54**	**0**	**3**	**3**	**241**

• Brother of Tim

Signed as a free agent by **Calgary**, August 16, 1983. Traded to **Hartford** by **Calgary** with Carey Wilson and rights to Lane MacDonald for Dana Murzyn and Shane Churla, January 3, 1988. Traded to **Washington** by **Hartford** with Mike Millar for Grant Jennings and Ed Kastelic, July 6, 1988. Signed as a free agent by **Calgary**, September 3, 1991.

SHEEHY, Tim

USHOF

Right wing. Shoots right. 6'1", 185 lbs. Born, Fort Frances, Ont., September 3, 1948.

Season	Club	GP	G	A	Pts	PIM	GP	G	A	Pts	PIM
1977-78	Detroit Red Wings	15	0	0	0	0	....	....	....	....	....
1979-80	Hartford Whalers	12	2	1	3	0	....	....	....	....	....
	NHL Totals	**27**	**2**	**1**	**3**	**0**	....	....	....	....	....

• Brother of Neil

Traded to **Detroit** by **Birmingham** (WHA) with Vaclav Nedomansky for the loan of Steve Durbano and Dave Hanson and future considerations, November 18, 1977. Traded to **New England** (WHA) by **Detroit** for cash, February 12, 1978.

SHELLEY, Jody

Left wing. Shoots left. 6'4", 225 lbs. Born, Thompson, Man., February 7, 1976.

Season	Club	GP	G	A	Pts	PIM	GP	G	A	Pts	PIM
2000-01	Columbus Blue Jackets	1	0	0	0	10	....	....	....	....	....
2001-02	Columbus Blue Jackets	52	3	3	6	206	....	....	....	....	....
2002-03	Columbus Blue Jackets	68	1	4	5	*249	....	....	....	....	....
	NHL Totals	**121**	**4**	**7**	**11**	**465**	....	....	....	....	....

Signed as a free agent by **Calgary**, September 1, 1998. Signed as a free agent by **Columbus**, January 31, 2001.

SHELTON, Doug

Right wing. Shoots right. 5'10", 175 lbs. Born, Woodstock, Ont., June 27, 1945.

Season	Club	GP	G	A	Pts	PIM	GP	G	A	Pts	PIM
1967-68	Chicago Black Hawks	5	0	1	1	2	....	....	....	....	....
	NHL Totals	**5**	**0**	**1**	**1**	**2**	....	....	....	....	....

Traded to **Minnesota** by **Chicago** to complete transaction that sent Andre Boudrias to Chicago (February 14, 1969), June, 1969. Claimed by **Denver** (WHL) from **Minnesota** in Reverse Draft, June 12, 1969. Traded to **Los Angeles** (Springfield-AHL) by **Denver** (WHL) for cash, February, 1970.

SHEPPARD, Frank

Center/Left wing. Shoots left. 5'6", 157 lbs. Born, Montreal, Que., October 19, 1907.

Season	Club	GP	G	A	Pts	PIM	GP	G	A	Pts	PIM
1927-28	Detroit Cougars	8	1	1	2	0	....	....	....	....	....
	NHL Totals	**8**	**1**	**1**	**2**	**0**	....	....	....	....	....

• Brother of Johnny

Signed as a free agent by **Detroit**, September 9, 1927. Traded to **St. Paul** (AHA) by **Detroit** for cash, December 19, 1927.

SHEPPARD, Gregg

Center. Shoots left. 5'8", 170 lbs. Born, North Battleford, Sask., April 23, 1949.

Season	Club	Regular Season GP	G	A	Pts	PIM	Playoffs GP	G	A	Pts	PIM
1972-73	Boston Bruins	64	24	26	50	18	5	2	1	3	0
1973-74	Boston Bruins	75	16	31	47	21	16	11	8	19	4
1974-75	Boston Bruins	76	30	48	78	19	3	3	1	4	5
1975-76	Boston Bruins	70	31	43	74	28	12	5	6	11	6
1976-77	Boston Bruins	77	31	36	67	20	14	5	7	12	8
1977-78	Boston Bruins	54	23	36	59	24	15	2	10	12	6
1978-79	Pittsburgh Penguins	60	15	22	37	9	7	1	2	3	0
1979-80	Pittsburgh Penguins	76	13	24	37	20	5	1	1	2	0
1980-81	Pittsburgh Penguins	47	11	17	28	49	5	2	4	6	2
1981-82	Pittsburgh Penguins	58	11	10	21	35	....	....	....	....	....
	NHL Totals	**657**	**205**	**293**	**498**	**243**	**82**	**32**	**40**	**72**	**31**

Played in NHL All-Star Game (1976)

Traded to **Atlanta** by **Boston** for Dick Redmond, September 6, 1978. Traded to **Pittsburgh** by **Atlanta** for Jean Pronovost, September 6, 1978.

SHEPPARD, Johnny

Left wing. Shoots left. 5'7", 165 lbs. Born, Montreal, Que., July 23, 1903.

Season	Club	Regular Season GP	G	A	Pts	PIM	Playoffs GP	G	A	Pts	PIM
1926-27	Detroit Cougars	43	13	8	21	60	....	....	....	....	....
1927-28	Detroit Cougars	44	10	10	20	40	....	....	....	....	....
1928-29	New York Americans	43	5	4	9	38	2	0	0	0	0
1929-30	New York Americans	43	14	15	29	32	....	....	....	....	....
1930-31	New York Americans	42	5	8	13	16	....	....	....	....	....
1931-32	New York Americans	5	1	0	1	2	....	....	....	....	....
1932-33	New York Americans	46	17	9	26	32	....	....	....	....	....
1933-34	Boston Bruins	4	0	0	0	0	....	....	....	....	....
	◆ Chicago Black Hawks	38	3	4	7	4	8	0	0	0	0
	NHL Totals	**308**	**68**	**58**	**126**	**224**	**10**	**0**	**0**	**0**	**0**

• Brother of Frank

Traded to **Detroit** by **Edmonton** (PrHL) for cash, October 5, 1926. Traded to **NY Americans** by **Detroit** for cash, October 14, 1928. Traded to **Boston** by **NY Americans** with Lloyd Gross and George Patterson for Bob Gracie and Art Chapman, September 8, 1933. Signed as a free agent by **Chicago** after securing release from **Boston**, November 24, 1933.

SHEPPARD, Ray

Right wing. Shoots right. 6'1", 195 lbs. Born, Pembroke, Ont., May 27, 1966.
(Buffalo's 3rd choice, 60th overall, in 1984 Entry Draft).

Season	Club	Regular Season GP	G	A	Pts	PIM	Playoffs GP	G	A	Pts	PIM
1987-88	Buffalo Sabres	74	38	27	65	14	6	1	1	2	2
1988-89	Buffalo Sabres	67	22	21	43	15	1	0	1	1	0
1989-90	Buffalo Sabres	18	4	2	6	0	....	....	....	....	....
1990-91	New York Rangers	59	24	23	47	21	....	....	....	....	....
1991-92	Detroit Red Wings	74	36	26	62	27	11	6	2	8	4
1992-93	Detroit Red Wings	70	32	34	66	29	7	2	3	5	0
1993-94	Detroit Red Wings	82	52	41	93	26	7	2	1	3	4
1994-95	Detroit Red Wings	43	30	10	40	17	17	4	3	7	5
1995-96	Detroit Red Wings	5	2	2	4	2	....	....	....	....	....
	San Jose Sharks	51	27	19	46	10	....	....	....	....	....
	Florida Panthers	14	8	2	10	4	21	8	8	16	4
1996-97	Florida Panthers	68	29	31	60	4	5	2	0	2	0
1997-98	Florida Panthers	61	14	17	31	21	....	....	....	....	....
	Carolina Hurricanes	10	4	2	6	2	....	....	....	....	....
1998-99	Carolina Hurricanes	74	25	33	58	16	6	5	1	6	2
99-2000	Florida Panthers	47	10	10	20	4	....	....	....	....	....
	NHL Totals	**817**	**357**	**300**	**657**	**212**	**81**	**30**	**20**	**50**	**21**

NHL All-Rookie Team (1988)

• Missed majority of 1989-90 season recovering from ankle injury suffered in game vs. Quebec, January 31, 1990. Traded to **NY Rangers** by **Buffalo** for cash and future considerations, July 9, 1990. Signed as a free agent by **Detroit**, August 5, 1991. Traded to **San Jose** by **Detroit** for Igor Larionov, October 24, 1995. Traded to **Florida** by **San Jose** with San Jose's 4th round choice (Joey Tetarenko) in 1996 Entry Draft for Florida's 2nd (later traded to Chicago – Chicago selected Geoff Peters) and 4th (Matt Bradley) round choices in 1996 Entry Draft, March 16, 1996. Traded to **Carolina** by **Florida** for Kirk McLean, March 24, 1998. Signed as a free agent by **Florida**, November 15, 1999.

SHERF, John

Left wing. Shoots left. 5'11", 178 lbs. Born, Calumet, MI, April 8, 1913.

Season	Club	Regular Season GP	G	A	Pts	PIM	Playoffs GP	G	A	Pts	PIM
1935-36	Detroit Red Wings	1	0	0	0	0	....	....	....	....	....
1936-37	◆ Detroit Red Wings	1	0	0	0	0	5	0	1	1	2
1937-38	Detroit Red Wings	6	0	0	0	2	....	....	....	....	....
1938-39	Detroit Red Wings	3	0	0	0	0	3	0	0	0	0
1943-44	Detroit Red Wings	8	0	0	0	6	....	....	....	....	....
	NHL Totals	**19**	**0**	**0**	**0**	**8**	**8**	**0**	**1**	**1**	**2**

Signed as a free agent by **Detroit**, October 15, 1935. Loaned to **NY Rangers** (Philadelphia-IAHL) by **Detroit** for remainder of 1937-38 season with cash for Eddie Wares, January 17, 1938. Traded to **Pittsburgh** (IAHL) by **Detroit** for cash, October 18, 1939.

SHERO, Fred

Defense. Shoots left. 5'10", 175 lbs. Born, Winnipeg, Man., October 23, 1925.

Season	Club	Regular Season GP	G	A	Pts	PIM	Playoffs GP	G	A	Pts	PIM
1947-48	New York Rangers	19	1	0	1	2	6	0	1	1	6
1948-49	New York Rangers	59	3	6	9	64	....	....	....	....	....
1949-50	New York Rangers	67	2	8	10	71	7	0	1	1	2
	NHL Totals	**145**	**6**	**14**	**20**	**137**	**13**	**0**	**2**	**2**	**8**

Lester Patrick Trophy (1980)

Traded to **Cleveland** (AHL) by **NY Rangers** with Ed Reigle, Jackie Gordon, Fern Perreault and cash for Hy Buller and Wally Hergesheimer, May 14, 1951.

SHERRITT, Gordon

Defense. Shoots left. 6'1", 195 lbs. Born, Oakville, Man., April 8, 1922.

Season	Club	Regular Season GP	G	A	Pts	PIM	Playoffs GP	G	A	Pts	PIM
1943-44	Detroit Red Wings	8	0	0	0	12	....	....	....	....	....
	NHL Totals	**8**	**0**	**0**	**0**	**12**	....	....	....	....	....

Signed as a free agent by **Detroit**, October 26, 1942. Loaned to **New Haven** (AHL) by **Detroit** (Indianapolis-AHL) for cash, December 11, 1942. Traded to **Cleveland** (AHL) by **Detroit** for cash, October 4, 1945.

SHERVEN, Gord

Center. Shoots right. 6', 185 lbs. Born, Gravelbourg, Sask., August 21, 1963.
(Edmonton's 9th choice, 197th overall, in 1981 Entry Draft).

Season	Club	Regular Season GP	G	A	Pts	PIM	Playoffs GP	G	A	Pts	PIM
1983-84	Edmonton Oilers	2	1	0	1	0	....	....	....	....	....
1984-85	Edmonton Oilers	37	9	7	16	10	....	....	....	....	....
	Minnesota North Stars	32	2	12	14	8	3	0	0	0	0
1985-86	Minnesota North Stars	13	0	2	2	11	....	....	....	....	....
	Edmonton Oilers	5	1	1	2	4	....	....	....	....	....
1986-87	Hartford Whalers	7	0	0	0	0	....	....	....	....	....
1987-88	Hartford Whalers	1	0	0	0	0	....	....	....	....	....
	NHL Totals	**97**	**13**	**22**	**35**	**33**	**3**	**0**	**0**	**0**	**0**

Traded to **Minnesota** by **Edmonton** with Terry Martin for Mark Napier, January 24, 1985. Traded to **Edmonton** by **Minnesota** with Don Biggs for Marc Habscheid, Don Barber and Emanuel Viveiros, December 20, 1985. Claimed by **Hartford** from **Edmonton** in Waiver Draft, October 6, 1986.

SHEVALIER, Jeff

Left wing. Shoots left. 5'11", 180 lbs. Born, Mississauga, Ont., March 14, 1974.
(Los Angeles' 4th choice, 111th overall, in 1992 Entry Draft).

Season	Club	Regular Season GP	G	A	Pts	PIM	Playoffs GP	G	A	Pts	PIM
1994-95	Los Angeles Kings	1	1	0	1	0	....	....	....	....	....
1996-97	Los Angeles Kings	26	4	9	13	6	....	....	....	....	....
99-2000	Tampa Bay Lightning	5	0	0	0	2	....	....	....	....	....
	NHL Totals	**32**	**5**	**9**	**14**	**8**	....	....	....	....	....

Signed as a free agent by **Tampa Bay**, July 8, 1999. Traded to **Ottawa** by **Tampa Bay** for future considerations, March 8, 2000.

SHEWCHUK, Jack

Defense. Shoots left. 6'1", 190 lbs. Born, Brantford, Ont., June 19, 1917.

Season	Club	Regular Season GP	G	A	Pts	PIM	Playoffs GP	G	A	Pts	PIM
1938-39	Boston Bruins	3	0	0	0	2	....	....	....	....	....
1939-40	Boston Bruins	47	2	4	6	55	6	0	0	0	0
1940-41	◆ Boston Bruins	20	2	2	4	8	....	....	....	....	....
1941-42	Boston Bruins	22	2	0	2	14	5	0	1	1	7
1942-43	Boston Bruins	48	2	6	8	50	9	0	0	0	12
1944-45	Boston Bruins	47	1	7	8	31	....	....	....	....	....
	NHL Totals	**187**	**9**	**19**	**28**	**160**	**20**	**0**	**1**	**1**	**19**

Signed as a free agent by **Boston**, October 26, 1937.

SHIBICKY, Alex

Right wing. Shoots right. 6', 180 lbs. Born, Winnipeg, Man., May 19, 1914.

Season	Club	Regular Season GP	G	A	Pts	PIM	Playoffs GP	G	A	Pts	PIM
1935-36	New York Rangers	18	4	2	6	6	....	....	....	....	....
1936-37	New York Rangers	47	14	8	22	30	9	1	4	5	0
1937-38	New York Rangers	48	17	18	35	26	3	2	0	2	2
1938-39	New York Rangers	48	24	9	33	24	7	3	1	4	2
1939-40	◆ New York Rangers	44	11	21	32	33	11	2	5	7	4
1940-41	New York Rangers	41	10	14	24	14	3	1	0	1	2
1941-42	New York Rangers	45	20	14	34	16	6	3	2	5	2
1945-46	New York Rangers	33	10	5	15	12	....	....	....	....	....
	NHL Totals	**324**	**110**	**91**	**201**	**161**	**39**	**12**	**12**	**24**	**12**

Signed as a free agent by **NY Rangers**, October 18, 1934.

SHIELDS, Al

Defense. Shoots right. 6', 188 lbs. Born, Ottawa, Ont., May 10, 1907.

Season	Club	Regular Season GP	G	A	Pts	PIM	Playoffs GP	G	A	Pts	PIM
1927-28	Ottawa Senators	7	0	1	1	2	2	0	0	0	0
1928-29	Ottawa Senators	42	0	1	1	10	....	....	....	....	....
1929-30	Ottawa Senators	44	6	3	9	32	2	0	0	0	0
1930-31	Philadelphia Quakers	43	7	3	10	98	....	....	....	....	....
1931-32	New York Americans	48	4	1	5	45	....	....	....	....	....
1932-33	Ottawa Senators	48	7	4	11	119	....	....	....	....	....
1933-34	Ottawa Senators	47	4	7	11	44	....	....	....	....	....
1934-35	◆ Montreal Maroons	42	4	8	12	45	7	0	1	1	6
1935-36	Montreal Maroons	45	2	7	9	81	3	0	0	0	6
1936-37	New York Americans	27	3	0	3	79	....	....	....	....	....
	Boston Bruins	18	0	4	4	15	3	0	0	0	2

Season	Club	GP	G	A	Pts	PIM	GP	G	A	Pts	PIM
		REGULAR SEASON					PLAYOFFS				
1937-38	Montreal Maroons	48	5	7	12	67	....	....	....	....	....
	NHL Totals	**459**	**42**	**46**	**88**	**637**	**17**	**0**	**1**	**1**	**14**

Played in NHL All-Star Game (1934)

Signed as a free agent by **Ottawa**, March 3, 1928. Traded to **Philadelphia** by **Ottawa** with Syd Howe and Wally Kilrea for $35,000, November 6, 1930. Claimed by **NY Americans** from **Ottawa** for 1931-32 season in Dispersal Draft, September 26, 1931. Traded to **Mtl. Maroons** by **Ottawa** for Irv Frew and future considerations (Normie Smith and Vern Ayres, October 22, 1934), September 20, 1934. Loaned to **NY Americans** by **Mtl. Maroons** for cash, September 15, 1936. Loaned to **Boston** by **NY Americans** with future considerations (rights to Terry Reardon and Tom Cooper, October 17, 1937) for Joe Jerwa, January 25, 1937. Returned to **Mtl. Maroons** July 1,1937. Signed as a free agent by **Montreal** (New Haven-IAHL), October 4, 1939. Loaned to **Buffalo** (AHL) by **Montreal** (New Haven-AHL) for cash, December 1, 1940 and recalled December 10, 1940. Traded to **Washington** (AHL) by **Montreal** for cash, October 9, 1941.

SHILL, Bill

Right wing. Shoots right. 6'1", 175 lbs. Born, Toronto, Ont., March 6, 1923.

Season	Club	GP	G	A	Pts	PIM	GP	G	A	Pts	PIM
1942-43	Boston Bruins	7	4	1	5	4	....	....	....	....	....
1945-46	Boston Bruins	45	15	12	27	12	7	1	2	3	2
1946-47	Boston Bruins	27	2	0	2	2	....	....	....	....	....
	NHL Totals	**79**	**21**	**13**	**34**	**18**	**7**	**1**	**2**	**3**	**2**

• Brother of Jack

Signed as a free agent by **Toronto**, March 1, 1934. Traded to **Montreal** by **Boston** for cash, February 15, 1947.

SHILL, Jack

Center. Shoots left. 5'9", 175 lbs. Born, Toronto, Ont., January 12, 1913.

Season	Club	GP	G	A	Pts	PIM	GP	G	A	Pts	PIM
1933-34	Toronto Maple Leafs	7	0	1	1	0	2	0	0	0	0
1934-35	Boston Bruins	45	4	4	8	22	2	0	0	0	0
1935-36	Toronto Maple Leafs	3	0	1	1	0	9	0	3	3	8
1936-37	Toronto Maple Leafs	32	4	4	8	26	2	0	0	0	0
1937-38	New York Americans	22	1	3	4	10	....	....	....	....	....
♦	Chicago Black Hawks	23	4	3	7	8	10	1	3	4	15
1938-39	Chicago Black Hawks	28	2	4	6	4	....	....	....	....	....
	NHL Totals	**160**	**15**	**20**	**35**	**70**	**25**	**1**	**6**	**7**	**23**

• Brother of Bill

Loaned to **Boston** by **Toronto** for 1934-35 season for cash, May 12, 1934. Traded to **NY Americans** by **Toronto** for the rights to Wally Stanowski, October 17, 1937. Traded to **Chicago** by **NY Americans** for cash, January 26, 1938. Traded to **Providence** (IAHL) by **Chicago** for cash, October 24, 1939.

SHINSKE, Rick

Center. Shoots left. 5'11", 165 lbs. Born, Weyburn, Sask., May 31, 1955.
(California's 7th choice, 111th overall, in 1975 Amateur Draft).

Season	Club	GP	G	A	Pts	PIM	GP	G	A	Pts	PIM
1976-77	Cleveland Barons	5	0	0	0	2	....	....	....	....	....
1977-78	Cleveland Barons	47	5	12	17	6	....	....	....	....	....
1978-79	St. Louis Blues	11	0	4	4	2	....	....	....	....	....
	NHL Totals	**63**	**5**	**16**	**21**	**10**	....	....	....	....	....

Rights transferred to **Cleveland** after **California** franchise relocated, August 26, 1976. Claimed by **Minnesota** in **Cleveland-Minnesota** Dispersal Draft, June 15, 1978. Claimed on waivers by **St. Louis** from **Minnesota**, August 12, 1978. Signed as a free agent by **Detroit**, September, 1979.

SHIRES, Jim

Left wing. Shoots left. 6', 180 lbs. Born, Edmonton, Alta., November 15, 1945.

Season	Club	GP	G	A	Pts	PIM	GP	G	A	Pts	PIM
1970-71	Detroit Red Wings	20	2	1	3	22	....	....	....	....	....
1971-72	St. Louis Blues	18	0	3	3	8	....	....	....	....	....
1972-73	Pittsburgh Penguins	18	1	2	3	2	....	....	....	....	....
	NHL Totals	**56**	**3**	**6**	**9**	**32**	....	....	....	....	....

Traded to **St. Louis** by **Detroit** for Rick Sentes, May 12, 1971. Traded to **Pittsburgh** by **St. Louis** for Joe Noris, January 8, 1973.

SHMYR, Paul

Defense. Shoots left. 5'11", 170 lbs. Born, Cudworth, Sask., January 18, 1946.

Season	Club	GP	G	A	Pts	PIM	GP	G	A	Pts	PIM
1968-69	Chicago Black Hawks	3	1	0	1	8	....	....	....	....	....
1969-70	Chicago Black Hawks	24	0	4	4	26	8	1	2	3	0
1970-71	Chicago Black Hawks	57	1	12	13	41	9	0	0	0	17
1971-72	California Golden Seals	69	6	21	27	156	....	....	....	....	....
1979-80	Minnesota North Stars	63	3	15	18	84	14	2	1	3	23
1980-81	Minnesota North Stars	61	1	9	10	79	3	0	0	0	4
1981-82	Hartford Whalers	66	1	11	12	134	....	....	....	....	....
	NHL Totals	**343**	**13**	**72**	**85**	**528**	**34**	**3**	**3**	**6**	**44**

Traded to **Chicago** by **NY Rangers** for Camille Henry, August 17, 1967. Traded to **California** by **Chicago** with Gilles Marotte for Gerry Desjardins, October 18, 1971. Claimed by **Minnesota** in **Cleveland-Minnesota** Dispersal Draft, June 15, 1978. Reclaimed by **Minnesota** from **Edmonton** prior to Expansion Draft, June 9, 1979. Signed as a free agent by **Hartford**, October, 1981.

SHOEBOTTOM, Bruce

Defense. Shoots left. 6'2", 200 lbs. Born, Windsor, Ont., August 20, 1965.
(Los Angeles' 1st choice, 47th overall, in 1983 Entry Draft).

Season	Club	GP	G	A	Pts	PIM	GP	G	A	Pts	PIM
1987-88	Boston Bruins	3	0	1	1	0	4	1	0	1	42
1988-89	Boston Bruins	29	1	3	4	44	10	0	2	2	35
1989-90	Boston Bruins	2	0	0	0	4	....	....	....	....	....
1990-91	Boston Bruins	1	0	0	0	5	....	....	....	....	....
	NHL Totals	**35**	**1**	**4**	**5**	**53**	**14**	**1**	**2**	**3**	**77**

Traded to **Washington** by **Los Angeles** for Bryan Erickson, October 31, 1985. Signed as a free agent by **Boston**, July 20, 1987.

SHORE, Eddie

HHOF

Defense. Shoots right. 5'11", 190 lbs. Born, Fort Qu'Appelle, Sask., November 25, 1902.

Season	Club	GP	G	A	Pts	PIM	GP	G	A	Pts	PIM
1926-27	Boston Bruins	40	12	6	18	130	8	1	1	2	*40
1927-28	Boston Bruins	43	11	6	17	*165	2	0	0	0	8
1928-29♦	Boston Bruins	39	12	7	19	96	5	1	1	2	*28
1929-30	Boston Bruins	42	12	19	31	105	6	1	0	1	*26
1930-31	Boston Bruins	44	15	16	31	105	5	2	1	3	24
1931-32	Boston Bruins	45	9	13	22	80	....	....	....	....	....
1932-33	Boston Bruins	48	8	27	35	102	5	0	1	1	14
1933-34	Boston Bruins	30	2	10	12	57	....	....	....	....	....
1934-35	Boston Bruins	48	7	26	33	32	4	0	1	1	2
1935-36	Boston Bruins	45	3	16	19	61	2	1	1	2	12
1936-37	Boston Bruins	20	3	1	4	12	....	....	....	....	....
1937-38	Boston Bruins	48	3	14	17	42	3	0	1	1	6
1938-39♦	Boston Bruins	44	4	14	18	47	12	0	4	4	19
1939-40	Boston Bruins	4	2	1	3	4	....	....	....	....	....
	New York Americans	10	2	3	5	9	3	0	2	2	2
	NHL Totals	**550**	**105**	**179**	**284**	**1047**	**55**	**6**	**13**	**19**	**181**

NHL First All-Star Team (1931, 1932, 1933, 1935, 1936, 1938, 1939) • Hart Trophy (1933, 1935, 1936, 1938) • NHL Second All-Star Team (1934) • Lester Patrick Trophy (1970)

Played in NHL All-Star Game (1934, 1937, 1939)

Traded to **Boston** by **Edmonton** (WHL) for cash, August 20, 1926. • Suspended indefinitely by NHL following on-ice assault against Ace Bailey of Toronto, December 12, 1933. Shore assessed a sixteen-game suspension by NHL, January, 1934. • Missed remainder of 1936-37 season after suffering a back injury vs. NY Rangers, January 28, 1937. Traded to **NY Americans** by **Boston** for Ed Wiseman and $5,000, January 25, 1940.

SHORE, Hamby

Defense/Left wing. Shoots left. 6', 175 lbs. Born, Ottawa, Ont., February 12, 1886.

Season	Club	GP	G	A	Pts	PIM	GP	G	A	Pts	PIM
1917-18	Ottawa Senators	18	3	8	11	51	....	....	....	....	....
	NHL Totals	**18**	**3**	**8**	**11**	**51**	....	....	....	....	....

Rights retained by **Ottawa** after NHA folded, November 26, 1917.

SHORT, Steve

Left wing. Shoots left. 6'2", 210 lbs. Born, Roseville, MN, April 6, 1954.
(Philadelphia's 7th choice, 142nd overall, in 1974 Amateur Draft).

Season	Club	GP	G	A	Pts	PIM	GP	G	A	Pts	PIM
1977-78	Los Angeles Kings	5	0	0	0	2	....	....	....	....	....
1978-79	Detroit Red Wings	1	0	0	0	0	....	....	....	....	....
	NHL Totals	**6**	**0**	**0**	**0**	**2**	....	....	....	....	....

Traded to **Los Angeles** by **Philadelphia** for future considerations (John Paul Evans, November 3, 1977), June 17, 1977. Traded to **Detroit** by **Los Angeles** for the rights to Steve Carlson, December 6, 1978.

SHUCHUK, Gary

Right wing. Shoots right. 5'11", 190 lbs. Born, Edmonton, Alta., February 17, 1967.
(Detroit's 1st choice, 22nd overall, in 1988 Supplemental Draft).

Season	Club	GP	G	A	Pts	PIM	GP	G	A	Pts	PIM
1990-91	Detroit Red Wings	6	1	2	3	6	3	0	0	0	0
1992-93	Los Angeles Kings	25	2	4	6	16	17	2	2	4	12
1993-94	Los Angeles Kings	56	3	4	7	30	....	....	....	....	....
1994-95	Los Angeles Kings	22	3	6	9	6	....	....	....	....	....
1995-96	Los Angeles Kings	33	4	10	14	12	....	....	....	....	....
	NHL Totals	**142**	**13**	**26**	**39**	**70**	**20**	**2**	**2**	**4**	**12**

Traded to **Los Angeles** by **Detroit** with Jimmy Carson and Marc Potvin for Paul Coffey, Sylvain Couturier and Jim Hiller, January 29, 1993.

SHUDRA, Ron

Defense. Shoots left. 6'2", 192 lbs. Born, Winnipeg, Man., November 28, 1967.
(Edmonton's 3rd choice, 63rd overall, in 1986 Entry Draft).

Season	Club	GP	G	A	Pts	PIM	GP	G	A	Pts	PIM
1987-88	Edmonton Oilers	10	0	5	5	6	....	....	....	....	....
	NHL Totals	**10**	**0**	**5**	**5**	**6**	....	....	....	....	....

Traded to **NY Rangers** by **Edmonton** for Jeff Crossman, October 27, 1988.

SHUTT, Steve

HHOF

Left wing. Shoots left. 5'11", 185 lbs. Born, Toronto, Ont., July 1, 1952.
(Montreal's 1st choice, 4th overall, in 1972 Amateur Draft).

Season	Club	GP	G	A	Pts	PIM	GP	G	A	Pts	PIM
1972-73♦	Montreal Canadiens	50	8	8	16	24	1	0	0	0	0
1973-74	Montreal Canadiens	70	15	20	35	17	6	5	3	8	9
1974-75	Montreal Canadiens	77	30	35	65	40	9	1	6	7	4
1975-76♦	Montreal Canadiens	80	45	34	79	47	13	7	8	15	2
1976-77♦	Montreal Canadiens	80	*60	45	105	28	14	8	10	18	2
1977-78♦	Montreal Canadiens	80	49	37	86	24	15	9	8	17	20
1978-79♦	Montreal Canadiens	72	37	40	77	31	11	4	7	11	6
1979-80	Montreal Canadiens	77	47	42	89	34	10	6	3	9	6
1980-81	Montreal Canadiens	77	35	38	73	51	3	2	1	3	4
1981-82	Montreal Canadiens	57	31	24	55	40	....	....	....	....	....
1982-83	Montreal Canadiens	78	35	22	57	26	3	1	0	1	0
1983-84	Montreal Canadiens	63	14	23	37	29	11	7	2	9	8

Season	Club	GP	G	A	Pts	PIM	GP	G	A	Pts	PIM
		REGULAR SEASON					PLAYOFFS				
1984-85	Montreal Canadiens	10	2	0	2	9	....	....	....	....	....
	Los Angeles Kings	59	16	25	41	10	3	0	0	0	4
	NHL Totals	**930**	**424**	**393**	**817**	**410**	**99**	**50**	**48**	**98**	**65**

NHL First All-Star Team (1977) • NHL Second All-Star Team (1978, 1980)
Played in NHL All-Star Game (1976, 1978, 1981)

Traded to **Los Angeles** by **Montreal** for future considerations, November 19, 1984. Claimed on waivers by **Montreal** from **Los Angeles**, June 18, 1985.

SHVIDKI, Denis

Right wing. Shoots left. 6'2", 215 lbs. Born, Kharkov, USSR, November 21, 1980.
(Florida's 1st choice, 12th overall, in 1999 Entry Draft).

Season	Club	GP	G	A	Pts	PIM	GP	G	A	Pts	PIM
2000-01	Florida Panthers	43	6	10	16	16	....	....	....	....	....
2001-02	Florida Panthers	8	1	2	3	2	....	....	....	....	....
2002-03	Florida Panthers	23	4	2	6	12	....	....	....	....	....
	NHL Totals	**74**	**11**	**14**	**25**	**30**	....	....	....	....	....

• Missed majority of 2001-02 season recovering from head injury suffered in game vs. Philadelphia, October 4, 2001.

SIEBERT, Babe

HHOF

Left wing/Defense. Shoots left. 5'10", 182 lbs. Born, Plattsville, Ont., January 14, 1904.

Season	Club	GP	G	A	Pts	PIM	GP	G	A	Pts	PIM
1925-26◆	Montreal Maroons	35	16	8	24	108	4	1	0	1	4
	Montreal Maroons (Cup)	....	....	....	....	....	*4*	*1*	*2*	*3*	*4*
1926-27	Montreal Maroons	42	5	3	8	116	2	1	0	1	2
1927-28	Montreal Maroons	39	8	9	17	109	9	2	0	2	26
1928-29	Montreal Maroons	40	3	5	8	52	....	....	....	....	....
1929-30	Montreal Maroons	39	14	19	33	94	3	0	0	0	0
1930-31	Montreal Maroons	43	16	12	28	76	2	0	0	0	6
1931-32	Montreal Maroons	48	21	18	39	64	4	0	1	1	4
1932-33◆	New York Rangers	43	9	10	19	38	8	1	0	1	12
1933-34	New York Rangers	13	0	1	1	18	....	....	....	....	....
	Boston Bruins	32	5	6	11	31	....	....	....	....	....
1934-35	Boston Bruins	48	6	18	24	80	4	0	0	0	6
1935-36	Boston Bruins	45	12	9	21	66	2	0	1	1	0
1936-37	Montreal Canadiens	44	8	20	28	38	5	1	2	3	2
1937-38	Montreal Canadiens	37	8	11	19	56	3	1	1	2	0
1938-39	Montreal Canadiens	44	9	7	16	36	3	0	0	0	0
	NHL Totals	**592**	**140**	**156**	**296**	**982**	**49**	**7**	**5**	**12**	**62**

NHL First All-Star Team (1936, 1937, 1938) • Hart Trophy (1937)
Played in NHL All-Star Game (1937)

Signed as a free agent by **Mtl. Maroons**, March 16, 1925. • 1925-26 Montreal Maroons playoff totals includes series against Ottawa and Pittsburgh. Traded to **NY Rangers** by **Mtl. Maroons** for cash, July 2, 1932. Traded to **Boston** by **NY Rangers** for Vic Ripley and Roy Burmeister, December 18, 1933. Traded to **Montreal** by **Boston** with Roger Jenkins for Leroy Goldsworthy, Sammy McManus and $10,000, September 10, 1936.

SIKLENKA, Mike

Right wing. Shoots right. 6'5", 224 lbs. Born, Meadow Lake, Sask., December 18, 1979.
(Washington's 5th choice, 118th overall, in 1998 Entry Draft).

Season	Club	GP	G	A	Pts	PIM	GP	G	A	Pts	PIM
2002-03	Philadelphia Flyers	1	0	0	0	0	....	....	....	....	....
	NHL Totals	**1**	**0**	**0**	**0**	**0**	....	....	....	....	....

Signed as a free agent by **Philadelphia**, January 27, 2002.

SILK, Dave

Right wing. Shoots right. 5'11", 190 lbs. Born, Scituate, MA, January 1, 1958.
(NY Rangers' 4th choice, 59th overall, in 1978 Amateur Draft).

Season	Club	GP	G	A	Pts	PIM	GP	G	A	Pts	PIM
1979-80	New York Rangers	2	0	0	0	0	....	....	....	....	....
1980-81	New York Rangers	59	14	12	26	58	....	....	....	....	....
1981-82	New York Rangers	64	15	20	35	39	9	2	4	6	4
1982-83	New York Rangers	16	1	1	2	15	....	....	....	....	....
1983-84	Boston Bruins	35	13	17	30	64	3	0	0	0	7
1984-85	Boston Bruins	29	7	5	12	22	....	....	....	....	....
	Detroit Red Wings	12	2	0	2	10	....	....	....	....	....
1985-86	Winnipeg Jets	32	2	4	6	63	1	0	0	0	2
	NHL Totals	**249**	**54**	**59**	**113**	**271**	**13**	**2**	**4**	**6**	**13**

Traded to **Boston** by **NY Rangers** for Dave Barr, October 5, 1983. Claimed on waivers by **Detroit** from **Boston**, December 21, 1984. Signed as a free agent by **Winnipeg**, September 30, 1985.

SILLINGER, Mike

Center. Shoots right. 5'11", 196 lbs. Born, Regina, Sask., June 29, 1971.
(Detroit's 1st choice, 11th overall, in 1989 Entry Draft).

Season	Club	GP	G	A	Pts	PIM	GP	G	A	Pts	PIM
1990-91	Detroit Red Wings	3	0	1	1	0	3	0	1	1	0
1991-92	Detroit Red Wings	....	....	....	....	....	8	2	2	4	2
1992-93	Detroit Red Wings	51	4	17	21	16	....	....	....	....	....
1993-94	Detroit Red Wings	62	8	21	29	10	....	....	....	....	....
1994-95	Detroit Red Wings	13	2	6	8	2	....	....	....	....	....
	Mighty Ducks of Anaheim	15	2	5	7	6	....	....	....	....	....
1995-96	Mighty Ducks of Anaheim	62	13	21	34	32	....	....	....	....	....
	Vancouver Canucks	12	1	3	4	6	6	0	0	0	2
1996-97	Vancouver Canucks	78	17	20	37	25	....	....	....	....	....
1997-98	Vancouver Canucks	48	10	9	19	34	....	....	....	....	....
	Philadelphia Flyers	27	11	11	22	16	3	1	0	1	0
1998-99	Philadelphia Flyers	25	0	3	3	8	....	....	....	....	....
	Tampa Bay Lightning	54	8	2	10	28	....	....	....	....	....
99-2000	Tampa Bay Lightning	67	19	25	44	86	....	....	....	....	....
	Florida Panthers	13	4	4	8	16	4	2	1	3	2
2000-01	Florida Panthers	55	13	21	34	44	....	....	....	....	....
	Ottawa Senators	13	3	4	7	4	4	0	0	0	2
2001-02	Columbus Blue Jackets	80	20	23	43	54	....	....	....	....	....
2002-03	Columbus Blue Jackets	75	18	25	43	52	....	....	....	....	....
	NHL Totals	**753**	**153**	**221**	**374**	**439**	**28**	**5**	**4**	**9**	**8**

Traded to **Anaheim** by **Detroit** with Jason York for Stu Grimson, Mark Ferner and Anaheim's 6th round choice (Magnus Nilsson) in 1996 Entry Draft, April 4, 1995. Traded to **Vancouver** by **Anaheim** for Roman Oksiuta, March 15, 1996. Traded to **Philadelphia** by **Vancouver** for Philadelphia's 5th round choice (later traded back to Philadelphia – Philadelphia selected Garrett Prosofsky) in 1998 Entry Draft, February 5, 1998. Traded to **Tampa Bay** by **Philadelphia** with Chris Gratton for Mikael Renberg and Daymond Langkow, December 12, 1998. Traded to **Florida** by **Tampa Bay** for Ryan Johnson and Dwayne Hay, March 14, 2000. Traded to **Ottawa** by **Florida** for future considerations, March 13, 2001. Signed as a free agent by **Columbus**, July 7, 2001. Traded to **Dallas** by **Columbus** with Columbus's 2nd round choice in 2004 Entry Draft for Darryl Sydor, July 22, 2003. Traded to **Phoenix** by **Dallas** with future considerations for Teppo Numminen, July 22, 2003.

SILTALA, Mike

Right wing. Shoots right. 5'9", 170 lbs. Born, Toronto, Ont., August 5, 1963.
(Washington's 4th choice, 89th overall, in 1981 Entry Draft).

Season	Club	GP	G	A	Pts	PIM	GP	G	A	Pts	PIM
1981-82	Washington Capitals	3	1	0	1	2	....	....	....	....	....
1986-87	New York Rangers	1	0	0	0	0	....	....	....	....	....
1987-88	New York Rangers	3	0	0	0	0	....	....	....	....	....
	NHL Totals	**7**	**1**	**0**	**1**	**2**	....	....	....	....	....

Signed as a free agent by **NY Rangers**, August 15, 1986. Traded to **Los Angeles** by **NY Rangers** with Gord Walker for Joe Paterson, January 21, 1988.

SILTANEN, Risto

Defense. Shoots right. 5'9", 158 lbs. Born, Tampere, Finland, October 31, 1958.
(St. Louis' 13th choice, 173rd overall, in 1978 Amateur Draft).

Season	Club	GP	G	A	Pts	PIM	GP	G	A	Pts	PIM
1979-80	Edmonton Oilers	64	6	29	35	26	2	0	0	0	2
1980-81	Edmonton Oilers	79	17	36	53	54	9	2	0	2	8
1981-82	Edmonton Oilers	63	15	48	63	26	5	3	2	5	10
1982-83	Hartford Whalers	74	5	25	30	28	....	....	....	....	....
1983-84	Hartford Whalers	75	15	38	53	34	....	....	....	....	....
1984-85	Hartford Whalers	76	12	33	45	30	....	....	....	....	....
1985-86	Hartford Whalers	52	8	22	30	30	....	....	....	....	....
	Quebec Nordiques	13	2	5	7	6	3	0	1	1	2
1986-87	Quebec Nordiques	66	10	29	39	32	13	1	9	10	8
	NHL Totals	**562**	**90**	**265**	**355**	**266**	**32**	**6**	**12**	**18**	**30**

Reclaimed by **St. Louis** from **Edmonton** prior to Expansion Draft, June 9, 1979. Traded to **Edmonton** by **St. Louis** with Tom Roulston for Joe Micheletti, August 7, 1979. Traded to **Hartford** by **Edmonton** with the rights to Brent Loney for Ken Linseman and Don Nachbaur, August 19, 1982. Traded to **Quebec** by **Hartford** for John Anderson, March 8, 1986.

SIM, Jon

Left wing. Shoots left. 5'10", 190 lbs. Born, New Glasgow, N.S., September 29, 1977.
(Dallas' 2nd choice, 70th overall, in 1996 Entry Draft).

Season	Club	GP	G	A	Pts	PIM	GP	G	A	Pts	PIM
1998-99◆	Dallas Stars	7	1	0	1	12	4	0	0	0	0
99-2000	Dallas Stars	25	5	3	8	10	7	1	0	1	6
2000-01	Dallas Stars	15	0	3	3	6	....	....	....	....	....
2001-02	Dallas Stars	26	3	0	3	10	....	....	....	....	....
2002-03	Dallas Stars	4	0	0	0	0	....	....	....	....	....
	Nashville Predators	4	1	0	1	0	....	....	....	....	....
	Los Angeles Kings	14	0	2	2	19	....	....	....	....	....
	NHL Totals	**95**	**10**	**8**	**18**	**57**	**11**	**1**	**0**	**1**	**6**

Traded to **Nashville** by **Dallas** for Bubba Berenzweig and future considerations, February 17, 2003. Claimed on waivers by **Los Angeles** from **Nashville**, March 8, 2003.

SIM, Trevor

Right wing. Shoots left. 6'2", 192 lbs. Born, Calgary, Alta., June 9, 1970.
(Edmonton's 3rd choice, 53rd overall, in 1988 Entry Draft).

Season	Club	GP	G	A	Pts	PIM	GP	G	A	Pts	PIM
1989-90	Edmonton Oilers	3	0	1	1	2	....	....	....	....	....
	NHL Totals	**3**	**0**	**1**	**1**	**2**	....	....	....	....	....

SIMARD, Martin

Right wing. Shoots right. 6'1", 215 lbs. Born, Montreal, Que., June 25, 1966.

Season	Club	GP	G	A	Pts	PIM	GP	G	A	Pts	PIM
1990-91	Calgary Flames	16	0	2	2	53	....	....	....	....	....
1991-92	Calgary Flames	21	1	3	4	119	....	....	....	....	....
1992-93	Tampa Bay Lightning	7	0	0	0	11	....	....	....	....	....
	NHL Totals	**44**	**1**	**5**	**6**	**183**	....	....	....	....	....

Signed as a free agent by **Calgary**, May 19, 1987. Traded to **Quebec** by **Calgary** for Greg Smyth, March 10, 1992. Traded to **Tampa Bay** by **Quebec** to complete transaction that sent Tim Hunter to Quebec (June 19, 1992), September 14, 1992. Traded to **Quebec** by **Tampa Bay** with Steve Tuttle and Michel Mongeau for Herb Raglan, February 12, 1993. Signed as a free agent by **Phoenix**, August 6, 1997.

SIMICEK, Roman

Center. Shoots left. 6'1", 190 lbs. Born, Ostrava, Czech., November 4, 1971.
(Pittsburgh's 9th choice, 273rd overall, in 2000 Entry Draft).

Season	Club	GP	G	A	Pts	PIM	GP	G	A	Pts	PIM
2000-01	Pittsburgh Penguins	29	3	6	9	30	....	....	....	....	....
	Minnesota Wild	28	2	4	6	21	....	....	....	....	....
2001-02	Minnesota Wild	6	2	0	2	8	....	....	....	....	....
	NHL Totals	**63**	**7**	**10**	**17**	**59**	....	....	....	....	....

Traded to **Minnesota** by **Pittsburgh** for Steve McKenna, January 13, 2001.

SIMMER, Charlie

Left wing. Shoots left. 6'3", 210 lbs. Born, Terrace Bay, Ont., March 20, 1954.
(California's 4th choice, 39th overall, in 1974 Amateur Draft).

Season	Club	Regular Season GP	G	A	Pts	PIM	Playoffs GP	G	A	Pts	PIM
1974-75	California Golden Seals	35	8	13	21	26	....	....	....	....	....
1975-76	California Golden Seals	21	1	1	2	22	....	....	....	....	....
1976-77	Cleveland Barons	24	2	0	2	16	....	....	....	....	....
1977-78	Los Angeles Kings	3	0	0	0	2	....	....	....	....	....
1978-79	Los Angeles Kings	38	21	27	48	16	2	1	0	1	2
1979-80	Los Angeles Kings	64	*56	45	101	65	3	2	0	2	0
1980-81	Los Angeles Kings	65	56	49	105	62	....	....	....	....	....
1981-82	Los Angeles Kings	50	15	24	39	42	10	4	7	11	22
1982-83	Los Angeles Kings	80	29	51	80	51	....	....	....	....	....
1983-84	Los Angeles Kings	79	44	48	92	78	....	....	....	....	....
1984-85	Los Angeles Kings	5	1	0	1	4	....	....	....	....	....
	Boston Bruins	63	33	30	63	35	5	2	2	4	2
1985-86	Boston Bruins	55	36	24	60	42	3	0	0	0	4
1986-87	Boston Bruins	80	29	40	69	59	1	0	0	0	2
1987-88	Pittsburgh Penguins	50	11	17	28	24	....	....	....	....	....
	NHL Totals	**712**	**342**	**369**	**711**	**544**	**24**	**9**	**9**	**18**	**32**

NHL First All-Star Team (1980, 1981) • Bill Masterton Trophy (1986)

Played in NHL All-Star Game (1981, 1984)

Transferred to **Cleveland** after **California** franchise relocated, August 26, 1976. Signed as a free agent by **Los Angeles**, August 8, 1977. Traded to **Boston** by **Los Angeles** for Boston's 1st round choice (Dan Gratton) in 1985 Entry Draft, October 24, 1984. Claimed by **Pittsburgh** from **Boston** in Waiver Draft, October 5, 1987.

SIMMONS, Al

Defense. Shoots right. 6', 170 lbs. Born, Winnipeg, Man., September 25, 1951.
(California's 6th choice, 85th overall, in 1971 Amateur Draft).

Season	Club	Regular Season GP	G	A	Pts	PIM	Playoffs GP	G	A	Pts	PIM
1971-72	California Golden Seals	1	0	0	0	0	....	....	....	....	....
1973-74	Boston Bruins	3	0	0	0	0	1	0	0	0	0
1975-76	Boston Bruins	7	0	1	1	21	....	....	....	....	....
	NHL Totals	**11**	**0**	**1**	**1**	**21**	**1**	**0**	**0**	**0**	**0**

Claimed by **San Diego** (WHL) from **California** in Reverse Draft, June 13, 1973. Traded to **Boston** by **San Diego** for cash, February 7, 1974. Traded to **NY Rangers** by **Boston** for cash, November 14, 1975.

SIMON, Ben

Left wing. Shoots left. 6', 195 lbs. Born, Shaker Heights, OH, June 14, 1978.
(Chicago's 5th choice, 110th overall, in 1997 Entry Draft).

Season	Club	Regular Season GP	G	A	Pts	PIM	Playoffs GP	G	A	Pts	PIM
2001-02	Atlanta Thrashers	6	0	0	0	6	....	....	....	....	....
2002-03	Atlanta Thrashers	10	0	1	1	9	....	....	....	....	....
	NHL Totals	**16**	**0**	**1**	**1**	**15**	....	....	....	....	....

Rights traded to **Atlanta** by **Chicago** for Atlanta's 9th round choice (Peter Flache) in 2000 Entry Draft, June 25, 2000. Signed as a free agent by **Nashville**, July 14, 2003.

SIMON, Chris

Left wing. Shoots left. 6'4", 235 lbs. Born, Wawa, Ont., January 30, 1972.
(Philadelphia's 2nd choice, 25th overall, in 1990 Entry Draft).

Season	Club	Regular Season GP	G	A	Pts	PIM	Playoffs GP	G	A	Pts	PIM
1992-93	Quebec Nordiques	16	1	1	2	67	5	0	0	0	26
1993-94	Quebec Nordiques	37	4	4	8	132	....	....	....	....	....
1994-95	Quebec Nordiques	29	3	9	12	106	6	1	1	2	19
1995-96◆	Colorado Avalanche	64	16	18	34	250	12	1	2	3	11
1996-97	Washington Capitals	42	9	13	22	165	....	....	....	....	....
1997-98	Washington Capitals	28	7	10	17	38	18	1	0	1	26
1998-99	Washington Capitals	23	3	7	10	48	....	....	....	....	....
99-2000	Washington Capitals	75	29	20	49	146	4	2	0	2	24
2000-01	Washington Capitals	60	10	10	20	109	6	0	1	1	4
2001-02	Washington Capitals	82	14	17	31	137	....	....	....	....	....
2002-03	Washington Capitals	10	0	2	2	23	....	....	....	....	....
	Chicago Blackhawks	61	12	6	18	125	....	....	....	....	....
	NHL Totals	**527**	**108**	**117**	**225**	**1346**	**51**	**5**	**4**	**9**	**110**

Traded to **Quebec** by **Philadelphia** with Philadelphia's 1st round choice (later traded to Toronto – later traded to Washington – Washington selected Nolan Baumgartner) in 1994 Entry Draft to complete transaction that sent Eric Lindros to Philadelphia (June 30, 1992), July 21, 1992. Transferred to **Colorado** after **Quebec** franchise relocated, June 21, 1995. Traded to **Washington** by **Colorado** with Curtis Leschyshyn for Keith Jones and Washington's 1st (Scott Parker) and 4th (later traded back to Washington – Washington selected Krys Barch) round choices in 1998 Entry Draft, November 2, 1996. Traded to **Chicago** by **Washington** with Andrei Nikolishin for Michael Nylander, Chicago's 3rd round choice (Stephen Werner) in 2003 Entry Draft and future considerations, November 1, 2002. Signed as a free agent by **NY Rangers**, July 25, 2003.

SIMON, Cully

Defense. Shoots left. 5'10", 190 lbs. Born, Brockville, Ont., May 8, 1918.

Season	Club	Regular Season GP	G	A	Pts	PIM	Playoffs GP	G	A	Pts	PIM
1942-43◆	Detroit Red Wings	34	1	1	2	34	9	1	0	1	4
1943-44	Detroit Red Wings	46	3	7	10	52	5	0	0	0	2
1944-45	Detroit Red Wings	21	0	2	2	26	....	....	....	....	....
	Chicago Black Hawks	29	0	1	1	9	....	....	....	....	....
	NHL Totals	**130**	**4**	**11**	**15**	**121**	**14**	**1**	**0**	**1**	**6**

• Brother of Thain

Signed as a free agent by **Detroit**, October 14, 1941. Loaned to **Washington** (AHL) by **Detroit** (Indianapolis-AHL) as an emergency injury replacement for cash, December 2, 1942. Traded to **Chicago** by **Detroit** with Don Grosso and Butch McDonald for Earl Seibert and future considerations (Fido Purpur, January 4, 1945), January 2, 1945.

SIMON, Jason

Left wing. Shoots left. 6'1", 210 lbs. Born, Sarnia, Ont., March 21, 1969.
(New Jersey's 9th choice, 215th overall, in 1989 Entry Draft).

Season	Club	Regular Season GP	G	A	Pts	PIM	Playoffs GP	G	A	Pts	PIM
1993-94	New York Islanders	4	0	0	0	34	....	....	....	....	....
1996-97	Phoenix Coyotes	1	0	0	0	0	....	....	....	....	....
	NHL Totals	**5**	**0**	**0**	**0**	**34**	....	....	....	....	....

Signed as a free agent by **NY Islanders**, January 6, 1994. Signed as a free agent by **Winnipeg**, August 9, 1995. Transferred to **Phoenix** after **Winnipeg** franchise relocated, July 1, 1996. Signed as a free agent by **Colorado**, August 22, 1997.

SIMON, Thain

Defense. Shoots left. 6', 200 lbs. Born, Brockville, Ont., April 24, 1922.

Season	Club	Regular Season GP	G	A	Pts	PIM	Playoffs GP	G	A	Pts	PIM
1946-47	Detroit Red Wings	3	0	0	0	0	....	....	....	....	....
	NHL Totals	**3**	**0**	**0**	**0**	**0**	....	....	....	....	....

• Brother of Cully

Traded to **Chicago** (St. Louis-AHL) by **Detroit** with Red Almas, Lloyd Doran, Barry Sullivan and Tony Licari for Joe Lund and Hec Highton, September 9, 1948.

SIMON, Todd

Center. Shoots right. 5'10", 188 lbs. Born, Toronto, Ont., April 21, 1972.
(Buffalo's 10th choice, 203rd overall, in 1992 Entry Draft).

Season	Club	Regular Season GP	G	A	Pts	PIM	Playoffs GP	G	A	Pts	PIM
1993-94	Buffalo Sabres	15	0	1	1	0	5	1	0	1	0
	NHL Totals	**15**	**0**	**1**	**1**	**0**	**5**	**1**	**0**	**1**	**0**

Signed as a free agent by **Carolina**, August 31, 1999.

SIMONETTI, Frank

Defense. Shoots right. 6'1", 190 lbs. Born, Melrose, MA, September 11, 1962.

Season	Club	Regular Season GP	G	A	Pts	PIM	Playoffs GP	G	A	Pts	PIM
1984-85	Boston Bruins	43	1	5	6	26	5	0	1	1	2
1985-86	Boston Bruins	17	1	0	1	14	3	0	0	0	0
1986-87	Boston Bruins	25	1	0	1	17	4	0	0	0	6
1987-88	Boston Bruins	30	2	3	5	19	....	....	....	....	....
	NHL Totals	**115**	**5**	**8**	**13**	**76**	**12**	**0**	**1**	**1**	**8**

Signed as a free agent by **Boston**, October 4, 1984.

SIMPSON, Bobby

Left wing. Shoots left. 6', 190 lbs. Born, Caughnawaga, Que., November 17, 1956.
(Atlanta's 3rd choice, 28th overall, in 1976 Amateur Draft).

Season	Club	Regular Season GP	G	A	Pts	PIM	Playoffs GP	G	A	Pts	PIM
1976-77	Atlanta Flames	72	13	10	23	45	2	0	1	1	0
1977-78	Atlanta Flames	55	10	8	18	49	2	0	0	0	2
1979-80	St. Louis Blues	18	2	2	4	0	....	....	....	....	....
1981-82	Pittsburgh Penguins	26	9	9	18	4	2	0	0	0	0
1982-83	Pittsburgh Penguins	4	1	0	1	0	....	....	....	....	....
	NHL Totals	**175**	**35**	**29**	**64**	**98**	**6**	**0**	**1**	**1**	**2**

Traded to **St. Louis** by **Atlanta** for Curt Bennett, May 24, 1979. Claimed by **St. Louis** as a fill-in during Expansion Draft, June 13, 1979. Signed as a free agent by **Pittsburgh**, October 1, 1981.

SIMPSON, Cliff

Center. Shoots right. 5'11", 175 lbs. Born, Toronto, Ont., April 4, 1923.

Season	Club	Regular Season GP	G	A	Pts	PIM	Playoffs GP	G	A	Pts	PIM
1946-47	Detroit Red Wings	6	0	1	1	0	1	0	0	0	0
1947-48	Detroit Red Wings	....	....	....	....	....	1	0	0	0	2
	NHL Totals	**6**	**0**	**1**	**1**	**0**	**2**	**0**	**0**	**0**	**2**

Signed as a free agent by **Detroit**, October 19, 1942. Traded to **St. Louis** (AHL) by **Detroit** with Fern Gauthier, Ed Nicholson and future considerations for Steve Black and Bill Brennan, August 29, 1949.

SIMPSON, Craig

Left wing. Shoots right. 6'2", 195 lbs. Born, London, Ont., February 15, 1967.
(Pittsburgh's 1st choice, 2nd overall, in 1985 Entry Draft).

Season	Club	Regular Season GP	G	A	Pts	PIM	Playoffs GP	G	A	Pts	PIM
1985-86	Pittsburgh Penguins	76	11	17	28	49	....	....	....	....	....
1986-87	Pittsburgh Penguins	72	26	25	51	57	....	....	....	....	....
1987-88	Pittsburgh Penguins	21	13	13	26	34	....	....	....	....	....
◆	Edmonton Oilers	59	43	21	64	43	19	13	6	19	26
1988-89	Edmonton Oilers	66	35	41	76	80	7	2	0	2	10
1989-90◆	Edmonton Oilers	80	29	32	61	180	22	*16	15	*31	8
1990-91	Edmonton Oilers	75	30	27	57	66	18	5	11	16	12
1991-92	Edmonton Oilers	79	24	37	61	80	1	0	0	0	0
1992-93	Edmonton Oilers	60	24	22	46	36	....	....	....	....	....
1993-94	Buffalo Sabres	22	8	8	16	8	....	....	....	....	....
1994-95	Buffalo Sabres	24	4	7	11	26	....	....	....	....	....
	NHL Totals	**634**	**247**	**250**	**497**	**659**	**67**	**36**	**32**	**68**	**56**

Traded to **Edmonton** by **Pittsburgh** with Dave Hannan, Moe Mantha and Chris Joseph for Paul Coffey, Dave Hunter and Wayne Van Dorp, November 24, 1987. Traded to **Buffalo** by **Edmonton** for Jozef Cierny and Buffalo's 4th round choice (Jussi Tarvainen) in 1994 Entry Draft, September 1, 1993. • Suffered eventual career-ending back injury in game vs. Tampa Bay, December 1, 1993.

SIMPSON, Joe

HHOF

Defense. Shoots right. 5'10", 175 lbs. Born, Selkirk, Man., August 13, 1893.

Season	Club	Regular Season GP	G	A	Pts	PIM	Playoffs GP	G	A	Pts	PIM
1925-26	New York Americans	32	2	2	4	2	....	....	....	....	....
1926-27	New York Americans	43	4	2	6	39	....	....	....	....	....
1927-28	New York Americans	24	2	0	2	32	....	....	....	....	....
1928-29	New York Americans	43	3	2	5	29	2	0	0	0	0
1929-30	New York Americans	44	8	13	21	41	....	....	....	....	....

Season	Club	Regular Season GP	G	A	Pts	PIM	Playoffs GP	G	A	Pts	PIM
1930-31	New York Americans	42	2	0	2	13	....	....	....	....	....
	NHL Totals	**228**	**21**	**19**	**40**	**156**	**2**	**0**	**0**	**0**	**0**

Traded to **NY Americans** by **Edmonton** (WHL) with John Morrison and Roy Rickey for $10,000, September 18, 1925.

SIMPSON, Reid

Left wing. Shoots left. 6'2", 216 lbs. Born, Flin Flon, Man., May 21, 1969.
(Philadelphia's 3rd choice, 72nd overall, in 1989 Entry Draft).

Season	Club	GP	G	A	Pts	PIM	GP	G	A	Pts	PIM
1991-92	Philadelphia Flyers	1	0	0	0	0	....	....	....	....	....
1992-93	Minnesota North Stars	1	0	0	0	5	....	....	....	....	....
1994-95	New Jersey Devils	9	0	0	0	27	....	....	....	....	....
1995-96	New Jersey Devils	23	1	5	6	79	....	....	....	....	....
1996-97	New Jersey Devils	27	0	4	4	60	5	0	0	0	29
1997-98	New Jersey Devils	6	0	0	0	16	....	....	....	....	....
	Chicago Blackhawks	38	3	2	5	102	....	....	....	....	....
1998-99	Chicago Blackhawks	53	5	4	9	145	....	....	....	....	....
99-2000	Tampa Bay Lightning	26	1	0	1	103	....	....	....	....	....
2000-01	St. Louis Blues	38	2	1	3	96	5	0	0	0	2
2001-02	Montreal Canadiens	25	1	1	2	63	....	....	....	....	....
	Nashville Predators	26	5	0	5	69	....	....	....	....	....
2002-03	Nashville Predators	26	0	1	1	56	....	....	....	....	....
	NHL Totals	**299**	**18**	**18**	**36**	**821**	**10**	**0**	**0**	**0**	**31**

Signed as a free agent by **Minnesota**, December 14, 1992. Transferred to **Dallas** after **Minnesota** franchise relocated, June 9, 1993. Traded to **New Jersey** by **Dallas** with Roy Mitchell for future considerations, March 21, 1994. Traded to **Chicago** by **New Jersey** for Chicago's 4th round choice (Mikko Jokela) in 1998 Entry Draft and future considerations, January 8, 1998. Traded to **Tampa Bay** by **Chicago** with Bryan Muir for Michael Nylander, November 12, 1999. • Missed majority of 1999-2000 season recovering from jaw injury suffered in game vs. NY Islanders, January 13, 2000. Signed as a free agent by **St. Louis**, August 24, 2000. • Missed majority of 2000-01 season recovering from groin injury originally suffered in game vs. Nashville, November 24, 2000. Signed as a free agent by **Montreal**, September 10, 2001. Claimed on waivers by **Nashville** from **Montreal**, January 28, 2002.

SIMPSON, Todd

Defense. Shoots left. 6'3", 218 lbs. Born, North Vancouver, B.C., May 28, 1973.

Season	Club	GP	G	A	Pts	PIM	GP	G	A	Pts	PIM
1995-96	Calgary Flames	6	0	0	0	32	....	....	....	....	....
1996-97	Calgary Flames	82	1	13	14	208	....	....	....	....	....
1997-98	Calgary Flames	53	1	5	6	109	....	....	....	....	....
1998-99	Calgary Flames	73	2	8	10	151	....	....	....	....	....
99-2000	Florida Panthers	82	1	6	7	202	4	0	0	0	4
2000-01	Florida Panthers	25	1	3	4	74	....	....	....	....	....
	Phoenix Coyotes	13	0	1	1	12	....	....	....	....	....
2001-02	Phoenix Coyotes	67	2	13	15	152	5	0	2	2	6
2002-03	Phoenix Coyotes	66	2	7	9	135	....	....	....	....	....
	NHL Totals	**467**	**10**	**56**	**66**	**1075**	**9**	**0**	**2**	**2**	**10**

Signed as free agent by **Calgary**, July 6, 1994. Traded to **Florida** by **Calgary** for Bill Lindsay, September 30, 1999. • Missed majority of 2000-01 season recovering from head injury suffered in game vs. NY Islanders, December 6, 2000. Traded to **Phoenix** by **Florida** for Phoenix's 2nd round choice (later traded to New Jersey – New Jersey selected Tuomas Pihlman) in 2001 Entry Draft, March 13, 2001.

SIMS, Al

Defense. Shoots left. 6', 182 lbs. Born, Toronto, Ont., April 18, 1953.
(Boston's 4th choice, 47th overall, in 1973 Amateur Draft).

Season	Club	GP	G	A	Pts	PIM	GP	G	A	Pts	PIM
1973-74	Boston Bruins	76	3	9	12	22	16	0	0	0	12
1974-75	Boston Bruins	75	4	8	12	73	....	....	....	....	....
1975-76	Boston Bruins	48	4	3	7	43	1	0	0	0	0
1976-77	Boston Bruins	1	0	0	0	0	2	0	0	0	0
1977-78	Boston Bruins	43	2	8	10	6	8	0	0	0	0
1978-79	Boston Bruins	67	9	20	29	28	11	0	2	2	0
1979-80	Hartford Whalers	76	10	31	41	30	3	0	0	0	2
1980-81	Hartford Whalers	80	16	36	52	68	....	....	....	....	....
1981-82	Los Angeles Kings	8	1	1	2	16	....	....	....	....	....
1982-83	Los Angeles Kings	1	0	0	0	0	....	....	....	....	....
	NHL Totals	**475**	**49**	**116**	**165**	**286**	**41**	**0**	**2**	**2**	**14**

Claimed by **Hartford** from **Boston** in Expansion Draft, June 13, 1979. Claimed by **Los Angeles** from **Hartford** in Waiver Draft, October 5, 1981.

SINCLAIR, Reg

Right wing/Center. Shoots right. 6', 165 lbs. Born, Lachine, Que., March 6, 1925.

Season	Club	GP	G	A	Pts	PIM	GP	G	A	Pts	PIM
1950-51	New York Rangers	70	18	21	39	70	....	....	....	....	....
1951-52	New York Rangers	69	20	10	30	33	....	....	....	....	....
1952-53	Detroit Red Wings	69	11	12	23	36	3	1	0	1	0
	NHL Totals	**208**	**49**	**43**	**92**	**139**	**3**	**1**	**0**	**1**	**0**

Played in NHL All-Star Game (1951, 1952)

Signed as a free agent by **NY Rangers**, October 3, 1950. Traded to **Detroit** by **NY Rangers** with John Morrison for Leo Reise Jr., August 18, 1952.

SINGBUSH, Alex

Defense. Shoots left. 5'11", 180 lbs. Born, January 31, 1914.

Season	Club	GP	G	A	Pts	PIM	GP	G	A	Pts	PIM
1940-41	Montreal Canadiens	32	0	5	5	15	3	0	0	0	4
	NHL Totals	**32**	**0**	**5**	**5**	**15**	**3**	**0**	**0**	**0**	**4**

Traded to **Washington** (AHL) by **Montreal** for cash, October 9, 1941.

SINISALO, Ilkka

Right wing. Shoots left. 6', 185 lbs. Born, Hauho, Finland, July 10, 1958.

Season	Club	GP	G	A	Pts	PIM	GP	G	A	Pts	PIM
1981-82	Philadelphia Flyers	66	15	22	37	22	4	0	2	2	0
1982-83	Philadelphia Flyers	61	21	29	50	16	3	1	1	2	0
1983-84	Philadelphia Flyers	73	29	17	46	29	2	2	0	2	0
1984-85	Philadelphia Flyers	70	36	37	73	16	19	6	1	7	0
1985-86	Philadelphia Flyers	74	39	37	76	31	5	2	2	4	2
1986-87	Philadelphia Flyers	42	10	21	31	8	18	5	1	6	4
1987-88	Philadelphia Flyers	68	25	17	42	30	7	4	2	6	0
1988-89	Philadelphia Flyers	13	1	6	7	2	8	1	1	2	0
1989-90	Philadelphia Flyers	59	23	23	46	26	....	....	....	....	....
1990-91	Minnesota North Stars	46	5	12	17	24	....	....	....	....	....
	Los Angeles Kings	7	0	0	0	2	2	0	1	1	0
1991-92	Los Angeles Kings	3	0	1	1	2	....	....	....	....	....
	NHL Totals	**582**	**204**	**222**	**426**	**208**	**68**	**21**	**11**	**32**	**6**

Signed as a free agent by **Philadelphia**, February 14, 1981. Signed as a free agent by **Minnesota**, July 3, 1990. Traded to **Los Angeles** by **Minnesota** for Los Angeles' 8th round choice (Michael Burkett) in 1991 Entry Draft, March 5, 1991.

SIREN, Ville

Defense. Shoots left. 6'2", 191 lbs. Born, Tampere, Finland, February 11, 1964.
(Hartford's 3rd choice, 23rd overall, in 1983 Entry Draft).

Season	Club	GP	G	A	Pts	PIM	GP	G	A	Pts	PIM
1985-86	Pittsburgh Penguins	60	4	8	12	32	....	....	....	....	....
1986-87	Pittsburgh Penguins	69	5	17	22	50	....	....	....	....	....
1987-88	Pittsburgh Penguins	58	1	20	21	62	....	....	....	....	....
1988-89	Pittsburgh Penguins	12	1	0	1	14	....	....	....	....	....
	Minnesota North Stars	38	2	10	12	58	4	0	0	0	4
1989-90	Minnesota North Stars	53	1	13	14	60	3	0	0	0	2
	NHL Totals	**290**	**14**	**68**	**82**	**276**	**7**	**0**	**0**	**0**	**6**

Rights traded to **Pittsburgh** by **Hartford** for Pat Boutette, November 16, 1984. Traded to **Minnesota** by **Pittsburgh** with Steve Gotaas for Gord Dineen and Scott Bjugstad, December 17, 1988.

SIROIS, Bob

Right wing. Shoots left. 6', 178 lbs. Born, Montreal, Que., February 6, 1954.
(Philadelphia's 2nd choice, 53rd overall, in 1974 Amateur Draft).

Season	Club	GP	G	A	Pts	PIM	GP	G	A	Pts	PIM
1974-75	Philadelphia Flyers	3	1	0	1	4	....	....	....	....	....
1975-76	Philadelphia Flyers	1	0	0	0	0	....	....	....	....	....
	Washington Capitals	43	10	19	29	6	....	....	....	....	....
1976-77	Washington Capitals	45	13	22	35	2	....	....	....	....	....
1977-78	Washington Capitals	72	24	37	61	6	....	....	....	....	....
1978-79	Washington Capitals	73	29	25	54	6	....	....	....	....	....
1979-80	Washington Capitals	49	15	17	32	18	....	....	....	....	....
	NHL Totals	**286**	**92**	**120**	**212**	**42**	....	....	....	....	....

Played in NHL All-Star Game (1978)

Traded to **Washington** by **Philadelphia** for future considerations (John Paddock, September 1, 1976), December 15, 1975.

SITTLER, Darryl

HHOF

Center. Shoots left. 6', 190 lbs. Born, Kitchener, Ont., September 18, 1950.
(Toronto's 1st choice, 8th overall, in 1970 Amateur Draft).

Season	Club	GP	G	A	Pts	PIM	GP	G	A	Pts	PIM
1970-71	Toronto Maple Leafs	49	10	8	18	37	6	2	1	3	31
1971-72	Toronto Maple Leafs	74	15	17	32	44	3	0	0	0	2
1972-73	Toronto Maple Leafs	78	29	48	77	69	....	....	....	....	....
1973-74	Toronto Maple Leafs	78	38	46	84	55	4	2	1	3	6
1974-75	Toronto Maple Leafs	72	36	44	80	47	7	2	1	3	15
1975-76	Toronto Maple Leafs	79	41	59	100	90	10	5	7	12	19
1976-77	Toronto Maple Leafs	73	38	52	90	89	9	5	16	21	4
1977-78	Toronto Maple Leafs	80	45	72	117	100	13	3	8	11	12
1978-79	Toronto Maple Leafs	70	36	51	87	69	6	5	4	9	17
1979-80	Toronto Maple Leafs	73	40	57	97	62	3	1	2	3	10
1980-81	Toronto Maple Leafs	80	43	53	96	77	3	0	0	0	4
1981-82	Toronto Maple Leafs	38	18	20	38	24	....	....	....	....	....
	Philadelphia Flyers	35	14	18	32	50	4	3	1	4	6
1982-83	Philadelphia Flyers	80	43	40	83	60	3	1	0	1	4
1983-84	Philadelphia Flyers	76	27	36	63	38	3	0	2	2	7
1984-85	Detroit Red Wings	61	11	16	27	37	2	0	2	2	0
	NHL Totals	**1096**	**484**	**637**	**1121**	**948**	**76**	**29**	**45**	**74**	**137**

NHL Second All-Star Team (1978)

Played in NHL All-Star Game (1975, 1978, 1980, 1983)

Traded to **Philadelphia** by **Toronto** for the rights to Rich Costello, Hartford's 2nd round choice (previously acquired, Toronto selected Peter Ihnacak) in 1982 Entry Draft and future considerations (Ken Strong, May, 1982), January 20, 1982. Traded to **Detroit** by **Philadelphia** for Murray Craven and Joe Paterson, October 10, 1984.

SIVEK, Michal

Center. Shoots left. 6'3", 209 lbs. Born, Nachod, Czech., January 21, 1981.
(Washington's 2nd choice, 29th overall, in 1999 Entry Draft).

Season	Club	GP	G	A	Pts	PIM	GP	G	A	Pts	PIM
2002-03	Pittsburgh Penguins	38	3	3	6	14	....	....	....	....	....
	NHL Totals	**38**	**3**	**3**	**6**	**14**	....	....	....	....	....

Traded to **Pittsburgh** by **Washington** with Kris Beech, Ross Lupaschuk and future considerations for Jaromir Jagr and Frantisek Kucera, July 11, 2001.

SJOBERG, Lars-Erik

Defense. Shoots left. 5'8", 179 lbs. Born, Falun, Sweden, April 5, 1944.

Season	Club	GP	G	A	Pts	PIM	GP	G	A	Pts	PIM
		REGULAR SEASON					PLAYOFFS				
1979-80	Winnipeg Jets	79	7	27	34	48	....	....	....	....	....
	NHL Totals	**79**	**7**	**27**	**34**	**48**	....	....	....	....	....

Rights retained by **Winnipeg** prior to Expansion Draft, June 9, 1979.

SJODIN, Tommy

Defense. Shoots right. 5'11", 190 lbs. Born, Timra, Sweden, August 13, 1965.
(Minnesota's 10th choice, 237th overall, in 1985 Entry Draft).

Season	Club	GP	G	A	Pts	PIM	GP	G	A	Pts	PIM
1992-93	Minnesota North Stars	77	7	29	36	30	....	....	....	....	....
1993-94	Dallas Stars	7	0	2	2	4	....	....	....	....	....
	Quebec Nordiques	22	1	9	10	18	....	....	....	....	....
	NHL Totals	**106**	**8**	**40**	**48**	**52**	....	....	....	....	....

Transferred to **Dallas** after **Minnesota** franchise relocated, June 9, 1993. Traded to **Quebec** by **Dallas** with Dallas' 3rd round choice (Chris Drury) in 1994 Entry Draft for the rights to Manny Fernandez, February 13, 1994.

SKAARE, Bjorn

Center. Shoots left. 6', 180 lbs. Born, Oslo, Norway, October 29, 1958.
(Detroit's 6th choice, 62nd overall, in 1978 Amateur Draft).

Season	Club	GP	G	A	Pts	PIM	GP	G	A	Pts	PIM
1978-79	Detroit Red Wings	1	0	0	0	0	....	....	....	....	....
	NHL Totals	**1**	**0**	**0**	**0**	**0**	....	....	....	....	....

SKALDE, Jarrod

Center. Shoots left. 6', 185 lbs. Born, Niagara Falls, Ont., February 26, 1971.
(New Jersey's 3rd choice, 26th overall, in 1989 Entry Draft).

Season	Club	GP	G	A	Pts	PIM	GP	G	A	Pts	PIM
1990-91	New Jersey Devils	1	0	1	1	0	....	....	....	....	....
1991-92	New Jersey Devils	15	2	4	6	4	....	....	....	....	....
1992-93	New Jersey Devils	11	0	2	2	4	....	....	....	....	....
1993-94	Mighty Ducks of Anaheim	20	5	4	9	10	....	....	....	....	....
1995-96	Calgary Flames	1	0	0	0	0	....	....	....	....	....
1997-98	San Jose Sharks	22	4	6	10	14	....	....	....	....	....
	Chicago Blackhawks	4	0	1	1	2	....	....	....	....	....
	Dallas Stars	1	0	0	0	0	....	....	....	....	....
	Chicago Blackhawks	3	0	0	0	2	....	....	....	....	....
1998-99	San Jose Sharks	17	1	1	2	4	....	....	....	....	....
2000-01	Atlanta Thrashers	19	1	2	3	20	....	....	....	....	....
2001-02	Philadelphia Flyers	1	0	0	0	2	....	....	....	....	....
	NHL Totals	**115**	**13**	**21**	**34**	**62**	....	....	....	....	....

Claimed by **Anaheim** from **New Jersey** in Expansion Draft, June 24, 1993. Traded to **Calgary** by **Anaheim** for Bobby Marshall, October 30, 1995. Signed as a free agent by **San Jose**, August 14, 1997. Claimed on waivers by **Chicago** from **San Jose**, January 8, 1998. Claimed on waivers by **San Jose** from **Chicago**, January 23, 1998. Claimed on waivers by **Dallas** from **San Jose**, January 27, 1998. Claimed on waivers by **Chicago** from **Dallas**, February 10, 1998. Claimed on waivers by **San Jose** from **Chicago**, March 6, 1998. Signed as a free agent by **Atlanta**, July 21, 2000. Traded to **Philadelphia** by **Atlanta** for Joe DiPenta, March 5, 2002. Signed as a free agent by **Dallas**, July 17, 2003.

SKARDA, Randy

Defense. Shoots right. 6'1", 205 lbs. Born, St. Paul, MN, May 5, 1968.
(St. Louis' 8th choice, 157th overall, in 1986 Entry Draft).

Season	Club	GP	G	A	Pts	PIM	GP	G	A	Pts	PIM
1989-90	St. Louis Blues	25	0	5	5	11	....	....	....	....	....
1991-92	St. Louis Blues	1	0	0	0	0	....	....	....	....	....
	NHL Totals	**26**	**0**	**5**	**5**	**11**	....	....	....	....	....

SKILTON, Raymie

Defense. Shoots right. 5'10", 190 lbs. Born, Cambridge, MA, September 26, 1889.

Season	Club	GP	G	A	Pts	PIM	GP	G	A	Pts	PIM
1917-18	Montreal Wanderers	1	0	0	0	0	....	....	....	....	....
	NHL Totals	**1**	**0**	**0**	**0**	**0**	....	....	....	....	....

Signed as a free agent by **Mtl. Wanderers**, December 21, 1917.

SKINNER, Alf

Right wing. Shoots right. 5'10", 180 lbs. Born, Toronto, Ont., January 26, 1896.

Season	Club	GP	G	A	Pts	PIM	GP	G	A	Pts	PIM
1917-18♦	Toronto Arenas	20	13	5	18	28	2	0	1	*1	9
	Toronto Arenas (Cup)	....	....	....	....	....	*5*	*8*	*2*	*10*	*0*
1918-19	Toronto Arenas	17	12	4	16	26	....	....	....	....	....
1924-25	Boston Bruins	10	0	0	0	15	....	....	....	....	....
	Montreal Maroons	17	1	1	2	16	....	....	....	....	....
1925-26	Pittsburgh Pirates	7	0	0	0	2	....	....	....	....	....
	NHL Totals	**71**	**26**	**10**	**36**	**87**	**2**	**0**	**1**	**1**	**9**

Signed as a free agent by **Toronto**, November 5, 1917. Traded to **Vancouver** (PCHA) by **Toronto** for cash, December 7, 1919. Traded to **Boston** by **Vancouver** (PCHA) for cash, November 2, 1924. Traded to **Mtl. Maroons** by **Boston** for Bernie Morris and Bobby Benson, January 3, 1925. Signed as a free agent by **Pittsburgh**, November 10, 1925.

SKINNER, Larry

Center. Shoots left. 5'11", 180 lbs. Born, Vancouver, B.C., April 21, 1956.
(Kansas City's 4th choice, 92nd overall, in 1976 Amateur Draft).

Season	Club	GP	G	A	Pts	PIM	GP	G	A	Pts	PIM
1976-77	Colorado Rockies	19	4	5	9	6	....	....	....	....	....
1977-78	Colorado Rockies	14	3	5	8	0	2	0	0	0	0
1978-79	Colorado Rockies	12	3	2	5	2	....	....	....	....	....
1979-80	Colorado Rockies	2	0	0	0	0	....	....	....	....	....
	NHL Totals	**47**	**10**	**12**	**22**	**8**	**2**	**0**	**0**	**0**	**0**

Transferred to **Colorado** after **Kansas City** franchise relocated, July 15, 1977. Selected by **Colorado** as a fill-in during Expansion Draft, June 13, 1979. Traded to **New Haven** (AHL) by **Colorado** with Dennis Owchar for Bobby Sheehan, May 12, 1979.

SKOPINTSEV, Andrei

Defense. Shoots right. 6', 185 lbs. Born, Elektrostal, USSR, September 28, 1971.
(Tampa Bay's 7th choice, 153rd overall, in 1997 Entry Draft).

Season	Club	GP	G	A	Pts	PIM	GP	G	A	Pts	PIM
1998-99	Tampa Bay Lightning	19	1	1	2	10	....	....	....	....	....
99-2000	Tampa Bay Lightning	4	0	0	0	6	....	....	....	....	....
2000-01	Atlanta Thrashers	17	1	3	4	16	....	....	....	....	....
	NHL Totals	**40**	**2**	**4**	**6**	**32**	....	....	....	....	....

Signed as a free agent by **Atlanta**, September 7, 2000.

SKOULA, Martin

Defense. Shoots left. 6'2", 195 lbs. Born, Litomerice, Czech., October 28, 1979.
(Colorado's 2nd choice, 17th overall, in 1998 Entry Draft).

Season	Club	GP	G	A	Pts	PIM	GP	G	A	Pts	PIM
99-2000	Colorado Avalanche	80	3	13	16	20	17	0	2	2	4
2000-01♦	Colorado Avalanche	82	8	17	25	38	23	1	4	5	8
2001-02	Colorado Avalanche	82	10	21	31	42	21	0	6	6	2
2002-03	Colorado Avalanche	81	4	21	25	68	7	0	1	1	4
	NHL Totals	**325**	**25**	**72**	**97**	**168**	**68**	**1**	**13**	**14**	**18**

SKOV, Glen

Center/Left wing. Shoots left. 6'2", 180 lbs. Born, Wheatley, Ont., January 26, 1931.

Season	Club	GP	G	A	Pts	PIM	GP	G	A	Pts	PIM
1949-50	Detroit Red Wings	2	0	0	0	0	....	....	....	....	....
1950-51	Detroit Red Wings	19	7	6	13	13	6	0	0	0	0
1951-52♦	Detroit Red Wings	70	12	14	26	48	8	1	4	5	16
1952-53	Detroit Red Wings	70	12	15	27	54	6	1	0	1	2
1953-54♦	Detroit Red Wings	70	17	10	27	95	12	1	2	3	16
1954-55♦	Detroit Red Wings	70	14	16	30	53	11	2	0	2	8
1955-56	Chicago Black Hawks	70	7	20	27	26	....	....	....	....	....
1956-57	Chicago Black Hawks	67	14	28	42	69	....	....	....	....	....
1957-58	Chicago Black Hawks	70	17	18	35	35	....	....	....	....	....
1958-59	Chicago Black Hawks	70	3	5	8	4	6	2	1	3	4
1959-60	Chicago Black Hawks	69	3	4	7	16	4	0	0	0	2
1960-61	Montreal Canadiens	3	0	0	0	0	....	....	....	....	....
	NHL Totals	**650**	**106**	**136**	**242**	**413**	**53**	**7**	**7**	**14**	**48**

Played in NHL All-Star Game (1954)

Traded to **Chicago** by **Detroit** with Tony Leswick, Johnny Wilson and Benny Woit for Dave Creighton, Gord Hollingworth, John McCormack and Jerry Toppazzini, May 27, 1955. Traded to **Montreal** by **Chicago** with Terry Gray, the rights to Danny Lewicki, Bob Bailey and Lorne Ferguson for Ab McDonald, Reggie Fleming, Bob Courcy and Cec Hoekstra, June 7, 1960.

SKRASTINS, Karlis

Defense. Shoots left. 6'1", 212 lbs. Born, Riga, USSR, July 9, 1974.
(Nashville's 8th choice, 230th overall, in 1998 Entry Draft).

Season	Club	GP	G	A	Pts	PIM	GP	G	A	Pts	PIM
1998-99	Nashville Predators	2	0	1	1	0	....	....	....	....	....
99-2000	Nashville Predators	59	5	6	11	20	....	....	....	....	....
2000-01	Nashville Predators	82	1	11	12	30	....	....	....	....	....
2001-02	Nashville Predators	82	4	13	17	36	....	....	....	....	....
2002-03	Nashville Predators	82	3	10	13	44	....	....	....	....	....
	NHL Totals	**307**	**13**	**41**	**54**	**130**	....	....	....	....	....

Traded to **Colorado** by **Nashville** for Colorado's 3rd round choice in 2004 Entry Draft, July 1, 2003.

SKRBEK, Pavel

Defense. Shoots left. 6'3", 217 lbs. Born, Kladno, Czech., August 9, 1978.
(Pittsburgh's 2nd choice, 28th overall, in 1996 Entry Draft).

Season	Club	GP	G	A	Pts	PIM	GP	G	A	Pts	PIM
1998-99	Pittsburgh Penguins	4	0	0	0	2	....	....	....	....	....
2000-01	Nashville Predators	5	0	0	0	4	....	....	....	....	....
2001-02	Nashville Predators	3	0	0	0	2	....	....	....	....	....
	NHL Totals	**12**	**0**	**0**	**0**	**8**	....	....	....	....	....

Traded to **Nashville** by **Pittsburgh** for Bob Boughner, March 13, 2000.

SKRIKO, Petri

Left wing. Shoots left. 5'10", 175 lbs. Born, Lappeenranta, Finland, March 12, 1962.
(Vancouver's 7th choice, 157th overall, in 1981 Entry Draft).

Season	Club	GP	G	A	Pts	PIM	GP	G	A	Pts	PIM
1984-85	Vancouver Canucks	72	21	14	35	10	....	....	....	....	....
1985-86	Vancouver Canucks	80	38	40	78	34	3	0	0	0	0
1986-87	Vancouver Canucks	76	33	41	74	44	....	....	....	....	....
1987-88	Vancouver Canucks	73	30	34	64	32	....	....	....	....	....
1988-89	Vancouver Canucks	74	30	36	66	57	7	1	5	6	0
1989-90	Vancouver Canucks	77	15	33	48	36	....	....	....	....	....
1990-91	Vancouver Canucks	20	4	4	8	8	....	....	....	....	....
	Boston Bruins	28	5	14	19	9	18	4	4	8	4
1991-92	Boston Bruins	9	1	0	1	6	....	....	....	....	....
	Winnipeg Jets	15	2	3	5	4	....	....	....	....	....
1992-93	San Jose Sharks	17	4	3	7	6	....	....	....	....	....
	NHL Totals	**541**	**183**	**222**	**405**	**246**	**28**	**5**	**9**	**14**	**4**

Traded to **Boston** by **Vancouver** for Boston's 2nd round choice (Michael Peca) in 1992 Entry Draft, January 16, 1991. Traded to **Winnipeg** by **Boston** for Brent Ashton, October 29, 1991. Signed as a free agent by **San Jose**, August 27, 1992.

SKRUDLAND, Brian

Center. Shoots left. 6', 195 lbs. Born, Peace River, Alta., July 31, 1963.

		REGULAR SEASON					PLAYOFFS				
Season	Club	GP	G	A	Pts	PIM	GP	G	A	Pts	PIM
1985-86 ♦	Montreal Canadiens	65	9	13	22	57	20	2	4	6	76
1986-87	Montreal Canadiens	79	11	17	28	107	14	1	5	6	29
1987-88	Montreal Canadiens	79	12	24	36	112	11	1	5	6	24
1988-89	Montreal Canadiens	71	12	29	41	84	21	3	7	10	40
1989-90	Montreal Canadiens	59	11	31	42	56	11	3	5	8	30
1990-91	Montreal Canadiens	57	15	19	34	85	13	3	10	13	42
1991-92	Montreal Canadiens	42	3	3	6	36	11	1	1	2	20
1992-93	Montreal Canadiens	23	5	3	8	55	....	....	....	....	....
	Calgary Flames	16	2	4	6	10	6	0	3	3	12
1993-94	Florida Panthers	79	15	25	40	136	....	....	....	....	....
1994-95	Florida Panthers	47	5	9	14	88	....	....	....	....	....
1995-96	Florida Panthers	79	7	20	27	129	21	1	3	4	18
1996-97	Florida Panthers	51	5	13	18	48	....	....	....	....	....
1997-98	New York Rangers	59	5	6	11	39	....	....	....	....	....
	Dallas Stars	13	2	0	2	10	17	0	1	1	16
1998-99 ♦	Dallas Stars	40	4	1	5	33	19	0	2	2	16
99-2000	Dallas Stars	22	1	2	3	22	....	....	....	....	....
	NHL Totals	**881**	**124**	**219**	**343**	**1107**	**164**	**15**	**46**	**61**	**323**

Signed as a free agent by **Montreal**, September 13, 1983. Traded to **Calgary** by **Montreal** for Gary Leeman, January 28, 1993. Claimed by **Florida** from **Calgary** in Expansion Draft, June 24, 1993. Signed as a free agent by **NY Rangers**, August 21, 1997. Traded to **Dallas** by **NY Rangers** with Mike Keane and NY Rangers' 6th round choice (Pavel Patera) in 1998 Entry Draft for Todd Harvey, Bob Errey and Dallas' 4th round choice (Boyd Kane) in 1998 Entry Draft, March 24, 1998. • Missed majority of 1999-2000 season recovering from rib injury originally suffered in game vs. Anaheim, October 8, 1999.

SLANEY, John

Defense. Shoots left. 6', 189 lbs. Born, St. John's, Nfld., February 2, 1972.
(Washington's 1st choice, 9th overall, in 1990 Entry Draft).

		REGULAR SEASON					PLAYOFFS				
Season	Club	GP	G	A	Pts	PIM	GP	G	A	Pts	PIM
1993-94	Washington Capitals	47	7	9	16	27	11	1	1	2	2
1994-95	Washington Capitals	16	0	3	3	6	....	....	....	....	....
1995-96	Colorado Avalanche	7	0	3	3	4	....	....	....	....	....
	Los Angeles Kings	31	6	11	17	10	....	....	....	....	....
1996-97	Los Angeles Kings	32	3	11	14	4	....	....	....	....	....
1997-98	Phoenix Coyotes	55	3	14	17	24	....	....	....	....	....
1998-99	Nashville Predators	46	2	12	14	14	....	....	....	....	....
99-2000	Pittsburgh Penguins	29	1	4	5	10	2	1	0	1	2
2001-02	Philadelphia Flyers	1	0	0	0	0	1	0	0	0	0
	NHL Totals	**264**	**22**	**67**	**89**	**99**	**14**	**2**	**1**	**3**	**4**

Traded to **Colorado** by **Washington** for Philadelphia's 3rd round choice (previously acquired, Washington selected Shawn McNeil) in 1996 Entry Draft, July 12, 1995. Traded to **Los Angeles** by **Colorado** for Winnipeg's 6th round choice (previously acquired, Colorado selected Brian Willsie) in 1996 Entry Draft, December 28, 1995. Signed as a free agent by **Phoenix**, August 19, 1997. Claimed by **Nashville** from **Phoenix** in Expansion Draft, June 26, 1998. Signed as a free agent by **Pittsburgh**, September 30, 1999. Traded to **Philadelphia** by **Pittsburgh** for Kevin Stevens, January 14, 2001.

SLEAVER, John

Center. Shoots right. 6'1", 180 lbs. Born, Copper Cliff, Ont., August 18, 1934.

		REGULAR SEASON					PLAYOFFS				
Season	Club	GP	G	A	Pts	PIM	GP	G	A	Pts	PIM
1953-54	Chicago Black Hawks	1	0	0	0	2	....	....	....	....	....
1956-57	Chicago Black Hawks	12	1	0	1	4	....	....	....	....	....
	NHL Totals	**13**	**1**	**0**	**1**	**6**	....	....	....	....	....

Signed as a free agent by **Detroit** (Sudbury-EPHL), October, 1959. Signed as a free agent by **Montreal** (North Bay-EPHL), October, 1961. NHL rights transferred to **Toronto** after NHL club purchased **Denver** (WHL) franchise and relocated team to Victoria, June, 1964. Claimed by **Providence** (AHL) from **Toronto** in Reverse Draft, June 15, 1966.

SLEGR, Jiri

Defense. Shoots left. 6', 216 lbs. Born, Jihlava, Czech., May 30, 1971.
(Vancouver's 3rd choice, 23rd overall, in 1990 Entry Draft).

		REGULAR SEASON					PLAYOFFS				
Season	Club	GP	G	A	Pts	PIM	GP	G	A	Pts	PIM
1992-93	Vancouver Canucks	41	4	22	26	109	5	0	3	3	4
1993-94	Vancouver Canucks	78	5	33	38	86	....	....	....	....	....
1994-95	Vancouver Canucks	19	1	5	6	32	....	....	....	....	....
	Edmonton Oilers	12	1	5	6	14	....	....	....	....	....
1995-96	Edmonton Oilers	57	4	13	17	74	....	....	....	....	....
1997-98	Pittsburgh Penguins	73	5	12	17	109	6	0	4	4	2
1998-99	Pittsburgh Penguins	63	3	20	23	86	13	1	3	4	12
99-2000	Pittsburgh Penguins	74	11	20	31	82	10	2	3	5	19
2000-01	Pittsburgh Penguins	42	5	10	15	60	....	....	....	....	....
	Atlanta Thrashers	33	3	16	19	36	....	....	....	....	....
2001-02	Atlanta Thrashers	38	3	5	8	51	....	....	....	....	....
	♦ Detroit Red Wings	8	0	1	1	8	1	0	0	0	2
	NHL Totals	**538**	**45**	**162**	**207**	**747**	**35**	**3**	**13**	**16**	**39**

• Son of Jiri Bubla

Traded to **Edmonton** by **Vancouver** for Roman Oksiuta, April 7, 1995. Traded to **Pittsburgh** by **Edmonton** for Pittsburgh's 3rd round choice (later traded to New Jersey – New Jersey selected Brian Gionta) in 1998 Entry Draft, August 12, 1997. Traded to **Atlanta** by **Pittsburgh** for San Jose's 3rd round choice (previously acquired, later traded to Columbus – Columbus selected Aaron Johnson) in 2001 Entry Draft, January 14, 2001. Traded to **Detroit** by **Atlanta** for Yuri Butsayev and Detroit's 3rd round choice (later traded to Columbus – Columbus selected Jeff Genovy) in 2002 Entry Draft, March 19, 2002.

SLEIGHER, Louis

Right wing. Shoots right. 5'11", 200 lbs. Born, Nouvelle, Que., October 23, 1958.
(Montreal's 24th choice, 233rd overall, in 1978 Amateur Draft).

		REGULAR SEASON					PLAYOFFS				
Season	Club	GP	G	A	Pts	PIM	GP	G	A	Pts	PIM
1979-80	Quebec Nordiques	2	0	1	1	0	....	....	....	....	....
1981-82	Quebec Nordiques	8	0	0	0	0	....	....	....	....	....
1982-83	Quebec Nordiques	51	14	10	24	49	4	0	0	0	4
1983-84	Quebec Nordiques	44	15	19	34	32	7	1	1	2	42
1984-85	Quebec Nordiques	6	1	2	3	0	....	....	....	....	....
	Boston Bruins	70	12	19	31	45	5	0	0	0	4
1985-86	Boston Bruins	13	4	2	6	20	1	0	0	0	14
	NHL Totals	**194**	**46**	**53**	**99**	**146**	**17**	**1**	**1**	**2**	**64**

Signed as a free agent by **Quebec**, September 11, 1980. Traded to **Boston** by **Quebec** for Luc Dufour and Boston's 4th round choice (Peter Massey) in 1985 Entry Draft, October 25, 1984. • Suffered eventual career-ending groin injury in game vs. Vancouver, October 16, 1985.

SLOAN, Blake

Right wing. Shoots right. 5'10", 196 lbs. Born, Park Ridge, IL, July 27, 1975.

		REGULAR SEASON					PLAYOFFS				
Season	Club	GP	G	A	Pts	PIM	GP	G	A	Pts	PIM
1998-99 ♦	Dallas Stars	14	0	0	0	10	19	0	2	2	8
99-2000	Dallas Stars	67	4	13	17	50	16	0	0	0	12
2000-01	Dallas Stars	33	2	2	4	4	....	....	....	....	....
	Columbus Blue Jackets	14	1	0	1	13	....	....	....	....	....
2001-02	Columbus Blue Jackets	60	2	7	9	46	....	....	....	....	....
	Calgary Flames	7	0	2	2	4	....	....	....	....	....
2002-03	Calgary Flames	67	2	8	10	28	....	....	....	....	....
	NHL Totals	**262**	**11**	**32**	**43**	**155**	**35**	**0**	**2**	**2**	**20**

Signed as a free agent by **Dallas**, March 10, 1998. Claimed on waivers by **Columbus** from **Dallas**, March 13, 2001. Traded to **Calgary** by **Columbus** for Jamie Allison, March 19, 2002.

SLOAN, Tod

Center/Right wing. Shoots right. 5'10", 152 lbs. Born, Pontiac, Que., November 30, 1927.

		REGULAR SEASON					PLAYOFFS				
Season	Club	GP	G	A	Pts	PIM	GP	G	A	Pts	PIM
1947-48	Toronto Maple Leafs	1	0	0	0	0	....	....	....	....	....
1948-49	Toronto Maple Leafs	29	3	4	7	0	....	....	....	....	....
1950-51 ♦	Toronto Maple Leafs	70	31	25	56	105	11	4	5	9	18
1951-52	Toronto Maple Leafs	68	25	23	48	89	4	0	0	0	10
1952-53	Toronto Maple Leafs	70	15	10	25	76	....	....	....	....	....
1953-54	Toronto Maple Leafs	67	11	32	43	100	5	1	1	2	4
1954-55	Toronto Maple Leafs	63	13	15	28	89	4	0	0	0	2
1955-56	Toronto Maple Leafs	70	37	29	66	100	2	0	0	0	5
1956-57	Toronto Maple Leafs	52	14	21	35	33	....	....	....	....	....
1957-58	Toronto Maple Leafs	59	13	25	38	58	....	....	....	....	....
1958-59	Chicago Black Hawks	59	27	35	62	79	6	3	5	8	0
1959-60	Chicago Black Hawks	70	20	20	40	54	3	0	0	0	0
1960-61 ♦	Chicago Black Hawks	67	11	23	34	48	12	1	1	2	8
	NHL Totals	**745**	**220**	**262**	**482**	**831**	**47**	**9**	**12**	**21**	**47**

NHL Second All-Star Team (1956)

Played in NHL All-Star Game (1951, 1952, 1956)

Signed as a free agent by **Toronto**, April 30, 1946. Loaned to **Cleveland** (AHL) by **Toronto** for the 1949-50 season with the trade of Ray Ceresino and Harry Taylor for Bob Solinger, September 6, 1949. Traded to **Chicago** by **Toronto** for cash, June 6, 1958.

SLOBODIAN, Peter

Defense. Shoots left. 6'1", 185 lbs. Born, Dauphin, Man., April 24, 1918.

		REGULAR SEASON					PLAYOFFS				
Season	Club	GP	G	A	Pts	PIM	GP	G	A	Pts	PIM
1940-41	New York Americans	41	3	2	5	54	....	....	....	....	....
	NHL Totals	**41**	**3**	**2**	**5**	**54**	....	....	....	....	....

Signed as a free agent by **NY Americans**, October 11, 1940.

SLOWINSKI, Ed

Right wing. Shoots right. 5'11", 195 lbs. Born, Winnipeg, Man., November 18, 1922.

		REGULAR SEASON					PLAYOFFS				
Season	Club	GP	G	A	Pts	PIM	GP	G	A	Pts	PIM
1947-48	New York Rangers	38	6	5	11	2	4	0	0	0	0
1948-49	New York Rangers	20	1	1	2	2	....	....	....	....	....
1949-50	New York Rangers	63	14	23	37	12	12	2	*6	8	6
1950-51	New York Rangers	69	14	18	32	15	....	....	....	....	....
1951-52	New York Rangers	64	21	22	43	18	....	....	....	....	....
1952-53	New York Rangers	37	2	5	7	14	....	....	....	....	....
	NHL Totals	**291**	**58**	**74**	**132**	**63**	**16**	**2**	**6**	**8**	**6**

Signed as a free agent by **NY Rangers**, October 7, 1947. Traded to **Detroit** by **NY Rangers** with future considerations for Roy Conacher, October 22, 1947. Transaction was voided when Conacher refused to report. Traded to **Montreal** by **NY Rangers** with Pete Babando for Ivan Irwin, August 8, 1953. Traded to **Buffalo** (AHL) by **Montreal** with Gaye Stewart and Pete Babando for Jack Leclair and cash, August 17, 1954.

SLY, Darryl

Defense. Shoots right. 5'11", 185 lbs. Born, Collingwood, Ont., April 3, 1939.

		REGULAR SEASON					PLAYOFFS				
Season	Club	GP	G	A	Pts	PIM	GP	G	A	Pts	PIM
1965-66	Toronto Maple Leafs	2	0	0	0	0	....	....	....	....	....
1967-68	Toronto Maple Leafs	17	0	0	0	4	....	....	....	....	....
1969-70	Minnesota North Stars	29	1	0	1	6	....	....	....	....	....
1970-71	Vancouver Canucks	31	0	2	2	10	....	....	....	....	....
	NHL Totals	**79**	**1**	**2**	**3**	**20**	....	....	....	....	....

Signed as a free agent by **Toronto**, June 5, 1961. Rights transferred to **Vancouver** (WHL) after WHL club purchased **Rochester** (AHL) franchise, August 13, 1968. Claimed by **Minnesota** from **Vancouver** (WHL) in Inter-League Draft, June 10, 1969. Claimed by **Vancouver** from **Minnesota** in Expansion Draft, June 10, 1970.

SMAIL, Doug

Left wing. Shoots left. 5'9", 175 lbs. Born, Moose Jaw, Sask., September 2, 1957.

Season	Club	REGULAR SEASON GP	G	A	Pts	PIM	PLAYOFFS GP	G	A	Pts	PIM
1980-81	Winnipeg Jets	30	10	8	18	45	....	....	....	....	....
1981-82	Winnipeg Jets	72	17	18	35	55	4	0	0	0	0
1982-83	Winnipeg Jets	80	15	29	44	32	3	0	0	0	6
1983-84	Winnipeg Jets	66	20	17	37	62	3	0	1	1	7
1984-85	Winnipeg Jets	80	31	35	66	45	8	2	1	3	4
1985-86	Winnipeg Jets	73	16	26	42	32	3	1	0	1	0
1986-87	Winnipeg Jets	78	25	18	43	36	10	4	0	4	10
1987-88	Winnipeg Jets	71	15	16	31	34	5	1	0	1	22
1988-89	Winnipeg Jets	47	14	15	29	52	....	....	....	....	....
1989-90	Winnipeg Jets	79	25	24	49	63	5	1	0	1	0
1990-91	Winnipeg Jets	15	1	2	3	10	....	....	....	....	....
	Minnesota North Stars	57	7	13	20	38	1	0	0	0	0
1991-92	Quebec Nordiques	46	10	18	28	47	....	....	....	....	....
1992-93	Ottawa Senators	51	4	10	14	51	....	....	....	....	....
	NHL Totals	**845**	**210**	**249**	**459**	**602**	**42**	**9**	**2**	**11**	**49**

Played in NHL All-Star Game (1990)

Signed as a free agent by **Winnipeg**, May 22, 1980. • Missed majority of 1980-81 season recovering from jaw injury suffered in game vs. Hartford, January 10, 1981. Traded to **Minnesota** by **Winnipeg** for Don Barber, November 7, 1990. Signed as a free agent by **Quebec**, August 30, 1991. Signed as a free agent by **Ottawa**, August 30, 1992.

SMART, Alex

Left wing. Shoots left. 5'10", 150 lbs. Born, Brandon, Man., May 29, 1918.

Season	Club	GP	G	A	Pts	PIM	GP	G	A	Pts	PIM
1942-43	Montreal Canadiens	8	5	2	7	0	....	....	....	....	....
	NHL Totals	**8**	**5**	**2**	**7**	**0**	....	....	....	....	....

Signed as a free agent by **Montreal**, February 1, 1943.

SMEDSMO, Dale

Left wing. Shoots left. 6'1", 195 lbs. Born, Roseau, MN, April 23, 1951.
(Toronto's 7th choice, 93rd overall, in 1971 Amateur Draft).

Season	Club	GP	G	A	Pts	PIM	GP	G	A	Pts	PIM
1972-73	Toronto Maple Leafs	4	0	0	0	0	....	....	....	....	....
	NHL Totals	**4**	**0**	**0**	**0**	**0**	....	....	....	....	....

SMEHLIK, Richard

Defense. Shoots left. 6'4", 222 lbs. Born, Ostrava, Czech., January 23, 1970.
(Buffalo's 3rd choice, 97th overall, in 1990 Entry Draft).

Season	Club	GP	G	A	Pts	PIM	GP	G	A	Pts	PIM
1992-93	Buffalo Sabres	80	4	27	31	59	8	0	4	4	2
1993-94	Buffalo Sabres	84	14	27	41	69	7	0	2	2	10
1994-95	Buffalo Sabres	39	4	7	11	46	5	0	0	0	2
1996-97	Buffalo Sabres	62	11	19	30	43	12	0	2	2	4
1997-98	Buffalo Sabres	72	3	17	20	62	15	0	2	2	6
1998-99	Buffalo Sabres	72	3	11	14	44	21	0	3	3	10
99-2000	Buffalo Sabres	64	2	9	11	50	5	1	0	1	0
2000-01	Buffalo Sabres	56	3	12	15	4	10	0	1	1	4
2001-02	Buffalo Sabres	60	3	6	9	22	....	....	....	....	....
2002-03	Atlanta Thrashers	43	2	9	11	16	....	....	....	....	....
	♦ New Jersey Devils	12	0	2	2	0	5	0	0	0	2
	NHL Totals	**644**	**49**	**146**	**195**	**415**	**88**	**1**	**14**	**15**	**40**

• Missed entire 1995-96 season recovering from knee surgery, August 11, 1995. Signed as a free agent by **Atlanta**, July 11, 2002. Traded to **New Jersey** by **Atlanta** with New Jersey's 6th and 8th round choices (previously acquired) in 2004 Entry Draft for New Jersey's 4th round choice (Michael Vannelli) in 2003 Entry Draft, March 10, 2003.

SMILLIE, Don

Left wing. Shoots left. 6', 185 lbs. Born, Toronto, Ont., September 13, 1910.

Season	Club	GP	G	A	Pts	PIM	GP	G	A	Pts	PIM
1933-34	Boston Bruins	12	2	2	4	4	....	....	....	....	....
	NHL Totals	**12**	**2**	**2**	**4**	**4**	....	....	....	....	....

Loaned to **Syracuse** (IHL) by **Boston** with Walter Harnott for cash, November 27, 1934. Traded to **Windsor** (IHL) by **Boston** for cash, December 27, 1934.

SMIRNOV, Alexei

Left wing. Shoots left. 6'3", 211 lbs. Born, Tver, USSR, January 28, 1982.
(Anaheim's 1st choice, 12th overall, in 2000 Entry Draft).

Season	Club	GP	G	A	Pts	PIM	GP	G	A	Pts	PIM
2002-03	Mighty Ducks of Anaheim	44	3	2	5	18	4	0	0	0	2
	NHL Totals	**44**	**3**	**2**	**5**	**18**	**4**	**0**	**0**	**0**	**2**

SMITH, Alex

Defense. Shoots left. 5'11", 176 lbs. Born, Liverpool, England, April 2, 1902.

Season	Club	GP	G	A	Pts	PIM	GP	G	A	Pts	PIM
1924-25	Ottawa Senators	7	0	0	0	4	....	....	....	....	....
1925-26	Ottawa Senators	36	0	0	0	36	2	0	0	0	2
1926-27♦	Ottawa Senators	42	4	1	5	58	6	0	0	0	8
1927-28	Ottawa Senators	44	9	4	13	90	2	0	0	0	4
1928-29	Ottawa Senators	44	1	7	8	96	....	....	....	....	....
1929-30	Ottawa Senators	43	2	6	8	91	2	0	0	0	4
1930-31	Ottawa Senators	37	5	6	11	73	....	....	....	....	....
1931-32	Detroit Falcons	48	6	8	14	47	2	0	0	0	4
1932-33	Ottawa Senators	34	2	0	2	42	....	....	....	....	....
	Boston Bruins	15	5	4	9	30	5	0	2	2	6
1933-34	Boston Bruins	45	4	6	10	32	....	....	....	....	....
1934-35	New York Americans	48	3	8	11	46	....	....	....	....	....
	NHL Totals	**443**	**41**	**50**	**91**	**645**	**19**	**0**	**2**	**2**	**28**

Signed as a free agent by **Ottawa**, February 10, 1925. Claimed by **Detroit** from **Ottawa** for 1931-32 season in Dispersal Draft, September 26, 1931. Traded to **Boston** by **Ottawa** for future considerations (Earl Roche), January 25, 1933. Traded to **NY Americans** by **Boston** for cash, October 18, 1934.

SMITH, Art

Defense. Shoots left. 5'10", 200 lbs. Born, Toronto, Ont., November 29, 1906.

Season	Club	GP	G	A	Pts	PIM	GP	G	A	Pts	PIM
1927-28	Toronto Maple Leafs	15	5	3	8	22	....	....	....	....	....
1928-29	Toronto Maple Leafs	43	5	0	5	91	4	1	1	2	8
1929-30	Toronto Maple Leafs	43	3	3	6	75	....	....	....	....	....
1930-31	Ottawa Senators	43	2	4	6	61	....	....	....	....	....
	NHL Totals	**144**	**15**	**10**	**25**	**249**	**4**	**1**	**1**	**2**	**8**

Signed as a free agent by **Toronto**, October 27, 1927. Traded to **Ottawa** by **Toronto** with Eric Pettinger and $35,000 for King Clancy, October 11, 1930.

SMITH, Barry

Center. Shoots left. 5'11", 178 lbs. Born, Surrey, B.C., April 25, 1955.
(Boston's 2nd choice, 32nd overall, in 1975 Amateur Draft).

Season	Club	GP	G	A	Pts	PIM	GP	G	A	Pts	PIM
1975-76	Boston Bruins	19	1	0	1	2	....	....	....	....	....
1979-80	Colorado Rockies	33	2	3	5	4	....	....	....	....	....
1980-81	Colorado Rockies	62	4	4	8	4	....	....	....	....	....
	NHL Totals	**114**	**7**	**7**	**14**	**10**	....	....	....	....	....

Signed as a free agent by **Colorado**, September 14, 1979.

SMITH, Bobby

Center. Shoots left. 6'4", 210 lbs. Born, North Sydney, N.S., February 12, 1958.
(Minnesota's 1st choice, 1st overall, in 1978 Amateur Draft).

Season	Club	GP	G	A	Pts	PIM	GP	G	A	Pts	PIM
1978-79	Minnesota North Stars	80	30	44	74	39	....	....	....	....	....
1979-80	Minnesota North Stars	61	27	56	83	24	15	1	13	14	9
1980-81	Minnesota North Stars	78	29	64	93	73	19	8	17	25	13
1981-82	Minnesota North Stars	80	43	71	114	82	4	2	4	6	5
1982-83	Minnesota North Stars	77	24	53	77	81	9	6	4	10	17
1983-84	Minnesota North Stars	10	3	6	9	9	....	....	....	....	....
	Montreal Canadiens	70	26	37	63	62	15	2	7	9	8
1984-85	Montreal Canadiens	65	16	40	56	59	12	5	6	11	30
1985-86♦	Montreal Canadiens	79	31	55	86	55	20	7	8	15	22
1986-87	Montreal Canadiens	80	28	47	75	72	17	9	9	18	19
1987-88	Montreal Canadiens	78	27	66	93	78	11	3	4	7	8
1988-89	Montreal Canadiens	80	32	51	83	69	21	11	8	19	46
1989-90	Montreal Canadiens	53	12	14	26	35	11	1	4	5	6
1990-91	Minnesota North Stars	73	15	31	46	60	23	8	8	16	56
1991-92	Minnesota North Stars	68	9	37	46	109	7	1	4	5	6
1992-93	Minnesota North Stars	45	5	7	12	10	....	....	....	....	....
	NHL Totals	**1077**	**357**	**679**	**1036**	**917**	**184**	**64**	**96**	**160**	**245**

Calder Memorial Trophy (1979)

Played in NHL All-Star Game (1981, 1982, 1989, 1991)

Traded to **Montreal** by **Minnesota** for Keith Acton, Mark Napier and Toronto's 3rd round choice (previously acquired, Minnesota selected Ken Hodge Jr.) in 1984 Entry Draft, October 28, 1983. Traded to **Minnesota** by **Montreal** for Minnesota's 4th round choice (Louis Bernard) in 1992 Entry Draft, August 7, 1990.

SMITH, Brad

Right wing. Shoots right. 6'1", 195 lbs. Born, Windsor, Ont., April 13, 1958.
(Vancouver's 5th choice, 57th overall, in 1978 Amateur Draft).

Season	Club	GP	G	A	Pts	PIM	GP	G	A	Pts	PIM
1978-79	Vancouver Canucks	2	0	0	0	2	....	....	....	....	....
1979-80	Vancouver Canucks	19	1	3	4	50	....	....	....	....	....
	Atlanta Flames	4	0	0	0	4	....	....	....	....	....
1980-81	Calgary Flames	45	7	4	11	65	....	....	....	....	....
	Detroit Red Wings	20	5	2	7	93	....	....	....	....	....
1981-82	Detroit Red Wings	33	2	0	2	80	....	....	....	....	....
1982-83	Detroit Red Wings	1	0	0	0	0	....	....	....	....	....
1983-84	Detroit Red Wings	8	2	1	3	36	....	....	....	....	....
1984-85	Detroit Red Wings	1	1	0	1	5	3	0	1	1	5
1985-86	Toronto Maple Leafs	42	5	17	22	84	6	2	1	3	20
1986-87	Toronto Maple Leafs	47	5	7	12	172	11	1	1	2	24
	NHL Totals	**222**	**28**	**34**	**62**	**591**	**20**	**3**	**3**	**6**	**49**

Traded to **Atlanta** by **Vancouver** with Don Lever for Ivan Boldirev and Darcy Rota, February 8, 1980. Transferred to **Calgary** after **Atlanta** franchise relocated, June 24, 1980. Traded to **Detroit** by **Calgary** for future considerations (Rick Vasko, May 28, 1981), February 24, 1981. Signed as a free agent by **Toronto**, July 2, 1985.

SMITH, Brandon

Defense. Shoots left. 6'1", 209 lbs. Born, Hazelton, B.C., February 25, 1973.

Season	Club	GP	G	A	Pts	PIM	GP	G	A	Pts	PIM
1998-99	Boston Bruins	5	0	0	0	0	....	....	....	....	....
99-2000	Boston Bruins	22	2	4	6	10	....	....	....	....	....
2000-01	Boston Bruins	3	1	0	1	0	....	....	....	....	....
2002-03	New York Islanders	3	0	0	0	0	....	....	....	....	....
	NHL Totals	**33**	**3**	**4**	**7**	**10**	....	....	....	....	....

Signed as a free agent by **Detroit**, July 22, 1997. Signed as a free agent by **Boston**, August 5, 1998. Signed as a free agent by **San Jose**, July 23, 2001. Signed as a free agent by **NY Islanders**, August 3, 2002.

SMITH, Brian

Left wing. Shoots left. 6', 180 lbs. Born, Creighton Mines, Ont., December 6, 1937.

Season	Club	GP	G	A	Pts	PIM	GP	G	A	Pts	PIM
		REGULAR SEASON					PLAYOFFS				
1957-58	Detroit Red Wings	4	0	1	1	0	....	....	....	....	....
1959-60	Detroit Red Wings	31	2	5	7	2	5	0	0	0	0
1960-61	Detroit Red Wings	26	0	2	2	10	....	....	....	....	....
	NHL Totals	**61**	**2**	**8**	**10**	**12**	**5**	**0**	**0**	**0**	**0**

• Son of Stu

Traded to **Chicago** by **Detroit** with Gerry Melnyk for Ed Litzenberger, June 12, 1961.

SMITH, Brian

Left wing. Shoots right. 5'11", 170 lbs. Born, Ottawa, Ont., September 6, 1940.

Season	Club	GP	G	A	Pts	PIM	GP	G	A	Pts	PIM
1967-68	Los Angeles Kings	58	10	9	19	33	7	0	0	0	0
1968-69	Minnesota North Stars	9	0	1	1	0	....	....	....	....	....
	NHL Totals	**67**	**10**	**10**	**20**	**33**	**7**	**0**	**0**	**0**	**0**

• Son of Des • Brother of Gary

Traded to **Springfield** (AHL) by **Montreal** with Wayne Boddy, Fred Hilts, Lorne O'Donnell and John Rodger for Terry Gray, Bruce Cline, Wayne Larkin, John Chasczewski, Ted Harris and the loan of Gary Bergman, June, 1963. NHL rights transferred to **Los Angeles** after NHL club purchased **Springfield** (AHL) franchise, May, 1967. Traded to **Montreal** by **Los Angeles** with Yves Locas for Larry Cahan, July 1, 1968. Traded to **Minnesota** by **Montreal** for cash, November 15, 1968. Traded to **Phoenix** (WHL) by **Minnesota** with Milan Marcetta for Tom Polanic, February 11, 1969.

SMITH, Carl

Right wing. Shoots left. 5'5", 150 lbs. Born, Cache Bay, Ont., September 18, 1917.

Season	Club	GP	G	A	Pts	PIM	GP	G	A	Pts	PIM
1943-44	Detroit Red Wings	7	1	1	2	2	....	....	....	....	....
	NHL Totals	**7**	**1**	**1**	**2**	**2**	....	....	....	....	....

• Brother of Nakina

Signed as a free agent by **Detroit**, September 28, 1939. Loaned to **New Haven** (AHL) by **Detroit** for cash, November, 1942. Loaned transferred to **Buffalo** (AHL) by **Detroit** for cash, January 21, 1943.

SMITH, Clint

HHOF

Center. Shoots left. 5'8", 165 lbs. Born, Assiniboia, Sask., December 12, 1913.

Season	Club	GP	G	A	Pts	PIM	GP	G	A	Pts	PIM
1936-37	New York Rangers	2	1	0	1	0	....	....	....	....	....
1937-38	New York Rangers	48	14	23	37	0	3	2	0	2	0
1938-39	New York Rangers	48	21	20	41	2	7	1	2	3	0
1939-40 ♦	New York Rangers	41	8	16	24	2	11	1	3	4	2
1940-41	New York Rangers	48	14	11	25	0	3	0	0	0	0
1941-42	New York Rangers	47	10	24	34	4	5	0	0	0	0
1942-43	New York Rangers	47	12	21	33	4	....	....	....	....	....
1943-44	Chicago Black Hawks	50	23	*49	72	4	9	4	8	12	0
1944-45	Chicago Black Hawks	50	23	31	54	0	....	....	....	....	....
1945-46	Chicago Black Hawks	50	26	24	50	2	4	2	1	3	0
1946-47	Chicago Black Hawks	52	9	17	26	6	....	....	....	....	....
	NHL Totals	**483**	**161**	**236**	**397**	**24**	**42**	**10**	**14**	**24**	**2**

Lady Byng Trophy (1939, 1944)

Signed as a free agent by **NY Rangers**, October 13, 1932. Signed as a free agent by **Chicago**, September, 1943.

SMITH, D.J.

Defense. Shoots left. 6'2", 205 lbs. Born, Windsor, Ont., May 13, 1977.
(NY Islanders' 3rd choice, 41st overall, in 1995 Entry Draft).

Season	Club	GP	G	A	Pts	PIM	GP	G	A	Pts	PIM
1996-97	Toronto Maple Leafs	8	0	1	1	7	....	....	....	....	....
99-2000	Toronto Maple Leafs	3	0	0	0	5	....	....	....	....	....
2002-03	Colorado Avalanche	34	1	0	1	55	....	....	....	....	....
	NHL Totals	**45**	**1**	**1**	**2**	**67**	....	....	....	....	....

Traded to **Toronto** by **NY Islanders** with Wendel Clark and Mathieu Schneider for Darby Hendrickson, Sean Haggerty, Kenny Jonsson and Toronto's 1st round choice (Roberto Luongo) in 1997 Entry Draft, March 13, 1996. Traded to **Nashville** by **Toronto** with Marty Wilford for Marc Moro, March 1, 2002. Traded to **Colorado** by **Nashville** for Tampa Bay's 9th round choice (previously acquired, Nashville selected Matt Davis) in 2002 Entry Draft, March 1, 2002.

SMITH, Dallas

Defense. Shoots left. 5'11", 180 lbs. Born, Hamiota, Man., October 10, 1941.

Season	Club	GP	G	A	Pts	PIM	GP	G	A	Pts	PIM
1959-60	Boston Bruins	5	1	1	2	0	....	....	....	....	....
1960-61	Boston Bruins	70	1	9	10	79	....	....	....	....	....
1961-62	Boston Bruins	7	0	0	0	10	....	....	....	....	....
1965-66	Boston Bruins	2	0	0	0	2	....	....	....	....	....
1966-67	Boston Bruins	33	0	1	1	24	....	....	....	....	....
1967-68	Boston Bruins	74	4	23	27	65	4	0	2	2	0
1968-69	Boston Bruins	75	4	24	28	74	10	0	3	3	16
1969-70 ♦	Boston Bruins	75	7	17	24	119	14	0	3	3	19
1970-71	Boston Bruins	73	7	38	45	68	7	0	3	3	26
1971-72 ♦	Boston Bruins	78	8	22	30	132	15	0	4	4	22
1972-73	Boston Bruins	78	4	27	31	72	5	0	2	2	2
1973-74	Boston Bruins	77	6	21	27	64	16	1	7	8	20
1974-75	Boston Bruins	79	3	20	23	84	3	0	2	2	4
1975-76	Boston Bruins	77	7	25	32	103	11	2	2	4	19
1976-77	Boston Bruins	58	2	20	22	40	....	....	....	....	....
1977-78	New York Rangers	29	1	4	5	23	1	0	1	1	0
	NHL Totals	**890**	**55**	**252**	**307**	**959**	**86**	**3**	**29**	**32**	**128**

NHL Plus/Minus Leader (1968)

Played in NHL All-Star Game (1971, 1972, 1973, 1974)

Loaned to **Montreal** (Hull-Ottawa-EPHL) by **Boston** with the loan of Bob Armstrong and cash for Wayne Connelly, October 26, 1961. Loaned to **San Francisco** (WHL) by **Boston** for the 1964-65 season to complete transaction that sent Cliff Pennington to Boston (December 17, 1963), July 8, 1964. Signed as a free agent by **NY Rangers**, December 19, 1977.

SMITH, Dan

Defense. Shoots left. 6'2", 200 lbs. Born, Fernie, B.C., October 19, 1976.
(Colorado's 7th choice, 181st overall, in 1995 Entry Draft).

Season	Club	GP	G	A	Pts	PIM	GP	G	A	Pts	PIM
1998-99	Colorado Avalanche	12	0	0	0	9	....	....	....	....	....
99-2000	Colorado Avalanche	3	0	0	0	0	....	....	....	....	....
	NHL Totals	**15**	**0**	**0**	**0**	**9**	....	....	....	....	....

SMITH, Dennis

Defense. Shoots left. 5'11", 190 lbs. Born, Detroit, MI, July 27, 1964.

Season	Club	GP	G	A	Pts	PIM	GP	G	A	Pts	PIM
1989-90	Washington Capitals	4	0	0	0	0	....	....	....	....	....
1990-91	Los Angeles Kings	4	0	0	0	4	....	....	....	....	....
	NHL Totals	**8**	**0**	**0**	**0**	**4**	....	....	....	....	....

Signed as a free agent by **Detroit**, December 2, 1986. Signed as a free agent by **Washington**, July 25, 1989. Signed as a free agent by **Los Angeles**, September 28, 1990. Signed as a free agent by **Boston**, August 2, 1991. Traded to **Washington** by **Boston** with John Byce for Brent Hughes and cash, February 24, 1992.

SMITH, Derek

Center/Left wing. Shoots left. 5'11", 180 lbs. Born, Quebec City, Que., July 31, 1954.
(Buffalo's 10th choice, 168th overall, in 1974 Amateur Draft).

Season	Club	GP	G	A	Pts	PIM	GP	G	A	Pts	PIM
1975-76	Buffalo Sabres	....	....	....	....	....	1	0	0	0	0
1976-77	Buffalo Sabres	5	0	0	0	0	....	....	....	....	....
1977-78	Buffalo Sabres	36	3	3	6	0	8	3	3	6	7
1978-79	Buffalo Sabres	43	14	12	26	8	....	....	....	....	....
1979-80	Buffalo Sabres	79	24	39	63	16	13	5	7	12	4
1980-81	Buffalo Sabres	69	21	43	64	12	8	1	4	5	2
1981-82	Buffalo Sabres	12	3	1	4	2	....	....	....	....	....
	Detroit Red Wings	49	6	14	20	10	....	....	....	....	....
1982-83	Detroit Red Wings	42	7	4	11	12	....	....	....	....	....
	NHL Totals	**335**	**78**	**116**	**194**	**60**	**30**	**9**	**14**	**23**	**13**

Traded to **Detroit** by **Buffalo** with Danny Gare and Jim Schoenfeld for Mike Foligno, Dale McCourt and Brent Peterson, December 2, 1981.

SMITH, Derrick

Left wing. Shoots left. 6'2", 215 lbs. Born, Scarborough, Ont., January 22, 1965.
(Philadelphia's 2nd choice, 44th overall, in 1983 Entry Draft).

Season	Club	GP	G	A	Pts	PIM	GP	G	A	Pts	PIM
1984-85	Philadelphia Flyers	77	17	22	39	31	19	2	5	7	16
1985-86	Philadelphia Flyers	69	6	6	12	57	4	0	0	0	10
1986-87	Philadelphia Flyers	71	11	21	32	34	26	6	4	10	26
1987-88	Philadelphia Flyers	76	16	8	24	104	7	0	0	0	6
1988-89	Philadelphia Flyers	74	16	14	30	43	19	5	2	7	12
1989-90	Philadelphia Flyers	55	3	6	9	32	....	....	....	....	....
1990-91	Philadelphia Flyers	72	11	10	21	37	....	....	....	....	....
1991-92	Minnesota North Stars	33	2	4	6	33	7	1	0	1	9
1992-93	Minnesota North Stars	9	0	1	1	2	....	....	....	....	....
1993-94	Dallas Stars	1	0	0	0	0	....	....	....	....	....
	NHL Totals	**537**	**82**	**92**	**174**	**373**	**82**	**14**	**11**	**25**	**79**

Claimed on waivers by **Minnesota** from **Philadelphia**, October 26, 1991. Transferred to **Dallas** after **Minnesota** franchise relocated, June 9, 1993.

SMITH, Des

Defense. Shoots left. 6', 185 lbs. Born, Ottawa, Ont., February 22, 1914.

Season	Club	GP	G	A	Pts	PIM	GP	G	A	Pts	PIM
1937-38	Montreal Maroons	40	3	1	4	47	....	....	....	....	....
1938-39	Montreal Canadiens	16	3	3	6	8	3	0	0	0	4
1939-40	Chicago Black Hawks	24	1	4	5	27	....	....	....	....	....
	Boston Bruins	20	2	2	4	23	6	0	0	0	0
1940-41 ♦	Boston Bruins	48	6	8	14	61	11	0	2	2	12
1941-42	Boston Bruins	48	7	7	14	70	5	1	2	3	2
	NHL Totals	**196**	**22**	**25**	**47**	**236**	**25**	**1**	**4**	**5**	**18**

• Brother of Rodger • Father of Brian and Gary

Signed as a free agent by **Mtl. Maroons**, October 7, 1937. Traded to **Montreal** by **Mtl. Maroons** for cash, September 14, 1938. Traded to **Chicago** by **Montreal** for cash, May 15, 1939. Traded to **Boston** by **Chicago** for Jack Portland, January 27, 1940.

SMITH, Don

Left wing/Center. Shoots left. 5'7", 160 lbs. Born, Cornwall, Ont., June 3, 1888.

Season	Club	GP	G	A	Pts	PIM	GP	G	A	Pts	PIM
1919-20	Montreal Canadiens	12	1	0	1	6	....	....	....	....	....
	NHL Totals	**12**	**1**	**0**	**1**	**6**	....	....	....	....	....

Signed as a free agent by **Montreal**, December 11, 1919.

SMITH, Don

Left wing/Center. Shoots left. 5'10", 165 lbs. Born, Regina, Sask., May 4, 1929.

Season	Club	GP	G	A	Pts	PIM	GP	G	A	Pts	PIM
1949-50	New York Rangers	11	1	1	2	0	1	0	0	0	0
	NHL Totals	**11**	**1**	**1**	**2**	**0**	**1**	**0**	**0**	**0**	**0**

• Brother of Ken

SMITH, Doug

Center. Shoots right. 5'11", 186 lbs. Born, Ottawa, Ont., May 17, 1963.
(Los Angeles' 1st choice, 2nd overall, in 1981 Entry Draft).

Season	Club	GP	G	A	Pts	PIM	GP	G	A	Pts	PIM
		REGULAR SEASON					PLAYOFFS				
1981-82	Los Angeles Kings	80	16	14	30	64	10	3	2	5	11
1982-83	Los Angeles Kings	42	11	11	22	12	....	....	....	....	....
1983-84	Los Angeles Kings	72	16	20	36	28	....	....	....	....	....
1984-85	Los Angeles Kings	62	21	20	41	58	3	1	0	1	4
1985-86	Los Angeles Kings	48	8	9	17	56	....	....	....	....	....
	Buffalo Sabres	30	10	11	21	73	....	....	....	....	....
1986-87	Buffalo Sabres	62	16	24	40	106	....	....	....	....	....
1987-88	Buffalo Sabres	70	9	19	28	117	1	0	0	0	0
1988-89	Edmonton Oilers	19	1	1	2	9	....	....	....	....	....
	Vancouver Canucks	10	3	4	7	4	4	0	0	0	6
1989-90	Vancouver Canucks	30	3	4	7	72	....	....	....	....	....
	Pittsburgh Penguins	10	1	1	2	25	....	....	....	....	....
	NHL Totals	**535**	**115**	**138**	**253**	**624**	**18**	**4**	**2**	**6**	**21**

Traded to **Buffalo** by **Los Angeles** with Brian Engblom for Sean McKenna, Larry Playfair and Ken Baumgartner, January 30, 1986. Claimed by **Edmonton** from **Buffalo** in NHL Waiver Draft, October 3, 1988. Traded to **Vancouver** by **Edmonton** with Greg Adams for John LeBlanc and Vancouver's 5th round choice (Peter White) in 1989 Entry Draft, March 7, 1989. Traded to **Pittsburgh** by **Vancouver** for cash, February 26, 1990.

SMITH, Floyd

Right wing. Shoots right. 5'10", 180 lbs. Born, Perth, Ont., May 16, 1935.

Season	Club	GP	G	A	Pts	PIM	GP	G	A	Pts	PIM
1954-55	Boston Bruins	3	0	1	1	0	....	....	....	....	....
1956-57	Boston Bruins	23	0	0	0	6	....	....	....	....	....
1960-61	New York Rangers	29	5	9	14	0	....	....	....	....	....
1962-63	Detroit Red Wings	51	9	17	26	10	11	2	3	5	4
1963-64	Detroit Red Wings	52	18	13	31	22	14	4	3	7	4
1964-65	Detroit Red Wings	67	16	29	45	44	7	1	3	4	4
1965-66	Detroit Red Wings	66	21	28	49	20	12	5	2	7	4
1966-67	Detroit Red Wings	54	11	14	25	8	....	....	....	....	....
1967-68	Detroit Red Wings	57	18	21	39	14	....	....	....	....	....
	Toronto Maple Leafs	6	6	1	7	0	....	....	....	....	....
1968-69	Toronto Maple Leafs	64	15	19	34	22	4	0	0	0	0
1969-70	Toronto Maple Leafs	61	4	14	18	13	....	....	....	....	....
1970-71	Buffalo Sabres	77	6	11	17	46	....	....	....	....	....
1971-72	Buffalo Sabres	6	0	1	1	2	....	....	....	....	....
	NHL Totals	**616**	**129**	**178**	**307**	**207**	**48**	**12**	**11**	**23**	**16**

Signed to a three-game amateur tryout contract by **Boston** during 1954-55 season. Signed as a free agent by **Boston**, August 23, 1955. Traded to **Springfield** (AHL) by **Boston** to complete transaction that sent Don Simmons to Boston (January 22, 1957), June, 1957. Claimed by **Detroit** from **NY Rangers** in Intra-League Draft, June 5, 1962. Traded to **Toronto** by **Detroit** with Norm Ullman, Paul Henderson and Doug Barrie for Frank Mahovlich, Pete Stemkowski, Garry Unger and the rights to Carl Brewer, March 3, 1968. Traded to **Buffalo** by **Toronto** with Brent Imlach for cash, August 31, 1970.

SMITH, Geoff

Defense. Shoots left. 6'3", 194 lbs. Born, Edmonton, Alta., March 7, 1969.
(Edmonton's 3rd choice, 63rd overall, in 1987 Entry Draft).

Season	Club	GP	G	A	Pts	PIM	GP	G	A	Pts	PIM
1989-90 ♦	Edmonton Oilers	74	4	11	15	52	3	0	0	0	0
1990-91	Edmonton Oilers	59	1	12	13	55	4	0	0	0	0
1991-92	Edmonton Oilers	74	2	16	18	43	5	0	1	1	6
1992-93	Edmonton Oilers	78	4	14	18	30	....	....	....	....	....
1993-94	Edmonton Oilers	21	0	3	3	12	....	....	....	....	....
	Florida Panthers	56	1	5	6	38	....	....	....	....	....
1994-95	Florida Panthers	47	2	4	6	22	....	....	....	....	....
1995-96	Florida Panthers	31	3	7	10	20	1	0	0	0	2
1996-97	Florida Panthers	3	0	0	0	2	....	....	....	....	....
1997-98	New York Rangers	15	1	1	2	6	....	....	....	....	....
1998-99	New York Rangers	4	0	0	0	2	....	....	....	....	....
	NHL Totals	**462**	**18**	**73**	**91**	**282**	**13**	**0**	**1**	**1**	**8**

NHL All-Rookie Team (1990)

Traded to **Florida** by **Edmonton** with Edmonton's 4th round choice (David Nemirovsky) in 1994 Entry Draft for Florida's 3rd round choice (Corey Neilson) in 1994 Entry Draft and St. Louis' 6th round choice (previously acquired by Florida – later traded to Winnipeg – Winnipeg selected Chris Kibermanis) in 1994 Entry Draft, December 6, 1993. Signed as a free agent by **NY Rangers**, September 29, 1997. Traded to **St. Louis** by **NY Rangers** with Jeff Finley for future considerations (Chris Kenady, February 22, 1999), February 13, 1999.

SMITH, Glen

Right wing. Shoots right. 5'8", 155 lbs. Born, Lucky Lake, Sask., March 19, 1931.

Season	Club	GP	G	A	Pts	PIM	GP	G	A	Pts	PIM
1950-51	Chicago Black Hawks	2	0	0	0	0	....	....	....	....	....
	NHL Totals	**2**	**0**	**0**	**0**	**0**	....	....	....	....	....

SMITH, Glenn

Defense. Shoots left. 5'8", 180 lbs. Born, Meaford, Ont., 1895.

Season	Club	GP	G	A	Pts	PIM	GP	G	A	Pts	PIM
1921-22	Toronto St. Pats	9	0	0	0	0	....	....	....	....	....
	NHL Totals	**9**	**0**	**0**	**0**	**0**	....	....	....	....	....

Signed as a free agent by **Toronto**, December 16, 1921.

SMITH, Gord

Defense. Shoots left. 5'10", 175 lbs. Born, Perth, Ont., November 17, 1949.

Season	Club	GP	G	A	Pts	PIM	GP	G	A	Pts	PIM
1974-75	Washington Capitals	63	3	8	11	56	....	....	....	....	....
1975-76	Washington Capitals	25	1	2	3	28	....	....	....	....	....
1976-77	Washington Capitals	79	1	12	13	92	....	....	....	....	....
1977-78	Washington Capitals	80	4	7	11	78	....	....	....	....	....
1978-79	Washington Capitals	39	0	1	1	22	....	....	....	....	....
1979-80	Winnipeg Jets	13	0	0	0	8	....	....	....	....	....
	NHL Totals	**299**	**9**	**30**	**39**	**284**	....	....	....	....	....

• Brother of Billy

Signed as a free agent by **Los Angeles**, May 22, 1970. Claimed by **Washington** from **Los Angeles** in Expansion Draft, June 12, 1974. Claimed by **Winnipeg** from **Washington** in Expansion Draft, June 13, 1979. Traded to **NY Rangers** by **Winnipeg** for cash, August 6, 1980.

SMITH, Greg

Defense. Shoots left. 6', 195 lbs. Born, Ponoka, Alta., July 8, 1955.
(California's 4th choice, 57th overall, in 1975 Amateur Draft).

Season	Club	GP	G	A	Pts	PIM	GP	G	A	Pts	PIM
1975-76	California Golden Seals	1	0	1	1	2	....	....	....	....	....
1976-77	Cleveland Barons	74	9	17	26	65	....	....	....	....	....
1977-78	Cleveland Barons	80	7	30	37	92	....	....	....	....	....
1978-79	Minnesota North Stars	80	5	27	32	147	....	....	....	....	....
1979-80	Minnesota North Stars	55	5	13	18	103	12	0	1	1	9
1980-81	Minnesota North Stars	74	5	21	26	126	19	1	5	6	39
1981-82	Detroit Red Wings	69	10	22	32	79	....	....	....	....	....
1982-83	Detroit Red Wings	73	4	26	30	79	....	....	....	....	....
1983-84	Detroit Red Wings	75	3	20	23	108	4	1	0	1	8
1984-85	Detroit Red Wings	73	2	18	20	117	3	0	0	0	7
1985-86	Detroit Red Wings	62	5	19	24	84	....	....	....	....	....
	Washington Capitals	14	0	3	3	10	9	2	1	3	9
1986-87	Washington Capitals	45	0	9	9	31	7	0	0	0	11
1987-88	Washington Capitals	54	1	6	7	67	9	0	0	0	23
	NHL Totals	**829**	**56**	**232**	**288**	**1110**	**63**	**4**	**7**	**11**	**106**

Signed as a free agent by **California**, March, 1975. Transferred to **Cleveland** after **California** franchise relocated, August 26, 1976. Protected by **Minnesota** prior to **Cleveland-Minnesota** Dispersal Draft, June 15, 1978. Traded to **Detroit** by **Minnesota** with the rights to Don Murdoch and Minnesota's 1st round choice (Murray Craven) in 1982 Entry Draft for Detroit's 1st round choice (Brian Bellows) in 1982 Entry Draft, August 21, 1981. Traded to **Washington** by **Detroit** with John Barrett for Darren Veitch, March 10, 1986.

SMITH, Hooley

HHOF

Center/Right wing. Shoots right. 5'10", 155 lbs. Born, Toronto, Ont., January 7, 1903.

Season	Club	GP	G	A	Pts	PIM	GP	G	A	Pts	PIM
1924-25	Ottawa Senators	30	10	13	23	81	....	....	....	....	....
1925-26	Ottawa Senators	28	16	9	25	53	2	0	0	0	14
1926-27 ♦	Ottawa Senators	43	9	6	15	125	6	1	0	1	16
1927-28	Montreal Maroons	34	14	5	19	72	9	2	1	3	23
1928-29	Montreal Maroons	41	10	9	19	120	....	....	....	....	....
1929-30	Montreal Maroons	42	21	9	30	83	4	1	1	2	14
1930-31	Montreal Maroons	39	12	14	26	68	....	....	....	....	....
1931-32	Montreal Maroons	43	11	33	44	49	4	2	1	3	2
1932-33	Montreal Maroons	48	20	21	41	66	2	2	0	2	2
1933-34	Montreal Maroons	47	18	19	37	58	4	0	1	1	6
1934-35 ♦	Montreal Maroons	46	5	22	27	41	6	0	0	0	14
1935-36	Montreal Maroons	47	19	19	38	75	3	0	0	0	2
1936-37	Boston Bruins	44	8	10	18	36	3	0	0	0	0
1937-38	New York Americans	47	10	10	20	23	6	0	3	3	0
1938-39	New York Americans	48	8	11	19	18	2	0	0	0	14
1939-40	New York Americans	47	7	8	15	41	3	3	1	4	2
1940-41	New York Americans	41	2	7	9	4	....	....	....	....	....
	NHL Totals	**715**	**200**	**225**	**425**	**1013**	**54**	**11**	**8**	**19**	**109**

NHL Second All-Star Team (1932) • NHL First All-Star Team (1936)

Played in NHL All-Star Game (1934)

Signed as a free agent by **Ottawa**, October 31, 1924. Traded to **Mtl. Maroons** by **Ottawa** for Harry Broadbent and $22,500, October 7, 1927. Traded to **Boston** by **Mtl. Maroons** for cash and future considerations (Gerry Shannon, December 4, 1936), October 26, 1936. Traded to **NY Americans** by **Boston** for cash, November, 5, 1937.

SMITH, Jason

Defense. Shoots right. 6'3", 210 lbs. Born, Calgary, Alta., November 2, 1973.
(New Jersey's 1st choice, 18th overall, in 1992 Entry Draft).

Season	Club	GP	G	A	Pts	PIM	GP	G	A	Pts	PIM
1993-94	New Jersey Devils	41	0	5	5	43	6	0	0	0	7
1994-95	New Jersey Devils	2	0	0	0	0	....	....	....	....	....
1995-96	New Jersey Devils	64	2	1	3	86	....	....	....	....	....
1996-97	New Jersey Devils	57	1	2	3	38	....	....	....	....	....
	Toronto Maple Leafs	21	0	5	5	16	....	....	....	....	....
1997-98	Toronto Maple Leafs	81	3	13	16	100	....	....	....	....	....
1998-99	Toronto Maple Leafs	60	2	11	13	40	....	....	....	....	....
	Edmonton Oilers	12	1	1	2	11	4	0	1	1	4
99-2000	Edmonton Oilers	80	3	11	14	60	5	0	1	1	4
2000-01	Edmonton Oilers	82	5	15	20	120	6	0	2	2	6
2001-02	Edmonton Oilers	74	5	13	18	103	....	....	....	....	....
2002-03	Edmonton Oilers	68	4	8	12	64	6	0	0	0	19
	NHL Totals	**642**	**26**	**85**	**111**	**681**	**27**	**0**	**4**	**4**	**40**

• Missed majority of 1994-95 season recovering from knee injury suffered in practice, November 5, 1994. Traded to **Toronto** by **New Jersey** with Steve Sullivan and the rights to Alyn McCauley for Doug Gilmour, Dave Ellett and New Jersey's 4th round choice (previously acquired, New Jersey selected Andre Lakos) in 1999 Entry Draft, February 25, 1997. Traded to **Edmonton** by **Toronto** for Edmonton's 4th round choice (Jonathon Zion) in 1999 Entry Draft and 2nd round choice (Kris Vernarsky) in 2000 Entry Draft, March 23, 1999.

SMITH, Ken

Left wing. Shoots left. 5'7", 150 lbs. Born, Moose Jaw, Sask., May 8, 1924.

Season	Club	GP	G	A	Pts	PIM	GP	G	A	Pts	PIM
1944-45	Boston Bruins	49	20	14	34	2	7	3	4	7	0

Season	Club	GP	G	A	Pts	PIM	GP	G	A	Pts	PIM
		REGULAR SEASON					PLAYOFFS				
1945-46	Boston Bruins	23	2	6	8	0	8	0	4	4	0
1946-47	Boston Bruins	60	14	7	21	4	5	3	0	3	2
1947-48	Boston Bruins	60	11	12	23	14	5	2	3	5	0
1948-49	Boston Bruins	59	20	20	40	6	5	0	2	2	4
1949-50	Boston Bruins	66	10	31	41	12	....	....	....	....	....
1950-51	Boston Bruins	14	1	3	4	11	....	....	....	....	....
	NHL Totals	**331**	**78**	**93**	**171**	**49**	**30**	**8**	**13**	**21**	**6**

• Brother of Don

Traded to **Toronto** by **Boston** with Fern Flaman, Phil Maloney and Leo Boivin for Bill Ezinicki and Vic Lynn, November 16, 1950. Traded to **Providence** (AHL) by **Toronto** for cash, November 10, 1951.

SMITH, Mark

Center. Shoots left. 5'10", 205 lbs. Born, Edmonton, Alta., October 24, 1977.
(San Jose's 7th choice, 219th overall, in 1997 Entry Draft).

Season	Club	GP	G	A	Pts	PIM	GP	G	A	Pts	PIM
2000-01	San Jose Sharks	42	2	2	4	51	....	....	....	....	....
2001-02	San Jose Sharks	49	3	3	6	72	....	....	....	....	....
2002-03	San Jose Sharks	75	4	11	15	64	....	....	....	....	....
	NHL Totals	**166**	**9**	**16**	**25**	**187**	....	....	....	....	....

SMITH, Nakina

Center. Shoots left. 5'10", 150 lbs. Born, Cache Bay, Ont., July 26, 1915.

Season	Club	GP	G	A	Pts	PIM	GP	G	A	Pts	PIM
1943-44	Detroit Red Wings	10	1	2	3	0	....	....	....	....	....
	NHL Totals	**10**	**1**	**2**	**3**	**0**	....	....	....	....	....

• Brother of Carl

Signed as a free agent by **Detroit**, October 19, 1943.

SMITH, Nick

Center. Shoots left. 6'2", 196 lbs. Born, Hamilton, Ont., March 23, 1979.
(Florida's 4th choice, 74th overall, in 1997 Entry Draft).

Season	Club	GP	G	A	Pts	PIM	GP	G	A	Pts	PIM
2001-02	Florida Panthers	15	0	0	0	0	....	....	....	....	....
	NHL Totals	**15**	**0**	**0**	**0**	**0**	....	....	....	....	....

Signed as a free agent by **Anaheim**, August 22, 2002.

SMITH, Randy

Center. Shoots left. 6'4", 200 lbs. Born, Saskatoon, Sask., July 7, 1965.
(St. Louis' 5th choice, 88th overall, in 1973 Amateur Draft)

Season	Club	GP	G	A	Pts	PIM	GP	G	A	Pts	PIM
1985-86	Minnesota North Stars	1	0	0	0	0	....	....	....	....	....
1986-87	Minnesota North Stars	2	0	0	0	0	....	....	....	....	....
	NHL Totals	**3**	**0**	**0**	**0**	**0**	....	....	....	....	....

Signed as a free agent by **Minnesota**, May 12, 1986.

SMITH, Rick

Defense. Shoots left. 5'11", 190 lbs. Born, Kingston, Ont., June 29, 1948.
(Boston's 2nd choice, 7th overall, in 1966 Amateur Draft).

Season	Club	GP	G	A	Pts	PIM	GP	G	A	Pts	PIM
1968-69	Boston Bruins	48	0	5	5	29	9	0	0	0	6
1969-70 ♦	Boston Bruins	69	2	8	10	65	14	1	3	4	17
1970-71	Boston Bruins	67	4	19	23	44	6	0	0	0	0
1971-72	Boston Bruins	61	2	12	14	46	....	....	....	....	....
	California Golden Seals	17	1	4	5	26	....	....	....	....	....
1972-73	California Golden Seals	64	9	24	33	77	....	....	....	....	....
1975-76	St. Louis Blues	24	1	7	8	18	3	0	1	1	4
1976-77	St. Louis Blues	18	0	1	1	6	....	....	....	....	....
	Boston Bruins	46	6	16	22	30	14	0	9	9	14
1977-78	Boston Bruins	79	7	29	36	69	15	1	5	6	18
1978-79	Boston Bruins	65	7	18	25	46	11	0	4	4	12
1979-80	Boston Bruins	78	8	18	26	62	6	1	1	2	2
1980-81	Detroit Red Wings	11	0	2	2	6	....	....	....	....	....
	Washington Capitals	40	5	4	9	36	....	....	....	....	....
	NHL Totals	**687**	**52**	**167**	**219**	**560**	**78**	**3**	**23**	**26**	**73**

Traded to **California** by **Boston** with Reggie Leach and Bob Stewart for Carol Vadnais and Don O'Donoghue, February 23, 1972. Traded to **St. Louis** by **California** for cash, October 22, 1975. Traded to **Boston** by **St. Louis** for Joe Zanussi, December 20, 1976. Claimed by **Detroit** from **Boston** in Waiver Draft, October 10, 1980. Claimed on waivers by **Washington** from **Detroit**, November 7, 1980.

SMITH, Rodger

Defense. Shoots left. 6', 175 lbs. Born, Ottawa, Ont., July 26, 1896.

Season	Club	GP	G	A	Pts	PIM	GP	G	A	Pts	PIM
1925-26	Pittsburgh Pirates	36	9	1	10	22	2	1	0	1	0
1926-27	Pittsburgh Pirates	36	4	0	4	6	....	....	....	....	....
1927-28	Pittsburgh Pirates	43	1	0	1	30	2	2	0	2	0
1928-29	Pittsburgh Pirates	44	4	2	6	49	....	....	....	....	....
1929-30	Pittsburgh Pirates	42	2	1	3	65	....	....	....	....	....
1930-31	Philadelphia Quakers	9	0	0	0	0	....	....	....	....	....
	NHL Totals	**210**	**20**	**4**	**24**	**172**	**4**	**3**	**0**	**3**	**0**

• Brother of Des

Signed as a free agent by **Pittsburgh**, September 26, 1925. Transferred to **Philadelphia** after **Pittsburgh** franchise relocated, October 18, 1930. Traded to **Pittsburgh** (IHL) by **Philadelphia**, December 16, 1930.

SMITH, Ron

Defense. Shoots right. 6', 185 lbs. Born, Port Hope, Ont., November 19, 1952.
(NY Islanders' 4th choice, 49th overall, in 1972 Amateur Draft).

Season	Club	GP	G	A	Pts	PIM	GP	G	A	Pts	PIM
1972-73	New York Islanders	11	1	1	2	14	....	....	....	....	....
	NHL Totals	**11**	**1**	**1**	**2**	**14**	....	....	....	....	....

SMITH, Sid

Left wing. Shoots left. 5'10", 173 lbs. Born, Toronto, Ont., July 11, 1925.

Season	Club	GP	G	A	Pts	PIM	GP	G	A	Pts	PIM
1946-47	Toronto Maple Leafs	14	2	1	3	0	....	....	....	....	....
1947-48 ♦	Toronto Maple Leafs	31	7	10	17	10	2	0	0	0	0
1948-49 ♦	Toronto Maple Leafs	1	0	0	0	0	6	5	2	7	0
1949-50	Toronto Maple Leafs	68	22	23	45	6	7	0	3	3	2
1950-51 ♦	Toronto Maple Leafs	70	30	21	51	10	11	7	3	10	0
1951-52	Toronto Maple Leafs	70	27	30	57	6	4	0	0	0	0
1952-53	Toronto Maple Leafs	70	20	19	39	6	....	....	....	....	....
1953-54	Toronto Maple Leafs	70	22	16	38	28	5	1	1	2	0
1954-55	Toronto Maple Leafs	70	33	21	54	14	4	3	1	4	0
1955-56	Toronto Maple Leafs	55	4	17	21	8	5	1	0	1	0
1956-57	Toronto Maple Leafs	70	17	24	41	4	....	....	....	....	....
1957-58	Toronto Maple Leafs	12	2	1	3	2	....	....	....	....	....
	NHL Totals	**601**	**186**	**183**	**369**	**94**	**44**	**17**	**10**	**27**	**2**

NHL Second All-Star Team (1951, 1952) • Lady Byng Trophy (1952, 1955) • NHL First All-Star Team (1955)

Played in NHL All-Star Game (1949, 1950, 1951, 1952, 1953, 1954, 1955)

Signed as a free agent by **Toronto**, December 8, 1946.

SMITH, Stan

Center. Shoots left. 5'10", 165 lbs. Born, Coal Creek, B.C., August 13, 1917.

Season	Club	GP	G	A	Pts	PIM	GP	G	A	Pts	PIM
1939-40 ♦	New York Rangers	1	0	0	0	0	1	0	0	0	0
1940-41	New York Rangers	8	2	1	3	0	....	....	....	....	....
	NHL Totals	**9**	**2**	**1**	**3**	**0**	**1**	**0**	**0**	**0**	**0**

Signed as a free agent by **NY Rangers**, October 23, 1939. Traded to **Cleveland** (AHL) by **NY Rangers** for cash, September 9, 1941.

SMITH, Steve

Defense. Shoots left. 5'9", 215 lbs. Born, Trenton, Ont., April 4, 1963.
(Philadelphia's 1st choice, 16th overall, in 1981 Entry Draft).

Season	Club	GP	G	A	Pts	PIM	GP	G	A	Pts	PIM
1981-82	Philadelphia Flyers	8	0	1	1	0	....	....	....	....	....
1984-85	Philadelphia Flyers	2	0	0	0	7	....	....	....	....	....
1985-86	Philadelphia Flyers	2	0	0	0	2	....	....	....	....	....
1986-87	Philadelphia Flyers	2	0	0	0	6	....	....	....	....	....
1987-88	Philadelphia Flyers	1	0	0	0	0	....	....	....	....	....
1988-89	Buffalo Sabres	3	0	0	0	0	....	....	....	....	....
	NHL Totals	**18**	**0**	**1**	**1**	**15**	....	....	....	....	....

Claimed by **Buffalo** from **Philadelphia** in Waiver Draft, October 3, 1988.

SMITH, Steve

Defense. Shoots left. 6'4", 215 lbs. Born, Glasgow, Scotland, April 30, 1963.
(Edmonton's 5th choice, 111th overall, in 1981 Entry Draft).

Season	Club	GP	G	A	Pts	PIM	GP	G	A	Pts	PIM
1984-85	Edmonton Oilers	2	0	0	0	2	....	....	....	....	....
1985-86	Edmonton Oilers	55	4	20	24	166	6	0	1	1	14
1986-87 ♦	Edmonton Oilers	62	7	15	22	165	15	1	3	4	45
1987-88 ♦	Edmonton Oilers	79	12	43	55	286	19	1	11	12	55
1988-89	Edmonton Oilers	35	3	19	22	97	7	2	2	4	20
1989-90 ♦	Edmonton Oilers	75	7	34	41	171	22	5	10	15	37
1990-91	Edmonton Oilers	77	13	41	54	193	18	1	2	3	45
1991-92	Chicago Blackhawks	76	9	21	30	304	18	1	11	12	16
1992-93	Chicago Blackhawks	78	10	47	57	214	4	0	0	0	10
1993-94	Chicago Blackhawks	57	5	22	27	174	....	....	....	....	....
1994-95	Chicago Blackhawks	48	1	12	13	128	16	0	1	1	26
1995-96	Chicago Blackhawks	37	0	9	9	71	6	0	0	0	16
1996-97	Chicago Blackhawks	21	0	0	0	29	3	0	0	0	4
1998-99	Calgary Flames	69	1	14	15	80	....	....	....	....	....
99-2000	Calgary Flames	20	0	4	4	42	....	....	....	....	....
2000-01	Calgary Flames	13	0	2	2	17	....	....	....	....	....
	NHL Totals	**804**	**72**	**303**	**375**	**2139**	**134**	**11**	**41**	**52**	**288**

Played in NHL All-Star Game (1991)

Traded to **Chicago** by **Edmonton** for Dave Manson and Chicago's 3rd round choice (Kirk Maltby) in 1992 Entry Draft, October 2, 1991. Signed as a free agent by **Calgary**, August 17, 1998. • Missed majority of 1999-2000 season recovering from neck injury suffered in game vs. Los Angeles, January 12, 2000. • Officially announced retirement, December 7, 2000.

SMITH, Stu

Left wing. Shoots left. 5'8", 165 lbs. Born, Basswood, Man., September 25, 1918.

Season	Club	GP	G	A	Pts	PIM	GP	G	A	Pts	PIM
1940-41	Montreal Canadiens	3	2	1	3	2	1	0	0	0	0
1941-42	Montreal Canadiens	1	0	1	1	0	....	....	....	....	....
	NHL Totals	**4**	**2**	**2**	**4**	**2**	**1**	**0**	**0**	**0**	**0**

• Father of Brian

Signed as a free agent by **Montreal**, October 16, 1941.

SMITH, Stu

Defense. Shoots right. 6'1", 205 lbs. Born, Toronto, Ont., March 17, 1960.
(Hartford's 2nd choice, 39th overall, in 1979 Entry Draft).

		REGULAR SEASON					PLAYOFFS				
Season	Club	GP	G	A	Pts	PIM	GP	G	A	Pts	PIM
1979-80	Hartford Whalers	4	0	0	0	0	....	....	....	....	....
1980-81	Hartford Whalers	38	1	7	8	55	....	....	....	....	....
1981-82	Hartford Whalers	17	0	3	3	15	....	....	....	....	....
1982-83	Hartford Whalers	18	1	0	1	25	....	....	....	....	....
	NHL Totals	**77**	**2**	**10**	**12**	**95**	....	....	....	....	....

Signed as a free agent by **Los Angeles**, November 8, 1984.

SMITH, Tommy

HHOF

Center. Shoots left. 5'6", 150 lbs. Born, Ottawa, Ont., September 27, 1886.

Season	Club	GP	G	A	Pts	PIM	GP	G	A	Pts	PIM
1919-20	Quebec Bulldogs	10	0	1	1	11	....	....	....	....	....
	NHL Totals	**10**	**0**	**1**	**1**	**11**	....	....	....	....	....

Rights retained by **Montreal** after NHA folded, November 26, 1917. Traded to **Ottawa** by **Montreal** for cash, November 28, 1918. Transferred to **Quebec** by **Ottawa** when Quebec franchise returned to NHL, November 25, 1919.

SMITH, Vern

Defense. Shoots left. 6'1", 190 lbs. Born, Winnipeg, Man., May 30, 1964.
(NY Islanders' 2nd choice, 42nd overall, in 1982 Entry Draft).

Season	Club	GP	G	A	Pts	PIM	GP	G	A	Pts	PIM
1984-85	New York Islanders	1	0	0	0	0	....	....	....	....	....
	NHL Totals	**1**	**0**	**0**	**0**	**0**	....	....	....	....	....

SMITH, Wayne

Defense. Shoots left. 6', 195 lbs. Born, Kamsack, Sask., February 12, 1943.

Season	Club	GP	G	A	Pts	PIM	GP	G	A	Pts	PIM
1966-67	Chicago Black Hawks	2	1	1	2	2	1	0	0	0	0
	NHL Totals	**2**	**1**	**1**	**2**	**2**	**1**	**0**	**0**	**0**	**0**

Rights traded to **Chicago** by **LA Blades** (WHL) to complete transaction that sent Howie Young to LA Blades (WHL) (February 11, 1964), July, 1964.

SMITH, Wyatt

Center. Shoots left. 5'11", 208 lbs. Born, Thief River Falls, MN, February 13, 1977.
(Phoenix's 6th choice, 233rd overall, in 1997 Entry Draft).

Season	Club	GP	G	A	Pts	PIM	GP	G	A	Pts	PIM
99-2000	Phoenix Coyotes	2	0	0	0	0	....	....	....	....	....
2000-01	Phoenix Coyotes	42	3	7	10	13	....	....	....	....	....
2001-02	Phoenix Coyotes	10	0	0	0	0	....	....	....	....	....
2002-03	Nashville Predators	11	1	0	1	0	....	....	....	....	....
	NHL Totals	**65**	**4**	**7**	**11**	**13**	....	....	....	....	....

Signed as a free agent by **Nashville**, July 15, 2002.

SMITHSON, Jerred

Center. Shoots right. 6'2", 190 lbs. Born, Vernon, B.C., February 4, 1979.

Season	Club	GP	G	A	Pts	PIM	GP	G	A	Pts	PIM
2002-03	Los Angeles Kings	22	0	2	2	21	....	....	....	....	....
	NHL Totals	**22**	**0**	**2**	**2**	**21**	....	....	....	....	....

Signed as a free agent by **Los Angeles**, February 18, 2000.

SMOLINSKI, Bryan

Center. Shoots right. 6'1", 208 lbs. Born, Toledo, OH, December 27, 1971.
(Boston's 1st choice, 21st overall, in 1990 Entry Draft).

Season	Club	GP	G	A	Pts	PIM	GP	G	A	Pts	PIM
1992-93	Boston Bruins	9	1	3	4	0	4	1	0	1	2
1993-94	Boston Bruins	83	31	20	51	82	13	5	4	9	4
1994-95	Boston Bruins	44	18	13	31	31	5	0	1	1	4
1995-96	Pittsburgh Penguins	81	24	40	64	69	18	5	4	9	10
1996-97	New York Islanders	64	28	28	56	25	....	....	....	....	....
1997-98	New York Islanders	81	13	30	43	34	....	....	....	....	....
1998-99	New York Islanders	82	16	24	40	49	....	....	....	....	....
99-2000	Los Angeles Kings	79	20	36	56	48	4	0	0	0	2
2000-01	Los Angeles Kings	78	27	32	59	40	13	1	5	6	14
2001-02	Los Angeles Kings	80	13	25	38	56	7	2	0	2	2
2002-03	Los Angeles Kings	58	18	20	38	18	....	....	....	....	....
	Ottawa Senators	10	3	5	8	2	18	2	7	9	6
	NHL Totals	**749**	**212**	**276**	**488**	**454**	**82**	**16**	**21**	**37**	**44**

Traded to **Pittsburgh** by **Boston** with Glen Murray and Boston's 3rd round choice (Boyd Kane) in 1996 Entry Draft for Kevin Stevens and Shawn McEachern, August 2, 1995. Traded to **NY Islanders** by **Pittsburgh** for Darius Kasparaitis and Andreas Johansson, November 17, 1996. Traded to **Los Angeles** by **NY Islanders** with Ziggy Palffy, Marcel Cousineau and New Jersey's 4th round choice (previously acquired, Los Angeles selected Daniel Johansson) in 1999 Entry Draft for Olli Jokinen, Josh Green, Mathieu Biron and Los Angeles' 1st round choice (Taylor Pyatt) in 1999 Entry Draft, June 20, 1999. Traded to **Ottawa** by **Los Angeles** for the rights to Tim Gleason and future considerations, March 11, 2003.

SMREK, Peter

Defense. Shoots left. 6'1", 215 lbs. Born, Martin, Czech., February 16, 1979.
(St. Louis' 2nd choice, 85th overall, in 1999 Entry Draft).

Season	Club	GP	G	A	Pts	PIM	GP	G	A	Pts	PIM
2000-01	St. Louis Blues	6	2	0	2	2	....	....	....	....	....
	New York Rangers	14	0	3	3	12	....	....	....	....	....
2001-02	New York Rangers	8	0	1	1	4	....	....	....	....	....
	NHL Totals	**28**	**2**	**4**	**6**	**18**	....	....	....	....	....

Traded to **NY Rangers** by **St. Louis** for Alexei Gusarov, March 5, 2001. Traded to **Nashville** by **NY Rangers** for Richard Lintner, March 19, 2002.

SMRKE, John

Left wing. Shoots left. 5'11", 205 lbs. Born, Chicoutimi, Que., February 25, 1956.
(St. Louis' 3rd choice, 25th overall, in 1976 Amateur Draft).

Season	Club	GP	G	A	Pts	PIM	GP	G	A	Pts	PIM
1977-78	St. Louis Blues	18	2	4	6	11	....	....	....	....	....
1978-79	St. Louis Blues	55	6	8	14	20	....	....	....	....	....
1979-80	Quebec Nordiques	30	3	5	8	2	....	....	....	....	....
	NHL Totals	**103**	**11**	**17**	**28**	**33**	....	....	....	....	....

• Son of Stan

Claimed by **Quebec** from **St. Louis** in Expansion Draft, June 13, 1979.

SMRKE, Stan

Left wing. Shoots left. 5'11", 180 lbs. Born, Belgrade, Yugoslavia, September 2, 1928.

Season	Club	GP	G	A	Pts	PIM	GP	G	A	Pts	PIM
1956-57	Montreal Canadiens	4	0	0	0	0	....	....	....	....	....
1957-58	Montreal Canadiens	5	0	3	3	0	....	....	....	....	....
	NHL Totals	**9**	**0**	**3**	**3**	**0**	....	....	....	....	....

• Father of John

Played in NHL All-Star Game (1957)

Traded to **Montreal** by **Chicoutimi** (QHL) for Jack Leclair, Jacques DesLauriers and Guy Rousseau, October 27, 1957. Traded to **Toronto** by **Montreal** for Al MacNeil, June 7, 1960.

SMYL, Stan

Right wing. Shoots right. 5'8", 185 lbs. Born, Glendon, Alta., January 28, 1958.
(Vancouver's 3rd choice, 40th overall, in 1978 Amateur Draft).

Season	Club	GP	G	A	Pts	PIM	GP	G	A	Pts	PIM
1978-79	Vancouver Canucks	62	14	24	38	89	2	1	1	2	0
1979-80	Vancouver Canucks	77	31	47	78	204	4	0	2	2	14
1980-81	Vancouver Canucks	80	25	38	63	171	3	1	2	3	0
1981-82	Vancouver Canucks	80	34	44	78	144	17	9	9	18	25
1982-83	Vancouver Canucks	74	38	50	88	114	4	3	2	5	12
1983-84	Vancouver Canucks	80	24	43	67	136	4	2	1	3	4
1984-85	Vancouver Canucks	80	27	37	64	100	....	....	....	....	....
1985-86	Vancouver Canucks	73	27	35	62	144	....	....	....	....	....
1986-87	Vancouver Canucks	66	20	23	43	84	....	....	....	....	....
1987-88	Vancouver Canucks	57	12	25	37	110	....	....	....	....	....
1988-89	Vancouver Canucks	75	7	18	25	102	7	0	0	0	9
1989-90	Vancouver Canucks	47	1	15	16	71	....	....	....	....	....
1990-91	Vancouver Canucks	45	2	12	14	87	....	....	....	....	....
	NHL Totals	**896**	**262**	**411**	**673**	**1556**	**41**	**16**	**17**	**33**	**64**

SMYLIE, Rod

Wing. Shoots right. 5'10", 170 lbs. Born, Toronto, Ont., September 28, 1895.

Season	Club	GP	G	A	Pts	PIM	GP	G	A	Pts	PIM
1920-21	Toronto St. Pats	23	2	1	3	2	2	0	0	0	0
1921-22 ◆	Toronto St. Pats	20	0	0	0	2	1	0	*0	0	2
	Toronto St. Pats (Cup)	....	....	....	....	....	*5*	*1*	*3*	*4*	*0*
1922-23	Toronto St. Pats	2	0	0	0	0	....	....	....	....	....
1923-24	Ottawa Senators	13	1	1	2	8	....	....	....	....	....
1924-25	Toronto St. Pats	11	1	0	1	0	1	0	0	0	0
1925-26	Toronto St. Pats	5	0	0	0	0	....	....	....	....	....
	NHL Totals	**74**	**4**	**2**	**6**	**12**	**4**	**0**	**0**	**0**	**2**

Signed as a free agent by **Toronto**, December 15, 1920. Signed as a free agent by **Ottawa**, January 2, 1924. Signed as a free agent by **Toronto**, January 27, 1925.

SMYTH, Brad

Right wing. Shoots right. 6', 195 lbs. Born, Ottawa, Ont., March 13, 1973.

Season	Club	GP	G	A	Pts	PIM	GP	G	A	Pts	PIM
1995-96	Florida Panthers	7	1	1	2	4	....	....	....	....	....
1996-97	Florida Panthers	8	1	0	1	2	....	....	....	....	....
	Los Angeles Kings	44	8	8	16	74	....	....	....	....	....
1997-98	Los Angeles Kings	9	1	3	4	4	....	....	....	....	....
	New York Rangers	1	0	0	0	0	....	....	....	....	....
1998-99	Nashville Predators	3	0	0	0	6	....	....	....	....	....
2000-01	New York Rangers	4	1	0	1	4	....	....	....	....	....
2002-03	Ottawa Senators	12	3	1	4	15	....	....	....	....	....
	NHL Totals	**88**	**15**	**13**	**28**	**109**	....	....	....	....	....

Signed as a free agent by **Florida**, October 4, 1993. Traded to **Los Angeles** by **Florida** for Los Angeles' 3rd round choice (Vratislav Cech) in 1997 Entry Draft, November 28, 1996. Traded to **NY Rangers** by **Los Angeles** for future considerations, November 14, 1997. Signed as a free agent by **Nashville**, July 16, 1998. Traded to **NY Rangers** by **Nashville** for future considerations, May 3, 1999. Signed as a free agent by **Ottawa**, August 1, 2002.

SMYTH, Greg

Defense. Shoots right. 6'3", 212 lbs. Born, Oakville, Ont., April 23, 1966.
(Philadelphia's 1st choice, 22nd overall, in 1984 Entry Draft).

Season	Club	GP	G	A	Pts	PIM	GP	G	A	Pts	PIM
1986-87	Philadelphia Flyers	1	0	0	0	0	1	0	0	0	2
1987-88	Philadelphia Flyers	48	1	6	7	192	5	0	0	0	38
1988-89	Quebec Nordiques	10	0	1	1	70	....	....	....	....	....
1989-90	Quebec Nordiques	13	0	0	0	57	....	....	....	....	....
1990-91	Quebec Nordiques	1	0	0	0	0	....	....	....	....	....
1991-92	Quebec Nordiques	29	0	2	2	138	....	....	....	....	....
	Calgary Flames	7	1	1	2	15	....	....	....	....	....
1992-93	Calgary Flames	35	1	2	3	95	....	....	....	....	....
1993-94	Florida Panthers	12	1	0	1	37	....	....	....	....	....
	Toronto Maple Leafs	11	0	1	1	38	....	....	....	....	....
	Chicago Blackhawks	38	0	0	0	108	6	0	0	0	0
1994-95	Chicago Blackhawks	22	0	3	3	33	....	....	....	....	....

Season	Club	GP	G	A	Pts	PIM	GP	G	A	Pts	PIM
		REGULAR SEASON					PLAYOFFS				
1996-97	Toronto Maple Leafs	2	0	0	0	0					
	NHL Totals	**229**	**4**	**16**	**20**	**783**	**12**	**0**	**0**	**0**	**40**

Traded to **Quebec** by **Philadelphia** with Philadelphia's 3rd round choice (John Tanner) in the 1989 Entry Draft for Terry Carkner, July 25, 1988. Traded to **Calgary** by **Quebec** for Martin Simard, March 10, 1992. Signed as a free agent by **Florida**, August 10, 1993. Traded to **Toronto** by **Florida** for cash, December 7, 1993. Claimed on waivers by **Chicago** from **Toronto**, January 8, 1994. Signed as a free agent by **Toronto**, August 22, 1996.

SMYTH, Kevin

Left wing. Shoots left. 6'2", 217 lbs. Born, Banff, Alta., November 22, 1973.
(Hartford's 4th choice, 79th overall, in 1992 Entry Draft).

Season	Club	GP	G	A	Pts	PIM	GP	G	A	Pts	PIM
1993-94	Hartford Whalers	21	3	2	5	10					
1994-95	Hartford Whalers	16	1	5	6	13					
1995-96	Hartford Whalers	21	2	1	3	8					
	NHL Totals	**58**	**6**	**8**	**14**	**31**					

• Brother of Ryan

Rights transferred to **Carolina** after **Hartford** franchise relocated, June 25, 1997.

SMYTH, Ryan

Left wing. Shoots left. 6'1", 195 lbs. Born, Banff, Alta., February 21, 1976.
(Edmonton's 2nd choice, 6th overall, in 1994 Entry Draft).

Season	Club	GP	G	A	Pts	PIM	GP	G	A	Pts	PIM
1994-95	Edmonton Oilers	3	0	0	0	0					
1995-96	Edmonton Oilers	48	2	9	11	28					
1996-97	Edmonton Oilers	82	39	22	61	76	12	5	5	10	12
1997-98	Edmonton Oilers	65	20	13	33	44	12	1	3	4	16
1998-99	Edmonton Oilers	71	13	18	31	62	3	3	0	3	0
99-2000	Edmonton Oilers	82	28	26	54	58	5	1	0	1	6
2000-01	Edmonton Oilers	82	31	39	70	58	6	3	4	7	4
2001-02	Edmonton Oilers	61	15	35	50	48					
2002-03	Edmonton Oilers	66	27	34	61	67	6	2	0	2	16
	NHL Totals	**560**	**175**	**196**	**371**	**441**	**44**	**15**	**12**	**27**	**54**

• Brother of Kevin

SNELL, Chris

Defense. Shoots left. 5'11", 200 lbs. Born, Regina, Sask., May 12, 1971.
(Buffalo's 8th choice, 145th overall, in 1991 Entry Draft).

Season	Club	GP	G	A	Pts	PIM	GP	G	A	Pts	PIM
1993-94	Toronto Maple Leafs	2	0	0	0	2					
1994-95	Los Angeles Kings	32	2	7	9	22					
	NHL Totals	**34**	**2**	**7**	**9**	**24**					

Signed as a free agent by **Toronto**, August 3, 1993. Traded to **Los Angeles** by **Toronto** with Eric Lacroix and Toronto's 4th round choice (Eric Belanger) in 1996 Entry Draft for Dixon Ward, Guy Leveque and Kelly Fairchild, October 3, 1994. Traded to **NY Rangers** by **Los Angeles** for Steve Larouche, January 14, 1996. Signed as a free agent by **Chicago**, August 16, 1996.

SNELL, Ron

Right wing. Shoots right. 5'10", 158 lbs. Born, Regina, Sask., August 11, 1948.
(Pittsburgh's 2nd choice, 14th overall, in 1968 Amateur Draft).

Season	Club	GP	G	A	Pts	PIM	GP	G	A	Pts	PIM
1968-69	Pittsburgh Penguins	4	3	1	4	6					
1969-70	Pittsburgh Penguins	3	0	1	1	0					
	NHL Totals	**7**	**3**	**2**	**5**	**6**					

Traded to **Hershey** (AHL) by **Pittsburgh** for cash, June, 1973.

SNELL, Ted

Right wing. Shoots right. 5'9", 190 lbs. Born, Ottawa, Ont., May 28, 1946.

Season	Club	GP	G	A	Pts	PIM	GP	G	A	Pts	PIM
1973-74	Pittsburgh Penguins	55	4	12	16	8					
1974-75	Kansas City Scouts	29	3	2	5	8					
	Detroit Red Wings	20	0	4	4	6					
	NHL Totals	**104**	**7**	**18**	**25**	**22**					

Claimed by **Springfield** (AHL) from **Boston** in Reverse Draft, June 13, 1968. Signed as a free agent by **Pittsburgh**, October, 1973. Claimed by **Kansas City** from **Pittsburgh** in Expansion Draft, June 12, 1974. Traded to **Detroit** by **Kansas City** with Bart Crashley and Larry Giroux for Guy Charron and Claude Houde, December 14, 1974.

SNEPSTS, Harold

Defense. Shoots left. 6'3", 210 lbs. Born, Edmonton, Alta., October 24, 1954.
(Vancouver's 3rd choice, 59th overall, in 1974 Amateur Draft).

Season	Club	GP	G	A	Pts	PIM	GP	G	A	Pts	PIM
1974-75	Vancouver Canucks	27	1	2	3	30					
1975-76	Vancouver Canucks	78	3	15	18	125	2	0	0	0	4
1976-77	Vancouver Canucks	79	4	18	22	149					
1977-78	Vancouver Canucks	75	4	16	20	118					
1978-79	Vancouver Canucks	76	7	24	31	130	3	0	0	0	0
1979-80	Vancouver Canucks	79	3	20	23	202	4	0	2	2	8
1980-81	Vancouver Canucks	76	3	16	19	212	3	0	0	0	8
1981-82	Vancouver Canucks	68	3	14	17	153	17	0	4	4	50
1982-83	Vancouver Canucks	46	2	8	10	80	4	1	1	2	8
1983-84	Vancouver Canucks	79	4	16	20	152	4	0	1	1	15
1984-85	Minnesota North Stars	71	0	7	7	232	9	0	0	0	24
1985-86	Detroit Red Wings	35	0	6	6	75					
1986-87	Detroit Red Wings	54	1	13	14	129	11	0	2	2	18
1987-88	Detroit Red Wings	31	1	4	5	67	10	0	0	0	40
1988-89	Vancouver Canucks	59	0	8	8	69	7	0	1	1	6
1989-90	Vancouver Canucks	39	1	3	4	26					
	St. Louis Blues	7	0	1	1	10	11	0	3	3	38
1990-91	St. Louis Blues	54	1	4	5	50	8	0	0	0	12
	NHL Totals	**1033**	**38**	**195**	**233**	**2009**	**93**	**1**	**14**	**15**	**231**

Played in NHL All-Star Game (1977, 1982)

Traded to **Minnesota** by **Vancouver** for Al MacAdam, June 21, 1984. Signed as a free agent by **Detroit**, July 31, 1985. Signed as a free agent by **Vancouver**, October 6, 1988. Traded to **St. Louis** by **Vancouver** with Rich Sutter and St. Louis' 2nd round choice (previously acquired, St. Louis selected Craig Johnson) in 1990 Entry Draft for Adrien Plavsic, Montreal's 1st round choice (previously acquired, Vancouver selected Shawn Antoski) in 1990 Entry Draft and St. Louis' 2nd round choice (later traded to Montreal – Montreal selected Craig Darby) in 1991 Entry Draft, March 6, 1990.

SNOW, Sandy

Right wing. Shoots right. 6', 175 lbs. Born, Glace Bay, N.S., November 11, 1946.

Season	Club	GP	G	A	Pts	PIM	GP	G	A	Pts	PIM
1968-69	Detroit Red Wings	3	0	0	0	2					
	NHL Totals	**3**	**0**	**0**	**0**	**2**					

Traded to **NY Rangers** by **Detroit** with Terry Sawchuk for Larry Jeffrey, June 17, 1969. Traded to **Phoenix** (WHL) by **NY Rangers** with Don Caley for Peter McDuffe, July 3, 1969.

SNUGGERUD, Dave

Right wing. Shoots left. 6', 190 lbs. Born, Minnetonka, MN, June 20, 1966.
(Buffalo's 1st choice, 1st overall, in 1987 Supplemental Draft).

Season	Club	GP	G	A	Pts	PIM	GP	G	A	Pts	PIM
1989-90	Buffalo Sabres	80	14	16	30	41	6	0	0	0	2
1990-91	Buffalo Sabres	80	9	15	24	32	6	1	3	4	4
1991-92	Buffalo Sabres	55	3	15	18	36					
	San Jose Sharks	11	0	1	1	4					
1992-93	San Jose Sharks	25	4	5	9	14					
	Philadelphia Flyers	14	0	2	2	0					
	NHL Totals	**265**	**30**	**54**	**84**	**127**	**12**	**1**	**3**	**4**	**6**

Traded to **San Jose** by **Buffalo** for Wayne Presley, March 9, 1992. Traded to **Philadelphia** by **San Jose** for Mark Pederson and future considerations, December 19, 1992.

SNYDER, Dan

Center. Shoots left. 6', 185 lbs. Born, Elmira, Ont., February 23, 1978.

Season	Club	GP	G	A	Pts	PIM	GP	G	A	Pts	PIM
2000-01	Atlanta Thrashers	2	0	0	0	0					
2001-02	Atlanta Thrashers	11	1	1	2	30					
2002-03	Atlanta Thrashers	36	10	4	14	34					
	NHL Totals	**49**	**11**	**5**	**16**	**64**					

Signed as a free agent by **Atlanta**, June 28, 1999.

SOBCHUK, Dennis

Center. Shoots left. 6'2", 176 lbs. Born, Lang, Sask., January 12, 1954.
(Philadelphia's 4th choice, 89th overall, in 1974 Amateur Draft).

Season	Club	GP	G	A	Pts	PIM	GP	G	A	Pts	PIM
1979-80	Detroit Red Wings	33	4	6	10	0					
1982-83	Quebec Nordiques	2	1	0	1	2					
	NHL Totals	**35**	**5**	**6**	**11**	**2**					

• Brother of Gene

Reclaimed by **Philadelphia** from **Edmonton** prior to Expansion Draft, June 9, 1979. Traded to **Detroit** by **Philadelphia** for Detroit's 5th round choice (Dave Michayluk) in 1981 Entry Draft, September 4, 1979. Signed as a free agent by **Quebec**, March 7, 1982.

SOBCHUK, Gene

Left wing/Center. Shoots left. 5'9", 160 lbs. Born, Lang, Sask., February 19, 1951.
(NY Rangers' 10th choice, 109th overall, in 1971 Amateur Draft).

Season	Club	GP	G	A	Pts	PIM	GP	G	A	Pts	PIM
1973-74	Vancouver Canucks	1	0	0	0	0					
	NHL Totals	**1**	**0**	**0**	**0**	**0**					

• Brother of Dennis

Claimed by **Vancouver** (Seattle-WHL) from **Vancouver** in Reverse Draft, June, 1973. Traded to **Detroit** (Virginia-AHL) by **Seattle** (WHL) for the loan of Ken Murray, February 18, 1974.

SOLHEIM, Ken

Left wing. Shoots left. 6'3", 210 lbs. Born, Hythe, Alta., March 27, 1961.
(Chicago's 4th choice, 30th overall, in 1980 Entry Draft).

Season	Club	GP	G	A	Pts	PIM	GP	G	A	Pts	PIM
1980-81	Chicago Black Hawks	5	2	0	2	0					
	Minnesota North Stars	5	2	1	3	0	2	1	0	1	0
1981-82	Minnesota North Stars	29	4	5	9	4	1	0	1	1	2
1982-83	Minnesota North Stars	25	2	4	6	4					
	Detroit Red Wings	10	0	0	0	2					
1984-85	Minnesota North Stars	55	8	10	18	19					
1985-86	Edmonton Oilers	6	1	0	1	5					
	NHL Totals	**135**	**19**	**20**	**39**	**34**	**3**	**1**	**1**	**2**	**2**

Traded to **Minnesota** by **Chicago** with Chicago's 2nd round choice (Tom Hirsch) in 1981 Entry Draft for Glen Sharpley, December 29, 1980. Traded to **Detroit** by **Minnesota** for future considerations, March 8, 1983. Traded to **Minnesota** by **Detroit** for future considerations, September 20, 1984. Signed as a free agent by **Edmonton**, August 15, 1985.

SOLINGER, Bob

Wing. Shoots left. 5'9", 170 lbs. Born, Star City, Sask., December 23, 1925.

Season	Club	GP	G	A	Pts	PIM	GP	G	A	Pts	PIM
1951-52	Toronto Maple Leafs	24	5	3	8	4					
1952-53	Toronto Maple Leafs	18	1	1	2	2					
1953-54	Toronto Maple Leafs	39	3	2	5	2					
1954-55	Toronto Maple Leafs	17	1	5	6	11					

Season	Club	GP	G	A	Pts	PIM	GP	G	A	Pts	PIM
		REGULAR SEASON					PLAYOFFS				
1959-60	Detroit Red Wings	1	0	0	0	0	....	....	....	....	....
	NHL Totals	**99**	**10**	**11**	**21**	**19**	....	....	....	....	....

Traded to **Toronto** by **Cleveland** (AHL) for Ray Ceresino, Harry Taylor and the loan of Tod Sloan for the 1949-50 season, September 6, 1949. Traded to **Detroit** (Hershey-AHL) by **Toronto** (Pittsburgh-AHL) with Gilles Mayer, Jack Price, Willie Marshall, Bob Hassard and Ray Gariepy for cash, July 7, 1956. Traded to **San Francisco** (WHL) by **Detroit** for cash, July, 1962. Traded to **NY Rangers** (LA Blades-WHL) by **San Francisco** (WHL) for Danny Belisle with NY Rangers holding right of recall, July, 1962.

SOMERS, Art

Center. Shoots left. 5'5", 167 lbs. Born, Winnipeg, Man., January 19, 1902.

Season	Club	GP	G	A	Pts	PIM	GP	G	A	Pts	PIM
1929-30	Chicago Black Hawks	44	11	13	24	74	2	0	0	0	2
1930-31	Chicago Black Hawks	33	3	6	9	33	9	0	0	0	0
1931-32	New York Rangers	48	11	15	26	45	7	0	1	1	8
1932-33 ♦	New York Rangers	48	7	15	22	28	8	1	*4	5	8
1933-34	New York Rangers	8	1	2	3	5	2	0	0	0	0
1934-35	New York Rangers	41	0	5	5	4	2	0	0	0	2
	NHL Totals	**222**	**33**	**56**	**89**	**189**	**30**	**1**	**5**	**6**	**20**

Traded to **NY Rangers** by **Chicago** with Vic Desjardins for Paul Thompson, September 27, 1931.

SOMIK, Radovan

Right wing. Shoots right. 6'2", 194 lbs. Born, Martin, Czech., May 5, 1977.
(Philadelphia's 3rd choice, 100th overall, in 1995 Entry Draft).

Season	Club	GP	G	A	Pts	PIM	GP	G	A	Pts	PIM
2002-03	Philadelphia Flyers	60	8	10	18	10	5	1	1	2	6
	NHL Totals	**60**	**8**	**10**	**18**	**10**	**5**	**1**	**1**	**2**	**6**

SOMMER, Roy

Left wing/Center. Shoots left. 6', 185 lbs. Born, Oakland, CA, April 5, 1957.
(Toronto's 7th choice, 101st overall, in 1977 Amateur Draft).

Season	Club	GP	G	A	Pts	PIM	GP	G	A	Pts	PIM
1980-81	Edmonton Oilers	3	1	0	1	7	....	....	....	....	....
	NHL Totals	**3**	**1**	**0**	**1**	**7**	....	....	....	....	....

Signed as a free agent by **Edmonton**, January 1, 1980. Signed as a free agent by **New Jersey**, September 25, 1982.

SONGIN, Tom

Right wing. Shoots right. 6'3", 195 lbs. Born, Norwood, MA, December 20, 1953.

Season	Club	GP	G	A	Pts	PIM	GP	G	A	Pts	PIM
1978-79	Boston Bruins	17	3	1	4	0	....	....	....	....	....
1979-80	Boston Bruins	17	1	3	4	16	....	....	....	....	....
1980-81	Boston Bruins	9	1	1	2	6	....	....	....	....	....
	NHL Totals	**43**	**5**	**5**	**10**	**22**	....	....	....	....	....

Signed as a free agent by **Boston**, October 10, 1978.

SONMOR, Glen

Left wing. Shoots left. 5'11", 165 lbs. Born, Moose Jaw, Sask., April 22, 1929.

Season	Club	GP	G	A	Pts	PIM	GP	G	A	Pts	PIM
1953-54	New York Rangers	15	2	0	2	17	....	....	....	....	....
1954-55	New York Rangers	13	0	0	0	4	....	....	....	....	....
	NHL Totals	**28**	**2**	**0**	**2**	**21**	....	....	....	....	....

Traded to **Cleveland** (AHL) by **NY Rangers** with Eric Pogue for Andy Bathgate and Vic Howe, November 15, 1954.

SONNENBERG, Martin

Left wing. Shoots left. 6', 197 lbs. Born, Wetaskiwin, Alta., January 23, 1978.

Season	Club	GP	G	A	Pts	PIM	GP	G	A	Pts	PIM
1998-99	Pittsburgh Penguins	44	1	1	2	19	7	0	0	0	0
99-2000	Pittsburgh Penguins	14	1	2	3	0	....	....	....	....	....
	NHL Totals	**58**	**2**	**3**	**5**	**19**	**7**	**0**	**0**	**0**	**0**

Signed as a free agent by **Pittsburgh**, October 9, 1998. Signed as a free agent by **Calgary**, July 9, 2002.

SOPEL, Brent

Defense. Shoots right. 6'1", 205 lbs. Born, Calgary, Alta., January 7, 1977.
(Vancouver's 6th choice, 144th overall, in 1995 Entry Draft).

Season	Club	GP	G	A	Pts	PIM	GP	G	A	Pts	PIM
1998-99	Vancouver Canucks	5	1	0	1	4	....	....	....	....	....
99-2000	Vancouver Canucks	18	2	4	6	12	....	....	....	....	....
2000-01	Vancouver Canucks	52	4	10	14	10	4	0	0	0	2
2001-02	Vancouver Canucks	66	8	17	25	44	6	0	2	2	2
2002-03	Vancouver Canucks	81	7	30	37	23	14	2	6	8	4
	NHL Totals	**222**	**22**	**61**	**83**	**93**	**24**	**2**	**8**	**10**	**8**

SOROCHAN, Lee

Defense. Shoots left. 5'11", 210 lbs. Born, Edmonton, Alta., September 9, 1975.
(NY Rangers' 2nd choice, 34th overall, in 1993 Entry Draft).

Season	Club	GP	G	A	Pts	PIM	GP	G	A	Pts	PIM
1998-99	Calgary Flames	2	0	0	0	0	....	....	....	....	....
99-2000	Calgary Flames	1	0	0	0	0	....	....	....	....	....
	NHL Totals	**3**	**0**	**0**	**0**	**0**	....	....	....	....	....

Traded to **Calgary** by **NY Rangers** for Chris O'Sullivan, March 23, 1999.

SORRELL, John

Left wing. Shoots left. 5'11", 155 lbs. Born, Chesterville, Ont., January 16, 1906.

Season	Club	GP	G	A	Pts	PIM	GP	G	A	Pts	PIM
1930-31	Detroit Falcons	39	9	7	16	10					
1931-32	Detroit Falcons	48	8	5	13	22	2	1	0	1	0
1932-33	Detroit Red Wings	47	14	10	24	11	4	2	2	4	4
1933-34	Detroit Red Wings	47	21	10	31	8	8	0	2	2	0
1934-35	Detroit Red Wings	47	20	16	36	12					
1935-36 ♦	Detroit Red Wings	48	13	15	28	8	7	3	4	7	0
1936-37 ♦	Detroit Red Wings	48	8	16	24	4	10	2	4	6	2
1937-38	Detroit Red Wings	23	3	7	10	0	....	....	....	....	....
	New York Americans	17	8	2	10	9	6	4	0	4	2
1938-39	New York Americans	48	13	9	22	10	2	0	0	0	0
1939-40	New York Americans	48	8	16	24	4	3	0	3	3	2
1940-41	New York Americans	30	2	6	8	2	....	....	....	....	....
	NHL Totals	**490**	**127**	**119**	**246**	**100**	**42**	**12**	**15**	**27**	**10**

Traded to **London** (IHL) by **Montreal** for cash, November 5, 1929. Traded to **Detroit** by **London** (IHL) for cash and future considerations (Herb Stuart, November 10, 1930), April 8, 1930. Traded to **NY Americans** by **Detroit** for Hap Emms, February 13, 1938. Traded to **Hershey** (AHL) by **NY Americans** (Springfield-AHL) for Joe Krol, February 14, 1941.

SOURAY, Sheldon

Defense. Shoots left. 6'4", 223 lbs. Born, Elk Point, Alta., July 13, 1976.
(New Jersey's 3rd choice, 71st overall, in 1994 Entry Draft).

Season	Club	GP	G	A	Pts	PIM	GP	G	A	Pts	PIM
1997-98	New Jersey Devils	60	3	7	10	85	3	0	1	1	2
1998-99	New Jersey Devils	70	1	7	8	110	2	0	1	1	0
99-2000	New Jersey Devils	52	0	8	8	70	....	....	....	....	....
	Montreal Canadiens	19	3	0	3	44	....	....	....	....	....
2000-01	Montreal Canadiens	52	3	8	11	95	....	....	....	....	....
2001-02	Montreal Canadiens	34	3	5	8	62	12	0	1	1	16
	NHL Totals	**287**	**13**	**35**	**48**	**466**	**17**	**0**	**3**	**3**	**18**

Traded to **Montreal** by **New Jersey** with Josh DeWolf and New Jersey's 2nd round choice (later traded to Washington – later traded to Tampa Bay – Tampa Bay selected Andreas Holmqvist) in 2001 Entry Draft for Vladimir Malakhov, March 1, 2000. • Missed majority of 2001-02 season recovering from wrist injury suffered in game vs. Tampa Bay, November 17, 2001.

SPACEK, Jaroslav

Defense. Shoots left. 5'11", 206 lbs. Born, Rokycany, Czech., February 11, 1974.
(Florida's 5th choice, 117th overall, in 1998 Entry Draft).

Season	Club	GP	G	A	Pts	PIM	GP	G	A	Pts	PIM
1998-99	Florida Panthers	63	3	12	15	28	....	....	....	....	....
99-2000	Florida Panthers	82	10	26	36	53	4	0	0	0	0
2000-01	Florida Panthers	12	2	1	3	8	....	....	....	....	....
	Chicago Blackhawks	50	5	18	23	20	....	....	....	....	....
2001-02	Chicago Blackhawks	60	3	10	13	29	....	....	....	....	....
	Columbus Blue Jackets	14	2	3	5	24	....	....	....	....	....
2002-03	Columbus Blue Jackets	81	9	36	45	70	....	....	....	....	....
	NHL Totals	**362**	**34**	**106**	**140**	**232**	**4**	**0**	**0**	**0**	**0**

Traded to **Chicago** by **Florida** for Anders Eriksson, November 6, 2000. Traded to **Columbus** by **Chicago** with Chicago's 2nd round choice (Dan Fritsche) in 2003 Entry Draft for Lyle Odelein, March 19, 2002.

SPANHEL, Martin

Left wing. Shoots left. 6'2", 206 lbs. Born, Zlin, Czech., July 1, 1977.
(Philadelphia's 6th choice, 152nd overall, in 1995 Entry Draft).

Season	Club	GP	G	A	Pts	PIM	GP	G	A	Pts	PIM
2000-01	Columbus Blue Jackets	6	1	0	1	2	....	....	....	....	....
2001-02	Columbus Blue Jackets	4	1	0	1	2	....	....	....	....	....
	NHL Totals	**10**	**2**	**0**	**2**	**4**	....	....	....	....	....

Traded to **San Jose** by **Philadelphia** with Philadelphia's 1st round choice (later traded to Buffalo – later traded to Phoenix – Phoenix selected Daniel Briere) in 1996 Entry Draft and Philadelphia's 4th round choice (later traded to Buffalo – Buffalo selected Mike Martone) in 1996 Entry Draft for Pat Falloon, November 16, 1995. Traded to **Buffalo** by **San Jose** with Vaclav Varada and Philadelphia's 1st (previously acquired, later traded to Phoenix – Phoenix selected Daniel Briere) and 4th (previously acquired, Buffalo selected Mike Martone) round choices in 1996 Entry Draft for Doug Bodger, November 16, 1995. Signed as a free agent by **Columbus**, May 30, 2000.

SPARROW, Emory

Right wing/Center. Shoots left. 5'11", 180 lbs. Born, Hartney, Man., September 15, 1898.

Season	Club	GP	G	A	Pts	PIM	GP	G	A	Pts	PIM
1924-25	Boston Bruins	8	0	0	0	4	....	....	....	....	....
	NHL Totals	**8**	**0**	**0**	**0**	**4**	....	....	....	....	....

Loaned to **Boston** by **Calgary** (WCHL) for cash, December 8, 1924. Returned to **Calgary** (WCHL) from **Boston** after breaking training rules, January 5, 1925. Traded to **Edmonton** (WHL) by **Calgary** (WHL) for cash, January 19, 1926. Traded to **Detroit** by **Edmonton** (WHL) for cash, October 5, 1926.

SPECK, Fred

Center. Shoots left. 5'9", 160 lbs. Born, Thorold, Ont., July 22, 1947.

Season	Club	GP	G	A	Pts	PIM	GP	G	A	Pts	PIM
1968-69	Detroit Red Wings	5	0	0	0	2	....	....	....	....	....
1969-70	Detroit Red Wings	5	0	0	0	0	....	....	....	....	....
1971-72	Vancouver Canucks	18	1	2	3	0	....	....	....	....	....
	NHL Totals	**28**	**1**	**2**	**3**	**2**	....	....	....	....	....

Claimed by **Vancouver** from **Detroit** in Intra-League Draft, June 8, 1971. Traded to **Minnesota** by **Vancouver** for cash, August, 1972.

SPEER, Bill

Defense. Shoots left. 5'11", 205 lbs. Born, Lindsay, Ont., March 20, 1942.

Season	Club	GP	G	A	Pts	PIM	GP	G	A	Pts	PIM
1967-68	Pittsburgh Penguins	68	3	13	16	44	....	....	....	....	....
1968-69	Pittsburgh Penguins	34	1	4	5	27	....	....	....	....	....
1969-70 ♦	Boston Bruins	27	1	3	4	4	8	1	0	1	4
1970-71	Boston Bruins	1	0	0	0	4	....	....	....	....	....
	NHL Totals	**130**	**5**	**20**	**25**	**79**	**8**	**1**	**0**	**1**	**4**

Traded to **Pittsburgh** by **Cleveland** (AHL) for cash, August 11, 1966. Loaned to **Buffalo** (AHL) by **Pittsburgh** for 1966-67 season, October, 1966. Claimed by **Boston** from **Pittsburgh** in Intra-League Draft, June 11, 1969. Traded to **Providence** (AHL) by **Boston** for cash, February, 1971. Claimed by **NY Islanders** from **Providence** (AHL) in Inter-League Draft, June, 1972.

SPEERS, Ted

Right wing. Shoots right. 5'11", 200 lbs. Born, Ann Arbor, MI, January 28, 1961.

Season	Club	GP	G	A	Pts	PIM	GP	G	A	Pts	PIM
		REGULAR SEASON					PLAYOFFS				
1985-86	Detroit Red Wings	4	1	1	2	0	....	....	....	....	....
	NHL Totals	**4**	**1**	**1**	**2**	**0**	....	....	....	....	....

Signed as a free agent by **Detroit**, September, 1983.

SPENCE, Gordon

Left wing. Shoots left. 5'7", 150 lbs. Born, Haileybury, Ont., July 25, 1897.

Season	Club	GP	G	A	Pts	PIM	GP	G	A	Pts	PIM
1925-26	Toronto St. Pats	3	0	0	0	0	....	....	....	....	....
	NHL Totals	**3**	**0**	**0**	**0**	**0**	....	....	....	....	....

Signed as a free agent by **Toronto**, December 31, 1925.

SPENCER, Brian

Left wing. Shoots left. 5'11", 185 lbs. Born, Fort St. James, B.C., September 3, 1949.
(Toronto's 5th choice, 55th overall, in 1969 Amateur Draft).

Season	Club	GP	G	A	Pts	PIM	GP	G	A	Pts	PIM
1969-70	Toronto Maple Leafs	9	0	0	0	12	....	....	....	....	....
1970-71	Toronto Maple Leafs	50	9	15	24	115	6	0	1	1	17
1971-72	Toronto Maple Leafs	36	1	5	6	65	....	....	....	....	....
1972-73	New York Islanders	78	14	24	38	90	....	....	....	....	....
1973-74	New York Islanders	54	5	16	21	65	....	....	....	....	....
	Buffalo Sabres	13	3	2	5	4	....	....	....	....	....
1974-75	Buffalo Sabres	73	12	29	41	77	16	0	4	4	8
1975-76	Buffalo Sabres	77	13	26	39	70	9	1	0	1	4
1976-77	Buffalo Sabres	77	14	15	29	55	6	0	0	0	0
1977-78	Pittsburgh Penguins	79	9	11	20	81	....	....	....	....	....
1978-79	Pittsburgh Penguins	7	0	0	0	0	....	....	....	....	....
	NHL Totals	**553**	**80**	**143**	**223**	**634**	**37**	**1**	**5**	**6**	**29**

Claimed by **NY Islanders** from **Toronto** in Expansion Draft, June 6, 1972. Traded to **Buffalo** by **NY Islanders** for Doug Rombough, March 10, 1974. Traded to **Pittsburgh** by **Buffalo** for Ron Schock, September 20, 1977.

SPENCER, Irv

Defense. Shoots left. 5'10", 180 lbs. Born, Sudbury, Ont., December 4, 1937.

Season	Club	GP	G	A	Pts	PIM	GP	G	A	Pts	PIM
1959-60	New York Rangers	32	1	2	3	20	....	....	....	....	....
1960-61	New York Rangers	56	1	8	9	30	....	....	....	....	....
1961-62	New York Rangers	43	2	10	12	31	1	0	0	0	2
1962-63	Boston Bruins	69	5	17	22	34	....	....	....	....	....
1963-64	Detroit Red Wings	25	3	0	3	8	11	0	0	0	0
1964-65	Detroit Red Wings	....	....	....	....	....	1	0	0	0	4
1965-66	Detroit Red Wings	....	....	....	....	....	3	0	0	0	2
1967-68	Detroit Red Wings	5	0	1	1	4	....	....	....	....	....
	NHL Totals	**230**	**12**	**38**	**50**	**127**	**16**	**0**	**0**	**0**	**8**

Claimed by **NY Rangers** from **Montreal** in Intra-League Draft, June 10, 1959. Claimed by **Boston** from **NY Rangers** in Intra-League Draft, June 4, 1962. Claimed by **Detroit** from **Boston** in Intra-League Draft, June 4, 1963. Traded to **San Diego** (WHL) by **Detroit** for cash, June 12, 1970. Traded to **Detroit** by **San Diego** (WHL) for cash, May, 1971. Claimed by **Vancouver** from **Tidewater** (AHL) in Inter-League Draft, June 7, 1971. Traded to **Detroit** by **Vancouver** with Bob Dillabough for John Cunniff and Gary Bredin, June 8, 1971.

SPEYER, Chris

Defense. Shoots left. 5'10", 170 lbs. Born, Toronto, Ont., February 6, 1907.

Season	Club	GP	G	A	Pts	PIM	GP	G	A	Pts	PIM
1923-24	Toronto St. Pats	3	0	0	0	0	....	....	....	....	....
1924-25	Toronto St. Pats	2	0	0	0	0	....	....	....	....	....
1933-34	New York Americans	9	0	0	0	0	....	....	....	....	....
	NHL Totals	**14**	**0**	**0**	**0**	**0**	....	....	....	....	....

Signed as a free agent by **Toronto**, February 23, 1924. Signed as a free agent by **NY Americans**, November 1, 1933.

SPEZZA, Jason

Center. Shoots right. 6'2", 211 lbs. Born, Mississauga, Ont., June 13, 1983.
(Ottawa's 1st choice, 2nd overall, in 2001 Entry Draft).

Season	Club	GP	G	A	Pts	PIM	GP	G	A	Pts	PIM
2002-03	Ottawa Senators	33	7	14	21	8	3	1	1	2	0
	NHL Totals	**33**	**7**	**14**	**21**	**8**	**3**	**1**	**1**	**2**	**0**

SPRING, Corey

Right wing. Shoots right. 6'4", 214 lbs. Born, Cranbrook, B.C., May 31, 1971.

Season	Club	GP	G	A	Pts	PIM	GP	G	A	Pts	PIM
1997-98	Tampa Bay Lightning	8	1	0	1	10	....	....	....	....	....
1998-99	Tampa Bay Lightning	8	0	1	1	2	....	....	....	....	....
	NHL Totals	**16**	**1**	**1**	**2**	**12**	....	....	....	....	....

Son of Frank

Signed as a free agent by **Tampa Bay**, July 24, 1995.

SPRING, Don

Defense. Shoots left. 5'11", 195 lbs. Born, Maracaibo, Venezuela, June 15, 1959.

Season	Club	GP	G	A	Pts	PIM	GP	G	A	Pts	PIM
1980-81	Winnipeg Jets	80	1	18	19	18	....	....	....	....	....
1981-82	Winnipeg Jets	78	0	16	16	21	4	0	0	0	4
1982-83	Winnipeg Jets	80	0	16	16	37	2	0	0	0	6
1983-84	Winnipeg Jets	21	0	4	4	4	....	....	....	....	....
	NHL Totals	**259**	**1**	**54**	**55**	**80**	**6**	**0**	**0**	**0**	**10**

Signed as a free agent by **Winnipeg**, May 22, 1980.

SPRING, Frank

Right wing. Shoots right. 6'3", 216 lbs. Born, Cranbrook, B.C., October 19, 1949.
(Boston's 2nd choice, 4th overall, in 1969 Amateur Draft).

Season	Club	GP	G	A	Pts	PIM	GP	G	A	Pts	PIM
1969-70	Boston Bruins	1	0	0	0	0	....	....	....	....	....
1973-74	St. Louis Blues	2	0	0	0	0	....	....	....	....	....
1974-75	St. Louis Blues	3	0	0	0	0	....	....	....	....	....
	California Golden Seals	28	3	8	11	6	....	....	....	....	....
1975-76	California Golden Seals	1	0	2	2	0	....	....	....	....	....
1976-77	Cleveland Barons	26	11	10	21	6	....	....	....	....	....
	NHL Totals	**61**	**14**	**20**	**34**	**12**	....	....	....	....	....

Claimed by **Philadelphia** from **Boston** in Intra-League Draft, June 8, 1971. Traded to **St. Louis** by **Philadelphia** for Ray Schultz, December, 1973. Traded to **California** by **St. Louis** for Bruce Affleck, January 9, 1975. Transferred to **Cleveland** after **California** franchise relocated, August 26, 1976. Traded to **NY Rangers** by **Indianapolis** (WHA) for Bill Goldsworthy, December, 1977.

SPRING, Jesse

Defense. Shoots left. 6', 185 lbs. Born, Alba, PA, January 18, 1901.

Season	Club	GP	G	A	Pts	PIM	GP	G	A	Pts	PIM
1923-24	Hamilton Tigers	20	3	3	6	20	....	....	....	....	....
1924-25	Hamilton Tigers	29	2	1	3	11	....	....	....	....	....
1925-26	Pittsburgh Pirates	32	5	0	5	23	2	0	2	2	2
1926-27	Toronto St. Pats/Maple Leafs	2	0	0	0	0	....	....	....	....	....
1928-29	New York Americans	23	0	0	0	0	....	....	....	....	....
	Pittsburgh Pirates	5	0	0	0	2	....	....	....	....	....
1929-30	Pittsburgh Pirates	22	1	0	1	18	....	....	....	....	....
	NHL Totals	**133**	**11**	**4**	**15**	**74**	**2**	**0**	**2**	**2**	**2**

Signed as a free agent by **Hamilton**, December 18, 1923. Transferred to **NY Americans** after NHL club purchased **Hamilton** franchise, September 26, 1925. Loaned to **Pittsburgh** by **NY Americans** for 1925-26 season for future considerations (Joe Miller, February 23, 1926), November 25, 1925. Traded to **Toronto** by **NY Americans** for Laurie Scott, November 15, 1926. Traded to **NY Americans** by **Toronto** for cash, January, 1927. Traded to **Pittsburgh** by **NY Americans** with the loan of Edmond Bouchard for remainder of 1928-29 season for the loan of Tex White for remainder of 1928-29 season, February 15, 1929. Signed as a free agent by **Detroit**, November 6, 1930.

SPRUCE, Andy

Left wing. Shoots left. 5'11", 178 lbs. Born, London, Ont., April 17, 1954.
(Vancouver's 5th choice, 95th overall, in 1974 Amateur Draft).

Season	Club	GP	G	A	Pts	PIM	GP	G	A	Pts	PIM
1976-77	Vancouver Canucks	51	9	6	15	37	....	....	....	....	....
1977-78	Colorado Rockies	74	19	21	40	43	2	0	2	2	0
1978-79	Colorado Rockies	47	3	15	18	31	....	....	....	....	....
	NHL Totals	**172**	**31**	**42**	**73**	**111**	**2**	**0**	**2**	**2**	**0**

Signed as a free agent by **Colorado**, October 5, 1977.

SRSEN, Tomas

Right wing. Shoots left. 5'11", 180 lbs. Born, Olomouc, Czech., August 25, 1966.
(Edmonton's 7th choice, 147th overall, in 1987 Entry Draft).

Season	Club	GP	G	A	Pts	PIM	GP	G	A	Pts	PIM
1990-91	Edmonton Oilers	2	0	0	0	0	....	....	....	....	....
	NHL Totals	**2**	**0**	**0**	**0**	**0**	....	....	....	....	....

STACKHOUSE, Ron

Defense. Shoots right. 6'3", 210 lbs. Born, Haliburton, Ont., August 26, 1949.
(Oakland's 2nd choice, 18th overall, in 1969 Amateur Draft).

Season	Club	GP	G	A	Pts	PIM	GP	G	A	Pts	PIM
1970-71	California Seals	78	8	24	32	73	....	....	....	....	....
1971-72	California Golden Seals	5	1	3	4	6	....	....	....	....	....
	Detroit Red Wings	74	5	25	30	83	....	....	....	....	....
1972-73	Detroit Red Wings	78	5	29	34	82	....	....	....	....	....
1973-74	Detroit Red Wings	33	2	14	16	33	....	....	....	....	....
	Pittsburgh Penguins	36	4	15	19	33	....	....	....	....	....
1974-75	Pittsburgh Penguins	72	15	45	60	52	9	2	6	8	10
1975-76	Pittsburgh Penguins	80	11	60	71	76	3	0	0	0	0
1976-77	Pittsburgh Penguins	80	7	34	41	72	3	2	1	3	0
1977-78	Pittsburgh Penguins	50	5	15	20	36	....	....	....	....	....
1978-79	Pittsburgh Penguins	75	10	33	43	54	7	0	0	0	4
1979-80	Pittsburgh Penguins	78	6	27	33	36	5	1	0	1	18
1980-81	Pittsburgh Penguins	74	6	29	35	86	4	0	1	1	6
1981-82	Pittsburgh Penguins	76	2	19	21	102	1	0	0	0	0
	NHL Totals	**889**	**87**	**372**	**459**	**824**	**32**	**5**	**8**	**13**	**38**

Played in NHL All-Star Game (1980)

Traded to **Detroit** by **California** for Tom Webster, October 22, 1971. Traded to **Pittsburgh** by **Detroit** for Jack Lynch and Jim Rutherford, January 17, 1974.

STACKHOUSE, Ted

Defense. Shoots right. 6'1", 200 lbs. Born, Wolfville, N.S.,

Season	Club	GP	G	A	Pts	PIM	GP	G	A	Pts	PIM
1921-22 ♦	Toronto St. Pats	13	0	0	0	2	1	0	0	0	0
	Toronto St. Pats (Cup)	....	....	....	....	....	*4*	*0*	*0*	*0*	*0*
	NHL Totals	**13**	**0**	**0**	**0**	**2**	**1**	**0**	**0**	**0**	**0**

Signed as a free agent by **Toronto**, December 23, 1921. • Released by **Toronto**, January 22, 1922. Signed as a free agent by **Toronto**, January 25, 1922.

STAHAN, Butch

Defense. Shoots left. 6'1", 195 lbs. Born, Minnedosa, Man., October 29, 1918.

Season	Club	GP	G	A	Pts	PIM	GP	G	A	Pts	PIM
		Regular Season					Playoffs				
1944-45	Montreal Canadiens	....	....	....	....	....	3	0	1	1	2
	NHL Totals	....	....	....	....	....	**3**	**0**	**1**	**1**	**2**

Traded to **Buffalo** (AHL) by **Montreal** with Jim McFadden for Tom Rockey and cash, October 8, 1946.

STAIOS, Steve

Defense. Shoots right. 6'1", 200 lbs. Born, Hamilton, Ont., July 28, 1973.
(St. Louis' 1st choice, 27th overall, in 1991 Entry Draft).

Season	Club	GP	G	A	Pts	PIM	GP	G	A	Pts	PIM
1995-96	Boston Bruins	12	0	0	0	4	3	0	0	0	0
1996-97	Boston Bruins	54	3	8	11	71	....	....	....	....	....
	Vancouver Canucks	9	0	6	6	20	....	....	....	....	....
1997-98	Vancouver Canucks	77	3	4	7	134	....	....	....	....	....
1998-99	Vancouver Canucks	57	0	2	2	54	....	....	....	....	....
99-2000	Atlanta Thrashers	27	2	3	5	66	....	....	....	....	....
2000-01	Atlanta Thrashers	70	9	13	22	137	....	....	....	....	....
2001-02	Edmonton Oilers	73	5	5	10	108	....	....	....	....	....
2002-03	Edmonton Oilers	76	5	21	26	96	6	0	0	0	4
	NHL Totals	**455**	**27**	**62**	**89**	**690**	**9**	**0**	**0**	**0**	**4**

Traded to **Boston** by **St. Louis** with Kevin Sawyer for Steve Leach, March 8, 1996. Claimed on waivers by **Vancouver** from **Boston**, March 18, 1997. Claimed by **Atlanta** from **Vancouver** in Expansion Draft, June 25, 1999. • Missed majority of 1999-2000 season recovering from knee injury suffered in game vs. Colorado, October 23, 1999. Traded to **New Jersey** by **Atlanta** for New Jersey's 9th round choice (Simon Gamache) in 2000 Entry Draft, June 12, 2000. Traded to **Atlanta** by **New Jersey** for future considerations, July 10, 2000. Signed as a free agent by **Edmonton**, July 12, 2001.

STAJAN, Matt

Center. Shoots left. 6'1", 178 lbs. Born, Mississauga, Ont., December 19, 1983.
(Toronto's 2nd choice, 57th overall, in 2002 Entry Draft).

Season	Club	GP	G	A	Pts	PIM	GP	G	A	Pts	PIM
2002-03	Toronto Maple Leafs	1	1	0	1	0	....	....	....	....	....
	NHL Totals	**1**	**1**	**0**	**1**	**0**	....	....	....	....	....

• One of only three players (Rolly Huard, Dean Morton) to score a goal in only NHL game.

STAJDUHAR, Nick

Defense. Shoots left. 6'3", 200 lbs. Born, Kitchener, Ont., December 6, 1974.
(Edmonton's 2nd choice, 16th overall, in 1993 Entry Draft).

Season	Club	GP	G	A	Pts	PIM	GP	G	A	Pts	PIM
1995-96	Edmonton Oilers	2	0	0	0	4	....	....	....	....	....
	NHL Totals	**2**	**0**	**0**	**0**	**4**	....	....	....	....	....

STALEY, Al

Center. Shoots right. 6'1", 175 lbs. Born, Regina, Sask., September 21, 1928.

Season	Club	GP	G	A	Pts	PIM	GP	G	A	Pts	PIM
1948-49	New York Rangers	1	0	1	1	0	....	....	....	....	....
	NHL Totals	**1**	**0**	**1**	**1**	**0**	....	....	....	....	....

STAMLER, Lorne

Left wing. Shoots left. 6', 190 lbs. Born, Winnipeg, Man., August 9, 1951.
(Los Angeles' 7th choice, 103rd overall, in 1971 Amateur Draft).

Season	Club	GP	G	A	Pts	PIM	GP	G	A	Pts	PIM
1976-77	Los Angeles Kings	7	2	1	3	2	....	....	....	....	....
1977-78	Los Angeles Kings	2	0	0	0	0	....	....	....	....	....
1978-79	Toronto Maple Leafs	45	4	3	7	2	....	....	....	....	....
1979-80	Winnipeg Jets	62	8	7	15	12	....	....	....	....	....
	NHL Totals	**116**	**14**	**11**	**25**	**16**	....	....	....	....	....

Traded to **Toronto** by **Los Angeles** with Dave Hutchison for Brian Glennie, Scott Garland, Kurt Walker and Toronto's 2nd round choice (Mark Hardy) in 1979 Entry Draft, June 14, 1978. Claimed by **Winnipeg** from **Toronto** in Expansion Draft, June 13, 1979. Signed as a free agent by **NY Islanders**, October 8, 1980.

STANDING, George

Right wing. Shoots right. 5'10", 190 lbs. Born, Toronto, Ont., August 3, 1941.

Season	Club	GP	G	A	Pts	PIM	GP	G	A	Pts	PIM
1967-68	Minnesota North Stars	2	0	0	0	0	....	....	....	....	....
	NHL Totals	**2**	**0**	**0**	**0**	**0**	....	....	....	....	....

Signed as a free agent by **Minnesota**, September, 1967.

STANFIELD, Fred

Left wing. Shoots left. 5'10", 185 lbs. Born, Toronto, Ont., May 4, 1944.

Season	Club	GP	G	A	Pts	PIM	GP	G	A	Pts	PIM
1964-65	Chicago Black Hawks	58	7	10	17	14	14	2	1	3	2
1965-66	Chicago Black Hawks	39	2	2	4	2	5	0	0	0	2
1966-67	Chicago Black Hawks	10	1	0	1	0	1	0	0	0	0
1967-68	Boston Bruins	73	20	44	64	10	4	0	1	1	0
1968-69	Boston Bruins	71	25	29	54	22	10	2	2	4	0
1969-70 ◆	Boston Bruins	73	23	35	58	14	14	4	12	16	6
1970-71	Boston Bruins	75	24	52	76	12	7	3	4	7	0
1971-72 ◆	Boston Bruins	78	23	56	79	12	15	7	9	16	0
1972-73	Boston Bruins	78	20	58	78	10	5	1	1	2	0
1973-74	Minnesota North Stars	71	16	28	44	10	....	....	....	....	....
1974-75	Minnesota North Stars	40	8	18	26	12	....	....	....	....	....
	Buffalo Sabres	32	12	21	33	4	17	2	4	6	0
1975-76	Buffalo Sabres	80	18	30	48	4	9	0	1	1	0
1976-77	Buffalo Sabres	79	9	14	23	6	5	0	0	0	0
1977-78	Buffalo Sabres	57	3	8	11	2	....	....	....	....	....
	NHL Totals	**914**	**211**	**405**	**616**	**134**	**106**	**21**	**35**	**56**	**10**

• Brother of Jack and Jim

Traded to **Boston** by **Chicago** with Phil Esposito and Ken Hodge for Gilles Marotte, Pit Martin and Jack Norris, May 15, 1967. Traded to **Minnesota** by **Boston** for Gilles Gilbert, May 22, 1973. Traded to **Buffalo** by **Minnesota** for Norm Gratton and Buffalo's 3rd round choice (Ron Zanussi) in 1976 Amateur Draft, January 27, 1975.

STANFIELD, Jack

Left wing. Shoots left. 5'11", 176 lbs. Born, Toronto, Ont., May 30, 1942.

Season	Club	GP	G	A	Pts	PIM	GP	G	A	Pts	PIM
1965-66	Chicago Black Hawks	....	....	....	....	....	1	0	0	0	0
	NHL Totals	....	....	....	....	....	**1**	**0**	**0**	**0**	**0**

• Brother of Fred and Jim

Claimed by **Vancouver** (WHL) from **Chicago** in Reverse Draft, June, 1969. NHL rights transferred to **Vancouver** after NHL club purchased **Vancouver** (WHL) franchise, December 19, 1969.

STANFIELD, Jim

Center/Right wing. Shoots left. 5'10", 160 lbs. Born, Toronto, Ont., January 1, 1947.

Season	Club	GP	G	A	Pts	PIM	GP	G	A	Pts	PIM
1969-70	Los Angeles Kings	1	0	0	0	0	....	....	....	....	....
1970-71	Los Angeles Kings	2	0	0	0	0	....	....	....	....	....
1971-72	Los Angeles Kings	4	0	1	1	0	....	....	....	....	....
	NHL Totals	**7**	**0**	**1**	**1**	**0**	....	....	....	....	....

• Brother of Fred and Jack

Traded to **Los Angeles** by **Chicago** with Gilles Marotte and Denis DeJordy for Bryan Campbell, Bill White and Gerry Desjardins, February 20, 1970. Traded to **Portland** (WHL) by **Los Angeles** with Mike Keeler and Glen Toner for John VanHorlick, December, 1972. Traded to **Philadelphia** by **Portland** (WHL) for cash, May, 1973. Traded to **San Diego** (WHL) by **Philadelphia** with Tom Trevelyan, Bob Currier and Bob Hurlburt for Bruce Cowick, May 25, 1973. Traded to **St. Louis** (Denver-WHL) by **San Diego** (WHL) for Bernie MacNeil, January 16, 1974.

STANKIEWICZ, Ed

Center. Shoots right. 5'9", 165 lbs. Born, Kitchener, Ont., December 1, 1929.

Season	Club	GP	G	A	Pts	PIM	GP	G	A	Pts	PIM
1953-54	Detroit Red Wings	1	0	0	0	2	....	....	....	....	....
1955-56	Detroit Red Wings	5	0	0	0	0	....	....	....	....	....
	NHL Totals	**6**	**0**	**0**	**0**	**2**	....	....	....	....	....

• Brother of Myron

Traded to **LA Blades** (WHL) by **Detroit** for cash, July, 1962.

STANKIEWICZ, Myron

Left wing. Shoots left. 5'11", 185 lbs. Born, Kitchener, Ont., December 4, 1935.

Season	Club	GP	G	A	Pts	PIM	GP	G	A	Pts	PIM
1968-69	St. Louis Blues	16	0	2	2	11	....	....	....	....	....
	Philadelphia Flyers	19	0	5	5	25	1	0	0	0	0
	NHL Totals	**35**	**0**	**7**	**7**	**36**	**1**	**0**	**0**	**0**	**0**

• Brother of Ed

Traded to **Quebec** (QHL) by **Detroit** (Edmonton-WHL) for Roger Dejordy, January, 1959. Traded to **Hershey** (AHL) by **Quebec** (AHL) with Al Millar for Claude Dufour, June, 1960. Claimed by **St. Louis** from **Hershey** (AHL) in Inter-League Draft, June 11, 1968. Traded to **Los Angeles** by **St. Louis** for Terry Gray, June 11, 1968. Claimed by **St. Louis** from **Los Angeles** in Intra-League Draft, June 12, 1968. Claimed on waivers by **Philadelphia** from **St. Louis**, January 16, 1969.

STANLEY, Allan

HHOF

Defense. Shoots left. 6'1", 170 lbs. Born, Timmins, Ont., March 1, 1926.

Season	Club	GP	G	A	Pts	PIM	GP	G	A	Pts	PIM
1948-49	New York Rangers	40	2	8	10	22	....	....	....	....	....
1949-50	New York Rangers	55	4	4	8	58	12	2	5	7	10
1950-51	New York Rangers	70	7	14	21	75	....	....	....	....	....
1951-52	New York Rangers	50	5	14	19	52	....	....	....	....	....
1952-53	New York Rangers	70	5	12	17	52	....	....	....	....	....
1953-54	New York Rangers	10	0	2	2	11	....	....	....	....	....
1954-55	New York Rangers	12	0	1	1	2	....	....	....	....	....
	Chicago Black Hawks	52	10	15	25	22	....	....	....	....	....
1955-56	Chicago Black Hawks	59	4	14	18	70	....	....	....	....	....
1956-57	Boston Bruins	60	6	25	31	45	....	....	....	....	....
1957-58	Boston Bruins	69	6	25	31	37	12	1	3	4	6
1958-59	Toronto Maple Leafs	70	1	22	23	47	12	0	3	3	2
1959-60	Toronto Maple Leafs	64	10	23	33	22	10	2	3	5	2
1960-61	Toronto Maple Leafs	68	9	25	34	42	5	0	3	3	0
1961-62 ◆	Toronto Maple Leafs	60	9	26	35	24	12	0	3	3	6
1962-63 ◆	Toronto Maple Leafs	61	4	15	19	22	10	1	6	7	8
1963-64 ◆	Toronto Maple Leafs	70	6	21	27	60	14	1	6	7	20
1964-65	Toronto Maple Leafs	64	2	15	17	30	6	0	1	1	12
1965-66	Toronto Maple Leafs	59	4	14	18	35	1	0	0	0	0
1966-67 ◆	Toronto Maple Leafs	53	1	12	13	20	12	0	2	2	10
1967-68	Toronto Maple Leafs	64	1	13	14	16	....	....	....	....	....
1968-69	Philadelphia Flyers	64	4	13	17	28	3	0	1	1	4
	NHL Totals	**1244**	**100**	**333**	**433**	**792**	**109**	**7**	**36**	**43**	**80**

NHL Second All-Star Team (1960, 1961, 1966)

Played in NHL All-Star Game (1955, 1957, 1960, 1962, 1963, 1967, 1968)

Traded to **NY Rangers** by **Providence** (AHL) for Eddie Kullman, Moe Morris, cash and future considerations (Buck Davies, June, 1949), December 9, 1948. Traded to **Chicago** by **NY Rangers** with Nick Mickoski and Rich Lamoureux for Bill Gadsby and Pete Conacher, November 23, 1954. Traded to **Boston** by **Chicago** for cash, October 8, 1956. Traded to **Toronto** by **Boston** for Jim Morrison, October 8, 1958. Claimed by **Philadelphia** (Quebec-AHL) from **Toronto** in Reverse Draft, June 13, 1968.

STANLEY, Barney

HHOF

Right wing. Shoots left. 6', 175 lbs. Born, Paisley, Ont., January 1, 1893.

Season	Club	Regular Season GP	G	A	Pts	PIM	Playoffs GP	G	A	Pts	PIM
1927-28	Chicago Black Hawks	1	0	0	0	0	....	....	....	....	....
	NHL Totals	**1**	**0**	**0**	**0**	**0**	....	....	....	....	....

Signed as a free agent by **Chicago** as manager/coach, September, 1927.

STANLEY, Daryl

Defense/Left wing. Shoots left. 6'2", 200 lbs. Born, Winnipeg, Man., December 2, 1962.

Season	Club	Regular Season GP	G	A	Pts	PIM	Playoffs GP	G	A	Pts	PIM
1983-84	Philadelphia Flyers	23	1	4	5	71	3	0	0	0	19
1985-86	Philadelphia Flyers	33	0	2	2	69	1	0	0	0	2
1986-87	Philadelphia Flyers	33	1	2	3	76	13	0	0	0	9
1987-88	Vancouver Canucks	57	2	7	9	151	....	....	....	....	....
1988-89	Vancouver Canucks	20	3	1	4	14	....	....	....	....	....
1989-90	Vancouver Canucks	23	1	1	2	27	....	....	....	....	....
	NHL Totals	**189**	**8**	**17**	**25**	**408**	**17**	**0**	**0**	**0**	**30**

Signed as a free agent by **Philadelphia**, October 9, 1981. Traded to **Vancouver** by **Philadelphia** with Darren Jensen for Wendell Young and Vancouver's 3rd round choice (Kimbi Daniels) in 1990 Entry Draft, August 31, 1987.

STANOWSKI, Wally

Defense. Shoots left. 5'11", 180 lbs. Born, Winnipeg, Man., April 28, 1919.

Season	Club	Regular Season GP	G	A	Pts	PIM	Playoffs GP	G	A	Pts	PIM
1939-40	Toronto Maple Leafs	27	2	7	9	11	10	1	0	1	2
1940-41	Toronto Maple Leafs	47	7	14	21	35	7	0	3	3	2
1941-42 ♦	Toronto Maple Leafs	24	1	7	8	10	13	2	8	10	2
1944-45 ♦	Toronto Maple Leafs	34	2	9	11	16	13	0	1	1	5
1945-46	Toronto Maple Leafs	45	3	10	13	10	....	....	....	....	....
1946-47 ♦	Toronto Maple Leafs	51	3	16	19	12	8	0	0	0	0
1947-48 ♦	Toronto Maple Leafs	54	2	11	13	12	9	0	2	2	2
1948-49	New York Rangers	60	1	8	9	16	....	....	....	....	....
1949-50	New York Rangers	37	1	1	2	10	....	....	....	....	....
1950-51	New York Rangers	49	1	5	6	28	....	....	....	....	....
	NHL Totals	**428**	**23**	**88**	**111**	**160**	**60**	**3**	**14**	**17**	**13**

NHL First All-Star Team (1941)

Played in NHL All-Star Game (1947)

Rights traded to **Toronto** by **NY Americans** for Jack Shill, October 17, 1937. Traded to **NY Rangers** by **Toronto** with Moe Morris for Cal Gardner, Bill Juzda, Rene Trudell and the rights to Frank Mathers, April 26, 1948.

STANTON, Paul

Defense. Shoots right. 6'1", 195 lbs. Born, Boston, MA, June 22, 1967.
(Pittsburgh's 8th choice, 149th overall, in 1985 Entry Draft).

Season	Club	Regular Season GP	G	A	Pts	PIM	Playoffs GP	G	A	Pts	PIM
1990-91 ♦	Pittsburgh Penguins	75	5	18	23	40	22	1	2	3	24
1991-92 ♦	Pittsburgh Penguins	54	2	8	10	62	21	1	7	8	42
1992-93	Pittsburgh Penguins	77	4	12	16	97	1	0	1	1	0
1993-94	Boston Bruins	71	3	7	10	54	....	....	....	....	....
1994-95	New York Islanders	18	0	4	4	9	....	....	....	....	....
	NHL Totals	**295**	**14**	**49**	**63**	**262**	**44**	**2**	**10**	**12**	**66**

Traded to **Boston** by **Pittsburgh** for Boston's 3rd round choice (Greg Crozier) in 1994 Entry Draft, October 8, 1993. Traded to **NY Islanders** by **Boston** for NY Islanders' 8th round choice (later traded to Ottawa – Ottawa selected Ray Schultz) in 1995 Entry Draft, February 10, 1995.

STAPLETON, Brian

Right wing. Shoots right. 6'2", 190 lbs. Born, Fort Erie, Ont., December 25, 1951.

Season	Club	Regular Season GP	G	A	Pts	PIM	Playoffs GP	G	A	Pts	PIM
1975-76	Washington Capitals	1	0	0	0	0	....	....	....	....	....
	NHL Totals	**1**	**0**	**0**	**0**	**0**	....	....	....	....	....

Signed as a free agent by **Washington** to three-game tryout contract, October, 1975.

STAPLETON, Mike

Center. Shoots right. 5'10", 183 lbs. Born, Sarnia, Ont., May 5, 1966.
(Chicago's 7th choice, 132nd overall, in 1984 Entry Draft).

Season	Club	Regular Season GP	G	A	Pts	PIM	Playoffs GP	G	A	Pts	PIM
1986-87	Chicago Blackhawks	39	3	6	9	6	4	0	0	0	2
1987-88	Chicago Blackhawks	53	2	9	11	59	....	....	....	....	....
1988-89	Chicago Blackhawks	7	0	1	1	7	....	....	....	....	....
1990-91	Chicago Blackhawks	7	0	1	1	2	....	....	....	....	....
1991-92	Chicago Blackhawks	19	4	4	8	8	....	....	....	....	....
1992-93	Pittsburgh Penguins	78	4	9	13	10	4	0	0	0	0
1993-94	Pittsburgh Penguins	58	7	4	11	18	....	....	....	....	....
	Edmonton Oilers	23	5	9	14	28	....	....	....	....	....
1994-95	Edmonton Oilers	46	6	11	17	21	....	....	....	....	....
1995-96	Winnipeg Jets	58	10	14	24	37	6	0	0	0	21
1996-97	Phoenix Coyotes	55	4	11	15	36	7	0	0	0	14
1997-98	Phoenix Coyotes	64	5	5	10	36	6	0	0	0	2
1998-99	Phoenix Coyotes	76	9	9	18	34	7	1	0	1	0
99-2000	Atlanta Thrashers	62	10	12	22	30	....	....	....	....	....
2000-01	New York Islanders	34	1	4	5	2	....	....	....	....	....
	Vancouver Canucks	18	1	2	3	8	....	....	....	....	....
	NHL Totals	**697**	**71**	**111**	**182**	**342**	**34**	**1**	**0**	**1**	**39**

• Son of Pat

Signed as a free agent by **Pittsburgh**, September 30, 1992. Claimed on waivers by **Edmonton** from **Pittsburgh**, February 19, 1994. Signed as a free agent by **Winnipeg**, August 18, 1995. Transferred to **Phoenix** after **Winnipeg** franchise relocated, July 1, 1996. Claimed by **Atlanta** from **Phoenix** in Expansion Draft, June 25, 1999. Signed as a free agent by **NY Islanders**, July 3, 2000. Traded to **Vancouver** by **NY Islanders** for Vancouver's 9th round choice (later traded to Washington – Washington selected Robert Muller) in 2001 Entry Draft, December 28, 2000.

STAPLETON, Pat

Defense. Shoots left. 5'8", 180 lbs. Born, Sarnia, Ont., July 4, 1940.

Season	Club	Regular Season GP	G	A	Pts	PIM	Playoffs GP	G	A	Pts	PIM
1961-62	Boston Bruins	69	2	5	7	42	....	....	....	....	....
1962-63	Boston Bruins	21	0	3	3	8	....	....	....	....	....
1965-66	Chicago Black Hawks	55	4	30	34	52	6	2	3	5	4
1966-67	Chicago Black Hawks	70	3	31	34	54	6	1	1	2	12
1967-68	Chicago Black Hawks	67	4	34	38	34	11	0	4	4	4
1968-69	Chicago Black Hawks	75	6	50	56	44	....	....	....	....	....
1969-70	Chicago Black Hawks	49	4	38	42	28	....	....	....	....	....
1970-71	Chicago Black Hawks	76	7	44	51	30	18	3	14	17	4
1971-72	Chicago Black Hawks	78	3	38	41	47	8	2	2	4	4
1972-73	Chicago Black Hawks	75	10	21	31	14	16	2	*15	17	10
	NHL Totals	**635**	**43**	**294**	**337**	**353**	**65**	**10**	**39**	**49**	**38**

• Father of Mike • NHL Second All-Star Team (1966, 1971, 1972)

Played in NHL All-Star Game (1967, 1969, 1971, 1972)

Claimed by **Boston** from **Chicago** in Intra-League Draft, June 13, 1961. Traded to **Toronto** by **Boston** with Orland Kurtenbach and Andy Hebenton for Ron Stewart, June 8, 1965. Claimed by **Chicago** from **Toronto** in Intra-League Draft, June 9, 1965.

STARIKOV, Sergei

Defense. Shoots left. 5'10", 225 lbs. Born, Chelyabinsk, Soviet Union, December 4, 1958.
(New Jersey's 7th choice, 152nd overall, in 1989 Entry Draft).

Season	Club	Regular Season GP	G	A	Pts	PIM	Playoffs GP	G	A	Pts	PIM
1989-90	New Jersey Devils	16	0	1	1	8	....	....	....	....	....
	NHL Totals	**16**	**0**	**1**	**1**	**8**	....	....	....	....	....

STARR, Harold

Defense. Shoots left. 5'11", 176 lbs. Born, Ottawa, Ont., July 6, 1906.

Season	Club	Regular Season GP	G	A	Pts	PIM	Playoffs GP	G	A	Pts	PIM
1929-30	Ottawa Senators	28	2	1	3	12	2	1	0	1	0
1930-31	Ottawa Senators	35	2	1	3	48	....	....	....	....	....
1931-32	Montreal Maroons	47	1	2	3	47	4	0	0	0	0
1932-33	Ottawa Senators	31	0	0	0	30	....	....	....	....	....
	Montreal Canadiens	15	0	0	0	6	2	0	0	0	2
1933-34	Montreal Maroons	....	....	....	....	....	3	0	0	0	0
1934-35	New York Rangers	33	1	1	2	31	4	0	0	0	2
1935-36	New York Rangers	16	0	0	0	12	....	....	....	....	....
	NHL Totals	**205**	**6**	**5**	**11**	**186**	**15**	**1**	**0**	**1**	**4**

Claimed by **Mtl. Maroons** from **Ottawa** for 1931-32 season in Dispersal Draft, September 26, 1931. Traded to **Montreal** by **Ottawa** with Leo Bourgeault for Marty Burke and future considerations (Nick Wasnie, March 23, 1933), February 14, 1933. Claimed on waivers by **Mtl. Maroons** from **Montreal**, December 5, 1933. Traded to **NY Rangers** by **Mtl. Maroons** for cash, December 23, 1934. Traded to **Cleveland** (IHL) by **NY Rangers** for cash, January 30, 1936.

STARR, Wilf

Center. Shoots left. 5'11", 190 lbs. Born, St. Boniface, Man., July 22, 1909.

Season	Club	Regular Season GP	G	A	Pts	PIM	Playoffs GP	G	A	Pts	PIM
1932-33	New York Americans	26	4	3	7	8	....	....	....	....	....
1933-34	Detroit Red Wings	28	2	2	4	17	7	0	2	2	2
1934-35	Detroit Red Wings	24	1	1	2	0	....	....	....	....	....
1935-36	Detroit Red Wings	9	1	0	1	0	....	....	....	....	....
	NHL Totals	**87**	**8**	**6**	**14**	**25**	**7**	**0**	**2**	**2**	**2**

Signed as a free agent by **NY Rangers**, October 29, 1930. Traded to **NY Americans** by **NY Rangers** for cash after Springfield (Can-Am) franchise folded, December 22, 1932. Traded to **Detroit** by **NY Americans** for cash, September, 1933. Loaned to **Windsor** (IHL) by **Detroit**, January 30, 1935.

STASIUK, Vic

Left wing. Shoots left. 6', 185 lbs. Born, Lethbridge, Alta., May 23, 1929.

Season	Club	Regular Season GP	G	A	Pts	PIM	Playoffs GP	G	A	Pts	PIM
1949-50	Chicago Black Hawks	17	1	1	2	2	....	....	....	....	....
1950-51	Chicago Black Hawks	20	5	3	8	6	....	....	....	....	....
	Detroit Red Wings	50	3	10	13	12	....	....	....	....	....
1951-52 ♦	Detroit Red Wings	58	5	9	14	19	7	0	2	2	0
1952-53	Detroit Red Wings	3	0	0	0	0	....	....	....	....	....
1953-54 ♦	Detroit Red Wings	42	5	2	7	4	....	....	....	....	....
1954-55 ♦	Detroit Red Wings	59	8	11	19	67	11	5	3	8	6
1955-56	Boston Bruins	59	19	18	37	118	....	....	....	....	....
1956-57	Boston Bruins	64	24	16	40	69	10	2	1	3	2
1957-58	Boston Bruins	70	21	35	56	55	12	0	5	5	13
1958-59	Boston Bruins	70	27	33	60	63	7	4	2	6	11
1959-60	Boston Bruins	69	29	39	68	121	....	....	....	....	....
1960-61	Boston Bruins	46	5	25	30	35	....	....	....	....	....
	Detroit Red Wings	23	10	13	23	16	11	2	5	7	4
1961-62	Detroit Red Wings	59	15	28	43	45	....	....	....	....	....
1962-63	Detroit Red Wings	36	6	11	17	37	11	3	0	3	4
	NHL Totals	**745**	**183**	**254**	**437**	**669**	**69**	**16**	**18**	**34**	**40**

Played in NHL All-Star Game (1960)

Traded to **Detroit** by **Chicago** with Bert Olmstead for Steve Black and Lee Fogolin, December 2, 1950. Traded to **Boston** by **Detroit** with Marcel Bonin, Lorne Davis and Terry Sawchuk for Gilles Boisvert, Real Chevrefils, Norm Corcoran, Warren Godfrey and Ed Sandford, June 3, 1955. Traded to **Detroit** by **Boston** with Leo Labine for Gary Aldcorn, Murray Oliver and Tom McCarthy, January 23, 1961.

STASTNY, Anton

Left wing. Shoots left. 6', 188 lbs. Born, Bratislava, Czech., August 5, 1959.
(Quebec's 4th choice, 83rd overall, in 1979 Entry Draft).

Season	Club	Regular Season GP	G	A	Pts	PIM	Playoffs GP	G	A	Pts	PIM
1980-81	Quebec Nordiques	80	39	46	85	12	5	4	3	7	2
1981-82	Quebec Nordiques	68	26	46	72	16	16	5	10	15	10

		REGULAR SEASON					PLAYOFFS				
Season	Club	GP	G	A	Pts	PIM	GP	G	A	Pts	PIM
1982-83	Quebec Nordiques	79	32	60	92	25	4	2	2	4	0
1983-84	Quebec Nordiques	69	25	37	62	14	9	2	5	7	7
1984-85	Quebec Nordiques	79	38	42	80	30	16	3	3	6	6
1985-86	Quebec Nordiques	74	31	43	74	19	3	1	1	2	0
1986-87	Quebec Nordiques	77	27	35	62	8	13	3	8	11	6
1987-88	Quebec Nordiques	69	27	45	72	14	....	....	....	....	....
1988-89	Quebec Nordiques	55	7	30	37	12	....	....	....	....	....
	NHL Totals	**650**	**252**	**384**	**636**	**150**	**66**	**20**	**32**	**52**	**31**

• Re-entered NHL Entry Draft. Originally Philadelphia's 19th choice, 198th overall, in 1978 Amateur Draft.

• Brother of Peter and Marian

STASTNY, Marian

Right wing. Shoots left. 5'10", 195 lbs. Born, Bratislava, Czech., January 8, 1953.

		REGULAR SEASON					PLAYOFFS				
Season	Club	GP	G	A	Pts	PIM	GP	G	A	Pts	PIM
1981-82	Quebec Nordiques	74	35	54	89	27	16	3	14	17	5
1982-83	Quebec Nordiques	60	36	43	79	32	2	0	0	0	0
1983-84	Quebec Nordiques	68	20	32	52	26	9	2	3	5	2
1984-85	Quebec Nordiques	50	7	14	21	4	2	0	0	0	0
1985-86	Toronto Maple Leafs	70	23	30	53	21	3	0	0	0	0
	NHL Totals	**322**	**121**	**173**	**294**	**110**	**32**	**5**	**17**	**22**	**7**

• Brother of Peter and Anton

Played in NHL All-Star Game (1983)

Signed as a free agent by **Quebec**, August 26, 1980. Signed as a free agent by **Toronto**, August 12, 1985.

STASTNY, Peter

HHOF

Center. Shoots left. 6'1", 200 lbs. Born, Bratislava, Czech., September 18, 1956.

		REGULAR SEASON					PLAYOFFS				
Season	Club	GP	G	A	Pts	PIM	GP	G	A	Pts	PIM
1980-81	Quebec Nordiques	77	39	70	109	37	5	2	8	10	7
1981-82	Quebec Nordiques	80	46	93	139	91	12	7	11	18	10
1982-83	Quebec Nordiques	75	47	77	124	78	4	3	2	5	10
1983-84	Quebec Nordiques	80	46	73	119	73	9	2	7	9	31
1984-85	Quebec Nordiques	75	32	68	100	95	18	4	19	23	24
1985-86	Quebec Nordiques	76	41	81	122	60	3	0	1	1	2
1986-87	Quebec Nordiques	64	24	53	77	43	13	6	9	15	12
1987-88	Quebec Nordiques	76	46	65	111	69	....	....	....	....	....
1988-89	Quebec Nordiques	72	35	50	85	117	....	....	....	....	....
1989-90	Quebec Nordiques	62	24	38	62	24	....	....	....	....	....
	New Jersey Devils	12	5	6	11	16	6	3	2	5	2
1990-91	New Jersey Devils	77	18	42	60	53	7	3	4	7	2
1991-92	New Jersey Devils	66	24	38	62	42	7	3	7	10	19
1992-93	New Jersey Devils	62	17	23	40	22	5	0	2	2	2
1993-94	St. Louis Blues	17	5	11	16	4	4	0	0	0	2
1994-95	St. Louis Blues	6	1	1	2	0	....	....	....	....	....
	NHL Totals	**977**	**450**	**789**	**1239**	**824**	**93**	**33**	**72**	**105**	**123**

• Brother of Marian and Anton • Calder Memorial Trophy (1981)

Played in NHL All-Star Game (1981, 1982, 1983, 1984, 1986, 1988)

Signed as a free agent by **Quebec**, August 26, 1980. Traded to **New Jersey** by **Quebec** for Craig Wolanin and future considerations (Randy Velischek, August 13, 1990), March 6, 1990. Signed as a free agent by **St. Louis**, March 9, 1994.

STASZAK, Ray

Right wing. Shoots right. 6', 200 lbs. Born, Philadelphia, PA, December 1, 1962.

		REGULAR SEASON					PLAYOFFS				
Season	Club	GP	G	A	Pts	PIM	GP	G	A	Pts	PIM
1985-86	Detroit Red Wings	4	0	1	1	7	....	....	....	....	....
	NHL Totals	**4**	**0**	**1**	**1**	**7**	....	....	....	....	....

Signed as a free agent by **Detroit**, July 31, 1985. • Suffered eventual career-ending groin injury in game vs. Minnesota, December 11, 1985.

STEELE, Frank

Right wing/Defense. Shoots right. 5'11", 170 lbs. Born, Niagara Falls, Ont., March 19, 1905.

		REGULAR SEASON					PLAYOFFS				
Season	Club	GP	G	A	Pts	PIM	GP	G	A	Pts	PIM
1930-31	Detroit Falcons	1	0	0	0	0	....	....	....	....	....
	NHL Totals	**1**	**0**	**0**	**0**	**0**	....	....	....	....	....

Signed as a free agent by **Detroit**, August 30, 1929.

STEEN, Anders

Center. Shoots left. 6'1", 204 lbs. Born, Nykoping, Sweden, April 28, 1955.

		REGULAR SEASON					PLAYOFFS				
Season	Club	GP	G	A	Pts	PIM	GP	G	A	Pts	PIM
1980-81	Winnipeg Jets	42	5	11	16	22	....	....	....	....	....
	NHL Totals	**42**	**5**	**11**	**16**	**22**	....	....	....	....	....

Signed as a free agent by **Winnipeg**, March 26, 1980.

STEEN, Thomas

Center. Shoots left. 5'11", 190 lbs. Born, Grums, Sweden, June 8, 1960.
(Winnipeg's 5th choice, 103rd overall, in 1979 Entry Draft).

		REGULAR SEASON					PLAYOFFS				
Season	Club	GP	G	A	Pts	PIM	GP	G	A	Pts	PIM
1981-82	Winnipeg Jets	73	15	29	44	42	4	0	4	4	2
1982-83	Winnipeg Jets	75	26	33	59	60	3	0	2	2	0
1983-84	Winnipeg Jets	78	20	45	65	69	3	0	1	1	9
1984-85	Winnipeg Jets	79	30	54	84	80	8	2	3	5	17
1985-86	Winnipeg Jets	78	17	47	64	76	3	1	1	2	4
1986-87	Winnipeg Jets	75	17	33	50	59	10	3	4	7	8
1987-88	Winnipeg Jets	76	16	38	54	53	5	1	5	6	2
1988-89	Winnipeg Jets	80	27	61	88	80	....	....	....	....	....
1989-90	Winnipeg Jets	53	18	48	66	35	7	2	5	7	16
1990-91	Winnipeg Jets	58	19	48	67	49	....	....	....	....	....
1991-92	Winnipeg Jets	38	13	25	38	29	7	2	4	6	2
1992-93	Winnipeg Jets	80	22	50	72	75	6	1	3	4	2
1993-94	Winnipeg Jets	76	19	32	51	32	....	....	....	....	....
1994-95	Winnipeg Jets	31	5	10	15	14	....	....	....	....	....
	NHL Totals	**950**	**264**	**553**	**817**	**753**	**56**	**12**	**32**	**44**	**62**

STEFAN, Patrik

Center. Shoots left. 6'3", 205 lbs. Born, Pribram, Czech., September 16, 1980.
(Atlanta's 1st choice, 1st overall, in 1999 Entry Draft).

		REGULAR SEASON					PLAYOFFS				
Season	Club	GP	G	A	Pts	PIM	GP	G	A	Pts	PIM
99-2000	Atlanta Thrashers	72	5	20	25	30	....	....	....	....	....
2000-01	Atlanta Thrashers	66	10	21	31	22	....	....	....	....	....
2001-02	Atlanta Thrashers	59	7	16	23	22	....	....	....	....	....
2002-03	Atlanta Thrashers	71	13	21	34	12	....	....	....	....	....
	NHL Totals	**268**	**35**	**78**	**113**	**86**	....	....	....	....	....

STEFANIW, Morris

Center. Shoots left. 5'11", 170 lbs. Born, North Battleford, Sask., January 10, 1948.

		REGULAR SEASON					PLAYOFFS				
Season	Club	GP	G	A	Pts	PIM	GP	G	A	Pts	PIM
1972-73	Atlanta Flames	13	1	1	2	2	....	....	....	....	....
	NHL Totals	**13**	**1**	**1**	**2**	**2**	....	....	....	....	....

Traded to **Phoenix** (WHL) by **Boston** for cash, February, 1968. Traded to **NY Rangers** by **Phoenix** (WHL) for cash, October, 1970. Claimed by **Atlanta** from **NY Rangers** in Expansion Draft, June 6, 1972. Traded to **Kansas City** by **Atlanta** for cash, September 17, 1974.

STEFANSKI, Bud

Center. Shoots left. 5'10", 170 lbs. Born, South Porcupine, Ont., April 28, 1955.
(NY Rangers' 9th choice, 154th overall, in 1975 Amateur Draft).

		REGULAR SEASON					PLAYOFFS				
Season	Club	GP	G	A	Pts	PIM	GP	G	A	Pts	PIM
1977-78	New York Rangers	1	0	0	0	0	....	....	....	....	....
	NHL Totals	**1**	**0**	**0**	**0**	**0**	....	....	....	....	....

Traded to **Winnipeg** by **NY Rangers** for cash and future considerations, October 12, 1979.

STEMKOWSKI, Pete

Center. Shoots left. 6'1", 196 lbs. Born, Winnipeg, Man., August 25, 1943.

		REGULAR SEASON					PLAYOFFS				
Season	Club	GP	G	A	Pts	PIM	GP	G	A	Pts	PIM
1963-64	Toronto Maple Leafs	1	0	0	0	2	....	....	....	....	....
1964-65	Toronto Maple Leafs	36	5	15	20	33	6	0	3	3	7
1965-66	Toronto Maple Leafs	56	4	12	16	55	4	0	0	0	26
1966-67 ◆	Toronto Maple Leafs	68	13	22	35	75	12	5	7	12	20
1967-68	Toronto Maple Leafs	60	7	15	22	82	....	....	....	....	....
	Detroit Red Wings	13	3	6	9	4	....	....	....	....	....
1968-69	Detroit Red Wings	71	21	31	52	81	....	....	....	....	....
1969-70	Detroit Red Wings	76	25	24	49	114	4	1	1	2	6
1970-71	Detroit Red Wings	10	2	2	4	8	....	....	....	....	....
	New York Rangers	68	16	29	45	61	13	3	2	5	6
1971-72	New York Rangers	59	11	17	28	53	16	4	8	12	18
1972-73	New York Rangers	78	22	37	59	71	10	4	2	6	6
1973-74	New York Rangers	78	25	45	70	74	13	6	6	12	35
1974-75	New York Rangers	77	24	35	59	63	3	1	0	1	10
1975-76	New York Rangers	75	13	28	41	49	....	....	....	....	....
1976-77	New York Rangers	61	2	13	15	8	....	....	....	....	....
1977-78	Los Angeles Kings	80	13	18	31	33	2	1	0	1	2
	NHL Totals	**967**	**206**	**349**	**555**	**866**	**83**	**25**	**29**	**54**	**136**

Played in NHL All-Star Game (1968)

Traded to **Detroit** by **Toronto** with Frank Mahovlich, Garry Unger and the rights to Carl Brewer for Norm Ullman, Paul Henderson, Floyd Smith and Doug Barrie, March 3, 1968. Traded to **NY Rangers** by **Detroit** for Larry Brown, October 31, 1970. Signed as a free agent by **Los Angeles**, August 31, 1977.

STENLUND, Vern

Center. Shoots left. 6'1", 178 lbs. Born, Thunder Bay, Ont., April 11, 1956.
(California's 2nd choice, 23rd overall, in 1976 Amateur Draft).

		REGULAR SEASON					PLAYOFFS				
Season	Club	GP	G	A	Pts	PIM	GP	G	A	Pts	PIM
1976-77	Cleveland Barons	4	0	0	0	0	....	....	....	....	....
	NHL Totals	**4**	**0**	**0**	**0**	**0**	....	....	....	....	....

Transferred to **Cleveland** after **California** franchise relocated, August 26, 1976.

STEPHENS, Charlie

Center/Right wing. Shoots right. 6'3", 225 lbs. Born, London, Ont., April 5, 1981.
(Colorado's 9th choice, 196th overall, in 2001 Entry Draft).

		REGULAR SEASON					PLAYOFFS				
Season	Club	GP	G	A	Pts	PIM	GP	G	A	Pts	PIM
2002-03	Colorado Avalanche	2	0	0	0	0	....	....	....	....	....
	NHL Totals	**2**	**0**	**0**	**0**	**0**	....	....	....	....	....

• Re-entered NHL Entry Draft. Originally Washington's 3rd choice, 31st overall, in 1999 Entry Draft.

STEPHENSON, Bob

Right wing. Shoots right. 6'1", 187 lbs. Born, Saskatoon, Sask., February 1, 1954.

		REGULAR SEASON					PLAYOFFS				
Season	Club	GP	G	A	Pts	PIM	GP	G	A	Pts	PIM
1979-80	Hartford Whalers	4	0	1	1	0	....	....	....	....	....
	Toronto Maple Leafs	14	2	2	4	4	....	....	....	....	....
	NHL Totals	**18**	**2**	**3**	**5**	**4**	....	....	....	....	....

Claimed by **Hartford** from **Birmingham** (WHA) in WHA Dispersal Draft, June, 1979. Traded to **Toronto** by **Hartford** for Pat Boutette, December 24, 1979.

STERN, Ron

Right wing. Shoots right. 6', 200 lbs. Born, Ste-Agathe, Que., January 11, 1967.
(Vancouver's 3rd choice, 70th overall, in 1986 Entry Draft).

		REGULAR SEASON					PLAYOFFS				
Season	Club	GP	G	A	Pts	PIM	GP	G	A	Pts	PIM
1987-88	Vancouver Canucks	15	0	0	0	52	....	....	....	....	....
1988-89	Vancouver Canucks	17	1	0	1	49	3	0	1	1	17
1989-90	Vancouver Canucks	34	2	3	5	208	....	....	....	....	....

Season	Club	GP	G	A	Pts	PIM	GP	G	A	Pts	PIM
		REGULAR SEASON					PLAYOFFS				
1990-91	Vancouver Canucks	31	2	3	5	171	....	....	....	....	....
	Calgary Flames	13	1	3	4	69	7	1	3	4	14
1991-92	Calgary Flames	72	13	9	22	338	....	....	....	....	....
1992-93	Calgary Flames	70	10	15	25	207	6	0	0	0	43
1993-94	Calgary Flames	71	9	20	29	243	7	2	0	2	12
1994-95	Calgary Flames	39	9	4	13	163	7	3	1	4	8
1995-96	Calgary Flames	52	10	5	15	111	4	0	2	2	8
1996-97	Calgary Flames	79	7	10	17	157	....	....	....	....	....
1998-99	San Jose Sharks	78	7	9	16	158	6	0	0	0	6
99-2000	San Jose Sharks	67	4	5	9	151	3	1	0	1	11
	NHL Totals	**638**	**75**	**86**	**161**	**2077**	**43**	**7**	**7**	**14**	**119**

Traded to **Calgary** by **Vancouver** with Kevan Guy for Dana Murzyn, March 5, 1991. • Missed entire 1997-98 season recovering from knee surgery, October, 1997. Signed as a free agent by **San Jose**, August 25, 1998. • Officially announced retirement, September 22, 2000.

STERNER, Ulf

Left wing. Shoots left. 6'2", 187 lbs. Born, Deje, Sweden, February 11, 1941.

Season	Club	GP	G	A	Pts	PIM	GP	G	A	Pts	PIM
1964-65	New York Rangers	4	0	0	0	0	....	....	....	....	....
	NHL Totals	**4**	**0**	**0**	**0**	**0**	....	....	....	....	....

Signed as a free agent by **NY Rangers**, October 1, 1964.

STEVENS, John

Defense. Shoots left. 6'1", 195 lbs. Born, Campbellton, N.B., May 4, 1966.
(Philadelphia's 5th choice, 47th overall, in 1984 Entry Draft).

Season	Club	GP	G	A	Pts	PIM	GP	G	A	Pts	PIM
1986-87	Philadelphia Flyers	6	0	2	2	14	....	....	....	....	....
1987-88	Philadelphia Flyers	3	0	0	0	0	....	....	....	....	....
1990-91	Hartford Whalers	14	0	1	1	11	....	....	....	....	....
1991-92	Hartford Whalers	21	0	4	4	19	....	....	....	....	....
1993-94	Hartford Whalers	9	0	3	3	4	....	....	....	....	....
	NHL Totals	**53**	**0**	**10**	**10**	**48**	....	....	....	....	....

Signed as a free agent by **Hartford**, July 30, 1990. Signed as a free agent by **Philadelphia**, August 6, 1996.

STEVENS, Kevin

Left wing. Shoots left. 6'3", 230 lbs. Born, Brockton, MA, April 15, 1965.
(Los Angeles' 6th choice, 112th overall, in 1983 Entry Draft).

Season	Club	GP	G	A	Pts	PIM	GP	G	A	Pts	PIM
1987-88	Pittsburgh Penguins	16	5	2	7	8	....	....	....	....	....
1988-89	Pittsburgh Penguins	24	12	3	15	19	11	3	7	10	16
1989-90	Pittsburgh Penguins	76	29	41	70	171	....	....	....	....	....
1990-91 ♦	Pittsburgh Penguins	80	40	46	86	133	24	*17	16	33	53
1991-92 ♦	Pittsburgh Penguins	80	54	69	123	254	21	13	15	28	28
1992-93	Pittsburgh Penguins	72	55	56	111	177	12	5	11	16	22
1993-94	Pittsburgh Penguins	83	41	47	88	155	6	1	1	2	10
1994-95	Pittsburgh Penguins	27	15	12	27	51	12	4	7	11	21
1995-96	Boston Bruins	41	10	13	23	49	....	....	....	....	....
	Los Angeles Kings	20	3	10	13	22	....	....	....	....	....
1996-97	Los Angeles Kings	69	14	20	34	96	....	....	....	....	....
1997-98	New York Rangers	80	14	27	41	130	....	....	....	....	....
1998-99	New York Rangers	81	23	20	43	64	....	....	....	....	....
99-2000	New York Rangers	38	3	5	8	43	....	....	....	....	....
2000-01	Philadelphia Flyers	23	2	7	9	18	....	....	....	....	....
	Pittsburgh Penguins	32	8	15	23	55	17	3	3	6	20
2001-02	Pittsburgh Penguins	32	1	4	5	25	....	....	....	....	....
	NHL Totals	**874**	**329**	**397**	**726**	**1470**	**103**	**46**	**60**	**106**	**170**

NHL Second All-Star Team (1991, 1993) • NHL First All-Star Team (1992)

Played in NHL All-Star Game (1991, 1992, 1993)

Rights traded to **Pittsburgh** by **Los Angeles** for Anders Hakansson, September 9, 1983. Traded to **Boston** by **Pittsburgh** with Shawn McEachern for Glen Murray, Bryan Smolinski and Boston's 3rd round choice (Boyd Kane) in 1996 Entry Draft, August 2, 1995. Traded to **Los Angeles** by **Boston** for Rick Tocchet, January 25, 1996. Traded to **NY Rangers** by **Los Angeles** for Luc Robitaille, August 28, 1997. • Missed majority of 1999-2000 season after entering NHL/NHLPA substance abuse program, January 23, 2000. Signed as a free agent by **Philadelphia**, July 7, 2000. Traded to **Pittsburgh** by **Philadelphia** for John Slaney, January 14, 2001. • Missed majority of 2001-02 season for personal reasons, January 30, 2002.

STEVENS, Mike

Left wing. Shoots left. 6', 202 lbs. Born, Kitchener, Ont., December 30, 1965.
(Vancouver's 5th choice, 58th overall, in 1984 Entry Draft).

Season	Club	GP	G	A	Pts	PIM	GP	G	A	Pts	PIM
1984-85	Vancouver Canucks	6	0	3	3	6	....	....	....	....	....
1987-88	Boston Bruins	7	0	1	1	9	....	....	....	....	....
1988-89	New York Islanders	9	1	0	1	14	....	....	....	....	....
1989-90	Toronto Maple Leafs	1	0	0	0	0	....	....	....	....	....
	NHL Totals	**23**	**1**	**4**	**5**	**29**	....	....	....	....	....

• Brother of Scott

Traded to **Boston** by **Vancouver** for cash, October 6, 1987. Signed as a free agent by **NY Islanders**, August 20, 1988. Traded to **Toronto** by **NY Islanders** with Gilles Thibaudeau for Jack Capuano, Paul Gagne and Derek Laxdal, December 20, 1989. Traded to **NY Rangers** by **Toronto** for Guy Larose, December 26, 1991. Signed as a free agent by **Calgary**, August 10, 1993.

STEVENS, Phil

Center/Defense. Shoots right. 5'11", 165 lbs. Born, St. Lambert, Ont., February 15, 1893.

Season	Club	GP	G	A	Pts	PIM	GP	G	A	Pts	PIM
1917-18	Montreal Wanderers	4	1	0	1	3	....	....	....	....	....
1921-22	Montreal Canadiens	4	0	0	0	0	....	....	....	....	....
1925-26	Boston Bruins	17	0	0	0	0	....	....	....	....	....
	NHL Totals	**25**	**1**	**0**	**1**	**3**	....	....	....	....	....

Rights retained by **Mtl. Wanderers** after NHA folded, November 26, 1917. Signed as a free agent by **Montreal**, December 6, 1921. Claimed on waivers by **Saskatoon** (WCHL) from **Montreal**, November 13, 1922. Signed as a free agent by **Boston**, November 14, 1925. Signed as a free agent by **NY Rangers**, October, 1926. Loaned to **Springfield** (Can-Am) by **NY Rangers** for cash, November 15, 1926.

STEVENS, Scott

Defense. Shoots left. 6'2", 215 lbs. Born, Kitchener, Ont., April 1, 1964.
(Washington's 1st choice, 5th overall, in 1982 Entry Draft).

Season	Club	GP	G	A	Pts	PIM	GP	G	A	Pts	PIM
1982-83	Washington Capitals	77	9	16	25	195	4	1	0	1	26
1983-84	Washington Capitals	78	13	32	45	201	8	1	8	9	21
1984-85	Washington Capitals	80	21	44	65	221	5	0	1	1	20
1985-86	Washington Capitals	73	15	38	53	165	9	3	8	11	12
1986-87	Washington Capitals	77	10	51	61	283	7	0	5	5	19
1987-88	Washington Capitals	80	12	60	72	184	13	1	11	12	46
1988-89	Washington Capitals	80	7	61	68	225	6	1	4	5	11
1989-90	Washington Capitals	56	11	29	40	154	15	2	7	9	25
1990-91	St. Louis Blues	78	5	44	49	150	13	0	3	3	36
1991-92	New Jersey Devils	68	17	42	59	124	7	2	1	3	29
1992-93	New Jersey Devils	81	12	45	57	120	5	2	2	4	10
1993-94	New Jersey Devils	83	18	60	78	112	20	2	9	11	42
1994-95 ♦	New Jersey Devils	48	2	20	22	56	20	1	7	8	24
1995-96	New Jersey Devils	82	5	23	28	100	....	....	....	....	....
1996-97	New Jersey Devils	79	5	19	24	70	10	0	4	4	2
1997-98	New Jersey Devils	80	4	22	26	80	6	1	0	1	8
1998-99	New Jersey Devils	75	5	22	27	64	7	2	1	3	10
99-2000 ♦	New Jersey Devils	78	8	21	29	103	23	3	8	11	6
2000-01	New Jersey Devils	81	9	22	31	71	25	1	7	8	37
2001-02	New Jersey Devils	82	1	16	17	44	6	0	0	0	4
2002-03 ♦	New Jersey Devils	81	4	16	20	41	24	3	6	9	14
	NHL Totals	**1597**	**193**	**703**	**896**	**2763**	**233**	**26**	**92**	**118**	**402**

• Brother of Mike • NHL All-Rookie Team (1983) • NHL First All-Star Team (1988, 1994) • NHL Second All-Star Team (1992, 1997, 2001) • Alka-Seltzer Plus Award (1994) • Conn Smythe Trophy (2000)

Played in NHL All-Star Game (1985, 1989, 1991, 1992, 1993, 1994, 1996, 1997, 1998, 1999, 2000, 2001, 2003)

Signed as a free agent by **St. Louis**, July 16, 1990. Transferred to **New Jersey** from **St. Louis** as compensation for St. Louis' signing of free agent Brendan Shanahan, September 3, 1991.

STEVENSON, Jeremy

Left wing. Shoots left. 6'2", 218 lbs. Born, San Bernardino, CA, July 28, 1974.
(Anaheim's 10th choice, 262nd overall, in 1994 Entry Draft).

Season	Club	GP	G	A	Pts	PIM	GP	G	A	Pts	PIM
1995-96	Mighty Ducks of Anaheim	3	0	1	1	12	....	....	....	....	....
1996-97	Mighty Ducks of Anaheim	5	0	0	0	14	....	....	....	....	....
1997-98	Mighty Ducks of Anaheim	45	3	5	8	101	....	....	....	....	....
99-2000	Mighty Ducks of Anaheim	3	0	0	0	7	....	....	....	....	....
2000-01	Nashville Predators	8	1	0	1	39	....	....	....	....	....
2001-02	Nashville Predators	4	0	0	0	9	....	....	....	....	....
2002-03	Minnesota Wild	32	5	6	11	69	14	0	5	5	12
	NHL Totals	**100**	**9**	**12**	**21**	**251**	**14**	**0**	**5**	**5**	**12**

• Re-entered NHL Entry Draft. Originally Winnipeg's 3rd choice, 60th overall, in 1992 Entry Draft.

Signed as a free agent by **Nashville**, September 25, 2000. Signed as a free agent by **Minnesota** November 26, 2002.

STEVENSON, Shayne

Right wing. Shoots right. 6'1", 190 lbs. Born, Newmarket, Ont., October 26, 1970.
(Boston's 1st choice, 17th overall, in 1989 Entry Draft).

Season	Club	GP	G	A	Pts	PIM	GP	G	A	Pts	PIM
1990-91	Boston Bruins	14	0	0	0	26	....	....	....	....	....
1991-92	Boston Bruins	5	0	1	1	2	....	....	....	....	....
1992-93	Tampa Bay Lightning	8	0	1	1	7	....	....	....	....	....
	NHL Totals	**27**	**0**	**2**	**2**	**35**	....	....	....	....	....

Claimed by **Tampa Bay** from **Boston** in Expansion Draft, June 18, 1992.

STEVENSON, Turner

Right wing. Shoots right. 6'3", 230 lbs. Born, Prince George, B.C., May 18, 1972.
(Montreal's 1st choice, 12th overall, in 1990 Entry Draft).

Season	Club	GP	G	A	Pts	PIM	GP	G	A	Pts	PIM
1992-93	Montreal Canadiens	1	0	0	0	0	....	....	....	....	....
1993-94	Montreal Canadiens	2	0	0	0	2	3	0	2	2	0
1994-95	Montreal Canadiens	41	6	1	7	86	....	....	....	....	....
1995-96	Montreal Canadiens	80	9	16	25	167	6	0	1	1	2
1996-97	Montreal Canadiens	65	8	13	21	97	5	1	1	2	2
1997-98	Montreal Canadiens	63	4	6	10	110	10	3	4	7	12
1998-99	Montreal Canadiens	69	10	17	27	88	....	....	....	....	....
99-2000	Montreal Canadiens	64	8	13	21	61	....	....	....	....	....
2000-01	New Jersey Devils	69	8	18	26	97	23	1	3	4	20
2001-02	New Jersey Devils	21	0	2	2	25	1	0	0	0	4
2002-03 ♦	New Jersey Devils	77	7	13	20	115	14	1	1	2	26
	NHL Totals	**552**	**60**	**99**	**159**	**848**	**62**	**6**	**12**	**18**	**66**

Selected by **Columbus** from **Montreal** in Expansion Draft, June 23, 2000. Traded to **New Jersey** by **Columbus** to complete transaction that sent Krzysztof Oliwa (June 12, 2000) and Deron Quint (June 23, 2000) to **Columbus**, June 23, 2000. • Missed majority of 2001-02 season recovering from knee injury suffered in game vs. Vancouver, December 29, 2001.

STEWART, Allan

Left wing. Shoots left. 6', 195 lbs. Born, Fort St. John, B.C., January 31, 1964.
(New Jersey's 9th choice, 213th overall, in 1983 Entry Draft).

		Regular Season					Playoffs				
Season	Club	GP	G	A	Pts	PIM	GP	G	A	Pts	PIM
1985-86	New Jersey Devils	4	0	0	0	21	....	....	....	....	....
1986-87	New Jersey Devils	7	1	0	1	26	....	....	....	....	....
1987-88	New Jersey Devils	1	0	0	0	0	....	....	....	....	....
1988-89	New Jersey Devils	6	0	2	2	15	....	....	....	....	....
1990-91	New Jersey Devils	41	5	2	7	159	....	....	....	....	....
1991-92	New Jersey Devils	1	0	0	0	5	....	....	....	....	....
	Boston Bruins	4	0	0	0	17	....	....	....	....	....
	NHL Totals	**64**	**6**	**4**	**10**	**243**	....	....	....	....	....

Traded to **Boston** by **New Jersey** for future considerations, October 16, 1991. Signed as a free agent by **Winnipeg**, October 5, 1992.

STEWART, Bill

Defense. Shoots right. 6'2", 190 lbs. Born, Toronto, Ont., October 6, 1957.
(Buffalo's 3rd choice, 68th overall, in 1977 Amateur Draft).

		Regular Season					Playoffs				
Season	Club	GP	G	A	Pts	PIM	GP	G	A	Pts	PIM
1977-78	Buffalo Sabres	13	2	0	2	15	8	0	2	2	0
1978-79	Buffalo Sabres	68	1	17	18	101	1	0	1	1	0
1980-81	St. Louis Blues	60	2	21	23	114	4	1	0	1	11
1981-82	St. Louis Blues	22	0	5	5	25	....	....	....	....	....
1982-83	St. Louis Blues	7	0	0	0	8	....	....	....	....	....
1983-84	Toronto Maple Leafs	56	2	17	19	116	....	....	....	....	....
1984-85	Toronto Maple Leafs	27	0	2	2	32	....	....	....	....	....
1985-86	Minnesota North Stars	8	0	2	2	13	....	....	....	....	....
	NHL Totals	**261**	**7**	**64**	**71**	**424**	**13**	**1**	**3**	**4**	**11**

Claimed by **Buffalo** as a fill-in during Expansion Draft, June 13, 1979. Traded to **St. Louis** by **Buffalo** for Bob Hess and St. Louis' 4th round choice (Anders Wikberg) in 1981 Entry Draft, October 30, 1980. Signed as a free agent by **Toronto**, September 10, 1983. Signed as a free agent by **Minnesota**, September 15, 1985.

STEWART, Blair

Center. Shoots right. 5'11", 185 lbs. Born, Winnipeg, Man., March 15, 1953.
(Detroit's 5th choice, 75th overall, in 1973 Amateur Draft).

		Regular Season					Playoffs				
Season	Club	GP	G	A	Pts	PIM	GP	G	A	Pts	PIM
1973-74	Detroit Red Wings	17	0	4	4	16	....	....	....	....	....
1974-75	Detroit Red Wings	19	0	5	5	38	....	....	....	....	....
	Washington Capitals	2	1	0	1	2	....	....	....	....	....
1975-76	Washington Capitals	74	13	14	27	113	....	....	....	....	....
1976-77	Washington Capitals	34	5	2	7	85	....	....	....	....	....
1977-78	Washington Capitals	8	0	1	1	9	....	....	....	....	....
1978-79	Washington Capitals	45	7	12	19	48	....	....	....	....	....
1979-80	Quebec Nordiques	30	8	6	14	15	....	....	....	....	....
	NHL Totals	**229**	**34**	**44**	**78**	**326**	....	....	....	....	....

Traded to **Washington** by **Detroit** for Mike Bloom, March 9, 1975. Claimed by **Quebec** from **Washington** in Expansion Draft, June 13, 1979.

STEWART, Bob

Defense. Shoots left. 6'1", 206 lbs. Born, Charlottetown, P.E.I., November 10, 1950.
(Boston's 4th choice, 13th overall, in 1970 Amateur Draft).

		Regular Season					Playoffs				
Season	Club	GP	G	A	Pts	PIM	GP	G	A	Pts	PIM
1971-72	Boston Bruins	8	0	0	0	15	....	....	....	....	....
	California Golden Seals	16	1	2	3	44	....	....	....	....	....
1972-73	California Golden Seals	63	4	17	21	181	....	....	....	....	....
1973-74	California Golden Seals	47	2	5	7	69	....	....	....	....	....
1974-75	California Golden Seals	67	5	12	17	93	....	....	....	....	....
1975-76	California Golden Seals	76	4	17	21	112	....	....	....	....	....
1976-77	Cleveland Barons	73	1	12	13	108	....	....	....	....	....
1977-78	Cleveland Barons	72	2	15	17	84	....	....	....	....	....
1978-79	St. Louis Blues	78	5	13	18	47	....	....	....	....	....
1979-80	St. Louis Blues	10	0	1	1	4	....	....	....	....	....
	Pittsburgh Penguins	65	3	7	10	52	5	1	1	2	2
	NHL Totals	**575**	**27**	**101**	**128**	**809**	**5**	**1**	**1**	**2**	**2**

Traded to **California** by **Boston** with Reggie Leach and Rick Smith for Carol Vadnais and Don O'Donoghue, February 23, 1972. Transferred to **Cleveland** after **California** franchise relocated, August 26, 1976. Claimed as a fill-in by **Minnesota** during **Cleveland-Minnesota** Dispersal Draft, June 15, 1978. Traded to **St. Louis** by **Minnesota** for St. Louis' 2nd round choice (Jali Wahlsten) in 1981 Entry Draft and future considerations, June 15, 1978. Traded to **Pittsburgh** by **St. Louis** for Blair Chapman, November 13, 1979.

STEWART, Cam

Left wing. Shoots right. 5'11", 196 lbs. Born, Kitchener, Ont., September 18, 1971.
(Boston's 2nd choice, 63rd overall, in 1990 Entry Draft).

		Regular Season					Playoffs				
Season	Club	GP	G	A	Pts	PIM	GP	G	A	Pts	PIM
1993-94	Boston Bruins	57	3	6	9	66	8	0	3	3	7
1994-95	Boston Bruins	5	0	0	0	2	....	....	....	....	....
1995-96	Boston Bruins	6	0	0	0	0	5	1	0	1	2
1996-97	Boston Bruins	15	0	1	1	4	....	....	....	....	....
99-2000	Florida Panthers	65	9	7	16	30	....	....	....	....	....
2000-01	Minnesota Wild	54	4	9	13	18	....	....	....	....	....
	NHL Totals	**202**	**16**	**23**	**39**	**120**	**13**	**1**	**3**	**4**	**9**

Signed as a free agent by **Florida**, July 21, 1999. Selected by **Minnesota** from **Florida** in Expansion Draft, June 23, 2000.

STEWART, Gaye

Left wing. Shoots left. 5'11", 175 lbs. Born, Fort William, Ont., June 28, 1923.

		Regular Season					Playoffs				
Season	Club	GP	G	A	Pts	PIM	GP	G	A	Pts	PIM
1941-42 ♦	Toronto Maple Leafs	....	....	....	....	....	1	0	0	0	0
1942-43	Toronto Maple Leafs	48	24	23	47	20	4	0	2	2	4
1945-46	Toronto Maple Leafs	50	*37	15	52	8	....	....	....	....	....
1946-47 ♦	Toronto Maple Leafs	60	19	14	33	15	11	2	5	7	8
1947-48	Toronto Maple Leafs	7	1	0	1	0	....	....	....	....	....
	Chicago Black Hawks	54	26	29	55	83	....	....	....	....	....
1948-49	Chicago Black Hawks	54	20	18	38	57	....	....	....	....	....
1949-50	Chicago Black Hawks	70	24	19	43	43	....	....	....	....	....
1950-51	Detroit Red Wings	67	18	13	31	18	6	0	2	2	4
1951-52	New York Rangers	69	15	25	40	22	....	....	....	....	....
1952-53	New York Rangers	18	1	1	2	8	....	....	....	....	....
	Montreal Canadiens	5	0	2	2	0	....	....	....	....	....
1953-54	Montreal Canadiens	....	....	....	....	....	3	0	0	0	0
	NHL Totals	**502**	**185**	**159**	**344**	**274**	**25**	**2**	**9**	**11**	**16**

Calder Trophy (1943) • NHL First All-Star Team (1946) • NHL Second All-Star Team (1948)

Played in NHL All-Star Game (1947, 1948, 1950, 1951)

Signed as a free agent by **Toronto**, March 6, 1942. Traded to **Chicago** by **Toronto** with Bud Poile, Bob Goldham, Gus Bodnar and Ernie Dickens for Max Bentley and Cy Thomas, November 2, 1947. Traded to **Detroit** by **Chicago** with Metro Prystai, Bob Goldham and Jim Henry for Harry Lumley, Jack Stewart, Al Dewsbury, Pete Babando and Don Morrison, July 13, 1950. Traded to **NY Rangers** by **Detroit** for Tony Leswick, June 8, 1951. Claimed on waivers by **Montreal** from **NY Rangers**, December 1, 1952. Traded to **Buffalo** (AHL) by **Montreal** with Ed Slowinski and Pete Babando for Jack Leclair and cash, August 17, 1954.

STEWART, Jack

HHOF

Defense. Shoots left. 5'10", 190 lbs. Born, Pilot Mound, Man., May 6, 1917.

		Regular Season					Playoffs				
Season	Club	GP	G	A	Pts	PIM	GP	G	A	Pts	PIM
1938-39	Detroit Red Wings	32	0	1	1	18	....	....	....	....	....
1939-40	Detroit Red Wings	48	1	0	1	40	5	0	0	0	4
1940-41	Detroit Red Wings	47	2	6	8	56	9	1	2	3	8
1941-42	Detroit Red Wings	44	4	7	11	93	12	0	1	1	12
1942-43 ♦	Detroit Red Wings	44	2	9	11	68	10	1	2	3	*35
1945-46	Detroit Red Wings	47	4	11	15	*73	5	0	0	0	14
1946-47	Detroit Red Wings	55	5	9	14	83	5	0	1	1	12
1947-48	Detroit Red Wings	60	5	14	19	91	9	1	3	4	6
1948-49	Detroit Red Wings	60	4	11	15	96	11	1	1	2	*32
1949-50 ♦	Detroit Red Wings	65	3	11	14	86	14	1	4	5	20
1950-51	Chicago Black Hawks	26	0	2	2	49	....	....	....	....	....
1951-52	Chicago Black Hawks	37	1	3	4	12	....	....	....	....	....
	NHL Totals	**565**	**31**	**84**	**115**	**765**	**80**	**5**	**14**	**19**	**143**

NHL First All-Star Team (1943, 1948, 1949) • NHL Second All-Star Team (1946, 1947)

Played in NHL All-Star Game (1947, 1948, 1949, 1950)

Signed as a free agent by **Detroit**, October 27, 1937. Traded to **Chicago** by **Detroit** with Harry Lumley, Al Dewsbury, Pete Babando and Don Morrison for Metro Prystai, Bob Goldham, Gaye Stewart and Jim Henry, July 13, 1950. • Missed remainder of 1950-51 season recovering from back injury suffered in game vs. Toronto, December 14, 1950.

STEWART, John

Center. Shoots left. 6', 180 lbs. Born, Toronto, Ont., January 2, 1954.
(Montreal's 11th choice, 105th overall, in 1974 Amateur Draft).

		Regular Season					Playoffs				
Season	Club	GP	G	A	Pts	PIM	GP	G	A	Pts	PIM
1979-80	Quebec Nordiques	2	0	0	0	0	....	....	....	....	....
	NHL Totals	**2**	**0**	**0**	**0**	**0**	....	....	....	....	....

Signed as a free agent by **Calgary**, August, 1980. Traded to **Hartford** by **Calgary** for future considerations, February, 1981.

STEWART, John

Left wing. Shoots left. 6', 180 lbs. Born, Eriksdale, Man., May 16, 1950.
(Pittsburgh's 2nd choice, 21st overall, in 1970 Amateur Draft).

		Regular Season					Playoffs				
Season	Club	GP	G	A	Pts	PIM	GP	G	A	Pts	PIM
1970-71	Pittsburgh Penguins	15	2	1	3	9	....	....	....	....	....
1971-72	Pittsburgh Penguins	25	2	8	10	23	....	....	....	....	....
1972-73	Atlanta Flames	68	17	17	34	30	....	....	....	....	....
1973-74	Atlanta Flames	74	18	15	33	41	4	0	0	0	10
1974-75	California Golden Seals	76	19	19	38	55	....	....	....	....	....
	NHL Totals	**258**	**58**	**60**	**118**	**158**	**4**	**0**	**0**	**0**	**10**

Claimed by **Atlanta** from **Pittsburgh** in Expansion Draft, June 6, 1972. Traded to **California** by **Atlanta** for Hilliard Graves, July 18, 1974.

STEWART, Ken

Defense. Shoots left. 6', 175 lbs. Born, Port Arthur, Ont., March 29, 1913.

		Regular Season					Playoffs				
Season	Club	GP	G	A	Pts	PIM	GP	G	A	Pts	PIM
1941-42	Chicago Black Hawks	6	1	1	2	2	....	....	....	....	....
	NHL Totals	**6**	**1**	**1**	**2**	**2**	....	....	....	....	....

STEWART, Nels

HHOF

Center. Shoots left. 6'1", 195 lbs. Born, Montreal, Que., December 29, 1902.

		Regular Season					Playoffs				
Season	Club	GP	G	A	Pts	PIM	GP	G	A	Pts	PIM
1925-26 ♦	Montreal Maroons	36	*34	8	*42	119	4	0	2	2	10
	Montreal Maroons (Cup)	....	....	....	....	....	*4*	*6*	*1*	*7*	*14*
1926-27	Montreal Maroons	43	17	4	21	*133	2	0	0	0	4
1927-28	Montreal Maroons	41	27	7	34	104	9	2	2	4	13
1928-29	Montreal Maroons	44	21	8	29	74	....	....	....	....	....
1929-30	Montreal Maroons	44	39	16	55	81	4	1	1	2	2
1930-31	Montreal Maroons	42	25	14	39	75	2	1	0	1	6
1931-32	Montreal Maroons	38	22	11	33	61	4	0	1	1	2
1932-33	Boston Bruins	47	18	18	36	62	5	2	0	2	4
1933-34	Boston Bruins	48	22	17	39	68	....	....	....	....	....
1934-35	Boston Bruins	47	21	18	39	45	4	0	1	1	0
1935-36	New York Americans	48	14	15	29	16	5	1	2	3	4
1936-37	Boston Bruins	11	*3	2	5	6	....	....	....	....	....
	New York Americans	32	*20	10	30	31	....	....	....	....	....
1937-38	New York Americans	48	19	17	36	29	6	2	3	5	2

Season	Club	GP	G	A	Pts	PIM	GP	G	A	Pts	PIM
		REGULAR SEASON					PLAYOFFS				
1938-39	New York Americans	46	16	19	35	43	2	0	0	0	0
1939-40	New York Americans	35	6	7	13	6	3	0	0	0	0
	NHL Totals	**650**	**324**	**191**	**515**	**953**	**50**	**9**	**12**	**21**	**47**

Hart Trophy (1926, 1930)
Played in NHL All-Star Game (1934)

Signed as a free agent by **Mtl. Maroons**, June 25, 1925. Traded to **Boston** by **Mtl. Maroons** for cash, October 17, 1932. Traded to **NY Americans** by **Boston** with Joe Jerwa for cash, September 28, 1935. Rights returned to **Boston** by **NY Americans** after NY Americans failed to complete purchase agreement, May 27, 1936. Traded to **NY Americans** by **Boston** for cash, December 19, 1936.

STEWART, Paul

Left wing/Defense. Shoots left. 6'1", 205 lbs. Born, Boston, MA, March 21, 1954.

Season	Club	GP	G	A	Pts	PIM	GP	G	A	Pts	PIM
1979-80	Quebec Nordiques	21	2	0	2	74	....	....	....	....	....
	NHL Totals	**21**	**2**	**0**	**2**	**74**	....	....	....	....	....

Claimed by **Quebec** from **Cincinnati** (WHA) in WHA Dispersal Draft, June 9, 1979.

STEWART, Ralph

USHOF

Center. Shoots left. 6'1", 190 lbs. Born, Fort William, Ont., December 2, 1948.

Season	Club	GP	G	A	Pts	PIM	GP	G	A	Pts	PIM
1970-71	Vancouver Canucks	3	0	1	1	0	....	....	....	....	....
1972-73	New York Islanders	31	4	10	14	4	....	....	....	....	....
1973-74	New York Islanders	67	23	20	43	6	....	....	....	....	....
1974-75	New York Islanders	70	16	24	40	12	13	3	3	6	2
1975-76	New York Islanders	31	6	7	13	2	6	1	1	2	0
1976-77	Vancouver Canucks	34	6	8	14	4	....	....	....	....	....
1977-78	Vancouver Canucks	16	2	3	5	0	....	....	....	....	....
	NHL Totals	**252**	**57**	**73**	**130**	**28**	**19**	**4**	**4**	**8**	**2**

Loaned to **Vancouver** (WHL) by **Montreal** for cash, September 27, 1968. Claimed by **Vancouver** from **Montreal** in Expansion Draft, June 10, 1970. Traded to **Detroit** by **Vancouver** for Jim Niekamp, March 6, 1972. Traded to **NY Islanders** by **Detroit** with Bob Cook for Ken Murray and Brian Lavender, January 17, 1973. Traded to **Vancouver** by **NY Islanders** with Dave Fortier for cash, October 6, 1976.

STEWART, Ron

Right wing. Shoots right. 6'1", 197 lbs. Born, Calgary, Alta., July 11, 1932.

Season	Club	GP	G	A	Pts	PIM	GP	G	A	Pts	PIM
1952-53	Toronto Maple Leafs	70	13	22	35	29	....	....	....	....	....
1953-54	Toronto Maple Leafs	70	14	11	25	72	5	0	1	1	10
1954-55	Toronto Maple Leafs	53	14	5	19	20	4	0	0	0	2
1955-56	Toronto Maple Leafs	69	13	14	27	35	5	1	1	2	2
1956-57	Toronto Maple Leafs	65	15	20	35	28	....	....	....	....	....
1957-58	Toronto Maple Leafs	70	15	24	39	51	....	....	....	....	....
1958-59	Toronto Maple Leafs	70	21	13	34	23	12	3	3	6	6
1959-60	Toronto Maple Leafs	67	14	20	34	28	10	0	2	2	2
1960-61	Toronto Maple Leafs	51	13	12	25	8	5	1	0	1	2
1961-62 ♦	Toronto Maple Leafs	60	8	9	17	14	11	1	6	7	4
1962-63 ♦	Toronto Maple Leafs	63	16	16	32	26	10	4	0	4	2
1963-64 ♦	Toronto Maple Leafs	65	14	5	19	46	14	0	4	4	24
1964-65	Toronto Maple Leafs	65	16	11	27	33	6	0	1	1	2
1965-66	Boston Bruins	70	20	16	36	17	....	....	....	....	....
1966-67	Boston Bruins	56	14	10	24	31	....	....	....	....	....
1967-68	St. Louis Blues	19	7	5	12	11	....	....	....	....	....
	New York Rangers	55	7	7	14	19	6	1	1	2	2
1968-69	New York Rangers	75	18	11	29	20	4	0	1	1	0
1969-70	New York Rangers	76	14	10	24	14	6	0	0	0	2
1970-71	New York Rangers	76	5	6	11	19	13	1	0	1	0
1971-72	Vancouver Canucks	42	3	1	4	10	....	....	....	....	....
	New York Rangers	13	0	2	2	2	8	2	1	3	0
1972-73	New York Rangers	11	0	1	1	0	....	....	....	....	....
	New York Islanders	22	2	2	4	4	....	....	....	....	....
	NHL Totals	**1353**	**276**	**253**	**529**	**560**	**119**	**14**	**21**	**35**	**60**

Played in NHL All-Star Game (1955, 1962, 1963, 1964)

Traded to **Boston** by **Toronto** for Orland Kurtenbach, Andy Hebenton and Pat Stapleton, June 8, 1965. Claimed by **St. Louis** from **Boston** in Expansion Draft, June 6, 1967. Traded to **NY Rangers** by **St. Louis** with Ron Attwell for Red Berenson and Barclay Plager, November 29, 1967. Traded to **Vancouver** by **NY Rangers** with Dave Balon and Wayne Connelly for Gary Doak and Jim Wiste, November 16, 1971. Traded to **NY Rangers** (Providence-AHL) by **Vancouver** (Rochester-AHL) for the loan of Mike McMahon for the remainder of the 1971-72 season, March 5, 1972. Traded to **NY Islanders** by **NY Rangers** for cash, November 14, 1972.

STEWART, Ryan

Center. Shoots right. 6'1", 175 lbs. Born, Houston, B.C., June 1, 1967.
(Winnipeg's 1st choice, 18th overall, in 1985 Entry Draft).

Season	Club	GP	G	A	Pts	PIM	GP	G	A	Pts	PIM
1985-86	Winnipeg Jets	3	1	0	1	0	....	....	....	....	....
	NHL Totals	**3**	**1**	**0**	**1**	**0**	....	....	....	....	....

STIENBURG, Trevor

Right wing. Shoots right. 6'1", 200 lbs. Born, Kingston, Ont., May 13, 1966.
(Quebec's 1st choice, 15th overall, in 1984 Entry Draft).

Season	Club	GP	G	A	Pts	PIM	GP	G	A	Pts	PIM
1985-86	Quebec Nordiques	2	1	0	1	0	1	0	0	0	0
1986-87	Quebec Nordiques	6	1	0	1	12	....	....	....	....	....
1987-88	Quebec Nordiques	8	0	1	1	24	....	....	....	....	....
1988-89	Quebec Nordiques	55	6	3	9	125	....	....	....	....	....
	NHL Totals	**71**	**8**	**4**	**12**	**161**	**1**	**0**	**0**	**0**	**0**

Signed as a free agent by **Hartford**, July 21, 1992.

STILES, Tony

Defense. Shoots left. 5'11", 200 lbs. Born, Carstairs, Alta., August 12, 1959.

Season	Club	GP	G	A	Pts	PIM	GP	G	A	Pts	PIM
1983-84	Calgary Flames	30	2	7	9	20	....	....	....	....	....
	NHL Totals	**30**	**2**	**7**	**9**	**20**	....	....	....	....	....

Signed as a free agent by **Calgary**, September 17, 1982. Traded to **Quebec** by **Calgary** for Tom Thornbury, January 16, 1986.

STILLMAN, Cory

Left wing. Shoots left. 6', 194 lbs. Born, Peterborough, Ont., December 20, 1973.
(Calgary's 1st choice, 6th overall, in 1992 Entry Draft).

Season	Club	GP	G	A	Pts	PIM	GP	G	A	Pts	PIM
1994-95	Calgary Flames	10	0	2	2	2	....	....	....	....	....
1995-96	Calgary Flames	74	16	19	35	41	2	1	1	2	0
1996-97	Calgary Flames	58	6	20	26	14	....	....	....	....	....
1997-98	Calgary Flames	72	27	22	49	40	....	....	....	....	....
1998-99	Calgary Flames	76	27	30	57	38	....	....	....	....	....
99-2000	Calgary Flames	37	12	9	21	12	....	....	....	....	....
2000-01	Calgary Flames	66	21	24	45	45	....	....	....	....	....
	St. Louis Blues	12	3	4	7	6	15	3	5	8	8
2001-02	St. Louis Blues	80	23	22	45	36	9	0	2	2	2
2002-03	St. Louis Blues	79	24	43	67	56	6	2	2	4	2
	NHL Totals	**564**	**159**	**195**	**354**	**290**	**32**	**6**	**10**	**16**	**12**

• Missed majority of 1999-2000 season recovering from shoulder injury suffered in game vs. Philadelphia, December 27, 1999. Traded to **St. Louis by Calgary** for Craig Conroy and St. Louis' 7th round choice (David Moss) in 2001 Entry Draft, March 13, 2001. Traded to **Tampa Bay** by **St. Louis** for Tampa Bay's 2nd round choice (David Backes) in 2003 Entry Draft, June 21, 2003.

STOCK, P.J.

Center. Shoots left. 5'10", 190 lbs. Born, Victoriaville, Que., May 26, 1975.

Season	Club	GP	G	A	Pts	PIM	GP	G	A	Pts	PIM
1997-98	New York Rangers	38	2	3	5	114	....	....	....	....	....
1998-99	New York Rangers	5	0	0	0	6	....	....	....	....	....
99-2000	New York Rangers	11	0	1	1	11	....	....	....	....	....
2000-01	Montreal Canadiens	20	1	2	3	32	....	....	....	....	....
	Philadelphia Flyers	31	1	3	4	78	2	0	0	0	0
2001-02	Boston Bruins	58	0	3	3	122	6	1	0	1	19
2002-03	Boston Bruins	71	1	9	10	160	....	....	....	....	....
	NHL Totals	**234**	**5**	**21**	**26**	**523**	**8**	**1**	**0**	**1**	**19**

Signed as a free agent by **NY Rangers**, November 18, 1997. Signed as a free agent by **Montreal**, July 7, 2000. Traded to **Philadelphia** by **Montreal** with Montreal's 6th round choice (Dennis Seidenberg) in 2001 Entry Draft for Gino Odjick, December 7, 2000. Signed as a free agent by **NY Rangers**, August 23, 2001. Claimed by **Boston** from **NY Rangers** in Waiver Draft, September 28, 2001.

STODDARD, Jack

Right wing. Shoots right. 6'3", 185 lbs. Born, Stoney Creek, Ont., September 26, 1926.

Season	Club	GP	G	A	Pts	PIM	GP	G	A	Pts	PIM
1951-52	New York Rangers	20	4	2	6	2	....	....	....	....	....
1952-53	New York Rangers	60	12	13	25	29	....	....	....	....	....
	NHL Totals	**80**	**16**	**15**	**31**	**31**	....	....	....	....	....

Traded to **NY Rangers** by **Providence** (AHL) for Pat Egan, Zellio Toppazzini and Jean-Paul Denis, January 1, 1952.

STOJANOV, Alek

Right wing. Shoots left. 6'4", 225 lbs. Born, Windsor, Ont., April 25, 1973.
(Vancouver's 1st choice, 7th overall, in 1991 Entry Draft).

Season	Club	GP	G	A	Pts	PIM	GP	G	A	Pts	PIM
1994-95	Vancouver Canucks	4	0	0	0	13	5	0	0	0	2
1995-96	Vancouver Canucks	58	0	1	1	123	....	....	....	....	....
	Pittsburgh Penguins	10	1	0	1	7	9	0	0	0	19
1996-97	Pittsburgh Penguins	35	1	4	5	79	....	....	....	....	....
	NHL Totals	**107**	**2**	**5**	**7**	**222**	**14**	**0**	**0**	**0**	**21**

Traded to **Pittsburgh** by **Vancouver** for Markus Naslund, March 20, 1996.

STOLL, Jarret

Center. Shoots right. 6'1", 199 lbs. Born, Melville, Sask., June 25, 1982.
(Edmonton's 3rd choice, 36th overall, in 2002 Entry Draft).

Season	Club	GP	G	A	Pts	PIM	GP	G	A	Pts	PIM
2002-03	Edmonton Oilers	4	0	1	1	0	....	....	....	....	....
	NHL Totals	**4**	**0**	**1**	**1**	**0**	....	....	....	....	....

• Re-entered NHL Entry Draft. Originally Calgary's 3rd choice, 46th overall, in 2000 Entry Draft.

STOLTZ, Roland

Right wing. Shoots right. 6'1", 191 lbs. Born, Oeverkalix, Sweden, August 15, 1954.

Season	Club	GP	G	A	Pts	PIM	GP	G	A	Pts	PIM
1981-82	Washington Capitals	14	2	2	4	14	....	....	....	....	....
	NHL Totals	**14**	**2**	**2**	**4**	**14**	....	....	....	....	....

Signed as a free agent by **Washington**, June 5, 1981.

STONE, Steve

Right wing. Shoots right. 5'8", 170 lbs. Born, Toronto, Ont., September 26, 1952.
(Vancouver's 9th choice, 131st overall, in 1972 Amateur Draft).

Season	Club	GP	G	A	Pts	PIM	GP	G	A	Pts	PIM
1973-74	Vancouver Canucks	2	0	0	0	0	....	....	....	....	....
	NHL Totals	**2**	**0**	**0**	**0**	**0**	....	....	....	....	....

STORM, Jim

Left wing. Shoots left. 6'2", 200 lbs. Born, Milford, MI, February 5, 1971.
(Hartford's 5th choice, 75th overall, in 1991 Entry Draft).

Season	Club	GP	G	A	Pts	PIM	GP	G	A	Pts	PIM
1993-94	Hartford Whalers	68	6	10	16	27	....	....	....	....	....

Season	Club	REGULAR SEASON GP	G	A	Pts	PIM	PLAYOFFS GP	G	A	Pts	PIM
1994-95	Hartford Whalers	6	0	3	3	0	....	....	....	....	....
1995-96	Dallas Stars	10	1	2	3	17	....	....	....	....	....
	NHL Totals	**84**	**7**	**15**	**22**	**44**	....	....	....	....	....

Signed as a free agent by **Dallas**, September 13, 1995. Signed as a free agent by **NY Islanders**, July 21, 1997.

STOTHERS, Mike

Defense. Shoots left. 6'4", 212 lbs. Born, Toronto, Ont., February 22, 1962.
(Philadelphia's 1st choice, 21st overall, in 1980 Entry Draft).

Season	Club	GP	G	A	Pts	PIM	GP	G	A	Pts	PIM
1984-85	Philadelphia Flyers	1	0	0	0	0	....	....	....	....	....
1985-86	Philadelphia Flyers	6	0	1	1	6	3	0	0	0	4
1986-87	Philadelphia Flyers	2	0	0	0	4	2	0	0	0	7
1987-88	Philadelphia Flyers	3	0	0	0	13	....	....	....	....	....
	Toronto Maple Leafs	18	0	1	1	42	....	....	....	....	....
	NHL Totals	**30**	**0**	**2**	**2**	**65**	**5**	**0**	**0**	**0**	**11**

Traded to **Toronto** by **Philadelphia** for future considerations, December 4, 1987. Traded to **Philadelphia** by **Toronto** for Bill Root, June 21, 1988.

STOUGHTON, Blaine

Right wing. Shoots right. 5'11", 185 lbs. Born, Gilbert Plains, Man., March 13, 1953.
(Pittsburgh's 1st choice, 7th overall, in 1973 Amateur Draft).

Season	Club	GP	G	A	Pts	PIM	GP	G	A	Pts	PIM
1973-74	Pittsburgh Penguins	34	5	6	11	8	....	....	....	....	....
1974-75	Toronto Maple Leafs	78	23	14	37	24	7	4	2	6	2
1975-76	Toronto Maple Leafs	43	6	11	17	8	....	....	....	....	....
1979-80	Hartford Whalers	80	*56	44	100	16	1	0	0	0	0
1980-81	Hartford Whalers	71	43	30	73	56	....	....	....	....	....
1981-82	Hartford Whalers	80	52	39	91	57	....	....	....	....	....
1982-83	Hartford Whalers	72	45	31	76	27	....	....	....	....	....
1983-84	Hartford Whalers	54	23	14	37	4	....	....	....	....	....
	New York Rangers	14	5	2	7	4	....	....	....	....	....
	NHL Totals	**526**	**258**	**191**	**449**	**204**	**8**	**4**	**2**	**6**	**2**

Played in NHL All-Star Game (1982)

Traded to **Toronto** by **Pittsburgh** with Pittsburgh's 1st round choice (Trevor Johansen) in 1977 Entry Draft for Rick Kehoe, September 13, 1974. Claimed by **Hartford** from **Toronto** in Expansion Draft, June 13, 1979. Traded to **NY Rangers** by **Hartford** for Scot Kleinendorst, February 27, 1984.

STOYANOVICH, Steve

Center. Shoots right. 6'2", 205 lbs. Born, London, Ont., May 2, 1957.
(NY Islanders' 5th choice, 69th overall, in 1977 Amateur Draft).

Season	Club	GP	G	A	Pts	PIM	GP	G	A	Pts	PIM
1983-84	Hartford Whalers	23	3	5	8	11	....	....	....	....	....
	NHL Totals	**23**	**3**	**5**	**8**	**11**	....	....	....	....	....

Traded to **Hartford** by **NY Islanders** for Hartford's 5th round choice (Tommy Hedlund) in 1985 Entry Draft, August 19, 1983.

STRAIN, Neil

Left wing/Center. Shoots left. 5'9", 165 lbs. Born, Kenora, Ont., February 24, 1926.

Season	Club	GP	G	A	Pts	PIM	GP	G	A	Pts	PIM
1952-53	New York Rangers	52	11	13	24	12	....	....	....	....	....
	NHL Totals	**52**	**11**	**13**	**24**	**12**	....	....	....	....	....

Traded to **NY Rangers** (Denver-USHL) by **Cleveland** (AHL) with Bill Richardson, Bob Jackson and Joe McArthur for Wally Hergesheimer, September 5, 1950. Traded to **Cleveland** (AHL) by **NY Rangers** with Emile Francis and cash for Johnny Bower and Eldred Kobussen, July 20, 1953.

STRAKA, Martin

Center. Shoots left. 5'9", 178 lbs. Born, Plzen, Czech., September 3, 1972.
(Pittsburgh's 1st choice, 19th overall, in 1992 Entry Draft).

Season	Club	GP	G	A	Pts	PIM	GP	G	A	Pts	PIM
1992-93	Pittsburgh Penguins	42	3	13	16	29	11	2	1	3	2
1993-94	Pittsburgh Penguins	84	30	34	64	24	6	1	0	1	2
1994-95	Pittsburgh Penguins	31	4	12	16	16	....	....	....	....	....
	Ottawa Senators	6	1	1	2	0	....	....	....	....	....
1995-96	Ottawa Senators	43	9	16	25	29	....	....	....	....	....
	New York Islanders	22	2	10	12	6	....	....	....	....	....
	Florida Panthers	12	2	4	6	6	13	2	2	4	2
1996-97	Florida Panthers	55	7	22	29	12	4	0	0	0	0
1997-98	Pittsburgh Penguins	75	19	23	42	28	6	2	0	2	2
1998-99	Pittsburgh Penguins	80	35	48	83	26	13	6	9	15	6
99-2000	Pittsburgh Penguins	71	20	39	59	26	11	3	9	12	10
2000-01	Pittsburgh Penguins	82	27	68	95	38	18	5	8	13	8
2001-02	Pittsburgh Penguins	13	5	4	9	0	....	....	....	....	....
2002-03	Pittsburgh Penguins	60	18	28	46	12	....	....	....	....	....
	NHL Totals	**676**	**182**	**322**	**504**	**252**	**82**	**21**	**29**	**50**	**32**

Played in NHL All-Star Game (1999)

Traded to **Ottawa** by **Pittsburgh** for Troy Murray and Norm Maciver, April 7, 1995. Traded to **NY Islanders** by **Ottawa** with Don Beaupre and Bryan Berard for Damian Rhodes and Wade Redden, January 23, 1996. Claimed on waivers by **Florida** from **NY Islanders**, March 15, 1996. Signed as a free agent by **Pittsburgh**, August 6, 1997. • Missed majority of 2001-02 season recovering from leg injury suffered in game vs. Florida, October 28, 2001.

STRATE, Gord

Defense. Shoots left. 6'1", 190 lbs. Born, Edmonton, Alta., May 28, 1935.

Season	Club	GP	G	A	Pts	PIM	GP	G	A	Pts	PIM
1956-57	Detroit Red Wings	5	0	0	0	4	....	....	....	....	....
1957-58	Detroit Red Wings	45	0	0	0	24	....	....	....	....	....
1958-59	Detroit Red Wings	11	0	0	0	6	....	....	....	....	....
	NHL Totals	**61**	**0**	**0**	**0**	**34**	....	....	....	....	....

STRATTON, Art

Center/Left wing. Shoots left. 5'11", 170 lbs. Born, Winnipeg, Man., October 8, 1935.

Season	Club	GP	G	A	Pts	PIM	GP	G	A	Pts	PIM
1959-60	New York Rangers	18	2	5	7	2	....	....	....	....	....
1963-64	Detroit Red Wings	5	0	3	3	2	....	....	....	....	....
1965-66	Chicago Black Hawks	2	0	0	0	0	....	....	....	....	....
1967-68	Pittsburgh Penguins	58	16	21	37	16	....	....	....	....	....
	Philadelphia Flyers	12	0	4	4	4	5	0	0	0	0
	NHL Totals	**95**	**18**	**33**	**51**	**24**	**5**	**0**	**0**	**0**	**0**

Traded to **NY Rangers** by **Cleveland** (AHL) for Aldo Guidolin and Ed Hoekstra with NY Rangers holding right of recall, June, 1959. Traded to **Chicago** (Buffalo-AHL) by **NY Rangers** for cash, September, 1961. Claimed by **Detroit** from **Chicago** (Buffalo-AHL) in Inter-League Draft, June 4, 1963. Traded to **Chicago** by **Detroit** with Ian Cushenan and John Miszuk for Ron Murphy and Aut Erickson, June 9, 1964. Claimed by **Pittsburgh** from **Chicago** in Expansion Draft, June 6, 1967. Traded to **Philadelphia** by **Pittsburgh** for Wayne Hicks, February 27, 1968. Traded to **Seattle** (WHL) by **Philadelphia** with John Hanna to complete transaction that sent Earl Heiskala to Philadelphia (May 19, 1968), June, 1968. Traded to **Detroit** by **Seattle** (WHL) for Bob Sneddon, November, 1971. Claimed by **Rochester** (AHL) from **Detroit** in Reverse Draft, June, 1973.

STROBEL, Art

Left wing. Shoots left. 5'6", 160 lbs. Born, Regina, Sask., November 28, 1922.

Season	Club	GP	G	A	Pts	PIM	GP	G	A	Pts	PIM
1943-44	New York Rangers	7	0	0	0	0	....	....	....	....	....
	NHL Totals	**7**	**0**	**0**	**0**	**0**	....	....	....	....	....

Signed as a free agent by **NY Rangers**, October 21, 1943.

STRONG, Ken

Left wing. Shoots left. 5'11", 185 lbs. Born, Toronto, Ont., May 9, 1963.
(Philadelphia's 4th choice, 58th overall, in 1981 Entry Draft).

Season	Club	GP	G	A	Pts	PIM	GP	G	A	Pts	PIM
1982-83	Toronto Maple Leafs	2	0	0	0	0	....	....	....	....	....
1983-84	Toronto Maple Leafs	2	0	2	2	2	....	....	....	....	....
1984-85	Toronto Maple Leafs	11	2	0	2	4	....	....	....	....	....
	NHL Totals	**15**	**2**	**2**	**4**	**6**	....	....	....	....	....

Traded to **Toronto** by **Philadelphia** to complete transaction that sent Darryl Sittler to Philadelphia (January 20, 1982), May, 1982.

STRUCH, David

Center. Shoots left. 5'10", 180 lbs. Born, Flin Flon, Man., February 11, 1971.
(Calgary's 11th choice, 195th overall, in 1991 Entry Draft).

Season	Club	GP	G	A	Pts	PIM	GP	G	A	Pts	PIM
1993-94	Calgary Flames	4	0	0	0	4	....	....	....	....	....
	NHL Totals	**4**	**0**	**0**	**0**	**4**	....	....	....	....	....

STRUDWICK, Jason

Defense. Shoots left. 6'3", 215 lbs. Born, Edmonton, Alta., July 17, 1975.
(NY Islanders' 3rd choice, 63rd overall, in 1994 Entry Draft).

Season	Club	GP	G	A	Pts	PIM	GP	G	A	Pts	PIM
1995-96	New York Islanders	1	0	0	0	7	....	....	....	....	....
1997-98	New York Islanders	17	0	1	1	36	....	....	....	....	....
	Vancouver Canucks	11	0	1	1	29	....	....	....	....	....
1998-99	Vancouver Canucks	65	0	3	3	114	....	....	....	....	....
99-2000	Vancouver Canucks	63	1	3	4	64	....	....	....	....	....
2000-01	Vancouver Canucks	60	1	4	5	64	2	0	0	0	0
2001-02	Vancouver Canucks	44	2	4	6	96	....	....	....	....	....
2002-03	Chicago Blackhawks	48	2	3	5	87	....	....	....	....	....
	NHL Totals	**309**	**6**	**19**	**25**	**497**	**2**	**0**	**0**	**0**	**0**

Traded to **Vancouver** by **NY Islanders** for Gino Odjick, March 23, 1998. Signed as a free agent by **Chicago**, July 15, 2002.

STRUEBY, Todd

Left wing. Shoots left. 6'1", 185 lbs. Born, Lanigan, Sask., June 15, 1963.
(Edmonton's 2nd choice, 29th overall, in 1981 Entry Draft).

Season	Club	GP	G	A	Pts	PIM	GP	G	A	Pts	PIM
1981-82	Edmonton Oilers	3	0	0	0	0	....	....	....	....	....
1982-83	Edmonton Oilers	1	0	0	0	0	....	....	....	....	....
1983-84	Edmonton Oilers	1	0	1	1	2	....	....	....	....	....
	NHL Totals	**5**	**0**	**1**	**1**	**2**	....	....	....	....	....

Traded to **NY Rangers** by **Edmonton** with Larry Melnyk for Mike Rogers, December 20, 1985.

STUART, Billy

Defense. Shoots left. 5'11", 190 lbs. Born, Sackville, N.B., February 1, 1900.

Season	Club	GP	G	A	Pts	PIM	GP	G	A	Pts	PIM
1920-21	Toronto St. Pats	19	2	1	3	4	2	0	0	0	0
1921-22 ♦	Toronto St. Pats	24	3	7	10	16	2	1	1	2	0
	Toronto St. Pats (Cup)	....	....	....	....	....	*5*	*0*	*2*	*2*	*6*
1922-23	Toronto St. Pats	23	7	3	10	16	....	....	....	....	....
1923-24	Toronto St. Pats	24	4	3	7	22	....	....	....	....	....
1924-25	Toronto St. Pats	4	0	1	1	2	....	....	....	....	....
	Boston Bruins	25	5	3	8	30	....	....	....	....	....
1925-26	Boston Bruins	33	6	1	7	41	....	....	....	....	....
1926-27	Boston Bruins	43	3	1	4	20	8	0	0	0	6
	NHL Totals	**195**	**30**	**20**	**50**	**151**	**12**	**1**	**1**	**2**	**6**

Signed as a free agent by **Toronto**, January 5, 1920. Traded to **Boston** by **Toronto** for cash, December 14, 1924. Traded to **Minneapolis** (AHA) by **Boston** with cash and future considerations for Nobby Clark and Norm Gainor, October 24, 1927.

STUART, Brad

Defense. Shoots left. 6'2", 215 lbs. Born, Rocky Mountain House, Alta., November 6, 1979.
(San Jose's 1st choice, 3rd overall, in 1998 Entry Draft).

Season	Club	REGULAR SEASON GP	G	A	Pts	PIM	PLAYOFFS GP	G	A	Pts	PIM
99-2000	San Jose Sharks	82	10	26	36	32	12	1	0	1	6
2000-01	San Jose Sharks	77	5	18	23	56	5	1	0	1	0
2001-02	San Jose Sharks	82	6	23	29	39	12	0	3	3	8
2002-03	San Jose Sharks	36	4	10	14	46	....	....	....	....	....
	NHL Totals	**277**	**25**	**77**	**102**	**173**	**29**	**2**	**3**	**5**	**14**

STUMPEL, Jozef

Center. Shoots right. 6'3", 225 lbs. Born, Nitra, Czech., July 20, 1972.
(Boston's 2nd choice, 40th overall, in 1991 Entry Draft).

Season	Club	REGULAR SEASON GP	G	A	Pts	PIM	PLAYOFFS GP	G	A	Pts	PIM
1991-92	Boston Bruins	4	1	0	1	0	....	....	....	....	....
1992-93	Boston Bruins	13	1	3	4	4	....	....	....	....	....
1993-94	Boston Bruins	59	8	15	23	14	13	1	7	8	4
1994-95	Boston Bruins	44	5	13	18	8	5	0	0	0	0
1995-96	Boston Bruins	76	18	36	54	14	5	1	2	3	0
1996-97	Boston Bruins	78	21	55	76	14	....	....	....	....	....
1997-98	Los Angeles Kings	77	21	58	79	53	4	1	2	3	2
1998-99	Los Angeles Kings	64	13	21	34	10	....	....	....	....	....
99-2000	Los Angeles Kings	57	17	41	58	10	4	0	4	4	8
2000-01	Los Angeles Kings	63	16	39	55	14	13	3	5	8	10
2001-02	Los Angeles Kings	9	1	3	4	4	....	....	....	....	....
	Boston Bruins	72	7	47	54	14	6	0	2	2	0
2002-03	Boston Bruins	78	14	37	51	12	5	0	2	2	0
	NHL Totals	**694**	**143**	**368**	**511**	**171**	**55**	**6**	**24**	**30**	**24**

Traded to **Los Angeles** by **Boston** with Sandy Moger and Boston's 4th round choice (later traded to New Jersey – New Jersey selected Pierre Dagenais) in 1998 Entry Draft for Dmitri Kristich and Byron Dafoe, August 29, 1997. Traded to **Boston** by **Los Angeles** with Glen Murray for Jason Allison and Mikko Eloranta, October 24, 2001. Traded to **Los Angeles** by **Boston** with Boston's 7th round choice (later traded to Nashville – Nashville selected Miroslav Hanuljak) in 2003 Entry Draft for Philadelphia's 4th round choice (previously acquired, Boston selected Patrick Valcak) in 2003 Entry Draft and Detroit's 2nd round choice (previously acquired) in 2004 Entry Draft, June 22, 2003.

STUMPF, Bob

Right wing/Defense. Shoots right. 6'1", 195 lbs. Born, Milo, Alta., April 25, 1953.
(Philadelphia's 3rd choice, 40th overall, in 1973 Amateur Draft).

Season	Club	REGULAR SEASON GP	G	A	Pts	PIM	PLAYOFFS GP	G	A	Pts	PIM
1974-75	St. Louis Blues	7	1	1	2	16	....	....	....	....	....
	Pittsburgh Penguins	3	0	0	0	4	....	....	....	....	....
	NHL Totals	**10**	**1**	**1**	**2**	**20**	....	....	....	....	....

Traded to **St. Louis** by **Philadelphia** for George Pesut, November, 1973. Traded to **Pittsburgh** by **St. Louis** for Bernie Lukowich, January 20, 1975.

STURGEON, Peter

Left wing. Shoots left. 6'2", 198 lbs. Born, Whitehorse, Yukon, February 12, 1954
(Boston's 3rd choice, 36th overall, in 1974 Amateur Draft).

Season	Club	REGULAR SEASON GP	G	A	Pts	PIM	PLAYOFFS GP	G	A	Pts	PIM
1979-80	Colorado Rockies	2	0	0	0	0	....	....	....	....	....
1980-81	Colorado Rockies	4	0	1	1	2	....	....	....	....	....
	NHL Totals	**6**	**0**	**1**	**1**	**2**	....	....	....	....	....

Signed as a free agent by **Colorado**, July 10, 1979.

STURM, Marco

Left wing. Shoots left. 6', 195 lbs. Born, Dingolfing, West Germany, September 8, 1978.
(San Jose's 2nd choice, 21st overall, in 1996 Entry Draft).

Season	Club	REGULAR SEASON GP	G	A	Pts	PIM	PLAYOFFS GP	G	A	Pts	PIM
1997-98	San Jose Sharks	74	10	20	30	40	2	0	0	0	0
1998-99	San Jose Sharks	78	16	22	38	52	6	2	2	4	4
99-2000	San Jose Sharks	74	12	15	27	22	12	1	3	4	6
2000-01	San Jose Sharks	81	14	18	32	28	6	0	2	2	0
2001-02	San Jose Sharks	77	21	20	41	32	12	3	2	5	2
2002-03	San Jose Sharks	82	28	20	48	16	....	....	....	....	....
	NHL Totals	**466**	**101**	**115**	**216**	**190**	**38**	**6**	**9**	**15**	**12**

Played in NHL All-Star Game (1999)

SUCHY, Radoslav

Defense. Shoots left. 6'2", 198 lbs. Born, Kezmarok, Czech., April 7, 1976.

Season	Club	REGULAR SEASON GP	G	A	Pts	PIM	PLAYOFFS GP	G	A	Pts	PIM
99-2000	Phoenix Coyotes	60	0	6	6	16	5	0	1	1	0
2000-01	Phoenix Coyotes	72	0	10	10	22	....	....	....	....	....
2001-02	Phoenix Coyotes	81	4	13	17	10	5	1	0	1	0
2002-03	Phoenix Coyotes	77	1	8	9	18	....	....	....	....	....
	NHL Totals	**290**	**5**	**37**	**42**	**66**	**10**	**1**	**1**	**2**	**0**

Signed as a free agent by **Phoenix**, September 26, 1997.

SUIKKANEN, Kai

Defense. Shoots left. 6'2", 205 lbs. Born, Parkano, Finland, June 29, 1959.

Season	Club	REGULAR SEASON GP	G	A	Pts	PIM	PLAYOFFS GP	G	A	Pts	PIM
1981-82	Buffalo Sabres	1	0	0	0	0	....	....	....	....	....
1982-83	Buffalo Sabres	1	0	0	0	0	....	....	....	....	....
	NHL Totals	**2**	**0**	**0**	**0**	**0**	....	....	....	....	....

Signed as a free agent by **Buffalo**, August 31, 1981.

SULLIMAN, Doug

Right wing. Shoots left. 6'2", 210 lbs. Born, Glace Bay, N.S., August 29, 1959.
(NY Rangers' 1st choice, 13th overall, in 1979 Entry Draft).

Season	Club	REGULAR SEASON GP	G	A	Pts	PIM	PLAYOFFS GP	G	A	Pts	PIM
1979-80	New York Rangers	31	4	7	11	2	....	....	....	....	....
1980-81	New York Rangers	32	4	1	5	32	3	1	0	1	0
1981-82	Hartford Whalers	77	29	40	69	39	....	....	....	....	....
1982-83	Hartford Whalers	77	22	19	41	14	....	....	....	....	....
1983-84	Hartford Whalers	67	6	13	19	20	....	....	....	....	....
1984-85	New Jersey Devils	57	22	16	38	4	....	....	....	....	....
1985-86	New Jersey Devils	73	21	22	43	20	....	....	....	....	....
1986-87	New Jersey Devils	78	27	26	53	14	....	....	....	....	....
1987-88	New Jersey Devils	59	16	14	30	22	9	0	3	3	2
1988-89	Philadelphia Flyers	52	6	6	12	8	4	0	0	0	0
1989-90	Philadelphia Flyers	28	3	4	7	0	....	....	....	....	....
	NHL Totals	**631**	**160**	**168**	**328**	**175**	**16**	**1**	**3**	**4**	**2**

Traded to **Hartford** by **NY Rangers** with Chris Kotsopoulos and Gerry McDonald for Mike Rogers and Hartford's 10th round choice (Simo Saarinen) in 1982 Entry Draft, October 2, 1981. Signed as a free agent by **New Jersey**, July 11, 1984. Claimed by **Philadelphia** from **New Jersey** in Waiver Draft, October 3, 1988.

SULLIVAN, Barry

Right wing. Shoots right. 6', 185 lbs. Born, Preston, Ont., September 21, 1927.

Season	Club	REGULAR SEASON GP	G	A	Pts	PIM	PLAYOFFS GP	G	A	Pts	PIM
1947-48	Detroit Red Wings	1	0	0	0	0	....	....	....	....	....
	NHL Totals	**1**	**0**	**0**	**0**	**0**	....	....	....	....	....

Traded to **Chicago** (St. Louis-AHL) by **Detroit** with Red Almas, Lloyd Doran, Tony Licari and Thain Simon for Joe Lund and Hec Highton, September 9, 1948. Loaned to **New Haven** (AHL) by **Chicago** (St. Louis-AHL) for cash, November 7, 1950 and recalled when New Haven franchise folded, December 11, 1950. Traded to **Providence** (AHL) by **Chicago** (St. Louis-AHL) for Jack Hamilton, January 29, 1951.

SULLIVAN, Bob

Left wing. Shoots right. 6', 210 lbs. Born, Noranda, Que., November 29, 1957.
(NY Rangers' 8th choice, 116th overall, in 1977 Amateur Draft).

Season	Club	REGULAR SEASON GP	G	A	Pts	PIM	PLAYOFFS GP	G	A	Pts	PIM
1982-83	Hartford Whalers	62	18	19	37	18	....	....	....	....	....
	NHL Totals	**62**	**18**	**19**	**37**	**18**	....	....	....	....	....

Signed as a free agent by **Hartford**, August 24, 1982.

SULLIVAN, Brian

Right wing. Shoots right. 6'4", 195 lbs. Born, South Windsor, CT, April 23, 1969.
(New Jersey's 3rd choice, 65th overall, in 1987 Entry Draft).

Season	Club	REGULAR SEASON GP	G	A	Pts	PIM	PLAYOFFS GP	G	A	Pts	PIM
1992-93	New Jersey Devils	2	0	1	1	0	....	....	....	....	....
	NHL Totals	**2**	**0**	**1**	**1**	**0**	....	....	....	....	....

Signed as a free agent by **Anaheim**, August 31, 1994.

SULLIVAN, Frank

Defense. Shoots right. 5'11", 178 lbs. Born, Toronto, Ont., June 16, 1929.

Season	Club	REGULAR SEASON GP	G	A	Pts	PIM	PLAYOFFS GP	G	A	Pts	PIM
1949-50	Toronto Maple Leafs	1	0	0	0	0	....	....	....	....	....
1952-53	Toronto Maple Leafs	5	0	0	0	2	....	....	....	....	....
1954-55	Chicago Black Hawks	1	0	0	0	0	....	....	....	....	....
1955-56	Chicago Black Hawks	1	0	0	0	0	....	....	....	....	....
	NHL Totals	**8**	**0**	**0**	**0**	**2**	....	....	....	....	....

• Brother of Peter

Traded to **Chicago** (Buffalo-AHL) by **Toronto** with Dusty Blair and Jack Leclair for Brian Cullen, May 4, 1954.

SULLIVAN, Mike

Center. Shoots left. 6'2", 204 lbs. Born, Marshfield, MA, February 27, 1968.
(NY Rangers' 4th choice, 69th overall, in 1987 Entry Draft).

Season	Club	REGULAR SEASON GP	G	A	Pts	PIM	PLAYOFFS GP	G	A	Pts	PIM
1991-92	San Jose Sharks	64	8	11	19	15	....	....	....	....	....
1992-93	San Jose Sharks	81	6	8	14	30	....	....	....	....	....
1993-94	San Jose Sharks	26	2	2	4	4	....	....	....	....	....
	Calgary Flames	19	2	3	5	6	7	1	1	2	8
1994-95	Calgary Flames	38	4	7	11	14	7	3	5	8	2
1995-96	Calgary Flames	81	9	12	21	24	4	0	0	0	0
1996-97	Calgary Flames	67	5	6	11	10	....	....	....	....	....
1997-98	Boston Bruins	77	5	13	18	34	6	0	1	1	2
1998-99	Phoenix Coyotes	63	2	4	6	24	5	0	0	0	2
99-2000	Phoenix Coyotes	79	5	10	15	10	5	0	1	1	0
2000-01	Phoenix Coyotes	72	5	4	9	16	....	....	....	....	....
2001-02	Phoenix Coyotes	42	1	2	3	16	....	....	....	....	....
	NHL Totals	**709**	**54**	**82**	**136**	**203**	**34**	**4**	**8**	**12**	**14**

Rights traded to **Minnesota** by **NY Rangers** with Mark Tinordi, Paul Jerrard, the rights to Bret Barnett and Los Angeles' 3rd round choice (previously acquired, Minnesota selected Murray Garbutt) in 1989 Entry Draft for Brian Lawton, Igor Liba and the rights to Eric Bennett, October 11, 1988. Signed as a free agent by **San Jose**, August 9, 1991. Claimed on waivers by **Calgary** from **San Jose**, January 6, 1994. Traded to **Boston** by **Calgary** for Boston's 7th round choice (Radek Duda) in 1998 Entry Draft, June 21, 1997. Claimed by **Nashville** from **Boston** in Expansion Draft, June 26, 1998. Traded to **Phoenix** by **Nashville** for Phoenix's 7th round choice (Kyle Kettles) in 1999 Entry Draft, June 30, 1998.

SULLIVAN, Peter

Center. Shoots right. 5'9", 165 lbs. Born, Toronto, Ont., July 25, 1951.
(Montreal's 12th choice, 95th overall, in 1971 Amateur Draft).

Season	Club	REGULAR SEASON GP	G	A	Pts	PIM	PLAYOFFS GP	G	A	Pts	PIM
1979-80	Winnipeg Jets	79	24	35	59	20	....	....	....	....	....
1980-81	Winnipeg Jets	47	4	19	23	20	....	....	....	....	....
	NHL Totals	**126**	**28**	**54**	**82**	**40**	....	....	....	....	....

• Brother of Frank

Rights retained by **Winnipeg** prior to Expansion Draft, June 9, 1979.

SULLIVAN, Red

Center. Shoots left. 5'11", 155 lbs. Born, Peterborough, Ont., December 24, 1929.

Season	Club	Regular Season GP	G	A	Pts	PIM	Playoffs GP	G	A	Pts	PIM
1949-50	Boston Bruins	3	0	1	1	0	....	....	....	....	....
1950-51	Boston Bruins	....	....	....	....	....	2	0	0	0	2
1951-52	Boston Bruins	67	12	12	24	24	7	0	0	0	0
1952-53	Boston Bruins	32	3	8	11	8	3	0	0	0	0
1954-55	Chicago Black Hawks	70	19	42	61	51	....	....	....	....	....
1955-56	Chicago Black Hawks	63	14	26	40	58	....	....	....	....	....
1956-57	New York Rangers	42	6	17	23	36	5	1	2	3	4
1957-58	New York Rangers	70	11	35	46	61	1	0	0	0	0
1958-59	New York Rangers	70	21	42	63	56	....	....	....	....	....
1959-60	New York Rangers	70	12	25	37	81	....	....	....	....	....
1960-61	New York Rangers	70	9	31	40	66	....	....	....	....	....
	NHL Totals	**557**	**107**	**239**	**346**	**441**	**18**	**1**	**2**	**3**	**6**

Played in NHL All-Star Game (1955, 1956, 1958, 1959, 1960)

Traded to **Chicago** by **Boston** for cash, September 10, 1954. Traded to **NY Rangers** by **Chicago** for Wally Hergesheimer, June 19, 1956.

SULLIVAN, Steve

Right wing. Shoots right. 5'9", 160 lbs. Born, Timmins, Ont., July 6, 1974.
(New Jersey's 10th choice, 233rd overall, in 1994 Entry Draft).

Season	Club	Regular Season GP	G	A	Pts	PIM	Playoffs GP	G	A	Pts	PIM
1995-96	New Jersey Devils	16	5	4	9	8	....	....	....	....	....
1996-97	New Jersey Devils	33	8	14	22	14	....	....	....	....	....
	Toronto Maple Leafs	21	5	11	16	23	....	....	....	....	....
1997-98	Toronto Maple Leafs	63	10	18	28	40	....	....	....	....	....
1998-99	Toronto Maple Leafs	63	20	20	40	28	13	3	3	6	14
99-2000	Toronto Maple Leafs	7	0	1	1	4	....	....	....	....	....
	Chicago Blackhawks	73	22	42	64	52	....	....	....	....	....
2000-01	Chicago Blackhawks	81	34	41	75	54	....	....	....	....	....
2001-02	Chicago Blackhawks	78	21	39	60	67	5	1	0	1	2
2002-03	Chicago Blackhawks	82	26	35	61	42	....	....	....	....	....
	NHL Totals	**517**	**151**	**225**	**376**	**332**	**18**	**4**	**3**	**7**	**16**

Traded to **Toronto** by **New Jersey** with Jason Smith and the rights to Alyn McCauley for Doug Gilmour, Dave Ellett and New Jersey's 3rd round choice (previously acquired, New Jersey selected Andre Lakos) in 1999 Entry Draft, February 25, 1997. Claimed on waivers by **Chicago** from **Toronto**, October 23, 1999.

SUMMANEN, Raimo

Left wing. Shoots left. 5'11", 185 lbs. Born, Jyvaskyla, Finland, March 2, 1962.
(Edmonton's 6th choice, 125th overall, in 1982 Entry Draft).

Season	Club	Regular Season GP	G	A	Pts	PIM	Playoffs GP	G	A	Pts	PIM
1983-84	Edmonton Oilers	2	1	4	5	2	5	1	4	5	0
1984-85	Edmonton Oilers	9	0	4	4	0	....	....	....	....	....
1985-86	Edmonton Oilers	73	19	18	37	16	5	1	1	2	0
1986-87	Edmonton Oilers	48	10	7	17	15	....	....	....	....	....
	Vancouver Canucks	10	4	4	8	0	....	....	....	....	....
1987-88	Vancouver Canucks	9	2	3	5	2	....	....	....	....	....
	NHL Totals	**151**	**36**	**40**	**76**	**35**	**10**	**2**	**5**	**7**	**0**

Traded to **Vancouver** by **Edmonton** for Moe Lemay, March 10, 1987.

SUMMERHILL, Bill

Right wing. Shoots right. 5'9", 170 lbs. Born, Toronto, Ont., July 9, 1915.

Season	Club	Regular Season GP	G	A	Pts	PIM	Playoffs GP	G	A	Pts	PIM
1937-38	Montreal Canadiens	....	....	....	....	....	1	0	0	0	0
1938-39	Montreal Canadiens	43	6	10	16	28	2	0	0	0	2
1939-40	Montreal Canadiens	13	3	2	5	24	....	....	....	....	....
1941-42	Brooklyn Americans	16	5	5	10	18	....	....	....	....	....
	NHL Totals	**72**	**14**	**17**	**31**	**70**	**3**	**0**	**0**	**0**	**2**

Traded to **Cleveland** (IAHL) by **Montreal** with Bill MacKenzie for Jim O'Neil, May 17, 1940. Traded to **Brooklyn** by **Cleveland** (AHL) for cash, October 6, 1941.

SUNDBLAD, Niklas

Right wing. Shoots right. 6'1", 200 lbs. Born, Stockholm, Sweden, January 3, 1973.
(Calgary's 1st choice, 19th overall, in 1991 Entry Draft).

Season	Club	Regular Season GP	G	A	Pts	PIM	Playoffs GP	G	A	Pts	PIM
1995-96	Calgary Flames	2	0	0	0	0	....	....	....	....	....
	NHL Totals	**2**	**0**	**0**	**0**	**0**	....	....	....	....	....

SUNDIN, Mats

Center. Shoots right. 6'4", 220 lbs. Born, Bromma, Sweden, February 13, 1971.
(Quebec's 1st choice, 1st overall, in 1989 Entry Draft).

Season	Club	Regular Season GP	G	A	Pts	PIM	Playoffs GP	G	A	Pts	PIM
1990-91	Quebec Nordiques	80	23	36	59	58	....	....	....	....	....
1991-92	Quebec Nordiques	80	33	43	76	103	....	....	....	....	....
1992-93	Quebec Nordiques	80	47	67	114	96	6	3	1	4	6
1993-94	Quebec Nordiques	84	32	53	85	60	....	....	....	....	....
1994-95	Toronto Maple Leafs	47	23	24	47	14	7	5	4	9	4
1995-96	Toronto Maple Leafs	76	33	50	83	46	6	3	1	4	4
1996-97	Toronto Maple Leafs	82	41	53	94	59	....	....	....	....	....
1997-98	Toronto Maple Leafs	82	33	41	74	49	....	....	....	....	....
1998-99	Toronto Maple Leafs	82	31	52	83	58	17	8	8	16	16
99-2000	Toronto Maple Leafs	73	32	41	73	46	12	3	5	8	10
2000-01	Toronto Maple Leafs	82	28	46	74	76	11	6	7	13	14
2001-02	Toronto Maple Leafs	82	41	39	80	94	8	2	5	7	4
2002-03	Toronto Maple Leafs	75	37	35	72	58	7	1	3	4	6
	NHL Totals	**1005**	**434**	**580**	**1014**	**817**	**74**	**31**	**34**	**65**	**64**

NHL Second All-Star Team (2002)

Played in NHL All-Star Game (1996, 1997, 1998, 1999, 2000, 2001, 2002)

Traded to **Toronto** by **Quebec** with Garth Butcher, Todd Warriner and Philadelphia's 1st round choice (previously acquired, later traded to Washington – Washington selected Nolan Baumgartner) in 1994 Entry Draft for Wendel Clark, Sylvain Lefebvre, Landon Wilson and Toronto's 1st round choice (Jeffrey Kealty) in 1994 Entry Draft, June 28, 1994.

SUNDIN, Ronnie

Defense. Shoots left. 6'1", 220 lbs. Born, Ludvika, Sweden, October 3, 1970.
(NY Rangers' 8th choice, 237th overall, in 1996 Entry Draft).

Season	Club	Regular Season GP	G	A	Pts	PIM	Playoffs GP	G	A	Pts	PIM
1997-98	New York Rangers	1	0	0	0	0	....	....	....	....	....
	NHL Totals	**1**	**0**	**0**	**0**	**0**	....	....	....	....	....

SUNDSTROM, Niklas

Right wing. Shoots left. 6', 190 lbs. Born, Ornskoldsvik, Sweden, June 6, 1975.
(NY Rangers' 1st choice, 8th overall, in 1993 Entry Draft).

Season	Club	Regular Season GP	G	A	Pts	PIM	Playoffs GP	G	A	Pts	PIM
1995-96	New York Rangers	82	9	12	21	14	11	4	3	7	4
1996-97	New York Rangers	82	24	28	52	20	9	0	5	5	2
1997-98	New York Rangers	70	19	28	47	24	....	....	....	....	....
1998-99	New York Rangers	81	13	30	43	20	....	....	....	....	....
99-2000	San Jose Sharks	79	12	25	37	22	12	0	2	2	2
2000-01	San Jose Sharks	82	10	39	49	28	6	0	3	3	2
2001-02	San Jose Sharks	73	9	30	39	50	12	1	6	7	6
2002-03	San Jose Sharks	47	2	10	12	22	....	....	....	....	....
	Montreal Canadiens	33	5	9	14	8	....	....	....	....	....
	NHL Totals	**629**	**103**	**211**	**314**	**208**	**50**	**5**	**19**	**24**	**16**

Traded to **Tampa Bay** by **NY Rangers** with Dan Cloutier and NY Rangers' 1st (Nikita Alexeev) and 3rd (later traded to San Jose – later traded to Chicago – Chicago selected Igor Radulov) round choices in 2000 Entry Draft for Chicago's 1st round choice (previously acquired, NY Rangers selected Pavel Brendl) in 1999 Entry Draft, June 26, 1999. Traded to **San Jose** by **Tampa Bay** with NY Rangers' 3rd round choice (previously acquired, later traded to Chicago – Chicago selected Igor Radulov) in 2000 Entry Draft for Bill Houlder, Andrei Zyuzin, Shawn Burr and Steve Guolla, August 4, 1999. Traded to **Montreal** by **San Jose** with San Jose's 3rd round choice in 2004 Entry Draft for Jeff Hackett, January 23, 2003.

SUNDSTROM, Patrik

Center. Shoots left. 6'1", 200 lbs. Born, Skelleftea, Sweden, December 14, 1961.
(Vancouver's 8th choice, 175th overall, in 1980 Entry Draft).

Season	Club	Regular Season GP	G	A	Pts	PIM	Playoffs GP	G	A	Pts	PIM
1982-83	Vancouver Canucks	74	23	23	46	30	4	0	0	0	2
1983-84	Vancouver Canucks	78	38	53	91	37	4	0	1	1	7
1984-85	Vancouver Canucks	71	25	43	68	46	....	....	....	....	....
1985-86	Vancouver Canucks	79	18	48	66	28	3	1	0	1	0
1986-87	Vancouver Canucks	72	29	42	71	40	....	....	....	....	....
1987-88	New Jersey Devils	78	15	36	51	42	18	7	13	20	14
1988-89	New Jersey Devils	65	28	41	69	36	....	....	....	....	....
1989-90	New Jersey Devils	74	27	49	76	34	6	1	3	4	2
1990-91	New Jersey Devils	71	15	31	46	48	2	0	0	0	0
1991-92	New Jersey Devils	17	1	3	4	8	....	....	....	....	....
	NHL Totals	**679**	**219**	**369**	**588**	**349**	**37**	**9**	**17**	**26**	**25**

• Brother of Peter

Traded to **New Jersey** by **Vancouver** with Vancouver's 2nd (Jeff Christian) and 4th (Matt Ruchty) round choices in 1988 Entry Draft for Kirk McLean, Greg Adams and New Jersey's 2nd round choice (Leif Rohlin) in 1988 Entry Draft, September 15, 1987.

SUNDSTROM, Peter

Left wing. Shoots left. 6', 180 lbs. Born, Skelleftea, Sweden, December 14, 1961.
(NY Rangers' 3rd choice, 50th overall, in 1981 Entry Draft).

Season	Club	Regular Season GP	G	A	Pts	PIM	Playoffs GP	G	A	Pts	PIM
1983-84	New York Rangers	77	22	22	44	24	5	1	3	4	0
1984-85	New York Rangers	76	18	25	43	34	3	0	0	0	0
1985-86	New York Rangers	53	8	15	23	12	1	0	0	0	2
1987-88	Washington Capitals	76	8	17	25	34	14	2	0	2	6
1988-89	Washington Capitals	35	4	2	6	12	....	....	....	....	....
1989-90	New Jersey Devils	21	1	2	3	4	....	....	....	....	....
	NHL Totals	**338**	**61**	**83**	**144**	**120**	**23**	**3**	**3**	**6**	**8**

• Brother of Patrik

Traded to **Washington** by **NY Rangers** for Washington's 5th round choice (Martin Bergeron) in 1988 Entry Draft, August 27, 1987. Traded to **New Jersey** by **Washington** for New Jersey's 10th round choice (Rob Leask) in 1991 Entry Draft, June 19, 1989.

SUOMI, Al

Left wing. Shoots left. 5'10", 170 lbs. Born, Eveleth, MN, October 29, 1913.

Season	Club	Regular Season GP	G	A	Pts	PIM	Playoffs GP	G	A	Pts	PIM
1936-37	Chicago Black Hawks	5	0	0	0	0	....	....	....	....	....
	NHL Totals	**5**	**0**	**0**	**0**	**0**	....	....	....	....	....

SURMA, Damian

Center. Shoots left. 5'9", 200 lbs. Born, Lincoln Park, MI, June 22, 1981.
(Carolina's 5th choice, 174th overall, in 1999 Entry Draft).

Season	Club	Regular Season GP	G	A	Pts	PIM	Playoffs GP	G	A	Pts	PIM
2002-03	Carolina Hurricanes	1	1	0	1	0	....	....	....	....	....
	NHL Totals	**1**	**1**	**0**	**1**	**0**	....	....	....	....	....

SUROVY, Tomas

Center. Shoots left. 6'1", 187 lbs. Born, Banska Bystrica, Czech., September 24, 1981.
(Pittsburgh's 5th choice, 120th overall, in 2001 Entry Draft).

Season	Club	Regular Season GP	G	A	Pts	PIM	Playoffs GP	G	A	Pts	PIM
2002-03	Pittsburgh Penguins	26	4	7	11	10	....	....	....	....	....
	NHL Totals	**26**	**4**	**7**	**11**	**10**	....	....	....	....	....

SUSHINSKY, Maxim

Right wing. Shoots left. 5'8", 165 lbs. Born, Leningrad, USSR, July 1, 1974.
(Minnesota's 4th choice, 132nd overall, in 2000 Entry Draft).

Season	Club	Regular Season GP	G	A	Pts	PIM	Playoffs GP	G	A	Pts	PIM
2000-01	Minnesota Wild	30	7	4	11	29	....	....	....	....	....
	NHL Totals	**30**	**7**	**4**	**11**	**29**	....	....	....	....	....

SUTER, Gary

Defense. Shoots left. 6', 215 lbs. Born, Madison, WI, June 24, 1964.
(Calgary's 9th choice, 180th overall, in 1984 Entry Draft).

Season	Club	Regular Season GP	G	A	Pts	PIM	Playoffs GP	G	A	Pts	PIM
1985-86	Calgary Flames	80	18	50	68	141	10	2	8	10	8
1986-87	Calgary Flames	68	9	39	48	70	6	0	3	3	10
1987-88	Calgary Flames	75	21	70	91	124	9	1	9	10	6
1988-89 ♦	Calgary Flames	63	13	49	62	78	5	0	3	3	10
1989-90	Calgary Flames	76	16	60	76	97	6	0	1	1	14
1990-91	Calgary Flames	79	12	58	70	102	7	1	6	7	12
1991-92	Calgary Flames	70	12	43	55	128	....	....	....	....	....
1992-93	Calgary Flames	81	23	58	81	112	6	2	3	5	8
1993-94	Calgary Flames	25	4	9	13	20	....	....	....	....	....
	Chicago Blackhawks	16	2	3	5	18	6	3	2	5	6
1994-95	Chicago Blackhawks	48	10	27	37	42	12	2	5	7	10
1995-96	Chicago Blackhawks	82	20	47	67	80	10	3	3	6	8
1996-97	Chicago Blackhawks	82	7	21	28	70	6	1	4	5	8
1997-98	Chicago Blackhawks	73	14	28	42	74	....	....	....	....	....
1998-99	San Jose Sharks	1	0	0	0	0	....	....	....	....	....
99-2000	San Jose Sharks	76	6	28	34	52	12	2	5	7	12
2000-01	San Jose Sharks	68	10	24	34	84	1	0	0	0	0
2001-02	San Jose Sharks	82	6	27	33	57	12	0	4	4	8
	NHL Totals	**1145**	**203**	**641**	**844**	**1349**	**108**	**17**	**56**	**73**	**120**

NHL All-Rookie Team (1986) • Calder Memorial Trophy (1986) • NHL Second All-Star Team (1988)
Played in NHL All-Star Game (1986, 1988, 1989, 1991)

Traded to **Hartford** by **Calgary** with Paul Ranheim and Ted Drury for James Patrick, Zarley Zalapski and Michael Nylander, March 10, 1994. Traded to **Chicago** by **Hartford** with Randy Cunneyworth and Hartford's 3rd round choice (later traded to Vancouver – Vancouver selected Larry Courville) in 1995 Entry Draft for Frantisek Kucera and Jocelyn Lemieux, March 11, 1994. Signed as a free agent by **San Jose**, July 1, 1998. • Missed majority of 1998-99 season recovering from tricep muscle injury suffered in game vs. Dallas, October 24, 1998. • Officially announced retirement, September 10, 2002.

SUTHERBY, Brian

Center. Shoots left. 6'2", 180 lbs. Born, Edmonton, Alta., March 1, 1982.
(Washington's 1st choice, 26th overall, in 2000 Entry Draft).

Season	Club	Regular Season GP	G	A	Pts	PIM	Playoffs GP	G	A	Pts	PIM
2001-02	Washington Capitals	7	0	0	0	2	....	....	....	....	....
2002-03	Washington Capitals	72	2	9	11	93	5	0	0	0	10
	NHL Totals	**79**	**2**	**9**	**11**	**95**	**5**	**0**	**0**	**0**	**10**

SUTHERLAND, Bill

Center. Shoots left. 5'10", 160 lbs. Born, Regina, Sask., November 10, 1934.

Season	Club	Regular Season GP	G	A	Pts	PIM	Playoffs GP	G	A	Pts	PIM
1962-63	Montreal Canadiens	....	....	....	....	....	2	0	0	0	0
1967-68	Philadelphia Flyers	60	20	9	29	6	7	1	3	4	0
1968-69	Toronto Maple Leafs	44	7	5	12	14	....	....	....	....	....
	Philadelphia Flyers	12	7	3	10	4	4	1	1	2	0
1969-70	Philadelphia Flyers	51	15	17	32	30	....	....	....	....	....
1970-71	Philadelphia Flyers	1	0	0	0	0	....	....	....	....	....
	St. Louis Blues	68	19	20	39	41	1	0	0	0	0
1971-72	St. Louis Blues	9	2	3	5	2	....	....	....	....	....
	Detroit Red Wings	5	0	1	1	2	....	....	....	....	....
	NHL Totals	**250**	**70**	**58**	**128**	**99**	**14**	**2**	**4**	**6**	**0**

Traded to **Quebec** (AHL) by **Montreal** for cash, July, 1962. NHL rights transferred to **Philadelphia** after NHL club purchased **Quebec** (AHL) franchise, May 8, 1967. Claimed by **Minnesota** from **Philadelphia** in Intra-League Draft, June 12, 1968. Claimed by **Toronto** from **Minnesota** in Intra-League Draft, June 12, 1968. Traded to **Philadelphia** by **Toronto** with Mike Byers and Gerry Meehan for Brit Selby and Forbes Kennedy, March 2, 1969. Claimed on waivers by **Buffalo** from **Philadelphia**, October 19, 1970. Traded to **St. Louis** by **Buffalo** for cash, October 19, 1970. Traded to **Detroit** by **St. Louis** for cash, November 9, 1971.

SUTHERLAND, Max

Left wing. Shoots left. 5'10", 165 lbs. Born, Grenfell, Sask., February 8, 1907.

Season	Club	Regular Season GP	G	A	Pts	PIM	Playoffs GP	G	A	Pts	PIM
1931-32	Boston Bruins	2	0	0	0	0	....	....	....	....	....
	NHL Totals	**2**	**0**	**0**	**0**	**0**	....	....	....	....	....

Traded to **Boston** by **Seattle** (PCHL) for cash, October 21, 1931.

SUTTER, Brent

Center. Shoots right. 6', 188 lbs. Born, Viking, Alta., June 10, 1962.
(NY Islanders' 1st choice, 17th overall, in 1980 Entry Draft).

Season	Club	Regular Season GP	G	A	Pts	PIM	Playoffs GP	G	A	Pts	PIM
1980-81	New York Islanders	3	2	2	4	0	....	....	....	....	....
1981-82 ♦	New York Islanders	43	21	22	43	114	19	2	6	8	36
1982-83 ♦	New York Islanders	80	21	19	40	128	20	10	11	21	26
1983-84	New York Islanders	69	34	15	49	69	20	4	10	14	18
1984-85	New York Islanders	72	42	60	102	51	10	3	3	6	14
1985-86	New York Islanders	61	24	31	55	74	3	0	1	1	2
1986-87	New York Islanders	69	27	36	63	73	5	1	0	1	4
1987-88	New York Islanders	70	29	31	60	55	6	2	1	3	18
1988-89	New York Islanders	77	29	34	63	77	....	....	....	....	....
1989-90	New York Islanders	67	33	35	68	65	5	2	3	5	2
1990-91	New York Islanders	75	21	32	53	49	....	....	....	....	....
1991-92	New York Islanders	8	4	6	10	6	....	....	....	....	....
	Chicago Blackhawks	61	18	32	50	30	18	3	5	8	22
1992-93	Chicago Blackhawks	65	20	34	54	67	4	1	1	2	4
1993-94	Chicago Blackhawks	73	9	29	38	43	6	0	0	0	2
1994-95	Chicago Blackhawks	47	7	8	15	51	16	1	2	3	4
1995-96	Chicago Blackhawks	80	13	27	40	56	10	1	1	2	6
1996-97	Chicago Blackhawks	39	7	7	14	18	2	0	0	0	6
1997-98	Chicago Blackhawks	52	2	6	8	28	....	....	....	....	....
	NHL Totals	**1111**	**363**	**466**	**829**	**1054**	**144**	**30**	**44**	**74**	**164**

• Brother of Brian, Darryl, Duane, Rich and Ron
Played in NHL All-Star Game (1985)

Traded to **Chicago** by **NY Islanders** with Brad Lauer for Adam Creighton and Steve Thomas, October 25, 1991.

SUTTER, Brian

Left wing. Shoots left. 5'11", 173 lbs. Born, Viking, Alta., October 7, 1956.
(St. Louis' 2nd choice, 20th overall, in 1976 Amateur Draft).

Season	Club	Regular Season GP	G	A	Pts	PIM	Playoffs GP	G	A	Pts	PIM
1976-77	St. Louis Blues	35	4	10	14	82	4	1	0	1	14
1977-78	St. Louis Blues	78	9	13	22	123	....	....	....	....	....
1978-79	St. Louis Blues	77	41	39	80	165	....	....	....	....	....
1979-80	St. Louis Blues	71	23	35	58	156	3	0	0	0	4
1980-81	St. Louis Blues	78	35	34	69	232	11	6	3	9	77
1981-82	St. Louis Blues	74	39	36	75	239	10	8	6	14	49
1982-83	St. Louis Blues	79	46	30	76	254	4	2	1	3	10
1983-84	St. Louis Blues	76	32	51	83	162	11	1	5	6	22
1984-85	St. Louis Blues	77	37	37	74	121	3	2	1	3	2
1985-86	St. Louis Blues	44	19	23	42	87	9	1	2	3	22
1986-87	St. Louis Blues	14	3	3	6	18	....	....	....	....	....
1987-88	St. Louis Blues	76	15	22	37	147	10	0	3	3	49
	NHL Totals	**779**	**303**	**333**	**636**	**1786**	**65**	**21**	**21**	**42**	**249**

• Brother of Brent, Darryl, Duane, Rich and Ron
Played in NHL All-Star Game (1982, 1983, 1985)

SUTTER, Darryl

Left wing. Shoots left. 5'11", 176 lbs. Born, Viking, Alta., August 19, 1958.
(Chicago's 11th choice, 179th overall, in 1978 Amateur Draft).

Season	Club	Regular Season GP	G	A	Pts	PIM	Playoffs GP	G	A	Pts	PIM
1979-80	Chicago Black Hawks	8	2	0	2	2	7	3	1	4	2
1980-81	Chicago Black Hawks	76	40	22	62	86	3	3	1	4	2
1981-82	Chicago Black Hawks	40	23	12	35	31	3	0	1	1	2
1982-83	Chicago Black Hawks	80	31	30	61	53	13	4	6	10	8
1983-84	Chicago Black Hawks	59	20	20	40	44	5	1	1	2	0
1984-85	Chicago Black Hawks	49	20	18	38	12	15	12	7	19	12
1985-86	Chicago Black Hawks	50	17	10	27	44	3	1	2	3	0
1986-87	Chicago Blackhawks	44	8	6	14	16	2	0	0	0	0
	NHL Totals	**406**	**161**	**118**	**279**	**288**	**51**	**24**	**19**	**43**	**26**

• Brother of Brian, Brent, Duane, Rich and Ron

SUTTER, Duane

Right wing. Shoots right. 6'1", 185 lbs. Born, Viking, Alta., March 16, 1960.
(NY Islanders' 1st choice, 17th overall, in 1979 Entry Draft).

Season	Club	Regular Season GP	G	A	Pts	PIM	Playoffs GP	G	A	Pts	PIM
1979-80 ♦	New York Islanders	56	15	9	24	55	21	3	7	10	74
1980-81 ♦	New York Islanders	23	7	11	18	26	12	3	1	4	10
1981-82 ♦	New York Islanders	77	18	35	53	100	19	5	5	10	57
1982-83 ♦	New York Islanders	75	13	19	32	118	20	9	12	21	43
1983-84	New York Islanders	78	17	23	40	94	21	1	3	4	48
1984-85	New York Islanders	78	17	24	41	174	10	0	2	2	47
1985-86	New York Islanders	80	20	33	53	157	3	0	0	0	16
1986-87	New York Islanders	80	14	17	31	169	14	1	0	1	26
1987-88	Chicago Blackhawks	37	7	9	16	70	5	0	0	0	21
1988-89	Chicago Blackhawks	75	7	9	16	214	16	3	1	4	15
1989-90	Chicago Blackhawks	72	4	14	18	156	20	1	1	2	48
	NHL Totals	**731**	**139**	**203**	**342**	**1333**	**161**	**26**	**32**	**58**	**405**

• Brother of Brian, Darryl, Brent, Rich and Ron

Traded to **Chicago** by **NY Islanders** for Chicago's 2nd round choice (Wayne Doucet) in 1988 Entry Draft, September 9, 1987.

SUTTER, Rich

Right wing. Shoots right. 5'11", 188 lbs. Born, Viking, Alta., December 2, 1963.
(Pittsburgh's 1st choice, 10th overall, in 1982 Entry Draft).

Season	Club	Regular Season GP	G	A	Pts	PIM	Playoffs GP	G	A	Pts	PIM
1982-83	Pittsburgh Penguins	4	0	0	0	0	....	....	....	....	....
1983-84	Pittsburgh Penguins	5	0	0	0	0	....	....	....	....	....
	Philadelphia Flyers	70	16	12	28	93	3	0	0	0	15
1984-85	Philadelphia Flyers	56	6	10	16	89	11	3	0	3	10
1985-86	Philadelphia Flyers	78	14	25	39	199	5	2	0	2	19
1986-87	Vancouver Canucks	74	20	22	42	113	....	....	....	....	....
1987-88	Vancouver Canucks	80	15	15	30	165	....	....	....	....	....
1988-89	Vancouver Canucks	75	17	15	32	122	7	2	1	3	12
1989-90	Vancouver Canucks	62	9	9	18	133	....	....	....	....	....
	St. Louis Blues	12	2	0	2	22	12	2	1	3	39

Season	Club	REGULAR SEASON GP	G	A	Pts	PIM	PLAYOFFS GP	G	A	Pts	PIM
1990-91	St. Louis Blues	77	16	11	27	122	13	4	2	6	16
1991-92	St. Louis Blues	77	9	16	25	107	6	0	0	0	8
1992-93	St. Louis Blues	84	13	14	27	100	11	0	1	1	10
1993-94	Chicago Blackhawks	83	12	14	26	108	6	0	0	0	2
1994-95	Chicago Blackhawks	15	0	0	0	28	....	....	....	....	....
	Tampa Bay Lightning	4	0	0	0	0	....	....	....	....	....
	Toronto Maple Leafs	18	0	3	3	10	4	0	0	0	2
	NHL Totals	**874**	**149**	**166**	**315**	**1411**	**78**	**13**	**5**	**18**	**133**

• Brother of Brent, Brian, Darryl, Duane, and Ron

Traded to **Philadelphia** by **Pittsburgh** with Pittsburgh's 2nd (Greg Smyth) and 3rd (David McLay) round choices in 1984 Entry Draft for Andy Brickley, Mark Taylor, Ron Flockhart and Philadelphia's 1st (Roger Belanger) and 3rd (later traded to Vancouver – Vancouver selected Mike Stevens) in 1984 Entry Draft, October 23, 1983. Traded to **Vancouver** by **Philadelphia** with Dave Richter and Vancouver's 3rd round choice (previously acquired, Vancouver selected Don Gibson) in 1986 Entry Draft for J.J. Daigneault, Vancouver's 2nd round choice (Kent Hawley) in 1986 Entry Draft and Vancouver's 5th round choice (later traded back to Vancouver – Vancouver selected Sean Fabian) in 1987 Entry Draft, June 6, 1986. Traded to **St. Louis** by **Vancouver** with Harold Snepsts and St. Louis' 2nd round choice (previously acquired, St. Louis selected Craig Johnson) in 1990 Entry Draft for Adrien Plavsic, Montreal's 1st round choice (previously acquired, Vancouver selected Shawn Antoski) in 1990 Entry Draft and St. Louis' 2nd round choice (later traded to Montreal – Montreal selected Craig Darby) in 1991 Entry Draft, March 6, 1990. Claimed by **Chicago** from **St. Louis** in Waiver Draft, October 3, 1993. Traded to **Tampa Bay** by **Chicago** with Paul Ysebaert for Jim Cummins, Tom Tilley and Jeff Buchanan, February 22, 1995. Traded to **Toronto** by **Tampa Bay** for cash, March 13, 1995.

SUTTER, Ron

Center. Shoots right. 6', 180 lbs. Born, Viking, Alta., December 2, 1963.
(Philadelphia's 1st choice, 4th overall, in 1982 Entry Draft).

Season	Club	GP	G	A	Pts	PIM	GP	G	A	Pts	PIM
1982-83	Philadelphia Flyers	10	1	1	2	9	....	....	....	....	....
1983-84	Philadelphia Flyers	79	19	32	51	101	3	0	0	0	22
1984-85	Philadelphia Flyers	73	16	29	45	94	19	4	8	12	28
1985-86	Philadelphia Flyers	75	18	42	60	159	5	0	2	2	10
1986-87	Philadelphia Flyers	39	10	17	27	69	16	1	7	8	12
1987-88	Philadelphia Flyers	69	8	25	33	146	7	0	1	1	26
1988-89	Philadelphia Flyers	55	26	22	48	80	19	1	9	10	51
1989-90	Philadelphia Flyers	75	22	26	48	104	....	....	....	....	....
1990-91	Philadelphia Flyers	80	17	28	45	92	....	....	....	....	....
1991-92	St. Louis Blues	68	19	27	46	91	6	1	3	4	8
1992-93	St. Louis Blues	59	12	15	27	99	....	....	....	....	....
1993-94	St. Louis Blues	36	6	12	18	46	....	....	....	....	....
	Quebec Nordiques	37	9	13	22	44	....	....	....	....	....
1994-95	New York Islanders	27	1	4	5	21	....	....	....	....	....
1995-96	Boston Bruins	18	5	7	12	24	5	0	0	0	8
1996-97	San Jose Sharks	78	5	7	12	65	....	....	....	....	....
1997-98	San Jose Sharks	57	2	7	9	22	6	1	0	1	14
1998-99	San Jose Sharks	59	3	6	9	40	6	0	0	0	4
99-2000	San Jose Sharks	78	5	6	11	34	12	0	2	2	10
2000-01	Calgary Flames	21	1	3	4	12	....	....	....	....	....
	NHL Totals	**1093**	**205**	**329**	**534**	**1352**	**104**	**8**	**32**	**40**	**193**

• Brother of Brent, Brian, Darryl, Duane and Rich

Traded to **St. Louis** by **Philadelphia** with Murray Baron for Dan Quinn and Rod Brind'Amour, September 22, 1991. Traded to **Quebec** by **St. Louis** with Garth Butcher and Bob Bassen for Steve Duchesne and Denis Chasse, January 23, 1994. Traded to **NY Islanders** by **Quebec** with Quebec's 1st round choice (Brett Lindros) in 1994 Entry Draft for Uwe Krupp and NY Islanders' 1st round choice (Wade Belak) in 1994 Entry Draft, June 28, 1994. Signed as a free agent by **Boston**, March 9, 1996. Signed as a free agent by **San Jose**, October 12, 1996. Signed as a free agent by **Calgary**, February 16, 2001.

SUTTON, Andy

Defense. Shoots left. 6'6", 245 lbs. Born, Edmonton, Alta., March 10, 1975.

Season	Club	GP	G	A	Pts	PIM	GP	G	A	Pts	PIM
1998-99	San Jose Sharks	31	0	3	3	65	....	....	....	....	....
99-2000	San Jose Sharks	40	1	1	2	80	....	....	....	....	....
2000-01	Minnesota Wild	69	3	4	7	131	....	....	....	....	....
2001-02	Minnesota Wild	19	2	4	6	35	....	....	....	....	....
	Atlanta Thrashers	24	0	4	4	46	....	....	....	....	....
2002-03	Atlanta Thrashers	53	3	18	21	114	....	....	....	....	....
	NHL Totals	**236**	**9**	**34**	**43**	**471**	....	....	....	....	....

Signed as a free agent by **San Jose**, March 20, 1998. Traded to **Minnesota** by **San Jose** with San Jose's 7th round choice (Peter Bartos) in 2000 Entry Draft and 3rd round choice (later traded to Atlanta – later traded to Pittsburgh – later traded to Columbus – Columbus selected Aaron Johnson) in 2001 Entry Draft for Minnesota's 8th round choice (later traded to Calgary – Calgary selected Joe Campbell) in 2001 Entry Draft and future considerations, June 12, 2000. Traded to **Atlanta** by **Minnesota** for Hnat Domenichelli, January 22, 2002.

SUTTON, Ken

Defense. Shoots left. 6'1", 205 lbs. Born, Edmonton, Alta., November 5, 1969.
(Buffalo's 4th choice, 98th overall, in 1989 Entry Draft).

Season	Club	GP	G	A	Pts	PIM	GP	G	A	Pts	PIM
1990-91	Buffalo Sabres	15	3	6	9	13	6	0	1	1	2
1991-92	Buffalo Sabres	64	2	18	20	71	7	0	2	2	4
1992-93	Buffalo Sabres	63	8	14	22	30	8	3	1	4	8
1993-94	Buffalo Sabres	78	4	20	24	71	4	0	0	0	2
1994-95	Buffalo Sabres	12	1	2	3	30	....	....	....	....	....
	Edmonton Oilers	12	3	1	4	12	....	....	....	....	....
1995-96	Edmonton Oilers	32	0	8	8	39	....	....	....	....	....
	St. Louis Blues	6	0	0	0	4	1	0	0	0	0
1997-98	New Jersey Devils	13	0	0	0	6	....	....	....	....	....
	San Jose Sharks	8	0	0	0	15	....	....	....	....	....
1998-99	New Jersey Devils	5	1	0	1	0	....	....	....	....	....
99-2000 ♦	New Jersey Devils	6	0	2	2	2	....	....	....	....	....
2000-01	New Jersey Devils	53	1	7	8	37	6	0	0	0	13
2001-02	New York Islanders	21	0	2	2	8	....	....	....	....	....
	NHL Totals	**388**	**23**	**80**	**103**	**338**	**32**	**3**	**4**	**7**	**29**

Traded to **Edmonton** by **Buffalo** for Scott Pearson, April 7, 1995. Traded to **St. Louis** by **Edmonton** with Igor Kravchuk for Jeff Norton and Donald Dufresne, January 4, 1996. Traded to **New Jersey** by **St. Louis** with St. Louis' 2nd round choice (Brett Clouthier) in 1999 Entry Draft for Mike Peluso and Ricard Persson, November 26, 1996. Traded to **San Jose** by **New Jersey** with John MacLean for Doug Bodger and Dody Wood, December 7, 1997. Traded to **New Jersey** by **San Jose** for future considerations, August 26, 1998. Claimed by **Washington** from **New Jersey** in Waiver Draft, September 27, 1999. Traded to **New Jersey** by **Washington** for future considerations, October 5, 1999. Signed as a free agent by **NY Islanders**, July 5, 2001. Signed as a free agent by **New Jersey**, August 27, 2002.

SUZOR, Mark

Defense. Shoots left. 6'1", 212 lbs. Born, Windsor, Ont., November 5, 1956.
(Philadelphia's 1st choice, 17th overall, in 1976 Amateur Draft).

Season	Club	GP	G	A	Pts	PIM	GP	G	A	Pts	PIM
1976-77	Philadelphia Flyers	4	0	1	1	4	....	....	....	....	....
1977-78	Colorado Rockies	60	4	15	19	56	....	....	....	....	....
	NHL Totals	**64**	**4**	**16**	**20**	**60**	....	....	....	....	....

Traded to **Colorado** by **Philadelphia** for Barry Dean, August 5, 1977. Traded to **Boston** by **Colorado** for Clayton Pachal, October 11, 1978.

SVARTVADET, Per

Center. Shoots left. 6'1", 195 lbs. Born, Solleftea, Sweden, May 17, 1975.
(Dallas' 5th choice, 139th overall, in 1993 Entry Draft).

Season	Club	GP	G	A	Pts	PIM	GP	G	A	Pts	PIM
99-2000	Atlanta Thrashers	38	3	4	7	6	....	....	....	....	....
2000-01	Atlanta Thrashers	69	10	11	21	20	....	....	....	....	....
2001-02	Atlanta Thrashers	78	3	12	15	24	....	....	....	....	....
2002-03	Atlanta Thrashers	62	1	7	8	8	....	....	....	....	....
	NHL Totals	**247**	**17**	**34**	**51**	**58**	....	....	....	....	....

Traded to **Atlanta** by **Dallas** for Ottawa's 6th round choice (previously acquired, Dallas selected Justin Cox) in 1999 Entry Draft, June 26, 1999.

SVEHLA, Robert

Defense. Shoots right. 6'1", 210 lbs. Born, Martin, Czech., January 2, 1969.
(Calgary's 4th choice, 78th overall, in 1992 Entry Draft).

Season	Club	GP	G	A	Pts	PIM	GP	G	A	Pts	PIM
1994-95	Florida Panthers	5	1	1	2	0	....	....	....	....	....
1995-96	Florida Panthers	81	8	49	57	94	22	0	6	6	32
1996-97	Florida Panthers	82	13	32	45	86	5	1	4	5	4
1997-98	Florida Panthers	79	9	34	43	113	....	....	....	....	....
1998-99	Florida Panthers	80	8	29	37	83	....	....	....	....	....
99-2000	Florida Panthers	82	9	40	49	64	4	0	1	1	4
2000-01	Florida Panthers	82	6	22	28	76	....	....	....	....	....
2001-02	Florida Panthers	82	7	22	29	87	....	....	....	....	....
2002-03	Toronto Maple Leafs	82	7	38	45	46	7	0	3	3	2
	NHL Totals	**655**	**68**	**267**	**335**	**649**	**38**	**1**	**14**	**15**	**42**

Played in NHL All-Star Game (1997)

Traded to **Florida** by **Calgary** with Magnus Svensson for Florida's 3rd round choice (Dmitri Vlasenkov) in 1996 Entry Draft and Florida's 4th round choice (Ryan Ready) in 1997 Entry Draft, September 29, 1994. Traded to **Toronto** by **Florida** for Dmitry Yushkevich, July 18, 2002.

SVEJKOVSKY, Jaroslav

Right wing. Shoots right. 6'1", 193 lbs. Born, Plzen, Czech., October 1, 1976.
(Washington's 2nd choice, 17th overall, in 1996 Entry Draft).

Season	Club	GP	G	A	Pts	PIM	GP	G	A	Pts	PIM
1996-97	Washington Capitals	19	7	3	10	4	....	....	....	....	....
1997-98	Washington Capitals	17	4	1	5	10	1	0	0	0	2
1998-99	Washington Capitals	25	6	8	14	12	....	....	....	....	....
99-2000	Washington Capitals	23	1	2	3	2	....	....	....	....	....
	Tampa Bay Lightning	29	5	5	10	28	....	....	....	....	....
	NHL Totals	**113**	**23**	**19**	**42**	**56**	**1**	**0**	**0**	**0**	**2**

Traded to **Tampa Bay** by **Washington** for Tampa Bay's 7th round choice (later traded to Los Angeles – Los Angeles selected Yevgeny Fedorov) in 2000 Entry Draft and 3rd round choice (later traded to Toronto – Toronto selected Brendan Bell) in 2001 Entry Draft, January 17, 2000.

SVENSSON, Leif

Defense. Shoots left. 6'3", 190 lbs. Born, Harnosand, Sweden, July 8, 1951.

Season	Club	GP	G	A	Pts	PIM	GP	G	A	Pts	PIM
1978-79	Washington Capitals	74	2	29	31	28	....	....	....	....	....
1979-80	Washington Capitals	47	4	11	15	21	....	....	....	....	....
	NHL Totals	**121**	**6**	**40**	**46**	**49**					

Signed as a free agent by **Washington**, June 10, 1978.

SVENSSON, Magnus

Defense. Shoots left. 5'11", 180 lbs. Born, Tranas, Sweden, March 1, 1963.
(Calgary's 13th choice, 250th overall, in 1987 Entry Draft).

Season	Club	GP	G	A	Pts	PIM	GP	G	A	Pts	PIM
1994-95	Florida Panthers	19	2	5	7	10	....	....	....	....	....
1995-96	Florida Panthers	27	2	9	11	21	....	....	....	....	....
	NHL Totals	**46**	**4**	**14**	**18**	**31**					

Traded to **Florida** by **Calgary** with Robert Svehla for Florida's 3rd round choice (Dmitri Vlasenkov) in 1996 Entry Draft and cash, September 29, 1994.

SVITOV, Alexander

Center. Shoots left. 6'3", 198 lbs. Born, Omsk, USSR, November 3, 1982.
(Tampa Bay's 1st choice, 3rd overall, in 2001 Entry Draft).

Season	Club	GP	G	A	Pts	PIM	GP	G	A	Pts	PIM
2002-03	Tampa Bay Lightning	63	4	4	8	58	7	0	0	0	6
	NHL Totals	**63**	**4**	**4**	**8**	**58**	**7**	**0**	**0**	**0**	**6**

SVOBODA, Jaroslav

Left wing. Shoots left. 6'2", 190 lbs. Born, Cervenka, Czech., June 1, 1980.
(Carolina's 8th choice, 208th overall, in 1998 Entry Draft).

Season	Club	GP	G	A	Pts	PIM	GP	G	A	Pts	PIM
		REGULAR SEASON					PLAYOFFS				
2001-02	Carolina Hurricanes	10	2	2	4	2	23	1	4	5	28
2002-03	Carolina Hurricanes	48	3	11	14	32	....	....	....	....	....
	NHL Totals	**58**	**5**	**13**	**18**	**34**	**23**	**1**	**4**	**5**	**28**

SVOBODA, Petr

Defense. Shoots left. 6'1", 198 lbs. Born, Most, Czech., February 14, 1966.
(Montreal's 1st choice, 5th overall, in 1984 Entry Draft).

Season	Club	GP	G	A	Pts	PIM	GP	G	A	Pts	PIM
1984-85	Montreal Canadiens	73	4	27	31	65	7	1	1	2	12
1985-86♦	Montreal Canadiens	73	1	18	19	93	8	0	0	0	21
1986-87	Montreal Canadiens	70	5	17	22	63	14	0	5	5	10
1987-88	Montreal Canadiens	69	7	22	29	149	10	0	5	5	12
1988-89	Montreal Canadiens	71	8	37	45	147	21	1	11	12	16
1989-90	Montreal Canadiens	60	5	31	36	98	10	0	5	5	7
1990-91	Montreal Canadiens	60	4	22	26	52	2	0	1	1	2
1991-92	Montreal Canadiens	58	5	16	21	94	....	....	....	....	....
	Buffalo Sabres	13	1	6	7	52	7	1	4	5	6
1992-93	Buffalo Sabres	40	2	24	26	59	....	....	....	....	....
1993-94	Buffalo Sabres	60	2	14	16	89	3	0	0	0	4
1994-95	Buffalo Sabres	26	0	5	5	60	....	....	....	....	....
	Philadelphia Flyers	11	0	3	3	10	14	0	4	4	8
1995-96	Philadelphia Flyers	73	1	28	29	105	12	0	6	6	22
1996-97	Philadelphia Flyers	67	2	12	14	94	16	1	2	3	16
1997-98	Philadelphia Flyers	56	3	15	18	83	3	0	1	1	4
1998-99	Philadelphia Flyers	25	4	2	6	28	....	....	....	....	....
	Tampa Bay Lightning	34	1	16	17	53	....	....	....	....	....
99-2000	Tampa Bay Lightning	70	2	23	25	170	....	....	....	....	....
2000-01	Tampa Bay Lightning	19	1	3	4	41	....	....	....	....	....
	NHL Totals	**1028**	**58**	**341**	**399**	**1605**	**127**	**4**	**45**	**49**	**140**

Played in NHL All-Star Game (2000)

Traded to **Buffalo** by **Montreal** for Kevin Haller, March 10, 1992. Traded to **Philadelphia** by **Buffalo** for Garry Galley, April 7, 1995. Traded to **Tampa Bay** by **Philadelphia** for Karl Dykhuis, December 28, 1998. • Missed majority of 2000-01 season recovering from head injury suffered in game vs. Los Angeles, December 16, 2000.

SVOBODA, Petr

Defense. Shoots right. 6'3", 200 lbs. Born, Jihlava, Czech., June 20, 1980.
(Toronto's 2nd choice, 35th overall, in 1998 Entry Draft).

Season	Club	GP	G	A	Pts	PIM	GP	G	A	Pts	PIM
2000-01	Toronto Maple Leafs	18	1	2	3	10	....	....	....	....	....
	NHL Totals	**18**	**1**	**2**	**3**	**10**	....	....	....	....	....

SWAIN, Garry

Center. Shoots left. 5'8", 164 lbs. Born, Welland, Ont., September 11, 1947.
(Pittsburgh's 1st choice, 4th overall, in 1968 Amateur Draft).

Season	Club	GP	G	A	Pts	PIM	GP	G	A	Pts	PIM
1968-69	Pittsburgh Penguins	9	1	1	2	0	....	....	....	....	....
	NHL Totals	**9**	**1**	**1**	**2**	**0**	....	....	....	....	....

SWANSON, Brian

Center. Shoots left. 5'10", 185 lbs. Born, Eagle River, AK, March 24, 1976.
(San Jose's 5th choice, 115th overall, in 1994 Entry Draft).

Season	Club	GP	G	A	Pts	PIM	GP	G	A	Pts	PIM
2000-01	Edmonton Oilers	16	1	1	2	6	....	....	....	....	....
2001-02	Edmonton Oilers	8	1	1	2	0	....	....	....	....	....
2002-03	Edmonton Oilers	44	2	10	12	10	....	....	....	....	....
	NHL Totals	**68**	**4**	**12**	**16**	**16**	....	....	....	....	....

Traded to **NY Rangers** by **San Jose** with Jayson More and San Jose's 4th round choice (later traded back to San Jose – San Jose selected Adam Colagiacomo) in 1997 Entry Draft for Marty McSorley, August 20, 1996. Signed as a free agent by **Edmonton**, August 19, 1999. Signed as a free agent by **Anaheim**, July 24, 2003.

SWARBRICK, George

Right wing. Shoots right. 5'10", 175 lbs. Born, Moose Jaw, Sask., February 16, 1942.

Season	Club	GP	G	A	Pts	PIM	GP	G	A	Pts	PIM
1967-68	Oakland Seals	49	13	5	18	62	....	....	....	....	....
1968-69	Oakland Seals	50	3	13	16	75	....	....	....	....	....
	Pittsburgh Penguins	19	1	6	7	28	....	....	....	....	....
1969-70	Pittsburgh Penguins	12	0	1	1	8	....	....	....	....	....
1970-71	Philadelphia Flyers	2	0	0	0	0	....	....	....	....	....
	NHL Totals	**132**	**17**	**25**	**42**	**173**	....	....	....	....	....

NHL rights transferred to **California** after owners of **San Francisco** (WHL) franchise awarded NHL expansion team, April 5, 1966. Traded to **Pittsburgh** by **Oakland** with Bryan Watson and Tracy Pratt for Earl Ingarfield, Gene Ubriaco and Dick Mattiussi, January 30, 1969. Traded to **Philadelphia** by **Pittsburgh** for Terry Ball, June 11, 1970. Signed as a free agent by **Atlanta** (Omaha-CHL), October 30, 1973. Traded to **Syracuse** (AHL) by **Atlanta** for cash, August, 1974.

SWEENEY, Bill

Center. Shoots left. 5'10", 165 lbs. Born, Guelph, Ont., January 30, 1937.

Season	Club	GP	G	A	Pts	PIM	GP	G	A	Pts	PIM
1959-60	New York Rangers	4	1	0	1	0	....	....	....	....	....
	NHL Totals	**4**	**1**	**0**	**1**	**0**	....	....	....	....	....

NHL rights transferred to **Los Angeles** after NHL club purchased **Springfield** (AHL) franchise, May, 1967. Traded to **Vancouver** (WHL) by **Los Angeles** with the loan of Mike Corbett and Larry Mavety for cash, October, 1967.

SWEENEY, Bob

Center/Right wing. Shoots right. 6'3", 200 lbs. Born, Concord, MA, January 25, 1964.
(Boston's 6th choice, 123rd overall, in 1982 Entry Draft).

Season	Club	GP	G	A	Pts	PIM	GP	G	A	Pts	PIM
1986-87	Boston Bruins	14	2	4	6	21	3	0	0	0	0
1987-88	Boston Bruins	80	22	23	45	73	23	6	8	14	66
1988-89	Boston Bruins	75	14	14	28	99	10	2	4	6	19
1989-90	Boston Bruins	70	22	24	46	93	20	0	2	2	30
1990-91	Boston Bruins	80	15	33	48	115	17	4	2	6	45
1991-92	Boston Bruins	63	6	14	20	103	14	1	0	1	25
1992-93	Buffalo Sabres	80	21	26	47	118	8	2	2	4	8
1993-94	Buffalo Sabres	60	11	14	25	94	1	0	0	0	0
1994-95	Buffalo Sabres	45	5	4	9	18	5	0	0	0	4
1995-96	New York Islanders	66	6	6	12	59	....	....	....	....	....
	Calgary Flames	6	1	1	2	6	2	0	0	0	0
	NHL Totals	**639**	**125**	**163**	**288**	**799**	**103**	**15**	**18**	**33**	**197**

Claimed on waivers by **Buffalo** from **Boston**, October 9, 1992. Claimed by **NY Islanders** from **Buffalo** in NHL Waiver Draft, October 2, 1995. Traded to **Calgary** by **NY Islanders** for Pat Conacher and Calgary's 6th round choice (later traded back to Calgary – Calgary selected Ilja Demidov) in 1997 Entry Draft, March 20, 1996.

SWEENEY, Don

Defense. Shoots left. 5'10", 185 lbs. Born, St. Stephen, N.B., August 17, 1966.
(Boston's 8th choice, 166th overall, in 1984 Entry Draft).

Season	Club	GP	G	A	Pts	PIM	GP	G	A	Pts	PIM
1988-89	Boston Bruins	36	3	5	8	20	....	....	....	....	....
1989-90	Boston Bruins	58	3	5	8	58	21	1	5	6	18
1990-91	Boston Bruins	77	8	13	21	67	19	3	0	3	25
1991-92	Boston Bruins	75	3	11	14	74	15	0	0	0	10
1992-93	Boston Bruins	84	7	27	34	68	4	0	0	0	4
1993-94	Boston Bruins	75	6	15	21	50	12	2	1	3	4
1994-95	Boston Bruins	47	3	19	22	24	5	0	0	0	4
1995-96	Boston Bruins	77	4	24	28	42	5	0	2	2	6
1996-97	Boston Bruins	82	3	23	26	39	....	....	....	....	....
1997-98	Boston Bruins	59	1	15	16	24	....	....	....	....	....
1998-99	Boston Bruins	81	2	10	12	64	11	3	0	3	6
99-2000	Boston Bruins	81	1	13	14	48	....	....	....	....	....
2000-01	Boston Bruins	72	2	10	12	26	....	....	....	....	....
2001-02	Boston Bruins	81	3	15	18	35	6	0	1	1	2
2002-03	Boston Bruins	67	3	5	8	24	5	0	1	1	0
	NHL Totals	**1052**	**52**	**210**	**262**	**663**	**103**	**9**	**10**	**19**	**79**

Signed as a free agent by **Dallas**, July 14, 2003.

SWEENEY, Tim

Left wing. Shoots left. 5'11", 185 lbs. Born, Boston, MA, April 12, 1967.
(Calgary's 7th choice, 122nd overall, in 1985 Entry Draft).

Season	Club	GP	G	A	Pts	PIM	GP	G	A	Pts	PIM
1990-91	Calgary Flames	42	7	9	16	8	....	....	....	....	....
1991-92	Calgary Flames	11	1	2	3	4	....	....	....	....	....
1992-93	Boston Bruins	14	1	7	8	6	3	0	0	0	0
1993-94	Mighty Ducks of Anaheim	78	16	27	43	49	....	....	....	....	....
1994-95	Mighty Ducks of Anaheim	13	1	1	2	2	....	....	....	....	....
1995-96	Boston Bruins	41	8	8	16	14	1	0	0	0	2
1996-97	Boston Bruins	36	10	11	21	14	....	....	....	....	....
1997-98	New York Rangers	56	11	18	29	26	....	....	....	....	....
	NHL Totals	**291**	**55**	**83**	**138**	**123**	**4**	**0**	**0**	**0**	**2**

Signed as a free agent by **Boston**, September 16, 1992. Claimed by **Anaheim** from **Boston** in Expansion Draft, June 24, 1993. Signed as a free agent by **Boston**, August 9, 1995. Signed as a free agent by **NY Rangers**, September 15, 1997. • Officially announced retirement, October 11, 1998.

SYDOR, Darryl

Defense. Shoots left. 6'1", 205 lbs. Born, Edmonton, Alta., May 13, 1972.
(Los Angeles' 1st choice, 7th overall, in 1990 Entry Draft).

Season	Club	GP	G	A	Pts	PIM	GP	G	A	Pts	PIM
1991-92	Los Angeles Kings	18	1	5	6	22	....	....	....	....	....
1992-93	Los Angeles Kings	80	6	23	29	63	24	3	8	11	16
1993-94	Los Angeles Kings	84	8	27	35	94	....	....	....	....	....
1994-95	Los Angeles Kings	48	4	19	23	36	....	....	....	....	....
1995-96	Los Angeles Kings	58	1	11	12	34	....	....	....	....	....
	Dallas Stars	26	2	6	8	41	....	....	....	....	....
1996-97	Dallas Stars	82	8	40	48	51	7	0	2	2	0
1997-98	Dallas Stars	79	11	35	46	51	17	0	5	5	14
1998-99♦	Dallas Stars	74	14	34	48	50	23	3	9	12	16
99-2000	Dallas Stars	74	8	26	34	32	23	1	6	7	6
2000-01	Dallas Stars	81	10	37	47	34	10	1	3	4	0
2001-02	Dallas Stars	78	4	29	33	50	....	....	....	....	....
2002-03	Dallas Stars	81	5	31	36	40	12	0	6	6	6
	NHL Totals	**863**	**82**	**323**	**405**	**598**	**116**	**8**	**39**	**47**	**58**

Played in NHL All-Star Game (1998, 1999)

Traded to **Dallas** by **Los Angeles** with Los Angeles' 5th round choice (Ryan Christie) in 1996 Entry Draft for Shane Churla and Doug Zmolek, February 17, 1996. Traded to **Columbus** by **Dallas** for Mike Sillinger and Columbus's 2nd round choice in 2004 Entry Draft, July 22, 2003.

SYKES, Bob

Left wing. Shoots left. 6', 200 lbs. Born, Sudbury, Ont., September 26, 1951.
(Toronto's 5th choice, 65th overall, in 1971 Amateur Draft).

Season	Club	GP	G	A	Pts	PIM	GP	G	A	Pts	PIM
1974-75	Toronto Maple Leafs	2	0	0	0	0	....	....	....	....	....
	NHL Totals	**2**	**0**	**0**	**0**	**0**	....	....	....	....	....

SYKES, Phil

Left wing. Shoots left. 6', 175 lbs. Born, Dawson Creek, B.C., March 18, 1959.

Season	Club	GP	G	A	Pts	PIM	GP	G	A	Pts	PIM
		REGULAR SEASON					PLAYOFFS				
1982-83	Los Angeles Kings	7	2	0	2	2	....	....	....	....	....
1983-84	Los Angeles Kings	3	0	0	0	2	....	....	....	....	....
1984-85	Los Angeles Kings	79	17	15	32	38	3	0	1	1	4
1985-86	Los Angeles Kings	76	20	24	44	97	....	....	....	....	....
1986-87	Los Angeles Kings	58	6	15	21	133	5	0	1	1	8
1987-88	Los Angeles Kings	40	9	12	21	82	4	0	0	0	0
1988-89	Los Angeles Kings	23	0	1	1	8	3	0	0	0	8
1989-90	Winnipeg Jets	48	9	6	15	26	4	0	0	0	0
1990-91	Winnipeg Jets	70	12	10	22	59	....	....	....	....	....
1991-92	Winnipeg Jets	52	4	2	6	72	7	0	1	1	9
	NHL Totals	**456**	**79**	**85**	**164**	**519**	**26**	**0**	**3**	**3**	**29**

Signed as a free agent by **Los Angeles**, April 5, 1982. Traded to **Winnipeg** by **Los Angeles** for Brad Jones, December 1, 1989.

SYKORA, Michal

Defense. Shoots left. 6'5", 225 lbs. Born, Pardubice, Czech., July 5, 1973.
(San Jose's 6th choice, 123rd overall, in 1992 Entry Draft).

Season	Club	GP	G	A	Pts	PIM	GP	G	A	Pts	PIM
1993-94	San Jose Sharks	22	1	4	5	14	....	....	....	....	....
1994-95	San Jose Sharks	16	0	4	4	10	....	....	....	....	....
1995-96	San Jose Sharks	79	4	16	20	54	....	....	....	....	....
1996-97	San Jose Sharks	35	2	5	7	59	....	....	....	....	....
	Chicago Blackhawks	28	1	9	10	10	1	0	0	0	0
1997-98	Chicago Blackhawks	28	1	3	4	12	....	....	....	....	....
1998-99	Tampa Bay Lightning	10	1	2	3	0	....	....	....	....	....
2000-01	Philadelphia Flyers	49	5	11	16	26	6	0	1	1	0
	NHL Totals	**267**	**15**	**54**	**69**	**185**	**7**	**0**	**1**	**1**	**0**

Traded to **Chicago** by **San Jose** with Chris Terreri and Ulf Dahlen for Ed Belfour, January 25, 1997. Traded to **Tampa Bay** by **Chicago** for Mark Fitzpatrick and Tampa Bay's 4th round choice (later traded to Montreal – Montreal selected Chris Dyment) in 1999 Entry Draft, July 17, 1998. Signed as a free agent by **Philadelphia**, July 6, 2000.

SYKORA, Petr

Center. Shoots right. 6'3", 206 lbs. Born, Pardubice, Czech., December 21, 1978.
(Detroit's 2nd choice, 76th overall, in 1997 Entry Draft).

Season	Club	GP	G	A	Pts	PIM	GP	G	A	Pts	PIM
1998-99	Nashville Predators	2	0	0	0	0	....	....	....	....	....
	NHL Totals	**2**	**0**	**0**	**0**	**0**	....	....	....	....	....

Traded to **Nashville** by **Detroit** with Detroit's 3rd round choice (later traded to Edmonton – Edmonton selected Mike Comrie) and 4th round compensatory choice (Alexander Krevsun) in 1999 Entry Draft for Doug Brown, July 14, 1998. Traded to **Washington** by **Nashville** for Washington's 3rd round choice (Paul Brown) in 2003 Entry Draft, June 22, 2002.

SYKORA, Petr

Right wing. Shoots left. 6', 190 lbs. Born, Plzen, Czech., November 19, 1976.
(New Jersey's 1st choice, 18th overall, in 1995 Entry Draft).

Season	Club	GP	G	A	Pts	PIM	GP	G	A	Pts	PIM
1995-96	New Jersey Devils	63	18	24	42	32	....	....	....	....	....
1996-97	New Jersey Devils	19	1	2	3	4	2	0	0	0	2
1997-98	New Jersey Devils	58	16	20	36	22	2	0	0	0	0
1998-99	New Jersey Devils	80	29	43	72	22	7	3	3	6	4
99-2000 ◆	New Jersey Devils	79	25	43	68	26	23	9	8	17	10
2000-01	New Jersey Devils	73	35	46	81	32	25	10	12	22	12
2001-02	New Jersey Devils	73	21	27	48	44	4	0	1	1	0
2002-03	Anaheim Mighty Ducks	82	34	25	59	24	21	4	9	13	12
	NHL Totals	**527**	**179**	**230**	**409**	**206**	**84**	**26**	**33**	**59**	**40**

NHL All-Rookie Team (1996)

Traded to **Anaheim** by **New Jersey** with Mike Commodore, Jean-Francois Damphousse and Igor Pohanka for Jeff Friesen, Oleg Tverdovsky and Maxim Balmochnykh, July 6, 2002.

SYLVESTER, Dean

Right wing. Shoots right. 6'2", 210 lbs. Born, Hanson, MA, December 30, 1972.

Season	Club	GP	G	A	Pts	PIM	GP	G	A	Pts	PIM
1998-99	Buffalo Sabres	1	0	0	0	0	4	0	0	0	0
99-2000	Atlanta Thrashers	52	16	10	26	24	....	....	....	....	....
2000-01	Atlanta Thrashers	43	5	6	11	8	....	....	....	....	....
	NHL Totals	**96**	**21**	**16**	**37**	**32**	**4**	**0**	**0**	**0**	**0**

Signed as a free agent by **Buffalo**, October 1, 1998. Traded to **Atlanta** by **Buffalo** for future considerations, June 25, 1999. • Officially announced retirement, June 25, 2001.

SZURA, Joe

Center. Shoots left. 6'3", 185 lbs. Born, Fort William, Ont., December 18, 1938.

Season	Club	GP	G	A	Pts	PIM	GP	G	A	Pts	PIM
1967-68	Oakland Seals	20	1	3	4	10	....	....	....	....	....
1968-69	Oakland Seals	70	9	12	21	20	7	2	3	5	2
	NHL Totals	**90**	**10**	**15**	**25**	**30**	**7**	**2**	**3**	**5**	**2**

Claimed by **California** (Oakland) from **Montreal** in Expansion Draft, June 6, 1967.

TAFFE, Jeff

Center. Shoots left. 6'3", 195 lbs. Born, Hastings, MN, February 19, 1981.
(St. Louis' 1st choice, 30th overall, in 2000 Entry Draft).

Season	Club	GP	G	A	Pts	PIM	GP	G	A	Pts	PIM
2002-03	Phoenix Coyotes	20	3	1	4	4	....	....	....	....	....
	NHL Totals	**20**	**3**	**1**	**4**	**4**	....	....	....	....	....

Rights traded to **Phoenix** by **St. Louis** with Michal Handzus, Ladislav Nagy and St. Louis' 1st round choice (Ben Eager) in 2002 Entry Draft for Keith Tkachuk, March 13, 2001.

TAFT, John

Defense. Shoots left. 6'2", 185 lbs. Born, Minneapolis, MN, March 8, 1954.
(Detroit's 5th choice, 81st overall, in 1974 Amateur Draft).

Season	Club	GP	G	A	Pts	PIM	GP	G	A	Pts	PIM
1978-79	Detroit Red Wings	15	0	2	2	4	....	....	....	....	....
	NHL Totals	**15**	**0**	**2**	**2**	**4**	....	....	....	....	....

Signed as a free agent by **St. Louis**, July 14, 1980.

TAGLIANETTI, Peter

Defense. Shoots left. 6'2", 195 lbs. Born, Framingham, MA, August 15, 1963.
(Winnipeg's 4th choice, 43rd overall, in 1983 Entry Draft).

Season	Club	GP	G	A	Pts	PIM	GP	G	A	Pts	PIM
1984-85	Winnipeg Jets	1	0	0	0	0	1	0	0	0	0
1985-86	Winnipeg Jets	18	0	0	0	48	3	0	0	0	2
1986-87	Winnipeg Jets	3	0	0	0	12	....	....	....	....	....
1987-88	Winnipeg Jets	70	6	17	23	182	5	1	1	2	12
1988-89	Winnipeg Jets	66	1	14	15	226	....	....	....	....	....
1989-90	Winnipeg Jets	49	3	6	9	136	5	0	0	0	6
1990-91	Minnesota North Stars	16	0	1	1	14	....	....	....	....	....
	◆ Pittsburgh Penguins	39	3	8	11	93	19	0	3	3	49
1991-92 ◆	Pittsburgh Penguins	44	1	3	4	57	....	....	....	....	....
1992-93	Tampa Bay Lightning	61	1	8	9	150	....	....	....	....	....
	Pittsburgh Penguins	11	1	4	5	34	11	1	2	3	16
1993-94	Pittsburgh Penguins	60	2	12	14	142	5	0	2	2	16
1994-95	Pittsburgh Penguins	13	0	1	1	12	4	0	0	0	2
	NHL Totals	**451**	**18**	**74**	**92**	**1106**	**53**	**2**	**8**	**10**	**103**

Traded to **Minnesota** by **Winnipeg** for future considerations, September 30, 1990. Traded to **Pittsburgh** by **Minnesota** with Larry Murphy for Chris Dahlquist and Jim Johnson, December 11, 1990. Claimed by **Tampa Bay** from **Pittsburgh** in Expansion Draft, June 18, 1992. Traded to **Pittsburgh** by **Tampa Bay** for Pittsburgh's 3rd round choice (later traded to Florida – Florida selected Steve Washburn) in 1993 Entry Draft, March 22, 1993. Signed as a free agent by **Boston**, August 9, 1995.

TALAFOUS, Dean

Right wing. Shoots right. 6'4", 180 lbs. Born, Duluth, MN, August 25, 1953.
(Atlanta's 4th choice, 53rd overall, in 1973 Amateur Draft).

Season	Club	GP	G	A	Pts	PIM	GP	G	A	Pts	PIM
1974-75	Atlanta Flames	18	1	4	5	13	....	....	....	....	....
	Minnesota North Stars	43	8	17	25	6	....	....	....	....	....
1975-76	Minnesota North Stars	79	18	30	48	18	....	....	....	....	....
1976-77	Minnesota North Stars	80	22	27	49	10	2	0	0	0	0
1977-78	Minnesota North Stars	75	13	16	29	25	....	....	....	....	....
1978-79	New York Rangers	68	13	16	29	29	....	....	....	....	....
1979-80	New York Rangers	55	10	20	30	26	5	1	2	3	9
1980-81	New York Rangers	50	13	17	30	28	14	3	5	8	2
1981-82	New York Rangers	29	6	7	13	8	....	....	....	....	....
	NHL Totals	**497**	**104**	**154**	**258**	**163**	**21**	**4**	**7**	**11**	**11**

Traded to **Minnesota** by **Atlanta** with Dwight Bialowas for Barry Gibbs, January 3, 1975. Signed as a free agent by **NY Rangers**, July 17, 1978. • Officially announced retirement, December 30, 1981.

TALAKOSKI, Ron

Right wing. Shoots right. 6'3", 220 lbs. Born, Thunder Bay, Ont., June 1, 1962.

Season	Club	GP	G	A	Pts	PIM	GP	G	A	Pts	PIM
1986-87	New York Rangers	3	0	0	0	21	....	....	....	....	....
1987-88	New York Rangers	6	0	1	1	12	....	....	....	....	....
	NHL Totals	**9**	**0**	**1**	**1**	**33**	....	....	....	....	....

Signed as a free agent by **NY Rangers**, October 3, 1986.

TALBOT, Jean-Guy

Defense. Shoots left. 5'11", 170 lbs. Born, Cap-de-la-Madeleine, Que., July 11, 1932.

Season	Club	GP	G	A	Pts	PIM	GP	G	A	Pts	PIM
1954-55	Montreal Canadiens	3	0	1	1	0	....	....	....	....	....
1955-56 ◆	Montreal Canadiens	66	1	13	14	80	9	0	2	2	4
1956-57 ◆	Montreal Canadiens	59	0	13	13	70	10	0	2	2	10
1957-58 ◆	Montreal Canadiens	55	4	15	19	65	10	0	3	3	12
1958-59 ◆	Montreal Canadiens	69	4	17	21	77	11	0	1	1	10
1959-60 ◆	Montreal Canadiens	69	1	14	15	60	8	1	1	2	8
1960-61	Montreal Canadiens	70	5	26	31	143	6	1	1	2	10
1961-62	Montreal Canadiens	70	5	42	47	90	6	1	1	2	10
1962-63	Montreal Canadiens	70	3	22	25	51	5	0	0	0	8
1963-64	Montreal Canadiens	66	1	13	14	83	7	0	2	2	10
1964-65 ◆	Montreal Canadiens	67	8	14	22	64	13	0	1	1	22
1965-66 ◆	Montreal Canadiens	59	1	14	15	50	10	0	2	2	8
1966-67	Montreal Canadiens	68	3	5	8	51	10	0	0	0	0
1967-68	Minnesota North Stars	4	0	0	0	4	....	....	....	....	....
	Detroit Red Wings	32	0	3	3	10	....	....	....	....	....
	St. Louis Blues	23	0	4	4	2	17	0	2	2	8
1968-69	St. Louis Blues	69	5	4	9	24	12	0	2	2	6
1969-70	St. Louis Blues	75	2	15	17	40	16	1	6	7	16
1970-71	St. Louis Blues	5	0	0	0	6	....	....	....	....	....
	Buffalo Sabres	57	0	7	7	36	....	....	....	....	....
	NHL Totals	**1056**	**43**	**242**	**285**	**1006**	**150**	**4**	**26**	**30**	**142**

NHL First All-Star Team (1962)

Played in NHL All-Star Game (1956, 1957, 1958, 1960, 1962, 1965, 1967)

Claimed by **Minnesota** from **Montreal** in Expansion Draft, June 6, 1967. Traded to **Detroit** by **Minnesota** with Dave Richardson for Bob McCord and Duke Harris, October 19, 1967. Claimed on waivers by **St. Louis** from **Detroit**, January 13, 1968. Traded to **Buffalo** by **St. Louis** with Larry Keenan for Bob Baun, November 4, 1970.

TALLINDER, Henrik

Defense. Shoots left. 6'3", 210 lbs. Born, Stockholm, Sweden, January 10, 1979.
(Buffalo's 2nd choice, 48th overall, in 1997 Entry Draft).

Season	Club	GP	G	A	Pts	PIM	GP	G	A	Pts	PIM
		REGULAR SEASON					PLAYOFFS				
2001-02	Buffalo Sabres	2	0	0	0	0	....	....	....	....	....
2002-03	Buffalo Sabres	46	3	10	13	28	....	....	....	....	....
	NHL Totals	**48**	**3**	**10**	**13**	**28**	....	....	....	....	....

TALLON, Dale

Defense. Shoots left. 6'1", 195 lbs. Born, Noranda, Que., October 19, 1950.
(Vancouver's 1st choice, 2nd overall, in 1970 Amateur Draft).

Season	Club	GP	G	A	Pts	PIM	GP	G	A	Pts	PIM
		REGULAR SEASON					PLAYOFFS				
1970-71	Vancouver Canucks	78	14	42	56	58	....	....	....	....	....
1971-72	Vancouver Canucks	69	17	27	44	78	....	....	....	....	....
1972-73	Vancouver Canucks	75	13	24	37	83	....	....	....	....	....
1973-74	Chicago Black Hawks	65	15	19	34	36	11	1	3	4	29
1974-75	Chicago Black Hawks	35	5	10	15	28	8	1	3	4	4
1975-76	Chicago Black Hawks	80	15	47	62	101	4	0	1	1	8
1976-77	Chicago Black Hawks	70	5	16	21	65	2	0	1	1	0
1977-78	Chicago Black Hawks	75	4	20	24	66	4	0	2	2	0
1978-79	Pittsburgh Penguins	63	5	24	29	35	....	....	....	....	....
1979-80	Pittsburgh Penguins	32	5	9	14	18	4	0	0	0	4
	NHL Totals	**642**	**98**	**238**	**336**	**568**	**33**	**2**	**10**	**12**	**45**

Played in NHL All-Star Game (1971, 1972)

Traded to **Chicago** by **Vancouver** for Jerry Korab and Gary Smith, May 14, 1973. Traded to **Pittsburgh** by **Chicago** for Pittsburgh's 2nd round choice (Ken Solheim) in 1980 Entry Draft, October 9, 1978. Claimed by **Pittsburgh** as a fill-in during Expansion Draft, June 13, 1979.

TAMBELLINI, Steve

Center. Shoots left. 6', 190 lbs. Born, Trail, B.C., May 14, 1958.
(NY Islanders' 1st choice, 15th overall, in 1978 Amateur Draft).

Season	Club	GP	G	A	Pts	PIM	GP	G	A	Pts	PIM
		REGULAR SEASON					PLAYOFFS				
1978-79	New York Islanders	1	0	0	0	0	....	....	....	....	....
1979-80 ♦	New York Islanders	45	5	8	13	4	....	....	....	....	....
1980-81	New York Islanders	61	19	17	36	17	....	....	....	....	....
	Colorado Rockies	13	6	12	18	2	....	....	....	....	....
1981-82	Colorado Rockies	79	29	30	59	14	....	....	....	....	....
1982-83	New Jersey Devils	73	25	18	43	14	....	....	....	....	....
1983-84	Calgary Flames	73	15	10	25	16	2	0	1	1	0
1984-85	Calgary Flames	47	19	10	29	4	....	....	....	....	....
1985-86	Vancouver Canucks	48	15	15	30	12	....	....	....	....	....
1986-87	Vancouver Canucks	72	16	20	36	14	....	....	....	....	....
1987-88	Vancouver Canucks	41	11	10	21	8	....	....	....	....	....
	NHL Totals	**553**	**160**	**150**	**310**	**105**	**2**	**0**	**1**	**1**	**0**

Traded to **Colorado** by **NY Islanders** with Glenn Resch for Mike McEwen and Jari Kaarela, March 10, 1981. Transferred to **New Jersey** after **Colorado** franchise relocated, June 30, 1982. Traded to **Calgary** by **New Jersey** with Joel Quenneville for Mel Bridgman and Phil Russell, June 20, 1983. Signed as a free agent by **Vancouver**, August 28, 1985.

TAMER, Chris

Defense. Shoots left. 6'2", 205 lbs. Born, Dearborn, MI, November 17, 1970.
(Pittsburgh's 3rd choice, 68th overall, in 1990 Entry Draft).

Season	Club	GP	G	A	Pts	PIM	GP	G	A	Pts	PIM
		REGULAR SEASON					PLAYOFFS				
1993-94	Pittsburgh Penguins	12	0	0	0	9	5	0	0	0	2
1994-95	Pittsburgh Penguins	36	2	0	2	82	4	0	0	0	18
1995-96	Pittsburgh Penguins	70	4	10	14	153	18	0	7	7	24
1996-97	Pittsburgh Penguins	45	2	4	6	131	4	0	0	0	4
1997-98	Pittsburgh Penguins	79	0	7	7	181	6	0	1	1	4
1998-99	Pittsburgh Penguins	11	0	0	0	32	....	....	....	....	....
	New York Rangers	52	1	5	6	92	....	....	....	....	....
99-2000	Atlanta Thrashers	69	2	8	10	91	....	....	....	....	....
2000-01	Atlanta Thrashers	82	4	13	17	128	....	....	....	....	....
2001-02	Atlanta Thrashers	78	3	3	6	111	....	....	....	....	....
2002-03	Atlanta Thrashers	72	1	9	10	118	....	....	....	....	....
	NHL Totals	**606**	**19**	**59**	**78**	**1128**	**37**	**0**	**8**	**8**	**52**

Traded to **NY Rangers** by **Pittsburgh** with Petr Nedved and Sean Pronger for Alexei Kovalev and Harry York, November 25, 1998. Claimed by **Atlanta** from **NY Rangers** in Expansion Draft, June 25, 1999.

TANABE, David

Defense. Shoots right. 6'1", 190 lbs. Born, White Bear Lake, MN, July 19, 1980.
(Carolina's 1st choice, 16th overall, in 1999 Entry Draft).

Season	Club	GP	G	A	Pts	PIM	GP	G	A	Pts	PIM
		REGULAR SEASON					PLAYOFFS				
99-2000	Carolina Hurricanes	31	4	0	4	14	....	....	....	....	....
2000-01	Carolina Hurricanes	74	7	22	29	42	6	2	0	2	12
2001-02	Carolina Hurricanes	78	1	15	16	35	1	0	1	1	0
2002-03	Carolina Hurricanes	68	3	10	13	24	....	....	....	....	....
	NHL Totals	**251**	**15**	**47**	**62**	**115**	**7**	**2**	**1**	**3**	**12**

Traded to **Phoenix** by **Carolina** with Igor Knyazev for Danny Markov and future considerations, June 21, 2003.

TANCILL, Chris

Center. Shoots left. 5'10", 185 lbs. Born, Livonia, MI, February 7, 1968.
(Hartford's 1st choice, 15th overall, in 1989 Supplemental Draft).

Season	Club	GP	G	A	Pts	PIM	GP	G	A	Pts	PIM
		REGULAR SEASON					PLAYOFFS				
1990-91	Hartford Whalers	9	1	1	2	4	....	....	....	....	....
1991-92	Hartford Whalers	10	0	0	0	2	....	....	....	....	....
	Detroit Red Wings	1	0	0	0	0	....	....	....	....	....
1992-93	Detroit Red Wings	4	1	0	1	2	....	....	....	....	....
1993-94	Dallas Stars	12	1	3	4	8	....	....	....	....	....
1994-95	San Jose Sharks	26	3	11	14	10	11	1	1	2	8
1995-96	San Jose Sharks	45	7	16	23	20	....	....	....	....	....
1996-97	San Jose Sharks	25	4	0	4	8	....	....	....	....	....
1997-98	Dallas Stars	2	0	1	1	0	....	....	....	....	....
	NHL Totals	**134**	**17**	**32**	**49**	**54**	**11**	**1**	**1**	**2**	**8**

Traded to **Detroit** by **Hartford** for Daniel Shank, December 18, 1991. Signed as a free agent by **Dallas**, August 28, 1993. Signed as a free agent by **San Jose**, August 24, 1994. Signed as a free agent by **Dallas**, August 6, 1997.

TANGUAY, Alex

Left wing. Shoots left. 6', 190 lbs. Born, Ste-Justine, Que., November 21, 1979.
(Colorado's 1st choice, 12th overall, in 1998 Entry Draft).

Season	Club	GP	G	A	Pts	PIM	GP	G	A	Pts	PIM
		REGULAR SEASON					PLAYOFFS				
99-2000	Colorado Avalanche	76	17	34	51	22	17	2	1	3	2
2000-01 ♦	Colorado Avalanche	82	27	50	77	37	23	6	15	21	8
2001-02	Colorado Avalanche	70	13	35	48	36	19	5	8	13	0
2002-03	Colorado Avalanche	82	26	41	67	36	7	1	2	3	4
	NHL Totals	**310**	**83**	**160**	**243**	**131**	**66**	**14**	**26**	**40**	**14**

TANGUAY, Christian

Right wing. Shoots right. 5'10", 190 lbs. Born, Beauport, Que., August 4, 1962.
(Quebec's 7th choice, 171st overall, in 1980 Entry Draft).

Season	Club	GP	G	A	Pts	PIM	GP	G	A	Pts	PIM
		REGULAR SEASON					PLAYOFFS				
1981-82	Quebec Nordiques	2	0	0	0	0	....	....	....	....	....
	NHL Totals	**2**	**0**	**0**	**0**	**0**	....	....	....	....	....

TANNAHILL, Don

Left wing. Shoots left. 5'11", 178 lbs. Born, Penetanguishene, Ont., February 21, 1949.
(Boston's 1st choice, 3rd overall, in 1969 Amateur Draft).

Season	Club	GP	G	A	Pts	PIM	GP	G	A	Pts	PIM
		REGULAR SEASON					PLAYOFFS				
1972-73	Vancouver Canucks	78	22	21	43	21	....	....	....	....	....
1973-74	Vancouver Canucks	33	8	12	20	4	....	....	....	....	....
	NHL Totals	**111**	**30**	**33**	**63**	**25**	....	....	....	....	....

Claimed by **Vancouver** from **Boston** in Intra-League Draft, June 5, 1972.

TANTI, Tony

Right wing. Shoots left. 5'9", 180 lbs. Born, Toronto, Ont., September 7, 1963.
(Chicago's 1st choice, 12th overall, in 1981 Entry Draft).

Season	Club	GP	G	A	Pts	PIM	GP	G	A	Pts	PIM
		REGULAR SEASON					PLAYOFFS				
1981-82	Chicago Black Hawks	2	0	0	0	0	....	....	....	....	....
1982-83	Chicago Black Hawks	1	1	0	1	0	....	....	....	....	....
	Vancouver Canucks	39	8	8	16	16	4	0	1	1	0
1983-84	Vancouver Canucks	79	45	41	86	50	4	1	2	3	0
1984-85	Vancouver Canucks	68	39	20	59	45	....	....	....	....	....
1985-86	Vancouver Canucks	77	39	33	72	85	3	0	1	1	11
1986-87	Vancouver Canucks	77	41	38	79	84	....	....	....	....	....
1987-88	Vancouver Canucks	73	40	37	77	90	....	....	....	....	....
1988-89	Vancouver Canucks	77	24	25	49	69	7	0	5	5	4
1989-90	Vancouver Canucks	41	14	18	32	50	....	....	....	....	....
	Pittsburgh Penguins	37	14	18	32	22	....	....	....	....	....
1990-91	Pittsburgh Penguins	46	6	12	18	44	....	....	....	....	....
	Buffalo Sabres	10	1	7	8	6	5	2	0	2	8
1991-92	Buffalo Sabres	70	15	16	31	100	7	0	3	3	4
	NHL Totals	**697**	**287**	**273**	**560**	**661**	**30**	**3**	**12**	**15**	**27**

Played in NHL All-Star Game (1986)

Traded to **Vancouver** by **Chicago** for Curt Fraser, January 6, 1983. Traded to **Pittsburgh** by **Vancouver** with Rod Buskas and Barry Pederson for Dave Capuano, Andrew McBain and Dan Quinn, January 8, 1990. Traded to **Buffalo** by **Pittsburgh** for Ken Priestlay, March 5, 1991.

TAPPER, Brad

Right wing. Shoots right. 6', 185 lbs. Born, Scarborough, Ont., April 28, 1978.

Season	Club	GP	G	A	Pts	PIM	GP	G	A	Pts	PIM
		REGULAR SEASON					PLAYOFFS				
2000-01	Atlanta Thrashers	16	2	3	5	6	....	....	....	....	....
2001-02	Atlanta Thrashers	20	2	4	6	43	....	....	....	....	....
2002-03	Atlanta Thrashers	35	10	4	14	23	....	....	....	....	....
	NHL Totals	**71**	**14**	**11**	**25**	**72**	....	....	....	....	....

Signed as a free agent by **Atlanta**, April 11, 2000.

TARDIF, Marc

Left wing. Shoots left. 6', 195 lbs. Born, Granby, Que., June 12, 1949.
(Montreal's 2nd choice, 2nd overall, in 1969 Amateur Draft).

Season	Club	GP	G	A	Pts	PIM	GP	G	A	Pts	PIM
		REGULAR SEASON					PLAYOFFS				
1969-70	Montreal Canadiens	18	3	2	5	27	....	....	....	....	....
1970-71 ♦	Montreal Canadiens	76	19	30	49	133	20	3	1	4	40
1971-72	Montreal Canadiens	75	31	22	53	81	6	2	3	5	9
1972-73 ♦	Montreal Canadiens	76	25	25	50	48	14	6	6	12	6
1979-80	Quebec Nordiques	58	33	35	68	30	....	....	....	....	....
1980-81	Quebec Nordiques	63	23	31	54	35	5	1	3	4	2
1981-82	Quebec Nordiques	75	39	31	70	55	13	1	2	3	16
1982-83	Quebec Nordiques	76	21	31	52	34	4	0	0	0	2
	NHL Totals	**517**	**194**	**207**	**401**	**443**	**62**	**13**	**15**	**28**	**75**

Played in NHL All-Star Game (1982)

Claimed by **Quebec** from **Montreal** in Expansion Draft, June 13, 1979.

TARDIF, Patrice

Center. Shoots left. 6'2", 202 lbs. Born, Thetford Mines, Que., October 30, 1970.
(St. Louis' 2nd choice, 54th overall, in 1990 Entry Draft).

Season	Club	GP	G	A	Pts	PIM	GP	G	A	Pts	PIM
		REGULAR SEASON					PLAYOFFS				
1994-95	St. Louis Blues	27	3	10	13	29	....	....	....	....	....

Season	Club	GP	G	A	Pts	PIM	GP	G	A	Pts	PIM
		REGULAR SEASON					PLAYOFFS				
1995-96	St. Louis Blues	23	3	0	3	12	....	....	....	....	....
	Los Angeles Kings	15	1	1	2	37	....	....	....	....	....
	NHL Totals	**65**	**7**	**11**	**18**	**78**	....	....	....	....	....

Traded to **Los Angeles** by **St. Louis** with Craig Johnson, Roman Vopat, St. Louis' 5th round choice (Peter Hogan) in 1996 Entry Draft and 1st round choice (Matt Zultek) in 1997 Entry Draft for Wayne Gretzky, February 27, 1996. Signed as a free agent by **Buffalo**, September 9, 1997.

TARNSTROM, Dick

Defense. Shoots left. 6'2", 200 lbs. Born, Sundbyberg, Sweden, January 20, 1975.
(NY Islanders' 12th choice, 272nd overall, in 1994 Entry Draft).

Season	Club	GP	G	A	Pts	PIM	GP	G	A	Pts	PIM
2001-02	New York Islanders	62	3	16	19	38	5	0	0	0	2
2002-03	Pittsburgh Penguins	61	7	34	41	50	....	....	....	....	....
	NHL Totals	**123**	**10**	**50**	**60**	**88**	**5**	**0**	**0**	**0**	**2**

Claimed on waivers by **Pittsburgh** from **NY Islanders**, August 6, 2002.

TATARINOV, Mikhail

Defense. Shoots left. 5'10", 195 lbs. Born, Angarsk, USSR, July 16, 1966.
(Washington's 10th choice, 225th overall, in 1984 Entry Draft).

Season	Club	GP	G	A	Pts	PIM	GP	G	A	Pts	PIM
1990-91	Washington Capitals	65	8	15	23	82	....	....	....	....	....
1991-92	Quebec Nordiques	66	11	27	38	72	....	....	....	....	....
1992-93	Quebec Nordiques	28	2	6	8	28	....	....	....	....	....
1993-94	Boston Bruins	2	0	0	0	2	....	....	....	....	....
	NHL Totals	**161**	**21**	**48**	**69**	**184**	....	....	....	....	....

Traded to **Quebec** by **Washington** for Toronto's 2nd round choice (previously acquired, Washington selected Eric Lavigne) in 1991 Entry Draft, June 22, 1991. Signed as a free agent by **Boston**, July 30, 1993.

TATCHELL, Spence

Defense. Shoots left. 5'11", 175 lbs. Born, Lloydminster, Sask., July 16, 1924.

Season	Club	GP	G	A	Pts	PIM	GP	G	A	Pts	PIM
1942-43	New York Rangers	1	0	0	0	0	....	....	....	....	....
	NHL Totals	**1**	**0**	**0**	**0**	**0**	....	....	....	....	....

Traded to **Montreal** (Buffalo-AHL) by **NY Rangers** with Hub Macey and Nestor Lubeck for Kilby MacDonald, January 12, 1944.

TAYLOR, Billy

Center. Shoots left. 6'1", 175 lbs. Born, Winnipeg, Man., October 14, 1942.

Season	Club	GP	G	A	Pts	PIM	GP	G	A	Pts	PIM
1964-65	New York Rangers	2	0	0	0	0	....	....	....	....	....
	NHL Totals	**2**	**0**	**0**	**0**	**0**	....	....	....	....	....

• Son of Billy

Traded to **Chicago** by **NY Rangers** with Camille Henry, Don Johns and Wally Chevrier for Doug Robinson, Wayne Hillman and John Brenneman, February 4, 1965. Claimed by **Minnesota** from **Chicago** in Intra-League Draft, June, 1967.

TAYLOR, Billy

Center. Shoots right. 5'9", 150 lbs. Born, Winnipeg, Man., May 3, 1919.

Season	Club	GP	G	A	Pts	PIM	GP	G	A	Pts	PIM
1939-40	Toronto Maple Leafs	29	4	6	10	9	2	1	0	1	0
1940-41	Toronto Maple Leafs	47	9	26	35	15	7	0	3	3	5
1941-42 ♦	Toronto Maple Leafs	48	12	26	38	20	13	2	*8	10	4
1942-43	Toronto Maple Leafs	50	18	42	60	2	6	2	2	4	0
1945-46	Toronto Maple Leafs	48	23	18	41	14	....	....	....	....	....
1946-47	Detroit Red Wings	60	17	*46	63	35	5	1	5	6	4
1947-48	Boston Bruins	39	4	16	20	25	....	....	....	....	....
	New York Rangers	2	0	0	0	0	....	....	....	....	....
	NHL Totals	**323**	**87**	**180**	**267**	**120**	**33**	**6**	**18**	**24**	**13**

• Father of Billy

Traded to **Detroit** by **Toronto** for Harry Watson, September 21, 1946. Traded to **Boston** by **Detroit** for Bep Guidolin, October 15, 1947. Traded to **NY Rangers** by **Boston** with future considerations (Pentti Lund and Ray Manson, June, 1948) for Grant Warwick, February 6, 1948. • Suspended for life by NHL for gambling infractions, March 9, 1948. • Suspension lifted by NHL, August 25, 1970.

TAYLOR, Bob

Right wing. Shoots right. 6'1", 190 lbs. Born, Newton, MA, August 12, 1904.

Season	Club	GP	G	A	Pts	PIM	GP	G	A	Pts	PIM
1929-30	Boston Bruins	8	0	0	0	6	....	....	....	....	....
	NHL Totals	**8**	**0**	**0**	**0**	**6**	....	....	....	....	....

Claimed by **Boston** from **Boston Tigers** (Can-Am) in Inter-League Draft, May 13, 1929.

TAYLOR, Chris

Center. Shoots left. 6'2", 192 lbs. Born, Stratford, Ont., March 6, 1972.
(NY Islanders' 2nd choice, 27th overall, in 1990 Entry Draft).

Season	Club	GP	G	A	Pts	PIM	GP	G	A	Pts	PIM
1994-95	New York Islanders	10	0	3	3	2	....	....	....	....	....
1995-96	New York Islanders	11	0	1	1	2	....	....	....	....	....
1996-97	New York Islanders	1	0	0	0	0	....	....	....	....	....
1998-99	Boston Bruins	37	3	5	8	12	....	....	....	....	....
99-2000	Buffalo Sabres	11	1	1	2	2	2	0	0	0	2
2000-01	Buffalo Sabres	14	0	2	2	6	....	....	....	....	....
2002-03	Buffalo Sabres	11	1	3	4	2	....	....	....	....	....
	NHL Totals	**95**	**5**	**15**	**20**	**26**	**2**	**0**	**0**	**0**	**2**

• Brother of Tim

Signed as a free agent by **Los Angeles**, July 25, 1997. Signed as a free agent by **Boston**, August 5, 1998. Signed as a free agent by **Buffalo**, August 13, 1999.

TAYLOR, Dave

Right wing. Shoots right. 6', 190 lbs. Born, Levack, Ont., December 4, 1955.
(Los Angeles' 14th choice, 210th overall, in 1975 Amateur Draft).

Season	Club	GP	G	A	Pts	PIM	GP	G	A	Pts	PIM
1977-78	Los Angeles Kings	64	22	21	43	47	2	0	0	0	5
1978-79	Los Angeles Kings	78	43	48	91	124	2	0	0	0	2
1979-80	Los Angeles Kings	61	37	53	90	72	4	2	1	3	4
1980-81	Los Angeles Kings	72	47	65	112	130	4	2	2	4	10
1981-82	Los Angeles Kings	78	39	67	106	130	10	4	6	10	20
1982-83	Los Angeles Kings	46	21	37	58	76	....	....	....	....	....
1983-84	Los Angeles Kings	63	20	49	69	91	....	....	....	....	....
1984-85	Los Angeles Kings	79	41	51	92	132	3	2	2	4	8
1985-86	Los Angeles Kings	76	33	38	71	110	....	....	....	....	....
1986-87	Los Angeles Kings	67	18	44	62	84	5	2	3	5	6
1987-88	Los Angeles Kings	68	26	41	67	129	5	3	3	6	6
1988-89	Los Angeles Kings	70	26	37	63	80	11	1	5	6	19
1989-90	Los Angeles Kings	58	15	26	41	96	6	4	4	8	2
1990-91	Los Angeles Kings	73	23	30	53	148	12	2	1	3	12
1991-92	Los Angeles Kings	77	10	19	29	63	6	1	1	2	20
1992-93	Los Angeles Kings	48	6	9	15	49	22	3	5	8	31
1993-94	Los Angeles Kings	33	4	3	7	28	....	....	....	....	....
	NHL Totals	**1111**	**431**	**638**	**1069**	**1589**	**92**	**26**	**33**	**59**	**145**

NHL Second All-Star Team (1981) • Bill Masterton Memorial Trophy (1991) • King Clancy Memorial Trophy (1991)

Played in NHL All-Star Game (1981, 1982, 1986, 1994)

TAYLOR, Harry

Center. Shoots right. 5'8", 165 lbs. Born, St. James, Man., March 28, 1926.

Season	Club	GP	G	A	Pts	PIM	GP	G	A	Pts	PIM
1946-47	Toronto Maple Leafs	9	0	2	2	0	....	....	....	....	....
1948-49 ♦	Toronto Maple Leafs	42	4	7	11	30	1	0	0	0	0
1951-52	Chicago Black Hawks	15	1	1	2	0	....	....	....	....	....
	NHL Totals	**66**	**5**	**10**	**15**	**30**	**1**	**0**	**0**	**0**	**0**

Signed as a free agent by **Toronto**, May 1, 1946. Traded to **Cleveland**, (AHL) by **Toronto** with Ray Ceresino and the loan of Tod Sloan for the 1949-50 season for Bob Solinger, September 6, 1949. Traded to **Chicago** (St. Louis-AHL) by **Cleveland** (AHL) for Jean-Paul Gladu, August 19, 1951.

TAYLOR, Mark

Center. Shoots left. 6', 190 lbs. Born, Vancouver, B.C., January 26, 1958.
(Philadelphia's 9th choice, 100th overall, in 1978 Amateur Draft).

Season	Club	GP	G	A	Pts	PIM	GP	G	A	Pts	PIM
1981-82	Philadelphia Flyers	2	0	0	0	0	....	....	....	....	....
1982-83	Philadelphia Flyers	61	8	25	33	24	3	0	0	0	0
1983-84	Philadelphia Flyers	1	0	0	0	0	....	....	....	....	....
	Pittsburgh Penguins	59	24	31	55	24	....	....	....	....	....
1984-85	Pittsburgh Penguins	47	7	10	17	19	....	....	....	....	....
	Washington Capitals	9	1	1	2	2	....	....	....	....	....
1985-86	Washington Capitals	30	2	1	3	4	3	0	0	0	0
	NHL Totals	**209**	**42**	**68**	**110**	**73**	**6**	**0**	**0**	**0**	**0**

Traded to **Pittsburgh** by **Philadelphia** with Ron Flockhart, Andy Brickley and Philadelphia's 1st (Roger Belanger) and 3rd (later traded to Vancouver – Vancouver selected Mike Stevens) round choices in 1984 Entry Draft for Ron Sutter and Pittsburgh's 2nd (Greg Smyth) and 3rd (David McLay) round choices in 1984 Entry Draft, October 23, 1983. Traded to **Washington** by **Pittsburgh** for Jim McGeough, March 12, 1985.

TAYLOR, Ralph

Defense. Shoots right. 5'9", 180 lbs. Born, Toronto, Ont., October 2, 1905.

Season	Club	GP	G	A	Pts	PIM	GP	G	A	Pts	PIM
1927-28	Chicago Black Hawks	22	1	1	2	39	....	....	....	....	....
1928-29	Chicago Black Hawks	38	0	0	0	56	....	....	....	....	....
1929-30	Chicago Black Hawks	17	1	0	1	42	....	....	....	....	....
	New York Rangers	22	2	0	2	32	4	0	0	0	10
	NHL Totals	**99**	**4**	**1**	**5**	**169**	**4**	**0**	**0**	**0**	**10**

Loaned to **St. Louis** (AHA) by **Chicago** for cash, November 23, 1928. Traded to **Tulsa** (AHA) by **Chicago** with cash for Teddy Graham, January 4, 1930. • Cash amount in January 4, 1930 transaction was increased after Taylor was not offered on waivers to other NHL clubs. Claimed on waivers by **NY Rangers** from **Chicago**, January 8, 1930. Traded to **Chicago Shamrocks** (AHA) by **NY Rangers** for $7,500, October 27, 1930. NHL rights transferred to **Detroit** from **Chicago Shamrocks** (AHA) after AHA club owners purchased Detroit (NHL and IHL) franchises, September 2, 1932.

TAYLOR, Ted

Left wing. Shoots left. 6', 175 lbs. Born, Oak Lake, Man., February 25, 1942.

Season	Club	GP	G	A	Pts	PIM	GP	G	A	Pts	PIM
1964-65	New York Rangers	4	0	0	0	4	....	....	....	....	....
1965-66	New York Rangers	4	0	1	1	2	....	....	....	....	....
1966-67	Detroit Red Wings	2	0	0	0	0	....	....	....	....	....
1967-68	Minnesota North Stars	31	3	5	8	34	....	....	....	....	....
1970-71	Vancouver Canucks	56	11	16	27	53	....	....	....	....	....
1971-72	Vancouver Canucks	69	9	13	22	88	....	....	....	....	....
	NHL Totals	**166**	**23**	**35**	**58**	**181**	....	....	....	....	....

Traded to **Montreal** by **NY Rangers** with Garry Peters for Red Berenson, June 13, 1966. Claimed by **Detroit** from **Montreal** in Intra-League Draft, June 15, 1966. Claimed by **Minnesota** from **Detroit** in Expansion Draft, June 6, 1967. Traded to **Toronto** (Rochester-AHL) by **Minnesota** with Murray Hall, Len Lunde, Don Johns, Duke Harris and the loan of Carl Wetzel for J.P. Parise and Milan Marcetta , December 23, 1967. Rights transferred to **Vancouver** (WHL) after WHL club purchased **Rochester** (AHL) franchise, August 13, 1968. NHL rights transferred to **Vancouver** after NHL club purchased **Vancouver** (WHL) franchise, December 19, 1969. Claimed by **NY Islanders** from **Vancouver** in Expansion Draft, June 6, 1972.

TAYLOR, Tim

Center. Shoots left. 6'1", 189 lbs. Born, Stratford, Ont., February 6, 1969.
(Washington's 2nd choice, 36th overall, in 1988 Entry Draft).

Season	Club	GP	G	A	Pts	PIM	GP	G	A	Pts	PIM
		REGULAR SEASON					PLAYOFFS				
1993-94	Detroit Red Wings	1	1	0	1	0	....	....	....	....	....
1994-95	Detroit Red Wings	22	0	4	4	16	6	0	1	1	12
1995-96	Detroit Red Wings	72	11	14	25	39	18	0	4	4	4
1996-97 ♦	Detroit Red Wings	44	3	4	7	52	2	0	0	0	0
1997-98	Boston Bruins	79	20	11	31	57	6	0	0	0	10
1998-99	Boston Bruins	49	4	7	11	55	12	0	3	3	8
99-2000	New York Rangers	76	9	11	20	72	....	....	....	....	....
2000-01	New York Rangers	38	2	5	7	16	....	....	....	....	....
2001-02	Tampa Bay Lightning	48	4	4	8	25	....	....	....	....	....
2002-03	Tampa Bay Lightning	82	4	8	12	38	11	0	1	1	6
	NHL Totals	**511**	**58**	**68**	**126**	**370**	**55**	**0**	**9**	**9**	**40**

• Brother of Chris

Traded to **Vancouver** by **Washington** for Eric Murano, January 29, 1993. Signed as a free agent by **Detroit**, July 28, 1993. Claimed by **Boston** from **Detroit** in Waiver Draft, September 28, 1997. Signed as a free agent by **NY Rangers**, July 30, 1999. • Missed majority of 2000-01 season recovering from abdominal injury suffered in game vs. Phoenix, January 4, 2001. Traded to **Tampa Bay** by **NY Rangers** for Kyle Freadrich and Nils Ekman, June 30, 2001.

TEAL, Jeff

Right wing. Shoots left. 6'3", 205 lbs. Born, Edina, MN, May 30, 1960.
(Montreal's 6th choice, 82nd overall, in 1980 Entry Draft).

Season	Club	GP	G	A	Pts	PIM	GP	G	A	Pts	PIM
1984-85	Montreal Canadiens	6	0	1	1	0	....	....	....	....	....
	NHL Totals	**6**	**0**	**1**	**1**	**0**	....	....	....	....	....

TEAL, Skip

Center. Shoots left. 5'8", 155 lbs. Born, Ridgeway, Ont., July 17, 1933.

Season	Club	GP	G	A	Pts	PIM	GP	G	A	Pts	PIM
1954-55	Boston Bruins	1	0	0	0	0	....	....	....	....	....
	NHL Totals	**1**	**0**	**0**	**0**	**0**	....	....	....	....	....

• Brother of Vic

TEAL, Vic

Right wing. Shoots right. 6'1", 160 lbs. Born, St. Catharines, Ont., August 10, 1949.
(St. Louis' 3rd choice, 42nd overall, in 1969 Amateur Draft).

Season	Club	GP	G	A	Pts	PIM	GP	G	A	Pts	PIM
1973-74	New York Islanders	1	0	0	0	0	....	....	....	....	....
	NHL Totals	**1**	**0**	**0**	**0**	**0**					

• Brother of Skip

Signed as a free agent by **NY Islanders**, September 29, 1973.

TEBBUTT, Greg

Defense. Shoots left. 6'3", 215 lbs. Born, North Vancouver, B.C., May 11, 1957.
(Minnesota's 7th choice, 130th overall, in 1977 Amateur Draft).

Season	Club	GP	G	A	Pts	PIM	GP	G	A	Pts	PIM
1979-80	Quebec Nordiques	2	0	1	1	4	....	....	....	....	....
1983-84	Pittsburgh Penguins	24	0	2	2	31	....	....	....	....	....
	NHL Totals	**26**	**0**	**3**	**3**	**35**	....	....	....	....	....

Reclaimed by **Minnesota** from **Birmingham** (WHA) prior to Expansion Draft, June 9, 1979. Claimed by **Quebec** from **Minnesota** on waivers, August 13, 1979. Signed as a free agent by **Pittsburgh**, July 22, 1983.

TENKRAT, Petr

Right wing. Shoots right. 5'11", 200 lbs. Born, Kladno, Czech., May 31, 1977.
(Anaheim's 6th choice, 230th overall, in 1999 Entry Draft).

Season	Club	GP	G	A	Pts	PIM	GP	G	A	Pts	PIM
2000-01	Mighty Ducks of Anaheim	46	5	9	14	16	....	....	....	....	....
2001-02	Mighty Ducks of Anaheim	9	0	0	0	6	....	....	....	....	....
	Nashville Predators	58	8	16	24	28	....	....	....	....	....
	NHL Totals	**113**	**13**	**25**	**38**	**50**	....	....	....	....	....

Traded to **Nashville** by **Anaheim** for Patrick Kjellberg, November 1, 2001. Claimed by **Florida** from **Nashville** in Waiver Draft, October 4, 2002. Traded to **Columbus** by **Florida** for Mathieu Biron, October 4, 2002.

TEPPER, Stephen

Right wing. Shoots right. 6'4", 215 lbs. Born, Santa Ana, CA, March 10, 1969.
(Chicago's 7th choice, 134th overall, in 1987 Entry Draft).

Season	Club	GP	G	A	Pts	PIM	GP	G	A	Pts	PIM
1992-93	Chicago Blackhawks	1	0	0	0	0	....	....	....	....	....
	NHL Totals	**1**	**0**	**0**	**0**	**0**	....	....	....	....	....

TERBENCHE, Paul

Defense. Shoots left. 5'10", 170 lbs. Born, Port Hope, Ont., September 16, 1945.

Season	Club	GP	G	A	Pts	PIM	GP	G	A	Pts	PIM
1967-68	Chicago Black Hawks	68	3	7	10	8	6	0	0	0	0
1970-71	Buffalo Sabres	3	0	0	0	2	....	....	....	....	....
1971-72	Buffalo Sabres	9	0	0	0	2	....	....	....	....	....
1972-73	Buffalo Sabres	42	0	7	7	8	6	0	0	0	0
1973-74	Buffalo Sabres	67	2	12	14	8	....	....	....	....	....
	NHL Totals	**189**	**5**	**26**	**31**	**28**	**12**	**0**	**0**	**0**	**0**

Claimed by **Buffalo** from **Chicago** in Expansion Draft, June, 1970. Claimed by **Kansas City** from **Buffalo** in Expansion Draft, June, 1974. Retained by **Winnipeg** prior to Expansion Draft, June 9, 1979. Traded to **Atlanta** by **Winnipeg** for future considerations, August, 1979.

TERRION, Greg

Left wing. Shoots left. 5'11", 190 lbs. Born, Marmora, Ont., May 2, 1960.
(Los Angeles' 3rd choice, 33rd overall, in 1980 Entry Draft).

Season	Club	GP	G	A	Pts	PIM	GP	G	A	Pts	PIM
		REGULAR SEASON					PLAYOFFS				
1980-81	Los Angeles Kings	73	12	25	37	99	3	1	0	1	4
1981-82	Los Angeles Kings	61	15	22	37	23	....	....	....	....	....
1982-83	Toronto Maple Leafs	74	16	16	32	59	4	1	2	3	2
1983-84	Toronto Maple Leafs	79	15	24	39	36	....	....	....	....	....
1984-85	Toronto Maple Leafs	72	14	17	31	20	....	....	....	....	....
1985-86	Toronto Maple Leafs	76	10	22	32	31	10	0	3	3	17
1986-87	Toronto Maple Leafs	67	7	8	15	6	13	0	2	2	14
1987-88	Toronto Maple Leafs	59	4	16	20	65	5	0	2	2	4
	NHL Totals	**561**	**93**	**150**	**243**	**339**	**35**	**2**	**9**	**11**	**41**

Traded to **Toronto** by **Los Angeles** for Toronto's 4th round choice (later traded to Detroit – Detroit selected David Korol) in 1983 Entry Draft, October 19, 1982.

TERRY, Bill

Center. Shoots right. 5'8", 175 lbs. Born, Toronto, Ont., July 13, 1961.

Season	Club	GP	G	A	Pts	PIM	GP	G	A	Pts	PIM
1987-88	Minnesota North Stars	5	0	0	0	0	....	....	....	....	....
	NHL Totals	**5**	**0**	**0**	**0**	**0**	....	....	....	....	....

Signed as a free agent by **Detroit**, September, 1986. Signed as a free agent by **Minnesota**, September, 1987.

TERTYSHNY, Dmitri

Defense. Shoots left. 6'1", 176 lbs. Born, Chelyabinsk, USSR, December 26, 1976.
(Philadelphia's 4th choice, 132nd overall, in 1995 Entry Draft).

Season	Club	GP	G	A	Pts	PIM	GP	G	A	Pts	PIM
1998-99	Philadelphia Flyers	62	2	8	10	30	1	0	0	0	0
	NHL Totals	**62**	**2**	**8**	**10**	**30**	**1**	**0**	**0**	**0**	**0**

• Died of injuries suffered in motor-boat accident, July 23, 1999.

TESSIER, Orval

Center. Shoots left. 5'8", 160 lbs. Born, Cornwall, Ont., June 30, 1933.

Season	Club	GP	G	A	Pts	PIM	GP	G	A	Pts	PIM
1954-55	Montreal Canadiens	4	0	0	0	0	....	....	....	....	....
1955-56	Boston Bruins	23	2	3	5	6	....	....	....	....	....
1960-61	Boston Bruins	32	3	4	7	0	....	....	....	....	....
	NHL Totals	**59**	**5**	**7**	**12**	**6**	....	....	....	....	....

Claimed by **Boston** from **Montreal** in Intra-League Draft, June 1, 1955. Traded to **Montreal** by **Boston** (Portland-WHL) for cash, August, 1964.

TETARENKO, Joey

Right wing. Shoots right. 6'2", 215 lbs. Born, Prince Albert, Sask., March 3, 1978.
(Florida's 4th choice, 82nd overall, in 1996 Entry Draft).

Season	Club	GP	G	A	Pts	PIM	GP	G	A	Pts	PIM
2000-01	Florida Panthers	29	3	1	4	44	....	....	....	....	....
2001-02	Florida Panthers	38	1	0	1	123	....	....	....	....	....
2002-03	Florida Panthers	2	0	0	0	4	....	....	....	....	....
	Ottawa Senators	2	0	0	0	5	....	....	....	....	....
	NHL Totals	**71**	**4**	**1**	**5**	**176**	....	....	....	....	....

Traded to **Ottawa** by **Florida** for Simon Lajeunesse, March 4, 2003. Signed as a free agent by **Carolina**, July 2, 2003.

TEZIKOV, Alexei

Defense. Shoots left. 6'1", 208 lbs. Born, Togliatti, USSR, June 22, 1978.
(Buffalo's 7th choice, 115th overall, in 1996 Entry Draft).

Season	Club	GP	G	A	Pts	PIM	GP	G	A	Pts	PIM
1998-99	Washington Capitals	5	0	0	0	0	....	....	....	....	....
99-2000	Washington Capitals	23	1	1	2	2	....	....	....	....	....
2001-02	Vancouver Canucks	2	0	0	0	0	....	....	....	....	....
	NHL Totals	**30**	**1**	**1**	**2**	**2**	....	....	....	....	....

Traded to **Washington** by **Buffalo** with Buffalo's 4th round compensatory choice (later traded to Calgary – Calgary selected Levente Szuper) in 2000 Entry Draft for Joe Juneau and Washington's 3rd round choice (Tim Preston) in 1999 Entry Draft, March 22, 1999. Traded to **Anaheim** by **Washington** with Edmonton's 4th round choice (previously acquired, Anaheim selected Brandon Rogers) in 2001 Entry Draft for Jason Marshall, March 13, 2001. Claimed on waivers by **Vancouver** from **Anaheim**, October 30, 2001. • Spent majority of 2001-02 season on practice roster, November 20, 2001.

THEBERGE, Greg

Defense. Shoots right. 5'10", 185 lbs. Born, Peterborough, Ont., September 3, 1959.
(Washington's 5th choice, 109th overall, in 1979 Entry Draft).

Season	Club	GP	G	A	Pts	PIM	GP	G	A	Pts	PIM
1979-80	Washington Capitals	12	0	1	1	0	....	....	....	....	....
1980-81	Washington Capitals	1	1	0	1	0	....	....	....	....	....
1981-82	Washington Capitals	57	5	32	37	49	....	....	....	....	....
1982-83	Washington Capitals	70	8	28	36	20	4	0	1	1	0
1983-84	Washington Capitals	13	1	2	3	4	....	....	....	....	....
	NHL Totals	**153**	**15**	**63**	**78**	**73**	**4**	**0**	**1**	**1**	**0**

THELIN, Mats

Defense. Shoots left. 5'10", 185 lbs. Born, Stockholm, Sweden, March 30, 1961.
(Boston's 6th choice, 140th overall, in 1981 Entry Draft).

Season	Club	GP	G	A	Pts	PIM	GP	G	A	Pts	PIM
1984-85	Boston Bruins	73	5	13	18	9	5	0	0	0	6
1985-86	Boston Bruins	31	2	3	5	29	....	....	....	....	....
1986-87	Boston Bruins	59	1	3	4	69	....	....	....	....	....
	NHL Totals	**163**	**8**	**19**	**27**	**107**	**5**	**0**	**0**	**0**	**6**

THELVEN, Michael

Defense. Shoots right. 5'11", 185 lbs. Born, Stockholm, Sweden, January 7, 1961.
(Boston's 8th choice, 186th overall, in 1980 Entry Draft).

Season	Club	Regular Season GP	G	A	Pts	PIM	Playoffs GP	G	A	Pts	PIM
1985-86	Boston Bruins	60	6	20	26	48	3	0	0	0	0
1986-87	Boston Bruins	34	5	15	20	18	....	....	....	....	....
1987-88	Boston Bruins	67	6	25	31	57	21	3	3	6	26
1988-89	Boston Bruins	40	3	18	21	71	10	1	7	8	8
1989-90	Boston Bruins	6	0	2	2	23	....	....	....	....	....
	NHL Totals	**207**	**20**	**80**	**100**	**217**	**34**	**4**	**10**	**14**	**34**

THERIEN, Chris

Defense. Shoots left. 6'5", 235 lbs. Born, Ottawa, Ont., December 14, 1971.
(Philadelphia's 7th choice, 47th overall, in 1990 Entry Draft).

Season	Club	Regular Season GP	G	A	Pts	PIM	Playoffs GP	G	A	Pts	PIM
1994-95	Philadelphia Flyers	48	3	10	13	38	15	0	0	0	10
1995-96	Philadelphia Flyers	82	6	17	23	89	12	0	0	0	18
1996-97	Philadelphia Flyers	71	2	22	24	64	19	1	6	7	6
1997-98	Philadelphia Flyers	78	3	16	19	80	5	0	1	1	4
1998-99	Philadelphia Flyers	74	3	15	18	48	6	0	0	0	6
99-2000	Philadelphia Flyers	80	4	9	13	66	18	0	1	1	12
2000-01	Philadelphia Flyers	73	2	12	14	48	6	1	0	1	8
2001-02	Philadelphia Flyers	77	4	10	14	30	5	0	0	0	2
2002-03	Philadelphia Flyers	67	1	6	7	36	13	0	2	2	2
	NHL Totals	**650**	**28**	**117**	**145**	**499**	**99**	**2**	**10**	**12**	**68**

NHL All-Rookie Team (1995)

THERRIEN, Gaston

Defense. Shoots right. 5'10", 185 lbs. Born, Montreal, Que., May 27, 1960.
(Quebec's 5th choice, 129th overall, in 1980 Entry Draft).

Season	Club	Regular Season GP	G	A	Pts	PIM	Playoffs GP	G	A	Pts	PIM
1980-81	Quebec Nordiques	3	0	1	1	2	....	....	....	....	....
1981-82	Quebec Nordiques	14	0	7	7	6	9	0	1	1	4
1982-83	Quebec Nordiques	5	0	0	0	4	....	....	....	....	....
	NHL Totals	**22**	**0**	**8**	**8**	**12**	**9**	**0**	**1**	**1**	**4**

THIBAUDEAU, Gilles

Center. Shoots left. 5'10", 165 lbs. Born, Montreal, Que., March 4, 1963.

Season	Club	Regular Season GP	G	A	Pts	PIM	Playoffs GP	G	A	Pts	PIM
1986-87	Montreal Canadiens	9	1	3	4	0	....	....	....	....	....
1987-88	Montreal Canadiens	17	5	6	11	0	8	3	3	6	2
1988-89	Montreal Canadiens	32	6	6	12	6	....	....	....	....	....
1989-90	New York Islanders	20	4	4	8	17	....	....	....	....	....
	Toronto Maple Leafs	21	7	11	18	13	....	....	....	....	....
1990-91	Toronto Maple Leafs	20	2	7	9	4	....	....	....	....	....
	NHL Totals	**119**	**25**	**37**	**62**	**40**	**8**	**3**	**3**	**6**	**2**

Signed as a free agent by **Montreal**, October 9, 1984. Signed as a free agent by **NY Islanders**, September, 1989. Traded to **Toronto** by **NY Islanders** with Mike Stevens for Jack Capuano, Paul Gagne and Derek Laxdal, December 20, 1989.

THIBEAULT, Lorrain

Left wing. Shoots left. 5'7", 180 lbs. Born, Charletone, Ont., October 2, 1918.

Season	Club	Regular Season GP	G	A	Pts	PIM	Playoffs GP	G	A	Pts	PIM
1944-45	Detroit Red Wings	4	0	2	2	2	....	....	....	....	....
1945-46	Montreal Canadiens	1	0	0	0	0	....	....	....	....	....
	NHL Totals	**5**	**0**	**2**	**2**	**2**	....	....	....	....	....

Signed as a free agent by **Detroit**, October 21, 1944. Traded to **Buffalo** (AHL) by **Detroit** for cash, October 17, 1945. Loaned to **Montreal** by **Buffalo** (AHL) for cash and the loan of Wilf Field, Kenny Mosdell and Frank Eddolls, October 29, 1945. Returned to **Buffalo** (AHL) from **Montreal** and requested that his amateur status be reinstated, November 6, 1945.

THIFFAULT, Leo

Left wing. Shoots left. 5'10", 175 lbs. Born, Drummondville, Que., December 16, 1944.

Season	Club	Regular Season GP	G	A	Pts	PIM	Playoffs GP	G	A	Pts	PIM
1967-68	Minnesota North Stars	....	....	....	....	....	5	0	0	0	0
	NHL Totals	....	....	....	....	....	**5**	**0**	**0**	**0**	**0**

Rights traded to **Minnesota** by **Montreal** with Bill Plager and the rights to Barrie Meissner for Bryan Watson, June 6, 1967. Traded to **Phoenix** (WHL) by **Minnesota** with Bob Charlebois to complete earlier transaction that sent Walt McKechnie to Minnesota (February 17, 1968), June, 1968.

THOMAS, Cy

Wing. Shoots left. 5'11", 185 lbs. Born, Dowlais, Wales, August 5, 1926.

Season	Club	Regular Season GP	G	A	Pts	PIM	Playoffs GP	G	A	Pts	PIM
1947-48	Chicago Black Hawks	6	1	0	1	8	....	....	....	....	....
	Toronto Maple Leafs	8	1	2	3	4	....	....	....	....	....
	NHL Totals	**14**	**2**	**2**	**4**	**12**	....	....	....	....	....

Traded to **Toronto** by **Chicago** with Max Bentley for Bob Goldham, Ernie Dickens, Bud Poile, Gus Bodnar and Gaye Stewart, November 2, 1947.

THOMAS, Reg

Left wing. Shoots left. 5'10", 185 lbs. Born, Lambeth, Ont., April 21, 1953.
(Chicago's 2nd choice, 29th overall, in 1973 Amateur Draft).

Season	Club	Regular Season GP	G	A	Pts	PIM	Playoffs GP	G	A	Pts	PIM
1979-80	Quebec Nordiques	39	9	7	16	6	....	....	....	....	....
	NHL Totals	**39**	**9**	**7**	**16**	**6**	....	....	....	....	....

Claimed by **Edmonton** from **Chicago** in Expansion Draft, June 13, 1979. Traded to **Toronto** by **Edmonton** for Toronto's 6th round choice (Steve Smith) in 1981 Entry Draft, August 22, 1979. Traded to **Quebec** by **Toronto** for Dave Farrish and Terry Martin, December 13, 1979. Signed as a free agent by **Toronto**, July 21, 1981.

THOMAS, Scott

Right wing. Shoots right. 6'2", 200 lbs. Born, Buffalo, NY, January 18, 1970.
(Buffalo's 2nd choice, 56th overall, in 1989 Entry Draft).

Season	Club	Regular Season GP	G	A	Pts	PIM	Playoffs GP	G	A	Pts	PIM
1992-93	Buffalo Sabres	7	1	1	2	15	....	....	....	....	....
1993-94	Buffalo Sabres	32	2	2	4	8	....	....	....	....	....
2000-01	Los Angeles Kings	24	3	1	4	9	12	1	0	1	4
	NHL Totals	**63**	**6**	**4**	**10**	**32**	**12**	**1**	**0**	**1**	**4**

Signed as a free agent by **Los Angeles**, July 30, 1999. Signed as a free agent by **San Jose**, September 5, 2002.

THOMAS, Steve

Left wing. Shoots left. 5'10", 185 lbs. Born, Stockport, England, July 15, 1963.

Season	Club	Regular Season GP	G	A	Pts	PIM	Playoffs GP	G	A	Pts	PIM
1984-85	Toronto Maple Leafs	18	1	1	2	2	....	....	....	....	....
1985-86	Toronto Maple Leafs	65	20	37	57	36	10	6	8	14	9
1986-87	Toronto Maple Leafs	78	35	27	62	114	13	2	3	5	13
1987-88	Chicago Blackhawks	30	13	13	26	40	3	1	2	3	6
1988-89	Chicago Blackhawks	45	21	19	40	69	12	3	5	8	10
1989-90	Chicago Blackhawks	76	40	30	70	91	20	7	6	13	33
1990-91	Chicago Blackhawks	69	19	35	54	129	6	1	2	3	15
1991-92	Chicago Blackhawks	11	2	6	8	26	....	....	....	....	....
	New York Islanders	71	28	42	70	71	....	....	....	....	....
1992-93	New York Islanders	79	37	50	87	111	18	9	8	17	37
1993-94	New York Islanders	78	42	33	75	139	4	1	0	1	8
1994-95	New York Islanders	47	11	15	26	60	....	....	....	....	....
1995-96	New Jersey Devils	81	26	35	61	98	....	....	....	....	....
1996-97	New Jersey Devils	57	15	19	34	46	10	1	1	2	18
1997-98	New Jersey Devils	55	14	10	24	32	6	0	3	3	2
1998-99	Toronto Maple Leafs	78	28	45	73	33	17	6	3	9	12
99-2000	Toronto Maple Leafs	81	26	37	63	68	12	6	3	9	10
2000-01	Toronto Maple Leafs	57	8	26	34	46	11	6	3	9	4
2001-02	Chicago Blackhawks	34	11	4	15	17	5	1	1	2	0
2002-03	Chicago Blackhawks	69	4	13	17	51	....	....	....	....	....
	Mighty Ducks of Anaheim	12	10	3	13	2	21	4	4	8	8
	NHL Totals	**1191**	**411**	**500**	**911**	**1281**	**168**	**54**	**52**	**106**	**185**

Signed as a free agent by **Toronto,** May 12, 1984. Traded to **Chicago** by **Toronto** with Rick Vaive and Bob McGill for Al Secord and Ed Olczyk, September 3, 1987. Traded to **NY Islanders** by **Chicago** with Adam Creighton for Brent Sutter and Brad Lauer, October 25, 1991. Traded to **New Jersey** by **NY Islanders** for Claude Lemieux, October 3, 1995. Signed as a free agent by **Toronto**, July 30, 1998. Signed as a free agent by **Chicago**, July 17, 2001. • Missed majority of 2001-02 season recovering from ankle injury suffered in game vs. Calgary, November 15, 2001. Traded to **Anaheim** by **Chicago** for Anaheim's 5th round choice (Alexei Ivanov) in 2003 Entry Draft, March 11, 2003.

THOMLINSON, Dave

Left wing. Shoots left. 6'1", 215 lbs. Born, Edmonton, Alta., October 22, 1966.
(Toronto's 3rd choice, 43rd overall, in 1985 Entry Draft).

Season	Club	Regular Season GP	G	A	Pts	PIM	Playoffs GP	G	A	Pts	PIM
1989-90	St. Louis Blues	19	1	2	3	12	....	....	....	....	....
1990-91	St. Louis Blues	3	0	0	0	0	9	3	1	4	4
1991-92	Boston Bruins	12	0	1	1	17	....	....	....	....	....
1993-94	Los Angeles Kings	7	0	0	0	21	....	....	....	....	....
1994-95	Los Angeles Kings	1	0	0	0	0	....	....	....	....	....
	NHL Totals	**42**	**1**	**3**	**4**	**50**	**9**	**3**	**1**	**4**	**4**

Signed as a free agent by **St. Louis**, June 4, 1987. Signed as a free agent by **Boston**, July 30, 1991. Signed as a free agent by **NY Rangers**, September 4, 1992. Signed as a free agent by **Los Angeles**, July 22, 1993.

THOMPSON, Brent

Defense. Shoots left. 6'2", 205 lbs. Born, Calgary, Alta., January 9, 1971.
(Los Angeles' 1st choice, 39th overall, in 1989 Entry Draft).

Season	Club	Regular Season GP	G	A	Pts	PIM	Playoffs GP	G	A	Pts	PIM
1991-92	Los Angeles Kings	27	0	5	5	89	4	0	0	0	4
1992-93	Los Angeles Kings	30	0	4	4	76	....	....	....	....	....
1993-94	Los Angeles Kings	24	1	0	1	81	....	....	....	....	....
1994-95	Winnipeg Jets	29	0	0	0	78	....	....	....	....	....
1995-96	Winnipeg Jets	10	0	1	1	21	....	....	....	....	....
1996-97	Phoenix Coyotes	1	0	0	0	7	....	....	....	....	....
	NHL Totals	**121**	**1**	**10**	**11**	**352**	**4**	**0**	**0**	**0**	**4**

Traded to **Winnipeg** by **Los Angeles** with cash for the rights to Ruslan Batyrshin and Winnipeg's 2nd round choice (Marian Cisar) in 1996 Entry Draft, August 8, 1994. Transferred to **Phoenix** after **Winnipeg** franchise relocated, July 1, 1996. Signed as a free agent by **NY Rangers**, August 26, 1997. Signed as a free agent by **Florida**, July 27, 1999. Traded to **Colorado** by **Florida** for future considerations, March 3, 2001.

THOMPSON, Cliff

Defense. Shoots left. 5'11", 185 lbs. Born, Winchester, MA, December 9, 1918.

Season	Club	Regular Season GP	G	A	Pts	PIM	Playoffs GP	G	A	Pts	PIM
1941-42	Boston Bruins	3	0	0	0	2	....	....	....	....	....
1948-49	Boston Bruins	10	0	1	1	0	....	....	....	....	....
	NHL Totals	**13**	**0**	**1**	**1**	**2**	....	....	....	....	....

Signed as a free agent by **Boston**, October 22, 1941.

THOMPSON, Errol

Left wing. Shoots left. 5'9", 185 lbs. Born, Summerside, P.E.I., May 28, 1950.
(Toronto's 2nd choice, 22nd overall, in 1970 Amateur Draft).

Season	Club	Regular Season GP	G	A	Pts	PIM	Playoffs GP	G	A	Pts	PIM
1970-71	Toronto Maple Leafs	1	0	0	0	0	....	....	....	....	....
1972-73	Toronto Maple Leafs	68	13	19	32	8	....	....	....	....	....
1973-74	Toronto Maple Leafs	56	7	8	15	6	2	0	1	1	0
1974-75	Toronto Maple Leafs	65	25	17	42	12	6	0	0	0	9

Season	Club	Regular Season GP	G	A	Pts	PIM	Playoffs GP	G	A	Pts	PIM
1975-76	Toronto Maple Leafs	75	43	37	80	26	10	3	3	6	0
1976-77	Toronto Maple Leafs	41	21	16	37	8	9	2	0	2	0
1977-78	Toronto Maple Leafs	59	17	22	39	10	....	....	....	....	....
	Detroit Red Wings	14	5	1	6	2	7	2	1	3	2
1978-79	Detroit Red Wings	70	23	31	54	26	....	....	....	....	....
1979-80	Detroit Red Wings	77	34	14	48	22	....	....	....	....	....
1980-81	Detroit Red Wings	39	14	12	26	52	....	....	....	....	....
	Pittsburgh Penguins	34	6	8	14	12	....	....	....	....	....
	NHL Totals	**599**	**208**	**185**	**393**	**184**	**34**	**7**	**5**	**12**	**11**

Traded to **Detroit** by **Toronto** with Toronto's 1st (Brent Peterson) and 2nd (Al Jensen) round choices in 1978 Amateur Draft and Toronto's 1st round choice (Mike Blaisdell) in 1980 Entry Draft for Dan Maloney and Detroit's 2nd round choice (Craig Muni) in 1980 Entry Draft, March 13, 1978. Traded to **Pittsburgh** by **Detroit** for Gary McAdam, January 8, 1981.

THOMPSON, Ken

Left wing/Center. Shoots left. 5'10", 160 lbs. Born, Oakengates, England, May 29, 1881.

Season	Club	GP	G	A	Pts	PIM	GP	G	A	Pts	PIM
1917-18	Montreal Wanderers	1	0	0	0	0	....	....	....	....	....
	NHL Totals	**1**	**0**	**0**	**0**	**0**	....	....	....	....	....

Rights retained by **Mtl. Wanderers** after NHA folded, November 26, 1917.

THOMPSON, Paul

Left wing. Shoots left. 5'11", 180 lbs. Born, Calgary, Alta., November 2, 1906.

Season	Club	GP	G	A	Pts	PIM	GP	G	A	Pts	PIM
1926-27	New York Rangers	43	7	3	10	12	2	0	0	0	0
1927-28 ♦	New York Rangers	42	4	4	8	22	8	0	0	0	30
1928-29	New York Rangers	44	10	7	17	38	6	0	*2	2	6
1929-30	New York Rangers	44	7	12	19	36	4	0	0	0	2
1930-31	New York Rangers	44	7	7	14	36	4	3	0	3	2
1931-32	Chicago Black Hawks	48	8	14	22	34	2	0	0	0	2
1932-33	Chicago Black Hawks	48	13	20	33	27	....	....	....	....	....
1933-34 ♦	Chicago Black Hawks	48	20	16	36	17	8	4	3	7	6
1934-35	Chicago Black Hawks	48	16	23	39	20	2	0	0	0	0
1935-36	Chicago Black Hawks	45	17	23	40	19	2	0	3	3	0
1936-37	Chicago Black Hawks	47	17	18	35	28	....	....	....	....	....
1937-38 ♦	Chicago Black Hawks	48	22	22	44	14	10	4	3	7	6
1938-39	Chicago Black Hawks	33	5	10	15	33	....	....	....	....	....
	NHL Totals	**582**	**153**	**179**	**332**	**336**	**48**	**11**	**11**	**22**	**54**

• Brother of Tiny • NHL Second All-Star Team (1936)

Signed as a free agent by **NY Rangers**, October 12, 1926. Traded to **Chicago** by **NY Rangers** for Art Somers and Vic Desjardins, September 27, 1931.

THOMPSON, Rocky

Right wing. Shoots right. 6'2", 205 lbs. Born, Calgary, Alta., August 8, 1977.
(Calgary's 3rd choice, 72nd overall, in 1995 Entry Draft).

Season	Club	GP	G	A	Pts	PIM	GP	G	A	Pts	PIM
1997-98	Calgary Flames	12	0	0	0	61	....	....	....	....	....
1998-99	Calgary Flames	3	0	0	0	25	....	....	....	....	....
2000-01	Florida Panthers	4	0	0	0	19	....	....	....	....	....
2001-02	Florida Panthers	6	0	0	0	12	....	....	....	....	....
	NHL Totals	**25**	**0**	**0**	**0**	**117**	....	....	....	....	....

Traded to **Florida** by **Calgary** for Filip Kuba, March 16, 2000. Signed as a free agent by **Edmonton**, July 20, 2003.

THOMS, Bill

Center. Shoots left. 5'9", 170 lbs. Born, Newmarket, Ont., March 5, 1910.

Season	Club	GP	G	A	Pts	PIM	GP	G	A	Pts	PIM
1932-33	Toronto Maple Leafs	29	3	9	12	15	9	1	1	2	4
1933-34	Toronto Maple Leafs	47	8	18	26	24	5	0	2	2	0
1934-35	Toronto Maple Leafs	47	9	13	22	15	7	2	0	2	0
1935-36	Toronto Maple Leafs	48	*23	15	38	29	9	3	*5	8	0
1936-37	Toronto Maple Leafs	48	10	9	19	14	2	0	0	0	0
1937-38	Toronto Maple Leafs	48	14	24	38	14	7	0	1	1	0
1938-39	Toronto Maple Leafs	12	1	4	5	4	....	....	....	....	....
	Chicago Black Hawks	36	6	11	17	16	....	....	....	....	....
1939-40	Chicago Black Hawks	47	9	13	22	2	1	0	0	0	0
1940-41	Chicago Black Hawks	47	13	19	32	4	....	....	....	....	....
1941-42	Chicago Black Hawks	47	15	30	45	4	3	0	1	1	0
1942-43	Chicago Black Hawks	47	15	28	43	3	....	....	....	....	....
1943-44	Chicago Black Hawks	7	3	5	8	2	....	....	....	....	....
1944-45	Chicago Black Hawks	21	2	6	8	8	....	....	....	....	....
	Boston Bruins	17	4	2	6	0	1	0	0	0	2
	NHL Totals	**548**	**135**	**206**	**341**	**154**	**44**	**6**	**10**	**16**	**6**

NHL Second All-Star Team (1936)
Played in NHL All-Star Game (1934)

Traded to **Toronto** by **Syracuse** (IHL) for Harold Darraugh, January 3, 1933. Traded to **Chicago** by **Toronto** for Doc Romnes, December 8, 1938. Traded to **Boston** by **Chicago** for cash, January 14, 1945.

THOMSON, Bill

Center/Right wing. Shoots right. 5'9", 162 lbs. Born, Troon, Scotland, March 23, 1914.

Season	Club	GP	G	A	Pts	PIM	GP	G	A	Pts	PIM
1938-39	Detroit Red Wings	4	0	0	0	0	....	....	....	....	....
1943-44	Detroit Red Wings	5	2	2	4	0	2	0	0	0	0
	NHL Totals	**9**	**2**	**2**	**4**	**0**	**2**	**0**	**0**	**0**	**0**

Signed as a free agent by **Toronto**, October 13, 1937. Traded to **Detroit** by **Toronto** with $10,000 for Bucko McDonald, December 19, 1938.

THOMSON, Floyd

Left wing. Shoots left. 6', 190 lbs. Born, Sudbury, Ont., June 14, 1949.

Season	Club	GP	G	A	Pts	PIM	GP	G	A	Pts	PIM
1971-72	St. Louis Blues	49	4	6	10	48	....	....	....	....	....
1972-73	St. Louis Blues	75	14	20	34	71	5	0	1	1	2
1973-74	St. Louis Blues	77	11	22	33	58	....	....	....	....	....
1974-75	St. Louis Blues	77	9	27	36	106	2	0	1	1	0
1975-76	St. Louis Blues	58	8	10	18	25	....	....	....	....	....
1976-77	St. Louis Blues	58	7	8	15	11	3	0	0	0	4
1977-78	St. Louis Blues	6	1	1	2	4	....	....	....	....	....
1979-80	St. Louis Blues	11	2	3	5	18	....	....	....	....	....
	NHL Totals	**411**	**56**	**97**	**153**	**341**	**10**	**0**	**2**	**2**	**6**

Signed as a free agent by **St. Louis**, October 1, 1970.

THOMSON, Jim

Right wing. Shoots right. 6'1", 220 lbs. Born, Edmonton, Alta., December 30, 1965.
(Washington's 8th choice, 185th overall, in 1984 Entry Draft).

Season	Club	GP	G	A	Pts	PIM	GP	G	A	Pts	PIM
1986-87	Washington Capitals	10	0	0	0	35	....	....	....	....	....
1988-89	Washington Capitals	14	2	0	2	53	....	....	....	....	....
	Hartford Whalers	5	0	0	0	14	....	....	....	....	....
1989-90	New Jersey Devils	3	0	0	0	31	....	....	....	....	....
1990-91	Los Angeles Kings	8	1	0	1	19	....	....	....	....	....
1991-92	Los Angeles Kings	45	1	2	3	162	....	....	....	....	....
1992-93	Ottawa Senators	15	0	1	1	41	....	....	....	....	....
	Los Angeles Kings	9	0	0	0	56	1	0	0	0	0
1993-94	Mighty Ducks of Anaheim	6	0	0	0	5	....	....	....	....	....
	NHL Totals	**115**	**4**	**3**	**7**	**416**	**1**	**0**	**0**	**0**	**0**

Traded to **Hartford** by **Washington** for Scot Kleinendorst, March 6, 1989. Traded to **New Jersey** by **Hartford** for Chris Cichocki, October 31, 1989. Signed as a free agent by **Los Angeles**, July 2, 1990. Claimed by **Minnesota** from **Los Angeles** in Expansion Draft, May 30, 1991. Traded to **Los Angeles** by **Minnesota** with Randy Gilhen, Charlie Huddy and NY Rangers' 4th round choice (previously acquired, Los Angeles selected Alexei Zhitnik) in 1991 Entry Draft for Todd Elik, June 22, 1991. Claimed by **Ottawa** from **Los Angeles** in Expansion Draft, June 18, 1992. Traded to **Los Angeles** by **Ottawa** with Marc Fortier for Bob Kudelski and Shawn McCosh, December 19, 1992. Claimed by **Anaheim** from **Los Angeles** in Expansion Draft, June 24, 1993.

THOMSON, Jimmy

Defense. Shoots right. 5'11", 175 lbs. Born, Winnipeg, Man., February 23, 1927.

Season	Club	GP	G	A	Pts	PIM	GP	G	A	Pts	PIM
1945-46	Toronto Maple Leafs	5	0	1	1	4	....	....	....	....	....
1946-47 ♦	Toronto Maple Leafs	60	2	14	16	97	11	0	1	1	22
1947-48 ♦	Toronto Maple Leafs	59	0	29	29	82	9	1	1	2	9
1948-49 ♦	Toronto Maple Leafs	60	4	16	20	56	9	1	5	6	10
1949-50	Toronto Maple Leafs	70	0	13	13	76	7	0	2	2	7
1950-51 ♦	Toronto Maple Leafs	69	3	33	36	76	11	0	1	1	*34
1951-52	Toronto Maple Leafs	70	0	25	25	86	4	0	0	0	25
1952-53	Toronto Maple Leafs	69	0	22	22	73	....	....	....	....	....
1953-54	Toronto Maple Leafs	61	2	24	26	86	3	0	0	0	2
1954-55	Toronto Maple Leafs	70	4	12	16	63	4	0	0	0	16
1955-56	Toronto Maple Leafs	62	0	7	7	96	5	0	3	3	10
1956-57	Toronto Maple Leafs	62	0	12	12	50	....	....	....	....	....
1957-58	Chicago Black Hawks	70	4	7	11	75	....	....	....	....	....
	NHL Totals	**787**	**19**	**215**	**234**	**920**	**63**	**2**	**13**	**15**	**135**

NHL Second All-Star Team (1951, 1952)
Played in NHL All-Star Game (1947, 1948, 1949, 1950, 1951, 1952, 1953)

Signed as a free agent by **Toronto**, October 16, 1945. Traded to **Chicago** by **Toronto** for cash, August, 1957. Traded to **Toronto** by **Chicago** for cash, July, 1958.

THOMSON, Rhys

Defense. Shoots left. 6'1", 195 lbs. Born, Toronto, Ont., August 9, 1918.

Season	Club	GP	G	A	Pts	PIM	GP	G	A	Pts	PIM
1939-40	Montreal Canadiens	7	0	0	0	16	....	....	....	....	....
1942-43	Toronto Maple Leafs	18	0	2	2	22	....	....	....	....	....
	NHL Totals	**25**	**0**	**2**	**2**	**38**	....	....	....	....	....

Signed as a free agent by **Montreal** (New Haven-IAHL), January 18, 1939. Traded to **NY Americans** (Springfield-AHL) by **Montreal** for cash, October, 1940. • Team name changed to **Brooklyn Americans** prior to 1941-42 season. Rights transferred to **Toronto** from **Brooklyn** in Special Dispersal Draw, September 11, 1942.

THORNBURY, Tom

Defense. Shoots right. 5'11", 175 lbs. Born, Lindsay, Ont., March 17, 1963.
(Pittsburgh's 2nd choice, 49th overall, in 1981 Entry Draft).

Season	Club	GP	G	A	Pts	PIM	GP	G	A	Pts	PIM
1983-84	Pittsburgh Penguins	14	1	8	9	16	....	....	....	....	....
	NHL Totals	**14**	**1**	**8**	**9**	**16**	....	....	....	....	....

Traded to **Quebec** by **Pittsburgh** for Brian Ford, December 6, 1984. Traded to **Calgary** by **Quebec** for Tony Stiles, January 16, 1986.

THORNTON, Joe

Center. Shoots left. 6'4", 220 lbs. Born, London, Ont., July 2, 1979.
(Boston's 1st choice, 1st overall, in 1997 Entry Draft).

Season	Club	GP	G	A	Pts	PIM	GP	G	A	Pts	PIM
1997-98	Boston Bruins	55	3	4	7	19	6	0	0	0	9
1998-99	Boston Bruins	81	16	25	41	69	11	3	6	9	4
99-2000	Boston Bruins	81	23	37	60	82	....	....	....	....	....
2000-01	Boston Bruins	72	37	34	71	107	....	....	....	....	....
2001-02	Boston Bruins	66	22	46	68	127	6	2	4	6	10

Season	Club	GP	G	A	Pts	PIM	GP	G	A	Pts	PIM
		REGULAR SEASON					PLAYOFFS				
2002-03	Boston Bruins	77	36	65	101	109	5	1	2	3	4
	NHL Totals	**432**	**137**	**211**	**348**	**513**	**28**	**6**	**12**	**18**	**27**

Played in NHL All-Star Game (2002, 2003)

THORNTON, Scott

Left wing. Shoots left. 6'3", 220 lbs. Born, London, Ont., January 9, 1971.
(Toronto's 1st choice, 3rd overall, in 1989 Entry Draft).

Season	Club	GP	G	A	Pts	PIM	GP	G	A	Pts	PIM
1990-91	Toronto Maple Leafs	33	1	3	4	30	....	....	....	....	....
1991-92	Edmonton Oilers	15	0	1	1	43	1	0	0	0	0
1992-93	Edmonton Oilers	9	0	1	1	0	....	....	....	....	....
1993-94	Edmonton Oilers	61	4	7	11	104	....	....	....	....	....
1994-95	Edmonton Oilers	47	10	12	22	89	....	....	....	....	....
1995-96	Edmonton Oilers	77	9	9	18	149	....	....	....	....	....
1996-97	Montreal Canadiens	73	10	10	20	128	5	1	0	1	2
1997-98	Montreal Canadiens	67	6	9	15	158	9	0	2	2	10
1998-99	Montreal Canadiens	47	7	4	11	87	....	....	....	....	....
99-2000	Montreal Canadiens	35	2	3	5	70	....	....	....	....	....
	Dallas Stars	30	6	3	9	38	23	2	7	9	28
2000-01	San Jose Sharks	73	19	17	36	114	6	3	0	3	8
2001-02	San Jose Sharks	77	26	16	42	116	12	3	3	6	6
2002-03	San Jose Sharks	41	9	12	21	41	....	....	....	....	....
	NHL Totals	**685**	**109**	**107**	**216**	**1167**	**56**	**9**	**12**	**21**	**54**

Traded to **Edmonton** by **Toronto** with Vincent Damphousse, Peter Ing and Luke Richardson for Grant Fuhr, Glenn Anderson and Craig Berube, September 19, 1991. Traded to **Montreal** by **Edmonton** for Andrei Kovalenko, September 6, 1996. Traded to **Dallas** by **Montreal** for Juha Lind, January 22, 2000. Signed as a free agent by **San Jose**, July 1, 2000.

THORNTON, Shawn

Right wing. Shoots right. 6'1", 210 lbs. Born, Oshawa, Ont., July 23, 1977.
(Toronto's 6th choice, 190th overall, in 1997 Entry Draft).

Season	Club	GP	G	A	Pts	PIM	GP	G	A	Pts	PIM
2002-03	Chicago Blackhawks	13	1	1	2	31	....	....	....	....	....
	NHL Totals	**13**	**1**	**1**	**2**	**31**	....	....	....	....	....

Traded to **Chicago** by **Toronto** for Marty Wilford, September 30, 2001.

THORSTEINSON, Joe

Right wing. Shoots right. 5'9", 157 lbs. Born, Winnipeg, Man., March 19, 1905.

Season	Club	GP	G	A	Pts	PIM	GP	G	A	Pts	PIM
1932-33	New York Americans	4	0	0	0	0	....	....	....	....	....
	NHL Totals	**4**	**0**	**0**	**0**	**0**	....	....	....	....	....

THURIER, Fred

Center. Shoots right. 5'11", 160 lbs. Born, Granby, Que., January 11, 1916.

Season	Club	GP	G	A	Pts	PIM	GP	G	A	Pts	PIM
1940-41	New York Americans	3	2	1	3	0	....	....	....	....	....
1941-42	Brooklyn Americans	27	7	7	14	4	....	....	....	....	....
1944-45	New York Rangers	50	16	19	35	14	....	....	....	....	....
	NHL Totals	**80**	**25**	**27**	**52**	**18**	....	....	....	....	....

Traded to **NY Americans** by **Springfield** (AHL) for cash, October 10, 1940. • Team name changed to **Brooklyn Americans** prior to 1941-42 season. Claimed by **NY Rangers** from **Brooklyn** in Special Dispersal Draw, September 11, 1943.

THURLBY, Tom

Defense. Shoots left. 5'10", 175 lbs. Born, Kingston, Ont., November 9, 1938.

Season	Club	GP	G	A	Pts	PIM	GP	G	A	Pts	PIM
1967-68	Oakland Seals	20	1	1	2	4	....	....	....	....	....
	NHL Totals	**20**	**1**	**1**	**2**	**4**	....	....	....	....	....

Claimed by **Boston** from **Montreal** in Intra-League Draft, June 8, 1960. NHL rights transferred to **California** after owners of **San Francisco** (WHL) franchise awarded NHL expansion team, April 5, 1966. Loaned to **Vancouver** (WHL) by **Oakland** for cash, October, 1967. Traded to **Montreal** by **Oakland** to complete transaction that sent Bryan Watson to Oakland (June 28, 1968), September, 1968.

THYER, Mario

Center. Shoots left. 5'11", 170 lbs. Born, Montreal, Que., September 29, 1966.

Season	Club	GP	G	A	Pts	PIM	GP	G	A	Pts	PIM
1989-90	Minnesota North Stars	5	0	0	0	0	1	0	0	0	2
	NHL Totals	**5**	**0**	**0**	**0**	**0**	**1**	**0**	**0**	**0**	**2**

Signed as a free agent by **Minnesota**, July 12, 1989. Traded to **NY Rangers** by **Minnesota** with Minnesota's 3rd round choice (Maxim Galanov) in 1993 Entry Draft for Mark Janssens, March 10, 1992. Traded to **Minnesota** by **NY Rangers** for cash, July 16, 1992.

TIBBETTS, Billy

Right wing. Shoots right. 6'2", 215 lbs. Born, Boston, MA, October 14, 1974.

Season	Club	GP	G	A	Pts	PIM	GP	G	A	Pts	PIM
2000-01	Pittsburgh Penguins	29	1	2	3	79	....	....	....	....	....
2001-02	Pittsburgh Penguins	33	1	5	6	109	....	....	....	....	....
	Philadelphia Flyers	9	0	1	1	69	....	....	....	....	....
2002-03	New York Rangers	11	0	0	0	12	....	....	....	....	....
	NHL Totals	**82**	**2**	**8**	**10**	**269**	....	....	....	....	....

Signed as a free agent by **Pittsburgh**, April 10, 2000. Traded to **Philadelphia** by **Pittsburgh** for Kent Manderville, March 17, 2002. Signed as a free agent by **NY Rangers**, December 16, 2002.

TICHY, Milan

Defense. Shoots left. 6'3", 198 lbs. Born, Plzen, Czech., September 22, 1969.
(Chicago's 6th choice, 153rd overall, in 1989 Entry Draft).

Season	Club	GP	G	A	Pts	PIM	GP	G	A	Pts	PIM
1992-93	Chicago Blackhawks	13	0	1	1	30	....	....	....	....	....
1994-95	New York Islanders	2	0	0	0	2	....	....	....	....	....
1995-96	New York Islanders	8	0	4	4	8	....	....	....	....	....
	NHL Totals	**23**	**0**	**5**	**5**	**40**	....	....	....	....	....

Claimed by **Florida** from **Chicago** in Expansion Draft, June 24, 1993. Traded to **Winnipeg** by **Florida** for Brent Severyn, October 3, 1993. Signed as a free agent by **NY Islanders**, August 2, 1994.

TIDEY, Alex

Right wing. Shoots right. 6', 182 lbs. Born, Vancouver, B.C., January 5, 1955.
(Buffalo's 9th choice, 143rd overall, in 1975 Amateur Draft).

Season	Club	GP	G	A	Pts	PIM	GP	G	A	Pts	PIM
1976-77	Buffalo Sabres	3	0	0	0	0	2	0	0	0	0
1977-78	Buffalo Sabres	1	0	0	0	0	....	....	....	....	....
1979-80	Edmonton Oilers	5	0	0	0	8	....	....	....	....	....
	NHL Totals	**9**	**0**	**0**	**0**	**8**	**2**	**0**	**0**	**0**	**0**

Traded to **Edmonton** by **Buffalo** for John Gould, November 13, 1979. Signed as a free agent by **Los Angeles**, August, 1980.

TIKKANEN, Esa

Left wing. Shoots left. 6'1", 190 lbs. Born, Helsinki, Finland, January 25, 1965.
(Edmonton's 4th choice, 82nd overall, in 1983 Entry Draft).

Season	Club	GP	G	A	Pts	PIM	GP	G	A	Pts	PIM
1984-85 ♦	Edmonton Oilers	....	....	....	....	....	3	0	0	0	2
1985-86	Edmonton Oilers	35	7	6	13	28	8	3	2	5	7
1986-87 ♦	Edmonton Oilers	76	34	44	78	120	21	7	2	9	22
1987-88 ♦	Edmonton Oilers	80	23	51	74	153	19	10	17	27	72
1988-89	Edmonton Oilers	67	31	47	78	92	7	1	3	4	12
1989-90 ♦	Edmonton Oilers	79	30	33	63	161	22	13	11	24	26
1990-91	Edmonton Oilers	79	27	42	69	85	18	12	8	20	24
1991-92	Edmonton Oilers	40	12	16	28	44	16	5	3	8	8
1992-93	Edmonton Oilers	66	14	19	33	76	....	....	....	....	....
	New York Rangers	15	2	5	7	18	....	....	....	....	....
1993-94 ♦	New York Rangers	83	22	32	54	114	23	4	4	8	34
1994-95	St. Louis Blues	43	12	23	35	22	7	2	2	4	20
1995-96	St. Louis Blues	11	1	4	5	18	....	....	....	....	....
	New Jersey Devils	9	0	2	2	4	....	....	....	....	....
	Vancouver Canucks	38	13	24	37	14	6	3	2	5	2
1996-97	Vancouver Canucks	62	12	15	27	66	....	....	....	....	....
	New York Rangers	14	1	2	3	6	15	9	3	12	26
1997-98	Florida Panthers	28	1	8	9	16	....	....	....	....	....
	Washington Capitals	20	2	10	12	2	21	3	3	6	20
1998-99	New York Rangers	32	0	3	3	38	....	....	....	....	....
	NHL Totals	**877**	**244**	**386**	**630**	**1077**	**186**	**72**	**60**	**132**	**275**

Traded to **NY Rangers** by **Edmonton** for Doug Weight, March 17, 1993. Traded to **St. Louis** by **NY Rangers** with Doug Lidster for Petr Nedved, July 24, 1994. Traded to **New Jersey** by **St. Louis** for New Jersey's 3rd round choice (later traded to Colorado – Colorado selected Ville Nieminen) in 1997 Entry Draft, November 1, 1995. Traded to **Vancouver** by **New Jersey** for Vancouver's 2nd round choice (Wes Mason) in 1996 Entry Draft, November 23, 1995. Traded to **NY Rangers** by **Vancouver** with Russ Courtnall for Sergei Nemchinov and Brian Noonan, March 8, 1997. Signed as a free agent by **Florida**, September 17, 1997. Traded to **Washington** by **Florida** for Dwayne Hay and future considerations, March 9, 1998. Signed as a free agent by **NY Rangers**, October 9, 1998.

TILEY, Brad

Defense. Shoots left. 6'1", 199 lbs. Born, Markdale, Ont., July 5, 1971.
(Boston's 4th choice, 84th overall, in 1991 Entry Draft).

Season	Club	GP	G	A	Pts	PIM	GP	G	A	Pts	PIM
1997-98	Phoenix Coyotes	1	0	0	0	0	....	....	....	....	....
1998-99	Phoenix Coyotes	8	0	0	0	0	1	0	0	0	0
2000-01	Philadelphia Flyers	2	0	0	0	0	....	....	....	....	....
	NHL Totals	**11**	**0**	**0**	**0**	**0**	**1**	**0**	**0**	**0**	**0**

Signed as a free agent by **NY Rangers**, September 4, 1992. Traded to **Los Angeles** by **NY Rangers** for Los Angeles' 11th round choice (Jamie Butt) in 1994 Entry Draft, January 28, 1994. Signed as a free agent by **Phoenix**, September 4, 1997. Signed as a free agent by **Philadelphia**, July 14, 2000.

TILLEY, Tom

Defense. Shoots right. 6', 190 lbs. Born, Trenton, Ont., March 28, 1965.
(St. Louis' 13th choice, 196th overall, in 1984 Entry Draft).

Season	Club	GP	G	A	Pts	PIM	GP	G	A	Pts	PIM
1988-89	St. Louis Blues	70	1	22	23	47	10	1	2	3	17
1989-90	St. Louis Blues	34	0	5	5	6	....	....	....	....	....
1990-91	St. Louis Blues	22	2	4	6	4	....	....	....	....	....
1993-94	St. Louis Blues	48	1	7	8	32	4	0	1	1	2
	NHL Totals	**174**	**4**	**38**	**42**	**89**	**14**	**1**	**3**	**4**	**19**

Traded to **Tampa Bay** by **St. Louis** for Adam Creighton, October 6, 1994. Traded to **Chicago** by **Tampa Bay** with Jim Cummins and Jeff Buchanan for Paul Ysebaert and Rich Sutter, February 22, 1995.

TIMANDER, Mattias

Defense. Shoots left. 6'2", 230 lbs. Born, Solleftea, Sweden, April 16, 1974.
(Boston's 7th choice, 208th overall, in 1992 Entry Draft).

Season	Club	GP	G	A	Pts	PIM	GP	G	A	Pts	PIM
1996-97	Boston Bruins	41	1	8	9	14	....	....	....	....	....
1997-98	Boston Bruins	23	1	1	2	6	....	....	....	....	....
1998-99	Boston Bruins	22	0	6	6	10	4	1	1	2	2
99-2000	Boston Bruins	60	0	8	8	22	....	....	....	....	....
2000-01	Columbus Blue Jackets	76	2	9	11	24	....	....	....	....	....
2001-02	Columbus Blue Jackets	78	4	7	11	44	....	....	....	....	....

		REGULAR SEASON					PLAYOFFS				
Season	Club	GP	G	A	Pts	PIM	GP	G	A	Pts	PIM
2002-03	New York Islanders	80	3	13	16	24	1	0	0	0	0
	NHL Totals	**380**	**11**	**52**	**63**	**144**	**5**	**1**	**1**	**2**	**2**

Selected by **Columbus** from **Boston** in Expansion Draft, June 23, 2000. Traded to **NY Islanders** by **Columbus** for NY Islanders' 4th round choice (Jekabs Redlihs) in 2002 Entry Draft, June 22, 2002.

TIMGREN, Ray

Left wing. Shoots left. 5'9", 150 lbs. Born, Windsor, Ont., September 29, 1928.

Season	Club	GP	G	A	Pts	PIM	GP	G	A	Pts	PIM
1948-49♦	Toronto Maple Leafs	36	3	12	15	9	9	3	3	6	2
1949-50	Toronto Maple Leafs	68	7	18	25	22	6	0	4	4	2
1950-51♦	Toronto Maple Leafs	70	1	9	10	20	11	0	1	1	2
1951-52	Toronto Maple Leafs	50	2	4	6	11	4	0	1	1	0
1952-53	Toronto Maple Leafs	12	0	0	0	4	....	....	....	....	....
1954-55	Chicago Black Hawks	14	1	1	2	2	....	....	....	....	....
	Toronto Maple Leafs	1	0	0	0	2	....	....	....	....	....
	NHL Totals	**251**	**14**	**44**	**58**	**70**	**30**	**3**	**9**	**12**	**6**

Played in NHL All-Star Game (1949)

Traded to **Chicago** by **Toronto** for Jack Price, October 4, 1954. Loaned to **Toronto** (Pittsburgh-AHL) by **Chicago**, November 16, 1954.

TIMONEN, Kimmo

Defense. Shoots left. 5'10", 196 lbs. Born, Kuopio, Finland, March 18, 1975.
(Los Angeles' 11th choice, 250th overall, in 1993 Entry Draft).

Season	Club	GP	G	A	Pts	PIM	GP	G	A	Pts	PIM
1998-99	Nashville Predators	50	4	8	12	30	....	....	....	....	....
99-2000	Nashville Predators	51	8	25	33	26	....	....	....	....	....
2000-01	Nashville Predators	82	12	13	25	50	....	....	....	....	....
2001-02	Nashville Predators	82	13	29	42	28	....	....	....	....	....
2002-03	Nashville Predators	72	6	34	40	46	....	....	....	....	....
	NHL Totals	**337**	**43**	**109**	**152**	**180**	....	....	....	....	....

Traded to **Nashville** by **Los Angeles** with Jan Vopat for future considerations, June 26, 1998.

TINORDI, Mark

Defense. Shoots left. 6'4", 213 lbs. Born, Red Deer, Alta., May 9, 1966.

Season	Club	GP	G	A	Pts	PIM	GP	G	A	Pts	PIM
1987-88	New York Rangers	24	1	2	3	50	....	....	....	....	....
1988-89	Minnesota North Stars	47	2	3	5	107	5	0	0	0	0
1989-90	Minnesota North Stars	66	3	7	10	240	7	0	1	1	16
1990-91	Minnesota North Stars	69	5	27	32	189	23	5	6	11	78
1991-92	Minnesota North Stars	63	4	24	28	179	7	1	2	3	11
1992-93	Minnesota North Stars	69	15	27	42	157					
1993-94	Dallas Stars	61	6	18	24	143	....	....	....	....	....
1994-95	Washington Capitals	42	3	9	12	71	1	0	0	0	2
1995-96	Washington Capitals	71	3	10	13	113	6	0	0	0	16
1996-97	Washington Capitals	56	2	6	8	118	....	....	....	....	....
1997-98	Washington Capitals	47	8	9	17	39	21	1	2	3	42
1998-99	Washington Capitals	48	0	6	6	108	....	....	....	....	....
	NHL Totals	**663**	**52**	**148**	**200**	**1514**	**70**	**7**	**11**	**18**	**165**

Played in NHL All-Star Game (1992)

Signed as a free agent by **NY Rangers**, January 4, 1987. Traded to **Minnesota** by **NY Rangers** with Paul Jerrard, the rights to Bret Barnett and Mike Sullivan and Los Angeles' 3rd round choice (previously acquired, Minnesota selected Murray Garbutt) in 1989 Entry Draft for Brian Lawton, Igor Liba and the rights to Eric Bennett, October 11, 1988. Transferred to **Dallas** after **Minnesota** franchise relocated, June 9, 1993. Traded to **Washington** by **Dallas** with Rich Mrozik for Kevin Hatcher, January 18, 1995. Claimed by **Atlanta** from **Washington** in Expansion Draft, June 25, 1999.

TIPPETT, Dave

Left wing. Shoots left. 5'10", 180 lbs. Born, Moosomin, Sask., August 25, 1961.

Season	Club	GP	G	A	Pts	PIM	GP	G	A	Pts	PIM
1983-84	Hartford Whalers	17	4	2	6	2	....	....	....	....	....
1984-85	Hartford Whalers	80	7	12	19	12	....	....	....	....	....
1985-86	Hartford Whalers	80	14	20	34	18	10	2	2	4	4
1986-87	Hartford Whalers	80	9	22	31	42	6	0	2	2	4
1987-88	Hartford Whalers	80	16	21	37	32	6	0	0	0	2
1988-89	Hartford Whalers	80	17	24	41	45	4	0	1	1	0
1989-90	Hartford Whalers	66	8	19	27	32	7	1	3	4	2
1990-91	Washington Capitals	61	6	9	15	24	10	2	3	5	8
1991-92	Washington Capitals	30	2	10	12	16	7	0	1	1	0
1992-93	Pittsburgh Penguins	74	6	19	25	56	12	1	4	5	14
1993-94	Philadelphia Flyers	73	4	11	15	38	....	....	....	....	....
	NHL Totals	**721**	**93**	**169**	**262**	**317**	**62**	**6**	**16**	**22**	**34**

Signed as a free agent by **Hartford**, February 29, 1984. Traded to **Washington** by **Hartford** for Washington's 6th round choice (Jarrett Reid) in 1992 Entry Draft, September 30, 1990. Signed as a free agent by **Pittsburgh**, August 25, 1992. Signed as a free agent by **Philadelphia**, August 30, 1993.

TITANIC, Morris

Left wing. Shoots left. 6'1", 180 lbs. Born, Toronto, Ont., January 7, 1953.
(Buffalo's 1st choice, 12th overall, in 1973 Amateur Draft).

Season	Club	GP	G	A	Pts	PIM	GP	G	A	Pts	PIM
1974-75	Buffalo Sabres	17	0	0	0	0	....	....	....	....	....
1975-76	Buffalo Sabres	2	0	0	0	0	....	....	....	....	....
	NHL Totals	**19**	**0**	**0**	**0**	**0**	....	....	....	....	....

TITOV, German

Left wing. Shoots left. 6'1", 203 lbs. Born, Moscow, USSR, October 16, 1965.
(Calgary's 10th choice, 252nd overall, in 1993 Entry Draft).

Season	Club	GP	G	A	Pts	PIM	GP	G	A	Pts	PIM
1993-94	Calgary Flames	76	27	18	45	28	7	2	1	3	4
1994-95	Calgary Flames	40	12	12	24	16	7	5	3	8	10
1995-96	Calgary Flames	82	28	39	67	24	4	0	2	2	0
1996-97	Calgary Flames	79	22	30	52	36	....	....	....	....	....
1997-98	Calgary Flames	68	18	22	40	38	....	....	....	....	....
1998-99	Pittsburgh Penguins	72	11	45	56	34	11	3	5	8	4
99-2000	Pittsburgh Penguins	63	17	25	42	34	....	....	....	....	....
	Edmonton Oilers	7	0	4	4	4	5	1	1	2	0
2000-01	Mighty Ducks of Anaheim	71	9	11	20	61	....	....	....	....	....
2001-02	Mighty Ducks of Anaheim	66	13	14	27	36	....	....	....	....	....
	NHL Totals	**624**	**157**	**220**	**377**	**311**	**34**	**11**	**12**	**23**	**18**

Traded to **Pittsburgh** by **Calgary** with Todd Hlushko for Ken Wregget and Dave Roche, June 17, 1998. Traded to **Edmonton** by **Pittsburgh** for Josef Beranek, March 14, 2000. Signed as a free agent by **Anaheim**, July 1, 2000.

TJARNQVIST, Daniel

Defense. Shoots left. 6'2", 190 lbs. Born, Umea, Sweden, October 14, 1976.
(Florida's 5th choice, 88th overall, in 1995 Entry Draft).

Season	Club	GP	G	A	Pts	PIM	GP	G	A	Pts	PIM
2001-02	Atlanta Thrashers	75	2	16	18	14	....	....	....	....	....
2002-03	Atlanta Thrashers	75	3	12	15	26	....	....	....	....	....
	NHL Totals	**150**	**5**	**28**	**33**	**40**	....	....	....	....	....

Traded to **Atlanta** by **Florida** with Gord Murphy, Herbert Vasiljevs and Ottawa's 6th round choice (previously acquired, later traded to Dallas – Dallas selected Justin Cox) in 1999 Entry Draft for Trevor Kidd, June 25, 1999.

TKACHUK, Keith

Left wing. Shoots left. 6'2", 225 lbs. Born, Melrose, MA, March 28, 1972.
(Winnipeg's 1st choice, 19th overall, in 1990 Entry Draft).

Season	Club	GP	G	A	Pts	PIM	GP	G	A	Pts	PIM
1991-92	Winnipeg Jets	17	3	5	8	28	7	3	0	3	30
1992-93	Winnipeg Jets	83	28	23	51	201	6	4	0	4	14
1993-94	Winnipeg Jets	84	41	40	81	255	....	....	....	....	....
1994-95	Winnipeg Jets	48	22	29	51	152	....	....	....	....	....
1995-96	Winnipeg Jets	76	50	48	98	156	6	1	2	3	22
1996-97	Phoenix Coyotes	81	*52	34	86	228	7	6	0	6	7
1997-98	Phoenix Coyotes	69	40	26	66	147	6	3	3	6	10
1998-99	Phoenix Coyotes	68	36	32	68	151	7	1	3	4	13
99-2000	Phoenix Coyotes	50	22	21	43	82	5	1	1	2	4
2000-01	Phoenix Coyotes	64	29	42	71	108	....	....	....	....	....
	St. Louis Blues	12	6	2	8	14	15	2	7	9	20
2001-02	St. Louis Blues	73	38	37	75	117	10	5	5	10	18
2002-03	St. Louis Blues	56	31	24	55	139	7	1	3	4	14
	NHL Totals	**781**	**398**	**363**	**761**	**1778**	**76**	**27**	**24**	**51**	**152**

NHL Second All-Star Team (1995, 1998)
Played in NHL All-Star Game (1997, 1998, 1999)

Transferred to **Phoenix** after **Winnipeg** franchise relocated, July 1, 1996. Traded to **St. Louis** by **Phoenix** for Michal Handzus, Ladislav Nagy, the rights to Jeff Taffe and St. Louis' 1st round choice (Ben Eager) in 2002 Entry Draft, March 13, 2001.

TKACZUK, Daniel

Center. Shoots left. 6'1", 197 lbs. Born, Toronto, Ont., June 10, 1979.
(Calgary's 1st choice, 6th overall, in 1997 Entry Draft).

Season	Club	GP	G	A	Pts	PIM	GP	G	A	Pts	PIM
2000-01	Calgary Flames	19	4	7	11	14	....	....	....	....	....
	NHL Totals	**19**	**4**	**7**	**11**	**14**	....	....	....	....	....

Traded to **St. Louis** by **Calgary** with Fred Brathwaite, Sergei Varlamov and Calgary's 9th round choice (Grant Jacobsen) in 2001 Entry Draft for Roman Turek and St. Louis' 4th round choice (Yegor Shastin) in 2001 Entry Draft, June 23, 2001.

TKACZUK, Walt

Center. Shoots left. 6', 185 lbs. Born, Emsdetten, West Germany, September 29, 1947.

Season	Club	GP	G	A	Pts	PIM	GP	G	A	Pts	PIM
1967-68	New York Rangers	2	0	0	0	0	....	....	....	....	....
1968-69	New York Rangers	71	12	24	36	28	4	0	1	1	6
1969-70	New York Rangers	76	27	50	77	38	6	2	1	3	17
1970-71	New York Rangers	77	26	49	75	48	13	1	5	6	14
1971-72	New York Rangers	76	24	42	66	65	16	4	6	10	35
1972-73	New York Rangers	76	27	39	66	59	10	7	2	9	8
1973-74	New York Rangers	71	21	42	63	58	13	0	5	5	22
1974-75	New York Rangers	62	11	25	36	34	3	1	2	3	5
1975-76	New York Rangers	78	8	28	36	56	....	....	....	....	....
1976-77	New York Rangers	80	12	38	50	38	....	....	....	....	....
1977-78	New York Rangers	80	26	40	66	30	3	0	2	2	0
1978-79	New York Rangers	77	15	27	42	38	18	4	7	11	10
1979-80	New York Rangers	76	12	25	37	36	7	0	1	1	2
1980-81	New York Rangers	43	6	22	28	28	....	....	....	....	....
	NHL Totals	**945**	**227**	**451**	**678**	**556**	**93**	**19**	**32**	**51**	**119**

Played in NHL All-Star Game (1970)

TOAL, Mike

Center. Shoots right. 6', 175 lbs. Born, Red Deer, Alta., March 23, 1959.
(Edmonton's 5th choice, 105th overall, in 1979 Entry Draft).

Season	Club	GP	G	A	Pts	PIM	GP	G	A	Pts	PIM
1979-80	Edmonton Oilers	3	0	0	0	0	....	....	....	....	....
	NHL Totals	**3**	**0**	**0**	**0**	**0**	....	....	....	....	....

TOBLER, Ryan

Left wing. Shoots left. 6'3", 227 lbs. Born, Calgary, Alta., May 13, 1976.

Season	Club	Regular Season GP	G	A	Pts	PIM	Playoffs GP	G	A	Pts	PIM
2001-02	Tampa Bay Lightning	4	0	0	0	5	....	....	....	....	....
	NHL Totals	**4**	**0**	**0**	**0**	**5**	....	....	....	....	....

Signed as a free agent by **Nashville**, May 1, 2000. Traded to **NY Rangers** by **Nashville** for Bert Robertsson, March 7, 2001. Signed as a free agent by **Tampa Bay**, August 21, 2001.

TOCCHET, Rick

Right wing. Shoots right. 6', 210 lbs. Born, Scarborough, Ont., April 9, 1964.
(Philadelphia's 5th choice, 125th overall, in 1983 Entry Draft).

Season	Club	Regular Season GP	G	A	Pts	PIM	Playoffs GP	G	A	Pts	PIM
1984-85	Philadelphia Flyers	75	14	25	39	181	19	3	4	7	72
1985-86	Philadelphia Flyers	69	14	21	35	284	5	1	2	3	26
1986-87	Philadelphia Flyers	69	21	28	49	288	26	11	10	21	72
1987-88	Philadelphia Flyers	65	31	33	64	299	5	1	4	5	55
1988-89	Philadelphia Flyers	66	45	36	81	183	16	6	6	12	69
1989-90	Philadelphia Flyers	75	37	59	96	196	....	....	....	....	....
1990-91	Philadelphia Flyers	70	40	31	71	150	....	....	....	....	....
1991-92	Philadelphia Flyers	42	13	16	29	102	....	....	....	....	....
	♦ Pittsburgh Penguins	19	14	16	30	49	14	6	13	19	24
1992-93	Pittsburgh Penguins	80	48	61	109	252	12	7	6	13	24
1993-94	Pittsburgh Penguins	51	14	26	40	134	6	2	3	5	20
1994-95	Los Angeles Kings	36	18	17	35	70	....	....	....	....	....
1995-96	Los Angeles Kings	44	13	23	36	117	....	....	....	....	....
	Boston Bruins	27	16	8	24	64	5	4	0	4	21
1996-97	Boston Bruins	40	16	14	30	67	....	....	....	....	....
	Washington Capitals	13	5	5	10	31	....	....	....	....	....
1997-98	Phoenix Coyotes	68	26	19	45	157	6	6	2	8	25
1998-99	Phoenix Coyotes	81	26	30	56	147	7	0	3	3	8
99-2000	Phoenix Coyotes	64	12	17	29	67	....	....	....	....	....
	Philadelphia Flyers	16	3	3	6	23	18	5	6	11	*49
2000-01	Philadelphia Flyers	60	14	22	36	83	6	0	1	1	6
2001-02	Philadelphia Flyers	14	0	2	2	28	....	....	....	....	....
	NHL Totals	**1144**	**440**	**512**	**952**	**2972**	**145**	**52**	**60**	**112**	**471**

Played in NHL All-Star Game (1989, 1990, 1991, 1993)

Traded to **Pittsburgh** by **Philadelphia** with Kjell Samuelsson, Ken Wregget and Philadelphia's 3rd round choice (Dave Roche) in 1993 Entry Draft for Mark Recchi, Brian Benning and Los Angeles' 1st round choice (previously acquired, Philadelphia selected Jason Bowen) in 1992 Entry Draft, February 19, 1992 Traded to **Los Angeles** by **Pittsburgh** with Pittsburgh's 2nd round choice (Pavel Rosa) in 1995 Entry Draft for Luc Robitaille, July 29, 1994. Traded to **Boston** by **Los Angeles** for Kevin Stevens, January 25, 1996. Traded to **Washington** by **Boston** with Bill Ranford and Adam Oates for Jim Carey, Anson Carter, Jason Allison and Washington's 3rd round choice (Lee Goren) in 1997 Entry Draft, March 1, 1997. Signed as a free agent by **Phoenix**, July 23, 1997. Traded to **Philadelphia** by **Phoenix** for Mikael Renberg, March 8, 2000. • Missed majority of 2001-02 season recovering from knee injury suffered in training camp, October 1, 2001.

TODD, Kevin

Center. Shoots left. 5'10", 180 lbs. Born, Winnipeg, Man., May 4, 1968.
(New Jersey's 7th choice, 129th overall, in 1986 Entry Draft).

Season	Club	Regular Season GP	G	A	Pts	PIM	Playoffs GP	G	A	Pts	PIM
1988-89	New Jersey Devils	1	0	0	0	0	....	....	....	....	....
1990-91	New Jersey Devils	1	0	0	0	0	1	0	0	0	6
1991-92	New Jersey Devils	80	21	42	63	69	7	3	2	5	8
1992-93	New Jersey Devils	30	5	5	10	16	....	....	....	....	....
	Edmonton Oilers	25	4	9	13	10	....	....	....	....	....
1993-94	Chicago Blackhawks	35	5	6	11	16	....	....	....	....	....
	Los Angeles Kings	12	3	8	11	8	....	....	....	....	....
1994-95	Los Angeles Kings	33	3	8	11	12	....	....	....	....	....
1995-96	Los Angeles Kings	74	16	27	43	38	....	....	....	....	....
1996-97	Mighty Ducks of Anaheim	65	9	21	30	44	4	0	0	0	2
1997-98	Mighty Ducks of Anaheim	27	4	7	11	12	....	....	....	....	....
	NHL Totals	**383**	**70**	**133**	**203**	**225**	**12**	**3**	**2**	**5**	**16**

Traded to **Edmonton** by **New Jersey** with Zdeno Ciger for Bernie Nicholls, January 13, 1993. Traded to **Chicago** by **Edmonton** for Adam Bennett, October 7, 1993. Traded to **Los Angeles** by **Chicago** for Los Angeles' 4th round choice (Steve McLaren) in 1994 Entry Draft, March 21, 1994. Signed as a free agent by **Pittsburgh**, July 10, 1996. Claimed on waivers by **Anaheim** from **Pittsburgh**, October 4, 1996.

TOMALTY, Glenn

Left wing. Shoots left. 6'1", 205 lbs. Born, Lachute, Que., July 23, 1954.

Season	Club	Regular Season GP	G	A	Pts	PIM	Playoffs GP	G	A	Pts	PIM
1979-80	Winnipeg Jets	1	0	0	0	0	....	....	....	....	....
	NHL Totals	**1**	**0**	**0**	**0**	**0**	....	....	....	....	....

Signed as a free agent by **Winnipeg**, October 1, 1979.

TOMLAK, Mike

Center/Left wing. Shoots left. 6'3", 205 lbs. Born, Thunder Bay, Ont., October 17, 1964.
(Toronto's 10th choice, 217th overall, in 1983 Entry Draft).

Season	Club	Regular Season GP	G	A	Pts	PIM	Playoffs GP	G	A	Pts	PIM
1989-90	Hartford Whalers	70	7	14	21	48	7	0	1	1	2
1990-91	Hartford Whalers	64	8	8	16	55	3	0	0	0	2
1991-92	Hartford Whalers	6	0	0	0	0	....	....	....	....	....
1993-94	Hartford Whalers	1	0	0	0	0	....	....	....	....	....
	NHL Totals	**141**	**15**	**22**	**37**	**103**	**10**	**0**	**1**	**1**	**4**

Signed as a free agent by **Hartford**, November 14, 1988.

TOMLINSON, Dave

Center. Shoots left. 5'11", 180 lbs. Born, North Vancouver, B.C., May 8, 1969.
(Toronto's 1st choice, 3rd overall, in 1989 Supplemental Draft).

Season	Club	Regular Season GP	G	A	Pts	PIM	Playoffs GP	G	A	Pts	PIM
1991-92	Toronto Maple Leafs	3	0	0	0	2	....	....	....	....	....
1992-93	Toronto Maple Leafs	3	0	0	0	2	....	....	....	....	....
1993-94	Winnipeg Jets	31	1	3	4	24	....	....	....	....	....
1994-95	Florida Panthers	5	0	0	0	0	....	....	....	....	....
	NHL Totals	**42**	**1**	**3**	**4**	**28**	....	....	....	....	....

Traded to **Florida** by **Toronto** for cash, July 30, 1993. Traded to **Winnipeg** by **Florida** for Jason Cirone, August 3, 1993. Signed as a free agent by **Florida**, June 23, 1994.

TOMLINSON, Kirk

Center. Shoots left. 5'10", 175 lbs. Born, Toronto, Ont., May 2, 1968.
(Minnesota's 7th choice, 75th overall, in 1986 Entry Draft).

Season	Club	Regular Season GP	G	A	Pts	PIM	Playoffs GP	G	A	Pts	PIM
1987-88	Minnesota North Stars	1	0	0	0	0	....	....	....	....	....
	NHL Totals	**1**	**0**	**0**	**0**	**0**	....	....	....	....	....

TOMS, Jeff

Center. Shoots left. 6'5", 200 lbs. Born, Swift Current, Sask., June 4, 1974.
(New Jersey's 10th choice, 210th overall, in 1992 Entry Draft).

Season	Club	Regular Season GP	G	A	Pts	PIM	Playoffs GP	G	A	Pts	PIM
1995-96	Tampa Bay Lightning	1	0	0	0	0	....	....	....	....	....
1996-97	Tampa Bay Lightning	34	2	8	10	10	....	....	....	....	....
1997-98	Tampa Bay Lightning	13	1	2	3	7	....	....	....	....	....
	Washington Capitals	33	3	4	7	8	1	0	0	0	0
1998-99	Washington Capitals	21	1	5	6	2	....	....	....	....	....
99-2000	Washington Capitals	20	1	2	3	4	....	....	....	....	....
2000-01	New York Islanders	39	2	4	6	10	....	....	....	....	....
	New York Rangers	15	1	1	2	0	....	....	....	....	....
2001-02	New York Rangers	38	7	4	11	10	....	....	....	....	....
	Pittsburgh Penguins	14	2	1	3	4	....	....	....	....	....
2002-03	Florida Panthers	8	2	2	4	4	....	....	....	....	....
	NHL Totals	**236**	**22**	**33**	**55**	**59**	**1**	**0**	**0**	**0**	**0**

Traded to **Tampa Bay** by **New Jersey** for Vancouver's 4th round choice (previously acquired, later traded to New Jersey – later traded to Calgary – Calgary selected Ryan Duthie) in 1994 Entry Draft, May 31, 1994. Claimed by on waivers by **Washington** from **Tampa Bay**, November 19, 1997. Signed as a free agent by **NY Islanders**, July 27, 2000. Claimed on waivers by **NY Rangers** from **NY Islanders**, January 13, 2001. Claimed on waivers by **Pittsburgh** from **NY Rangers**, March 16, 2002. Signed as a free agent by **Florida**, July 11, 2002.

TOMSON, Jack

Defense. Shoots right. 6'1", 175 lbs. Born, Uxbridge, England, January 31, 1918.

Season	Club	Regular Season GP	G	A	Pts	PIM	Playoffs GP	G	A	Pts	PIM
1938-39	New York Americans	....	....	....	....	....	2	0	0	0	0
1939-40	New York Americans	12	1	1	2	0	....	....	....	....	....
1940-41	New York Americans	3	0	0	0	0	....	....	....	....	....
	NHL Totals	**15**	**1**	**1**	**2**	**0**	**2**	**0**	**0**	**0**	**0**

Signed as a free agent by **NY Americans**, October 24, 1938. Loaned to **Seattle** (PCHL) by **NY Americans** for cash, November, 1938. Loaned to **Philadelphia** (IAHL) by **NY Americans** for cash, November 25, 1938.

TONELLI, John

Left wing. Shoots left. 6'1", 200 lbs. Born, Milton, Ont., March 23, 1957.
(NY Islanders' 2nd choice, 33rd overall, in 1977 Amateur Draft).

Season	Club	Regular Season GP	G	A	Pts	PIM	Playoffs GP	G	A	Pts	PIM
1978-79	New York Islanders	73	17	39	56	44	10	1	6	7	0
1979-80♦	New York Islanders	77	14	30	44	49	21	7	9	16	18
1980-81♦	New York Islanders	70	20	32	52	57	16	5	8	13	16
1981-82♦	New York Islanders	80	35	58	93	57	19	6	10	16	18
1982-83♦	New York Islanders	76	31	40	71	55	20	7	11	18	20
1983-84	New York Islanders	73	27	40	67	66	17	1	3	4	31
1984-85	New York Islanders	80	42	58	100	95	10	1	8	9	10
1985-86	New York Islanders	65	20	41	61	50	....	....	....	....	....
	Calgary Flames	9	3	4	7	10	22	7	9	16	49
1986-87	Calgary Flames	78	20	31	51	72	3	0	0	0	4
1987-88	Calgary Flames	74	17	41	58	84	6	2	5	7	8
1988-89	Los Angeles Kings	77	31	33	64	110	6	0	0	0	8
1989-90	Los Angeles Kings	73	31	37	68	62	10	1	2	3	6
1990-91	Los Angeles Kings	71	14	16	30	49	12	2	4	6	12
1991-92	Chicago Blackhawks	33	1	7	8	37	....	....	....	....	....
	Quebec Nordiques	19	2	4	6	14	....	....	....	....	....
	NHL Totals	**1028**	**325**	**511**	**836**	**911**	**172**	**40**	**75**	**115**	**200**

NHL Second All-Star Team (1982, 1985)

Played in NHL All-Star Game (1982, 1985)

NHL rights reclaimed by **NY Islanders** after **Houston** (WHA) franchise folded, July 6, 1978. Traded to **Calgary** by **NY Islanders** for Richard Kromm and Steve Konroyd, March 11, 1986. Signed as a free agent by **Los Angeles**, June 29, 1988. Signed as a free agent by **Chicago**, June 30, 1991. Traded to **Quebec** by **Chicago** for future considerations, February 18, 1992.

TOOKEY, Tim

Center. Shoots left. 5'11", 185 lbs. Born, Edmonton, Alta., August 29, 1960.
(Washington's 4th choice, 88th overall, in 1979 Entry Draft).

Season	Club	Regular Season GP	G	A	Pts	PIM	Playoffs GP	G	A	Pts	PIM
1980-81	Washington Capitals	29	10	13	23	18	....	....	....	....	....
1981-82	Washington Capitals	28	8	8	16	35	....	....	....	....	....
1982-83	Quebec Nordiques	12	1	6	7	4	....	....	....	....	....
1983-84	Pittsburgh Penguins	8	0	2	2	2	....	....	....	....	....
1986-87	Philadelphia Flyers	2	0	0	0	0	10	1	3	4	2
1987-88	Los Angeles Kings	20	1	6	7	8	....	....	....	....	....

Season	Club	Regular Season GP	G	A	Pts	PIM	Playoffs GP	G	A	Pts	PIM
1988-89	Los Angeles Kings	7	2	1	3	4	....	....	....	....	....
	NHL Totals	**106**	**22**	**36**	**58**	**71**	**10**	**1**	**3**	**4**	**2**

Traded to **Quebec** by **Washington** with Washington's 7th round choice (Daniel Poudrier) in 1982 Entry Draft for Lee Norwood and Quebec's 6th round choice (later traded to Calgary – Calgary selected Mats Kihlstrom) in 1982 Entry Draft, February 1, 1982. Signed as a free agent by **Pittsburgh**, September 12, 1983. Signed as a free agent by **Philadelphia**, July 11, 1985. Claimed by **Los Angeles** from **Philadelphia** in Waiver Draft, October 5, 1987. Traded to **Pittsburgh** by **Los Angeles** for Pat Mayer, March 7, 1989. Signed as a free agent by **Philadelphia**, June 30, 1989.

TOOMEY, Sean

Left wing. Shoots left. 6'1", 200 lbs. Born, St. Paul, MN, June 27, 1965.
(Minnesota's 8th choice, 141st overall, in 1983 Entry Draft).

Season	Club	GP	G	A	Pts	PIM	GP	G	A	Pts	PIM
1986-87	Minnesota North Stars	1	0	0	0	0	....	....	....	....	....
	NHL Totals	**1**	**0**	**0**	**0**	**0**	....	....	....	....	....

TOPOROWSKI, Shayne

Right wing. Shoots right. 6'2", 216 lbs. Born, Paddockwood, Sask., August 6, 1975.
(Los Angeles' 1st choice, 42nd overall, in 1993 Entry Draft).

Season	Club	GP	G	A	Pts	PIM	GP	G	A	Pts	PIM
1996-97	Toronto Maple Leafs	3	0	0	0	7	....	....	....	....	....
	NHL Totals	**3**	**0**	**0**	**0**	**7**	....	....	....	....	....

Traded to **Toronto** by **Los Angeles** with Dixon Ward, Guy Leveque and Kelly Fairchild for Eric Lacroix, Chris Snell and Toronto's 4th round choice (Eric Belanger) in 1996 Entry Draft, October 3, 1994. Signed as a free agent by **St. Louis**, September 9, 1997. Signed as a free agent by **Phoenix**, August 17, 1999.

TOPPAZZINI, Jerry

Right wing. Shoots right. 6', 180 lbs. Born, Copper Cliff, Ont., July 29, 1931.

Season	Club	GP	G	A	Pts	PIM	GP	G	A	Pts	PIM
1952-53	Boston Bruins	69	10	13	23	36	11	0	3	3	9
1953-54	Boston Bruins	37	0	5	5	24	....	....	....	....	....
	Chicago Black Hawks	14	5	3	8	18	....	....	....	....	....
1954-55	Chicago Black Hawks	70	9	18	27	59	....	....	....	....	....
1955-56	Detroit Red Wings	40	1	7	8	31	....	....	....	....	....
	Boston Bruins	28	7	7	14	22	....	....	....	....	....
1956-57	Boston Bruins	55	15	23	38	26	10	0	1	1	2
1957-58	Boston Bruins	64	25	24	49	51	12	9	3	12	2
1958-59	Boston Bruins	70	21	23	44	61	7	4	2	6	0
1959-60	Boston Bruins	69	12	33	45	26	....	....	....	....	....
1960-61	Boston Bruins	67	15	35	50	35	....	....	....	....	....
1961-62	Boston Bruins	70	19	31	50	26	....	....	....	....	....
1962-63	Boston Bruins	65	17	18	35	6	....	....	....	....	....
1963-64	Boston Bruins	65	7	4	11	15	....	....	....	....	....
	NHL Totals	**783**	**163**	**244**	**407**	**436**	**40**	**13**	**9**	**22**	**13**

• Brother of Zellio

Played in NHL All-Star Game (1955, 1958, 1959)

Traded to **Chicago** by **Boston** for Gus Bodnar, February 16, 1954. Traded to **Detroit** by **Chicago** with Dave Creighton, Gord Hollingworth and John McCormack for Tony Leswick, Glen Skov, Johnny Wilson and Benny Woit, May 27, 1955. Traded to **Boston** by **Detroit** with Real Chevrefils for Murray Costello and Lorne Ferguson, January 17, 1956. Traded to **Chicago** by **Boston** with Matt Ravlich for Murray Balfour and Mike Draper, June 9, 1964. Traded to **Detroit** (Pittsburgh-AHL) by **Chicago** (Buffalo-AHL) for Hank Ciesla, October 10, 1964. Claimed by **LA Blades** (WHL) from **Detroit** in Reverse Draft, June 9, 1965.

TOPPAZZINI, Zellio

Right wing. Shoots right. 5'11", 180 lbs. Born, Copper Cliff, Ont., January 5, 1930.

Season	Club	GP	G	A	Pts	PIM	GP	G	A	Pts	PIM
1948-49	Boston Bruins	5	1	1	2	0	2	0	0	0	0
1949-50	Boston Bruins	36	5	5	10	18	....	....	....	....	....
1950-51	Boston Bruins	4	0	1	1	0	....	....	....	....	....
	New York Rangers	55	14	14	28	27	....	....	....	....	....
1951-52	New York Rangers	16	1	1	2	4	....	....	....	....	....
1956-57	Chicago Black Hawks	7	0	0	0	0	....	....	....	....	....
	NHL Totals	**123**	**21**	**22**	**43**	**49**	**2**	**0**	**0**	**0**	**0**

• Brother of Jerry

Traded to **NY Rangers** by **Boston** with Ed Harrison for Dunc Fisher and future considerations (loan of Alex Kaleta to Hershey-AHL, November 20, 1950), November 16, 1950. Traded to **Providence** (AHL) by **NY Rangers** with Pat Egan and Jean-Paul Denis for Jack Stoddard, January 1, 1952. Claimed by **Chicago** from **Providence** (AHL) in Inter-League Draft, June 5, 1956.

TORGAEV, Pavel

Left wing. Shoots left. 6'1", 187 lbs. Born, Gorky, USSR, January 25, 1966.
(Calgary's 13th choice, 279th overall, in 1994 Entry Draft).

Season	Club	GP	G	A	Pts	PIM	GP	G	A	Pts	PIM
1995-96	Calgary Flames	41	6	10	16	14	1	0	0	0	0
99-2000	Calgary Flames	9	0	2	2	4	....	....	....	....	....
	Tampa Bay Lightning	5	0	2	2	2	....	....	....	....	....
	NHL Totals	**55**	**6**	**14**	**20**	**20**	**1**	**0**	**0**	**0**	**0**

Claimed on waivers by **Tampa Bay** from **Calgary**, November 26, 1999. • Suspended by **Tampa Bay** for refusing assignment to **Detroit** (IHL), December 21, 1999.

TORKKI, Jari

Left wing. Shoots left. 5'11", 185 lbs. Born, Rauma, Finland, August 11, 1965.
(Chicago's 6th choice, 119th overall, in 1983 Entry Draft).

Season	Club	GP	G	A	Pts	PIM	GP	G	A	Pts	PIM
1988-89	Chicago Blackhawks	4	1	0	1	0	....	....	....	....	....
	NHL Totals	**4**	**1**	**0**	**1**	**0**	....	....	....	....	....

TORMANEN, Antti

Right wing. Shoots left. 6'1", 198 lbs. Born, Espoo, Finland, September 19, 1970.
(Ottawa's 10th choice, 274th overall, in 1994 Entry Draft).

Season	Club	GP	G	A	Pts	PIM	GP	G	A	Pts	PIM
1995-96	Ottawa Senators	50	7	8	15	28	....	....	....	....	....
	NHL Totals	**50**	**7**	**8**	**15**	**28**	....	....	....	....	....

TORRES, Raffi

Left wing. Shoots left. 6', 218 lbs. Born, Toronto, Ont., October 8, 1981.
(NY Islanders' 2nd choice, 5th overall, in 2000 Entry Draft).

Season	Club	GP	G	A	Pts	PIM	GP	G	A	Pts	PIM
2001-02	New York Islanders	14	0	1	1	6	....	....	....	....	....
2002-03	New York Islanders	17	0	5	5	10	....	....	....	....	....
	NHL Totals	**31**	**0**	**6**	**6**	**16**	....	....	....	....	....

Traded to **Edmonton** by **NY Islanders** with Brad Isbister for Janne Niinimaa and Washington's 2nd round choice (previously acquired, NY Islanders selected Evgeni Tunik) in 2003 Entry Draft, March 11, 2003.

TOUHEY, Bill

Left wing. Shoots left. 5'9", 155 lbs. Born, Ottawa, Ont., March 23, 1906.

Season	Club	GP	G	A	Pts	PIM	GP	G	A	Pts	PIM
1927-28	Montreal Maroons	29	2	0	2	2	....	....	....	....	....
1928-29	Ottawa Senators	44	9	3	12	28	....	....	....	....	....
1929-30	Ottawa Senators	44	10	3	13	24	2	1	0	1	0
1930-31	Ottawa Senators	44	15	15	30	8	....	....	....	....	....
1931-32	Boston Bruins	26	5	4	9	12	....	....	....	....	....
1932-33	Ottawa Senators	47	12	7	19	12	....	....	....	....	....
1933-34	Ottawa Senators	46	12	8	20	21	....	....	....	....	....
	NHL Totals	**280**	**65**	**40**	**105**	**107**	**2**	**1**	**0**	**1**	**0**

Signed as a free agent by **Mtl. Maroons**, November 2, 1927. Traded to **Stratford** (Can-Pro) by **Mtl. Maroons** for Fred Brown with Montreal holding right of recall, February 14, 1928. Traded to **Ottawa** by **Mtl. Maroons** for cash, October 25, 1928. Claimed by **Boston** from **Ottawa** for 1931-32 season in Dispersal Draft, September 26, 1931. Transferred to **St. Louis** after **Ottawa** franchise relocated, May 14, 1934. Loaned to **Syracuse** (IHL) by **St. Louis**, December 28, 1934.

TOUPIN, Jacques

Right wing. Shoots right. 5'7", 155 lbs. Born, Trois-Rivieres, Que., November 10, 1910.

Season	Club	GP	G	A	Pts	PIM	GP	G	A	Pts	PIM
1943-44	Chicago Black Hawks	8	1	2	3	0	4	0	0	0	0
	NHL Totals	**8**	**1**	**2**	**3**	**0**	**4**	**0**	**0**	**0**	**0**

Traded to **Chicago** by **Providence** (AHL) for cash, February 28, 1944.

TOWNSEND, Art

Defense. Shoots left. 5'10", 185 lbs. Born, Souris, Man., October 9, 1905.

Season	Club	GP	G	A	Pts	PIM	GP	G	A	Pts	PIM
1926-27	Chicago Black Hawks	5	0	0	0	0	....	....	....	....	....
	NHL Totals	**5**	**0**	**0**	**0**	**0**	....	....	....	....	....

NHL rights transferred to **Chicago** after NHL club purchased **Portland** (WHL) franchise, May 16, 1926.

TOWNSHEND, Graeme

Right wing. Shoots right. 6'2", 225 lbs. Born, Kingston, Jamaica, October 2, 1965.

Season	Club	GP	G	A	Pts	PIM	GP	G	A	Pts	PIM
1989-90	Boston Bruins	4	0	0	0	7	....	....	....	....	....
1990-91	Boston Bruins	18	2	5	7	12	....	....	....	....	....
1991-92	New York Islanders	7	1	2	3	0	....	....	....	....	....
1992-93	New York Islanders	2	0	0	0	0	....	....	....	....	....
1993-94	Ottawa Senators	14	0	0	0	9	....	....	....	....	....
	NHL Totals	**45**	**3**	**7**	**10**	**28**	....	....	....	....	....

Signed as a free agent by **Boston**, May 12, 1989. Signed as a free agent by **NY Islanders**, September 3, 1991. Signed as a free agent by **Ottawa**, August 24, 1993.

TRADER, Larry

Defense. Shoots left. 6'1", 180 lbs. Born, Barry's Bay, Ont., July 7, 1963.
(Detroit's 3rd choice, 86th overall, in 1981 Entry Draft).

Season	Club	GP	G	A	Pts	PIM	GP	G	A	Pts	PIM
1982-83	Detroit Red Wings	15	0	2	2	6	....	....	....	....	....
1984-85	Detroit Red Wings	40	3	7	10	39	3	0	0	0	0
1986-87	St. Louis Blues	5	0	0	0	8	....	....	....	....	....
1987-88	St. Louis Blues	1	0	0	0	2	....	....	....	....	....
	Montreal Canadiens	30	2	4	6	19	....	....	....	....	....
	NHL Totals	**91**	**5**	**13**	**18**	**74**	**3**	**0**	**0**	**0**	**0**

Traded to **St. Louis** by **Detroit** for Lee Norwood, August 7, 1986. Traded to **Montreal** by **St. Louis** with St. Louis' 3rd round choice (Pierre Sevigny) in 1989 Entry Draft for Gaston Gingras and Montreal's 3rd round choice (later traded to Winnipeg – Winnipeg selected Kris Draper) in 1989 Entry Draft, October 13, 1987. Signed as a free agent by **Hartford**, August 3, 1988.

TRAINOR, Wes

Center/Left wing. Shoots right. 5'8", 180 lbs. Born, Charlottetown, P.E.I., September 11, 1922.

Season	Club	GP	G	A	Pts	PIM	GP	G	A	Pts	PIM
1948-49	New York Rangers	17	1	2	3	6	....	....	....	....	....
	NHL Totals	**17**	**1**	**2**	**3**	**6**	....	....	....	....	....

Signed as a free agent by **NY Rangers**, September, 1947.

TRAPP, Bob

Defense. Shoots left. 5'10", 170 lbs. Born, Pembroke, Ont., December 16, 1899.

Season	Club	GP	G	A	Pts	PIM	GP	G	A	Pts	PIM
1926-27	Chicago Black Hawks	44	4	2	6	92	2	0	0	0	4

Season	Club	GP	G	A	Pts	PIM	GP	G	A	Pts	PIM
		REGULAR SEASON					PLAYOFFS				
1927-28	Chicago Black Hawks	38	0	2	2	37	....	....	....	....	....
	NHL Totals	**82**	**4**	**4**	**8**	**129**	**2**	**0**	**0**	**0**	**4**

NHL rights transferred to **Chicago** after NHL club purchased **Portland** (WHL) franchise, May 16, 1926.

TRAPP, Doug

Left wing. Shoots left. 6', 180 lbs. Born, Balcarres, Sask., November 28, 1965.
(Buffalo's 2nd choice, 39th overall, in 1984 Entry Draft).

Season	Club	GP	G	A	Pts	PIM	GP	G	A	Pts	PIM
1986-87	Buffalo Sabres	2	0	0	0	0	....	....	....	....	....
	NHL Totals	**2**	**0**	**0**	**0**	**0**	....	....	....	....	....

TRAUB, Percy

Defense. Shoots left. 5'9", 175 lbs. Born, Elmwood, Ont., August 23, 1896.

Season	Club	GP	G	A	Pts	PIM	GP	G	A	Pts	PIM
1926-27	Chicago Black Hawks	42	0	2	2	93	2	0	0	0	6
1927-28	Detroit Cougars	44	3	1	4	78	....	....	....	....	....
1928-29	Detroit Cougars	44	0	0	0	46	2	0	0	0	0
	NHL Totals	**130**	**3**	**3**	**6**	**217**	**4**	**0**	**0**	**0**	**6**

NHL rights transferred to **Chicago** after NHL club purchased **Portland** (WHL) franchise, May 16, 1926. Traded to **Detroit** by **Chicago** with George Hay for $15,000, April 11, 1927.

TRAVERSE, Patrick

Defense. Shoots left. 6'4", 207 lbs. Born, Montreal, Que., March 14, 1974.
(Ottawa's 3rd choice, 50th overall, in 1992 Entry Draft).

Season	Club	GP	G	A	Pts	PIM	GP	G	A	Pts	PIM
1995-96	Ottawa Senators	5	0	0	0	2	....	....	....	....	....
1998-99	Ottawa Senators	46	1	9	10	22	....	....	....	....	....
99-2000	Ottawa Senators	66	6	17	23	21	6	0	0	0	2
2000-01	Mighty Ducks of Anaheim	15	1	0	1	6	....	....	....	....	....
	Boston Bruins	37	2	6	8	14	....	....	....	....	....
	Montreal Canadiens	19	2	3	5	10	....	....	....	....	....
2001-02	Montreal Canadiens	25	2	3	5	14	....	....	....	....	....
2002-03	Montreal Canadiens	65	0	13	13	24	....	....	....	....	....
	NHL Totals	**278**	**14**	**51**	**65**	**113**	**6**	**0**	**0**	**0**	**2**

Traded to **Anaheim** by **Ottawa** for Joel Kwiatkowski, June 12, 2000. Traded to **Boston** by **Anaheim** with Andrei Nazarov for Samuel Pahlsson, November 18, 2000. • Missed majority of 2001-02 season recovering from knee (November 3, 2001 vs. Calgary) and head (January 10, 2002 vs. NY Islanders) injuries. Traded to **Montreal** by **Boston** for Eric Weinrich, February 21, 2001.

TREBIL, Dan

Defense. Shoots right. 6'3", 210 lbs. Born, Bloomington, MN, April 10, 1974.
(New Jersey's 7th choice, 138th overall, in 1992 Entry Draft).

Season	Club	GP	G	A	Pts	PIM	GP	G	A	Pts	PIM
1996-97	Mighty Ducks of Anaheim	29	3	3	6	23	9	0	1	1	6
1997-98	Mighty Ducks of Anaheim	21	0	1	1	2	....	....	....	....	....
1998-99	Mighty Ducks of Anaheim	6	0	0	0	0	1	0	0	0	2
99-2000	Pittsburgh Penguins	3	1	0	1	0	....	....	....	....	....
2000-01	Pittsburgh Penguins	16	0	0	0	7	....	....	....	....	....
	St. Louis Blues	10	0	0	0	0	....	....	....	....	....
	NHL Totals	**85**	**4**	**4**	**8**	**32**	**10**	**0**	**1**	**1**	**8**

Signed as a free agent by **Anaheim**, May 30, 1996. Traded to **Pittsburgh** by **Anaheim** for Pittsburgh's 5th round choice (Bill Cass) in 2000 Entry Draft, March 14, 2000. Signed as a free agent by **NY Islanders**, July 31, 2000. Traded to **Pittsburgh** by **NY Islanders** for Pittsburgh's 9th round choice (Roman Kuhtinov) in 2001 Entry Draft, November 14, 2000. Traded to **St. Louis** by **Pittsburgh** for Marc Bergevin, December 28, 2000.

TREDWAY, Brock

Right wing. Shoots right. 6', 180 lbs. Born, Highland Creek, Ont., June 23, 1959.

Season	Club	GP	G	A	Pts	PIM	GP	G	A	Pts	PIM
1981-82	Los Angeles Kings	....	....	....	....	....	1	0	0	0	0
	NHL Totals	....	....	....	....	....	**1**	**0**	**0**	**0**	**0**

Signed as a free agent by **Los Angeles**, May 11, 1981.

TREMBLAY, Brent

Defense. Shoots left. 6'2", 192 lbs. Born, North Bay, Ont., November 1, 1957.
(Washington's 8th choice, 127th overall, in 1977 Amateur Draft).

Season	Club	GP	G	A	Pts	PIM	GP	G	A	Pts	PIM
1978-79	Washington Capitals	1	0	0	0	0	....	....	....	....	....
1979-80	Washington Capitals	9	1	0	1	6	....	....	....	....	....
	NHL Totals	**10**	**1**	**0**	**1**	**6**	....	....	....	....	....

TREMBLAY, Gilles

Left wing. Shoots left. 5'10", 170 lbs. Born, Montmorency, Que., December 17, 1938.

Season	Club	GP	G	A	Pts	PIM	GP	G	A	Pts	PIM
1960-61	Montreal Canadiens	45	7	11	18	4	6	1	3	4	0
1961-62	Montreal Canadiens	70	32	22	54	28	6	1	0	1	2
1962-63	Montreal Canadiens	60	25	24	49	42	5	2	0	2	0
1963-64	Montreal Canadiens	61	22	15	37	21	2	0	0	0	0
1964-65	Montreal Canadiens	26	9	7	16	16	....	....	....	....	....
1965-66 ♦	Montreal Canadiens	70	27	21	48	24	10	4	5	9	0
1966-67	Montreal Canadiens	62	13	19	32	16	10	0	1	1	0
1967-68 ♦	Montreal Canadiens	71	23	28	51	8	9	1	5	6	2
1968-69 ♦	Montreal Canadiens	44	10	15	25	2	....	....	....	....	....
	NHL Totals	**509**	**168**	**162**	**330**	**161**	**48**	**9**	**14**	**23**	**4**

Played in NHL All-Star Game (1965, 1967)

• Missed remainder of 1964-65 season recovering from leg injury suffered in game vs. Toronto, December 17, 1964.

TREMBLAY, J.C.

Defense. Shoots left. 5'11", 170 lbs. Born, Bagotville, Que., January 22, 1939.

Season	Club	GP	G	A	Pts	PIM	GP	G	A	Pts	PIM
1959-60	Montreal Canadiens	11	0	1	1	0	....	....	....	....	....
1960-61	Montreal Canadiens	29	1	3	4	18	5	0	0	0	2
1961-62	Montreal Canadiens	70	3	17	20	18	6	0	2	2	2
1962-63	Montreal Canadiens	69	1	17	18	10	5	0	0	0	0
1963-64	Montreal Canadiens	70	5	16	21	24	7	2	1	3	9
1964-65 ♦	Montreal Canadiens	68	3	17	20	22	13	1	*9	10	18
1965-66 ♦	Montreal Canadiens	59	6	29	35	8	10	2	9	11	2
1966-67	Montreal Canadiens	60	8	26	34	14	10	2	4	6	2
1967-68 ♦	Montreal Canadiens	73	4	26	30	18	13	3	6	9	2
1968-69 ♦	Montreal Canadiens	75	7	32	39	18	13	1	4	5	6
1969-70	Montreal Canadiens	58	2	19	21	7	....	....	....	....	....
1970-71 ♦	Montreal Canadiens	76	11	52	63	23	20	3	14	17	15
1971-72	Montreal Canadiens	76	6	51	57	24	6	0	2	2	0
	NHL Totals	**794**	**57**	**306**	**363**	**204**	**108**	**14**	**51**	**65**	**58**

NHL Second All-Star Team (1968) • NHL First All-Star Team (1971)
Played in NHL All-Star Game (1959, 1965, 1967, 1968, 1969, 1971, 1972)

TREMBLAY, Marcel

Right wing. Shoots right. 5'11", 165 lbs. Born, St. Boniface, Man., July 4, 1915.

Season	Club	GP	G	A	Pts	PIM	GP	G	A	Pts	PIM
1938-39	Montreal Canadiens	10	0	2	2	0	....	....	....	....	....
	NHL Totals	**10**	**0**	**2**	**2**	**0**	....	....	....	....	....

TREMBLAY, Mario

Right wing. Shoots right. 6', 185 lbs. Born, Montreal, Que., February 9, 1956.
(Montreal's 4th choice, 12th overall, in 1974 Amateur Draft).

Season	Club	GP	G	A	Pts	PIM	GP	G	A	Pts	PIM
1974-75	Montreal Canadiens	63	21	18	39	108	11	0	1	1	7
1975-76 ♦	Montreal Canadiens	71	11	16	27	88	10	0	1	1	27
1976-77 ♦	Montreal Canadiens	74	18	28	46	61	14	3	0	3	9
1977-78 ♦	Montreal Canadiens	56	10	14	24	44	5	2	1	3	16
1978-79 ♦	Montreal Canadiens	76	30	29	59	74	13	3	4	7	13
1979-80	Montreal Canadiens	77	16	26	42	105	10	0	11	11	14
1980-81	Montreal Canadiens	77	25	38	63	123	3	0	0	0	9
1981-82	Montreal Canadiens	80	33	40	73	66	5	4	1	5	24
1982-83	Montreal Canadiens	80	30	37	67	87	3	0	1	1	7
1983-84	Montreal Canadiens	67	14	25	39	112	15	6	3	9	31
1984-85	Montreal Canadiens	75	31	35	66	120	12	2	6	8	30
1985-86 ♦	Montreal Canadiens	56	19	20	39	55	....	....	....	....	....
	NHL Totals	**852**	**258**	**326**	**584**	**1043**	**101**	**20**	**29**	**49**	**187**

• Suffered career-ending shoulder injury in game vs. Quebec, March 17, 1986.

TREMBLAY, Nils

Center. Shoots right. 5'9", 170 lbs. Born, Matane, Que., July 26, 1923.

Season	Club	GP	G	A	Pts	PIM	GP	G	A	Pts	PIM
1944-45	Montreal Canadiens	1	0	1	1	0	2	0	0	0	0
1945-46	Montreal Canadiens	2	0	0	0	0	....	....	....	....	....
	NHL Totals	**3**	**0**	**1**	**1**	**0**	**2**	**0**	**0**	**0**	**0**

Signed as a free agent by **Montreal**, November 14, 1944.

TREMBLAY, Yannick

Defense. Shoots right. 6'2", 200 lbs. Born, Pointe-aux-Trembles, Que., November 15, 1975.
(Toronto's 4th choice, 145th overall, in 1995 Entry Draft).

Season	Club	GP	G	A	Pts	PIM	GP	G	A	Pts	PIM
1996-97	Toronto Maple Leafs	5	0	0	0	0	....	....	....	....	....
1997-98	Toronto Maple Leafs	38	2	4	6	6	....	....	....	....	....
1998-99	Toronto Maple Leafs	35	2	7	9	16	....	....	....	....	....
99-2000	Atlanta Thrashers	75	10	21	31	22	....	....	....	....	....
2000-01	Atlanta Thrashers	46	4	8	12	30	....	....	....	....	....
2001-02	Atlanta Thrashers	66	9	15	24	47	....	....	....	....	....
2002-03	Atlanta Thrashers	75	8	22	30	32	....	....	....	....	....
	NHL Totals	**340**	**35**	**77**	**112**	**153**	....	....	....	....	....

Claimed by **Atlanta** from **Toronto** in Expansion Draft, June 25, 1999.

TREPANIER, Pascal

Defense. Shoots right. 6', 210 lbs. Born, Gaspe, Que., September 4, 1973.

Season	Club	GP	G	A	Pts	PIM	GP	G	A	Pts	PIM
1997-98	Colorado Avalanche	15	0	1	1	18	....	....	....	....	....
1998-99	Mighty Ducks of Anaheim	45	2	4	6	48	....	....	....	....	....
99-2000	Mighty Ducks of Anaheim	37	0	4	4	54	....	....	....	....	....
2000-01	Mighty Ducks of Anaheim	57	6	4	10	73	....	....	....	....	....
2001-02	Colorado Avalanche	74	4	9	13	59	2	0	0	0	0
2002-03	Nashville Predators	1	0	0	0	0	....	....	....	....	....
	NHL Totals	**229**	**12**	**22**	**34**	**252**	**2**	**0**	**0**	**0**	**0**

Signed as a free agent by **Colorado**, August 30, 1995. Claimed by **Anaheim** from **Colorado** in Waiver Draft, October 5, 1998. Signed as a free agent by **Colorado**, September, 2001. Signed as a free agent by **Nashville**, July 16, 2002. Traded to **Florida** by **Nashville** for Wade Flaherty, March 9, 2003. Signed as a free agent by **Tampa Bay**, July 23, 2003.

TRIMPER, Tim

Left wing. Shoots left. 5'9", 184 lbs. Born, Windsor, Ont., September 28, 1959.
(Chicago's 2nd choice, 28th overall, in 1979 Entry Draft).

Season	Club	GP	G	A	Pts	PIM	GP	G	A	Pts	PIM
1979-80	Chicago Black Hawks	30	6	10	16	10	1	0	0	0	2
1980-81	Winnipeg Jets	56	15	14	29	28	....	....	....	....	....
1981-82	Winnipeg Jets	74	8	8	16	100	1	0	0	0	0
1982-83	Winnipeg Jets	5	0	0	0	0	....	....	....	....	....

Season	Club	GP	G	A	Pts	PIM	GP	G	A	Pts	PIM
		REGULAR SEASON					PLAYOFFS				
1983-84	Winnipeg Jets	5	0	0	0	0	....	....	....	....	....
1984-85	Minnesota North Stars	20	1	4	5	15	....	....	....	....	....
	NHL Totals	**190**	**30**	**36**	**66**	**153**	**2**	**0**	**0**	**0**	**2**

Traded to **Winnipeg** by **Chicago** with Doug Lecuyer for Peter Marsh, December 1, 1980. Traded to **Minnesota** by **Winnipeg** for Jordy Douglas, January 12, 1984.

TRIPP, John

Right wing. Shoots right. 6'2", 215 lbs. Born, Kingston, Ont., May 4, 1977.
(Calgary's 3rd choice, 42nd overall, in 1997 Entry Draft).

Season	Club	GP	G	A	Pts	PIM	GP	G	A	Pts	PIM
2002-03	New York Rangers	9	1	2	3	2	....	....	....	....	....
	NHL Totals	**9**	**1**	**2**	**3**	**2**	....	....	....	....	....

• Re-entered NHL Entry Draft. Originally Colorado's 3rd choice, 77th overall, in 1995 Entry Draft.

TRNKA, Pavel

Defense. Shoots left. 6'2", 200 lbs. Born, Plzen, Czech., July 27, 1976.
(Anaheim's 5th choice, 106th overall, in 1994 Entry Draft).

Season	Club	GP	G	A	Pts	PIM	GP	G	A	Pts	PIM
1997-98	Mighty Ducks of Anaheim	48	3	4	7	40	....	....	....	....	....
1998-99	Mighty Ducks of Anaheim	63	0	4	4	60	4	0	1	1	2
99-2000	Mighty Ducks of Anaheim	57	2	15	17	34	....	....	....	....	....
2000-01	Mighty Ducks of Anaheim	59	1	7	8	42	....	....	....	....	....
2001-02	Mighty Ducks of Anaheim	71	2	11	13	66	....	....	....	....	....
2002-03	Mighty Ducks of Anaheim	24	3	6	9	6	....	....	....	....	....
	Florida Panthers	22	0	3	3	24	....	....	....	....	....
	NHL Totals	**344**	**11**	**50**	**61**	**272**	**4**	**0**	**1**	**1**	**2**

Traded to **Florida** by **Anaheim** with Matt Cullen and Anaheim's 4th round choice (James Pemberton) in 2003 Entry Draft for Sandis Ozolinsh and Lance Ward, January 30, 2003.

TROTTIER, Bryan

HHOF

Center. Shoots left. 5'11", 195 lbs. Born, Val Marie, Sask., July 17, 1956.
(NY Islanders' 2nd choice, 22nd overall, in 1974 Amateur Draft).

Season	Club	GP	G	A	Pts	PIM	GP	G	A	Pts	PIM
1975-76	New York Islanders	80	32	63	95	21	13	1	7	8	8
1976-77	New York Islanders	76	30	42	72	34	12	2	8	10	2
1977-78	New York Islanders	77	46	*77	123	46	7	0	3	3	4
1978-79	New York Islanders	76	47	*87	*134	50	10	2	4	6	13
1979-80 ♦	New York Islanders	78	42	62	104	68	21	*12	17	*29	16
1980-81 ♦	New York Islanders	73	31	72	103	74	*18	11	*18	29	34
1981-82 ♦	New York Islanders	80	50	79	129	88	19	6	*23	*29	40
1982-83 ♦	New York Islanders	80	34	55	89	68	17	8	12	20	18
1983-84	New York Islanders	68	40	71	111	59	21	8	6	14	49
1984-85	New York Islanders	68	28	31	59	47	10	4	2	6	8
1985-86	New York Islanders	78	37	59	96	72	3	1	1	2	2
1986-87	New York Islanders	80	23	64	87	50	14	8	5	13	12
1987-88	New York Islanders	77	30	52	82	48	6	0	0	0	10
1988-89	New York Islanders	73	17	28	45	44	....	....	....	....	....
1989-90	New York Islanders	59	13	11	24	29	4	1	0	1	4
1990-91 ♦	Pittsburgh Penguins	52	9	19	28	24	23	3	4	7	49
1991-92 ♦	Pittsburgh Penguins	63	11	18	29	54	21	4	3	7	8
1993-94	Pittsburgh Penguins	41	4	11	15	36	2	0	0	0	0
	NHL Totals	**1279**	**524**	**901**	**1425**	**912**	**221**	**71**	**113**	**184**	**277**

• Brother of Rocky • Calder Memorial Trophy (1976) • NHL First All-Star Team (1978, 1979) • NHL Plus/Minus Leader (1979) • Art Ross Trophy (1979) • Hart Trophy (1979) • Conn Smythe Trophy (1980) • NHL Second All-Star Team (1982, 1984) • Bud Man of the Year Award (1988) • King Clancy Memorial Trophy (1989)

Played in NHL All-Star Game (1976, 1978, 1980, 1982, 1983, 1985, 1986, 1992)

Signed as a free agent by **Pittsburgh**, July 20, 1990. Signed as a free agent by **Pittsburgh**, June 22, 1993.

TROTTIER, Dave

Left wing. Shoots left. 5'10", 170 lbs. Born, Pembroke, Ont., June 25, 1906.

Season	Club	GP	G	A	Pts	PIM	GP	G	A	Pts	PIM
1928-29	Montreal Maroons	37	2	4	6	69	....	....	....	....	....
1929-30	Montreal Maroons	41	17	10	27	73	4	0	2	2	8
1930-31	Montreal Maroons	43	9	8	17	58	2	0	0	0	6
1931-32	Montreal Maroons	48	26	18	44	94	4	1	0	1	0
1932-33	Montreal Maroons	48	16	15	31	38	2	0	0	0	6
1933-34	Montreal Maroons	48	9	17	26	47	4	0	0	0	6
1934-35 ♦	Montreal Maroons	34	10	9	19	22	7	2	1	3	4
1935-36	Montreal Maroons	46	10	10	20	25	3	0	0	0	4
1936-37	Montreal Maroons	43	12	11	23	33	5	1	0	1	5
1937-38	Montreal Maroons	47	9	10	19	42	....	....	....	....	....
1938-39	Detroit Red Wings	11	1	1	2	16	....	....	....	....	....
	NHL Totals	**446**	**121**	**113**	**234**	**517**	**31**	**4**	**3**	**7**	**39**

Played in NHL All-Star Game (1937)

Signed as a free agent by **Mtl. Maroons**, April 8, 1928. Rights later awarded to **Toronto**. Traded to **Mtl. Maroons** by **Toronto** for $15,000, November 28, 1928. Traded to **Detroit** by **Mtl. Maroons** for cash, December 13, 1938.

TROTTIER, Guy

Right wing. Shoots right. 5'8", 165 lbs. Born, Hull, Que., April 1, 1941.

Season	Club	GP	G	A	Pts	PIM	GP	G	A	Pts	PIM
1968-69	New York Rangers	2	0	0	0	0	....	....	....	....	....
1970-71	Toronto Maple Leafs	61	19	5	24	21	5	0	0	0	0
1971-72	Toronto Maple Leafs	52	9	12	21	16	4	1	0	1	16
	NHL Totals	**115**	**28**	**17**	**45**	**37**	**9**	**1**	**0**	**1**	**16**

Traded to **NY Rangers** by **Buffalo** (AHL) for cash, December, 1968. Claimed by **Toronto** from **NY Rangers** in Intra-League Draft, June 9, 1970.

TROTTIER, Rocky

Right wing. Shoots left. 5'11", 185 lbs. Born, Climax, Sask., April 11, 1964.
(New Jersey's 1st choice, 8th overall, in 1982 Entry Draft).

Season	Club	GP	G	A	Pts	PIM	GP	G	A	Pts	PIM
1983-84	New Jersey Devils	5	1	1	2	0	....	....	....	....	....
1984-85	New Jersey Devils	33	5	3	8	2	....	....	....	....	....
	NHL Totals	**38**	**6**	**4**	**10**	**2**	....	....	....	....	....

• Brother of Bryan

TRUDEL, Jean-Guy

Left wing. Shoots left. 5'11", 202 lbs. Born, Sudbury, Ont., October 18, 1975.

Season	Club	GP	G	A	Pts	PIM	GP	G	A	Pts	PIM
99-2000	Phoenix Coyotes	1	0	0	0	0	....	....	....	....	....
2001-02	Phoenix Coyotes	3	0	0	0	2	....	....	....	....	....
2002-03	Minnesota Wild	1	0	0	0	2	....	....	....	....	....
	NHL Totals	**5**	**0**	**0**	**0**	**4**	....	....	....	....	....

Signed as a free agent by **Phoenix**, July 17, 1999. Signed as a free agent by **Minnesota**, July 16, 2002.

TRUDEL, Lou

Left wing. Shoots left. 5'11", 167 lbs. Born, Salem, MA, July 21, 1912.

Season	Club	GP	G	A	Pts	PIM	GP	G	A	Pts	PIM
1933-34 ♦	Chicago Black Hawks	31	1	3	4	13	7	0	0	0	0
1934-35	Chicago Black Hawks	47	11	11	22	28	2	0	0	0	0
1935-36	Chicago Black Hawks	47	3	4	7	27	2	0	0	0	2
1936-37	Chicago Black Hawks	45	6	12	18	11	....	....	....	....	....
1937-38 ♦	Chicago Black Hawks	42	6	16	22	15	10	0	3	3	2
1938-39	Montreal Canadiens	31	8	13	21	2	3	1	0	1	0
1939-40	Montreal Canadiens	47	12	7	19	24	....	....	....	....	....
1940-41	Montreal Canadiens	16	2	3	5	2	....	....	....	....	....
	NHL Totals	**306**	**49**	**69**	**118**	**122**	**24**	**1**	**3**	**4**	**4**

Played in NHL All-Star Game (1939)

Traded to **Montreal** by **Chicago** for Joffre Desilets, August 26, 1938. Traded to **Washington** (AHL) by **Montreal** for cash, October 9, 1941.

TRUDELL, Rene

Right wing. Shoots right. 5'9", 165 lbs. Born, Mariapolis, Man., January 31, 1919.

Season	Club	GP	G	A	Pts	PIM	GP	G	A	Pts	PIM
1945-46	New York Rangers	16	3	5	8	4	....	....	....	....	....
1946-47	New York Rangers	59	8	16	24	38	....	....	....	....	....
1947-48	New York Rangers	54	13	7	20	30	5	0	0	0	2
	NHL Totals	**129**	**24**	**28**	**52**	**72**	**5**	**0**	**0**	**0**	**2**

Traded to **Toronto** by **NY Rangers** with Cal Gardner, Bill Juzda and the rights to Frank Mathers for Wally Stanowski and Moe Morris, April 26, 1948. Traded to **Springfield** (AHL) by **Toronto** (Pittsburgh-AHL) for $5,000 and future considerations, November 17, 1948.

TSELIOS, Nikos

Defense. Shoots left. 6'5", 210 lbs. Born, Oak Park, IL, January 20, 1979.
(Carolina's 1st choice, 22nd overall, in 1997 Entry Draft).

Season	Club	GP	G	A	Pts	PIM	GP	G	A	Pts	PIM
2001-02	Carolina Hurricanes	2	0	0	0	6	....	....	....	....	....
	NHL Totals	**2**	**0**	**0**	**0**	**6**	....	....	....	....	....

Signed as a free agent by **Phoenix**, July 21, 2003.

TSULYGIN, Nikolai

Defense. Shoots right. 6'3", 210 lbs. Born, Ufa, USSR, May 29, 1975.
(Anaheim's 2nd choice, 30th overall, in 1993 Entry Draft).

Season	Club	GP	G	A	Pts	PIM	GP	G	A	Pts	PIM
1996-97	Mighty Ducks of Anaheim	22	0	1	1	8	....	....	....	....	....
	NHL Totals	**22**	**0**	**1**	**1**	**8**	....	....	....	....	....

TSYGUROV, Denis

Defense. Shoots left. 6'3", 198 lbs. Born, Chelyabinsk, USSR, February 26, 1971.
(Buffalo's 1st choice, 38th overall, in 1993 Entry Draft).

Season	Club	GP	G	A	Pts	PIM	GP	G	A	Pts	PIM
1993-94	Buffalo Sabres	8	0	0	0	8	....	....	....	....	....
1994-95	Buffalo Sabres	4	0	0	0	4	....	....	....	....	....
	Los Angeles Kings	21	0	0	0	11	....	....	....	....	....
1995-96	Los Angeles Kings	18	1	5	6	22	....	....	....	....	....
	NHL Totals	**51**	**1**	**5**	**6**	**45**	....	....	....	....	....

Traded to **Los Angeles** by **Buffalo** with Philippe Boucher and Grant Fuhr for Alexei Zhitnik, Robb Stauber, Charlie Huddy and Los Angeles' 5th round choice (Marian Menhart) in 1995 Entry Draft, February 14, 1995.

TSYPLAKOV, Vladimir

Left wing. Shoots left. 6'1", 197 lbs. Born, Inta, USSR, April 18, 1969.
(Los Angeles' 4th choice, 59th overall, in 1995 Entry Draft).

Season	Club	GP	G	A	Pts	PIM	GP	G	A	Pts	PIM
1995-96	Los Angeles Kings	23	5	5	10	4	....	....	....	....	....
1996-97	Los Angeles Kings	67	16	23	39	12	....	....	....	....	....
1997-98	Los Angeles Kings	73	18	34	52	18	4	0	1	1	8
1998-99	Los Angeles Kings	69	11	12	23	32	....	....	....	....	....
99-2000	Los Angeles Kings	29	6	7	13	4	....	....	....	....	....
	Buffalo Sabres	34	6	13	19	10	5	0	1	1	4
2000-01	Buffalo Sabres	36	7	7	14	10	9	1	0	1	4
	NHL Totals	**331**	**69**	**101**	**170**	**90**	**18**	**1**	**2**	**3**	**16**

Traded to **Buffalo** by **Los Angeles** for Buffalo's 8th round choice (Dan Welch) in 2000 Entry Draft, January 24, 2000. • Missed majority of 2000-01 season recovering from knee injury suffered in game vs. Edmonton, October 13, 2000.

TUCKER, Darcy

Right wing. Shoots left. 5'11", 185 lbs. Born, Castor, Alta., March 15, 1975.
(Montreal's 8th choice, 151st overall, in 1993 Entry Draft).

Season	Club	Regular Season GP	G	A	Pts	PIM	Playoffs GP	G	A	Pts	PIM
1995-96	Montreal Canadiens	3	0	0	0	0	....	....	....	....	....
1996-97	Montreal Canadiens	73	7	13	20	110	4	0	0	0	0
1997-98	Montreal Canadiens	39	1	5	6	57	....	....	....	....	....
	Tampa Bay Lightning	35	6	8	14	89	....	....	....	....	....
1998-99	Tampa Bay Lightning	82	21	22	43	176	....	....	....	....	....
99-2000	Tampa Bay Lightning	50	14	20	34	108	....	....	....	....	....
	Toronto Maple Leafs	27	7	10	17	55	12	4	2	6	15
2000-01	Toronto Maple Leafs	82	16	21	37	141	11	0	2	2	6
2001-02	Toronto Maple Leafs	77	24	35	59	92	17	4	4	8	38
2002-03	Toronto Maple Leafs	77	10	26	36	119	6	0	3	3	6
	NHL Totals	**545**	**106**	**160**	**266**	**947**	**50**	**8**	**11**	**19**	**65**

Traded to **Tampa Bay** by **Montreal** with Stephane Richer and David Wilkie for Patrick Poulin, Mick Vukota and Igor Ulanov, January 15, 1998. Traded to **Toronto** by **Tampa Bay** with Tampa Bay's 4th round choice (Miguel Delisle) in 2000 Entry Draft and future considerations for Mike Johnson, Marek Posmyk, Toronto's 5th (Pavel Sedov) and 6th (Aaron Gionet) round choices in 2000 Entry Draft and future considerations, February 9, 2000.

TUCKER, John

Center. Shoots right. 6', 200 lbs. Born, Windsor, Ont., September 29, 1964.
(Buffalo's 4th choice, 31st overall, in 1983 Entry Draft).

Season	Club	Regular Season GP	G	A	Pts	PIM	Playoffs GP	G	A	Pts	PIM
1983-84	Buffalo Sabres	21	12	4	16	4	3	1	0	1	0
1984-85	Buffalo Sabres	64	22	27	49	21	5	1	5	6	0
1985-86	Buffalo Sabres	75	31	34	65	39	....	....	....	....	....
1986-87	Buffalo Sabres	54	17	34	51	21	....	....	....	....	....
1987-88	Buffalo Sabres	45	19	19	38	20	6	7	3	10	18
1988-89	Buffalo Sabres	60	13	31	44	31	3	0	3	3	0
1989-90	Buffalo Sabres	8	1	2	3	2	....	....	....	....	....
	Washington Capitals	38	9	19	28	10	12	1	7	8	4
1990-91	Buffalo Sabres	18	1	3	4	4	....	....	....	....	....
	New York Islanders	20	3	4	7	4	....	....	....	....	....
1992-93	Tampa Bay Lightning	78	17	39	56	69	....	....	....	....	....
1993-94	Tampa Bay Lightning	66	17	23	40	28	....	....	....	....	....
1994-95	Tampa Bay Lightning	46	12	13	25	14	....	....	....	....	....
1995-96	Tampa Bay Lightning	63	3	7	10	18	2	0	0	0	2
	NHL Totals	**656**	**177**	**259**	**436**	**285**	**31**	**10**	**18**	**28**	**24**

Traded to **Washington** by **Buffalo** for future considerations, January 5, 1990. Traded to **Buffalo** by **Washington** for cash, July 3, 1990. Traded to **NY Islanders** by **Buffalo** for future considerations, January 21, 1991. Signed as a free agent by **Tampa Bay**, August 5, 1992.

TUDIN, Connie

Center. Shoots left. 5'11", 170 lbs. Born, Ottawa, Ont., September 21, 1917.

Season	Club	Regular Season GP	G	A	Pts	PIM	Playoffs GP	G	A	Pts	PIM
1941-42	Montreal Canadiens	4	0	1	1	4	....	....	....	....	....
	NHL Totals	**4**	**0**	**1**	**1**	**4**	....	....	....	....	....

Signed as a free agent by **Montreal**, October 16, 1941.

TUDOR, Rob

Right wing/Center. Shoots right. 5'11", 188 lbs. Born, Cupar, Sask., June 30, 1956.
(Vancouver's 5th choice, 98th overall, in 1976 Amateur Draft).

Season	Club	Regular Season GP	G	A	Pts	PIM	Playoffs GP	G	A	Pts	PIM
1978-79	Vancouver Canucks	24	4	4	8	19	2	0	0	0	0
1979-80	Vancouver Canucks	2	0	0	0	0	1	0	0	0	0
1982-83	St. Louis Blues	2	0	0	0	0	....	....	....	....	....
	NHL Totals	**28**	**4**	**4**	**8**	**19**	**3**	**0**	**0**	**0**	**0**

Signed as a free agent by **St. Louis**, July 22, 1982.

TUER, Allan

Defense. Shoots left. 6', 190 lbs. Born, North Battleford, Sask., July 19, 1963.
(Los Angeles' 8th choice, 186th overall, in 1981 Entry Draft).

Season	Club	Regular Season GP	G	A	Pts	PIM	Playoffs GP	G	A	Pts	PIM
1985-86	Los Angeles Kings	45	0	1	1	150	....	....	....	....	....
1987-88	Minnesota North Stars	6	1	0	1	29	....	....	....	....	....
1988-89	Hartford Whalers	4	0	0	0	23	....	....	....	....	....
1989-90	Hartford Whalers	2	0	0	0	6	....	....	....	....	....
	NHL Totals	**57**	**1**	**1**	**2**	**208**	....	....	....	....	....

Signed as a free agent by **Edmonton**, August 18, 1986. Claimed by **Minnesota** from **Edmonton** in Waiver Draft, October 5, 1987. Signed as a free agent by **Hartford**, July 12, 1988.

TUOMAINEN, Marko

Right wing. Shoots right. 6'3", 230 lbs. Born, Kuopio, Finland, April 25, 1972.
(Edmonton's 10th choice, 205th overall, in 1992 Entry Draft).

Season	Club	Regular Season GP	G	A	Pts	PIM	Playoffs GP	G	A	Pts	PIM
1994-95	Edmonton Oilers	4	0	0	0	0	....	....	....	....	....
99-2000	Los Angeles Kings	63	9	8	17	80	1	0	0	0	0
2000-01	Los Angeles Kings	11	0	1	1	4	....	....	....	....	....
2001-02	New York Islanders	1	0	0	0	0	....	....	....	....	....
	NHL Totals	**79**	**9**	**9**	**18**	**84**	**1**	**0**	**0**	**0**	**0**

Signed as a free agent by **Los Angeles**, June 20, 1999. Signed as a free agent by **Los Angeles**, January 4, 2001. Signed as a free agent by **NY Islanders**, July 18, 2001.

TURCOTTE, Alfie

Center. Shoots left. 5'11", 185 lbs. Born, Gary, IN, June 5, 1965.
(Montreal's 1st choice, 17th overall, in 1983 Entry Draft).

Season	Club	Regular Season GP	G	A	Pts	PIM	Playoffs GP	G	A	Pts	PIM
1983-84	Montreal Canadiens	30	7	7	14	10	....	....	....	....	....
1984-85	Montreal Canadiens	53	8	16	24	35	5	0	0	0	0
1985-86	Montreal Canadiens	2	0	0	0	2	....	....	....	....	....
1987-88	Winnipeg Jets	3	0	0	0	0	....	....	....	....	....
1988-89	Winnipeg Jets	14	1	3	4	2	....	....	....	....	....
1989-90	Washington Capitals	4	0	2	2	0	....	....	....	....	....
1990-91	Washington Capitals	6	1	1	2	0	....	....	....	....	....
	NHL Totals	**112**	**17**	**29**	**46**	**49**	**5**	**0**	**0**	**0**	**0**

Traded to **Edmonton** by **Montreal** for future considerations, June 25, 1986. Traded to **Montreal** by **Edmonton** for cash, May 14, 1987. Traded to **Winnipeg** by **Montreal** for future considerations, January 14, 1988. Signed as a free agent by **Boston**, June 27, 1989. Traded to **Washington** by **Boston** for Mike Millar, October 2, 1989.

TURCOTTE, Darren

Center. Shoots left. 6', 182 lbs. Born, Boston, MA, May 2, 1968.
(NY Rangers' 6th choice, 114th overall, in 1986 Entry Draft).

Season	Club	Regular Season GP	G	A	Pts	PIM	Playoffs GP	G	A	Pts	PIM
1988-89	New York Rangers	20	7	3	10	4	1	0	0	0	0
1989-90	New York Rangers	76	32	34	66	32	10	1	6	7	4
1990-91	New York Rangers	74	26	41	67	37	6	1	2	3	0
1991-92	New York Rangers	71	30	23	53	57	8	4	0	4	6
1992-93	New York Rangers	71	25	28	53	40	....	....	....	....	....
1993-94	New York Rangers	13	2	4	6	13	....	....	....	....	....
	Hartford Whalers	19	2	11	13	4	....	....	....	....	....
1994-95	Hartford Whalers	47	17	18	35	22	....	....	....	....	....
1995-96	Winnipeg Jets	59	16	16	32	26	....	....	....	....	....
	San Jose Sharks	9	6	5	11	4	....	....	....	....	....
1996-97	San Jose Sharks	65	16	21	37	16	....	....	....	....	....
1997-98	St. Louis Blues	62	12	6	18	26	10	0	0	0	2
1998-99	Nashville Predators	40	4	5	9	16	....	....	....	....	....
99-2000	Nashville Predators	9	0	1	1	4	....	....	....	....	....
	NHL Totals	**635**	**195**	**216**	**411**	**301**	**35**	**6**	**8**	**14**	**12**

Played in NHL All-Star Game (1991)

Traded to **Hartford** by **NY Rangers** with James Patrick for Steve Larmer, Nick Kypreos, Barry Richter and Hartford's 6th round choice (Yuri Litvinov) in 1994 Entry Draft, November 2, 1993. Traded to **Winnipeg** by **Hartford** for Nelson Emerson, October 6, 1995. Traded to **San Jose** by **Winnipeg** with Dallas' 2nd round choice (previously acquired and later traded to Chicago – Chicago selected Remi Royer) in 1996 Entry Draft for Craig Janney, March 18, 1996. Traded to **St. Louis** by **San Jose** for Stephane Matteau, July 24, 1997. Traded to **Nashville** by **St. Louis** for future considerations, June 26, 1998. • Missed majority of 1999-2000 season recovering from knee injury suffered in game vs. Montreal, November 18, 1999. • Officially announced retirement, March 14, 2000.

TURGEON, Pierre

Center. Shoots left. 6'1", 199 lbs. Born, Rouyn, Que., August 28, 1969.
(Buffalo's 1st choice, 1st overall, in 1987 Entry Draft).

Season	Club	Regular Season GP	G	A	Pts	PIM	Playoffs GP	G	A	Pts	PIM
1987-88	Buffalo Sabres	76	14	28	42	34	6	4	3	7	4
1988-89	Buffalo Sabres	80	34	54	88	26	5	3	5	8	2
1989-90	Buffalo Sabres	80	40	66	106	29	6	2	4	6	2
1990-91	Buffalo Sabres	78	32	47	79	26	6	3	1	4	6
1991-92	Buffalo Sabres	8	2	6	8	4	....	....	....	....	....
	New York Islanders	69	38	49	87	16	....	....	....	....	....
1992-93	New York Islanders	83	58	74	132	26	11	6	7	13	0
1993-94	New York Islanders	69	38	56	94	18	4	0	1	1	0
1994-95	New York Islanders	34	13	14	27	10	....	....	....	....	....
	Montreal Canadiens	15	11	9	20	4	....	....	....	....	....
1995-96	Montreal Canadiens	80	38	58	96	44	6	2	4	6	2
1996-97	Montreal Canadiens	9	1	10	11	2	....	....	....	....	....
	St. Louis Blues	69	25	49	74	12	5	1	1	2	2
1997-98	St. Louis Blues	60	22	46	68	24	10	4	4	8	2
1998-99	St. Louis Blues	67	31	34	65	36	13	4	9	13	6
99-2000	St. Louis Blues	52	26	40	66	8	7	0	7	7	0
2000-01	St. Louis Blues	79	30	52	82	37	15	5	10	15	2
2001-02	Dallas Stars	66	15	32	47	16	....	....	....	....	....
2002-03	Dallas Stars	65	12	30	42	18	5	0	1	1	0
	NHL Totals	**1139**	**480**	**754**	**1234**	**390**	**99**	**34**	**57**	**91**	**28**

• Brother of Sylvain • Lady Byng Memorial Trophy (1993)

Played in NHL All-Star Game (1990, 1993, 1994, 1996)

Traded to **NY Islanders** by **Buffalo** with Uwe Krupp, Benoit Hogue and Dave McLlwain for Pat LaFontaine, Randy Hillier, Randy Wood and NY Islanders' 4th round choice (Dean Melanson) in 1992 Entry Draft, October 25, 1991. Traded to **Montreal** by **NY Islanders** with Vladimir Malakhov for Kirk Muller, Mathieu Schneider and Craig Darby, April 5, 1995. Traded to **St. Louis** by **Montreal** with Rory Fitzpatrick and Craig Conroy for Murray Baron, Shayne Corson and St. Louis' 5th round choice (Gennady Razin) in 1997 Entry Draft, October 29, 1996. Signed as a free agent by **Dallas**, July 1, 2001.

TURGEON, Sylvain

Left wing. Shoots left. 6', 200 lbs. Born, Noranda, Que., January 17, 1965.
(Hartford's 1st choice, 2nd overall, in 1983 Entry Draft).

Season	Club	Regular Season GP	G	A	Pts	PIM	Playoffs GP	G	A	Pts	PIM
1983-84	Hartford Whalers	76	40	32	72	55	....	....	....	....	....
1984-85	Hartford Whalers	64	31	31	62	67	....	....	....	....	....
1985-86	Hartford Whalers	76	45	34	79	88	9	2	3	5	4
1986-87	Hartford Whalers	41	23	13	36	45	6	1	2	3	4
1987-88	Hartford Whalers	71	23	26	49	71	6	0	0	0	4
1988-89	Hartford Whalers	42	16	14	30	40	4	0	2	2	4
1989-90	New Jersey Devils	72	30	17	47	81	1	0	0	0	0
1990-91	Montreal Canadiens	19	5	7	12	20	5	0	0	0	2
1991-92	Montreal Canadiens	56	9	11	20	39	5	1	0	1	4
1992-93	Ottawa Senators	72	25	18	43	104	....	....	....	....	....
1993-94	Ottawa Senators	47	11	15	26	52	....	....	....	....	....

Season	Club	Regular Season GP	G	A	Pts	PIM	Playoffs GP	G	A	Pts	PIM
1994-95	Ottawa Senators	33	11	8	19	29	....	....	....	....	....
	NHL Totals	**669**	**269**	**226**	**495**	**691**	**36**	**4**	**7**	**11**	**22**

• Brother of Pierre • NHL All-Rookie Team (1984)

Played in NHL All-Star Game (1986)

Traded to **New Jersey** by **Hartford** for Pat Verbeek, June 17, 1989. • Missed majority of 1990-91 season recovering from hernia surgery (August 23, 1990) and kneecap injury suffered in game vs. Chicago, February 6, 1991. Traded to **Montreal** by **New Jersey** for Claude Lemieux, September 4, 1990. Claimed by **Ottawa** from **Montreal** in Expansion Draft, June 18, 1992.

TURLICK, Gord

Left wing/Center. Shoots left. 6'1", 170 lbs. Born, Miskel, B.C., September 17, 1939.

Season	Club	GP	G	A	Pts	PIM	GP	G	A	Pts	PIM
1959-60	Boston Bruins	2	0	0	0	2	....	....	....	....	....
	NHL Totals	**2**	**0**	**0**	**0**	**2**	....	....	....	....	....

TURNBULL, Ian

Defense. Shoots left. 6', 200 lbs. Born, Montreal, Que., December 22, 1953.
(Toronto's 3rd choice, 15th overall, in 1973 Amateur Draft).

Season	Club	GP	G	A	Pts	PIM	GP	G	A	Pts	PIM
1973-74	Toronto Maple Leafs	78	8	27	35	74	4	0	0	0	8
1974-75	Toronto Maple Leafs	22	6	7	13	44	7	0	2	2	4
1975-76	Toronto Maple Leafs	76	20	36	56	90	10	2	9	11	29
1976-77	Toronto Maple Leafs	80	22	57	79	84	9	4	4	8	10
1977-78	Toronto Maple Leafs	77	14	47	61	77	13	6	10	16	10
1978-79	Toronto Maple Leafs	80	12	51	63	80	6	0	4	4	27
1979-80	Toronto Maple Leafs	75	11	28	39	90	3	0	3	3	2
1980-81	Toronto Maple Leafs	80	19	47	66	104	3	1	0	1	4
1981-82	Toronto Maple Leafs	12	0	2	2	8	....	....	....	....	....
	Los Angeles Kings	42	11	15	26	81	....	....	....	....	....
1982-83	Pittsburgh Penguins	6	0	0	0	4	....	....	....	....	....
	NHL Totals	**628**	**123**	**317**	**440**	**736**	**55**	**13**	**32**	**45**	**94**

Played in NHL All-Star Game (1977)

• Missed majority of 1974-75 season recovering from knee injury suffered in game vs. St. Louis, November 25, 1974. Traded to **Los Angeles** by **Toronto** for Billy Harris and John Gibson, November 11, 1981. Signed as a free agent by **Pittsburgh**, October 4, 1982.

TURNBULL, Perry

Center. Shoots left. 6'2", 200 lbs. Born, Bentley, Alta., March 9, 1959.
(St. Louis' 1st choice, 2nd overall, in 1979 Entry Draft).

Season	Club	GP	G	A	Pts	PIM	GP	G	A	Pts	PIM
1979-80	St. Louis Blues	80	16	19	35	124	3	1	1	2	2
1980-81	St. Louis Blues	75	34	22	56	209	....	....	....	....	....
1981-82	St. Louis Blues	79	33	26	59	161	5	3	2	5	11
1982-83	St. Louis Blues	79	32	15	47	172	4	1	0	1	14
1983-84	St. Louis Blues	32	14	8	22	81	....	....	....	....	....
	Montreal Canadiens	40	6	7	13	59	9	1	2	3	10
1984-85	Winnipeg Jets	66	22	21	43	130	8	0	1	1	26
1985-86	Winnipeg Jets	80	20	31	51	183	3	0	1	1	11
1986-87	Winnipeg Jets	26	1	5	6	44	1	0	0	0	10
1987-88	St. Louis Blues	51	10	9	19	82	1	0	0	0	2
	NHL Totals	**608**	**188**	**163**	**351**	**1245**	**34**	**6**	**7**	**13**	**86**

Traded to **Montreal** by **St. Louis** for Doug Wickenheiser, Gilbert Delorme and Greg Paslawski, December 21, 1983. Traded to **Winnipeg** by **Montreal** for Lucien DeBlois, June 13, 1984. Traded to **St. Louis** by **Winnipeg** for St. Louis' 5th round choice (Ken Gernander) in 1987 Entry Draft, June 5, 1987.

TURNBULL, Randy

Defense. Shoots right. 6', 185 lbs. Born, Bentley, Alta., February 7, 1962.
(Calgary's 6th choice, 97th overall, in 1980 Entry Draft).

Season	Club	GP	G	A	Pts	PIM	GP	G	A	Pts	PIM
1981-82	Calgary Flames	1	0	0	0	2	....	....	....	....	....
	NHL Totals	**1**	**0**	**0**	**0**	**2**	....	....	....	....	....

TURNER, Bob

Defense. Shoots left. 6', 170 lbs. Born, Regina, Sask., January 31, 1934.

Season	Club	GP	G	A	Pts	PIM	GP	G	A	Pts	PIM
1955-56◆	Montreal Canadiens	33	1	4	5	35	10	0	1	1	10
1956-57◆	Montreal Canadiens	58	1	4	5	48	6	0	1	1	0
1957-58◆	Montreal Canadiens	66	0	3	3	30	10	0	0	0	2
1958-59◆	Montreal Canadiens	68	4	24	28	66	11	0	2	2	20
1959-60◆	Montreal Canadiens	54	0	9	9	40	8	0	0	0	0
1960-61	Montreal Canadiens	60	2	2	4	16	5	0	0	0	0
1961-62	Chicago Black Hawks	69	8	2	10	52	12	1	0	1	6
1962-63	Chicago Black Hawks	70	3	3	6	20	6	0	0	0	6
	NHL Totals	**478**	**19**	**51**	**70**	**307**	**68**	**1**	**4**	**5**	**44**

Played in NHL All-Star Game (1956, 1957, 1958, 1959, 1960, 1961)

Traded to **Chicago** by **Montreal** for Fred Hilts, June, 1961. Traded to **LA Blades** (WHL) by **Chicago** for cash, August 6, 1964.

TURNER, Brad

Defense. Shoots right. 6'2", 205 lbs. Born, Winnipeg, Man., May 25, 1968.
(Minnesota's 6th choice, 58th overall, in 1986 Entry Draft).

Season	Club	GP	G	A	Pts	PIM	GP	G	A	Pts	PIM
1991-92	New York Islanders	3	0	0	0	0	....	....	....	....	....
	NHL Totals	**3**	**0**	**0**	**0**	**0**	....	....	....	....	....

Signed as a free agent by **NY Islanders**, June 4, 1991.

TURNER, Dean

Defense. Shoots left. 6'2", 215 lbs. Born, Dearborn, MI, June 22, 1958.
(NY Rangers' 3rd choice, 44th overall, in 1978 Amateur Draft).

Season	Club	GP	G	A	Pts	PIM	GP	G	A	Pts	PIM
1978-79	New York Rangers	1	0	0	0	0	....	....	....	....	....
1979-80	Colorado Rockies	27	1	0	1	51	....	....	....	....	....
1980-81	Colorado Rockies	4	0	0	0	4	....	....	....	....	....
1982-83	Los Angeles Kings	3	0	0	0	4	....	....	....	....	....
	NHL Totals	**35**	**1**	**0**	**1**	**59**	....	....	....	....	....

Traded to **Colorado** by **NY Rangers** with Pat Hickey, Mike McEwen, Lucien DeBlois and future considerations (Bobby Crawford, January 15, 1980) for Barry Beck, November 2, 1979. Signed as a free agent by **Buffalo**, September 24, 1981. Traded to **Los Angeles** by **Buffalo** for cash, September 9, 1982.

TUSTIN, Norm

Left wing. Shoots left. 5'11", 175 lbs. Born, Regina, Sask., January 3, 1919.

Season	Club	GP	G	A	Pts	PIM	GP	G	A	Pts	PIM
1941-42	New York Rangers	18	2	4	6	0	....	....	....	....	....
	NHL Totals	**18**	**2**	**4**	**6**	**0**	....	....	....	....	....

TUTEN, Aud

Defense. Shoots left. 5'10", 180 lbs. Born, Enterprize, AL, January 14, 1915.

Season	Club	GP	G	A	Pts	PIM	GP	G	A	Pts	PIM
1941-42	Chicago Black Hawks	5	1	1	2	10	....	....	....	....	....
1942-43	Chicago Black Hawks	34	3	7	10	38	....	....	....	....	....
	NHL Totals	**39**	**4**	**8**	**12**	**48**	....	....	....	....	....

TUTT, Brian

Defense. Shoots left. 6'1", 195 lbs. Born, Swalwell, Alta., June 9, 1962.
(Philadelphia's 6th choice, 126th overall, in 1980 Entry Draft).

Season	Club	GP	G	A	Pts	PIM	GP	G	A	Pts	PIM
1989-90	Washington Capitals	7	1	0	1	2	....	....	....	....	....
	NHL Totals	**7**	**1**	**0**	**1**	**2**	....	....	....	....	....

Signed as a free agent by **Washington**, July 25, 1989.

TUTTLE, Steve

Right wing. Shoots right. 6'1", 197 lbs. Born, Vancouver, B.C., January 5, 1966.
(St. Louis' 8th choice, 113th overall, in 1984 Entry Draft).

Season	Club	GP	G	A	Pts	PIM	GP	G	A	Pts	PIM
1988-89	St. Louis Blues	53	13	12	25	6	6	1	2	3	0
1989-90	St. Louis Blues	71	12	10	22	4	5	0	1	1	2
1990-91	St. Louis Blues	20	3	6	9	2	6	0	3	3	0
	NHL Totals	**144**	**28**	**28**	**56**	**12**	**17**	**1**	**6**	**7**	**2**

Traded to **Tampa Bay** by **St. Louis** with Pat Jablonski, Darin Kimble, and Rob Robinson for future considerations, June 19, 1992. Traded to **Quebec** by **Tampa Bay** with Martin Simard and Michel Mongeau for Herb Raglan, February 12, 1993.

TUZZOLINO, Tony

Right wing. Shoots right. 6'2", 208 lbs. Born, Buffalo, NY, October 9, 1975.
(Quebec's 7th choice, 113th overall, in 1994 Entry Draft).

Season	Club	GP	G	A	Pts	PIM	GP	G	A	Pts	PIM
1997-98	Mighty Ducks of Anaheim	1	0	0	0	2	....	....	....	....	....
2000-01	New York Rangers	6	0	0	0	5	....	....	....	....	....
2001-02	Boston Bruins	2	0	0	0	0	....	....	....	....	....
	NHL Totals	**9**	**0**	**0**	**0**	**7**	....	....	....	....	....

Rights transferred to **Colorado** after **Quebec** franchise relocated, June 21, 1995. Signed as a free agent by **NY Islanders**, April 26, 1997. Traded to **Anaheim** by **NY Islanders** with Travis Green and Doug Houda for Joe Sacco, J.J. Daigneault and Mark Janssens, February 6, 1998. Loaned to **Hartford** (AHL) by **Anaheim**, January 25, 2000. Signed as a free agent by **NY Rangers**, February 9, 2001. Signed as a free agent by **Boston**, July 23, 2001. Signed as a free agent by **Minnesota**, July 9, 2002.

TVERDOVSKY, Oleg

Defense. Shoots left. 6'1", 205 lbs. Born, Donetsk, USSR, May 18, 1976.
(Anaheim's 1st choice, 2nd overall, in 1994 Entry Draft).

Season	Club	GP	G	A	Pts	PIM	GP	G	A	Pts	PIM
1994-95	Mighty Ducks of Anaheim	36	3	9	12	14	....	....	....	....	....
1995-96	Mighty Ducks of Anaheim	51	7	15	22	35	....	....	....	....	....
	Winnipeg Jets	31	0	8	8	6	6	0	1	1	0
1996-97	Phoenix Coyotes	82	10	45	55	30	7	0	1	1	0
1997-98	Phoenix Coyotes	46	7	12	19	12	6	0	7	7	0
1998-99	Phoenix Coyotes	82	7	18	25	32	6	0	2	2	6
99-2000	Mighty Ducks of Anaheim	82	15	36	51	30	....	....	....	....	....
2000-01	Mighty Ducks of Anaheim	82	14	39	53	32	....	....	....	....	....
2001-02	Mighty Ducks of Anaheim	73	6	26	32	31	....	....	....	....	....
2002-03◆	New Jersey Devils	50	5	8	13	22	15	0	3	3	0
	NHL Totals	**615**	**74**	**216**	**290**	**244**	**40**	**0**	**14**	**14**	**6**

Played in NHL All-Star Game (1997)

Traded to **Winnipeg** by **Anaheim** with Chad Kilger and Anaheim's 3rd round choice (Per-Anton Lundstrom) in 1996 Entry Draft for Teemu Selanne, Marc Chouinard and Winnipeg's 4th round choice (later traded to Toronto – later traded to Montreal – Montreal selected Kim Staal) in 1996 Entry Draft, February 7, 1996. Transferred to **Phoenix** after **Winnipeg** franchise relocated, July 1, 1996. Traded to **Anaheim** by **Phoenix** for Travis Green and Anaheim's 1st round choice (Scott Kelman) in 1999 Entry Draft, June 26, 1999. Traded to **New Jersey** by **Anaheim** with Jeff Friesen and Maxim Balmochnykh for Petr Sykora, Mike Commodore, Jean-Francois Damphousse and Igor Pohanka, July 6, 2002.

TWIST, Tony

Left wing. Shoots left. 6'1", 220 lbs. Born, Sherwood Park, Alta., May 9, 1968.
(St. Louis' 9th choice, 177th overall, in 1988 Entry Draft).

Season	Club	GP	G	A	Pts	PIM	GP	G	A	Pts	PIM
1989-90	St. Louis Blues	28	0	0	0	124	....	....	....	....	....
1990-91	Quebec Nordiques	24	0	0	0	104	....	....	....	....	....

Season	Club	REGULAR SEASON GP	G	A	Pts	PIM	PLAYOFFS GP	G	A	Pts	PIM
1991-92	Quebec Nordiques	44	0	1	1	164	....	....	....	....	....
1992-93	Quebec Nordiques	34	0	2	2	64	....	....	....	....	....
1993-94	Quebec Nordiques	49	0	4	4	101	....	....	....	....	....
1994-95	St. Louis Blues	28	3	0	3	89	1	0	0	0	6
1995-96	St. Louis Blues	51	3	2	5	100	10	1	1	2	16
1996-97	St. Louis Blues	64	1	2	3	121	6	0	0	0	0
1997-98	St. Louis Blues	60	1	1	2	105	....	....	....	....	....
1998-99	St. Louis Blues	63	2	6	8	149	1	0	0	0	0
	NHL Totals	**445**	**10**	**18**	**28**	**1121**	**18**	**1**	**1**	**2**	**22**

Traded to **Quebec** by **St. Louis** with Herb Raglan and Andy Rymsha for Darin Kimble, February 4, 1991. Signed as a free agent by **St. Louis**, August 16, 1994. • Missed entire 1999-2000 season recovering from injuries suffered in motorcycle accident, July, 1999.

UBRIACO, Gene

Left wing/Center. Shoots left. 5'8", 157 lbs. Born, Sault Ste. Marie, Ont., December 26, 1937.

Season	Club	GP	G	A	Pts	PIM	GP	G	A	Pts	PIM
1967-68	Pittsburgh Penguins	65	18	15	33	16	....	....	....	....	....
1968-69	Pittsburgh Penguins	49	15	11	26	14	....	....	....	....	....
	Oakland Seals	26	4	7	11	14	7	2	0	2	2
1969-70	Oakland Seals	16	1	1	2	4	....	....	....	....	....
	Chicago Black Hawks	21	1	1	2	2	4	0	0	0	2
	NHL Totals	**177**	**39**	**35**	**74**	**50**	**11**	**2**	**0**	**2**	**4**

Traded to **Hershey** (AHL) by **Toronto** with future considerations (Bruce Draper, September, 1964) for Les Duff, September, 1963. Traded to **Pittsburgh** by **Hershey** (AHL) for Jeannot Gilbert, October, 1967. Traded to **Oakland** by **Pittsburgh** with Earl Ingarfield and Dick Mattiussi for Bryan Watson, George Swarbrick and Tracy Pratt, January 30, 1969. Traded to **Chicago** by **Oakland** for Howie Menard, December 15, 1969.

ULANOV, Igor

Defense. Shoots left. 6'3", 220 lbs. Born, Krasnokamsk, USSR, October 1, 1969.
(Winnipeg's 8th choice, 203rd overall, in 1991 Entry Draft).

Season	Club	GP	G	A	Pts	PIM	GP	G	A	Pts	PIM
1991-92	Winnipeg Jets	27	2	9	11	67	7	0	0	0	39
1992-93	Winnipeg Jets	56	2	14	16	124	4	0	0	0	4
1993-94	Winnipeg Jets	74	0	17	17	165	....	....	....	....	....
1994-95	Winnipeg Jets	19	1	3	4	27	....	....	....	....	....
	Washington Capitals	3	0	1	1	2	2	0	0	0	4
1995-96	Chicago Blackhawks	53	1	8	9	92	....	....	....	....	....
	Tampa Bay Lightning	11	2	1	3	24	5	0	0	0	15
1996-97	Tampa Bay Lightning	59	1	7	8	108	....	....	....	....	....
1997-98	Tampa Bay Lightning	45	2	7	9	85	....	....	....	....	....
	Montreal Canadiens	4	0	1	1	12	10	1	4	5	12
1998-99	Montreal Canadiens	76	3	9	12	109	....	....	....	....	....
99-2000	Montreal Canadiens	43	1	5	6	76	....	....	....	....	....
	Edmonton Oilers	14	0	3	3	10	5	0	0	0	6
2000-01	Edmonton Oilers	67	3	20	23	90	6	0	0	0	4
2001-02	New York Rangers	39	0	6	6	53	....	....	....	....	....
	Florida Panthers	14	0	4	4	11	....	....	....	....	....
2002-03	Florida Panthers	56	1	1	2	39	....	....	....	....	....
	NHL Totals	**660**	**19**	**116**	**135**	**1094**	**39**	**1**	**4**	**5**	**84**

Traded to **Washington** by **Winnipeg** with Mike Eagles for Washington's 3rd (later traded to Dallas – Dallas selected Sergey Gusev) and 5th (Brian Elder) round choices in 1995 Entry Draft, April 7, 1995. Traded to **Chicago** by **Washington** for Chicago's 3rd round choice (Dave Weninger) in 1996 Entry Draft, October 17, 1995. Traded to **Tampa Bay** by **Chicago** with Patrick Poulin and Chicago's 2nd round choice (later traded to New Jersey – New Jersey selected Pierre Dagenais) in 1996 Entry Draft for Enrico Ciccone and Tampa Bay's 2nd round choice (Jeff Paul) in 1996 Entry Draft, March 20, 1996. Traded to **Montreal** by **Tampa Bay** with Patrick Poulin and Mick Vukota for Stephane Richer, Darcy Tucker and David Wilkie, January 15, 1998. Traded to **Edmonton** by **Montreal** with Alain Nasreddine for Christian Laflamme and Matthieu Descoteaux, March 9, 2000. Signed as a free agent by **NY Rangers**, July 20, 2001. Traded to **Florida** by **NY Rangers** with Filip Novak, NY Rangers' 1st (later traded to Calgary – Calgary selected Eric Nystrom) and 2nd (Rob Globke) round choices in 2002 Entry Draft and NY Rangers' 4th round choice (later traded to Atlanta – Atlanta selected Guillaume Desbiens) in 2003 Entry Draft for Pavel Bure and Florida's 2nd round choice (Lee Falardeau) in 2002 Entry Draft, March 18, 2002.

ULLMAN, Norm

HHOF

Center. Shoots left. 5'10", 175 lbs. Born, Provost, Alta., December 26, 1935.

Season	Club	GP	G	A	Pts	PIM	GP	G	A	Pts	PIM
1955-56	Detroit Red Wings	66	9	9	18	26	10	1	3	4	13
1956-57	Detroit Red Wings	64	16	36	52	47	5	1	1	2	6
1957-58	Detroit Red Wings	69	23	28	51	38	4	0	2	2	4
1958-59	Detroit Red Wings	69	22	36	58	42	....	....	....	....	....
1959-60	Detroit Red Wings	70	24	34	58	46	6	2	2	4	0
1960-61	Detroit Red Wings	70	28	42	70	34	11	0	4	4	4
1961-62	Detroit Red Wings	70	26	38	64	54	....	....	....	....	....
1962-63	Detroit Red Wings	70	26	30	56	53	11	4	*12	*16	14
1963-64	Detroit Red Wings	61	21	30	51	55	14	7	10	17	6
1964-65	Detroit Red Wings	70	*42	41	83	70	7	6	4	10	2
1965-66	Detroit Red Wings	70	31	41	72	35	12	*6	9	*15	12
1966-67	Detroit Red Wings	68	26	44	70	26	....	....	....	....	....
1967-68	Detroit Red Wings	58	30	25	55	26	....	....	....	....	....
	Toronto Maple Leafs	13	5	12	17	2	....	....	....	....	....
1968-69	Toronto Maple Leafs	75	35	42	77	41	4	1	0	1	0
1969-70	Toronto Maple Leafs	74	18	42	60	37	....	....	....	....	....
1970-71	Toronto Maple Leafs	73	34	51	85	24	6	0	2	2	2
1971-72	Toronto Maple Leafs	77	23	50	73	26	5	1	3	4	2
1972-73	Toronto Maple Leafs	65	20	35	55	10	....	....	....	....	....
1973-74	Toronto Maple Leafs	78	22	47	69	12	4	1	1	2	0
1974-75	Toronto Maple Leafs	80	9	26	35	8	7	0	0	0	2
	NHL Totals	**1410**	**490**	**739**	**1229**	**712**	**106**	**30**	**53**	**83**	**67**

NHL First All-Star Team (1965) • NHL Second All-Star Team (1967)

Played in NHL All-Star Game (1955, 1960, 1961, 1962, 1963, 1964, 1965, 1967, 1968, 1969, 1974)

Traded to **Toronto** by **Detroit** with Floyd Smith, Paul Henderson and Doug Barrie for Frank Mahovlich, Pete Stemkowski, Garry Unger and the rights to Carl Brewer, March 3, 1968.

ULMER, Jeff

Right wing. Shoots right. 5'11", 195 lbs. Born, Wilcox, Sask., April 27, 1977.

Season	Club	GP	G	A	Pts	PIM	GP	G	A	Pts	PIM
2000-01	New York Rangers	21	3	0	3	8	....	....	....	....	....
	NHL Totals	**21**	**3**	**0**	**3**	**8**	....	....	....	....	....

Signed as a free agent by **NY Rangers**, July 27, 2000. Traded to **Ottawa** by **NY Rangers** with Jason Doig for Sean Gagnon, June 29, 2001.

UNGER, Garry

Center. Shoots left. 5'11", 170 lbs. Born, Calgary, Alta., December 7, 1947.

Season	Club	GP	G	A	Pts	PIM	GP	G	A	Pts	PIM
1967-68	Toronto Maple Leafs	15	1	1	2	4	....	....	....	....	....
	Detroit Red Wings	13	5	10	15	2	....	....	....	....	....
1968-69	Detroit Red Wings	76	24	20	44	33	....	....	....	....	....
1969-70	Detroit Red Wings	76	42	24	66	67	4	0	1	1	6
1970-71	Detroit Red Wings	51	13	14	27	63	....	....	....	....	....
	St. Louis Blues	28	15	14	29	41	6	3	2	5	20
1971-72	St. Louis Blues	78	36	34	70	104	11	4	5	9	35
1972-73	St. Louis Blues	78	41	39	80	119	5	1	2	3	2
1973-74	St. Louis Blues	78	33	35	68	96	....	....	....	....	....
1974-75	St. Louis Blues	80	36	44	80	123	2	1	3	4	6
1975-76	St. Louis Blues	80	39	44	83	95	3	2	1	3	7
1976-77	St. Louis Blues	80	30	27	57	56	4	0	1	1	2
1977-78	St. Louis Blues	80	32	20	52	66	....	....	....	....	....
1978-79	St. Louis Blues	80	30	26	56	44	....	....	....	....	....
1979-80	Atlanta Flames	79	17	16	33	39	4	0	3	3	2
1980-81	Los Angeles Kings	58	10	10	20	40	....	....	....	....	....
	Edmonton Oilers	13	0	0	0	6	8	0	0	0	2
1981-82	Edmonton Oilers	46	7	13	20	69	4	1	0	1	23
1982-83	Edmonton Oilers	16	2	0	2	8	1	0	0	0	0
	NHL Totals	**1105**	**413**	**391**	**804**	**1075**	**52**	**12**	**18**	**30**	**105**

Played in NHL All-Star Game (1972, 1973, 1974, 1975, 1976, 1977, 1978)

Traded to **Detroit** by **Toronto** with Frank Mahovlich, Pete Stemkowski and the rights to Carl Brewer for Norm Ullman, Paul Henderson, Floyd Smith and Doug Barrie, March 3, 1968. Traded to **St. Louis** by **Detroit** with Wayne Connelly for Red Berenson and Tim Ecclestone, February 6, 1971. Traded to **Atlanta** by **St. Louis** for Ed Kea, Don Laurence and Atlanta's 2nd round choice (Hakan Nordin) in 1981 Entry Draft, October 10, 1979. Transferred to **Calgary** after **Atlanta** franchise relocated, June 24, 1980. Traded to **Los Angeles** by **Calgary** for Bert Wilson and Randy Holt, June 6, 1980. Traded to **Edmonton** by **Los Angeles** for Edmonton's 7th round choice (Craig Hurley) in 1981 Entry Draft, March 10, 1981.

UPSHALL, Scottie

Right wing. Shoots left. 6', 184 lbs. Born, Fort McMurray, Alta., October 7, 1983.
(Nashville's 1st choice, 6th overall, in 2002 Entry Draft).

Season	Club	GP	G	A	Pts	PIM	GP	G	A	Pts	PIM
2002-03	Nashville Predators	8	1	0	1	0	....	....	....	....	....
	NHL Totals	**8**	**1**	**0**	**1**	**0**	....	....	....	....	....

USTORF, Stefan

Center. Shoots left. 6', 195 lbs. Born, Kaufbeuren, West Germany, January 3, 1974.
(Washington's 3rd choice, 53rd overall, in 1992 Entry Draft).

Season	Club	GP	G	A	Pts	PIM	GP	G	A	Pts	PIM
1995-96	Washington Capitals	48	7	10	17	14	5	0	0	0	0
1996-97	Washington Capitals	6	0	0	0	2	....	....	....	....	....
	NHL Totals	**54**	**7**	**10**	**17**	**16**	**5**	**0**	**0**	**0**	**0**

Signed as a free agent by **Washington**, July 13, 2000.

VAANANEN, Ossi

Defense. Shoots left. 6'4", 215 lbs. Born, Vantaa, Finland, August 18, 1980.
(Phoenix's 2nd choice, 43rd overall, in 1998 Entry Draft).

Season	Club	GP	G	A	Pts	PIM	GP	G	A	Pts	PIM
2000-01	Phoenix Coyotes	81	4	12	16	90	....	....	....	....	....
2001-02	Phoenix Coyotes	76	2	12	14	74	5	0	0	0	6
2002-03	Phoenix Coyotes	67	2	7	9	82	....	....	....	....	....
	NHL Totals	**224**	**8**	**31**	**39**	**246**	**5**	**0**	**0**	**0**	**6**

VACHON, Nick

Center. Shoots left. 5'10", 185 lbs. Born, Montreal, Que., July 20, 1972.
(Toronto's 11th choice, 241st overall, in 1990 Entry Draft).

Season	Club	GP	G	A	Pts	PIM	GP	G	A	Pts	PIM
1996-97	New York Islanders	1	0	0	0	0	....	....	....	....	....
	NHL Totals	**1**	**0**	**0**	**0**	**0**	....	....	....	....	....

• Son of Rogie

Signed as a free agent by **Los Angeles**, September 12, 1995. Traded to **NY Islanders** by **Los Angeles** for Chris Marinucci, November 19, 1996.

VADNAIS, Carol

Defense. Shoots left. 6'1", 185 lbs. Born, Montreal, Que., September 25, 1945.

Season	Club	GP	G	A	Pts	PIM	GP	G	A	Pts	PIM
1966-67	Montreal Canadiens	11	0	3	3	35	1	0	0	0	2
1967-68 ♦	Montreal Canadiens	31	1	1	2	31	1	0	0	0	0
1968-69	Oakland Seals	76	15	27	42	151	7	1	4	5	10
1969-70	Oakland Seals	76	24	20	44	212	4	2	1	3	15

Season	Club	GP	G	A	Pts	PIM	GP	G	A	Pts	PIM
		REGULAR SEASON					PLAYOFFS				
1970-71	California Seals	42	10	16	26	91	....	....	....	....	....
1971-72	California Golden Seals	52	14	20	34	106	....	....	....	....	....
	♦ Boston Bruins	16	4	6	10	37	15	0	2	2	43
1972-73	Boston Bruins	78	7	24	31	127	5	0	0	0	8
1973-74	Boston Bruins	78	16	43	59	123	16	1	12	13	42
1974-75	Boston Bruins	79	18	56	74	129	3	1	5	6	0
1975-76	Boston Bruins	12	2	5	7	17	....	....	....	....	....
	New York Rangers	64	20	30	50	104	....	....	....	....	....
1976-77	New York Rangers	74	11	37	48	131	....	....	....	....	....
1977-78	New York Rangers	80	6	40	46	115	3	0	2	2	16
1978-79	New York Rangers	77	8	37	45	86	18	2	9	11	13
1979-80	New York Rangers	66	3	20	23	118	9	1	2	3	6
1980-81	New York Rangers	74	3	20	23	91	14	1	3	4	26
1981-82	New York Rangers	50	5	6	11	45	10	1	0	1	4
1982-83	New Jersey Devils	51	2	7	9	64	....	....	....	....	....
	NHL Totals	**1087**	**169**	**418**	**587**	**1813**	**106**	**10**	**40**	**50**	**185**

Played in NHL All-Star Game (1969, 1970, 1972, 1975, 1976, 1978)

Claimed by **Oakland** from **Montreal** in Intra-League Draft, June 12, 1968. Traded to **Boston** by **California** with Don O'Donoghue for Reggie Leach, Rick Smith and Bob Stewart, February 23, 1972. Traded to **NY Rangers** by **Boston** with Phil Esposito for Brad Park, Jean Ratelle and Joe Zanussi, November 7, 1975. Claimed by **New Jersey** from **NY Rangers** in Waiver Draft, October 4, 1982.

VAIC, Lubomir

Center. Shoots left. 5'9", 178 lbs. Born, Spisska Nova Ves, Czech., March 6, 1977.
(Vancouver's 8th choice, 227th overall, in 1996 Entry Draft).

Season	Club	GP	G	A	Pts	PIM	GP	G	A	Pts	PIM
1997-98	Vancouver Canucks	5	1	1	2	2	....	....	....	....	....
99-2000	Vancouver Canucks	4	0	0	0	0	....	....	....	....	....
	NHL Totals	**9**	**1**	**1**	**2**	**2**	....	....	....	....	....

VAIL, Eric

Left wing. Shoots left. 6'1", 220 lbs. Born, Timmins, Ont., September 16, 1953.
(Atlanta's 3rd choice, 21st overall, in 1973 Amateur Draft).

Season	Club	GP	G	A	Pts	PIM	GP	G	A	Pts	PIM
1973-74	Atlanta Flames	23	2	9	11	30	1	0	0	0	2
1974-75	Atlanta Flames	72	39	21	60	46	....	....	....	....	....
1975-76	Atlanta Flames	60	16	31	47	34	2	0	0	0	0
1976-77	Atlanta Flames	78	32	39	71	22	3	1	3	4	0
1977-78	Atlanta Flames	79	22	36	58	16	2	1	1	2	0
1978-79	Atlanta Flames	80	35	48	83	53	2	0	1	1	2
1979-80	Atlanta Flames	77	28	25	53	22	4	3	1	4	2
1980-81	Calgary Flames	64	28	36	64	23	6	0	0	0	0
1981-82	Calgary Flames	6	4	1	5	0	....	....	....	....	....
	Detroit Red Wings	52	10	14	24	35	....	....	....	....	....
	NHL Totals	**591**	**216**	**260**	**476**	**281**	**20**	**5**	**6**	**11**	**6**

Calder Memorial Trophy (1975)

Played in NHL All-Star Game (1977)

Transferred to **Calgary** after **Atlanta** franchise relocated, June 24, 1980. Traded to **Detroit** by **Calgary** for Gary McAdam and Detroit's 4th round choice (John Bekkers) in 1983 Entry Draft, November 10, 1981.

VAIL, Sparky

Defense/Left wing. Shoots left. 6', 185 lbs. Born, Meaford, Ont., July 5, 1906.

Season	Club	GP	G	A	Pts	PIM	GP	G	A	Pts	PIM
1928-29	New York Rangers	18	3	0	3	16	6	0	0	0	2
1929-30	New York Rangers	32	1	1	2	2	4	0	0	0	0
	NHL Totals	**50**	**4**	**1**	**5**	**18**	**10**	**0**	**0**	**0**	**2**

Signed as a free agent by **NY Rangers**, September 2, 1926. Traded to **Providence** (Can-Am) by **NY Rangers** for cash, October 27, 1930. Traded to **Detroit** (Detroit-IHL) by **Providence** (Can-Am) for Frank Peters, October 30, 1933.

VAIVE, Rick

Right wing. Shoots right. 6'1", 198 lbs. Born, Ottawa, Ont., May 14, 1959.
(Vancouver's 1st choice, 5th overall, in 1979 Entry Draft).

Season	Club	GP	G	A	Pts	PIM	GP	G	A	Pts	PIM
1979-80	Vancouver Canucks	47	13	8	21	111	....	....	....	....	....
	Toronto Maple Leafs	22	9	7	16	77	3	1	0	1	11
1980-81	Toronto Maple Leafs	75	33	29	62	229	3	1	0	1	4
1981-82	Toronto Maple Leafs	77	54	35	89	157	....	....	....	....	....
1982-83	Toronto Maple Leafs	78	51	28	79	105	4	2	5	7	6
1983-84	Toronto Maple Leafs	76	52	41	93	114	....	....	....	....	....
1984-85	Toronto Maple Leafs	72	35	33	68	112	....	....	....	....	....
1985-86	Toronto Maple Leafs	61	33	31	64	85	9	6	2	8	9
1986-87	Toronto Maple Leafs	73	32	34	66	61	13	4	2	6	23
1987-88	Chicago Blackhawks	76	43	26	69	108	5	6	2	8	38
1988-89	Chicago Blackhawks	30	12	13	25	60	....	....	....	....	....
	Buffalo Sabres	28	19	13	32	64	5	2	1	3	8
1989-90	Buffalo Sabres	70	29	19	48	74	6	4	2	6	6
1990-91	Buffalo Sabres	71	25	27	52	74	6	1	2	3	6
1991-92	Buffalo Sabres	20	1	3	4	14	....	....	....	....	....
	NHL Totals	**876**	**441**	**347**	**788**	**1445**	**54**	**27**	**16**	**43**	**111**

Played in NHL All-Star Game (1982, 1983, 1984)

Traded to **Toronto** by **Vancouver** with Bill Derlago for Tiger Williams and Jerry Butler, February 18, 1980. Traded to **Chicago** by **Toronto** with Steve Thomas and Bob McGill for Al Secord and Ed Olczyk, September 3, 1987. Traded to **Buffalo** by **Chicago** for Adam Creighton, December 26, 1988. Signed as a free agent by **Vancouver**, September 2, 1992.

VALENTINE, Chris

Center. Shoots right. 6', 190 lbs. Born, Belleville, Ont., December 6, 1961.
(Washington's 10th choice, 194th overall, in 1981 Entry Draft).

Season	Club	GP	G	A	Pts	PIM	GP	G	A	Pts	PIM
1981-82	Washington Capitals	60	30	37	67	92	....	....	....	....	....
1982-83	Washington Capitals	23	7	10	17	14	2	0	0	0	4
1983-84	Washington Capitals	22	6	5	11	21	....	....	....	....	....
	NHL Totals	**105**	**43**	**52**	**95**	**127**	**2**	**0**	**0**	**0**	**4**

VALICEVIC, Rob

Right wing. Shoots right. 6'1", 198 lbs. Born, Detroit, MI, January 6, 1971.
(NY Islanders' 6th choice, 114th overall, in 1991 Entry Draft).

Season	Club	GP	G	A	Pts	PIM	GP	G	A	Pts	PIM
1998-99	Nashville Predators	19	4	2	6	2	....	....	....	....	....
99-2000	Nashville Predators	80	14	11	25	21	....	....	....	....	....
2000-01	Nashville Predators	60	8	6	14	26	....	....	....	....	....
2001-02	Los Angeles Kings	17	1	1	2	8	....	....	....	....	....
2002-03	Mighty Ducks of Anaheim	10	1	0	1	2	....	....	....	....	....
	NHL Totals	**186**	**28**	**20**	**48**	**59**	....	....	....	....	....

Signed as a free agent by **Nashville**, May 28, 1998. Signed as a free agent by **Los Angeles**, August 16, 2001. Signed as a free agent by **Anaheim**, July 24, 2002.

VALIQUETTE, Jack

Center. Shoots left. 6'2", 195 lbs. Born, St. Thomas, Ont., March 18, 1954.
(Toronto's 1st choice, 13th overall, in 1974 Amateur Draft).

Season	Club	GP	G	A	Pts	PIM	GP	G	A	Pts	PIM
1974-75	Toronto Maple Leafs	1	0	0	0	0	....	....	....	....	....
1975-76	Toronto Maple Leafs	45	10	23	33	30	10	2	3	5	2
1976-77	Toronto Maple Leafs	66	15	30	45	7	....	....	....	....	....
1977-78	Toronto Maple Leafs	60	8	13	21	15	13	1	3	4	2
1978-79	Colorado Rockies	76	23	34	57	12	....	....	....	....	....
1979-80	Colorado Rockies	77	25	25	50	8	....	....	....	....	....
1980-81	Colorado Rockies	25	3	9	12	7	....	....	....	....	....
	NHL Totals	**350**	**84**	**134**	**218**	**79**	**23**	**3**	**6**	**9**	**4**

Traded to **Colorado** by **Toronto** for Colorado's 2nd round choice (Gary Yaremchuk) in 1981 Entry Draft, October 19, 1978.

VALK, Garry

Right wing. Shoots left. 6'1", 200 lbs. Born, Edmonton, Alta., November 27, 1967.
(Vancouver's 5th choice, 108th overall, in 1987 Entry Draft).

Season	Club	GP	G	A	Pts	PIM	GP	G	A	Pts	PIM
1990-91	Vancouver Canucks	59	10	11	21	67	5	0	0	0	20
1991-92	Vancouver Canucks	65	8	17	25	56	4	0	0	0	5
1992-93	Vancouver Canucks	48	6	7	13	77	7	0	1	1	12
1993-94	Mighty Ducks of Anaheim	78	18	27	45	100	....	....	....	....	....
1994-95	Mighty Ducks of Anaheim	36	3	6	9	34	....	....	....	....	....
1995-96	Mighty Ducks of Anaheim	79	12	12	24	125	....	....	....	....	....
1996-97	Mighty Ducks of Anaheim	53	7	7	14	53	....	....	....	....	....
	Pittsburgh Penguins	17	3	4	7	25	....	....	....	....	....
1997-98	Pittsburgh Penguins	39	2	1	3	33	....	....	....	....	....
1998-99	Toronto Maple Leafs	77	8	21	29	53	17	3	4	7	22
99-2000	Toronto Maple Leafs	73	10	14	24	44	12	1	2	3	14
2000-01	Toronto Maple Leafs	74	8	18	26	46	5	1	0	1	2
2001-02	Toronto Maple Leafs	63	5	10	15	28	11	1	0	1	4
2002-03	Chicago Blackhawks	16	0	1	1	6	....	....	....	....	....
	NHL Totals	**777**	**100**	**156**	**256**	**747**	**61**	**6**	**7**	**13**	**79**

Claimed by **Anaheim** from **Vancouver** in Waiver Draft, October 3, 1993. Traded to **Pittsburgh** by **Anaheim** for J.J. Daigneault, February 21, 1997. Signed as a free agent by **Toronto**, October 8, 1998. Signed as a free agent by **Chicago**, October 9, 2002. • Spent majority of 2002-03 season as a healthy reserve.

VALLIS, Lindsay

Defense. Shoots right. 6'3", 207 lbs. Born, Winnipeg, Man., January 12, 1971.
(Montreal's 1st choice, 13th overall, in 1989 Entry Draft).

Season	Club	GP	G	A	Pts	PIM	GP	G	A	Pts	PIM
1993-94	Montreal Canadiens	1	0	0	0	0	....	....	....	....	....
	NHL Totals	**1**	**0**	**0**	**0**	**0**	....	....	....	....	....

VAN ALLEN, Shaun

Center. Shoots left. 6'1", 205 lbs. Born, Calgary, Alta., August 29, 1967.
(Edmonton's 5th choice, 105th overall, in 1987 Entry Draft).

Season	Club	GP	G	A	Pts	PIM	GP	G	A	Pts	PIM
1990-91	Edmonton Oilers	2	0	0	0	0	....	....	....	....	....
1992-93	Edmonton Oilers	21	1	4	5	6	....	....	....	....	....
1993-94	Mighty Ducks of Anaheim	80	8	25	33	64	....	....	....	....	....
1994-95	Mighty Ducks of Anaheim	45	8	21	29	32	....	....	....	....	....
1995-96	Mighty Ducks of Anaheim	49	8	17	25	41	....	....	....	....	....
1996-97	Ottawa Senators	80	11	14	25	35	7	0	1	1	4
1997-98	Ottawa Senators	80	4	15	19	48	11	0	1	1	10
1998-99	Ottawa Senators	79	6	11	17	30	4	0	0	0	0
99-2000	Ottawa Senators	75	9	19	28	37	6	0	1	1	9
2000-01	Dallas Stars	59	7	16	23	16	8	0	2	2	8
2001-02	Dallas Stars	19	2	4	6	6	....	....	....	....	....
	Montreal Canadiens	54	6	9	15	20	7	0	1	1	2
2002-03	Ottawa Senators	78	12	20	32	66	18	1	1	2	12
	NHL Totals	**721**	**82**	**175**	**257**	**401**	**61**	**1**	**7**	**8**	**45**

Signed as a free agent by **Anaheim**, July 22, 1993. Traded to **Ottawa** by **Anaheim** with Jason York for Ted Drury and the rights to Marc Moro, October 1, 1996. Signed as a free agent by **Dallas**, July 12, 2000. Traded to **Montreal** by **Dallas** with Donald Audette for Martin Rucinsky and Benoit Brunet, November 21, 2001. Signed as a free agent by **Ottawa**, July 24, 2002.

VAN BOXMEER, John

Defense. Shoots right. 6', 190 lbs. Born, Petrolia, Ont., November 20, 1952.
(Montreal's 4th choice, 14th overall, in 1972 Amateur Draft).

Season	Club	Regular Season GP	G	A	Pts	PIM	Playoffs GP	G	A	Pts	PIM
1973-74	Montreal Canadiens	20	1	4	5	18	1	0	0	0	0
1974-75	Montreal Canadiens	9	0	2	2	0	....	....	....	....	....
1975-76 ♦	Montreal Canadiens	46	6	11	17	31	....	....	....	....	....
1976-77	Montreal Canadiens	4	0	1	1	0	....	....	....	....	....
	Colorado Rockies	41	2	11	13	32	....	....	....	....	....
1977-78	Colorado Rockies	80	12	42	54	87	2	0	1	1	2
1978-79	Colorado Rockies	76	9	34	43	46	....	....	....	....	....
1979-80	Buffalo Sabres	80	11	40	51	55	14	3	5	8	12
1980-81	Buffalo Sabres	80	18	51	69	69	8	1	8	9	7
1981-82	Buffalo Sabres	69	14	54	68	62	4	0	1	1	6
1982-83	Buffalo Sabres	65	6	21	27	53	9	1	0	1	10
1983-84	Quebec Nordiques	18	5	3	8	12	....	....	....	....	....
	NHL Totals	**588**	**84**	**274**	**358**	**465**	**38**	**5**	**15**	**20**	**37**

Traded to **Colorado** by **Montreal** for Colorado's 3rd round choice (Craig Levie) in 1979 Entry Draft and cash, November 24, 1976. Traded to **Buffalo** by **Colorado** for Rene Robert, October 5, 1979. Claimed by **Quebec** from **Buffalo** in Waiver Draft, October 3, 1983.

VANDENBUSSCHE, Ryan

Right wing. Shoots right. 6', 200 lbs. Born, Simcoe, Ont., February 28, 1973.
(Toronto's 9th choice, 173rd overall, in 1992 Entry Draft).

Season	Club	Regular Season GP	G	A	Pts	PIM	Playoffs GP	G	A	Pts	PIM
1996-97	New York Rangers	11	1	0	1	30	....	....	....	....	....
1997-98	New York Rangers	16	1	0	1	38	....	....	....	....	....
	Chicago Blackhawks	4	0	1	1	5	....	....	....	....	....
1998-99	Chicago Blackhawks	6	0	0	0	17	....	....	....	....	....
99-2000	Chicago Blackhawks	52	0	1	1	143	....	....	....	....	....
2000-01	Chicago Blackhawks	64	2	5	7	146	....	....	....	....	....
2001-02	Chicago Blackhawks	50	1	2	3	103	1	0	0	0	0
2002-03	Chicago Blackhawks	22	0	0	0	58	....	....	....	....	....
	NHL Totals	**225**	**5**	**9**	**14**	**540**	**1**	**0**	**0**	**0**	**0**

Signed as a free agent by **NY Rangers**, August 22, 1995. Traded to **Chicago** by **NY Rangers** for Ryan Risidore, March 24, 1998. • Missed majority of 2002-03 season recovering from hand injury suffered in game vs. Detroit, January 5, 2003.

VANDERMEER, Jim

Defense. Shoots left. 6'1", 208 lbs. Born, Caroline, Alta., February 21, 1980.

Season	Club	Regular Season GP	G	A	Pts	PIM	Playoffs GP	G	A	Pts	PIM
2002-03	Philadelphia Flyers	24	2	1	3	27	8	0	1	1	9
	NHL Totals	**24**	**2**	**1**	**3**	**27**	**8**	**0**	**1**	**1**	**9**

Signed as a free agent by **Philadelphia**, December 21, 2000.

VAN DORP, Wayne

Left wing. Shoots left. 6'4", 225 lbs. Born, Vancouver, B.C., May 19, 1961.

Season	Club	Regular Season GP	G	A	Pts	PIM	Playoffs GP	G	A	Pts	PIM
1986-87	Edmonton Oilers	3	0	0	0	25	3	0	0	0	2
1987-88	Pittsburgh Penguins	25	1	3	4	75	....	....	....	....	....
1988-89	Chicago Blackhawks	8	0	0	0	23	16	0	1	1	17
1989-90	Chicago Blackhawks	61	7	4	11	303	8	0	0	0	23
1990-91	Quebec Nordiques	4	1	0	1	30	....	....	....	....	....
1991-92	Quebec Nordiques	24	3	5	8	109	....	....	....	....	....
	NHL Totals	**125**	**12**	**12**	**24**	**565**	**27**	**0**	**1**	**1**	**42**

Signed as a free agent by **Buffalo**, October, 1986. Traded to **Edmonton** by **Buffalo** with Normand Lacombe and Buffalo's 4th round choice (Peter Eriksson) in 1987 Entry Draft for Lee Fogolin, Mark Napier and Edmonton's 4th round choice (John Bradley) in 1987 Entry Draft, March 6, 1987. Traded to **Pittsburgh** by **Edmonton** with Paul Coffey and Dave Hunter for Craig Simpson, Dave Hannan, Moe Mantha and Chris Joseph, November 24, 1987. Traded to **Buffalo** by **Pittsburgh** for future considerations, September 30, 1988. Traded to **Chicago** by **Buffalo** for Chicago's 7th round choice (Viktor Gordiouk) in 1990 Entry Draft, February 16, 1989. Claimed by **Quebec** from **Chicago** in Waiver Draft, October 1, 1990. • Missed remainder of 1990-91 season recovering from shoulder injury originally suffered in training camp and re-injured in game vs. Hartford, November 21, 1990.

VAN DRUNEN, David

Defense. Shoots right. 6', 204 lbs. Born, Sherwood Park, Alta., January 31, 1976.

Season	Club	Regular Season GP	G	A	Pts	PIM	Playoffs GP	G	A	Pts	PIM
99-2000	Ottawa Senators	1	0	0	0	0	....	....	....	....	....
	NHL Totals	**1**	**0**	**0**	**0**	**0**	....	....	....	....	....

Signed as a free agent by **Ottawa**, May 2, 1997.

VAN IMPE, Darren

Defense. Shoots left. 6'1", 205 lbs. Born, Saskatoon, Sask., May 18, 1973.
(NY Islanders' 7th choice, 170th overall, in 1993 Entry Draft).

Season	Club	Regular Season GP	G	A	Pts	PIM	Playoffs GP	G	A	Pts	PIM
1994-95	Mighty Ducks of Anaheim	1	0	1	1	4	....	....	....	....	....
1995-96	Mighty Ducks of Anaheim	16	1	2	3	14	....	....	....	....	....
1996-97	Mighty Ducks of Anaheim	74	4	19	23	90	9	0	2	2	16
1997-98	Mighty Ducks of Anaheim	19	1	3	4	4	....	....	....	....	....
	Boston Bruins	50	2	8	10	36	6	2	1	3	0
1998-99	Boston Bruins	60	5	15	20	66	11	1	2	3	4
99-2000	Boston Bruins	79	5	23	28	73	....	....	....	....	....
2000-01	Boston Bruins	31	3	10	13	41	....	....	....	....	....
2001-02	New York Rangers	17	1	0	1	12	....	....	....	....	....
	Florida Panthers	36	1	6	7	31	....	....	....	....	....
	New York Islanders	14	1	2	3	16	7	0	4	4	8
2002-03	Columbus Blue Jackets	14	1	1	2	10	....	....	....	....	....
	NHL Totals	**411**	**25**	**90**	**115**	**397**	**33**	**3**	**9**	**12**	**28**

Traded to **Anaheim** by **NY Islanders** for Anaheim's 8th round choice (Mike Broda) in 1995 Entry Draft, August 31, 1994. Claimed on waivers by **Boston** from **Anaheim**, November 26, 1997. • Missed majority of 2000-01 season recovering from shoulder injury suffered in game vs. Detroit, December 23, 2000. Claimed on waivers by **NY Rangers** from **Boston**, August 7, 2001. Claimed on waivers by **Florida** from **NY Rangers**, December 18, 2001. Traded to **NY Islanders** by **Florida** for NY Islanders' 5th round choice (later traded to Los Angeles – Los Angeles selected Brady Murray) in 2003 Entry Draft, March 19, 2002. Signed as a free agent by **Columbus**, January 20, 2003.

VAN IMPE, Ed

Defense. Shoots left. 5'10", 205 lbs. Born, Saskatoon, Sask., May 27, 1940.

Season	Club	Regular Season GP	G	A	Pts	PIM	Playoffs GP	G	A	Pts	PIM
1966-67	Chicago Black Hawks	61	8	11	19	111	6	0	0	0	8
1967-68	Philadelphia Flyers	67	4	13	17	141	7	0	4	4	11
1968-69	Philadelphia Flyers	68	7	12	19	112	1	0	0	0	17
1969-70	Philadelphia Flyers	65	0	10	10	117	....	....	....	....	....
1970-71	Philadelphia Flyers	77	0	11	11	80	4	0	1	1	8
1971-72	Philadelphia Flyers	73	4	9	13	78	....	....	....	....	....
1972-73	Philadelphia Flyers	72	1	11	12	76	11	0	0	0	16
1973-74 ♦	Philadelphia Flyers	77	2	16	18	119	17	1	2	3	41
1974-75 ♦	Philadelphia Flyers	78	1	17	18	109	17	0	4	4	28
1975-76	Philadelphia Flyers	40	0	8	8	60	....	....	....	....	....
	Pittsburgh Penguins	12	0	5	5	16	3	0	1	1	2
1976-77	Pittsburgh Penguins	10	0	3	3	6	....	....	....	....	....
	NHL Totals	**700**	**27**	**126**	**153**	**1025**	**66**	**1**	**12**	**13**	**131**

Played in NHL All-Star Game (1969, 1974, 1975)

Claimed by **Philadelphia** from **Chicago** in Expansion Draft, June 6, 1967. Traded to **Pittsburgh** by **Philadelphia** with Bobby Taylor for Gary Inness and cash, March 9, 1976.

VAN RYN, Mike

Defense. Shoots right. 6'1", 190 lbs. Born, London, Ont., May 14, 1979.
(New Jersey's 1st choice, 26th overall, in 1998 Entry Draft).

Season	Club	Regular Season GP	G	A	Pts	PIM	Playoffs GP	G	A	Pts	PIM
2000-01	St. Louis Blues	1	0	0	0	0	....	....	....	....	....
2001-02	St. Louis Blues	48	2	8	10	18	9	0	0	0	0
2002-03	St. Louis Blues	20	0	3	3	8	....	....	....	....	....
	NHL Totals	**69**	**2**	**11**	**13**	**26**	**9**	**0**	**0**	**0**	**0**

Signed as a free agent by **St. Louis**, June 30, 2000. • Missed majority of 2000-01 season recovering from shoulder injury suffered in game vs. Phoenix, October 5, 2000. Traded to **Florida** by **St. Louis** for Valeri Bure and future considerations, March 11, 2003.

VARADA, Vaclav

Right wing. Shoots left. 6', 208 lbs. Born, Vsetin, Czech., April 26, 1976.
(San Jose's 4th choice, 89th overall, in 1994 Entry Draft).

Season	Club	Regular Season GP	G	A	Pts	PIM	Playoffs GP	G	A	Pts	PIM
1995-96	Buffalo Sabres	1	0	0	0	0	....	....	....	....	....
1996-97	Buffalo Sabres	5	0	0	0	2	....	....	....	....	....
1997-98	Buffalo Sabres	27	5	6	11	15	15	3	4	7	18
1998-99	Buffalo Sabres	72	7	24	31	61	21	5	4	9	14
99-2000	Buffalo Sabres	76	10	27	37	62	5	0	0	0	8
2000-01	Buffalo Sabres	75	10	21	31	81	13	0	4	4	8
2001-02	Buffalo Sabres	76	7	16	23	82	....	....	....	....	....
2002-03	Buffalo Sabres	44	7	4	11	23	....	....	....	....	....
	Ottawa Senators	11	2	6	8	8	18	2	4	6	18
	NHL Totals	**387**	**48**	**104**	**152**	**334**	**72**	**10**	**16**	**26**	**66**

Traded to **Buffalo** by **San Jose** with Martin Spahnel and Philadelphia's 1st (previously acquired, later traded to Phoenix – Phoenix selected Daniel Briere) and 4th (previously acquired, Buffalo selected Mike Martone) round choices in 1996 Entry Draft for Doug Bodger, November 16, 1995. Traded to **Ottawa** by **Buffalo** with Buffalo's 5th round choice (Tim Cook) in 2003 Entry Draft for Jakub Klepis, February 25, 2003.

VARIS, Petri

Left wing. Shoots left. 6'1", 200 lbs. Born, Varkaus, Finland, May 13, 1969.
(San Jose's 7th choice, 132nd overall, in 1993 Entry Draft).

Season	Club	Regular Season GP	G	A	Pts	PIM	Playoffs GP	G	A	Pts	PIM
1997-98	Chicago Blackhawks	1	0	0	0	0	....	....	....	....	....
	NHL Totals	**1**	**0**	**0**	**0**	**0**	....	....	....	....	....

Rights traded to **Chicago** by **San Jose** with San Jose's 6th round choice (Jari Viuhkola) in 1998 Entry Draft for Murray Craven, July 25, 1997.

VARLAMOV, Sergei

Left wing. Shoots left. 5'11", 195 lbs. Born, Kiev, USSR, July 21, 1978.

Season	Club	Regular Season GP	G	A	Pts	PIM	Playoffs GP	G	A	Pts	PIM
1997-98	Calgary Flames	1	0	0	0	0	....	....	....	....	....
99-2000	Calgary Flames	7	3	0	3	0	....	....	....	....	....
2001-02	St. Louis Blues	52	5	7	12	26	1	0	0	0	2
2002-03	St. Louis Blues	3	0	0	0	0	....	....	....	....	....
	NHL Totals	**63**	**8**	**7**	**15**	**26**	**1**	**0**	**0**	**0**	**2**

Signed as a free agent by **Calgary**, September 18, 1996. Traded to **St. Louis** by **Calgary** with Fred Brathwaite, Daniel Tkaczuk and Calgary's 9th round choice (Grant Jacobsen) in 2001 Entry Draft for Roman Turek and St. Louis' 4th round choice (Yegor Shastin) in 2001 Entry Draft, June 23, 2001.

VARVIO, Jarkko

Right wing. Shoots right. 5'9", 175 lbs. Born, Tampere, Finland, April 28, 1972.
(Minnesota's 1st choice, 34th overall, in 1992 Entry Draft).

Season	Club	Regular Season GP	G	A	Pts	PIM	Playoffs GP	G	A	Pts	PIM
1993-94	Dallas Stars	8	2	3	5	4	....	....	....	....	....

Season	Club	REGULAR SEASON GP	G	A	Pts	PIM	PLAYOFFS GP	G	A	Pts	PIM
1994-95	Dallas Stars	5	1	1	2	0	....	....	....	....	....
	NHL Totals	**13**	**3**	**4**	**7**	**4**	....	....	....	....	....

Rights transferred to **Dallas** after **Minnesota** franchise relocated, June 9, 1993.

VASICEK, Josef

Center. Shoots left. 6'4", 200 lbs. Born, Havlickuv Brod, Czech., September 12, 1980.
(Carolina's 4th choice, 91st overall, in 1998 Entry Draft).

Season	Club	REGULAR SEASON GP	G	A	Pts	PIM	PLAYOFFS GP	G	A	Pts	PIM
2000-01	Carolina Hurricanes	76	8	13	21	53	6	2	0	2	0
2001-02	Carolina Hurricanes	78	14	17	31	53	23	3	2	5	12
2002-03	Carolina Hurricanes	57	10	10	20	33	....	....	....	....	....
	NHL Totals	**211**	**32**	**40**	**72**	**139**	**29**	**5**	**2**	**7**	**12**

VASILEVSKI, Alexander

Right wing. Shoots left. 5'11", 190 lbs. Born, Kiev, USSR, January 8, 1975.
(St. Louis' 9th choice, 271st overall, in 1993 Entry Draft).

Season	Club	REGULAR SEASON GP	G	A	Pts	PIM	PLAYOFFS GP	G	A	Pts	PIM
1995-96	St. Louis Blues	1	0	0	0	0	....	....	....	....	....
1996-97	St. Louis Blues	3	0	0	0	2	....	....	....	....	....
	NHL Totals	**4**	**0**	**0**	**0**	**2**	....	....	....	....	....

VASILIEV, Alexei

Defense. Shoots left. 6'1", 192 lbs. Born, Yaroslavl, USSR, September 1, 1977.
(NY Rangers' 4th choice, 110th overall, in 1995 Entry Draft).

Season	Club	REGULAR SEASON GP	G	A	Pts	PIM	PLAYOFFS GP	G	A	Pts	PIM
99-2000	New York Rangers	1	0	0	0	2	....	....	....	....	....
	NHL Totals	**1**	**0**	**0**	**0**	**2**	....	....	....	....	....

Traded to **Nashville** by **NY Rangers** for future considerations, September 25, 2000.

VASILJEVS, Herbert

Right wing. Shoots right. 5'11", 180 lbs. Born, Riga, Latvia, May 27, 1976.

Season	Club	REGULAR SEASON GP	G	A	Pts	PIM	PLAYOFFS GP	G	A	Pts	PIM
1998-99	Florida Panthers	5	0	0	0	2	....	....	....	....	....
99-2000	Atlanta Thrashers	7	1	0	1	4	....	....	....	....	....
2000-01	Atlanta Thrashers	21	4	5	9	14	....	....	....	....	....
2001-02	Vancouver Canucks	18	3	2	5	2	....	....	....	....	....
	NHL Totals	**51**	**8**	**7**	**15**	**22**	....	....	....	....	....

Signed as a free agent by **Florida**, October 3, 1996. Traded to **Atlanta** by **Florida** with Gord Murphy, Daniel Tjarnqvist and Ottawa's 6th round choice (previously acquired, later traded to Dallas – Dallas selected Justin Cox) in 1999 Entry Draft for Trevor Kidd, June 25, 1999. Signed as a free agent by **Vancouver**, August 11, 2001.

VASILYEV, Andrei

Left wing. Shoots right. 5'9", 180 lbs. Born, Voskresensk, USSR, March 30, 1972.
(NY Islanders' 11th choice, 248th overall, in 1992 Entry Draft).

Season	Club	REGULAR SEASON GP	G	A	Pts	PIM	PLAYOFFS GP	G	A	Pts	PIM
1994-95	New York Islanders	2	0	0	0	2	....	....	....	....	....
1995-96	New York Islanders	10	2	5	7	2	....	....	....	....	....
1996-97	New York Islanders	3	0	0	0	2	....	....	....	....	....
1998-99	Phoenix Coyotes	1	0	0	0	0	....	....	....	....	....
	NHL Totals	**16**	**2**	**5**	**7**	**6**	....	....	....	....	....

Signed as a free agent by **Phoenix**, August 26, 1998.

VASKE, Dennis

Defense. Shoots left. 6'2", 210 lbs. Born, Rockford, IL, October 11, 1967.
(NY Islanders' 2nd choice, 38th overall, in 1986 Entry Draft).

Season	Club	REGULAR SEASON GP	G	A	Pts	PIM	PLAYOFFS GP	G	A	Pts	PIM
1990-91	New York Islanders	5	0	0	0	2	....	....	....	....	....
1991-92	New York Islanders	39	0	1	1	39	....	....	....	....	....
1992-93	New York Islanders	27	1	5	6	32	18	0	6	6	14
1993-94	New York Islanders	65	2	11	13	76	4	0	1	1	2
1994-95	New York Islanders	41	1	11	12	53	....	....	....	....	....
1995-96	New York Islanders	19	1	6	7	21	....	....	....	....	....
1996-97	New York Islanders	17	0	4	4	12	....	....	....	....	....
1997-98	New York Islanders	19	0	3	3	12	....	....	....	....	....
1998-99	Boston Bruins	3	0	0	0	6	....	....	....	....	....
	NHL Totals	**235**	**5**	**41**	**46**	**253**	**22**	**0**	**7**	**7**	**16**

• Missed remainder of 1995-96 season recovering from head injury suffered in game vs. Los Angeles, November 22, 1995. • Missed majority of 1996-97 season recovering from head injury suffered in game vs. Washington, November 29, 1996. • Missed remainder of 1997-98 season recovering from head injury suffered in game vs. Buffalo, November 22, 1997. Signed as a free agent by **Boston**, September 10, 1998.

VASKO, Moose

Defense. Shoots left. 6'2", 200 lbs. Born, Duparquet, Que., December 11, 1935.

Season	Club	REGULAR SEASON GP	G	A	Pts	PIM	PLAYOFFS GP	G	A	Pts	PIM
1956-57	Chicago Black Hawks	64	3	12	15	31	....	....	....	....	....
1957-58	Chicago Black Hawks	59	6	20	26	51	....	....	....	....	....
1958-59	Chicago Black Hawks	63	6	10	16	52	6	0	1	1	4
1959-60	Chicago Black Hawks	69	3	27	30	110	4	0	0	0	0
1960-61 ♦	Chicago Black Hawks	63	4	18	22	40	12	1	1	2	23
1961-62	Chicago Black Hawks	64	2	22	24	87	12	0	0	0	4
1962-63	Chicago Black Hawks	64	4	9	13	70	6	0	1	1	8
1963-64	Chicago Black Hawks	70	2	18	20	65	7	0	0	0	4
1964-65	Chicago Black Hawks	69	1	10	11	56	14	1	2	3	20
1965-66	Chicago Black Hawks	56	1	7	8	44	3	0	0	0	4
1967-68	Minnesota North Stars	70	1	6	7	45	14	0	2	2	6
1968-69	Minnesota North Stars	72	1	7	8	68	....	....	....	....	....
1969-70	Minnesota North Stars	3	0	0	0	0	....	....	....	....	....
	NHL Totals	**786**	**34**	**166**	**200**	**719**	**78**	**2**	**7**	**9**	**73**

NHL Second All-Star Team (1963, 1964)
Played in NHL All-Star Game (1961, 1963, 1964, 1969)
Claimed by **Minnesota** from **Chicago** in Expansion Draft, June 6, 1967.

VASKO, Rick

Defense. Shoots left. 6', 185 lbs. Born, St. Catharines, Ont., January 12, 1957.
(Detroit's 2nd choice, 37th overall, in 1977 Amateur Draft).

Season	Club	REGULAR SEASON GP	G	A	Pts	PIM	PLAYOFFS GP	G	A	Pts	PIM
1977-78	Detroit Red Wings	3	0	0	0	7	....	....	....	....	....
1979-80	Detroit Red Wings	8	0	0	0	2	....	....	....	....	....
1980-81	Detroit Red Wings	20	3	7	10	20	....	....	....	....	....
	NHL Totals	**31**	**3**	**7**	**10**	**29**	....	....	....	....	....

Traded to **Calgary** by **Detroit** to complete transaction that sent Brad Smith to Detroit (February 24, 1981), May 28, 1981.

VAUTOUR, Yvon

Right wing. Shoots right. 6', 200 lbs. Born, St. John, N.B., September 10, 1956.
(NY Islanders' 6th choice, 104th overall, in 1976 Amateur Draft).

Season	Club	REGULAR SEASON GP	G	A	Pts	PIM	PLAYOFFS GP	G	A	Pts	PIM
1979-80	New York Islanders	17	3	1	4	24	....	....	....	....	....
1980-81	Colorado Rockies	74	15	19	34	143	....	....	....	....	....
1981-82	Colorado Rockies	14	1	2	3	18	....	....	....	....	....
1982-83	New Jersey Devils	52	4	7	11	136	....	....	....	....	....
1983-84	New Jersey Devils	42	3	4	7	78	....	....	....	....	....
1984-85	Quebec Nordiques	5	0	0	0	2	....	....	....	....	....
	NHL Totals	**204**	**26**	**33**	**59**	**401**	....	....	....	....	....

Claimed by **NY Islanders** as a fill-in during Expansion Draft, June 13, 1979. Claimed by **Colorado** from **NY Islanders** in Waiver Draft, October 8, 1980. Transferred to **New Jersey** after **Colorado** franchise relocated, June 30, 1982. Signed as a free agent by **Quebec**, October 18, 1984.

VAYDIK, Greg

Center. Shoots left. 6'1", 190 lbs. Born, Yellowknife, N.W.T., October 9, 1955.
(Chicago's 1st choice, 7th overall, in 1975 Amateur Draft).

Season	Club	REGULAR SEASON GP	G	A	Pts	PIM	PLAYOFFS GP	G	A	Pts	PIM
1976-77	Chicago Black Hawks	5	0	0	0	0	....	....	....	....	....
	NHL Totals	**5**	**0**	**0**	**0**	**0**	....	....	....	....	....

VEILLEUX, Stephane

Left wing. Shoots left. 6'1", 187 lbs. Born, Beaureville, Que., November 16, 1981.
(Minnesota's 4th choice, 93rd overall, in 2001 Entry Draft).

Season	Club	REGULAR SEASON GP	G	A	Pts	PIM	PLAYOFFS GP	G	A	Pts	PIM
2002-03	Minnesota Wild	38	3	2	5	23	....	....	....	....	....
	NHL Totals	**38**	**3**	**2**	**5**	**23**	....	....	....	....	....

VEITCH, Darren

Defense. Shoots right. 5'11", 195 lbs. Born, Saskatoon, Sask., April 24, 1960.
(Washington's 1st choice, 5th overall, in 1980 Entry Draft).

Season	Club	REGULAR SEASON GP	G	A	Pts	PIM	PLAYOFFS GP	G	A	Pts	PIM
1980-81	Washington Capitals	59	4	21	25	46	....	....	....	....	....
1981-82	Washington Capitals	67	9	44	53	54	....	....	....	....	....
1982-83	Washington Capitals	10	0	8	8	0	....	....	....	....	....
1983-84	Washington Capitals	46	6	18	24	17	5	0	1	1	15
1984-85	Washington Capitals	75	3	18	21	37	5	0	1	1	4
1985-86	Washington Capitals	62	3	9	12	27	....	....	....	....	....
	Detroit Red Wings	13	0	5	5	2	....	....	....	....	....
1986-87	Detroit Red Wings	77	13	45	58	52	12	3	4	7	8
1987-88	Detroit Red Wings	63	7	33	40	45	11	1	5	6	6
1988-89	Toronto Maple Leafs	37	3	7	10	16	....	....	....	....	....
1990-91	Toronto Maple Leafs	2	0	1	1	0	....	....	....	....	....
	NHL Totals	**511**	**48**	**209**	**257**	**296**	**33**	**4**	**11**	**15**	**33**

• Missed majority of 1982-83 season recovering from collarbone injury suffered in game vs. Vancouver, October 28, 1982. Traded to **Detroit** by **Washington** for John Barrett and Greg Smith, March 10, 1986. Traded to **Toronto** by **Detroit** for Miroslav Frycer, June 10, 1988. Traded to **St. Louis** by **Toronto** for Keith Osborne, March 5, 1991. Signed as a free agent by **Phoenix Mustangs**, October 6, 1997.

VELISCHEK, Randy

Defense. Shoots left. 6', 200 lbs. Born, Montreal, Que., February 10, 1962.
(Minnesota's 3rd choice, 53rd overall, in 1980 Entry Draft).

Season	Club	REGULAR SEASON GP	G	A	Pts	PIM	PLAYOFFS GP	G	A	Pts	PIM
1982-83	Minnesota North Stars	3	0	0	0	2	9	0	0	0	0
1983-84	Minnesota North Stars	33	2	2	4	10	1	0	0	0	0
1984-85	Minnesota North Stars	52	4	9	13	26	9	2	3	5	8
1985-86	New Jersey Devils	47	2	7	9	39	....	....	....	....	....
1986-87	New Jersey Devils	64	2	16	18	52	....	....	....	....	....
1987-88	New Jersey Devils	51	3	9	12	66	19	0	2	2	20
1988-89	New Jersey Devils	80	4	14	18	70	....	....	....	....	....
1989-90	New Jersey Devils	62	0	6	6	72	6	0	0	0	4
1990-91	Quebec Nordiques	79	2	10	12	42	....	....	....	....	....
1991-92	Quebec Nordiques	38	2	3	5	22	....	....	....	....	....
	NHL Totals	**509**	**21**	**76**	**97**	**401**	**44**	**2**	**5**	**7**	**32**

Claimed by **New Jersey** from **Minnesota** in Waiver Draft, October 7, 1985. Traded to **Quebec** by **New Jersey** to complete transaction that sent Peter Stastny to New Jersey (March 6, 1990), August 13, 1990.

VELLUCCI, Mike

Defense. Shoots left. 6'1", 180 lbs. Born, Farmington, MI, August 11, 1966.
(Hartford's 3rd choice, 131st overall, in 1984 Entry Draft).

Season	Club	Regular Season GP	G	A	Pts	PIM	Playoffs GP	G	A	Pts	PIM
1987-88	Hartford Whalers	2	0	0	0	11	....	....	....	....	....
	NHL Totals	**2**	**0**	**0**	**0**	**11**	....	....	....	....	....

VENASKY, Vic

Center. Shoots right. 5'11", 185 lbs. Born, Thunder Bay, Ont., June 3, 1951.
(Los Angeles' 1st choice, 34th overall, in 1971 Amateur Draft).

Season	Club	Regular Season GP	G	A	Pts	PIM	Playoffs GP	G	A	Pts	PIM
1972-73	Los Angeles Kings	77	15	19	34	10	....	....	....	....	....
1973-74	Los Angeles Kings	32	6	5	11	12	....	....	....	....	....
1974-75	Los Angeles Kings	17	1	2	3	0	....	....	....	....	....
1975-76	Los Angeles Kings	80	18	26	44	12	9	0	1	1	6
1976-77	Los Angeles Kings	80	14	26	40	18	9	1	4	5	6
1977-78	Los Angeles Kings	71	3	10	13	6	1	0	0	0	0
1978-79	Los Angeles Kings	73	4	13	17	8	2	0	0	0	0
	NHL Totals	**430**	**61**	**101**	**162**	**66**	**21**	**1**	**5**	**6**	**12**

VENERUZZO, Gary

Wing. Shoots left. 5'8", 165 lbs. Born, Fort William, Ont., June 28, 1943.

Season	Club	Regular Season GP	G	A	Pts	PIM	Playoffs GP	G	A	Pts	PIM
1967-68	St. Louis Blues	5	1	1	2	0	9	0	2	2	2
1971-72	St. Louis Blues	2	0	0	0	0	....	....	....	....	....
	NHL Totals	**7**	**1**	**1**	**2**	**0**	**9**	**0**	**2**	**2**	**2**

Claimed by **St. Louis** from **Toronto** in Expansion Draft, June 6, 1967.

VERBEEK, Pat

Right wing. Shoots right. 5'9", 192 lbs. Born, Sarnia, Ont., May 24, 1964.
(New Jersey's 3rd choice, 43rd overall, in 1982 Entry Draft).

Season	Club	Regular Season GP	G	A	Pts	PIM	Playoffs GP	G	A	Pts	PIM
1982-83	New Jersey Devils	6	3	2	5	8	....	....	....	....	....
1983-84	New Jersey Devils	79	20	27	47	158	....	....	....	....	....
1984-85	New Jersey Devils	78	15	18	33	162	....	....	....	....	....
1985-86	New Jersey Devils	76	25	28	53	79	....	....	....	....	....
1986-87	New Jersey Devils	74	35	24	59	120	....	....	....	....	....
1987-88	New Jersey Devils	73	46	31	77	227	20	4	8	12	51
1988-89	New Jersey Devils	77	26	21	47	189	....	....	....	....	....
1989-90	Hartford Whalers	80	44	45	89	228	7	2	2	4	26
1990-91	Hartford Whalers	80	43	39	82	246	6	3	2	5	40
1991-92	Hartford Whalers	76	22	35	57	243	7	0	2	2	12
1992-93	Hartford Whalers	84	39	43	82	197	....	....	....	....	....
1993-94	Hartford Whalers	84	37	38	75	177	....	....	....	....	....
1994-95	Hartford Whalers	29	7	11	18	53	....	....	....	....	....
	New York Rangers	19	10	5	15	18	10	4	6	10	20
1995-96	New York Rangers	69	41	41	82	129	11	3	6	9	12
1996-97	Dallas Stars	81	17	36	53	128	7	1	3	4	16
1997-98	Dallas Stars	82	31	26	57	170	17	3	2	5	26
1998-99 ♦	Dallas Stars	78	17	17	34	133	18	3	4	7	14
99-2000	Detroit Red Wings	68	22	26	48	95	9	1	1	2	2
2000-01	Detroit Red Wings	67	15	15	30	73	5	2	0	2	6
2001-02	Dallas Stars	64	7	13	20	72	....	....	....	....	....
	NHL Totals	**1424**	**522**	**541**	**1063**	**2905**	**117**	**26**	**36**	**62**	**225**

Played in NHL All-Star Game (1991, 1996)

Traded to **Hartford** by **New Jersey** for Sylvain Turgeon, June 17, 1989. Traded to **NY Rangers** by **Hartford** for Glen Featherstone, Michael Stewart, NY Rangers' 1st round choice (Jean-Sebastien Giguere) in 1995 Entry Draft and 4th round choice (Steve Wasylko) in 1996 Entry Draft, March 23, 1995. Signed as a free agent by **Dallas**, August 21, 1996. Signed as a free agent by **Detroit**, November 11, 1999. Signed as a free agent by **Dallas**, August 31, 2001.

VERMETTE, Mark

Right wing. Shoots right. 6'1", 203 lbs. Born, Cochenour, Ont., October 3, 1967.
(Quebec's 8th choice, 134th overall, in 1986 Entry Draft).

Season	Club	Regular Season GP	G	A	Pts	PIM	Playoffs GP	G	A	Pts	PIM
1988-89	Quebec Nordiques	12	0	4	4	7	....	....	....	....	....
1989-90	Quebec Nordiques	11	1	5	6	8	....	....	....	....	....
1990-91	Quebec Nordiques	34	3	4	7	10	....	....	....	....	....
1991-92	Quebec Nordiques	10	1	0	1	8	....	....	....	....	....
	NHL Totals	**67**	**5**	**13**	**18**	**33**	....	....	....	....	....

VERNARSKY, Kris

Center. Shoots left. 6'3", 201 lbs. Born, Detroit, MI, April 5, 1982.
(Toronto's 2nd choice, 51st overall, in 2000 Entry Draft).

Season	Club	Regular Season GP	G	A	Pts	PIM	Playoffs GP	G	A	Pts	PIM
2002-03	Boston Bruins	14	1	0	1	2	....	....	....	....	....
	NHL Totals	**14**	**1**	**0**	**1**	**2**	....	....	....	....	....

Rights traded to **Boston** by **Toronto** for Richard Jackman, May 13, 2002.

VERRET, Claude

Center. Shoots left. 5'9", 165 lbs. Born, Lachine, Que., April 20, 1963.
(Buffalo's 12th choice, 163rd overall, in 1982 Entry Draft).

Season	Club	Regular Season GP	G	A	Pts	PIM	Playoffs GP	G	A	Pts	PIM
1983-84	Buffalo Sabres	11	2	5	7	2	....	....	....	....	....
1984-85	Buffalo Sabres	3	0	0	0	0	....	....	....	....	....
	NHL Totals	**14**	**2**	**5**	**7**	**2**	....	....	....	....	....

VERSTRAETE, Leigh

Right wing. Shoots right. 5'11", 185 lbs. Born, Pincher Creek, Alta., January 6, 1962.
(Toronto's 13th choice, 192nd overall, in 1982 Entry Draft).

Season	Club	Regular Season GP	G	A	Pts	PIM	Playoffs GP	G	A	Pts	PIM
1982-83	Toronto Maple Leafs	3	0	0	0	5	....	....	....	....	....
1984-85	Toronto Maple Leafs	2	0	0	0	0	....	....	....	....	....
1987-88	Toronto Maple Leafs	3	0	1	1	9	....	....	....	....	....
	NHL Totals	**8**	**0**	**1**	**1**	**14**	....	....	....	....	....

VERVERGAERT, Dennis

Right wing. Shoots right. 6', 185 lbs. Born, Hamilton, Ont., March 30, 1953.
(Vancouver's 1st choice, 3rd overall, in 1973 Amateur Draft).

Season	Club	Regular Season GP	G	A	Pts	PIM	Playoffs GP	G	A	Pts	PIM
1973-74	Vancouver Canucks	78	26	31	57	25	....	....	....	....	....
1974-75	Vancouver Canucks	57	19	32	51	25	1	0	0	0	0
1975-76	Vancouver Canucks	80	37	34	71	53	2	1	0	1	4
1976-77	Vancouver Canucks	79	27	18	45	38	....	....	....	....	....
1977-78	Vancouver Canucks	80	21	33	54	23	....	....	....	....	....
1978-79	Vancouver Canucks	35	9	17	26	13	....	....	....	....	....
	Philadelphia Flyers	37	9	7	16	6	3	0	2	2	2
1979-80	Philadelphia Flyers	58	14	17	31	24	2	0	0	0	0
1980-81	Washington Capitals	79	14	27	41	40	....	....	....	....	....
	NHL Totals	**583**	**176**	**216**	**392**	**247**	**8**	**1**	**2**	**3**	**6**

Played in NHL All-Star Game (1976, 1978)

Traded to **Philadelphia** by **Vancouver** for Drew Callander and Kevin McCarthy, December 29, 1978. Signed as a free agent by **Washington**, October 6, 1980.

VESEY, Jim

Center/Right wing. Shoots right. 6'1", 202 lbs. Born, Columbus, MA, October 29, 1965.
(St. Louis' 11th choice, 155th overall, in 1984 Entry Draft).

Season	Club	Regular Season GP	G	A	Pts	PIM	Playoffs GP	G	A	Pts	PIM
1988-89	St. Louis Blues	5	1	1	2	7	....	....	....	....	....
1989-90	St. Louis Blues	6	0	1	1	0	....	....	....	....	....
1991-92	Boston Bruins	4	0	0	0	0	....	....	....	....	....
	NHL Totals	**15**	**1**	**2**	**3**	**7**	....	....	....	....	....

Traded to **Winnipeg** by **St. Louis** to complete transaction that sent Tom Draper to St. Louis (February 28, 1991), May 24, 1991. Traded to **Boston** by **Winnipeg** for future considerations, June 20, 1991.

VEYSEY, Sid

Center. Shoots left. 5'11", 175 lbs. Born, Woodstock, N.B., July 30, 1955.
(Vancouver's 10th choice, 182nd overall, in 1975 Amateur Draft).

Season	Club	Regular Season GP	G	A	Pts	PIM	Playoffs GP	G	A	Pts	PIM
1977-78	Vancouver Canucks	1	0	0	0	0	....	....	....	....	....
	NHL Totals	**1**	**0**	**0**	**0**	**0**	....	....	....	....	....

VIAL, Dennis

Defense/Left wing. Shoots left. 6'1", 220 lbs. Born, Sault Ste. Marie, Ont., April 10, 1969.
(NY Rangers' 5th choice, 110th overall, in 1988 Entry Draft).

Season	Club	Regular Season GP	G	A	Pts	PIM	Playoffs GP	G	A	Pts	PIM
1990-91	New York Rangers	21	0	0	0	61	....	....	....	....	....
	Detroit Red Wings	9	0	0	0	16	....	....	....	....	....
1991-92	Detroit Red Wings	27	1	0	1	72	....	....	....	....	....
1992-93	Detroit Red Wings	9	0	1	1	20	....	....	....	....	....
1993-94	Ottawa Senators	55	2	5	7	214	....	....	....	....	....
1994-95	Ottawa Senators	27	0	4	4	65	....	....	....	....	....
1995-96	Ottawa Senators	64	1	4	5	276	....	....	....	....	....
1996-97	Ottawa Senators	11	0	1	1	25	....	....	....	....	....
1997-98	Ottawa Senators	19	0	0	0	45	....	....	....	....	....
	NHL Totals	**242**	**4**	**15**	**19**	**794**	....	....	....	....	....

Traded to **Detroit** by **NY Rangers** with Kevin Miller and Jim Cummins for Joe Kocur and Per Djoos, March 5, 1991. Traded to **Quebec** by **Detroit** with Doug Crossman for cash, June 15, 1992. Traded to **Detroit** by **Quebec** for cash, September 9, 1992. Traded to **Tampa Bay** by **Detroit** for Steve Maltais, June 8, 1993. Claimed by **Anaheim** from **Tampa Bay** in Expansion Draft, June 24, 1993. Claimed by **Ottawa** from **Anaheim** in Phase II of Expansion Draft, June 25, 1993.

VICKERS, Steve

Left wing. Shoots left. 6', 180 lbs. Born, Toronto, Ont., April 21, 1951.
(NY Rangers' 1st choice, 10th overall, in 1971 Amateur Draft).

Season	Club	Regular Season GP	G	A	Pts	PIM	Playoffs GP	G	A	Pts	PIM
1972-73	New York Rangers	61	30	23	53	37	10	5	4	9	4
1973-74	New York Rangers	75	34	24	58	18	13	4	4	8	17
1974-75	New York Rangers	80	41	48	89	64	3	2	4	6	6
1975-76	New York Rangers	80	30	53	83	40	....	....	....	....	....
1976-77	New York Rangers	75	22	31	53	26	....	....	....	....	....
1977-78	New York Rangers	79	19	44	63	30	3	2	1	3	0
1978-79	New York Rangers	66	13	34	47	24	18	5	3	8	13
1979-80	New York Rangers	75	29	33	62	38	9	2	2	4	4
1980-81	New York Rangers	73	19	39	58	40	12	4	7	11	14
1981-82	New York Rangers	34	9	11	20	13	....	....	....	....	....
	NHL Totals	**698**	**246**	**340**	**586**	**330**	**68**	**24**	**25**	**49**	**58**

Calder Memorial Trophy (1973) • NHL Second All-Star Team (1975)
Played in NHL All-Star Game (1975, 1976)

VIGIER, J.P.

Right wing. Shoots right. 6'1", 190 lbs. Born, Notre Dame de Lourdes, Man., September 11, 1976.

Season	Club	Regular Season GP	G	A	Pts	PIM	Playoffs GP	G	A	Pts	PIM
2000-01	Atlanta Thrashers	2	0	0	0	0	....	....	....	....	....
2001-02	Atlanta Thrashers	15	4	1	5	4	....	....	....	....	....
2002-03	Atlanta Thrashers	13	0	0	0	4	....	....	....	....	....
	NHL Totals	**30**	**4**	**1**	**5**	**8**	....	....	....	....	....

Signed as a free agent by **Atlanta**, April 20, 2000.

VIGNEAULT, Alain

Defense. Shoots right. 5'11", 195 lbs. Born, Quebec City, Que., May 14, 1961.
(St. Louis' 7th choice, 167th overall, in 1981 Entry Draft).

Season	Club	Regular Season					Playoffs				
		GP	G	A	Pts	PIM	GP	G	A	Pts	PIM
1981-82	St. Louis Blues	14	1	2	3	43	....	....	....	....	....
1982-83	St. Louis Blues	28	1	3	4	39	4	0	1	1	26
	NHL Totals	**42**	**2**	**5**	**7**	**82**	**4**	**0**	**1**	**1**	**26**

VIITAKOSKI, Vesa

Left wing. Shoots left. 6'3", 215 lbs. Born, Lappeenranta, Finland, February 13, 1971.
(Calgary's 3rd choice, 32nd overall, in 1990 Entry Draft).

Season	Club	Regular Season					Playoffs				
		GP	G	A	Pts	PIM	GP	G	A	Pts	PIM
1993-94	Calgary Flames	8	1	2	3	0	....	....	....	....	....
1994-95	Calgary Flames	10	1	2	3	6	....	....	....	....	....
1995-96	Calgary Flames	5	0	0	0	2	....	....	....	....	....
	NHL Totals	**23**	**2**	**4**	**6**	**8**	....	....	....	....	....

Traded to **Colorado** by **Calgary** for Paxton Schulte, March 19, 1996.

VILGRAIN, Claude

Right wing. Shoots right. 6'1", 205 lbs. Born, Port-au-Prince, Haiti, March 1, 1963.
(Detroit's 6th choice, 107th overall, in 1982 Entry Draft).

Season	Club	Regular Season					Playoffs				
		GP	G	A	Pts	PIM	GP	G	A	Pts	PIM
1987-88	Vancouver Canucks	6	1	1	2	0	....	....	....	....	....
1989-90	New Jersey Devils	6	1	2	3	4	4	0	0	0	0
1991-92	New Jersey Devils	71	19	27	46	74	7	1	1	2	17
1992-93	New Jersey Devils	4	0	2	2	0	....	....	....	....	....
1993-94	Philadelphia Flyers	2	0	0	0	0	....	....	....	....	....
	NHL Totals	**89**	**21**	**32**	**53**	**78**	**11**	**1**	**1**	**2**	**17**

Signed as a free agent by **Vancouver**, June 18, 1987. Traded to **New Jersey** by **Vancouver** for Tim Lenardon, March 7, 1989. Signed as a free agent by **Philadelphia**, August 3, 1993.

VINCELETTE, Dan

Left wing. Shoots left. 6'2", 202 lbs. Born, Verdun, Que., August 1, 1967.
(Chicago's 3rd choice, 74th overall, in 1985 Entry Draft).

Season	Club	Regular Season					Playoffs				
		GP	G	A	Pts	PIM	GP	G	A	Pts	PIM
1986-87	Chicago Blackhawks	....	....	....	....	....	3	0	0	0	0
1987-88	Chicago Blackhawks	69	6	11	17	109	4	0	0	0	0
1988-89	Chicago Blackhawks	66	11	4	15	119	5	0	0	0	4
1989-90	Chicago Blackhawks	2	0	0	0	4	....	....	....	....	....
	Quebec Nordiques	11	0	1	1	25	....	....	....	....	....
1990-91	Quebec Nordiques	16	0	1	1	38	....	....	....	....	....
1991-92	Chicago Blackhawks	29	3	5	8	56	....	....	....	....	....
	NHL Totals	**193**	**20**	**22**	**42**	**351**	**12**	**0**	**0**	**0**	**4**

Traded to **Quebec** by **Chicago** with Mario Doyon and Everett Sanipass for Greg Millen, Michel Goulet and Quebec's 6th round choice (Kevin St. Jacques) in 1991 Entry Draft, March 5, 1990. Traded to **Chicago** by **Quebec** with Paul Gillis for Ryan McGill and Mike McNeill, March 5, 1991. Claimed by **Tampa Bay** from **Chicago** in Expansion Draft, June 18, 1992. Traded to **Philadelphia** by **Tampa Bay** for Steve Kasper, December 8, 1992.

VIPOND, Pete

Left wing. Shoots left. 5'10", 175 lbs. Born, Oshawa, Ont., December 8, 1949.
(Oakland's 7th choice, 76th overall, in 1969 Amateur Draft).

Season	Club	Regular Season					Playoffs				
		GP	G	A	Pts	PIM	GP	G	A	Pts	PIM
1972-73	California Golden Seals	3	0	0	0	0	....	....	....	....	....
	NHL Totals	**3**	**0**	**0**	**0**	**0**	....	....	....	....	....

VIRTA, Hannu

Defense. Shoots left. 5'11", 183 lbs. Born, Turku, Finland, March 22, 1963.
(Buffalo's 2nd choice, 38th overall, in 1981 Entry Draft).

Season	Club	Regular Season					Playoffs				
		GP	G	A	Pts	PIM	GP	G	A	Pts	PIM
1981-82	Buffalo Sabres	3	0	1	1	4	4	0	1	1	0
1982-83	Buffalo Sabres	74	13	24	37	18	10	1	2	3	4
1983-84	Buffalo Sabres	70	6	30	36	12	3	0	0	0	2
1984-85	Buffalo Sabres	51	1	23	24	16	....	....	....	....	....
1985-86	Buffalo Sabres	47	5	23	28	16	....	....	....	....	....
	NHL Totals	**245**	**25**	**101**	**126**	**66**	**17**	**1**	**3**	**4**	**6**

VIRTA, Tony

Right wing. Shoots left. 5'10", 187 lbs. Born, Hameenlinna, Finland, June 28, 1972.
(Minnesota's 5th choice, 103rd overall, in 2001 Entry Draft).

Season	Club	Regular Season					Playoffs				
		GP	G	A	Pts	PIM	GP	G	A	Pts	PIM
2001-02	Minnesota Wild	8	2	3	5	0	....	....	....	....	....
	NHL Totals	**8**	**2**	**3**	**5**	**0**	....	....	....	....	....

VIRTUE, Terry

Defense. Shoots right. 6', 207 lbs. Born, Scarborough, Ont., August 12, 1970.

Season	Club	Regular Season					Playoffs				
		GP	G	A	Pts	PIM	GP	G	A	Pts	PIM
1998-99	Boston Bruins	4	0	0	0	0	....	....	....	....	....
99-2000	New York Rangers	1	0	0	0	0	....	....	....	....	....
	NHL Totals	**5**	**0**	**0**	**0**	**0**	....	....	....	....	....

Signed as a free agent by **St. Louis**, January 29, 1996. Signed as a free agent by **Boston**, August 28, 1998. Signed as a free agent by **NY Rangers**, July 29, 1999.

VISHEAU, Mark

Defense. Shoots right. 6'6", 222 lbs. Born, Burlington, Ont., June 27, 1973.
(Winnipeg's 4th choice, 84th overall, in 1992 Entry Draft).

Season	Club	Regular Season					Playoffs				
		GP	G	A	Pts	PIM	GP	G	A	Pts	PIM
1993-94	Winnipeg Jets	1	0	0	0	0	....	....	....	....	....
1998-99	Los Angeles Kings	28	1	3	4	107	....	....	....	....	....
	NHL Totals	**29**	**1**	**3**	**4**	**107**	....	....	....	....	....

Signed as a free agent by **Los Angeles**, July 30, 1997.

VISHNEVSKI, Vitaly

Defense. Shoots left. 6'2", 206 lbs. Born, Kharkov, USSR, March 18, 1980.
(Anaheim's 1st choice, 5th overall, in 1998 Entry Draft).

Season	Club	Regular Season					Playoffs				
		GP	G	A	Pts	PIM	GP	G	A	Pts	PIM
99-2000	Mighty Ducks of Anaheim	31	1	1	2	26	....	....	....	....	....
2000-01	Mighty Ducks of Anaheim	76	1	10	11	99	....	....	....	....	....
2001-02	Mighty Ducks of Anaheim	74	0	3	3	60	....	....	....	....	....
2002-03	Mighty Ducks of Anaheim	80	2	6	8	76	21	0	1	1	6
	NHL Totals	**261**	**4**	**20**	**24**	**261**	**21**	**0**	**1**	**1**	**6**

VISNOVSKY, Lubomir

Defense. Shoots left. 5'10", 183 lbs. Born, Topolcany, Czech., August 11, 1976.
(Los Angeles' 4th choice, 118th overall, in 2000 Entry Draft).

Season	Club	Regular Season					Playoffs				
		GP	G	A	Pts	PIM	GP	G	A	Pts	PIM
2000-01	Los Angeles Kings	81	7	32	39	36	8	0	0	0	0
2001-02	Los Angeles Kings	72	4	17	21	14	4	0	1	1	0
2002-03	Los Angeles Kings	57	8	16	24	28	....	....	....	....	....
	NHL Totals	**210**	**19**	**65**	**84**	**78**	**12**	**0**	**1**	**1**	**0**

NHL All-Rookie Team (2001)

VITOLINSH, Harijs

Center. Shoots left. 6'3", 212 lbs. Born, Riga, Latvia, April 30, 1968.
(Winnipeg's 12th choice, 228th overall, in 1993 Entry Draft).

Season	Club	Regular Season					Playoffs				
		GP	G	A	Pts	PIM	GP	G	A	Pts	PIM
1993-94	Winnipeg Jets	8	0	0	0	4	....	....	....	....	....
	NHL Totals	**8**	**0**	**0**	**0**	**4**	....	....	....	....	....

• Re-entered NHL Entry Draft. Originally Montreal's 10th choice, 188th overall, in 1988 Entry Draft.

VIVEIROS, Emanuel

Defense. Shoots left. 6', 175 lbs. Born, St. Albert, Alta., January 8, 1966.
(Edmonton's 6th choice, 106th overall, in 1984 Entry Draft).

Season	Club	Regular Season					Playoffs				
		GP	G	A	Pts	PIM	GP	G	A	Pts	PIM
1985-86	Minnesota North Stars	4	0	1	1	0	....	....	....	....	....
1986-87	Minnesota North Stars	1	0	1	1	0	....	....	....	....	....
1987-88	Minnesota North Stars	24	1	9	10	6	....	....	....	....	....
	NHL Totals	**29**	**1**	**11**	**12**	**6**	....	....	....	....	....

Traded to **Minnesota** by **Edmonton** with Marc Habscheid and Don Barber for Gord Sherven and Don Biggs, December 20, 1985. Signed as a free agent by **Hartford**, February 9, 1990.

VLASAK, Tomas

Center. Shoots right. 5'10", 175 lbs. Born, Prague, Czech., February 1, 1975.
(Los Angeles' 6th choice, 120th overall, in 1993 Entry Draft).

Season	Club	Regular Season					Playoffs				
		GP	G	A	Pts	PIM	GP	G	A	Pts	PIM
2000-01	Los Angeles Kings	10	1	3	4	2	....	....	....	....	....
	NHL Totals	**10**	**1**	**3**	**4**	**2**	....	....	....	....	....

VOKES, Ed

Left wing. Shoots left. 5'9", 160 lbs. Born, Quill Lake, Sask., 1904.

Season	Club	Regular Season					Playoffs				
		GP	G	A	Pts	PIM	GP	G	A	Pts	PIM
1930-31	Chicago Black Hawks	5	0	0	0	0	....	....	....	....	....
	NHL Totals	**5**	**0**	**0**	**0**	**0**	....	....	....	....	....

Traded to **Chicago** by **Oakland** (Cal-Pro) for cash, December 15, 1930. Traded to **Pittsburgh** (IHL) by **Chicago** for cash, February 12, 1931.

VOLCAN, Mickey

Defense. Shoots right. 6', 190 lbs. Born, Edmonton, Alta., March 3, 1962.
(Hartford's 3rd choice, 50th overall, in 1980 Entry Draft).

Season	Club	Regular Season					Playoffs				
		GP	G	A	Pts	PIM	GP	G	A	Pts	PIM
1980-81	Hartford Whalers	49	2	11	13	26	....	....	....	....	....
1981-82	Hartford Whalers	26	1	5	6	29	....	....	....	....	....
1982-83	Hartford Whalers	68	4	13	17	73	....	....	....	....	....
1983-84	Calgary Flames	19	1	4	5	18	....	....	....	....	....
	NHL Totals	**162**	**8**	**33**	**41**	**146**	....	....	....	....	....

Traded to **Calgary** by **Hartford** for Joel Quenneville and Richie Dunn, July 5, 1983.

VOLCHENKOV, Anton

Defense. Shoots left. 6', 209 lbs. Born, Moscow, USSR, February 25, 1982.
(Ottawa's 1st choice, 21st overall, in 2000 Entry Draft).

Season	Club	Regular Season					Playoffs				
		GP	G	A	Pts	PIM	GP	G	A	Pts	PIM
2002-03	Ottawa Senators	57	3	13	16	40	17	1	1	2	4
	NHL Totals	**57**	**3**	**13**	**16**	**40**	**17**	**1**	**1**	**2**	**4**

VOLCHKOV, Alexandre

Center. Shoots left. 6'2", 204 lbs. Born, Moscow, USSR, September 25, 1977.
(Washington's 1st choice, 4th overall, in 1996 Entry Draft).

Season	Club	Regular Season					Playoffs				
		GP	G	A	Pts	PIM	GP	G	A	Pts	PIM
99-2000	Washington Capitals	3	0	0	0	0	....	....	....	....	....
	NHL Totals	**3**	**0**	**0**	**0**	**0**	....	....	....	....	....

Traded to **Edmonton** by **Washington** for a Edmonton's 4th round choice (later traded to Anaheim – Anaheim selected Brandon Rogers) in 2001 Entry Draft, February 4, 2000.

VOLEK, David

Wing. Shoots left. 6', 185 lbs. Born, Prague, Czech., June 18, 1966.
(NY Islanders' 11th choice, 208th overall, in 1984 Entry Draft).

Season	Club	Regular Season					Playoffs				
		GP	G	A	Pts	PIM	GP	G	A	Pts	PIM
1988-89	New York Islanders	77	25	34	59	24	....	....	....	....	....
1989-90	New York Islanders	80	17	22	39	41	5	1	4	5	0
1990-91	New York Islanders	77	22	34	56	57	....	....	....	....	....
1991-92	New York Islanders	74	18	42	60	35	....	....	....	....	....
1992-93	New York Islanders	56	8	13	21	34	10	4	1	5	2

Season	Club	GP	G	A	Pts	PIM	GP	G	A	Pts	PIM
		REGULAR SEASON					PLAYOFFS				
1993-94	New York Islanders	32	5	9	14	10	....	....	....	....	....
	NHL Totals	**396**	**95**	**154**	**249**	**201**	**15**	**5**	**5**	**10**	**2**

NHL All-Rookie Team (1989)

VOLMAR, Doug

Right wing. Shoots right. 6'1", 215 lbs. Born, Cleveland, OH, January 9, 1945.

Season	Club	GP	G	A	Pts	PIM	GP	G	A	Pts	PIM
1969-70	Detroit Red Wings	....	....	....	....	....	2	1	0	1	0
1970-71	Detroit Red Wings	2	0	1	1	2	....	....	....	....	....
1971-72	Detroit Red Wings	39	9	5	14	8	....	....	....	....	....
1972-73	Los Angeles Kings	21	4	2	6	16	....	....	....	....	....
	NHL Totals	**62**	**13**	**8**	**21**	**26**	**2**	**1**	**0**	**1**	**0**

Claimed by **San Diego** (WHL) from **Detroit** in Reverse Draft, June 12, 1969. Traded to **Detroit** by **San Diego** (WHL) for cash, July, 1969. Claimed by **Los Angeles** from **Detroit** in Intra-League Draft, June 5, 1972.

VON ARX, Reto

Center. Shoots left. 5'10", 190 lbs. Born, Egerkingen, Switz., September 13, 1976.
(Chicago's 14th choice, 271st overall, in 2000 Entry Draft).

Season	Club	GP	G	A	Pts	PIM	GP	G	A	Pts	PIM
2000-01	Chicago Blackhawks	19	3	1	4	4	....	....	....	....	....
	NHL Totals	**19**	**3**	**1**	**4**	**4**	....	....	....	....	....

VON STEFENELLI, Phil

Defense. Shoots left. 6'1", 200 lbs. Born, Vancouver, B.C., April 10, 1969.
(Vancouver's 5th choice, 122nd overall, in 1988 Entry Draft).

Season	Club	GP	G	A	Pts	PIM	GP	G	A	Pts	PIM
1995-96	Boston Bruins	27	0	4	4	16	....	....	....	....	....
1996-97	Ottawa Senators	6	0	1	1	7	....	....	....	....	....
	NHL Totals	**33**	**0**	**5**	**5**	**23**	....	....	....	....	....

Signed as a free agent by **Boston**, September 10, 1994. Signed as a free agent by **Ottawa**, July 17, 1996. Signed as a free agent by **Tampa Bay**, July 22, 1999.

VOPAT, Jan

Defense. Shoots left. 6', 205 lbs. Born, Most, Czech., March 22, 1973.
(Hartford's 3rd choice, 57th overall, in 1992 Entry Draft).

Season	Club	GP	G	A	Pts	PIM	GP	G	A	Pts	PIM
1995-96	Los Angeles Kings	11	1	4	5	4	....	....	....	....	....
1996-97	Los Angeles Kings	33	4	5	9	22	....	....	....	....	....
1997-98	Los Angeles Kings	21	1	5	6	10	2	0	1	1	2
1998-99	Nashville Predators	55	5	6	11	28	....	....	....	....	....
99-2000	Nashville Predators	6	0	0	0	6	....	....	....	....	....
	NHL Totals	**126**	**11**	**20**	**31**	**70**	**2**	**0**	**1**	**1**	**2**

• Brother of Roman

Rights traded to **Los Angeles** by **Hartford** for Los Angeles' 4th round choice (Ian MacNeil) in 1995 Entry Draft, May 31, 1995. Traded to **Nashville** by **Los Angeles** with Kimmo Timonen for future considerations, June 26, 1998.

VOPAT, Roman

Center. Shoots left. 6'3", 223 lbs. Born, Litvinov, Czech., April 21, 1976.
(St. Louis' 4th choice, 172nd overall, in 1994 Entry Draft).

Season	Club	GP	G	A	Pts	PIM	GP	G	A	Pts	PIM
1995-96	St. Louis Blues	25	2	3	5	48	....	....	....	....	....
1996-97	Los Angeles Kings	29	4	5	9	60	....	....	....	....	....
1997-98	Los Angeles Kings	25	0	3	3	55	....	....	....	....	....
1998-99	Los Angeles Kings	3	0	0	0	6	....	....	....	....	....
	Chicago Blackhawks	3	0	0	0	4	....	....	....	....	....
	Philadelphia Flyers	48	0	3	3	80	....	....	....	....	....
	NHL Totals	**133**	**6**	**14**	**20**	**253**	....	....	....	....	....

• Brother of Jan

Traded to **Los Angeles** by **St. Louis** with Craig Johnson, Patrice Tardif, St. Louis' 5th round choice (Peter Hogan) in 1996 Entry Draft and 1st round choice (Matt Zultek) in 1997 Entry Draft for Wayne Gretzky, February 27, 1996. Traded to **Colorado** by **Los Angeles** with Los Angeles' 6th round choice (later traded to Chicago, later traded to Ottawa – Ottawa selected Martin Prusek) in 1999 Entry Draft for Eric Lacroix, October 29, 1998. Traded to **Chicago** by **Colorado** with Los Angeles' 6th round choice (previously acquired, later traded to Ottawa – Ottawa selected Martin Prusek) in 1999 Entry Draft for Cam Russell, November 10, 1998. Traded to **Philadelphia** by **Chicago** for Mike Maneluk, November 17, 1998.

VOROBIEV, Vladimir

Left wing. Shoots right. 6', 184 lbs. Born, Cherepovets, USSR, October 2, 1972.
(NY Rangers' 10th choice, 240th overall, in 1992 Entry Draft).

Season	Club	GP	G	A	Pts	PIM	GP	G	A	Pts	PIM
1996-97	New York Rangers	16	5	5	10	6	....	....	....	....	....
1997-98	New York Rangers	15	2	2	4	6	....	....	....	....	....
1998-99	Edmonton Oilers	2	2	0	2	2	1	0	0	0	0
	NHL Totals	**33**	**9**	**7**	**16**	**14**	**1**	**0**	**0**	**0**	**0**

Traded to **Edmonton** by **NY Rangers** for Kevin Brown, March 23, 1999.

VOSS, Carl

HHOF

Center. Shoots left. 5'9", 168 lbs. Born, Chelsea, MA, January 6, 1907.

Season	Club	GP	G	A	Pts	PIM	GP	G	A	Pts	PIM
1926-27	Toronto St. Pats/Maple Leafs	12	0	0	0	0	....	....	....	....	....
1928-29	Toronto Maple Leafs	2	0	0	0	0	....	....	....	....	....
1932-33	New York Rangers	10	2	1	3	4	....	....	....	....	....
	Detroit Red Wings	38	6	14	20	6	4	1	1	2	0
1933-34	Detroit Red Wings	8	0	2	2	2	....	....	....	....	....
	Ottawa Senators	40	7	16	23	10	....	....	....	....	....
1934-35	St. Louis Eagles	48	13	18	31	14	....	....	....	....	....
1935-36	New York Americans	46	3	9	12	10	5	0	0	0	0
1936-37	Montreal Maroons	20	0	2	2	4	5	1	0	1	0
1937-38	Montreal Maroons	3	0	0	0	0	....	....	....	....	....
	◆ Chicago Black Hawks	34	3	8	11	0	10	3	2	5	0
	NHL Totals	**261**	**34**	**70**	**104**	**50**	**24**	**5**	**3**	**8**	**0**

NHL Rookie of the Year (1933)

Signed as a free agent by **Toronto**, February 16, 1927. Traded to **Buffalo** (IHL) by **Toronto** with Wes King for Gord Brydson, October 10, 1929. Traded to **NY Rangers** by **Buffalo** (IHL) for Lorne Carr and $15,000, October 4, 1932. Traded to **Detroit** by **NY Rangers** for cash, December 11, 1932. Traded to **Ottawa** by **Detroit** with cash for Cooney Weiland, November 26, 1933. Transferred to **St. Louis** after **Ottawa** franchise relocated, September 22, 1934. Claimed by **Detroit** from **St. Louis** in Dispersal Draft, October 15, 1935. Traded to **NY Americans** by **Detroit** for Pete Kelly, October 16, 1935. Traded to **Mtl. Maroons** by **NY Americans** for Joe Lamb and $10,000, September 6, 1936. Signed as a free agent by **Chicago**, December 6, 1937. • Suffered career-ending knee injury in training camp, September 30, 1938.

VRBATA, Radim

Right wing. Shoots right. 6'1", 185 lbs. Born, Boleslav, Czech., June 13, 1981.
(Colorado's 10th choice, 212th overall, in 1999 Entry Draft).

Season	Club	GP	G	A	Pts	PIM	GP	G	A	Pts	PIM
2001-02	Colorado Avalanche	52	18	12	30	14	9	0	0	0	0
2002-03	Colorado Avalanche	66	11	19	30	16	....	....	....	....	....
	Carolina Hurricanes	10	5	0	5	2	....	....	....	....	....
	NHL Totals	**128**	**34**	**31**	**65**	**32**	**9**	**0**	**0**	**0**	**0**

Traded to **Carolina** by **Colorado** for Bates Battaglia, March 11, 2003.

VUJTEK, Vladimir

Left wing. Shoots left. 6'2", 200 lbs. Born, Ostrava, Czech., February 17, 1972.
(Montreal's 5th choice, 73rd overall, in 1991 Entry Draft).

Season	Club	GP	G	A	Pts	PIM	GP	G	A	Pts	PIM
1991-92	Montreal Canadiens	2	0	0	0	0	....	....	....	....	....
1992-93	Edmonton Oilers	30	1	10	11	8	....	....	....	....	....
1993-94	Edmonton Oilers	40	4	15	19	14	....	....	....	....	....
1997-98	Tampa Bay Lightning	30	2	4	6	16	....	....	....	....	....
99-2000	Atlanta Thrashers	3	0	0	0	0	....	....	....	....	....
2002-03	Pittsburgh Penguins	5	0	1	1	0	....	....	....	....	....
	NHL Totals	**110**	**7**	**30**	**37**	**38**	....	....	....	....	....

Traded to **Edmonton** by **Montreal** with Shayne Corson and Brent Gilchrist for Vincent Damphousse and Edmonton's 4th round choice (Adam Wiesel) in 1993 Entry Draft, August 27, 1992. Traded to **Tampa Bay** by **Edmonton** with Edmonton's 3rd round choice (Dmitry Afanasenkov) in 1998 Entry Draft for Brantt Myhres and Toronto's 3rd round choice (previously acquired, Edmonton selected Alex Henry) in 1998 Entry Draft, July 16, 1997. • Missed majority of 1997-98 season recovering from Epstein-Barr Virus, December, 1997. Signed as a free agent by **Atlanta**, July 29, 1999. • Missed majority of 1999-2000 season recovering from facial injuries suffered in exhibition game vs. NY Rangers, September 18, 1999. Signed as a free agent by **Pittsburgh**, July 15, 2002.

VUKOTA, Mick

Right wing. Shoots right. 6'1", 225 lbs. Born, Saskatoon, Sask., September 14, 1966.

Season	Club	GP	G	A	Pts	PIM	GP	G	A	Pts	PIM
1987-88	New York Islanders	17	1	0	1	82	2	0	0	0	23
1988-89	New York Islanders	48	2	2	4	237	....	....	....	....	....
1989-90	New York Islanders	76	4	8	12	290	1	0	0	0	17
1990-91	New York Islanders	60	2	4	6	238	....	....	....	....	....
1991-92	New York Islanders	74	0	6	6	293	....	....	....	....	....
1992-93	New York Islanders	74	2	5	7	216	15	0	0	0	16
1993-94	New York Islanders	72	3	1	4	237	4	0	0	0	17
1994-95	New York Islanders	40	0	2	2	109	....	....	....	....	....
1995-96	New York Islanders	32	1	1	2	106	....	....	....	....	....
1996-97	New York Islanders	17	1	0	1	71	....	....	....	....	....
1997-98	Tampa Bay Lightning	42	1	0	1	116	....	....	....	....	....
	Montreal Canadiens	22	0	0	0	76	1	0	0	0	0
	NHL Totals	**574**	**17**	**29**	**46**	**2071**	**23**	**0**	**0**	**0**	**73**

Signed as a free agent by **NY Islanders**, March 2, 1987. Claimed by **Tampa Bay** from **NY Islanders** in NHL Waiver Draft, September 28, 1997. Traded to **Montreal** by **Tampa Bay** with Patrick Poulin and Igor Ulanov for Stephane Richer, Darcy Tucker and David Wilkie, January 15, 1998.

VYAZMIKIN, Igor

Wing. Shoots left. 6'1", 194 lbs. Born, Moscow, USSR, January 8, 1966.
(Edmonton's 13th choice, 252nd overall, in 1987 Entry Draft).

Season	Club	GP	G	A	Pts	PIM	GP	G	A	Pts	PIM
1990-91	Edmonton Oilers	4	1	0	1	0	....	....	....	....	....
	NHL Totals	**4**	**1**	**0**	**1**	**0**	....	....	....	....	....

VYBORNY, David

Right wing. Shoots left. 5'10", 189 lbs. Born, Jihlava, Czech., June 2, 1975.
(Edmonton's 3rd choice, 33rd overall, in 1993 Entry Draft).

Season	Club	GP	G	A	Pts	PIM	GP	G	A	Pts	PIM
2000-01	Columbus Blue Jackets	79	13	19	32	22	....	....	....	....	....
2001-02	Columbus Blue Jackets	75	13	18	31	6	....	....	....	....	....
2002-03	Columbus Blue Jackets	79	20	26	46	16	....	....	....	....	....
	NHL Totals	**233**	**46**	**63**	**109**	**44**	....	....	....	....	....

Signed as a free agent by **Columbus**, June 8, 2000.

VYSHEDKEVICH, Sergei

Defense. Shoots left. 6', 195 lbs. Born, Dedovsk, USSR, January 3, 1975.
(New Jersey's 3rd choice, 70th overall, in 1995 Entry Draft).

Season	Club	GP	G	A	Pts	PIM	GP	G	A	Pts	PIM
99-2000	Atlanta Thrashers	7	1	3	4	2	....	....	....	....	....
2000-01	Atlanta Thrashers	23	1	2	3	14	....	....	....	....	....
	NHL Totals	**30**	**2**	**5**	**7**	**16**	....	....	....	....	....

Traded to **Atlanta** by **New Jersey** for future considerations, June 25, 1999. Traded to **Anaheim** by **Atlanta** with Scott Langkow for Ladislav Kohn, February 9, 2001.

WADDELL, Don

Defense. Shoots left. 5'10", 180 lbs. Born, Detroit, MI, August 19, 1958.
(Los Angeles' 3rd choice, 111th overall, in 1978 Amateur Draft).

Season	Club	Regular Season GP	G	A	Pts	PIM	Playoffs GP	G	A	Pts	PIM
1980-81	Los Angeles Kings	1	0	0	0	0	....	....	....	....	....
	NHL Totals	**1**	**0**	**0**	**0**	**0**	....	....	....	....	....

WAITE, Frank

Center. Shoots left. 5'11", 150 lbs. Born, Fort Qu'Appelle, Sask., April 9, 1905.

Season	Club	Regular Season GP	G	A	Pts	PIM	Playoffs GP	G	A	Pts	PIM
1930-31	New York Rangers	17	1	3	4	4	....	....	....	....	....
	NHL Totals	**17**	**1**	**3**	**4**	**4**	....	....	....	....	....

Signed as a free agent by **NY Rangers**, September 2, 1926. Traded to **Boston** by **NY Rangers** for cash, September, 1928. Traded to **Springfield** (Can-Am) by **Boston** for cash, September, 1930. Traded to **NY Rangers** by **Springfield** (Can-Am) for cash, November 4, 1930. Traded to **Syracuse** (IAHL) by **NY Rangers** for cash, October 21, 1931. Signed as a free agent by **Cleveland** (IHL), November 5, 1932. Traded to **Detroit** by **Cleveland** (IHL) for Jack Riley and Tony Prelesnik, December 2, 1932. Traded to **Chicago** (London-IHL) by **Detroit** with Leroy Goldsworthy for Gene Carrigan, October 19, 1933.

WALKER, Gord

Right wing. Shoots left. 6', 175 lbs. Born, Castlegar, B.C., August 12, 1965.
(NY Rangers' 4th choice, 54th overall, in 1983 Entry Draft).

Season	Club	Regular Season GP	G	A	Pts	PIM	Playoffs GP	G	A	Pts	PIM
1986-87	New York Rangers	1	1	0	1	4	....	....	....	....	....
1987-88	New York Rangers	18	1	4	5	17	....	....	....	....	....
1988-89	Los Angeles Kings	11	1	0	1	2	....	....	....	....	....
1989-90	Los Angeles Kings	1	0	0	0	0	....	....	....	....	....
	NHL Totals	**31**	**3**	**4**	**7**	**23**	....	....	....	....	....

Traded to **Los Angeles** by **NY Rangers** with Mike Siltala for Joe Paterson, January 21, 1988.

WALKER, Howard

Defense. Shoots left. 6', 205 lbs. Born, Grande Prairie, Alta., August 5, 1958.

Season	Club	Regular Season GP	G	A	Pts	PIM	Playoffs GP	G	A	Pts	PIM
1980-81	Washington Capitals	64	2	11	13	100	....	....	....	....	....
1981-82	Washington Capitals	16	0	2	2	26	....	....	....	....	....
1982-83	Calgary Flames	3	0	0	0	7	....	....	....	....	....
	NHL Totals	**83**	**2**	**13**	**15**	**133**	....	....	....	....	....

Signed as a free agent by **Washington**, June 5, 1980. Traded to **Calgary** by **Washington** with George White, Washington's 6th round choice (Mats Kihlstrom) in 1982 Entry Draft, 3rd round choice (Perry Berezan) in 1983 Entry Draft and 2nd round choice (Paul Ranheim) in 1984 Entry Draft for Pat Riggin and Ken Houston, June 9, 1982.

WALKER, Jack

HHOF

Forward. Shoots left. 5'8", 153 lbs. Born, Silver Mountain, Ont., November 29, 1888.

Season	Club	Regular Season GP	G	A	Pts	PIM	Playoffs GP	G	A	Pts	PIM
1926-27	Detroit Cougars	37	3	4	7	6	....	....	....	....	....
1927-28	Detroit Cougars	43	2	4	6	12	....	....	....	....	....
	NHL Totals	**80**	**5**	**8**	**13**	**18**	....	....	....	....	....

Traded to **Detroit** by **Victoria** (WHL) for cash, May 15, 1926.

WALKER, Kurt

Defense. Shoots right. 6'3", 200 lbs. Born, Weymouth, MA, June 10, 1954.

Season	Club	Regular Season GP	G	A	Pts	PIM	Playoffs GP	G	A	Pts	PIM
1975-76	Toronto Maple Leafs	5	0	0	0	49	6	0	0	0	24
1976-77	Toronto Maple Leafs	26	2	3	5	24	....	....	....	....	....
1977-78	Toronto Maple Leafs	40	2	2	4	69	10	0	0	0	10
	NHL Totals	**71**	**4**	**5**	**9**	**142**	**16**	**0**	**0**	**0**	**34**

Signed as a free agent by **Toronto**, September, 1975. Traded to **Los Angeles** by **Toronto** with Scott Garland, Brian Glennie and Toronto's 2nd round choice (Mark Hardy) in 1979 Entry Draft for Dave Hutchison and Lorne Stamler, June 14, 1978.

WALKER, Matt

Defense. Shoots right. 6'2", 222 lbs. Born, Beaverlodge, Alta., April 7, 1980.
(St. Louis' 3rd choice, 83rd overall, in 1998 Entry Draft).

Season	Club	Regular Season GP	G	A	Pts	PIM	Playoffs GP	G	A	Pts	PIM
2002-03	St. Louis Blues	16	0	1	1	38	....	....	....	....	....
	NHL Totals	**16**	**0**	**1**	**1**	**38**	....	....	....	....	....

WALKER, Russ

Right wing. Shoots right. 6'2", 185 lbs. Born, Red Deer, Alta., May 24, 1953.
(Los Angeles' 1st choice, 38th overall, in 1973 Amateur Draft).

Season	Club	Regular Season GP	G	A	Pts	PIM	Playoffs GP	G	A	Pts	PIM
1976-77	Los Angeles Kings	16	1	0	1	35	....	....	....	....	....
1977-78	Los Angeles Kings	1	0	0	0	6	....	....	....	....	....
	NHL Totals	**17**	**1**	**0**	**1**	**41**	....	....	....	....	....

WALKER, Scott

Right wing. Shoots right. 5'10", 196 lbs. Born, Cambridge, Ont., July 19, 1973.
(Vancouver's 4th choice, 124th overall, in 1993 Entry Draft).

Season	Club	Regular Season GP	G	A	Pts	PIM	Playoffs GP	G	A	Pts	PIM
1994-95	Vancouver Canucks	11	0	1	1	33	....	....	....	....	....
1995-96	Vancouver Canucks	63	4	8	12	137	....	....	....	....	....
1996-97	Vancouver Canucks	64	3	15	18	132	....	....	....	....	....
1997-98	Vancouver Canucks	59	3	10	13	164	....	....	....	....	....
1998-99	Nashville Predators	71	15	25	40	103	....	....	....	....	....
99-2000	Nashville Predators	69	7	21	28	90	....	....	....	....	....
2000-01	Nashville Predators	74	25	29	54	66	....	....	....	....	....
2001-02	Nashville Predators	28	4	5	9	18	....	....	....	....	....
2002-03	Nashville Predators	60	15	18	33	58	....	....	....	....	....
	NHL Totals	**499**	**76**	**132**	**208**	**801**	....	....	....	....	....

Claimed by **Nashville** from **Vancouver** in Expansion Draft, June 26, 1998.

WALL, Bob

Defense. Shoots left. 5'10", 171 lbs. Born, Richmond Hill, Ont., December 1, 1942.

Season	Club	Regular Season GP	G	A	Pts	PIM	Playoffs GP	G	A	Pts	PIM
1964-65	Detroit Red Wings	1	0	0	0	0	1	0	0	0	0
1965-66	Detroit Red Wings	8	1	1	2	8	6	0	0	0	2
1966-67	Detroit Red Wings	31	2	2	4	26	....	....	....	....	....
1967-68	Los Angeles Kings	71	5	18	23	66	7	0	1	1	0
1968-69	Los Angeles Kings	71	13	13	26	16	8	0	2	2	0
1969-70	Los Angeles Kings	70	5	13	18	26	....	....	....	....	....
1970-71	St. Louis Blues	25	2	4	6	4	....	....	....	....	....
1971-72	Detroit Red Wings	45	2	4	6	9	....	....	....	....	....
	NHL Totals	**322**	**30**	**55**	**85**	**155**	**22**	**0**	**3**	**3**	**2**

Claimed by **Los Angeles** from **Detroit** in Expansion Draft, June 6, 1967. Traded to **St. Louis** by **Los Angeles** for Ray Fortin, May 11, 1970. Traded to **Detroit** by **St. Louis** with Ab McDonald and Mike Lowe to complete transaction that sent Carl Brewer to Detroit (February 22, 1971), May 12, 1971.

WALLIN, Jesse

Defense. Shoots left. 6'2", 190 lbs. Born, Saskatoon, Sask., March 10, 1978.
(Detroit's 1st choice, 26th overall, in 1996 Entry Draft).

Season	Club	Regular Season GP	G	A	Pts	PIM	Playoffs GP	G	A	Pts	PIM
99-2000	Detroit Red Wings	1	0	0	0	0	....	....	....	....	....
2000-01	Detroit Red Wings	1	0	0	0	2	....	....	....	....	....
2001-02	Detroit Red Wings	15	0	1	1	13	....	....	....	....	....
2002-03	Detroit Red Wings	32	0	1	1	19	....	....	....	....	....
	NHL Totals	**49**	**0**	**2**	**2**	**34**	....	....	....	....	....

WALLIN, Niclas

Defense. Shoots left. 6'3", 220 lbs. Born, Boden, Sweden, February 20, 1975.
(Carolina's 3rd choice, 97th overall, in 2000 Entry Draft).

Season	Club	Regular Season GP	G	A	Pts	PIM	Playoffs GP	G	A	Pts	PIM
2000-01	Carolina Hurricanes	37	2	3	5	21	3	0	0	0	2
2001-02	Carolina Hurricanes	52	1	2	3	36	23	2	1	3	12
2002-03	Carolina Hurricanes	77	2	8	10	71	....	....	....	....	....
	NHL Totals	**166**	**5**	**13**	**18**	**128**	**26**	**2**	**1**	**3**	**14**

• Missed most of 2000-01 season recovering from shoulder injury suffered in game vs. Florida, January 12, 2001.

WALLIN, Peter

Right wing. Shoots right. 5'9", 170 lbs. Born, Stockholm, Sweden, April 30, 1957.

Season	Club	Regular Season GP	G	A	Pts	PIM	Playoffs GP	G	A	Pts	PIM
1980-81	New York Rangers	12	1	5	6	2	14	2	6	8	6
1981-82	New York Rangers	40	2	9	11	12	....	....	....	....	....
	NHL Totals	**52**	**3**	**14**	**17**	**14**	**14**	**2**	**6**	**8**	**6**

Signed as a free agent by **NY Rangers**, March 8, 1981.

WALLIN, Rickard

Center. Shoots left. 6'2", 185 lbs. Born, Stockholm, Sweden, April 19, 1980.
(Phoenix's 8th choice, 160th overall, in 1998 Entry Draft).

Season	Club	Regular Season GP	G	A	Pts	PIM	Playoffs GP	G	A	Pts	PIM
2002-03	Minnesota Wild	4	1	0	1	0	....	....	....	....	....
	NHL Totals	**4**	**1**	**0**	**1**	**0**	....	....	....	....	....

Rights traded to **Minnesota** by **Phoenix** for Joe Juneau, June 23, 2000.

WALSER, Derrick

Defense. Shoots left. 5'10", 196 lbs. Born, New Glasgow, N.S., May 12, 1978.

Season	Club	Regular Season GP	G	A	Pts	PIM	Playoffs GP	G	A	Pts	PIM
2001-02	Columbus Blue Jackets	2	1	0	1	0	....	....	....	....	....
2002-03	Columbus Blue Jackets	53	4	13	17	34	....	....	....	....	....
	NHL Totals	**55**	**5**	**13**	**18**	**34**	....	....	....	....	....

Signed as a free agent by **Calgary**, October 16, 1998. Signed as a free agent by **Columbus**, September 17, 2001.

WALSH, Jim

Defense. Shoots right. 6'1", 185 lbs. Born, Norfolk, VA, October 26, 1956.

Season	Club	Regular Season GP	G	A	Pts	PIM	Playoffs GP	G	A	Pts	PIM
1981-82	Buffalo Sabres	4	0	1	1	4	....	....	....	....	....
	NHL Totals	**4**	**0**	**1**	**1**	**4**	....	....	....	....	....

Signed as a free agent by **Buffalo**, September 5, 1979.

WALSH, Mike

Wing. Shoots right. 6'2", 195 lbs. Born, New York, NY, April 3, 1962.

Season	Club	Regular Season GP	G	A	Pts	PIM	Playoffs GP	G	A	Pts	PIM
1987-88	New York Islanders	1	0	0	0	0	....	....	....	....	....
1988-89	New York Islanders	13	2	0	2	4	....	....	....	....	....
	NHL Totals	**14**	**2**	**0**	**2**	**4**	....	....	....	....	....

Signed as a free agent by **NY Islanders**, August, 1986.

WALTER, Ryan

Center/Left wing. Shoots left. 6', 200 lbs. Born, New Westminster, B.C., April 23, 1958.
(Washington's 1st choice, 2nd overall, in 1978 Amateur Draft).

Season	Club	Regular Season GP	G	A	Pts	PIM	Playoffs GP	G	A	Pts	PIM
1978-79	Washington Capitals	69	28	28	56	70	....	....	....	....	....
1979-80	Washington Capitals	80	24	42	66	106	....	....	....	....	....
1980-81	Washington Capitals	80	24	44	68	150	....	....	....	....	....
1981-82	Washington Capitals	78	38	49	87	142	....	....	....	....	....
1982-83	Montreal Canadiens	80	29	46	75	40	3	0	0	0	11
1983-84	Montreal Canadiens	73	20	29	49	83	15	2	1	3	4
1984-85	Montreal Canadiens	72	19	19	38	59	12	2	7	9	13
1985-86 ♦	Montreal Canadiens	69	15	34	49	45	5	0	1	1	2
1986-87	Montreal Canadiens	76	23	23	46	34	17	7	12	19	10

Season	Club	REGULAR SEASON GP	G	A	Pts	PIM	PLAYOFFS GP	G	A	Pts	PIM
1987-88	Montreal Canadiens	61	13	23	36	39	11	2	4	6	6
1988-89	Montreal Canadiens	78	14	17	31	48	21	3	5	8	6
1989-90	Montreal Canadiens	70	8	16	24	59	11	0	2	2	0
1990-91	Montreal Canadiens	25	0	1	1	12	5	0	0	0	2
1991-92	Vancouver Canucks	67	6	11	17	49	13	0	3	3	8
1992-93	Vancouver Canucks	25	3	0	3	10	....	....	....	....	....
	NHL Totals	**1003**	**264**	**382**	**646**	**946**	**113**	**16**	**35**	**51**	**62**

Played in NHL All-Star Game (1983)

Traded to **Montreal** by **Washington** with Rick Green for Rod Langway, Brian Engblom, Doug Jarvis and Craig Laughlin, September 9, 1982. • Missed majority of 1990-91 season recovering from wrist injury suffered in game vs. Hartford, October 13, 1990. Signed as a free agent by **Vancouver**, July 26, 1991.

WALTON, Bobby

Center/Right wing. Shoots right. 5'9", 165 lbs. Born, Ottawa, Ont., August 5, 1912.

Season	Club	GP	G	A	Pts	PIM	GP	G	A	Pts	PIM
1943-44	Montreal Canadiens	4	0	0	0	0	....	....	....	....	....
	NHL Totals	**4**	**0**	**0**	**0**	**0**	....	....	....	....	....

• Father of Mike

Signed as a free agent by **Montreal**, February 2, 1942.

WALTON, Mike

Center. Shoots left. 5'10", 175 lbs. Born, Kirkland Lake, Ont., January 3, 1945.

Season	Club	GP	G	A	Pts	PIM	GP	G	A	Pts	PIM
1965-66	Toronto Maple Leafs	6	1	3	4	0	....	....	....	....	....
1966-67 ♦	Toronto Maple Leafs	31	7	10	17	13	12	4	3	7	2
1967-68	Toronto Maple Leafs	73	30	29	59	48	....	....	....	....	....
1968-69	Toronto Maple Leafs	66	22	21	43	34	4	0	0	0	4
1969-70	Toronto Maple Leafs	58	21	34	55	68	....	....	....	....	....
1970-71	Toronto Maple Leafs	23	3	10	13	21	....	....	....	....	....
	Boston Bruins	22	3	5	8	10	5	2	0	2	19
1971-72 ♦	Boston Bruins	76	28	28	56	45	15	6	6	12	13
1972-73	Boston Bruins	56	25	22	47	37	5	1	1	2	2
1975-76	Vancouver Canucks	10	8	8	16	9	2	0	0	0	5
1976-77	Vancouver Canucks	40	7	24	31	32	....	....	....	....	....
1977-78	Vancouver Canucks	65	29	37	66	30	....	....	....	....	....
1978-79	St. Louis Blues	22	7	11	18	6	....	....	....	....	....
	Boston Bruins	14	4	2	6	0	....	....	....	....	....
	Chicago Black Hawks	26	6	3	9	4	4	1	0	1	0
	NHL Totals	**588**	**201**	**247**	**448**	**357**	**47**	**14**	**10**	**24**	**45**

• Son of Bobby

Played in NHL All-Star Game (1968)

Traded to **Philadelphia** by **Toronto** with Bruce Gamble and Toronto's 1st round choice (Pierre Plante) in 1971 Amateur Draft for Bernie Parent and Philadelphia's 2nd round choice (Rick Kehoe) in 1971 Amateur Draft, February 1, 1971. Traded to **Boston** by **Philadelphia** for Danny Schock and Rick MacLeish, February 1, 1971. NHL rights traded to **Vancouver** by **Boston** with the trade of Chris Oddleifson and Fred O'Donnell for Bobby Schmautz, February 7, 1974. Traded to **St. Louis** by **Vancouver** for St. Louis' 4th round choice (Harald Luckner) in 1978 Amateur Draft and future considerations, June 12, 1978. Signed as a free agent by **Boston**, December 5, 1978. Signed as a free agent by **Chicago**, January 22, 1979.

WALZ, Wes

Center. Shoots right. 5'10", 180 lbs. Born, Calgary, Alta., May 15, 1970.
(Boston's 3rd choice, 57th overall, in 1989 Entry Draft).

Season	Club	GP	G	A	Pts	PIM	GP	G	A	Pts	PIM
1989-90	Boston Bruins	2	1	1	2	0	....	....	....	....	....
1990-91	Boston Bruins	56	8	8	16	32	2	0	0	0	0
1991-92	Boston Bruins	15	0	3	3	12	....	....	....	....	....
	Philadelphia Flyers	2	1	0	1	0	....	....	....	....	....
1993-94	Calgary Flames	53	11	27	38	16	6	3	0	3	2
1994-95	Calgary Flames	39	6	12	18	11	1	0	0	0	0
1995-96	Detroit Red Wings	2	0	0	0	0	....	....	....	....	....
2000-01	Minnesota Wild	82	18	12	30	37	....	....	....	....	....
2001-02	Minnesota Wild	64	10	20	30	43	....	....	....	....	....
2002-03	Minnesota Wild	80	13	19	32	63	18	7	6	13	14
	NHL Totals	**395**	**68**	**102**	**170**	**214**	**27**	**10**	**6**	**16**	**16**

Traded to **Philadelphia** by **Boston** with Garry Galley and Boston's 3rd round choice (Milos Holan) in 1993 Entry Draft for Gord Murphy, Brian Dobbin, Philadelphia's 3rd round choice (Sergei Zholtok) in 1992 Entry Draft and 4th round choice (Charles Paquette) in 1993 Entry Draft, January 2, 1992. Signed as a free agent by **Calgary**, August 26, 1993. Signed as a free agent by **Detroit**, September 6, 1995. Signed as a free agent by **Minnesota**, June 28, 2000.

WANVIG, Kyle

Right wing. Shoots right. 6'2", 219 lbs. Born, Calgary, Alta., January 29, 1981.
(Minnesota's 2nd choice, 36th overall, in 2001 Entry Draft).

Season	Club	GP	G	A	Pts	PIM	GP	G	A	Pts	PIM
2002-03	Minnesota Wild	7	1	0	1	13	....	....	....	....	....
	NHL Totals	**7**	**1**	**0**	**1**	**13**	....	....	....	....	....

• Re-entered NHL Entry Draft. Originally Boston's 3rd choice, 89th overall, in 1999 Entry Draft.

WAPPEL, Gord

Defense. Shoots left. 6'2", 205 lbs. Born, Regina, Sask., July 26, 1958.
(Atlanta's 4th choice, 80th overall, in 1978 Amateur Draft).

Season	Club	GP	G	A	Pts	PIM	GP	G	A	Pts	PIM
1979-80	Atlanta Flames	2	0	0	0	0	2	0	0	0	4
1980-81	Calgary Flames	7	0	1	1	4	....	....	....	....	....
1981-82	Calgary Flames	11	1	0	1	6	....	....	....	....	....
	NHL Totals	**20**	**1**	**1**	**2**	**10**	**2**	**0**	**0**	**0**	**4**

Transferred to **Calgary** after **Atlanta** franchise relocated, June 24, 1980.

WARD, Aaron

Defense. Shoots right. 6'2", 200 lbs. Born, Windsor, Ont., January 17, 1973.
(Winnipeg's 1st choice, 5th overall, in 1991 Entry Draft).

Season	Club	GP	G	A	Pts	PIM	GP	G	A	Pts	PIM
1993-94	Detroit Red Wings	5	1	0	1	4	....	....	....	....	....
1994-95	Detroit Red Wings	1	0	1	1	2	....	....	....	....	....
1996-97 ♦	Detroit Red Wings	49	2	5	7	52	19	0	0	0	17
1997-98 ♦	Detroit Red Wings	52	5	5	10	47	....	....	....	....	....
1998-99	Detroit Red Wings	60	3	8	11	52	8	0	1	1	8
99-2000	Detroit Red Wings	36	1	3	4	24	3	0	0	0	0
2000-01	Detroit Red Wings	73	4	5	9	57	....	....	....	....	....
2001-02	Carolina Hurricanes	79	3	11	14	74	23	1	1	2	22
2002-03	Carolina Hurricanes	77	3	6	9	90	....	....	....	....	....
	NHL Totals	**432**	**22**	**44**	**66**	**402**	**53**	**1**	**2**	**3**	**47**

Traded to **Detroit** by **Winnipeg** with Toronto's 4th round choice (previously acquired, later traded to Detroit – Detroit selected John Jakopin) in 1993 Entry Draft for Paul Ysebaert and future considerations (Alan Kerr, June 18, 1993), June 11, 1993. • Missed majority of 1999-2000 season recovering from shoulder injury suffered in game vs. Vancouver, January 19, 2000. Traded to **Carolina** by **Detroit** for Carolina's 2nd round choice (Jiri Hudler) in 2002 Entry Draft, July 9, 2001.

WARD, Dixon

Right wing. Shoots right. 6', 200 lbs. Born, Leduc, Alta., September 23, 1968.
(Vancouver's 6th choice, 128th overall, in 1988 Entry Draft).

Season	Club	GP	G	A	Pts	PIM	GP	G	A	Pts	PIM
1992-93	Vancouver Canucks	70	22	30	52	82	9	2	3	5	0
1993-94	Vancouver Canucks	33	6	1	7	37	....	....	....	....	....
	Los Angeles Kings	34	6	2	8	45	....	....	....	....	....
1994-95	Toronto Maple Leafs	22	0	3	3	31	....	....	....	....	....
1995-96	Buffalo Sabres	8	2	2	4	6	....	....	....	....	....
1996-97	Buffalo Sabres	79	13	32	45	36	12	2	3	5	6
1997-98	Buffalo Sabres	71	10	13	23	42	15	3	8	11	6
1998-99	Buffalo Sabres	78	20	24	44	44	21	7	5	12	32
99-2000	Buffalo Sabres	71	11	9	20	41	5	0	1	1	2
2000-01	Boston Bruins	63	5	13	18	65	....	....	....	....	....
2002-03	New York Rangers	8	0	0	0	2	....	....	....	....	....
	NHL Totals	**537**	**95**	**129**	**224**	**431**	**62**	**14**	**20**	**34**	**46**

Traded to **Los Angeles** by **Vancouver** for Jimmy Carson, January 8, 1994. Traded to **Toronto** by **Los Angeles** with Guy Leveque, Kelly Fairchild and Shayne Toporowski for Eric Lacroix, Chris Snell and Toronto's 4th round choice (Eric Belanger) in 1996 Entry Draft, October 3, 1994. Signed as a free agent by **Buffalo**, September 20, 1995. Signed as a free agent by **Boston**, November 8, 2000. Signed as a free agent by **NY Rangers**, October 1, 2002.

WARD, Don

Defense. Shoots left. 6'2", 200 lbs. Born, Sarnia, Ont., October 19, 1935.

Season	Club	GP	G	A	Pts	PIM	GP	G	A	Pts	PIM
1957-58	Chicago Black Hawks	3	0	0	0	0	....	....	....	....	....
1959-60	Boston Bruins	31	0	1	1	16	....	....	....	....	....
	NHL Totals	**34**	**0**	**1**	**1**	**16**	....	....	....	....	....

• Father of Joe

Claimed by **Boston** from **Calgary** (WHL) in Inter-League Draft, June 9, 1959. Traded to **Portland** (WHL) by **Boston** with Gene Achtymichuk as part of transaction that sent Don Head to Boston (May, 1961), August, 1961.

WARD, Ed

Right wing. Shoots right. 6'3", 220 lbs. Born, Edmonton, Alta., November 10, 1969.
(Quebec's 7th choice, 108th overall, in 1988 Entry Draft).

Season	Club	GP	G	A	Pts	PIM	GP	G	A	Pts	PIM
1993-94	Quebec Nordiques	7	1	0	1	5	....	....	....	....	....
1994-95	Calgary Flames	2	1	1	2	2	....	....	....	....	....
1995-96	Calgary Flames	41	3	5	8	44	....	....	....	....	....
1996-97	Calgary Flames	40	5	8	13	49	....	....	....	....	....
1997-98	Calgary Flames	64	4	5	9	122	....	....	....	....	....
1998-99	Calgary Flames	68	3	5	8	67	....	....	....	....	....
99-2000	Atlanta Thrashers	44	5	1	6	44	....	....	....	....	....
	Mighty Ducks of Anaheim	8	1	0	1	15	....	....	....	....	....
2000-01	New Jersey Devils	4	0	1	1	6	....	....	....	....	....
	NHL Totals	**278**	**23**	**26**	**49**	**354**	....	....	....	....	....

Traded to **Calgary** by **Quebec** for Francois Groleau, March 23, 1995. Claimed by **Atlanta** from **Calgary** in Expansion Draft, June 25, 1999. Traded to **Anaheim** by **Atlanta** for Anaheim's 7th round choice (Colin Fitzrandolph) in 2001 Entry Draft, March 14, 2000. Traded to **New Jersey** by **Anaheim** for New Jersey's 7th round choice (Tony Martensson) in 2001 Entry Draft, June 12, 2000.

WARD, Jason

Right wing. Shoots right. 6'3", 200 lbs. Born, Chapleau, Ont., January 16, 1979.
(Montreal's 1st choice, 11th overall, in 1997 Entry Draft).

Season	Club	GP	G	A	Pts	PIM	GP	G	A	Pts	PIM
99-2000	Montreal Canadiens	32	2	1	3	10	....	....	....	....	....
2000-01	Montreal Canadiens	12	0	0	0	12	....	....	....	....	....
2002-03	Montreal Canadiens	8	3	2	5	0	....	....	....	....	....
	NHL Totals	**52**	**5**	**3**	**8**	**22**	....	....	....	....	....

WARD, Jimmy

Right wing. Shoots right. 5'11", 167 lbs. Born, Fort William, Ont., September 1, 1906.

Season	Club	GP	G	A	Pts	PIM	GP	G	A	Pts	PIM
1927-28	Montreal Maroons	42	10	2	12	44	9	1	1	2	6
1928-29	Montreal Maroons	43	14	8	22	46	....	....	....	....	....
1929-30	Montreal Maroons	44	10	7	17	54	4	0	1	1	12
1930-31	Montreal Maroons	41	14	8	22	52	2	0	0	0	2
1931-32	Montreal Maroons	48	19	19	38	39	4	2	1	3	0
1932-33	Montreal Maroons	48	16	17	33	52	2	0	0	0	0

Season	Club	Regular Season GP	G	A	Pts	PIM	Playoffs GP	G	A	Pts	PIM
1933-34	Montreal Maroons	48	14	9	23	46	4	0	0	0	0
1934-35♦	Montreal Maroons	41	9	6	15	24	7	1	1	2	0
1935-36	Montreal Maroons	48	12	19	31	30	3	0	0	0	6
1936-37	Montreal Maroons	40	14	14	28	34	....	....	....	....	....
1937-38	Montreal Maroons	48	11	15	26	34	....	....	....	....	....
1938-39	Montreal Canadiens	36	4	3	7	0	1	0	0	0	0
	NHL Totals	**527**	**147**	**127**	**274**	**455**	**36**	**4**	**4**	**8**	**26**

Played in NHL All-Star Game (1934, 1937)

Signed as a free agent by **Mtl. Maroons**, August 26, 1927. Traded to **Montreal** by **Mtl. Maroons** for cash, September 14, 1938.

WARD, Joe

Center. Shoots left. 6', 180 lbs. Born, Sarnia, Ont., February 11, 1961.
(Colorado's 2nd choice, 22nd overall, in 1980 Entry Draft).

Season	Club	GP	G	A	Pts	PIM	GP	G	A	Pts	PIM
1980-81	Colorado Rockies	4	0	0	0	2	....	....	....	....	....
	NHL Totals	**4**	**0**	**0**	**0**	**2**	....	....	....	....	....

• Son of Don

WARD, Lance

Defense. Shoots left. 6'3", 220 lbs. Born, Lloydminster, Alta., June 2, 1978.
(Florida's 3rd choice, 63rd overall, in 1998 Entry Draft).

Season	Club	GP	G	A	Pts	PIM	GP	G	A	Pts	PIM
2000-01	Florida Panthers	30	0	2	2	45	....	....	....	....	....
2001-02	Florida Panthers	68	1	4	5	131	....	....	....	....	....
2002-03	Florida Panthers	36	3	1	4	78	....	....	....	....	....
	Mighty Ducks of Anaheim	29	0	1	1	43	....	....	....	....	....
	NHL Totals	**163**	**4**	**8**	**12**	**297**	....	....	....	....	....

• Re-entered NHL Entry Draft. Originally New Jersey's 1st choice, 10th overall, in 1996 Entry Draft.

Traded to **Anaheim** by **Florida** with Sandis Ozolinsh for Pavel Trnka, Matt Cullen and Anaheim's 4th round choice (James Pemberton) in 2003 Entry Draft, January 30, 2003.

WARD, Ron

Center. Shoots right. 5'11", 175 lbs. Born, Cornwall, Ont., September 12, 1944.

Season	Club	GP	G	A	Pts	PIM	GP	G	A	Pts	PIM
1969-70	Toronto Maple Leafs	18	0	1	1	2	....	....	....	....	....
1971-72	Vancouver Canucks	71	2	4	6	4	....	....	....	....	....
	NHL Totals	**89**	**2**	**5**	**7**	**6**	....	....	....	....	....

Traded to **Toronto** by **Vancouver** (WHL) for Brad Selwood and Rene Robert, May, 1969. Claimed by **Vancouver** from **Toronto** in Expansion Draft, June 10, 1970.

WARE, Jeff

Defense. Shoots left. 6'4", 220 lbs. Born, Toronto, Ont., May 19, 1977.
(Toronto's 1st choice, 15th overall, in 1995 Entry Draft).

Season	Club	GP	G	A	Pts	PIM	GP	G	A	Pts	PIM
1996-97	Toronto Maple Leafs	13	0	0	0	6	....	....	....	....	....
1997-98	Toronto Maple Leafs	2	0	0	0	0	....	....	....	....	....
1998-99	Florida Panthers	6	0	1	1	6	....	....	....	....	....
	NHL Totals	**21**	**0**	**1**	**1**	**12**	....	....	....	....	....

Traded to **Florida** by **Toronto** for David Nemirovsky, February 17, 1999. Signed as a free agent by **Columbus**, May 31, 2001.

WARE, Michael

Right wing. Shoots right. 6'5", 216 lbs. Born, York, Ont., March 22, 1967.
(Edmonton's 3rd choice, 62nd overall, in 1985 Entry Draft).

Season	Club	GP	G	A	Pts	PIM	GP	G	A	Pts	PIM
1988-89	Edmonton Oilers	2	0	1	1	11	....	....	....	....	....
1989-90	Edmonton Oilers	3	0	0	0	4	....	....	....	....	....
	NHL Totals	**5**	**0**	**1**	**1**	**15**	....	....	....	....	....

WARES, Eddie

Defense/Right wing. Shoots right. 5'11", 182 lbs. Born, Calgary, Alta., March 19, 1915.

Season	Club	GP	G	A	Pts	PIM	GP	G	A	Pts	PIM
1936-37	New York Rangers	2	2	0	2	0	....	....	....	....	....
1937-38	Detroit Red Wings	21	9	7	16	2	....	....	....	....	....
1938-39	Detroit Red Wings	28	8	8	16	10	6	1	0	1	8
1939-40	Detroit Red Wings	33	2	6	8	19	5	0	0	0	0
1940-41	Detroit Red Wings	42	10	16	26	34	9	0	0	0	0
1941-42	Detroit Red Wings	43	9	29	38	31	12	1	3	4	22
1942-43♦	Detroit Red Wings	47	12	18	30	10	10	3	3	6	4
1945-46	Chicago Black Hawks	45	4	11	15	34	3	0	1	1	0
1946-47	Chicago Black Hawks	60	4	7	11	21	....	....	....	....	....
	NHL Totals	**321**	**60**	**102**	**162**	**161**	**45**	**5**	**7**	**12**	**34**

Signed as a free agent by **Mtl. Maroons**, September 30, 1935. Traded to **NY Rangers** by **Mtl. Maroons** for the rights to George Brown, October 30, 1935. Traded to **Detroit** by **NY Rangers** (Philadelphia-IAHL) for cash and the loan of John Sherf for the remainder of the 1937-38 season, January 17, 1938. Traded to **Chicago** by **Detroit** for cash, October 11, 1945. Traded to **Cleveland** (AHL) by **Chicago** for cash, September, 1947. Traded to **Chicago** (Kansas City-USHL) by **Cleveland** (AHL) for Doug Baldwin, January 28, 1949.

WARNER, Bob

Defense. Shoots left. 5'11", 180 lbs. Born, Grimsby, Ont., December 13, 1950.

Season	Club	GP	G	A	Pts	PIM	GP	G	A	Pts	PIM
1975-76	Toronto Maple Leafs	....	....	....	....	....	2	0	0	0	0
1976-77	Toronto Maple Leafs	10	1	1	2	4	2	0	0	0	0
	NHL Totals	**10**	**1**	**1**	**2**	**4**	**4**	**0**	**0**	**0**	**0**

Signed as a free agent by **Toronto**, September 3, 1975.

WARNER, Jim

Right wing. Shoots right. 5'11", 180 lbs. Born, Minneapolis, MN, March 26, 1954.
(NY Rangers' 23rd choice, 245th overall, in 1974 Amateur Draft).

Season	Club	GP	G	A	Pts	PIM	GP	G	A	Pts	PIM
1979-80	Hartford Whalers	32	0	3	3	10	....	....	....	....	....
	NHL Totals	**32**	**0**	**3**	**3**	**10**	....	....	....	....	....

Rights retained by **Hartford** prior to Expansion Draft, June 9, 1979.

WARRENER, Rhett

Defense. Shoots right. 6'2", 217 lbs. Born, Shaunavon, Sask., January 27, 1976.
(Florida's 2nd choice, 27th overall, in 1994 Entry Draft).

Season	Club	GP	G	A	Pts	PIM	GP	G	A	Pts	PIM
1995-96	Florida Panthers	28	0	3	3	46	21	0	1	1	0
1996-97	Florida Panthers	62	4	9	13	88	5	0	0	0	0
1997-98	Florida Panthers	79	0	4	4	99	....	....	....	....	....
1998-99	Florida Panthers	48	0	7	7	64	....	....	....	....	....
	Buffalo Sabres	13	1	0	1	20	20	1	3	4	32
99-2000	Buffalo Sabres	61	0	3	3	89	5	0	0	0	2
2000-01	Buffalo Sabres	77	3	16	19	78	13	0	2	2	4
2001-02	Buffalo Sabres	65	5	5	10	113	....	....	....	....	....
2002-03	Buffalo Sabres	50	0	9	9	63	....	....	....	....	....
	NHL Totals	**483**	**13**	**56**	**69**	**660**	**64**	**1**	**6**	**7**	**38**

Traded to **Buffalo** by **Florida** with Florida's 5th round choice (Ryan Miller) in 1999 Entry Draft for Mike Wilson, March 23, 1999. Traded to **Calgary** by **Buffalo** with Steve Reinprecht for Chris Drury and Steve Begin, July 3, 2003.

WARRINER, Todd

Left wing. Shoots left. 6'1", 200 lbs. Born, Blenheim, Ont., January 3, 1974.
(Quebec's 1st choice, 4th overall, in 1992 Entry Draft).

Season	Club	GP	G	A	Pts	PIM	GP	G	A	Pts	PIM
1994-95	Toronto Maple Leafs	5	0	0	0	0	....	....	....	....	....
1995-96	Toronto Maple Leafs	57	7	8	15	26	6	1	1	2	2
1996-97	Toronto Maple Leafs	75	12	21	33	41	....	....	....	....	....
1997-98	Toronto Maple Leafs	45	5	8	13	20	....	....	....	....	....
1998-99	Toronto Maple Leafs	53	9	10	19	28	9	0	0	0	2
99-2000	Toronto Maple Leafs	18	3	1	4	2	....	....	....	....	....
	Tampa Bay Lightning	55	11	13	24	34	....	....	....	....	....
2000-01	Tampa Bay Lightning	64	10	11	21	46	....	....	....	....	....
2001-02	Phoenix Coyotes	18	0	3	3	8	....	....	....	....	....
	Vancouver Canucks	14	2	4	6	12	6	1	0	1	2
2002-03	Vancouver Canucks	30	4	6	10	22	....	....	....	....	....
	Philadelphia Flyers	13	2	3	5	6	....	....	....	....	....
	Nashville Predators	6	0	1	1	4	....	....	....	....	....
	NHL Totals	**453**	**65**	**89**	**154**	**249**	**21**	**2**	**1**	**3**	**6**

Traded to **Toronto** by **Quebec** with Mats Sundin, Garth Butcher and Philadelphia's 1st round choice (previously acquired, later traded to Washington – Washington selected Nolan Baumgartner) in 1994 Entry Draft for Wendel Clark, Sylvain Lefebvre, Landon Wilson and Toronto's 1st round choice (Jeffrey Kealty) in 1994 Entry Draft, June 28, 1994. Traded to **Tampa Bay** by **Toronto** for Tampa Bay's 3rd round choice (Mikael Tellqvist) in 2000 Entry Draft, November 29, 1999. Traded to **Phoenix** by **Tampa Bay** for Juha Ylonen, June 18, 2001. Traded to **Vancouver** by **Phoenix** with Trevor Letowski, Tyler Bouck and Phoenix's 3rd round choice (later traded back to Phoenix – Phoenix selected Dimitri Pestunov) in 2003 Entry Draft for Drake Berehowsky and Denis Pederson, December 28, 2001. Traded to **Philadelphia** by **Vancouver** for future considerations, February 5, 2003. Claimed on waivers by **Nashville** from **Philadelphia**, March 11, 2003.

WARWICK, Bill

Left wing. Shoots left. 5'7", 155 lbs. Born, Regina, Sask., November 17, 1924.

Season	Club	GP	G	A	Pts	PIM	GP	G	A	Pts	PIM
1942-43	New York Rangers	1	0	1	1	4	....	....	....	....	....
1943-44	New York Rangers	13	3	2	5	12	....	....	....	....	....
	NHL Totals	**14**	**3**	**3**	**6**	**16**	....	....	....	....	....

• Brother of Grant

WARWICK, Grant

Right wing. Shoots right. 5'6", 155 lbs. Born, Regina, Sask., October 11, 1921.

Season	Club	GP	G	A	Pts	PIM	GP	G	A	Pts	PIM
1941-42	New York Rangers	44	16	17	33	36	6	0	1	1	2
1942-43	New York Rangers	50	17	18	35	31	....	....	....	....	....
1943-44	New York Rangers	18	8	9	17	14	....	....	....	....	....
1944-45	New York Rangers	42	20	22	42	25	....	....	....	....	....
1945-46	New York Rangers	45	19	18	37	19	....	....	....	....	....
1946-47	New York Rangers	54	20	20	40	24	....	....	....	....	....
1947-48	New York Rangers	40	17	12	29	30	....	....	....	....	....
	Boston Bruins	18	6	5	11	8	5	0	3	3	4
1948-49	Boston Bruins	58	22	15	37	14	5	2	0	2	0
1949-50	Montreal Canadiens	26	2	6	8	19	....	....	....	....	....
	NHL Totals	**395**	**147**	**142**	**289**	**220**	**16**	**2**	**4**	**6**	**6**

• Brother of Bill • Calder Trophy (1942)

Played in NHL All-Star Game (1947)

Claimed by **NY Rangers** from **Cleveland** (AHL) in Inter-League Draft, June 27, 1941. • Missed majority of 1943-44 season recovering from head injury suffered in game vs. Detroit, December 23, 1943. Traded to **Boston** by **NY Rangers** for Billy Taylor and future considerations (Pentti Lund and Ray Manson, June, 1948), February 6, 1948. Traded to **Montreal** by **Boston** for cash, October 10, 1949.

WASHBURN, Steve

Center. Shoots left. 6'2", 198 lbs. Born, Ottawa, Ont., April 10, 1975.
(Florida's 5th choice, 78th overall, in 1993 Entry Draft).

Season	Club	GP	G	A	Pts	PIM	GP	G	A	Pts	PIM
1995-96	Florida Panthers	1	0	1	1	0	1	0	1	1	0
1996-97	Florida Panthers	18	3	6	9	4	....	....	....	....	....

Season	Club	Regular Season GP	G	A	Pts	PIM	Playoffs GP	G	A	Pts	PIM
1997-98	Florida Panthers	58	11	8	19	32	....	....	....	....	....
1998-99	Florida Panthers	4	0	0	0	4	....	....	....	....	....
	Vancouver Canucks	8	0	0	0	2	....	....	....	....	....
99-2000	Philadelphia Flyers	1	0	0	0	0	....	....	....	....	....
2000-01	Philadelphia Flyers	3	0	0	0	0	....	....	....	....	....
	NHL Totals	**93**	**14**	**15**	**29**	**42**	**1**	**0**	**1**	**1**	**0**

Claimed on waivers by **Vancouver** from **Florida**, February 18, 1999. Signed as a free agent by **Nashville**, August 11, 1999. Traded to **Philadelphia** by **Nashville** for future considerations, November 16, 1999.

WASNIE, Nick

Right wing. Shoots right. 5'11", 174 lbs. Born, Winnipeg, Man., January 1, 1904.

Season	Club	GP	G	A	Pts	PIM	GP	G	A	Pts	PIM
1927-28	Chicago Black Hawks	14	1	0	1	22	....	....	....	....	....
1929-30 ♦	Montreal Canadiens	44	12	11	23	64	6	2	2	4	12
1930-31 ♦	Montreal Canadiens	44	9	2	11	26	10	4	1	5	8
1931-32	Montreal Canadiens	48	10	2	12	16	4	0	0	0	0
1932-33	New York Americans	48	11	12	23	36	....	....	....	....	....
1933-34	Ottawa Senators	37	11	6	17	10	....	....	....	....	....
1934-35	St. Louis Eagles	13	3	1	4	2	....	....	....	....	....
	NHL Totals	**248**	**57**	**34**	**91**	**176**	**20**	**6**	**3**	**9**	**20**

Signed as a free agent by **Chicago**, October 12, 1927. Traded to **Saskatoon** (PrHL) by **Chicago** with Corb Denneny for Eddie McCalmon and Earl Miller, January 11, 1928. Signed as a free agent by **Montreal**, November 10, 1929. Loaned to **NY Americans** by **Montreal** for the 1932-33 season, October, 1932. Traded to **Ottawa** by **Montreal** for cash to complete the transaction that sent Harold Starr and Leo Bourgeault to the Montreal Canadiens (February 14, 1933), March 23, 1933. Transferred to **St. Louis** after **Ottawa** franchise relocated, 1934. Traded to **Minneapolis** (CHL) by **St. Louis** with $1,600 for Fido Purpur, December 28, 1934.

WATSON, Bill

Right wing. Shoots right. 6', 185 lbs. Born, Pine Falls, Man., March 30, 1964.
(Chicago's 4th choice, 70th overall, in 1982 Entry Draft).

Season	Club	GP	G	A	Pts	PIM	GP	G	A	Pts	PIM
1985-86	Chicago Black Hawks	52	8	16	24	2	2	0	1	1	0
1986-87	Chicago Blackhawks	51	13	19	32	6	4	0	1	1	0
1987-88	Chicago Blackhawks	9	2	0	2	0	....	....	....	....	....
1988-89	Chicago Blackhawks	3	0	1	1	4	....	....	....	....	....
	NHL Totals	**115**	**23**	**36**	**59**	**12**	**6**	**0**	**2**	**2**	**0**

WATSON, Bryan

Defense. Shoots right. 5'9", 175 lbs. Born, Bancroft, Ont., November 14, 1942.

Season	Club	GP	G	A	Pts	PIM	GP	G	A	Pts	PIM
1963-64	Montreal Canadiens	39	0	2	2	18	6	0	0	0	2
1964-65	Montreal Canadiens	5	0	1	1	7	....	....	....	....	....
1965-66	Detroit Red Wings	70	2	7	9	133	12	2	0	2	30
1966-67	Detroit Red Wings	48	0	1	1	66	....	....	....	....	....
1967-68	Montreal Canadiens	12	0	1	1	9	....	....	....	....	....
1968-69	Oakland Seals	50	2	3	5	97	....	....	....	....	....
	Pittsburgh Penguins	18	0	4	4	35	....	....	....	....	....
1969-70	Pittsburgh Penguins	61	1	9	10	189	10	0	0	0	17
1970-71	Pittsburgh Penguins	43	2	6	8	119	....	....	....	....	....
1971-72	Pittsburgh Penguins	75	3	17	20	*212	4	0	0	0	21
1972-73	Pittsburgh Penguins	69	1	17	18	179	....	....	....	....	....
1973-74	Pittsburgh Penguins	38	1	4	5	137	....	....	....	....	....
	St. Louis Blues	11	0	1	1	19	....	....	....	....	....
	Detroit Red Wings	21	0	4	4	99	....	....	....	....	....
1974-75	Detroit Red Wings	70	1	13	14	238	....	....	....	....	....
1975-76	Detroit Red Wings	79	0	18	18	322	....	....	....	....	....
1976-77	Detroit Red Wings	14	0	1	1	39	....	....	....	....	....
	Washington Capitals	56	1	14	15	91	....	....	....	....	....
1977-78	Washington Capitals	79	3	11	14	167	....	....	....	....	....
1978-79	Washington Capitals	20	0	1	1	36	....	....	....	....	....
	NHL Totals	**878**	**17**	**135**	**152**	**2212**	**32**	**2**	**0**	**2**	**70**

Traded to **Chicago** by **Montreal** for Don Johns, June 8, 1965. Claimed by **Detroit** from **Chicago** in Intra-League Draft, June 9, 1965. Claimed by **Minnesota** from **Detroit** in Expansion Draft, June 6, 1967. Traded to **Montreal** by **Minnesota** for Bill Plager and the rights to Leo Thiffault and Barrie Meissner, June 6, 1967. Traded to **Oakland** by **Montreal** with cash for Oakland's 1st round choice (Michel Larocque) in 1972 Amateur Draft and future considerations (Tom Thurlby, September, 1968), June 28, 1968. Traded to **Pittsburgh** by **Oakland** with George Swarbrick and Tracy Pratt for Earl Ingarfield, Gene Ubriaco and Dick Mattiussi, January 30, 1969. Traded to **St. Louis** by **Pittsburgh** with Greg Polis and Pittsburgh's 2nd round choice (Bob Hess) in 1974 Amateur Draft for Steve Durbano, Ab DeMarco Jr. and Bob Kelly, January 17, 1974. Traded to **Detroit** by **St. Louis** with Chris Evans and Jean Hamel for Ted Harris, Bill Collins and Garnet Bailey, February 14, 1974. Traded to **Washington** by **Detroit** for Greg Joly, November 30, 1976. Claimed by **Edmonton** from **Cincinnati** (WHA) in WHA Dispersal Draft, June 9, 1979.

WATSON, Dave

Left wing. Shoots left. 6'2", 190 lbs. Born, Kirkland Lake, Ont., May 19, 1958.
(Colorado's 4th choice, 58th overall, in 1978 Amateur Draft).

Season	Club	GP	G	A	Pts	PIM	GP	G	A	Pts	PIM
1979-80	Colorado Rockies	5	0	0	0	2	....	....	....	....	....
1980-81	Colorado Rockies	13	0	1	1	8	....	....	....	....	....
	NHL Totals	**18**	**0**	**1**	**1**	**10**	....	....	....	....	....

Missed entire 1978-79 season recovering from knee injury suffered in training camp, September, 1978.

WATSON, Harry

HHOF

Left wing. Shoots left. 6'1", 207 lbs. Born, Saskatoon, Sask., May 6, 1923.

Season	Club	GP	G	A	Pts	PIM	GP	G	A	Pts	PIM
1941-42	Brooklyn Americans	47	10	8	18	6					
1942-43 ♦	Detroit Red Wings	50	13	18	31	10	7	0	0	0	0
1945-46	Detroit Red Wings	44	14	10	24	4	5	2	0	2	0
1946-47 ♦	Toronto Maple Leafs	44	19	15	34	10	11	3	2	5	6
1947-48 ♦	Toronto Maple Leafs	57	21	20	41	16	9	5	2	7	9
1948-49 ♦	Toronto Maple Leafs	60	26	19	45	0	9	4	2	6	2
1949-50	Toronto Maple Leafs	60	19	16	35	11	7	0	0	0	2
1950-51 ♦	Toronto Maple Leafs	68	18	19	37	18	5	1	2	3	4
1951-52	Toronto Maple Leafs	70	22	17	39	18	4	1	0	1	2
1952-53	Toronto Maple Leafs	63	16	8	24	8	....	....	....	....	....
1953-54	Toronto Maple Leafs	70	21	7	28	30	5	0	1	1	2
1954-55	Toronto Maple Leafs	8	1	1	2	0	....	....	....	....	....
	Chicago Black Hawks	43	14	16	30	4	....	....	....	....	....
1955-56	Chicago Black Hawks	55	11	14	25	6	....	....	....	....	....
1956-57	Chicago Black Hawks	70	11	19	30	9	....	....	....	....	....
	NHL Totals	**809**	**236**	**207**	**443**	**150**	**62**	**16**	**9**	**25**	**27**

Played in NHL All-Star Game (1947, 1948, 1949, 1951, 1952, 1953, 1955)

Signed as a free agent by **Brooklyn**, October 10, 1941. Rights transferred to **Detroit** from **Brooklyn** in Special Dispersal Draft October 9, 1942. Traded to **Toronto** by **Detroit** for Billy Taylor, September 21, 1946. Traded to **Chicago** by **Toronto** for cash, December 10, 1954.

WATSON, Jim

Defense. Shoots left. 6'2", 186 lbs. Born, Malartic, Que., June 28, 1943.

Season	Club	GP	G	A	Pts	PIM	GP	G	A	Pts	PIM
1963-64	Detroit Red Wings	1	0	0	0	0	....	....	....	....	....
1964-65	Detroit Red Wings	1	0	0	0	2	....	....	....	....	....
1965-66	Detroit Red Wings	2	0	0	0	4	....	....	....	....	....
1967-68	Detroit Red Wings	61	0	3	3	87	....	....	....	....	....
1968-69	Detroit Red Wings	8	0	1	1	4	....	....	....	....	....
1969-70	Detroit Red Wings	4	0	0	0	0	....	....	....	....	....
1970-71	Buffalo Sabres	78	2	9	11	147	....	....	....	....	....
1971-72	Buffalo Sabres	66	2	6	8	101	....	....	....	....	....
	NHL Totals	**221**	**4**	**19**	**23**	**345**	....	....	....	....	....

Claimed by **Buffalo** from **Detroit** in Expansion Draft, June 10, 1970.

WATSON, Jimmy

Defense. Shoots left. 6', 195 lbs. Born, Smithers, B.C., August 19, 1952.
(Philadelphia's 3rd choice, 39th overall, in 1972 Amateur Draft).

Season	Club	GP	G	A	Pts	PIM	GP	G	A	Pts	PIM
1972-73	Philadelphia Flyers	4	0	1	1	5	2	0	0	0	0
1973-74 ♦	Philadelphia Flyers	78	2	18	20	44	17	1	2	3	41
1974-75 ♦	Philadelphia Flyers	68	7	18	25	72	17	1	8	9	10
1975-76	Philadelphia Flyers	79	2	34	36	66	16	1	8	9	6
1976-77	Philadelphia Flyers	71	3	23	26	35	10	1	2	3	2
1977-78	Philadelphia Flyers	71	5	12	17	62	12	1	7	8	6
1978-79	Philadelphia Flyers	77	9	13	22	52	8	0	2	2	2
1979-80	Philadelphia Flyers	71	5	18	23	51	15	0	4	4	20
1980-81	Philadelphia Flyers	18	2	2	4	6	....	....	....	....	....
1981-82	Philadelphia Flyers	76	3	9	12	99	4	0	1	1	2
	NHL Totals	**613**	**38**	**148**	**186**	**492**	**101**	**5**	**34**	**39**	**89**

• Brother of Joe • NHL Plus/Minus Leader (1980)

Played in NHL All-Star Game (1975, 1976, 1977, 1978, 1980)

• Missed majority of 1980-81 season recovering from back injury that required surgery, January, 1981.

WATSON, Joe

Defense. Shoots right. 5'10", 185 lbs. Born, Smithers, B.C., July 6, 1943.

Season	Club	GP	G	A	Pts	PIM	GP	G	A	Pts	PIM
1964-65	Boston Bruins	4	0	1	1	0	....	....	....	....	....
1966-67	Boston Bruins	69	2	13	15	38	....	....	....	....	....
1967-68	Philadelphia Flyers	73	5	14	19	56	7	1	1	2	28
1968-69	Philadelphia Flyers	60	2	8	10	14	4	0	0	0	0
1969-70	Philadelphia Flyers	54	3	11	14	28	....	....	....	....	....
1970-71	Philadelphia Flyers	57	3	7	10	50	1	0	0	0	0
1971-72	Philadelphia Flyers	65	3	7	10	38	....	....	....	....	....
1972-73	Philadelphia Flyers	63	2	24	26	46	11	0	2	2	12
1973-74 ♦	Philadelphia Flyers	74	1	17	18	34	17	1	4	5	24
1974-75 ♦	Philadelphia Flyers	80	6	17	23	42	17	0	4	4	6
1975-76	Philadelphia Flyers	78	2	22	24	28	16	1	1	2	10
1976-77	Philadelphia Flyers	77	4	26	30	39	10	0	0	0	2
1977-78	Philadelphia Flyers	65	5	9	14	22	1	0	0	0	0
1978-79	Colorado Rockies	16	0	2	2	12	....	....	....	....	....
	NHL Totals	**835**	**38**	**178**	**216**	**447**	**84**	**3**	**12**	**15**	**82**

• Brother of Jimmy

Played in NHL All-Star Game (1974, 1977)

Claimed by **Philadelphia** from **Boston** in Expansion Draft, June 6, 1967. Traded to **Colorado** by **Philadelphia** for cash, August 31, 1978.

WATSON, Phil

Right wing/Center. Shoots right. 5'11", 165 lbs. Born, Montreal, Que., April 24, 1914.

Season	Club	GP	G	A	Pts	PIM	GP	G	A	Pts	PIM
1935-36	New York Rangers	24	0	2	2	24	....	....	....	....	....
1936-37	New York Rangers	48	11	17	28	22	9	0	2	2	9
1937-38	New York Rangers	48	7	25	32	52	3	0	2	2	0
1938-39	New York Rangers	48	15	22	37	42	7	1	1	2	7
1939-40 ♦	New York Rangers	48	7	28	35	42	12	3	6	*9	16
1940-41	New York Rangers	40	11	25	36	49	3	0	2	2	9
1941-42	New York Rangers	48	15	*37	52	58	6	1	4	5	8
1942-43	New York Rangers	46	14	28	42	44	....	....	....	....	....
1943-44 ♦	Montreal Canadiens	44	17	32	49	61	9	3	5	8	16
1944-45	New York Rangers	45	11	8	19	24	....	....	....	....	....

Season	Club	REGULAR SEASON GP	G	A	Pts	PIM	PLAYOFFS GP	G	A	Pts	PIM
1945-46	New York Rangers	49	12	14	26	43	....	....	....	....	....
1946-47	New York Rangers	48	6	12	18	17	....	....	....	....	....
1947-48	New York Rangers	54	18	15	33	54	5	2	3	5	2
	NHL Totals	**590**	**144**	**265**	**409**	**532**	**54**	**10**	**25**	**35**	**67**

NHL Second All-Star Team (1942)

Signed as a free agent by **NY Rangers** for $4,500, October 27, 1935. Loaned to **Montreal** by **NY Rangers** for the 1943-44 season for the loan of Charlie Sands, Fern Gauthier, Dutch Hiller, John Mahaffy and future considerations (Tony Demers, December, 1943), October 27, 1943.

WATT, Mike

Left wing. Shoots left. 6'2", 212 lbs. Born, Seaforth, Ont., March 31, 1976.
(Edmonton's 3rd choice, 32nd overall, in 1994 Entry Draft).

Season	Club	GP	G	A	Pts	PIM	GP	G	A	Pts	PIM
1997-98	Edmonton Oilers	14	1	2	3	4	....	....	....	....	....
1998-99	New York Islanders	75	8	17	25	12	....	....	....	....	....
99-2000	New York Islanders	45	5	6	11	17	....	....	....	....	....
2000-01	Nashville Predators	18	1	1	2	8	....	....	....	....	....
2002-03	Carolina Hurricanes	5	0	0	0	0	....	....	....	....	....
	NHL Totals	**157**	**15**	**26**	**41**	**41**	....	....	....	....	....

Traded to **NY Islanders** by **Edmonton** for Eric Fichaud, June 18, 1998. Claimed on waivers by **Nashville** from **NY Islanders**, May 23, 2000. Traded to **Philadelphia** by **Nashville** for Mikhail Chernov, May 24, 2001. Signed as a free agent by **Carolina**, August 7, 2002.

WATTERS, Tim

Defense. Shoots left. 5'11", 185 lbs. Born, Kamloops, B.C., July 25, 1959.
(Winnipeg's 6th choice, 124th overall, in 1979 Entry Draft).

Season	Club	GP	G	A	Pts	PIM	GP	G	A	Pts	PIM
1981-82	Winnipeg Jets	69	2	22	24	97	4	0	1	1	8
1982-83	Winnipeg Jets	77	5	18	23	98	3	0	0	0	2
1983-84	Winnipeg Jets	74	3	20	23	169	3	1	0	1	2
1984-85	Winnipeg Jets	63	2	20	22	74	8	0	1	1	16
1985-86	Winnipeg Jets	56	6	8	14	97	....	....	....	....	....
1986-87	Winnipeg Jets	63	3	13	16	119	10	0	0	0	21
1987-88	Winnipeg Jets	36	0	0	0	106	4	0	0	0	4
1988-89	Los Angeles Kings	76	3	18	21	168	11	0	1	1	6
1989-90	Los Angeles Kings	62	1	10	11	92	4	0	0	0	6
1990-91	Los Angeles Kings	45	0	4	4	92	7	0	0	0	12
1991-92	Los Angeles Kings	37	0	7	7	92	6	0	0	0	8
1992-93	Los Angeles Kings	22	0	2	2	18	22	0	2	2	30
1993-94	Los Angeles Kings	60	1	9	10	67	....	....	....	....	....
1994-95	Los Angeles Kings	1	0	0	0	0	....	....	....	....	....
	NHL Totals	**741**	**26**	**151**	**177**	**1380**	**82**	**1**	**3**	**4**	**115**

Signed as a free agent by **Los Angeles**, June 27, 1988.

WATTS, Brian

Left wing. Shoots left. 6', 180 lbs. Born, Hagersville, Ont., September 10, 1947.
(Detroit's 2nd choice, 7th overall, in 1964 Amateur Draft).

Season	Club	GP	G	A	Pts	PIM	GP	G	A	Pts	PIM
1975-76	Detroit Red Wings	4	0	0	0	0	....	....	....	....	....
	NHL Totals	**4**	**0**	**0**	**0**	**0**	....	....	....	....	....

WEAVER, Mike

Defense. Shoots right. 5'9", 180 lbs. Born, Bramalea, Ont., May 2, 1978.

Season	Club	GP	G	A	Pts	PIM	GP	G	A	Pts	PIM
2001-02	Atlanta Thrashers	16	0	1	1	10	....	....	....	....	....
2002-03	Atlanta Thrashers	40	0	5	5	20	....	....	....	....	....
	NHL Totals	**56**	**0**	**6**	**6**	**30**	....	....	....	....	....

Signed as a free agent by **Atlanta**, June 15, 2000.

WEBB, Steve

Right wing. Shoots right. 6', 211 lbs. Born, Peterborough, Ont., April 30, 1975.
(Buffalo's 8th choice, 176th overall, in 1994 Entry Draft).

Season	Club	GP	G	A	Pts	PIM	GP	G	A	Pts	PIM
1996-97	New York Islanders	41	1	4	5	144	....	....	....	....	....
1997-98	New York Islanders	20	0	0	0	35	....	....	....	....	....
1998-99	New York Islanders	45	0	0	0	32	....	....	....	....	....
99-2000	New York Islanders	65	1	3	4	103	....	....	....	....	....
2000-01	New York Islanders	31	0	2	2	35	....	....	....	....	....
2001-02	New York Islanders	60	2	4	6	104	7	0	0	0	12
2002-03	New York Islanders	49	1	0	1	75	5	0	0	0	10
	NHL Totals	**311**	**5**	**13**	**18**	**528**	**12**	**0**	**0**	**0**	**22**

Signed as a free agent by **NY Islanders**, October 10, 1996. • Missed majority of 2000-01 season recovering from knee injury suffered in game vs. Anaheim, November 19, 2000.

WEBSTER, Aubrey

Right wing. Shoots right. 5'9", 168 lbs. Born, Kenora, Ont., September 25, 1912.

Season	Club	GP	G	A	Pts	PIM	GP	G	A	Pts	PIM
1930-31	Philadelphia Quakers	1	0	0	0	0	....	....	....	....	....
1934-35	Montreal Maroons	4	0	0	0	0	....	....	....	....	....
	NHL Totals	**5**	**0**	**0**	**0**	**0**	....	....	....	....	....

Signed as a free agent by **Mtl. Maroons**, August, 1934. Traded to **Windsor** (IHL) by **Mtl. Maroons** for cash, December 26, 1934.

WEBSTER, Don

Left wing. Shoots left. 5'8", 180 lbs. Born, Toronto, Ont., July 3, 1924.

Season	Club	GP	G	A	Pts	PIM	GP	G	A	Pts	PIM
1943-44	Toronto Maple Leafs	27	7	6	13	28	5	0	0	0	12
	NHL Totals	**27**	**7**	**6**	**13**	**28**	**5**	**0**	**0**	**0**	**12**

• Brother of John

Traded to **Buffalo** (AHL) by **Toronto** with George Boothman for the rights to Bill Ezinicki, October 13, 1944.

WEBSTER, John

Center. Shoots left. 5'11", 160 lbs. Born, Toronto, Ont., November 3, 1920.

Season	Club	GP	G	A	Pts	PIM	GP	G	A	Pts	PIM
1949-50	New York Rangers	14	0	0	0	4	....	....	....	....	....
	NHL Totals	**14**	**0**	**0**	**0**	**4**	....	....	....	....	....

• Brother of Don

WEBSTER, Tom

Right wing. Shoots right. 5'10", 170 lbs. Born, Kirkland Lake, Ont., October 4, 1948.
(Boston's 4th choice, 19th overall, in 1966 Amateur Draft).

Season	Club	GP	G	A	Pts	PIM	GP	G	A	Pts	PIM
1968-69	Boston Bruins	9	0	2	2	9	1	0	0	0	0
1969-70	Boston Bruins	2	0	1	1	2	....	....	....	....	....
1970-71	Detroit Red Wings	78	30	37	67	40	....	....	....	....	....
1971-72	Detroit Red Wings	5	1	1	2	4	....	....	....	....	....
	California Golden Seals	7	2	1	3	6	....	....	....	....	....
1979-80	Detroit Red Wings	1	0	0	0	0	....	....	....	....	....
	NHL Totals	**102**	**33**	**42**	**75**	**61**	**1**	**0**	**0**	**0**	**0**

Claimed by **Buffalo** from **Boston** in Expansion Draft, June 10, 1970. Traded to **Detroit** by **Buffalo** for Roger Crozier, June 10, 1970. Traded to **California** by **Detroit** for Ron Stackhouse, October 22, 1971. • Missed remainder of 1971-72 season recovering from back injury suffered in game vs. NY Rangers, November 5, 1971. Signed as a free agent by **Detroit**, September 15, 1979.

WEIGHT, Doug

Center. Shoots left. 5'11", 200 lbs. Born, Warren, MI, January 21, 1971.
(NY Rangers' 2nd choice, 34th overall, in 1990 Entry Draft).

Season	Club	GP	G	A	Pts	PIM	GP	G	A	Pts	PIM
1990-91	New York Rangers	....	....	....	....	....	1	0	0	0	0
1991-92	New York Rangers	53	8	22	30	23	7	2	2	4	0
1992-93	New York Rangers	65	15	25	40	55	....	....	....	....	....
	Edmonton Oilers	13	2	6	8	10	....	....	....	....	....
1993-94	Edmonton Oilers	84	24	50	74	47	....	....	....	....	....
1994-95	Edmonton Oilers	48	7	33	40	69	....	....	....	....	....
1995-96	Edmonton Oilers	82	25	79	104	95	....	....	....	....	....
1996-97	Edmonton Oilers	80	21	61	82	80	12	3	8	11	8
1997-98	Edmonton Oilers	79	26	44	70	69	12	2	7	9	14
1998-99	Edmonton Oilers	43	6	31	37	12	4	1	1	2	15
99-2000	Edmonton Oilers	77	21	51	72	54	5	3	2	5	4
2000-01	Edmonton Oilers	82	25	65	90	91	6	1	5	6	17
2001-02	St. Louis Blues	61	15	34	49	40	10	1	1	2	4
2002-03	St. Louis Blues	70	15	32	67	52	7	5	8	13	2
	NHL Totals	**837**	**210**	**553**	**763**	**697**	**64**	**18**	**34**	**52**	**64**

Played in NHL All-Star Game (1996, 1998, 2001, 2003)

Traded to **Edmonton** by **NY Rangers** for Esa Tikkanen, March 17, 1993. Traded to **St. Louis** by **Edmonton** with Michel Riesen for Marty Reasoner, Jochen Hecht and Jan Horacek, July 1, 2001.

WEILAND, Cooney

HHOF

Center. Shoots left. 5'7", 150 lbs. Born, Seaforth (Edmondville), Ont., November 5, 1904.

Season	Club	GP	G	A	Pts	PIM	GP	G	A	Pts	PIM
1928-29♦	Boston Bruins	42	11	7	18	16	5	2	0	2	2
1929-30	Boston Bruins	44	*43	30	*73	27	6	1	*5	*6	2
1930-31	Boston Bruins	44	25	13	38	14	5	*6	3	*9	2
1931-32	Boston Bruins	46	14	12	26	20	....	....	....	....	....
1932-33	Ottawa Senators	48	16	11	27	4	....	....	....	....	....
1933-34	Ottawa Senators	9	2	0	2	4	....	....	....	....	....
	Detroit Red Wings	39	11	19	30	6	9	2	2	4	4
1934-35	Detroit Red Wings	48	13	25	38	10	....	....	....	....	....
1935-36	Boston Bruins	48	14	13	27	15	2	1	0	1	2
1936-37	Boston Bruins	48	6	9	15	6	3	0	0	0	0
1937-38	Boston Bruins	48	11	12	23	16	3	0	0	0	0
1938-39♦	Boston Bruins	45	7	9	16	9	12	0	0	0	0
	NHL Totals	**509**	**173**	**160**	**333**	**147**	**45**	**12**	**10**	**22**	**12**

NHL Second All-Star Team (1935) • Lester Patrick Trophy (1972)

Traded to **Boston** by **Minneapolis** (AHA) for cash, December 23, 1927. • Remained with Minneapolis (AHA) for the duration of the 1927-28 season. Traded to **Ottawa** by **Boston** for Joe Lamb and $7,000, July 25, 1932. Traded to **Detroit** by **Ottawa** for Carl Voss and cash, November 26, 1933. Traded to **Boston** by **Detroit** with Walt Buswell for Marty Barry and Art Giroux, July 11, 1935.

WEINHANDL, Mattias

Right wing. Shoots right. 6', 183 lbs. Born, Ljungby, Sweden, June 1, 1980.
(NY Islanders' 5th choice, 78th overall, in 1999 Entry Draft).

Season	Club	GP	G	A	Pts	PIM	GP	G	A	Pts	PIM
2002-03	New York Islanders	47	6	17	23	10	....	....	....	....	....
	NHL Totals	**47**	**6**	**17**	**23**	**10**	....	....	....	....	....

WEINRICH, Eric

Defense. Shoots left. 6'1", 213 lbs. Born, Roanoke, VA, December 19, 1966.
(New Jersey's 3rd choice, 32nd overall, in 1985 Entry Draft).

Season	Club	GP	G	A	Pts	PIM	GP	G	A	Pts	PIM
1988-89	New Jersey Devils	2	0	0	0	0	....	....	....	....	....
1989-90	New Jersey Devils	19	2	7	9	11	6	1	3	4	17
1990-91	New Jersey Devils	76	4	34	38	48	7	1	2	3	6
1991-92	New Jersey Devils	76	7	25	32	55	7	0	2	2	4
1992-93	Hartford Whalers	79	7	29	36	76	....	....	....	....	....
1993-94	Hartford Whalers	8	1	1	2	2	....	....	....	....	....
	Chicago Blackhawks	54	3	23	26	31	6	0	2	2	6
1994-95	Chicago Blackhawks	48	3	10	13	33	16	1	5	6	4
1995-96	Chicago Blackhawks	77	5	10	15	65	10	1	4	5	10
1996-97	Chicago Blackhawks	81	7	25	32	62	6	0	1	1	4

Season	Club	REGULAR SEASON GP	G	A	Pts	PIM	PLAYOFFS GP	G	A	Pts	PIM
1997-98	Chicago Blackhawks	82	2	21	23	106	....	....	....	....	....
1998-99	Chicago Blackhawks	14	1	3	4	12	....	....	....	....	....
	Montreal Canadiens	66	6	12	18	77	....	....	....	....	....
99-2000	Montreal Canadiens	77	4	25	29	39	....	....	....	....	....
2000-01	Montreal Canadiens	60	6	19	25	34	....	....	....	....	....
	Boston Bruins	22	1	5	6	10	....	....	....	....	....
2001-02	Philadelphia Flyers	80	4	20	24	26	5	0	0	0	4
2002-03	Philadelphia Flyers	81	2	18	20	40	13	2	3	5	12
	NHL Totals	**1002**	**65**	**287**	**352**	**727**	**76**	**6**	**22**	**28**	**67**

NHL All-Rookie Team (1991)

Traded to **Hartford** by **New Jersey** with Sean Burke for Bobby Holik and Hartford's 2nd round choice (Jay Pandolfo) in 1993 Entry Draft, August 28, 1992. Traded to **Chicago** by **Hartford** with Patrick Poulin for Steve Larmer and Bryan Marchment, November 2, 1993. Traded to **Montreal** by **Chicago** with Jeff Hackett, Alain Nasreddine and Tampa Bay's 4th round choice (previously acquired, Montreal selected Chris Dyment) in 1999 Entry Draft for Jocelyn Thibault, Dave Manson and Brad Brown, November 16, 1998. Traded to **Boston** by **Montreal** for Patrick Traverse, February 21, 2001. Signed as a free agent by **Philadelphia**, July 5, 2001.

WEIR, Stan

Center. Shoots left. 6'1", 180 lbs. Born, Ponoka, Alta., March 17, 1952.
(California's 2nd choice, 28th overall, in 1972 Amateur Draft).

Season	Club	GP	G	A	Pts	PIM	GP	G	A	Pts	PIM
1972-73	California Golden Seals	78	15	24	39	16	....	....	....	....	....
1973-74	California Golden Seals	58	9	7	16	10	....	....	....	....	....
1974-75	California Golden Seals	80	18	27	45	12	....	....	....	....	....
1975-76	Toronto Maple Leafs	64	19	32	51	22	9	1	3	4	0
1976-77	Toronto Maple Leafs	65	11	19	30	14	7	2	1	3	0
1977-78	Toronto Maple Leafs	30	12	5	17	4	13	3	1	4	0
1979-80	Edmonton Oilers	79	33	33	66	40	3	0	0	0	2
1980-81	Edmonton Oilers	70	12	20	32	40	5	0	0	0	2
1981-82	Edmonton Oilers	51	3	13	16	13	....	....	....	....	....
	Colorado Rockies	10	2	3	5	10	....	....	....	....	....
1982-83	Detroit Red Wings	57	5	24	29	2	....	....	....	....	....
	NHL Totals	**642**	**139**	**207**	**346**	**183**	**37**	**6**	**5**	**11**	**4**

Traded to **Toronto** by **California** for Gary Sabourin, June 20, 1975. Reclaimed by **Toronto** from **Edmonton** prior to Expansion Draft, June 9, 1979. Claimed on waivers by **Edmonton** from **Toronto**, July 4, 1979. Traded to **Colorado** by **Edmonton** for Ed Cooper, March 9, 1982. Traded to **Edmonton** by **Colorado** for Ed Cooper, July 2, 1982. Traded to **Detroit** by **Edmonton** for cash, September 14, 1982.

WEIR, Wally

Defense. Shoots right. 6'2", 200 lbs. Born, Verdun, Que., June 3, 1954.

Season	Club	GP	G	A	Pts	PIM	GP	G	A	Pts	PIM
1979-80	Quebec Nordiques	73	3	12	15	133	....	....	....	....	....
1980-81	Quebec Nordiques	54	6	8	14	77	3	0	0	0	15
1981-82	Quebec Nordiques	62	3	5	8	173	15	0	0	0	45
1982-83	Quebec Nordiques	58	5	11	16	135	4	0	1	1	19
1983-84	Quebec Nordiques	25	2	3	5	17	1	0	0	0	17
1984-85	Hartford Whalers	34	2	3	5	56	....	....	....	....	....
	Pittsburgh Penguins	14	0	3	3	34	....	....	....	....	....
	NHL Totals	**320**	**21**	**45**	**66**	**625**	**23**	**0**	**1**	**1**	**96**

Claimed by **Hartford** from **Quebec** in Waiver Draft, October 9, 1984. Claimed on waivers by **Pittsburgh** from **Hartford**, March 1, 1985.

WEISS, Stephen

Center. Shoots left. 5'11", 183 lbs. Born, Toronto, Ont., April 3, 1983.
(Florida's 1st choice, 4th overall, in 2001 Entry Draft).

Season	Club	GP	G	A	Pts	PIM	GP	G	A	Pts	PIM
2001-02	Florida Panthers	7	1	1	2	0	....	....	....	....	....
2002-03	Florida Panthers	77	6	15	21	17	....	....	....	....	....
	NHL Totals	**84**	**7**	**16**	**23**	**17**	....	....	....	....	....

WELLINGTON, Alex

Right wing. Shoots right. , Born, Port Arthur, Ont.,

Season	Club	GP	G	A	Pts	PIM	GP	G	A	Pts	PIM
1919-20	Quebec Bulldogs	1	0	0	0	0	....	....	....	....	....
	NHL Totals	**1**	**0**	**0**	**0**	**0**	....	....	....	....	....

Signed as a free agent by **Quebec**, January 9, 1920.

WELLS, Chris

Center. Shoots left. 6'6", 223 lbs. Born, Calgary, Alta., November 12, 1975.
(Pittsburgh's 1st choice, 24th overall, in 1994 Entry Draft).

Season	Club	GP	G	A	Pts	PIM	GP	G	A	Pts	PIM
1995-96	Pittsburgh Penguins	54	2	2	4	59	....	....	....	....	....
1996-97	Florida Panthers	47	2	6	8	42	3	0	0	0	0
1997-98	Florida Panthers	61	5	10	15	47	....	....	....	....	....
1998-99	Florida Panthers	20	0	2	2	31	....	....	....	....	....
99-2000	Florida Panthers	13	0	0	0	14	....	....	....	....	....
	NHL Totals	**195**	**9**	**20**	**29**	**193**	**3**	**0**	**0**	**0**	**0**

Traded to **Florida** by **Pittsburgh** for Stu Barnes and Jason Woolley, November 19, 1996. Traded to **NY Rangers** by **Florida** for future considerations, March 13, 2000. Signed as a free agent by **Dallas**, July 28, 2000.

WELLS, Jay

Defense. Shoots left. 6'1", 210 lbs. Born, Paris, Ont., May 18, 1959.
(Los Angeles' 1st choice, 16th overall, in 1979 Entry Draft).

Season	Club	GP	G	A	Pts	PIM	GP	G	A	Pts	PIM
1979-80	Los Angeles Kings	43	0	0	0	113	4	0	0	0	11
1980-81	Los Angeles Kings	72	5	13	18	155	4	0	0	0	27
1981-82	Los Angeles Kings	60	1	8	9	145	10	1	3	4	41
1982-83	Los Angeles Kings	69	3	12	15	167	....	....	....	....	....
1983-84	Los Angeles Kings	69	3	18	21	141	....	....	....	....	....
1984-85	Los Angeles Kings	77	2	9	11	185	3	0	1	1	0
1985-86	Los Angeles Kings	79	11	31	42	226	....	....	....	....	....
1986-87	Los Angeles Kings	77	7	29	36	155	5	1	2	3	10
1987-88	Los Angeles Kings	58	2	23	25	159	5	1	2	3	21
1988-89	Philadelphia Flyers	67	2	19	21	184	18	0	2	2	51
1989-90	Philadelphia Flyers	59	3	16	19	129	....	....	....	....	....
	Buffalo Sabres	1	0	1	1	0	6	0	0	0	12
1990-91	Buffalo Sabres	43	1	2	3	86	1	0	1	1	0
1991-92	Buffalo Sabres	41	2	9	11	157	....	....	....	....	....
	New York Rangers	11	0	0	0	24	13	0	2	2	10
1992-93	New York Rangers	53	1	9	10	107	....	....	....	....	....
1993-94♦	New York Rangers	79	2	7	9	110	23	0	0	0	20
1994-95	New York Rangers	43	2	7	9	36	10	0	0	0	8
1995-96	St. Louis Blues	76	0	3	3	67	12	0	1	1	2
1996-97	Tampa Bay Lightning	21	0	0	0	13	....	....	....	....	....
	NHL Totals	**1098**	**47**	**216**	**263**	**2359**	**114**	**3**	**14**	**17**	**213**

Traded to **Philadelphia** by **Los Angeles** for Doug Crossman, September 29, 1988. Traded to **Buffalo** by **Philadelphia** with Philadelphia's 4th round choice (Peter Ambroziak) in 1991 Entry Draft for Kevin Maguire and Buffalo's 2nd round choice (Mikael Renberg) in 1990 Entry Draft, March 5, 1990. Traded to **NY Rangers** by **Buffalo** for Randy Moller, March 9, 1992. Traded to **St. Louis** by **NY Rangers** for Doug Lidster, July 31, 1995. Signed as a free agent by **Tampa Bay**, August 3, 1996.

WENSINK, John

Left wing. Shoots left. 6', 200 lbs. Born, Pincher Creek, Alta., April 1, 1953.
(St. Louis' 6th choice, 104th overall, in 1973 Amateur Draft).

Season	Club	GP	G	A	Pts	PIM	GP	G	A	Pts	PIM
1973-74	St. Louis Blues	3	0	0	0	0	....	....	....	....	....
1976-77	Boston Bruins	23	4	6	10	32	13	0	3	3	8
1977-78	Boston Bruins	80	16	20	36	181	15	2	2	4	54
1978-79	Boston Bruins	76	28	18	46	106	8	0	1	1	19
1979-80	Boston Bruins	69	9	11	20	110	4	0	0	0	5
1980-81	Quebec Nordiques	53	6	3	9	124	3	0	0	0	0
1981-82	Colorado Rockies	57	5	3	8	152	....	....	....	....	....
1982-83	New Jersey Devils	42	2	7	9	135	....	....	....	....	....
	NHL Totals	**403**	**70**	**68**	**138**	**840**	**43**	**2**	**6**	**8**	**86**

Signed as a free agent by **Boston**, October 12, 1976. Claimed by **Quebec** from **Boston** in Waiver Draft, October 10, 1980. Signed as a free agent by **Colorado**, September 21, 1981. Transferred to **New Jersey** after **Colorado** franchise relocated, June 30, 1982.

WENTWORTH, Cy

Defense. Shoots right. 5'10", 170 lbs. Born, Grimsby, Ont., January 24, 1905.

Season	Club	GP	G	A	Pts	PIM	GP	G	A	Pts	PIM
1927-28	Chicago Black Hawks	43	5	5	10	31	....	....	....	....	....
1928-29	Chicago Black Hawks	44	2	1	3	44	....	....	....	....	....
1929-30	Chicago Black Hawks	37	3	4	7	28	....	....	....	....	....
1930-31	Chicago Black Hawks	44	4	4	8	12	9	1	1	2	14
1931-32	Chicago Black Hawks	48	3	10	13	30	2	0	0	0	0
1932-33	Montreal Maroons	47	4	10	14	48	2	0	1	1	0
1933-34	Montreal Maroons	48	2	5	7	31	4	0	2	2	2
1934-35♦	Montreal Maroons	48	4	9	13	28	7	3	2	*5	0
1935-36	Montreal Maroons	48	4	5	9	24	3	0	0	0	0
1936-37	Montreal Maroons	43	3	4	7	29	5	1	0	1	0
1937-38	Montreal Maroons	48	4	5	9	32	....	....	....	....	....
1938-39	Montreal Canadiens	45	0	3	3	12	3	0	0	0	4
1939-40	Montreal Canadiens	32	1	3	4	6	....	....	....	....	....
	NHL Totals	**575**	**39**	**68**	**107**	**355**	**35**	**5**	**6**	**11**	**20**

NHL Second All-Star Team (1935)

Played in NHL All-Star Game (1937, 1939)

Traded to **Chicago** by **Windsor** (Can-Pro) for cash, December, 20, 1926. Traded to **Mtl. Maroons** by **Chicago** for $10,000, October 24, 1932. Traded to **Montreal** by **Mtl. Maroons** for cash, September 14, 1938.

WERENKA, Brad

Defense. Shoots left. 6'1", 221 lbs. Born, Two Hills, Alta., February 12, 1969.
(Edmonton's 2nd choice, 42nd overall, in 1987 Entry Draft).

Season	Club	GP	G	A	Pts	PIM	GP	G	A	Pts	PIM
1992-93	Edmonton Oilers	27	5	4	9	24	....	....	....	....	....
1993-94	Edmonton Oilers	15	0	4	4	14	....	....	....	....	....
	Quebec Nordiques	11	0	7	7	8	....	....	....	....	....
1995-96	Chicago Blackhawks	9	0	0	0	8	....	....	....	....	....
1997-98	Pittsburgh Penguins	71	3	15	18	46	6	1	0	1	8
1998-99	Pittsburgh Penguins	81	6	18	24	93	13	1	1	2	6
99-2000	Pittsburgh Penguins	61	3	8	11	69	....	....	....	....	....
	Calgary Flames	12	1	1	2	21	....	....	....	....	....
2000-01	Calgary Flames	33	1	4	5	16	....	....	....	....	....
	NHL Totals	**320**	**19**	**61**	**80**	**299**	**19**	**2**	**1**	**3**	**14**

Traded to **Quebec** by **Edmonton** for Steve Passmore, March 21, 1994. Signed as a free agent by **Chicago**, July 20, 1995. Signed as a free agent by **Pittsburgh**, July 31, 1997. Traded to **Calgary** by **Pittsburgh** for Tyler Moss and Rene Corbet, March 14, 2000. • Missed majority of 2000-01 season recovering from head injury suffered in game vs. Dallas, December 29, 2000.

WESENBERG, Brian

Right wing. Shoots right. 6'3", 187 lbs. Born, Peterborough, Ont., May 9, 1977.
(Anaheim's 2nd choice, 29th overall, in 1995 Entry Draft).

Season	Club	GP	G	A	Pts	PIM	GP	G	A	Pts	PIM
1998-99	Philadelphia Flyers	1	0	0	0	5	....	....	....	....	....
	NHL Totals	**1**	**0**	**0**	**0**	**5**	....	....	....	....	....

Traded to **Philadelphia** by **Anaheim** for Anatoli Semenov and Mike Crowley, March 19, 1996. Traded to **Atlanta** by **Philadelphia** for Eric Bertrand, December 9, 1999.

WESLEY, Blake

Defense. Shoots left. 6'1", 200 lbs. Born, Red Deer, Alta., July 10, 1959.
(Philadelphia's 2nd choice, 22nd overall, in 1979 Entry Draft).

Season	Club	Regular Season GP	G	A	Pts	PIM	Playoffs GP	G	A	Pts	PIM
1979-80	Philadelphia Flyers	2	0	1	1	2	....	....	....	....	....
1980-81	Philadelphia Flyers	50	3	7	10	107	....	....	....	....	....
1981-82	Hartford Whalers	78	9	18	27	123	....	....	....	....	....
1982-83	Hartford Whalers	22	0	1	1	46	....	....	....	....	....
	Quebec Nordiques	52	4	8	12	84	4	0	0	0	2
1983-84	Quebec Nordiques	46	2	8	10	75	9	1	2	3	20
1984-85	Quebec Nordiques	21	0	2	2	28	6	1	0	1	8
1985-86	Toronto Maple Leafs	27	0	1	1	21	....	....	....	....	....
	NHL Totals	**298**	**18**	**46**	**64**	**486**	**19**	**2**	**2**	**4**	**30**

• Brother of Glen

Traded to **Hartford** by **Philadelphia** with Rick MacLeish, Don Gillen and Philadelphia's 1st (Paul Lawless), 2nd (Mark Paterson) and 3rd (Kevin Dineen) round choices in 1982 Entry Draft for Ray Allison, Fred Arthur and Hartford's 1st (Ron Sutter), 2nd (later traded to Toronto – Toronto selected Peter Ihnacak) and 3rd (Miroslav Dvorak) round choices in 1982 Entry Draft, July 3, 1981. Traded to **Quebec** by **Hartford** for Pierre Lacroix, December 3, 1982. Signed as a free agent by **Toronto**, July 31, 1985.

WESLEY, Glen

Defense. Shoots left. 6'1", 205 lbs. Born, Red Deer, Alta., October 2, 1968.
(Boston's 1st choice, 3rd overall, in 1987 Entry Draft).

Season	Club	Regular Season GP	G	A	Pts	PIM	Playoffs GP	G	A	Pts	PIM
1987-88	Boston Bruins	79	7	30	37	69	23	6	8	14	22
1988-89	Boston Bruins	77	19	35	54	61	10	0	2	2	4
1989-90	Boston Bruins	78	9	27	36	48	21	2	6	8	36
1990-91	Boston Bruins	80	11	32	43	78	19	2	9	11	19
1991-92	Boston Bruins	78	9	37	46	54	15	2	4	6	16
1992-93	Boston Bruins	64	8	25	33	47	4	0	0	0	0
1993-94	Boston Bruins	81	14	44	58	64	13	3	3	6	12
1994-95	Hartford Whalers	48	2	14	16	50	....	....	....	....	....
1995-96	Hartford Whalers	68	8	16	24	88	....	....	....	....	....
1996-97	Hartford Whalers	68	6	26	32	40	....	....	....	....	....
1997-98	Carolina Hurricanes	82	6	19	25	36	....	....	....	....	....
1998-99	Carolina Hurricanes	74	7	17	24	44	6	0	0	0	2
99-2000	Carolina Hurricanes	78	7	15	22	38	....	....	....	....	....
2000-01	Carolina Hurricanes	71	5	16	21	42	6	0	0	0	0
2001-02	Carolina Hurricanes	77	5	13	18	56	22	0	2	2	12
2002-03	Carolina Hurricanes	63	1	7	8	40	....	....	....	....	....
	Toronto Maple Leafs	7	0	3	3	4	5	0	1	1	2
	NHL Totals	**1173**	**124**	**376**	**500**	**859**	**144**	**15**	**35**	**50**	**125**

• Brother of Blake • NHL All-Rookie Team (1988)

Played in NHL All-Star Game (1989)

Traded to **Hartford** by **Boston** for Hartford's 1st round choices in 1995 (Kyle McLaren), 1996 (Johnathan Aitken) and 1997 (Sergei Samsonov) Entry Drafts, August 26, 1994. Transferred to **Carolina** after **Hartford** franchise relocated, June 25, 1997. Traded to **Toronto** by **Carolina** for Toronto's 2nd round choice in 2004 Entry Draft, March 9, 2003. Signed as a free agent by **Carolina**, July 8, 2003.

WESTCOTT, Duvie

Defense. Shoots right. 5'11", 192 lbs. Born, Winnipeg, Man., October 30, 1977.

Season	Club	Regular Season GP	G	A	Pts	PIM	Playoffs GP	G	A	Pts	PIM
2001-02	Columbus Blue Jackets	4	0	0	0	2	....	....	....	....	....
2002-03	Columbus Blue Jackets	39	0	7	7	77	....	....	....	....	....
	NHL Totals	**43**	**0**	**7**	**7**	**79**	....	....	....	....	....

Signed as a free agent by **Columbus**, May 10, 2001.

WESTFALL, Ed

Defense/Right wing. Shoots right. 6'1", 197 lbs. Born, Belleville, Ont., September 19, 1940.

Season	Club	Regular Season GP	G	A	Pts	PIM	Playoffs GP	G	A	Pts	PIM
1961-62	Boston Bruins	63	2	9	11	53	....	....	....	....	....
1962-63	Boston Bruins	48	1	11	12	34	....	....	....	....	....
1963-64	Boston Bruins	55	1	5	6	35	....	....	....	....	....
1964-65	Boston Bruins	68	12	15	27	65	....	....	....	....	....
1965-66	Boston Bruins	59	9	21	30	42	....	....	....	....	....
1966-67	Boston Bruins	70	12	24	36	26	....	....	....	....	....
1967-68	Boston Bruins	73	14	22	36	38	4	2	0	2	2
1968-69	Boston Bruins	70	18	24	42	22	10	3	7	10	11
1969-70 ♦	Boston Bruins	72	14	22	36	28	14	3	5	8	4
1970-71	Boston Bruins	78	25	34	59	48	7	1	2	3	2
1971-72 ♦	Boston Bruins	71	18	26	44	19	15	4	3	7	10
1972-73	New York Islanders	67	15	31	46	25	....	....	....	....	....
1973-74	New York Islanders	68	19	23	42	28	....	....	....	....	....
1974-75	New York Islanders	73	22	33	55	28	17	5	10	15	12
1975-76	New York Islanders	80	25	31	56	27	8	2	3	5	0
1976-77	New York Islanders	79	14	33	47	8	12	1	5	6	0
1977-78	New York Islanders	71	5	19	24	14	2	0	0	0	0
1978-79	New York Islanders	55	5	11	16	4	6	1	2	3	0
	NHL Totals	**1220**	**231**	**394**	**625**	**544**	**95**	**22**	**37**	**59**	**41**

Bill Masterton Trophy (1977)

Played in NHL All-Star Game (1971, 1973, 1974, 1975)

Claimed by **NY Islanders** from **Boston** in Expansion Draft, June 6, 1972.

WESTLUND, Tommy

Right wing. Shoots right. 6', 210 lbs. Born, Fors, Sweden, December 29, 1974.
(Carolina's 5th choice, 93rd overall, in 1998 Entry Draft).

Season	Club	Regular Season GP	G	A	Pts	PIM	Playoffs GP	G	A	Pts	PIM
99-2000	Carolina Hurricanes	81	4	8	12	19	....	....	....	....	....
2000-01	Carolina Hurricanes	79	5	3	8	23	6	0	0	0	17
2001-02	Carolina Hurricanes	40	0	2	2	6	19	1	0	1	0
2002-03	Carolina Hurricanes	3	0	0	0	0	....	....	....	....	....
	NHL Totals	**203**	**9**	**13**	**22**	**48**	**25**	**1**	**0**	**1**	**17**

• Missed majority of 2001-02 season recovering from back injury suffered in game vs. Columbus, November 19, 2001.

WHARRAM, Kenny

Right wing/Center. Shoots right. 5'9", 160 lbs. Born, North Bay, Ont., July 2, 1933.

Season	Club	Regular Season GP	G	A	Pts	PIM	Playoffs GP	G	A	Pts	PIM
1951-52	Chicago Black Hawks	1	0	0	0	0	....	....	....	....	....
1953-54	Chicago Black Hawks	29	1	7	8	8	....	....	....	....	....
1955-56	Chicago Black Hawks	3	0	0	0	0	....	....	....	....	....
1958-59	Chicago Black Hawks	66	10	9	19	14	6	0	2	2	2
1959-60	Chicago Black Hawks	59	14	11	25	16	4	1	1	2	0
1960-61 ♦	Chicago Black Hawks	64	16	29	45	12	12	3	5	8	12
1961-62	Chicago Black Hawks	62	14	23	37	24	12	3	4	7	8
1962-63	Chicago Black Hawks	55	20	18	38	17	6	1	5	6	0
1963-64	Chicago Black Hawks	70	39	32	71	18	7	2	2	4	6
1964-65	Chicago Black Hawks	68	24	20	44	27	12	2	3	5	4
1965-66	Chicago Black Hawks	69	26	17	43	28	6	1	0	1	4
1966-67	Chicago Black Hawks	70	31	34	65	21	6	2	2	4	2
1967-68	Chicago Black Hawks	74	27	42	69	18	9	1	3	4	0
1968-69	Chicago Black Hawks	76	30	39	69	19	....	....	....	....	....
	NHL Totals	**766**	**252**	**281**	**533**	**222**	**80**	**16**	**27**	**43**	**38**

NHL First All-Star Team (1964, 1967) • Lady Byng Trophy (1964)

Played in NHL All-Star Game (1961, 1968)

Traded to **Buffalo** (AHL) by **Chicago** for cash, August, 1956. Traded to **Chicago** by **Buffalo** (AHL) for Wally Hergesheimer and Frank Martin, May 5, 1958. • Suffered career-ending heart attack during training camp, September 18, 1969.

WHARTON, Len

Defense. Shoots left. 6', 170 lbs. Born, Winnipeg, Man., December 13, 1927.

Season	Club	Regular Season GP	G	A	Pts	PIM	Playoffs GP	G	A	Pts	PIM
1944-45	New York Rangers	1	0	0	0	0	....	....	....	....	....
	NHL Totals	**1**	**0**	**0**	**0**	**0**	....	....	....	....	....

Signed as a free agent by **NY Rangers** , October 10, 1944.

WHEELDON, Simon

Center. Shoots left. 5'11", 170 lbs. Born, Vancouver, B.C., August 30, 1966.
(Edmonton's 11th choice, 229th overall, in 1984 Entry Draft).

Season	Club	Regular Season GP	G	A	Pts	PIM	Playoffs GP	G	A	Pts	PIM
1987-88	New York Rangers	5	0	1	1	4	....	....	....	....	....
1988-89	New York Rangers	6	0	1	1	2	....	....	....	....	....
1990-91	Winnipeg Jets	4	0	0	0	4	....	....	....	....	....
	NHL Totals	**15**	**0**	**2**	**2**	**10**	....	....	....	....	....

Signed as a free agent by **NY Rangers**, September 8, 1986. Traded to **Winnipeg** by **NY Rangers** for Brian McReynolds, July 9, 1990. Traded to **Washington** by **Winnipeg** with Craig Duncanson and Brent Hughes for Bob Joyce, Tyler Larter and Kent Paynter, May 21, 1991.

WHELDON, Don

Defense. Shoots right. 6'2", 185 lbs. Born, Falmouth, MA, December 28, 1954.
(St. Louis' 4th choice, 87th overall, in 1974 Amateur Draft).

Season	Club	Regular Season GP	G	A	Pts	PIM	Playoffs GP	G	A	Pts	PIM
1974-75	St. Louis Blues	2	0	0	0	0	....	....	....	....	....
	NHL Totals	**2**	**0**	**0**	**0**	**0**	....	....	....	....	....

WHELTON, Bill

Defense. Shoots left. 6'1", 180 lbs. Born, Everett, MA, August 28, 1959.
(Winnipeg's 3rd choice, 61st overall, in 1979 Entry Draft).

Season	Club	Regular Season GP	G	A	Pts	PIM	Playoffs GP	G	A	Pts	PIM
1980-81	Winnipeg Jets	2	0	0	0	0	....	....	....	....	....
	NHL Totals	**2**	**0**	**0**	**0**	**0**	....	....	....	....	....

WHISTLE, Rob

Defense. Shoots right. 6'2", 195 lbs. Born, Thunder Bay, Ont., April 4, 1961.

Season	Club	Regular Season GP	G	A	Pts	PIM	Playoffs GP	G	A	Pts	PIM
1985-86	New York Rangers	32	4	2	6	10	3	0	0	0	2
1987-88	St. Louis Blues	19	3	3	6	6	1	0	0	0	0
	NHL Totals	**51**	**7**	**5**	**12**	**16**	**4**	**0**	**0**	**0**	**2**

Signed as a free agent by **NY Rangers**, August 13, 1985. Traded to **St. Louis** by **NY Rangers** with Tony McKegney for Bruce Bell and future considerations, May 28, 1987. Traded to **Washington** by **St. Louis** for Washington's 6th round choice (Derek Frenette) in 1989 Entry Draft, October 19, 1988.

WHITE, Bill

Defense. Shoots right. 6'2", 195 lbs. Born, Toronto, Ont., August 26, 1939.

Season	Club	Regular Season GP	G	A	Pts	PIM	Playoffs GP	G	A	Pts	PIM
1967-68	Los Angeles Kings	74	11	27	38	100	7	2	2	4	4
1968-69	Los Angeles Kings	75	5	28	33	38	11	1	4	5	8
1969-70	Los Angeles Kings	40	4	11	15	21	....	....	....	....	....
	Chicago Black Hawks	21	0	5	5	18	8	1	2	3	8
1970-71	Chicago Black Hawks	67	4	21	25	64	18	1	4	5	20
1971-72	Chicago Black Hawks	76	7	22	29	58	8	0	3	3	6
1972-73	Chicago Black Hawks	72	9	38	47	80	16	1	6	7	10
1973-74	Chicago Black Hawks	69	5	31	36	52	11	1	7	8	14
1974-75	Chicago Black Hawks	51	4	23	27	20	8	0	3	3	4

		REGULAR SEASON					PLAYOFFS				
Season	Club	GP	G	A	Pts	PIM	GP	G	A	Pts	PIM
1975-76	Chicago Black Hawks	59	1	9	10	44	4	0	1	1	2
	NHL Totals	**604**	**50**	**215**	**265**	**495**	**91**	**7**	**32**	**39**	**76**

NHL Second All-Star Team (1972, 1973, 1974)

Played in NHL All-Star Game (1969, 1970, 1971, 1972, 1973, 1974)

Traded to **Springfield** (AHL) by **Toronto** (Rochester-AHL) with Dick Mattiussi, Jim Wilcox, Roger Cote and the loan of Wally Boyer for Kent Douglas, June 7, 1962. NHL rights transferred to **Los Angeles** after NHL club purchased **Springfield** (AHL) franchise, May, 1967. Traded to **Chicago** by **Los Angeles** with Bryan Campbell and Gerry Desjardins for Gilles Marotte, Jim Stanfield and Denis DeJordy, February 20, 1970. • Suffered eventual career-ending neck injury in game vs. Montreal, April 16, 1976.

WHITE, Brian

Defense. Shoots right. 6'1", 195 lbs. Born, Winchester, MA, February 7, 1976.
(Tampa Bay's 11th choice, 268th overall, in 1994 Entry Draft).

Season	Club	GP	G	A	Pts	PIM	GP	G	A	Pts	PIM
1998-99	Colorado Avalanche	2	0	0	0	0	....	....	....	....	....
	NHL Totals	**2**	**0**	**0**	**0**	**0**	....	....	....	....	....

Signed as a free agent by **Colorado**, July 7, 1998. Signed as a free agent by **Anaheim**, August 14, 2001.

WHITE, Colin

Defense. Shoots left. 6'4", 215 lbs. Born, New Glasgow, N.S., December 12, 1977.
(New Jersey's 5th choice, 49th overall, in 1996 Entry Draft).

Season	Club	GP	G	A	Pts	PIM	GP	G	A	Pts	PIM
99-2000 ♦	New Jersey Devils	21	2	1	3	40	23	1	5	6	18
2000-01	New Jersey Devils	82	1	19	20	155	25	0	3	3	42
2001-02	New Jersey Devils	73	2	3	5	133	6	0	0	0	2
2002-03 ♦	New Jersey Devils	72	5	8	13	98	24	0	5	5	29
	NHL Totals	**248**	**10**	**31**	**41**	**426**	**78**	**1**	**13**	**14**	**91**

NHL All-Rookie Team (2001)

WHITE, Moe

Left wing/Center. Shoots left. 5'11", 178 lbs. Born, Verdun, Que., July 28, 1919.

Season	Club	GP	G	A	Pts	PIM	GP	G	A	Pts	PIM
1945-46	Montreal Canadiens	4	0	1	1	2	....	....	....	....	....
	NHL Totals	**4**	**0**	**1**	**1**	**2**	....	....	....	....	....

Traded to **Buffalo** (AHL) by **Montreal** with John Adams for Murdo MacKay with Montreal holding right of recall, January 14, 1946. Traded to **Buffalo** (AHL) by **Montreal** for cash, October 8, 1946.

WHITE, Peter

Center. Shoots left. 5'11", 200 lbs. Born, Montreal, Que., March 15, 1969.
(Edmonton's 4th choice, 92nd overall, in 1989 Entry Draft).

Season	Club	GP	G	A	Pts	PIM	GP	G	A	Pts	PIM
1993-94	Edmonton Oilers	26	3	5	8	2	....	....	....	....	....
1994-95	Edmonton Oilers	9	2	4	6	0	....	....	....	....	....
1995-96	Edmonton Oilers	26	5	3	8	0	....	....	....	....	....
	Toronto Maple Leafs	1	0	0	0	0	....	....	....	....	....
1998-99	Philadelphia Flyers	3	0	0	0	0	....	....	....	....	....
99-2000	Philadelphia Flyers	21	1	5	6	6	16	0	2	2	0
2000-01	Philadelphia Flyers	77	9	16	25	16	3	0	0	0	0
2001-02	Chicago Blackhawks	48	3	3	6	10	....	....	....	....	....
2002-03	Chicago Blackhawks	6	0	1	1	0	....	....	....	....	....
	NHL Totals	**217**	**23**	**37**	**60**	**34**	**19**	**0**	**2**	**2**	**0**

Traded to **Toronto** by **Edmonton** with Edmonton's 4th round choice (Jason Sessa) in 1996 Entry Draft for Kent Manderville, December 4, 1995. Signed as a free agent by **Philadelphia**, August 19, 1996. Signed as a free agent by **Chicago**, September 10, 2001. Traded to **Philadelphia** by **Chicago** for future considerations, March 11, 2003.

WHITE, Sherman

Center. Shoots left. 5'10", 165 lbs. Born, Cape Tormentine, N.B., May 12, 1923.

Season	Club	GP	G	A	Pts	PIM	GP	G	A	Pts	PIM
1946-47	New York Rangers	1	0	0	0	0	....	....	....	....	....
1949-50	New York Rangers	3	0	2	2	0	....	....	....	....	....
	NHL Totals	**4**	**0**	**2**	**2**	**0**	....	....	....	....	....

Traded to **St. Louis** (AHL) by **NY Rangers** for cash, September 19, 1950.

WHITE, Tex

Right wing. Shoots right. 5'11", 155 lbs. Born, Hillbrough, Ont., June 26, 1900.

Season	Club	GP	G	A	Pts	PIM	GP	G	A	Pts	PIM
1925-26	Pittsburgh Pirates	35	7	1	8	22	....	....	....	....	....
1926-27	Pittsburgh Pirates	43	5	4	9	21	....	....	....	....	....
1927-28	Pittsburgh Pirates	44	5	1	6	54	2	0	0	0	2
1928-29	Pittsburgh Pirates	30	3	4	7	18	....	....	....	....	....
	New York Americans	13	2	1	3	8	2	0	0	0	2
1929-30	Pittsburgh Pirates	29	8	1	9	16	....	....	....	....	....
1930-31	Philadelphia Quakers	9	3	0	3	2	....	....	....	....	....
	NHL Totals	**203**	**33**	**12**	**45**	**141**	**4**	**0**	**0**	**0**	**4**

Signed as a free agent by **Pittsburgh**, September 26, 1925. Loaned to **NY Americans** by **Pittsburgh** for remainder of 1928-29 season for Jesse Spring and the loan of Edmond Bouchard for remainder of 1928-29 season, February 15, 1929. Transferred to **Philadelphia** after **Pittsburgh** franchise relocated, September 27, 1930. Traded to **Pittsburgh** (IHL) by **Philadelphia** for cash, December 16, 1930.

WHITE, Todd

Center. Shoots left. 5'10", 194 lbs. Born, Kanata, Ont., May 21, 1975.

Season	Club	GP	G	A	Pts	PIM	GP	G	A	Pts	PIM
1997-98	Chicago Blackhawks	7	1	0	1	2	....	....	....	....	....
1998-99	Chicago Blackhawks	35	5	8	13	20	....	....	....	....	....
99-2000	Chicago Blackhawks	1	0	0	0	0	....	....	....	....	....
	Philadelphia Flyers	3	1	0	1	0	....	....	....	....	....
2000-01	Ottawa Senators	16	4	1	5	4	2	0	0	0	0
2001-02	Ottawa Senators	81	20	30	50	24	12	2	2	4	6
2002-03	Ottawa Senators	80	25	35	60	28	18	5	1	6	6
	NHL Totals	**223**	**56**	**74**	**130**	**78**	**32**	**7**	**3**	**10**	**12**

Signed as a free agent by **Chicago**, August 27, 1997. Traded to **Philadelphia** by **Chicago** for future considerations, January 26, 2000. Signed as a free agent by **Ottawa**, July 12, 2000.

WHITE, Tony

Left wing. Shoots left. 5'10", 175 lbs. Born, Grand Falls, Nfld., June 16, 1954.
(Washington's 10th choice, 161st overall, in 1974 Amateur Draft).

Season	Club	GP	G	A	Pts	PIM	GP	G	A	Pts	PIM
1974-75	Washington Capitals	5	0	2	2	0	....	....	....	....	....
1975-76	Washington Capitals	80	25	17	42	56	....	....	....	....	....
1976-77	Washington Capitals	72	12	9	21	44	....	....	....	....	....
1977-78	Washington Capitals	1	0	0	0	0	....	....	....	....	....
1979-80	Minnesota North Stars	6	0	0	0	4	....	....	....	....	....
	NHL Totals	**164**	**37**	**28**	**65**	**104**	....	....	....	....	....

Signed as a free agent by **Minnesota**, September 17, 1979.

WHITELAW, Bob

Defense. Shoots left. 5'11", 185 lbs. Born, Motherwell, Scotland, October 5, 1916.

Season	Club	GP	G	A	Pts	PIM	GP	G	A	Pts	PIM
1940-41	Detroit Red Wings	23	0	2	2	2	8	0	0	0	0
1941-42	Detroit Red Wings	9	0	0	0	0	....	....	....	....	....
	NHL Totals	**32**	**0**	**2**	**2**	**2**	**8**	**0**	**0**	**0**	**0**

Signed as a free agent by **Detroit**, October 13, 1939. Traded to **Providence** (AHL) by **Detroit** with Buck Jones for Eddie Bush and future considerations, February 3, 1942.

WHITFIELD, Trent

Center. Shoots left. 5'11", 204 lbs. Born, Estevan, Sask., June 17, 1977.
(Boston's 5th choice, 100th overall, in 1996 Entry Draft).

Season	Club	GP	G	A	Pts	PIM	GP	G	A	Pts	PIM
99-2000	Washington Capitals	....	....	....	....	....	3	0	0	0	0
2000-01	Washington Capitals	61	2	4	6	35	5	0	0	0	2
2001-02	Washington Capitals	24	0	1	1	28	....	....	....	....	....
	New York Rangers	1	0	0	0	0	....	....	....	....	....
2002-03	Washington Capitals	14	1	1	2	6	6	0	0	0	10
	NHL Totals	**100**	**3**	**6**	**9**	**69**	**14**	**0**	**0**	**0**	**12**

Signed as a free agent by **Washington**, September 1, 1998. Claimed on waivers by **NY Rangers** from **Washington**, January 16, 2002. Claimed on waivers by **Washington** from **NY Rangers**, February 1, 2002.

WHITLOCK, Bob

Center. Shoots right. 5'10", 175 lbs. Born, Charlottetown, P.E.I., July 16, 1949.

Season	Club	GP	G	A	Pts	PIM	GP	G	A	Pts	PIM
1969-70	Minnesota North Stars	1	0	0	0	0	....	....	....	....	....
	NHL Totals	**1**	**0**	**0**	**0**	**0**	....	....	....	....	....

Signed as a free agent by **Minnesota**, October 2, 1969.

WHITNEY, Ray

Left wing. Shoots right. 5'10", 175 lbs. Born, Fort Saskatchewan, Alta., May 8, 1972.
(San Jose's 2nd choice, 23rd overall, in 1991 Entry Draft).

Season	Club	GP	G	A	Pts	PIM	GP	G	A	Pts	PIM
1991-92	San Jose Sharks	2	0	3	3	0	....	....	....	....	....
1992-93	San Jose Sharks	26	4	6	10	4	....	....	....	....	....
1993-94	San Jose Sharks	61	14	26	40	14	14	0	4	4	8
1994-95	San Jose Sharks	39	13	12	25	14	11	4	4	8	2
1995-96	San Jose Sharks	60	17	24	41	16	....	....	....	....	....
1996-97	San Jose Sharks	12	0	2	2	4	....	....	....	....	....
1997-98	Edmonton Oilers	9	1	3	4	0	....	....	....	....	....
	Florida Panthers	68	32	29	61	28	....	....	....	....	....
1998-99	Florida Panthers	81	26	38	64	18	....	....	....	....	....
99-2000	Florida Panthers	81	29	42	71	35	4	1	0	1	4
2000-01	Florida Panthers	43	10	21	31	28	....	....	....	....	....
	Columbus Blue Jackets	3	0	3	3	2	....	....	....	....	....
2001-02	Columbus Blue Jackets	67	21	40	61	12	....	....	....	....	....
2002-03	Columbus Blue Jackets	81	24	52	76	22	....	....	....	....	....
	NHL Totals	**633**	**191**	**301**	**492**	**197**	**29**	**5**	**8**	**13**	**14**

Played in NHL All-Star Game (2000, 2003)

Signed as a free agent by **Edmonton**, October 1, 1997. Claimed on waivers by **Florida** from **Edmonton**, November 6, 1997. Traded to **Columbus** by **Florida** with future considerations for Kevyn Adams and Coliumbus's 4th round choice (Michael Woodford) in 2001 Entry Draft, March 13, 2001. Signed as a free agent by **Detroit**, July 30, 2003.

WHYTE, Sean

Right wing. Shoots right. 6', 198 lbs. Born, Sudbury, Ont., May 4, 1970.
(Los Angeles' 7th choice, 165th overall, in 1989 Entry Draft).

Season	Club	GP	G	A	Pts	PIM	GP	G	A	Pts	PIM
1991-92	Los Angeles Kings	3	0	0	0	0	....	....	....	....	....
1992-93	Los Angeles Kings	18	0	2	2	12	....	....	....	....	....
	NHL Totals	**21**	**0**	**2**	**2**	**12**	....	....	....	....	....

WICKENHEISER, Doug

Center. Shoots left. 6'1", 200 lbs. Born, Regina, Sask., March 30, 1961.
(Montreal's 1st choice, 1st overall, in 1980 Entry Draft).

Season	Club	GP	G	A	Pts	PIM	GP	G	A	Pts	PIM
1980-81	Montreal Canadiens	41	7	8	15	20	....	....	....	....	....
1981-82	Montreal Canadiens	56	12	23	35	43	....	....	....	....	....
1982-83	Montreal Canadiens	78	25	30	55	49	....	....	....	....	....
1983-84	Montreal Canadiens	27	5	5	10	6	....	....	....	....	....
	St. Louis Blues	46	7	21	28	19	11	2	2	4	2
1984-85	St. Louis Blues	68	23	20	43	36	....	....	....	....	....

Season	Club	GP	G	A	Pts	PIM	GP	G	A	Pts	PIM
		REGULAR SEASON					PLAYOFFS				
1985-86	St. Louis Blues	36	8	11	19	16	19	2	5	7	12
1986-87	St. Louis Blues	80	13	15	28	37	6	0	0	0	2
1987-88	Vancouver Canucks	80	7	19	26	36	....	....	....	....	....
1988-89	New York Rangers	1	1	0	1	0	....	....	....	....	....
	Washington Capitals	16	2	5	7	4	5	0	0	0	2
1989-90	Washington Capitals	27	1	8	9	20	....	....	....	....	....
	NHL Totals	**556**	**111**	**165**	**276**	**286**	**41**	**4**	**7**	**11**	**18**

Traded to **St. Louis** by **Montreal** with Gilbert Delorme and Greg Paslawski for Perry Turnbull, December 21, 1983. Claimed by **Hartford** from **St. Louis** in Waiver Draft, October 5, 1987. Claimed by **Vancouver** from **Hartford** in Waiver Draft, October 5, 1987. Signed as a free agent by **NY Rangers**, August 12, 1988. Signed as a free agent by **Washington**, February 28, 1989.

WIDING, Juha

Center. Shoots left. 6', 180 lbs. Born, Oulu, Finland, July 4, 1947.

Season	Club	GP	G	A	Pts	PIM	GP	G	A	Pts	PIM
1969-70	New York Rangers	44	7	7	14	10	....	....	....	....	....
	Los Angeles Kings	4	0	2	2	2	....	....	....	....	....
1970-71	Los Angeles Kings	78	25	40	65	24	....	....	....	....	....
1971-72	Los Angeles Kings	78	27	28	55	26	....	....	....	....	....
1972-73	Los Angeles Kings	77	16	54	70	30	....	....	....	....	....
1973-74	Los Angeles Kings	71	27	30	57	26	5	1	0	1	2
1974-75	Los Angeles Kings	80	26	34	60	46	3	0	2	2	0
1975-76	Los Angeles Kings	67	7	15	22	26	....	....	....	....	....
1976-77	Los Angeles Kings	47	3	8	11	8	....	....	....	....	....
	Cleveland Barons	29	6	8	14	10	....	....	....	....	....
	NHL Totals	**575**	**144**	**226**	**370**	**208**	**8**	**1**	**2**	**3**	**2**

Traded to **Los Angeles** by **NY Rangers** with Real Lemieux for Ted Irvine, February 28, 1970. Traded to **Cleveland** by **Los Angeles** with Gary Edwards for Jim Moxey and Gary Simmons, January 22, 1977.

WIDMER, Jason

Defense. Shoots left. 6', 200 lbs. Born, Calgary, Alta., August 1, 1973.
(NY Islanders' 8th choice, 176th overall, in 1992 Entry Draft).

Season	Club	GP	G	A	Pts	PIM	GP	G	A	Pts	PIM
1994-95	New York Islanders	1	0	0	0	0	....	....	....	....	....
1995-96	New York Islanders	4	0	0	0	7	....	....	....	....	....
1996-97	San Jose Sharks	2	0	1	1	0	....	....	....	....	....
	NHL Totals	**7**	**0**	**1**	**1**	**7**	....	....	....	....	....

Signed as a free agent by **San Jose**, September 11, 1996. Signed as a free agent by **St. Louis**, July 28, 1998.

WIEBE, Art

Defense. Shoots left. 5'10", 180 lbs. Born, Rosthern, Sask., September 28, 1912.

Season	Club	GP	G	A	Pts	PIM	GP	G	A	Pts	PIM
1932-33	Chicago Black Hawks	4	0	0	0	0	....	....	....	....	....
1934-35	Chicago Black Hawks	42	2	1	3	27	2	0	0	0	2
1935-36	Chicago Black Hawks	46	1	0	1	25	2	0	0	0	0
1936-37	Chicago Black Hawks	43	0	2	2	6	....	....	....	....	....
1937-38♦	Chicago Black Hawks	43	0	3	3	24	10	0	1	1	2
1938-39	Chicago Black Hawks	47	1	2	3	24	....	....	....	....	....
1939-40	Chicago Black Hawks	47	2	2	4	20	2	1	0	1	2
1940-41	Chicago Black Hawks	45	3	2	5	28	4	0	0	0	0
1941-42	Chicago Black Hawks	43	2	4	6	20	3	0	0	0	0
1942-43	Chicago Black Hawks	33	1	7	8	25	....	....	....	....	....
1943-44	Chicago Black Hawks	21	2	4	6	2	8	0	2	2	4
	NHL Totals	**414**	**14**	**27**	**41**	**201**	**31**	**1**	**3**	**4**	**10**

Traded to **Chicago** by **St. Paul** (AHA) for Helge Bostrom, December 29, 1932.

WIEMER, Jason

Center. Shoots left. 6'1", 225 lbs. Born, Kimberley, B.C., April 14, 1976.
(Tampa Bay's 1st choice, 8th overall, in 1994 Entry Draft).

Season	Club	GP	G	A	Pts	PIM	GP	G	A	Pts	PIM
1994-95	Tampa Bay Lightning	36	1	4	5	44	....	....	....	....	....
1995-96	Tampa Bay Lightning	66	9	9	18	81	6	1	0	1	28
1996-97	Tampa Bay Lightning	63	9	5	14	134	....	....	....	....	....
1997-98	Tampa Bay Lightning	67	8	9	17	132	....	....	....	....	....
	Calgary Flames	12	4	1	5	28	....	....	....	....	....
1998-99	Calgary Flames	78	8	13	21	177	....	....	....	....	....
99-2000	Calgary Flames	64	11	11	22	120	....	....	....	....	....
2000-01	Calgary Flames	65	10	5	15	177	....	....	....	....	....
2001-02	Florida Panthers	70	11	20	31	178	....	....	....	....	....
2002-03	New York Islanders	81	9	19	28	116	5	0	0	0	23
	NHL Totals	**602**	**80**	**96**	**176**	**1187**	**11**	**1**	**0**	**1**	**51**

Traded to **Calgary** by **Tampa Bay** for Sandy McCarthy and Calgary's 3rd (Brad Richards) and 5th (Curtis Rich) round choices in 1998 Entry Draft, March 24, 1998. Traded to **Florida** by **Calgary** with Valeri Bure for Rob Neidermayer and Philadelphia's 2nd round choice (previously acquired, Calgary selected Andrei Medvedev) in 2001 Entry Draft, June 24, 2001. Traded to **NY Islanders** by **Florida** for Branislav Mezei, July 3, 2002.

WIEMER, Jim

Defense. Shoots left. 6'4", 216 lbs. Born, Sudbury, Ont., January 9, 1961.
(Buffalo's 5th choice, 83rd overall, in 1980 Entry Draft).

Season	Club	GP	G	A	Pts	PIM	GP	G	A	Pts	PIM
1982-83	Buffalo Sabres	....	....	....	....	....	1	0	0	0	0
1983-84	Buffalo Sabres	64	5	15	20	48	....	....	....	....	....
1984-85	Buffalo Sabres	10	3	2	5	4	....	....	....	....	....
	New York Rangers	22	4	3	7	30	1	0	0	0	0
1985-86	New York Rangers	7	3	0	3	2	8	1	0	1	6
1987-88	Edmonton Oilers	12	1	2	3	15	2	0	0	0	2
1988-89	Los Angeles Kings	9	2	3	5	20	10	2	1	3	19
1989-90	Boston Bruins	61	5	14	19	63	8	0	1	1	4
1990-91	Boston Bruins	61	4	19	23	62	16	1	3	4	14
1991-92	Boston Bruins	47	1	8	9	84	15	1	3	4	14
1992-93	Boston Bruins	28	1	6	7	48	1	0	0	0	4
1993-94	Boston Bruins	4	0	0	0	2	....	....	....	....	....
	NHL Totals	**325**	**29**	**72**	**101**	**378**	**62**	**5**	**8**	**13**	**63**

Traded to **NY Rangers** by **Buffalo** with Steve Patrick for Dave Maloney and Chris Renaud, December 6, 1984. Traded to **Edmonton** by **NY Rangers** with Reijo Ruotsalainen, Clark Donatelli and Ville Kentala for Don Jackson, Mike Golden, Miloslav Horova and future considerations (Stu Kulak, March 10, 1987), October 23, 1986. Traded to **Los Angeles** by **Edmonton** with Alan May for Brian Wilks and John English, March 7, 1989. Signed as a free agent by **Boston**, July 6, 1989.

WILCOX, Archie

Right wing/Defense. Shoots left. 5'11", 195 lbs. Born, Montreal, Que., May 9, 1903.

Season	Club	GP	G	A	Pts	PIM	GP	G	A	Pts	PIM
1929-30	Montreal Maroons	42	3	5	8	38	4	1	0	1	2
1930-31	Montreal Maroons	39	2	2	4	42	2	0	0	0	2
1931-32	Montreal Maroons	48	3	3	6	37	4	0	0	0	4
1932-33	Montreal Maroons	47	0	3	3	37	2	0	0	0	0
1933-34	Montreal Maroons	10	0	0	0	2	....	....	....	....	....
	Boston Bruins	14	0	1	1	2	....	....	....	....	....
1934-35	St. Louis Eagles	8	0	0	0	0	....	....	....	....	....
	NHL Totals	**208**	**8**	**14**	**22**	**158**	**12**	**1**	**0**	**1**	**8**

Traded to **Mtl. Maroons** by **Providence** (Can-Am) for cash, September 23, 1929. Claimed on waivers by **Boston** from **Mtl. Maroons**, January 29, 1934. Traded to **St. Louis** by **Boston** for Burr Williams, December 2, 1934. Traded to **Syracuse** (IHL) by **St. Louis** for cash, January 4, 1934.

WILCOX, Barry

Right wing. Shoots left. 6'1", 190 lbs. Born, New Westminster, B.C., April 23, 1948.

Season	Club	GP	G	A	Pts	PIM	GP	G	A	Pts	PIM
1972-73	Vancouver Canucks	31	3	2	5	15	....	....	....	....	....
1974-75	Vancouver Canucks	2	0	0	0	0	....	....	....	....	....
	NHL Totals	**33**	**3**	**2**	**5**	**15**	....	....	....	....	....

Signed as a free agent by **Vancouver**, September, 1971.

WILDER, Arch

Left wing. Shoots left. 5'9", 155 lbs. Born, Melville, Sask., April 30, 1917.

Season	Club	GP	G	A	Pts	PIM	GP	G	A	Pts	PIM
1940-41	Detroit Red Wings	18	0	2	2	2	....	....	....	....	....
	NHL Totals	**18**	**0**	**2**	**2**	**2**	....	....	....	....	....

Signed as a free agent by **Detroit**, October 28, 1937.

WILEY, Jim

Center. Shoots left. 6'2", 200 lbs. Born, Sault Ste. Marie, Ont., April 28, 1950.

Season	Club	GP	G	A	Pts	PIM	GP	G	A	Pts	PIM
1972-73	Pittsburgh Penguins	4	0	1	1	0	....	....	....	....	....
1973-74	Pittsburgh Penguins	22	0	3	3	2	....	....	....	....	....
1974-75	Vancouver Canucks	1	0	0	0	0	....	....	....	....	....
1975-76	Vancouver Canucks	2	0	0	0	2	....	....	....	....	....
1976-77	Vancouver Canucks	34	4	6	10	4	....	....	....	....	....
	NHL Totals	**63**	**4**	**10**	**14**	**8**	....	....	....	....	....

Signed as a free agent by **Pittsburgh**, June 25, 1972. Claimed by **Vancouver** from **Pittsburgh** in Intra-League Draft, June 10, 1974.

WILKIE, Bob

Defense. Shoots right. 6'2", 215 lbs. Born, Calgary, Alta., February 11, 1969.
(Detroit's 3rd choice, 41st overall, in 1987 Entry Draft).

Season	Club	GP	G	A	Pts	PIM	GP	G	A	Pts	PIM
1990-91	Detroit Red Wings	8	1	2	3	2	....	....	....	....	....
1993-94	Philadelphia Flyers	10	1	3	4	8	....	....	....	....	....
	NHL Totals	**18**	**2**	**5**	**7**	**10**	....	....	....	....	....

Traded to **Philadelphia** by **Detroit** for future considerations, February 2, 1993. Traded to **Chicago** by **Philadelphia** with Philadelphia's 5th round choice (Kyle Calder) in 1997 Entry Draft for Karl Dykhuis, February 16, 1995.

WILKIE, David

Defense. Shoots right. 6'3", 215 lbs. Born, Ellensburgh, WA, May 30, 1974.
(Montreal's 1st choice, 20th overall, in 1992 Entry Draft).

Season	Club	GP	G	A	Pts	PIM	GP	G	A	Pts	PIM
1994-95	Montreal Canadiens	1	0	0	0	0	....	....	....	....	....
1995-96	Montreal Canadiens	24	1	5	6	10	6	1	2	3	12
1996-97	Montreal Canadiens	61	6	9	15	63	2	0	0	0	2
1997-98	Montreal Canadiens	5	1	0	1	4	....	....	....	....	....
	Tampa Bay Lightning	29	1	5	6	17	....	....	....	....	....
1998-99	Tampa Bay Lightning	46	1	7	8	69	....	....	....	....	....
2000-01	New York Rangers	1	0	0	0	2	....	....	....	....	....
	NHL Totals	**167**	**10**	**26**	**36**	**165**	**8**	**1**	**2**	**3**	**14**

Traded to **Tampa Bay** by **Montreal** with Stephane Richer and Darcy Tucker for Patrick Poulin, Mick Vukota and Igor Ulanov, January 15, 1998. Signed as a free agent by **NY Rangers**, September 29, 1999.

WILKINS, Barry

Defense. Shoots left. 6', 190 lbs. Born, Toronto, Ont., February 28, 1947.

Season	Club	GP	G	A	Pts	PIM	GP	G	A	Pts	PIM
1966-67	Boston Bruins	1	0	0	0	0	....	....	....	....	....
1968-69	Boston Bruins	1	1	0	1	0	....	....	....	....	....
1969-70	Boston Bruins	6	0	0	0	2	....	....	....	....	....
1970-71	Vancouver Canucks	70	5	18	23	131	....	....	....	....	....
1971-72	Vancouver Canucks	45	2	5	7	65	....	....	....	....	....
1972-73	Vancouver Canucks	76	11	17	28	133	....	....	....	....	....
1973-74	Vancouver Canucks	78	3	28	31	123	....	....	....	....	....

Season	Club	Regular Season GP	G	A	Pts	PIM	Playoffs GP	G	A	Pts	PIM
1974-75	Vancouver Canucks	7	0	1	1	6	....	....	....	....	....
	Pittsburgh Penguins	59	5	29	34	97	3	0	0	0	0
1975-76	Pittsburgh Penguins	75	0	27	27	106	3	0	1	1	4
	NHL Totals	**418**	**27**	**125**	**152**	**663**	**6**	**0**	**1**	**1**	**4**

Claimed by **Vancouver** from **Boston** in Expansion Draft, June 10, 1970. Traded to **Pittsburgh** by **Vancouver** for Ab Demarco Jr., November 4, 1974.

WILKINSON, John

Defense. Shoots left. 5'11", 195 lbs. Born, Ottawa, Ont., July 9, 1911.

Season	Club	GP	G	A	Pts	PIM	GP	G	A	Pts	PIM
1943-44	Boston Bruins	9	0	0	0	6	....	....	....	....	....
	NHL Totals	**9**	**0**	**0**	**0**	**6**	....	....	....	....	....

WILKINSON, Neil

Defense. Shoots right. 6'3", 194 lbs. Born, Selkirk, Man., August 15, 1967.
(Minnesota's 2nd choice, 30th overall, in 1986 Entry Draft).

Season	Club	GP	G	A	Pts	PIM	GP	G	A	Pts	PIM
1989-90	Minnesota North Stars	36	0	5	5	100	7	0	2	2	11
1990-91	Minnesota North Stars	50	2	9	11	117	22	3	3	6	12
1991-92	San Jose Sharks	60	4	15	19	107	....	....	....	....	....
1992-93	San Jose Sharks	59	1	7	8	96	....	....	....	....	....
1993-94	Chicago Blackhawks	72	3	9	12	116	4	0	0	0	0
1994-95	Winnipeg Jets	40	1	4	5	75	....	....	....	....	....
1995-96	Winnipeg Jets	21	1	4	5	33	....	....	....	....	....
	Pittsburgh Penguins	41	2	10	12	87	15	0	1	1	14
1996-97	Pittsburgh Penguins	23	0	0	0	36	5	0	0	0	4
1997-98	Pittsburgh Penguins	34	2	4	6	24	....	....	....	....	....
1998-99	Pittsburgh Penguins	24	0	0	0	22	....	....	....	....	....
	NHL Totals	**460**	**16**	**67**	**83**	**813**	**53**	**3**	**6**	**9**	**41**

Claimed by **San Jose** from **Minnesota** in Dispersal Draft, May 30, 1991. Traded to **Chicago** by **San Jose** to complete transaction that sent Jimmy Waite to San Jose (June 18, 1993), July 9, 1993. Traded to **Winnipeg** by **Chicago** for Chicago's 3rd round choice (previously acquired, Chicago selected Kevin McKay) in 1995 Entry Draft, June 3, 1994. Traded to **Pittsburgh** by **Winnipeg** for Norm Maciver, December 28, 1995.

WILKS, Brian

Center. Shoots right. 5'11", 175 lbs. Born, North York, Ont., February 27, 1966.
(Los Angeles' 2nd choice, 24th overall, in 1984 Entry Draft).

Season	Club	GP	G	A	Pts	PIM	GP	G	A	Pts	PIM
1984-85	Los Angeles Kings	2	0	0	0	0	....	....	....	....	....
1985-86	Los Angeles Kings	43	4	8	12	25	....	....	....	....	....
1986-87	Los Angeles Kings	1	0	0	0	0	....	....	....	....	....
1988-89	Los Angeles Kings	2	0	0	0	2	....	....	....	....	....
	NHL Totals	**48**	**4**	**8**	**12**	**27**	....	....	....	....	....

Traded to **Edmonton** by **Los Angeles** with John English for Jim Wiemer and Alan May, March 7, 1989. Traded to **Pittsburgh** by **Edmonton** for future considerations, March 6, 1990.

WILLARD, Rod

Left wing. Shoots left. 6', 190 lbs. Born, New Liskeard, Ont., May 1, 1960.

Season	Club	GP	G	A	Pts	PIM	GP	G	A	Pts	PIM
1982-83	Toronto Maple Leafs	1	0	0	0	0	....	....	....	....	....
	NHL Totals	**1**	**0**	**0**	**0**	**0**	....	....	....	....	....

Signed as a free agent by **Toronto**, September 14, 1982. Traded to **Chicago** by **Toronto** for Dave Snopek, January 23, 1983.

WILLIAMS, Burr

Defense. Shoots right. 5'10", 183 lbs. Born, Okemah, OK, August 30, 1909.

Season	Club	GP	G	A	Pts	PIM	GP	G	A	Pts	PIM
1933-34	Detroit Red Wings	1	0	1	1	12	7	0	0	0	8
1934-35	St. Louis Eagles	9	0	0	0	6	....	....	....	....	....
	Boston Bruins	7	0	0	0	6	....	....	....	....	....
1936-37	Detroit Red Wings	2	0	0	0	4	....	....	....	....	....
	NHL Totals	**19**	**0**	**1**	**1**	**28**	**7**	**0**	**0**	**0**	**8**

Claimed by **Toronto** from **Tulsa** (AHA) in Inter-League Draft, April 15, 1930. • Rights returned to **Tulsa** (AHA) when American Hockey Association severed working relationship with NHL. Traded to **St. Louis** (AHA) by **Tulsa** (AHA) for cash, December, 1931. Claimed by **Chicago** from **St. Louis** (AHA) in Inter-League Draft, September 2, 1932. Traded to **Duluth** (AHA) by **Chicago** for cash, October, 1932. Traded to **Detroit** by **Duluth** (AHA) for cash, January 29, 1933. Traded to **St. Louis** by **Detroit** for Normie Smith, October 22, 1934. Traded to **Boston** by **St. Louis** for Archie Wilcox, December 2, 1934. Traded to **Detroit** by **Boston** for cash, December 31, 1934.

WILLIAMS, Butch

Right wing. Shoots right. 5'11", 195 lbs. Born, Duluth, MN, September 11, 1952.

Season	Club	GP	G	A	Pts	PIM	GP	G	A	Pts	PIM
1973-74	St. Louis Blues	31	3	10	13	6	....	....	....	....	....
1974-75	California Golden Seals	63	11	21	32	118	....	....	....	....	....
1975-76	California Golden Seals	14	0	4	4	7	....	....	....	....	....
	NHL Totals	**108**	**14**	**35**	**49**	**131**	....	....	....	....	....

• Brother of Tommy

Signed as a free agent by **St. Louis**, August, 1972. Traded to **California** by **St. Louis** with Dave Gardner for Craig Patrick and Stan Gilbertson, November 11, 1974.

WILLIAMS, Darryl

Left wing. Shoots left. 5'11", 185 lbs. Born, Mt. Pearl, Nfld., February 9, 1968.

Season	Club	GP	G	A	Pts	PIM	GP	G	A	Pts	PIM
1992-93	Los Angeles Kings	2	0	0	0	10	....	....	....	....	....
	NHL Totals	**2**	**0**	**0**	**0**	**10**	....	....	....	....	....

Signed as a free agent by **Los Angeles**, May 19, 1989.

WILLIAMS, David

Defense. Shoots right. 6'2", 195 lbs. Born, Plainfield, NJ, August 25, 1967.
(New Jersey's 12th choice, 234th overall, in 1985 Entry Draft).

Season	Club	GP	G	A	Pts	PIM	GP	G	A	Pts	PIM
1991-92	San Jose Sharks	56	3	25	28	40	....	....	....	....	....
1992-93	San Jose Sharks	40	1	11	12	49	....	....	....	....	....
1993-94	Mighty Ducks of Anaheim	56	5	15	20	42	....	....	....	....	....
1994-95	Mighty Ducks of Anaheim	21	2	2	4	26	....	....	....	....	....
	NHL Totals	**173**	**11**	**53**	**64**	**157**	....	....	....	....	....

Signed as a free agent by **San Jose**, August 9, 1991. Claimed by **Anaheim** from **San Jose** in Expansion Draft, June 24, 1993. Signed as a free agent by **Hartford**, August 25, 1995. Signed as a free agent by **St. Louis**, July 29, 1996.

WILLIAMS, Fred

Center. Shoots left. 5'11", 178 lbs. Born, Saskatoon, Sask., July 1, 1956.
(Detroit's 1st choice, 4th overall, in 1976 Amateur Draft).

Season	Club	GP	G	A	Pts	PIM	GP	G	A	Pts	PIM
1976-77	Detroit Red Wings	44	2	5	7	10	....	....	....	....	....
	NHL Totals	**44**	**2**	**5**	**7**	**10**	....	....	....	....	....

• Brother of Gord

Signed as a free agent by **Philadelphia**, September 15, 1979.

WILLIAMS, Gord

Right wing. Shoots right. 5'11", 190 lbs. Born, Saskatoon, Sask., April 10, 1960.
(Philadelphia's 7th choice, 119th overall, in 1979 Entry Draft).

Season	Club	GP	G	A	Pts	PIM	GP	G	A	Pts	PIM
1981-82	Philadelphia Flyers	1	0	0	0	2	....	....	....	....	....
1982-83	Philadelphia Flyers	1	0	0	0	0	....	....	....	....	....
	NHL Totals	**2**	**0**	**0**	**0**	**2**	....	....	....	....	....

• Brother of Fred

WILLIAMS, Jason

Center. Shoots right. 5'11", 185 lbs. Born, London, Ont., August 11, 1980.

Season	Club	GP	G	A	Pts	PIM	GP	G	A	Pts	PIM
2000-01	Detroit Red Wings	5	0	3	3	2	2	0	0	0	0
2001-02 ♦	Detroit Red Wings	25	8	2	10	4	9	0	0	0	2
2002-03	Detroit Red Wings	16	3	3	6	2	....	....	....	....	....
	NHL Totals	**46**	**11**	**8**	**19**	**8**	**11**	**0**	**0**	**0**	**2**

Signed as a free agent by **Detroit**, September 18, 2000.

WILLIAMS, Justin

Right wing. Shoots right. 6'1", 190 lbs. Born, Cobourg, Ont., October 4, 1981.
(Philadelphia's 1st choice, 28th overall, in 2000 Entry Draft).

Season	Club	GP	G	A	Pts	PIM	GP	G	A	Pts	PIM
2000-01	Philadelphia Flyers	63	12	13	25	22	....	....	....	....	....
2001-02	Philadelphia Flyers	75	17	23	40	32	5	0	0	0	4
2002-03	Philadelphia Flyers	41	8	16	24	22	12	1	5	6	8
	NHL Totals	**179**	**37**	**52**	**89**	**76**	**17**	**1**	**5**	**6**	**12**

• Missed majority of 2002-03 season recovering from shoulder (November 15, 2002 vs. Carolina) and knee (January 18, 2003 vs. Tampa Bay) injuries.

WILLIAMS, Sean

Center. Shoots left. 6'1", 182 lbs. Born, Oshawa, Ont., January 28, 1968.
(Chicago's 11th choice, 245th overall, in 1986 Entry Draft).

Season	Club	GP	G	A	Pts	PIM	GP	G	A	Pts	PIM
1991-92	Chicago Blackhawks	2	0	0	0	4	....	....	....	....	....
	NHL Totals	**2**	**0**	**0**	**0**	**4**	....	....	....	....	....

WILLIAMS, Tiger

Left wing. Shoots left. 5'11", 190 lbs. Born, Weyburn, Sask., February 3, 1954.
(Toronto's 2nd choice, 31st overall, in 1974 Amateur Draft).

Season	Club	GP	G	A	Pts	PIM	GP	G	A	Pts	PIM
1974-75	Toronto Maple Leafs	42	10	19	29	187	7	1	3	4	25
1975-76	Toronto Maple Leafs	78	21	19	40	299	10	0	0	0	75
1976-77	Toronto Maple Leafs	77	18	25	43	*338	9	3	6	9	29
1977-78	Toronto Maple Leafs	78	19	31	50	351	12	1	2	3	*63
1978-79	Toronto Maple Leafs	77	19	20	39	*298	6	0	0	0	*48
1979-80	Toronto Maple Leafs	55	22	18	40	197	....	....	....	....	....
	Vancouver Canucks	23	8	5	13	81	3	0	0	0	20
1980-81	Vancouver Canucks	77	35	27	62	*343	3	0	0	0	20
1981-82	Vancouver Canucks	77	17	21	38	341	17	3	7	10	*116
1982-83	Vancouver Canucks	68	8	13	21	265	4	0	3	3	12
1983-84	Vancouver Canucks	67	15	16	31	294	4	1	0	1	13
1984-85	Detroit Red Wings	55	3	8	11	158	....	....	....	....	....
	Los Angeles Kings	12	4	3	7	43	3	0	0	0	4
1985-86	Los Angeles Kings	72	20	29	49	320	....	....	....	....	....
1986-87	Los Angeles Kings	76	16	18	34	358	5	3	2	5	30
1987-88	Los Angeles Kings	2	0	0	0	6	....	....	....	....	....
	Hartford Whalers	26	6	0	6	87	....	....	....	....	....
	NHL Totals	**962**	**241**	**272**	**513**	**3966**	**83**	**12**	**23**	**35**	**455**

Played in NHL All-Star Game (1981)

Traded to **Vancouver** by **Toronto** with Jerry Butler for Rick Vaive and Bill Derlago, February 18, 1980. Traded to **Detroit** by **Vancouver** for Rob McClanahan, August 8, 1984. Traded to **Los Angeles** by **Detroit** for future considerations, March 12, 1985. Traded to **Hartford** by **Los Angeles** for cash, October 15, 1987.

WILLIAMS, Tom

Left wing. Shoots right. 5'11", 187 lbs. Born, Windsor, Ont., February 7, 1951.
(NY Rangers' 3rd choice, 27th overall, in 1971 Amateur Draft).

Season	Club	GP	G	A	Pts	PIM	GP	G	A	Pts	PIM
1971-72	New York Rangers	3	0	0	0	2	....	....	....	....	....

Season	Club	GP	G	A	Pts	PIM	GP	G	A	Pts	PIM
		REGULAR SEASON					PLAYOFFS				
1972-73	New York Rangers	8	0	1	1	0	....	....	....	....	....
1973-74	New York Rangers	14	1	2	3	4	....	....	....	....	....
	Los Angeles Kings	46	11	17	28	6	5	3	1	4	0
1974-75	Los Angeles Kings	74	24	22	46	16	3	0	0	0	0
1975-76	Los Angeles Kings	70	19	20	39	14	9	2	2	4	2
1976-77	Los Angeles Kings	80	35	39	74	14	9	3	4	7	2
1977-78	Los Angeles Kings	58	15	22	37	9	2	0	0	0	0
1978-79	Los Angeles Kings	44	10	15	25	8	1	0	0	0	0
	NHL Totals	**397**	**115**	**138**	**253**	**73**	**29**	**8**	**7**	**15**	**4**

Traded to **Los Angeles** by **NY Rangers** with Mike Murphy and Sheldon Kannegiesser for Gilles Marotte and Real Lemieux, November 30, 1973. Traded to **St. Louis** by **Los Angeles** to complete three-team transaction that sent Barry Gibbs to Los Angeles (June 9, 1979) and Terry Richardson to NY Islanders (June 9, 1979), August 16, 1979.

WILLIAMS, Tommy

USHOF

Right wing. Shoots right. 5'11", 180 lbs. Born, Duluth, MN, April 17, 1940.

Season	Club	GP	G	A	Pts	PIM	GP	G	A	Pts	PIM
1961-62	Boston Bruins	26	6	6	12	2	....	....	....	....	....
1962-63	Boston Bruins	69	23	20	43	11	....	....	....	....	....
1963-64	Boston Bruins	37	8	15	23	8	....	....	....	....	....
1964-65	Boston Bruins	65	13	21	34	28	....	....	....	....	....
1965-66	Boston Bruins	70	16	22	38	31	....	....	....	....	....
1966-67	Boston Bruins	29	8	13	21	2	....	....	....	....	....
1967-68	Boston Bruins	68	18	32	50	14	4	1	0	1	2
1968-69	Boston Bruins	26	4	7	11	19	....	....	....	....	....
1969-70	Minnesota North Stars	75	15	52	67	18	6	1	5	6	0
1970-71	Minnesota North Stars	41	10	13	23	16	....	....	....	....	....
	California Seals	18	7	10	17	8	....	....	....	....	....
1971-72	California Golden Seals	32	3	9	12	2	....	....	....	....	....
1974-75	Washington Capitals	73	22	36	58	12	....	....	....	....	....
1975-76	Washington Capitals	34	8	13	21	6	....	....	....	....	....
	NHL Totals	**663**	**161**	**269**	**430**	**177**	**10**	**2**	**5**	**7**	**2**

• Missed majority of 1968-69 season recovering from knee injury suffered in game vs. Chicago, December 13, 1968. Traded to **Minnesota** by **Boston** with Barry Gibbs for Minnesota's 1st round choice (Don Tannahill) in 1969 Amateur Draft and future considerations (Fred O'Donnell, May 7, 1971), May 7, 1969. Traded to **California** by **Minnesota** with Dick Redmond for Ted Hampson and Wayne Muloin, March 7, 1971. Traded to **Boston** by **California** for cash, March 5, 1972. Traded to **Washington** by **Boston** for cash, July 22, 1974.

WILLIS, Shane

Right wing. Shoots right. 6'1", 190 lbs. Born, Edmonton, Alta., June 13, 1977.
(Carolina's 4th choice, 88th overall, in 1997 Entry Draft).

Season	Club	GP	G	A	Pts	PIM	GP	G	A	Pts	PIM
1998-99	Carolina Hurricanes	7	0	0	0	0	....	....	....	....	....
99-2000	Carolina Hurricanes	2	0	0	0	0	....	....	....	....	....
2000-01	Carolina Hurricanes	73	20	24	44	45	2	0	0	0	0
2001-02	Carolina Hurricanes	59	7	10	17	24	....	....	....	....	....
	Tampa Bay Lightning	21	4	3	7	6	....	....	....	....	....
	NHL Totals	**162**	**31**	**37**	**68**	**75**	**2**	**0**	**0**	**0**	**0**

• Re-entered NHL Entry Draft. Originally Tampa Bay's 3rd choice, 56th overall, in 1995 Entry Draft.

NHL All-Rookie Team (2001)

Traded to **Tampa Bay** by **Carolina** with Chris Dingman for Kevin Weekes, March 5, 2002.

WILLSIE, Brian

Right wing. Shoots right. 6'1", 195 lbs. Born, London, Ont., March 16, 1978.
(Colorado's 7th choice, 146th overall, in 1996 Entry Draft).

Season	Club	GP	G	A	Pts	PIM	GP	G	A	Pts	PIM
99-2000	Colorado Avalanche	1	0	0	0	0	....	....	....	....	....
2001-02	Colorado Avalanche	56	7	7	14	14	4	0	1	1	2
2002-03	Colorado Avalanche	12	0	1	1	15	6	1	0	1	2
	NHL Totals	**69**	**7**	**8**	**15**	**29**	**10**	**1**	**1**	**2**	**4**

WILLSON, Don

Center. Shoots left. 5'8", 157 lbs. Born, Chatham, Ont., January 1, 1914.

Season	Club	GP	G	A	Pts	PIM	GP	G	A	Pts	PIM
1937-38	Montreal Canadiens	18	2	7	9	0	3	0	0	0	0
1938-39	Montreal Canadiens	4	0	0	0	0	....	....	....	....	....
	NHL Totals	**22**	**2**	**7**	**9**	**0**	**3**	**0**	**0**	**0**	**0**

WILM, Clarke

Center. Shoots left. 6', 202 lbs. Born, Central Butte, Sask., October 24, 1976.
(Calgary's 5th choice, 150th overall, in 1995 Entry Draft).

Season	Club	GP	G	A	Pts	PIM	GP	G	A	Pts	PIM
1998-99	Calgary Flames	78	10	8	18	53	....	....	....	....	....
99-2000	Calgary Flames	78	10	12	22	67	....	....	....	....	....
2000-01	Calgary Flames	81	7	8	15	69	....	....	....	....	....
2001-02	Calgary Flames	66	4	14	18	61	....	....	....	....	....
2002-03	Nashville Predators	82	5	11	16	36	....	....	....	....	....
	NHL Totals	**385**	**36**	**53**	**89**	**286**	....	....	....	....	....

Signed as a free agent by **Nashville**, July 11, 2002.

WILSON, Behn

Defense. Shoots left. 6'3", 210 lbs. Born, Toronto, Ont., December 19, 1958.
(Philadelphia's 1st choice, 6th overall, in 1978 Amateur Draft).

Season	Club	GP	G	A	Pts	PIM	GP	G	A	Pts	PIM
1978-79	Philadelphia Flyers	80	13	36	49	197	5	1	0	1	8
1979-80	Philadelphia Flyers	61	9	25	34	212	19	4	9	13	66
1980-81	Philadelphia Flyers	77	16	47	63	237	12	2	10	12	36
1981-82	Philadelphia Flyers	59	13	23	36	135	4	1	4	5	10
1982-83	Philadelphia Flyers	62	8	24	32	92	3	0	1	1	2
1983-84	Chicago Black Hawks	59	10	22	32	143	4	0	0	0	0
1984-85	Chicago Black Hawks	76	10	23	33	185	15	4	5	9	60
1985-86	Chicago Black Hawks	69	13	37	50	113	2	0	0	0	2
1987-88	Chicago Blackhawks	58	6	23	29	166	3	0	0	0	6
	NHL Totals	**601**	**98**	**260**	**358**	**1480**	**67**	**12**	**29**	**41**	**190**

Played in NHL All-Star Game (1981)

Traded to **Chicago** by **Philadelphia** for Doug Crossman and Chicago's 2nd round choice (Scott Mellanby) in 1984 Entry Draft, June 8, 1983. • Missed entire 1986-87 season and entire 1988-89 season recovering from back injury originally suffered in game vs. Toronto, April 5, 1986. Claimed by **Vancouver** from **Chicago** in Waiver Draft, October 3, 1988.

WILSON, Bert

Left wing. Shoots left. 6', 178 lbs. Born, Orangeville, Ont., October 17, 1949.
(NY Rangers' 3rd choice, 23rd overall, in 1969 Amateur Draft).

Season	Club	GP	G	A	Pts	PIM	GP	G	A	Pts	PIM
1973-74	New York Rangers	5	1	1	2	2	....	....	....	....	....
1974-75	New York Rangers	61	5	1	6	66	....	....	....	....	....
1975-76	St. Louis Blues	45	2	3	5	47	....	....	....	....	....
	Los Angeles Kings	13	0	0	0	17	8	0	0	0	24
1976-77	Los Angeles Kings	77	4	3	7	64	8	0	2	2	12
1977-78	Los Angeles Kings	79	7	16	23	127	2	0	0	0	2
1978-79	Los Angeles Kings	73	9	10	19	138	....	....	....	....	....
1979-80	Los Angeles Kings	75	4	3	7	91	2	0	0	0	4
1980-81	Calgary Flames	50	5	7	12	94	1	0	0	0	0
	NHL Totals	**478**	**37**	**44**	**81**	**646**	**21**	**0**	**2**	**2**	**42**

Traded to **St. Louis** by **NY Rangers** with Ted Irvine and Jerry Butler for Bill Collins and John Davidson, June 18, 1975. Traded to **Los Angeles** by **St. Louis** with rights to Curt Brackenbury for cash, March 6, 1976. Traded to **Calgary** by **Los Angeles** with Randy Holt for Garry Unger, June 6, 1980.

WILSON, Bob

Defense. Shoots left. 5'9", 165 lbs. Born, Sudbury, Ont., February 18, 1934.

Season	Club	GP	G	A	Pts	PIM	GP	G	A	Pts	PIM
1953-54	Chicago Black Hawks	1	0	0	0	0	....	....	....	....	....
	NHL Totals	**1**	**0**	**0**	**0**	**0**	....	....	....	....	....

Claimed by **Baltimore** (AHL) from **Chicago** in Reverse Draft, June 15, 1966.

WILSON, Carey

Center. Shoots right. 6'2", 195 lbs. Born, Winnipeg, Man., May 19, 1962.
(Chicago's 8th choice, 67th overall, in 1980 Entry Draft).

Season	Club	GP	G	A	Pts	PIM	GP	G	A	Pts	PIM
1983-84	Calgary Flames	15	2	5	7	2	6	3	1	4	2
1984-85	Calgary Flames	74	24	48	72	27	4	0	0	0	0
1985-86	Calgary Flames	76	29	29	58	24	9	0	2	2	2
1986-87	Calgary Flames	80	20	36	56	42	6	1	1	2	6
1987-88	Calgary Flames	34	9	21	30	18	....	....	....	....	....
	Hartford Whalers	36	18	20	38	22	6	2	4	6	2
1988-89	Hartford Whalers	34	11	11	22	14	....	....	....	....	....
	New York Rangers	41	21	34	55	45	4	1	2	3	2
1989-90	New York Rangers	41	9	17	26	57	10	2	1	3	0
1990-91	Hartford Whalers	45	8	15	23	16	....	....	....	....	....
	Calgary Flames	12	3	3	6	2	7	2	2	4	0
1991-92	Calgary Flames	42	11	12	23	37	....	....	....	....	....
1992-93	Calgary Flames	22	4	7	11	8	....	....	....	....	....
	NHL Totals	**552**	**169**	**258**	**427**	**314**	**52**	**11**	**13**	**24**	**14**

• Son of Jerry

Rights traded to **Calgary** by **Chicago** for Denis Cyr, November 8, 1982. Traded to **Hartford** by **Calgary** with Neil Sheehy and rights to Lane MacDonald for Dana Murzyn and Shane Churla, January 3, 1988. Traded to **NY Rangers** by **Hartford** with Hartford's 5th round choice (Lubos Rob) in 1990 Entry Draft for Brian Lawton, Norm MacIver and Don Maloney, December 26, 1988. Traded to **Hartford** by **NY Rangers** with NY Rangers' 3rd round choice (Michael Nylander) in 1991 Entry Draft for Jody Hull, July 9, 1990. Traded to **Calgary** by **Hartford** for Mark Hunter, March 5, 1991. • Suffered eventual career-ending knee injury in game vs. St. Louis, December 4, 1992.

WILSON, Cully

Right wing. Shoots right. 5'8", 180 lbs. Born, Winnipeg, Man.,

Season	Club	GP	G	A	Pts	PIM	GP	G	A	Pts	PIM
1919-20	Toronto St. Pats	23	20	6	26	*86	....	....	....	....	....
1920-21	Toronto St. Pats	8	2	3	5	22	....	....	....	....	....
	Montreal Canadiens	11	6	1	7	29	....	....	....	....	....
1921-22	Hamilton Tigers	23	7	9	16	20	....	....	....	....	....
1922-23	Hamilton Tigers	23	16	5	21	46	....	....	....	....	....
1926-27	Chicago Black Hawks	39	8	4	12	40	2	1	0	1	6
	NHL Totals	**127**	**59**	**28**	**87**	**243**	**2**	**1**	**0**	**1**	**6**

Signed as a free agent by **Toronto**, November 27, 1919. Loaned to **Montreal** by **Toronto**, January 21, 1921. • Suspended for remainder of the 1920-21 season by **Toronto** for refusing to report to NHL club after being recalled from Montreal, February 11, 1921. Traded to **Hamilton** by **Toronto** for Ed Carpenter, November 9, 1921. Traded to **Calgary** (WCHL) by **Hamilton** for cash, November 22, 1923. Traded to **Chicago** by **Calgary** (WHL) for cash, October 25, 1926. Traded to **St. Paul** (AHA) by **Chicago**, September, 1927.

WILSON, Doug

Defense. Shoots left. 6'1", 187 lbs. Born, Ottawa, Ont., July 5, 1957.
(Chicago's 1st choice, 6th overall, in 1977 Amateur Draft).

Season	Club	GP	G	A	Pts	PIM	GP	G	A	Pts	PIM
1977-78	Chicago Black Hawks	77	14	20	34	72	4	0	0	0	0
1978-79	Chicago Black Hawks	56	5	21	26	37	....	....	....	....	....
1979-80	Chicago Black Hawks	73	12	49	61	70	7	2	8	10	6
1980-81	Chicago Black Hawks	76	12	39	51	80	3	0	3	3	2
1981-82	Chicago Black Hawks	76	39	46	85	54	15	3	10	13	32
1982-83	Chicago Black Hawks	74	18	51	69	58	13	4	11	15	12
1983-84	Chicago Black Hawks	66	13	45	58	64	5	0	3	3	2

Season	Club	GP	G	A	Pts	PIM	GP	G	A	Pts	PIM
		REGULAR SEASON					PLAYOFFS				
1984-85	Chicago Black Hawks	78	22	54	76	44	12	3	10	13	12
1985-86	Chicago Black Hawks	79	17	47	64	80	3	1	1	2	2
1986-87	Chicago Blackhawks	69	16	32	48	36	4	0	0	0	0
1987-88	Chicago Blackhawks	27	8	24	32	28	....	....	....	....	....
1988-89	Chicago Blackhawks	66	15	47	62	69	4	1	2	3	0
1989-90	Chicago Blackhawks	70	23	50	73	40	20	3	12	15	18
1990-91	Chicago Blackhawks	51	11	29	40	32	5	2	1	3	2
1991-92	San Jose Sharks	44	9	19	28	26	....	....	....	....	....
1992-93	San Jose Sharks	42	3	17	20	40	....	....	....	....	....
	NHL Totals	**1024**	**237**	**590**	**827**	**830**	**95**	**19**	**61**	**80**	**88**

• Brother of Murray • NHL First All-Star Team (1982) • James Norris Trophy (1982) • NHL Second All-Star Team (1985, 1990)

Played in NHL All-Star Game (1982, 1983, 1984, 1985, 1986, 1990, 1992)

• Missed majority of 1987-88 season recovering from shoulder surgery, December, 1987. Traded to **San Jose** by **Chicago** for Kerry Toporowski and San Jose's 2nd round choice (later traded to Winnipeg – Winnipeg selected Boris Mironov) in 1992 Entry Draft, September 6, 1991.

WILSON, Gord

Left wing. Shoots left. 6', 175 lbs. Born, Port Arthur, Ont., August 13, 1932.

Season	Club	GP	G	A	Pts	PIM	GP	G	A	Pts	PIM
1954-55	Boston Bruins	....	....	....	....	....	2	0	0	0	0
	NHL Totals	....	....	....	....	....	**2**	**0**	**0**	**0**	**0**

WILSON, Hub

Left wing. Shoots left. 5'10", 180 lbs. Born, Ottawa, Ont., May 13, 1909.

Season	Club	GP	G	A	Pts	PIM	GP	G	A	Pts	PIM
1931-32	New York Americans	2	0	0	0	0	....	....	....	....	....
	NHL Totals	**2**	**0**	**0**	**0**	**0**	....	....	....	....	....

Traded to **Philadelphia** (Can-Am) by **NY Americans** with Norm Clooings for Eddie Burke, February 11, 1933.

WILSON, Jerry

Center. Shoots left. 6'2", 200 lbs. Born, Edmonton, Alta., April 10, 1937.

Season	Club	GP	G	A	Pts	PIM	GP	G	A	Pts	PIM
1956-57	Montreal Canadiens	3	0	0	0	2	....	....	....	....	....
	NHL Totals	**3**	**0**	**0**	**0**	**2**	....	....	....	....	....

• Father of Carey

WILSON, Johnny

Left wing. Shoots left. 5'11", 168 lbs. Born, Kincardine, Ont., June 14, 1929.

Season	Club	GP	G	A	Pts	PIM	GP	G	A	Pts	PIM
1949-50 ♦	Detroit Red Wings	1	0	0	0	0	8	0	1	1	0
1950-51	Detroit Red Wings	....	....	....	....	....	1	0	0	0	0
1951-52 ♦	Detroit Red Wings	28	4	5	9	18	8	4	1	5	5
1952-53	Detroit Red Wings	70	23	19	42	22	6	2	5	7	0
1953-54 ♦	Detroit Red Wings	70	17	17	34	22	12	3	0	3	0
1954-55 ♦	Detroit Red Wings	70	12	15	27	14	11	0	1	1	0
1955-56	Chicago Black Hawks	70	24	9	33	12	....	....	....	....	....
1956-57	Chicago Black Hawks	70	18	30	48	24	....	....	....	....	....
1957-58	Detroit Red Wings	70	12	27	39	14	4	2	1	3	0
1958-59	Detroit Red Wings	70	11	17	28	18	....	....	....	....	....
1959-60	Toronto Maple Leafs	70	15	16	31	8	10	1	2	3	2
1960-61	Toronto Maple Leafs	3	0	1	1	0	....	....	....	....	....
	New York Rangers	56	14	12	26	24	....	....	....	....	....
1961-62	New York Rangers	40	11	3	14	14	6	2	2	4	4
	NHL Totals	**688**	**161**	**171**	**332**	**190**	**66**	**14**	**13**	**27**	**11**

• Brother of Larry

Played in NHL All-Star Game (1954, 1956)

Traded to **Chicago** by **Detroit** with Tony Leswick, Glen Skov and Benny Woit for Dave Creighton, Gord Hollingworth, John McCormack and Jerry Toppazzini, May 27, 1955. Traded to **Detroit** by **Chicago** with Forbes Kennedy, Bill Preston and Hank Bassen for Ted Lindsay and Glenn Hall, July 23, 1957. Traded to **Toronto** by **Detroit** with Frank Roggeveen for Barry Cullen, June 9, 1959. Traded to **NY Rangers** by **Toronto** with Pat Hannigan for Eddie Shack, November 7, 1960.

WILSON, Landon

Right wing. Shoots right. 6'3", 232 lbs. Born, St. Louis, MO, March 13, 1975.
(Toronto's 2nd choice, 19th overall, in 1993 Entry Draft).

Season	Club	GP	G	A	Pts	PIM	GP	G	A	Pts	PIM
1995-96	Colorado Avalanche	7	1	0	1	6	....	....	....	....	....
1996-97	Colorado Avalanche	9	1	2	3	23	....	....	....	....	....
	Boston Bruins	40	7	10	17	49	....	....	....	....	....
1997-98	Boston Bruins	28	1	5	6	7	1	0	0	0	0
1998-99	Boston Bruins	22	3	3	6	17	8	1	1	2	8
99-2000	Boston Bruins	40	1	3	4	18	....	....	....	....	....
2000-01	Phoenix Coyotes	70	18	13	31	92	....	....	....	....	....
2001-02	Phoenix Coyotes	47	7	12	19	46	4	0	0	0	12
2002-03	Phoenix Coyotes	31	6	8	14	26	....	....	....	....	....
	NHL Totals	**294**	**45**	**56**	**101**	**284**	**13**	**1**	**1**	**2**	**20**

• Son of Rick

Traded to **Quebec** by **Toronto** with Wendel Clark, Sylvain Lefebvre and Toronto's 1st round choice (Jeffrey Kealty) in 1994 Entry Draft for Mats Sundin, Garth Butcher, Todd Warriner and Philadelphia's 1st round choice (previously acquired, later traded to Washington – Washington selected Nolan Baumgartner) in 1994 Entry Draft, June 28, 1994. Transferred to **Colorado** after **Quebec** franchise relocated, June 21, 1995. Traded to **Boston** by **Colorado** with Anders Myrvold for Boston's 1st round choice (Robyn Regehr) in 1998 Entry Draft, November 22, 1996. Signed as a free agent by **Phoenix**, July 7, 2000. • Missed majority of 2002-03 season recovering from eye injury suffered in game vs. Los Angeles, December 26, 2002.

WILSON, Larry

Center. Shoots left. 5'11", 160 lbs. Born, Kincardine, Ont., October 23, 1930.

Season	Club	GP	G	A	Pts	PIM	GP	G	A	Pts	PIM
1949-50 ♦	Detroit Red Wings	1	0	0	0	2	4	0	0	0	0
1951-52	Detroit Red Wings	5	0	0	0	4	....	....	....	....	....
1952-53	Detroit Red Wings	15	0	4	4	6	....	....	....	....	....
1953-54	Chicago Black Hawks	66	9	33	42	22	....	....	....	....	....
1954-55	Chicago Black Hawks	63	12	11	23	39	....	....	....	....	....
1955-56	Chicago Black Hawks	2	0	0	0	2	....	....	....	....	....
	NHL Totals	**152**	**21**	**48**	**69**	**75**	**4**	**0**	**0**	**0**	**0**

• Brother of Johnny • Father of Ron

Traded to **Chicago** by **Detroit** with Larry Zeidel and Lou Jankowski for cash, August 12, 1953. Traded to **Buffalo** (AHL) by **Chicago** for cash, August 12, 1957.

WILSON, Mike

Defense. Shoots left. 6'6", 229 lbs. Born, Brampton, Ont., February 26, 1975.
(Vancouver's 1st choice, 20th overall, in 1993 Entry Draft).

Season	Club	GP	G	A	Pts	PIM	GP	G	A	Pts	PIM
1995-96	Buffalo Sabres	58	4	8	12	41	....	....	....	....	....
1996-97	Buffalo Sabres	77	2	9	11	51	10	0	1	1	2
1997-98	Buffalo Sabres	66	4	4	8	48	15	0	1	1	13
1998-99	Buffalo Sabres	30	1	2	3	47	....	....	....	....	....
	Florida Panthers	4	0	0	0	0	....	....	....	....	....
99-2000	Florida Panthers	60	4	16	20	35	4	0	0	0	0
2000-01	Florida Panthers	19	0	1	1	25	....	....	....	....	....
2001-02	Pittsburgh Penguins	21	1	1	2	17	....	....	....	....	....
2002-03	New York Rangers	1	0	0	0	0	....	....	....	....	....
	NHL Totals	**336**	**16**	**41**	**57**	**264**	**29**	**0**	**2**	**2**	**15**

Traded to **Buffalo** by **Vancouver** with Michael Peca and Vancouver's 1st round choice (Jay McKee) in 1995 Entry Draft for Alexander Mogilny and Buffalo's 5th round choice (Todd Norman) in 1995 Entry Draft, July 8, 1995. Traded to **Florida** by **Buffalo** for Rhett Warrener and Florida's 5th round choice (Ryan Miller) in 1999 Entry Draft, March 23, 1999. Signed as a free agent by **Pittsburgh**, July 5, 2001. Traded to **NY Rangers** by **Pittsburgh** with Alexei Kovalev, Janne Laukkanen and Dan LaCouture for Joel Bouchard, Richard Lintner, Rico Fata, Mikael Samuelsson and future considerations, February 10, 2003.

WILSON, Mitch

Center. Shoots right. 5'8", 190 lbs. Born, Kelowna, B.C., February 15, 1962.

Season	Club	GP	G	A	Pts	PIM	GP	G	A	Pts	PIM
1984-85	New Jersey Devils	9	0	2	2	21	....	....	....	....	....
1986-87	Pittsburgh Penguins	17	2	1	3	83	....	....	....	....	....
	NHL Totals	**26**	**2**	**3**	**5**	**104**	....	....	....	....	....

Signed as a free agent by **New Jersey**, October 12, 1982. Signed as a free agent by **Pittsburgh**, July 24, 1986.

WILSON, Murray

Left wing. Shoots left. 6'1", 185 lbs. Born, Toronto, Ont., November 7, 1951.
(Montreal's 3rd choice, 11th overall, in 1971 Amateur Draft).

Season	Club	GP	G	A	Pts	PIM	GP	G	A	Pts	PIM
1972-73 ♦	Montreal Canadiens	52	18	9	27	16	16	2	4	6	6
1973-74	Montreal Canadiens	72	17	14	31	26	5	1	0	1	2
1974-75	Montreal Canadiens	73	24	18	42	44	5	0	3	3	4
1975-76 ♦	Montreal Canadiens	59	11	24	35	36	12	1	1	2	6
1976-77 ♦	Montreal Canadiens	60	13	14	27	26	14	1	6	7	14
1977-78 ♦	Montreal Canadiens	12	0	1	1	0	....	....	....	....	....
1978-79	Los Angeles Kings	58	11	15	26	14	1	0	0	0	0
	NHL Totals	**386**	**94**	**95**	**189**	**162**	**53**	**5**	**14**	**19**	**32**

• Brother of Doug

• Missed majority of 1977-78 season recovering from spinal fusion surgery, October, 1977. Traded to **Los Angeles** by **Montreal** with Montreal's 1st round choice (Jay Wells) in 1979 Entry Draft for Los Angeles' 1st round choice (Gilbert Delorme) in 1981 Entry Draft, October 5, 1978.

WILSON, Rick

Defense. Shoots left. 6'1", 195 lbs. Born, Prince Albert, Sask., August 10, 1950.
(Montreal's 6th choice, 66th overall, in 1970 Amateur Draft).

Season	Club	GP	G	A	Pts	PIM	GP	G	A	Pts	PIM
1973-74	Montreal Canadiens	21	0	2	2	6	....	....	....	....	....
1974-75	St. Louis Blues	76	2	5	7	83	2	0	0	0	0
1975-76	St. Louis Blues	65	1	6	7	20	1	0	0	0	0
1976-77	Detroit Red Wings	77	3	13	16	56	....	....	....	....	....
	NHL Totals	**239**	**6**	**26**	**32**	**165**	**3**	**0**	**0**	**0**	**0**

• Father of Landon

Traded to **St. Louis** by **Montreal** with Montreal's 5th round choice (Don Wheldon) in 1974 Amateur Draft for St. Louis' 4th round choice (Barry Legge) in 1974 Amateur Draft and future considerations (Glen Sather, June 14, 1974), May 27, 1974. Traded to **Detroit** by **St. Louis** to complete transaction that sent Doug Grant to St. Louis (March 9, 1976), June 16, 1976.

WILSON, Rik

Defense. Shoots right. 6', 180 lbs. Born, Long Beach, CA, June 17, 1962.
(St. Louis' 1st choice, 12th overall, in 1980 Entry Draft).

Season	Club	GP	G	A	Pts	PIM	GP	G	A	Pts	PIM
1981-82	St. Louis Blues	48	3	18	21	24	9	0	3	3	14
1982-83	St. Louis Blues	56	3	11	14	50	....	....	....	....	....
1983-84	St. Louis Blues	48	7	11	18	53	11	0	0	0	9
1984-85	St. Louis Blues	51	8	16	24	39	2	0	1	1	0
1985-86	St. Louis Blues	32	0	4	4	48	....	....	....	....	....
	Calgary Flames	2	0	0	0	0	....	....	....	....	....

Season	Club	REGULAR SEASON GP	G	A	Pts	PIM	PLAYOFFS GP	G	A	Pts	PIM
1987-88	Chicago Blackhawks	14	4	5	9	6	....	....	....	....	....
	NHL Totals	**251**	**25**	**65**	**90**	**220**	**22**	**0**	**4**	**4**	**23**

Traded to **Calgary** by **St. Louis** with Joe Mullen and Terry Johnson for Eddy Beers, Charlie Bourgeois and Gino Cavallini, February 1, 1986. Traded to **Chicago** by **Calgary** for Tom McMurchy, March 11, 1986. Signed as free agent by **St. Louis** July 19, 1989.

WILSON, Roger

Defense. Shoots right. 5'11", 175 lbs. Born, Sudbury, Ont., September 18, 1946.

Season	Club	GP	G	A	Pts	PIM	GP	G	A	Pts	PIM
1974-75	Chicago Black Hawks	7	0	2	2	6	....	....	....	....	....
	NHL Totals	**7**	**0**	**2**	**2**	**6**	....	....	....	....	....

WILSON, Ron

Center. Shoots left. 5'9", 180 lbs. Born, Toronto, Ont., May 13, 1956.
(Montreal's 15th choice, 133rd overall, in 1976 Amateur Draft).

Season	Club	GP	G	A	Pts	PIM	GP	G	A	Pts	PIM
1979-80	Winnipeg Jets	79	21	36	57	28	....	....	....	....	....
1980-81	Winnipeg Jets	77	18	33	51	55	....	....	....	....	....
1981-82	Winnipeg Jets	39	3	13	16	49	....	....	....	....	....
1982-83	Winnipeg Jets	12	6	3	9	4	3	2	2	4	2
1983-84	Winnipeg Jets	51	3	12	15	12	....	....	....	....	....
1984-85	Winnipeg Jets	75	10	9	19	31	8	4	2	6	2
1985-86	Winnipeg Jets	54	6	7	13	16	1	0	0	0	0
1986-87	Winnipeg Jets	80	3	13	16	13	10	1	2	3	0
1987-88	Winnipeg Jets	69	5	8	13	28	1	0	0	0	2
1989-90	St. Louis Blues	33	3	17	20	23	12	3	5	8	18
1990-91	St. Louis Blues	73	10	27	37	54	7	0	0	0	28
1991-92	St. Louis Blues	64	12	17	29	46	6	0	1	1	0
1992-93	St. Louis Blues	78	8	11	19	44	11	0	0	0	12
1993-94	Montreal Canadiens	48	2	10	12	12	4	0	0	0	0
	NHL Totals	**832**	**110**	**216**	**326**	**415**	**63**	**10**	**12**	**22**	**64**

Traded to **Winnipeg** by **Montreal** for cash, October 4, 1979. Traded to **St. Louis** by **Winnipeg** for Doug Evans, January 22, 1990. Signed as a free agent by **Montreal**, August 20, 1993.

WILSON, Ron

Defense. Shoots right. 5'10", 170 lbs. Born, Windsor, Ont., May 28, 1955.
(Toronto's 7th choice, 132nd overall, in 1975 Amateur Draft).

Season	Club	GP	G	A	Pts	PIM	GP	G	A	Pts	PIM
1977-78	Toronto Maple Leafs	13	2	1	3	0	....	....	....	....	....
1978-79	Toronto Maple Leafs	46	5	12	17	4	3	0	1	1	0
1979-80	Toronto Maple Leafs	5	0	2	2	2	3	1	2	3	2
1984-85	Minnesota North Stars	13	4	8	12	2	9	1	6	7	2
1985-86	Minnesota North Stars	11	1	3	4	8	3	2	4	6	4
1986-87	Minnesota North Stars	65	12	29	41	36	....	....	....	....	....
1987-88	Minnesota North Stars	24	2	12	14	16	....	....	....	....	....
	NHL Totals	**177**	**26**	**67**	**93**	**68**	**20**	**4**	**13**	**17**	**8**

• Son of Larry

Signed as a free agent by **Minnesota**, March 7, 1985.

WILSON, Wally

Center. Shoots right. 5'11", 165 lbs. Born, Berwick, N.S., May 25, 1921.

Season	Club	GP	G	A	Pts	PIM	GP	G	A	Pts	PIM
1947-48	Boston Bruins	53	11	8	19	18	1	0	0	0	0
	NHL Totals	**53**	**11**	**8**	**19**	**18**	**1**	**0**	**0**	**0**	**0**

Claimed by **Toronto** from **Hershey** (AHL) in Inter-League Draft, June 14, 1945. Traded to **Boston** by **Toronto** for cash, August 17, 1947.

WING, Murray

Defense. Shoots right. 5'11", 180 lbs. Born, Thunder Bay, Ont., October 14, 1950.
(Boston's 9th choice, 83rd overall, in 1970 Amateur Draft).

Season	Club	GP	G	A	Pts	PIM	GP	G	A	Pts	PIM
1973-74	Detroit Red Wings	1	0	1	1	0	....	....	....	....	....
	NHL Totals	**1**	**0**	**1**	**1**	**0**	....	....	....	....	....

Traded to **Detroit** by **Boston** to complete transaction that sent Gary Doak to Boston (March 1, 1973), June 4, 1973.

WINNES, Chris

Right wing. Shoots right. 6', 201 lbs. Born, Ridgefield, CT, February 12, 1968.
(Boston's 9th choice, 161st overall, in 1987 Entry Draft).

Season	Club	GP	G	A	Pts	PIM	GP	G	A	Pts	PIM
1990-91	Boston Bruins	....	....	....	....	....	1	0	0	0	0
1991-92	Boston Bruins	24	1	3	4	6	....	....	....	....	....
1992-93	Boston Bruins	5	0	1	1	0	....	....	....	....	....
1993-94	Philadelphia Flyers	4	0	2	2	0	....	....	....	....	....
	NHL Totals	**33**	**1**	**6**	**7**	**6**	**1**	**0**	**0**	**0**	**0**

Signed as a free agent by **Philadelphia**, August 4, 1993. Signed as a free agent by **NY Rangers**, July 21, 1998.

WISEMAN, Brian

Center. Shoots left. 5'8", 175 lbs. Born, Chatham, Ont., July 13, 1971.
(NY Rangers' 11th choice, 257th overall, in 1991 Entry Draft).

Season	Club	GP	G	A	Pts	PIM	GP	G	A	Pts	PIM
1996-97	Toronto Maple Leafs	3	0	0	0	0	....	....	....	....	....
	NHL Totals	**3**	**0**	**0**	**0**	**0**	....	....	....	....	....

Signed as a free agent by **Toronto**, August 14, 1996.

WISEMAN, Chad

Left wing. Shoots left. 6', 205 lbs. Born, Burlington, Ont., March 25, 1981.
(San Jose's 8th choice, 246th overall, in 2000 Entry Draft).

Season	Club	GP	G	A	Pts	PIM	GP	G	A	Pts	PIM
2002-03	San Jose Sharks	4	0	0	0	4	....	....	....	....	....
	NHL Totals	**4**	**0**	**0**	**0**	**4**	....	....	....	....	....

WISEMAN, Eddie

Right wing. Shoots right. 5'7", 160 lbs. Born, Newcastle, N.B., December 28, 1912.

Season	Club	GP	G	A	Pts	PIM	GP	G	A	Pts	PIM
1932-33	Detroit Red Wings	43	8	8	16	16	2	0	0	0	0
1933-34	Detroit Red Wings	48	5	9	14	13	7	0	1	1	4
1934-35	Detroit Red Wings	39	11	13	24	14	....	....	....	....	....
1935-36	Detroit Red Wings	1	0	0	0	0	....	....	....	....	....
	New York Americans	44	12	16	28	15	4	2	1	3	0
1936-37	New York Americans	44	14	19	33	12	....	....	....	....	....
1937-38	New York Americans	48	18	14	32	32	6	0	4	4	10
1938-39	New York Americans	47	12	21	33	8	2	0	0	0	0
1939-40	New York Americans	31	5	13	18	8	....	....	....	....	....
	Boston Bruins	18	2	6	8	0	6	2	1	3	2
1940-41 ♦	Boston Bruins	48	16	24	40	10	11	*6	2	8	0
1941-42	Boston Bruins	45	12	22	34	8	5	0	1	1	0
	NHL Totals	**456**	**115**	**165**	**280**	**136**	**43**	**10**	**10**	**20**	**16**

NHL rights transferred to **Detroit** from **Chicago Shamrocks** (AHA) after AHA club owners purchased Detroit (NHL and IHL) franchises, September 2, 1932. Traded to **NY Americans** by **Detroit** for Fred Hergert and $7,500, November 21, 1935. Traded to **Boston** by **NY Americans** with $5,000 for Eddie Shore, January 25, 1940.

WISTE, Jim

Center. Shoots left. 5'10", 185 lbs. Born, Moose Jaw, Sask., February 18, 1946.

Season	Club	GP	G	A	Pts	PIM	GP	G	A	Pts	PIM
1968-69	Chicago Black Hawks	3	0	0	0	0	....	....	....	....	....
1969-70	Chicago Black Hawks	26	0	8	8	8	....	....	....	....	....
1970-71	Vancouver Canucks	23	1	2	3	0	....	....	....	....	....
	NHL Totals	**52**	**1**	**10**	**11**	**8**	....	....	....	....	....

Signed as a free agent by **Chicago**, September 27, 1968. Claimed by **Vancouver** from **Chicago** in Expansion Draft, June 10, 1970. Loaned to **Seattle** (WHL) by **Vancouver** with Ed Hatoum for the remainder of the 1970-71 season for Bobby Schmautz, February 9, 1971. Traded to **NY Rangers** by **Vancouver** with Gary Doak for Dave Balon, Wayne Connelly and Ron Stewart, November 16, 1971.

WITEHALL, Johan

Left wing. Shoots left. 6'1", 198 lbs. Born, Goteborg, Sweden, January 7, 1972.
(NY Rangers' 8th choice, 207th overall, in 1998 Entry Draft).

Season	Club	GP	G	A	Pts	PIM	GP	G	A	Pts	PIM
1998-99	New York Rangers	4	0	0	0	0	....	....	....	....	....
99-2000	New York Rangers	9	1	1	2	2	....	....	....	....	....
2000-01	New York Rangers	15	0	3	3	8	....	....	....	....	....
	Montreal Canadiens	26	1	1	2	6	....	....	....	....	....
	NHL Totals	**54**	**2**	**5**	**7**	**16**	....	....	....	....	....

Claimed on waivers by **Montreal** from **NY Rangers**, January 12, 2001.

WITHERSPOON, Jim

Defense. Shoots right. 6'3", 205 lbs. Born, Toronto, Ont., October 3, 1951.

Season	Club	GP	G	A	Pts	PIM	GP	G	A	Pts	PIM
1975-76	Los Angeles Kings	2	0	0	0	2	....	....	....	....	....
	NHL Totals	**2**	**0**	**0**	**0**	**2**	....	....	....	....	....

Signed as a free agent by **Los Angeles**, August, 1974.

WITIUK, Steve

Right wing. Shoots right. 5'7", 165 lbs. Born, Winnipeg, Man., January 8, 1929.

Season	Club	GP	G	A	Pts	PIM	GP	G	A	Pts	PIM
1951-52	Chicago Black Hawks	33	3	8	11	14	....	....	....	....	....
	NHL Totals	**33**	**3**	**8**	**11**	**14**	....	....	....	....	....

Signed as a free agent by **Chicago**, October 1, 1951. Traded to **Toronto** (Winnipeg-WHL) by **Chicago** (Calgary-WHL) for George Ford and Murray Wilkie, January, 1958. Rights transferred to **Toronto** after NHL club purchased **Spokane** (WHL) franchise, June 4, 1963. Transferred to **Phoenix** (WHL) after **Victoria** (WHL) franchise relocated, August, 1967. Traded to **Toronto** by **Phoenix** (WHL) for Walt McKechnie, October 15, 1967.

WITT, Brendan

Defense. Shoots left. 6'2", 229 lbs. Born, Humboldt, Sask., February 20, 1975.
(Washington's 1st choice, 11th overall, in 1993 Entry Draft).

Season	Club	GP	G	A	Pts	PIM	GP	G	A	Pts	PIM
1995-96	Washington Capitals	48	2	3	5	85	....	....	....	....	....
1996-97	Washington Capitals	44	3	2	5	88	....	....	....	....	....
1997-98	Washington Capitals	64	1	7	8	112	16	1	0	1	14
1998-99	Washington Capitals	54	2	5	7	87	....	....	....	....	....
99-2000	Washington Capitals	77	1	7	8	114	3	0	0	0	0
2000-01	Washington Capitals	72	3	3	6	101	6	2	0	2	12
2001-02	Washington Capitals	68	3	7	10	78	....	....	....	....	....
2002-03	Washington Capitals	69	2	9	11	106	6	1	0	1	0
	NHL Totals	**496**	**17**	**43**	**60**	**771**	**31**	**4**	**0**	**4**	**26**

• Missed entire 1994-95 season after failing to come to contract terms with **Washington**.

WOIT, Benny

Right wing/Defense. Shoots right. 5'11", 195 lbs. Born, Fort William, Ont., January 7, 1928.

Season	Club	GP	G	A	Pts	PIM	GP	G	A	Pts	PIM
1950-51	Detroit Red Wings	2	0	0	0	2	4	0	0	0	2
1951-52 ♦	Detroit Red Wings	58	3	8	11	20	8	1	1	2	2
1952-53	Detroit Red Wings	70	1	5	6	40	6	1	3	4	0
1953-54 ♦	Detroit Red Wings	70	0	2	2	38	12	0	1	1	8

		REGULAR SEASON					PLAYOFFS				
Season	Club	GP	G	A	Pts	PIM	GP	G	A	Pts	PIM
1954-55 ♦	Detroit Red Wings	62	2	3	5	22	11	0	1	1	6
1955-56	Chicago Black Hawks	63	1	8	9	46	....	....	....	....	....
1956-57	Chicago Black Hawks	9	0	0	0	2	....	....	....	....	....
	NHL Totals	**334**	**7**	**26**	**33**	**170**	**41**	**2**	**6**	**8**	**18**

Played in NHL All-Star Game (1954)

Traded to **Chicago** by **Detroit** with Tony Leswick, Glen Skov and Johnny Wilson for Dave Creighton, Gord Hollingworth, John McCormack and Jerry Toppazzini, May 27, 1955. Claimed on waivers by **Montreal** from **Chicago**, November, 1956.

WOJCIECHOWSKI, Steve

Right wing. Shoots right. 5'8", 158 lbs. Born, Fort William, Ont., December 25, 1922.

1944-45	Detroit Red Wings	49	19	20	39	17	6	0	1	1	0
1946-47	Detroit Red Wings	5	0	0	0	0	....	....	....	....	....
	NHL Totals	**54**	**19**	**20**	**39**	**17**	**6**	**0**	**1**	**1**	**0**

• Also known as Steve Wochy

Traded to **Cleveland** (AHL) by **Detroit** for cash, June 15, 1947.

WOLANIN, Craig

Defense. Shoots left. 6'4", 215 lbs. Born, Grosse Pointe, MI, July 27, 1967.
(New Jersey's 1st choice, 3rd overall, in 1985 Entry Draft).

1985-86	New Jersey Devils	44	2	16	18	74	....	....	....	....	....
1986-87	New Jersey Devils	68	4	6	10	109	....	....	....	....	....
1987-88	New Jersey Devils	78	6	25	31	170	18	2	5	7	51
1988-89	New Jersey Devils	56	3	8	11	69	....	....	....	....	....
1989-90	New Jersey Devils	37	1	7	8	47	....	....	....	....	....
	Quebec Nordiques	13	0	3	3	10	....	....	....	....	....
1990-91	Quebec Nordiques	80	5	13	18	89	....	....	....	....	....
1991-92	Quebec Nordiques	69	2	11	13	80	....	....	....	....	....
1992-93	Quebec Nordiques	24	1	4	5	49	4	0	0	0	4
1993-94	Quebec Nordiques	63	6	10	16	80	....	....	....	....	....
1994-95	Quebec Nordiques	40	3	6	9	40	6	1	1	2	4
1995-96 ♦	Colorado Avalanche	75	7	20	27	50	7	1	0	1	8
1996-97	Tampa Bay Lightning	15	0	0	0	8	....	....	....	....	....
	Toronto Maple Leafs	23	0	4	4	13	....	....	....	....	....
1997-98	Toronto Maple Leafs	10	0	0	0	6	....	....	....	....	....
	NHL Totals	**695**	**40**	**133**	**173**	**894**	**35**	**4**	**6**	**10**	**67**

Traded to **Quebec** by **New Jersey** with future considerations (Randy Velischek, August 13, 1990) for Peter Stastny, March 6, 1990. Transferred to **Colorado** after **Quebec** franchise relocated, June 21, 1995. Traded to **Tampa Bay** by **Colorado** for Tampa Bay's 2nd round choice (Ramzi Abid) in 1998 Entry Draft, July 29, 1996. Traded to **Toronto** by **Tampa Bay** for Toronto's 3rd round choice (later traded to Edmonton – Edmonton selected Alex Henry) in 1998 Entry Draft, January 31, 1997.

WOLF, Bennett

Defense. Shoots right. 6'3", 205 lbs. Born, Kitchener, Ont., October 23, 1959.
(Pittsburgh's 2nd choice, 52nd overall, in 1979 Entry Draft).

1980-81	Pittsburgh Penguins	24	0	1	1	94	....	....	....	....	....
1981-82	Pittsburgh Penguins	1	0	0	0	2	....	....	....	....	....
1982-83	Pittsburgh Penguins	5	0	0	0	37	....	....	....	....	....
	NHL Totals	**30**	**0**	**1**	**1**	**133**	....	....	....	....	....

WONG, Mike

Center. Shoots left. 6'3", 204 lbs. Born, Minneapolis, MN, January 14, 1955.
(Detroit's 7th choice, 77th overall, in 1975 Amateur Draft).

1975-76	Detroit Red Wings	22	1	1	2	12	....	....	....	....	....
	NHL Totals	**22**	**1**	**1**	**2**	**12**	....	....	....	....	....

WOOD, Dody

Center. Shoots left. 6', 200 lbs. Born, Chetwynd, B.C., March 18, 1972.
(San Jose's 4th choice, 45th overall, in 1991 Entry Draft).

1992-93	San Jose Sharks	13	1	1	2	71	....	....	....	....	....
1994-95	San Jose Sharks	9	1	1	2	29	....	....	....	....	....
1995-96	San Jose Sharks	32	3	6	9	138	....	....	....	....	....
1996-97	San Jose Sharks	44	3	2	5	193	....	....	....	....	....
1997-98	San Jose Sharks	8	0	0	0	40	....	....	....	....	....
	NHL Totals	**106**	**8**	**10**	**18**	**471**	....	....	....	....	....

Traded to **New Jersey** by **San Jose** with Doug Bodger for John MacLean and Ken Sutton, December 7, 1997. Signed as a free agent by **Vancouver**, September 5, 2000.

WOOD, Randy

Left wing/Center. Shoots left. 6', 195 lbs. Born, Princeton, NJ, October 12, 1963.

1986-87	New York Islanders	6	1	0	1	4	13	1	3	4	14
1987-88	New York Islanders	75	22	16	38	80	5	1	0	1	6
1988-89	New York Islanders	77	15	13	28	44	....	....	....	....	....
1989-90	New York Islanders	74	24	24	48	39	5	1	1	2	4
1990-91	New York Islanders	76	24	18	42	45	....	....	....	....	....
1991-92	New York Islanders	8	2	2	4	21	....	....	....	....	....
	Buffalo Sabres	70	20	16	36	65	7	2	1	3	6
1992-93	Buffalo Sabres	82	18	25	43	77	8	1	4	5	4
1993-94	Buffalo Sabres	84	22	16	38	71	6	0	0	0	0
1994-95	Toronto Maple Leafs	48	13	11	24	34	7	2	0	2	6
1995-96	Toronto Maple Leafs	46	7	9	16	36	....	....	....	....	....
	Dallas Stars	30	1	4	5	26	....	....	....	....	....
1996-97	New York Islanders	65	6	5	11	61	....	....	....	....	....
	NHL Totals	**741**	**175**	**159**	**334**	**603**	**51**	**8**	**9**	**17**	**40**

Signed as a free agent by **NY Islanders**, September 17, 1986. Traded to **Buffalo** by **NY Islanders** with Pat LaFontaine, Randy Hillier and NY Islanders' 4th round choice (Dean Melanson) in 1992 Entry Draft for Pierre Turgeon, Uwe Krupp, Benoit Hogue and Dave McLlwain, October 25, 1991. Claimed by **Toronto** from **Buffalo** in NHL Waiver Draft, January 18, 1995. Traded to **Dallas** by **Toronto** with Benoit Hogue for Dave Gagner and Dallas' 6th round choice (Dmitri Yakushin) in 1996 Entry Draft, January 29, 1996. Signed as a free agent by **NY Islanders**, October 2, 1996.

WOOD, Robert

Defense. Shoots left. 6'1", 185 lbs. Born, Lethbridge, Alta., July 9, 1930.

1950-51	New York Rangers	1	0	0	0	0	....	....	....	....	....
	NHL Totals	**1**	**0**	**0**	**0**	**0**	....	....	....	....	....

WOODLEY, Dan

Right wing. Shoots right. 5'11", 185 lbs. Born, Oklahoma City, OK, December 29, 1967.
(Vancouver's 1st choice, 7th overall, in 1986 Entry Draft).

1987-88	Vancouver Canucks	5	2	0	2	17	....	....	....	....	....
	NHL Totals	**5**	**2**	**0**	**2**	**17**	....	....	....	....	....

Traded to **Montreal** by **Vancouver** for Jose Charbonneau, January 25, 1989.

WOODS, Paul

Left wing. Shoots left. 5'10", 175 lbs. Born, Hespeler, Ont., April 12, 1955.
(Montreal's 5th choice, 51st overall, in 1975 Amateur Draft).

1977-78	Detroit Red Wings	80	19	23	42	52	7	0	5	5	4
1978-79	Detroit Red Wings	80	14	23	37	59	....	....	....	....	....
1979-80	Detroit Red Wings	79	6	20	26	24	....	....	....	....	....
1980-81	Detroit Red Wings	67	8	16	24	45	....	....	....	....	....
1981-82	Detroit Red Wings	75	10	17	27	48	....	....	....	....	....
1982-83	Detroit Red Wings	63	13	20	33	30	....	....	....	....	....
1983-84	Detroit Red Wings	57	2	5	7	18	....	....	....	....	....
	NHL Totals	**501**	**72**	**124**	**196**	**276**	**7**	**0**	**5**	**5**	**4**

Claimed by **Detroit** from **Montreal** in Waiver Draft, October 10, 1977.

WOOLLEY, Jason

Defense. Shoots left. 6', 203 lbs. Born, Toronto, Ont., July 27, 1969.
(Washington's 4th choice, 61st overall, in 1989 Entry Draft).

1991-92	Washington Capitals	1	0	0	0	0	....	....	....	....	....
1992-93	Washington Capitals	26	0	2	2	10	....	....	....	....	....
1993-94	Washington Capitals	10	1	2	3	4	4	1	0	1	4
1994-95	Florida Panthers	34	4	9	13	18	....	....	....	....	....
1995-96	Florida Panthers	52	6	28	34	32	13	2	6	8	14
1996-97	Florida Panthers	3	0	0	0	2	....	....	....	....	....
	Pittsburgh Penguins	57	6	30	36	28	5	0	3	3	0
1997-98	Buffalo Sabres	71	9	26	35	35	15	2	9	11	12
1998-99	Buffalo Sabres	80	10	33	43	62	21	4	11	15	10
99-2000	Buffalo Sabres	74	8	25	33	52	5	0	2	2	2
2000-01	Buffalo Sabres	67	5	18	23	46	8	1	5	6	2
2001-02	Buffalo Sabres	59	8	20	28	34	....	....	....	....	....
2002-03	Buffalo Sabres	14	0	3	3	29	....	....	....	....	....
	Detroit Red Wings	62	6	17	23	22	4	1	0	1	0
	NHL Totals	**610**	**63**	**213**	**276**	**374**	**75**	**11**	**36**	**47**	**44**

Signed as a free agent by **Florida**, February 15, 1995. Traded to **Pittsburgh** by **Florida** with Stu Barnes for Chris Wells, November 19, 1996. Traded to **Buffalo** by **Pittsburgh** for Buffalo's 5th round choice (Robert Scuderi) in 1998 Entry Draft, September 24, 1997. Traded to **Detroit** by **Buffalo** for future considerations, November 16, 2002.

WORRELL, Peter

Left wing. Shoots left. 6'6", 235 lbs. Born, Pierrefonds, Que., August 18, 1977.
(Florida's 7th choice, 166th overall, in 1995 Entry Draft).

1997-98	Florida Panthers	19	0	0	0	153	....	....	....	....	....
1998-99	Florida Panthers	62	4	5	9	258	....	....	....	....	....
99-2000	Florida Panthers	48	3	6	9	169	4	1	0	1	8
2000-01	Florida Panthers	71	3	7	10	248	....	....	....	....	....
2001-02	Florida Panthers	79	4	5	9	*354	....	....	....	....	....
2002-03	Florida Panthers	63	2	3	5	193	....	....	....	....	....
	NHL Totals	**342**	**16**	**26**	**42**	**1375**	**4**	**1**	**0**	**1**	**8**

Traded to **Colorado** by **Florida** with Florida's 2nd round choice in 2004 Entry Draft for Eric Messier and Vaclav Nedorost, July 19, 2003.

WORTMAN, Kevin

Defense. Shoots right. 6', 200 lbs. Born, Saugus, MA, February 22, 1969.
(Calgary's 9th choice, 168th overall, in 1989 Entry Draft).

1993-94	Calgary Flames	5	0	0	0	2	....	....	....	....	....
	NHL Totals	**5**	**0**	**0**	**0**	**2**	....	....	....	....	....

Signed as a free agent by **San Jose**, August 25, 1994.

WOTTON, Mark

Defense. Shoots left. 6'1", 195 lbs. Born, Foxwarren, Man., November 16, 1973.
(Vancouver's 11th choice, 237th overall, in 1992 Entry Draft).

1994-95	Vancouver Canucks	1	0	0	0	0	5	0	0	0	4
1996-97	Vancouver Canucks	36	3	6	9	19	....	....	....	....	....
1997-98	Vancouver Canucks	5	0	0	0	6	....	....	....	....	....

Season	Club	Regular Season GP	G	A	Pts	PIM	Playoffs GP	G	A	Pts	PIM
2000-01	Dallas Stars	1	0	0	0	0	....	....	....	....	....
	NHL Totals	**43**	**3**	**6**	**9**	**25**	**5**	**0**	**0**	**0**	**4**

Signed as a free agent by **Dallas**, July 9, 1999.

WOYTOWICH, Bob

Defense. Shoots right. 6', 185 lbs. Born, Winnipeg, Man., August 18, 1941.

Season	Club	GP	G	A	Pts	PIM	GP	G	A	Pts	PIM
1964-65	Boston Bruins	21	2	10	12	16	....	....	....	....	....
1965-66	Boston Bruins	68	2	17	19	75	....	....	....	....	....
1966-67	Boston Bruins	64	2	7	9	43	....	....	....	....	....
1967-68	Minnesota North Stars	66	4	17	21	63	14	0	1	1	18
1968-69	Pittsburgh Penguins	71	9	20	29	62	....	....	....	....	....
1969-70	Pittsburgh Penguins	68	8	25	33	49	10	1	2	3	2
1970-71	Pittsburgh Penguins	78	4	22	26	30	....	....	....	....	....
1971-72	Pittsburgh Penguins	31	1	4	5	8	....	....	....	....	....
	Los Angeles Kings	36	0	4	4	6	....	....	....	....	....
	NHL Totals	**503**	**32**	**126**	**158**	**352**	**24**	**1**	**3**	**4**	**20**

Played in NHL All-Star Game (1970)

Claimed by **Boston** from **NY Rangers** in Intra-League Draft, June 10, 1964. Claimed by **Minnesota** from **Boston** in Expansion Draft, June 6, 1967. Traded to **Pittsburgh** by **Minnesota** for Pittsburgh's 1st round choice (later traded to Montreal – Montreal selected Dave Gardner) in 1972 Amateur Draft, October 1, 1968. Traded to **Los Angeles** by **Pittsburgh** for Al McDonough, January 11, 1972.

WREN, Bob

Center. Shoots left. 5'10", 185 lbs. Born, Preston, Ont., September 16, 1974.
(Los Angeles' 3rd choice, 94th overall, in 1993 Entry Draft).

Season	Club	GP	G	A	Pts	PIM	GP	G	A	Pts	PIM
1997-98	Mighty Ducks of Anaheim	3	0	0	0	0	....	....	....	....	....
2000-01	Mighty Ducks of Anaheim	1	0	0	0	0	....	....	....	....	....
2001-02	Toronto Maple Leafs	1	0	0	0	0	1	0	0	0	0
	NHL Totals	**5**	**0**	**0**	**0**	**0**	**1**	**0**	**0**	**0**	**0**

Signed as a free agent by **Hartford**, September 6, 1994. Signed as a free agent by **Anaheim**, August 1, 1997. Signed as a free agent by **Toronto**, July 24, 2001. Traded to **Nashville** by **Toronto** for Nathan Perrott, December 31, 2002. Traded to **Ottawa** by **Nashville** for future considerations, March 10, 2003.

WRIGHT, Jamie

Left wing. Shoots left. 6', 195 lbs. Born, Kitchener, Ont., May 13, 1976.
(Dallas' 3rd choice, 98th overall, in 1994 Entry Draft).

Season	Club	GP	G	A	Pts	PIM	GP	G	A	Pts	PIM
1997-98	Dallas Stars	21	4	2	6	2	5	0	0	0	0
1998-99	Dallas Stars	11	0	0	0	0	....	....	....	....	....
99-2000	Dallas Stars	23	1	4	5	16	....	....	....	....	....
2000-01	Dallas Stars	2	1	0	1	0	....	....	....	....	....
2001-02	Calgary Flames	44	4	12	16	20	....	....	....	....	....
2002-03	Calgary Flames	19	2	2	4	12	....	....	....	....	....
	Philadelphia Flyers	4	0	0	0	4	....	....	....	....	....
	NHL Totals	**124**	**12**	**20**	**32**	**54**	**5**	**0**	**0**	**0**	**0**

Signed as a free agent by **Calgary**, August 2, 2001. Traded to **Philadelphia** by **Calgary** for future considerations, January 22, 2003.

WRIGHT, John

Center. Shoots right. 5'11", 175 lbs. Born, Toronto, Ont., November 9, 1948.
(Toronto's 1st choice, 4th overall, in 1966 Amateur Draft).

Season	Club	GP	G	A	Pts	PIM	GP	G	A	Pts	PIM
1972-73	Vancouver Canucks	71	10	27	37	32	....	....	....	....	....
1973-74	Vancouver Canucks	20	3	3	6	11	....	....	....	....	....
	St. Louis Blues	32	3	6	9	22	....	....	....	....	....
1974-75	Kansas City Scouts	4	0	0	0	2	....	....	....	....	....
	NHL Totals	**127**	**16**	**36**	**52**	**67**	....	....	....	....	....

Claimed by **Vancouver** (WHL) from **Toronto** in Reverse Draft, June, 1970. NHL rights transferred to **Vancouver** when owners of **Vancouver** (WHL) club awarded NHL expansion team, May 20, 1970. Traded to **St. Louis** by **Vancouver** for Mike Lampman, December 10, 1973. Claimed by **Kansas City** from **St. Louis** in Expansion Draft, June, 1974.

WRIGHT, Keith

Left wing. Shoots left. 6', 180 lbs. Born, Aurora, Ont., April 13, 1944.

Season	Club	GP	G	A	Pts	PIM	GP	G	A	Pts	PIM
1967-68	Philadelphia Flyers	1	0	0	0	0	....	....	....	....	....
	NHL Totals	**1**	**0**	**0**	**0**	**0**	....	....	....	....	....

Claimed by **Omaha** (CPHL) from **Montreal** in Reverse Draft, June 10, 1964. Claimed by **NY Rangers** from **Omaha** (CPHL) in Intra-League Draft, June 8, 1965. Claimed on waivers by **Boston** from **NY Rangers** June 9, 1965. Claimed by **Philadelphia** from **Boston** in Expansion Draft, June 6, 1967. Traded to **Quebec** (AHL) by **Philadelphia** for cash, December, 1968.

WRIGHT, Larry

Center. Shoots left. 6'2", 180 lbs. Born, Regina, Sask., October 8, 1951.
(Philadelphia's 1st choice, 8th overall, in 1971 Amateur Draft).

Season	Club	GP	G	A	Pts	PIM	GP	G	A	Pts	PIM
1971-72	Philadelphia Flyers	27	0	1	1	2	....	....	....	....	....
1972-73	Philadelphia Flyers	9	0	1	1	4	....	....	....	....	....
1974-75	California Golden Seals	2	0	0	0	0	....	....	....	....	....
1975-76	Philadelphia Flyers	2	1	0	1	0	....	....	....	....	....
1977-78	Detroit Red Wings	66	3	6	9	13	....	....	....	....	....
	NHL Totals	**106**	**4**	**8**	**12**	**19**	....	....	....	....	....

Traded to **California** by **Philadelphia** with Al MacAdam and Philadelphia's 1st round choice (Ron Chipperfield) in 1974 Amateur Draft for Reggie Leach, May 24, 1974. Signed as a free agent by **Philadelphia**, September, 1975. Signed as a free agent by **Detroit**, October 22, 1977.

WRIGHT, Tyler

Center. Shoots right. 6', 190 lbs. Born, Kamsack, Sask., April 6, 1973.
(Edmonton's 1st choice, 12th overall, in 1991 Entry Draft).

Season	Club	GP	G	A	Pts	PIM	GP	G	A	Pts	PIM
1992-93	Edmonton Oilers	7	1	1	2	19	....	....	....	....	....
1993-94	Edmonton Oilers	5	0	0	0	4	....	....	....	....	....
1994-95	Edmonton Oilers	6	1	0	1	14	....	....	....	....	....
1995-96	Edmonton Oilers	23	1	0	1	33	....	....	....	....	....
1996-97	Pittsburgh Penguins	45	2	2	4	70	....	....	....	....	....
1997-98	Pittsburgh Penguins	82	3	4	7	112	6	0	1	1	4
1998-99	Pittsburgh Penguins	61	0	0	0	90	13	0	0	0	19
99-2000	Pittsburgh Penguins	50	12	10	22	45	11	3	1	4	17
2000-01	Columbus Blue Jackets	76	16	16	32	140	....	....	....	....	....
2001-02	Columbus Blue Jackets	77	13	11	24	100	....	....	....	....	....
2002-03	Columbus Blue Jackets	70	19	11	30	113	....	....	....	....	....
	NHL Totals	**502**	**68**	**55**	**123**	**740**	**30**	**3**	**2**	**5**	**40**

Traded to **Pittsburgh** by **Edmonton** for Pittsburgh's 7th round choice (Brandon Lafrance) in 1996 Entry Draft, June 22, 1996. Selected by **Columbus** from **Pittsburgh** in Expansion Draft, June 23, 2000.

WYCHERLEY, Ralph

Left wing. Shoots left. 6', 185 lbs. Born, Saskatoon, Sask., February 26, 1920.

Season	Club	GP	G	A	Pts	PIM	GP	G	A	Pts	PIM
1940-41	New York Americans	26	4	5	9	4	....	....	....	....	....
1941-42	Brooklyn Americans	2	0	2	2	2	....	....	....	....	....
	NHL Totals	**28**	**4**	**7**	**11**	**6**	....	....	....	....	....

Signed as a free agent by **NY Americans**, October 11, 1940. • Team name changed to **Brooklyn Americans** prior to 1941-42 season. Traded to **Chicago** (Kansas City-USHL) by **Cleveland** (AHL) with Doug Baldwin for Al Rollins, September 13, 1949.

WYLIE, Bill

Center. Shoots left. 5'7", 145 lbs. Born, Galt, Ont., July 15, 1928.

Season	Club	GP	G	A	Pts	PIM	GP	G	A	Pts	PIM
1950-51	New York Rangers	1	0	0	0	0	....	....	....	....	....
	NHL Totals	**1**	**0**	**0**	**0**	**0**	....	....	....	....	....

WYLIE, Duane

Center. Shoots left. 5'8", 170 lbs. Born, Spokane, WA, November 10, 1950.
(NY Rangers' 6th choice, 81st overall, in 1970 Amateur Draft).

Season	Club	GP	G	A	Pts	PIM	GP	G	A	Pts	PIM
1974-75	Chicago Black Hawks	6	1	3	4	2	....	....	....	....	....
1976-77	Chicago Black Hawks	8	2	0	2	0	....	....	....	....	....
	NHL Totals	**14**	**3**	**3**	**6**	**2**	....	....	....	....	....

Signed as a free agent by **Chicago**, October 12, 1972.

WYROZUB, Randy

Center. Shoots left. 5'11", 180 lbs. Born, Lacombe, Alta., April 8, 1950.
(Buffalo's 4th choice, 43rd overall, in 1970 Amateur Draft).

Season	Club	GP	G	A	Pts	PIM	GP	G	A	Pts	PIM
1970-71	Buffalo Sabres	16	2	2	4	6	....	....	....	....	....
1971-72	Buffalo Sabres	34	3	4	7	0	....	....	....	....	....
1972-73	Buffalo Sabres	45	3	3	6	4	....	....	....	....	....
1973-74	Buffalo Sabres	5	0	1	1	0	....	....	....	....	....
	NHL Totals	**100**	**8**	**10**	**18**	**10**	....	....	....	....	....

Claimed by **Washington** from **Buffalo** in Expansion Draft, June 12, 1974.

YACHMENEV, Vitali

Left wing. Shoots left. 5'11", 200 lbs. Born, Chelyabinsk, USSR, January 8, 1975.
(Los Angeles' 3rd choice, 59th overall, in 1994 Entry Draft).

Season	Club	GP	G	A	Pts	PIM	GP	G	A	Pts	PIM
1995-96	Los Angeles Kings	80	19	34	53	16	....	....	....	....	....
1996-97	Los Angeles Kings	65	10	22	32	10	....	....	....	....	....
1997-98	Los Angeles Kings	4	0	1	1	4	....	....	....	....	....
1998-99	Nashville Predators	55	7	10	17	10	....	....	....	....	....
99-2000	Nashville Predators	68	16	16	32	12	....	....	....	....	....
2000-01	Nashville Predators	78	15	19	34	10	....	....	....	....	....
2001-02	Nashville Predators	75	11	16	27	14	....	....	....	....	....
2002-03	Nashville Predators	62	5	15	20	12	....	....	....	....	....
	NHL Totals	**487**	**83**	**133**	**216**	**88**	....	....	....	....	....

Traded to **Nashville** by **Los Angeles** for future considerations, July 7, 1998.

YACKEL, Ken

USHOF

Right wing. Shoots right. 5'11", 195 lbs. Born, St. Paul, MN, March 5, 1932.

Season	Club	GP	G	A	Pts	PIM	GP	G	A	Pts	PIM
1958-59	Boston Bruins	6	0	0	0	2	2	0	0	0	2
	NHL Totals	**6**	**0**	**0**	**0**	**2**	**2**	**0**	**0**	**0**	**2**

Traded to **Boston** by **NY Rangers** (Saskatoon-WHL) for cash, September 30, 1958.

YAKE, Terry

Center. Shoots right. 5'11", 190 lbs. Born, New Westminster, B.C., October 22, 1968.
(Hartford's 3rd choice, 81st overall, in 1987 Entry Draft).

Season	Club	GP	G	A	Pts	PIM	GP	G	A	Pts	PIM
1988-89	Hartford Whalers	2	0	0	0	0	....	....	....	....	....
1989-90	Hartford Whalers	2	0	1	1	0	....	....	....	....	....
1990-91	Hartford Whalers	19	1	4	5	10	6	1	1	2	16
1991-92	Hartford Whalers	15	1	1	2	4	....	....	....	....	....
1992-93	Hartford Whalers	66	22	31	53	46	....	....	....	....	....
1993-94	Mighty Ducks of Anaheim	82	21	31	52	44	....	....	....	....	....
1994-95	Toronto Maple Leafs	19	3	2	5	2	....	....	....	....	....
1997-98	St. Louis Blues	65	10	15	25	38	10	2	1	3	6
1998-99	St. Louis Blues	60	9	18	27	34	13	1	2	3	14

Season	Club	GP	G	A	Pts	PIM	GP	G	A	Pts	PIM
		REGULAR SEASON					PLAYOFFS				
99-2000	St. Louis Blues	26	4	9	13	22	....	....	....	....	....
	Washington Capitals	35	6	5	11	12	3	0	0	0	0
2000-01	Washington Capitals	12	0	3	3	8	....	....	....	....	....
	NHL Totals	**403**	**77**	**120**	**197**	**220**	**32**	**4**	**4**	**8**	**36**

Claimed by **Anaheim** from **Hartford** in Expansion Draft, June 24, 1993. Traded to **Toronto** by **Anaheim** for David Sacco, September 28, 1994. Loaned to **Denver** (IHL) by **Toronto**, April 5, 1995. Signed as a free agent by **Buffalo**, September 17, 1996. Signed as a free agent by **St. Louis**, July 24, 1997. Claimed by **Atlanta** from **St. Louis** in Expansion Draft, June 25, 1999. Claimed by **St. Louis** from **Atlanta** in Waiver Draft, September 27, 1999. Claimed on waivers by **Washington** from **St. Louis**, January 18, 2000.

YAKUSHIN, Dmitri

Defense. Shoots left. 6', 200 lbs. Born, Kharkov, USSR, January 21, 1978.
(Toronto's 9th choice, 140th overall, in 1996 Entry Draft).

Season	Club	GP	G	A	Pts	PIM	GP	G	A	Pts	PIM
99-2000	Toronto Maple Leafs	2	0	0	0	2	....	....	....	....	....
	NHL Totals	**2**	**0**	**0**	**0**	**2**	....	....	....	....	....

YAREMCHUK, Gary

Center. Shoots left. 6', 185 lbs. Born, Edmonton, Alta., August 15, 1961.
(Toronto's 2nd choice, 24th overall, in 1981 Entry Draft).

Season	Club	GP	G	A	Pts	PIM	GP	G	A	Pts	PIM
1981-82	Toronto Maple Leafs	18	0	3	3	10	....	....	....	....	....
1982-83	Toronto Maple Leafs	3	0	0	0	2	....	....	....	....	....
1983-84	Toronto Maple Leafs	1	0	0	0	0	....	....	....	....	....
1984-85	Toronto Maple Leafs	12	1	1	2	16	....	....	....	....	....
	NHL Totals	**34**	**1**	**4**	**5**	**28**	....	....	....	....	....

• Brother of Ken

Signed as a free agent by **Detroit**, August 13, 1985.

YAREMCHUK, Ken

Center. Shoots right. 5'11", 185 lbs. Born, Edmonton, Alta., January 1, 1964.
(Chicago's 1st choice, 7th overall, in 1982 Entry Draft).

Season	Club	GP	G	A	Pts	PIM	GP	G	A	Pts	PIM
1983-84	Chicago Black Hawks	47	6	7	13	19	1	0	0	0	0
1984-85	Chicago Black Hawks	63	10	16	26	16	15	5	5	10	37
1985-86	Chicago Black Hawks	78	14	20	34	43	3	1	1	2	2
1986-87	Toronto Maple Leafs	20	3	8	11	16	6	0	0	0	0
1987-88	Toronto Maple Leafs	16	2	5	7	10	6	0	2	2	10
1988-89	Toronto Maple Leafs	11	1	0	1	2	....	....	....	....	....
	NHL Totals	**235**	**36**	**56**	**92**	**106**	**31**	**6**	**8**	**14**	**49**

• Brother of Gary

Transferred to **Toronto** by **Chicago** with Jerome Dupont and Chicago's 4th round choice (Joe Sacco) in 1987 Entry Draft as compensation for Chicago's signing of free agent Gary Nylund, September 6, 1986.

YASHIN, Alexei

Center. Shoots right. 6'3", 225 lbs. Born, Sverdlovsk, USSR, November 5, 1973.
(Ottawa's 1st choice, 2nd overall, in 1992 Entry Draft).

Season	Club	GP	G	A	Pts	PIM	GP	G	A	Pts	PIM
1993-94	Ottawa Senators	83	30	49	79	22	....	....	....	....	....
1994-95	Ottawa Senators	47	21	23	44	20	....	....	....	....	....
1995-96	Ottawa Senators	46	15	24	39	28	....	....	....	....	....
1996-97	Ottawa Senators	82	35	40	75	44	7	1	5	6	2
1997-98	Ottawa Senators	82	33	39	72	24	11	5	3	8	8
1998-99	Ottawa Senators	82	44	50	94	54	4	0	0	0	10
2000-01	Ottawa Senators	82	40	48	88	30	4	0	1	1	0
2001-02	New York Islanders	78	32	43	75	25	7	3	4	7	2
2002-03	New York Islanders	81	26	39	65	32	5	2	2	4	2
	NHL Totals	**663**	**276**	**355**	**631**	**279**	**38**	**11**	**15**	**26**	**24**

NHL Second All-Star Team (1999)

Played in NHL All-Star Game (1994, 1999, 2002)

• Suspended for entire 1999-2000 season by **Ottawa** for refusing to report to team, November 9, 1999. Traded to **NY Islanders** by **Ottawa** for Bill Muckalt, Zdeno Chara and NY Islanders' 1st round choice (Jason Spezza) in 2001 Entry Draft, June 23, 2001.

YATES, Ross

Center. Shoots right. 5'11", 170 lbs. Born, Montreal, Que., June 18, 1959.

Season	Club	GP	G	A	Pts	PIM	GP	G	A	Pts	PIM
1983-84	Hartford Whalers	7	1	1	2	4	....	....	....	....	....
	NHL Totals	**7**	**1**	**1**	**2**	**4**	....	....	....	....	....

Signed as a free agent by **Hartford**, August 6, 1981.

YAWNEY, Trent

Defense. Shoots left. 6'3", 195 lbs. Born, Hudson Bay, Sask., September 29, 1965.
(Chicago's 2nd choice, 45th overall, in 1984 Entry Draft).

Season	Club	GP	G	A	Pts	PIM	GP	G	A	Pts	PIM
1987-88	Chicago Blackhawks	15	2	8	10	15	5	0	4	4	8
1988-89	Chicago Blackhawks	69	5	19	24	116	15	3	6	9	20
1989-90	Chicago Blackhawks	70	5	15	20	82	20	3	5	8	27
1990-91	Chicago Blackhawks	61	3	13	16	77	1	0	0	0	0
1991-92	Calgary Flames	47	4	9	13	45	....	....	....	....	....
1992-93	Calgary Flames	63	1	16	17	67	6	3	2	5	6
1993-94	Calgary Flames	58	6	15	21	60	7	0	0	0	16
1994-95	Calgary Flames	37	0	2	2	108	2	0	0	0	2
1995-96	Calgary Flames	69	0	3	3	88	4	0	0	0	2
1996-97	St. Louis Blues	39	0	2	2	17	....	....	....	....	....
1997-98	Chicago Blackhawks	45	1	0	1	76	....	....	....	....	....
1998-99	Chicago Blackhawks	20	0	0	0	32	....	....	....	....	....
	NHL Totals	**593**	**27**	**102**	**129**	**783**	**60**	**9**	**17**	**26**	**81**

Traded to **Calgary** by **Chicago** for Stephane Matteau, December 16, 1991. Signed as a free agent by **St. Louis**, July 31, 1996. Signed as a free agent by **Chicago**, September 25, 1997.
• Missed remainder of 1998-99 season recovering from arm injury suffered in game vs. Colorado, January 9, 1999.

YEGOROV, Alexei

Right wing. Shoots left. 5'11", 185 lbs. Born, Leningrad, USSR, May 21, 1975.
(San Jose's 3rd choice, 66th overall, in 1994 Entry Draft).

Season	Club	GP	G	A	Pts	PIM	GP	G	A	Pts	PIM
1995-96	San Jose Sharks	9	3	2	5	2	....	....	....	....	....
1996-97	San Jose Sharks	2	0	1	1	0	....	....	....	....	....
	NHL Totals	**11**	**3**	**3**	**6**	**2**	....	....	....	....	....

Claimed by **Atlanta** from **San Jose** in Expansion Draft, June 25, 1999.

YELLE, Stephane

Center. Shoots left. 6'1", 190 lbs. Born, Ottawa, Ont., May 9, 1974.
(New Jersey's 9th choice, 186th overall, in 1992 Entry Draft).

Season	Club	GP	G	A	Pts	PIM	GP	G	A	Pts	PIM
1995-96 ◆	Colorado Avalanche	71	13	14	27	30	22	1	4	5	8
1996-97	Colorado Avalanche	79	9	17	26	38	12	1	6	7	2
1997-98	Colorado Avalanche	81	7	15	22	48	7	1	0	1	12
1998-99	Colorado Avalanche	72	8	7	15	40	10	0	1	1	6
99-2000	Colorado Avalanche	79	8	14	22	28	17	1	2	3	4
2000-01 ◆	Colorado Avalanche	50	4	10	14	20	23	1	2	3	8
2001-02	Colorado Avalanche	73	5	12	17	48	20	0	2	2	14
2002-03	Calgary Flames	82	10	15	25	50	....	....	....	....	....
	NHL Totals	**587**	**64**	**104**	**168**	**302**	**111**	**5**	**17**	**22**	**54**

Traded to **Quebec** by **New Jersey** with New Jersey's 11th round choice (Steven Low) in 1994 Entry Draft for Quebec's 11th round choice (Mike Hanson) in 1994 Entry Draft, June 1, 1994. Transferred to **Colorado** after **Quebec** franchise relocated, June 21, 1995. Traded to **Calgary** by **Colorado** with Chris Drury for Derek Morris, Jeff Shantz and Dean McAmmond, October 1, 2002.

YLONEN, Juha

Center. Shoots left. 6'1", 189 lbs. Born, Helsinki, Finland, February 13, 1972.
(Winnipeg's 3rd choice, 91st overall, in 1991 Entry Draft).

Season	Club	GP	G	A	Pts	PIM	GP	G	A	Pts	PIM
1996-97	Phoenix Coyotes	2	0	0	0	0	....	....	....	....	....
1997-98	Phoenix Coyotes	55	1	11	12	10	....	....	....	....	....
1998-99	Phoenix Coyotes	59	6	17	23	20	2	0	2	2	2
99-2000	Phoenix Coyotes	76	6	23	29	12	1	0	0	0	0
2000-01	Phoenix Coyotes	69	9	14	23	38	....	....	....	....	....
2001-02	Tampa Bay Lightning	65	3	10	13	8	....	....	....	....	....
	Ottawa Senators	15	1	1	2	2	12	0	5	5	2
	NHL Totals	**341**	**26**	**76**	**102**	**90**	**15**	**0**	**7**	**7**	**4**

Rights transferred to **Phoenix** after **Winnipeg** franchise relocated, July 1, 1996. Traded to **Tampa Bay** by **Phoenix** for Todd Warriner, June 18, 2001. Traded to **Ottawa** by **Tampa Bay** for Andre Roy and Ottawa's 6th round choice (Paul Ranger) in 2002 Entry Draft, March 15, 2002.

YONKMAN, Nolan

Defense. Shoots right. 6'6", 236 lbs. Born, Punnicht, Sask., April 1, 1981.
(Washington's 5th choice, 37th overall, in 1999 Entry Draft).

Season	Club	GP	G	A	Pts	PIM	GP	G	A	Pts	PIM
2001-02	Washington Capitals	11	1	0	1	4	....	....	....	....	....
	NHL Totals	**11**	**1**	**0**	**1**	**4**	....	....	....	....	....

YORK, Harry

Center. Shoots left. 6'2", 215 lbs. Born, Ponoka, Alta., April 16, 1974.

Season	Club	GP	G	A	Pts	PIM	GP	G	A	Pts	PIM
1996-97	St. Louis Blues	74	14	18	32	24	5	0	0	0	2
1997-98	St. Louis Blues	58	4	6	10	31	....	....	....	....	....
	New York Rangers	2	0	0	0	0	....	....	....	....	....
1998-99	New York Rangers	5	0	0	0	4	....	....	....	....	....
	Pittsburgh Penguins	2	0	0	0	0	....	....	....	....	....
	Vancouver Canucks	49	7	9	16	20	....	....	....	....	....
99-2000	Vancouver Canucks	54	4	13	17	20	....	....	....	....	....
	NHL Totals	**244**	**29**	**46**	**75**	**99**	**5**	**0**	**0**	**0**	**2**

Signed as a free agent by **St. Louis**, May 1, 1996. Traded to **NY Rangers** by **St. Louis** for Mike Eastwood, March 24, 1998. Traded to **Pittsburgh** by **NY Rangers** with Alexei Kovalev for Petr Nedved, Chris Tamer and Sean Pronger, November 25, 1998. Claimed on waivers by **Vancouver** from **Pittsburgh**, December 7, 1998.

YORK, Jason

Defense. Shoots right. 6'1", 208 lbs. Born, Nepean, Ont., May 20, 1970.
(Detroit's 6th choice, 129th overall, in 1990 Entry Draft).

Season	Club	GP	G	A	Pts	PIM	GP	G	A	Pts	PIM
1992-93	Detroit Red Wings	2	0	0	0	0	....	....	....	....	....
1993-94	Detroit Red Wings	7	1	2	3	2	....	....	....	....	....
1994-95	Detroit Red Wings	10	1	2	3	2	....	....	....	....	....
	Mighty Ducks of Anaheim	15	0	8	8	12	....	....	....	....	....
1995-96	Mighty Ducks of Anaheim	79	3	21	24	88	....	....	....	....	....
1996-97	Ottawa Senators	75	4	17	21	67	7	0	0	0	4
1997-98	Ottawa Senators	73	3	13	16	62	7	1	1	2	7
1998-99	Ottawa Senators	79	4	31	35	48	4	1	1	2	4
99-2000	Ottawa Senators	79	8	22	30	60	6	0	2	2	2
2000-01	Ottawa Senators	74	6	16	22	72	4	0	0	0	4
2001-02	Mighty Ducks of Anaheim	74	5	20	25	60	....	....	....	....	....

Season	Club	REGULAR SEASON GP	G	A	Pts	PIM	PLAYOFFS GP	G	A	Pts	PIM
2002-03	Nashville Predators	74	4	15	19	52	....	....	....	....	....
	NHL Totals	**641**	**39**	**167**	**206**	**525**	**28**	**2**	**4**	**6**	**21**

Traded to **Anaheim** by **Detroit** with Mike Sillinger for Stu Grimson, Mark Ferner and Anaheim's 6th round choice (Magnus Nilsson) in 1996 Entry Draft, April 4, 1995. Traded to **Ottawa** by **Anaheim** with Shaun Van Allen for Ted Drury and the rights to Marc Moro, October 1, 1996. Signed as a free agent by **Anaheim**, July 3, 2001. Traded to **Nashville** by **Anaheim** for future considerations, October 23, 2002.

YORK, Mike

Left wing. Shoots right. 5'10", 185 lbs. Born, Waterford, MI, January 3, 1978.
(NY Rangers' 7th choice, 136th overall, in 1997 Entry Draft).

Season	Club	GP	G	A	Pts	PIM	GP	G	A	Pts	PIM
99-2000	New York Rangers	82	26	24	50	18	....	....	....	....	....
2000-01	New York Rangers	79	14	17	31	20	....	....	....	....	....
2001-02	New York Rangers	69	18	39	57	16	....	....	....	....	....
	Edmonton Oilers	12	2	2	4	0	....	....	....	....	....
2002-03	Edmonton Oilers	71	22	29	51	10	6	0	2	2	2
	NHL Totals	**313**	**82**	**111**	**193**	**64**	**6**	**0**	**2**	**2**	**2**

NHL All-Rookie Team (2000)

Played in NHL All-Star Game (2002)

Traded to **Edmonton** by **NY Rangers** with NY Rangers' 4th round choice (Ivan Koltsov) in 2002 Entry Draft for Tom Poti and Rem Murray, March 19, 2002.

YOUNG, B.J.

Right wing. Shoots right. 5'10", 178 lbs. Born, Anchorage, AK, July 23, 1977.
(Detroit's 5th choice, 157th overall, in 1997 Entry Draft).

Season	Club	GP	G	A	Pts	PIM	GP	G	A	Pts	PIM
99-2000	Detroit Red Wings	1	0	0	0	0	....	....	....	....	....
	NHL Totals	**1**	**0**	**0**	**0**	**0**	....	....	....	....	....

YOUNG, Brian

Defense. Shoots right. 6'1", 183 lbs. Born, Jasper, Alta., October 2, 1958.
(Chicago's 4th choice, 63rd overall, in 1978 Amateur Draft).

Season	Club	GP	G	A	Pts	PIM	GP	G	A	Pts	PIM
1980-81	Chicago Black Hawks	8	0	2	2	6	....	....	....	....	....
	NHL Totals	**8**	**0**	**2**	**2**	**6**	....	....	....	....	....

YOUNG, C.J.

Right wing. Shoots right. 5'10", 180 lbs. Born, Waban, MA, January 1, 1968.
(New Jersey's 1st choice, 5th overall, in 1989 Supplemental Draft).

Season	Club	GP	G	A	Pts	PIM	GP	G	A	Pts	PIM
1992-93	Calgary Flames	28	3	2	5	20	....	....	....	....	....
	Boston Bruins	15	4	5	9	12	....	....	....	....	....
	NHL Totals	**43**	**7**	**7**	**14**	**32**	....	....	....	....	....

Signed as a free agent by **Calgary**, October 5, 1990. Traded to **Boston** by **Calgary** for Brent Ashton, February 1, 1993.

YOUNG, Doug

Defense. Shoots right. 5'10", 190 lbs. Born, Medicine Hat, Alta., October 1, 1908.

Season	Club	GP	G	A	Pts	PIM	GP	G	A	Pts	PIM
1931-32	Detroit Falcons	47	10	2	12	45	2	0	0	0	2
1932-33	Detroit Red Wings	48	5	6	11	59	4	1	1	2	0
1933-34	Detroit Red Wings	47	4	0	4	36	9	0	0	0	10
1934-35	Detroit Red Wings	48	4	6	10	37	....	....	....	....	....
1935-36 ◆	Detroit Red Wings	47	5	12	17	54	7	0	2	2	0
1936-37 ◆	Detroit Red Wings	11	0	0	0	6	....	....	....	....	....
1937-38	Detroit Red Wings	48	3	5	8	24	....	....	....	....	....
1938-39	Detroit Red Wings	42	1	5	6	16	6	0	2	2	4
1939-40	Montreal Canadiens	47	3	9	12	22	....	....	....	....	....
1940-41	Montreal Canadiens	3	0	0	0	4	....	....	....	....	....
	NHL Totals	**388**	**35**	**45**	**80**	**303**	**28**	**1**	**5**	**6**	**16**

Played in NHL All-Star Game (1939)

Claimed by **Philadelphia** from **Cleveland** (IHL) in Inter-League Draft, May 9, 1931. Claimed by **NY Americans** from **Philadelphia** in Dispersal Draft, September 17, 1931. Traded to **Detroit** by **NY Americans** for Ron Martin, October 18, 1931. • Missed remainder of 1936-37 season recovering from ankle injury suffered in game vs. NY Americans, December 6, 1936. Signed as a free agent by **Montreal**, October 30, 1939. Traded to **Buffalo** (AHL) by **Montreal** for cash pending waiver claim, November 27, 1940. Claimed on waivers by **Toronto** from **Montreal** and assigned to **Providence** (AHL), November 29, 1940.

YOUNG, Howie

Defense/Right wing. Shoots right. 5'11", 175 lbs. Born, Toronto, Ont., August 2, 1937.

Season	Club	GP	G	A	Pts	PIM	GP	G	A	Pts	PIM
1960-61	Detroit Red Wings	29	0	8	8	108	11	2	2	4	*30
1961-62	Detroit Red Wings	30	0	2	2	67	....	....	....	....	....
1962-63	Detroit Red Wings	64	4	5	9	*273	8	0	2	2	16
1963-64	Chicago Black Hawks	39	0	7	7	99	....	....	....	....	....
1966-67	Detroit Red Wings	44	3	14	17	100	....	....	....	....	....
1967-68	Detroit Red Wings	62	2	17	19	112	....	....	....	....	....
1968-69	Chicago Black Hawks	57	3	7	10	67	....	....	....	....	....
1970-71	Vancouver Canucks	11	0	2	2	25	....	....	....	....	....
	NHL Totals	**336**	**12**	**62**	**74**	**851**	**19**	**2**	**4**	**6**	**46**

Loaned to **New Westminster** (WHL) by **Toronto** for cash, October, 1958. Transferred to **Chicoutimi** (QHL) by **Toronto** for cash, October 26, 1958. Traded to **Hershey** (AHL) by **Toronto** (Rochester-AHL) for cash, August, 1960. Traded to **Detroit** by **Hershey** (AHL) for Jack McIntyre, Marc Reaume and Pete Conacher, January, 1961. Traded to **Chicago** by **Detroit** for Ron Ingram and Roger Crozier, June 5, 1963. Traded to **LA Blades** (WHL) by **Chicago** for cash and future considerations (rights to Wayne Smith, July, 1964) with Chicago retaining NHL rights, February 11, 1964. Traded to **Detroit** by **Chicago** (LA Blades-WHL) for loan of Murray Hall and Al Lebrun for remainder of 1966-67 season and future considerations (Murray Hall, Al Lebrun and Rick Morris, June, 1967), December 20, 1966. Traded to **Oakland** by **Detroit** with Gary Jarrett, Doug Roberts and Chris Worthy for Bob Baun and Ron Harris, May 27, 1968. Claimed on waivers by **Chicago** from **Oakland**, October 2, 1968. • Rights transferred to **Vancouver** after NHL club purchased Vancouver (WHL) franchise, December 19, 1969. Loaned to **Phoenix** (WHL) by **Vancouver** for remainder of 1970-71 season, November 7, 1970. Claimed by **San Diego** (WHL) from **Vancouver** in Reverse Draft, June, 1971.

YOUNG, Scott

Right wing. Shoots right. 6'1", 200 lbs. Born, Clinton, MA, October 1, 1967.
(Hartford's 1st choice, 11th overall, in 1986 Entry Draft).

Season	Club	GP	G	A	Pts	PIM	GP	G	A	Pts	PIM
1987-88	Hartford Whalers	7	0	0	0	2	4	1	0	1	0
1988-89	Hartford Whalers	76	19	40	59	27	4	2	0	2	4
1989-90	Hartford Whalers	80	24	40	64	47	7	2	0	2	2
1990-91	Hartford Whalers	34	6	9	15	8	....	....	....	....	....
	◆ Pittsburgh Penguins	43	11	16	27	33	17	1	6	7	2
1992-93	Quebec Nordiques	82	30	30	60	20	6	4	1	5	0
1993-94	Quebec Nordiques	76	26	25	51	14	....	....	....	....	....
1994-95	Quebec Nordiques	48	18	21	39	14	6	3	3	6	2
1995-96 ◆	Colorado Avalanche	81	21	39	60	50	22	3	12	15	10
1996-97	Colorado Avalanche	72	18	19	37	14	17	4	2	6	14
1997-98	Mighty Ducks of Anaheim	73	13	20	33	22	....	....	....	....	....
1998-99	St. Louis Blues	75	24	28	52	27	13	4	7	11	10
99-2000	St. Louis Blues	75	24	15	39	18	6	6	2	8	8
2000-01	St. Louis Blues	81	40	33	73	30	15	6	7	13	2
2001-02	St. Louis Blues	67	19	22	41	26	10	3	0	3	2
2002-03	Dallas Stars	79	23	19	42	30	10	4	3	7	6
	NHL Totals	**1049**	**316**	**376**	**692**	**382**	**137**	**43**	**43**	**86**	**62**

Traded to **Pittsburgh** by **Hartford** for Rob Brown, December 21, 1990. Traded to **Quebec** by **Pittsburgh** for Bryan Fogarty, March 10, 1992. Transferred to **Colorado** after **Quebec** franchise relocated, June 21, 1995. Traded to **Anaheim** by **Colorado** for Anaheim's 3rd round choice (later traded to Florida – Florida selected Lance Ward) in 1998 Entry Draft, September 17, 1997. Signed as a free agent by **St. Louis**, July 28, 1998. Signed as a free agent by **Dallas**, July 5, 2002.

YOUNG, Tim

Center. Shoots right. 6'1", 190 lbs. Born, Scarborough, Ont., February 22, 1955.
(Los Angeles' 1st choice, 16th overall, in 1975 Amateur Draft).

Season	Club	GP	G	A	Pts	PIM	GP	G	A	Pts	PIM
1975-76	Minnesota North Stars	63	18	33	51	71	....	....	....	....	....
1976-77	Minnesota North Stars	80	29	66	95	58	2	1	1	2	2
1977-78	Minnesota North Stars	78	23	35	58	64	....	....	....	....	....
1978-79	Minnesota North Stars	73	24	32	56	46	....	....	....	....	....
1979-80	Minnesota North Stars	77	31	43	74	24	15	2	5	7	4
1980-81	Minnesota North Stars	74	25	41	66	40	12	3	14	17	9
1981-82	Minnesota North Stars	49	10	31	41	67	4	1	1	2	10
1982-83	Minnesota North Stars	70	18	35	53	31	2	0	2	2	2
1983-84	Winnipeg Jets	44	15	19	34	25	1	0	1	1	0
1984-85	Philadelphia Flyers	20	2	6	8	12	....	....	....	....	....
	NHL Totals	**628**	**195**	**341**	**536**	**438**	**36**	**7**	**24**	**31**	**27**

Played in NHL All-Star Game (1977)

Traded to **Minnesota** by **Los Angeles** for Minnesota's 2nd round choice (Steve Clippingdale) in 1976 Amateur Draft, August 15, 1975. Traded to **Winnipeg** by **Minnesota** for Craig Levie and Tom Ward, August 3, 1983. Traded to **Philadelphia** by **Winnipeg** for future considerations, October 16, 1984.

YOUNG, Warren

Center. Shoots left. 6'3", 195 lbs. Born, Toronto, Ont., January 11, 1956.
(California's 4th choice, 59th overall, in 1976 Amateur Draft).

Season	Club	GP	G	A	Pts	PIM	GP	G	A	Pts	PIM
1981-82	Minnesota North Stars	1	0	0	0	0	....	....	....	....	....
1982-83	Minnesota North Stars	4	1	1	2	0	....	....	....	....	....
1983-84	Pittsburgh Penguins	15	1	7	8	19	....	....	....	....	....
1984-85	Pittsburgh Penguins	80	40	32	72	174	....	....	....	....	....
1985-86	Detroit Red Wings	79	22	24	46	161	....	....	....	....	....
1986-87	Pittsburgh Penguins	50	8	13	21	103	....	....	....	....	....
1987-88	Pittsburgh Penguins	7	0	0	0	15	....	....	....	....	....
	NHL Totals	**236**	**72**	**77**	**149**	**472**	....	....	....	....	....

NHL All-Rookie Team (1985)

Signed as a free agent by **Minnesota**, October 22, 1981. Signed as a free agent by **Pittsburgh**, August 12, 1983. Signed as a free agent by **Detroit**, July 10, 1985. Traded to **Pittsburgh** by **Detroit** for cash, October 8, 1986.

YOUNGHANS, Tom

Right wing. Shoots right. 5'11", 175 lbs. Born, St. Paul, MN, January 22, 1953.

Season	Club	GP	G	A	Pts	PIM	GP	G	A	Pts	PIM
1976-77	Minnesota North Stars	78	8	6	14	35	2	0	0	0	0
1977-78	Minnesota North Stars	72	10	8	18	100	....	....	....	....	....
1978-79	Minnesota North Stars	76	8	10	18	50	....	....	....	....	....
1979-80	Minnesota North Stars	79	10	6	16	92	15	2	1	3	17
1980-81	Minnesota North Stars	74	4	6	10	79	5	0	0	0	4

		REGULAR SEASON					PLAYOFFS				
Season	Club	GP	G	A	Pts	PIM	GP	G	A	Pts	PIM
1981-82	Minnesota North Stars	3	1	0	1	0	....	....	....	....	....
	New York Rangers	47	3	5	8	17	2	0	0	0	0
	NHL Totals	**429**	**44**	**41**	**85**	**373**	**24**	**2**	**1**	**3**	**21**

Signed as a free agent by **Minnesota**, September 14, 1976. Traded to **NY Rangers** by **Minnesota** for cash, October 30, 1981.

YSEBAERT, Paul

Center. Shoots left. 6'1", 194 lbs. Born, Sarnia, Ont., May 15, 1966.
(New Jersey's 4th choice, 74th overall, in 1984 Entry Draft).

		REGULAR SEASON					PLAYOFFS				
Season	Club	GP	G	A	Pts	PIM	GP	G	A	Pts	PIM
1988-89	New Jersey Devils	5	0	4	4	0	....	....	....	....	....
1989-90	New Jersey Devils	5	1	2	3	0	....	....	....	....	....
1990-91	New Jersey Devils	11	4	3	7	6	....	....	....	....	....
	Detroit Red Wings	51	15	18	33	16	2	0	2	2	0
1991-92	Detroit Red Wings	79	35	40	75	55	10	1	0	1	10
1992-93	Detroit Red Wings	80	34	28	62	42	7	3	1	4	2
1993-94	Winnipeg Jets	60	9	18	27	18	....	....	....	....	....
	Chicago Blackhawks	11	5	3	8	8	6	0	0	0	8
1994-95	Chicago Blackhawks	15	4	5	9	6	....	....	....	....	....
	Tampa Bay Lightning	29	8	11	19	12	....	....	....	....	....
1995-96	Tampa Bay Lightning	55	16	15	31	16	5	0	0	0	0
1996-97	Tampa Bay Lightning	39	5	12	17	4	....	....	....	....	....
1997-98	Tampa Bay Lightning	82	13	27	40	32	....	....	....	....	....
1998-99	Tampa Bay Lightning	10	0	1	1	2	....	....	....	....	....
	NHL Totals	**532**	**149**	**187**	**336**	**217**	**30**	**4**	**3**	**7**	**20**

Alka-Seltzer Plus Award (1992)

Traded to **Detroit** by **New Jersey** for Lee Norwood and Detroit's 4th round choice (Scott McCabe) in 1992 Entry Draft, November 27, 1990. Traded to **Winnipeg** by **Detroit** with future considerations (Alan Kerr, June 18, 1993) for Aaron Ward and Toronto's 4th round choice (previously acquired by Winnipeg – later traded to Detroit – Detroit selected John Jakopin) in 1993 Entry Draft, June 11, 1993. Traded to **Chicago** by **Winnipeg** for Chicago's 3rd round choice (later traded back to Chicago – Chicago selected Kevin McKay) in 1995 Entry Draft, March 21, 1994. Traded to **Tampa Bay** by **Chicago** with Rich Sutter for Jim Cummins, Tom Tilley and Jeff Buchanan, February 22, 1995.

YUSHKEVICH, Dmitry

Defense. Shoots right. 5'11", 208 lbs. Born, Cherepovets, USSR, November 19, 1971.
(Philadelphia's 6th choice, 122nd overall, in 1991 Entry Draft).

		REGULAR SEASON					PLAYOFFS				
Season	Club	GP	G	A	Pts	PIM	GP	G	A	Pts	PIM
1992-93	Philadelphia Flyers	82	5	27	32	71	....	....	....	....	....
1993-94	Philadelphia Flyers	75	5	25	30	86	....	....	....	....	....
1994-95	Philadelphia Flyers	40	5	9	14	47	15	1	5	6	12
1995-96	Toronto Maple Leafs	69	1	10	11	54	4	0	0	0	0
1996-97	Toronto Maple Leafs	74	4	10	14	56	....	....	....	....	....
1997-98	Toronto Maple Leafs	72	0	12	12	78	....	....	....	....	....
1998-99	Toronto Maple Leafs	78	6	22	28	88	17	1	5	6	22
99-2000	Toronto Maple Leafs	77	3	24	27	55	12	1	1	2	4
2000-01	Toronto Maple Leafs	81	5	19	24	52	11	0	4	4	12
2001-02	Toronto Maple Leafs	55	6	13	19	26	....	....	....	....	....
2002-03	Florida Panthers	23	1	6	7	14	....	....	....	....	....
	Los Angeles Kings	42	0	3	3	24	....	....	....	....	....
	Philadelphia Flyers	18	2	2	4	8	13	1	4	5	2
	NHL Totals	**786**	**43**	**182**	**225**	**659**	**72**	**4**	**19**	**23**	**52**

Played in NHL All-Star Game (2000)

Traded to **Toronto** by **Philadelphia** with Philadelphia's 2nd round choice (Francis Larivee) in 1996 Entry Draft for Toronto's 1st round choice (Dainius Zubrus) in 1996 Entry Draft, 2nd round choice (Jean-Marc Pelletier) in 1997 Entry Draft and Los Angeles' 4th round choice (previously acquired, later traded to Los Angeles – Los Angeles selected Mikael Simons) in 1996 Entry Draft, August 30, 1995. Traded to **Florida** by **Toronto** for Robert Svehla, July 18, 2002. Traded to **Los Angeles** by **Florida** with NY Islanders' 5th round choice (previously acquired, Los Angeles selected Brady Murray) in 2003 Entry Draft for Jaroslav Bednar and Andreas Lilja, November 26, 2002. Traded to **Philadelphia** by **Los Angeles** for Philadelphia's 4th round choice (later traded to Boston – Boston selected Patrick Valcak) in 2003 Entry Draft and Philadelphia's 7th round choice in 2004 Entry Draft, March 1, 2003.

YZERMAN, Steve

Center. Shoots right. 5'11", 185 lbs. Born, Cranbrook, B.C., May 9, 1965.
(Detroit's 1st choice, 4th overall, in 1983 Entry Draft).

		REGULAR SEASON					PLAYOFFS				
Season	Club	GP	G	A	Pts	PIM	GP	G	A	Pts	PIM
1983-84	Detroit Red Wings	80	39	48	87	33	4	3	3	6	0
1984-85	Detroit Red Wings	80	30	59	89	58	3	2	1	3	2
1985-86	Detroit Red Wings	51	14	28	42	16	....	....	....	....	....
1986-87	Detroit Red Wings	80	31	59	90	43	16	5	13	18	8
1987-88	Detroit Red Wings	64	50	52	102	44	3	1	3	4	6
1988-89	Detroit Red Wings	80	65	90	155	61	6	5	5	10	2
1989-90	Detroit Red Wings	79	62	65	127	79	....	....	....	....	....
1990-91	Detroit Red Wings	80	51	57	108	34	7	3	3	6	4
1991-92	Detroit Red Wings	79	45	58	103	64	11	3	5	8	12
1992-93	Detroit Red Wings	84	58	79	137	44	7	4	3	7	4
1993-94	Detroit Red Wings	58	24	58	82	36	3	1	3	4	0
1994-95	Detroit Red Wings	47	12	26	38	40	15	4	8	12	0
1995-96	Detroit Red Wings	80	36	59	95	64	18	8	12	20	4
1996-97 ♦	Detroit Red Wings	81	22	63	85	78	20	7	6	13	4
1997-98 ♦	Detroit Red Wings	75	24	45	69	46	22	6	*18	*24	22
1998-99	Detroit Red Wings	80	29	45	74	42	10	9	4	13	0
99-2000	Detroit Red Wings	78	35	44	79	34	8	0	4	4	0
2000-01	Detroit Red Wings	54	18	34	52	18	1	0	0	0	0
2001-02 ♦	Detroit Red Wings	52	13	35	48	18	23	6	17	23	10
2002-03	Detroit Red Wings	16	2	6	8	8	4	0	1	1	2
	NHL Totals	**1378**	**660**	**1010**	**1670**	**860**	**181**	**67**	**109**	**176**	**80**

NHL All-Rookie Team (1984) • Lester B. Pearson Award (1989) • Conn Smythe Trophy (1998) • NHL First All-Star Team (2000) • Frank J. Selke Trophy (2000) • Bill Masterton Memorial Trophy (2003)

Played in NHL All-Star Game (1984, 1988, 1989, 1990, 1991, 1992, 1993, 1997, 2000)

• Missed majority of 2002-03 season recovering from off-season knee surgery, August 2, 2002.

ZABRANSKY, Libor

Defense. Shoots left. 6'3", 196 lbs. Born, Brno, Czech., November 25, 1973.
(St. Louis' 8th choice, 209th overall, in 1995 Entry Draft).

		REGULAR SEASON					PLAYOFFS				
Season	Club	GP	G	A	Pts	PIM	GP	G	A	Pts	PIM
1996-97	St. Louis Blues	34	1	5	6	44	....	....	....	....	....
1997-98	St. Louis Blues	6	0	1	1	6	....	....	....	....	....
	NHL Totals	**40**	**1**	**6**	**7**	**50**	....	....	....	....	....

ZAHARKO, Miles

Defense. Shoots left. 6', 197 lbs. Born, Mannville, Alta., April 30, 1957.
(Atlanta's 1st choice, 20th overall, in 1977 Amateur Draft).

		REGULAR SEASON					PLAYOFFS				
Season	Club	GP	G	A	Pts	PIM	GP	G	A	Pts	PIM
1977-78	Atlanta Flames	71	1	19	20	26	1	0	0	0	0
1978-79	Chicago Black Hawks	1	0	0	0	0	....	....	....	....	....
1980-81	Chicago Black Hawks	42	3	11	14	40	2	0	0	0	0
1981-82	Chicago Black Hawks	15	1	2	3	18	....	....	....	....	....
	NHL Totals	**129**	**5**	**32**	**37**	**84**	**3**	**0**	**0**	**0**	**0**

Traded to **Chicago** by **Atlanta** with Tom Lysiak, Pat Ribble, Greg Fox and Harold Phillipoff for Ivan Boldirev, Phil Russell and Darcy Rota, March 13, 1979. Claimed by **Chicago** as fill in Expansion Draft, June 13, 1979.

ZAINE, Rod

Center. Shoots left. 5'10", 180 lbs. Born, Ottawa, Ont., May 18, 1946.

		REGULAR SEASON					PLAYOFFS				
Season	Club	GP	G	A	Pts	PIM	GP	G	A	Pts	PIM
1970-71	Pittsburgh Penguins	37	8	5	13	21	....	....	....	....	....
1971-72	Buffalo Sabres	24	2	1	3	4	....	....	....	....	....
	NHL Totals	**61**	**10**	**6**	**16**	**25**	....	....	....	....	....

Traded to **Pittsburgh** by **Baltimore** AHL) for cash, July, 1970. Claimed by **Buffalo** from **Pittsburgh** in Intra-League Draft, June 8, 1971. Claimed by **Atlanta** from **Buffalo** in Expansion Draft, June 6, 1972.

ZALAPSKI, Zarley

Defense. Shoots left. 6'1", 215 lbs. Born, Edmonton, Alta., April 22, 1968.
(Pittsburgh's 1st choice, 4th overall, in 1986 Entry Draft).

		REGULAR SEASON					PLAYOFFS				
Season	Club	GP	G	A	Pts	PIM	GP	G	A	Pts	PIM
1987-88	Pittsburgh Penguins	15	3	8	11	7	....	....	....	....	....
1988-89	Pittsburgh Penguins	58	12	33	45	57	11	1	8	9	13
1989-90	Pittsburgh Penguins	51	6	25	31	37	....	....	....	....	....
1990-91	Pittsburgh Penguins	66	12	36	48	59	....	....	....	....	....
	Hartford Whalers	11	3	3	6	6	6	1	3	4	8
1991-92	Hartford Whalers	79	20	37	57	120	7	2	3	5	6
1992-93	Hartford Whalers	83	14	51	65	94	....	....	....	....	....
1993-94	Hartford Whalers	56	7	30	37	56	....	....	....	....	....
	Calgary Flames	13	3	7	10	18	7	0	3	3	2
1994-95	Calgary Flames	48	4	24	28	46	7	0	4	4	4
1995-96	Calgary Flames	80	12	17	29	115	4	0	1	1	10
1996-97	Calgary Flames	2	0	0	0	0	....	....	....	....	....
1997-98	Calgary Flames	35	2	7	9	41	....	....	....	....	....
	Montreal Canadiens	28	1	5	6	22	6	0	1	1	4
99-2000	Philadelphia Flyers	12	0	2	2	6	....	....	....	....	....
	NHL Totals	**637**	**99**	**285**	**384**	**684**	**48**	**4**	**23**	**27**	**47**

NHL All-Rookie Team (1989)

Played in NHL All-Star Game (1993)

Traded to **Hartford** by **Pittsburgh** with John Cullen and Jeff Parker for Ron Francis, Grant Jennings and Ulf Samuelsson, March 4, 1991. Traded to **Calgary** by **Hartford** with James Patrick and Michael Nylander for Gary Suter, Paul Ranheim and Ted Drury, March 10, 1994. • Missed majority of 1996-97 season recovering from knee injury suffered during practice, October 7, 1996. Traded to **Montreal** by **Calgary** with Jonas Hoglund for Valeri Bure and Montreal's 4th round choice (Shaun Sutter) in 1998 Entry Draft, February 1, 1998. Signed as a free agent by **NY Rangers**, August 31, 1998. Signed as a free agent by **Philadelphia**, February 15, 2000.

ZALESAK, Miroslav

Right wing. Shoots left. 6', 185 lbs. Born, Skalica, Czech., January 2, 1980.
(San Jose's 5th choice, 104th overall, in 1998 Entry Draft).

		REGULAR SEASON					PLAYOFFS				
Season	Club	GP	G	A	Pts	PIM	GP	G	A	Pts	PIM
2002-03	San Jose Sharks	10	1	2	3	0	....	....	....	....	....
	NHL Totals	**10**	**1**	**2**	**3**	**0**	....	....	....	....	....

ZAMUNER, Rob

Left wing. Shoots left. 6'3", 203 lbs. Born, Oakville, Ont., September 17, 1969.
(NY Rangers' 3rd choice, 45th overall, in 1989 Entry Draft).

		REGULAR SEASON					PLAYOFFS				
Season	Club	GP	G	A	Pts	PIM	GP	G	A	Pts	PIM
1991-92	New York Rangers	9	1	2	3	2	....	....	....	....	....
1992-93	Tampa Bay Lightning	84	15	28	43	74	....	....	....	....	....
1993-94	Tampa Bay Lightning	59	6	6	12	42	....	....	....	....	....
1994-95	Tampa Bay Lightning	43	9	6	15	24	....	....	....	....	....
1995-96	Tampa Bay Lightning	72	15	20	35	62	6	2	3	5	10
1996-97	Tampa Bay Lightning	82	17	33	50	56	....	....	....	....	....
1997-98	Tampa Bay Lightning	77	14	12	26	41	....	....	....	....	....
1998-99	Tampa Bay Lightning	58	8	11	19	24	....	....	....	....	....
99-2000	Ottawa Senators	57	9	12	21	32	6	2	0	2	2
2000-01	Ottawa Senators	79	19	18	37	52	4	0	0	0	6
2001-02	Boston Bruins	66	12	13	25	24	6	0	2	2	4

Season	Club	GP	G	A	Pts	PIM	GP	G	A	Pts	PIM
		REGULAR SEASON					PLAYOFFS				
2002-03	Boston Bruins	55	10	6	16	18	5	0	0	0	4
	NHL Totals	**741**	**135**	**167**	**302**	**451**	**27**	**4**	**5**	**9**	**26**

Signed as a free agent by **Tampa Bay**, July 13, 1992. Traded to **Ottawa** by **Tampa Bay** with Tampa Bay's 2nd round choice (later traded to Philadelphia – later traded back to Tampa Bay – later traded to Dallas – Dallas selected Tobias Stephan) in 2002 Entry Draft for Andreas Johansson, June 29, 1999. Signed as a free agent by **Boston**, July 6, 2001.

ZANUSSI, Joe

Defense. Shoots right. 5'10", 180 lbs. Born, Rossland, B.C., September 25, 1947.

Season	Club	GP	G	A	Pts	PIM	GP	G	A	Pts	PIM
1974-75	New York Rangers	8	0	2	2	4	....	....	....	....	....
1975-76	Boston Bruins	60	1	7	8	30	4	0	1	1	2
1976-77	Boston Bruins	8	0	1	1	8	....	....	....	....	....
	St. Louis Blues	11	0	3	3	4	....	....	....	....	....
	NHL Totals	**87**	**1**	**13**	**14**	**46**	**4**	**0**	**1**	**1**	**2**

• Brother of Ron

Traded to **NY Rangers** by **Detroit** with Detroit's 1st round choice (Al Blanchard) in 1972 Amateur Draft for Gary Doak and Rick Newell, May 24, 1972. Selected by **Winnipeg** (WHA) in 1972 WHA General Player Draft, February 12, 1972. Traded to **Boston** by **NY Rangers** with Brad Park and Jean Ratelle for Phil Esposito and Carol Vadnais, November 7, 1975. Traded to **St. Louis** by **Boston** for Rick Smith, December 20, 1976.

ZANUSSI, Ron

Right wing. Shoots right. 5'11", 180 lbs. Born, Toronto, Ont., August 31, 1956.
(Minnesota's 4th choice, 51st overall, in 1976 Amateur Draft).

Season	Club	GP	G	A	Pts	PIM	GP	G	A	Pts	PIM
1977-78	Minnesota North Stars	68	15	17	32	89	....	....	....	....	....
1978-79	Minnesota North Stars	63	14	16	30	82	....	....	....	....	....
1979-80	Minnesota North Stars	72	14	31	45	93	14	0	4	4	17
1980-81	Minnesota North Stars	41	6	11	17	89	....	....	....	....	....
	Toronto Maple Leafs	12	3	0	3	6	3	0	0	0	0
1981-82	Toronto Maple Leafs	43	0	8	8	14	....	....	....	....	....
	NHL Totals	**299**	**52**	**83**	**135**	**373**	**17**	**0**	**4**	**4**	**17**

• Brother of Joe

Claimed by **Minnesota** as a fill-in during **Cleveland-Minnesota** Dispersal Draft, June 15, 1978. Traded to **Toronto** by **Minnesota** with Minnesota's 3rd round choice (Ernie Godden) in 1981 Entry Draft for Toronto's 2nd round choice (Dave Donnelly) in 1981 Entry Draft, March 10, 1981.

ZAVISHA, Brad

Left wing. Shoots left. 6'2", 205 lbs. Born, Hines Creek, Alta., January 4, 1972.
(Quebec's 3rd choice, 43rd overall, in 1990 Entry Draft).

Season	Club	GP	G	A	Pts	PIM	GP	G	A	Pts	PIM
1993-94	Edmonton Oilers	2	0	0	0	0	....	....	....	....	....
	NHL Totals	**2**	**0**	**0**	**0**	**0**	....	....	....	....	....

Traded to **Edmonton** by **Quebec** with Ron Tugnutt for Martin Rucinsky, March 10, 1992. • Missed entire 1992-93 season recovering from knee injury suffered in training camp, September 23, 1992. Traded to **Philadelphia** by **Edmonton** with Edmonton's 6th round choice (Jamie Sokolsky) in 1995 Entry Draft for Ryan McGill, March 13, 1995.

ZEDNIK, Richard

Right wing. Shoots left. 6', 200 lbs. Born, Bystrica, Czech., January 6, 1976.
(Washington's 10th choice, 249th overall, in 1994 Entry Draft).

Season	Club	GP	G	A	Pts	PIM	GP	G	A	Pts	PIM
1995-96	Washington Capitals	1	0	0	0	0	....	....	....	....	....
1996-97	Washington Capitals	11	2	1	3	4	....	....	....	....	....
1997-98	Washington Capitals	65	17	9	26	28	17	7	3	10	16
1998-99	Washington Capitals	49	9	8	17	50	....	....	....	....	....
99-2000	Washington Capitals	69	19	16	35	54	5	0	0	0	5
2000-01	Washington Capitals	62	16	19	35	61	....	....	....	....	....
	Montreal Canadiens	12	3	6	9	10	....	....	....	....	....
2001-02	Montreal Canadiens	82	22	22	44	59	4	4	4	8	6
2002-03	Montreal Canadiens	80	31	19	50	79	....	....	....	....	....
	NHL Totals	**431**	**119**	**100**	**219**	**345**	**26**	**11**	**7**	**18**	**27**

Traded to **Montreal** by **Washington** with Jan Bulis and Washington's 1st round choice (Alexander Perezhogin) in 2001 Entry Draft for Trevor Linden, Dainius Zubrus and New Jersey's 2nd round choice (previously acquired, later traded to Tampa Bay – Tampa Bay selected Andreas Holmqvist) in 2001 Entry Draft, March 13, 2001.

ZEHR, Jeff

Left wing. Shoots left. 6'3", 195 lbs. Born, Woodstock, Ont., December 10, 1978.
(NY Islanders' 3rd choice, 31st overall, in 1997 Entry Draft).

Season	Club	GP	G	A	Pts	PIM	GP	G	A	Pts	PIM
99-2000	Boston Bruins	4	0	0	0	2	....	....	....	....	....
	NHL Totals	**4**	**0**	**0**	**0**	**2**	....	....	....	....	....

Signed as a free agent by **Boston**, June 21, 1999.

ZEIDEL, Larry

Defense. Shoots left. 5'11", 185 lbs. Born, Montreal, Que., June 1, 1928.

Season	Club	GP	G	A	Pts	PIM	GP	G	A	Pts	PIM
1951-52 ♦	Detroit Red Wings	19	1	0	1	14	5	0	0	0	0
1952-53	Detroit Red Wings	9	0	0	0	8	....	....	....	....	....
1953-54	Chicago Black Hawks	64	1	6	7	102	....	....	....	....	....
1967-68	Philadelphia Flyers	57	1	10	11	68	7	0	1	1	12
1968-69	Philadelphia Flyers	9	0	0	0	6	....	....	....	....	....
	NHL Totals	**158**	**3**	**16**	**19**	**198**	**12**	**0**	**1**	**1**	**12**

Traded to **Chicago** by **Detroit** with Larry Wilson and Lou Jankowski for cash, August 12, 1953. Traded to **Detroit** by **Chicago** for cash, June, 1954. Traded to **Hershey** (AHL) by **Detroit** (Edmonton-WHL) with Jimmy Uniac for Hugh Coflin, August 14, 1955. Traded to **Montreal** by **Seattle** (WHL) for cash, June, 1965. Traded to **Cleveland** (AHL) by **Montreal** for cash, June, 1965. Traded to **Philadelphia** by **Cleveland** (AHL) for cash, October 23, 1967.

ZELEPUKIN, Valeri

Left wing. Shoots left. 6'1", 200 lbs. Born, Voskresensk, USSR, September 17, 1968.
(New Jersey's 13th choice, 221st overall, in 1990 Entry Draft).

Season	Club	GP	G	A	Pts	PIM	GP	G	A	Pts	PIM
1991-92	New Jersey Devils	44	13	18	31	28	4	1	1	2	2
1992-93	New Jersey Devils	78	23	41	64	70	5	0	2	2	0
1993-94	New Jersey Devils	82	26	31	57	70	20	5	2	7	14
1994-95 ♦	New Jersey Devils	4	1	2	3	6	18	1	2	3	12
1995-96	New Jersey Devils	61	6	9	15	107	....	....	....	....	....
1996-97	New Jersey Devils	71	14	24	38	36	8	3	2	5	2
1997-98	New Jersey Devils	35	2	8	10	32	....	....	....	....	....
	Edmonton Oilers	33	2	10	12	57	8	1	2	3	2
1998-99	Philadelphia Flyers	74	16	9	25	48	4	1	0	1	4
99-2000	Philadelphia Flyers	77	11	21	32	55	18	1	2	3	12
2000-01	Chicago Blackhawks	36	3	4	7	18	....	....	....	....	....
	NHL Totals	**595**	**117**	**177**	**294**	**527**	**85**	**13**	**13**	**26**	**48**

• Missed majority of 1994-95 season recovering from eye injury suffered in practice, January 24, 1995. Traded to **Edmonton** by **New Jersey** with Bill Guerin for Jason Arnott and Bryan Muir, January 4, 1998. Traded to **Philadelphia** by **Edmonton** for Daniel Lacroix, October 5, 1998. Signed as a free agent by **Chicago**, July 18, 2000.

ZEMLAK, Richard

Right wing. Shoots right. 6'2", 190 lbs. Born, Wynard, Sask., March 3, 1963.
(St. Louis' 9th choice, 209th overall, in 1981 Entry Draft).

Season	Club	GP	G	A	Pts	PIM	GP	G	A	Pts	PIM
1986-87	Quebec Nordiques	20	0	2	2	47	....	....	....	....	....
1987-88	Minnesota North Stars	54	1	4	5	307	....	....	....	....	....
1988-89	Minnesota North Stars	3	0	0	0	13	....	....	....	....	....
	Pittsburgh Penguins	31	0	0	0	135	1	0	0	0	10
1989-90	Pittsburgh Penguins	19	1	5	6	43	....	....	....	....	....
1991-92	Calgary Flames	5	0	1	1	42	....	....	....	....	....
	NHL Totals	**132**	**2**	**12**	**14**	**587**	**1**	**0**	**0**	**0**	**10**

Rights traded to **Quebec** by **St. Louis** with rights to Dan Wood and Roger Hagglund for cash, June 22, 1984. Claimed by **Minnesota** from **Quebec** in Waiver Draft, October 5, 1987. Traded to **Pittsburgh** by **Minnesota** for the rights to Rob Gaudreau, November 1, 1988. Signed as a free agent by **Calgary**, November 8, 1990.

ZENIUK, Ed

Defense. Shoots left. 5'11", 180 lbs. Born, Landis, Sask., March 8, 1933.

Season	Club	GP	G	A	Pts	PIM	GP	G	A	Pts	PIM
1954-55	Detroit Red Wings	2	0	0	0	0	....	....	....	....	....
	NHL Totals	**2**	**0**	**0**	**0**	**0**	....	....	....	....	....

ZENT, Jason

Left wing. Shoots left. 5'11", 204 lbs. Born, Buffalo, NY, April 15, 1971.
(NY Islanders' 3rd choice, 44th overall, in 1989 Entry Draft).

Season	Club	GP	G	A	Pts	PIM	GP	G	A	Pts	PIM
1996-97	Ottawa Senators	22	3	3	6	9	....	....	....	....	....
1997-98	Ottawa Senators	3	0	0	0	4	....	....	....	....	....
1998-99	Philadelphia Flyers	2	0	0	0	0	....	....	....	....	....
	NHL Totals	**27**	**3**	**3**	**6**	**13**	....	....	....	....	....

Traded to **Ottawa** by **NY Islanders** for Ottawa's 5th round choice (Bubba Berenzweig) in 1996 Entry Draft, October 15, 1994. Signed as a free agent by **Philadelphia**, July 28, 1998. • Officially released by **Philadelphia**, December 12, 1999.

ZETTERBERG, Henrik

Left wing. Shoots left. 5'11", 176 lbs. Born, Njurunda, Sweden, October 9, 1980.
(Detroit's 4th choice, 210th overall, in 1999 Entry Draft).

Season	Club	GP	G	A	Pts	PIM	GP	G	A	Pts	PIM
2002-03	Detroit Red Wings	79	22	22	44	8	4	1	0	1	0
	NHL Totals	**79**	**22**	**22**	**44**	**8**	**4**	**1**	**0**	**1**	**0**

NHL All-Rookie Team (2003)

ZETTERSTROM, Lars

Defense. Shoots left. 6'1", 198 lbs. Born, Stockholm, Sweden, November 6, 1953.

Season	Club	GP	G	A	Pts	PIM	GP	G	A	Pts	PIM
1978-79	Vancouver Canucks	14	0	1	1	2	....	....	....	....	....
	NHL Totals	**14**	**0**	**1**	**1**	**2**	....	....	....	....	....

Signed as a free agent by **Vancouver**, June 5, 1978. Claimed by **Quebec** from **Vancouver** in Expansion Draft, June 13, 1979.

ZETTLER, Rob

Defense. Shoots left. 6'3", 200 lbs. Born, Sept-Iles, Que., March 8, 1968.
(Minnesota's 5th choice, 55th overall, in 1986 Entry Draft).

Season	Club	GP	G	A	Pts	PIM	GP	G	A	Pts	PIM
1988-89	Minnesota North Stars	2	0	0	0	0	....	....	....	....	....
1989-90	Minnesota North Stars	31	0	8	8	45	....	....	....	....	....
1990-91	Minnesota North Stars	47	1	4	5	119	....	....	....	....	....
1991-92	San Jose Sharks	74	1	8	9	99	....	....	....	....	....
1992-93	San Jose Sharks	80	0	7	7	150	....	....	....	....	....
1993-94	San Jose Sharks	42	0	3	3	65	....	....	....	....	....
	Philadelphia Flyers	33	0	4	4	69	....	....	....	....	....
1994-95	Philadelphia Flyers	32	0	1	1	34	1	0	0	0	2
1995-96	Toronto Maple Leafs	29	0	1	1	48	2	0	0	0	0
1996-97	Toronto Maple Leafs	48	2	12	14	51	....	....	....	....	....
1997-98	Toronto Maple Leafs	59	0	7	7	108	....	....	....	....	....
1998-99	Nashville Predators	2	0	0	0	2	....	....	....	....	....
99-2000	Washington Capitals	12	0	2	2	19	5	0	0	0	2
2000-01	Washington Capitals	29	0	4	4	55	6	0	0	0	0

		REGULAR SEASON					PLAYOFFS				
Season	Club	GP	G	A	Pts	PIM	GP	G	A	Pts	PIM
2001-02	Washington Capitals	49	1	4	5	56	....	....	....	....	....
	NHL Totals	**569**	**5**	**65**	**70**	**920**	**14**	**0**	**0**	**0**	**4**

Claimed by **San Jose** from **Minnesota** in Dispersal Draft, May 30, 1991. Traded to **Philadelphia** by **San Jose** for Viacheslav Butsayev, February 1, 1994. Traded to **Toronto** by **Philadelphia** for Toronto's 5th round choice (Per-Ragna Bergqvist) in 1996 Entry Draft, July 8, 1995. Claimed by **Nashville** from **Toronto** in Expansion Draft, June 26, 1998. Signed as a free agent by **Washington**, September 7, 1999.

ZEZEL, Peter

Center. Shoots left. 5'11", 220 lbs. Born, Toronto, Ont., April 22, 1965.
(Philadelphia's 1st choice, 41st overall, in 1983 Entry Draft).

Season	Club	GP	G	A	Pts	PIM	GP	G	A	Pts	PIM
1984-85	Philadelphia Flyers	65	15	46	61	26	19	1	8	9	28
1985-86	Philadelphia Flyers	79	17	37	54	76	5	3	1	4	4
1986-87	Philadelphia Flyers	71	33	39	72	71	25	3	10	13	10
1987-88	Philadelphia Flyers	69	22	35	57	42	7	3	2	5	7
1988-89	Philadelphia Flyers	26	4	13	17	15	....	....	....	....	....
	St. Louis Blues	52	17	36	53	27	10	6	6	12	4
1989-90	St. Louis Blues	73	25	47	72	30	12	1	7	8	4
1990-91	Washington Capitals	20	7	5	12	10	....	....	....	....	....
	Toronto Maple Leafs	32	14	14	28	4	....	....	....	....	....
1991-92	Toronto Maple Leafs	64	16	33	49	26	....	....	....	....	....
1992-93	Toronto Maple Leafs	70	12	23	35	24	20	2	1	3	6
1993-94	Toronto Maple Leafs	41	8	8	16	19	18	2	4	6	8
1994-95	Dallas Stars	30	6	5	11	19	3	1	0	1	0
1995-96	St. Louis Blues	57	8	13	21	12	10	3	0	3	2
1996-97	St. Louis Blues	35	4	9	13	12	....	....	....	....	....
	New Jersey Devils	18	0	3	3	4	2	0	0	0	10
1997-98	New Jersey Devils	5	0	3	3	0	....	....	....	....	....
	Vancouver Canucks	25	5	12	17	2	....	....	....	....	....
1998-99	Vancouver Canucks	41	6	8	14	16	....	....	....	....	....
	NHL Totals	**873**	**219**	**389**	**608**	**435**	**131**	**25**	**39**	**64**	**83**

Traded to **St. Louis** by **Philadelphia** for Mike Bullard, November 29, 1988. Traded to **Washington** by **St. Louis** with Mike Lalor for Geoff Courtnall, July 13, 1990. Traded to **Toronto** by **Washington** with Bob Rouse for Al Iafrate, January 16, 1991. Transferred to **Dallas** by **Toronto** with Grant Marshall as compensation for Toronto's signing of free agent Mike Craig, August 10, 1994. Signed as a free agent by **St. Louis**, October 19, 1995. Traded to **New Jersey** by **St. Louis** for Chris McAlpine and New Jersey's 9th round choice (James Desmarais) in 1999 Entry Draft, February 11, 1997. Traded to **Vancouver** by **New Jersey** for Vancouver's 5th round choice (Anton But) in 1998 Entry Draft, February 5, 1998.

ZHAMNOV, Alexei

Center. Shoots left. 6'1", 200 lbs. Born, Moscow, USSR, October 1, 1970.
(Winnipeg's 5th choice, 77th overall, in 1990 Entry Draft).

Season	Club	GP	G	A	Pts	PIM	GP	G	A	Pts	PIM
1992-93	Winnipeg Jets	68	25	47	72	58	6	0	2	2	2
1993-94	Winnipeg Jets	61	26	45	71	62	....	....	....	....	....
1994-95	Winnipeg Jets	48	30	35	65	20	....	....	....	....	....
1995-96	Winnipeg Jets	58	22	37	59	65	6	2	1	3	8
1996-97	Chicago Blackhawks	74	20	42	62	56	....	....	....	....	....
1997-98	Chicago Blackhawks	70	21	28	49	61	....	....	....	....	....
1998-99	Chicago Blackhawks	76	20	41	61	50	....	....	....	....	....
99-2000	Chicago Blackhawks	71	23	37	60	61	....	....	....	....	....
2000-01	Chicago Blackhawks	63	13	36	49	40	....	....	....	....	....
2001-02	Chicago Blackhawks	77	22	45	67	67	5	0	0	0	0
2002-03	Chicago Blackhawks	74	15	43	58	70	....	....	....	....	....
	NHL Totals	**740**	**237**	**436**	**673**	**610**	**17**	**2**	**3**	**5**	**10**

NHL Second All-Star Team (1995)
Played in NHL All-Star Game (2002)

Traded to **Chicago** by **Phoenix** with Craig Mills and Phoenix's 1st round choice (Ty Jones) in 1997 Entry Draft for Jeremy Roenick, August 16, 1996.

ZHITNIK, Alexei

Defense. Shoots left. 5'11", 215 lbs. Born, Kiev, USSR, October 10, 1972.
(Los Angeles' 3rd choice, 81st overall, in 1991 Entry Draft).

Season	Club	GP	G	A	Pts	PIM	GP	G	A	Pts	PIM
1992-93	Los Angeles Kings	78	12	36	48	80	24	3	9	12	26
1993-94	Los Angeles Kings	81	12	40	52	101	....	....	....	....	....
1994-95	Los Angeles Kings	11	2	5	7	27	....	....	....	....	....
	Buffalo Sabres	21	2	5	7	34	5	0	1	1	14
1995-96	Buffalo Sabres	80	6	30	36	58	....	....	....	....	....
1996-97	Buffalo Sabres	80	7	28	35	95	12	1	0	1	16
1997-98	Buffalo Sabres	78	15	30	45	102	15	0	3	3	36
1998-99	Buffalo Sabres	81	7	26	33	96	21	4	11	15	*52
99-2000	Buffalo Sabres	74	2	11	13	95	4	0	0	0	8
2000-01	Buffalo Sabres	78	8	29	37	75	13	1	6	7	12
2001-02	Buffalo Sabres	82	1	33	34	80	....	....	....	....	....
2002-03	Buffalo Sabres	70	3	18	21	85	....	....	....	....	....
	NHL Totals	**814**	**77**	**291**	**368**	**928**	**94**	**9**	**30**	**39**	**164**

Played in NHL All-Star Game (1999, 2002)

Traded to **Buffalo** by **Los Angeles** with Robb Stauber, Charlie Huddy and Los Angeles' 5th round choice (Marian Menhart) in 1995 Entry Draft for Philippe Boucher, Denis Tsygurov and Grant Fuhr, February 14, 1995.

ZHOLTOK, Sergei

Center. Shoots right. 6'2", 191 lbs. Born, Riga, Latvia, December 2, 1972.
(Boston's 2nd choice, 55th overall, in 1992 Entry Draft).

Season	Club	GP	G	A	Pts	PIM	GP	G	A	Pts	PIM
1992-93	Boston Bruins	1	0	1	1	0	....	....	....	....	....
1993-94	Boston Bruins	24	2	1	3	2	....	....	....	....	....
1996-97	Ottawa Senators	57	12	16	28	19	7	1	1	2	0
1997-98	Ottawa Senators	78	10	13	23	16	11	0	2	2	0
1998-99	Montreal Canadiens	70	7	15	22	6	....	....	....	....	....
99-2000	Montreal Canadiens	68	26	12	38	28	....	....	....	....	....
2000-01	Montreal Canadiens	32	1	10	11	8	....	....	....	....	....
	Edmonton Oilers	37	4	16	20	22	3	0	0	0	0
2001-02	Minnesota Wild	73	19	20	39	28	....	....	....	....	....
2002-03	Minnesota Wild	78	16	26	42	18	18	2	11	13	0
	NHL Totals	**518**	**97**	**130**	**227**	**147**	**39**	**3**	**14**	**17**	**0**

Signed as a free agent by **Ottawa**, July 10, 1996. Signed as a free agent by **Montreal**, September 9, 1998. Traded to **Edmonton** by **Montreal** for Chad Kilger, December 18, 2000. Traded to **Minnesota** by **Edmonton** for Minnesota's 7th round choice (J.F. Dufort) in 2002 Entry Draft, June 29, 2001.

ZIEGLER, Thomas

Right wing. Shoots left. 5'11", 174 lbs. Born, Zurich, Switz., June 9, 1978.
(Tampa Bay's 10th choice, 263rd overall, in 2000 Entry Draft).

Season	Club	GP	G	A	Pts	PIM	GP	G	A	Pts	PIM
2000-01	Tampa Bay Lightning	5	0	0	0	0	....	....	....	....	....
	NHL Totals	**5**	**0**	**0**	**0**	**0**	....	....	....	....	....

ZIGOMANIS, Mike

Center. Shoots right. 6'1", 189 lbs. Born, North York, Ont., January 17, 1981.
(Carolina's 2nd choice, 46th overall, in 2001 Entry Draft).

Season	Club	GP	G	A	Pts	PIM	GP	G	A	Pts	PIM
2002-03	Carolina Hurricanes	19	2	1	3	0	....	....	....	....	....
	NHL Totals	**19**	**2**	**1**	**3**	**0**	....	....	....	....	....

• Re-entered NHL Entry Draft. Originally Buffalo's 4th choice, 64th overall, in 1999 Entry Draft.

ZIZKA, Tomas

Defense. Shoots left. 6'1", 198 lbs. Born, Sternberk, Czech., October 10, 1979.
(Los Angeles' 6th choice, 163rd overall, in 1998 Entry Draft).

Season	Club	GP	G	A	Pts	PIM	GP	G	A	Pts	PIM
2002-03	Los Angeles Kings	10	0	3	3	4	....	....	....	....	....
	NHL Totals	**10**	**0**	**3**	**3**	**4**	....	....	....	....	....

ZMOLEK, Doug

Defense. Shoots left. 6'2", 222 lbs. Born, Rochester, MN, November 3, 1970.
(Minnesota's 1st choice, 7th overall, in 1989 Entry Draft).

Season	Club	GP	G	A	Pts	PIM	GP	G	A	Pts	PIM
1992-93	San Jose Sharks	84	5	10	15	229	....	....	....	....	....
1993-94	San Jose Sharks	68	0	4	4	122	....	....	....	....	....
	Dallas Stars	7	1	0	1	11	7	0	1	1	4
1994-95	Dallas Stars	42	0	5	5	67	5	0	0	0	10
1995-96	Dallas Stars	42	1	5	6	65	....	....	....	....	....
	Los Angeles Kings	16	1	0	1	22	....	....	....	....	....
1996-97	Los Angeles Kings	57	1	0	1	116	....	....	....	....	....
1997-98	Los Angeles Kings	46	0	8	8	111	2	0	0	0	2
1998-99	Chicago Blackhawks	62	0	14	14	102	....	....	....	....	....
99-2000	Chicago Blackhawks	43	2	7	9	60	....	....	....	....	....
	NHL Totals	**467**	**11**	**53**	**64**	**905**	**14**	**0**	**1**	**1**	**16**

Claimed by **San Jose** from **Minnesota** in Dispersal Draft, May 30, 1991. Traded to **Dallas** by **San Jose** with Mike Lalor for Ulf Dahlen and Dallas' 7th round choice (Brad Mehalko) in 1995 Entry Draft, March 19, 1994. Traded to **Los Angeles** by **Dallas** with Shane Churla for Darryl Sydor and Los Angeles' 5th round choice (Ryan Christie) in 1996 Entry Draft, February 17, 1996. Traded to **Chicago** by **Los Angeles** for Chicago's 3rd round choice (Frantisek Kaberle) in 1999 Entry Draft, September 3, 1998.

ZOBOROSKY, Marty

Defense. Shoots right. 5'10", 180 lbs. Born, Moose Jaw, Sask.,

Season	Club	GP	G	A	Pts	PIM	GP	G	A	Pts	PIM
1944-45	Chicago Black Hawks	1	0	0	0	2	....	....	....	....	....
	NHL Totals	**1**	**0**	**0**	**0**	**2**	....	....	....	....	....

ZOMBO, Rick

Defense. Shoots right. 6'1", 202 lbs. Born, Des Plaines, IL, May 8, 1963.
(Detroit's 6th choice, 149th overall, in 1981 Entry Draft).

Season	Club	GP	G	A	Pts	PIM	GP	G	A	Pts	PIM
1984-85	Detroit Red Wings	1	0	0	0	0	....	....	....	....	....
1985-86	Detroit Red Wings	14	0	1	1	16	....	....	....	....	....
1986-87	Detroit Red Wings	44	1	4	5	59	7	0	1	1	9
1987-88	Detroit Red Wings	62	3	14	17	96	16	0	6	6	55
1988-89	Detroit Red Wings	75	1	20	21	106	6	0	1	1	16
1989-90	Detroit Red Wings	77	5	20	25	95	....	....	....	....	....
1990-91	Detroit Red Wings	77	4	19	23	55	7	1	0	1	10
1991-92	Detroit Red Wings	3	0	0	0	15	....	....	....	....	....
	St. Louis Blues	64	3	15	18	46	6	0	2	2	12
1992-93	St. Louis Blues	71	0	15	15	78	11	0	1	1	12
1993-94	St. Louis Blues	74	2	8	10	85	4	0	0	0	11
1994-95	St. Louis Blues	23	1	4	5	24	3	0	0	0	2
1995-96	Boston Bruins	67	4	10	14	53	....	....	....	....	....
	NHL Totals	**652**	**24**	**130**	**154**	**728**	**60**	**1**	**11**	**12**	**127**

Traded to **St. Louis** by **Detroit** for Vincent Riendeau, October 18, 1991. Traded to **Boston** by **St. Louis** for Fred Knipscheer, October 2, 1995. Signed as a free agent by **Los Angeles**, December 13, 1996.

ZUBOV, Sergei

Defense. Shoots right. 6'1", 200 lbs. Born, Moscow, USSR, July 22, 1970.
(NY Rangers' 6th choice, 85th overall, in 1990 Entry Draft).

Season	Club	GP	G	A	Pts	PIM	GP	G	A	Pts	PIM
1992-93	New York Rangers	49	8	23	31	4	....	....	....	....	....
1993-94◆	New York Rangers	78	12	77	89	39	22	5	14	19	0
1994-95	New York Rangers	38	10	26	36	18	10	3	8	11	2

Season	Club	GP	G	A	Pts	PIM	GP	G	A	Pts	PIM
		REGULAR SEASON					PLAYOFFS				
1995-96	Pittsburgh Penguins	64	11	55	66	22	18	1	14	15	26
1996-97	Dallas Stars	78	13	30	43	24	7	0	3	3	2
1997-98	Dallas Stars	73	10	47	57	16	17	4	5	9	2
1998-99♦	Dallas Stars	81	10	41	51	20	23	1	12	13	4
99-2000	Dallas Stars	77	9	33	42	18	18	2	7	9	6
2000-01	Dallas Stars	79	10	41	51	24	10	1	5	6	4
2001-02	Dallas Stars	80	12	32	44	22	....	....	....	....	....
2002-03	Dallas Stars	82	11	44	55	26	12	4	10	14	4
	NHL Totals	**779**	**116**	**449**	**565**	**233**	**137**	**21**	**78**	**99**	**50**

Played in NHL All-Star Game (1998, 1999, 2000)

Traded to **Pittsburgh** by **NY Rangers** with Petr Nedved for Luc Robitaille and Ulf Samuelsson, August 31, 1995. Traded to **Dallas** by **Pittsburgh** for Kevin Hatcher, June 22, 1996.

ZUBRUS, Dainius

Right wing. Shoots left. 6'4", 231 lbs. Born, Elektrenai, USSR, June 16, 1978.
(Philadelphia's 1st choice, 15th overall, in 1996 Entry Draft).

Season	Club	GP	G	A	Pts	PIM	GP	G	A	Pts	PIM
1996-97	Philadelphia Flyers	68	8	13	21	22	19	5	4	9	12
1997-98	Philadelphia Flyers	69	8	25	33	42	5	0	1	1	2
1998-99	Philadelphia Flyers	63	3	5	8	25	....	....	....	....	....
	Montreal Canadiens	17	3	5	8	4	....	....	....	....	....
99-2000	Montreal Canadiens	73	14	28	42	54	....	....	....	....	....
2000-01	Montreal Canadiens	49	12	12	24	30	....	....	....	....	....
	Washington Capitals	12	1	1	2	7	6	0	0	0	2
2001-02	Washington Capitals	71	17	26	43	38	....	....	....	....	....
2002-03	Washington Capitals	63	13	22	35	43	6	2	2	4	4
	NHL Totals	**485**	**79**	**137**	**216**	**265**	**36**	**7**	**7**	**14**	**20**

Traded to **Montreal** by **Philadelphia** with Philadelphia's 2nd round choice (Matt Carkner) in 1999 Entry Draft and NY Islanders' 6th round choice (previously acquired, Montreal selected Scott Selig) in 2000 Entry Draft for Mark Recchi, March 10, 1999. Traded to **Washington** by **Montreal** with Trevor Linden and New Jersey's 2nd round choice (previously acquired, later traded to Tampa Bay – Tampa Bay selected Andreas Holmqvist) in 2001 Entry Draft for Richard Zednik, Jan Bulis and Washington's 1st round choice (Alexander Perezhogin) in 2001 Entry Draft, March 13, 2001.

ZUKE, Mike

Center. Shoots right. 6', 180 lbs. Born, Sault Ste. Marie, Ont., April 16, 1954.
(St. Louis' 3rd choice, 79th overall, in 1974 Amateur Draft).

Season	Club	GP	G	A	Pts	PIM	GP	G	A	Pts	PIM
1978-79	St. Louis Blues	34	9	17	26	18	....	....	....	....	....
1979-80	St. Louis Blues	69	22	42	64	30	3	0	0	0	2
1980-81	St. Louis Blues	74	24	44	68	57	11	4	5	9	4
1981-82	St. Louis Blues	76	13	40	53	41	8	1	1	2	2
1982-83	St. Louis Blues	43	8	16	24	14	4	1	0	1	4
1983-84	Hartford Whalers	75	6	23	29	36	....	....	....	....	....
1984-85	Hartford Whalers	67	4	12	16	12	....	....	....	....	....
1985-86	Hartford Whalers	17	0	2	2	12	....	....	....	....	....
	NHL Totals	**455**	**86**	**196**	**282**	**220**	**26**	**6**	**6**	**12**	**12**

Signed as a free agent by **St. Louis**, September 29, 1978. Claimed by **Hartford** from **St. Louis** in Waiver Draft, October 3, 1983.

ZUNICH, Rudy

Defense. Shoots left. 5'9", 170 lbs. Born, Calumet, MI, November 24, 1910.

Season	Club	GP	G	A	Pts	PIM	GP	G	A	Pts	PIM
1943-44	Detroit Red Wings	2	0	0	0	2	....	....	....	....	....
	NHL Totals	**2**	**0**	**0**	**0**	**2**	....	....	....	....	....

Signed as a free agent by **Detroit** to a three-game tryout contract, October 31, 1943.

ZYUZIN, Andrei

Defense. Shoots right. 6'1", 215 lbs. Born, Ufa, USSR, January 21, 1978.
(San Jose's 1st choice, 2nd overall, in 1996 Entry Draft).

Season	Club	GP	G	A	Pts	PIM	GP	G	A	Pts	PIM
1997-98	San Jose Sharks	56	6	7	13	66	6	1	0	1	14
1998-99	San Jose Sharks	25	3	1	4	38	....	....	....	....	....
99-2000	Tampa Bay Lightning	34	2	9	11	33	....	....	....	....	....
2000-01	Tampa Bay Lightning	64	4	16	20	76	....	....	....	....	....
2001-02	Tampa Bay Lightning	9	0	2	2	6	....	....	....	....	....
	New Jersey Devils	38	1	2	3	25	....	....	....	....	....
2002-03	New Jersey Devils	1	0	1	1	2	....	....	....	....	....
	Minnesota Wild	66	4	12	16	34	18	0	1	1	14
	NHL Totals	**293**	**20**	**50**	**70**	**280**	**24**	**1**	**1**	**2**	**28**

• Suspended for remainder of 1998-99 season by **San Jose** for leaving team without permission, April 1, 1999. Traded to **Tampa Bay** by **San Jose** with Bill Houlder, Shawn Burr and Steve Guolla for Niklas Sundstrom and NY Rangers' 3rd round choice (previously acquired, later traded to Chicago – Chicago selected Igor Radulov) in 2000 Entry Draft, August 4, 1999. • Missed majority of 1999-2000 season recovering from shoulder injury suffered in game vs. NY Islanders, January 13, 2000. Traded to **New Jersey** by **Tampa Bay** for Josef Boumedienne, Sascha Goc and the rights to Anton But, November 9, 2001. Claimed on waivers by **Minnesota** from **New Jersey**, November 2, 2002.

CHAPTER 10

All-Time NHL Goaltender Register

NHL Statistics for Every Goaltender, 1917–18 to 2002–03

Note: The All-Time NHL Goaltender Register lists the NHL statistics of every goaltender who has appeared in an NHL regular-season or playoff game from 1917–18 to 2002–03. Trades current as of July 29, 2003.

Abbreviations: GP - games played, **W** - wins, **L** - losses (including overtime losses), **T** - ties, **Mins** - minutes played, ***** - league leading total, **◆** - member of Stanley Cup winning team. **(Cup)** - Stanley Cup games vs. non-NHL opponents, 1917-18 to 1925-26. These statistics not included in career NHL playoff totals.

All-time NHL Player Register begins on page 447.

All-Time NHL Coach Register begins on page 909.

Late Trades and Transactions are found on page 446.

ABBOTT, George

Goaltender. Catches Left. 5'7", 153 lbs. Born, Sydenham, Ont., August 3, 1911

Season	Club	GP	W	L	T	Mins	GA	SO	Avg	GP	W	L	Mins	GA	SO	Avg
		REGULAR SEASON								PLAYOFFS						
1943-44	Boston	1	0	1	0	60	7	0	7.00	....	....	....	....	....	....	....
	NHL Totals	**1**	**0**	**1**	**0**	**60**	**7**	**0**	**7.00**	....	....	....	....	....	....	....

• **Toronto's** practice goaltender loaned to **Boston** to replace injured Bert Gardiner, November 27, 1943. (Toronto 7, Boston 4)

ADAMS, John

Goaltender. Catches left. 6', 200 lbs. Born, Port Arthur, Ont., July 27, 1946

Season	Club	GP	W	L	T	Mins	GA	SO	Avg	GP	W	L	Mins	GA	SO	Avg
1972-73	Boston	14	9	3	1	780	39	1	3.00	....	....	....	....	....	....	....
1974-75	Washington	8	0	7	0	400	46	0	6.90	....	....	....	....	....	....	....
	NHL Totals	**22**	**9**	**10**	**1**	**1180**	**85**	**1**	**4.32**	....	....	....	....	....	....	....

Traded to **San Diego** (WHL) by **Boston** to complete transaction that sent Ken Broderick to Boston (March 10, 1973), June 12, 1973. Traded to **Washington** by **San Diego** (WHL) for cash, July 11, 1974.

AEBISCHER, David

Goaltender. Catches left. 6'1", 190 lbs. Born, Fribourg, Switz., February 7, 1978
(Colorado's 7th choice, 161st overall, in 1997 Entry Draft).

Season	Club	GP	W	L	T	Mins	GA	SO	Avg	GP	W	L	Mins	GA	SO	Avg
2000-01◆	Colorado	26	12	7	3	1393	52	3	2.24	1	0	0	1	0	0	0.00
2001-02	Colorado	21	13	6	0	1184	37	2	1.88	1	0	0	34	1	0	1.76
2002-03	Colorado	22	7	12	0	1235	50	1	2.43	....	....	....	....	....	....	....
	NHL Totals	**69**	**32**	**25**	**3**	**3812**	**139**	**6**	**2.19**	**2**	**0**	**0**	**35**	**1**	**0**	**1.71**

AIKEN, Don

Goaltender. Catches Left. 5'11", 165 lbs. Born, Arlington, MA, January 1, 1932

Season	Club	GP	W	L	T	Mins	GA	SO	Avg	GP	W	L	Mins	GA	SO	Avg
1957-58	Montreal	1	0	1	0	34	6	0	10.59	....	....	....	....	....	....	....
	NHL Totals	**1**	**0**	**1**	**0**	**34**	**6**	**0**	**10.59**	....	....	....	....	....	....	....

• **Boston's** practice goaltender loaned to **Montreal** to replace injured Jacques Plante in 2nd period, March 13, 1958. (Boston 7, Montreal 3) • At the time of his appearance with Montreal, he was employed as a mathematician with the U.S. Air Force. • Served as Boston's practice goaltender for 13 seasons.

AITKENHEAD, Andy

Goaltender. Catches left. 5'9", 145 lbs. Born, Glasgow, Scotland, March 6, 1904

Season	Club	GP	W	L	T	Mins	GA	SO	Avg	GP	W	L	Mins	GA	SO	Avg
1932-33◆	NY Rangers	*48	23	17	8	2970	107	3	2.16	8	*6	1	488	13	*2	1.60
1933-34	NY Rangers	*48	21	19	8	2990	113	7	2.27	2	0	1	120	2	1	1.00
1934-35	NY Rangers	10	3	7	0	610	37	1	3.64	....	....	....	....	....	....	....
	NHL Totals	**106**	**47**	**43**	**16**	**6570**	**257**	**11**	**2.35**	**10**	**6**	**2**	**608**	**15**	**3**	**1.48**

Claimed by **NY Rangers** from **Saskatoon** (PrHL) in Inter-League Draft, May 12, 1928. Traded to **Portland** (PCHL) by **NY Rangers** for cash, October, 1929. Traded to **NY Rangers** by **Portland** (PCHL) for cash, April 19, 1931. Loaned to **Portland** (NWHL) by **NY Rangers** for cash, December 30, 1934.

ALMAS, Red

Goaltender. Catches right. 5'9", 160 lbs. Born, Saskatoon, Sask., April 26, 1924

Season	Club	GP	W	L	T	Mins	GA	SO	Avg	GP	W	L	Mins	GA	SO	Avg
1946-47	Detroit	1	0	1	0	60	5	0	5.00	5	1	3	263	13	0	2.97
1950-51	Chicago	1	0	1	0	60	5	0	5.00	....	....	....	....	....	....	....
1952-53	Detroit	1	0	0	1	60	3	0	3.00	....	....	....	....	....	....	....
	NHL Totals	**3**	**0**	**2**	**1**	**180**	**13**	**0**	**4.33**	**5**	**1**	**3**	**263**	**13**	**0**	**2.97**

Traded to **Chicago** (St. Louis-AHL) by **Detroit** with Barry Sullivan, Lloyd Doran, Tony Licari and Thain Simon for Hec Highton and Joe Lund, September 9, 1948. Traded to **Detroit** by **Chicago** with Guyle Fielder and Steve Hrymnak for cash, September 23, 1952.

ANDERSON, Craig

Goaltender. Catches left. 6'2", 174 lbs. Born, Park Ridge, IL, May 21, 1981
(Chicago's 4th choice, 73rd overall, in 2001 Entry Draft).

Season	Club	GP	W	L	T	Mins	GA	SO	Avg	GP	W	L	Mins	GA	SO	Avg
2002-03	Chicago	6	0	3	2	270	18	0	4.00	....	....	....	....	....	....	....
	NHL Totals	**6**	**0**	**3**	**2**	**270**	**18**	**0**	**4.00**	....	....	....	....	....	....	....

• Re-entered NHL Entry Draft. Originally Calgary's 3rd choice, 77th overall, in 1999 Entry Draft.

ANDERSON, Lorne

Goaltender. Catches right. 5'11", 166 lbs. Born, Renfrew, Ont., July 26, 1931

Season	Club	GP	W	L	T	Mins	GA	SO	Avg	GP	W	L	Mins	GA	SO	Avg
1951-52	NY Rangers	3	1	2	0	180	18	0	6.00	....	....	....	....	....	....	....
	NHL Totals	**3**	**1**	**2**	**0**	**180**	**18**	**0**	**6.00**	....	....	....	....	....	....	....

ASKEY, Tom

Goaltender. Catches left. 6'1", 195 lbs. Born, Kenmore, NY, October 4, 1974
(Anaheim's 8th choice, 186th overall, in 1993 Entry Draft).

Season	Club	GP	W	L	T	Mins	GA	SO	Avg	GP	W	L	Mins	GA	SO	Avg
1997-98	Anaheim	7	0	1	2	273	12	0	2.64	....	....	....	....	....	....	....
1998-99	Anaheim	....	....	....	....	....	....	....	....	1	0	1	30	2	0	4.00
	NHL Totals	**7**	**0**	**1**	**2**	**273**	**12**	**0**	**2.64**	**1**	**0**	**1**	**30**	**2**	**0**	**4.00**

Signed as a free agent by **Buffalo**, August 10, 2001.

ASTROM, Hardy

Goaltender. Catches left. 6', 170 lbs. Born, Skelleftea, Sweden, March 29, 1951

Season	Club	GP	W	L	T	Mins	GA	SO	Avg	GP	W	L	Mins	GA	SO	Avg
1977-78	NY Rangers	4	2	2	0	240	14	0	3.50	....	....	....	....	....	....	....
1979-80	Colorado	49	9	27	6	2574	161	0	3.75	....	....	....	....	....	....	....
1980-81	Colorado	30	6	15	6	1642	103	0	3.76	....	....	....	....	....	....	....
	NHL Totals	**83**	**17**	**44**	**12**	**4456**	**278**	**0**	**3.74**	....	....	....	....	....	....	....

Signed as a free agent by **NY Rangers**, March 15, 1977. Rights traded to **Colorado** by **NY Rangers** for Bill Lochead, July 2, 1979.

AUBIN, Jean-Sebastien

Goaltender. Catches right. 5'11", 180 lbs. Born, Montreal, Que., July 19, 1977
(Pittsburgh's 2nd choice, 76th overall, in 1995 Entry Draft).

Season	Club	GP	W	L	T	Mins	GA	SO	Avg	GP	W	L	Mins	GA	SO	Avg
1998-99	Pittsburgh	17	4	3	6	756	28	2	2.22	....	....	....	....	....	....	....
99-2000	Pittsburgh	51	23	21	3	2789	120	2	2.58	....	....	....	....	....	....	....
2000-01	Pittsburgh	36	20	14	1	2050	107	0	3.13	1	0	0	1	0	0	0.00
2001-02	Pittsburgh	21	3	12	1	1094	65	0	3.56	....	....	....	....	....	....	....
2002-03	Pittsburgh	21	6	13	0	1132	59	1	3.13	....	....	....	....	....	....	....
	NHL Totals	**146**	**56**	**63**	**11**	**7821**	**379**	**5**	**2.91**	**1**	**0**	**0**	**1**	**0**	**0**	**0.00**

AULD, Alexander

Goaltender. Catches left. 6'4", 197 lbs. Born, Cold Lake, Alta., January 7, 1981
(Florida's 2nd choice, 40th overall, in 1999 Entry Draft).

Season	Club	GP	W	L	T	Mins	GA	SO	Avg	GP	W	L	Mins	GA	SO	Avg
2001-02	Vancouver	1	1	0	0	60	2	0	2.00	....	....	....	....	....	....	....
2002-03	Vancouver	7	3	3	0	382	10	1	1.57	1	0	0	20	1	0	3.00
	NHL Totals	**8**	**4**	**3**	**0**	**442**	**12**	**1**	**1.63**	**1**	**0**	**0**	**20**	**1**	**0**	**3.00**

Rights traded to **Vancouver** by **Florida** for Vancouver's compensatory 2nd round choice (later traded to New Jersey – New Jersey selected Tuomas Pihlman) in 2001 Entry Draft and Vancouver's 3rd round choice (later traded to Atlanta – later traded to Buffalo – Buffalo selected John Adams) in 2002 Entry Draft, May 31, 2001.

BACH, Ryan

Goaltender. Catches left. 6'1", 185 lbs. Born, Sherwood Park, Alta., October 21, 1973
(Detroit's 11th choice, 262nd overall, in 1992 Entry Draft).

Season	Club	GP	W	L	T	Mins	GA	SO	Avg	GP	W	L	Mins	GA	SO	Avg
1998-99	Los Angeles	3	0	3	0	108	8	0	4.44	....	....	....	....	....	....	....
	NHL Totals	**3**	**0**	**3**	**0**	**108**	**8**	**0**	**4.44**	....	....	....	....	....	....	....

Traded to **Los Angeles** by **Detroit** for Los Angeles' 6th round choice (Per Backer) in 2000 Entry Draft, October 22, 1998. Signed as a free agent by **Florida**, July 27, 1999.

BAILEY, Scott

Goaltender. Catches left. 6', 195 lbs. Born, Calgary, Alta., May 2, 1972
(Boston's 3rd choice, 112th overall, in 1992 Entry Draft).

Season	Club	GP	W	L	T	Mins	GA	SO	Avg	GP	W	L	Mins	GA	SO	Avg
1995-96	Boston	11	5	1	2	571	31	0	3.26	....	....	....	....	....	....	....
1996-97	Boston	8	1	5	0	394	24	0	3.65	....	....	....	....	....	....	....
	NHL Totals	**19**	**6**	**6**	**2**	**965**	**55**	**0**	**3.42**	....	....	....	....	....	....	....

BAKER, Steve

Goaltender. Catches left. 6'3", 200 lbs. Born, Boston, MA, May 6, 1957
(NY Rangers' 4th choice, 44th overall, in 1977 Amateur Draft).

Season	Club	GP	W	L	T	Mins	GA	SO	Avg	GP	W	L	Mins	GA	SO	Avg
1979-80	NY Rangers	27	9	8	6	1391	79	1	3.41	....	....	....	....	....	....	....
1980-81	NY Rangers	21	10	6	5	1260	73	2	3.48	14	7	7	826	55	0	4.00
1981-82	NY Rangers	6	1	5	0	328	33	0	6.04	....	....	....	....	....	....	....
1982-83	NY Rangers	3	0	1	0	102	5	0	2.94	....	....	....	....	....	....	....
	NHL Totals	**57**	**20**	**20**	**11**	**3081**	**190**	**3**	**3.70**	**14**	**7**	**7**	**826**	**55**	**0**	**4.00**

BALES, Mike

Goaltender. Catches left. 6'1", 200 lbs. Born, Prince Albert, Sask., August 6, 1971
(Boston's 4th choice, 105th overall, in 1990 Entry Draft).

Season	Club	Regular Season GP	W	L	T	Mins	GA	SO	Avg	Playoffs GP	W	L	Mins	GA	SO	Avg
1992-93	Boston	1	0	0	0	25	1	0	2.40	....	....	....	....	....	....	....
1994-95	Ottawa	1	0	0	0	3	0	0	0.00	....	....	....	....	....	....	....
1995-96	Ottawa	20	2	14	1	1040	72	0	4.15	....	....	....	....	....	....	....
1996-97	Ottawa	1	0	1	0	52	4	0	4.62	....	....	....	....	....	....	....
	NHL Totals	**23**	**2**	**15**	**1**	**1120**	**77**	**0**	**4.13**	....	....	....	....	....	....	....

Signed as a free agent by **Ottawa**, July 4, 1994. Signed as a free agent by **Buffalo**, September 9, 1997. Signed as a free agent by **Dallas**, July 8, 1998.

BANNERMAN, Murray

Goaltender. Catches left. 5'11", 185 lbs. Born, Fort Frances, Ont., April 27, 1957
(Vancouver's 5th choice, 58th overall, in 1977 Amateur Draft).

Season	Club	Regular Season GP	W	L	T	Mins	GA	SO	Avg	Playoffs GP	W	L	Mins	GA	SO	Avg
1977-78	Vancouver	1	0	0	0	20	0	0	0.00	....	....	....	....	....	....	....
1980-81	Chicago	15	2	10	2	865	62	0	4.30	....	....	....	....	....	....	....
1981-82	Chicago	29	11	12	4	1671	116	1	4.17	10	5	4	555	35	0	3.78
1982-83	Chicago	41	24	12	5	2460	127	4	3.10	8	4	4	480	32	0	4.00
1983-84	Chicago	56	23	29	4	3335	188	2	3.38	5	2	3	300	17	0	3.40
1984-85	Chicago	60	27	25	4	3371	215	0	3.83	15	9	6	906	72	0	4.77
1985-86	Chicago	48	20	19	6	2689	201	1	4.48	2	0	1	81	9	0	6.67
1986-87	Chicago	39	9	18	8	2059	142	0	4.14	....	....	....	....	....	....	....
	NHL Totals	**289**	**116**	**125**	**33**	**16470**	**1051**	**8**	**3.83**	**40**	**20**	**18**	**2322**	**165**	**0**	**4.26**

Played in NHL All-Star Game (1983, 1984)

Traded to **Chicago** by **Vancouver** to complete transaction that sent Pit Martin to Vancouver (November 4, 1977), May 27, 1978.

BARON, Marco

Goaltender. Catches left. 5'11", 180 lbs. Born, Montreal, Que., April 8, 1959
(Boston's 6th choice, 99th overall, in 1979 Entry Draft).

Season	Club	Regular Season GP	W	L	T	Mins	GA	SO	Avg	Playoffs GP	W	L	Mins	GA	SO	Avg
1979-80	Boston	1	0	0	0	40	2	0	3.00	....	....	....	....	....	....	....
1980-81	Boston	10	3	4	1	507	24	0	2.84	1	0	1	20	3	0	9.00
1981-82	Boston	44	22	16	4	2515	144	1	3.44	....	....	....	....	....	....	....
1982-83	Boston	9	6	3	0	516	33	0	3.84	....	....	....	....	....	....	....
1983-84	Los Angeles	21	3	14	4	1211	87	0	4.31	....	....	....	....	....	....	....
1984-85	Edmonton	1	0	1	0	33	2	0	3.64	....	....	....	....	....	....	....
	NHL Totals	**86**	**34**	**38**	**9**	**4822**	**292**	**1**	**3.63**	**1**	**0**	**1**	**20**	**3**	**0**	**9.00**

Traded to **Los Angeles** by **Boston** for Bob LaForest, January 3, 1984. Signed as a free agent by **Edmonton**, February 21, 1985.

BARRASSO, Tom

Goaltender. Catches right. 6'3", 210 lbs. Born, Boston, MA, March 31, 1965
(Buffalo's 1st choice, 5th overall, in 1983 Entry Draft).

Season	Club	Regular Season GP	W	L	T	Mins	GA	SO	Avg	Playoffs GP	W	L	Mins	GA	SO	Avg
1983-84	Buffalo	42	26	12	3	2475	117	2	2.84	3	0	2	139	8	0	3.45
1984-85	Buffalo	54	25	18	10	3248	144	*5	*2.66	5	2	3	300	22	0	4.40
1985-86	Buffalo	60	29	24	5	3561	214	2	3.61	....	....	....	....	....	....	....
1986-87	Buffalo	46	17	23	2	2501	152	2	3.65	....	....	....	....	....	....	....
1987-88	Buffalo	54	25	18	8	3133	173	2	3.31	4	1	3	224	16	0	4.29
1988-89	Buffalo	10	2	7	0	545	45	0	4.95	....	....	....	....	....	....	....
	Pittsburgh	44	18	15	7	2406	162	0	4.04	11	7	4	631	40	0	3.80
1989-90	Pittsburgh	24	7	12	3	1294	101	0	4.68	....	....	....	....	....	....	....
1990-91 ♦	Pittsburgh	48	27	16	3	2754	165	1	3.59	20	12	7	1175	51	*1	*2.60
1991-92 ♦	Pittsburgh	57	25	22	9	3329	196	1	3.53	*21	*16	5	*1233	58	1	2.82
1992-93	Pittsburgh	63	*43	14	5	3702	186	4	3.01	12	7	5	722	35	*2	2.91
1993-94	Pittsburgh	44	22	15	5	2482	139	2	3.36	6	2	4	356	17	0	2.87
1994-95	Pittsburgh	2	0	1	1	125	8	0	3.84	2	0	1	80	8	0	6.00
1995-96	Pittsburgh	49	29	16	2	2799	160	2	3.43	10	4	5	558	26	1	2.80
1996-97	Pittsburgh	5	0	5	0	270	26	0	5.78	....	....	....	....	....	....	....
1997-98	Pittsburgh	63	31	14	13	3542	122	7	2.07	6	2	4	376	17	0	2.71
1998-99	Pittsburgh	43	19	16	3	2306	98	4	2.55	13	6	7	787	35	1	2.67
99-2000	Pittsburgh	18	5	7	2	870	46	1	3.17	....	....	....	....	....	....	....
	Ottawa	7	3	4	0	418	22	0	3.16	6	2	4	372	16	0	2.58
2001-02	Carolina	34	13	12	5	1908	83	2	2.61	....	....	....	....	....	....	....
	Toronto	4	2	2	0	219	10	0	2.74	....	....	....	....	....	....	....
2002-03	St. Louis	6	1	4	0	293	16	1	3.28	....	....	....	....	....	....	....
	NHL Totals	**777**	**369**	**277**	**86**	**44180**	**2385**	**38**	**3.24**	**119**	**61**	**54**	**6953**	**349**	**6**	**3.01**

NHL All-Rookie Team (1984) • NHL First All-Star Team (1984) • Calder Memorial Trophy (1984) • Vezina Trophy (1984) • NHL Second All-Star Team (1985, 1993) • Shared William M. Jennings Trophy with Bob Sauve (1985)

Played in NHL All-Star Game (1985)

Traded to **Pittsburgh** by **Buffalo** with Buffalo's 3rd round choice (Joe Dziedzic) in 1990 Entry Draft for Doug Bodger and Darrin Shannon, November 12, 1988. • Missed majority of 1994-95 season recovering from wrist surgery, January 20, 1995. • Missed majority of 1996-97 season recovering from shoulder injury suffered in game vs. Montreal, February 5, 1996. Traded to **Ottawa** by **Pittsburgh** for Ron Tugnutt and Janne Laukkanen, March 14, 2000. • Missed entire 2000-01 season for personal reasons. Signed as a free agent by **Carolina**, July 17, 2001. Traded to **Toronto** by **Carolina** for Toronto's 4th round choice (Kevin Nastiuk) in 2003 Entry Draft, March 15, 2002. Signed as a free agent by **St. Louis**, November 1, 2002. Signed as a free agent by **Pittsburgh**, June 18, 2003. • Officially announced retirement, June 18, 2003.

BASSEN, Hank

Goaltender. Catches left. 5'10", 180 lbs. Born, Calgary, Alta., December 6, 1932

Season	Club	Regular Season GP	W	L	T	Mins	GA	SO	Avg	Playoffs GP	W	L	Mins	GA	SO	Avg
1954-55	Chicago	21	4	9	8	1260	63	0	3.00	....	....	....	....	....	....	....
1955-56	Chicago	12	2	9	1	720	40	1	3.33	....	....	....	....	....	....	....
1960-61	Detroit	35	13	13	8	2050	100	0	2.93	4	1	2	220	9	0	2.45
1961-62	Detroit	27	9	12	6	1620	75	3	2.78	....	....	....	....	....	....	....
1962-63	Detroit	16	6	5	5	960	51	0	3.19	....	....	....	....	....	....	....
1963-64	Detroit	1	0	1	0	60	4	0	4.00	....	....	....	....	....	....	....
1965-66	Detroit	11	3	3	0	406	17	0	2.51	1	0	1	54	2	0	2.22
1966-67	Detroit	8	2	4	0	384	22	0	3.44	....	....	....	....	....	....	....
1967-68	Pittsburgh	25	7	10	3	1299	62	1	2.86	....	....	....	....	....	....	....
	NHL Totals	**156**	**46**	**66**	**31**	**8759**	**434**	**5**	**2.97**	**5**	**1**	**3**	**274**	**11**	**0**	**2.41**

• Father of Bob

Traded to **Detroit** by **Chicago** with Johnny Wilson, Forbes Kennedy and Bill Preston for Ted Lindsay and Glenn Hall, July 23, 1957. Traded to **Springfield** (AHL) by **Detroit** with Dennis Olson and Bill McCreary for Gerry Ehman, May 1, 1958. Traded to **Vancouver** (WHL) by **Springfield** (AHL) for Colin Kilburn and $7,500, July, 1959. Claimed by **Detroit** from **Vancouver** (WHL) in Inter-League Draft, June, 1960. Traded to **Pittsburgh** by **Detroit** for Roy Edwards, September 7, 1967.

BASTIEN, Baz

Goaltender. Catches left. 5'7", 160 lbs. Born, Timmins, Ont., August 29, 1919

Season	Club	Regular Season GP	W	L	T	Mins	GA	SO	Avg	Playoffs GP	W	L	Mins	GA	SO	Avg
1945-46	Toronto	5	0	4	1	300	20	0	4.00	....	....	....	....	....	....	....
	NHL Totals	**5**	**0**	**4**	**1**	**300**	**20**	**0**	**4.00**	....	....	....	....	....	....	....

BAUMAN, Gary

Goaltender. Catches left. 5'11", 175 lbs. Born, Innisfail, Alta., July 21, 1940

Season	Club	Regular Season GP	W	L	T	Mins	GA	SO	Avg	Playoffs GP	W	L	Mins	GA	SO	Avg
1966-67	Montreal	2	1	1	0	120	5	0	2.50	....	....	....	....	....	....	....
1967-68	Minnesota	26	5	13	5	1294	75	0	3.48	....	....	....	....	....	....	....
1968-69	Minnesota	7	0	4	1	304	22	0	4.34	....	....	....	....	....	....	....
	NHL Totals	**35**	**6**	**18**	**6**	**1718**	**102**	**0**	**3.56**	....	....	....	....	....	....	....

Played in NHL All-Star Game (1967)

Signed as a free agent by **Montreal**, September 20, 1964. Claimed by **Minnesota** from **Montreal** in Expansion Draft, June 6, 1967. Claimed by **Vancouver** (WHL) from **Minnesota** in Reverse Draft, June 12, 1969.

BEAUPRE, Don

Goaltender. Catches left. 5'10", 172 lbs. Born, Waterloo, Ont., September 19, 1961
(Minnesota's 2nd choice, 37th overall, in 1980 Entry Draft).

Season	Club	Regular Season GP	W	L	T	Mins	GA	SO	Avg	Playoffs GP	W	L	Mins	GA	SO	Avg
1980-81	Minnesota	44	18	14	11	2585	138	0	3.20	6	4	2	360	26	0	4.33
1981-82	Minnesota	29	11	8	9	1634	101	0	3.71	2	0	1	60	4	0	4.00
1982-83	Minnesota	36	19	10	5	2011	120	0	3.58	4	2	2	245	20	0	4.90
1983-84	Minnesota	33	16	13	2	1791	123	0	4.12	13	6	7	782	40	1	3.07
1984-85	Minnesota	31	10	17	3	1770	109	1	3.69	4	1	1	184	12	0	3.91
1985-86	Minnesota	52	25	20	6	3073	182	1	3.55	5	2	3	300	17	0	3.40
1986-87	Minnesota	47	17	20	6	2622	174	1	3.98	....	....	....	....	....	....	....
1987-88	Minnesota	43	10	22	3	2288	161	0	4.22	....	....	....	....	....	....	....
1988-89	Minnesota	1	0	1	0	59	3	0	3.05	....	....	....	....	....	....	....
	Washington	11	5	4	0	578	28	1	2.91	....	....	....	....	....	....	....
1989-90	Washington	48	23	18	5	2793	150	2	3.22	8	4	3	401	18	0	2.69
1990-91	Washington	45	20	18	3	2572	113	*5	2.64	11	5	5	624	29	*1	2.79
1991-92	Washington	54	29	17	6	3108	166	1	3.20	7	3	4	419	22	0	3.15
1992-93	Washington	58	27	23	5	3282	181	1	3.31	2	1	1	119	9	0	4.54
1993-94	Washington	53	24	16	8	2853	135	2	2.84	8	5	2	429	21	1	2.94
1994-95	Ottawa	38	8	25	3	2161	121	1	3.36	....	....	....	....	....	....	....
1995-96	Ottawa	33	6	23	0	1770	110	1	3.73	....	....	....	....	....	....	....
	Toronto	8	0	5	0	336	26	0	4.64	2	0	0	20	2	0	6.00
1996-97	Toronto	3	0	3	0	110	10	0	5.45	....	....	....	....	....	....	....
	NHL Totals	**667**	**268**	**277**	**75**	**37396**	**2151**	**17**	**3.45**	**72**	**33**	**31**	**3943**	**220**	**3**	**3.35**

Played in NHL All-Star Game (1981, 1992)

Traded to **Washington** by **Minnesota** for the rights to Claudio Scremin, November 1, 1988. Traded to **Ottawa** by **Washington** for Ottawa's 5th round choice (Benoit Gratton) in 1995 Entry Draft, January 18, 1995. Traded to **NY Islanders** by **Ottawa** with Martin Straka and Bryan Berard for Damian Rhodes and Wade Redden, January 23, 1996. Traded to **Toronto** by **NY Islanders** with Kirk Muller to complete transaction that sent Damian Rhodes and Ken Belanger to NY Islanders (January 23, 1996), January 23, 1996.

BEAUREGARD, Stephane

Goaltender. Catches right. 5'11", 190 lbs. Born, Cowansville, Que., January 10, 1968
(Winnipeg's 3rd choice, 52nd overall, in 1988 Entry Draft).

Season	Club	Regular Season GP	W	L	T	Mins	GA	SO	Avg	Playoffs GP	W	L	Mins	GA	SO	Avg
1989-90	Winnipeg	19	7	8	3	1079	59	0	3.28	4	1	3	238	12	0	3.03
1990-91	Winnipeg	16	3	10	1	836	55	0	3.95	....	....	....	....	....	....	....
1991-92	Winnipeg	26	6	8	6	1267	61	2	2.89	....	....	....	....	....	....	....
1992-93	Philadelphia	16	3	9	0	802	59	0	4.41	....	....	....	....	....	....	....
1993-94	Winnipeg	13	0	4	1	418	34	0	4.88	....	....	....	....	....	....	....
	NHL Totals	**90**	**19**	**39**	**11**	**4402**	**268**	**2**	**3.65**	**4**	**1**	**3**	**238**	**12**	**0**	**3.03**

Traded to **Buffalo** by **Winnipeg** for Christian Ruuttu and future considerations, June 15, 1992. Traded to **Chicago** by **Buffalo** with Buffalo's 4th round choice (Eric Daze) in 1993 Entry Draft for Dominik Hasek, August 7, 1992. Traded to **Winnipeg** by **Chicago** for Christian Ruuttu, August 10, 1992. Traded to **Philadelphia** by **Winnipeg** for future considerations, October 1, 1992. Traded to **Winnipeg** by **Philadelphia** for future considerations, June 11, 1993. Signed as a free agent by **Washington**, August 20, 1997.

BEDARD, Jim

Goaltender. Catches left. 5'10", 181 lbs. Born, Niagara Falls, Ont., November 14, 1956
(Washington's 6th choice, 91st overall, in 1976 Amateur Draft).

Season	Club	Regular Season GP	W	L	T	Mins	GA	SO	Avg	Playoffs GP	W	L	Mins	GA	SO	Avg
1977-78	Washington	43	11	23	7	2492	152	1	3.66	....	....	....	....	....	....	....
1978-79	Washington	30	6	17	6	1740	126	0	4.34	....	....	....	....	....	....	....
	NHL Totals	**73**	**17**	**40**	**13**	**4232**	**278**	**1**	**3.94**	....	....	....	....	....	....	....

BEHREND, Marc

Goaltender. Catches left. 6'1", 180 lbs. Born, Madison, WI, January 11, 1961
(Winnipeg's 5th choice, 85th overall, in 1981 Entry Draft).

Season	Club	Regular Season GP	W	L	T	Mins	GA	SO	Avg	Playoffs GP	W	L	Mins	GA	SO	Avg
1983-84	Winnipeg	6	2	4	0	351	32	0	5.47	2	0	2	121	9	0	4.46
1984-85	Winnipeg	24	8	10	3	1218	87	1	4.45	4	1	1	179	10	0	3.35

		REGULAR SEASON								PLAYOFFS						
Season	Club	GP	W	L	T	Mins	GA	SO	Avg	GP	W	L	Mins	GA	SO	Avg
1985-86	Winnipeg	9	2	5	0	422	41	0	5.83	1	0	0	12	0	0	0.00
	NHL Totals	**39**	**12**	**19**	**3**	**1991**	**160**	**1**	**4.82**	**7**	**1**	**3**	**312**	**19**	**0**	**3.65**

BELANGER, Yves

Goaltender. Catches left. 5'11", 170 lbs. Born, Baie Comeau, Que., September 30, 1952

Season	Club	GP	W	L	T	Mins	GA	SO	Avg	GP	W	L	Mins	GA	SO	Avg
1974-75	St. Louis	11	6	3	2	640	29	1	2.72	....	....	....	....	....	....	....
1975-76	St. Louis	31	11	17	1	1763	113	0	3.85	....	....	....	....	....	....	....
1976-77	St. Louis	3	2	0	0	140	7	0	3.00	....	....	....	....	....	....	....
1977-78	St. Louis	3	0	3	0	144	15	0	6.25	....	....	....	....	....	....	....
	Atlanta	17	7	8	0	937	55	1	3.52	....	....	....	....	....	....	....
1978-79	Atlanta	5	1	2	0	182	21	0	6.92	....	....	....	....	....	....	....
1979-80	Boston	8	2	0	3	328	19	0	3.48	....	....	....	....	....	....	....
	NHL Totals	**78**	**29**	**33**	**6**	**4134**	**259**	**2**	**3.76**	....	....	....	....	....	....	....

Traded to **St. Louis** by **Cleveland** (WHA) for cash, August, 1974. Traded to **Atlanta** by **St. Louis** with Bob MacMillan, Dick Redmond and St. Louis' 2nd round choice (Mike Perovich) in 1979 Entry Draft for Phil Myre, Curt Bennett and Barry Gibbs, December 12, 1977. Signed as a free agent by **Boston**, October 8, 1979.

BELFOUR, Ed

Goaltender. Catches left. 5'11", 192 lbs. Born, Carman, Man., April 21, 1965

Season	Club	GP	W	L	T	Mins	GA	SO	Avg	GP	W	L	Mins	GA	SO	Avg
1988-89	Chicago	23	4	12	3	1148	74	0	3.87	....	....	....	....	....	....	....
1989-90	Chicago	....	....	....	....	....	....	....	....	9	4	2	409	17	0	2.49
1990-91	Chicago	*74	*43	19	7	*4127	170	4	*2.47	6	2	4	295	20	0	4.07
1991-92	Chicago	52	21	18	10	2928	132	*5	2.70	18	12	4	949	39	1	*2.47
1992-93	Chicago	*71	41	18	11	*4106	177	*7	2.59	4	0	4	249	13	0	3.13
1993-94	Chicago	70	37	24	6	3998	178	*7	2.67	6	2	4	360	15	0	2.50
1994-95	Chicago	42	22	15	3	2450	93	*5	2.28	16	9	7	1014	37	1	2.19
1995-96	Chicago	50	22	17	10	2956	135	1	2.74	9	6	3	666	23	1	*2.07
1996-97	Chicago	33	11	15	6	1966	88	1	2.69	....	....	....	....	....	....	....
	San Jose	13	3	9	0	757	43	1	3.41	....	....	....	....	....	....	....
1997-98	Dallas	61	37	12	10	3581	112	9	*1.88	17	10	7	1039	31	1	*1.79
1998-99◆	Dallas	61	35	15	9	3536	117	5	1.99	*23	*16	7	*1544	43	*3	*1.67
99-2000	Dallas	62	32	21	7	3620	127	4	2.10	*23	14	9	1443	45	*4	1.87
2000-01	Dallas	63	35	20	7	3687	144	8	2.34	10	4	6	671	25	0	2.24
2001-02	Dallas	60	21	27	11	3467	153	1	2.65	....	....	....	....	....	....	....
2002-03	Toronto	62	37	20	5	3738	141	7	2.26	7	3	4	532	24	0	2.71
	NHL Totals	**797**	**401**	**262**	**105**	**46065**	**1884**	**65**	**2.45**	**148**	**82**	**61**	**9171**	**332**	**11**	**2.17**

NHL All-Rookie Team (1991) • NHL First All-Star Team (1991, 1993) • Trico Goaltender Award (1991) • Calder Memorial Trophy (1991) • William M. Jennings Trophy (1991, 1993, 1995) • Vezina Trophy (1991, 1993) • NHL Second All-Star Team (1995) • Shared William M. Jennings Trophy with Roman Turek (1999) • MBNA Roger Crozier Saving Grace Award (2000)

Played in NHL All-Star Game (1992, 1993, 1996, 1998, 1999)

Signed as a free agent by **Chicago**, September 25, 1987. Traded to **San Jose** by **Chicago** for Chris Terreri, Ulf Dahlen and Michal Sykora, January 25, 1997. Signed as a free agent by **Dallas**, July 2, 1997. Traded to **Nashville** by **Dallas** with Cameron Mann for David Gosselin and Nashville's 5th round choice (Eero Kilpelainen) in 2003 Entry Draft, June 29, 2002. Signed as a free agent by **Toronto**, July 2, 2002.

BELHUMEUR, Michel

Goaltender. Catches left. 5'10", 160 lbs. Born, Sorel, Que., September 2, 1949
(Philadelphia's 4th choice, 40th overall, in 1969 Amateur Draft).

Season	Club	GP	W	L	T	Mins	GA	SO	Avg	GP	W	L	Mins	GA	SO	Avg
1972-73	Philadelphia	23	9	7	3	1117	60	0	3.22	1	0	0	10	1	0	6.00
1974-75	Washington	35	0	24	3	1812	162	0	5.36	....	....	....	....	....	....	....
1975-76	Washington	7	0	5	1	377	32	0	5.09	....	....	....	....	....	....	....
	NHL Totals	**65**	**9**	**36**	**7**	**3306**	**254**	**0**	**4.61**	**1**	**0**	**0**	**10**	**1**	**0**	**6.00**

Claimed by **Washington** from **Philadelphia** in Expansion Draft, June 12, 1974. Signed as a free agent by **Atlanta**, October 7, 1976.

BELL, Gordie

Goaltender. Catches left. 5'10", 164 lbs. Born, Portage la Prairie, Man., March 13, 1925

Season	Club	GP	W	L	T	Mins	GA	SO	Avg	GP	W	L	Mins	GA	SO	Avg
1945-46	Toronto	8	3	5	0	480	31	0	3.88	....	....	....	....	....	....	....
1955-56	NY Rangers	....	....	....	....	....	....	....	....	2	1	1	120	9	0	4.50
	NHL Totals	**8**	**3**	**5**	**0**	**480**	**31**	**0**	**3.88**	**2**	**1**	**1**	**120**	**9**	**0**	**4.50**

• Brother of Joe

Claimed by **NY Rangers** from **Buffalo** (AHL) in Inter-League Draft, May 8, 1943. • Rights returned to **Buffalo** (AHL) by **NY Rangers** after failing to come to contract terms. Traded to **Toronto** by **Buffalo** (AHL) for cash, September 22, 1945. Traded to **Washington** (AHL) by **Toronto** for cash with Toronto retaining right of recall, October 5, 1947. Traded to **Springfield** (AHL) by **Toronto** with Armand Lemieux, Leo Curick and Rod Roy for Eldie Kobussen, April 20, 1948. Traded to **Montreal** (Buffalo-AHL) by **Springfield** (AHL) with the rights to Sid McNabney for Hub Macey, December 21, 1948. Signed as a free agent by **NY Rangers**, March 22, 1956.

BENEDICT, Clint

HHOF

Goaltender. Catches left. Born, Ottawa, Ont., September 26, 1892

Season	Club	GP	W	L	T	Mins	GA	SO	Avg	GP	W	L	Mins	GA	SO	Avg
1917-18	Ottawa	*22	9	13	0	*1337	114	*1	5.12	....	....	....	....	....	....	....
1918-19	Ottawa	*18	*12	6	0	*1152	53	*2	*2.76	5	1	4	300	26	0	5.20
1919-20◆	Ottawa	*24	*19	5	0	1443	64	*5	*2.66	....	....	....	....	....	....	....
	Ottawa (Cup)	....	....	....	....	....	....	....	....	*5*	*3*	*2*	*300*	*11*	*1*	*2.20*
1920-21◆	Ottawa	*24	*14	10	0	*1462	75	*2	*3.08	2	2	0	120	0	2	*0.00
	Ottawa (Cup)	....	....	....	....	....	....	....	....	*5*	*3*	*2*	*300*	*12*	*0*	*2.40*
1921-22	Ottawa	*24	*14	8	2	*1510	84	*2	*3.34	2	0	1	120	5	1	2.50
1922-23◆	Ottawa	*24	*14	9	1	1486	54	*4	*2.18	2	1	1	120	2	1	*1.00
	Ottawa (Cup)	....	....	....	....	....	....	....	....	*6*	*5*	*1*	*361*	*8*	*1*	*1.33*
1923-24	Ottawa	22	*15	7	0	1356	45	*3	1.99	2	0	2	120	5	0	2.50
1924-25	Mtl. Maroons	*30	9	19	2	1843	65	2	2.12	....	....	....	....	....	....	....
1925-26◆	Mtl. Maroons	*36	20	11	5	*2288	73	6	1.91	4	2	0	240	5	1	1.25
	Maroons (Cup)	....	....	....	....	....	....	....	....	*4*	*3*	*1*	*240*	*3*	*3*	*0.75*
1926-27	Mtl. Maroons	43	20	19	4	2748	65	13	*1.42	2	0	1	132	2	0	0.91
1927-28	Mtl. Maroons	*44	24	14	6	2690	76	7	1.70	*9	*5	3	*555	8	*4	*0.86
1928-29	Mtl. Maroons	37	14	16	7	2300	57	11	1.49	....	....	....	....	....	....	....
1929-30	Mtl. Maroons	14	6	6	1	752	38	0	3.03	....	....	....	....	....	....	....
	NHL Totals	**362**	**190**	**143**	**28**	**22367**	**863**	**58**	**2.32**	**28**	**11**	**12**	**1707**	**53**	**9**	**1.86**

Rights retained by **Ottawa** after NHA folded, November 26, 1917. • 1922-23 Stanley Cup totals includes series with Regina (WCHL) and Edmonton (PCHA). Traded to **Mtl. Maroons** by **Ottawa** with Punch Broadbent for cash, October 20, 1924. • First goaltender to wear a facemask in a NHL game, February 20, 1930. (Mtl. Maroons 3, NY Americans 3)

BENNETT, Harvey

Goaltender. Catches left. 6', 175 lbs. Born, Edington, Sask., July 23, 1925

Season	Club	GP	W	L	T	Mins	GA	SO	Avg	GP	W	L	Mins	GA	SO	Avg
1944-45	Boston	25	10	12	2	1470	103	0	4.20	....	....	....	....	....	....	....
	NHL Totals	**25**	**10**	**12**	**2**	**1470**	**103**	**0**	**4.20**	....	....	....	....	....	....	....

• Father of Harvey Jr., Curt and Bill

BERGERON, Jean-Claude

Goaltender. Catches left. 6'2", 192 lbs. Born, Hauterive, Que., October 14, 1968
(Montreal's 6th choice, 104th overall, in 1988 Entry Draft).

Season	Club	GP	W	L	T	Mins	GA	SO	Avg	GP	W	L	Mins	GA	SO	Avg
1990-91	Montreal	18	7	6	2	941	59	0	3.76	....	....	....	....	....	....	....
1992-93	Tampa Bay	21	8	10	1	1163	71	0	3.66	....	....	....	....	....	....	....
1993-94	Tampa Bay	3	1	1	1	134	7	0	3.13	....	....	....	....	....	....	....
1994-95	Tampa Bay	17	3	9	1	883	49	1	3.33	....	....	....	....	....	....	....
1995-96	Tampa Bay	12	2	6	2	595	42	0	4.24	....	....	....	....	....	....	....
1996-97	Los Angeles	1	0	1	0	56	4	0	4.29	....	....	....	....	....	....	....
	NHL Totals	**72**	**21**	**33**	**7**	**3772**	**232**	**1**	**3.69**	....	....	....	....	....	....	....

Traded to **Tampa Bay** by **Montreal** for Frederic Chabot, June 19, 1992. Signed as a free agent by **Los Angeles**, August 28, 1996.

BERNHARDT, Tim

Goaltender. Catches left. 5'9", 160 lbs. Born, Sarnia, Ont., January 17, 1958
(Atlanta's 2nd choice, 47th overall, in 1978 Amateur Draft).

Season	Club	GP	W	L	T	Mins	GA	SO	Avg	GP	W	L	Mins	GA	SO	Avg
1982-83	Calgary	6	0	5	0	280	21	0	4.50	....	....	....	....	....	....	....
1984-85	Toronto	37	13	19	4	2182	136	0	3.74	....	....	....	....	....	....	....
1985-86	Toronto	23	4	12	3	1266	107	0	5.07	....	....	....	....	....	....	....
1986-87	Toronto	1	0	0	0	20	3	0	9.00	....	....	....	....	....	....	....
	NHL Totals	**67**	**17**	**36**	**7**	**3748**	**267**	**0**	**4.27**	....	....	....	....	....	....	....

Transferred to **Calgary** after **Atlanta** franchise relocated, June 24, 1980. Signed as a free agent by **Toronto**, December 5, 1984.

BERTHIAUME, Daniel

Goaltender. Catches left. 5'9", 155 lbs. Born, Longueuil, Que., January 26, 1966
(Winnipeg's 3rd choice, 60th overall, in 1985 Entry Draft).

Season	Club	GP	W	L	T	Mins	GA	SO	Avg	GP	W	L	Mins	GA	SO	Avg
1985-86	Winnipeg	....	....	....	....	....	....	....	....	1	0	1	68	4	0	3.53
1986-87	Winnipeg	31	18	7	3	1758	93	1	3.17	8	4	4	439	21	0	2.87
1987-88	Winnipeg	56	22	19	7	3010	176	2	3.51	5	1	4	300	25	0	5.00
1988-89	Winnipeg	9	0	8	0	443	44	0	5.96	....	....	....	....	....	....	....
1989-90	Winnipeg	24	10	11	3	1387	86	1	3.72	....	....	....	....	....	....	....
	Minnesota	5	1	3	0	240	14	0	3.50	....	....	....	....	....	....	....
1990-91	Los Angeles	37	20	11	4	2119	117	1	3.31	....	....	....	....	....	....	....
1991-92	Los Angeles	19	7	10	1	979	66	0	4.04	....	....	....	....	....	....	....
	Boston	8	1	4	2	399	21	0	3.16	....	....	....	....	....	....	....
1992-93	Ottawa	25	2	17	1	1326	95	0	4.30	....	....	....	....	....	....	....
1993-94	Ottawa	1	0	0	0	1	2	0	120.00	....	....	....	....	....	....	
....																
	NHL Totals	**215**	**81**	**90**	**21**	**11662**	**714**	**5**	**3.67**	**14**	**5**	**9**	**807**	**50**	**0**	**3.72**

Traded to **Minnesota** by **Winnipeg** for future considerations, January 22, 1990. Traded to **Los Angeles** by **Minnesota** for Craig Duncanson, September 6, 1990. Traded to **Boston** by **Los Angeles** for future considerations, January 18, 1992. Traded to **Winnipeg** by **Boston** for Doug Evans, June 10, 1992. Signed as a free agent by **Ottawa**, December 15, 1992. Traded to **Detroit** by **Ottawa** for Steve Konroyd, March 21, 1994.

BESTER, Allan

Goaltender. Catches left. 5'7", 155 lbs. Born, Hamilton, Ont., March 26, 1964
(Toronto's 3rd choice, 49th overall, in 1983 Entry Draft).

Season	Club	GP	W	L	T	Mins	GA	SO	Avg	GP	W	L	Mins	GA	SO	Avg
1983-84	Toronto	32	11	16	4	1848	134	0	4.35	....	....	....	....	....	....	....
1984-85	Toronto	15	3	9	1	767	54	1	4.22	....	....	....	....	....	....	....
1985-86	Toronto	1	0	0	0	20	2	0	6.00	....	....	....	....	....	....	....
1986-87	Toronto	36	10	14	3	1808	110	2	3.65	1	0	0	39	1	0	1.54
1987-88	Toronto	30	8	12	5	1607	102	2	3.81	5	2	3	253	21	0	4.98
1988-89	Toronto	43	17	20	3	2460	156	2	3.80	....	....	....	....	....	....	....
1989-90	Toronto	42	20	16	0	2206	165	0	4.49	4	0	3	196	14	0	4.29
1990-91	Toronto	6	0	4	0	247	18	0	4.37	....	....	....	....	....	....	....
	Detroit	3	0	3	0	178	13	0	4.38	1	0	0	20	1	0	3.00
1991-92	Detroit	1	0	0	0	31	2	0	3.87	....	....	....	....	....	....	....
1995-96	Dallas	10	4	5	1	601	30	0	3.00	....	....	....	....	....	....	....
	NHL Totals	**219**	**73**	**99**	**17**	**11773**	**786**	**7**	**4.01**	**11**	**2**	**6**	**508**	**37**	**0**	**4.37**

Traded to **Detroit** by **Toronto** for Detroit's 6th round choice (Alexander Kuzminsky) in 1991 Entry Draft, March 5, 1991. Signed as a free agent by **Anaheim**, September 9, 1993. Signed as a free agent by **Dallas**, January 21, 1996.

BEVERIDGE, Bill

Goaltender. Catches left. 5'8", 170 lbs. Born, Ottawa, Ont., July 1, 1909

Season	Club	GP	W	L	T	Mins	GA	SO	Avg	GP	W	L	Mins	GA	SO	Avg
1929-30	Detroit	39	14	20	5	2410	109	2	2.71	....	....	....	....	....	....	....
1930-31	Ottawa	9	0	8	0	520	32	0	3.69	....	....	....	....	....	....	....
1932-33	Ottawa	35	7	19	8	2195	95	5	2.60	....	....	....	....	....	....	....
1933-34	Ottawa	*48	13	29	6	3000	143	3	2.86	....	....	....	....	....	....	....
1934-35	St. Louis	*48	11	31	6	2990	144	3	2.89	....	....	....	....	....	....	....

Season	Club	GP	W	L	T	Mins	GA	SO	Avg	GP	W	L	Mins	GA	SO	Avg
		REGULAR SEASON								PLAYOFFS						
1935-36	Mtl. Maroons	32	14	13	5	1970	71	1	2.16							
1936-37	Mtl. Maroons	21	12	6	3	1290	47	1	2.19	5	2	3	300	11	0	2.20
1937-38	Mtl. Maroons	*48	12	30	6	2980	149	2	3.00							
1942-43	NY Rangers	17	4	10	3	1020	89	1	5.24							
	NHL Totals	**297**	**87**	**166**	**42**	**18375**	**879**	**18**	**2.87**	**5**	**2**	**3**	**300**	**11**	**0**	**2.20**

Loaned to **Detroit** by **Ottawa** for the 1929-30 season for cash, November 27, 1929. Transferred to **St. Louis** after **Ottawa** franchise relocated, September 22, 1934. Claimed by **Montreal** from **St. Louis** in Dispersal Draft, October 15, 1935. Traded to **Mtl. Maroons** by **Montreal** for cash, October, 1935. Loaned to **NY Rangers** by **Cleveland** (AHL) to replace injured Jimmy Franks, January 26, 1943.

BIBEAULT, Paul

Goaltender. Catches left. 5'9", 160 lbs. Born, Montreal, Que., April 13, 1919

Season	Club	GP	W	L	T	Mins	GA	SO	Avg	GP	W	L	Mins	GA	SO	Avg
1940-41	Montreal	4	1	2	0	210	15	0	4.29							
1941-42	Montreal	38	17	19	2	2380	131	1	3.30	3	1	2	180	8	*1	2.67
1942-43	Montreal	*50	19	19	12	3010	191	1	3.81	5	1	4	320	18	1	3.38
1943-44	Toronto	29	13	14	2	1740	87	*5	3.00	5	1	4	300	23	0	4.60
1944-45	Boston	26	6	18	2	1530	116	0	4.55	7	3	4	437	22	0	3.02
1945-46	Boston	16	8	4	4	960	45	2	2.81							
	Montreal	10	4	6	0	600	30	0	3.00							
1946-47	Chicago	41	13	25	3	2460	170	1	4.15							
	NHL Totals	**214**	**81**	**107**	**25**	**12890**	**785**	**10**	**3.65**	**20**	**6**	**14**	**1237**	**71**	**2**	**3.44**

Signed as a free agent by **Montreal**, March 6, 1941. Loaned to **Toronto** by **Montreal** for remainder of 1943-44 season, December 22, 1943. Loaned to **Boston** by **Montreal** as a war-time replacement for Frank Brimsek, December 27, 1944. Returned to **Montreal** by **Boston** as an injury replacement for Bill Durnan, January 6, 1946. Mike McMahon was loaned to **Boston** on January 8, 1946 as compensation for recalling Bibeault. Traded to **Chicago** by **Montreal** for George Allen with both teams holding right of recall, September 23, 1946. • Players returned to original teams, June 2, 1947.

BIERK, Zac

Goaltender. Catches left. 6'4", 205 lbs. Born, Peterborough, Ont., September 17, 1976
(Tampa Bay's 8th choice, 212th overall, in 1995 Entry Draft).

Season	Club	GP	W	L	T	Mins	GA	SO	Avg	GP	W	L	Mins	GA	SO	Avg
1997-98	Tampa Bay	13	1	4	1	433	30	0	4.16							
1998-99	Tampa Bay	1	0	1	0	59	2	0	2.03							
99-2000	Tampa Bay	12	4	4	1	509	31	0	3.65							
2000-01	Minnesota	1	0	1	0	60	6	0	6.00							
2002-03	Phoenix	16	4	9	1	884	32	1	2.17							
	NHL Totals	**43**	**9**	**19**	**3**	**1945**	**101**	**1**	**3.12**							

Claimed by **Minnesota** from **Tampa Bay** in Expansion Draft, June 23, 2000. Signed as a free agent by **Phoenix**, August 30, 2001.

BILLINGTON, Craig

Goaltender. Catches left. 5'10", 170 lbs. Born, London, Ont., September 11, 1966
(New Jersey's 2nd choice, 23rd overall, in 1984 Entry Draft).

Season	Club	GP	W	L	T	Mins	GA	SO	Avg	GP	W	L	Mins	GA	SO	Avg
1985-86	New Jersey	18	4	9	1	901	77	0	5.13							
1986-87	New Jersey	22	4	13	2	1114	89	0	4.79							
1988-89	New Jersey	3	1	1	0	140	11	0	4.71							
1991-92	New Jersey	26	13	7	1	1363	69	2	3.04							
1992-93	New Jersey	42	21	16	4	2389	146	2	3.67	2	0	1	78	5	0	3.85
1993-94	Ottawa	63	11	41	4	3319	254	0	4.59							
1994-95	Ottawa	9	0	6	2	472	32	0	4.07							
	Boston	8	5	1	0	373	19	0	3.06	1	0	0	25	1	0	2.40
1995-96	Boston	27	10	13	3	1380	79	1	3.43	1	0	1	60	6	0	6.00
1996-97	Colorado	23	11	8	2	1200	53	1	2.65	1	0	0	20	1	0	3.00
1997-98	Colorado	23	8	7	4	1162	45	1	2.32	1	0	0	1	0	0	0.00
1998-99	Colorado	21	11	8	1	1086	52	0	2.87	1	0	0	9	1	0	6.67
99-2000	Washington	13	3	6	1	611	28	2	2.75	1	0	0	20	1	0	3.00
2000-01	Washington	12	3	5	2	660	27	0	2.45							
2001-02	Washington	17	4	5	3	710	36	0	3.04							
2002-03	Washington	5	1	3	1	217	17	0	4.70							
	NHL Totals	**332**	**110**	**149**	**31**	**17097**	**1034**	**9**	**3.63**	**8**	**0**	**2**	**213**	**15**	**0**	**4.23**

Played in NHL All-Star Game (1993)

Traded to **Ottawa** by **New Jersey** with Troy Mallette and New Jersey's 4th round choice (Cosmo Dupaul) in 1993 Entry Draft for Peter Sidorkiewicz and future considerations (Mike Peluso, June 26, 1993), June 20, 1993. Traded to **Boston** by **Ottawa** for NY Islanders' 8th round choice (previously acquired, Ottawa selected Ray Schultz) in 1995 Entry Draft, April 7, 1995. Signed as a free agent by **Florida**, September 5, 1996. Claimed by **Colorado** from **Florida** in Waiver Draft, September 30, 1996. Traded to **Washington** by **Colorado** for future considerations, July 16, 1999. • Officially announced retirement, January 7, 2003.

BINETTE, Andre

Goaltender. Catches left. 5'8", 140 lbs. Born, Montreal, Que., December 2, 1933

Season	Club	GP	W	L	T	Mins	GA	SO	Avg	GP	W	L	Mins	GA	SO	Avg
1954-55	Montreal	1	1	0	0	60	4	0	4.00							
	NHL Totals	**1**	**1**	**0**	**0**	**60**	**4**	**0**	**4.00**							

Promoted to **Montreal** from **Montreal Royals** (QHL) to replace injured Jacques Plante, November 11, 1954. (Montreal 7, Chicago 4)

BINKLEY, Les

Goaltender. Catches right. 6', 175 lbs. Born, Owen Sound, Ont., June 6, 1934

Season	Club	GP	W	L	T	Mins	GA	SO	Avg	GP	W	L	Mins	GA	SO	Avg
1967-68	Pittsburgh	54	20	24	10	3141	151	6	2.88							
1968-69	Pittsburgh	50	10	31	8	2885	158	0	3.29							
1969-70	Pittsburgh	27	10	13	1	1477	79	3	3.21	7	5	2	428	15	0	2.10
1970-71	Pittsburgh	34	11	11	10	1870	89	2	2.86							
1971-72	Pittsburgh	31	7	15	5	1673	98	0	3.51							
	NHL Totals	**196**	**58**	**94**	**34**	**11046**	**575**	**11**	**3.12**	**7**	**5**	**2**	**428**	**15**	**0**	**2.10**

Traded to **Pittsburgh** by **San Diego** (WHL) for cash, October, 1967.

BIRON, Martin

Goaltender. Catches left. 6'2", 168 lbs. Born, Lac-St-Charles, Que., August 15, 1977
(Buffalo's 2nd choice, 16th overall, in 1995 Entry Draft).

Season	Club	GP	W	L	T	Mins	GA	SO	Avg	GP	W	L	Mins	GA	SO	Avg
1995-96	Buffalo	3	0	2	0	119	10	0	5.04							
1998-99	Buffalo	6	1	2	1	281	10	0	2.14							
99-2000	Buffalo	41	19	18	2	2229	90	5	2.42							
2000-01	Buffalo	18	7	7	1	918	39	2	2.55							
2001-02	Buffalo	72	31	28	10	4085	151	4	2.22							
2002-03	Buffalo	54	17	28	6	3170	135	4	2.56							
	NHL Totals	**194**	**75**	**85**	**20**	**10802**	**435**	**15**	**2.42**							

• Brother of Mathieu

BITTNER, Richard

Goaltender. Catches left. 6', 170 lbs. Born, New Haven, CT, January 12, 1922

Season	Club	GP	W	L	T	Mins	GA	SO	Avg	GP	W	L	Mins	GA	SO	Avg
1949-50	Boston	1	0	0	1	60	3	0	3.00							
	NHL Totals	**1**	**0**	**0**	**1**	**60**	**3**	**0**	**3.00**							

Promoted to **Boston** from **Boston** (EAHL) to replace injured Jack Gelineau, February 12, 1950. (Montreal 3, Boston 3)

BLACKBURN, Dan

Goaltender. Catches left. 6', 180 lbs. Born, Montreal, Que., May 20, 1983
(NY Rangers' 1st choice, 10th overall, in 2001 Entry Draft).

Season	Club	GP	W	L	T	Mins	GA	SO	Avg	GP	W	L	Mins	GA	SO	Avg
2001-02	NY Rangers	31	12	16	0	1737	95	0	3.28							
2002-03	NY Rangers	32	8	16	4	1762	93	1	3.17							
	NHL Totals	**63**	**20**	**32**	**4**	**3499**	**188**	**1**	**3.22**							

NHL All-Rookie Team (2002)

BLAKE, Mike

Goaltender. Catches left. 6', 185 lbs. Born, Kitchener, Ont., April 6, 1956

Season	Club	GP	W	L	T	Mins	GA	SO	Avg	GP	W	L	Mins	GA	SO	Avg
1981-82	Los Angeles	2	0	0	0	51	2	0	2.35							
1982-83	Los Angeles	9	4	4	0	432	30	0	4.17							
1983-84	Los Angeles	29	9	11	5	1634	118	0	4.33							
	NHL Totals	**40**	**13**	**15**	**5**	**2117**	**150**	**0**	**4.25**							

Signed as a free agent by **Los Angeles**, January 5, 1982.

BLUE, John

Goaltender. Catches left. 5'10", 185 lbs. Born, Huntington Beach, CA, February 19, 1966
(Winnipeg's 9th choice, 197th overall, in 1986 Entry Draft).

Season	Club	GP	W	L	T	Mins	GA	SO	Avg	GP	W	L	Mins	GA	SO	Avg
1992-93	Boston	23	9	8	4	1322	64	1	2.90	2	0	1	96	5	0	3.13
1993-94	Boston	18	5	8	3	944	47	0	2.99							
1995-96	Buffalo	5	2	2	0	255	15	0	3.53							
	NHL Totals	**46**	**16**	**18**	**7**	**2521**	**126**	**1**	**3.00**	**2**	**0**	**1**	**96**	**5**	**0**	**3.13**

Traded to **Minnesota** by **Winnipeg** for Minnesota's 7th round choice (Markus Akerblom) in 1988 Entry Draft, March 7, 1988. Signed as a free agent by **Boston**, August 1, 1991. Signed as a free agent by **Buffalo**, December 28, 1995.

BOISVERT, Gilles

Goaltender. Catches left. 5'8", 152 lbs. Born, Trois-Rivieres, Que., February 15, 1933

Season	Club	GP	W	L	T	Mins	GA	SO	Avg	GP	W	L	Mins	GA	SO	Avg
1959-60	Detroit	3	0	3	0	180	9	0	3.00							
	NHL Totals	**3**	**0**	**3**	**0**	**180**	**9**	**0**	**3.00**							

Claimed by **Boston** (Hershey-AHL) from **Mtl. Royals** (QHL) in Inter-League Draft, June 1, 1955. Traded to **Detroit** by **Boston** with Real Chevrefils, Norm Corcoran, Warren Godfrey and Ed Sandford for Terry Sawchuk, Marcel Bonin, Lorne Davis and Vic Stasiuk, June 3, 1955. Loaned to **Cleveland** (AHL) by **Detroit** (Sudbury-EPHL) for cash, November, 1959. Promoted to **Detroit** from **Cleveland** (AHL) to replace Terry Sawchuk in games on November 26, 28, 29, 1959. Traded to **Baltimore** (AHL) by **Detroit** for cash, June, 1963.

BOUCHARD, Dan

Goaltender. Catches left. 6', 190 lbs. Born, Val-d'Or, Que., December 12, 1950
(Boston's 5th choice, 27th overall, in 1970 Amateur Draft).

Season	Club	GP	W	L	T	Mins	GA	SO	Avg	GP	W	L	Mins	GA	SO	Avg
1972-73	Atlanta	34	9	15	10	1944	100	2	3.09							
1973-74	Atlanta	46	19	18	8	2660	123	5	2.77	1	0	1	60	4	0	4.00
1974-75	Atlanta	40	20	15	5	2400	111	3	2.78							
1975-76	Atlanta	47	19	17	8	2671	113	2	2.54	2	0	2	120	3	0	1.50
1976-77	Atlanta	42	17	17	5	2378	139	1	3.51	1	0	1	60	5	0	5.00
1977-78	Atlanta	58	25	12	19	3340	153	2	2.75	2	0	2	120	7	0	3.50
1978-79	Atlanta	*64	*32	21	7	3624	201	3	3.33	2	0	2	100	9	0	5.40
1979-80	Atlanta	53	23	19	10	3076	163	2	3.18	4	1	3	241	14	0	3.49
1980-81	Calgary	14	4	5	3	760	51	0	4.03							
	Quebec	29	19	5	5	1740	92	2	3.17	5	2	3	286	19	*1	3.99
1981-82	Quebec	60	27	22	11	3572	230	1	3.86	11	4	7	677	38	0	3.37
1982-83	Quebec	50	20	21	8	2947	197	1	4.01	4	1	3	242	11	0	2.73
1983-84	Quebec	57	29	18	8	3373	180	1	3.20	9	5	4	543	25	0	2.76
1984-85	Quebec	29	12	13	4	1738	101	0	3.49	1	0	1	60	7	0	7.00
1985-86	Winnipeg	32	11	14	2	1696	107	2	3.79	1	0	1	40	5	0	7.50
	NHL Totals	**655**	**286**	**232**	**113**	**37919**	**2061**	**27**	**3.26**	**43**	**13**	**30**	**2549**	**147**	**1**	**3.46**

Claimed by **Atlanta** from **Boston** in Expansion Draft, June 6, 1972. Transferred to **Calgary** after **Atlanta** franchise relocated, June 24, 1980. Traded to **Quebec** by **Calgary** for Jamie Hislop, January 30, 1981. Traded to **Winnipeg** by **Quebec** for Winnipeg's 7th round choice (Mark Vermette) in 1986 Entry Draft, October 14, 1985.

BOUCHER, Brian

Goaltender. Catches left. 6'2", 190 lbs. Born, Woonsocket, RI, January 2, 1977
(Philadelphia's 1st choice, 22nd overall, in 1995 Entry Draft).

Season	Club	GP	W	L	T	Mins	GA	SO	Avg	GP	W	L	Mins	GA	SO	Avg
99-2000	Philadelphia	35	20	10	3	2038	65	4	*1.91	18	11	7	1183	40	1	2.03

Season	Club	GP	W	L	T	Mins	GA	SO	Avg	GP	W	L	Mins	GA	SO	Avg
		REGULAR SEASON								PLAYOFFS						
2000-01	Philadelphia	27	8	12	5	1470	80	1	3.27	1	0	0	37	3	0	4.86
2001-02	Philadelphia	41	18	16	4	2295	92	2	2.41	2	0	1	88	2	0	1.36
2002-03	Phoenix	45	15	20	8	2544	128	0	3.02	....	....	....	....	....	....	....
	NHL Totals	**148**	**61**	**58**	**20**	**8347**	**365**	**7**	**2.62**	**21**	**11**	**8**	**1308**	**45**	**1**	**2.06**

NHL All-Rookie Team (2000)

Traded to **Phoenix** by **Philadelphia** with Nashville's 3rd round choice (previously acquired, Phoenix selected Joe Callahan) in 2002 Entry Draft for Michal Handzus and Robert Esche, June 12, 2002.

BOURQUE, Claude

Goaltender. Catches left. 5'6", 140 lbs. Born, Oxford, N.S., March 31, 1915

Season	Club	GP	W	L	T	Mins	GA	SO	Avg	GP	W	L	Mins	GA	SO	Avg
1938-39	Montreal	25	7	13	5	1560	69	2	2.65	3	1	2	188	8	1	2.55
1939-40	Montreal	36	9	24	3	2210	121	2	3.29	....	....	....	....	....	....	....
	Detroit	1	0	1	0	60	3	0	3.00	....	....	....	....	....	....	....
	NHL Totals	**62**	**16**	**38**	**8**	**3830**	**193**	**4**	**3.02**	**3**	**1**	**2**	**188**	**8**	**1**	**2.55**

Rights traded to **Montreal** by **Mtl. Maroons** for cash, September 14, 1938. Loaned to **Detroit** by **Montreal** to replace injured Tiny Thompson, February 15, 1940. (NY Rangers 3, Detroit 1). Traded to **NY Rangers** by **Montreal** for Bert Gardiner and cash, April 26, 1940.

BOUTIN, Rollie

Goaltender. Catches left. 5'9", 179 lbs. Born, Westlock, Alta., November 6, 1957
(Washington's 7th choice, 111th overall, in 1977 Amateur Draft).

Season	Club	GP	W	L	T	Mins	GA	SO	Avg	GP	W	L	Mins	GA	SO	Avg
1978-79	Washington	2	0	1	0	90	10	0	6.67	....	....	....	....	....	....	....
1979-80	Washington	18	7	7	1	927	54	0	3.50	....	....	....	....	....	....	....
1980-81	Washington	2	0	2	0	120	11	0	5.50	....	....	....	....	....	....	....
	NHL Totals	**22**	**7**	**10**	**1**	**1137**	**75**	**0**	**3.96**	....	....	....	....	....	....	....

Traded to **Minnesota** by **Washington** with Wes Jarvis for Robbie Moore and Minnesota's 11th round choice (Anders Huss) in 1983 Entry Draft, August 4, 1982. Signed as a free agent by **Hartford**, December 8, 1983.

BOUVRETTE, Lionel

Goaltender. Catches left. 5'9", 165 lbs. Born, Hawkesbury, Ont., June 10, 1914

Season	Club	GP	W	L	T	Mins	GA	SO	Avg	GP	W	L	Mins	GA	SO	Avg
1942-43	NY Rangers	1	0	1	0	60	6	0	6.00	....	....	....	....	....	....	....
	NHL Totals	**1**	**0**	**1**	**0**	**60**	**6**	**0**	**6.00**	....	....	....	....	....	....	....

Loaned to **NY Rangers** by **Montreal** (Quebec-QSHL) to replace injured Jimmy Franks, March 18, 1943. (Montreal 6, NY Rangers 3)

BOWER, Johnny

HHOF

Goaltender. Catches left. 5'11", 189 lbs. Born, Prince Albert, Sask., November 8, 1924

Season	Club	GP	W	L	T	Mins	GA	SO	Avg	GP	W	L	Mins	GA	SO	Avg
1953-54	NY Rangers	*70	29	31	10	*4200	182	5	2.60	....	....	....	....	....	....	....
1954-55	NY Rangers	5	2	2	1	300	13	0	2.60	....	....	....	....	....	....	....
1956-57	NY Rangers	2	0	2	0	120	6	0	3.00	....	....	....	....	....	....	....
1958-59	Toronto	39	15	17	7	2340	106	3	2.72	*12	5	7	*746	38	0	3.06
1959-60	Toronto	66	34	24	8	3960	177	5	2.68	*10	4	6	*645	31	0	2.88
1960-61	Toronto	58	*33	15	10	3480	145	2	*2.50	3	0	3	180	8	0	2.67
1961-62♦	Toronto	59	31	18	10	3540	151	2	2.56	10	*6	3	579	20	0	*2.07
1962-63♦	Toronto	42	20	15	7	2520	109	1	2.60	10	*8	2	600	16	*2	*1.60
1963-64♦	Toronto	51	24	16	11	3009	106	5	*2.11	*14	*8	6	*850	30	*2	*2.12
1964-65	Toronto	34	13	13	8	2040	81	3	*2.38	5	2	3	321	13	0	2.43
1965-66	Toronto	35	18	10	5	1998	75	3	*2.25	2	0	2	120	8	0	4.00
1966-67♦	Toronto	27	12	9	3	1431	63	2	2.64	4	2	0	183	5	*1	1.64
1967-68	Toronto	43	14	18	7	2239	84	4	2.25	....	....	....	....	....	....	....
1968-69	Toronto	20	5	4	3	779	37	2	2.85	4	0	2	154	11	0	4.29
1969-70	Toronto	1	0	1	0	60	5	0	5.00	....	....	....	....	....	....	....
	NHL Totals	**552**	**250**	**195**	**90**	**32016**	**1340**	**37**	**2.51**	**74**	**35**	**34**	**4378**	**180**	**5**	**2.47**

NHL First All-Star Team (1961) • Vezina Trophy (1961) • Shared Vezina Trophy with Terry Sawchuk (1965)

Played in NHL All-Star Game (1961, 1962, 1963, 1964)

• Also known as John Kizkan. Traded to **NY Rangers** by **Cleveland** (AHL) with Eldred Kobussen for Emile Francis, Neil Strain and cash, July 20, 1953. Traded to **Cleveland** (AHL) by **NY Rangers** for Ed MacQueen and cash, July 31, 1957. Claimed by **Toronto** from **Cleveland** (AHL) in Inter-League Draft, June 3, 1958.

BRATHWAITE, Fred

Goaltender. Catches left. 5'7", 175 lbs. Born, Ottawa, Ont., November 24, 1972

Season	Club	GP	W	L	T	Mins	GA	SO	Avg	GP	W	L	Mins	GA	SO	Avg
1993-94	Edmonton	19	3	10	3	982	58	0	3.54	....	....	....	....	....	....	....
1994-95	Edmonton	14	2	5	1	601	40	0	3.99	....	....	....	....	....	....	....
1995-96	Edmonton	7	0	2	0	293	12	0	2.46	....	....	....	....	....	....	....
1998-99	Calgary	28	11	9	7	1663	68	1	2.45	....	....	....	....	....	....	....
99-2000	Calgary	61	25	25	7	3448	158	5	2.75	....	....	....	....	....	....	....
2000-01	Calgary	49	15	17	10	2742	106	5	2.32	....	....	....	....	....	....	....
2001-02	St. Louis	25	9	11	4	1446	54	2	2.24	1	0	0	1	0	0	0.00
2002-03	St. Louis	30	12	9	4	1615	74	2	2.75	....	....	....	....	....	....	....
	NHL Totals	**233**	**77**	**88**	**36**	**12790**	**570**	**15**	**2.67**	**1**	**0**	**0**	**1**	**0**	**0**	**0.00**

Signed as a free agent by **Edmonton**, October 6, 1993. Signed as a free agent by **Calgary**, January 6, 1999. Traded to **St. Louis** by **Calgary** with Daniel Tkaczuk, Sergei Varlamov and Calgary's 9th round choice (Grant Jacobsen) in 2001 Entry Draft for Roman Turek and St. Louis' 4th round choice (Yegor Shastin) in 2001 Entry Draft, June 23, 2001. • Played 6 seconds of playoff game vs. Detroit, May 4, 2002. Signed as a free agent by **Columbus**, June 2, 2003.

BRIMSEK, Frank

USHOF HHOF

Goaltender. Catches left. 5'9", 170 lbs. Born, Eveleth, MN, September 26, 1915

Season	Club	GP	W	L	T	Mins	GA	SO	Avg	GP	W	L	Mins	GA	SO	Avg
1938-39♦	Boston	43	*33	9	1	2610	68	*10	*1.56	*12	*8	4	*863	18	1	*1.25
1939-40	Boston	*48	*31	12	5	2950	98	6	1.99	6	2	4	360	15	0	2.50
1940-41♦	Boston	*48	27	8	13	*3040	102	*6	2.01	*11	*8	3	*678	23	*1	*2.04
1941-42	Boston	47	24	17	6	2930	115	3	*2.35	5	2	3	307	16	0	3.13
1942-43	Boston	*50	24	17	9	3000	176	1	3.52	9	4	5	560	33	0	3.54
1945-46	Boston	34	16	14	4	2040	111	2	3.26	*10	5	5	*651	29	0	2.67
1946-47	Boston	*60	26	23	11	*3600	175	3	2.92	5	1	4	343	16	0	2.80
1947-48	Boston	*60	23	24	13	*3600	168	3	2.80	5	1	4	317	20	0	3.79
1948-49	Boston	54	26	20	8	3240	147	1	2.72	5	1	4	316	16	0	3.04
1949-50	Chicago	*70	22	38	10	*4200	244	5	3.49	....	....	....	....	....	....	....
	NHL Totals	**514**	**252**	**182**	**80**	**31210**	**1404**	**40**	**2.70**	**68**	**32**	**36**	**4395**	**186**	**2**	**2.54**

NHL First All-Star Team (1939, 1942) • Calder Trophy (1939) • Vezina Trophy (1939, 1942) • NHL Second All-Star Team (1940, 1941, 1943, 1946, 1947, 1948)

Played in NHL All-Star Game (1939, 1947, 1948)

Signed as a free agent by **Boston**, October 27, 1938. Traded to **Chicago** by **Boston** for cash, September 8, 1949.

BROCHU, Martin

Goaltender. Catches left. 6', 199 lbs. Born, Anjou, Que., March 10, 1973

Season	Club	GP	W	L	T	Mins	GA	SO	Avg	GP	W	L	Mins	GA	SO	Avg
1998-99	Washington	2	0	2	0	120	6	0	3.00	....	....	....	....	....	....	....
2001-02	Vancouver	6	0	3	0	216	15	0	4.17	....	....	....	....	....	....	....
	NHL Totals	**8**	**0**	**5**	**0**	**336**	**21**	**0**	**3.75**	....	....	....	....	....	....	....

Signed as a free agent by **Montreal**, September 22, 1992. Traded to **Washington** by **Montreal** for future considerations, March 15, 1996. Signed as a free agent by **Calgary**, August 25, 2000. Signed as a free agent by **Minnesota**, July 17, 2001. Claimed by **Vancouver** from **Minnesota** in Waiver Draft, September 28, 2001.

BRODA, Turk

HHOF

Goaltender. Catches left. 5'9", 180 lbs. Born, Brandon, Man., May 15, 1914

Season	Club	GP	W	L	T	Mins	GA	SO	Avg	GP	W	L	Mins	GA	SO	Avg
1936-37	Toronto	45	22	19	4	2770	106	3	2.30	2	0	2	133	5	0	2.26
1937-38	Toronto	*48	24	15	9	2980	127	6	2.56	7	4	3	452	13	1	1.73
1938-39	Toronto	*48	19	20	9	*2990	107	8	2.15	10	5	5	617	20	*2	1.94
1939-40	Toronto	47	25	17	5	2900	108	4	2.23	10	6	4	657	19	1	1.74
1940-41	Toronto	*48	*28	14	6	2970	99	5	*2.00	7	3	4	438	15	0	2.05
1941-42♦	Toronto	*48	27	18	3	*2960	136	*6	2.76	*13	*8	5	*780	31	*1	2.38
1942-43	Toronto	*50	22	19	9	3000	159	1	3.18	6	2	4	439	20	0	2.73
1945-46	Toronto	15	6	6	3	900	53	0	3.53	....	....	....	....	....	....	....
1946-47♦	Toronto	*60	31	19	10	*3600	172	4	2.87	*11	*8	3	680	27	*1	2.38
1947-48♦	Toronto	*60	*32	15	13	*3600	143	5	*2.38	9	*8	1	557	20	*1	*2.15
1948-49♦	Toronto	*60	22	25	13	*3600	161	5	2.68	9	*8	1	574	15	*1	*1.57
1949-50	Toronto	68	30	25	12	4040	167	*9	2.48	7	3	4	450	10	*3	*1.33
1950-51♦	Toronto	31	14	11	5	1827	68	6	2.23	8	*5	1	492	9	*2	1.10
1951-52	Toronto	1	0	1	0	30	3	0	6.00	2	0	2	120	7	0	3.50
	NHL Totals	**629**	**302**	**224**	**101**	**38167**	**1609**	**62**	**2.53**	**101**	**60**	**39**	**6389**	**211**	**13**	**1.98**

NHL First All-Star Team (1941, 1948) • Vezina Trophy (1941, 1948) • NHL Second All-Star Team (1942)

Played in NHL All-Star Game (1947, 1948, 1949, 1950)

Traded to **Toronto** by **Detroit** (Detroit-IHL) for $8,000, May 6, 1936.

BRODERICK, Ken

Goaltender. Catches right. 5'10", 178 lbs. Born, Toronto, Ont., February 16, 1942

Season	Club	GP	W	L	T	Mins	GA	SO	Avg	GP	W	L	Mins	GA	SO	Avg
1969-70	Minnesota	7	2	4	0	360	26	0	4.33	....	....	....	....	....	....	....
1973-74	Boston	5	2	2	1	300	16	0	3.20	....	....	....	....	....	....	....
1974-75	Boston	15	7	6	0	804	32	1	2.39	....	....	....	....	....	....	....
	NHL Totals	**27**	**11**	**12**	**1**	**1464**	**74**	**1**	**3.03**	....	....	....	....	....	....	....

• Brother of Len

Rights traded to **Minnesota** by **Toronto** for cash, June 6, 1967. Signed as a free agent by **San Diego** (WHL), June 12, 1971. Traded to **Boston** by **San Diego** (WHL) for cash and future considerations (John Adams, June 12, 1973), March 10, 1973.

BRODERICK, Len

Goaltender. Catches left. 5'11", 175 lbs. Born, Toronto, Ont., October 11, 1938

Season	Club	GP	W	L	T	Mins	GA	SO	Avg	GP	W	L	Mins	GA	SO	Avg
1957-58	Montreal	1	1	0	0	60	2	0	2.00	....	....	....	....	....	....	....
	NHL Totals	**1**	**1**	**0**	**0**	**60**	**2**	**0**	**2.00**	....	....	....	....	....	....	....

• Brother of Ken

Loaned to **Montreal** by **Toronto** (Toronto/OHA-Jr.) to replace Jacques Plante, October 30, 1957. (Montreal 6, Toronto 2)

BRODEUR, Martin

Goaltender. Catches left. 6'2", 210 lbs. Born, Montreal, Que., May 6, 1972
(New Jersey's 1st choice, 20th overall, in 1990 Entry Draft).

Season	Club	GP	W	L	T	Mins	GA	SO	Avg	GP	W	L	Mins	GA	SO	Avg
1991-92	New Jersey	4	2	1	0	179	10	0	3.35	1	0	1	32	3	0	5.63
1993-94	New Jersey	47	27	11	8	2625	105	3	2.40	17	8	9	1171	38	1	1.95
1994-95♦	New Jersey	40	19	11	6	2184	89	3	2.45	*20	*16	4	*1222	34	*3	*1.67
1995-96	New Jersey	77	34	30	12	*4433	173	6	2.34	....	....	....	....	....	....	....
1996-97	New Jersey	67	37	14	13	3838	120	*10	*1.88	10	5	5	659	19	2	*1.73
1997-98	New Jersey	70	*43	17	8	4128	130	10	1.89	6	2	4	366	12	0	1.97
1998-99	New Jersey	*70	*39	21	10	*4239	162	4	2.29	7	3	4	425	20	0	2.82
99-2000♦	New Jersey	72	*43	20	8	4312	161	6	2.24	*23	*16	7	*1450	39	2	*1.61
2000-01	New Jersey	72	*42	17	11	4297	166	9	2.32	*25	15	10	*1505	52	*4	2.07
2001-02	New Jersey	*73	38	26	9	*4347	156	4	2.15	6	2	4	381	9	1	1.42
2002-03♦	New Jersey	73	*41	23	9	4374	147	*9	2.02	24	*16	8	*1491	41	*7	1.65
	NHL Totals	**665**	**365**	**191**	**94**	**38956**	**1419**	**64**	**2.19**	**139**	**83**	**56**	**8702**	**267**	**20**	**1.84**

NHL All-Rookie Team (1994) • Calder Memorial Trophy (1994) • NHL Second All-Star Team (1997, 1998) • Shared William M. Jennings Trophy with Mike Dunham (1997) • William M. Jennings Trophy (1998) • NHL First All-Star Team (2003) • William M. Jennings Trophy (tied with Roman Cechmanek/Robert Esche) (2003) • Vezina Trophy (2003)

Played in NHL All-Star Game (1996, 1997, 1998, 1999, 2000, 2001, 2003)

• Scored a goal in playoffs vs. Montreal, April 17, 1997.

BRODEUR, Richard

Goaltender. Catches left. 5'7", 160 lbs. Born, Longueuil, Que., September 15, 1952
(NY Islanders' 7th choice, 97th overall, in 1972 Amateur Draft).

Season	Club	GP	W	L	T	Mins	GA	SO	Avg	GP	W	L	Mins	GA	SO	Avg
		REGULAR SEASON								PLAYOFFS						
1979-80	NY Islanders	2	1	0	0	80	6	0	4.50	....	....	....	....	....	....	....
1980-81	Vancouver	52	17	18	16	3024	177	0	3.51	3	0	3	185	13	0	4.22
1981-82	Vancouver	52	20	18	12	3010	168	2	3.35	17	11	6	1089	49	0	2.70
1982-83	Vancouver	58	21	26	8	3291	208	0	3.79	3	0	3	193	13	0	4.04
1983-84	Vancouver	36	10	21	5	2110	141	1	4.01	4	1	3	222	12	1	3.24
1984-85	Vancouver	51	16	27	6	2930	228	0	4.67	....	....	....	....	....	....	....
1985-86	Vancouver	*64	19	32	8	*3541	240	2	4.07	2	0	2	120	12	0	6.00
1986-87	Vancouver	53	20	25	5	2972	178	1	3.59	....	....	....	....	....	....	....
1987-88	Vancouver	11	3	6	2	670	49	0	4.39	....	....	....	....	....	....	....
	Hartford	6	4	2	0	340	15	0	2.65	4	1	3	200	12	0	3.60
	NHL Totals	**385**	**131**	**175**	**62**	**21968**	**1410**	**6**	**3.85**	**33**	**13**	**20**	**2009**	**111**	**1**	**3.32**

Reclaimed by **NY Islanders** from **Quebec** prior to Expansion Draft, June 9, 1979. Claimed as a priority selection by **Quebec**, June 9, 1979. Traded to **NY Islanders** by **Quebec** for Goran Hogasta, August, 1979. Traded to **Vancouver** by **NY Islanders** with NY Islanders' 5th round choice (Moe Lemay) in 1981 Entry Draft for Vancouver's 5th round choice (Jacques Sylvestre) in 1981 Entry Draft, October 6, 1980. Traded to **Hartford** by **Vancouver** for Steve Weeks, March 8, 1988.

BROMLEY, Gary

Goaltender. Catches left. 5'10", 160 lbs. Born, Edmonton, Alta., January 19, 1950

Season	Club	GP	W	L	T	Mins	GA	SO	Avg	GP	W	L	Mins	GA	SO	Avg
1973-74	Buffalo	12	3	5	3	598	33	0	3.31	....	....	....	....	....	....	....
1974-75	Buffalo	50	26	11	11	2787	144	4	3.10	....	....	....	....	....	....	....
1975-76	Buffalo	1	0	1	0	60	7	0	7.00	....	....	....	....	....	....	....
1978-79	Vancouver	38	11	19	6	2144	136	2	3.81	3	1	2	180	14	0	4.67
1979-80	Vancouver	15	8	2	4	860	43	1	3.00	4	1	3	180	11	0	3.67
1980-81	Vancouver	20	6	6	4	978	62	0	3.80	....	....	....	....	....	....	....
	NHL Totals	**136**	**54**	**44**	**28**	**7427**	**425**	**7**	**3.43**	**7**	**2**	**5**	**360**	**25**	**0**	**4.17**

Signed as a free agent by **Buffalo**, September 29, 1971. Signed as a free agent by **Vancouver**, May 23, 1978. Traded to **Los Angeles** by **Vancouver** to complete transaction that sent Doug Halward to Vancouver (March 8, 1981), May 12, 1981.

BROOKS, Art

Goaltender. Born, Guelph, Ont., 1892

Season	Club	GP	W	L	T	Mins	GA	SO	Avg	GP	W	L	Mins	GA	SO	Avg
1917-18	Toronto	4	2	2	0	220	23	0	6.27	....	....	....	....	....	....	....
	NHL Totals	**4**	**2**	**2**	**0**	**220**	**23**	**0**	**6.27**	....	....	....	....	....	....	....

Signed as a free agent by **Toronto**, December 15, 1917.

BROOKS, Ross

Goaltender. Catches left. 5'8", 173 lbs. Born, Toronto, Ont., October 17, 1937

Season	Club	GP	W	L	T	Mins	GA	SO	Avg	GP	W	L	Mins	GA	SO	Avg
1972-73	Boston	16	11	1	3	910	40	1	2.64	1	0	0	20	3	0	9.00
1973-74	Boston	21	16	3	0	1170	46	3	2.36	....	....	....	....	....	....	....
1974-75	Boston	17	10	3	3	967	48	0	2.98	....	....	....	....	....	....	....
	NHL Totals	**54**	**37**	**7**	**6**	**3047**	**134**	**4**	**2.64**	**1**	**0**	**0**	**20**	**3**	**0**	**9.00**

Signed as a free agent by **Boston**, October 2, 1971.

BROPHY, Frank

Goaltender. Catches left. 5'6", 150 lbs. Born, Quebec City, Que., 1900

Season	Club	GP	W	L	T	Mins	GA	SO	Avg	GP	W	L	Mins	GA	SO	Avg
1919-20	Quebec	21	3	18	0	1249	148	0	7.11	....	....	....	....	....	....	....
	NHL Totals	**21**	**3**	**18**	**0**	**1249**	**148**	**0**	**7.11**	....	....	....	....	....	....	....

Signed as a free agent by **Quebec**, November 25, 1919.

BROWN, Andy

Goaltender. Catches left. 6', 185 lbs. Born, Hamilton, Ont., February 15, 1944

Season	Club	GP	W	L	T	Mins	GA	SO	Avg	GP	W	L	Mins	GA	SO	Avg
1971-72	Detroit	10	4	5	1	560	37	0	3.96	....	....	....	....	....	....	....
1972-73	Detroit	7	2	1	2	337	20	0	3.56	....	....	....	....	....	....	....
	Pittsburgh	9	3	4	2	520	41	0	4.73	....	....	....	....	....	....	....
1973-74	Pittsburgh	36	13	16	4	1956	115	1	3.53	....	....	....	....	....	....	....
	NHL Totals	**62**	**22**	**26**	**9**	**3373**	**213**	**1**	**3.79**	....	....	....	....	....	....	....

• Son of Adam

Claimed by **Detroit** from **Baltimore** (AHL) in Inter-League Draft, June 7, 1971. Traded to **Pittsburgh** by **Detroit** for Pittsburgh's 3rd round choice (Nelson Pyatt) in 1973 Amateur Draft and cash, February 25, 1973. • Last NHL goaltender to play without a facemask.

BROWN, Ken

Goaltender. Catches left. 5'11", 175 lbs. Born, Port Arthur, Ont., December 19, 1948

Season	Club	GP	W	L	T	Mins	GA	SO	Avg	GP	W	L	Mins	GA	SO	Avg
1970-71	Chicago	1	0	0	0	18	1	0	3.33	....	....	....	....	....	....	....
	NHL Totals	**1**	**0**	**0**	**0**	**18**	**1**	**0**	**3.33**	....	....	....	....	....	....	....

BRUNETTA, Mario

Goaltender. Catches left. 6'3", 180 lbs. Born, Quebec City, Que., January 25, 1967
(Quebec's 9th choice, 162nd overall, in 1985 Entry Draft).

Season	Club	GP	W	L	T	Mins	GA	SO	Avg	GP	W	L	Mins	GA	SO	Avg
1987-88	Quebec	29	10	12	1	1550	96	0	3.72	....	....	....	....	....	....	....
1988-89	Quebec	5	1	3	0	226	19	0	5.04	....	....	....	....	....	....	....
1989-90	Quebec	6	1	2	0	191	13	0	4.08	....	....	....	....	....	....	....
	NHL Totals	**40**	**12**	**17**	**1**	**1967**	**128**	**0**	**3.90**	....	....	....	....	....	....	....

BRYZGALOV, Ilja

Goaltender. Catches left. 6'3", 198 lbs. Born, Togliatti, USSR, June 22, 1980
(Anaheim's 2nd choice, 44th overall, in 2000 Entry Draft).

Season	Club	GP	W	L	T	Mins	GA	SO	Avg	GP	W	L	Mins	GA	SO	Avg
		REGULAR SEASON								PLAYOFFS						
2001-02	Anaheim	1	0	0	0	32	1	0	1.88	....	....	....	....	....	....	....
	NHL Totals	**1**	**0**	**0**	**0**	**32**	**1**	**0**	**1.88**	....	....	....	....	....	....	....

BULLOCK, Bruce

Goaltender. Catches right. 5'7", 160 lbs. Born, Toronto, Ont., May 9, 1949

Season	Club	GP	W	L	T	Mins	GA	SO	Avg	GP	W	L	Mins	GA	SO	Avg
1972-73	Vancouver	14	3	8	3	840	67	0	4.79	....	....	....	....	....	....	....
1974-75	Vancouver	1	0	1	0	60	4	0	4.00	....	....	....	....	....	....	....
1976-77	Vancouver	1	0	0	0	27	3	0	6.67	....	....	....	....	....	....	....
	NHL Totals	**16**	**3**	**9**	**3**	**927**	**74**	**0**	**4.79**	....	....	....	....	....	....	....

Traded to **Vancouver** (Seattle-WHL) by **Chicago** (Dallas-CHL) for cash, February 26, 1972.

BURKE, Sean

Goaltender. Catches left. 6'4", 211 lbs. Born, Windsor, Ont., January 29, 1967
(New Jersey's 2nd choice, 24th overall, in 1985 Entry Draft).

Season	Club	GP	W	L	T	Mins	GA	SO	Avg	GP	W	L	Mins	GA	SO	Avg
1987-88	New Jersey	13	10	1	0	689	35	1	3.05	17	9	8	1001	57	*1	3.42
1988-89	New Jersey	62	22	31	9	3590	230	3	3.84	....	....	....	....	....	....	....
1989-90	New Jersey	52	22	22	6	2914	175	0	3.60	2	0	2	125	8	0	3.84
1990-91	New Jersey	35	8	12	8	1870	112	0	3.59	....	....	....	....	....	....	....
1992-93	Hartford	50	16	27	3	2656	184	0	4.16	....	....	....	....	....	....	....
1993-94	Hartford	47	17	24	5	2750	137	2	2.99	....	....	....	....	....	....	....
1994-95	Hartford	42	17	19	4	2418	108	0	2.68	....	....	....	....	....	....	....
1995-96	Hartford	66	28	28	6	3669	190	4	3.11	....	....	....	....	....	....	....
1996-97	Hartford	51	22	22	6	2985	134	4	2.69	....	....	....	....	....	....	....
1997-98	Carolina	25	7	11	5	1415	66	1	2.80	....	....	....	....	....	....	....
	Vancouver	16	2	9	4	838	49	0	3.51	....	....	....	....	....	....	....
	Philadelphia	11	7	3	0	632	27	1	2.56	5	1	4	283	17	0	3.60
1998-99	Florida	59	21	24	14	3402	151	3	2.66	....	....	....	....	....	....	....
99-2000	Florida	7	2	5	0	418	18	0	2.58	....	....	....	....	....	....	....
	Phoenix	35	17	14	3	2074	88	3	2.55	5	1	4	296	16	0	3.24
2000-01	Phoenix	62	25	22	13	3644	138	4	2.27	....	....	....	....	....	....	....
2001-02	Phoenix	60	33	21	6	3587	137	5	2.29	5	1	4	297	13	0	2.63
2002-03	Phoenix	22	12	6	2	1248	44	2	2.12	....	....	....	....	....	....	....
	NHL Totals	**715**	**288**	**301**	**94**	**40799**	**2023**	**33**	**2.98**	**34**	**12**	**22**	**2002**	**111**	**1**	**3.33**

Played in NHL All-Star Game (1989, 2001, 2002)

Traded to **Hartford** by **New Jersey** with Eric Weinrich for Bobby Holik and Hartford's 2nd round choice (Jay Pandolfo) in 1993 Entry Draft, August 28, 1992. Transferred to **Carolina** after **Hartford** franchise relocated, June 25, 1997. Traded to **Vancouver** by **Carolina** with Geoff Sanderson and Enrico Ciccone for Kirk McLean and Martin Gelinas, January 3, 1998. Traded to **Philadelphia** by **Vancouver** for Garth Snow, March 4, 1998. Signed as a free agent by **Florida**, September 12, 1998. Traded to **Phoenix** by **Florida** with Florida's 5th round choice (Nate Kiser) in 2000 Entry Draft for Mikhail Shtalenkov and Phoenix's 4th round choice (Chris Eade) in 2000 Entry Draft, November 18, 1999.

BUZINSKI, Steve

Goaltender. Catches left. 5'8", 140 lbs. Born, Dunblane, Sask., October 15, 1917

Season	Club	GP	W	L	T	Mins	GA	SO	Avg	GP	W	L	Mins	GA	SO	Avg
1942-43	NY Rangers	9	2	6	1	560	55	0	5.89	....	....	....	....	....	....	....
	NHL Totals	**9**	**2**	**6**	**1**	**560**	**55**	**0**	**5.89**	....	....	....	....	....	....	....

Signed as a free agent by **NY Rangers** as a war-time replacement for Jim Henry, October, 1942.

CALEY, Don

Goaltender. Catches left. 5'10", 160 lbs. Born, Dauphin, Man., October 9, 1945

Season	Club	GP	W	L	T	Mins	GA	SO	Avg	GP	W	L	Mins	GA	SO	Avg
1967-68	St. Louis	1	0	0	0	30	3	0	6.00	....	....	....	....	....	....	....
	NHL Totals	**1**	**0**	**0**	**0**	**30**	**3**	**0**	**6.00**	....	....	....	....	....	....	....

Claimed by **St. Louis** from **Detroit** in Expansion Draft, June 6, 1967. Traded to **NY Rangers** by **St. Louis** with Wayne Rivers for Camille Henry, Bill Plager and Robbie Irons, June 13, 1968. Traded to **Phoenix** (WHL) by **NY Rangers** with Sandy Snow for Peter McDuffe, July 3, 1969.

CAPRICE, Frank

Goaltender. Catches left. 5'9", 150 lbs. Born, Hamilton, Ont., May 2, 1962
(Vancouver's 8th choice, 178th overall, in 1981 Entry Draft).

Season	Club	GP	W	L	T	Mins	GA	SO	Avg	GP	W	L	Mins	GA	SO	Avg
1982-83	Vancouver	1	0	0	0	20	3	0	9.00	....	....	....	....	....	....	....
1983-84	Vancouver	19	8	8	2	1098	62	1	3.39	....	....	....	....	....	....	....
1984-85	Vancouver	28	8	14	3	1523	122	0	4.81	....	....	....	....	....	....	....
1985-86	Vancouver	7	0	3	2	308	28	0	5.45	....	....	....	....	....	....	....
1986-87	Vancouver	25	8	11	2	1390	89	0	3.84	....	....	....	....	....	....	....
1987-88	Vancouver	22	7	10	2	1250	87	0	4.18	....	....	....	....	....	....	....
	NHL Totals	**102**	**31**	**46**	**11**	**5589**	**391**	**1**	**4.20**	....	....	....	....	....	....	....

CAREY, Jim

Goaltender. Catches left. 6'2", 205 lbs. Born, Dorchester, MA, May 31, 1974
(Washington's 2nd choice, 32nd overall, in 1992 Entry Draft).

Season	Club	GP	W	L	T	Mins	GA	SO	Avg	GP	W	L	Mins	GA	SO	Avg
1994-95	Washington	28	18	6	3	1604	57	4	2.13	7	2	4	358	25	0	4.19
1995-96	Washington	71	35	24	9	4069	153	*9	2.26	3	0	1	97	10	0	6.19
1996-97	Washington	40	17	18	3	2293	105	1	2.75	....	....	....	....	....	....	....
	Boston	19	5	13	0	1004	64	0	3.82	....	....	....	....	....	....	....
1997-98	Boston	10	3	2	1	496	24	2	2.90	....	....	....	....	....	....	....
1998-99	St. Louis	4	1	2	0	202	13	0	3.86	....	....	....	....	....	....	....
	NHL Totals	**172**	**79**	**65**	**16**	**9668**	**416**	**16**	**2.58**	**10**	**2**	**5**	**455**	**35**	**0**	**4.62**

NHL All-Rookie Team (1995) • NHL First All-Star Team (1996) • Vezina Trophy (1996)

Traded to **Boston** by **Washington** with Anson Carter, Jason Allison and Washington's 3rd round choice (Lee Goren) in 1997 Entry Draft for Bill Ranford, Adam Oates and Rick Tocchet, March 1, 1997. Signed as a free agent by **St. Louis**, March 1, 1999.

CARON, Jacques

Goaltender. Catches left. 6'2", 185 lbs. Born, Noranda, Que., April 21, 1940

		REGULAR SEASON								PLAYOFFS						
Season	Club	GP	W	L	T	Mins	GA	SO	Avg	GP	W	L	Mins	GA	SO	Avg
1967-68	Los Angeles	1	0	1	0	60	4	0	4.00							
1968-69	Los Angeles	3	0	1	0	140	9	0	3.86							
1971-72	St. Louis	28	14	8	5	1619	68	1	2.52	9	4	5	499	26	0	3.13
1972-73	St. Louis	30	8	14	5	1562	92	1	3.53	3	0	2	140	8	0	3.43
1973-74	Vancouver	10	2	5	1	465	38	0	4.90							
	NHL Totals	**72**	**24**	**29**	**11**	**3846**	**211**	**2**	**3.29**	**12**	**4**	**7**	**639**	**34**	**0**	**3.19**

Rights transferred to **Los Angeles** when NHL club purchased **Springfield** (AHL) franchise, May, 1967. Claimed by **St. Louis** (Denver-WHL) from **Los Angeles** in Reverse Draft, June 12, 1969. Claimed by **Vancouver** (Seattle-WHL) from **St. Louis** in Reverse Draft, June 15, 1973. Traded to **Buffalo** by **Vancouver** for future considerations, September 15, 1974.

CARON, Sebastian

Goaltender. Catches left. 6'1", 167 lbs. Born, Amqui, Que., June 25, 1980
(Pittsburgh's 4th choice, 86th overall, in 1999 Entry Draft).

Season	Club	GP	W	L	T	Mins	GA	SO	Avg	GP	W	L	Mins	GA	SO	Avg
2002-03	Pittsburgh	24	7	14	2	1408	62	2	2.64							
	NHL Totals	**24**	**7**	**14**	**2**	**1408**	**62**	**2**	**2.64**							

NHL All-Rookie Team (2003)

CARTER, Lyle

Goaltender. Catches left. 6'1", 185 lbs. Born, Truro, N.S., April 29, 1945

Season	Club	GP	W	L	T	Mins	GA	SO	Avg	GP	W	L	Mins	GA	SO	Avg
1971-72	California	15	4	7	0	721	50	0	4.16							
	NHL Totals	**15**	**4**	**7**	**0**	**721**	**50**	**0**	**4.16**							

Signed as a free agent by **Montreal** (Cleveland-AHL), March 30, 1968. Traded to **California** by **Montreal** with John French for Randy Rota, October, 1971. Claimed by **Minnesota** (Jacksonville-AHL) from **California** in Reverse Draft, June 10, 1973. Traded to **Syracuse** (AHL) by **Minnesota** for cash, August, 1974.

CASEY, Jon

Goaltender. Catches left. 5'10", 155 lbs. Born, Grand Rapids, MN, March 29, 1962

Season	Club	GP	W	L	T	Mins	GA	SO	Avg	GP	W	L	Mins	GA	SO	Avg
1983-84	Minnesota	2	1	0	0	84	6	0	4.29							
1985-86	Minnesota	26	11	11	1	1402	91	0	3.89							
1987-88	Minnesota	14	1	7	4	663	41	0	3.71							
1988-89	Minnesota	55	18	17	12	2961	151	1	3.06	4	1	3	211	16	0	4.55
1989-90	Minnesota	61	*31	22	4	3407	183	3	3.22	7	3	4	415	21	1	3.04
1990-91	Minnesota	55	21	20	11	3185	158	3	2.98	*23	*14	7	*1205	61	*1	3.04
1991-92	Minnesota	52	19	23	5	2911	165	2	3.40	7	3	4	437	22	0	3.02
1992-93	Minnesota	60	26	26	5	3476	193	3	3.33							
1993-94	Boston	57	30	15	9	3192	153	4	2.88	11	5	6	698	34	0	2.92
1994-95	St. Louis	19	7	5	4	872	40	0	2.75	2	0	1	30	2	0	4.00
1995-96	St. Louis	9	2	3	0	395	25	0	3.80	12	6	6	747	36	1	2.89
1996-97	St. Louis	15	3	8	0	707	40	0	3.39							
	NHL Totals	**425**	**170**	**157**	**55**	**23255**	**1246**	**16**	**3.21**	**66**	**32**	**31**	**3743**	**192**	**3**	**3.08**

Played in NHL All-Star Game (1993)

Signed as a free agent by **Minnesota**, April 1, 1984. Transferred to **Dallas** after **Minnesota** franchise relocated, June 9, 1993. Traded to **Boston** by **Dallas** for Andy Moog to complete transaction that sent Gord Murphy to Dallas (June 20, 1993), June 25, 1993. Signed as a free agent by **St. Louis**, June 29, 1994.

CASSIVI, Frederic

Goaltender. Catches left. 6'4", 220 lbs. Born, Sorel, Que., June 12, 1975
(Ottawa's 7th choice, 210th overall, in 1994 Entry Draft).

Season	Club	GP	W	L	T	Mins	GA	SO	Avg	GP	W	L	Mins	GA	SO	Avg
2001-02	Atlanta	6	2	3	0	307	17	0	3.32							
2002-03	Atlanta	2	1	1	0	123	11	0	5.37							
	NHL Totals	**8**	**3**	**4**	**0**	**430**	**28**	**0**	**3.91**							

Signed as a free agent by **Colorado**, August 17, 1999. Traded to **Atlanta** by **Colorado** for Brett Clark, January 24, 2002.

CECHMANEK, Roman

Goaltender. Catches left. 6'3", 187 lbs. Born, Gottwaldov, Czech., March 2, 1971
(Philadelphia's 3rd choice, 171st overall, in 2000 Entry Draft).

Season	Club	GP	W	L	T	Mins	GA	SO	Avg	GP	W	L	Mins	GA	SO	Avg
2000-01	Philadelphia	59	35	15	6	3431	115	10	2.01	6	2	4	347	18	0	3.11
2001-02	Philadelphia	46	24	13	6	2603	89	4	2.05	4	1	3	227	7	1	1.85
2002-03	Philadelphia	58	33	15	10	3350	102	6	1.83	13	6	7	867	31	2	2.15
	NHL Totals	**163**	**92**	**43**	**22**	**9384**	**306**	**20**	**1.96**	**23**	**9**	**14**	**1441**	**56**	**3**	**2.33**

NHL Second All-Star Team (2001) • Shared William M. Jennings Trophy with Robert Esche (tied with Martin Brodeur) (2003)

Played in NHL All-Star Game (2001)

Traded to **Los Angeles** by **Philadelphia** for Los Angeles' 2nd round choice in 2004 Entry Draft, May 28, 2003.

CENTOMO, Sebastien

Goaltender. Catches right. 6'1", 193 lbs. Born, Montreal, Que., March 26, 1981

Season	Club	GP	W	L	T	Mins	GA	SO	Avg	GP	W	L	Mins	GA	SO	Avg
2001-02	Toronto	1	0	0	0	40	3	0	4.50							
	NHL Totals	**1**	**0**	**0**	**0**	**40**	**3**	**0**	**4.50**							

Signed as a free agent by **Toronto**, September 10, 1999.

CHABOT, Frederic

Goaltender. Catches left. 5'11", 187 lbs. Born, Hebertville-Station, Que., February 12, 1968
(New Jersey's 10th choice, 192nd overall, in 1986 Entry Draft).

Season	Club	GP	W	L	T	Mins	GA	SO	Avg	GP	W	L	Mins	GA	SO	Avg
1990-91	Montreal	3	0	0	1	108	6	0	3.33							
1992-93	Montreal	1	0	0	0	40	1	0	1.50							
1993-94	Montreal	1	0	1	0	60	5	0	5.00							
	Philadelphia	4	0	1	1	70	5	0	4.29							
1997-98	Los Angeles	12	3	3	2	554	29	0	3.14							
1998-99	Montreal	11	1	3	0	430	16	0	2.23							
	NHL Totals	**32**	**4**	**8**	**4**	**1262**	**62**	**0**	**2.95**							

Signed as a free agent by **Montreal**, January 16, 1990. Claimed by **Tampa Bay** from **Montreal** in Expansion Draft, June 18, 1992. Traded to **Montreal** by **Tampa Bay** for Jean-Claude Bergeron, June 19, 1992. Traded to **Philadelphia** by **Montreal** for cash, February 21, 1994. Signed as a free agent by **Florida**, August 11, 1994. Signed as a free agent by **Los Angeles**, September 3, 1997. Claimed by **Nashville** from **Los Angeles** in Expansion Draft, June 26, 1998. Claimed on waivers by **Los Angeles** from **Nashville**, July 18, 1998. Claimed by **Montreal** from **Los Angeles** in Waiver Draft, October 5, 1998. Claimed by **Columbus** from **Montreal** in Expansion Draft, June 23, 2000.

CHABOT, Lorne

Goaltender. Catches left. 6'1", 185 lbs. Born, Montreal, Que., October 5, 1900

Season	Club	GP	W	L	T	Mins	GA	SO	Avg	GP	W	L	Mins	GA	SO	Avg
1926-27	NY Rangers	36	22	9	5	2307	56	10	1.46	2	0	1	120	3	1	1.50
1927-28◆	NY Rangers	*44	19	16	9	2730	79	11	1.74	6	2	2	321	8	1	1.50
1928-29	Toronto	43	20	18	5	2458	66	12	1.61	4	2	2	242	5	0	1.24
1929-30	Toronto	42	16	20	6	2620	113	6	2.59							
1930-31	Toronto	37	21	8	8	2300	80	6	2.09	2	0	1	139	4	0	1.73
1931-32◆	Toronto	44	22	16	6	2698	106	4	2.36	*7	*5	1	438	15	0	2.05
1932-33	Toronto	*48	24	18	6	2946	111	5	2.26	*9	4	5	*686	18	*2	1.57
1933-34	Montreal	47	21	20	6	2928	101	8	2.07	2	0	1	131	4	0	1.83
1934-35	Chicago	*48	26	17	5	2940	88	8	*1.80	2	0	1	124	1	1	0.48
1935-36	Mtl. Maroons	16	8	3	5	1010	35	2	2.08	3	0	3	297	6	0	*1.21
1936-37	NY Americans	6	2	3	1	370	25	1	4.05							
	NHL Totals	**411**	**201**	**148**	**62**	**25307**	**860**	**73**	**2.04**	**37**	**13**	**17**	**2498**	**64**	**5**	**1.54**

NHL First All-Star Team (1935) • Vezina Trophy (1935)

Signed as a free agent by **NY Rangers**, September 2, 1926. • Recorded shutout (2-0) in NHL debut vs. Montreal Canadiens, November 27, 1926. Traded to **Toronto** by **NY Rangers** with $10,000 for John Ross Roach, October 18, 1928. Traded to **Montreal** by **Toronto** for George Hainsworth, October 1, 1933. Traded to **Chicago** by **Montreal** with Howie Morenz and Marty Burke for Lionel Conacher, Roger Jenkins and Leroy Goldsworthy, October 3, 1934. • Missed majority of 1935-36 season recovering from knee injury suffered in training camp, October 23, 1935. Traded to **Montreal** by **Chicago** for cash, February 8, 1936. Traded to **Mtl. Maroons** by **Montreal** for Bill Miller, Toe Blake and the rights to Ken Grivel, February, 1936. Traded to **NY Americans** by **Mtl. Maroons** for cash, October 22, 1936.

CHADWICK, Ed

Goaltender. Catches left. 5'11", 184 lbs. Born, Fergus, Ont., May 8, 1933

Season	Club	GP	W	L	T	Mins	GA	SO	Avg	GP	W	L	Mins	GA	SO	Avg
1955-56	Toronto	5	2	0	3	300	3	2	0.60							
1956-57	Toronto	*70	21	34	15	*4200	186	5	2.66							
1957-58	Toronto	*70	21	38	11	*4200	223	4	3.19							
1958-59	Toronto	31	12	15	4	1860	92	3	2.97							
1959-60	Toronto	4	1	2	1	240	15	0	3.75							
1961-62	Boston	4	0	3	1	240	22	0	5.50							
	NHL Totals	**184**	**57**	**92**	**35**	**11040**	**541**	**14**	**2.94**							

Recalled by **Toronto** from **Winnipeg** (WHL) to replace injured Harry Lumley in games from February 8 – 15, 1956. Traded to **Boston** by **Toronto** for Don Simmons, January 31, 1961. Traded to **Detroit** (Hershey-AHL) by **Boston** with Barry Ashbee for Bob Perreault, June, 1962. Traded to **Chicago** by **Hershey** (AHL) for cash, August, 1964.

CHAMPOUX, Bob

Goaltender. Catches left. 5'10", 175 lbs. Born, Ste-Hilaire, Que., December 2, 1942

Season	Club	GP	W	L	T	Mins	GA	SO	Avg	GP	W	L	Mins	GA	SO	Avg
1963-64	Detroit									1	1	0	55	4	0	4.36
1973-74	California	17	2	11	3	923	80	0	5.20							
	NHL Totals	**17**	**2**	**11**	**3**	**923**	**80**	**0**	**5.20**	**1**	**1**	**0**	**55**	**4**	**0**	**4.36**

• **Detroit's** spare goaltender replaced injured Terry Sawchuk, March 29, 1964. (Detroit 5, Chicago 4). Loaned to **San Diego** (WHL) by **Detroit**, September, 1966. Traded to **San Diego** (WHL) by **Detroit** for cash, October, 1967. Loaned to **St. Louis** (Kansas City-CHL) by **San Diego** (WHL) for the loan of Gary Edwards, November, 1969. Signed as a free agent by **California** (Salt Lake-CHL) after securing release from **San Diego** (WHL), November, 1973.

CHARPENTIER, Sebastien

Goaltender. Catches left. 5'9", 177 lbs. Born, Drummondville, Que., April 18, 1977
(Washington's 4th choice, 93rd overall, in 1995 Entry Draft).

Season	Club	GP	W	L	T	Mins	GA	SO	Avg	GP	W	L	Mins	GA	SO	Avg
2001-02	Washington	2	1	1	0	122	5	0	2.46							
2002-03	Washington	17	5	7	1	859	40	0	2.79							
	NHL Totals	**19**	**6**	**8**	**1**	**981**	**45**	**0**	**2.75**							

CHEEVERS, Gerry

HHOF

Goaltender. Catches left. 5'11", 185 lbs. Born, St. Catharines, Ont., December 7, 1940

Season	Club	GP	W	L	T	Mins	GA	SO	Avg	GP	W	L	Mins	GA	SO	Avg
1961-62	Toronto	2	1	1	0	120	6	0	3.00							
1965-66	Boston	7	0	4	1	340	34	0	6.00							
1966-67	Boston	22	5	10	6	1298	72	1	3.33							
1967-68	Boston	47	23	17	5	2646	125	3	2.83	4	0	4	240	15	0	3.75
1968-69	Boston	52	28	12	12	3112	145	3	2.80	9	6	3	572	16	*3	1.68
1969-70◆	Boston	41	24	8	8	2384	108	4	2.72	*13	*12	1	*781	29	0	2.23
1970-71	Boston	40	27	8	5	2400	109	3	2.73	6	3	3	360	21	0	3.50
1971-72◆	Boston	41	27	5	8	2420	101	2	2.50	8	*6	2	483	21	*2	2.61
1975-76	Boston	15	8	2	5	900	41	1	2.73	6	2	4	392	14	1	2.14
1976-77	Boston	45	30	10	5	2700	137	3	3.04	*14	8	5	*858	44	1	3.08
1977-78	Boston	21	10	5	2	1086	48	1	2.65	12	8	4	731	35	1	2.87
1978-79	Boston	43	23	9	10	2509	132	1	3.16	6	4	2	360	15	0	2.50

		REGULAR SEASON								PLAYOFFS						
Season	Club	GP	W	L	T	Mins	GA	SO	Avg	GP	W	L	Mins	GA	SO	Avg
1979-80	Boston	42	24	11	7	2479	116	4	2.81	10	4	6	619	32	0	3.10
	NHL Totals	**418**	**230**	**102**	**74**	**24394**	**1174**	**26**	**2.89**	**88**	**53**	**34**	**5396**	**242**	**8**	**2.69**

Played in NHL All-Star Game (1969)

Promoted to **Toronto** from **Sault Ste. Marie** (EPHL) to replace injured Johnny Bower in games on December 2 (Toronto 6, Chicago 4) and December 3 (Detroit 3, Toronto 1), 1961. Claimed by **Boston** from **Toronto** in Intra-League Draft, June 9, 1965. Signed as a free agent by **Boston** after securing his release from **Cleveland** (WHA), January 27, 1976.

CHEVELDAE, Tim

Goaltender. Catches left. 5'10", 195 lbs. Born, Melville, Sask., February 15, 1968
(Detroit's 4th choice, 64th overall, in 1986 Entry Draft).

Season	Club	GP	W	L	T	Mins	GA	SO	Avg	GP	W	L	Mins	GA	SO	Avg
1988-89	Detroit	2	0	2	0	122	9	0	4.43	....	....	....	....	....	....	....
1989-90	Detroit	28	10	9	8	1600	101	0	3.79	....	....	....	....	....	....	....
1990-91	Detroit	65	30	26	5	3615	214	2	3.55	7	3	4	398	22	0	3.32
1991-92	Detroit	*72	*38	23	9	*4236	226	2	3.20	11	3	7	597	25	*2	2.51
1992-93	Detroit	67	34	24	7	3880	210	4	3.25	7	3	4	423	24	0	3.40
1993-94	Detroit	30	16	9	1	1572	91	1	3.47	....	....	....	....	....	....	....
	Winnipeg	14	5	8	1	788	52	1	3.96	....	....	....	....	....	....	....
1994-95	Winnipeg	30	8	16	3	1571	97	0	3.70	....	....	....	....	....	....	....
1995-96	Winnipeg	30	8	18	3	1695	111	0	3.93	....	....	....	....	....	....	....
1996-97	Boston	2	0	1	0	93	5	0	3.23	....	....	....	....	....	....	....
	NHL Totals	**340**	**149**	**136**	**37**	**19172**	**1116**	**10**	**3.49**	**25**	**9**	**15**	**1418**	**71**	**2**	**3.00**

Played in NHL All-Star Game (1992)

Traded to **Winnipeg** by **Detroit** with Dallas Drake for Bob Essensa and Sergei Bautin, March 8, 1994. Traded to **Philadelphia** by **Winnipeg** with Winnipeg's 3rd round choice (Chester Gallant) in 1996 Entry Draft for Dominic Roussel, February 27, 1996. Signed as a free agent by **Boston**, August 27, 1996.

CHEVRIER, Alain

Goaltender. Catches left. 5'8", 180 lbs. Born, Cornwall, Ont., April 23, 1961

Season	Club	GP	W	L	T	Mins	GA	SO	Avg	GP	W	L	Mins	GA	SO	Avg
1985-86	New Jersey	37	11	18	2	1862	143	0	4.61	....	....	....	....	....	....	....
1986-87	New Jersey	58	24	26	2	3153	227	0	4.32	....	....	....	....	....	....	....
1987-88	New Jersey	45	18	19	3	2354	148	1	3.77	....	....	....	....	....	....	....
1988-89	Winnipeg	22	8	8	2	1092	78	1	4.29	....	....	....	....	....	....	....
	Chicago	27	13	11	2	1573	92	0	3.51	16	9	7	1013	44	0	2.61
1989-90	Chicago	39	16	14	3	1894	132	0	4.18	....	....	....	....	....	....	....
	Pittsburgh	3	1	2	0	166	14	0	5.06	....	....	....	....	....	....	....
1990-91	Detroit	3	0	2	0	108	11	0	6.11	....	....	....	....	....	....	....
	NHL Totals	**234**	**91**	**100**	**14**	**12202**	**845**	**2**	**4.16**	**16**	**9**	**7**	**1013**	**44**	**0**	**2.61**

Signed as a free agent by **New Jersey**, May 31, 1985. Traded to **Winnipeg** by **New Jersey** with New Jersey's 7th round choice (Doug Evans) in 1989 Entry Draft for Steve Rooney and Winnipeg's 3rd round choice (Brad Bombardir) in 1990 Entry Draft, July 19, 1988. Traded to **Chicago** by **Winnipeg** for Chicago's 4th round choice (Allain Roy) in 1989 Entry Draft, January 19, 1989. Traded to **Pittsburgh** by **Chicago** for future considerations, March 6, 1990. Signed as a free agent by **Detroit**, July 5, 1990.

CLEMMENSEN, Scott

Goaltender. Catches left. 6'2", 205 lbs. Born, Des Moines, IA, July 23, 1977
(New Jersey's 7th choice, 215th overall, in 1997 Entry Draft).

Season	Club	GP	W	L	T	Mins	GA	SO	Avg	GP	W	L	Mins	GA	SO	Avg
2001-02	New Jersey	2	0	0	0	20	1	0	3.00	....	....	....	....	....	....	....
	NHL Totals	**2**	**0**	**0**	**0**	**20**	**1**	**0**	**3.00**	....	....	....	....	....	....	....

CLIFFORD, Chris

Goaltender. Catches left. 5'9", 167 lbs. Born, Kingston, Ont., May 26, 1966
(Chicago's 6th choice, 111th overall, in 1984 Entry Draft).

Season	Club	GP	W	L	T	Mins	GA	SO	Avg	GP	W	L	Mins	GA	SO	Avg
1984-85	Chicago	1	0	0	0	20	0	0	0.00	....	....	....	....	....	....	....
1988-89	Chicago	1	0	0	0	4	0	0	0.00	....	....	....	....	....	....	....
	NHL Totals	**2**	**0**	**0**	**0**	**24**	**0**	**0**	**0.00**	....	....	....	....	....	....	....

Signed as a free agent by **Pittsburgh**, September 6, 1989.

CLOUTIER, Dan

Goaltender. Catches left. 6'1", 182 lbs. Born, Mont-Laurier, Que., April 22, 1976
(NY Rangers' 1st choice, 26th overall, in 1994 Entry Draft).

Season	Club	GP	W	L	T	Mins	GA	SO	Avg	GP	W	L	Mins	GA	SO	Avg
1997-98	NY Rangers	12	4	5	1	551	23	0	2.50	....	....	....	....	....	....	....
1998-99	NY Rangers	22	6	8	3	1097	49	0	2.68	....	....	....	....	....	....	....
99-2000	Tampa Bay	52	9	30	3	2492	145	0	3.49	....	....	....	....	....	....	....
2000-01	Tampa Bay	24	3	13	3	1005	59	1	3.52	....	....	....	....	....	....	....
	Vancouver	16	4	6	5	914	37	0	2.43	2	0	2	117	9	0	4.62
2001-02	Vancouver	62	31	22	5	3502	142	7	2.43	6	2	3	273	16	0	3.52
2002-03	Vancouver	57	33	16	7	3376	136	2	2.42	14	7	7	833	45	0	3.24
	NHL Totals	**245**	**90**	**100**	**27**	**12937**	**591**	**10**	**2.74**	**22**	**9**	**12**	**1223**	**70**	**0**	**3.43**

• Brother of Sylvain

Traded to **Tampa Bay** by **NY Rangers** with Niklas Sundstrom and NY Rangers' 1st (Nikita Alexeev) and 3rd (later traded to San Jose – later traded to Chicago – Chicago selected Igor Radulov) round choices in 2000 Entry Draft for Chicago's 1st round choice (previously acquired, NY Rangers selected Pavel Brendl) in 1999 Entry Draft, June 26, 1999. Traded to **Vancouver** by **Tampa Bay** for Adrian Aucoin and Vancouver's 2nd round choice (Alexander Polushin) in 2001 Entry Draft, February 7, 2001.

CLOUTIER, Jacques

Goaltender. Catches left. 5'7", 168 lbs. Born, Noranda, Que., January 3, 1960
(Buffalo's 4th choice, 55th overall, in 1979 Entry Draft).

Season	Club	GP	W	L	T	Mins	GA	SO	Avg	GP	W	L	Mins	GA	SO	Avg
1981-82	Buffalo	7	5	1	0	311	13	0	2.51	....	....	....	....	....	....	....
1982-83	Buffalo	25	10	7	6	1390	81	0	3.50	....	....	....	....	....	....	....
1984-85	Buffalo	1	0	0	1	65	4	0	3.69	....	....	....	....	....	....	....
1985-86	Buffalo	15	5	9	1	872	49	1	3.37	....	....	....	....	....	....	....
1986-87	Buffalo	40	11	19	5	2167	137	0	3.79	....	....	....	....	....	....	....
1987-88	Buffalo	20	4	8	2	851	67	0	4.72	....	....	....	....	....	....	....
1988-89	Buffalo	36	15	14	0	1786	108	0	3.63	4	1	3	238	10	1	2.52
1989-90	Chicago	43	18	15	2	2178	112	2	3.09	4	0	2	175	8	0	2.74
1990-91	Chicago	10	2	3	0	403	24	0	3.57	....	....	....	....	....	....	....
	Quebec	15	3	8	2	829	61	0	4.41	....	....	....	....	....	....	....
1991-92	Quebec	26	6	14	3	1345	88	0	3.93	....	....	....	....	....	....	....
1992-93	Quebec	3	0	2	1	154	10	0	3.90	....	....	....	....	....	....	....
1993-94	Quebec	14	3	2	1	475	24	0	3.03	....	....	....	....	....	....	....
	NHL Totals	**255**	**82**	**102**	**24**	**12826**	**778**	**3**	**3.64**	**8**	**1**	**5**	**413**	**18**	**1**	**2.62**

Traded to **Chicago** by **Buffalo** with Chicago's 5th round choice (Todd Bojcun) in 1990 Entry Draft for Steve Ludzik and Buffalo's 6th round choice (Derek Edgerly) in 1990 Entry Draft, September 28, 1989. Traded to **Quebec** by **Chicago** for Tony McKegney, January 29, 1991.

COLVIN, Les

Goaltender. Catches left. 5'6", 150 lbs. Born, Oshawa, Ont., February 8, 1921

Season	Club	GP	W	L	T	Mins	GA	SO	Avg	GP	W	L	Mins	GA	SO	Avg
1948-49	Boston	1	0	1	0	60	4	0	4.00	....	....	....	....	....	....	....
	NHL Totals	**1**	**0**	**1**	**0**	**60**	**4**	**0**	**4.00**	....	....	....	....	....	....	....

Loaned to **Boston** by **Shawinigan** (QSHL) to replace Frank Brimsek, January 22, 1949. (Montreal 4, Boston 2)

CONKLIN, Ty

Goaltender. Catches left. 6', 180 lbs. Born, Anchorage, AK, March 30, 1976

Season	Club	GP	W	L	T	Mins	GA	SO	Avg	GP	W	L	Mins	GA	SO	Avg
2001-02	Edmonton	4	2	0	0	148	4	0	1.62	....	....	....	....	....	....	....
	NHL Totals	**4**	**2**	**0**	**0**	**148**	**4**	**0**	**1.62**	....	....	....	....	....	....	....

Signed as a free agent by **Edmonton**, April 18, 2001.

CONNELL, Alex

HHOF

Goaltender. Catches right. 5'9", 150 lbs. Born, Ottawa, Ont., February 8, 1902

Season	Club	GP	W	L	T	Mins	GA	SO	Avg	GP	W	L	Mins	GA	SO	Avg
1924-25	Ottawa	*30	17	12	1	1852	66	*7	2.14	....	....	....	....	....	....	....
1925-26	Ottawa	*36	*24	8	4	2251	42	*15	*1.12	2	0	1	120	2	0	*1.00
1926-27 ♦	Ottawa	*44	*30	10	4	2782	69	13	1.49	6	*3	0	400	4	*2	*0.60
1927-28	Ottawa	*44	20	14	10	2760	57	*15	1.24	2	0	2	120	3	0	1.50
1928-29	Ottawa	*44	14	17	13	*2820	67	7	1.43	....	....	....	....	....	....	....
1929-30	Ottawa	*44	21	15	8	2780	118	3	2.55	2	0	1	120	6	0	3.00
1930-31	Ottawa	36	10	22	4	2190	110	3	3.01	....	....	....	....	....	....	....
1931-32	Detroit	*48	18	20	10	*3050	108	6	2.12	2	0	1	120	3	0	1.50
1932-33	Ottawa	15	4	8	2	845	36	1	2.56	....	....	....	....	....	....	....
1933-34	NY Americans	1	1	0	0	40	2	0	3.00	....	....	....	....	....	....	....
1934-35 ♦	Mtl. Maroons	*48	24	19	5	2970	92	*9	1.86	*7	*5	0	429	8	*2	*1.12
1936-37	Mtl. Maroons	27	10	11	6	1710	63	2	2.21	....	....	....	....	....	....	....
	NHL Totals	**417**	**193**	**136**	**67**	**26050**	**830**	**81**	**1.91**	**21**	**8**	**5**	**1309**	**26**	**4**	**1.19**

Signed as a free agent by **Ottawa**, November 18, 1924. • Established NHL record for consecutive shutouts (6), January 31 – February 18, 1928. Claimed by **Detroit** from **Ottawa** in Dispersal Draft for 1931-32 season, September 26, 1931. Loaned to **NY Americans** by **Ottawa** to replace injured Roy Worters, March 15, 1934. (NY Americans 3, Ottawa 2). Traded to **Mtl. Maroons** by **Ottawa** for future considerations (Glenn Brydson, October 22, 1934), October 2, 1934.

CORSI, Jim

Goaltender. Catches left. 5'10", 180 lbs. Born, Montreal, Que., June 19, 1954

Season	Club	GP	W	L	T	Mins	GA	SO	Avg	GP	W	L	Mins	GA	SO	Avg
1979-80	Edmonton	26	8	14	3	1366	83	0	3.65	....	....	....	....	....	....	....
	NHL Totals	**26**	**8**	**14**	**3**	**1366**	**83**	**0**	**3.65**	....	....	....	....	....	....	....

Signed as a free agent by **Edmonton**, October 4, 1979. Traded to **Minnesota** by **Edmonton** for future considerations, March 11, 1980.

COURTEAU, Maurice

Goaltender. Catches left. 5'8", 162 lbs. Born, Quebec City, Que., February 18, 1920

Season	Club	GP	W	L	T	Mins	GA	SO	Avg	GP	W	L	Mins	GA	SO	Avg
1943-44	Boston	6	2	4	0	360	33	0	5.50	....	....	....	....	....	....	....
	NHL Totals	**6**	**2**	**4**	**0**	**360**	**33**	**0**	**5.50**	....	....	....	....	....	....	....

COUSINEAU, Marcel

Goaltender. Catches left. 5'9", 183 lbs. Born, Delson, Que., April 30, 1973
(Boston's 3rd choice, 62nd overall, in 1991 Entry Draft).

Season	Club	GP	W	L	T	Mins	GA	SO	Avg	GP	W	L	Mins	GA	SO	Avg
1996-97	Toronto	13	3	5	1	566	31	1	3.29	....	....	....	....	....	....	....
1997-98	Toronto	2	0	0	0	17	0	0	0.00	....	....	....	....	....	....	....
1998-99	NY Islanders	6	0	4	0	293	14	0	2.87	....	....	....	....	....	....	....
99-2000	Los Angeles	5	1	1	0	171	6	0	2.11	....	....	....	....	....	....	....
	NHL Totals	**26**	**4**	**10**	**1**	**1047**	**51**	**1**	**2.92**	....	....	....	....	....	....	....

Signed as a free agent by **Toronto**, November 13, 1993. Signed as a free agent by **NY Islanders**, July 29, 1998. Traded to **Los Angeles** by **NY Islanders** with Ziggy Palffy, Brian Smolinski and New Jersey's 4th round choice (previously acquired, Los Angeles selected Daniel Johansson) in 1999 Entry Draft for Olli Jokinen, Josh Green, Mathieu Biron and Los Angeles' 1st round choice (Taylor Pyatt) in 1999 Entry Draft, June 20, 1999.

COWLEY, Wayne

Goaltender. Catches left. 6', 185 lbs. Born, Scarborough, Ont., December 4, 1964

Season	Club	GP	W	L	T	Mins	GA	SO	Avg	GP	W	L	Mins	GA	SO	Avg
1993-94	Edmonton	1	0	1	0	57	3	0	3.16	....	....	....	....	....	....	....
	NHL Totals	**1**	**0**	**1**	**0**	**57**	**3**	**0**	**3.16**	....	....	....	....	....	....	....

Signed as a free agent by **Calgary**, May 1, 1988. Signed as a free agent by **Edmonton**, September 13, 1993.

COX, Abbie

Goaltender. Catches left. 5'6", 140 lbs. Born, London, Ont., July 19, 1904

Season	Club	GP	W	L	T	Mins	GA	SO	Avg	GP	W	L	Mins	GA	SO	Avg
1929-30	Mtl. Maroons	1	1	0	0	60	2	0	2.00	....	....	....	....	....	....	....
1933-34	NY Americans	1	0	1	0	24	3	0	7.50	....	....	....	....	....	....	....
	Detroit	2	0	0	1	109	5	0	2.75	....	....	....	....	....	....	....

		REGULAR SEASON								PLAYOFFS						
Season	Club	GP	W	L	T	Mins	GA	SO	Avg	GP	W	L	Mins	GA	SO	Avg
1935-36	Montreal	1	0	0	1	70	1	0	0.86	....	....	....	....	....	....	....
	NHL Totals	**5**	**1**	**1**	**2**	**263**	**11**	**0**	**2.51**	....	....	....	....	....	....	....

Signed as a free agent by **NY Rangers**, November 9, 1926. Traded to **Windsor** (Can-Pro) by **NY Rangers** for cash, September, 1928. Loaned to **Mtl. Maroons** by **Windsor** (IHL) to replace injured Clint Benedict and Flat Walsh, February 1, 1930. (Mtl. Maroons 7, NY Americans 2). Loaned to **Detroit** (IHL) by **Windsor** (IHL) for cash, November 21, 1930. Loaned to **NY Americans** by **Windsor** (IHL) to replace injured Roy Worters, November 12, 1933. (Detroit 5, NY Americans 2). Loaned to **Detroit** by **Windsor** (IHL) to replace injured John Ross Roach, December 10, 1933 (Detroit 4, Mtl. Maroons 1) and December 17, 1933. (NY Americans 4, Detroit 4). Loaned to **Montreal** by **Springfield** (Can-Am) to replace injured Wilf Cude, February 16, 1936. (Montreal 1, NY Rangers 1)

CRAIG, Jim

Goaltender. Catches left. 6'1", 190 lbs. Born, North Easton, MA, May 31, 1957
(Atlanta's 4th choice, 72nd overall, in 1977 Amateur Draft).

Season	Club	GP	W	L	T	Mins	GA	SO	Avg	GP	W	L	Mins	GA	SO	Avg
1979-80	Atlanta	4	1	2	1	206	13	0	3.79	....	....	....	....	....	....	....
1980-81	Boston	23	9	7	6	1272	78	0	3.68	....	....	....	....	....	....	....
1983-84	Minnesota	3	1	1	0	110	9	0	4.91	....	....	....	....	....	....	....
	NHL Totals	**30**	**11**	**10**	**7**	**1588**	**100**	**0**	**3.78**	....	....	....	....	....	....	....

Traded to **Boston** by **Atlanta** for Boston's 2nd round choice (Steve Konroyd) in 1980 Entry Draft and Boston's 3rd round choice (Mike Vernon) in 1981 Entry Draft, June 2, 1980. Signed as a free agent by **Minnesota**, March 2, 1983.

CRHA, Jiri

Goaltender. Catches left. 5'11", 170 lbs. Born, Pardubice, Czech., April 13, 1950

Season	Club	GP	W	L	T	Mins	GA	SO	Avg	GP	W	L	Mins	GA	SO	Avg
1979-80	Toronto	15	8	7	0	830	50	0	3.61	2	0	2	121	10	0	4.96
1980-81	Toronto	54	20	20	11	3112	211	0	4.07	3	0	2	65	11	0	10.15
	NHL Totals	**69**	**28**	**27**	**11**	**3942**	**261**	**0**	**3.97**	**5**	**0**	**4**	**186**	**21**	**0**	**6.77**

Signed as a free agent by **Toronto**, February 4, 1980.

CROZIER, Roger

Goaltender. Catches right. 5'8", 165 lbs. Born, Bracebridge, Ont., March 16, 1942

Season	Club	GP	W	L	T	Mins	GA	SO	Avg	GP	W	L	Mins	GA	SO	Avg
1963-64	Detroit	15	5	6	4	900	51	2	3.40	3	0	2	126	5	0	2.38
1964-65	Detroit	*70	*40	22	7	*4168	168	*6	2.42	7	3	4	420	23	0	3.29
1965-66	Detroit	*64	27	24	12	3734	173	*7	2.78	*12	6	5	*668	26	*1	2.34
1966-67	Detroit	58	22	29	4	3256	182	4	3.35	....	....	....	....	....	....	....
1967-68	Detroit	34	9	18	2	1729	95	1	3.30	....	....	....	....	....	....	....
1968-69	Detroit	38	12	16	3	1820	101	0	3.33	....	....	....	....	....	....	....
1969-70	Detroit	34	16	6	9	1877	83	0	2.65	1	0	1	34	3	0	5.29
1970-71	Buffalo	44	9	20	7	2198	135	1	3.69	....	....	....	....	....	....	....
1971-72	Buffalo	63	13	34	14	3654	214	2	3.51	....	....	....	....	....	....	....
1972-73	Buffalo	49	23	13	7	2633	121	3	2.76	4	2	2	249	11	0	2.65
1973-74	Buffalo	12	4	5	0	615	39	0	3.80	....	....	....	....	....	....	....
1974-75	Buffalo	23	17	2	1	1260	55	3	2.62	5	3	2	292	14	0	2.88
1975-76	Buffalo	11	8	2	0	620	27	1	2.61	....	....	....	....	....	....	....
1976-77	Washington	3	1	0	0	103	2	0	1.17	....	....	....	....	....	....	....
	NHL Totals	**518**	**206**	**197**	**70**	**28567**	**1446**	**30**	**3.04**	**32**	**14**	**16**	**1789**	**82**	**1**	**2.75**

NHL First All-Star Team (1965) • Calder Memorial Trophy (1965) • Conn Smythe Trophy (1966)

Traded to **Detroit** by **Chicago** with Ron Ingram for Howie Young, June 5, 1963. Traded to **Buffalo** by **Detroit** for Tom Webster, June 10, 1970. Traded to **Washington** by **Buffalo** for cash, March 3, 1977.

CUDE, Wilf

Goaltender. Catches left. 5'9", 146 lbs. Born, Barry, Wales, July 4, 1910

Season	Club	GP	W	L	T	Mins	GA	SO	Avg	GP	W	L	Mins	GA	SO	Avg
1930-31	Philadelphia	30	2	25	3	1850	130	1	4.22	....	....	....	....	....	....	....
1931-32	Boston	2	1	1	0	120	6	1	3.00	....	....	....	....	....	....	....
	Chicago	1	0	0	0	41	9	0	13.17	....	....	....	....	....	....	....
1933-34	Montreal	1	1	0	0	60	0	1	*0.00	....	....	....	....	....	....	....
	Detroit	29	15	6	8	1860	47	4	*1.52	*9	4	5	*593	21	1	2.12
1934-35	Montreal	*48	19	23	6	2960	145	1	2.94	2	0	1	120	6	0	3.00
1935-36	Montreal	47	11	26	10	2940	122	6	2.49	....	....	....	....	....	....	....
1936-37	Montreal	44	22	17	5	2730	99	5	2.18	5	2	3	352	13	0	2.22
1937-38	Montreal	47	18	17	12	2990	126	3	2.53	3	1	2	192	11	0	3.44
1938-39	Montreal	23	8	11	4	1440	77	2	3.21	....	....	....	....	....	....	....
1939-40	Montreal	7	1	5	1	415	24	0	3.47	....	....	....	....	....	....	....
1940-41	Montreal	3	2	1	0	180	13	0	4.33	....	....	....	....	....	....	....
	NHL Totals	**282**	**100**	**132**	**49**	**17586**	**798**	**24**	**2.72**	**19**	**7**	**11**	**1257**	**51**	**1**	**2.43**

NHL Second All-Star Team (1936, 1937)

Played in NHL All-Star Game (1937, 1939)

Signed as a free agent by **Pittsburgh**, February 18, 1930. Transferred to **Philadelphia** after **Pittsburgh** franchise relocated, October 18, 1930. • Signed as a utility back-up goaltender by **NHL** for 1931-32 season after **Philadelphia** franchise suspended operations, September 27, 1931. Traded to **Montreal** by **Philadelphia** for cash, October 19, 1933. Loaned to **Detroit** by **Montreal** for balance of 1933-34 season for cash, January 2, 1934.

CUTTS, Don

Goaltender. Catches left. 6'3", 190 lbs. Born, Edmonton, Alta., February 24, 1953
(NY Islanders' 6th choice, 97th overall, in 1973 Amateur Draft).

Season	Club	GP	W	L	T	Mins	GA	SO	Avg	GP	W	L	Mins	GA	SO	Avg
1979-80	Edmonton	6	1	2	1	269	16	0	3.57	....	....	....	....	....	....	....
	NHL Totals	**6**	**1**	**2**	**1**	**269**	**16**	**0**	**3.57**	....	....	....	....	....	....	....

Signed as a free agent by **Edmonton**, January 12, 1980.

CYR, Claude

Goaltender. Catches left. 5'10", 180 lbs. Born, Montreal, Que., March 27, 1939

Season	Club	GP	W	L	T	Mins	GA	SO	Avg	GP	W	L	Mins	GA	SO	Avg
1958-59	Montreal	1	0	0	0	20	1	0	3.00	....	....	....	....	....	....	....
	NHL Totals	**1**	**0**	**0**	**0**	**20**	**1**	**0**	**3.00**	....	....	....	....	....	....	....

Promoted to **Montreal** from **Hull-Ottawa** (EOHL) and replaced Claude Pronovost at start of 3rd period, March 19, 1959. (Toronto 6, Montreal 3)

DADSWELL, Doug

Goaltender. Catches left. 5'10", 180 lbs. Born, Scarborough, Ont., February 7, 1964

Season	Club	GP	W	L	T	Mins	GA	SO	Avg	GP	W	L	Mins	GA	SO	Avg
1986-87	Calgary	2	0	1	1	125	10	0	4.80	....	....	....	....	....	....	....
1987-88	Calgary	25	8	7	2	1221	89	0	4.37	....	....	....	....	....	....	....
	NHL Totals	**27**	**8**	**8**	**3**	**1346**	**99**	**0**	**4.41**	....	....	....	....	....	....	....

Signed as a free agent by **Calgary**, August 6, 1986.

DAFOE, Byron

Goaltender. Catches left. 5'11", 200 lbs. Born, Sussex, England, February 25, 1971
(Washington's 2nd choice, 35th overall, in 1989 Entry Draft).

Season	Club	GP	W	L	T	Mins	GA	SO	Avg	GP	W	L	Mins	GA	SO	Avg
1992-93	Washington	1	0	0	0	1	0	0	0.00	....	....	....	....	....	....	....
1993-94	Washington	5	2	2	0	230	13	0	3.39	2	0	2	118	5	0	2.54
1994-95	Washington	4	1	1	1	187	11	0	3.53	1	0	0	20	1	0	3.00
1995-96	Los Angeles	47	14	24	8	2666	172	1	3.87	....	....	....	....	....	....	....
1996-97	Los Angeles	40	13	17	5	2162	112	0	3.11	....	....	....	....	....	....	....
1997-98	Boston	65	30	25	9	3693	138	6	2.24	6	2	4	422	14	1	1.99
1998-99	Boston	68	32	23	11	4001	133	*10	1.99	12	6	6	768	26	2	2.03
99-2000	Boston	41	13	16	10	2307	114	3	2.96	....	....	....	....	....	....	....
2000-01	Boston	45	22	14	7	2536	101	2	2.39	....	....	....	....	....	....	....
2001-02	Boston	64	35	26	3	3827	141	4	2.21	6	2	4	358	19	0	3.18
2002-03	Atlanta	17	5	11	1	895	65	0	4.36	....	....	....	....	....	....	....
	NHL Totals	**397**	**167**	**159**	**55**	**22505**	**1000**	**26**	**2.67**	**27**	**10**	**16**	**1686**	**65**	**3**	**2.31**

NHL Second All-Star Team (1999)

Traded to **Los Angeles** by **Washington** with Dmitri Khristich for Los Angeles' 1st round choice (Alexandre Volchkov) in 1996 Entry Draft and Dallas' 4th round choice (previously acquired, Washington selected Justin Davis) in 1996 Entry Draft, July 8, 1995. Traded to **Boston** by **Los Angeles** with Dimitri Khristich for Jozef Stumpel, Sandy Moger and Boston's 4th round choice (later traded to New Jersey – New Jersey selected Pierre Dagenais) in 1998 Entry Draft, August 29, 1997. Signed as a free agent by **Atlanta**, November 19, 2002.

D'ALESSIO, Corrie

Goaltender. Catches left. 5'11", 155 lbs. Born, Cornwall, Ont., September 9, 1969
(Vancouver's 4th choice, 107th overall, in 1988 Entry Draft).

Season	Club	GP	W	L	T	Mins	GA	SO	Avg	GP	W	L	Mins	GA	SO	Avg
1992-93	Hartford	1	0	0	0	11	0	0	0.00	....	....	....	....	....	....	....
	NHL Totals	**1**	**0**	**0**	**0**	**11**	**0**	**0**	**0.00**	....	....	....	....	....	....	....

Traded to **Hartford** by **Vancouver** with cash for Kay Whitmore, October 1, 1992.

DALEY, Joe

Goaltender. Catches left. 5'10", 170 lbs. Born, Winnipeg, Man., February 20, 1943

Season	Club	GP	W	L	T	Mins	GA	SO	Avg	GP	W	L	Mins	GA	SO	Avg
1968-69	Pittsburgh	29	10	13	3	1615	87	2	3.23	....	....	....	....	....	....	....
1969-70	Pittsburgh	9	1	5	3	528	26	0	2.95	....	....	....	....	....	....	....
1970-71	Buffalo	38	12	16	8	2073	128	1	3.70	....	....	....	....	....	....	....
1971-72	Detroit	29	11	10	5	1620	85	0	3.15	....	....	....	....	....	....	....
	NHL Totals	**105**	**34**	**44**	**19**	**5836**	**326**	**3**	**3.35**	....	....	....	....	....	....	....

Claimed by **Pittsburgh** from **Detroit** in Expansion Draft, June 6, 1967. Claimed on waivers by **Buffalo** from **Pittsburgh**, June 9, 1970. Traded to **Detroit** by **Buffalo** for Don Luce and Mike Robitaille, May 25, 1971. Claimed by **Cleveland** (AHL) from **Detroit** in Reverse Draft, June, 1972.

DAMORE, Nick

Goaltender. Catches left. 5'6", 160 lbs. Born, Niagara Falls, Ont., July 10, 1916

Season	Club	GP	W	L	T	Mins	GA	SO	Avg	GP	W	L	Mins	GA	SO	Avg
1941-42	Boston	1	1	0	0	60	3	0	3.00	....	....	....	....	....	....	....
	NHL Totals	**1**	**1**	**0**	**0**	**60**	**3**	**0**	**3.00**	....	....	....	....	....	....	....

• Brother of Hank

Promoted to **Boston** from **Hershey** (AHL) to replace injured Frank Brimsek, January 25, 1942. (Boston 7, Montreal 3)

D'AMOUR, Marc

Goaltender. Catches left. 5'9", 190 lbs. Born, Sudbury, Ont., May 29, 1961

Season	Club	GP	W	L	T	Mins	GA	SO	Avg	GP	W	L	Mins	GA	SO	Avg
1985-86	Calgary	15	2	4	2	560	32	0	3.43	....	....	....	....	....	....	....
1988-89	Philadelphia	1	0	0	0	19	0	0	0.00	....	....	....	....	....	....	....
	NHL Totals	**16**	**2**	**4**	**2**	**579**	**32**	**0**	**3.32**	....	....	....	....	....	....	....

Signed as a free agent by **Calgary**, June 7, 1982. Signed as a free agent by **Philadelphia**, September 30, 1988.

DAMPHOUSSE, Jean-Francois

Goaltender. Catches left. 6', 180 lbs. Born, St-Alexis-des-Monts, Que., July 21, 1979
(New Jersey's 1st choice, 24th overall, in 1997 Entry Draft).

Season	Club	GP	W	L	T	Mins	GA	SO	Avg	GP	W	L	Mins	GA	SO	Avg
2001-02	New Jersey	6	1	3	0	294	12	0	2.45	....	....	....	....	....	....	....
	NHL Totals	**6**	**1**	**3**	**0**	**294**	**12**	**0**	**2.45**	....	....	....	....	....	....	....

Traded to **Anaheim** by **New Jersey** with Petr Sykora, Mike Commodore and Igor Pohanka for Jeff Friesen, Oleg Tverdovsky and Maxim Balmochnykh, July 6, 2002. Traded to **Calgary** by **Anaheim** with Mike Commodore for Rob Niedermayer, March 11, 2003. Signed as a free agent by **Montreal**, July 4, 2003.

DASKALAKIS, Cleon

Goaltender. Catches left. 5'9", 175 lbs. Born, Boston, MA, September 29, 1962

Season	Club	GP	W	L	T	Mins	GA	SO	Avg	GP	W	L	Mins	GA	SO	Avg
1984-85	Boston	8	1	2	1	289	24	0	4.98	....	....	....	....	....	....	....

Season	Club	GP	W	L	T	Mins	GA	SO	Avg	GP	W	L	Mins	GA	SO	Avg
		REGULAR SEASON								PLAYOFFS						
1985-86	Boston	2	0	2	0	120	10	0	5.00	....	....	....	....	....	....	....
1986-87	Boston	2	2	0	0	97	7	0	4.33	....	....	....	....	....	....	....
	NHL Totals	**12**	**3**	**4**	**1**	**506**	**41**	**0**	**4.86**	....	....	....	....	....	....	....

Signed as a free agent by **Boston**, June 1, 1984.

DAVIDSON, John

Goaltender. Catches left. 6'3", 205 lbs. Born, Ottawa, Ont., February 27, 1953
(St. Louis' 1st choice, 5th overall, in 1973 Amateur Draft).

Season	Club	GP	W	L	T	Mins	GA	SO	Avg	GP	W	L	Mins	GA	SO	Avg
1973-74	St. Louis	39	13	19	7	2300	118	0	3.08	....	....	....	....	....	....	....
1974-75	St. Louis	40	17	15	7	2360	144	0	3.66	1	0	1	60	4	0	4.00
1975-76	NY Rangers	56	22	28	5	3207	212	3	3.97	....	....	....	....	....	....	....
1976-77	NY Rangers	39	14	14	6	2116	125	1	3.54	....	....	....	....	....	....	....
1977-78	NY Rangers	34	14	13	4	1848	98	1	3.18	2	1	1	122	7	0	3.44
1978-79	NY Rangers	39	20	12	5	2232	131	0	3.52	*18	11	7	*1106	42	*1	2.28
1979-80	NY Rangers	41	20	15	4	2306	122	2	3.17	9	4	5	541	21	0	2.33
1980-81	NY Rangers	10	1	7	1	560	48	0	5.14	....	....	....	....	....	....	....
1981-82	NY Rangers	1	1	0	0	60	1	0	1.00	1	0	0	33	3	0	5.45
1982-83	NY Rangers	2	1	1	0	120	5	0	2.50	....	....	....	....	....	....	....
	NHL Totals	**301**	**123**	**124**	**39**	**17109**	**1004**	**7**	**3.52**	**31**	**16**	**14**	**1862**	**77**	**1**	**2.48**

• First goaltender to spend full season in NHL directly from junior without minor league experience. Traded to **NY Rangers** by **St. Louis** with Bill Collins for Jerry Butler, Ted Irvine and Bert Wilson, June 18, 1975.

DECOURCY, Bob

Goaltender. Catches right. 5'11", 160 lbs. Born, Toronto, Ont., June 12, 1927

Season	Club	GP	W	L	T	Mins	GA	SO	Avg	GP	W	L	Mins	GA	SO	Avg
1947-48	NY Rangers	1	0	1	0	29	6	0	12.41	....	....	....	....	....	....	....
	NHL Totals	**1**	**0**	**1**	**0**	**29**	**6**	**0**	**12.41**	....	....	....	....	....	....	....

• **NY Rangers'** spare goaltender replaced injured Chuck Rayner in 2nd period, November 12, 1947. (Boston 8, NY Rangers 2)

DEFELICE, Norm

Goaltender. Catches left. 5'10", 150 lbs. Born, Schumacher, Ont., January 19, 1933

Season	Club	GP	W	L	T	Mins	GA	SO	Avg	GP	W	L	Mins	GA	SO	Avg
1956-57	Boston	10	3	5	2	600	30	0	3.00	....	....	....	....	....	....	....
	NHL Totals	**10**	**3**	**5**	**2**	**600**	**30**	**0**	**3.00**	....	....	....	....	....	....	....

Loaned to **Sydney** (MMHL) by **Boston** for cash, October 5, 1953. Promoted to **Boston** from **Hershey** (AHL) to replace Terry Sawchuk who was hospitalized for nervous exhaustion, December 13, 1956. Traded to **Springfield** (AHL) by **Boston** with future considerations (Floyd Smith, June, 1957) and the loan of Jack Bionda for Don Simmons, January 22, 1957.

DeJORDY, Denis

Goaltender. Catches left. 5'9", 185 lbs. Born, St-Hyacinthe, Que., November 12, 1938

Season	Club	GP	W	L	T	Mins	GA	SO	Avg	GP	W	L	Mins	GA	SO	Avg
1960-61	Chicago	DID NOT PLAY – SPARE GOALTENDER														
1962-63	Chicago	5	2	1	2	290	12	0	2.48	....	....	....	....	....	....	....
1963-64	Chicago	6	2	3	1	340	19	0	3.35	1	0	0	20	2	0	6.00
1964-65	Chicago	30	16	11	3	1760	74	3	2.52	2	0	1	80	9	0	6.75
1966-67	Chicago	44	22	12	7	2536	104	4	2.46	4	1	2	184	10	0	3.26
1967-68	Chicago	50	23	15	11	2838	128	4	2.71	11	5	6	662	34	0	3.08
1968-69	Chicago	53	22	22	7	2981	156	2	3.14	....	....	....	....	....	....	....
1969-70	Chicago	10	3	5	1	557	25	0	2.69	....	....	....	....	....	....	....
	Los Angeles	21	5	11	4	1147	62	0	3.24	....	....	....	....	....	....	....
1970-71	Los Angeles	60	18	29	11	3375	214	1	3.80	....	....	....	....	....	....	....
1971-72	Los Angeles	5	0	5	0	291	23	0	4.74	....	....	....	....	....	....	....
	Montreal	7	3	2	1	332	25	0	4.52	....	....	....	....	....	....	....
1972-73	Detroit	24	8	11	3	1331	83	1	3.74	....	....	....	....	....	....	....
1973-74	Detroit	1	0	1	0	20	4	0	12.00	....	....	....	....	....	....	....
	NHL Totals	**316**	**124**	**128**	**51**	**17798**	**929**	**15**	**3.13**	**18**	**6**	**9**	**946**	**55**	**0**	**3.49**

Shared Vezina Trophy with Glenn Hall (1967)

Traded to **Los Angeles** by **Chicago** with Gilles Marotte and Jim Stanfield for Bill White, Bryan Campbell and Gerry Desjardins, February 20, 1970. Traded to **Montreal** by **Los Angeles** with Dale Hoganson, Noel Price and Doug Robinson for Rogie Vachon, November 4, 1971. Traded to **NY Islanders** by **Montreal** with Glenn Resch, Alex Campbell and future considerations (Germain Gagnon, June 26, 1972) for cash and NY Islanders' 2nd round choice (Glenn Goldup) in 1973 Amateur Draft, June 6, 1972. Traded to **Detroit** by **NY Islanders** with Don McLaughlin for Arnie Brown and Gerry Gray, October 4, 1972.

DELGUIDICE, Matt

Goaltender. Catches right. 5'9", 170 lbs. Born, West Haven, CT, March 5, 1967
(Boston's 5th choice, 77th overall, in 1987 Entry Draft).

Season	Club	GP	W	L	T	Mins	GA	SO	Avg	GP	W	L	Mins	GA	SO	Avg
1990-91	Boston	1	0	0	0	10	0	0	0.00	....	....	....	....	....	....	....
1991-92	Boston	10	2	5	1	424	28	0	3.96	....	....	....	....	....	....	....
	NHL Totals	**11**	**2**	**5**	**1**	**434**	**28**	**0**	**3.87**	....	....	....	....	....	....	....

DENIS, Marc

Goaltender. Catches left. 6'1", 190 lbs. Born, Montreal, Que., August 1, 1977
(Colorado's 1st choice, 25th overall, in 1995 Entry Draft).

Season	Club	GP	W	L	T	Mins	GA	SO	Avg	GP	W	L	Mins	GA	SO	Avg
1996-97	Colorado	1	0	1	0	60	3	0	3.00	....	....	....	....	....	....	....
1998-99	Colorado	4	1	1	1	217	9	0	2.49	....	....	....	....	....	....	....
99-2000	Colorado	23	9	8	3	1203	51	3	2.54	....	....	....	....	....	....	....
2000-01	Columbus	32	6	20	4	1830	99	0	3.25	....	....	....	....	....	....	....
2001-02	Columbus	42	9	24	5	2335	121	1	3.11	....	....	....	....	....	....	....
2002-03	Columbus	77	27	41	8	*4511	232	5	3.09	....	....	....	....	....	....	....
	NHL Totals	**179**	**52**	**95**	**21**	**10156**	**515**	**9**	**3.04**	....	....	....	....	....	....	....

Traded to **Columbus** by **Colorado** for Columbus' 2nd round choice (later traded to Carolina – Carolina selected Tomas Kurka) in 2000 Entry Draft, June 7, 2000.

DeROUVILLE, Philippe

Goaltender. Catches left. 6'1", 185 lbs. Born, Victoriaville, Que., August 7, 1974
(Pittsburgh's 5th choice, 115th overall, in 1992 Entry Draft).

Season	Club	GP	W	L	T	Mins	GA	SO	Avg	GP	W	L	Mins	GA	SO	Avg
1994-95	Pittsburgh	1	1	0	0	60	3	0	3.00	....	....	....	....	....	....	....
1996-97	Pittsburgh	2	0	2	0	111	6	0	3.24	....	....	....	....	....	....	....
	NHL Totals	**3**	**1**	**2**	**0**	**171**	**9**	**0**	**3.16**	....	....	....	....	....	....	....

DESJARDINS, Gerry

Goaltender. Catches left. 5'11", 190 lbs. Born, Sudbury, Ont., July 22, 1944

Season	Club	GP	W	L	T	Mins	GA	SO	Avg	GP	W	L	Mins	GA	SO	Avg
1968-69	Los Angeles	60	18	34	6	3499	190	4	3.26	9	3	4	431	28	0	3.90
1969-70	Los Angeles	43	7	29	5	2453	159	3	3.89	....	....	....	....	....	....	....
	Chicago	4	4	0	0	240	8	0	2.00	....	....	....	....	....	....	....
1970-71	Chicago	22	12	6	3	1217	49	0	2.42	....	....	....	....	....	....	....
1971-72	Chicago	6	1	2	3	360	21	0	3.50	1	1	0	60	5	0	5.00
1972-73	NY Islanders	44	5	35	3	2498	195	0	4.68	....	....	....	....	....	....	....
1973-74	NY Islanders	36	9	17	6	1945	101	0	3.12	....	....	....	....	....	....	....
1974-75	Buffalo	9	6	2	1	540	25	0	2.78	*15	7	5	760	43	0	3.39
1975-76	Buffalo	55	29	15	11	3280	161	2	2.95	9	4	5	563	28	0	2.98
1976-77	Buffalo	49	31	12	6	2871	126	3	2.63	1	0	1	60	4	0	4.00
1977-78	Buffalo	3	0	1	0	111	7	0	3.78	....	....	....	....	....	....	....
	NHL Totals	**331**	**122**	**153**	**44**	**19014**	**1042**	**12**	**3.29**	**35**	**15**	**15**	**1874**	**108**	**0**	**3.46**

Played in NHL All-Star Game (1977)

Traded to **Los Angeles** by **Montreal** for Los Angeles' 1st round choices in 1969 (later traded to Minnesota – Minnesota selected Dick Redmond) and 1972 (Steve Shutt) Amateur Drafts, June 11, 1968. Traded to **Chicago** by **Los Angeles** with Bill White and Bryan Campbell for Denis DeJordy, Gilles Marotte and Jim Stanfield, February 20, 1970. Traded to **California** by **Chicago** with Kerry Bond and Gerry Pinder for Gary Smith, September 9, 1971. Traded to **Chicago** by **California** for Paul Shmyr and Gilles Meloche, October 18, 1971. Claimed by **NY Islanders** from **Chicago** in Expansion Draft, June 6, 1972. Rights traded to **Buffalo** by **NY Islanders** for the rights to Garry Lariviere, February 19, 1975.

DesROCHERS, Patrick

Goaltender. Catches left. 6'3", 209 lbs. Born, Penetanguishene, Ont., October 27, 1979
(Phoenix's 1st choice, 14th overall, in 1998 Entry Draft).

Season	Club	GP	W	L	T	Mins	GA	SO	Avg	GP	W	L	Mins	GA	SO	Avg
2001-02	Phoenix	5	1	2	1	243	15	0	3.70	....	....	....	....	....	....	....
2002-03	Phoenix	4	0	3	0	175	11	0	3.77	....	....	....	....	....	....	....
	Carolina	2	1	1	0	122	7	0	3.44	....	....	....	....	....	....	....
	NHL Totals	**11**	**2**	**6**	**1**	**540**	**33**	**0**	**3.67**	....	....	....	....	....	....	....

Traded to **Carolina** by **Phoenix** for Jean-Marc Pelletier and future considerations, December 31, 2002.

DICKIE, Bill

Goaltender. Catches right. 5'8", 185 lbs. Born, Campbellton, N.B., February 20, 1916

Season	Club	GP	W	L	T	Mins	GA	SO	Avg	GP	W	L	Mins	GA	SO	Avg
1941-42	Chicago	1	1	0	0	60	3	0	3.00	....	....	....	....	....	....	....
	NHL Totals	**1**	**1**	**0**	**0**	**60**	**3**	**0**	**3.00**	....	....	....	....	....	....	....

Loaned to **Chicago** by **Montreal** (Mtl. Pats-MCSHL) to replace injured Sam LoPresti, February 5, 1942. (Chicago 4, Montreal 3)

DION, Connie

Goaltender. Catches right. 5'4", 140 lbs. Born, St-Remi-de-Rinqwick, Que., August 11, 1918

Season	Club	GP	W	L	T	Mins	GA	SO	Avg	GP	W	L	Mins	GA	SO	Avg
1943-44	Detroit	26	17	7	2	1560	80	1	3.08	5	1	4	300	17	0	3.40
1944-45	Detroit	12	6	4	2	720	39	0	3.25	....	....	....	....	....	....	....
	NHL Totals	**38**	**23**	**11**	**4**	**2280**	**119**	**1**	**3.13**	**5**	**1**	**4**	**300**	**17**	**0**	**3.40**

Traded to **Washington** (AHL) by **Montreal** for cash, October 9, 1941. Signed as a free agent by **Detroit**, January 25, 1944. Traded to **St. Louis** (AHL) by **Detroit** for cash, August 24, 1945.

DION, Michel

Goaltender. Catches left. 5'10", 185 lbs. Born, Granby, Que., February 11, 1954

Season	Club	GP	W	L	T	Mins	GA	SO	Avg	GP	W	L	Mins	GA	SO	Avg
1979-80	Quebec	50	15	25	6	2773	171	2	3.70	....	....	....	....	....	....	....
1980-81	Quebec	12	0	8	3	688	61	0	5.32	....	....	....	....	....	....	....
	Winnipeg	14	3	6	3	757	61	0	4.83	....	....	....	....	....	....	....
1981-82	Pittsburgh	62	25	24	12	3580	226	0	3.79	5	2	3	304	22	0	4.34
1982-83	Pittsburgh	49	12	30	4	2791	198	0	4.26	....	....	....	....	....	....	....
1983-84	Pittsburgh	30	2	19	4	1553	138	0	5.33	....	....	....	....	....	....	....
1984-85	Pittsburgh	10	3	6	0	553	43	0	4.67	....	....	....	....	....	....	....
	NHL Totals	**227**	**60**	**118**	**32**	**12695**	**898**	**2**	**4.24**	**5**	**2**	**3**	**304**	**22**	**0**	**4.34**

Played in NHL All-Star Game (1982)

Claimed by **Quebec** from **Cincinnati** (WHA) in WHA Dispersal Draft, June 9, 1979. Traded to **Winnipeg** by **Quebec** for cash, February 10, 1981. Signed as a free agent by **Pittsburgh**, June 30, 1981.

DiPIETRO, Rick

Goaltender. Catches right. 5'11", 185 lbs. Born, Winthrop, MA, September 19, 1981
(NY Islanders' 1st choice, 1st overall, in 2000 Entry Draft).

Season	Club	GP	W	L	T	Mins	GA	SO	Avg	GP	W	L	Mins	GA	SO	Avg
2000-01	NY Islanders	20	3	15	1	1083	63	0	3.49	....	....	....	....	....	....	....
2002-03	NY Islanders	10	2	5	2	585	29	0	2.97	1	0	0	15	0	0	0.00
	NHL Totals	**30**	**5**	**20**	**3**	**1668**	**92**	**0**	**3.31**	**1**	**0**	**0**	**15**	**0**	**0**	**0.00**

DIVIS, Reinhard

Goaltender. Catches left. 5'11", 200 lbs. Born, Vienna, Austria, July 4, 1975
(St. Louis' 8th choice, 261st overall, in 2000 Entry Draft).

Season	Club	GP	W	L	T	Mins	GA	SO	Avg	GP	W	L	Mins	GA	SO	Avg
2001-02	St. Louis	1	0	0	0	25	0	0	0.00	....	....	....	....	....	....	....
2002-03	St. Louis	2	2	0	0	83	1	0	0.72	....	....	....	....	....	....	....
	NHL Totals	**3**	**2**	**0**	**0**	**108**	**1**	**0**	**0.56**	....	....	....	....	....	....	....

DOLSON, Dolly

Goaltender. Catches left. 5'7", 160 lbs. Born, Hespeler, Ont., May 23, 1897

Season	Club	GP	W	L	T	Mins	GA	SO	Avg	GP	W	L	Mins	GA	SO	Avg
		REGULAR SEASON								PLAYOFFS						
1928-29	Detroit	*44	19	16	9	2750	63	10	1.37	2	0	2	120	7	0	3.50
1929-30	Detroit	5	0	4	1	320	24	0	4.50	....	....	....	....	....	....	....
1930-31	Detroit	*44	16	21	7	2750	105	6	2.29	....	....	....	....	....	....	....
	NHL Totals	**93**	**35**	**41**	**17**	**5820**	**192**	**16**	**1.98**	**2**	**0**	**2**	**120**	**7**	**0**	**3.50**

Claimed by **Detroit** from **Stratford** (Can-Pro) in Inter-League Draft, May 12, 1928.

DOPSON, Rob

Goaltender. Catches left. 6', 200 lbs. Born, Smiths Falls, Ont., August 21, 1967

Season	Club	GP	W	L	T	Mins	GA	SO	Avg	GP	W	L	Mins	GA	SO	Avg
1993-94	Pittsburgh	2	0	0	0	45	3	0	4.00	....	....	....	....	....	....	....
	NHL Totals	**2**	**0**	**0**	**0**	**45**	**3**	**0**	**4.00**	....	....	....	....	....	....	....

Signed as a free agent by **Pittsburgh**, July 6, 1991.

DOWIE, Bruce

Goaltender. Catches left. 5'10", 170 lbs. Born, Oakville, Ont., December 9, 1962

Season	Club	GP	W	L	T	Mins	GA	SO	Avg	GP	W	L	Mins	GA	SO	Avg
1983-84	Toronto	2	0	1	0	72	4	0	3.33	....	....	....	....	....	....	....
	NHL Totals	**2**	**0**	**1**	**0**	**72**	**4**	**0**	**3.33**	....	....	....	....	....	....	....

Signed as a free agent by **Toronto**, May 6, 1983.

DRAPER, Tom

Goaltender. Catches left. 5'11", 185 lbs. Born, Outremont, Que., November 20, 1966
(Winnipeg's 8th choice, 165th overall, in 1985 Entry Draft).

Season	Club	GP	W	L	T	Mins	GA	SO	Avg	GP	W	L	Mins	GA	SO	Avg
1988-89	Winnipeg	2	1	1	0	120	12	0	6.00	....	....	....	....	....	....	....
1989-90	Winnipeg	6	2	4	0	359	26	0	4.35	....	....	....	....	....	....	....
1991-92	Buffalo	26	10	9	5	1403	75	1	3.21	7	3	4	433	19	1	2.63
1992-93	Buffalo	11	5	6	0	664	41	0	3.70	....	....	....	....	....	....	....
1993-94	NY Islanders	7	1	3	0	227	16	0	4.23	....	....	....	....	....	....	....
1995-96	Winnipeg	1	0	0	0	34	3	0	5.29	....	....	....	....	....	....	....
	NHL Totals	**53**	**19**	**23**	**5**	**2807**	**173**	**1**	**3.70**	**7**	**3**	**4**	**433**	**19**	**1**	**2.63**

Traded to **St. Louis** by **Winnipeg** for future considerations (Jim Vesey, May 24, 1991), February 28, 1991. Traded to **Winnipeg** by **St. Louis** for future considerations, May 24, 1991. Traded to **Buffalo** by **Winnipeg** for Buffalo's 7th round choice (Artur Oktyabrev) in 1992 Entry Draft, June 22, 1991. Traded to **NY Islanders** by **Buffalo** for NY Islanders' 7th round choice (Steve Plouffe) in 1994 Entry Draft, September 30, 1993. Signed as a free agent by **Winnipeg**, December 14, 1995.

DRYDEN, Dave

Goaltender. Catches left. 6'1", 186 lbs. Born, Hamilton, Ont., September 5, 1941

Season	Club	GP	W	L	T	Mins	GA	SO	Avg	GP	W	L	Mins	GA	SO	Avg
1961-62	NY Rangers	1	0	1	0	40	3	0	4.50	....	....	....	....	....	....	....
1965-66	Chicago	11	3	4	1	453	23	0	3.05	1	0	0	13	0	0	0.00
1967-68	Chicago	27	7	8	5	1268	69	1	3.26	....	....	....	....	....	....	....
1968-69	Chicago	30	11	11	2	1479	79	3	3.20	....	....	....	....	....	....	....
1970-71	Buffalo	10	3	3	0	409	23	1	3.37	....	....	....	....	....	....	....
1971-72	Buffalo	20	3	9	5	1026	68	0	3.98	....	....	....	....	....	....	....
1972-73	Buffalo	37	14	13	7	2018	89	3	2.65	2	0	2	120	9	0	4.50
1973-74	Buffalo	53	23	20	8	2987	148	1	2.97	....	....	....	....	....	....	....
1979-80	Edmonton	14	2	7	3	744	53	0	4.27	....	....	....	....	....	....	....
	NHL Totals	**203**	**66**	**76**	**31**	**10424**	**555**	**9**	**3.19**	**3**	**0**	**2**	**133**	**9**	**0**	**4.06**

• Brother of Ken

Played in NHL All-Star Game (1974)

Loaned to **NY Rangers** by **Toronto** (Toronto-MTJHL) to replace injured Gump Worsley in 2nd period, February 3, 1962. (Toronto 4, NY Rangers 1). Signed as a free agent by **Chicago** (Buffalo-AHL), March 12, 1965. • Suspended by **Chicago** (Dallas-CHL) after refusing assignment to minors, October, 1969. Traded to **Pittsburgh** by **Chicago** for cash, June 10, 1970. Traded to **Buffalo** by **Pittsburgh** for cash, October 9, 1970. Reclaimed by **Buffalo** from **Edmonton** prior to Expansion Draft, June 9, 1979. Claimed as a priority selection by **Edmonton**, June 9, 1979.

DRYDEN, Ken HHOF

Goaltender. Catches left. 6'4", 205 lbs. Born, Hamilton, Ont., August 8, 1947
(Boston's 3rd choice, 14th overall, in 1964 Amateur Draft).

Season	Club	GP	W	L	T	Mins	GA	SO	Avg	GP	W	L	Mins	GA	SO	Avg
1970-71♦	Montreal	6	6	0	0	327	9	0	1.65	*20	*12	8	*1221	61	0	3.00
1971-72	Montreal	*64	*39	8	15	*3800	142	8	2.24	6	2	4	360	17	0	2.83
1972-73♦	Montreal	54	*33	7	13	3165	119	*6	*2.26	*17	*12	5	*1039	50	1	2.89
1974-75	Montreal	56	30	9	16	3320	149	4	2.69	11	6	5	688	29	2	2.53
1975-76♦	Montreal	62	*42	10	8	3580	121	*8	*2.03	*13	*12	1	*780	25	1	*1.92
1976-77♦	Montreal	56	*41	6	8	3275	117	*10	2.14	*14	*12	2	849	22	*4	*1.55
1977-78♦	Montreal	52	37	7	7	3071	105	5	*2.05	*15	*12	3	*919	29	*2	*1.89
1978-79♦	Montreal	47	30	10	7	2814	108	*5	*2.30	16	*12	4	990	41	0	2.48
	NHL Totals	**397**	**258**	**57**	**74**	**23352**	**870**	**46**	**2.24**	**112**	**80**	**32**	**6846**	**274**	**10**	**2.40**

• Brother of Dave • Conn Smythe Trophy (1971) • NHL Second All-Star Team (1972) • Calder Memorial Trophy (1972) • NHL First All-Star Team (1973, 1976, 1977, 1978, 1979) • Vezina Trophy (1973, 1976) • Shared Vezina Trophy with Michel Larocque (1977, 1978, 1979)

Played in NHL All-Star Game (1972, 1975, 1976, 1977, 1978)

Rights traded to **Montreal** by **Boston** with Alex Campbell for Guy Allen and Paul Reid, June, 1964. Promoted to **Montreal** from **Mtl. Voyageurs** (AHL), March, 1971. • Sat out entire 1973-74 season after failing to come to contract terms with Montreal.

DUFFUS, Parris

Goaltender. Catches left. 6'2", 192 lbs. Born, Denver, CO, January 27, 1970
(St. Louis' 6th choice, 180th overall, in 1990 Entry Draft).

Season	Club	GP	W	L	T	Mins	GA	SO	Avg	GP	W	L	Mins	GA	SO	Avg
1996-97	Phoenix	1	0	0	0	29	1	0	2.07	....	....	....	....	....	....	....
	NHL Totals	**1**	**0**	**0**	**0**	**29**	**1**	**0**	**2.07**	....	....	....	....	....	....	....

Signed as a free agent by **Winnipeg**, August 4, 1995. Transferred to **Phoenix** after **Winnipeg** franchise relocated, July 1, 1996.

DUMAS, Michel

Goaltender. Catches left. 5'9", 180 lbs. Born, St-Antoine-de-Pontbriand, Que., July 8, 1949

Season	Club	GP	W	L	T	Mins	GA	SO	Avg	GP	W	L	Mins	GA	SO	Avg
1974-75	Chicago	3	2	0	0	121	7	0	3.47	1	0	0	19	1	0	3.16
1975-76	Chicago	DID NOT PLAY – SPARE GOALTENDER														
1976-77	Chicago	5	0	1	2	241	17	0	4.23	....	....	....	....	....	....	....
	NHL Totals	**8**	**2**	**1**	**2**	**362**	**24**	**0**	**3.98**	**1**	**0**	**0**	**19**	**1**	**0**	**3.16**

Signed as a free agent by **Chicago**, October 7, 1971. • On active roster for entire 1975-76 season but did not play. • Suffered career-ending eye injury in game vs. Colorado, December 26, 1976.

DUNHAM, Mike

Goaltender. Catches left. 6'3", 200 lbs. Born, Johnson City, NY, June 1, 1972
(New Jersey's 4th choice, 53rd overall, in 1990 Entry Draft).

Season	Club	GP	W	L	T	Mins	GA	SO	Avg	GP	W	L	Mins	GA	SO	Avg
1996-97	New Jersey	26	8	7	1	1013	43	2	2.55	....	....	....	....	....	....	....
1997-98	New Jersey	15	5	5	3	773	29	1	2.25	....	....	....	....	....	....	....
1998-99	Nashville	44	16	23	3	2472	127	1	3.08	....	....	....	....	....	....	....
99-2000	Nashville	52	19	27	6	3077	146	0	2.85	....	....	....	....	....	....	....
2000-01	Nashville	48	21	21	4	2810	107	4	2.28	....	....	....	....	....	....	....
2001-02	Nashville	58	23	24	9	3316	144	3	2.61	....	....	....	....	....	....	....
2002-03	Nashville	15	2	9	2	819	43	0	3.15	....	....	....	....	....	....	....
	NY Rangers	43	19	17	5	2467	94	5	2.29	....	....	....	....	....	....	....
	NHL Totals	**301**	**113**	**133**	**33**	**16747**	**733**	**16**	**2.63**	....	....	....	....	....	....	....

Claimed by **Nashville** from **New Jersey** in Expansion Draft, June 26, 1998. Traded to **NY Rangers** by **Nashville** for Rem Murray, Tomas Kloucek and Marek Zidlicky, December 12, 2002.

DUPUIS, Bob

Goaltender. Catches left. 5'11", 167 lbs. Born, North Bay, Ont., August 26, 1952

Season	Club	GP	W	L	T	Mins	GA	SO	Avg	GP	W	L	Mins	GA	SO	Avg
1979-80	Edmonton	1	0	1	0	60	4	0	4.00	....	....	....	....	....	....	....
	NHL Totals	**1**	**0**	**1**	**0**	**60**	**4**	**0**	**4.00**	....	....	....	....	....	....	....

Signed as a free agent by **Edmonton**, March, 1980.

DURNAN, Bill HHOF

Goaltender. Catches r/l. 6', 190 lbs. Born, Toronto, Ont., January 22, 1916

Season	Club	GP	W	L	T	Mins	GA	SO	Avg	GP	W	L	Mins	GA	SO	Avg
1943-44♦	Montreal	*50	*38	5	7	*3000	109	2	*2.18	*9	*8	1	*549	14	*1	*1.53
1944-45	Montreal	*50	*38	8	4	*3000	121	1	*2.42	6	2	4	373	15	0	2.41
1945-46♦	Montreal	40	*24	11	5	2400	104	*4	*2.60	9	*8	1	581	20	0	*2.07
1946-47	Montreal	*60	*34	16	10	*3600	138	4	*2.30	*11	6	5	*720	23	*1	*1.92
1947-48	Montreal	59	20	28	10	3505	162	5	2.77	....	....	....	....	....	....	....
1948-49	Montreal	*60	28	23	9	*3600	126	*10	*2.10	7	3	4	468	17	0	2.18
1949-50	Montreal	64	26	21	17	3840	141	8	*2.20	3	0	3	180	10	0	3.33
	NHL Totals	**383**	**208**	**112**	**62**	**22945**	**901**	**34**	**2.36**	**45**	**27**	**18**	**2871**	**99**	**2**	**2.07**

NHL First All-Star Team (1944, 1945, 1946, 1947, 1949, 1950) • Vezina Trophy (1944, 1945, 1946, 1947, 1949, 1950)

Played in NHL All-Star Game (1947, 1948, 1949)

Signed as a free agent by **Montreal**, October 30, 1943.

DYCK, Ed

Goaltender. Catches left. 5'11", 160 lbs. Born, Warman, Sask., October 29, 1950
(Vancouver's 3rd choice, 30th overall, in 1970 Amateur Draft).

Season	Club	GP	W	L	T	Mins	GA	SO	Avg	GP	W	L	Mins	GA	SO	Avg
1971-72	Vancouver	12	1	6	2	573	35	0	3.66	....	....	....	....	....	....	....
1972-73	Vancouver	25	5	17	1	1297	98	1	4.53	....	....	....	....	....	....	....
1973-74	Vancouver	12	2	5	2	583	45	0	4.63	....	....	....	....	....	....	....
	NHL Totals	**49**	**8**	**28**	**5**	**2453**	**178**	**1**	**4.35**	....	....	....	....	....	....	....

EDWARDS, Don

Goaltender. Catches left. 5'9", 160 lbs. Born, Hamilton, Ont., September 28, 1955
(Buffalo's 6th choice, 89th overall, in 1975 Amateur Draft).

Season	Club	GP	W	L	T	Mins	GA	SO	Avg	GP	W	L	Mins	GA	SO	Avg
1976-77	Buffalo	25	16	7	2	1480	62	2	2.51	5	2	3	300	15	0	3.00
1977-78	Buffalo	*72	*38	16	17	*4209	185	5	2.64	8	3	5	482	22	0	2.74
1978-79	Buffalo	54	26	18	9	3160	159	2	3.02	....	....	....	....	....	....	....
1979-80	Buffalo	49	27	9	12	2920	125	2	2.57	6	3	3	360	17	1	2.83
1980-81	Buffalo	45	23	10	12	2700	133	*3	2.96	8	4	4	503	28	0	3.34
1981-82	Buffalo	62	26	23	9	3500	205	0	3.51	4	1	3	214	16	0	4.49
1982-83	Calgary	39	16	15	6	2209	148	1	4.02	5	1	2	226	22	0	5.84
1983-84	Calgary	41	13	19	5	2303	157	0	4.09	6	2	1	217	12	0	3.32
1984-85	Calgary	34	11	15	2	1691	115	1	4.08	....	....	....	....	....	....	....
1985-86	Toronto	38	12	23	0	2009	160	0	4.78	....	....	....	....	....	....	....
	NHL Totals	**459**	**208**	**155**	**74**	**26181**	**1449**	**16**	**3.32**	**42**	**16**	**21**	**2302**	**132**	**1**	**3.44**

NHL Second All-Star Team (1978, 1980) • Shared Vezina Trophy with Bob Sauve (1980)

Played in NHL All-Star Game (1980, 1982)

Traded to **Calgary** by **Buffalo** with Richie Dunn, Buffalo's 2nd round choice (Richard Kromm) in 1982 Entry Draft and Buffalo's 1st round choice (Dan Quinn) in 1983 Entry Draft for Calgary's 1st (Paul Cyr) and 2nd (Jens Johansson) round choices in 1982 Entry Draft and Calgary's 1st (Normand Lacombe) and 2nd (John Tucker) round choices in 1983 Entry Draft, June 9, 1982. Traded to **Toronto** by **Calgary** for Toronto's 4th round choice (Tim Harris) in 1987 Entry Draft, May 29, 1985.

EDWARDS, Gary

Goaltender. Catches left. 5'9", 165 lbs. Born, Toronto, Ont., October 5, 1947
(St. Louis' 1st choice, 6th overall, in 1968 Amateur Draft).

Season	Club	GP	W	L	T	Mins	GA	SO	Avg	GP	W	L	Mins	GA	SO	Avg
1968-69	St. Louis	1	0	0	0	4	0	0	0.00	....	....	....	....	....	....	....
1969-70	St. Louis	1	0	1	0	60	4	0	4.00	....	....	....	....	....	....	....
1971-72	Los Angeles	44	13	23	5	2503	150	2	3.60	....	....	....	....	....	....	....
1972-73	Los Angeles	27	9	16	1	1560	94	1	3.62	....	....	....	....	....	....	....
1973-74	Los Angeles	18	5	7	2	929	50	1	3.23	1	1	0	60	1	0	1.00
1974-75	Los Angeles	27	15	3	8	1561	61	3	2.34	....	....	....	....	....	....	....

Season	Club	GP	W	L	T	Mins	GA	SO	Avg	GP	W	L	Mins	GA	SO	Avg
		REGULAR SEASON								PLAYOFFS						
1975-76	Los Angeles	29	12	13	4	1740	103	0	3.55	2	1	1	120	9	0	4.50
1976-77	Los Angeles	10	0	6	2	501	39	0	4.67	....	....	....	....	....	....	....
	Cleveland	17	4	10	3	999	68	2	4.08	....	....	....	....	....	....	....
1977-78	Cleveland	30	6	18	5	1700	128	0	4.52	....	....	....	....	....	....	....
1978-79	Minnesota	25	6	11	5	1337	83	0	3.72	....	....	....	....	....	....	....
1979-80	Minnesota	26	9	7	10	1539	82	0	3.20	7	3	3	337	22	0	3.92
1980-81	Edmonton	15	5	3	4	729	44	0	3.62	1	0	0	20	2	0	6.00
1981-82	St. Louis	10	1	5	1	480	45	0	5.63	....	....	....	....	....	....	....
	Pittsburgh	6	3	2	1	360	22	1	3.67	....	....	....	....	....	....	....
	NHL Totals	**286**	**88**	**125**	**51**	**16002**	**973**	**10**	**3.65**	**11**	**5**	**4**	**537**	**34**	**0**	**3.80**

Loaned to **San Diego** (WHL) by **St. Louis** (Kansas City-CHL) for the loan of Bob Champoux, November, 1969. Claimed by **Buffalo** from **St. Louis** in Expansion Draft, June 10, 1970. Loaned to **St. Louis** (Kansas City-CHL) by **Buffalo** for cash, October, 1970. Claimed by **Los Angeles** from **Buffalo** in Intra-League Draft, June 8, 1971. Traded to **Cleveland** by **Los Angeles** with Juha Widing for Gary Simmons and Jim Moxey, January 22, 1977. Placed on **Minnesota** reserve list after Cleveland-Minnesota Dispersal Draft, June 15, 1978. Traded to **Edmonton** by **Minnesota** for future considerations, February 2, 1981. Claimed by **St. Louis** from **Edmonton** in Waiver Draft, October 8, 1981. Claimed on waivers by **Pittsburgh** from **St. Louis**, February 14, 1982.

EDWARDS, Marv

Goaltender. Catches left. 5'8", 155 lbs. Born, St. Catharines, Ont., August 15, 1935

Season	Club	GP	W	L	T	Mins	GA	SO	Avg	GP	W	L	Mins	GA	SO	Avg
1968-69	Pittsburgh	1	0	1	0	60	3	0	3.00	....	....	....	....	....	....	....
1969-70	Toronto	25	10	9	4	1420	77	1	3.25	....	....	....	....	....	....	....
1972-73	California	21	4	14	2	1207	87	1	4.32	....	....	....	....	....	....	....
1973-74	California	14	1	10	1	780	51	0	3.92	....	....	....	....	....	....	....
	NHL Totals	**61**	**15**	**34**	**7**	**3467**	**218**	**2**	**3.77**	....	....	....	....	....	....	....

Signed as a free agent by **Pittsburgh**, September, 1967. Claimed by **Toronto** from **Pittsburgh** in Intra-League Draft, June 11, 1969. Claimed by **California** (Salt Lake-WHL) from **Toronto** in Reverse Draft, June 8, 1972.

EDWARDS, Roy

Goaltender. Catches right. 5'8", 165 lbs. Born, Seneca Township, Ont., March 12, 1937

Season	Club	GP	W	L	T	Mins	GA	SO	Avg	GP	W	L	Mins	GA	SO	Avg
1967-68	Detroit	41	15	15	8	2177	127	0	3.50	....	....	....	....	....	....	....
1968-69	Detroit	40	18	11	6	2099	89	4	2.54	....	....	....	....	....	....	....
1969-70	Detroit	47	24	15	6	2683	116	2	2.59	4	0	3	206	11	0	3.20
1970-71	Detroit	37	11	19	7	2104	119	0	3.39	....	....	....	....	....	....	....
1971-72	Pittsburgh	15	2	8	4	847	36	0	2.55	....	....	....	....	....	....	....
1972-73	Detroit	52	27	17	7	3012	132	*6	2.63	....	....	....	....	....	....	....
1973-74	Detroit	4	0	3	0	187	18	0	5.78	....	....	....	....	....	....	....
	NHL Totals	**236**	**97**	**88**	**38**	**13109**	**637**	**12**	**2.92**	**4**	**0**	**3**	**206**	**11**	**0**	**3.20**

Claimed by **Pittsburgh** from **Chicago** in Expansion Draft, June 6, 1967. Traded to **Detroit** by **Pittsburgh** for Hank Bassen, September 7, 1967. Claimed on waivers by **Pittsburgh** from **Detroit**, June 7, 1971 • Retired to recover from stress and nervous exhaustion, December 30, 1971. Traded to **Detroit** by **Pittsburgh** for cash, October 6, 1972 . Claimed on waivers by **Buffalo** from **Detroit**, May 20, 1974.

ELIOT, Darren

Goaltender. Catches right. 6'1", 175 lbs. Born, Hamilton, Ont., November 26, 1961
(Los Angeles' 8th choice, 115th overall, in 1980 Entry Draft).

Season	Club	GP	W	L	T	Mins	GA	SO	Avg	GP	W	L	Mins	GA	SO	Avg
1984-85	Los Angeles	33	12	11	6	1882	137	0	4.37	....	....	....	....	....	....	....
1985-86	Los Angeles	27	5	17	3	1481	121	0	4.90	....	....	....	....	....	....	....
1986-87	Los Angeles	24	8	13	2	1404	103	1	4.40	1	0	0	40	7	0	10.50
1987-88	Detroit	3	0	0	1	97	9	0	5.57	....	....	....	....	....	....	....
1988-89	Buffalo	2	0	0	0	67	7	0	6.27	....	....	....	....	....	....	....
	NHL Totals	**89**	**25**	**41**	**12**	**4931**	**377**	**1**	**4.59**	**1**	**0**	**0**	**40**	**7**	**0**	**10.50**

Signed as a free agent by **Detroit**, June 30, 1987. Signed as a free agent by **Buffalo**, February 27, 1989.

ELLACOTT, Ken

Goaltender. Catches left. 5'8", 160 lbs. Born, Paris, Ont., March 3, 1959
(Vancouver's 3rd choice, 47th overall, in 1979 Entry Draft).

Season	Club	GP	W	L	T	Mins	GA	SO	Avg	GP	W	L	Mins	GA	SO	Avg
1982-83	Vancouver	12	2	3	4	555	41	0	4.43	....	....	....	....	....	....	....
	NHL Totals	**12**	**2**	**3**	**4**	**555**	**41**	**0**	**4.43**	....	....	....	....	....	....	....

EMERY, Ray

Goaltender. Catches left. 6'3", 192 lbs. Born, Cayuga, Ont., September 28, 1982
(Ottawa's 4th choice, 99th overall, in 2001 Entry Draft).

Season	Club	GP	W	L	T	Mins	GA	SO	Avg	GP	W	L	Mins	GA	SO	Avg
2002-03	Ottawa	3	1	0	0	85	2	0	1.41	....	....	....	....	....	....	....
	NHL Totals	**3**	**1**	**0**	**0**	**85**	**2**	**0**	**1.41**	....	....	....	....	....	....	....

ERICKSON, Chad

Goaltender. Catches right. 5'10", 175 lbs. Born, Minneapolis, MN, August 21, 1970
(New Jersey's 8th choice, 138th overall, in 1988 Entry Draft).

Season	Club	GP	W	L	T	Mins	GA	SO	Avg	GP	W	L	Mins	GA	SO	Avg
1991-92	New Jersey	2	1	1	0	120	9	0	4.50	....	....	....	....	....	....	....
	NHL Totals	**2**	**1**	**1**	**0**	**120**	**9**	**0**	**4.50**	....	....	....	....	....	....	....

ESCHE, Robert

Goaltender. Catches left. 6'1", 210 lbs. Born, Whitesboro, NY, January 22, 1978
(Phoenix's 5th choice, 139th overall, in 1996 Entry Draft).

Season	Club	GP	W	L	T	Mins	GA	SO	Avg	GP	W	L	Mins	GA	SO	Avg
1998-99	Phoenix	3	0	1	0	130	7	0	3.23	....	....	....	....	....	....	....
99-2000	Phoenix	8	2	5	0	408	23	0	3.38	....	....	....	....	....	....	....
2000-01	Phoenix	25	10	8	4	1350	68	2	3.02	....	....	....	....	....	....	....
2001-02	Phoenix	22	6	10	2	1145	52	1	2.72	....	....	....	....	....	....	....
2002-03	Philadelphia	30	12	9	3	1638	60	2	2.20	1	0	0	30	1	0	2.00
	NHL Totals	**88**	**30**	**33**	**9**	**4671**	**210**	**5**	**2.70**	**1**	**0**	**0**	**30**	**1**	**0**	**2.00**

Shared William M. Jennings Trophy with Roman Cechmanek (tied with Martin Brodeur) (2003)

Traded to **Philadelphia** by **Phoenix** with Michal Handzus for Brian Boucher and Nashville's 3rd round choice (previously acquired, Phoenix selected Joe Callahan) in 2002 Entry Draft, June 12, 2002.

ESPOSITO, Tony — HHOF

Goaltender. Catches right. 5'11", 185 lbs. Born, Sault Ste. Marie, Ont., April 23, 1943

Season	Club	GP	W	L	T	Mins	GA	SO	Avg	GP	W	L	Mins	GA	SO	Avg
1968-69♦	Montreal	13	5	4	4	746	34	2	2.73	....	....	....	....	....	....	....
1969-70	Chicago	63	*38	17	8	3763	136	*15	2.17	8	4	4	480	27	0	3.38
1970-71	Chicago	57	*35	14	6	3325	126	6	2.27	18	11	7	1151	42	*2	*2.19
1971-72	Chicago	48	31	10	6	2780	82	*9	*1.77	5	2	3	300	16	0	3.20
1972-73	Chicago	56	32	17	7	3340	140	4	2.51	15	10	5	895	46	1	3.08
1973-74	Chicago	70	34	14	21	4143	141	10	2.04	10	6	4	584	28	*2	2.88
1974-75	Chicago	71	34	30	7	*4219	193	6	2.74	8	3	5	472	34	0	4.32
1975-76	Chicago	*68	30	23	13	*4003	198	4	2.97	4	0	4	240	13	0	3.25
1976-77	Chicago	*69	25	36	8	*4067	234	2	3.45	2	0	2	120	6	0	3.00
1977-78	Chicago	64	28	22	14	3840	168	5	2.63	4	0	4	252	19	0	4.52
1978-79	Chicago	63	24	28	11	*3780	206	4	3.27	4	0	4	243	14	0	3.46
1979-80	Chicago	*69	31	22	16	*4140	205	*6	2.97	6	3	3	373	14	0	2.25
1980-81	Chicago	*66	29	23	14	*3935	246	0	3.75	3	0	3	215	15	0	4.19
1981-82	Chicago	52	19	25	8	3069	231	1	4.52	7	3	3	381	16	*1	2.52
1982-83	Chicago	39	23	11	5	2340	135	1	3.46	5	3	2	311	18	0	3.47
1983-84	Chicago	18	5	10	3	1095	88	1	4.82	....	....	....	....	....	....	....
	NHL Totals	**886**	**423**	**306**	**151**	**52585**	**2563**	**76**	**2.92**	**99**	**45**	**53**	**6017**	**308**	**6**	**3.07**

• Brother of Phil • NHL First All-Star Team (1970, 1972, 1980) • Calder Memorial Trophy (1970) • Vezina Trophy (1970) • Shared Vezina Trophy with Gary Smith (1972) • NHL Second All-Star Team (1973, 1974) • Vezina Trophy (tied with Bernie Parent) (1974)

Played in NHL All-Star Game (1970, 1971, 1972, 1973, 1974, 1980)

Signed as a free agent by **Montreal** (Cleveland-AHL), September 29, 1967. Claimed by **Chicago** from **Montreal** in Intra-League Draft, June 11, 1969.

ESSENSA, Bob

Goaltender. Catches left. 6', 190 lbs. Born, Toronto, Ont., January 14, 1965
(Winnipeg's 5th choice, 71st overall, in 1983 Entry Draft).

Season	Club	GP	W	L	T	Mins	GA	SO	Avg	GP	W	L	Mins	GA	SO	Avg
1988-89	Winnipeg	20	6	8	3	1102	68	1	3.70	....	....	....	....	....	....	....
1989-90	Winnipeg	36	18	9	5	2035	107	1	3.15	4	2	1	206	12	0	3.50
1990-91	Winnipeg	55	19	24	6	2916	153	4	3.15	....	....	....	....	....	....	....
1991-92	Winnipeg	47	21	17	6	2627	126	*5	2.88	1	0	0	33	3	0	5.45
1992-93	Winnipeg	67	33	26	6	3855	227	2	3.53	6	2	4	367	20	0	3.27
1993-94	Winnipeg	56	19	30	6	3136	201	1	3.85	....	....	....	....	....	....	....
	Detroit	13	4	7	2	778	34	1	2.62	2	0	2	109	9	0	4.95
1996-97	Edmonton	19	4	8	0	868	41	1	2.83	....	....	....	....	....	....	....
1997-98	Edmonton	16	6	6	1	825	35	0	2.55	1	0	0	27	1	0	2.22
1998-99	Edmonton	39	12	14	6	2091	96	0	2.75	....	....	....	....	....	....	....
99-2000	Phoenix	30	13	10	3	1573	73	1	2.78	....	....	....	....	....	....	....
2000-01	Vancouver	39	18	12	3	2059	92	1	2.68	2	0	2	122	6	0	2.95
2001-02	Buffalo	9	0	5	0	350	17	0	2.91	....	....	....	....	....	....	....
	NHL Totals	**446**	**173**	**176**	**47**	**24215**	**1270**	**18**	**3.15**	**16**	**4**	**9**	**864**	**51**	**0**	**3.54**

NHL All-Rookie Team (1990)

Traded to **Detroit** by **Winnipeg** with Sergei Bautin for Tim Cheveldae and Dallas Drake, March 8, 1994. Traded to **Edmonton** by **Detroit** for future considerations, June 14, 1996. Signed as a free agent by **Phoenix**, September 5, 1999. Signed as a free agent by **Vancouver**, July 26, 2000. Signed as a free agent by **Buffalo**, August 3, 2001.

EVANS, Claude

Goaltender. Catches left. 5'8", 165 lbs. Born, Longueuil, Que., April 28, 1933

Season	Club	GP	W	L	T	Mins	GA	SO	Avg	GP	W	L	Mins	GA	SO	Avg
1954-55	Montreal	4	1	2	0	200	12	0	3.60	....	....	....	....	....	....	....
1957-58	Boston	1	0	0	1	60	4	0	4.00	....	....	....	....	....	....	....
	NHL Totals	**5**	**1**	**2**	**1**	**260**	**16**	**0**	**3.69**	....	....	....	....	....	....	....

Promoted to **Montreal** from **Mtl. Royals** (QHL) to replace injured Jacques Plante in games from November 13 through 18, 1954. Promoted to **Boston** from **Springfield** (AHL) to replace injured Harry Lumley, March 6, 1958. (Chicago 4, Boston 4)

EXELBY, Randy

Goaltender. Catches left. 5'9", 170 lbs. Born, Toronto, Ont., August 13, 1965
(Montreal's 1st choice, 20th overall, in 1986 Supplemental Draft).

Season	Club	GP	W	L	T	Mins	GA	SO	Avg	GP	W	L	Mins	GA	SO	Avg
1988-89	Montreal	1	0	0	0	3	0	0	0.00	....	....	....	....	....	....	....
1989-90	Edmonton	1	0	1	0	60	5	0	5.00	....	....	....	....	....	....	....
	NHL Totals	**2**	**0**	**1**	**0**	**63**	**5**	**0**	**4.76**	....	....	....	....	....	....	....

Traded to **Edmonton** by **Montreal** for cash, October 2, 1989.

FANKHOUSER, Scott

Goaltender. Catches left. 6'2", 205 lbs. Born, Bismark, ND, July 1, 1975
(St. Louis' 8th choice, 276th overall, in 1994 Entry Draft).

Season	Club	GP	W	L	T	Mins	GA	SO	Avg	GP	W	L	Mins	GA	SO	Avg
99-2000	Atlanta	16	2	11	2	920	49	0	3.20	....	....	....	....	....	....	....
2000-01	Atlanta	7	2	1	0	260	16	0	3.69	....	....	....	....	....	....	....
	NHL Totals	**23**	**4**	**12**	**2**	**1180**	**65**	**0**	**3.31**	....	....	....	....	....	....	....

Signed as a free agent by **Atlanta**, August 24, 1999.

FARR, Rocky

Goaltender. Catches right. 5'10", 175 lbs. Born, Toronto, Ont., April 7, 1947

Season	Club	GP	W	L	T	Mins	GA	SO	Avg	GP	W	L	Mins	GA	SO	Avg
1972-73	Buffalo	1	0	1	0	29	3	0	6.21	....	....	....	....	....	....	....
1973-74	Buffalo	11	2	4	1	480	25	0	3.13	....	....	....	....	....	....	....

Season	Club	GP	W	L	T	Mins	GA	SO	Avg	GP	W	L	Mins	GA	SO	Avg
		REGULAR SEASON								PLAYOFFS						
1974-75	Buffalo	7	0	1	2	213	14	0	3.94							
	NHL Totals	**19**	**2**	**6**	**3**	**722**	**42**	**0**	**3.49**							

Claimed by **Cleveland** (AHL) (Montreal) from **Montreal** in Reverse Draft, June 13, 1968. Claimed by **Buffalo** from **Montreal** in Expansion Draft, June 10, 1970. Traded to **Kansas City** by **Buffalo** for cash, October 1, 1975.

FAVELL, Doug

Goaltender. Catches left. 5'10", 172 lbs. Born, St. Catharines, Ont., April 5, 1945

Season	Club	GP	W	L	T	Mins	GA	SO	Avg	GP	W	L	Mins	GA	SO	Avg
1967-68	Philadelphia	37	15	15	6	2192	83	4	2.27	2	1	1	120	8	0	4.00
1968-69	Philadelphia	21	3	12	5	1195	71	1	3.56	1	0	1	60	5	0	5.00
1969-70	Philadelphia	15	4	5	4	820	43	1	3.15							
1970-71	Philadelphia	44	16	15	9	2434	108	2	2.66	2	0	2	120	8	0	4.00
1971-72	Philadelphia	54	18	25	9	2993	140	5	2.81							
1972-73	Philadelphia	44	20	15	4	2419	114	3	2.83	11	5	6	669	29	1	2.60
1973-74	Toronto	32	14	7	9	1752	79	0	2.71	3	0	3	181	10	0	3.31
1974-75	Toronto	39	12	17	6	2149	145	1	4.05							
1975-76	Toronto	3	0	2	1	160	15	0	5.63							
1976-77	Colorado	30	8	15	3	1614	105	0	3.90							
1977-78	Colorado	47	13	20	11	2663	159	1	3.58	2	0	2	120	6	0	3.00
1978-79	Colorado	7	0	5	2	380	34	0	5.37							
	NHL Totals	**373**	**123**	**153**	**69**	**20771**	**1096**	**18**	**3.17**	**21**	**6**	**15**	**1270**	**66**	**1**	**3.12**

Claimed by **Philadelphia** from **Boston** in Expansion Draft, June 6, 1967. • Missed remainder of 1969-70 season recovering from heel injury suffered in dressing room accident, February 11, 1970. Traded to **Toronto** by **Philadelphia** to complete transaction that sent Bernie Parent to Philadelphia (May 15, 1973), July 27, 1973. Traded to **Colorado** by **Toronto** for cash, September 15, 1976. Claimed by **Edmonton** from **Colorado** in Expansion Draft, June 13, 1979. • Only player to be claimed in both the 1967 and 1979 Expansion Drafts.

FERNANDEZ, Manny

Goaltender. Catches left. 6', 180 lbs. Born, Etobicoke, Ont., August 27, 1974
(Quebec's 4th choice, 52nd overall, in 1992 Entry Draft).

Season	Club	GP	W	L	T	Mins	GA	SO	Avg	GP	W	L	Mins	GA	SO	Avg
1994-95	Dallas	1	0	1	0	59	3	0	3.05							
1995-96	Dallas	5	0	1	1	249	19	0	4.58							
1997-98	Dallas	2	1	0	0	69	2	0	1.74	1	0	0	2	0	0	0.00
1998-99	Dallas	1	0	1	0	60	2	0	2.00							
99-2000	Dallas	24	11	8	3	1353	48	1	2.13	1	0	0	17	1	0	3.53
2000-01	Minnesota	42	19	17	4	2461	92	4	2.24							
2001-02	Minnesota	44	12	24	5	2463	125	1	3.05							
2002-03	Minnesota	35	19	13	2	1979	74	2	2.24	9	3	4	552	18	0	1.96
	NHL Totals	**154**	**62**	**65**	**15**	**8693**	**365**	**8**	**2.52**	**11**	**3**	**4**	**571**	**19**	**0**	**2.00**

Rights traded to **Dallas** by **Quebec** for Tommy Sjodin and Dallas' 3rd round choice (Chris Drury) in 1994 Entry Draft, February 13, 1994. Traded to **Minnesota** by **Dallas** with Brad Lukowich for Minnesota's 3rd round choice (Joel Lundqvist) in 2000 Entry Draft and Minnesota's 4th round choice (later traded back to Minnesota – later traded to Los Angeles – Los Angeles selected Aaron Rome) in 2002 Entry Draft, June 12, 2000.

FICHAUD, Eric

Goaltender. Catches left. 5'11", 171 lbs. Born, Anjou, Que., November 4, 1975
(Toronto's 1st choice, 16th overall, in 1994 Entry Draft).

Season	Club	GP	W	L	T	Mins	GA	SO	Avg	GP	W	L	Mins	GA	SO	Avg
1995-96	NY Islanders	24	7	12	2	1234	68	1	3.31							
1996-97	NY Islanders	34	9	14	4	1759	91	0	3.10							
1997-98	NY Islanders	17	3	8	3	807	40	0	2.97							
1998-99	Nashville	9	0	6	0	447	24	0	3.22							
99-2000	Carolina	9	3	5	1	490	24	1	2.94							
2000-01	Montreal	2	0	2	0	62	4	0	3.87							
	NHL Totals	**95**	**22**	**47**	**10**	**4799**	**251**	**2**	**3.14**							

Traded to **NY Islanders** by **Toronto** for Benoit Hogue, NY Islanders' 3rd round choice (Ryan Pepperall) in 1995 Entry Draft and NY Islanders' 5th round choice (Brandon Sugden) in 1996 Entry Draft, April 6, 1995. Traded to **Edmonton** by **NY Islanders** for Mike Watt, June 18, 1998. Traded to **Nashville** by **Edmonton** with Drake Berehowsky and Greg de Vries for Mikhail Shtalenkov and Jim Dowd, October 1, 1998. Traded to **Carolina** by **Nashville** for Toronto's 4th round choice (previously acquired, Nashville selected Yevgeny Pavlov) in 1999 Entry Draft and future considerations, June 26, 1999. Claimed on waivers by **Montreal** from **Carolina**, February 11, 2000. Signed as a free agent by **Montreal**, September 10, 2002.

FINLEY, Brian

Goaltender. Catches right. 6'3", 205 lbs. Born, Sault Ste. Marie, Ont., July 13, 1981
(Nashville's 1st choice, 6th overall, in 1999 Entry Draft).

Season	Club	GP	W	L	T	Mins	GA	SO	Avg	GP	W	L	Mins	GA	SO	Avg
2002-03	Nashville	1	0	0	0	47	3	0	3.83							
	NHL Totals	**1**	**0**	**0**	**0**	**47**	**3**	**0**	**3.83**							

FISET, Stephane

Goaltender. Catches left. 6'1", 215 lbs. Born, Montreal, Que., June 17, 1970
(Quebec's 3rd choice, 24th overall, in 1988 Entry Draft).

Season	Club	GP	W	L	T	Mins	GA	SO	Avg	GP	W	L	Mins	GA	SO	Avg
1989-90	Quebec	6	0	5	1	342	34	0	5.96							
1990-91	Quebec	3	0	2	1	186	12	0	3.87							
1991-92	Quebec	23	7	10	2	1133	71	1	3.76							
1992-93	Quebec	37	18	9	4	1939	110	0	3.40	1	0	0	21	1	0	2.86
1993-94	Quebec	50	20	25	4	2798	158	2	3.39							
1994-95	Quebec	32	17	10	3	1879	87	2	2.78	4	1	2	209	16	0	4.59
1995-96♦	Colorado	37	22	6	7	2107	103	1	2.93	1	0	0	1	0	0	0.00
1996-97	Los Angeles	44	13	24	5	2482	132	4	3.19							
1997-98	Los Angeles	60	26	25	8	3497	158	2	2.71	2	0	2	93	7	0	4.52
1998-99	Los Angeles	42	18	21	1	2403	104	3	2.60							
99-2000	Los Angeles	47	20	15	7	2592	119	1	2.75	4	0	3	200	10	0	3.00
2000-01	Los Angeles	7	3	0	1	318	19	0	3.58	1	0	0	1	0	0	0.00
2001-02	Montreal	2	0	1	0	109	7	0	3.85	1	0	0	38	3	0	4.74
	NHL Totals	**390**	**164**	**153**	**44**	**21785**	**1114**	**16**	**3.07**	**14**	**1**	**7**	**563**	**37**	**0**	**3.94**

Transferred to **Colorado** after **Quebec** franchise relocated, June 21, 1995. Traded to **Los Angeles** by **Colorado** with Colorado's 1st round choice (Mathieu Biron) in 1998 Entry Draft for Eric Lacroix and Los Angeles' 1st round choice (Martin Skoula) in 1998 Entry Draft, June 20, 1996. • Missed majority of 2000-01 season recovering from knee injury suffered in exhibition game vs. Anaheim, September 22, 2000. • Played 12 seconds of playoff game vs. Colorado, April 28, 2001. Traded to **Montreal** by **Los Angeles** for future considerations, March 19, 2002. • Officially announced retirement, September 9, 2002.

FITZPATRICK, Mark

Goaltender. Catches left. 6'2", 195 lbs. Born, Toronto, Ont., November 13, 1968
(Los Angeles' 2nd choice, 27th overall, in 1987 Entry Draft).

Season	Club	GP	W	L	T	Mins	GA	SO	Avg	GP	W	L	Mins	GA	SO	Avg
1988-89	Los Angeles	17	6	7	3	957	64	0	4.01							
	NY Islanders	11	3	5	2	627	41	0	3.92							
1989-90	NY Islanders	47	19	19	5	2653	150	3	3.39	4	0	2	152	13	0	5.13
1990-91	NY Islanders	2	1	1	0	120	6	0	3.00							
1991-92	NY Islanders	30	11	13	5	1743	93	0	3.20							
1992-93	NY Islanders	39	17	15	5	2253	130	0	3.46	3	0	1	77	4	0	3.12
1993-94	Florida	28	12	8	6	1603	73	1	2.73							
1994-95	Florida	15	6	7	2	819	36	2	2.64							
1995-96	Florida	34	15	11	3	1786	88	0	2.96	2	0	0	60	6	0	6.00
1996-97	Florida	30	8	9	9	1680	66	0	2.36							
1997-98	Florida	12	2	7	2	640	32	1	3.00							
	Tampa Bay	34	7	24	1	1938	102	1	3.16							
1998-99	Chicago	27	6	8	6	1403	64	0	2.74							
99-2000	Carolina	3	0	2	0	107	8	0	4.49							
	NHL Totals	**329**	**113**	**136**	**49**	**18329**	**953**	**8**	**3.12**	**9**	**0**	**3**	**289**	**23**	**0**	**4.78**

Bill Masterton Memorial Trophy (1992)

Traded to **NY Islanders** by **Los Angeles** with Wayne McBean and future considerations (Doug Crossman, May 23, 1989) for Kelly Hrudey, February 22, 1989. Traded to **Quebec** by **NY Islanders** with NY Islanders' 1st round choice (Adam Deadmarsh) in 1993 Entry Draft for Ron Hextall and Quebec's 1st round choice (Todd Bertuzzi) in 1993 Entry Draft, June 20, 1993. Claimed by **Florida** from **Quebec** in Expansion Draft, June 24, 1993. Traded to **Tampa Bay** by **Florida** with Jody Hull for Dino Ciccarelli and Jeff Norton, January 15, 1998. Traded to **Chicago** by **Tampa Bay** with Tampa Bay's 4th round choice (later traded to Montreal – Montreal selected Chris Dyment) in 1999 Entry Draft for Michal Sykora, July 17, 1998. Signed as a free agent by **Carolina**, August 19, 1999.

FLAHERTY, Wade

Goaltender. Catches left. 6', 170 lbs. Born, Terrace, B.C., January 11, 1968
(Buffalo's 10th choice, 181st overall, in 1988 Entry Draft).

Season	Club	GP	W	L	T	Mins	GA	SO	Avg	GP	W	L	Mins	GA	SO	Avg
1991-92	San Jose	3	0	3	0	178	13	0	4.38							
1992-93	San Jose	1	0	1	0	60	5	0	5.00							
1994-95	San Jose	18	5	6	1	852	44	1	3.10	7	2	3	377	31	0	4.93
1995-96	San Jose	24	3	12	1	1137	92	0	4.85							
1996-97	San Jose	7	2	4	0	359	31	0	5.18							
1997-98	NY Islanders	16	4	4	3	694	23	3	1.99							
1998-99	NY Islanders	20	5	11	2	1048	53	0	3.03							
99-2000	NY Islanders	4	0	1	1	182	7	0	2.31							
2000-01	NY Islanders	20	6	10	0	1017	56	1	3.30							
	Tampa Bay	2	0	2	0	118	8	0	4.07							
2001-02	Florida	4	2	1	1	245	12	0	2.94							
2002-03	Nashville	1	0	1	0	51	4	0	4.71							
	NHL Totals	**120**	**27**	**56**	**9**	**5941**	**348**	**5**	**3.51**	**7**	**2**	**3**	**377**	**31**	**0**	**4.93**

Signed as a free agent by **San Jose**, September 3, 1991. Signed as a free agent by **NY Islanders**, July 22, 1997. Traded to **Tampa Bay** by **NY Islanders** for future considerations, February 16, 2001. Signed as a free agent by **Florida**, August 2, 2001. Traded to **Nashville** by **Florida** for Pascal Trepanier, March 9, 2003.

FORBES, Jake

Goaltender. Catches left. 5'6", 140 lbs. Born, Toronto, Ont., July 4, 1897

Season	Club	GP	W	L	T	Mins	GA	SO	Avg	GP	W	L	Mins	GA	SO	Avg
1919-20	Toronto	5	2	3	0	300	21	0	4.20							
1920-21	Toronto	20	13	7	0	1221	78	0	3.83	2	0	2	120	7	0	3.50
1922-23	Hamilton	*24	6	18	0	1470	110	0	4.49							
1923-24	Hamilton	*24	9	15	0	1483	68	1	2.75							
1924-25	Hamilton	*30	*19	10	1	1833	60	6	1.96							
1925-26	NY Americans	*36	12	20	4	2240	86	2	2.30							
1926-27	NY Americans	*44	17	25	2	2715	91	8	2.01							
1927-28	NY Americans	16	3	11	2	980	51	2	3.12							
1928-29	NY Americans	1	1	0	0	60	3	0	3.00							
1929-30	NY Americans	1	0	0	1	70	1	0	0.86							
1930-31	Philadelphia	2	0	2	0	120	7	0	3.50							
1931-32	NY Americans	6	3	3	0	360	16	0	2.67							
1932-33	NY Americans	1	0	0	1	70	2	0	1.71							
	NHL Totals	**210**	**85**	**114**	**11**	**12922**	**594**	**19**	**2.76**	**2**	**0**	**2**	**120**	**7**	**0**	**3.50**

Signed as a free agent by **Toronto**, February 28, 1920. • Suspended for entire 1921-22 season by **Toronto** for refusing to accept contract terms, December 12, 1921. Traded to **Hamilton** by **Toronto** for cash, May 27, 1922. Rights transferred to **NY Americans** after NHL club purchased **Hamilton** franchise, November 7, 1925. Loaned to **Providence** (Can-Am) by **NY Americans** for cash, December 7, 1927. Loan transferred to **Niagara Falls** (Can-Pro) from **Providence** (Can-Am) by **NY Americans**, January 12, 1928. Loaned to **Philadelphia** by **NY Americans** (New Haven-AHL) to replace injured Wilf Cude, January 13 (Montreal 2, Philadelphia 1) and January 17 (Detroit 5, Philadelphia 2), 1931.

FORD, Brian

Goaltender. Catches left. 5'10", 170 lbs. Born, Edmonton, Alta., September 22, 1961

Season	Club	GP	W	L	T	Mins	GA	SO	Avg	GP	W	L	Mins	GA	SO	Avg
1983-84	Quebec	3	1	1	0	123	13	0	6.34							

		REGULAR SEASON								PLAYOFFS						
Season	Club	GP	W	L	T	Mins	GA	SO	Avg	GP	W	L	Mins	GA	SO	Avg
1984-85	Pittsburgh	8	2	6	0	457	48	0	6.30	....	....	....	....	....	....	....
	NHL Totals	**11**	**3**	**7**	**0**	**580**	**61**	**0**	**6.31**	....	....	....	....	....	....	....

Signed as a free agent by **Quebec**, August 1, 1982. Traded to **Pittsburgh** by **Quebec** for Tom Thornbury, December 6, 1984.

FOSTER, Norm

Goaltender. Catches left. 5'9", 175 lbs. Born, Vancouver, B.C., February 10, 1965
(Boston's 11th choice, 231st overall, in 1983 Entry Draft).

Season	Club	GP	W	L	T	Mins	GA	SO	Avg	GP	W	L	Mins	GA	SO	Avg
1990-91	Boston	3	2	1	0	184	14	0	4.57	....	....	....	....	....	....	....
1991-92	Edmonton	10	5	3	0	439	20	0	2.73	....	....	....	....	....	....	....
	NHL Totals	**13**	**7**	**4**	**0**	**623**	**34**	**0**	**3.27**	....	....	....	....	....	....	....

Traded to **Edmonton** by **Boston** for Edmonton's 6th round choice (Jiri Dopita) in 1992 Entry Draft, September 11, 1991. Signed as a free agent by **Philadelphia**, August 4, 1993.

FOUNTAIN, Mike

Goaltender. Catches left. 6'1", 180 lbs. Born, North York, Ont., January 26, 1972
(Vancouver's 3rd choice, 45th overall, in 1992 Entry Draft).

Season	Club	GP	W	L	T	Mins	GA	SO	Avg	GP	W	L	Mins	GA	SO	Avg
1996-97	Vancouver	6	2	2	0	245	14	1	3.43	....	....	....	....	....	....	....
1997-98	Carolina	3	0	3	0	163	10	0	3.68	....	....	....	....	....	....	....
99-2000	Ottawa	1	0	0	0	16	1	0	3.75	....	....	....	....	....	....	....
2000-01	Ottawa	1	0	1	0	59	3	0	3.05	....	....	....	....	....	....	....
	NHL Totals	**11**	**2**	**6**	**0**	**483**	**28**	**1**	**3.48**	....	....	....	....	....	....	....

• Recorded shutout (3-0) in NHL debut vs. **New Jersey**, November 14, 1996. Signed as a free agent by **Carolina**, August 19, 1997. Signed as a free agent by **Ottawa**, July 30, 1999.

FOWLER, Hec

Goaltender. Catches left. 5'11", 190 lbs. Born, Saskatoon, Sask., October 14, 1892

Season	Club	GP	W	L	T	Mins	GA	SO	Avg	GP	W	L	Mins	GA	SO	Avg
1924-25	Boston	7	1	6	0	409	42	0	6.16	....	....	....	....	....	....	....
	NHL Totals	**7**	**1**	**6**	**0**	**409**	**42**	**0**	**6.16**	....	....	....	....	....	....	....

Traded to **Boston** by **Victoria** (PCHA) for cash, October 29, 1924.

FRANCIS, Emile

HHOF

Goaltender. Catches left. 5'6", 145 lbs. Born, North Battleford, Sask., September 13, 1926

Season	Club	GP	W	L	T	Mins	GA	SO	Avg	GP	W	L	Mins	GA	SO	Avg
1946-47	Chicago	19	6	12	1	1140	104	0	5.47	....	....	....	....	....	....	....
1947-48	Chicago	54	18	31	5	3240	183	1	3.39	....	....	....	....	....	....	....
1948-49	NY Rangers	2	2	0	0	120	4	0	2.00	....	....	....	....	....	....	....
1949-50	NY Rangers	1	0	1	0	60	8	0	8.00	....	....	....	....	....	....	....
1950-51	NY Rangers	5	1	1	2	260	14	0	3.23	....	....	....	....	....	....	....
1951-52	NY Rangers	14	4	7	3	840	42	0	3.00	....	....	....	....	....	....	....
	NHL Totals	**95**	**31**	**52**	**11**	**5660**	**355**	**1**	**3.76**	....	....	....	....	....	....	....

• Father of Bobby • Lester Patrick Trophy (1982)

Traded to **NY Rangers** by **Chicago** with Alex Kaleta for Jim Henry, October 7, 1948. Traded to **Cleveland** (AHL) by **NY Rangers** with Neil Strain and cash for Johnny Bower and Eldred Kobussen, July 20, 1953.

FRANKS, Jimmy

Goaltender. Catches left. 5'11", 150 lbs. Born, Melville, Sask., November 8, 1914

Season	Club	GP	W	L	T	Mins	GA	SO	Avg	GP	W	L	Mins	GA	SO	Avg
1936-37♦	Detroit	....	....	....	....	....	....	....	....	1	0	1	30	2	0	4.00
1937-38	Detroit	1	1	0	0	60	3	0	3.00	....	....	....	....	....	....	....
1942-43	NY Rangers	23	5	14	4	1380	103	0	4.48	....	....	....	....	....	....	....
1943-44	Detroit	17	6	8	3	1020	69	1	4.06	....	....	....	....	....	....	....
	Boston	1	0	1	0	60	6	0	6.00	....	....	....	....	....	....	....
	NHL Totals	**42**	**12**	**23**	**7**	**2520**	**181**	**1**	**4.31**	**1**	**0**	**1**	**30**	**2**	**0**	**4.00**

Signed as a free agent by **Detroit**, May 7, 1936. Loaned to **NY Rangers** by **Detroit** for 1942-43 season as a war-time replacement for Jim Henry, October, 1942. • Suspended by **Detroit** for refusing assignment to **Indianapolis** (AHL), October, 1943. Suspension lifted after Franks agreed to play "road games only" for club, December, 1943. Loaned to **Boston** by **Detroit** to replace injured Bert Gardiner, January 29, 1944. (Detroit 6, Boston 1).

FREDERICK, Ray

Goaltender. Catches left. 6', 154 lbs. Born, Fort Frances, Ont., July 31, 1929

Season	Club	GP	W	L	T	Mins	GA	SO	Avg	GP	W	L	Mins	GA	SO	Avg
1954-55	Chicago	5	0	4	1	300	22	0	4.40	....	....	....	....	....	....	....
	NHL Totals	**5**	**0**	**4**	**1**	**300**	**22**	**0**	**4.40**	....	....	....	....	....	....	....

Traded to **Chicago** by **Ottawa** (QHL) for cash, February 10, 1955.

FRIESEN, Karl

Goaltender. Catches left. 6', 185 lbs. Born, Winnipeg, Man., June 30, 1958

Season	Club	GP	W	L	T	Mins	GA	SO	Avg	GP	W	L	Mins	GA	SO	Avg
1986-87	New Jersey	4	0	2	1	130	16	0	7.38	....	....	....	....	....	....	....
	NHL Totals	**4**	**0**	**2**	**1**	**130**	**16**	**0**	**7.38**	....	....	....	....	....	....	....

Signed as a free agent by **New Jersey**, April 24, 1985.

FROESE, Bob

Goaltender. Catches left. 5'11", 176 lbs. Born, St. Catharines, Ont., June 30, 1958
(St. Louis' 11th choice, 160th overall, in 1978 Amateur Draft).

Season	Club	GP	W	L	T	Mins	GA	SO	Avg	GP	W	L	Mins	GA	SO	Avg
1982-83	Philadelphia	25	17	4	2	1407	59	4	2.52	....	....	....	....	....	....	....
1983-84	Philadelphia	48	28	13	7	2863	150	2	3.14	3	0	2	154	11	0	4.29
1984-85	Philadelphia	17	13	2	0	923	37	1	2.41	4	0	1	146	11	0	4.52
1985-86	Philadelphia	51	*31	10	3	2728	116	*5	*2.55	5	2	3	293	15	0	3.07
1986-87	Philadelphia	3	3	0	0	180	8	0	2.67	....	....	....	....	....	....	....
	NY Rangers	28	14	11	0	1474	92	0	3.74	4	1	1	165	10	0	3.64
1987-88	NY Rangers	25	8	11	3	1443	85	0	3.53	....	....	....	....	....	....	....
1988-89	NY Rangers	30	9	14	4	1621	102	1	3.78	2	0	2	72	8	0	6.67
1989-90	NY Rangers	15	5	7	1	812	45	0	3.33	....	....	....	....	....	....	....
	NHL Totals	**242**	**128**	**72**	**20**	**13451**	**694**	**13**	**3.10**	**18**	**3**	**9**	**830**	**55**	**0**	**3.98**

NHL Second All-Star Team (1986) • Shared William M. Jennings Trophy with Darren Jensen (1986)

Played in NHL All-Star Game (1986)

Signed as a free agent by **Philadelphia**, June 18, 1981. Traded to **NY Rangers** by **Philadelphia** for Kjell Samuelsson and NY Rangers' 2nd round choice (Patrik Juhlin) in 1989 Entry Draft, December 18, 1986.

FUHR, Grant

HHOF

Goaltender. Catches right. 5'10", 201 lbs. Born, Spruce Grove, Alta., September 28, 1962
(Edmonton's 1st choice, 8th overall, in 1981 Entry Draft).

Season	Club	GP	W	L	T	Mins	GA	SO	Avg	GP	W	L	Mins	GA	SO	Avg
1981-82	Edmonton	48	28	5	14	2847	157	0	3.31	5	2	3	309	26	0	5.05
1982-83	Edmonton	32	13	12	5	1803	129	0	4.29	1	0	0	11	0	0	0.00
1983-84♦	Edmonton	45	30	10	4	2625	171	1	3.91	16	11	4	883	44	1	2.99
1984-85♦	Edmonton	46	26	8	7	2559	165	1	3.87	*18	*15	3	1064	55	0	3.10
1985-86	Edmonton	40	29	8	0	2184	143	0	3.93	9	5	4	541	28	0	3.11
1986-87♦	Edmonton	44	22	13	3	2388	137	0	3.44	19	14	5	1148	47	0	2.46
1987-88♦	Edmonton	*75	*40	24	9	*4304	246	*4	3.43	*19	*16	2	*1136	55	0	2.90
1988-89	Edmonton	59	23	26	6	3341	213	1	3.83	7	3	4	417	24	1	3.45
1989-90♦	Edmonton	21	9	7	3	1081	70	1	3.89	....	....	....	....	....	....	....
1990-91	Edmonton	13	6	4	3	778	39	1	3.01	17	8	7	1019	51	0	3.00
1991-92	Toronto	66	25	33	5	3774	230	2	3.66	....	....	....	....	....	....	....
1992-93	Toronto	29	13	9	4	1665	87	1	3.14	....	....	....	....	....	....	....
	Buffalo	29	11	15	2	1694	98	0	3.47	8	3	4	474	27	1	3.42
1993-94	Buffalo	32	13	12	3	1726	106	2	3.68	....	....	....	....	....	....	....
1994-95	Buffalo	3	1	2	0	180	12	0	4.00	....	....	....	....	....	....	....
	Los Angeles	14	1	7	3	698	47	0	4.04	....	....	....	....	....	....	....
1995-96	St. Louis	*79	30	28	16	4365	209	3	2.87	2	1	0	69	1	0	0.87
1996-97	St. Louis	73	33	27	11	4261	193	3	2.72	6	2	4	357	13	2	2.18
1997-98	St. Louis	58	29	21	6	3274	138	3	2.53	10	6	4	616	28	0	2.73
1998-99	St. Louis	39	16	11	8	2193	89	2	2.44	13	6	6	790	31	1	2.35
99-2000	Calgary	23	5	13	2	1205	77	0	3.83	....	....	....	....	....	....	....
	NHL Totals	**868**	**403**	**295**	**114**	**48945**	**2756**	**25**	**3.38**	**150**	**92**	**50**	**8834**	**430**	**6**	**2.92**

NHL Second All-Star Team (1982) • NHL First All-Star Team (1988) • Vezina Trophy (1988) • Shared William M. Jennings Trophy with Dominik Hasek (1994)

Played in NHL All-Star Game (1982, 1984, 1985, 1986, 1988, 1989)

Traded to **Toronto** by **Edmonton** with Glenn Anderson and Craig Berube for Vincent Damphousse, Peter Ing, Scott Thornton and Luke Richardson, September 19, 1991. Traded to **Buffalo** by **Toronto** with Toronto's 5th round choice (Kevin Popp) in 1995 Entry Draft for Dave Andreychuk, Daren Puppa and Buffalo's 1st round choice (Kenny Jonsson) in 1993 Entry Draft, February 2, 1993. Traded to **Los Angeles** by **Buffalo** with Philippe Boucher and Denis Tsygurov for Alexei Zhitnik, Robb Stauber, Charlie Huddy and Los Angeles' 5th round choice (Marian Menhart) in 1995 Entry Draft, February 14, 1995. Signed as a free agent by **St. Louis**, July 14, 1995. Traded to **Calgary** by **St. Louis** for Calgary's 3rd round choice (Justin Papineau) in 2000 Entry Draft, September 4, 1999. • Statistics for suspended game vs. Boston on May 24, 1988 are included in playoff record. • Officially announced retirement, September 6, 2000.

GAGE, Joaquin

Goaltender. Catches left. 6', 200 lbs. Born, Vancouver, B.C., October 19, 1973
(Edmonton's 6th choice, 109th overall, in 1992 Entry Draft).

Season	Club	GP	W	L	T	Mins	GA	SO	Avg	GP	W	L	Mins	GA	SO	Avg
1994-95	Edmonton	2	0	2	0	99	7	0	4.24	....	....	....	....	....	....	....
1995-96	Edmonton	16	2	8	1	717	45	0	3.77	....	....	....	....	....	....	....
2000-01	Edmonton	5	2	2	0	260	15	0	3.46	....	....	....	....	....	....	....
	NHL Totals	**23**	**4**	**12**	**1**	**1076**	**67**	**0**	**3.74**	....	....	....	....	....	....	....

Signed as a free agent by **Edmonton**, July 25, 2000.

GAGNON, David

Goaltender. Catches left. 6', 185 lbs. Born, Windsor, Ont., October 31, 1967

Season	Club	GP	W	L	T	Mins	GA	SO	Avg	GP	W	L	Mins	GA	SO	Avg
1990-91	Detroit	2	0	1	0	35	6	0	10.29	....	....	....	....	....	....	....
	NHL Totals	**2**	**0**	**1**	**0**	**35**	**6**	**0**	**10.29**	....	....	....	....	....	....	....

Signed as a free agent by **Detroit**, June 11, 1990.

GAMBLE, Bruce

Goaltender. Catches left. 5'9", 200 lbs. Born, Port Arthur, Ont., May 24, 1938

Season	Club	GP	W	L	T	Mins	GA	SO	Avg	GP	W	L	Mins	GA	SO	Avg
1958-59	NY Rangers	2	0	2	0	120	6	0	3.00	....	....	....	....	....	....	....
1960-61	Boston	52	12	33	7	3120	193	0	3.71	....	....	....	....	....	....	....
1961-62	Boston	28	6	18	4	1680	121	1	4.32	....	....	....	....	....	....	....
1965-66	Toronto	10	5	2	3	501	21	4	2.51	....	....	....	....	....	....	....
1966-67♦	Toronto	23	5	10	4	1185	67	0	3.39	....	....	....	....	....	....	....
1967-68	Toronto	41	19	13	3	2201	85	5	2.32	....	....	....	....	....	....	....
1968-69	Toronto	61	28	20	11	3446	161	3	2.80	3	0	2	86	13	0	9.07
1969-70	Toronto	52	19	24	9	3057	156	5	3.06	....	....	....	....	....	....	....
1970-71	Toronto	23	6	14	1	1286	83	2	3.87	....	....	....	....	....	....	....
	Philadelphia	11	3	6	2	660	37	0	3.36	2	0	2	120	12	0	6.00
1971-72	Philadelphia	24	7	8	2	1186	58	2	2.93	....	....	....	....	....	....	....
	NHL Totals	**327**	**110**	**150**	**46**	**18442**	**988**	**22**	**3.21**	**5**	**0**	**4**	**206**	**25**	**0**	**7.28**

Played in NHL All-Star Game (1968)

Promoted to **NY Rangers** from **Vancouver** (WHL) to replace injured Gump Worsley in games on February 11 (Boston 5, NY Rangers 3) and February 12 (Detroit 1, NY Rangers 0), 1959. Claimed by **Boston** from **NY Rangers** in Intra-League Draft, June 10, 1959. Loaned to **Portland** (WHL) by **Boston** to complete transaction that sent Don Head to Boston (May, 1961), September, 1961. Traded to **Springfield** (AHL) by **Boston** with Terry Gray, Randy Miller and Dale Rolfe for Bob McCord, June, 1963. Traded to **Toronto** by **Springfield** (AHL) for Larry Johnston and Bill Smith, September, 1965. Traded to **Philadelphia** by **Toronto** with Mike Walton and Toronto's 1st round choice (Pierre Plante) in 1971 Amateur Draft for Bernie Parent and Philadelphia's 2nd round choice (Rick Kehoe) in 1971 Amateur Draft, February 1, 1971. • Suffered career-ending heart attack during game vs. Vancouver, February 9, 1972.

GAMBLE, Troy

Goaltender. Catches left. 5'11", 195 lbs. Born, New Glasgow, N.S., April 7, 1967
(Vancouver's 2nd choice, 25th overall, in 1985 Entry Draft).

Season	Club	GP	W	L	T	Mins	GA	SO	Avg	GP	W	L	Mins	GA	SO	Avg
		Regular Season								Playoffs						
1986-87	Vancouver	1	0	1	0	60	4	0	4.00							
1988-89	Vancouver	5	2	3	0	302	12	0	2.38							
1990-91	Vancouver	47	16	16	6	2433	140	1	3.45	4	1	3	249	16	0	3.86
1991-92	Vancouver	19	4	9	3	1009	73	0	4.34							
	NHL Totals	**72**	**22**	**29**	**9**	**3804**	**229**	**1**	**3.61**	**4**	**1**	**3**	**249**	**16**	**0**	**3.86**

Signed as a free agent by **Dallas**, August 28, 1993.

GARDINER, Bert

Goaltender. Catches left. 5'11", 160 lbs. Born, Saskatoon, Sask., March 25, 1913

Season	Club	GP	W	L	T	Mins	GA	SO	Avg	GP	W	L	Mins	GA	SO	Avg
1935-36	NY Rangers	1	1	0	0	60	1	0	1.00							
1938-39	NY Rangers									6	3	3	433	12	0	1.66
1940-41	Montreal	42	13	23	6	2600	119	2	2.75	3	1	2	214	8	0	2.24
1941-42	Montreal	10	1	8	1	620	42	0	4.06							
1942-43	Chicago	*50	17	18	15	*3020	180	1	3.58							
1943-44	Boston	41	17	19	5	2460	212	1	5.17							
	NHL Totals	**144**	**49**	**68**	**27**	**8760**	**554**	**4**	**3.79**	**9**	**4**	**5**	**647**	**20**	**0**	**1.85**

Signed as a free agent by **NY Rangers**, October 18, 1935. Traded to **Montreal** by **NY Rangers** with cash for Claude Bourque, April 26, 1940. Loaned to **Chicago** by **Montreal** for cash, October 12, 1942. Traded to **Boston** by **Montreal** for cash with Montreal holding right of repurchase, October 30, 1943.

GARDINER, Charlie

HHOF

Goaltender. Catches right. , 176 lbs. Born, Edinburgh, Scotland, December 31, 1904

Season	Club	GP	W	L	T	Mins	GA	SO	Avg	GP	W	L	Mins	GA	SO	Avg
1927-28	Chicago	40	6	32	2	2420	114	3	2.83							
1928-29	Chicago	*44	7	29	8	2758	85	5	1.85							
1929-30	Chicago	*44	21	18	5	2750	111	3	2.42	2	0	1	172	3	0	1.05
1930-31	Chicago	*44	24	17	3	2710	78	*12	1.73	9	5	3	638	14	*2	1.32
1931-32	Chicago	*48	18	19	11	2989	92	4	*1.85	2	1	1	120	6	*1	3.00
1932-33	Chicago	*48	16	20	12	*3010	101	5	2.01							
1933-34♦	Chicago	*48	20	17	11	3050	83	*10	1.63	8	*6	1	542	12	*2	*1.33
	NHL Totals	**316**	**112**	**152**	**52**	**19687**	**664**	**42**	**2.02**	**21**	**12**	**6**	**1472**	**35**	**5**	**1.43**

NHL First All-Star Team (1931, 1932, 1934) • Vezina Trophy (1932, 1934) • NHL Second All-Star Team (1933)

Played in NHL All-Star Game (1934)

Traded to **Chicago** by **Winnipeg** (AHA) with Cecil Browne for cash, April 8, 1927.

GARDNER, George

Goaltender. Catches left. 5'8", 165 lbs. Born, Lachine, Que., October 8, 1942

Season	Club	GP	W	L	T	Mins	GA	SO	Avg	GP	W	L	Mins	GA	SO	Avg
1965-66	Detroit	1	1	0	0	60	1	0	1.00							
1966-67	Detroit	11	3	6	0	560	36	0	3.86							
1967-68	Detroit	12	3	2	2	534	32	0	3.60							
1970-71	Vancouver	18	6	8	1	922	52	0	3.38							
1971-72	Vancouver	24	3	14	3	1237	86	0	4.17							
	NHL Totals	**66**	**16**	**30**	**6**	**3313**	**207**	**0**	**3.75**							

Claimed by **Boston** from **Kingston** (EPHL) in Inter-League Draft, June 4, 1963. Claimed by **Detroit** from **Boston** in Intra-League Draft, June 10, 1964. Promoted to **Detroit** from **Pittsburgh** (AHL) to replace Roger Crozier, March 20, 1966. (Detroit 6, Toronto 1). Claimed by **Rochester** (AHL) from **Detroit** in Reverse Draft, June 13, 1968. Rights transferred to **Vancouver** (WHL) after WHL club purchased **Rochester** (AHL) franchise, August 13, 1968. NHL rights transferred to **Vancouver** after NHL club purchased **Vancouver** (WHL) franchise, December 19, 1969.

GARNER, Tyrone

Goaltender. Catches left. 6'1", 200 lbs. Born, Stoney Creek, Ont., July 27, 1978
(NY Islanders' 4th choice, 83rd overall, in 1996 Entry Draft).

Season	Club	GP	W	L	T	Mins	GA	SO	Avg	GP	W	L	Mins	GA	SO	Avg
1998-99	Calgary	3	0	2	0	139	12	0	5.18							
	NHL Totals	**3**	**0**	**2**	**0**	**139**	**12**	**0**	**5.18**							

Traded to **Calgary** by **NY Islanders** with Marty McInnis and Calgary's 6th round choice (previously acquired, Calgary selected Ilja Demidov) in 1997 Entry Draft for Robert Reichel, March 18, 1997. Signed as a free agent by **Florida**, July 31, 2002.

GARON, Mathieu

Goaltender. Catches right. 6'2", 192 lbs. Born, Chandler, Que., January 9, 1978
(Montreal's 2nd choice, 44th overall, in 1996 Entry Draft).

Season	Club	GP	W	L	T	Mins	GA	SO	Avg	GP	W	L	Mins	GA	SO	Avg
2000-01	Montreal	11	4	5	1	589	24	2	2.44							
2001-02	Montreal	5	1	4	0	261	19	0	4.37							
2002-03	Montreal	8	3	5	0	482	16	2	1.99							
	NHL Totals	**24**	**8**	**14**	**1**	**1332**	**59**	**4**	**2.66**							

GARRETT, John

Goaltender. Catches left. 5'8", 175 lbs. Born, Trenton, Ont., June 17, 1951
(St. Louis' 2nd choice, 38th overall, in 1971 Amateur Draft).

Season	Club	GP	W	L	T	Mins	GA	SO	Avg	GP	W	L	Mins	GA	SO	Avg
1979-80	Hartford	52	16	24	11	3046	202	0	3.98	1	0	1	60	8	0	8.00
1980-81	Hartford	54	15	27	12	3152	241	0	4.59							
1981-82	Hartford	16	5	6	4	898	63	0	4.21							
	Quebec	12	4	5	3	720	62	0	5.17	5	3	2	323	21	0	3.90
1982-83	Quebec	17	6	8	2	953	64	0	4.03							
	Vancouver	17	7	6	3	934	48	1	3.08	1	1	0	60	4	0	4.00
1983-84	Vancouver	29	14	10	2	1653	113	0	4.10	2	0	0	18	0	0	0.00
1984-85	Vancouver	10	1	5	0	407	44	0	6.49							
	NHL Totals	**207**	**68**	**91**	**37**	**11763**	**837**	**1**	**4.27**	**9**	**4**	**3**	**461**	**33**	**0**	**4.30**

Played in NHL All-Star Game (1983)

Rights traded to **Chicago** by **St. Louis** to complete transaction that sent Danny O'Shea to St. Louis (February 8, 1972), September 19, 1972. Reclaimed by **Chicago** from **Hartford** prior to Expansion Draft, June 9, 1979. Claimed by **Hartford** as a priority selection, June 9, 1979. Traded to **Quebec** by **Hartford** for Michel Plasse and Quebec's 4th round choice (Ron Chyzowski) in 1983 Entry Draft, January 12, 1982. Traded to **Vancouver** by **Quebec** for Anders Eldebrink, February 4, 1983.

GATHERUM, Dave

Goaltender. Catches left. 5'8", 170 lbs. Born, Fort William, Ont., March 28, 1932

Season	Club	GP	W	L	T	Mins	GA	SO	Avg	GP	W	L	Mins	GA	SO	Avg
1953-54♦	Detroit	3	2	0	1	180	3	1	1.00							
	NHL Totals	**3**	**2**	**0**	**1**	**180**	**3**	**1**	**1.00**							

Promoted to **Detroit** from **Sherbrooke** (QHL) to replace injured Terry Sawchuk in games on October 11, 16, 17, 1953. • Recorded a shutout (4-0) in NHL debut vs. Toronto, October 11, 1953. • NHL record for longest shutout sequence by a goaltender from start of career (100:21), October 11, 16, 1953.

GAUTHIER, Paul

Goaltender. Catches right. 5'5", 125 lbs. Born, Winnipeg, Man., March 6, 1915

Season	Club	GP	W	L	T	Mins	GA	SO	Avg	GP	W	L	Mins	GA	SO	Avg
1937-38	Montreal	1	0	0	1	70	2	0	1.71							
	NHL Totals	**1**	**0**	**0**	**1**	**70**	**2**	**0**	**1.71**							

Signed as a free agent by **Montreal**, October, 1937. Loaned to **New Haven** (AHL) by **Montreal** for cash, October, 1937. • Promoted to **Montreal** from **New Haven** (AHL) to replace injured Wilf Cude, January 13, 1938. (Montreal 2, Chicago 2). Loaned to **Kansas City** (AHA) by **Montreal** for cash, October, 1939. Loaned to **Seattle** (PCHL) by **Montreal** for cash, October, 1940. NHL rights loaned to **Boston** by **Montreal** for remainder of 1941-42 season for loan of Terry Reardon, November 5, 1941.

GAUTHIER, Sean

Goaltender. Catches left. 5'11", 200 lbs. Born, Sudbury, Ont., March 28, 1971
(Winnipeg's 7th choice, 181st overall, in 1991 Entry Draft).

Season	Club	GP	W	L	T	Mins	GA	SO	Avg	GP	W	L	Mins	GA	SO	Avg
1998-99	San Jose	1	0	0	0	3	0	0	0.00							
	NHL Totals	**1**	**0**	**0**	**0**	**3**	**0**	**0**	**0.00**							

Signed as a free agent by **San Jose**, July 23, 1998. Signed as a free agent by **Florida**, January 13, 2000.

GELINEAU, Jack

Goaltender. Catches left. 6', 180 lbs. Born, Toronto, Ont., November 11, 1924

Season	Club	GP	W	L	T	Mins	GA	SO	Avg	GP	W	L	Mins	GA	SO	Avg
1948-49	Boston	4	2	2	0	240	12	0	3.00							
1949-50	Boston	67	22	30	15	4020	220	3	3.28							
1950-51	Boston	*70	22	30	18	*4200	197	4	2.81	4	1	2	260	7	1	1.62
1953-54	Chicago	2	0	2	0	120	18	0	9.00							
	NHL Totals	**143**	**46**	**64**	**33**	**8580**	**447**	**7**	**3.13**	**4**	**1**	**2**	**260**	**7**	**1**	**1.62**

Calder Memorial Trophy (1950)

NHL rights traded to **Chicago** by **Boston** for cash, November 28, 1953.

GERBER, Martin

Goaltender. Catches left. 6', 185 lbs. Born, Burgdorf, Switz., September 3, 1974
(Anaheim's 10th choice, 232nd overall, in 2001 Entry Draft).

Season	Club	GP	W	L	T	Mins	GA	SO	Avg	GP	W	L	Mins	GA	SO	Avg
2002-03	Anaheim	22	6	11	3	1203	39	1	1.95	2	0	0	20	1	0	3.00
	NHL Totals	**22**	**6**	**11**	**3**	**1203**	**39**	**1**	**1.95**	**2**	**0**	**0**	**20**	**1**	**0**	**3.00**

GIACOMIN, Ed

HHOF

Goaltender. Catches left. 5'11", 180 lbs. Born, Sudbury, Ont., June 6, 1939

Season	Club	GP	W	L	T	Mins	GA	SO	Avg	GP	W	L	Mins	GA	SO	Avg
1965-66	NY Rangers	35	8	20	6	2036	125	0	3.68							
1966-67	NY Rangers	*68	*30	27	11	*3981	173	*9	2.61	4	0	4	246	14	0	3.41
1967-68	NY Rangers	*66	*36	20	10	*3940	160	*8	2.44	6	2	4	360	18	0	3.00
1968-69	NY Rangers	*70	*37	23	7	*4114	175	7	2.55	3	0	3	180	10	0	3.33
1969-70	NY Rangers	*70	35	21	14	*4148	163	6	2.36	5	2	3	280	19	0	4.07
1970-71	NY Rangers	45	27	10	7	2641	95	*8	2.16	12	7	5	759	28	0	2.21
1971-72	NY Rangers	44	24	10	9	2551	115	1	2.70	*10	*6	4	*600	27	0	2.70
1972-73	NY Rangers	43	26	11	6	2580	125	4	2.91	10	5	4	539	23	1	2.56
1973-74	NY Rangers	56	30	15	10	3286	168	5	3.07	13	7	6	788	37	0	2.82
1974-75	NY Rangers	37	13	12	8	2069	120	1	3.48	2	0	2	86	4	0	2.79
1975-76	NY Rangers	4	0	3	1	240	19	0	4.75							
	Detroit	29	12	14	3	1740	100	2	3.45							
1976-77	Detroit	33	8	18	3	1791	107	3	3.58							
1977-78	Detroit	9	3	5	1	516	27	0	3.14							
	NHL Totals	**609**	**289**	**209**	**96**	**35633**	**1672**	**54**	**2.82**	**65**	**29**	**35**	**3838**	**180**	**1**	**2.81**

NHL First All-Star Team (1967, 1971) • NHL Second All-Star Team (1968, 1969, 1970) • Shared Vezina Trophy with Gilles Villemure (1971)

Played in NHL All-Star Game (1967, 1968, 1969, 1970, 1971, 1973)

Traded to **NY Rangers** by **Providence** (AHL) for Marcel Paille, Aldo Guidolin, Sandy McGregor and Jim Mikol, May 18, 1965. • McGregor refused to report to Providence and was replaced with Buzz Deschamps. Claimed on waivers by **Detroit** from **NY Rangers**, October 31, 1975.

GIGUERE, Jean-Sebastien

Goaltender. Catches left. 6'1", 199 lbs. Born, Montreal, Que., May 16, 1977
(Hartford's 1st choice, 13th overall, in 1995 Entry Draft).

Season	Club	GP	W	L	T	Mins	GA	SO	Avg	GP	W	L	Mins	GA	SO	Avg
1996-97	Hartford	8	1	4	0	394	24	0	3.65							
1998-99	Calgary	15	6	7	1	860	46	0	3.21							
99-2000	Calgary	7	1	3	1	330	15	0	2.73							
2000-01	Anaheim	34	11	17	5	2031	87	4	2.57							
2001-02	Anaheim	53	20	25	6	3127	111	4	2.13							

Season	Club	GP	W	L	T	Mins	GA	SO	Avg	GP	W	L	Mins	GA	SO	Avg
		REGULAR SEASON								PLAYOFFS						
2002-03	Anaheim	65	34	22	6	3775	145	8	2.30	21	15	6	1407	38	5	*1.62
	NHL Totals	**182**	**73**	**78**	**19**	**10517**	**428**	**16**	**2.44**	**21**	**15**	**6**	**1407**	**38**	**5**	**1.62**

Conn Smythe Trophy (2003)

Transferred to **Carolina** after **Hartford** franchise relocated, June 25, 1997. Traded to **Calgary** by **Carolina** with Andrew Cassels for Gary Roberts and Trevor Kidd, August 25, 1997. Traded to **Anaheim** by **Calgary** for Anaheim's 2nd round choice (later traded to Washington – Washington selected Matt Pettinger) in 2000 Entry Draft, June 10, 2000.

GILBERT, Gilles

Goaltender. Catches left. 6'1", 175 lbs. Born, St-Esprit, Que., March 31, 1949
(Minnesota's 3rd choice, 25th overall, in 1969 Amateur Draft).

Season	Club	GP	W	L	T	Mins	GA	SO	Avg	GP	W	L	Mins	GA	SO	Avg
1969-70	Minnesota	1	0	1	0	60	6	0	6.00	....	....	....	....	....	....	....
1970-71	Minnesota	17	5	9	2	931	59	0	3.80	....	....	....	....	....	....	....
1971-72	Minnesota	4	1	2	1	218	11	0	3.03	....	....	....	....	....	....	....
1972-73	Minnesota	22	10	10	2	1320	67	2	3.05	1	0	1	60	4	0	4.00
1973-74	Boston	54	34	12	8	3210	158	6	2.95	16	10	6	977	43	1	2.64
1974-75	Boston	53	23	17	11	3029	158	3	3.13	3	1	2	188	12	0	3.83
1975-76	Boston	55	33	8	10	3123	151	3	2.90	6	3	3	360	19	*2	3.17
1976-77	Boston	34	18	13	3	2040	97	1	2.85	1	0	1	20	3	0	9.00
1977-78	Boston	25	15	6	2	1326	56	2	2.53	....	....	....	....	....	....	....
1978-79	Boston	23	12	8	2	1254	74	0	3.54	5	3	2	314	16	0	3.06
1979-80	Boston	33	20	9	3	1933	88	1	2.73	....	....	....	....	....	....	....
1980-81	Detroit	48	11	24	9	2618	175	0	4.01	....	....	....	....	....	....	....
1981-82	Detroit	27	6	10	6	1478	105	0	4.26	....	....	....	....	....	....	....
1982-83	Detroit	20	4	14	1	1137	85	0	4.49	....	....	....	....	....	....	....
	NHL Totals	**416**	**192**	**143**	**60**	**23677**	**1290**	**18**	**3.27**	**32**	**17**	**15**	**1919**	**97**	**3**	**3.03**

Played in NHL All-Star Game (1974)

Traded to **Boston** by **Minnesota** for Fred Stanfield, May 22, 1973. Traded to **Detroit** by **Boston** for Rogie Vachon, July 15, 1980.

GILL, Andre

Goaltender. Catches left. 5'7", 145 lbs. Born, Sorel, Que., September 19, 1941

Season	Club	GP	W	L	T	Mins	GA	SO	Avg	GP	W	L	Mins	GA	SO	Avg
1967-68	Boston	5	3	2	0	270	13	1	2.89	....	....	....	....	....	....	....
	NHL Totals	**5**	**3**	**2**	**0**	**270**	**13**	**1**	**2.89**	....	....	....	....	....	....	....

Promoted to **Boston** by **Hershey** (AHL) to replace injured Gerry Cheevers, December 23, 1967.
• Recorded a shutout (4-0) in NHL debut vs. NY Rangers, December 23, 1967.

GOODMAN, Paul

Goaltender. Catches left. 5'10", 165 lbs. Born, Selkirk, Man., February 25, 1905

Season	Club	GP	W	L	T	Mins	GA	SO	Avg	GP	W	L	Mins	GA	SO	Avg
1937-38♦	Chicago	....	....	....	....	....	....	....	....	1	0	1	60	5	0	5.00
1939-40	Chicago	31	16	10	5	1920	62	4	1.94	2	0	2	127	5	0	2.36
1940-41	Chicago	21	7	10	4	1320	55	2	2.50	....	....	....	....	....	....	....
	NHL Totals	**52**	**23**	**20**	**9**	**3240**	**117**	**6**	**2.17**	**3**	**0**	**3**	**187**	**10**	**0**	**3.21**

GORDON, Scott

Goaltender. Catches left. 5'10", 175 lbs. Born, Brockton, MA, February 6, 1963

Season	Club	GP	W	L	T	Mins	GA	SO	Avg	GP	W	L	Mins	GA	SO	Avg
1989-90	Quebec	10	2	8	0	597	53	0	5.33	....	....	....	....	....	....	....
1990-91	Quebec	13	0	8	0	485	48	0	5.94	....	....	....	....	....	....	....
	NHL Totals	**23**	**2**	**16**	**0**	**1082**	**101**	**0**	**5.60**	....	....	....	....	....	....	....

Signed as a free agent by **Quebec**, October 2, 1986.

GOSSELIN, Mario

Goaltender. Catches left. 5'8", 160 lbs. Born, Thetford Mines, Que., June 15, 1963
(Quebec's 3rd choice, 55th overall, in 1982 Entry Draft).

Season	Club	GP	W	L	T	Mins	GA	SO	Avg	GP	W	L	Mins	GA	SO	Avg
1983-84	Quebec	3	2	0	0	148	3	1	1.22	....	....	....	....	....	....	....
1984-85	Quebec	35	19	11	3	1960	109	1	3.34	17	9	8	1059	54	0	3.06
1985-86	Quebec	31	14	14	1	1726	111	2	3.86	1	0	1	40	5	0	7.50
1986-87	Quebec	30	13	11	1	1625	86	0	3.18	11	7	4	654	37	0	3.39
1987-88	Quebec	54	20	28	4	3002	189	2	3.78	....	....	....	....	....	....	....
1988-89	Quebec	39	11	19	3	2064	146	0	4.24	....	....	....	....	....	....	....
1989-90	Los Angeles	26	7	11	1	1226	79	0	3.87	3	0	2	63	3	0	2.90
1992-93	Hartford	16	5	9	1	867	57	0	3.94	....	....	....	....	....	....	....
1993-94	Hartford	7	0	4	0	239	21	0	5.27	....	....	....	....	....	....	....
	NHL Totals	**241**	**91**	**107**	**14**	**12857**	**801**	**6**	**3.74**	**32**	**16**	**15**	**1816**	**99**	**0**	**3.27**

Played in NHL All-Star Game (1986)

• Recorded a shutout (5-0) in NHL debut vs. St. Louis, February 26, 1984. Signed as a free agent by **Los Angeles**, June 14, 1989. Signed as a free agent by **Hartford**, September 4, 1991.
• Suffered eventual career-ending knee injury in game vs. Florida, November 27, 1993.

GOVERDE, David

Goaltender. Catches right. 6', 210 lbs. Born, Toronto, Ont., April 9, 1970
(Los Angeles' 4th choice, 91st overall, in 1990 Entry Draft).

Season	Club	GP	W	L	T	Mins	GA	SO	Avg	GP	W	L	Mins	GA	SO	Avg
1991-92	Los Angeles	2	1	1	0	120	9	0	4.50	....	....	....	....	....	....	....
1992-93	Los Angeles	2	0	2	0	98	13	0	7.96	....	....	....	....	....	....	....
1993-94	Los Angeles	1	0	1	0	60	7	0	7.00	....	....	....	....	....	....	....
	NHL Totals	**5**	**1**	**4**	**0**	**278**	**29**	**0**	**6.26**	....	....	....	....	....	....	....

GRAHAME, John

Goaltender. Catches left. 6'2", 214 lbs. Born, Denver, CO, August 31, 1975
(Boston's 7th choice, 229th overall, in 1994 Entry Draft).

Season	Club	GP	W	L	T	Mins	GA	SO	Avg	GP	W	L	Mins	GA	SO	Avg
		REGULAR SEASON								PLAYOFFS						
99-2000	Boston	24	7	10	5	1344	55	2	2.46	....	....	....	....	....	....	....
2000-01	Boston	10	3	4	0	471	28	0	3.57	....	....	....	....	....	....	....
2001-02	Boston	19	8	7	2	1079	52	1	2.89	....	....	....	....	....	....	....
2002-03	Boston	23	11	9	2	1352	61	1	2.71	....	....	....	....	....	....	....
	Tampa Bay	17	6	5	4	914	34	2	2.23	1	0	1	111	2	0	1.08
	NHL Totals	**93**	**35**	**35**	**13**	**5160**	**230**	**6**	**2.67**	**1**	**0**	**1**	**111**	**2**	**0**	**1.08**

• Son of Ron

Traded to **Tampa Bay** by **Boston** for Tampa Bay's 4th round choice in 2004 Entry Draft, January 13, 2003.

GRAHAME, Ron

Goaltender. Catches left. 5'11", 175 lbs. Born, Victoria, B.C., June 7, 1950

Season	Club	GP	W	L	T	Mins	GA	SO	Avg	GP	W	L	Mins	GA	SO	Avg
1977-78	Boston	40	26	6	7	2328	107	3	2.76	4	2	1	202	7	0	2.08
1978-79	Los Angeles	34	11	19	2	1940	136	0	4.21	....	....	....	....	....	....	....
1979-80	Los Angeles	26	9	11	4	1405	98	2	4.19	....	....	....	....	....	....	....
1980-81	Los Angeles	6	3	2	1	360	28	0	4.67	....	....	....	....	....	....	....
	Quebec	8	1	5	1	439	40	0	5.47	....	....	....	....	....	....	....
	NHL Totals	**114**	**50**	**43**	**15**	**6472**	**409**	**5**	**3.79**	**4**	**2**	**1**	**202**	**7**	**0**	**2.08**

• Father of John

Signed as a free agent by **Boston**, October 13, 1977. Traded to **Los Angeles** by **Boston** for Los Angeles' 1st round choice (Raymond Bourque) in 1979 Entry Draft, October 9, 1978. Sold to **Quebec** by **Los Angeles** for cash, December 12, 1980.

GRANT, Benny

Goaltender. Catches left. 5'11", 160 lbs. Born, Owen Sound, Ont., July 14, 1908

Season	Club	GP	W	L	T	Mins	GA	SO	Avg	GP	W	L	Mins	GA	SO	Avg
1928-29	Toronto	3	1	0	0	110	3	0	1.64	....	....	....	....	....	....	....
1929-30	Toronto	2	1	1	0	130	11	0	5.08	....	....	....	....	....	....	....
	NY Americans	7	3	4	0	420	25	0	3.57	....	....	....	....	....	....	....
1930-31	Toronto	7	1	5	1	430	19	2	2.65	....	....	....	....	....	....	....
1931-32	Toronto	5	1	2	1	320	18	1	3.38	....	....	....	....	....	....	....
1933-34	NY Americans	5	1	4	0	320	18	1	3.38	....	....	....	....	....	....	....
1943-44	Toronto	20	9	9	2	1200	83	0	4.15	....	....	....	....	....	....	....
	Boston	1	0	1	0	60	10	0	10.00	....	....	....	....	....	....	....
	NHL Totals	**50**	**17**	**26**	**4**	**2990**	**187**	**4**	**3.75**	....	....	....	....	....	....	....

Traded to **Toronto** by **London** (Can-Pro) for cash, January, 1928. Loaned to **NY Americans** by **Toronto** for cash, December 18, 1929. Loaned to **Minneapolis** (AHA) by **Toronto** for cash, January 24, 1930. Loaned to **Boston** (Can-Am) by **Toronto** for cash, December 26, 1930. Loaned to **NY Americans** by **Toronto** to replace injured Moe Roberts, December 9, 1933. Signed as a free agent by **Toronto** as a war-time replacement for Turk Broda, October, 1942. Loaned to **Boston** by **Toronto** to replace Maurice Courteau, March 18, 1944. (Toronto 10, Boston 2)

GRANT, Doug

Goaltender. Catches left. 6'1", 200 lbs. Born, Corner Brook, Nfld., July 27, 1948

Season	Club	GP	W	L	T	Mins	GA	SO	Avg	GP	W	L	Mins	GA	SO	Avg
1973-74	Detroit	37	15	16	2	2018	140	1	4.16	....	....	....	....	....	....	....
1974-75	Detroit	7	1	5	0	380	34	0	5.37	....	....	....	....	....	....	....
1975-76	Detroit	2	1	1	0	120	8	0	4.00	....	....	....	....	....	....	....
1976-77	St. Louis	17	7	7	3	960	50	1	3.13	....	....	....	....	....	....	....
1977-78	St. Louis	9	3	3	2	500	24	0	2.88	....	....	....	....	....	....	....
1978-79	St. Louis	4	0	2	1	190	23	0	7.26	....	....	....	....	....	....	....
1979-80	St. Louis	1	0	0	0	31	1	0	1.94	....	....	....	....	....	....	....
	NHL Totals	**77**	**27**	**34**	**8**	**4199**	**280**	**2**	**4.00**	....	....	....	....	....	....	....

Signed as a free agent by **Detroit**, March 1, 1972. Traded to **St. Louis** by **Detroit** for future considerations (Rick Wilson, June 16, 1976), March 9, 1976.

GRATTON, Gilles

Goaltender. Catches left. 5'11", 160 lbs. Born, LaSalle, Que., July 28, 1952
(Buffalo's 5th choice, 69th overall, in 1972 Amateur Draft).

Season	Club	GP	W	L	T	Mins	GA	SO	Avg	GP	W	L	Mins	GA	SO	Avg
1975-76	St. Louis	6	2	0	2	265	11	0	2.49	....	....	....	....	....	....	....
1976-77	NY Rangers	41	11	18	7	2034	143	0	4.22	....	....	....	....	....	....	....
	NHL Totals	**47**	**13**	**18**	**9**	**2299**	**154**	**0**	**4.02**	....	....	....	....	....	....	....

• Brother of Norm

Rights traded to **St. Louis** by **Buffalo** for cash, July 3, 1975. • Placed on "voluntary retired" list after walking out on the team following game vs. NY Islanders, November 28, 1975. • **St. Louis** refused to place Gratton on waivers, blocking his attempt to sign with Toronto (WHA). Signed as a free agent by **NY Rangers** after securing release from **St. Louis**, March 24, 1976.

GRAY, Gerry

Goaltender. Catches left. 6', 165 lbs. Born, Brantford, Ont., January 28, 1948

Season	Club	GP	W	L	T	Mins	GA	SO	Avg	GP	W	L	Mins	GA	SO	Avg
1970-71	Detroit	7	1	4	1	380	30	0	4.74	....	....	....	....	....	....	....
1972-73	NY Islanders	1	0	1	0	60	5	0	5.00	....	....	....	....	....	....	....
	NHL Totals	**8**	**1**	**5**	**1**	**440**	**35**	**0**	**4.77**	....	....	....	....	....	....	....

Traded to **NY Islanders** by **Detroit** with Arnie Brown for Denis DeJordy and Don McLaughlin, October 4, 1972.

GRAY, Harrison

Goaltender. 5'11", 165 lbs. Born, Calgary, Alta., September 5, 1941

Season	Club	GP	W	L	T	Mins	GA	SO	Avg	GP	W	L	Mins	GA	SO	Avg
1963-64	Detroit	1	0	1	0	40	5	0	7.50	....	....	....	....	....	....	....
	NHL Totals	**1**	**0**	**1**	**0**	**40**	**5**	**0**	**7.50**	....	....	....	....	....	....	....

• **Detroit's** spare goaltender replaced injured Terry Sawchuk at start of 2nd period, November 28, 1963. (Montreal 7, Detroit 3).

GREENLAY, Mike

Goaltender. Catches left. 6'3", 200 lbs. Born, Vitoria, Brazil, September 15, 1968
(Edmonton's 9th choice, 189th overall, in 1986 Entry Draft).

Season	Club	GP	W	L	T	Mins	GA	SO	Avg	GP	W	L	Mins	GA	SO	Avg
1989-90	Edmonton	2	0	0	0	20	4	0	12.00	....	....	....	....	....	....	....
	NHL Totals	**2**	**0**	**0**	**0**	**20**	**4**	**0**	**12.00**	....	....	....	....	....	....	....

Signed as a free agent by **Tampa Bay**, July 29, 1992. Traded to **Philadelphia** by **Tampa Bay** for Scott Lagrand, February 2, 1995.

GUENETTE, Steve

Goaltender. Catches left. 5'10", 175 lbs. Born, Gloucester, Ont., November 13, 1965

Season	Club	GP	W	L	T	Mins	GA	SO	Avg	PO GP	PO W	PO L	PO Mins	PO GA	PO SO	PO Avg
1986-87	Pittsburgh	2	0	2	0	113	8	0	4.25							
1987-88	Pittsburgh	19	12	7	0	1092	61	1	3.35							
1988-89	Pittsburgh	11	5	6	0	574	41	0	4.29							
1989-90	Calgary	2	1	1	0	119	8	0	4.03							
1990-91	Calgary	1	1	0	0	60	4	0	4.00							
	NHL Totals	**35**	**19**	**16**	**0**	**1958**	**122**	**1**	**3.74**							

Signed as a free agent by **Pittsburgh**, April 6, 1985. Traded to **Calgary** by **Pittsburgh** for Calgary's 6th round choice (Mike Needham) in 1989 Entry Draft, January 9, 1989. Traded to **Minnesota** by **Calgary** for Minnesota's 7th round choice (Matt Hoffman) in 1991 Entry Draft, May 30, 1991.

GUSTAFSON, Derek

Goaltender. Catches left. 5'11", 210 lbs. Born, Gresham, OR, June 21, 1979

Season	Club	GP	W	L	T	Mins	GA	SO	Avg	PO GP	PO W	PO L	PO Mins	PO GA	PO SO	PO Avg
2000-01	Minnesota	4	1	3	0	239	10	0	2.51							
2001-02	Minnesota	1	0	0	0	26	0	0	0.00							
	NHL Totals	**5**	**1**	**3**	**0**	**265**	**10**	**0**	**2.26**							

Signed as a free agent by **Minnesota**, June 9, 2000.

HACKETT, Jeff

Goaltender. Catches left. 6'1", 198 lbs. Born, London, Ont., June 1, 1968
(NY Islanders' 2nd choice, 34th overall, in 1987 Entry Draft).

Season	Club	GP	W	L	T	Mins	GA	SO	Avg	PO GP	PO W	PO L	PO Mins	PO GA	PO SO	PO Avg
1988-89	NY Islanders	13	4	7	0	662	39	0	3.53							
1990-91	NY Islanders	30	5	18	1	1508	91	0	3.62							
1991-92	San Jose	42	11	27	1	2314	148	0	3.84							
1992-93	San Jose	36	2	30	1	2000	176	0	5.28							
1993-94	Chicago	22	2	12	3	1084	62	0	3.43							
1994-95	Chicago	7	1	3	2	328	13	0	2.38	2	0	0	26	1	0	2.31
1995-96	Chicago	35	18	11	4	2000	80	4	2.40	1	0	1	60	5	0	5.00
1996-97	Chicago	41	19	18	4	2473	89	2	2.16	6	2	4	345	25	0	4.35
1997-98	Chicago	58	21	25	11	3441	126	8	2.20							
1998-99	Chicago	10	2	6	1	524	33	0	3.78							
	Montreal	53	24	20	9	3091	117	5	2.27							
99-2000	Montreal	56	23	25	7	3301	132	3	2.40							
2000-01	Montreal	19	4	10	2	998	54	0	3.25							
2001-02	Montreal	15	5	5	2	717	38	0	3.18							
2002-03	Montreal	18	7	8	2	1063	45	0	2.54							
	Boston	18	8	9	0	991	53	1	3.21	3	1	2	179	5	0	1.68
	NHL Totals	**473**	**156**	**234**	**50**	**26495**	**1296**	**23**	**2.93**	**12**	**3**	**7**	**610**	**36**	**0**	**3.54**

Claimed by **San Jose** from **NY Islanders** in Expansion Draft, May 30, 1991. Traded to **Chicago** by **San Jose** for Chicago's 3rd round choice (Alexei Yegorov) in 1994 Entry Draft, July 13, 1993. Traded to **Montreal** by **Chicago** with Eric Weinrich, Alain Nasreddine and Tampa Bay's 4th round choice (previously acquired, Montreal selected Chris Dyment) in 1999 Entry Draft for Jocelyn Thibault, Dave Manson and Brad Brown, November 16, 1998. • Missed majority of 2000-01 season recovering from hand injury suffered in game vs. Minnesota, October 24, 2000. • Missed majority of 2001-02 season recovering from shoulder injury suffered in game vs. Buffalo, October 20, 2001. Traded to **San Jose** by **Montreal** for Niklas Sundstrom and San Jose's 3rd round choice in 2004 Entry Draft, January 23, 2003. Traded to **Boston** by **San Jose** with Jeff Jillson for Kyle McLaren and Boston's 4th round choice in 2004 Entry Draft, January 23, 2003. Signed as a free agent by **Philadelphia**, July 1, 2003.

HAINSWORTH, George — HHOF

Goaltender. Catches left. 5'6", 150 lbs. Born, Toronto, Ont., June 26, 1895

Season	Club	GP	W	L	T	Mins	GA	SO	Avg	PO GP	PO W	PO L	PO Mins	PO GA	PO SO	PO Avg
1926-27	Montreal	*44	28	14	2	2732	67	*14	1.47	4	1	1	252	6	1	1.43
1927-28	Montreal	*44	*26	11	7	2730	48	13	*1.05	2	0	1	128	3	0	1.41
1928-29	Montreal	*44	22	7	15	2800	43	*22	*0.92	3	0	3	180	5	0	1.67
1929-30♦	Montreal	42	20	13	9	2680	108	*4	2.42	*6	*5	0	*481	6	*3	*0.75
1930-31♦	Montreal	*44	26	10	8	2740	89	8	1.95	*10	*6	4	*722	21	*2	1.75
1931-32	Montreal	*48	*25	16	7	2998	110	6	2.20	4	1	3	300	13	0	2.60
1932-33	Montreal	*48	18	25	5	2980	115	8	2.32	2	0	1	120	8	0	4.00
1933-34	Toronto	*48	*26	13	9	*3010	119	3	2.37	5	2	3	302	11	0	2.19
1934-35	Toronto	*48	*30	14	4	2957	111	8	2.25	*7	3	4	*460	12	*2	1.57
1935-36	Toronto	*48	23	19	6	3000	106	8	2.12	*9	4	5	*541	27	0	2.99
1936-37	Toronto	3	0	2	1	190	9	0	2.84							
	Montreal	4	2	1	1	270	12	0	2.67							
	NHL Totals	**465**	**246**	**145**	**74**	**29087**	**937**	**94**	**1.93**	**52**	**22**	**25**	**3486**	**112**	**8**	**1.93**

Vezina Trophy (1927, 1928, 1929)

Played in NHL All-Star Game (1934)

Traded to **Montreal** by **Saskatoon** (WHL) for cash, August 23, 1926. Traded to **Toronto** by **Montreal** for Lorne Chabot, October 1, 1933. Signed as a free agent by **Montreal**, November 24, 1936.

HALL, Glenn — HHOF

Goaltender. Catches left. 5'11", 180 lbs. Born, Humboldt, Sask., October 3, 1931

Season	Club	GP	W	L	T	Mins	GA	SO	Avg	PO GP	PO W	PO L	PO Mins	PO GA	PO SO	PO Avg
1951-52	Detroit	DID NOT PLAY – SPARE GOALTENDER														
1952-53	Detroit	6	4	1	1	360	10	1	1.67							
1954-55	Detroit	2	2	0	0	120	2	0	1.00							
1955-56	Detroit	*70	30	24	16	*4200	147	*12	2.10	*10	5	5	*604	28	0	2.78
1956-57	Detroit	*70	*38	20	12	*4200	155	4	2.21	5	1	4	300	15	0	3.00
1957-58	Chicago	*70	24	39	7	*4200	200	7	2.86							
1958-59	Chicago	*70	28	29	13	*4200	208	1	2.97	6	2	4	360	21	0	3.50
1959-60	Chicago	*70	28	29	13	*4200	179	*6	2.56	4	0	4	249	14	0	3.37
1960-61♦	Chicago	*70	29	24	17	*4200	176	*6	2.51	*12	*8	4	*772	26	*2	*2.02
1961-62	Chicago	*70	31	26	13	*4200	184	*9	2.63	*12	*6	6	*720	31	*2	2.58
1962-63	Chicago	66	*30	20	15	3910	161	*5	2.47	6	2	4	360	25	0	4.17
1963-64	Chicago	65	*34	19	11	3860	148	7	2.30	7	3	4	408	22	0	3.24
1964-65	Chicago	41	18	17	5	2440	99	4	2.43	*13	*7	6	*760	28	1	2.21
1965-66	Chicago	*64	*34	21	7	*3747	164	4	2.63	6	2	4	347	22	0	3.80
1966-67	Chicago	32	19	5	5	1664	66	2	*2.38	3	1	2	176	8	0	2.73
1967-68	St. Louis	49	19	21	9	2858	118	5	2.48	*18	8	10	*1111	45	*1	2.43
1968-69	St. Louis	41	19	12	8	2354	85	*8	2.17	3	0	2	131	5	0	2.29
1969-70	St. Louis	18	7	8	3	1010	49	1	2.91	7	4	3	421	21	0	2.99
1970-71	St. Louis	32	13	11	8	1761	71	2	2.42	3	0	3	180	9	0	3.00
	NHL Totals	**906**	**407**	**326**	**163**	**53484**	**2222**	**84**	**2.49**	**115**	**49**	**65**	**6899**	**320**	**6**	**2.78**

NHL Second All-Star Team (1956, 1961, 1962, 1967) • Calder Memorial Trophy (1956) • NHL First All-Star Team (1957, 1958, 1960, 1963, 1964, 1966, 1969) • Vezina Trophy (1963) • Shared Vezina Trophy with Denis DeJordy (1967) • Conn Smythe Trophy (1968) • Shared Vezina Trophy with Jacques Plante (1969)

Played in NHL All-Star Game (1955, 1956, 1957, 1958, 1960, 1961, 1962, 1963, 1964, 1965, 1967, 1968, 1969)

Promoted to **Detroit** from **Edmonton** (WHL) to replace injured Terry Sawchuk in games from December 27, 1952 through January 11, 1953 and February 12, 13, 1955. Traded to **Chicago** by **Detroit** with Ted Lindsay for Johnny Wilson, Forbes Kennedy, Bill Preston and Hank Bassen, July 23, 1957. Claimed by **St. Louis** from **Chicago** in Expansion Draft, June 6, 1967.

HAMEL, Pierre

Goaltender. Catches left. 5'9", 170 lbs. Born, Montreal, Que., September 16, 1952

Season	Club	GP	W	L	T	Mins	GA	SO	Avg	PO GP	PO W	PO L	PO Mins	PO GA	PO SO	PO Avg
1974-75	Toronto	4	1	2	0	195	18	0	5.54							
1978-79	Toronto	1	0	0	0	1	0	0	0.00							
1979-80	Winnipeg	35	9	19	3	1947	130	0	4.01							
1980-81	Winnipeg	29	3	20	4	1623	128	0	4.73							
	NHL Totals	**69**	**13**	**41**	**7**	**3766**	**276**	**0**	**4.40**							

Signed as a free agent by **Toronto**, September 27, 1974. Claimed by **Winnipeg** from **Toronto** in Expansion Draft, June 13, 1979.

HANLON, Glen

Goaltender. Catches right. 6', 185 lbs. Born, Brandon, Man., February 20, 1957
(Vancouver's 3rd choice, 40th overall, in 1977 Amateur Draft).

Season	Club	GP	W	L	T	Mins	GA	SO	Avg	PO GP	PO W	PO L	PO Mins	PO GA	PO SO	PO Avg
1977-78	Vancouver	4	1	2	1	200	9	0	2.70							
1978-79	Vancouver	31	12	13	5	1821	94	3	3.10							
1979-80	Vancouver	57	17	29	10	3341	193	0	3.47	2	0	0	60	3	0	3.00
1980-81	Vancouver	17	5	8	0	798	59	1	4.44							
1981-82	Vancouver	28	8	14	5	1610	106	1	3.95							
	St. Louis	2	0	1	0	76	8	0	6.32	3	0	2	109	9	0	4.95
1982-83	St. Louis	14	3	8	1	671	50	0	4.47							
	NY Rangers	21	9	10	1	1173	67	0	3.43	1	0	1	60	5	0	5.00
1983-84	NY Rangers	50	28	14	4	2837	166	1	3.51	5	2	3	308	13	1	2.53
1984-85	NY Rangers	44	14	20	7	2510	175	0	4.18	3	0	3	168	14	0	5.00
1985-86	NY Rangers	23	5	12	1	1170	65	0	3.33	3	0	0	75	6	0	4.80
1986-87	Detroit	36	11	16	5	1963	104	1	3.18	8	5	2	467	13	*2	*1.67
1987-88	Detroit	47	22	17	5	2623	141	*4	3.23	8	4	3	431	22	*1	3.06
1988-89	Detroit	39	13	14	8	2092	124	1	3.56	2	0	1	78	7	0	5.38
1989-90	Detroit	45	15	18	5	2290	154	1	4.03							
1990-91	Detroit	19	4	6	3	862	46	0	3.20							
	NHL Totals	**477**	**167**	**202**	**61**	**26037**	**1561**	**13**	**3.60**	**35**	**11**	**15**	**1756**	**92**	**4**	**3.14**

Traded to **St. Louis** by **Vancouver** for Rick Heinz, Tony Currie, Jim Nill and St. Louis' 4th round choice (Shawn Kilroy) in 1982 Entry Draft, March 9, 1982. Traded to **NY Rangers** by **St. Louis** with Vaclav Nedomansky for Andre Dore, January 4, 1983. Traded to **Detroit** by **NY Rangers** with NY Rangers' 3rd round choices in 1987 (Dennis Holland) and 1988 (Guy Dupuis) Entry Drafts for Kelly Kisio, Lane Lambert, Jim Leavins and Detroit's 5th round choice (later traded to Winnipeg – Winnipeg selected Benoit Lebeau) in 1988 Entry Draft, July 29, 1986.

HARRISON, Paul

Goaltender. Catches left. 6'1", 196 lbs. Born, Timmins, Ont., February 11, 1955
(Minnesota's 2nd choice, 40th overall, in 1975 Amateur Draft).

Season	Club	GP	W	L	T	Mins	GA	SO	Avg	PO GP	PO W	PO L	PO Mins	PO GA	PO SO	PO Avg
1975-76	Minnesota	6	0	4	1	307	28	0	5.47							
1976-77	Minnesota	2	0	2	0	120	11	0	5.50							
1977-78	Minnesota	27	6	16	2	1555	99	1	3.82							
1978-79	Toronto	25	8	12	3	1403	82	1	3.51	2	0	1	91	7	0	4.62
1979-80	Toronto	30	9	17	2	1492	110	0	4.42							
1980-81	Toronto									1	0	0	40	1	0	1.50
1981-82	Pittsburgh	13	3	7	0	700	64	0	5.49							
	Buffalo	6	2	1	1	229	14	0	3.67	1	0	0	26	1	0	2.31
	NHL Totals	**109**	**28**	**59**	**9**	**5806**	**408**	**2**	**4.22**	**4**	**0**	**1**	**157**	**9**	**0**	**3.44**

Traded to **Toronto** by **Minnesota** for Toronto's 4th round choice (Terry Tait) in 1981 Entry Draft, June 14, 1978. Traded to **Pittsburgh** by **Toronto** for future considerations, September 11, 1981. Claimed on waivers by **Buffalo** from **Pittsburgh**, February 8, 1982.

HASEK, Dominik

Goaltender. Catches left. 5'11", 180 lbs. Born, Pardubice, Czech., January 29, 1965
(Chicago's 11th choice, 207th overall, in 1983 Entry Draft).

Season	Club	GP	W	L	T	Mins	GA	SO	Avg	PO GP	PO W	PO L	PO Mins	PO GA	PO SO	PO Avg
1990-91	Chicago	5	3	0	1	195	8	0	2.46	3	0	0	69	3	0	2.61
1991-92	Chicago	20	10	4	1	1014	44	1	2.60	3	0	2	158	8	0	3.04
1992-93	Buffalo	28	11	10	4	1429	75	0	3.15	1	1	0	45	1	0	1.33
1993-94	Buffalo	58	30	20	6	3358	109	*7	*1.95	7	3	4	484	13	2	*1.61
1994-95	Buffalo	41	19	14	7	2416	85	*5	*2.11	5	1	4	309	18	0	3.50
1995-96	Buffalo	59	22	30	6	3417	161	2	2.83							
1996-97	Buffalo	67	37	20	10	4037	153	5	2.27	3	1	1	153	5	0	1.96
1997-98	Buffalo	*72	33	23	13	*4220	147	*13	2.09	15	10	5	948	32	1	2.03
1998-99	Buffalo	64	30	18	14	3817	119	9	1.87	19	13	6	1217	36	2	1.77
99-2000	Buffalo	35	15	11	6	2066	76	3	2.21	5	1	4	301	12	0	2.39
2000-01	Buffalo	67	37	24	4	3904	137	*11	2.11	13	7	6	833	29	1	2.09

Season	Club	GP	W	L	T	Mins	GA	SO	Avg	GP	W	L	Mins	GA	SO	Avg
		REGULAR SEASON								PLAYOFFS						
2001-02◆	Detroit	65	*41	15	8	3872	140	5	2.17	*23	*16	7	*1455	45	*6	1.86
	NHL Totals	**581**	**288**	**189**	**80**	**33745**	**1254**	**61**	**2.23**	**97**	**53**	**39**	**5972**	**202**	**12**	**2.03**

NHL All-Rookie Team (1992) • NHL First All-Star Team (1994, 1995, 1997, 1998, 1999, 2001) • Shared William M. Jennings Trophy with Grant Fuhr (1994) • Vezina Trophy (1994, 1995, 1997, 1998, 1999, 2001) • Lester B. Pearson Award (1997, 1998) • Hart Trophy (1997, 1998) • William M. Jennings Trophy (2001)

Played in NHL All-Star Game (1996, 1997, 1998, 1999, 2001, 2002)

Traded to **Buffalo** by **Chicago** for Stephane Beauregard and Buffalo's 4th round choice (Eric Daze) in 1993 Entry Draft, August 7, 1992. Traded to **Detroit** by **Buffalo** for Vyacheslav Kozlov, Detroit's 1st round choice (later traded to Columbus – later traded to Atlanta – Atlanta selected Jim Slater) in 2002 Entry Draft and future considerations, July 1, 2001. • Officially announced retirement, June 25, 2002.

HAYWARD, Brian

Goaltender. Catches left. 5'10", 180 lbs. Born, Toronto, Ont., June 25, 1960

Season	Club	GP	W	L	T	Mins	GA	SO	Avg	GP	W	L	Mins	GA	SO	Avg
1982-83	Winnipeg	24	10	12	2	1440	89	1	3.71	3	0	3	160	14	0	5.25
1983-84	Winnipeg	28	7	18	2	1530	124	0	4.86	....	....	....	....	....	....	....
1984-85	Winnipeg	61	33	17	7	3436	220	0	3.84	6	2	4	309	23	0	4.47
1985-86	Winnipeg	52	13	28	5	2721	217	0	4.79	2	0	1	68	6	0	5.29
1986-87	Montreal	37	19	13	4	2178	102	1	*2.81	13	6	5	708	32	0	2.71
1987-88	Montreal	39	22	10	4	2247	107	2	2.86	4	2	2	230	9	0	2.35
1988-89	Montreal	36	20	13	3	2091	101	1	2.90	2	1	1	124	7	0	3.39
1989-90	Montreal	29	10	12	6	1674	94	1	3.37	1	0	0	33	2	0	3.64
1990-91	Minnesota	26	6	15	3	1473	77	2	3.14	6	0	2	171	11	0	3.86
1991-92	San Jose	7	1	4	0	305	25	0	4.92	....	....	....	....	....	....	....
1992-93	San Jose	18	2	14	1	930	86	0	5.55	....	....	....	....	....	....	....
	NHL Totals	**357**	**143**	**156**	**37**	**20025**	**1242**	**8**	**3.72**	**37**	**11**	**18**	**1803**	**104**	**0**	**3.46**

Signed as a free agent by **Winnipeg**, May 5, 1982. Traded to **Montreal** by **Winnipeg** for Steve Penney and the rights to Jan Ingman, August 19, 1986. Traded to **Minnesota** by **Montreal** for Jayson More, November 7, 1990. Claimed by **San Jose** from **Minnesota** in Dispersal Draft, May 30, 1991. • Missed majority of 1991-92 season recovering from back injury suffered in game vs. Buffalo, October 19, 1991. • Suffered eventual career-ending back injury in game vs. Detroit, January 15, 1993.

HEAD, Don

Goaltender. Catches left. 5'10", 200 lbs. Born, Mt. Dennis, Ont., June 30, 1933

Season	Club	GP	W	L	T	Mins	GA	SO	Avg	GP	W	L	Mins	GA	SO	Avg
1961-62	Boston	38	9	26	3	2280	158	2	4.16	....	....	....	....	....	....	....
	NHL Totals	**38**	**9**	**26**	**3**	**2280**	**158**	**2**	**4.16**	....	....	....	....	....	....	....

Traded to **Boston** by **Portland** (WHL) for Jack Bionda and future considerations (Gene Achtymichuk and Don Ward (August, 1961) and the loan of Bruce Gamble (September, 1961), May, 1961. Traded to **Portland** (WHL) by **Boston** for cash, June 10, 1962.

HEALY, Glenn

Goaltender. Catches left. 5'9", 190 lbs. Born, Pickering, Ont., August 23, 1962

Season	Club	GP	W	L	T	Mins	GA	SO	Avg	GP	W	L	Mins	GA	SO	Avg
1985-86	Los Angeles	1	0	0	0	51	6	0	7.06	....	....	....	....	....	....	....
1987-88	Los Angeles	34	12	18	1	1869	135	1	4.33	4	1	3	240	20	0	5.00
1988-89	Los Angeles	48	25	19	2	2699	192	0	4.27	3	0	1	97	6	0	3.71
1989-90	NY Islanders	39	12	19	6	2197	128	2	3.50	4	1	2	166	9	0	3.25
1990-91	NY Islanders	53	18	24	9	2999	166	0	3.32	....	....	....	....	....	....	....
1991-92	NY Islanders	37	14	16	4	1960	124	1	3.80	....	....	....	....	....	....	....
1992-93	NY Islanders	47	22	20	2	2655	146	1	3.30	18	9	8	1109	59	0	3.19
1993-94◆	NY Rangers	29	10	12	2	1368	69	2	3.03	2	0	0	68	1	0	0.88
1994-95	NY Rangers	17	8	6	1	888	35	1	2.36	5	2	1	230	13	0	3.39
1995-96	NY Rangers	44	17	14	11	2564	124	2	2.90	....	....	....	....	....	....	....
1996-97	NY Rangers	23	5	12	4	1357	59	1	2.61	....	....	....	....	....	....	....
1997-98	Toronto	21	4	10	2	1068	53	0	2.98	....	....	....	....	....	....	....
1998-99	Toronto	9	6	3	0	546	27	0	2.97	1	0	0	20	0	0	0.00
99-2000	Toronto	20	9	10	0	1164	59	2	3.04	....	....	....	....	....	....	....
2000-01	Toronto	15	4	7	3	871	38	0	2.62	....	....	....	....	....	....	....
	NHL Totals	**437**	**166**	**190**	**47**	**24256**	**1361**	**13**	**3.37**	**37**	**13**	**15**	**1930**	**108**	**0**	**3.36**

Signed as a free agent by **Los Angeles**, June 13, 1985. Signed as a free agent by **NY Islanders**, August 16, 1989. Claimed by **Anaheim** from **NY Islanders** in Expansion Draft, June 24, 1993. Claimed by **Tampa Bay** from **Anaheim** in Phase II of Expansion Draft, June 25, 1993. Traded to **NY Rangers** by **Tampa Bay** for Tampa Bay's 3rd round choice (previously acquired, Tampa Bay selected Allan Egeland) in 1993 Entry Draft, June 25, 1993. Signed as a free agent by **Toronto**, August 8, 1997.

HEBERT, Guy

Goaltender. Catches left. 5'11", 186 lbs. Born, Troy, NY, January 7, 1967
(St. Louis' 8th choice, 159th overall, in 1987 Entry Draft).

Season	Club	GP	W	L	T	Mins	GA	SO	Avg	GP	W	L	Mins	GA	SO	Avg
1991-92	St. Louis	13	5	5	1	738	36	0	2.93	....	....	....	....	....	....	....
1992-93	St. Louis	24	8	8	2	1210	74	1	3.67	1	0	0	2	0	0	0.00
1993-94	Anaheim	52	20	27	3	2991	141	2	2.83	....	....	....	....	....	....	....
1994-95	Anaheim	39	12	20	4	2092	109	2	3.13	....	....	....	....	....	....	....
1995-96	Anaheim	59	28	23	5	3326	157	4	2.83	....	....	....	....	....	....	....
1996-97	Anaheim	67	29	25	12	3863	172	4	2.67	9	4	4	534	18	1	2.02
1997-98	Anaheim	46	13	24	6	2660	130	3	2.93	....	....	....	....	....	....	....
1998-99	Anaheim	69	31	29	9	4083	165	6	2.42	4	0	3	208	15	0	4.33
99-2000	Anaheim	68	28	31	9	3976	166	4	2.51	....	....	....	....	....	....	....
2000-01	Anaheim	41	12	23	4	2215	115	2	3.12	....	....	....	....	....	....	....
	NY Rangers	13	5	7	1	735	42	0	3.43	....	....	....	....	....	....	....
	NHL Totals	**491**	**191**	**222**	**56**	**27889**	**1307**	**28**	**2.81**	**14**	**4**	**7**	**744**	**33**	**1**	**2.66**

Played in NHL All-Star Game (1997)

Claimed by **Anaheim** from **St. Louis** in Expansion Draft, June 24, 1993. Claimed on waivers by **NY Rangers** from **Anaheim**, March 7, 2001.

HEBERT, Sammy

Goaltender. Catches right. 5'10", 145 lbs. Born, Ottawa, Ont., March 31, 1894

Season	Club	GP	W	L	T	Mins	GA	SO	Avg	GP	W	L	Mins	GA	SO	Avg
1917-18◆	Toronto	2	1	0	0	80	10	0	7.50	....	....	....	....	....	....	....
1923-24	Ottawa	2	1	1	0	120	9	0	4.50	....	....	....	....	....	....	....
	NHL Totals	**4**	**2**	**1**	**0**	**200**	**19**	**0**	**5.70**	....	....	....	....	....	....	....

Signed as a free agent by **Toronto**, December 5, 1917. Traded to **Ottawa** by **Toronto** for cash, February 11, 1918. Rights awarded to **Quebec** when team returned to NHL, November 25, 1919. Signed as a free agent by **Ottawa**, February 29, 1924.

HEDBERG, Johan

Goaltender. Catches left. 6', 184 lbs. Born, Leksand, Sweden, May 3, 1973
(Philadelphia's 8th choice, 218th overall, in 1994 Entry Draft).

Season	Club	GP	W	L	T	Mins	GA	SO	Avg	GP	W	L	Mins	GA	SO	Avg
2000-01	Pittsburgh	9	7	1	1	545	24	0	2.64	18	9	9	1123	43	2	2.30
2001-02	Pittsburgh •	66	25	34	7	3877	178	6	2.75	....	....	....	....	....	....	....
2002-03	Pittsburgh	41	14	22	4	2410	126	1	3.14	....	....	....	....	....	....	....
	NHL Totals	**116**	**46**	**57**	**12**	**6832**	**328**	**7**	**2.88**	**18**	**9**	**9**	**1123**	**43**	**2**	**2.30**

Rights traded to **San Jose** by **Philadelphia** for San Jose's 7th round choice (Pavel Kasparik) in 1999 Entry Draft, August 6, 1998. Traded to **Pittsburgh** by **San Jose** with Bobby Dollas for Jeff Norton, March 12, 2001.

HEINZ, Rick

Goaltender. Catches left. 5'10", 165 lbs. Born, Essex, Ont., May 30, 1955

Season	Club	GP	W	L	T	Mins	GA	SO	Avg	GP	W	L	Mins	GA	SO	Avg
1980-81	St. Louis	4	2	1	1	220	8	0	2.18	....	....	....	....	....	....	....
1981-82	St. Louis	9	2	5	0	433	35	0	4.85	....	....	....	....	....	....	....
	Vancouver	3	2	1	0	180	9	1	3.00	....	....	....	....	....	....	....
1982-83	St. Louis	9	1	5	1	335	24	1	4.30	....	....	....	....	....	....	....
1983-84	St. Louis	22	7	7	3	1118	80	0	4.29	1	0	0	8	1	0	7.50
1984-85	St. Louis	2	0	0	0	70	3	0	2.57	....	....	....	....	....	....	....
	NHL Totals	**49**	**14**	**19**	**5**	**2356**	**159**	**2**	**4.05**	**1**	**0**	**0**	**8**	**1**	**0**	**7.50**

Signed as a free agent by **St. Louis**, April 16, 1979. Traded to **Vancouver** by **St. Louis** with Tony Currie, Jim Nill and St. Louis' 4th round choice (Shawn Kilroy) in 1982 Entry Draft for Glen Hanlon, March 9, 1982. Traded to **St. Louis** by **Vancouver** for cash, June 3, 1982.

HENDERSON, John

Goaltender. Catches left. 6'1", 174 lbs. Born, Toronto, Ont., March 25, 1933

Season	Club	GP	W	L	T	Mins	GA	SO	Avg	GP	W	L	Mins	GA	SO	Avg
1954-55	Boston	45	15	14	15	2628	109	5	2.49	2	0	2	120	8	0	4.00
1955-56	Boston	1	0	1	0	60	4	0	4.00	....	....	....	....	....	....	....
	NHL Totals	**46**	**15**	**15**	**15**	**2688**	**113**	**5**	[illegible]	**2**	**0**	**2**	**120**	**8**	**0**	**4.00**

Traded to **Boston** by **Toronto** for Ray Gariepy, September 23, 1954. Promoted to **Boston** from **Hershey** (AHL) to replace injured Terry Sawchuk, January 15, 1956. (Toronto 4, Boston 1). • Suspended by **Boston** for refusing to report to training camp, September, 1956.

HENRY, Gord

Goaltender. Catches left. 6', 185 lbs. Born, Owen Sound, Ont., August 17, 1926

Season	Club	GP	W	L	T	Mins	GA	SO	Avg	GP	W	L	Mins	GA	SO	Avg
1948-49	Boston	1	1	0	0	60	0	1	0.00	....	....	....	....	....	....	....
1949-50	Boston	2	0	2	0	120	5	0	2.50	....	....	....	....	....	....	....
1950-51	Boston	....	....	....	....	....	....	....	....	2	0	2	120	10	0	5.00
1952-53	Boston	....	....	....	....	....	....	....	....	3	0	2	163	11	0	4.05
	NHL Totals	**3**	**1**	**2**	**0**	**180**	**5**	**1**	**1.67**	**5**	**0**	**4**	**283**	**21**	**0**	**4.45**

• Recorded shutout (3-0) in NHL debut vs. Montreal, January 23, 1949.

HENRY, Jim

Goaltender. Catches left. 5'9", 165 lbs. Born, Winnipeg, Man., October 23, 1920

Season	Club	GP	W	L	T	Mins	GA	SO	Avg	GP	W	L	Mins	GA	SO	Avg
1941-42	NY Rangers	*48	*29	17	2	*2960	143	1	2.90	6	2	4	360	13	*1	*2.17
1945-46	NY Rangers	11	1	7	2	623	42	1	4.04	....	....	....	....	....	....	....
1946-47	NY Rangers	2	0	2	0	120	9	0	4.50	....	....	....	....	....	....	....
1947-48	NY Rangers	48	17	18	13	2880	153	2	3.19	....	....	....	....	....	....	....
1948-49	Chicago	*60	21	31	8	*3600	211	0	3.52	....	....	....	....	....	....	....
1951-52	Boston	*70	25	29	16	*4200	176	7	2.51	7	3	4	448	18	1	2.41
1952-53	Boston	*70	28	29	13	*4200	172	7	2.46	*9	5	4	*510	26	0	3.06
1953-54	Boston	*70	32	28	10	*4200	181	8	2.59	4	0	4	240	16	0	4.00
1954-55	Boston	27	8	12	6	1572	79	1	3.02	3	1	2	183	8	0	2.62
	NHL Totals	**406**	**161**	**173**	**70**	**24355**	**1166**	**27**	**2.87**	**29**	**11**	**18**	**1741**	**81**	**2**	**2.79**

NHL Second All-Star Team (1952)

Played in NHL All-Star Game (1952)

Signed as a free agent by **NY Rangers**, October 28, 1941. Traded to **Chicago** by **NY Rangers** for Emile Francis and Alex Kaleta, October 7, 1948. Traded to **Detroit** by **Chicago** with Metro Prystai, Gaye Stewart and Bob Goldham for Harry Lumley, Jack Stewart, Al Dewsbury, Pete Babando and Don Morrison, July 13, 1950. Traded to **Boston** by **Detroit** for cash, September 28, 1951.

HERRON, Denis

Goaltender. Catches left. 5'11", 165 lbs. Born, Chambly, Que., June 18, 1952
(Pittsburgh's 3rd choice, 40th overall, in 1972 Amateur Draft).

Season	Club	GP	W	L	T	Mins	GA	SO	Avg	GP	W	L	Mins	GA	SO	Avg
1972-73	Pittsburgh	18	6	7	2	967	55	2	3.41	....	....	....	....	....	....	....
1973-74	Pittsburgh	5	1	3	0	260	18	0	4.15	....	....	....	....	....	....	....
1974-75	Pittsburgh	3	1	1	0	108	11	0	6.11	....	....	....	....	....	....	....
	Kansas City	22	4	13	4	1280	80	0	3.75	....	....	....	....	....	....	....
1975-76	Kansas City	64	11	39	11	3620	243	0	4.03	....	....	....	....	....	....	....
1976-77	Pittsburgh	34	15	11	5	1920	94	1	2.94	3	1	2	180	11	0	3.67
1977-78	Pittsburgh	60	20	25	15	3534	210	0	3.57	....	....	....	....	....	....	....
1978-79	Pittsburgh	56	22	19	12	3208	180	0	3.37	7	2	5	421	24	0	3.42
1979-80	Montreal	34	25	3	3	1909	80	0	2.51	5	2	3	300	15	0	3.00
1980-81	Montreal	25	6	9	6	1147	67	1	3.50	....	....	....	....	....	....	....
1981-82	Montreal	27	12	6	8	1547	68	*3	*2.64	....	....	....	....	....	....	....
1982-83	Pittsburgh	31	5	18	5	1707	151	1	5.31	....	....	....	....	....	....	....

Season	Club	GP	W	L	T	Mins	GA	SO	Avg	GP	W	L	Mins	GA	SO	Avg
		REGULAR SEASON								PLAYOFFS						
1983-84	Pittsburgh	38	8	24	2	2028	138	1	4.08							
1984-85	Pittsburgh	42	10	22	3	2193	170	1	4.65							
1985-86	Pittsburgh	3	0	3	0	180	14	0	4.67							
	NHL Totals	**462**	**146**	**203**	**76**	**25608**	**1579**	**10**	**3.70**	**15**	**5**	**10**	**901**	**50**	**0**	**3.33**

Shared Vezina Trophy with Richard Sevigny and Michel Larocque (1981) • Shared William M. Jennings Trophy with Rick Wamsley (1982)

Traded to **Kansas City** by **Pittsburgh** with Jean-Guy Lagace for Michel Plasse, January 10, 1975. Signed as a free agent by **Pittsburgh**, August 7, 1976. Traded to **Montreal** by **Pittsburgh** with Pittsburgh's 2nd round choice (Jocelyn Gauvreau) in 1982 Entry Draft for Pat Hughes and Robbie Holland, August 30, 1979. Traded to **Pittsburgh** by **Montreal** for Pittsburgh's 3rd round choice (later traded to St. Louis – St. Louis selected Nelson Emerson) in 1985 Entry Draft, September 15, 1982.

HEXTALL, Ron

Goaltender. Catches left. 6'3", 192 lbs. Born, Brandon, Man., May 3, 1964
(Philadelphia's 6th choice, 119th overall, in 1982 Entry Draft).

Season	Club	GP	W	L	T	Mins	GA	SO	Avg	GP	W	L	Mins	GA	SO	Avg
1986-87	Philadelphia	*66	*37	21	6	*3799	190	1	3.00	*26	15	11	*1540	71	*2	2.77
1987-88	Philadelphia	62	30	22	7	3561	208	0	3.50	7	2	4	379	30	0	4.75
1988-89	Philadelphia	64	30	28	6	3756	202	0	3.23	15	8	7	886	49	0	3.32
1989-90	Philadelphia	8	4	2	1	419	29	0	4.15							
1990-91	Philadelphia	36	13	16	5	2035	106	0	3.13							
1991-92	Philadelphia	45	16	21	6	2668	151	3	3.40							
1992-93	Quebec	54	29	16	5	2988	172	0	3.45	6	2	4	372	18	0	2.90
1993-94	NY Islanders	65	27	26	6	3581	184	5	3.08	3	0	3	158	16	0	6.08
1994-95	Philadelphia	31	17	9	4	1824	88	1	2.89	15	10	5	897	42	0	2.81
1995-96	Philadelphia	53	31	13	7	3102	112	4	*2.17	12	6	6	760	27	0	2.13
1996-97	Philadelphia	55	31	16	5	3094	132	5	2.56	8	4	3	444	22	0	2.97
1997-98	Philadelphia	46	21	17	7	2688	97	4	2.17	1	0	0	20	1	0	3.00
1998-99	Philadelphia	23	10	7	4	1235	52	0	2.53							
	NHL Totals	**608**	**296**	**214**	**69**	**34750**	**1723**	**23**	**2.97**	**93**	**47**	**43**	**5456**	**276**	**2**	**3.04**

• Son of Bryan Jr. • NHL All-Rookie Team (1987) • NHL First All-Star Team (1987) • Vezina Trophy (1987) • Conn Smythe Trophy (1987) • Scored a goal vs. Boston, December 8, 1987 • Scored a goal in playoffs vs. Washington, April 11, 1989.

Played in NHL All-Star Game (1988)

Traded to **Quebec** by **Philadelphia** with Steve Duchesne, Peter Forsberg, Kerry Huffman, Mike Ricci, Philadelphia's 1st round choice (Jocelyn Thibault) in 1993 Entry Draft, $15,000,000 and future considerations (Chris Simon and Philadelphia's 1st round choice (later traded to Toronto – later traded to Washington – Washington selected Nolan Baumgartner) in 1994 Entry Draft, July 21, 1992) for Eric Lindros, June 30, 1992. Traded to **NY Islanders** by **Quebec** with Quebec's 1st round choice (Todd Bertuzzi) in 1993 Entry Draft for Mark Fitzpatrick and NY Islanders' 1st round choice (Adam Deadmarsh) in 1993 Entry Draft, June 20, 1993. Traded to **Philadelphia** by **NY Islanders** with NY Islanders' 6th round choice (Dmitri Tertyshny) in 1995 Entry Draft for Tommy Soderstrom, September 22, 1994.

HIGHTON, Hec

Goaltender. Catches right. 6', 175 lbs. Born, Medicine Hat, Alta., December 10, 1923

Season	Club	GP	W	L	T	Mins	GA	SO	Avg	GP	W	L	Mins	GA	SO	Avg
1943-44	Chicago	24	10	14	0	1440	108	0	4.50							
	NHL Totals	**24**	**10**	**14**	**0**	**1440**	**108**	**0**	**4.50**							

Traded to **Providence** (AHL) by **Chicago** with Gord Buttrey and $10,000 for Mike Karakas, January 7, 1944. Traded to **Chicago** (St. Louis-AHL) by **Providence** (AHL) for cash, February 4, 1945. Traded to **Detroit** by **Chicago** (St. Louis-AHL) with Joe Lund for Red Almas, Lloyd Doran, Tony Licari, Barry Sullivan and Thain Simon, September 9, 1948.

HIRSCH, Corey

Goaltender. Catches left. 5'10", 175 lbs. Born, Medicine Hat, Alta., August 10, 1972
(NY Rangers' 7th choice, 169th overall, in 1991 Entry Draft).

Season	Club	GP	W	L	T	Mins	GA	SO	Avg	GP	W	L	Mins	GA	SO	Avg
1992-93	NY Rangers	4	1	2	1	224	14	0	3.75							
1995-96	Vancouver	41	17	14	6	2338	114	1	2.93	6	2	3	338	21	0	3.73
1996-97	Vancouver	39	12	20	4	2127	116	2	3.27							
1997-98	Vancouver	1	0	0	0	50	5	0	6.00							
1998-99	Vancouver	20	3	8	3	919	48	1	3.13							
2000-01	Washington	1	1	0	0	20	0	0	0.00							
2002-03	Dallas	2	0	1	0	97	4	0	2.47							
	NHL Totals	**108**	**34**	**45**	**14**	**5775**	**301**	**4**	**3.13**	**6**	**2**	**3**	**338**	**21**	**0**	**3.73**

NHL All-Rookie Team (1996)

Traded to **Vancouver** by **NY Rangers** for Nathan LaFayette, April 7, 1995. Signed as a free agent by **Nashville**, August 10, 1999. Traded to **Anaheim** by **Nashville** for future considerations, March 14, 2000. Signed as a free agent by **Washington**, October 27, 2000. Signed as a free agent by **Dallas**, August 14, 2002.

HNILICKA, Milan

Goaltender. Catches left. 5'11", 190 lbs. Born, Kladno, Czech., June 25, 1973
(NY Islanders' 4th choice, 70th overall, in 1991 Entry Draft).

Season	Club	GP	W	L	T	Mins	GA	SO	Avg	GP	W	L	Mins	GA	SO	Avg
99-2000	NY Rangers	2	0	1	0	86	5	0	3.49							
2000-01	Atlanta	36	12	19	2	1879	105	2	3.35							
2001-02	Atlanta	60	13	33	10	3367	179	3	3.19							
2002-03	Atlanta	21	4	13	1	1097	65	0	3.56							
	NHL Totals	**119**	**29**	**66**	**13**	**6429**	**354**	**5**	**3.30**							

Signed as a free agent by **NY Rangers**, July 15, 1999. Signed as a free agent by **Atlanta**, July 28, 2000.

HODGE, Charlie

Goaltender. Catches left. 5'6", 150 lbs. Born, Lachine, Que., July 28, 1933

Season	Club	GP	W	L	T	Mins	GA	SO	Avg	GP	W	L	Mins	GA	SO	Avg
1954-55	Montreal	14	6	4	4	820	31	1	2.27	4	1	2	84	6	0	4.29
1955-56	Montreal	DID NOT PLAY – SPARE GOALTENDER														
1957-58	Montreal	12	8	2	2	720	31	1	2.58							
1958-59♦	Montreal	2	1	1	0	120	6	0	3.00							
1959-60♦	Montreal	1	0	1	0	60	3	0	3.00							
1960-61	Montreal	30	18	8	4	1800	74	4	2.47							
1963-64	Montreal	62	33	18	11	3720	140	*8	2.26	7	3	4	420	16	1	2.29
1964-65♦	Montreal	53	26	16	10	3180	135	3	2.55	5	3	2	300	10	1	2.00
1965-66♦	Montreal	26	12	7	2	1301	56	1	2.58							
1966-67	Montreal	37	11	15	7	2055	88	3	2.57							
1967-68	Oakland	58	13	29	13	3311	158	3	2.86							
1968-69	Oakland	14	4	6	1	781	48	0	3.69							
1969-70	Oakland	14	3	5	2	738	43	0	3.50							
1970-71	Vancouver	35	15	13	5	1967	112	0	3.42							
	NHL Totals	**358**	**150**	**125**	**61**	**20573**	**925**	**24**	**2.70**	**16**	**7**	**8**	**804**	**32**	**2**	**2.39**

NHL Second All-Star Team (1964, 1965) • Vezina Trophy (1964) • Shared Vezina Trophy with Gump Worsley (1966)

Played in NHL All-Star Game (1964, 1965, 1967)

Promoted to **Montreal** from **Mtl. Royals** (QHL) to replace Jacques Plante, March 21, 22, 1959 and March 13, 1960. Claimed by **California** (Oakland) from **Montreal** in Expansion Draft, June 6, 1967. Claimed by **Vancouver** from **Oakland** in Expansion Draft, June 10, 1970.

HODSON, Kevin

Goaltender. Catches left. 6', 182 lbs. Born, Winnipeg, Man., March 27, 1972

Season	Club	GP	W	L	T	Mins	GA	SO	Avg	GP	W	L	Mins	GA	SO	Avg
1995-96	Detroit	4	2	0	0	163	3	1	1.10							
1996-97♦	Detroit	6	2	2	1	294	8	1	1.63							
1997-98♦	Detroit	21	9	3	3	988	44	2	2.67	1	0	0	1	0	0	0.00
1998-99	Detroit	4	0	2	0	175	9	0	3.09							
	Tampa Bay	5	2	1	1	238	11	0	2.77							
99-2000	Tampa Bay	24	2	7	4	769	47	0	3.67							
2002-03	Tampa Bay	7	0	3	1	283	12	0	2.54							
	NHL Totals	**71**	**17**	**18**	**10**	**2910**	**134**	**4**	**2.76**	**1**	**0**	**0**	**1**	**0**	**0**	**0.00**

Signed as a free agent by **Chicago**, August 17, 1992. Signed as a free agent by **Detroit**, June 16, 1993. • Played 16 seconds in playoff game vs. St. Louis, May 17, 1998. Traded to **Tampa Bay** by **Detroit** with San Jose's 2nd round choice (previously acquired, Tampa Bay selected Sheldon Keefe) in 1999 Entry Draft for Wendel Clark and Detroit's 6th round choice (previously acquired, Detroit selected Kent McDonell) in 1999 Entry Draft, March 23, 1999. Traded to **Montreal** by **Tampa Bay** for Montreal's 7th round choice (later traded to Philadelphia – Philadelphia selected John Eichelberger) in 2000 Entry Draft, June 2, 2000. Signed as a free agent by **Tampa Bay**, May 28, 2002.

HOFFORT, Bruce

Goaltender. Catches left. 5'10", 185 lbs. Born, North Battleford, Sask., July 30, 1966

Season	Club	GP	W	L	T	Mins	GA	SO	Avg	GP	W	L	Mins	GA	SO	Avg
1989-90	Philadelphia	7	3	0	2	329	19	0	3.47							
1990-91	Philadelphia	2	1	0	1	39	3	0	4.62							
	NHL Totals	**9**	**4**	**0**	**3**	**368**	**22**	**0**	**3.59**							

Signed as a free agent by **Philadelphia**, June 30, 1989.

HOGANSON, Paul

Goaltender. Catches right. 5'11", 175 lbs. Born, Toronto, Ont., November 12, 1949
(Pittsburgh's 5th choice, 62nd overall, in 1969 Amateur Draft).

Season	Club	GP	W	L	T	Mins	GA	SO	Avg	GP	W	L	Mins	GA	SO	Avg
1970-71	Pittsburgh	2	0	1	0	57	7	0	7.37							
	NHL Totals	**2**	**0**	**1**	**0**	**57**	**7**	**0**	**7.37**							

HOGOSTA, Goran

Goaltender. Catches left. 6'1", 179 lbs. Born, Appelbo, Sweden, April 15, 1954

Season	Club	GP	W	L	T	Mins	GA	SO	Avg	GP	W	L	Mins	GA	SO	Avg
1977-78	NY Islanders	1	0	0	0	9	0	0	0.00							
1979-80	Quebec	21	5	12	3	1199	83	1	4.15							
	NHL Totals	**22**	**5**	**12**	**3**	**1208**	**83**	**1**	**4.12**							

Signed as a free agent by **NY Islanders**, June 17, 1977. • Shared shutout (9-0) with Billy Smith in NHL debut vs. Atlanta, November 1, 1977. Traded to **Quebec** by **NY Islanders** for Richard Brodeur, August, 1979.

HOLDEN, Mark

Goaltender. Catches left. 5'10", 165 lbs. Born, Weymouth, MA, June 12, 1957
(Montreal's 16th choice, 160th overall, in 1977 Amateur Draft).

Season	Club	GP	W	L	T	Mins	GA	SO	Avg	GP	W	L	Mins	GA	SO	Avg
1981-82	Montreal	1	0	0	0	20	0	0	0.00							
1982-83	Montreal	2	0	1	1	87	6	0	4.14							
1983-84	Montreal	1	0	1	0	52	4	0	4.62							
1984-85	Winnipeg	4	2	0	0	213	15	0	4.23							
	NHL Totals	**8**	**2**	**2**	**1**	**372**	**25**	**0**	**4.03**							

Traded to **Winnipeg** by **Montreal** for Doug Soetaert, October 9, 1984.

HOLLAND, Ken

Goaltender. Catches left. 5'8", 160 lbs. Born, Vernon, B.C., November 10, 1955
(Toronto's 13th choice, 188th overall, in 1975 Amateur Draft).

Season	Club	GP	W	L	T	Mins	GA	SO	Avg	GP	W	L	Mins	GA	SO	Avg
1980-81	Hartford	1	0	1	0	60	7	0	7.00							
1983-84	Detroit	3	0	1	1	146	10	0	4.11							
	NHL Totals	**4**	**0**	**2**	**1**	**206**	**17**	**0**	**4.95**							

Signed as a free agent by **Hartford**, July 17, 1980. Signed as a free agent by **Detroit**, July 6, 1983.

HOLLAND, Robbie

Goaltender. Catches left. 6'1", 180 lbs. Born, Montreal, Que., September 10, 1957
(Montreal's 8th choice, 64th overall, in 1977 Amateur Draft).

Season	Club	GP	W	L	T	Mins	GA	SO	Avg	GP	W	L	Mins	GA	SO	Avg
1979-80	Pittsburgh	34	10	17	6	1974	126	1	3.83							
1980-81	Pittsburgh	10	1	5	3	539	45	0	5.01							
	NHL Totals	**44**	**11**	**22**	**9**	**2513**	**171**	**1**	**4.08**							

Traded to **Pittsburgh** by **Montreal** with Pat Hughes for Denis Herron and Pittsburgh's 2nd round choice (Jocelyn Gauvreau) in 1982 Entry Draft, August 30, 1979. Rights traded to **NY Islanders** by **Pittsburgh** for future considerations, September 28, 1981.

HOLMES, Hap

HHOF

Goaltender. Catches left. 5'10", 170 lbs. Born, Aurora, Ont., February 21, 1892

		Regular Season								Playoffs						
Season	Club	GP	W	L	T	Mins	GA	SO	Avg	GP	W	L	Mins	GA	SO	Avg
1917-18◆	Toronto	16	9	7	0	965	76	0	4.73	*2	*1	1	*120	7	0	*3.50
	Toronto (Cup)									*5*	*3*	*2*	*300*	*21*	*0*	*4.20*
1918-19	Toronto	2	0	2	0	120	9	0	4.50							
1926-27	Detroit	41	11	26	4	2685	100	6	2.23							
1927-28	Detroit	*44	19	19	6	2740	79	11	1.73							
	NHL Totals	**103**	**39**	**54**	**10**	**6510**	**264**	**17**	**2.43**	**2**	**1**	**1**	**120**	**7**	**0**	**3.50**

Signed as a free agent by **Mtl. Wanderers**, November, 1917. Loaned to **Seattle** (PCHA) by **Mtl. Wanderers**, December 12, 1917. Loaned to **Toronto** by **Seattle** (PCHA), January 4, 1918 and recalled December 27, 1918. Signed as a free agent by **Victoria** (WCHL), November 7, 1924. Rights transferred to **Detroit** after NHL club purchased **Victoria** (WHL) franchise, May 26, 1926.

HOLMQVIST, Johan

Goaltender. Catches left. 6'3", 190 lbs. Born, Tolfta, Sweden, May 24, 1978
(NY Rangers' 9th choice, 175th overall, in 1997 Entry Draft).

		Regular Season								Playoffs						
Season	Club	GP	W	L	T	Mins	GA	SO	Avg	GP	W	L	Mins	GA	SO	Avg
2000-01	NY Rangers	2	0	2	0	119	10	0	5.04							
2001-02	NY Rangers	1	0	0	0	9	0	0	0.00							
2002-03	NY Rangers	1	0	1	0	39	2	0	3.08							
	NHL Totals	**4**	**0**	**3**	**0**	**167**	**12**	**0**	**4.31**							

Traded to **Minnesota** by **NY Rangers** for Lawrence Nycholat, March 11, 2003.

HRIVNAK, Jim

Goaltender. Catches left. 6'2", 195 lbs. Born, Montreal, Que., May 28, 1968
(Washington's 4th choice, 61st overall, in 1986 Entry Draft).

		Regular Season								Playoffs						
Season	Club	GP	W	L	T	Mins	GA	SO	Avg	GP	W	L	Mins	GA	SO	Avg
1989-90	Washington	11	5	5	0	609	36	0	3.55							
1990-91	Washington	9	4	2	1	432	26	0	3.61							
1991-92	Washington	12	6	3	0	605	35	0	3.47							
1992-93	Washington	27	13	9	2	1421	83	0	3.50							
	Winnipeg	3	2	1	0	180	13	0	4.33							
1993-94	St. Louis	23	4	10	0	970	69	0	4.27							
	NHL Totals	**85**	**34**	**30**	**3**	**4217**	**262**	**0**	**3.73**							

Traded to **Winnipeg** by **Washington** with Washington's 2nd round choice (Alexei Budayev) in 1993 Entry Draft for Rick Tabaracci, March 22, 1993. Traded to **St. Louis** by **Winnipeg** for St. Louis' 6th round choice (later traded to Florida – later traded to Edmonton – later traded to Winnipeg – Winnipeg selected Chris Kibermanis) in 1994 Entry Draft and future considerations, July 29, 1993.

HRUDEY, Kelly

Goaltender. Catches left. 5'10", 189 lbs. Born, Edmonton, Alta., January 13, 1961
(NY Islanders' 2nd choice, 38th overall, in 1980 Entry Draft).

		Regular Season								Playoffs						
Season	Club	GP	W	L	T	Mins	GA	SO	Avg	GP	W	L	Mins	GA	SO	Avg
1983-84	NY Islanders	12	7	2	0	535	28	0	3.14							
1984-85	NY Islanders	41	19	17	3	2335	141	2	3.62	5	1	3	281	8	0	1.71
1985-86	NY Islanders	45	19	15	8	2563	137	1	3.21	2	0	2	120	6	0	3.00
1986-87	NY Islanders	46	21	15	7	2634	145	0	3.30	14	7	7	842	38	0	2.71
1987-88	NY Islanders	47	22	17	5	2751	153	3	3.34	6	2	4	381	23	0	3.62
1988-89	NY Islanders	*50	18	24	3	*2800	183	0	3.92							
	Los Angeles	*16	10	4	2	*974	47	1	2.90	10	4	6	566	35	0	3.71
1989-90	Los Angeles	52	22	21	6	2860	194	2	4.07	9	4	4	539	39	0	4.34
1990-91	Los Angeles	47	26	13	6	2730	132	3	2.90	12	6	6	798	37	0	2.78
1991-92	Los Angeles	60	26	17	13	3509	197	1	3.37	6	2	4	355	22	0	3.72
1992-93	Los Angeles	50	18	21	6	2718	175	2	3.86	20	10	10	1261	74	0	3.52
1993-94	Los Angeles	64	22	31	7	3713	228	1	3.68							
1994-95	Los Angeles	35	14	13	5	1894	99	0	3.14							
1995-96	Los Angeles	36	7	15	10	2077	113	0	3.26							
1996-97	San Jose	48	16	24	5	2631	140	0	3.19							
1997-98	San Jose	28	4	16	2	1360	62	1	2.74	1	0	0	20	1	0	3.00
	NHL Totals	**677**	**271**	**265**	**88**	**38084**	**2174**	**17**	**3.43**	**85**	**36**	**46**	**5163**	**283**	**0**	**3.29**

Traded to **Los Angeles** by **NY Islanders** for Mark Fitzpatrick, Wayne McBean and future considerations (Doug Crossman, May 23, 1989) February 22, 1989. Signed as a free agent by **San Jose**, August 18, 1996.

HUET, Cristobal

Goaltender. Catches left. 6', 194 lbs. Born, St-Martin-d'Heres, France, September 3, 1975
(Los Angeles' 9th choice, 214th overall, in 2001 Entry Draft).

		Regular Season								Playoffs						
Season	Club	GP	W	L	T	Mins	GA	SO	Avg	GP	W	L	Mins	GA	SO	Avg
2002-03	Los Angeles	12	4	4	1	541	21	1	2.33							
	NHL Totals	**12**	**4**	**4**	**1**	**541**	**21**	**1**	**2.33**							

HURME, Jani

Goaltender. Catches left. 6', 187 lbs. Born, Turku, Finland, January 7, 1975
(Ottawa's 2nd choice, 58th overall, in 1997 Entry Draft).

		Regular Season								Playoffs						
Season	Club	GP	W	L	T	Mins	GA	SO	Avg	GP	W	L	Mins	GA	SO	Avg
99-2000	Ottawa	1	1	0	0	60	2	0	2.00							
2000-01	Ottawa	22	12	5	4	1296	54	2	2.50							
2001-02	Ottawa	25	12	9	1	1309	54	3	2.48							
2002-03	Florida	28	4	11	6	1376	66	1	2.88							
	NHL Totals	**76**	**29**	**25**	**11**	**4041**	**176**	**6**	**2.61**							

Traded to **Florida** by **Ottawa** for Billy Thompson and Greg Watson, October 1, 2002.

ING, Peter

Goaltender. Catches left. 6'2", 170 lbs. Born, Toronto, Ont., April 28, 1969
(Toronto's 3rd choice, 48th overall, in 1988 Entry Draft).

		Regular Season								Playoffs						
Season	Club	GP	W	L	T	Mins	GA	SO	Avg	GP	W	L	Mins	GA	SO	Avg
1989-90	Toronto	3	0	2	1	182	18	0	5.93							
1990-91	Toronto	56	16	29	8	3126	200	1	3.84							
1991-92	Edmonton	12	3	4	0	463	33	0	4.28							
1993-94	Detroit	3	1	2	0	170	15	0	5.29							
	NHL Totals	**74**	**20**	**37**	**9**	**3941**	**266**	**1**	**4.05**							

Traded to **Edmonton** by **Toronto** with Vincent Damphousse, Scott Thornton and Luke Richardson for Grant Fuhr, Glenn Anderson and Craig Berube, September 19, 1991. Traded to **Detroit** by **Edmonton** for Detroit's 7th round choice (Chris Wickenheiser) in 1994 Entry Draft and future considerations, August 30, 1993.

INNESS, Gary

Goaltender. Catches left. 6', 195 lbs. Born, Toronto, Ont., May 28, 1949

		Regular Season								Playoffs						
Season	Club	GP	W	L	T	Mins	GA	SO	Avg	GP	W	L	Mins	GA	SO	Avg
1973-74	Pittsburgh	20	7	10	1	1032	56	0	3.26							
1974-75	Pittsburgh	57	24	18	10	3122	161	2	3.09	9	5	4	540	24	0	2.67
1975-76	Pittsburgh	23	8	9	2	1212	82	0	4.06							
	Philadelphia	2	2	0	0	120	3	0	1.50							
1976-77	Philadelphia	6	1	0	2	210	9	0	2.57							
1978-79	Washington	37	14	14	8	2107	130	0	3.70							
1979-80	Washington	14	2	9	2	727	44	0	3.63							
1980-81	Washington	3	0	1	2	180	9	0	3.00							
	NHL Totals	**162**	**58**	**61**	**27**	**8710**	**494**	**2**	**3.40**	**9**	**5**	**4**	**540**	**24**	**0**	**2.67**

Signed as a free agent by **Pittsburgh**, June, 1973. Traded to **Philadelphia** by **Pittsburgh** with future considerations for Bobby Taylor and Ed Van Impe, March 9, 1976. Signed as a free agent by **Washington**, December 19, 1978.

IRBE, Arturs

Goaltender. Catches left. 5'8", 190 lbs. Born, Riga, Latvia, February 2, 1967
(Minnesota's 11th choice, 196th overall, in 1989 Entry Draft).

		Regular Season								Playoffs						
Season	Club	GP	W	L	T	Mins	GA	SO	Avg	GP	W	L	Mins	GA	SO	Avg
1991-92	San Jose	13	2	6	3	645	48	0	4.47							
1992-93	San Jose	36	7	26	0	2074	142	1	4.11							
1993-94	San Jose	*74	30	28	16	*4412	209	3	2.84	14	7	7	806	50	0	3.72
1994-95	San Jose	38	14	19	3	2043	111	4	3.26	6	2	4	316	27	0	5.13
1995-96	San Jose	22	4	12	4	1112	85	0	4.59							
1996-97	Dallas	35	17	12	3	1965	88	3	2.69	1	0	0	13	0	0	0.00
1997-98	Vancouver	41	14	11	6	1999	91	2	2.73							
1998-99	Carolina	62	27	20	12	3643	135	6	2.22	6	2	4	408	15	0	2.21
99-2000	Carolina	*75	34	28	9	4345	175	5	2.42							
2000-01	Carolina	*77	37	29	9	*4406	180	6	2.45	6	2	4	360	20	0	3.33
2001-02	Carolina	51	20	19	11	2974	126	3	2.54	18	10	8	1078	30	1	1.67
2002-03	Carolina	34	7	24	2	1884	100	0	3.18							
	NHL Totals	**558**	**213**	**234**	**78**	**31502**	**1490**	**33**	**2.84**	**51**	**23**	**27**	**2981**	**142**	**1**	**2.86**

Played in NHL All-Star Game (1994, 1999)

Claimed by **San Jose** from **Minnesota** in Dispersal Draft, May 30, 1991. Signed as a free agent by **Dallas**, August 13, 1996. Signed as a free agent by **Vancouver**, August 25, 1997. Signed as a free agent by **Carolina**, September 14, 1998.

IRELAND, Randy

Goaltender. Catches left. 6', 165 lbs. Born, Rosetown, Sask., April 5, 1957
(Buffalo's 5th choice, 82nd overall, in 1978 Amateur Draft).

		Regular Season								Playoffs						
Season	Club	GP	W	L	T	Mins	GA	SO	Avg	GP	W	L	Mins	GA	SO	Avg
1978-79	Buffalo	2	0	0	0	30	3	0	6.00							
	NHL Totals	**2**	**0**	**0**	**0**	**30**	**3**	**0**	**6.00**							

• Re-entered NHL Entry Draft. Originally Chicago's 3rd choice, 60th overall, in 1977 Amateur Draft.

IRONS, Robbie

Goaltender. Catches left. 5'8", 150 lbs. Born, Toronto, Ont., November 19, 1946

		Regular Season								Playoffs						
Season	Club	GP	W	L	T	Mins	GA	SO	Avg	GP	W	L	Mins	GA	SO	Avg
1968-69	St. Louis	1	0	0	0	3	0	0	0.00							
	NHL Totals	**1**	**0**	**0**	**0**	**3**	**0**	**0**	**0.00**							

Traded to **St. Louis** by **NY Rangers** with Camille Henry and Bill Plager for Don Caley and Wayne Rivers, June 13, 1968. • Replaced Glenn Hall in 1st period vs. NY Rangers after Hall was given a game misconduct, November 13, 1968. Shares NHL record with Christian Soucy for having shortest career (three minutes) in league history.

IRONSTONE, Joe

Goaltender. Catches right. 5'6", 180 lbs. Born, Sudbury, Ont., June 28, 1898

		Regular Season								Playoffs						
Season	Club	GP	W	L	T	Mins	GA	SO	Avg	GP	W	L	Mins	GA	SO	Avg
1924-25	Ottawa	DID NOT PLAY – SPARE GOALTENDER														
1925-26	NY Americans	1	0	0	0	40	3	0	4.50							
1927-28	Toronto	1	0	0	1	70	0	1	0.00							
	NHL Totals	**2**	**0**	**0**	**1**	**110**	**3**	**1**	**1.64**							

Signed as a free agent by **Ottawa**, October 30, 1924. Signed as a free agent by **NY Americans**, October 30, 1925. Traded to **Toronto** (Can-Pro) by **NY Americans** for cash, January 6, 1928. Loaned to **Toronto** by **Toronto** (Can-Pro) to replace injured John Ross Roach, March 3, 1928. (Toronto 0, NY Americans 0). Claimed by **NY Americans** from **Toronto** (Can-Pro) in Inter-League Draft, May 12, 1928. Traded to **London** (Can-Pro) by **NY Americans** for cash, October 30, 1928.

JABLONSKI, Pat

Goaltender. Catches right. 6', 180 lbs. Born, Toledo, OH, June 20, 1967
(St. Louis' 6th choice, 138th overall, in 1985 Entry Draft).

		Regular Season								Playoffs						
Season	Club	GP	W	L	T	Mins	GA	SO	Avg	GP	W	L	Mins	GA	SO	Avg
1989-90	St. Louis	4	0	3	0	208	17	0	4.90							
1990-91	St. Louis	8	2	3	3	492	25	0	3.05	3	0	0	90	5	0	3.33
1991-92	St. Louis	10	3	6	0	468	38	0	4.87							
1992-93	Tampa Bay	43	8	24	4	2268	150	1	3.97							
1993-94	Tampa Bay	15	5	6	3	834	54	0	3.88							
1995-96	St. Louis	1	0	0	0	8	1	0	7.50							
	Montreal	23	5	9	6	1264	62	0	2.94	1	0	0	49	1	0	1.22
1996-97	Montreal	17	4	6	2	754	50	0	3.98							
	Phoenix	2	0	1	0	59	2	0	2.03							

		REGULAR SEASON								PLAYOFFS						
Season	Club	GP	W	L	T	Mins	GA	SO	Avg	GP	W	L	Mins	GA	SO	Avg
1997-98	Carolina	5	1	4	0	279	14	0	3.01	....	....	....	....	....	....	....
	NHL Totals	**128**	**28**	**62**	**18**	**6634**	**413**	**1**	**3.74**	**4**	**0**	**0**	**139**	**6**	**0**	**2.59**

Traded to **Tampa Bay** by **St. Louis** with Steve Tuttle, Darin Kimble and Rob Robinson for future considerations, June 19, 1992. Traded to **Toronto** by **Tampa Bay** for cash, February 21, 1994. Claimed by **St. Louis** from **Toronto** in Waiver Draft, October 2, 1995. Traded to **Montreal** by **St. Louis** for J.J. Daigneault, November 7, 1995. Traded to **Phoenix** by **Montreal** for Steve Cheredaryk, March 18, 1997. Signed as a free agent by **Carolina**, August 12, 1997.

JACKSON, Doug

Goaltender. Catches left. 5'10", 150 lbs. Born, Winnipeg, Man., December 12, 1924

Season	Club	GP	W	L	T	Mins	GA	SO	Avg	GP	W	L	Mins	GA	SO	Avg
1947-48	Chicago	6	2	3	1	360	42	0	7.00	....	....	....	....	....	....	....
	NHL Totals	**6**	**2**	**3**	**1**	**360**	**42**	**0**	**7.00**	....	....	....	....	....	....	....

Traded to **Vancouver** (PCHL) by **Chicago** for cash, May 31, 1948.

JACKSON, Percy

Goaltender. Catches left. 5'9", 165 lbs. Born, Canmore, Alta., September 21, 1907

Season	Club	GP	W	L	T	Mins	GA	SO	Avg	GP	W	L	Mins	GA	SO	Avg
1931-32	Boston	4	1	1	1	232	8	0	2.07	....	....	....	....	....	....	....
1933-34	NY Americans	1	0	1	0	60	9	0	9.00	....	....	....	....	....	....	....
1934-35	NY Rangers	1	0	1	0	60	8	0	8.00	....	....	....	....	....	....	....
1935-36	Boston	1	0	0	0	40	1	0	1.50	....	....	....	....	....	....	....
	NHL Totals	**7**	**1**	**3**	**1**	**392**	**26**	**0**	**3.98**	....	....	....	....	....	....	....

Loaned to **NY Americans** by **Boston** to replace injured Roy Worters, March 18, 1934. (NY Americans 9, Boston 5). Traded to **NY Rangers** by **Boston** for Jean Pusie, November 1, 1934. Traded to **Boston** by **NY Rangers** for cash, November 18, 1934.

JAKS, Pauli

Goaltender. Catches left. 6', 194 lbs. Born, Schaffhausen, Switz., January 25, 1972
(Los Angeles' 4th choice, 108th overall, in 1991 Entry Draft).

Season	Club	GP	W	L	T	Mins	GA	SO	Avg	GP	W	L	Mins	GA	SO	Avg
1994-95	Los Angeles	1	0	0	0	40	2	0	3.00	....	....	....	....	....	....	....
	NHL Totals	**1**	**0**	**0**	**0**	**40**	**2**	**0**	**3.00**	....	....	....	....	....	....	....

JANASZAK, Steve

Goaltender. Catches right. 6'1", 210 lbs. Born, St. Paul, MN, January 7, 1957

Season	Club	GP	W	L	T	Mins	GA	SO	Avg	GP	W	L	Mins	GA	SO	Avg
1979-80	Minnesota	1	0	0	1	60	2	0	2.00	....	....	....	....	....	....	....
1981-82	Colorado	2	0	1	0	100	13	0	7.80	....	....	....	....	....	....	....
	NHL Totals	**3**	**0**	**1**	**1**	**160**	**15**	**0**	**5.63**	....	....	....	....	....	....	....

Signed as a free agent by **Minnesota**, March, 1980. Signed as a free agent by **Colorado**, April 14, 1980. Traded to **Calgary** by **Colorado** for future considerations, September 18, 1982.

JANECYK, Bob

Goaltender. Catches left. 6'1", 180 lbs. Born, Chicago, IL, May 18, 1957

Season	Club	GP	W	L	T	Mins	GA	SO	Avg	GP	W	L	Mins	GA	SO	Avg
1983-84	Chicago	8	2	3	1	412	28	0	4.08	....	....	....	....	....	....	....
1984-85	Los Angeles	51	22	21	8	3002	183	2	3.66	3	0	3	184	10	0	3.26
1985-86	Los Angeles	38	14	16	4	2083	162	0	4.67	....	....	....	....	....	....	....
1986-87	Los Angeles	7	4	3	0	420	34	0	4.86	....	....	....	....	....	....	....
1987-88	Los Angeles	5	1	4	0	303	23	0	4.55	....	....	....	....	....	....	....
1988-89	Los Angeles	1	0	0	0	30	2	0	4.00	....	....	....	....	....	....	....
	NHL Totals	**110**	**43**	**47**	**13**	**6250**	**432**	**2**	**4.15**	**3**	**0**	**3**	**184**	**10**	**0**	**3.26**

Signed as a free agent by **Chicago**, June 3, 1980. Traded to **Los Angeles** by **Chicago** with Chicago's 1st (Craig Redmond), 3rd (John English) and 4th (Tom Glavine) round choices in 1984 Entry Draft for Los Angeles' 1st (Ed Olczyk) and 4th (Tommy Eriksson) round choices in 1984 Entry Draft, June 9, 1984.

JENSEN, Al

Goaltender. Catches left. 5'10", 180 lbs. Born, Hamilton, Ont., November 27, 1958
(Detroit's 4th choice, 31st overall, in 1978 Amateur Draft).

Season	Club	GP	W	L	T	Mins	GA	SO	Avg	GP	W	L	Mins	GA	SO	Avg
1980-81	Detroit	1	0	1	0	60	7	0	7.00	....	....	....	....	....	....	....
1981-82	Washington	26	8	8	4	1274	81	0	3.81	....	....	....	....	....	....	....
1982-83	Washington	40	22	12	6	2358	135	1	3.44	3	1	2	139	10	0	4.32
1983-84	Washington	43	25	13	3	2414	117	4	2.91	6	3	1	258	14	0	3.26
1984-85	Washington	14	10	3	1	803	34	1	2.54	3	1	2	201	8	0	2.39
1985-86	Washington	44	28	9	3	2437	129	2	3.18	....	....	....	....	....	....	....
1986-87	Washington	6	1	3	1	328	27	0	4.94	....	....	....	....	....	....	....
	Los Angeles	5	1	4	0	300	27	0	5.40	....	....	....	....	....	....	....
	NHL Totals	**179**	**95**	**53**	**18**	**9974**	**557**	**8**	**3.35**	**12**	**5**	**5**	**598**	**32**	**0**	**3.21**

Shared William M. Jennings Trophy with Pat Riggin (1984)

Traded to **Washington** by **Detroit** for Mark Lofthouse, July 23, 1981. Traded to **Los Angeles** by **Washington** for Garry Galley, February 14, 1987.

JENSEN, Darren

Goaltender. Catches left. 5'9", 165 lbs. Born, Creston, B.C., May 27, 1960
(Hartford's 5th choice, 92nd overall, in 1980 Entry Draft).

Season	Club	GP	W	L	T	Mins	GA	SO	Avg	GP	W	L	Mins	GA	SO	Avg
1984-85	Philadelphia	1	0	1	0	60	7	0	7.00	....	....	....	....	....	....	....
1985-86	Philadelphia	29	15	9	1	1436	88	2	3.68	....	....	....	....	....	....	....
	NHL Totals	**30**	**15**	**10**	**1**	**1496**	**95**	**2**	**3.81**	....	....	....	....	....	....	....

Signed as a free agent by **Philadelphia**, May 1, 1984. Traded to **Vancouver** by **Philadelphia** with Daryl Stanley for Wendell Young and Vancouver's 3rd round choice (Kimbi Daniels) in 1990 Entry Draft, August 31, 1987.

JOHNSON, Bob

Goaltender. Catches left. 6'1", 185 lbs. Born, Farmington, MI, November 12, 1948

Season	Club	GP	W	L	T	Mins	GA	SO	Avg	GP	W	L	Mins	GA	SO	Avg
1972-73	St. Louis	12	6	5	0	583	26	0	2.68	....	....	....	....	....	....	....
1974-75	Pittsburgh	12	3	4	1	476	40	0	5.04	....	....	....	....	....	....	....
	NHL Totals	**24**	**9**	**9**	**1**	**1059**	**66**	**0**	**3.74**	....	....	....	....	....	....	....

• Father of Brent

Signed as a free agent by **Detroit**, September 29, 1970. Traded to **St. Louis** (Denver-WHL) by **Detroit** for cash, October 1, 1971. Traded to **Pittsburgh** by **St. Louis** for Nick Harbaruk, October 4, 1973.

JOHNSON, Brent

Goaltender. Catches left. 6'2", 200 lbs. Born, Farmington, MI, March 12, 1977
(Colorado's 5th choice, 129th overall, in 1995 Entry Draft).

Season	Club	GP	W	L	T	Mins	GA	SO	Avg	GP	W	L	Mins	GA	SO	Avg
1998-99	St. Louis	6	3	2	0	286	10	0	2.10	....	....	....	....	....	....	....
2000-01	St. Louis	31	19	9	2	1744	63	4	2.17	2	0	1	62	2	0	1.94
2001-02	St. Louis	58	34	20	4	3491	127	5	2.18	10	5	5	590	18	3	1.83
2002-03	St. Louis	38	16	13	5	2042	84	2	2.47	....	....	....	....	....	....	....
	NHL Totals	**133**	**72**	**44**	**11**	**7563**	**284**	**11**	**2.25**	**12**	**5**	**6**	**652**	**20**	**3**	**1.84**

• Son of Bob

Traded to **St. Louis** by **Colorado** for San Jose's 3rd round choice (previously acquired, Colorado selected Rick Berry) in 1997 Entry Draft, May 30, 1997.

JOHNSTON, Eddie

Goaltender. Catches left. 6', 190 lbs. Born, Montreal, Que., November 24, 1935

Season	Club	GP	W	L	T	Mins	GA	SO	Avg	GP	W	L	Mins	GA	SO	Avg
1962-63	Boston	50	11	27	10	2913	193	1	3.98	....	....	....	....	....	....	....
1963-64	Boston	*70	18	40	12	*4200	211	6	3.01	....	....	....	....	....	....	....
1964-65	Boston	47	11	32	4	2820	163	3	3.47	....	....	....	....	....	....	....
1965-66	Boston	33	10	19	2	1744	108	1	3.72	....	....	....	....	....	....	....
1966-67	Boston	34	8	21	2	1880	116	0	3.70	....	....	....	....	....	....	....
1967-68	Boston	28	11	8	5	1524	73	0	2.87	....	....	....	....	....	....	....
1968-69	Boston	24	14	6	4	1440	74	2	3.08	1	0	1	65	4	0	3.69
1969-70♦	Boston	37	16	9	11	2176	108	3	2.98	1	0	1	60	4	0	4.00
1970-71	Boston	38	30	6	2	2280	96	4	2.53	1	0	1	60	7	0	7.00
1971-72♦	Boston	38	27	8	3	2260	102	2	2.71	7	*6	1	420	13	1	*1.86
1972-73	Boston	45	24	17	1	2510	137	5	3.27	3	1	2	160	9	0	3.38
1973-74	Toronto	26	12	9	4	1516	78	1	3.09	1	0	1	60	6	0	6.00
1974-75	St. Louis	30	12	13	5	1800	93	2	3.10	1	0	1	60	5	0	5.00
1975-76	St. Louis	38	11	17	9	2152	130	1	3.62	....	....	....	....	....	....	....
1976-77	St. Louis	38	13	16	5	2111	108	1	3.07	3	0	2	138	9	0	3.91
1977-78	St. Louis	12	5	6	1	650	45	0	4.15	....	....	....	....	....	....	....
	Chicago	4	1	3	0	240	17	0	4.25	....	....	....	....	....	....	....
	NHL Totals	**592**	**234**	**257**	**80**	**34216**	**1852**	**32**	**3.25**	**18**	**7**	**10**	**1023**	**57**	**1**	**3.34**

Traded to **Chicago** by **Montreal** for cash, September 10, 1959. Claimed by **Boston** from **Spokane** (WHL) in Inter-League Draft, June 4, 1962. Traded to **Toronto** by **Boston** to complete transaction that sent Jacques Plante to Boston (March 3, 1973), May 22, 1973. Traded to **St. Louis** by **Toronto** for Gary Sabourin, May 27, 1974. Traded to **Chicago** by **St. Louis** for cash, January 27, 1978.

JOSEPH, Curtis

Goaltender. Catches left. 5'11", 190 lbs. Born, Keswick, Ont., April 29, 1967

Season	Club	GP	W	L	T	Mins	GA	SO	Avg	GP	W	L	Mins	GA	SO	Avg
1989-90	St. Louis	15	9	5	1	852	48	0	3.38	6	4	1	327	18	0	3.30
1990-91	St. Louis	30	16	10	2	1710	89	0	3.12	....	....	....	....	....	....	....
1991-92	St. Louis	60	27	20	10	3494	175	2	3.01	6	2	4	379	23	0	3.64
1992-93	St. Louis	68	29	28	9	3890	196	1	3.02	11	7	4	715	27	*2	2.27
1993-94	St. Louis	71	36	23	11	4127	213	1	3.10	4	0	4	246	15	0	3.66
1994-95	St. Louis	36	20	10	1	1914	89	1	2.79	7	3	3	392	24	0	3.67
1995-96	Edmonton	34	15	16	2	1936	111	0	3.44	....	....	....	....	....	....	....
1996-97	Edmonton	72	32	29	9	4100	200	6	2.93	12	5	7	767	36	2	2.82
1997-98	Edmonton	71	29	31	9	4132	181	8	2.63	12	5	7	716	23	3	1.93
1998-99	Toronto	67	35	24	7	4001	171	3	2.56	17	9	8	1011	41	1	2.43
99-2000	Toronto	63	36	20	7	3801	158	4	2.49	12	6	6	729	25	1	2.06
2000-01	Toronto	68	33	27	8	4100	163	6	2.39	11	7	4	685	24	3	2.10
2001-02	Toronto	51	29	17	5	3065	114	4	2.23	20	10	10	1253	48	3	2.30
2002-03	Detroit	61	34	19	6	3566	148	5	2.49	4	0	4	289	10	0	2.08
	NHL Totals	**767**	**380**	**279**	**87**	**44688**	**2056**	**41**	**2.76**	**122**	**58**	**62**	**7509**	**314**	**15**	**2.51**

King Clancy Memorial Trophy (2000)

Played in NHL All-Star Game (1994, 2000)

Signed as a free agent by **St. Louis**, June 16, 1989. Traded to **Edmonton** by **St. Louis** with the rights to Mike Grier for St. Louis' 1st round choices (previously acquired) in 1996 (Marty Reasoner) and 1997 (later traded to Los Angeles – Los Angeles selected Matt Zultek) Entry Drafts, August 4, 1995. Signed as a free agent by **Toronto**, July 15, 1998. Traded to **Calgary** by **Toronto** for Calgary's 3rd round choice (later traded to Minnesota – Minnesota selected Danny Irmen) in 2003 Entry Draft and future considerations, June 30, 2002. Signed as a free agent by **Detroit**, July 2, 2002.

JUNKIN, Joe

Goaltender. Catches left. 5'11", 180 lbs. Born, Lindsay, Ont., September 8, 1946

Season	Club	GP	W	L	T	Mins	GA	SO	Avg	GP	W	L	Mins	GA	SO	Avg
1968-69	Boston	1	0	0	0	8	0	0	0.00	....	....	....	....	....	....	....
	NHL Totals	**1**	**0**	**0**	**0**	**8**	**0**	**0**	**0.00**	....	....	....	....	....	....	....

Signed as a free agent by **Boston**, September 12, 1968.

KAARELA, Jari

Goaltender. Catches left. 5'10", 165 lbs. Born, Tampere, Finland, August 8, 1958

Season	Club	GP	W	L	T	Mins	GA	SO	Avg	GP	W	L	Mins	GA	SO	Avg
1980-81	Colorado	5	2	2	0	220	22	0	6.00	....	....	....	....	....	....	....
	NHL Totals	**5**	**2**	**2**	**0**	**220**	**22**	**0**	**6.00**	....	....	....	....	....	....	....

Signed as a free agent by **Colorado**, February 9, 1981. Traded to **NY Islanders** by **Colorado** with Mike McEwen for Glenn Resch and Steve Tambellini, March 10, 1981.

KAMPPURI, Hannu

Goaltender. Catches right. 6', 175 lbs. Born, Helsinki, Finland, June 1, 1957

Season	Club	GP	W	L	T	Mins	GA	SO	Avg	GP	W	L	Mins	GA	SO	Avg
		REGULAR SEASON								PLAYOFFS						
1984-85	New Jersey	13	1	10	1	645	54	0	5.02							
	NHL Totals	**13**	**1**	**10**	**1**	**645**	**54**	**0**	**5.02**							

Signed as a free agent by **New Jersey**, August 1, 1984.

KARAKAS, Mike

USHOF

Goaltender. Catches left. 5'11", 147 lbs. Born, Aurora, MN, December 12, 1911

Season	Club	GP	W	L	T	Mins	GA	SO	Avg	GP	W	L	Mins	GA	SO	Avg
1935-36	Chicago	*48	21	19	8	2990	92	9	1.85	2	1	1	120	7	0	3.50
1936-37	Chicago	*48	14	*27	7	2978	131	5	2.64							
1937-38♦	Chicago	*48	14	25	9	2980	139	1	2.80	*8	*6	2	*525	15	*2	1.71
1938-39	Chicago	*48	12	*28	8	2988	132	5	2.65							
1939-40	Chicago	17	7	9	1	1050	58	0	3.31							
	Montreal	5	0	4	1	310	18	0	3.48							
1943-44	Chicago	26	12	9	5	1560	79	3	3.04	*9	4	5	*549	24	*1	2.62
1944-45	Chicago	48	12	*29	7	2880	187	*4	3.90							
1945-46	Chicago	48	22	19	7	2880	166	1	3.46	4	0	4	240	26	0	6.50
	NHL Totals	**336**	**114**	**169**	**53**	**20616**	**1002**	**28**	**2.92**	**23**	**11**	**12**	**1434**	**72**	**3**	**3.01**

NHL Rookie of the Year (1936) • NHL Second All-Star Team (1945)

Signed as a free agent by **Chicago**, October 28, 1935. • Suspended by **Chicago** for remainder of 1939-40 season after refusing assignment to **Providence** (AHL), December 30, 1939. • Suspension lifted by NHL President Frank Calder and rights loaned to **Montreal** for remainder of 1939-40 season after Montreal goaltender Wilf Cude suffered shoulder injury, February 23, 1940. Traded to **Providence** (AHL) by **Chicago** for cash, May 14, 1940. Traded to **Chicago** by **Providence** (AHL) for Hec Highton, Gord Buttrey and $10,000, January 7, 1944.

KEANS, Doug

Goaltender. Catches left. 5'7", 185 lbs. Born, Pembroke, Ont., January 7, 1958
(Los Angeles' 2nd choice, 94th overall, in 1978 Amateur Draft).

Season	Club	GP	W	L	T	Mins	GA	SO	Avg	GP	W	L	Mins	GA	SO	Avg
1979-80	Los Angeles	10	3	3	3	559	23	0	2.47	1	0	1	40	7	0	10.50
1980-81	Los Angeles	9	2	3	1	454	37	0	4.89							
1981-82	Los Angeles	31	8	10	7	1436	103	0	4.30	2	0	1	32	1	0	1.88
1982-83	Los Angeles	6	0	2	2	304	24	0	4.74							
1983-84	Boston	33	19	8	3	1779	92	2	3.10							
1984-85	Boston	25	16	6	3	1497	82	1	3.29	4	2	2	240	15	0	3.75
1985-86	Boston	30	14	13	3	1757	107	0	3.65							
1986-87	Boston	36	18	8	4	1942	108	0	3.34	2	0	2	120	11	0	5.50
1987-88	Boston	30	16	11	0	1660	90	1	3.25							
	NHL Totals	**210**	**96**	**64**	**26**	**11388**	**666**	**4**	**3.51**	**9**	**2**	**6**	**432**	**34**	**0**	**4.72**

Claimed on waivers by **Boston** from **Los Angeles**, May 24, 1983.

KEENAN, Don

Goaltender. Catches left. 6', 170 lbs. Born, Toronto, Ont., August 8, 1938

Season	Club	GP	W	L	T	Mins	GA	SO	Avg	GP	W	L	Mins	GA	SO	Avg
1958-59	Boston	1	0	1	0	60	4	0	4.00							
	NHL Totals	**1**	**0**	**1**	**0**	**60**	**4**	**0**	**4.00**							

Loaned to **Boston** by **Toronto** (St. Michael's/OHA Jr.) to replace Harry Lumley, March 7, 1959. (Toronto 4, Boston 1).

KERR, Dave

Goaltender. Catches right. 5'10", 160 lbs. Born, Toronto, Ont., January 11, 1910

Season	Club	GP	W	L	T	Mins	GA	SO	Avg	GP	W	L	Mins	GA	SO	Avg
1930-31	Mtl. Maroons	29	13	11	4	1769	70	1	2.37	2	0	2	120	8	0	4.00
1931-32	NY Americans	1	0	1	0	60	6	0	6.00							
1932-33	Mtl. Maroons	25	14	8	3	1520	58	4	2.29	2	0	2	120	5	0	2.50
1933-34	Mtl. Maroons	*48	19	18	11	3060	122	6	2.39	4	1	2	240	7	1	1.75
1934-35	NY Rangers	37	19	12	6	2290	94	4	2.46	4	1	1	240	10	0	2.50
1935-36	NY Rangers	47	18	17	12	2980	95	8	1.91							
1936-37	NY Rangers	*48	19	20	9	3020	106	4	2.11	*9	*6	3	*553	10	*4	*1.08
1937-38	NY Rangers	*48	27	15	6	2960	96	*8	1.95	3	1	2	262	8	0	1.83
1938-39	NY Rangers	*48	26	16	6	2970	105	6	2.12	1	0	1	119	2	0	1.01
1939-40♦	NY Rangers	*48	27	11	10	3000	77	*8	*1.54	*12	*8	4	*770	20	*3	*1.56
1940-41	NY Rangers	*48	21	19	8	3010	125	2	2.49	3	1	2	192	6	0	1.88
	NHL Totals	**427**	**203**	**148**	**75**	**26639**	**954**	**51**	**2.15**	**40**	**18**	**19**	**2616**	**76**	**8**	**1.74**

NHL Second All-Star Team (1938) • NHL First All-Star Team (1940) • Vezina Trophy (1940)

Signed as a free agent by **Mtl. Maroons**, September 2, 1930. Loaned to **NY Americans** by **Mtl. Maroons** to replace injured Roy Worters, March 8, 1932. (Montreal 6, NY Americans 1). Traded to **NY Rangers** by **Mtl. Maroons** for cash, December 14, 1934.

KHABIBULIN, Nikolai

Goaltender. Catches left. 6'1", 203 lbs. Born, Sverdlovsk, USSR, January 13, 1973
(Winnipeg's 8th choice, 204th overall, in 1992 Entry Draft).

Season	Club	GP	W	L	T	Mins	GA	SO	Avg	GP	W	L	Mins	GA	SO	Avg
1994-95	Winnipeg	26	8	9	4	1339	76	0	3.41							
1995-96	Winnipeg	53	26	20	3	2914	152	2	3.13	6	2	4	359	19	0	3.18
1996-97	Phoenix	72	30	33	6	4091	193	7	2.83	7	3	4	426	15	1	2.11
1997-98	Phoenix	70	30	28	10	4026	184	4	2.74	4	2	1	185	13	0	4.22
1998-99	Phoenix	63	32	23	7	3657	130	8	2.13	7	3	4	449	18	0	2.41
2000-01	Tampa Bay	2	1	1	0	123	6	0	2.93							
2001-02	Tampa Bay	70	24	32	10	3896	153	7	2.36							
2002-03	Tampa Bay	65	30	22	11	3787	156	4	2.47	10	5	5	644	26	0	2.42
	NHL Totals	**421**	**181**	**168**	**51**	**23833**	**1050**	**32**	**2.64**	**34**	**15**	**18**	**2063**	**91**	**1**	**2.65**

Played in NHL All-Star Game (1998, 1999, 2002, 2003)

Transferred to **Phoenix** after **Winnipeg** franchise relocated, July 1, 1996. • Missed entire 1999-2000 NHL season and majority of 2000-01 season after failing to come to contract terms with **Phoenix**. Traded to **Tampa Bay** by **Phoenix** with Stan Neckar for Mike Johnson, Paul Mara, Ruslan Zainullin and NY Islanders' 2nd round choice (previously acquired, Phoenix selected Matthew Spiller) in 2001 Entry Draft, March 5, 2001.

KIDD, Trevor

Goaltender. Catches left. 6'2", 210 lbs. Born, Dugald, Man., March 26, 1972
(Calgary's 1st choice, 11th overall, in 1990 Entry Draft).

Season	Club	GP	W	L	T	Mins	GA	SO	Avg	GP	W	L	Mins	GA	SO	Avg
1991-92	Calgary	2	1	1	0	120	8	0	4.00							
1993-94	Calgary	31	13	7	6	1614	85	0	3.16							
1994-95	Calgary	*43	22	14	6	*2463	107	3	2.61	7	3	4	434	26	1	3.59
1995-96	Calgary	47	15	21	8	2570	119	3	2.78	2	0	1	83	9	0	6.51
1996-97	Calgary	55	21	23	6	2979	141	4	2.84							
1997-98	Carolina	47	21	21	3	2685	97	3	2.17							
1998-99	Carolina	25	7	10	6	1358	61	2	2.70							
99-2000	Florida	28	14	11	2	1574	69	1	2.63							
2000-01	Florida	42	10	23	6	2354	130	1	3.31							
2001-02	Florida	33	4	16	5	1683	90	1	3.21							
2002-03	Toronto	19	6	10	2	1143	59	0	3.10							
	NHL Totals	**372**	**134**	**157**	**50**	**20543**	**966**	**18**	**2.82**	**9**	**3**	**5**	**517**	**35**	**1**	**4.06**

Traded to **Carolina** by **Calgary** with Gary Roberts for Andrew Cassels and Jean-Sebastien Giguere, August 25, 1997. Claimed by **Atlanta** from **Carolina** in Expansion Draft, June 25, 1999. Traded to **Florida** by **Atlanta** for Gord Murphy, Herbert Vasiljevs, Daniel Tjarnqvist and Ottawa's 6th round choice (previously acquired, later traded to Dallas – Dallas selected Justin Cox) in 1999 Entry Draft, June 25, 1999. Signed as a free agent by **Toronto**, August 26, 2002.

KING, Scott

Goaltender. Catches left. 6'1", 185 lbs. Born, Thunder Bay, Ont., June 25, 1967
(Detroit's 10th choice, 190th overall, in 1986 Entry Draft).

Season	Club	GP	W	L	T	Mins	GA	SO	Avg	GP	W	L	Mins	GA	SO	Avg
1990-91	Detroit	1	0	0	0	45	2	0	2.67							
1991-92	Detroit	1	0	0	0	16	1	0	3.75							
	NHL Totals	**2**	**0**	**0**	**0**	**61**	**3**	**0**	**2.95**							

KIPRUSOFF, Miikka

Goaltender. Catches left. 6'2", 190 lbs. Born, Turku, Finland, October 26, 1976
(San Jose's 5th choice, 116th overall, in 1995 Entry Draft).

Season	Club	GP	W	L	T	Mins	GA	SO	Avg	GP	W	L	Mins	GA	SO	Avg
2000-01	San Jose	5	2	1	0	154	5	0	1.95	3	1	1	149	5	0	2.01
2001-02	San Jose	20	7	6	3	1037	43	2	2.49	1	0	0	8	0	0	0.00
2002-03	San Jose	22	5	14	0	1199	65	1	3.25							
	NHL Totals	**47**	**14**	**21**	**3**	**2390**	**113**	**3**	**2.84**	**4**	**1**	**1**	**157**	**5**	**0**	**1.91**

KLEISINGER, Terry

Goaltender. Catches right. 6', 190 lbs. Born, Regina, Sask., October 10, 1960

Season	Club	GP	W	L	T	Mins	GA	SO	Avg	GP	W	L	Mins	GA	SO	Avg
1985-86	NY Rangers	4	0	2	0	191	14	0	4.40							
	NHL Totals	**4**	**0**	**2**	**0**	**191**	**14**	**0**	**4.40**							

Signed as a free agent by **NY Rangers**, October 8, 1985.

KLYMKIW, Julian

Goaltender. Catches right. 5'11", 180 lbs. Born, Winnipeg, Man., July 16, 1933

Season	Club	GP	W	L	T	Mins	GA	SO	Avg	GP	W	L	Mins	GA	SO	Avg
1958-59	NY Rangers	1	0	0	0	19	2	0	6.32							
	NHL Totals	**1**	**0**	**0**	**0**	**19**	**2**	**0**	**6.32**							

• **Detroit's** assistant trainer/practice goaltender loaned to **NY Rangers** to replace injured Gump Worsley in 3rd period, October 12, 1958. (Detroit 3, NY Rangers 0).

KNICKLE, Rick

Goaltender. Catches left. 5'10", 175 lbs. Born, Chatham, N.B., February 26, 1960
(Buffalo's 7th choice, 116th overall, in 1979 Entry Draft).

Season	Club	GP	W	L	T	Mins	GA	SO	Avg	GP	W	L	Mins	GA	SO	Avg
1992-93	Los Angeles	10	6	4	0	532	35	0	3.95							
1993-94	Los Angeles	4	1	2	0	174	9	0	3.10							
	NHL Totals	**14**	**7**	**6**	**0**	**706**	**44**	**0**	**3.74**							

Signed as a free agent by **Montreal**, February 8, 1985. Signed as a free agent by **Los Angeles**, February 16, 1993.

KOCHAN, Dieter

Goaltender. Catches left. 6'1", 180 lbs. Born, Saskatoon, Sask., May 11, 1974
(Vancouver's 3rd choice, 98th overall, in 1993 Entry Draft).

Season	Club	GP	W	L	T	Mins	GA	SO	Avg	GP	W	L	Mins	GA	SO	Avg
99-2000	Tampa Bay	5	1	4	0	238	17	0	4.29							
2000-01	Tampa Bay	10	0	3	0	314	18	0	3.44							
2001-02	Tampa Bay	5	0	3	1	237	16	0	4.05							
2002-03	Minnesota	1	0	1	0	60	5	0	5.00							
	NHL Totals	**21**	**1**	**11**	**1**	**849**	**56**	**0**	**3.96**							

Signed as a free agent by **Tampa Bay**, March 27, 2000. Signed as a free agent by **Minnesota**, August 5, 2002.

KOLZIG, Olaf

Goaltender. Catches left. 6'3", 225 lbs. Born, Johannesburg, South Africa, April 9, 1970
(Washington's 1st choice, 19th overall, in 1989 Entry Draft).

Season	Club	GP	W	L	T	Mins	GA	SO	Avg	GP	W	L	Mins	GA	SO	Avg
1989-90	Washington	2	0	2	0	120	12	0	6.00							
1992-93	Washington	1	0	0	0	20	2	0	6.00							
1993-94	Washington	7	0	3	0	224	20	0	5.36							
1994-95	Washington	14	2	8	2	724	30	0	2.49	2	1	0	44	1	0	1.36
1995-96	Washington	18	4	8	2	897	46	0	3.08	5	2	3	341	11	0	*1.94
1996-97	Washington	29	8	15	4	1645	71	2	2.59							
1997-98	Washington	64	33	18	10	3788	139	5	2.20	21	12	9	1351	44	*4	1.95
1998-99	Washington	64	26	31	3	3586	154	4	2.58							
99-2000	Washington	73	41	20	11	*4371	163	5	2.24	5	1	4	284	16	0	3.38
2000-01	Washington	72	37	26	8	4279	177	5	2.48	6	2	4	375	14	1	2.24
2001-02	Washington	71	31	29	8	4131	192	6	2.79							

Season	Club	GP	W	L	T	Mins	GA	SO	Avg	GP	W	L	Mins	GA	SO	Avg
		REGULAR SEASON								PLAYOFFS						
2002-03	Washington	66	33	25	6	3894	156	4	2.40	6	2	4	404	14	1	2.08
	NHL Totals	**481**	**215**	**185**	**54**	**27679**	**1162**	**31**	**2.52**	**45**	**20**	**24**	**2799**	**100**	**6**	**2.14**

NHL First All-Star Team (2000) • Vezina Trophy (2000)
Played in NHL All-Star Game (1998, 2000)

KONSTANTINOV, Evgeny

Goaltender. Catches left. 6', 176 lbs. Born, Kazan, USSR, March 29, 1981
(Tampa Bay's 2nd choice, 67th overall, in 1999 Entry Draft).

Season	Club	GP	W	L	T	Mins	GA	SO	Avg	GP	W	L	Mins	GA	SO	Avg
2000-01	Tampa Bay	1	0	0	0	1	0	0	0.00							
2002-03	Tampa Bay	1	0	0	0	20	1	0	3.00							
	NHL Totals	**2**	**0**	**0**	**0**	**21**	**1**	**0**	**2.86**							

• Played 24 seconds of game vs. Colorado, December 8, 2000.

KUNTAR, Les

Goaltender. Catches left. 6'2", 195 lbs. Born, Elma, NY, July 28, 1969
(Montreal's 8th choice, 122nd overall, in 1987 Entry Draft).

Season	Club	GP	W	L	T	Mins	GA	SO	Avg	GP	W	L	Mins	GA	SO	Avg
1993-94	Montreal	6	2	2	0	302	16	0	3.18							
	NHL Totals	**6**	**2**	**2**	**0**	**302**	**16**	**0**	**3.18**							

Signed as a free agent by **Philadelphia**, June 30, 1995.

KURT, Gary

Goaltender. Catches left. 6'3", 205 lbs. Born, Kitchener, Ont., March 9, 1947

Season	Club	GP	W	L	T	Mins	GA	SO	Avg	GP	W	L	Mins	GA	SO	Avg
1971-72	California	16	1	7	5	838	60	0	4.30							
	NHL Totals	**16**	**1**	**7**	**5**	**838**	**60**	**0**	**4.30**							

Claimed by **Cleveland** (AHL) from **NY Rangers** in Reverse Draft, June 12, 1969. Claimed by **California** from **Cleveland** (AHL) in Inter-League Draft, June 7, 1971.

LABARBERA, Jason

Goaltender. Catches left. 6'2", 205 lbs. Born, Prince George, B.C., January 18, 1980
(NY Rangers' 3rd choice, 66th overall, in 1998 Entry Draft).

Season	Club	GP	W	L	T	Mins	GA	SO	Avg	GP	W	L	Mins	GA	SO	Avg
2000-01	NY Rangers	1	0	0	0	10	0	0	0.00							
	NHL Totals	**1**	**0**	**0**	**0**	**10**	**0**	**0**	**0.00**							

LABBE, Jean-Francois

Goaltender. Catches left. 5'10", 175 lbs. Born, Sherbrooke, Que., June 15, 1972

Season	Club	GP	W	L	T	Mins	GA	SO	Avg	GP	W	L	Mins	GA	SO	Avg
99-2000	NY Rangers	1	0	1	0	60	3	0	3.00							
2001-02	Columbus	3	1	1	0	117	6	0	3.08							
2002-03	Columbus	11	2	4	0	451	27	0	3.59							
	NHL Totals	**15**	**3**	**6**	**0**	**628**	**36**	**0**	**3.44**							

Signed as a free agent by **Ottawa**, May 12, 1994. Traded to **Colorado** by **Ottawa** for future considerations, September 20, 1995. Signed as a free agent by **Edmonton**, September 2, 1997. Signed as a free agent by **NY Rangers**, July 30, 1998. Traded to **Columbus** by **NY Rangers** for Bert Robertsson, November 9, 2000.

LABRECQUE, Patrick

Goaltender. Catches left. 6', 190 lbs. Born, Laval, Que., March 6, 1971
(Quebec's 5th choice, 90th overall, in 1991 Entry Draft).

Season	Club	GP	W	L	T	Mins	GA	SO	Avg	GP	W	L	Mins	GA	SO	Avg
1995-96	Montreal	2	0	1	0	98	7	0	4.29							
	NHL Totals	**2**	**0**	**1**	**0**	**98**	**7**	**0**	**4.29**							

Signed as a free agent by **Montreal**, June 21, 1994.

LACHER, Blaine

Goaltender. Catches left. 6'1", 205 lbs. Born, Medicine Hat, Alta., September 5, 1970

Season	Club	GP	W	L	T	Mins	GA	SO	Avg	GP	W	L	Mins	GA	SO	Avg
1994-95	Boston	35	19	11	2	1965	79	4	2.41	5	1	4	283	12	0	2.54
1995-96	Boston	12	3	5	2	671	44	0	3.93							
	NHL Totals	**47**	**22**	**16**	**4**	**2636**	**123**	**4**	**2.80**	**5**	**1**	**4**	**283**	**12**	**0**	**2.54**

Signed as a free agent by **Boston**, June 2, 1994.

LACROIX, Frenchy

Goaltender. Catches left. 5'7", 136 lbs. Born, Newton, MA, October 21, 1897

Season	Club	GP	W	L	T	Mins	GA	SO	Avg	GP	W	L	Mins	GA	SO	Avg
1925-26	Montreal	5	1	4	0	280	16	0	3.43							
1926-27	Montreal	DID NOT PLAY – SPARE GOALTENDER														
	NHL Totals	**5**	**1**	**4**	**0**	**280**	**16**	**0**	**3.43**							

Signed as a free agent by **Montreal**, November 10, 1925.

LaFERRIERE, Rick

Goaltender. Catches left. 5'8", 165 lbs. Born, Hawkesbury, Ont., January 3, 1961
(Colorado's 3rd choice, 64th overall, in 1980 Entry Draft).

Season	Club	GP	W	L	T	Mins	GA	SO	Avg	GP	W	L	Mins	GA	SO	Avg
1981-82	Colorado	1	0	0	0	20	1	0	3.00							
	NHL Totals	**1**	**0**	**0**	**0**	**20**	**1**	**0**	**3.00**							

• **Colorado's** spare goaltender replaced Glenn Resch at start of 3rd period, February 23, 1982. (Detroit 6, Colorado 3).

LaFOREST, Mark

Goaltender. Catches left. 5'11", 190 lbs. Born, Welland, Ont., July 10, 1962

Season	Club	GP	W	L	T	Mins	GA	SO	Avg	GP	W	L	Mins	GA	SO	Avg
1985-86	Detroit	28	4	21	0	1383	114	1	4.95							
1986-87	Detroit	5	2	1	0	219	12	0	3.29							
1987-88	Philadelphia	21	5	9	2	972	60	1	3.70	2	1	0	48	1	0	1.25
1988-89	Philadelphia	17	5	7	2	933	64	0	4.12							
1989-90	Toronto	27	9	14	0	1343	87	0	3.89							
1993-94	Ottawa	5	0	2	0	182	17	0	5.60							
	NHL Totals	**103**	**25**	**54**	**4**	**5032**	**354**	**2**	**4.22**	**2**	**1**	**0**	**48**	**1**	**0**	**1.25**

• Brother of Bob

Signed as a free agent by **Detroit**, April 29, 1983. Traded to **Philadelphia** by **Detroit** for Philadelphia's 2nd round choice (Bob Wilkie) in 1987 Entry Draft, June 13, 1987. Traded to **Toronto** by **Philadelphia** for Toronto's 5th round choice (later traded to Winnipeg – Winnipeg selected Juha Ylonen) in 1991 Entry Draft and Philadelphia's 7th round choice (previously acquired, Philadelphia selected Andrei Lomakin) in 1991 Entry Draft, September 8, 1989. Traded to **NY Rangers** by **Toronto** with Tie Domi for Greg Johnston, June 28, 1990. Claimed by **Ottawa** from **NY Rangers** in Expansion Draft, June 18, 1992.

LAJEUNESSE, Simon

Goaltender. Catches left. 6', 175 lbs. Born, Quebec City, Que., January 22, 1981
(Ottawa's 2nd choice, 48th overall, in 1999 Entry Draft).

Season	Club	GP	W	L	T	Mins	GA	SO	Avg	GP	W	L	Mins	GA	SO	Avg
2001-02	Ottawa	1	0	0	0	24	0	0	0.00							
	NHL Totals	**1**	**0**	**0**	**0**	**24**	**0**	**0**	**0.00**							

Traded to **Florida** by **Ottawa** for Joey Tetarenko, March 4, 2003.

LALIME, Patrick

Goaltender. Catches left. 6'3", 185 lbs. Born, St-Bonaventure, Que., July 7, 1974
(Pittsburgh's 6th choice, 156th overall, in 1993 Entry Draft).

Season	Club	GP	W	L	T	Mins	GA	SO	Avg	GP	W	L	Mins	GA	SO	Avg
1996-97	Pittsburgh	39	21	12	2	2058	101	3	2.94							
99-2000	Ottawa	38	19	14	3	2038	79	3	2.33							
2000-01	Ottawa	60	36	19	5	3607	141	7	2.35	4	0	4	251	10	0	2.39
2001-02	Ottawa	61	27	24	8	3583	148	7	2.48	12	7	5	778	18	4	*1.39
2002-03	Ottawa	67	39	20	7	3943	142	8	2.16	18	11	7	1122	34	1	1.82
	NHL Totals	**265**	**142**	**89**	**25**	**15229**	**611**	**28**	**2.41**	**34**	**18**	**16**	**2151**	**62**	**5**	**1.73**

NHL All-Rookie Team (1997)
Played in NHL All-Star Game (2003)

Rights traded to **Anaheim** by **Pittsburgh** for Sean Pronger, March 24, 1998. Traded to **Ottawa** by **Anaheim** for Ted Donato and the rights to Antti-Jussi Niemi, June 18, 1999.

LAMOTHE, Marc

Goaltender. Catches left. 6'2", 210 lbs. Born, New Liskeard, Ont., February 27, 1974
(Montreal's 6th choice, 92nd overall, in 1992 Entry Draft).

Season	Club	GP	W	L	T	Mins	GA	SO	Avg	GP	W	L	Mins	GA	SO	Avg
99-2000	Chicago	2	1	1	0	116	10	0	5.17							
	NHL Totals	**2**	**1**	**1**	**0**	**116**	**10**	**0**	**5.17**							

Signed as a free agent by **Chicago**, September 26, 1996. Signed as a free agent by **Edmonton**, August 16, 2001. Signed as a free agent by **Detroit**, August 5, 2002.

LANGKOW, Scott

Goaltender. Catches left. 5'11", 190 lbs. Born, Sherwood Park, Alta., April 21, 1975
(Winnipeg's 2nd choice, 31st overall, in 1993 Entry Draft).

Season	Club	GP	W	L	T	Mins	GA	SO	Avg	GP	W	L	Mins	GA	SO	Avg
1995-96	Winnipeg	1	0	0	0	6	0	0	0.00							
1997-98	Phoenix	3	0	1	1	137	10	0	4.38							
1998-99	Phoenix	1	0	0	0	35	3	0	5.14							
99-2000	Atlanta	15	3	11	0	765	55	0	4.31							
	NHL Totals	**20**	**3**	**12**	**1**	**943**	**68**	**0**	**4.33**							

• Brother of Daymond

Transferred to **Phoenix** after **Winnipeg** franchise relocated, July 1, 1996. Traded to **Atlanta** by **Phoenix** for future considerations, June 25, 1999. Traded to **Anaheim** by **Atlanta** with Sergei Vyshedkevich for Ladislav Kohn, February 9, 2001.

LAROCQUE, Michel

Goaltender. Catches left. 5'11", 200 lbs. Born, Lahr, West Germany, October 3, 1976
(San Jose's 5th choice, 137th overall, in 1996 Entry Draft).

Season	Club	GP	W	L	T	Mins	GA	SO	Avg	GP	W	L	Mins	GA	SO	Avg
2000-01	Chicago	3	0	2	0	152	9	0	3.55							
	NHL Totals	**3**	**0**	**2**	**0**	**152**	**9**	**0**	**3.55**							

Traded to **Chicago** by **San Jose** for Chicago's 5th round choice (Michael Pinc) in 2000 Entry Draft, August 23, 1999.

LAROCQUE, Michel

Goaltender. Catches left. 5'10", 200 lbs. Born, Hull, Que., April 6, 1952
(Montreal's 2nd choice, 6th overall, in 1972 Amateur Draft).

Season	Club	GP	W	L	T	Mins	GA	SO	Avg	GP	W	L	Mins	GA	SO	Avg
1973-74	Montreal	27	15	8	2	1431	69	0	2.89	6	2	4	364	18	0	2.97
1974-75	Montreal	25	17	5	3	1480	74	3	3.00							
1975-76♦	Montreal	22	16	1	3	1220	50	2	2.46							
1976-77♦	Montreal	26	19	2	4	1525	53	4	*2.09							
1977-78♦	Montreal	30	22	3	4	1729	77	1	2.67							
1978-79♦	Montreal	34	22	7	4	1986	94	3	2.84	1	0	0	20	0	0	0.00
1979-80	Montreal	39	17	13	8	2259	125	3	3.32	5	4	1	300	11	1	2.20
1980-81	Montreal	28	16	9	3	1623	82	1	3.03							
	Toronto	8	3	3	2	460	40	0	5.22	2	0	1	75	8	0	6.40
1981-82	Toronto	50	10	24	8	2647	207	0	4.69							
1982-83	Toronto	16	3	8	3	835	68	0	4.89							
	Philadelphia	2	0	1	1	120	8	0	4.00							
1983-84	St. Louis	5	0	5	0	300	31	0	6.20							
	NHL Totals	**312**	**160**	**89**	**45**	**17615**	**978**	**17**	**3.33**	**14**	**6**	**6**	**759**	**37**	**1**	**2.92**

Shared Vezina Trophy with Ken Dryden (1977, 1978, 1979) • Shared Vezina Trophy with Denis Herron and Richard Sevigny (1981)

Traded to **Toronto** by **Montreal** for Robert Picard, March 10, 1981. Traded to **Philadelphia** by **Toronto** for Rick St. Croix, January 11, 1983. Traded to **St. Louis** by **Philadelphia** for cash, January 5, 1984.

LASAK, Jan

Goaltender. Catches left. 6'1", 204 lbs. Born, Zvolen, Czech., April 10, 1979
(Nashville's 6th choice, 65th overall, in 1999 Entry Draft).

		REGULAR SEASON								PLAYOFFS						
Season	Club	GP	W	L	T	Mins	GA	SO	Avg	GP	W	L	Mins	GA	SO	Avg
2001-02	Nashville	3	0	3	0	177	13	0	4.41	....	....	....	....	....	....	....
2002-03	Nashville	3	0	1	0	90	5	0	3.33	....	....	....	....	....	....	....
	NHL Totals	**6**	**0**	**4**	**0**	**267**	**18**	**0**	**4.04**	....	....	....	....	....	....	....

LASKOWSKI, Gary

Goaltender. Catches left. 6'1", 175 lbs. Born, Ottawa, Ont., June 6, 1959

		REGULAR SEASON								PLAYOFFS						
Season	Club	GP	W	L	T	Mins	GA	SO	Avg	GP	W	L	Mins	GA	SO	Avg
1982-83	Los Angeles	46	15	20	4	2277	173	0	4.56	....	....	....	....	....	....	....
1983-84	Los Angeles	13	4	7	1	665	55	0	4.96	....	....	....	....	....	....	....
	NHL Totals	**59**	**19**	**27**	**5**	**2942**	**228**	**0**	**4.65**	....	....	....	....	....	....	....

Signed as a free agent by **Los Angeles**, October 22, 1982.

LAXTON, Gord

Goaltender. Catches left. 5'10", 195 lbs. Born, Montreal, Que., March 16, 1955
(Pittsburgh's 1st choice, 13th overall, in 1975 Amateur Draft).

		REGULAR SEASON								PLAYOFFS						
Season	Club	GP	W	L	T	Mins	GA	SO	Avg	GP	W	L	Mins	GA	SO	Avg
1975-76	Pittsburgh	8	3	4	0	414	31	0	4.49	....	....	....	....	....	....	....
1976-77	Pittsburgh	6	1	3	0	253	26	0	6.17	....	....	....	....	....	....	....
1977-78	Pittsburgh	2	0	1	0	73	9	0	7.40	....	....	....	....	....	....	....
1978-79	Pittsburgh	1	0	1	0	60	8	0	8.00	....	....	....	....	....	....	....
	NHL Totals	**17**	**4**	**9**	**0**	**800**	**74**	**0**	**5.55**	....	....	....	....	....	....	....

LeBLANC, Ray

Goaltender. Catches left. 5'10", 170 lbs. Born, Fitchburg, MA, October 24, 1964

		REGULAR SEASON								PLAYOFFS						
Season	Club	GP	W	L	T	Mins	GA	SO	Avg	GP	W	L	Mins	GA	SO	Avg
1991-92	Chicago	1	1	0	0	60	1	0	1.00	....	....	....	....	....	....	....
	NHL Totals	**1**	**1**	**0**	**0**	**60**	**1**	**0**	**1.00**	....	....	....	....	....	....	....

Signed as a free agent by **Chicago**, July 5, 1989.

LEGACE, Manny

Goaltender. Catches left. 5'9", 162 lbs. Born, Toronto, Ont., February 4, 1973
(Hartford's 5th choice, 188th overall, in 1993 Entry Draft).

		REGULAR SEASON								PLAYOFFS						
Season	Club	GP	W	L	T	Mins	GA	SO	Avg	GP	W	L	Mins	GA	SO	Avg
1998-99	Los Angeles	17	2	9	2	899	39	0	2.60	....	....	....	....	....	....	....
99-2000	Detroit	4	4	0	0	240	11	0	2.75	....	....	....	....	....	....	....
2000-01	Detroit	39	24	5	5	2136	73	2	2.05	....	....	....	....	....	....	....
2001-02 ♦	Detroit	20	10	6	2	1117	45	1	2.42	1	0	0	11	1	0	5.45
2002-03	Detroit	25	14	5	4	1406	51	0	2.18	....	....	....	....	....	....	....
	NHL Totals	**105**	**54**	**25**	**13**	**5798**	**219**	**3**	**2.27**	**1**	**0**	**0**	**11**	**1**	**0**	**5.45**

Rights transferred to **Carolina** after **Hartford** franchise relocated, June 25, 1997. Traded to **Los Angeles** by **Carolina** for future considerations, July 31, 1998. Signed as a free agent by **Detroit**, August 9, 1999. Claimed on waivers by **Vancouver** from **Detroit**, September 30, 1999. Claimed on waivers by **Detroit** from **Vancouver**, October 13, 1999.

LEGRIS, Claude

Goaltender. Catches left. 5'9", 160 lbs. Born, Verdun, Que., November 6, 1956
(Detroit's 8th choice, 120th overall, in 1976 Amateur Draft).

		REGULAR SEASON								PLAYOFFS						
Season	Club	GP	W	L	T	Mins	GA	SO	Avg	GP	W	L	Mins	GA	SO	Avg
1980-81	Detroit	3	0	1	0	63	4	0	3.81	....	....	....	....	....	....	....
1981-82	Detroit	1	0	0	1	28	0	0	0.00	....	....	....	....	....	....	....
	NHL Totals	**4**	**0**	**1**	**1**	**91**	**4**	**0**	**2.64**	....	....	....	....	....	....	....

LEHMAN, Hugh

HHOF

Goaltender. Catches left. 5'8", 168 lbs. Born, Pembroke, Ont., October 27, 1885

		REGULAR SEASON								PLAYOFFS						
Season	Club	GP	W	L	T	Mins	GA	SO	Avg	GP	W	L	Mins	GA	SO	Avg
1926-27	Chicago	*44	19	22	3	*2797	116	5	2.49	2	0	1	120	10	0	5.00
1927-28	Chicago	4	1	2	1	250	20	1	4.80	....	....	....	....	....	....	....
	NHL Totals	**48**	**20**	**24**	**4**	**3047**	**136**	**6**	**2.68**	**2**	**0**	**1**	**120**	**10**	**0**	**5.00**

Traded to **Chicago** by **Vancouver** (WHL) for cash, October 9, 1926.

LEIGHTON, Michael

Goaltender. Catches left. 6'2", 175 lbs. Born, Petrolia, Ont., May 19, 1981
(Chicago's 5th choice, 165th overall, in 1999 Entry Draft).

		REGULAR SEASON								PLAYOFFS						
Season	Club	GP	W	L	T	Mins	GA	SO	Avg	GP	W	L	Mins	GA	SO	Avg
2002-03	Chicago	8	2	3	2	447	21	1	2.82	....	....	....	....	....	....	....
	NHL Totals	**8**	**2**	**3**	**2**	**447**	**21**	**1**	**2.82**	....	....	....	....	....	....	....

LEMELIN, Reggie

Goaltender. Catches left. 5'11", 170 lbs. Born, Quebec City, Que., November 19, 1954
(Philadelphia's 6th choice, 125th overall, in 1974 Amateur Draft).

		REGULAR SEASON								PLAYOFFS						
Season	Club	GP	W	L	T	Mins	GA	SO	Avg	GP	W	L	Mins	GA	SO	Avg
1978-79	Atlanta	18	8	8	1	994	55	0	3.32	1	0	0	20	0	0	0.00
1979-80	Atlanta	3	0	2	0	150	15	0	6.00	....	....	....	....	....	....	....
1980-81	Calgary	29	14	6	7	1629	88	2	3.24	6	3	3	366	22	0	3.61
1981-82	Calgary	34	10	15	6	1866	135	0	4.34	....	....	....	....	....	....	....
1982-83	Calgary	39	16	12	8	2211	133	0	3.61	7	3	3	327	27	0	4.95
1983-84	Calgary	51	21	12	9	2568	150	0	3.50	8	4	4	448	32	0	4.29
1984-85	Calgary	56	30	12	10	3176	183	1	3.46	4	1	3	248	15	1	3.63
1985-86	Calgary	60	29	24	4	3369	229	1	4.08	3	0	1	109	7	0	3.85
1986-87	Calgary	34	16	9	1	1735	94	2	3.25	2	0	1	101	6	0	3.56
1987-88	Boston	49	24	17	6	2828	138	3	2.93	17	11	6	1027	45	*1	*2.63
1988-89	Boston	40	19	15	6	2392	120	0	3.01	4	1	3	252	16	0	3.81
1989-90	Boston	43	22	15	2	2310	108	2	2.81	3	0	1	135	13	0	5.78
1990-91	Boston	33	17	10	3	1829	111	1	3.64	2	0	0	32	0	0	0.00
1991-92	Boston	8	5	1	0	407	23	0	3.39	2	0	0	54	3	0	3.33
1992-93	Boston	10	5	4	0	542	31	0	3.43	....	....	....	....	....	....	....
	NHL Totals	**507**	**236**	**162**	**63**	**28006**	**1613**	**12**	**3.46**	**59**	**23**	**25**	**3119**	**186**	**2**	**3.58**

Played in NHL All-Star Game (1989)

Signed as a free agent by **Atlanta**, August 17, 1978. Transferred to **Calgary** after **Atlanta** franchise relocated, June 24, 1980. Signed as a free agent by **Boston**, August 13, 1987.

LENARDUZZI, Mike

Goaltender. Catches left. 6'1", 165 lbs. Born, London, Ont., September 14, 1972
(Hartford's 3rd choice, 57th overall, in 1990 Entry Draft).

		REGULAR SEASON								PLAYOFFS						
Season	Club	GP	W	L	T	Mins	GA	SO	Avg	GP	W	L	Mins	GA	SO	Avg
1992-93	Hartford	3	1	1	1	168	9	0	3.21	....	....	....	....	....	....	....
1993-94	Hartford	1	0	0	0	21	1	0	2.86	....	....	....	....	....	....	....
	NHL Totals	**4**	**1**	**1**	**1**	**189**	**10**	**0**	**3.17**	....	....	....	....	....	....	....

LESSARD, Mario

Goaltender. Catches left. 5'9", 190 lbs. Born, East Broughton, Que., June 25, 1954
(Los Angeles' 7th choice, 154th overall, in 1974 Amateur Draft).

		REGULAR SEASON								PLAYOFFS						
Season	Club	GP	W	L	T	Mins	GA	SO	Avg	GP	W	L	Mins	GA	SO	Avg
1978-79	Los Angeles	49	23	15	10	2860	148	4	3.10	2	0	2	126	8	0	3.81
1979-80	Los Angeles	50	18	22	7	2836	185	0	3.91	4	1	2	207	14	0	4.06
1980-81	Los Angeles	64	*35	18	11	3746	203	2	3.25	4	1	3	220	20	0	5.45
1981-82	Los Angeles	52	13	28	8	2933	213	2	4.36	10	4	5	583	41	0	4.22
1982-83	Los Angeles	19	3	10	2	888	68	1	4.59	....	....	....	....	....	....	....
1983-84	Los Angeles	6	0	4	1	266	26	0	5.86	....	....	....	....	....	....	....
	NHL Totals	**240**	**92**	**97**	**39**	**13529**	**843**	**9**	**3.74**	**20**	**6**	**12**	**1136**	**83**	**0**	**4.38**

NHL Second All-Star Team (1981)

Played in NHL All-Star Game (1981)

• Recorded shutout (6-0) in NHL debut vs. Buffalo, October 26, 1978.

LEVASSEUR, Jean-Louis

Goaltender. Catches left. 5'10", 160 lbs. Born, Noranda, Que., June 16, 1949

		REGULAR SEASON								PLAYOFFS						
Season	Club	GP	W	L	T	Mins	GA	SO	Avg	GP	W	L	Mins	GA	SO	Avg
1979-80	Minnesota	1	0	1	0	60	7	0	7.00	....	....	....	....	....	....	....
	NHL Totals	**1**	**0**	**1**	**0**	**60**	**7**	**0**	**7.00**	....	....	....	....	....	....	....

Signed as a free agent by **Minnesota**, October 2, 1979.

LINDBERGH, Pelle

Goaltender. Catches left. 5'9", 165 lbs. Born, Stockholm, Sweden, May 24, 1959
(Philadelphia's 3rd choice, 35th overall, in 1979 Entry Draft).

		REGULAR SEASON								PLAYOFFS						
Season	Club	GP	W	L	T	Mins	GA	SO	Avg	GP	W	L	Mins	GA	SO	Avg
1981-82	Philadelphia	8	2	4	2	480	35	0	4.38	....	....	....	....	....	....	....
1982-83	Philadelphia	40	23	13	3	2333	116	3	2.98	3	0	3	180	18	0	6.00
1983-84	Philadelphia	36	16	13	3	1999	135	1	4.05	2	0	1	26	3	0	6.92
1984-85	Philadelphia	*65	*40	17	7	*3858	194	2	3.02	*18	12	6	1008	42	*3	*2.50
1985-86	Philadelphia	8	6	2	0	480	23	1	2.88	....	....	....	....	....	....	....
	NHL Totals	**157**	**87**	**49**	**15**	**9150**	**503**	**7**	**3.30**	**23**	**12**	**10**	**1214**	**63**	**3**	**3.11**

NHL First All-Star Team (1985) • Vezina Trophy (1985)

Played in NHL All-Star Game (1983, 1985)

Died of injuries suffered in automobile accident, November 10, 1985.

LINDSAY, Bert

Goaltender. Catches right. 5'7", 160 lbs. Born, Garafraxa County, Ont., July 23, 1881

		REGULAR SEASON								PLAYOFFS						
Season	Club	GP	W	L	T	Mins	GA	SO	Avg	GP	W	L	Mins	GA	SO	Avg
1917-18	Mtl. Wanderers	4	1	3	0	240	35	0	8.75	....	....	....	....	....	....	....
1918-19	Toronto	16	5	11	0	998	83	0	4.99	....	....	....	....	....	....	....
	NHL Totals	**20**	**6**	**14**	**0**	**1238**	**118**	**0**	**5.72**	....	....	....	....	....	....	....

• Father of Ted

Signed as a free agent by **Toronto**, December 28, 1918.

LITTLE, Neil

Goaltender. Catches left. 6'1", 193 lbs. Born, Medicine Hat, Alta., December 18, 1971
(Philadelphia's 10th choice, 226th overall, in 1991 Entry Draft).

		REGULAR SEASON								PLAYOFFS						
Season	Club	GP	W	L	T	Mins	GA	SO	Avg	GP	W	L	Mins	GA	SO	Avg
2001-02	Philadelphia	1	0	1	0	60	4	0	4.00	....	....	....	....	....	....	....
	NHL Totals	**1**	**0**	**1**	**0**	**60**	**4**	**0**	**4.00**	....	....	....	....	....	....	....

LITTMAN, David

Goaltender. Catches left. 6', 183 lbs. Born, Cranston, RI, June 13, 1967
(Buffalo's 12th choice, 211th overall, in 1987 Entry Draft).

		REGULAR SEASON								PLAYOFFS						
Season	Club	GP	W	L	T	Mins	GA	SO	Avg	GP	W	L	Mins	GA	SO	Avg
1990-91	Buffalo	1	0	0	0	36	3	0	5.00	....	....	....	....	....	....	....
1991-92	Buffalo	1	0	1	0	60	4	0	4.00	....	....	....	....	....	....	....
1992-93	Tampa Bay	1	0	1	0	45	7	0	9.33	....	....	....	....	....	....	....
	NHL Totals	**3**	**0**	**2**	**0**	**141**	**14**	**0**	**5.96**	....	....	....	....	....	....	....

Signed as a free agent by **Tampa Bay**, August 27, 1992. Signed as a free agent by **Boston**, August 6, 1993.

LIUT, Mike

Goaltender. Catches left. 6'2", 195 lbs. Born, Weston, Ont., January 7, 1956
(St. Louis' 5th choice, 56th overall, in 1976 Amateur Draft).

		REGULAR SEASON								PLAYOFFS						
Season	Club	GP	W	L	T	Mins	GA	SO	Avg	GP	W	L	Mins	GA	SO	Avg
1979-80	St. Louis	64	*32	23	9	3661	194	2	3.18	3	0	3	193	12	0	3.73
1980-81	St. Louis	61	33	14	13	3570	199	1	3.34	11	5	6	685	50	0	4.38
1981-82	St. Louis	*64	28	28	7	*3691	250	2	4.06	10	5	3	494	27	0	3.28
1982-83	St. Louis	*68	21	27	13	*3794	235	1	3.72	4	1	3	240	15	0	3.75
1983-84	St. Louis	58	25	29	4	3425	197	3	3.45	11	6	5	714	29	1	2.44
1984-85	St. Louis	32	12	12	6	1869	119	1	3.82	....	....	....	....	....	....	....
	Hartford	13	5	7	1	791	38	1	2.88	....	....	....	....	....	....	....
1985-86	Hartford	57	27	23	4	3282	198	2	3.62	8	5	2	441	14	*1	*1.90
1986-87	Hartford	59	31	22	5	3476	187	*4	3.23	6	2	4	332	25	0	4.52
1987-88	Hartford	60	25	28	5	3532	187	2	3.18	3	1	1	160	11	0	4.13

		REGULAR SEASON								PLAYOFFS						
Season	Club	GP	W	L	T	Mins	GA	SO	Avg	GP	W	L	Mins	GA	SO	Avg
1988-89	Hartford	35	13	19	1	2006	142	1	4.25							
1989-90	Hartford	29	15	12	1	1683	74	*3	*2.64							
	Washington	8	4	4	0	478	17	*1	*2.13	9	4	4	507	28	0	3.31
1990-91	Washington	35	13	16	3	1834	114	0	3.73	2	0	1	48	4	0	5.00
1991-92	Washington	21	10	7	2	1123	70	1	3.74							
	NHL Totals	**664**	**294**	**271**	**74**	**38215**	**2221**	**25**	**3.49**	**67**	**29**	**32**	**3814**	**215**	**2**	**3.38**

NHL First All-Star Team (1981) • Lester B. Pearson Award (1981) • NHL Second All-Star Team (1987)

Played in NHL All-Star Game (1981)

Reclaimed by **St. Louis** from **Cincinnati** (WHA) prior to Expansion Draft, June 9, 1979. Traded to **Hartford** by **St. Louis** with Jorgen Pettersson for Mark Johnson and Greg Millen, February 21, 1985. Traded to **Washington** by **Hartford** for Yvon Corriveau, March 6, 1990.

LOCKETT, Ken

Goaltender. Catches left. 6', 160 lbs. Born, Toronto, Ont., August 30, 1947

Season	Club	GP	W	L	T	Mins	GA	SO	Avg	GP	W	L	Mins	GA	SO	Avg
1974-75	Vancouver	25	6	7	1	912	48	2	3.16	1	0	1	60	6	0	6.00
1975-76	Vancouver	30	7	8	7	1436	83	0	3.47							
	NHL Totals	**55**	**13**	**15**	**8**	**2348**	**131**	**2**	**3.35**	**1**	**0**	**1**	**60**	**6**	**0**	**6.00**

Traded to **Vancouver** by **Baltimore** (AHL), August, 1974.

LOCKHART, Howard

Goaltender. Catches left. 5'8", 180 lbs. Born, North Bay, Ont., 1895

Season	Club	GP	W	L	T	Mins	GA	SO	Avg	GP	W	L	Mins	GA	SO	Avg
1919-20	Toronto	7	4	2	0	310	25	0	4.84							
	Quebec	1	0	1	0	60	11	0	11.00							
1920-21	Hamilton	*24	6	18	0	1454	132	1	5.45							
1921-22	Hamilton	*24	6	17	0	1409	103	0	4.39							
1923-24	Toronto	1	0	1	0	60	5	0	5.00							
1924-25	Boston	2	0	2	0	120	11	0	5.50							
	NHL Totals	**59**	**16**	**41**	**0**	**3413**	**287**	**1**	**5.05**							

Signed as a free agent by **Toronto**, December 15, 1919. Loaned to **Quebec** by **Toronto**, March 6, 1920. (Toronto 11, Quebec 2). Traded to **Hamilton** by **Toronto** for cash, December 16, 1920. Signed as a free agent by **Toronto**, December 18, 1923. Traded to **Boston** by **Toronto** for cash, December 24, 1924.

LoPRESTI, Pete

Goaltender. Catches left. 6'1", 195 lbs. Born, Virginia, MN, May 23, 1954
(Minnesota's 3rd choice, 42nd overall, in 1974 Amateur Draft).

Season	Club	GP	W	L	T	Mins	GA	SO	Avg	GP	W	L	Mins	GA	SO	Avg
1974-75	Minnesota	35	9	20	3	1964	137	1	4.19							
1975-76	Minnesota	34	7	22	1	1789	123	1	4.13							
1976-77	Minnesota	44	13	20	10	2590	156	1	3.61	2	0	2	77	6	0	4.68
1977-78	Minnesota	53	12	35	6	3065	216	2	4.23							
1978-79	Minnesota	7	2	4	0	345	28	0	4.87							
1980-81	Edmonton	2	0	1	0	105	8	0	4.57							
	NHL Totals	**175**	**43**	**102**	**20**	**9858**	**668**	**5**	**4.07**	**2**	**0**	**2**	**77**	**6**	**0**	**4.68**

• Son of Sam

Claimed by **Edmonton** from **Minnesota** in Expansion Draft, June 13, 1979.

LoPRESTI, Sam

USHOF

Goaltender. Catches left. 5'11", 200 lbs. Born, Eveleth, MN, January 30, 1917

Season	Club	GP	W	L	T	Mins	GA	SO	Avg	GP	W	L	Mins	GA	SO	Avg
1940-41	Chicago	27	9	15	3	1670	84	1	3.02	5	2	3	343	12	0	2.10
1941-42	Chicago	47	21	23	3	2860	152	3	3.19	3	1	2	187	5	*1	1.60
	NHL Totals	**74**	**30**	**38**	**6**	**4530**	**236**	**4**	**3.13**	**8**	**3**	**5**	**530**	**17**	**1**	**1.92**

• Father of Pete

LORENZ, Danny

Goaltender. Catches left. 5'10", 187 lbs. Born, Murrayville, B.C., December 12, 1969
(NY Islanders' 4th choice, 58th overall, in 1988 Entry Draft).

Season	Club	GP	W	L	T	Mins	GA	SO	Avg	GP	W	L	Mins	GA	SO	Avg
1990-91	NY Islanders	2	0	1	0	80	5	0	3.75							
1991-92	NY Islanders	2	0	2	0	120	10	0	5.00							
1992-93	NY Islanders	4	1	2	0	157	10	0	3.82							
	NHL Totals	**8**	**1**	**5**	**0**	**357**	**25**	**0**	**4.20**							

Signed as a free agent by **Florida**, June 14, 1994.

LOUSTEL, Ron

Goaltender. Catches left. 5'11", 185 lbs. Born, Winnipeg, Man., March 7, 1962
(Winnipeg's 6th choice, 107th overall, in 1980 Entry Draft).

Season	Club	GP	W	L	T	Mins	GA	SO	Avg	GP	W	L	Mins	GA	SO	Avg
1980-81	Winnipeg	1	0	1	0	60	10	0	10.00							
	NHL Totals	**1**	**0**	**1**	**0**	**60**	**10**	**0**	**10.00**							

LOW, Ron

Goaltender. Catches left. 6'1", 205 lbs. Born, Birtle, Man., June 21, 1950
(Toronto's 8th choice, 103rd overall, in 1970 Amateur Draft).

Season	Club	GP	W	L	T	Mins	GA	SO	Avg	GP	W	L	Mins	GA	SO	Avg
1972-73	Toronto	42	12	24	4	2343	152	1	3.89							
1974-75	Washington	48	8	36	2	2588	235	1	5.45							
1975-76	Washington	43	6	31	2	2289	208	0	5.45							
1976-77	Washington	54	16	27	5	2918	188	0	3.87							
1977-78	Detroit	32	9	12	9	1816	102	1	3.37	4	1	3	240	17	0	4.25
1979-80	Quebec	15	5	7	2	828	51	0	3.70							
	Edmonton	11	8	2	1	650	37	0	3.42	3	0	3	212	12	0	3.40
1980-81	Edmonton	24	5	13	3	1260	93	0	4.43							
1981-82	Edmonton	29	17	7	1	1554	100	0	3.86							
1982-83	Edmonton	3	0	1	0	104	10	0	5.77							
	New Jersey	11	2	7	1	608	41	0	4.05							
1983-84	New Jersey	44	8	25	4	2218	161	0	4.36							
1984-85	New Jersey	26	6	11	4	1326	85	1	3.85							
	NHL Totals	**382**	**102**	**203**	**38**	**20502**	**1463**	**4**	**4.28**	**7**	**1**	**6**	**452**	**29**	**0**	**3.85**

Claimed by **Washington** from **Toronto** in Expansion Draft, June 12, 1974. Rights traded to **Detroit** by **Washington** with Washington's 3rd round choice (Boris Fistric) in 1979 Amateur Draft for Walt McKechnie, Detroit's 3rd round choice (Jay Johnston) in 1978 Amateur Draft and Detroit's 2nd round choice (Errol Rausse) in 1979 Amateur Draft, August 17, 1977. Claimed by **Quebec** from **Detroit** in Expansion Draft, June 13, 1979. Traded to **Edmonton** by **Quebec** for Ron Chipperfield, March 11, 1980. Traded to **New Jersey** by **Edmonton** with Jim McTaggart for Lindsay Middlebrook and Paul Miller, February 19, 1983.

LOZINSKI, Larry

Goaltender. Catches right. 5'11", 175 lbs. Born, Hudson Bay, Sask., March 11, 1958
(Detroit's 16th choice, 219th overall, in 1978 Amateur Draft).

Season	Club	GP	W	L	T	Mins	GA	SO	Avg	GP	W	L	Mins	GA	SO	Avg
1980-81	Detroit	30	6	11	7	1459	105	0	4.32							
	NHL Totals	**30**	**6**	**11**	**7**	**1459**	**105**	**0**	**4.32**							

LUMLEY, Harry

HHOF

Goaltender. Catches left. 6', 195 lbs. Born, Owen Sound, Ont., November 11, 1926

Season	Club	GP	W	L	T	Mins	GA	SO	Avg	GP	W	L	Mins	GA	SO	Avg
1943-44	Detroit	2	0	2	0	120	13	0	6.50							
	NY Rangers	1	0	0	0	20	0	0	0.00							
1944-45	Detroit	37	24	10	3	2220	119	1	3.22	*14	7	7	*871	31	2	*2.14
1945-46	Detroit	*50	20	20	10	*3000	159	2	3.18	5	1	4	310	16	*1	3.10
1946-47	Detroit	52	22	20	10	3120	159	3	3.06							
1947-48	Detroit	*60	30	18	12	3592	147	*7	2.46	*10	4	6	*600	30	0	3.00
1948-49	Detroit	*60	*34	19	7	*3600	145	6	2.42	*11	4	7	*726	26	0	2.15
1949-50♦	Detroit	63	*33	16	14	3780	148	7	2.35	*14	*8	6	910	28	*3	1.85
1950-51	Chicago	64	12	41	10	3785	246	3	3.90							
1951-52	Chicago	*70	17	44	9	4180	241	2	3.46							
1952-53	Toronto	*70	27	30	13	*4200	167	*10	2.39							
1953-54	Toronto	69	32	24	13	4140	128	*13	*1.86	5	1	4	321	15	0	2.80
1954-55	Toronto	*69	23	24	22	*4140	134	8	*1.94	4	0	4	240	14	0	3.50
1955-56	Toronto	59	21	28	10	3527	157	3	2.67	5	1	4	304	13	1	2.57
1957-58	Boston	24	11	10	3	1440	70	3	2.92	1	0	1	60	5	0	5.00
1958-59	Boston	11	8	2	1	660	27	1	2.45	7	3	4	436	20	0	2.75
1959-60	Boston	42	16	21	5	2520	146	2	3.48							
	NHL Totals	**803**	**330**	**329**	**142**	**48044**	**2206**	**71**	**2.75**	**76**	**29**	**47**	**4778**	**198**	**7**	**2.49**

NHL First All-Star Team (1954, 1955) • Vezina Trophy (1954)

Played in NHL All-Star Game (1951, 1954, 1955)

Loaned to **NY Rangers** by **Detroit** to replace injured Ken McAuley, December 23, 1943. (Detroit 5, NY Rangers 3). Traded to **Chicago** by **Detroit** with Jack Stewart, Al Dewsbury, Pete Babando and Don Morrison for Metro Prystai, Gaye Stewart, Bob Goldham and Jim Henry, July 13, 1950. Traded to **Toronto** by **Chicago** for Al Rollins, Gus Mortson, Cal Gardner and Ray Hannigan, September 11, 1952. Traded to **Chicago** by **Toronto** with Eric Nesterenko for $40,000, May 21, 1956. Traded to **Boston** by **Chicago** for cash, January, 1958.

LUONGO, Roberto

Goaltender. Catches left. 6'3", 205 lbs. Born, Montreal, Que., April 4, 1979
(NY Islanders' 1st choice, 4th overall, in 1997 Entry Draft).

Season	Club	GP	W	L	T	Mins	GA	SO	Avg	GP	W	L	Mins	GA	SO	Avg
99-2000	NY Islanders	24	7	14	1	1292	70	1	3.25							
2000-01	Florida	47	12	24	7	2628	107	5	2.44							
2001-02	Florida	58	16	33	4	3030	140	4	2.77							
2002-03	Florida	65	20	34	7	3627	164	6	2.71							
	NHL Totals	**194**	**55**	**105**	**19**	**10577**	**481**	**16**	**2.73**							

Traded to **Florida** by **NY Islanders** with Olli Jokinen for Mark Parrish and Oleg Kvasha, June 24, 2000.

MacKENZIE, Shawn

Goaltender. Catches left. 5'10", 175 lbs. Born, Bedford, N.S., August 22, 1962
(Colorado's 8th choice, 169th overall, in 1980 Entry Draft).

Season	Club	GP	W	L	T	Mins	GA	SO	Avg	GP	W	L	Mins	GA	SO	Avg
1982-83	New Jersey	4	0	1	0	130	15	0	6.92							
	NHL Totals	**4**	**0**	**1**	**0**	**130**	**15**	**0**	**6.92**							

Transferred to **New Jersey** after **Colorado** franchise relocated, June 30, 1982.

MADELEY, Darrin

Goaltender. Catches left. 5'11", 170 lbs. Born, Holland Landing, Ont., February 25, 1968

Season	Club	GP	W	L	T	Mins	GA	SO	Avg	GP	W	L	Mins	GA	SO	Avg
1992-93	Ottawa	2	0	2	0	90	10	0	6.67							
1993-94	Ottawa	32	3	18	5	1583	115	0	4.36							
1994-95	Ottawa	5	1	3	0	255	15	0	3.53							
	NHL Totals	**39**	**4**	**23**	**5**	**1928**	**140**	**0**	**4.36**							

Signed as a free agent by **Ottawa**, June 20, 1992. Signed as a free agent by **San Jose**, October 22, 1996.

MALARCHUK, Clint

Goaltender. Catches left. 6', 185 lbs. Born, Grande Prairie, Alta., May 1, 1961
(Quebec's 3rd choice, 74th overall, in 1981 Entry Draft).

Season	Club	GP	W	L	T	Mins	GA	SO	Avg	GP	W	L	Mins	GA	SO	Avg
1981-82	Quebec	2	0	1	1	120	14	0	7.00							
1982-83	Quebec	15	8	5	2	900	71	0	4.73							
1983-84	Quebec	23	10	9	2	1215	80	0	3.95							
1985-86	Quebec	46	26	12	4	2657	142	4	3.21	3	0	2	143	11	0	4.62
1986-87	Quebec	54	18	26	9	3092	175	1	3.40	3	0	2	140	8	0	3.43
1987-88	Washington	54	24	20	4	2926	154	*4	3.16	4	0	2	193	15	0	4.66
1988-89	Washington	42	16	18	7	2428	141	1	3.48							
	Buffalo	7	3	1	1	326	13	1	2.39	1	0	1	59	5	0	5.08
1989-90	Buffalo	29	14	11	2	1596	89	0	3.35							
1990-91	Buffalo	37	12	14	10	2131	119	1	3.35	4	2	2	246	17	0	4.15

Season	Club	Regular Season GP	W	L	T	Mins	GA	SO	Avg	Playoffs GP	W	L	Mins	GA	SO	Avg
1991-92	Buffalo	29	10	13	3	1639	102	0	3.73	....	....	....	....	....	....	....
	NHL Totals	**338**	**141**	**130**	**45**	**19030**	**1100**	**12**	**3.47**	**15**	**2**	**9**	**781**	**56**	**0**	**4.30**

Traded to **Washington** by **Quebec** with Dale Hunter for Gaetan Duchesne, Alan Haworth and Washington's 1st round choice (Joe Sakic) in 1987 Entry Draft, June 13, 1987. Traded to **Buffalo** by **Washington** with Grant Ledyard and Washington's 6th round choice (Brian Holzinger) in 1991 Entry Draft for Calle Johansson and Buffalo's 2nd round choice (Byron Dafoe) in 1989 Entry Draft, March 7, 1989.

MANELUK, George

Goaltender. Catches left. 5'11", 185 lbs. Born, Winnipeg, Man., July 25, 1967
(NY Islanders' 4th choice, 76th overall, in 1987 Entry Draft).

Season	Club	GP	W	L	T	Mins	GA	SO	Avg	GP	W	L	Mins	GA	SO	Avg
1990-91	NY Islanders	4	1	1	0	140	15	0	6.43	....	....	....	....	....	....	....
	NHL Totals	**4**	**1**	**1**	**0**	**140**	**15**	**0**	**6.43**	....	....	....	....	....	....	....

MANIAGO, Cesare

Goaltender. Catches left. 6'3", 195 lbs. Born, Trail, B.C., January 13, 1939

Season	Club	GP	W	L	T	Mins	GA	SO	Avg	GP	W	L	Mins	GA	SO	Avg
1960-61	Toronto	7	4	2	1	420	17	0	2.43	2	1	1	145	6	0	2.48
1962-63	Montreal	14	5	5	4	820	42	0	3.07	....	....	....	....	....	....	....
1965-66	NY Rangers	28	9	14	4	1613	94	2	3.50	....	....	....	....	....	....	....
1966-67	NY Rangers	6	0	1	1	219	14	0	3.84	....	....	....	....	....	....	....
1967-68	Minnesota	52	21	17	9	2877	133	6	2.77	14	7	7	893	39	0	2.62
1968-69	Minnesota	64	18	33	10	3599	198	1	3.30	....	....	....	....	....	....	....
1969-70	Minnesota	50	9	24	16	2887	163	2	3.39	3	1	2	180	6	*1	2.00
1970-71	Minnesota	40	19	15	6	2380	107	5	2.70	8	3	5	480	28	0	3.50
1971-72	Minnesota	43	20	17	4	2539	112	3	2.65	4	1	3	238	12	0	3.03
1972-73	Minnesota	47	21	18	6	2736	132	5	2.89	5	2	3	309	9	*2	*1.75
1973-74	Minnesota	40	12	18	10	2378	138	1	3.48	....	....	....	....	....	....	....
1974-75	Minnesota	37	11	21	4	2129	149	1	4.20	....	....	....	....	....	....	....
1975-76	Minnesota	47	13	27	5	2704	151	2	3.35	....	....	....	....	....	....	....
1976-77	Vancouver	47	17	21	9	2699	151	1	3.36	....	....	....	....	....	....	....
1977-78	Vancouver	46	10	24	8	2570	172	1	4.02	....	....	....	....	....	....	....
	NHL Totals	**568**	**189**	**257**	**97**	**32570**	**1773**	**30**	**3.27**	**36**	**15**	**21**	**2245**	**100**	**3**	**2.67**

Claimed by **Montreal** from **Toronto** (Rochester-AHL) in Inter-League Draft, June 12, 1961. Traded to **NY Rangers** by **Montreal** with Garry Peters for Noel Price, Earl Ingarfield, Gord Labossiere, Dave McComb and cash, June 8, 1965. Claimed by **Minnesota** from **NY Rangers** in Expansion Draft, June 6, 1967. Traded to **Vancouver** by **Minnesota** for Gary Smith, August 23, 1976.

MARACLE, Norm

Goaltender. Catches left. 5'9", 195 lbs. Born, Belleville, Ont., October 2, 1974
(Detroit's 6th choice, 126th overall, in 1993 Entry Draft).

Season	Club	GP	W	L	T	Mins	GA	SO	Avg	GP	W	L	Mins	GA	SO	Avg
1997-98	Detroit	4	2	0	1	178	6	0	2.02	....	....	....	....	....	....	....
1998-99	Detroit	16	6	5	2	821	31	0	2.27	2	0	0	58	3	0	3.10
99-2000	Atlanta	32	4	19	2	1618	94	1	3.49	....	....	....	....	....	....	....
2000-01	Atlanta	13	2	8	3	753	43	0	3.43	....	....	....	....	....	....	....
2001-02	Atlanta	1	0	1	0	60	3	0	3.00	....	....	....	....	....	....	....
	NHL Totals	**66**	**14**	**33**	**8**	**3430**	**177**	**1**	**3.10**	**2**	**0**	**0**	**58**	**3**	**0**	**3.10**

Claimed by **Atlanta** from **Detroit** in Expansion Draft, June 25, 1999.

MARKKANEN, Jussi

Goaltender. Catches left. 5'11", 183 lbs. Born, Imatra, Finland, May 8, 1975
(Edmonton's 5th choice, 133rd overall, in 2001 Entry Draft).

Season	Club	GP	W	L	T	Mins	GA	SO	Avg	GP	W	L	Mins	GA	SO	Avg
2001-02	Edmonton	14	6	4	2	784	24	2	1.84	....	....	....	....	....	....	....
2002-03	Edmonton	22	7	8	3	1180	51	3	2.59	1	0	0	14	1	0	4.29
	NHL Totals	**36**	**13**	**12**	**5**	**1964**	**75**	**5**	**2.29**	**1**	**0**	**0**	**14**	**1**	**0**	**4.29**

Traded to **NY Rangers** by **Edmonton** with future considerations for the rights to Brian Leetch, June 30, 2003.

MAROIS, Jean

Goaltender. Catches left. 5'8", 155 lbs. Born, Quebec City, Que., May 11, 1924

Season	Club	GP	W	L	T	Mins	GA	SO	Avg	GP	W	L	Mins	GA	SO	Avg
1943-44	Toronto	1	1	0	0	60	4	0	4.00	....	....	....	....	....	....	....
1953-54	Chicago	2	0	2	0	120	11	0	5.50	....	....	....	....	....	....	....
	NHL Totals	**3**	**1**	**2**	**0**	**180**	**15**	**0**	**5.00**	....	....	....	....	....	....	....

Promoted to **Toronto** from **St. Michael's** (OHA-Jr.) to replace injured Benny Grant, November 18, 1943. (Montreal 5, Toronto 2). Loaned to **Chicago** by **Quebec** (QHL), November 21, 1953.

MARTIN, Seth

Goaltender. Catches left. 5'11", 180 lbs. Born, Rossland, B.C., May 4, 1933

Season	Club	GP	W	L	T	Mins	GA	SO	Avg	GP	W	L	Mins	GA	SO	Avg
1967-68	St. Louis	30	8	10	7	1552	67	1	2.59	2	0	0	73	5	0	4.11
	NHL Totals	**30**	**8**	**10**	**7**	**1552**	**67**	**1**	**2.59**	**2**	**0**	**0**	**73**	**5**	**0**	**4.11**

Signed as a free agent by **St. Louis**, June 6, 1967. Claimed by **Buffalo** (AHL) from **St. Louis** in Reverse Draft, June 13, 1968. Traded to **St. Louis** by **Buffalo** (AHL) for cash, June 27, 1968.

MASON, Bob

Goaltender. Catches right. 6'1", 180 lbs. Born, International Falls, MN, April 22, 1961

Season	Club	GP	W	L	T	Mins	GA	SO	Avg	GP	W	L	Mins	GA	SO	Avg
1983-84	Washington	2	2	0	0	120	3	0	1.50	....	....	....	....	....	....	....
1984-85	Washington	12	8	2	1	661	31	1	2.81	....	....	....	....	....	....	....
1985-86	Washington	1	1	0	0	16	0	0	0.00	....	....	....	....	....	....	....
1986-87	Washington	45	20	18	5	2536	137	0	3.24	4	2	2	309	9	1	1.75
1987-88	Chicago	41	13	18	8	2312	160	0	4.15	1	0	1	60	3	0	3.00
1988-89	Quebec	22	5	14	1	1168	92	0	4.73	....	....	....	....	....	....	....
1989-90	Washington	16	4	9	1	822	48	0	3.50	....	....	....	....	....	....	....
1990-91	Vancouver	6	2	4	0	353	29	0	4.93	....	....	....	....	....	....	....
	NHL Totals	**145**	**55**	**65**	**16**	**7988**	**500**	**1**	**3.76**	**5**	**2**	**3**	**369**	**12**	**1**	**1.95**

Signed as a free agent by **Washington**, February 21, 1984. Signed as a free agent by **Chicago**, June 12, 1987. Traded to **Quebec** by **Chicago** for Mike Eagles, July 5, 1988. Traded to **Washington** by **Quebec** for future considerations, June 17, 1989. Signed as a free agent by **Vancouver**, December 1, 1990.

MASON, Chris

Goaltender. Catches left. 6', 195 lbs. Born, Red Deer, Alta., April 20, 1976
(New Jersey's 7th choice, 122nd overall, in 1995 Entry Draft).

Season	Club	GP	W	L	T	Mins	GA	SO	Avg	GP	W	L	Mins	GA	SO	Avg
1998-99	Nashville	3	0	0	0	69	6	0	5.22	....	....	....	....	....	....	....
2000-01	Nashville	1	0	1	0	59	2	0	2.03	....	....	....	....	....	....	....
	NHL Totals	**4**	**0**	**1**	**0**	**128**	**8**	**0**	**3.75**	....	....	....	....	....	....	....

Signed as a free agent by **Anaheim**, June 27, 1997. Traded to **Nashville** by **Anaheim** with Marc Moro for Dominic Roussel, October 5, 1998. Signed as a free agent by **Florida**, August 20, 2002.

MATTSSON, Markus

Goaltender. Catches right. 6', 180 lbs. Born, Suoneiemi, Finland, July 30, 1957
(NY Islanders' 6th choice, 87th overall, in 1977 Amateur Draft).

Season	Club	GP	W	L	T	Mins	GA	SO	Avg	GP	W	L	Mins	GA	SO	Avg
1979-80	Winnipeg	21	5	11	4	1200	65	2	3.25	....	....	....	....	....	....	....
1980-81	Winnipeg	31	3	21	4	1707	128	1	4.50	....	....	....	....	....	....	....
1982-83	Minnesota	2	1	1	0	100	6	1	3.60	....	....	....	....	....	....	....
	Los Angeles	19	5	5	4	899	65	1	4.34	....	....	....	....	....	....	....
1983-84	Los Angeles	19	7	8	2	1101	79	1	4.31	....	....	....	....	....	....	....
	NHL Totals	**92**	**21**	**46**	**14**	**5007**	**343**	**6**	**4.11**	....	....	....	....	....	....	....

Reclaimed by **NY Islanders** from **Winnipeg** prior to Expansion Draft, June 9, 1979. Claimed as a priority selection by **Winnipeg**, June 9, 1979. Signed as a free agent by **Minnesota**, September 24, 1982. Traded to **Los Angeles** by **Minnesota** for Los Angeles' 3rd round choice (Stephane Roy) in 1985 Entry Draft, February 1, 1983.

MAY, Darrell

Goaltender. Catches left. 6', 175 lbs. Born, Edmonton, Alta., March 6, 1962
(Vancouver's 4th choice, 91st overall, in 1980 Entry Draft).

Season	Club	GP	W	L	T	Mins	GA	SO	Avg	GP	W	L	Mins	GA	SO	Avg
1985-86	St. Louis	3	1	2	0	184	13	0	4.24	....	....	....	....	....	....	....
1987-88	St. Louis	3	0	3	0	180	18	0	6.00	....	....	....	....	....	....	....
	NHL Totals	**6**	**1**	**5**	**0**	**364**	**31**	**0**	**5.11**	....	....	....	....	....	....	....

Signed as a free agent by **St. Louis**, October 9, 1985. Traded to **Montreal** by **St. Louis** with Jocelyn Lemieux and St. Louis' 2nd round choice (Patrice Brisebois) in 1989 Entry Draft for Sergio Momesso and Vincent Riendeau, August 9, 1988.

MAYER, Gilles

Goaltender. Catches left. 5'6", 135 lbs. Born, Ottawa, Ont., August 24, 1930

Season	Club	GP	W	L	T	Mins	GA	SO	Avg	GP	W	L	Mins	GA	SO	Avg
1949-50	Toronto	1	0	1	0	60	2	0	2.00	....	....	....	....	....	....	....
1953-54	Toronto	1	0	0	1	60	3	0	3.00	....	....	....	....	....	....	....
1954-55	Toronto	1	1	0	0	60	1	0	1.00	....	....	....	....	....	....	....
1955-56	Toronto	6	1	5	0	360	18	0	3.00	....	....	....	....	....	....	....
	NHL Totals	**9**	**2**	**6**	**1**	**540**	**24**	**0**	**2.67**	....	....	....	....	....	....	....

Promoted to **Toronto** from **Pittsburgh** (AHL) to replace Turk Broda, December 1, 1949. (Detroit 2, Toronto 1). Promoted to **Toronto** from **Pittsburgh** (AHL) to replace Harry Lumley, March 4, 1954 (Toronto 3, Detroit 3) and October 21, 1954 (Toronto 3, Montreal 1). Traded to **Detroit** (Hershey-AHL) by **Toronto** (Pittsburgh-AHL) with Jack Price, Willie Marshall, Bob Hassard, Bob Solinger and Ray Gariepy for cash, July 7, 1956.

McAULEY, Ken

Goaltender. Catches right. 5'10", 190 lbs. Born, Edmonton, Alta., January 9, 1921

Season	Club	GP	W	L	T	Mins	GA	SO	Avg	GP	W	L	Mins	GA	SO	Avg
1943-44	NY Rangers	*50	6	39	5	2980	310	0	6.24	....	....	....	....	....	....	....
1944-45	NY Rangers	46	11	25	10	2760	227	1	4.93	....	....	....	....	....	....	....
	NHL Totals	**96**	**17**	**64**	**15**	**5740**	**537**	**1**	**5.61**	....	....	....	....	....	....	....

Signed as a free agent by **NY Rangers**, October 16, 1943.

McCARTAN, Jack

USHOF

Goaltender. 6'1", 195 lbs. Born, St. Paul, MN, August 5, 1935

Season	Club	GP	W	L	T	Mins	GA	SO	Avg	GP	W	L	Mins	GA	SO	Avg
1959-60	NY Rangers	4	1	1	2	240	7	0	1.75	....	....	....	....	....	....	....
1960-61	NY Rangers	8	1	6	1	440	35	1	4.77	....	....	....	....	....	....	....
	NHL Totals	**12**	**2**	**7**	**3**	**680**	**42**	**1**	**3.71**	....	....	....	....	....	....	....

Signed to five-game amateur tryout contract by **NY Rangers** following 1960 Winter Olympic Games, March 2, 1960. Traded to **LA Blades** (WHL) by **NY Rangers** for cash, October 2, 1962. Claimed by **Chicago** from **LA Blades** (WHL) in Inter-League Draft, June 4, 1963. Traded to **LA Blades** (WHL) by **Chicago** for cash, January, 1965. Traded to **San Francisco** (WHL) by **LA Blades** (WHL) for Paul Jackson, June, 1965. NHL rights transferred to **California** after owners of **San Francisco** (WHL) franchise granted expansion team, April 6, 1966. Claimed by **San Diego** (WHL) from **Oakland** in Reverse Draft, June 13, 1968.

McCOOL, Frank

Goaltender. Catches left. 6', 170 lbs. Born, Calgary, Alta., October 27, 1918

Season	Club	GP	W	L	T	Mins	GA	SO	Avg	GP	W	L	Mins	GA	SO	Avg
1944-45♦	Toronto	*50	24	22	4	*3000	161	*4	3.22	13	*8	5	807	30	*4	2.23
1945-46	Toronto	22	10	9	3	1320	81	0	3.68	....	....	....	....	....	....	....
	NHL Totals	**72**	**34**	**31**	**7**	**4320**	**242**	**4**	**3.36**	**13**	**8**	**5**	**807**	**30**	**4**	**2.23**

Calder Memorial Trophy (1945)

Signed as a free agent by **Toronto**, October 25, 1944.

McDUFFE, Peter

Goaltender. Catches left. 5'9", 180 lbs. Born, Milton, Ont., February 16, 1948

Season	Club	GP	W	L	T	Mins	GA	SO	Avg	GP	W	L	Mins	GA	SO	Avg
1971-72	St. Louis	10	0	6	0	467	29	0	3.73	1	0	1	60	7	0	7.00
1972-73	NY Rangers	1	1	0	0	60	1	0	1.00	....	....	....	....	....	....	....
1973-74	NY Rangers	6	3	2	1	340	18	0	3.18	....	....	....	....	....	....	....

		REGULAR SEASON								PLAYOFFS						
Season	Club	GP	W	L	T	Mins	GA	SO	Avg	GP	W	L	Mins	GA	SO	Avg
1974-75	Kansas City	36	7	25	4	2100	148	0	4.23	....	....	....	....	....	....	....
1975-76	Detroit	4	0	3	1	240	22	0	5.50	....	....	....	....	....	....	....
	NHL Totals	**57**	**11**	**36**	**6**	**3207**	**218**	**0**	**4.08**	**1**	**0**	**1**	**60**	**7**	**0**	**7.00**

Claimed by **Phoenix** (WHL) from **Chicago** in Reverse Draft, June 12, 1969. Traded to **NY Rangers** by **Phoenix** (WHL) for Don Caley and Sandy Snow, July 3, 1969. Traded to **St. Louis** by **NY Rangers** for St. Louis' 1st round choice (Steve Vickers) in 1971 Amateur Draft, May 25, 1971. Traded to **NY Rangers** by **St. Louis** with Curt Bennett to complete transaction that sent Steve Durbano to St. Louis (May 24, 1972), June 7, 1972. Claimed by **Kansas City** from **NY Rangers** in Expansion Draft, June 12, 1974. Traded to **Detroit** by **Kansas City** with Glen Burdon for Gary Bergman and Bill McKenzie, August 22, 1975.

McGRATTAN, Tom

Goaltender. Catches left. 6'2", 170 lbs. Born, Brantford, Ont., October 19, 1927

Season	Club	GP	W	L	T	Mins	GA	SO	Avg	GP	W	L	Mins	GA	SO	Avg
1947-48	Detroit	1	0	0	0	8	1	0	7.50	....	....	....	....	....	....	....
	NHL Totals	**1**	**0**	**0**	**0**	**8**	**1**	**0**	**7.50**	....	....	....	....	....	....	....

Signed as a free agent by **Detroit**, March 20, 1945. • **Detroit's** spare goaltender replaced injured Harry Lumley in 3rd period, November 9, 1947. (Toronto 6, Detroit 0)

McKAY, Ross

Goaltender. Catches right. 5'11", 175 lbs. Born, Edmonton, Alta., March 3, 1964

Season	Club	GP	W	L	T	Mins	GA	SO	Avg	GP	W	L	Mins	GA	SO	Avg
1990-91	Hartford	1	0	0	0	35	3	0	5.14	....	....	....	....	....	....	....
	NHL Totals	**1**	**0**	**0**	**0**	**35**	**3**	**0**	**5.14**	....	....	....	....	....	....	....

Signed as a free agent by **Hartford**, May 2, 1988.

McKENZIE, Bill

Goaltender. Catches right. 5'11", 180 lbs. Born, St. Thomas, Ont., March 12, 1949

Season	Club	GP	W	L	T	Mins	GA	SO	Avg	GP	W	L	Mins	GA	SO	Avg
1973-74	Detroit	13	4	4	4	720	43	1	3.58	....	....	....	....	....	....	....
1974-75	Detroit	13	1	9	2	740	58	0	4.70	....	....	....	....	....	....	....
1975-76	Kansas City	22	1	16	1	1120	97	0	5.20	....	....	....	....	....	....	....
1976-77	Colorado	5	0	2	1	200	8	0	2.40	....	....	....	....	....	....	....
1977-78	Colorado	12	3	6	2	654	42	0	3.85	....	....	....	....	....	....	....
1979-80	Colorado	26	9	12	3	1342	78	1	3.49	....	....	....	....	....	....	....
	NHL Totals	**91**	**18**	**49**	**13**	**4776**	**326**	**2**	**4.10**	....	....	....	....	....	....	....

Signed as a free agent by **Detroit**, October 4, 1972. Traded to **Kansas City** by **Detroit** with Gary Bergman for Peter McDuffe and Glen Burdon, August 22, 1975. Transferred to **Colorado** after **Kansas City** franchise relocated, July 15, 1976.

McKICHAN, Steve

Goaltender. Catches left. 5'11", 180 lbs. Born, Strathroy, Ont., May 29, 1967
(Vancouver's 2nd choice, 7th overall, in 1988 Supplemental Draft).

Season	Club	GP	W	L	T	Mins	GA	SO	Avg	GP	W	L	Mins	GA	SO	Avg
1990-91	Vancouver	1	0	0	0	20	2	0	6.00	....	....	....	....	....	....	....
	NHL Totals	**1**	**0**	**0**	**0**	**20**	**2**	**0**	**6.00**	....	....	....	....	....	....	....

McLACHLAN, Murray

Goaltender. Catches left. 6', 195 lbs. Born, London, Ont., October 20, 1948

Season	Club	GP	W	L	T	Mins	GA	SO	Avg	GP	W	L	Mins	GA	SO	Avg
1970-71	Toronto	2	0	1	0	25	4	0	9.60	....	....	....	....	....	....	....
	NHL Totals	**2**	**0**	**1**	**0**	**25**	**4**	**0**	**9.60**	....	....	....	....	....	....	....

Signed as a free agent by **Toronto**, October 1, 1970.

McLEAN, Kirk

Goaltender. Catches left. 6', 180 lbs. Born, Willowdale, Ont., June 26, 1966
(New Jersey's 6th choice, 107th overall, in 1984 Entry Draft).

Season	Club	GP	W	L	T	Mins	GA	SO	Avg	GP	W	L	Mins	GA	SO	Avg
1985-86	New Jersey	2	1	1	0	111	11	0	5.95	....	....	....	....	....	....	....
1986-87	New Jersey	4	1	1	0	160	10	0	3.75	....	....	....	....	....	....	....
1987-88	Vancouver	41	11	27	3	2380	147	1	3.71	....	....	....	....	....	....	....
1988-89	Vancouver	42	20	17	3	2477	127	4	3.08	5	2	3	302	18	0	3.58
1989-90	Vancouver	*63	21	30	10	*3739	216	0	3.47	....	....	....	....	....	....	....
1990-91	Vancouver	41	10	22	3	1969	131	0	3.99	2	1	1	123	7	0	3.41
1991-92	Vancouver	65	*38	17	9	3852	176	*5	2.74	13	6	7	785	33	*2	2.52
1992-93	Vancouver	54	28	21	5	3261	184	3	3.39	12	6	6	754	42	0	3.34
1993-94	Vancouver	52	23	26	3	3128	156	3	2.99	*24	15	9	*1544	59	*4	2.29
1994-95	Vancouver	40	18	12	10	2374	109	1	2.75	11	4	7	660	36	0	3.27
1995-96	Vancouver	45	15	21	9	2645	156	2	3.54	1	0	1	21	3	0	8.57
1996-97	Vancouver	44	21	18	3	2581	138	0	3.21	....	....	....	....	....	....	....
1997-98	Vancouver	29	6	17	4	1583	97	1	3.68	....	....	....	....	....	....	....
	Carolina	8	4	2	0	401	22	0	3.29	....	....	....	....	....	....	....
	Florida	7	4	2	1	406	22	0	3.25	....	....	....	....	....	....	....
1998-99	Florida	30	9	10	4	1597	73	2	2.74	....	....	....	....	....	....	....
99-2000	NY Rangers	22	7	8	4	1206	58	0	2.89	....	....	....	....	....	....	....
2000-01	NY Rangers	23	8	10	1	1220	71	0	3.49	....	....	....	....	....	....	....
	NHL Totals	**612**	**245**	**262**	**72**	**35090**	**1904**	**22**	**3.26**	**68**	**34**	**34**	**4189**	**198**	**6**	**2.84**

NHL Second All-Star Team (1992)

Played in NHL All-Star Game (1990, 1992)

Traded to **Vancouver** by **New Jersey** with Greg Adams and New Jersey's 2nd round choice (Leif Rohlin) in 1988 Entry Draft for Patrik Sundstrom and Vancouver's 2nd (Jeff Christian) and 4th (Matt Ruchty) round choices in 1988 Entry Draft, September 15, 1987. Traded to **Carolina** by **Vancouver** with Martin Gelinas for Sean Burke, Geoff Sanderson and Enrico Ciccone, January 3, 1998. Traded to **Florida** by **Carolina** for Ray Sheppard, March 24, 1998. Signed as a free agent by **NY Rangers**, July 20, 1999.

McLELLAND, Dave

Goaltender. Catches left. 5'9", 165 lbs. Born, Penticton, B.C., November 20, 1952
(Vancouver's 6th choice, 83rd overall, in 1972 Amateur Draft).

Season	Club	GP	W	L	T	Mins	GA	SO	Avg	GP	W	L	Mins	GA	SO	Avg
1972-73	Vancouver	2	1	1	0	120	10	0	5.00	....	....	....	....	....	....	....
	NHL Totals	**2**	**1**	**1**	**0**	**120**	**10**	**0**	**5.00**	....	....	....	....	....	....	....

McLENNAN, Jamie

Goaltender. Catches left. 6', 190 lbs. Born, Edmonton, Alta., June 30, 1971
(NY Islanders' 3rd choice, 48th overall, in 1991 Entry Draft).

		REGULAR SEASON								PLAYOFFS						
Season	Club	GP	W	L	T	Mins	GA	SO	Avg	GP	W	L	Mins	GA	SO	Avg
1993-94	NY Islanders	22	8	7	6	1287	61	0	2.84	2	0	1	82	6	0	4.39
1994-95	NY Islanders	21	6	11	2	1185	67	0	3.39	....	....	....	....	....	....	....
1995-96	NY Islanders	13	3	9	1	636	39	0	3.68	....	....	....	....	....	....	....
1997-98	St. Louis	30	16	8	2	1658	60	2	2.17	1	0	0	14	1	0	4.29
1998-99	St. Louis	33	13	14	4	1763	70	3	2.38	1	0	1	37	0	0	0.00
99-2000	St. Louis	19	9	5	2	1009	33	2	1.96	....	....	....	....	....	....	....
2000-01	Minnesota	38	5	23	9	2230	98	2	2.64	....	....	....	....	....	....	....
2002-03	Calgary	22	2	11	4	1165	58	0	2.99	....	....	....	....	....	....	....
	NHL Totals	**198**	**62**	**88**	**30**	**10933**	**486**	**9**	**2.67**	**4**	**0**	**2**	**133**	**7**	**0**	**3.16**

Bill Masterton Memorial Trophy (1998)

Signed as a free agent by **St. Louis**, July 15, 1996. Claimed by **Minnesota** from **St. Louis** in Expansion Draft, June 23, 2000. Traded to **Calgary** by **Minnesota** for Calgary's 9th round choice (Mika Hannula) in 2002 Entry Draft, June 22, 2002.

McLEOD, Don

Goaltender. Catches left. 6', 190 lbs. Born, Trail, B.C., August 24, 1946
(Pittsburgh's 11th choice, 164th overall, in 1973 Amateur Draft).

Season	Club	GP	W	L	T	Mins	GA	SO	Avg	GP	W	L	Mins	GA	SO	Avg
1970-71	Detroit	14	3	7	0	698	60	0	5.16	....	....	....	....	....	....	....
1971-72	Philadelphia	4	0	3	1	181	14	0	4.64	....	....	....	....	....	....	....
	NHL Totals	**18**	**3**	**10**	**1**	**879**	**74**	**0**	**5.05**	....	....	....	....	....	....	....

Claimed by **Philadelphia** (Quebec-AHL) from **Detroit** in Reverse Draft, June, 1971.

McLEOD, Jim

Goaltender. Catches left. 5'8", 170 lbs. Born, Port Arthur, Ont., April 7, 1937

Season	Club	GP	W	L	T	Mins	GA	SO	Avg	GP	W	L	Mins	GA	SO	Avg
1971-72	St. Louis	16	6	6	4	880	44	0	3.00	....	....	....	....	....	....	....
	NHL Totals	**16**	**6**	**6**	**4**	**880**	**44**	**0**	**3.00**	....	....	....	....	....	....	....

Claimed by **St. Louis** from **Portland** (WHL) in Inter-League Draft, June 7, 1971.

McNAMARA, Gerry

Goaltender. Catches left. 6'2", 190 lbs. Born, Sturgeon Falls, Ont., September 22, 1934

Season	Club	GP	W	L	T	Mins	GA	SO	Avg	GP	W	L	Mins	GA	SO	Avg
1960-61	Toronto	5	2	2	1	300	12	0	2.40	....	....	....	....	....	....	....
1969-70	Toronto	2	0	0	0	23	2	0	5.22	....	....	....	....	....	....	....
	NHL Totals	**7**	**2**	**2**	**1**	**323**	**14**	**0**	**2.60**	....	....	....	....	....	....	....

McNEIL, Gerry

Goaltender. Catches left. 5'7", 155 lbs. Born, Quebec City, Que., April 17, 1926

Season	Club	GP	W	L	T	Mins	GA	SO	Avg	GP	W	L	Mins	GA	SO	Avg
1947-48	Montreal	2	0	1	1	95	7	0	4.42	....	....	....	....	....	....	....
1949-50	Montreal	6	3	1	2	360	9	1	1.50	2	1	1	135	5	0	2.22
1950-51	Montreal	*70	25	30	15	*4200	184	6	2.63	*11	*5	6	*785	25	1	1.91
1951-52	Montreal	*70	34	26	10	*4200	164	5	2.34	*11	4	7	*688	23	1	2.01
1952-53 ♦	Montreal	66	25	23	18	3960	140	*10	2.12	8	*5	3	486	16	*2	1.98
1953-54	Montreal	53	28	19	6	3180	114	6	2.15	3	2	1	190	3	1	0.95
1956-57 ♦	Montreal	9	4	5	0	540	31	0	3.44	....	....	....	....	....	....	....
1957-58	Montreal	DID NOT PLAY – SPARE GOALTENDER														
	NHL Totals	**276**	**119**	**105**	**52**	**16535**	**649**	**28**	**2.36**	**35**	**17**	**18**	**2284**	**72**	**5**	**1.89**

NHL Second All-Star Team (1953)

Played in NHL All-Star Game (1951, 1952, 1953)

McRAE, Gord

Goaltender. Catches left. 6', 180 lbs. Born, Sherbrooke, Que., April 12, 1948

Season	Club	GP	W	L	T	Mins	GA	SO	Avg	GP	W	L	Mins	GA	SO	Avg
1972-73	Toronto	11	7	3	0	620	39	0	3.77	....	....	....	....	....	....	....
1974-75	Toronto	20	10	3	6	1063	57	0	3.22	7	2	5	441	21	0	2.86
1975-76	Toronto	20	6	5	2	956	59	0	3.70	1	0	0	13	1	0	4.62
1976-77	Toronto	2	0	1	1	120	9	0	4.50	....	....	....	....	....	....	....
1977-78	Toronto	18	7	10	1	1040	57	1	3.29	....	....	....	....	....	....	....
	NHL Totals	**71**	**30**	**22**	**10**	**3799**	**221**	**1**	**3.49**	**8**	**2**	**5**	**454**	**22**	**0**	**2.91**

Signed as a free agent by **Toronto** (Tulsa – CHL), December 18, 1971.

MELANSON, Roland

Goaltender. Catches left. 5'10", 185 lbs. Born, Moncton, N.B., June 28, 1960
(NY Islanders' 4th choice, 59th overall, in 1979 Entry Draft).

Season	Club	GP	W	L	T	Mins	GA	SO	Avg	GP	W	L	Mins	GA	SO	Avg
1980-81 ♦	NY Islanders	11	8	1	1	620	32	0	3.10	3	1	0	92	6	0	3.91
1981-82 ♦	NY Islanders	36	22	7	6	2115	114	0	3.23	3	0	1	64	5	0	4.69
1982-83 ♦	NY Islanders	44	24	12	5	2460	109	1	2.66	5	2	2	238	10	0	2.52
1983-84	NY Islanders	37	20	11	2	2019	110	0	3.27	6	0	1	87	5	0	3.45
1984-85	NY Islanders	8	3	3	0	425	35	0	4.94	....	....	....	....	....	....	....
	Minnesota	20	5	10	3	1142	78	0	4.10	....	....	....	....	....	....	....
1985-86	Minnesota	6	2	1	2	325	24	0	4.43	....	....	....	....	....	....	....
	Los Angeles	22	4	16	1	1246	87	0	4.19	....	....	....	....	....	....	....
1986-87	Los Angeles	46	18	21	6	2734	168	1	3.69	5	1	4	260	24	0	5.54
1987-88	Los Angeles	47	17	20	7	2676	195	2	4.37	1	0	1	60	9	0	9.00
1988-89	Los Angeles	4	1	1	0	178	19	0	6.40	....	....	....	....	....	....	....
1990-91	New Jersey	1	0	0	0	20	2	0	6.00	....	....	....	....	....	....	....

Season	Club	GP	W	L	T	Mins	GA	SO	Avg	GP	W	L	Mins	GA	SO	Avg
		REGULAR SEASON								PLAYOFFS						
1991-92	Montreal	9	5	3	0	492	22	2	2.68							
	NHL Totals	**291**	**129**	**106**	**33**	**16452**	**995**	**6**	**3.63**	**23**	**4**	**9**	**801**	**59**	**0**	**4.42**

NHL Second All-Star Team (1983) • Shared William M. Jennings Trophy with Billy Smith (1983)

Traded to **Minnesota** by **NY Islanders** for Minnesota's 1st round choice (Brad Dalgarno) in 1985 Entry Draft, November 19, 1984. Traded to **NY Rangers** by **Minnesota** for NY Rangers' 2nd round choice (Neil Wilkinson) in 1986 Entry Draft and NY Rangers' 4th round choice (John Weisbrod) in 1987 Entry Draft, December 9, 1985. Traded to **Los Angeles** by **NY Rangers** with Grant Ledyard for Brian MacLellan and Los Angeles' 4th round choice (Mike Sullivan) in 1987 Entry Draft, December 9, 1985. Signed as a free agent by **New Jersey**, August 10, 1989. Traded to **Montreal** by **New Jersey** with Kirk Muller for Stephane Richer and Tom Chorske, September 20, 1991.

MELOCHE, Gilles

Goaltender. Catches left. 5'9", 185 lbs. Born, Montreal, Que., July 12, 1950
(Chicago's 5th choice, 70th overall, in 1970 Amateur Draft).

Season	Club	GP	W	L	T	Mins	GA	SO	Avg	GP	W	L	Mins	GA	SO	Avg
1970-71	Chicago	2	2	0	0	120	6	0	3.00							
1971-72	California	56	16	25	13	3121	173	4	3.33							
1972-73	California	*59	12	32	14	*3473	235	1	4.06							
1973-74	California	47	9	33	5	2800	198	1	4.24							
1974-75	California	47	9	27	10	2771	186	1	4.03							
1975-76	California	41	12	23	6	2440	140	1	3.44							
1976-77	Cleveland	51	19	24	6	2961	171	2	3.47							
1977-78	Cleveland	54	16	27	8	3100	195	1	3.77							
1978-79	Minnesota	53	20	25	7	3118	173	2	3.33							
1979-80	Minnesota	54	27	20	5	3141	160	1	3.06	11	5	4	564	34	1	3.62
1980-81	Minnesota	38	17	14	6	2215	120	2	3.25	13	8	5	802	47	0	3.52
1981-82	Minnesota	51	26	15	9	3026	175	1	3.47	4	1	2	184	8	0	2.61
1982-83	Minnesota	47	20	13	11	2689	160	1	3.57	5	2	3	319	18	0	3.39
1983-84	Minnesota	52	21	17	8	2883	201	2	4.18	4	1	2	200	11	0	3.30
1984-85	Minnesota	32	10	13	6	1817	115	0	3.80	8	4	3	395	25	1	3.80
1985-86	Pittsburgh	34	13	15	5	1989	119	0	3.59							
1986-87	Pittsburgh	43	13	19	7	2343	134	0	3.43							
1987-88	Pittsburgh	27	8	9	5	1394	95	0	4.09							
	NHL Totals	**788**	**270**	**351**	**131**	**45401**	**2756**	**20**	**3.64**	**45**	**21**	**19**	**2464**	**143**	**2**	**3.48**

Played in NHL All-Star Game (1980, 1982)

Traded to **California** by **Chicago** with Paul Shmyr for Gerry Desjardins, October 18, 1971. Transferred to **Cleveland** after **California** franchise relocated, August 26, 1976. Protected by **Minnesota** prior to Cleveland – Minnesota Dispersal Draft, June 15, 1978. Traded to **Edmonton** by **Minnesota** for Paul Houck, May 31, 1985. Traded to **Pittsburgh** by **Edmonton** for Marty McSorley, Tim Hrynewich and future considerations (Craig Muni, October 6, 1986), September 11, 1985.

MICALEF, Corrado

Goaltender. Catches right. 5'8", 172 lbs. Born, Montreal, Que., April 20, 1961
(Detroit's 2nd choice, 44th overall, in 1981 Entry Draft).

Season	Club	GP	W	L	T	Mins	GA	SO	Avg	GP	W	L	Mins	GA	SO	Avg
1981-82	Detroit	18	4	10	1	809	63	0	4.67							
1982-83	Detroit	34	11	13	5	1756	106	2	3.62							
1983-84	Detroit	14	5	8	1	808	52	0	3.86	1	0	0	7	2	0	17.14
1984-85	Detroit	36	5	19	7	1856	136	0	4.40	2	0	0	42	6	0	8.57
1985-86	Detroit	11	1	9	1	565	52	0	5.52							
	NHL Totals	**113**	**26**	**59**	**15**	**5794**	**409**	**2**	**4.24**	**3**	**0**	**0**	**49**	**8**	**0**	**9.80**

MICHAUD, Alfie

Goaltender. Catches left. 5'10", 177 lbs. Born, Selkirk, Man., November 6, 1976

Season	Club	GP	W	L	T	Mins	GA	SO	Avg	GP	W	L	Mins	GA	SO	Avg
99-2000	Vancouver	2	0	1	0	69	5	0	4.35							
	NHL Totals	**2**	**0**	**1**	**0**	**69**	**5**	**0**	**4.35**							

Signed as a free agent by **Vancouver**, July 12, 1999.

MICHAUD, Olivier

Goaltender. Catches left. 5'11", 160 lbs. Born, Beloeil, Que., September 14, 1983

Season	Club	GP	W	L	T	Mins	GA	SO	Avg	GP	W	L	Mins	GA	SO	Avg
2001-02	Montreal	1	0	0	0	18	0	0	0.00							
	NHL Totals	**1**	**0**	**0**	**0**	**18**	**0**	**0**	**0.00**							

Signed as a free agent by **Montreal**, September 18, 2001. • Promoted to **Montreal** from **Shawinigan** (QMJHL) and replaced injured Jose Theodore, October 26, 2001.

MIDDLEBROOK, Lindsay

Goaltender. Catches right. 5'7", 160 lbs. Born, Collingwood, Ont., September 7, 1955

Season	Club	GP	W	L	T	Mins	GA	SO	Avg	GP	W	L	Mins	GA	SO	Avg
1979-80	Winnipeg	10	2	8	0	580	40	0	4.14							
1980-81	Winnipeg	14	0	9	3	653	65	0	5.97							
1981-82	Minnesota	3	0	0	2	140	7	0	3.00							
1982-83	New Jersey	9	0	6	1	412	37	0	5.39							
	Edmonton	1	1	0	0	60	3	0	3.00							
	NHL Totals	**37**	**3**	**23**	**6**	**1845**	**152**	**0**	**4.94**							

Signed as a free agent by **NY Rangers**, October 12, 1977. Claimed by **Winnipeg** from **NY Rangers** in Expansion Draft, June 13, 1979. Traded to **Minnesota** by **Winnipeg** for cash, July 31, 1981. Signed as a free agent by **New Jersey**, September 25, 1982. Traded to **Edmonton** by **New Jersey** with Paul Miller for Ron Low and Jim McTaggart, February 19, 1983.

MILLAR, Al

Goaltender. Catches left. 5'11", 175 lbs. Born, Winnipeg, Man., September 18, 1929

Season	Club	GP	W	L	T	Mins	GA	SO	Avg	GP	W	L	Mins	GA	SO	Avg
1957-58	Boston	6	1	4	1	360	25	0	4.17							
	NHL Totals	**6**	**1**	**4**	**1**	**360**	**25**	**0**	**4.17**							

Traded to **Quebec** (QMHL) by **Detroit** for cash, September 16, 1951. Promoted to **Boston** from **Quebec** (AHL) to replace injured Don Simmons in games from January 1 through 12, 1958. Traded to **Detroit** (Hershey-AHL) by **Boston** (Quebec-AHL) with Myron Stankiewicz for Claude Dufour, June, 1960. Transferred to **Seattle** (WHL) by **Detroit** as compensation for the loss of Les Hunt and Marc Boileau, November 5, 1961. Traded to **Toronto** (Denver-WHL) by **Seattle** (WHL) for cash, September, 1963. Traded to **Philadelphia** by **Toronto** for cash, September, 1967. Traded to **Vancouver** (WHL) by **Philadelphia** for cash, October, 1968. Rights transferred to **Vancouver** after NHL club purchased **Vancouver** (WHL) franchise, December 19, 1969.

MILLEN, Greg

Goaltender. Catches right. 5'9", 175 lbs. Born, Toronto, Ont., June 25, 1957
(Pittsburgh's 4th choice, 102nd overall, in 1977 Amateur Draft).

Season	Club	GP	W	L	T	Mins	GA	SO	Avg	GP	W	L	Mins	GA	SO	Avg
1978-79	Pittsburgh	28	14	11	1	1532	86	2	3.37							
1979-80	Pittsburgh	44	18	18	7	2586	157	2	3.64	5	2	3	300	21	0	4.20
1980-81	Pittsburgh	63	25	27	10	3721	258	0	4.16	5	2	3	325	19	0	3.51
1981-82	Hartford	55	11	30	12	3201	229	0	4.29							
1982-83	Hartford	60	14	38	6	3520	282	1	4.81							
1983-84	Hartford	*60	21	30	9	*3583	221	2	3.70							
1984-85	Hartford	44	16	22	6	2659	187	1	4.22							
	St. Louis	10	2	7	1	607	35	0	3.46	1	0	1	60	2	0	2.00
1985-86	St. Louis	36	14	16	6	2168	129	1	3.57	10	6	3	586	29	0	2.97
1986-87	St. Louis	42	15	18	9	2482	146	0	3.53	4	1	3	250	10	0	2.40
1987-88	St. Louis	48	21	19	7	2854	167	1	3.51	10	5	5	600	38	0	3.80
1988-89	St. Louis	52	22	20	7	3019	170	*6	3.38	10	5	5	649	34	0	3.14
1989-90	St. Louis	21	11	7	3	1245	61	1	2.94							
	Quebec	18	3	14	1	1080	95	0	5.28							
	Chicago	10	5	4	1	575	32	0	3.34	14	6	6	613	40	0	3.92
1990-91	Chicago	3	0	1	0	58	4	0	4.14							
1991-92	Detroit	10	3	2	3	487	22	0	2.71							
	NHL Totals	**604**	**215**	**284**	**89**	**35377**	**2281**	**17**	**3.87**	**59**	**27**	**29**	**3383**	**193**	**0**	**3.42**

Signed as a free agent by **Hartford**, June 15, 1981. Traded to **St. Louis** by **Hartford** with Mark Johnson for Mike Liut and Jorgen Pettersson, February 21, 1985. Traded to **Quebec** by **St. Louis** with Tony Hrkac for Jeff Brown, December 13, 1989. Traded to **Chicago** by **Quebec** with Michel Goulet and Quebec's 6th round choice (Kevin St. Jacques) in 1991 Entry Draft for Mario Doyon, Everett Sanipass and Dan Vincelette, March 5, 1990. Traded to **NY Rangers** by **Chicago** for future considerations, September 24, 1991. Traded to **Detroit** by **NY Rangers** for future considerations, December 26, 1991.

MILLER, Joe

Goaltender. 5'9", 170 lbs. Born, Morrisburg, Ont., October 6, 1900

Season	Club	GP	W	L	T	Mins	GA	SO	Avg	GP	W	L	Mins	GA	SO	Avg
1927-28	NY Americans	28	8	16	4	1721	77	5	2.68							
	♦ NY Rangers									3	2	1	180	3	1	1.00
1928-29	Pittsburgh	*44	9	27	8	2780	80	11	1.73							
1929-30	Pittsburgh	43	5	35	3	2630	179	0	4.08							
1930-31	Philadelphia	12	2	9	1	740	47	0	3.81							
	NHL Totals	**127**	**24**	**87**	**16**	**7871**	**383**	**16**	**2.92**	**3**	**2**	**1**	**180**	**3**	**1**	**1.00**

NHL rights traded to **NY Americans** by **Pittsburgh** for the rights to Odie Cleghorn and the loan of Jesse Spring, January 23, 1926. Loaned to **NY Rangers** by **NY Americans** to replace injured Lorne Chabot for remainder of Stanley Cup Finals, April 10, 1928. Traded to **Pittsburgh** by **NY Americans** with $20,000 for Roy Worters, November 1, 1928. Transferred to **Philadelphia** after **Pittsburgh** franchise relocated, October 26, 1930.

MILLER, Ryan

Goaltender. Catches left. 6'2", 150 lbs. Born, East Lansing, MI, July 17, 1980
(Buffalo's 7th choice, 138th overall, in 1999 Entry Draft).

Season	Club	GP	W	L	T	Mins	GA	SO	Avg	GP	W	L	Mins	GA	SO	Avg
2002-03	Buffalo	15	6	8	1	912	40	1	2.63							
	NHL Totals	**15**	**6**	**8**	**1**	**912**	**40**	**1**	**2.63**							

MINARD, Mike

Goaltender. Catches left. 6'3", 205 lbs. Born, Owen Sound, Ont., November 1, 1976
(Edmonton's 4th choice, 83rd overall, in 1995 Entry Draft).

Season	Club	GP	W	L	T	Mins	GA	SO	Avg	GP	W	L	Mins	GA	SO	Avg
99-2000	Edmonton	1	1	0	0	60	3	0	3.00							
	NHL Totals	**1**	**1**	**0**	**0**	**60**	**3**	**0**	**3.00**							

Signed as a free agent by **Toronto**, March 16, 2001.

MIO, Eddie

Goaltender. Catches left. 5'10", 180 lbs. Born, Windsor, Ont., January 31, 1954
(Chicago's 7th choice, 124th overall, in 1974 Amateur Draft).

Season	Club	GP	W	L	T	Mins	GA	SO	Avg	GP	W	L	Mins	GA	SO	Avg
1979-80	Edmonton	34	9	13	5	1711	120	1	4.21							
1980-81	Edmonton	43	16	15	9	2393	155	0	3.89							
1981-82	NY Rangers	25	13	6	5	1500	89	0	3.56	8	4	3	443	28	0	3.79
1982-83	NY Rangers	41	16	18	6	2365	136	2	3.45	8	5	3	480	32	0	4.00
1983-84	Detroit	24	7	11	3	1295	95	1	4.40	1	0	1	63	3	0	2.86
1984-85	Detroit	7	1	3	2	376	27	0	4.31							
1985-86	Detroit	18	2	7	0	788	83	0	6.32							
	NHL Totals	**192**	**64**	**73**	**30**	**10428**	**705**	**4**	**4.06**	**17**	**9**	**7**	**986**	**63**	**0**	**3.83**

NHL rights traded to **Minnesota** by **Chicago** with future considerations (Pierre Plante, May 4, 1978) for Doug Hicks and Minnesota's 3rd round choice (Marcel Frere) in 1980 Entry Draft, March 14, 1978. Traded to **Edmonton** (WHA) by **Indianapolis** (WHA) with Wayne Gretzky and Peter Driscoll for $700,000 and future considerations, November 2, 1978. Reclaimed by **Minnesota** from **Edmonton** prior to Expansion Draft, June 9, 1979. Claimed as priority selection by **Edmonton**, June 9, 1979. Traded to **NY Rangers** by **Edmonton** for Lance Nethery, December 11, 1981. Traded to **Detroit** by **NY Rangers** with Ron Duguay and Eddie Johnstone for Willie Huber, Mike Blaisdell and Mark Osborne, June 13, 1983.

MITCHELL, Ivan

Goaltender. , Born, 1896

		REGULAR SEASON								PLAYOFFS						
Season	Club	GP	W	L	T	Mins	GA	SO	Avg	GP	W	L	Mins	GA	SO	Avg
1919-20	Toronto	16	6	7	0	830	60	0	4.34							
1920-21	Toronto	4	2	2	0	240	22	0	5.50							
1921-22♦	Toronto	2	2	0	0	120	6	0	3.00							
	NHL Totals	**22**	**10**	**9**	**0**	**1190**	**88**	**0**	**4.44**							

Signed as a free agent by **Toronto**, December 15, 1919. Signed as a free agent by **Hamilton**, December 5, 1921. Loaned to **Toronto** by **Hamilton** to replace injured John Ross Roach, December 13, 1921. • Missed remainder of 1921-22 season recovering from eventual career-ending illness that required treatment at Mayo Clinic in Baltimore, MD.

MOFFAT, Mike

Goaltender. Catches left. 5'10", 165 lbs. Born, Galt, Ont., February 4, 1962
(Boston's 7th choice, 165th overall, in 1980 Entry Draft).

		REGULAR SEASON								PLAYOFFS						
Season	Club	GP	W	L	T	Mins	GA	SO	Avg	GP	W	L	Mins	GA	SO	Avg
1981-82	Boston	2	2	0	0	120	6	0	3.00	11	6	5	663	38	0	3.44
1982-83	Boston	13	4	6	1	673	49	0	4.37							
1983-84	Boston	4	1	1	1	186	15	0	4.84							
	NHL Totals	**19**	**7**	**7**	**2**	**979**	**70**	**0**	**4.29**	**11**	**6**	**5**	**663**	**38**	**0**	**3.44**

MOOG, Andy

Goaltender. Catches left. 5'8", 175 lbs. Born, Penticton, B.C., February 18, 1960
(Edmonton's 6th choice, 132nd overall, in 1980 Entry Draft).

		REGULAR SEASON								PLAYOFFS						
Season	Club	GP	W	L	T	Mins	GA	SO	Avg	GP	W	L	Mins	GA	SO	Avg
1980-81	Edmonton	7	3	3	0	313	20	0	3.83	9	5	4	526	32	0	3.65
1981-82	Edmonton	8	3	5	0	399	32	0	4.81							
1982-83	Edmonton	50	33	8	7	2833	167	1	3.54	16	11	5	949	48	0	3.03
1983-84♦	Edmonton	38	27	8	1	2212	139	1	3.77	7	4	0	263	12	0	2.74
1984-85♦	Edmonton	39	22	9	3	2019	111	1	3.30	2	0	0	20	0	0	0.00
1985-86	Edmonton	47	27	9	7	2664	164	1	3.69	1	1	0	60	1	0	1.00
1986-87♦	Edmonton	46	28	11	3	2461	144	0	3.51	2	2	0	120	8	0	4.00
1987-88	Boston	6	4	2	0	360	17	1	2.83	7	1	4	354	25	0	4.24
1988-89	Boston	41	18	14	8	2482	133	1	3.22	6	4	2	359	14	0	2.34
1989-90	Boston	46	24	10	7	2536	122	3	2.89	20	13	7	1195	44	*2	*2.21
1990-91	Boston	51	25	13	9	2844	136	4	2.87	19	10	9	1133	60	0	3.18
1991-92	Boston	62	28	22	9	3640	196	1	3.23	15	8	7	866	46	1	3.19
1992-93	Boston	55	37	14	3	3194	168	3	3.16	3	0	3	161	14	0	5.22
1993-94	Dallas	55	24	20	7	3121	170	2	3.27	4	1	3	246	12	0	2.93
1994-95	Dallas	31	10	12	7	1770	72	2	2.44	5	1	4	277	16	0	3.47
1995-96	Dallas	41	13	19	7	2228	111	1	2.99							
1996-97	Dallas	48	28	13	5	2738	98	3	2.15	7	3	4	449	21	0	2.81
1997-98	Montreal	42	18	17	5	2337	97	3	2.49	9	4	5	474	24	1	3.04
	NHL Totals	**713**	**372**	**209**	**88**	**40151**	**2097**	**28**	**3.13**	**132**	**68**	**57**	**7452**	**377**	**4**	**3.04**

Shared William Jennings Trophy with Reggie Lemelin (1990)
Played in NHL All-Star Game (1985, 1986, 1991, 1997)
• Statistics for suspended game vs. Edmonton on May 24, 1988 are included in playoff record.
Traded to **Boston** by **Edmonton** for Geoff Courtnall, Bill Ranford and Boston's 2nd round choice (Petro Koivunen) in 1988 Entry Draft, March 8, 1988. Traded to **Dallas** by **Boston** for Jon Casey to complete transaction that sent Gord Murphy to Dallas (June 20, 1993), June 25, 1993. Signed as a free agent by **Montreal**, July 17, 1997.

MOORE, Alfie

Goaltender. Catches right. 5'11", 155 lbs. Born, Toronto, Ont., December 1, 1905

		REGULAR SEASON								PLAYOFFS						
Season	Club	GP	W	L	T	Mins	GA	SO	Avg	GP	W	L	Mins	GA	SO	Avg
1936-37	NY Americans	18	7	11	0	1110	64	1	3.46							
1937-38♦	Chicago									1	1	0	60	1	0	1.00
1938-39	NY Americans	2	0	2	0	120	14	0	7.00	2	0	2	120	6	0	3.00
1939-40	Detroit	1	0	1	0	60	3	0	3.00							
	NHL Totals	**21**	**7**	**14**	**0**	**1290**	**81**	**1**	**3.77**	**3**	**1**	**2**	**180**	**7**	**0**	**2.33**

Claimed by **NY Rangers** from **Cleveland** (IHL) in Inter-League Draft, April 15, 1930. Loaned to **Springfield** (Can-Am) by **NY Rangers** for cash, October, 1930. Traded to **Cleveland** (IHL) by **NY Rangers** after Springfield (Can-Am) folded, December 18, 1932. Signed as a free agent by **New Haven** (Can-Am), October, 1933. Traded to **NY Americans** by **New Haven** (IAHL) for Lloyd Jackson and cash, November, 1936. • Recorded a shutout (4-0) in NHL debut vs. Montreal , January 30, 1937. Loaned to **Chicago** by **NY Americans** (Pittsburgh-IAHL) to replace injured Mike Karakas for game one of Stanley Cup Finals, April 5, 1938 (Chicago 3, Toronto 1). Traded to **Detroit** by **NY Americans** for cash, November 7, 1939. Promoted to **Detroit** by **Indianapolis** (IAHL) to replace injured Tiny Thompson, January 9, 1940. (Boston 3, Detroit 1).

MOORE, Robbie

Goaltender. Catches right. 5'5", 155 lbs. Born, Sarnia, Ont., May 3, 1954

		REGULAR SEASON								PLAYOFFS						
Season	Club	GP	W	L	T	Mins	GA	SO	Avg	GP	W	L	Mins	GA	SO	Avg
1978-79	Philadelphia	5	3	0	1	237	7	2	1.77	5	3	2	268	18	0	4.03
1982-83	Washington	1	0	1	0	20	1	0	3.00							
	NHL Totals	**6**	**3**	**1**	**1**	**257**	**8**	**2**	**1.87**	**5**	**3**	**2**	**268**	**18**	**0**	**4.03**

Signed as a free agent by **Philadelphia**, November 7, 1978. • Recorded a shutout (5-0) in NHL debut vs. Colorado, March 6, 1979. Signed as a free agent by **Minnesota**, July 27, 1981. Traded to **Washington** by **Minnesota** with Minnesota's 11th round choice (Anders Huss) in 1983 Entry Draft for Wes Jarvis and Rollie Boutin, August 4, 1982.

MORISSETTE, Jean-Guy

Goaltender. Catches left. 5'8", 140 lbs. Born, Causapscal, N.B., December 16, 1937

		REGULAR SEASON								PLAYOFFS						
Season	Club	GP	W	L	T	Mins	GA	SO	Avg	GP	W	L	Mins	GA	SO	Avg
1963-64	Montreal	1	0	1	0	36	4	0	6.67							
	NHL Totals	**1**	**0**	**1**	**0**	**36**	**4**	**0**	**6.67**							

• **Montreal's** spare goaltender replaced injured Gump Worsley in 2nd period, October 30, 1963. (Toronto 6, Montreal 3). • Missed majority of 1963-64 season recovering from broken cheekbone suffered in practice, October 31, 1963. Loaned to **NY Rangers** by **Montreal** for remainder of 1964-65 season with the trade of Bill Hicke for Dick Duff and Dave McComb, December 22, 1964. Claimed by **Hershey** (AHL) from **Montreal** in Reverse Draft, June 15, 1966.

MOSS, Tyler

Goaltender. Catches right. 6', 185 lbs. Born, Ottawa, Ont., June 29, 1975
(Tampa Bay's 2nd choice, 29th overall, in 1993 Entry Draft).

		REGULAR SEASON								PLAYOFFS						
Season	Club	GP	W	L	T	Mins	GA	SO	Avg	GP	W	L	Mins	GA	SO	Avg
1997-98	Calgary	6	2	3	1	367	20	0	3.27							
1998-99	Calgary	11	3	7	0	550	23	0	2.51							
2000-01	Carolina	12	1	6	0	557	37	0	3.99							
2002-03	Vancouver	1	0	0	0	22	1	0	2.73							
	NHL Totals	**30**	**6**	**16**	**1**	**1496**	**81**	**0**	**3.25**							

Traded to **Calgary** by **Tampa Bay** for Jamie Huscroft, March 18, 1997. Traded to **Pittsburgh** by **Calgary** with Rene Corbet for Brad Werenka, March 14, 2000. Signed as a free agent by **Carolina**, August 9, 2000. Signed as a free agent by **Vancouver**, July 5, 2002.

MOWERS, Johnny

Goaltender. Catches left. 5'11", 185 lbs. Born, Niagara Falls, Ont., October 29, 1916

		REGULAR SEASON								PLAYOFFS						
Season	Club	GP	W	L	T	Mins	GA	SO	Avg	GP	W	L	Mins	GA	SO	Avg
1940-41	Detroit	*48	21	16	11	*3040	102	4	2.01	9	4	5	561	20	0	2.14
1941-42	Detroit	47	19	25	3	2880	144	5	3.00	12	7	5	720	38	0	3.17
1942-43♦	Detroit	*50	*25	14	11	3010	124	*6	*2.47	*10	*8	2	*679	22	*2	*1.94
1946-47	Detroit	7	0	6	1	420	29	0	4.14	1	0	1	40	5	0	7.50
	NHL Totals	**152**	**65**	**61**	**26**	**9350**	**399**	**15**	**2.56**	**32**	**19**	**13**	**2000**	**85**	**2**	**2.55**

NHL First All-Star Team (1943) • Vezina Trophy (1943)
Signed as a free agent by **Detroit**, October 2, 1939.

MRAZEK, Jerome

Goaltender. Catches left. 5'9", 160 lbs. Born, Prince Albert, Sask., October 15, 1951
(Philadelphia's 8th choice, 106th overall, in 1971 Amateur Draft).

		REGULAR SEASON								PLAYOFFS						
Season	Club	GP	W	L	T	Mins	GA	SO	Avg	GP	W	L	Mins	GA	SO	Avg
1975-76	Philadelphia	1	0	0	0	6	1	0	10.00							
	NHL Totals	**1**	**0**	**0**	**0**	**6**	**1**	**0**	**10.00**							

MURPHY, Hal

Goaltender. Catches right. 5'9", 140 lbs. Born, Montreal, Que., July 6, 1927

		REGULAR SEASON								PLAYOFFS						
Season	Club	GP	W	L	T	Mins	GA	SO	Avg	GP	W	L	Mins	GA	SO	Avg
1952-53	Montreal	1	1	0	0	60	4	0	4.00							
	NHL Totals	**1**	**1**	**0**	**0**	**60**	**4**	**0**	**4.00**							

Promoted to **Montreal** from **Mtl. Royals** (QMHL) to replace injured Gerry McNeil, November 8, 1952. (Montreal 6, Chicago 4)

MURRAY, Mickey

Goaltender. Catches right. 5'10", 168 lbs. Born, Peterborough, Ont., October 14, 1898

		REGULAR SEASON								PLAYOFFS						
Season	Club	GP	W	L	T	Mins	GA	SO	Avg	GP	W	L	Mins	GA	SO	Avg
1929-30	Montreal	1	0	1	0	60	4	0	4.00							
	NHL Totals	**1**	**0**	**1**	**0**	**60**	**4**	**0**	**4.00**							

Promoted to **Montreal** from **Providence** (Can-Am) to replace injured George Hainsworth, February 25, 1930. (NY Americans 4, Montreal 2)

MUZZATTI, Jason

Goaltender. Catches left. 6'2", 210 lbs. Born, Toronto, Ont., February 3, 1970
(Calgary's 1st choice, 21st overall, in 1988 Entry Draft).

		REGULAR SEASON								PLAYOFFS						
Season	Club	GP	W	L	T	Mins	GA	SO	Avg	GP	W	L	Mins	GA	SO	Avg
1993-94	Calgary	1	0	1	0	60	8	0	8.00							
1994-95	Calgary	1	0	0	0	10	0	0	0.00							
1995-96	Hartford	22	4	8	3	1013	49	1	2.90							
1996-97	Hartford	31	9	13	5	1591	91	0	3.43							
1997-98	NY Rangers	6	0	3	2	313	17	0	3.26							
	San Jose	1	0	0	0	27	2	0	4.44							
	NHL Totals	**62**	**13**	**25**	**10**	**3014**	**167**	**1**	**3.32**							

Claimed on waivers by **Hartford** from **Calgary**, October 6, 1995. Transferred to **Carolina** after **Hartford** franchise relocated, June 25, 1997. Traded to **NY Rangers** by **Carolina** for NY Rangers' 4th round choice (Tommy Westlund) in 1998 Entry Draft, August 8, 1997. Traded to **San Jose** by **NY Rangers** for Rich Brennan, March 24, 1998.

MYLLYS, Jarmo

Goaltender. Catches left. 5'8", 160 lbs. Born, Savonlinna, Finland, May 29, 1965
(Minnesota's 9th choice, 172nd overall, in 1987 Entry Draft).

		REGULAR SEASON								PLAYOFFS						
Season	Club	GP	W	L	T	Mins	GA	SO	Avg	GP	W	L	Mins	GA	SO	Avg
1988-89	Minnesota	6	1	4	0	238	22	0	5.55							
1989-90	Minnesota	4	0	3	0	156	16	0	6.15							
1990-91	Minnesota	2	0	2	0	78	8	0	6.15							
1991-92	San Jose	27	3	18	1	1374	115	0	5.02							
	NHL Totals	**39**	**4**	**27**	**1**	**1846**	**161**	**0**	**5.23**							

Claimed by **San Jose** from **Minnesota** in Dispersal Draft, May 30, 1991. Traded to **Toronto** by **San Jose** for cash, June 15, 1992.

MYLNIKOV, Sergei

Goaltender. Catches left. 5'10", 176 lbs. Born, Chelyabinsk, USSR, October 6, 1958
(Quebec's 9th choice, 127th overall, in 1989 Entry Draft).

		REGULAR SEASON								PLAYOFFS						
Season	Club	GP	W	L	T	Mins	GA	SO	Avg	GP	W	L	Mins	GA	SO	Avg
1989-90	Quebec	10	1	7	2	568	47	0	4.96							
	NHL Totals	**10**	**1**	**7**	**2**	**568**	**47**	**0**	**4.96**							

MYRE, Phil

Goaltender. Catches left. 6'1", 185 lbs. Born, Ste-Anne-de-Bellevue, Que., November 1, 1948
(Montreal's 1st choice, 5th overall, in 1966 Amateur Draft).

		REGULAR SEASON								PLAYOFFS						
Season	Club	GP	W	L	T	Mins	GA	SO	Avg	GP	W	L	Mins	GA	SO	Avg
1969-70	Montreal	10	4	3	2	503	19	0	2.27							
1970-71♦	Montreal	30	13	11	4	1677	87	1	3.11							
1971-72	Montreal	9	4	5	0	528	32	0	3.64							
1972-73	Atlanta	46	16	23	5	2736	138	2	3.03							
1973-74	Atlanta	36	11	16	6	2020	112	0	3.33	3	0	3	186	13	0	4.19
1974-75	Atlanta	40	14	16	10	2400	114	5	2.85							
1975-76	Atlanta	37	16	16	4	2129	123	1	3.47							

Season	Club	GP	W	L	T	Mins	GA	SO	Avg	GP	W	L	Mins	GA	SO	Avg
		REGULAR SEASON								PLAYOFFS						
1976-77	Atlanta	43	17	17	7	2422	124	3	3.07	2	1	1	120	5	0	2.50
1977-78	Atlanta	9	2	7	0	523	43	0	4.93	....	....	....	....	....	....	....
	St. Louis	44	11	25	8	2620	159	1	3.64	....	....	....	....	....	....	....
1978-79	St. Louis	39	9	22	8	2259	163	1	4.33	....	....	....	....	....	....	....
1979-80	Philadelphia	41	18	7	15	2367	141	0	3.57	6	5	1	384	16	1	2.50
1980-81	Philadelphia	16	6	5	4	900	61	0	4.07	....	....	....	....	....	....	....
	Colorado	10	3	6	1	580	33	0	3.41	....	....	....	....	....	....	....
1981-82	Colorado	24	2	17	2	1256	112	0	5.35	....	....	....	....	....	....	....
1982-83	Buffalo	5	3	2	0	300	21	0	4.20	1	0	0	57	7	0	7.37
	NHL Totals	**439**	**149**	**198**	**76**	**25220**	**1482**	**14**	**3.53**	**12**	**6**	**5**	**747**	**41**	**1**	**3.29**

Claimed by **Atlanta** from **Montreal** in Expansion Draft, June 6, 1972. Traded to **St. Louis** by **Atlanta** with Curt Bennett and Barry Gibbs for Yves Belanger, Dick Redmond, Bob MacMillan and St. Louis' 2nd round choice (Mike Perovich) in 1979 Entry Draft, December 12, 1977. Traded to **Philadelphia** by **St. Louis** for Blake Dunlop and Rick Lapointe, June 7, 1979. Traded to **Colorado** by **Philadelphia** for cash, February 26, 1981. Signed as a free agent by **Buffalo**, September 11, 1982.

NABOKOV, Evgeni

Goaltender. Catches left. 6', 200 lbs. Born, Ust-Kamenogorsk, USSR, July 25, 1975
(San Jose's 9th choice, 219th overall, in 1994 Entry Draft).

Season	Club	GP	W	L	T	Mins	GA	SO	Avg	GP	W	L	Mins	GA	SO	Avg
99-2000	San Jose	11	2	2	1	414	15	1	2.17	1	0	0	20	0	0	0.00
2000-01	San Jose	66	32	21	7	3700	135	6	2.19	4	1	3	218	10	1	2.75
2001-02	San Jose	67	37	24	5	3901	149	7	2.29	12	7	5	712	31	0	2.61
2002-03	San Jose	55	19	28	8	3227	146	3	2.71	....	....	....	....	....	....	....
	NHL Totals	**199**	**90**	**75**	**21**	**11242**	**445**	**17**	**2.38**	**17**	**8**	**8**	**950**	**41**	**1**	**2.59**

NHL All-Rookie Team (2001) • Calder Memorial Trophy (2001)

Played in NHL All-Star Game (2001)

• Scored a goal vs. Vancouver, March 10, 2002.

NAUMENKO, Gregg

Goaltender. Catches left. 6'1", 201 lbs. Born, Chicago, IL, March 30, 1977

Season	Club	GP	W	L	T	Mins	GA	SO	Avg	GP	W	L	Mins	GA	SO	Avg
2000-01	Anaheim	2	0	1	0	70	7	0	6.00	....	....	....	....	....	....	....
	NHL Totals	**2**	**0**	**1**	**0**	**70**	**7**	**0**	**6.00**	....	....	....	....	....	....	....

Signed as a free agent by **Anaheim**, March 31, 1999.

NEWTON, Cam

Goaltender. Catches left. 5'11", 170 lbs. Born, Peterborough, Ont., February 25, 1950
(Pittsburgh's 8th choice, 102nd overall, in 1970 Amateur Draft).

Season	Club	GP	W	L	T	Mins	GA	SO	Avg	GP	W	L	Mins	GA	SO	Avg
1970-71	Pittsburgh	5	1	3	1	281	16	0	3.42	....	....	....	....	....	....	....
1972-73	Pittsburgh	11	3	4	0	533	35	0	3.94	....	....	....	....	....	....	....
	NHL Totals	**16**	**4**	**7**	**1**	**814**	**51**	**0**	**3.76**	....	....	....	....	....	....	....

NORONEN, Mika

Goaltender. Catches left. 6'2", 196 lbs. Born, Tampere, Finland, June 17, 1979
(Buffalo's 1st choice, 21st overall, in 1997 Entry Draft).

Season	Club	GP	W	L	T	Mins	GA	SO	Avg	GP	W	L	Mins	GA	SO	Avg
2000-01	Buffalo	2	2	0	0	108	5	0	2.78	....	....	....	....	....	....	....
2001-02	Buffalo	10	4	3	1	518	23	0	2.66	....	....	....	....	....	....	....
2002-03	Buffalo	16	4	9	3	891	36	1	2.42	....	....	....	....	....	....	....
	NHL Totals	**28**	**10**	**12**	**4**	**1517**	**64**	**1**	**2.53**	....	....	....	....	....	....	....

NORRIS, Jack

Goaltender. Catches left. 5'10", 185 lbs. Born, Saskatoon, Sask., August 5, 1942

Season	Club	GP	W	L	T	Mins	GA	SO	Avg	GP	W	L	Mins	GA	SO	Avg
1964-65	Boston	23	10	11	2	1380	85	1	3.70	....	....	....	....	....	....	....
1967-68	Chicago	7	2	3	0	334	22	1	3.95	....	....	....	....	....	....	....
1968-69	Chicago	3	1	0	0	100	10	0	6.00	....	....	....	....	....	....	....
1970-71	Los Angeles	25	7	11	2	1305	85	0	3.91	....	....	....	....	....	....	....
	NHL Totals	**58**	**20**	**25**	**4**	**3119**	**202**	**2**	**3.89**	....	....	....	....	....	....	....

Promoted to **Boston** from **Los Angeles** (WHL) after Eddie Johnston suffered hand injury in game vs. Toronto, January 30, 1965. Traded to **Chicago** by **Boston** with Gilles Marotte and Pit Martin for Phil Esposito, Ken Hodge and Fred Stanfield, May 15, 1967. Claimed by **Montreal** from **Chicago** in Intra-League Draft, June 11, 1969. Traded to **Los Angeles** by **Montreal** with Larry Mickey and Lucien Grenier for Leon Rochefort, Gregg Boddy and Wayne Thomas, May 22, 1970. Claimed by **Seattle** (WHL) from **Los Angeles** in Reverse Draft, June, 1971.

NURMINEN, Pasi

Goaltender. Catches left. 5'10", 190 lbs. Born, Lahti, Finland, December 17, 1975
(Atlanta's 6th choice, 189th overall, in 2001 Entry Draft).

Season	Club	GP	W	L	T	Mins	GA	SO	Avg	GP	W	L	Mins	GA	SO	Avg
2001-02	Atlanta	9	2	5	0	465	28	0	3.61	....	....	....	....	....	....	....
2002-03	Atlanta	52	21	19	5	2856	137	2	2.88	....	....	....	....	....	....	....
	NHL Totals	**61**	**23**	**24**	**5**	**3321**	**165**	**2**	**2.98**	....	....	....	....	....	....	....

OLESCHUK, Bill

Goaltender. Catches left. 6'3", 194 lbs. Born, Edmonton, Alta., July 20, 1955
(Kansas City's 7th choice, 110th overall, in 1975 Amateur Draft).

Season	Club	GP	W	L	T	Mins	GA	SO	Avg	GP	W	L	Mins	GA	SO	Avg
1975-76	Kansas City	1	0	1	0	60	4	0	4.00	....	....	....	....	....	....	....
1977-78	Colorado	2	0	2	0	100	9	0	5.40	....	....	....	....	....	....	....
1978-79	Colorado	40	6	19	8	2118	136	1	3.85	....	....	....	....	....	....	....
1979-80	Colorado	12	1	6	2	557	39	0	4.20	....	....	....	....	....	....	....
	NHL Totals	**55**	**7**	**28**	**10**	**2835**	**188**	**1**	**3.98**	....	....	....	....	....	....	....

Transferred to **Colorado** after **Kansas City** franchise relocated, July 15, 1976.

Season	Club	GP	W	L	T	Mins	GA	SO	Avg	GP	W	L	Mins	GA	SO	Avg
		REGULAR SEASON								PLAYOFFS						

OLESEVICH, Dan

Goaltender. Catches left. 6', 170 lbs. Born, Port Colborne, Ont., September 16, 1937

Season	Club	GP	W	L	T	Mins	GA	SO	Avg	GP	W	L	Mins	GA	SO	Avg
1961-62	NY Rangers	1	0	0	1	29	2	0	4.14	....	....	....	....	....	....	....
	NHL Totals	**1**	**0**	**0**	**1**	**29**	**2**	**0**	**4.14**	....	....	....	....	....	....	....

Loaned to **NY Rangers** by **Detroit** to replace injured Gump Worsley in 2nd period, October 21, 1961. (NY Rangers 4, Detroit 4)

O'NEILL, Mike

Goaltender. Catches left. 5'7", 155 lbs. Born, LaSalle, Que., November 3, 1967
(Winnipeg's 1st choice, 15th overall, in 1988 Supplemental Draft).

Season	Club	GP	W	L	T	Mins	GA	SO	Avg	GP	W	L	Mins	GA	SO	Avg
1991-92	Winnipeg	1	0	0	0	13	1	0	4.62	....	....	....	....	....	....	....
1992-93	Winnipeg	2	0	0	1	73	6	0	4.93	....	....	....	....	....	....	....
1993-94	Winnipeg	17	0	9	1	738	51	0	4.15	....	....	....	....	....	....	....
1996-97	Anaheim	1	0	0	0	31	3	0	5.81	....	....	....	....	....	....	....
	NHL Totals	**21**	**0**	**9**	**2**	**855**	**61**	**0**	**4.28**	....	....	....	....	....	....	....

Signed as a free agent by **Anaheim**, July 14, 1995. Signed as a free agent by **Washington**, August 20, 1997. Signed as a free agent by **Los Angeles**, July 21, 1999.

OSGOOD, Chris

Goaltender. Catches left. 5'10", 175 lbs. Born, Peace River, Alta., November 26, 1972
(Detroit's 3rd choice, 54th overall, in 1991 Entry Draft).

Season	Club	GP	W	L	T	Mins	GA	SO	Avg	GP	W	L	Mins	GA	SO	Avg
1993-94	Detroit	41	23	8	5	2206	105	2	2.86	6	3	2	307	12	1	2.35
1994-95	Detroit	19	14	5	0	1087	41	1	2.26	2	0	0	68	2	0	1.76
1995-96	Detroit	50	*39	6	5	2933	106	5	2.17	15	8	7	936	33	2	2.12
1996-97♦	Detroit	47	23	13	9	2769	106	6	2.30	2	0	0	47	2	0	2.55
1997-98♦	Detroit	64	33	20	11	3807	140	6	2.21	*22	*16	6	*1361	48	2	2.12
1998-99	Detroit	63	34	25	4	3691	149	3	2.42	6	4	2	358	14	1	2.35
99-2000	Detroit	53	30	14	8	3148	126	6	2.40	9	5	4	547	18	2	1.97
2000-01	Detroit	52	25	19	4	2834	127	1	2.69	6	2	4	365	15	1	2.47
2001-02	NY Islanders	66	32	25	6	3743	156	4	2.50	7	3	4	392	17	0	2.60
2002-03	NY Islanders	37	17	14	4	1993	97	2	2.92	....	....	....	....	....	....	....
	St. Louis	9	4	3	2	532	27	2	3.05	7	3	4	417	17	1	2.45
	NHL Totals	**501**	**274**	**152**	**58**	**28743**	**1180**	**38**	**2.46**	**82**	**44**	**33**	**4798**	**178**	**10**	**2.23**

NHL Second All-Star Team (1996) • Shared William M. Jennings Trophy with Mike Vernon (1996)

Played in NHL All-Star Game (1996, 1997, 1998)

• Scored a goal vs. Hartford, March 6, 1996. Claimed by **NY Islanders** from **Detroit** in Waiver Draft, September 28, 2001. Traded to **St. Louis** by **NY Islanders** with NY Islanders' 3rd round choice (Konstantin Barulin) in 2003 Entry Draft for Justin Papineau and St. Louis' 2nd round choice (Jeremy Colliton) in 2003 Entry Draft, March 11, 2003.

OUELLET, Maxime

Goaltender. Catches left. 6'2", 195 lbs. Born, Beauport, Que., June 17, 1981
(Philadelphia's 1st choice, 22nd overall, in 1999 Entry Draft).

Season	Club	GP	W	L	T	Mins	GA	SO	Avg	GP	W	L	Mins	GA	SO	Avg
2000-01	Philadelphia	2	0	1	0	76	3	0	2.37	....	....	....	....	....	....	....
	NHL Totals	**2**	**0**	**1**	**0**	**76**	**3**	**0**	**2.37**	....	....	....	....	....	....	....

Traded to **Washington** by **Philadelphia** with Philadelphia's 1st (later traded to Dallas – Dallas selected Martin Vagner), 2nd (Maxime Daigneault) and 3rd (Derek Krestanovich) round choices in 2002 Entry Draft for Adam Oates, March 19, 2002.

OUIMET, Ted

Goaltender. 5'9", 165 lbs. Born, Noranda, Que., July 6, 1947

Season	Club	GP	W	L	T	Mins	GA	SO	Avg	GP	W	L	Mins	GA	SO	Avg
1968-69	St. Louis	1	0	1	0	60	2	0	2.00	....	....	....	....	....	....	....
	NHL Totals	**1**	**0**	**1**	**0**	**60**	**2**	**0**	**2.00**	....	....	....	....	....	....	....

Traded to **St. Louis** by **Montreal** for cash, June 11, 1968.

PAGEAU, Paul

Goaltender. Catches right. 5'9", 160 lbs. Born, Montreal, Que., October 1, 1959

Season	Club	GP	W	L	T	Mins	GA	SO	Avg	GP	W	L	Mins	GA	SO	Avg
1980-81	Los Angeles	1	0	1	0	60	8	0	8.00	....	....	....	....	....	....	....
	NHL Totals	**1**	**0**	**1**	**0**	**60**	**8**	**0**	**8.00**	....	....	....	....	....	....	....

QMJHL First All-Star Team (1980)

Signed as a free agent by **Los Angeles**, May 6, 1980.

PAILLE, Marcel

Goaltender. Catches left. 5'8", 175 lbs. Born, Shawinigan Falls, Que., December 8, 1932

Season	Club	GP	W	L	T	Mins	GA	SO	Avg	GP	W	L	Mins	GA	SO	Avg
1957-58	NY Rangers	33	11	15	7	1980	102	1	3.09	....	....	....	....	....	....	....
1958-59	NY Rangers	1	0	0	1	60	4	0	4.00	....	....	....	....	....	....	....
1959-60	NY Rangers	17	6	9	2	1020	67	1	3.94	....	....	....	....	....	....	....
1960-61	NY Rangers	4	1	2	1	240	16	0	4.00	....	....	....	....	....	....	....
1961-62	NY Rangers	10	4	4	2	600	28	0	2.80	....	....	....	....	....	....	....
1962-63	NY Rangers	3	0	1	2	180	10	0	3.33	....	....	....	....	....	....	....
1964-65	NY Rangers	39	10	21	7	2262	135	0	3.58	....	....	....	....	....	....	....
	NHL Totals	**107**	**32**	**52**	**22**	**6342**	**362**	**2**	**3.42**	....	....	....	....	....	....	....

Claimed by **NY Rangers** from **Chicoutimi** (QHL) in Inter-League Draft, June 5, 1956. • Recorded a shutout (5-0) in NHL debut vs. Boston, November 2, 1957. Traded to **Providence** (AHL) by **NY Rangers** with Aldo Guidolin, Sandy McGregor and Jim Mikol for Ed Giacomin, May 18, 1965. • McGregor refused to report and was replaced with Buzz Deschamps.

PALMATEER, Mike

Goaltender. Catches right. 5'9", 170 lbs. Born, Toronto, Ont., January 13, 1954
(Toronto's 5th choice, 85th overall, in 1974 Amateur Draft).

Season	Club	GP	W	L	T	Mins	GA	SO	Avg	GP	W	L	Mins	GA	SO	Avg
1976-77	Toronto	50	23	18	8	2877	154	4	3.21	6	3	3	360	16	0	2.67
1977-78	Toronto	63	34	19	9	3760	172	5	2.74	13	6	7	795	32	*2	2.42
1978-79	Toronto	58	26	21	10	3396	167	4	2.95	5	2	3	298	17	0	3.42
1979-80	Toronto	38	16	14	3	2039	125	2	3.68	1	0	1	60	7	0	7.00

Season	Club	GP	W	L	T	Mins	GA	SO	Avg	GP	W	L	Mins	GA	SO	Avg
		REGULAR SEASON								PLAYOFFS						
1980-81	Washington	49	18	19	9	2679	172	2	3.85							
1981-82	Washington	11	2	7	2	584	47	0	4.83							
1982-83	Toronto	53	21	23	7	2965	197	0	3.99	4	1	3	252	17	0	4.05
1983-84	Toronto	34	9	17	4	1831	149	0	4.88							
	NHL Totals	**356**	**149**	**138**	**52**	**20131**	**1183**	**17**	**3.53**	**29**	**12**	**17**	**1765**	**89**	**2**	**3.03**

Traded to **Washington** by **Toronto** with Toronto's 3rd round choice (Torrie Robertson) in 1980 Entry Draft for Robert Picard, Tim Coulis and Washington's 2nd round choice (Bob McGill) in 1980 Entry Draft, June 11, 1980. • Missed majority of 1981-82 season recovering from knee surgery, September, 1981. Traded to **Toronto** by **Washington** for cash, September 9, 1982.

PANG, Darren

Goaltender. Catches left. 5'5", 155 lbs. Born, Meaford, Ont., February 17, 1964

Season	Club	GP	W	L	T	Mins	GA	SO	Avg	GP	W	L	Mins	GA	SO	Avg
1984-85	Chicago	1	0	1	0	60	4	0	4.00							
1987-88	Chicago	45	17	23	1	2548	163	0	3.84	4	1	3	240	18	0	4.50
1988-89	Chicago	35	10	11	6	1644	120	0	4.38	2	0	0	10	0	0	0.00
	NHL Totals	**81**	**27**	**35**	**7**	**4252**	**287**	**0**	**4.05**	**6**	**1**	**3**	**250**	**18**	**0**	**4.32**

NHL All-Rookie Team (1988)

Signed as a free agent by **Chicago**, August 15, 1984.

PARENT, Bernie

HHOF

Goaltender. Catches left. 5'10", 180 lbs. Born, Montreal, Que., April 3, 1945

Season	Club	GP	W	L	T	Mins	GA	SO	Avg	GP	W	L	Mins	GA	SO	Avg
1965-66	Boston	39	11	20	3	2083	128	1	3.69							
1966-67	Boston	18	4	12	2	1022	62	0	3.64							
1967-68	Philadelphia	38	16	17	5	2248	93	4	2.48	5	2	3	355	8	0	*1.35
1968-69	Philadelphia	58	17	23	16	3365	151	1	2.69	3	0	3	180	12	0	4.00
1969-70	Philadelphia	62	13	29	20	3680	171	3	2.79							
1970-71	Philadelphia	30	9	12	6	1586	73	2	2.76							
	Toronto	18	7	7	3	1040	46	0	2.65	4	2	2	235	9	0	2.30
1971-72	Toronto	47	17	18	9	2715	116	3	2.56	4	1	3	243	13	0	3.21
1973-74♦	Philadelphia	*73	*47	13	12	*4314	136	*12	*1.89	*17	*12	5	*1042	35	*2	2.02
1974-75♦	Philadelphia	68	*44	14	10	4041	137	*12	*2.03	*15	*10	5	*922	29	*4	*1.89
1975-76	Philadelphia	11	6	2	3	615	24	0	2.34	8	4	4	480	27	0	3.38
1976-77	Philadelphia	61	35	13	12	3525	159	5	2.71	3	0	3	123	8	0	3.90
1977-78	Philadelphia	49	29	6	13	2923	108	*7	2.22	12	7	5	722	33	0	2.74
1978-79	Philadelphia	36	16	12	7	1979	89	4	2.70							
	NHL Totals	**608**	**271**	**198**	**121**	**35136**	**1493**	**54**	**2.55**	**71**	**38**	**33**	**4302**	**174**	**6**	**2.43**

NHL First All-Star Team (1974, 1975) • Vezina Trophy (tied with Tony Esposito) (1974) • Conn Smythe Trophy (1974, 1975) • Vezina Trophy (1975)

Played in NHL All-Star Game (1969, 1970, 1974, 1975, 1977)

Claimed by **Philadelphia** from **Boston** in Expansion Draft, June 6, 1967. Traded to **Toronto** by **Philadelphia** with Philadelphia's 2nd round choice (Rick Kehoe) in 1971 Amateur Draft for Bruce Gamble, Mike Walton and Toronto's 1st round choice (Pierre Plante) in 1971 Amateur Draft, February 1, 1971. Traded to **Philadelphia** by **Toronto** with Toronto's 2nd round choice (Larry Goodenough) in 1973 Amateur Draft for Philadelphia's 1st round choice (Bob Neely) in 1973 Amateur Draft and future considerations (Doug Favell, July 27, 1973), May 15, 1973. • Missed majority of 1975-76 season recovering from a back injury suffered during training camp, September, 1975. • Suffered career-ending eye injury in game vs. NY Rangers, February 17, 1979.

PARENT, Bob

Goaltender. Catches right. 5'9", 175 lbs. Born, Windsor, Ont., February 19, 1958
(Toronto's 3rd choice, 65th overall, in 1978 Amateur Draft).

Season	Club	GP	W	L	T	Mins	GA	SO	Avg	GP	W	L	Mins	GA	SO	Avg
1981-82	Toronto	2	0	2	0	120	13	0	6.50							
1982-83	Toronto	1	0	0	0	40	2	0	3.00							
	NHL Totals	**3**	**0**	**2**	**0**	**160**	**15**	**0**	**5.63**							

PARENT, Rich

Goaltender. Catches left. 6'3", 195 lbs. Born, Montreal, Que., January 12, 1973

Season	Club	GP	W	L	T	Mins	GA	SO	Avg	GP	W	L	Mins	GA	SO	Avg
1997-98	St. Louis	1	0	0	0	12	0	0	0.00							
1998-99	St. Louis	10	4	3	1	519	22	1	2.54							
99-2000	Tampa Bay	14	2	7	1	698	43	0	3.70							
2000-01	Pittsburgh	7	1	1	3	332	17	0	3.07							
	NHL Totals	**32**	**7**	**11**	**5**	**1561**	**82**	**1**	**3.15**							

Signed as a free agent by **St. Louis**, July 31, 1997. Traded to **Tampa Bay** by **St. Louis** with Chris McAlpine for Stephane Richer, January 13, 2000. Traded to **Ottawa** by **Tampa Bay** for Ottawa's 7th round choice (later traded to NY Islanders – later traded to Buffalo – Buffalo selected Paul Gaustad) in 2000 Entry Draft, June 4, 2000. Signed as a free agent by **Pittsburgh**, September 20, 2000.

PARRO, Dave

Goaltender. Catches left. 5'11", 165 lbs. Born, Saskatoon, Sask., April 30, 1957
(Boston's 2nd choice, 34th overall, in 1977 Amateur Draft).

Season	Club	GP	W	L	T	Mins	GA	SO	Avg	GP	W	L	Mins	GA	SO	Avg
1980-81	Washington	18	4	7	2	811	49	1	3.63							
1981-82	Washington	52	16	26	7	2942	206	1	4.20							
1982-83	Washington	6	1	3	1	261	19	0	4.37							
1983-84	Washington	1	0	0	0	1	0	0	0.00							
	NHL Totals	**77**	**21**	**36**	**10**	**4015**	**274**	**2**	**4.09**							

Claimed by **Quebec** from **Boston** in Expansion Draft, June 13, 1979. Traded to **Washington** by **Quebec** for Nelson Burton, June 15, 1979.

PASSMORE, Steve

Goaltender. Catches left. 5'9", 165 lbs. Born, Thunder Bay, Ont., January 29, 1973
(Quebec's 10th choice, 196th overall, in 1992 Entry Draft).

Season	Club	GP	W	L	T	Mins	GA	SO	Avg	GP	W	L	Mins	GA	SO	Avg
1998-99	Edmonton	6	1	4	1	362	17	0	2.82							
99-2000	Chicago	24	7	12	3	1388	63	1	2.72							
2000-01	Los Angeles	14	3	8	1	718	37	1	3.09							
	Chicago	6	0	4	1	340	14	0	2.47							
2001-02	Chicago	23	8	5	4	1142	43	0	2.26	3	0	2	138	6	0	2.61
2002-03	Chicago	11	2	5	2	617	38	0	3.70							
	NHL Totals	**84**	**21**	**38**	**12**	**4567**	**212**	**2**	**2.79**	**3**	**0**	**2**	**138**	**6**	**0**	**2.61**

Traded to **Edmonton** by **Quebec** for Brad Werenka, March 21, 1994. Signed as a free agent by **Chicago**, July 8, 1999. Traded to **Los Angeles** by **Chicago** for Los Angeles' 4th round choice (Olli Malmivaara) in 2000 Entry Draft, May 1, 2000. Traded to **Chicago** by **Los Angeles** for Chicago's 8th round choice (Mike Gabinet) in 2001 Entry Draft, February 28, 2001.

PEETERS, Pete

Goaltender. Catches left. 6'1", 195 lbs. Born, Edmonton, Alta., August 17, 1957
(Philadelphia's 9th choice, 135th overall, in 1977 Amateur Draft).

Season	Club	GP	W	L	T	Mins	GA	SO	Avg	GP	W	L	Mins	GA	SO	Avg
1978-79	Philadelphia	5	1	2	1	280	16	0	3.43							
1979-80	Philadelphia	40	29	5	5	2373	108	1	2.73	13	8	5	799	37	1	2.78
1980-81	Philadelphia	40	22	12	5	2333	115	2	2.96	3	2	1	180	12	0	4.00
1981-82	Philadelphia	44	23	18	3	2591	160	0	3.71	4	1	2	220	17	0	4.64
1982-83	Boston	62	*40	11	9	3611	142	*8	*2.36	*17	9	8	*1024	61	1	3.57
1983-84	Boston	50	29	16	2	2868	151	0	3.16	3	0	3	180	10	0	3.33
1984-85	Boston	51	19	26	4	2975	172	1	3.47	1	0	1	60	4	0	4.00
1985-86	Boston	8	3	4	1	485	31	0	3.84							
	Washington	34	19	11	3	2021	113	1	3.35	9	5	4	544	24	0	2.65
1986-87	Washington	37	17	11	4	2002	107	0	3.21	3	1	2	180	9	0	3.00
1987-88	Washington	35	14	12	5	1896	88	2	*2.78	12	7	5	654	34	0	3.12
1988-89	Washington	33	20	7	3	1854	88	4	2.85	6	2	4	359	24	0	4.01
1989-90	Philadelphia	24	1	13	5	1140	72	1	3.79							
1990-91	Philadelphia	26	9	7	1	1270	61	1	2.88							
	NHL Totals	**489**	**246**	**155**	**51**	**27699**	**1424**	**21**	**3.08**	**71**	**35**	**35**	**4200**	**232**	**2**	**3.31**

NHL First All-Star Team (1983) • Vezina Trophy (1983)

Played in NHL All-Star Game (1980, 1981, 1983, 1984)

Traded to **Boston** by **Philadelphia** for Brad McCrimmon, June 9, 1982. Traded to **Washington** by **Boston** for Pat Riggin, November 14, 1985. Signed as a free agent by **Philadelphia**, June 17, 1989. Traded to **Winnipeg** by **Philadelphia** with Keith Acton for future considerations, September 28, 1989. Traded to **Philadelphia** by **Winnipeg** with Keith Acton for Toronto's 5th round choice (previously acquired, Winnipeg selected Juha Ylonen) in 1991 Entry Draft and the cancellation of future considerations owed Philadelphia from the trade for Shawn Cronin (July 21, 1989), October 3, 1989.

PELLETIER, Jean-Marc

Goaltender. Catches left. 6'3", 200 lbs. Born, Atlanta, GA, March 4, 1978
(Philadelphia's 1st choice, 30th overall, in 1997 Entry Draft).

Season	Club	GP	W	L	T	Mins	GA	SO	Avg	GP	W	L	Mins	GA	SO	Avg
1998-99	Philadelphia	1	0	1	0	60	5	0	5.00							
2002-03	Phoenix	2	0	2	0	119	6	0	3.03							
	NHL Totals	**3**	**0**	**3**	**0**	**179**	**11**	**0**	**3.69**							

Traded to **Carolina** by **Philadelphia** with Rod Brind'Amour and Philadelphia's 2nd round choice (later traded to Colorado – Colorado selected Argis Saviels) in 2000 Entry Draft for Keith Primeau and Carolina's 5th round choice (later traded to NY Islanders – NY Islanders selected Kristofer Ottosson) in 2000 Entry Draft, January 23, 2000. Traded to **Phoenix** by **Carolina** with future considerations for Patrick DesRochers, December 31, 2002.

PELLETIER, Marcel

Goaltender. Catches right. 5'11", 180 lbs. Born, Drummondville, Que., December 6, 1927

Season	Club	GP	W	L	T	Mins	GA	SO	Avg	GP	W	L	Mins	GA	SO	Avg
1950-51	Chicago	6	1	5	0	355	29	0	4.90							
1962-63	NY Rangers	2	0	1	0	40	3	0	4.50							
	NHL Totals	**8**	**1**	**6**	**0**	**395**	**32**	**0**	**4.86**							

Loaned to **Chicago** by **Milwaukee** (USHL) to replace injured Harry Lumley, January, 1951. Signed as a free agent by **NY Rangers**, June, 1962.

PENNEY, Steve

Goaltender. Catches left. 6'1", 190 lbs. Born, Ste-Foy, Que., February 2, 1961
(Montreal's 10th choice, 166th overall, in 1980 Entry Draft).

Season	Club	GP	W	L	T	Mins	GA	SO	Avg	GP	W	L	Mins	GA	SO	Avg
1983-84	Montreal	4	0	4	0	240	19	0	4.75	15	9	6	871	32	*3	*2.20
1984-85	Montreal	54	26	18	8	3252	167	1	3.08	12	6	6	733	40	1	3.27
1985-86	Montreal	18	6	8	2	990	72	0	4.36							
1986-87	Winnipeg	7	1	4	1	327	25	0	4.59							
1987-88	Winnipeg	8	2	4	1	385	30	0	4.68							
	NHL Totals	**91**	**35**	**38**	**12**	**5194**	**313**	**1**	**3.62**	**27**	**15**	**12**	**1604**	**72**	**4**	**2.69**

NHL All-Rookie Team (1985)

Traded to **Winnipeg** by **Montreal** with the rights to Jan Ingman for Brian Hayward, August 19, 1986.

PERREAULT, Bob

Goaltender. Catches left. 5'8", 170 lbs. Born, Trois-Rivieres, Que., January 28, 1931

Season	Club	GP	W	L	T	Mins	GA	SO	Avg	GP	W	L	Mins	GA	SO	Avg
1955-56	Montreal	6	3	3	0	360	12	1	2.00							
1958-59	Detroit	3	2	1	0	180	9	1	3.00							
1962-63	Boston	22	3	12	7	1287	82	1	3.82							
	NHL Totals	**31**	**8**	**16**	**7**	**1827**	**103**	**3**	**3.38**							

Traded to **Montreal** by **Providence** (AHL) for George McAvoy and cash, June 11, 1953. Promoted to **Montreal** from **Shawinigan** (QHL) to replace injured Jacques Plante in games from December 17 through 28, 1955. • Recorded a shutout (5-0) in NHL debut vs. Chicago, December 17, 1955. Claimed by **Detroit** (Hershey-AHL) from **Montreal** (Shawinigan-QHL) in Inter-League Draft, June 4, 1957. Promoted to **Detroit** from **Hershey** (AHL) to replace injured Terry Sawchuk in games from January 21 through 25, 1959. Traded to **Boston** by **Detroit** (Hershey-AHL) for Ed Chadwick and Barry Ashbee, June, 1962. Traded to **San Francisco** (WHL) by **Boston** for $25,000, June 4, 1963. Claimed by **Toronto** (Victoria-WHL) from **Boston** in Reverse Draft, June 9, 1965.

PETTIE, Jim

Goaltender. Catches left. 6', 195 lbs. Born, Toronto, Ont., October 24, 1953
(Boston's 10th choice, 142nd overall, in 1973 Amateur Draft).

Season	Club	GP	W	L	T	Mins	GA	SO	Avg	GP	W	L	Mins	GA	SO	Avg
1976-77	Boston	1	1	0	0	60	3	0	3.00							
1977-78	Boston	1	0	1	0	60	6	0	6.00							

Season	Club	Regular Season GP	W	L	T	Mins	GA	SO	Avg	Playoffs GP	W	L	Mins	GA	SO	Avg
1978-79	Boston	19	8	6	2	1037	62	1	3.59	....	....	....	....	....	....	....
	NHL Totals	**21**	**9**	**7**	**2**	**1157**	**71**	**1**	**3.68**	....	....	....	....	....	....	....

PIETRANGELO, Frank

Goaltender. Catches left. 5'10", 185 lbs. Born, Niagara Falls, Ont., December 17, 1964
(Pittsburgh's 4th choice, 64th overall, in 1983 Entry Draft).

Season	Club	GP	W	L	T	Mins	GA	SO	Avg	GP	W	L	Mins	GA	SO	Avg
1987-88	Pittsburgh	21	9	11	0	1207	80	1	3.98	....	....	....	....	....	....	....
1988-89	Pittsburgh	15	5	3	0	669	45	0	4.04	....	....	....	....	....	....	....
1989-90	Pittsburgh	21	8	6	2	1066	77	0	4.33	....	....	....	....	....	....	....
1990-91◆	Pittsburgh	25	10	11	1	1311	86	0	3.94	5	4	1	288	15	*1	3.13
1991-92	Pittsburgh	5	2	1	0	225	20	0	5.33	....	....	....	....	....	....	....
	Hartford	5	3	1	1	306	12	0	2.35	7	3	4	425	19	0	2.68
1992-93	Hartford	30	4	15	1	1373	111	0	4.85	....	....	....	....	....	....	....
1993-94	Hartford	19	5	11	1	984	59	0	3.60	....	....	....	....	....	....	....
	NHL Totals	**141**	**46**	**59**	**6**	**7141**	**490**	**1**	**4.12**	**12**	**7**	**5**	**713**	**34**	**1**	**2.86**

Traded to **Hartford** by **Pittsburgh** for Hartford's 3rd (Sven Butenschon) and 7th (Serge Aubin) round choices in 1994 Entry Draft, March 10, 1992. Signed as a free agent by **NY Islanders**, July 28, 1994.

PLANTE, Jacques

HHOF

Goaltender. Catches left. 6', 175 lbs. Born, Shawinigan Falls, Que., January 17, 1929

Season	Club	GP	W	L	T	Mins	GA	SO	Avg	GP	W	L	Mins	GA	SO	Avg
1952-53◆	Montreal	3	2	0	1	180	4	0	1.33	4	3	1	240	7	1	*1.75
1953-54	Montreal	17	7	5	5	1020	27	5	1.59	8	5	3	480	15	*2	1.88
1954-55	Montreal	52	33	12	7	3080	110	5	2.14	*12	6	3	639	30	0	2.82
1955-56◆	Montreal	64	*42	12	10	3840	119	7	*1.86	*10	*8	2	600	18	*2	*1.80
1956-57◆	Montreal	61	31	18	12	3660	122	*9	*2.00	*10	*8	2	*616	17	1	*1.66
1957-58◆	Montreal	57	*34	14	8	3386	119	*9	*2.11	10	*8	2	618	20	*1	*1.94
1958-59◆	Montreal	67	*38	16	13	4000	144	*9	*2.16	11	*8	3	670	26	0	*2.33
1959-60◆	Montreal	69	*40	17	12	4140	175	3	*2.54	8	*8	0	489	11	*3	*1.35
1960-61	Montreal	40	23	11	6	2400	112	2	2.80	6	2	4	412	16	0	2.33
1961-62	Montreal	*70	*42	14	14	*4200	166	4	*2.37	6	2	4	360	19	0	3.17
1962-63	Montreal	56	22	14	19	3320	138	*5	*2.49	5	1	4	300	14	0	2.80
1963-64	NY Rangers	65	22	36	7	3900	220	3	3.38	....	....	....	....	....	....	....
1964-65	NY Rangers	33	10	17	5	1938	109	2	3.37	....	....	....	....	....	....	....
1968-69	St. Louis	37	18	12	6	2139	70	5	*1.96	*10	*8	2	*589	14	*3	1.43
1969-70	St. Louis	32	18	9	5	1839	67	5	2.19	6	4	1	324	8	*1	*1.48
1970-71	Toronto	40	24	11	4	2329	73	4	*1.88	3	0	2	134	7	0	3.13
1971-72	Toronto	34	16	13	5	1965	86	2	2.63	1	0	1	60	5	0	5.00
1972-73	Toronto	32	8	14	6	1717	87	1	3.04	....	....	....	....	....	....	....
	Boston	8	7	1	0	480	16	2	2.00	2	0	2	120	10	0	5.00
	NHL Totals	**837**	**437**	**246**	**145**	**49533**	**1964**	**82**	**2.38**	**112**	**71**	**36**	**6651**	**237**	**14**	**2.14**

NHL First All-Star Team (1956, 1959, 1962) • Vezina Trophy (1956, 1957, 1958, 1959, 1960, 1962) • NHL Second All-Star Team (1957, 1958, 1960, 1971) • Hart Trophy (1962) • Shared Vezina Trophy with Glenn Hall (1969)

Played in NHL All-Star Game (1956, 1957, 1958, 1959, 1960, 1962, 1969, 1970)

Signed to a three-game amateur tryout contract by **Montreal** and replaced injured Gerry McNeil in games from November 1 through 6, 1952. Signed as a free agent by **Montreal** (Buffalo-AHL), December 29, 1952. • Recorded a shutout (3-0) in NHL playoff debut at Chicago, April 4, 1953. Traded to **NY Rangers** by **Montreal** with Don Marshall and Phil Goyette for Gump Worsley, Dave Balon, Leon Rochefort and Len Ronson, June 4, 1963. • Signed to tryout contract by **California**, September, 1967. • Ordered to leave training camp when it was confirmed his rights were still property of **NY Rangers**, September, 1967. Claimed by **St. Louis** from **NY Rangers** in Intra-League Draft, June 12, 1968. Traded to **Toronto** by **St. Louis** for cash, May 18, 1970. Traded to **Boston** by **Toronto** with Toronto's 3rd round choice (Doug Gibson) in 1973 Amateur Draft for Boston's 1st round choice (Ian Turnbull) in 1973 Amateur Draft and future considerations (Eddie Johnston, May 22, 1973), March 3, 1973.

PLASSE, Michel

Goaltender. Catches left. 5'11", 172 lbs. Born, Montreal, Que., June 1, 1948
(Montreal's 1st choice, 1st overall, in 1968 Amateur Draft).

Season	Club	GP	W	L	T	Mins	GA	SO	Avg	GP	W	L	Mins	GA	SO	Avg
1970-71	St. Louis	1	1	0	0	60	3	0	3.00	....	....	....	....	....	....	....
1972-73◆	Montreal	17	11	2	3	932	40	0	2.58	....	....	....	....	....	....	....
1973-74	Montreal	15	7	4	2	839	57	0	4.08	....	....	....	....	....	....	....
1974-75	Kansas City	24	4	16	3	1420	96	0	4.06	....	....	....	....	....	....	....
	Pittsburgh	20	9	5	4	1094	73	0	4.00	....	....	....	....	....	....	....
1975-76	Pittsburgh	55	24	19	10	3096	178	2	3.45	3	1	2	180	8	1	2.67
1976-77	Colorado	54	12	29	10	2986	190	0	3.82	....	....	....	....	....	....	....
1977-78	Colorado	25	3	12	8	1383	90	0	3.90	....	....	....	....	....	....	....
1978-79	Colorado	41	9	29	2	2302	152	0	3.96	....	....	....	....	....	....	....
1979-80	Colorado	6	0	3	2	327	26	0	4.77	....	....	....	....	....	....	....
1980-81	Quebec	33	10	14	9	1933	118	0	3.66	1	0	0	15	1	0	4.00
1981-82	Quebec	8	2	3	1	388	35	0	5.41	....	....	....	....	....	....	....
	NHL Totals	**299**	**92**	**136**	**54**	**16760**	**1058**	**2**	**3.79**	**4**	**1**	**2**	**195**	**9**	**1**	**2.77**

Loaned to **Kansas City** (CHL) by **Montreal**, October 1, 1970. Traded to **St. Louis** by **Montreal** for cash, December 11, 1970. Traded to **Montreal** by **St. Louis** for cash, August 23, 1971. Claimed by **Kansas City** from **Montreal** in Expansion Draft, June 12, 1974. Traded to **Pittsburgh** by **Kansas City** for Denis Herron and Jean-Guy Lagace, January 10, 1975. Transferred to **Colorado** from **Pittsburgh** with Simon Nolet and the loan of Colin Campbell for the 1976-77 season (September 1, 1976) as compensation for Pittsburgh's signing of free agent Denis Herron, August 7, 1976. Signed as a free agent by **Quebec**, September 14, 1980. Traded to **Hartford** by **Quebec** with Quebec's 4th round choice (Ron Chyzowski) in 1983 Entry Draft for John Garrett, January 12, 1982.

POTVIN, Felix

Goaltender. Catches left. 6'1", 190 lbs. Born, Anjou, Que., June 23, 1971
(Toronto's 2nd choice, 31st overall, in 1990 Entry Draft).

Season	Club	GP	W	L	T	Mins	GA	SO	Avg	GP	W	L	Mins	GA	SO	Avg
1991-92	Toronto	4	0	2	1	210	8	0	2.29	....	....	....	....	....	....	....
1992-93	Toronto	48	25	15	7	2781	116	2	*2.50	*21	11	10	*1308	62	1	2.84
1993-94	Toronto	66	34	22	9	3883	187	3	2.89	18	9	9	1124	46	3	2.46
1994-95	Toronto	36	15	13	7	2144	104	0	2.91	7	3	4	424	20	1	2.83
1995-96	Toronto	69	30	26	11	4009	192	2	2.87	6	2	4	350	19	0	3.26
1996-97	Toronto	*74	27	36	7	*4271	224	0	3.15	....	....	....	....	....	....	....
1997-98	Toronto	67	26	33	7	3864	176	5	2.73	....	....	....	....	....	....	....
1998-99	Toronto	5	3	2	0	299	19	0	3.81	....	....	....	....	....	....	....
	NY Islanders	11	2	7	1	606	37	0	3.66	....	....	....	....	....	....	....
99-2000	NY Islanders	22	5	14	3	1273	68	1	3.21	....	....	....	....	....	....	....
	Vancouver	34	12	13	7	1966	85	0	2.59	....	....	....	....	....	....	....
2000-01	Vancouver	35	14	17	3	2006	103	1	3.08	....	....	....	....	....	....	....
	Los Angeles	23	13	5	5	1410	46	5	1.96	13	7	6	812	33	2	2.44
2001-02	Los Angeles	71	31	27	8	4071	157	6	2.31	7	3	4	417	15	1	2.16
2002-03	Los Angeles	42	17	20	3	2367	105	3	2.66	....	....	....	....	....	....	....
	NHL Totals	**607**	**254**	**252**	**79**	**35160**	**1627**	**28**	**2.78**	**72**	**35**	**37**	**4435**	**195**	**8**	**2.64**

NHL All-Rookie Team (1993)

Played in NHL All-Star Game (1994, 1996)

Traded to **NY Islanders** by **Toronto** with Toronto's 6th round choice (later traded to Tampa Bay – Tampa Bay selected Fedor Fedorov) in 1999 Entry Draft for Bryan Berard and NY Islanders' 6th round choice (Jan Sochor) in 1999 Entry Draft, January 9, 1999. Traded to **Vancouver** by **NY Islanders** with NY Islanders' compensatory 2nd round choice (later traded to New Jersey – New Jersey selected Teemu Laine) in 2000 Entry Draft and NY Islanders' 3rd round choice (Thatcher Bell) in 2000 Entry Draft for Kevin Weekes, Dave Scatchard and Bill Muckalt, December 19, 1999. Traded to **Los Angeles** by **Vancouver** for future considerations, February 15, 2001.

PRONOVOST, Claude

Goaltender. Catches left. 5'9", 190 lbs. Born, Shawinigan Falls, Que., July 22, 1935

Season	Club	GP	W	L	T	Mins	GA	SO	Avg	GP	W	L	Mins	GA	SO	Avg
1955-56	Boston	1	1	0	0	60	0	1	0.00	....	....	....	....	....	....	....
1958-59	Montreal	2	0	1	0	60	7	0	7.00	....	....	....	....	....	....	....
	NHL Totals	**3**	**1**	**1**	**0**	**120**	**7**	**1**	**3.50**	....	....	....	....	....	....	....

• Brother of Marcel and Jean

Loaned to **Boston** by **Montreal** (Mtl. Royals-QHL) to replace John Henderson, January 14, 1956. • Recorded shutout (2-0) in NHL debut vs. Montreal, January 14, 1956. Traded to **Chicago** by **Montreal** for cash, September 10, 1959.

PRUSEK, Martin

Goaltender. Catches left. 6'1", 176 lbs. Born, Ostrava, Czech., December 11, 1975
(Ottawa's 6th choice, 164th overall, in 1999 Entry Draft).

Season	Club	GP	W	L	T	Mins	GA	SO	Avg	GP	W	L	Mins	GA	SO	Avg
2001-02	Ottawa	1	0	1	0	62	3	0	2.90	....	....	....	....	....	....	....
2002-03	Ottawa	18	12	2	1	935	37	0	2.37	....	....	....	....	....	....	....
	NHL Totals	**19**	**12**	**3**	**1**	**997**	**40**	**0**	**2.41**	....	....	....	....	....	....	....

PUPPA, Daren

Goaltender. Catches right. 6'4", 205 lbs. Born, Kirkland Lake, Ont., March 23, 1965
(Buffalo's 6th choice, 76th overall, in 1983 Entry Draft).

Season	Club	GP	W	L	T	Mins	GA	SO	Avg	GP	W	L	Mins	GA	SO	Avg
1985-86	Buffalo	7	3	4	0	401	21	1	3.14	....	....	....	....	....	....	....
1986-87	Buffalo	3	0	2	1	185	13	0	4.22	....	....	....	....	....	....	....
1987-88	Buffalo	17	8	6	1	874	61	0	4.19	3	1	1	142	11	0	4.65
1988-89	Buffalo	37	17	10	6	1908	107	1	3.36	....	....	....	....	....	....	....
1989-90	Buffalo	56	*31	16	6	3241	156	1	2.89	6	2	4	370	15	0	2.43
1990-91	Buffalo	38	15	11	6	2092	118	2	3.38	2	0	1	81	10	0	7.41
1991-92	Buffalo	33	11	14	4	1757	114	0	3.89	....	....	....	....	....	....	....
1992-93	Buffalo	24	11	5	4	1306	78	0	3.58	....	....	....	....	....	....	....
	Toronto	8	6	2	0	479	18	2	2.25	1	0	0	20	1	0	3.00
1993-94	Tampa Bay	63	22	33	6	3653	165	4	2.71	....	....	....	....	....	....	....
1994-95	Tampa Bay	36	14	19	2	2013	90	1	2.68	....	....	....	....	....	....	....
1995-96	Tampa Bay	57	29	16	9	3189	131	5	2.46	4	1	3	173	14	0	4.86
1996-97	Tampa Bay	6	1	1	2	325	14	0	2.58	....	....	....	....	....	....	....
1997-98	Tampa Bay	26	5	14	6	1456	66	0	2.72	....	....	....	....	....	....	....
1998-99	Tampa Bay	13	5	6	1	691	33	2	2.87	....	....	....	....	....	....	....
99-2000	Tampa Bay	5	1	2	0	249	19	0	4.58	....	....	....	....	....	....	....
	NHL Totals	**429**	**179**	**161**	**54**	**23819**	**1204**	**19**	**3.03**	**16**	**4**	**9**	**786**	**51**	**0**	**3.89**

NHL Second All-Star Team (1990)

Played in NHL All-Star Game (1990)

• Recorded shutout (2-0) in NHL debut vs. Edmonton, November 1, 1985. Traded to **Toronto** by **Buffalo** with Dave Andreychuk and Buffalo's 1st round choice (Kenny Jonsson) in 1993 Entry Draft for Grant Fuhr and Toronto's 5th round choice (Kevin Popp) in 1995 Entry Draft, February 2, 1993. Claimed by **Florida** from **Toronto** in Expansion Draft, June 24, 1993. Claimed by **Tampa Bay** from **Florida** in Phase II of Expansion Draft, June 25, 1993. • Missed majority of 1996-97 season recovering from groin injury suffered in training camp, September, 1997. • Missed majority of 1997-98 and 1998-99 seasons recovering from back injury suffered in game vs. Boston on December 27, 1997.

PUSEY, Chris

Goaltender. Catches left. 6', 180 lbs. Born, Brantford, Ont., June 30, 1965
(Detroit's 7th choice, 109th overall, in 1983 Entry Draft).

Season	Club	GP	W	L	T	Mins	GA	SO	Avg	GP	W	L	Mins	GA	SO	Avg
1985-86	Detroit	1	0	0	0	40	3	0	4.50	....	....	....	....	....	....	....
	NHL Totals	**1**	**0**	**0**	**0**	**40**	**3**	**0**	**4.50**	....	....	....	....	....	....	....

RACICOT, Andre

Goaltender. Catches left. 5'11", 165 lbs. Born, Rouyn-Noranda, Que., June 9, 1969
(Montreal's 5th choice, 83rd overall, in 1989 Entry Draft).

Season	Club	GP	W	L	T	Mins	GA	SO	Avg	GP	W	L	Mins	GA	SO	Avg
1989-90	Montreal	1	0	0	0	13	3	0	13.85	....	....	....	....	....	....	....
1990-91	Montreal	21	7	9	2	975	52	1	3.20	2	0	1	12	2	0	10.00
1991-92	Montreal	9	0	3	3	436	23	0	3.17	1	0	0	1	0	0	0.00
1992-93◆	Montreal	26	17	5	1	1433	81	1	3.39	1	0	0	18	2	0	6.67
1993-94	Montreal	11	2	6	2	500	37	0	4.44	....	....	....	....	....	....	....
	NHL Totals	**68**	**26**	**23**	**8**	**3357**	**196**	**2**	**3.50**	**4**	**0**	**1**	**31**	**4**	**0**	**7.74**

Signed as a free agent by **Los Angeles**, September 22, 1994. Signed as a free agent by **Chicago**, August 25, 1995.

RACINE, Bruce

Goaltender. Catches left. 6', 170 lbs. Born, Cornwall, Ont., August 9, 1966
(Pittsburgh's 3rd choice, 58th overall, in 1985 Entry Draft).

Season	Club	GP	W	L	T	Mins	GA	SO	Avg	GP	W	L	Mins	GA	SO	Avg
		Regular Season								Playoffs						
1995-96	St. Louis	11	0	3	0	230	12	0	3.13	1	0	0	1	0	0	0.00
	NHL Totals	**11**	**0**	**3**	**0**	**230**	**12**	**0**	**3.13**	**1**	**0**	**0**	**1**	**0**	**0**	**0.00**

Signed as a free agent by **Toronto**, August 11, 1993. Signed as a free agent by **St. Louis**, August 10, 1995. Signed as a free agent by **San Jose**, September 8, 1998.

RAM, Jamie

Goaltender. Catches left. 5'11", 175 lbs. Born, Scarborough, Ont., January 18, 1971
(NY Rangers' 9th choice, 213th overall, in 1991 Entry Draft).

Season	Club	GP	W	L	T	Mins	GA	SO	Avg	GP	W	L	Mins	GA	SO	Avg
1995-96	NY Rangers	1	0	0	0	27	0	0	0.00							
	NHL Totals	**1**	**0**	**0**	**0**	**27**	**0**	**0**	**0.00**							

Signed as a free agent by **San Jose**, August 19, 1997. Signed as a free agent by **Anaheim**, July 30, 1998.

RANFORD, Bill

Goaltender. Catches left. 5'11", 185 lbs. Born, Brandon, Man., December 14, 1966
(Boston's 2nd choice, 52nd overall, in 1985 Entry Draft).

Season	Club	GP	W	L	T	Mins	GA	SO	Avg	GP	W	L	Mins	GA	SO	Avg
1985-86	Boston	4	3	1	0	240	10	0	2.50	2	0	2	120	7	0	3.50
1986-87	Boston	41	16	20	2	2234	124	3	3.33	2	0	2	123	8	0	3.90
1987-88♦	Edmonton	6	3	0	2	325	16	0	2.95							
1988-89	Edmonton	29	15	8	2	1509	88	1	3.50							
1989-90♦	Edmonton	56	24	16	9	3107	165	1	3.19	*22	*16	6	*1401	59	1	2.53
1990-91	Edmonton	60	27	27	3	3415	182	0	3.20	3	1	2	135	8	0	3.56
1991-92	Edmonton	67	27	26	10	3822	228	1	3.58	16	8	8	909	51	*2	3.37
1992-93	Edmonton	67	17	38	6	3753	240	1	3.84							
1993-94	Edmonton	71	22	34	11	4070	236	1	3.48							
1994-95	Edmonton	40	15	20	3	2203	133	2	3.62							
1995-96	Edmonton	37	13	18	5	2015	128	1	3.81							
	Boston	40	21	12	4	2307	109	1	2.83	4	1	3	239	16	0	4.02
1996-97	Boston	37	12	16	8	2147	125	2	3.49							
	Washington	18	8	7	2	1009	46	0	2.74							
1997-98	Washington	22	7	12	2	1183	55	0	2.79							
1998-99	Tampa Bay	32	3	18	3	1568	102	1	3.90							
	Detroit	4	3	0	1	244	8	0	1.97	4	2	2	183	10	1	3.28
99-2000	Edmonton	16	4	6	3	785	47	0	3.59							
	NHL Totals	**647**	**240**	**279**	**76**	**35936**	**2042**	**15**	**3.41**	**53**	**28**	**25**	**3110**	**159**	**4**	**3.07**

Conn Smythe Trophy (1990)

Played in NHL All-Star Game (1991)

Traded to **Edmonton** by **Boston** with Geoff Courtnall and Boston's 2nd round choice (Petro Koivunen) in 1988 Entry Draft for Andy Moog, March 8, 1988. Traded to **Boston** by **Edmonton** for Mariusz Czerkawski, Sean Brown and Boston's 1st round choice (Matthieu Descoteaux) in 1996 Entry Draft, January 11, 1996. Traded to **Washington** by **Boston** with Adam Oates and Rick Tocchet for Jim Carey, Anson Carter, Jason Allison and Washington's 3rd round choice (Lee Goren) in 1997 Entry Draft, March 1, 1997. Traded to **Tampa Bay** by **Washington** for Tampa Bay's 3rd round choice (Todd Hornung) in 1998 Entry Draft and Tampa Bay's 2nd round choice (Michal Sivek) in 1999 Entry Draft, June 18, 1998. Traded to **Detroit** by **Tampa Bay** for future considerations, March 23, 1999. Signed as a free agent by **Edmonton**, August 4, 1999. • Officially announced retirement, April 24, 2000.

RAYCROFT, Andrew

Goaltender. Catches left. 6', 174 lbs. Born, Belleville, Ont., May 4, 1980
(Boston's 4th choice, 135th overall, in 1998 Entry Draft).

Season	Club	GP	W	L	T	Mins	GA	SO	Avg	GP	W	L	Mins	GA	SO	Avg
2000-01	Boston	15	4	6	0	649	32	0	2.96							
2001-02	Boston	1	0	0	1	65	3	0	2.77							
2002-03	Boston	5	2	3	0	300	12	0	2.40							
	NHL Totals	**21**	**6**	**9**	**1**	**1014**	**47**	**0**	**2.78**							

RAYMOND, Alain

Goaltender. Catches left. 5'10", 180 lbs. Born, Rimouski, Que., June 24, 1965
(Washington's 7th choice, 224th overall, in 1983 Entry Draft).

Season	Club	GP	W	L	T	Mins	GA	SO	Avg	GP	W	L	Mins	GA	SO	Avg
1987-88	Washington	1	0	1	0	40	2	0	3.00							
	NHL Totals	**1**	**0**	**1**	**0**	**40**	**2**	**0**	**3.00**							

Signed as a free agent by **St. Louis**, September 12, 1990.

RAYNER, Chuck

HHOF

Goaltender. Catches left. 5'11", 190 lbs. Born, Sutherland, Sask., August 11, 1920

Season	Club	GP	W	L	T	Mins	GA	SO	Avg	GP	W	L	Mins	GA	SO	Avg
1940-41	NY Americans	12	2	7	3	773	44	0	3.42							
1941-42	Brooklyn	36	13	21	2	2230	129	1	3.47							
1945-46	NY Rangers	40	12	21	7	2377	149	1	3.76							
1946-47	NY Rangers	58	22	30	6	3480	177	*5	3.05							
1947-48	NY Rangers	12	4	7	0	691	42	0	3.65	6	2	4	360	17	0	2.83
1948-49	NY Rangers	58	16	31	11	3480	168	7	2.90							
1949-50	NY Rangers	69	28	30	11	4140	181	6	2.62	12	7	5	775	29	1	2.25
1950-51	NY Rangers	66	19	28	19	3940	187	2	2.85							
1951-52	NY Rangers	53	18	25	10	3180	159	2	3.00							
1952-53	NY Rangers	20	4	8	8	1200	58	1	2.90							
	NHL Totals	**424**	**138**	**208**	**77**	**25491**	**1294**	**25**	**3.05**	**18**	**9**	**9**	**1135**	**46**	**1**	**2.43**

NHL Second All-Star Team (1949, 1950, 1951) • Hart Trophy (1950)

Played in NHL All-Star Game (1949, 1950, 1951)

Signed as a free agent by **NY Americans**, October 11, 1939. • Team name changed to **Brooklyn Americans** prior to 1941-42 season. Signed as a free agent by **NY Rangers** after **Brooklyn** franchise folded, 1945.

REAUGH, Daryl

Goaltender. Catches left. 6'4", 200 lbs. Born, Prince George, B.C., February 13, 1965
(Edmonton's 2nd choice, 42nd overall, in 1984 Entry Draft).

Season	Club	GP	W	L	T	Mins	GA	SO	Avg	GP	W	L	Mins	GA	SO	Avg
1984-85	Edmonton	1	0	1	0	60	5	0	5.00							
1987-88	Edmonton	6	1	1	0	176	14	0	4.77							
1990-91	Hartford	20	7	7	1	1010	53	1	3.15							
	NHL Totals	**27**	**8**	**9**	**1**	**1246**	**72**	**1**	**3.47**							

Signed as a free agent by **Hartford**, October 9, 1989.

REDDICK, Pokey

Goaltender. Catches left. 5'8", 170 lbs. Born, Halifax, N.S., October 6, 1964

Season	Club	GP	W	L	T	Mins	GA	SO	Avg	GP	W	L	Mins	GA	SO	Avg
1986-87	Winnipeg	48	21	21	4	2762	149	0	3.24	3	0	2	166	10	0	3.61
1987-88	Winnipeg	28	9	13	3	1487	102	0	4.12							
1988-89	Winnipeg	41	11	17	7	2109	144	0	4.10							
1989-90♦	Edmonton	11	5	4	2	604	31	0	3.08	1	0	0	2	0	0	0.00
1990-91	Edmonton	2	0	2	0	120	9	0	4.50							
1993-94	Florida	2	0	1	0	80	8	0	6.00							
	NHL Totals	**132**	**46**	**58**	**16**	**7162**	**443**	**0**	**3.71**	**4**	**0**	**2**	**168**	**10**	**0**	**3.57**

Signed as a free agent by **Winnipeg**, September 27, 1985. Traded to **Edmonton** by **Winnipeg** for future considerations, September 28, 1989. Signed as a free agent by **Florida**, July 12, 1993.

REDQUEST, Greg

Goaltender. Catches left. 5'10", 190 lbs. Born, Toronto, Ont., July 30, 1956
(Pittsburgh's 5th choice, 65th overall, in 1976 Amateur Draft).

Season	Club	GP	W	L	T	Mins	GA	SO	Avg	GP	W	L	Mins	GA	SO	Avg
1977-78	Pittsburgh	1	0	0	0	13	3	0	13.85							
	NHL Totals	**1**	**0**	**0**	**0**	**13**	**3**	**0**	**13.85**							

REECE, Dave

Goaltender. Catches right. 6'1", 190 lbs. Born, Troy, NY, September 13, 1948

Season	Club	GP	W	L	T	Mins	GA	SO	Avg	GP	W	L	Mins	GA	SO	Avg
1975-76	Boston	14	7	5	2	777	43	2	3.32							
	NHL Totals	**14**	**7**	**5**	**2**	**777**	**43**	**2**	**3.32**							

Signed as a free agent by **Boston** (Boston-AHL), November 24, 1972.

REESE, Jeff

Goaltender. Catches left. 5'9", 180 lbs. Born, Brantford, Ont., March 24, 1966
(Toronto's 3rd choice, 67th overall, in 1984 Entry Draft).

Season	Club	GP	W	L	T	Mins	GA	SO	Avg	GP	W	L	Mins	GA	SO	Avg
1987-88	Toronto	5	1	2	1	249	17	0	4.10							
1988-89	Toronto	10	2	6	1	486	40	0	4.94							
1989-90	Toronto	21	9	6	3	1101	81	0	4.41	2	1	1	108	6	0	3.33
1990-91	Toronto	30	6	13	3	1430	92	1	3.86							
1991-92	Toronto	8	1	5	1	413	20	1	2.91							
	Calgary	12	3	2	2	587	37	0	3.78							
1992-93	Calgary	26	14	4	1	1311	70	1	3.20	4	1	3	209	17	0	4.88
1993-94	Calgary	1	0	0	0	13	1	0	4.62							
	Hartford	19	5	9	3	1086	56	1	3.09							
1994-95	Hartford	11	2	5	1	477	26	0	3.27							
1995-96	Hartford	7	2	3	0	275	14	1	3.05							
	Tampa Bay	19	7	7	1	994	54	0	3.26	5	1	1	198	12	0	3.64
1996-97	New Jersey	3	0	2	0	139	13	0	5.61							
1998-99	Toronto	2	1	1	0	106	8	0	4.53							
	NHL Totals	**174**	**53**	**65**	**17**	**8667**	**529**	**5**	**3.66**	**11**	**3**	**5**	**515**	**35**	**0**	**4.08**

Traded to **Calgary** by **Toronto** with Craig Berube, Alexander Godynyuk, Gary Leeman and Michel Petit for Doug Gilmour, Jamie Macoun, Ric Nattress, Rick Wamsley and Kent Manderville, January 2, 1992. Traded to **Hartford** by **Calgary** for Dan Keczmer, November 19, 1993. Traded to **Tampa Bay** by **Hartford** for Tampa Bay's 9th round choice (Ashkat Rakhmatullin) in 1996 Entry Draft, December 1, 1995. Traded to **New Jersey** by **Tampa Bay** with Chicago's 2nd round choice (previously acquired, New Jersey selected Pierre Dagenais) in 1996 Entry Draft and Tampa Bay's 8th round choice (Jason Bertsch) in 1996 Entry Draft for Corey Schwab, June 22, 1996. Signed as a free agent by **Toronto**, January 5, 1999. Traded to **Tampa Bay** by **Toronto** with Toronto's 9th round choice (later traded to Philadelphia – Philadelphia selected Milan Kopecky) in 2000 Entry Draft for Tampa Bay's 9th round choice (Jean-Philippe Cote) in 2000 Entry Draft, August 6, 1999.

RESCH, Glenn

Goaltender. Catches left. 5'9", 165 lbs. Born, Moose Jaw, Sask., July 10, 1948

Season	Club	GP	W	L	T	Mins	GA	SO	Avg	GP	W	L	Mins	GA	SO	Avg
1973-74	NY Islanders	2	1	1	0	120	6	0	3.00							
1974-75	NY Islanders	25	12	7	5	1432	59	3	2.47	12	8	4	692	25	1	2.17
1975-76	NY Islanders	44	23	11	8	2546	88	7	2.07	7	3	3	357	18	0	3.03
1976-77	NY Islanders	46	26	13	6	2711	103	4	2.28	3	1	1	144	5	0	2.08
1977-78	NY Islanders	45	28	9	7	2637	112	3	2.55	7	3	4	388	15	0	2.32
1978-79	NY Islanders	43	26	7	10	2539	106	2	2.50	5	2	3	300	11	*1	2.20
1979-80♦	NY Islanders	45	23	14	6	2606	132	3	3.04	4	0	2	120	9	0	4.50
1980-81	NY Islanders	32	18	7	5	1817	93	*3	3.07							
	Colorado	8	2	4	2	449	28	0	3.74							
1981-82	Colorado	61	16	31	11	3424	230	0	4.03							
1982-83	New Jersey	65	15	35	12	3650	242	0	3.98							
1983-84	New Jersey	51	9	31	3	2641	184	1	4.18							
1984-85	New Jersey	51	15	27	5	2884	200	0	4.16							
1985-86	New Jersey	31	10	20	0	1769	126	0	4.27							
	Philadelphia	5	1	2	0	187	10	0	3.21	1	0	0	7	1	0	8.57

Season	Club	GP	W	L	T	Mins	GA	SO	Avg	GP	W	L	Mins	GA	SO	Avg
		REGULAR SEASON								PLAYOFFS						
1986-87	Philadelphia	17	6	5	2	867	42	0	2.91	2	0	0	36	1	0	1.67
	NHL Totals	**571**	**231**	**224**	**82**	**32279**	**1761**	**26**	**3.27**	**41**	**17**	**17**	**2044**	**85**	**2**	**2.50**

NHL Second All-Star Team (1976, 1979) • Bill Masterton Trophy (1982)

Played in NHL All-Star Game (1976, 1977, 1984)

Traded to **NY Islanders** by **Montreal** with Denis DeJordy, Alex Campbell and future considerations (Germain Gagnon, June 26, 1972) for cash and NY Islanders' 2nd round choice (Glenn Goldup) in 1973 Amateur Draft, June 6, 1972. Traded to **Colorado** by **NY Islanders** with Steve Tambellini for Mike McEwen and Jari Kaarela, March 10, 1981. Transferred to **New Jersey** after **Colorado** franchise relocated, June 30, 1982. Traded to **Philadelphia** by **New Jersey** for Philadelphia's 3rd round choice (Marc Laniel) in 1986 Entry Draft, March 11, 1986.

RHEAUME, Herb

Goaltender. Catches left. 6', 200 lbs. Born, Mason, Que., January 12, 1900

Season	Club	GP	W	L	T	Mins	GA	SO	Avg	GP	W	L	Mins	GA	SO	Avg
1925-26	Montreal	31	10	20	1	1889	92	0	2.92	....	....	....	....	....	....	....
	NHL Totals	**31**	**10**	**20**	**1**	**1889**	**92**	**0**	**2.92**	....	....	....	....	....	....	....

Signed as a free agent by **Montreal**, December 13, 1925.

RHODES, Damian

Goaltender. Catches left. 5'11", 195 lbs. Born, St. Paul, MN, May 28, 1969
(Toronto's 6th choice, 112th overall, in 1987 Entry Draft).

Season	Club	GP	W	L	T	Mins	GA	SO	Avg	GP	W	L	Mins	GA	SO	Avg
1990-91	Toronto	1	1	0	0	60	1	0	1.00	....	....	....	....	....	....	....
1993-94	Toronto	22	9	7	3	1213	53	0	2.62	1	0	0	1	0	0	0.00
1994-95	Toronto	13	6	6	1	760	34	0	2.68	....	....	....	....	....	....	....
1995-96	Toronto	11	4	5	1	624	29	0	2.79	....	....	....	....	....	....	....
	Ottawa	36	10	22	4	2123	98	2	2.77	....	....	....	....	....	....	....
1996-97	Ottawa	50	14	20	14	2934	133	1	2.72	....	....	....	....	....	....	....
1997-98	Ottawa	50	19	19	7	2743	107	5	2.34	10	5	5	590	21	0	2.14
1998-99	Ottawa	45	22	13	7	2480	101	3	2.44	2	0	2	150	6	0	2.40
99-2000	Atlanta	28	5	19	3	1561	101	1	3.88	....	....	....	....	....	....	....
2000-01	Atlanta	38	7	19	7	2072	116	0	3.36	....	....	....	....	....	....	....
2001-02	Atlanta	15	2	10	1	769	47	0	3.67	....	....	....	....	....	....	....
	NHL Totals	**309**	**99**	**140**	**48**	**17339**	**820**	**12**	**2.84**	**13**	**5**	**7**	**741**	**27**	**0**	**2.19**

• Played 10 seconds of playoff game vs. San Jose, May 6, 1994. • Credited with scoring a goal vs. New Jersey, January 2, 1999.

Traded to **NY Islanders** by **Toronto** with Ken Belanger for future considerations (Kirk Muller and Don Beaupre, January 23, 1996), January 23, 1996. Traded to **Ottawa** by **NY Islanders** with Wade Redden for Don Beaupre, Martin Straka and Bryan Berard, January 23, 1996. Traded to **Atlanta** by **Ottawa** for future considerations, June 18, 1999.

RICCI, Nick

Goaltender. Catches left. 5'10", 160 lbs. Born, Niagara Falls, Ont., June 3, 1959
(Pittsburgh's 4th choice, 94th overall, in 1979 Entry Draft).

Season	Club	GP	W	L	T	Mins	GA	SO	Avg	GP	W	L	Mins	GA	SO	Avg
1979-80	Pittsburgh	4	2	2	0	240	14	0	3.50	....	....	....	....	....	....	....
1980-81	Pittsburgh	9	4	5	0	540	35	0	3.89	....	....	....	....	....	....	....
1981-82	Pittsburgh	3	0	3	0	160	14	0	5.25	....	....	....	....	....	....	....
1982-83	Pittsburgh	3	1	2	0	147	16	0	6.53	....	....	....	....	....	....	....
	NHL Totals	**19**	**7**	**12**	**0**	**1087**	**79**	**0**	**4.36**	....	....	....	....	....	....	....

Traded to **Toronto** by **Pittsburgh** with Pat Graham for Vincent Tremblay and Rocky Saganiuk, August 15, 1983.

RICHARDSON, Terry

Goaltender. Catches right. 6'1", 190 lbs. Born, Powell River, B.C., May 7, 1953
(Detroit's 1st choice, 11th overall, in 1973 Amateur Draft).

Season	Club	GP	W	L	T	Mins	GA	SO	Avg	GP	W	L	Mins	GA	SO	Avg
1973-74	Detroit	9	1	4	0	315	28	0	5.33	....	....	....	....	....	....	....
1974-75	Detroit	4	1	2	0	202	23	0	6.83	....	....	....	....	....	....	....
1975-76	Detroit	1	0	1	0	60	7	0	7.00	....	....	....	....	....	....	....
1976-77	Detroit	5	1	3	0	269	18	0	4.01	....	....	....	....	....	....	....
1978-79	St. Louis	1	0	1	0	60	9	0	9.00	....	....	....	....	....	....	....
	NHL Totals	**20**	**3**	**11**	**0**	**906**	**85**	**0**	**5.63**	....	....	....	....	....	....	....

Signed as a free agent by **St. Louis**, July 26, 1978. Traded to **NY Islanders** by **St. Louis** with Barry Gibbs for future considerations, June 9, 1979. Traded to **Hartford** by **NY Islanders** for Ralph Klassen, June 14, 1979.

RICHTER, Mike

Goaltender. Catches left. 5'11", 185 lbs. Born, Abington, PA, September 22, 1966
(NY Rangers' 2nd choice, 28th overall, in 1985 Entry Draft).

Season	Club	GP	W	L	T	Mins	GA	SO	Avg	GP	W	L	Mins	GA	SO	Avg
1988-89	NY Rangers	....	....	....	....	....	....	....	....	1	0	1	58	4	0	4.14
1989-90	NY Rangers	23	12	5	5	1320	66	0	3.00	6	3	2	330	19	0	3.45
1990-91	NY Rangers	45	21	13	7	2596	135	0	3.12	6	2	4	313	14	*1	2.68
1991-92	NY Rangers	41	23	12	2	2298	119	3	3.11	7	4	2	412	24	1	3.50
1992-93	NY Rangers	38	13	19	3	2105	134	1	3.82	....	....	....	....	....	....	....
1993-94♦	NY Rangers	68	*42	12	6	3710	159	5	2.57	23	*16	7	1417	49	*4	2.07
1994-95	NY Rangers	35	14	17	2	1993	97	2	2.92	7	2	5	384	23	0	3.59
1995-96	NY Rangers	41	24	13	3	2396	107	3	2.68	11	5	6	661	36	0	3.27
1996-97	NY Rangers	61	33	22	6	3598	161	4	2.68	15	9	6	939	33	*3	2.11
1997-98	NY Rangers	*72	21	31	15	4143	184	0	2.66	....	....	....	....	....	....	....
1998-99	NY Rangers	68	27	30	8	3878	170	4	2.63	....	....	....	....	....	....	....
99-2000	NY Rangers	61	22	31	8	3622	173	0	2.87	....	....	....	....	....	....	....
2000-01	NY Rangers	45	20	21	3	2635	144	0	3.28	....	....	....	....	....	....	....
2001-02	NY Rangers	55	24	26	4	3195	157	2	2.95	....	....	....	....	....	....	....
2002-03	NY Rangers	13	5	6	1	694	34	0	2.94	....	....	....	....	....	....	....
	NHL Totals	**666**	**301**	**258**	**73**	**38183**	**1840**	**24**	**2.89**	**76**	**41**	**33**	**4514**	**202**	**9**	**2.68**

Played in NHL All-Star Game (1992, 1994, 2000)

Claimed by **Nashville** from **NY Rangers** in Expansion Draft, June 26, 1998. Signed as a free agent by **NY Rangers**, July 15, 1998. Traded to **Edmonton** by **NY Rangers** for Edmonton's 4th round choice (Corey Potter) in 2003 Entry Draft, June 30, 2002. Signed as a free agent by **NY Rangers**, July 4, 2002.

RIDLEY, Curt

Goaltender. Catches left. 6', 190 lbs. Born, Minnedosa, Man., September 24, 1951
(Boston's 3rd choice, 28th overall, in 1971 Amateur Draft).

Season	Club	GP	W	L	T	Mins	GA	SO	Avg	GP	W	L	Mins	GA	SO	Avg
1974-75	NY Rangers	2	1	1	0	81	7	0	5.19	....	....	....	....	....	....	....
1975-76	Vancouver	9	6	0	2	500	19	1	2.28	2	0	2	120	8	0	4.00
1976-77	Vancouver	37	8	21	4	2074	134	0	3.88	....	....	....	....	....	....	....
1977-78	Vancouver	40	9	17	8	2010	136	0	4.06	....	....	....	....	....	....	....
1979-80	Vancouver	10	2	6	2	599	39	0	3.91	....	....	....	....	....	....	....
	Toronto	3	0	1	0	110	8	0	4.36	....	....	....	....	....	....	....
1980-81	Toronto	3	1	1	0	124	12	0	5.81	....	....	....	....	....	....	....
	NHL Totals	**104**	**27**	**47**	**16**	**5498**	**355**	**1**	**3.87**	**2**	**0**	**2**	**120**	**8**	**0**	**4.00**

Claimed by **NY Rangers** (Providence-AHL) from **Boston** in Reverse Draft, June 13, 1973. Traded to **Atlanta** by **NY Rangers** for Jerry Byers, September 9, 1975. Traded to **Vancouver** by **Atlanta** for Vancouver's 1st round choice (Dave Shand) in 1976 Amateur Draft, January 20, 1976. Traded to **Toronto** by **Vancouver** for cash, February 10, 1980.

RIENDEAU, Vincent

Goaltender. Catches left. 5'10", 185 lbs. Born, St-Hyacinthe, Que., April 20, 1966

Season	Club	GP	W	L	T	Mins	GA	SO	Avg	GP	W	L	Mins	GA	SO	Avg
1987-88	Montreal	1	0	0	0	36	5	0	8.33	....	....	....	....	....	....	....
1988-89	St. Louis	32	11	15	5	1842	108	0	3.52	....	....	....	....	....	....	....
1989-90	St. Louis	43	17	19	5	2551	149	1	3.50	8	3	4	397	24	0	3.63
1990-91	St. Louis	44	29	9	6	2671	134	3	3.01	13	6	7	687	35	*1	3.06
1991-92	St. Louis	3	1	2	0	157	11	0	4.20	....	....	....	....	....	....	....
	Detroit	2	2	0	0	87	2	0	1.38	2	1	0	73	4	0	3.29
1992-93	Detroit	22	13	4	2	1193	64	0	3.22	....	....	....	....	....	....	....
1993-94	Detroit	8	2	4	0	345	23	0	4.00	....	....	....	....	....	....	....
	Boston	18	7	6	1	976	50	1	3.07	2	1	1	120	8	0	4.00
1994-95	Boston	11	3	6	1	565	27	0	2.87	....	....	....	....	....	....	....
	NHL Totals	**184**	**85**	**65**	**20**	**10423**	**573**	**5**	**3.30**	**25**	**11**	**12**	**1277**	**71**	**1**	**3.34**

Signed as a free agent by **Montreal**, October 9, 1985. Traded to **St. Louis** by **Montreal** with Sergio Momesso for Jocelyn Lemieux, Darrell May and St. Louis' 2nd round choice (Patrice Brisebois) in 1989 Entry Draft, August 9, 1988. Traded to **Detroit** by **St. Louis** for Rick Zombo, October 18, 1991. Traded to **Boston** by **Detroit** for Boston's 5th round choice (Chad Wilchynski) in 1995 Entry Draft, January 17, 1994.

RIGGIN, Dennis

Goaltender. Catches left. 5'11", 156 lbs. Born, Kincardine, Ont., April 11, 1936

Season	Club	GP	W	L	T	Mins	GA	SO	Avg	GP	W	L	Mins	GA	SO	Avg
1959-60	Detroit	9	2	6	1	540	30	1	3.33	....	....	....	....	....	....	....
1962-63	Detroit	9	4	4	1	459	22	0	2.88	....	....	....	....	....	....	....
	NHL Totals	**18**	**6**	**10**	**2**	**999**	**52**	**1**	**3.12**	....	....	....	....	....	....	....

• Father of Pat

RIGGIN, Pat

Goaltender. Catches right. 5'9", 170 lbs. Born, Kincardine, Ont., May 26, 1959
(Atlanta's 3rd choice, 33rd overall, in 1979 Entry Draft).

Season	Club	GP	W	L	T	Mins	GA	SO	Avg	GP	W	L	Mins	GA	SO	Avg
1979-80	Atlanta	25	11	9	2	1368	73	2	3.20	....	....	....	....	....	....	....
1980-81	Calgary	42	21	16	4	2411	154	0	3.83	11	6	4	629	37	0	3.53
1981-82	Calgary	52	19	19	11	2934	207	2	4.23	3	0	3	194	10	0	3.09
1982-83	Washington	38	16	9	9	2161	121	0	3.36	3	0	1	101	8	0	4.75
1983-84	Washington	41	21	14	2	2299	102	*4	*2.66	5	1	3	230	9	0	2.35
1984-85	Washington	57	28	20	7	3388	168	2	2.98	2	1	1	122	5	0	2.46
1985-86	Washington	7	2	3	1	369	23	0	3.74	....	....	....	....	....	....	....
	Boston	39	17	11	8	2272	127	1	3.35	1	0	1	60	3	0	3.00
1986-87	Boston	10	3	5	1	513	29	0	3.39	....	....	....	....	....	....	....
	Pittsburgh	17	8	6	3	988	55	0	3.34	....	....	....	....	....	....	....
1987-88	Pittsburgh	22	7	8	4	1169	76	0	3.90	....	....	....	....	....	....	....
	NHL Totals	**350**	**153**	**120**	**52**	**19872**	**1135**	**11**	**3.43**	**25**	**8**	**13**	**1336**	**72**	**0**	**3.23**

• Son of Dennis • NHL Second All-Star Team (1984) • Shared William M. Jennings Trophy with Al Jensen (1984)

Transferred to **Calgary** after **Atlanta** franchise relocated, June 24, 1980. Traded to **Washington** by **Calgary** with Ken Houston for Howard Walker, George White, Washington's 6th round choice (Mats Kihlstrom) in 1982 Entry Draft, Washington's 3rd round choice (Perry Berezan) in 1983 Entry Draft and Washington's 2nd round choice (Paul Ranheim) in 1984 Entry Draft, June 9, 1982. Traded to **Boston** by **Washington** for Pete Peeters, November 14, 1985. Traded to **Pittsburgh** by **Boston** for Roberto Romano, February 6, 1987.

RING, Bob

Goaltender. Catches left. 5'10", 170 lbs. Born, Winchester, MA, October 6, 1946

Season	Club	GP	W	L	T	Mins	GA	SO	Avg	GP	W	L	Mins	GA	SO	Avg
1965-66	Boston	1	0	0	0	33	4	0	7.27	....	....	....	....	....	....	....
	NHL Totals	**1**	**0**	**0**	**0**	**33**	**4**	**0**	**7.27**	....	....	....	....	....	....	....

• **Boston's** spare goaltender replaced injured Eddie Johnston in 2nd period, October 30, 1965. (NY Rangers 8, Boston 2)

RIVARD, Fern

Goaltender. Catches left. 5'9", 160 lbs. Born, Grand'Mere, Que., January 18, 1946

Season	Club	GP	W	L	T	Mins	GA	SO	Avg	GP	W	L	Mins	GA	SO	Avg
1968-69	Minnesota	13	0	6	4	657	48	0	4.38	....	....	....	....	....	....	....
1969-70	Minnesota	14	3	5	5	800	42	1	3.15	....	....	....	....	....	....	....
1973-74	Minnesota	13	3	6	2	701	50	1	4.28	....	....	....	....	....	....	....
1974-75	Minnesota	15	3	9	0	707	50	0	4.24	....	....	....	....	....	....	....
	NHL Totals	**55**	**9**	**26**	**11**	**2865**	**190**	**2**	**3.98**	....	....	....	....	....	....	....

Rights transferred to **Philadelphia** after NHL club purchased **Quebec** (AHL) franchise, May 8, 1967. Claimed by **Minnesota** from **Philadelphia** in Intra-League Draft, June 12, 1968.

ROACH, John Ross

Goaltender. Catches left. 5'5", 130 lbs. Born, Port Perry, Ont., June 23, 1900

Season	Club	GP	W	L	T	Mins	GA	SO	Avg	GP	W	L	Mins	GA	SO	Avg
		REGULAR SEASON								PLAYOFFS						
1921-22 ◆	Toronto	22	11	10	1	1340	91	0	4.07	2	1	0	120	4	1	*2.00
	Toronto (Cup)	....	....	....	....	....	....	....	....	*5*	*3*	*2*	*305*	*9*	*1*	*1.77*
1922-23	Toronto	*24	13	10	1	1469	88	1	3.59	....	....	....	....	....	....	....
1923-24	Toronto	23	10	13	0	1380	80	1	3.48	....	....	....	....	....	....	....
1924-25	Toronto	*30	*19	11	0	1800	84	1	2.80	2	0	2	120	5	0	*2.50
1925-26	Toronto	*36	12	21	3	2231	114	2	3.07	....	....	....	....	....	....	....
1926-27	Toronto	*44	15	24	5	2764	94	4	2.04	....	....	....	....	....	....	....
1927-28	Toronto	43	18	18	7	2690	88	4	1.96	....	....	....	....	....	....	....
1928-29	NY Rangers	*44	21	13	10	2760	65	13	1.41	*6	3	2	*392	5	*3	0.77
1929-30	NY Rangers	*44	17	17	10	2770	143	1	3.10	4	1	2	309	7	0	1.36
1930-31	NY Rangers	*44	19	16	9	*2760	87	7	1.89	4	2	2	240	4	1	*1.00
1931-32	NY Rangers	*48	23	17	8	3020	112	*9	2.23	*7	3	4	*480	27	*1	3.38
1932-33	Detroit	*48	*25	15	8	2970	93	10	1.88	4	2	2	240	8	1	2.00
1933-34	Detroit	19	9	8	1	1030	45	1	2.62	....	....	....	....	....	....	....
1934-35	Detroit	23	7	11	5	1460	62	4	2.55	....	....	....	....	....	....	....
	NHL Totals	**492**	**219**	**204**	**68**	**30444**	**1246**	**58**	**2.46**	**29**	**12**	**14**	**1901**	**60**	**7**	**1.89**

NHL First All-Star Team (1933)

Signed as a free agent by **Toronto**, December 5, 1921. Traded to **NY Rangers** by **Toronto** for Lorne Chabot and $10,000, October 18, 1928. Traded to **Detroit** by **NY Rangers** for cash, October 25, 1932.

ROBERTS, Moe

Goaltender. Catches right. 5'9", 165 lbs. Born, Waterbury, CT, December 13, 1905

Season	Club	GP	W	L	T	Mins	GA	SO	Avg	GP	W	L	Mins	GA	SO	Avg
1925-26	Boston	2	1	1	0	85	5	0	3.53	....	....	....	....	....	....	....
1931-32	NY Americans	1	1	0	0	60	1	0	1.00	....	....	....	....	....	....	....
1933-34	NY Americans	6	1	4	0	336	25	0	4.46	....	....	....	....	....	....	....
1951-52	Chicago	1	0	0	0	20	0	0	0.00	....	....	....	....	....	....	....
	NHL Totals	**10**	**3**	**5**	**0**	**501**	**31**	**0**	**3.71**	....	....	....	....	....	....	....

Signed as a free agent by **Boston**, December 8, 1925. Signed as a free agent by **NY Americans**, October 18, 1931. Promoted to **NY Americans** from **New Haven** (Can-Am) to replace injured Roy Worters, March 10, 1932. (NY Americans 5, NY Rangers 1). • **Chicago's** assistant trainer replaced injured Harry Lumley, November 25, 1951. (Detroit 5, Chicago 2)

ROBERTSON, Earl

Goaltender. Catches left. 5'10", 165 lbs. Born, Bengough, Sask., November 24, 1910

Season	Club	GP	W	L	T	Mins	GA	SO	Avg	GP	W	L	Mins	GA	SO	Avg
1936-37 ◆	Detroit	....	....	....	....	....	....	....	....	6	3	2	340	8	2	1.41
1937-38	NY Americans	*48	19	18	11	*3000	111	6	2.22	6	3	3	475	12	0	*1.52
1938-39	NY Americans	46	17	18	10	2850	136	3	2.86	....	....	....	....	....	....	....
1939-40	NY Americans	*48	15	29	4	2960	140	6	2.84	3	1	2	180	9	0	3.00
1940-41	NY Americans	36	6	22	8	2260	142	1	3.77	....	....	....	....	....	....	....
1941-42	Brooklyn	12	3	8	1	750	46	0	3.68	....	....	....	....	....	....	....
	NHL Totals	**190**	**60**	**95**	**34**	**11820**	**575**	**16**	**2.92**	**15**	**7**	**7**	**995**	**29**	**2**	**1.75**

NHL Second All-Star Team (1939)

Traded to **Detroit** by **Windsor** (IAHL) for $1,500, October 21, 1936. Traded to **NY Americans** by **Detroit** for John Doran and $7,500, May 9, 1937. • Recorded a shutout (3-0) in NHL regular season debut vs. Chicago, November 4, 1937. • Team name changed to **Brooklyn Americans** prior to 1941-42 season.

ROLLINS, Al

Goaltender. Catches left. 6'2", 175 lbs. Born, Vanguard, Sask., October 9, 1926

Season	Club	GP	W	L	T	Mins	GA	SO	Avg	GP	W	L	Mins	GA	SO	Avg
1949-50	Toronto	2	1	1	0	100	4	1	2.40	....	....	....	....	....	....	....
1950-51 ◆	Toronto	40	*27	5	8	2373	70	5	*1.77	4	3	1	210	6	0	1.71
1951-52	Toronto	*70	29	24	16	4170	154	5	2.22	2	0	2	120	6	0	3.00
1952-53	Chicago	*70	27	28	15	*4200	175	6	2.50	7	3	4	425	18	0	2.54
1953-54	Chicago	66	12	47	7	3960	213	5	3.23	....	....	....	....	....	....	....
1954-55	Chicago	44	9	27	8	2640	150	0	3.41	....	....	....	....	....	....	....
1955-56	Chicago	58	17	30	11	3480	171	3	2.95	....	....	....	....	....	....	....
1956-57	Chicago	*70	16	39	15	*4200	224	3	3.20	....	....	....	....	....	....	....
1959-60	NY Rangers	10	3	4	3	600	31	0	3.10	....	....	....	....	....	....	....
	NHL Totals	**430**	**141**	**205**	**83**	**25723**	**1192**	**28**	**2.78**	**13**	**6**	**7**	**755**	**30**	**0**	**2.38**

Vezina Trophy (1951) • Hart Trophy (1954)

Played in NHL All-Star Game (1954)

Traded to **Cleveland** (AHL) by **Chicago** (Kansas City-USHL) for Doug Baldwin and Ralph Wycherley, September 13, 1949. Traded to **Toronto** by **Cleveland** (AHL) for Bobby Dawes, $40,000 and future considerations (Phil Samis, Eric Pogue and the rights to Bob Shropshire), April 6, 1950), November 29, 1949. Traded to **Chicago** by **Toronto** with Gus Mortson, Cal Gardner and Ray Hannigan for Harry Lumley, September 11, 1952. Loaned to **NY Rangers** by **Chicago** (Winnipeg-WHL) for the loan of Ray Mikulan, future considerations and cash, February 20, 1960.

ROLOSON, Dwayne

Goaltender. Catches left. 6'1", 178 lbs. Born, Simcoe, Ont., October 12, 1969

Season	Club	GP	W	L	T	Mins	GA	SO	Avg	GP	W	L	Mins	GA	SO	Avg
1996-97	Calgary	31	9	14	3	1618	78	1	2.89	....	....	....	....	....	....	....
1997-98	Calgary	39	11	16	8	2205	110	0	2.99	....	....	....	....	....	....	....
1998-99	Buffalo	18	6	8	2	911	42	1	2.77	4	1	1	139	10	0	4.32
99-2000	Buffalo	14	1	7	3	677	32	0	2.84	....	....	....	....	....	....	....
2001-02	Minnesota	45	14	20	7	2506	112	5	2.68	....	....	....	....	....	....	....
2002-03	Minnesota	50	23	16	8	2945	98	4	2.00	11	5	6	579	25	0	2.59
	NHL Totals	**197**	**64**	**81**	**31**	**10862**	**472**	**11**	**2.61**	**15**	**6**	**7**	**718**	**35**	**0**	**2.92**

Signed as a free agent by **Calgary**, July 4, 1994. Signed as a free agent by **Buffalo**, July 15, 1998. Claimed by **Columbus** from **Buffalo** in Expansion Draft, June 23, 2000. Signed as a free agent by **St. Louis**, July 14, 2000. Signed as a free agent by **Minnesota**, July 2, 2001.

ROMANO, Roberto

Goaltender. Catches left. 5'6", 170 lbs. Born, Montreal, Que., October 10, 1962

Season	Club	GP	W	L	T	Mins	GA	SO	Avg	GP	W	L	Mins	GA	SO	Avg
1982-83	Pittsburgh	3	0	3	0	155	18	0	6.97	....	....	....	....	....	....	....
1983-84	Pittsburgh	18	6	11	0	1020	78	1	4.59	....	....	....	....	....	....	....
1984-85	Pittsburgh	31	9	17	2	1629	120	1	4.42	....	....	....	....	....	....	....
1985-86	Pittsburgh	46	21	20	3	2684	159	2	3.55	....	....	....	....	....	....	....
1986-87	Pittsburgh	25	9	11	2	1438	87	0	3.63	....	....	....	....	....	....	....
	Boston	1	0	1	0	60	6	0	6.00	....	....	....	....	....	....	....
1993-94	Pittsburgh	2	1	0	1	125	3	0	1.44	....	....	....	....	....	....	....
	NHL Totals	**126**	**46**	**63**	**8**	**7111**	**471**	**4**	**3.97**	....	....	....	....	....	....	....

Signed as a free agent by **Pittsburgh**, December 6, 1982. Traded to **Boston** by **Pittsburgh** for Pat Riggin, February 6, 1987. Signed as a free agent by **Pittsburgh**, October 7, 1993.

ROSATI, Mike

Goaltender. Catches left. 5'10", 170 lbs. Born, Toronto, Ont., January 7, 1968
(NY Rangers' 6th choice, 131st overall, in 1988 Entry Draft).

Season	Club	GP	W	L	T	Mins	GA	SO	Avg	GP	W	L	Mins	GA	SO	Avg
1998-99	Washington	1	1	0	0	28	0	0	0.00	....	....	....	....	....	....	....
	NHL Totals	**1**	**1**	**0**	**0**	**28**	**0**	**0**	**0.00**	....	....	....	....	....	....	....

Signed as a free agent by **Washington**, July 15, 1998.

ROUSSEL, Dominic

Goaltender. Catches left. 6'1", 200 lbs. Born, Hull, Que., February 22, 1970
(Philadelphia's 4th choice, 63rd overall, in 1988 Entry Draft).

Season	Club	GP	W	L	T	Mins	GA	SO	Avg	GP	W	L	Mins	GA	SO	Avg
1991-92	Philadelphia	17	7	8	2	922	40	1	2.60	....	....	....	....	....	....	....
1992-93	Philadelphia	34	13	11	5	1769	111	1	3.76	....	....	....	....	....	....	....
1993-94	Philadelphia	60	29	20	5	3285	183	1	3.34	....	....	....	....	....	....	....
1994-95	Philadelphia	19	11	7	0	1075	42	1	2.34	1	0	0	23	0	0	0.00
1995-96	Philadelphia	9	2	3	2	456	22	1	2.89	....	....	....	....	....	....	....
	Winnipeg	7	2	2	0	285	16	0	3.37	....	....	....	....	....	....	....
1998-99	Anaheim	18	4	5	4	884	37	1	2.51	....	....	....	....	....	....	....
99-2000	Anaheim	20	6	5	3	988	52	1	3.16	....	....	....	....	....	....	....
2000-01	Anaheim	13	2	5	2	653	31	0	2.85	....	....	....	....	....	....	....
	Edmonton	8	1	4	0	348	21	0	3.62	....	....	....	....	....	....	....
	NHL Totals	**205**	**77**	**70**	**23**	**10665**	**555**	**7**	**3.12**	**1**	**0**	**0**	**23**	**0**	**0**	**0.00**

Traded to **Winnipeg** by **Philadelphia** for Tim Cheveldae and Winnipeg's 3rd round choice (Chester Gallant) in 1996 Entry Draft, February 27, 1996. Signed as a free agent by **Philadelphia**, July 3, 1996. Traded to **Nashville** by **Philadelphia** with Jeff Staples for Nashville's 7th round choice (Cam Ondrik) in 1998 Entry Draft, June 26, 1998. Traded to **Anaheim** by **Nashville** for Chris Mason and Marc Moro, October 5, 1998. Claimed on waivers by **Edmonton** from **Anaheim**, January 10, 2001.

ROY, Patrick

Goaltender. Catches left. 6'2", 185 lbs. Born, Quebec City, Que., October 5, 1965
(Montreal's 4th choice, 51st overall, in 1984 Entry Draft).

Season	Club	GP	W	L	T	Mins	GA	SO	Avg	GP	W	L	Mins	GA	SO	Avg
1984-85	Montreal	1	1	0	0	20	0	0	0.00	....	....	....	....	....	....	....
1985-86 ◆	Montreal	47	23	18	3	2651	148	1	3.35	20	*15	5	1218	39	*1	1.92
1986-87	Montreal	46	22	16	6	2686	131	1	2.93	6	4	2	330	22	0	4.00
1987-88	Montreal	45	23	12	9	2586	125	3	2.90	8	3	4	430	24	0	3.35
1988-89	Montreal	48	33	5	6	2744	113	4	*2.47	19	13	6	1206	42	2	*2.09
1989-90	Montreal	54	*31	16	5	3173	134	3	2.53	11	5	6	641	26	1	2.43
1990-91	Montreal	48	25	15	6	2835	128	1	2.71	13	7	5	785	40	0	3.06
1991-92	Montreal	67	36	22	8	3935	155	*5	*2.36	11	4	7	686	30	1	2.62
1992-93 ◆	Montreal	62	31	25	5	3595	192	2	3.20	20	*16	4	1293	46	0	*2.13
1993-94	Montreal	68	35	17	11	3867	161	*7	2.50	6	3	3	375	16	0	2.56
1994-95	Montreal	43	17	20	6	2566	127	1	2.97	....	....	....	....	....	....	....
1995-96	Montreal	22	12	9	1	1260	62	1	2.95	....	....	....	....	....	....	....
◆	Colorado	39	22	15	1	2305	103	1	2.68	*22	*16	6	*1454	51	*3	2.10
1996-97	Colorado	62	*38	15	7	3698	143	7	2.32	17	10	7	1034	38	*3	2.21
1997-98	Colorado	65	31	19	13	3835	153	4	2.39	7	3	4	430	18	0	2.51
1998-99	Colorado	61	32	19	8	3648	139	5	2.29	19	11	8	1173	52	1	2.66
99-2000	Colorado	63	32	21	8	3704	141	2	2.28	17	11	6	1039	31	3	1.79
2000-01 ◆	Colorado	62	40	13	7	3585	132	4	2.21	23	*16	7	1451	41	*4	*1.70
2001-02	Colorado	63	32	23	8	3773	122	*9	*1.94	21	11	10	1241	52	3	2.51
2002-03	Colorado	63	35	15	13	3769	137	5	2.18	7	3	4	423	16	1	2.27
	NHL Totals	**1029**	**551**	**315**	**131**	**60235**	**2546**	**66**	**2.54**	**247**	**151**	**94**	**15209**	**584**	**23**	**2.30**

• Brother of Stephane • NHL All-Rookie Team (1986) • Conn Smythe Trophy (1986, 1993, 2001) • Shared William M. Jennings Trophy with Brian Hayward (1987, 1988, 1989) • NHL Second All-Star Team (1988, 1991) • NHL First All-Star Team (1989, 1990, 1992, 2002) • Trico Goaltending Award (1989, 1990) • Vezina Trophy (1989, 1990, 1992) • William M. Jennings Trophy (1992, 2002)

Played in NHL All-Star Game (1988, 1990, 1991, 1992, 1993, 1994, 1997, 1998, 2001, 2002, 2003)

Traded to **Colorado** by **Montreal** with Mike Keane for Andrei Kovalenko, Martin Rucinsky and Jocelyn Thibault, December 6, 1995. • Officially announced retirement, May 28, 2003.

RUDKOWSKY, Cody

Goaltender. Catches left. 6'1", 206 lbs. Born, Willingdon, Alta., July 21, 1978

Season	Club	GP	W	L	T	Mins	GA	SO	Avg	GP	W	L	Mins	GA	SO	Avg
2002-03	St. Louis	1	1	0	0	30	0	0	0.00	....	....	....	....	....	....	....
	NHL Totals	**1**	**1**	**0**	**0**	**30**	**0**	**0**	**0.00**	....	....	....	....	....	....	....

Signed as a free agent by **St. Louis**, March 25, 1999.

RUPP, Pat

Goaltender. Catches left. 5'11", 180 lbs. Born, Detroit, MI, August 12, 1942

Season	Club	GP	W	L	T	Mins	GA	SO	Avg	GP	W	L	Mins	GA	SO	Avg
		Regular Season								Playoffs						
1963-64	Detroit	1	0	1	0	60	4	0	4.00	....	....	....	....	....	....	....
	NHL Totals	**1**	**0**	**1**	**0**	**60**	**4**	**0**	**4.00**	....	....	....	....	....	....	....

Loaned to **Detroit** by **Philadelphia** (EHL) to replace injured Terry Sawchuk, March 22, 1964. (Toronto 4, Detroit 1)

RUTHERFORD, Jim

Goaltender. Catches left. 5'8", 168 lbs. Born, Beeton, Ont., February 17, 1949
(Detroit's 1st choice, 10th overall, in 1969 Amateur Draft).

Season	Club	GP	W	L	T	Mins	GA	SO	Avg	GP	W	L	Mins	GA	SO	Avg
1970-71	Detroit	29	7	15	3	1498	94	1	3.77	....	....	....	....	....	....	....
1971-72	Pittsburgh	40	17	15	5	2160	116	1	3.22	4	0	4	240	14	0	3.50
1972-73	Pittsburgh	49	20	22	5	2660	129	3	2.91	....	....	....	....	....	....	....
1973-74	Pittsburgh	26	7	12	4	1432	82	0	3.44	....	....	....	....	....	....	....
	Detroit	25	9	11	4	1420	86	0	3.63	....	....	....	....	....	....	....
1974-75	Detroit	59	20	29	10	3478	217	2	3.74	....	....	....	....	....	....	....
1975-76	Detroit	44	13	25	6	2640	158	4	3.59	....	....	....	....	....	....	....
1976-77	Detroit	48	7	34	6	2740	180	0	3.94	....	....	....	....	....	....	....
1977-78	Detroit	43	20	17	4	2468	134	1	3.26	3	2	1	180	12	0	4.00
1978-79	Detroit	32	13	14	5	1892	103	1	3.27	....	....	....	....	....	....	....
1979-80	Detroit	23	6	13	3	1326	92	1	4.16	....	....	....	....	....	....	....
1980-81	Detroit	10	2	6	2	600	43	0	4.30	....	....	....	....	....	....	....
	Toronto	18	4	10	2	961	82	0	5.12	....	....	....	....	....	....	....
	Los Angeles	3	3	0	0	180	10	0	3.33	1	0	0	20	2	0	6.00
1981-82	Los Angeles	7	3	3	0	380	43	0	6.79	....	....	....	....	....	....	....
1982-83	Detroit	1	0	1	0	60	7	0	7.00	....	....	....	....	....	....	....
	NHL Totals	**457**	**151**	**227**	**59**	**25895**	**1576**	**14**	**3.65**	**8**	**2**	**5**	**440**	**28**	**0**	**3.82**

Claimed by **Pittsburgh** from **Detroit** in Intra-League Draft, June 8, 1971. Traded to **Detroit** by **Pittsburgh** with Jack Lynch for Ron Stackhouse, January 17, 1974. Traded to **Toronto** by **Detroit** for Mark Kirton, December 4, 1980. Traded to **Los Angeles** by **Toronto** for Los Angeles' 5th round choice (Barry Brigley) in 1981 Entry Draft, March 10, 1981. Signed as a free agent by **Detroit**, September 13, 1982.

RUTLEDGE, Wayne

Goaltender. Catches left. 6'2", 200 lbs. Born, Barrie, Ont., January 5, 1942

Season	Club	GP	W	L	T	Mins	GA	SO	Avg	GP	W	L	Mins	GA	SO	Avg
1967-68	Los Angeles	45	20	18	4	2444	117	2	2.87	3	1	1	149	8	0	3.22
1968-69	Los Angeles	17	6	7	4	921	56	0	3.65	5	1	3	229	12	0	3.14
1969-70	Los Angeles	20	2	12	1	960	68	0	4.25	....	....	....	....	....	....	....
	NHL Totals	**82**	**28**	**37**	**9**	**4325**	**241**	**2**	**3.34**	**8**	**2**	**4**	**378**	**20**	**0**	**3.17**

Claimed by **Los Angeles** from **NY Rangers** in Expansion Draft, June 6, 1967. Claimed by **Salt Lake** (WHL) from **Los Angeles** in Reverse Draft, June, 1971.

ST. CROIX, Rick

Goaltender. Catches left. 5'10", 160 lbs. Born, Kenora, Ont., January 3, 1955
(Philadelphia's 3rd choice, 72nd overall, in 1975 Amateur Draft).

Season	Club	GP	W	L	T	Mins	GA	SO	Avg	GP	W	L	Mins	GA	SO	Avg
1977-78	Philadelphia	7	2	4	1	395	20	0	3.04	....	....	....	....	....	....	....
1978-79	Philadelphia	2	0	1	1	117	6	0	3.08	....	....	....	....	....	....	....
1979-80	Philadelphia	1	1	0	0	60	2	0	2.00	....	....	....	....	....	....	....
1980-81	Philadelphia	27	13	7	6	1567	65	2	2.49	9	4	5	541	27	*1	2.99
1981-82	Philadelphia	29	13	9	6	1729	112	0	3.89	1	0	1	20	1	0	3.00
1982-83	Philadelphia	16	9	5	2	940	54	0	3.45	....	....	....	....	....	....	....
	Toronto	17	4	9	2	920	58	0	3.78	1	0	0	1	1	0	60.00
1983-84	Toronto	20	5	10	0	939	80	0	5.11	....	....	....	....	....	....	....
1984-85	Toronto	11	2	9	0	628	54	0	5.16	....	....	....	....	....	....	....
	NHL Totals	**130**	**49**	**54**	**18**	**7295**	**451**	**2**	**3.71**	**11**	**4**	**6**	**562**	**29**	**1**	**3.10**

Traded to **Toronto** by **Philadelphia** for Michel Larocque, January 11, 1983.

ST. LAURENT, Sam

Goaltender. Catches left. 5'10", 190 lbs. Born, Arvida, Que., February 16, 1959

Season	Club	GP	W	L	T	Mins	GA	SO	Avg	GP	W	L	Mins	GA	SO	Avg
1985-86	New Jersey	4	2	1	0	188	13	1	4.15	....	....	....	....	....	....	....
1986-87	Detroit	6	1	2	2	342	16	0	2.81	....	....	....	....	....	....	....
1987-88	Detroit	6	2	2	0	294	16	0	3.27	1	0	0	10	1	0	6.00
1988-89	Detroit	4	0	1	1	141	9	0	3.83	....	....	....	....	....	....	....
1989-90	Detroit	14	2	6	1	607	38	0	3.76	....	....	....	....	....	....	....
	NHL Totals	**34**	**7**	**12**	**4**	**1572**	**92**	**1**	**3.51**	**1**	**0**	**0**	**10**	**1**	**0**	**6.00**

Signed as a free agent by **Philadelphia**, October 10, 1979. Traded to **New Jersey** by **Philadelphia** for future considerations, September 27, 1984. Traded to **Detroit** by **New Jersey** for Steve Richmond, August 18, 1986. Traded to **NY Rangers** by **Detroit** for cash, June 26, 1990.

SALO, Tommy

Goaltender. Catches left. 5'11", 173 lbs. Born, Surahammar, Sweden, February 1, 1971
(NY Islanders' 5th choice, 118th overall, in 1993 Entry Draft).

Season	Club	GP	W	L	T	Mins	GA	SO	Avg	GP	W	L	Mins	GA	SO	Avg
1994-95	NY Islanders	6	1	5	0	358	18	0	3.02	....	....	....	....	....	....	....
1995-96	NY Islanders	10	1	7	1	523	35	0	4.02	....	....	....	....	....	....	....
1996-97	NY Islanders	58	20	27	8	3208	151	5	2.82	....	....	....	....	....	....	....
1997-98	NY Islanders	62	23	29	5	3461	152	4	2.64	....	....	....	....	....	....	....
1998-99	NY Islanders	51	17	26	7	3018	132	5	2.62	....	....	....	....	....	....	....
	Edmonton	13	8	2	2	700	27	0	2.31	4	0	4	296	11	0	2.23
99-2000	Edmonton	70	27	28	13	4164	162	2	2.33	5	1	4	297	14	0	2.83
2000-01	Edmonton	73	36	25	12	4364	179	8	2.46	6	2	4	406	15	0	2.22
2001-02	Edmonton	69	30	28	10	4035	149	6	2.22	....	....	....	....	....	....	....
2002-03	Edmonton	65	29	27	8	3814	172	4	2.71	6	2	4	343	18	0	3.15
	NHL Totals	**477**	**192**	**204**	**66**	**27645**	**1177**	**34**	**2.55**	**21**	**5**	**16**	**1342**	**58**	**0**	**2.59**

Played in NHL All-Star Game (2000, 2002)

Traded to **Edmonton** by **NY Islanders** for Mats Lindgren and Edmonton's 8th round choice (Radek Martinek) in 1999 Entry Draft, March 20, 1999.

SANDS, Mike

Goaltender. Catches left. 5'9", 170 lbs. Born, Mississauga, Ont., April 6, 1963
(Minnesota's 3rd choice, 31st overall, in 1981 Entry Draft).

Season	Club	GP	W	L	T	Mins	GA	SO	Avg	GP	W	L	Mins	GA	SO	Avg
1984-85	Minnesota	3	0	3	0	139	14	0	6.04	....	....	....	....	....	....	....
1986-87	Minnesota	3	0	2	0	163	12	0	4.42	....	....	....	....	....	....	....
	NHL Totals	**6**	**0**	**5**	**0**	**302**	**26**	**0**	**5.17**	....	....	....	....	....	....	....

SANFORD, Curtis

Goaltender. Catches right. 5'10", 187 lbs. Born, Owen Sound, Ont., October 5, 1979

Season	Club	GP	W	L	T	Mins	GA	SO	Avg	GP	W	L	Mins	GA	SO	Avg
2002-03	St. Louis	8	5	1	0	397	13	1	1.96	....	....	....	....	....	....	....
	NHL Totals	**8**	**5**	**1**	**0**	**397**	**13**	**1**	**1.96**	....	....	....	....	....	....	....

Signed as a free agent by **St. Louis**, October 1, 2000.

SARJEANT, Geoff

Goaltender. Catches left. 5'9", 180 lbs. Born, Newmarket, Ont., November 30, 1969
(St. Louis' 1st choice, 17th overall, in 1990 Supplemental Draft).

Season	Club	GP	W	L	T	Mins	GA	SO	Avg	GP	W	L	Mins	GA	SO	Avg
1994-95	St. Louis	4	1	0	0	120	6	0	3.00	....	....	....	....	....	....	....
1995-96	San Jose	4	0	2	1	171	14	0	4.91	....	....	....	....	....	....	....
	NHL Totals	**8**	**1**	**2**	**1**	**291**	**20**	**0**	**4.12**	....	....	....	....	....	....	....

Signed as a free agent by **San Jose**, September 23, 1995.

SAUVE, Bob

Goaltender. Catches left. 5'8", 175 lbs. Born, Ste-Genevieve, Que., June 17, 1955
(Buffalo's 1st choice, 17th overall, in 1975 Amateur Draft).

Season	Club	GP	W	L	T	Mins	GA	SO	Avg	GP	W	L	Mins	GA	SO	Avg
1976-77	Buffalo	4	1	2	0	184	11	0	3.59	....	....	....	....	....	....	....
1977-78	Buffalo	11	6	2	0	480	20	0	2.50	....	....	....	....	....	....	....
1978-79	Buffalo	29	10	10	7	1610	100	0	3.73	3	1	2	181	9	0	2.98
1979-80	Buffalo	32	20	8	4	1880	74	4	*2.36	8	6	2	501	17	*2	*2.04
1980-81	Buffalo	35	16	10	9	2100	111	2	3.17	....	....	....	....	....	....	....
1981-82	Buffalo	14	6	1	5	760	35	0	2.76	....	....	....	....	....	....	....
	Detroit	41	11	25	4	2365	165	0	4.19	....	....	....	....	....	....	....
1982-83	Buffalo	54	25	20	7	3110	179	1	3.45	10	6	4	545	28	*2	3.08
1983-84	Buffalo	40	22	13	4	2375	138	0	3.49	2	0	1	41	5	0	7.32
1984-85	Buffalo	27	13	10	3	1564	84	0	3.22	....	....	....	....	....	....	....
1985-86	Chicago	38	19	13	2	2099	138	0	3.94	2	0	2	99	8	0	4.85
1986-87	Chicago	46	19	19	5	2660	159	1	3.59	4	0	4	245	15	0	3.67
1987-88	New Jersey	34	10	16	3	1804	107	0	3.56	5	2	1	238	13	0	3.28
1988-89	New Jersey	15	4	5	1	720	56	0	4.67	....	....	....	....	....	....	....
	NHL Totals	**420**	**182**	**154**	**54**	**23711**	**1377**	**8**	**3.48**	**34**	**15**	**16**	**1850**	**95**	**4**	**3.08**

• Brother of Jean-Francois • Father of Phillipe • Shared Vezina Trophy with Don Edwards (1980)
• Shared William M. Jennings Trophy with Tom Barrasso (1985)

Traded to **Detroit** by **Buffalo** for future considerations, December 2, 1981. Signed as a free agent by **Buffalo**, June 1, 1982. Traded to **Chicago** by **Buffalo** for Chicago's 3rd round choice (Kevin Kerr) in 1986 Entry Draft, October 15, 1985. Signed as a free agent by **New Jersey**, July 10, 1987.

SAWCHUK, Terry HHOF

Goaltender. Catches left. 5'11", 195 lbs. Born, Winnipeg, Man., December 28, 1929

Season	Club	GP	W	L	T	Mins	GA	SO	Avg	GP	W	L	Mins	GA	SO	Avg
1949-50	Detroit	7	4	3	0	420	16	1	2.29	....	....	....	....	....	....	....
1950-51	Detroit	*70	*44	13	13	*4200	139	*11	1.99	6	2	4	463	13	1	1.68
1951-52♦	Detroit	*70	*44	14	12	*4200	133	*12	*1.90	*8	*8	0	480	5	*4	*0.63
1952-53	Detroit	63	*32	15	16	3780	120	9	*1.90	6	2	4	372	21	1	3.39
1953-54♦	Detroit	67	*35	19	13	4004	129	12	1.93	*12	*8	4	*751	20	*2	*1.60
1954-55♦	Detroit	68	*40	17	11	4040	132	*12	1.96	11	*8	3	*660	26	*1	*2.36
1955-56	Boston	68	22	33	13	4080	177	9	2.60	....	....	....	....	....	....	....
1956-57	Boston	34	18	10	6	2040	81	2	2.38	....	....	....	....	....	....	....
1957-58	Detroit	*70	29	29	12	*4200	206	3	2.94	4	0	4	252	19	0	4.52
1958-59	Detroit	67	23	36	8	4020	207	5	3.09	....	....	....	....	....	....	....
1959-60	Detroit	58	24	20	14	3480	155	5	2.67	6	2	4	405	20	0	2.96
1960-61	Detroit	37	12	16	8	2150	112	2	3.13	8	5	3	465	18	1	2.32
1961-62	Detroit	43	14	21	8	2580	141	5	3.28	....	....	....	....	....	....	....
1962-63	Detroit	48	22	16	7	2781	118	3	2.55	*11	5	6	*660	35	0	3.18
1963-64	Detroit	53	25	20	7	3140	138	5	2.64	13	6	5	677	31	1	2.75
1964-65	Toronto	36	17	13	6	2160	92	1	2.56	1	0	1	60	3	0	3.00
1965-66	Toronto	27	10	11	3	1521	80	1	3.16	2	0	2	120	6	0	3.00
1966-67♦	Toronto	28	15	5	4	1409	66	2	2.81	*10	*6	4	*565	25	0	2.65
1967-68	Los Angeles	36	11	14	6	1936	99	2	3.07	5	2	3	280	18	*1	3.86
1968-69	Detroit	13	3	4	3	641	28	0	2.62	....	....	....	....	....	....	....

Season	Club	GP	W	L	T	Mins	GA	SO	Avg	GP	W	L	Mins	GA	SO	Avg
		REGULAR SEASON								PLAYOFFS						
1969-70	NY Rangers	8	3	1	2	412	20	1	2.91	3	0	1	80	6	0	4.50
	NHL Totals	**971**	**447**	**330**	**172**	**57194**	**2389**	**103**	**2.51**	**106**	**54**	**48**	**6290**	**266**	**12**	**2.54**

NHL First All-Star Team (1951, 1952, 1953) • Calder Memorial Trophy (1951) • Vezina Trophy (1952, 1953, 1955) • NHL Second All-Star Team (1954, 1955, 1959, 1963) • Shared Vezina Trophy with Johnny Bower (1965) • Lester Patrick Trophy (1971)

Played in NHL All-Star Game (1950, 1951, 1952, 1953, 1954, 1955, 1956, 1959, 1963, 1964, 1968)

Traded to **Boston** by **Detroit** with Marcel Bonin, Lorne Davis and Vic Stasiuk for Gilles Boisvert, Real Chevrefils, Norm Corcoran, Warren Godfrey and Ed Sandford, June 3, 1955. • Missed remainder of 1956-57 season recovering from nervous exhaustion, January 16, 1957. Traded to **Detroit** by **Boston** for John Bucyk and cash, July 10, 1957. Claimed by **Toronto** from **Detroit** in Intra-League Draft, June 10, 1964. Claimed by **Los Angeles** from **Toronto** in Expansion Draft, June 6, 1967. Traded to **Detroit** by **Los Angeles** for Jimmy Peters, October 10, 1968. Traded to **NY Rangers** by **Detroit** with Sandy Snow for Larry Jeffrey, June 17, 1969.

SCHAEFER, Joe

Goaltender. Catches left. 5'8", 165 lbs. Born, Long Island, NY, December 21, 1924

Season	Club	GP	W	L	T	Mins	GA	SO	Avg	GP	W	L	Mins	GA	SO	Avg
1959-60	NY Rangers	1	0	1	0	39	5	0	7.69							
1960-61	NY Rangers	1	0	1	0	47	3	0	3.83							
	NHL Totals	**2**	**0**	**2**	**0**	**86**	**8**	**0**	**5.58**							

• **NY Rangers'** assistant trainer/practice goaltender replaced injured Gump Worsley in 2nd period, February 17, 1960 (Chicago 5, NY Rangers 1) and in 1st period, March 8, 1961 (Chicago 4, NY Rangers 3).

SCHAFER, Paxton

Goaltender. Catches left. 5'9", 164 lbs. Born, Medicine Hat, Alta., February 26, 1976
(Boston's 3rd choice, 47th overall, in 1995 Entry Draft).

Season	Club	GP	W	L	T	Mins	GA	SO	Avg	GP	W	L	Mins	GA	SO	Avg
1996-97	Boston	3	0	0	0	77	6	0	4.68							
	NHL Totals	**3**	**0**	**0**	**0**	**77**	**6**	**0**	**4.68**							

SCHWAB, Corey

Goaltender. Catches left. 6', 180 lbs. Born, North Battleford, Sask., November 4, 1970
(New Jersey's 12th choice, 200th overall, in 1990 Entry Draft).

Season	Club	GP	W	L	T	Mins	GA	SO	Avg	GP	W	L	Mins	GA	SO	Avg
1995-96	New Jersey	10	0	3	0	331	12	0	2.18							
1996-97	Tampa Bay	31	11	12	1	1462	74	2	3.04							
1997-98	Tampa Bay	16	2	9	1	821	40	1	2.92							
1998-99	Tampa Bay	40	8	25	3	2146	126	0	3.52							
99-2000	Vancouver	6	2	1	1	269	16	0	3.57							
2001-02	Toronto	30	12	10	5	1646	75	1	2.73	1	0	0	12	0	0	0.00
2002-03♦	New Jersey	11	5	3	1	614	15	1	1.47	2	0	0	28	0	0	0.00
	NHL Totals	**144**	**40**	**63**	**12**	**7289**	**358**	**5**	**2.95**	**3**	**0**	**0**	**40**	**0**	**0**	**0.00**

Traded to **Tampa Bay** by **New Jersey** for Jeff Reese, Chicago's 2nd round choice (previously acquired, New Jersey selected Pierre Dagenais) in 1996 Entry Draft and Tampa Bay's 8th round choice (Jay Bertsch) in 1996 Entry Draft, June 22, 1996. Claimed by **Atlanta** from **Tampa Bay** in Expansion Draft, June 25, 1999. Traded to **Vancouver** by **Atlanta** for Vancouver's 4th round choice (Carl Mallette) in 2000 Entry Draft, October 29, 1999. Signed as a free agent by **Toronto**, October 1, 2001. Signed as a free agent by **New Jersey**, July 8, 2002.

SCOTT, Ron

Goaltender. Catches left. 5'8", 155 lbs. Born, Guelph, Ont., July 21, 1960

Season	Club	GP	W	L	T	Mins	GA	SO	Avg	GP	W	L	Mins	GA	SO	Avg
1983-84	NY Rangers	9	2	3	3	485	29	0	3.59							
1985-86	NY Rangers	4	0	3	0	156	11	0	4.23							
1986-87	NY Rangers	1	0	0	1	65	5	0	4.62							
1987-88	NY Rangers	2	1	1	0	90	6	0	4.00							
1989-90	Los Angeles	12	5	6	0	654	40	0	3.67	1	0	0	32	4	0	7.50
	NHL Totals	**28**	**8**	**13**	**4**	**1450**	**91**	**0**	**3.77**	**1**	**0**	**0**	**32**	**4**	**0**	**7.50**

Signed as a free agent by **NY Rangers**, May 25, 1983. Signed as a free agent by **Los Angeles**, January 12, 1990.

SCOTT, Travis

Goaltender. Catches left. 6'2", 185 lbs. Born, Kanata, Ont., September 14, 1975

Season	Club	GP	W	L	T	Mins	GA	SO	Avg	GP	W	L	Mins	GA	SO	Avg
2000-01	Los Angeles	1	0	0	0	25	3	0	7.20							
	NHL Totals	**1**	**0**	**0**	**0**	**25**	**3**	**0**	**7.20**							

Signed as a free agent by **St. Louis**, December 30, 1996. Signed as a free agent by **Los Angeles**, February 18, 2000.

SEVIGNY, Richard

Goaltender. Catches left. 5'8", 172 lbs. Born, Montreal, Que., April 11, 1957
(Montreal's 11th choice, 124th overall, in 1977 Amateur Draft).

Season	Club	GP	W	L	T	Mins	GA	SO	Avg	GP	W	L	Mins	GA	SO	Avg
1978-79	Montreal	DID NOT PLAY – SPARE GOALTENDER														
1979-80	Montreal	11	5	4	2	632	31	0	2.94							
1980-81	Montreal	33	20	4	3	1777	71	2	*2.40	3	0	3	180	13	0	4.33
1981-82	Montreal	19	11	4	2	1027	53	0	3.10							
1982-83	Montreal	38	15	11	8	2130	122	1	3.44	1	0	0	28	0	0	0.00
1983-84	Montreal	40	16	18	2	2203	124	1	3.38							
1984-85	Quebec	20	10	6	2	1104	62	1	3.37							
1985-86	Quebec	11	3	5	1	468	33	0	4.23							
1986-87	Quebec	4	0	2	0	144	11	0	4.58							
	NHL Totals	**176**	**80**	**54**	**20**	**9485**	**507**	**5**	**3.21**	**4**	**0**	**3**	**208**	**13**	**0**	**3.75**

Shared Vezina Trophy with Denis Herron and Michel Larocque (1981)

Signed as a free agent by **Quebec**, July 4, 1984.

SHARPLES, Scott

Goaltender. Catches left. 6', 180 lbs. Born, Montreal, Que., March 1, 1968
(Calgary's 8th choice, 184th overall, in 1986 Entry Draft).

Season	Club	GP	W	L	T	Mins	GA	SO	Avg	GP	W	L	Mins	GA	SO	Avg
1991-92	Calgary	1	0	0	1	65	4	0	3.69							
	NHL Totals	**1**	**0**	**0**	**1**	**65**	**4**	**0**	**3.69**							

SHIELDS, Steve

Goaltender. Catches left. 6'3", 215 lbs. Born, Toronto, Ont., July 19, 1972
(Buffalo's 5th choice, 101st overall, in 1991 Entry Draft).

Season	Club	GP	W	L	T	Mins	GA	SO	Avg	GP	W	L	Mins	GA	SO	Avg
1995-96	Buffalo	2	1	0	0	75	4	0	3.20							
1996-97	Buffalo	13	3	8	2	789	39	0	2.97	10	4	6	570	26	1	2.74
1997-98	Buffalo	16	3	6	4	785	37	0	2.83							
1998-99	San Jose	37	15	11	8	2162	80	4	2.22	1	0	1	60	6	0	6.00
99-2000	San Jose	67	27	30	8	3797	162	4	2.56	12	5	7	696	36	0	3.10
2000-01	San Jose	21	6	8	5	1135	47	2	2.48							
2001-02	Anaheim	33	9	20	2	1777	79	0	2.67							
2002-03	Boston	36	12	13	9	2112	97	0	2.76	2	0	2	119	6	0	3.03
	NHL Totals	**225**	**76**	**96**	**38**	**12632**	**545**	**10**	**2.59**	**25**	**9**	**16**	**1445**	**74**	**1**	**3.07**

Traded to **San Jose** by **Buffalo** with Buffalo's 4th round choice (Miroslav Zalesak) in 1998 Entry Draft for Kay Whitmore, Colorado's 2nd round choice (previously acquired, Buffalo selected Jaroslav Kristek) in 1998 Entry Draft and San Jose's 5th round choice (later traded to Columbus – Columbus selected Tyler Kolarik) in 2000 Entry Draft, June 18, 1998. Traded to **Anaheim** by **San Jose** with Jeff Friesen and San Jose's 2nd round choice (later traded to Dallas – Dallas selected Vojtech Polak) in 2003 Entry Draft for Teemu Selanne, March 5, 2001. Traded to **Boston** by **Anaheim** for Boston's 3rd round choice (Shane Hynes) in 2003 Entry Draft, June 25, 2002.

SHTALENKOV, Mikhail

Goaltender. Catches left. 6'2", 185 lbs. Born, Moscow, USSR, October 20, 1965
(Anaheim's 5th choice, 108th overall, in 1993 Entry Draft).

Season	Club	GP	W	L	T	Mins	GA	SO	Avg	GP	W	L	Mins	GA	SO	Avg
1993-94	Anaheim	10	3	4	1	543	24	0	2.65							
1994-95	Anaheim	18	4	7	1	810	49	0	3.63							
1995-96	Anaheim	30	7	16	3	1637	85	0	3.12							
1996-97	Anaheim	24	7	8	1	1079	52	2	2.89	4	0	3	211	10	0	2.84
1997-98	Anaheim	40	13	18	5	2049	110	1	3.22							
1998-99	Edmonton	34	12	17	3	1819	81	3	2.67							
	Phoenix	4	1	2	1	243	9	0	2.22							
99-2000	Phoenix	15	7	6	2	904	36	2	2.39							
	Florida	15	8	4	2	882	34	0	2.31							
	NHL Totals	**190**	**62**	**82**	**19**	**9966**	**480**	**8**	**2.89**	**4**	**0**	**3**	**211**	**10**	**0**	**2.84**

Claimed by **Nashville** from **Anaheim** in Expansion Draft, June 26, 1998. Traded to **Edmonton** by **Nashville** with Jim Dowd for Eric Fichaud, Drake Berehowsky and Greg de Vries, October 1, 1998. Traded to **Phoenix** by **Edmonton** for Phoenix's 5th round choice (later traded to Nashville – Nashville selected Matt Koalska) in 2000 Entry Draft, March 11, 1999. Traded to **Florida** by **Phoenix** with Phoenix's 4th round choice (Chris Eade) in 2000 Entry Draft for Sean Burke and Florida's 5th round choice (Nate Kiser) in 2000 Entry Draft, November 18, 1999.

SHULMISTRA, Richard

Goaltender. Catches right. 6'2", 185 lbs. Born, Sudbury, Ont., April 1, 1971
(Quebec's 1st choice, 4th overall, in 1992 Supplemental Draft).

Season	Club	GP	W	L	T	Mins	GA	SO	Avg	GP	W	L	Mins	GA	SO	Avg
1997-98	New Jersey	1	0	1	0	62	2	0	1.94							
99-2000	Florida	1	1	0	0	60	1	0	1.00							
	NHL Totals	**2**	**1**	**1**	**0**	**122**	**3**	**0**	**1.48**							

Rights transferred to **Colorado** after **Quebec** franchise relocated, June 21, 1995. Signed as a free agent by **New Jersey**, December 31, 1997. Signed as a free agent by **Florida**, July 27, 1999.

SIDORKIEWICZ, Peter

Goaltender. Catches left. 5'9", 180 lbs. Born, Dabrowa Bialostocka, Poland, June 29, 1963
(Washington's 5th choice, 91st overall, in 1981 Entry Draft).

Season	Club	GP	W	L	T	Mins	GA	SO	Avg	GP	W	L	Mins	GA	SO	Avg
1987-88	Hartford	1	0	1	0	60	6	0	6.00							
1988-89	Hartford	44	22	18	4	2635	133	4	3.03	2	0	2	124	8	0	3.87
1989-90	Hartford	46	19	19	7	2703	161	1	3.57	7	3	4	429	23	0	3.22
1990-91	Hartford	52	21	22	7	2953	164	1	3.33	6	2	4	359	24	0	4.01
1991-92	Hartford	35	9	19	6	1995	111	2	3.34							
1992-93	Ottawa	64	8	46	3	3388	250	0	4.43							
1993-94	New Jersey	3	0	3	0	130	6	0	2.77							
1997-98	New Jersey	1	0	0	0	20	1	0	3.00							
	NHL Totals	**246**	**79**	**128**	**27**	**13884**	**832**	**8**	**3.60**	**15**	**5**	**10**	**912**	**55**	**0**	**3.62**

NHL All-Rookie Team (1989)

Played in NHL All-Star Game (1993)

Traded to **Hartford** by **Washington** with Dean Evason for David Jensen, March 12, 1985. Claimed by **Ottawa** from **Hartford** in Expansion Draft, June 18, 1992. Traded to **New Jersey** by **Ottawa** with future considerations (Mike Peluso, June 26, 1993) for Craig Billington, Troy Mallette and New Jersey's 4th round choice (Cosmo Dupaul) in 1993 Entry Draft, June 20, 1993.

SIMMONS, Don

Goaltender. Catches right. 5'10", 150 lbs. Born, Port Colborne, Ont., September 13, 1931

Season	Club	GP	W	L	T	Mins	GA	SO	Avg	GP	W	L	Mins	GA	SO	Avg
1956-57	Boston	26	13	9	4	1560	63	4	2.42	*10	5	5	600	29	*2	2.90
1957-58	Boston	39	15	14	9	2288	92	5	2.41	*11	6	5	*671	25	*1	2.24
1958-59	Boston	58	24	26	8	3480	183	3	3.16							
1959-60	Boston	28	12	13	3	1680	91	2	3.25							
1960-61	Boston	18	3	9	6	1079	58	1	3.23							
1961-62♦	Toronto	9	5	3	1	540	21	1	2.33	3	2	1	165	8	0	2.91
1962-63♦	Toronto	28	15	8	5	1680	69	1	*2.46							
1963-64♦	Toronto	21	9	9	1	1191	63	3	3.17							
1965-66	NY Rangers	12	1	7	1	551	40	0	4.36							
1967-68	NY Rangers	5	2	1	2	300	13	0	2.60							

Season	Club	GP	W	L	T	Mins	GA	SO	Avg	GP	W	L	Mins	GA	SO	Avg
		REGULAR SEASON								PLAYOFFS						
1968-69	NY Rangers	5	2	2	1	206	8	0	2.33	....	....	....	....	....	....	....
	NHL Totals	**249**	**101**	**101**	**41**	**14555**	**701**	**20**	**2.89**	**24**	**13**	**11**	**1436**	**62**	**3**	**2.59**

Played in NHL All-Star Game (1963)

Traded to **Boston** by **Springfield** (AHL) for Norm Defelice, future considerations (Floyd Smith), June, 1957) and the loan of Jack Bionda, January 22, 1957. Traded to **Toronto** by **Boston** for Ed Chadwick, January 31, 1961. Claimed by **NY Rangers** from **Toronto** (Tulsa – CHL) in Inter-League Draft, June 8, 1965. Traded to **Buffalo** (AHL) by **NY Rangers** for cash, June 10, 1969.

SIMMONS, Gary

Goaltender. Catches left. 6'2", 200 lbs. Born, Charlottetown, P.E.I., July 19, 1944

Season	Club	GP	W	L	T	Mins	GA	SO	Avg	GP	W	L	Mins	GA	SO	Avg
1974-75	California	34	10	21	3	2029	124	2	3.67	....	....	....	....	....	....	....
1975-76	California	40	15	19	5	2360	131	2	3.33	....	....	....	....	....	....	....
1976-77	Cleveland	15	2	8	4	840	51	1	3.64	....	....	....	....	....	....	....
	Los Angeles	4	1	2	1	240	16	0	4.00	1	0	0	20	1	0	3.00
1977-78	Los Angeles	14	2	7	2	693	44	0	3.81	....	....	....	....	....	....	....
	NHL Totals	**107**	**30**	**57**	**15**	**6162**	**366**	**5**	**3.56**	**1**	**0**	**0**	**20**	**1**	**0**	**3.00**

Traded to **California** by **Phoenix** (WHA) for cash, October 1, 1974. • Recorded shutout (3-0) in NHL debut vs. Atlanta, October 11, 1974. Transferred to **Cleveland** after **California** franchise relocated, August 26, 1976. Traded to **Los Angeles** by **Cleveland** with Jim Moxey for Gary Edwards and Juha Widing, January 22, 1977.

SKIDMORE, Paul

Goaltender. Catches left. 6', 180 lbs. Born, Smithtown, NY, July 22, 1956
(St. Louis' 6th choice, 61st overall, in 1976 Amateur Draft).

Season	Club	GP	W	L	T	Mins	GA	SO	Avg	GP	W	L	Mins	GA	SO	Avg
1981-82	St. Louis	2	1	1	0	120	6	0	3.00	....	....	....	....	....	....	....
	NHL Totals	**2**	**1**	**1**	**0**	**120**	**6**	**0**	**3.00**	....	....	....	....	....	....	....

SKORODENSKI, Warren

Goaltender. Catches left. 5'8", 165 lbs. Born, Winnipeg, Man., March 22, 1960

Season	Club	GP	W	L	T	Mins	GA	SO	Avg	GP	W	L	Mins	GA	SO	Avg
1981-82	Chicago	1	0	1	0	60	5	0	5.00	....	....	....	....	....	....	....
1984-85	Chicago	27	11	9	3	1396	75	2	3.22	2	0	0	33	6	0	10.91
1985-86	Chicago	1	0	1	0	60	6	0	6.00	....	....	....	....	....	....	....
1986-87	Chicago	3	1	0	1	155	7	0	2.71	....	....	....	....	....	....	....
1987-88	Edmonton	3	0	0	0	61	7	0	6.89	....	....	....	....	....	....	....
	NHL Totals	**35**	**12**	**11**	**4**	**1732**	**100**	**2**	**3.46**	**2**	**0**	**0**	**33**	**6**	**0**	**10.91**

Signed as a free agent by **Chicago**, August 12, 1979. Signed as a free agent by **Edmonton**, October 8, 1987.

SKUDRA, Peter

Goaltender. Catches left. 6'1", 189 lbs. Born, Riga, Latvia, April 24, 1973

Season	Club	GP	W	L	T	Mins	GA	SO	Avg	GP	W	L	Mins	GA	SO	Avg
1997-98	Pittsburgh	17	6	4	3	851	26	0	1.83	....	....	....	....	....	....	....
1998-99	Pittsburgh	37	15	11	5	1914	89	3	2.79	....	....	....	....	....	....	....
99-2000	Pittsburgh	20	5	7	3	922	48	1	3.12	1	0	0	20	1	0	3.00
2000-01	Buffalo	1	0	0	0	1	0	0	0.00	....	....	....	....	....	....	....
	Boston	25	6	12	1	1116	62	0	3.33	....	....	....	....	....	....	....
2001-02	Vancouver	23	10	8	2	1166	47	1	2.42	2	0	1	96	5	0	3.13
2002-03	Vancouver	23	9	5	6	1192	54	1	2.72	....	....	....	....	....	....	....
	NHL Totals	**146**	**51**	**47**	**20**	**7162**	**326**	**6**	**2.73**	**3**	**0**	**1**	**116**	**6**	**0**	**3.10**

Signed as a free agent by **Pittsburgh**, September 25, 1997. Signed as a free agent by **Boston**, October 3, 2000. Claimed on waivers by **Buffalo** from **Boston**, October 6, 2000. • Played 27 seconds of game vs. Anaheim, October 20, 2000. Claimed on waivers by **Boston** from **Buffalo**, November 14, 2000. Signed as a free agent by **Vancouver**, November 7, 2001.

SMITH, Al

Goaltender. Catches left. 6'1", 200 lbs. Born, Toronto, Ont., November 10, 1945

Season	Club	GP	W	L	T	Mins	GA	SO	Avg	GP	W	L	Mins	GA	SO	Avg
1965-66	Toronto	2	1	0	0	62	2	0	1.94	....	....	....	....	....	....	....
1966-67	Toronto	1	0	1	0	60	5	0	5.00	....	....	....	....	....	....	....
1968-69	Toronto	7	2	2	1	335	16	0	2.87	....	....	....	....	....	....	....
1969-70	Pittsburgh	46	15	20	8	2555	129	2	3.03	3	1	2	180	10	0	3.33
1970-71	Pittsburgh	46	9	22	9	2472	128	2	3.11	....	....	....	....	....	....	....
1971-72	Detroit	43	18	20	4	2500	135	4	3.24	....	....	....	....	....	....	....
1975-76	Buffalo	14	9	3	2	840	43	0	3.07	1	0	0	17	1	0	3.53
1976-77	Buffalo	7	0	3	0	265	19	0	4.30	....	....	....	....	....	....	....
1979-80	Hartford	30	11	10	8	1754	107	2	3.66	2	0	2	120	10	0	5.00
1980-81	Colorado	37	9	18	4	1909	151	0	4.75	....	....	....	....	....	....	....
	NHL Totals	**233**	**74**	**99**	**36**	**12752**	**735**	**10**	**3.46**	**6**	**1**	**4**	**317**	**21**	**0**	**3.97**

Played in NHL All-Star Game (1968)

Promoted to **Toronto** from **Toronto** (OHA-Jr.) and replaced Gary Smith in third period, February 20, 1966 (Detroit 4, Toronto 1) and in first period, February 23, 1966. (Toronto 3, Chicago 2). Claimed by **Pittsburgh** from **Toronto** in Intra-League Draft, June 11, 1969. Claimed by **Detroit** from **Pittsburgh** in Intra-League Draft, June 8, 1971. Traded to **Buffalo** by **Detroit** for future considerations, March 10, 1975. NHL rights retained by **Hartford** prior to Expansion Draft, June 9, 1979. Traded to **Colorado** by **Hartford** for cash, September 4, 1980.

SMITH, Billy

HHOF

Goaltender. Catches left. 5'10", 185 lbs. Born, Perth, Ont., December 12, 1950
(Los Angeles' 3rd choice, 59th overall, in 1970 Amateur Draft).

Season	Club	GP	W	L	T	Mins	GA	SO	Avg	GP	W	L	Mins	GA	SO	Avg
1971-72	Los Angeles	5	1	3	1	300	23	0	4.60	....	....	....	....	....	....	....
1972-73	NY Islanders	37	7	24	3	2122	147	0	4.16	....	....	....	....	....	....	....
1973-74	NY Islanders	46	9	23	12	2615	134	0	3.07	....	....	....	....	....	....	....
1974-75	NY Islanders	58	21	18	17	3368	156	3	2.78	6	1	4	333	23	0	4.14
1975-76	NY Islanders	39	19	10	9	2254	98	3	2.61	8	4	3	437	21	0	2.88
1976-77	NY Islanders	36	21	8	6	2089	87	2	2.50	10	7	3	580	27	0	2.79
1977-78	NY Islanders	38	20	8	8	2154	95	2	2.65	1	0	0	47	1	0	1.28
1978-79	NY Islanders	40	25	8	4	2261	108	1	2.87	5	4	1	315	10	*1	*1.90
1979-80♦	NY Islanders	38	15	14	7	2114	104	2	2.95	*20	*15	4	*1198	56	1	2.80
1980-81♦	NY Islanders	41	22	10	8	2363	129	2	3.28	*17	*14	3	*994	42	0	*2.54
1981-82♦	NY Islanders	46	*32	9	4	2685	133	0	2.97	*18	*15	3	*1120	47	*1	2.52
1982-83♦	NY Islanders	41	18	14	7	2340	112	1	2.87	*17	*13	3	962	43	*2	*2.68
1983-84	NY Islanders	42	23	13	2	2279	130	2	3.42	*21	*12	8	*1190	54	0	2.72
1984-85	NY Islanders	37	18	14	3	2090	133	0	3.82	6	3	3	342	19	0	3.33
1985-86	NY Islanders	41	20	14	4	2308	143	1	3.72	1	0	1	60	4	0	4.00
1986-87	NY Islanders	40	14	18	5	2252	132	1	3.52	2	0	0	67	1	0	0.90
1987-88	NY Islanders	38	17	14	5	2107	113	2	3.22	....	....	....	....	....	....	....
1988-89	NY Islanders	17	3	11	0	730	54	0	4.44	....	....	....	....	....	....	....
	NHL Totals	**680**	**305**	**233**	**105**	**38431**	**2031**	**22**	**3.17**	**132**	**88**	**36**	**7645**	**348**	**5**	**2.73**

• Brother of Gord • NHL First All-Star Team (1982) • Vezina Trophy (1982) • Shared William M. Jennings Trophy with Roland Melanson (1983) • Conn Smythe Trophy (1983)

Played in NHL All-Star Game (1978)

Claimed by **NY Islanders** from **Los Angeles** in Expansion Draft, June 6, 1972. • Credited with scoring a goal vs. Colorado, November 28, 1979.

SMITH, Gary

Goaltender. Catches left. 6'4", 215 lbs. Born, Ottawa, Ont., February 4, 1944

Season	Club	GP	W	L	T	Mins	GA	SO	Avg	GP	W	L	Mins	GA	SO	Avg
1965-66	Toronto	3	0	2	0	118	7	0	3.56	....	....	....	....	....	....	....
1966-67	Toronto	2	0	2	0	115	7	0	3.65	....	....	....	....	....	....	....
1967-68	Oakland	21	2	13	4	1129	60	1	3.19	....	....	....	....	....	....	....
1968-69	Oakland	54	21	24	7	2993	148	4	2.97	7	3	4	420	23	0	3.29
1969-70	Oakland	65	19	34	12	3762	195	2	3.11	4	0	4	248	13	0	3.15
1970-71	California	*71	19	48	4	*3975	256	2	3.86	....	....	....	....	....	....	....
1971-72	Chicago	28	14	5	6	1540	62	5	2.42	2	1	1	120	3	1	1.50
1972-73	Chicago	23	10	10	2	1340	79	0	3.54	2	0	1	65	5	0	4.62
1973-74	Vancouver	66	20	33	8	3632	208	3	3.44	....	....	....	....	....	....	....
1974-75	Vancouver	*72	32	24	9	3828	197	6	3.09	4	1	3	257	14	0	3.27
1975-76	Vancouver	51	20	24	6	2864	167	2	3.50	....	....	....	....	....	....	....
1976-77	Minnesota	36	10	17	8	2090	139	1	3.99	1	0	0	43	4	0	5.58
1977-78	Washington	17	2	12	3	980	68	0	4.16	....	....	....	....	....	....	....
	Minnesota	3	0	2	1	180	9	0	3.00	....	....	....	....	....	....	....
1979-80	Winnipeg	20	4	11	4	1073	73	0	4.08	....	....	....	....	....	....	....
	NHL Totals	**532**	**173**	**261**	**74**	**29619**	**1675**	**26**	**3.39**	**20**	**5**	**13**	**1153**	**62**	**1**	**3.23**

• Son of Des • Brother of Brian • Shared Vezina Trophy with Tony Esposito (1972)

Played in NHL All-Star Game (1975)

Promoted to **Toronto** from **Rochester** (AHL) to replace injured Terry Sawchuk and played in games on February 19, 20, 23, 1966. Claimed by **California** (Oakland) from **Toronto** in Expansion Draft, June 6, 1967. Traded to **Chicago** by **California** for Kerry Bond, Gerry Pinder and Gerry Desjardins, September 9, 1971. Traded to **Vancouver** by **Chicago** with Jerry Korab for Dale Tallon, May 14, 1973. Traded to **Minnesota** by **Vancouver** for Cesare Maniago, August 23, 1976. Signed as a free agent by **Washington**, September 3, 1977. Traded to **Minnesota** by **Washington** for cash, February 19, 1978. NHL rights retained by **Winnipeg** prior to Expansion Draft, June 9, 1979.

SMITH, Normie

Goaltender. Catches left. 5'7", 165 lbs. Born, Toronto, Ont., March 18, 1908

Season	Club	GP	W	L	T	Mins	GA	SO	Avg	GP	W	L	Mins	GA	SO	Avg
1931-32	Mtl. Maroons	21	5	12	4	1267	62	0	2.94	....	....	....	....	....	....	....
1934-35	Detroit	25	12	11	2	1550	52	2	2.01	....	....	....	....	....	....	....
1935-36♦	Detroit	*48	*24	16	8	*3030	103	6	2.04	7	*6	1	538	12	*2	1.34
1936-37♦	Detroit	*48	*25	14	9	2980	102	*6	*2.05	5	3	1	282	6	1	1.28
1937-38	Detroit	47	11	25	11	2930	130	3	2.66	....	....	....	....	....	....	....
1938-39	Detroit	4	0	4	0	240	12	0	3.00	....	....	....	....	....	....	....
1943-44	Detroit	5	3	1	1	300	15	0	3.00	....	....	....	....	....	....	....
1944-45	Detroit	1	1	0	0	60	3	0	3.00	....	....	....	....	....	....	....
	NHL Totals	**199**	**81**	**83**	**35**	**12357**	**479**	**17**	**2.33**	**12**	**9**	**2**	**820**	**18**	**3**	**1.32**

NHL First All-Star Team (1937) • Vezina Trophy (1937)

Signed as a free agent by **Mtl. Maroons**, July 29, 1930. Traded to **St. Louis** by **Mtl. Maroons** with Vern Ayres to complete transaction that sent Al Shields to Mtl. Maroons (September 20, 1934), October 22, 1934. Traded to **Detroit** by **St. Louis** for Burr Williams, October 22, 1934. • Suspended by **Detroit** for refusing to play following game vs. NY Rangers, November 15, 1938. Rights traded to **Boston** by **Detroit** with $15,000 for Tiny Thompson, November 28, 1938. • Officially announced retirement, November 29, 1938.

SNEDDON, Bob

Goaltender. Catches right. 6'2", 190 lbs. Born, Montreal, Que., May 31, 1944

Season	Club	GP	W	L	T	Mins	GA	SO	Avg	GP	W	L	Mins	GA	SO	Avg
1970-71	California	5	0	2	0	225	21	0	5.60	....	....	....	....	....	....	....
	NHL Totals	**5**	**0**	**2**	**0**	**225**	**21**	**0**	**5.60**	....	....	....	....	....	....	....

Traded to **Philadelphia** by **Chicago** for Brian Bradley, December, 1968. Claimed by **Los Angeles** (Springfield-AHL) from **Philadelphia** in Reverse Draft, June 12, 1969. Claimed by **California** (Providence-AHL) from **Los Angeles** in Reverse Draft, June, 1970. Claimed by **Detroit** (Tidewater-AHL) from **California** (Cleveland-AHL) in Reverse Draft, June, 1971. Traded to **Seattle** (WHL) by **Detroit** for Art Stratton, November, 1971.

SNOW, Garth

Goaltender. Catches left. 6'3", 200 lbs. Born, Wrentham, MA, July 28, 1969
(Quebec's 6th choice, 114th overall, in 1987 Entry Draft).

Season	Club	GP	W	L	T	Mins	GA	SO	Avg	GP	W	L	Mins	GA	SO	Avg
1993-94	Quebec	5	3	2	0	279	16	0	3.44	....	....	....	....	....	....	....
1994-95	Quebec	2	1	1	0	119	11	0	5.55	1	0	0	9	1	0	6.67
1995-96	Philadelphia	26	12	8	4	1437	69	0	2.88	1	0	0	1	0	0	0.00
1996-97	Philadelphia	35	14	8	8	1884	79	2	2.52	12	8	4	699	33	0	2.83
1997-98	Philadelphia	29	14	9	4	1651	67	1	2.43	....	....	....	....	....	....	....
	Vancouver	12	3	6	0	504	26	0	3.10	....	....	....	....	....	....	....
1998-99	Vancouver	65	20	31	8	3501	171	6	2.93	....	....	....	....	....	....	....
99-2000	Vancouver	32	10	15	3	1712	76	0	2.66	....	....	....	....	....	....	....
2000-01	Pittsburgh	35	14	15	4	2032	101	3	2.98	....	....	....	....	....	....	....
2001-02	NY Islanders	25	10	7	2	1217	55	2	2.71	1	0	0	26	2	0	4.62

Season	Club	GP	W	L	T	Mins	GA	SO	Avg	GP	W	L	Mins	GA	SO	Avg
		REGULAR SEASON								PLAYOFFS						
2002-03	NY Islanders	43	16	17	5	2390	92	1	2.31	5	1	4	305	12	1	2.36
	NHL Totals	**309**	**117**	**119**	**38**	**16726**	**763**	**15**	**2.74**	**20**	**9**	**8**	**1040**	**48**	**1**	**2.77**

Transferred to **Colorado** after **Quebec** franchise relocated, June 21, 1995. Traded to **Philadelphia** by **Colorado** for Philadelphia's 3rd (later traded to Washington – Washington selected Shawn McNeil) and 6th (Kai Fischer) round choices in 1996 Entry Draft, July 12, 1995. Traded to **Vancouver** by **Philadelphia** for Sean Burke, March 4, 1998. Signed as a free agent by **Pittsburgh**, October 10, 2000. Signed as a free agent by **NY Islanders**, July 14, 2001.

SODERSTROM, Tommy

Goaltender. Catches left. 5'7", 157 lbs. Born, Stockholm, Sweden, July 17, 1969
(Philadelphia's 14th choice, 214th overall, in 1990 Entry Draft).

Season	Club	GP	W	L	T	Mins	GA	SO	Avg	GP	W	L	Mins	GA	SO	Avg
1992-93	Philadelphia	44	20	17	6	2512	143	5	3.42							
1993-94	Philadelphia	34	6	18	4	1736	116	2	4.01							
1994-95	NY Islanders	26	8	12	3	1350	70	1	3.11							
1995-96	NY Islanders	51	11	22	6	2590	167	2	3.87							
1996-97	NY Islanders	1	0	0	0	1	0	0	0.00							
	NHL Totals	**156**	**45**	**69**	**19**	**8189**	**496**	**10**	**3.63**							

Traded to **NY Islanders** by **Philadelphia** for Ron Hextall and NY Islanders' 6th round choice (Dmitri Tertyshny) in 1995 Entry Draft, September 22, 1994. • Played 10 seconds in game on October 17, 1996.

SOETAERT, Doug

Goaltender. Catches left. 6', 180 lbs. Born, Edmonton, Alta., April 21, 1955
(NY Rangers' 2nd choice, 30th overall, in 1975 Amateur Draft).

Season	Club	GP	W	L	T	Mins	GA	SO	Avg	GP	W	L	Mins	GA	SO	Avg
1975-76	NY Rangers	8	2	2	0	273	24	0	5.27							
1976-77	NY Rangers	12	3	4	1	570	28	1	2.95							
1977-78	NY Rangers	6	2	2	2	360	20	0	3.33							
1978-79	NY Rangers	17	5	7	3	900	57	0	3.80							
1979-80	NY Rangers	8	5	2	0	435	33	0	4.55							
1980-81	NY Rangers	39	16	16	7	2320	152	0	3.93							
1981-82	Winnipeg	39	13	14	8	2157	155	2	4.31	2	1	1	120	8	0	4.00
1982-83	Winnipeg	44	19	19	6	2533	174	0	4.12	1	0	0	20	0	0	0.00
1983-84	Winnipeg	47	18	15	7	2539	182	0	4.30	1	0	1	20	5	0	15.00
1984-85	Montreal	28	14	9	4	1606	91	0	3.40	1	0	0	20	1	0	3.00
1985-86♦	Montreal	23	11	7	2	1215	56	3	2.77							
1986-87	NY Rangers	13	2	7	2	675	58	0	5.16							
	NHL Totals	**284**	**110**	**104**	**42**	**15583**	**1030**	**6**	**3.97**	**5**	**1**	**2**	**180**	**14**	**0**	**4.67**

Traded to **Winnipeg** by **NY Rangers** for Winnipeg's 3rd round choice (Vesa Salo) in 1983 Entry Draft, September 8, 1981. Traded to **Montreal** by **Winnipeg** for Mark Holden, October 9, 1984. Signed as a free agent by **NY Rangers**, July 24, 1986.

SOUCY, Christian

Goaltender. Catches left. 5'11", 160 lbs. Born, Gatineau, Que., September 14, 1970

Season	Club	GP	W	L	T	Mins	GA	SO	Avg	GP	W	L	Mins	GA	SO	Avg
1993-94	Chicago	1	0	0	0	3	0	0	0.00							
	NHL Totals	**1**	**0**	**0**	**0**	**3**	**0**	**0**	**0.00**							

Signed as a free agent by **Chicago**, June 21, 1993. • Shares NHL record with Robbie Irons for having shortest career (three minutes) in league history.

SPOONER, Red

Goaltender. Catches left. 5'8", 170 lbs. Born, Port Arthur, Ont., August 24, 1910

Season	Club	GP	W	L	T	Mins	GA	SO	Avg	GP	W	L	Mins	GA	SO	Avg
1929-30	Pittsburgh	1	0	1	0	60	6	0	6.00							
	NHL Totals	**1**	**0**	**1**	**0**	**60**	**6**	**0**	**6.00**							

Loaned to **Pittsburgh** by **Fort William** (TBSHL) to replace injured Joe Miller, January 18, 1930. (NY Rangers 6, Pittsburgh 5).

STANIOWSKI, Ed

Goaltender. Catches left. 5'9", 170 lbs. Born, Moose Jaw, Sask., July 7, 1955
(St. Louis' 1st choice, 27th overall, in 1975 Amateur Draft).

Season	Club	GP	W	L	T	Mins	GA	SO	Avg	GP	W	L	Mins	GA	SO	Avg
1975-76	St. Louis	11	5	3	2	620	33	0	3.19	3	1	2	206	7	0	2.04
1976-77	St. Louis	29	10	16	1	1589	108	0	4.08	3	0	2	102	9	0	5.29
1977-78	St. Louis	17	1	10	2	886	57	0	3.86							
1978-79	St. Louis	39	9	25	3	2291	146	0	3.82							
1979-80	St. Louis	22	2	11	3	1108	80	0	4.33							
1980-81	St. Louis	19	10	3	3	1010	72	0	4.28							
1981-82	Winnipeg	45	20	19	6	2643	174	1	3.95	2	0	2	120	12	0	6.00
1982-83	Winnipeg	17	4	8	0	827	65	1	4.72							
1983-84	Winnipeg	1	0	0	0	40	8	0	12.00							
	Hartford	18	6	9	1	1041	74	0	4.27							
1984-85	Hartford	1	0	0	0	20	1	0	3.00							
	NHL Totals	**219**	**67**	**104**	**21**	**12075**	**818**	**2**	**4.06**	**8**	**1**	**6**	**428**	**28**	**0**	**3.93**

Traded to **Winnipeg** by **St. Louis** with Bryan Maxwell and Paul MacLean for Scott Campbell and John Markell, July 3, 1981. Traded to **Hartford** by **Winnipeg** for Mike Veisor, November 10, 1983.

STAUBER, Robb

Goaltender. Catches left. 5'11", 180 lbs. Born, Duluth, MN, November 25, 1967
(Los Angeles' 5th choice, 107th overall, in 1986 Entry Draft).

Season	Club	GP	W	L	T	Mins	GA	SO	Avg	GP	W	L	Mins	GA	SO	Avg
1989-90	Los Angeles	2	0	1	0	83	11	0	7.95							
1992-93	Los Angeles	31	15	8	4	1735	111	0	3.84	4	3	1	240	16	0	4.00
1993-94	Los Angeles	22	4	11	5	1144	65	1	3.41							
1994-95	Los Angeles	1	0	0	0	16	2	0	7.50							
	Buffalo	6	2	3	0	317	20	0	3.79							
	NHL Totals	**62**	**21**	**23**	**9**	**3295**	**209**	**1**	**3.81**	**4**	**3**	**1**	**240**	**16**	**0**	**4.00**

Traded to **Buffalo** by **Los Angeles** with Alexei Zhitnik, Charlie Huddy and Los Angeles' 5th round choice (Marian Menhart) in 1995 Entry Draft for Philippe Boucher, Denis Tsygurov and Grant Fuhr, February 14, 1995. Signed as a free agent by **Washington**, August 27, 1996. Signed as a free agent by **NY Rangers**, September 2, 1997.

STEFAN, Greg

Goaltender. Catches left. 5'11", 180 lbs. Born, Brantford, Ont., February 11, 1961
(Detroit's 5th choice, 128th overall, in 1981 Entry Draft).

Season	Club	GP	W	L	T	Mins	GA	SO	Avg	GP	W	L	Mins	GA	SO	Avg
1981-82	Detroit	2	0	2	0	120	10	0	5.00							
1982-83	Detroit	35	6	16	9	1847	139	0	4.52							
1983-84	Detroit	50	19	22	2	2600	152	2	3.51	3	1	2	210	8	0	2.29
1984-85	Detroit	46	21	19	3	2635	190	0	4.33	3	0	3	138	17	0	7.39
1985-86	Detroit	37	10	20	5	2068	155	1	4.50							
1986-87	Detroit	43	20	17	3	2351	135	1	3.45	9	4	5	508	24	0	2.83
1987-88	Detroit	33	17	9	5	1854	96	1	3.11	10	5	4	531	32	*1	3.62
1988-89	Detroit	46	21	17	3	2499	167	0	4.01	5	2	3	294	18	0	3.67
1989-90	Detroit	7	1	5	0	359	24	0	4.01							
	NHL Totals	**299**	**115**	**127**	**30**	**16333**	**1068**	**5**	**3.92**	**30**	**12**	**17**	**1681**	**99**	**1**	**3.53**

• Suffered eventual career-ending knee injury in game vs. Edmonton, November 25, 1989.

STEIN, Phil

Goaltender. Catches left. 5'11", Born, Toronto, Ont., September 13, 1913

Season	Club	GP	W	L	T	Mins	GA	SO	Avg	GP	W	L	Mins	GA	SO	Avg
1939-40	Toronto	1	0	0	1	70	2	0	1.71							
	NHL Totals	**1**	**0**	**0**	**1**	**70**	**2**	**0**	**1.71**							

Signed as a free agent by **Toronto**, October 30, 1934. Promoted to **Toronto** from **Providence** (IAHL) to replace injured Turk Broda, January 18, 1940. (NY Americans 2, Toronto 2). Traded to **New Haven** (AHL) by **Toronto** for cash, October 22, 1940.

STEPHENSON, Wayne

Goaltender. Catches left. 5'9", 175 lbs. Born, Fort William, Ont., January 29, 1945

Season	Club	GP	W	L	T	Mins	GA	SO	Avg	GP	W	L	Mins	GA	SO	Avg
1971-72	St. Louis	2	0	1	0	100	9	0	5.40							
1972-73	St. Louis	45	18	15	7	2535	128	1	3.03	3	1	2	160	14	0	5.25
1973-74	St. Louis	40	13	21	5	2360	123	2	3.13							
1974-75♦	Philadelphia	12	7	2	1	639	29	1	2.72	2	2	0	123	4	1	1.95
1975-76	Philadelphia	66	40	10	13	3819	164	1	2.58	8	4	4	494	22	0	2.67
1976-77	Philadelphia	21	12	3	2	1065	41	3	2.31	9	4	3	532	23	1	2.59
1977-78	Philadelphia	26	14	10	1	1482	68	3	2.75							
1978-79	Philadelphia	40	20	10	5	2187	122	2	3.35	4	0	3	213	16	0	4.51
1979-80	Washington	56	18	24	10	3146	187	0	3.57							
1980-81	Washington	20	4	7	5	1010	66	1	3.92							
	NHL Totals	**328**	**146**	**103**	**49**	**18343**	**937**	**14**	**3.06**	**26**	**11**	**12**	**1522**	**79**	**2**	**3.11**

Played in NHL All-Star Game (1976, 1978)

Signed as a free agent by **St. Louis**, January 2, 1972. Traded to **Philadelphia** by **St. Louis** for Philadelphia's 2nd round choice (Jamie Masters) in 1975 Amateur Draft and the rights to Randy Andreachuk, September 16, 1974. Traded to **Washington** by **Philadelphia** for Washington's 3rd round choice (Barry Tabobondung) in 1981 Entry Draft, August 16, 1979.

STEVENSON, Doug

Goaltender. Catches left. 5'8", 170 lbs. Born, Regina, Sask., April 6, 1924

Season	Club	GP	W	L	T	Mins	GA	SO	Avg	GP	W	L	Mins	GA	SO	Avg
1944-45	NY Rangers	4	0	4	0	240	20	0	5.00							
	Chicago	2	1	1	0	120	7	0	3.50							
1945-46	Chicago	2	1	1	0	120	12	0	6.00							
	NHL Totals	**8**	**2**	**6**	**0**	**480**	**39**	**0**	**4.88**							

Loaned to **Chicago** by **NY Rangers** to replace injured Mike Karakas, March 17, 1945. (Montreal 4, Chicago 3)

STEWART, Charles

Goaltender. Catches left. 5'7", 140 lbs. Born, Carleton Place, Ont., November 13, 1895

Season	Club	GP	W	L	T	Mins	GA	SO	Avg	GP	W	L	Mins	GA	SO	Avg
1924-25	Boston	21	5	16	0	1266	65	2	3.08							
1925-26	Boston	35	16	14	4	2173	80	6	2.21							
1926-27	Boston	21	9	11	1	1303	49	2	2.26							
	NHL Totals	**77**	**30**	**41**	**5**	**4742**	**194**	**10**	**2.45**							

Signed as a free agent by **Boston**, December 25, 1924. Loaned to **Hamilton** (Can-Pro) by **Boston**, January 28, 1927.

STEWART, Jim

Goaltender. Catches left. 5'11", 170 lbs. Born, Cambridge, MA, April 23, 1957

Season	Club	GP	W	L	T	Mins	GA	SO	Avg	GP	W	L	Mins	GA	SO	Avg
1979-80	Boston	1	0	1	0	20	5	0	15.00							
	NHL Totals	**1**	**0**	**1**	**0**	**20**	**5**	**0**	**15.00**							

Signed as a free agent by **Boston**, September, 1979.

STORR, Jamie

Goaltender. Catches left. 6'2", 195 lbs. Born, Brampton, Ont., December 28, 1975
(Los Angeles' 1st choice, 7th overall, in 1994 Entry Draft).

Season	Club	GP	W	L	T	Mins	GA	SO	Avg	GP	W	L	Mins	GA	SO	Avg
1994-95	Los Angeles	5	1	3	1	263	17	0	3.88							
1995-96	Los Angeles	5	3	1	0	262	12	0	2.75							
1996-97	Los Angeles	5	2	1	1	265	11	0	2.49							
1997-98	Los Angeles	17	9	5	1	920	34	2	2.22	3	0	2	145	9	0	3.72
1998-99	Los Angeles	28	12	12	2	1525	61	4	2.40							
99-2000	Los Angeles	42	18	15	5	2206	93	1	2.53	1	0	1	36	2	0	3.33
2000-01	Los Angeles	45	19	18	6	2498	114	4	2.74							
2001-02	Los Angeles	19	9	4	3	886	28	2	1.90	1	0	0	1	0	0	0.00
2002-03	Los Angeles	39	12	19	2	2027	86	3	2.55							
	NHL Totals	**205**	**85**	**78**	**21**	**10852**	**456**	**16**	**2.52**	**5**	**0**	**3**	**182**	**11**	**0**	**3.63**

NHL All-Rookie Team (1998, 1999)

• Played 8 seconds of playoff game vs. Colorado, April 29, 2002.

STUART, Herb

Goaltender. Catches left. 5'6", 175 lbs. Born, Brantford, Ont., March 30, 1899

Season	Club	GP	W	L	T	Mins	GA	SO	Avg	GP	W	L	Mins	GA	SO	Avg
		REGULAR SEASON								PLAYOFFS						
1926-27	Detroit	3	1	2	0	180	5	0	1.67	....	....	....	....	....	....	....
	NHL Totals	**3**	**1**	**2**	**0**	**180**	**5**	**0**	**1.67**	....	....	....	....	....	....	....

Traded to **Detroit** by **Edmonton** (WHL) for cash, October 5, 1926. Traded to **London** (IHL) by **Detroit** for cash, November 10, 1930.

SYLVESTRI, Don

Goaltender. Catches left. 6', 180 lbs. Born, Sudbury, Ont., June 2, 1961
(Boston's 8th choice, 182nd overall, in 1981 Entry Draft).

Season	Club	GP	W	L	T	Mins	GA	SO	Avg	GP	W	L	Mins	GA	SO	Avg
1984-85	Boston	3	0	0	2	102	6	0	3.53	....	....	....	....	....	....	....
	NHL Totals	**3**	**0**	**0**	**2**	**102**	**6**	**0**	**3.53**	....	....	....	....	....	....	....

TABARACCI, Rick

Goaltender. Catches left. 6'1", 190 lbs. Born, Toronto, Ont., January 2, 1969
(Pittsburgh's 2nd choice, 26th overall, in 1987 Entry Draft).

Season	Club	GP	W	L	T	Mins	GA	SO	Avg	GP	W	L	Mins	GA	SO	Avg
1988-89	Pittsburgh	1	0	0	0	33	4	0	7.27	....	....	....	....	....	....	....
1990-91	Winnipeg	24	4	9	4	1093	71	1	3.90	....	....	....	....	....	....	....
1991-92	Winnipeg	18	6	7	3	966	52	0	3.23	7	3	4	387	26	0	4.03
1992-93	Winnipeg	19	5	10	0	959	70	0	4.38	....	....	....	....	....	....	....
	Washington	6	3	2	0	343	10	2	1.75	4	1	3	304	14	0	2.76
1993-94	Washington	32	13	14	2	1770	91	2	3.08	2	0	2	111	6	0	3.24
1994-95	Washington	8	1	3	2	394	16	0	2.44	....	....	....	....	....	....	....
	Calgary	5	2	0	1	202	5	0	1.49	1	0	0	19	0	0	0.00
1995-96	Calgary	43	19	16	3	2391	117	3	2.94	3	0	3	204	7	0	2.06
1996-97	Calgary	7	2	4	0	361	14	1	2.33	....	....	....	....	....	....	....
	Tampa Bay	55	20	25	6	3012	138	4	2.75	....	....	....	....	....	....	....
1997-98	Calgary	42	13	22	6	2419	116	0	2.88	....	....	....	....	....	....	....
1998-99	Washington	23	4	12	3	1193	50	2	2.51	....	....	....	....	....	....	....
99-2000	Atlanta	1	0	1	0	59	4	0	4.07	....	....	....	....	....	....	....
	Colorado	2	1	0	0	60	2	0	2.00	....	....	....	....	....	....	....
	NHL Totals	**286**	**93**	**125**	**30**	**15255**	**760**	**15**	**2.99**	**17**	**4**	**12**	**1025**	**53**	**0**	**3.10**

Traded to **Winnipeg** by **Pittsburgh** with Randy Cunneyworth and Dave McLlwain for Jim Kyte, Andrew McBain and Randy Gilhen, June 17, 1989. Traded to **Washington** by **Winnipeg** for Jim Hrivnak and Washington's 2nd round choice (Alexei Budayev) in 1993 Entry Draft, March 22, 1993. Traded to **Calgary** by **Washington** for Calgary's 5th round choice (Joel Cort) in 1995 Entry Draft, April 7, 1995. Traded to **Tampa Bay** by **Calgary** for Aaron Gavey, November 19, 1996. Traded to **Calgary** by **Tampa Bay** for Calgary's 4th round choice (Eric Beaudoin) in 1998 Entry Draft, June 21, 1997. Traded to **Washington** by **Calgary** for future considerations, August 7, 1998. Signed as a free agent by **Atlanta**, November 3, 1999. Traded to **Colorado** by **Atlanta** for Shean Donovan, December 8, 1999. Claimed by **Columbus** from **Colorado** in Expansion Draft, June 23, 2000. Signed as a free agent by **Dallas**, July 12, 2000.

TAKKO, Kari

Goaltender. Catches left. 6'2", 189 lbs. Born, Uusikaupunki, Finland, June 23, 1962
(Minnesota's 5th choice, 97th overall, in 1984 Entry Draft).

Season	Club	GP	W	L	T	Mins	GA	SO	Avg	GP	W	L	Mins	GA	SO	Avg
1985-86	Minnesota	1	0	1	0	60	3	0	3.00	....	....	....	....	....	....	....
1986-87	Minnesota	38	13	18	4	2075	119	0	3.44	....	....	....	....	....	....	....
1987-88	Minnesota	37	8	19	6	1919	143	1	4.47	....	....	....	....	....	....	....
1988-89	Minnesota	32	8	15	4	1603	93	0	3.48	3	0	1	105	7	0	4.00
1989-90	Minnesota	21	4	12	0	1012	68	0	4.03	1	0	0	4	0	0	0.00
1990-91	Minnesota	2	0	2	0	119	12	0	6.05	....	....	....	....	....	....	....
	Edmonton	11	4	4	0	529	37	0	4.20	....	....	....	....	....	....	....
	NHL Totals	**142**	**37**	**71**	**14**	**7317**	**475**	**1**	**3.90**	**4**	**0**	**1**	**109**	**7**	**0**	**3.85**

• Re-entered NHL Entry Draft. Originally Quebec's 8th choice, 200th overall, in 1981 Entry Draft.

Traded to **Edmonton** by **Minnesota** for Bruce Bell, November 22, 1990.

TALLAS, Robbie

Goaltender. Catches left. 6', 170 lbs. Born, Edmonton, Alta., March 20, 1973

Season	Club	GP	W	L	T	Mins	GA	SO	Avg	GP	W	L	Mins	GA	SO	Avg
1995-96	Boston	1	1	0	0	60	3	0	3.00	....	....	....	....	....	....	....
1996-97	Boston	28	8	12	1	1244	69	1	3.33	....	....	....	....	....	....	....
1997-98	Boston	14	6	3	3	788	24	1	1.83	....	....	....	....	....	....	....
1998-99	Boston	17	7	7	2	987	43	1	2.61	....	....	....	....	....	....	....
99-2000	Boston	27	4	13	4	1363	72	0	3.17	....	....	....	....	....	....	....
2000-01	Chicago	12	2	7	0	627	35	0	3.35	....	....	....	....	....	....	....
	NHL Totals	**99**	**28**	**42**	**10**	**5069**	**246**	**3**	**2.91**	....	....	....	....	....	....	....

Signed as a free agent by **Boston**, September 13, 1995. Signed as a free agent by **Chicago**, July 31, 2000. Signed as a free agent by **Pittsburgh**, August 14, 2001.

TANNER, John

Goaltender. Catches left. 6'3", 182 lbs. Born, Cambridge, Ont., March 17, 1971
(Quebec's 4th choice, 54th overall, in 1989 Entry Draft).

Season	Club	GP	W	L	T	Mins	GA	SO	Avg	GP	W	L	Mins	GA	SO	Avg
1989-90	Quebec	1	0	1	0	60	3	0	3.00	....	....	....	....	....	....	....
1990-91	Quebec	6	1	3	1	228	16	0	4.21	....	....	....	....	....	....	....
1991-92	Quebec	14	1	7	4	796	46	1	3.47	....	....	....	....	....	....	....
	NHL Totals	**21**	**2**	**11**	**5**	**1084**	**65**	**1**	**3.60**	....	....	....	....	....	....	....

Traded to **Anaheim** by **Quebec** for Anaheim's 4th round choice (Tomi Kallio) in 1995 Entry Draft, February 20, 1994.

TATARYN, Dave

Goaltender. Catches left. 5'9", 160 lbs. Born, Sudbury, Ont., July 17, 1950
(St. Louis' 8th choice, 104th overall, in 1970 Amateur Draft).

Season	Club	GP	W	L	T	Mins	GA	SO	Avg	GP	W	L	Mins	GA	SO	Avg
1976-77	NY Rangers	2	1	1	0	80	10	0	7.50	....	....	....	....	....	....	....
	NHL Totals	**2**	**1**	**1**	**0**	**80**	**10**	**0**	**7.50**	....	....	....	....	....	....	....

Signed as a free agent by **NY Rangers** (New Haven-AHL) after Southern Hockey League folded, January 30, 1977.

TAYLOR, Bobby

Goaltender. Catches left. 6'1", 180 lbs. Born, Calgary, Alta., January 24, 1945

Season	Club	GP	W	L	T	Mins	GA	SO	Avg	GP	W	L	Mins	GA	SO	Avg
1971-72	Philadelphia	6	1	2	2	320	16	0	3.00	....	....	....	....	....	....	....
1972-73	Philadelphia	23	8	8	4	1144	78	0	4.09	....	....	....	....	....	....	....
1973-74♦	Philadelphia	8	3	3	0	366	26	0	4.26	....	....	....	....	....	....	....
1974-75	Philadelphia	3	0	2	0	120	13	0	6.50	....	....	....	....	....	....	....
1975-76	Philadelphia	4	3	1	0	240	15	0	3.75	....	....	....	....	....	....	....
	Pittsburgh	2	0	1	0	78	7	0	5.38	....	....	....	....	....	....	....
	NHL Totals	**46**	**15**	**17**	**6**	**2268**	**155**	**0**	**4.10**	....	....	....	....	....	....	....

Signed as a free agent by **Philadelphia**, September, 1968. Traded to **Pittsburgh** by **Philadelphia** with Ed Van Impe for Gary Inness and future considerations, March 9, 1976.

TELLQVIST, Mikael

Goaltender. Catches left. 5'11", 185 lbs. Born, Sundbyberg, Sweden, September 19, 1979
(Toronto's 3rd choice, 70th overall, in 2000 Entry Draft).

Season	Club	GP	W	L	T	Mins	GA	SO	Avg	GP	W	L	Mins	GA	SO	Avg
2002-03	Toronto	3	1	1	0	86	4	0	2.79	....	....	....	....	....	....	....
	NHL Totals	**3**	**1**	**1**	**0**	**86**	**4**	**0**	**2.79**	....	....	....	....	....	....	....

TENO, Harvey

Goaltender. Catches left. 5'7", 175 lbs. Born, Windsor, Ont., February 15, 1915

Season	Club	GP	W	L	T	Mins	GA	SO	Avg	GP	W	L	Mins	GA	SO	Avg
1938-39	Detroit	5	2	3	0	300	15	0	3.00	....	....	....	....	....	....	....
	NHL Totals	**5**	**2**	**3**	**0**	**300**	**15**	**0**	**3.00**	....	....	....	....	....	....	....

Signed as a free agent by **Detroit**, October 21, 1938. Promoted to **Detroit** from **Pittsburgh** (IAHL) to replace suspended Normie Smith, November 17, 1938. Loaned to **Boston** by **Detroit** for remainder of 1938-39 season, December 28, 1938. Traded to **Pittsburgh** (IAHL) by **Detroit** for cash, October 5, 1939.

TERRERI, Chris

Goaltender. Catches left. 5'9", 170 lbs. Born, Providence, RI, November 15, 1964
(New Jersey's 3rd choice, 87th overall, in 1983 Entry Draft).

Season	Club	GP	W	L	T	Mins	GA	SO	Avg	GP	W	L	Mins	GA	SO	Avg
1986-87	New Jersey	7	0	3	1	286	21	0	4.41	....	....	....	....	....	....	....
1988-89	New Jersey	8	0	4	2	402	18	0	2.69	....	....	....	....	....	....	....
1989-90	New Jersey	35	15	12	3	1931	110	0	3.42	4	2	2	238	13	0	3.28
1990-91	New Jersey	53	24	21	7	2970	144	1	2.91	7	3	4	428	21	0	2.94
1991-92	New Jersey	54	22	22	10	3186	169	1	3.18	7	3	3	386	23	0	3.58
1992-93	New Jersey	48	19	21	3	2672	151	2	3.39	4	1	3	219	17	0	4.66
1993-94	New Jersey	44	20	11	4	2340	106	2	2.72	4	3	0	200	9	0	2.70
1994-95♦	New Jersey	15	3	7	2	734	31	0	2.53	1	0	0	8	0	0	0.00
1995-96	New Jersey	4	3	0	0	210	9	0	2.57	....	....	....	....	....	....	....
	San Jose	46	13	29	1	2516	155	0	3.70	....	....	....	....	....	....	....
1996-97	San Jose	22	6	10	3	1200	55	0	2.75	....	....	....	....	....	....	....
	Chicago	7	4	1	2	429	19	0	2.66	2	0	0	44	3	0	4.09
1997-98	Chicago	21	8	10	2	1222	49	2	2.41	....	....	....	....	....	....	....
1998-99	New Jersey	12	8	3	1	726	30	1	2.48	....	....	....	....	....	....	....
99-2000♦	New Jersey	12	2	9	0	649	37	0	3.42	....	....	....	....	....	....	....
2000-01	New Jersey	10	2	5	1	453	21	0	2.78	....	....	....	....	....	....	....
	NY Islanders	8	2	4	1	443	18	0	2.44	....	....	....	....	....	....	....
	NHL Totals	**406**	**151**	**172**	**43**	**22369**	**1143**	**9**	**3.07**	**29**	**12**	**12**	**1523**	**86**	**0**	**3.39**

Traded to **San Jose** by **New Jersey** for San Jose's 2nd round choice (later traded to Pittsburgh – Pittsburgh selected Pavel Skrbek) in 1996 Entry Draft, November 15, 1995. Traded to **Chicago** by **San Jose** with Ulf Dahlen and Michal Sykora for Ed Belfour, January 25, 1997. Traded to **New Jersey** by **Chicago** for New Jersey's 2nd round choice (Stepan Mokhov) in 1999 Entry Draft, August 25, 1998. Claimed by **Minnesota** from **New Jersey** in Expansion Draft, June 23, 2000. Traded to **New Jersey** by **Minnesota** with Minnesota's 9th round choice (later traded to Tampa Bay – Tampa Bay selected Thomas Ziegler) in 2000 Entry Draft for Brad Bombardir, June 23, 2000. Traded to **NY Islanders** by **New Jersey** with New Jersey's 9th round choice (Juha-Pekka Ketola) in 2001 Entry Draft for John Vanbiesbrouck, March 12, 2001.

THEODORE, Jose

Goaltender. Catches right. 5'11", 182 lbs. Born, Laval, Que., September 13, 1976
(Montreal's 2nd choice, 44th overall, in 1994 Entry Draft).

Season	Club	GP	W	L	T	Mins	GA	SO	Avg	GP	W	L	Mins	GA	SO	Avg
1995-96	Montreal	1	0	0	0	9	1	0	6.67	....	....	....	....	....	....	....
1996-97	Montreal	16	5	6	2	821	53	0	3.87	2	1	1	168	7	0	2.50
1997-98	Montreal	....	....	....	....	....	....	....	....	3	0	1	120	1	0	0.50
1998-99	Montreal	18	4	12	0	913	50	1	3.29	....	....	....	....	....	....	....
99-2000	Montreal	30	12	13	2	1655	58	5	2.10	....	....	....	....	....	....	....
2000-01	Montreal	59	20	29	5	3298	141	2	2.57	....	....	....	....	....	....	....
2001-02	Montreal	67	30	24	10	3864	136	7	2.11	12	6	6	686	35	0	3.06
2002-03	Montreal	57	20	31	6	3419	165	2	2.90	....	....	....	....	....	....	....
	NHL Totals	**248**	**91**	**115**	**25**	**13979**	**604**	**17**	**2.59**	**17**	**7**	**8**	**974**	**43**	**0**	**2.65**

NHL Second All-Star Team (2002) • MBNA Roger Crozier Saving Grace Award (2002) • Vezina Trophy (2002) • Hart Trophy (2002)

Played in NHL All-Star Game (2002)

• Scored a goal vs. NY Islanders, January 2, 2001.

THIBAULT, Jocelyn

Goaltender. Catches left. 5'11", 170 lbs. Born, Montreal, Que., January 12, 1975
(Quebec's 1st choice, 10th overall, in 1993 Entry Draft).

Season	Club	GP	W	L	T	Mins	GA	SO	Avg	GP	W	L	Mins	GA	SO	Avg
1993-94	Quebec	29	8	13	3	1504	83	0	3.31	....	....	....	....	....	....	....
1994-95	Quebec	18	12	2	2	898	35	1	2.34	3	1	2	148	8	0	3.24
1995-96	Colorado	10	3	4	2	558	28	0	3.01	....	....	....	....	....	....	....
	Montreal	40	23	13	3	2334	110	3	2.83	6	2	4	311	18	0	3.47
1996-97	Montreal	61	22	24	11	3397	164	1	2.90	3	0	3	179	13	0	4.36
1997-98	Montreal	47	19	15	8	2652	109	2	2.47	2	0	0	43	4	0	5.58
1998-99	Montreal	10	3	4	2	529	23	1	2.61	....	....	....	....	....	....	....
	Chicago	52	21	26	5	3014	136	4	2.71	....	....	....	....	....	....	....
99-2000	Chicago	60	25	26	7	3438	158	3	2.76	....	....	....	....	....	....	....

Season	Club	GP	W	L	T	Mins	GA	SO	Avg	GP	W	L	Mins	GA	SO	Avg
		REGULAR SEASON								PLAYOFFS						
2000-01	Chicago	66	27	32	7	3844	180	6	2.81	....	....	....	....	....	....	....
2001-02	Chicago	67	33	23	9	3838	159	6	2.49	3	1	2	159	7	0	2.64
2002-03	Chicago	62	26	28	7	3650	144	8	2.37	....	....	....	....	....	....	....
	NHL Totals	**522**	**222**	**210**	**66**	**29656**	**1329**	**35**	**2.69**	**17**	**4**	**11**	**840**	**50**	**0**	**3.57**

Played in NHL All-Star Game (2003)

Transferred to **Colorado** after **Quebec** franchise relocated, June 21, 1995. Traded to **Montreal** by **Colorado** with Andrei Kovalenko and Martin Rucinsky for Patrick Roy and Mike Keane, December 6, 1995. Traded to **Chicago** by **Montreal** with Dave Manson and Brad Brown for Jeff Hackett, Eric Weinrich, Alain Nasreddine and Tampa Bay's 4th round choice (previously acquired, Montreal selected Chris Dyment) in 1999 Entry Draft, November 16, 1998.

THOMAS, Tim

Goaltender. Catches left. 5'11", 181 lbs. Born, Flint, MI, April 15, 1974
(Quebec's 11th choice, 217th overall, in 1994 Entry Draft).

Season	Club	GP	W	L	T	Mins	GA	SO	Avg	GP	W	L	Mins	GA	SO	Avg
2002-03	Boston	4	3	1	0	220	11	0	3.00	....	....	....	....	....	....	....
	NHL Totals	**4**	**3**	**1**	**0**	**220**	**11**	**0**	**3.00**	....	....	....	....	....	....	....

Signed as a free agent by **Edmonton**, June 4, 1998. Signed as a free agent by **Boston**, August 8, 2002.

THOMAS, Wayne

Goaltender. Catches left. 6'2", 195 lbs. Born, Ottawa, Ont., October 9, 1947

Season	Club	GP	W	L	T	Mins	GA	SO	Avg	GP	W	L	Mins	GA	SO	Avg
1972-73	Montreal	10	8	1	0	583	23	1	2.37	....	....	....	....	....	....	....
1973-74	Montreal	42	23	12	5	2410	111	1	2.76	....	....	....	....	....	....	....
1974-75	Montreal	DID NOT PLAY – SPARE GOALTENDER														
1975-76	Toronto	64	28	24	12	3684	196	2	3.19	10	5	5	587	34	1	3.48
1976-77	Toronto	33	10	13	6	1803	116	1	3.86	4	1	2	202	12	0	3.56
1977-78	NY Rangers	41	12	20	7	2352	141	4	3.60	1	0	1	60	4	0	4.00
1978-79	NY Rangers	31	15	10	3	1668	101	1	3.63	....	....	....	....	....	....	....
1979-80	NY Rangers	12	4	7	0	668	44	0	3.95	....	....	....	....	....	....	....
1980-81	NY Rangers	10	3	6	1	600	34	0	3.40	....	....	....	....	....	....	....
	NHL Totals	**243**	**103**	**93**	**34**	**13768**	**766**	**10**	**3.34**	**15**	**6**	**8**	**849**	**50**	**1**	**3.53**

Played in NHL All-Star Game (1976)

Traded to **Los Angeles** by **Toronto** with Brian Murphy and Gary Croteau for Grant Moore and Lou Deveault, October 15, 1968. Traded to **Montreal** by **Los Angeles** with Leon Rochefort and Gregg Boddy for Jack Norris, Larry Mickey and Lucien Grenier, May 22, 1970. • Recorded shutout (3-0) in NHL debut vs. Vancouver, January 14, 1973. • On active roster for entire 1974-75 season but did not play. Traded to **Toronto** by **Montreal** for Toronto's 1st round choice (Peter Lee) in 1976 Amateur Draft, June 17, 1975. Claimed by **NY Rangers** from **Toronto** in Waiver Draft, October 10, 1977.

THOMPSON, Tiny

HHOF

Goaltender. Catches left. 5'10", 160 lbs. Born, Sandon, B.C., May 31, 1905

Season	Club	GP	W	L	T	Mins	GA	SO	Avg	GP	W	L	Mins	GA	SO	Avg
1928-29♦	Boston	*44	*26	13	5	2710	52	12	1.15	5	*5	0	300	3	*3	*0.60
1929-30	Boston	*44	*38	5	1	2680	98	3	*2.19	*6	3	3	432	12	0	1.67
1930-31	Boston	*44	*28	10	6	2730	90	3	1.98	5	2	3	343	13	0	2.27
1931-32	Boston	43	13	19	11	2698	103	*9	2.29	....	....	....	....	....	....	....
1932-33	Boston	*48	*25	15	8	3000	88	*11	*1.76	5	2	3	438	9	0	*1.23
1933-34	Boston	*48	18	25	5	2980	130	5	2.62	....	....	....	....	....	....	....
1934-35	Boston	*48	26	16	6	2970	112	8	2.26	4	1	3	275	7	1	1.53
1935-36	Boston	*48	22	20	6	2930	82	*10	*1.68	2	1	1	120	8	1	4.00
1936-37	Boston	*48	23	18	7	2970	110	*6	2.22	3	1	2	180	8	1	2.67
1937-38	Boston	*48	*30	11	7	2970	89	7	*1.80	3	0	3	212	6	0	1.70
1938-39	Boston	5	3	1	1	310	8	0	1.55	....	....	....	....	....	....	....
	Detroit	39	16	17	6	2397	101	4	2.53	6	3	3	374	15	1	2.41
1939-40	Detroit	46	16	24	6	2830	120	3	2.54	5	2	3	300	12	0	2.40
	NHL Totals	**553**	**284**	**194**	**75**	**34175**	**1183**	**81**	**2.08**	**44**	**20**	**24**	**2974**	**93**	**7**	**1.88**

• Brother of Paul • Vezina Trophy (1930, 1933, 1936, 1938) • NHL Second All-Star Team (1931, 1935) • NHL First All-Star Team (1936, 1938)

Played in NHL All-Star Game (1937)

Traded to **Boston** by **Minneapolis** (AHA) for cash, May 12, 1928. • Recorded shutout (1-0) in NHL debut vs. Pittsburgh, November 15, 1928. Traded to **Detroit** by **Boston** for the rights to Normie Smith and $15,000, November 28, 1938.

TORCHIA, Mike

Goaltender. Catches left. 5'11", 215 lbs. Born, Toronto, Ont., February 23, 1972
(Minnesota's 2nd choice, 74th overall, in 1991 Entry Draft).

Season	Club	GP	W	L	T	Mins	GA	SO	Avg	GP	W	L	Mins	GA	SO	Avg
1994-95	Dallas	6	3	2	1	327	18	0	3.30	....	....	....	....	....	....	....
	NHL Totals	**6**	**3**	**2**	**1**	**327**	**18**	**0**	**3.30**	....	....	....	....	....	....	....

Transferred to **Dallas** after **Minnesota** franchise relocated, June 9, 1993. Traded to **Washington** by **Dallas** for cash, July 14, 1995. Traded to **Anaheim** by **Washington** for Todd Krygier, March 8, 1996.

TOSKALA, Vesa

Goaltender. Catches left. 5'10", 190 lbs. Born, Tampere, Finland, May 20, 1977
(San Jose's 4th choice, 90th overall, in 1995 Entry Draft).

Season	Club	GP	W	L	T	Mins	GA	SO	Avg	GP	W	L	Mins	GA	SO	Avg
2001-02	San Jose	1	0	0	0	10	0	0	0.00	....	....	....	....	....	....	....
2002-03	San Jose	11	4	3	1	537	21	1	2.35	....	....	....	....	....	....	....
	NHL Totals	**12**	**4**	**3**	**1**	**547**	**21**	**1**	**2.30**	....	....	....	....	....	....	....

TREFILOV, Andrei

Goaltender. Catches left. 6', 190 lbs. Born, Kirovo-Chepetsk, USSR, August 31, 1969
(Calgary's 14th choice, 261st overall, in 1991 Entry Draft).

Season	Club	GP	W	L	T	Mins	GA	SO	Avg	GP	W	L	Mins	GA	SO	Avg
1992-93	Calgary	1	0	0	1	65	5	0	4.62	....	....	....	....	....	....	....
1993-94	Calgary	11	3	4	2	623	26	2	2.50	....	....	....	....	....	....	....
1994-95	Calgary	6	0	3	0	236	16	0	4.07	....	....	....	....	....	....	....
1995-96	Buffalo	22	8	8	1	1094	64	0	3.51	....	....	....	....	....	....	....
1996-97	Buffalo	3	0	2	0	159	10	0	3.77	1	0	0	5	0	0	0.00
1997-98	Chicago	6	1	4	0	299	17	0	3.41	....	....	....	....	....	....	....
1998-99	Chicago	1	0	1	0	25	4	0	9.60	....	....	....	....	....	....	....
	Calgary	4	0	3	0	162	11	0	4.07	....	....	....	....	....	....	....
	NHL Totals	**54**	**12**	**25**	**4**	**2663**	**153**	**2**	**3.45**	**1**	**0**	**0**	**5**	**0**	**0**	**0.00**

Signed as a free agent by **Buffalo**, July 11, 1995. Traded to **Chicago** by **Buffalo** for future considerations, November 12, 1997. Traded to **Calgary** by **Chicago** for future considerations, December 29, 1998.

TREMBLAY, Vincent

Goaltender. Catches left. 6'1", 180 lbs. Born, Quebec City, Que., October 21, 1959
(Toronto's 3rd choice, 72nd overall, in 1979 Entry Draft).

Season	Club	GP	W	L	T	Mins	GA	SO	Avg	GP	W	L	Mins	GA	SO	Avg
1979-80	Toronto	10	2	1	0	329	28	0	5.11	....	....	....	....	....	....	....
1980-81	Toronto	3	0	3	0	143	16	0	6.71	....	....	....	....	....	....	....
1981-82	Toronto	40	10	18	8	2033	153	1	4.52	....	....	....	....	....	....	....
1982-83	Toronto	1	0	0	0	40	2	0	3.00	....	....	....	....	....	....	....
1983-84	Pittsburgh	4	0	4	0	240	24	0	6.00	....	....	....	....	....	....	....
	NHL Totals	**58**	**12**	**26**	**8**	**2785**	**223**	**1**	**4.80**	....	....	....	....	....	....	....

Traded to **Pittsburgh** by **Toronto** with Rocky Saganiuk for Nick Ricci and Pat Graham, August 15, 1983. Signed as a free agent by **Buffalo**, March 7, 1985.

TUCKER, Ted

Goaltender. Catches left. 5'11", 165 lbs. Born, Fort William, Ont., May 7, 1949

Season	Club	GP	W	L	T	Mins	GA	SO	Avg	GP	W	L	Mins	GA	SO	Avg
1973-74	California	5	1	1	1	177	10	0	3.39	....	....	....	....	....	....	....
	NHL Totals	**5**	**1**	**1**	**1**	**177**	**10**	**0**	**3.39**	....	....	....	....	....	....	....

Traded to **Atlanta** by **Montreal** for cash, June, 1972. Traded to **California** by **Atlanta** for cash, June 10, 1973.

TUGNUTT, Ron

Goaltender. Catches left. 5'11", 160 lbs. Born, Scarborough, Ont., October 22, 1967
(Quebec's 4th choice, 81st overall, in 1986 Entry Draft).

Season	Club	GP	W	L	T	Mins	GA	SO	Avg	GP	W	L	Mins	GA	SO	Avg
1987-88	Quebec	6	2	3	0	284	16	0	3.38	....	....	....	....	....	....	....
1988-89	Quebec	26	10	10	3	1367	82	0	3.60	....	....	....	....	....	....	....
1989-90	Quebec	35	5	24	3	1978	152	0	4.61	....	....	....	....	....	....	....
1990-91	Quebec	56	12	29	10	3144	212	0	4.05	....	....	....	....	....	....	....
1991-92	Quebec	30	6	17	3	1583	106	1	4.02	....	....	....	....	....	....	....
	Edmonton	3	1	1	0	124	10	0	4.84	2	0	0	60	3	0	3.00
1992-93	Edmonton	26	9	12	2	1338	93	0	4.17	....	....	....	....	....	....	....
1993-94	Anaheim	28	10	15	1	1520	76	1	3.00	....	....	....	....	....	....	....
	Montreal	8	2	3	1	378	24	0	3.81	1	0	1	59	5	0	5.08
1994-95	Montreal	7	1	3	1	346	18	0	3.12	....	....	....	....	....	....	....
1996-97	Ottawa	37	17	15	1	1991	93	3	2.80	7	3	4	425	14	1	1.98
1997-98	Ottawa	42	15	14	8	2236	84	3	2.25	2	0	1	74	6	0	4.86
1998-99	Ottawa	43	22	10	8	2508	75	3	*1.79	2	0	2	118	6	0	3.05
99-2000	Ottawa	44	18	12	8	2435	103	4	2.54	....	....	....	....	....	....	....
	Pittsburgh	7	4	2	0	374	15	0	2.41	11	6	5	746	22	2	1.77
2000-01	Columbus	53	22	25	5	3129	127	4	2.44	....	....	....	....	....	....	....
2001-02	Columbus	44	12	27	3	2502	119	2	2.85	....	....	....	....	....	....	....
2002-03	Dallas	31	15	10	5	1701	70	4	2.47	....	....	....	....	....	....	....
	NHL Totals	**526**	**183**	**232**	**62**	**28938**	**1475**	**25**	**3.06**	**25**	**9**	**13**	**1482**	**56**	**3**	**2.27**

Played in NHL All-Star Game (1999)

Traded to **Edmonton** by **Quebec** with Brad Zavisha for Martin Rucinsky, March 10, 1992. Claimed by **Anaheim** from **Edmonton** in Expansion Draft, June 24, 1993. Traded to **Montreal** by **Anaheim** for Stephan Lebeau, February 20, 1994. Signed as a free agent by **Washington**, September 25, 1995. Signed as a free agent by **Ottawa**, August 14, 1996. Traded to **Pittsburgh** by **Ottawa** with Janne Laukkanen for Tom Barrasso, March 14, 2000. Signed as a free agent by **Columbus**, July 4, 2000. Traded to **Dallas** by **Columbus** with Columbus' 2nd round choice (Janos Vas) in 2002 Entry Draft for New Jersey's 1st round choice (previously acquired, later traded to Buffalo – Buffalo selected Dan Paille) in 2002 Entry Draft, June 18, 2002.

TURCO, Marty

Goaltender. Catches left. 5'11", 183 lbs. Born, Sault Ste. Marie, Ont., August 13, 1975
(Dallas' 4th choice, 124th overall, in 1994 Entry Draft).

Season	Club	GP	W	L	T	Mins	GA	SO	Avg	GP	W	L	Mins	GA	SO	Avg
2000-01	Dallas	26	13	6	1	1266	40	3	*1.90	....	....	....	....	....	....	....
2001-02	Dallas	31	15	6	2	1519	53	2	2.09	....	....	....	....	....	....	....
2002-03	Dallas	55	31	10	10	3203	92	7	*1.72	12	6	6	798	25	0	1.88
	NHL Totals	**112**	**59**	**22**	**13**	**5988**	**185**	**12**	**1.85**	**12**	**6**	**6**	**798**	**25**	**0**	**1.88**

MBNA Roger Crozier Saving Grace Award (2001, 2003) • NHL Second All-Star Team (2003)

Played in NHL All-Star Game (2003)

TUREK, Roman

Goaltender. Catches right. 6'3", 220 lbs. Born, Strakonice, Czech., May 21, 1970
(Minnesota's 6th choice, 113th overall, in 1990 Entry Draft).

Season	Club	GP	W	L	T	Mins	GA	SO	Avg	GP	W	L	Mins	GA	SO	Avg
1996-97	Dallas	6	3	1	0	263	9	0	2.05	....	....	....	....	....	....	....
1997-98	Dallas	23	11	10	1	1324	49	1	2.22	....	....	....	....	....	....	....
1998-99♦	Dallas	26	16	3	3	1382	48	1	2.08	....	....	....	....	....	....	....
99-2000	St. Louis	67	42	15	9	3960	129	*7	1.95	7	3	4	415	19	0	2.75
2000-01	St. Louis	54	24	18	10	3232	123	6	2.28	14	9	5	908	31	0	2.05
2001-02	Calgary	69	30	28	11	4081	172	5	2.53	....	....	....	....	....	....	....
2002-03	Calgary	65	27	29	9	3822	164	4	2.57	....	....	....	....	....	....	....
	NHL Totals	**310**	**153**	**104**	**43**	**18064**	**694**	**24**	**2.31**	**21**	**12**	**9**	**1323**	**50**	**0**	**2.27**

Shared William M. Jennings Trophy with Ed Belfour (1999) • NHL Second All-Star Team (2000) • William M. Jennings Trophy (2000)

Played in NHL All-Star Game (2000)

Rights transferred to **Dallas** after **Minnesota** franchise relocated, June 9, 1993. Traded to **St. Louis** by **Dallas** for St. Louis' compensatory 2nd round choice (Dan Jancevski) in 1999 Entry Draft, June 20, 1999. Traded to **Calgary** by **St. Louis** with St. Louis' 4th round choice (Yegor Shastin) in 2001 Entry Draft for Fred Brathwaite, Daniel Tkaczuk, Sergei Varlamov and Calgary's 9th round choice (Grant Jacobsen) in 2001 Entry Draft, June 23, 2001.

TURNER, Joe

Goaltender. Catches left. 5'10", 182 lbs. Born, Windsor, Ont., March 28, 1919

Season	Club	GP	W	L	T	Mins	GA	SO	Avg	GP	W	L	Mins	GA	SO	Avg
		REGULAR SEASON								PLAYOFFS						
1941-42	Detroit	1	0	0	1	70	3	0	2.57	....	....	....	....	....	....	....
	NHL Totals	**1**	**0**	**0**	**1**	**70**	**3**	**0**	**2.57**	....	....	....	....	....	....	....

Promoted to **Detroit** from **Indianapolis** (AHL) to replace injured Johnny Mowers, February 5, 1942. (Toronto 3, Detroit 3). • Killed in action in Holland while serving with U.S. Marine Corps., January 12, 1945.

VACHON, Rogie

Goaltender. Catches left. 5'7", 170 lbs. Born, Palmarolle, Que., September 8, 1945

Season	Club	GP	W	L	T	Mins	GA	SO	Avg	GP	W	L	Mins	GA	SO	Avg
1966-67	Montreal	19	11	3	4	1137	47	1	2.48	9	*6	3	555	22	0	*2.38
1967-68♦	Montreal	39	23	13	2	2227	92	4	2.48	2	1	1	113	4	0	2.12
1968-69♦	Montreal	36	22	9	3	2051	98	2	2.87	8	7	1	507	12	1	*1.42
1969-70	Montreal	64	31	18	12	3697	162	4	2.63	....	....	....	....	....	....	....
1970-71♦	Montreal	47	23	12	9	2676	118	2	2.65	....	....	....	....	....	....	....
1971-72	Montreal	1	0	1	0	20	4	0	12.00	....	....	....	....	....	....	....
	Los Angeles	28	6	18	3	1586	107	0	4.05	....	....	....	....	....	....	....
1972-73	Los Angeles	53	22	20	10	3120	148	4	2.85	....	....	....	....	....	....	....
1973-74	Los Angeles	65	28	26	10	3751	175	5	2.80	4	0	4	240	7	0	*1.75
1974-75	Los Angeles	54	27	14	13	3239	121	6	2.24	3	1	2	199	7	0	2.11
1975-76	Los Angeles	51	26	20	5	3060	160	5	3.14	7	4	3	438	17	1	2.33
1976-77	Los Angeles	68	33	23	12	4059	184	8	2.72	9	4	5	520	36	0	4.15
1977-78	Los Angeles	70	29	27	13	4107	196	4	2.86	2	0	2	120	11	0	5.50
1978-79	Detroit	50	10	27	11	2908	189	0	3.90	....	....	....	....	....	....	....
1979-80	Detroit	59	20	30	8	3474	209	4	3.61	....	....	....	....	....	....	....
1980-81	Boston	53	25	19	6	3021	168	1	3.34	3	0	2	164	16	0	5.85
1981-82	Boston	38	19	11	6	2165	132	1	3.66	1	0	0	20	1	0	3.00
	NHL Totals	**795**	**355**	**291**	**127**	**46298**	**2310**	**51**	**2.99**	**48**	**23**	**23**	**2876**	**133**	**2**	**2.77**

• Father of Nick • Shared Vezina Trophy with Gump Worsley (1968) • NHL Second All-Star Team (1975, 1977)

Played in NHL All-Star Game (1973, 1975, 1978)

Traded to **Los Angeles** by **Montreal** for Denis DeJordy, Dale Hoganson, Noel Price and Doug Robinson, November 4, 1971. Signed as a free agent by **Detroit**, August 8, 1978. Traded to **Boston** by **Detroit** for Gilles Gilbert, July 15, 1980.

VALIQUETTE, Steve

Goaltender. Catches left. 6'5", 190 lbs. Born, Etobicoke, Ont., August 20, 1977
(Los Angeles' 8th choice, 190th overall, in 1996 Entry Draft).

Season	Club	GP	W	L	T	Mins	GA	SO	Avg	GP	W	L	Mins	GA	SO	Avg
99-2000	NY Islanders	6	2	0	0	193	6	0	1.87	....	....	....	....	....	....	....
	NHL Totals	**6**	**2**	**0**	**0**	**193**	**6**	**0**	**1.87**	....	....	....	....	....	....	....

Signed as a free agent by **NY Islanders**, August 18, 1998. Signed as a free agent by **Edmonton**, July 20, 2003.

VANBIESBROUCK, John

Goaltender. Catches left. 5'8", 176 lbs. Born, Detroit, MI, September 4, 1963
(NY Rangers' 5th choice, 72nd overall, in 1981 Entry Draft).

Season	Club	GP	W	L	T	Mins	GA	SO	Avg	GP	W	L	Mins	GA	SO	Avg
1981-82	NY Rangers	1	1	0	0	60	1	0	1.00	....	....	....	....	....	....	....
1983-84	NY Rangers	3	2	1	0	180	10	0	3.33	1	0	0	1	0	0	0.00
1984-85	NY Rangers	42	12	24	3	2358	166	1	4.22	1	0	0	20	0	0	0.00
1985-86	NY Rangers	61	*31	21	5	3326	184	3	3.32	16	8	8	899	49	*1	3.27
1986-87	NY Rangers	50	18	20	5	2656	161	0	3.64	4	1	3	195	11	1	3.38
1987-88	NY Rangers	56	27	22	7	3319	187	2	3.38	....	....	....	....	....	....	....
1988-89	NY Rangers	56	28	21	4	3207	197	0	3.69	2	0	1	107	6	0	3.36
1989-90	NY Rangers	47	19	19	7	2734	154	1	3.38	6	2	3	298	15	0	3.02
1990-91	NY Rangers	40	15	18	6	2257	126	3	3.35	1	0	0	52	1	0	1.15
1991-92	NY Rangers	45	27	13	3	2526	120	2	2.85	7	2	5	368	23	0	3.75
1992-93	NY Rangers	48	20	18	7	2757	152	4	3.31	....	....	....	....	....	....	....
1993-94	Florida	57	21	25	11	3440	145	1	2.53	....	....	....	....	....	....	....
1994-95	Florida	37	14	15	4	2087	86	4	2.47	....	....	....	....	....	....	....
1995-96	Florida	57	26	20	7	3178	142	2	2.68	*22	12	10	1332	50	1	2.25
1996-97	Florida	57	27	19	10	3347	128	2	2.29	5	1	4	328	13	1	2.38
1997-98	Florida	60	18	29	11	3451	165	4	2.87	....	....	....	....	....	....	....
1998-99	Philadelphia	62	27	18	15	3712	135	6	2.18	6	2	4	369	9	1	1.46
99-2000	Philadelphia	50	25	15	9	2950	108	3	2.20	....	....	....	....	....	....	....
2000-01	NY Islanders	44	10	25	5	2390	120	1	3.01	....	....	....	....	....	....	....
	New Jersey	4	4	0	0	240	6	1	1.50	....	....	....	....	....	....	....
2001-02	New Jersey	5	2	3	0	300	10	0	2.00	....	....	....	....	....	....	....
	NHL Totals	**882**	**374**	**346**	**119**	**50475**	**2503**	**40**	**2.98**	**71**	**28**	**38**	**3969**	**177**	**5**	**2.68**

NHL First All-Star Team (1986) • Vezina Trophy (1986) • NHL Second All-Star Team (1994)

Played in NHL All-Star Game (1994, 1996, 1997)

Traded to **Vancouver** by **NY Rangers** for future considerations (Doug Lidster, June 25, 1993), June 20, 1993. Claimed by **Florida** from **Vancouver** in Expansion Draft, June 24, 1993. Signed as a free agent by **Philadelphia**, July 16, 1998. Traded to **NY Islanders** by **Philadelphia** for NY Islanders' 4th round choice (later traded to Nashville – Nashville selected Jordin Tootoo) in 2001 Entry Draft, June 25, 2000. Traded to **New Jersey** by **NY Islanders** for Chris Terreri and New Jersey's 9th round choice (Juha-Pekka Ketola) in 2001 Entry Draft, March 12, 2001. • Officially announced retirement, June 10, 2001. Signed as a free agent by **New Jersey**, February 4, 2002. • Officially announced retirement, May 22, 2002.

VEISOR, Mike

Goaltender. Catches left. 5'9", 160 lbs. Born, Toronto, Ont., August 25, 1952
(Chicago's 3rd choice, 45th overall, in 1972 Amateur Draft).

Season	Club	GP	W	L	T	Mins	GA	SO	Avg	GP	W	L	Mins	GA	SO	Avg
1973-74	Chicago	10	7	0	2	537	20	1	2.23	2	0	1	80	5	0	3.75
1974-75	Chicago	9	1	5	1	460	36	0	4.70	....	....	....	....	....	....	....
1976-77	Chicago	3	1	2	0	180	13	0	4.33	....	....	....	....	....	....	....
1977-78	Chicago	12	3	4	5	720	31	2	2.58	....	....	....	....	....	....	....
1978-79	Chicago	17	5	8	4	1020	60	0	3.53	....	....	....	....	....	....	....
1979-80	Chicago	11	3	5	3	660	37	0	3.36	1	0	1	60	6	0	6.00
1980-81	Hartford	29	6	13	6	1588	118	1	4.46	....	....	....	....	....	....	....
1981-82	Hartford	13	5	5	2	701	53	0	4.54	....	....	....	....	....	....	....
1982-83	Hartford	23	5	16	1	1280	118	1	5.53	....	....	....	....	....	....	....
1983-84	Hartford	4	1	3	0	240	20	0	5.00	....	....	....	....	....	....	....
	Winnipeg	8	4	1	2	420	26	0	3.71	1	0	0	40	4	0	6.00
	NHL Totals	**139**	**41**	**62**	**26**	**7806**	**532**	**5**	**4.09**	**4**	**0**	**2**	**180**	**15**	**0**	**5.00**

Traded to **Hartford** by **Chicago** for Hartford's 2nd round choice (Kevin Griffin) in 1981 Entry Draft, June 19, 1980. Traded to **Winnipeg** by **Hartford** for Ed Staniowski, November 10, 1983.

VERNON, Mike

Goaltender. Catches left. 5'9", 180 lbs. Born, Calgary, Alta., February 24, 1963
(Calgary's 2nd choice, 56th overall, in 1981 Entry Draft).

Season	Club	GP	W	L	T	Mins	GA	SO	Avg	GP	W	L	Mins	GA	SO	Avg
1982-83	Calgary	2	0	2	0	100	11	0	6.59	....	....	....	....	....	....	....
1983-84	Calgary	1	0	1	0	11	4	0	22.22	....	....	....	....	....	....	....
1985-86	Calgary	18	9	3	3	921	52	1	3.39	*21	12	*9	*1229	60	0	2.93
1986-87	Calgary	54	30	21	1	2957	178	1	3.61	5	2	3	263	16	0	3.65
1987-88	Calgary	64	39	16	7	3565	210	1	3.53	9	4	4	515	34	0	3.96
1988-89♦	Calgary	52	*37	6	5	2938	130	0	2.65	*22	*16	5	*1381	52	*3	2.26
1989-90	Calgary	47	23	14	9	2795	146	0	3.13	6	2	3	342	19	0	3.33
1990-91	Calgary	54	31	19	3	3121	172	1	3.31	7	3	4	427	21	0	2.95
1991-92	Calgary	63	24	30	9	3640	217	0	3.58	....	....	....	....	....	....	....
1992-93	Calgary	64	29	26	9	3732	203	2	3.26	4	1	1	150	15	0	6.00
1993-94	Calgary	48	26	17	5	2798	131	3	2.81	7	3	4	466	23	0	2.96
1994-95	Detroit	30	19	6	4	1807	76	1	2.52	18	12	6	1063	41	1	2.31
1995-96	Detroit	32	21	7	2	1855	70	3	2.26	4	2	2	243	11	0	2.72
1996-97♦	Detroit	33	13	11	8	1952	79	0	2.43	*20	*16	4	*1229	36	1	1.76
1997-98	San Jose	62	30	22	8	3564	146	5	2.46	6	2	4	348	14	1	2.41
1998-99	San Jose	49	16	22	10	2831	107	4	2.27	5	2	3	321	13	0	2.43
99-2000	San Jose	15	6	5	1	772	32	0	2.49	....	....	....	....	....	....	....
	Florida	34	18	13	2	2019	83	1	2.47	4	0	4	237	12	0	3.04
2000-01	Calgary	41	12	23	5	2246	121	3	3.23	....	....	....	....	....	....	....
2001-02	Calgary	18	2	9	1	825	38	1	2.76	....	....	....	....	....	....	....
	NHL Totals	**781**	**385**	**273**	**92**	**44449**	**2206**	**27**	**2.98**	**138**	**77**	**56**	**8214**	**367**	**6**	**2.68**

NHL Second All-Star Team (1989) • Shared William M. Jennings Trophy with Chris Osgood (1996) • Conn Smythe Trophy (1997)

Played in NHL All-Star Game (1988, 1989, 1990, 1991, 1993)

Traded to **Detroit** by **Calgary** for Steve Chiasson, June 29, 1994. Traded to **San Jose** by **Detroit** with Detroit's 5th round choice (later traded back to Detroit – Detroit selected Andrei Maximenko) in 1999 Entry Draft for San Jose's 2nd round choice (later traded to St. Louis – St. Louis selected Maxim Linnik) in 1998 Entry Draft and San Jose's 2nd round choice (later traded to Tampa Bay – Tampa Bay selected Sheldon Keefe) in 1999 Entry Draft, August 18, 1997. Traded to **Florida** by **San Jose** with San Jose's 3rd round choice (Sean O'Connor) in 2000 Entry Draft for Radek Dvorak, December 30, 1999. Claimed by **Minnesota** from **Florida** in Expansion Draft, June 23, 2000. Traded to **Calgary** by **Minnesota** for Calgary's 8th round choice (Jake Riddle) in 2001 Entry Draft and the rights to Dan Cavanaugh, June 23, 2000. • Officially announced retirement, September 13, 2002.

VEZINA, Georges

HHOF

Goaltender. Catches left. 5'6", 185 lbs. Born, Chicoutimi, Que., January 21, 1887

Season	Club	GP	W	L	T	Mins	GA	SO	Avg	GP	W	L	Mins	GA	SO	Avg
1917-18	Montreal	21	*12	9	0	1282	84	*1	*3.93	2	1	1	120	10	0	5.00
1918-19	Montreal	*18	10	8	0	1117	78	1	4.19	*5	*4	1	*300	18	*0	*3.60
	Montreal (Cup)	....	....	....	....	....	....	....	....	*5*	*2*	*2*	*356*	*19*	*1*	*2.74*
1919-20	Montreal	*24	13	11	0	*1456	113	0	4.66	....	....	....	....	....	....	....
1920-21	Montreal	*24	13	11	0	1441	99	1	4.12	....	....	....	....	....	....	....
1921-22	Montreal	*24	12	11	1	1469	94	0	3.84	....	....	....	....	....	....	....
1922-23	Montreal	*24	13	9	2	1488	61	2	2.46	2	1	1	120	3	0	1.50
1923-24♦	Montreal	*24	13	11	0	1459	48	*3	*1.97	2	2	0	120	2	1	*1.00
	Montreal (Cup)	....	....	....	....	....	....	....	....	*4*	*4*	*0*	*240*	*4*	*1*	*1.00*
1924-25	Montreal	*30	17	11	2	*1860	56	5	*1.81	2	2	0	120	2	1	*1.00
	Montreal (Cup)	....	....	....	....	....	....	....	....	*4*	*1*	*3*	*240*	*16*	*0*	*4.00*
1925-26	Montreal	1	0	0	0	20	0	0	0.00	....	....	....	....	....	....	....
	NHL Totals	**190**	**103**	**81**	**5**	**11592**	**633**	**13**	**3.28**	**13**	**10**	**3**	**780**	**35**	**2**	**2.69**

Rights retained by **Montreal** after NHA folded, November 26, 1917. • 1923-24 Stanley Cup totals includes series with Calgary (WCHL) and Vancouver (PCHA). • Forced to retire because of tuberculosis after appearing in 325 consecutive regular-season games for Montreal, November 28, 1925.

VILLEMURE, Gilles

Goaltender. Catches right. 5'8", 185 lbs. Born, Trois-Rivieres, Que., May 30, 1940

Season	Club	GP	W	L	T	Mins	GA	SO	Avg	GP	W	L	Mins	GA	SO	Avg
1963-64	NY Rangers	5	0	2	3	300	18	0	3.60	....	....	....	....	....	....	....
1967-68	NY Rangers	4	1	2	0	200	8	1	2.40	....	....	....	....	....	....	....
1968-69	NY Rangers	4	2	1	1	240	9	0	2.25	1	0	1	60	4	0	4.00
1970-71	NY Rangers	34	22	8	4	2039	78	4	2.30	2	0	1	80	6	0	4.50
1971-72	NY Rangers	37	24	7	4	2129	74	3	2.09	6	4	2	360	14	0	2.33
1972-73	NY Rangers	34	20	12	2	2040	78	3	2.29	2	0	1	61	2	0	1.97
1973-74	NY Rangers	21	7	7	3	1054	62	0	3.53	1	0	0	1	0	0	0.00
1974-75	NY Rangers	45	22	14	6	2470	130	2	3.16	2	1	0	94	6	0	3.83
1975-76	Chicago	15	2	7	5	797	57	0	4.29	....	....	....	....	....	....	....
1976-77	Chicago	6	0	4	1	312	28	0	5.38	....	....	....	....	....	....	....
	NHL Totals	**205**	**100**	**64**	**29**	**11581**	**542**	**13**	**2.81**	**14**	**5**	**5**	**656**	**32**	**0**	**2.93**

Shared Vezina Trophy with Ed Giacomin (1971)

Played in NHL All-Star Game (1971, 1972, 1973)

Promoted to **NY Rangers** from **Baltimore** (AHL) to replace injured Jacques Plante, November 20, 1963. (Boston 1, NY Rangers 1). • Played 22 seconds in playoff game vs. Philadelphia, April 23, 1974. Traded to **Chicago** by **NY Rangers** for Doug Jarrett, October 28, 1975.

VOKOUN, Tomas

Goaltender. Catches right. 6', 195 lbs. Born, Karlovy Vary, Czech., July 2, 1976
(Montreal's 11th choice, 226th overall, in 1994 Entry Draft).

		REGULAR SEASON								PLAYOFFS						
Season	Club	GP	W	L	T	Mins	GA	SO	Avg	GP	W	L	Mins	GA	SO	Avg
1996-97	Montreal	1	0	0	0	20	4	0	12.00	....	....	....	....	....	....	....
1998-99	Nashville	37	12	18	4	1954	96	1	2.95	....	....	....	....	....	....	....
99-2000	Nashville	33	9	20	1	1879	87	1	2.78	....	....	....	....	....	....	....
2000-01	Nashville	37	13	17	5	2088	85	2	2.44	....	....	....	....	....	....	....
2001-02	Nashville	29	5	14	4	1471	66	2	2.69	....	....	....	....	....	....	....
2002-03	Nashville	69	25	31	11	3974	146	3	2.20	....	....	....	....	....	....	....
	NHL Totals	**206**	**64**	**100**	**25**	**11386**	**484**	**9**	**2.55**	....	....	....	....	....	....	....

Claimed by **Nashville** from **Montreal** in Expansion Draft, June 26, 1998.

WAITE, Jimmy

Goaltender. Catches left. 6'1", 180 lbs. Born, Sherbrooke, Que., April 15, 1969
(Chicago's 1st choice, 8th overall, in 1987 Entry Draft).

		REGULAR SEASON								PLAYOFFS						
Season	Club	GP	W	L	T	Mins	GA	SO	Avg	GP	W	L	Mins	GA	SO	Avg
1988-89	Chicago	11	0	7	1	494	43	0	5.22	....	....	....	....	....	....	....
1989-90	Chicago	4	2	0	0	183	14	0	4.59	....	....	....	....	....	....	....
1990-91	Chicago	1	1	0	0	60	2	0	2.00	....	....	....	....	....	....	....
1991-92	Chicago	17	4	7	4	877	54	0	3.69	....	....	....	....	....	....	....
1992-93	Chicago	20	6	7	1	996	49	2	2.95	....	....	....	....	....	....	....
1993-94	San Jose	15	3	7	0	697	50	0	4.30	2	0	0	40	3	0	4.50
1994-95	Chicago	2	1	1	0	119	5	0	2.52	....	....	....	....	....	....	....
1995-96	Chicago	1	0	0	0	31	0	0	0.00	....	....	....	....	....	....	....
1996-97	Chicago	2	0	1	1	105	7	0	4.00	....	....	....	....	....	....	....
1997-98	Phoenix	17	5	6	1	793	28	1	2.12	4	0	3	171	11	0	3.86
1998-99	Phoenix	16	6	5	4	898	41	1	2.74	....	....	....	....	....	....	....
	NHL Totals	**106**	**28**	**41**	**12**	**5253**	**293**	**4**	**3.35**	**6**	**0**	**3**	**211**	**14**	**0**	**3.98**

Traded to **San Jose** by **Chicago** for future considerations (Neil Wilkinson, July 9, 1993), June 18, 1993. Traded to **Chicago** by **San Jose** for Chicago's 4th round choice (later traded to NY Rangers – NY Rangers selected Tomi Kallarsson) in 1997 Entry Draft, February 5, 1995. Claimed by **Phoenix** from **Chicago** in Waiver Draft, September 28, 1997. Signed as a free agent by **Toronto**, August 19, 1999.

WAKALUK, Darcy

Goaltender. Catches left. 5'11", 180 lbs. Born, Pincher Creek, Alta., March 14, 1966
(Buffalo's 7th choice, 144th overall, in 1984 Entry Draft).

		REGULAR SEASON								PLAYOFFS						
Season	Club	GP	W	L	T	Mins	GA	SO	Avg	GP	W	L	Mins	GA	SO	Avg
1988-89	Buffalo	6	1	3	0	214	15	0	4.21	....	....	....	....	....	....	....
1990-91	Buffalo	16	4	5	3	630	35	0	3.33	2	0	1	37	2	0	3.24
1991-92	Minnesota	36	13	19	1	1905	104	1	3.28	....	....	....	....	....	....	....
1992-93	Minnesota	29	10	12	5	1596	97	1	3.65	....	....	....	....	....	....	....
1993-94	Dallas	36	18	9	6	2000	88	3	2.64	5	4	1	307	15	0	2.93
1994-95	Dallas	15	4	8	0	754	40	2	3.18	1	0	0	20	1	0	3.00
1995-96	Dallas	37	9	16	5	1875	106	1	3.39	....	....	....	....	....	....	....
1996-97	Phoenix	16	8	3	1	782	39	1	2.99	....	....	....	....	....	....	....
	NHL Totals	**191**	**67**	**75**	**21**	**9756**	**524**	**9**	**3.22**	**8**	**4**	**2**	**364**	**18**	**0**	**2.97**

Traded to **Minnesota** by **Buffalo** for Minnesota's 8th round choice (Jiri Kuntos) in 1991 Entry Draft and Minnesota's 5th round choice (later traded to Toronto – Toronto selected Chris Deruiter) in 1992 Entry Draft, May 26, 1991. Transferred to **Dallas** after **Minnesota** franchise relocated, June 9, 1993. Signed as a free agent by **Phoenix**, July 23, 1996. • Suffered career-ending knee injury in game vs. Washington, January 4, 1997.

WAKELY, Ernie

Goaltender. Catches left. 5'11", 160 lbs. Born, Flin Flon, Man., November 27, 1940

		REGULAR SEASON								PLAYOFFS						
Season	Club	GP	W	L	T	Mins	GA	SO	Avg	GP	W	L	Mins	GA	SO	Avg
1962-63	Montreal	1	1	0	0	60	3	0	3.00	....	....	....	....	....	....	....
1968-69	Montreal	1	0	1	0	60	4	0	4.00	....	....	....	....	....	....	....
1969-70	St. Louis	30	12	9	4	1651	58	4	*2.11	4	0	4	216	17	0	4.72
1970-71	St. Louis	51	20	14	11	2859	133	3	2.79	3	2	1	180	7	1	2.33
1971-72	St. Louis	30	8	18	2	1614	92	1	3.42	3	0	1	113	13	0	6.90
	NHL Totals	**113**	**41**	**42**	**17**	**6244**	**290**	**8**	**2.79**	**10**	**2**	**6**	**509**	**37**	**1**	**4.36**

Played in NHL All-Star Game (1971)

Traded to **St. Louis** by **Montreal** for Norm Beaudin and Bobby Schmautz, June 27, 1969.

WALSH, Flat

Goaltender. Catches left. 5'11", 180 lbs. Born, Kingston, Ont., March 23, 1897

		REGULAR SEASON								PLAYOFFS						
Season	Club	GP	W	L	T	Mins	GA	SO	Avg	GP	W	L	Mins	GA	SO	Avg
1926-27	Mtl. Maroons	1	0	1	0	60	3	0	3.00	....	....	....	....	....	....	....
1927-28	Mtl. Maroons	1	0	0	0	40	1	0	1.50	....	....	....	....	....	....	....
1928-29	NY Americans	4	2	0	2	260	1	3	0.23	....	....	....	....	....	....	....
	Mtl. Maroons	7	1	4	2	450	8	1	1.07	....	....	....	....	....	....	....
1929-30	Mtl. Maroons	30	16	10	4	1897	74	2	2.34	4	1	3	312	11	1	2.12
1930-31	Mtl. Maroons	16	7	7	2	961	36	2	2.25	....	....	....	....	....	....	....
1931-32	Mtl. Maroons	27	14	10	3	1670	77	2	2.77	4	1	1	258	5	*1	*1.16
1932-33	Mtl. Maroons	22	8	11	3	1303	56	2	2.58	....	....	....	....	....	....	....
	NHL Totals	**108**	**48**	**43**	**16**	**6641**	**256**	**12**	**2.31**	**8**	**2**	**4**	**570**	**16**	**2**	**1.68**

Signed as a free agent by **Mtl. Maroons** after **Detroit** (AHA) franchise folded, December, 1926. Loaned to **NY Americans** by **Mtl. Maroons** until NHL and club resolved the status of Roy Worters' contract, November 15, 1928.

WAMSLEY, Rick

Goaltender. Catches left. 5'11", 185 lbs. Born, Simcoe, Ont., May 25, 1959
(Montreal's 5th choice, 58th overall, in 1979 Entry Draft).

		REGULAR SEASON								PLAYOFFS						
Season	Club	GP	W	L	T	Mins	GA	SO	Avg	GP	W	L	Mins	GA	SO	Avg
1980-81	Montreal	5	3	0	1	253	8	1	1.90	....	....	....	....	....	....	....
1981-82	Montreal	38	23	7	7	2206	101	2	2.75	5	2	3	300	11	0	*2.20
1982-83	Montreal	46	27	12	5	2583	151	0	3.51	3	0	3	152	7	0	2.76
1983-84	Montreal	42	19	17	3	2333	144	2	3.70	1	0	0	32	0	0	0.00
1984-85	St. Louis	40	23	12	5	2319	126	0	3.26	2	0	2	120	7	0	3.50
1985-86	St. Louis	42	22	16	3	2517	144	1	3.43	10	4	6	569	37	0	3.90
1986-87	St. Louis	41	17	15	6	2410	142	0	3.54	2	1	1	120	5	0	2.50
1987-88	St. Louis	31	13	16	1	1818	103	2	3.40	....	....	....	....	....	....	....
	Calgary	2	1	0	0	73	5	0	4.11	1	0	1	33	2	0	3.64
1988-89♦	Calgary	35	17	11	4	1927	95	2	2.96	1	0	1	20	2	0	6.00
1989-90	Calgary	36	18	8	6	1969	107	2	3.26	1	0	1	49	9	0	11.02
1990-91	Calgary	29	14	7	5	1670	85	0	3.05	1	0	0	2	1	0	30.00
1991-92	Calgary	9	3	4	0	457	34	0	4.46	....	....	....	....	....	....	....
	Toronto	8	4	3	0	428	27	0	3.79	....	....	....	....	....	....	....
1992-93	Toronto	3	0	3	0	160	15	0	5.63	....	....	....	....	....	....	....
	NHL Totals	**407**	**204**	**131**	**46**	**23123**	**1287**	**12**	**3.34**	**27**	**7**	**18**	**1397**	**81**	**0**	**3.48**

Shared William M. Jennings Trophy with Denis Herron (1982)

Traded to **St. Louis** by **Montreal** with Hartford's 2nd round choice (previously acquired, St. Louis selected Brian Benning) in 1984 Entry Draft, Montreal's 2nd (Tony Hrkac) and 3rd (Robert Dirk) round choices in 1984 Entry Draft for St. Louis' 1st (Shayne Corson) and 2nd (Stephane Richer) round choices in 1984 Entry Draft, June 9, 1984. Traded to **Calgary** by **St. Louis** with Rob Ramage for Brett Hull and Steve Bozek, March 7, 1988. Traded to **Toronto** by **Calgary** with Doug Gilmour, Jamie Macoun, Kent Manderville and Ric Nattress for Gary Leeman, Alexander Godynyuk, Jeff Reese, Michel Petit and Craig Berube, January 2, 1992.

WATT, Jim

Goaltender. Catches left. 5'11", 180 lbs. Born, Duluth, MN, May 11, 1950

		REGULAR SEASON								PLAYOFFS						
Season	Club	GP	W	L	T	Mins	GA	SO	Avg	GP	W	L	Mins	GA	SO	Avg
1973-74	St. Louis	1	0	0	0	20	2	0	6.00	....	....	....	....	....	....	....
	NHL Totals	**1**	**0**	**0**	**0**	**20**	**2**	**0**	**6.00**	....	....	....	....	....	....	....

Signed as a free agent by **St. Louis** (Fort Worth-CHL), October 1, 1972.

WEEKES, Kevin

Goaltender. Catches left. 6', 195 lbs. Born, Toronto, Ont., April 4, 1975
(Florida's 2nd choice, 41st overall, in 1993 Entry Draft).

		REGULAR SEASON								PLAYOFFS						
Season	Club	GP	W	L	T	Mins	GA	SO	Avg	GP	W	L	Mins	GA	SO	Avg
1997-98	Florida	11	0	5	1	485	32	0	3.96	....	....	....	....	....	....	....
1998-99	Vancouver	11	0	8	1	532	34	0	3.83	....	....	....	....	....	....	....
99-2000	Vancouver	20	6	7	4	987	47	1	2.86	....	....	....	....	....	....	....
	NY Islanders	36	10	20	4	2026	115	1	3.41	....	....	....	....	....	....	....
2000-01	Tampa Bay	61	20	33	3	3378	177	4	3.14	....	....	....	....	....	....	....
2001-02	Tampa Bay	19	3	9	0	830	40	2	2.89	....	....	....	....	....	....	....
	Carolina	2	2	0	0	120	3	0	1.50	8	3	2	408	11	2	1.62
2002-03	Carolina	51	14	24	9	2965	126	5	2.55	....	....	....	....	....	....	....
	NHL Totals	**211**	**55**	**106**	**22**	**11323**	**574**	**13**	**3.04**	**8**	**3**	**2**	**408**	**11**	**2**	**1.62**

Traded to **Vancouver** by **Florida** with Ed Jovanovski, Dave Gagner, Mike Brown and Florida's 1st round choice (Nathan Smith) in 2000 Entry Draft for Pavel Bure, Bret Hedican, Brad Ference and Vancouver's 3rd round choice (Robert Fried) in 2000 Entry Draft, January 17, 1999. Traded to **NY Islanders** by **Vancouver** with Dave Scatchard and Bill Muckalt for Felix Potvin, NY Islanders' compensatory 2nd round choice (later traded to New Jersey – New Jersey selected Teemu Laine) in 2000 Entry Draft and NY Islanders' 3rd round choice (Thatcher Bell) in 2000 Entry Draft, December 19, 1999. Traded to **Tampa Bay** by **NY Islanders** with the rights to Kristian Kudroc and NY Islanders' 2nd round choice (later traded to Phoenix – Phoenix selected Matthew Spiller) in 2001 Entry Draft for Tampa Bay's 1st round choice (Raffi Torres) in 2000 Entry Draft, Calgary's 4th round choice (previously acquired, NY Islanders selected Vladimir Gorbunov) in 2000 Entry Draft and NY Islanders' 7th round choice (previously acquired, NY Islanders selected Ryan Caldwell) in 2000 Entry Draft, June 24, 2000. Traded to **Carolina** by **Tampa Bay** for Shane Willis and Chris Dingman, March 5, 2002.

WEEKS, Steve

Goaltender. Catches left. 5'11", 170 lbs. Born, Scarborough, Ont., June 30, 1958
(NY Rangers' 12th choice, 176th overall, in 1978 Amateur Draft).

		REGULAR SEASON								PLAYOFFS						
Season	Club	GP	W	L	T	Mins	GA	SO	Avg	GP	W	L	Mins	GA	SO	Avg
1980-81	NY Rangers	1	0	1	0	60	2	0	2.00	1	0	0	14	1	0	4.29
1981-82	NY Rangers	49	23	16	9	2852	179	1	3.77	4	1	2	127	9	0	4.25
1982-83	NY Rangers	18	9	5	3	1040	68	0	3.92	....	....	....	....	....	....	....
1983-84	NY Rangers	26	10	11	2	1361	90	0	3.97	....	....	....	....	....	....	....
1984-85	Hartford	23	9	12	2	1397	91	2	3.91	....	....	....	....	....	....	....
1985-86	Hartford	27	13	13	0	1544	99	1	3.85	3	1	2	169	8	0	2.84
1986-87	Hartford	25	12	8	2	1367	78	1	3.42	1	0	0	36	1	0	1.67
1987-88	Hartford	18	6	7	2	918	55	0	3.59	....	....	....	....	....	....	....
	Vancouver	9	4	3	2	550	31	0	3.38	....	....	....	....	....	....	....
1988-89	Vancouver	35	11	19	5	2056	102	0	2.98	3	1	1	140	8	0	3.43
1989-90	Vancouver	21	4	11	4	1142	79	0	4.15	....	....	....	....	....	....	....
1990-91	Vancouver	1	0	1	0	59	6	0	6.10	....	....	....	....	....	....	....
1991-92	NY Islanders	23	9	4	2	1032	62	0	3.60	....	....	....	....	....	....	....
	Los Angeles	7	1	3	0	252	17	0	4.05	....	....	....	....	....	....	....
1992-93	Ottawa	7	0	5	0	249	30	0	7.23	....	....	....	....	....	....	....
	NHL Totals	**290**	**111**	**119**	**33**	**15879**	**989**	**5**	**3.74**	**12**	**3**	**5**	**486**	**27**	**0**	**3.33**

Traded to **Hartford** by **NY Rangers** for future considerations, September 5, 1984. Traded to **Vancouver** by **Hartford** for Richard Brodeur, March 8, 1988. Traded to **Buffalo** by **Vancouver** for future considerations, March 5, 1991. Signed as a free agent by **NY Islanders**, September 16, 1991. Traded to **Los Angeles** by **NY Islanders** for Los Angeles' 7th round choice (Steve O'Rourke) in 1992 Entry Draft, February 18, 1992. Signed as a free agent by **Washington**, June 16, 1992. Traded to **Ottawa** by **Washington** for future considerations, August 13, 1992.

WETZEL, Carl

Goaltender. Catches left. 6'1", 170 lbs. Born, Detroit, MI, December 12, 1938

		REGULAR SEASON								PLAYOFFS						
Season	Club	GP	W	L	T	Mins	GA	SO	Avg	GP	W	L	Mins	GA	SO	Avg
1964-65	Detroit	2	0	1	0	32	4	0	7.50	....	....	....	....	....	....	....
1967-68	Minnesota	5	1	2	1	269	18	0	4.01	....	....	....	....	....	....	....
	NHL Totals	**7**	**1**	**3**	**1**	**301**	**22**	**0**	**4.39**	....	....	....	....	....	....	....

Claimed by **Montreal** (Quebec-AHL) from **Detroit** in Reverse Draft, June 9, 1965. Traded to **Minnesota** by **Montreal** for cash, June 14, 1967. Loaned to **Toronto** (Rochester-AHL) by **Minnesota** with the trade of Murray Hall, Ted Taylor, Len Lunde, Don Johns and Duke Harris for J.P. Parise and Milan Marcetta, December 23, 1967.

WHITMORE, Kay

Goaltender. Catches left. 5'11", 175 lbs. Born, Sudbury, Ont., April 10, 1967
(Hartford's 2nd choice, 26th overall, in 1985 Entry Draft).

Season	Club	Regular Season GP	W	L	T	Mins	GA	SO	Avg	Playoffs GP	W	L	Mins	GA	SO	Avg
1988-89	Hartford	3	2	1	0	180	10	0	3.33	2	0	2	135	10	0	4.44
1989-90	Hartford	9	4	2	1	442	26	0	3.53	....	....	....	....	....	....	....
1990-91	Hartford	18	3	9	3	850	52	0	3.67	....	....	....	....	....	....	....
1991-92	Hartford	45	14	21	6	2567	155	3	3.62	1	0	0	19	1	0	3.16
1992-93	Vancouver	31	18	8	4	1817	94	1	3.10	....	....	....	....	....	....	....
1993-94	Vancouver	32	18	14	0	1921	113	0	3.53	....	....	....	....	....	....	....
1994-95	Vancouver	11	0	6	2	558	37	0	3.98	1	0	0	20	2	0	6.00
2000-01	Boston	5	1	2	0	203	18	0	5.32	....	....	....	....	....	....	....
2001-02	Calgary	1	0	1	0	58	3	0	3.10	....	....	....	....	....	....	....
	NHL Totals	**155**	**60**	**64**	**16**	**8596**	**508**	**4**	**3.55**	**4**	**0**	**2**	**174**	**13**	**0**	**4.48**

Traded to **Vancouver** by **Hartford** for Corrie D'Alessio and cash, October 1, 1992. Traded to **NY Rangers** by **Vancouver** for Joe Kocur, March 20, 1996. Signed as a free agent by **San Jose**, September 10, 1997. Traded to **Buffalo** by **San Jose** with Colorado's 2nd round choice (previously acquired, Buffalo selected Jaroslav Kristek) in 1998 Entry Draft and San Jose's 5th round choice (later traded to Columbus – Columbus selected Tyler Kolarik) in 2000 Entry Draft for Steve Shields and Buffalo's 4th round choice (Miroslav Zalesak) in 1998 Entry Draft, June 18, 1998. Signed as a free agent by **NY Rangers**, August 17, 1998. Signed as a free agent by **Boston**, August 25, 1999. Traded to **Edmonton** by **Boston** for Mike Matteucci, December 28, 1999. Traded to **Boston** by **Edmonton** for future considerations, July 20, 2000. Signed as a free agent by **Calgary**, July 9, 2001.

WILKINSON, Derek

Goaltender. Catches left. 6', 170 lbs. Born, Lasalle, Que., July 29, 1974
(Tampa Bay's 7th choice, 145th overall, in 1992 Entry Draft).

Season	Club	Regular Season GP	W	L	T	Mins	GA	SO	Avg	Playoffs GP	W	L	Mins	GA	SO	Avg
1995-96	Tampa Bay	4	0	3	0	200	15	0	4.50	....	....	....	....	....	....	....
1996-97	Tampa Bay	5	0	2	1	169	12	0	4.26	....	....	....	....	....	....	....
1997-98	Tampa Bay	8	2	4	1	311	17	0	3.28	....	....	....	....	....	....	....
1998-99	Tampa Bay	5	1	3	1	253	13	0	3.08	....	....	....	....	....	....	....
	NHL Totals	**22**	**3**	**12**	**3**	**933**	**57**	**0**	**3.67**	....	....	....	....	....	....	....

WILLIS, Jordan

Goaltender. Catches left. 5'9", 155 lbs. Born, Kincardine, Ont., February 28, 1975
(Dallas' 8th choice, 243rd overall, in 1993 Entry Draft).

Season	Club	Regular Season GP	W	L	T	Mins	GA	SO	Avg	Playoffs GP	W	L	Mins	GA	SO	Avg
1995-96	Dallas	1	0	1	0	19	1	0	3.16	....	....	....	....	....	....	....
	NHL Totals	**1**	**0**	**1**	**0**	**19**	**1**	**0**	**3.16**	....	....	....	....	....	....	....

WILSON, Dunc

Goaltender. 5'11", 175 lbs. Born, Toronto, Ont., March 22, 1948

Season	Club	Regular Season GP	W	L	T	Mins	GA	SO	Avg	Playoffs GP	W	L	Mins	GA	SO	Avg
1969-70	Philadelphia	1	0	1	0	60	3	0	3.00	....	....	....	....	....	....	....
1970-71	Vancouver	35	3	25	2	1791	128	0	4.29	....	....	....	....	....	....	....
1971-72	Vancouver	53	16	30	3	2870	173	1	3.62	....	....	....	....	....	....	....
1972-73	Vancouver	43	13	21	5	2423	159	1	3.94	....	....	....	....	....	....	....
1973-74	Toronto	24	9	11	3	1412	68	1	2.89	....	....	....	....	....	....	....
1974-75	Toronto	25	8	11	4	1393	86	0	3.70	....	....	....	....	....	....	....
	NY Rangers	3	1	2	0	180	13	0	4.33	....	....	....	....	....	....	....
1975-76	NY Rangers	20	5	9	3	1080	76	0	4.22	....	....	....	....	....	....	....
1976-77	Pittsburgh	45	18	19	8	2627	129	5	2.95	....	....	....	....	....	....	....
1977-78	Pittsburgh	21	5	11	3	1180	95	0	4.83	....	....	....	....	....	....	....
1978-79	Vancouver	17	2	10	2	835	58	0	4.17	....	....	....	....	....	....	....
	NHL Totals	**287**	**80**	**150**	**33**	**15851**	**988**	**8**	**3.74**	....	....	....	....	....	....	....

Claimed by **Philadelphia** from **Boston** (Oshawa/OHA-Jr.) in Special Internal Amateur Draft, June, 1968. Claimed by **Vancouver** from **Philadelphia** in Expansion Draft, June 10, 1970. Traded to **Toronto** by **Vancouver** for Larry McIntyre and Murray Heatley, May 29, 1973. Claimed on waivers by **NY Rangers** from **Toronto**, February 15, 1975. Traded to **Pittsburgh** by **NY Rangers** for Pittsburgh's 4th round choice (Dave Silk) in 1978 Amateur Draft, October 8, 1976. Traded to **Vancouver** by **Pittsburgh** for cash, November 17, 1978.

WILSON, Lefty

Goaltender. Catches left. 5'11", 178 lbs. Born, Toronto, Ont., October 15, 1919

Season	Club	Regular Season GP	W	L	T	Mins	GA	SO	Avg	Playoffs GP	W	L	Mins	GA	SO	Avg
1953-54	Detroit	1	0	0	0	16	0	0	0.00	....	....	....	....	....	....	....
1955-56	Toronto	1	0	0	0	13	0	0	0.00	....	....	....	....	....	....	....
1957-58	Boston	1	0	0	1	52	1	0	1.15	....	....	....	....	....	....	....
	NHL Totals	**3**	**0**	**0**	**1**	**81**	**1**	**0**	**0.74**	....	....	....	....	....	....	....

• **Detroit's** assistant trainer/practice goaltender replaced injured Terry Sawchuk in 3rd period, October 10, 1953. (Montreal 4, Detroit 1). Loaned to **Toronto** by **Detroit** to replace injured Harry Lumley in 3rd period, January 22, 1956. (Detroit 4, Toronto 1). Loaned to **Boston** by **Detroit** to replace injured Don Simmons in 1st period, December 29, 1957. (Boston 2, Detroit 2)

WINKLER, Hal

Goaltender. 5'8", 150 lbs. Born, Gretna, Man., March 20, 1892

Season	Club	Regular Season GP	W	L	T	Mins	GA	SO	Avg	Playoffs GP	W	L	Mins	GA	SO	Avg
1926-27	NY Rangers	8	3	4	1	514	16	2	1.87	....	....	....	....	....	....	....
	Boston	23	12	9	2	1445	40	4	1.66	*8	2	2	*520	13	*2	1.50
1927-28	Boston	*44	20	13	11	*2780	70	*15	1.51	2	0	1	120	5	0	2.50
	NHL Totals	**75**	**35**	**26**	**14**	**4739**	**126**	**21**	**1.60**	**10**	**2**	**3**	**640**	**18**	**2**	**1.69**

Traded to **NY Rangers** by **Calgary** (WHL) for cash, October 27, 1926. • Recorded shutout (1-0) in NHL debut vs. Mtl. Maroons, November 16, 1926. Traded to **Boston** by **NY Rangers** for $5,000, January 17, 1927. Signed as a free agent by **Seattle** (PCHL), October 28, 1929. Traded to **Boston** (Can-Am) by **Seattle** (PCHL) for cash, October 10, 1930.

WOLFE, Bernie

Goaltender. Catches left. 5'9", 165 lbs. Born, Montreal, Que., December 18, 1951

Season	Club	Regular Season GP	W	L	T	Mins	GA	SO	Avg	Playoffs GP	W	L	Mins	GA	SO	Avg
1975-76	Washington	40	5	23	7	2134	148	0	4.16	....	....	....	....	....	....	....
1976-77	Washington	37	7	15	9	1779	114	1	3.84	....	....	....	....	....	....	....
1977-78	Washington	25	4	14	4	1328	94	0	4.25	....	....	....	....	....	....	....
1978-79	Washington	18	4	9	1	863	68	0	4.73	....	....	....	....	....	....	....
	NHL Totals	**120**	**20**	**61**	**21**	**6104**	**424**	**1**	**4.17**	....	....	....	....	....	....	....

Signed as a free agent by **Washington**, October 1, 1974.

WOOD, Alex

Goaltender. Catches left. 5'11", 165 lbs. Born, Falkirk, Scotland, January 15, 1911

Season	Club	Regular Season GP	W	L	T	Mins	GA	SO	Avg	Playoffs GP	W	L	Mins	GA	SO	Avg
1936-37	NY Americans	1	0	1	0	70	3	0	2.57	....	....	....	....	....	....	....
	NHL Totals	**1**	**0**	**1**	**0**	**70**	**3**	**0**	**2.57**	....	....	....	....	....	....	....

Signed as a free agent by **Chicago**, June 27, 1930. Signed as a free agent by **NY Americans**, December 31, 1936. Promoted to **NY Americans** from **New Haven** (IAHL) to replace Alfie Moore, January 31, 1937. (Mtl. Maroons 3, NY Americans 2). Traded to **Chicago** by **St. Louis** (AHA) with Leo Carbol for cash, October 9, 1942.

WORSLEY, Gump

HHOF

Goaltender. Catches left. 5'7", 180 lbs. Born, Montreal, Que., May 14, 1929

Season	Club	Regular Season GP	W	L	T	Mins	GA	SO	Avg	Playoffs GP	W	L	Mins	GA	SO	Avg
1952-53	NY Rangers	50	13	29	8	3000	153	2	3.06	....	....	....	....	....	....	....
1954-55	NY Rangers	65	15	33	17	3900	197	4	3.03	....	....	....	....	....	....	....
1955-56	NY Rangers	*70	32	28	10	*4200	198	4	2.83	3	0	3	180	14	0	4.67
1956-57	NY Rangers	68	26	28	14	4080	216	3	3.18	5	1	4	316	21	0	3.99
1957-58	NY Rangers	37	21	10	6	2220	86	4	2.32	6	2	4	365	28	0	4.60
1958-59	NY Rangers	67	26	30	11	4001	198	2	2.97	....	....	....	....	....	....	....
1959-60	NY Rangers	39	7	23	8	2301	135	0	3.52	....	....	....	....	....	....	....
1960-61	NY Rangers	59	20	29	8	3473	190	1	3.28	....	....	....	....	....	....	....
1961-62	NY Rangers	60	22	27	9	3531	172	2	2.92	6	2	4	384	21	0	3.28
1962-63	NY Rangers	*67	22	34	10	*3980	217	2	3.27	....	....	....	....	....	....	....
1963-64	Montreal	8	3	2	2	444	22	1	2.97	....	....	....	....	....	....	....
1964-65♦	Montreal	19	10	7	1	1020	50	1	2.94	8	5	3	501	14	*2	*1.68
1965-66♦	Montreal	51	29	14	6	2899	114	2	2.36	10	*8	2	602	20	*1	*1.99
1966-67	Montreal	18	9	6	2	888	47	1	3.18	2	0	1	80	2	0	1.50
1967-68♦	Montreal	40	19	9	8	2213	73	6	*1.98	12	*11	0	672	21	*1	1.88
1968-69♦	Montreal	30	19	5	4	1703	64	5	2.25	7	5	1	370	14	0	2.27
1969-70	Montreal	6	3	1	2	360	14	0	2.33	....	....	....	....	....	....	....
	Minnesota	8	5	1	1	453	20	1	2.65	3	1	2	180	14	0	4.67
1970-71	Minnesota	24	4	10	8	1369	57	0	2.50	4	3	1	240	13	0	3.25
1971-72	Minnesota	34	16	10	7	1923	68	2	2.12	4	2	1	194	7	1	2.16
1972-73	Minnesota	12	6	2	3	624	30	0	2.88	....	....	....	....	....	....	....
1973-74	Minnesota	29	8	14	5	1601	86	0	3.22	....	....	....	....	....	....	....
	NHL Totals	**861**	**335**	**352**	**150**	**50183**	**2407**	**43**	**2.88**	**70**	**40**	**26**	**4084**	**189**	**5**	**2.78**

Calder Memorial Trophy (1953) • NHL Second All-Star Team (1966) • Shared Vezina Trophy with Charlie Hodge (1966) • NHL First All-Star Team (1968) • Shared Vezina Trophy with Rogie Vachon (1968)

Played in NHL All-Star Game (1961, 1962, 1965, 1972)

Traded to **Montreal** by **NY Rangers** with Dave Balon, Leon Rochefort and Len Ronson for Jacques Plante, Don Marshall and Phil Goyette, June 4, 1963. Traded to **Minnesota** by **Montreal** for cash, February 27, 1970.

WORTERS, Roy

HHOF

Goaltender. Catches left. 5'3", 135 lbs. Born, Toronto, Ont., October 19, 1900

Season	Club	Regular Season GP	W	L	T	Mins	GA	SO	Avg	Playoffs GP	W	L	Mins	GA	SO	Avg
1925-26	Pittsburgh	35	18	16	1	2145	68	7	1.90	2	0	1	120	6	0	3.00
1926-27	Pittsburgh	*44	15	26	3	2711	108	4	2.39	....	....	....	....	....	....	....
1927-28	Pittsburgh	*44	19	17	8	2740	76	11	1.66	2	1	1	120	6	0	3.00
1928-29	NY Americans	38	16	12	10	2390	46	13	1.15	2	0	1	150	1	1	0.40
1929-30	NY Americans	36	11	21	4	2270	135	2	3.57	....	....	....	....	....	....	....
	Montreal	1	1	0	0	60	2	0	2.00	....	....	....	....	....	....	....
1930-31	NY Americans	*44	18	16	10	*2760	74	8	*1.61	....	....	....	....	....	....	....
1931-32	NY Americans	40	12	20	8	2459	110	5	2.68	....	....	....	....	....	....	....
1932-33	NY Americans	47	15	22	10	2970	116	5	2.34	....	....	....	....	....	....	....
1933-34	NY Americans	36	12	13	10	2240	75	4	2.01	....	....	....	....	....	....	....
1934-35	NY Americans	*48	12	27	9	*3000	142	3	2.84	....	....	....	....	....	....	....
1935-36	NY Americans	*48	16	25	7	3000	122	3	2.44	5	2	3	300	11	*2	2.20
1936-37	NY Americans	23	6	14	3	1430	69	2	2.90	....	....	....	....	....	....	....
	NHL Totals	**484**	**171**	**229**	**83**	**30175**	**1143**	**67**	**2.27**	**11**	**3**	**6**	**690**	**24**	**3**	**2.09**

Hart Trophy (1929) • Vezina Trophy (1931) • NHL Second All-Star Team (1932, 1934)

Signed as a free agent by **Pittsburgh**, September 26, 1925. Traded to **NY Americans** by **Pittsburgh** for Joe Miller and $20,000, November 1, 1928. • Suspended by NHL President Frank Calder for refusing to report to **NY Americans**, November 12, 1928. • Was re-instated at a special Board of Governors meeting in December, 1928. Loaned to **Montreal** by **NY Americans** to replace George Hainsworth, February 27, 1930. (Montreal 6, Toronto 2). • Missed remainder of 1936-37 season recovering from hernia surgery, January 25, 1937.

WORTHY, Chris

Goaltender. Catches left. 6', 180 lbs. Born, Bristol, England, October 23, 1947

Season	Club	Regular Season GP	W	L	T	Mins	GA	SO	Avg	Playoffs GP	W	L	Mins	GA	SO	Avg
1968-69	Oakland	14	4	6	3	786	54	0	4.12	....	....	....	....	....	....	....
1969-70	Oakland	1	0	1	0	60	5	0	5.00	....	....	....	....	....	....	....
1970-71	California	11	1	3	1	480	39	0	4.88	....	....	....	....	....	....	....
	NHL Totals	**26**	**5**	**10**	**4**	**1326**	**98**	**0**	**4.43**	....	....	....	....	....	....	....

Traded to **Oakland** by **Detroit** with Gary Jarrett, Howie Young and Doug Roberts for Bob Baun and Ron Harris, May 27, 1968. Claimed by **Denver** (WHL) from **California** in Reverse Draft, June, 1972.

WREGGET, Ken

Goaltender. Catches left. 6'1", 201 lbs. Born, Brandon, Man., March 25, 1964
(Toronto's 4th choice, 45th overall, in 1982 Entry Draft).

Season	Club	Regular Season GP	W	L	T	Mins	GA	SO	Avg	Playoffs GP	W	L	Mins	GA	SO	Avg
1983-84	Toronto	3	1	1	1	165	14	0	5.09	....	....	....	....	....	....	....
1984-85	Toronto	23	2	15	3	1278	103	0	4.84	....	....	....	....	....	....	....
1985-86	Toronto	30	9	13	4	1566	113	0	4.33	10	6	4	607	32	*1	3.16
1986-87	Toronto	56	22	28	3	3026	200	0	3.97	13	7	6	761	29	1	2.29

Season	Club	Regular Season GP	W	L	T	Mins	GA	SO	Avg	Playoffs GP	W	L	Mins	GA	SO	Avg
1987-88	Toronto	56	12	35	4	3000	222	2	4.44	2	0	1	108	11	0	6.11
1988-89	Toronto	32	9	20	2	1888	139	0	4.42	....	....	....	....	....	....	....
	Philadelphia	3	1	1	0	130	13	0	6.00	5	2	2	268	10	0	2.24
1989-90	Philadelphia	51	22	24	3	2961	169	0	3.42	....	....	....	....	....	....	....
1990-91	Philadelphia	30	10	14	3	1484	88	0	3.56	....	....	....	....	....	....	....
1991-92	Philadelphia	23	9	8	3	1259	75	0	3.57	....	....	....	....	....	....	....
◆	Pittsburgh	9	5	3	0	448	31	0	4.15	1	0	0	40	4	0	6.00
1992-93	Pittsburgh	25	13	7	2	1368	78	0	3.42	....	....	....	....	....	....	....
1993-94	Pittsburgh	42	21	12	7	2456	138	1	3.37	....	....	....	....	....	....	....
1994-95	Pittsburgh	38	*25	9	2	2208	118	0	3.21	11	5	6	661	33	1	3.00
1995-96	Pittsburgh	37	20	13	2	2132	115	3	3.24	9	7	2	599	23	0	2.30
1996-97	Pittsburgh	46	17	17	6	2514	136	2	3.25	5	1	4	297	18	0	3.64
1997-98	Pittsburgh	15	3	6	2	611	28	0	2.75	....	....	....	....	....	....	....
1998-99	Calgary	27	10	12	4	1590	67	1	2.53	....	....	....	....	....	....	....
99-2000	Detroit	29	14	10	2	1579	70	0	2.66	....	....	....	....	....	....	....
	NHL Totals	**575**	**225**	**248**	**53**	**31663**	**1917**	**9**	**3.63**	**56**	**28**	**25**	**3341**	**160**	**3**	**2.87**

Traded to **Philadelphia** by **Toronto** for Philadelphia's 1st round choice (Rob Pearson) in 1989 Entry Draft and Calgary's 1st round choice (previously acquired, Toronto selected Steve Bancroft) in 1989 Entry Draft, March 6, 1989. Traded to **Pittsburgh** by **Philadelphia** with Rick Tocchet, Kjell Samuelsson and Philadelphia's 3rd round choice (Dave Roche) in 1993 Entry Draft for Mark Recchi, Brian Benning and Los Angeles' 1st round choice (previously acquired, Philadelphia selected Jason Bowen) in 1992 Entry Draft, February 19, 1992. Traded to **Calgary** by **Pittsburgh** with Dave Roche for German Titov and Todd Hlushko, June 17, 1998. Signed as a free agent by **Detroit**, July 23, 1999.

YEREMEYEV, Vitali

Goaltender. Catches left. 5'10", 167 lbs. Born, Ust-Kamenogorsk, USSR, September 23, 1975
(NY Rangers' 11th choice, 209th overall, in 1994 Entry Draft).

Season	Club	Regular Season GP	W	L	T	Mins	GA	SO	Avg	Playoffs GP	W	L	Mins	GA	SO	Avg
2000-01	NY Rangers	4	0	4	0	212	16	0	4.53	....	....	....	....	....	....	....
	NHL Totals	**4**	**0**	**4**	**0**	**212**	**16**	**0**	**4.53**	....	....	....	....	....	....	....

YOUNG, Wendell

Goaltender. Catches left. 5'9", 181 lbs. Born, Halifax, N.S., August 1, 1963
(Vancouver's 3rd choice, 73rd overall, in 1981 Entry Draft).

Season	Club	Regular Season GP	W	L	T	Mins	GA	SO	Avg	Playoffs GP	W	L	Mins	GA	SO	Avg
1985-86	Vancouver	22	4	9	3	1023	61	0	3.58	1	0	1	60	5	0	5.00
1986-87	Vancouver	8	1	6	1	420	35	0	5.00	....	....	....	....	....	....	....
1987-88	Philadelphia	6	3	2	0	320	20	0	3.75	....	....	....	....	....	....	....
1988-89	Pittsburgh	22	12	9	0	1150	92	0	4.80	1	0	0	39	1	0	1.54
1989-90	Pittsburgh	43	16	20	3	2318	161	1	4.17	....	....	....	....	....	....	....
1990-91 ◆	Pittsburgh	18	4	6	2	773	52	0	4.04	....	....	....	....	....	....	....
1991-92 ◆	Pittsburgh	18	7	6	0	838	53	0	3.79	....	....	....	....	....	....	....
1992-93	Tampa Bay	31	7	19	2	1591	97	0	3.66	....	....	....	....	....	....	....
1993-94	Tampa Bay	9	2	3	1	480	20	1	2.50	....	....	....	....	....	....	....
1994-95	Pittsburgh	10	3	6	0	497	27	0	3.26	....	....	....	....	....	....	....
	NHL Totals	**187**	**59**	**86**	**12**	**9410**	**618**	**2**	**3.94**	**2**	**0**	**1**	**99**	**6**	**0**	**3.64**

Traded to **Philadelphia** by **Vancouver** with Vancouver's 3rd round choice (Kimbi Daniels) in 1990 Entry Draft for Darren Jensen and Daryl Stanley, August 31, 1987. Traded to **Pittsburgh** by **Philadelphia** with Philadelphia's 7th round choice (Mika Valila) in 1990 Entry Draft for Pittsburgh's 3rd round choice (Chris Therien) in 1990 Entry Draft, Steptember 1, 1988. Claimed by **Tampa Bay** from **Pittsburgh** in Expansion Draft, June 18, 1992. Traded to **Pittsburgh** by **Tampa Bay** for future considerations, February 16, 1995.

• Only goaltender in hockey history to win Memorial Cup (1982); Calder Cup (1988); Stanley Cup (1991, 1992) and Turner Cup (1998, 2000).

ZANIER, Mike

Goaltender. Catches left. 5'11", 183 lbs. Born, Trail, B.C., August 22, 1962

Season	Club	Regular Season GP	W	L	T	Mins	GA	SO	Avg	Playoffs GP	W	L	Mins	GA	SO	Avg
1984-85	Edmonton	3	1	1	1	185	12	0	3.89	....	....	....	....	....	....	....
	NHL Totals	**3**	**1**	**1**	**1**	**185**	**12**	**0**	**3.89**	....	....	....	....	....	....	....

Signed as a free agent by **Edmonton**, October 4, 1983.

CHAPTER 11

All-Time NHL Coach Register

NHL Statistics for Every Coach, 1917–18 to 2002–03

Note: The All-Time NHL Coach Register lists the NHL statistics of every coach who has worked a regular-season or playoff game in the National Hockey League from 1917–18 to 2002–03.

Team Points (TP) include points from overtime losses beginning in 1999–2000.

Abbreviations: GC - games coached, **W** - wins, **L** - losses (including overtime losses), **T** - ties, **TP** - team points earned, ♦ - coach of Stanley Cup winning team, **(Cup)** - Stanley Cup games vs. non-NHL opponents, 1917-18 to 1925-26. These statistics not included in career NHL playoff totals.

All-time NHL Player Register begins on page 447.

All-Time NHL Goaltender Register begins on page 864.

ABEL, Sid — HHOF

Born: Melville, Sask., February 22, 1918. Died: February 7, 2000.
Played in NHL. See Player Register for career statistics.

Season	Club	Regular Season GC	W	L	T	TP	Playoffs GC	W	L	T
1952-53	Chicago	70	27	28	15	69	7	3	4	0
1953-54	Chicago	70	12	51	7	31	....	....	....	....
1957-58	Detroit	33	16	12	5	37	4	0	4	0
1958-59	Detroit	70	25	37	8	58	....	....	....	....
1959-60	Detroit	70	26	29	15	67	6	2	4	0
1960-61	Detroit	70	25	29	16	66	11	6	5	0
1961-62	Detroit	70	23	33	14	60	....	....	....	....
1962-63	Detroit	70	32	25	13	77	14	7	7	0
1963-64	Detroit	70	30	29	11	71	11	5	6	0
1964-65	Detroit	70	40	23	7	87	7	3	4	0
1965-66	Detroit	70	31	27	12	74	12	6	6	0
1966-67	Detroit	70	27	39	4	58	....	....	....	....
1967-68	Detroit	74	27	35	12	66	....	....	....	....
1969-70	Detroit	74	38	21	15	91	4	0	4	0
1971-72	St. Louis	10	3	6	1	7	....	....	....	....
1975-76	Kansas City	3	0	3	0	0	....	....	....	....
	NHL Totals	**964**	**382**	**427**	**155**	....	**76**	**32**	**44**	**0**

ADAMS, Jack — HHOF

Born: Fort William, Ont., June 14, 1895. Died: May 1, 1968.
Played in NHL. See Player Register for career statistics.

Season	Club	Regular Season GC	W	L	T	TP	Playoffs GC	W	L	T
1927-28	Detroit	44	19	19	6	44	....	....	....	....
1928-29	Detroit	44	19	16	9	47	2	0	2	0
1929-30	Detroit	44	14	24	6	34	....	....	....	....
1930-31	Detroit	44	16	21	7	39	....	....	....	....
1931-32	Detroit	48	18	20	10	46	2	0	1	1
1932-33	Detroit	48	25	15	8	58	4	2	2	0
1933-34	Detroit	48	24	14	10	58	9	4	5	0
1934-35	Detroit	48	19	22	7	45	....	....	....	....
1935-36♦	Detroit	48	24	16	8	56	7	6	1	0
1936-37♦	Detroit	48	25	14	9	59	10	6	4	0
1937-38	Detroit	48	12	25	11	35	....	....	....	....
1938-39	Detroit	48	18	24	6	42	6	3	3	0
1939-40	Detroit	48	16	26	6	38	5	2	3	0
1940-41	Detroit	48	21	16	11	53	9	4	5	0
1941-42	Detroit	48	19	25	4	42	12	7	5	0
1942-43♦	Detroit	50	25	14	11	61	10	8	2	0
1943-44	Detroit	50	26	18	6	58	5	1	4	0
1944-45	Detroit	50	31	14	5	67	14	7	7	0
1945-46	Detroit	50	20	20	10	50	5	1	4	0
1946-47	Detroit	60	22	27	11	55	5	1	4	0
	NHL Totals	**964**	**413**	**390**	**161**	....	**105**	**52**	**52**	**1**

ALLEN, Keith — HHOF

Born: Saskatoon, Sask., August 21, 1923.
Played in NHL. See Player Register for career statistics.

Season	Club	Regular Season GC	W	L	T	TP	Playoffs GC	W	L	T
1967-68	Philadelphia	74	31	32	11	73	7	3	4	0
1968-69	Philadelphia	76	20	35	21	61	4	0	4	0
	NHL Totals	**150**	**51**	**67**	**32**	....	**11**	**3**	**8**	**0**

ALLISON, Dave

Born: Fort Frances, Ont., April 14, 1959.
Played in NHL. See Player Register for career statistics.

Season	Club	Regular Season GC	W	L	T	TP	Playoffs GC	W	L	T
1995-96	Ottawa	25	2	22	1	5	....	....	....	....
	NHL Totals	**25**	**2**	**22**	**1**	....	....	....	....	....

ANDERSON, Jim

Born: Pembroke, Ont., December 1, 1930.
Played in NHL. See Player Register for career statistics.

Season	Club	Regular Season GC	W	L	T	TP	Playoffs GC	W	L	T
1974-75	Washington	54	4	45	5	13	....	....	....	....
	NHL Totals	**54**	**4**	**45**	**5**	....	....	....	....	....

ANGOTTI, Lou

Born: Toronto, Ont., January 16, 1938.
Played in NHL. See Player Register for career statistics.

Season	Club	Regular Season GC	W	L	T	TP	Playoffs GC	W	L	T
1973-74	St. Louis	23	4	15	4	12	....	....	....	....
1974-75	St. Louis	9	2	5	2	6	....	....	....	....
1983-84	Pittsburgh	80	16	58	6	38	....	....	....	....
	NHL Totals	**112**	**22**	**78**	**12**	....	....	....	....	....

ARBOUR, Al — HHOF

Born: Sudbury, Ont., November 1, 1932.
Played in NHL. See Player Register for career statistics.

Season	Club	Regular Season GC	W	L	T	TP	Playoffs GC	W	L	T
1970-71	St. Louis	50	21	15	14	56		....	....	....
1971-72	St. Louis	44	19	19	6	44	11	4	7	0
1972-73	St. Louis	13	2	6	5	9	....	....	....	....
1973-74	NY Islanders	78	19	41	18	56	....	....	....	....
1974-75	NY Islanders	80	33	25	22	88	17	9	8	0
1975-76	NY Islanders	80	42	21	17	101	13	7	6	0
1976-77	NY Islanders	80	47	21	12	106	12	8	4	0
1977-78	NY Islanders	80	48	17	15	111	7	3	4	0
1978-79	NY Islanders	80	51	15	14	116	10	6	4	0
1979-80♦	NY Islanders	80	39	28	13	91	21	15	6	0
1980-81♦	NY Islanders	80	48	18	14	110	18	15	3	0
1981-82♦	NY Islanders	80	54	16	10	118	19	15	4	0
1982-83♦	NY Islanders	80	42	26	12	96	20	15	5	0
1983-84	NY Islanders	80	50	26	4	104	21	12	9	0
1984-85	NY Islanders	80	40	34	6	86	10	4	6	0
1985-86	NY Islanders	80	39	29	12	90	3	0	3	0
1988-89	NY Islanders	53	21	29	3	45	....	....	....	....
1989-90	NY Islanders	80	31	38	11	73	5	1	4	0
1990-91	NY Islanders	80	25	45	10	60	....	....	....	....
1991-92	NY Islanders	80	34	35	11	79	....	....	....	....
1992-93	NY Islanders	84	40	37	7	87	18	9	9	0
1993-94	NY Islanders	84	36	36	12	84	4	0	4	0
	NHL Totals	**1606**	**781**	**577**	**248**	....	**209**	**123**	**86**	**0**

• Won Jack Adams Award (1979)

ARMSTRONG, George — HHOF

Born: Skead, Ontario, July 6, 1930.
Played in NHL. See Player Register for career statistics.

Season	Club	Regular Season GC	W	L	T	TP	Playoffs GC	W	L	T
1988-89	Toronto	47	17	26	4	38	....	....	....	....
	NHL Totals	**47**	**17**	**26**	**4**	....	....	....	....	....

BABCOCK, Mike

Born: Manitouwadge, ON, April 29, 1963.

Season	Club	Regular Season GC	W	L	T	TP	Playoffs GC	W	L	T
2002-03	Anaheim	82	40	33	9	95	21	15	6	0
	NHL Totals	**82**	**40**	**33**	**9**	....	**21**	**15**	**6**	**0**

BARBER, Bill — HHOF

Born: Callander, Ont., July 11, 1952.
Played in NHL. See Player Register for career statistics.

Season	Club	Regular Season GC	W	L	T	TP	Playoffs GC	W	L	T
2000-01	Philadelphia	54	31	16	7	72	6	2	4	0
2001-02	Philadelphia	82	42	30	10	97	5	1	4	0
	NHL Totals	**136**	**73**	**46**	**17**	....	**11**	**3**	**8**	**0**

• Won Jack Adams Award (2001)

BARKLEY, Doug

Born: Lethbridge, Alta., January 6, 1937.
Played in NHL. See Player Register for career statistics.

Season	Club	Regular Season GC	W	L	T	TP	Playoffs GC	W	L	T
1970-71	Detroit	40	10	23	7	27	....	....	....	....
1971-72	Detroit	11	3	8	0	6	....	....	....	....
1975-76	Detroit	26	7	15	4	18	....	....	....	....
	NHL Totals	**77**	**20**	**46**	**11**	....	....	....	....	....

BEAULIEU, Andre

Born: Montreal, Que., January 22, 1940.

Season	Club	Regular Season GC	W	L	T	TP	Playoffs GC	W	L	T
1977-78	Minnesota	32	6	23	3	15	....	....	....	....
	NHL Totals	**32**	**6**	**23**	**3**	....	....	....	....	....

BELISLE, Danny

Born: South Porcupine, Ont., May 9, 1937.
Played in NHL. See Player Register for career statistics.

Season	Club	Regular Season GC	W	L	T	TP	Playoffs GC	W	L	T
1978-79	Washington	80	24	41	15	63	....	....	....	....
1979-80	Washington	16	4	10	2	10	....	....	....	....
	NHL Totals	**96**	**28**	**51**	**17**	....	....	....	....	....

BERENSON, Red

Born: Regina, Sask., December 8, 1939.
Played in NHL. See Player Register for career statistics.

Season	Club	Regular Season GC	W	L	T	TP	Playoffs GC	W	L	T
1979-80	St. Louis	56	27	20	9	63	3	0	3	0
1980-81	St. Louis	80	45	18	17	107	11	5	6	0
1981-82	St. Louis	68	28	34	6	62	....	....	....	....
	NHL Totals	**204**	**100**	**72**	**32**	....	**14**	**5**	**9**	**0**

• Won Jack Adams Award (1981)

BERGERON, Michel

Born: Montreal, Que., June 12, 1946.

Season	Club	Regular Season GC	W	L	T	TP	Playoffs GC	W	L	T
1980-81	Quebec	74	29	29	16	74	5	2	3	0
1981-82	Quebec	80	33	31	16	82	16	7	9	0
1982-83	Quebec	80	34	34	12	80	4	1	3	0
1983-84	Quebec	80	42	28	10	94	9	5	4	0
1984-85	Quebec	80	41	30	9	91	18	9	9	0
1985-86	Quebec	80	43	31	6	92	3	0	3	0
1986-87	Quebec	80	31	39	10	72	13	7	6	0
1987-88	NY Rangers	80	36	34	10	82	....	....	....	....
1988-89	NY Rangers	78	37	33	8	82	....	....	....	....
1989-90	Quebec	80	12	61	7	31	....	....	....	....
	NHL Totals	**792**	**338**	**350**	**104**	....	**68**	**31**	**37**	**0**

BERRY, Bob

Born: Montreal, Que., November 29, 1943.
Played in NHL. See Player Register for career statistics.

Season	Club	Regular Season GC	W	L	T	TP	Playoffs GC	W	L	T
1978-79	Los Angeles	80	34	34	12	80	2	0	2	0
1979-80	Los Angeles	80	30	36	14	74	4	1	3	0
1980-81	Los Angeles	80	43	24	13	99	4	1	3	0
1981-82	Montreal	80	46	17	17	109	5	2	3	0
1982-83	Montreal	80	42	24	14	98	3	0	3	0
1983-84	Montreal	63	28	30	5	61	....	....	....	....
1984-85	Pittsburgh	80	24	51	5	53	....	....	....	....
1985-86	Pittsburgh	80	34	38	8	76	....	....	....	....
1986-87	Pittsburgh	80	30	38	12	72	....	....	....	....
1992-93	St. Louis	73	33	30	10	76	11	7	4	0
1993-94	St. Louis	84	40	33	11	91	4	0	4	0
	NHL Totals	**860**	**384**	**355**	**121**	....	**33**	**11**	**22**	**0**

BEVERLEY, Nick

Born: Toronto, Ont., April 21, 1947.
Played in NHL. See Player Register for career statistics.

Season	Club	Regular Season GC	W	L	T	TP	Playoffs GC	W	L	T
1995-96	Toronto	17	9	6	2	20	6	2	4	0
	NHL Totals	**17**	**9**	**6**	**2**	....	**6**	**2**	**4**	**0**

BLACKBURN, Don

Born: Kirkland Lake, Ont., May 14, 1938.
Played in NHL. See Player Register for career statistics.

Season	Club	Regular Season GC	W	L	T	TP	Playoffs GC	W	L	T
1979-80	Hartford	80	27	34	19	73	3	0	3	0
1980-81	Hartford	60	15	29	16	46	....	....	....	....
	NHL Totals	**140**	**42**	**63**	**35**	....	**3**	**0**	**3**	**0**

BLAIR, Wren

Born: Lindsay, Ont., October 2, 1925.

Season	Club	Regular Season GC	W	L	T	TP	Playoffs GC	W	L	T
1967-68	Minnesota	74	27	32	15	69	14	7	7	0
1968-69	Minnesota	41	12	20	9	33	....	....	....	....
1969-70	Minnesota	32	9	13	10	28	....	....	....	....
	NHL Totals	**147**	**48**	**65**	**34**	....	**14**	**7**	**7**	**0**

BLAKE, Toe — HHOF

Born: Victoria Mines, Ont., August 21, 1912. Died: May 17, 1995.
Played in NHL. See Player Register for career statistics.

Season	Club	Regular Season GC	W	L	T	TP	Playoffs GC	W	L	T
1955-56◆	Montreal	70	45	15	10	100	10	8	2	0
1956-57◆	Montreal	70	35	23	12	82	10	8	2	0
1957-58◆	Montreal	70	43	17	10	96	10	8	2	0
1958-59◆	Montreal	70	39	18	13	91	11	8	3	0
1959-60◆	Montreal	70	40	18	12	92	8	8	0	0
1960-61	Montreal	70	41	19	10	92	6	2	4	0
1961-62	Montreal	70	42	14	14	98	6	2	4	0
1962-63	Montreal	70	28	19	23	79	7	3	4	0
1963-64	Montreal	70	36	21	13	85	5	1	4	0
1964-65◆	Montreal	70	36	23	11	83	13	8	5	0
1965-66◆	Montreal	70	41	21	8	90	10	8	2	0
1966-67	Montreal	70	32	25	13	77	10	6	4	0
1967-68◆	Montreal	74	42	22	10	94	13	12	1	0
	NHL Totals	**914**	**500**	**255**	**159**	....	**119**	**82**	**37**	**0**

BOILEAU, Marc

Born: Pointe Claire, Que., September 3, 1932.
Played in NHL. See Player Register for career statistics.

Season	Club	Regular Season GC	W	L	T	TP	Playoffs GC	W	L	T
1973-74	Pittsburgh	28	14	10	4	32	....	....	....	....
1974-75	Pittsburgh	80	37	28	15	89	9	5	4	0
1975-76	Pittsburgh	43	15	23	5	35	....	....	....	....
	NHL Totals	**151**	**66**	**61**	**24**	....	**9**	**5**	**4**	**0**

BOIVIN, Leo — HHOF

Born: Prescott, Ont., August 2, 1932.
Played in NHL. See Player Register for career statistics.

Season	Club	Regular Season GC	W	L	T	TP	Playoffs GC	W	L	T
1975-76	St. Louis	43	17	17	9	43	3	1	2	0
1977-78	St. Louis	54	11	36	7	29	....	....	....	....
	NHL Totals	**97**	**28**	**53**	**16**	....	**3**	**1**	**2**	**0**

BOUCHER, Frank — HHOF

Born: Ottawa, Ont., October 7, 1901. Died: December 12, 1977.
Played in NHL. See Player Register for career statistics.

Season	Club	Regular Season GC	W	L	T	TP	Playoffs GC	W	L	T
1939-40◆	NY Rangers	48	27	11	10	64	12	8	4	0
1940-41	NY Rangers	48	21	19	8	50	3	1	2	0
1941-42	NY Rangers	48	29	17	2	60	6	2	4	0
1942-43	NY Rangers	50	11	31	8	30	....	....	....	....
1943-44	NY Rangers	50	6	39	5	17	....	....	....	....
1944-45	NY Rangers	50	11	29	10	32	....	....	....	....
1945-46	NY Rangers	50	13	28	9	35	....	....	....	....
1946-47	NY Rangers	60	22	32	6	50	....	....	....	....
1947-48	NY Rangers	60	21	26	13	55	6	2	4	0
1948-49	NY Rangers	23	6	11	6	18	....	....	....	....
1953-54	NY Rangers	40	14	20	6	34	....	....	....	....
	NHL Totals	**527**	**181**	**263**	**83**	....	**27**	**13**	**14**	**0**

BOUCHER, Georges — HHOF

Born: Ottawa, Ont., August 19, 1896. Died: October 17, 1960.
Played in NHL. See Player Register for career statistics.

Season	Club	Regular Season GC	W	L	T	TP	Playoffs GC	W	L	T
1930-31	Mtl. Maroons	12	6	5	1	13	2	0	2	0
1933-34	Ottawa	48	13	29	6	32	....	....	....	....
1934-35	St. Louis	35	9	20	6	24	....	....	....	....
1949-50	Boston	70	22	32	16	60	....	....	....	....
	NHL Totals	**165**	**50**	**86**	**29**	....	**2**	**0**	**2**	**0**

BOWMAN, Scotty — HHOF

Born: Montreal, Que., September 18, 1933.

Season	Club	Regular Season GC	W	L	T	TP	Playoffs GC	W	L	T
1967-68	St. Louis	58	23	21	14	60	18	8	10	0
1968-69	St. Louis	76	37	25	14	88	12	8	4	0
1969-70	St. Louis	76	37	27	12	86	16	8	8	0
1970-71	St. Louis	28	13	10	5	31	6	2	4	0
1971-72	Montreal	78	46	16	16	108	6	2	4	0
1972-73◆	Montreal	78	52	10	16	120	17	12	5	0
1973-74	Montreal	78	45	24	9	99	6	2	4	0
1974-75	Montreal	80	47	14	19	113	11	6	5	0
1975-76◆	Montreal	80	58	11	11	127	13	12	1	0
1976-77◆	Montreal	80	60	8	12	132	14	12	2	0
1977-78◆	Montreal	80	59	10	11	129	15	12	3	0
1978-79◆	Montreal	80	52	17	11	115	16	12	4	0
1979-80	Buffalo	80	47	17	16	110	14	9	5	0
1981-82	Buffalo	35	18	10	7	43	4	1	3	0
1982-83	Buffalo	80	38	29	13	89	10	6	4	0
1983-84	Buffalo	80	48	25	7	103	3	0	3	0
1984-85	Buffalo	80	38	28	14	90	5	2	3	0
1985-86	Buffalo	37	18	18	1	37	....	....	....	....
1986-87	Buffalo	12	3	7	2	8	....	....	....	....
1991-92◆	Pittsburgh	80	39	32	9	87	21	16	5	0
1992-93	Pittsburgh	84	56	21	7	119	12	7	5	0
1993-94	Detroit	84	46	30	8	100	7	3	4	0
1994-95	Detroit	48	33	11	4	70	18	12	6	0
1995-96	Detroit	82	62	13	7	131	19	10	9	0

Season	Club	Regular Season GC	W	L	T	TP	Playoffs GC	W	L	T
1996-97♦	Detroit	82	38	26	18	94	20	16	4	0
1997-98♦	Detroit	82	44	23	15	103	22	16	6	0
1998-99	Detroit	77	39	32	6	84	10	6	4	0
99-2000	Detroit	82	48	24	10	108	9	5	4	0
2000-01	Detroit	82	49	24	9	111	6	2	4	0
2001-02♦	Detroit	82	51	21	10	116	23	16	7	0
	NHL Totals	**2141**	**1244**	**584**	**313**	....	**353**	**223**	**130**	**0**

• Won Jack Adams Award (1977, 1996)

Associate coaches Dave Lewis and Barry Smith shared a 4-1-0 record while combining as co-head coaches until Scotty Bowman received medical clearance and decided to return to coaching on October 23, 1998.

BOWNESS, Rick

Born: Moncton, N.B., January 25, 1955.
Played in NHL. See Player Register for career statistics.

Season	Club	GC	W	L	T	TP	GC	W	L	T
1988-89	Winnipeg	28	8	17	3	19	....	....	....	....
1991-92	Boston	80	36	32	12	84	15	8	7	0
1992-93	Ottawa	84	10	70	4	24	....	....	....	....
1993-94	Ottawa	84	14	61	9	37	....	....	....	....
1994-95	Ottawa	48	9	34	5	23	....	....	....	....
1995-96	Ottawa	19	6	13	0	12	....	....	....	....
1996-97	NY Islanders	37	16	18	3	35	....	....	....	....
1997-98	NY Islanders	63	22	32	9	53	....	....	....	....
	NHL Totals	**443**	**121**	**277**	**45**	....	**15**	**8**	**7**	**0**

BROOKS, Herb

USHOF

Born: St. Paul, MN, August 5, 1937.

Season	Club	GC	W	L	T	TP	GC	W	L	T
1981-82	NY Rangers	80	39	27	14	92	10	5	5	0
1982-83	NY Rangers	80	35	35	10	80	9	5	4	0
1983-84	NY Rangers	80	42	29	9	93	5	2	3	0
1984-85	NY Rangers	45	15	22	8	38	....	....	....	....
1987-88	Minnesota	80	19	48	13	51	....	....	....	....
1992-93	New Jersey	84	40	37	7	87	5	1	4	0
99-2000	Pittsburgh	58	29	24	5	65	11	6	5	0
	NHL Totals	**507**	**219**	**222**	**66**	....	**40**	**19**	**21**	**0**

BROPHY, John

Born: Antigonish, N.S., January 20, 1933.

Season	Club	GC	W	L	T	TP	GC	W	L	T
1986-87	Toronto	80	32	42	6	70	13	7	6	0
1987-88	Toronto	80	21	49	10	52	6	2	4	0
1988-89	Toronto	33	11	20	2	24	....	....	....	....
	NHL Totals	**193**	**64**	**111**	**18**	....	**19**	**9**	**10**	**0**

BURNETT, George

Born: Port Perry, Ont., March 25, 1962.

Season	Club	GC	W	L	T	TP	GC	W	L	T
1994-95	Edmonton	35	12	20	3	27	....	....	....	....
	NHL Totals	**35**	**12**	**20**	**3**	....	....	....	....	....

BURNS, Charlie

Born: Detroit, MI, February 14, 1936.
Played in NHL. See Player Register for career statistics.

Season	Club	GC	W	L	T	TP	GC	W	L	T
1969-70	Minnesota	44	10	22	12	32	6	2	4	0
1974-75	Minnesota	42	12	28	2	26	....	....	....	....
	NHL Totals	**86**	**22**	**50**	**14**	....	**6**	**2**	**4**	**0**

BURNS, Pat

Born: St-Henri, Que., April 4, 1952.

Season	Club	GC	W	L	T	TP	GC	W	L	T
1988-89	Montreal	80	53	18	9	115	21	14	7	0
1989-90	Montreal	80	41	28	11	93	11	5	6	0
1990-91	Montreal	80	39	30	11	89	13	7	6	0
1991-92	Montreal	80	41	28	11	93	11	4	7	0
1992-93	Toronto	84	44	29	11	99	21	11	10	0
1993-94	Toronto	84	43	29	12	98	18	9	9	0
1994-95	Toronto	48	21	19	8	50	7	3	4	0
1995-96	Toronto	65	25	30	10	60	....	....	....	....
1997-98	Boston	82	39	30	13	91	6	2	4	0
1998-99	Boston	82	39	30	13	91	12	6	6	0
99-2000	Boston	82	24	39	19	73	....	....	....	....
2000-01	Boston	8	3	4	1	7	....	....	....	....
2002-03♦	New Jersey	82	46	26	10	108	24	16	8	0
	NHL Totals	**937**	**458**	**340**	**139**	....	**144**	**77**	**67**	**0**

• Won Jack Adams Award (1989, 1993, 1998)

BUSH, Eddie

Born: Collingwood, Ont., July 11, 1918. Died: May 31, 1984.
Played in NHL. See Player Register for career statistics.

Season	Club	GC	W	L	T	TP	GC	W	L	T
1975-76	Kansas City	32	1	23	8	10	....	....	....	....
	NHL Totals	**32**	**1**	**23**	**8**	....	....	....	....	....

CAMPBELL, Colin

Born: London, Ont., January 28, 1953.
Played in NHL. See Player Register for career statistics.

Season	Club	GC	W	L	T	TP	GC	W	L	T
1994-95	NY Rangers	48	22	23	3	47	10	4	6	0
1995-96	NY Rangers	82	41	27	14	96	11	5	6	0
1996-97	NY Rangers	82	38	34	10	86	15	9	6	0
1997-98	NY Rangers	57	17	24	16	50	....	....	....	....
	NHL Totals	**269**	**118**	**108**	**43**	....	**36**	**18**	**18**	**0**

CARPENTER, Doug

Born: Cornwall, Ont., July 1, 1942.

Season	Club	GC	W	L	T	TP	GC	W	L	T
1984-85	New Jersey	80	22	48	10	54	....	....	....	....
1985-86	New Jersey	80	28	49	3	59	....	....	....	....
1986-87	New Jersey	80	29	45	6	64	....	....	....	....
1987-88	New Jersey	50	21	24	5	47	....	....	....	....
1989-90	Toronto	80	38	38	4	80	5	1	4	0
1990-91	Toronto	11	1	9	1	3	....	....	....	....
	NHL Totals	**381**	**139**	**213**	**29**	....	**5**	**1**	**4**	**0**

CARROLL, Dick

Born: Guelph, Ont., 1888. Died: January 21, 1952.

Season	Club	GC	W	L	T	TP	GC	W	L	T
1917-18♦	Toronto	22	13	9	0	26	2	1	1	0
	Toronto (Cup)	....	....	....	....	....	*5*	*3*	*2*	*0*
1918-19	Toronto	18	5	13	0	10	....	....	....	....
	NHL Totals	**40**	**18**	**22**	**0**	....	**2**	**1**	**1**	**0**

CARROLL, Frank

Born: unknown Deceased

Season	Club	GC	W	L	T	TP	GC	W	L	T
1920-21	Toronto	24	15	9	0	30	2	0	2	0
	NHL Totals	**24**	**15**	**9**	**0**	....	**2**	**0**	**2**	**0**

CASHMAN, Wayne

Born: Kingston, Ont., June 24, 1945.
Played in NHL. See Player Register for career statistics.

Season	Club	GC	W	L	T	TP	GC	W	L	T
1997-98	Philadelphia	61	32	20	9	73	....	....	....	....
	NHL Totals	**61**	**32**	**20**	**9**	....	....	....	....	....

Shared an 0-2-0 record as co-coach with Ed Giacomin when Tom Webster was ill, suffering a 4-3 loss to Minnesota at New York on December 15, 1986, and a 7-4 loss at Edmonton on January 23, 1987. All games are credited to Webster's coaching record.

CASSIDY, Bruce

Born: Ottawa, Ont., May 20, 1965.
Played in NHL. See Player Register for career statistics.

Season	Club	GC	W	L	T	TP	GC	W	L	T
2002-03	Washington	82	39	35	8	92	6	2	4	0
	NHL Totals	**82**	**39**	**35**	**8**	....	**6**	**2**	**4**	**0**

CHAMBERS, Dave

Born: Leaside, Ont., May 7, 1940.

Season	Club	GC	W	L	T	TP	GC	W	L	T
1990-91	Quebec	80	16	50	14	46	....	....	....	....
1991-92	Quebec	18	3	14	1	7	....	....	....	....
	NHL Totals	**98**	**19**	**64**	**15**	....	....	....	....	....

CHARRON, Guy

Born: Verdun, Que., January 24, 1949.
Played in NHL. See Player Register for career statistics.

Season	Club	GC	W	L	T	TP	GC	W	L	T
1991-92	Calgary	16	6	7	3	15	....	....	....	....
2000-01	Anaheim	49	14	28	7	37	....	....	....	....
	NHL Totals	**65**	**20**	**35**	**10**	....	....	....	....	....

CHEEVERS, Gerry

HHOF

Born: St. Catharines, Ont., December 7, 1940.
Played in NHL. See Goaltender Register for career statistics.

Season	Club	GC	W	L	T	TP	GC	W	L	T
1980-81	Boston	80	37	30	13	87	3	0	3	0
1981-82	Boston	80	43	27	10	96	11	6	5	0
1982-83	Boston	80	50	20	10	110	17	9	8	0
1983-84	Boston	80	49	25	6	104	3	0	3	0
1984-85	Boston	56	25	24	7	57	....	....	....	....
	NHL Totals	**376**	**204**	**126**	**46**	....	**34**	**15**	**19**	**0**

CHERRY, Don

Born: Kingston, Ont., February 5, 1934.
Played in NHL. See Player Register for career statistics.

Season	Club	GC	W	L	T	TP	GC	W	L	T
1974-75	Boston	80	40	26	14	94	3	1	2	0
1975-76	Boston	80	48	15	17	113	12	5	7	0
1976-77	Boston	80	49	23	8	106	14	8	6	0
1977-78	Boston	80	51	18	11	113	15	10	5	0
1978-79	Boston	80	43	23	14	100	11	7	4	0
1979-80	Colorado	80	19	48	13	51	....	....	....	....
	NHL Totals	**480**	**250**	**153**	**77**	....	**55**	**31**	**24**	**0**

• Won Jack Adams Award (1976)

CLANCY, King

HHOF

Born: Ottawa, Ont., February 25, 1903. Died: November 8, 1986.
Played in NHL. See Player Register for career statistics.

Season	Club	GC	W	L	T	TP	GC	W	L	T
1937-38	Mtl. Maroons	18	6	11	1	13	....	....	....	....
1953-54	Toronto	70	32	24	14	78	5	1	4	0
1954-55	Toronto	70	24	24	22	70	4	0	4	0

Season	Club	Regular Season GC	W	L	T	TP	Playoffs GC	W	L	T
1955-56	Toronto	70	24	33	13	61	5	1	4	0
	NHL Totals	**228**	**86**	**92**	**50**	....	**14**	**2**	**12**	**0**

Posted a 7-1-2 record as replacement coach when Punch Imlach was sidelined with heart problems, February 18 to March 11, 1967. All games are credited to Imlach's coaching record. Posted a 6-2-3 record as replacement coach when John McLellan was sidelined with a duodenal ulcer, February 23 to March 22, 1972. Posted a 3-1-0 regular season record and a 1-4 playoff record as replacement coach when John McLellan was again sidelined with a duodenal ulcer, March 25 to April 11, 1972. All games are credited to McLellan's coaching record.

CLAPPER, Dit — HHOF

Born: Newmarket, Ont., February 9, 1907. Died: January 21, 1978.
Played in NHL. See Player Register for career statistics.

Season	Club	GC	W	L	T	TP	GC	W	L	T
1945-46	Boston	50	24	18	8	56	10	5	5	0
1946-47	Boston	60	26	23	11	63	5	1	4	0
1947-48	Boston	60	23	24	13	59	5	1	4	0
1948-49	Boston	60	29	23	8	66	5	1	4	0
	NHL Totals	**230**	**102**	**88**	**40**	....	**25**	**8**	**17**	**0**

CLEGHORN, Odie

Born: Montreal, Que., September 19, 1891. Died: July 13, 1956.
Played in NHL. See Player Register for career statistics.

Season	Club	GC	W	L	T	TP	GC	W	L	T
1925-26	Pittsburgh	36	19	16	1	39	2	0	1	1
1926-27	Pittsburgh	44	15	26	3	33	....	....	....	....
1927-28	Pittsburgh	44	19	17	8	46	2	1	1	0
1928-29	Pittsburgh	44	9	27	8	26	....	....	....	....
	NHL Totals	**168**	**62**	**86**	**20**	....	**4**	**1**	**2**	**1**

CLEGHORN, Sprague — HHOF

Born: Montreal, Que., March 11, 1890. Died: July 11, 1956.
Played in NHL. See Player Register for career statistics.

Season	Club	GC	W	L	T	TP	GC	W	L	T
1931-32	Mtl. Maroons	48	19	22	7	45	4	1	1	2
	NHL Totals	**48**	**19**	**22**	**7**	....	**4**	**1**	**1**	**2**

COLVILLE, Neil — HHOF

Born: Edmonton, Alta., August 4, 1914. Died: December 26, 1987.
Played in NHL. See Player Register for career statistics.

Season	Club	GC	W	L	T	TP	GC	W	L	T
1950-51	NY Rangers	70	20	29	21	61	....	....	....	....
1951-52	NY Rangers	23	6	12	5	17	....	....	....	....
	NHL Totals	**93**	**26**	**41**	**26**	....	....	....	....	....

CONACHER, Charlie — HHOF

Born: Toronto, Ont., December 20, 1910. Died: December 30, 1967.
Played in NHL. See Player Register for career statistics.

Season	Club	GC	W	L	T	TP	GC	W	L	T
1947-48	Chicago	32	13	15	4	30	....	....	....	....
1948-49	Chicago	60	21	31	8	50	....	....	....	....
1949-50	Chicago	70	22	38	10	54	....	....	....	....
	NHL Totals	**162**	**56**	**84**	**22**	....	....	....	....	....

CONACHER, Lionel — HHOF

Born: Toronto, Ont., May 24, 1901. Died: May 26, 1954.
Played in NHL. See Player Register for career statistics.

Season	Club	GC	W	L	T	TP	GC	W	L	T
1929-30	NY Americans	44	14	25	5	33	....	....	....	....
	NHL Totals	**44**	**14**	**25**	**5**	....	....	....	....	....

CONSTANTINE, Kevin

Born: International Falls, MN, December 27, 1958.

Season	Club	GC	W	L	T	TP	GC	W	L	T
1993-94	San Jose	84	33	35	16	82	14	7	7	0
1994-95	San Jose	48	19	25	4	42	11	4	7	0
1995-96	San Jose	25	3	18	4	10	....	....	....	....
1997-98	Pittsburgh	82	40	24	18	98	6	2	4	0
1998-99	Pittsburgh	82	38	30	14	90	13	6	7	0
99-2000	Pittsburgh	24	8	13	3	23	....	....	....	....
2000-01	New Jersey	31	20	9	2	43	6	2	4	....
	NHL Totals	**376**	**161**	**154**	**61**	....	**50**	**21**	**29**	**0**

COOK, Bill — HHOF

Born: Brantford, Ont., October 9, 1896. Died: April 6, 1986.
Played in NHL. See Player Register for career statistics.

Season	Club	GC	W	L	T	TP	GC	W	L	T
1951-52	NY Rangers	47	17	22	8	42	....	....	....	....
1952-53	NY Rangers	70	17	37	16	50	....	....	....	....
	NHL Totals	**117**	**34**	**59**	**24**	....	....	....	....	....

CRAWFORD, Marc

Born: Belleville, Ont., February 13, 1961.
Played in NHL. See Player Register for career statistics.

Season	Club	GC	W	L	T	TP	GC	W	L	T
1994-95	Quebec	48	30	13	5	65	6	2	4	0
1995-96♦	Colorado	82	47	25	10	104	22	16	6	0
1996-97	Colorado	82	49	24	9	107	17	10	7	0
1997-98	Colorado	82	39	26	17	95	7	3	4	0
1998-99	Vancouver	37	8	23	6	22	....	....	....	....
99-2000	Vancouver	82	30	37	15	83	....	....	....	....
2000-01	Vancouver	82	36	35	11	90	....	....	....	....
2001-02	Vancouver	82	42	33	7	94	6	2	4	0
2002-03	Vancouver	82	45	24	13	104	14	7	7	0
	NHL Totals	**659**	**326**	**240**	**93**	....	**72**	**40**	**32**	**0**

Won Jack Adams Award (1995)

CREAMER, Pierre

Born: Chomedy, Que, July 6, 1944.

Season	Club	GC	W	L	T	TP	GC	W	L	T
1987-88	Pittsburgh	80	36	35	9	81	....	....	....	....
	NHL Totals	**80**	**36**	**35**	**9**	....	....	....	....	....

CREIGHTON, Fred

Born: Hamiota, Man., July 14, 1933.

Season	Club	GC	W	L	T	TP	GC	W	L	T
1974-75	Atlanta	28	12	11	5	29	....	....	....	....
1975-76	Atlanta	80	35	33	12	82	2	1	1	0
1976-77	Atlanta	80	34	34	12	80	3	1	2	0
1977-78	Atlanta	80	34	27	19	87	2	0	2	0
1978-79	Atlanta	80	41	31	8	90	2	0	2	0
1979-80	Boston	73	40	20	13	93	....	....	....	....
	NHL Totals	**421**	**196**	**156**	**69**	....	**9**	**2**	**7**	**0**

CRISP, Terry

Born: Parry Sound, Ont., May 28, 1943.
Played in NHL. See Player Register for career statistics.

Season	Club	GC	W	L	T	TP	GC	W	L	T
1987-88	Calgary	80	48	23	9	105	9	4	5	0
1988-89♦	Calgary	80	54	17	9	117	22	16	6	0
1989-90	Calgary	80	42	23	15	99	6	2	4	0
1992-93	Tampa Bay	84	23	54	7	53	....	....	....	....
1993-94	Tampa Bay	84	30	43	11	71	....	....	....	....
1994-95	Tampa Bay	48	17	28	3	37	....	....	....	....
1995-96	Tampa Bay	82	38	32	12	88	6	2	4	0
1996-97	Tampa Bay	82	32	40	10	74	....	....	....	....
1997-98	Tampa Bay	11	2	7	2	6	....	....	....	....
	NHL Totals	**631**	**286**	**267**	**78**	....	**43**	**24**	**19**	**0**

CROZIER, Joe

Born: Winnipeg, Man., February 19, 1929.
Played in NHL. See Player Register for career statistics.

Season	Club	GC	W	L	T	TP	GC	W	L	T
1971-72	Buffalo	36	8	19	9	25	....	....	....	....
1972-73	Buffalo	78	37	27	14	88	6	2	4	0
1973-74	Buffalo	78	32	34	12	76	....	....	....	....
1980-81	Toronto	40	13	22	5	31	....	....	....	....
	NHL Totals	**232**	**90**	**102**	**40**	....	**6**	**2**	**4**	**0**

CROZIER, Roger

Born: Bracebridge, Ont., March 16, 1942. Died: January 11, 1996.
Played in NHL. See Goaltender Register for career statistics.

Season	Club	GC	W	L	T	TP	GC	W	L	T
1981-82	Washington	1	0	1	0	0	....	....	....	....
	NHL Totals	**1**	**0**	**1**	**0**	....	....	....	....	....

CUNNIFF, John — USHOF

Born: South Boston, MA, July 9, 1943. Died: May 9, 2002.

Season	Club	GC	W	L	T	TP	GC	W	L	T
1982-83	Hartford	13	3	9	1	7	....	....	....	....
1989-90	New Jersey	66	31	28	7	69	6	2	4	0
1990-91	New Jersey	67	28	28	11	67	....	....	....	....
	NHL Totals	**146**	**62**	**65**	**19**	....	**6**	**2**	**4**	**0**

CURRY, Alex

Born: unknown Deceased

Season	Club	GC	W	L	T	TP	GC	W	L	T
1925-26	Ottawa	36	24	8	4	52	2	0	1	1
	NHL Totals	**36**	**24**	**8**	**4**	....	**2**	**0**	**1**	**1**

DANDURAND, Leo — HHOF

Born: Bourbonnais, IL, July 9, 1889. Died: June 26, 1964.

Season	Club	GC	W	L	T	TP	GC	W	L	T
1921-22	Montreal	17	10	6	1	21	....	....	....	....
1922-23	Montreal	24	13	9	2	28	2	1	1	0
1923-24♦	Montreal	24	13	11	0	26	2	2	0	0
	Montreal (Cup)	....	....	....	....	....	*4*	*4*	*0*	*0*
1924-25	Montreal	30	17	11	2	36	2	2	0	0
	Montreal (Cup)	....	....	....	....	....	*4*	*1*	*3*	*0*
1925-26	Montreal	36	11	24	1	23	....	....	....	....
1934-35	Montreal	32	14	15	3	31	2	0	2	0
	NHL Totals	**163**	**78**	**76**	**9**	....	**8**	**5**	**3**	**0**

DAY, Hap — HHOF

Born: Owen Sound, Ont., June 14, 1901. Died: February 17, 1990.
Played in NHL. See Player Register for career statistics.

Season	Club	GC	W	L	T	TP	GC	W	L	T
1940-41	Toronto	48	28	14	6	62	7	3	4	0
1941-42♦	Toronto	48	27	18	3	57	13	8	5	0
1942-43	Toronto	50	22	19	9	53	6	2	4	0
1943-44	Toronto	50	23	23	4	50	5	1	4	0
1944-45♦	Toronto	50	24	22	4	52	13	8	5	0
1945-46	Toronto	50	19	24	7	45	....	....	....	....
1946-47♦	Toronto	60	31	19	10	72	11	8	3	0
1947-48♦	Toronto	60	32	15	13	77	9	8	1	0

Season	Club	Regular Season GC	W	L	T	TP	Playoffs GC	W	L	T
1948-49◆	Toronto	60	22	25	13	57	9	8	1	0
1949-50	Toronto	70	31	27	12	74	7	3	4	0
	NHL Totals	**546**	**259**	**206**	**81**	....	**80**	**49**	**31**	**0**

DEA, Billy

Born: Edmonton, Alta., April 3, 1933.
Played in NHL. See Player Register for career statistics.

Season	Club	GC	W	L	T	TP	GC	W	L	T
1981-82	Detroit	11	3	8	0	6	....	....	....	....
	NHL Totals	**11**	**3**	**8**	**0**	....	....	....	....	....

DELVECCHIO, Alex

HHOF

Born: Fort William, Ont., December 4, 1932.
Played in NHL. See Player Register for career statistics.

Season	Club	GC	W	L	T	TP	GC	W	L	T
1973-74	Detroit	67	27	31	9	63	....	....	....	....
1974-75	Detroit	80	23	45	12	58	....	....	....	....
1975-76	Detroit	54	19	29	6	44	....	....	....	....
1976-77	Detroit	44	13	26	5	31	....	....	....	....
	NHL Totals	**245**	**82**	**131**	**32**	....	....	....	....	....

DEMERS, Jacques

Born: Montreal, Que., August 25, 1944.

Season	Club	GC	W	L	T	TP	GC	W	L	T
1979-80	Quebec	80	25	44	11	61	....	....	....	....
1983-84	St. Louis	80	32	41	7	71	11	6	5	0
1984-85	St. Louis	80	37	31	12	86	3	0	3	0
1985-86	St. Louis	80	37	34	9	83	19	10	9	0
1986-87	Detroit	80	34	36	10	78	16	9	7	0
1987-88	Detroit	80	41	28	11	93	16	9	7	0
1988-89	Detroit	80	34	34	12	80	6	2	4	0
1989-90	Detroit	80	28	38	14	70	....	....	....	....
1992-93◆	Montreal	84	48	30	6	102	20	16	4	0
1993-94	Montreal	84	41	29	14	96	7	3	4	0
1994-95	Montreal	48	18	23	7	43	....	....	....	....
1995-96	Montreal	5	0	5	0	0	....	....	....	....
1997-98	Tampa Bay	63	15	40	8	38	....	....	....	....
1998-99	Tampa Bay	82	19	54	9	47	....	....	....	....
	NHL Totals	**1006**	**409**	**467**	**130**	....	**98**	**55**	**43**	**0**

• Won Jack Adams Award (1987, 1988)

DENNENY, Cy

HHOF

Born: Farrow's Point, Ont., December 23, 1891. Died: October 12, 1970.
Played in NHL. See Player Register for career statistics.

Season	Club	GC	W	L	T	TP	GC	W	L	T
1928-29◆	Boston	44	26	13	5	57	5	5	0	0
1932-33	Ottawa	48	11	27	10	32	....	....	....	....
	NHL Totals	**92**	**37**	**40**	**15**	....	**5**	**5**	**0**	**0**

DINEEN, Bill

Born: Arvida, Que., September 18, 1932.
Played in NHL. See Player Register for career statistics.

Season	Club	GC	W	L	T	TP	GC	W	L	T
1991-92	Philadelphia	56	24	23	9	57	....	....	....	....
1992-93	Philadelphia	84	36	37	11	83	....	....	....	....
	NHL Totals	**140**	**60**	**60**	**20**	....	....	....	....	....

DUDLEY, Rick

Born: Toronto, Ont., January 31, 1949.
Played in NHL. See Player Register for career statistics.

Season	Club	GC	W	L	T	TP	GC	W	L	T
1989-90	Buffalo	80	45	27	8	98	6	2	4	0
1990-91	Buffalo	80	31	30	19	81	6	2	4	0
1991-92	Buffalo	28	9	15	4	22	....	....	....	....
	NHL Totals	**188**	**85**	**72**	**31**	....	**12**	**4**	**8**	**0**

DUFF, Dick

Born: Kirkland Lake, Ont., February 18, 1936.
Played in NHL. See Player Register for career statistics.

Season	Club	GC	W	L	T	TP	GC	W	L	T
1979-80	Toronto	2	0	2	0	0	....	....	....	....
	NHL Totals	**2**	**0**	**2**	**0**	....	....	....	....	....

DUGAL, Jules

Born: unknown Deceased

Season	Club	GC	W	L	T	TP	GC	W	L	T
1938-39	Montreal	18	9	6	3	21	3	1	2	0
	NHL Totals	**18**	**9**	**6**	**3**	....	**3**	**1**	**2**	**0**

DUNCAN, Art

Born: Sault Ste. Marie, Ont., July 4, 1894. Died: April 13, 1975.
Played in NHL. See Player Register for career statistics.

Season	Club	GC	W	L	T	TP	GC	W	L	T
1926-27	Detroit	33	10	21	2	22	....	....	....	....
1930-31	Toronto	42	21	13	8	50	2	0	1	1
1931-32	Toronto	5	0	3	2	2	....	....	....	....
	NHL Totals	**80**	**31**	**37**	**12**	....	**2**	**0**	**1**	**1**

DUTTON, Red

HHOF

Born: Russell, Man., July 23, 1898. Died: March 15, 1987.
Played in NHL. See Player Register for career statistics.

Season	Club	GC	W	L	T	TP	GC	W	L	T
1935-36	NY Americans	48	16	25	7	39	5	2	3	0
1936-37	NY Americans	48	15	29	4	34	....	....	....	....
1937-38	NY Americans	48	19	18	11	49	6	3	3	0
1938-39	NY Americans	48	17	21	10	44	2	0	2	0
1939-40	NY Americans	48	15	29	4	34	3	1	2	0
1940-41	NY Americans	48	8	29	11	27	....	....	....	....
1941-42	Brooklyn	48	16	29	3	35	....	....	....	....
	NHL Totals	**336**	**106**	**180**	**50**	....	**16**	**6**	**10**	**0**

EDDOLLS, Frank

Born: Lachine, Que., July 5, 1921. Died: August 13, 1961.
Played in NHL. See Player Register for career statistics.

Season	Club	GC	W	L	T	TP	GC	W	L	T
1954-55	Chicago	70	13	40	17	43	....	....	....	....
	NHL Totals	**70**	**13**	**40**	**17**	....	....	....	....	....

ESPOSITO, Phil

HHOF

Born: Sault Ste. Marie, Ont., February 20, 1942.
Played in NHL. See Player Register for career statistics.

Season	Club	GC	W	L	T	TP	GC	W	L	T
1986-87	NY Rangers	43	24	19	0	48	6	2	4	0
1988-89	NY Rangers	2	0	2	0	0	4	0	4	0
	NHL Totals	**45**	**24**	**21**	**0**	....	**10**	**2**	**8**	**0**

EVANS, Jack

Born: Morriston, South Wales, April 21, 1928. Died: November 10, 1996.
Played in NHL. See Player Register for career statistics.

Season	Club	GC	W	L	T	TP	GC	W	L	T
1975-76	California	80	27	42	11	65	....	....	....	....
1976-77	Cleveland	80	25	42	13	63	....	....	....	....
1977-78	Cleveland	80	22	45	13	57	....	....	....	....
1983-84	Hartford	80	28	42	10	66	....	....	....	....
1984-85	Hartford	80	30	41	9	69	....	....	....	....
1985-86	Hartford	80	40	36	4	84	10	6	4	0
1986-87	Hartford	80	43	30	7	93	6	2	4	0
1987-88	Hartford	54	22	25	7	51	....	....	....	....
	NHL Totals	**614**	**237**	**303**	**74**	....	**16**	**8**	**8**	**0**

FASHOWAY, Gordie

Born: Portage La Prairie, Man., June 16, 1926.
Played in NHL. See Player Register for career statistics.

Season	Club	GC	W	L	T	TP	GC	W	L	T
1967-68	Oakland	10	4	5	1	9	....	....	....	....
	NHL Totals	**10**	**4**	**5**	**1**	....	....	....	....	....

FERGUSON, John

Born: Vancouver, B.C., September 5, 1938.
Played in NHL. See Player Register for career statistics.

Season	Club	GC	W	L	T	TP	GC	W	L	T
1975-76	NY Rangers	41	14	22	5	33	....	....	....	....
1976-77	NY Rangers	80	29	37	14	72	....	....	....	....
1985-86	Winnipeg	14	7	6	1	15	3	0	3	0
	NHL Totals	**135**	**50**	**65**	**20**	....	**3**	**0**	**3**	**0**

FILION, Maurice

Born: Montreal, Que., February 12, 1932.

Season	Club	GC	W	L	T	TP	GC	W	L	T
1980-81	Quebec	6	1	3	2	4	....	....	....	....
	NHL Totals	**6**	**1**	**3**	**2**	....	....	....	....	....

FRANCIS, Bob

Born: North Battleford, Sask., December 5, 1958.
Played in NHL. See Player Register for career statistics.

Season	Club	GC	W	L	T	TP	GC	W	L	T
99-2000	Phoenix	82	39	35	8	90	5	1	4	0
2000-01	Phoenix	82	35	30	17	90	....	....	....	....
2001-02	Phoenix	82	40	33	9	95	5	1	4	0
2002-03	Phoenix	82	31	40	11	78	....	....	....	....
	NHL Totals	**328**	**145**	**138**	**45**	....	**10**	**2**	**8**	**0**

• Won Jack Adams Award (2002)

FRANCIS, Emile

HHOF

Born: North Battleford, Sask., September 13, 1926.
Played in NHL. See Goaltender Register for career statistics.

Season	Club	GC	W	L	T	TP	GC	W	L	T
1965-66	NY Rangers	50	13	31	6	32	....	....	....	....
1966-67	NY Rangers	70	30	28	12	72	4	0	4	0
1967-68	NY Rangers	74	39	23	12	90	6	2	4	0
1968-69	NY Rangers	33	19	8	6	44	4	0	4	0
1969-70	NY Rangers	76	38	22	16	92	6	2	4	0
1970-71	NY Rangers	78	49	18	11	109	13	7	6	0
1971-72	NY Rangers	78	48	17	13	109	16	10	6	0
1972-73	NY Rangers	78	47	23	8	102	10	5	5	0
1973-74	NY Rangers	37	22	10	5	49	13	7	6	0
1974-75	NY Rangers	80	37	29	14	88	3	1	2	0
1976-77	St. Louis	80	32	39	9	73	4	0	4	0
1981-82	St. Louis	12	4	6	2	10	10	5	5	0
1982-83	St. Louis	32	10	19	3	23	....	....	....	....
	NHL Totals	**778**	**388**	**273**	**117**	....	**89**	**39**	**50**	**0**

FRASER, Curt

Born: Cincinnati, OH, January 12, 1958.
Played in NHL. See Player Register for career statistics.

Season	Club	Regular Season GC	W	L	T	TP	Playoffs GC	W	L	T
99-2000	Atlanta	82	14	61	7	39	....	....	....	....
2000-01	Atlanta	82	23	47	12	60	....	....	....	....
2001-02	Atlanta	82	19	52	11	54	....	....	....	....
2002-03	Atlanta	33	8	24	1	21	....	....	....	....
	NHL Totals	**279**	**64**	**184**	**31**	....	....	....	....	....

FREDRICKSON, Frank — HHOF

Born: Winnipeg, Man., June 11, 1895. Died: May 28, 1979.
Played in NHL. See Player Register for career statistics.

Season	Club	Regular Season GC	W	L	T	TP	Playoffs GC	W	L	T
1929-30	Pittsburgh	44	5	36	3	13	....	....	....	....
	NHL Totals	**44**	**5**	**36**	**3**	....	....	....	....	....

FTOREK, Robbie — USHOF

Born: Needham, MA, January 2, 1952.
Played in NHL. See Player Register for career statistics.

Season	Club	Regular Season GC	W	L	T	TP	Playoffs GC	W	L	T
1987-88	Los Angeles	52	23	25	4	50	5	1	4	0
1988-89	Los Angeles	80	42	31	7	91	11	4	7	0
1998-99	New Jersey	82	47	24	11	105	7	3	4	0
99-2000	New Jersey	74	41	25	8	95	....	....	....	....
2001-02	Boston	82	43	33	6	101	6	2	4	0
2002-03	Boston	73	33	32	8	78	....	....	....	....
	NHL Totals	**443**	**229**	**170**	**44**	....	**29**	**10**	**19**	**0**

GADSBY, Bill — HHOF

Born: Calgary, Alta., August 8, 1927.
Played in NHL. See Player Register for career statistics.

Season	Club	Regular Season GC	W	L	T	TP	Playoffs GC	W	L	T
1968-69	Detroit	76	33	31	12	78	....	....	....	....
1969-70	Detroit	2	2	0	0	4	....	....	....	....
	NHL Totals	**78**	**35**	**31**	**12**	....	....	....	....	....

GAINEY, Bob — HHOF

Born: Peterborough, Ont., December 13, 1953.
Played in NHL. See Player Register for career statistics.

Season	Club	Regular Season GC	W	L	T	TP	Playoffs GC	W	L	T
1990-91	Minnesota	80	27	39	14	68	23	14	9	0
1991-92	Minnesota	80	32	42	6	70	7	3	4	0
1992-93	Minnesota	84	36	38	10	82	....	....	....	....
1993-94	Dallas	84	42	29	13	97	9	5	4	0
1994-95	Dallas	48	17	23	8	42	5	1	4	0
1995-96	Dallas	39	11	19	9	31	....	....	....	....
	NHL Totals	**415**	**165**	**190**	**60**	....	**44**	**23**	**21**	**0**

GARDINER, Herb — HHOF

Born: Winnipeg, Man., May 8, 1891. Died: January 11, 1972.
Played in NHL. See Player Register for career statistics.

Season	Club	Regular Season GC	W	L	T	TP	Playoffs GC	W	L	T
1928-29	Chicago	32	5	23	4	14	....	....	....	....
	NHL Totals	**32**	**5**	**23**	**4**	....	....	....	....	....

GARDNER, Jimmy — HHOF

Born: Montreal, Que., November 18, 1881. Died: November 7, 1940.

Season	Club	Regular Season GC	W	L	T	TP	Playoffs GC	W	L	T
1924-25	Hamilton	30	19	10	1	39	....	....	....	....
	NHL Totals	**30**	**19**	**10**	**1**	....	....	....	....	....

GARVIN, Ted

Born: Sarnia, Ont., August 20, 1923.

Season	Club	Regular Season GC	W	L	T	TP	Playoffs GC	W	L	T
1973-74	Detroit	11	2	8	1	5	....	....	....	....
	NHL Totals	**11**	**2**	**8**	**1**	....	....	....	....	....

GEOFFRION, Bernie — HHOF

Born: Montreal, Que., February 14, 1931.
Played in NHL. See Player Register for career statistics.

Season	Club	Regular Season GC	W	L	T	TP	Playoffs GC	W	L	T
1968-69	NY Rangers	43	22	18	3	47	....	....	....	....
1972-73	Atlanta	78	25	38	15	65	....	....	....	....
1973-74	Atlanta	78	30	34	14	74	4	0	4	0
1974-75	Atlanta	52	22	20	10	54	....	....	....	....
1979-80	Montreal	30	15	9	6	36	....	....	....	....
	NHL Totals	**281**	**114**	**119**	**48**	....	**4**	**0**	**4**	**0**

GERARD, Eddie — HHOF

Born: Ottawa, Ont., February 22, 1890. Died: December 7, 1937.
Played in NHL. See Player Register for career statistics.

Season	Club	Regular Season GC	W	L	T	TP	Playoffs GC	W	L	T
1917-18	Ottawa	22	9	13	0	18	....	....	....	....
1924-25	Mtl. Maroons	30	9	19	2	20	....	....	....	....
1925-26 ♦	Mtl. Maroons	36	20	11	5	45	4	2	0	2
	Mtl. Maroons (Cup)	....	....	....	....	....	*4*	*3*	*1*	*0*
1926-27	Mtl. Maroons	44	20	20	4	44	2	0	1	1
1927-28	Mtl. Maroons	44	24	14	6	54	9	5	3	1
1928-29	Mtl. Maroons	44	15	20	9	39	....	....	....	....
1930-31	NY Americans	44	18	16	10	46	....	....	....	....
1931-32	NY Americans	48	16	24	8	40	....	....	....	....
1932-33	Mtl. Maroons	48	22	20	6	50	2	0	2	0
1933-34	Mtl. Maroons	48	19	18	11	49	4	1	2	1
1934-35	St. Louis	13	2	11	0	4	....	....	....	....
	NHL Totals	**421**	**174**	**186**	**61**	....	**21**	**8**	**8**	**5**

GILBERT, Greg

Born: Mississauga, Ont., January 22, 1962.
Played in NHL. See Player Register for career statistics.

Season	Club	Regular Season GC	W	L	T	TP	Playoffs GC	W	L	T
2000-01	Calgary	14	4	8	2	10	....	....	....	....
2001-02	Calgary	82	32	38	12	79	....	....	....	....
2002-03	Calgary	25	6	16	3	18	....	....	....	....
	NHL Totals	**121**	**42**	**62**	**17**	....	....	....	....	....

GILL, David

Born: unknown Deceased

Season	Club	Regular Season GC	W	L	T	TP	Playoffs GC	W	L	T
1926-27 ♦	Ottawa	44	30	10	4	64	6	3	0	3
1927-28	Ottawa	44	20	14	10	50	2	0	2	0
1928-29	Ottawa	44	14	17	13	41	....	....	....	....
	NHL Totals	**132**	**64**	**41**	**27**	....	**8**	**3**	**2**	**3**

GLOVER, Fred

Born: Toronto, Ont., January 5, 1928.
Played in NHL. See Player Register for career statistics.

Season	Club	Regular Season GC	W	L	T	TP	Playoffs GC	W	L	T
1968-69	Oakland	76	29	36	11	69	7	3	4	0
1969-70	Oakland	76	22	40	14	58	4	0	4	0
1970-71	California	78	20	53	5	45	....	....	....	....
1971-72	California	3	0	1	2	2	....	....	....	....
	Los Angeles	68	18	42	8	44	....	....	....	....
1972-73	California	66	14	39	13	41	....	....	....	....
1973-74	California	57	11	38	8	30	....	....	....	....
	NHL Totals	**424**	**114**	**249**	**61**	....	**11**	**3**	**8**	**0**

GOODFELLOW, Ebbie — HHOF

Born: Ottawa, Ont., April 9, 1907. Died: September 10, 1965.
Played in NHL. See Player Register for career statistics.

Season	Club	Regular Season GC	W	L	T	TP	Playoffs GC	W	L	T
1950-51	Chicago	70	13	47	10	36	....	....	....	....
1951-52	Chicago	70	17	44	9	43	....	....	....	....
	NHL Totals	**140**	**30**	**91**	**19**	....	....	....	....	....

GORDON, Jackie

Born: Winnipeg, Man., March 3, 1928.
Played in NHL. See Player Register for career statistics.

Season	Club	Regular Season GC	W	L	T	TP	Playoffs GC	W	L	T
1970-71	Minnesota	78	28	34	16	72	12	6	6	0
1971-72	Minnesota	78	37	29	12	86	7	3	4	0
1972-73	Minnesota	78	37	30	11	85	6	2	4	0
1973-74	Minnesota	17	3	8	6	12	....	....	....	....
1974-75	Minnesota	38	11	22	5	27	....	....	....	....
	NHL Totals	**289**	**116**	**123**	**50**	....	**25**	**11**	**14**	**0**

GORING, Butch

Born: St. Boniface, Man., October 22, 1949.
Played in NHL. See Player Register for career statistics.

Season	Club	Regular Season GC	W	L	T	TP	Playoffs GC	W	L	T
1985-86	Boston	80	37	31	12	86	3	0	3	0
1986-87	Boston	13	5	7	1	11	....	....	....	....
99-2000	NY Islanders	82	24	49	9	58	....	....	....	....
2000-01	NY Islanders	65	17	43	5	42	....	....	....	....
	NHL Totals	**240**	**83**	**130**	**27**	....	**3**	**0**	**3**	**0**

GORMAN, Tommy — HHOF

Born: Ottawa, Ont., June 9, 1886. Died: May 15, 1961.

Season	Club	Regular Season GC	W	L	T	TP	Playoffs GC	W	L	T
1925-26	NY Americans	36	12	20	4	28	....	....	....	....
1928-29	NY Americans	44	19	13	12	50	2	0	1	1
1932-33	Chicago	25	8	11	6	22	....	....	....	....
1933-34 ♦	Chicago	48	20	17	11	51	8	6	1	1
1934-35 ♦	Mtl. Maroons	48	24	19	5	53	7	5	0	2
1935-36	Mtl. Maroons	48	22	16	10	54	3	0	3	0
1936-37	Mtl. Maroons	48	22	17	9	53	5	2	3	0
1937-38	Mtl. Maroons	30	6	19	5	17	....	....	....	....
	NHL Totals	**327**	**133**	**132**	**62**	....	**25**	**13**	**8**	**4**

GOTTSELIG, Johnny

Born: Odessa, Russia, June 24, 1905. Died: May 15, 1986.
Played in NHL. See Player Register for career statistics.

Season	Club	Regular Season GC	W	L	T	TP	Playoffs GC	W	L	T
1944-45	Chicago	49	13	29	7	33	....	....	....	....
1945-46	Chicago	50	23	20	7	53	4	0	4	0
1946-47	Chicago	60	19	37	4	42	....	....	....	....
1947-48	Chicago	28	7	19	2	16	....	....	....	....
	NHL Totals	**187**	**62**	**105**	**20**	....	**4**	**0**	**4**	**0**

GOYETTE, Phil

Born: Lachine, Que., October 31, 1933.
Played in NHL. See Player Register for career statistics.

Season	Club	Regular Season GC	W	L	T	TP	Playoffs GC	W	L	T
1972-73	NY Islanders	48	6	38	4	16	....	....	....	....
	NHL Totals	**48**	**6**	**38**	**4**	....	....	....	....	....

GRAHAM, Dirk

Born: Regina, Sask., July 29, 1959.
Played in NHL. See Player Register for career statistics.

Season	Club	Regular Season GC	W	L	T	TP	Playoffs GC	W	L	T
1998-99	Chicago	59	16	35	8	40	....	....	....	....
	NHL Totals	**59**	**16**	**35**	**8**	....	....	....	....	....

GRANATO, Tony

Born: Downers Grove, IL, July 25, 1964.
Played in NHL. See Player Register for career statistics.

Season	Club	Regular Season GC	W	L	T	TP	Playoffs GC	W	L	T
2002-03	Colorado	51	32	15	4	72	7	3	4	0
	NHL Totals	**51**	**32**	**15**	**4**	....	**7**	**3**	**4**	**0**

GREEN, Gary

Born: Tillsonburg, Ont., August 23, 1953.

Season	Club	Regular Season GC	W	L	T	TP	Playoffs GC	W	L	T
1979-80	Washington	64	23	30	11	57	....	....	....	....
1980-81	Washington	80	26	36	18	70	....	....	....	....
1981-82	Washington	13	1	12	0	2	....	....	....	....
	NHL Totals	**157**	**50**	**78**	**29**	....	....	....	....	....

GREEN, Pete

Born: unknown Deceased

Season	Club	Regular Season GC	W	L	T	TP	Playoffs GC	W	L	T
1919-20♦	Ottawa	24	19	5	0	38	....	....	....	....
	Ottawa (Cup)	....	....	....	....	....	*5*	*3*	*2*	*0*
1920-21♦	Ottawa	24	14	10	0	28	2	2	0	0
	Ottawa (Cup)	....	....	....	....	....	*5*	*3*	*2*	*0*
1921-22	Ottawa	24	14	8	2	30	2	0	1	1
1922-23♦	Ottawa	24	14	9	1	29	2	1	1	0
	Ottawa (Cup)	....	....	....	....	....	*6*	*5*	*1*	*0*
1923-24	Ottawa	24	16	8	0	32	2	0	2	0
1924-25	Ottawa	30	17	12	1	35	....	....	....	....
	NHL Totals	**150**	**94**	**52**	**4**	....	**8**	**3**	**4**	**1**

GREEN, Shorty

HHOF

Born: Sudbury, Ont., July 17, 1896. Died: April 19, 1960.
Played in NHL. See Player Register for career statistics.

Season	Club	Regular Season GC	W	L	T	TP	Playoffs GC	W	L	T
1927-28	NY Americans	44	11	27	6	28	....	....	....	....
	NHL Totals	**44**	**11**	**27**	**6**	....	....	....	....	....

GREEN, Ted

Born: Eriksdale, Man., March 23, 1940.
Played in NHL. See Player Register for career statistics.

Season	Club	Regular Season GC	W	L	T	TP	Playoffs GC	W	L	T
1991-92	Edmonton	80	36	34	10	82	16	8	8	0
1992-93	Edmonton	84	26	50	8	60	....	....	....	....
1993-94	Edmonton	24	3	18	3	9	....	....	....	....
	NHL Totals	**188**	**65**	**102**	**21**	....	**16**	**8**	**8**	**0**

GUIDOLIN, Aldo

Born: Forks of Credit, Ont., June 6, 1932.
Played in NHL. See Player Register for career statistics.

Season	Club	Regular Season GC	W	L	T	TP	Playoffs GC	W	L	T
1978-79	Colorado	59	12	39	8	32	....	....	....	....
	NHL Totals	**59**	**12**	**39**	**8**	....	....	....	....	....

GUIDOLIN, Bep

Born: Thorold, Ont., December 9, 1925.
Played in NHL. See Player Register for career statistics.

Season	Club	Regular Season GC	W	L	T	TP	Playoffs GC	W	L	T
1972-73	Boston	26	20	6	0	40	5	1	4	0
1973-74	Boston	78	52	17	9	113	16	10	6	0
1974-75	Kansas City	80	15	54	11	41	....	....	....	....
1975-76	Kansas City	45	11	30	4	26	....	....	....	....
	NHL Totals	**229**	**98**	**107**	**24**	....	**21**	**11**	**10**	**0**

HARKNESS, Ned

USHOF

Born: Ottawa, Ont., September 19, 1921.

Season	Club	Regular Season GC	W	L	T	TP	Playoffs GC	W	L	T
1970-71	Detroit	38	12	22	4	28	....	....	....	....
	NHL Totals	**38**	**12**	**22**	**4**	....	....	....	....	....

HARRIS, Ted

Born: Winnipeg, Man., July 18, 1936.
Played in NHL. See Player Register for career statistics.

Season	Club	Regular Season GC	W	L	T	TP	Playoffs GC	W	L	T
1975-76	Minnesota	80	20	53	7	47	....	....	....	....
1976-77	Minnesota	80	23	39	18	64	2	0	2	0
1977-78	Minnesota	19	5	12	2	12	....	....	....	....
	NHL Totals	**179**	**48**	**104**	**27**	....	**2**	**0**	**2**	**0**

HART, Cecil

Born: 1883. Died: 1940

Season	Club	Regular Season GC	W	L	T	TP	Playoffs GC	W	L	T
1926-27	Montreal	44	28	14	2	58	4	1	1	2
1927-28	Montreal	44	26	11	7	59	2	0	1	1
1928-29	Montreal	44	22	7	15	59	3	0	3	0
1929-30♦	Montreal	44	21	14	9	51	6	5	0	1
1930-31♦	Montreal	44	26	10	8	60	10	6	4	0
1931-32	Montreal	48	25	16	7	57	4	1	3	0
1936-37	Montreal	48	24	18	6	54	5	2	3	0
1937-38	Montreal	48	18	17	13	49	3	1	2	0
1938-39	Montreal	30	6	18	6	18	....	....	....	....
	NHL Totals	**394**	**196**	**125**	**73**	....	**37**	**16**	**17**	**4**

HARTLEY, Bob

Born: Hawkesbury, Ont., September 9, 1960.

Season	Club	Regular Season GC	W	L	T	TP	Playoffs GC	W	L	T
1998-99	Colorado	82	44	28	10	98	19	11	8	0
99-2000	Colorado	82	42	29	11	96	17	11	6	0
2000-01♦	Colorado	82	52	20	10	118	23	16	7	....
2001-02	Colorado	82	45	29	8	99	21	11	10	0
2002-03	Colorado	31	10	12	9	33	....	....	....	....
	Atlanta	39	19	15	5	44	....	....	....	....
	NHL Totals	**398**	**212**	**133**	**53**	....	**80**	**49**	**31**	**0**

HARTSBURG, Craig

Born: Stratford, Ont., June 29, 1959.
Played in NHL. See Player Register for career statistics.

Season	Club	Regular Season GC	W	L	T	TP	Playoffs GC	W	L	T
1995-96	Chicago	82	40	28	14	94	10	6	4	0
1996-97	Chicago	82	34	35	13	81	6	2	4	0
1997-98	Chicago	82	30	39	13	73	....	....	....	....
1998-99	Anaheim	82	35	34	13	83	4	0	4	0
99-2000	Anaheim	82	34	36	12	83	....	....	....	....
2000-01	Anaheim	33	11	18	4	29	....	....	....	....
	NHL Totals	**443**	**184**	**190**	**69**	....	**20**	**8**	**12**	**0**

HARVEY, Doug

HHOF

Born: Montreal, Que., December 19, 1924. Died: December 26, 1989.
Played in NHL. See Player Register for career statistics.

Season	Club	Regular Season GC	W	L	T	TP	Playoffs GC	W	L	T
1961-62	NY Rangers	70	26	32	12	64	6	2	4	0
	NHL Totals	**70**	**26**	**32**	**12**	....	**6**	**2**	**4**	**0**

HAY, Don

Born: Kamloops, B.C., February 13, 1954.
Played in NHL. See Player Register for career statistics.

Season	Club	Regular Season GC	W	L	T	TP	Playoffs GC	W	L	T
1996-97	Phoenix	82	38	37	7	83	7	3	4	0
2000-01	Calgary	68	23	32	13	63	....	....	....	....
	NHL Totals	**150**	**61**	**69**	**20**	....	**7**	**3**	**4**	**0**

HEFFERNAN, Frank

Born: Peterborough, Ont., Deceased
Played in NHL. See Player Register for career statistics.

Season	Club	Regular Season GC	W	L	T	TP	Playoffs GC	W	L	T
1919-20	Toronto	12	5	7	0	10	....	....	....	....
	NHL Totals	**12**	**5**	**7**	**0**	....	....	....	....	....

HENNING, Lorne

Born: Melfort, Sask., February 22, 1952.
Played in NHL. See Player Register for career statistics.

Season	Club	Regular Season GC	W	L	T	TP	Playoffs GC	W	L	T
1985-86	Minnesota	80	38	33	9	85	5	2	3	0
1986-87	Minnesota	78	30	39	9	69	....	....	....	....
1994-95	NY Islanders	48	15	28	5	35	....	....	....	....
2000-01	NY Islanders	17	4	11	2	10	....	....	....	....
	NHL Totals	**223**	**87**	**111**	**25**	....	**5**	**2**	**3**	**0**

HITCHCOCK, Ken

Born: Edmonton, Alta., December 17, 1951.

Season	Club	Regular Season GC	W	L	T	TP	Playoffs GC	W	L	T
1995-96	Dallas	43	15	23	5	35	....	....	....	....
1996-97	Dallas	82	48	26	8	104	7	3	4	0
1997-98	Dallas	82	49	22	11	109	17	10	7	0
1998-99♦	Dallas	82	51	19	12	114	23	16	7	0
99-2000	Dallas	82	43	29	10	102	23	14	9	0
2000-01	Dallas	82	48	26	8	106	10	4	6	0
2001-02	Dallas	50	23	21	6	56	....	....	....	....
2002-03	Philadelphia	82	45	24	13	107	13	6	7	0
	NHL Totals	**585**	**322**	**190**	**73**	....	**93**	**53**	**40**	**0**

HLINKA, Ivan

Born: Most, Czechoslavakia, January 26, 1950.
Played in NHL. See Player Register for career statistics.

Season	Club	Regular Season GC	W	L	T	TP	Playoffs GC	W	L	T
2000-01	Pittsburgh	82	42	31	9	96	18	9	9	0
2001-02	Pittsburgh	4	0	4	0	0	....	....	....	....
	NHL Totals	**86**	**42**	**35**	**9**	....	**18**	**9**	**9**	**0**

HOLMGREN, Paul

Born: St. Paul, MN, December 2, 1955.
Played in NHL. See Player Register for career statistics.

Season	Club	Regular Season GC	W	L	T	TP	Playoffs GC	W	L	T
1988-89	Philadelphia	80	36	36	8	80	19	10	9	0
1989-90	Philadelphia	80	30	39	11	71	....	....	....	....
1990-91	Philadelphia	80	33	37	10	76	....	....	....	....
1991-92	Philadelphia	24	8	14	2	18	....	....	....	....
1992-93	Hartford	84	26	52	6	58	....	....	....	....
1993-94	Hartford	17	4	11	2	10	....	....	....	....
1994-95	Hartford	48	19	24	5	43	....	....	....	....

Season	Club	Regular Season GC	W	L	T	TP	Playoffs GC	W	L	T
1995-96	Hartford	12	5	6	1	11	....	....	....	....
	NHL Totals	**425**	**161**	**219**	**45**	....	**19**	**10**	**9**	**0**

HOWELL, Harry
HHOF

Born: Hamilton, Ont., December 28, 1932.
Played in NHL. See Player Register for career statistics.

Season	Club	GC	W	L	T	TP	GC	W	L	T
1978-79	Minnesota	11	3	6	2	8	....	....	....	....
	NHL Totals	**11**	**3**	**6**	**2**	....	....	....	....	....

IMLACH, Punch
HHOF

Born: Toronto, Ont., March 15, 1918. Died: December 1, 1987.

Season	Club	GC	W	L	T	TP	GC	W	L	T
1958-59	Toronto	50	22	20	8	52	12	5	7	0
1959-60	Toronto	70	35	26	9	79	10	4	6	0
1960-61	Toronto	70	39	19	12	90	5	1	4	0
1961-62♦	Toronto	70	37	22	11	85	12	8	4	0
1962-63♦	Toronto	70	35	23	12	82	14	8	6	0
1963-64♦	Toronto	70	33	25	12	78	10	8	2	0
1964-65	Toronto	70	30	26	14	74	6	2	4	0
1965-66	Toronto	70	34	25	11	79	4	0	4	0
1966-67♦	Toronto	70	32	27	11	75	12	8	4	0
1967-68	Toronto	74	33	31	10	76	....	....	....	....
1968-69	Toronto	76	35	26	15	85	4	0	4	0
1970-71	Buffalo	78	24	39	15	63	....	....	....	....
1971-72	Buffalo	41	8	23	10	26	....	....	....	....
1979-80	Toronto	10	5	5	0	10	3	0	3	0
	NHL Totals	**889**	**402**	**337**	**150**	....	**92**	**44**	**48**	**0**

Assistant general manager King Clancy posted a 7-1-2 record as replacement coach when Punch Imlach was sidelined with heart problems, February 18 to March 11, 1967. All games are credited to Imlach's coaching record.

INGARFIELD, Earl

Born: Lethbridge, Alta., October 25, 1934.
Played in NHL. See Player Register for career statistics.

Season	Club	GC	W	L	T	TP	GC	W	L	T
1972-73	NY Islanders	30	6	22	2	14	....	....	....	....
	NHL Totals	**30**	**6**	**22**	**2**	....	....	....	....	....

INGLIS, Bill

Born: Ottawa, Ont., May 11, 1943.
Played in NHL. See Player Register for career statistics.

Season	Club	GC	W	L	T	TP	GC	W	L	T
1978-79	Buffalo	56	28	18	10	66	3	1	2	0
	NHL Totals	**56**	**28**	**18**	**10**	....	**3**	**1**	**2**	**0**

IRVIN, Dick
HHOF

Born: Hamilton, Ont., July 19, 1892. Died: March 16, 1957.
Played in NHL. See Player Register for career statistics.

Season	Club	GC	W	L	T	TP	GC	W	L	T
1928-29	Chicago	12	2	6	4	8	....	....	....	....
1930-31	Chicago	44	24	17	3	51	9	5	3	1
1931-32♦	Toronto	43	23	15	5	51	7	5	1	1
1932-33	Toronto	48	24	18	6	54	9	4	5	0
1933-34	Toronto	48	26	13	9	61	5	2	3	0
1934-35	Toronto	48	30	14	4	64	7	3	4	0
1935-36	Toronto	48	23	19	6	52	9	4	5	0
1936-37	Toronto	48	22	21	5	49	2	0	2	0
1937-38	Toronto	48	24	15	9	57	7	4	3	0
1938-39	Toronto	48	19	20	9	47	10	5	5	0
1939-40	Toronto	48	25	17	6	56	10	6	4	0
1940-41	Montreal	48	16	26	6	38	3	1	2	0
1941-42	Montreal	48	18	27	3	39	3	1	2	0
1942-43	Montreal	50	19	19	12	50	5	1	4	0
1943-44♦	Montreal	50	38	5	7	83	9	8	1	0
1944-45	Montreal	50	38	8	4	80	6	2	4	0
1945-46♦	Montreal	50	28	17	5	61	9	8	1	0
1946-47	Montreal	60	34	16	10	78	11	6	5	0
1947-48	Montreal	60	20	29	11	51	....	....	....	....
1948-49	Montreal	60	28	23	9	65	7	3	4	0
1949-50	Montreal	70	29	22	19	77	5	1	4	0
1950-51	Montreal	70	25	30	15	65	11	5	6	0
1951-52	Montreal	70	34	26	10	78	11	4	7	0
1952-53♦	Montreal	70	28	23	19	75	12	8	4	0
1953-54	Montreal	70	35	24	11	81	11	7	4	0
1954-55	Montreal	70	41	18	11	93	12	7	5	0
1955-56	Chicago	70	19	39	12	50	....	....	....	....
	NHL Totals	**1449**	**692**	**527**	**230**	....	**190**	**100**	**88**	**2**

IVAN, Tommy
HHOF

Born: Toronto, Ont., January 31, 1911. Died: June 25, 1999.

Season	Club	GC	W	L	T	TP	GC	W	L	T
1947-48	Detroit	60	30	18	12	72	10	4	6	0
1948-49	Detroit	60	34	19	7	75	11	4	7	0
1949-50♦	Detroit	70	37	19	14	88	14	8	6	0
1950-51	Detroit	70	44	13	13	101	6	2	4	0
1951-52♦	Detroit	70	44	14	12	100	8	8	0	0
1952-53	Detroit	70	36	16	18	90	6	2	4	0
1953-54♦	Detroit	70	37	19	14	88	12	8	4	0
1956-57	Chicago	70	16	39	15	47	....	....	....	....
1957-58	Chicago	33	10	17	6	26	....	....	....	....
	NHL Totals	**573**	**288**	**174**	**111**	....	**67**	**36**	**31**	**0**

IVERSON, Emil

Born: unknown Deceased

Season	Club	GC	W	L	T	TP	GC	W	L	T
1932-33	Chicago	21	8	7	6	22	....	....	....	....
	NHL Totals	**21**	**8**	**7**	**6**	....	....	....	....	....

JOHNSON, Bob
USHOF HHOF

Born: Farmington, MI, November 12, 1948. Died: November 26, 1991.

Season	Club	GC	W	L	T	TP	GC	W	L	T
1982-83	Calgary	80	32	34	14	78	9	4	5	0
1983-84	Calgary	80	34	32	14	82	11	6	5	0
1984-85	Calgary	80	41	27	12	94	4	1	3	0
1985-86	Calgary	80	40	31	9	89	22	12	10	0
1986-87	Calgary	80	46	31	3	95	6	2	4	0
1990-91♦	Pittsburgh	80	41	33	6	88	24	16	8	0
	NHL Totals	**480**	**234**	**188**	**58**	....	**76**	**41**	**35**	**0**

JOHNSON, Tom
HHOF

Born: Baldur, Man., February 18, 1928.
Played in NHL. See Player Register for career statistics.

Season	Club	GC	W	L	T	TP	GC	W	L	T
1970-71	Boston	78	57	14	7	121	7	3	4	0
1971-72♦	Boston	78	54	13	11	119	15	12	3	0
1972-73	Boston	52	31	16	5	67	....	....	....	....
	NHL Totals	**208**	**142**	**43**	**23**	....	**22**	**15**	**7**	**0**

JOHNSTON, Eddie

Born: Montreal, Que., November 24, 1935.
Played in NHL. See Goaltender Register for career statistics.

Season	Club	GC	W	L	T	TP	GC	W	L	T
1979-80	Chicago	80	34	27	19	87	7	3	4	0
1980-81	Pittsburgh	80	30	37	13	73	5	2	3	0
1981-82	Pittsburgh	80	31	36	13	75	5	2	3	0
1982-83	Pittsburgh	80	18	53	9	45	....	....	....	....
1993-94	Pittsburgh	84	44	27	13	101	6	2	4	0
1994-95	Pittsburgh	48	29	16	3	61	12	5	7	0
1995-96	Pittsburgh	82	49	29	4	102	18	11	7	0
1996-97	Pittsburgh	62	31	26	5	67	....	....	....	....
	NHL Totals	**596**	**266**	**251**	**79**	....	**53**	**25**	**28**	**0**

JOHNSTON, Marshall

Born: Birch Hills, Sask., June 6, 1941.
Played in NHL. See Player Register for career statistics.

Season	Club	GC	W	L	T	TP	GC	W	L	T
1973-74	California	21	2	17	2	6	....	....	....	....
1974-75	California	48	11	28	9	31	....	....	....	....
1981-82	Colorado	56	15	32	9	39	....	....	....	....
	NHL Totals	**125**	**28**	**77**	**20**	....	....	....	....	....

JULIEN, Claude

Born: Blind River, Ont., April 23, 1960.
Played in NHL. See Player Register for career statistics.

Season	Club	GC	W	L	T	TP	GC	W	L	T
2002-03	Montreal	36	12	21	3	32	....	....	....	....
	NHL Totals	**36**	**12**	**21**	**3**	....	....	....	....	....

KASPER, Steve

Born: Montreal, Que., September 28, 1961.
Played in NHL. See Player Register for career statistics.

Season	Club	GC	W	L	T	TP	GC	W	L	T
1995-96	Boston	82	40	31	11	91	5	1	4	0
1996-97	Boston	82	26	47	9	61	....	....	....	....
	NHL Totals	**164**	**66**	**78**	**20**	....	**5**	**1**	**4**	**0**

KEATS, Duke
HHOF

Born: Montreal, Que., March 1, 1895. Died: January 16, 1971.
Played in NHL. See Player Register for career statistics.

Season	Club	GC	W	L	T	TP	GC	W	L	T
1926-27	Detroit	11	2	7	2	6	....	....	....	....
	NHL Totals	**11**	**2**	**7**	**2**	....	....	....	....	....

KEENAN, Mike

Born: Bowmanville, Ont., October 21, 1949.

Season	Club	GC	W	L	T	TP	GC	W	L	T
1984-85	Philadelphia	80	53	20	7	113	19	12	7	0
1985-86	Philadelphia	80	53	23	4	110	5	2	3	0
1986-87	Philadelphia	80	46	26	8	100	26	15	11	0
1987-88	Philadelphia	80	38	33	9	85	7	3	4	0
1988-89	Chicago	80	27	41	12	66	16	9	7	0
1989-90	Chicago	80	41	33	6	88	20	10	10	0
1990-91	Chicago	80	49	23	8	106	6	2	4	0
1991-92	Chicago	80	36	29	15	87	18	12	6	0
1993-94♦	NY Rangers	84	52	24	8	112	23	16	7	0
1994-95	St. Louis	48	28	15	5	61	7	3	4	0
1995-96	St. Louis	82	32	34	16	80	13	7	6	0
1996-97	St. Louis	33	15	17	1	31	....	....	....	....
1997-98	Vancouver	63	21	30	12	54	....	....	....	....
1998-99	Vancouver	45	15	24	6	36	....	....	....	....
2000-01	Boston	74	33	34	7	81	....	....	....	....

Season	Club	Regular Season GC	W	L	T	TP	Playoffs GC	W	L	T
2001-02	Florida	56	16	32	8	43	....	....	....	....
2002-03	Florida	82	24	45	13	70	....	....	....	....
	NHL Totals	**1207**	**579**	**483**	**145**	....	**160**	**91**	**69**	**0**

• Won Jack Adams Award (1985)

KEHOE, Rick

Born: Windsor, Ont, July 15, 1951.
Played in NHL. See Player Register for career statistics.

Season	Club	GC	W	L	T	TP	GC	W	L	T
2001-02	Pittsburgh	78	28	40	8	67	....	....	....	....
2002-03	Pittsburgh	82	27	49	6	65	....	....	....	....
	NHL Totals	**160**	**55**	**89**	**14**	....	....	....	....	....

KELLY, Pat

Born: Sioux Lookout, Ont., September 8, 1935.

Season	Club	GC	W	L	T	TP	GC	W	L	T
1977-78	Colorado	80	19	40	21	59	2	0	2	0
1978-79	Colorado	21	3	14	4	10	....	....	....	....
	NHL Totals	**101**	**22**	**54**	**25**	....	**2**	**0**	**2**	**0**

KELLY, Red

HHOF

Born: Simcoe, Ont., July 9, 1927.
Played in NHL. See Player Register for career statistics.

Season	Club	GC	W	L	T	TP	GC	W	L	T
1967-68	Los Angeles	74	31	33	10	72	7	3	4	0
1968-69	Los Angeles	76	24	42	10	58	11	4	7	0
1969-70	Pittsburgh	76	26	38	12	64	10	6	4	0
1970-71	Pittsburgh	78	21	37	20	62	....	....	....	....
1971-72	Pittsburgh	78	26	38	14	66	4	0	4	0
1972-73	Pittsburgh	42	17	19	6	40	....	....	....	....
1973-74	Toronto	78	35	27	16	86	4	0	4	0
1974-75	Toronto	80	31	33	16	78	7	2	5	0
1975-76	Toronto	80	34	31	15	83	10	5	5	0
1976-77	Toronto	80	33	32	15	81	9	4	5	0
	NHL Totals	**742**	**278**	**330**	**134**	....	**62**	**24**	**38**	**0**

KING, Dave

Born: Saskatoon, Sask., December 22, 1947.

Season	Club	GC	W	L	T	TP	GC	W	L	T
1992-93	Calgary	84	43	30	11	97	6	2	4	0
1993-94	Calgary	84	42	29	13	97	7	3	4	0
1994-95	Calgary	48	24	17	7	55	7	3	4	0
2000-01	Columbus	82	28	45	9	71	....	....	....	....
2001-02	Columbus	82	22	52	8	57	....	....	....	....
2002-03	Columbus	40	14	22	4	34	....	....	....	....
	NHL Totals	**420**	**173**	**195**	**52**	....	**20**	**8**	**12**	**0**

KINGSTON, George

Born: Biggar, Sask., August 20, 1939.

Season	Club	GC	W	L	T	TP	GC	W	L	T
1991-92	San Jose	80	17	58	5	39	....	....	....	....
1992-93	San Jose	84	11	71	2	24	....	....	....	....
	NHL Totals	**164**	**28**	**129**	**7**	....	....	....	....	....

KISH, Larry

Born: Welland, Ont., December 11, 1941.

Season	Club	GC	W	L	T	TP	GC	W	L	T
1982-83	Hartford	49	12	32	5	29	....	....	....	....
	NHL Totals	**49**	**12**	**32**	**5**	....	....	....	....	....

KROMM, Bobby

Born: Calgary, Alta., June 8, 1928.

Season	Club	GC	W	L	T	TP	GC	W	L	T
1977-78	Detroit	80	32	34	14	78	7	3	4	0
1978-79	Detroit	80	23	41	16	62	....	....	....	....
1979-80	Detroit	71	24	36	11	59	....	....	....	....
	NHL Totals	**231**	**79**	**111**	**41**	....	**7**	**3**	**4**	**0**

• Won Jack Adams Award (1978)

KURTENBACH, Orland

Born: Cudworth, Sask., September 7, 1936.
Played in NHL. See Player Register for career statistics.

Season	Club	GC	W	L	T	TP	GC	W	L	T
1976-77	Vancouver	45	16	19	10	42	....	....	....	....
1977-78	Vancouver	80	20	43	17	57	....	....	....	....
	NHL Totals	**125**	**36**	**62**	**27**	....	....	....	....	....

LAFORGE, Bill

Born: Edmonton, Alta., September 2, 1951.

Season	Club	GC	W	L	T	TP	GC	W	L	T
1984-85	Vancouver	20	4	14	2	10	....	....	....	....
	NHL Totals	**20**	**4**	**14**	**2**	....	....	....	....	....

LALONDE, Newsy

HHOF

Born: Cornwall, Ont., October 31, 1888. Died: November 21, 1971.
Played in NHL. See Player Register for career statistics.

Season	Club	GC	W	L	T	TP	GC	W	L	T
1917-18	Montreal	22	13	9	0	26	2	1	1	0
1918-19	Montreal	18	10	8	0	20	5	4	1	0
	Montreal (Cup)	....	....	....	....	....	*5*	*2*	*2*	*1*
1919-20	Montreal	24	13	11	0	26	....	....	....	....
1920-21	Montreal	24	13	11	0	26	....	....	....	....
1921-22	Montreal	7	2	5	0	4	....	....	....	....
1926-27	NY Americans	44	17	25	2	36	....	....	....	....
1929-30	Ottawa	44	21	15	8	50	2	0	1	1
1930-31	Ottawa	44	10	30	4	24	....	....	....	....
1932-33	Montreal	48	18	25	5	41	2	0	1	1
1933-34	Montreal	48	22	20	6	50	2	0	1	1
1934-35	Montreal	16	5	8	3	13	....	....	....	....
	NHL Totals	**339**	**144**	**167**	**28**	....	**13**	**5**	**5**	**3**

LAPOINTE, Ron

Born: Verdun, Que., November 12, 1949. Died: March 23, 1992.

Season	Club	GC	W	L	T	TP	GC	W	L	T
1987-88	Quebec	56	22	30	4	48	....	....	....	....
1988-89	Quebec	33	11	20	2	24	....	....	....	....
	NHL Totals	**89**	**33**	**50**	**6**	....	....	....	....	....

LAVIOLETTE, Peter

Born: Norwood, MA, December 7, 1964.
Played in NHL. See Player Register for career statistics.

Season	Club	GC	W	L	T	TP	GC	W	L	T
2001-02	NY Islanders	82	42	32	8	96	7	3	4	0
2002-03	NY Islanders	82	35	36	11	83	5	1	4	0
	NHL Totals	**164**	**77**	**68**	**19**	....	**12**	**4**	**8**	**0**

LAYCOE, Hal

Born: Sutherland, Sask., June 23, 1922. Died: April 29, 1997.
Played in NHL. See Player Register for career statistics.

Season	Club	GC	W	L	T	TP	GC	W	L	T
1969-70	Los Angeles	24	5	18	1	11	....	....	....	....
1970-71	Vancouver	78	24	46	8	56	....	....	....	....
1971-72	Vancouver	78	20	50	8	48	....	....	....	....
	NHL Totals	**180**	**49**	**114**	**17**	....	....	....	....	....

LEHMAN, Hugh

HHOF

Born: Pembroke, Ont., October 27, 1885. Died: April 8, 1961.
Played in NHL. See Goaltender Register for career statistics.

Season	Club	GC	W	L	T	TP	GC	W	L	T
1927-28	Chicago	21	3	17	1	7	....	....	....	....
	NHL Totals	**21**	**3**	**17**	**1**	....	....	....	....	....

LEMAIRE, Jacques

HHOF

Born: LaSalle, Que., September 7, 1945.
Played in NHL. See Player Register for career statistics.

Season	Club	GC	W	L	T	TP	GC	W	L	T
1983-84	Montreal	17	7	10	0	14	15	9	6	0
1984-85	Montreal	80	41	27	12	94	12	6	6	0
1993-94	New Jersey	84	47	25	12	106	20	11	9	0
1994-95 ♦	New Jersey	48	22	18	8	52	20	16	4	0
1995-96	New Jersey	82	37	33	12	86	....	....	....	....
1996-97	New Jersey	82	45	23	14	104	10	5	5	0
1997-98	New Jersey	82	48	23	11	107	6	2	4	0
2000-01	Minnesota	82	25	44	13	68	....	....	....	....
2001-02	Minnesota	82	26	44	12	73	....	....	....	....
2002-03	Minnesota	82	42	30	10	95	18	8	10	0
	NHL Totals	**721**	**340**	**277**	**104**	....	**101**	**57**	**44**	**0**

• Won Jack Adams Award (1994, 2003)

LEPINE, Pit

Born: St. Anne de Bellevue, Que., July 30, 1901. Died: August 2, 1955.
Played in NHL. See Player Register for career statistics.

Season	Club	GC	W	L	T	TP	GC	W	L	T
1939-40	Montreal	48	10	33	5	25	....	....	....	....
	NHL Totals	**48**	**10**	**33**	**5**	....	....	....	....	....

LeSUEUR, Percy

HHOF

Born: Quebec City, Que., November 18, 1881. Died: January 27, 1962.

Season	Club	GC	W	L	T	TP	GC	W	L	T
1923-24	Hamilton	10	3	7	0	6	....	....	....	....
	NHL Totals	**10**	**3**	**7**	**0**	....	....	....	....	....

LEWIS, Dave

Born: Kindersley, Sask., July 3, 1953.
Played in NHL. See Player Register for career statistics.

Season	Club	GC	W	L	T	TP	GC	W	L	T
1998-99	Detroit	5	4	1	0	8	....	....	....	....
2002-03	Detroit	82	48	24	10	110	4	0	4	0
	NHL Totals	**87**	**52**	**25**	**10**	....	**4**	**0**	**4**	**0**

Shared a 4-1-0 record with associate coach Barry Smith while serving as co-head coaches until Scotty Bowman received medical clearance and decided to return to coaching on October 23, 1998.

LEY, Rick

Born: Orillia, Ont., November 2, 1948.
Played in NHL. See Player Register for career statistics.

Season	Club	GC	W	L	T	TP	GC	W	L	T
1989-90	Hartford	80	38	33	9	85	7	3	4	0
1990-91	Hartford	80	31	38	11	73	6	2	4	0
1994-95	Vancouver	48	18	18	12	48	11	4	7	0
1995-96	Vancouver	76	29	32	15	73	....	....	....	....
	NHL Totals	**284**	**116**	**121**	**47**	....	**24**	**9**	**15**	**0**

Posted a 1-1 playoff record as replacement coach when Pat Quinn was sidelined with heart arrythmia, May 21 and 25, 2002. All games are credited to Quinn's coaching record.

LINDSAY, Ted — HHOF

Born: Renfrew, Ont., July 29, 1925.
Played in NHL. See Player Register for career statistics.

Season	Club	GC	W	L	T	TP	Playoffs GC	W	L	T
1979-80	Detroit	9	2	7	0	4	....	....	....	....
1980-81	Detroit	20	3	14	3	9	....	....	....	....
	NHL Totals	**29**	**5**	**21**	**3**	....	....	....	....	....

LONG, Barry

Born: Brantford, Ont., January 3, 1949.
Played in NHL. See Player Register for career statistics.

Season	Club	GC	W	L	T	TP	Playoffs GC	W	L	T
1983-84	Winnipeg	59	25	25	9	59	3	0	3	0
1984-85	Winnipeg	80	43	27	10	96	8	3	5	0
1985-86	Winnipeg	66	19	41	6	44	....	....	....	....
	NHL Totals	**205**	**87**	**93**	**25**	....	**11**	**3**	**8**	**0**

LOUGHLIN, Clem

Born: Carroll, Man., November 15, 1894. Deceased
Played in NHL. See Player Register for career statistics.

Season	Club	GC	W	L	T	TP	Playoffs GC	W	L	T
1934-35	Chicago	48	26	17	5	57	2	0	1	1
1935-36	Chicago	48	21	19	8	50	2	1	1	0
1936-37	Chicago	48	14	27	7	35	....	....	....	....
	NHL Totals	**144**	**61**	**63**	**20**	....	**4**	**1**	**2**	**1**

LOW, Ron

Born: Birtle, Man., June 21, 1950.
Played in NHL. See Goaltender Register for career statistics.

Season	Club	GC	W	L	T	TP	Playoffs GC	W	L	T
1994-95	Edmonton	13	5	7	1	11	....	....	....	....
1995-96	Edmonton	82	30	44	8	68	....	....	....	....
1996-97	Edmonton	82	36	37	9	81	12	5	7	0
1997-98	Edmonton	82	35	37	10	80	12	5	7	0
1998-99	Edmonton	82	33	37	12	78	4	0	4	0
2000-01	NY Rangers	82	33	44	5	72	....	....	....	....
2001-02	NY Rangers	82	36	42	4	80	....	....	....	....
	NHL Totals	**505**	**208**	**248**	**49**	....	**28**	**10**	**18**	**0**

LOWE, Kevin

Born: Lachute, Que., April 15, 1959.
Played in NHL. See Player Register for career statistics.

Season	Club	GC	W	L	T	TP	Playoffs GC	W	L	T
99-2000	Edmonton	82	32	34	16	88	5	1	4	0
	NHL Totals	**82**	**32**	**34**	**16**	....	**5**	**1**	**4**	**0**

LUDZIK, Steve

Born: Toronto, Ont., April 3, 1962.
Played in NHL. See Player Register for career statistics.

Season	Club	GC	W	L	T	TP	Playoffs GC	W	L	T
99-2000	Tampa Bay	82	19	54	9	54	....	....	....	....
2000-01	Tampa Bay	39	12	22	5	31	....	....	....	....
	NHL Totals	**121**	**31**	**76**	**14**	....	....	....	....	....

MacDONALD, Parker

Born: Sydney, N.S., June 14, 1933.
Played in NHL. See Player Register for career statistics.

Season	Club	GC	W	L	T	TP	Playoffs GC	W	L	T
1973-74	Minnesota	61	20	30	11	51	....	....	....	....
1981-82	Los Angeles	42	13	24	5	31	....	....	....	....
	NHL Totals	**103**	**33**	**54**	**16**	....	....	....	....	....

MacLEAN, Doug

Born: Summerside, PEI, April 12, 1954.

Season	Club	GC	W	L	T	TP	Playoffs GC	W	L	T
1995-96	Florida	82	41	31	10	92	22	12	10	0
1996-97	Florida	82	35	28	19	89	5	1	4	0
1997-98	Florida	23	7	12	4	18	....	....	....	....
2002-03	Columbus	42	15	23	4	35	....	....	....	....
	NHL Totals	**229**	**98**	**94**	**37**	....	**27**	**13**	**14**	**0**

MacMILLAN, Bill

Born: Charlottetown, P.E.I., March 7, 1943.
Played in NHL. See Player Register for career statistics.

Season	Club	GC	W	L	T	TP	Playoffs GC	W	L	T
1980-81	Colorado	80	22	45	13	57	....	....	....	....
1982-83	New Jersey	80	17	49	14	48	....	....	....	....
1983-84	New Jersey	20	2	18	0	4	....	....	....	....
	NHL Totals	**180**	**41**	**112**	**27**	....	....	....	....	....

MacNEIL, Al

Born: Sydney, N.S., September 27, 1935.
Played in NHL. See Player Register for career statistics.

Season	Club	GC	W	L	T	TP	Playoffs GC	W	L	T
1970-71	♦ Montreal	55	31	15	9	71	20	12	8	0
1979-80	Atlanta	80	35	32	13	83	4	1	3	0
1980-81	Calgary	80	39	27	14	92	16	9	7	0
1981-82	Calgary	80	29	34	17	75	3	0	3	0
2002-03	Calgary	11	4	5	2	10	....	....	....	....
	NHL Totals	**306**	**138**	**113**	**55**	....	**43**	**22**	**21**	**0**

MacTAVISH, Craig

Born: London, Ont., August 15, 1958.
Played in NHL. See Player Register for career statistics.

Season	Club	GC	W	L	T	TP	Playoffs GC	W	L	T
2000-01	Edmonton	82	39	31	12	93	....	....	....	....
2001-02	Edmonton	82	38	32	12	92	....	....	....	....
2002-03	Edmonton	82	36	35	11	92	6	2	4	0
	NHL Totals	**246**	**113**	**98**	**35**	....	**6**	**2**	**4**	**0**

MAGNUSON, Keith

Born: Saskatoon, Sask., April 27, 1947.
Played in NHL. See Player Register for career statistics.

Season	Club	GC	W	L	T	TP	Playoffs GC	W	L	T
1980-81	Chicago	80	31	33	16	78	3	0	3	0
1981-82	Chicago	52	18	24	10	46	....	....	....	....
	NHL Totals	**132**	**49**	**57**	**26**	....	**3**	**0**	**3**	**0**

MAHONEY, Bill

Born: Peterborough, Ont., June 23, 1939.

Season	Club	GC	W	L	T	TP	Playoffs GC	W	L	T
1983-84	Minnesota	80	39	31	10	88	16	7	9	0
1984-85	Minnesota	13	3	8	2	8	....	....	....	....
	NHL Totals	**93**	**42**	**39**	**12**	....	**16**	**7**	**9**	**0**

MALONEY, Dan

Born: Barrie, Ont., September 24, 1950.
Played in NHL. See Player Register for career statistics.

Season	Club	GC	W	L	T	TP	Playoffs GC	W	L	T
1984-85	Toronto	80	20	52	8	48	....	....	....	....
1985-86	Toronto	80	25	48	7	57	10	6	4	0
1986-87	Winnipeg	80	40	32	8	88	10	4	6	0
1987-88	Winnipeg	80	33	36	11	77	5	1	4	0
1988-89	Winnipeg	52	18	25	9	45	....	....	....	....
	NHL Totals	**372**	**136**	**193**	**43**	....	**25**	**11**	**14**	**0**

MALONEY, Phil

Born: Ottawa, Ont., October 6, 1927.
Played in NHL. See Player Register for career statistics.

Season	Club	GC	W	L	T	TP	Playoffs GC	W	L	T
1973-74	Vancouver	37	15	18	4	34	....	....	....	....
1974-75	Vancouver	80	38	32	10	86	5	1	4	0
1975-76	Vancouver	80	33	32	15	81	2	0	2	0
1976-77	Vancouver	35	9	23	3	21	....	....	....	....
	NHL Totals	**232**	**95**	**105**	**32**	....	**7**	**1**	**6**	**0**

MANTHA, Sylvio — HHOF

Born: Montreal, Que., April 14, 1902. Died: August 7, 1974.
Played in NHL. See Player Register for career statistics.

Season	Club	GC	W	L	T	TP	Playoffs GC	W	L	T
1935-36	Montreal	48	11	26	11	33	....	....	....	....
	NHL Totals	**48**	**11**	**26**	**11**	....	....	....	....	....

MARSHALL, Bert

Born: Kamloops, B.C., November 22, 1943.
Played in NHL. See Player Register for career statistics.

Season	Club	GC	W	L	T	TP	Playoffs GC	W	L	T
1981-82	Colorado	24	3	17	4	10	....	....	....	....
	NHL Totals	**24**	**3**	**17**	**4**	....	....	....	....	....

MARTIN, Jacques

Born: St. Pascal, Ont., October 1, 1952.

Season	Club	GC	W	L	T	TP	Playoffs GC	W	L	T
1986-87	St. Louis	80	32	33	15	79	6	2	4	0
1987-88	St. Louis	80	34	38	8	76	10	5	5	0
1995-96	Ottawa	38	10	24	4	24	....	....	....	....
1996-97	Ottawa	82	31	36	15	77	7	3	4	0
1997-98	Ottawa	82	34	33	15	83	11	5	6	0
1998-99	Ottawa	82	44	23	15	103	4	0	4	0
99-2000	Ottawa	82	41	30	11	95	6	2	4	0
2000-01	Ottawa	82	48	25	9	109	4	0	4	0
2001-02	Ottawa	80	38	33	9	92	12	7	5	0
2002-03	Ottawa	82	52	22	8	113	18	11	7	0
	NHL Totals	**770**	**364**	**297**	**109**	....	**78**	**35**	**43**	**0**

• Won Jack Adams Award (1999)

Martin stepped aside (with NHL permission) during the final two games of the 2001-02 season in order to allow assistant coach Roger Neilson to reach the 1,000-game plateau, April 11 and 13, 2002.

MATHESON, Godfrey

Born: unknown

Season	Club	GC	W	L	T	TP	Playoffs GC	W	L	T
1932-33	Chicago	2	0	2	0	0	....	....	....	....
	NHL Totals	**2**	**0**	**2**	**0**	....	....	....	....	....

MAURICE, Paul

Born: Sault Ste. Marie, Ont., January 30, 1967.

Season	Club	GC	W	L	T	TP	Playoffs GC	W	L	T
1995-96	Hartford	70	29	33	8	66	....	....	....	....
1996-97	Hartford	82	32	39	11	75	....	....	....	....
1997-98	Carolina	82	33	41	8	74	....	....	....	....
1998-99	Carolina	82	34	30	18	86	6	2	4	0
99-2000	Carolina	82	37	35	10	84	....	....	....	....

Season	Club	Regular Season GC	W	L	T	TP	Playoffs GC	W	L	T
2000-01	Carolina	82	38	35	9	88	6	2	4	0
2001-02	Carolina	82	35	31	16	91	23	13	10	0
2002-03	Carolina	82	22	49	11	61	....	....	....	....
	NHL Totals	**644**	**260**	**293**	**91**	....	**35**	**17**	**18**	**0**

MAXNER, Wayne

Born: Halifax, N.S., September 27, 1942.
Played in NHL. See Player Register for career statistics.

Season	Club	GC	W	L	T	TP	GC	W	L	T
1980-81	Detroit	60	16	29	15	47	....	....	....	....
1981-82	Detroit	69	18	39	12	48	....	....	....	....
	NHL Totals	**129**	**34**	**68**	**27**	....	....	....	....	....

McCAMMON, Bob

Born: Kenora, Ont., April 14, 1941.

Season	Club	GC	W	L	T	TP	GC	W	L	T
1978-79	Philadelphia	50	22	17	11	55	....	....	....	....
1981-82	Philadelphia	8	4	2	2	10	4	1	3	0
1982-83	Philadelphia	80	49	23	8	106	3	0	3	0
1983-84	Philadelphia	80	44	26	10	98	3	0	3	0
1987-88	Vancouver	80	25	46	9	59	....	....	....	....
1988-89	Vancouver	80	33	39	8	74	7	3	4	0
1989-90	Vancouver	80	25	41	14	64	....	....	....	....
1990-91	Vancouver	54	19	30	5	43	....	....	....	....
	NHL Totals	**512**	**221**	**224**	**67**	....	**17**	**4**	**13**	**0**

McCREARY, Bill

Born: Sundridge, Ont., December 2, 1934.
Played in NHL. See Player Register for career statistics.

Season	Club	GC	W	L	T	TP	GC	W	L	T
1971-72	St. Louis	24	6	14	4	16	....	....	....	....
1973-74	Vancouver	41	9	25	7	25	....	....	....	....
1974-75	California	32	8	20	4	20	....	....	....	....
	NHL Totals	**97**	**23**	**59**	**15**	....	....	....	....	....

McGUIRE, Pierre

Born: Englewood, NJ, August 8, 1961.

Season	Club	GC	W	L	T	TP	GC	W	L	T
1993-94	Hartford	67	23	37	7	53	....	....	....	....
	NHL Totals	**67**	**23**	**37**	**7**	....	....	....	....	....

McLELLAN, John

Born: South Porcupine, Ont., August 6, 1928. Died: October 27, 1979.
Played in NHL. See Player Register for career statistics.

Season	Club	GC	W	L	T	TP	GC	W	L	T
1969-70	Toronto	76	29	34	13	71	....	....	....	....
1970-71	Toronto	78	37	33	8	82	6	2	4	0
1971-72	Toronto	78	33	31	14	80	5	1	4	0
1972-73	Toronto	78	27	41	10	64	....	....	....	....
	NHL Totals	**310**	**126**	**139**	**45**	....	**11**	**3**	**8**	**0**

Assistant general manager King Clancy posted a 6-2-3 record as replacement coach when John McLellan was sidelined with a duodenal ulcer, February 23 to March 22, 1972. King Clancy posted a 3-1-0 record and a 1-4 playoff record as replacement coach when John McLellan was again sidelined with a duodenal ulcer, March 25 to April 11, 1972. All games are credited to McLellan's coaching record.

McVIE, Tom

Born: Trail, B.C., June 6, 1935.

Season	Club	GC	W	L	T	TP	GC	W	L	T
1975-76	Washington	44	8	31	5	21	....	....	....	....
1976-77	Washington	80	24	42	14	62	....	....	....	....
1977-78	Washington	80	17	49	14	48	....	....	....	....
1979-80	Winnipeg	77	19	47	11	49	....	....	....	....
1980-81	Winnipeg	28	1	20	7	9	....	....	....	....
1983-84	New Jersey	60	15	38	7	37	....	....	....	....
1990-91	New Jersey	13	4	5	4	12	7	3	4	0
1991-92	New Jersey	80	38	31	11	87	7	3	4	0
	NHL Totals	**462**	**126**	**263**	**73**	....	**14**	**6**	**8**	**0**

MEEKER, Howie

Born: Kitchener, Ont., November 4, 1924.
Played in NHL. See Player Register for career statistics.

Season	Club	GC	W	L	T	TP	GC	W	L	T
1956-57	Toronto	70	21	34	15	57	....	....	....	....
	NHL Totals	**70**	**21**	**34**	**15**	....	....	....	....	....

MELROSE, Barry

Born: Kelvington, Sask., July 15, 1956.
Played in NHL. See Player Register for career statistics.

Season	Club	GC	W	L	T	TP	GC	W	L	T
1992-93	Los Angeles	84	39	35	10	88	24	13	11	0
1993-94	Los Angeles	84	27	45	12	66	....	....	....	....
1994-95	Los Angeles	41	13	21	7	33	....	....	....	....
	NHL Totals	**209**	**79**	**101**	**29**	....	**24**	**13**	**11**	**0**

MILBURY, Mike

Born: Brighton, MA, June 17, 1952.
Played in NHL. See Player Register for career statistics.

Season	Club	GC	W	L	T	TP	GC	W	L	T
1989-90	Boston	80	46	25	9	101	21	13	8	0
1990-91	Boston	80	44	24	12	100	19	10	9	0
1995-96	NY Islanders	82	22	50	10	54	....	....	....	....
1996-97	NY Islanders	45	13	23	9	35	....	....	....	....
1997-98	NY Islanders	19	8	9	2	18	....	....	....	....
1998-99	NY Islanders	45	13	29	3	29	....	....	....	....
	NHL Totals	**351**	**146**	**160**	**45**	....	**40**	**23**	**17**	**0**

MOLLEKEN, Lorne

Born: Regina, Sask., June 11, 1956.

Season	Club	GC	W	L	T	TP	GC	W	L	T
1998-99	Chicago	23	13	6	4	30	....	....	....	....
99-2000	Chicago	24	5	15	4	16	....	....	....	....
	NHL Totals	**47**	**18**	**21**	**8**	....	....	....	....	....

MUCKLER, John

Born: Midland, Ont., April 3, 1934.

Season	Club	GC	W	L	T	TP	GC	W	L	T
1968-69	Minnesota	35	6	23	6	18	....	....	....	....
1989-90♦	Edmonton	80	38	28	14	90	22	16	6	0
1990-91	Edmonton	80	37	37	6	80	18	9	9	0
1991-92	Buffalo	52	22	22	8	52	7	3	4	0
1992-93	Buffalo	84	38	36	10	86	8	4	4	0
1993-94	Buffalo	84	43	32	9	95	7	3	4	0
1994-95	Buffalo	48	22	19	7	51	5	1	4	0
1997-98	NY Rangers	25	8	15	2	18	....	....	....	....
1998-99	NY Rangers	82	33	38	11	77	....	....	....	....
99-2000	NY Rangers	78	29	38	11	72	....	....	....	....
	NHL Totals	**648**	**276**	**288**	**84**	....	**67**	**36**	**31**	**0**

MULDOON, Pete

Born: St. Mary, Ont., 1881. Died: March 13, 1929.

Season	Club	GC	W	L	T	TP	GC	W	L	T
1926-27	Chicago	44	19	22	3	41	2	0	1	1
	NHL Totals	**44**	**19**	**22**	**3**	....	**2**	**0**	**1**	**1**

MUNRO, Dunc

Born: Moray, Scotland, January 19, 1901. Died: January 3, 1958.
Played in NHL. See Player Register for career statistics.

Season	Club	GC	W	L	T	TP	GC	W	L	T
1929-30	Mtl. Maroons	44	23	16	5	51	4	1	3	0
1930-31	Mtl. Maroons	32	14	13	5	33	....	....	....	....
	NHL Totals	**76**	**37**	**29**	**10**	....	**4**	**1**	**3**	**0**

MURDOCH, Bob

Born: Kirkland Lake, Ont., November 20, 1946.
Played in NHL. See Player Register for career statistics.

Season	Club	GC	W	L	T	TP	GC	W	L	T
1987-88	Chicago	80	30	41	9	69	5	1	4	0
1989-90	Winnipeg	80	37	32	11	85	7	3	4	0
1990-91	Winnipeg	80	26	43	11	63	....	....	....	....
	NHL Totals	**240**	**93**	**116**	**31**	....	**12**	**4**	**8**	**0**

• Won Jack Adams Award (1990)

MURPHY, Mike

Born: Toronto, Ont., September 12, 1950.
Played in NHL. See Player Register for career statistics.

Season	Club	GC	W	L	T	TP	GC	W	L	T
1986-87	Los Angeles	38	13	21	4	30	5	1	4	0
1987-88	Los Angeles	27	7	16	4	18	....	....	....	....
1996-97	Toronto	82	30	44	8	68	....	....	....	....
1997-98	Toronto	82	30	43	9	69	....	....	....	....
	NHL Totals	**229**	**80**	**124**	**25**	....	**5**	**1**	**4**	**0**

MURRAY, Andy

Born: Gladstone, Man., March 3, 1951.

Season	Club	GC	W	L	T	TP	GC	W	L	T
99-2000	Los Angeles	82	39	31	12	94	4	0	4	0
2000-01	Los Angeles	82	38	31	13	92	13	7	6	0
2001-02	Los Angeles	82	40	31	11	95	7	3	4	0
2002-03	Los Angeles	82	33	43	6	78	....	....	....	....
	NHL Totals	**328**	**150**	**136**	**42**	....	**24**	**10**	**14**	**0**

Assistant coach Dave Tippett posted a 2-1-1 record as replacement coach when Andy Murray was sidelined following a car accident, February 26 to March 6, 2002, All games are credited to Murray's coaching record.

MURRAY, Bryan

Born: Shawville, Que., December 5, 1942.

Season	Club	GC	W	L	T	TP	GC	W	L	T
1981-82	Washington	66	25	28	13	63	....	....	....	....
1982-83	Washington	80	39	25	16	94	4	1	3	0
1983-84	Washington	80	48	27	5	101	8	4	4	0
1984-85	Washington	80	46	25	9	101	5	2	3	0
1985-86	Washington	80	50	23	7	107	9	5	4	0
1986-87	Washington	80	38	32	10	86	7	3	4	0
1987-88	Washington	80	38	33	9	85	14	7	7	0
1988-89	Washington	80	41	29	10	92	6	2	4	0
1989-90	Washington	46	18	24	4	40	....	....	....	....
1990-91	Detroit	80	34	38	8	76	7	3	4	0
1991-92	Detroit	80	43	25	12	98	11	4	7	0
1992-93	Detroit	84	47	28	9	103	7	3	4	0
1997-98	Florida	59	17	31	11	45	....	....	....	....
2001-02	Anaheim	82	29	45	8	69	....	....	....	....
	NHL Totals	**1057**	**513**	**413**	**131**	....	**78**	**34**	**44**	**0**

• Won Jack Adams Award (1984)

MURRAY, Terry

Born: Shawville, Que., July 20, 1950.
Played in NHL. See Player Register for career statistics.

Season	Club	Regular Season GC	W	L	T	TP	Playoffs GC	W	L	T
1989-90	Washington	34	18	14	2	38	15	8	7	0
1990-91	Washington	80	37	36	7	81	11	5	6	0
1991-92	Washington	80	45	27	8	98	7	3	4	0
1992-93	Washington	84	43	34	7	93	6	2	4	0
1993-94	Washington	47	20	23	4	44	....	....	....	....
1994-95	Philadelphia	48	28	16	4	60	15	10	5	0
1995-96	Philadelphia	82	45	24	13	103	12	6	6	0
1996-97	Philadelphia	82	45	24	13	103	19	12	7	0
1998-99	Florida	82	30	34	18	78	....	....	....	....
99-2000	Florida	82	43	33	6	98	4	0	4	0
2000-01	Florida	36	6	23	7	24	....	....	....	....
	NHL Totals	**737**	**360**	**288**	**89**	....	**89**	**46**	**43**	**0**

NANNE, Lou

USHOF

Born: Sault Ste. Marie, Ont., June 2, 1941.
Played in NHL. See Player Register for career statistics.

Season	Club	Regular Season GC	W	L	T	TP	Playoffs GC	W	L	T
1977-78	Minnesota	29	7	18	4	18	....	....	....	....
	NHL Totals	**29**	**7**	**18**	**4**	....	....	....	....	....

NEALE, Harry

Born: Sarnia, Ont., March 9, 1937.

Season	Club	Regular Season GC	W	L	T	TP	Playoffs GC	W	L	T
1978-79	Vancouver	80	25	42	13	63	3	1	2	0
1979-80	Vancouver	80	27	37	16	70	4	1	3	0
1980-81	Vancouver	80	28	32	20	76	3	0	3	0
1981-82	Vancouver	75	26	33	16	68	....	....	....	....
1983-84	Vancouver	32	15	13	4	34	4	1	3	0
1984-85	Vancouver	60	21	32	7	49	....	....	....	....
1985-86	Detroit	35	8	23	4	20	....	....	....	....
	NHL Totals	**442**	**150**	**212**	**80**	....	**14**	**3**	**11**	**0**

NEILSON, Roger

HHOF

Born: Toronto, Ont., June 16, 1934. Died: June 21, 2003.

Season	Club	Regular Season GC	W	L	T	TP	Playoffs GC	W	L	T
1977-78	Toronto	80	41	29	10	92	13	6	7	0
1978-79	Toronto	80	34	33	13	81	6	2	4	0
1980-81	Buffalo	80	39	20	21	99	8	4	4	0
1981-82	Vancouver	5	4	0	1	9	17	11	6	0
1982-83	Vancouver	80	30	35	15	75	4	1	3	0
1983-84	Vancouver	48	17	26	5	39	....	....	....	....
	Los Angeles	28	8	17	3	19	....	....	....	....
1989-90	NY Rangers	80	36	31	13	85	10	5	5	0
1990-91	NY Rangers	80	36	31	13	85	6	2	4	0
1991-92	NY Rangers	80	50	25	5	105	13	6	7	0
1992-93	NY Rangers	40	19	17	4	42	....	....	....	....
1993-94	Florida	84	33	34	17	83	....	....	....	....
1994-95	Florida	48	20	22	6	46	....	....	....	....
1997-98	Philadelphia	21	10	9	2	22	5	1	4	0
1998-99	Philadelphia	82	37	26	19	93	6	2	4	0
99-2000	Philadelphia	82	45	25	12	105	18	11	7	0
2001-02	Ottawa	2	1	1	0	2	....	....	....	....
	NHL Totals	**1000**	**460**	**381**	**159**	....	**106**	**51**	**55**	**0**

Assistant coach Craig Ramsay posted a 16-10-1 regular-season record and an 11-7 playoff record as interim coach after Roger Neilson was sidelined for treatment of bone marrow cancer on February 20, 2000. All games are credited to Neilson's coaching record. Head coach Jacques Martin stepped aside (with NHL permission) during the final two games of the 2001-02 season in order to allow assistant coach Roger Neilson to reach the 1,000-game plateau, April 11 and 13, 2002.

NOLAN, Ted

Born: Sault Ste. Marie, Ont., April 7, 1958.
Played in NHL. See Player Register for career statistics.

Season	Club	Regular Season GC	W	L	T	TP	Playoffs GC	W	L	T
1995-96	Buffalo	82	33	42	7	73	....	....	....	....
1996-97	Buffalo	82	40	30	12	92	12	5	7	0
	NHL Totals	**164**	**73**	**72**	**19**	....	**12**	**5**	**7**	**0**

• Won Jack Adams Award (1997)

NYKOLUK, Mike

Born: Toronto, Ont., December 11, 1934.
Played in NHL. See Player Register for career statistics.

Season	Club	Regular Season GC	W	L	T	TP	Playoffs GC	W	L	T
1980-81	Toronto	40	15	15	10	40	3	0	3	0
1981-82	Toronto	80	20	44	16	56	....	....	....	....
1982-83	Toronto	80	28	40	12	68	4	1	3	0
1983-84	Toronto	80	26	45	9	61	....	....	....	....
	NHL Totals	**280**	**89**	**144**	**47**	....	**7**	**1**	**6**	**0**

O'CONNELL, Mike

Born: Chicago, IL, November 25, 1955.
Played in NHL. See Player Register for career statistics.

Season	Club	Regular Season GC	W	L	T	TP	Playoffs GC	W	L	T
2002-03	Boston	9	3	3	3	9	5	1	4	0
	NHL Totals	**9**	**3**	**3**	**3**	....	**5**	**1**	**4**	**0**

O'DONOGHUE, George

Born: unknown Deceased

Season	Club	Regular Season GC	W	L	T	TP	Playoffs GC	W	L	T
1921-22 ♦	Toronto	24	13	10	1	27	2	1	0	1
	Toronto (Cup)	....	....	....	....	....	*5*	*3*	*2*	*0*
1922-23	Toronto	5	2	3	0	4	....	....	....	....
	NHL Totals	**29**	**15**	**13**	**1**	....	**2**	**1**	**0**	**1**

OLIVER, Murray

Born: Hamilton, Ont., November 14, 1937.
Played in NHL. See Player Register for career statistics.

Season	Club	Regular Season GC	W	L	T	TP	Playoffs GC	W	L	T
1981-82	Minnesota	4	3	0	1	7	4	1	3	0
1982-83	Minnesota	37	18	12	7	43	9	4	5	0
	NHL Totals	**41**	**21**	**12**	**8**	....	**13**	**5**	**8**	**0**

OLMSTEAD, Bert

HHOF

Born: Sceptre, Sask., September 4, 1926.
Played in NHL. See Player Register for career statistics.

Season	Club	Regular Season GC	W	L	T	TP	Playoffs GC	W	L	T
1967-68	Oakland	64	11	37	16	38	....	....	....	....
	NHL Totals	**64**	**11**	**37**	**16**	....	....	....	....	....

O'REILLY, Terry

Born: Niagara Falls, Ont., June 7, 1951.
Played in NHL. See Player Register for career statistics.

Season	Club	Regular Season GC	W	L	T	TP	Playoffs GC	W	L	T
1986-87	Boston	67	34	27	6	74	4	0	4	0
1987-88	Boston	80	44	30	6	94	23	12	10	1
1988-89	Boston	80	37	29	14	88	10	5	5	0
	NHL Totals	**227**	**115**	**86**	**26**	....	**37**	**17**	**19**	**1**

PADDOCK, John

Born: Brandon, Man., June 9, 1954.
Played in NHL. See Player Register for career statistics.

Season	Club	Regular Season GC	W	L	T	TP	Playoffs GC	W	L	T
1991-92	Winnipeg	80	33	32	15	81	7	3	4	0
1992-93	Winnipeg	84	40	37	7	87	6	2	4	0
1993-94	Winnipeg	84	24	51	9	57	....	....	....	....
1994-95	Winnipeg	33	9	18	6	24	....	....	....	....
	NHL Totals	**281**	**106**	**138**	**37**	....	**13**	**5**	**8**	**0**

PAGE, Pierre

Born: St-Hermas, Que., April 30, 1948.

Season	Club	Regular Season GC	W	L	T	TP	Playoffs GC	W	L	T
1988-89	Minnesota	80	27	37	16	70	5	1	4	0
1989-90	Minnesota	80	36	40	4	76	7	3	4	0
1991-92	Quebec	62	17	34	11	45	....	....	....	....
1992-93	Quebec	84	47	27	10	104	6	2	4	0
1993-94	Quebec	84	34	42	8	76	....	....	....	....
1995-96	Calgary	82	34	37	11	79	4	0	4	0
1996-97	Calgary	82	32	41	9	73	....	....	....	....
1997-98	Anaheim	82	26	43	13	65	....	....	....	....
	NHL Totals	**636**	**253**	**301**	**82**	....	**22**	**6**	**16**	**0**

PARK, Brad

HHOF

Born: Toronto, Ont., July 6, 1948.
Played in NHL. See Player Register for career statistics.

Season	Club	Regular Season GC	W	L	T	TP	Playoffs GC	W	L	T
1985-86	Detroit	45	9	34	2	20	....	....	....	....
	NHL Totals	**45**	**9**	**34**	**2**	....	....	....	....	....

PATERSON, Rick

Born: Kingston, Ont., February 10, 1958.
Played in NHL. See Player Register for career statistics.

Season	Club	Regular Season GC	W	L	T	TP	Playoffs GC	W	L	T
1997-98	Tampa Bay	8	0	8	0	0	....	....	....	....
	NHL Totals	**8**	**0**	**8**	**0**	....	....	....	....	....

PATRICK, Craig

USHOF HHOF

Born: Detroit, MI, May 20, 1946.
Played in NHL. See Player Register for career statistics.

Season	Club	Regular Season GC	W	L	T	TP	Playoffs GC	W	L	T
1980-81	NY Rangers	60	26	23	11	63	14	7	7	0
1984-85	NY Rangers	35	11	22	2	24	3	0	3	0
1989-90	Pittsburgh	54	22	26	6	50	....	....	....	....
1996-97	Pittsburgh	20	7	10	3	17	5	1	4	0
	NHL Totals	**169**	**66**	**81**	**22**	....	**22**	**8**	**14**	**0**

PATRICK, Frank

HHOF

Born: Ottawa, Ont., December 21, 1885. Died: June 29, 1960.

Season	Club	Regular Season GC	W	L	T	TP	Playoffs GC	W	L	T
1934-35	Boston	48	26	16	6	58	4	1	3	0
1935-36	Boston	48	22	20	6	50	2	1	1	0
	NHL Totals	**96**	**48**	**36**	**12**	....	**6**	**2**	**4**	**0**

PATRICK, Lester

HHOF

Born: Drummondville, Que., December 30, 1883. Died: June 1, 1960.
Played in NHL. See Player Register for career statistics.

Season	Club	Regular Season GC	W	L	T	TP	Playoffs GC	W	L	T
1926-27	NY Rangers	44	25	13	6	56	2	0	1	1
1927-28 ♦	NY Rangers	44	19	16	9	47	9	5	3	1
1928-29	NY Rangers	44	21	13	10	52	6	3	2	1

Season	Club	Regular Season GC	W	L	T	TP	Playoffs GC	W	L	T
1929-30	NY Rangers	44	17	17	10	44	4	1	2	1
1930-31	NY Rangers	44	19	16	9	47	4	2	2	0
1931-32	NY Rangers	48	23	17	8	54	7	3	4	0
1932-33 ♦	NY Rangers	48	23	17	8	54	8	6	1	1
1933-34	NY Rangers	48	21	19	8	50	2	0	1	1
1934-35	NY Rangers	48	22	20	6	50	4	2	1	1
1935-36	NY Rangers	48	19	17	12	50	....	....	....	....
1936-37	NY Rangers	48	19	20	9	47	9	6	3	0
1937-38	NY Rangers	48	27	15	6	60	3	1	2	0
1938-39	NY Rangers	48	26	16	6	58	7	3	4	0
	NHL Totals	**604**	**281**	**216**	**107**	....	**65**	**32**	**26**	**7**

PATRICK, Lynn

HHOF

Born: Victoria, B.C., February 3, 1912. Died: January 26, 1980.
Played in NHL. See Player Register for career statistics.

Season	Club	GC	W	L	T	TP	GC	W	L	T
1948-49	NY Rangers	37	12	20	5	29	....	....	....	....
1949-50	NY Rangers	70	28	31	11	67	12	7	5	0
1950-51	Boston	70	22	30	18	62	6	1	4	1
1951-52	Boston	70	25	29	16	66	7	3	4	0
1952-53	Boston	70	28	29	13	69	11	5	6	0
1953-54	Boston	70	32	28	10	74	4	0	4	0
1954-55	Boston	30	10	14	6	26	....	....	....	....
1967-68	St. Louis	16	4	10	2	10	....	....	....	....
1974-75	St. Louis	2	1	0	1	3	....	....	....	....
1975-76	St. Louis	8	3	5	0	6	....	....	....	....
	NHL Totals	**443**	**165**	**196**	**82**	....	**40**	**16**	**23**	**1**

PATRICK, Muzz

Born: Victoria, B.C., June 28, 1915. Died: July 23, 1998.
Played in NHL. See Player Register for career statistics.

Season	Club	GC	W	L	T	TP	GC	W	L	T
1953-54	NY Rangers	30	15	11	4	34	....	....	....	....
1954-55	NY Rangers	70	17	35	18	52	....	....	....	....
1959-60	NY Rangers	2	0	1	1	1	....	....	....	....
1962-63	NY Rangers	34	11	19	4	26	....	....	....	....
	NHL Totals	**136**	**43**	**66**	**27**	....	....	....	....	....

PERRON, Jean

Born: St-Isidore d'Auckland, Que., October 5, 1946.

Season	Club	GC	W	L	T	TP	GC	W	L	T
1985-86 ♦	Montreal	80	40	33	7	87	20	15	5	0
1986-87	Montreal	80	41	29	10	92	17	10	7	0
1987-88	Montreal	80	45	22	13	103	11	5	6	0
1988-89	Quebec	47	16	26	5	37	....	....	....	....
	NHL Totals	**287**	**142**	**110**	**35**	....	**48**	**30**	**18**	**0**

PERRY, Don

Born: Edmonton, Alta., March 16, 1930.

Season	Club	GC	W	L	T	TP	GC	W	L	T
1981-82	Los Angeles	38	11	17	10	32	10	4	6	0
1982-83	Los Angeles	80	27	41	12	66	....	....	....	....
1983-84	Los Angeles	50	14	27	9	37	....	....	....	....
	NHL Totals	**168**	**52**	**85**	**31**	....	**10**	**4**	**6**	**0**

PIKE, Alf

Born: Winnipeg, Man., September 15, 1917.
Played in NHL. See Player Register for career statistics.

Season	Club	GC	W	L	T	TP	GC	W	L	T
1959-60	NY Rangers	53	14	28	11	39	....	....	....	....
1960-61	NY Rangers	70	22	38	10	54	....	....	....	....
	NHL Totals	**123**	**36**	**66**	**21**	....	....	....	....	....

PILOUS, Rudy

Born: Winnipeg, Man., August 11, 1914. Died: December 11, 1994.

Season	Club	GC	W	L	T	TP	GC	W	L	T
1957-58	Chicago	37	14	22	1	29	....	....	....	....
1958-59	Chicago	70	28	29	13	69	6	2	4	0
1959-60	Chicago	70	28	29	13	69	4	0	4	0
1960-61 ♦	Chicago	70	29	24	17	75	12	8	4	0
1961-62	Chicago	70	31	26	13	75	12	6	6	0
1962-63	Chicago	70	32	21	17	81	7	3	4	0
	NHL Totals	**387**	**162**	**151**	**74**	....	**41**	**19**	**22**	**0**

PLAGER, Barclay

Born: Kirkland Lake, Ont., March 26, 1941. Died: February 6, 1988.
Played in NHL. See Player Register for career statistics.

Season	Club	GC	W	L	T	TP	GC	W	L	T
1977-78	St. Louis	26	9	11	6	24	....	....	....	....
1978-79	St. Louis	80	18	50	12	48	....	....	....	....
1979-80	St. Louis	24	7	14	3	17	....	....	....	....
1982-83	St. Louis	48	15	21	12	42	4	1	3	0
	NHL Totals	**178**	**49**	**96**	**33**	....	**4**	**1**	**3**	**0**

PLAGER, Bob

Born: Kirkland Lake, Ont., March 11, 1943.
Played in NHL. See Player Register for career statistics.

Season	Club	GC	W	L	T	TP	GC	W	L	T
1992-93	St. Louis	11	4	6	1	9	....	....	....	....
	NHL Totals	**11**	**4**	**6**	**1**	....	....	....	....	....

PLEAU, Larry

USHOF

Born: Lynn, MA, January 29, 1947.
Played in NHL. See Player Register for career statistics.

Season	Club	GC	W	L	T	TP	GC	W	L	T
1980-81	Hartford	20	6	12	2	14	....	....	....	....
1981-82	Hartford	80	21	41	18	60	....	....	....	....
1982-83	Hartford	18	4	13	1	9	....	....	....	....
1987-88	Hartford	26	13	13	0	26	6	2	4	0
1988-89	Hartford	80	37	38	5	79	4	0	4	0
	NHL Totals	**224**	**81**	**117**	**26**	....	**10**	**2**	**8**	**0**

POLANO, Nick

Born: Sudbury, Ont., March 25, 1941.

Season	Club	GC	W	L	T	TP	GC	W	L	T
1982-83	Detroit	80	21	44	15	57	....	....	....	....
1983-84	Detroit	80	31	42	7	69	4	1	3	0
1984-85	Detroit	80	27	41	12	66	3	0	3	0
	NHL Totals	**240**	**79**	**127**	**34**	....	**7**	**1**	**6**	**0**

POPEIN, Larry

Born: Yorkton, Sask., August 11, 1930.
Played in NHL. See Player Register for career statistics.

Season	Club	GC	W	L	T	TP	GC	W	L	T
1973-74	NY Rangers	41	18	14	9	45	....	....	....	....
	NHL Totals	**41**	**18**	**14**	**9**	....	....	....	....	....

POWERS, Eddie

Born: Toronto, Ont., Died: January 18, 1943.

Season	Club	GC	W	L	T	TP	GC	W	L	T
1924-25	Toronto	30	19	11	0	38	2	0	2	0
1925-26	Toronto	36	12	21	3	27	....	....	....	....
	NHL Totals	**66**	**31**	**32**	**3**	....	**2**	**0**	**2**	**0**

PRIMEAU, Joe

HHOF

Born: Lindsay, Ont., January 29, 1906. Died: May 14, 1989.
Played in NHL. See Player Register for career statistics.

Season	Club	GC	W	L	T	TP	GC	W	L	T
1950-51 ♦	Toronto	70	41	16	13	95	11	8	2	1
1951-52	Toronto	70	29	25	16	74	4	0	4	0
1952-53	Toronto	70	27	30	13	67	....	....	....	....
	NHL Totals	**210**	**97**	**71**	**42**	....	**15**	**8**	**6**	**1**

PRONOVOST, Marcel

HHOF

Born: Shawinigan Falls, Que., June 15, 1930.
Played in NHL. See Player Register for career statistics.

Season	Club	GC	W	L	T	TP	GC	W	L	T
1977-78	Buffalo	80	44	19	17	105	8	3	5	0
1978-79	Buffalo	24	8	10	6	22	....	....	....	....
	NHL Totals	**104**	**52**	**29**	**23**	....	**8**	**3**	**5**	**0**

PULFORD, Bob

HHOF

Born: Newton Robinson, Ont., March 31, 1936.
Played in NHL. See Player Register for career statistics.

Season	Club	GC	W	L	T	TP	GC	W	L	T
1972-73	Los Angeles	78	31	36	11	73	....	....	....	....
1973-74	Los Angeles	78	33	33	12	78	5	1	4	0
1974-75	Los Angeles	80	42	17	21	105	3	1	2	0
1975-76	Los Angeles	80	38	33	9	85	9	4	5	0
1976-77	Los Angeles	80	34	31	15	83	9	4	5	0
1977-78	Chicago	80	32	29	19	83	4	0	4	0
1978-79	Chicago	80	29	36	15	73	4	0	4	0
1981-82	Chicago	28	12	14	2	26	15	8	7	0
1984-85	Chicago	27	16	7	4	36	15	9	6	0
1985-86	Chicago	80	39	33	8	86	3	0	3	0
1986-87	Chicago	80	29	37	14	72	4	0	4	0
99-2000	Chicago	58	28	24	6	62	....	....	....	....
	NHL Totals	**829**	**363**	**330**	**136**	....	**71**	**27**	**44**	**0**

• Won Jack Adams Award (1975)

QUENNEVILLE, Joel

Born: Windsor, Ont., September 15, 1958.
Played in NHL. See Player Register for career statistics.

Season	Club	GC	W	L	T	TP	GC	W	L	T
1996-97	St. Louis	40	18	15	7	43	6	2	4	0
1997-98	St. Louis	82	45	29	8	98	10	6	4	0
1998-99	St. Louis	82	37	32	13	87	13	6	7	0
99-2000	St. Louis	82	51	20	11	114	7	3	4	0
2000-01	St. Louis	82	43	27	12	103	15	9	6	0
2001-02	St. Louis	82	43	31	8	98	10	5	5	0
2002-03	St. Louis	82	41	30	11	99	7	3	4	0
	NHL Totals	**532**	**278**	**184**	**70**	....	**68**	**34**	**34**	**0**

• Won Jack Adams Award (2000)

QUERRIE, Charles

Born: unknown Deceased

Season	Club	GC	W	L	T	TP	GC	W	L	T
1922-23	Toronto	19	11	7	1	23	....	....	....	....
1923-24	Toronto	24	10	14	0	20	....	....	....	....
1926-27	Toronto	29	8	17	4	20	....	....	....	....
	NHL Totals	**72**	**29**	**38**	**5**	....	....	....	....	....

QUINN, Mike

Born: unknown Deceased

Season	Club	Regular Season GC	W	L	T	TP	Playoffs GC	W	L	T
1919-20	Quebec	24	4	20	0	8	....	....	....	....
	NHL Totals	**24**	**4**	**20**	**0**	....	....	....	....	....

QUINN, Pat

Born: Hamilton, Ont., January 29, 1943.
Played in NHL. See Player Register for career statistics.

Season	Club	Regular Season GC	W	L	T	TP	Playoffs GC	W	L	T
1978-79	Philadelphia	30	18	8	4	40	8	3	5	0
1979-80	Philadelphia	80	48	12	20	116	19	13	6	0
1980-81	Philadelphia	80	41	24	15	97	12	6	6	0
1981-82	Philadelphia	72	34	29	9	77	....	....	....	....
1984-85	Los Angeles	80	34	32	14	82	3	0	3	0
1985-86	Los Angeles	80	23	49	8	54	....	....	....	....
1986-87	Los Angeles	42	18	20	4	40	....	....	....	....
1990-91	Vancouver	26	9	13	4	22	6	2	4	0
1991-92	Vancouver	80	42	26	12	96	13	6	7	0
1992-93	Vancouver	84	46	29	9	101	12	6	6	0
1993-94	Vancouver	84	41	40	3	85	24	15	9	0
1995-96	Vancouver	6	3	3	0	6	6	2	4	0
1998-99	Toronto	82	45	30	7	97	17	9	8	0
99-2000	Toronto	82	45	30	7	100	12	6	6	0
2000-01	Toronto	82	37	34	11	90	11	7	4	0
2001-02	Toronto	82	43	29	10	100	20	10	10	0
2002-03	Toronto	82	44	31	7	98	7	3	4	0
	NHL Totals	**1154**	**571**	**439**	**144**	....	**170**	**88**	**82**	**0**

• Won Jack Adams Award (1980, 1992)

Assistant coach Rick Ley posted a 1-1 playoff record as replacement coah when Pat Quinn was sidelined with heart arrythmia, May 21 and 25, 2002. All games are credited to Quinn's coaching record.

RAEDER, Cap

Born: Portland, ME, October 8, 1953.

Season	Club	Regular Season GC	W	L	T	TP	Playoffs GC	W	L	T
2002-03	San Jose	1	1	0	0	2	....	....	....	....
	NHL Totals	**1**	**1**	**0**	**0**	....	....	....	....	....

RAMSAY, Craig

Born: Weston, Ont., March 17, 1951.
Played in NHL. See Player Register for career statistics.

Season	Club	Regular Season GC	W	L	T	TP	Playoffs GC	W	L	T
1986-87	Buffalo	21	4	15	2	10	....	....	....	....
2000-01	Philadelphia	28	12	12	4	28	....	....	....	....
	NHL Totals	**49**	**16**	**27**	**6**	....	....	....	....	....

Posted a 16-10-1 regular-season record and an 11-7 playoff record as interim coach when Roger Neilson was sidelined for treatment of bone-marrow cancer after February 20, 2000. All games are credited to Neilson's coaching record.

RANDALL, Ken

Born: Kingston, Ont., Deceased
Played in NHL. See Player Register for career statistics.

Season	Club	Regular Season GC	W	L	T	TP	Playoffs GC	W	L	T
1923-24	Hamilton	14	6	8	0	12	....	....	....	....
	NHL Totals	**14**	**6**	**8**	**0**	....	....	....	....	....

REAY, Billy

Born: Winnipeg, Man., August 21, 1918.
Played in NHL. See Player Register for career statistics.

Season	Club	Regular Season GC	W	L	T	TP	Playoffs GC	W	L	T
1957-58	Toronto	70	21	38	11	53	....	....	....	....
1958-59	Toronto	20	5	12	3	13	....	....	....	....
1963-64	Chicago	70	36	22	12	84	6	2	4	0
1964-65	Chicago	70	34	28	8	76	14	7	7	0
1965-66	Chicago	70	37	25	8	82	6	2	4	0
1966-67	Chicago	70	41	17	12	94	6	2	4	0
1967-68	Chicago	74	32	26	16	80	11	5	6	0
1968-69	Chicago	76	34	33	9	77	....	....	....	....
1969-70	Chicago	76	45	22	9	99	8	4	4	0
1970-71	Chicago	78	49	20	9	107	18	11	7	0
1971-72	Chicago	78	46	17	15	107	8	4	4	0
1972-73	Chicago	78	42	27	9	93	16	10	6	0
1973-74	Chicago	78	41	14	23	105	11	6	5	0
1974-75	Chicago	80	37	35	8	82	8	3	5	0
1975-76	Chicago	80	32	30	18	82	4	0	4	0
1976-77	Chicago	34	10	19	5	25	....	....	....	....
	NHL Totals	**1102**	**542**	**385**	**175**	....	**116**	**56**	**60**	**0**

REGAN, Larry

Born: North Bay, Ont., August 9, 1930.
Played in NHL. See Player Register for career statistics.

Season	Club	Regular Season GC	W	L	T	TP	Playoffs GC	W	L	T
1970-71	Los Angeles	78	25	40	13	63	....	....	....	....
1971-72	Los Angeles	10	2	7	1	5	....	....	....	....
	NHL Totals	**88**	**27**	**47**	**14**	....	....	....	....	....

RENNEY, Tom

Born: Cranbrooke, B.C., March 1, 1955.

Season	Club	Regular Season GC	W	L	T	TP	Playoffs GC	W	L	T
1996-97	Vancouver	82	35	40	7	77	....	....	....	....
1997-98	Vancouver	19	4	13	2	10	....	....	....	....
	NHL Totals	**101**	**39**	**53**	**9**	....	....	....	....	....

RISEBROUGH, Doug

Born: Guelph, Ont., January 29, 1954.
Played in NHL. See Player Register for career statistics.

Season	Club	Regular Season GC	W	L	T	TP	Playoffs GC	W	L	T
1990-91	Calgary	80	46	26	8	100	7	3	4	0
1991-92	Calgary	64	25	30	9	59	....	....	....	....
	NHL Totals	**144**	**71**	**56**	**17**	....	**7**	**3**	**4**	**0**

ROBERTS, Jim

Born: Toronto, Ont., April 9, 1940.
Played in NHL. See Player Register for career statistics.

Season	Club	Regular Season GC	W	L	T	TP	Playoffs GC	W	L	T
1981-82	Buffalo	45	21	16	8	50	....	....	....	....
1991-92	Hartford	80	26	41	13	65	7	3	4	0
1996-97	St. Louis	9	3	3	3	9	....	....	....	....
	NHL Totals	**134**	**50**	**60**	**24**	....	**7**	**3**	**4**	**0**

ROBINSON, Larry

HHOF

Born: Winchester, Ont., June 2, 1951.
Played in NHL. See Player Register for career statistics.

Season	Club	Regular Season GC	W	L	T	TP	Playoffs GC	W	L	T
1995-96	Los Angeles	82	24	40	18	66	....	....	....	....
1996-97	Los Angeles	82	28	43	11	67	....	....	....	....
1997-98	Los Angeles	82	38	33	11	87	4	0	4	0
1998-99	Los Angeles	82	32	45	5	69	....	....	....	....
99-2000 ♦	New Jersey	8	4	4	0	8	23	16	7	0
2000-01	New Jersey	82	48	22	12	111	25	15	10	0
2001-02	New Jersey	51	21	23	7	52	....	....	....	....
	NHL Totals	**469**	**195**	**210**	**64**	....	**52**	**31**	**21**	**0**

RODDEN, Mike

HHOF

Born: April 24, 1891. Died: January 11, 1978.

Season	Club	Regular Season GC	W	L	T	TP	Playoffs GC	W	L	T
1926-27	Toronto	2	0	2	0	0	....	....	....	....
	NHL Totals	**2**	**0**	**2**	**0**	....	....	....	....	....

ROMERIL, Alex

Born: unknown

Season	Club	Regular Season GC	W	L	T	TP	Playoffs GC	W	L	T
1926-27	Toronto	13	7	5	1	15	....	....	....	....
	NHL Totals	**13**	**7**	**5**	**1**	....	....	....	....	....

ROSS, Art

HHOF

Born: Naughton, Ont., January 13, 1886. Died: August 5, 1964.
Played in NHL. See Player Register for career statistics.

Season	Club	Regular Season GC	W	L	T	TP	Playoffs GC	W	L	T
1917-18	Mtl. Wanderers	6	1	5	0	2	....	....	....	....
1922-23	Hamilton	24	6	18	0	12	....	....	....	....
1924-25	Boston	30	6	24	0	12	....	....	....	....
1925-26	Boston	36	17	15	4	38	....	....	....	....
1926-27	Boston	44	21	20	3	45	8	2	2	4
1927-28	Boston	44	20	13	11	51	2	0	1	1
1929-30	Boston	44	38	5	1	77	6	3	3	0
1930-31	Boston	44	28	10	6	62	5	2	3	0
1931-32	Boston	48	15	21	12	42	....	....	....	....
1932-33	Boston	48	25	15	8	58	5	2	3	0
1933-34	Boston	48	18	25	5	41	....	....	....	....
1936-37	Boston	48	23	18	7	53	3	1	2	0
1937-38	Boston	48	30	11	7	67	3	0	3	0
1938-39 ♦	Boston	48	36	10	2	74	12	8	4	0
1941-42	Boston	48	25	17	6	56	5	2	3	0
1942-43	Boston	50	24	17	9	57	9	4	5	0
1943-44	Boston	50	19	26	5	43	....	....	....	....
1944-45	Boston	50	16	30	4	36	7	3	4	0
	NHL Totals	**758**	**368**	**300**	**90**	....	**65**	**27**	**33**	**5**

RUEL, Claude

Born: Sherbrooke, Que., September 12, 1938.

Season	Club	Regular Season GC	W	L	T	TP	Playoffs GC	W	L	T
1968-69 ♦	Montreal	76	46	19	11	103	14	12	2	0
1969-70	Montreal	76	38	22	16	92	....	....	....	....
1970-71	Montreal	23	11	8	4	26	....	....	....	....
1979-80	Montreal	50	32	11	7	71	10	6	4	0
1980-81	Montreal	80	45	22	13	103	3	0	3	0
	NHL Totals	**305**	**172**	**82**	**51**	....	**27**	**18**	**9**	**0**

RUFF, Lindy

Born: Warburg, Alta., February 17, 1960.
Played in NHL. See Player Register for career statistics.

Season	Club	Regular Season GC	W	L	T	TP	Playoffs GC	W	L	T
1997-98	Buffalo	82	36	29	17	89	15	10	5	0
1998-99	Buffalo	82	37	28	17	91	21	14	7	0
99-2000	Buffalo	82	35	36	11	85	5	1	4	0
2000-01	Buffalo	82	46	31	5	98	13	7	6	0
2001-02	Buffalo	82	35	36	11	82	....	....	....	....
2002-03	Buffalo	82	27	45	10	72	....	....	....	....
	NHL Totals	**492**	**216**	**205**	**71**	....	**54**	**32**	**22**	**0**

SATHER, Glen — HHOF

Born: High River, Alta., September 2, 1943.
Played in NHL. See Player Register for career statistics.

Season	Club	Regular Season GC	W	L	T	TP	Playoffs GC	W	L	T
1979-80	Edmonton	80	28	39	13	69	3	0	3	0
1980-81	Edmonton	62	25	26	11	61	9	5	4	0
1981-82	Edmonton	80	48	17	15	111	5	2	3	0
1982-83	Edmonton	80	47	21	12	106	16	11	5	0
1983-84♦	Edmonton	80	57	18	5	119	19	15	4	0
1984-85♦	Edmonton	80	49	20	11	109	18	15	3	0
1985-86	Edmonton	80	56	17	7	119	10	6	4	0
1986-87♦	Edmonton	80	50	24	6	106	21	16	5	0
1987-88♦	Edmonton	80	44	25	11	99	19	16	2	1
1988-89	Edmonton	80	38	34	8	84	7	3	4	0
1993-94	Edmonton	60	22	27	11	55	....	....	....	....
2002-03	NY Rangers	28	11	13	4	29	....	....	....	....
	NHL Totals	**870**	**475**	**281**	**114**	....	**127**	**89**	**37**	**1**

• Won Jack Adams Award (1986)

SATOR, Ted

Born: Utica, NY, November 18, 1949.

Season	Club	GC	W	L	T	TP	GC	W	L	T
1985-86	NY Rangers	80	36	38	6	78	16	8	8	0
1986-87	NY Rangers	19	5	10	4	14	....	....	....	....
	Buffalo	47	21	22	4	46	....	....	....	....
1987-88	Buffalo	80	37	32	11	85	6	2	4	0
1988-89	Buffalo	80	38	35	7	83	5	1	4	0
	NHL Totals	**306**	**137**	**137**	**32**	....	**27**	**11**	**16**	**0**

SAVARD, Andre

Born: Temiscamingue, Que., February 9, 1953.
Played in NHL. See Player Register for career statistics.

Season	Club	GC	W	L	T	TP	GC	W	L	T
1987-88	Quebec	24	10	13	1	21	....	....	....	....
	NHL Totals	**24**	**10**	**13**	**1**	....	....	....	....	....

SCHINKEL, Ken

Born: Jansen, Sask., November 27, 1932.
Played in NHL. See Player Register for career statistics.

Season	Club	GC	W	L	T	TP	GC	W	L	T
1972-73	Pittsburgh	36	15	18	3	33	....	....	....	....
1973-74	Pittsburgh	50	14	31	5	33	....	....	....	....
1975-76	Pittsburgh	37	20	10	7	47	3	1	2	0
1976-77	Pittsburgh	80	34	33	13	81	3	1	2	0
	NHL Totals	**203**	**83**	**92**	**28**	....	**6**	**2**	**4**	**0**

SCHMIDT, Milt — HHOF

Born: Kitchener, Ont., March 5, 1918.
Played in NHL. See Player Register for career statistics.

Season	Club	GC	W	L	T	TP	GC	W	L	T
1954-55	Boston	40	13	12	15	41	5	1	4	0
1955-56	Boston	70	23	34	13	59	....	....	....	....
1956-57	Boston	70	34	24	12	80	10	5	5	0
1957-58	Boston	70	27	28	15	69	12	6	6	0
1958-59	Boston	70	32	29	9	73	7	3	4	0
1959-60	Boston	70	28	34	8	64	....	....	....	....
1960-61	Boston	70	15	42	13	43	....	....	....	....
1962-63	Boston	56	13	31	12	38	....	....	....	....
1963-64	Boston	70	18	40	12	48	....	....	....	....
1964-65	Boston	70	21	43	6	48	....	....	....	....
1965-66	Boston	70	21	43	6	48	....	....	....	....
1974-75	Washington	8	2	6	0	4	....	....	....	....
1975-76	Washington	36	3	28	5	11	....	....	....	....
	NHL Totals	**770**	**250**	**394**	**126**	....	**34**	**15**	**19**	**0**

SCHOENFELD, Jim

Born: Galt, Ont., September 4, 1952.
Played in NHL. See Player Register for career statistics.

Season	Club	GC	W	L	T	TP	GC	W	L	T
1985-86	Buffalo	43	19	19	5	43	....	....	....	....
1987-88	New Jersey	30	17	12	1	35	20	11	9	0
1988-89	New Jersey	80	27	41	12	66	....	....	....	....
1989-90	New Jersey	14	6	6	2	14	....	....	....	....
1993-94	Washington	37	19	12	6	44	11	5	6	0
1994-95	Washington	48	22	18	8	52	7	3	4	0
1995-96	Washington	82	39	32	11	89	6	2	4	0
1996-97	Washington	82	33	40	9	75	....	....	....	....
1997-98	Phoenix	82	35	35	12	82	6	2	4	0
1998-99	Phoenix	82	39	31	12	90	7	3	4	0
	NHL Totals	**580**	**256**	**246**	**78**	....	**57**	**26**	**31**	**0**

SHAUGHNESSY, Tom

Born: unknown   Died: September 21, 1938.

Season	Club	GC	W	L	T	TP	GC	W	L	T
1929-30	Chicago	21	10	8	3	23	....	....	....	....
	NHL Totals	**21**	**10**	**8**	**3**	....	....	....	....	....

SHERO, Fred

Born: Winnipeg, Man., October 23, 1925.   Died: November 24, 1990.
Played in NHL. See Player Register for career statistics.

Season	Club	GC	W	L	T	TP	GC	W	L	T
1971-72	Philadelphia	78	26	38	14	66	....	....	....	....
1972-73	Philadelphia	78	37	30	11	85	11	5	6	0
1973-74♦	Philadelphia	78	50	16	12	112	17	12	5	0
1974-75♦	Philadelphia	80	51	18	11	113	17	12	5	0
1975-76	Philadelphia	80	51	13	16	118	16	8	8	0
1976-77	Philadelphia	80	48	16	16	112	10	4	6	0
1977-78	Philadelphia	80	45	20	15	105	12	7	5	0
1978-79	NY Rangers	80	40	29	11	91	18	11	7	0
1979-80	NY Rangers	80	38	32	10	86	9	4	5	0
1980-81	NY Rangers	20	4	13	3	11	....	....	....	....
	NHL Totals	**734**	**390**	**225**	**119**	....	**110**	**63**	**47**	**0**

• Won Jack Adams Award (1974)

SIMPSON, Joe — HHOF

Born: Selkirk, Man., August 13, 1893.   Died: December 25, 1973.
Played in NHL. See Player Register for career statistics.

Season	Club	GC	W	L	T	TP	GC	W	L	T
1932-33	NY Americans	48	15	22	11	41	....	....	....	....
1933-34	NY Americans	48	15	23	10	40	....	....	....	....
1934-35	NY Americans	48	12	27	9	33	....	....	....	....
	NHL Totals	**144**	**42**	**72**	**30**	....	....	....	....	....

SIMPSON, Terry

Born: Brantford, Ont., August 30, 1943.

Season	Club	GC	W	L	T	TP	GC	W	L	T
1986-87	NY Islanders	80	35	33	12	82	14	7	7	0
1987-88	NY Islanders	80	39	31	10	88	6	2	4	0
1988-89	NY Islanders	27	7	18	2	16	....	....	....	....
1993-94	Philadelphia	84	35	39	10	80	....	....	....	....
1994-95	Winnipeg	15	7	7	1	15	....	....	....	....
1995-96	Winnipeg	82	36	40	6	78	6	2	4	0
	NHL Totals	**368**	**159**	**168**	**41**	....	**26**	**11**	**15**	**0**

SIMS, Al

Born: Toronto, Ont., April 18, 1953.
Played in NHL. See Player Register for career statistics.

Season	Club	GC	W	L	T	TP	GC	W	L	T
1996-97	San Jose	82	27	47	8	62	....	....	....	....
	NHL Totals	**82**	**27**	**47**	**8**	....	....	....	....	....

SINDEN, Harry — HHOF

Born: Collins Bay, Ont., September 14, 1932.

Season	Club	GC	W	L	T	TP	GC	W	L	T
1966-67	Boston	70	17	43	10	44	....	....	....	....
1967-68	Boston	74	37	27	10	84	4	0	4	0
1968-69	Boston	76	42	18	16	100	10	6	4	0
1969-70♦	Boston	76	40	17	19	99	14	12	2	0
1979-80	Boston	7	6	1	0	12	10	4	6	0
1984-85	Boston	24	11	10	3	25	5	2	3	0
	NHL Totals	**327**	**153**	**116**	**58**	....	**43**	**24**	**19**	**0**

SKINNER, Jimmy

Born: Selkirk, Man., January 12, 1918.

Season	Club	GC	W	L	T	TP	GC	W	L	T
1954-55♦	Detroit	70	42	17	11	95	11	8	3	0
1955-56	Detroit	70	30	24	16	76	10	5	5	0
1956-57	Detroit	70	38	20	12	88	5	1	4	0
1957-58	Detroit	37	13	17	7	33	....	....	....	....
	NHL Totals	**247**	**123**	**78**	**46**	....	**26**	**14**	**12**	**0**

SMEATON, Cooper — HHOF

Born: Carleton Place, Ont., July 22, 1890.   Died: October 3, 1978.

Season	Club	GC	W	L	T	TP	GC	W	L	T
1930-31	Philadelphia	44	4	36	4	12	....	....	....	....
	NHL Totals	**44**	**4**	**36**	**4**	....	....	....	....	....

SMITH, Alf — HHOF

Born: Ottawa, Ont., June 3, 1873.   Died: August 21, 1953.

Season	Club	GC	W	L	T	TP	GC	W	L	T
1918-19	Ottawa	18	12	6	0	24	5	1	4	0
	NHL Totals	**18**	**12**	**6**	**0**	....	**5**	**1**	**4**	**0**

SMITH, Barry

Born: Buffalo, NY, August 21, 1950.

Season	Club	GC	W	L	T	TP	GC	W	L	T
1998-99	Detroit	5	4	1	0	8	....	....	....	....
	NHL Totals	**5**	**4**	**1**	**0**	....	....	....	....	....

Shared a 4-1-0 record with associate coach Dave Lewis while serving as co-head coaches until Scotty Bowman received medical clearance and decided to return to coaching on October 23, 1998.

SMITH, Floyd

Born: Perth, Ont., May 16, 1935.
Played in NHL. See Player Register for career statistics.

Season	Club	GC	W	L	T	TP	GC	W	L	T
1971-72	Buffalo	1	0	1	0	0	....	....	....	....
1974-75	Buffalo	80	49	16	15	113	17	10	7	0
1975-76	Buffalo	80	46	21	13	105	9	4	5	0

Season	Club	Regular Season GC	W	L	T	TP	Playoffs GC	W	L	T
1976-77	Buffalo	80	48	24	8	104	6	2	4	0
1979-80	Toronto	68	30	33	5	65	....	....	....	....
	NHL Totals	**309**	**173**	**95**	**41**	....	**32**	**16**	**16**	**0**

SMITH, Mike

Born: Potsdam, NY, August 31, 1945.

Season	Club	GC	W	L	T	TP	GC	W	L	T
1980-81	Winnipeg	23	2	17	4	8	....	....	....	....
	NHL Totals	**23**	**2**	**17**	**4**	....	....	....	....	....

SMITH, Ron

Born: Port Hope, Ont., November 19, 1952.
Played in NHL. See Player Register for career statistics.

Season	Club	GC	W	L	T	TP	GC	W	L	T
1992-93	NY Rangers	44	15	22	7	37	....	....	....	....
	NHL Totals	**44**	**15**	**22**	**7**	....	....	....	....	....

SMYTHE, Conn

HHOF

Born: Toronto, Ont., February 1, 1895. Died: November 18, 1980.

Season	Club	GC	W	L	T	TP	GC	W	L	T
1927-28	Toronto	44	18	18	8	44	....	....	....	....
1928-29	Toronto	44	21	18	5	47	4	2	2	0
1929-30	Toronto	44	17	21	6	40	....	....	....	....
1930-31	Toronto	2	1	0	1	3	....	....	....	....
	NHL Totals	**134**	**57**	**57**	**20**	....	**4**	**2**	**2**	**0**

SONMOR, Glen

Born: Moose Jaw, Sask., April 22, 1929.
Played in NHL. See Player Register for career statistics.

Season	Club	GC	W	L	T	TP	GC	W	L	T
1978-79	Minnesota	69	25	34	10	60	....	....	....	....
1979-80	Minnesota	80	36	28	16	88	15	8	7	0
1980-81	Minnesota	80	35	28	17	87	19	12	7	0
1981-82	Minnesota	76	34	23	19	87	....	....	....	....
1982-83	Minnesota	43	22	12	9	53	....	....	....	....
1984-85	Minnesota	67	22	35	10	54	9	5	4	0
1986-87	Minnesota	2	0	1	1	1	....	....	....	....
	NHL Totals	**417**	**174**	**161**	**82**	....	**43**	**25**	**18**	**0**

SPROULE, Harvey

Born: unknown Deceased

Season	Club	GC	W	L	T	TP	GC	W	L	T
1919-20	Toronto	12	7	5	0	14	....	....	....	....
	NHL Totals	**12**	**7**	**5**	**0**	....	....	....	....	....

STANLEY, Barney

HHOF

Born: Paisley, Ont., January 1, 1893. Died: May 14, 1971.
Played in NHL. See Player Register for career statistics.

Season	Club	GC	W	L	T	TP	GC	W	L	T
1927-28	Chicago	23	4	17	2	10	....	....	....	....
	NHL Totals	**23**	**4**	**17**	**2**	....	....	....	....	....

STASIUK, Vic

Born: Lethbridge, Alta., May 23, 1929.
Played in NHL. See Player Register for career statistics.

Season	Club	GC	W	L	T	TP	GC	W	L	T
1969-70	Philadelphia	76	17	35	24	58	....	....	....	....
1970-71	Philadelphia	78	28	33	17	73	4	0	4	0
1971-72	California	75	21	38	16	58	....	....	....	....
1972-73	Vancouver	78	22	47	9	53	....	....	....	....
	NHL Totals	**307**	**88**	**153**	**66**	....	**4**	**0**	**4**	**0**

STEWART, Bill

Born: Toronto, Ont., October 6, 1957.
Played in NHL. See Player Register for career statistics.

Season	Club	GC	W	L	T	TP	GC	W	L	T
1998-99	NY Islanders	37	11	19	7	29	....	....	....	....
	NHL Totals	**37**	**11**	**19**	**7**	....	....	....	....	....

STEWART, Bill

USHOF

Born: Fitchburg, MA, September 26, 1894. Died: February 14, 1964.

Season	Club	GC	W	L	T	TP	GC	W	L	T
1937-38 ♦	Chicago	48	14	25	9	37	10	7	3	0
1938-39	Chicago	21	8	10	3	19	....	....	....	....
	NHL Totals	**69**	**22**	**35**	**12**	....	**10**	**7**	**3**	**0**

STEWART, Ron

Born: Calgary, Alta., July 11, 1932.
Played in NHL. See Player Register for career statistics.

Season	Club	GC	W	L	T	TP	GC	W	L	T
1975-76	NY Rangers	39	15	20	4	34	....	....	....	....
1977-78	Los Angeles	80	31	34	15	77	2	0	2	0
	NHL Totals	**119**	**46**	**54**	**19**	....	**2**	**0**	**2**	**0**

SUHONEN, Alpo

Born: Valkeakoski, Finland, June 17, 1948.

Season	Club	GC	W	L	T	TP	GC	W	L	T
2000-01	Chicago	82	29	45	8	70	....	....	....	....
	NHL Totals	**82**	**29**	**45**	**8**	....	....	....	....	....

Assistant coaches Denis Savard and Al MacAdam posted an 0-6-1 record as interim coaches after Alpo Suhonen was sidelined with heart problems, March 27 to April 8, 2001. All games are credited to Suhonen's coaching record.

SULLIVAN, Red

Born: Peterborough, Ont., December 24, 1929.
Played in NHL. See Player Register for career statistics.

Season	Club	GC	W	L	T	TP	GC	W	L	T
1962-63	NY Rangers	36	11	17	8	30	....	....	....	....
1963-64	NY Rangers	70	22	38	10	54	....	....	....	....
1964-65	NY Rangers	70	20	38	12	52	....	....	....	....
1965-66	NY Rangers	20	5	10	5	15	....	....	....	....
1967-68	Pittsburgh	74	27	34	13	67	....	....	....	....
1968-69	Pittsburgh	76	20	45	11	51	....	....	....	....
1974-75	Washington	18	2	16	0	4	....	....	....	....
	NHL Totals	**364**	**107**	**198**	**59**	....	....	....	....	....

SUTHERLAND, Bill

Born: Regina, Sask., November 10, 1934.
Played in NHL. See Player Register for career statistics.

Season	Club	GC	W	L	T	TP	GC	W	L	T
1979-80	Winnipeg	3	1	2	0	2	....	....	....	....
1980-81	Winnipeg	29	6	20	3	15	....	....	....	....
	NHL Totals	**32**	**7**	**22**	**3**	....	....	....	....	....

SUTTER, Brian

Born: Viking, Alta., October 7, 1956.
Played in NHL. See Player Register for career statistics.

Season	Club	GC	W	L	T	TP	GC	W	L	T
1988-89	St. Louis	80	33	35	12	78	10	5	5	0
1989-90	St. Louis	80	37	34	9	83	12	7	5	0
1990-91	St. Louis	80	47	22	11	105	13	6	7	0
1991-92	St. Louis	80	36	33	11	83	6	2	4	0
1992-93	Boston	84	51	26	7	109	4	0	4	0
1993-94	Boston	84	42	29	13	97	13	6	7	0
1994-95	Boston	48	27	18	3	57	5	1	4	0
1997-98	Calgary	82	26	41	15	67	....	....	....	....
1998-99	Calgary	82	30	40	12	72	....	....	....	....
99-2000	Calgary	82	31	41	10	77	....	....	....	....
2001-02	Chicago	82	41	28	13	96	5	1	4	0
2002-03	Chicago	82	30	39	13	79	....	....	....	....
	NHL Totals	**946**	**431**	**386**	**129**	....	**68**	**28**	**40**	**0**

• Won Jack Adams Award (1991)

SUTTER, Darryl

Born: Viking, Alta., August 19, 1958.
Played in NHL. See Player Register for career statistics.

Season	Club	GC	W	L	T	TP	GC	W	L	T
1992-93	Chicago	84	47	25	12	106	4	0	4	0
1993-94	Chicago	84	39	36	9	87	6	2	4	0
1994-95	Chicago	48	24	19	5	53	16	9	7	0
1997-98	San Jose	82	34	38	10	78	6	2	4	0
1998-99	San Jose	82	31	33	18	80	6	2	4	0
99-2000	San Jose	82	35	37	10	87	12	5	7	0
2000-01	San Jose	82	40	30	12	95	6	2	4	0
2001-02	San Jose	82	44	30	8	99	12	7	5	0
2002-03	San Jose	24	8	14	2	20	....	....	....	....
	Calgary	46	19	19	8	47	....	....	....	....
	NHL Totals	**696**	**321**	**281**	**94**	....	**68**	**29**	**39**	**0**

SUTTER, Duane

Born: Viking, Alberta, March 16, 1960.
Played in NHL. See Player Register for career statistics.

Season	Club	GC	W	L	T	TP	GC	W	L	T
2000-01	Florida	46	16	24	6	42	....	....	....	....
2001-02	Florida	26	6	18	2	17	....	....	....	....
	NHL Totals	**72**	**22**	**42**	**8**	....	....	....	....	....

TALBOT, Jean-Guy

Born: Cap de La Madeliene, Que., July 11, 1932.
Played in NHL. See Player Register for career statistics.

Season	Club	GC	W	L	T	TP	GC	W	L	T
1972-73	St. Louis	65	30	28	7	67	5	1	4	0
1973-74	St. Louis	55	22	25	8	52	....	....	....	....
1977-78	NY Rangers	80	30	37	13	73	3	1	2	0
	NHL Totals	**200**	**82**	**90**	**28**	....	**8**	**2**	**6**	**0**

TESSIER, Orval

Born: Cornwall, Ont., June 30, 1933.
Played in NHL. See Player Register for career statistics.

Season	Club	GC	W	L	T	TP	GC	W	L	T
1982-83	Chicago	80	47	23	10	104	13	7	6	0
1983-84	Chicago	80	30	42	8	68	5	2	3	0
1984-85	Chicago	53	22	28	3	47	....	....	....	....
	NHL Totals	**213**	**99**	**93**	**21**	....	**18**	**9**	**9**	**0**

• Won Jack Adams Award (1983)

THERRIEN, Michel

Born: Montreal, Que., November 4, 1963.

Season	Club	GC	W	L	T	TP	GC	W	L	T
2000-01	Montreal	62	23	33	6	58	....	....	....	....
2001-02	Montreal	82	36	34	12	87	12	6	6	0
2002-03	Montreal	46	18	23	5	45	....	....	....	....
	NHL Totals	**190**	**77**	**90**	**23**	....	**12**	**6**	**6**	**0**

THOMPSON, Paul

Born: Calgary, Alta., November 2, 1906. Deceased
Played in NHL. See Player Register for career statistics.

Season	Club	Regular Season GC	W	L	T	TP	Playoffs GC	W	L	T
1938-39	Chicago	27	4	18	5	13	....	....	....	....
1939-40	Chicago	48	23	19	6	52	2	0	2	0
1940-41	Chicago	48	16	25	7	39	5	2	3	0
1941-42	Chicago	48	22	23	3	47	3	1	2	0
1942-43	Chicago	50	17	18	15	49	....	....	....	....
1943-44	Chicago	50	22	23	5	49	9	4	5	0
1944-45	Chicago	1	0	1	0	0	....	....	....	....
	NHL Totals	**272**	**104**	**127**	**41**	....	**19**	**7**	**12**	**0**

THOMPSON, Percy

Born: unknown Deceased

Season	Club	Regular Season GC	W	L	T	TP	Playoffs GC	W	L	T
1920-21	Hamilton	24	6	18	0	12	....	....	....	....
1921-22	Hamilton	24	7	17	0	14	....	....	....	....
	NHL Totals	**48**	**13**	**35**	**0**	....	....	....	....	....

TIPPETT, Dave

Born: Moosomin, Sask., August 25, 1961.
Played in NHL. See Player Register for career statistics.

Season	Club	Regular Season GC	W	L	T	TP	Playoffs GC	W	L	T
2002-03	Dallas	82	46	21	15	111	12	6	6	0
	NHL Totals	**82**	**46**	**21**	**15**	....	**12**	**6**	**6**	**0**

Posted a 2-2-1 record as replacement coach when Andy Murray was sidelined following a car accident, February 26 to March 6, 2002, All games are credited to Murray's coaching record.

TOBIN, Bill

Born: Ottawa, Ont., May 20, 1895. Died: May 8, 1963.

Season	Club	Regular Season GC	W	L	T	TP	Playoffs GC	W	L	T
1929-30	Chicago	23	11	10	2	24	2	0	1	1
1931-32	Chicago	48	18	19	11	47	2	1	1	0
	NHL Totals	**71**	**29**	**29**	**13**	....	**4**	**1**	**2**	**1**

TORTORELLA, John

Born: Boston, MA, June 24, 1958.

Season	Club	Regular Season GC	W	L	T	TP	Playoffs GC	W	L	T
99-2000	NY Rangers	4	0	3	1	1	....	....	....	....
2000-01	Tampa Bay	43	12	30	1	28	....	....	....	....
2001-02	Tampa Bay	82	27	44	11	69	....	....	....	....
2002-03	Tampa Bay	82	36	30	16	93	11	5	6	....
	NHL Totals	**211**	**75**	**107**	**29**		**11**	**5**	**6**	....

TREMBLAY, Mario

Born: Montreal, Que., February 9, 1956.
Played in NHL. See Player Register for career statistics.

Season	Club	Regular Season GC	W	L	T	TP	Playoffs GC	W	L	T
1995-96	Montreal	77	40	27	10	90	6	2	4	0
1996-97	Montreal	82	31	36	15	77	5	1	4	0
	NHL Totals	**159**	**71**	**63**	**25**	....	**11**	**3**	**8**	**0**

TROTTIER, Bryan HHOF

Born: Val Marie, Sask., July 17, 1956.
Played in NHL. See Player Register for career statistics.

Season	Club	Regular Season GC	W	L	T	TP	Playoffs GC	W	L	T
2002-03	NY Rangers	54	21	27	6	49	....	....	....	....
	NHL Totals	**54**	**21**	**27**	**6**	....	....	....	....	....

TROTZ, Barry

Born: Winnipeg, Man., July 15, 1962.

Season	Club	Regular Season GC	W	L	T	TP	Playoffs GC	W	L	T
1998-99	Nashville	82	28	47	7	63	....	....	....	....
99-2000	Nashville	82	28	47	7	70	....	....	....	....
2000-01	Nashville	82	34	39	9	80	....	....	....	....
2001-02	Nashville	82	28	41	13	69	....	....	....	....
2002-03	Nashville	82	27	42	13	74	....	....	....	....
	NHL Totals	**410**	**145**	**216**	**49**	....	....	....	....	....

UBRIACO, Gene

Born: Sault Ste. Marie, Ont., December 26, 1937.
Played in NHL. See Player Register for career statistics.

Season	Club	Regular Season GC	W	L	T	TP	Playoffs GC	W	L	T
1988-89	Pittsburgh	80	40	33	7	87	11	7	4	0
1989-90	Pittsburgh	26	10	14	2	22	....	....	....	....
	NHL Totals	**106**	**50**	**47**	**9**	....	**11**	**7**	**4**	**0**

VACHON, Rogie

Born: Palmarolle, Que., September 8, 1945.
Played in NHL. See Goaltender Register for career statistics.

Season	Club	Regular Season GC	W	L	T	TP	Playoffs GC	W	L	T
1983-84	Los Angeles	2	1	0	1	3	....	....	....	....
1987-88	Los Angeles	1	0	1	0	0	....	....	....	....
1994-95	Los Angeles	7	3	2	2	8	....	....	....	....
	NHL Totals	**10**	**4**	**3**	**3**	....	....	....	....	....

VIGNEAULT, Alain

Born: Quebec City, Que., May 14, 1961.
Played in NHL. See Player Register for career statistics.

Season	Club	Regular Season GC	W	L	T	TP	Playoffs GC	W	L	T
1997-98	Montreal	82	37	32	13	87	10	4	6	0
1998-99	Montreal	82	32	39	11	75	....	....	....	....
99-2000	Montreal	82	35	38	9	83	....	....	....	....
2000-01	Montreal	20	5	13	2	12	....	....	....	....
	NHL Totals	**266**	**109**	**122**	**35**	....	**10**	**4**	**6**	**0**

WADDELL, Don

Born: Detroit, MI, August 19, 1958.
Played in NHL. See Player Register for career statistics.

Season	Club	Regular Season GC	W	L	T	TP	Playoffs GC	W	L	T
2002-03	Atlanta	10	4	5	1	9	....	....	....	....
	NHL Totals	**10**	**4**	**5**	**1**	....	....	....	....	....

WATSON, Bryan

Born: Bancroft, Ont., November 14, 1942.
Played in NHL. See Player Register for career statistics.

Season	Club	Regular Season GC	W	L	T	TP	Playoffs GC	W	L	T
1980-81	Edmonton	18	4	9	5	13	....	....	....	....
	NHL Totals	**18**	**4**	**9**	**5**	....	....	....	....	....

WATSON, Phil

Born: Montreal, Que., April 24, 1914. Deceased
Played in NHL. See Player Register for career statistics.

Season	Club	Regular Season GC	W	L	T	TP	Playoffs GC	W	L	T
1955-56	NY Rangers	70	32	28	10	74	5	1	4	0
1956-57	NY Rangers	70	26	30	14	66	5	1	4	0
1957-58	NY Rangers	70	32	25	13	77	6	2	4	0
1958-59	NY Rangers	70	26	32	12	64	....	....	....	....
1959-60	NY Rangers	15	3	9	3	9	....	....	....	....
1961-62	Boston	70	15	47	8	38	....	....	....	....
1962-63	Boston	14	1	8	5	7	....	....	....	....
	NHL Totals	**379**	**135**	**179**	**65**	....	**16**	**4**	**12**	**0**

WATT, Tom

Born: Toronto, Ont., June 17, 1935.

Season	Club	Regular Season GC	W	L	T	TP	Playoffs GC	W	L	T
1981-82	Winnipeg	80	33	33	14	80	4	1	3	0
1982-83	Winnipeg	80	33	39	8	74	3	0	3	0
1983-84	Winnipeg	21	6	13	2	14	....	....	....	....
1985-86	Vancouver	80	23	44	13	59	3	0	3	0
1986-87	Vancouver	80	29	43	8	66	....	....	....	....
1990-91	Toronto	69	22	37	10	54	....	....	....	....
1991-92	Toronto	80	30	43	7	67	....	....	....	....
	NHL Totals	**490**	**176**	**252**	**62**	....	**10**	**1**	**9**	**0**

• Won Jack Adams Award (1982)

WEBSTER, Tom

Born: Kirkland Lake, Ont., October 4, 1948.
Played in NHL. See Player Register for career statistics.

Season	Club	Regular Season GC	W	L	T	TP	Playoffs GC	W	L	T
1986-87	NY Rangers	18	5	9	4	14	....	....	....	....
1989-90	Los Angeles	80	34	39	7	75	10	4	6	0
1990-91	Los Angeles	80	46	24	10	102	12	6	6	0
1991-92	Los Angeles	80	35	31	14	84	6	2	4	0
	NHL Totals	**258**	**120**	**103**	**35**	....	**28**	**12**	**16**	**0**

Assistant coaches Wayne Cashman and Ed Giacomin posted 0-2-0 record when Tom Webster was ill, a 4-3 loss to Minnesota at New York on December 15, 1986, and a 7-4 loss at Edmonton on January 23, 1987. All games are credited to Webster's coaching record.

WEILAND, Cooney HHOF

Born: Seaforth (Edmondville), Ont., November 5, 1904. Died: July 3, 1985.
Played in NHL. See Player Register for career statistics.

Season	Club	Regular Season GC	W	L	T	TP	Playoffs GC	W	L	T
1939-40	Boston	48	31	12	5	67	6	2	4	0
1940-41	♦ Boston	48	27	8	13	67	11	8	3	0
	NHL Totals	**96**	**58**	**20**	**18**	....	**17**	**10**	**7**	**0**

WHITE, Bill

Born: Toronto, Ont., August 26, 1939.
Played in NHL. See Player Register for career statistics.

Season	Club	Regular Season GC	W	L	T	TP	Playoffs GC	W	L	T
1976-77	Chicago	46	16	24	6	38	2	0	2	0
	NHL Totals	**46**	**16**	**24**	**6**	....	**2**	**0**	**2**	**0**

WILEY, Jim

Born: Sault Ste. Marie, Ont., April 28, 1950.
Played in NHL. See Player Register for career statistics.

Season	Club	Regular Season GC	W	L	T	TP	Playoffs GC	W	L	T
1995-96	San Jose	57	17	37	3	37	....	....	....	....
	NHL Totals	**57**	**17**	**37**	**3**	....	....	....	....	....

WILSON, Johnny

Born: Kincardine, Ont., June 14, 1929.
Played in NHL. See Player Register for career statistics.

Season	Club	Regular Season GC	W	L	T	TP	Playoffs GC	W	L	T
1969-70	Los Angeles	52	9	34	9	27	....	....	....	....
1971-72	Detroit	67	30	27	10	70	....	....	....	....
1972-73	Detroit	78	37	29	12	86	....	....	....	....
1976-77	Colorado	80	20	46	14	54	....	....	....	....
1977-78	Pittsburgh	80	25	37	18	68	....	....	....	....
1978-79	Pittsburgh	80	36	31	13	85	7	2	5	0
1979-80	Pittsburgh	80	30	37	13	73	5	2	3	0
	NHL Totals	**517**	**187**	**241**	**89**	....	**12**	**4**	**8**	**0**

WILSON, Larry

Born: Kincardine, Ont., October 23, 1930. Died: August 16, 1979.
Played in NHL. See Player Register for career statistics.

Season	Club	Regular Season GC	W	L	T	TP	Playoffs GC	W	L	T
1976-77	Detroit	36	3	29	4	10	....	....	....	....
	NHL Totals	**36**	**3**	**29**	**4**	....	....	....	....	....

WILSON, Rick

Born: Prince Albert, Sask, August 10, 1950.
Played in NHL. See Player Register for career statistics.

Season	Club	Regular Season GC	W	L	T	TP	Playoffs GC	W	L	T
2001-02	Dallas	32	13	12	7	34	....	....	....	....
	NHL Totals	**32**	**13**	**12**	**7**	....	....	....	....	....

WILSON, Ron

Born: Toronto, Ont., May 13, 1956.
Played in NHL. See Player Register for career statistics.

Season	Club	Regular Season GC	W	L	T	TP	Playoffs GC	W	L	T
1993-94	Anaheim	84	33	46	5	71	....	....	....	....
1994-95	Anaheim	48	16	27	5	37	....	....	....	....
1995-96	Anaheim	82	35	39	8	78	....	....	....	....
1996-97	Anaheim	82	36	33	13	85	11	4	7	0
1997-98	Washington	82	40	30	12	92	21	12	9	0
1998-99	Washington	82	31	45	6	68	....	....	....	....
99-2000	Washington	82	44	26	12	102	5	1	4	0
2000-01	Washington	82	41	31	10	96	6	2	4	0
2001-02	Washington	82	36	35	11	85	....	....	....	....
2002-03	San Jose	57	19	31	7	51	....	....	....	....
	NHL Totals	**763**	**331**	**343**	**89**	....	**43**	**19**	**24**	**0**

YOUNG, Garry

Born: Toronto, Ont., January 2, 1936.

Season	Club	Regular Season GC	W	L	T	TP	Playoffs GC	W	L	T
1972-73	California	12	2	7	3	7	....	....	....	....
1974-75	St. Louis	69	32	26	11	75	2	0	2	0
1975-76	St. Louis	29	9	15	5	23	....	....	....	....
	NHL Totals	**110**	**43**	**48**	**19**	....	**2**	**0**	**2**	**0**

Notes on Contributors and Acknowledgments

Contributors

Paul Bontje (managing editor) is a member of the editorial team that produces the *NHL Official Guide and Record Book* and *Total Hockey*.

Bob Borgen (contributing editor/statistician) produces Los Angeles Kings television broadcasts for Fox Sports West. He is a member of the Society for International Hockey Research.

Dan Diamond (editor) redesigned the *NHL Official Guide & Record Book* in 1984 and has edited numerous books about the sport including the *Official NHL Stanley Cup Centennial Book* and *Total Hockey*. He has asked Gordie Howe for his autograph in five different decades.

Ralph Dinger (managing editor) is an experienced researcher and editor who has specialized in goaltending records. He is managing editor of the *NHL Official Guide & Record Book.*

James Duplacey (assistant editor) is a former curator of the Hockey Hall of Fame. He is the author of the Hockey Superstars series of children's books and frequently consulted on matters of hockey history by broadcasters and journalists.

Brian McFarlane has worked as a commentator on "Hockey Night in Canada," NBC and CBS. He is a recipient of the Foster Hewitt Memorial Award for broadcasting and has written more than 30 books about hockey. He is a member of the Society for International Hockey Research and has operated his own hockey museum.

Gary Meagher has worked with the National Hockey League since 1981. He is currently vice president, public relations and media services.

Mark Paddock (contributing editor) wrote for both editions of *Total Hockey*. He co-edited *Coolest Game on the Road: A Travel Guide to the NHL*, and has served as assistant editor of the *NHL Official Guide and Record Book.*

John Pasternak (data management) developed the data base of player and goaltender statistics used to create the registers in *Total NHL*. He lives and works in Hillsburgh, Ontario.

Eric Zweig (managing editor) is the author of the historical novel *Hockey Night in the Dominion of Canada* and three non-fiction books for children. He has written about sports history for several Canadian media outlets including *The Beaver* and CBC Radio.

Acknowledgments

Thanks to the following contributors:

For the National Hockey League

Pat Armstrong, Frank Brown, Bill Daly, Lisa Crompton, Amy Early, Benny Ercolani, Denise Gomez, Greg Inglis, David Keon, Bernadette Mansur, Dave McCarthy, Steve Pellegrini, George Puro, Julie Young.

For the Hockey Hall of Fame

Craig Campbell, Peter Jagla, Phil Pritchard, Tyler Wolosewich.

Special Thanks

Sean Baines, Tom Bast, Michael Berger, Pat Cairns, Tuan Doan, Alex Dubiel, Joe Fonseca, Kevin Harper, Michelle Hayles, Natalie King, Warren Mackey, Bill Masuda, Peter Mikos, North 49 Books, Mitch Rogatz, Scott Rowan, Dox San Agustin, Randy Savoie, Catherine Slavin, Society for International Hockey Research, Phil Springstead, Lisa Stevenson, Bill Swanson, Dave Therrien, Triumph Books, Diane and Peter Waldock Fred Waldock, Chris Whalen, Danny Yip, Jonathan Zweig.

Contributors

Tim Bateman, Paul R. Carroll, Jr., Bob Duff, Jason Farris, Ernie Fitzsimmons, Peter Fillman, Hal Knudsen, Al Mason, Gary J. Pearce, Stephen Schmidt-Stutzman, Erik Schwetje, John Storrisere, Donald Teplyske, Jussi Uotila, Chris Wilkie, Ian Wilson.

References

Books: (Author/editor names follow book titles where appropriate) *NHL Entry Draft Book, NHL Official Guide & Record Book, NHL Guide, NHL Playoff Fact Guide, NHL Official Rule Book, NHL Year in Review, The Hockey News, Total Hockey editions I and II, Total Stanley Cup, The Hockey Encyclopedia* (Stan and Shirley Fischler with Bob Duff), *The Sporting News,* media guides from NHL teams, *The Trail of the Stanley Cup* (Charles Coleman), *Mackie's Hockey Atlas* (Roy W. Mackie), *Deceptions and Doublecross* (Morey Holzman and Joseph Nieforth).

Web sites:

www.nhl.com
www.hhof.com
www.hockeydb.com

Photo Credits

Photos from the collections of the Hockey Hall of Fame, including the Steve and Brian Babineau collection, Paul Bereswill collection, Joe DiMaggio and JoAnne Kalish collection, Graphic Artists collection, Doug MacLellan Collection, Jack and Peter Mecca Collection, Miles Nadal collection, O-Pee-Chee collection, London Life Lewis Portnoy collection, Frank Prazak collection, James Rice collection, Dave Sandford collection and the Imperial Oil Turofsky collection. Additional photos from the Dan Diamond and Associates collection, NHL Images and Phoenix Coyotes.

To Contact *Total NHL*

E-mail: dda.nhl@sympatico.ca
Fax: 416 531-3939
Mail: *Total Hockey*
194 Dovercourt Road
Toronto, Ontario
Canada M6J 3C8

Contributors will be acknowledged in future editions.